SAUNDERS MEDICAL AND NURSING DICTIONARIES AND VOCABULARY AIDS

Dorland's Illustrated Medical Dictionary

Dorland's Pocket Medical Dictionary

Cole: The Doctor's Shorthand

Jablonski: Illustrated Dictionary of Eponymic Syndromes and Diseases

Leader & Leader: Dictionary of Comparative Pathology and Experimental Biology

Miller–Keane: Encyclopedia and Dictionary of Medicine and Nursing

Sloane: The Medical Word Book – A Spelling and Vocabulary Guide to Medical Transcription

DORLAND'S ILLUSTRATED

MEDICAL DICTIONARY

EDITORIAL CONSULTANTS

DORLAND'S ILLUSTRATED

MEDICAL DICTIONARY

24th edition

W. B. SAUNDERS COMPANY
Philadelphia and London

Some of the words appearing in this Dictionary are proprietary names even though no reference to this fact is made in the text. The appearance of any name without designation as proprietary is therefore not to be regarded as a representation by the editors or publisher that it is not a proprietary name or is not the subject of proprietary rights.

The use of portions of the text of the *Pharmacopeia of the United States of America*, Sixteenth Revision, official from October 1, 1960, is by permission received from the Board of Trustees of the United States Pharmacopeial Convention. The said Board is not responsible for any inaccuracies of the text thus used.

Permission to use portions of the text of the *National Formulary*, Eleventh Edition, official October 1, 1960, has been granted by the American Pharmaceutical Association. The American Pharmaceutical Association is not responsible for any inaccuracy of quotation, or for false implications that may arise by reason of the separation of excerpts from the original context.

The use of certain portions of the text of *New and Nonofficial Drugs* in this volume is by virtue of permission received from the Council on Drugs of the American Medical Association. The said Council is not responsible for any inaccuracy of quotation or for errors in the statement of quantities or percentage strengths.

Listed here is the latest translated edition of this book together with the language for the translation and the publisher.

Spanish (24th Edition) (Adaptation) – El Ateneo, Buenos Aires, Argentina

Made in the United States of America

Press of W. B. Saunders Company

SBN 0-7216-3146-0
SBN 0-7216-3147-9 Deluxe edition

LIBRARY OF CONGRESS CATALOG CARD NUMBER: 0-6383

Print No.: 15 14

Dedicated

To All Who Have Helped

in the

Revision of This Dictionary

Preface

So EXTENSIVE HAS BEEN THE REVISION for this, the twenty-fourth edition of Dorland's Illustrated Medical Dictionary, that it seems appropriate to explain not only the lexicographic principles upon which this Dictionary is built but also the specific measures which have been taken to make this the most changed of all the editions in a sixty-five-year period of service to biomedical scientists, students, and physicians.

All learning in science is based on education in vocabulary, for the imagery of words and symbols is the only means to expression of scientific data and concepts. For the continuing successful interchange of ideas, the words and ideographs of science must have precise and specific meanings and these must be recorded in a carefully arranged repository of such information. Accuracy, comprehensiveness, ease of understanding, and typographic legibility are obvious standards of usefulness in such a work. The occasional assembly of related data in tables and illustrations serves the additional purpose of grouping information under broad headings of reference or educative value.

Codification of knowledge is made increasingly difficult by the steadily broadening scope and mounting complexity of contemporary medical science. In this trying situation we believe that writers and editors constitute the first line of defense, particularly against erosion and adulteration of the language. We believe that editors should not be unmindful of the advisability of safeguarding the faithful transmission of ideas, by insuring the integrity of the words in which they are expressed. In furtherance of this purpose, we believe that the exercise of judgment is a legitimate activity of the compiler of a dictionary of scientific terms: to lend support to words properly compounded of properly derived stems, and to favor such terms over words which may bear the taint of ambiguity or even of illegitimacy.

The function of a dictionary must then be something more than that of a record of usage. It is our belief that maintenance of certain standards of etymological propriety and of selection is also a responsibility of the lexicographer—no less in the language of science than in that of imaginative or creative writing. Validity of formation of a word supplies its best assurance of intact passage across language barriers that are fast disappearing in medicine, as in other sciences. And the extensive usage of this Dictionary outside the United States makes us all the more aware of this responsibility.

Certain questions that arise in writing or editing may be entirely a matter of style, and their answers are not primarily to be established by recourse to a dictionary—such questions as that regarding hyphenation of a word, or whether, in instances not covered by official pronouncement, a word should be spelled with a diphthong. It would be impossible, except in unabridged volumes, to present every variation on such themes that might be completely acceptable and proper.

Within the framework of these principles, certain areas of information have received particular attention in this new edition. The greatest revision has been in the anatomical entries, with major overhauling of the definitions. This activity, under the supervision of Dr. C. Murphy Combs, Professor of Anatomy at Northwestern University Medical School, was assisted by

Dr. Carolyn E. Thomas, Assistant Professor of Anatomy, and Miss Hope C. Smith, research fellow in the department.

Consistent with the desire of most anatomists to achieve universal adoption of the new Nomina Anatomica, approved by the Sixth and Seventh International Congresses of Anatomists held in Paris in 1955, and New York in 1960, the definitions of the various anatomical structures are placed on the N A terms. Definitions are also placed on common terms which are more frequently encountered in clinical literature. Hence, elaboration is placed on both "stomach" and "ventriculus," "liver" and "hepar," "gallbladder" and "vesica fellea," "lung" and "pulmo," and on many other similar pairs of equivalent common and N A terms. Many common names for specific anatomical structures having circulation almost exclusively among anatomists are cross referred to the official terms, where the definitions appear.

Dr. L. R. C. Agnew, Professor of the History of Medicine at the University of Kansas, was responsible for revision of the entries on historical figures and concepts. Names of winners of Nobel prizes in medicine and physiology since publication of the last edition have been added.

Hundreds of drug names were added or deleted on the advice of Dr. Domingo M. Aviado, Associate Professor of Pharmacology at the University of Pennsylvania School of Medicine.

Dr. Jerome I. Brody, Assistant Professor of Medicine at the University of Pennsylvania Graduate School of Medicine, examined the terms relating to hematology, and Dr. William Burrows, Professor of Microbiology at the University of Chicago, again gave his excellent assistance in updating the microbiological nomenclature.

Dr. Maynard K. Hine, Dean of the Indiana University School of Dentistry, and members of his department accepted the task of going over dental terms. Indebtedness in this area is also acknowledged to the Glossary of Prosthodontic Terms, published by the C. V. Mosby Company and edited by The Nomenclature Committee of The Academy of Denture Prosthetics: Carl O. Boucher, Chairman, with Richard Kingery, LeRoy E. Kurth, Victor H. Sears, Vincent R. Trapozzano, Jack Werner, Arthur A. Frechette, and Daniel H. Gehl, all Doctors of Dental Surgery.

Terms relating to dermatology were the special object of the attention of Dr. Walter B. Shelley, Professor of Dermatology at the University of Pennsylvania School of Medicine.

Dr. Carl M. Gambill of the Section of Publications of Mayo Clinic was the greatest single source of information in clinical medicine, giving immeasurable help in other areas as well. Dr. Roy F. Butler, Professor of Classics at Baylor University, gave unstintingly of help on questions of etymology. Dr. Otto Glasser, Late Emeritus Consultant in Biophysics at Cleveland Clinic Foundation, was an unfailing source of help and encouragement.

In this complex endeavor, wisdom of selection, contemporaneity of definition, and accuracy of information would have been impossible without the dedicated help of those listed on the title page as Consultants and those included in the list of Contributors. Hundreds of others, not specifically named, have made valuable suggestions for the improvement of this book of words. To these persons, named and unnamed, we gratefully acknowledge our great debt for help beyond measure. This help can be repaid only insofar as we have succeeded in combining these separate threads of knowledge into a fabric useful and authoritative to all.

THE PUBLISHER

Contributors

FRANCIS HEED ADLER, M.D.
Emeritus Professor of Ophthalmology, University of Pennsylvania Medical School

LESLIE BRAINERD AREY, Ph.D., Sc.D., LL.D.
Robert Laughlin Rea Professor of Anatomy, Emeritus, Northwestern University

MURRAY L. BARR, M.Sc., M.D., LL.D., F.R.S.(C), F.R.C.P.(C)
Professor and Head, Department of Anatomy, Faculty of Medicine, University of Western Ontario

BARUCH S. BLUMBERG, M.D., Ph.D.
Associate Director for Clinical Research, The Institute for Cancer Research; Associate Professor of Medicine, The University of Pennsylvania

SIR MACFARLANE BURNET, M.D., F.R.S.
Director, Walter & Eliza Hall Institute of Medical Research, Melbourne, Australia

CHARLES JUSTIN BURSTONE, D.D.S., M.S.
Chairman, Department of Orthodontics, Indiana University School of Dentistry

THELMA CHAREN, M.A.
National Library of Medicine

H. O. J. COLLIER, B.A., Ph.D., F.I.Biol.
Director of Pharmacological Research, Parke, Davis & Company, Hounslow, Middlesex, England

ROSS M. COLVIN, B.A.
Librarian, C. J. Marshall Memorial Library, University of Pennsylvania School of Veterinary Medicine

BERNARD D. DAVIS, M.D.
Head, Department of Bacteriology and Immunology, Harvard Medical School

RICHARD V. ECK
Laboratory of Biology, National Cancer Institute

JAMES R. ECKMAN, M.A., Ph.D.
Section of Publications, Mayo Clinic

J. H. EDWARDS, M.R.C.P.
Senior Lecturer in Social Medicine, University of Birmingham

A. REBEKAH FISK, R.D.H., B.S., M.S.
Director of the Public Health Dental Hygiene Program, and Assistant Professor in Clinic, Indiana University School of Dentistry

BERNARD K. FORSCHER, Ph.D.
Section of Publications, Mayo Clinic

H. WILLIAM GILMORE, D.D.S., M.S.D.
Associate Professor and Chairman, Department of Operative Dentistry, Indiana University School of Dentistry

BRUCE W. HALSTEAD, M.D.
Director, World Life Research Institute, Colton, California

WEBB HAYMAKER, M.D.
Ames Research Center, Moffett Field, California

HARRY J. HEALEY, A.B., D.D.S., M.S.D.
Professor of Endodontics, Indiana University School of Dentistry

WERNER HEIDEL, M.D.
Section of Publications, Mayo Clinic

Robert D. Knapp, Jr., M.D.
Section of Publications, Mayo Clinic

Robert T. Lentz, B.S., M.S.(L.S.)
Librarian, Jefferson Medical College

W. B. McDaniel, 2d, Ph.D.
Curator of Historical Collections, Library of The College of Physicians of Philadelphia

Ralph E. McDonald, D.D.S., M.S.
Assistant Dean and Professor of Pedodontics, Indiana University School of Dentistry

Lawrence MacKenzie, B.A.

Paul D. MacLean, M.D.
Chief, Section on Limbic Integration and Behavior, Laboratory of Neurophysiology, National Institute of Mental Health

Henry Clinton Maguire, Jr., B.A., M.D.
Assistant Professor of Dermatology, University of Pennsylvania School of Medicine

Rolland J. Main, Ph.D.
Assistant Director, Department of Drugs, American Medical Association

Adam G. N. Moore, A.B., M.B., Ch.B.
Resident Physician, Aberdeen Royal Infirmary, Aberdeen, Scotland

Joseph C. Muhler, D.D.S., Ph.D.
Research Professor of Basic Sciences, Indiana University School of Dentistry

Elsie Murray, Ph.D.
Formerly Director of Color Research Laboratory, Department of Psychology, Cornell University, Ithaca, New York

Richard D. Norman, A.B., D.D.S., M.S.D.
Assistant Professor of Dental Materials, Indiana University School of Dentistry

Ronan O'Rahilly, M.S., M.D.
Professor and Director, Department of Anatomy, St. Louis University

Gerald T. Perkoff, M.D.
Chief, Unit I (Washington University) Medical Service, St. Louis City Hospital; Associate Professor of Medicine, Washington University School of Medicine

Ralph W. Phillips, M.S., D.Sc.
Research Professor of Dental Materials, Indiana University School of Dentistry

Ronald S. Ping, D.D.S.
Associate Professor and Acting Chairman, Department of Oral Surgery, Indiana University School of Dentistry

Oscar W. Richards, B.A., M.A., Ph.D.
Chief Biologist, American Optical Company

Jacob Robbins, M.D.
Chief, Clinical Endocrinology Branch, National Institute of Arthritis and Metabolic Diseases

Richard E. Rosenfield, M.D.
Attending Hematologist, The Mount Sinai Hospital; Hematologist, New York City Department of Health

Ernest H. Runyon, Ph.D.
Research Microbiologist, Veterans Administration, Salt Lake City

Frederick Sargent, II, S.B., M.D.
Professor of Physiology, Department of Physiology and Biophysics; Senior Staff Member for the Center for Zoonoses Research; Professorial Lecturer in Medicine in Department of Medicine, University of Illinois

Florence L. Schmidt, B.S.E.
Section of Publications, Mayo Clinic

William G. Shafer, B.S., D.D.S., M.S.
Professor and Chairman, Department of Oral Pathology, Indiana University School of Dentistry

Marc A. Shampo, M.S., Ph.D.
Section of Publications, Mayo Clinic

Hope C. Smith, B.A.
Research Fellow, Department of Anatomy, Northwestern University Medical School

M. Katharine Smith, B.A.
Section of Publications, Mayo Clinic

Harold F. Stimson, A.M., Ph.D.
Physicist, National Bureau of Standards, Retired

Henry M. Swenson, D.D.S.
Professor of Periodontics, Indiana University School of Dentistry

Carolyn E. Thomas, Ph.D.
Assistant Professor of Anatomy, Northwestern University Medical School

P. C. Trexler, B.S., M.S.
Gnotobiotic Research Foundation, North Wilmington, Massachusetts

Marshall R. Urist, M.D.
Associate Clinical Professor of Surgery (Orthopedics) and Director of Bone Research Laboratory, University of California

Grant Van Huysen, D.D.S.
Professor of Oral Anatomy, Indiana University School of Dentistry

C. J. Watson, M.D., Ph.D.
Distinguished Service Professor and Head, Department of Medicine, University of Minnesota

Thomas H. Weller, A.B., S.M., M.D., LL.D.
Richard Pearson Strong Professor of Tropical Public Health and Chairman of the Department, Harvard University School of Public Health

Guy Whitehead, M.A., Ph.D.
Section of Publications, Mayo Clinic

Ernest Witebsky, M.D.
Professor of Bacteriology and Immunology at the School of Medicine, State University of New York at Buffalo

A. V. Wolf, Ph.D.
Professor of Physiology and Head of the Department, University of Illinois College of Medicine

Irving S. Wright, M.D.
Professor of Clinical Medicine, Cornell University Medical College, New York City

Contents

NOTES ON USE OF THIS DICTIONARY xv

- Arrangement of Entries xv
- Sequence of Entries xvi
- Indication of Pronunciation xvi
- Presentation of Plural Forms xvii
- Etymology xviii
- Anatomical Entries xviii
- Abbreviations xix

FUNDAMENTALS OF MEDICAL ETYMOLOGY xxi

INDEX TO PLATES xxxvii

VOCABULARY 1–1724

- Naturally Occurring Amino Acids 15
- Cavity Angles 92
- Tooth Angles 93
- Chief Malaria-Carrying Anopheles Species of the World 99
- Table of Arteriae 134
- Chemical Elements 476
- Gram-Negative and Gram-Positive Bacteria 629
- Table of Ligamenta 825
- Endocardial Murmurs 951
- Table of Musculi 956
- Table of Nervi 995
- Positions of the Child in Utero in Various Presentations 1203
- Equivalents of Celsius (Centigrade) and Fahrenheit Temperature Scales 1346
- Important Poisonous Snakes of the World 1398
- Stains and Staining Methods 1432
- Tests 1518
- Table of Venae 1672
- Tables of Weights and Measures 1706
- Metric Doses with Approximate Apothecary Equivalents 1709

Notes on Use of This Dictionary

THE NEW USER of this Dictionary, we believe, will profit from an understanding of the policies that have been followed in its actual construction. This section is therefore presented to explain some of the mechanics which were involved in the compilation of the material.

It is our hope that a corollary of the conventional use of this Dictionary, to discover the spelling, meaning, and derivation of specific terms, will be assistance in the reverse direction—to aid in the creation of words desired to express new concepts. To this end individual elements—prefixes, suffixes, and stems—may be found both in the vocabulary portion and in the section entitled Fundamentals of Medical Etymology. An understanding of the elements of a term encountered for the first time, if the term is too new to be in any dictionary, will aid one in arriving at an approximation if not an exact distillation of its meaning. Similarly, knowledge of these elements and of the conventions governing their combination will be of help to a person seeking to construct a new word. We believe the serious user of the Dictionary will find familiarity with these features highly rewarding.

ARRANGEMENT OF ENTRIES

Quick simple usefulness continues to be one of the principal objectives of this work. Words appearing as main entries are recognizable at a glance, not being distorted by accents or other indication of syllabication. Accents and syllables are shown in the phonetic respelling immediately following the bold face entry. Subentries—terms consisting of two words which are ordinarily defined under the second (or principal) word, the *noun*—are immediately apparent as subentries, run on in the same paragraph, and set in the same bold face type as the word constituting the main entry. For example, acetic acid, acetrizoic acid, iopanoic acid, neuraminic acid, shikimic acid, and the like, are included as subentries under acid, regardless of the pH of the specific compounds. Absorption bands, Büngner's bands, Lane's band, Parham band are defined under band; Heinz-Ehrlich bodies, Howell-Jolly bodies, Leishman-Donovan bodies are defined under body.

The space-imposed practice of defining a term only once accounts for the cross references necessitated on eponymic terms where biographical information is given. Thus you will find such entries as "Apgar score . . . See under *score*" and "Aran's cancer, law . . . See under *cancer* and *law*." When the entry combines several terms, the words under which the definitions appear are not separately specified: the instruction instead is to "See under the nouns." Thus "Huguier's canal, circle, disease, glands . . . See under the nouns" directs the reader to look within the subentries under canal, circle, disease, and gland, respectively, for definition of the term desired. An exception to this policy of arrangement occurs in the case of specific chemical terms embodying the name of the element: aluminum acetate, aluminum hydroxide, aluminum sulfate, and the like are defined under aluminum; calcium carbonate, calcium oxide, calcium sulfate under calcium.

If biographical information is not given for an individual named in an eponymic term, such as Kortzeborn's operation, the definition should be sought directly under the noun, in this case under operation. For certain phrases, because of prevalent multiplicity of terminology, it may be necessary to look in more than one place. For example, what one man may speak of as a disease may originally have been called a syndrome; if the desired term does not appear under one, it should be sought under the alternative term. Similarly for phenomenon and sign, and numerous other entities.

SEQUENCE OF ENTRIES

Entries will be found alphabetized on the sequence of the letters, regardless of space or hyphens which may occur between them. Thus sequences such as

bitemporal,	or	serum,
bite-rim,		serumal,
biterminal,		serum-fast,
bite-wing		serum identical

appear in that order. An exception to this occurs in the case of compound eponymic terms: Bard-Pic's syndrome precedes Bardach's test. In eponymic terms, the apostrophe s ('s) is ignored in determining the alphabetical sequence, thus *Hahn's cannula* precedes *hahnemannian*, *Sabouraud's agar* precedes *Sabouraudia*, and *Förster's operation* precedes *Förster-Penfield operation*, both as a main entry and under operation. Similarly umlauts (ö, ü) are ignored in alphabetizing the entries, and *Löwenthal's reaction*, *Lower's rings*, *Löwi's reaction*, *Löwitt's bodies*, and *Lowman balance board* appear in that sequence. Proper names beginning with "Mc" or "Mac" are alphabetized as though spelled "mac" in every instance, the sequence being determined by the letters immediately following the *c*.

Proper names (or capitalized entries) commonly appear before a common noun (or lower case entry) with the identical spelling. Thus *Diplococcus* precedes *diplococcus*, *Micrococcus* precedes *micrococcus*.

INDICATION OF PRONUNCIATION

As in the twenty-three preceding editions, phonetic respelling of a term appears in parentheses immediately following the main bold face entry. As a rule only the most commonly heard pronunciation is given, with no effort to represent any variants. Such phonetic respelling is presented in the simplest possible manner, with a minimum of diacritical markings. The basic rule is this: An unmarked vowel ending a syllable is long; an unmarked vowel in a syllable ending with a consonant is short. By this same token, a long vowel in a syllable which must end with a consonant is indicated by a macron (ā, ē, ī, ō, ū, and o͞o): for example ah-bāt′, lēd, la′bīl, mi′o-fōn, mol′e-kūl, to͞oth. A short vowel ending or alone constituting a syllable is usually indicated by use of the breve (ĕ, ĭ, ŏ, ŭ, o͝o): for example ĕ-fish′ent, ĭ-mu′nĭ-te, ŏ-kloo′zhun. However, such vowels constituting an unaccented syllable following a syllable which bears a major accent may appear without the breve, as in jen′e-sis, ther-mom′e-ter, and the like.

The use of the syllable *ah* for the sound of *a* in open, unaccented syllables (ah-bāt′, ah-lu′mĭ-num, ah-pof′ĭ-sis, ah-tak′se-ah) has been continued;

ah is also used in syllables ending with a consonant, to indicate a broader *a* sound (fahr′mah-se, in contrast to am-ne′se-ah). No effort has been made to complicate the system by introduction of additional diacritical marks showing the finer gradations of sound, such as the circumflex (â, ô), diaeresis (ä, ü), tilde (ẽ). The primary (′) and secondary (″) accents are indicated in polysyllabic words (as pol″e-sĭ-lab′ik); an unstressed syllable is followed by a hyphen.

To recapitulate, unmarked vowels not followed by a consonant have the long sound:

ba, da, ka, la, ma, na, etc., are all pronounced to rhyme with *fay* (bāt, kām, mān, etc., have the same vowel sound).
be, de, le, re, te, we, etc., are all pronounced to rhyme with *fee* (bēm, dēp, rēt, etc., have the same vowel sound).
bi, di, ni, pi, ti, zi, etc., are all pronounced to rhyme with *sigh* (bīd, pīnt, tīm, etc., have the same vowel sound).
bo, do, lo, mo, to, wo, etc., are all pronounced to rhyme with *go* (bōd, lōm, tōt, etc., have the same vowel sound).
bu, du, hu, mu, nu, su, etc., are all pronounced to rhyme with *few* (kūt, mūt, etc., have the same vowel sound).

Short vowels terminating syllables are affected by the value or the consonantal sounds of the adjoining syllables. For example, as usually pronounced, the sound of *i* in the second syllable more closely approaches that of long *e* in mult*i*articular than it does in mult*i*gravida, although in either word it may show any gradation between the long *e* and an indeterminate vowel sound. Combinations of vowels are also indicated: *oi* as in oil; *ou* as in out; *aw* as in paw.

It has been impossible, within the framework of this simplified system, to represent the exact pronunciation of many foreign words and proper names which have entered the medical vocabulary. They have been represented as well as possible by an English approximation.

The important key to remember in interpreting the phonetic respelling is that an unmarked vowel not followed by a consonant has the long value; one followed by a consonant has the short. A long vowel which must perforce be followed by a consonant is indicated by use of the macron; a short vowel ending its respective syllable is indicated by use of the breve.

PRESENTATION OF PLURAL FORMS

The plural of a word which is irregularly formed or of a foreign word is given following the phonetic respelling and often, but not invariably, is given a separate bold face listing in proper alphabetical order. Alternate plurals (e.g., exanthemas, exanthemata) are frequently shown. Subentries appear in proper alphabetical order, determined by the subsequent, modifying word or phrases, regardless of whether they are singular or plural. For example, under *ligamentum*, the entries

l. annulare baseos stapedis
ligamenta annularia digitorum manus
ligamenta annularia digitorum pedis
l. annulare radii
ligamenta annularia (trachealia)

appear in that order.

ETYMOLOGY

Information on the derivation of a word appears in square brackets following the phonetic respelling, or following the plural form of the word, when that is given. Greek characters are no longer used in presentation of the etymological information in the vocabulary portion of this book,* being transliterated into the English alphabet as shown in the following tabulation:

	Greek		English
	α	=	a
initial	ἀ	=	a
"	ἁ	=	ha
diphthong	αι	=	ai
initial	αἰ	=	ai
"	αἱ	=	hai
diphthong	αυ	=	au
initial	αὐ	=	au
"	αὑ	=	hau
	β	=	b
	γ	=	g
	γγ	=	ng [as in "angeion"]
	γκ	=	nk [as in "ankyle"]
	γξ	=	nx [as in "salpinx"]
	γχ	=	nch [as in "anchousa"]
	δ	=	d
	ε	=	e
initial	ἐ	=	e
"	ἑ	=	he
diphthong	ει	=	ei
initial	εἰ	=	ei
"	εἱ	=	hei
diphthong	ευ	=	eu
initial	εὐ	=	eu
"	εὑ	=	heu
	ζ	=	z
	η	=	ē
initial	ἠ	=	ē
"	ἡ	=	hē
	θ	=	th
	ι	=	i
initial	ἰ	=	i
"	ἱ	=	hi
	κ	=	k

	Greek		English
	λ	=	l
	μ	=	m
	ν	=	n
	ξ	=	x
	ο	=	o
initial	ὀ	=	o
"	ὁ	=	ho
diphthong	οι	=	oi
initial	οἰ	=	oi
"	οἱ	=	hoi
diphthong	ου	=	ou
initial	οὐ	=	ou
"	οὑ	=	hou
	π	=	p
	ρ	=	r
initial	ῥ	=	rh
	ρρ	=	rrh [used in compounds, although the root has only initial rh, e.g. diarrhoia—(English) diarrhea]
	σ, ς	=	s
	τ	=	t
	υ	=	y
[initial	ὐ		does not occur]
"	ὑ	=	hy
diphthong	υι	=	ui
initial	υἱ	=	hui
	φ	=	ph
	χ	=	ch
	ψ	=	ps
	ω	=	ō
initial	ὠ	=	ō
"	ὡ	=	hō

The original words from which the terms presented in this dictionary are derived are reproduced in italic, the language of their origin being indicated by one of the following abbreviations:

Ar.	= Arabic
A.S.	= Anglo-Saxon
Dan.	= Danish
Fin.	= Finnish
Fr.	= French
Ger.	= German
Gr.	= Greek
Hind.	= Hindu
It.	= Italian
Jap.	= Japanese
L.	= Latin
Mex.	= Mexican
Peruv.	= Peruvian
Port.	= Portuguese
Russ.	= Russian
Sp.	= Spanish

As a guide to related vocabulary, especially on anatomical terms, the main entry may be followed in brackets by its Latin and/or Greek equivalent, such as "liver [L. *jecur;* Gr. *hepar*]" and "kidney [L. *ren;* Gr. *nephros*]."

ANATOMICAL ENTRIES

Because the major revision in this edition has been in the anatomical vocabulary, it may be well to repeat here the principles that have governed that activity. A definition (as opposed to a cross reference) appears on every

* The Greek characters do appear, however, in the section entitled Fundamentals of Medical Etymology (pp. xxi—xxxvi).

term official in the Nomina Anatomica as approved by the International Anatomical Nomenclature Committee appointed by the Fifth International Congress of Anatomists held at Oxford in 1950, and approved by the Sixth and Seventh International Congresses of Anatomists, held in Paris, 1955 and New York, 1960. Such terms, when unchanged from the Basle Nomina Anatomica, are indicated "[N A, B N A]." BNA terms which have been changed in the new nomenclature are listed but not defined: there is simply reference to the NA term. Definitions are also placed on the common names by which various structures are universally referred to in clinical medicine, such as gallbladder, heart, kidney, liver, lung, and stomach. Other common names are cross referred to the official names. Thus the reader will find on the anglicized common names of anatomical structures, as those under artery, ligament, muscle, nerve, and vein, a cross reference to the official name of the specific structure. The complete descriptions, in these particular instances, are given in the tables of arteriae, ligamenta, musculi, nervi, and venae.

On many entries in this Dictionary (unrelated as well as related to anatomy) the "definition" will be found to consist of only a single word or phrase, to which the reader should turn to find elaboration of the meaning. Such practice is followed for earlier terms which have been supplanted in the vocabulary, without further indication being given of their obsolescence, as well as for terms which are currently used with the same meaning as the word referred to. In some of these instances the shade of preference for the term on which the definition is placed may be slight, or even denied by some persons. In such cases the policy has been adhered to as a means of keeping down the size of the Dictionary by avoiding duplication or possibly even triplication of definitions.

ABBREVIATIONS

Numerous abbreviations have been employed in the vocabulary portion of this book. They include:

a.	artery (L. *arteria*)
ant.	anterior
C.	cervical
ca.	about (L. *circa*)
cf.	compare (L. *confer*)
Coc.	coccygeal
def.	definition
dim.	diminutive
inf.	inferior
L.	lumbar
lat.	lateral
lt.	left
m.	muscle (L. *musculus*)
med.	medial, median
n.	nerve (L. *nervus*)
pl.	plural
q.v.	which see (L. *quod vide*)
rt.	right
S.	sacral
sing.	singular
sup.	superior
Th.	thoracic

Fundamentals of Medical Etymology

By Lloyd W. Daly, A.M., Ph.D., Litt.D.
Allen Memorial Professor of Greek, University of Pennsylvania

The very size of current medical dictionaries is evidence of the massive proportions which the medical, scientific, and technical vocabulary has attained within the English language. As this vocabulary grows, its mastery by each succeeding generation becomes increasingly difficult. It is popularly believed that the study of Latin at least, if not also of Greek, is prerequisite for the study of medicine. Although this is no longer literally true, the composition of the medical vocabulary makes it evident why such study was formerly considered necessary. At least fifty per cent of the general English vocabulary is of Greek and Latin derivation, and it is a conservative estimate that as much as seventy-five per cent of the scientific element is of such origin.

Some familiarity with these two languages which contribute so largely to the terminology must obviously simplify the task of learning a basic vocabulary and of comprehending new words as they are encountered. Experience shows that it does. However, since it no longer seems economical to learn to read the two languages for this purpose, some short cut to the necessary information is needed, and again experience has shown that certain fundamentals of vocabulary and linguistic principle can easily be mastered and are of great assistance. The purpose of the present introduction is to present those fundamentals in as practical and concise a form as possible; any statements in the following pages which are contrary to historical linguistic fact are made deliberately, in keeping with this purpose.

GREEK

Alphabet and transcription

The Latin alphabet as we use it is derived, with slight modifications, from the Greek alphabet, which is almost completely phonetic. The table (p. xxii) shows as nearly as possible the sound equivalent of each letter in terms of our own alphabet, the names of the letters, and their transcribed equivalents in English. The first syllable of the name of each letter, properly pronounced, also gives its sound equivalent.

Greek words are written with an accent (θέσις, φῦλον); for present purposes, the two kinds of accent mark may be regarded simply as indicating the syllable on which the stress of accent is placed. Words beginning with a vowel, diphthong, or *rho* (ρ) are written with a breathing mark over the initial vowel or *rho*, or over the second vowel of the diphthong (ἄλλος, ῥυθμός, αὐτός). The so-called rough breathing mark (῾) indicates that the syllable over which it is placed should be initiated in pronunciation with an *h* sound, and words beginning with such a sound are usually transcribed into English with an initial *h*. Rarely they may appear with or without the *h*.* The smooth breathing mark (᾿) has no effect on pronunciation.

* For example, in the Analytical Word List, following, compare -em- and hem(at)-, -aph- and hapt-, -elc- and helc-; such forms without the *h* rarely appear as the initial element of a compound.

Capital	Small Letter	Sound	Name	Transcription
Α	α	*a*ha	alpha	a
Β	β	*b*et	beta	b
Γ	γ	*g*et	gamma	g
Δ	δ	*d*o	delta	d
Ε	ε	*e*gg	epsilon	e
Ζ	ζ	a*dz*e	zeta	z
Η	η	f*ê*te	eta	ē
Θ	θ	*th*in	theta	th
Ι	ι	*i*t / mach*i*ne	iota	i
Κ	κ	*k*ey	kappa	k
Λ	λ	*l*et	lambda	l
Μ	μ	*m*et	mu	m
Ν	ν	*n*et	nu	n
Ξ	ξ	he*x*	xi	x
Ο	ο	*o*ho	omicron	o
Π	π	*p*et	pi	p
Ρ	ρ	r (trilled)	rho	r
Σ	σ, ς*	*s*et	sigma	s
Τ	τ	*t*ell	tau	t
Υ	υ	ü (German)	upsilon	y
Φ	φ	*ph*oto	phi	ph
Χ	χ	a*ch* (German)	chi	ch
Ψ	ψ	ti*ps*	psi	ps
Ω	ω	*o*ho	omega	ō

* Sigma is written σ at the beginning or in the middle of a word and ς at the end of a word. E.g., σύνδεσις.

The vowels are α, ε, η, ι, ο, υ, and ω, which may be combined to give the diphthongs shown in the listing below. The letter *iota* (ι) may also be written as a subscript (ᾳ, ῃ, ῳ), but as such it has no effect on pronunciation.

Diphthong	Sound	Transcription
αι	*ai*sle	ae, e, or ai
αυ	*ou*t	au
ει	*ei*ght	i, e, or ei
ευ	*eh-oo*	eu
οι	*oi*l	oe or e
ου	gh*ou*l	ou or u
υι	q*ui*t	ui

Words are transcribed from Greek into our own alphabet as indicated in the foregoing tables, with the following exceptions: *Gamma* (γ) before *gamma* (γ), *kappa* (κ), *chi* (χ), or *xi* (ξ) is nasal and so is transcribed as *n*. Initial *rho* (ῥ) is transcribed as *rh*, and double *rho* (ρρ) as *rrh*. *Upsilon* (υ) is transcribed as *y* except in diphthongs, where it is reproduced by *u*, as indicated in the table.

Many Greek words have come into English through Latin, in which they have undergone some change (Greek στέρνον, Latin *sternum*), or through a second intermediary language, such as French, with still further change (Greek χειρουργία, Latin *chirurgia*, French *cirurgerie*, English *surgery*). Such evolution explains many of the apparent peculiarities of Greek words in English. Other changes are accounted for by our tendency to drop inflectional terminations which indicate grammatical function in Greek but have no function in English (σπέρμα, sperm), or to simplify the termination (γονοφόρος, gonophore).

Combining forms The most constant change, however, in the transition of Greek words to English, is the loss of termination which produces what we may call the *combining form.* This combining form, which is used when the word enters into a compound with another word, may differ markedly from the *lexical form,* under which the word would be located in a dictionary of the Greek language.

For most nouns (those ending in -η, -α, -ος, -ον), the combining form may be derived by dropping the termination from the lexical form. For another large class the combining form must be derived from a secondary form of the word (indicated in parentheses in the following table) by dropping the ending -ος. For most words ending in -ις only ς need be dropped. In some instances, as in terms derived from the words for blood (hemat-) and body (somat-), different combining forms are used, derived from either the lexical or the secondary form. Adjectives are similar in formation to nouns. For those ending in -υς only the ς need be dropped.

LEXICAL FORM	COMBINING FORM	ENGLISH
ἀρχή	ἀρχ-	*arch*enteron
ἰδέα	ἰδε-	*ide*ology
τόπος	τοπ-	*top*esthesia
ὀστέον	ὀστε-	*oste*otome
βάσις	βασι-	*basi*cranial
μῦς (μυός)	μυ-	*my*ectomy
αἷμα (αἵματος)	αἱμ-, αἱματ-	*hem*angioma, *hemat*ophyte
παῖς (παιδός)	παιδ-	*ped*iatrics

For verbs the combining form may be derived from several of the six principal parts, which may show a variable vowel just as English verbs do (sing, sang, sung). Thus the verb meaning *to stretch* has the forms τείνω and τέτακα, and English words may be derived from either, e.g. *tein*oscope, ec*tas*is. In most cases, however, the combining form may be derived from the lexical form ending in -ω, -μαι, or -μι, or from the infinitive form ending in -ειν, -αν, -ουν, -σθαι, or -ναι, the latter being the form often cited in the etymology given in dictionaries. The commonest vowel variation is from ϵ to ο, as in the verb τρέφω, which frequently shows the combining form τροφ-, as in a*trophy*.

Compounds Most derivatives are composed not of single Greek words but of a combination of two or more words or word elements. Thus the word *osteotome* is composed of the noun ὀστέον (oste) plus τέμνω (tom). When the second member of the compound begins with a consonant, as in this instance, a connective *o* is usually inserted between the two members to facilitate pronunciation.

Prefixes Many compounds consist of a word preceded by a prefix, commonly a preposition. As shown in the table, most of these prepositions have a final vowel, which is dropped when the word to which it is affixed begins with a vowel, the prefix περί (peri-) being an exception. A final consonant may also be changed as indicated, to accommodate it to a succeeding initial consonant. The negative prefix ἀν- before a vowel (*an*omaly) must not be confused with the preposition ἀνά with the final vowel dropped (*an*ode).

PREPOSITION	COMBINING FORMS	ENGLISH
ἀμφί	ἀμφι-	*amphi*crania
	ἀμφ-	*amph*eclexis
ἀνά	ἀνα-	*ana*bolism
	ἀν-	*an*ode
ἀντί	ἀντι-	*anti*gen
	ἀντ-	*ant*helminthic
ἀπό	ἀπο-	*apo*physis
	ἀπ-	*ap*andria
διά	δια-	*dia*thermy
	δι-	*di*uretic
ἐκ	ἐκ-	*ec*topia
ἐξ	ἐξ-	*ex*osmosis
ἐν	ἐν-	*en*ostosis
	ἐμ-	*em*bolus
ἐπί	ἐπι-	*epi*nephrin
	ἐπ-	*ep*arterial
κατά	κατα-	*cata*lepsy
	κατ-	*cat*ion
μετά	μετα-	*meta*morphosis
	μετ-	*met*encephalon
παρά	παρα-	*para*mastoid
	παρ-	*par*otid
περί	περι-	*peri*toneum
πρό	προ-	*pro*gnosis
σύν	συν-	*syn*thesis
	συμ-	*sym*physis
	συλ-	*syl*lepsis
	συ-	*sy*stole
ὑπέρ	ὑπερ-	*hyper*trophy
ὑπό	ὑπο-	*hypo*dermic
	ὑπ-	*hyp*axial

Suffixes Suffixes, which constitute a third element in the formation of compounds, are added directly to the combining forms of words without insertion of a connective *o*, but when the result would be a combination of consonants difficult to pronounce, certain euphonic changes are made in the final consonant of the combining form. The combinations shown

CONSONANT CHANGES	ENGLISH
β or $\varphi + \tau = \pi\tau$	epile*pt*ic
γ or $\chi + \tau = \kappa\tau$	ta*ct*ic
δ or $\theta + \tau = \sigma\tau$	schi*st*
π, β or $\varphi + \mu = \mu\mu$	le*mm*a
κ, γ or $\chi + \mu = \gamma\mu$	paradi*gm*
τ, δ or $\theta + \mu = \sigma\mu$	pla*sm*a
π, β or $\varphi + \sigma = \psi$	auto*ps*y
κ, γ or $\chi + \sigma = \xi$	cache*x*ia
τ, δ or $\theta + \sigma = \sigma$	do*s*e

in the table represent the results of the addition of those suffixes which are the commonest in the vocabulary. The suffixes -τηs (*-t*), -τηρ (*-ter*), -σις (*-sis*), -σια (*-sia* or *-sy*), -μος (*-m*), -μα (*-ma* or *-m*) are usually added to verbal combining forms to produce nouns; -τος (*-t*, *-te*) and -τικος (*-tic*) are added to verbal combining forms to produce adjectives or nouns; -ιζω (*-ize*) is added to noun or adjective combining forms to produce verbs; -ια (*-ia* or *-y*) is added to noun or verb combining forms to produce nouns; -ιτις (*-itis*) and -κος or -ικος (*-c* or *-ic*) are added to noun combining forms to produce nouns or adjectives. The following examples illustrate such compounding and indicate some of the possibilities of adding one suffix to another. It should be noted that nouns ending with the suffix -μα have a combining form ending in -ματ- and that verbs ending with the suffix -ιζω have a combining form ending in -ιδ-.

GREEK COMPONENTS	ENGLISH
ὀστέον + κλάω + -της	osteocla*st*
σφίγγω + -τηρ	sphinc*ter*
ἐμέω + -σις	eme*sis*
κινέω + -σια	cine*sia*
ἐπί + λαμβάνω + -σια	epilep*sy*
σπάω + -μος	spas*m*
καρκινόω + -μα	carcino*ma*
ὁράω + -τος + μέτρον	op*t*ometer
ζυγόω + -τος	zygo*te*
ἵστημι + -τικος	sta*tic*
κρύσταλλος + -ιζω	crystall*ize*
μαίνω + -ια	man*ia*
νεῦρον + γράφω + -ια	neurograph*y*
οὖς + -ιτις	ot*itis*
κόλον + -ικος	col*ic*
φύσις + -κος	physi*c*
ἄρθρον + -ιτις + -κος	arthr*itic*
συμπίπτω + -μα + -ικος	sympto*matic*
κρέας + φαγεῖν + -ιζω + -μος	creophag*ism*
φύω + -σις + -κος + -ιζω + -της	phy*sicist*

In the formation of compounds English follows natural tendencies of the Greek language but often goes far beyond the actual Greek vocabulary. For example, there is no such Greek verb as φυσικίζω nor even such an English verb as *physicize*, yet the word physicist is formed as though there were, on the analogy of such verbs as *stigmatize*, which actually have Greek counterparts. In a similar manner, the need for new terms is met by coining new words composed of prefixes, combining forms, and suffixes, on the basis of analogy.

LATIN

A high percentage of medical terms is of Latin origin, but a good proportion of this element, being in the form of anatomical nomenclature, is original Latin and not derivative. The purpose of this introduction is to explain derivatives, words which have undergone some change in the transfer to English. For original Latin words the reader may refer to the body of the dictionary.

Alphabet The Latin alphabet is a modification of the Greek which has been adopted for English with the addition of the characters *J*, *U*, and *W*, which were developed during the Middle Ages. The ease with which the Romans adapted the Greek alphabet is evidence of the close relationship of the two languages.

The inflectional terminations of Latin words, as of Greek, tend to be modified or to be dropped in English. Thus *nervus* becomes nerve, *spina* becomes spine, *penicillum* becomes pencil, and *oleum* appears usually as -ol. However, Latin terminations are more frequently tolerated than those of Greek, and are adopted into English, as occurred with the terms *fetus*, *rectum*, *pelvis*, and *vagina*.

Combining forms Combining forms of Latin words, as of Greek, are derived by dropping an inflectional termination. Thus for most nouns ending in *-a*, *-us*, or *-um*, this ending must be dropped from the lexical form, whereas for others *-is* must be dropped from a secondary form (indicated in parentheses in the table).

Lexical Form	Combining Form	English
retina	*retin-*	*retin*opapillitis
bulbus	*bulb-*	*bulb*iform
ovum	*ov-*	*ov*iduct
frons (*frontis*)	*front-*	*front*oparietal
cortex (*corticis*)	*cortic-*	*cortic*ipetal

Adjectives follow these same patterns. The comparative form, ending in *-ior*, frequently appears in English without change, as in *inferior*.

The lexical forms of all regular Latin verbs end in either *-o* or *-or*, but the forms most commonly used in English derivatives are the participles, or verbal adjectives, present and past. Whereas the English present participle ends in *-ing*, the combining form of the Latin ends in *-nt* preceded by a vowel, either *a* or *e*. Whereas the English past participle usually ends in *-ed* or *-en*, the combining form of the Latin regularly ends in *-t* or *-s*, which may be preceded by a vowel, either *a* or *i*. The *-us* termination of these past participles is regularly modified to an *e*, thus producing the common English ending *-ate*.

Lexical Form	English (From Pres. Part.)	English (From Past Part.)
consulto	*consultant*	*consultat*ion
aperio	*aperient*	*apert*ure
nutrio	*nutrient*	*nutrit*ive
sentio	*sentient*	*sens*ory

Use of the past participial form ending in *-atus* is greatly extended in English by the formation of numerous derivatives, including not only such verbs as rotate, from the Latin verb *roto* but also, by analogy, such verbs as aerate, although there is no such Latin verb as *aero*.

Compounds In the formation of compound derivatives from Latin words a combining form is linked to the following element by what may be called, regardless of its origin, a connective vowel. This vowel is most commonly either *o* (lumb*o*costal, genit*o*urinary) or *i* (nerv*i*motor, bil*i*rubin), or less frequently *u* (gran*u*lation).

Prefixes As in Greek, most of the prefixes in Latin are prepositions. Most of these may be added to other words without change, but some of those which end in a consonant assimilate this consonant to the initial sound of the word to which it is affixed.

Consonant Changes		English
ad-	before *c* becomes *ac-*	*ac*celerate
ad-	before *f* becomes *af-*	*af*finity
ad-	before *g* becomes *ag-*	*ag*glutinant
ad-	before *p* becomes *ap-*	*ap*pendix
ad-	before *s* becomes *as-*	*as*similate
ad-	before *t* becomes *at-*	*at*trition
ex-	before *f* becomes *ef-*	*ef*fusion
in-	before *l* becomes *il-*	*il*linition
in-	before *m* becomes *im-*	*im*mersion
in-	before *r* becomes *ir-*	*ir*radiation
ob-	before *c* becomes *oc-*	*oc*clusion
sub-	before *f* becomes *suf-*	*suf*focate
sub-	before *p* becomes *sup-*	*sup*pository
trans-	before *s* becomes *tran-*	*tran*spiration

The addition of a prefix may also affect the following word by changing its characteristic vowel; thus *ob* + *caput* becomes *occiput*, and *in* + *iactus* becomes *inject*.

Suffixes The commonest Latin suffixes used in forming nouns are: *-arium*, *-orium* (-ary, -ory), *-io* (-ion added to past participles), *-or* (-or added to past participles), and *-tas* (-ty). Those used in forming adjectives are: *-abilis*, *-ibilis* (-able, -ible), *-alis*, *-ilis* (-al, -ile), *-aris* (-ar), *-arius*, *-orius* (-ary, -ory), *-atus* (-ate), *-idus* (-id), *-ivus* (-ive), and *-osus* (-ous or -ose).

LATIN COMPONENTS	ENGLISH
avis + *-arium*	avi*ary*
dormio (*dormitus*) + *-orium*	dormit*ory*
nutrio (*nutritus*) + *-io*	nutrit*ion*
moveo (*motus*) + *-or*	mot*or*
porosus + *-tas*	poros*ity*
frio + *-abilis*	fri*able*
edo + *-ibilis*	ed*ible*
corpus (*corporis*) + *-alis*	corpor*al*
febris + *-ilis*	febr*ile*
oculus + *-aris*	ocul*ar*
cilium + *-arius*	cili*ary*
sensus + *-orius*	sens*ory*
reticulum + *-atus*	reticul*ate*
morbus + *-idus*	morb*id*
aborior (*abortus*) + *-ivus*	abort*ive*
squama + *-osus*	squam*ous*
adeps (*adipis*) + *-osus*	adip*ose*
prae + *caveo* (*cautus*) + *-io* + *-arius*	precaut*ionary*

HYBRID TERMS

The examples hitherto cited have been purely Greek or purely Latin, but elements from the two languages are often combined in one compound word, which is called a hybrid. A prefix from one language may be added to a word from the other (*de* + ὕδωρ + *-atus* = dehydrate), or a Greek and a Latin word may be combined (δόλιχος + *facialis* = dolichofacial). However, the most productive source of such hybrids is the addition of a Latin suffix to a Greek word (κρανίον + *-alis* = cranial) or vice versa (*cerebellum* + -ιτις = cerebellitis).

ANALYTICAL WORD LIST

The following list includes those Greek and Latin words which an actual count* shows occur most frequently in the vocabulary of this dictionary, arranged alphabetically under their English combining forms as rubrics. The dash appended to a combining form indicates that it is not a complete word and, if the dash precedes the combining form, that it commonly appears as the terminal element of a compound. Infrequently a combining form is both preceded and followed by a dash, showing that it usually appears between two other elements. Closely related forms are shown in one entry by the use of parentheses: thus carbo(n)-, showing it may be either carbo-, as in *carbo*hydrate, or carbon-, as in *carbon*uria.

* For the count upon which the selection was based, thanks are due to my wife, Bernadine A. Daly, whose expert work will, I am sure, greatly increase the practical usefulness of the list.

Following each combining form the first item of information is the Greek or Latin word from which it is derived. Those words which are not printed in Greek characters are Latin. Occasionally both a Greek and a Latin word are given. Presence of a dash before or after such an element indicates that it does not occur as an independent word in the original language. Information necessary to the understanding of the form appears next in parentheses. Then the meaning or meanings of the word are given, followed where appropriate by reference to a synonymous combining form in the other language, that is, on a combining form of Latin derivation, to the synonymous form of Greek derivation, and vice versa. Finally, an example is given to illustrate use of the combining form in a compound English derivative.

If this list is used in close conjunction with the etymological information given in the body of the dictionary, no confusion should be caused by the similarity of elements in such words as *mel*algia, *mel*ancholia, and *mel*icera, where the similarity is only apparent and the derivation of each word is different.

a- — α- (*n* is added before words beginning with a vowel) negative prefix. Cf. in-[3]. *a*metria
ab- — *ab* away from. Cf. apo-. *ab*ducent
abdomin- — *abdomen, abdominis*. *abdomi*noscopy
ac- — See ad-. *ac*cretion
acet- — *acetum* vinegar. *acet*ometer
acid- — *acidus* sour. *acid*uric
acou- — ἀκούω hear. *acou*esthesia. (Also spelled acu-)
acr- — ἄκρον extremity, peak. *acro*megaly
act- — *ago, actus* do, drive, act. re*action*
actin- — ἀκτίς, ἀκτῖνος ray, radius. Cf. radi-. *actin*ogenesis
acu- — See acou-. osteo*acu*sis
ad- — *ad* (*d* changes to *c*, *f*, *g*, *p*, *s*, or *t* before words beginning with those consonants) to. *ad*renal
aden- — ἀδήν gland. Cf. gland-. *ade*noma
adip- — *adeps, adipis* fat. Cf. lip- and stear-. *adip*ocellular
aer- — ἀήρ air. an*aer*obiosis
aesthe- — See esthe-. *aesthe*sioneurosis
af- — See ad-. *af*ferent
ag- — See ad-. *ag*glutinant
-agogue — ἀγωγός leading, inducing. galact*agogue*
-agra — ἄγρα catching, seizure. pod*agra*
alb- — *albus* white. Cf. leuk-. *albo*cinereous
alg- — ἄλγος pain. neur*alg*ia
all- — ἄλλος other, different. *all*ergy
alve- — *alveus* trough, channel, cavity. *alve*olar
amph- — See amphi-. *amph*eclexis
amphi- — ἀμφί (*i* is dropped before words beginning with a vowel) both, doubly. *amphi*celous
amyl- — ἄμυλον starch. *amyl*osynthesis
an-[1] — See ana-. *an*agogic
an-[2] — See a-. *an*omalous
ana- — ἀνά (final *a* is dropped before words beginning with a vowel) up, positive. *ana*phoresis
ancyl- — See ankyl-. *ancyl*ostomiasis
andr- — ἀνήρ, ἀνδρός man. gyn*andr*oid
angi- — ἀγγεῖον vessel. Cf. vas-. *angi*emphraxis
ankyl- — ἀγκύλος crooked, looped. *anky*lodactylia. (Also spelled ancyl-)
ant- — See anti-. *ant*ophthalmic
ante- — *ante* before. *ante*flexion
anti- — ἀντί (*i* is dropped before words beginning with a vowel) against, counter. Cf. contra-. *anti*pyogenic
antr- — ἄντρον cavern. *antr*odynia
ap-[1] — See apo-. *ap*heter
ap-[2] — See ad-. *ap*pend
-aph- — ἅπτω, ἀφ- touch. dys*aph*ia. (See also hapt-)
apo- — ἀπό (*o* is dropped before words beginning with a vowel) away from, detached. Cf. ab-. *apo*physis
arachn- — ἀράχνη spider. *arachn*odactyly
arch- — ἀρχή beginning, origin. *arch*enteron
arter(i)- — ἀρτηρία elevator (?), artery. *arteri*osclerosis, peri*arter*itis
arthr- — ἄρθρον joint. Cf. articul-. syn*arthr*osis
articul- — *articulus* joint. Cf. arthr-. dis*articul*ation
as- — See ad-. *as*similation
at- — See ad-. *at*trition
aur- — *auris* ear. Cf. ot-. *aur*inasal
aux- — αὔξω increase. enter*auxe*
ax- — ἄξων or *axis* axis. *ax*ofugal
axon- — ἄξων axis. *axon*ometer

ba-	βαίνω, βα- go, walk, stand. hypno*bat*ia
bacill-	*bacillus* small staff, rod. Cf. bacter-. actino*bacill*osis
bacter-	βακτήριον small staff, rod. Cf. bacill-. *bacter*iophage
ball-	βάλλω, βολ- throw. *ball*istics. (See also bol-)
bar-	βάρος weight. pedo*bar*ometer
bi-[1]	βίος life. Cf. vit-. aero*bic*
bi-[2]	*bi-* two (see also di-[1]). *bi*lobate
bil-	*bilis* bile. Cf. chol-. *bil*iary
blast-	βλαστός bud, child, a growing thing in its early stages. Cf. germ-. *blast*oma, zygoto*blast*.
blep-	βλέπω look, see. hemia*bleps*ia
blephar-	βλέφαρον (from βλέπω; see blep-) eyelid. Cf. cili-. *blepharoncus*
bol-	See ball-. em*bol*ism
brachi-	βραχίων arm. *brachi*ocephalic
brachy-	βραχύς short. *brachy*cephalic
brady-	βραδύς slow. *brady*cardia
brom-	βρῶμος stench. podo*brom*idrosis
bronch-	βρόγχος windpipe. *bronch*oscopy
bry-	βρύω be full of life. em*bry*onic
bucc-	*bucca* cheek. disto*bucc*al
cac-	κακός bad, abnormal. Cf. mal-. *cac*odontia, arthro*cace*. (See also dys-)
calc-[1]	*calx, calcis* stone (cf. lith-), limestone, lime. *calc*ipexy
calc-[2]	*calx, calcis* heel. *calc*aneotibial
calor-	*calor* heat. Cf. therm-. *calo*rimeter
cancr-	*cancer, cancri* crab, cancer. Cf. carcin-. *cancr*ology. (Also spelled chancr-)
capit-	*caput, capitis* head. Cf. cephal-. de*capit*ator
caps-	*capsa* (from *capio;* see cept-) container. en*caps*ulation
carbo(n)-	*carbo, carbonis* coal, charcoal. *carbo*hydrate, *carbon*uria
carcin-	καρκίνος crab, cancer. Cf. cancr-. *carcin*oma
cardi-	καρδία heart. lipo*cardi*ac
cary-	See kary-. *cary*okinesis
cat-	See cata-. *cat*hode
cata-	κατά (final *a* is dropped before words beginning with a vowel) down, negative. *cata*batic
caud-	*cauda* tail. *caud*ad
cav-	*cavus* hollow. Cf. coel-. con*cav*e
cec-	*caecus* blind. Cf. typhl-. *ceco*pexy
cel-[1]	See coel-. amphi*cel*ous
cel-[2]	See -cele. *cel*ectome
-cele	κήλη tumor, hernia. gastro*cele*
cell-	*cella* room, cell. Cf. cyt-. *cell*iferous
cen-	κοινός common. *cen*esthesia
cent-	*centum* hundred. Cf. hect-. Indicates fraction in metric system. [This exemplifies the custom in the metric system of identifying fractions of units by stems from the Latin, as centimeter, decimeter, millimeter, and multiples of units by the similar stems from the Greek, as hectometer, decameter, and kilometer.] *cent*imeter, *centi*pede
cente-	κεντέω puncture. Cf. punct-. entero*cente*sis
centr-	κέντρον or *centrum* point, center. neuro*centr*al
cephal-	κεφαλή head. Cf. capit-. en*cephal*itis
cept-	*capio, -cipientis, -ceptus* take, receive. re*cept*or
cer-	κηρός or *cera* wax. *cer*oplasty, *cer*omel
cerat-	See kerat-. a*cerat*osis
cerebr-	*cerebrum*. *cerebr*ospinal
cervic-	*cervix, cervicis* neck. Cf. trachel-. *cervic*itis
chancr-	See cancr-. *chancr*iform
cheil-	χεῖλος lip. Cf. labi-. *chei*loschisis
cheir-	χείρ hand. Cf. man-. macro*cheir*ia. (Also spelled chir-)
chir-	See cheir-. *chir*omegaly
chlor-	χλωρός green. a*chlor*opsia
chol-	χολή bile. Cf. bil-. hepato*chol*angeitis
chondr-	χόνδρος cartilage. *chondro*malacia
chord-	χορδή string, cord. peri*chord*al
chori-	χόριον protective fetal membrane. endo*chori*on
chro-	χρώς color. poly*chro*matic
chron-	χρόνος time. syn*chron*ous
chy-	χέω, χυ- pour. ec*chy*mosis
-cid(e)	*caedo, -cisus* cut, kill. infanti*cide*, germi*cid*al
cili-	*cilium* eyelid. Cf. blephar-. super*cili*ary
cine-	See kine-. auto*cine*sis
-cipient	See cept-. in*cipient*
circum-	*circum* around. Cf. peri-. *circum*ferential
-cis-	*caedo, -cisus* cut, kill. ex*cis*ion
clas-	κλάω, κλασ- break. cranio*clast*
clin-	κλίνω bend, incline, make lie down. *clin*ometer
clus-	*claudo, -clusus* shut. Maloc*clus*ion
co-	See con-. *co*hesion
cocc-	κόκκος seed, pill. gono*cocc*us
coel-	κοῖλος hollow. Cf. cav-. *coel*enteron. (Also spelled cel-)
col-[1]	See colon-. *col*ic
col-[2]	See con-. *col*lapse
colon-	κόλον lower intestine. *colon*ic
colp-	κόλπος hollow, vagina. Cf. sin-. endo*colp*itis
com-	See con-. *com*masculation
con-	*con-* (becomes co- before vowels or *h;* col- before *l;* com- be-

fore *b*, *m*, or *p*; cor- before *r*) with, together. Cf. syn-. *con*traction
contra- *contra* against, counter. Cf. anti-. *contra*indication
copr- κόπρος dung. Cf. sterco-. *copr*oma
cor-[1] κόρη doll, little image, pupil. iso*cor*ia
cor-[2] See con-. *cor*rugator
corpor- *corpus*, *corporis* body. Cf. somat-. intra*corpor*al
cortic- *cortex*, *corticis* bark, rind. *cortic*osterone
cost- *costa* rib. Cf. pleur-. inter*cost*al
crani- κρανίον or *cranium* skull. peri*crani*um
creat- κρέας, κρεατ- meat, flesh. *creat*orrhea
-crescent *cresco*, *crescentis*, *cretus* grow. ex*crescent*
cret-[1] *cerno*, *cretus* distinguish, separate off. Cf. crin-. dis*crete*
cret-[2] See -crescent. ac*cret*ion
crin- κρίνω distinguish, separate off. Cf. cret-[1]. endo*crin*ology
crur- *crus*, *cruris* shin, leg. brachio*crur*al
cry- κρύος cold. *cry*esthesia
crypt- κρύπτω hide, conceal. *crypt*orchism
cult- *colo*, *cultus* tend, cultivate. *cult*ure
cune- *cuneus* wedge. Cf. sphen-. *cune*iform
cut- *cutis* skin. Cf. derm(at)-. sub*cut*aneous
cyan- κύανος blue. antho*cyan*in
cycl- κύκλος circle, cycle. *cycl*ophoria
cyst- κύστις bladder. Cf. vesic-. nephro*cyst*itis
cyt- κύτος cell. Cf. cell-. plasmo*cyt*oma
dacry- δάκρυ tear. *dacry*ocyst
dactyl- δάκτυλος finger, toe. Cf. digit-. hexa*dactyl*ism
de- *de* down from. *de*composition
dec-[1] δέκα ten. Indicates multiple in metric system. Cf. dec-[2]. *dec*agram
dec-[2] *decem* ten. Indicates fraction in metric system. Cf. dec-[1]. *dec*ipara, *dec*imeter
dendr- δένδρον tree. neuro*dendr*ite
dent- *dens*, *dentis* tooth. Cf. odont-. inter*dent*al
derm(at)- δέρμα, δέρματος skin. Cf. cut-. endo*derm*, *dermat*itis
desm- δεσμός band, ligament. syn*desm*opexy
dextr- *dexter*, *dextr*- right-hand. ambi*dextr*ous
di-[1] *di*- two. *di*morphic. (See also bi-[2])
di-[2] See dia-. *di*uresis.
di-[3] See dis-. *di*vergent.
dia- διά (*a* is dropped before words beginning with a vowel) through, apart. Cf. per-. *dia*gnosis
didym- δίδυμος twin. Cf. gemin-. epi*didym*al
digit- *digitus* finger, toe. Cf. dactyl-. *digit*igrade
diplo- διπλόος double. *diplo*myelia
dis- *dis*- (*s* may be dropped before a word beginning with a consonant) apart, away from. *dis*location
disc- δίσκος or *discus* disk. *disc*oplacenta
dors- *dorsum* back. ventro*dors*al
drom- δρόμος course. hemo*drom*ometer
-ducent See duct-. ad*ducent*
duct- *duco*, *ducentis*, *ductus* lead, conduct. ovi*duct*
dur- *durus* hard. Cf. scler-. in*dur*ation
dynam(i)- δύναμις power. *dynam*oneure, neuro*dynamic*
dys- δυσ- bad, improper. Cf. mal-. *dys*trophic. (See also cac-)
e- *e* out from. Cf. ec- and ex-. *e*mission
ec- ἐκ out of. Cf. e- *ec*centric
-ech- ἔχω have, hold, be. syn*ech*otomy
ect- ἐκτός outside. Cf. extra-. *ect*oplasm
ede- οἰδέω swell. *ede*matous
ef- See ex-. *ef*florescent
-elc- ἕλκος sore, ulcer. enter*elc*osis. (See also *helc*-)
electr- ἤλεκτρον amber. *electr*otherapy
em- See en-. *em*bolism, *em*pathy, *em*phlysis
-em- αἷμα blood. an*em*ia. (See also hem(at)-)
en- ἐν (*n* changes to *m* before *b*, *p*, or *ph*) in, on. Cf. in-[2]. *en*celitis
end- ἔνδον inside. Cf. intra-. *end*angium.
enter- ἔντερον intestine. dys*enter*y
ep- See epi-. *ep*axial
epi- ἐπί (*i* is dropped before words beginning with a vowel) upon, after, in addition. *epi*glottis
erg- ἔργον work, deed. en*erg*y
erythr- ἐρυθρός red. Cf. rub(r)-. *erythr*ochromia
eso- ἔσω inside. Cf. intra-. *eso*phylactic
esthe- αἰσθάνομαι, αἰσθη- perceive, feel. Cf. sens-. an*esthe*sia
eu- εὖ good, normal. *eu*pepsia
ex- ἐξ or *ex* out of. Cf. e-. *ex*cretion
exo- ἔξω outside. Cf. extra-. *exo*pathic
extra- *extra* outside of, beyond. Cf. ect- and exo-. *extra*cellular
faci- *facies* face. Cf. prosop-. brachio*faci*olingual

-facient *facio, facientis, factus, -fectus* make. Cf. poie-. cale*facient*
-fact- See facient-. arte*fact*
fasci- *fascia* band. *fasci*orrhaphy
febr- *febris* fever. Cf. pyr-. *febr*icide
-fect- See -facient. de*fect*ive
-ferent *fero, ferentis, latus* bear, carry. Cf. phor-. ef*ferent*
ferr- *ferrum* iron. *ferr*oprotein
fibr- *fibra* fibre. Cf. in-[1]. chondro*fibr*oma
fil- *filum* thread. *fil*iform
fiss- *findo, fissus* split. Cf. schis-. *fiss*ion
flagell- *flagellum* whip. *flagell*ation
flav- *flavus* yellow. Cf. xanth-. ribo*flav*in
-flect- *flecto, flexus* bend, divert. de*flect*ion
-flex- See -flect-. re*flex*ometer
flu- *fluo, fluxus* flow. Cf. rhe-. *flu*id
flux- See flu-. af*flux*ion
for- *foris* door, opening. per*for*ated
-form *forma* shape. Cf. -oid. ossi*form*
fract- *frango, fractus* break. re*fract*ive
front- *frons, frontis* forehead, front. naso*front*al
-fug(e) *fugio* flee, avoid. vermi*fuge*, centri*fug*al
funct- *fungor, functus* perform, serve, function. mal*funct*ion
fund- *fundo, fusus* pour. in*fund*ibulum
fus- See fund-. dif*fus*ible
galact- γάλα, γάλακτος milk. Cf. lact-. dys*galact*ia
gam- γάμος marriage, reproductive union. a*gam*ont
gangli- γάγγλιον swelling, plexus. neuro*gangli*itis
gastr- γαστήρ, γαστρός stomach. cholangio*gastr*ostomy
gelat- *gelo, gelatus* freeze, congeal. *gelat*in
gemin- *geminus* twin, double. Cf. didym-. quadri*gemin*al
gen- γίγνομαι, γεν-, γον- become, be produced, originate, or γεννάω produce, originate. cyto*gen*ic
germ- *germen, germinis* bud, a growing thing in its early stages. Cf. blast-. *germ*inal, ovi*germ*
gest- *gero, gerentis, gestus* bear, carry. con*gest*ion
gland- *glans, glandis* acorn. Cf. aden-. intra*gland*ular
-glia γλία glue. neuro*glia*
gloss- γλῶσσα tongue. Cf. lingu-. tricho*gloss*ia
glott- γλῶττα tongue, language. *glott*ic
gluc- See glyc(y)-. *gluc*ophenetidin
glutin- *gluten, glutinis* glue. ag*glutin*ation
glyc(y)- γλυκύς sweet. *glyc*emia, *glycyr*rhizin. (Also spelled gluc-)
gnath- γνάθος jaw. ortho*gnath*ous
gno- γιγνώσκω, γνω- know, discern. dia*gno*sis
gon- See gen-. amphi*gon*y
grad- *gradior* walk, take steps. retro*grad*e
-gram γράφω, γραφ- + -μα scratch, write, record. cardio*gram*
gran- *granum* grain, particle. lipo*gran*uloma
graph- γράφω scratch, write, record. histo*graph*y
grav- *gravis* heavy. multi*grav*ida
gyn(ec)- γυνή, γυναικός woman, wife. andro*gyn*y, *gynec*ologic
gyr- γῦρος ring, circle. *gyr*ospasm
haem(at)- See hem(at)-. *haem*orrhagia, *haemat*oxylon
hapt- ἅπτω touch. *hapt*ometer
hect- ἑκτ- hundred. Cf. cent-. Indicates multiple in metric system. *hect*ometer
helc- ἕλκος sore, ulcer. *helc*osis
hem(at)- αἷμα, αἵματος blood. Cf. sanguin-. *hem*angioma, *hemat*ocyturia. (See also -em-)
hemi- ἡμι- half. Cf. semi-. *hemi*ageusia
hen- εἷς, ἑνός one. Cf. un-. *hen*ogenesis
hepat- ἧπαρ, ἥπατος liver. gastro*hepat*ic
hept(a)- ἑπτά seven. Cf. sept-[2]. *hept*atomic, *hepta*valent
hered- *heres, heredis* heir. *hered*oimmunity
hex-[1] ἕξ six. Cf. sex-. *hex*yl-. An *a* is added in some combinations.
hex-[2] ἔχω, ἐχ- (added to σ becomes ἑξ-) have, hold, be. cac*hex*y
hexa- See hex-[1]. *hexa*chromic
hidr- ἱδρώς sweat. hyper*hidr*osis
hist- ἱστός web, tissue. *hist*odialysis
hod- ὁδός road, path. *hod*oneuromere. (See also od- and -ode[1])
hom- ὁμός common, same. *homo*morphic
horm- ὁρμή impetus, impulse. *horm*one
hydat- ὕδωρ, ὕδατος water. *hydat*ism
hydr- ὕδωρ, ὑδρ- water. Cf. lymph-. achlor*hydr*ia
hyp- See hypo-. *hyp*axial
hyper- ὑπέρ above, beyond, extreme. Cf. super-. *hyper*trophy
hypn- ὕπνος sleep. *hypn*otic
hypo- ὑπό (*o* is dropped before words beginning with a vowel) under, below. Cf. sub-. *hypo*metabolism
hyster- ὑστέρα womb. colpo*hyster*opexy
iatr- ἰατρός physician. ped*iatr*ics
idi- ἴδιος peculiar, separate, distinct. *idi*osyncrasy
il- See in-[2, 3]. *il*linition (in, on), *il*legible (negative prefix)
ile- See ili- [ile- is commonly used to refer to the portion of the

intestines known as the ileum]. *ileo*stomy

ili- *ilium* (*ileum*) lower abdomen, intestines [ili- is commonly used to refer to the flaring part of the hip bone known as the ilium]. *ilio*sacral

im- See in-[2, 3]. *im*mersion (in, on), *im*perforation (negative prefix)

in-[1] ἴς, ἰνός fiber. Cf. fibr-. *in*osteatoma

in-[2] *in* (*n* changes to *l*, *m*, or *r* before words beginning with those consonants) in, on. Cf. en-. *in*sertion

in-[3] *in-* (*n* changes to *l*, *m*, or *r* before words beginning with those consonants) negative prefix. Cf. a-. *in*valid

infra- *infra* beneath. *infra*orbital

insul- *insula* island. *insul*in

inter- *inter* among, between. *inter*carpal

intra- *intra* inside. Cf. end- and eso-. *intra*venous

ir- See in-[2, 3]. *ir*radiation (in, on), *ir*reducible (negative prefix)

irid- ἶρις, ἴριδος rainbow, colored circle. kerato*irido*cyclitis

is- ἴσος equal. *is*otope

ischi- ἰσχίον hip, haunch. *ischi*opubic

jact- *iacio*, *iactus* throw. *jact*itation

ject- *iacio*, *-iectus* throw. in*jection*

jejun- *ieiunus* hungry, not partaking of food. gastro*jejuno*stomy

jug- *iugum* yoke. con*jug*ation

junct- *iungo*, *iunctus* yoke, join. con*junct*iva

kary- κάρυον nut, kernel, nucleus. Cf. nucle-. mega*karyo*cyte. (Also spelled cary-)

kerat- κέρας, κέρατος horn. *kerat*olysis. (Also spelled cerat-)

kil- χίλιοι one thousand. Cf. mill-. Indicates multiple in metric system. *kil*ogram

kine- κινέω move. *kine*matograph. (Also spelled cine-)

labi- *labium* lip. Cf. cheil-. gingivo*labi*al

lact- *lac*, *lactis* milk. Cf. galact-. gluco*lact*one

lal- λαλέω talk, babble. glosso*lal*ia

lapar- λαπάρα flank. *lapar*otomy

laryng- λάρυγξ, λάρυγγος windpipe. *laryng*endoscope

lat- *fero*, *latus* bear, carry. See -ferent. trans*lat*ion

later- *latus*, *lateris* side. ventro*later*al

lent- *lens*, *lentis* lentil. Cf. phac-. *lent*iconus

lep- λαμβάνω, ληπ- take, seize. cata*lep*tic

leuc- See leuk-. *leuc*inuria

leuk- λευκός white. Cf. alb-. *leuk*orrhea. (Also spelled leuc-)

lien- *lien* spleen. Cf. splen-. *lieno*cele

lig- *ligo* tie, bind. *lig*ate

lingu- *lingua* tongue. Cf. gloss-. sub*lingu*al

lip- λίπος fat. Cf. adip-. glyco*lip*in

lith- λίθος stone. Cf. calc-[1]. nephro*litho*tomy

loc- *locus* place. Cf. top-. *loco*motion

log- λέγω, λογ- speak, give an account. *log*orrhea, embry*ology*

lumb- *lumbus* loin. dorso*lumb*ar

lute- *luteus* yellow. Cf. xanth-. *lute*oma

ly- λύω loose, dissolve. Cf. solut-. kerato*lys*is

lymph- *lympha* water. Cf. hydr-. *lymph*adenosis

macr- μακρός long, large. *macr*omyeloblast

mal- *malus* bad, abnormal. Cf. cac- and dys-. *mal*function

malac- μαλακός soft. osteo*malac*ia

mamm- *mamma* breast. Cf. mast-. sub*mamm*ary

man- *manus* hand. Cf. cheir-. *man*iphalanx

mani- μανία mental aberration. *ma-ni*graphy, klepto*mania*

mast- μαστός breast. Cf. mamm-. hyper*mast*ia

medi- *medius* middle. Cf. mes-. *medi*frontal

mega- μέγας great, large. Also indicates multiple (1,000,000) in metric system. *mega*colon, *mega*dyne. (See also megal-)

megal- μέγας, μεγάλου great, large. acro*megal*y

mel- μέλος limb, member. sym*mel*ia

melan- μέλας, μέλανος black. hippo*melan*in

men- μήν month. dys*men*orrhea

mening- μῆνιγξ, μήνιγγος membrane. encephalo*mening*itis

ment- *mens*, *mentis* mind. Cf. phren-, psych- and thym-. de*ment*ia

mer- μέρος part. poly*mer*ic

mes- μέσος middle. Cf. medi-. *meso*derm

met- See meta-. *met*allergy

meta- μετά (*a* is dropped before words beginning with a vowel) after, beyond, accompanying. *meta*carpal

metr-[1] μέτρον measure. stereo*metr*y

metr-[2] μήτρα womb. endo*metr*itis

micr- μικρός small. photo*micr*ograph

mill- *mille* one thousand. Cf. kil-. Indicates fraction in metric system. *milli*gram, *milli*pede

miss- See -mittent. intro*miss*ion

-mittent *mitto*, *mittentis*, *missus* send. inter*mittent*

mne- μιμνήσκω, μνη- remember. pseudo*mnes*ia
mon- μόνος only, sole. *mono*plegia
morph- μορφή form, shape. poly*morph*onuclear
mot- *moveo, motus* move. vaso*mot*or
my- μῦς, μυός muscle. inoleio*my*oma
-myces μύκης, μύκητος fungus. myelo*myces*
myc(et)- See -myces. asco*mycet*es, strepto*myc*in
myel- μυελός marrow. polio*myel*itis
myx- μύξα mucus. *myx*edema
narc- νάρκη numbness. topo*narc*osis
nas- *nasus* nose. Cf. rhin-. palato*nas*al
ne- νέος new, young. *ne*ocyte
necr- νεκρός corpse. *necr*ocytosis
nephr- νεφρός kidney. Cf. ren-. para*nephr*ic
neur- νεῦρον nerve. esthesio*neur*e
nod- *nodus* knot. *nod*osity
nom- νόμος (from νέμω deal out, distribute) law, custom. tax*onom*y
non- *nona* nine. *non*acosane
nos- νόσος disease. *nos*ology
nucle- *nucleus* (from *nux, nucis* nut) kernel. Cf. kary-. *nucle*ide
nutri- *nutrio* nourish. mal*nutri*tion
ob- *ob* (*b* changes to *c* before words beginning with that consonant) against, toward, etc. *ob*tuse
oc- See ob-. *oc*clude.
ocul- *oculus* eye. Cf. ophthalm-. *ocul*omotor
-od- See -ode[1]. peri*od*ic
-ode[1] ὁδός road, path. cath*ode*. (See also hod-)
-ode[2] See -oid. nemat*ode*
odont- ὀδούς, ὀδόντος tooth. Cf. dent-. orth*odont*ia
-odyn- ὀδύνη pain, distress. gastr*odyn*ia
-oid εἶδος form. Cf. -form. hy*oid*
-ol See ole-. cholester*ol*
ole- *oleum* oil. *ole*oresin
olig- ὀλίγος few, small. *olig*ospermia
omphal- ὀμφαλός navel. peri*omphal*ic
onc- ὄγκος bulk, mass. hemato*n*cometry
onych- ὄνυξ, ὄνυχος claw, nail. an*onych*ia
oo- ᾠόν egg. Cf. ov-. peri*oo*thecitis
op- ὁράω, ὀπ- see. erythr*op*sia
ophthalm- ὀφθαλμός eye. Cf. ocul-. ex*ophthalm*ic
or- *os, oris* mouth. Cf. stom(at)-. intra*or*al
orb- *orbis* circle. sub*orb*ital
orchi- ὄρχις testicle. Cf. test-. *orchi*opathy
organ- ὄργανον implement, instrument. *organ*oleptic
orth- ὀρθός straight, right, normal. *orth*opedics
oss- *os, ossis* bone. Cf. ost(e)-. *oss*iphone
ost(e)- ὀστέον bone. Cf. oss-. en*ost*osis, *oste*anaphysis
ot- οὖς, ὠτός ear. Cf. aur-. par*ot*id
ov- *ovum* egg. Cf. oo-. syn*ov*ia
oxy- ὀξύς sharp. *oxy*cephalic
pachy(n)- παχύνω thicken. *pachy*derma, myo*pachyn*sis
pag- πήγνυμι, παγ- fix, make fast. thoraco*pag*us
par-[1] *pario* bear, give birth to. primi*par*ous
par-[2] See para-. *par*epigastric
para- παρά (final *a* is dropped before words beginning with a vowel) beside, beyond. *para*mastoid
part- *pario, partus* bear, give birth to. *part*urition
path- πάθος that which one undergoes, sickness. psycho*path*ic
pec- πήγνυμι, πηγ- (πηκ- before τ) fix, make fast. sym*pec*tothiene. (See also pex-)
ped- παῖς, παιδός child. ortho*ped*ic
pell- *pellis* skin, hide. *pell*agra
-pellent *pello, pellentis, pulsus* drive. re*pellent*
pen- πένομαι need, lack. erythrocyto*pen*ia
pend- *pendeo* hang down. ap*pend*ix
pent(a)- πέντε five. Cf. quinque-. *pen*tose, *penta*ploid
peps- πέπτω, πεψ- (before σ) digest brady*peps*ia
pept- πέπτω digest. dys*pept*ic
per- *per* through. Cf. dia-. *per*nasal
peri- περί around. Cf. circum-. *peri*phery
pet- *peto* seek, tend toward. centri*pet*al
pex- πήγνυμι, πηγ- (added to σ becomes πηξ-) fix, make fast. hepato*pex*y
pha- φημί, φα- say, speak. dys*pha*sia
phac- φακός lentil, lens. Cf. lent-. *phac*osclerosis. (Also spelled phak-)
phag- φαγεῖν eat. lipo*phag*ic
phak- See phac-. *phak*itis
phan- See phen-. dia*phan*oscopy
pharmac- φάρμακον drug. *pharmac*ognosy
pharyng- φάρυγξ, φαρυγγ- throat. glosso*pharyng*eal
phen- φαίνω, φαν- show, be seen. phos*phen*e
pher- φέρω, φορ- bear, support. peri*pher*y
phil- φιλέω like, have affinity for. eosino*phil*ia
phleb- φλέψ, φλεβός vein. peri*phleb*itis
phleg- φλέγω, φλογ- burn, inflame. adeno*phleg*mon
phlog- See phleg-. anti*phlog*istic
phob- φόβος fear, dread. claustro*phob*ia
phon- φωνή sound. echo*phon*y

phor- See pher-. Cf. -ferent. exo*phor*ia
phos- See phot-. *phos*phorus
phot- φῶς, φωτός light. *phot*erythrous
phrag- φράσσω, φραγ- fence, wall off, stop up. Cf. sept-[1]. dia*phrag*m
phrax- φράσσω, φραγ- (added to σ becomes φραξ-) fence, wall off, stop up. em*phrax*is
phren- φρήν mind, midriff. Cf. ment-. meta*phren*ia, meta*phren*on
phthi- φθίνω decay, waste away. ophthalmo*phthi*sis
phy- φύω beget, bring forth, produce, be by nature. noso*phy*te
phyl- φῦλον tribe, kind. *phyl*ogeny
-phyll φύλλον leaf. xantho*phyll*
phylac- φύλαξ guard. pro*phylac*tic
phys(a)- φυσάω blow, inflate. *phys*ocele, *phys*alis
physe- φυσάω, φυση- blow, inflate. em*physe*ma
pil- *pilus* hair. e*pil*ation
pituit- *pituita* phlegm, rheum. *pitui*tous
placent- *placenta* (from πλακοῦς) cake. extra*placent*al
plas- πλάσσω mold, shape. cine*plas*ty
platy- πλατύς broad, flat. *platy*rrhine
pleg- πλήσσω, πληγ- strike. di*pleg*ia
plet- *pleo, -pletus* fill. de*plet*ion
pleur- πλευρά rib, side. Cf. cost-. peri*pleur*al
plex- πλήσσω, πληγ- (added to σ becomes πληξ-) strike. apo*plex*y
plic- *plico* fold. com*plic*ation
pne- πνοιά breathing. traumato*pne*a
pneum(at)- πνεῦμα, πνεύματος breath, air. *pneum*odynamics, *pneumat*othorax
pneumo(n)- πνεύμων lung. Cf. pulmo(n)-. *pneumo*centesis, *pneumon*otomy
pod- πούς, ποδός foot. *pod*iatry
poie- ποιέω make, produce. Cf. -facient. sarco*poie*tic
pol- πόλος axis of a sphere. peri*pol*ar
poly- πολύς much, many. *poly*spermia
pont- *pons, pontis* bridge. *ponto*cerebellar
por-[1] πόρος passage. myelo*pore*
por-[2] πῶρος callus. *por*ocele
posit- *pono, positus* put, place. re*posit*or
post- *post* after, behind in time or place. *post*natal, *post*oral
pre- *prae* before in time or place. *pre*natal, *pre*vesical
press- *premo, pressus* press. *press*oreceptive
pro- πρό or *pro* before in time or place. *pro*gamous, *pro*cheilon, *pro*lapse
proct- πρωκτός anus. entero*proct*ia
prosop- πρόσωπον face. Cf. faci-. di*prosop*us
pseud- ψευδής false. *pseud*oparaplegia
psych- ψυχή soul, mind. Cf. ment-. *psych*osomatic
pto- πίπτω, πτω- fall. nephro*pto*sis
pub- *pubes* & *puber, puberis* adult. ischio*pub*ic. (See also puber-)
puber- *puber* adult. *puber*ty
pulmo(n)- *pulmo, pulmonis* lung. Cf. pneumo(n)-. *pulmo*lith, cardio*pulmon*ary
puls- *pello, pellentis, pulsus* drive. pro*puls*ion
punct- *pungo, punctus* prick, pierce. Cf. cente-. *punct*iform
pur- *pus, puris* pus. Cf. py-. sup*pur*ation
py- πύον pus. Cf. pur-. nephro*py*osis
pyel- πύελος trough, basin, pelvis. nephro*pyel*itis
pyl- πύλη door, orifice. *pyl*ephlebitis
pyr- πῦρ fire. Cf. febr-. galacto*pyr*a
quadr- *quadr-* four. Cf. tetra-. *quadr*igeminal
quinque- *quinque* five. Cf. pent(a)-. *quinque*cuspid
rachi- ῥαχίς spine. Cf. spin-. encephalo*rachi*dian
radi- *radius* ray. Cf. actin-. ir*radi*ation
re- *re-* back, again. *re*traction
ren- *renes* kidneys. Cf. nephr-. ad*ren*al
ret- *rete* net. *ret*othelium
retro- *retro* backwards. *retro*deviation
rhag- ῥήγνυμι, ῥαγ- break, burst. hemor*rhag*ic
rhaph- ῥαφή suture. gastror*rhaph*y
rhe- ῥέω flow. Cf. flu-. diar*rhe*al
rhex- ῥήγνυμι, ῥηγ- (added to σ becomes ῥηξ-) break, burst. metror*rhex*is
rhin- ῥίς, ῥινός nose. Cf. nas-. basi*rhin*al
rot- *rota* wheel. *rot*ator
rub(r)- *ruber, rubri* red. Cf. erythr-. bili*rub*in, *rubr*ospinal
salping- σάλπιγξ, σάλπιγγος tube, trumpet. *salping*itis
sanguin- *sanguis, sanguinis* blood. Cf. hem(at)-. *sanguin*eous
sarc- σάρξ, σαρκός flesh. *sarc*oma
schis- σχίζω, σχιδ- (before τ or added to σ becomes σχισ-) split. Cf. fiss-. *schis*torachis, rachi*schis*is
scler- σκληρός hard. Cf. dur-. *scler*osis
scop- σκοπέω look at, observe. endo*scop*e
sect- *seco, sectus* cut. Cf. tom-. *sect*ile
semi- *semi-* half. Cf. hemi-. *semi*flexion
sens- *sentio, sensus* perceive, feel. Cf. esthe-. *sens*ory

sep- σήπω rot, decay. *sep*sis
sept-[1] *saepio*, *saeptus* fence, wall off, stop up. Cf. phrag-. naso*sept*al
sept-[2] *septem* seven. Cf. hept(a)-. *sept*an
ser- *serum* whey, watery substance. *ser*osynovitis
sex- *sex* six. Cf. hex-[1]. *sex*digitate
sial- σίαλον saliva. poly*sial*ia
sin- *sinus* hollow, fold. Cf. colp-. *sin*obronchitis
sit- σῖτος food. para*sit*ic
solut- *solvo*, *solventis*, *solutus* loose, dissolve, set free. Cf. ly-. dis*solut*ion
-solvent See solut-. dis*solvent*
somat- σῶμα, σώματος body. Cf. corpor-. psycho*somat*ic
-some See somat-. dictyo*some*
spas- σπάω, σπασ- draw, pull. *spas*m, *spas*tic
spectr- *spectrum* appearance, what is seen. micro*spectr*oscope
sperm(at)- σπέρμα, σπέρματος seed. *sperm*acrasia, *spermat*ozoon
spers- *spargo*, *-spersus* scatter. dis*pers*ion
sphen- σφήν wedge. Cf. cune-. *sphen*oid
spher- σφαῖρα ball. hemi*sphere*
sphygm- σφυγμός pulsation. *sphygmo*manometer
spin- *spina* spine. Cf. rachi-. cerebro*spin*al
spirat- *spiro*, *spiratus* breathe. in*spirat*ory
splanchn- σπλάγχνα entrails, viscera. neuro*splanchn*ic
splen- σπλήν spleen. Cf. lien-. *splen*omegaly
spor- σπόρος seed. *spor*ophyte, zygo*spore*
squam- *squama* scale. de*squam*ation
sta- ἵστημι, στα- make stand, stop. genesi*sta*sis
stal- στέλλω, σταλ- send. peri*stal*sis. (See also stol-)
staphyl- σταφυλή bunch of grapes, uvula. *staphyl*ococcus, *staphyl*ectomy
stear- στέαρ, στέατος fat. Cf. adip-. *stear*odermia
steat- See stear-. *steat*opygous
sten- στενός narrow, compressed. *sten*ocardia
ster- στερεός solid. chole*ster*ol
sterc- *stercus* dung. Cf. copr-. *sterco*porphyrin
sthen- σθένος strength. a*sthen*ia
stol- στέλλω, στολ- send. dia*stol*e
stom(at)- στόμα, στόματος mouth, orifice. Cf. or-. ana*stom*osis, *stomat*ogastric
strep(h)- στρέφω, στρεπ- (before τ) twist. Cf. tors-. *streph*osymbolia, *strep*tomycin. (See also stroph-)
strict- *stringo*, *stringentis*, *strictus* draw tight, compress, cause pain. con*strict*ion
-stringent See strict-. a*stringent*
stroph- στρέφω, στροφ- twist. ana*stroph*ic. (See also strep(h)-)
struct- *struo*, *structus* pile up (against). ob*struct*ion
sub- *sub* (*b* changes to *f* or *p* before words beginning with those consonants) under, below. Cf. hypo-. *sub*lumbar
suf- See sub-. *suf*fusion
sup- See sub-. *sup*pository
super- *super* above, beyond, extreme. Cf. hyper-. *super*motility
sy- See syn-. *sy*stole
syl- See syn-. *syl*lepsiology
sym- See syn-. *sym*biosis, *sym*metry, *sym*pathetic, *sym*physis
syn- σύν (*n* disappears before *s*, changes to *l* before *l*, and changes to *m* before *b*, *m*, *p*, and *ph*) with, together. Cf. con-. myo*syn*izesis
ta- See ton-. ec*ta*sis
tac- τάσσω, ταγ- (τακ- before τ) order, arrange. a*tac*tic
tact- *tango*, *tactus* touch. con*tact*
tax- τάσσω, ταγ- (added to σ becomes ταξ-) order, arrange. a*tax*ia
tect- See teg-. pro*tect*ive
teg- *tego*, *tectus* cover. in*teg*ument
tel- τέλος end. *tel*osynapsis
tele- τῆλε at a distance. *tele*ceptor
tempor- *tempus*, *temporis* time, timely or fatal spot, temple. *tempo*romalar
ten(ont)- τένων, τένοντος (from τείνω stretch) tight stretched band. *ten*odynia, *tenon*itis, *tenon*tagra
tens- *tendo*, *tensus* stretch. Cf. ton-. ex*tens*or
test- *testis* testicle. Cf. orchi-. *test*itis
tetra- τετρα- four. Cf. quadr-. *tetrag*enous
the- τίθημι, θη- put, place. syn*the*sis
thec- θήκη repository, case. *theco*stegnosis
thel- θηλή teat, nipple. *thel*erethism
therap- θεραπεία treatment. hydro*therapy*
therm- θέρμη heat. Cf. calor-. dia*thermy*
thi- θεῖον sulfur. *thi*ogenic
thorac- θώραξ, θώρακος chest. *thoraco*plasty
thromb- θρόμβος lump, clot. *thrombo*penia
thym- θυμός spirit. Cf. ment-. dys*thym*ia
thyr- θυρεός shield (shaped like a door θύρα). *thyr*oid

tme- *τέμνω, τμη-* cut. axono*tme*sis
toc- *τόκος* childbirth. dys*toc*ia
tom- *τέμνω, τομ-* cut. Cf. sect-. appendec*tomy*
ton- *τείνω, τον-* stretch, put under tension. Cf. tens-. peri*tone*um
top- *τόπος* place. Cf. loc-. *top*esthesia
tors- *torqueo, torsus* twist. Cf. strep-. ex*tors*ion
tox- *τοξικόν* (from *τόξον* bow) arrow poison, poison. *tox*emia
trache- *τραχεῖα* windpipe. *trache*otomy
trachel- *τράχηλος* neck. Cf. cervic-. *trachel*opexy
tract- *traho, tractus* draw, drag. pro*tract*ion
traumat- *τραῦμα, τραύματος* wound. *traumat*ic
tri- *τρεῖς, τρία* or *tri-* three. *tri*gonid
trich- *θρίξ, τριχός* hair. *trich*oid
trip- *τρίβω* rub. en*trip*sis
trop- *τρέπω, τροπ-* turn, react. sito*trop*ism
troph- *τρέφω, τροφ-* nurture. a*trophy*
tuber- *tuber* swelling, node. *tuber*cle
typ- *τύπος* (from *τύπτω* strike) type. a*typ*ical
typh- *τῦφος* fog, stupor. adeno*typh*us
typhl- *τυφλός* blind. Cf. cec-. *typhl*ectasis
un- *unus* one. Cf. hen-. *un*ioval
ur- *οὖρον* urine. poly*ur*ia
vacc- *vacca* cow. *vacc*ine
vagin- *vagina* sheath. in*vagin*ated
vas- *vas* vessel. Cf. angi-. *vas*cular
vers- See vert-. in*vers*ion
vert- *verto, versus* turn. di*vert*iculum
vesic- *vesica* bladder. Cf. cyst-. *vesic*ovaginal
vit- *vita* life. Cf. bi-[1]. de*vit*alize
vuls- *vello, vulsus* pull, twitch. con*vuls*ion
xanth- *ξανθός* yellow, blond. Cf. flav- and lute-. *xanth*ophyll
-yl- *ὕλη* substance. cacod*yl*
zo- *ζωή* life, *ζῷον* animal. micro*zo*aria
zyg- *ζυγόν* yoke, union. *zyg*odactyly
zym- *ζύμη* ferment. en*zym*e

Index to Plates

Plate I	Principal Arteries of Body, and Pulmonary Veins	*facing* 136
II	Arteries of Head, Neck, and Base of Brain	*following Plate I*
III	Arteries of Thorax and Axilla	*following Plate II*
IV	Arteries of Abdomen and Pelvis	*following Plate III*
V	Arteries of Upper Extremity	*following Plate IV*
VI	Arteries of Lower Extremity	*facing* 137
VII	Bacteria	*facing* 176
VIII	Bandages	181
IX	Brain	*facing* 218
X	Brain	*facing* 219
XI	Cells	271
XII	Cycles	373
XIII	Dislocations	439
XIV	Ear	462
XV	Eye	530
XVI	Fractures	583
XVII	Endocrine Glands	612
XVIII	Heart	648
XIX	Hernias	671
XX	Kidney	779
XXI	Ligaments	*facing* 822
XXII	Ligaments	*facing* 823
XXIII	Lung (segments)	855
XXIV	Lymph (drainage)	857
XXV	Molds	*facing* 936
XXVI	Muscles of Head and Face	*facing* 952
XXVII	Muscles of Trunk (anterior view)	*following Plate XXVI*
XXVIII	Muscles of Trunk (posterior view)	*following Plate XXVII*
XXIX	Muscles of Upper Extremity	*following Plate XXVIII*
XXX	Muscles of Lower Extremity	*following Plate XXIX*
XXXI	Nerves (structure)	992
XXXII	Nerves of Head and Neck	*facing* 994
XXXIII	Nerves of Face	*following Plate XXXII*
XXXIV	Nerves of Neck, Axilla, and Upper Thorax	*following Plate XXXIII*
XXXV	Nerves of Lower Trunk	*following Plate XXXIV*
XXXVI	Nerves of Upper Extremity	*following Plate XXXV*
XXXVII	Nerves of Lower Extremity	*facing* 995
XXXVIII	Positions	1204
XXXIX	Respiration (mouth-to-mouth)	1311
XL	Skeleton	1395
XLI	Splints	1424
XLII	Strapping	1447
XLIII	Sutures and Knots	1476
XLIV	Autonomic Nervous System	1498
XLV	Respiratory System	1499
XLVI	Urogenital System	1500
XLVII	Veins of Head and Neck	*facing* 1676
XLVIII	Veins of Trunk	*following Plate XLVII*
XLIX	Veins of Extremities	*following Plate XLVIII*
L	Viruses	*facing* 1692
LI	Viscera	1695

DORLAND'S ILLUSTRATED

Medical Dictionary

A. Abbreviation for *absorbance, accommodation, acetum, Angstrom unit, anode, anterior, arteria,* and *axial.*

Å. Abbreviation for *Angstrom unit.*

A_2. Abbreviation for *aortic second sound.*

a. 1. Abbreviation for *accommodation, ampere, anode, anterior, aqua,* and *arteria.* 2. Symbol for *total acidity.*

a- 1. [Gr.]. An inseparable prefix signifying want or absence; appears as *an* before stems beginning with a vowel. 2. [L.]. A prefix signifying separation, or away from.

α. The first letter of the Greek alphabet. See *alpha.*

A.A. Abbreviation for *achievement age* and *Alcoholics Anonymous.*

$\overline{AA}$, $\overline{aa}$ [Gr. *ana* of each]. An abbreviation used in prescription writing, following the names of two or more ingredients and signifying "of each."

aaa. Abbreviation for *amalgama,* amalgam.

A.A.A.S. Abbreviation for *American Association for the Advancement of Science.*

A.A.B.B. Abbreviation for *American Association of Blood Banks.*

A.A.D.P. Abbreviation for *American Academy of Denture Prosthetics.*

A.A.D.S. Abbreviation for *American Association of Dental Schools.*

A.A.E. Abbreviation for *American Association of Endodontists.*

A.A.G.P. Abbreviation for *American Academy of General Practice.*

A.A.O. Abbreviation for *American Association of Orthodontists.*

A.A.O.P. Abbreviation for *American Academy of Oral Pathology.*

A.A.P. Abbreviation for *American Academy of Pediatrics, American Academy of Pedodontics,* and *American Academy of Periodontology.*

Aaron (ār′on) **of Alexandria** (7th century A.D.). A physician who wrote medical works in the Syriac language, all of which are lost except fragments (e.g., on smallpox) preserved by Rhazes.

Aaron's sign (ār′onz) [Charles D. *Aaron,* American physician, 1866–1951]. See under *sign.*

aasmus (a-as′mus) [Gr. *aasmos* breathing]. Asthma.

A.B. Abbreviation for L. *Artium Baccalaureus,* Bachelor of Arts, and for *axiobuccal.*

ab. Latin preposition meaning from.

ab- [L. *ab* of, off]. Prefix signifying from, off, away from.

abacterial (a″bak-te′re-al). Nonbacterial; free from bacteria.

abactio (ah-bak′she-o) [L.]. Induced abortion.

abactus venter (ah-bak′tus ven′ter) [L.]. Induced abortion.

Abadie's sign (ah-bah-dēz′) [1. Charles A. *Abadie,* ophthalmologist in Paris, 1842–1932. 2. Jean *Abadie,* Bordeaux neurologist, 1873–1946]. See under *sign.*

abaissement (ah-bās-mon′) [Fr.]. 1. A lowering or a depressing. 2. Couching.

abalienated (ab-āl′yen-āt″ed). Mentally deranged.

abalienatio (ab-āl″yen-a′she-o) [L. "made alien," "deprived"]. Abalienation. **a. men′tis,** mental derangement.

abalienation (ab-āl″yen-a′shun) [L. *abalienatio*]. Mental derangement.

Abano (ah-ba′no), **Peter of.** See *Peter of Abano.*

abaptiston (ah″bap-tis′ton), pl. *abaptis′ta* [*a* neg. + Gr. *baptein* to dip]. A trephine so shaped that it will not penetrate the brain.

abarognosis (a″bar-og-no′sis) [*a* neg. + Gr. *baros* weight + *gnōsis* knowledge]. Loss of weight sense; baragnosis.

abarthrosis (ab″ar-thro′sis) [*ab-* + L. *arthrosis*]. Diarthrosis.

abarticular (ab″ar-tik′u-lar). 1. Not affecting a joint. 2. Remote from a joint.

abarticulation (ab″ar-tik″u-la′shun) [*ab-* + L. *articulatio* joint]. 1. A dislocation of a joint. 2. Diarthrosis.

abasia (ah-ba′zhe-ah) [*a* neg. + Gr. *basis* step + *-ia*]. Inability to walk from a defect of coordination. **a. asta′sia,** astasia-abasia. **a. atac′tica,** abasia characterized by uncertainty of movement. **choreic a.,** a form due to chorea of the legs. **paralytic a.,** a form due to paralysis of the leg muscles. **paroxysmal trepidant a.,** astasia-abasia caused by spastic stiffening of the legs on attempting to stand. **spastic a.,** paroxysmal trepidant a. **trembling a., a. trep′idans,** abasia due to trembling of the legs.

abasic (ah-ba′sik). Pertaining to abasia.

abatardissement (ah-bah″tar-dēs-mon′) [Fr.]. Deterioration of a race or breed.

abate (ah-bāt′). To lessen or decrease.

abatement (ah-bāt′ment). A decrease in the severity of a pain or a symptom.

abatic (ah-bat′ik). Abasic.

abaxial (ab-ak′se-al) [*ab-* + L. *axis* axis]. Not situated in the axis of the body or of a particular part or organ.

abaxile (ab-ak′sīl). Abaxial.

abbau (ab′ow) [Ger.]. Catabolic products.

Abbe's condenser, illuminator (ah-bez′) [Ernst-Karl *Abbe,* German physicist, 1840–1905]. See under *condenser.*

Abbe's operation, rings, string method (ab′ēz) [Robert *Abbe,* New York surgeon, 1851–1928]. See under *operation, ring,* and *treatment.*

Abbe-Zeiss counting cell, chamber [E.-K. *Abbe;* Carl *Zeiss,* German optician, 1816–1888]. See under *chamber.*

abbocillin (ab″bo-sil′lin). Trade mark for preparations of penicillin G procaine.

Abbott's method (ab′ots) [Edville Gerhardt *Ab-*

bott, surgeon in Portland, Maine, 1870–1938]. See under *method.*

Abbott-Miller tube [W. Osler *Abbott,* American physician, 1902–1943; T. Grier *Miller,* American physician, born 1886]. See *Miller-Abbott tube,* under *tube.*

Abbott-Rawson tube [W. Osler *Abbott;* Arthur J. *Rawson,* American medical physicist]. See under *tube.*

A.B.C. Abbreviation for *axiobuccocervical.*

Abderhalden's reaction (ahb′der-hal″denz) [Emil *Abderhalden,* Swiss physiologist, 1877–1950]. See under *reaction.*

Abdollatif (ab″dol-lat′if) (1162–1231). An Arabian physician and traveler who criticized Galen's anatomical observations.

abdom. Abbreviation for *abdomen.*

abdomen (ab-do′men) [L., possibly from *abdere* to hide]. That portion of the body which lies between the thorax and the pelvis [N A, B N A]. Called also *venter.* It consists of a cavity (*abdominal cavity*) separated by the diaphragm from the thoracic cavity, and lined with a serous membrane, the

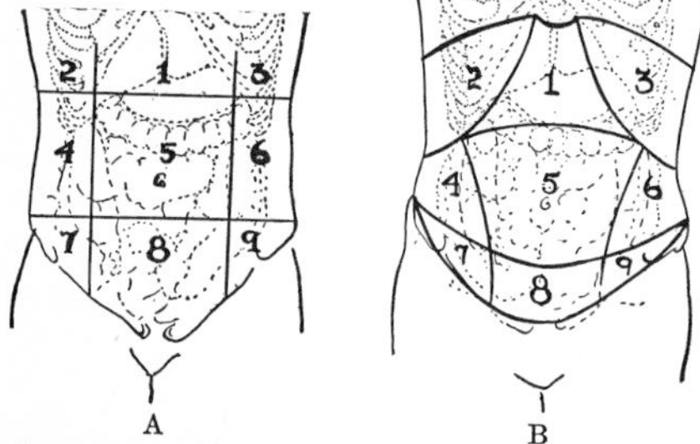

Regions of abdomen bounded according to (A) earlier and (B) later systems: 1, epigastric; 2, right hypochondriac; 3, left hypochondriac; 4, right lateral (or lumbar); 5, umbilical; 6, left lateral (or lumbar); 7, right inguinal (or iliac); 8, pubic (hypogastric); 9, left inguinal (or iliac).

peritoneum. This cavity contains the viscera, and is inclosed by a wall (*abdominal wall* or *parietes*) formed by the abdominal muscles, vertebral column, and the ilia. It is divided into nine regions by four imaginary lines, of which two pass horizontally around the body (the upper at the level of the cartilages of the ninth ribs, the lower at the top of the crests of the ilia), and two extend vertically on each side of the body from the cartilage of the eighth rib to the center of the inguinal ligament, as in A above. The regions are: three upper—right hypochondriac, epigastric, left hypochondriac; three middle (*regio mesogastrica* [B N A])—right lateral, umbilical, left lateral; and three lower (*regio hypogastrica* [B N A])—right inguinal, pubic, left inguinal. **accordion a.,** a nervous pseudotympany; swelling of the abdomen, due neither to distention with gas nor to a tumor, and appearing and disappearing rapidly. **acute a.,** medical jargon for an acute condition within the abdomen demanding immediate operation. **boat-shaped a.,** scaphoid a. **burst a.,** injury to the abdominal viscera without penetration, as by concussion (blast) or by falling debris. **carinate a.,** scaphoid a. **navicular a.,** scaphoid a. **a. obsti′pum,** congenital shortness of the rectus abdominis muscle. **pendulous a.,** a relaxed condition of the abdominal walls, so that the anterior abdominal wall hangs over the pubis. **scaphoid a.,** an abdomen whose anterior wall is hollowed out: seen in children with cerebral disease. **surgical a.,** acute a.

abdominal (ab-dom′ĭ-nal) [L. *abdominalis*]. Pertaining to the abdomen.

abdominalgia (ab″dom-ĭ-nal′je-ah) [*abdomen* + Gr. *algos* pain + *-ia*]. Pain in the abdomen.

abdomino- (ab-dom′ĭ-no) [L. *abdomen* the belly]. A combining form denoting relationship to the abdomen.

abdomino-anterior (ab-dom″ĭ-no-an-te′re-or). With the abdomen forward (noting a position of the fetus in utero).

abdominocentesis (ab-dom″ĭ-no-sen-te′sis) [*abdomino-* + Gr. *kentēsis* puncture]. Paracentesis of the abdomen.

abdominocystic (ab-dom″ĭ-no-sis′tik). Pertaining to the abdomen and gallbladder.

abdominogenital (ab-dom″ĭ-no-jen′ĭ-tal). Pertaining to the abdomen and the reproductive organs.

abdominohysterectomy (ab-dom″ĭ-no-his″ter-ek′to-me). Hysterectomy performed through an abdominal incision.

abdominohysterotomy (ab-dom″ĭ-no-his″ter-ot′o-me). Hysterotomy performed through an abdominal incision.

abdominoposterior (ab-dom″ĭ-no-pos-te′re-or). Having the abdomen turned backward (noting a position of the fetus in utero).

abdominoscopy (ab-dom″ĭ-nos′ko-pe) [*abdomino-* + Gr. *skopein* to inspect]. Inspection or examination of the abdomen; particularly direct examination of the abdominal organs by endoscopy; peritoneoscopy.

abdominoscrotal (ab-dom″ĭ-no-skro′tal). Pertaining to the abdomen and scrotum.

abdominothoracic (ab-dom″ĭ-no-tho-ras′ik). Pertaining to the abdomen and thorax.

abdominous (ab-dom′ĭ-nus). Having a large abdomen.

abdominouterotomy (ab-dom″ĭ-no-u″ter-ot′o-me). Abdominohysterotomy.

abdominovaginal (ab-dom″ĭ-no-vaj′ĭ-nal). Pertaining to the abdomen and the vagina.

abdominovesical (ab-dom″ĭ-no-ves′ĭ-k'l). Pertaining to the abdomen and urinary bladder.

abduce (ab-dūs′). To draw away; abduct.

abducens (ab-du′senz) [L. "drawing away"]. Latin adjective used in names of structures (e.g. muscles, nerves) which serve to abduct a part.

abducent (ab-du′sent) [L. *abducens*]. Abducting, or effecting a separation.

abduct (ab-dukt′) [*ab-* + L. *ducere* to draw]. To draw away from the median line or from a neighboring part or limb.

abduction (ab-duk′shun). The withdrawal of a part from the axis of the body; the act of turning outward; the act of abducting or state of being abducted.

abductor (ab-duk′tor) [L.]. That which or one who abducts. See *Table of Musculi.*

Abée's support (ab′āz) [Ernst *Abée,* physician in Nauheim, 1843–1913]. See under *support.*

Abegg's rule (ab′egz) [Richard *Abegg,* Danish chemist, 1869–1910]. See under *rule.*

Abelin's reaction, test (ab′e-linz) [Isaak *Abelin,* Swiss physiologist, born 1883]. See under *reaction.*

abembryonic (ab″em-bre-on′ik) [*ab-* + Gr. *embryon* embryo]. Away from the embryo.

abenteric (ab″en-ter′ik) [*ab-* + Gr. *enteron* intestine]. Situated in a part other than the intestine; apenteric.

abepithymia (ab″ep-ĭ-thi′me-ah) [*ab-* + Gr. *epithymia* desire]. Paralysis of the solar plexus.

Abercrombie's degeneration (ab′er-krom″-bēz) [John *Abercrombie,* Scottish physician, 1780–1844]. See under *degeneration.*

Abernethy's fascia, operation, sarcoma (ab′er-ne″thēz) [John *Abernethy,* British surgeon and anatomist, 1764–1831]. See under the nouns.

aberrant (ab-er′ant) [L. *aberrans; ab* from + *errare* to wander]. Wandering or deviating from the usual or normal course.

aberratio (ab″er-a′she-o) [L.]. Aberration. **a. lac′tis,** metastasis of milk secretion. **a. tes′tis,**

situation of the testis in a part distant from the path which it takes in normal descent.

aberration (ab″er-a′shun) [*ab-* + L. *errare* to wander]. 1. Deviation from the usual course or condition. 2. Imperfect refraction or focalization of light rays by a lens, resulting in degradation of the image they produce. **chromatic a.,** imperfect refraction by a lens of light rays of different wavelengths passing through it, resulting in fringes of color around the image produced by them. **chromatic a., lateral,** difference in magnification due to differences in position of the principal points for light of different wavelength, also a difference of focal length. **chromatic a., longitudinal,** difference in position along the axis for the focal points of light, produced by imperfect refraction of the rays by a lens. **chromosome a.,** an irregularity in the number or constitution of chromosomes that may alter the course of development of the embryo. **dioptric a.,** *spherical a.* **distantial a.,** a blurring of vision of distant objects. **mental a.,** unsoundness of mind of mild degree. **meridional a.,** imperfect refraction of light rays as a result of variation of refractive power in different portions of the same meridian of a lens. **newtonian a.,** *chromatic a.* **spherical a.,** zonal aberration in relation to an axial point. See *spherical a., negative,* and *spherical a., positive.* **spherical a., negative,** imperfect refraction of light rays by a lens, those passing through the outer zones of the lens being focused farther from the lens than those passing through the central zones. **spherical a., positive,** imperfect refraction of light rays by a lens, those passing through the outer zones of the lens being focused closer to the lens than those passing through the central zones. **zonal a.,** imperfect refraction of light rays by a lens, the rays passing through different zones being focused at different distances from the lens.

aberrometer (ab″er-om′e-ter) [*aberration* + Gr. *metron* measure]. An instrument for measuring errors in delicate experiments or observations.

a-beta-lipoproteinemia (a-ba″tah-lip″o-pro″te″in-e′me-ah). A condition characterized by the lack of β-lipoproteins in the blood. See *acanthocytosis.*

abevacuation (ab″e-vak″u-a′shun) [*ab-* + L. *evacuatio* an emptying]. 1. Evacuation that is abnormal in respect to either excess or deficiency. 2. Metastasis.

abeyance (ah-ba′ans). A suspension of function or of action; a state of suspended activity.

A.B.G. Abbreviation for *axiobuccogingival.*

abiatrophy (ah″bi-at′ro-fe). Premature and endogenous loss of vitality.

abient (ab′e-ent). Avoiding the source of stimulation: said of a response to a stimulus. Cf. *adient.*

abietate (ab′e-ĕ-tāt). A salt of abietic acid.

abietene (ab′e-ĕ-tēn). A colorless liquid hydrocarbon distilled from pine resin and consisting largely of heptane.

abiochemistry (ab″e-o-kem′is-tre) [*a* neg. + Gr. *bios* life + *chemistry*]. Inorganic chemistry as distinguished from the chemistry of vital processes.

abiogenesis (ab″e-o-jen′ĕ-sis) [*a* neg. + Gr. *bios* life + Gr. *genesis* generation]. The spontaneous generation of life; the origin of living things from things inanimate. Cf. *biogenesis.*

abiogenetic (ab″e-o-jĕ-net′ik). Pertaining to, or marked by, spontaneous generation.

abiogenous (ab″e-oj′ĕ-nus). Abiogenetic.

abiologic (a″bi-o-loj′ik). Abiological.

abiological (a″bi-o-loj′e-k′l). Pertaining to abiology.

abiology (a″bi-ol′o-je) [*a* neg. + Gr. *bios* life + *-logy*]. The study of nonliving things; anorganology.

abionarce (ab″e-o-nar′se) [*a* neg. + Gr. *bios* life + *narkē* stupor]. Inactivity due to infirmity.

abionergy (ab″e-on′er-je) [*a* neg. + Gr. *bios* life + *ergon* work]. Abiotrophy.

abiophysiology (ab″e-o-fiz″e-ol′o-je) [*a* neg. + Gr. *bios* life + *physiology*]. The study of inorganic processes in living organisms.

abiosis (ab″e-o′sis) [*a* neg. + Gr. *bios* life + *-osis*]. 1. Absence or deficiency of life. 2. Abiotrophy.

abiotic (ab″e-ot′ik). Pertaining to or characterized by absence of life; incapable of living; antagonistic to life.

abiotrophia (ab″e-o-tro′fe-ah). Abiotrophy.

abiotrophic (ab″e-o-trof′ik). Pertaining to or characterized by abiotrophy.

abiotrophy (ab″e-ot′ro-fe) [*a* neg. + Gr. *bios* life + *trophē* nutrition]. Trophic failure; degeneration or failure of vitality resulting in loss of specific resistance, etc. Called also *abionergy* and *hypotrophy.* **retinal a.,** a general term for a group of degenerative diseases of the retina such as retinitis pigmentosa and amaurotic familial idiocy.

abirritant (ab-ir′rĭ-tant) [*ab-* + L. *irritans* irritating]. 1. Diminishing or relieving irritation; soothing. 2. An agent which relieves irritation.

abirritation (ab″ir-rĭ-ta′shun). Diminished responsiveness to stimulation; atony.

abirritative (ab-ir′rĭ-ta″tiv). Reducing irritability; soothing.

abiuret (ah-bi′u-ret) [*a* neg. + *biuret*]. Not giving the biuret reaction.

abiuretic (ah-bi″u-ret′ik). Not responsive to the biuret test.

A.B.L. Abbreviation for *axiobuccolingual.*

ablactation (ab″lak-ta′shun) [L. *ablactatio,* from *ab* from + *lactare* to give milk]. The weaning of a child or the cessation of milk secretion.

ablastemic (a-blas-tem′ik) [*a* neg. + Gr. *blastēma* a shoot]. Not concerned with germination.

ablastin (ah-blas′tin). An antibody which prevents the multiplication of invading microorganisms.

ablate (ab-lāt′) [L. *ablatus* removed]. To remove, especially by cutting.

ablatio (ab-la′she-o) [L.]. Ablation. **a. placen′tae,** premature detachment of a normal placenta. **a. ret′inae,** detachment of the retina.

ablation (ab-la′shun) [L. *ablatio*]. 1. Separation or detachment. 2. Removal of a part, especially by cutting.

ablepharia (ah″blef-a′re-ah) [*a* neg. + Gr. *blepharon* eyelid + *-ia*]. Congenital reduction or absence of the eyelids.

ablepharon (ah-blef′ah-ron). Ablepharia.

ablepharous (ah-blef′ah-rus). Lacking eyelids; pertaining to ablepharia.

ablephary (ah-blef′ah-re). Ablepharia.

ablepsia (ah-blep′se-ah) [*a* neg. + Gr. *blepsis* sight + *-ia*]. Lack or loss of sight; blindness.

ablepsy (ah-blep′se). Ablepsia.

abluent (ab′lu-ent) [*ab-* + L. *luens* washing]. 1. Detergent or cleansing. 2. A cleansing agent.

ablution (ab-lu′shun) [L. *ablutio* a washing]. The act of washing or cleansing.

ablutomania (ab-lu″to-ma′ne-ah) [L. *ablutio* a washing + *mania*]. Abnormal interest in washing or bathing.

abman (ab′man) [*ab-* + L. *manus* hand]. Anything that is believed to act as a carrier for human effluvium.

abmortal (ab-mor′tal). Situated or directed away from a dead or injured part; a term applied especially to electric currents set up in the injured tissue.

abnerval (ab-ner′val). Passing from a nerve to and through a muscle: said of electric currents.

abneural (ab-nu′ral) [*ab-* + Gr. *neuron* nerve]. 1. Distant from the central nervous system; ventral. 2. Abnerval.

abnormal (ab-nor′mal) [*ab-* + L. *norma* rule]. Not

normal; contrary to the usual structure, position, or condition.

abnormality (ab″nor-mal′ĭ-te). 1. The quality or fact of being abnormal. 2. A malformation.

abnormity (ab-nor′mĭ-te). Abnormality.

abocclusion (ab″o-kloo′zhun). The relation of the teeth of a dentition in which the mandibular teeth are not in contact with the maxillary teeth.

aboiement (ah-bwah-mon′) [Fr.]. The utterance of barking sounds.

abomasitis (ab″o-mah-si′tis). Inflammation of the abomasum.

abomasum (ab″o-ma′sum) [*ab-* + L. *oma′sum* paunch]. The fourth stomach of a ruminant animal.

abomasus (ab″o-ma′sus). Abomasum.

aborad (ab-o′rad). Directed away from the mouth.

aboral (ab-o′ral). Opposite to, away from, or remote from, the mouth.

aboriginal (ab-ŏ-rij′ĭ-nal). Native to the place inhabited.

abort (ah-bort′) [L. *aboriri* to miscarry]. 1. To check the usual course of a disease. 2. To miscarry before the fetus is viable. 3. An abortion. 4. To become checked in development.

aborticide (ah-bor′tĭ-sīd) [L. *aboriri* to miscarry + *caedere* to kill]. 1. The killing of a fetus within the uterus. 2. An agent which kills the fetus and causes abortion.

abortient (ah-bor′shent). Abortifacient.

abortifacient (ah-bor″tĭ-fa′shent) [L. *abortio* abortion + *facere* to make]. 1. Causing abortion. 2. An agent which causes abortion.

abortin (ah-bor′tin). A glycerin extract of the *Brucella abortus*, prepared and used as is tuberculin, but in the diagnosis of contagious abortion of cattle.

abortion (ah-bor′shun) [L. *abortio*]. 1. The premature expulsion from the uterus of the products of conception—of the embryo, or of a nonviable fetus. The four classic symptoms, usually present in each type of abortion, are uterine pain, uterine hemorrhage, softening and dilatation of the cervix, and presentation or expulsion of all or part of the ovum. 2. Products of conception that have been expelled prematurely. 3. Premature stoppage of a natural or a morbid process. **accidental a.,** an abortion which is due to accident. **afebrile a.,** abortion in which the temperature is rarely elevated above 100.4°F. **ampullar a.,** a variety of tubal abortion occurring from the ampulla of the oviduct. **artificial a.,** induced abortion; an abortion which is brought on purposely. **cervical a.,** abortion in which the ovum is retained in the cervix uteri because the external os resists dilatation. **complete a.,** abortion in which all of the products of conception have been expelled from the uterus and identified. **contagious a.,** infectious a. **criminal a.,** an abortion that is not justified by the circumstances; an illegal attempt to produce an abortion. **early a.,** expulsion from the uterus of an embryo weighing less than 400 Gm., measuring less than 28 cm., and of less than 22 weeks gestation. **epizootic a.,** infectious a. **habitual a.,** the expulsion of a dead or nonviable fetus at about the same period of development in at least three successive pregnancies. **imminent a.,** impending abortion in which the bleeding is profuse, the cervix softened and dilated, and the cramps approach the character of labor pains. **incomplete a.,** abortion in which the uterus is not entirely rid of its contents. **induced a.,** abortion brought on intentionally. **inevitable a.,** abortion in progress. **infectious a.** 1. An infectious disease of cattle caused by *Brucella abortus*, marked by inflammatory changes in the uterine mucosa and fetal membranes, resulting in premature expulsion of the fetus. Called also *warping*. 2. An infectious disease of horses due to *Salmonella abortus equi* and of sheep due to *S. abortus ovis*. **justifiable a.,** abortion induced to save the life of the mother. **late a.,** expulsion from the uterus of an embryo weighing 400–1000 Gm., measuring 28–35 cm., and of 22–28 weeks gestation. **missed a.,** retention of a dead ovum in the uterus for at least two months, indicated either by cessation of growth and hardening of the uterus, or by actual diminution of its size; absence of fetal heart tones after they have been heard is also definitive. **natural a.,** any abortion except one which has been artificially produced. **a. in progress,** a condition marked by profuse hemorrhage from the uterus and pains resembling those of labor, with softening and dilatation of the cervix, going on to expulsion of the ovum. **septic a.,** abortion in which there is infection of the tissue of the uterus. **spontaneous a.,** abortion occurring naturally. **therapeutic a.,** abortion induced to save the life of the mother. **threatened a.,** a condition in which discharge of the ovum is threatened, with bloody discharge from the uterus, and sometimes softening and dilatation of the cervix; it may go on to abortion in progress, or the symptoms may subside and the pregnancy go to full term. **tubal a.,** extrusion of the conceptus through the open end of the uterine tube into the abdominal cavity, occurring in tubal (ectopic) pregnancy. **vibrio a.,** infectious a., def. 2.

abortionist (ah-bor′shun-ist). One who makes a business of inducing criminal abortions.

abortive (ah-bor′tiv) [L. *abortivus*]. 1. Prematurely born; incompletely developed. 2. Effecting an abortion; abortifacient. 3. Cutting short the course of a disease; ending without completing.

abortoscope (ah-bor′to-skōp) [Brucella *abortus* + Gr. *skopein* to examine]. An instrument for performing the agglutination test for undulant fever due to *Brucella abortus*.

abortus (ah-bor′tus) [L.]. A fetus weighing less than 500 Gm. (17 oz.) at time of expulsion from the uterus, having no chance of survival.

abouchement (ah-boosh-mon′) [Fr.]. The termination of a vessel in a larger one.

ab-oukine. The native name in Gabun of *frambesia*.

aboulia (ah-boo′le-ah). Abulia.

aboulomania (ah-boo″lo-ma′ne-ah). Abulomania.

abrachia (ah-bra′ke-ah) [*a* neg. + Gr. *brachiōn* arm + *-ia*]. A developmental anomaly characterized by complete absence of the arms.

abrachiatism (ah-bra′ke-ah-tizm″). Abrachia.

abrachiocephalia (ah-bra″ke-o-sĕ-fa′le-ah) [*a* neg. + Gr. *brachiōn* arm + *kephalē* head + *-ia*]. A developmental anomaly characterized by absence of the arms and head.

abrachiocephalus (ah-bra″ke-o-sef′ah-lus). A fetal monster exhibiting abrachiocephalia.

abrachius (ah-bra′ke-us). An individual exhibiting abrachia.

abradant (ah-bra′dant). Abrasive.

abrade (ah-brād′). To rub away the external covering or layer of a part.

Abrahams' sign (a′brah-hamz) [Robert *Abrahams*, New York physician, 1861–1935]. See under *sign*.

Abrami's disease (ah-brahm′ēz) [Pierre *Abrami*, French physician, 1879–1943]. See under *disease*.

Abrams' reflex (a′bramz) [Albert *Abrams*, physician in San Francisco, 1864–1924]. See under *reflex*.

abrasio (ah-bra′se-o) [L.]. Abrasion. **a. cor′neae,** a rubbing off of the superficial layers of the cornea. **a. den′tium,** a wearing away of tooth substance.

abrasion (ah-bra′zhun) [L. *abrasio*]. 1. The wearing away of a substance or structure (such as the skin or the teeth) through some unusual or abnormal mechanical process. 2. An area of body surface denuded of skin or mucous membrane by some unusual or abnormal mechanical process.

abrasive (ah-bra′siv). 1. Causing abrasion. 2. A substance used for abrading, grinding, or polishing.

abrasor (ah-bra′zor). An instrument used for abrasion.

abreaction (ab″re-ak′shun) [*ab-* + *reaction*]. The process of working off a repressed disagreeable experience by living through it again in speech and action in the presence of the psychoanalyst. Called also *psychocatharsis* and *catharsis*. **motor a.,** an abreaction achieved through motor or muscular expression.

abreuography (ab″roo-og′rah-fe) [Manoel de *Abreu*, Brazilian physician, 1892–1962]. Photofluorography.

Abrikossoff's (Abrikosov's) tumor (ab″rĭ-kos′ofs) [Aleksey Ivanovich *Abrikosov*, Moscow pathologist, 1875–1955]. Myoblastoma.

abrin (a′brin). A poisonous substance (phytotoxin) found in the seeds of jequirity (*Abrus precatorius*).

abrism (a′brizm). Poisoning by jequirity.

abrosia (ah-bro′ze-ah) [Gr. *abrōsia* fasting]. Lack of food.

abruptio (ab-rup′she-o) [L.]. A rending asunder. **a. placen′tae,** premature detachment of a normally implanted placenta, occurring in the region of maternal transdecidual arterial blood supply and attended by maternal systemic reactions in the form of shock, oliguria, and fibrinopenia. **a. placen′tae margina′lis,** premature separaof the placenta at its margin, resulting in venous bleeding at that site.

abs-. A prefix signifying away, from.

abscess (ab′ses) [L. *abscessus*, from *ab* away + *cedere* to go]. A localized collection of pus in a cav-

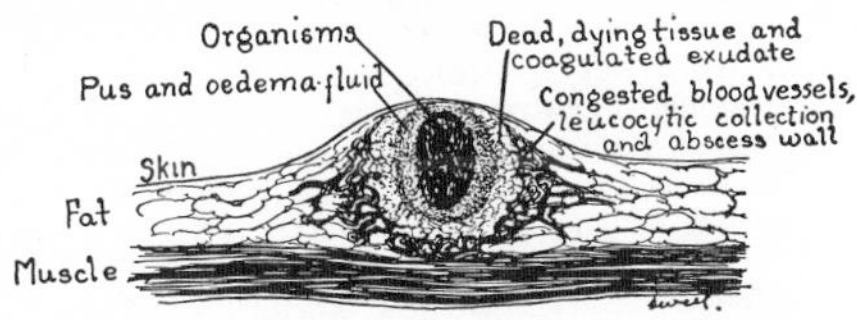

Abscess: diagram of tissue changes (Woolf).

ity formed by the disintegration of tissues. **acute a.,** one which runs a relatively short course, producing some fever and a painful local inflammation. **alveolar a.,** a collection of pus at the alveolar border, resulting from infection of the periodontal membrane and the bony tissues surrounding the root of a tooth. **amebic a., amoebic a.,** suppurative hepatitis caused by *Entamoeba histolytica*. **anorectal a.,** one in the cellulo-adipose tissue near the anus. **apical a.,** one situated at the apex of the root of a tooth, or at the apex of an organ. **apical periodontal a., acute,** a localized infection of short duration, arising at or near the apex of a tooth root, resulting in pain, swelling, and a collection of pus. **apical periodontal a., chronic,** a localized collection of inflammatory tissue and occasionally a little pus in the alveolar bone at or near the apex of a tooth root, usually resulting from infection or the presence of pulpal degradation products within the root canal; the process may progress to dental granuloma. **appendiceal a., appendicular a.,** a formation of pus around or near the vermiform appendix. **arthrifluent a.,** a wandering abscess which has its point of origin in a diseased joint. **atheromatous a.,** an area of softening in the wall of a blood vessel occurring as a result of sclerotic endarteritis. **axillary a.,** abscess, usually multiple, in the axilla. **bartholinian a.,** an abscess of Bartholin's gland. **Bezold's a.,** subperiosteal abscess of the temporal bone. **bicameral a.,** one which has two chambers or pockets. **bile duct a.,** cholangitic a. **bilharziasis a.,** one in the wall of the intestine caused by *Schistosoma* (*Bilharzia*) *mansoni*. **biliary a.,** abscess of the gallbladder or some part of the biliary tract. **bone a.,** osteomyelitis; suppurative periostitis. **broad ligament a.,** an abscess between the folds of the broad ligament of the uterus. **Brodie's a.,** a roughly spherical region of bone destruction, filled with pus or connective tissue, usually found in the metaphyseal region of long bones and caused by *Staphylococcus aureus*. **bursal a.,** one occurring in a bursa. **canalicular a.,** a mammary abscess communicating with a milk duct. **carniform a.,** a hard sarcoma of a joint. **caseous a.,** one that contains cheesy matter. **cerebral a.,** one in the brain substance. **cheesy a.,** caseous a. **cholangitic a.,** abscess of a bile duct. **chronic a.,** cold a. **circumscribed a.,** an abscess limited by a layer of fibroblasts. **circumtonsillar a.,** quinsy. **cold a.,** an abscess of comparatively slow development with little evidence of inflammation; it is usually tuberculous. **collar-button a.,** shirt-stud a. **congestive a.,** one which, because of the resistance of the tissues, cannot gather, but forms at a point distant from the seat of inflammation. **constitutional a.,** one resulting from a general disease, such as pyemia, tuberculosis, or erysipelas. **deep a.,** one occurring below the deep fascia. **Delpech's a.,** rapidly developing abscess with great prostration but little fever. **dental a.,** an abscess in or about a tooth. **dento-alveolar a.,** alveolar a. **diathetic a.,** one whose predisposing cause is a diathesis. **diffuse a.,** an abscess the pus of which, or a part of it, is widely diffused in the surrounding tissues. **Douglas' a.,** an abscess in Douglas' pouch. **dry a.,** one that disappears without pointing or breaking. **Dubois's a.,** abscess of the thymus in congenital syphilis. **embolic a.,** one caused by the lodging of an infected embolus. **emphysematous a.,** tympanitic a. **encysted a.,** one in which pus is circumscribed in a serous cavity. **endamebic a., entamebic a.,** amebic a. **epidural a.,** extradural a. **epiploic a.,** an abscess in the omentum. **extradural a.,** an abscess of the brain situated between the dura and the cranial bone. **fecal a.,** one which communicates with the large intestine and contains feces. **filarial a.,** an abscess caused by filaria. **fixation a.,** an abscess produced artificially (as by the injection of turpentine) for the purpose of attracting and fixing at the site of the abscess the bacteria of an acute infection. **Fochier's a.,** fixation a. **follicular a.,** one developing in a follicle. **frontal a.,** one in the frontal lobe of the brain. **fungal a.,** one caused by a fungus, such as Nocardia. **gangrenous a.,** one attended with gangrene of the surrounding parts. **gas a.,** tympanitic a. **gastric a.,** phlegmonous gastritis. **gingival a.,** one situated in the oral gingival tissues. **glandular a.,** one formed around a lymph gland. **gravitation a., gravity a.,** one in which the pus migrates or gravitates to a lower or deeper portion of the body. **helminthic a.,** one caused by a worm, such as filaria or ascaris. **hematic a.,** one due to an extravasated blood clot. **hemorrhagic a.,** one which contains blood. **hepatic a.,** an abscess of the liver. **hot a.,** an acute abscess with symptoms of local inflammation. **hypostatic a.,** wandering a. **idiopathic a.,** one due to unknown causes. **iliac a.,** one in the iliac region. **intradural a.,** one within the layers of the dura mater. **intramammary a.,** one in the substance of the mammary gland. **intramastoid a.,** an abscess of the mastoid process of the temporal bone. **ischiorectal a.,** one seated in the ischiorectal fossa. **lacrimal a.,** one in the areolar tissue around the lacrimal sac. **lacunar a.,** one in the lacunae of the urethra. **lateral a., lateral alveolar a.,** a periodontal abscess. **lumbar a.,** one in the lumbar region. **lymphatic a.,** a cold abscess of a lymphatic gland. **mammary a.,** abscess of the mammary gland. **marginal a.,** one near the orifice of the anus. **mastoid a.,** suppuration within the cells of the mastoid portion of the temporal bone. **mediastinal a.,** suppura-

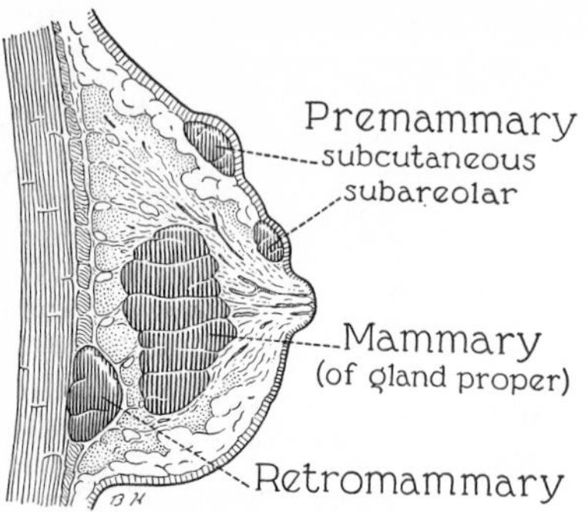

Abscesses of Breast.

tion in the mediastinum. **metastatic a.,** a secondary abscess, usually of embolic origin, in which organisms are carried by the circulation to a point distant from the primary focus. **migrating a.,** wandering a. **miliary a.,** one of a set of small multiple abscesses. **milk a.,** an abscess of the mammary gland during lactation. **Monro's a's,** minute intra-epidermal accumulations of cellular débris in the upper part of the epidermis: seen in psoriasis. **mother a.,** a primary abscess from which other abscesses arise. **multiple a.,** one of a set of many abscesses usually accompanying pyemia. **mural a.,** one in the abdominal wall. **nocardial a.,** one caused by a species of Nocardia. **orbital a.,** suppuration in the orbit. **ossifluent a.,** an abscess dependent on a breaking down of bone tissue. **Paget's a.,** one recurring about the residue of a former abscess. **palatal a.,** a dento-alveolar abscess of a maxillary tooth which erupts or extends toward the palate. **palmar a.,** a purulent effusion into the tissues of the palm of the hand. **parafrenal a.,** abscess of Tyson's gland. **parametric a.,** broad ligament a. **paranephric a.,** one in the tissues around the kidney. **parapancreatic a.,** one in the tissues around the pancreas. **parietal a.,** periodontal a. **parotid a.,** an abscess of the parotid gland. **pelvic a.,** abscess of the pelvic peritoneum, usually of Douglas' pouch. **pelvirectal a.,** one lying immediately above the levator ani muscle, in close relation to the wall of the rectum. **perianal a.,** one located immediately beneath the skin of the anus and of the lowermost part of the anal canal. **periapical a.,** apical periodontal a. **pericemental a.,** one situated in the pericemental tissue which has undergone no previous loss of continuity and which is not an extension of a periclasial pocket. **pericoronal a.,** an abscess around the crown of a partially erupted tooth. **peridental a.,** periodontal a. **perinephric a.,** one in the tissues immediately around the kidney. **periodontal a.,** a localized purulent inflammation situated in the periodontal tissues. **peripleuritic a.,** one beneath the parietal pleura. **perirectal a.,** one in the areolar tissue around the rectum. **perisinus a., perisinuous a.,** an abscess around a lateral sinus. **peritoneal a.,** an encysted mass of exudate in peritonitis. **peritonsillar a.,** an abscess in the connective tissue of the tonsil capsule, resulting from suppuration of the tonsil. **periureteral a.,** one around the ureter. **periurethral a.,** one formed around the urethra. **perivesical a.,** one in the tissues around the bladder. **phlegmonous a.,** one associated with an inflammation seated in the connective tissues. **pneumococcic a.,** one due to infection with pneumococci. **postanal a.,** one located posterior to the anal canal, between the coccygeal attachments of the superficial part of the external sphincter and of the levator ani muscle. **postcecal a.,** one sometimes occurring in appendicitis. **post-typhoid a.,** a chronic abscess following typhoid fever. **Pott's a.,** one developing in Pott's disease of the hip. **prelacrimal a.,** one of the lacrimal bone causing a swelling near the inner canthus. **premammary a.,** a small cutaneous abscess on the mammary gland. **primary a.,** one formed at the seat of a pyogenic infection. **protozoal a.,** one caused by a protozoan. **psoas a.,** one which arises from disease of the lumbar or lower dorsal vertebrae, the pus descending in the sheath of the psoas muscle. **pulmonary a.,** an abscess of the lungs. **pulp a.** 1. A cavity discharging pus formed in the pulp tissue of a tooth. 2. An abscess of the tissues of the pulp of a finger. **pyemic a.,** a constitutional abscess due to pyemia. **residual a.,** one seated near the residue of a former inflammation. **retrocecal a.,** one behind the cecum. **retromammary a.,** one situated between the mammary gland, and the chest wall. **retroperitoneal a.,** subperitoneal a. **retropharyngeal a.,** a suppurative inflammation of the lymph nodes in the posterior and lateral walls of the pharynx. **ring a.,** a ring-shaped purulent infiltration at the periphery of the cornea: called also *peripheral annular infiltration.* **root a.,** acute periodontitis circumscribed to a root surface, which may be a focus of infection. **sacrococcygeal a.,** one over the sacrum and coccyx. **satellite a.,** a secondary abscess arising from a primary one and situated near the latter. **scrofulous a.,** cold a. **secondary a.,** one occurring as the result of another process. **septal a.,** one at the proximal surface of the root of a tooth. **septicemic a.,** one resulting from septicemia. **serous a.,** periostitis albuminosa. **shirt-stud a.,** a superficial abscess connected with a deeper one by a passage. **spermatic a.,** one in the seminiferous tubules. **spinal a.,** one due to necrosis of a vertebra. **spirillar a.,** one containing spirilla. **spleen a., splenic a.,** an abscess of the spleen. **stercoraceous a., stercoral a.,** fecal a. **sterile a.,** one which contains no microorganisms. **stitch a.,** one which develops at or near a stitch or suture. **streptococcal a.,** one caused by streptococci. **strumous a.,** cold a. **subaponeurotic a.,** one beneath an aponeurosis or fascia. **subareolar a.,** a subcutaneous abscess of the areola of the nipple. **subdiaphragmatic a.,** one beneath the diaphragm. **subdural a.,** a brain abscess situated just under the dura mater. **subepidermal a.,** one situated just beneath the epidermis. **subfascial a.,** one beneath a fascia. **subgaleal a.,** one under the galea aponeurotica. **subhepatic a.,** one situated beneath the liver. **submammary a.,** one beneath the mammary gland. **subpectoral a.,** one beneath the pectoral muscles. **subperiosteal a.,** a bone abscess situated just below the periosteum. **subperitoneal a.,** one between the parietal peritoneum and the abdominal wall. **subphrenic a.,** one beneath the diaphragm. **subscapular a.,** one between the serratus anterior and the posterior thoracic wall. **subungual a.,** one situated underneath the nail. **sudoriparous a.,** an abscess of a sweat gland. **superficial a.,** one occurring above the deep fascia. **suprahepatic a.,** one situated in the suspensory ligament between the liver and the diaphragm. **sympathetic a.,** one arising some distance from the exciting cause. **syphilitic a.,** one occurring in the bones during tertiary syphilis. **thecal a.,** one in the sheath of a tendon. **thymus a.,** Dubois's a. **tonsillar a.,** acute suppurative tonsillitis. **tooth a.,** dental a. **traumatic a.,** one provoked by injury. **tropical a.,** an abscess of the liver in residents in the tropics, usually due to *Entamoeba histolytica.* **tuberculous a.,** one produced by infection with tubercle bacilli. **tympanitic a.,** one that contains air or gas. **tympanocervical a.,** one arising in the tympanum and extending to the neck. **tympanomastoid a.,** a combined abscess of the tympanum and the mastoid. **urethral a.,** an abscess of the urethra. **urinary a.,** one caused by extravasation of urine. **urinous a.,** one which contains pus mixed with urine. **verminous a.,** one which contains insect larvae or other animal parasites. **von Bezold's** a., Bezold's a. **wandering a.,** one that burrows in the tissues and finally points at a distance from the site of origin. **web-space a.,** one in the loose connective tissue and fat between the bases of the fingers. **worm a.,** one caused by or containing worms.

abscessus (ab-ses'us) [L.]. Abscess. **a. sic'cus cor'neae,** disciform keratitis.

abscissa (ab-sis'ah) [L. *ab* from + *scindere* to cut]. One of two coordinates, the other of which is called ordinate, used as a frame of reference. The abscissa is usually horizontal and the ordinate vertical and when suitable values have been assigned to them the corresponding data can be plotted.

abscission (ab-sish'un) [L. *ab* from + *scindere* to cut]. Removal by cutting. **corneal a.,** excision of the prominence of the cornea in staphyloma.

absconsio (ab-skon'se-o), pl. *absconsio'nes* [L.]. The cavity of a bone receiving and concealing the head of another bone.

absence (ab'sens). Temporary loss of consciousness, as may occur in a hysterical or epileptic attack.

absentia (ab-sen'she-ah) [L.]. Absence. **a. epilep'tica,** temporary loss of consciousness in mild epilepsy.

abs. feb. Abbreviation for L. *absen'te feb're,* while fever is absent.

Absidia (ab-sid'e-ah). A genus of pathogenic fungi of the order Phycomycetes. *A. corymbif'era* is pathogenic for laboratory animals and may cause localized or generalized mycosis in man.

absolute (ab'so-lūt) [L. *absolutus,* from *absolvere* to set loose]. Free from limitations; unlimited; uncombined.

absorbefacient (ab-sor"be-fa'shent) [L. *absorbere* to absorb + *facere* to make]. 1. Causing or promoting absorption. 2. A medicine or an agent that promotes absorption.

absorbent (ab-sor'bent) [L. *absorbens,* from *ab* away + *sorbere* to suck]. 1. Sucking up, or taking up by suction. 2. A lacteal, lymphatic or other absorbing vessel. 3. A medicine or dressing that promotes absorption.

absorptiometer (ab-sorp"she-om'e-ter) [*absorption* + Gr. *metron* measure]. 1. An instrument for measuring the solubility of gas in a liquid. 2. A device for measuring the layer of liquid absorbed between two glass plates: used as a hematoscope.

absorption (ab-sorp'shun) [L. *absorptio*]. 1. The taking up of fluids or other substances by the skin, mucous surfaces, or absorbent vessels; the term is applied to a net increase in the content of a certain substance in the blood, occurring when its insorption exceeds its exsorption. 2. In psychology, devotion of the thought to one object or activity, with inattention to others. **agglutinin a.,** the removal of antibody from an immune serum by treatment with particulate antigen (usually bacteria) homologous to that antibody, followed by centrifugation and separation of the antigen-antibody complex. **cutaneous a.,** absorption by the skin. **disjunctive a.,** the process by which a slough separates from healthy tissue by the absorption of the thin layer of the latter which is in direct contact with the necrosed portion. **enteral a.,** internal a. **excrementitial a.,** pathologic a. **external a.,** the absorption of foods, poisons, or other agents through the skin or mucous membrane. **internal a.,** the normal absorption of foods, water, etc. in digestion. **interstitial a.,** removal of waste matter by the absorbent system. **parenteral a.,** absorption otherwise than through the digestive tract. **pathologic a., pathological a.,** the absorption into the blood of any bodily excretion or morbid product, such as bile and pus.

absorptive (ab-sorp'tiv). Capable of absorbing.

abst., abstr. Abbreviation for *abstract.*

abstergent (ab-ster'jent) [L. *abstergere* to cleanse]. 1. Cleansing or purifying. 2. A cleansing application or medicine.

abstinence (ab'stĭ-nens). A refraining from the use of or indulgence in food, stimulants, or sexual intercourse. **alimentary a.,** fasting, hunger or starvation.

abstinyl (ab'stĭ-nil). A trade mark for tetraethylthiuram disulfide.

abstr. Abbreviation for *abstract.*

abstract (ab'strakt) [L. *abstractum,* from *abstrahere* to draw off]. 1. A powder made from a drug or its fluidextract with lactose, and brought to twice the strength of the original drug or extract. 2. A summary or epitome of a book, paper, or case history.

abstraction (ab-strak'shun) [L. *abstractio*]. 1. The withdrawal of any ingredient from a compound. 2. The letting of blood. 3. In dentistry, malocclusion in which the occlusal plane is further than normal from the eye-ear plane. It causes lengthening of the face. Cf. *attraction,* def. 2.

abterminal (ab-ter'mĭ-nal) [*ab* + L. *terminus* end]. Moving from the terminus toward the center: said of electric currents in muscular substance.

abtorsion (ab-tor'shun). Disclination.

Abulcasis (ah"bool-kas'is). See *Albucasis.*

abulia (ah-bu'le-ah) [*a* neg. + Gr. *boulē* will + *-ia*]. Loss or deficiency of will power. **cyclic a.,** abulia occurring periodically.

abulic (ah-bu'lik). Affected with, or pertaining to, abulia.

Abulkasim (ah"bool-kas'im). See *Albucasis.*

abulomania (ah-bu"lo-ma'ne-ah) [*abulia* + Gr. *mania* madness]. Mental disorder characterized by weakness of the will or indecision of character.

abuse (ah-būs'). Misuse or wrong use, particularly excessive use of anything.

abut (ah-but'). To touch, adjoin, or border upon.

abutment (ah-but'ment). A supporting structure to sustain lateral or horizontal pressure; applied in dentistry to any tooth to which either a fixed or a removable partial denture is attached. **intermediate a.,** a natural tooth, without other natural teeth in proximal contact, used for the support or anchorage of a fixed or removable partial denture, in addition to two primary abutments. **primary a.,** a tooth with other natural teeth in proximal contact, used for the support or anchorage of a fixed or removable partial denture.

abuttal (ah-but'al). Abutment.

abwehrfermente (ahb-vair'fer-men"te) [Ger.]. Protective ferments.

A.C. Abbreviation for *air conduction, alternating current, anodal closure,* and *axiocervical.*

Ac. Chemical symbol for *actinium.*

a. c. Abbreviation for L. *an'te ci'bum,* before meals.

a-c., A-C. Abbreviation for *auriculocarotid* and *atriocarotid.*

Acacia (ah-ka'she-ah) [L.; Gr. *akakia*]. A genus of leguminous trees of many species, some of which produce gum arabic and others catechu.

acacia (ah-ka'shah). The dried, gummy exudate from the stems and branches of *Acacia senegal* and other species, prepared as a mucilage or syrup. Uses: 1. suspending agent for drugs in pharmaceutical preparations; 2. emollient and demulcent; 3. in solution, injected intravenously in shock.

acalcerosis (ah-kal"ser-o'sis). A deficiency of calcium in the system.

acalcicosis (ah-kal"si-ko'sis). A condition caused by a deficiency of calcium in the diet.

acalculia (ah"kal-ku'le-ah) [*a* neg. + L. *calculare* to reckon + *-ia*]. Inability to do simple arithmetical calculations.

acampsia (ah-kamp'se-ah) [*a* neg. + Gr. *kamptein* to bend + *-ia*]. Rigidity or inflexibility of a part or of a joint.

acantha (ah-kan'thah) [Gr. *akantha* thorn]. 1. The spine. 2. The spinous process of a vertebra.

acanthaceous (ak″an-tha′shus). Bearing prickles or spines.

acanthesthesia (ah-kan″thes-the′ze-ah) [*acantho-* + Gr. *aisthēsis* sensation + *-ia*]. Perverted sensibility with a feeling as of pressure of a sharp point.

Acanthia lectularia (ah-kan′the-ah lek″tu-la′re-ah). The bedbug.

acanthion (ah-kan′the-on) [Gr. *akanthion* little thorn]. A point at the base of the anterior nasal spine.

acantho- (ah-kan′tho) [Gr. *akantha* a thorn or prickle]. A combining form meaning thorny or spiny, or denoting a relationship to a sharp spine or thorn.

Acanthobdellidea (ah-kan″tho-del-lid′e-ah). An order of leeches of the class Hirudinea, characterized by the presence of spines on the surface of the body.

Acanthocephala (ah-kan″tho-sef′ah-lah) [*acantho-* + Gr. *kephalē* head]. A division (class) of nematode animal parasites, the thorn-head worms, so called because of the proboscis which projects anteriorly, and is covered with thornlike recurved spines for attachment to the host.

acanthocephaliasis (ah-kan″tho-sef″ah-li′ah-sis). Infestation with any species of the class Acanthocephala.

Acanthocheilone′ma per′stans. A filarial nematode up to 80 mm. long found in the tropical regions of South America, Africa and New Guinea and transmitted by the bites of small flies of the genus *Culicoides*. The adult forms inhabit the pleural and peritoneal cavities, pericardium, mesentery and retroperitoneal tissues, while the larval forms are in the peripheral blood. Formerly called *Filaria perstans* and *Dipetalonema perstans*.

acanthocheilonemiasis (ah-kan″tho-ki″lo-ne-mi′ah-sis). Infection with *Acanthocheilonema perstans*.

acanthocyte (ah-kan′tho-sīt) [*acantho-* + Gr. *kytos* cell]. An erythrocyte characterized by protoplasmic projections of varying sizes and shapes, which give the cell a distorted, "thorny" appearance.

acanthocytosis (ah-kan″tho-si-to′sis). Presence in the blood of acanthocytes, characteristically associated, in a familial manner, with a neurologic disorder, retinitis pigmentosa, a celiac syndrome, hypocholesterolemia, absence of β-lipoprotein, and altered intracellular red cell lipids. See also *Bassen-Kornzweig syndrome*, under *syndrome*.

acanthoid (ah-kan′thoid) [*acantho-* + Gr. *eidos* form]. Resembling a spine; spinous.

acanthokeratodermia (ah-kan″tho-ker″ah-to-der′me-ah) [*acantho-* + Gr. *keras* horn + *derma* skin + *-ia*]. Hyperkeratosis.

acantholysis (ak″an-thol′ĭ-sis) [*acantho-* + Gr. *lysis* a loosening]. Atrophy and detachment of the prickle layer of the skin (Auspitz). **a. bullo′sa,** epidermolysis bullosa.

acanthoma (ak″an-tho′mah), pl. *acantho′mas* or *acantho′mata* [*acantho-* + *-oma*]. Adult cornifying squamous carcinoma. **a. adenoi′des cys′ticum,** epithelioma adenoides cysticum. **a. inguina′le, a. trop′icum,** papilloma inguinale tropicum. **a. verruco′sa seborrhoe′ica,** senile warts.

acanthopelvis (ah-kan″tho-pel′vis) [*acantho-* + Gr. *pelyx* bowl]. A pelvis with the crest of the pubes very sharp.

acanthopelyx (ak″an-thop′ĕ-liks). Acanthopelvis.

Acanthophacetus (ah-kan″tho-fa-se′tus). A genus of small fish. **A. reticula′tus,** *Lebistes reticulatus*.

Acanthophis (ah-kan′tho-fis). A genus of elapid snakes. **A. antarc′tica,** a poisonous elapid snake of Australia and New Guinea; called also *death adder*.

acanthosis (ak″an-tho′sis) [*acantho-* + *-osis*]. Hypertrophy or thickening of the prickle cell layer of the skin. **a. ni′gricans,** hyperpigmentation and roughness of the skin, either generalized or in the axillae or body folds. In about half the cases there is associated internal cancer. Called also *keratosis nigricans*. **a. papulo′sa ni′gra,** a papular eruption on the face, commonly seen in Negroes. **a. seborrhoe′ica, a. verruco′sa,** verruca senilis.

acanthotic (ak″an-thot′ik). Marked by acanthosis.

acanthrocyte (ah-kan′thro-sīt). Acanthocyte.

acanthrocytosis (ah-kan″thro-si-to′sis). Acanthocytosis.

a cap′ite ad cal′cem [L.]. From head to heel, the classic order for describing symptoms.

acapnia (ah-kap′ne-ah) [*a* neg. + Gr. *kapnos* smoke + *-ia*]. A condition of diminished carbon dioxide in blood.

acapnial (ah-kap′ne-al). Acapnic.

acapnic (a-kap′nik). Pertaining to or characterized by acapnia.

Acarapis (a-kar′ah-pis). A genus of mites. **A. wood′i,** the tracheal mite of the honey bee, which causes Isle of Wight disease.

acarbia (ah-kar′be-ah). A condition in which the blood bicarbonate is lowered.

acardia (a-kar′de-ah) [*a* neg. + Gr. *kardia* heart]. A developmental anomaly characterized by absence of the heart.

acardiac (a-kar′de-ak). 1. Having no heart. 2. Acardius.

acardiacus (ah″kar-di′ah-kus) [L. "without a heart"]. Acardius.

acardiohemia (ah-kar″de-o-he′me-ah) [*a* neg. + Gr. *kardia* heart + *haima* blood + *-ia*]. Lack of blood in the heart.

acardionervia (ah-kar″de-o-ner′ve-ah) [*a* neg. + Gr. *kardia* heart + *neuron* sinew + *-ia*]. Lack of nerve stimulus to the heart.

acardiotrophia (ah-kar″de-o-tro′fe-ah) [*a* neg. + Gr. *kardia* heart + *trophē* nutrition + *-ia*]. Atrophy of the heart.

acardius (ah-kar′de-us) [*a* neg. + Gr. *kardia* heart]. An imperfectly formed free twin fetus, lacking a heart and invariably lacking other body parts as well. **a. aceph′alus,** holoacardius acephalus. **a. acor′mus,** holoacardius acormus. **a. amor′phus,** holoacardius amorphus. **a. an′ceps,** hemiacardius.

acari (ak′ah-ri) [L.]. Plural of *acarus*.

acarian (ah-ka′re-an). Pertaining to the acarids or mites.

acariasis (ak″ah-ri′ah-sis) [Gr. *akari* mite + *-iasis*]. An infestation with mites. **chorioptic a.** See *Chorioptes*. **demodectic a.,** infestation of the hair follicles with the mite *Demodex folliculorum*. It affects man, dogs, horses, cattle, and sheep. In animals it is also called *follicular mange*. **psoroptic a.,** infestation with mites which deposit their eggs on the skin of the host and produce scabs, e.g., *Psoroptes*. **pulmonary a.,** disease of monkeys produced by mites which live in the lungs of the host. **sarcoptic a.,** an infestation with mites of species which burrow into the skin, producing channels in which their eggs are deposited, e.g., *Sarcoptes*. See *scabies*.

acaricide (ah-kar′ĭ-sīd) [L. *acarus* mite + *caedere* to slay]. 1. Destructive to mites. 2. An agent that destroys mites.

acarid (ak′ah-rid). A mite or tick of the family Acaridae, or order Acarina.

Acaridae (ah-kar′i-de). A family of small mites belonging to the order Acarina. Several species cause skin rashes, such as grocers' itch, copra itch and vanillism.

acaridan (ah-kar′i-dan). Acarid.

acaridiasis (ah-kar″i-di′ah-sis). Acariasis.

Acarina (ak″ah-ri′nah). An order of the class *Arachnida*, including the ticks and mites.

acarinosis (ah-kar″i-no′sis). Any disease caused by acari; acariasis.

acariosis (ah-kar″e-o′sis). Acarinosis.

acaro- (ak′ah-ro) [Gr. *akari;* L. *acarus,* a mite]. Combining form denoting relationship to mites.

acarodermatitis (ak″ah-ro-der″mah-ti′tis). Any skin inflammation caused by acari. **a. urticarioi′des,** grain itch.

acaroid (ak′ah-roid) [Gr. *akari* a mite + *eidos* form]. Resembling a mite.

acarology (ak″ah-rol′o-je) [*acaro-* + *-logy*]. The scientific study of mites and ticks.

acarophobia (ak″ah-ro-fo′be-ah) [*acaro-* + *phobia*]. Morbid dread of mites (Acarus), or of small objects.

acarotoxic (ak″ah-ro-tok′sik). Destructive to mites.

Acartomyia (ah-kar″to-mi′yah). A genus of culicine mosquitoes.

Acarus (ak′ah-rus) [L.; Gr. *akari* a mite]. A genus of small animals, often ectoparasitic, and called mites. They cause itch, mange, and other skin diseases. **A. folliculo′rum,** *Demodex folliculorum.* **A. galli′nae,** *Dermanyssus gallinae.* **A. hor′dei,** the barley bug, a mite which burrows under the skin of man. **A. rhyzoglyp′ticus hyacin′thi,** the onion mite which occurs on decaying onions and produces a dermatitis on persons who handle them. **A. scabi′ei,** *Sarcoptes scabiei.* **A. trit′ici,** *Pediculoides ventricosus.*

acarus (ak′ah-rus), pl. *ac′ari* [L.]. A mite.

acaryote (ah-kăr′e-ōt) [*a* neg. + Gr. *karyon* kernel]. 1. Non-nucleated. 2. A non-nucleated cell.

acatalasemia (a″kat-ah-la-se′me-ah). Deficiency of catalase in the blood. See *acatalasia.*

acatalasia (a″kat-ah-la′ze-ah). A rare disease characterized by congenital absence of the enzyme catalase, due to homozygosity for a Mendelian gene and occurring mostly in Japanese persons. Only about half of the patients have symptoms, which consist of recurrent infections of the gingiva and associated oral structures. Originally called *acatalasemia* because the absence of catalase was first detected in the red blood cells.

acatalepsia (ah-kat″ah-lep′se-ah) [*a* neg. + Gr. *katalēpsis* comprehension]. 1. Lack of understanding. 2. Uncertainty of diagnosis.

acatalepsy (ah-kat′ah-lep″se). Acatalepsia.

acataleptic (ah-kat″ah-lep′tik). 1. Mentally deficient. 2. Doubtful or uncertain.

acatamathesia (a-kat″ah-mah-the′ze-ah) [*a* neg. + Gr. *katamathēsis* understanding + *-ia*]. 1. Loss or impairment of the power to understand speech. 2. Impairment of any one of the perceptive faculties, due to a central lesion.

acataphasia (a-kat″ah-fa′ze-ah) [*a* neg. + Gr. *kataphasis* orderly utterance + *-ia*]. Inability to express one's thoughts in a connected manner, due to a central lesion.

acataposis (a-kat″ah-po′sis) [*a* neg. + Gr. *kata* down + *posis* drinking]. Difficulty in swallowing.

acatastasia (ak″ah-tas-ta′se-ah) [*a* neg. + Gr. *katastasis* stability + *-ia*]. Irregularity; variation from the normal.

acatastatic (ak″ah-tas-tat′ik). Irregular; varying from the normal.

acatharsia (ak″ah-thar′se-ah). Failure to obtain purgation.

acathectic (ak″ah-thek′tik) [*a* neg. + Gr. *kathexis* a retention]. Pertaining to or characterized by a cathexia.

acathexia (ak″ah-thek′se-ah). Inability to retain bodily secretions.

acathisia (ak″ah-the′ze-ah). Akathisia.

acaudal (a-kaw′dal). Acaudate.

acaudate (a-kaw′dāt) [*a* neg. + L. *cauda* tail]. Having no tail.

acauline (a-kaw′lin) [*a* neg. + L. *caulis* stem]. Having no stem: a term applied to certain fungi.

acaulinosis (a-kaw″li-no′sis). A mycotic disease characterized by an erythematous eruption with purulent discharges and crusts: due to species of *Acaulium.*

Acaulium (ah-kaw′le-um). A genus of fungi, which may cause infection in man.

ACC. Abbreviation for *anodal closure contraction.*

Acc. Abbreviation for *accommodation.*

accelerans (ak-sel′er-anz) [L. "hastening"]. A nerve, stimulation of which hastens the heart's action.

accelerant (ak-sel′er-ant). A catalyzer.

acceleration (ak-sel″er-a′shun) [L. *acceleratio;* from *ad* intensification + *celerare* to quicken]. A quickening, as of the pulse rate or respiration. **negative a.,** a slowing.

accelerator (ak-sel′er-a″tor) [L. "hastener"]. 1. An agent or apparatus that is used to increase the rate at which an object proceeds or a substance acts, or at which some reaction occurs. 2. Any nerve or muscle which hastens the performance of a function. **linear a.,** an apparatus for the acceleration of subatomic particles, using alternating hollow electrodes in a straight vacuum tube, so arranged that when their high frequency potentials are properly varied the particles traveling through them receive successive increases in energy. **serum prothrombin conversion a.,** factor VII. See under *coagulation factors.* **serum thrombotic a.,** a factor in serum which possesses procoagulant properties and the ability, when infused experimentally into locally arrested flow systems, to induce blood coagulation; not yet assigned a number in the scheme of coagulation factors. **thromboplastin generation a.,** a moderately heat-labile component, present in fresh plasma but not in serum, which appears to influence primarily the rate of formation of intrinsic thromboplastin and may be responsible for the acceleration of coagulation observed in some patients with intravascular thrombosis; not yet assigned a number in the scheme of blood coagulation.

accelerin (ak-sel′er-in). Factor V. See under *coagulation factors.*

accentuation (ak-sen″chu-a′shun) [L. *accentus* accent]. Increased loudness or distinctness; intensification.

accentuator (ak-sen′chu-a″tor). A substance which intensifies the action of a tissue stain.

acceptor (ak-sep′tor). A substance which unites with another substance; specifically a substance which unites with hydrogen or oxygen, in an oxido-reduction reaction, and so enables the reaction to proceed. **hydrogen a.,** the substance which is reduced in the oxidation and reduction occurring anaerobically in the body tissues. **oxygen a.,** the substance which is oxidized.

accès pernicieux (ak-sa′ păr-nis-yuh′) [Fr. "pernicious attack"]. A sudden and severe paroxysm in falciparum malaria.

accessiflexor (ak-ses′e-flek″sor). Any accessory flexor muscle.

accessorius (ak″ses-o′re-us) [L. "supplementary"]. Accessory; used in B N A in naming certain structures thought to serve a supplementary function.

accessory (ak-ses′o-re) [L. *accessorius*]. Supplementary or affording aid to another similar and generally more important thing.

accident (ak′si-dent). An unforeseen occurrence, especially one of an injurious character; an unexpected complicating occurrence in the regular course of a disease. **cerebral vascular a.,** apoplexy.

accidentalism (ak″si-den′tal-izm). The theory of medicine that attends only the symptoms of disease, ignoring the etiology and pathology.

accipiter (ak-sip′ĭ-ter) [L. "hawk"]. A facial bandage with tails like the talons of a hawk.

ACCl. Abbreviation for *anodal closure clonus.*

acclimatation (ah-kli″mah-ta′shun). Acclimation.

acclimation (ak″li-ma′shun). The process of becoming accustomed to a new climate, soil, and conditions.

acclimatization (ah-kli″mah-ti-za′shun). Acclimation.

accommodation (ah-kom″o-da′shun) [L. *accommodere* to fit to]. Adjustment, especially that of the eye for various distances. **absolute a.,** the accommodation of either eye separately. **binocular a.,** like accommodation in both eyes in coordination with convergence. **excessive a.,** accommodation of the eye which is persistently above the normal. **histologic a.,** a group of changes in the morphology and function of cells following changed conditions. **negative a.,** adjustment of the eye for long distances by relaxation. **nerve a.,** the rise in the threshold during the passage of a constant, direct electric current because of which only the make and break of the current stimulates the nerve. **positive a.,** adjustment of the eye for short distances by contraction. **relative a.,** the change in accommodation that is possible with a fixed amount of convergence. **subnormal a.,** insufficient power of accommodation of the eye.

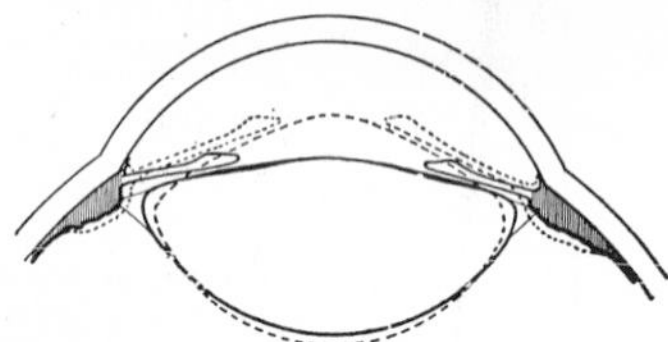

Changes during accommodation: Contraction of ciliary muscle; approximation of ciliary muscle to lens; relaxation of suspensory ligament; increased curvature of anterior surface of lens. (Helmholtz.)

accommodative (ah-kom′o-da″tiv). Pertaining to, of the nature of, or affecting accommodation.

accommodometer (ah-kom″o-dom′e-ter). A device for measuring the accommodative capacity of the eye.

accomplice (ak-om-plēs′) [Fr.]. A bacterium which accompanies the chief infecting agent in a mixed infection and which influences the virulence of the chief organism.

accouchement (ah-koosh-mon′) [Fr.]. Delivery in childbed; labor. **a. forcé** (ah-koosh-mon′ for-sa′), rapid delivery from below by any one of several methods; originally applied to rapid dilation of the cervix with the hands, with version and forcible extraction of the fetus.

accoucheur (ah-koosh-er′) [Fr.]. One skilled in midwifery; an obstetrician.

accoucheuse (ah-koosh-ez′) [Fr.]. A midwife.

accrementition (ak″re-men-tish′un) [L. *ad* to + *crementum* increase]. Growth or increase by the addition of similar tissue.

accretio (ah-kre′she-o) [L.]. Abnormal adhesion of parts normally separate. **a. cor′dis, a. pericar′dii,** a form of adhesive pericarditis in which there are adhesions extending from the pericardium to the pleurae, diaphragm, and chest wall.

accretion (ah-kre′shun) [L. *ad* to + *crescere* to grow]. 1. The normal increase in size of a tissue through the provision of nutrient material. 2. The adherence of parts naturally separate. 3. A mass of foreign matter which has accumulated in a cavity.

accumulator (ah-ku′mu-la″tor). An apparatus for collecting and storing electricity; a storage cell or storage battery.

A.C.D. Abbreviation for *absolute cardiac dulness,* and *acid citrate dextrose* (see under *solution*).

ACE. Abbreviation for *adrenocortical extract.*

acedia (ah-se′de-ah) [*a* neg. + Gr. *kēdos* care + *-ia*]. A mental disorder characterized by apathy and melancholy.

acellular (a-sel′u-lar). Not made up of or containing cells.

acelomate (ah-se′lo-māt). Not having a celom or body cavity.

acenesthesia (ah-sen″es-the′ze-ah) [*a* neg. + *cenesthesia*]. Abolition of the sense of well being, seen in melancholia and hypochondriasis.

acenocoumarol (ah-se″no-koo′mah-rol). Chemical name: 3-(α-acetonyl-p-nitrobenzyl)-4-hydroxycoumarin. Use: anticoagulant which acts by reducing formation of prothrombin by the liver.

acentric (ah-sen′trik) [Gr. *akentrikos* not centric]. 1. Not central; not located in the center. 2. Not originating in a nerve center.

acephalia (ah″sĕ-fa′le-ah) [*a* neg. + Gr. *kephalē* head]. A developmental anomaly characterized by absence of the head.

acephalism (ah-sef′ah-lizm). Acephalia.

acephalobrachia (ah-sef″ah-lo-bra′ke-ah) [*a* neg. + Gr. *kephalē* head + *brachiōn* arm + *-ia*]. A developmental anomaly characterized by absence of the head and arms.

acephalobrachius (ah-sef″ah-lo-bra′ke-us). A fetal monster exhibiting acephalobrachia.

acephalocardia (ah-sef″ah-lo-kar′de-ah) [*a* neg. + Gr. *kephalē* head + *kardia* heart + *-ia*]. A developmental anomaly characterized by absence of the head and heart.

acephalocardius (ah-sef″ah-lo-kar′de-us). A fetal monster exhibiting acephalocardia.

acephalochiria (ah-sef″ah-lo-ki′re-ah) [*a* neg. + Gr. *kephalē* head + *cheir* hand + *-ia*]. A developmental anomaly characterized by absence of the head and hands.

acephalochirus (ah-sef″ah-lo-ki′rus). A fetal monster exhibiting acephalochiria.

acephalocyst (ah-sef″ah-lo′sist) [*a* neg. + Gr. *kephalē* head + *kystis* bladder]. A headless, bag-like hydatid filled with a liquid, it being one of the stages of the existence of a sterile cestoid worm (Laennec, 1804).

acephalocystis racemosa (ah-sef″ah-lo-sis′tis ra-se-mo′sah). A hydatid mole of the uterus.

acephalogaster (ah-sef″ah-lo-gas′ter) [*a* neg. + Gr. *kephalē* head + *gastēr* belly]. A fetal monster exhibiting acephalogastria.

acephalogastria (ah-sef″ah-lo-gas′tre-ah). A developmental anomaly characterized by absence of the head, chest, and upper part of the abdomen.

acephalopodia (ah-sef″ah-lo-po′de-ah) [*a* neg. + Gr. *kephalē* head + *pous* foot + *-ia*]. A developmental anomaly characterized by absence of the head and feet.

acephalopodius (ah-sef″ah-lo-po′de-us). A fetal monster exhibiting acephalopodia.

acephalorhachia (ah-sef″ah-lo-ra′ke-ah) [*a* neg. + Gr. *kephalē* head + *rhachis* spine + *-ia*]. A developmental anomaly characterized by absence of the head and spinal column.

acephalostomia (ah-sef″ah-lo-sto′me-ah) [*a* neg. + Gr. *kephalē* head + *stoma* mouth + *-ia*]. A developmental anomaly characterized by absence of the head, and with a kind of mouth on the superior aspect.

acephalostomus (ah-sef″ah-los′to-mus). A fetal monster exhibiting acephalostomia.

acephalothoracia (ah-sef″ah-lo-tho-ra′se-ah) [*a* neg. + Gr. *kephalē* head + *thōrax* chest + *-ia*]. A developmental anomaly characterized by absence of the head and chest.

acephalothorus (ah-sef″ah-lo-tho′rus). A fetal monster exhibiting acephalothoracia.

acephalous (ah-sef′ah-lus). Without a head.

acephalus (ah-sef′ah-lus), pl. *aceph′ali* [*a* neg. + Gr. *kephalē* head]. A fetal monster without a head.

a. dibra'chius, an acephalus with both upper limbs more or less undeveloped. **a. di'pus,** an acephalus with both lower limbs more or less undeveloped. **a. monobra'chius,** an acephalus with only one upper limb. **a. mon'opus,** an acephalus with only one lower limb. **a. paraceph'alus,** a fetal monster with a partially formed skull but no brain. **a. sym'pus,** an acephalus with the two lower limbs fused into one.

acephaly (ah-sef'ah-le). Acephalia.

Aceraria (as″ĕ-ra're-ah). A genus of nematode parasites. **A. spira'lis,** a nematode parasite occurring in growths in the esophagus of fowls.

aceratosis (ah-ser″ah-to'sis) [*a* neg. + Gr. *keras* horn + *-osis*]. Deficiency of the horny tissue.

acervuli (ah-ser'vu-li) [L.]. Plural of *acervulus.*

acervuline (ah-ser'vu-lin) [L. *acervulus* little heap]. Aggregated, like certain glands.

acervuloma (ah-ser″vu-lo'mah) [L. *acervulus* little heap + *-oma*]. A meningioma containing psammoma bodies.

acervulus (ah-ser'vu-lus), pl. *acer'vuli* [L., dim. of *acervus* a heap]. [B N A] The mass of gritty matter which lies in or near the pineal body, the choroid plexus, and other parts of the brain. Called also *acervulus cerebri* and *brain sand.*

acescence (ah-ses'ens) [L. *acescere* to become sour]. 1. Sourness. 2. The process of becoming sour.

acescent (ah-ses'ent). Somewhat or slightly acid.

acesodyne (ah-ses'o-dīn) [Gr. *akesis* cure + *odynē* pain]. Anodyne; allaying pain.

acestoma (ah″ses-to'mah) [Gr. *akesis* cure + *-oma*]. A mass of granulations.

acetabular (as″e-tab'u-lar). Pertaining to the acetabulum.

acetabulectomy (as″e-tab″u-lek'to-me) [*acetabulum* + Gr. *ektomē* excision]. Excision of the acetabulum along with the rest of the hip joint.

acetabuloplasty (as″e-tab'u-lo-plas″te) [*acetabulum* + Gr. *plassein* to form]. Plastic reconstruction of the acetabulum.

acetabulum (as″e-tab'u-lum), pl. *acetab'ula* [L. "vinegar-cruet," from *acetum* vinegar]. [N A, B N A] The large cup-shaped cavity on the lateral surface of the os coxae in which the head of the femur articulates.

acetaldehydase (as″et-al'de-hi″dās). An enzyme which catalyzes the oxidation of acetic aldehyde to acetic acid.

acetaldehyde (as″et-al'de-hīd″). Acetic aldehyde.

acetamide (as″et-am'īd). A white, crystalline substance, CH_3CONH_2.

acetamidine (as″et-am'i-din). The amine, $CH_3C(NH)NH_2$, of acetic acid.

p-acetamidobenzene sulfonamide. One of the conjugated forms in which benzene sulfonamide is excreted in the urine.

acetaminofluorene (as″et-am″i-no-floo'o-rēn). A compound $C_6H_4CH_2C_6H_3NH.CO.CH_3$, which is carcinogenic when ingested.

acetaminophen (as″et-am'ĭ-no-fen). Chemical name: N-acetyl-p-aminophenol. Uses: 1. analgesic; 2. antipyretic.

acetanilid (as″e-tan'i-lid) [*acetic* + *aniline*]. A white, crystalline, sublimable solid, phenylacetamide, $C_6H_5NH.OC.CH_3$, produced by combining glacial acetic acid with aniline. It is analgesic and antipyretic, and is used in neuralgia and rheumatism. Called also *antifebrin.*

acetannin (as″e-tan'in). Acetyltannic acid.

acetarsol (as″et-ar'sol). Acetarsone.

acetarsone (as″et-ar'sōn). A white or slightly yellow, odorless powder, $CH_3.CO.NH.C_6H_4(OH).AsO(OH)_2$. It is used in the treatment of amebiasis and locally in trichomonas vaginitis. It has been proposed for use in sarcoid and in certain cases of syphilis.

acetas (ah-se'tas) [L.]. Acetate.

acetate (as'e-tāt). Any salt of acetic acid.

acetazolamide (as″et-ah-zol'ah-mīd). Chemical name: 5-acetamido-1,3,4-thiadiazole-2-sulfonamide; a diuretic of the carbonic anhydrase inhibitor type, useful in treatment of carbon dioxide retention in chronic lung disease; as an adjunct in treatment of epilepsy; and to reduce intraocular pressure in glaucoma.

acetenyl (ah-se'tĕ-nil). The group—$C{\equiv}CH$, when it occurs in organic compounds.

aceteugenol (as″et-u'je-nol). An essential oil from oil of cloves: it is 1-ethyl, 3-methoxy, 4-acetoxy benzene.

acethemin (as″et-he'min). A preparation of hemin, $C_{34}H_{33}O_4N_4ClFe$, derived from the coloring matter of the blood.

acetic (ah-se'tik). Pertaining to vinegar or its acid; sour.

aceticoceptor (ah-se″te-ko-sep'tor). A ceptor or side chain having specific affinity for the acetic acid radical.

acetify (ah-set'ĭ-fi). To turn into acetic acid or vinegar.

acetimeter (as″e-tim'e-ter) [L. *acetum* vinegar + Gr. *metron* measure]. An apparatus for determining the amount of acetic acid present in a solution.

acetin (as'ĕ-tin). A glyceryl acetate; it may contain one, two, or three acetic acid radicals.

Acetobacter (ah-se″to-bak'ter) [L. *acetum* vinegar + *bactrum* (Gr. *baktērion*) little rod]. A genus of microorganisms of the family Pseudomonadaceae, suborder Pseudomonadineae, order Pseudomonadales, occurring as ellipsoidal to rod-shaped cells, singly, or in pairs or short or long chains, important for their role in completion of the carbon cycle and in production of vinegar. It includes seven species, *A. ace'ti, A. melano'genus, A. ox'ydans, A. ran'cens, A. ro'seus, A. subox'ydans,* and *A. xy'linum; A. kuetzingia'nus* and *A. pasteuria'nus* are considered varieties of *A. rancens.*

acetobromanilide (as″e-to-brōm-an'ĭ-lid). A compound, $CH_3CONH.C_6H_4Br$, which possesses hypnotic, antipyretic and antineuralgic properties.

acetochloral (as″e-to-klo'ral). Chloral.

acetoform (ah-se'to-form). Methenamine.

acetolase (ah-set'o-lās). An enzyme which catalyzes the conversion of alcohol into acetic acid.

acetolysis (as″e-tol'ĭ-sis). Combined hydrolysis and acetylation.

acetomeroctol (as″e-to-mer-ok'tol). Chemical name: 2-acetoxymercuri-4(1,1,3,3-tetramethylbutyl) phenol. Use: applied locally to the skin as an antiseptic for the prevention and control of superficial infection.

acetometer (as″e-tom'e-ter). Acetimeter.

acetomorphine (as″e-to-mor'fin). Diacetylmorphine.

acetonal (ah-set'o-nal). Aluminum and sodium acetate, $Al_2(OH)_2(C_2H_3O_2)_5Na$.

acetonaphthone (as″e-to-naf'thōn). An acetyl derivative of naphthalene, $C_{10}H_7COCH_3$, occurring in two isomeric forms.

acetonasthma (as″e-tōn-az'mah). Asthma accompanied with acetonuria and probably due to it, and marked by headache, vomiting, restlessness, and amaurosis.

acetonation (as″e-to-na'shun). The combination with acetone.

acetone (as'e-tōn) [*acetic* + *ketone*]. 1. Dimethyl ketone, $CH_3.CO.CH_3$, a colorless liquid with a pleasant ethereal odor. Found in small quantities in normal urine, it occurs in larger amounts in diabetic urine. It is acrid and inflammable, and is used as a solvent for fats, resins, rubber, and plastic. 2. Any member of the series to which the normal or typical acetone belongs. See *acetone bodies.* **a. diethyl-sulfone,** sulfonmethane.

acetonemia (as″e-to-ne'me-ah) [*acetone* + Gr. *haima* blood + *-ia*]. The presence of acetone bodies in the blood.

acetonemic (as″e-to-ne′mik). Pertaining to or marked by acetonemia.

acetonglycosuria (as″e-tōn″gli-ko-su′re-ah). Glycosuria following acetone poisoning.

acetonitrate (as″e-to-ni′trāt). A compound of a base with acetic and nitric acids.

acetonitrile (as″e-to-ni′tril). Methyl cyanide, CH_3CN, a colorless liquid.

acetonum (as″e-to′num) [L.]. Acetone.

acetonumerator (as″e-to-nu′mer-a″tor). An instrument for estimating the amount of acetone in the urine.

acetonuria (as″e-to-nu′re-ah). Excess of acetone bodies in the urine. It occurs in diabetes, fever, carcinoma, and digestive disorders.

acetophenazine (as″e-to-fen′ah-zēn). A substance with a mild sedative effect, used as a tranquilizer.

acetophenetidin (as″e-to-fĕ-net′ĭ-din). A compound, $C_2H_5O.C_6H_4.NH.CO.CH_3$, occurring as white glistening crystals or a fine white crystalline powder, without odor and with a slightly bitter taste: antipyretic and analgesic.

acetosal (ah-se′to-sal). Acetylsalicylic acid.

acetosoluble (as″e-to-sol′u-b'l). Soluble in acetic acid.

acetous (as′e-tus) [L. *acetosus*]. Pertaining to, producing, or resembling acetic acid.

acetphenarsine (as″et-fen-ar′sēn). Acetarsone.

acetphenetidin (as″et-fĕ-net′ĭ-din). Acetophenetidin.

acetpyrogall (as″et-pi′ro-gal). A white, crystalline compound, $C_6H_3(CH_3CO_2)_3$: antipruritic, used as a powder or in ointment.

acetract (as′e-trakt). An extract of a drug made with a menstruum containing acetic acid.

acetrozoate sodium (as″e-tro′zo-āt so′de-um). Chemical name: 3-acetamido-2,4,6-triiodobenzoic acid sodium salt. Use: radiopaque medium for roentgenographic visualization of blood vessels and kidneys.

acetum (ah-se′tum), pl. *ace′ta* [L.]. 1. Vinegar. 2. A medicinal solution of a drug in dilute acetic acid. **a. plum′bi, a. satur′ni,** lead subacetate solution.

acetyl (as′e-til) [L. *acetum* vinegar + Gr. *hylē* matter]. The monovalent radical, CH_3CO, the form in which acetic acid enters into various compounds. **a. chloride,** a colorless liquid, $CH_3.CO.Cl$, used as a reagent. **a. dioxide,** a thick liquid $(C_2H_3O)_2O_2$, a powerful oxidizing agent. **a. peroxide,** a powerful oxidizing substance, CH_3COOOH. **a. sulfisoxazole,** chemical name: N-acetyl-N′-(3,4-dimethyl-5-isoxazolyl) sulfanilamide: used as an anti-infective.

acetylaminobenzene sulfonate (as″e-til-am″ĭ-no-ben′zēn sul′fo-nāt). A compound, $CH_3.CO.NH.C_6H_4.SO_2.NH_2$, the form in which sulfanilamide is excreted.

acetylaminobenzine (as″e-til-am″ĭ-no-ben′zēn). Acetanilid.

acetylaniline (as″e-til-an′ĭ-lin). Acetanilid.

acetylation (ah-set″ĭ-la′shun). The introduction of an acetyl group into the molecule of an organic compound.

acetyl-beta-methylcholine (as″e-til-ba″tah-meth″il-ko′lin). A choline compound $(CH_3)_3NCH_2CH(CH_3)OCOCH_3$ which increases the tone and movement of the gastrointestinal tract and has a vasodilating effect: suggested for use in tachycardia. See *methacholine*.

acetylcarbromal (as″e-til-kar-bro′mal). Chemical name: N-acetyl-N-bromodiethylacetylurea. Use: sedative.

acetylcholine (as″e-til-ko′lēn). A reversible acetic acid ester of choline, $CH_3.CO.O.CH_2.CH_2.N(CH_3)_3.OH$, normally present in many parts of the body and having important physiological functions, such as playing a role in the transmission of an impulse from one nerve fiber to another across a synaptic junction: used also in medicine as a parasympathomimetic agent.

acetyldigitoxin-α (as″e-til-dij″ĭ-tok′sin al-fah). A digitalis preparation composed of the aglycone digitoxigenin and 3 molecules of digitoxose, to one of which an acetyl group is attached. Use: to improve function of failing heart.

acetylene (ah-set′ĭ-lēn). 1. A colorless, volatile, and explosive gas, ethine, C_2H_2, with a garlic-like odor. It is formed by the action of water on calcium carbide and burns with a brilliant white flame. It has been employed as a general anesthetic. 2. The type of a class of unsaturated (triple bonded) organic compounds.

acetylization (ah-set″il-i-za′shun). Acetylation.

acetylphenylhydrazine (as″e-til-fen″il-hi-dra′-zen). Chemical name: B-acetylphenylhydrazine: used as a hemolytic agent in the treatment of polycythemia.

acetylphosphatase (as″e-til-fos′fah-tās). An enzyme in muscle which catalyzes the splitting of acetylphosphate.

acetylsulfadiazine (as″e-til-sul″fah-di′ah-zēn). The form in which sulfadiazine is excreted in the urine, often occurring in dark green crystalline spheres.

acetylsulfaguanidine (as″e-til-sul″fah-gwan′i-dēn). The form in which sulfaguanidine is excreted in the urine, often occurring in thin oblong crystalline plates.

acetylsulfanilamide (as″e-til-sul″fah-nil′ah-mid). Acetylated (conjugated) sulfanilamide as it appears in the body after administration.

acetylsulfathiazole (as″e-til-sul″fah-thi′ah-zōl). The form in which sulfathiazole is excreted in the urine, often occurring in the form of sheaves-of-wheat crystals.

acetyltannin (as″e-til-tan′in). Acetyltannic acid.

Ac-G. Abbreviation for *accelerator globulin*.

ACH. Abbreviation for *adrenal cortical hormone*.

ACh. Abbreviation for *acetylcholine*.

achalasia (ak″ah-la′ze-ah) [*a* neg. + Gr. *chalasis* relaxation + *-ia*]. Failure to relax of the smooth muscle fibers of the gastrointestinal tract at any point of junction of one part with another, such as the failure to relax of the smooth muscle fibers of the lower esophagus, called *achalasia of the esophagus*, characterized by dilatation and hypertrophy of the esophagus above an atrophic lower segment (mega-esophagus). **pelvirectal a.,** congenital hypertrophic dilatation of the colon (megacolon). **sphincteral a.,** failure of relaxation of any sphincter of a tubular organ.

Achard-Castaigne method (ash-ar′ kas-tān′) [Emile Charles *Achard*, Paris physician, 1860–1944; Joseph *Castaigne*, French physician, 1871–1951]. The methylene blue test.

Achard-Thiers syndrome (ash-ar′ tērz′) [Emile Charles *Achard;* Joseph *Thiers*]. Diabetes occurring with hirsutism in women.

ache (āk). A continuous, fixed pain.

acheilia (ah-ki′le-ah) [*a* neg. + Gr. *cheilos* lip + *-ia*]. A developmental anomaly characterized by absence of one or both lips.

acheilous (ah-ki′lus). Having no lips; exhibiting or pertaining to acheilia.

acheiria (ah-ki′re-ah) [*a* neg. + Gr. *cheir* hand + *-ia*]. A developmental anomaly characterized by absence of one or both hands.

acheiropodia (ah-ki″ro-po′de-ah) [*a* neg. + Gr. *cheir* hand + *pous* foot + *-ia*]. A developmental anomaly characterized by absence of hands and feet.

acheirus (ah-ki′rus) [L.]. An individual exhibiting acheiria.

Achillea (ak″i-le′ah) [L.; Gr. *achilleia*]. A genus of

composite-flowered plants. *A. millefolium*, milfoil, or yarrow, is a good bitter and stimulant tonic.

Achilles bursa, tendon (ak-kil'ēz) [Gr. *Achilleus* Greek hero, whose mother held him by the ankle to dip him in the Styx]. See *bursa tendinis calcanei* (*achillis*) and *tendo calcaneus* (*achillis*).

Achillini (ak"ĭ-le'ne), Alessandro (1463–1512). A celebrated Bolognese physician and philosopher, who left several works on anatomy.

achilloburs itis (ah-kil"o-bur-si'tis) [*Achilles* + Gr. *byrsa* bursa + *-itis*]. Inflammation and thickening of the bursae about the Achilles tendon, especially of the bursa in front of it.

achillodynia (ak"i-lo-din'e-ah) [*Achilles* (tendon) + Gr. *odynē* pain + *-ia*]. Pain in the Achilles tendon or in its bursa; achillobursitis.

achillorrhaphy (ak"i-lor'ah-fe) [*Achilles* (tendon) + Gr. *rhaphē* suture]. The operation of suturing the Achilles tendon.

achillotenotomy (ah-kil"o-ten-ot'o-me) [*Achilles* + Gr. *tenōn* tendon + *tomē* cut]. Surgical division of the Achilles tendon. **plastic a.,** elongation of the Achilles tendon by plastic operation.

achillotomy (ak"ĭ-lot'o-me). Achillotenotomy.

achiria (ah-ki're-ah). Acheiria.

achirus (ah-ki'rus). Acheirus.

Achlea (ak'le-ah). A genus of fungi which form molds on certain fish and insects.

achlorhydria (ah"klor-hid're-ah) [*a* neg. + *chlorhydria*]. Absence of hydrochloric acid from the gastric secretions. **a. apep'sia,** absence of the digestive secretions of the stomach.

achloride (ah-klo'rīd). A salt which is not a chloride.

achloroblepsia (ah-klo"ro-blep'se-ah). Achloropsia.

achloropsia (ah"klo-rop'se-ah) [*a* neg. + Gr. *chlōros* green + *opsis* vision + *-ia*]. Inability to distinguish green tints; deuteranopia.

achlys (ak'lis) [Gr. *achlys* darkness]. A mild corneal opacity (Himly).

acholia (ah-ko'le-ah) [*a* neg. + Gr. *cholē* bile + *-ia*]. Lack or absence of the secretion of bile.

acholic (ah-kol'ik). Free from bile.

acholuria (ah-ko-lu're-ah) [*a* neg. + Gr. *cholē* bile + *ouron* urine + *-ia*]. Absence of bile pigment from the urine.

acholuric (ah-ko-lu'rik). Pertaining to or characterized by acholuria.

achondroplasia (ah-kon"dro-pla'ze-ah) [*a* neg. + Gr. *chondros* cartilage + *plassein* to form + *-ia*]. A hereditary, congenital, familial disturbance of epiphyseal chondroblastic growth and maturation, causing inadequate enchondral bone formation and resulting in a peculiar type of dwarfism. It may be accompanied by other anomalies.

achondroplastic (ah-kon"dro-plas'tik). Pertaining to, or affected with, achondroplasia.

achondroplasty (ah-kon'dro-plas"te). Achondroplasia.

achor (a'kor) [Gr. *achōr* dandruff]. 1. An eruption of small papules on the hairy parts. 2. A scaly or scabby eruption on the face and scalp in infants. 3. An acuminate pustule.

achordal (ah-kor'dal). Achordate.

achordate (ah-kor'dāt). Without a notochord; used with reference to animals below the chordates.

achoresis (ak"o-re'sis) [*a* neg. + Gr. *chōrein* to hold]. Diminution of the capacity of a hollow organ.

Achorion (ah-ko're-on). Trichophyton.

achreocythemia (ah-kre"o-si-the'me-ah). Achroiocythemia.

achrestic (ah-kres'tik) [Gr. *achrēstia* the nonusance of a thing]. Pertaining to the lack of use of a principle which is present in the body.

achroacyte (ah-kro'ah-sīt). A lymphocyte.

achroacytosis (ah-kro"ah-si-to'sis) [*a* neg. + Gr. *chroa* color + *kytos* hollow vessel + *-osis*]. Excessive development of the colorless or lymph cells, as in Mikulicz's disease (q.v.).

achroglobin (ak"ro-glo'bin). A respiratory pigment found in certain invertebrates.

achroiocythemia (ah-kroi"o-si-the'me-ah) [Gr. *achroios* colorless + *kytos* hollow vessel + *haima* blood + *-ia*]. Deficiency or lack of hemoglobin in the red blood corpuscles.

achroma (ah-kro'mah) [*a* neg. + Gr. *chrōma* color]. Absence of color or of normal pigmentation.

achromachia (ah"kro-mak'e-ah). Grayness or whiteness of the hair.

achromacyte (ah-kro'mah-sīt) [*a* neg. + Gr. *chrōma* color + *kytos* hollow vessel]. A decolorized red blood corpuscle.

achromasia (ak"ro-ma'se-ah) [*a* neg. + Gr. *chrōma* color + *-ia*]. 1. Lack of normal pigmentation of the skin. 2. Absence of the usual staining reaction from a tissue or cell.

achromat (a'kro-mat) [*a* neg. + *chromatic*]. 1. An achromatic objective. 2. An individual who lacks the ability to discriminate hues, seeing the entire solar spectrum in terms of neutral grays of different shades of light and dark; able to match any of the visible wavelengths with any other with suitable adjustment of light intensities. There are two types, a cone achromat, and a second, less severely affected type, with some central vision.

achromate (ah-kro'māt). Achromat, def. 2.

Achromatiaceae (ak"ro-ma"she-a'se-e). A systematic family of schizomycetes (order Beggiatoales), made up of cells which are spherical to ovoid, or short cylinders with hemispherical ends, not possessing photosynthetic pigments. It includes a single genus, *Achromatium*.

achromatic (ak"ro-mat'ik) [*a* neg. + Gr. *chrōmatikos* pertaining to color]. 1. Producing no discoloration. 2. Staining with difficulty. 3. Containing achromatin. 4. Refracting light without decomposing it into its component colors. 5. Pertaining to or characterized by complete absence of color vision (achromatopia).

achromatin (ah-kro'mah-tin) [*a* neg. + Gr. *chrōma* color]. The faintly staining substance forming the nuclear sap, linin, and nuclear membrane of the nucleus of a cell.

achromatinic (ah-kro"mah-tin'ik). Pertaining to or containing achromatin.

achromatism (ah-kro'mah-tizm"). 1. The quality or condition of being achromatic. 2. Achromatopia.

achromatistous (ah-kro"mah-tis'tus). Deficient in pigment or coloring matter.

Achromatium (ak"ro-ma'she-um). A genus of microorganisms of the family Achromatiaceae.

achromatize (ah-kro'mah-tīz). To render achromatic.

achromatocyte (ak"ro-mat'o-sīt) [*a* neg. + Gr. *chrōma* color + *kytos* hollow vessel]. A decolorized erythrocyte.

achromatolysis (ah-kro"mah-tol'ĭ-sis) [*achromatin* + Gr. *lysis* dissolution]. Disorganization of the achromatin of a cell.

achromatophil (ah"kro-mat'o-fil) [*a* neg. + Gr. *chrōma* color + *philein* to love]. 1. Having no affinity for stains. 2. An organism or tissue element that does not stain easily.

achromatophilia (ah-kro"mah-to-fil'e-ah). The property of resisting the coloring action of stains.

achromatopia (ah"kro-mah-to'pe-ah) [*a* neg. + Gr. *chrōma* color + *ōpē* vision + *-ia*]. Inability to differentiate any of the rainbow hues, violet, indigo, blue, green, yellow, orange, red, or their intermediates.

achromatopic (ah"kro-mah-top'ik). Pertaining to or exhibiting achromatopia.

achromatopsia (ah-kro″mah-top′se-ah). Achromatopia.

achromatosis (ah-kro″mah-to′sis) [*a* neg. + Gr. *chrōma* color + *-osis*]. 1. Deficiency of pigmentation in the tissues, as in the skin and the iris. 2. Loss of staining power in a cell or tissue.

achromatous (ah-kro′mah-tus). Having no color; colorless.

achromaturia (ah-kro″mah-tu′re-ah) [*a* neg. + Gr. *chrōma* color + *ouron* urine + *-ia*]. The excretion of colorless urine.

achromia (ah-kro′me-ah) [*a* neg. + Gr. *chrōma* color + *-ia*]. Absence of normal color: specifically, a condition of the red cells of the blood in which the centers of the cells are paler than normal (**central a.**). **congenital a.,** albinism. **cortical a.,** a condition in which an area of the cerebral cortex shows disappearance of ganglion cells. **a. parasit′ica,** a disease of the skin marked by white or dirty white spots, usually on the face and neck. **a. un′guium,** leukonychia.

achromic (ah-kro′mik). Pertaining to or characterized by achromia.

achromin (ah-kro′min). Achromatin.

Achromobacter (ah-kro″mo-bak′ter) [*a* neg. + Gr. *chrōma* color + *baktērion* little rod]. A genus of microorganisms of the family Achromobacteraceae, order Eubacteriales, made up of non-pigment-forming gram-negative rod-shaped bacteria occurring in soil or in fresh or salt water. Fifteen species have been described.

Achromobacteraceae (ah-kro″mo-bak″tĕ-ra′se-e). A family of Schizomycetes (order Eubacteriales), made up of motile or non-motile small to medium-sized rods, generally in soil or in fresh or salt water. Some are parasitic or pathogenic. It includes five genera, *Achromobacter, Agarbacterium, Alcaligenes, Berneckea,* and *Flavobacterium.*

achromocyte (ah-kro′mo-sīt). A morphologic red cell artifact which stains more faintly than intact erythrocytes; thought to be derived from ruptured erythrocytes. Called also *selenoid* or *crescent body.* Not to be confused with the sickle cells present in sickle cell anemia.

achromoderma (ah-kro″mo-der′mah) [*a* neg. + Gr. *chrōma* color + *derma* skin]. A colorless state of the skin; leukoderma.

achromodermia (ah-kro″mo-der′me-ah). Achromoderma.

achromophil (ah-kro′mo-fil) [*a* neg. + Gr. *chrōma* color + *philein* to love]. Achromatophil.

achromophilous (ah″kro-mof′ĭ-lus). Having no affinity for stains.

achromotrichia (ah-kro″mo-trik′e-ah) [*a* neg. + Gr. *chrōma* color + *thrix* hair + *-ia*]. Absence of normal pigmentation of the hair. **nutritional a.,** lack of normal pigmentation of the hair attributed to a deficiency of certain factors in the diet.

Achromycin (ak′ro-mi″sin). Trade mark for preparations of tetracycline.

achrooamyloid (ah-kro″o-am′i-loid). Amyloid in its early nonstainable stage.

achroocytosis (ah-kro″o-si-to′sis). Achroacytosis.

achroodextrin (ah-kro″o-dek′strin) [Gr. *achroos* uncolored + *dextrin*]. A kind of dextrin not colored by iodine.

Achucárro's stain (ach″oo-kah′rōz) [Nicolás *Achucárro,* Spanish histologist, 1851–1918]. See *stains, table of.*

achylanemia (ah-ki″lah-ne′me-ah). A condition in which gastric achylia is associated with simple or hypochromic anemia; it does not necessarily indicate an etiologic correlation between the two conditions.

achylia (ah-ki′le-ah) [Gr. *achylos* juiceless + *-ia*]. Absence of the chyle; specifically absence of hydrochloric acid and rennin from the gastric juice (**a. gas′trica**). **a. gas′trica haemorrha′gica,** absence of hydrochloric acid from, and presence of occult blood in, the stomach. **a. pancreat′ica,** absence or deficiency of the pancreatic secretion; chronic pancreatitis.

achylosis (ah″ki-lo′sis). Achylia.

achylous (ah-ki′lus) [Gr. *achylos* juiceless]. Deficient in chyle.

achymia (ah-ki′me-ah). Imperfect or insufficient formation of chyme.

achymosis (ak″i-mo′sis). Achymia.

acicular (ah-sik′u-lar) [L. *acicularis*]. Shaped like a needle or needle point.

acid (as′id). 1. [L. *acidus,* from *acere* to be sour.] Sour; having properties opposed to those of the alkalis. 2. [L. *acidum.*] Any compound of an electronegative element with one or more hydrogen atoms that are replaceable by electropositive atoms; a compound which, in aqueous solution, undergoes dissociation with the formation of hydrogen ions. Acids have a sour taste, turn blue litmus red, and unite with bases to form salts. Acids are distinguished as *binary* or *hydracids,* and *ternary* or *oxacids:* the former contain no oxygen; in the latter the hydrogen is united to the electronegative element by oxygen. The hydracids are distinguished by the prefix *hydro-*. The names of acids end in "ic," except in the case where there are two degrees of oxygenation, when the acid containing the greater amount of oxygen has the termination *-ic,* the one having the lesser amount, the termination *-ous.* Acids ending in *-ic* form salts with the termination *-ate;* those ending in *-ous* form salts ending in *-ite.* The salts of hydracids end in *-id.* Acids are called *monobasic, dibasic, tribasic,* and *tetrabasic,* according as they contain one, two, three, or four replaceable hydrogen atoms. **abietic a., abietinic a.,** an acid resin, $C_{20}H_{30}O_2$, forming about 83 per cent of American rosin. **abietolic a.,** a crystalline acid resin, $C_{20}H_{28}O_2$, forming about 1.5 to 2 per cent of Chian turpentine. **abric a.,** a crystalline acid, $C_{21}H_{24}N_3O$, from jequirity. **absinthic a.,** an acid obtained from oil of wormwood. **aceric a.,** an acid from the juice of *Acer campestre,* the European maple. **acetic a.,** a colorless, crystalline acid, $CH_3.COOH$, the acid of vinegar. **acetic a., dilute,** an aqueous solution containing 6 per cent of the pure acid. **acetic a., glacial,** a clear, colorless liquid, with a pungent, characteristic odor, containing not less than 99.4 per cent, by weight, of $CH_3.COOH$. **acetoacetic a.,** a colorless syrupy compound, $CH_3.CO.CH_2.COOH$, one of the acetone bodies, occurring in traces in the normal urine and in abnormal amounts in the urine of diabetics. **acetrizoic a.,** an odorless white powder, $C_9H_6I_3NO_3$, soluble in alcohol and slightly soluble in water, ether, and chloroform. **acetylaminobenzoic a.,** $CH_3.CO.NH.C_6H_4.COOH$, the form in which aminobenzoic acid is detoxicated by acetylation and eliminated. **acetylenic a.,** an unsaturated fatty acid having the general formula C_nH_{2n-3}-COOH. **acetylpropionic a.,** levulinic acid. **acetylsalicylic a.,** $CH_3CO_2C_6H_4CO_2H$, a white, crystalline compound, soluble in 100 parts of water and in alcohol: antipyretic and analgesic. **acetyltannic a.,** a diacetic ester of tannic acid, a grayish or white powder, insoluble in water, soluble in alcohol. It is presumed to pass through the stomach unchanged, but to dissolve in alkaline intestinal juice, with subsequent slow hydrolysis, thereby permitting the tannic acid component to act as an astringent in chronic diarrhea. **aconitic a.,** a crystalline acid, 1,2,3-tricarboxylpropylene, $COOH.CH:C(COOH)CH_2.COOH$, from aconite and other plants. **acrylic a.,** an olefinic acid, $CH_2:CH.COOH$, found in animal and vegetable tissues. **adenosine triphosphoric a., adenyl-pyrophosphoric a.,** a normal constituent of muscle, $C_5H_4N_5.C_5H_8O_4.PO_3H_2.P_2O_3(OH)_4$, which participates in carbohydrate and phosphorus metabolism. **adenylic a.,** a mononucleotide, $NH_2.C_5H_2N_4.C_4H_3O(OH)_2.CH_2OH.PO_2(OH)_2$, made up of adenine, ribose, and phosphoric acid. It is one of the decomposition products of nucleic acid and occurs in muscle, blood corpuscles, yeast and other nuclear material. It is one of the factors in the vitamin B complex. *Yeast adenylic a.* is adenosine 3-phosphoric acid; *muscle adenylic a.* is adenosine 5-phosphoric acid. **adipic a.,** a crystalline acid, $COOH(CH_2)_4COOH$, formed by oxidizing fats with nitric acid. **agaric a., agaricic a.,** a resinous acid, $C_{19}H_{36}(OH)(COOH)_3.1\frac{1}{2}H_2O$, from the fungus *Polyporus officinalis*, or white agaric. **ailantic a.,** a bitter acid from *Ailantus excelsa;* tonic. **alantic a.,** an acid, $C_{15}H_{23}O_3$, from *Inulo helenium.* **aldepalmitic a.,** an acid, $C_{16}H_{30}O_2$, from cow's butter. **aldobionic a.,** $C_{11}H_{19}O_{10}.COOH$, a disaccharide which contains a uronic acid as one of its component sugars. It occurs in various plant gums and certain pathogenic organisms. It results from the hydrolysis of the specific polysaccharide of Type III pneumococcus. **alepric a.,** a homologue of chaulmoogric acid. **aleprylic a.,** a homologue of chaulmoogric acid. **alginic a.,** an organic acid from various species of algae. **aliphatic a.,** an organic acid with an open carbon chain. **allanic a., allanturic a.,** an acid, glyoxalyl urea, $NH_2CO.N:CH.COOH$, formed along with urea by the action of nitric acid on allantoin. **allonic a.,** one of the isomeric forms of pentahydroxycaproic acid, $CH_3(CHOH)_4COOH$, formed by the gentle oxidation of allose. **allophanic a.,** an acid, urea carbonic acid, $NH_2CO.NH.COOH$, not known in the free state. Its amide is biuret. It combines with various substances and makes them less disagreeable to take. **alloxanic a.,** a crystalline acid, $NH_2CO.NH.CO.COOH$, obtainable from alloxan. **alloxyproteic a.,** a sulfur compound sometimes found in the urine. **alluranic a.,** an acid, $C_5H_4N_4O_4$, derived from alloxan and urea. **aloitinic a.,** a yellow and nearly insoluble substance, $C_7H_2N_2O_5$, obtainable from aloes. **alpha-amino-beta-hydroxypropionic a.,** serine. **alpha-glucoheptonic a.,** a heptahydroxy acid, $CH_2OH(CHOH)_5COOH$. **alpha-hydroxypropionic a.,** lactic a. **alpha-oxynaphthoic a.,** a crystalline acid, $OH.C_{10}H_6COOH$, antiseptic and deodorant. **alpharsonic a.,** an arsonic acid containing an alphyl radical. **alphatoluic a.,** phenylacetic a. **altronic a.,** one of the isomeric forms of pentahydroxycaproic acid, $CH_3OH(CHOH)_4COOH$. **amalic a.,** a crystalline acid, $C_8(CH_3)_4N_4O_7$, formed by the reduction of dimethyl alloxan with hydrogen disulfide. **ambrettolic a.,** an unsaturated hydroxy acid, 16-hydroxyhexadecen-7-oic acid, $CH_2OH(CH_2)_7CH:CH(CH_2)_5COOH$, that occurs as a lactone in musk. **amic a.,** any amide of an organic acid. **amido a.,** amino a. **amino a.,** any one of a class of organic compounds containing the amino (NH_2) group and the carboxyl

NATURALLY OCCURRING AMINO ACIDS

The substances listed below have been found either free as components of plant or animal tissues or as products of the hydrolysis of proteins. The year refers to the earliest occasion upon which the substance was characterized. As found in nature, all belong to the L family, being configurationally related to L-glyceraldehyde. However, in recent years, the D-enantiomorphs of a few of these substances have been detected in complex polypeptides produced by bacterial metabolism.

Year	Common Name	Systematic Name	Discoverer
1806	Asparagine	2-amino-4-succinamic acid	Vauquelin and Robiquet
1810	Cystine	3,3′-dithiobis-(2-aminopropionic acid)	Wollaston
1819	Leucine	2-aminoisocaproic acid	Proust
1820	Glycine	aminoacetic acid	Braconnot
1846	Tyrosine	2-amino-3-(4-hydroxyphenyl)-propionic acid	Liebig
1856	Valine	2-aminoisovaleric acid	von Gorup-Besanez
1865	Serine	2-amino-3-hydroxypropionic acid	Cramer
1866	Glutamic acid	2-aminoglutaric acid	Ritthausen
1869	Aspartic acid[1]	2-aminosuccinic acid	Ritthausen
1879	Phenylalanine	2-amino-3-phenylpropionic acid	Schulze
1883	Glutamine	2-amino-5-glutaramic acid	Schulze and Bosshard
1884	Cysteine	2-amino-3-mercaptopropionic acid	Baumann
1886	Arginine	2-amino-5-guanidinovaleric acid	Schulze
1888	Alanine[2]	2-aminopropionic acid	Weyl
1889	Lysine	2,6-diaminohexanoic acid	Drechsel
1896	3,5-Diiodotyrosine (Iodogorgoic acid)	2-amino-3-(3,5-diiodo-4-hydroxyphenyl)-propionic acid	Drechsel
1896	Histidine	2-amino-3-(5-imidazolyl)-propionic acid	Hedin: Kossel
1898	Ornithine[3]	2,5-diaminovaleric acid	Schulze and Winterstein
1901	Proline[4]	2-pyrrolidinecarboxylic acid	Fischer
1901	Tryptophan	2-amino-3-(3-indo yl)-propionic acid	Hopkins and Cole
1902	Hydroxyproline	4 hydroxy-2-pyrrolidinecarboxylic acid	Fischer
1903	Isoleucine	2-amino-3-methylvaleric acid	Ehrlich
1913	3,5-Dibromotyrosine[5]	2-amino-3-(3,5-dibromo-4-hydroxyphenyl)-propionic acid	Morner
1913	3,4-Dihydroxyphenylalanine	2-amino-3-3,4-(dihydroxyphenyl)-propionic acid	Guggenheim
1915	Thyroxine	2-amino-3[(3,5-diiodo-4-hydroxyphenoxy)-3,5-diiodophenyl]-propionic acid	Kendall
1922	Methionine	2-amino-4-methylmercaptobutyric acid	Mueller
1929	Canavanine	2-amino-4-guanidinoöxy-butyric acid	Kitagawa and Tomita
1930	Citrulline[6]	2-amino-5-ureidovaleric acid	Wada
1935	Djenkolic acid	3,3′-methylenedithiobis-(2-aminopropionic acid)	van Veen and Hyman
1936	Threonine	2-amino-3-hydroxybutyric acid	Meyer and Rose
1938	Hydroxylysine[7]	2,6-diamino-5-hydroxyhexanoic acid	Van Slyke, Hiller, Dillon, and MacFadyen
1948	α,γ-Diaminobutyric acid	2,4-diaminobutyric acid	Catch, Jones, and Wilkenson
1950	α,ϵ-Diaminopimelic acid	2,6-diaminopimelic acid	Work

1 Aspartic acid was prepared from asparagine by Plisson in 1827.
2 Synthesized by Strecker, 1850.
3 Ornithuric acid, the dibenzoyl derivative of ornithine, was discovered by Jaffé in 1877. The base was first characterized as a decomposition product of arginine by Schulze and Winterstein in 1898 and in 1943 was shown to be a product of the hydrolysis of tyrocidine by Gordon, Martin, and Synge.
4 Synthesized by Willstätter, 1900.
5 3,5-Dibromotyrosine was synthesized from tyrosine by von Gorup-Besanez in 1863.
6 Isolated but not characterized by Koga and Odake in 1914.
7 Van Slyke and Hiller announced the probable presence of a new basic amino acid in gelatin in 1921. It was identified as an hydroxylysine in 1938.

(COOH) group. The amino acids form the chief structure of proteins, and several of them are essential in human nutrition. (See table listing names of amino acids occurring in nature.) **amino a., essential,** one that is essential for optimal growth in a young animal, or for nitrogen equilibrium in an adult. Those essential for nitrogen equilibrium in man are isoleucine, leucine, lysine, methionine, phenylalanine, threonine, tryptophan, and valine; histidine, in addition to these eight, is required by infants. **aminoacetic a.,** a colorless crystalline powder, $CH_2.NH_2.$-COOH, derivable from many proteins: used as a dietary supplement. **aminobenzoic a.,** the para form of this acid, $C_6H_4(NH_2)COOH$, lessens the bacteriostatic activity of sulfanilamide and apparently is a factor in several forms of metabolism. **aminobutyric a.,** an alpha amino acid found in small amounts in some proteins. **aminocaproic a.,** leucine. **aminoglutaric a.,** glutaminic acid. **aminoguanidine valerianic a.,** arginine. **amino-indole propionic a.,** tryptophan. **amino-isovalerianic a.,** valine. **aminolthanoic a.,** aminoacetic a. **aminopropionic a.,** alanine. **aminopteroylglutamic a.,** aminopterin. **aminosalicylic a.,** a white, or nearly white, bulky powder, $C_7H_7NO_3$, odorless, or with a slightly acetous odor: antibacterial and tuberculostatic. **aminosuccinic a.,** aspartic acid. **aminothiopropionic a.,** cysteine. **aminovaleric a.,** an amino acid, $CH_3.CH_2.CH_2.CH(NH_2).$-COOH, occurring in protein. **amygdalic a.,** one formed by the decomposition of amygdalin, the result of boiling with an alkali. **anacardic a.,** a crystalline principle, normal pentadecylene salicylic acid, $C_{15}H_{27}.C_6H_3(OH).COOH$, from *Anacardium occidentale:* anthelmintic. **angelic a.,** an unsaturated fatty acid, $CH_3CH{:}C(CH_3).$-COOH, from the roots of *Angelica archangelica.* **anilinparasulfonic a.,** sulfanilic acid. **anisic a.,** a crystalline acid, $CH_3O.C_6H_4.CO_2H$, from anise and fennel, forming anisates: antiseptic and antirheumatic. **anisuric a.,** an acid, $C_{10}H_{11}NO_2$, in leafy crystals, obtainable from urine after the ingestion of anisic acid. **anthranilic a.,** a crystalline acid, orthoaminobenzoic acid, NH_2C_6-$H_4.COOH$, obtained by oxidizing indigo by boiling it with sodium hydroxide and magnesium dioxide. **anticyclic a.,** a fragrant powdery acid: antipyretic. **antimonic a.,** antimonium pentoxide, Sb_2O_5, or, more correctly, antimonium hydroxide, $Sb(OH)_5$ or $SbO(OH)_3$. **antimonious a.** 1. Antimony trioxide. 2. More correctly, antimony hydroxide, $HSbO_2$. **antiscorbic a.,** ascorbic a. **antitartaric a.,** mesotartaric a. **antoxyproteic a.,** an organic acid obtained from urine. **apocrenic a.,** an acid, $C_{48}H_{12}O_{24}$, from certain spring waters and from the soil. **aposorbic a.,** a crystalline acid, $C_5H_8O_7$, obtained by oxidizing sorbin with HNO_3. **arabic a.,** arabin. **arabonic a.,** one of the forms of tetra-hydroxy-normal valeric acid, CH_2OH $(CHOH)_3COOH$, formed by the action of bromine water on arabinose. **arachic a., arachidic a.,** a fatty acid, $CH_3(CH_2)_{18}COOH$, from the oil of the peanut, *Arachis hypogaea.* **arachidonic a.,** an unsaturated fatty acid, $CH_3(CH_2)_4(CH{:}CH{:}CH_2)_4(CH_2)_2COOH$, an important constituent of lecithin. **aristic a.,** an acid, $C_{18}H_{13}NO_7$, from serpentaria. **aristidic a.,** a resinous acid, $C_{17}H_{10}(CH_3)NO_7$, from serpentaria. **aristolic a.,** an acid, $C_{15}H_{13}.NO_7$, from serpentaria. **aristolochic a.,** a volatile acid obtainable from various species of *Aristolochia.* **aromatic a.,** any one of a group of acids derivable from various balsams and resins and containing the benzene or other ring. **arsanilic a.,** a compound, $NH_2.C_6H_4.AsO(OH)_2$, or arsenic acid in which an hydroxyl group is replaced by an aminobenzene, aminophenol, or aniline group. **arsellic a.,** an unsaturated fatty acid, $C_{17}H_{32}O_2$, from cod liver oil. **arsenic a.,** the acid, H_3AsO_4, some of whose salts, called arsenates, are used as medicines. See *metarsenic a., pyro-arsenic a.* **arsenous a.** 1. A monobasic acid, $HAsO_2$, forming arsenites. 2. Arsenic trioxide, or arsenous anhydride. **arsinic a.,** an organic compound containing the group —As-$(OH)_2$. **arsinosalicylic a.,** a colorless, crystalline substance, used in African sleeping sickness. **arsonic a.,** an organic compound containing the group —SO_2OH. **arylarsonic a.,** arsonic acid combined with an aryl radical. **ascorbic a.,** an organic compound, $C_6H_8O_6$, known also as vitamin C, cevitamic acid, and avitamic acid. It is present in citrus fruits, and in tomatoes, strawberries, and in many other fruits, and is also made synthetically. Deficiency of this substance tends to produce scurvy. **aseptic a.,** an antiseptic mixture of boric acid, water, hydrogen dioxide, and salicylic acid. **asparaginic a.,** aspartic a. **aspartic a.,** a dibasic amino acid, COOH.-$CH(NH_2).CH_2.COOH$, derivable from asparagine, and found in the body as one of the products of pancreatic digestion. It is actively anticoagulant. **aspergillic a.,** an antibiotic substance isolated from cultures of *Aspergillus flavus,* which inhibits the growth of the tubercle bacillus. **atractylic a.,** a poisonous glycoside, $C_{30}H_{25}O_{18}S_2$, from *Atractylis gummifer.* **auric a.** 1. The acid, $Au(HO)_3$, forming salts called aurates. 2. Less correctly, gold peroxide, Au_2O_2, or auric anhydride. **avitamic a.,** ascorbic a. **avivitellinic a.,** a paranuclein found in ovovitellin. **axinic a.,** an acid, $C_{18}H_{28}O_2$, from axin. **azelaic a.,** an acid, $COOH.(CH_2)_7COOH$, formed by oxidation of oleic acid. **barbituric a.,** a crystalline substance, $CO(NHCO)_2CH_2$; known in medicine chiefly because of its derivatives, such as barbital and phenobarbital. **behenic a.,** a fatty acid, $CH_3(CH_2)_{20}$-COOH, present in oil of black mustard. **benzenesulfonic a.,** a soluble crystalline substance, $C_6H_5SO_3H$. **benzoboric a.,** a compound used as an antizymotic. **benzoic a.,** a white, crystalline acid, $C_6H_5.COOH$, from benzoin and other resins and from coal tar: used as an antibacterial preservative in pharmacopeial preparations. **benzoyl-aminoacetic a.,** hippuric a. **benzoylglucuronic a.,** a conjugate of benzoic acid and glucuronic acid, by which the former is detoxicated and eliminated. **beta-acetylpropionic a.,** levulinic a. **beta-aminobutyric a.,** an acid, $CH_3.CH(NH_2).CH_2COOH$, which causes profound narcotism and symptoms resembling coma. **beta-hydroxybutyric a.,** beta-oxybutyric a. **beta-ketobutyric a.,** diacetic a. **beta-ketopalmitic a.,** an oxidized form of palmitic acid, $CH_3(CH_2)_{12}CO.CH_2.COOH$. **beta-naphthol-sulfonic a.,** white pearly scales tinged with red, $OH.C_{10}H_6SO_2.OH$, used as a test for albumin in the urine; an agent which causes profound narcotism and symptoms resembling diabetic coma. **beta-oxybutyric a.,** an acid, $CH_3CHOH.CH_2.COOH$, occurring in diabetic urine and forming one of the acetone bodies. **beta-parahydroxy-phenylpropionic a.,** tyrosine. **beta-phenylpropionic a.,** a cinnamic acid derivative in colorless crystals, $C_6H_5.CH_2.CH_2.COOH$: used in tuberculosis. **bichloracetic a.,** dichloracetic a. **bile a.,** an acid of the bile: glycocholic or taurocholic acid. **bilianic a.,** an acid, $C_{24}H_{34}O_8$, formed by oxidizing dehydrocholic acid. **bilic a.,** a crystalline acid, $C_{16}H_{22}O_6$, formed by oxidizing cholic acid with chromium trioxide. **bilirubinic a.,** bilirubin. **biliverdinic a.** 1. Biliverdin. 2. An acid, $C_8H_9NO_4$, formed by the oxidation of biliverdin. **binary a.,** an acid which contains only two elements. **bioluric a.,** a compound derivable from uric acid. **bionic a., biotic a.,** a compound which stimulates the growth of yeast cells. **bismuthic a.,** the monobasic acid, $HBiO_3$. **blattic a.,** an active diuretic, derivable from cockroaches. **boheic a.,** an acid, $C_7H_{10}O_6$, found in tea. **boracic a.,** boric a. **boric a.,** a white, crystalline powder, H_3BO_3: used as a bactericide and fungicide for skin and conjunctiva. **borobenzoic a.,** $B(OH)_2$-$C_6H_4.COOH$, occurring in brilliant white needles.

borocitric a., a white, crystalline combination of boric and citric acids, employed as a solvent for urates and phosphates. **borophenylic a.,** a white aromatic powder, $C_6H_5.OB(OH)_2$, used as an antiseptic. **borosalicylic a.,** a white powder, $BOH(OC_6H_4COOH)_2$, prepared by evaporating a mixture of aqueous solution of boric acid and alcoholic solution of salicylic acid. **boswellinic a.,** a constituent, $C_{32}H_{52}O_4$, of olibanum. **botulinic a.,** an acid found in putrid sausages, believed to consist of allantotoxicon mixed with other substances. **brassic a., brassidic a.,** $CH_3.(CH_2)_7.CH:CH.(CH_2)_{11}.COOH$, an isomer of erucic acid produced by treating erucic acid with nitric acid. **brassilic a.,** a dibasic fatty acid, $COOH(CH_2)_{11}COOH$, obtained by the oxidation of erucic acid. **brenz-catechin sulfuric a.,** pyrocatechin sulfuric acid, $OH.C_6H_4.O.SO_2OH$, found in the urine after the administration of salicin, hydroquinone, etc. **bromauric a.,** a brownish, crystalline acid, $HAuBr_4 + 5H_2O$. **brom-phenylmercapturic a.,** a compound, brom-phenylacetyl-cysteine, $C_6H_4Br.S.CH_2.CH(NH.CO.CH_3)COOH$, found conjugated with glycuronic acid in the urine of dogs fed bromo-benzene. **bursic a., bursinic a.,** a pale yellow astringent agent derived from *Capsella bursa-pastoris.* **butylcarboxylic a.,** valeric a. **butylethylbarbituric a.,** a white crystalline powder, $CO(NHCO)_2C(C_2H_5)(C_4H_9)$: used as a hypnotic like barbital. **butyric a.,** a rancid, sticky acid, $CH_3CH_2CH_2COOH$, a product of the putrefaction of protein: found in butter, sweat, feces, and urine, and in traces in the spleen and in blood. **cacodylic a.,** a crystalline deliquescent solid, dimethylarsinic acid, $(CH_3)_2.AsO.OH$. **caffeic a.,** a crystalline solid, dihydroxy cinnamic acid, $(OH)_2C_6H_3CH:CH.COOH$, obtained from coffee. **caffetannic a.,** a glycoside, $C_{15}H_{18}O_8$, found in coffee. It is resolvable into dextrose and caffeic acid. **caffuric a.,** a crystalline acid, $C_6H_9N_3O_4$, formed by the oxidation of caffeine. **calumbic a.,** a yellow, bitter substance, $C_{21}H_{24}O_7$, from calumba. **camphoglycuronic a.,** $C_{16}H_{24}O_8$, a combination of glycuronic acid and camphor, found in the urine after the use of camphor. **campholic a.,** a compound, $C_{10}H_{18}O_2$, formed by distilling camphor with alcoholic potash. **camphoric a.,** a colorless, crystalline substance, $C_8H_{14}(COOH)_2$, from the oxidation of camphor. **camphoronic a.,** an antiseptic compound, $C_9H_{14}O_2$, in white needles, formed by the oxidation of camphor. **canadinic a.,** an acid resin, $C_{19}H_{34}O_6$, soluble in ammonium carbonate, found in Canada turpentine. **canadinolic a.,** an acid resin, $C_{19}H_{30}O_2$, found in Canada turpentine. **canadolic a.,** an acid resin, $C_{19}H_{28}O_2$, found in Canada turpentine. **cantharic a.,** a crystalline acid, $C_{10}H_{12}O_4$, derivable from cantharidin. **cantharidic a.,** a dibasic acid, $C_{10}H_{14}O_5$, formed by the combination of cantharidin with water. **capric a.,** a crystalline fatty acid, $CH_3(CH_2)_8COOH$, from butter. **caproic a.,** a fatty acid, $CH_3(CH_2)_4COOH$, forming caproates. **caprylic a.,** a fatty acid, $CH_3(CH_2)_6COOH$, from butter; it forms caprylates. **capsic a.,** an irritating principle existing in pimenta. **carbamic a.,** a monobasic acid, the mono-amide of carbonic acid, or aminoformic acid, $NH_2CO.OH$; its ethyl ester is urethan. **carbamino-carboxylic a.,** an acid, $COOH.NH.CH_2.COOH$, formed by CO_2 in the presence of amino acids and alkalis. **carbazotic a.,** trinitrophenol. **carbolic a.,** phenol. **carbonaphthoic a.,** hydroxynaphthoic a. **carbonic a.** 1. An acidulous unstable liquid, H_2CO_3, made by dissolving carbon dioxide in water; it forms carbonates. 2. Carbon dioxide. **carmic a.,** a red glucoside which forms the red pigment of the cochineal insect. **carminic a.,** a brilliant purplish-red solid, dioxymethylalphanaphthoquinone, $C_{12}H_{11}O_7$, from carmine. **carnaubic a.,** an acid, $CH_3(CH_2)_{22}COOH$, from carnauba wax or from wool fat. **carnic a.,** a compound, probably a dipeptide, $C_{10}H_{15}N_3O_5$, formed by the decomposition of carniferrin. It is found in the muscles in the form of phosphocarnic acid. **carolic a.,** a metabolic product of *Penicillium charlesii.* **caronic a.,** a solid dibasic acid, $(CH_3)_2C(CH.COOH)_2$, derived by oxidation from carone. **carthamic a.,** a red stain, $C_{14}H_{16}O_7$, from safflower. **caryophyllic a.,** eugenol. **caseanic a.,** an acid, $C_9H_{16}N_2O_7$, found in casein. **caseinic a.,** an acid, $C_{12}H_{24}N_2O_5$, found in casein. **catechuic a.,** catechin. **catechutannic a.,** a variety of tannic acid from catechu. **cathartic a., cathartinic a.,** a laxative principle from senna. **cellulosic a.,** oxidized cellulose. **cephalinic a.,** an unsaturated acid of the linolinic acid series in cephalin. **cephalylphosphoric a.,** a substance derived from cephalin, by the loss of neurin. **cerebric a.,** a compound derived from the brain tissue and containing cerebrose. **cerebronic a.,** a fatty acid, $C_{24}H_{48}O_3$, derived from sphingomyelin. **cerotic a., cerotinic a.,** a fatty acid, $CH_3(CH_2)_{24}.COOH$, from beeswax and other waxes. **cetraric a.,** cetrarin. **cevitamic a.,** ascorbic a. **chaulmoogric a.,** an unsaturated fatty acid, $CH_2.CH_2.CH:CH.CH(CH_2)_{12}COOH$, from chaulmoogra and hydnocarpus oils. Its ethyl ester is used in the treatment of leprosy. **chelidonic a.,** a crystalline acid, $C_5H_2O_2(COOH)_2$, from *Chelidonium majus.* **chelidoninic a.,** succinic a. **chenocholalic a.,** a compound, $C_{27}H_{44}O_4$, occurring in the bile of geese. **chenodesoxycholic a.,** an acid, 3,7-dihydroxycholanic acid, occurring in the bile of geese. **chenotaurocholic a.,** a crystalline compound, $C_{29}H_{49}NSO_6$, occurring in the bile of geese. **chinovic a.,** quinovic a. **chitonic a.,** an acid, trihydroxymethyl-tetrahydrofurfurane-carboxylic acid, $CH_2OH.CHO(CHOH)_2.CH.COOH$, formed by the oxidation of chitose. **chloracetic a.,** an acid in which the three hydrogen atoms of acetic acid are wholly or partly replaced by chlorine; it occurs, therefore, in three forms, called respectively monochloracetic, dichloracetic, and trichloracetic acid, all being strongly caustic: the more chlorine, the more caustic the acid. **chloranilic a.,** a compound, 2,5-dihydroxy-3,6-dichloroquinone, used in tests of liver function. **chlorauric a.,** yellow hygroscopic crystals of gold chloride, $AuCl_3.HCl.4H_2O$, which contain 48 per cent of metallic gold. **chlorhydric a.,** hydrochloric a. **chlorogenic a.,** a simple phenolic compound of low molecular weight isolated from raw coffee bean, castor bean, and oranges, minute quantities of which give a positive reaction when injected intracutaneously in persons allergic to those plant materials. **chloropeptic a.,** peptohydrochloric a. **chloroplatinic a.,** $H_2PtCl_6.6H_2O$, made by dissolving metallic platinum in nitrohydrochloric acid. **chlorosulfonic a.,** an irritant war smoke, $Cl.SO_2.OH$, used in hand grenades. **chlorous a.,** a feebly acid compound, $HClO_2$, forming salts called chlorites. **cholalic a.,** cholic a. **cholanic a.** 1. The product, $C_{20}H_{28}O_6$, of the oxidation of cholalic acid. 2. The product, $C_{24}H_{34}O_8$, of the oxidation of choleic acid. **choleic a's,** compounds of fatty acids with bile acids. **choleocamphoric a.,** a compound, $C_{10}H_{16}O_4$, formed by the oxidation of cholalic acid. **cholesterinic a.,** an acid, $C_8H_{10}O_5$, obtained by oxidizing cholic acid. **cholic a.,** an acid, 3,7,12-trihydroxycholanic acid, $C_{24}H_{40}O_4$, from bile. **cholodinic a.,** an acid, $C_{24}H_{38}O_4$, derived from cholic acid. **choloidanic a.,** an acid, $C_{16}H_{24}O_7$, derived from cholic acid. **cholonic a.,** an acid, $C_{26}H_{41}NO_5$, formed by dehydration of glycocholic acid. **chondroitic a., chondroitin-sulfuric a.,** a mucopolysaccharide occurring in cartilage. **chondrosaminic a.,** an oxidation product of chondrosamine. **chromic a.** 1. A dibasic acid, H_2CrO_4; its salts are called chromates. 2. Chromium trioxide, CrO_3; a crystalline anhydride used as an escharotic for the removal of warty growths. **chromonucleic a.,** deoxyribonucleic a. **chry-**

senic a., a crystalline compound, $C_{17}H_{12}O_3$. **chrysophanic a.,** a yellow crystalline acid, dioxymethyl-anthraquinone, $CH_3(OH).C_6H_2(CO)_2$-C_6H_3OH, from a glycoside in senna, rhubarb, certain lichens, etc., and from chrysarobin, whose therapeutic properties it shares. **cinchomeronic a.,** pyridine-dicarboxylic acid, C_5H_3N-$(COOH)_2$, formed from cinchonine by oxidation. **cinchonic a.,** quinolin-carboxylic acid, C_9H_6-$N(COOH)$, formed from cinchonine by oxidation. **cinchoninic a.,** an acid, $C_{10}H_7O_2N$, produced in the oxidation of cinchonine. **cinnamic a.,** a white, crystalline acid, phenyl acrylic acid, C_6H_5-$(CH)_2COOH$, from cinnamon, storax, the balsams, and other aromatic resins. **citraconic a.,** a crystalline compound, $COOH.C.(CH_3)$:-$CH.COOH$, formed by distilling citric acid. **citric a.,** a tribasic, crystalline acid, $COOH.$-$C(OH)(CH_2COOH)_2$, from lemons, limes, etc. It forms citrates; is antiscorbutic, refrigerant, and diuretic. **clupanodonic a.,** $C_{17}H_{27}.COOH$, from cod liver oil and oils of other fish. **cocatannic a.,** a compound found in the leaves of *Erythroxylon coca*. **cojic a.,** kojic a. **colchicinic a.,** an acid, $C_{16}H_{15}O_5$, formed from colchicine by heating it with hydrochloric acid. **comanic a.,** an acid, $C_6H_4O_4$, derived from chelidonic acid. **comenic a.,** a crystalline acid, oxypyrone-carboxylic acid, $OH.C_5H_2O_2.COOH$, from opium. **copaibic a.,** an acid nearly identical with the resin of copaiba. **coumaric a.,** an acid, $OH.C_6H_4.(CH)_2.COOH$, from coumarin, readily convertible into salicylic acid. **coumarilic a.,** a crystalline acid, $C_9H_6O_3$, from coumarin. **crenic a.,** an acid, $C_{24}H_{12}O_{16}$, from certain spring waters and from the soil. **cresolsulfuric a.,** a substance, $CH_3C_6H_4SO_2.OH$, found in small quantities in the urine. **cresotic a., cresotinic a.,** an acid, $CH_3C_6H_3(OH).COOH$, oxytoluic acid, occurring in three modified forms, ortho-, meta-, and para-; its sodium salt is antipyretic. **cresylic a.,** cresol. **croconic a.,** a yellow crystalline acid, $CO(CO.C.OH)_2.3H_2O$. **crotonic a.,** an unsaturated fatty acid, $CH_3.CH{:}CH.COOH$, found in croton oil. **crotonoleic a.,** an unsaturated fatty acid found in croton oil; it closely resembles ricinoleic acid, but is more irritant. **crotonolic a.,** crotonol. **cryptophanic a.,** an amorphous acid, $C_{10}H_{18}O_{10}N_2$, said to be found in the urine. **cubebic a.,** a strongly diuretic principle, $C_{13}H_{14}O_7$, from cubeb: purgative. **cumic a., cuminic a.,** an acid, $C_6H_4(C_3H_7)COOH$, formed by the oxidation of cuminol. **cuminuric a.,** the excretion product of cumic acid and glycocoll, $(CH_3)_2.CH.$-$C_6H_4.CO.NH.CH_2.COOH$. **cyanhydric a.,** hydrocyanic a. **cyanic a.,** an acid, $H.CNO$, stable at low temperatures: has vesicant properties. **cyanuric a.,** a white crystalline compound, formed by heating urea. **cynurenic a.,** kynurenic a. **cysteic a.,** an acid, $SO_2OH.CH_2CH.$-$(NH_2)COOH$. **damalic a.,** C_7H_8O, said to occur in urine. **damaluric a.,** $C_7H_{12}O_2$, found in human urine and in that of cows. **decenoic a.,** an acid, $C_{10}H_{20}O_2$, found in milk and butter. **decoic a.,** capric a. **dehydro-ascorbic a.,** an acid resulting from the oxidation of ascorbic acid. **dehydrocholalic a.,** dehydrocholic a. **dehydrocholeic a.,** an acid, $C_{24}H_{34}O_4$, formed by the oxidation of choleic acid. **dehydrocholic a.,** an acid, $C_{24}H_{34}O_5$, formed by the oxidation of cholic acid and derived from natural bile acids: it has cholagogue action. **dekacrylic a.,** a yellow acid, $C_{10}H_{18}O_2$, from cork. **deoxypentosenucleic a.,** deoxyribonucleic a. **deoxyribonucleic a.,** a nucleic acid originally isolated from fish sperm and thymus gland, but later found in all living cells; on hydrolysis it yields adenine, guanine, cytosine, thymine, deoxyribose, and phosphoric acid. Abbreviated DNA. **desoxalic a.,** a crystalline acid, $COOH.$-$CHOH.C(OH)(COOH)_2$. **desoxycholeic a.,** one of the bile acids. **desoxycholic a.,** an acid, 3,12-dihydroxycholanic acid, $C_{24}H_{40}O_4$, formed by the reduction of cholic acid. **desoxyribonucleic a., desoxyribose nucleic a.,** deoxyribonucleic a. **dextrotartaric a.,** ordinary tartaric acid, which turns the plane of polarization to the right. **diacetic a.,** acetoacetic a. **diacetyltannic a.,** acetyltannic a. **diallyl barbituric a.,** 5,5-diallylbarbituric acid, used as a hypnotic and sedative. **dialuric a.,** a crystalline acid, $CO(NH.CO)_2$-$CH.OH$, obtainable from alloxan. **diamino a.,** one containing two amino, or NH_2, groups. **diamino-acetic a.,** an acid, $CH(NH_2)_2COOH$, formed by heating casein in sealed tubes with concentrated hydrochloric acid. **α,γ-diaminobutyric a.,** a naturally occurring amino acid discovered in 1948. **diaminocaproic a.,** lysine. **diaminocarboxylic a., diaminotrihydroxydodecanoic a.,** an amino acid obtained from casein, $C_{12}H_{26}N_2O_5$. **α,ϵ-diaminopimelic a.,** a naturally occurring amino acid discovered in 1950. **diaminovaleric a.,** ornithine. **diazobenzene-sulfonic a.,** an aromatic acid, $C_6H_5.$-$N_2.SO_2OH$, used in Ehrlich's diazo reaction. **dichloracetic a.,** $CHCl_2.COOH$, an acid formed from acetic acid by substitution: used for the removal of warts, corns, and calluses. **diethylbarbituric a.,** barbital. **digallic a.,** tannic a. **diglycoldisalicylic a.,** a compound, $O(CH_2$-$COOC_6H_4COOH)_2$, used like acetylsalicylic acid. **4,8-dihydroxyquinaldic a.,** xanthurenic a. **dihydroxystearic a.,** an acid, $CH_3(CH_2)_7$-$(CHOH)_2(CH_2)_7COOH$, obtained by oxidizing oleic acid, and found in castor oil. **diiodosalicylic a.,** a yellowish-white crystalline powder, $OH.C_6H_2I_2.COOH$. **dimethylarsinic a.,** cacodylic a. **dimethyl-colchicinic a.,** an acid, $C_{18}H_{19}O_5N$, formed from colchicine by heating it with hydrochloric acid. **diolic a.,** an acid, $C_{10}H_{18}O_3.H_2O$, produced by boiling diosphenol with alcoholic potash. **dioxy-diaminosuberic a.,** an acid, $C_8H_{16}N_2O_6$, obtained from casein. **dioxy-phenyl-acetic a.,** homogentisic a. **dioxy-salicylic a.,** gallic a. **dithioaminolactic a.,** cysteine. **dithiochloralsalicylic a.,** a reddish-yellow powder, $S_2C_6H.Cl.OH.COOH$: antiseptic. **dithionous a.,** hyposulfurous acid, $H_2S_2O_4$. **djenkolic a.,** an alpha-diamino acid, $CH_2(S.CH_2.CH(NH_2)COOH)_2$, obtained by hydrolyzing djenkol nuts. **doeglic a.,** an oleic acid, $C_{19}H_{36}O_2$, from doegling oil: it is isomeric with jecoleic acid. **dracilic a., dracylic a.,** para-aminobenzoic a. **draconic a.,** anisic a. **durylic a.,** a crystalline compound, trimethylbenzoic acid, $(CH_3)_3C_6H_2.COOH$. **elaidic a.,** an unsaturated fatty acid, $CH_3(CH_2)_7.CH{:}CH$-$(CH_2)_7.COOH$, isomeric with oleic acid, and formed by treating the latter with nitrous acid. **elaieimic a.,** a fatty acid from mutton tallow. **ellagic a.,** an acid, $C_{14}H_6O_8$, occurring in Oriental bezoars and prepared from gallic acid. **embelic a.,** a compound, $C_9H_{14}O_2$, from *Embelia ribes*. **emulcic a.,** an acid derived from the albumin of almonds. **enanthylic a.,** a compound formed by the action of nitric acid on fatty substances. **eosolic a.,** acetyl-creosote-trisulfonic acid, whose salts are called eosolates. **episaccharic a.,** a saccharic acid obtained when nucleic acid is hydrolyzed with nitric acid. It is the oxidized form of an unknown hexose. **ergotic a.,** a principle contained in ergot. **ergotinic a.,** an acid from ergot, not poisonous when given by the mouth, but toxic if injected through the skin. **erucic a.,** an unsaturated fatty acid, $CH_3(CH_2)_7CH$:-$CH(CH_2)_{11}COOH$, the cis-isomer of brassic acid. It exists as a glyceride in oil of rape seed and of mustard. **ethanal a.,** glyoxylic a. **ethanoic a.,** acetic a. **ethylamine sulfonic a.,** taurine. **ethylene lactic a., ethylidene lactic a.** See under *lactic a.* **5-ethyl-5-isoamylbarbituric a.,** amobarbital. **ethylsulfonic a.,** an acid, $CH_3.CH_2.SO_2.OH$, found in the urine after administration of sulfonmethane. **eugenic a.,** eugenol. **excretoleic a., excretolic a.,** a fatty acid derived from feces. **fatty a.,** any monobasic aliphatic acid containing only carbon, hydrogen and oxygen and made up of an alkyl radical attached to the carboxyl group. The saturated fatty acids have the general formula $C_nH_{2n}O_2$. There are also several series of unsaturated fatty acids having one or more double bonds. **fellic a.,** an acid, $C_{23}H_{40}O_4$, said to be obtainable from human bile. **ferulic a.,** an acid, methyl-caffeic acid, $CH_3O.C_6H_3.(OH)(CH)_2.COOH$, obtained from asafetida by precipitation with lead acetate. **fibril a.,** an amorphous, colorless horny compound dissolving in acidified alcohol, contained in the neurofibrils. It stains an intense violet with toluidine blue. See *Nissl a.* **filicic a.,** a tasteless, white, amorphous powder, $(CH_3)_2C_6HO(OH)_2$, from male fern: anthelmintic. **filixic a.,** a principle from male fern. **flavaspidic a.,** a compound from the root of *Aspidium.* **fluoric a.,** hydrofluoric a. **fluosilic a.,** hydrofluosilicic a. **folic a.,** a widely distributed vitamin, existing in a number of natural products in free form or in various conjugates, which have been designated by various names, including *pteroylglutamic acid, fermentation Lactobacillus casei factor, liver L. casei factor, Norit eluate factor, factor R, Streptococcus lactis R* (or *SLR*) *factor, factor U, yeast L. casei factor, vitamin* B_c, *vitamin* B_c *conjugate,* and *vitamin M.* It is an essential growth factor for many animals and microorganisms, and has a hematopoietic influence in certain types of macrocytic anemias. Synthetic folic acid is pteroylglutamic acid, $COOH.(CH_2)_2.CH.(COOH).NH.CO.C_6HN_4.(NH_3).OH$. **folinic a.,** 5-formyl-5,6,7,8-tetrahydropteroyl-L-glutamic acid: used in treatment of megaloblastic anemia, and to correct toxic effects of folic acid antagonists. **formic a.,** a colorless pungent liquid, HCOOH, from nettles; derivable from oxalic acid and from glycerin, and from the oxidation of formaldehyde. It is a vesicant and counterirritant, but has no advantage over mustard. **formiminoglutamic a.,** an intermediate product in the metabolism of histidine which accumulates in the urine of humans and rats deficient in folic acid. Its appearance, although probably not completely specific, may be employed clinically as a test for folic acid deficiency. **frangulic a.,** a yellowish-brown, crystalline substance, $C_{14}H_8O_4$, from frangulin; aperient. **fulminic a.,** an unstable acid, carbyloxime, C:N.OH, isomeric with cyanic acid. It has the odor of hydrocyanic acid and is equally poisonous. **fumaric a.,** a transisomeric form of maleic acid. **gadelaidic a.,** the transisomer of gadoleic acid. **gadoleic a.,** a fatty acid, $C_{20}H_{38}O_2$, from cod liver oil. **gaidic a.,** a crystalline compound, $C_{16}H_{30}O_2$, from hypogeic acid. **galactonic a.,** lactonic acid. **galacturonic a.,** an acid isomeric with glucuronic acid, being an oxidized form of galactose, $COH.(CHOH)_4COOH$. It is the principal constituent of pectin. **gallhumic a.,** melanogallic a. **gallic a.,** a white crystalline acid, trihydroxybenzoic acid, $(OH)_3C_6H_2.COOH.H_2O$, from nutgalls and tannic acid. **gallotannic a.,** tannic a. **gambogic a.,** a resin, $C_{29}H_{23}O_4$, obtainable in large quantities from gamboge. **gentiotannic a.,** a variety of tannic acid, $C_{14}H_{10}O_5$, from gentian root; gentianin. **gentisic a.,** dihydroxy-benzoic acid, $(OH)_2C_6H_3.COOH$, obtained by melting gentianin with potassium hydroxide. **geronic a.,** a compound, $(CH_3)_2.(COOH).(CH_2)_3.CO.CH_3$. **gigantic a.,** an antibiotic substance isolated from *Aspergillus giganteus.* **glucic a.,** a colorless soluble acid formed from cane sugar by the action of potassium hydroxide. **glucoascorbic a.,** an analogue of ascorbic acid, which competitively inhibits the activity of the latter. **gluconic a.,** one of the isomeric forms of pentahydroxy-caproic acid, $CH_2OH(CHOH)_4COOH$. It is made by the gentle oxidation of dextrose, cane sugar, etc. **glucothionic a.,** a sulfuric acid ester of an unknown carbohydrate isolated from the mammary gland. **glucuronic a.,** a uronic acid formed by oxidation in animal metabolism. It is a tetrahydroxy-aldehyde acid, $CHO(CHOH)_4COOH$, with the configuration of glucose. It is found in the urine combined with camphor, chloroform, chloral, and other aromatic bodies. **glutamic a.,** a crystalline dibasic amino acid, $COOH.(CH_2)_2.CH(NH_2).COOH$, obtained by the digestion or hydrolytic decomposition of proteins. **glutamic a. hydrochloride,** 2-aminopentanedioic hydrochloride, used as a gastric acidifier. **glutaric a.,** normal pyrotartaric acid, $CH_2(CH_2.COOH)_2$. **glyceric a.,** a dihydroxymonobasic acid formed by the oxidation of glycerol. It is dihydroxypropionic acid, $CH_2OH.CHOH.COOH$. **glyceroarsenic a.,** an acid, $AsO(OH)_2OC_3H_5(OH)_2$. **glycerophosphoric a.,** a pale yellow, oily liquid, $CH_2OH.CHOH.CH_2.O.PO(OH)_2$, an acid certain of whose salts are nerve tonics and are serviceable in phosphaturia. **glycocholeic a.,** an acid, $C_{26}H_{43}NO_5$, found in bile. **glycocholic a.,** one of the bile acids that yields glycocoll and cholic acid on hydrolysis. **glycolic a.,** an acid, $CH_2OH.COOH$, formed by treating oxalic acid with nascent hydrogen; oxyacetic acid. **glycoluric a.,** a crystalline acid, a ureid of glycollic acid, $NH_2CO.NH.CH_2.COOH$, formed by heating urea with glycocoll. **glycosuric a.,** an acid found in the urine in certain conditions. It causes the urine to turn black on exposure to the air. **glycuronic a.,** glucuronic a. **glycyrrhizic a.,** glycyrrhizin. **glyoxylic a.,** a crystalline acid, dihydroxyacetic acid, $(O:HC.COOH)_2$, used in Hopkins-Cole test for protein. **gorlic a.,** a dehydrochaulmoogric acid, $C_5H_7(CH_2)_6CH:CH(CH_2)_4.COOH$, from *Corpotroche brasiliensis* and *Oncoba echinata.* **granatotannic a.,** the tannic acid, $C_{20}H_{16}O_{13}$, of pomegranate bark, a greenish-yellow, amorphous powder. **guaiacolcarbonic a.,** a white, crystalline powder, $C_6H_3(OH)(OCH_3)COOH + 2H_2O$. **guaiaconic a.,** an acid, $C_{20}H_{24}O_5$, from guaiac resin. **guaiaretic a.,** an acid, $C_{20}H_{26}O_4$, the chief constituent of guaiacum. **guanylic a.,** a mononucleotid made up of guanine, phosphoric acid, and a pentose. **gulonic a.,** one of the isomeric forms of pentahydroxycaproic acid, $CH_3OH(CHOH)_4COOH$, formed by the gentle oxidation of gulose. **gummic a.,** arabin. **gurjunic a.,** a compound, $C_{22}H_{34}O_4$, from the resin of gurjun balsam. **gymnemic a.,** an acid, $C_{32}H_{55}O_{12}$, from *Gymnema sylvestre,* a southern Asiatic shrub: placed in the mouth, it temporarily abolishes the sense of taste for sweetness. **gynocardic a.,** an oily acid, $C_{18}H_{34}O_2$, from the seeds of *Gynocardia odorata.* **haloid a.,** an acid which contains no oxygen in the molecule, but is composed of hydrogen and a halogen element. **helvellic a.,** the active, poisonous constituent of the fungus *Morchella helvella.* **helvolic a.,** a monobasic acid, $C_{32}H_{44}O_8$, from cultures of *Aspergillus fumigatus* mut. *Helvola.* **hemipinic a.,** an acid, $(CH_3O)_2C_6H_2(COOH)$, obtained by oxidizing narcotine. **hepta-iodic a.,** a periodic acid. **hexamethylenamine-salicyl-sulfonic a.,** a white, crystalline compound, $(CH_2)_6N_4.SO_2.OH.C_6H_3.(OH)COOH$. **hexonic a.,** any one of several isomeric forms of pentahydroxycaproic acid. **hexosediphosphoric a.,** a compound occurring in the products of fermentation of sugars by yeast accelerated by phosphates. **hexuronic a.,** ascorbic a. **hidrolic a., hidrotic a.,** sudoric a. **hippuric a.,** a crystallizable acid, benzoyl amino-acetic acid, $C_6H_5.CO.NH.CH_2.COOH$, from the urine of domestic animals; more rarely found in human urine. **hircic a.,** an acid with a peculiar odor, found in goat's milk. **hirsutic a.,** an antibacterial compound obtained from cultures of a fungus, *Stereum hirsutum.* **homogentisic a.,** an intermediate product of the catabolism of tyrosine and phenylalanine, which is ultimately metabolized to acetone. **homophthalic a.,** a crystalline acid, phenyl-acetocarboxylic acid, $COOH.C_6H_4.CH_2.COOH$, formed by fusing gamboge with potassium hydroxide. **homopiperidinic a.,** an amino acid, $NH_2(CH_2)_4.COOH$, found in decomposing meat. **humic a.,** an acid, $C_{40}H_{15}O_5$, from peat, soil, certain waters, etc. **humulotannic a.,** the tannic acid of hops, $C_{50}H_{48}O_{26}$. **hyaluronic a.,** a mucopolysaccharide which is a polymer of acetylglucosamine and glucuronic acid. It occurs as a gel in the intercellular substance of various tissues, especially the skin, and has also been isolated from the vitreous humor, the umbilical cord, and synovial fluids. **hydantoic a.,** glycoluric a. **hydnocarpic a.,** an unsaturated fatty acid obtained from chaulmoogra and hynocarpus oils. Its ethyl ester is used in the treatment of leprosy. **hydracrylic a.** See under *lactic a.* **hydrazoic a.,** triazoic a. **hydriodic a.,** a gaseous, haloid acid, HI. Its aqueous solution and its syrup are used as alteratives, but with no material advantage over the alkali iodides. **hydrobromic a.,** a gaseous, haloid acid, HBr: its 10 per cent aqueous solution is used like the bromides. **hydrocaffeic a.,** an acid, dihydroxy-phenyl-propionic acid, $(OH)_2.C_6H_3.CH_2.CH_2.COOH$, formed by treating caffeic acid with sodium amalgam. **hydrochloric a.,** a normal constituent of the gastric juice in man and other mammals, HCl. **hydrochloroplatinic a.,** a compound occurring in reddish-brown, deliquescent crystals, $H_2PtCl_6.6H_2O$. **hydrocinnamic a.,** a balsamic cinnamic acid derivative, beta-phenyl-propionic acid, $C_6H_5.CH_2.CH_2.COOH$, in white needles. **hydrocumaric a.,** an acid, beta-phenol-propionic acid, $OH.C_6H_4.(CH_2)_2.COOH$, sometimes found in the urine and derived from the putrefaction of protein. **hydrocyanic a.,** a colorless liquid, HCN, extremely poisonous because it checks the oxidation process in protoplasm. **hydrodesoxycholic a.,** the cholic acid of hog bile, $C_{25}H_{40}O_4$, or 3,6-dihydroxycholanic acid. **hydrofluoric a.,** a gaseous, haloid acid, HF, extremely poisonous. **hydrofluosilicic a.,** an acid, H_2SiF_6, formed by passing silicon tetrafluoride into water. **hydroparacumaric a.,** an isomer of hydrocumaric acid, sometimes found in the urine of dogs. **hydroquinone-acetic a.,** homogentisic acid. **hydrosulfuric a.,** an offensive and poisonous gas, H_2S, much used as a chemical reagent. **hydrosulfurous a.,** thiosulfuric a. **hydroxyacetic a.,** glycolic a. **hydroxybutyric a.,** a poisonous acid, $CH_3CHOHCH_2COOH$, sometimes occurring in the urine in diabetes and sometimes in the blood. It frequently occurs in several isomeric forms. See *beta-oxybutyric a.* **hydroxyformobenzoylic a.,** a crystalline compound parahydroxyphenylglycolic acid, $OH.C_6H_4.CHOH.COOH$, sometimes occurring in the urine in acute yellow atrophy of the liver. **hydroxyglutamic a.,** an amino acid, $COOH.CH_2.CHOH.CH(NH_2).COOH$. **hydroxymandelic a.,** parahydroxyphenylglycolic acid. **hydroxy-n-decanic a.,** a saturated, monohydroxy fatty acid found in brain phospholipids. It is $CH_3(CH_2)_7(CHOH)COOH$. **hydroxynaphthoic a.,** alpha-naphtholcarboxylic acid, $OH.C_{10}H_6.COOH$, a naphthylene homologue of salicylic acid. **hydroxypentacosanic a.,** cerebronic a. **2-hydroxypropionic a.,** lactic a. **hydroxystearic a.,** a monohydroxy acid, $CH_3(CH_2)_7CHOH(CH_2)_8COOH$, found in castor oil. **hydrozosophalic a.,** a toxic agent obtainable from artificial salicylic acid. **hydrurilic a.,** an acid, $C_8H_7N_4O_6.2H_2O$, obtained as the ammonium salt on boiling alloxantin with dilute sulfuric acid. **hygric a.,** an acid that results from the oxidation of hygrine. **hyodesoxycholic a.,** a bile acid, $C_{24}H_{40}O_4$, from the hog. **hyoglycocholic a.,** an acid, $C_{27}H_{43}NO_5$, occurring in the bile of pigs. **hyotaurocholic a.,** an acid, $C_{26}H_{45}NSO_6$, occurring in pigs' bile in the form of its sodium salt. **hypobromous a.,** the acid, HBrO, forming hypobromites, which are used in testing for urea. **hypochlorous a.,** an unstable compound, HClO, a disinfectant and bleaching agent. Its salts (hypochlorites) are used as medicinal agents, particularly as surgical solution of chlorinated soda. **hypogeic a.,** an unsaturated, fatty acid, $CH_3(CH_2)_7.CH:CH(CH_2)_5COOH$, found in the oil of the peanut, *Arachis hypogaea.* **hyponitrous a.,** a monobasic acid, NHO. **hypophosphoric a.,** an acid $H_4P_2O_6$, of phosphorus, forming salts called hypophosphates. **hypophosphorous a.,** the acid, H_3PO_2, forming hypophosphites. **hypophosphorous a., dilute,** a 10 per cent solution of the acid in water: used like the hypophosphites. **hyposulfurous a.,** dithionous acid. **hypoxanthylic a.,** inosinic a. **ichthulinic a.,** an acid derived from ichthulin by treating the latter with alkalis. **ichthyolsulfonic a.,** an ichthyol derivative. **idonic a.,** an acid, $CH_2OH(CHOH)_3C(OH)_2COOH$, resulting from the catalytic reduction of ascorbic acid. **indoleacetic a.,** a compound occurring in the urine in minute quantities in pathological conditions of the digestive tract; a decomposition product of tryptophan. **indopropionic a.,** a decomposition product of tryptophan. **indoxylic a.,** an acid, $C_9H_7NO_3$, formed by fusing its ethyl ester with sodium hydroxide. **indoxylsulfonic a.,** one of the ethereal sulfates found in the urine. **inosinic a.,** a mononucleotide made up of hypoxanthine, ribose, and phosphoric acid. It is one of the decomposition products of nucleic acid and is also found in muscle tissue. **inositol hexaphosphoric a.,** phytic a. **iodic a.,** a monobasic acid, HIO_3. **iodoacetic a.,** CH_2ICOOH, whose sodium salt is used in physiological study of muscle contraction. **iodoalphionic a.,** an iodine compound, $C_{15}H_{12}I_2O_3$, occurring as white crystals or a white or faintly yellowish powder: used as a radiopaque medium in roentgenography of the gallbladder. **iodogorgoric a.,** 3,5-diiodotyrosine. **iodopanoic a.,** iopanoic a. **iodophenyl-arsenic a.,** a proposed substitute for atoxyl. It is similar to atoxyl, but the amino group has been replaced with iodine, $C_6H_4I.AsO(OH)_2$. **iodosalicylic a.,** an antipyretic, analgesic, and antiseptic compound, $OH.C_6H_3I.COOH$. **iodosobenzoic a.,** an antiseptic agent, $C_6H_4(IO)COOH$, used like iodoform. **iodoxybenzoic a.,** a compound, $C_6H_4(IO_2)COOH$. The salts of ortho-iodoxybenzoic acid are indicated chiefly in arthritis. Cf. *amidoxyl benzoate.* **iodoxyquinoline sulfonic a.,** loretin. **iopanoic a.,** a tasteless, cream-colored powder, with a characteristic odor, $C_{11}H_{12}I_3NO_2$: used as a radiopaque medium in cholecystography. **iophenoxic a.,** α-ethyl-3-hydroxy-2,4,6-triiodohydrocinnamic acid. Use: radiopaque medium for cholecystography. **iridic a.,** an acid, $C_{16}H_{12}O_5$, from orris root. **isanic a.,** a crystalline acid, $C_{14}H_{20}O_2$, from isano oil: a violent purgative. **isethionic a.,** a thick, liquid, hydroxy-ethyl-sulfonic acid, $CH_2(OH).CH_2.SO_2.OH$, isomeric with ethyl-sulfuric acid; formed by the action of nitrous acid on taurine. **isoamyl-ethylbarbituric a.,** amytal. **isobilianic a.,** an acid, $C_{24}H_{34}O_8$, derived along with bilianic acid by the oxidation of dehydrocholalic acid. **isobutylallyl barbituric a.,** a hypnotic compound, $(C_4H_9)(C_3H_5)C(CO.NH)_2CO$: used like barbital. **isobutyl-aminoacetic a.,** leucine. **isobutyric a.,** an acid, $(CH_3)_2CH.COOH$, a product of putrefaction of protein found in the urine. **isodialuric a.,** an acid, $CO.(NH.CO)_2.CHOH$, isomeric with dilauric acid and formed from oxyuracil by the action of bromine water. **iso-erucic a.,** brassic acid. **isolysergic a.,** $C_{16}H_{16}N_2O_2$, one of the main cleavage products of the alkaline hydrolysis of the alkaloids characteristic of ergot, and the parent compound of the ergotinine group of alkaloids. **isopentoic a.,** isovaleric a. **isopropyl-aminoacetic a.,** valine. **isosaccharic a.,** an acid, $COOH.CH(O).(CHOH)_2.CH.COOH$, resulting from the oxidation of glycosamine with nitric acid. **isosulfocyanic a., isothiocyanic a.,** an acid, HNCS, whose salts are isosulfocyanates or isothiocyanates. **isouric a.,** an acid, $NC.NH.CH.(CO.NH)_2CO$, formed by the combination of cyanamide and alloxantin and which yields uric acid when boiled with hydrochloric acid. **isovalerianic a.,** an acid, $(CH_3)_2CHCH_2COOH$, of unpleasant odor, found in cheese, in the sweat of the feet, in the urine of smallpox, in typhus, and in acute yellow atrophy of the liver. Called also *isopentoic a.* **japonic a.,** a variety of tannic acid from catechu. **jervic a.,** an acid, $C_{14}H_{10}O_{12}.2H_2O$, from *Veratrum album.* **juglandic a.,** an acid from the bark of *Juglans cinerea,* considered to be the same as juglone. **kenurenic a.,** kynurenic a. **kephalophosphoric a.,** cephalylphosphoric a. **kermisic a.,** a red coloring matter from kermes insects. **keto a.,** a chemical compound containing the group CO and COOH. **ketocholanic a.,** an oxidized form of cholanic acid. **ketostearic a.,** an oxidized form of stearic acid, $CH_3(CH_2)_{11}$-$CO(CH_2)_4COOH$, found in mushrooms. **kinic a.,** quinic acid. **kinotannic a.,** the tannic acid of kino. **kojic a.,** a pyrone, formed under certain conditions by molds and aerobic bacteria: it has a toxic action on animals. **krameric a.,** ratanhiatannic a. **kynurenic a.,** a crystalline acid, $C_9H_5N(OH)COOH$ (4-hydroxyquinaldic acid), a metabolite of tryptophan found in microorganisms and in the urine of normal mammals. **laccic a.,** a brownish-red, crystalline compound, obtained from lac dye. **lactic a.,** a monobasic acid, hydroxypropionic acid, $C_3H_6O_3$, alpha-hydroxy-propionic acid known in three stereoisomeric forms: (*a*) Dextrolactic acid (paralactic acid), called also sarcolactic acid because it occurs in flesh, can be obtained conveniently from beef extract. (*b*) Levolactic acid is produced by the fermentation of dextrose by *Micrococcus acidi levolactici.* (*c*) Inactive, ethylidene, racemic or fermentation lactic acid is the ordinary kind found in sour milk, in the stomach, and in certain fermented foods, such as sauerkraut, silage, etc. Beta-hydroxy-propionic acid, $CHOH.CH_2.COOH$, called also ethylene-lactic acid, is not found in the body. **lactonic a.,** a crystallizable monobasic acid, $CH_2OH.(CHOH)_4.COOH$, produced by the oxidation of milk sugar, gum arabic, or galactose. **lactucic a.,** a bitter principle from lactucarium. **lanoceric a.,** a saturated dihydroxy fatty acid present in wool fat, $CH_3(CH_2)_{26}$-$(CHOH)_2COOH$. **lanopalmic a.,** a saturated monohydroxy fatty acid present in wool fat, $CH_3(CH_2)_{13}(CHOH)COOH$. **laricic a., larixinic a.,** a crystallizable acid, $C_{10}H_{10}O_5$, from the bark of the European larch; called also *larixin.* **laricinolic a.,** an acid resin, $C_{20}H_{30}O_2$, found in Venice turpentine. **larinolic a.,** an amorphous acid resin, $C_{18}H_{26}O_2$, forming one of the principal constituents of Venice turpentine. **lauric a., laurostearic a.,** a compound, $C_{12}H_{24}O_2$, from oil of laurel and other oils. **leuconic a.,** a crystalline acid obtained by oxidizing crotonic acid. **levotartaric a.,** a form of tartaric acid which turns the plane of polarization to the left. **levulinic a.,** an acid, $CH_3COCH_2CH_2COOH$, or β-acetyl-propionic acid, from the nucleic acid of the thymus gland. It occurs in the form of hygroscopical scales. **lignoceric a.,** an acid, CH_3-$(CH_2)_{22}.COOH$, obtained from kerasin by hydrolysis. **lignulmic a.,** a dark brown, crystalline acid, $C_{54}H_{28}O_6$, allied to ulmic acid. **linoleic a.,** an unsaturated fatty acid, $C_{18}H_{32}O_2$, from linseed oil and various animal tissues. **linolenic a.,** an unsaturated fatty acid, $C_{18}H_{30}O_2$, from linseed oil. **linolic a.,** linoleic a. **lithic a.,** uric acid. **lithobilic a.,** an acid derivable from bile products. **lithocholic a.,** an acid, $C_{24}H_{40}O_3$, from bile of the ox. **lithofellic a.,** an acid, $C_{20}H_{36}O_4$, found in intestinal concretions of ruminants. **luteic a.,** a highly mucilaginous polysaccharide acid produced by the growth of *Penicillium luteum* on liquid media that contain sugar. It seems to be a malonyl ester of luteose. **lymphokentric a.,** a hydroxy acid from the urine of patients with lymphoid leukemia, which stimulates the proliferation of cells of the leukopoietic system. **lysalbic a.,** a compound formed by treating egg-albumin with caustic alkali. **lysergic a.,** a constituent of the ergot alkaloids. It is $C_6H_4.NH.C_5H_2N(CH_3)(CH$:-$CH.CH_3).COOH$. **lysuric a.,** a crystalline, dibenzoyl lysine, $C_6H_5.CO.NH(CH_2)_4.CH(COOH)$.-$NH.CO.C_6H_5$, obtained from lysine. **lyxonic a.,** one of the isomeric forms of tetrahydroxy valeric acid, $CH_2OH(CHOH)_3COOH$, formed by the gentle oxidation of lyxose. **maizenic a.,** a compound from the silk of Indian corn (*Zea mays*). **maleic a.,** an unsaturated dibasic acid, $(CH.$-$COOH)_2$; the cis form of which fumaric acid is the trans form. **malic a.,** an acid, hydroxysuccinic acid, $COOH.CH_2CH(OH).COOH$, found in unripe and sour apples and in many other fruits. It has been prescribed for scurvy, and its iron salt, ferric malate, has been employed in medicine. **malonic a.,** a crystalline dibasic acid, $COOH$.-CH_2COOH, formed by oxidizing malic acid with chromium trioxide. **mandelic a.,** an acid, phenylglycolic acid, $C_6H_5.CHOH.COOH$, from oil of bitter almonds. It is one of the constituents of homatropine. Its salts are used in the treatment of urinary infection. **manganic a.,** an acid, H_2-MnO_4, formed by fusing manganese dioxide with potassium or sodium hydroxide. **mannitic a.,** a compound, $CH_2OH(CHOH)_4.COOH$, derived from mannitol by the action of platinum black. **mannonic a.,** a compound, $CH_2OH(CHOH)_4$.-$COOH$, formed by oxidizing mannose. **mannosaccharic a.,** a dicarboxylic acid, $COOH$-$(CHOH)_4COOH$. **margaric a.** 1. An artificial fatty acid, $CH_3(CH_2)_{15}.COOH$. 2. The incorrect name of a mixture of stearic and palmitic acids. **margosic a.,** an acid derived from the oil of the seeds of the margosa tree. **meconic a.,** a white, crystalline acid, derived from opium: feebly narcotic. **medullic a.,** a colorless compound, $C_{20}H_{41}COOH$, found in beef suet and beef marrow. **melanogallic a.,** an amorphous, tasteless compound, $C_6H_4O_2$, formed by heating gallic or tannic acid. **melassic a.,** a dark colored insoluble acid formed from cane sugar by the action of potassium hydroxide. **melilotic a.,** an acid, phenolpropionic acid, $OH.C_6H_4(CH_2)_2.COOH$, from coumarin. **melissic a.,** a crystalline, fatty acid, $CH_3(CH_2)_{29}COOH$, from beeswax. **mellitic a.,** benzene-hexacarboxylic acid, $C_6(COOH)_6$. **mercapturic a.,** one of a series of acids formed in the body on the introduction of a halogen derivative of benzol. They are formed by combination with cysteine. See *bromphenyl mercapturic a.* **mesitonic a.,** a homologue of levulinic acid, $CH_3.CO.CH_2.C(CH_3)_2COOH$. **mesitylenic a.,** $C_6H_3(CH_3)_2COOH$, an oxidized form of mesitylene. **mesityluric a.,** the form in which mesitylene is excreted in the urine combined with glycocoll, $C_6H_3(CH_3)_2CO.NH.CH_2.COOH$. **mesotartaric a.,** an optically inactive form of tartaric acid by internal compensation, $COOH$-$(CHOH)_2COOH$. **mesoxalic a.,** $(OH)_2C$-$(COOH)_2$, an oxidation product of glycerol. **metagallic a.,** melanogallic a. **metaphosphoric a.,** a glassy solid substance, HPO_3, soluble in water: used as a test for albumin in the urine. **metarsenic a.,** the acid, $HAsO_3$, which forms metarsenates. **metasaccharic a.,** a dibasic tetrahydroxy acid formed by the oxidation of mannitol. It is $COOH(CHOH)_4COOH$, and in the free state passes into a double lactone. **metastannic a's,** two acids from the oxidation of tin: the alpha-acid is $H_4SnO_4[Sn(OH)_4]$, the beta-acid is $H_2SnO_3[SnO(OH)_2]$. **metatartaric a.,** one of the modifications of tartaric acid produced by heat. **metavanadic a.,** vanadic a. **methacrylic a.,** alpha methyl acrylic acid, CH_2:C-$(CH_3).COOH$. **methionic a.,** an acid, CH_2-$(SO_2OH)_2$: used in the preparation of ether. **methyl-aminoacetic a.,** sarcosine. **methyl-arsinic a.,** a white, crystalline compound, $CH_3.AsO(OH)_2$, an organic derivative of arsenic. **methylene-hippuric a.,** a compound readily giving off formaldehyde. **methyl-guanidine-acetic a.,** creatine. **methyl-hydantoic a.,** an acid, glycoluric acid, $NH_2CO.N(CH_3).CH_2$.-$COOH$, obtained by boiling creatine with barium hydroxide. **methyl-maleic a.,** citraconic acid. **methylprotocatechuic a.,** vanillic a. **methylsuccinic a.,** pyrotartaric a. **molybdenic a., molybdic a.,** the acid, H_2MoO_4: used homeopathically. **monamino a., monoamino a.,** an organic acid which contains an NH_2 group. **mono-amino-dicarboxylic a.,** an acid containing one amino group and two carboxyl groups in the molecule. Glutamic acid is an example. **mono-amino-monocarboxylic a.,** an acid having one amino group and one carboxyl group in the molecule. Alanine is one. **monobasic a.,** a monatomic acid. **monochloracetic a.,** $CH_2Cl.COOH$. See *chloracetic a.* **moritannic a.,** the tannic acid of fustic, *Morus tinctoria*, $C_{13}H_{19}O_6$. **morphoxylacetic a.,** a narcotic agent, $C_{17}H_{16}NO_3.CH_2.COOH$: only one fiftieth as toxic as morphine. **morrhuic a.,** an hydroxy acid, $C_9H_{13}O_3N$, found in small quantities in cod liver oil. **mucic a.,** a tetrahydroxy dibasic acid, $COOH(CHOH)_4COOH$, produced by oxidizing galactose or any carbohydrate containing galactose, such as milk sugar, agar, galactitol, or the galactans. **mucoitin-sulfuric a.,** a mucopolysaccharide occurring in gastric mucus and in the cornea of the eye. It is isomeric with chondroitin sulfuric acid but contains glucosamine in place of galactosamine. **mucolic a's,** the acid-fast hydroxy acids of high molecular weight, which are specific metabolic products of acid-fast bacteria. **muconic a.,** a dibasic acid, $COOH.(CH)_4.COOH$, found in the urine of dogs that have been given benzene. **muriatic a.,** hydrochloric acid. **muscle adenosine phosphoric a.,** a substance obtained from striated muscle which is said to facilitate muscular contraction in the presence of deficient circulation. **mycophenolic a.,** a crystalline antibiotic substance from cultures of *Penicillium brevi-compactum*, which is both bacteriostatic and fungistatic. **myelokentric a.,** a keto acid from the urine of patients with myeloid leukemia, which stimulates the proliferation of cells of the leukopoietic system. **myristic a.,** an acid, $CH_3.(CH_2)_{12}.COOH$, found in spermaceti, nutmeg butter, and other fats under the form of myristin. **myronic a.,** a glycoside, $C_{10}H_{19}NS_2O_{10}$, found in black mustard: this acid, by the myrosin present, is changed into allyl mustard oil, glucose, and potassium sulfate on the addition of water. **naphthionic a.,** a white powder, naphthyl-amino-sulfonic acid, $NH_2.C_{10}H_6SO_2OH$: used in iodism and nitrite poisoning and in bladder diseases. **naphthol-carboxylic a.,** a white, crystalline substance, $C_{10}H_6(OH)CO_2H$: antiseptic and antiparasitic. **naphtholdisulfonic a.,** an acid, $C_{10}H_5(OH)(SO_2OH)_2$, derived from naphthol. **naphtholsulfonic a.,** an acid, $C_{10}H_6(OH)SO_2OH$, derived from naphthol. **naphthyl-amino-sulfonic a.,** naphthionic a. **naphthylmercapturic a.,** a compound found in the urine of rabbits to which naphthalene has been administered. **nastinic a.,** a fatty acid of high molecular weight found in nastin. **nervonic a.,** a fatty acid, $CH_3(CH_2)_7.CH:CH(CH_2)_{13}:COOH$, associated with sphingomyelin. **neuraminic a.,** a widely distributed 9-carbon aminosugar acid, one of the sialic acids. **neurostearic a.,** a fatty acid, $C_{18}H_{36}O_2$, formed by the decomposition of phrenosin, found in cerebral tissue. **nicotinic a.,** an acid, $C_5H_4N(COOH)$, produced by oxidizing nicotine or by oxidizing quinoline to quinolic acid which, on heating, loses carbon dioxide to yield nicotinic acid. It is a component of certain coenzymes of oxidation-reduction systems, and forms part of the vitamin B complex. Called also *niacin*, and *antipellagra vitamin.* **nicotinuric a.,** the form in which absorbed nicotine is excreted in the urine. It is $C_5H_4.N.CO.NH.CH_2.COOH$. **Nissl a.,** a compound occurring along with fibril acid in the neurofibrils. It is soluble in acidified water and in ammonia. See *fibril a.* **nitric a.,** a colorless liquid, HNO_3, extremely caustic and escharotic, decomposing most organic substances, and combining with bases to form nitrates. Nitric acid has been used as a caustic for ulcers, chancres, nasal growths, etc., and as an astringent and stimulant. *Fuming nitric acid* is a brownish liquid giving off a suffocating vapor, and containing some nitrogen peroxide. **nitroferrocyanic a.,** a complex cyano-acid, $H_2[Fe(NO)Cy_6]$, formed by the action of nitric acid on potassium ferrocyanide. It is used as a salt in several tests. **nitrohydrochloric a.,** a yellowish mixture of concentrated nitric acid and hydrochloric acid. **nitromuriatic a.,** nitrohydrochloric a. **nitroprussic a.,** nitro-ferrocyanic a. **nitrosonitric a.,** fuming nitric acid. **nitrous a.,** an unstable compound having the formula HNO_2. **normal fatty a.,** a fatty acid that has a straight chain, or at least one that is not branched. **norpinic a.,** an acid that results from the oxidation of pinene. **nucleic a's,** substances of high molecular weight which constitute the prosthetic groups of the nucleoproteins, and contain phosphoric acid, sugars, and purine and pyrimidine bases. Two types, ribonucleic a. and deoxyribonucleic a., are distinguished on the basis of the contained sugar and a difference in the pyrimidine bases. **nucleinic a.,** nucleic a. **nucleothymimic a.,** a patented yellowish-white powder prepared from the pancreas of the calf or from nucleic acid: used therapeutically. **oenanthylic a.,** enanthylic a. **olefinic a.,** an unsaturated fatty acid having the general formula $C_nH_{2n-1}COOH$. **oleic a.,** a colorless, liquid, unsaturated fatty acid, $CH_3(CH_2)_7CH:CH(CH_2)_7COOH$, which is a constituent of most of the common fats and oils: insoluble in water, but soluble in alcohol and ether. **oleophosphoric a.,** a viscid yellow fluid, $C_{78}H_{143}PO_{12}$, occurring in the brain and believed to be a product of the decomposition of lecithin. **opianic a.,** a compound, $CHO.C_6H_2(CH_3O)_2.COOH$, obtained from narcotine. **organic a.,** any acid the radical of which is a carbon derivative; a compound in which a hydrocarbon radical is united to carboxyl, COOH. **ornithuric a.,** an acid, $C_6H_5.CO.NH(CH_2)_3.CH.NH.CO.C_6H_5$, or dibenzoylornithin, occurring in the urine of birds fed on benzoic acid. **orotic a.,** an acid found in milk. **orsellinic a.,** a crystalline acid, $C_8H_8O_4$, from certain lichens. **ortho-aminosalicylic a.,** a grayish powder, $C_6H_3(NH_2)(OH)COOH$. **ortho-arsenic a.,** arsenic acid. **orthoboric a.,** boric a. **orthohydroxybenzoic a.,** salicylic a. **ortho-oxybenzoic a.,** salicylic a. **orthophosphoric a.,** the ordinary phosphoric acid, H_3PO_4. **orylic a.,** an acid, $C_{18}H_{28}O_5N_4$, obtained by boiling carniferrin with baryta water. **oshaic a.,** a principle resembling angelic acid, and found in osha. **osmic a.** 1. A dibasic acid, H_2OsO_4, forming salts called osmates. 2. The perosmic anhydride, a crystalline, odorous compound, OsO_4: used as a caustic, a stain for fats, and an analgesic. **oxalic a.,** a poisonous, crystalline, dibasic acid, $(COOH)_2 + 2H_2O$: used as a disinfectant for the skin, in pharmacy and the arts, and as a chemical reagent. **oxaluric a.,** an acid, $NH_2.CO.NH.CO.COOH$, found in healthy urine. **oxamic a.,** it is the mono-amide of oxalic acid; a monobasic crystalline acid, $NH_2.CO.COOH$. **oxy a.,** an acid that contains oxygen. **oxyacetic a.,** glycolic a. **oxyamygdalic a.,** hydroxyformobenzoylic a. **oxybenzoic a.,** salicylic a. **oxybutyric a.,** hydroxybutyric a. **oxycarnic a.,** an acid, $C_{30}H_{41}N_9O_{15}$, derived from carnic acid. **oxyformobenzoylic a.,** hydroxyformobenzoylic a. **oxygen a.,** an acid that contains oxygen; an oxacid. **oxylic a.,** an acid, $C_{18}H_{28}N_4O_8$, from carniferrin. **oxymandelic a.,** hydroxyformobenzoylic a. **oxynaphthoic a.,** hydroxynaphthoic a. **oxyphenylacetic a.,** parahydroxyphenylacetic a. **oxyphenylaminopropionic a.,** tyrosine. **oxypropionic a.** See under *lactic a.* **oxyproteic a.,** a nitrogenous substance of unknown constitution, perhaps a peptide, sometimes found in the urine. **oxyproteinic a.,** a compound occurring in normal urine. **oxyprotonic a.,** an acid formed by oxidizing proteins; called also *oxyprotosulfonic a.* **oxytoluic a.,** cresotinic a. **palmitic a.,** a fatty acid, $CH_3(CH_2)_{14}COOH$, found in most of the common fats and oils. **palmitoleic a.,** an acid found as a glyceride in the oil of whales, walrus, seals and various fish. It is $CH_3(CH_2)_5CH$:-$CH(CH_2)_7COOH$. **palmitolic a.,** an acid isomeric with linoleic acid. **pangamic a.,** an amino derivative of glycuronic acid, $C_{10}H_{19}O_8N$, a water-soluble substance originally discovered in the kernel of the apricot; tentatively assigned to the fifteenth position in the list of vitamins in the B complex. **pantothenic a.,** the antidermatitis factor of chicks essential for the normal development of rats and chicks. It is alpha gamma dihydroxy beta beta dimethyl butyroalanine, CH_2-OH.C $(CH_3)_2$.CHOH.CO.NH.CH_2.CH_2.CO_2OH, and is widely distributed in foods and tissues; it stimulates the growth of yeast. It is a vitamin of the B complex, and has been reported as an antigray hair factor in experimental animals. **paraaminobenzoic a.,** $NH_2.C_6H_4.COOH$; a member of the group of B vitamins. It is a growth factor for rats, chicks and yeast and an essential constituent of bacterial culture media. It nullifies the bacteriostatic effects of the sulfonamide drugs and opposes gray hair in rats. It has been used in the treatment of tsutsugamushi disease (scrub typhus). Often abbreviated PABA. **paraaminohippuric a.,** the N-acetic acid of paraaminobenzoic acid, $C_9H_{10}N_2O_3$: used to measure the effective renal plasma flow and to determine the functional capacity of the tubular excretory mechanism. Often abbreviated PAH. **paraaminosalicylic a.,** a salicylic-acid derivative which has been used in the treatment of tuberculosis. Often abbreviated PAS or PASA. **parabanic a.,** a solid acid, $CO(NH.CO)_2$, derivable from uric acid by oxidation. **paracresotic a.,** an antipyretic substance, oxytoluic acid, CH_3C_6-$H_3(OH)$.COOH. **paraffinic a.,** an acid, C_{24}-$H_{48}O_2$, formed when paraffin is oxidized with strong nitric acid. **parahydroxybenzoic a.,** an acid isomeric with salicylic acid, produced by boiling phenol with carbon tetrachloride. **parahydroxyhydratropic a.,** hydrocumaric acid. **parahydroxyphenylacetic a.,** an acid, OH.-C_6H_4.CH_2.COOH, derived from tyrosine by putrefactive changes in the intestines and sometimes found in the urine. **parahydroxyphenylglycolic a.,** an acid, OH.C_6H_4.CHOH.COOH, derived from tyrosine by deaminization and oxidation. It is found in the urine at times, especially in cases of acute yellow atrophy of the liver. **parahydroxyphenyl-propionic a.,** an acid, OH.$C_6H_4(CH_2)_2$COOH, sometimes found in the urine. **para-iodo-phenyl-arsenic a.,** a colorless crystalline compound, $C_6H_4I.AsO(OH)_2$. **paralactic a.** See under *lactic a.* **paranucleic a.,** any one of a set of nucleic acids from which no nuclein bases are derivable. **pararosolic a.,** trihydroxyphenylmethane, CH-$(C_6H_4OH)_3$: used as an indicator. **parasaccharic a.,** a dibasic acid, $COOH(CHOH)_4$-COOH, obtained when glycyrrhizic acid is hydrolyzed. It is isomeric with saccharic acid. **paratartaric a.** See under *tartaric a.* **parillic a.,** parillin. **pectic a.,** a complex polysaccharide present in pectin. It is composed of four mols of galacturonic acid, one of arabinose, one of galactose, two of acetic acid, and two of methyl alcohol. **pelargonic a.,** a normal fatty acid, $CH_3(CH_2)_7COOH$, found in oil of the garden geranium (pelargonium) and other plants. **penicillic a.,** an antibiotic compound, CH_3.C:(CH_2).-CO.C$(O.CH_3)$:CH.COOH, isolated from cultures of *Penicillium puberulum* and *P. cyclopeum.* **pentacosanic a.,** an acid, $C_{25}H_{50}O_2$, from phrenosin. **pentonic a.,** any one of several isomeric forms of tetrahydroxy-valeric acid. **pentosenucleic a.,** ribonucleic a. **peptohydrochloric a.,** the acid supposed to be formed by the combination of pepsin and dilute hydrochloric acid. **perboric a.,** an oxidized form of boric acid, $HBO_3.4H_2O$. **perchloric a.,** a volatile colorless fuming liquid, $HClO_4$, highly caustic and explosive. **periodic a.,** a series of acids formed by the union of different amounts of water with periodic anhydride (I_2O_7) varying from HIO_4 to H_7IO_7. **permanganic a.,** a monobasic acid, $HMnO_4$. Its salts are permanganates. **perosmic a.,** a yellow, crystalline acid anhydride, OsO_4, with suffocating odor. **peroxymonosulfuric a.,** persulfuric a. **peroxyprotonic a.,** a compound produced by oxidizing oxyprotonic acid. **persulfuric a.,** an oxidized form, $H_2S_2O_8$, of sulfuric acid. **petroselinic a.,** an unsaturated acid, $CH_3(CH_2)_{10}$-CH:$CH(CH_2)_4COOH$, which is the principal constituent of the fatty oil from Coriander seed. **phenaceturic a.,** an alpha amino acid, C_6H_5-CH_2.CO.NH.CH_2.COOH, found in horse and dog urine. **phenic a.,** phenol. **phenylacetic a.,** a crystalline acid, $C_6H_5.CH_2$.COOH, formed in the putrefaction of proteins. **phenylaminopropionic a.,** phenylalanine. **phenylcinchoninic a.,** cinchophen. **phenylethylbarbituric a.,** phenobarbital. **phenylglycolic a.,** mandelic a. **phenylglycuronic a.,** a compound of phenol and glycuronic acid, C_6H_5.O.CO.-$(CHOH)_4$.CHO, found in the urine after the ingestion of phenol. **phenylic a.,** phenol. **phenylmercapturic a.,** brom-phenylmercapturic a. **phenyloboric a.,** a white powder, $C_6H_5.B(OH)_2$, used as a germicide. **phenylpropionic a.,** hydrocinnamic a. **phenylpyruvic a.,** an intermediary product, $C_6H_5CH_2COCOOH$, in the metabolism of phenylalanine. **phenyl quinoline carboxylic a.,** cinchophen. **phenylsalicylic a.,** a white powder, $C_6H_3(OH)$-(C_6H_5)COOH, used as an antiseptic dusting powder. **phloretic a.,** hydrocumaric a. **phocenic a.,** valeric a. **phosphatidic a.,** a compound formed by an indirect union of fatty acid and phosphoric acid: it is derivable from leaf cytoplasm where it occurs in the form of the calcium salt of diglyceridephosphoric acid. **phosphocarnic a.,** an acid consisting of carnic acid united with phosphorus, found in muscle, blood, and milk. **phosphoglyceric a.,** glycerophosphoric a. **phosphomolybdic a.,** an acid, $H_3PO_4.12MoO_3 + H_2O$, important as being a precipitant for all the alkaloids. **phosphoric a.,** a crystalline acid, H_3PO_4, formed by the oxidation of phosphorus. See also *metaphosphoric a.* and *pyrophosphoric a.* **phosphoric a., glacial,** metaphosphoric a. **phosphorous a.,** the acid, H_3PO_3, whose salts are called phosphites. **phosphotungstic a.,** an acid, $H_3PO_4.12WO_3$, used in preparing histological stains and testing for ptomaines. **phrenosinic a.,** an acid, $C_{25}H_{50}O_3$, obtained from phrenosin by hydrolysis. **phthalic a.,** a crystalline dibasic acid, benzene dicarboxylic acid, $C_6H_4(COOH)_2$, formed by oxidizing naphthalin. **phthioic a.,** an optically active fraction of the phosphatide portion of the tubercle bacillus. **phyllocyanic a.,** a compound, homologous with bilirubin, formed by treating chlorophyll with hydrochloric acid. **physetoleic a.,** an unsaturated acid, $C_{16}H_{30}O_2$, from seal oil. **phytic a.,** inositol hexaphosphoric acid, $6CHOPO(OH)_2$, occurring in the leaves of plants. **picramic a.,** an acid found in the blood after poisoning with picric acid, forming red granules, free or in the leukocytes. It is monaminodinitrophenol, NH_2.-$C_6H_2(NO_2)_2$.OH. **picric a.,** trinitrophenol. **picric-nitric a.,** an agent used as a fixing agent in histological work. **picropodophyllic a.,** a resinous acid derivable from podophyllotoxin. **picrosulfuric a.,** a mixture used as a fixing agent in histological work. **pimaric a.,** an acid resin, $C_{20}H_{30}O_2$, soluble in sodium hydroxide solution and forming 8 to 10 per cent of European turpentine. **pimarinic a.,** an acid resin, C_{14}-$H_{22}O_2$, soluble in ammonium carbonate solution and forming 6 to 8 per cent of European turpentine. **pimarobic a.,** an acid resin, $C_{18}H_{26}O_2$, soluble in sodium hydroxide solution and forming 48 to 50 per cent of European turpentine. **pimelic a.,** a dibasic acid, $COOH(CH_2)_5COOH$, homologous with adipic acid. **piperic a., piperidic a.,** a crystalline unsaturated acid, dioxymethylenylacrylic acid, $CH_2O_2.C_6H_3.(CH)_4$.-

COOH, formed when piperine is boiled with alcoholic potassium hydroxide. **pipitzahoic a.,** a golden yellow compound, $C_{15}H_{19}(OH)O_2$, found in the root of *Trixis pipitzahuac.* **pivalic a.** See under *valeric a.* **plasminic a.,** an acid obtained by splitting up nucleic acids. It may be decomposed into phosphoric acid and nucleic bases. **plasmonucleic a.,** ribose nucleic a. **platinochloric a.,** hydrochloroplatinic a. **plumbodithio-pyridine carboxylic a.,** a yellow powder, soluble in water, contains 42.4 per cent of lead: used in the treatment of cancer. **podophyllic a.,** a principle contained in podophyllum: medicinally inert. **polyatomic a., polybasic a.,** an acid which contains two or more hydrogen atoms which may be replaced by radicals. **polygalic a.,** polygalin. **propiolic a.,** an unsaturated fatty acid, CH:C.COOH, called also *propargylic a.* **propionic a.,** an acid, CH_3-CH_2.COOH, found in chyme and in sweat, and one of the products of alcoholic and propionic fermentation. **propionylsalicylic a.,** the salicylic ester of propionic acid, $CH_3.CH_2.CO.O.C_6$-H_4.COOH. **protic a.,** an acid derived from the albuminous constituents of fish muscle. **protocatechuic a.,** dioxybenzoic acid, $(OH)_2C_6H_3$.-COOH, sometimes found in the urine. **prussic a.,** hydrocyanic a. **pteroic a.,** folic acid with glutamic acid removed. **pteroyldiglutamic a.,** See *diopterin.* **pteroylglutamic a.,** folic a. **pteroylmonoglutamic a.,** folic a. **pteroyltriglutamic a.** See *teropterin.* **puberolonic a.,** an acid, $C_8H_4O_6$, isolated from cultures of *Penicillium:* bacteriostatic for gram-positive bacteria. **puberulic a.,** an acid, $C_8H_6O_6$, isolated from cultures of *Penicillium puberulum:* bacteriostatic to gram-positive bacteria. **punico-tannic a.,** the tannic acid of pomegranate root. **purpuric a.,** an imino-condensation product of alloxan, $CO(NH.CO)_2C.NH.C(NH.CO)_2CO$, found in the murexide test for uric acid. See *ammonium purpurate.* **pyolipic a.,** an antibiotic substance isolated from *Pseudomonas aeruginosa.* **pyridine-tricarboxylic a.,** an antiseptic, antipyretic, and antispasmodic agent, C_5H_2N-$(COOH)_3$. **pyridoxic a.,** a pyridine compound sometimes occurring in the urine. **pyroarsenic a.,** the acid, $H_4As_2O_7$ forming pyroarsenates. **pyroboric a.,** a dibasic acid, $H_2B_4O_7$, obtained by heating boric acid. **pyrocechatuic a.,** an acid formerly thought to be concerned in the reaction of alkapton urine. **pyrocholesteric a.,** a compound, $C_{11}H_{16}O_7$, formed by the action of potassium dichromate and sulfuric acid on cholalic acid. **pyrocinchonic a.,** an acid, dimethylmaleic acid, $(CH_3.C.COOH)_2$, known as an anhydride, which is formed when cinchonic acid is heated, and by its salts. **pyrocitric a.,** citraconic acid. **pyrogallic a.,** pyrogallol. **pyroligneous a.,** the dark brown volatile fraction obtained when wood is heated without access of air; its acid constituent is mainly acetic acid. **pyrophosphoric a.,** a crystalline acid, H_4P_2-O_7; its salts are pyrophosphates. **pyroracemic a.,** pyruvic acid. **pyrosulfuric a.,** $H_2SO_4SO_3$, a compound of sulfuric acid and sulfur trioxide. **pyrotartaric a.,** an acid, methylsuccinic acid, $COOH.CH_2CH(CH_3)COOH$, produced in the dry distillation of tartaric acid. **pyrrolidin carboxylic a.,** proline. **pyruvic a.,** a colorless liquid, $CH_3CO.CO_2H$, with an odor like acetic acid, formed by the dry distillation of racemic or tartaric acid. **quercitannic a.,** the tannic acid of oak bark, $C_{17}H_{16}O_9$, differing in its properties slightly from ordinary tannic acid. **quillaic a.,** an acid, $C_{30}H_{46}O_5$, from a saponin in quillaia bark. **quinaldinic a.,** a crystalline acid, $C_9H_6N(CO_2$-$H)$. **quinic a.,** an acid, $CH_2.(CHOH)_3CH_2.C$-(OH).COOH, found in cinchona bark, coffee, cranberries, and in many other plants; in man, largely transformed into benzoic acid and excreted as hippuric acid. **quininic a.,** a crystalline acid, $CH_3O.C_9H_5N.COOH$, formed by oxidizing quinine and quinidine. **quinotannic a.,** a variety of tannic acid from cinchona bark. **quinovic a.,** an acid, $C_{30}H_{46}O_5$, from a cinchona glucoside. **ratanhiatannic a.,** the tannic acid of ratany. Called also *krameric a.* **reductic a.,** a reducing compound developed in sugar solutions. **Reinecke's a.,** tetrathiocyanodiaminochromic acid, $(SCN)_4Cr(NH_3)_2.NH_4$, used as a reagent for the isolation of proline and other basic substances. **rheic a.,** chrysophanic acid. **rheotannic a.,** the tannic acid of rhubarb, C_{26}-$H_{26}O_{11}$. **rheumic a.,** an acid, $C_{20}H_{16}O_9$, derivable from rheotannic acid. **rhodanic a.,** thiocyanic a. **ribonic a.,** an acid, $CH_2OH(CHOH)_3$-COOH, which results from oxidation of ribose. **ribonucleic a.,** a nucleic acid originally isolated from yeast, but later found in all living cells; on hydrolysis it yields adenine, guanine, cytosine, uracil, ribose, and phosphoric acid. Abbreviated RNA. *messenger RNA* is an RNA fraction of intermediate molecular weight, with a base ratio corresponding to the DNA of the same organism, which transfers information from DNA to the protein-forming system of the cell. In bacteria it turns over rapidly. *soluble RNA.* See *transfer RNA. transfer RNA* is an RNA fraction of low molecular weight (S = 4), existing in 20 species, each of which combines with one amino acid species, transferring it from activating enzyme to ribosome. **ribose nucleic a.,** ribonucleic a. **ricinoleic a., ricinolic a.,** an unsaturated hydroxyacid, $CH_3(CH_2)_5.CHOH.CH_2.CH:CH$-$(CH_2)_7$.COOH, found as a glyceride in castor oil. **rosacic a.,** purpurin. **rosolic a.** 1. Dihydroxyphenylmonohydroxytolylmethane, $CH_3.C_6$-$H_3OH.C(C_6H_4OH)_2$. 2. A mixture of rosolic and pararosolic acids used as an indicator. **ruberythric a.,** a glycoside found in madder root which on hydrolysis yields alizarin. **rufigallic a.,** a brownish, crystalline acid, $C_{24}H_8O_6 + 2H_2O$, derived from anthracene. **rutic a.,** a fatty acid, $C_{10}H_{20}O_2$, whose salts are called rutates. **sabinenic a.,** an acid, $C_{10}H_{16}O_3$, derivable from sabinene by oxidation. **saccharic a.** 1. A dibasic acid, $COOH.(CHOH)_4CO.OH$, formed by the action of nitric acid on dextrose or carbohydrates containing dextrose. 2. A monobasic acid, $C_6H_{12}O_6$, or tetraoxycaproic acid, not existing in the free state. **saccharonic a.,** an acid, methyltrihydroxyglutaric acid, $CH_3.C(OH)(COOH)$-$(CHOH)_2COOH$, formed by the oxidation of saccharin (2) with nitric acid. **salicylacetic a.,** salicylo-acetic acid. **salicylic a.,** a crystalline acid, $OH.C_6H_4.COOH$, orthohydroxy benzoic acid, made from phenol, from oil of gaultheria, from salicin, etc.; used as a keratolytic agent. **salicylo-acetic a.,** a compound, $C_9H_8O_5$, used as an antiseptic. **salicylous a.** See *salicylic aldehyde,* under *aldehyde.* **salicylsulfonic a.,** sulfosalicylic a. **salicyluric a.,** an acid, CH_2.-$NH_2.CO.O.C_6H_4$.COOH, found in urine after the exhibition of salicylic acid. **santalinic a.,** a crystalline compound from oil of sandalwood, produced by oxidation with solution of potassium permanganate. **santonic a.,** the acid, $C_{15}H_{20}O_4$, from santonica. **santoninic a.,** santonin. **sapocholic a.,** a weak acid, $C_{29}H_{46}O_3$, obtained from the bile of cattle. **sarcolactic a.** See *lactic a.* **sarcylic a.,** inosinic acid. **Scheele's a.,** hydrocyanic acid 4 per cent. **sclerotic a., sclerotinic a.,** an acid found in ergot, of which it is one of the active principles. **sebacic a.,** a crystalline dibasic acid, COOH.-$(CH_2)_8$.COOH, derivable from olein and various fixed oils. **selenic a.,** a clear liquid, H_2SeO_4, resembling sulfuric acid. **selenious a.** 1. An acid, H_2SeO_3, forming selenites. 2. Less correctly, selenium oxide, SeO_2. **shikimic a.,** a compound, 3,4,5-trihydroxycyclohexene-1-carboxylic acid, found in the fruits of the star anise, *Illicium verum,* which serves as a precursor in the biosynthesis of several aromatic compounds. **silicic a.** 1. An acid of which silicon is the base, forming silicates. It is of several kinds, as orthosilicic acid, H_4SiO_4; metasilicic acid, H_2SiO_3; and parasilicic acid, H_6SiO_6. 2. Less correctly, silica, SiO, or silicic anhydride. **silicotungstic a.,** an acid, $12WO_3SiO_2 + 2H_2O$, in white or yellow crystals: used as a reagent for alkaloids. **sinapinic a.,** an aromatic acid, $(CH_3O)_2C_6H_2OH(CH)_2$-COOH, from the seeds of white mustard. **skatol carboxylic a.,** a compound, $C_8H_5(CH_3)N$.-COOH, formed during the putrefaction of proteins. **skatoxyl-glycuronic a.,** a detoxicated form of skatoxyl produced by conjugation with glycuronic acid. **skatoxyl-sulfuric a.,** one of the ethereal sulfates, $C_9H_8N.O.SO_3OH$, found in the urine in the form of its potassium salt. **sorbic a.,** an acid, $CH_3.(CH)_4.COOH$, found in berries of mountain-ash. **spermanucleic a.,** nucleic acid from the spermatozoa of various animals. **sphacelinic a.,** a poisonous substance from ergot. **sphingomyelinic a.,** an acid obtained from sphingomyelin by hydrolysis. **sphingostearic a.,** a fatty acid, $C_{18}H_{36}O_2$, probably an isomer of stearic acid obtained from sphingomyelinic acid by hydrolysis. **stannic a.,** a gelatinous compound, H_2SnO_3. **stearic a.,** an acid, $CH_3(CH_2)_{16}COOH$, from the solid animal fats. A pharmaceutical preparation of solid organic acids obtained from fats, consisting chiefly of stearic acid and palmitic acid, is used as a constituent of glycerin suppository. **stearoleic a.,** an unsaturated fatty acid, $CH_3(CH_2)_6$-$C{\equiv}C(CH_2)_7COOH$, from oleic and elaidic acids. **stibanilic a.,** an acid, $NH_2.CH_2.CH_2.CH(NH_2)$-COOH.HCl. **suberic a.,** a dibasic fatty acid, $COOH(CH_2)_6COOH$, obtained from cork by boiling it with nitric acid. **succinic a.,** an acid, ethylene-dicarboxylic acid, $COOH(CH_2)_2$-COOH, from amber, etc.; found in certain hydatid cysts; it is diuretic, antispasmodic, and stimulant. **sudoric a.,** an acid, $C_5H_9O_7N$, said to exist in perspiration. **sulfacetic a.,** acetylsalicylic acid. **sulfaminic a.,** an amino-sulfonic acid, $NH_2.SO_2OH$, at one time used in the treatment of cholera. **sulfanilic a.,** a white, crystalline compound, para-amino benzene sulfonic acid, $NH_2.C_6H_4.SO_2.OH.2H_2O$, used in Ehrlich's test for typhoid fever. **sulfhydric a.,** hydrosulfuric a. **sulfichthyolic a.,** ichthyolsulfonic a. **sulfindigotic a.,** an acid, $C_{16}H_8(SO_2.OH)_2N_2O_2$, produced by the action of sulfuric acid upon indigo blue. **sulfinic a.,** an organic compound containing the group —SO.OH. **sulfo-a.,** an acid in which oxygen or carbon is replaced by sulfur. **sulfo-aminolactic a.,** cysteine. **sulfoconjugate a.,** the compound sulfuric acid formed in the urine after the ingestion of cresol, phenol, etc. **sulfocyanic a.,** thiocyanic acid. **sulfo-ichthyolic a.,** ichthyolsulfonic acid. **sulfoleic a.,** a colorless compound, $CH_3(CH_2)_{15}$.-$CH(SO_2OH).COOH$, formed by the action of concentrated sulfuric acid upon oleic acid; called also *stearin-sulfuric a.* **sulfonic a.,** a compound of SO_2OH, with another radical, especially a hydrocarbon. **sulforicinic a.,** an acid derived from castor oil by the action of sulfuric acid. **sulforicinoleic a.,** an acid formed by treating castor oil with sulfuric acid. **sulfosalicylic a.,** a compound, $C_6H_3(OH)(SO_3H)COOH.2H_2O$, occurring as white or slightly pinkish needle-like crystals, or crystalline powder, soluble in water and alcohol: used as a reagent for protein. **sulfovinic a.,** ethylsulfuric acid, $C_2H_5.HSO_4$, formed by the action of sulfuric acid in alcohol. **sulfuric a.,** an oily, highly caustic, and poisonous acid, H_2SO_4. Used in chemistry and the arts. **sulfuric a., fuming,** pyrosulfuric a. **sulfurous a.** 1. A dibasic acid, H_2SO_3, produced by combining sulfurous anhydride, a gas, SO_2, with water. Its salts are called sulfites. 2. Sulfurous anhydride, SO_2, a colorless gas: disinfectant and a bleaching agent. **talonic a.,** one of the isomeric forms of pentahydroxy-caproic acid; formed by the gentle oxidation of talose. **tannic a.,** a white or yellowish astringent powder, $(OH)_3C_6$-$H_2.CO.O.C_6H_2(OH)_2COOH$, usually obtained from nutgalls, the excrescences produced on young twigs of *Quercus infectoria* and other species of Quercus: used as an astringent. **tariric a.,** a complex organic acid, $C_{17}H_{31}COOH$, from a species of *Picramnia.* **tartaric a.,** a white powder from the lees of wine and from various plants, dihydroxy-ethylene-succinic acid, $COOH(CHOH)_2$-COOH. It is known in four forms: (*a*) ordinary or dextro-tartaric acid; (*b*) levo-tartaric acid; these two are so called because their solutions rotate the plane of polarized light to the right and the left respectively; (*c*) paratartaric acid, a mixture of (*a*) and (*b*), and hence optically inactive; and (*d*) mesotartaric acid, optically inactive from internal compensation. **tartronic a.,** a dibasic acid, COOH.CHOH.COOH, produced by the oxidation of glycerin. **taurocarbamic a.,** the form in which taurine when fed is excreted in the urine. It is taurine paired with carbamic acid, $NH_2.CO.NH(CH_2)_2.SO_2OH$. **taurocholeic a.,** an acid obtained from the bile of the dog and ox. **taurocholic a.,** one of the bile acids, $C_{26}H_{45}$-NSO_7; when hydrolyzed it splits into taurine and cholic acid. **taurylic a.,** a compound, $C_7H_{14}O$, found in urine. **telluric a.,** an acid, H_2TeO_4. **teracrylic a.,** an unsaturated acid, $CH_3(CH_2)_2$-$CH{:}CH.CH_2.COOH$. **terebic a.,** a monobasic acid, $C_7H_{10}O_4$, from oxidizing turpentine. **terrestric a.,** a metabolic product of *Penicillium terrestre.* **testicular nucleic a.,** an acid derivable from testicular nuclein. **tetraboric a.,** pyroboric acid. **tetracosanic a.,** an acid, C_{24}-$H_{48}O_2$, from phrenosin. **tetradeconic a.,** an acid occurring in small amounts in milk. **tetramethyluric a.,** a methylated purine found in tea. **tetrodonic a.,** a poisonous acid from various fishes of the genus *Tetrodon.* **thapsic a.,** an acid said to occur in *Thapsia garganica.* **thebolactic a.,** the lactic acid found in opium. **therapic a.,** a member of the oleo-acid group, $C_{17}H_{26}O_2$, from cod liver oil. **thioaminopropionic a.,** cysteine. **thiocyanic a.,** an unstable acid, HCNS. It forms salts called thiocyanates or sulfocyanides, which give a blood-red color with ferric salts. **thiolactic a.,** an acid, $CH_3CH(SH)COOH$, derived from keratin. **thiolinic a.,** a derivative of sulfur and of linseed oil. **thiopanic a.,** a compound, (dihydroxy dimethyl butyryl) taurine, $CH_2OH.C(CH_3)_2.CHOH.CO$.-$NH.CH_2.CH_2.SO_2OH$, which inhibits bacterial growth in competition with pantothenic acid. **thiopyruvic a.,** one of the intermediary products in the metabolism of cysteines. **thiosalicylic a.,** sulfosalicylic a. **thiosulfuric a.,** a very unstable acid, $H_2S_2O_3$, not known in the free state, but it forms salts called thiosulfates. The sodium salt is the photographer's "hypo." **thiuretic a.,** a colorless or yellowish liquid, $CH_3.CO.SH$, produced when phosphorus pentoxide acts on acetic acid. **thymic a.,** the residue left after partial acid hydrolysis of nucleic acid. It is a combination of phosphoric acid, carbohydrate, and pyrimidine bases. **thyminic a.,** an acid formed by the splitting up of thymonucleic acid. **thymonucleic a., thymus nucleic a.,** deoxyribonucleic a. **tiglic a.,** an unsaturated acid, methyl crotonic acid, CH_3.-$CH{:}C(CH_3).COOH$, found in croton oil. **toluic a.,** $CH_3.C_6H_4.COOH$, produced by the oxidation of xylene. **toluric a.,** the form in which toluic acid, paired with glycine, is excreted in the urine. **toxicodendric a.,** a volatile acid from *Rhus toxicodendron*, supposed to be poisonous. **traumatic a.,** an acid, 1-decene 1,10-dicarboxylic acid, $COOH.CH{:}CH(CH_2)_8COOH$, which functions as a plant-wound hormone, stimulating the production of wound periderm. **triatomic a.,** an acid that has three replaceable acid atoms or groups. **triazoic a.,** a strong monobasic acid, N_3H, a colorless liquid with an unpleasant odor; it is explosive and forms salts that are called hydrazoates, azides, or trinitrides. **trichlorethyl-glucuronic a.,** $CHCl_2.CHCl.C_6H_9O_7$, the conjugated form of chloral hydrate, the form in which it is excreted in the urine. **trichloroacetic a.,** a caustic crystalline substance, CCl_3.-COOH. **tricyanic a.,** a crystalline acid, C_3N_3-$(OH)_3$, formed when urea is heated dry. **trihydroxybenzoic a.,** gallic a. **triiodoethionic**

a., iophenoxic a. **trimethylamino-acetic a.,** a methylated glycocoll, $OH(CH_3)_3N.CH_2.COOH$. Its anhydride is betaine. **triticonucleic a.,** the nucleic acid of the wheat embryo. **tropic a.,** a crystalline acid, alphaphenyl betahydroxy propionic acid, $C_6H_5.CH(CH_2OH)-COOH$, obtained from atropine by digesting it with baryta water. **tuberculinic a.,** a nucleic acid obtained from fat-free tubercle bacilli decomposed by superheated steam, and said to be the toxic principle of the bacilli. **tuberculostearic a.,** an acid, $CH_3(CH_2)_7.CH(CH_3).(CH_2)_8.COOH$, isolated from the acetone-soluble fat of tubercle bacilli. **tungstic a.,** a yellow crystalline compound, H_2WO_4. **ulmic a.,** a gummy acid, $C_{20}H_{14}O_6$, from elm sap, peat, and other sources. **umbellic a.,** dioxycinnamic acid, $(OH)_2C_6H_3(CH_2)COOH$. **umbelliferic a.,** an acid derivable from asafetida and other fetid gum-resins. **undecylenic a.,** an acid, $CH_2:CH(CH_2)_8.COOH$; an ointment or a powder containing it, along with its zinc salt, has been used in fungus infections, and in psoriasis and neurodermatitis. **uramilic a.,** an acid, $C_8H_9N_5O_2$, obtained by treating uramil with sulfuric acid. **uramino-acetic a.,** glycoluric a. **uraminobenzoic a.,** an acid found in the urine after the ingestion of aminobenzoic acid. This last is paired with carbamic acid, giving $NH_2.CO.NH.C_6H_4.COOH$. **uraminotauric a.,** a compound occurring in the urine after the administration of taurine. **uric a.,** a crystallizable acid, $C_5H_4N_4O_3$, from the urine of man and animals, being one of the products of nuclein metabolism. It is nearly insoluble in water, alcohol, and ether, but soluble in solutions of alkaline salts. It forms a large portion of certain calculi, and in the blood it causes morbid symptoms, among which are those of gout. **urobenzoic a.,** hippuric a. **urocanic a.,** an acid, iminazolyl-acrylic acid, $C_3H_3N_2(CH)_2COOH$, found in dogs' urine. **urochloralic a., urochloric a.,** an acid, $C_{14}H_{12}Cl_2O_{12}.[C_7H_{12}Cl_2O_6]$, found in the urine after the exhibition of chloral. **uroferric a.,** a substance found in urine. **uroleucic a., uroleucinic a.,** a crystalline acid, $C_9H_{10}O_5$, found in the urine in alkaptonuria. **uronic a.,** any one of certain aldehyde acids derived from simple sugars by oxidation of the alcohol end of the chain. See *glucuronic acid* and *galacturonic acid*. **uroproteic a.,** a constituent of dogs' urine. **uroxanic a.,** an oxidized form of uric acid. **ursolic a.,** ursone. **usnic a.,** an acid occurring in the lichen, *Usnea barbata*. **uvitic a.,** a crystalline acid, methyl-iso-phthalic acid, $CH_3.C_6H_3.(COOH)_2$, obtained by oxidizing mesitylene. **vaccenic a.,** an unsaturated fatty acid, $CH_3(CH_2)_5CH:CH-(CH_2)_9.COOH$, isomeric with oleic acid. **valerianic a.,** valeric a. **valeric a.,** an organic acid found in the roots of *Valeriana officinalis* and *Angelica archangelica*, and which may be synthesized in various ways. There are four valeric acids: (*a*) normal valeric acid, $CH_3(CH_2)_3COOH$, (*b*) isovaleric acid, $(CH_3)_2CH.CH_2.COOH$, (*c*) methyl-ethyl-acetic acid, $CH_3(C_2H_5).CH.COOH$, and (*d*) trimethylacetic acid (pivalic acid), $(CH_3)_3.C.COOH$. The salts are medicinal. **vanadic a.,** an acid, HVO_3, formed by the oxidation of vanadium. It may cause chronic poisoning in certain industries. **vanillic a.,** an acid, methylprotocatechuic acid, $CH_3.O.C_6H_3(OH)COOH$, obtained by the oxidation of vanillin. **veratric a.,** a white, crystalline acid, dimethyl-oxybenzoic acid, $(CH_3.O)_2C_6H_3.COOH$, found in sabadilla seeds. **viburnic a.,** acid from bark of *Viburnum prunifolium*, identical with valeric a. **violuric a.,** a synthetic barbituric acid compound, 5-isonitrosobarbituric acid, $OHN:C(CO.NH)_2CO$. **vulpic a., vulpinic a.,** a yellow, crystalline acid, $C_{19}H_{14}O_5$, from the lichen, *Cetraria vulpina*. **xanthic a.,** an oily liquid, $C_2H_5O.CS.SH$, with a penetrating odor. **xanthogenic a.,** xanthic a. **xanthoproteic a.,** a yellow compound obtained by treating protein with nitric acid. **xanthurenic a.,** $C_9H_5N(OH)_2COOH_2$, a metabolite of L-tryptophan, present in normal urine and found in increased amounts in vitamin B_6–deficiency. L-kynurenine is a precursor. **xanthylic a.,** one of the nucleic acids. **xanthylic-nucleic a.,** a nucleic acid which may be made to afford xanthine. **xylic a.,** a crystalline acid, dimethylbenzoic acid, $(CH_3)_2C_6H_3.COOH$. **xylidic a.,** a dibasic acid, methylisophthalic acid, $CH_3.C_6H_3.(COOH)_2$. **xylonic a.,** one of the isomeric forms of tetrahydroxyvaleric acid, $CH_2OH(CHOH)_3COOH$, formed by the gentle oxidation of xylose. **yeast nucleic a.,** ribonucleic a.

acidalbumin (as″id-al′bu-min). A protein which dissolves in acids and shows an acid reaction.

acidaminuria (as″id-am″ĭ-nu′re-ah). An excess of amino acids in the urine.

acidemia (as″ĭ-de′me-ah) [*acid* + Gr. *haima* blood + *-ia*]. A decreased pH of the blood, irrespective of changes in the blood bicarbonate.

acid-fast (as′id-fast). Not readily decolorized by acids or other means when stained; said of bacteria.

acidifiable (ah-sid′ĭ-fi″ah-b′l). Susceptible of being made acid.

acidifier (ah-sid″ĭ-fi′er). An agent that causes acidity; a substance used to increase gastric acidity.

acidify (ah-sid′ĭ-fi). 1. To render acid. 2. To become acid.

acidimeter (as″ĭ-dim′ĕ-ter) [L. *acidum* acid + Gr. *metron* measure]. An instrument used in performing acidimetry.

acidimetry (as-ĭ-dim′ĕ-tre). The determination of the amount of free acid in a solution.

acidism (as′ĭ-dizm). A condition due to introduction into the body of acids from outside.

acidismus (as″ĭ-diz′mus). Acidism.

acidity (ah-sid′ĭ-te) [L. *aciditas*]. The quality of being acid or sour; excess of an acid.

acidocyte (as′ĭ-do-sīt″). 1. An acidophilic cell. 2. An eosinophil leukocyte.

acidocytopenia (as″ĭ-do-si″to-pe′ne-ah) [*acidocyte* + Gr. *penia* poverty]. Abnormal reduction in the eosinophil leukocytes of the blood.

acidocytosis (as″ĭ-do-si-to′sis). The presence in the blood of an abnormally large proportion of eosinophil leukocytes.

acidogenic (as″ĭ-do-jen′ik). Producing acid or acidity, especially acidity of the urine.

acidol (a′sĭ-dol). Trade mark for a preparation of betaine.

acidology (as″ĭ-dol′o-je) [Gr. *akis* bandage + *-logy*]. The science of surgical appliances.

acidopenia (as″ĭ-do-pe′ne-ah). Acidocytopenia.

acidophil (ah-sid′o-fil) [L. *acidum* acid + Gr. *philein* to love]. 1. Acidophilic. 2. One of the acid-staining cells of the anterior pituitary. 3. An organism that grows well in highly acid media.

acidophile (ah-sid′o-fil). Acidophil.

acidophilic (as″ĭ-do-fil′ik). 1. Readily stained with acid dyes. 2. Growing in highly acid media: said of microorganisms.

acidophilism (as″ĭ-dof′ĭ-lizm). The condition produced by acidophil adenoma of the hypophysis, resulting in acromegaly.

acidophilous (as″ĭ-dof′ĭ-lus). Acidophilic.

acidoproteolytic (as″ĭ-do-pro″te-o-lit′ik). Producing acid and digesting protein.

acidoresistance (as″ĭ-do-re-zis′tans). Resistance to acid.

acidoresistant (as″ĭ-do-re-zis′tant). Resistant to decolorization by acids: said of certain bacteria.

acidosic (as″ĭ-do′sik). Affected with acidosis.

acidosis (as″ĭ-do′sis). A pathologic condition resulting from accumulation of acid or loss of base in the body, and characterized by increase in hydrogen ion concentration (decrease in pH). **compensated a.,** a condition in which the compensatory mechanisms have returned the pH toward normal. See *metabolic a., compensated*, and *respiratory a., compensated*. **diabetic a.,** a variety of metabolic acidosis produced by accumulation of ketones resulting from uncontrolled diabetes. **hypercapnic a.,** respiratory a. **hyperchloremic a.,** renal tubular a. **metabolic a.,** a disturbance in which the acid-base status of the body shifts toward the acid side because of changes in the fixed (non-volatile) acids and bases. **metabolic a., compensated,** a state of acidosis in which the pH of the blood has been returned toward normal by loss of carbonic acid through pulmonary mechanisms. **nonrespiratory a.,** metabolic a. **renal tubular a.,** a variety of metabolic acidosis resulting from impairment of the reabsorption of bicarbonate by the renal tubules, the urine being alkaline. **respiratory a.,** a state due to excess retention of carbon dioxide in the body. **respiratory a., compensated,** a respiratory acidosis in which the pH of the blood has been returned toward normal through retention of base or excretion of acid by renal mechanisms. **starvation a.,** a variety of metabolic acidosis produced by accumulation of ketones following a caloric deficit.

acidosteophyte (as″ĭ-dos′te-o-fīt″) [Gr. *akis* point + *osteon* bone + *phyton* plant]. A sharp-pointed osteophyte.

acidotic (as″ĭ-dot′ik). Pertaining to or characterized by acidosis.

acid-proof. Acid-fast.

acidulated (ah-sid′u-lāt″ed). Rendered acid in reaction.

acidulin (ah-sid′u-lin). Trade mark for a preparation of glutamic acid hydrochloride.

acidulous (ah-sid′u-lus). Somewhat acid.

acidum (as′ĭ-dum) [L.]. Acid.

aciduria (as″ĭ-du′re-ah). The presence of acid in the urine.

aciduric (as″ĭ-du′rik) [L. *acidum* acid + *durare* to endure]. Acid-tolerant; said of bacteria which are able to withstand a degree of acidity usually fatal to non-sporulating bacteria.

acidyl (as′ĭ-dil). Any acid radical.

acidylation (ah-sid″ĭ-la′shun). Acylation.

acies (a′se-ēz) [L.]. Edge, margin, or border. **a. thal′ami op′tici,** stria medullaris thalami.

acinar (as′ĭ-nar). Pertaining to or affecting an acinus or acini.

acinesia (as″ĭ-ne′ze-ah). Akinesia.

acinetic (as″ĭ-net′ik). Akinetic.

acini (as′ĭ-ne) [L.]. Plural of *acinus*.

acinic (ah-sin′ik). Pertaining to an acinus.

aciniform (ah-sin′ĭ-form) [L. *acinus* grape + *forma* form]. Shaped like an acinus or grape.

acinitis (as″ĭ-ni′tis). Inflammation of the acini of a gland.

acinose (as′ĭ-nos) [L. *acinosus* grape-like]. 1. Made up of acini. 2. Acinar.

acinotubular (as″ĭ-no-tu′bu-lar). Composed of tubular acini.

acinous (as′ĭ-nus). 1. Resembling a grape. 2. Acinar.

acinus (as′ĭ-nus), pl. *ac′ini* [L. "grape"]. A general term used in anatomical nomenclature to designate a small saclike dilatation, particularly one found in various glands; commonly used as being synonymous with alveolus. **ac′ini hep′atis,** lobuli hepatis. **a. liena′lis, a. lie′nis.** See *folliculi lymphatici lienales*. **a. rena′lis [malpig′hii].** See *corpuscula renis*. **a. re′nis,** a glomerulus of the kidney. **a. re′nis [malpig′hii].** See *corpuscula renis*.

Acipenser (as″ĭ-pen′ser). A genus of fishes, among which *A. hu′so*, the Russian sturgeon, and other species furnish ichthyocolla.

acipenserin (as″ĭ-pen′ser-in). A toxic substance from the gonads of the sturgeon, Acipenser.

acladiosis (ak-lad″e-o′sis). An ulcerative dermatomycosis caused by *Acladium castellani*, occurring in Ceylon, the Malay States and Macedonia, and marked by the formation of roundish or oval ulcers with sharply defined edges and a granulating fundus.

acladiotic (ak-lad″e-ot′ik). Caused by *Acladium.*

Acladium (ah-kla′de-um). A genus of fungi sometimes causing human infection.

aclasis (ak′lah-sis) [*a* neg. + Gr. *klasis* a breaking]. Pathologic continuity of structure, as in dyschondroplasia. **diaphyseal a.,** a condition marked by the imperfect formation of bone in the cartilage between the diaphysis and epiphysis. See *dyschondroplasia*. **tarsoepiphyseal a.,** dysplasia epiphysealis hemimelica.

aclastic (a-klas′tik) [*a* neg. + Gr. *klan* to break]. 1. Pertaining to or characterized by aclasis. 2. Not refracting.

acleistocardia (ah-klīs″to-kar′de-ah) [*a* neg. + Gr. *kleistos* closed + *kardia* heart]. An open condition of the foramen ovale.

aclinic (ah-klin′ik). Having no inclination.

aclusion (ah-klu′zhun) [*a* neg. + *occlusion*]. Absence of occlusion of the opposing surfaces of teeth.

acmastic (ak-mas′tik). Pertaining to acme; having a period of increase (epacmastic) followed by a period of decline (*paracmastic*).

acme (ak′me) [Gr. *akmē* point]. The crisis or critical stage of a disease.

acmesthesia (ak″mes-the′ze-ah) [Gr. *akmē* + *aisthēsis* perception + *-ia*]. A sensation of a sharp point touching the skin.

acne (ak′ne) [possibly a corruption of Greek *akmē* a point or of *achnē* chaff]. A name applied to any inflammatory disease of the sebaceous glands, the specific type usually being indicated by a modifying term. Frequently used alone to designate common acne, or *acne vulgaris*. **adenoid a.,** disseminated follicular lupus. **a. aggrega′ta seu congloba′ta,** a form of acne in men after puberty, marked by the presence of numerous comedones and comedo scars with follicular inflammatory infiltrations. **a. agmina′ta,** tuberculosis papulonecrotica. **a. al′bida,** milium. **a. artificia′lis,** that which is due to external irritation. **a. atroph′ica,** acne in which, after the disappearance of small papular lesions, there is left a stippling of tiny atrophic pits and scars. **bromine a.,** acne which is one of the most constant symptoms of bromism. **a. cachectico′rum** (Hebra), a form of acne which accompanies wasting diseases, and is situated chiefly on the trunk and legs. The lesions are flat and livid and leave scars. **a. chéloidique,** keloidal folliculitis. **chlorine a.,** chloracne. **a. cilia′ris,** acne of the edges of the eyelids. **common a.,** a. vulgaris. **a. congloba′ta,** a rare form of acne in which the comedones are accompanied by indolent abscesses, cysts and sinuses which leave marked scarring. **cystic a.,** acne with the formation of cysts enclosing hard deposits of sebum. **a. decal′vans,** Quinquaud's disease. **a. dissemina′ta,** common acne. **a. dorsa′lis,** acne of the back. **epileptic a.,** acne in an epileptic subject, due sometimes to anticonvulsant compounds, and sometimes to an unknown cause. **a. erythemato′sa,** rosacea. **a. excoriée des jeunes filles,** Brocq's name for a superficial acne of the face of girls caused by the patient's picking at and squeezing out small blackheads. **a. fronta′lis,** a. varioliformis. **a. genera′lis,** acne over the whole surface of the body. **halogen a.,** acne caused by the use of or exposure to halogens, such as chlorine, bromine, or iodine, or their salts. **halowax a.,** chloracne. **a. hordeola′ris,** acne in which the tubercles are hard, tough, and arranged in rows. **a. hypertroph′ica,** acne rosacea, with a thickening of the lips and of the sides of the nose. **a. indura′ta,** acne vulgaris with chronic livid indurations. **iodine a.,** an eruption caused by the use of iodine compounds. **a. ke′loid,** keloidal folliculitis. **lupoid a.,** a. varioliformis. **a. menta′gra,** sycosis. **a.**

necrot'ica milia'ris, a rare and chronic form of folliculitis of the scalp, occurring principally in adults, with formation of tiny superficial pustules which are destroyed by scratching; antibacterial treatment usually produces a rapid, although often only temporary, response. **a. necrot'icans et exul'cerans serpigino'sa na'si,** a grouped and spreading papular eruption in the nose, undergoing necrosis or purulent change and leaving conspicuous scarring. **a. neonato'rum,** a condition found in infants with oily skins, characterized by comedones, papules and pustules on nose, cheeks, and forehead. **pancreatic a.,** a condition in which the pancreas contains small cysts, caused by distention of the finer divisions of the pancreatic duct. **a. papulo'sa,** acne vulgaris in which the lesions are papular. **petroleum a.,** acne-like lesions sometimes seen in workers in petroleum. **a. picea'lis,** a form of acne caused by contact with tar, or exposure to its vapors. **a. puncta'ta,** acne in which the lesions are pointed papules, in the centers of which are black-tipped comedones. **a. pustulo'sa,** acne in which the lesions show central suppuration. **a. ro'dens,** a. varioliformis. **a. rosa'cea,** rosacea. **a. scorbu'tica,** a papular eruption in scurvy. **a. scrofuloso'rum** (Bazin), tuberculosis papulonecrotica. **a. seborrhe'ica,** seborrhea oleosum. **a. sim'plex,** common acne. **a. syphilit'ica,** an acuminated pustular syphiloderm. **tar a.,** a. picealis. **a. tar'si,** acne of the sebaceous glands of the eyelids. **a. variolifor'mis,** a somewhat rare condition, with persistent brown papulopustules, usually localized to the brow and scalp; probably a deep variant of acne necrotica miliaris. **a. vulga'ris,** a chronic inflammatory disease of the sebaceous glands, the lesions occurring most frequently on the face, chest, and back. The inflamed glands may form small pink papules which sometimes surround comedones so as to have black centers, or form pustules or hypertrophied nodules.

acneform (ak'ne-form). Acneiform.

acnegenic (ak"ne-jen'ĭk) [*acne* + Gr. *gennan* to produce]. Causing, or capable of producing, acne.

acneiform (ak-ne'ĭ-form"). Resembling acne.

acnemia (ak-ne'me-ah) [*a* neg. + Gr. *knēmē* leg]. 1. Atrophy of the calves of the legs. 2. Congenital absence of the legs.

acnitis (ak-ni'tis). Tuberculosis papulonecrotica.

acnitrazole (ak-ni'trah-zōl). Aminitrozole.

ACO. Abbreviation for *anodal closing odor.*

acoasma (a"ko-as'mah). Acousma.

Acocanthera (ak"o-kan-the'rah). A genus of apocynaceous plants growing in Africa, several species of which furnish an arrow poison used by the natives.

acocantherin (ak"o-kan'ther-in). Ouabain.

acoenesthesia (ah-sen"es-the'ze-ah). Acenesthesia.

acognosia (ak"og-no'se-ah) [Gr. *akos* cure + *gnōsis* knowledge]. Knowledge of or study of remedies.

acognosy (ah-kog'no-se). Acognosia.

acology (ah-kol'o-je) [Gr. *akos* cure + *-logy*]. The science of remedies; therapeutics.

acolous (ak'o-lus) [*a* neg. + Gr. *kōlon* limb]. Having no limbs.

acomia (ah-ko'me-ah) [*a* neg. + Gr. *komē* hair + *-ia*]. Baldness; absence or defect of hair.

aconative (ah-kon'ah-tiv). Without conation; not involving desire or volition.

aconine (ak'o-nin). An alkaloid, $C_{25}H_{41}NO_9$, from aconitine; much less toxic than aconitine.

aconitase (ah-kon'ĭ-tās). An enzyme which catalyzes the transformation of citric acid into cis-aconitic acid and l-isocitric acid.

aconite (ak'o-nit) [L. *aconitum;* Gr. *akoniton*]. A poisonous drug, the dried tuberous root of *Aconitum napellus.* **benzoyl a.,** benzaconine.

aconitine (ah-kon'ĭ-tin) [L. *aconitina, aconitia*]. A poisonous white crystalline alkaloid, $C_{34}H_{47}O_{11}N$, the active principle of aconite.

Aconitum (ak-o-ni'tum), gen. *aconi'ti* [L.]. A genus of poisonous ranunculaceous herbs, species of which are the source of aconite.

aconuresis (ak"on-u-re'sis) [Gr. *akōn* unwilling + *ourēsis* urination]. The involuntary passage of urine.

acoprosis (ak"o-pro'sis) [*a* neg. + Gr. *kopros* excrement]. Absence of fecal matter from the intestine.

acoprous (ah-kop'rus). Having no fecal matter in the intestine.

acor (a'kor) [L.]. 1. Acidity. 2. Acrimony or bitterness.

acorea (ah-ko-re'ah) [*a* neg. + Gr. *korē* pupil]. Absence of the pupil of the eye.

acoria (ah-ko're-ah) [*a* neg. + Gr. *koros* satiety + *-ia*]. A form of polyphagia due to loss of the sensation of satiety; a condition in which the patient never feels that he has enough, although the appetite may not be large.

acorin (ak'o-rin). A bitter glycoside, $C_{36}H_{60}O_6$, from calamus. It splits into oil of calamus and sugar.

acormia (a-kor'me-ah) [*a* neg. + Gr. *kormos* trunk + *-ia*]. A developmental anomaly in which the trunk is very rudimentary.

acormus (ah-kor'mus). A monster fetus exhibiting acormia.

Acorus (ak'o-rus) [L.; Gr. *akoros*]. A genus of araceous plants.

acosmia (a-koz'me-ah) [*a* neg. + Gr. *kosmos* order + *-ia*]. 1. Ill health. 2. An irregularity in the course of a disease.

Acosta's disease (ah-kos'tas) [José *d'Acosta,* a Jesuit father who first described it after his travels in Peru in 1590]. Mountain sickness.

acou- (ah-koo') [Gr. *akouein* to hear]. A combining form denoting relationship to hearing.

acouasm (ah-koo'azm). Acousma.

acouesthesia (ah-koo"es-the'ze-ah) [*acou-* + Gr. *aisthēsis* perception + *-ia*]. Acoustic sensibility.

acoumeter (ah-koo'mĕ-ter) [*acou-* + Gr. *metron* to measure]. An instrument for use in testing the accuracy or acuteness of the hearing.

acoumetry (ah-koo'mĕ-tre). The testing of the accuracy or acuteness of the sense of hearing.

acouometer (ah"koo-om'e-ter). Acoumeter.

acouophone (ak'oo-o-fōn) [*acou-* + Gr. *phōnē* voice]. An electric appliance for aiding the deaf to hear.

acouophonia (ah-koo"o-fo'ne-ah) [*acou-* + Gr. *phōnē* voice + *-ia*]. Auscultation combined with percussion.

acousma (ah-ko͞os'mah), pl. *acous'mata* [Gr. *akousma* a thing heard]. An auditory hallucination or imaginary sound.

acousmatagnosis (ah-ko͞os"mat-ag-no'sis) [Gr. *akousma* hearing + *a* neg. + *gnōsis* recognition]. Failure to recognize sounds due to mental disorder; mind deafness.

acousmatamnesia (ah-ko͞os"mat-am-ne'ze-ah) [Gr. *akousma* hearing + *amnēsia* forgetfulness]. Failure of the memory to call up the images of sounds.

acoustic (ah-ko͞os'tik) [Gr. *akoustikos*]. Pertaining to sound or to the sense of hearing.

acousticon (ah-koo'ste-kon). The proprietary name of an apparatus for aiding the deaf to hear.

acousticophobia (ah-koos"te-ko-fo'be-ah) [Gr. *akoustos* heard + *phobia*]. Morbid fear of sounds.

acoustics (ah-ko͞os'tiks). The science of sounds or of hearing.

acoustigram (ah-koos'tĭ-gram). Acoustogram.

acoustogram (ah-koos'to-gram). The graphic tracing of the curves, delineated in frequencies per second and decibel levels, of sounds produced by motion of a joint. Applied to the knee joint, an acoustogram will show the sound of the moving semilunar cartilages, the moving contact between the articular surfaces of the femur and tibia, and the circulation of the synovia.

acoutometer (ah″koo-tom′e-ter). Acoumeter.

ACP. Abbreviation for *anodal closing picture.*

acquired (ah-kwīrd′) [L. *acquirere* to obtain]. Not genetic, but produced by influences originating outside the organism.

acquisitus (ah-kwis′e-tus) [L.]. Acquired.

acra (ak′rah). The distal parts of the extremities.

acragnosis (ak″rag-no′sis). Acro-agnosis.

acral (ak′ral) [Gr. *akron* extremity]. Pertaining to the extremities or apex; affecting the extremities.

acrania (ah-kra′ne-ah) [*a* neg. + Gr. *kranion* skull + *-ia*]. A developmental anomaly characterized by partial or complete absence of the cranium, or skull.

acranial (ah-kra′ne-al). Having no cranium.

acranius (ah-kra′ne-us). A fetal monster exhibiting acrania.

acrasia (ah-kra′ze-ah). Lack of self-control; intemperance.

acratia (ah-kra′she-ah) [*a* neg. + Gr. *kratos* power + *-ia*]. Loss of power or strength.

acraturesis (ah-krat″u-re′sis) [Gr. *akratēs* feeble + *ourēsis* urination]. Difficult urination due to atony of the bladder.

Acrel's ganglion (ak′relz) [Olof *Acrel*, Swedish surgeon, 1717–1807]. See under *ganglion.*

Acremoniella (ak″re-mo-ne-el′ah). A genus of fungi resembling *Acremonium.*

acremoniosis (ak″re-mo-ne-o′sis). Infection with the fungus *Acremonium*, producing a state marked by fever and the formation of gumma-like swellings.

Acremonium (ak″re-mo′ne-um). A genus of fungi capable of producing infection.

acribometer (ak″re-bom′e-ter) [Gr. *akribēs* exact + *metron* measure]. An instrument for measuring minute objects.

acrid (ak′rid) [L. *acer, acris* sharp]. Pungent; producing an irritation.

acridine (ak′rĭ-din). A hydrocarbon, $CH:(C_6H_4)_2:N$, used in the synthesis of dyes and drugs. Its derivatives are mostly yellow dyes (**acridine dyes**) and those used in medicine are acriflavine hydrochloride, acriflavine base, and proflavine. **a. orange,** tetramethyl acridine, $CH[N(CH_3)_2C_6H_3]_2N$.

acriflavine (ak″rĭ-fla′vin). A granular, odorless, deep orange powder; a mixture of 2,8-diamino-10-methylacridinium chloride and 2,8-diamino-acridine: antiseptic and germicide. **a. hydrochloride,** a brownish-red crystalline acridine dye; the hydrochloride of diaminomethyl-acridinium chloride, $CH(NH_2.C_6H_3)_2N(CH_3)Cl.HCl$: antiseptic and germicide. This substance was originally prepared by Benda in 1911 for use in trypanosomiasis, and was by him given the name of *trypaflavine.* It has also been called *flavine.* **neutral a.,** acriflavine.

acrimony (ak′rĭ-mo″ne) [L. *acrimonia*]. An acrid quality, property, or condition.

acrinyl sulfocyanate (ak-ri′nil sul″fo-si′ah-nāt). An acrid vesicating principle found in white mustard.

acrisia (ah-kri′se-ah). Uncertainty in the nature or character of a disease.

acritical (ah-krit′e-kal) [*a* neg. + Gr. *krisis* a crisis]. Having no crisis.

acritochromacy (ah-krit″o-kro′mah-se) [*a* neg. + Gr. *krinein* to judge + *chrōma* color]. Defective perception of color.

acro- (ak′ro) [Gr. *akron* extremity; *akros* extreme]. A combining form denoting relation to an extremity, top, or summit, or to an extreme.

acro-agnosis (ak″ro-ag-no′sis) [*acro-* + *a* neg. + Gr. *gnōsis* knowledge]. Lack of sensory recognition of a limb; lack of acrognosis.

acro-agonines (ak″ro-ag′o-nīnz) [*acro-* + Gr. *agōn* struggle]. Substances formed in the body when it is stimulated to extreme effort, as in shock treatment.

acro-anesthesia (ak″ro-an″es-the′ze-ah) [*acro-* + *anesthesia*]. Anesthesia of the extremities.

acro-arthritis (ak″ro-ar-thri′tis) [*acro-* + *arthritis*]. Arthritis affecting the extremities.

acro-asphyxia (ak″ro-as-fik′se-ah) [*acro-* + *asphyxia*]. Acrocyanosis.

acro-ataxia (ak″ro-ah-tak′se-ah) [*acro-* + *ataxia*]. Ataxia affecting the fingers and toes.

acroblast (ak′ro-blast) [*acro-* + Gr. *blastos* germ]. Golgi material in the spermatid from which arises the acrosome.

acrobrachycephaly (ak″ro-brak″e-sef′ah-le) [*acro-* + Gr. *brachys* short + *kephalē* head]. A condition resulting from fusion of the coronal suture, causing abnormal shortening of the anteroposterior diameter of the skull.

acrobystiolith (ak″ro-bis′te-o-lith) [Gr. *akrobystia* prepuce + *lithos* stone]. A preputial calculus.

acrobystitis (ak″ro-bis-ti′tis) [Gr. *akrobystia* prepuce + *-itis*]. Inflammation of the prepuce.

acrocephalia (ak″ro-sĕ-fa′le-ah) [Gr. *akra* point + *kephalē* head + *-ia*]. Oxycephaly.

acrocephalic (ak″ro-sĕ-fal′ik). Oxycephalic.

acrocephalosyndactylia (ak″ro-sef″ah-lo-sin″-dak-til′e-ah) [*acrocephalia* + *syndactylia*]. A congenital malformation consisting of a pointed shape of the top of the head and syndactylia of the four extremities. Called also *acrosphenosyndactylia* and *Apert's syndrome.*

acrocephalosyndactylism (ak″ro-sef″ah-lo-sin-dak′tĭ-lizm). Acrocephalosyndactylia.

acrocephalosyndactyly (ak″ro-sef″ah-lo-sin-dak′tĭ-le). Acrocephalosyndactylia.

acrocephalous (ak″ro-sef′ah-lus). Oxycephalic.

acrocephaly (ak″ro-sef′ah-le). Oxycephaly. **a.-syndactyly,** acrocephalosyndactylia.

acrochordon (ak″ro-kor′don) [*acro-* + Gr. *chordē* string]. A soft, pendulous growth on the neck or eyelids.

acrocinesis (ak″ro-si-ne′sis) [*acro-* + Gr. *kinēsis* motion]. Excessive motility; abnormal freedom of movement.

acrocinetic (ak″ro-si-net′ik). Affected with acrocinesis.

acrocontracture (ak″ro-kon-trak′tūr) [*acro-* + *contracture*]. Contracture of an extremity; contracture of muscles of the hand or foot.

acrocyanosis (ak″ro-si″ah-no′sis) [*acro-* + *cyanosis*]. A condition marked by symmetrical cyanosis of the extremities, with persistent, uneven, mottled blue or red discoloration of the skin of the digits, wrists, and ankles, with profuse sweating and coldness of the digits.

acrodermatitis (ak″ro-der″mah-ti′tis) [*acro-* + *dermatitis*]. Inflammation of the skin of the hands or feet. **a. chron′ica atroph′icans,** a diffuse, idiopathic atrophy of the skin, usually confined to the extremities, and occurring in two forms: the early, erythematous, edematous phase, and the more characteristic later, atrophic phase. **a. contin′ua,** a chronic inflammation of the skin of the extremities, in some cases becoming more generalized. **a. enteropath′ica,** a severe gastrointestinal and cutaneous disease of early childhood, frequently familial, and characterized by a pustulous dermatitis, preferentially located around the body orifices and on the head, hands and feet, with diarrhea and true steatorrhea. **Hallopeau's a.,** a. continua. **a. hiema′lis,** inflammation of the skin of the hands or feet, occurring in winter. **a. per′stans,** a. continua. **a. vesiculo′sa trop′ica,** inflammation of the skin of the fingers, which becomes glossy and covered with small vesicles.

acrodermatoses (ak″ro-der″mah-to′sēz). Plural of *acrodermatosis.*

acrodermatosis (ak″ro-der″mah-to′sis), pl. *acrodermato′ses* [*acro-* + *dermatosis*]. Any disease of the skin of the hands or feet.

acrodolichomelia (ak″ro-dol″e-ko-me′le-ah) [*acro-* + Gr. *dolichos* long + *melos* limb + *-ia*]. Abnormal or disproportionate length of hands and feet.

acrodont (ak′ro-dont) [*acro-* + Gr. *odous* tooth]. Having the teeth fused to the outer surface of the bone or the summit of the jaws: a condition seen in lizards.

acrodynia (ak″ro-din′e-ah) [*acro-* + Gr. *odynē* pain + *-ia*]. Erythredema polyneuropathy. **rat a.,** a condition in rats, dogs and pigs due to deficiency of pyridoxine, and marked by swelling and necrosis of the paws, the tips of ears and nose and of the lips.

acro-edema (ak″ro-e-de′mah) [*acro-* + *edema*]. Permanent edema of the hand or foot.

acro-esthesia (ak″ro-es-the′ze-ah) [*acro-* + Gr. *aisthēsis* sensation + *-ia*]. 1. Increased sensitiveness. 2. Pain in the extremities.

acrogenous (ak-roj′e-nus) [*acro-* + Gr. *gennan* to produce]. Increasing by growth at the apex: said of some plants.

acrogeria (ak″ro-je′re-ah) [*acro-* + Gr. *gerōn* old man + *-ia*]. A condition marked by premature aging of the skin of the hands and feet.

acrognosis (ak″rog-no′sis) [*acro-* + Gr. *gnōsis* knowledge]. Sensory recognition of the limbs and of the different portions of each limb in relation to each other; limb knowledge.

acrohyperhidrosis (ak″ro-hi″per-hĭ-dro′sis) [*acro-* + *hyperhidrosis*]. Excessive sweating of the hands and feet.

acrohypothermy (ak″ro-hi″po-ther′me) [*acro-* + Gr. *hypo* under + *thermē* heat]. Abnormal coldness of the hands and feet.

acrohysterosalpingectomy (ak″ro-his″ter-o-sal″pin-jek′to-me) [*acro-* + Gr. *hystera* uterus + *salpinx* tube + *ektomē* excision]. Excision of both fallopian tubes and part of the fundus uteri: done for pelvic inflammatory disease.

acrokeratosis (ak″ro-ker″ah-to′sis). A condition involving the skin of the extremities, with the appearance of horny growths. **a. verrucifor′mis,** a condition closely resembling epidermodysplasia verruciformis, but with the lesions appearing only on the palms and soles, and not on the face.

acrokinesia (ak″ro-ki-ne′ze-ah). Acrocinesis.

acrolein (ak-ro′le-in) [L. *acer* acrid + *oleum* oil]. A volatile acrid liquid, CH_2:CHCHO, from the decomposition of glycerin.

acromacria (ak″ro-mak′re-ah) [*acro-* + Gr. *makros* long]. Arachnodactyly.

acromania (ak″ro-ma′ne-ah) [*acro-* + Gr: *mania* madness]. Mania marked by great motor activity.

acromastitis (ak″ro-mas-ti′tis) [*acro-* + Gr. *mastos* mamma + *-itis*]. Inflammation of the nipple.

acromegalia (ak″ro-mĕ-ga′le-ah). Acromegaly.

acromegalic (ak″ro-mĕ-gal′ik). Pertaining to or characterized by acromegaly.

acromegalogigantism (ak″ro-meg″ah-lo-ji′-gan-tizm). Gigantism due to acromegaly developing in the period of life between puberty and maturity.

acromegaloidism (ak″ro-meg′ah-loid-izm). A bodily condition resembling acromegaly but not due to pituitary disorder.

acromegaly (ak″ro-meg′ah-le) [*acro-* + Gr. *megalē* great]. A condition characterized by hyperplasia of the extremities of the skeleton—the nose, jaws, fingers, and toes; the converse of acromicria.

acromelalgia (ak″ro-mĕ-lal′je-ah). Erythromelalgia.

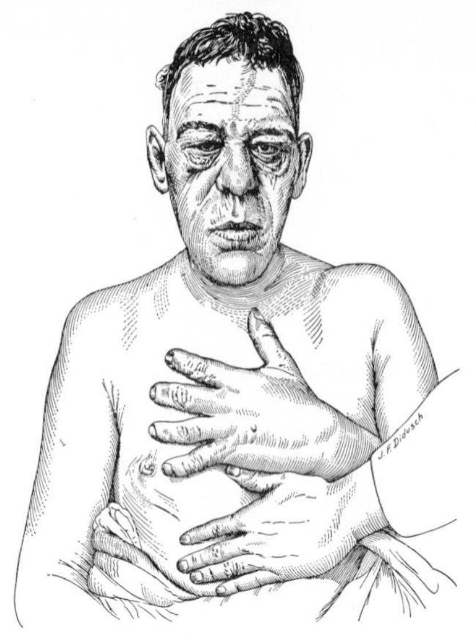

Acromegaly (Dunphy and Botsford).

acromelic (ak″ro-me′lik) [*acro-* + Gr. *melos* limb]. Pertaining to or affecting the end of a limb.

acrometagenesis (ak″ro-met″ah-jen′ĕ-sis) [*acro-* + Gr. *meta* beyond + *genesis* production]. Undue growth of the extremities.

acromial (ah-kro′me-al). Pertaining to the acromion.

acromicria (ak″ro-mik′re-ah) [*acro-* + Gr. *mikros* small + *-ia*]. A condition characterized by hypoplasia of the extremities of the skeleton—the nose, jaws, fingers, and toes; the converse of acromegaly.

acromikria (ak″ro-mik′re-ah). Acromicria.

acromioclavicular (ah-kro″me-o-klah-vik′u-lar). Pertaining to the acromion and clavicle.

acromiocoracoid (ah-kro″me-o-kor′ah-koid). Pertaining to the acromion and the coracoid process.

acromiohumeral (ah-kro″me-o-hu′mer-al). Pertaining to the acromion and humerus.

acromion (ah-kro′me-on) [*acro-* + Gr. *ōmos* shoulder]. [N A, B N A] The lateral extension of the spine of the scapula, forming the highest point of the shoulder. Called also *acromion scapulae.*

acromionectomy (ah-kro″me-on-ek′to-me). Resection of the distal end of the clavicle, used in treatment of acromioclavicular arthritis.

acromioscapular (ah-kro″me-o-skap′u-lar). Pertaining to the acromion and scapula.

acromiothoracic (ah-kro″me-o-tho-ras′ik). Pertaining to the acromion and thorax.

acromphalus (ah-krom′fah-lus) [*acro-* + Gr. *omphalos* navel]. 1. Undue prominence of the navel: sometimes a sign of the approach of umbilical hernia. 2. The center of the navel.

acromycosis (ak″ro-mi-ko′sis). Mycosis of the limbs.

acromyotonia (ak″ro-mi-o-to′ne-ah) [*acro-* + Gr. *mys* muscle + *tonos* contraction + *-ia*]. Contracture of the hand or foot resulting in spastic deformity (Sicard, 1915).

acromyotonus (ak″ro-mi-ot′o-nus). Acromyotonia.

acronarcotic (ak″ro-nar-kot′ik). Both acrid and narcotic.

acroneuropathy (ak″ro-nu-rop′ah-the). A familial form of neuropathy, affecting the distal parts of the extremities and producing anesthetic ulcers.

acroneurosis (ak″ro-nu-ro′sis) [*acro-* + *neurosis*]. Any neurosis of the extremities.

acronym (ak′ro-nym) [*acro-* + Gr. *onoma* name]. A word formed by the initial letters of the principal components of a compound term, as laser or maser.

acronyx (ak′ro-niks) [*acro-* + Gr. *onyx* nail]. An ingrowing nail.

acropachy (ak′ro-pak″e) [*acro-* + Gr. *pachys* thick]. Clubbing of the fingers and toes, with distal periosteal bone changes and swelling of the overlying soft tissues.

acropachyderma (ak″ro-pak″e-der′mah) [*acro-* + Gr. *pachys* thick + *derma* skin]. A condition marked by thickening of the skin over the face, scalp, and extremities, clubbing of the extremities, and deformities of the long bones. Called also *pachyacria* and *Brugsch's syndrome.*

acroparalysis (ak″ro-pah-ral′ĭ-sis) [*acro-* + *paralysis*]. Paralysis of the extremities.

acroparesthesia (ak″ro-par″es-the′ze-ah) [*acro-* + *paresthesia*]. A disease marked by attacks of tingling, numbness, and stiffness in the extremities, chiefly the fingers, hands, and forearms. Sometimes there is pain, pallor of the skin, or slight cyanosis. Two forms have been described—the simple form (Schultze's type), which tends to end in acrocyanosis, and the vasomotor or angiospastic form (Nothnagel's type), which may end in recovery or go on to gangrene.

acropathology (ak″ro-pah-thol′o-je) [*acro-* + *pathology*]. The pathology of diseases affecting the extremities.

acropathy (ak-rop′ah-the) [*acro-* + Gr. *pathos* disorder]. Any disease of the extremities.

acropeptide (ak″ro-pep′tid). A protein fraction obtained by heating protein to above 140°C. in nonaqueous solvents.

acropetal (ah-krop′e-tal) [*acro-* + L. *petere* to seek]. Rising toward the summit.

acrophobia (ak″ro-fo′be-ah). Morbid dread of high places.

acroposthitis (ak″ro-pos-thi′tis) [Gr. *acroposthia* prepuce + *-itis*]. Inflammation of the prepuce.

acroscleriasis (ak″ro-skle-ri′ah-sis). Acrosclerosis.

acroscleroderma (ak″ro-skle″ro-der′mah). Scleroderma of the extremities; sclerodactylia.

acrosclerosis (ak″ro-skle-ro′sis) [*acro-* + *sclerosis*]. A condition combining the features of Raynaud's disease with scleroderma of the distal parts of the extremities and of the neck and upper parts of the face.

acrose (ak′rōs). An optically inactive sugar produced by the action of weak alkali on formaldehyde.

acrosome (ak′ro-sōm) [*acro-* + Gr. *sōma* body]. A cap-like structure investing the anterior half of the head of a spermatozoon.

acrosphacelus (ak″ro-sfas′e-lus) [*acro-* + Gr. *sphakelos* gangrene]. Gangrene of the digits.

acrosphenosyndactylia (ak″ro-sfe″no-sin″dak-til′e-ah). Acrocephalosyndactylia.

acrostealgia (ak″ros-te-al′je-ah) [*acro-* + Gr. *osteon* bone + *algos* pain + *-ia*]. A painful apophysitis of the bones of the extremities.

acrosyndactyly (ak″ro-sin-dak′tĭ-le) [*acro-* + Gr. *syn* with + *daktylos* finger]. Fusion of the terminal portion of two or more digits, with clefts or sinuses present between their proximal phalanges.

acroteric (ak″ro-ter′ik). Pertaining to the periphery or outermost parts (Hutchinson).

Acrotheca pedrosoi (ak″ro-the′kah pĕ-dro′soi). *Hormodendrum pedrosoi.*

Acrothesium floccosum (ak″ro-the′se-um flok-ko′sum). *Epidermophyton floccosum.*

acrotic (ah-krot′ik). 1. [Gr. *akros* extreme]. Affecting the surface. 2. [*a* neg. + Gr. *krotos* beat]. Characterized by absence or weakness of the pulse.

acrotism (ak′ro-tizm) [*a* neg. + Gr. *krotos* beat + *-ism*]. Absence or imperceptibility of the pulse.

acrotrophodynia (ak″ro-trof″o-din′e-ah) [*acro-* + Gr. *trophē* nutrition + *odynē* pain + *-ia*]. A trophic disorder with neuritis and paresthesia from exposure of extremities to cold and moisture.

acrotrophoneurosis (ak″ro-trof″o-nu-ro′sis). Trophoneurotic disturbance of the extremities.

acrylaldehyde (ak″ril-al′de-hīd). Acrolein.

acrylic (ah-kril′ik). An acrylic resin.

acrylonitrile (ak″rĭ-lo-ni′tril). A compound, CH_2:CH.CN, used in the making of plastics.

ACS. Abbreviation for *anodal closing sound.*

A.C.S. Abbreviation for *American Chemical Society,* and *antireticular cytotoxic serum.*

act (akt). A doing, or a thing done; a performance involving motor activity. **compulsive a.,** an act performed by a person which seems to him to be done because of another and dominant will. **imperious a.,** compulsive a. **impulsive a.,** an act performed by a person, not so much because he wills it, but because of strong impulses which seem to arise within him.

Actaea (ak-te′ah) [L.; Gr. *aktē* elder-tree]. A genus of ranunculaceous plants. **A. odora′ta,** bitter weed, a plant that causes heavy losses of sheep and goats in the Southwest. **A. richardso′ni,** rubber weed which is poisonous to sheep. **A. spica′ta,** red cohosh.

ACTe. Abbreviation for *anodal closure tetanus.*

ACTH. Adrenocorticotropic hormone. See *corticotropin.*

acthar (ak′thar). Trade mark for preparations of corticotropin.

actidil (ak′tĭ-dil). Trade mark for preparations of triprolidine.

acti-dione (ak″tĭ-di′ōn). Trade mark for an antibiotic substance derived from *Streptomyces griseus:* active against certain yeasts and fungi.

actin (ak′tin). A protein discovered in muscle by Szent-Györgi. It occurs in filaments which, acting along with myosin particles, are responsible for the contraction and relaxation of muscle. See *actomyosin.*

actinic (ak-tin′ik) [Gr. *aktis* ray]. Pertaining to the rays of light beyond the violet end of the spectrum that produce chemical effects.

actinicity (ak″tĭ-nis′ĭ-te). Actinism.

actiniform (ak-tin′ĭ-form) [Gr. *aktis* ray]. Formed like a ray; radiate.

actinine (ak′tĭ-nin). A compound occurring in the sea anemone *Actinia equina:* it is identical with γ-butyrobetaine.

actinism (ak′tĭ-nizm) [Gr. *aktis* ray]. That property of radiant energy which produces chemical changes, as in photography or heliotherapy.

actinium (ak-tin′e-um) [Gr. *aktis* ray]. A chemical element occurring in the ore of uranium and having radioactive properties. Its atomic number is 89, its atomic weight 227, and its symbol Ac.

actino- (ak′tĭ-no) [Gr. *aktis, aktinos* a ray]. A combining form denoting relation to a ray, as ray-shaped, or pertaining to some form of radiation.

actinobacillosis (ak″tĭ-no-bas″ĭ-lo′sis). A disease of domestic animals resembling actinomycosis and caused by *Actinobacillus lignieresii,* sometimes seen in man; the bacillus forms radiating structures in the tissues.

Actinobacillus (ak″tĭ-no-bah-sil′lus). A genus of microorganisms of the family Brucellaceae, order Eubacteriales. **A. actinoi′des,** an organism isolated from chronic pneumonias in calves and rats; of uncertain relation to the disease. **A. actinomycetemcom′itans,** a microorganism found in the actinomycotic granules in bovine actinomycosis, and of doubtful relation to the disease. **A. equu′li,** the causative agent of a disease of foals; considered to be identical with *A. lignieresii.* **A. ligniere′sii,** the causative agent of actinomycosis-like disease of cattle and other domestic animals. **A. mal′lei,** *Pseudomonas mallei.* **A. pseudomal′lei,** *Pseudomonas pseudomallei.*

actinocardiogram (ak″tĭ-no-kar′de-o-gram) [*actino-* + Gr. *kardia* heart + *gramma* mark]. A cardiogram produced by utilizing the changes in density on the fluoroscopic screen.

actinochemistry (ak″tĭ-no-kem′is-tre) [*actino-* + *chemistry*]. Chemistry dealing with action of rays of light; photochemistry.

actinocongestin (ak″tĭ-no-kon-jĕs′tin). Congestin.

actinocutitis (ak″tĭ-no-ku-ti′tis) [*actino-* + *cutitis*]. Roentgen-ray dermatitis.

actinocymography (ak″tĭ-no-si-mog′rah-fe). Actinokymography.

actinodaphnine (ak″tĭ-no-daf′nin). A crystalline alkaloid, $C_{18}H_{17}O_4N$, from *Actinodaphne hookeri.*

actinodermatitis (ak″tĭ-no-der″mah-ti′tis). Roentgen-ray dermatitis.

actinodiastase (ak″tĭ-no-di′as-tās). An enzyme found in the body of coelenterate animals which performs the intracellular digestion characteristic of these animals.

actino-erythrin (ak″tĭ-no-er′ĭ-thrin). An ester of violerythrin, which gives the color to sea anemones.

actinogen (ak-tin′o-jen). A substance which produces radiation.

actinogenesis (ak″tĭ-no-jen′e-sis) [*actino-* + Gr. *genesis* production]. The production of rays; radiogenesis.

actinogenic (ak″tĭ-no-jen′ik). Producing or forming rays; radiogenic.

actinogenics (ak″tĭ-no-jen′iks). The science or study of radiation.

actinogram (ak-tin′o-gram). Roentgenogram.

actinograph (ak-tin′o-graf) [*actino-* + Gr. *graphein* to write]. 1. Roentgenogram. 2. An instrument for recording variations in the actinic effect of the sun's rays.

actinographema (ak-tin″o-grah-fe′mah). Roentgenogram.

actinography (ak″tĭ-nog′rah-fe). Roentgenography.

actinohematin (ak″tĭ-no-hem′ah-tin). A red respiratory pigment (hemochromogen) occurring in certain actinias (sea anemones).

actinokymography (ak″tĭ-no-ki-mog′rah-fe) [*actino-* + Gr. *kyma* wave + *graphein* to write]. Motion picture radiography.

actinolite (ak-tin′o-līt). Any substance that is markedly changed by light.

actinology (ak″tĭ-nol′o-je) [*actino-* + *-logy*]. 1. The science of photochemistry; the science of the chemical effects of light. 2. The study of radiant energy.

actinolyte (ak-tin′o-līt). An apparatus for concentrating the rays of electric light, or for generating the ultraviolet rays.

actinometer (ak″tĭ-nom′ĕ-ter) [*actino-* + Gr. *metron* measure]. 1. An instrument for measuring the intensity of actinic effects. 2. An apparatus for measuring the penetrating power of actinic rays.

actinometry (ak″tĭ-nom′ĕ-tre). The measurement of the photochemical power of light.

actinomycelial (ak″tĭ-no-mi-se′le-al). 1. Pertaining to the mycelium of an actinomyces. 2. Actinomycetic.

Actinomyces (ak″tĭ-no-mi′sēz) [*actino-* + Gr. *mykēs* fungus]. A genus of microorganisms of the family Actinomycetaceae, order Actinomycetales, made up of three pathogenic species. **A. baudet′ii,** an etiologic agent of actinomycosis in cats and dogs. **A. bo′vis,** a non-acid-fast anaerobic or microaerophilic microorganism; the specific etiologic agent of actinomycosis in cattle. **A. israe′lii,** a non-acid-fast anaerobic actinomyces parasitic in the mouth, proliferating in necrotic tissue, and occurring as the etiologic agent in some cases of human actinomycosis.

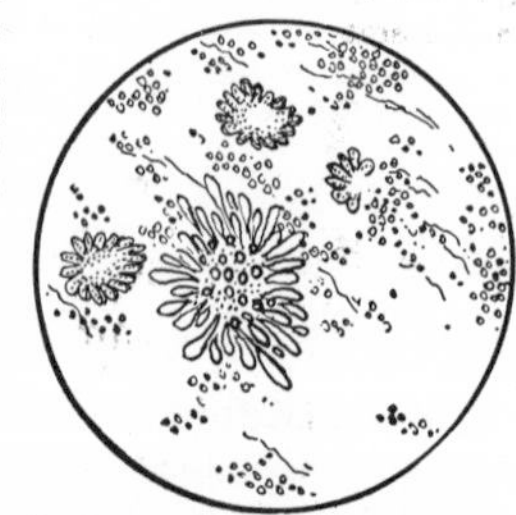
Actinomyces bovis (de Rivas)

actinomyces (ak″tĭ-no-mi′sēz), pl. *actinomyce′tes.* An organism of the genus Actinomyces.

Actinomycetaceae (ak″tĭ-no-mi″se-ta′se-e). A family of Schizomycetes, order Actinomycetales, divided into two genera, Nocardia, or aerobic forms, and Actinomyces, or anaerobic forms.

Actinomycetales (ak″tĭ-no-mi″se-ta′lēz). An order of class Schizomycetes, made up of elongated cells which have a definite tendency to branch. It includes four families, *Actinomycetaceae, Actinoplanaceae, Mycobacteriaceae,* and *Streptomycetaceae.*

actinomycetes (ak″tĭ-no-mi-se′tēz). Plural of *actinomyces.*

actinomycetic (ak″tĭ-no-mi-set′ik). Of, or caused by, actinomyces.

actinomycetin (ak″tĭ-no-mi-se′tin). An antibiotic enzyme from Actinomycetes which lyses especially dead bacteria.

actinomycin (ak″tĭ-no-mi′sin). An antibiotic substance obtained from cultures of *Streptomyces antibioticus.* Actinomycin A is soluble in ether and alcohol, is bright red in color and is bacteriostatic; actinomycin B is soluble in ether but not in alcohol, is colorless, and is bactericidal.

actinomycoma (ak″tĭ-no-mi-ko′mah) [*actinomyces* + *-oma*]. A tumor formed by the action of actinomycetes.

actinomycosis (ak″tĭ-no-mi-ko′sis) [*actino-* + Gr. *mykēs* fungus]. Any infection with Actinomyces; especially a chronic infectious disease of cattle, sometimes transmitted to man, caused by *Actinomyces bovis,* and characterized by the formation of granulomatous lesions that break down and form abscesses discharging through numerous sinuses a pus which contains yellow granules (sulfur granules). The lesions appear in the neck, thorax or abdomen. Called also *lumpy jaw, big jaw, clams, clyers, wooden tongue.*

actinomycotic (ak″tĭ-no-mi-kot′ik). Pertaining to or affected with actinomycosis.

actinomycotin (ak″tĭ-no-mi′ko-tin). A therapeutic preparation of cultures of Actinomyces: used in treating actinomycosis.

actinon (ak′tĭ-non). See *actinium emanation,* under *emanation.*

actinoneuritis (ak″tĭ-no-nu-ri′tis) [*actino-* + *neuritis*]. Neuritis caused by exposure to the rays of radioactive substances.

actinophage (ak-tin′o-fāj). A virus which causes the lysis of actinomycetes.

actinophor (ak-tin′o-fōr) [*actino-* + Gr. *phoros* bearing]. A mixture of 3 parts cerium dioxide and 1 part thorium dioxide: used in roentgen-ray diagnosis.

actinophytosis (ak″tĭ-no-fi-to′sis). Streptothricosis.

Actinoplanaceae (ak″tĭ-no-plah-na′se-e). A family of Schizomycetes, order Actinomycetales.

Actinoplanes (ak″tĭ-no-pla′nēz) [*actino-* + Gr. *planēs* one who wanders]. A genus of microorganisms of the family Actinoplanaceae, order Actinomycetales, made up of saprophytic forms found in soil and water.

Actinopoda (ak″tĭ-nop′o-dah) [*actino-* + Gr. *pous* foot]. A subclass of Sarcodina distinguished by slender, radiating, unbranched pseudopodia.

actinopraxis (ak″tĭ-no-prak′sis) [*actino-* + Gr. *praxis* doing]. The diagnostic and therapeutic use of the rays of radioactive substances.

actinoscopy (ak″tĭ-nos′ko-pe) [*actino-* + Gr. *skopein* to view]. Examination by means of the roentgen ray.

actinostereoscopy (ak″tĭ-no-ste″re-os′ko-pe). Actinoscopy.

actinotherapeutics (ak″tĭ-no-ther″ah-pu′tiks). Actinotherapy.

actinotherapy (ak″tĭ-no-ther′ah-pe) [*actino-* + Gr. *therapeia* treatment]. Treatment of disease by rays of light, especially actinic or ultraviolet light.

actinotoxemia (ak″tĭ-no-tok-se′me-ah) [*actino-* + *toxemia*]. Toxemia from the tissue destruction caused by roentgen rays or other radioactivity.

actinotoxin (ak″tĭ-no-tok′sin). A crude poison derived from alcoholic extracts of the tentacles of sea anemones.

action (ak′shun) [L. *actio*]. Any performance of function or movement either of any part or organ or of the whole body. **ball-valve a.,** the intermittent obstruction caused by a free or partially attached foreign body in a tubular structure, as by a foreign body in a bronchus, or a stone in a bile duct. **buffer a.,** the action exerted by a buffer in regulating the change in pH. **calorigenic a.** 1. Specific dynamic action. 2. The total energy released in the body by a food or food constituent. **capillary a.,** capillary attraction. **contact a.,** contact catalysis. **cumulative a.,** action of suddenly increased intensity, as may be evidenced after administration of several doses of a drug. **diastasic a., diastatic a.,** the action of diastase of converting starch into glucose. **opsonic a.,** the effect which opsonins exert on bacteria and other cells making them subject to phagocytosis. **reflex a.,** an action that results when some sensation or stimulation passes over a reflex arc to a peripheral organ which is thus stimulated to activity without the aid of volition or, in many cases, without even entering consciousness. **specific a.,** the action of a drug which is exerted on a certain definite pathogenic organism. **specific dynamic a.,** the increase in metabolism over the basal rate brought about by the ingestion and assimilation of food, varying from 4 to 6 per cent for fats and carbohydrates to 30 per cent for protein. **tampon a.,** buffer a. **thermogenic a.,** the action of a food or drug in increasing the production of heat or the temperature of the body. **trigger a.,** an action which releases energy whose character has no relation to the process which released it. **vitaminoid a.,** an action resembling the action of vitamins.

activate (ak′tĭ-vāt). To render active.

activation (ak″tĭ-va′shun). The act or process of rendering active, as in the transformation of a zymogen into an active enzyme by the action of a kinase or zymogen; or again in the purifying of sewage by means of activated sludge. **embryonic a.,** the liberation of activators from inactive combinations. **plasma a.,** the stimulation of the cellular metabolism produced by the successful application of nonspecific agents, such as the injection of foreign proteins or of colloidal metals.

activator (ak′tĭ-va″tor). 1. A substance which renders some other substance active; especially a substance which combines with an inactive enzyme to render it capable of effecting its proper action. Cf. *co-enzyme.* 2. A substance that stimulates the development of a particular structure in the embryo. Cf. *inductor* and *organizer.* **plasminogen a.,** a substance that has the ability to activate plasminogen and convert it into plasmin, its active form. **tissue a.,** fibrinokinase.

active (ak′tiv). Characterized by action; not passive; not expectant. **optically a.,** having the power of rotating the plane of polarization.

actomyosin (ak″to-mi′o-sin). The system of actin filaments and myosin particles constituting muscle fibers and responsible for the contraction and relaxation of muscle. Cf. *actin* and *myosin.*

Actonia (ak-to′ne-ah). A fungus of the family Endomycetales, which may produce creamy patches in the throat resembling diphtheria.

actor (ak′tor). A substance which takes part in both primary and secondary chemical reactions.

ACTP. Adrenocorticotropic polypeptide, a hydrolysate of ACTH.

actual (ak′chu-al) [L. *actualis*]. Real; not potential.

actuary (ak′chu-a″re). A person whose business is the calculation of premiums and risks in insurance.

acu- (ak′u) [L. *acus* needle]. Combining form denoting relationship to a needle.

Acuaria spiralis (ak″u-a′re-ah spi-ra′lis). A filaroid parasite in the proventriculus and esophagus of fowls.

acuclosure (ak″u-klo′zhur). Arrest of hemorrhage by means of a needle.

acuesthesia (ak″u-es-the′ze-ah). Acouesthesia.

acufilopressure (ak″u-fi′lo-presh″er) [*acu-* + L. *filum* thread + *pressura* pressure]. A combination of acupressure and ligation.

acuity (ah-ku′ĭ-te) [L. *acuitas* sharpness]. Acuteness or clearness, especially of the vision. **Vernier a.,** displacement threshold.

aculeate (ah-ku′le-āt) [L. *aculeatus* thorny]. Covered with sharp points; pointed.

acumeter (ah-koo′mĕ-ter). Acoumeter.

acuminate (ah-ku′mĭ-nāt) [L. *acuminatus*]. Sharp pointed.

acupression (ak″u-presh′un). Acupressure.

acupressure (ak′u-presh″er) [*acu-* + L. *pressio* or *pressura* pressure]. Compression of a bleeding vessel by inserting needles into adjacent tissue.

acupuncture (ak″u-pungk′tūr) [*acu-* + L. *punctura* a prick]. The insertion of needles into a part for the production of counterirritation.

acus (a′kus) [L.]. A needle or needle-like process.

acusection (ak″u-sek′shun). Cutting by means of the electrosurgical needle.

acusector (ak″u-sek′tor) [*acu-* + L. *sectere* to cut]. An electric needle used like a scalpel in dividing tissues.

acute (ah-kūt′) [L. *acutus* sharp]. 1. Sharp; poignant. 2. Having a short and relatively severe course.

acutenaculum (ak″u-tĕ-nak′u-lum) [L.]. Needle holder.

acutorsion (ak″u-tor′shun) [*acu-* + L. *torsio* a twisting]. The twisting of an artery with a needle for the control of hemorrhage.

acyanoblepsia (ah-si″ah-no-blep′se-ah) [*a* neg. + Gr. *kyanos* blue + *blepsia* vision]. Inability to distinguish blue tints.

acyanopsia (ah-si″ah-nop′se-ah). Acyanoblepsia.

acyanotic (ah-si″ah-not′ik). Not characterized or accompanied by cyanosis.

acyclia (ah-si′kle-ah). Arrest of circulation of body fluids.

acyclic (ah-si′klik). 1. In chemistry, having an open-chain structure; aliphatic. 2. Occurring independently of a cycle, as of the menstrual cycle.

acyesis (ah″si-e′sis) [*a* neg. + Gr. *kyēsis* pregnancy]. 1. Sterility in women. 2. Absence of pregnancy.

acyl (as′il). An organic radical derived from an organic acid by removal of the hydroxyl group.

acylanid (as″il-an′id). Trade mark for a preparation derived from digitalis glycosides, lanatosides A, B, and C.

acylation (as″e-la′shun). The introduction of an acid radical into the molecule of a chemical compound.

acystia (ah-sis′te-ah) [*a* neg. + Gr. *kystis* bladder]. Congenital absence of the bladder.

acystinervia (ah-sis″te-ner′ve-ah) [*a* neg. + Gr. *kystis* bladder + L. *nervus* nerve + *-ia*]. Defective nervous tone in the bladder.

acystineuria (ah-sis″te-nu′re-ah). Acystinervia.

Acystosporidia (ah-sis″to-spo-rid′e-ah) [*a* neg. + Gr. *kystis* bladder + *sporidia*]. A group or order of animal parasites closely related to the Haemosporidia.

acytotoxin (ah-si″to-tok′sin). A toxin in a crystalline form.

AD. Abbreviation for *diphenylchlorarsine* and *anodal duration.*

A.D. Abbreviation for L. *au′ris dex′tra,* right ear, and *axiodistal.*

ad- [L. *ad* to]. A prefix expressing *to* or *toward, addition to, nearness,* or *intensification.*

-ad. A suffix expressing direction *toward,* as cephalad, caudad.

ad. Abbreviation for L. *ad′de,* add, or *adde′tur,* let there be added: used in writing prescriptions.

A.D.A. Abbreviation for *American Dental Association, American Diabetic Association,* and *American Dietetic Association.*

adactylia (ah″dak-til′e-ah) [*a* neg. + Gr. *daktylos* finger + *-ia*]. A developmental anomaly characterized by the absence of digits on the hand or foot.

adactylism (a-dak′tĭ-lizm). Adactylia.

adactylous (a-dak′tĭ-lus). Pertaining to adactylia; lacking digits on the hand or foot.

adactyly (a-dak′tĭ-le). Adactylia.

adamantine (ad″ah-man′tin). Pertaining to the enamel of the teeth.

adamantinocarcinoma (ad″ah-man″tĭ-no-kar″sĭ-no′mah). Odontogenic fibrosarcoma.

adamantinoma (ad″ah-man″tĭ-no′mah). Ameloblastoma. **pituitary a.,** craniopharyngioma. **a. polycys′ticum,** an adamantinoma (ameloblastoma) that has undergone cystic degeneration.

adamantoblast (ad″ah-man′to-blast) [Gr. *adamas* a hard substance + *blastos* germ]. Ameloblast.

adamantoblastoma (ad″ah-man″to-blas-to′mah). Ameloblastoma.

adamantoma (ad″ah-man-to′mah). Ameloblastoma.

adamas (ad′ah-mas) [Gr. "unconquerable"]. Anything fixed or unalterable. **a. den′tis,** the enamel of the teeth.

Adami's theory (ad-am′ēz) [John George *Adami,* Canadian pathologist, 1862–1926]. See under *theory.*

Adamkiewicz's demilunes, reaction, test (ah-dam-ke′viks) [Albert *Adamkiewicz,* Polish pathologist, 1850–1921]. See under *demilune* and *test.*

Adams' operation, saw (ad′amz). 1. [William *Adams,* English surgeon, 1820–1900]. See under *operation,* 2nd def., and under *saw.* 2. [Sir William *Adams,* British surgeon, 1760–1829]. See under *operation,* 3rd def.

Adams-Stokes disease, syndrome [Robert *Adams,* Irish physician, 1791–1875; William *Stokes,* Irish physician, 1804–1878]. See under *disease.*

adamsite (ad′amz-īt). Diphenylaminearsine chloride.

Adansonia (ad″an-so′ne-ah) [after Michel *Adanson,* French naturalist, 1727–1806]. A genus of sterculiaceous trees. *A. digita′ta* is the baobob, a huge tree of Africa, found also in India; the leaves are febrifugal.

adaptation (ad″ap-ta′shun) [L. *adaptare* to fit]. 1. The normal power of the eye to adjust itself to variations in the intensity of light. 2. Immunization. 3. The fitness of an organism for its environment, or the process by which it becomes fit. 4. A condition in reflex activity marked by a decline in the frequency of impulses when sensory stimuli are repeated several times. 5. In dentistry (*a*) the proper fitting of a denture; (*b*) the degree of proximity and interlocking of filling material to a cavity wall; (*c*) the exact adjustment of bands to teeth. 6. In microbiology, the adjustment of bacterial physiology to a new environment, especially an unfavorable one, as in the development of a tolerance for or resistance to chemotherapeutic drugs (drug-resistance, drug-fastness). Adaptation may arise as a consequence of the selective effect of the new environment on spontaneously occurring mutants, of adaptive enzyme formation, or of the pre-existence of a minute portion of resistant cells. **color a.** 1. Fading of hue and dulling of brightness of visual perceptions with prolonged stimulation. 2. Adjustment of vision to degree of brightness or color tone of illumination indoors or out; includes *dark adaptation.* **dark a.,** the adaptation of the eye to vision in the dark or in reduced illumination (scotopia), with build-up of rhodopsin in the retinal rods. **light a.,** adaptation of the eye to vision in the sunlight or in bright illumination (photopia), with reduction in the concentration of the photosensitive pigments of the eye. **negative a.** See *habituation,* def. 2. **retinal a.,** the complete adjustment of the eyes to the surrounding illumination.

adapter (ah-dap′ter). A device by which different parts of an apparatus or instrument are connected.

adaptometer (ad″ap-tom′ĕ-ter) [*adaptation* + Gr. *metron* measure]. An instrument for measuring the time required for retinal adaptation: i.e., for regeneration of the visual purple. It is used to detect night blindness and vitamin A deficiency. **color a.,** an instrument using colored and neutral filters and control of illuminant to demonstrate adaptation of eye to color or light.

adatom (ad′at-om). An atom which is adsorbed on a surface.

adaxial (ad-ak′se-al). Located on the side of, or directed toward the axis.

ADC. Abbreviation for *anodal duration contraction.*

A.D.C. Abbreviation for *axiodistocervical.*

add. Abbreviation for L. *ad′de* add, or *adde′tur* let there be added; used in writing prescriptions.

adde (ad′e) [L.]. Add.

Ad def. an. Abbreviation for L. *ad defectio′nem an′imi,* to the point of fainting.

Ad deliq. Abbreviation for L. *ad deli′quium,* to fainting.

addict (ad′ikt). An individual who is given up to a habit, especially to the habitual use of alcohol or of a drug.

addiction (ah-dik′shun). The state of being given up to some habit. **drug a.,** a state characterized by an overwhelming desire or need (compulsion) to continue use of a drug and to obtain it by any means, with a tendency to increase the dosage, a psychological and usually a physical dependence on its effects, and a detrimental effect on the individual and on society. **polysurgical a.,** habitual seeking of surgical treatment for physical disorders.

addictologist (ad″ik-tol′o-jist). A physician who specializes in treatment of persons addicted to use of alcohol, drugs, or tobacco.

addictology (ad″ik-tol′o-je). The branch of medicine which deals with addiction to drugs, alcohol, and tobacco.

addiment (ad′ĭ-ment). Complement.

Addis count (ad′is) [Thomas *Addis,* San Francisco physician, 1881–1949]. See under *count.*

addisin (ad′ĭ-sin). A substance present in the gastric juice which has stimulating power on bone-marrow formation. Such an extract from the gastric juice of the hog is used in pernicious anemia.

Addison's anemia, disease, keloid, etc. (ad′ĭ-sonz) [Thomas *Addison,* English physician, 1793–1860: he was a colleague of Bright at Guy's Hospital]. See under the nouns.

Addison's planes (ad′ĭ-sonz) [Christopher *Addison,* English anatomist, 1869–1951]. See under *plane.*

addisonian (ad″dĭ-so′ne-an). Named for Thomas *Addison.* See *Addison's anemia, disease.*

addisonism (ad′ĭ-son-izm″). A group of symptoms in pulmonary tuberculosis consisting of pigmentation and debility, but falling short of those of Addison's disease.

additive (ad'ĭ-tiv). Characterized by addition.

adducent (ah-du'sent). Performing adduction.

adduct (ah-dukt') [L. *adducere* to draw toward]. To draw toward the median line of the body or toward a neighboring part.

adduction (ah-duk'shun). The act of drawing toward a center or toward a median line: also the state of being adducted.

adductor (ah-duk'tor) [L.]. That which or one who adducts.

Adelmann's maneuver or **method, operation** (ad'el-manz) [Georg Franz Blasius *Adelmann*, German surgeon, 1811–1888]. See under *method* and *operation*.

adelomorphic (ah-del"o-mor'fik). Adelomorphous.

adelomorphous (ah-del"o-mor'fus) [Gr. *adēlos* not evident + *morphē* form]. Not having a clearly defined form. See under *cell*.

adelphotaxis (ah-del'fo-tak"sis). Adelphotaxy.

adelphotaxy (ah-del'fo-tak"se) [Gr. *adelphos* brother + *taxis* arrangement]. The assumption by certain motile cells of a definite position and arrangement in relation to each other.

ademol (ad'ĕ-mol). Trade mark for a preparation of flumethiazide.

aden-. See *adeno-*.

adenalgia (ad"ĕ-nal'je-ah) [*aden-* + Gr. *algos* pain + *-ia*]. Pain in a gland.

adenase (ad'ĕ-nās) [*aden-* + *-ase*]. A deaminizing enzyme which catalyzes the conversion of adenine into hypoxanthine and ammonia.

adenasthenia (ad"en-as-the'ne-ah) [*aden-* + *a* neg. + Gr. *sthenos* strength + *-ia*]. Deficient glandular activity. **a. gas'trica,** deficient glandular secretion in the stomach.

adendric (ah-den'drik) [*a* neg. + Gr. *dendron* tree]. Lacking dendrons or branches.

adendritic (ah"den-drit'ik). Adendric.

adenectomy (ad"ĕ-nek'to-me) [*aden-* + Gr. *ektomē* excision]. 1. Surgical removal of a gland. 2. Excision of adenoid growths.

adenectopia (ad"ĕ-nek-to'pe-ah) [*aden-* + Gr. *ektopos* displaced + *-ia*]. Malposition or displacement of a gland.

adenemphraxis (ad"ĕ-nem-frak'sis) [*aden-* + Gr. *emphraxis* stoppage]. Glandular obstruction.

adenia (ah-de'ne-ah). 1. A chronic affection marked by great enlargement of the lymphatic glands. See *lymphoma*. 2. Pseudoleukemia. **angibromic a.,** any disease of the glandular adnexa of the digestive tract. **leukemic a.,** adenia with a leukemic state of the blood. **simple a.,** Hodgkin's disease.

adenic (ah-de'nik). Pertaining to or resembling a gland.

adeniform (ah-den'ĭ-form) [*aden-* + L. *forma* shape]. Resembling a gland.

adenine (ad'ĕ-nīn). A white crystalline base, 6-aminopurine, $C_5H_5N_5$, found in various animal and vegetable tissues. It is one of the decomposition products of nuclein and may be found in the urine. Adenine is nonpoisonous, and occurs in the form of pearly crystals. **a. hypoxanthine,** a leukomaine, $C_5H_5N_5 + C_4H_4N_4O$, being a compound of adenine and hypoxanthine. **a. nucleotide,** adenylic acid. **a. sulfate,** $C_5H_5N_5(SO_4)$, used in nucleotide therapy for agranulocytosis and in pneumonia.

adenitis (ad"ĕ-ni'tis). Inflammation of a gland. **acute epidemic infectious a.,** infectious mononucleosis. **acute salivary a.,** Pirera's name for an epidemic disease in Naples and vicinity, marked by inflammation of the parotid and other salivary glands, enlargement of the spleen, and pain in the axillary glands. **cervical a.,** a condition characterized by enlarged, inflamed, and tender lymph nodes of the neck: seen in certain infectious diseases of children, such as scarlet fever. **phlegmonous a.,** inflammation of a gland and the surrounding connective tissue. **a. tropica'lis,** venereal lymphogranuloma.

adenization (ad"ĕ-ni-za'shun). The assumption by other tissue of an abnormal glandlike appearance; adenoid degeneration.

adeno-, aden- (ad'ĕ-no, ad'en) [Gr. *adēn, adenos* gland]. Combining form denoting relationship to a gland or glands.

adenoacanthoma (ad"ĕ-no-ak"an-tho'mah). An adenocarcinoma in which some of the constituent elements exhibit malignant metaplasia to cells of a squamous type.

adenoameloblastoma (ad"ĕ-no-ah-mel"o-blasto'mah). Ameloblastoma characterized by the formation of ductlike structures in place of or in addition to the typical odontogenic pattern.

adenoangiosarcoma (ad"ĕ-no-an"je-o-sar-ko'mah). An angiosarcoma involving gland structures.

adenoblast (ad'ĕ-no-blast") [*adeno-* + Gr. *blastos* germ]. An embryonic cell that gives rise to glandular tissue.

adenocancroid (ad"ĕ-no-kang'kroid). Adenoacanthoma.

adenocarcinoma (ad"ĕ-no-kar"sĭ-no'mah). A carcinoma in which the cells are arranged in the form of glands; a malignant adenoma. **papillary a., polypoid a.,** a soft and friable malignant growth, composed of long, delicate fronds of epithelium with little stroma; usually found in the rectum.

adenocele (ad'ĕ-no-sēl") [*adeno-* + Gr. *kēlē* tumor]. An adenomatous cystic tumor.

adenocellulitis (ad"ĕ-no-sel"u-li'tis). Inflammation of a gland and the cellular tissue around it.

adenochirapsology (ad"ĕ-no-ki"rap-sol'o-je) [*adeno-* + Gr. *cheir* hand + *hapsis* touch + *-logy*]. See *royal touch*, under *touch*.

adenochondroma (ad"ĕ-no-kon-dro'mah). Adenoma blended with chondroma.

adenochondrosarcoma (ad"ĕ-no-kon"dro-sar-ko'mah). A tumor containing the elements of adenoma, chondroma, and sarcoma.

adenocyst (ad'ĕ-no-sist") [*adeno-* + Gr. *kystis* bladder]. Adenocystoma.

adenocystoma (ad"ĕ-no-sis-to'mah). Adenoma associated with cysts. **papillary a. lymphomato'sum,** a rare cystic tumor of the parotid and submaxillary glands.

adenocyte (ad'ĕ-no-sīt") [*adeno-* + Gr. *kytos* hollow vessel]. A mature secretory cell of a gland.

adenodynia (ad"ĕ-no-din'e-ah) [*adeno-* + Gr. *odynē* pain + *-ia*]. Pain in a gland.

adenoepithelioma (ad"ĕ-no-ep"ĭ-the"le-o'mah). A tumor composed of glandular and epithelial elements.

adenofibroma (ad"ĕ-no-fi-bro'mah). A tumor composed of connective tissue containing glandular structures. **a. edemato'des,** a nasal polyp in which formation of glandular tissue is prominent.

adenofibrosis (ad"ĕ-no-fi-bro'sis). Fibroid degeneration of a gland.

adenogenous (ad"ĕ-noj'ĕ-nus) [*adeno-* + Gr. *gennan* to produce]. Originating from glandular tissue.

adenographic (ad"ĕ-no-graf'ik). Pertaining to adenography.

adenography (ad"ĕ-nog'rah-fe) [*adeno-* + Gr. *graphein* to write]. 1. A treatise on the glands. 2. Roentgenography of a gland or glands.

adenohypersthenia (ad"ĕ-no-hi"per-sthe'ne-ah) [*adeno-* + Gr. *hyper* over + *sthenos* strength + *-ia*]. Excessive glandular activity. **a. gas'trica,** excessive glandular secretion in the stomach.

adenohypophyseal (ad"ĕ-no-hi"po-fiz'e-al). Pertaining to the adenohypophysis.

adenohypophysial (ad"ĕ-no-hi"po-fiz'e-al). Adenohypophyseal.

adenohypophysis (ad″ĕ-no-hi-pof′ĭ-sis) [*adeno-* + *hypophysis*]. The anterior or glandular portion of the hypophysis cerebri, as distinguished from the neurohypophysis.

adenoid (ad′ĕ-noid) [*aden-* + Gr. *eidos* form]. 1. Resembling a gland. 2. In the plural, hypertrophy of the adenoid tissue that normally exists in the nasopharynx of children and is known as the pharyngeal tonsil.

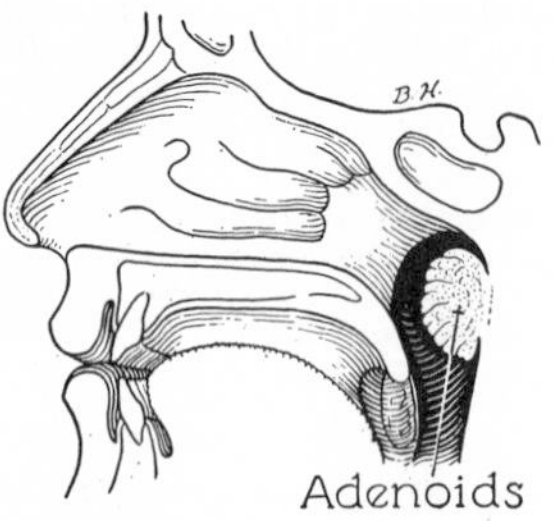

Adenoids

adenoidectomy (ad″ĕ-noid-ek′to-me) [*adenoid* + Gr. *ektomē* excision]. Excision of the adenoids.

adenoidism (ad′ĕ-noid-izm). The symptom-complex which results from the presence of greatly enlarged adenoids.

adenoiditis (ad″ĕ-noid-i′tis). Inflammation of the adenoid tissue of the nasopharynx.

adenoleiomyofibroma (ad″ĕ-no-li″o-mi″o-fi-bro′mah). A leiomyofibroma containing adenomatous elements.

adenolipoma (ad″ĕ-no-lip-o′mah). A glandular tumor made up largely of fatty tissue.

adenolipomatosis (ad″ĕ-no-lip″o-mah-to′sis). A condition characterized by the development of multiple adenolipomas.

adenologaditis (ad″ĕ-no-log″ah-di′tis) [*adeno-* + Gr. *logades* whites of the eyes + *-itis*]. 1. Ophthalmia neonatorum. 2. Inflammation of the glands of the eyes and conjunctiva.

adenology (ad″ĕ-nol′o-je) [*adeno-* + *-logy*]. The scientific study of or the body of knowledge relating to glands.

adenolymphitis (ad″ĕ-no-lim-fi′tis). Lymphadenitis.

adenolymphocele (ad″ĕ-no-lim′fo-sēl) [*adeno-* + *lymphocele*]. A cyst of a lymph node.

adenolymphoma (ad″ĕ-no-lim-fo′mah). Adenoma of a lymph organ.

adenoma (ad″ĕ-no′mah) [*adeno-* + *-oma*]. An epithelial tumor, usually benign, with a glandlike structure (the cells lining glandlike depressions or cavities in the stroma). **acidophilic a.,** a tumor of the hypophysis whose cells stain with acid dyes. **a. adamanti′num,** ameloblastoma. **a. alveola′re,** an adenoma formed on the type of an alveolar gland. **basophil a., basophilic a.,** a tumor of the hypophysis whose cells stain with basic dyes. **chromophobe a.,** a tumor of the hypophysis whose cells do not stain readily with either basic or acid dyes and whose presence is associated with hypopituitarism. **cortical a's,** minute adenomas in the cortex of the kidney, arising from the renal tubules. **a. des′truens,** a malignant adenoma in the walls of the stomach. **a. endometrioi′des ova′rii,** ovarian endometriosis. **eosinophil a.,** a tumor of eosinophilic cells of the anterior hypophysis whose presence is associated with acromegaly and gigantism. **a. fibro′sum,** fibroadenoma. **a. gelatino′sum,** colloid goiter. **Getsowa's a.,** struma postbranchialis. **a. hidradenoi′des,** syringocystadenoma. **Hürthle cell a.,** malignant adenoma of the thyroid containing Hürthle cells. **islet a., langerhansian a.,** insuloma. **malignant a.,** adenocarcinoma. **a. ova′rii testicula′re,** a. tubulare testiculare ovarii. **oxyphilic granular cell a.,** an adenoma of the parotid gland containing oxyphilic granular cells. Called also *oncocytoma, Hürthle cell tumor,* and *pyknocytoma.* **papillary cystic a.,** a form of adenoma in which the alveoli are distended by fluid or by outgrowths of tissue. **racemose a.,** an adenoma whose structure resembles that of a racemose gland. **a. seba′ceum,** a neoplastic growth of the face, containing a mass of sebaceous glands and forming a reddish-yellow collection of papules. It is frequently associated with mental deficiency. In the Balzer type the sebaceous glands are chiefly affected; in the Pringle type the blood vessels are involved. **a. sim′plex,** simple hyperplasia of a gland. **a. sudorip′arum,** adenoma of the sweat glands; spiradenoma. **tubular a.,** an adenoma formed on the type of a tubular gland. **a. tubula′re testicula′re ova′rii,** adenoma of the ovary in which the cells resemble and are arranged in a manner similar to that of the cells of the testes.

adenomalacia (ad″ĕ-no-mah-la′she-ah) [*adeno-* + Gr. *malakia* softness]. Abnormal softening of a gland.

adenomammectomy (ad″ĕ-no-mam-mek′to-me) [*adeno-* + *mamma* + Gr. *ektomē* excision]. Excision of part or all of the glandular tissue of the breast, leaving the fibrous capsule and the overlying skin and subcutaneous tissue.

adenomatoid (ad″ĕ-no′mah-toid). Resembling adenoma.

adenomatome (ad″ĕ-no′mah-tōm) [*adenoma* + Gr. *tomē* cut]. A kind of scissors used in removing adenoid and adenomatous growths.

adenomatosis (ad″ĕ-no-mah-to′sis). A condition characterized by development of numerous adenomatous growths. **epizootic a.,** a fatal contagious disease of sheep in Iceland, resembling jagziekte.

adenomatous (ad″ĕ-nom′ah-tus). Pertaining to adenoma or to glandular hyperplasia.

adenomere (ad′ĕ-no-mēr″) [*adeno-* + Gr. *meros* part]. The blind terminal portion of a developing gland, becoming the functional portion of the organ.

adenomyofibroma (ad″ĕ-no-mi″o-fi-bro′mah). A fibroma containing adenomatous and myomatous tissue.

adenomyoma (ad″ĕ-no-mi-o′mah) [*adeno-* + Gr. *mys* muscle + *-oma*]. 1. Adenomyosis. 2. A tumor made up of endometrium and muscle tissue, found in the uterus or, more frequently, in the uterine ligaments. **a. psammopapilla′re,** a multiple papillary tumor in the broad ligament described by Pick.

adenomyomatosis (ad″ĕ-no-mi″o-mah-to′sis). A condition in which adenomyoma has extended to neighboring tissues.

adenomyometritis (ad″ĕ-no-mi″o-mĕ-tri′tis). Inflammatory hyperplasia of the uterus resembling adenomyoma.

adenomyosarcoma (ad″ĕ-no-mi″o-sar-ko′mah). Adenosarcoma containing striated muscle. **embryonal a.,** embryonal carcinosarcoma.

adenomyosis (ad″ĕ-no-mi-o′sis). A condition characterized by benign invasion of the endometrium into the uterine musculature, with diffuse overgrowth of the latter. **a. exter′na,** the presence of endometrial growths outside of the uterus. **stromal a.,** stromatosis.

adenomyositis (ad″ĕ-no-mi″o-si′tis). An inflammatory hypertrophy of the uterus resembling adenomyoma.

adenomyxoma (ad″ĕ-no-mik-so′mah). A tumor that is composed of both glandular and mucous elements.

adenomyxosarcoma (ad″ĕ-no-mik″so-sar-ko′mah). A sarcoma containing both glandular and mucous elements.

adenoncus (ad″ĕ-nong′kus) [*adeno-* + Gr. *onkos* weight]. Enlargement of a gland.

adenoneural (ad″ĕ-no-nu′ral). Pertaining to a gland and a nerve.

adenoneure (ad′ĕ-no-nūr″) [*adeno-* + Gr. *neuron* nerve]. A neuron controlling glandular action.

adenopathy (ad″ĕ-nop′ah-the) [*adeno-* + Gr. *pathos* disease]. Any disease of the glands, especially of the lymphatic glands.

adenopharyngitis (ad″ĕ-no-far″in-ji′tis) [*adeno-* + Gr. *pharynx* pharynx + *-itis*]. Inflammation of the tonsils and pharynx.

adenophlegmon (ad″ĕ-no-fleg′mon) [*adeno-* + *phlegmon*]. Phlegmonous adenitis.

adenophthalmia (ad″ĕ-nof-thal′me-ah) [*adeno-* + Gr. *ophthalmos* eye + *-ia*]. Inflammation of the meibomian glands.

adenosarcoma (ad″ĕ-no-sar-ko′mah). A sarcoma containing glandular elements. **embryonal a.,** a congenital growth of the kidney or adrenal gland of very complex structure, resembling a sarcoma.

adenosarcorhabdomyoma (ad″ĕ-no-sar″ko-rab″do-mi-o′mah) [*adeno-* + Gr. *sarx* flesh + *rhabdos* rod + *mys* muscle + *-oma*]. A tumor made up of elements of adenoma, sarcoma, and rhabdomyoma.

adenosclerosis (ad″ĕ-no-skle-ro′sis) [*adeno-* + Gr. *sklērōsis* hardening]. The hardening of a gland.

adenosinase (ad-ĕ-no′sin-ās). An enzyme which splits adenosine.

adenosine (ah-den′o-sin). A nucleotide, adenine-d-ribose, $C_5H_5N_5.CH(CHOH)_2.CH.CH_2OH$, derived from nucleic acid. **a. deaminase,** an enzyme which converts adenosine into inosine. **a. diphosphate,** a product, along with organic phosphate, of the hydrolysis of adenosine triphosphate. **a. hydrolase,** an enzyme which converts adenosine into adenine and sugar. **a. triphosphate,** adenyl-pyrophosphoric acid, a nucleotide compound occurring in all cells but chiefly in striated muscle tissue: it represents the energy reserve of the muscle (myosin).

adenosinetriphosphatase (ah-den″o-sin-tri-fos′fah-tas). An enzyme which catalyzes the splitting of adenosine triphosphate, with liberation of inorganic phosphate.

adenosis (ad″ĕ-no′sis). 1. Any disease of the glands. 2. The development or formation of gland tissue.

adenositis (ad″ĕ-no-si′tis). The formation of glandular tissue regarded as an inflammatory reaction.

adenotome (ad′ĕ-no-tōm″) [*adeno-* + Gr. *tomē* cutting]. 1. An instrument for cutting glands. 2. An instrument for excision of the adenoids.

adenotomy (ad″ĕ-not′o-me) [*adeno-* + Gr. *tomē* cutting]. 1. The anatomy, incision, or dissection of glands, 2. Excision of adenoids.

adenotonsillectomy (ad″ĕ-no-ton″sil-lek′to-me). Removal of the tonsils and adenoids.

adenotyphus (ad″ĕ-no-ti′fus) [*adeno-* + *typhus*]. Typhus fever in which the lesions appear chiefly in the mesenteric glands and spleen. Called also *adenotyphus fever.*

adenous (ad′ĕ-nus). Pertaining to a gland.

adenovirus (ad″ĕ-no-vi′rus). One of a group of viruses causing upper respiratory disease and present also in latent infections in normal persons. Some 28 differentiable serotypes have been described and given numbers. Types 1, 2, and 5 have been recovered from tonsils and adenoids of persons not ill with respiratory disease, as well as from patients with febrile respiratory infections; types 3, 4, and 7 have been isolated from patients with acute respiratory disease. Adenovirus type 3 is the specific etiologic agent of pharyngoconjunctival fever, and adenovirus type 8 is thought to be the specific cause of epidemic keratoconjunctivitis.

adenyl (ad′ĕ-nil). A radical, $C_5H_4N_4$, contained in adenine.

adenyl-pyrophosphate (ad″ĕ-nil-pi″ro-fos′fāt). Adenosine triphosphate.

adephagia (ad″ĕ-fa′jĭ-ah) [Gr. *adēn* enough + *phagein* to eat + *-ia*]. 1. Gluttony. 2. Insatiable hunger.

adeps (ad′eps), gen. *ad′ipis* [L.]. Lard; the purified omental fat of the hog: used in the preparation of ointments. **a. anseri′nus,** goose grease. **a. benzoina′tus,** benzoinated lard; lard containing 1 per cent of benzoin. **a. la′nae,** wool fat; the purified fat from the wool of sheep. **a. la′nae hydro′sus,** lanolin. **a. ovil′lus,** sheep suet, or tallow. **a. por′ci,** hog lard. **a. re′nis,** the fatty capsule of the kidney. **a. suil′lus,** hog lard.

adermia (ah-der′me-ah) [*a* neg. + Gr. *derma* skin + *-ia*]. Congenital defect or absence of the skin.

adermine (ah-der′min). Pyridoxine.

adermogenesis (ah-der″mo-jen′ĕ-sis) [*a* neg. + Gr. *derma* skin + *genesis* production]. Imperfect development of the skin.

A.D.G. Abbreviation for *axiodistogingival.*

Ad grat. acid. Abbreviation for L. *ad gra′tum acidita′tem,* to an agreeable sourness.

ADH. Abbreviation for *antidiuretic hormone.*

Adhatoda (ad-hat′o-dah). A genus of plants. The leaves of *A. justicia* or *A. vasica* are used in asthma and as an expectorant, either by smoking in cigarets or internally in powder or tincture.

adhere (ad-hēr′). To cling together; to become fastened.

adhesio (ad-he′ze-o), pl. *adhesio′nes* [L. "clinging together"]. A connecting band or structure. **a. interthalam′ica** [N A], a band of gray matter connecting the two halves of the thalamus across the third ventricle. Called also *intermediate mass* and *massa intermedia* [B N A].

adhesion (ad-he′zhun) [L. *adhaesio,* from *adhaerere* to stick to]. 1. The property of remaining in close approximation, as that resulting from the physical attraction of unlike molecules, or the molecular attraction existing between the surfaces of contacting bodies. 2. The stable joining of parts to each other, which may occur abnormally. 3. A fibrous band or structure by which parts abnormally adhere. **attic a's,** adhesions about the gallbladder and pyloric region. **primary a.,** healing by the first intention. **secondary a.,** healing by the second intention.

adhesiotomy (ad-he″ze-ot′o-me). The cutting or division of adhesions.

adhesive (ad-he′siv). 1. Pertaining to, characterized by, or causing close adherence of adjoining surfaces. 2. A substance which causes close adherence of adjoining surfaces. **denture a.,** a compound of natural or artificial gums, used to stabilize denture bases.

adhesiveness (ad-he′siv-nes). The condition or quality of remaining in close approximation. **platelet a.,** a reversible viscidity of the platelet surface which may be induced by cooling or by chemical means, the latter requiring the presence of divalent metallic ions, such as calcium or magnesium, and certain soluble plasma factors. Also called *platelet stickiness.*

Adhib. Abbreviation for L. *adhiben′dus,* to be administered.

A.D.I. Abbreviation for *axiodistoincisal.*

adiabatic (ah-di″ah-bat′ik). Conducted without the evolution or absorption of heat.

adiactinic (ah-di″ak-tin′ik) [*a* neg. + Gr. *dia* through + *aktis* ray]. Not permitting the passage of actinic rays.

adiadochocinesia (ah-di″ah-do″ko-si-ne′se-ah). Adiadochokinesia.

adiadochocinesis (ah-di″ah-do″ko-si-ne′sis). Adiadochokinesia.

adiadochokinesia (ah-di″ah-do″ko-ki-ne′se-ah) [*a* neg. + Gr. *diadochos* succeeding + *kinesis* motion + *-ia*]. Inability to perform rapid alternating movements. Cf. *diadochokinesia.*

adiadochokinesis (ah-di″ah-do″ko-ki-ne′sis). Adiadochokinesia.

adiadokokinesia (ah-di″ah-do″ko-ki-ne′se-ah). Adiadochokinesia.

adiadokokinesis (ah-di″ah-do″ko-ki-ne′sis). Adiadochokinesia.

adiaemorrhysis (ah-di″ĕ-mor′ĭ-sis). Adiemorrhysis.

Adiantum (ad″e-an′tum) [*a* neg. + Gr. *dianein* to moisten]. A genus of ferns, popularly called maidenhair: pectoral demulcents.

adiaphanous (ah″di-af′ah-nus). Opaque.

adiaphoresis (ah-di″ah-fo-re′sis) [*a* neg. + Gr. *diaphorein* to perspire]. Deficiency or absence of the perspiration.

adiaphoretic (ah-di″ah-fo-ret′ik). Pertaining to, characterized by, or causing adiaphoresis.

adiaphoria (ah-di″ah-fo′re-ah) [Gr. "indifference"]. Nonresponse to stimuli as a result of previous similar stimuli.

adiapneustia (ah″di-ap-nūs′te-ah) [*a* neg. + Gr. *diapnein* to breathe through + *-ia*]. Adiaphoresis.

adiastole (ah″di-as′to-le). Absence of diastole.

adiathermance (ah-di″ah-ther′mans). Adiathermancy.

adiathermancy (ah-di″ah-ther′man-se) [*a* neg. + Gr. *dia* through + *thermansis* heating]. The condition of being impervious to heat waves.

adiathetic (ah-di″ah-thet′ik). Occurring without reference to diathesis or constitutional tendency.

adicity (ah-dis′ĭ-te). Valence.

Adie's syndrome (a′dēz) [William John *Adie*, British neurologist, 1886–1935]. See under *syndrome*.

adiemorrhysis (ah-di″ĕ-mor′ĭ-sis) [*a* neg. + Gr. *dia* through + *haima* blood + *rhysis* flow]. Stoppage of circulation of blood.

adient (ad′e-ent). Tending toward the source of stimulation; positive. Cf. *abient.*

Adinida (ah-din′ĭ-dah). An order of Flagellata marked by the flagella being free and not enclosed in furrows.

adipectomy (ad″ĭ-pek′to-me) [L. *adeps* + Gr. *ektomē* excision]. The excision of a mass of adipose tissue, as from the abdomen or buttocks.

adiphenine (ad″ĭ-fen′ēn). Chemical name: 2-diethylaminoethyl diphenylacetate. Uses: 1. parasympathetic blockade; 2. antispasmodic for gastrointestinal, genitourinary, and biliary tracts.

adipic (ah-dip′ik) [L. *adeps* fat]. Pertaining to fat.

adipo- (ad′ĭ-po) [L. *adeps, adipis* fat]. A combining form denoting relationship to fat.

adipocele (ad′ĭ-po-sēl) [*adipo-* + Gr. *kēlē* hernia]. A hernia containing fat or fatty tissue.

adipocellular (ad″ĭ-po-sel′u-lar). Composed of connective tissue and fat.

adipoceratous (ad″ĭ-po-ser′ah-tus). Pertaining to or resembling adipocere.

adipocere (ad′ĭ-po-sēr″) [*adipo-* + L. *cera* wax]. A peculiar waxy substance formed during the decomposition of animal bodies, and seen especially in human bodies buried in moist places. It consists principally of insoluble salts of fatty acids. Called also *grave-wax.*

adipochrome (ah-dip′o-krōm). A hypothetical pigment said to be manufactured directly by the fat of the body, which is increased in some diseases.

adipofibroma (ad″ĭ-po-fi-bro′mah), pl. *adipofibro′mas.* A fibroma containing fatty elements.

adipogenesis (ad″ĭ-po-jen′e-sis). The formation of fat.

adipogenic (ad″ĭ-po-jen′ik) [*adipo-* + Gr. *gennan* to produce]. Producing fat or fatness.

adipogenous (ad″ĭ-poj′ĕ-nus). Adipogenic.

adipohepatic (ad″ĭ-po-hĕ-pat′ik). Pertaining to or marked by fatty degeneration of the liver.

adipoid (ad′ĭ-poid) [*adipo-* + Gr. *eidos* form]. Lipoid.

adipokinesis (ad″ĭ-po-ki-ne′sis). The mobilization of fat in the body, with the liberation of free fatty acids into the blood plasma.

adipokinetic (ad″ĭ-po-ki-net′ik). Pertaining to, characterized by, or promoting adipokinesis.

adipokinin (ad″ĭ-po-ki′nin). A fat-burning hormone isolated from the anterior lobe of the pituitary gland.

adipolysis (ad″ĭ-pol′ĭ-sis) [*adipo-* + Gr. *lysis* dissolution]. The digestion or hydrolysis of fats.

adipolytic (ad″ĭ-po-lit′ik). Pertaining to, characterized by, or promoting adipolysis.

adipoma (ad″ĭ-po′mah). Lipoma.

adipometer (ad″ĭ-pom′e-ter). An instrument for measuring the thickness of the skin fold, as a means of determining the presence of obesity.

adiponecrosis (ad″ĭ-po-ne-kro′sis). Necrosis of fatty tissue in the body. **a. subcuta′nea neonato′rum,** subcutaneous fat induration in newborn and young infants: called also *subcutaneous fat necrosis* and *pseudosclerema.*

adipopectic (ad″ĭ-po-pek′tik). Pertaining to, characterized by, or promoting adipopexis.

adipopexia (ad″ĭ-po-pek′se-ah). Adipopexis.

adipopexic (ad″ĭ-po-pek′sik). Adipopectic.

adipopexis (ad″ĭ-po-pek′sis) [*adipo-* + Gr. *pēxis* fixation]. The fixation or storing of fats.

adiposalgia (ad″ĭ-pōs-al′je-ah) [*adipo-* + Gr. *algos* pain + *-ia*]. A neurotic state in which there are painful areas of subcutaneous fat.

adipose (ad′ĭ-pōs) [L. *adiposus* fatty]. 1. Of a fatty nature; fatty; fat. 2. The fat present in the cells of adipose tissue.

adiposis (ad″ĭ-po′sis) [L. *adeps* fat + *-osis*]. 1. Obesity or corpulence; an excessive accumulation of fat in the body. 2. Fatty infiltration. **a. cerebra′lis,** cerebral adiposity. **a. doloro′sa,** a disease accompanied by painful localized fatty swellings and by various nerve lesions. The disease is usually seen in women, and may cause death from pulmonary complications. Called also *Dercum's disease* and *paratrophy.* **a. hepat′ica,** fatty infiltration or degeneration of the liver. **a. orcha′lis, a. or′chica,** a condition of marked obesity developing in the course of tumor of the brain and associated with defective genital development. **a. tubero′sa sim′plex,** a disorder resembling adiposis dolorosa, marked by development in the subcutaneous tissue of fatty masses which are sometimes painful to pressure. Called also *Anders' disease.* **a. universa′lis,** a deposit of fat generally throughout the body, including the internal organs and ductless glands.

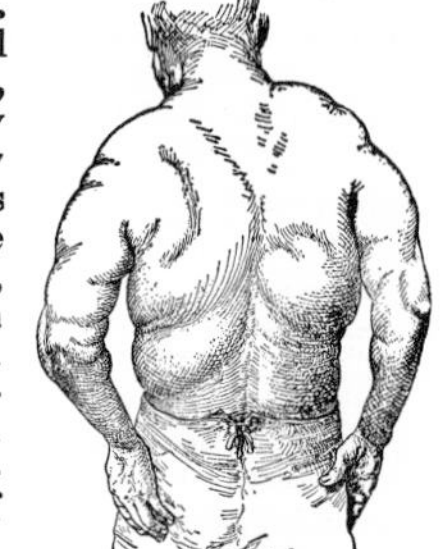

Adiposis dolorosa (Homans).

adipositas (ad″ĭ-pos′ĭ-tas) [L.]. Fatness. **a. cerebra′lis,** cerebral adiposity. **a. cor′dis,** fatty heart, def. 2. **a. ex vac′uo,** fatty atrophy.

adipositis (ad″ĭ-po-si′tis). Inflammation of the subcutaneous adipose tissue.

adiposity (ad″ĭ-pos′ĭ-te). The state of being fat; fatness; obesity. **cerebral a.,** fatness due to cerebral disease, especially disease of the pituitary body. See *Fröhlich's syndrome,* under *syndrome.* **pituitary a.,** obesity due to pituitary insufficiency.

adiposuria (ad″ĭ-po-su′re-ah) [*adipo-* + Gr. *ouron* urine + *-ia*]. The occurrence of fat in the urine; lipuria.

adipsia (ah-dip′se-ah) [*a* neg. + Gr. *dipsa* thirst + *-ia*]. Absence of thirst, or abnormal avoidance of drinking.

adipsy (ah-dip′se). Adipsia.

aditus (ad′e-tus), pl. *aditus* [L.]. A general term used in anatomical nomenclature to designate the entrance or approach to an organ or part. **a. ad an′trum,** recessus epitympanicus. **a. ad an′trum mastoi′deum** [N A], the entrance to the mastoid antrum. **a. ad an′trum tympan′icum,** recessus epitympanicus. **a. ad aquaeduc′tum cer′ebri** [B N A], the posterior portion of the third ventricle where it passes over into the aqueductus cerebri. **a. ad infundib′ulum,** recessus infundibuli. **a. ad pel′vis,** the pelvic inlet. **a. ad sac′cum peritonae′i mino′rem,** epiploic foramen. **a. glot′tidis infe′rior** [B N A], the inferior opening of the glottis. **a. glot′tidis supe′rior** [B N A], the superior opening of the glottis. **a. laryn′gis** [N A, B N A], the aperture by which the pharynx communicates with the larynx. **a. or′bitae** [B N A], the opening to the orbit in the cranium. **a. vagi′nae,** ostium vaginae.

adjection (ad-jek′shun). Addition; specifically, the principle that as many microbes can be added to the living microbes in the body as will form in combination with the latter the proper dose to immunize the patient.

adjunct (ad′junkt). An accessory or auxiliary agent or measure, used in the treatment of disease or in other procedures.

adjunctive (ad-junk′tiv). Assisting or aiding.

adjustment (ad-just′ment). 1. A rearrangement of physical parts or revision of mental attitudes made in response to changing conditions. 2. In chiropractic, manipulation of the spine, said to restore normal nerve function and cure disease. 3. The mechanism for raising and lowering the tube of a microscope, for bringing the object being examined into proper focus. 4. A modification made in a dental prosthesis after its completion and insertion in the mouth. **occlusal a.,** modification of the occluding surfaces of teeth to develop more harmonious relationships between these surfaces.

adjustor (ad-jus′tor). The ganglionic portion of a reflex arc.

adjuvant (ad′ju-vant) [L. *adjuvans* aiding]. 1. Assisting, or aiding. 2. A substance which aids another, such as an auxiliary remedy. In immunology, any substance that, when mixed with an antigen, enhances antigenicity and gives a superior immune response. **Freund a.,** a mixture consisting of a mineral oil and an emulsifying agent, used as a vehicle for antigens and injected as a depot to increase the immunizing stimulus. **Freund a., complete,** Freund adjuvant which has been enriched by the addition of heat-killed, acid-fast bacteria.

Adler's test (ad′lerz) [Oscar *Adler*, German physician, 1879–1932, and his brother Rudolph, born 1882]. Benzidine test. See under *tests*.

Adler's theory (ad′lerz) [Alfred *Adler*, Vienna psychiatrist, 1870–1937]. See under *theory*.

ad lib. Abbreviation of L. *ad lib′itum*, at pleasure.

adlumidine (ad-loo′mi-din). A crystalline alkaloid, $C_{19}H_{15}O_6H$, from *Adlu′mina cirrho′sa.*

adlumine (ad-loo′min). A crystalline alkaloid, $OHC_{37}H_{34}NO_9(OCH_3)_2$, from *Adlu′mina cirrho′sa.*

admedial (ad-me′de-al). Situated near the median plane.

admedian (ad-me′de-an). Toward the median plane or midline of the body.

adminicula (ad″mĭ-nik′u-lah) [L.]. Plural of *adminiculum.*

adminiculum (ad″mĭ-nik′u-lum), pl. *adminic′ula* [L.]. A prop or support. **a. lin′eae al′bae** [N A, B N A], the expansion of fibers extending from the superior pubic ligament to the posterior surface of the linea alba.

admov. Abbreviation for L. *ad′move, admovea′tur,* add, let there be added.

ad nauseam (ad naw′se-am) [L.]. To the extent of producing nausea.

adnerval (ad-ner′val). 1. Situated near a nerve. 2. Toward a nerve, said of an electric current which passes through muscle toward the entrance point of a nerve.

adneural (ad-nu′ral) [*ad-* + Gr. *neuron* nerve]. Adnerval.

adnexa (ad-nek′sah) [L., pl.]. Appendages or adjunct parts. **a. oc′uli,** the lacrimal apparatus and other appendages of the eye. **a. u′teri,** the uterine appendages, the ovaries, uterine tubes, and ligaments of the uterus.

adnexal (ad-nek′sal). Pertaining to adnexa, especially the adnexa uteri.

adnexectomy (ad″nek-sek′to-me) [*adnexa* + Gr. *ektomē* excision]. Excision or removal of the adnexa.

adnexitis (ad″nek-si′tis). Inflammation of the adnexa uteri.

adnexogenesis (ad-nek″so-jen′ĕ-sis) [L. *adnexa* + Gr. *genesis* production]. The development in the embryo of the adnexa or accessory structures.

adnexopexy (ad-nek′so-pek″se) [L. *adnexa* + Gr. *pēxis* fixation]. The operation of elevating and fixing the adnexa uteri to the abdominal wall.

adnexorganogenic (ad-neks″or-gah-no-jen′ik). Having its origin in the adnexa uteri.

A.D.O. Abbreviation for *axiodisto-occlusal.*

adolescence (ad″o-les′ens) [L. *adolescentia*]. The period of life beginning with the appearance of secondary sex characters and terminating with the cessation of somatic growth.

adolescent (ad″o-les′ent). 1. Pertaining to adolescence. 2. An individual during the period of adolescence.

adonidin (ah-don′i-din). A poisonous glycoside, $C_{24}H_{42}O_9$, from *Adonis vernalis*, not unlike digitalin in its effects.

adonin (ah-do′nin). A glucoside, $C_{20}H_{40}O_9$, from *Ado′nis amuren′sis*, a plant of Asia.

Adonis (ah-do′nis) [L.]. A genus of poisonous ranunculaceous plants, natives of Europe, Asia, and Africa. *A. aestiva′lis* and *A. verna′lis* are valuable cardiac stimulants.

adonit (ad′o-nit). Adonitol.

adonitol (ah-don′i-tol). A pentahydric alcohol found in *Adonis vernalis*. By oxidation it yields ribose.

adoral (ad-o′ral) [L. *ad* near + *os, oris* mouth]. 1. Toward the mouth. 2. Near the mouth.

A.D.P. Abbreviation for *adenosine diphosphate.*

Ad pond. om. Abbreviation for L. *ad pon′dus om′nium*, to the weight of the whole.

adrenal (ad-re′nal) [L. *ad* near + *ren* kidney]. 1. Situated near the kidney. 2. An adrenal gland. **Marchand's a's,** accessory adrenal bodies in the broad ligament.

adrenalectomize (ad-re″nal-ek′to-mīz). To deprive of one or both adrenal glands by surgical removal.

adrenalectomy (ad-re″nal-ek′to-me) [*adrenal* + Gr. *ektomē* excision]. Excision of the adrenal glands.

adrenalin (ad-ren′ah-lin). Trade mark for preparations of epinephrine.

adrenalinemia (ad-ren″ah-lin-e′me-ah) [*adrenalin* + Gr. *haima* blood + *-ia*]. Presence of epinephrine in the blood.

adrenalinogenesis (ad-ren″ah-lin-o-jen′ĕ-sis). The formation of epinephrine.

adrenalinuria (ad-ren″ah-lin-u′re-ah). The presence of epinephrine in the urine.

adrenalism (ad-ren′al-izm). Ill health due to adrenal dysfunction.

adrenalitis (ad-re″nal-i′tis). Inflammation of the adrenal glands.

adrenalone (ad-ren′ah-lōn). A ketone, $(HO)_2C_6$-

$H_3COCH_2NHCH_3$, obtained by oxidation of an epinephrine derivative. It has vasoconstrictor activity and raises the blood pressure.

adrenalopathy (ad-re″nal-op′ah-the) [*adrenal* + Gr. *pathos* disease]. Any disease of the adrenal glands.

adrenalotropic (ad-ren″ah-lo-trop′ik) [*adrenal* + Gr. *tropos* a turning]. Having a special affinity for the adrenal glands.

adrenarche (ad″ren-ar′ke) [*adrenal* + Gr. *archē* beginning]. Augmentation (via the pituitary gland) of adrenal cortex function, involving both androgens and glucocorticoids, a physiological change which occurs at approximately the age of eight years.

adrenergic (ad″ren-er′jik). Activated or transmitted by epinephrine: a term applied to those nerve fibers that liberate sympathin at a synapse when a nerve impulse passes, i.e., the sympathetic fibers. Cf. *cholinergic*.

adrenic (ad-ren′ik). Pertaining to the adrenal glands.

adrenin (ad-re′nin). The internal secretion (hormone) of the adrenal medulla.

adreninemia (ad-ren″in-e′me-ah). Epinephrinemia.

adrenitis (ad″re-ni′tis). Adrenalitis.

adreno- [L. *ad* near + *ren* kidney]. Combining form denoting relationship to the adrenal gland.

adrenochrome (ad-re′no-krōm″). An oxidation product of epinephrine, used as an adjunct in the insulin treatment of diabetes and for the internal treatment of skin diseases.

adrenocortical (ad-re″no-kor′te-kal). Pertaining to or arising from the cortex of the adrenal gland.

adrenocorticomimetic (ad-re″no-kor″te-ko-mi-met′ik). Producing effects similar to those of hormones of the cortex of the adrenal glands.

adrenocorticotrophic (ad-re″no-kor″te-ko-trof′ik). Adrenocorticotropic.

adrenocorticotrophin (ad-re″no-kor″te-ko-trof′in). Adrenocorticotropin.

adrenocorticotropic (ad-re″no-kor″te-ko-trop′-ik). Having a hormonic influence on the cortex of the adrenal gland.

adrenocorticotropin (ad-re″no-kor″te-ko-trop′-in). Corticotropin.

adrenodont (ad-ren′o-dont″). A person showing adrenodontia.

adrenodontia (ad-ren″o-don′she-ah) [*adreno-* + Gr. *odous* tooth]. Tooth form indicative of adrenal predominance. The canines are large and sharp, and the occlusal surfaces of the teeth have a brownish coloration.

adrenogenous (ad″ren-oj′ĕ-nus) [*adreno-* + Gr. *gennan* to produce]. Produced or arising in the adrenals.

adrenoglomerulotropin (ah-dre″no-glo-mer″u-lo-tro′pin). A hormone which stimulates the production of aldosterone by the adrenal cortex.

adrenogram (ad-ren′o-gram). A roentgenogram of the adrenals.

adrenokinetic (ad-re″no-kĭ-net′ik) [*adreno-* + Gr. *kinētikos* moving]. Stimulating the adrenal gland.

adrenolytic (ad″ren-o-lit′ik) [*adreno-* + Gr. *lysis* a loosening]. Inhibiting the action of adrenergic nerves; inhibiting the response to epinephrine.

adrenomedullotropic (ad-re″no-med″u-lo-trop′ik). Having a hormonic influence on the adrenal medulla.

adrenomegaly (ad-ren″o-meg′ah-le) [*adreno-* + Gr. *megaleia* bigness]. Enlargement of one or both of the adrenal glands.

adrenopathy (ad″ren-op′ah-the) [*adreno-* + Gr. *pathos* disease]. Adrenalopathy.

adrenopause (ad-ren′o-pawz). Cessation or suppression of function of the adrenal glands.

adrenoprival (ad-ren′o-pri″val). Pertaining to or characterized by deprivation of the adrenal glands, as a result of their removal or suppression of their function.

adrenosem (ah-dren′o-sem). Trade mark for preparations of carbazochrome.

adrenostatic (ad-re″no-stat′ik). 1. Inhibiting activity of the adrenal glands. 2. An agent which inhibits the activity of the adrenal glands.

adrenosterone (ad″re-no′ster-ōn″). A crystalline androgenic steroid, $C_{19}H_{24}O_3$, isolated from the adrenal cortex.

adrenotoxin (ad-ren″o-tok′sin). Any substance that is toxic for adrenals.

adrenotrope (ad-ren′o-trōp). A person exhibiting adrenotropism.

adrenotrophic (ad-ren″o-trof′ik) [*adreno-* + Gr. *trophē* nutrition]. Adrenotropic.

adrenotrophin (ad-ren″o-trof′in). Adrenotropin.

adrenotropic (ad-ren″o-trop′ik) [*adreno-* + Gr. *tropos* a turning]. Having specific affinity for or influence on the adrenal glands.

adrenotropin (ad-ren″o-trop′in). A substance in extracts of anterior pituitary having affinity for or a stimulating effect on the adrenal gland, more specifically, affecting the adrenal cortex.

adrenotropism (ad″ren-ot′ro-pizm) [*adreno-* + Gr. *tropos* a turning]. That type of endocrine constitution in which the influence of the adrenals predominates.

adrenoxidase (ad″ren-ok′sĭ-dās). Oxygenized adrenal secretion.

adrenoxin (ad″ren-ok′sin). A substance supposed to give blood plasma its oxidizing powers, being formed in the lungs by combination of oxygen with the internal secretion of the adrenals.

Adrian, Edward Douglas (a′dre-an). An English biologist, born 1889; co-winner, with Sir Charles Scott Sherrington, of the Nobel prize for medicine and physiology in 1932, for their work on the neuron.

adromia (ah-dro′me-ah) [*a* neg. + Gr. *dromos* a running + *-ia*]. Absence of conduction in nerve of muscle.

adroyd (ad′roid). Trade mark for a preparation of oxymetholone.

adrue (ad-ru′a). The *Cyperus articulatus*, a grass-like plant of the West Indies, with a tonic, antiemetic, and anthelmintic root.

ADS. Abbreviation for *antidiuretic substance*.

adsorbate (ad-sor′bāt). A substance taken up on a surface by adsorption.

adsorbent (ad-sor′bent). The substance which takes up another substance by adsorption.

adsorption (ad-sorp′shun) [L. *ad* to + *sorbere* to suck]. The attachment of one substance to the surface of another; the concentration of a gas or a substance in solution in a liquid on a surface in contact with the gas or liquid, resulting in a relatively high concentration of the gas or solution at the surface.

Adst. feb. Abbreviation for L. *adstan′te feb′re*, while fever is present.

adsternal (ad-ster′nal). Toward the sternum; situated near the sternum.

ADT. 1. Adenosine triphosphate. 2. An abbreviation placed on the label of a placebo prescription: A for "any," D for "what you desire," T for "thing."

ADTe. Symbol for *tetanic contraction*, produced by an application of the positive pole with the circuit closed.

adterminal (ad-ter′mĭ-nal). Passing toward the end of a muscle; said of an electric current.

adtorsion (ad-tor′shun). Conclination.

Ad 2 vic. Abbreviation of L. *ad du′as vi′ces*, at two times, for two doses.

adult (ah-dult′) [L. *adultus* grown up]. 1. Having attained full growth or maturity. 2. A living organism which has attained full growth or maturity.

adulterant (ah-dul′ter-ant″). A substance used as an addition to another substance for sophistication or adulteration.

adulteration (ah-dul″ter-a′shun). Addition of an impure, cheap, or unnecessary ingredient to cheat, cheapen, or falsify a preparation.

Adv. Abbreviation for L. *adver′sum*, against.

advance (ad-vans′). To perform the operation of advancement on.

advancement (ad-vans′ment). Surgical detachment, as of a muscle or tendon, followed by reattachment at an advanced point; chiefly an operation for strabismus. The round ligaments of the uterus have sometimes been advanced for retrodisplacement. **capsular a.,** the artificial attachment of a part of Tenon's capsule in such a way as to draw forward the insertion of an ocular muscle. **tendon a.,** advancement applied to a tendon.

adventitia (ad″ven-tish′e-ah) [L. *adventicious* from without]. Outermost. See *tunica adventitia.*

adventitial (ad″ven-tish′al). 1. Pertaining to the tunica adventitia. 2. Adventitious.

adventitious (ad″ven-tish′us) [L. *ad* to + *venire* to come]. 1. Accidental or acquired; not natural or hereditary. 2. Found out of the normal or usual place.

advitant (ad′vi-tant). Vitamin.

adynamia (ad″i-na′me-ah) [*a* neg. + Gr. *dynamis* might + *-ia*]. Lack or loss of the normal or vital powers; asthenia. **a. episod′ica hered′itaria,** a hereditary form of periodic paralysis.

adynamic (ad″i-nam′ik). Characterized by adynamia; asthenic.

A.E. Abbreviation for Ger. *antitoxineinheit* (antitoxin unit).

ae-. For words beginning thus, see also those beginning *e-*.

Aeby's muscle, plane (a′bēz) [Christopher Theodore *Aeby*, Swiss anatomist, 1835–1885]. See under *muscle* and *plane.*

aec-. For words beginning thus see words beginning with *ec-*.

Aedes (a-e′dēz) [Gr. *aēdēs* unpleasant]. A genus of culicine mosquitoes with broad appressed scales on the head and scutellum. The palpi in the female are short, sparsely tufted, and have three segments of equal length. In the male the palpi are long and tufted. **A. aegyp′ti,** a species of mosquito which breeds near houses and transmits yellow fever and dengue. It may also transmit filariasis and encephalitis. **A. albopic′tus,** a species that transmits yellow fever, equine encephalomyelitis and dengue. **A. cine′reus,** a species occurring in certain parts of the United States which transmits equine encephalomyelitis. **A. flaves′cens,** a species of the Pacific Islands which transmits filariasis. **A. leucocelae′nus,** a species of South America which transmits jungle yellow fever. **A. scutella′ris pseudoscutella′ris,** a species in the Pacific Islands which is a vector for filaria. **A. sollic′itans,** the common salt-marsh mosquito of the Atlantic and Gulf coasts. It may transmit equine encephalomyelitis. **A. spen′cerii,** a species of mosquito found on the Saskatchewan prairies. **A. taeniorhyn′chus,** a species which transmits dengue in Florida. Other species which are annoying because of their bites are *A. aldrichi, A. communis, A. excrucians, A. punctor, A. stimulans* and *A. vexans.*

aedoeocephalus (ed″e-o-sef′ah-lus) [Gr. *aidoia* genitals + *kephalē* head]. A fetal monster with no mouth, nose like a penis, and but one orbit.

Aeg. Abbreviation for L. *aeger, aegra,* the patient.

Aegyptianella pullorum (e-jip″she-ah-nel′ah pul-lo′rum). A parasite found in the blood of fowls.

aelurophobia (e-loo″ro-fo′be-ah) [Gr. *ailouros* cat + *phobia*]. Ailurophobia.

aeluropsis (e″loo-rop′sis) [Gr. *ailouros* cat + *opsis* vision]. A slanting palpebral fissure like that of a cat.

aequator (e-kwa′tor) [L. "equalizer"] [B N A]. See *equator.*

aequum (e′kwum) [L. "equal"]. Pirquet's term for the amount of food required to maintain weight under a given condition of activity.

aer (a′er) [Gr. *aēr*]. Atmos.

aer-. See *aero-*.

aerarium (a″er-a′re-um), pl. *aera′ria* [L.]. An apparatus or arrangement for providing or securing fresh air.

aerase (a′er-ās) [*aer-* + *-ase*]. The hypothetical respiratory enzyme of aerobic bacteria. Cf. *anaerase.*

aerasthenia (a″er-as-the′ne-ah) [*aer-* + *asthenia*]. Psychasthenia with loss of self-confidence and mental worry, seen in pilots of airplanes.

aerated (a′er-āt″ed) [L. *aeratus*]. 1. Charged with air. 2. Charged with carbon dioxide.

aeration (a″er-a′shun). 1. The exchange of carbon dioxide for oxygen by the blood in the lungs. 2. The charging of a liquid with air or gas.

aeremia (a″er-e′me-ah) [*aer-* + Gr. *haima* blood + *-ia*]. The presence of air in the blood vessels; aero-embolism. See also *compressed air illness.*

aerendocardia (a″er-en″do-kar′de-ah) [*aer-* + Gr. *endon* in + *kardia* heart]. The presence of gas or air within the heart.

aerenterectasia (a″er-en″ter-ek-ta′ze-ah) [*aer-* + Gr. *enteron* intestine + *ektasis* distention + *-ia*]. Distention of the intestines with air or gas.

aerial (a-e′re-al). Pertaining to the air.

aeriferous (a″er-if′er-us) [*aer-* + L. *ferre* to bear]. Conveying air.

aeriform (a-er′e-form) [*aer-* + L. *forma* form]. Like the air; gaseous.

aero-, aer- (a′er-o, a′er) [Gr. *aēr;* L. *aer* air or gas]. Combining form denoting relationship to air or gas.

aero-asthenia (a″er-o-as-the′ne-ah). Aeroneurosis.

Aerobacter (a″er-o-bak′ter) [*aero-* + Gr. *baktērion* little rod]. A genus of microorganisms of the tribe Escherichieae, family Enterobacteriaceae, order Eubacteriales, made up of short, motile or non-motile, gram-negative rods, which ferment glucose and lactose to produce acid and gas. It includes two species, *A. aero′genes* and *A. cloa′cae.*

aerobe (a′er-ob) [*aero-* + Gr. *bios* life]. A microorganism which can live and grow in the presence of free oxygen. **facultative a's,** microorganisms which are able to live under either aerobic or anaerobic conditions. **obligate a's,** microorganisms which require free access to molecular oxygen for growth.

aerobia (a″er-o′be-ah). Plural of *aerobion.*

aerobian (a″er-o′be-an). 1. Aerobic. 2. Aerobe.

aerobic (a-er-o′bik). Growing only in the presence of molecular oxygen.

aerobiology (a″er-o-bi-ol′o-je) [*aero-* + *biology*]. That branch of biology which deals with the distribution of living organisms by the air, either the exterior or outdoor air (**extramural a.**) or the indoor air (**intramural a.**).

aerobion (a″er-o′be-on), pl. *aero′bia.* Aerobe.

aerobioscope (a″er-o-bi′o-skōp) [*aero-* + Gr. *bios* life + *skopein* to view]. An apparatus for analyzing the bacterial composition of air.

aerobiosis (a″er-o-bi-o′sis). Life in the presence of oxygen.

aerobiotic (a″er-o-bi-ot′ik). Aerobic.

aerobium (a″er-o′be-um) [L.]. Aerobe.

aerocele (a′er-o-sēl″) [*aero-* + Gr. *kēlē* tumor]. A tumor formed by air filling an adventitious pouch, such as laryngocele and tracheocele.

aerochir (a′er-o-kēr″). An airplane carrying a surgeon and radiologist with their equipment.

aerocolia (a″er-o-ko′le-ah). Aerocoly.

aerocolic (a″er-o-kol′ik). Pertaining to aerocoly.

aerocolpos (a″e-ro-kol′pos) [*aero-* + Gr. *kolpos* bosom or fold]. Distention of the vagina with gas.

aerocoly (a″er-o′ko-le) [*aero-* + *colon*]. Distention of the colon with gas.

aerocystography (a″er-o-sis-tog′rah-fe). Roentgenography of the bladder after it has been injected with air.

aerocystoscope (a″er-o-sis′to-skōp). Aero-urethroscope.

aerocystoscopy (a″er-o-sis-tos′ko-pe) [*aero-* + Gr. *kystis* bladder + *skopein* to inspect]. Examination of the bladder with the aero-urethroscope.

aerodermectasia (a″er-o-der″mek-ta′ze-ah) [*aero-* + Gr. *derma* skin + *ektasis* extension + *-ia*]. Subcutaneous or surgical emphysema.

aerodontalgia (a″er-o-don-tal′je-ah). Pain experienced in the teeth at lowered atmospheric pressures, as in aircraft flight or ascent of high mountains; sometimes simulated by pain arising from maxillary aerosinusitis which occurs during recompression.

aerodontia (a″er-o-don′she-ah). Aerodontics.

aerodontics (a″er-o-don′tiks). That branch of dentistry which is concerned with effects on the teeth of high altitude flying.

aerodromophobia (a″er-o-dro″mo-fo′be-ah) [*aero* + Gr. *dromos* quick movement + *phobos* fear + *-ia*]. Morbid fear of traveling by air.

aerodynamics (a″er-o-di-nam′iks) [*aero-* + Gr. *dynamis* might]. The science of air and gases in motion.

aero-embolism (a″er-o-em′bo-lizm). A condition in aviators who rise to high altitudes, due to the formation of bubbles of nitrogen in the blood and spinal fluid, and characterized by rash, pain in the joints and in the lungs, neuritis, and paresthesia.

aero-emphysema (a″er-o-em″fi-ze′mah). Pulmonary emphysema and edema due to the collection of nitrogen bubbles in the arterioles of the lung.

aerogastria (a″er-o-gas′tre-ah). The presence of gas in the stomach. **blocked a.,** retention of air in the stomach due to spasm of the esophagus.

aerogastrocolia (a″er-o-gas″tro-ko′le-ah). The presence of air or gas in the stomach and colon.

aerogel (a′er-o-jel″). A solid formed by replacing the liquid of a gel with a gas.

aerogen (a′er-o-jen″). An aerogenic or gas-producing bacterium.

aerogenesis (a″er-o-jen′ĕ-sis) [*aero-* + Gr. *genesis* production]. Gas production.

aerogenic (a″er-o-jen′ik). Producing gas: said of bacteria which liberate free gaseous products by their metabolism.

aerogenous (a″er-oj′e-nus). Aerogenic.

aerogram (a′er-o-gram″) [*aero-* + Gr. *gramma* mark]. A roentgenogram of an organ after it has been injected with air.

aerohydropathy (a″er-o-hi-drop′ah-the). Aerohydrotherapy.

aerohydrotherapy (a″er-o-hi″dro-ther′ah-pe) [*aero-* + Gr. *hydōr* water + *therapeia* treatment]. The therapeutic use of air and water.

aero-ionotherapy (a″er-o-i″o-no-ther′ah-pe) [*aero-* + *ionotherapy*]. Treatment of respiratory conditions by the inhalation of electrical charges.

aeromammography (a″er-o-mam-mog′rah-fe). Mammography after injecting carbon dioxide into the retromammary space.

aeromedicine (a″er-o-med′e-sin). Aviation medicine.

aerometer (a″er-om′e-ter) [*aero-* + Gr. *metron* measure]. An instrument for weighing air or for estimating the density of air.

aeromicrobe (a″er-o-mi′krōb) [*aero-* + Gr. *mikros* small + *bios* life]. Aerobe.

Aeromonas (a″er-o-mo′nas). A genus of microorganisms of the family Pseudomonadaceae, suborder Pseudomonadineae, order Pseudomonadales, occurring as small rod-shaped cells and usually found in water, some being pathogenic for fish and amphibians. It includes four species, *A. hydro′phila*, *A. liquefa′ciens*, *A. puncta′ta*, and *A. salmoni′cida*.

aeroneurosis (a″er-o-nu-ro′sis) [*aero-* + *neurosis*]. A functional nervous disorder occurring in aviators, characterized by gastric distress, nervous irritability, insomnia, emotional instability and increased motor activity. It is due to prolonged anoxia and the emotional anxieties of flying.

aero-odontalgia (a″er-o-o″don-tal′je-ah). Aerodontalgia.

aero-odontodynia (a″er-o-o-don″to-din′e-ah). Aerodontalgia.

aero-otitis (a″er-o-o-ti′tis) [*aero-* + *otitis*]. Barotitis.

aeropathy (a″er-op′ah-the) [*aero-* + Gr. *pathos* disease]. Any disease due to change in atmospheric pressure, such as compressed air illness or air sickness.

aeropause (a′er-o-paws″). The region between the stratosphere and outer space, where to all practical purposes the atmosphere does not exist.

aeroperitoneum (a″er-o-per″ĭ-to-ne′um) [*aero-* + *peritoneum*]. Air or gas in the peritoneum.

aeroperitonia (a″er-o-per″ĭ-to′ne-ah). Aeroperitoneum.

aerophagia (a″er-o-fa′je-ah). Aerophagy.

aerophagy (a″er-of′ah-je) [*aero-* + Gr. *phagein* to eat]. Spasmodic swallowing of air, followed by eructations; seen in hysteria.

aerophil (a′er-o-fil″) [*aero-* + Gr. *philein* to love]. An aerophilic organism.

aerophilic (a″er-o-fil′ik). Requiring air for proper growth.

aerophilous (a″er-of′ĭ-lus). Aerophilic.

aerophobia (a″er-o-fo′be-ah) [*aero-* + *phobia*]. 1. Morbid dread of air, drafts of air, air-borne influences, or bad air (body odor). 2. Morbid dread of being up in the air; acrophobia.

aerophore (a′er-o-fōr″) [*aero-* + Gr. *phoros* bearing]. A device used in inflating with air the lungs of stillborn children, for treating asphyxia, etc.

aerophyte (a′er-o-fīt″) [*aero-* + Gr. *phyton* plant]. An air plant; any microbe or other plant organism that derives its sustenance from the air.

aeropiesotherapy (a″er-o-pi-e″so-ther′ah-pe) [*aero-* + Gr. *piesis* pressure + *therapy*]. The therapeutic use of compressed or rarefied air.

aeroplankton (a″er-o-plank′ton). The organisms (bacteria, pollen, etc.) present in the air.

aeroplast (ăr′o-plast). Trade mark for vibesate.

aeroplethysmograph (a″er-o-plĕ-thiz′mo-graf) [*aero-* + Gr. *plēthysmos* enlargement + *graphein* to record]. An apparatus for registering the amount of air respired.

aeropleura (a″er-o-plu′rah) [*aero-* + Gr. *pleura* side]. Pneumothorax.

aeroporotomy (a″er-o-po-rot′o-me) [*aero-* + Gr. *poros* passage + *tomē* cutting]. Operation of letting air into the air passages, as by intubation or tracheostomy.

aeroscope (a′er-o-skōp″) [*aero-* + Gr. *skopein* to inspect]. An instrument for the microscopic examination of the air in respect to its purity.

aerosialophagy (a″er-o-si″ah-lof′ah-je). Sialoaerophagy.

aerosinusitis (a″er-o-si″nus-i′tis). Barosinusitis.

aerosis (a″er-o′sis). The production of gas in the tissues or organs of the body.

aerosol (a′er-o-sol″). 1. A colloid system in which the continuous phase (dispersion medium) is a gas. 2. A bactericidal solution which can be finely atomized for the purpose of sterilizing the air of a room. 3. A solution of a drug which can be atomized into a fine mist for inhalation therapy.

aerosolization (a″er-o-sol″ĭ-za′shun). The process of dispersing in a fine mist.

aerosolology (a″er-o-sol-ol′o-je). The scientific study of aerosol therapy.

aerosome (a′er-o-sōm″) [*aero-* + Gr. *sōma* body]. One of the hypothetical bodies in the air of tropical climates which affect the acclimatization of Europeans.

aerosporin (a″er-os′po-rin). Trade mark for a preparation of polymyxin B sulfate.

aerostatics (a″er-o-stat′iks) [*aero-* + Gr. *statikos* causing to stand]. The science of gases in equilibrium.

aerotaxis (a″er-o-tak′sis) [*aero-* + Gr. *taxis* arrangement]. A movement of a motile organism in reaction to the presence of molecular oxygen.

aerotherapeutics (a″er-o-ther″ah-pu′tiks) [*aero-* + Gr. *therapeia* treatment]. The use of air in treating diseases.

aerotherapy (a″er-o-ther′ah-pe). Aerotherapeutics.

aerothermotherapy (a″er-o-ther″mo-ther′ah-pe) [*aero-* + Gr. *thermē* heat + *therapeia* treatment]. Treatment with currents of hot air.

aerothorax (a″er-o-tho′raks) [*aero-* + Gr. *thōrax* chest]. Pneumothorax.

aerotitis (a″er-o-ti′tis). Barotitis.

aerotonometer (a″er-o-to-nom′e-ter) [*aero-* + Gr. *tonos* tension + *metron* measure]. An instrument for measuring the tension of the gases in the blood.

aerotropism (a″er-ot′ro-pizm) [*aero-* + Gr. *tropos* a turning]. The movement of organisms toward (*positive a.*) or away from (*negative a.*) a supply of air.

aerotympanal (a″er-o-tim′pah-nal) [*aero-* + L. *tympanum* drum]. Pertaining to atmospheric pressure (air) and the middle ear.

aero-urethroscope (a″er-o-u-re′thro-skōp″) [*aero-* + *urethroscope*]. A urethroscope by which the urethra is dilated with air before inspection.

aero-urethroscopy (a″er-o-u″re-thros′ko-pe). The use of the aero-urethroscope.

aertryckosis (a″er-trĭ-ko′sis). Infection with *Salmonella aertrycke.*

aes-, aet-. For words beginning thus, see also those beginning *es-*, *et-*.

aesculapian (es″ku-la′pe-an). 1. Pertaining to Æsculapius, the god of medicine, or to the art of medicine. 2. A physician.

Æsculapius (es″ku-la′pe-us) [Gr. *Asklēpios*]. The mythical god of healing, son of Apollo and the nymph Coronis. See *Asclepiad* and *asclepion.*

Aesculus (es′ku-lus). A genus of trees. *A. hippocas′tanum*, the horse chestnut, the bark and seeds of which were formerly used in treatment of rheumatism and malaria; used also as an anticoagulant.

aet. Abbreviation for L. *aetas*, age.

Aethusa (e-thoo′sah). A genus of plants. **A. cyna′pium,** a plant which resembles parsley and has caused poisoning.

aethylenum (eth″ĭ-le′num) [L.]. Ethylene. **a. pro narco′si,** ethylene used for producing surgical anesthesia.

Aëtius (a-e′she-us) **of Amida** (6th century A.D.). A Byzantine Greek writer, whose *Tetrabiblion* gives details of the works of Rufus (of Ephesus), Leonides, Soranus, and Philumenus, and good accounts of diseases of the eye, ear, nose, and throat, and also of technical procedures (e.g., tonsillectomy, urethrotomy, and the treatment of hemorrhoids).

afebrile (ah-feb′ril). Without symptoms of fever.

afetal (ah-fe′tal). Without a fetus.

affect (af′fekt). A Freudian term for the feeling of pleasantness or unpleasantness evoked by a stimulus; also the emotional complex associated with a mental state; the feeling experienced in connection with an emotion.

affection (ah-fek′shun). 1. The mental element common to all states of emotion or feeling. 2. A morbid condition or diseased state. **celiac a.,** intestinal infantilism.

affective (ah-fek′tiv). Pertaining to a feeling or mental state.

affectivity (af″ek-tiv′ĭ-te). The affective faculty. In psychology, the feeling tone; the basal tone or tendency of the feeling life.

affectomotor (ah-fek″to-mo′tor). Combining emotional disturbance with muscular activity.

affektepilepsie (af″fekt-ep″ĭ-lep′se). Bratz's name for a psychogenic convulsion occurring in psychasthenia and obsessive states.

affenspalte (af′en-spahl″te) [Ger. "ape fissure"]. Sulcus lunatus.

afferent (af′er-ent) [L. *ad* to + *ferre* to carry]. Centripetal; conveying toward a center.

afferentia (af″er-en′she-ah) [L.]. 1. Any afferent vessels, whether blood or lymph vessels. 2. The lymph vessels in general.

affinity (ah-fin′ĭ-te) [L. *affinitas* relationship]. 1. Inherent likeness or relationship. 2. A special attraction for a specific element, organ, or structure. **chemical a.,** the force that unites atoms into molecules. **elective a.,** that force by which a substance chooses or elects to unite with one substance rather than with another. **residual a.,** the force which enables molecules to combine into larger aggregates.

affirmation (af″er-ma′shun). One of the stages in autosuggestion by which is secured a positive reactive tendency.

afflux (af′luks) [L. *affluxus, affluxio*]. The rush of blood or liquid to a part.

affluxion (ah-fluk′shun). Afflux.

affusion (ah-fu′zhun) [L. *affusio*]. The pouring of water upon a part or upon the body for reducing fever or correcting nervous symptoms.

afibrinogenemia (ah-fi″brin-o-jĕ-ne′me-ah). Deficiency of fibrinogen in the blood, which may be either congenital or acquired.

aflatoxin (af″lah-tok′sin). A toxic factor produced by *Aspergillus flavus*, a pathogenic mold on ground nut seedlings, responsible in Britain for deaths of fowl and other farm animals fed with infected ground nut meal.

after-action (af″ter-ak′shun). An effect occurring after cessation of the causative stimulus, such as the negative variation of the electric current continuing for a short time in a tetanized muscle.

after-birth (af′ter-berth″). The mass, consisting of the placenta and allied membranes, cast from the uterus after the birth of the child.

afterbrain (af′ter-brān″). Myelencephalon.

after-care (af′ter-kār). After-treatment.

after-condensation (af″ter-kon″den-sa′shun). Condensation occurring in filling material after its placement in a dental cavity.

after-current (af″ter-kur′ent). A current produced in a muscle and nerve after cessation of an electric current which has been flowing through it.

after-discharge (af″ter-dis′charj). A response to stimulation in a sensory nerve which persists after the stimulus has ceased.

after-gilding (af″ter-gild′ing). The histologic application of gold salts to nerve tissue after fixation and hardening.

after-hearing (af″ter-hēr′ing). An auditory sensation persisting after the stimulus producing it has ceased.

after-image (af′ter-im″ij). A visual impression persisting briefly after cessation of the stimuli causing the original image. A *positive* after-image is one in which the bright parts of the appearance remain bright, the dark parts dark. In a *negative* after-image the bright parts appear dark and the dark parts bright.

after-impression (af″ter-im-presh′un). After-sensation.

after-movement (af″ter-mo͞ov′ment). Spontaneous elevation of the arm by idiomuscular contraction after benumbing it by powerful pressure against a rigid object. Called also *Kohnstamm's phenomenon.*

after-pains (af″ter-pānz″). The cramplike pains felt after the birth of the child, due to the contractions of the uterus.

after-perception (af″ter-per-sep′shun). The perception of a sensation after the stimulus producing it has ceased.

after-potential (af″ter-po-ten′shal). See under *spike.*

after-sensation (af″ter-sen-sa′shun). A sensation lasting after the stimulus that produced it has been removed.

after-sound (af′ter-sownd″). An auditory impression persisting after the cessation of the vibration that produced it.

after-stain (af′ter-stān″). A stain used after another stain for the purpose of producing greater differentiation of details.

after-taste (af′ter-tāst″). A taste continuing after the substance producing it has been removed.

after-treatment (af″ter-trēt′ment). The care and treatment of a convalescent patient; especially that of a patient who has undergone surgery.

after-vision (af″ter-vizh′un). Persistence of visual sensation after cessation of the stimuli producing it.

aftosa (af-to′sah) [Mexican]. Foot-and-mouth disease.

afunction (a-funk′shun). Loss of function.

A.G. Abbreviation for *axiogingival.*

Ag. Chemical symbol for *silver* (L. *argentum*).

agalactia (ah″gah-lak′she-ah) [*a* neg. + Gr. *gala* milk + *-ia*]. Absence or failure of the secretion of milk. **contagious a.,** a contagious disease of goats and sometimes of sheep, marked by inflammation of the udder, eyes and joints and caused by a pleuropneumonia-like organism.

agalactosis (ah-gal″ak-to′sis). Agalactia.

agalactosuria (ah-gal″ak-to-su′re-ah) [*a* neg. + *galactose* + Gr. *ouron* urine + *-ia*]. Absence of galactose from the urine.

agalactous (ah″gah-lak′tus). 1. Checking the secretion of milk. 2. Not nursed; artificially fed.

agalorrhea (ah-gal″o-re′ah) [*a* neg. + Gr. *gala* milk + *rhoia* flow]. Absence or arrest of the milk flow.

agamete (ag′ah-mēt) [*a* neg. + Gr. *gamos* marriage]. A protozoon reproducing asexually by spores.

agamic (ah-gam′ik) [*a* neg. + Gr. *gamos* marriage]. 1. Asexual. 2. Reproducing without impregnation.

agammaglobulinemia (a-gam″mah-glob″u-line′me-ah) [*a* neg. + *gamma globulin* + Gr. *haima* blood + *-ia*]. Deficiency or absence of gamma globulin in the blood, which may be idiopathic or occur secondarily to a disease of the lymphatic or reticuloendothelial system.

agamobium (ag″ah-mo′be-um) [*a* neg. + Gr. *gamos* marriage + *bios* life]. The asexual stage in the alternation of generations. Cf. *gamobium.*

agamocytogeny (ah-gam″o-si-toj′ĕ-ne). Schizogony.

Agamodistomum (ag″ah-mo-dis′to-mum). A genus of trematode parasites. **A. ophthalmo′bium,** a trematode parasite that has been found in the crystalline lens of the human eye.

Agamofilaria (ah-gam″o-fi-la′re-ah). A genus of immature nematode parasites only imperfectly known.

agamogenesis (ag″ah-mo-jen′ĕ-sis) [*a* neg. + Gr. *gamos* marriage + *genesis* production]. Schizogony.

agamogenetic (ag″ah-mo-jĕ-net′ik). Reproducing asexually.

agamogony (ag″ah-mog′ŏ-ne) [*a* neg. + Gr. *gamos* marriage + *gonos* offspring]. Schizogony.

Agamomermis culicis (ag″ah-mo-mer′mis ku′lĭ-sis). A nematode parasitic in the mosquito.

Agamonema (ag″ah-mo-ne′mah). A group of immature and unidentified nematodes from fish, which have been found in urine.

Agamonematodum migrans (ag″ah-mo-ne″mah-to′dum mi′grans). A minute nematode larva found in cases of creeping eruption in the southern United States.

agamont (ag′ah-mont) [*a* neg. + Gr. *gamos* marriage + *on* being]. Schizont.

agamous (ag′ah-mus). 1. Agamic. 2. Having no recognizable sexual organs.

aganglionic (a-gang″gle-on′ik). Pertaining to or characterized by the absence of ganglion cells.

aganglionosis (ah-gang″gle-on-o′sis). Congenital absence of parasympathetic ganglion cells.

agar (ag′ar). A dried mucilaginous substance extracted from *Gelidium cartilagineum, Gracilaria confervoides,* and related red algae. Uses: 1. bulk laxative; 2. making emulsions; 3. nutrient media for bacterial cultures. **ascitic a.** See *serum a.* **ascitic fluid a.,** nutrient agar to which have been added distilled water, ascitic fluid, and nutrose. **Ashby's a.,** a synthetic culture medium containing mannite, dipotassium phosphate, magnesium sulfate, sodium chloride, calcium sulfate, calcium carbonate, water, and agar. **Avery's sodium oleate a.** See *sodium oleate a.* **beer wort a.,** beer wort made from crushed malt to which agar is added. **bile salt a.** (MacConkey), an agar culture medium containing peptone, sodium taurocholate, lactose, and sufficient neutral red to color it. **Blaxall's English proof a.** See *English proof a.* **blood a.** 1. Nutrient agar containing citrated blood: used as a bacteriologic culture medium especially for the gonococcus. 2. (Washbourn). Inclined nutrient agar tubes over which fresh sterile blood has been flowed. **Bordet-Gengou potato blood a.,** a glycerin potato agar containing blood. **Braun's fuchsin a.** See *fuchsin a.* **brilliant green a.** 1. (Conradi). A nutrient agar containing brilliant green and picric acid. 2. (Krumwiede). A beef extract agar containing Andrade indicator, lactose, glucose, and brilliant green. The reaction should be neutral to Andrade's indicator. **brilliant green-bile salt a.,** a nutrient agar containing peptone, sodium taurocholate, lactose, brilliant green solution, and picric acid. **brilliant green-eosin a.,** a nutrient agar containing lactose, saccharose, eosin, and brilliant green. **carbolized a.,** a nutrient agar containing phenol. **China green a.,** a nutrient agar containing China green. **chocolate a.** See under *culture medium.* **Conradi's brilliant green a.** See *brilliant green a.,* def. 1. **Conradi-Drigalski's litmus nutrose a.** See *litmus nutrose a.* **cystine blood a.,** an infusion agar containing cystine, glucose, and horse blood. **dextrose a.,** nutrient agar containing dextrose. **Dieudonné's alkaline blood a.,** a nutrient agar containing an alkali-blood mixture. **Drigalski-Conradi's litmus nutrose a.** See *litmus nutrose a.* **egg albumin a.,** a mixture of egg albumin broth and nutrient agar. **egg yolk a.,** a mixture of egg yolk and agar. **E.-M. B. a.** See *eosin-methylene blue a.* and *Holt-Harris and Teague's E.-M. B. a.* **English proof a.,** a nutrient agar containing Witte's peptone. **eosin-methylene blue a.,** an agar containing peptone, dipotassium phosphate, lactose, eosin, and methylene blue. **Eyre's nutrose a.** See *nutrose a.* **Fawcus' brilliant green-bile salt a.** See *brilliant green-bile salt a.* **fish gelatin a.,** fish bouillon solidified with agar and gelatin. **French mannite a.** See *French proof* *a.* **French proof a.,** a nutrient agar containing Chassaing's peptone and maltose or mannite. **fuchsin a.,** a nutrient agar containing lactose, fuchsin, and sodium sulfite. **fuchsin-sulfite a.** See *fuchsin a.* **gelatin a.,** nutrient bouillon solidified with gelatin and agar. **glucose a.** See *dextrose a.* **glucose formate a.,** nutrient agar containing glucose and sodium formate. **glycerin a.,** nutrient agar containing glycerin. **Guy's citrated blood a.** See *blood a.* **haricot a.,** haricot bouillon solidified with agar. **Heiman's serum a.** See *serum a.,* def. 1. **Hitchens's a.,** a nutrient medium containing only 0.1 per cent of agar. **Holt-Harris and Teague's E.-M. B. a.,** nutrient agar to which have been added saccharose, lactose, eosin solution, and methylene blue. **hydrocele a.** See *serum a.* **Japan a.,** agar. **Jordan's tartrate a.,** a peptone agar containing sodium and potassium tartrate and an indicator. **Kanthack and Stephens' serum a.** See *serum a.,* def. 2. **Kitasato's glucose formate a.** See *glucose formate a.* **lactose litmus a.,** nutrient agar containing lactose and sufficient litmus to color the medium a bluish-purple color when cool. The reaction should be pH 7.5 to 7.8. **lead acetate a.,** a nutrient agar containing basic lead acetate. Paratyphoid A does not change the color of this medium; the other members of the group blacken it. **Levine's eosin-methylene blue a.,** a buffered peptone agar containing lactose, eosin, and methylene blue: for use in detecting organisms of the colon-aerogenes type. **Libman's serum a.** See *serum a.,* def. 3. **litmus nutrose a.,** nutrose agar made up with 3 per cent of agar and with meat extract in place of serum water. **Löffler's malachite green a.** See *malachite green a.* **MacConkey's bile salt a.** See *bile salt a.* **malachite green a.,** nutrient agar containing dextrose and malachite green. **meat extract a.,** meat extract bouillon solidified with agar. **meat infusion a.,** meat infusion bouillon solidified with agar. **Moor's nitrogen-free a.** See *nitrogen-free a.* **nitrogen-free a.,** a culture medium containing magnesium sulfate, monopotassium acid phosphate, sugar, and agar. **Novy-MacNeal blood a.,** a nutrient agar containing defibrinated rabbit's blood: recommended especially for cultures of trypanosomes. **nutrient a.,** nutrient bouillon solidified with 1 per cent of agar. **nutrose a.,** a nutrient agar containing blood serum, nutrose, lactose, litmus solution, and crystal violet solution. **phenolphthalein a.,** agar impregnated with phenolphthalein to augment its action in relieving constipation. **plain a.,** nutrient a. **pleuritic a.** See *serum a.* **potato a.** a medium prepared from potato and solidified with agar. **potato blood a.** See *Bordet-Gengou potato blood agar.* **Russell's double sugar a.,** nutrient agar containing dextrose, lactose, and sufficient litmus to color it. **Russell's double sugar a. with lead acetate,** nutrient agar to which have been added Andrade's indicator, lactose, glucose, and basic lead acetate. **Sabouraud's French mannite a., Sabouraud's French proof a.** See *French proof a.* **saccharose-mannitol a.,** nutrient agar containing saccharose, mannitol, and Andrade's indicator: used in the study of intestinal bacteria. **serum a.** 1. (Heiman). A mixture of ascitic, pleuritic, or hydrocele fluid with nutrient agar. The latter should be made up with 3 per cent of agar so that it will solidify after diluting with the fluid. 2. (Kanthack and Stephens). Ascitic, pleuritic, or hydrocele fluid is first heated with sodium hydroxide and then solidified with agar. Either glucose or glycerin, or both, may be added. 3. (Libman). Two volumes of agar containing 1.5 per cent of agar and 2 per cent of dextrose are mixed with one volume of ascitic, pleuritic, or hydrocele fluid. 4. (Wertheimer). A mixture of equal volumes of double strength nutrient agar and human blood serum. **serum nutrose a.** (Wassermann), a mixture containing glycerin, water, hog serum, and nutrose, added to peptone agar. **serum tellurite a.,** a preparation of agar, beef infusion broth, and human or hog serum: used for the isolation of pneumococci. **Simmons' citrate a.,** a salt agar containing sodium citrate and an indicator for determining the utilization of citrate. **sodium oleate a.,** a preparation of sodium oleate and a red blood cell suspension in nutrient bouillon: used for growing influenza organisms. **starch a.,** a beef infusion agar made without either salt or peptone, but containing cornstarch. **sulfindigotate a.,** nutrient agar containing glucose and sodium sulfindigotate. **tryp a.,** a meat infusion agar prepared from chopped meat which has been digested with trypsin for five or six hours. **urine a.,** freshly passed urine solidified with agar. **Vedder's starch a.** See *starch a.* **Washbourn's blood a.,** blood a., def. 2. **Wassermann's ascitic fluid a.** See *ascitic fluid a.* **Weil's meat-potato a.,** potato juice and bouillon with agar. **Werbitski's China green a.** See *China green a.* **Wertheimer's serum a.** See *serum a.,* def. 4. **whey a.,** whey obtained by curdling fresh milk with rennet and solidified with agar. **wort a.,** beer wort solidified with agar. **Würtz lactose litmus a.** See *lactose litmus a.*

agar-agar (ag″ar-ag′ar) [Singhalese]. Agar.

Agarbacterium (ag″ar-bak-te′re-um). A genus of microorganisms of the family Achromobacteraceae, order Eubacteriales, made up of short to medium-sized, motile or non-motile rod-shaped bacteria which characteristically digest agar; found primarily on decomposing seaweed and in sea water, it occurs also in soil and fresh water. It includes 12 species.

agaric (ah-gar′ik) [Gr. *agarikon* a sort of tree fungus]. 1. Any mushroom; more especially any species of *Agaricus.* 2. The tinder or punk prepared from dried mushrooms. **fly a.,** a poisonous species used like white agaric. **larch a., purging a., white a.,** the *Polyporus officinalis,* a spongy mass growing on larch trees. **surgeons' a.,** the *Polyporus officinalis* from beech and oak trees: used as a hemostatic.

Agaricus (ah-gar′ĭ-kus). A genus of mushrooms. See *agaric.* **A. campes′tris,** the common edible mushroom. **A. musca′rius,** *Amanita muscaria.*

agastria (ah-gas′tre-ah). Absence of the stomach.

agastric (ah-gas′trik) [*a* neg. + Gr. *gastēr* stomach]. Having no alimentary canal.

agastroneuria (ah-gas″tro-nu′re-ah) [*a* neg. + Gr. *gastēr* stomach + *neuron* nerve + *-ia*]. Defective nervous tone in the stomach.

Agathinus (ag″ah-thi′nus) **of Sparta** (1st century A.D.). A Greek physician who was a pupil of Athenaeus and, like his master, a Pneumatist.

AgCl. Silver chloride.

AgCN. Silver cyanide.

age (āj). 1. The duration of individual existence measured in units of time. 2. The measure of some individual attribute in terms of the chronological age of an average normal individual showing the same degree of proficiency. 3. To undergo change as the result of the passage of time. **achievement a.,** proficiency in study expressed in terms of the chronological age of an average child showing the same degree of attainment. **anatomical a.,** age expressed in terms of the chronological age of the average individual showing the same body development. **Binet a.,** mental age as determined by the Binet tests. **bone a.,** osseous development shown roentgenographically, stated in terms of the chronological age at which the development is ordinarily attained. **chronological a.,** the age of a person expressed in terms of the period elapsed from the time of birth. **coital a.,** the age of an embryo expressed in terms of the period elapsed from the time of coitus which resulted in fertilization of the ovum. **emotional a.,** the age of an individual expressed in terms of the chronological age of an average, normal individual showing the same degree of emotional maturity. **fertilization a.,** the age of an embryo expressed in terms of the period elapsed from the calculated time of fertilization of the ovum. **functional a.,** the combined expression of the chronological, emotional, mental, and physiological ages of an individual. **menstrual a.,** the age of an embryo expressed in terms of the period elapsed from the time of the last menstruation of the mother. **mental a.,** the score achieved by a person in an intelligence test, expressed in terms of the chronological age of an average, normal individual showing the same degree of attainment. **ovulational a.,** the age of an embryo expressed in terms of the period elapsed from the presumed time of release of the ovum from the maternal ovary. **physical a., physiological a.,** the age of an individual expressed in terms of the chronological age of a normal individual showing the same degree of anatomical and physiological development.

agenesia (ah″jĕ-ne′se-ah). Agenesis. **a. cortica′lis,** congenital failure of development of the cortical cells, especially the pyramidal cells, of the brain, resulting in infantile cerebral paralysis and idiocy.

agenesis (ah-jen′ĕ-sis) [*a* neg. + Gr. *genesis* production]. 1. Absence of an organ; frequently used to designate such absence resulting from failure of appearance of the primordium of an organ in embryonic development. Cf. *aplasia*. 2. Sterility or impotence. **callosal a.,** defect of the callosal structures of the brain.

agenitalism (ah-jen′ĕ-tal-izm). A condition due to lack of the internal secretion of the testicles or ovaries.

agenized (a′jĕn-īzd″). Treated with nitrogen trichloride, for bleaching purposes: said of flour.

agenosomia (ah-jen″o-so′me-ah). A developmental anomaly characterized by absence or rudimentary development of the genitals and eventration of the lower part of the abdomen.

agenosomus (ah-jen″o-so′mus) [*a* neg. + Gr. *gennan* to beget + *sōma* body]. A fetal monster exhibiting agenosomia.

agent (a′jent) [L. *agens* acting]. Any power, principle, or substance capable of acting upon the organism, whether curative, morbific, or other. **alkylating a.,** a compound with two or more end groups (alkyl groups) that are either unsaturated or cyclic or that can be converted to such forms, and hence combine readily with other molecules. **bacteriolytic a.** See *bacteriophage*. **chelating a.,** a compound which combines with metals to form weakly dissociated complexes in which the metal is part of a ring. **chimpanzee coryza a.,** respiratory syncytial virus. **Eaton a.,** a member of the group of pleuropneumonia-like organisms, which is one of the principal etiologic agents of primary atypical pneumonia. **mammary tumor a., mouse mammary tumor a.,** one of the factors, the virus factor, which cooperate in the production of mammary tumors in mice. It comes to the mouse through its mother's milk. **Marcy a.,** a virus causing afebrile diarrhea in man.

agerasia (ah″jer-a′se-ah) [*a* neg. + Gr. *gēras* old age]. An unusually youthful appearance in a person of advanced years.

ageusia (ah-gu′se-ah) [*a* neg. + Gr. *geusis* taste]. Lack or impairment of the sense of taste.

ageusic (ah-gu′sik). Pertaining to ageusia.

ageustia (ah-gōōs′te-ah). Ageusia.

agger (aj′er), pl. *ag′geres* [L.]. An eminence. **a. na′si** [L. "ridge of the nose"] [N A, B N A], a ridgelike elevation midway between the anterior extremity of the middle nasal concha and the inner surface of the dorsum of the nose. Called also *ridge of nose*. **a. perpendicula′ris,** eminentia fossae triangularis auriculae. **a. val′vae venae,** an elevation of the wall of a vein over the site of a valve.

aggeres (aj′er-ēz) [L.]. Plural of *agger*.

agglomerated (ah-glom′er-āt″ed) [L. *agglomeratus*, from *ad* together + *glomus* mass]. Crowded into a mass.

agglomerin (ah-glom′er-in). A plasma protein which, on the addition of complement, causes an increase in sedimentation rate.

agglutinable (ah-gloo′tĭ-nah-bl). Capable of agglutination.

agglutinant (ah-gloo′tĭ-nant) [L. *agglutinans* gluing]. 1. Promoting repair by adhesion. 2. A plaster or gluey application which holds parts together during the process of healing. 3. Agglutinin.

agglutination (ah-gloo″tĭ-na′shun) [L. *agglutinatio*]. 1. The action of an agglutinant substance. 2. A process of union in the healing of a wound. 3. A phenomenon consisting of the collection into clumps of the cells distributed in a fluid. It is believed to be caused by specific substances called agglutinins, the molecules of which become attached to the cells. The phenomenon is seen when a bacterial culture is treated with serum immunized against the particular organism. It also occurs when the spermatozoa of marine animals encounter the fertilizin of egg-water. Called also *clumping*. See also *Gruber-Widal reaction*, under *reaction*. **acid a.,** the agglutination of microorganisms at low hydrogen ion concentration. **bacteriogenic a.,** clumping of erythrocytes due to bacterial action; Hübner-Thomson phenomenon. **chief a.** See *chief agglutinin*, under *agglutinin*. **cross a.,** group a. **group a.,** agglutination of various members of a group of biologically related organisms or corpuscles by an agglutinin specific for one of that group. For instance, the specific agglutinin of typhoid bacilli may agglutinate other members of the colon-typhoid group, such as *Escherichia coli* and *Salmonella enteritidis*. **H a.,** the agglutination of motile bacteria in the presence of antibody to the heat-labile flagellar antigens. **immediate a.,** healing by the first intention. **intravascular a.,** agglutination of red corpuscles in the intact blood vessels, occurring in response to injury or in certain diseases, and interfering with adequate blood flow. Called also *sludging of blood*. **macroscopic a.,** agglutination done in test tubes or other containers large enough so that the flocculation and sedimentation of the organisms or corpuscles can be seen with the unaided eye. **mediate a.,** healing by the formation of plastic material. **microscopic a.,** agglutination so done, usually by means of a hanging drop, that the clumping of the microorganisms or corpuscles can be observed with the microscope. **minor a., part a.** See *partial agglutinin*, under *agglutinin*. **O a.,** the agglutination of bacteria in the presence of antibody to the heat-stable somatic antigen. **platelet a.,** the clumping together of platelets resulting from the action of antiplatelet agglutinins. **salt a.,** agglutination that occurs in concentrations of certain salts. **spontaneous a.,** the agglutina-

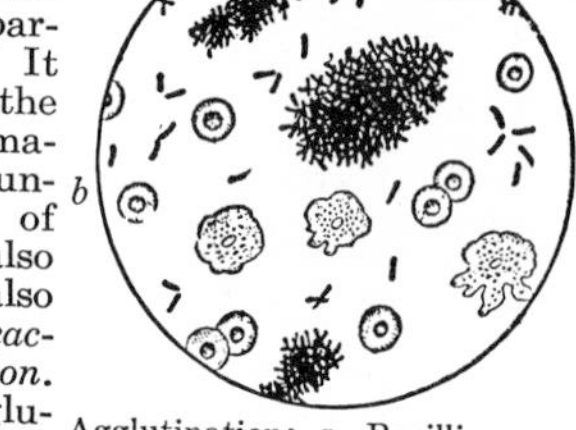

Agglutination: *a*, Bacilli unagglutinated; *b*, bacilli agglutinated.

tion of bacteria in physiological salt solution due to the lack of sufficient surface polar groups to give stable suspensions in the presence of electrolytes. **T-a.,** bacteriogenic a. **Vi a.,** bacterial agglutination produced by Vi antigen.

agglutinative (ah-gloo′tĭ-na″tiv). Promoting adhesion, or adhering.

agglutinator (ah-gloo′tĭ-na″tor). Something which agglutinates; an agglutinin.

agglutinin (ah-gloo′tĭ-nin). Antibody which aggregates a particulate antigen, e.g., bacteria, following combination with the homologous antigen in vivo or in vitro. **anti-Rh a.,** an agglutinin not normally present in human plasma but which may be produced in Rh— mothers carrying an Rh+ fetus or after transfusion of Rh+ blood into an Rh— patient. See *blood type.* **chief a.,** the specific immune agglutinin in the blood of an animal immunized against a disease or microorganism. It is active at a higher dilution of the blood serum than are the partial agglutinins. Called also *haupt-a.* and *major a.* **cold a.,** an agglutinin which acts only at a low temperature. Cf. *autoagglutinin.* **cross a.,** group a. **flagellar a.,** an agglutinin specific for the flagella of an organism. **group a.,** an agglutinin which has a specific action on certain organisms or corpuscles, but which will agglutinate other closely related species as well. **H a.,** an agglutinin produced by the motile strain of an organism. Cf. *H.* **haupt-a.,** chief a. **immune a.,** a specific agglutinin found in the blood as a result of recovering from the disease or of having been injected with the microorganism. **incomplete a.,** an agglutinin, demonstrable only when suspended in high molecular weight media or by the Coombs antiglobulin reaction, considered to be univalent and capable of uniting with only one antigenic site. Called also *blocking antibody.* **leukocyte a.,** a type of agglutinin, directed against neutrophilic and other leukocytes, found in a variety of disorders, the presence of which may not necessarily be related to the manifestations of a particular clinical entity or to the pathogenesis of the manifest leukopenic state. **major a.,** chief a. **minor a.,** partial a. **normal a.,** a specific agglutinin found in the blood of an animal or of man that has neither had the disease nor been injected with the causative organism. **O a.,** an agglutinin produced by the non-motile strain of an organism. **partial a.,** an agglutinin present in an agglutinative serum which acts on organisms and corpuscles that are closely related to the specific antigen, but in a lower dilution. Called also *minor a., mitagglutinin, neben-agglutinin, para-agglutinin,* and *coagglutinin.* **platelet a.,** an agglutinin directed against platelets, observed in a number of disorders, the presence of which may not always be correlated with demonstrable thrombocytopenia. **Rh a.** See *blood type.* **somatic a.,** an agglutinin specific for the body of a bacterium. **warm a.,** an incomplete antibody, detectable by the Coombs (antiglobulin) test, that sensitizes and reacts optimally with erythrocytes at body temperature (37°C.).

agglutinogen (ag″loo-tin′o-jen). 1. Any substance which, acting as an antigen, stimulates the production of agglutinin. 2. The antigen or suspensions of cells used in conducting agglutination tests.

agglutinogenic (ah-gloo″tĭ-no-jen′ik). Pertaining to the production of agglutinin; producing agglutinin.

agglutinoid (ah-gloo′tĭ-noid″). An agglutinin which has lost the power to agglutinate, but can still unite with its agglutinogen.

agglutinophilic (ah-gloo″tĭ-no-fil′ik). Agglutinating readily.

agglutinophore (ah-gloo′tĭ-no-fōr″) [*agglutinin* + Gr. *phoros* bearing]. That constituent of an agglutinin to which its agglutinating property is believed to be due.

agglutinoscope (ah-gloo′tĭ-no-skōp″) [*agglutinin* + Gr. *skopein* to view]. An apparatus for examining test tubes to ascertain the agglutination in the agglutination reaction.

agglutinum (ah-gloo′tĭ-num). The agglutinable part of a bacillus.

agglutinumoid (ag″loo-tin′u-moid). An agglutinin which has been heated, yet still retains its agglutinating power.

agglutogenic (ah-gloo″to-jen′ik). Agglutinogenic.

agglutometer (ag″loo-tom′e-ter). An apparatus for performing the Gruber-Widal test without the use of a microscope.

aggred. feb. Abbreviation for L. *aggredien′te feb′re,* while the fever is coming on.

aggregate (ag′re-gāt) [L. *aggregatus,* from *ad* to + *grex* flock]. 1. To crowd or cluster together. 2. Crowded or clustered together. 3. A mass or assemblage.

aggregation (ag″re-ga′shun). 1. Massing of materials together; clumping. 2. A clumped mass of material. **platelet a.,** a clumping together of platelets resulting from agitation and stickiness induced in the presence of metallic ions and plasma factors, occurring at 37° C. and reversed upon removal of the metallic ions. Also called *platelet clumping.*

aggressin (ah-gres′in). Bail's term for substances formed by pathogenic bacteria that facilitate invasion of the host tissue and dissemination of the infectious agent within the body in event of infection. Cf. *virulin.*

aggressinogen (ag″res-sin′o-jen). A substance which stimulates the formation of aggressins.

aggression (ah-gresh′un) [L. *aggressus,* from *ad* to + *gradi* to step]. A forceful action, usually directed toward another, often an unprovoked assault. In psychiatry, such action considered inseparable from its emotional association.

aggressivity (ag″res-siv′ĭ-te). The force by which an invading microorganism strives to maintain itself against the defensive forces of the host.

AgI. Silver iodide.

aging (āj′ing). Progressive changes produced with the passage of time.

agitated (aj′e-tāt″ed). Marked by restlessness, increased activity, and a certain amount of anxiety, fear, and tension.

agitation (aj″e-ta′shun). 1. Exceeding restlessness with motion or mental disturbance. 2. A shaking.

agitographia (aj″e-to-graf′e-ah) [L. *agitare* to hurry + Gr. *graphein* to write + *-ia*]. Excessive rapidity of writing with unconscious omission of words or parts of words. It is usually associated with agitophasia.

agitolalia (aj″e-to-la′le-ah). Agitophasia.

agitophasia (aj″e-to-fa′ze-ah) [L. *agitare* to hurry + Gr. *phasis* speech + *-ia*]. Excessive rapidity of speech in which words or syllables are unconsciously omitted or imperfectly uttered.

Agit. vas. Abbreviation for L. *agita′to va′se,* the vial being shaken.

Agkistrodon (ag-kis′tro-don). Ancistrodon.

aglaucopsia (ah″glaw-kop′se-ah) [*a* neg. + Gr. *glaukos* green + *opsis* vision + *-ia*]. Green blindness.

aglaukopsia (ah″glaw-kop′se-ah). Aglaucopsia.

aglobulia (ah″glo-bu′le-ah) [*a* neg. + L. *globulus* globule + *-ia*]. Decrease in the proportion of red blood corpuscles.

aglobuliosis (ah″glo-bu″le-o′sis). Aglobulia.

aglobulism (ah-glob′u-lizm). Aglobulia.

aglomerular (ah″glo-mer′u-lar). Having no glomeruli: said of a kidney in which the glomeruli have been absorbed or in which they have never formed (as in some fishes).

aglossia (ah-glos′e-ah) [*a* neg. + Gr. *glōssa* tongue + *-ia*]. 1. Congenital absence of the tongue. 2. Absence of the power of speech.

aglossostomia (ah″glos-o-sto′me-ah) [*a* neg. + Gr. *glōssa* tongue + *stoma* mouth + *-ia*]. A developmental anomaly characterized by absence of the tongue and mouth opening.

aglucone (ah-gloo′kōn). Aglycone.

aglutition (ag-loo-tish′un). Inability to swallow.

aglycemia (ah″gli-se′me-ah) [*a* neg. + Gr. *glykys* sweet + *haima* blood + *-ia*]. Absence of sugar from the blood.

aglycone (ah-gli′kōn) [*a* neg. + Gr. *glykys* sweet + *ōn* being]. The noncarbohydrate group of a glycoside molecule: called also *genin*.

aglycosuric (ah-gli″ko-su′rik). Free from glycosuria.

agmatology (ag″mah-tol′o-je) [Gr. *agmos* fracture + *-logy*]. The sum of what is known regarding fractures.

agmen (ag′men), pl. *ag′mina* [L. "a group"]. An aggregation. **a. peyeria′num,** Peyer's patches.

agmina (ag′mĭ-nah) [L.]. Plural of *agmen*.

agminated (ag′min-āt″ed) [L. *agmen* a group]. Clustered.

agnail (ag′nāl). Hangnail.

agnate (ag′nāt). In Scotch law, the nearest relative on the father's side of one adjudged insane, and appointed guardian of the same.

agnathia (ag-na′the-ah) [*a* neg. + Gr. *gnathos* jaw + *-ia*]. A developmental anomaly characterized by total or virtual absence of the lower jaw.

agnathus (ag-na′thus). A fetus exhibiting agnathia.

agnea (ag-ne′ah). A condition in which objects are not recognized.

Agnew's splint (ag′nūz) [David Hayes *Agnew*, Philadelphia surgeon, 1818–1892]. See under *splint*.

$AgNO_3$. Silver nitrate.

agnogenic (ag″no-jen′ik) [Gr. *agnōs* unknown, obscure + *genesis* origin]. Of unknown origin or etiology.

agnosia (ag-no′se-ah) [*a* neg. + Gr. *gnōsis* perception]. Loss of the power to recognize the import of sensory stimuli. The varieties correspond with the several senses and are distinguished as *auditory, visual, olfactory, gustatory,* and *tactile*. **body-image a.,** autotopagnosia. **ideational a.,** loss of the special associations which make up the idea of an object from its component ideas.

agnosterol (ag-nos′ter-ol″). An unsaturated sterol, $C_{30}H_{48}O$, present in wool fat.

agnus castus (ag′nus kas′tus) [L. "chaste lamb"]. The chaste-tree, *Vi′tex ag′nus-cas′tus:* said to be anaphrodisiac.

Ag_2O. Silver oxide.

-agogue [Gr. *agōgos* leading, inducing]. Word termination meaning an agent which leads or induces.

agomphiasis (ag″om-fi′ah-sis) [*a* neg. + Gr. *gomphios* molar + *-ia*]. Looseness of the teeth; also, absence of the teeth.

agomphious (ah-gom′fe-us). Without teeth.

agonad (ah-go′nad) [*a* neg. + *gonad*]. An individual without gonads.

agonadal (ah-gon′ah-dal). Having no sex glands; due to absence of sex glands.

agonal (ag′o-nal). 1. Pertaining to the death agony; occurring at the moment of or just before death. 2. Pertaining to terminal infection.

agoniadin (ag″o-ni′ah-din). A glycoside from *Plume′ria suc′cuba*.

agonist (ag′o-nist). A prime mover; a muscle opposed in action by another muscle, called the antagonist.

agony (ag′o-ne) [Gr. *agōnia*]. 1. Severe pain or extreme suffering. 2. The death struggle.

agoraphobia (ag″o-rah-fo′be-ah) [Gr. *agora* marketplace + *phobia*]. A feeling of fear at the thought of being alone in a large open space (Westphal, 1871).

Agostini's reaction, test (ag-os-te′nēz). See under *tests*.

agouti (ah-goo′te). A rodent of the genus *Dasyprocta*, about the size of a rabbit, found in tropical America.

Ag_3PO_4. Silver orthophosphate.

-agra (ag′rah) [Gr. *agra* a catching, seizure]. Word termination meaning a seizure of acute pain.

agraffe (ah-graf′) [Fr.]. A clamplike instrument for keeping together the edges of a wound.

agrammatica (ag″rah-mat′e-kah). Agrammatism.

agrammatism (ah-gram′ah-tizm″) [Gr. *agrammatos* unlettered]. Absence of the ability to speak grammatically because of brain injury or disease.

agrammatologia (ah-gram″ah-to-lo′je-ah). Agrammatism.

agranulemia (ah-gran″u-le′me-ah). Agranulocytosis.

agranulocyte (ah-gran′u-lo-sīt″). A nongranular leukocyte.

agranulocytopenia (ah-gran″u-lo-si″to-pe′ne-ah). Agranulocytosis.

agranulocytosis (ah-gran″u-lo-si-to′sis). An acute disease characterized by marked leukopenia and neutropenia and with ulcerative lesions of the throat and other mucous membranes, of the gastrointestinal tract and of the skin. It frequently follows the use of aminopyrine, the sulfonamides, or other drugs. Called also *agranulocytic angina, essential granulopenia, sepsis agranulocytica, malignant leukopenia, malignant neutropenia, granulopenia, granulophthisis, mucositis necroticans agranulocytica, Schultz's angina*. **infectious feline a.,** panleukopenia.

agranuloplastic (ah-gran″u-lo-plas′tik) [*a* neg. + *granule* + Gr. *plassein* to form]. Forming nongranular cells only; not forming granular cells.

agranulosis (ah-gran″u-lo′sis). Agranulocytosis.

agraphia (ah-graf′e-ah) [*a* neg. + Gr. *graphein* to write + *-ia*]. Inability to express thoughts in writing, due to a central lesion. **absolute a.,** loss of the power to form even single letters. **acoustic a.,** loss of the power of writing from dictation. **a. amnemon′ica,** agraphia in which letters and words can be written, but not so arranged as to express any idea. **a. atac′tica,** absolute agraphia. **cerebral a.,** mental a. **jargon a.,** agraphia in which the patient can write, but forms only senseless combinations of letters. **literal a.,** inability to write letters of the alphabet. **mental a.,** agraphia due to inability to put thought into phrases. **motor a.,** inability to write because of lack of motor coordination. **musical a.,** loss of the power to write musical symbols. **optic a.,** inability to copy written or printed words, but with ability to write from dictation. **verbal a.,** ability to write single letters, with loss of ability to combine them into words.

agraphic (ah-graf′ik). Pertaining to, affected with, or of the nature of, agraphia.

agremia (ah-gre′me-ah) [Gr. *agra* seizure + *haima* blood + *-ia*]. That condition of the blood which characterizes gout.

agria (ag′re-ah) [L.; Gr. *agrios* wild]. An obstinate pustular eruption.

agriothymia (ag″re-o-thim′e-ah) [Gr. *agrios* wild + *thymos* spirit + *-ia*]. Insane ferocity.

agrius (a′gre-us) [L. "wild"]. Very severe; said of skin eruptions.

Agrobacterium (ag″ro-bak-te′re-um) [Gr. *agros* field + *bacterium*]. A genus of microorganisms of the family Rhizobiaceae, order Eubacteriales, made up of small, short, flagellated rods, found in soil or in the roots or stems of plants. Seven species have been named; the type species is *A. tumefa′ciens*.

agromania (ag″ro-ma′ne-ah) [Gr. *agros* field + *mania* madness]. Insane passion for solitude or for wandering in the fields.

agronomy (ah-gron′o-me) [Gr. *agros* field + *nomos* law]. Rural economy; husbandry.

Agropyrum (ag″ro-pi′rum). See *Triticum.*

Agrostem′ma githa′go. Corn cockle, *Lychnis githago*, a plant whose seeds may cause poisoning.

agrypnia (ah-grip′ne-ah) [Gr. *agrypnos* sleepless + *-ia*]. Sleeplessness, or insomnia.

agrypnocoma (ah-grip″no-ko′mah). Wakeful coma; lethargy with wakefulness and muttering delirium.

agrypnode (ah-grip′nōd). Agrypnotic.

agrypnotic (ah″grip-not′ik) [Gr. *agrypnotikos*]. 1. Promoting wakefulness. 2. A drug that prevents sleep.

Ag_2S. Silver sulfide.

Ag_2SO_4. Silver sulfate.

aguamiel (ag″wah-me-el′). The sap from which pulque is made.

ague (a′gu) [Fr. *aigu* sharp]. 1. Malarial fever, or any other severe recurrent symptom of malarial origin. 2. A chill. **brass-founders' a.,** a disease of brass-founders, with symptoms resembling those of malarial fever. **catenating a.,** that which is associated with some other disease. **dumb a.,** ague with no well-marked chill, and with only a slight periodicity. **face a.,** tic douloureux. **quartan a.,** that in which paroxysms are seventy-two hours apart. **quintan a.,** that in which the paroxysms are ninety-six hours apart. **quotidian a.,** that in which there is a twenty-four-hour interval between the paroxysms. **shaking a.,** a severe form of malarial paroxysm, beginning with a marked chill. **tertian a.,** that in which the paroxysms are forty-eight hours apart.

A.G.V. Abbreviation for *aniline gentian violet.*

agyria (ah-ji′re-ah) [*a* neg. + Gr. *gyros* ring + *-ia*]. A malformation in which the convolutions of the cerebral cortex are not normally developed.

agyric (ah-ji′rik). 1. Pertaining to or characterized by agyria. 2. Having no gyri.

ah. Symbol for *hypermetropic astigmatism.*

A.H.A. Abbreviation for *American Heart Association.*

ahaptoglobinemia (a-hap″to-glo″bĭ-ne′me-ah). The presence of little or no haptoglobin in the blood serum.

AHF. Abbreviation for *antihemophilic factor* (blood coagulation factor VIII).

AHG. Abbreviation for *antihemophilic globulin* (blood coagulation factor VIII).

Ahlfeld's sign (ahl′felts) [Friedrich *Ahlfeld*, German obstetrician, 1843–1929]. See *Hicks's sign,* under *sign.*

ahypnia (ah-hip′ne-ah). Ahypnosis.

ahypnosis (ah″hip-no′sis) [*a* neg. + Gr. *hypnos* sleep + *-osis*]. Morbid wakefulness, or insomnia.

A.I. Abbreviation for *axioincisal.*

aichmophobia (āk″mo-fo′be-ah) [Gr. *aichmē* spearpoint + *phobos* fear + *-ia*]. Abnormal fear of sharp-pointed objects.

aid (ād). Help, or assistance. By extension, applied to any device by which a function can be improved or augmented. **first a.,** emergency assistance and treatment furnished in cases of accident, injury or illness pending regular surgical or medical treatment. **hearing a.,** a device which makes better hearing possible for patients with deafness. **speech a.,** an appliance used to improve an individual's speech, or therapy which is designed to promote the improvement of speech. **speech a., prosthetic,** an appliance which is used to close a cleft in the hard or soft palate, or both, or to restore other tissue necessary to the production of vocal sounds.

aidoiitis (a″doy-i′tis). Inflammation of the genitals; vulvitis or balanitis.

aidoiomania (a″doy-o-ma′ne-ah) [Gr. *aidoia* genitals + *mania* madness]. Abnormal sexual desire.

Ailanthus (a-lan′thus) [L. from Malacca name]. A genus of simarubaceous trees. The bark of *A. glandulosa* is purgative, tonic, and anthelmintic.

Ailantus (a-lan′tus). Ailanthus.

ailment (āl′ment). Any disease or affection of the body.

ailurophilia (a-lu″ro-fil′e-ah) [Gr. *ailouros* cat + *philein* to love]. A morbid or inordinate fondness for cats.

ailurophobia (a-lu″ro-fo′be-ah) [Gr. *ailouros* cat + *phobia*]. Pathologic fear of cats (Weir Mitchell).

ainhum (ān′hum, or, Portuguese, īn-yoon′) [African]. A condition, occurring chiefly in Negroes in tropical countries, marked by linear constriction of a toe, especially the little one, which constriction by its contraction gradually amputates the toe.

Ainsworth's punch (ānz′worths) [George C. *Ainsworth*, Boston dentist, 1852–1948]. An instrument for punching holes in rubber dam for application to teeth.

air (ār) [L. *a′er;* Gr. *aēr*]. The gaseous mixture which makes up the earth's atmosphere. It is an odorless, colorless gas, consisting of about 1 part by volume of oxygen and 4 parts of nitrogen, the proportion varying somewhat according to conditions. It also contains a small amount of carbon dioxide, ammonia, argon, nitrites, and organic matter. **alkaline a.,** free ammonia. **alveolar a., arterial alveolar a.,** air in the lungs, mostly below the level of tidal air, that is in CO_2 equilibrium with arterial blood. It consists of residual air, reserve air and portions of tidal air. **complemental a.,** the air in excess of the tidal air which may be drawn into the lungs by forced inspiration. **dephlogisticated a.,** oxygen. **factitious a.,** nitrous oxide. **fixed a.,** carbon dioxide. **functional residual a.,** the amount of air remaining in the lungs at the end of a normal expiration. It consists of both supplemental and residual air. **liquid a.,** air liquefied by great pressure. On evaporation it produces intense cold. Liquid air has been used to produce local anesthesia; also in the treatment of neuralgia and zoster. **minimal a.,** the small amount of air caught in the alveoli of the excised or collapsed lungs. **reserve a.,** supplemental a. **residual a.,** air that stays in the lungs after the strongest possible expiration. **stationary a.,** that which remains in the lungs during normal respiration. **supplemental a.,** air which may be expelled from the lungs in excess of that normally breathed out. **tidal a.,** the air that is carried to and fro in normal respiration. **venous alveolar a.,** alveolar air in CO_2 equilibrium with venous blood.

airbrasive (ār′bra-siv). An instrument for preparing a cavity in a tooth or removing deposits from teeth by application of a mixture of sand and aluminum oxide by air blast.

airdent (ār′dent). Registered trade mark of a dental unit which utilizes abrasive particles applied by air blast for the preparation of dental cavities.

airway (ār′wa). 1. The route for passage of air into and out of the lungs. 2. A device for securing unobstructed passage of air into and out of the lungs during general anesthesia.

ak-. For words beginning thus, see also words beginning *ac-*.

akaryocyte (ah-kar′e-o-sīt″) [*a* neg. + Gr. *karyon* kernel + *kytos* hollow vessel]. 1. A non-nucleated cell. 2. Osgood's name for erythrocyte or red blood corpuscle.

akaryota (ah-kar″e-o′tah). Akaryote.

akaryote (ah-kar′e-ōt) [*a* neg. + Gr. *karyon* kernel]. A non-nucleated cell.

akatama (ak″ah-tam′ah). A form of chronic peripheral neuritis occurring in West Africa. It is marked by swelling, erythema, prickling sensations, burning, numbness, and sometimes excessive sweating.

akatamathesia (ah-kat″ah-mah-the′zhe-ah) [*a* neg. + Gr. *katamathēsis* understanding]. Inability to understand.

akatanoesis (ah-kat″ah-no′e-sis) [*a* neg. + Gr. *katanoein* to understand]. Inability to understand oneself (Heveroch, 1914).

akathisia (ak″ah-the′ze-ah) [*a* neg. + Gr. *kathisis* a sitting down + *-ia*]. A condition of motor restlessness, ranging from a feeling of inner disquiet to inability to sit or lie quietly, or to sleep. Called also *acathisia* and *kathisophobia*.

akee (ah-ke′). A small tree of the West Indies, *Blighia sapida*, the fruit of which may cause poisoning.

akembe (ah-kem′be). Onyalai.

Åkerlund deformity (ek′er-loond) [Åke *Åkerlund*, Swedish roentgenologist, 1885–1958]. See under *deformity*.

akidogalvanocautery (ak″i-do-gal″vah-no-kaw′ter-e). Cauterization by the needle electrode.

akidopeirastic (ak″i-do-pi-ras′tik) [Gr. *akis* needle + *peirastikos* testing]. Pertaining to or characterized by exploratory puncture with a needle.

akinesia (ak″i-ne′se-ah) [*a* neg. + Gr. *kinēsis* motion + *-ia*]. 1. Abnormal absence or poverty of movements. 2. The temporary paralysis of a muscle by the injection of procaine. **a. al′gera,** paralysis or voluntary abstinence from motion caused by neuroticism or by the intense pain accompanying muscular movements (Moebius). It is often seen in neurasthenic states. **a. amnes′tica,** loss of the power of movement from disuse. **crossed a.,** motor paralysis on the side opposite the lesion. **O'Brien a.,** paralysis of the orbicularis oculi muscle produced by injection of an anesthetic solution directly over the orbital branch of the seventh nerve as it emerges from behind the ear and extends toward the orbital region along the ramus of the jaw, permitting better exposure of the bulb of the eye. **reflex a.,** loss of reflex movement.

akinesis (ak″i-ne′sis). Akinesia.

akinesthesia (ah-kin″es-the′zhe-ah). Absence of kinesthesia; absence of the movement sense.

akinetic (ah″ki-net′ik). 1. Pertaining to, characterized by, or causing akinesia. 2. Amitotic.

akineton (a″ki-ne′ton). Trade mark for preparations of biperiden.

akiyami (ah″ke-yah′me). Nanukayami.

aknephascopia (ak″nef-ah-sko′pe-ah) [*a* neg. + Gr. *knephas* twilight + *skopein* to view]. Twilight blindness; reduced visual acuity with weak daylight, such as twilight, or with inadequate artificial illumination.

Akokanthera (ak″o-kan-the′rah). Acocanthera.

akrencephalon (ak″ren-sef′ah-lon). Telencephalon.

akromikrie (ak″ro-mik′re). Brugsch's term for a disease marked by thinning of the extremities, subnormal growth, falling hair, thrist, amenorrhea and acrocyanosis.

aktinine (ak′ti-nin). Actinine.

A.L. Abbreviation for *axiolingual*.

Al. Chemical symbol for *aluminum*.

-al. A suffix used in forming the names of chemical compounds, indicating presence of the aldehyde group, —CHO, as *chloral*.

A.La. Abbreviation for *axiolabial*.

ala (a′lah), pl. *a′lae* [L. "wing"]. A general term used in anatomical nomenclature to designate a winglike structure or process. Called also *wing*. **a. al′ba latera′lis,** fovea inferior fossae rhomboideae. **a. al′ba media′lis,** area vestibularis. **a. au′ris,** the pinna of the ear. **a. cerebel′li,** a. lobuli centralis. **a. cine′rea** [B N A], trigonum nervi vagi. **a. cris′tae gal′li** [N A], a small winglike process on the anterior part of the crista galli of the ethmoid bone. Called also *processus alaris ossis ethmoidalis* [B N A]. **a. il′ii,** a. ossis illi. **a′lae lin′gulae cerebel′li,** vincula lingulae cerebelli. **a. lob′uli centra′lis cerebel′li** [N A, B N A], the lateral portion of the central lobe of the cerebellum. **a. mag′na os′sis sphenoida′lis** [B N A], a. major ossis sphenoidalis. **a. ma′jor os′sis sphenoida′lis** [N A], a large wing-shaped process arising from either side of the body of the sphenoid bone. Its cerebral surface forms the anterior part of the floor of the middle cranial fossa, and its orbital surface forms the chief part of the lateral wall of the orbit. Called also *great wing of sphenoid bone*. **a. mi′nor os′sis sphenoida′lis** [N A], the thin triangular plate of bone that extends horizontally and laterally from either side of the anterior part of the body of the sphenoid bone. It articulates with the frontal bone and helps form the roof of the orbit and the floor of the anterior cranial fossa. Called also *small wing of sphenoid bone*. **a. na′si** [N A, B N A], the flaring cartilaginous expansion forming the outer side of each nostril. **a. os′sis il′ii** [N A], the superior, winglike portion of the ilium. **a. os′sis il′ium** [B N A], a. ossis ilii. **a. par′va os′sis sphenoida′lis** [B N A], a. minor ossis sphenoidalis. **a. pon′tis,** tenia ventriculi quarti. **a. sacra′lis, a. sa′cri, a. of the sacrum,** pars lateralis ossis sacri. **a. tempora′lis os′sis sphenoida′lis,** a. major ossis sphenoidalis. **a. vespertilio′nis** ["bat's wing"], mesosalpinx. **a. of vomer, a. vo′meris** [N A, B N A], one of the two lateral expansions on the superior border of the vomer, coming into contact with the sphenoidal process of the palate and the vaginal process of the medial pterygoid plate.

ala-azar. Kala-azar.

alae (a′le) [L.]. Plural of *ala*.

A.La.G. Abbreviation for *axiolabiogingival*.

A.La.L. Abbreviation for *axiolabiolingual*.

alalia (ah-la′le-ah) [*a* neg. + Gr. *lalein* to speak + *-ia*]. Lack of ability to talk. **a. coph′ica,** deaf-mutism. **a. organ′ica,** alalia due to organic disease. **a. physiolo′gica,** deaf-mutism. **a. prolonga′ta,** delayed speech.

alalic (ah-lal′ik). Pertaining to, affected with, or of the nature of, alalia.

alangine (ah-lan′jin). A yellowish, amorphous alkaloid from *Alangium lamarckii*.

Alangium lamarckii (ah-lan′je-um lah-mark′e-e). An East Indian plant whose root is emetic, antipyretic, and diuretic.

alanine (al′ah-nin). An amino acid, $CH_3CH(NH_2).COOH$, or alpha-aminopropionic acid. **a. mercury,** mercury aminopropionate, $[CH_3.CH(NH_2)COO]_2Hg$.

Alanson's amputation [Edward *Alanson*, British surgeon, 1747–1823]. See under *amputation*.

alantin (ah-lan′tin). See *inulin*.

alanyl-leucine (al″ah-nil-loo′sin). A dipeptide, $CH_3.CH(NH_2).CO.NH(COOH).CH.CH_2.CH(CH_3)_2$.

alar (a′lar) [L. *alaris*]. 1. Pertaining to a wing or ala. 2. Pertaining to the armpit; axillary.

alastrim (ah-las′trim). Variola minor.

alastrimic (al″as-trim′ik). Pertaining to alastrim.

alastrinic (al″as-trin′ik). Alastrimic.

alate (a′lāt) [L. *alatus* winged]. Having wings; winged.

alba (al′bah) [L.]. White. Used as an adjective in names of certain anatomical tissues or structures.

albamycin (al′bah-mi″sin). Trade mark for preparations of novobiocin.

Albarran's disease, gland, test (al″bar-anz′) [Joaquin *Albarran*, Cuban surgeon in Paris, 1860–1912]. See *colibacilluria*, and under *gland* and *test*.

albation (al-ba′shun) [L. *albare* to whiten]. The

act of bleaching, or rendering white, as of discolored teeth.

albedo (al-be′do) [L.]. Whiteness. **a. ret′inae,** edema of the retina.

Albee's operation (awl′bēz) [Fred. Houdlett *Albee,* New York surgeon, 1876–1945]. See under *operation.*

albefaction (al″be-fak′shun) [L. *albus* white + *facere* to make]. The process of making white or bleaching.

Albers-Schönberg disease [Heinrich Ernst *Albers-Schönberg,* Hamburg roentgenologist, 1865–1921]. Osteopetrosis.

Albert's disease, operation, suture [Eduard *Albert,* Austrian surgeon, 1841–1900]. See *achillobursitis,* and under *operation* and *suture.*

albicans (al′bĭ-kanz), pl. *albican′tia* [L.]. White.

albiduria (al″bĭ-du′re-ah) [L. *albidus* whitish + Gr. *ouron* urine + *-ia*]. The discharge of white or pale urine.

albidus (al′bĭ-dus) [L.]. Whitish.

albine (al′ben). The diamidophosphide of egg yolk.

Albini's nodules (al-be′nēz) [Giuseppe *Albini,* Italian physiologist, 1830–1911]. See under *nodule.*

albinic (al-bin′ik). Pertaining to, or affected with albinism.

albinism (al′bĭ-nizm) [L. *albus* white + *-ism*]. Congenital absence of pigment in the skin, hair, and eyes. **localized a.,** partial a. **partial a.,** absence of pigment in local areas only; called also *localized albinism* and *naevus anaemicus.* **total a.,** complete absence of pigment in the eyes and in the skin and its appendages, often attended with astigmatism, photophobia, and nystagmus.

albinismus (al″bĭ-niz′mus) [L.]. Albinism. **a. conscrip′tus,** partial albinism manifested as piebaldism, white forelock, or circumscribed areas of depigmentation of the skin. **a. tota′lis, a. universa′lis,** total albinism.

albino (al-bi′no). An individual affected with albinism.

albinoism (al-bi′no-izm). Albinism.

albinotic (al″bĭ-not′ik). Pertaining to or characterized by albinism.

albinuria (al″bĭ-nu′re-ah). Albiduria.

Albinus's muscle (al-bi′nus-ez) [Bernhard Siegfried *Albinus,* anatomist and surgeon in Leyden, 1697–1770]. See under *muscle.*

albocinereous (al″bo-sĭ-ne′re-us) [L. *albus* white + *cinereus* gray]. Containing both white and gray matter.

Albrecht's bone (al′brektz) [Karl Martin Paul *Albrecht,* German anatomist, 1851–1894]. Basiotic bone.

Albright's disease, syndrome (awl′brīts) [Fuller *Albright,* Boston physician, born 1900]. See *osteitis fibrosa cystica,* and under *syndrome.*

Albucasis (al″boo-kas′is) (936–1013). The most famous Arabic writer upon surgery. The surgical part of his encyclopedic *Altasrif* greatly influenced medieval European medicine.

albugin (al′bu-jin). A collective name for the albumins and globulins.

albuginea (al″bu-jin′e-ah) [L. from *albus* white]. A tough, whitish layer of fibrous tissue investing a part; especially a dense white membrane forming immediate covering of the testicle. Called also *tunica albuginea testis.* **a. oc′uli,** the sclera. **a. ova′rii,** the outer layer of the stroma of the ovary. **a. pe′nis,** the outer envelope of the corpora cavernosa.

albugineotomy (al″bu-jin″e-ot′o-me) [*albuginea* + Gr. *tomē* a cutting]. Incision of the tunica albuginea of the testicle.

albugineous (al″bu-jin′e-us) [L. *albugineus*]. Pertaining to or resembling a tough whitish layer of fibrous tissue (tunica albuginea [NA]).

albuginitis (al″bu-jĭ-ni′tis). Inflammation of any one of the albugineous tissues or tunics.

albugo (al-bu′go) [L. from *albus* white]. A white corneal opacity.

albukalin (al″bu-ka′lin). A substance, $C_8H_{16}N_2O_6$, found in leukemic blood.

albumen (al-bu′men) [L., from *albus* white]. Albumin.

albumimeter (al″bu-mim′e-ter). Albuminimeter.

albumin (al-bu′min). A protein found in nearly every animal and in many vegetable tissues, and characterized by being soluble in water and coagulable by heat. It contains carbon, hydrogen, nitrogen, oxygen, and sulfur, but its exact composition has not yet been determined, although the formula for crystallized albumin has been given as $C_{720}H_{1134}N_{218}S_5O_{248}$. **a. A,** a certain constituent of the blood serum which in cancer patients is reduced in amount but which gathers abundantly in cancer cells. See *Kahn test* (2nd def.), under *test.* **acetosoluble a.,** a form of albumin soluble in acetic acid, sometimes found in the urine; called also *Patein's a.* **acid a.,** albumin altered by the action of an acid. **alkali a.,** any albumin which has been treated with an alkali. **a. of Bence Jones.** See *Bence Jones protein,* under *protein.* **blood a.,** serum a. **caseiniform a.,** a variety coagulated by acids, but not by heat. **circulating a.,** that which is found in the fluids of the body. **coagulated a.,** albumin altered by heat or chemical action so as to be insoluble in water, neutral salt solutions, or dilute acid and alkaline solutions. **derived a.,** any albumin altered by chemical action. **egg a.,** a principle which constitutes 20 per cent of the white of hens' eggs; called also *ovalbumin.* **hematin a.,** a preparation of ox blood rich in iron. **iodinated serum a.,** radio-iodinated serum a. **Mayer's a.,** white of egg 50 cc., glycerol 50 cc., sodium salicylate 1 Gm. **muscle a.,** a variety found in muscle juice. **native a.,** any albumin normally present in the body. **normal human serum a.,** a preparation of serum albumin obtained by fractionation of pooled normal human plasma: used in prevention and treatment of shock, and in treatment of hypoproteinemia. **organ a.,** any albumin normally present in a particular organ. **Patein's a.,** acetosoluble a. **radio-iodinated serum a.,** a substance obtained by treatment of normal human serum albumin with I 131: used as a diagnostic aid for measuring blood volume, and for determining output of blood by the heart. **serum a.,** the chief protein of human blood plasma: it is used intravenously in the treatment of shock. **soap a.,** a combination of soap and albumin which is supposed to constitute the intracellular granules of soap; called also *protein fat.* **a. tannate,** a yellowish-white astringent powder containing about 50 per cent tannic acid combined with protein. Used in diarrhea. **triphenyl a.,** a preparation of egg albumin and phenol; used as a nutrient in bacteriological study. **vegetable a.,** any albumin derived from a plant or of vegetable origin.

albuminate (al-bu′mĭ-nāt). Any compound of albumin with a base or an acid; one of a class of proteins characterized by their solubility in dilute acids or alkalis, and by being insoluble in dilute salt solutions, water, or alcohol; called also *derived albumin* and *derived protein. acid a's* are obtained by the action of a dilute acid on native proteins; *alkali a's,* by the action of alkalis on native proteins.

albuminaturia (al-bu″mĭ-na-tu′re-ah) [*albuminate* + *urine*]. The presence of an excessive amount of albuminates in the urine.

albuminemia (al-bu″mĭ-ne′me-ah) [*albumin* + Gr. *haima* blood + *-ia*]. The presence of an abnormally large amount of albumin in the blood plasma.

albuminiferous (al-bu″mĭ-nif′er-us) [*albumin* + L. *ferre* to bear]. Producing albumin.

albuminimeter (al-bu″mĭ-nim′e-ter) [*albumin* +

meter]. An instrument used in determining the proportion of albumin present, as in the urine.

albuminimetry (al-bu″mĭ-nim′e-tre). The determination of the proportion of albumin present.

albuminiparous (al-bu″mĭ-nip′ah-rus) [*albumin* + L. *parere* to produce]. Producing albumin.

albuminocholia (al-bu″mĭ-no-ko′le-ah) [*albumin* + Gr. *cholē* bile + *-ia*]. The presence of albumin in the bile.

albuminogenous (al-bu″mĭ-noj′e-nus) [*albumin* + Gr. *gennan* to produce]. Producing or forming albumin.

albuminoid (al-bu′mĭ-noid) [*albumin* + Gr. *eidos* form]. 1. Resembling albumin. 2. Protein. 3. A scleroprotein.

albuminolysin (al″bu-mĭ-nol′ĭ-sin) [*albumin* + *lysin*]. 1. A lysin which produces disintegration of albumins. 2. Sensibilisin.

albuminolysis (al-bu″mĭ-nol′ĭ-sis). The splitting up of albumins.

albuminometer (al-bu″mĭ-nom′e-ter). Albuminimeter.

albuminone (al-bu′mĭ-nōn). A principle from various albuminoids, soluble in alcohol and not coagulated by heat.

albuminoptysis (al″bu-mĭ-nop′tĭ-sis) [*albumin* + Gr. *ptyein* to spit]. Presence of albumin in the sputum.

albuminoreaction (al-bu″mĭ-no-re-ak′shun). The reaction of the sputum to tests for albumin; the presence of albumin (positive reaction) is indicative of pulmonary inflammation.

albuminorrhea (al-bu″mi-no-re′ah) [*albumin* + Gr. *rhoia* flow]. Excessive excretion of albumins.

albuminose (al-bu′mĭ-nōs). Albumose.

albuminosis (al-bu″mĭ-no′sis). An abnormal increase of the albuminous elements of the blood, or a condition resulting from such an increase.

albuminous (al-bu′mĭ-nus). Containing, charged with, or of the nature of, an albumin.

albuminuretic (al-bu″mĭ-nu-ret′ik) [*albumin* + Gr. *ourētikos* diuretic]. 1. Pertaining to, characterized by, or promoting albuminuria. 2. An agent that promotes albuminuria.

albuminuria (al″bu-mĭ-nu′re-ah) [*albumin* + Gr. *ouron* urine + *-ia*]. Presence in the urine of serum albumin or serum globulin. **accidental a.,** adventitious a. **a. of adolescence,** cyclic a. **adventitious a.,** that which is not due to a kidney disease. **athletic a.,** functional albuminuria occurring in athletes. **Bamberger's hematogenic a.,** albuminuria during the latter periods of severe anemia. **cardiac a.,** that which is caused by valvular disease. **colliquative a.,** albuminuria which is at first mild, but increases suddenly and markedly during convalescence; seen in typhoid fever. **cyclic a.,** a term used in the past to denote the appearance, at stated times each day, of a small amount of albumin in the urine; observed principally in young persons. **dietetic a., digestive a.,** albuminuria produced by the use of certain foods. **emulsion a.,** albuminuria in which the turbidity does not disappear on filtration, heating, or adding acid, seen in puerperal eclampsia. **essential a.,** a form of functional albuminuria which is not associated with or followed by renal disease: it includes cyclic, postural, and orthostatic albuminuria, etc. **false a.,** adventitious a. **febrile a.,** albuminuria due to fever. **functional a.,** any albuminuria which is not truly pathologic, such as the transient albuminurias of pregnancy or of adolescence. **globular a.,** albuminuria due to destruction of red blood corpuscles and dependent on blood in the urine. **gouty a.,** physiologic albuminuria, with excessive secretion of urea. **hematogenous a., hemic a.,** a variety due to abnormal condition of the blood. **hypostatic a.,** a form of postural albuminuria present when the patient is reclining and absent when he is in the erect posture. **intermittent a.,** functional a. **intrinsic a.,** true a. **lordotic a.,** orthostatic albuminuria due to lordotic deformity of the spine. **mixed a.,** serous albuminuria occurring concurrently with adventitious albuminuria. **nephrogenous a.,** that caused by renal disease. **neurotic a.,** a variety dependent on nervous diseases. **orthostatic a., orthotic a.,** a type of albuminuria which appears only when the patient is standing or sitting and disappears on reclining; called also *postural a.* **palpatory a.,** temporary albuminuria produced by bimanual palpation of the kidneys. **paroxysmal a.,** functional a. **physiological a.,** functional a. **postrenal a.,** albuminuria which has arisen at some point beyond the uriniferous tubule, such as the renal pelvis, ureter, bladder, prostate or urethra. **postural a.,** orthostatic a. **a. praetuberculo′sa,** that occurring in the incipient stage of pulmonary tuberculosis. **prerenal a.,** albuminuria due primarily to a disease other than one of the kidney, such as heart disease, liver disease, fever, hyperthyroidism. **pseudo-a.,** adventitious a. **recurrent a.,** cyclic albuminuria. **regulatory a.,** albuminuria or the transitory elimination of albumin after excessive physical exercise, etc. **renal a.,** albuminuria due to disease of the kidneys. **residual a.,** persistence of albumin in the urine after an attack of acute nephritis. **serous a.,** true a. **transient a.,** functional a. **true a.,** that which is characterized by the discharge with the urine of some of the albuminous elements of the blood.

albuminuric (al″bu-mĭ-nu′rik). Pertaining to or marked by albuminuria.

albuminurophobia (al-bu″min-u″ro-fo′be-ah) [*albuminuria* + *phobia*]. 1. An exaggerated fear of acquiring albuminuria. 2. Overemphasis on the significance of albumin in the urine.

albumisol (al-bu′mĭ-sol). Trade mark for a preparation of normal human serum albumin.

albumoid (al′bu-moid″). Albuminoid.

albumone (al′bu-mōn″). A compound resembling proteose, supposed to occur in the blood.

albumoscope (al-bu′mo-skōp″) [*albumin* + Gr. *skopein* to view]. An instrument for determining the presence and amount of albumin in the urine.

albumose (al′bu-mōs). Any primary product of the digestion of a protein, differing from albumin in not being coagulable by heat. The albumoses are convertible by further digestion into peptones. **Bence Jones a.** See *Bence Jones protein*, under *protein.*

albumosease (al′bu-mōs-ās″). An enzyme which splits up albumose.

albumosemia (al″bu-mo-se′me-ah) [*albumose* + Gr. *haima* blood + *-ia*]. Presence of albumose in the blood.

albumosuria (al″bu-mo-su′re-ah). The presence of an albumose (proteose) in the urine. **Bence Jones a.,** the presence of Bence Jones protein in the urine. See *multiple myeloma*, under *myeloma.* **Bradshaw's a.** Same as *Bence Jones a.* **enterogenic a.,** albumosuria due to intestinal decomposition. **hematogenic a.,** albumosuria due to some intoxication. **myelopathic a.,** Bence Jones a. See *multiple myeloma*, under *myeloma.* **pyogenic a.,** albumosuria due to the absorption of pus cells or exudate, as in pneumonia, septic processes, etc.

A.L.C. Abbreviation for *axiolinguocervical.*

Alcaligenes (al″kah-lij′e-nēz). A genus of microorganisms of the family Achromobacteraceae, order Eubacteriales, made up of gram-negative rod-shaped bacteria generally found in the intestinal tracts of vertebrates or in dairy products. It includes six species, *A. boo′keri, A. faeca′lis, A. marshal′lii, A. metalcalig′enes, A. rec′ti,* and *A. viscolac′tis.*

alcapton (al-kap′ton). Alkapton. See *alkapton body.*

alcaptonuria (al-kap″to-nu′re-ah). Alkaptonuria.

alchemy (al′kĕ-me). The supposed art of transmutation of baser metals into gold; also chemical magic.

Alcmaeon (alk-me′on) **of Crotona** (c. 500 B.C.). Famous physician, a pupil of Pythagoras, and the reputed discoverer of the optic nerve and the eustachian tube.

Alcock's canal (al′koks) [Benjamin *Alcock*, Professor of Anatomy, Queen's College, Cork, from 1849 to 1855; born 1801, date of death in America unknown]. See under *canal.*

alcohol (al′ko-hol) [Arabic *al-koh'l* something subtle]. 1. A transparent, colorless, mobile, volatile liquid, C_2H_5OH, miscible with water, ether, and chloroform: used internally as a cardiac stimulant and locally as an antiseptic and astringent. It is also used for the preservation of anatomical and biological specimens. The alcohol of the pharmacopeia contains not less than 92.3 per cent by weight or 94.9 per cent by volume, at 15.56°C., of C_2H_5OH. 2. Any one of a class of organic compounds formed from the hydrocarbons by the substitution of one or more hydroxyl groups for an equal number of hydrogen atoms; the term is extended to various substitution products which are neutral in reaction and which contain one or more of the alcohol groups. They are distinguished as *monatomic* or *monohydric, diatomic* or *dihydric, triatomic* or *trihydric*, etc., depending on the number of hydroxyl groups present. **absolute a.,** dehydrated a. **amyl a.,** a colorless, oily liquid, $C_5H_{11}OH$, with characteristic odor; miscible with alcohol, ether, and chloroform, and slightly soluble in water. **amyl a., tertiary,** amylene hydrate. **anisyl a.,** an alcohol, paramethoxybenzyl alcohol, $CH_3O.C_6H_4.CH_2.OH$, in pungent, shining prisms. **aromatic a.,** any fatty alcohol in which a hydrocarbon of the phenyl series replaces a part of the hydrogen of the alcohol radical. **batyl a.,** a compound alcohol, $C_{21}H_{42}O(OH)_2$, found in fish liver oil. **benzyl a.,** a clear, colorless oily liquid, $C_6H_5.CH_2.OH$, occurring in balsam of Peru, balsam of Tolu, and styrax; used as a local anesthetic. **butyl a.,** a clear liquid, C_4H_9OH, from the molasses of beets; four isomeric forms are known. **camphyl a.,** borneol, or Borneo camphor. **carnaubyl a.,** a constituent, $CH_3(CH_2)_{23}OH$, of carnauba wax and of wool fat. **caustic a.,** sodium ethylate. **ceryl a.,** a fatty alcohol, $CH_3(CH_2)_{24}CH_2OH$, from Chinese wool. **cetyl a.,** a fatty alcohol, $CH_3(CH_2)_{14}CH_2OH$, from spermaceti; used as an emollient. **cinnamyl a.,** styrone. **dehydrated a.,** an extremely hygroscopic, transparent, colorless, volatile liquid with characteristic odor and burning taste, containing not less than 99 per cent by volume of C_2H_5OH. **denatured a.,** alcohol which has been rendered unfit for beverage or medicinal purposes by addition of methanol or acetone, but which may still be used for industrial purposes or as a solvent. **deodorized a.,** one that contains 92.5 per cent of absolute alcohol, and is free from fusel oil (amyl alcohol) and organic impurities. **diatomic a., dihydric a.,** an alcohol containing two hydroxyl groups. **diluted a.,** a mixture of alcohol and water containing 41–42 per cent by weight, or 48.4–49.5 per cent by volume, at 15.56°C., of C_2H_5OH. **ethyl a.,** alcohol. **fatty a.,** any hydroxide of a hydrocarbon derived from the paraffin series. **glyceryl a., glycyl a.,** glycerin. **iso-amyl a.,** amyl a. **isobutyl a.,** a clear, colorless liquid, with a characteristic odor, $(CH_3)_2CHCH_2OH$; miscible with alcohol and with ether. **isopropyl a.,** a colorless liquid with slight odor resembling that of ethanol, $(CH_3)_2CHOH$; miscible with water, alcohol, and other organic liquids. **ketone a.,** an alcohol which contains the ketone (carbonyl) group. **methyl a.,** methanol. **monatomic a., monohydric a.,** an alcohol containing only one hydroxyl group. **palmityl a.,** cetyl a. **phenacyl a.,** benzoyl carbinol. **phenylethyl a.,** 2-phenylethanol, $C_8H_{10}O$; used as an antibacterial and preservative for drug solutions. **phenylic a.,** phenol. **polyglucosic a.,** an alcohol having the formula $C_{6n}H_{10n} + 2O_{5n}$. **primary a.,** an alcohol containing the monovalent carbinol group, $—CH_2OH$. ***n*-propyl a.,** a clear colorless liquid with an alcohol-like odor, $CH_3.CH_2.CH_2OH$, miscible with water and most organic solvents. **rubbing a.,** a preparation containing acetone, methyl isobutyl ketone, and ethyl alcohol. Use: rubefacient. **secondary a.,** an alcohol containing the divalent group, $=CHOH$. **stearyl a.,** a solid alcohol $[CH_3(CH_2)_{16}CH_2OH]$, prepared from stearic acid by catalytic hydrogenation; a pharmaceutical preparation of a mixture of solid alcohols, consisting chiefly of stearyl alcohol, is used as an ingredient of hydrophilic ointment and hydrophilic petrolatum. **sugar a's,** alcohols that result from the reduction of the functional group (aldehyde or ketone) of sugars. **tertiary a.,** an alcohol containing the trivalent group, $\equiv COH$. **triatomic a., trihydric a.,** an alcohol containing three hydroxyl groups. **tribromoethyl a.,** tribromoethanol. **unsaturated a.,** alcohol that is derived from unsaturated alkylenes. **wood a.,** methanol.

alcoholase (al′ko-hol-ās). A ferment which converts lactic acid into alcohol.

alcoholemia (al″ko-hol-e′me-ah) [*alcohol* + Gr. *haima* blood + *-ia*]. The presence of alcohol in the blood.

alcoholic (al″ko-hol′ik) [L. *alcoholicus*]. 1. Pertaining to or containing alcohol. 2. A person who is addicted to alcohol.

alcoholism (al′ko-hol-izm). A chronic behavioral disorder manifested by repeated drinking of alcoholic beverages in excess of the dietary and social uses of the community and to an extent that interferes with the drinker's health or his social or economic functioning.

alcoholization (al″ko-hol″i-za′shun). Treatment by application or injection of alcohol.

alcoholize (al′ko-hol-īz″). 1. To treat with alcohol. 2. To transform into alcohol.

alcoholomania (al″ko-hol″o-ma′ne-ah) [*alcohol* + Gr. *mania* mania]. Maniacal craving for intoxication by alcoholic beverages.

alcoholometer (al″ko-hol-om′e-ter) [*alcohol* + Gr. *metron* measure]. An instrument used in determining the percentage of alcohol in a solution.

alcoholophilia (al″ko-hol-o-fil′e-ah) [*alcohol* + Gr. *philein* to love]. A morbid appetite for alcoholic drinks.

alcoholuria (al″ko-hol-u′re-ah). The presence of alcohol in the urine.

alcoholysis (al″ko-hol′ĭ-sis) [*alcohol* + Gr. *lysis* dissolution]. A process analogous to hydrolysis, but in which alcohol takes the place of water.

aldactazide (al-dak′tah-zīd). Trade mark for a preparation of spironolactone with hydrochlorothiazide.

aldactone (al-dak′tōn). Trade mark for a preparation of spironolactone.

aldamine (al′dah-min). A name given by Loele to the stable oxidases.

aldebaranium (al-deb″ah-ra′ne-um). Thulium.

aldehydase (al″de-hi′dās). An enzyme from the liver which oxidizes certain aldehydes into their corresponding acids.

aldehyde (al′de-hīd) [*alcohol* + L. *de* away from + *hyd*rogen]. 1. Any one of a large class of substances derived from the primary alcohols by oxidation and containing the group $—CHO$. 2. Acetic aldehyde. **acetic a.,** a volatile liquid, $CH_3.CHO$, with a peculiar pungent odor. It is found in freshly distilled spirits, produces profound narcosis, and deleterious after-effects. It has anesthetic and antiseptic properties, and produces narcosis when inhaled. **acrylic a.,** acrolein. **amylic a.,** valeral. **anisic a.,** a volatile oil, methoxybenzaldehyde, $CH_3.O.C_6H_4.CHO$, obtainable from oil of anise and other volatile oils. **benzoic a.,** benzaldehyde. **butylic a.,** a substance, isobutylaldehyde, $(CH_3)_2CH.CHO$. **cinnamic a.,** a colorless aldehyde, $C_6H_5(CH)_2CHO$, obtained from oil of cinnamon. **cumic a.,** an aromatic volatile oil, para-iso-propyl-benzaldehyde, $C_3H_7.C_6H_4.CHO$, from several essential oils. **formic a.,** formaldehyde. **glyceric a., glycerin a.,** one of the allomeric forms of triose, it is $CH_2OH.CHOH.CHO$. **glycollic a.** See *diose.* **keto a.,** an aldehyde that contains the keto group CO and COOH. **salicylic a.,** a fragrant, colorless liquid, $C_6H_4OH.CHO$, soluble in water, from volatile oil of species of *Spiraea.* **trichloracetic a.,** chloral. **valeric a.,** a colorless liquid, isovaleric aldehyde, $(CH_3)_2CH.-CH_2CHO$, having a pungent apple-like odor.

aldin (al′din). An aldehyde base.

aldohexose (al″do-hek′sōs). A hexose which is an aldehyde derivative; any of a class of sugars which contain six carbon atoms and an aldehyde group, as glucose or mannose.

aldoketomutase (al″do-ke″to-mu′tās). Glyoxalase.

aldolase (al′do-lās). An enzyme in muscle extract which causes aldol condensations between phosphodihydroxyacetone and aldehydes to produce ketophosphoric acid.

aldopentose (al″do-pen′tōs). Any one of a class of sugars which contain five carbon atoms and an aldehyde group, as arabinose.

aldose (al′dōs). A sugar containing an aldehyde group, —CHO.

aldoside (al′do-sīd). A glycoside which on hydrolysis yields an aldose sugar.

aldosterone (al″do-stĕr′ōn). The principal electrolyte-regulating steroid (18-aldo-corticosterone) secreted by the adrenal cortex.

aldosteronism (al″do-stĕr′ōn-izm″). An abnormality of electrolyte metabolism produced by excessive secretion of aldosterone. Such secretion may be primary (*primary a.*) or occur secondarily in response to extra-adrenal disease (*secondary a.*).

aldosteronogenesis (al″do-stĕr-o-no-jen′e-sis). The production of aldosterone by the adrenal glands.

aldosteronoma (al″do-stĕr″ōn-o′mah). An aldosterone-secreting tumor of the adrenal cortex.

aldosteronopenia (al″do-stĕr-o-no-pe′ne-ah). A deficiency of aldosterone in the body.

aldosteronuria (al″do-stĕr″ōn-u′re-ah). The presence of aldosterone in the urine.

aldotetrose (al″do-tet′rōs). An aldehyde sugar containing 4 atoms of carbon.

aldoxime (al-dok′sīm). A compound formed by the union of an aldehyde with hydroxylamine.

Aldrich mixture (awl′drich) [Robert Henry *Aldrich,* American surgeon, born 1902]. See under *mixture.*

Aldrich syndrome (awl′drich) [Robert A. *Aldrich,* American pediatrician, born 1917]. See under *syndrome.*

alecithal (ah-les′ĭ-thal) [*a* neg. + Gr. *lekithos* yolk]. Having only a small amount of yolk. See under *ovum.*

Alectorobius talaje. The chinche; a tick common in Mexico and Central and South America. It is a great pest, as it bites at night and suppuration often results.

alembic (ah-lem′bik) [Arabic *al-imbīq,* the still, from Gr. *ambix* cup]. A retort with a removable cap formerly used by chemists.

alembroth (ah-lem′broth). A compound, $(NH_4Cl)_2HgCl_2 + 2H_2O$, of mercuric and ammonium chlorides. It is used as an antiseptic dressing.

alemmal (ah-lem′al) [*a* neg. + Gr. *lemma* husk]. Having no neurilemma; said of a nerve fiber.

alethia (ah-le′the-ah) [*a* neg. + Gr. *lēthē* forgetfulness]. The inability to forget.

aletocyte (ah-le′to-sīt) [Gr. *alētēs* wanderer + *kytos* hollow vessel]. A wandering cell.

aleucemia (ah″lu-se′me-ah). Aleukemia.

aleucia (ah-lu′se-ah). Aleukia.

aleukemia (ah-lu-ke′me-ah) [*a* neg. + Gr. *leukos* white + *haima* blood + *-ia*]. Absence or deficiency of leukocytes in the blood; aleukemic leukemia.

aleukemic (ah″lu-ke′mik). 1. Marked by aleukemia. 2. Not marked by leukemia.

aleukemoid (ah″lu-ke′moid). Resembling aleukemia.

aleukia (ah-lu′ke-ah) [*a* neg. + Gr. *leukos* white + *-ia*]. 1. Absence of leukocytes from the blood. Called *aleukemic myelosis* and *aleukemic lymphadenosis.* 2. Absence of blood platelets. **congenital a.,** absence of leukocytes from the blood in the newborn. **a. hemorrha′gica,** an accessory or auxiliary term which actually refers to the condition of primary refractory anemia, the features of which are persistent anemia, granulocytopenia, and thrombocytopenia. Called also *aregenerative anemia, hypoplastic anemia,* and *panmyelophthisis.*

aleukocytic (ah-lu″ko-sit′ik). Showing no leukocytes.

aleukocytosis (ah-lu″ko-si-to′sis) [*a* neg. + *leukocyte* + *-osis*]. Deficiency in the proportion of white cells in the blood.

Aleurisma (al″u-riz′mah). A genus of fungi several species of which have been isolated from superficial skin lesions in man.

Aleuro′bius fari′nae. Tyroglyphus farinae.

aleurometer (al″u-rom′e-ter) [Gr. *aleuron* flour + *metron* measure]. An instrument for determining the value of flour for bread-making purposes.

aleuronat (ah-lu′ro-nat″). A proprietary wheat flour from which most of the starch has been removed: used by diabetics.

aleuronoid (ah-lu′ro-noid″). Resembling flour.

aleuroscope (ah-lu′ro-skōp″). Aleurometer.

Alexander (al″ek-san′der) **of Tralles** (c. 525 A.D.). A Byzantine Greek physician and compiler who practiced latterly in Rome. His writings were mainly on pathology and the treatment of internal diseases, his descriptions of parasites being outstanding.

Alexander's operation (al″ek-zan′derz). 1. [Samuel *Alexander,* American surgeon, 1859–1910.] See under *operation* (def. 3). 2. [William *Alexander,* Liverpool surgeon, 1844–1919.] See under *operation* (defs. 1 and 2).

Alexander-Adams operation [William *Alexander;* James A. *Adams,* gynecologist in Glasgow, 1857–1930]. See *Alexander's operation* (def. 1).

alexanderism (al″ek-zan′der-izm). The insanity of conquest, or an insane belief that one is a great conqueror.

alexeteric (ah-lek″se-ter′ik) [Gr. *alexētēr* defender]. Effective against infection or poison.

alexia (ah-lek′se-ah) [*a* neg. + Gr. *lexis* word + *-ia*]. Visual aphasia or word blindness; inability to read due to a central lesion. **cortical a.,** a form of sensory aphasia due to lesions of the left gyrus angularis. **motor a.,** alexia in which the patient understands what he sees written or printed, but cannot read it aloud. **musical a.,** loss of the ability to read music; music blindness. **optical a.,** alexia in which the patient has lost the power to comprehend the significance of what he sees written or printed. Called also *sensory aphasia* and *visual aphasia.* **subcortical a.,** a form due to interruption of the connection between the optic center and the gyrus angularis.

alexic (ah-lek′sik). 1. Having the properties of an alexin. 2. Pertaining to alexia.

alexin (ah-lek′sin) [Gr. *alexein* to ward off]. A nonspecific thermolabile ferment-like substance which in the presence of specific sensitizer exerts a lytic action on bacteria and other cells. It is not increased by immunization and is present in plasma and serum. See *complement* and *cytase,* 1st def. **leukocytic a.** See *leukin,* 1st def.

alexinic (al″ek-sin′ik). Pertaining to, or having the properties of, an alexin.

alexipharmac (ah-lek″se-far′mak) [Gr. *alexein* to ward off + *pharmakon* poison]. 1. Warding off the ill effects of a poison. 2. An antidote or remedy for poisoning.

alexipyretic (ah-lek″sĭ-pi-ret′ik) [Gr. *alexein* to ward off + *pyretos* fever]. 1. Dispelling or preventing fever. 2. An agent which dispels or prevents fever.

alexocyte (ah-lek′so-sīt″) [Gr. *alexein* to ward off + *kytos* hollow vessel]. A cell of the animal organism secreting alexins. The term was formerly applied to eosinophil cells.

alexofixagen (ah-lek″so-fik′sah-jen). An antigen which induces the production of complement-fixing antibodies.

alexofixagin (ah-lek″so-fik′sah-jin). The complement-fixing antibody produced by injecting alexofixagen.

alexofixin (ah-lek″so-fik′sin). Alexofixagin.

aleydigism (ah-li′dig-izm″). Absence of androgen secretion of the interstitial cells of Leydig.

alflorone (al′flo-rōn). Trade mark for preparations of fludrocortisone.

A.L.G. Abbreviation for *axiolinguogingival.*

algae (al′je) [L., pl., "seaweeds"]. A group of cryptogamous plants, in which the body is unicellular or consists of a thallus; it includes the seaweed and many unicellular fresh-water plants.

algal (al′gal). Of, pertaining to, or caused by algae.

alganesthesia (al-gan″es-the′ze-ah) [Gr. *algos* pain + *anesthesia*]. Analgesia.

alge-. See *algesi-.*

algedonic (al″je-don′ik) [*alge-* + Gr. *hēdonē* pleasure]. Pertaining to both pleasure and pain.

algefacient (al″je-fa′shent) [L. *algere* to be cold + *faciens* making]. Cooling; refrigerant.

algeoscopy (al″je-os′ko-pe). 1. [Gr. *algos* pain + *skopein* to view]. Physical examination by pressure, to ascertain whether such pressure produces pain. 2. [L. *algor* cold + Gr. *skopein* to view]. Cryoscopy.

algesi-, alge-, algo- (al-je′ze, al′je, al′go) [Gr. *algos* pain]. Combining form denoting relationship to pain.

algesia (al-je′ze-ah). Sensitiveness to pain; hyperesthesia.

algesic (al-je′sik). Painful.

algesichronometer (al-je″ze-kro-nom′e-ter) [*algesi-* + Gr. *chronos* time + *metron* measure]. An instrument for recording the time required to produce a painful impression.

algesimeter (al″je-sim′e-ter) [*algesi-* + Gr. *metron* measure]. An instrument used in measuring the sensitiveness to pain as produced by pricking with a sharp point. **Björnström's a.,** an apparatus for determining the sensitiveness of the skin. **Boas' a.,** an instrument for determining the sensitiveness over the epigastrium.

algesimetry (al″je-sim′e-tre). The measurement of sensitiveness to pain.

algesiogenic (al-je″ze-o-jen′ik) [*algesi-* + Gr. *gennan* to produce]. Producing pain.

algesiometer (al-je″ze-om′e-ter). Algesimeter.

algesthesia (al″jes-the′ze-ah). Pain sensibility; algesthesis.

algesthesis (al″jes-the′sis) [*algesi-* + Gr. *aisthēsis* perception]. The perception of pain; any painful sensation.

algetic (al-jet′ik). Painful.

-algia (al′je-ah) [Gr. *algos* pain + *-ia* condition]. A word termination indicating a painful condition.

algicide (al′jĭ-sīd) [*algae* + L. *caedere* to kill]. A substance which is destructive to algae.

algid (al′jid) [L. *algidus*]. Chilly or cold.

algin (al′jin). See *alginic acid,* under *acid.*

alginate (al′jĭ-nāt). A salt of alginic acid, which is extracted from marine kelp. Calcium, sodium, and ammonium alginates have been used as foam, clot, or gauze for absorbable surgical dressings. Soluble alginates, such as sodium, potassium, and magnesium alginates, form a viscous sol which can be changed into a gel by a chemical reaction with compounds such as calcium sulfate, a property which makes them useful as materials for taking dental impressions.

Alginobacter (al″jĭ-no-bak′ter). A genus of microorganisms of the tribe Escherichieae, family Enterobacteriaceae, order Eubacteriales, made up of short, motile rods, found in the soil. The type species is *A. acidofa′ciens.*

Alginomonas (al″jĭ-no-mo′nas). A genus of microorganisms of the family Pseudomonadaceae, suborder Pseudomonadineae, order Pseudomonadales, occurring as motile coccoid rods, found on algae and in sea water and soil. It includes five species, *A. algi′nica, A. algino′vora, A. fuci′cola, A. nonfermen′tans, A. terrestralgi′nica.*

alginuresis (al″jin-u-re′sis) [Gr. *algos* pain + *ourēsis* urination]. Painful urination.

algioglandular (al″je-o-glan′du-lar). Pertaining to glandular action resulting from painful stimulation.

algiometabolic (al″je-o-met″ah-bol′ik). Pertaining to metabolic changes resulting from painful stimulation.

algiomotor (al″je-o-mo′tor). Producing painful movements, such as spasm or dysperistalsis.

algiomuscular (al″je-o-mus′ku-lar). Causing painful muscular movements.

algiovascular (al″je-o-vas′ku-lar). Pertaining to vascular action resulting from painful stimulation.

algo-. See *algesi-.*

algogenesia (al″go-jĕ-ne′ze-ah) [*algo-* + Gr. *gennan* to produce]. The production of pain.

algogenesis (al″go-jen′e-sis). Algogenesia.

algogenic (al-go-jen′ik). 1. [*algo-* + Gr. *gennan* to produce.] Causing pain. 2. [L. *algor* cold + Gr. *gennan* to produce.] Producing cold.

algolagnia (al″go-lag′ne-ah) [*algo-* + Gr. *lagneia* lust]. Abnormal and distorted activity of sexual impulse toward persons of opposite sex with a desire for experiencing or causing pain. **active a.,** sadism. **passive a.,** masochism.

algologist (al-gol′o-jist). A specialist in algology.

algology (al-gol′o-je). The scientific study of algae.

algomenorrhea (al″go-men-o-re′ah) [*algo-* + *menorrhea*]. Painful menstruation.

algometer (al-gom′e-ter) [*algo-* + Gr. *metron* measure]. An instrument for testing sensitivity to painful stimuli. **pressure a.,** an instrument for measuring sensitivity to pressure.

algometry (al-gom′ĕ-tre). The measurement of sensitivity to painful stimuli, as with an algometer.

algophilia (al″go-fil′e-ah). Algophily.

algophily (al-gof′ĭ-le) [*algo-* + Gr. *philein* to love]. Sexual perversion marked by a desire for experiencing pain.

algophobia (al″go-fo′be-ah) [*algo-* + *phobia*]. Morbid dread of experiencing or of witnessing pain.

algopsychalia (al″go-si-ka′le-ah) [*algo-* + Gr. *psychē* soul]. A condition of melancholia with perverted imaginary perceptions of sounds and sights which cause dread, despair, and inclination to suicide. Called also *psychoalgalia.*

algor (al′gor) [L.]. A chill or rigor; coldness. **a. mor′tis** ["chill of death"], the gradual decrease of temperature of the body after death.

algoscopy (al-gos′ko-pe) [L. *algor* cold + Gr. *skopein* to view]. Cryoscopy.

algosis (al-go′sis). Presence of algae or fungi in a part of the body.

algospasm (al′go-spazm) [*algo-* + *spasm*]. Painful spasm or cramp.

algovascular (al″go-vas′ku-lar). Algiovascular.

ALH. Abbreviation for the combined sex hormone of the anterior lobe of the hypophysis.

Ali Abbas (ah′le ab′bas) (10th century A.D.). A celebrated Persian physician who wrote *Al-Maliki* (the "Royal Book"), a comprehensive treatise on medicine.

Ali ben Iza (ah′le ben i′zah) (11th century A.D.). A noted Arabic ophthalmologist, who wrote *Tadhkirat* (or *risala*) *al-kah-halin* (the "Book of Memoranda for Eye-doctors"), the earliest Arabic work on ophthalmology which is completely extant.

Alibert's disease, keloid (al-e-berz′) [Jean Louis *Alibert*, French dermatologist, 1768–1837]. See *mycosis fungoides*, and under *keloid*.

alible (al′ĭ-bl) [L. *alibilis*]. Nutritive; assimilable as a food.

alices (al′ĭ-sēz) [pl.]. The red spots that appear before the pustules in smallpox.

alicyclic (al″ĭ-sik′lik). Having the properties of both aliphatic and cyclic substances.

alidase (al′ĭ-dās). Trade mark for a preparation of hyaluronidase for injection.

alienation (āl″yen-a′shun) [L. *alienatio*]. Mental derangement.

alienia (ah″li-e′ne-ah) [*a* neg. + L. *lien* spleen]. Absence of the spleen.

alienism (āl′yen-izm) [L. *alienus* alien]. 1. Mental disorder. 2. The study or treatment of mental disorders.

alienist (āl′yen-ist). An expert in the diagnosis and treatment of mental disorders; a psychiatrist.

aliform (al′ĭ-form) [L. *ala* wing + *forma* shape]. Shaped like a wing.

alignment (ah-līn′ment) [Fr. *aligner* to put in a straight line]. The act of arranging in a line; the state of being arranged in a line. In dentistry, the bringing of natural teeth into normal articulation, or the arranging of artificial teeth in normal articulation.

alima (al′e-mah). Alimentary substances.

aliment (al′e-ment) [L. *alimentum*]. Food, or nutritive material.

alimentary (al″e-men′tar-e). Pertaining to or caused by food, or nutritive material.

alimentation (al″e-men-ta′shun). The act of giving or receiving nutriment. **artificial a.,** the giving of food or nourishment to persons who cannot take it in the usual way. **forced a.** 1. The feeding of a person against his will. 2. The giving of more food to a person than his appetite calls for. **rectal a.,** the administration of concentrated nourishment by injection into the rectum.

alimentology (al″e-men-tol′o-je). The science of nutrition.

alimentotherapy (al″e-men″to-ther′ah-pe) [*aliment* + Gr. *therapeia* treatment]. Dietetic treatment; treatment by systematic feeding.

alinasal (al″e-na′sal). Pertaining to the ala nasi.

alinement (ah-līn′ment). Alignment.

alinjection (al″in-jek′shun). Repeated injection of alcohol for preserving anatomic specimens.

aliphatic (al″e-fat′ik) [Gr. *aleiphar*, *aleiphatos* oil]. Pertaining to an oil; a term applied to the "open-chain" or fatty series of hydrocarbons.

alipogenetic (ah-li″po-jĕ-net′ik). Not lipogenetic; not forming fat.

alipoidic (ah″lip-oi′dik). Free from lipoids.

alipotropic (ah″lip-o-trop′ik). Having no influence on the metabolism of fat.

aliquot (al′e-kwot). The part of a number which will divide it without a remainder, e.g., 2 is an aliquot of 6. By extension, used to indicate any portion that bears a known quantitative relationship to a whole, or to other portions of the same whole.

alismin (ah-lis′min). An extractive from *Alisma plantago*, or water plantain.

alisphenoid (al-e-sfe′noid) [*ala* + *sphenoid*]. 1. Pertaining to the greater wing of the sphenoid. 2. A cartilage in the fetus on each side of the basisphenoid. It afterward develops into the greater part of the great wing of the sphenoid.

alizarin (ah-liz′ah-rin) [Arabic *ala sara* extract]. A red, crystalline dye, 1,2-dihydroxyanthraquinone, $C_6H_4(CO)_2C_6H_2(OH)_2$, obtained from coal tar and from madder. Its compounds are used as indicators. **a. monosulfonate,** an indicator with a pH range of 3.7 to 4.2. **a. No. 6,** purpurin. **a. red.** See under *red*. **a. yellow, a. yellow g.** See under *yellow*.

alizarinopurpurin (al″ĭ-zar″ĭ-no-pur′pu-rin). Purpurin.

alkalemia (al″kah-le′me-ah) [*alkali* + Gr. *haima* blood + *-ia*]. Increased pH of the blood, irrespective of changes in the blood bicarbonate.

alkalescence (al″kah-les′ens). Slight or incipient alkalinity.

alkalescent (al″kah-les′ent). Having a tendency to alkalinity.

alkali (al′kah-li) [Arabic *al-qalīy* potash]. Any one of a class of compounds which form soluble soaps with fatty acids, turn red litmus blue, and form soluble carbonates. Essentially the hydroxides of cesium, lithium, potassium, rubidium, and sodium, they include also the carbonates of these metals and of ammonia. **caustic a.,** any solid hydroxide of a fixed alkali. **fixed a.,** any of the alkalis except ammonium. **volatile a.,** ammonia, NH_3; also ammonium hydroxide.

alkalify (al-kal′e-fi). To make alkaline.

Alkaligenes (al″kah-lij′e-nēz). Alcaligenes.

alkaligenous (al″kah-lij′e-nus). Yielding an alkali.

alkalimeter (al″kah-lim′e-ter) [*alkali* + *meter*]. An instrument for measuring the alkali contained in any mixture.

alkalimetry (al″kah-lim′e-tre). The measurement of the alkalis present in any substance. **Engel's a.,** a method of determining the alkalinity of the blood by titrating a diluted specimen with normal tartaric acid solution until it reddens litmus paper. The amount of tartaric solution necessary to produce the result indicates the degree of alkalinity of the blood.

alkaline (al′kah-līn) [L. *alkalinus*]. Having the reactions of an alkali.

alkalinity (al″kah-lin′ĭ-te). The fact or quality of being alkaline.

alkalinization (al″kah-lin″ĭ-za′shun). Alkalization.

alkalinize (al′kah-lin-īz″). Alkalize.

alkalinuria (al″kah-lin-u′re-ah) [*alkaline* + *urine*]. An alkaline condition of the urine.

alkalion (al-kal′e-on). Hydroxyl ion.

alkalipenia (al″kah-li-pe′ne-ah) [*alkali* + Gr. *penia* poverty]. A condition in which the alkali reserve of the body is below normal.

alkalitherapy (al″kah-li-ther′ah-pe). Treatment by alkalis; the administration of large amounts of alkali in the treatment of peptic ulcer and hyperchlorhydria.

alkalization (al″kah-li-za′shun). The act of making alkaline.

alkalize (al′kah-līz). To render alkaline.

alkalizer (al″kah-līz′er). An agent that causes alkalization.

alkalogenic (al″kah-lo-jen′ik). Producing alkalinity, especially alkalinity of the urine.

alkaloid (al′kah-loid″) [*alkali* + Gr. *eidos* form]. One of a large group of organic, basic substances found in plants. They are usually bitter in taste and physiologically active. Examples are: atropine, caffeine, coniine, morphine, nicotine, quinine, strychnine. The term is also applied to synthetic substances (*synthetic a's*) which have structures similar to plant alkaloids, such as procaine. **animal a.,** a ptomaine or leukomaine. **artificial a.,** an alkaloid that is made artificially by chemical processes. **cadaveric a., putrefactive a.,** a ptomaine.

alkalometry (al″kah-lom′e-tre) [*alkaloid* + Gr. *metron* measure]. The dosimetric administration of alkaloids.

alkalosis (al″kah-lo′sis). A pathologic condition resulting from accumulation of base or loss of acid in the body, and characterized by decrease in hydrogen ion concentration (increase in pH). **compensated a.,** a condition in which compensatory mechanisms have returned the pH toward normal. See *metabolic a., compensated,* and *respiratory a., compensated.* **hypokalemic a.,** a variety of metabolic alkalosis resulting from losses of potassium, and associated with a low serum potassium level. **metabolic a.,** a disturbance in which the acid-base status of the body shifts toward the alkaline side because of changes in the fixed (nonvolatile) acids and bases. **metabolic a., compensated,** a state of alkalosis in which the pH of the blood has been returned toward normal by retention of carbonic acid through pulmonary mechanisms. **respiratory a.,** a state due to excess loss of carbon dioxide from the body. **respiratory a., compensated,** a respiratory alkalosis in which the pH of the blood has been returned toward normal through retention of acid or excretion of base by renal mechanisms.

alkalotherapy (al″kah-lo-ther′ah-pe). Alkalitherapy.

alkalotic (al″kah-lot′ik). Pertaining to, or characterized by, alkalosis.

alkaluria (al″kah-lu′re-ah). The presence of an alkali in the urine.

alkamine (al′kah-min). An alcohol which contains an amido group.

alkane (al′kān). A paraffin hydrocarbon.

alkapton (al-kap′tōn) [*alk*ali + Gr. *haptō* to fasten or bind to]. See *alkapton bodies,* under *body.*

alkaptone (al-kap′tōn). See *alkapton bodies.*

alkaptonuria (al″kap-to-nu′re-ah) [*alkaptone* + Gr. *ouron* urine + *-ia*]. Excretion in the urine of alkapton bodies, which cause the urine to turn dark on standing, or on addition of alkali. It may occur without other symptoms, or it may in long-standing cases be associated with ochronosis and arthritic symptoms. **spontaneous a.,** a hereditary, familial, and congenital anomaly of the metabolism of tyrosine and alanine, with excretion in the urine of homogentisic acid.

alkaptonuric (al-kap″to-nu′rik). Pertaining to, characterized by, or causing alkaptonuria. By extension, sometimes used as a noun to designate an individual with alkaptonuria.

alkatriene (al″kah-tri′ēn). An unsaturated aliphatic hydrocarbon containing three double bonds.

alkavervir (al″kah-ver′vir). A mixture of alkaloids obtained from selective extraction of *Veratrum viride.* Use: to lower blood pressure.

alkene (al′kēn). An unsaturated aliphatic hydrocarbon containing one double bond.

alkyl (al′kil). The radical which results when an aliphatic hydrocarbon loses one hydrogen atom.

alkylate (al′kĭ-lāt). To treat with an alkylating agent.

alkylogen (al-kil′o-jen). An alkyl ester of any one of the halogen acids, e.g., ethyl chloride.

allachesthesia (al″ah-kes-the′ze-ah) [Gr. *allachē* elsewhere + *aisthēsis* perception + *-ia*]. The sensation of touch experienced at a point remote from the point touched. **optical a.,** the illusory projection of a real object from one quadrant of the visual field into the diagonally opposite quadrant.

allantiasis (al″an-ti′ah-sis) [*allanto-* + *-iasis*]. Sausage poisoning; poisoning from sausages containing the toxins of *Clostridium botulinum.* Cf. *botulism.*

allanto- (ah-lan′to) [Gr. *allas, allantos* sausage]. Combining form denoting relationship to a sausage, or to the allantois.

allantochorion (ah-lan″to-ko′re-on). A compound membrane formed by fusion of the allantois and chorion.

allantogenesis (al″an-to-jen′e-sis). The formation and development of the allantois.

allantoic (al″an-to′ik). Pertaining to the allantois.

allantoicase (al″an-to′i-kās). A substance necessary in the conversion by allantoinase of allantoin into glyoxylic acid.

allantoid (ah-lan′toid) [*allanto-* + Gr. *eidos* form]. 1. Resembling the allantois. 2. Sausage shaped.

allantoidean (al″an-toi′de-an). Any animal which in the embryo possesses an allantois.

allantoido-angiopagus (al″an-toi″do-an″je-op′ah-gus). Omphalo-angiopagus.

allantoin (ah-lan′to-in). A crystallizable substance, the diureide of glyoxylic acid, NHCONH.CO.CH.NH.CO.NH_2, from allantoic fluid, fetal urine, and many plants. Allantoin may also be formed by the oxidation of uric acid. It has been employed to encourage epithelial formation in wounds and ulcers and in osteomyelitis. It is the active substance in maggot treatment, being secreted by the maggots.

allantoinase (al″an-to′ĭ-nās). An enzyme which in connection with allantoicase catalyzes the change of allantoin into glyoxylic acid.

allantoinuria (ah-lan″to-in-u′re-ah). The presence of allantoin in the urine.

allantois (ah-lan′to-is) [*allanto-* + Gr. *eidos* form]. A tubular diverticulum of the posterior part of the hind-gut of the embryo. It passes into the body stalk through which it is accompanied by the allantoic (umbilical) blood vessels, thus taking part in the formation of the umbilical cord, and later, fusing with the chorion, it helps to form the placenta.

allantotoxicon (ah-lan″to-tok′se-kon) [*allanto-* + Gr. *toxikon* poison]. A hypothetical poison formerly supposed to cause sausage poisoning.

allassotherapy (ah-las″o-ther′ah-pe) [Gr. *allassein* to alter + *therapy*]. Treatment based on producing a change in the general biologic conditions of the organism.

allaxis (ah-lak′sis) [Gr. "exchange"]. Transformation.

allel (ah-lēl′). Allele.

allele (ah-lēl′) [Gr. *allēlōn* of one another]. 1. One of two or more contrasting genes, situated at the same locus in homologous chromosomes, which determine alternative characters in inheritance (short or tall, smooth or rough, etc.). See *Mendel's law,* under *law.* 2. One of two or more contrasting characters transmitted by alternative genes.

allelic (ah-le′lik). Pertaining to alleles; produced by alternative genes.

allelism (al′e-lizm). The existence of alleles, or their relationship to one another.

allelo- (ah-le′lo) [Gr. *allēlōn* to one another]. Combining form denoting relationship to another.

allelocatalysis (ah-le″lo-kah-tal′ĭ-sis) [*allelo-* + *catalysis*]. Mutual stimulation of cells to growth; stimulation of growth in a bacterial culture by the addition to it of other cells of the same type.

allelocatalytic (ah-le″lo-kat-ah-lit′ik). Catalyzing each other; causing or marked by allelocatalysis.

allelomorph (ah-le′lo-morf) [*allelo-* + Gr. *morphē* form]. Allele.

allelomorphic (ah-le″lo-mor′fik). Allelic.

allelomorphism (ah-le″lo-mor′fizm). Allelism.

allelotaxis (ah-le″lo-tak′sis) [*allelo-* + Gr. *taxis*

arrangement]. The development of an organ from several embryonic structures.

allelotaxy (ah-le′lo-tak″se). Allelotaxis.

Allen's cement [John *Allen*, New York dentist, 1810–1892]. See under *cement*.

Allen's fossa [Harrison *Allen*, Philadelphia anatomist, 1841–1897]. See under *fossa*.

Allen's paradoxic law, treatment [Frederick M. *Allen*, American physician, 1879–1964]. See under *law* and *treatment*.

Allen's root pliers [Albert Bromley *Allen*, American dentist, 1862–1943]. See under *pliers*.

Allen's test [Charles Warren *Allen*, American physician, 1854–1906]. See *Allen's test* (4th def.), under *tests*.

Allen-Doisy test, unit (al′en doi′se) [Edgar V. *Allen*, American anatomist, 1892–1943; Edward A. *Doisy*, American biochemist, born 1893]. See under *test*, and *mouse unit* and *rat unit*, under *unit*.

allenthesis (ah-len′the-sis). Introduction into the body of a foreign substance.

allergen (al′er-jen) [*allergy* + Gr. *gennan* to produce]. 1. A substance which is capable of inducing allergy or specific susceptibility. Such a substance may be a protein or a nonprotein. Called also *sensitinogen* and *sensibilisinogen*. 2. The purified protein or proteins of some food, bacterium or pollen. For example, the proteins of milk, egg, or wheat. They are used to test whether a patient is hypersensitive to certain substances. **bacterial a.,** the essential protein extracted from the bacterial cell. **pollen a.** See *pollen antigen*, under *antigen*.

allergenic (al″er-jen′ik). Acting as an allergen; inducing allergy.

allergia (ah-ler′je-ah). Allergy.

allergic (ah-ler′jik). Pertaining to, caused by, affected with, or of the nature of, allergy.

allergid (al′er-jid). A nodular allergic skin reaction.

allergie (al′er-je). Allergy.

allergin (al′er-jin). 1. The antibody responsible for anaphylaxis. 2. A sterilized standardized solution of tuberculin used in a 1 to 5 per cent solution in the ophthalmoreaction and in a 25 per cent solution in the cutaneous reaction.

allergist (al′er-jist). A physician who specializes in the diagnosis and treatment of allergic conditions.

allergization (al″er-jĭ-za′shun). Active sensitization or the introduction of allergens into the body.

allergodermia (al″er-go-der′me-ah) [*allergy* + Gr. *derma* skin + *-ia*]. An allergic skin disease.

allergologist (al″ler-gol′o-jist). One who specializes in allergology.

allergology (al″ler-gol′o-je). The science dealing with the problems of hypersensitivity.

allergometry (al″er-gom′e-tre). Determination of the allergic condition of the body in relation to certain allergens.

allergosis (al″er-go′sis), pl. *allergo′ses*. Any allergic disease.

allergy (al′er-je) [Gr. *allos* other + *ergon* work]. A hypersensitive state acquired through exposure to a particular allergen, re-exposure bringing to light an altered capacity to react. Cf. *anaphylaxis* and *hypersensitiveness*. **bacterial a.,** specific hypersensitiveness to a particular bacterial antigen. It is dependent on previous infection with the specific organism, and shows no circulating antibodies. **bronchial a.,** asthma. **cold a.,** a condition manifested by local and systemic reactions, mediated by histamine, which is released from mast cells and basophils as a result of exposure to cold. **contact a.,** hypersensitiveness marked by an eczematous reaction to contact between the epidermis and the allergen. **delayed a.,** an allergic response which appears after hours or days. **drug a.,** an allergic manifestation occurring as the result of unusual sensitivity to a drug. **endocrine a.,** allergy to an endogenous hormone. **hereditary a.,** allergy existing as a result of heredity, as contrasted with *induced a.* **immediate a.,** an allergic response which appears within a short time, i.e., from a few minutes up to an hour. **induced a.,** allergy resulting from the injection of an antigen, contact with an antigen or infection with a bacterium. **latent a.,** allergy which is not manifested by symptoms but which may be detected by tests. **mental a.,** a condition resembling allergy but in which the allergen is a mental or emotional state. **normal a.,** induced a. **pathologic a.,** hereditary a. **physical a.,** a condition in which the patient is sensitive to the effects of physical agents, such as heat, cold, light, etc. **physiologic a.,** induced a. **polyvalent a.** See *pathergia*, 2nd def. **spontaneous a.,** hereditary a.

Allescheria (al″es-ke′re-ah). A genus of moldlike fungi. **A. boy′dii** has been found in human lesions.

allesthesia (al″es-the′ze-ah) [Gr. *allos* other + *aisthēsis* perception + *-ia*]. Allachesthesia.

alliaceous (al″e-a′shus). Pertaining to or resembling garlic.

alligation (al″ĭ-ga′shun). The process of finding the value of a mixture of known quantities of ingredients, each of known value.

Allingham's operation [Herbert William *Allingham*, English surgeon, 1862–1904]. See under *operation*, def. 1.

Allingham's operation, ulcer [William *Allingham*, English surgeon, 1830–1908]. See under *operation*, def. 2, and under *ulcer*.

Allis's inhaler, sign (al′is-iz) [Oscar H. *Allis*, Philadelphia surgeon, 1833–1921]. See under *inhaler* and *sign*.

alliteration (ah-lit″er-a′shun) [L. *ad* to + *litera* letter]. A dysphrasia in which the patient uses words containing the same consonant sounds.

Allium (al′e-um) [L. "garlic"]. 1. A genus of liliaceous plants, including the garlic, onion, etc. 2. The bulb of *A. sati′vum*, or garlic, a digestive stimulant and pectoral.

allo- (al′o) [Gr. *allos* other]. A combining form denoting a condition differing from the normal, or reversal, or referring to another.

allobarbital (al″o-bar′bĭ-tal). A slightly bitter, white crystalline powder, $(C_3H_5)_2C(CO.NH)_2CO$: hypnotic and sedative.

allobiosis (al″o-bi-o′sis) [*allo-* + Gr. *bios* life]. The condition of altered reactivity which an organism manifests under changed environmental or physiologic conditions.

Alloboph′ora agric′ola. A parasitic worm which may enter the human intestine by the medium of water or green vegetables.

allocentric (al″o-sen′trik). Having all one's ideas centered on others, rather than on one's self. Cf. *egocentric*.

allocheiria (al″o-ki′re-ah). Allochiria.

allochesthesia (al″o-kes-the′ze-ah). Allachesthesia.

allochezia (al″o-ke′ze-ah) [*allo-* + Gr. *chezein* to defecate]. The discharge of nonfecal matter by the anus, or the discharge of fecal matter by an abnormal passage.

allochiral (al″o-ki′ral) [*allo-* + Gr. *cheir* hand]. Pertaining to allochiria.

allochiria (al″o-ki′re-ah) [*allo-* + Gr. *cheir* hand + *-ia*]. A condition, chiefly in tabes, during which, if one extremity is pricked, the sensation is referred to the opposite side (Obersteiner).

allocholesterol (al″o-ko-les′ter-ol). An isomer of cholesterol.

allochroic (al″o-kro′ik). Changeable in color.

allochroism (al″o-kro′izm) [*allo-* + Gr. *chroa* color + *-ism*]. Change or variation in color.

allochromasia (al″o-kro-ma′se-ah). Change of color of the hair or skin.

allocinesia (al″o-si-ne′ze-ah) [*allo-* + Gr. *kinēsis* motion + *-ia*]. A condition in which the patient performs a movement on the side of the body opposite to that directed.

allocolloid (al″o-kol′oid) [*allo-* + *colloid*]. A colloid in which a single element in its allotropic forms makes up the colloid system.

allocortex (al″o-kor′teks) [*allo-* + *cortex*]. That portion of the cerebral cortex which is not laminated and which represents the more primitive areas of the cortex such as the olfactory cortex. Cf. *isocortex*.

allocrine (al′o-krin) [*allo-* + Gr. *krīnein* to separate]. Heterocrine.

allodesmism (al″o-des′mizm) [*allo-* + Gr. *desmos* bond]. Allomerism based on a difference in the bonds uniting the atoms.

allodiploid (al″o-dip′loid) [*allo-* + *diploid*]. 1. Having two sets of chromosomes derived from different parental species. 2. An individual or cell having two sets of chromosomes derived from different parental species.

allodiploidy (al″o-dip′loi-de). The state of having two sets of chromosomes derived from different parental species.

allodromy (al-lod′ro-me) [*allo-* + Gr. *dromos* running]. Disturbed rhythm of the heart.

alloeosis (al″e-o′sis). Change in the character of a disease.

allo-eroticism (al″o-e-rot′i-sizm). Allo-erotism.

allo-erotism (al″o-er′o-tizm) [*allo-* + *erotism*]. Sexuality directed to another, in contrast to autoerotism.

alloesthesia (al″o-es-the′ze-ah). Allachesthesia.

allogamy (al-log′ah-me) [*allo-* + Gr. *gamos* marriage]. Cross fertilization.

allogotrophia (al″o-go-tro′fe-ah). Nourishment of one part of the body at the expense of another part.

Allogromia (al″o-gro′me-ah). A genus of parasites found in protozoan animals, such as *Amoeba proteus*.

allo-isomerism (al″o-i-som′er-izm). Isomerism which does not appear in the formula.

allokeratoplasty (al″o-ker′ah-to-plas″te) [*allo-* + *keratoplasty*]. Repair of the cornea by the use of foreign material.

allokinesis (al″o-ki-ne′sis). Movement that is not performed voluntarily but is produced passively or occurs reflexly.

allokinetic (al″o-ki-net′ik) [*allo-* + Gr. *kinēsis* movement]. Pertaining to or characterized by allokinesis.

allolactose (al″o-lak′tōs). A disaccharide, isomeric with lactose, occurring in milk.

allolalia (al″o-la′le-ah) [*allo-* + Gr. *lalein* to speak + *-ia*]. Any defect of speech of central origin.

allomerism (al-lom′er-izm) [*allo-* + Gr. *meros* part]. Change of chemical constitution without change in the crystalline form.

allometron (al″o-met′ron) [*allo-* + Gr. *metron* measure]. An evolutionary change in bodily form or proportion as expressed in measurements and indices.

allometropia (al″o-mĕ-tro′pe-ah) [*allo-* + Gr. *metron* measure + *ōps* eye + *-ia*]. The refraction of the eye in indirect, as opposed to direct, vision (Matthiessen).

allomorphism (al″o-mor′fizm) [*allo-* + Gr. *morphē* form]. Change of crystalline form without change in chemical constitution.

allongement (al-onzh-mon′) [Fr.]. Elongation; especially any procedure for elongating a uterine tumor after it has been severed from its connections, so as to admit of its extraction. This is usually done by making a spiral incision into its substance while it is being pulled down.

allonomous (al-lon′o-mus) [*allo-* + Gr. *nomos* law]. Regulated by stimuli from the outside.

allopath (al′o-path). A term sometimes applied to a practitioner of allopathy.

allopathic (al″o-path′ik). Pertaining to, or characteristic of, allopathy.

allopathist (al-lop′ah-thist). Allopath.

allopathy (al-lop′ah-the) [*allo-* + Gr. *pathos* disease]. A term frequently applied to the method of treatment practiced by recipients of the degree of doctor of medicine but specifically excluding homeopathy.

allophanamide (al-o-fan-am′id). Biuret.

allophasis (al-lof′ah-sis) [*allo-* + Gr. *phasis* speech]. Incoherent speech; delirium.

allophore (al′o-fōr). Erythrophore.

allophthalmia (al″of-thal′me-ah). Heterophthalmia.

alloplasia (al″o-pla′ze-ah) [*allo-* + Gr. *plasis* formation + *-ia*]. Heteroplasia.

alloplasmatic (al″o-plaz-mat′ik) [*allo-* + Gr. *plassein* to form]. Formed by differentiation from the protoplasm.

alloplast (al′o-plast). An idorgan consisting of more than one kind of tissue.

alloplastic (al″o-plas′tik) [*allo-* + Gr. *plassein* to form]. Pertaining to or characterized by alloplasty.

alloplasty (al′o-plas-te) [*allo-* + Gr. *plassein* to form]. 1. Plastic surgery in which use is made of material not from the human body, such as bone, ivory or silver. Cf. *autoplasty*, 1st def., and *heteroplasty*. 2. The developmental direction of the libido away from self to other people or objects.

alloploid (al′o-ploid) [*allo-* + *-ploid*]. 1. Having any number (two or many) of chromosome sets derived from different ancestral species. 2. An individual or cell having any number (two or many) of chromosome sets derived from different ancestral species.

alloploidy (al″o-ploi′de). The state of having any number (two or many) of chromosome sets derived from different ancestral species. See *allodiploidy* and *allopolyploidy*.

allopolyploid (al″lo-pol′e-ploid) [*allo-* + *polyploid*]. 1. Having more than two chromosome sets derived from different ancestral species. 2. An individual or cell having more than two chromosome sets derived from different ancestral species.

allopolyploidy (al″lo-pol′e-ploi-de). The state of having more than two chromosome sets derived from different ancestral species.

allopregnandiol (al″o-preg-nan′de-ol). An isomer of pregnandiol occurring in female urine.

allopregnenolone (al″o-preg-nen′o-lōn). A chemical compound which can be transformed into progesterone or testosterone.

allopsychic (al″o-si′kik) [*allo-* + Gr. *psychē* soul]. Pertaining to mind in its relation to the external world.

allopsychosis (al″o-si-ko′sis). A psychosis marked by disorganization of the perceptive powers for the outer world (hallucinations and illusions), but without disorder of the motor powers such as speech and action (Wernicke).

allorhythmia (al″o-rith′me-ah) [*allo-* + Gr. *rhythmos* rhythm + *-ia*]. Irregularity in the rhythm of the heart beat or pulse.

allorhythmic (al″o-rith′mik). Affected with or of the nature of allorhythmia.

all or none. The fact, discovered by Bowditch (1871), that the heart muscle, under whatever stimulus, will contract to the fullest extent or not at all. Called also *all-or-none law*.

allorphine (al′lor-fēn). Nalorphine.

allose (al′ōs). A sugar, $C_6H_{12}O_6$, isomeric with glucose.

allosome (al′o-sōm) [*allo-* + Gr. *sōma* body]. 1. A special kind of chromosome distinguished from the autosome; a sex chromosome. See under *chromosome*. 2. A foreign constituent of the cytoplasm of a cell which has entered from the outside.

paired a., a diplosome. **unpaired a.,** a monosome.

allotherm (al′o-therm) [*allo-* + Gr. *thermē* heat]. 1. Poikilotherm. 2. Heterotherm.

allotopia (al″o-to′pe-ah). Dystopia.

allotopic (al″o-top′ik). Dystopic.

allotoxin (al″o-tok′sin) [*allo-* + *toxin*]. Any substance formed by tissue change within the body which serves as a defense against toxins by neutralizing their poisonous properties.

allotransplantation (al″o-trans″plan-ta′shun) [*allo-* + *transplantation*]. Transplantation of tissue from one individual into the body of another.

allotrio- (ah-lot′re-o) [Gr. *allotrios* strange]. A combining form meaning strange or foreign.

allotriodontia (ah-lot″re-o-don′she-ah) [*allotrio-* + Gr. *odous* tooth + *-ia*]. 1. The transplantation of teeth from one person to another. 2. The existence of teeth in abnormal places, as in tumors.

allotriogeustia (ah-lot″re-o-gu′ste-ah) [*allotrio-* + Gr. *geusis* taste + *-ia*]. A perverted condition of the sense of taste.

allotriolith (al″o-tri′o-lith) [*allotrio-* + Gr. *lithos* stone]. A calculus in an abnormal situation, or one composed of unusual materials.

allotriophagia (ah-lot″re-o-fa′je-ah). Allotriophagy.

allotriophagy (ah-lot″re-of′ah-je) [*allotrio-* + Gr. *phagein* to eat]. A craving for unnatural food; pica.

allotriosmia (al″o-tri-os′me-ah). Heterosmia.

allotriuria (ah-lot″re-u′re-ah) [*allotrio-* + Gr. *ouron* urine + *-ia*]. A strange or perverted condition of the urine.

allotrope (al′o-trōp). An allotropic form.

allotrophic (al″o-trof′ik). Rendered innutritious by the process of digestion.

allotropic (al″o-trop′ik). 1. Exhibiting allotropism. 2. Concerned with others: said of a type of personality which is inclined to be preoccupied by others than oneself; not self-centered.

allotropism (ah-lot′ro-pizm) [*allo-* + Gr. *tropos* a turning]. 1. The existence of an element in two or more distinct forms (allotropic forms) with distinct physical properties. Examples of allotropism are furnished by carbon and sulfur. 2. A tropism between different structures, e.g., between spermatozoa and ova (Roux).

allotropy (ah-lot′ro-pe). Allotropism.

allotrylic (al″o-tril′ik) [*allotrio-* + Gr. *hylē* matter]. Produced by the presence of a foreign body or principle.

alloxan (al′ok-san). A reddish, crystalline substance, mesoxalyl urea, CO.NH.CO:NH.CO (ring closed by —CO—), an oxidized product of uric acid. It has been obtained from the mucus of the intestine in diarrhea. It tends to destroy the islet cells of the pancreas, thus producing diabetes.

alloxantin (al″ok-san′tin). A crystalline derivative of alloxan and dialuric acid, $[CO(NH.CO)_2C(OH)—]_2$, obtained by reduction.

alloxazine (ah-lok′sah-zēn). A compound, $C_{10}H_6N_4O_2$, being the chief constituent of lipochrome.

alloxin (ah-lok′sin). Any one of a class of basic substances derived from the nuclein of cell nuclei, and on oxidation producing uric acid. The alloxins include xanthine, guanine, adenine, and hypoxanthine.

alloxuremia (al″ok-su-re′me-ah) [*alloxur* + Gr. *haima* blood + *-ia*]. The presence of purine bases in the blood, causing a form of intoxication.

alloxuria (al″ok-su′re-ah) [*alloxur* + Gr. *ouron* urine + *-ia*]. Presence of purine bases in the urine.

alloxuric (al″ok-su′rik). Pertaining to or characterized by alloxuria.

alloy (ah-loi′) [Fr. *aloyer* to mix metals]. A solid mixture of two or more metals or metalloids that are mutually soluble in the molten condition; distinguished as binary, ternary, quaternary, etc., depending on the number of metals in the mixture. **amalgam a.,** a metal in the form of filings or chips which is to be blended with mercury to form an amalgam. **Bean's a.,** an alloy of tin and silver. **contour a.,** an alloy especially suitable for creating anatomically shaped fillings. **Newton's a.,** Melotte's metal.

alloyage (ah-loi′ij). The combining of metals into alloys.

allyl (al′il) [L. *allium* garlic + Gr. *hylē* matter]. A univalent radical, C_3H_5 or $CH_2.CH:CH_2$, from garlic and other plants. **a. aldehyde,** acrolein. **a. cyanamide,** sinamin. **a. isothiocyanate,** volatile oil of mustard, C_3H_5NCS. **a. sulfide,** an artificially prepared compound, $(C_3H_5)S$, used in cholera and subcutaneously in phthisis. **a. sulfocarbamide, a. thiocarbamide, a. thiourea,** thiosinamine. **a tribromide,** a colorless or yellowish liquid, $C_3H_5Br_3$: antispasmodic and anodyne.

allylamine (al″il-am′in). A caustic liquid with an ammoniacal odor, 3-amino-1-propylene, $CH_2:CH.CH_2.NH_2$.

allylguaiacol (al″lil-gwi′ah-kol). Eugenol.

almagacin (al″mah-ga′sin). A combination of gastric mucin, aluminum hydroxide gel, and magnesium trisilicate: used as an antacid.

Almeida's disease (al-ma-ēd′ahz) [F. P. de *Almeida*, Brazilian physician]. South American blastomycosis. See under *blastomycosis*.

Almén's reagent, solution, test (al-mānz′) [August Theodor *Almén*, Swedish physiologist, 1833–1903]. See under *reagent* and *tests*.

almond (ah′mund) [Fr. *amande*, from L. *amygdala* almond]. The fruit of *Prunus amygdalus*. **bitter a.,** the fruit of *P. amygdalus* var. *amara*. **sweet a.,** the fruit of *P. amygdalus* var. *dulcis*.

almoner (al′mo-ner). A person who dispenses alms. **hospital a.,** a person trained in dispensing the social service funds of a hospital, and in administering social service work.

A.L.O. Abbreviation for *axiolinguo-occlusal*.

Al_2O_3. Aluminum oxide.

alochia (ah-lo′ke-ah) [L.; *a* neg. + Gr. *lochia* lochia]. Absence of the lochia.

Alocimua (al″o-sim′u-ah). A genus of snails. **A. longicor′nis,** a fresh-water snail which ingests the eggs of *Clonorchis sinensis* and in whose body the eggs hatch.

aloe (al′o). The dried juice of the leaves of various species of liliaceous plants of the genus Aloe.

aloetic (al″o-et′ik) [L. *aloeticus*]. Pertaining to or containing aloe.

alogia (ah-lo′je-ah) [*a* neg. + Gr. *logos* word + *-ia*]. Inability to speak, due to a central nerve lesion.

$Al(OH)_3$. Aluminum hydroxide.

aloin (al′o-in). A mixture of active principles obtained from aloe: used as a cathartic.

alopecia (al″o-pe′she-ah) [Gr. *alōpekia* a disease, like the mange in foxes, in which the hair falls out]. Absence of the hair from skin areas where it normally is present. **androgenetic a.,** an androgen-dependent alopecia occurring in hereditarily predisposed individuals. See *female pattern a.* and *male pattern a.* **a. area′ta,** an inflammatory, potentially reversible loss of hair occurring in sharply defined areas, and usually involving the scalp. **a. cap′itis tota′lis,** complete loss of hair from the scalp. **cicatricial a., a. cicatrisa′ta,** an irreversible loss of hair associated with some degree of scarring, usually occurring on the scalp. **a. circumscrip′ta,** a. areata. **congenital a., a. congenita′lis,** atrichosis congenitalis. **a. dissemina′ta,** patchy loss of hair on various areas of the body. **drug a.,** a. medicamentosa. **female pattern a.,** loss of scalp hair in the female, analogous to male pattern alopecia, but more benign. **follicular a., a. follicula′ris,** loss of hair as a result of inflammation of the hair follicles. **a. heredita'ria, hereditary a.,** absence or premature loss of hair occurring as a hereditary trait. **a. limina'ris,** loss of hair along the front and back margins of the scalp, occurring as the result of trauma or pressure. **male pattern a.,** a progressive, diffuse, symmetrical loss of scalp hair, beginning with characteristic frontal recession and leaving ultimately only a sparse peripheral rim of scalp hair (the hippocratic wreath); the condition is androgen dependent and is caused by a dominant autosome of variable expressivity. **marginal a., a. margina'lis,** a. liminaris. **a. medicamento'sa,** loss of hair caused by the ingestion of a drug, such as heparin, thallium, or one of the radiomimetic drugs. **a. mucino'sa,** a patchy loss of hair associated with follicular mucinosis. **a. orbicula'ris,** a. cicatrisata. **a. perinev'ica,** a circumscribed area of hair loss surrounding a nevus pigmentosus. **physiologic a.,** the normal shedding of hair at the end of telogen. **postpartum a.,** a common diffuse, temporary loss of resting scalp hair (telogen effluvium), beginning soon after parturition. **a. prematu'ra, a. preseni'lis,** early, rapidly progressive male pattern alopecia. **pressure a.,** loss of hair from a body area subjected to constant or prolonged pressure. **roentgen a.,** x-ray a. **a. seborrhe'ica,** loss of scalp hair associated with chronic disorder of the scalp, marked by itching, hyperemia, and dandruff. **senile a., a. seni'lis,** loss of hair accompanying old age. **symptomatic a., a. symptomat'ica,** loss of hair occurring after fever or childbirth, as a result of systemic or psychogenic causes, or after some other stress of which the effluvium is symptomatic. **syphilitic a., a. syphilit'ica,** loss of hair resulting from either secondary or tertiary syphilis. **a. tota'lis,** complete loss of hair from the entire scalp, especially that resulting from alopecia areata. **toxic a., a. tox'ica,** loss of hair occurring as a result of toxins, such as bacterial toxins during an infectious disease. **traction a.,** loss of scalp hair as a consequence of continuous or prolonged traction, as produced by braiding or use of tight curlers. **traumatic a., a. traumat'ica,** loss of hair occurring as the result of injury. See *traction a.* **a. triangula'ris congenita'lis,** the absence of hair in a triangular area of normal skin at the margin of the scalp, over the junction of the frontal and temporal regions. **a. universa'lis,** loss of hair over the entire body, especially that resulting from alopecia areata. **x-ray a.,** loss of hair after exposure to roentgen radiation, the extent and permanence of which are dependent on the field and dosage.

alopecic (al″o-pe'sik). Pertaining to or characterized by alopecia.

aloxanthine (al″ok-san'thin). A yellow principle, $C_{15}H_{10}O_6$, derivable from aloes by the action of potassium dichromate.

aloxidione (al-ok″sĭ-di'ōn). Chemical name: 3-allyl-5-methyl-2,4-oxazolidinedione. Use: anticonvulsant for petit mal epilepsy.

alpenstich (ahl'pen-stikh″) [Ger. "alpine stab"]. Epidemic pneumonia in Alpine valleys.

alpha (al'fah). The first letter of the Greek alphabet, α or *a;* used as a part of a chemical name to denote the first of a series of isomeric compounds, or the carbon atom next to the carboxyl group. The succeeding letters of the Greek alphabet, beta (β), gamma (γ), delta (δ), etc., are used to name, in order, succeeding compounds or carbon atoms.

alphadinitrophenol (al″fah-di-ni″tro-fe'nol). See under *dinitrophenol.*

alphadrol (al'fah-drol). Trade mark for a preparation of fluprednisolone.

alpha-hypophamine (al″fah-hi-pof'ah-min). An oxytocic principle formerly thought to be secreted by the posterior lobe of the pituitary gland.

alpha-leukocyte (al″fah-lu'ko-sit). A name formerly given to a leukocyte which disintegrates during the coagulation of the blood.

alpha-lobeline (al″fah-lob'e-lin). See *lobeline.*

alphanaphthol (al″fah-naf'thol). A form of naphthol, occurring as a white or pinkish crystalline compound, soluble in alcohol, ether, and hot water; slightly soluble in cold water: used mainly in the arts.

alphaprodine (al″fah-pro'dēn). Chemical name: 1,3-dimethyl-4-phenyl-4-piperidyl propionate: used to relieve pain and as a narcotic.

alpha-tocopherol (al″fah-to-kof'er-ol). See under *tocopherol.*

alpha-tropeine (al″fah-tro'pe-in). A substance derivable from scopolamine and hyoscine.

alphelasma (al″fel-as'mah). Leukoplakia.

alphitomorphous (al″fit-o-mor'fus) [Gr. *alphiton* barley-meal + *morphē* form]. Having a mealy appearance: said of certain fungous parasites.

alphodermia (al″fo-der'me-ah). Absence of pigmentation of the skin.

alphonsin (al-fon'sin) [named for *Alphonse* Ferri, Italian surgeon, 1515–1595]. A bullet-forceps having three prongs.

alphos (al'fos) [L.; Gr. *alphos*]. A variety of lepra or psoriasis.

alphosis (al-fo'sis). Alphodermia.

Alpinia (al-pin'e-ah) [after Prospero *Alpini,* 1553–1617]. A genus of zingiberaceous plants, source of a substance once used as a stimulant aromatic.

alseroxylon (al″ser-ok'sĭ-lon). A purified extract of *Rauwolfia serpentina,* containing reserpine and other amorphous alkaloids: used to reduce blood pressure, as a tranquilizing agent, and to slow the heart rate.

altauna (al-taw'nah) [Arabic]. A malignant carbuncle, bubo, or endemic ulcer.

Alt. dieb. Abbreviation for L. *alter'nis die'bus,* every other day.

alter (awl'ter). To castrate.

alterant (awl'ter-ant). Alterative.

alterative (awl'ter-a″tiv) [L. *alterare* to change]. An obsolete term originally used for drugs said to re-establish healthy functions of the system.

alteregoism (awl″ter-e'go-izm). Interest and sympathy only for persons who are in the same situation as one's self.

alternans (awl-ter'nanz) [L.]. Alternating; alternation. **a. of the heart,** heart block appearing at every alternate heart beat.

Alternaria (awl″ter-na're-ah). A genus of the fungi imperfecti with dark colored conidia somewhat resembling Trichophyton. It causes several diseases of plants and has been found in diseases of the lungs and in skin infection in man.

alternating (awl'ter-nāt″ing). Occurring in regular succession; alternately direct and reversed.

alternation (awl″ter-na'shun) [L. *alternatio*]. Interrupted occurrence, being interspersed with different or opposite events. **a. of generations,** alternate occurrence in regular sequence of asexual and sexual methods of reproduction in the same species; metagenesis.

Althaea (al-the'ah) [L.]. A genus of malvaceous plants. The root and leaves of *A. officinalis,* or marshmallow, are demulcent and furnish a mucilage.

Althausen test (awlt'how-zen) [Theodore L. *Althausen,* San Francisco physician, born 1897]. See under *tests.*

althea (al-the'ah). The dried root of *Althaea officinalis,* or marshmallow root: a decoction has been used as a demulcent, and the boiled root as a poultice.

Alt. hor. Abbreviation for L. *alter'nis ho'ris,* every other hour.

Altmann's fluid, granule, theory (ahlt'manz)

[Richard *Altmann*, German histologist, 1852–1900]. See under the nouns.

Altmann-Gersh method (ahlt′man gersh) [Richard *Altmann;* Isidore *Gersh*, American anatomist, born 1907]. See under *method.*

altofrequent (al″to-fre′quent) [L. *altus* high + *frequent*]. Marked by high frequency. See *high-frequency current*, under *current.*

altricious (al-trish′us). Requiring a long period of nursing.

altrose (al′trōs). A sugar, $C_6H_{12}O_6$, isomeric with glucose.

aludrine (ah-lu′drin). A brand of isopropylepinephrine, a bronchial dilator used in asthma.

alum (al′um) [L. *alumen*]. 1. A colorless, crystalline substance, with astringent and styptic properties, and soluble in water, but insoluble in alcohol: potassium alum, $AlK(SO_4)_2 + 12H_2O$, or ammonium alum, $AlNH_4(SO_4)_2 + 12H_2O$. 2. Any member of a class of double sulfates formed on the type of the foregoing compounds. 3. Any member of a class of double aluminum-containing compounds. **ammonioferric a.,** a powerfully styptic alum, sulfate of iron, and ammonium. **ammonium a.** See *alum*, def. 1. **burnt a.,** exsiccated a. **chrome a.,** chromium and potassium sulfate; a violet pigment. **concentrated a., patent a.,** ammonium sulfate, incorrectly called an alum. **dried a.,** exsiccated a. **exsiccated a.,** a white, odorless powder, with a sweetish, astringent taste: exsiccated ammonium alum, $AlNH_4(SO_4)_2$, or exsiccated potassium alum, $AlK(SO_4)_2$, as indicated on the label, and containing at least 96.5 per cent of the labeled product. **iron a.,** iron and potassium sulfate. **potassium a.** See *alum*, def. 1. **Roman a.,** a special make of common alum. **sodium a.,** aluminum and sodium sulfate.

alumen (ah-loo′men), gen. *alu′minis* [L.]. Alum. **a. exsicca′tum,** exsiccated alum.

alumina (ah-loo′mi-nah). Aluminum oxide, Al_2O_3, found in clay and in many minerals.

aluminated (ah-loo′mi-nāt″ed). Charged with alum.

aluminium (al″u-min′e-um) [L.]. Aluminum.

aluminoid (ah-loo′mĭ-noid). A proprietary colloidal aluminum hydroxide in capsular form for use in gastric ulcers and hyperacidity.

aluminosis (ah-loo″mĭ-no′sis). A form of pneumoconiosis due to the presence of aluminum-bearing dust in the lungs, especially that of alum, bauxite or clay. Called also *a. pulmonum.*

aluminum (ah-loo′mĭ-num). An extremely light, whitish, lustrous, metallic element, obtainable from clay: specific gravity, 2.699; atomic weight, 26.982; atomic number, 13; symbol, Al. It is very malleable and ductile, and is used for the manufacture of instruments; also as a base for artificial dentures. The aluminum of the pharmacopeia is a fine, free-flowing, silvery powder, free from gritty or discolored particles. Aluminum compounds are used chiefly for their antacid and astringent properties. **a. acetate,** a compound, $C_6H_9AlO_6$, used in solution as an astringent and antiseptic. **a. aminoacetate,** dihydroxyaluminum aminoacetate. **a. ammonium sulfate,** ammonium alum. **a. carbonate,** a mild antiseptic, styptic, $Al_2(CO_3)_3$. **a. carbonate basic,** a complex of aluminum hydroxide and carbonate: used in control of gastric hyperacidity. **a. chloride,** an odorless, white or yellowish white, deliquescent powder, with a sweet astringent taste, $AlCl_3 + 6H_2O$: used in 10 to 25 per cent solution to stop perspiration or as a deodorant or astringent. **a. glycinate,** dihydroxyaluminum aminoacetate. **a. hydrate,** a. hydroxide. **a. hydroxide,** a white, tasteless powder, $Al(OH)_3$, mildly astringent, and used externally as a drying powder and internally as an antacid and absorbent. See also under *gel.* **a. hydroxide, colloidal,** aluminum hydroxide gel. **a. monostearate,** a combination of aluminum with variable proportions of stearic acid and palmitic acid; used in preparation of a suspension of procaine penicillin G. **a. oxide,** a pure compound, Al_2O_3, produced in various grain sizes and used as an abrasive agent in dentistry. **a. potassium sulfate,** potassium alum. **a. subacetate,** $Al(C_2H_3O_2)_2OH$: used as an astringent wash, diluted with 10 parts of water. **a. sulfate,** an odorless, white, crystalline powder, with a sweet taste, $Al_2(SO_4)_3 + 18H_2O$: astringent and antiperspirant.

alundum (ah-lun′dum). Electrically fused alumina: used in making laboratory appliances which are to be subjected to intense heat.

alurate (al′ūr-āt). Trade mark for a preparation of aprobarbital.

Alv. adst. Abbreviation for L. *al′vo adstric′ta,* when the bowels are constipated.

Alv. deject. Abbreviation for L. *al′vi dejectio′nes,* alvine dejections.

alvei (al′ve-i) [L]. Plural of *alveus.*

alveobronchiolitis (al″ve-o-brong″ke-o-li′tis). Inflammation of the bronchioles and alveoli of the lungs; bronchopneumonia.

alveolalgia (al″ve-o-lal′je-ah) [*alveolus* + *-algia*]. Pain occuring in a dental alveolus.

alveolar (al-ve′o-lar) [L. *alveolaris*]. Pertaining to an alveolus.

alveolate (al-ve′o-lāt). Marked by honeycomb-like pits.

alveolectomy (al″ve-o-lek′to-me) [*alveolus* + Gr. *ektomē* excision]. Surgical preparation of the jaw for prosthesis, with removal of remaining teeth and roots of teeth and excision of diseased tissue and alveolar process. **partial a.,** alveolectomy involving the site of only one or a few teeth, or a portion of the jaw in which no teeth are present.

alveoli (al-ve′o-li). Plural of *alveolus.*

alveolitis (al″ve-o-li′tis). Inflammation of an alveolus.

alveolo- (al-ve′o-lo) [L. *alveolus*]. Combining form denoting relationship to an alveolus, probably most often used in reference to a dental alveolus.

alveoloclasia (al-ve″o-lo-kla′ze-ah) [*alveolo-* + Gr. *klasis* breaking]. Disintegration or absorption of the inner wall of a tooth alveolus, causing looseness of the teeth.

alveolocondylean (al-ve″o-lo″kon-dil′e-an). Pertaining to the alveolus and condyle.

alveolodental (al-ve″o-lo-den′tal). Pertaining to a tooth and its alveolus.

alveololabial (al-ve″o-lo-la′be-al). Pertaining to the alveolar processes and the lips.

alveololabialis (al-ve″o-lo-la″be-a′lis). The buccinator muscle.

alveololingual (al-ve″o-lo-ling′gwal). Pertaining to the alveolar processes and the tongue.

alveolomerotomy (al-ve″o-lo″mĕ-rot′o-me) [*alveolus* + Gr. *meros* part + *tomē* a cutting]. Excision of a portion of the alveolar process.

alveolonasal (al-ve″o-lo-na′sal). Pertaining to the alveolar point and the nasion.

alveolopalatal (al-ve″o-lo-pal′ah-tal). Pertaining to the alveolar process and palate.

alveoloplasty (al-ve′o-lo-plas″te) [*alveolo-* + Gr. *plassein* to form]. The surgical improvement of the shape and condition of the alveolar process, in preparation for immediate or future denture construction.

alveolotomy (al″ve-o-lot′o-me) [*alveolo-* + Gr. *tomē* a cutting]. Incision into a dental alveolus.

alveolus (al-ve′o-lus), pl. *alve′oli* [L., dim. of *alveus* hollow]. A general term used in anatomical nomenclature to designate a small saclike dilatation. See also *acinus.* **dental alveoli,** the cavities or sockets of either jaw, in which the roots of the teeth are embedded. See *alveoli dentales mandibulae* and *alveoli dentales maxillae.* **alve′oli denta′les mandib′ulae** [N A, B N A], the cavities or sockets in the alveolar process of the mandible in which the roots of the teeth are held by the periodontal membrane. Called also *dental alveoli of mandible.* **alve'oli denta'les maxil'lae** [N A, B N A], the cavities or sockets in the alveolar process of the maxilla in which the roots of the teeth are held by the periodontal membrane. Called also *dental alveoli of maxilla.* **alve'oli pulmo'nis** [N A], small outpocketings of the alveolar sacs, through whose walls the gaseous exchange takes place. Called also *pulmonary alveoli* and *a. pulmonum* [B N A]. **alveoli pulmo'num** [B N A], alveoli pulmonis.

alveolysis (al″ve-ol'ĭ-sis) [*alveolus* + Gr. *lysis* dissolution]. Periodontal disease.

alveus (al've-us), pl. *al'vei* [L.]. A trough or a canal. **a. commu'nis,** utriculus. **a. hippocam'pi** [N A], **a. of hippocampus,** the thin layer of white matter that covers the ventricular surface of the hippocampus.

alvine (al'vīn) [L. *alvinus*]. Pertaining to the belly or intestines.

alvinolith (al'vi-no-lith″) [L. *alvus* abdomen + Gr. *lithos* stone]. An intestinal concretion, especially one formed from calcareous salts, oatmeal or other débris.

alvodine (al'vo-dīn). Trade mark for preparations of piminodine ethanesulfonate.

alvus (al'vus) [L.]. The abdomen with its contained viscera.

A.L.W. Abbreviation for *arch-loop-whorl.*

alymphia (ah-lim'fe-ah) [*a* neg. + L. *lympha* lymph]. Deficiency or absence of the lymph.

alymphocytosis (ah-lim″fo-si-to'sis). Complete or nearly complete absence of lymphocytes from the blood.

alymphopotent (ah-lim″fo-po'tent) [*a* neg. + *lymphoid* + L. *potens* able]. Incapable of producing lymphocytes or lymphoid cells.

alyssous (ah-lis'us). Preventing or curing rabies.

Alzheimer's baskets, cells, dementia, disease, sclerosis, stain (altz'hi-merz) [Alois *Alzheimer*, German neurologist, 1864–1915]. See under the nouns.

alzinox (al'zĭ-noks). Trade mark for preparations of dihydroxyaluminum aminoacetate.

A.M. Abbreviation for *amperemeter, axiomesial,* and *meter-angle.*

Am. Chemical symbol for *americium.*

am. A symbol for *myopic astigmatism,* for *meter-angle,* and for *ametropia.*

A.M.A. Abbreviation for *American Medical Association,* and *Australian Medical Association.*

ama (a'mah), pl. *a'mae* [L.]. An enlargement of a semicircular canal of the internal ear at the end opposite the ampulla.

amaas (ah'mahs). Variola minor.

amacratic (am″ah-krat'ik) [Gr. *hama* together + *kratos* strength]. Amasthenic.

amacrinal (am″ah-kri'nal). Of the nature of amacrines.

amacrine (am'ah-krīn) [*a* neg. + Gr. *makros* long + *is, inos* fiber]. 1. Having no long processes. 2. Any one of a group of branched retinal structures regarded as modified nerve cells.

amadil (am'ah-dil). Trade mark for a preparation of acetaminophen.

amadin (am'ah-din). A globulin derived from almonds.

amadou (am'ah-doo) [Fr.]. Touchwood or punk; the fungus *Boletus igniarius,* which grows on old trees, formerly used as a wound dressing and a hemostatic.

amakebe (am″ah-ke'be). A disease affecting calves in Uganda, due to a parasite, *Theileria parva,* which is transmitted by the bite of a tick, *Rhipicephalus appendiculatus.*

amakrine (am'ah-krīn). Amacrine.

AMAL. Abbreviation for *Aero-Medical Acceleration Laboratory.*

amalgam (ah-mal'gam) [Gr. *malagma* poultice or soft mass]. An alloy of which mercury is one of the metals. **dental a.,** an amalgam of silver, tin, and mercury ($Ag_3Sn + Hg$), with low concentrations of copper and zinc: used for filling cavities in teeth.

amalgamable (ah-mal'gah-mah-b'l). Capable of forming an amalgam with mercury.

amalgamate (ah-mal'gah-māt″). To unite a metal in an alloy with mercury; to form an amalgam.

amalgamation (ah-mal″gah-ma'shun). 1. The formation of an amalgam. 2. The creation of a homogeneous whole by mixing. Called also *trituration.*

amalgamator (ah-mal'gah-ma″tor). Triturator.

amandin (am'an-din). A protein from the almond nut.

Amanita (am″ah-ni'tah). A genus of mushrooms. *A. musca'ria,* the fly agaric, a poisonous mushroom. *A. phalloi'des,* the white or deadly amanita; a very poisonous mushroom. *A. rubes'cens,* a species considered edible. It contains a powerful hemolysin. *A. ver'na* is poisonous.

amanitine (ah-man'ĭ-tin). A poisonous alkaloid from fly agaric; also a poisonous glycoside from the various mushrooms, especially from *Amanita phalloides.*

amanitotoxin (ah-man″ĭ-to-tok'sin). Amanita toxin.

amara (ah-ma'rah) [L., pl.]. Bitters.

amaranth (am'ah-ranth). A dark, red brown powder, $C_{10}H_6(SO_2.ONa).N{:}N.C_{10}H_4(SO_2.ONa)_2.OH$, used as a coloring agent for food and cosmetics, or for drugs.

amaril (am'ah-ril) [Sp. *amarillo*]. Yellow; a name formerly given to a hypothetical poison that was considered at that time to be a cause of yellow fever. **virus a.,** yellow fever.

amarillic (am″ah-ril'ik). Pertaining to amaril.

amarine (am'ah-rin) [L. *amarus* bitter]. A poisonous, crystalline base, triphenyl dihydroglyoxaline, $C_6H_5.CH.NH.C{:}(C_6H_5)N.CH.C_6H_5$, from oil of bitter almonds, and also prepared artificially.

amaroid (am'ah-roid). A bitter principle; a general name for vegetable extractives other than alkaloids and glycosides.

amaroidal (am-ah-roi'dal). Somewhat bitter; also resembling a bitter in properties.

amarthritis (am″ar-thri'tis) [Gr. *hama* together + *arthron* joint + *-itis*]. Inflammation of several joints at the same time.

amasesis (am″ah-se'sis) [*a* neg. + Gr. *masēsis* chewing]. Inability to chew the food.

amasthenic (am″as-then'ik) [Gr. *hama* together + *sthenos* strength]. Bringing the rays of light into one focus: said of a lens.

amastia (ah-mas'te-ah) [*a* neg. + Gr. *mastos* breast]. A developmental anomaly characterized by absence of the mammae.

amathophobia (ah-math″o-fo'be-ah) [Gr. *amathos* sand + *phobia*]. Morbid dread of dust.

amativeness (am'ah-tiv″nes) [L. *amare* to love]. Inclination to love.

amatol (am'ah-tol). A war explosive, being a mixture of trinitrotoluene and ammonium nitrate.

amatory (am'ah-to″re) [L. *amatorius*]. Pertaining to love or sexual desire.

amaurosis (am″aw-ro'sis) [L. from Gr. *amaurōsis* darkening]. Blindness (Hippocrates); especially blindness occurring without apparent lesion of the eye, from disease of the optic nerve, retina, spine, or brain. Cf. *amblyopia.* **albuminuric a.,** that which is due to renal disease. **Burns's a.,** postmarital amblyopia. **cat's eye a.,** blindness of one eye, with bright reflection from the pupil, as from the tapetum of a cat (Beer). **central a., a. centra'lis,** amaurosis due to disease of the central nervous system. **cerebral a.,** that which is due to cerebral or brain disease. **congenital a.,** that which exists from birth. **diabetic a.,** that which is associated with diabetes. **a. fu'gax,** a transient episode of monocular blindness, or partial blindness, lasting 10 minutes or less. **hysteric a.,** that which is associated with hysteria. **intoxication a.,** amaurosis caused by some systemic poison, as alcohol or tobacco. **reflex a.,** that which is caused by the reflex action of a remote irritation. **saburral a.,** that which occurs in an attack of acute gastritis. **uremic a.,** an amaurotic condition due to uremia: sometimes attendant on nephritis.

amaurotic (am"aw-rot'ik). Pertaining to, or of the nature of, amaurosis.

amaxophobia (ah-mak"so-fo'be-ah) [Gr. *hamaxa* carriage + *phobia*]. Insane dread of vehicles.

amazia (ah-ma'ze-ah) [*a* neg. + Gr. *mazos* breast + *-ia*]. A developmental anomaly characterized by absence of the mammary gland.

amazon (am'ah-zon). An individual exhibiting amazia.

amb-. A prefix signifying both or on both sides.

Ambard's constant, formula, laws (ahm-barz') [Léon *Ambard*, physiologist in Strassburg]. See under *formula* and *law*.

ambenonium (am"be-no'ne-um). Chemical name: N,N'-bis-2 [(2-chlorobenzyl) diethylammonium]-ethyloxamide. Uses: 1. cholinesterase inhibitor; 2. increase muscular strength in myasthenic patient.

amber (am'ber). A yellowish fossil resin, the gum of several species of coniferous trees, found in the alluvial deposits of northeastern Prussia.

Amberg's line (am'bergz) [Emil *Amberg*, Detroit otologist, 1869–1948]. See under *line*.

ambergris (am'ber-gris) [L. *ambra grisea* gray amber]. A gray substance from the sperm whale's intestines: used as a perfuming agent and as a stimulant.

ambi-. A prefix signifying on both sides.

ambidexter (am"bĭ-dek'ster) [*ambi-* + L. *dexter* right]. 1. Ambidextrous. 2. An individual exhibiting ambidexterity.

ambidexterity (am"bĭ-deks-ter'ĭ-te). The ability to perform acts requiring manual skill with either hand, some ordinarily being performed with one and some with the other.

ambidextrality (am"bĭ-deks-tral'ĭ-te). Ambidexterity.

ambidextrism (am"bĭ-deks'trizm). Ambidexterity.

ambidextrous (am"bĭ-dek'strus). Pertaining to or characterized by ambidexterity.

ambient (am'be-ent) [L. *ambire* to surround]. Surrounding; encompassing; prevailing.

ambilateral (am"bĭ-lat'er-al) [*ambi-* + L. *latus* side]. Pertaining to or affecting both the right and the left side.

ambilevosity (am"bĭ-lĕ-vos'ĭ-te). The inability to perform acts requiring manual skill with either hand.

ambilevous (am"bĭ-le'vus) [*ambi-* + L. *laevus* left-handed]. Pertaining to or characterized by ambilevosity.

ambiopia (am"be-o'pe-ah) [L.]. Diplopia.

ambisexual (am"bĭ-seks'u-al). Bisexual; pertaining to or affecting both sexes.

ambisinister (am"bĭ-sin'is-ter) [*ambi-* + L. *sinister* left]. 1. Ambilevous. 2. An individual exhibiting ambilevosity.

ambisinistrous (am"bĭ-sĭ-nis'trus). Ambilevous.

ambivalence (am-biv'ah-lens) [*ambi-* + L. *valentia* strength, power]. The simultaneous existence of opposite attitudes, as of love and hate, toward the same object.

ambivalent (am-biv'ah-lent). 1. Characterized by or pertaining to ambivalence. 2. Having equal power in two opposite directions.

ambiversion (am"bĭ-ver'zhun). A personality type which is intermediate between introversion and extroversion.

ambivert (am'bĭ-vert). A person who is intermediate between an extrovert and an introvert.

ambly- (am'ble) [Gr. *amblys* dull]. A combining form denoting dulness.

amblyacousia (am"ble-ah-koo'se-ah) [*ambly-* + Gr. *akousis* hearing + *-ia*]. Dulness of hearing.

amblyaphia (am-ble-a'fe-ah) [*ambly-* + Gr. *haphe* touch + *-ia*]. Bluntness or dulness of the sense of touch.

amblychromasia (am"ble-kro-ma'ze-ah). The condition of staining faintly or of having little chromatin.

amblychromatic (am"ble-kro-mat'ik) [*ambly-* + Gr. *chrōma* color]. Feebly staining.

amblygeustia (am"ble-gu'ste-ah) [*ambly-* + Gr. *geusis* taste + *-ia*]. Dulness of the sense of taste.

amblykusis (am"ble-ku'sis) [*ambly-* + Gr. *akouein* to hear]. Amblyacousia.

Amblyomma (am"ble-om'ah) [*ambly-* + Gr. *omma* eye]. A genus of ticks. **A. america'num,** the Lone Star tick of the southern United States, particularly Texas and Louisiana: a vector of Rocky Mountain spotted fever. **A. cajennen'se,** a particularly obnoxious species of tropical America: it transmits São Paulo fever. **A. hebrae'um,** the bont tick; an African species which transmits the disease known as "heartwater" as well as the South African tick-bite fever of man. **A. macula'tum** is found on the gulf coast. **A. ova'le,** a tropical tick of dogs and tapirs. **A. tubercula'tum,** a species found in Florida. **A. variega'tum,** a species which carries the same infection as *A. hebraeum*.

amblyopia (am"ble-o'pe-ah) [*ambly-* + Gr. *ōps* eye + *-ia*]. Dimness of vision without detectable organic lesion of the eye. **a. alcohol'ica,** impairment of the vision as a result of alcohol poisoning. **arsenic a.,** disturbance of vision due to the use of arsenic. **astigmatic a.,** amblyopia due to imperfect development of the finer elements of the retina. **color a.,** impairment of color vision, caused by toxic or other influences. **a. crapulo'sa,** a. alcoholica. **crossed a., a. crucia'ta,** that which affects one eye, with hemianesthesia of the same side. **a. ex anop'sia,** that which results from long disuse. **hysteric a.,** that which is associated with hysteria. **nocturnal a.,** abnormal dimness of vision at night. **postmarital a.,** that which is caused by sexual excess. **quinine a.,** amblyopia following large doses of quinine. It is due to anemia of the retina. **reflex a.,** that which results from peripheral irritation. **toxic a.,** amblyopia due to poisoning, as from tobacco or alcohol. **traumatic a.,** amblyopia due to injury. **uremic a.,** loss of visual power sometimes seen during a uremic attack.

amblyopiatrics (am"ble-o"pe-at'riks) [*amblyopia* + Gr. *iatreia* healing]. The therapeutics or treatment of amblyopia.

amblyoscope (am'ble-o-skōp") [*amblyopia* + Gr. *skopein* to view]. An instrument for training an amblyopic eye to take part in vision.

Amblystoma (am-blis'to-mah). Ambystoma.

ambo (am'bo). Ambon.

ambo-. A prefix signifying both, or on both sides.

amboceptoid (am"bo-sep'toid). A modified amboceptor which has lost its cytophilic power.

amboceptor (am"bo-sep'tor) [*ambo* + L. *capere* to take]. A substance in the blood and lymph serving as one of the active elements in cytolysis, the other element being the complement (Ehrlich and Morgenroth). It serves to connect the cell with the complement, being composed of two elements, the *cytophile* group, which has an affinity for the cell, and a *complementophile* group, which has an affinity for the complement. The amboceptor normally present in serum is called *natural a.;* that which is produced by inoculation of foreign cells is called *immune a.* Called also *immune body, immunism, intermediary body, copula, sensitizer, sensibilizer, desmon, philocytase, preparative, preparator, thermostable body, fixative,* and *fixator.* See *Ehrlich's side-chain theory,* under *theory.* **bacteriolytic a.,** an amboceptor that takes part in bacteriolysis. **Bordet's a.,** an alexin-fixing amboceptor. **hemolytic a.,** an amboceptor which takes part in hemolysis.

amboceptorgen (am″bo-sep′tor-jen). An antigen giving rise to amboceptors.

ambodryl (am′bo-dril). Trade mark for preparations of bromodiphenhydramine.

ambomalleal (am″bo-mal′e-al). Pertaining to the incus and the malleus.

ambon (am′bon). The ring of fibrocartilage forming the edge of the sockets in which the heads of long bones are lodged.

ambosexual (am″bo-seks′u-al) [*ambo-* + *sexual*]. Bisexual; pertaining to or affecting both sexes.

ambotoxoid (am″bo-tok′soid). A toxoid prepared from several strains of staphylococci combined with bacterial antigen.

ambrain (am-bra′in). Ambrin.

ambrein (am-bre′in). Ambrin.

ambrin (am′brin). A white crystalline fatty substance resembling cholesterol. It is the chief constituent of ambergris.

ambrine (am′brēn). A proprietary preparation of paraffin, rosin, and wax: used as a dressing in the treatment of extensive burns and in rheumatic disorders, introduced by Barthe de Sandfort (1913).

Ambrosia (am-bro′zhe-ah) [L. and Gr., from Gr. *ambrotos* immortal]. A genus of annual weeds which produce quantities of wind-borne pollen and so cause much hay fever. *A. artemisiaefo'lia* is the common or small ragweed; *A. trif'ida* is the giant ragweed.

ambrosin (am-bro′sin). A substance contained in the pollen of ragweed (*Ambrosia*), which is probably the cause of autumnal hay fever.

ambrosterol (am-bros′te-rol). A phytosterol, $C_{20}H_{34}O$, with a melting point of 147 to 149° C. found in the pollen of *ambrosia.*

ambulance (am′bu-lans) [Fr.]. A vehicle for conveying the sick and wounded.

ambulant (am′bu-lant) [L. *ambulans* walking]. Walking or able to walk; not confined to bed.

ambulatorium (am″bu-lah-to′re-um). A place where ambulant patients are treated.

ambulatory (am′bu-lah-to″re). Ambulant.

ambustion (am-bust′yun). A burn or scald.

ambutonium (am″bu-to′ne-um). Chemical name: 3-carbomoyl-3,3 diphenylpropyl ethyldimethylammonium. Uses: 1. parasympathetic blockade; 2. antispasmodic; 3. reduce gastric acid secretion.

Ambystoma (am-bis′to-mah). A genus of salamanders used for experimental purposes. See *axolotl.*

A.M.C. Abbreviation for *axiomesiocervical.*

A.M.D. Abbreviation for *axiomesiodistal.*

A.M.D.S. Abbreviation for *Association of Military Dental Surgeons.*

ameba (ah-me′bah), pl. *amebae* or *amebas* [L., from Gr. *amoibē* change]. A minute one-celled protozoan animal organism; a single-celled nucleated mass of protoplasm which is constantly changing its shape by extending from its circumference processes of protoplasm called pseudopodia. By these processes it moves about and also absorbs nourishment. The following amebae are parasitic in man: *Entamoeba coli, Entamoeba histolytica, Entamoeba gingivalis, Dientamoeba fragilis, Endolimax nana,* and *Iodamoeba buetschlii.* **artificial a.,** combinations of chemicals which behave somewhat like living amebae. For example, a drop of mercury will move toward a crystal of potassium dichromate if they are close together in dilute nitric acid. **coprozoic a.,** free-living amebae, mostly of the limax type, sometimes found in human feces and characterized by the fact that they grow readily on artificial media. There are four genera: Dimastigamoeba, Hartmanella, Sappinia, and Vahlkampfia.

amebacidal (ah-me″bah-si′dal). Amebicidal.

amebacide (ah-me′bah-sīd). Amebicide.

amebadiastase (ah-me″bah-di′as-tās). An intracellular enzyme found in amebae which digests the bacteria engulfed by the latter.

amebaism (ah-me′bah-izm). The power or property of ameboid motion.

amebiasis (am″e-bi′ah-sis). The state of being infected with amebae, especially with *Entamoeba histolytica.* **intestinal a.,** amebic dysentery.

amebic (ah-me′bik). Pertaining to, or of the nature of, an ameba.

amebicidal (ah-me″bĭ-si′dal). Destructive to amebae.

amebicide (ah-me′bĭ-sīd) [*ameba* + L. *caedere* to kill]. An agent which is destructive to amebae.

amebiform (ah-me′bĭ-form). Shaped like or resembling an ameba.

amebiosis (am″e-bi-o′sis). Infection with amebae.

amebism (am′e-bizm). 1. Ameboid movement. 2. Invasion of the system with amebae.

amebocyte (ah-me′bo-sīt″) [*ameba* + Gr. *kytos* hollow vessel]. An ameba-like cell, frequently containing granules, found among the tissues of various invertebrate animals.

amebocytogenous (ah-me″bo-si-toj′e-nus). Producing or caused by amebocytes.

amebodiastase (ah-me″bo-di′as-tās). A proteolytic enzyme extracted from the bodies of protozoa.

ameboid (ah-me′boid) [*ameba* + Gr. *eidos* form]. Resembling an ameba in form or in movements.

ameboididity (am″e-boi-did′i-te). The power of moving by means of ameboid movements.

ameboidism (ah-me′boid-izm). A characteristic observed in certain cells, with displacement occurring as a result of protrusion of pseudopods.

ameboma (am″e-bo′mah). A tumor-like mass produced by localized inflammation due to amebiasis.

amebula (ah-me′bu-lah) [dim. of L. *amoeba*]. A swarm spore of a protozoan having pseudopodia: as the spore of the malarial parasite after it has entered the red blood corpuscle and become amebiform. Called also *pseudopodiospore.*

ameburia (am″e-bu′re-ah) [*ameba* + Gr. *ouron* urine + *-ia*]. The discharge or presence of amebae in the urine.

AMEL. Abbreviation for *Aero-Medical Equipment Laboratory.*

amelanotic (ah″mel-ah-not′ik). Containing no melanin; unpigmented.

amelia (ah-me′le-ah) [*a* neg. + Gr. *melos* limb + *-ia*]. A developmental anomaly characterized by absence of a limb or limbs.

amelification (ah-mel″ĭ-fi-ka′shun) [Old Fr. *amel* enamel + L. *facere* to make]. The development of enamel cells into enamel.

amelioration (ah-mēl″yo-ra′shun) [L. *ad* to + *melior* better]. Improvement, as of the condition of a patient.

ameloblast (ah-mel′o-blast) [Old Fr. *amel* enamel + Gr. *blastos* germ]. A cylindrical epithelial cell in the innermost layer of the enamel organ which takes part in the elaboration of the enamel prism. The ameloblasts cover

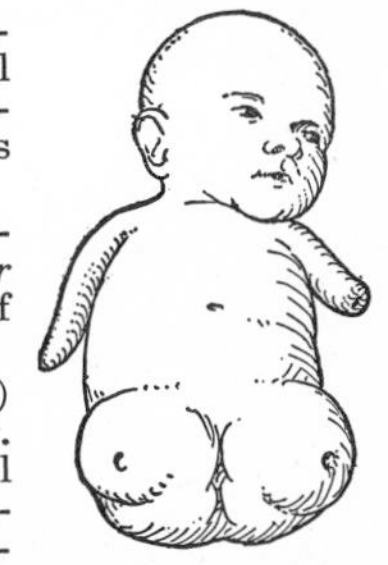

Amelia in legs; hemimelia in arms (Arey)

the dental papilla. Called also *adamantoblast*, *ganoblast*, and *enamel builder*.

ameloblastoma (ah-mel″o-blas-to′mah). A true neoplasm of tissue of the type characteristic of the enamel organ, but which does not undergo differentiation to the point of enamel formation. Formerly called *adamantinoma*. **pituitary a.**, craniopharyngioma.

amelodentinal (am″ĕ-lo-den′tĭ-nal). Pertaining to the enamel and dentin of a tooth.

amelogenesis (am″ĕ-lo-jen′e-sis). The formation of enamel. **a. imperfec′ta**, a hereditary condition resulting in poor development or complete absence of enamel of the teeth, caused by improper differentiation of the ameloblasts and characterized by a brown color of the teeth.

amelogenic (am″ĕ-lo-jen′ik). Forming enamel.

amelus (am′ĕ-lus). An individual exhibiting amelia.

amenia (ah-me′ne-ah) [*a* neg. + *menses* + *-ia*]. Absence of the menses.

amenomania (am″ĕ-no-ma′ne-ah) [L. *amoenus* pleasant + *mania*]. Insanity with agreeable hallucinations.

amenorrhea (ah-men″o-re′ah) [*a* neg. + Gr. *mēn* month + *rhoia* flow]. Absence or abnormal stoppage of the menses. **absolute a.**, total suppression of the menses. **dysponderal a.**, amenorrhea associated with disorder of weight, such as obesity or extreme underweight. **hypothalamic a.**, amenorrhea associated with disorders of the hypothalamus. **lactation a.**, the absence of the menses incidental to lactation. **ovarian a.**, amenorrhea resulting from deficiency of ovarian (estrus-producing) hormone. **physiologic a.**, absence of menses not due to organic disorder. **pituitary a.**, absence of the menses owing to pituitary deficiency. **premenopausal a.**, physiologic decrease of menstruation during establishment of the climacterium. **primary a.**, failure of menstruation to occur at puberty. **relative a.**, menstrual flow which is less than normal for the individual. **secondary a.**, cessation of menstruation after it has once been established at puberty.

amenorrheal (ah-men-o-re′al). Pertaining to amenorrhea.

amensalism (a-men′sal-izm). Symbiosis in which one population (or individual) is inhibited and the other is not affected.

ament (a′ment) [L. *a* away + *mens* mind]. An idiot; a person with no mind.

amentia (ah-men′she-ah) [L. *a* away + *mens* mind + *-ia*]. 1. Mental deficiency; a congenital lack of the ordinary mental ability, of varying extent. 2. A mental disorder characterized by mental confusion of varying degree, sometimes so severe as to approach stupor; called also *confusion* and *confusional insanity*. **a. agita′ta**, amentia attended by great excitement and continuous hallucinations. **a. atton′ita**, amentia marked by stupor, immobility, and indifference. **nevoid a.**, amentia with a nevoid condition of the trigeminal region (face or scalp), calcification of the brain substance, glaucoma, signs of damage to the pyramidal system, and epilepsy. Called also *Sturge's disease, Kalischer's disease, Weber's disease, Krabbe's disease, Dimitri's disease* and *Brushfield-Wyatt disease*. **a. occul′ta**, mild melancholia with sudden violent actions. **a. paranoi′des**, amentia with mild symptoms. **phenylpyruvic a.**, idiocy attended by the secretion of phenylpyruvic acid in the urine. **Stearn's alcoholic a.**, a form of temporary alcoholic insanity marked by less emotional disturbance than delirium tremens, but of longer duration and characterized by greater mental clouding and amnesia.

amential (ah-men′she-al). Pertaining to or characterized by amentia.

americium (am″ĕ-ris′e-um). The chemical element of atomic number 95, atomic weight 243, symbol Am, obtained by cyclotron bombardment of uranium and plutonium.

amerisia (am″ĕ-ris′e-ah) [*a* neg. + Gr. *merizein* to divide + *-ia*]. Inability to articulate words in speaking or writing; a form of aphasia (Heveroch, 1914).

amerism (am′er-izm) [*a* neg. + Gr. *meros* part]. The quality of not splitting into segments or fragments.

ameristic (am″er-is′tik) [*a* neg. + Gr. *meristos* divided]. Not split into segments.

ametabolon (ah″mĕ-tab′o-lon). An animal which develops without undergoing metamorphosis.

ametabolous (ah″mĕ-tab′o-lus). Not undergoing metamorphoses.

ametachromophil (ah″met-ah-kro′mo-fil). Orthochromophil.

ametamorphosis (ah-met″ah-mor′fo-sis). Undue activity of thought leading to a condition of mental absorption and abstraction.

ametaneutrophil (ah-met-ah-nu′tro-fil). Orthochromophil.

amethone (am′ĕ-thōn). Proprietary name of 3-β-diethylaminoethyl-3-phenyl-2-benzofuranone hydrochloride, a smooth muscle antispasmodic.

ametria (ah-me′tre-ah) [*a* neg. + Gr. *mētra* uterus]. Congenital absence of the uterus.

ametrometer (am″e-trom′e-ter) [*ametropia* + Gr. *metron* measure]. An instrument for measuring the degree of ametropia.

ametropia (am″e-tro′pe-ah) [Gr. *ametros* disproportionate + *ōps* eye + *-ia*]. Imperfection in the refractive powers of the eye, so that images are not brought to a proper focus on the retina, producing hypermetropia, myopia, or astigmatism. **axial a.**, ametropia due to lengthening of the eyeball on the optic axis. **curvature a.**, ametropia due to variations in the curvature of the surface of the eye. **index a.**, ametropia due to alterations in the refractive index media of the eye. **position a.**, ametropia due to faulty position of the crystalline lens. **refractive a.**, ametropia due to fault in the dioptric system of the eye.

ametropic (am″e-trop′ik). Affected with, or pertaining to, ametropia.

A.M.G. Abbreviation for *axiomesiogingival*.

Amh. Abbreviation for *mixed astigmatism with myopia predominating*.

A.M.I. Abbreviation for *axiomesioincisal*.

amianthoid (am″e-an′thoid) [Gr. *amianthos* asbestos + *eidos* form]. Having the appearance of asbestos: a term applied to certain fibers seen in degenerated costal and laryngeal cartilage.

amianthosis (am″e-an-tho′sis) [Gr. *amianthos* asbestos + *-osis*]. Asbestosis.

amic (am′ik). Relating to, or derived from, ammonia. The *amic acids* are the amido derivatives of the inorganic acids.

Amici's disk (ah-me′chēz) [Giovanni Battista *Amici*, Italian physicist, 1784–1863]. The membrane of Krause.

amicine (am′ĭ-sin). A substance in the posterior lobe of the hypophysis which inhibits the growth of both plants and animals.

amicrobic (ah″mi-kro′bik) [*a* neg. + *microbe*]. Not caused by microbes.

amicron (ah-mi′kron). A colloid particle about 10^{-7} cm. in diameter. Such particles are just visible with the ultramicroscope.

amicrone (ah-mi′krōn). Amicron.

amicroscopic (ah-mi″kro-skop′ik). Too small to be observed by the ultramicroscope.

amidase (am′ĭ-dās). A deamidizing enzyme.

amide (am′īd) [*ammonia* + *-ide*]. An organic compound derived from ammonia by substituting an acyl radical for hydrogen, or from an acid by replacing the —OH group by —NH_2. **niacin a.**, **nicotinic acid a.**, nicotinamide.

amidin (am′ĭ-din) [Fr. *amidon* starch]. One of the constituents of starch granules—the portion that is soluble in water.

amidine (am′ĭ-din). Any compound containing the monovalent group .C(:NH).NH_2. **insoluble a., tegumentary a.,** the cellular lining of a starch granule; amylin.

amido-. A prefix indicating the presence of the radical NH_2 along with the radical CO.

amido-acetal (am″e-do-as′e-tal). A highly poisonous substance, $NH_2.CH_2.CH(OC_2H_5)_2$, which acts by paralyzing the respiratory center.

amido-azotoluene (am″e-do-a″zo-tol′u-ēn). A reddish-brown powder, $CH_3.C_6H_4.N_2.C_6H_3.CH_2.$-$NH_2$, derived from scarlet red: used in an 8 per cent ointment to stimulate the growth of epithelium.

amidobenzene (am″e-do-ben′zēn). Aniline.

amidocephalin (am″e-do-sef′ah-lin). A form of cephalin found in the brain substance.

amidogen (am′e-do-jen″). The hypothetic radical, NH_2, found in amido compounds.

amidohexose (am″e-do-hek′sōs). A hexose combined with the amido group NH_2.

amidomyelin (am″e-do-mi′ĕ-lin). A base, $C_{44}H_{92}$-N_2PO_{10}, from the brain substance; also any member of the group to which it belongs.

amidopurine (am″e-do-pu′rēn). Adenine.

amidopyrine (am″e-do-pi′rēn). Aminopyrine.

Amidostomum (am″ĭ-dos′to-mum). A genus of round worms. **A. an′seris,** a round worm parasitic in the mucous membrane of the intestinal tract of geese, particularly underneath the cuticle of the gizzard. Called also *Strongylus nodularis* and *gizzard worm.*

amidoxime (am-ĭ-dok′sīm). Any one of a class of compounds formed from the amidines by substituting hydroxyl for a hydrogen atom of the amido group.

amidulin (ah-mid′u-lin). The granulose of starch freed from its envelope of amylocellulose by the action of hydrochloric acid; soluble starch.

amigen (am′ĭ-jen). Trade mark for a protein hydrolysate preparation for intravenous injection.

amimia (ah-mim′e-ah) [*a* neg. + Gr. *mimos* mimic + *-ia*]. Loss of the power of expression by the use of signs or gestures. **amnesic a.,** a condition in which gestures can be made, but their meaning cannot be remembered. **ataxic a.,** absolute loss of the power of making signs.

aminase (am′ĭ-nās). An enzyme which releases the amino group in amino compounds, liberating nitrogen.

amine (am′in). An organic compound containing nitrogen; any member of a group of chemical compounds formed from ammonia by replacement of one or more of the hydrogen atoms by organic (hydrocarbon) radicals. The amines are distinguished as *primary, secondary,* and *tertiary,* according to whether one, two, or three hydrogen atoms are replaced. The amines include allylamine, amylamine, ethylamine, methylamine, phenylamine, propylamine, and many other compounds. **catechol a.** See *catecholamine.*

aminitrozole (am″ĭ-ni′tro-zōl). Chemical name: 2-acetamido-5-nitrothiazole: used in treatment of trichomoniasis.

amino (am′ĭ-no). The monovalent chemical group —NH_2. As a prefix (amino-) it indicates the presence in a compound of the group —NH_2.

amino-acidemia (am″ĭ-no-as″ĭ-de′me-ah) [*amino acid* + Gr. *haima* blood + *-ia*]. Presence of amino acids in the blood.

amino-aciduria (am″ĭ-no-as″ĭ-du′re-ah) [*amino acid* + Gr. *ouron* urine + *-ia*]. Presence of amino acids in the urine.

amino-azotoluene (am″ĭ-no-az″o-tol′u-ēn). A red crystalline solid, $CH_3.C_6H_4.N_2.C_6H_3(CH_3)$-$NH_2$. It is actively carcinogenic and is used to stimulate epithelial growth.

aminobenzene (am″ĭ-no-ben′zēn). Aniline.

aminofluorene (am″ĭ-no-floo′o-rēn). A carcinogenic compound, $C_6H_4.CH_2.C_6H_3.NH_2$.

aminoform (ah-min′o-form). Methenamine.

aminoglutethimide (am″ĭ-no-gloo-teth′ĭ-mīd). Chemical name: alpha (p-aminophenyl)-alpha ethyl-glutarimide: used in treatment of most forms of epilepsy.

aminogram (am-i′no-gram). A graphic representation of the pattern of amino acids present in a substance as determined quantitatively.

aminolipid (am″ĭ-no-lip′id). Aminolipin.

aminolipin (am″ĭ-no-li′pin). Any one of a class of fatty substances containing amino nitrogen and fatty acids.

aminolysis (am″ĭ-nol′ĭ-sis) [*amine* + Gr. *lysis* dissolution]. A process of decomposition of a substance analogous to hydrolysis, but which involves recombination of the elements constituting an amino group.

aminometradine (am″ĭ-no-met′rah-dēn). Chemical name: 1-allyl-3-ethyl-6-aminotetrahydroxypyrimidinedione: used to increase urine formation, and in treatment of edema of heart failure.

aminometramide (am″ĭ-no-met′rah-mīd). Aminometradine.

aminomyelin (am″ĭ-no-mi′ĕ-lin). A phosphatide, $C_{44}H_{82}N_2PO_{10}$, from brain substance.

amino-nitrogen (am″ĭ-no-ni′tro-jen). See under *nitrogen.*

aminopentamide (am″ĭ-no-pen′tah-mīd). Chemical name: 4-dimethylamino-2,2-diphenylvaleramide. Uses: 1. parasympathetic blockade; 2. locally applied to the eye for dilatation of the pupil.

aminopeptidase (am″ĭ-no-pep′ti-dās). An exopeptidase that acts on the peptide bond of terminal amino acids possessing a free amino group. **leucine a.,** an enzyme that acts preferentially on peptides in which the free amino group is that of an L-leucine residue; found in all human tissues analyzed, with high activity in duodenum, liver, and kidney.

aminopherase (am″ĭ-nof′er-ās). An enzyme by which transamination is effected; transaminase.

aminophylline (am″ĭ-no-fil′in). A compound, $C_{16}H_{24}NO_4.2H_2O$, occurring as a white or slightly yellowish powder or granules, with a slight ammoniacal odor and bitter taste: used to relax spasm of smooth muscle in air passages, blood vessels, and biliary passages, to stimulate respiration, and to increase urine production.

aminopolypeptidase (am″ĭ-no-pol″e-pep′ti-dās). An enzyme which hydrolyzes polypeptides by loosing the peptide linkage adjacent to a free amino group.

aminoprotease (am″ĭ-no-pro′te-ās). An enzyme which hydrolyzes a protein and unites with the free amino group of its substrate, i.e., pepsin.

aminopterin (am″ĭ-nop′ter-in). Trade name for 4-aminopteroyl glutamic acid: used as a folic acid antagonist in treatment of leukemia. **sodium a.,** sodium 4-aminopteroylglutamate, a derivative of folic acid, a folic acid antagonist used in treatment of acute leukemia in children.

aminopurine (am″ĭ-no-pu′rin). See under *purine.*

aminopyrine (am″ĭ-no-pi′rin). An antipyretic and anodyne, dimethylaminophenyl dimethyl pyrazolon (pyramidon), $C_6H_5.N.CO.CN(CH_3)_2$:-$C(CH_3)N(CH_3)$.

aminosaccharide (am″ĭ-no-sak′ah-rīd). A sugar in which the OH group has been replaced by an amino group, —NH_2.

aminosis (am″ĭ-no′sis). A condition characterized by the pathologic production of amino acids in the body.

aminosol (ah-me′no-sol). Trade mark for an amino acid preparation for intravenous injection.

aminostiburia (am″ĭ-no-sti-bu′re-ah). A chemotherapeutic antimony compound, the glycoside of urea stibamine.

aminosuria (am″ĭ-no-su′re-ah) [*amine* + Gr. *ouron* urine + *-ia*]. The presence of amines in the urine.

aminothiazole (am″ĭ-no-thi′ah-zol). A sulfonamide compound, $NH_2.C:N.CH:CH.S$, that has been used in the treatment of hyperthyroidism.

aminotransferase (am″ĭ-no-trans′fer-ās). Transaminase.

aminotrate (am′ĭ-no-trāt). Trolnitrate.

aminuria (am″ĭ-nu′re-ah). The presence of amines in the urine.

amisometradine (am-i″so-met′rah-dēn). Chemical name: 6-amino-3-methyl-(2-methylallyl) uracil: used as a diuretic.

amitosis (am″ĭ-to′sis) [*a* neg. + Gr. *mitos* thread + *-osis*]. Direct cell division; cell division by simple cleavage of the nucleus without the formation of spireme spindle figure or chromosomes.

amitotic (am″ĭ-tot′ik). Of the nature of amitosis; not occurring by mitosis.

ammeter (am′e-ter) [*ampere* + Gr. *metron* measure]. An instrument calibrated to read in amperes the strength of a current flowing in a circuit. For medical purposes the ampere is too large a unit; hence it is divided into a thousand parts or *milliamperes.*

Ammi (am′me). A genus of umbelliferous plants. **A. visna′ga.** See *khellin.*

ammo-aciduria (am″o-as″ĭ-du′re-ah). Presence of ammonia and amino acids in the urine.

Ammon's fissure, operation (am′unz) [Friedrich August von *Ammon*, ophthalmologist and pathologist in Dresden, 1799–1861]. See under *fissure* and *operation.*

Ammon's horn (am′unz) [*Ammon*, a ram-headed god of the Egyptians]. See *cornu Ammonis.*

ammonemia (am″mo-ne′me-ah) [*ammonia* + Gr. *haima* blood + *-ia*]. An abnormal condition marked by the presence of ammonia or its compounds in the blood.

ammonia (ah-mo′ne-ah) [named from Jupiter *Ammon*, near whose temple in Libya it was formerly obtained]. A colorless alkaline gas, NH_3, of a penetrating odor, and soluble in water, forming ammonia water. **a. hemate,** a compound of ammonia and hematein, used as a violet-black stain for microscopic specimens.

ammoniac (ah-mo′ne-ak) [L. *ammoniacum*]. A fetid gum-resin, stimulant and expectorant, from a Persian umbelliferous plant, *Dorema ammoniacum*, used in bronchitis and asthma. Ammoniac plaster and plaster of ammoniac and mercury are used as counterirritants in pleurisy and rheumatism.

ammoniacal (am″o-ni′ah-kal). Containing ammonia.

ammoniated (ah-mo′ne-āt″ed). Combined with ammonia.

ammoniemia (ah-mo″ne-e′me-ah). Ammonemia.

ammonification (ah-mo″nĭ-fi-ka′shun). The formation of ammonia by the action of bacteria on proteins.

ammonirrhea (am″o-nĭ-re′ah) [*ammonia* + Gr. *rhoia* flow]. The excretion of ammonia by the urine or sweat.

ammonium (ah-mo′ne-um). The hypothetical radical, NH_4. It forms salts analogous to those of the alkaline metals. These are stimulant to the heart and respiration. **a. acetate,** a compound, $NH_4C_2H_3O_2$, used as a diaphoretic and refrigerant. **a. alum.** See *alum.* **a. benzoate,** a white crystalline salt, $C_6H_5.CO.ONH_4$, stimulant and diuretic. **a. bromide,** a compound, NH_4Br occurring as colorless crystals or a yellowish white crystalline powder: used as a sedative and diuretic. **a. carbamate,** a compound, $NH_2.COONH_4$. **a. carbonate,** a white powder, or hard white or translucent masses, with a strong odor of ammonia and a sharp ammoniacal taste, the official salt consisting of ammonium acid carbonate (NH_4HCO_3) and ammonium carbamate in varying proportions, yielding 30–33 per cent of NH_3. **a. chloride,** a hygroscopic compound, NH_4Cl, occurring as colorless crystals or as a fine or coarse, white crystalline powder, with a cool, saline taste: used to promote expulsion of secretion in air passages, increase production of urine, acidify urine, and to promote excretion of lead deposits in patients with lead poisoning. **ferric a. citrate, brown,** a preparation containing 16.5 to 18.5 per cent iron, about 9 per cent ammonia, and about 65 per cent hydrated citric acid: used in treatment of iron deficiency anemia. **ferric a. citrate, green,** a preparation containing 14.5 to 16 per cent iron, about 7.5 per cent ammonia, and about 75 per cent hydrated citric acid: used in treatment of iron deficiency anemia. **a. hypophosphite,** $NH_4H_2PO_2$: expectorant. **a. ichthyolate,** a reddish-brown viscous fluid: used like ichthyol. **a. ichthyosulfonate,** ichthyol. **a. iodide,** an odorless compound, NH_4I, occurring as minute, colorless, cubic crystals or as a white, granular powder, with a sharp, salty taste: expectorant. **a. mandelate,** a urinary antiseptic, $C_6H_5CH(OH)CO_2NH_4$. **a. muriate,** a. chloride. **a. nitrate,** a colorless, crystalline compound, NH_4NO_3: used in making nitrous oxide gas. It is readily soluble in water and soluble in 20 parts of alcohol. **a. oxalate,** $(NH_4)_2C_2O_4 + H_2O$: is used as a test solution. **a. persulfate,** a colorless, crystalline substance, $(NH_4)_2S_2O_8$: deodorant and disinfectant. **a. phosphate,** a compound occurring in colorless, translucent prisms, $(NH_4)_2HPO_4$ and $NH_4H_2PO_4$: used in gout and rheumatism. **a. purpurate,** the substance which gives the red color in the murexide test for uric acid. **a. rhodanilate,** a reagent for proline. It is $NH_4[Cr(CNS)_4(C_6H_4.NH_2)_2]$. **a. salicylate,** an odorless compound, $C_7H_5NH_4O_3$, occurring as colorless, lustrous prisms or plates, or as a faintly pink crystalline powder: analgetic. **a. sulfoichthyolate,** ichthyol.

ammoniuria (ah-mo″ne-u′re-ah) [*ammonia* + Gr. *ouron* urine + *-ia*]. Excess of ammonia in the urine.

Ammonius (ah-mo′ne-us) (3rd century B.C.). An Alexandrian surgeon who, according to Celsus, devised a lithotrite.

ammonol (am′o-nol). Ammoniated phenylacetamide, $C_6H_5NH_2$: analgesic.

ammonolysis (am″o-nol′ĭ-sis). A process analogous to hydrolysis, but in which ammonia takes the place of water.

ammonotelic (ah-mo″no-tel′ik) [*ammonia* + Gr. *telikos* belonging to the completion, or end]. Having ammonia as the chief excretory product of nitrogen metabolism.

Ammospermophilus (am″mo-sper-mof′ĭ-lus). A genus of burrowing rodents. **a. leucu′rus,** the desert antelope ground squirrel which is a natural host of the plague-transmitting flea, *Thrassis francisi.*

ammotherapy (am″o-ther′ah-pe) [Gr. *ammos* sand + *therapeia* healing]. Treatment of disease by the sand bath.

amnalgesia (am″nal-je′ze-ah) [*amnesia* + *algesia*]. A technique by which all pain and memory of a potentially painful procedure are abolished, involving the use of drugs or, for minor procedures, hypnosis.

amnemonic (am″ne-mon′ik) [*a* neg. + Gr. *mnēmē* a remembrance, record]. Pertaining to, characterized by, or causing loss of memory.

amnesia (am-ne′se-ah) [Gr. *amnēsia* forgetfulness]. Lack or loss of memory, especially inability to remember past experiences. **anterograde a.,** amnesia for events occurring after the trauma or disease which caused the condition. **auditory a.,** word deafness. **Broca's a.,** inability to remember spoken words. **infantile a.,** the usual inability to recall the events of the first five or six years of life. **lacunar a.,** loss of memory for certain isolated events only. **localized a.,** amnesia for events connected with a certain place, time, or incident. **olfactory a.,** loss of the sense of smell. **patchy a.,** lacunar a. **post-hypnotic a.,** a directed forgetfulness of the subject for experiences undergone while he was in the hypnotic state. **retro-active a., retrograde a.,** amnesia for events which occurred before the trauma or disease causing the condition. **tactile a.,** astereognosis. **tropic a., tropical a.,** loss of memory frequently affecting white men in the tropics; a condition very prevalent on the west coast of Africa, where it is called *coast memory.* **verbal a.,** loss of memory for words. **visual a.,** word blindness.

amnesiac (am-ne′se-ak). A person affected with amnesia.

amnesic (am-ne′sik). Affected with or characterized by amnesia.

amnestic (am-nes′tik). 1. Amnesic. 2. Causing amnesia.

amnio- (am′ne-o) [Gr. *amnion* lamb]. Combining form denoting relationship to the amnion.

amniocentesis (am″ne-o-sen-te′sis). Transabdominal perforation of the uterus, to permit drainage of amniotic fluid.

amniochorial (am″ne-o-ko′re-al). Pertaining to the amnion and chorion.

amniogenesis (am″ne-o-jen′e-sis) [*amnio-* + Gr. *genesis* formation]. The development of the amnion.

amniography (am″ne-og′rah-fe) [*amnio-* + Gr. *graphein* to record]. Roentgenography of the gravid uterus after injection of opaque media into the amniotic fluid, outlining the uterine cavity and permitting study of maternal and fetal physiology.

amnioma (am″ne-o′mah) [*amnio-* + *-oma*]. A tumor formed from the amnion.

amnion (am′ne-on) [Gr. *amnion* lamb]. The thin, transparent, silvery and tough membrane lining the chorion laeve and chorion frondosum (placenta), which produces, at the very earliest period of fetation, the amniotic fluid.

Amnion and chorion: *A*, Amnion; 1, 2, chorion; *P*, allantois; *U*, umbilical vesicle (Dorland).

amnionic (am″ne-on′ik). Pertaining to the amnion.

amnionitis (am″ne-o-ni′tis). Inflammation of the amnion.

amnioplastin (am-ne-o-plas′-tin). Proprietary name for dried and sterilized amnionic membrane applied to prevent adhesions after craniotomy.

amniorrhea (am″ne-o-re′ah) [*amnion* + Gr. *rhoia* flow]. The escape of the amniotic fluid, or liquor amnii.

amniorrhexis (am″ne-o-rek′sis) [*amnion* + Gr. *rhēxis* rupture]. Rupture of the amnion.

Amniota (am-ne-o′tah). A major group of vertebrates comprising those which develop an amnion: opposed to *Anamniota.*

amniote (am′ne-ōt). Any animal or group belonging to the Amniota.

amniotic (am″ne-ot′ik). Pertaining to or developing an amnion.

amniotin (am-ni′o-tin). Trade mark for an estrogenic preparation derived from the urine of pregnant mares.

amniotome (am′ne-o-tōm″) [*amnion* + Gr. *tomē* a cutting]. An instrument for cutting the fetal membranes.

amniotomy (am″ne-ot′o-me). Surgical rupture of the fetal membranes in induction of labor.

A.M.O. Abbreviation for *axiomesio-occlusal.*

amobarbital (am″o-bar′bi-tal). An odorless, white crystalline powder with a bitter taste, $C_{11}H_{18}N_2O_3$: used as a sedative and hypnotic. **a. sodium,** an odorless white, friable, granular powder with a bitter taste, $C_{11}H_{17}N_2NaO_3$.

amodiaquine (am″o-di′ah-kwin). Chemical name: 4-(7-chloro-4-quinolylamino)-α-diethyl-amino-o-cresol): used to suppress malaria, to treat malaria due to *Plasmodium falciparum,* and to treat liver abscess due to ameba.

Amoeba (ah-me′bah). A name given various protozoa of the subphylum Sarcodina, many of them now assigned to other taxonomic categories. **A. bucca′lis,** *Entamoeba gingivalis.* **A. cachex′ica,** a name given to an amoeba-like cell found in carcinoma. **A. co′li,** *Entamoeba coli.* **A. co′li mi′tis,** a nonpathogenic form. **A. denta′lis,** *Entamoeba gingivalis.* **A. dysente′riae,** *Entamoeba histolytica.* **A. histolyt′ica,** *Entamoeba histolytica.* **A. li′max,** *Endolimax nana.* **A. meleag′ridis,** *Histomonas meleagridis.* **A. uri′nae granula′ta,** a name given an ameba-like cell found in the urine in case of infective jaundice with albuminuria. **A. urogenita′lis,** a name given an ameba-like cell found in the urine and the vaginal secretions. **A. verruco′sa,** a name given an ameba-like cell having a large knobby nucleus and a deeply staining nucleolus.

Amoebobacter (ah-me″bo-bak′ter). A genus of microorganisms of the family Thiorhodaceae, suborder Rhodobacteriineae, order Pseudomonadales, made up of cells usually occurring without a common capsule. It includes three species, *A. bacillo′sus, A. gran′ula,* and *A. ro′seus.*

Amoebotaenia (ah-me″bo-te′ne-ah). A tapeworm parasitic in chickens.

amok (ah-mok′) [Malay "impulse to murder"]. A psychic disturbance marked by a period of depression, followed by violent attempts to kill people.

amolanone (ah-mo′lah-nōn). Chemical name: 3-(B-diethylaminolthyl)-3-phenyl-2-benzofuranone: used for parasympathetic blockade, relaxation of spasm of the urinary tract, and as a topical anesthetic.

Amomum (ah-mo′mum) [L.; Gr. *amōmon*]. A genus of scitamineous plants which afford cardamoms and grains of paradise. See *cardamom* and *grains of paradise.*

amor (a′mor) [L.]. Love. **a. les′bicus,** sapphism.

amoralia (ah″mo-ra′le-ah) [*a* neg. + *moral*]. Moral imbecility.

amoralis (ah″mo-ra′lis) [*a* neg. + L. *moralis* moral]. A moral imbecile.

amorpha (ah-mor′fah) [*a* neg. + Gr. *morphē* form]. Diseases that evince no definite pathologic changes.

amorphia (ah-mor′fe-ah) [*a* neg. + Gr. *morphē* form + *-ia*]. The fact or quality of being amorphous.

amorphinism (ah-mor′fĭ-nizm). The state produced by depriving a morphine addict of his drug.

amorphism (ah-mor′fizm). Amorphia.

amorphous (ah-mor′fus) [*a* neg. + Gr. *morphē* form]. Having no definite form; shapeless; in pharmacy, not crystallized.

amorphus (ah-mor′fus) [*a* neg. + Gr. *morphē* form]. A shapeless acardiac fetal monster.

Amoss′ sign (a′mos) [Harold Lindsay *Amoss,* American physician, 1886–1956]. See under *sign.*

amotio (ah-mo′she-o) [L.]. A removing. **a. ret′inae,** detachment of the retina.

amp. Abbreviation for *ampere.*

Ampelopsis (am″pě-lop′sis) [Gr. *ampelos* grape + *opsis* appearance]. A genus of vitaceous climbing shrubs.

ampelotherapy (am″pě-lo-ther′ah-pe) [Gr. *ampelos* grape + *therapy*]. The therapeutic use of grape products; grape cure.

amperage (am′per-ij). The strength of an electric current expressed in amperes or milliamperes.

ampere (am′pēr) [André M. *Ampère*, 1775–1836]. The unit of electric current in the M.K.S. system of measurement, being the current produced by one volt acting through a resistance of one ohm. The international ampere is the unvarying electrical current which, when passed through a solution of silver nitrate in accordance with certain specifications, deposits silver at the rate of 0.001118 Gm. per second.

amperemeter (am′pēr-me″ter). An instrument for measuring amperage.

amphamphoterodiplopia (am″fam-fo″ter-o-dĭ-plo′pe-ah) [Gr. *amphi* on both sides + *amphoteros* both together + *diplopia*]. Double vision with both eyes together, or with either eye separately.

ampheclexis (am″fĕ-klek′sis) [Gr. *amphi* on both sides + *eklexis* selection]. Sexual selection on the part of both male and female.

amphedroxyn (am″fe-drok′sin). Trade mark for a preparation of methamphetamine.

amphemerous (am-fem′er-us). Quotidian; occurring daily.

amphenidone (am-fen′ĭ-dōn). Chemical name: aminophenylpyridone: used as a tranquilizer.

amphetamine (am-fet′ah-min). Synthetic racemic desoxy-nor-ephedrine or alpha-methylphenethylamine, $C_6H_5.CH_2CHNH_2CH_3$: used to stimulate the central nervous system, increase blood pressure, reduce appetite, and reduce nasal congestion. **a. sulfate,** an odorless, white, crystalline powder, with a slightly bitter taste, $(C_9H_{13}N)_2.H_2SO_4$: central nervous system stimulant. **a. sulfate, dextro,** the dextrorotatory isomer of amphetamine sulfate.

amphi- (am′fe) [Gr. *amphi* on both sides]. A prefix signifying on both sides; around or about; double.

amphiarkyochrome (am″fe-ar′ke-o-krōm″) [*amphi-* + Gr. *arkys* net + *chrōma* color]. A nerve cell, the stainable portion of whose body is a pale network, of which the nodal points are joined by a readily and intensely stainable network.

amphiarthrodial (am″fe-ar-thro′de-al). Pertaining to amphiarthrosis.

amphiarthrosis (am″fe-ar-thro′sis) [*amphi-* + Gr. *arthrōsis* joint]. [B N A] A form of articulation permitting little motion, the apposed surfaces of bone being connected by fibrocartilage. Called *junctura cartilaginea* [N A].

amphiaster (am″fe-as′ter) [*amphi-* + Gr. *astēr* star]. The figure of achromatin fibers formed in karyokinesis, consisting of two asters joined by a spindle. Called also *diaster.*

Amphibia (am-fib′e-ah) [*amphi-* + Gr. *bios* life]. A class of vertebrated animals that are able to live both on land and in water: it includes frogs, toads, newts and salamanders.

amphibious (am-fib′e-us) [see *Amphibia*]. Capable of living both on land and in water.

amphiblastic (am″fe-blas′tik) [*amphi-* + Gr. *blastos* germ]. Denoting the complete but unequal cleavage of a telolecithal egg.

amphiblastula (am″fe-blas′tu-lah) [*amphi-* + *blastula*]. A blastula with unequal blastomeres.

amphiblestritis (am″fe-bles-tri′tis) [Gr. *amphiblēstron* net + *-itis*]. Retinitis.

amphibolia (am″fe-bo′le-ah) [Gr. *amphibolia* uncertainty]. The uncertain stage of a fever or disease: a period of doubtful prognosis.

amphibolic (am″fe-bol′ik). 1. Uncertain; vacillating; of doubtful prognosis. 2. Having both a catabolic and an anabolic function.

amphibolous (am-fib′o-lus) [Gr. *amphibolos*]. Amphibolic.

amphicarcinogenic (am″fe-kar″sĭ-no-jen′ik). Tending, optionally, to increase or to decrease carcinogenic activity.

amphicelous (am″fe-se′lus) [*amphi-* + Gr. *koilos* hollow]. Concave at both ends or sides.

amphicentric (am″fe-sen′trik) [*amphi-* + Gr. *kentron* center]. Beginning and ending in the same vessel, as a branch of a rete mirabile.

amphichroic (am″fe-kro′ik) [*amphi-* + Gr. *chrōma* color]. Exhibiting two colors; affecting both red and blue litmus.

amphichromatic (am″fe-kro-mat′ik). Amphichroic.

amphicrania (am″fe-kra′ne-ah) [*amphi-* + Gr. *kranion* head + *-ia*]. Pain in both sides of the head.

amphicreatine (am″fe-kre′ah-tin) [*amphi-* + *creatine*]. A leukomaine, $C_9H_{19}N_7O_4$, from muscle, occurring in the form of opaque, yellowish-white crystals.

amphicreatinine (am″fe-kre-at′ĭ-nin) [*amphi-* + *creatinine*]. A poisonous leukomaine, $C_9H_{19}N_7O_4$, from muscle.

amphicroic (am″fe-kro′ik) [*amphi-* + Gr. *krouein* to test]. Turning red litmus paper blue, and blue litmus paper red.

amphicyte (am′fe-sit) [*amphi-* + Gr. *kytos* hollow vessel]. One of the cells forming the capsule which surrounds a cerebrospinal ganglion cell.

amphicytula (am″fe-sit′u-lah) [*amphi-* + *cytula*]. A fertilized telolecithal ovum.

amphidiarthrosis (am″fe-di″ar-thro′sis) [*amphi-* + *diarthrosis*]. A joint having the nature of both a ginglymus and arthrodia, as the articulation of the lower jaw.

amphigastrula (am″fe-gas′tru-lah) [*amphi-* + *gastrula*]. A gastrula composed of cells unequal in size in its upper and lower hemispheres.

amphigenetic (am″fe-je-net′ik). Produced by means of both sexes; as, *amphigenetic* reproduction.

amphigonium (am″fe-go′ne-um) [*amphi-* + Gr. *gonos* generation]. That stage of the life of a malaria parasite which is passed in the mosquito.

amphigony (am-fig′o-ne). Sexual reproduction.

amphikaryon (am″fe-kar′e-on) [*amphi-* + Gr. *karyon* kernel]. A diploid nucleus.

Amphileptus (am″fe-lep′tus). A genus of ciliate parasitic organisms. **A. branchia′rum,** a ciliate parasite on the gills of frog tadpoles.

amphileucemic (am″fe-lu-se′mik). Amphileukemic.

amphileukemic (am″fe-lu-ke′mik) [*amphi-* + *leukemic*]. Showing leukemic changes which vary in degree with the changes in the organ.

Amphimerus (am-fim′er-us). A genus of trematodes. *A. nover′ca* infects dogs in India and has been reported in man. *A. pseudofelin′eus* infects cats and coyotes in the central United States.

amphimicrobian (am″fe-mi-kro′be-an) [*amphi-* + *microbe*]. Both aerobic and anaerobic.

amphimixis (am″fe-mik′sis) [*amphi-* + Gr. *mixis* a mingling]. 1. The intermingling of the paternal and maternal hereditary characters in the offspring. 2. In psychiatry, the direction of early energies toward the genital organs in psychosexual development.

amphimorula (am″fe-mor′u-lah) [*amphi-* + *morula*]. The morula resulting from unequal cleavage, the cells of the two hemispheres being of unequal size.

amphinucleus (am″fe-nu′kle-us) [*amphi-* + *nucleus*]. A nucleus that consists of a single body made of spindle fibers and centrosome, around which the chromatin is massed. It is the ordinary form of protozoan nucleus. Called also *centronucleus.*

Amphioxus (am″fe-ok′sus). A primitive fishlike marine chordate, considered similar to the ancestor of the vertebrates.

amphipeptone (am″fe-pep′tōn) [*amphi-* + *peptone*]. A mixture of antipeptone with hemipeptone formed in the digestion of proteins.

amphiporine (am″fe-po′rin). An alkaloid of the nicotine group found in certain nemertean worms.

amphipyrenin (am″fe-pi′re-nin) [*amphi-* + Gr. *pyrēn* stone of a fruit]. The substance of the nuclear membrane of a cell.

Amphistoma (am-fis′to-mah) [*amphi-* + Gr. *stoma* mouth]. A genus of parasitic trematode worms. **A. con′icum,** a species found in the rumen of sheep, cattle, etc. **A. hom′inis,** *Gastrodiscoides hominis.* **A. watso′ni,** *Watsonius watsoni.*

amphistomiasis (am″fe-sto-mi′ah-sis). The condition of being infected with trematodes of the genus *Amphistoma.*

amphitene (am′fe-tēn). Denoting the synaptic stage of miosis.

amphitheater (am″fe-the′ah-ter). An operating room or lecture room with seats arranged in tiers for students or spectators.

amphithymia (am″fe-thi′me-ah) [*amphi-* + Gr. *thymos* spirit + *-ia*]. A mental state characterized by both depression and elation.

amphitrichate (am″fe-tri′kāt). Having a single flagellum at each end.

amphitrichous (am-fit′rĕ-kus) [*amphi-* + Gr. *thrix* hair]. Having a single flagellum, or a single tuft of flagella, at each end: applied to a bacterial cell.

amphitropic (am″fe-trop′ik). Passing into the abdomen or other cavity from one side.

amphitypy (am-fit′ĭ-pe). The condition of showing both types.

ampho- (am′fo) [Gr. *amphō* both]. A prefix signifying both.

ampho-albumose (am″fo-al′bu-mōs). Any albumose which is converted by digestion into amphopeptone.

amphochromatophil (am″fo-kro-mat′o-fil). Amphophil.

amphochromophil (am″fo-kro′mo-fil) [*ampho-* + Gr. *chrōma* color + *philein* to love]. Amphophil.

amphocyte (am′fo-sīt). An amphophilic cell.

amphodiplopia (am″fo-dĭ-plo′pe-ah) [*ampho-* + *diplopia*]. Double vision in both eyes.

amphogenic (am″fo-jen′ik) [*ampho-* + Gr. *gennan* to produce]. Producing offspring of both sexes.

amphojel (am′fo-jel). Trade mark for preparations of aluminum hydroxide gel.

ampholyte (am′fo-līt) [*ampho-* + *electrolyte*]. An amphoteric electrolyte.

amphopeptone (am″fo-pep′tōn). Amphipeptone.

amphophil (am′fo-fil). 1. Amphophilic. 2. An amphophilic cell.

amphophilic (am-fo-fil′ik) [*ampho-* + Gr. *philein* to love]. Stainable with either acid or basic dyes. **a.-basophil,** staining with both acid and basic stains, but having a greater affinity for basic ones. **gram-a.,** tending to stain both positive and negative with gram stain. **a.-oxyphil,** staining with both acid and basic dyes, but having a greater affinity for the acid ones.

amphophilous (am-fof′i-lus). Amphophilic.

amphoric (am-for′ik) [L. *amphoricus,* from L. *amphora,* Gr. *amphoreus* jar]. Pertaining to a bottle; resembling the sound made by blowing across the mouth of a bottle.

amphoricity (am″fo-ris′ĭ-te). The condition of giving off amphoric sounds on percussion or auscultation.

amphoriloquy (am″fo-ril′o-kwe) [L. *amphora* jar + *loqui* to speak]. The production of amphoric sounds in speaking.

amphorophony (am″fo-rof′o-ne) [Gr. *amphoreus* jar + *phonē* voice]. An amphoric sound of the voice.

amphoteric (am-fo-ter′ik) [Gr. *amphoteros* pertaining to both]. Having opposite characters; capable of acting either as an acid or as a base; combining with both acids and bases; affecting both red and blue litmus.

amphotericin (am″fo-ter′ĭ-sin). A name given an antibiotic substance. **a. B,** an antibiotic substance derived from strains of *Streptomyces nodosus:* used in treatment of meningitis caused by cryptococcus, and of systemic fungus infections.

amphotericity (am″fo-ter-is′ĭ-te). Amphoterism.

amphoterism (am-fo′ter-izm). The condition or quality of possessing both basic and acid properties.

amphoterodiplopia (am-fot″er-o-dĭ-plo′pe-ah) [Gr. *amphoteros* pertaining to both + *diplopia*]. Amphodiplopia.

amphoterous (am-fot′er-us). Amphoteric.

amphotony (am-fot′o-ne) [*ampho-* + Gr. *tonos* tension]. A condition in which both sympathicotonia and vagotony exist; hypertonia of the entire sympathetic nervous system.

amplexation (am″plek-sa′shun) [L. *amplexus* embrace]. Treatment of fractured clavicle by an apparatus which fixes the shoulder and embraces the chest and neck.

amplexus (am-plek′sus) [L.]. An embrace, as in the sexual clasping of the female by the male frog.

amplification (am″plĭ-fi-ka′shun) [L. *amplifica′tio*]. The process of making larger, as the increase of an auditory or visual stimulus, as a means of improving its perception.

amplifier (am′ple-fi″er). An apparatus for increasing the volume of sound, or the magnification of a microscope.

amplitude (am′ple-tūd) [L. *amplitudo*]. Largeness or fulness: wideness or breadth of range or extent. **a. of accommodation,** the total amount of accommodative power of the eye; the difference in refractive power of the eye when adjusted for farthest vision and that when adjusted for nearest vision. **a. of convergence,** the power required to turn the eyes from their far point to their near point of convergence.

amprotropine (am″pro-tro′pēn). Chemical name: 3-diethylamino-2,2-dimethylpropyl tropate: used for parasympathetic blockade, and as an antispasmodic.

ampul (am′pūl). Ampule.

ampule (am′pūl) [Fr. *ampoule*]. A small glass container capable of being sealed so as to preserve its contents in a sterile condition: used principally for containing hypodermic solutions.

ampulla (am-pul′lah), pl. *ampul′lae* [L. "a jug"]. A general term used in anatomical nomenclature to designate a flasklike dilatation of a tubular structure. **a. canalic′uli lacrima′lis** [N A], a dilatation of a lacrimal canaliculus just before it opens into the lacrimal sac. Called also *ampulla ductus lacrimalis* [B N A], and *a. of lacrimal canaliculus.* **a. chy′li,** receptaculum chyli. **a. duc′tus deferen′tis** [N A, B N A], the enlarged and tortuous distal end of the ductus deferens. **a. ductus lacrimalis** [B N A], a. canaliculi lacrimalis. **Henle′s a.,** a. ductus deferentis. **a. hepatopancreat′ica** [N A], the dilatation formed by junction of the common bile and the pancreatic duct proximal to their opening on the wall of the duodenum. Called also *hepatopancreatic a.* **ampul′lae lactif′erae,** sinus lactiferi. **Lieberkühn′s a.,** the termination of a lacteal in an intestinal villus. **ampul′lae membrana′ceae** [N A, B N A], the dilatations at one end of each of the three semicircular ducts, each named according to the duct of which it forms a part. Called also *membranaceous ampullae.* **a. membrana′cea ante′rior** [N A], the dilatation at the end of the anterior semicircular duct. Called also *anterior membranaceous a.* **a. membrana′cea latera′lis** [N A, B N A], the dilatation at the end of the lateral semicircular duct. Called also *lateral membranaceous a.* **a. membrana′cea poste′rior** [N A, B N A], the dilatation at the end of the posterior semicircular duct. Called also *posterior membranaceous a.* **ampul′lae os′seae** [N A, B N A], the dilatations at one of the ends of the semicircular canals, each named according to the duct of which it forms a part, and lodging the correspondingly named ampulla of a semicircular duct. Called also *osseous ampullae*. **a. os'sea ante'rior** [N A], the dilatation at one end of the anterior semicircular canal. See *ampullae osseae*. **a. os'sea latera'lis** [N A, B N A], the dilatation at one end of the lateral semicircular canal. See *ampullae osseae*. **a. os'sea poste'rior** [N A, B N A], the dilatation at one end of the posterior semicircular canal. See *ampullae osseae*. **phrenic a.,** the dilatation at the lower end of the esophagus. **a. rec'ti** [N A, B N A], the dilated portion of the rectum just proximal to the anal canal. Called also *rectal a.* **a. of Thoma,** one of the small terminal expansions of an interlobar artery in the pulp of the spleen. **a. tu'bae uteri'nae** [N A, B N A], the part of the uterine tube between the isthmus and the infundibulum. Called also *a. of uterine tube*. **a. of vas deferens,** a. ductus deferentis. **a. of Vater,** a. hepatopancreatica.

ampullae (am-pul'le) [L.]. Plural of *ampulla*.

ampullar (am-pul'ar). Pertaining to an ampulla, especially to the ampulla of Vater.

ampullary (am'pu-la″re). Ampullar.

ampullate (am-pul'āt). Flask shaped.

ampullitis (am″pul-li'tis). Inflammation of an ampulla, especially of the ampulla ductus deferentis.

ampullula (am-pul'u-lah) [L.]. Any minute ampulla, like many of those of the lymphatic and lacteal vessels.

amputation (am″pu-ta'shun) [L. *amputare* to cut off, or to prune]. The removal of a limb or other appendage or outgrowth of the body. **Alanson's a.,** circular amputation, the stump shaped like a hollow cone. **Alouette's a.,** amputation at the hip, with a semicircular outer flap to the great trochanter, and a large internal flap from within outward. **amniotic a.,** the alleged amputation of a fetal extremity by a band of amnion. **aperiosteal a.,** amputation with complete removal of the periosteum from the end of the stump of the bone. **Béclard's a.,** amputation at hip joint by cutting the posterior flap first. **Bier's a.,** osteoplastic amputation of the leg with a bone flap cut out of the tibia and fibula above the stump. **bloodless a.,** one in which there is little or no loss of blood, the circulation being controlled by mechanical means. **Bunge's a.,** aperiosteal a. **Callander's a.,** a tendoplastic amputation at the knee joint with long anterior and posterior flaps, the patella being removed to leave a fossa for the end of the divided femur. **Carden's a.,** a single-flap operation, cutting through the femur just above the knee. **central a.,** one in which the scar is situated at or near the center of the stump. **chop a.,** amputation by a circular cut through the parts without the formation of a flap. **Chopart's a.,** amputation of the foot, the calcaneus, talus, and other parts of the tarsus being retained. **cinematic a., cineplastic a.,** kineplasty. **circular a.,** one performed by means of a single flap and by a circular cut in a direction vertical to the long axis of a limb. **coat-sleeve a.,** a circular amputation, with a single skin flap made very long, the end being closed with a tape. **complete a.,** amputation in which the entire limb or segment of the limb is removed. **congenital a.,** the alleged amputation of a fetal extremity in utero by a constricting band. **consecutive a.,** amputation performed during or after the period of suppuration. **a. in contiguity,** an amputation at a joint. **a. in continuity,** an amputation elsewhere than at a joint. **cutaneous a.,** amputation in which the flaps are composed entirely of skin. **diaclastic a.,** an amputation in which the bone is broken by the osteoclast and the soft tissues divided by the écraseur. **Dieffenbach's a.** See under *operation*. **double-flap a.,** one in which two flaps are formed. **dry a.,** bloodless a. **Dupuytren's a.,** amputation of the arm at the shoulder joint. **eccentric a.,** one in which the scar is not at the center of the stump. **elliptic a.,** one in which the cut has an elliptic outline on account of the oblique direction of the incision. **Farabeuf's a.,** amputation of the leg at the "place of choice" by a large external flap. **flap a.,** one in which flaps are made from the soft tissues, the division being oblique. **flapless a.,** one in which no flaps are formed, and the wound must heal by granulation. **Forbe's a.,** a foot amputation which retains the calcaneum, astragalus, scaphoid, and a part of the cuboid bones. **forequarter a.,** interscapulothoracic a. **galvanocaustic a.,** one in which the soft parts are divided with the galvanocautery. **Gritti's a.,** amputation of the leg through the knee, using the patella as an osteoplastic flap over the end of the femur. **Gritti-Stokes a.,** a modification of Gritti's amputation, using an oval anterior flap. **guillotine a.,** rapid amputation of a limb by a circular sweep of the knife and a cut of the saw, the entire cross section being left open for dressing. **Guyon's a.,** amputation above the malleoli. **Hancock's a.,** a modification of Pirogoff's amputation, a part of the astragalus (talus) being retained in the flap, the lower surface being sawed off and the cut surface of the calcaneus being brought into contact with it. **Hey's a.,** disarticulation of the metatarsus from the tarsus, with removal of a part of the medial cuneiform bone. **hindquarter a.,** interilioabdominal a. **immediate a.,** one performed within 12 hours after the injury which made it necessary. **interilio-abdominal a., interinnomino-abdominal a.,** amputation of an entire lower limb, including the whole or part of the innominate bone. **intermediary a., intermediate a.,** one done during the period of reaction and before suppuration. **interpelviabdominal a.,** amputation of thigh with excision of the lateral half of the pelvis. **interscapulothoracic a.,** amputation of the upper extremity, including the scapula and external part of the clavicle. **intrapyretic a.,** intermediary a. **intra-uterine a.,** congenital a. **Jaboulay's a.,** interpelviabdominal a. **kineplastic a.,** kineplasty. **Kirk's a.,** a tendoplastic amputation just above the femoral condyles. The tendon of the quadriceps extensor muscle is sutured over the end of the divided femur. **Langenbeck's a.,** amputation in which the flaps are cut from without inward. **Larrey's a.,** a method of disarticulation of the humerus at the shoulder joint by an incision extending from the acromion about three inches down the arm, splitting the deltoid muscle, and from this point about the arm to the center of the axilla. **Le Fort's a.,** a modification of Pirogoff's amputation in which the calcaneus is sawed through horizontally instead of vertically. **linear a.,** amputation by a simple straight division of all the tissues. **Lisfranc's a.** 1. *Dupuytren's a.* 2. A division of the foot between the tarsus and the metatarsus. **MacKenzie's a.,** amputation like that of Syme except that the flap is taken from the inner side of the ankle. **Maisonneuve's a.,** amputation by breaking the bone, followed by cutting of the soft parts. **major a.,** amputation of a leg above the ankle or of an arm above the wrist. **Malgaigne's a.,** subastragalar a. **mediate a.,** intermediary a. **mediotarsal a.,** Chopart's a. **minor a.,** amputation of a small part, as a finger or toe. **mixed a.,** that which is performed by a combination of the circular and flap methods. **multiple a.,** amputation of two or more parts at the same time. **musculocutaneous a.,** one in which the flap consists of muscle and skin. **natural a.,** congenital a. **oblique a.,** oval a. **operative a.,** removal of a part by surgery. **osteoplastic a.,** one in which the two severed surfaces of bone are brought into contact so as to unite. **oval a.,** one in which the incision consists of two reversed spirals. **partial a.,** amputation of only a portion or segment of a limb. **pathological a.,** amputation for a diseased condition of the part, as tumor. **periosteoplastic a.,** subperiosteal a.

phalangophalangeal a., amputation of a digit at a phalangeal joint. **Pirogoff's a.,** amputation of the foot at the ankle, part of the calcaneus being left in the lower end of the stump. **primary a.,** one performed after the period of shock, and before the development of inflammation. **pulp a.,** pulpotomy. **quadruple a.,** amputation of all four extremities. **racket a.,** one in which there is a single longitudinal incision continuous below with a spiral incision on each side of the limb. **rectangular a.,** one with a long and a short rectangular skin flap. See *Teale's a.* **Ricard's a.,** intertibiocalcaneal disarticulation, astragalectomy, and the placing of the os calcis in the tibiofibular mortise. **root a.,** apicoectomy. **secondary a.,** one performed during the period of suppuration. **spontaneous a.,** loss of a part which occurs without surgical intervention. **Stokes's a.,** Gritti-Stokes a. **subastragalar a.,** amputation of the foot, leaving the astragalus (talus) in the lower end of the stump. **subperiosteal a.,** one in which the cut end of the bone is covered with a flap of periosteum. **Syme's a.,** amputation of the foot at the ankle joint with removal of both malleoli. **synchronous a.,** multiple amputation, especially multiple amputation in which two or more parts are removed simultaneously by different operators. **Teale's a.,** amputation with preservation of a long rectangular flap of muscle and integument on one side of the limb and a short rectangular flap on the other. **tertiary a.,** amputation done after the stage of inflammatory reaction has subsided. **a. by transfixion,** one performed by thrusting a long knife through the limb and cutting the flaps from within outward. **traumatic a.,** amputation of a part by accidental injury. **Tripier's a.,** one like Chopart's, except that a part of the tarsus is removed. **triple a.,** amputation of three extremities. **Vladimiroff-Mikulicz a.,** osteoplastic resection of foot with incision of the calcaneus and talus.

amputee (am″pu-te′). A person who has one or more of his limbs amputated.

Amsler's marker (am′slerz). A form of caliper compass used for marking with a dot of India ink the point for the application of the cautery in the Gonin operation.

amsustain (am′sus-tān). Trade mark for a preparation of dextroamphetamine.

amuck (ah-muk′). Amok.

amusia (ah-mu′ze-ah) [Gr. *amousia* want of harmony]. Inability to produce (**motor a.**) or to comprehend (**sensory a.**) musical sounds (Knoblunch). **instrumental a.,** that in which the patient has lost the power of playing a musical instrument. **vocal motor a.,** that in which the patient cannot sing in tune.

Amussat's operation, probe, valve (am″oo-saz′) [Jean Zuléma *Amussat*, French surgeon, 1796–1856]. See under the nouns.

amyasthenia (ah-mi″as-the′ne-ah). Amyosthenia.

amyasthenic (ah-mi″as-then′ik). Amyosthenic.

amychophobia (ah-mi″ko-fo′be-ah) [Gr. *amychē* a scratch + *phobia*]. Morbid fear of being scratched, as by the claws of a cat.

amyctic (ah-mik′tik). Caustic or irritating.

amydricaine (ah-mi′drĭ-kān). Chemical name: 2-benzoxy-2-dimethylaminomethyl-1-dimethylaminobutane: used as a surface or spinal anesthetic agent.

amyelencephalia (ah-mi″el-en-seh-fa′le-ah) [*a* neg. + Gr. *myelos* marrow + *enkephalos* brain + *-ia*]. A developmental anomaly characterized by absence of both brain and spinal cord.

amyelencephalus (ah-mi″el-en-sef′ah-lus). A fetal monster exhibiting amyelencephalia.

amyelia (ah″mi-e′le-ah) [*a* neg. + Gr. *myelos* marrow + *-ia*]. A developmental anomaly characterized by absence of the spinal cord.

amyelic (ah″mi-el′ik). Having no spinal cord.

amyelineuria (ah-mi″e-lin-u′re-ah) [*a* neg. + Gr. *myelos* marrow + *neuron* nerve + *-ia*]. Paralysis or defective function of the spine.

amyelinic (ah-mi″e-lin′ik). Without myelin; having no medullary sheath.

amyeloidemia (ah-mi″e-loi-de′me-ah) [*a* neg. + *myeloid* + Gr. *haima* blood + *-ia*]. Absence of myelocytes from the blood.

amyelonic (ah-mi″e-lon′ik) [*a* neg. + Gr. *myelos* marrow]. 1. Having no spinal cord. 2. Having no bone marrow.

amyelotrophy (ah-mi″e-lot′ro-fe) [*a* neg. + Gr. *myelos* marrow + *trophē* nourishment]. Atrophy of the spinal cord.

amyelus (ah-mi′e-lus) [*a* neg. + Gr. *myelos* marrow]. A fetal monster exhibiting amyelia.

amygdala (ah-mig′dah-lah) [Gr. *amygdalē* almond]. An almond; used in anatomical nomenclature to designate an almond-shaped structure. **a. accesso′ria, accessory a.,** tonsilla lingualis. **a. ama′ra,** the bitter almond. **a. ceraso′rum,** the kernels of cherry stones. **a. of cerebellum,** tonsilla cerebelli. **a. dul′cis,** the sweet almond of many varieties.

amygdalase (ah-mig′dah-lās). An enzyme which splits amygdalose.

amygdalectomy (ah-mig″dah-lek′to-me) [*amygdalo-* + Gr. *ektomē* excision]. 1. Excision of the nucleus amygdalae. 2. Excision of a tonsil.

amygdalin (ah-mig′dah-lin). A glycoside from bitter almond and the leaves of cherry laurel, $C_6H_5CH(CN).O.C_{12}H_{21}O_{10}$. It is split by the enzyme emulsin into glucose, benzaldehyde, and hydrocyanic acid.

amygdaline (ah-mig′dah-lin) [L. *amygdalinus*]. 1. Like an almond. 2. Pertaining to a tonsil.

amygdalitis (ah-mig″dah-li′tis). Inflammation of a tonsil.

amygdalo- (ah-mig′dah-lo) [Gr. *amygdalē* almond]. Combining form denoting relationship to an almond-shaped structure or to the tonsil.

amygdaloid (ah-mig′dah-loid) [*amygdalo-* + Gr. *eidos* form]. Resembling an almond, or tonsil.

amygdalolith (ah-mig′dah-lo-lith″) [*amygdalo-* + Gr. *lithos* stone]. A concretion in a tonsil.

amygdalopathy (ah-mig″dah-lop′ah-the) [*amygdalo-* + Gr. *pathos* illness]. Any disease of a tonsil.

amygdalophenin (ah-mig″dah-lof′ĕ-nin). Salicyl phenetidin, $C_6H_4(OC_2H_5)NH.OC.CH(OH)C_6H_5$.

amygdalose (ah-mig′dah-los). A disaccharide from amygdalin. It splits into two molecules of dextrose.

amygdalothrypsis (ah-mig″dah-lo-thrip′sis) [*amygdalo-* + Gr. *thrypsis* crushing]. Removal of a hypertrophied tonsil by crushing with a strong forceps.

amygdalotome (ah-mig′dah-lo-tōm″) [*amygdalo-* + Gr. *tomē* cut]. Tonsillotome.

amygdalotomy (ah-mig″dah-lot′o-me). 1. Incision of the nucleus amygdalae. 2. Tonsillotomy.

amygdalo-uvular (ah-mig″dah-lo-u′vu-lar). Pertaining to the amygdala (tonsilla) and the uvula of the cerebellum.

amyl (am′il) [Gr. *amylon* starch]. The univalent radical, C_5H_{11}. **a. acetate,** a colorless, limpid liquid, the acetic acid ester of amyl alcohol, $CH_3.CO.OC_5H_{11}$, prepared by distilling 1 part of amylic alcohol, 2 parts of potassium acetate, and 1 of concentrated sulfuric acid. It has the odor of bananas and is called *banana oil.* **a. chloride,** a colorless liquid, $C_5H_{11}Cl$: a slow but profound anesthetic. **a. hydride,** pentane. **a. iodide,** a volatile compound, $C_5H_{11}I$, used in dyspnea and heart affections by inhalation. **a. nitrite,** a flammable, clear, yellowish liquid with a peculiar, ethereal, fruity odor, which is volatile at low temperatures, $C_5H_{11}NO_2$: inhaled as a vapor during pain of heart disease; also used to relax spasm of smooth muscles of various organs, and in treatment of cyanide poisoning. **a. salicylate,** a compound, $C_5H_{11}.O_2C.C_6H_4.OH$: used in rheumatism and locally as an analgesic for burns and scalds. **a. valerate, a. valerianate,** a colorless liquid, $(CH_3)_2CH.CH_2.CO.O.(CH_2)_2.CH(CH_3)_2$: used as an artificial flavoring substance.

amylaceous (am″ĭ-la′she-us) [L. *amylaceus*]. Starchy; containing starch; of the nature of starch.

amylamine (am″il-am′in). A poisonous liquid base, $C_5H_{11}NH_2$, sometimes found in cod liver oil, and formed by the decomposition of yeast.

amylase (am′ĭ-lās) [*amyl* + *-ase*]. An enzyme that catalyzes the hydrolysis of starch into smaller molecules. **pancreatic a.,** amylopsin. **salivary a.,** ptyalin.

amylatic (am-ĭ-lat′ik). Characterized by conversion of starch into sugar.

amylcaine hydrochloride (am″il-kān hi″dro-klo′rīd). Amylsine hydrochloride.

amylemia (am″ĭ-le′me-ah) [Gr. *amylon* starch + *haima* blood + *-ia*]. Presence of starch in the blood.

amylene (am′ĭ-lēn). A liquid hydrocarbon of five isomeric forms, C_5H_{10}: an unsafe anesthetic. **a. chloral,** an oily, colorless liquid, composed of chloral and amylene hydrate: used as a hypnotic. **a. hydrate,** a clear, colorless liquid, with camphoraceous odor, $C_2H_5.C(CH_3)_2OH$; miscible with alcohol, chloroform, ether, and glycerin: used in preparation of tribromoethanol solution.

amylenization (am″ĭ-len-i-za′shun). Anesthesia produced by amylene.

amylic (ah-mil′ik [L. *amylicus*]. Pertaining to amyl.

amylin (am′ĭ-lin). Insoluble amidin.

amylism (am′ĭ-lizm). Poisoning by amyl alcohol.

amylo- (am′ĭ-lo) [Gr. *amylon* starch]. A combining form denoting relationship to starch.

amylobarbitone (am″ĭ-lo-bar′bĭ-tōn). Amobarbital.

amylocellulose (am″ĭ-lo-sel′u-lōs). Amylose.

amyloclast (am′ĭ-lo-klast″). A starch-splitting enzyme.

amyloclastic (am″ĭ-lo-klas′tik) [*amylo-* + Gr. *klastikos* breaking up]. Digesting or splitting up starch.

amylocoagulase (am″ĭ-lo-ko-ag′u-lās). A ferment occurring in cereals which coagulates soluble starch.

amylodextrin (am″ĭ-lo-deks′trin). A compound, colored yellow by iodine, formed during the change of starch into sugar.

amylodyspepsia (am″ĭ-lo-dis-pep′se-ah) [*amylo-* + *dyspepsia*]. Inability to digest starch foods.

amylogen (ah-mil′o-jen). The portion of the starch granule that is soluble in water.

amylogenesis (am″ĭ-lo-jen′e-sis) [*amylo-* + Gr. *gennan* to produce]. The formation of starch.

amylogenic (am″ĭ-lo-jen′ik). Producing starch.

amylohemicellulose (am″ĭ-lo-hem″e-sel′u-lōs). A polysaccharide found in the cell wall of plants. It is much like the amylose of starch in that it is insoluble in water and stains blue with iodine.

amylohydrolysis (am″ĭ-lo-hi-drol′ĭ-sis). Hydrolysis of starch; amylolysis.

amyloid (am′ĭ-loid) [*amylo-* + Gr. *eidos* form]. 1. Resembling starch; characterized by a starchlike formation. 2. An abnormal complex material, most probably a glycoprotein, the exact biochemical composition of which has not been defined. Its protein component may be related to the immunoglobulins (gamma globulins), and it bears only a superficial resemblance to starch. 3. A substance produced by the action of sulfuric acid on cellulose. It gives a blue color when treated with iodine.

amyloidemia (am″ĭ-loi-de′me-ah). The presence of amyloid in the blood.

amyloidosis (am″ĭ-loi-do′sis). The accumulation of amyloid in various body tissues, better called *tissue proteinosis;* divided, mainly for descriptive purposes, into the following categories: (1) primary; (2) secondary; (3) familial; (4) associated with multiple myeloma; and (5) associated with familial Mediterranean fever. **cutaneous a., a. cu′tis,** amyloid degeneration of the skin characterized by an eruption of papules, nodules, plaques, and pigmentation, associated with itching.

amylolysis (am″ĭ-lol′ĭ-sis) [*amylo-* + Gr. *lysis* solution]. The digestion and disintegration of starch, or its conversion into sugar.

amylolytic (am″ĭ-lo-lit′ik). Pertaining to, characterized by, or promoting amylolysis.

amylopectin (am″ĭ-lo-pek′tin). The insoluble constituent of starch. It stains violet red with iodine and forms a paste with hot water. The soluble constituent of starch is amylose. Called also *alpha-amylose* and *starch cellulose.*

amylopectinosis (am″ĭ-lo-pek′tĭ-no′sis). A form of hepatic glycogen disease resulting from deficiency of glycogen "brancher" enzyme (amylo 1:4, 1:6 transglucosidase) and associated with a form of cirrhosis of the liver, an abnormal polysaccharide, with less branching than normal, accumulating in that organ.

amylophagia (am″ĭ-lo-fa′je-ah) [*amylo-* + Gr. *phagein* to eat + *-ia*]. Starch eating; an abnormal craving for starch.

amyloplast (ah-mil′o-plast″) [*amylo-* + Gr. *plassein* to form]. A starch-forming vegetable leukoplastid.

amyloplastic (am″ĭ-lo-plas′tik). Forming starch.

amylopsin (am″ĭ-lop′sin) [*amylo-* + try*psin*]. A pancreatic enzyme which changes starch into maltose.

amylorrhea (am″ĭ-lo-re′ah) [*amylo-* + Gr. *rhoia* flow]. The presence of an abnormal amount of starch in the stools.

amylorrhexis (am″ĭ-lo-rek′sis) [*amylo-* + Gr. *rhēxis* a breaking]. The enzymatic hydrolysis of starch.

amylose (am′ĭ-lōs). 1. Any carbohydrate of the starch group; a polysaccharide. 2. The soluble constituent of starch. It stains blue with iodine and does not form a paste with hot water. The other constituent is amylopectin. Called also *amylocellulose, beta-amylose,* and *granulose.* **alpha a.** Same as *amylopectin.* **crystalline a's,** beautifully crystalline compounds, produced by the growth of *Bacillus macerans* in a solution of starch or glycogen. The degree of polymerization may vary from 4 to 8.

amylosis (am″ĭ-lo′sis). Amyloidosis.

amylosuria (am″ĭ-lo-su′re-ah). The presence of amylose in the urine.

amylosynthease (am″ĭ-lo-sin′the-ās). An enzyme in starch which converts dextrin into starch.

amylosynthesis (am″ĭ-lo-sin′the-sis). The synthesis of starch from sugar.

amylsine hydrochloride (am′il-sin hi″dro-klo′rid). Proprietary name for mono-*n*-amyl-amino-ethyl-*p*-aminobenzoate hydrochloride, formerly known as amylcaine hydrochloride: used to produce corneal anesthesia.

amylum (am′ĭ-lum) [L.; Gr. *amylon*]. Starch. **a. ioda′tum,** iodized starch: used as an alterant.

amyluria (am″ĭ-lu′re-ah) [*amylo-* + Gr. *ouron* urine + *-ia*]. Presence of starch in the urine.

amynologic (ah-min″o-loj′ik). Immunologic.

amynology (am″ĭ-nol′o-je). Immunology.

amyocardia (ah-mi″o-kar′de-ah) [*a* neg. + Gr. *mys* muscle + *kardia* heart]. Weakness of the heart muscle.

amyo-esthesis (ah-mi″o-es-the′sis) [*a* neg. + Gr. *mys* muscle + *aisthēsis* sensation]. The lack of muscle sense.

amyoplasia (ah-mi″o-pla′se-ah) [*a* neg. + Gr.

mys muscle + *plassein* to form]. Lack of muscle formation. **a. congen'ita,** a generalized lack of muscular development and growth, with contracture and deformity at most of the joints.

amyostasia (ah-mi"o-sta'se-ah) [*a* neg. + Gr. *mys* muscle + *stasis* a standing still]. A tremor of the muscles, seen especially in locomotor ataxia.

amyostatic (ah-mi"o-stat'ik). Marked by amyostasia or muscular tremors.

amyosthenia (ah-mi"os-the'ne-ah) [*a* neg. + Gr. *mys* muscle + *sthenos* strength]. Deficient muscular power, especially a feeling of weakness in the arms and legs, often seen in hysteria.

amyosthenic (ah-mi"os-then'ik). Pertaining to, characterized by, or causing amyosthenia.

amyotaxia (ah-mi"o-tak'se-ah). Amyotaxy.

amyotaxy (ah-mi'o-tak"se) [*a* neg. + Gr. *mys* muscle + *tassein* to arrange]. Muscular ataxia.

amyotonia (ah-mi"o-to'ne-ah) [*a* neg. + Gr. *mys* muscle + *tonos* tension + *-ia*]. Atonic condition of the musculature of the body; myatonia. **a. congen'ita** (Oppenheim, 1900), myatonia congenita; Oppenheim's disease; a rare congenital disease of children marked by general hypotonia of the muscles. Called also *congenital atonic pseudoparalysis.*

amyotrophia (ah-mi"o-tro'fe-ah) [*a* neg. + Gr. *mys* muscle + *trophē* nourishment + *-ia*]. Amyotrophy. **neuralgic a.,** neuralgic amyotrophy. **a. spina'lis progressi'va,** progressive muscular atrophy.

amyotrophic (ah-mi"o-trof'ik). Pertaining to or characterized by amyotrophy.

amyotrophy (ah"mi-ot'ro-fe). Atrophy of muscle tissue. **diabetic a.,** progressive weakening and wasting of muscles accompanied by an aching or stabbing pain, usually limited to the muscles of the pelvic girdle and thigh, associated with poorly controlled diabetes. **neuralgic a.,** a condition characterized by pain across the shoulder and upper arm, with atrophy and paralysis of the muscles of the shoulder girdle.

amyous (am'e-us) [*a* neg. + Gr. *mys* muscle]. Deficient in muscular tissue.

amyrol (am'ĭ-rol). Two isomeric principles, C_5H_{26}-O, from sandalwood oil.

amytal (am'ĭ-tal). Trade mark for preparations of amobarbital. **sodium a.,** trade mark for the monosodium salt of isoamyl-ethylbarbituric acid, $NaC_5H_{11}(C_2H_5)C(CO.NH)_2CO$, used as a sedative before general anesthesia.

amyxia (ah-mik'se-ah) [*a* neg. + Gr. *myxa* mucus + *-ia*]. Absence of mucus.

amyxorrhea (ah-mik"so-re'ah) [*a* neg. + Gr. *myxa* mucus + *rhoia* flow]. Absence of mucous secretion. **a. gas'trica,** deficiency of mucus in the gastric secretion.

An. Abbreviation for *anode, anodal* and *anisometropia.*

an-. See *a-* (def. 1).

A.N.A. Abbreviation for *American Nurses' Association.*

ana (an'ah) [Gr.]. So much of each; usually written aa.

ana- (an'ah) [Gr. *ana* up, back, again]. A prefix indicating upward, backward, excessive, or again.

anabacteria (an"ah-bak-te're-ah). A formalin-treated autolysate from aqueous suspensions of bacteria: used for curative or protective vaccination.

anabasine (ah-nab'ah-sin). An alkaloid, C_5H_4N.-$C_5H_{10}N$, from the plant, *Anabasis aphylla,* which closely resembles nicotine.

anabasis (ah-nab'ah-sis) [Gr. "ascent"]. The stage of increase in a disease.

anabatic (an"ah-bat'ik) [Gr. *anabatikos*]. 1. Increasing or growing more intense. 2. Pertaining to or characterized by anabasis.

Anabena (ah-nab'e-nah). A genus of blue-green algae which sometimes imparts an objectionable odor to a water supply.

anabiosis (an"ah-bi-o'sis) [Gr. *anabiōsis* a reviving]. Restoration of life processes after their apparent cessation.

anabiotic (an"ah-bi-ot'ik). Apparently lifeless, but still capable of living.

anabolergy (an"ah-bol'er-je) [Gr. *anabolē* a throwing up + *ergon* work]. Force expended in anabolism or in anabolic processes.

anabolic (an"ah-bol'ik) [Gr. *anabolikos*]. Pertaining to, characteristic of, or promoting anabolism, or constructive metabolism.

anabolin (ah-nab'o-lin). Anabolite.

anabolism (ah-nab'o-lizm) [Gr. *anabole* a throwing up]. Any constructive process by which simple substances are converted by living cells into more complex compounds, especially conversion of simple compounds into protoplasm; constructive metabolism.

anabolistic (ah-nab"o-lis'tik). Pertaining to anabolism.

anabolite (ah-nab'o-līt"). Any product of anabolism, or of a constructive metabolic process.

anabrosis (an"ah-bro'sis) [Gr.]. Ulceration or erosion of the surface.

anabrotic (an"ah-brot'ik). Pertaining to or marked by anabrosis.

anacamptic (an"ah-kamp'tik). Pertaining to reflection, as of sound or light.

anacamptometer (an"ah-kamp-tom'e-ter) [Gr. *anakampsis* reflection + *metron* measure]. An instrument for measuring the reflexes (Duprat, 1886).

Anacardium (an"ah-kar'de-um) [L.; *ana-* + Gr. *kardia* heart]. A genus of tropical trees with a poisonous juice. *A. occidentale,* the cashew tree, affords the cashew nut and a useful gum, as well as cardol.

anacardol (an"ah-kar'dol). A constituent, 3-pentadecadienylphenol, $C_{15}H_{27}.C_6H_4OH$, of cashew nut shell liquid: it causes reactions in persons sensitive to poison ivy.

anacatadidymus (an"ah-kat-ah-did'ĭ-mus). Anakatadidymus.

anacatesthesia (an"ah-kat"es-the'ze-ah). Anakatesthesia.

anacatharsis (an"ah-kah-thar'sis) [*ana-* + *catharsis*]. Severe vomiting.

anachlorhydria (an"ah-klor-hi'dre-ah). Absence of hydrochloric acid from the gastric juice.

anacholia (an"ah-ko'le-ah). Decreased secretion of bile.

anachoresis (an"ah-ko-re'sis) [Gr. *anachōrēsis* a retreating]. The preferential collection or deposits of particles at a certain site, as of bacteria or of metals which have localized out of the blood stream in areas of inflammation.

anachoretic (an"ah-ko-ret'ik). Pertaining to, characterized by, or resulting from anachoresis.

anachoric (an"ah-ko'rik). Anachoretic.

anachronobiology (an"ah-kron"o-bi-ol'o-je). A term suggested to denote the study of the constructive effects (growth, development, and maturation) of time on a living system. Cf. *catachronobiology.*

anacidity (an"ah-sid'ĭ-te) [*an* neg. + *acidity*]. Lack of normal acidity. **gastric a.,** achlorhydria.

anaclasimeter (an"ah-klah-sim'e-ter) [Gr. *anaklasis* reflection + *metron* measure]. An instrument for measuring eye refraction.

anaclasis (ah-nak'lah-sis) [Gr. *anaklasis* reflection]. 1. Reflection or refraction of light. 2. Reflex action. 3. Refracture. 4. Forcible flexion of a limb; the breaking up of an ankylosis.

anaclitic (an"ah-klit'ik) [*ana-* + Gr. *klinein* to lean]. Leaning against or depending on something: a term applied to the first love object on account of the original dependence on such a person (the mother) for care and feeding.

anacmesis (an-ak′me-sis). Anakmesis.

anacobra (an″ah-ko′brah). Cobra venom which has been treated with formaldehyde and heat.

anacousia (an″ah-ku′se-ah). Anakusis.

anacroasia (an″ah-kro-a′ze-ah) [*an* neg. + Gr. *akroasis* hearing + *-ia*]. Inability to understand language, due to cerebral disease.

anacrotic (an″ah-krot′ik). Pertaining to or characterized by anacrotism.

anacrotism (ah-nak′ro-tizm) [*ana-* + Gr. *krotos* beat + *-ism*]. An anomaly of the pulse evidenced by appearance of a small additional wave or notch in the ascending limb of the pulse tracing.

anaculture (an″ah-kul′cher). A bacterial whole culture treated with formalin and incubated: used for prophylactic vaccination.

anacusis (an″ah-ku′sis). Anakusis.

Anacyclus pyrethrum (an″ah-si′klus pi-re′-thrum). See *pyrethrum*.

anadenia (an″ah-de′ne-ah) [*an* neg. + Gr. *adēn* gland + *-ia*]. 1. Absence of glands. 2. Insufficiency of glandular function. **a. ventric′uli,** absence or destruction of the glands of the stomach.

anadicrotic (an″ah-di-krot′ik). Pertaining to or characterized by anadicrotism.

anadicrotism (an″ah-dik′ro-tizm) [*ana-* + Gr. *dis* twice + *krotos* beat + *-ism*]. An anomaly of the pulse evidenced by appearance of two small additional waves or notches in the ascending limb of the pulse tracing.

anadidymus (an″ah-did′ĭ-mus) [*ana-* + Gr. *didymos* twin]. A twin fetal monster, divided below, but single toward the cephalic pole (monstra duplicia anadidyma—Förster).

anadipsia (an″ah-dip′se-ah) [*ana-* + Gr. *dipsa* thirst + *-ia*]. Intense thirst.

anadrenalism (an″ah-dre′nal-izm). Absence or failure of adrenal functioning.

anadrenia (an″ah-dre′ne-ah). Anadrenalism.

anaerase (an-a′er-ās″) [*an* neg. + Gr. *aēr* air + *-ase*]. The hypothetical respiratory enzyme of anaerobic bacteria. Cf. *aerase*.

anaerobe (an-a′er-ōb) [*an* neg. + Gr. *aēr* air + *bios* life]. A microorganism that lives and grows only in the complete, or almost complete, absence of molecular oxygen. **facultative a's,** microorganisms which are able to live under either anaerobic or aerobic conditions. **obligate a's,** microorganisms that can live only in the complete absence of molecular oxygen, oxygen being toxic to them.

anaerobia (an″a-er-o′be-ah). Plural of *anaerobion*.

anaerobian (an″a-er-o′be-an). 1. Living without air. 2. An anaerobe.

anaerobiase (an-a″er-o-bi′ās). A proteolytic enzyme from *Clostridium welchii* and other anaerobes which is fully active under anaerobic conditions.

anaerobic (an″a-er-o′bik). Growing only in the absence of molecular oxygen.

anaerobion (an″a-er-o′be-on), pl. *anaerobia*. Anaerobe.

anaerobiosis (an-a″er-o-bi-o′sis) [*an* neg. + Gr. *aēr* air + *bios* life + *-osis*]. Life without free oxygen; anoxybiosis.

anaerobiotic (an-a″er-o-bi-ot′ik). Anaerobic.

anaerobism (an-a′er-o-bizm″). The ability to live without oxygen.

anaerogenic (an-a″er-o-jen′ik) [*an* neg. + Gr. *aēr* air + *gennan* to produce]. 1. Producing little or no gas. 2. Suppressing the formation of gas by the gas-producing bacteria.

anaerophyte (an-a′er-o-fit″) [*an* neg. + Gr. *aēr* air + *phyton* plant]. A vegetable anaerobic microorganism.

anaeroplasty (an-a′er-o-plas″te) [*an* neg. + Gr. *aēr* air + *plassein* to form]. Exclusion of the air from wounds by applying water.

anaerosis (an″a-er-o′sis) [*an* neg. + Gr. *aēr* air + *-osis*]. Interruption of the respiratory function, especially in the newborn. **desquamative a.,** idiopathic respiratory distress of newborn.

anagen (an′ah-jen). The phase of the hair cycle during which synthesis of hair takes place.

anagenesis (an″ah-jen′e-sis) [*ana-* + Gr. *genesis* production]. Reproduction or regeneration of tissue.

anagenetic (an″ah-jĕ-net′ik). Pertaining to or producing anagenesis.

anagnosasthenia (an-ag″nōs-as-the′ne-ah) [Gr. *anagnōsis* reading + *asthenia*]. Neurasthenia with distress at any attempt to read; also inability to read, although the eye can distinguish printed words.

Anagnostakis' operation (ah-nag″nos-ta′kis) [Andrei *Anagnostakis*, Greek ophthalmologist, 1826–1897]. See under *operation*.

anagocytic (an-ag″o-si′tik). Retarding or inhibiting the growth of cells.

anagoge (an″ah-go′je). Anagogy.

anagogic (an″ah-goj′ik) [*ana-* + Gr. *agogē* leading]. Pertaining to the moral, uplifting, progressive strivings of the unconscious.

anagogy (an″ah-go′je). Psychic material that has an idealistic quality.

anagotoxic (an-ag″o-tok′sik). Acting antagonistically to toxin; counteracting toxic action.

anakatadidymus (an″ah-kat″ah-did′ĭ-mus) [*ana-* + Gr. *kata* down + *didymos* twin]. A twin fetal monster separate above and below, but united in the middle (monstra duplicia anakatadidyma—Förster).

anakatesthesia (an″ah-kat″es-the′ze-ah) [*ana-* + Gr. *kata* down + *aisthēsis* perception + *-ia*]. A hovering feeling or sensation.

anakhre (an-ak′er) See *goundou*.

anakinetomere (an″ah-kin′e-to-mēr″) [*ana-* + Gr. *kinētos* moved + *meros* part]. A. P. Mathews' term for matter in which the molecules and atoms are rich in energy content so that such matter is alive. Cf. *katakinetomere*.

anakinetomeric (an″ah-kin″e-to-mer′ik). Rich in energy content and therefore living. Cf. *katakinetomeric*.

anakmesis (an-ak′me-sis) [*an* neg + Gr. *akmēnos* full grown]. Arrest of maturation; specifically, increase of early granular cells (stem cells) in the marrow with lack of further maturation, as observed in the marrow in agranulocytosis.

anakusis (an″ah-koo′sis) [*an* neg. + Gr. *akouein* to hear]. Total deafness.

anal (a′nal) [L. *analis*]. Pertaining to the anus.

analbuminemia (an″al-bu″mĭ-ne′me-ah). A state characterized by deficiency or absence of albumins in the blood serum.

analeptic (an″ah-lep′tik) [Gr. *analepsis* a repairing]. 1. A drug which acts as a stimulant of the central nervous system, such as caffeine, amphetamine, etc. 2. A restorative medicine or agent.

analexin (an″ah-lek′sin). Trade mark for preparations of phenyramidol.

analgesia (an″al-je′ze-ah) [*an* neg. + Gr. *algēsis* pain + *-ia*]. Absence of sensibility to pain; designating particularly the relief of pain without loss of consciousness. **a. al′gera, a. doloro′sa,** acute pain in a part, with loss of sensibility. **audio a.,** production of insensitivity to pain by the use of loud sound, particularly in dentistry. **continuous caudal a.,** the relief of the pain of labor and childbirth by the continuous bathing of the sacral and lumbar plexuses within the epidural space by the injection of an anesthetic solution (1.5 per cent solution of metycaine). This method is used also in general surgery to block the pain pathways below the navel. **infiltration a.,** paralysis of the nerve endings at the site of operation by subcutaneous injection of an anesthetic. **narcolocal a.,** local analgesia preceded by premedication. **paretic a.,** loss of the sense of pain accompanied by partial paralysis. **permeation a.,** surface a. **surface a.,** local analgesia produced by an anesthetic applied to the surface of such mucous membranes as those of the eye, nose, throat, larynx, and urethra.

analgesic (an″al-je′zik). 1. Relieving pain. 2. Not sensitive as to pain. 3. An agent that alleviates pain without causing loss of consciousness.

analgesin (an″al-je′sin). Trade mark for a preparation of antipyrine.

analgetic (an″al-jet′ik). Analgesic.

analgia (an-al′je-ah) [*an* neg. + Gr. *algos* pain + *-ia*]. Absence of pain.

analgic (an-al′jik). Insensible to pain.

anallergic (an″ah-ler′jik). Not allergic; not causing anaphylaxis.

analogous (ah-nal′o-gus) [Gr. *analogos* according to a due ratio, conformable, proportionate]. Resembling or similar in some respects, as in function or appearance, but not in origin or development. Cf. *homologous*.

analogue (an′ah-log). 1. A part or organ having the same function as another, but of a different evolutionary origin. See *homologue*, def. 1. 2. A chemical compound with a structure similar to that of another but differing from it in respect to a certain component; it may have a similar or opposite action metabolically. **homologous a.,** a part that is similar to another in both function and structure. **metabolic a.,** a closely similar but inactive compound which tends to replace an essential metabolite.

analogy (ah-nal′o-je) [Gr. *analogia* equality of ratios, proportion]. The quality of being analogous; resemblance or similarity in function or appearance, but not in origin or development.

analysand (ah-nal′ĭ-sand). The person who is being psychoanalyzed.

analysis (ah-nal′ĭ-sis), pl. *anal′yses* [*ana-* + Gr. *lysis* dissolution]. Separation into component parts or elements; the act of determining the component parts of a substance. **bite a.,** occlusal a. **bradycinetic a.,** cinematographic study of motor activity. **chromatographic a.** See *chromatography*. **colorimetric a.,** analysis by means of the various color tests. **densimetric a.,** analysis by ascertaining the specific gravity of a solution and estimating the amount of matter dissolved. **distributive a.,** psychobiologic treatment by the directed study and interpretation of the patient's present and past behavior. **gasometric a.,** the measurement of the different components of a gaseous mixture. **gravimetric a.,** the quantitative analysis of a body weight. **occlusal a.,** a study of the relations of the occlusal surfaces of opposing teeth. **organic a.,** the analysis of animal and vegetable tissues. **polariscopic a.,** analysis by means of the polariscope. **proximate a.,** the determination of the simpler constituents of a substance. **qualitative a., qualitive a.,** the determination of the nature of the constituents of a compound. **quantitative a., quantitive a.,** the determination of the proportionate quantities of the constituents of a compound. **spectroscopic a., spectrum a.,** analysis by means of the spectroscope. **ultimate a.,** the determination of the ultimate elements of a compound. **volumetric a.,** quantitative analysis by measuring volumes of liquids.

analysor (an′ah-li″zor). 1. Pavlov's name for a specialized part of the nervous system which controls the reactions of the organism to changing external conditions. 2. A nervous receptor together with its central connections, by means of which sensitivity to stimulations is differentiated.

analytic (an″ah-lit′ik). Pertaining to analysis.

analyzer (an′ah-li″zer). A Nicol prism attached to a polarizing apparatus which extinguishes the ray of light polarized by the polarizer.

Aname (an′ah-me). A genus of poisonous spiders, known as the "bird spiders."

anamirtin (an″ah-mer′tin). An oily glyceride, $C_{19}H_{24}O_{10}$, from *Cocculus indicus*.

anamnesis (an″am-ne′sis) [Gr. *anamnēsis* a recalling]. 1. The faculty of memory. 2. The collected data concerning a patient, his family, previous environment, and experiences, including any abnormal sensations, moods, or acts observed by the patient himself or by others, with the dates of their appearance and duration, as well as any results of treatment. 3. Anamnestic reaction. See under *reaction*.

anamnestic (an″am-nes′tik). Pertaining to anamnesis.

Anamniota (an″am-ne-o′tah) [*an* priv. + Gr. *amnion*]. A major group of vertebrates comprising those which develop no amnion. Opposed to *Amniota*.

anamniote (an-am′ne-ōt″). Any animal or group belonging to the Anamniota.

anamniotic (an″am-ne-ot′ik) [*an* neg. + *amnion*]. Having no amnion.

anamorphosis (an″ah-mor-fo′sis) [*ana-* + Gr. *morphē* form]. An ascending progression or change of form in the evolution of a group of animals or plants.

ananabasia (an-an″ah-ba′se-ah) [*an* neg. + Gr. *anabasis* ascent + *-ia*]. Inability to ascend high places.

ananabolic (an″an-ah-bol′ik) [*an* neg. + *anabolic*]. Characterized by absence of anabolism.

ananaphylaxis (an-an″ah-fĭ-lak′sis). Antianaphylaxis.

ananase (an′ah-nās). Trade mark for a plant protease concentrate.

ananastasia (an-an″as-ta′se-ah) [*an* neg. + Gr. *anastasis* a standing up + *-ia*]. Inability to stand up or to rise from a sitting posture.

anancastic (an″an-kas′tik) [Gr. *anankastos* forced]. Obsessive-compulsive.

anandia (an-an′de-ah). Aphemia.

anandria (an-an′dre-ah) [*an* neg. + Gr. *anēr* man]. The loss of masculinity or virility.

anangioid (an-an′je-oid) [*an* neg. + Gr. *angeion* vessel + *eidos* form]. Seemingly without blood vessels.

anangioplasia (an-an″je-o-pla′ze-ah) [*an* neg. + Gr. *angeion* vessel + *plassein* to form + *-ia*]. Congenital diminution of the lumen of the arteries.

anangioplastic (an-an″je-o-plas′tik). Pertaining to or characterized by anangioplasia.

anapeiratic (an″ah-pi-rat′ik) [Gr. *anapeirasthai* to try again]. Due to excessive use.

anapepsia (an″ah-pep′se-ah). Complete absence of pepsin from the stomach secretion.

anaphalantiasis (an-af″ah-lan-ti′ah-sis) [Gr. "forehead-baldness']. Absence of the eyebrows.

anaphase (an′ah-fāz) [*ana-* + Gr. *phasis* phase]. That stage in mitosis, following the metaphase, in which the halves of the divided chromosomes move apart toward the poles of the spindle to form the diaster. See *mitosis*.

anaphia (an-a′fe-ah) [*an* neg. + Gr. *haphē* touch + *-ia*]. Lack or loss of the sense of touch.

anaphoresis (an″ah-fo-re′sis). 1. Transmission of electropositive substances into the tissues by passage of electric current. The flow is toward the positive pole. 2. Diminution in the activity of the sweat glands.

anaphoria (an″ah-fo′re-ah) [*ana-* + Gr. *pherein* to bear + *-ia*]. A tendency for the visual axes of both eyes to divert above the horizontal plane.

anaphrodisia (an″af-ro-diz′e-ah) [*an* neg. + Gr. *Aphroditē* Venus + *-ia*]. Absence or loss of sexual desire.

anaphrodisiac (an″af-ro-diz′e-ak). 1. Repressing sexual desire. 2. A drug or medicine that allays sexual desire.

anaphylactia (an″ah-fi-lak′she-ah). The condition produced as a result of anaphylaxis; any anaphylactic disease.

anaphylactic (an″ah-fi-lak′tik). Decreasing immunity instead of increasing it; pertaining to anaphylaxis; possessing anaphylaxis.

anaphylactin (an″ah-fi-lak′tin). Sensibilisin.

anaphylactogen (an″ah-fi-lak′to-jen). A substance which is capable of inducing a condition of anaphylaxis. Called also *allergen* and *sensitinogen*.

anaphylactogenesis (an″ah-fi-lak″to-jen′e-sis). The production of anaphylaxis.

anaphylactogenic (an″ah-fi-lak-to-jen′ik). Producing anaphylaxis

anaphylactoid (an″ah-fi-lak′toid). Resembling anaphylaxis.

anaphylactotoxin (an″ah-fi-lak″to-tok′sin). Anaphylatoxin.

anaphylatoxin (an″ah-fi″lah-tok′sin). The poisonous substance in anaphylaxis (Friedberger).

anaphylatoxis (an″ah-fi″lah-tok′sis). The reaction produced by an anaphylatoxin.

anaphylaxin (an″ah-fi-lak′sin). Sensibilisin.

anaphylaxis (an″ah-fi-lak′sis) [*ana-* + Gr. *phylaxis* protection]. An unusual or exaggerated reaction of the organism to foreign protein or other substances. Use of the term has been restricted to a condition of sensitization in laboratory animals produced by the injection of foreign matter, such as horse serum. Such an injection renders the animal hypersusceptible to a subsequent injection. This is termed *active a.* Anaphylaxis produced in an animal by injecting the blood of a sensitized animal is termed *passive a.* Anaphylaxis is an antigen-antibody reaction. Called also *Theobald Smith phenomenon*, *hypersusceptibility*, and *protein sensitization*. **acquired a.,** anaphylaxis in which sensitization is known to have been produced by the administration of a foreign protein. **active a.,** the anaphylactic state produced in an animal by the injection of a foreign protein; distinguished from passive a. **antiserum a.,** passive anaphylaxis. **chronic a.,** Richet's term for enteritis anaphylactica. **heterologous a.,** a passive anaphylaxis induced by the transference of serum from an animal of a different species. **homologous a.,** a passive anaphylaxis induced by the transference of serum from an animal of the same species. **indirect a.,** anaphylaxis induced by an animal's own protein modified in some way. **inverse a.,** an anaphylactic shock produced by a single intravenous injection of Forssman's antibody. **passive a.,** anaphylaxis occurring in a normal individual as a result of the injection of the serum of a previously sensitized individual. **psychic a.,** liability to the development of neurotic symptoms as a result of early psychic trauma. **reverse a.,** anaphylaxis following the injection of antigen succeeded by the injection of antiserum; also local reactions from the union of circulating antibodies with antigen fixed by tissue cells.

anaphylodiagnosis (an″ah-fi″lo-di″ag-no′sis). Diagnosis of disease by means of anaphylactic reactions.

anaphylotoxin (an″ah-fi″lo-tok′sin). Anaphylatoxin.

anaplasia (an″ah-pla′ze-ah) [Gr. *ana* backward + *plassein* to form]. A condition in tumor cells in which there is loss of normal differentiation, organization, and specific function (Hansemann). Called also *reversionary atrophy* and *undifferentiation*. **monophasic a.,** reversion of a cell form to embryonic type as in cancer formation. **polyphasic a.,** change of a cell into a cell of more complex character.

Anaplasma (an″ah-plaz′mah) [Gr. *anaplasma* something formed]. A genus of microorganisms of the family Anaplasmataceae, including three species, *A. centra′le*, *A. margina′le*, and *A. ovis*.

Anaplasmataceae (an″ah-plaz″mah-ta′se-e). A family of the order Rickettsiales, class Microtatobiotes, made up of microorganisms parasitic in red blood cells, in which they appear as spherical granules staining a deep reddish violet; naturally parasitic in ruminants and transmitted by arthropods. It includes a single genus, *Anaplasma*.

anaplasmosis (an″ah-plaz-mo′sis). The condition of being infected with *Anaplasma*. See *gall-sickness*.

anaplastia (an″ah-plas′te-ah). Anaplasia.

anaplastic (an″ah-plas′tik) [*ana-* + Gr. *plassein* to form]. 1. Restoring a lost or absent part. 2. Characterized by anaplasia or reversed development: said of cells.

anaplasty (an′ah-plas″te) [*ana-* + Gr. *plassein* to form]. Restorative or plastic surgery.

anaplerosis (an″ah-ple-ro′sis). The repair or replacement of lost or defective parts.

Anaplocephala (an″ah-plo-sef′ah-lah). A genus of tapeworms that infect horses, donkeys, and mules.

anapnograph (an-ap′no-graf) [Gr. *anapnoē* respiration + *graphein* to record]. A device which registers the speed and pressure of the respired air current.

anapnoic (an″ap-no′ik). 1. [*ana-* + Gr. *apnoia* breathlessness.] Relieving dyspnea. 2. [Gr. *anapnoē* respiration.] Pertaining to the respiration.

anapnometer (an″ap-nom′e-ter) [Gr. *anapnoē* respiration + *metron* measure]. A spirometer.

anapnotherapy (an″ap-no-ther′ah-pe) [Gr. *anapnein* to inhale + *therapeia* treatment]. Treatment by inhalation of gas, as in resuscitation.

anapophysis (an″ah-pof′ĭ-sis) [*ana-* + Gr. *apophysis* process of a bone]. An accessory vertebral process; especially an accessory process of a dorsal or lumbar vertebra.

anaptic (an-ap′tik) [*an* neg. + Gr. *haphē* touch]. Marked by anaphia.

anaraxia (an″ah-rak′se-ah) [*an* neg. + Gr. *araxis* a dashing, beating]. Malocclusion.

anarchic (an-ar′kik). Of the nature of anarchy: against rule; different from the usual.

anaric (ah-na′rik) [*a* neg. + L. *naris* nose]. Having no nose.

anarithmia (an″ah-rith′me-ah) [*an* neg. + Gr. *arithmos* number]. Inability to count, due to a central lesion.

anarrhea (an″ah-re′ah) [*ana-* + Gr. *rhoia* flow]. A flowing or flux to an upper part.

anarrhexis (an″ah-rek′sis) [*ana-* + Gr. *rhēxis* fracture]. The operation of refracturing a bone.

anarthria (an-ar′thre-ah) [*an* neg. + Gr. *arthroun* to articulate + *-ia*]. Inability to articulate words properly. Cf. *dysarthria*. **a. litera′lis,** stuttering.

anasarca (an″ah-sar′kah) [*ana-* + Gr. *sarx* flesh]. Generalized massive edema; all parts of the body, including the genitalia, chest wall, arms, and, rarely, the face are affected.

anasarcous (an″ah-sar′kus). Affected with, or of the nature of, anasarca.

anascitic (an″ah-sit′ik). Without ascites.

anaspadia (an″ah-spa′de-ah) [*ana-* + Gr. *spadōn* a rent + *-ia*]. Epispadias.

anaspadias (an″ah-spa′de-as). Epispadias.

anastalsis (an″ah-stal′sis) [*ana-* + Gr. *stalsis* contraction]. 1. An upward moving wave of contraction without a preceding wave of inhibition, occurring in the digestive tube in addition to the peristaltic wave. Cf. *catastalsis* and *diastalsis*. 2. Styptic action.

anastaltic (an″ah-stal′tik) [Gr. *anastaltikos* contracting]. 1. Highly astringent; styptic. 2. A styptic medicine.

anastate (an′ah-stāt″) [Gr. *anastatos* raised up].

Any substance or condition characteristic of, or resulting from, an anabolic process.

anastatic (an″ah-stat′ik). Restorative; inclining to recovery.

anastigmatic (an″as-tig-mat′ik). Not astigmatic; corrected for astigmatism.

anastole (ah-nas′to-le) [Gr. *anastolē*]. Retraction, as of the lips of a wound.

anastomat (ah-nas′to-mat). An apparatus for securing an anastomosis between a remnant of the sigmoid and the lower end of the rectum.

anastomose (ah-nas′to-mōs). 1. To communicate with one another, as arteries and veins. 2. To create a communication between two formerly separate structures.

anastomosis (ah-nas″to-mo′sis), pl. *anastomo′ses* [Gr. *anastomōsis* opening, outlet]. 1. A communication between two vessels. 2. The surgical or pathological formation of a passage between any two normally distinct spaces or organs. **antiperistaltic a.,** enterostomy in which the intestinal segments are so joined that the peristaltic waves in the two parts are in opposite directions. **a. arterioveno′sa** [N A], a vessel that directly interconnects an artery and a vein, and that acts

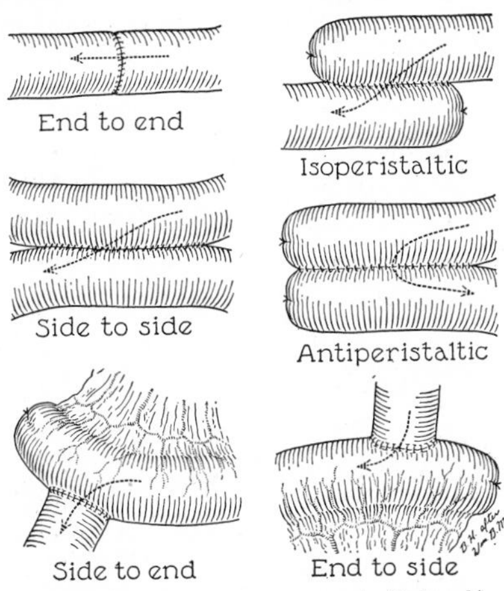

Methods of intestinal anastomosis (Babcock).

as a shunt to bypass the capillary bed. **arteriovenous a.** 1. Anastomosis arteriovenosa [N A]. 2. A communication created between an artery and a vein. **Braun's a.,** formation of an anastomosis between the afferent and efferent intestinal loops in gastro-enterostomy to prevent a vicious cycle. **Clado's a.,** the anastomosis between the appendicular and ovarian arteries in the appendiculo-ovarian ligament. **crucial a.,** an arterial anastomosis in the proximal part of the thigh, formed by the anastomotic branch of the sciatic, the internal circumflex, the first perforating, and the transverse portion of the external circumflex. **Galen's a.,** the anastomosis between the superior and inferior laryngeal nerves. **heterocladic a.,** an anastomosis between branches of different arteries. **homocladic a.,** an anastomosis between branches of the same artery. **Hyrtl's a.** See *Hyrtl's loop,* under *loop.* **intestinal a.,** the establishment of a communication between two portions of the intestines. **isoperistaltic a.,** enterostomy in which the intestinal segments are so joined that the peristaltic waves in the two parts are in the same direction. **Jacobson's a.,** the anastomosing part of the tympanic plexus. **postcostal a.,** a longitudinal linkage of the seven highest intersegmental arteries that gives rise to the vertebral artery. **precapillary a.,** anastomosis between small arteries just before they become capillaries. **precostal a.,** a longitudinal anastomosis of intersegmental arteries that gives rise to the thyrocervical and costocervical trunks. **pyeloileocutaneous a.,** direct connection of the renal pelvis to an isolated loop of the ileum, which is then anchored to the abdominal wall at the stoma, to drain exteriorly. **Schmidel's a's,** abnormal communications between the vena cava and the portal system. **sinusoido-arterial a., sinusoido-venous a.,** anastomotic connections between the sinusoids of the heart and the arteries and veins, respectively. **stirrup a.,** an arterial branch joining the dorsalis pedis with the external plantar artery. **Sucquet-Hoyer a.,** regulatory connections between small peripheral arteries and veins, especially in the hands and feet. **terminoterminal a.,** anastomosis between the peripheral end of an artery and the central end of the corresponding vein, and between the central end of the artery and the terminal end of the vein. **transuretero-ureteral a.,** the operation of transplanting one ureter into the ureter on the opposite side. **ureteroileocutaneous a.,** connection of the transected ureter to an isolated loop of the ileum, which is then anchored to the abdominal wall at the stoma, to drain exteriorly. **uretero-tubal a.,** an anastomosis between the ureter and the fallopian tube. **uretero-ureteral a.,** the operation of joining portions of the same ureter.

anastomotic (ah-nas″to-mot′ik). Pertaining to, or of the nature of, an anastomosis.

anastral (an-as′tral) [*an* neg. + Gr. *astēr* star]. Lacking, or pertaining to the lack of, an aster: used in reference to a mitotic figure.

anastrophic (an″ah-stof′ik) [Gr. *anastrophē* a turning back, reversal]. Capable of being inactivated and then reactivated: said of certain proteinases.

anat. Abbreviation for *anatomy* or *anatomical.*

anatabine (ah-nat′ah-bin). An alkaloid, $C_{10}H_{12}N_2$, from tobacco.

anatherapeusis (an″ah-ther″ah-pu′sis) [Gr. *ana* upward + *therapeusis*]. Treatment by increasing doses.

anatomic (an″ah-tom′ik). Anatomical.

anatomical (an″ah-tom′e-kal). Pertaining to anatomy, or to the structure of the organism.

anatomicomedical (an-ah-tom″e-ko-med′e-kal). Pertaining to anatomy and medicine or to medical anatomy.

anatomicopathological (an″ah-tom″e-ko-path″o-loj′e-kal). Pertaining to pathological anatomy.

anatomicophysiological (an-ah-tom″e-ko-fiz″-e-o-loj′e-kal). Pertaining to anatomy and physiology.

anatomicosurgical (an-ah-tom″e-ko-ser′je-kal). Pertaining to anatomy and surgery.

anatomist (ah-nat′o-mist). A person who is skilled or learned in anatomy; a specialist in the study of anatomy.

anatomist's snuff-box. Tabatière anatomique.

anatomy (ah-nat′o-me) [*ana-* + Gr. *temnein* to cut]. 1. The science of the structure of the animal body and the relation of its parts. It is largely based on dissection, from which it obtains its name. 2. Dissection of an organized body. **applied a.,** anatomy as applied to diagnosis and treatment. **artificial a.,** the study of artificial dissection made in wax. **artistic a.,** the study of anatomy as applied to painting and sculpture. **clastic a.,** anatomy studied by the aid of models in which various layers can be removed to show the position of organs and parts underneath. **comparative a.,** a comparative view of the structure of different animals and plants one with another. **corrosion a.,** anatomy by means of corrosive agents that remove the tissues which it is not intended to observe. **dental a.,** the study of the structure of the teeth and their correlated parts. **descriptive a.,** the study or description of individual parts of the body. **developmental a.,** embryology. **general a.,** the study of the structure and composition of the body, and its tissues and fluids in general. **gross a.,** that which deals with structures that can be distinguished with the naked eye. **histological a.,** histology. **homological a.,** the study of the correlated parts of the body. **macroscopical a.** Same as *gross a.* **medical a.,** anatomy concerned with the study of points connected with the diagnosis and situation of internal diseases. **microscopical a., minute a.,** histology. **morbid a., pathological a.,** the anatomy of diseased tissues. **physiognomonic a.,** the study of the external expression of the body surface, especially of the face. **physiological a.,** the study of the organs with respect to their normal functions. **plastic a.,** the study of anatomy by the aid of models and manikins that can be taken apart. **practical a.,** anatomy studied by means of demonstration and dissection. **regional a.,** the study of limited portions or regions of the body. **special a.,** the study of particular organs or parts. **surface a.,** the study of the form and markings of the surface of the body. **surgical a.,** the study of limited portions or regions of the body, with a view to the diagnosis and treatment of surgical conditions. **systematic a.,** descriptive a. **topographic a.,** the study of parts in their relation to surrounding parts. **transcendental a.,** the study of the general design and morphology of the body and the analogies and homologies of its parts. **veterinary a.,** the anatomy of the domestic animals.

anatopism (ah-nat′o-pizm) [*ana-* + Gr. *topos* place + *-ism*]. A mental condition in which the patient fails to conform to the customs of the social group to which he belongs: called also *ectopism.*

anatoxic (an″ah-tok′sik). Pertaining to anatoxin.

anatoxin (an″ah-tok′sin) [*ana-* + *toxin*]. Formol toxoid. **diphtheria a., a.-Ramon,** diphtheria toxoid.

anatoxireaction (an″ah-tok″se-re-ak′shun). Moloney's test. See under *tests.*

anatricrotic (an″ah-tri-krot′ik). Pertaining to or characterized by anatricrotism.

anatricrotism (an″ah-trik′ro-tizm) [*ana-* + Gr. *treis* three + *krotos* beat + *-ism*]. An anomaly of the pulse evidenced by the appearance of three small additional waves or notches in the ascending limb of the pulse tracing.

anatripsis (an″ah-trip′sis) [Gr. "rubbing"]. Therapeutic rubbing or friction.

anatriptic (an″ah-trip′tik) [Gr. *anatriptos* rubbed up]. 1. Pertaining to anatripsis. 2. A medication applied by rubbing.

anatrophic (an″ah-trof′ik). 1. Correcting or preventing atrophy. 2. A remedy that prevents waste of the tissues.

anatropia (an″ah-tro′pe-ah) [*ana-* + Gr. *trepein* to turn]. Upward deviation of the visual axis of one eye when the other eye is fixing.

anatropic (an″ah-trop′ik). Pertaining to anatropia; deviating upward.

anavenin (an″ah-ven′in). A venom which has become inactivated by the addition of formaldehyde.

anaxon (an-ak′son) [*an* neg. + Gr. *axōn* axis]. A neuron, or nerve cell, which appears to be devoid of axis-cylinder processes.

anaxone (an-ak′sōn). Anaxon.

anazoturia (an″az-o-tu′re-ah) [*an* neg. + *azote* + Gr. *ouron* urine + *-ia*]. Absence or deficiency in the secretion of nitrogen, and especially of urea in the urine.

anazoturic (an″az-o-tu′rik). Pertaining to or characterized by anazoturia.

AnCC. Abbreviation for *anodal closure contraction.*

anchone (ang-ko′ne). Spasmodic constriction of the throat in hysteria.

anchor (ang′ker). A means by which something is held securely. See *convenience point.*

anchorage (ang′ker-ij). Fixation, such as the surgical fixation of a displaced viscus. In operative dentistry, the fixation of fillings or of artificial crowns or bridges; in orthodontics, the support used for a regulating apparatus, which may be *intramaxillary*, by means of teeth located in the same arch; *intermaxillary*, by means of both maxillary and mandibular teeth; or *extramaxillary*, by means of a device that is located outside of the mouth.

Anchusa (an-ku′zah) [L.; Gr. *anchousa*]. The genus of plants from which alkanet is obtained.

anchusin (an-ku′sin). A red coloring matter $C_{35}H_{40}O_8$, from alkanet.

anchylo-. For words beginning thus, see those beginning *ankylo-.*

ancillary (an′sil-lăr″e) [L. *ancillaris* relating to a maid servant]. Assisting in the performance of a service or the achievement of a result.

ancipital (an-sip′ĭ-tal) [L. *an′ceps* two headed]. Having two heads or two edges.

Ancistrodon (an-sis′tro-don) [Gr. *ankistron* fishhook + *odous* tooth]. A genus of poisonous serpents of the family Crotalidae. *A. contor′trix* is the copperhead, and *A. pisciv′orus,* the water moccasin, of North America.

ancistroid (an-sis′troid) [Gr. *ankistron* fishhook + *eidos* form]. Hook shaped.

anconad (an′ko-nad) [Gr. *ankōn* elbow + L. *ad* toward]. Toward the elbow or olecranon.

anconagra (an″kon-ag′rah) [Gr. *ankōn* elbow + *agra* seizure]. Gout of the elbow.

anconal (an′kŏ-nal). Anconeal.

anconeal (an-ko′ne-al). Pertaining to the elbow.

anconitis (an″ko-ni′tis). Inflammation of the elbow joint.

anconoid (an′ko-noid). Resembling the elbow.

ancylo-. For words beginning thus, see also words beginning *ankylo-.*

Ancylostoma (an″sĭ-los′to-mah) [Gr. *ankylos* crooked + *stoma* mouth]. A genus of nematode parasites, the old world hookworms. **A. america′num,** *Necator americanus.* **A. brazilien′se,** a species found in cats and dogs in the southeastern United States, Brazil and other tropical countries: it may cause a creeping eruption in man and its larvae produce a dermatitis. **A. cani′num,** the common hookworm of dogs and cats. **A. ceylon′icum,** a species infesting felines and canines in India. **A. duodena′le** (Dubini, 1843), the common hookworm, a nematode worm, the male being 10–12 mm. ($\frac{1}{3}$–$\frac{1}{2}$ inch) long and 0.4 mm. ($\frac{1}{60}$ inch) broad, the female somewhat larger. The mature parasites inhabit the small intestine, producing the condition known as ancylostomiasis.

ancylostomatic (an″sĭ-lo-sto-mat′ik). Caused by Ancylostoma.

ancylostome (an-sĭl′o-stōm). An individual organism of the genus Ancylostoma.

ancylostomiasis (an″sĭ-lo-sto-mi′ah-sis). Hookworm disease; a condition due to the presence of *Ancylostoma duodenale* or *Necator americanus,* nematode worms which closely resemble each other. The disease occurs in practically all tropical and subtropical countries and is especially prevalent in the southern United States and in the West Indies. In temperate regions it occurs in mines and tunnels where conditions of temperature and moisture resemble the tropics. The larvae of the parasite live in earth and gain entrance to the digestive tract either directly with contaminated food or water, or indirectly by way of the skin of the feet or legs. The latter infection is followed by a transitory eruption known as "ground itch" or "mazamorra" (**a. cu′tis**). From here the parasites are carried by the blood to the lungs, ascend the trachea, are swallowed, and settle in the small intestine. The infection is marked by gastrointestinal disturbance, abdominal pain, intermittent fever, progressive anemia, pallor, and emaciation which may be marked or concealed by a dropsical condition. Called also *dochmiasis, uncinariasis, hookworm disease, miners' anemia, St. Gotthard's tunnel disease, tunnel anemia, Egyptian chlorosis.*

ancylostomo-anemia (an″sĭ-los″to-mo″ah-ne′me-ah). Ancylostomiasis.

Ancylostomum (an″sĭ-los-to′mum). Ancylostoma.

ancyroid (an′sĭ-roid) [Gr. *ankyra* anchor + *eidos* form]. Shaped like an anchor or hook.

Anda (an′dah) [Brazilian]. A genus of euphorbiaceous trees. *A. as′su* and *A. gome′sii*, of Brazil, afford purgative oils.

Andernach's ossicles (ahn′der-nahks) [Johann Winther von *Andernach*, German physician, 1487–1574]. The wormian bones.

Anders' disease (an′ders) [James M. *Anders*, Philadelphia physician, 1854–1936]. Adiposis tuberosa simplex.

Andersch's ganglion, nerve (an′dersh-ez) [Carol Samuel *Andersch*, German anatomist of the 18th Century]. See under *ganglion* and *nerve.*

Andersen's syndrome or **triad** (an′der-sonz) [Dorothy Hansine *Andersen*, New York pathologist, born 1901]. See under *syndrome.*

Anderson splint (an′der-son) [Roger *Anderson*, Seattle orthopedic surgeon, born 1891]. See under *splint.*

Andira (an-di′rah). Genus of tropical leguminous trees. Goa powder (q.v.) and chrysarobin (q.v.) are derived from *A. araro′ba*, of Brazil. Many species afford poisons, and several are anthelmintic.

andirine (an-di′rin). Surinamine.

andr-. See *andro-.*

Andrade's indicator (an-drah′dēz) [Eduardo Penny *Andrade*, American bacteriologist, 1872–1906]. See under *indicator.*

Andral's decubitus (an-dralz′) [Gabriel *Andral*, French physician, 1797–1876]. See under *decubitus.*

andranatomy (an″dran-at′o-me) [*andr-* + *anatomy*]. Male anatomy.

andrase (an′drās) [*andr-* + *-ase* enzyme]. A hypothetical enzyme-like substance regarded as the material basis of maleness in heredity. Cf. *gynase.*

andreioma (an″dre-o′mah) [*andr-* + *-oma*]. Arrhenoblastoma.

andreoblastoma (an″dre-o-blas-to′mah). Arrhenoblastoma.

Andrewes' test (an′dro͞oz) [C. H. *Andrewes*, British physician]. See under *tests.*

Andrews' disease [George Clinton *Andrews*, New York dermatologist, born 1891]. Pustular bacterid.

Andrews' operation [E. Wyllys *Andrews*, American surgeon, 1857–1927]. See under *operation.*

andriatrics (an″dre-at′riks) [Gr. *anēr* man + *iatrikos* healing]. That branch of medicine which deals with diseases of men and their treatment.

andriatry (an-dri′ah-tre). Andriatrics.

andrin (an′drin) [Gr. *anēr* man]. A general term for the androgens of the testicle, namely testosterone, androsterone and dehydro-androsterone.

andro-, andr- (an′dro) [Gr. *anēr, andros* man]. Combining form denoting relationship to man, or to the male.

androcyte (an′dro-sīt) [*andro-* + Gr. *kytos* hollow vessel]. Spermatid.

androdedotoxin (an″dro-de″do-tok′sin). A poisonous principle from the leaves of rhododendrons.

androgalactozemia (an″dro-gah-lak″to-ze′me-ah) [*andro-* + Gr. *gala* milk + *zēmia* loss]. The secretion or escape of milk from the male breast.

androgen (an′dro-jen) [*andro-* + Gr. *gennan* to produce]. Any substance which possesses masculinizing activities, such as the testis hormone. See *androsterone* and *testosterone.*

androgenesis (an″dro-jen′e-sis) [*andro-* + Gr. *genesis* production]. Development of an egg which contains only paternal chromosomes.

androgenic (an″dro-jen′ik). Producing masculine characteristics.

androgenicity (an″dro-je-nis′ĭ-te). The quality of exerting a masculinizing effect.

androgenous (an-droj′e-nus) [*andro-* + Gr. *gennan* to beget]. Pertaining or tending to the production of male rather than female offspring.

androglossia (an″dro-glos′e-ah) [*andro-* + Gr. *glōssa* tongue]. A quality of maleness in a woman's voice.

androgone (an′dro-gōn) [*andro-* + Gr. *gonos* seed]. A spermatogenous cell.

androgyne (an′dro-jīn). Androgynus.

androgyneity (an″dro-jĭ-ne′ĭ-te). Androgynism.

androgynism (an-droj′ĭ-nizm). The possession of masculine characteristics by a genetically pure female; female pseudohermaphroditism.

androgynoid (an-droj′ĭ-noid). 1. A pseudohermaphrodite. 2. Pertaining to androgynism.

androgynous (an-droj′ĭ-nus). Pertaining to or characterized by androgynism.

androgynus (an-droj′ĭ-nus) [*andro-* + Gr. *gynē* woman]. A genetically pure female with masculine characteristics; a female pseudohermaphrodite.

androgyny (an-droj′ĭ-ne). Androgynism.

android (an′droid) [*andro-* + Gr. *eidos* shape]. Resembling a man; manlike.

androidal (an-droi′dal). Android.

androkinin (an″dro-kin′in) [*andro-* + Gr. *kinein* to move]. A general term for androgenic substances; no longer in good usage.

andrology (an-drol′o-je) [*andro-* + *-logy*]. Scientific study of the masculine constitution and of the diseases of the male sex; especially the study of diseases of the male organs of generation.

androma (an-dro′mah) [*andr-* + *-oma*]. Arrhenoma.

Andromachus (an-drom′ah-kus) (1st century A.D.). Known as Andromachus the Elder, of Crete, he was body physician to the Emperor Nero, and supposedly the originator of a famous universal remedy, *theriaca andromachi.*

andromania (an″dro-ma′ne-ah) [*andro-* + Gr. *mania* madness]. Nymphomania.

Andromeda (an-drom′e-dah) [L.]. A genus of ericaceous shrubs and trees, some of which afford a poisonous narcotic principle. *A. maria′na, A. nit′ida*, and *A. polifo′lia* are among the poisonous species.

andromedotoxin (an-drom″e-do-tok′sin) [*Andromeda* + *toxin*]. A poisonous crystalline principle from various ericaceous plants: it inhibits the respiratory centers and is hypnotic.

andromerogon (an″dro-mer′o-gon) [*andro-* + Gr. *meros* part + *gonē* seed]. An organism developed from an ovum containing the male pronucleus only, the cells, as a result, containing only the paternal set of chromosomes.

andromerogone (an″dro-mer′o-gon). Andromerogon.

andromerogony (an″dro-mĕ-rog′o-ne) [*andro-* + Gr. *meros* a part + *gonos* procreation]. Development of a portion of an ovum containing the male pronucleus only, the nucleus of the ovum having been removed before fusion of the male and female pronuclei occurred.

andromimetic (an″dro-mĭ-met′ik) [*andro-* + Gr. *mimētikos* imitating]. Producing male characteristics; having a masculinizing effect. Cf. *arrhenomimetic.*

andromorphous (an″dro-mor′fus) [*andro-* + Gr. *morphē* form]. Having a masculine appearance.

andropathy (an-drop′ah-the) [*andro-* + Gr. *pathos* disease]. Any disease peculiar to man.

androphany (an-drof′ah-ne) [*andro-* + Gr *phainein* to show]. Virilism.

androphile (an′dro-fil). Anthropophilic.

androphilous (an-drof′ĭ-lus). Anthropophilic.

androphobia (an″dro-fo′be-ah) [*andro-* + *phobia*]. Morbid dislike of the male sex.

androphonomania (an″dro-fo″no-ma′ne-ah) [Gr. *androphonos* man killing + *mania* madness]. Homicidal insanity.

Andropogon (an″dro-po′gon). A genus of grasses. *A. sor′ghum* includes broom corn, kafir corn, and sorghum.

androstane (an′dro-stān). A tetracyclic hydrocarbon, $C_{19}H_{32}$, the nucleus from which the androgens are derived.

androstanediol (an″dro-stān′de-ol). An androgen, $C_{19}H_{32}O_2$, prepared by reducing androsterone.

androstanedione (an″dro-stān′de-ōn). An androgen, $C_{19}H_{28}O_2$ (3,17-diketo androstane), formed in the testes.

androstanolone (an″dro-stan′o-lōn). An androgen, $C_{19}H_{30}O_2$, occurring in two isomeric forms. See *androsterone.*

androstene (an′dro-stēn). An unsaturated cyclic hydrocarbon, $C_{19}H_{30}$, with one double bond; a steroid occurring in two isomeric forms forming the nucleus of testosterone and some other androgens.

androstenediol (an″dro-stēn′de-ol). An androgen, $C_{19}H_{30}O_2$, occurring in two isomeric forms, 3-trans, 17-dihydroxy $\triangle^5$-androstene and 3-cis, 17-dihydroxy $\triangle^5$-androstene.

androstenedione (an″dro-stēn′de-ōn). An androgen, $C_{19}H_{26}O_2$, 3,17-diketo $\triangle^4$-androstene.

androsterone (an-dros′ter-ōn). An androgen excreted in the urine of both men and women. It is 3-trans-hydroxy-17-keto-androstene, $C_{19}H_{30}O_2$. When injected it counteracts the effects of castration.

androtermone (an-dro′ter-mōn). The gamete hormone given off from the male gametes which tends to cause the zygote to be male.

androtin (an′dro-tin). A generic term for androgenic substances, no longer in good usage.

AnDTe. Abbreviation for *anodal duration tetanus.*

anectasin (an-ek′tah-sin) [*an* neg. + Gr. *ektasis* distention]. A substance produced by bacteria, having an effect on the vasomotor nerves opposite to that of ectasin.

anectine (an-ek′tin). Trade mark for preparations of succinylcholine.

anedeous (an-e′de-us) [*an* neg. + Gr. *aidoia* genitals]. Lacking genitals.

Anel's operation, probe, etc. [Dominique *Anel,* French surgeon, 1679–1730]. See under the nouns.

anelectrode (an″e-lek′trōd) [Gr. *ana* up + *electrode*]. The positive pole of a galvanic battery.

anelectrotonic (an″e-lek-tro-ton′ik). Pertaining to anelectrotonus.

anelectrotonus (an″e-lek-trot′o-nus) [Gr. *ana* up + *electrotonus*]. Lessened irritability of a nerve in the region of the positive pole or anode during the passage of an electric current.

anematize (ah-ne′mah-tiz). To make or render anemic.

anematosis (ah-ne″mah-to′sis). General anemia.

anemia (ah-ne′me-ah) (Gr. *an* neg. + *haima* blood + *-ia*]. A reduction below normal in the number of erythrocytes per cu. mm., the quantity of hemoglobin, or the volume of packed red cells per 100 ml. blood which occurs when the equilibrium between blood loss and blood production is disturbed. **achlorhydric a.,** hypochromic a., idiopathic. **achrestic a.,** a fatal form of macrocytic anemia, similar morphologically to Addisonian pernicious anemia but not responsive to the same therapy. The etiology is unknown but may reflect inability to utilize the anti-pernicious anemia principle. **achylic a., a. achy′lica,** hypochromic a., idiopathic. **acute a.,** anemia of short duration due to hemorrhage. **Addison's a., Addison-Biermer a., addisonian a.,** pernicious a. **agastric a.,** a non-definitive term applied to anemia which follows extensive resection of the stomach. **alimentary a.,** deficiency a. **angiospastic a.,** anemia due to local blood vessel spasm. **anhematopoietic a., anhemopoietic a.,** anemia due to defective formation of erythrocytes. **aplastic a.,** a persistent form of anemia generally unresponsive to specific antianemia therapy, often accompanied by granulocytopenia and thrombocytopenia, in which the bone marrow may not necessarily be acellular or hypoplastic but fails to produce adequate numbers of peripheral blood elements. The term actually is all-inclusive and most probably it encompasses several clinical syndromes. Also called *aregenerative a., hypoplastic a.,* and *refractory a.* **aplastic a., atrophic,** myelophthisic a. **aplastic a., pure,** anemia in which there is complete absence of reticulocytes in the blood and of all types of erythroblasts in the bone marrow. **aregenerative a.** 1. Aplastic anemia. 2. Aleukia hemorrhagica. **aregenerative a., chronic congenital,** hypoplastic a., congenital (def. 1). **asiderotic a.,** hypochromic a. **atrophic a.,** anemia secondary to atrophy of the bone marrow. **Bagdad Spring a.,** a type of hemolytic anemia most probably due to a red cell deficiency of glucose-6-phosphate dehydrogenase. **Bartonella a.** 1. Oroya fever. 2. The anemia in rats that follows splenectomy. A latent Bartonella infection seems to be activated by loss of the spleen. **Biermer's a., Biermer-Ehrlich a.,** pernicious a. **a. of Blackfan and Diamond,** hypoplastic a., congenital (def. 1). **bothriocephalus a.,** anemia caused by the *Bothriocephalus latus.* **brickmakers' a.,** ancylostomiasis. **cameloid a.,** elliptocytosis. **cattle a.,** a condition caused by infection with *Theileria parva.* **chlorotic a.,** chlorosis. **Chvostek's a.,** applied originally to anemia of apparent pancreatic origin, without designation of the morphologic characteristics or the cause of the condition. **congenital hypoplastic a.** See *hypoplastic a., congenital.* **congenital nonspherocytic hemolytic a.** See *hemolytic a., congenital non-spherocytic.* **Cooley's a.,** thalassemia. **costogenic a.,** anemia due to disorder of the bone marrow of the ribs. **cow's milk a.,** chlorotic anemia in infants due to lack of iron in a cow's milk diet. **crescent cell a.,** sickle cell a. Not to be confused with a condition in which the blood contains crescent (or solenoid) bodies which are probably derived from rupture of erythrocytes. **cytogenic a.,** progressive pernicious anemia. **Czerny's a.,** alimentary anemia of infants caused by inadequate nourishment. **deficiency a.,** anemia caused by a lack of a specific substance required for normal hemoglobin synthesis and erythrocytic maturation arising by several means, such as malabsorption or poor dietary intake. **dilution a.,** a condition in which anemia is more apparent than real, being due to an increased plasma volume rather than to decreased total circulating cell mass. **dimorphic a.,** a condition characterized by a dual erythrocyte population, as defined by a double peak of the diameter frequency curve, observed when combined deficiencies of vitamin B_{12} or analogous substance and of iron exist concurrently in the same patient. **drepanocytic a.,** sickle cell a. **Dresbach's a.,** sickle cell a. **Edelmann's a.,** a type of chronic infectious anemia. **Egyptian a.,** ancylostomiasis. **elliptocytary a., elliptocytotic a.,** elliptocytosis. **equine infectious a.,** an infectious disease of horses marked by recurring attacks of malaise with abrupt rises of temperature, and spread through feed and water contaminated by the urine of infected animals; also suggested as transmissible to man, in whom it causes anemia, neutropenia, and relative lymphocytosis. Called also *infectious anemia of horses, Vallee's disease,* and *swamp fever.* **erythroblastic a. of childhood.** 1. Anemia pseudoleukemica infantum. 2. Thalassemia. **erythroblastic a., familial,** thalassemia.

erythroblastotic a. of childhood, thalassemia. **erythronoclastic a.,** hemolytic a. **erythronormoblastic a.,** hypochromic a. **essential a.,** primary a. **Faber's a.,** achylanemia. **familial erythroblastic a.,** thalassemia. **familial splenic a.,** Gaucher's disease. **febrile a., acute,** a term which originally described an illness resembling thrombotic thrombocytopenic purpura. **fertilizer a.,** acute hemolytic anemia occurring among fertilizer workers. **globe cell a.,** anemia characterized by the presence of spherocytes or elliptocytes. Called also *hereditary spherocytosis, congenital hemolytic icterus, chronic familial icterus,* and *chronic acholuric jaundice.* **globular a.,** anemia from deficiency of red blood corpuscles. **glucose-6-phosphate dehydrogenase deficiency a.,** a genetically determined hemolytic anemia caused by a red cell deficiency of this enzyme which follows ingestion of drugs of certain groups (such as antimalarials, sulfonamides, nitrofurans, antipyretics and analgesics, and sulfones), fava beans, and a number of other agents. Recent studies imply that this predisposition to hemolysis may be expressed in varying degrees, and that other biochemical defects, in addition to that involving glucose-6-phosphate dehydrogenase, may also be present in the red cells. **goat's milk a.,** a macrocytic anemia, observed particularly in Germany and Italy, occurring in infants fed exclusively on goat's milk, associated with a megaloblastic bone marrow, thrombocytopenia, leukopenia, hyperbilirubinemia, and hyperferremia. **ground itch a.,** ancylostomiasis. **hemolytic a.,** anemia due to shortened *in vivo* survival of the erythrocytes and inability of the bone marrow to compensate for their decreased life span. **hemolytic a., acute,** a condition characterized by sudden destruction of erythrocytes by hemolysis. **hemolytic a., congenital non-spherocytic,** a hereditary hemolytic anemia secondary to a biochemical defect of the red cell glycolytic mechanism such that *in vitro* erythrocyte autohemolysis will vary with the concentrations of glucose or adenosine triphosphate present in the incubation mixture; an associated deficiency of glucose-6-phosphate dehydrogenase has been demonstrated in some patients and, in others, a defect in pyruvate kinase. **hemorrhagic a.,** anemia that is caused by the sudden and acute loss of blood. Called also *acute posthemorrhagic anemia.* **hereditary sex-linked a.,** an obscure form of anemia, which may not necessarily represent an individual entity; it is limited to males, possibly transmitted by the female, is associated with anisocytosis and poikilocytosis of the red cells, hemosiderosis, hyperferremia, decreased red cell survival, and splenomegaly, and is refractory to the usual therapeutic hematinics. **Herrick's a.,** sickle cell a. **hookworm a.,** ancylostomiasis. **hyperchromic a.,** a misleading term, no longer in general use, which implies that the red cell may carry more hemoglobin than its surface area may tolerate. This does not occur except in hereditary spherocytosis. **hypochromic a.,** a condition characterized by a disproportionate reduction of red cell hemoglobin, compared with the volume of packed red cells; generally, the red cells are also reduced in size, so that the designation *hypochromic, microcytic anemia* is more appropriate. **hypochromic a., idiopathic,** a syndrome occurring mainly in females in the third to fifth decades, associated with achlorhydria, hypochromic red cells, and, in some instances, certain of the clinical features of pernicious anemia. There is usually therapeutic response to iron salts. Called also *chronic hypochromic a.* and *simple achlorhydric a.* **a. hypochro'mica siderochres'tica heredita'ria,** a refractory anemia, beginning in childhood, displaying a chronic course, with hyperplastic bone marrow, iron-containing erythroblasts, normal red cell survival, and normal serum iron, but rapid plasma iron clearance and turnover; possibly related to impaired iron utilization. **hypoferric a.,** iron deficiency a. **hypoplastic a.** 1. Aplastic anemia. 2. Aleukia hemorrhagica. **hypoplastic a., congenital.** 1. A progressive anemia of unknown etiology encountered in the first year of life, unaccompanied by leukopenia and thrombocytopenia, unresponsive to hematinics, and requiring multiple blood transfusions to sustain life. Called also *chronic congenital aregenerative anemia, erythrogenesis imperfecta, anemia of Blackfan and Diamond,* and *pure red cell anemia.* 2. A rare, fatal childhood anemia, probably familial and hereditary, characterized by pancytopenia and congenital anomalies of the neuromusculoskeletal and urogenital systems. Also called *Fanconi syndrome.* **icterohemolytic a.,** hemolytic jaundice. **idiopathic a.,** primary a. **inclusion body a.,** a hemolytic anemia characterized by abnormal pigments in the urine, red cells with basophilic stippling, siderotic granules, and inclusion bodies similar to but not identical with Heinz-Ehrlich bodies, increased *in vitro* autohemolysis, and an abnormal, undefined hemoglobin component. **a. infan'tum pseudoleuke'mica.** See *a. pseudoleukemica infantum.* **infectious a. of horses,** equine infectious a. **intertropical a.,** ancylostomiasis. **isochromic a.,** normochromic a. **Jaksch's a.,** a. pseudoleukemica infantum. **kennel a.,** a disease of dogs caused by *Ancylostoma caninum.* **Larzel's a.,** a. pseudoleukemica infantum. **Lederer's a.,** an acute hemolytic anemia of short duration and unknown etiology, possibly autoimmune, which, when originally described, further helped to establish the concept of acquired hemolytic anemia as distinct from the congenital spherocytic type. **Leishman's a.,** kala-azar. **leukoerythroblastic a.,** agnogenic myeloid metaplasia. **Luzet's a.,** a. pseudoleukemica infantum. **a. lymphat'ica,** Hodgkin's disease. **macrocytic a.,** a name applied to a category of anemias, of varying etiologies, characterized by larger than normal red cells, absence of the customary central area of pallor, and an increased mean corpuscular volume and mean corpuscular hemoglobin. **macrocytic a., tropical,** a type of macrocytic anemia occurring in India, China, and the African west coast; resembling pernicious anemia in many respects but without achlorhydria and only erratically responsive to vitamin B_{12}. Folic acid produces marked improvement in most cases. **malignant a.,** primary pernicious a. **Mediterranean a.,** thalassemia. **megaloblastic a.,** anemia characterized by the presence of megaloblasts in the bone marrow. **megaloblastic a., familial,** a rare familial form of anemia observed in Norwegian and Finnish children, characterized by selective intestinal malabsorption of vitamin B_{12} uninfluenced by intrinsic factor, and associated with proteinuria, and structural genitourinary tract anomalies. **megalocytic a.,** macrocytic a. **metaplastic a.,** pernicious anemia marked by change in the plastic elements of the blood. **microcytic a.,** anemia characterized by erythrocytes the majority of which are smaller than normal. **microelliptopoikilocytic a. of Rietti, Greppi, and Micheli,** one of the thalassemic syndromes, caused by presence of abnormal hemoglobins and characterized by abnormally small erythrocytes of elliptical and other irregular shapes. **milk a.,** an anemia, generally hypochromic, which probably results from prolonged maintenance of infants on milk as the sole or major dietary constituent. **miners' a.,** ancylostomiasis. **monkey a.,** a macrocytic anemia produced in monkeys by feeding them a generally deficient diet. **mountain a.,** mountain sickness. **myelopathic a., myelophthisic a.,** anemia due to the destruction, or crowding out, of the hematopoietic tissues by various space-occupying lesions. **a. neonato'rum,** the mildest form of erythroblastosis fetalis in which anemia is the chief manifestation. Now replaced by the term erythroblastosis qualified by an adjective indicating the degree of severity. **normocytic a.,** an anemia characterized by a proportionate decrease in the hemoglobin content, the packed red cell volume, and the number of erythrocytes per cubic millimeter of blood. **nutritional a.,** deficiency a. **osteosclerotic a.,** anemia occurring in association with osteosclerosis, as a result of effect on bone marrow of changes in the bones. **ovalocytary a.,** anemia with oval or elliptical red cells in the blood. **perniciosiform a.,** a subacute disease affecting infants about one year of age, resembling pernicious anemia in the adult, but ending in recovery, sometimes with anti-anemic therapy alone. **pernicious a.,** a megaloblastic anemia generally occurring in later adult life, characterized by histamine-fast achlorhydria, in which the laboratory and clinical manifestations are predicated on the reduced ability to absorb vitamin B_{12} from the gastrointestinal tract due to a failure of gastric mucosal secretion of intrinsic factor. **phenylhydrazine a.,** a hemolytic anemia resulting from ingestion of phenylhydrazine, which most probably is converted to a compound that, by acting as an oxidant, transforms oxyhemoglobin to methemoglobin, and then sulfhemoglobin, and finally produces Heinz-Ehrlich bodies. In certain instances, due to an intracellular deficiency of reduced glutathione, and enzymes such as glucose-6-phosphate dehydrogenase, the red cell may be particularly sensitive to this agent. **physiologic a.,** the normocytic, normochromic anemia that occurs in infants at the age of 2 or 3 months, owing to normal depression of erythropoiesis and hemoglobin synthesis, probably resulting as an adjustment to the change-over from placental to pulmonary oxygenation. **pleiochromic a., febrile,** a disease characterized by wide-spread hyaline thrombi in the terminal arterioles and capillaries, the thrombi being composed of agglutinated red blood cells. **polar a.,** an anemic condition that occurs during exposure to low temperature; initially microcytic, but subsequently becoming normocytic. The basic mechanism is not defined precisely, but it may be due to loss of circulating erythrocytes secondary to trauma or capillary wall diapedesis, in addition to failure of compensatory bone marrow response. Called also *arctic a.* **posthemorrhagic a., acute,** hemorrhagic a. **primaquine-sensitive a.,** glucose-6-phosphate dehydrogenase a.; so called because the initial studies characterizing the condition were made during investigation of the hemolytic properties of primaquine. **primary a.,** any form of anemia in which there is alteration of function of bone marrow, leading to reduction in erythrocytic output. Called also *essential* or *idiopathic a.* **progressive pernicious a.** See *pernicious a.* **pseudoaplastic a.,** a term implying pancytopenia in which the bone marrow is hypercellular and contains bizarre red and white cell precursors; actually not a specific entity. **a. pseudoleuke′mica infan′tum,** a condition originally described as a specific entity in children under age three, with anisocytosis, poikilocytosis, peripheral blood red cell immaturity, leukocytosis, lymphadenopathy and hepatosplenomegaly; now considered to be a syndrome produced by many factors such as malnutrition, chronic infection, malabsorption, and hemoglobinopathies. **Puerto Rican a.,** an extreme form of anemia caused by hookworm infection. **pure red cell a.,** hypoplastic a., congenital (def. 1). **pyridoxine-responsive a.,** an anemia characterized by hypochromia, microcytosis, anisocytosis, poikilocytosis, targeting, hyperferremia, increased tissue iron stores, abnormal urinary excretion of xanthurenic acid and related compounds; occurring after administration of L-tryptophane and showing improvement and reticulocytosis after treatment with pyridoxine. **a. refracto′ria sideroblas′tica,** a condition occurring in adults, similar to anemia hypochromica siderochrestica hereditaria in children, which, like the childhood condition, is thought to be related to impaired utilization of iron. **Santesson's a.,** a fatal aplastic anemia due to benzene occurring in bicycle tire workers. **scorbutic a.,** anemia due to deficiency of vitamin C; in naturally occurring human scurvy the anemia is generally normocytic, although in experimentally induced vitamin C deficiency the anemia is of the megaloblastic type. **secondary a.,** anemia originally used to include all types of anemia, now used to designate anemia resulting from antecedent or associated disease. Called also *simple, chronic anemia.* **sickle cell a.,** a hereditary, genetically determined hemolytic anemia, one of the hemoglobinopathies, occurring in the Negro, characterized by arthralgia, acute attacks of abdominal pain, ulcerations of the lower extremities, oat-shaped erythrocytes in the blood, and, for full clinical expression, the homozygous presence of S hemoglobin as defined by hemoglobin electrophoresis. Also called *sicklemia, Dresbach's a.* and *Herrick's a.* **slaty a.,** a term applied to a grayish color of the face in poisoning by acetanilid or silver. **spastic a.,** angiospastic a. **spherocytic a.** See *hemolytic a., congenital.* **splenic a., a. splenet′ica,** Banti's disease. **splenic a. of infants,** a. pseudoleukemica infantum. **thrombopenic a.,** thrombopenia. **toxic a.,** anemia due to destruction of the blood cells by poisons or disease toxins, actually representing a form of aplastic anemia. Called also *toxic paralytic a.* **tropical a.** 1. Anemia affecting persons visiting the tropics and who have not become acclimatized. 2. Ancylostomiasis. **tunnel a.,** ancylostomiasis. **von Jaksch's a.,** a. pseudoleukemica infantum.

anemic (ah-ne′mik). Pertaining to or characterized by anemia.

anemize (ah-ne′mīz). To render anemic.

anemo- (ah-nem′o) [Gr. *anemos* wind]. A combining form denoting relationship to wind.

anemometer (an″e-mom′e-ter) [*anemo-* + Gr. *metron* measure]. An instrument for measuring the velocity of the wind.

Anemone (ah-nem′o-ne). A genus of plants. See *pulsatilla.*

anemonin (ah-nem′o-nin). The active principle of *Anemone pulsatilla*, a colorless crystalline substance, $C_{10}H_8O_4$, or pulsatilla camphor.

anemonism (ah-nem′o-nizm). Poisoning by the plants of the genus *Anemone.*

anemonol (ah-nem′o-nol). An exceedingly poisonous volatile oil from various species of *Anemone* and from other ranunculaceous plants.

anemopathy (an″e-mop′ah-the) [*anemo-* + Gr. *pathos* disease]. The treatment of disease by inhalation.

anemophilous (an″e-mof′ĭ-lus) [*anemo-* + Gr. *philein* to love]. Pollinated by the wind: said of certain flowers.

anemophobia (an″e-mo-fo′be-ah) [*anemo-* + *phobia*]. Morbid fear of wind or of drafts.

anemotaxis (an″e-mo-tak′sis) [*anemo-* + Gr. *taxis* arrangement]. Adjustment with reference to the wind.

anemotrophy (an″e-mot′ro-fe) [*an* neg. + Gr. *haima* blood + *trophē* nourishment]. Deficiency of blood nourishment.

anemotropism (an″e-mot′ro-pism) [*anemo-* + Gr. *tropos* a turning]. A turning toward or away from the wind.

anempeiria (an″em-pi′re-ah) [*an* neg. + Gr. *empeiria* experience]. Loss of acquired capacities; inability to apply what has been learned, e.g., speech or writing (Heveroch, 1914).

anencephalia (an″en-se-fa′le-ah) [*an* neg. + Gr. *enkephalos* brain + *-ia*]. A developmental anomaly characterized by absence of the cranial vault and cerebral hemispheres completely missing or reduced to small masses attached to the base of the skull.

anencephalic (an″en-se-fal′ik). Exhibiting anencephalia; having no brain.

anencephalohemia (an″en-sef″ah-lo-he′me-ah) [*an* neg. + Gr. *enkephalos* brain + *haima* blood +

-*ia*]. An insufficient supply of blood to the brain.

anencephalous (an″en-sef′ah-lus). Having no brain.

anencephalus (an″en-sef′ah-lus). A fetal monster exhibiting anencephalia.

anencephaly (an″en-sef′ah-le). Anencephalia.

anenteroneuria (an-en″ter-o-nu′re-ah) [*an* neg. + Gr. *enteron* intestine + *neuron* nerve + -*ia*]. Intestinal atony.

anenterous (an-en′ter-us) [*an* neg. + Gr. *enteron* intestine]. Lacking intestines.

anenzymia (an″en-zi′me-ah). A morbid condition resulting from absence of an enzyme normally present in the body. **a. catala′sea,** acatalasia.

aneosinophilia (an″e-o-sin-o-fil′e-ah). Decrease in the number of eosinophils of the blood; eosinopenia, hypo-eosinophilia.

anephrogenesis (a″nef-ro-jen′e-sis) [*a* neg. + Gr. *nephros* kidney + *genesis*]. A developmental anomaly characterized by the absence of kidney tissue.

anepia (an-e′pe-ah) [*an* neg. + Gr. *epos* word + -*ia*]. Inability to speak.

anepiploic (an-ep″e-plo′ik). Devoid of omentum.

anepithymia (an-ep″e-thim′e-ah). Loss of any natural appetite.

anerethisia (an-er″e-thiz′e-ah) [*an* neg. + Gr. *erethizein* to excite + -*ia*] Deficient irritability.

aneretic (an″e-ret′ik) [Gr. *anairetikos*]. Destructive.

anergasia (an″er-ga′ze-ah) [*an* neg. + Gr. *ergasia* work]. Lack of functional activity; a psychosis associated with a structural lesion of the central nervous system.

anergastic (an″er-gas′tik). Meyer's term for psychic disorders from structural loss of brain function (loss of memory and judgment, fits, contractures, palsies, etc.).

anergia (an-er′je-ah). Anergy.

anergic (an-er′jik) [*an* neg. + Gr. *ergon* work]. 1. Characterized by abnormal inactivity; inactive. 2. Marked by asthenia or lack of energy. 3. Pertaining to anergy (1st def.).

anergy (an′er-je). 1. A condition in which there is no response to the injection of an antigen, *anti-anaphylaxis*. 2. Asthenia.

aneroid (an′er-oid) [*a* neg. + Gr. *nēros* liquid + *eidos* form]. Not containing liquid.

anerythroblepsia (an″e-rith″ro-blep′se-ah). Anerythropsia.

anerythrocyte (an″e-rith′ro-sit) [*an* neg. + *erythrocyte*]. A red blood corpuscle having no hemoglobin; called also *lympho-erythrocyte*.

anerythroplasia (an″e-rith″ro-pla′ze-ah) [*an* neg. + Gr. *erythros* red + *plassein* to form + -*ia*]. Absence of red blood corpuscle formation.

anerythroplastic (an″e-rith″ro-plas′tik). Pertaining to or characterized by anerythroplasia.

anerythropoiesis (an″e-rith″ro-poi-e′sis) [*an* neg. + *erythropoiesis*]. Deficient production of red blood corpuscles.

anerythropsia (an″er-e-throp′se-ah) [*an* neg. + Gr. *erythros* red + *opsis* sight + -*ia*]. Impaired perception of red tints.

anerythroregenerative (an″e-rith″ro-re-jen′-er-a″tiv). Marked by the absence of regeneration of red blood corpuscles.

anesthecinesia (an-es″the-sĭ-ne′ze-ah) [*an* neg. + Gr. *aisthēsis* perception + *kinēsis* movement + -*ia*]. Loss of sensibility and motor power.

anesthekinesia (an-es″the-kĭ-ne′ze-ah). Anesthecinesia.

anesthesia (an″es-the′ze-ah) [*an* neg. + Gr. *aisthēsis* sensation]. Loss of feeling or sensation. Although the term is used for loss of tactile sensibility, or of any of the other senses, it is applied especially to loss of the sensation of pain, as it is induced to permit performance of surgery or other painful procedures. **angiospastic a.,** loss of sensibility dependent on spasm of the blood vessels. **balanced a.,** anesthesia which utilizes a combination of drugs, each in an amount sufficient to produce its major or desired effect to the optimum degree and keep its undesirable or unnecessary effects to a minimum. **basal a.,** an anesthesia which acts as a basis for further and deeper anesthesia; a state of narcosis produced by preliminary medication so profound that the added inhalation anesthetic necessary to produce surgical anesthesia is greatly reduced. **Bier's local a.,** local anesthesia produced by injection of a 0.5 per cent solution of procaine in the veins of a limb that has been rendered bloodless by elevation and constriction. **block a.** See *regional a.* and *block*. **bulbar a.,** lack of sensation caused by a lesion of the pons. **caudal a.,** anesthesia produced by injection of a local anesthetic into the caudal or sacral canal. **central a.,** lack of sensation caused by disease of the nerve centers. **cerebral a.,** lack of sensation caused by a cerebral lesion. **closed a.,** inhalational anesthesia maintained indefinitely by the continuous rebreathing of a relatively small amount of the anesthetic gas, normally used with an absorption apparatus for the removal of carbon dioxide. **colonic a.,** anesthesia induced by injection of the anesthetic agent into the rectum and lower colon. **compression a.,** loss of sensation resulting from pressure on a nerve. **conduction a.,** regional a. **continuous caudal a.** See under *analgesia*. **Corning's a.** See *spinal a.*, def. 1. **crossed a.,** hemianesthesia cruciata. **dissociated a., dissociation a.,** loss of certain sensations while others remain intact. **doll's head a.,** loss of sensation affecting the head, neck, and upper part of the thorax. **a. doloro′sa,** tactile anesthesia with severe pain in the part, occurring after paralysis, and seen in certain diseases of the spinal cord. **electric a.,** anesthesia induced by passage of an electric current. **endobronchial a.,** anesthesia produced by introduction of a gaseous mixture through a slender tube placed in a large bronchus. **endotracheal a.,** anesthesia produced by introduction of a gaseous mixture through a wide-bore tube inserted into the trachea. **epidural a.,** anesthesia produced by injection of the anesthetic agent between the vertebral spines and beneath the ligamentum flavum into the extradural space. **facial a.,** loss of sensation caused by a lesion of the facial nerve. **gauntlet a.,** loss of sensation in the hand and wrist. **general a.,** a state of unconsciousness, produced by anesthetic agents, with absence of pain sensation over the entire body, and a greater or lesser degree of muscular relaxation. The drugs producing this state can be administered by inhalation, intravenously, intramuscularly, or via the gastrointestinal tract. **girdle a.,** loss of sensation in a zone encircling the body. **glove a.,** gauntlet a. **gustatory a.,** loss of the sense of taste. **Gwathmey's oil-ether a.,** anesthesia produced by introduction into the rectum of a mixture of liquid ether and olive oil. **high pressure a.,** anesthesia produced by a local anesthetic forced into the tissues under high pressure, as into the dentin of a tooth. **hypnosis a.,** production of insensibility to pain during surgical procedures by means of hypnotism. **hypotensive a.,** anesthesia accompanied by the deliberate lowering of the blood pressure, a procedure claimed to reduce blood loss. **hypothermic a.,** anesthesia accompanied by the deliberate lowering of the body temperature. **hysterical a.,** loss of sensation occurring in hysteria. **infiltration a.,** local anesthesia produced by the injection of a solution, such as procaine, lidocaine, and the like, into the tissues. **inhalation a.,** anesthesia produced by the respiration of a volatile liquid or gaseous anesthetic agent. **insufflation a.,** anesthesia produced by administration of a gaseous mixture through a slender tube introduced into the respiratory tract. **intercostal a.,** anesthesia produced by blocking intercostal nerves with a local anesthetic. **intranasal a.,**

local anesthesia, produced by insertion into the nasal fossae of pledgets soaked in a solution of an anesthetic agent which is effective after topical application. **intra-oral a.,** anesthesia produced by the injection of an anesthetic agent around a nerve through a needle inserted into the tissues in the oral cavity. **intraspinal a.,** subarachnoid a. **intravenous a.,** anesthesia produced by introduction of an anesthetic agent into a vein. **Kulenkampff's a.,** anesthesia of the upper extremity produced by injection of a local anesthetic around the brachial plexus. **local a.,** anesthesia which is confined to one part of the body. **Meltzer's a.,** anesthesia induced by endotracheal insufflation. **mental a.,** loss of ability to recognize or identify sensory stimulations. **mixed a.,** anesthesia which is produced by administration of more than one anesthetic agent. See also *balanced a.* **muscular a.,** loss of the muscular sense. **nausea a.,** loss of the sensation of nausea usually stimulated by noxious and disgusting substances. **nerve blocking a.,** regional a. **olfactory a.,** loss of the sense of smell. **open a.,** general inhalation anesthesia in which there is no rebreathing of expired gases. **paraneural a.,** anesthesia produced by injection of the anesthetic agent around a nerve. **parasacral a.,** regional anesthesia produced by injection of a local anesthetic around the sacral nerves as they emerge from the sacral foramina. **paravertebral a.,** regional anesthesia produced by injection of a local anesthetic around the spinal nerves at their exit from the spinal column, and outside the spinal dura. **partial a.,** anesthesia with retention of some degree of sensibility. **peridural a.,** epidural a. **perineural a.,** regional anesthesia produced by injection of the anesthetic agent close to the nerve. **periodontal a.,** anesthesia produced by introduction of the anesthetic agent into the periodontal membrane. **peripheral a.,** loss of sensation which is due to changes in the peripheral nerves. **permeation a.,** analgesia of a body surface produced by the application of a local anesthetic, most commonly to mucous membranes. **plexus a.,** anesthesia produced by the injection of a local anesthetic around a nerve plexus. **pressure a.,** anesthesia produced by a local anesthetic forced into the tissues by pressure. **rectal a.,** anesthesia induced by introduction of the anesthetic agent into the rectum. **refrigeration a.,** local anesthesia produced by chilling the part to near freezing temperature and applying a tourniquet. Called also *crymo-anesthesia.* **regional a.,** the production of insensibility of a part by interrupting the sensory nerve conductivity from that region of the body. It may be produced by (1) *field block*, that is, the creation of walls of anesthesia encircling the operative field by means of injections of a local anesthetic; or (2) *nerve block*, that is, injection of the anesthetic agent close to the nerves whose conductivity is to be cut off. Called also *block a.* and *conduction a.* **sacral a.,** anesthesia produced by injection of a local anesthetic into the extradural space of the sacral canal. **saddle block a.,** the production of anesthesia in a region corresponding roughly with the areas of the buttocks, perineum, and inner aspects of the thighs which impinge on the saddle in riding, by introducing the anesthetic agent low in the dural sac. **segmental a.,** loss of sensation caused by a lesion of a single nerve root, and affecting only a segment of the body. **semi-closed a.,** general inhalation anesthesia in which there is partial rebreathing of the expired gases, with a carbon dioxide absorber in the circuit. **semi-open a.,** general inhalation anesthesia in which there is partial rebreathing of the expired gases, without a carbon dioxide absorber in the circuit. **sexual a.,** anaphrodisia. **spinal a.** 1. Anesthesia produced by injection of a local anesthetic into the subarachnoid space around the spinal cord. 2. Loss of sensation due to a spinal lesion. **splanchnic a.,** anesthesia produced by injection of a local anesthetic around the semilunar ganglia. **subarachnoid a.,** spinal a., def. 1. **surface a.,** permeation a. **surgical a.,** that degree of anesthesia at which surgery may safely be performed; ordinarily used to designate such depth of general anesthesia. **tactile a.,** loss or impairment of the sense of touch. **thalamic hyperesthetic a.** See *thalamic syndrome*, under *syndrome.* **thermal a., thermic a.,** loss of the heat sense. **topical a.,** anesthesia produced by application of a local anesthetic directly to the area involved, as to the oral mucosa or the cornea. **total a.,** loss of all sensibility in the affected part. **transsacral a.,** spinal anesthesia produced by injection of the anesthetic agent into the sacral canal and about the sacral nerves through each of the posterior sacral foramina. **traumatic a.,** loss of sensation caused by injury to a nerve. **twilight a.,** twilight sleep. **unilateral a.,** hemianesthesia. **vein a.,** Bier's local a. **visceral a.,** loss of visceral sensations.

anesthesimeter (an″es-the-sim′e-ter) [*anesthesia* + Gr. *metron* measure]. 1. An instrument to regulate the amount of an anesthetic administered. 2. An instrument for taking the degree of insensitiveness.

anesthesin (ah-nes′the-sin). Trade mark for a preparation of ethyl aminobenzoate.

anesthesiologist (an″es-the″ze-ol′o-jist). A specialist in anesthesiology.

anesthesiology (an″es-the″ze-ol′o-je) [*anesthesia* + *-logy*]. The study of anesthesia and anesthetics.

anesthesiophore (an″es-the′ze-o-fōr″) [*anesthesia* + Gr. *phoros* bearing]. 1. Conveying the anesthetic action. 2. The portion of the molecule of a chemical compound which is responsible for its anesthetic action.

anesthetic (an″es-thet′ik). 1. Pertaining to, characterized by, or producing anesthesia. 2. A drug or agent that is used to abolish the sensation of pain. **general a.,** an agent which produces general anesthesia. **local a.,** an agent whose anesthetic action is limited to an area of the body around the site of its application.

anesthetist (ah-nes′the-tist). A person trained in the administration of anesthetics.

anesthetization (ah-nes″thĕ-tĭ-za′shun). The production of insensibility to pain.

anesthetize (ah-nes′the-tīz). To put under the influence of anesthetics.

anesthetometer (an″es-the-tom′e-ter). An apparatus for measuring and mixing anesthetic vapors and gases.

anesthetospasm (an″es-thet′o-spazm). Spasm with anesthesia.

anesthone (an′es-thōn). Trade mark for a preparation containing epinephrine, ephedrine hydrochloride, and ethyl aminobenzoate: used as a local anesthetic and astringent, analgesic and nasal decongestant.

anestrum (an-es′trum). Anestrus.

anestrus (an-es′trus). A period of sexual inactivity intervening between two estrous cycles.

anethene (an′e-thēn). A hydrocarbon, $C_{10}H_{16}$, from oil of dill.

anethole (an′e-thōl). A colorless, or faintly yellow liquid, $C_{10}H_{12}O$, obtained from anise oil and other sources, or prepared synthetically: used as a flavoring agent for drugs, to expel secretions from the air passages, and to stimulate intestinal peristalsis.

anethopathy (an″e-thop′ah-the) [*an* neg. + Gr. *ēthos* character + *pathos* disease]. A form of psychopathic personality in which the patient apparently knows perfectly well the difference between right and wrong and the consequences of transgression yet persistently gets into trouble.

Anethum (ah-ne′thum) [L.; Gr. *anēthon*]. A genus of plants, including fennel and dill. The fruit of *A.* or *Peucedanum graveolens*, or dill, is carminative and stimulant.

anetic (ah-net′ik). Relaxing or soothing.

anetiological (an-e″te-o-loj′e-kal) [*an* neg. + *etiologic*]. Not conforming to etiological principles.

anetoderma (an″e-to-der′mah) [Gr. *anetos* slack + *derma* skin]. Atrophy and looseness of the skin; primary macular atrophy. There are two forms: that of Schweninger and Buzzi in which the skin becomes loosened, gray, thickened and stiff, and contains multiple new growths; that of Jadassohn in which erythematous lesions develop which become baglike protrusions.

anetus (an′e-tus). An intermittent fever.

aneugamy (an-u′gah-me) [*an-* neg. + Gr. *eu* well + *gamos* marriage]. Union of gametes in one or both of which the chromosomes have not been reduced to the normal haploid number, resulting in an abnormal number of chromosomes in the zygote.

aneuploid (an′u-ploid) [*an-* + *euploid*]. 1. Having more or less than the normal diploid number of chromosomes. 2. An individual or cell having more or less than the normal diploid number of chromosomes.

aneuploidy (an″u-ploi′de). The state of having more or less than the normal diploid number of chromosomes.

aneuria (ah-nu′re-ah) [*an* neg. + Gr. *neuron* nerve + *-ia*]. Failure or lack of nervous energy.

aneuric (ah-nu′rik). Pertaining to or characterized by aneuria.

aneurilemmic (ah-nu″rĭ-lem′ik). Marked by the absence of neurilemma.

aneurin (ah-nu′rin) [*an* neg. + Gr. *neuron* nerve]. Thiamine.

aneurysm (an′u-rizm) [Gr. *aneurysma* a widening]. A sac formed by the dilatation of the walls of an artery or of a vein and filled with blood. The chief symptoms of arterial aneurysm are the formation of a pulsating tumor, a peculiar bruit (*aneurysmal bruit*) heard over the swelling, and pressure symptoms, consisting of pain and paralysis from pressure on nerves and absorption of contiguous parts. **abdominal a.,** an aneurysm of the abdominal aorta. **ampullary a.,** sacculated a. **a. by anastomosis, a. anastomot′ica,** a dilatation of several arteries which forms a pulsating tumor under the skin. **aortic a.,** aneurysm of the aorta. **arteriovenous a.** (William Hunter, 1761), the rupture simultaneously of an artery and a vein in which the blood flows directly into a neighboring vein (*aneurysmal varix*) or else is carried into such a vein by a connecting sac (*varicose aneurysm*). **axial a.,** an aneurysm in which the entire circumference of the vessel is dilated. **axillary a.,** aneurysm of the axillary artery. **bacterial a.,** mycotic a. **Bérard's a.,** an arteriovenous aneurysm in the tissues outside of the injured vein; aneurysm in the tissues around a vein. **berry a.,** a small saccular aneurysm of a cerebral artery, having a narrow opening into the artery. Such aneurysms frequently rupture, causing subarachnoid hemorrhage. **bone a.,** a pulsating vascular tumor of a bone. **branching a.,** a cirsoid aneurysm. **cardiac a.,** thinning and dilatation of a portion of the wall of the heart. It may follow coronary occlusion. **circumscribed a.,** true aneurysm. **cirsoid a.** Same as *racemose a.* **compound a.,** one in which some of the coats are ruptured and others merely dilated. **consecutive a.** Same as *false a.* **Crisp's a.,** aneurysm of the splenic artery. **cylindroid a.,** the uniform dilatation of a considerable part of an artery; called also *tubular a.* **cystogenic a.,** one formed by the rupture of a cyst into an artery. **diffuse a.,** false aneurysm. **dissecting a.,** one in which the blood is forced between the coats of an artery. **ectatic a.,** one formed by distention of a section of an artery without rupture of any of its coats. **embolic a.,** one caused by embolism. **embolomycotic a.,** aneurysm due to embolism from some vegetative condition in the heart. **endogenous a.,** one due to disease of the coats of the vessel. **erosive a.,** an aortic aneurysm resulting from the extension of disease from the heart valves, producing ulcerative endarteritis with destruction of the intima. **exogenous a.,** one that is due to a wound or to violence. **external a.,** one not situated in a body cavity. **false a.,** one in which all the coats are ruptured and the blood is retained by the surrounding tissues. **fusiform a.,** a spindle-shaped arterial dilatation. **hernial a.,** one in which the sac is formed by an inner coat projecting through the outer. **innominate a.,** aneurysm of the brachiocephalic trunk. **internal a.,** one situated in any one of the body cavities. **intracranial a.,** any aneurysm situated within the cranium. **intramural a.,** an aneurysm in which the blood is within the wall of the artery. **lateral a.,** one that projects from one side of an artery. **medical a.,** a deep-seated aneurysm (as in the thorax) not accessible by a surgical operation. **miliary a.,** aneurysm of a minute artery, chiefly intracranial. **mixed a.,** compound a. **mural a.,** aneurysm of the heart wall. **mycotic a.,** aneurysm produced by growth of microorganisms in the vessel wall. **orbital a.,** one situated within the orbit of the eye. **osteoid a.,** bone a. **Park's a.,** an arteriovenous aneurysm in which the arterial dilatation communicates with two veins. **pelvic a.,** one situated within the pelvis. **phantom a.,** a condition in which the aorta is palpable and the patient complains of throbbing in the region of the aorta; called also *students' a.* and *aortismus abdominalis.* **Pott's a.,** an aneurysmal varix. **racemose a.,** a condition in which the blood vessels become dilated, lengthened, and tortuous. **Rasmussen's a.,** a dilatation of a terminal artery in a tuberculous cavity. Its rupture produces hemorrhage in the third stage of pulmonary tuberculosis. **renal a.,** renal epistaxis. **Richet's a.,** fusiform a. **Rodrigues's a.,** a varicose aneurysm with the sac lying contiguous to the artery. **sacculated a.,** a saclike arterial dilatation which opens into the artery by an opening that is small compared with the size of the sac. **secondary a.,** one that recurs after having apparently been cured. **serpentine a.,** an elongated and varicose senile condition of certain arteries, such as the splenic, iliac, and temporal. **Shekelton's a.,** dissecting a. **silent a.,** an aneurysm that produces no signs or symptoms. **spongy a.,** an angioma. **spontaneous a.,** an endogenous aneurysm. **spurious a.,** false a. **students' a.,** phantom a. **surgical a.,** one that may be treated by a surgical procedure. **thoracic a.,** one situated within the thorax. **traction a.,** aneurysm produced by traction on the aorta by an incompletely atrophied ductus arteriosus. **traumatic a.,** an aneurysm due to injury. **true a.,** an aneurysm in which the sac is formed by the arterial walls one of which, at least, is unbroken. **tubular a.,** cylindroid a. **valvular a.,** an aneurysm between the layers of a valve of the heart. **varicose a.,** an aneurysm in which the artery communicates with a contiguous vein by means of an intervening sac. **venous a.,** aneurysm of a vein. **ventricular a.,** aneurysmal dilatation of a ventricle of the heart. **verminous a.,** one that contains hematozoa. **worm a.,** aneurysm in horses caused by the larvae of Strongylus.

Cirsoid or racemose aneurysm (Homans).

aneurysmal (an″u-riz′mal). Pertaining to or resembling an aneurysm.

aneurysmatic (an″u-riz-mat′ik). Aneurysmal.

aneurysmectomy (an″u-riz-mek′to-me) [*aneurysm* + Gr. *ektomē* excision]. Extirpation of an aneurysm by removal of the sac.

aneurysmogram (an″u-riz′mo-gram). A roentgenogram of an aneurysm.

aneurysmoplasty (an″u-riz′mo-plas″te) [*aneurysm* + Gr. *plassein* to form]. Plastic restoration of the artery in the treatment of aneurysm.

aneurysmorrhaphy (an″u-riz-mor′ah-fe) [*aneurysm* + Gr. *rhaphē* suture]. The operation of suturing an aneurysm.

aneurysmotomy (an″u-riz-mot′o-me) [*aneurysm* + Gr. *tomē* cut]. The operation of incising the sac of an aneurysm and allowing it to heal by granulation.

an. ex. Abbreviation for *anode excitation.*

anfractuosity (an-frak″tu-os′ĭ-te) [L. *anfractus* a bending]. A cerebral sulcus.

anfractuous (an-frak′tu-us). Convoluted or sinuous.

angei-. For words beginning thus, see those beginning *angi-*.

Angelica (an-jel′e-kah) [L., from Gr. *angelikos* angelic]. A genus of umbelliferous plants.

angeline (an′jĕ-lin). Surinamine.

Angelucci's syndrome (an″jĕ-loo′chēz) [Arnaldo *Angelucci*, Naples ophthalmologist, 1854–1934]. See under *syndrome.*

Anghelescu's sign (ahn-jĕ-les′ko͞oz) [Constantin *Anghelescu*, Roumanian surgeon, 1869–1948]. See under *sign.*

angi-. See *angio-*.

angialgia (an″je-al′je-ah) [*angi-* + Gr. *algos* pain + *-ia*]. Pain in a blood vessel.

angiasthenia (an″je-as-the′ne-ah) [*angi-* + *a* neg. + Gr. *sthenos* strength + *-ia*]. Loss of tone in the vascular system; vascular instability.

angiectasis (an″je-ek′tah-sis) [*angi-* + Gr. *ektasis* dilatation]. The dilatation of a blood vessel, whether from aneurysm, varix, or angioparalysis.

angiectatic (an″je-ek-tat′ik). Pertaining to or characterized by angiectasis.

angiectid (an″je-ek′tid). An intradermal, elevated, circumscribed conglomerant mass of dark bluish venules that is frequently warm, tender, and tense.

angiectomy (an″je-ek′to-me) [*angi-* + Gr. *ektomē* excision]. The excision or resection of a vessel.

angiectopia (an″je-ek-to′pe-ah) [*angi-* + Gr. *ek* out + Gr. *topos* place + *-ia*]. Abnormal position or course of a vessel.

angiemphraxis (an″je-em-frak′sis) [*angi-* + Gr. *emphraxis* stoppage]. The stopping up of a vessel.

angiitis (an″je-i′tis) [*angi-* + *-itis*]. Inflammation of a vessel, chiefly of a blood or a lymph vessel. **consecutive a.,** inflammation of a vessel caused by extension of the inflammation from the neighboring tissues. **visceral a.,** a term proposed for a group of disorders marked by peculiar lesions of the small arteries, such as periarteritis nodosa, lupus erythematosus disseminatus, and Libman-Sacks disease.

angileucitis (an″je-lu-si′tis). Angioleucitis.

angina (an′jĭ-nah, an-ji′nah) [L.]. Spasmodic, choking or suffocative pain: often used for the disease or condition producing such pain. **abdominal a., a. abdomina′lis, a. abdom′inis,** intestinal a. **a. acu′ta,** simple sore throat. **agranulocytic a., a. agranulocytot′ica,** agranulocytosis. **a. arthrit′ica,** pharyngitis of a gouty nature. **benign croupous a.,** pharyngitis herpetica. **a. cap′itis,** headache due to refractive errors. **a. catarrha′lis,** catarrhal pharyngitis. **a. cor′dis,** a. pectoris. **a. croupo′sa,** pseudomembranous or croupous sore throat. **a. cru′ris,** intermittent claudication. **a. decu′bitus,** cardiac pain occurring in a recumbent position. **a. diphtherit′ica,** diphtheritic pharyngitis or laryngitis. **a. dyspep′tica,** a condition resembling angina pectoris, due to distention of the stomach with gas. **a. epiglottide′a,** inflammation of the epiglottis. **a. erysipela-to′sa,** pharyngitis due to erysipelas. **exudative a.,** croup. **false a.,** a. pectoris vasomotoria. **a. follicula′ris,** follicular tonsillitis. **fusospirochetal a.,** Vincent's a. **a. gangreno′sa,** gangrenous inflammation of the fauces. **hippocratic a.,** retropharyngeal abscess. **hypercyanotic a.,** angina pectoris accompanied by cyanosis. **hypoleukocytic a.,** a severe leukopenia clinically resembling agranulocytic angina and marked by great decrease in total leukocytes with a high percentage of nonsegmented neutrophils. **hysteric a.,** a. pectoris vasomotoria. **a. in′nocens,** a. pectoris vasomotoria. **intestinal a.,** generalized cramping abdominal pain that may extend to the back, occurring shortly after a meal and persisting for one to three hours, caused by ischemia of the smooth muscle of the bowel. **lacunar a.,** tonsillitis. **a. laryn′gea,** laryngitis. **a. ludovi′ci, a. ludwig′ii, Ludwig's a.,** purulent inflammation seated around the submaxillary gland, beneath the jaw and about the floor of the mouth, usually due to streptococcus infection. **a. lymphomato′sa,** agranulocytosis. **malignant a.,** a. gangrenosa. **a. membrana′cea,** croup. **a. mi′nor,** a mild form of angina pectoris. **mock a.,** a. pectoris vasomotoria. **monocytic a.,** infectious mononucleosis. **nerve a.,** neuralgia due to spasm of the sclerotic arteries of the nerves. **a. nervo′sa,** anginal attacks in nervous persons. **neutropenic a.,** agranulocytosis. **a. nosoco′mii,** pharyngitis ulcerosa. **a. no′tha,** a. pectoris vasomotoria. **a. parotid′ea,** epidemic parotitis. **a. pec′toris,** a paroxysmal thoracic pain, with a feeling of suffocation and impending death, due, most often, to anoxia of the myocardium and precipitated by effort or excitement (Heberden, 1768). **a. pec′toris vasomoto′ria,** a condition marked by precordial pain due to vasomotor disturbance and showing no organic disease of the heart. **a. phlegmono′sa,** quinsy. **Plaut's a.,** ulceromembranous stomatitis. **pseudomembranous a.,** ulceromembranous stomatitis. **a. rheumat′ica,** a pharyngitis associated with the rheumatic diathesis. **a. scarlatino′sa,** pharyngitis due to scarlatina. **Schultz's a.,** agranulocytosis. **a. sim′plex,** simple sore throat. **a. sine dolo′re,** a slight anginal attack in which no pain is experienced. **a. spu′ria, spurious a.,** a. pectoris vasomotoria. **streptococcus a.,** angina due to a streptococcus. **a. tonsilla′ris,** quinsy. **a. trachea′lis,** croup. **ulceromembranous a.,** Vincent's infection. **a. ulcero′sa,** pharyngitis ulcerosa. **a. urat′ica,** gouty pharyngitis. **vasomotor a.,** a. pectoris vasomotoria. **Vincent's a.,** Vincent's infection.

anginal (an′jĭ-nal). Pertaining to, or characteristic of, angina.

anginiform (an-jin′ĭ-form). Resembling angina.

anginoid (an′jĭ-noid). Resembling angina.

anginophobia (an″jin-o-fo′be-ah) [*angina* + *phobia*]. Morbid dread of angina pectoris.

anginose (an′jĭ-nōs) [L. *anginosus*]. Pertaining to or affected with angina, especially angina pectoris.

anginosis (an″jĭ-no′sis). A general term for anginal conditions; angina.

anginous (an′jĭ-nus). Anginose.

angio-, angi- (an′je-o, an′je) [Gr. *angeion* vessel]. Combining form denoting relationship to a vessel, usually a blood vessel.

angio-asthenia (an″je-o-as-the′ne-ah). Angiasthenia.

angio-ataxia (an″je-o-ah-tak′se-ah) [*angio-* + *ataxia*]. Irregular tension of the blood vessels.

angioblast (an′je-o-blast) [*angio-* + Gr. *blastos* germ]. 1. The formative mesenchymal tissue from which the blood cells and blood vessels differentiate. 2. An individual vessel-forming cell.

angioblastic (an″je-o-blas′tik). Pertaining to angioblast.

angioblastoma (an″je-o-blas-to′mah). Angioblastic meningioma; a blood-vessel tumor arising from the meninges of the brain and spinal cord.

angiocardiography (an″je-o-kar″de-og′rah-fe) [*angio-* + Gr. *kardia* heart + *graphein* to write]. Roentgenography of the heart and great vessels after intravenous injection of opaque fluid.

angiocardiokinetic (an″je-o-kar″de-o-ki-net′ik) [*angio-* + Gr. *kardia* heart + *kinēsis* motion]. 1. Affecting the motions or movements of the heart and blood vessels. 2. Any agent that affects the movements of the heart and vessels.

angiocardiopathy (an″je-o-kar″de-op′ah-the). Any disease of the heart and blood vessels.

angiocarditis (an″je-o-kar-di′tis) [*angio-* + Gr. *kardia* heart + *-itis*]. Inflammation of the heart and great blood vessels.

angiocavernous (an″je-o-kav′er-nus). Of the nature of angioma and cavernoma.

angioceratoma (an″je-o-ser″ah-to′mah). Angiokeratoma.

angiocheiloscope (an″je-o-ki′lo-skōp″) [*angio-* + Gr. *cheilos* lip + *skopein* to view]. An instrument for observing blood circulation of the lips under magnification.

angiocholecystitis (an″je-o-ko″le-sis-ti′tis) [*angio-* + Gr. *cholē* bile + *kystis* bladder + *-itis*]. Inflammation of the gallbladder and bile ducts.

angiocholitis (an″je-o-ko-li′tis) [*angio-* + Gr. *cholē* bile + *-itis*]. Inflammation of the bile ducts; cholangitis. **a. prolif′erans,** proliferating inflammation of the bile ducts leading frequently to carcinoma.

angiochondroma (an″je-o-kon-dro′mah). A chondroma about which there is an excessive development of blood vessels.

angioclast (an′je-o-klast) [*angio-* + Gr. *klastos* broken]. A forceps-like instrument for compressing a bleeding artery.

Angiococcus (an″je-o-kok′us) [Gr. *angeion* vessel + *kokkos* berry]. A genus of microorganisms of the family Myxococcaceae, with two species, *A. cellulosum* and *A. discoformis.*

angiocrine (an′je-o-krīn) [*angio-* + *endocrine*]. Noting vasomotor disorders of endocrine origin.

angiocrinosis (an″je-o-kri-no′sis). A vasomotor disorder of endocrine origin.

angiocyst (an′je-o-sist″) [*angio-* + *cyst*]. An ingrowth of mesothelial tissue in the embryo having blood-forming power.

angioderm (an′je-o-derm). Angioblast, def. 1.

angiodermatitis (an″je-o-der-mah-ti′tis). Inflammation of the vessels of the skin.

angiodiascopy (an″je-o-di-as′ko-pe) [*angio-* + Gr. *dia* through + *skopein* to view]. Direct visual inspection of blood vessels of the extremities, a light being held behind the part.

angiodiathermy (an″je-o-di′ah-ther″me) [*angio-* + *diathermy*]. Coagulation by diathermy of the long posterior ciliary arteries: performed in treatment of glaucoma.

angiodynia (an″je-o-din′e-ah) [*angio-* + Gr. *odynē* pain + *-ia*]. Angialgia.

angiodystrophia (an″je-o-dis-tro′fe-ah) [*angio-* + *dystrophy*]. Defective nutrition of blood vessels. **a. ova′rii,** disease and increase in the number of blood vessels of the ovary.

angiodystrophy (an″je-o-dis′tro-fe). Angiodystrophia.

angio-ectatic (an″je-o-ek-tat′ik). Angiectatic.

angio-edema (an″je-o-e-de′mah). Angioneurotic edema.

angio-elephantiasis (an″je-o-el″e-fan-ti′ah-sis). Extensive angiomatous condition of the subcutaneous tissues.

angio-endothelioma (an″je-o-en″do-the″le-o′-mah). An endothelioma rich in blood vessels.

angiofibroma (an″je-o-fi-bro′mah). An angioma containing fibrous tissue. **a. contagio′sum trop′icum,** a skin disease of Brazil characterized by an eruption of red papules which develop into bluish nodules.

angiogenesis (an″je-o-jen′e-sis) [*angio-* + *genesis*]. The development of the vessels.

angiogenic (an″je-o-jen′ik). 1. Arising in the vascular system. 2. Developing into blood vessels.

angioglioma (an″je-o-gli-o′mah). A very vascular form of glioma.

angiogliomatosis (an″je-o-gli″o-mah-to′sis). A condition marked by the formation of multiple vascular gliomas.

angiogliosis (an″je-o-gli-o′sis). A condition marked by the development of angiogliomas.

angiogram (an′ji-o-gram). A roentgenogram of a blood vessel.

angiograph (an′je-o-graf″) [*angio-* + Gr. *graphein* to record]. A form of sphygmograph.

angiography (an″je-og′rah-fe) [*angio-* + Gr. *graphein* to record]. 1. A treatise upon the vessels; the study of the vessels. 2. The roentgenological visualization of blood vessels. **cerebral a.,** roentgenography of the vascular system of the brain after injection of radiopaque material into the arterial blood stream. **coronary a.,** roentgenographic visualization of the coronary arteries.

angiohemophilia (an″je-o-he″mo-fil′e-ah). A congenital hemorrhagic diathesis, inherited as an autosomal dominant and characterized by integumentary and mucosal surface bleeding, in which the faulty hemostasis is due to abnormal blood vessels with or without associated platelet defects or deficiencies of blood coagulation factor VIII or IX. Called also *vascular hemophilia, pseudohemophilia,* and *von Willebrand's disease.*

angiohyalinosis (an″je-o-hi″ah-lĭ-no′sis) [*angio-* + *hyalinosis*]. Hyaline degeneration of the muscularis of blood vessels. **a. haemorrhag′ica,** a variety characterized by congenital hemorrhage.

angiohypertonia (an″je-o-hi″per-to′ne-ah) [*angio-* + Gr. *hyper* over + *tonos* tension]. Angiospasm; vasoconstriction.

angiohypotonia (an″je-o-hi″po-to′ne-ah) [*angio-* + Gr. *hypo* under + *tonos* tension]. Lack of tone in the walls of the blood vessels, without any corresponding lack in the heart; vasodilatation.

angioid (an′je-oid) [*angio-* + Gr. *eidos* form]. Resembling a blood vessel.

angioinvasive (an″je-o-in-va′siv). Tending to invade the walls of blood vessels.

angiokeratoma (an″je-o-ker″ah-to′mah) [*angio-* + Gr. *keras* horn + *-oma*]. A disease of the skin characterized by telangiectases or warty growths, in groups, together with thickening of the epidermis (Mibelli). The dorsal aspect of the fingers and toes, and the scrotum are sites of predilection. Called also *telangiectatic warts.* **a. cor′poris diffu′sum,** a condition affecting many systems of the body, with vasomotor disturbances, edema, enlargement of the heart, especially of the left ventricle, and moderately increased blood pressure; urinary abnormalities (albuminuria, and some erythrocytes, leukocytes, and casts), and cutaneous lesions (diffuse, purpuric and nodular, or generalized angiomatous); muscles also may be affected, with vacuolated muscle bundles.

angiokeratosis (an″je-o-ker″ah-to′sis). Angiokeratoma.

angiokinesis (an″je-o-kĭ-ne′sis) [*angio-* + Gr. *kinēsis* movement]. Vascular activity.

angiokinetic (an″je-o-kĭ-net′ik). Pertaining to vascular activity; vasomotor.

angioleucitis (an″je-o-lu-si′tis) [*angio-* + Gr. *leukos* white + *-itis*]. Inflammation of a lymph vessel.

angioleukitis (an″je-o-lu-ki′tis). Angioleucitis.

angiolipoma (an″je-o-lip-o′mah). An angioma containing fatty tissue, often seen in the subcutaneous tissue.

angiolith (an′je-o-lith″) [*angio-* + Gr. *lithos* stone].

A calculus or concretion in the wall of a blood vessel.

angiolithic (an″je-o-lith′ik) [*angio-* + Gr. *lithos* stone]. Pertaining to or characterized by angioliths.

angiologia (an″je-o-lo′je-ah). Angiology; in N A terminology *angiologia* encompasses the nomenclature relating to the heart arteries, veins, lymphatic system, and spleen.

angiology (an″je-ol′o-je) [*angio-* + Gr. *logos* treatise]. The scientific study of the vessels of the body; applied also to the sum of knowledge relating to the blood vessels and lymph vessels.

angiolupoid (an″je-o-lu′poid). A tuberculous skin lesion consisting of small red oval infiltrated plaques with telangiectases over the surface and occurring chiefly on the sides of the nose.

angiolymphangioma (an″je-o-lim-fan″je-o′-mah). A mixed angioma in which lymph vessels and blood vessels are involved.

angiolymphitis (an″je-o-lim-fi′tis). Lymphangitis.

angiolymphoma (an″je-o-lim-fo′mah). A tumor made up of lymph vessels.

angiolysis (an″je-ol′ĭ-sis) [*angio-* + Gr. *lysis* dissolution]. Retrogression or obliteration of blood vessels, such as occurs during embryonic development.

angioma (an″je-o′mah) [*angio-* + *-oma*]. A tumor whose cells tend to form blood vessels (*hemangioma*) or lymph vessels (*lymphangioma*); a tumor made up of blood vessels or lymph vessels. **a. arteria′le racemo′sum,** a dilatation and complex intertwining of many new-formed and altered vessels of small caliber with subsequent involvement of normal vessels. **a. caverno′sum, cavernous a.,** an erectile tumor; a tumor made up of a connective-tissue framework inclosing large spaces filled with blood. Called also *cavernous hemangioma* and *erectile tumor.* **a. cu′tis,** a kind of nevus made up of a network of dilated blood vessels. **encephalic a.,** a mass of dilated arteries in the brain. **fissural a.,** angioma occurring in embryonal fissures of the face, neck, or lips. **hereditary hemorrhagic a.,** hereditary hemorrhagic telangiectasia. **hypertrophic a.,** an angioma containing solid matter formed by hyperplasia of the endothelium. **infective a.,** a. serpiginosum. **a. lymphat′icum,** lymphangioma. **a. pigmento′sum atroph′icum,** xeroderma pigmentosum. **plexiform a.,** ordinary angioma made up of dilated and tortuous capillaries usually located in the skin. **a. serpigino′sum,** a skin disease characterized by minute vascular points, looking like grains of cayenne pepper, arranged in rings on the skin. **simple a.,** a nevus or telangiectasis: a tumor composed of a network of small vessels or of distended capillaries bound together by connective tissue. **spider a.,** nevus araneus. **telangiectatic a.,** an angioma made up of dilated blood vessels. **a. veno′sum racemo′sum,** the swellings caused by severe varicosity of superficial veins.

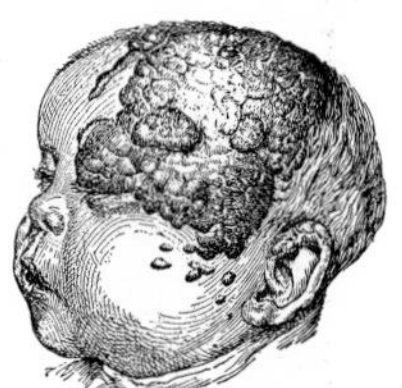

Cavernous angioma (Homans).

angiomalacia (an″je-o-mah-la′she-ah) [*angio-* + Gr. *malakia* softness]. Morbid softening of the walls of the vessels.

angiomatosis (an″je-o-mah-to′sis). A diseased state of the vessels with the formation of multiple angiomas. **hemorrhagic familial a.,** hereditary hemorrhagic angioma. **a. of retina,** Lindau-von Hippel disease.

angiomatous (an″je-om′ah-tus). Of the nature of angioma.

angiomegaly (an″je-o-meg′ah-le) [*angio-* + Gr. *megas* large]. Enlargement of blood vessels; especially a condition of the eyelid marked by great increase in its volume.

angiometer (an″je-om′e-ter) [*angio-* + Gr. *metron* measure]. An instrument for measuring the diameter of caliber and tension of the blood vessels.

angiomyocardiac (an″je-o-mi″o-kar′de-ak). Affecting the vessels and the heart muscle.

angiomyoma (an″je-o-mi-o′mah). A myoma containing many vessels.

angiomyoneuroma (an″je-o-mi″o-nu-ro′mah). Glomangioma.

angiomyopathy (an″je-o-mi-op′ah-the). Disturbances of blood vessels involving the muscle layer.

angiomyosarcoma (an″je-o-mi″o-sar-ko′mah). A tumor made up of elements of angioma, myoma, and sarcoma.

angiomyxoma (an″je-o-mik-so′mah). A tumor of the placenta composed of numerous capillary-like blood vessels often extending into the cord and containing myxomatous tissue resembling that in the normal cord.

angionecrosis (an″je-o-nĕ-kro′sis) [*angio-* + Gr. *nekros* dead + *-osis*]. Necrosis of the walls of blood vessels.

angioneoplasm (an″je-o-ne′o-plazm) [*angio-* + *neoplasm*]. A tumor or neoplasm of blood vessels.

angioneuralgia (an″je-o-nu-ral′je-ah) [*angio-* + *neuralgia*]. A condition marked by pain in an extremity attended by edema and redness of the part.

angioneurectomy (an″je-o-nu-rek′to-me) [*angio-* + Gr. *neuron* nerve + *ektomē* excision]. Excision of vessels and nerves.

angioneuro-edema (an″je-o-nu″ro-e-de′mah) [*angio-* + Gr. *neuron* nerve + *oidēma* swelling]. Angioneurotic edema.

angioneuroma (an″je-o-nu-ro′mah). Glomangioma.

angioneuromyoma (an″je-o-nu″ro-mi-o′mah). Glomangioma.

angioneuro-oedema (an″je-o-nu″ro-e-de′mah). Angioneurotic edema.

angioneurosis (an″je-o-nu-ro′sis) [*angio-* + *neurosis*]. Any neurosis affecting primarily the blood vessels; a disorder of the vasomotor system, as angiospasm, angioparesis, or angioparalysis.

angioneurotic (an″je-o-nu-rot′ik). Caused by or of the nature of an angioneurosis.

angioneurotomy (an″je-o-nu-rot′o-me) [*angio-* + Gr. *neuron* nerve + *tomē* cutting]. The operation of cutting vessels and nerves.

angionoma (an″je-o-no′mah) [*angio-* + Gr. *nomē* ulcer]. Ulceration of a blood vessel.

angiopancreatitis (an″je-o-pan″kre-ah-ti′tis). Inflammation of the pancreatic vessels or of the vascular tissue of the pancreas.

angioparalysis (an″je-o-pah-ral′ĭ-sis) [*angio-* + *paralysis*]. Paralysis of blood vessels from vasomotor defect.

angioparesis (an″je-o-par′e-sis) [*angio-* + *paresis*]. Vasomotor paralysis.

angiopathology (an″je-o-pah-thol′o-je). The pathology of, or the morbid changes seen in, diseases of the blood vessels.

angiopathy (an-je-op′ah-the) [*angio-* + Gr. *pathos* disease]. Any disease of the vessels.

angiophakomatosis (an″je-o-fak″o-mah-to′sis) [*angio-* + Gr. *phakos* lens + *-oma*]. A general development of angiomatous cysts of the cerebellum and of the retina; Lindau's disease.

angioplany (an′je-o-plan″e) [*angio-* + Gr. *planē* wandering]. Abnormality in position, course, or structure of a vessel.

angioplasty (an′je-o-plas″te) [*angio-* + Gr. *plassein* to form]. Plastic surgery of blood vessels.

angiopneumography (an″je-o-nu-mog′rah-fe) [*angio-* + Gr. *pneumōn* lung + *graphein* to record].

Roentgenographic photography of the pulmonary vessels.

angiopoiesis (an″je-o-poi-e′sis) [*angio-* + Gr. *poiein* to make]. The process of vessel formation.

angiopoietic (an″je-o-poi-et′ik). Pertaining to or causing angiopoiesis.

angiopressure (an′je-o-presh″ur). Control of hemorrhage from a vessel by the application of hemostatic forceps with pressure.

angiopsathyrosis (an″je-o-sath″ĭ-ro′sis). Fragility of the blood vessels as in some forms of purpura.

angioreticuloma (an″je-o-re-tik″u-lo′mah). A hemangioma, especially one of the brain.

angiorhigosis (an″je-o-rĭ-go′sis) [*angio-* + Gr. *rhigos* frost]. Rigidity of the wall of a blood vessel.

angiorrhaphy (an″je-or′ah-fe) [*angio-* + Gr. *rhaphē* suture]. Suture of a vessel or vessels. **arteriovenous a.,** the suturing of an artery to a vein, so as to divert the arterial current into the vein.

angiorrhea (an″je-o-re′ah) [*angio-* + Gr. *rhoia* flow]. Oozing of blood from the vessels.

angiorrhexis (an″je-o-rek′sis) [*angio-* + Gr. *rhēxis* rupture]. Rupture of a vessel.

angiosarcoma (an″je-o-sar-ko′mah) [*angio-* + *sarcoma*]. A sarcoma containing very many fine blood vessels. **a. myxomato′des,** an angiosarcoma in which the walls of the vessels are affected with mucous degeneration.

angiosclerosis (an″je-o-skle-ro′sis) [*angio-* + *sclerosis*]. Hardening of the walls of the blood vessels; a combined sclerosis of arteries, veins, and capillaries.

angiosclerotic (an″je-o-skle-rot′ik). Pertaining to or marked by angiosclerosis.

angioscope (an′je-o-skōp) [*angio-* + Gr. *skopein* to view]. A microscope for observing capillary blood vessels.

angioscotoma (an″je-o-sko-to′mah). A scotoma, or defect in the visual field, caused by shadows of the retinal blood vessels.

angioscotometry (an″je-o-sko-tom′e-tre) [*angio-* + *scotoma* + Gr. *metron* measure]. The plotting or mapping of the scotoma caused by the shadow of retinal blood vessels.

angiosialitis (an″je-o-si″ah-li′tis) [*angio-* + Gr. *sialon* saliva + *-itis*]. Inflammation of a salivary duct.

angiosis (an″je-o′sis). Angiopathy.

angiospasm (an′je-o-spazm) [*angio-* + Gr. *spasmos* spasm]. Spasmodic contraction of the blood vessels.

angiospastic (an″je-o-spas′tik). Of the nature of angiospasm; causing contraction of the blood vessels.

angiosperm (an′je-o-sperm″) [*angio-* + Gr. *sperma* seed]. A true flowering plant; a plant having its seeds in an inclosed ovary.

angiospermin (an″je-o-sper′min). A substance derived from flowering plants: claimed to have hormone-like properties.

angiostaxis (an″je-o-stak′sis) [*angio-* + Gr. *staxis* hemorrhage]. Hemorrhagic diathesis.

angiostegnosis (an″je-o-steg-no′sis). Angiostenosis.

angiostenosis (an″je-o-ste-no′sis) [*angio-* + *stenosis*]. Narrowing of the caliber of a vessel.

angiosteosis (an″je-os″te-o′sis) [*angio-* + Gr. *osteon* bone]. Ossification or calcification of a vessel.

angiosthenia (an″je-os-the′ne-ah) [*angio-* + Gr. *sthenos* strength + *-ia*]. Arterial tension.

Angiostomidae (an″je-o-sto′mĭ-de). A family of the Nematoda characterized by heterogony. There is only one important genus, *Strongyloides.*

angiostomy (an″je-os′to-me) [*angio-* + Gr. *stoma* mouth]. The operation of making an opening into a blood vessel and inserting a cannula therein.

angiostrophe (an″je-os′tro-fe) [*angio-* + Gr. *strophē* a twist]. The twisting of a vessel for the arrest of hemorrhage.

angiostrophy (an″je-os′tro-fe). Angiostrophe.

angiosynizesis (an″je-o-sin″ĭ-ze′sis). Collapse of blood vessel walls with subsequent adhesions.

angiotelectasis (an″je-o-tĕ-lek′tah-sis) [*angio-* + Gr. *telos* end + *ektasis* dilatation]. Dilatation of the capillary vessels and the minute arteries and veins.

angiotenic (an″je-o-ten′ik) [*angio-* + Gr. *teinein* to stretch]. Marked by or caused by distention of blood vessels.

angiotensin (an″je-o-ten′sin). A vasoconstrictor substance present in the blood, and formed by the action of renin on a globulin of the blood plasma. Formerly called *angiotonin* or *hypertensin.*

angiotitis (an″je-o-ti′tis) [*angio-* + *otitis*]. Inflammation of the vessels of the ear.

angiotome (an′je-o-tōm″) [*angio-* + Gr. *tomē* a cutting]. Any one of the segments of the vascular system of the embryo: called also *vascular segment.*

angiotomy (an″je-ot′o-me) [*angio-* + Gr. *tomē* a cutting]. 1. The cutting or severing of a blood or lymph vessel. 2. Anatomy of vessels.

angiotonase (an″je-o-to′nās). An enzyme formed by the kidneys which inactivates angiotonin.

angiotonia (an″je-o-to′ne-ah). Vasotonia.

angiotonic (an″je-o-ton′ik) [*angio-* + Gr. *tonos* tension]. Increasing the vascular tension.

angiotonin (an″je-o-to′nin). Angiotensin.

angiotribe (an′je-o-trīb″) [*angio-* + Gr. *tribein* to crush]. An exceedingly strong pair of forceps in which pressure is exercised by means of a screw. It is used for crushing tissue containing an artery for the purpose of closing the artery and checking hemorrhage. Called also *vasotribe.*

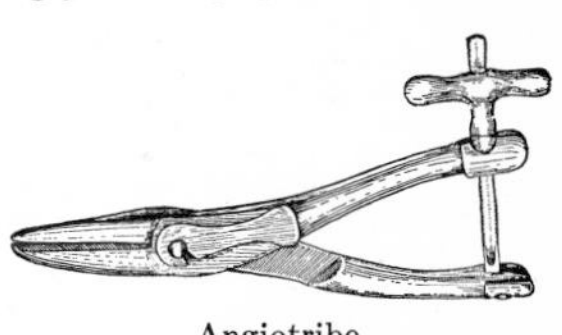

Angiotribe.

angiotripsy (an′je-o-trip″se). Production of hemostasis by means of the angiotribe. Called also *vasotripsy.*

angiotrophic (an″je-o-trof′ik) [*angio-* + Gr. *trophē* nutrition]. Pertaining to vascular nutrition.

angiotrophoneurosis (an″je-o-trof″o-nu-ro′sis). A neurosis of the vessels with trophic disturbances.

angitis (an-ji′tis). Angiitis.

angle (ang′g'l) [L. *angulus*]. 1. The area or point of junction of two intersecting borders or surfaces. See *angulus.* 2. The degree of divergence of two intersecting lines or planes. **a. of aberration,** a. of deviation. **Ackermann's a's,** certain angles of the base of the skull, characteristic of kyphosis, encephalocele, and hydrocephalus. **acromial a.,** angulus acromialis. **acromial a. of scapula,** angulus lateralis scapulae. **alpha a.,** that formed by the intersection of the visual line with the optic axis at the nodal point. **Alsberg's a.** See *Alsberg's triangle,* under *triangle.* **alveolar a.,** the angle between a line running through a point beneath the nasal spine and the most prominent point of the lower border of the alveolar process of the superior maxilla and the cephalic horizontal. **anterior a. of petrous portion of temporal bone,** angulus anterior pyramidis ossis temporalis. **a. of aperture,** the angle between two lines from the focus of a lens to the ends of its diameter. **auriculo-occipital a.,** the angle between lines from the auricular point to the lambda and opisthion. **axial a.,** any angle the formation of which is partially dependent on the axial wall of a tooth cavity. **axial line a.,** any line angle which is parallel with the long axis of a tooth. For names of various angles see the tables of

Cavity Angles and *Tooth Angles*. **Bennett a.,** the angle formed by the sagittal plane and the path of the advancing condyle during lateral movement of the mandible, as viewed in the horizontal plane. **beta a.,** that between the radius fixus and a line joining the bregma and hormion. **biorbital a.,** the angle formed by intersection of the axes of the two orbits. **buccal a's,** the angles formed between the buccal surface and the other surfaces of a posterior tooth, or between the buccal wall of a tooth cavity and other walls, named according to the surfaces which participate in their formation. See the tables of *Cavity Angles* and *Tooth Angles*. **Camper's a.** 1. Facial angle. 2. Maxillary angle. **cardiodiaphragmatic a.,** the angle formed by the junction of the shadows of the heart and diaphragm in posteroanterior roentgenograms of the chest. **cardiohepatic a.,** the angle formed by the horizontal limit of hepatic dulness with the upright line of cardiac dulness in the fifth right intercostal space, close to the sternal border. **carrying a.,** the angle formed by the axes of the arm and forearm when the forearm is extended. **cavity a's,** the angles formed by the junction of two or more walls of a tooth cavity, named according to the walls participating in their formation. See table of *Cavity*

CAVITY ANGLES

Line Angles

(Formed by the junction of two walls)

axiodistal	gingivoaxial
axiogingival	labiogingival
axioincisal	linguoaxial
axiolabial	linguodistal
axiolingual	linguogingival
axiomesial	linguomesial
axio-occlusal	linguopulpal
axiopulpal	mesiobuccal
buccoaxial	mesiogingival
buccodistal	mesiolabial
buccogingival	mesiolingual
buccomesial	mesio-occlusal
buccopulpal	mesiopulpal
distobuccal	pulpoaxial
distogingival	pulpodistal
distolabial	pulpolabial
distolingual	pulpolingual
disto-occlusal	pulpomesial
distopulpal	

Point Angles

(Formed by the junction of three walls)

axiodistogingival	distopulpolingual
axiodisto-occlusal	gingivobuccoaxial
axiolabiogingival	gingivolinguoaxial
axiolinguogingival	mesiobuccopulpal
axiomesiogingival	mesiolinguopulpal
axiomesio-occlusal	mesiopulpolabial
distobuccopulpal	mesiopulpolingual
distolinguopulpal	pulpobuccoaxial
distopulpolabial	pulpolinguoaxial

Angles. **cavosurface a.,** the angle formed by junction of a wall of a cavity and a surface of the crown of the tooth. **cephalic a.,** any angle of the skull or face. **cephalic-medullar a.,** the angle at which the brain is attached to its stalk. **cerebellopontile a.,** that between the cerebellum and the pons. **chi a.,** that between two lines from the hormion to the staphylion and to the basion, respectively. **collodiaphysial a.,** the angle formed by the intersection of the long axes of the neck and shaft of the femur. **condylar a.,** that between the planes of the basilar clivus and the foramen magnum. **a. of convergence,** that between the visual axis and the median line when an object is looked at. **coronary a.,** that between the sagittal and the coronary suture. **costal a.,** angulus costae. **costophrenic a.,** the angle formed at the junction of the costal and diaphragmatic pleurae. **costovertebral a.,** the angle formed on either side of the vertebral column, between the last rib and the lumbar vertebrae. **craniofacial a.,** that between the basifacial and basicranial axes at the middle of the ethmoidosphenoid suture. **critical a.,** the angle of incidence at which a ray of light passing from one medium to another of different density changes from refraction to total reflection. **cusp a.,** an angle made by the slope of the cusp of a tooth. **Daubenton's a.,** an angle formed by junction of the opisthiobasal and opisthionasial lines. **a. of declination,** Mikulicz's a. **a. of deviation,** the angle between a refracted ray and the incident ray prolonged. **a. of direction,** the angle through which the eye must move to bring the image onto the fovea. **distal a's,** the angles formed between the distal surface and other surfaces of a tooth, or between the distal wall of a tooth cavity and other walls; named according to the surfaces which participate in their formation. See the tables of *Cavity Angles* and *Tooth Angles*. **Ebstein's a.,** cardiohepatic a. **elevation a.** 1. The angle made by the visual plane when moved upward or downward with its normal position. 2. See *Alsberg's triangle*, under *triangle*. **epigastric a.,** the angle made by the xiphoid process with the body of the sternum. **ethmocranial a.,** the angle included between the plane of the cribriform plate of the ethmoid bone prolonged and the basicranial axis. **external a. of border of tibia,** margo interosseus tibiae. **external a. of scapula,** angulus lateralis scapulae. **facial a.,** an expression of the degree of recession or protrusion of the chin, determined by a line drawn from the nasion to the pogonion. **filtration a.,** angulus iridocornealis. **frontal a. of parietal bone,** angulus frontalis ossis parietalis. **gamma a.,** the angle formed by junction of the line of fixation and the optic axis at the center of rotation of the eye. **impedance a.,** the ratio between the resistance of the body to an electric current and its condensor function. Cf. *impedance*. **a. of incidence,** the angle made with the perpendicular by a ray of light which strikes a denser or a rarer medium. See *refraction*. **incisal a.,** one of the angles formed by junction of the incisal and the mesial or distal surface of an anterior tooth; called the *mesial* and the *distal incisal angle*, respectively **a. of inclination,** inclinatio pelvis. **inferior a. of duodenum,** flexura duodeni inferior. **inferior a. of parietal bone, anterior,** angulus sphenoidalis ossis parietalis. **inferior a. of parietal bone, posterior,** angulus mastoideus ossis parietalis. **inferior a. of scapula,** angulus inferior scapulae. **infrasternal a. of thorax,** angulus infrasternalis thoracis. **inner a. of humerus,** margo medialis humeri. **internal a. of tibia,** margo medialis tibiae. **iridial a., iridocorneal a., a. of iris,** angulus iridocornealis. **Jacquart's a.,** ophryospinal a. **a. of jaw,** angulus mandibularis. **kappa a.,** the angle between the pupillary axes. **kyphotic a.,** the superior angle formed by intersection of two lines drawn on the lateral chest roentgenogram, tangential to the anterior borders of the second and eleventh intervertebral spaces, an index of the degree of deformity in thoracic kyphosis. **labial a's,** the angles formed between the labial surface and other surfaces of an anterior tooth, or between the labial wall of a tooth cavity and other walls; named according to the surfaces participating in their formation. See tables of *Cavity Angles* and *Tooth Angles*. **lambda a.,** the angle between the pupillary axis and the line of sight. **lateral a. of border of tibia,** margo interosseus tibiae. **lateral a. of eye,** angulus oculi lateralis. **lateral a. of humerus,** margo lateralis humeri. **lateral a. of scapula,** angulus lateralis scapulae. **limiting a.,** critical a. **line a.,** an angle formed by junction of two planes. Used in dentistry to designate the junction of two surfaces of a tooth, or of two walls of a tooth cavity; named according to the tooth surfaces or the cavity walls which participate in its formation. See tables of *Cavity Angles* and *Tooth Angles*. **lingual a's,** the angles formed between the lingual and other surfaces of a tooth, or between the lingual wall of a tooth cavity and other walls; named according to the surfaces which participate in their formation. See tables of *Cavity Angles* and *Tooth Angles*. **Louis's a., Ludwig's a.,** angulus sterni. **lumbosacral a.,** sacrovertebral a. **a. of mandible, mandibular a.,** angulus mandibulae. **mastoid a.,** angulus mastoideus ossis parietalis. **maxillary a.** (*of Camper*), the angle between two lines extending from the point of contact of the upper and lower central incisors to the ophryon and the most prominent point of the lower jaw. **medial a. of eye,** angulus oculi medialis. **medial a. of humerus,** margo medialis humeri. **medial a. of scapula,** angulus superior scapulae. **medial a. of tibia,** margo medialis tibiae. **mesial a's,** the angles formed between the mesial surface and other surfaces of a tooth, or between the mesial wall of a tooth cavity and other walls, named according to the surfaces participating with the mesial in their formation. See tables of *Cavity Angles* and *Tooth Angles*. **metafacial a.,** the angle between the base of the skull and the pterygoid process. **meter a.,** the angle traversed by the visual axis of the eye from its position at rest to its position when fixed on an object one meter distant. **Mikulicz's a.,** an angle formed by two planes, one passing through the long axis of the epiphysis of the femur and the other through the long axis of the diaphysis. It is normally 130 degrees. Called also *angle of declination*. **minimum visual a.,** the angle which the minimum separabile subtends at the eye. Sixty seconds of arc is usually taken as standard for a normal eye. **a. of Mulder,** the angle between the facial line of Camper and a line from the root of the nose to the spheno-occipital suture and intersecting the first line. **nu a.,** the angle between the radius fixus and a line joining the hormion and nasion. **occipital a.,** Daubenton's a. **occipital a. of parietal bone,** angulus occipitalis ossis parietalis. **ocular a's.** See *angulus oculi lateralis* and *angulus oculi medialis*. **olfactive a.,** the angle formed by the line of the olfactory fossa and the os planum of the sphenoid bone. **ophryospinal a.,** the angle at the anterior nasal spine between lines from the auricular point and the glabella. **optic a.,** visual a. **orifacial a.,** the angle formed by junction of the plane determined by the occlusal surfaces of the teeth of the maxilla with the facial line. **parietal a.,** the angle formed by junction of lines passing through the extremities of the transverse bizygomatic diameter and the maximum transverse frontal diameter. **parietal a. of sphenoid bone,** margo parietalis alae majoris. **a. of pelvis,** inclinatio pelvis. **pelvivertebral a.,** a. of inclination. **phrenopericardial a.,** the space or angle between the pericardium and the diaphragm. **Pirogoff's a.,** venous a. **point a.,** an angle that is formed by the junction of two lines or of three planes. Used in dentistry to designate the junction of three surfaces of a tooth, or of three walls of a tooth cavity; named according to the tooth surfaces or the cavity walls participating in its formation. See tables of *Cavity Angles* and *Tooth Angles*. **a. of polarization,** the angle at which light is most completely polarized. **posterior a. of petrous portion of temporal bone,** angulus posterior pyramidis ossis temporalis. **principal a.,** refracting a. **a. of pubis,** angulus subpubicus. **pulpal line a.,** a line angle which is horizontal to the long axis of a tooth. **Quatrefage's a.,** parietal a. **Ranke's a.,** the angle between the horizontal plane of the skull and a line through the center of the alveolar margin and the center of the nasofrontal suture. **a. of reflection,** that which a reflected ray makes with a line perpendicular to the reflecting surface. **refracting a.,** that between the two refracting faces of a prism: called also *principal a*. **a. of refraction,** the angle between a refracted ray and a line perpendicular to the refracting surface. See *refraction*. **a. of rib,** angulus costae. **rolandic a., a. of Rolando,** the angle formed by junction of the mesial plane and the fissure of Rolando. **sacrovertebral a.,** the angle formed at the junction of the sacrum with the lowest lumbar vertebra. **Serres's a.,** metafacial a. **sigma a.,** the angle between the radius fixus and a line from the staphylion to the hormion. **solid a.,** point a. **somatosplanchnic a.,** the angle formed by junction of the somatic and splanchnic layers of the mesoblast in the embryo. **sphenoid a., sphenoidal a.,** an angle at the top of the sella turcica between lines from the nasal point and from the tip of the rostrum of the sphenoid. **sphenoidal a. of parietal bone,** angulus sphenoidalis ossis parietalis. **squint a.,** the angle by which the visual line of the squinting eye deviates from the object which should be fixed. **sternal a.,** angulus sterni. **sternoclavicular a.,** the angle formed by junction of the sternum and clavicle. **a. of sternum,** angulus sterni. **subcostal a.,** angulus infrasternalis thoracis. **subpubic a.,** angulus subpubicus. **subscapular a.,** a transverse depression on the costal or ventral surface of the scapula, where the bone appears bent on itself perpendicular to and passing through the glenoid cavity. **substernal a.,** angulus infrasternalis thoracis. **superior a. of duodenum,** flexura duodeni superior. **superior a. of parietal bone, anterior,** angulus frontalis ossis parietalis. **superior a. of parietal bone, posterior,** angulus occipitalis ossis parietalis. **superior a. of petrous portion of temporal bone,** angulus superior pyramidis ossis temporalis. **superior a. of scapula,** angulus superior scapulae. **a. of Sylvius,** the angle formed by junction of the fissure of Sylvius and a line perpendicular to the superior edge of the cerebral hemisphere. **tentorial a.,** the angle between the basicranial axis and the plane of the tentorium. **tooth a's,** the angles formed by the junction of two or more surfaces of a tooth, named according to the surfaces participating in their formation (see table).

TOOTH ANGLES

Line Angles

(Formed by the junction of two surfaces)

bucco-occlusal	linguoincisal
distobuccal	linguo-occlusal
distolabial	mesiobuccal
distolingual	mesiolabial
disto-occlusal	mesiolingual
labioincisal	mesio-occlusal

Point Angles

(Formed by the junction of three surfaces)

distobucco-occlusal	mesiobucco-occlusal
distolabioincisal	mesiolabioincisal
distolinguoincisal	mesiolinguoincisal
distolinguo-occlusal	mesiolinguo-occlusal

Topinard's a., ophryospinal a. **a. of torsion,** the angle between the axes of different portions of long bones. **tuber a.,** the angle formed by junction of two lines, one parallel with the superior surface of the tuber calcanei and the other joining the anterior and posterior articular facets; normally about 30 degrees. **venous a.,** the angle formed by junction of the internal jugular and subclavian veins. **vesicourethral a.,** the angle formed by junction of the bladder wall and the urethra. **vesicourethral a., anterior,** the angle formed by junction of the anterior wall of the bladder and the urethra. **vesicourethral a., posterior,** the angle formed by junction of the posterior wall of the bladder and the urethra. **a. of Virchow,** the angle between the nasobasilar line and the nasosubnasal line. **visual a.,** the angle formed between two lines extending from the nodal point of the eye to the extremities of the object seen. **Vogt's a.,** the angle between the nasobasilar and alveolonasal lines. **Weisbach's a.,** the angle at the alveolar point between lines passing from the basion and from the middle of the frontonasal suture. **Welcher's a.,** sphenoid a. **xiphoid a's,** the angles formed by the borders of the xiphoid notch. **Y a.,** the angle between the radius fixus and line joining the lambda and the inion.

Angle's classification, splint (ang′elz) [Edward Hartley *Angle*, American orthodontist, 1855–1930]. See under *malocclusion* and *splint*.

Anglesey leg (ang′g'l-se) [Marquis of *Anglesey*, 1768–1854, for whom the leg was made]. See under *leg*.

anglicus sudor (ang′le-kus su′dor). The English sweating fever; a deadly pestilential fever which has several times ravaged England.

angophrasia (ang″go-fra′zhe-ah) [Gr. *anchein* to choke + *phrasis* utterance + *-ia*]. A drawling and broken form of speech occurring in dementia (Kussmaul).

angor (ang′gōr) [L. "a strangling"]. Angina. **a. an′imi,** a feeling of impending dissolution. **a. noctur′nus.** Same as *pavor nocturnus*. **a. ocula′ris,** a condition marked by fear of imminent blindness, and by sudden attacks of mist before the eyes: due to angiospasm of ocular vessels. **a. pec′toris,** angina pectoris.

angostura (ang″gos-too′rah). [Sp. *Angostura*, "narrows," a town of Venezuela]. The bark of *Galipe′a cuspa′ria*, a tree of South America: a bitter tonic and stimulant.

angosturine (ang″gos-too′rin). A tonic alkaloid, $C_{10}H_{40}N_{14}$, from angostura.

angstrom (awng′strem). The unit of wavelength of electromagnetic and corpuscular radiations: equal to 10^{-7} mm. Called also *Angström unit*. Abbreviated Å or A.

Angström law, unit (awng′strem) [Anders Jonas *Angström*, Swedish physicist, 1814–1874]. See *Angström law*, under *law*, and *angstrom*.

Anguillula (ang-gwil′u-lah) [L. "little eel"]. A genus of nematode parasites. **A. ace′ti,** a species found in vinegar, and sometimes in the urine. **A. intestina′lis, A. stercora′lis,** *Strongyloides stercoralis*.

anguilluliasis (ang″gwil-u-li′ah-sis). The presence of an anguillula in the body.

Anguilluli′na putrefa′ciens. A nematode normally parasitic in the bulb of onions, and sometimes found in man.

anguillulosis (ang″gwil-u-lo′sis). Anguilluliasis.

angular (ang′gu-lar) [L. *angula′ris*]. Sharply bent; having corners or angles.

angulation (ang″gu-la′shun) [L. *angula′tus* bent]. The formation of a sharp obstructive angle, as in the intestine, the ureter, or similar tubes.

anguli (ang′gu-li) [L.]. Plural of *angulus*.

angulus (ang′gu-lus), pl *an′guli* [L.]. An angle; used as a general term in anatomical nomenclature to designate a triangular area, or the angle of a particular body structure or part. **a. acromia′lis** [N A], the easily palpable subcutaneous bony point where the lateral border of the acromion becomes continuous with the spine of the scapula. Called also *acromial angle*. **a. ante′rior pyram′idis os′sis tempora′lis** [B N A], a short area on the petrous part of the temporal bone consisting of two parts: one, adjoined to the squamous part of the bone at the petrosquamous suture; the other, a free part articulating with the great wing of the sphenoid. Called also *anterior angle of petrous portion of temporal bone*. **a. cos′tae** [N A, B N A], a prominent line on the external surface of a rib, a little in front of the tubercle, where the rib is bent in two directions and at the same time twisted on its long axis. Called also *angle of rib*. **a. fronta′lis os′sis parieta′lis** [N A, B N A], the anterosuperior angle of the parietal bone, which is membranous at birth and forms part of the anterior fontanelle. Called also *frontal angle of parietal bone*. **a. infectio′sus,** perlèche. **a. infe′rior scap′ulae** [N A, B N A], the angle formed by the junction of the medial and lateral borders of the scapula. Called also *inferior angle of scapula*. **a. infrasterna′lis thora′cis** [N A, B N A], the angle on the anteroinferior surface of the thorax, the apex of which is the sternoxiphoid junction, and the sides of which are the seventh, eighth and ninth costal cartilages. It partially delimits two sides of the triangular epigastric region on the ventral body surface. Called also *infrasternal angle of thorax*. **a. i′ridis** [B N A], a. iridocornealis. **a. iridocornea′lis** [N A], a narrow recess between the sclerocorneal junction and the attached margin of the iris, marking the periphery of the anterior chamber of the eye. Called also *iridocorneal angle* and *angulus iridis* [B N A]. **a. latera′lis scap′ulae** [N A, B N A], the head of the scapula, which bears the glenoid cavity and articulates with the head of the humerus. Called also *lateral angle of scapula*. **a. latera′lis tib′iae,** margo interosseus tibiae. **a. Ludovi′ci,** a. sterni. **a. mandib′ulae** [N A, B N A], the angle created at the junction of the posterior edge of the ramus and the lower edge of the mandible. Called also *angle of mandible*. **a. mastoi′deus os′sis parieta′lis** [N A, B N A], the posteroinferior angle of the parietal bone, which articulates with the posterior part of the temporal bone and the occipital bone. Called also *mastoid angle of parietal bone*. **a. media′lis scap′ulae** [B N A], a. superior scapulae. **a. media′lis tib′iae,** margo medialis tibiae. **a. occipita′lis os′sis parieta′lis** [N A, B N A], the posterosuperior angle of the parietal bone, which during fetal life participates in the formation of the posterior fontanelle. Called also *occipital angle of parietal bone*. **a. oc′uli latera′lis** [N A, B N A], the angle formed by the lateral junction of the superior and inferior eyelids. Called also *lateral angle of eye*. **a. oc′uli media′lis** [N A, B N A], the angle formed by the medial junction of the superior and inferior eyelids. Called also *medial angle of eye*. **a. o′ris** [N A, B N A], the angle formed at either side of the mouth by junction of the upper and the lower lip. Called also *angle of mouth*. **a. parieta′lis os′sis sphenoida′lis** [B N A], margo parietalis alae majoris. **a. poste′rior pyram′idis os′sis tempora′lis** [B N A], the angle on the petrous portion of the temporal bone that separates the posterior from the inferior surface. Called also *posterior angle of petrous portion of temporal bone*. **a. pu′bis** [B N A], a. subpubicus. **a. sphenoida′lis os′sis parieta′lis** [N A, B N A], the anteroinferior angle of the parietal bone, which articulates with the great wing of the sphenoid bone and the frontal bone. Called also *sphenoid angle of parietal bone*. **a. ster′ni** [N A, B N A], the angle formed on the anterior surface of the sternum at the junction of its body and manubrium. Called also *sternal angle*. **a. subpu′bicus** [N A], the apex of the pubic arch; the angle formed at the point of meeting of the conjoined rami of the ischial and pubic bones of the two sides of the body. Called also *subpubic angle* and *angulus pubis* [B N A]. **a. supe′rior pyram′idis os′sis tempora′lis** [B N A], the angle on the internal surface of the petrous portion of the temporal bone that separates its posterior and anterior surfaces. Called also *superior angle of petrous portion of temporal bone*. **a. supe′rior scap′ulae** [N A], the angle made by the superior and medial borders of the scapula. Called also *superior angle of scapula* and *angulus medialis scapulae* [B N A]. **a. veno′sus,** the angle at the junction of the common jugular vein and the subclavian vein.

angustura (ang″gus-too′rah). Angostura.

angusty (ang-gus′te) [L. *angustus* narrow]. Narrowness.

anhalamine (an-hal′ah-min). A crystalline alkaloid, $C_{11}H_{15}NO_3$, from *Lophophora williamsii*.

anhaline (an′hah-lin). An alkaloid from *Lophophora williamsii* which is identical with hordenine.

anhalonine (an″hah-lo′nin). A crystalline alkaloid, $C_{12}H_{15}NO_3$, from *Lophophora williamsii*, with the physiological properties of mezcaline.

Anhalonium lewinii (an″hah-lo′ne-um lu-win′e-e). *Lophophora williamsii*.

anhaphia (an-ha′fe-ah). Anaphia.

anhedonia (an″he-do′ne-ah) [*an* neg. + Gr.

hēdonē pleasure + *-ia*]. Total loss of feeling of pleasure in acts that normally give pleasure.

anhelation (an-hĕ-la′shun) [L. *anhela′tio*]. Dyspnea, with panting; shortness of breath.

anhelous (an-he′lus). Short of breath; marked by dyspnea.

anhematopoiesis (an-hem″ah-to″poi-e′sis) [*an* neg. + Gr. *haima* blood + *poiein* to make]. Anhematosis.

anhematopoietic (an-hem″ah-to″poi-et′ik) [*an* neg. + Gr. *haima* blood + *poiein* to make]. Pertaining to anhematosis (anhematopoiesis).

anhematosis (an″hem-ah-to′sis) [*an* neg. + Gr. *haimatoun* to make bloody + *-osis*]. Defect in the formation of blood, due to hypofunction of the bone marrow.

anhemolytic (an″hem-o-lit′ik) [*an* neg. + Gr. *haima* blood + *lytikos* dissolving]. Not causing hemolysis; not destructive to blood corpuscles.

anhemothigmic (an″hem-o-thig′mik) [*an* neg. + Gr. *haima* blood + *thigma* touch]. A term applied to those tissues on contact with which blood undergoes coagulation. Cf. *hemothigmic*.

anhepatia (an″he-pat′e-ah) [*an* neg. + Gr. *hēpar* liver + *-ia*]. Absence or suppression of liver function.

anhepatic (an″he-pat′ik). 1. Pertaining to or characterized by anhepatia. 2. Anhepatogenic.

anhepatogenic (an-hep″ah-to-jen′ik) [*an* neg. + Gr. *hēpar* liver + *gennan* to produce]. Not originating in the liver; not due to any morbid process within the liver.

anhidrosis (an″hĭ-dro′sis) [*an* neg. + Gr. *hidrōs* sweat + *-osis*]. An abnormal deficiency of sweat.

anhidrotic (an″hĭ-drot′ik). 1. Checking the secretion of sweat. 2. An agent that checks the secretion of sweat.

anhistic (an-his′tik) [*an* neg. + Gr. *histos* web]. Structureless or of unknown structure.

anhistous (an-his′tus). Anhistic.

anhormonia (an″hor-mo′ne-ah). Hormone deficiency.

anhydrase (an-hi′drās). An enzyme which catalyzes the removal of water from a compound. **carbonic a.,** an enzyme which catalyzes the decomposition of carbonic acid into carbon dioxide and water, and which thus facilitates the transfer of carbon dioxide from tissues to blood and to alveolar air.

anhydration (an″hi-dra′shun). Dehydration.

anhydremia (an″hi-dre′me-ah) [*an* neg. + Gr. *hydōr* water + *haima* blood + *-ia*]. Lack of water in the blood.

anhydride (an-hi′drīd) [*an* neg. + Gr. *hydōr* water]. A chemical compound derived from a substance, especially an acid, by the abstraction of a molecule of water. The anhydrides of bases are oxides; those of alcohols are ethers. **abietic acid a.,** a resinous substance, $C_{44}H_{62}O_4$, found in rosin. **acetic a.,** a colorless mobile liquid of a pungent acetic odor. It is the anhydride of acetic acid $(CH_3CO)_2O$. **arsenious a.,** arsenic trioxide. **carbonic a.,** carbon dioxide. **chromic a.,** chromic acid.

anhydrochloric (an″hi-dro-klo′rik). Characterized by the absence of hydrochloric acid.

anhydrohydroxyprogesterone (an-hi″dro-hi-drok″se-pro-jes′ter-ōn). Pregneninolone.

anhydromuscarine (an″hi-dro-mus′kah-rin). A synthetic alkaloid, $OH(CH_3)_3N.CH_2.CHO$, which has no action on a frog's heart.

anhydromyelia (an″hi-dro-mi-e′le-ah) [*an* neg. + Gr. *hydōr* water + *myelos* marrow + *-ia*]. A deficiency of the fluid that is normally found in the spinal canal.

anhydrosugar (an″hi-dro-shug′ar). A substance produced from cane sugar by heating it under diminished pressure to about 170°C. It does not ferment nor reduce copper solutions, and it has been used as a food in diabetes.

anhydrous (an-hi′drus) [*an* neg. + Gr. *hydōr* water]. Deprived or destitute of water.

anhypnia (an-hip′ne-ah) [*an* neg. + Gr. *hypnos* sleep + *-ia*]. Insomnia.

anhypnosis (an″hip-no′sis). Insomnia.

aniacinamidosis (ah-ni″ah-sin-am″i-do′sis). Any disorder due to nicotinic acid amide deficiency.

aniacinosis (ah-ni″ah-sĭ-no′sis). Nicotinic acid (niacin) deficiency.

anianthinopsy (an″e-an′thĭ-nop″se) [*an* neg. + Gr. *ianthinos* violet + *opsis* vision]. Inability to distinguish violet tints.

anicteric (an″ik-ter′ik). Without icterus; not associated with jaundice.

anidean (ah-nid′e-an). Pertaining to anideus.

anideation (an″i-de-a′shun). The negation of ideation.

anideus (ah-nid′e-us) [*an* neg. + Gr. *idea* form]. Holoacardius amorphous. **embryonic a.,** a blastoderm in which no embryonic axis develops.

anidous (ah-ni′dus). Without form due to arrested development.

anidrosis (an-ĭ-dro′sis). Anhidrosis.

anile (a′nīl) [L. *anus*, old woman]. Like an old woman; imbecilic.

anileridine (an″ĭ-ler′ĭ-dēn). Chemical name: 1-(4-aminophenethyl)-4-phenylisonipecotic acid ethyl ester: used as a narcotic, analgesic, and sedative.

anilid (an′ĭ-lid). Anilide.

anilide (an′ĭ-lid). Any compound formed from aromatic amines by substitution of an acyl group for the hydrogen of NH_2.

anilinction (a″nĭ-link′shun) [L. *anus* + *lingere, linctum* to lick]. Application of the mouth to, or licking of, the anus.

anilinctus (a″nĭ-link′tus). Anilinction.

aniline (an′ĭ-lin) [Arabic *an′nil* indigo, *nīl* blue; L. *nil* indigo]. A colorless oily liquid, $C_6H_5NH_2$, from coal tar and from indigo, made commercially by reducing nitrobenzene. It is slightly soluble in water; freely so in ether and alcohol. It frequently produces symptoms of poisoning (anilinism). The drug itself and its sulfate have been used in epilepsy and chorea. Combined with other substances, especially chlorine and the chlorates, it forms the aniline colors or dyes that are derived from coal tar. **a. sulfate,** a white, crystalline substance, $(C_6H_5NH_2)_2H_2SO_4$.

anilingus (a″nĭ-lin′gus). An individual who practices anilinction.

anilinism (an′ĭ-lin-izm). A condition produced by exposure to aniline, and marked by methemoglobinemia and anemia, vertigo, muscular weakness, cyanosis, and digestive derangement.

anilinophil (an-ĭ-lin′o-fil) [*aniline* + Gr. *philein* to love]. An anilinophilous element or structure.

anilinophile (an″ĭ-lin′o-fīl). 1. Anilinophilous. 2. Anilinophil.

anilinophilous (an″ĭ-lin-of′ĭ-lus). Staining readily with aniline dyes.

anilism (an′ĭ-lizm). Anilinism.

anility (ah-nil′ĭ-te) [L. *anus*, old woman]. The state of being like an old woman; imbecility.

anil-quinoline (an″il-kwin′o-lin). Synthetic quinoline prepared from aniline.

anima (an′e-mah) [L. "air"]. 1. The soul. 2. The active principle of a drug. 3. Jung's term for the inner being or personality as contrasted with the outer character of the personality or persona. 4. In psychoanalysis, the female ideal or image existing in the unconscious of a woman. Cf. *animus*.

animal (an′ĭ-mal) [L. *animalis*, from *anima* life, breath]. 1. A living organism having sensation and the power of voluntary movement, and requiring for its existence oxygen and organic food.

2. Pertaining to such an organism. **control a.** See *control.* **decerebrate a.,** one from which the cerebral hemispheres have been removed along with more or less of the basal ganglia. **experimental a.,** an animal which is used as a subject of experimental procedures in the laboratory. **Houssay a.,** an experimental animal deprived of both hypophysis cerebri and pancreas. **immune a.,** an animal in a control experiment made immune by inoculation with some specific antisubstance. **Long-Lukens a.,** an experimental animal which has been deprived of both pancreas and adrenal glands. **normal a.,** an animal used in experiments which there is full reason to regard as healthy and free from the effects of infection or immunization, artificial or natural. **nuclein a.,** an animal into which a certain amount of nuclein has been injected. **spinal a.,** an animal whose spinal cord has been severed, thus cutting off communication with the brain. **thalamic a.,** an animal in which the brain stem has been sectioned just above the thalamus.

animalcule (an″ĭ-mal′kūl) [L. *animalculum*]. Any minute or microscopic animal organism.

animalculist (an″ĭ-mal′ku-list). A believer in the theory that the undeveloped embryo exists preformed in the spermatozoon. Cf. *ovist.*

animality (an″ĭ-mal′ĭ-te). The distinguishing characteristics of animals.

animalized (an′ĭ-mal-īzd). Cultivated in the animal body or on animal secretions, such as blood, milk, etc.; said of bacteria.

animation (an″ĭ-ma′shun). 1. The state of being alive. 2. Liveliness of spirits. **suspended a.,** a temporary state of apparent death.

anime, animi (an′ĭ-me, an′ĭ-mi) [Fr. *animé*]. A name of various resins, especially that of *Hymenaea courbaril* and *H. stilbocarpa*, trees of tropical America.

animism (an′ĭ-mizm) [L. *anima* soul]. 1. The obsolete doctrine that the soul is the source of all organic development. 2. The belief that all objects are endowed with inner life and purpose.

animus (an′ĭ-mus). The male ideal or image existing in the unconscious of a man.

anincretinasis (an-in″kre-tĭ-na′sis). Anincretinosis.

anincretinosis (an-in″kre-tĭ-no′sis) [*an* neg. + *incretion*]. A disorder due to defect or lack of some internal secretion.

anion (an′i-on) [Gr. *ana* up + *iōn* going]. An ion carrying a negative charge. Hence, as unlike forms of electricity attract each other, it is attracted by, and travels to, the anode or positive pole. See *ion.* The anions include all the nonmetals, the acid radicals, and the hydroxyl ion. They are indicated by an accent mark, or a minus sign, as Cl' or Cl^-.

anionic (an″i-on′ik). Pertaining to or containing an anion.

anionotrophy (an″e-on-ot′ro-pe) [*anion* + Gr. *tropos* a turning]. A type of tautomerism in which the migrating group is a negative ion rather than the more usual hydrogen ion.

aniridia (an″ĭ-rid′e-ah) [*an* neg. + *iris*]. Absence of the iris.

anisate (an′ĭ-sāt). A salt of anisic acid.

anischuria (an″is-ku′re-ah) [*an* neg. + Gr. *ischouria* retention of the urine]. Incontinence of the urine; enuresis.

anise (an′is) [L. *anisum*]. The fruit of *Pimpinella anisum*, an umbelliferous plant. It is carminative and expectorant, and has a slightly stimulative action on the heart. **Chinese a., Indian a., star a.,** the fruit of *Illicium verum* or of *I. anisatum*, magnoliaceous trees of Asia.

aniseikonia (an″ĭ-si-ko′ne-ah) [Gr. *anisos* unequal + *eikōn* image + *-ia*]. A condition in which the ocular image of an object as seen by one eye differs in size and shape from that seen by the other.

aniseikonic (an″ĭ-si-kon′ik). Pertaining to or correcting aniseikonia.

anisergy (an-is′er-je) [Gr. *anisos* unequal + *ergon* work]. The existence of different degrees of blood pressure in different sections of the circulatory system.

anisine (an′ĭ-sin). A crystalline alkaloid, $C_{22}H_{24}N_2O_3$, from anise.

aniso- (an-i′so) [Gr. *anisos* unequal, uneven]. Combining form denoting *unequal* or *dissimilar.*

aniso-accommodation (an-i″so-ah-kom″mo-da′shun). A difference in the accommodative capacity of the two eyes.

anisochromasia (an-i″so-kro-ma′ze-ah) [*aniso-* + Gr. *chrōma* color]. A condition in which only the peripheral zone of a red blood corpuscle is colored.

anisochromatic (an-i″so-kro-mat′ik) [*aniso-* + Gr. *chrōma* color]. Not of the same color throughout: applied to solutions used for testing color blindness, containing two pigments which are distinguished by both the normal and the colorblind eye.

anisochromia (an″ĭ-so-kro′me-ah) [*aniso-* + Gr. *chrōma* color + *-ia*]. Variation in the color of the red corpuscles due to unequal hemoglobin content.

anisocoria (an″ĭ-so-ko′re-ah) [*aniso-* + Gr. *korē* pupil + *-ia*]. Inequality of the pupils in diameter.

anisocytosis (an-i″so-si-to′sis) [*aniso-* + Gr. *kytos* hollow vessel + *-osis*]. Presence in the blood of erythrocytes showing abnormal variation in size.

anisodactylous (an″ĭ-so-dak′tĭ-lus) [*aniso-* + Gr. *daktylos* finger]. Having digits of unequal lengths.

anisodactyly (an″ĭ-so-dak′tĭ-le). A condition characterized by having digits of unequal lengths.

anisodont (an-i′so-dont) [*aniso-* + Gr. *odous* tooth]. Having teeth of unequal size or length.

anisogamy (an″ĭ-sog′ah-me) [*aniso-* + Gr. *gamos* marriage]. Sexual conjugation in protozoa in which the gametes differ in structure and size.

anisognathous (an″ĭ-sog′nah-thus) [*aniso-* + Gr. *gnathos* jaw]. Having the upper jaw much wider relatively than the lower one.

anisohypercytosis (an-i″so-hi″per-si-to′sis) [*aniso-* + Gr. *hyper* over + *kytos* hollow vessel + *-osis*]. Increase in the number of leukocytes of the blood, with abnormality in the proportion of the various forms of neutrophil cells.

anisohypocytosis (an-i″so-hi″po-si-to′sis) [*aniso-* + Gr. *hypo* under + *kytos* hollow vessel + *-osis*]. Decrease in the number of leukocytes of the blood, with abnormality in the proportion of the various forms of neutrophil cells.

anisoic (an″ĭ-so′ik). Pertaining to anise.

anisoiconia (an-i″so-i-ko′ne-ah). Aniseikonia.

anisokaryosis (an-i″so-kar″e-o′sis) [*aniso-* + Gr. *karyon* nucleus + *-osis*]. Inequality in the size of the nuclei of cells.

anisoleukocytosis (an-i″so-lu″ko-si-to′sis) [*aniso-* + *leukocytosis*]. A condition in which the proportion of the various forms of neutrophilic leukocytes in the blood is abnormal.

anisomastia (an-i″so-mas′te-ah) [*aniso-* + Gr. *mastos* breast + *-ia*]. Inequality of the breasts.

anisomelia (an-i″so-me′le-ah) [*aniso-* + Gr. *melos* limb + *-ia*]. Inequality between paired limbs.

anisomeric (an-i″so-mer′ik). Not isomeric.

anisometrope (an-i″so-met′rōp). A person affected with anisometropia.

anisometropia (an-i″so-me-tro′pe-ah) [*aniso-* + Gr. *metron* measure + *ōps* eye + *-ia*]. A difference in the refractive power of the two eyes which can be corrected by ordinary lenses.

anisometropic (an-i″so-me-trop′ik). Pertaining to or characterized by anisometropia.

Anisomorpha (an-i″so-mor′fah). A genus of insects. **A. buprestoi'des,** the walking stick; an orthopterous insect which is capable of discharging an irritating fluid.

anisonormocytosis (an-i″so-nor″mo-si-to′sis) [*aniso-* + *normocyte*]. A condition in which the number of leukocytes in the blood is normal but the proportion of the various forms of neutrophilic cells is abnormal.

anisophoria (an″i-so-fo′re-ah) [*aniso-* + *phoria*]. A condition in which the tension of the vertical muscles of one eye differs from that of the other eye, so that the visual lines do not lie in the same horizontal plane.

anisopia (an″i-so′pe-ah) [*aniso-* + Gr. *ōps* eye + *-ia*]. Inequality of vision in the two eyes.

anisopiesis (an-i″so-pi-e′sis) [*aniso-* + Gr. *piesis* pressure]. Variation or inequality in the blood pressure as registered in different parts of the body.

anisopoikilocytosis (an-i″so-poi″kĭ-lo-si-to′sis). The presence in the blood of erythrocytes of varying sizes and abnormal shape.

anisorhythmia (an-i″so-rith′me-ah) [*aniso-* + Gr. *rhythmos* rhythm + *-ia*]. Irregular heart action marked by lack of synchronism in the rhythm of atria and ventricles.

anisosphygmia (an-i″so-sfig′me-ah) [*aniso-* + Gr. *sphygmos* pulse + *-ia*]. Inequality of the pulse, either in volume, time or force, in symmetrical arteries of the body, as in the two radial arteries.

anisospore (an-i′so-spōr″) [*aniso-* + Gr. *sporos* spore]. A sexual spore that unites with a spore of opposite sex to form a new individual.

anisosthenic (an-i″sos-then′ik) [*aniso-* + Gr. *sthenos* strength]. Not having equal strength: said of paired muscles.

anisotonic (an-i″so-ton′ik). 1. Showing a variation in tonicity or tension. 2. Having an osmotic pressure differing from that of a solution with which it is compared.

anisotropal (an″i-sot′ro-pal). Anisotropic.

anisotropic (an-i″so-trop′ik) [*aniso-* + Gr. *tropos* a turning]. 1. Having unlike properties in different directions, as in any unit lacking spherical symmetry. 2. Doubly refracting or having a double polarizing power.

anisotropy (an″i-sot′ro-pe). The quality or condition of being anisotropic.

anisum (an-i′sum), gen. *ani′si* [L.]. Anise.

anisuria (an″i-su′re-ah) [*aniso-* + Gr. *ouron* urine + *-ia*]. A condition marked by alternating oliguria and polyuria.

anitrogenous (ah″ni-troj′e-nus). Not nitrogenous.

Anitschkow's cell, myocyte (ah-nich′kofs) [Nikolai Nikolaiewitsch *Anitschkow*, Russian pathologist, born 1885]. See under *myocyte.*

ankle (ang′kl). The part of the leg just above the foot; also the joint between the foot and the leg; ankle joint. **cocked a.,** a partial dislocation of the fetlock joint of a horse. **deck a's,** edema of the ankles observed on troop ships. **tailors' a.,** an abnormal bursa over the head of the fibula in tailors, from pressure caused by sitting on the floor with the legs crossed in front.

ankylo- (ang′kĭ-lo) [Gr. *ankylē* the bend of the arm, hence bent or crooked; also noose or loop]. Combining form meaning bent, or in the form of a noose or loop.

ankyloblepharon (ang″kĭ-lo-blef′ah-ron) [*ankylo-* + Gr. *blepharon* eyelid]. The adhesion of the ciliary edges of the eyelid to each other. **a. filifor'me adna'tum,** congenital adhesion of the margins of the upper and lower lid by filamentous bands. **a. tota'le,** cryptophthalmos.

ankylochilia (ang″kĭ-lo-ki′le-ah) [*ankylo-* + Gr. *cheilos* lip + *-ia*]. Adhesion of the lips to each other.

ankylocolpos (ang-kĭ-lo-kol′pos) [*ankylo-* + Gr. *kolpos* vagina]. Atresia or imperforation of the vagina.

ankylodactylia (ang″kĭ-lo-dak-til′e-ah) [*ankylo-* + Gr. *daktylos* finger + -ia]. Adhesion of fingers or toes to one another.

ankyloglossia (ang″kĭ-lo-glos′e-ah) [*ankylo-* + Gr. *glōssa* tongue + *-ia*]. Tonguetie.

ankylomele (ang″kĭ-lo-me′le) [*ankylo-* + Gr. *mēlē* probe]. A curved probe.

ankylophobia (ang″kĭ-lo-fo′be-ah) [*ankylo-* + *phobia*]. Morbid fear of ankylosis in cases of fracture or joint affection.

ankylopoietic (ang″kĭ-lo-poi-et′ik) [*ankylo-* + Gr. *poiein* to make]. Producing or characterized by ankylosis.

ankyloproctia (ang″kĭ-lo-prok′she-ah) [*ankylo-* + Gr. *prōktos* anus + *-ia*]. A stricture of the anus.

ankylosed (ang′kĭ-lōsd). Affected with ankylosis.

ankyloses (ang″kĭ-lo′sēz). Plural of *ankylosis.*

ankylosis (ang″kĭ-lo′sis), pl. *ankylo′ses* [Gr. *ankylōsis*]. Abnormal immobility and consolidation of a joint. **artificial a.,** arthrodesis. **bony a.,** the abnormal union of the bones of a joint. **dental a.** 1. Solid fixation of a tooth, resulting from fusion of the cementum and alveolar bone, with obliteration of the periodontal membrane. 2. Fusion of the head of the condyle of the mandible to the mandibular fossa, occurring congenitally or as the result of trauma. **extracapsular a.,** ankylosis due to rigidity of structures exterior to the joint capsule. **false a.,** ankylosis that is not due to abnormal union of the bones comprising the joint, but to some other cause. **fibrous a.,** that due to the formation of fibrous bands within a joint. **intracapsular a.,** ankylosis due to the undue rigidity of structures interior to the joint capsule. **ligamentous a.,** ankylosis resulting from rigidity of the ligaments. **spurious a.,** false a. **true a.,** bony a.

Ankylostoma (ang″kĭ-los′to-mah). Ancylostoma.

ankylostomiasis (ang″kĭ-lo-sto-mi′ah-sis). Ancylostomiasis.

ankylotia (ang″kĭ-lo′she-ah) [*ankylo-* + Gr. *ous* (*ōtos*) ear + *-ia*]. Closure of the external meatus of the ear.

ankylotic (ang″kĭ-lot′ik). Pertaining to or marked by ankylosis.

ankylotome (ang-kil′o-tōm) [*ankylo-* + Gr. *tomē* cut]. A knife for operating for tonguetie.

ankylotomy (ang″kĭ-lot′o-me) [*ankylo-* + Gr. *tomē* cut]. A cutting operation for curing tonguetie.

ankylurethria (ang″kil-u-re′thre-ah) [*ankylo-* + *urethra* + *-ia*]. Stricture of the urethra.

ankyrism (ang′kĭ-rizm) [Gr. *ankyra* hook + *-ism*]. A hooklike articulation or suture.

ankyroid (ang′kĭ-roid) [Gr. *ankyra* hook + *eidos* form]. Hook-shaped.

anlage (ahn′lah-geh, or an′lāj), pl. *anla′gen* [Ger. "a laying on"]. Primordium.

Annandale's operation (an′an-dālz) [Thomas *Annandale*, Scottish surgeon, 1838–1907]. See under *operation.*

anneal (an-nēl′). To soften a material, such as a metal, by controlled heating and cooling, making it less brittle and more easily adapted, bent, or swaged.

annectent (ah-nek′tent) [L. *annectens*]. Connecting or joining.

Annelida (ah-nel′ĭ-dah). A phylum of metazoan invertebrates, the segmented worms. It contains only one class of medical interest, *Hirudinea*, the leeches.

annotto (ah-not′o). A red color or stain from the fruit of *Bixa orellana*, a South American tree: used for coloring butter and other foods.

annoyer (ah-noi′er). A stimulus which arouses an unpleasant feeling reaction.

annular (an′u-lar) [L. *annularis*]. Shaped like a ring.

annuli (an′u-li) [L.]. Plural of *annulus.*

annulorrhaphy (an″u-lor′ah-fe) [L. *annulus* ring + Gr. *rhaphē* suture]. Closure of a hernial ring or sac by sutures.

annulus (an′u-lus), *pl. an′nuli* [L. "a ring"; dim. of *annus* a year, originally a circuit]. A ring, or ringlike or circular structure. This word, official in B N A, was changed to *anulus* in N A terminology. For official names which were otherwise unchanged, see under *anulus.* **a. abdomina′lis.** See *anulus inguinalis profundus* and *anulus inguinalis superficialis.* **a. abdomina′lis abdom′inis,** anulus abdominalis profundus. **a. cilia′ris,** orbiculus ciliaris. **a. haemorrhoid-a′lis** [B N A], zona hemorrhoidalis. **a. inguin-a′lis abdomina′lis** [B N A], anulus inguinalis profundus. **a. inguina′lis subcuta′neus** [B N A], anulus inguinalis superficialis. **a. mi′grans,** a disease marked by formation on the tongue of raised red patches with a yellow border, which spread in eccentric circles over the upper and under surfaces. **a. ova′lis,** limbus fossae ovalis. **a. tra′cheae,** any one of the rings of the trachea. **tympanic a.,** anulus tympanicus. **a. urethra′lis** [B N A], a thickening around the urethral opening of the bladder formed by a thickening of the middle muscular coat. Omitted in N A. **Vieussens′ a.** 1. Limbus fossae ovalis. 2. Ansa subclavia. **a. zin′nii,** anulus tendineus communis.

AnOC. Abbreviation for *anodal opening contraction.*

anochlesia (an″o-kle′ze-ah). 1. Tranquillity. 2. Catalepsy.

anochromasia (an″o-kro-ma′se-ah). 1. Absence of the usual staining reaction from a tissue or cell. 2. A condition in which the erythrocytes show a piling up of hemoglobin at the periphery so that the center is pale.

anoci-association (ah-no″se-ah-so″se-a′shun) [*a* neg. + L. *nocere* to injure + *association*]. The blunting of harmful association impulses; a method of anesthesia designed to minimize the effect of surgical shock. The mind of the patient is calmed by an injection of scopolamine and morphine one hour before the operation. The general anesthetic employed is usually nitrous oxide and oxygen. The field of operation is blocked by infiltration with procaine and every division of sensitive tissue during the operation is preceded by the injection of procaine. Sharp dissection and gentle manipulations are employed. To minimize postoperative discomfort in serious cases quinine and urea hydrochloride solution is injected at some distance from the wound (Crile).

anociated (ah-no′se-āt″ed). In a condition of anoci-association.

anociation (ah-no″se-a′shun). Anoci-association.

anocithesia (ah-no″se-the′ze-ah). Anoci-association.

anococcygeal (a″no-kok-sij′e-al). Pertaining to the anus and coccyx.

anodal (an-o′dal). Pertaining to the anode.

anode (an′ōd) [Gr. *ana* up + *hodos* way]. The positive pole of a galvanic battery or other electric source. Cf. *cathode.*

anoderm (a′no-derm). The epithelial lining of the anal canal.

anodinia (an″o-din′e-ah) [*an* neg. + Gr. *ōdis* pain of childbirth + *-ia*]. Absence of labor pains.

anodmia (an-od′me-ah) [*an* neg. + Gr. *odmē* smell + *-ia*]. Lack of the sense of smell.

anodontia (an″o-don′she-ah) [*an* neg. + Gr. *odous* tooth + *-ia*]. Congenital absence of the teeth. It may involve all or only some of the teeth, and both the deciduous and the permanent dentition, or only teeth of the permanent dentition. **partial a., a. partia′lis,** congenital absence of some of the teeth, some of them being present. **total a., a. tota′lis,** congenital absence of all of the teeth. **a. ve′ra,** total failure of development of the teeth, usually associated with other anomalies, such as absence of sebaceous glands and deficiency of the sweat, lacrimal, pharyngeal, conjunctival and salivary glands, and other congenital defects.

anodontism (an″o-don′tizm). Anodontia.

anodyne (an′o-dīn) [*an* neg. + Gr. *odynē* pain]. 1. Relieving pain. 2. A medicine that relieves pain. The anodynes include opium, morphine, codeine, hyoscine, atropine, coniine, ether, lupulin, potassium bromide. **Hoffmann's a.,** compound ether spirit.

anodynia (an″o-din′e-ah) [*an* neg. + Gr. *odynē* pain + *-ia*]. Freedom from pain.

anoesia (an″o-e′ze-ah) [Gr. *anoēsia*]. Want of understanding; idiocy.

anoetic (an″o-et′ik) [*a* neg. + Gr. *noētos* thinkable]. 1. Not subject to conscious attention; not clearly conscious. 2. Characterized by anoesia.

anoia (ah-noi′ah) [Gr. *anoia*]. Idiocy; amentia.

anol (a′nol). A compound, *p*-hydroxy propenyl benzene, which is readily polymerized to form active carcinogenic and estrogenic substances. It is also a synthetic sex hormone which stimulates the growth of the duct system of the mammary gland and also the lobular alveolar system.

anomalo- (ah-nom′ah-lo) [Gr. *anōmalos* irregular, *anōmalia* irregularity, unevenness; from *an* neg. + Gr. *homalos* even]. Combining form meaning irregular or uneven.

anomalopia (ah-nom″ah-lo′pe-ah) [*anomalo-* + Gr. *ōpe* vision + *-ia*]. A slight anomaly of visual perception. **color a.,** a minor deviation of color vision, without loss of ability to distinguish the four primary colors. See *deuteranomalopia* and *protanomalopia.*

anomaloscope (ah-nom′ah-lo-skōp) [*anomalo-* + Gr. *skopein* to view]. An instrument used in testing for anomalies of color vision by having the subject match mixed spectral lines.

anomalotrophy (ah-nom″al-ot′ro-fe) [*anomalo-* + Gr. *trophē* nutrition]. Abnormality of nutrition.

anomalous (ah-nom′ah-lus) [Gr. *anōmalos*]. Irregular; marked by deviation from the natural order.

anomaly (ah-nom′ah-le) [Gr. *anōmalia*]. Marked deviation from the normal standard. **Alder's a.,** a condition in which all leukocytes, but mainly those of the myelocytic series, contain coarse, azurophilic granules. Called also *Alder's constitutional granulation anomaly.* **Aristotle's a.,** if the first and second fingers are crossed and a pencil is placed between them, the person feels two pencils. **Chediak-Higashi a.,** a hereditary disorder, occurring in children of either sex, characterized by abnormalities in the nuclear structure of the leukocytes, which also contain giant, peroxidase-positive cytoplasmic granules and inclusions. Albinism, photophobia, lymphadenopathy, hepatosplenomegaly, and a course punctuated by repeated skin infections, with death ensuing generally before the eighth year, are the clinical features. Also called *Chediak-Steinbrinck-Higashi anomaly.* **developmental a.,** a defect which is the result of imperfect development of the embryo. **Ebstein's a.,** a malformation of the tricuspid valve, the septal and posterior leaflets being attached at the apex of the right ventricle and the anterior leaflet being normally attached to the anulus fibrosis; usually associated with an atrial septal defect. **Freund's a.,** stenosis of the upper thoracic aperture from shortening of the first rib, resulting in deficient expansion of the apex of the lung. **May-Hegglin a.,** a hereditary disorder of blood cell morphology, consisting of large, poorly granulated platelets and cytoplasmic collections of ribonucleic acid in the polymorphonuclear leukocytes, without associated distinguishing clinical features; transmitted as an autosomal dominant. **Pelger's nuclear a.** 1. A hereditary anomaly in the form of the nuclei of the leukocytes. The segmentation of the neutrophils does not exceed two segments, and numerous staff cells appear. The nucleus of all segmented cells has the same well-rounded pear-shaped outline. The nuclear structure is coarse and lumpy. Called also *Pelger-Huët anomaly.* 2. An acquired condition with changes similar to those observed in the genetically determined abnormality, occurring in certain types of anemia and leukemia.

anomia (ah-no′me-ah) [*an* neg. + Gr. *anoma* name + *-ia*]. Loss of the power of naming objects or of recognizing and recalling their names.

Anona (ah-no′nah). A genus of trees and shrubs of tropical America: the bark, fruit, and leaves of various species are used in native medicine, and the seeds are poisonous for fish and insects.

anonacein (an″o-na′se-in). An alkaloid of *Hylopia aethiopica*, an African aphrodisiac.

anonaine (an″o-na′in). An alkaloid, $C_{17}H_{17}O_3N$, from *Anona reticulata*.

anoneme (an′o-nēm″) [Gr. *anō* upward + *nēma* a thread]. A delicate filament from kinetoplast to cell wall, as observed in *Leishmania donovani*.

anonychia (an″o-nik′e-ah) [*an* neg. + Gr. *onyx* nail + *-ia*]. Congenital absence of a nail or nails.

anonymous (ah-non′ĭ-mus). Nameless; innominate.

anoopsia (an″o-op′se-ah) [Gr. *anō* upward + *opsis* vision + *-ia*]. Hypertropia.

anoperineal (a″no-per-ĭ-ne′al). Pertaining to the anus and perineum.

Anopheles (ah-nof′ĕ-lēz) [Gr. *anōphelēs* hurtful]. A genus of mosquitoes characterized by long slender palpi, nearly as long as the beak, and by holding the body at an angle with the surface on which it rests while the head and beak are in line with the body, whose members are the hosts of malarial parasites, their bite being the means of transmitting malaria. Some species are vectors of *Wuchereria bancrofti*.

CHIEF MALARIA-CARRYING ANOPHELES SPECIES OF THE WORLD

Modified from Russell et al., *Practical Malariology*.

A. aconitus	*A. maculatus maculatus*
A. albimanus	*A. maculipennis freeborni*
A. albitarsis	*A. mangyanus*
A. amictus	*A. messeae*
A. annularis	*A. minimus*
A. annulipes annulipes	*A. minimus flavirostris*
A. aquasalis	*A. moucheti moucheti*
A. bancroftii	*A. moucheti nigeriensis*
A. barbirostris barbirostris	*A. multicolor*
A. bellator	*A. nili*
A. claviger	*A. pattoni*
A. culicifacies	*A. pharoensis*
A. darlingi	*A. philippinensis*
A. farauti	*A. pretoriensis*
A. fluviatilis	*A. pseudopunctipennis pseudopunctipennis*
A. funestus	*A. punctimacula*
A. gambiae	*A. punctulatus punctulatus*
A. hancocki	*A. quadrimaculatus*
A. hargreavesi	*A. sacharovi*
A. hyrcanus nigerrimus	*A. sergentii*
A. hyrcanus sinensis	*A. stephensi stephensi*
A. jeyporiensis candidiensis	*A. subpictus subpictus*
A. jeyporiensis jeyporiensis	*A. sundaicus*
A. kochi	*A. superpictus*
A. labranchiae atroparvus	*A. umbrosus*
A. labranchiae labranchiae	*A. varuna*
A. leucosphyrus leucosphyrus	
A. lungae	

anophelicide (ah-nof′ĕ-lĭ-sīd″) [*anopheles* + L. *caedere* to kill]. Destructive to anopheles mosquitoes.

anophelifuge (ah-nof′ĕ-lĭ-fūj) [*anopheles* + L. *fugare* to put to flight]. Preventing the bite or attack of anopheles mosquitoes.

anopheline (ah-nof′ĭ-līn). 1. Pertaining to or caused by mosquitoes of the tribe Anophelini. 2. An agent that is destructive to Anopheles mosquitoes.

Anophelini (ah-nof″ĭ-li′ni). A tribe of the *Culicidae,* or mosquitoes, including several genera whose members act as carriers of the malarial parasite.

anophelism (ah-nof′ĕ-lizm). Infestation of a district with anopheles.

anophoria (an-o-fo′re-ah) [Gr. *anō* upward + Gr. *pherein* to bear]. See *anotropia*.

anophthalmia (an″of-thal′me-ah) [*an* neg. + Gr. *ophthalmos* eye]. A developmental defect characterized by absence of the eyes.

anophthalmos (an″of-thal′mos). Anophthalmia.

anophthalmus (an″of-thal′mus). An individual exhibiting anophthalmia.

anopia (an-o′pe-ah) [*an* neg. + Gr. *ōpē* sight + *-ia*]. 1. Absence or rudimentary condition of the eye. 2. Anopsia. 3. Hypertropia.

anoplasty (a′no-plas″te) [L. *anus* anus + Gr. *plassein* to form]. A plastic or restorative operation on the anus.

Anoplocephala (an″op-lo-sef′ah-lah) [Gr. *anoplos* unarmed + Gr. *kephalē* head]. A genus of tapeworms found in horses.

Anoplura (an″o-plu′rah) [Gr. *anoplos* unarmed + *oura* tail]. An order of insects, the sucking lice, characterized by the absence of wings. It includes only two genera of medical interest, *Pediculus* and *Phthirus*. Cf. *Mallophaga*.

anopsia (an-op′se-ah). [*an-* neg. + Gr. *opsis* vision + *-ia*]. 1. Nonuse of or suppression of vision in one eye, as in heterotropia. 2. Hypertropia.

anorchia (an-or′ke-ah). Anorchism.

anorchid (an-or′kid) [*an* neg. + Gr. *orchis* testis]. An individual with no testes in the scrotum.

anorchidic (an″or-kid′ik). Pertaining to anorchism; having no testes in the scrotum.

anorchidism (an-or′kĭ-dizm″). Anorchism.

anorchis (an-or′kis). Anorchid.

anorchism (an-or′kizm). Congenital absence of the testis, which may occur unilaterally or bilaterally.

anorectal (a″no-rek′tal). Pertaining to the anus and rectum.

anorectic (an″o-rek′tik) [Gr. *anorektos* without appetite for]. 1. Pertaining to anorexia; having no appetite. 2. A substance which diminishes the appetite.

anorectocolonic (a″no-rek″to-ko-lon′ik). Pertaining to the anus, rectum, and colon.

anorectum (a″no-rek′tum) [*anus* + *rectum*]. The anus and rectum considered as a single continuous structure.

anoretic (an″o-ret′ik). Anorectic.

anorexia (an″o-rek′se-ah) [Gr. "want of appetite"]. Lack or loss of the appetite for food. **a. nervo′sa,** a serious nervous condition in which the patient loses his appetite and systematically takes but little food, so that he becomes greatly emaciated.

anorexiant (an″o-rek′se-ant). Anorexigenic.

anorexic (an″o-rek′sik). Anorectic.

anorexigenic (an″o-rek″sĭ-jen′ik) [*anorexia* + Gr. *gennan* to produce]. 1. Producing anorexia, or diminishing the appetite. 2. An agent that produces anorexia, or controls the appetite.

anorganology (an″or-gan-ol′o-je). The study of nonliving things; abiology.

anorgasmy (an-or-gaz′me) [*an* neg. + *orgasm*]. Failure to experience orgasm in coitus.

anorthography (an″or-thog′rah-fe) [*an* neg. + Gr. *orthos* straight + *graphein* to write]. Loss of the power of writing correctly.

anorthopia (an″or-tho′pe-ah) [*an* neg. + Gr. *orthos* straight + *opsis* vision + *-ia*]. Distorted vision.

anorthoscope (an-or′tho-skōp″) [*an* neg. + Gr. *orthos* straight + *skopein* to examine]. An instrument for combining two disconnected pictures in one perfect visual image.

anorthosis (an″or-tho′sis) [*an* neg. + Gr. *orthos* straight + *-osis*]. Absence of erectility.

anoscope (a′no-skōp) [*anus* + Gr. *skopein* to examine]. A speculum for examining the anus and lower rectum. **Bacon's a.,** a self-retaining instrument with an electric light in the head of a detachable handle and a slit in the opposite side, providing adequate visualization and illumination for examination and treatment of the anorectal area.

anoscopy (ah-nos′ko-pe). Examination of the anus and lower rectum by means of an anoscope.

anosigmoidoscopic (a″no-sig-moi″do-skop′ik). Pertaining to anosigmoidoscopy.

anosigmoidoscopy (a″no-sig″moi-dos′ko-pe) [*anus* + *sigmoid* + Gr. *skopein* to examine]. Visual examination of the anus and sigmoid by means of a speculum.

anosmatic (an″oz-mat′ik) [*an* neg. + Gr. *osmasthai* to smell]. Having no sense of smell, or only an imperfect sense of smell.

anosmia (an-oz′me-ah) [*an* neg. + Gr. *osmē* smell + *-ia*]. Absence of the sense of smell. **a. gusta-to′ria,** the loss of the power to smell foods which are being eaten. **preferential a.,** lack of ability to sense certain odors only. **a. respirato′-ria,** loss of smell due to nasal obstruction.

anosmic (an-oz′mik). 1. Pertaining to or characterized by anosmia. 2. Odorless.

anosodiaphoria (an-o″so-di-ah-fo′re-ah) [*a* neg. + Gr. *nosos* disease + *diaphoria* difference]. Indifference to the existence of disease.

anosognosia (an-o″so-no′se-ah) [*a* neg. + Gr. *nosos* disease + *gnosis* knowledge + *-ia*]. Loss of ability in a person to recognize that he has a disease or bodily defect.

anosphrasia (an″os-fra′ze-ah) [*an* neg. + Gr. *osphrasis* sense of smell]. Anosmia.

anospinal (a″no-spi′nal). Pertaining to the anus and the spinal cord.

anosteoplasia (an-os″te-o-pla′se-ah) [*an* neg. + Gr. *osteon* bone + *plasis* formation + *-ia*]. Defective bone formation.

anostosis (an″os-to′sis) [*an* neg. + Gr. *osteon* bone + *-osis*]. Defective development of bone.

anotia (an-o′she-ah) [*an* neg. + Gr. *ous* ear + *-ia*]. Congenital absence of the external ears.

anotropia (an″o-tro′pe-ah) [Gr. *anō* upward + *trepein* to turn]. A condition in which the visual axes tend to rise above the object looked at: called also *anophoria*.

anotus (an-o′tus) [*an* neg. + Gr. *ous* ear]. An earless fetus.

anovaginal (a″no-vaj′ĭ-nal). Pertaining to the anus and vagina, or communicating with the anal canal and vagina, as an anovaginal fistula.

anovaria (an″o-va′re-ah). Anovarism.

anovarism (an-o′var-izm) [*an* neg. + *ovary*]. Absence of the ovaries.

anovesical (a″no-ves′ĭ-kal) [L. *anus* fundament + *vesica* bladder]. Pertaining to the anus and urinary bladder.

anovular (an-ov′u-lar). Not accompanied with the discharge of an ovum.

anovulation (an″ov-u-la′shun). Suspension or cessation of ovulation.

anovulatory (an-ov′u-lah-to″re). Anovular.

anovulia (an″ov-u′le-ah). Anovulation.

anovulomenorrhea (an-ov″u-lo-men″o-re′ah). Anovular menstruation.

anoxemia (an-ok-se′me-ah) [*an* neg. + *oxygen* + Gr. *haima* blood + *-ia*]. Reduction of oxygen content of the blood below physiologic levels.

anoxemic (an″ok-se′mik). Characterized by or due to a lack of the normal proportion of oxygen in the blood.

anoxia (an-ok′se-ah). Absence or lack of oxygen; reduction of oxygen in body tissues below physiologic levels. **altitude a.,** sickness in aviators due to anoxia during flying at high altitudes. **anemic a.,** anoxia resulting from decrease in amount of hemoglobin or number of erythrocytes in the blood. **anoxic a.,** anoxia resulting from interference with the source of oxygen. **fulminating a.,** a rapid fall in the O_2 content of the blood causing collapse and unconsciousness. **histotoxic a.,** anoxia resulting from disturbance in the cells that makes utilization of oxygen impossible. **a. neonato′rum,** anoxia of the newborn. **stagnant a.,** anoxia resulting from failure of the circulation to move blood through the vessels at a sufficient rate of speed.

anoxiate (an-ok′se-āt). To put into a state of anoxia.

anoxic (an-ok′sik). Pertaining to or characterized by anoxia.

anoxoluin (an″oks-ol′u-in). A substance, insoluble in glacial acetic acid, occurring in albumin, fibrin, casein, and globulin.

anoxolyin (an″oks-ol′e-in). Anoxoluin.

anoxybiontic (an-ok″se-bi-on′tik). Anaerobic.

anoxybiosis (an-ok″se-bi-o′sis) [*an* neg. + *oxygen* + Gr. *bios* life]. Anaerobiosis.

ansa (an′sah), pl. *an′sae* [L. "handle"]. A general term used in anatomical nomenclature to designate a looplike structure. Called also *loop*. **a. cervica′lis** [N A], a nerve loop in the neck attached in front and above to the hypoglossal nerve and behind to the upper cervical spinal nerves. Its hypoglossal attachment is misleading since this part of the loop ultimately rejoins the upper spinal nerves. It has a superior and an inferior root and a thyrohyoid branch. Called also *ansa hypoglossi* [B N A]. **Haller's a.,** ramus communicans nervi facialis cum nervi glossopharyngeo. **Henle's a.,** a. peduncularis. **a. hypoglos′si** [B N A], a. cervicalis. **a. of lenticular nucleus, a. lenticula′ris** [N A, B N A], a small fiber tract arising in the globus pallidus of the lenticular nucleus and extending around the medial border of the internal capsule to reach the anterior portion of the ventral thalamic nucleus. **an′sae nervo′rum spina′-lium** [N A, B N A], loops of nerve fibers joining the anterior spinal nerves. **a. peduncula′ris** [N A, B N A], a group of fiber bundles that bend around the posterior limb of the internal capsule. **a. of Reil, a. Rei′lii,** a. peduncularis. **an′sae sacra′les,** loops of nerve fibers joining the anterior sacral nerves. **a. subcla′via** [N A], nerve filaments that pass anterior and posterior to the subclavian artery to form a loop interconnecting the middle and inferior cervical ganglia. Called also *ansa of Vieussens*. **a. of Vieussens,** a. subclavia. **a. vitelli′na,** an embryonic vein from the yolk sac to the umbilical vein.

ansae (an′se) [L.]. Plural of *ansa*.

ansate (an′sāt) [L. *ansatus*, from *ansa* handle]. Having a handle; loop-shaped.

anserine (an′ser-in) [L. *anserinus*]. 1. Pertaining to or like a goose. 2. A basic substance, beta-alanyl-methyl-histidine, occurring in goose muscle.

ansiform (an′sĭ-form). Loop-shaped.

ansolysen (an″so-li′sen). Trade mark for preparations of pentolinium.

ansotomy (an-sot′o-me) [*ansa* + *-tomy*]. Cutting of the ansa lenticularis, used particularly for treatment of tremor in paralysis agitans and parkinsonism.

Anstie's limit, reagent, rule, test (an′stēz) [Francis Edmund *Anstie*, English physician, 1833–1874]. See under *reagent*, *rule*, and *tests*.

ant-. See *anti-*.

antabuse (an′tah-būs″). Trade mark for a preparation of disulfiram.

antacid (ant-as′id) [*ant-* + L. *acidus* sour]. 1. Correcting acidity. 2. A substance that counteracts or neutralizes acidity.

antagonism (an-tag′o-nizm″) [Gr. *antagōnisma* struggle]. Opposition or contrariety, as between muscles, medicines, or organisms. Cf. *antibiosis*. **bacterial a.,** the antagonistic (inhibiting) effect of one bacterial organism on another, as of the colon bacillus on the bacilli of anthrax and typhoid or streptococcus. **induced bacterial a.,** the interaction between two bacteria, induced by close association, which results in antagonism between them.

antagonist (an-tag′o-nist) [Gr. *antagōnistēs* an opponent]. 1. A muscle that acts in opposition to the action of another muscle, its agonist. 2. An agent that tends to nullify the action of another agent. 3. A tooth in one jaw that articulates with a tooth in the other jaw. **associated a's,** muscles that act on different parts, and by their combined actions move the parts in parallel directions. **competitive a.,** a substance that competes with another for a material which is essential for its usual metabolic activity. See *antimetabolite.* **direct a's,** muscles that act on the same part, and by their combined actions keep the part at rest. **enzyme a.,** a substance that interferes with the normal action of an enzyme. See *antimetabolite.* **insulin a.,** a low-molecular weight compound, attached to serum albumin and circulating in the blood, which blocks the action of insulin. **metabolic a.,** a substance that interferes with the utilization of another substance essential in metabolism. See *antimetabolite.* **sulfonamide a.,** para-aminobenzoic acid.

antalgesic (ant-al-je′zik). Analgesic.

antalgic (ant-al′jik). Analgesic.

antalkaline (ant-al′kah-līn″) [*ant-* + *alkali*]. 1. Neutralizing alkalinity. 2. An agent that neutralizes the alkalis.

antaphrodisiac (ant″af-ro-diz′e-ak). 1. Abrogating the sexual instinct. 2. An agent that allays sexual impulses.

antapoplectic (ant″ap-o-plek′tik) [*ant-* + Gr. *apoplēxia* apoplexy]. 1. Alleviating apoplexy. 2. An agent for alleviating apoplexy.

antarthritic (ant″ar-thrit′ik) [*ant-* + Gr. *arthritikos* gouty]. 1. Alleviating arthritis. 2. An agent that alleviates arthritis.

antasthenic (ant″as-then′ik) [*ant-* + Gr. *astheneia* weakness]. 1. Alleviating weakness, or restoring strength. 2. An agent that alleviates weakness and restores strength.

antasthmatic (ant″az-mat′ik) [*ant-* + Gr. *asthma* asthma]. 1. Affording relief in asthma. 2. An agent that relieves the spasm of asthma.

antatrophic (ant″ah-trof′ik). Correcting or opposing the progress of atrophy.

antazoline (ant-az′o-lēn). Chemical name: 2-(N-benzylanilinomethyl)-2-imidazoline. Use: antihistaminic.

ante- (an′te) [L. *ante* before]. A prefix signifying "before" in time or place.

antebrachium (an″te-bra′ke-um) [*ante-* + L. *brachium* arm]. [N A] The part of the upper member of the body, between the elbow and the wrist. Called also *antibrachium* [B N A], and *forearm.*

antecardium (an-te-kar′de-um). Epigastrium.

antecedent (an″te-ce′dent) [L. *antecedere* to go before, precede]. A precursor. **plasma thromboplastin a.,** factor XI. See under *coagulation factors.*

ante cibum (an′te si′bum) [L.]. Before meals.

antecornu (an″te-kor′nu). The anterior cornu of a lateral ventricle of the brain.

antecubital (an″te-ku′bĭ-tal). Situated in front of the cubitus or forearm.

antecurvature (an″te-kur′vah-tūr″) [*ante-* + L. *curvatura* bend]. A slight anteflexion.

antefebrile (an″te-feb′rīl) [*ante-* + L. *febris* fever]. Before the onset of fever.

anteflect (an′te-flekt). To bend forward.

anteflexed. In a condition of anteflexion.

anteflexio (an″te-flek′se-o) [L.]. Anteflexion. **a. u′teri,** anteflexion, def. 2.

anteflexion (an-te-flek′shun) [*ante-* + L. *flexio* bend]. 1. An abnormal forward curvature; a form of displacement in which the upper part of the organ is bent forward. 2. The normal forward curvature of the uterus.

antegrade (an′te-grād). Anterograde.

antehypophysis (an″te-hi-pof′ĭ-sis). The anterior lobe of the hypophysis or pituitary body.

antelocation (an″te-lo-ka′shun) [*ante-* + L. *locatio* placement]. The forward displacement of an organ.

antemetic (ant″e-met′ik). Antiemetic.

ante mortem (an′te mor′tem) [L.]. Before death.

antenatal (an″te-na′tal) [*ante-* + L. *natus* born]. Occurring or formed before birth.

antenna (an-ten′ah), pl. *anten′nae.* A feeler of an arthropod; one of the two lateral appendages on the anterior segment of the head of arthropods.

antepar (an′te-par). Trade mark for a preparation of piperazine citrate and piperazine phosphate.

antepartal (an″te-par′tal). Occurring before parturition, or childbirth.

ante partum (an′te par′tum) [L.]. Before parturition, or childbirth.

antepartum (an″te-par′tum) [L.]. Antepartal.

antephase (an′te-fāz). The portion of interphase immediately preceding mitosis, when energy is being produced and stored for mitosis and chromosome reproduction is taking place.

antephialtic (ant″ef-e-al′tik) [*ant-* + Gr. *ephialtēs* nightmare]. Good against or preventing nightmare.

anteposition (an″te-po-zish′un). Forward displacement, as of the uterus.

anteprostate (an″te-pros′tāt) [*ante-* + *prostate*]. One of Cowper's glands.

anteprostatitis (an″te-pros-tah-ti′tis). Inflammation of Cowper's glands.

antepyretic (an″te-pi-ret′ik) [*ante-* + *pyretic*]. Occurring before the stage of fever.

antergan (ant′er-gan). A proprietary antihistamine compound, dimethyl-amino-ethyl benzylaniline.

antergia (ant-er′je-ah) [*ant-* + Gr. *ergon* work]. Antagonism; resistance.

antergic (ant-er′jik). Working in opposite directions: a term applied to antagonistic muscles.

antergy (ant′er-je). Antergia.

anteriad (an-te′re-ad). Toward the anterior surface of the body.

anterior (an-te′re-or). Situated in front of or in the forward part of, affecting the forward part of an organ, toward the head end of the body; in official anatomical nomenclature, used in reference to the ventral or belly surface of the body.

antero- [L. *anterior* before]. A prefix signifying "before."

anteroclusion (an″ter-o-kloo′zhun). A malrelation of the dental arches in which the mandibular arch is in an anterior position in relation to the maxillary arch.

antero-external (an″ter-o-eks-ter′nal). Situated on the front and to the outer side.

anterograde (an′ter-o-grād″) [*antero-* + L. *gredi* to go]. Moving or extending forward.

antero-inferior (an″ter-o-in-fe′re-or). Situated in front and below.

antero-internal (an″ter-o-in-ter′nal). Situated on the front and to the inner side.

anterolateral (an″ter-o-lat′er-al). Situated in front and to one side.

anteromedian (an″ter-o-me′de-an). Situated in front and on the median line.

anteron (an′ter-on). A proprietary gonadotropic extract from pregnant mare serum.

anteroposterior (an″ter-o-pos-te′re-or). From front to back, or from the anterior (ventral) to the posterior (dorsal) surface; in roentgenology, it denotes the direction of the beam, from the x-ray source to the beam exit surface.

anterosuperior (an″ter-o-su-pe′re-or). Situated in front and above.

anterotic (ant″e-rot′ik). Antaphrodisiac.

anteroventral (an″ter-o-ven′tral). Situated in front and toward the ventral surface.

anteversion (an″te-ver′zhun) [*ante-* + L. *versio* a turning]. The forward tipping or tilting of an organ; displacement in which the organ is tipped forward, but is not bent at an angle, as occurs in anteflexion.

anteverted (an″te-vert′ed). Tipped or bent forward.

antexed (an-tekst′). Bent forward.

antexion (an-tek′shun). An abnormal forward bending, as of the spine.

anthelix (ant′he-liks) [*ant-* + Gr. *helix* coil]. [N A, B N A] The prominent semicircular ridge seen on the lateral aspect of the auricle of the external ear, anteroinferior to the helix.

anthelminthic (ant″hel-min′thik). Anthelmintic.

anthelmintic (ant″hel-min′tik) [*ant-* + Gr. *helmins* worm]. 1. Destructive to worms. 2. An agent that is destructive to worms.

anthelone (ant-he′lōn) [*ant-* + Gr. *helkos* ulcer]. Urogastrone.

anthelotic (ant″he-lot′ik) [*ant-* + Gr. *hēlos* nail]. 1. Effective against corns. 2. A remedy for corns.

anthema (an′the-mah). An exanthem; a skin eruption.

Anthemis (an′the-mis) [L.; Gr. *anthemis*]. 1. A genus of composite-flowered plants. 2. The flower heads of *A. nobilis*, or common camomile: tonic and febrifuge, and used in coughs, spasmodic conditions in infants, and as a stomachic tonic.

anthemorrhagic (ant″hem-o-raj′ik) [*ant-* + *hemorrhage*]. Antihemorrhagic.

anther (an′ther) [Gr. *anthēros* blooming]. The male sexual organ in a flowering plant; it is the portion of the stamen which contains the pollen sacs.

antheridium (an″ther-id′e-um). The male organ of a cryptogamic plant taking part in the formation of sexually produced spores. Cf. *archegonium*.

antherozoid (an′ther-o-zoid″). The motile fertilizing cell of fungi.

antherpetic (ant″her-pet′ik). Curing or preventing herpes.

anthiomaline (an″the-o-mal′in). A proprietary name for antimony sodium thiomalate, $[Li.O.CO.CH_2.CH(S).CO.OLi]_3Sb.9H_2O$. It is a powerful anthelmintic for schistosomiasis and is used in lymphogranuloma venereum.

anthocyanidin (an″tho-si-an′ĭ-din). Any one of a group of compounds occurring in the coloring matter of flowers.

anthocyanin (an″tho-si′ah-nin). Any one of a class of pigments of blue, red and violet flowers. They are glycosides, yielding anthocyanidin and a sugar on hydrolysis.

anthocyaninemia (an″tho-si″ah-nin-e′me-ah). The presence of anthocyanin in the blood.

anthocyaninuria (an″tho-si″ah-nin-u′re-ah). The presence of anthocyanin in the urine.

Anthomyia (an″tho-mi′yah). A genus of small black houseflies, the larvae of which sometimes infest the intestine of man. Species found in the stools include *A. canicularis*, *A. incisura*, *A. manicata*, *A. saltatrix*, *A. scalaris*.

Anthomyiidae (an″tho-mi-i′id-e) [Gr. *anthos* flower + *myia* fly]. A systematic family of flies which sometimes infest man. It includes three genera: *Fannia*, *Hylemyia*, and *Hydrotea*.

anthophobia (an″tho-fo′be-ah) [Gr. *anthos* flower + *phobia*]. A morbid dislike or dread of flowers.

anthorisma (an″tho-riz′mah) [*ant-* + Gr. *horisma* boundary]. A diffuse swelling.

anthormon (an-thor′mōn). Colyone.

anthracemia (an″thrah-se′me-ah) [Gr. *anthrax* coal + *haima* blood + *-ia*]. 1. Asphyxia from carbon monoxide poisoning. 2. The presence of *Bacil′lus anthra′cis* in the blood.

anthracene (an′thrah-sen). 1. A colorless crystalline hydrocarbon, $C_{14}H_{10}[C_6H_4(CH)_2C_6H_4]$, from coal tar: used in the manufacture of anthracene dyes. It is slightly soluble in ether and alcohol, and freely soluble in hot vinegar. 2. A ptomaine obtained from cultures of the bacillus of anthrax.

anthracia (an-thra′she-ah) [L. *anthrax* carbuncle]. A diseased condition characterized by the formation of carbuncles.

anthracic (an-thras′ik). Pertaining to or resembling anthrax.

anthracidal (an″thrah-si′dal). Destructive to *Bacillus anthracis*.

anthracin (an′thrah-sin). A poisonous ptomaine from anthrax cultures.

anthraco- (an′thrah-ko) [Gr. *anthrax* coal]. Combining form denoting relationship to coal or to a carbuncle; also to carbon dioxide.

anthracoid (an′thrah-koid) [*anthraco-* + Gr. *eidos* form]. Resembling anthrax or a carbuncle.

anthracometer (an″thrah-kom′e-ter) [*anthraco-* + Gr. *metron* measure]. An instrument for measuring the carbon dioxide of the air.

anthracomucin (an″thrah-ko-mu′sin). A protective substance against anthrax existing in the tissues.

anthraconecrosis (an″thrah-ko-nĕ-kro′sis) [*anthraco-* + Gr. *nekrōsis* death]. Necrotic transformation of a tissue into a black, dry mass.

anthracosilicosis (an″thrah-ko-sil″ĭ-ko′sis) [*anthraco-* + *silicon*]. A mixed condition of anthracosis and silicosis.

anthracosis (an-thrah-ko′sis) [*anthraco-* + *-osis*]. A form of pneumoconiosis caused by the inhalation of coal dust, thus causing the lungs and the regional lymph glands to become dark or even black in color. **a. lin′guae,** black tongue.

anthracotherapy (an″thrah-ko-ther′ah-pe) [Gr. *anthrax* coal + *therapy*]. Treatment with charcoal.

anthracotic (an″thrah-kot′ik). Pertaining to or affected with anthracosis.

anthragallol (an″thrah-gal′ol). A product of the interaction of gallic, benzoic, and sulfuric acids, $C_{14}H_8O_5$.

anthralin (an′thrah-lin). A compound, 1,8,9-anthratriol, used externally in the treatment of psoriasis and chronic dermatoses.

anthramucin (an″thrah-mu′sin). A capsular substance from *Bacillus anthracis*, which is capable of neutralizing the anthracidal substance of the host.

anthraquinone (an″thrah-kwin′ōn). A yellow substance, $C_6H_4(CO)_2C_6H_4$, from anthracene.

anthrarobin (an″thrah-ro′bin) [*anthracene* + *araroba*]. A yellowish-white powder from alizarin, $C_6H_4{:}C(OH).CH{:}C_6H_2(OH)_2$. It is useful in psoriasis and various skin diseases in 10 to 20 per cent ointment.

anthrax (an′thraks) [Gr. *anthrax* coal, carbuncle]. 1. A carbuncle or other infection caused by the anthrax bacillus. 2. Malignant anthrax. **cerebral a.,** anthrax in which the bacilli invade the brain. **emphysematous a.,** symptomatic anthrax. **intestinal a.,** a severe form of anthrax in which the intestine is affected. **malignant a.,** a fatal infectious disease of cattle and sheep, due to *Bacillus anthracis* and characterized by the formation of hard edema or ulcers at the point of inoculation and by symptoms of collapse. It may occur in man. Called also *contagious anthrax*, *splenic fever*, *woolsorters' disease*, *ragsorters' disease*, *malignant pustule*, *milzbrand*, and *charbon*. **pulmonary a.** Same as *woolsorters' disease*. **symptomatic a.,** a disease of sheep, cattle, and goats, characterized by emphysematous and subcutaneous swellings and nodules and

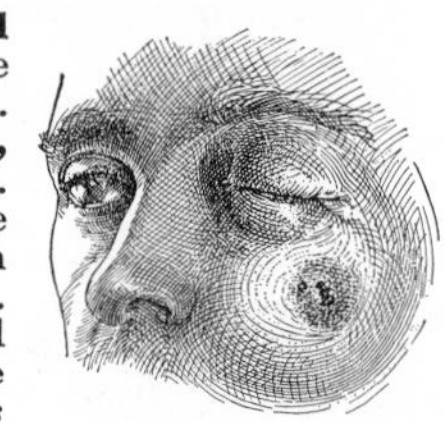

Anthrax: showing the malignant pustule (Homans).

caused by *Clostridium chauvoei*. Called also *black-leg, quarter evil, black quarter, black spaul, rausch-brand,* and *bloody murrain.*

anthropo- (an′thro-po) [Gr. *anthrōpos* man]. Combining form denoting a relationship to man, or to a human being.

anthropobiology (an″thro-po-bi-ol′o-je). The biological study of man and the anthropoid apes.

anthropocentric (an″thro-po-sen′trik) [*anthropo-* + Gr. *kentrikos* of or from the center]. With a human bias; considering man the center of the universe.

anthropocracy (an″thro-pok′rah-se) [*anthropo-* + Gr. *kratein* to rule]. The tendency in therapeutics to actively interfere in the course of disease. Cf. *physiocracy.*

anthropogeny (an″thro-poj′ĕ-ne) [*anthropo-* + Gr. *gennan* to produce]. The evolution and development of man.

anthropography (an″thro-pog′rah-fe) [*anthropo-* + Gr. *graphein* to write]. That branch of anthropology which deals with the distribution of the varieties of man, as distinguished by physical character, institutions, customs, etc. Cf. *ethnography.*

anthropoid (an′thro-poid) [*anthropo-* + Gr. *eidos* form]. Resembling man. The anthropoid apes are the tailless apes, including chimpanzee, gibbon, gorilla, and orang-utan.

Anthropoidea (an″thro-poi′de-ah). A suborder of *Primates,* including the monkeys, apes, and man.

anthropokinetics (an″thro-po-ki-net′iks) [*anthropo-* + Gr. *kinētikos* for putting in motion]. The study of the total human being in action, with integrated applications from the special fields of the biological and physical sciences, psychology, and sociology.

anthropology (an″thro-pol′o-je) [*anthropo-* + *-ology*]. The science that treats of man. **criminal a.,** that branch of anthropology which treats of criminals and crimes. **cultural a.,** that branch of anthropology which treats of man in relation to his fellows and to his environment. **physical a.,** that branch of anthropology which treats of the physical characteristics of man.

anthropometer (an″thro-pom′e-ter). An instrument especially designed for measuring various dimensions of the body.

anthropometric (an″thro-po-met′rik). Pertaining to or connected with anthropometry.

anthropometrist (an″thro-pom′ĕ-trist). A person skilled in anthropometry.

anthropometry (an″thro-pom′e-tre) [*anthropo-* + Gr. *metron* measure]. The science which deals with the measurement of the size, weight, and proportions of the human body.

anthropomorphism (an″thro-po-mor′fizm) [*anthropo-* + Gr. *morphē* form]. The attribution of human form or character to nonhuman objects.

anthroponomy (an″thro-pon′o-me) [*anthropo-* + Gr. *nomos* law]. The science that deals with the laws of human development in relation to environment and to other organisms.

anthropopathy (an″thro-pop′ah-the) [*anthropo-* + Gr. *pathos* suffering]. The ascription of human emotions to nonhuman subjects.

anthropophagy (an″thro-pof′ah-je) [*anthropo-* + Gr. *phagein* to eat]. 1. Cannibalism. 2. A sexual perversion with cannibalistic tendencies.

anthropophilic (an″thro-po-fil′ik) [*anthropo-* + Gr. *philein* to love]. Preferring human beings to other animals: said of certain mosquitoes. Cf. *zoophilic.*

anthropophobia (an″thro-po-fo′be-ah) [*anthropo-* + *phobia*]. Morbid dread of human society.

anthroposcopy (an″thro-pos′ko-pe) [*anthropo-* + Gr. *skopein* to examine]. The judging of the type of body build by inspection rather than by anthropometry.

anthroposomatology (an″thro-po″so-mah-tol′o-je) [*anthropo-* + Gr. *sōma* body + *-logy*]. The sum of knowledge regarding the human body.

anthroposophy (an″thro-pos′o-fe) [*anthropo-* + Gr. *sophos* wise]. Knowledge of the nature of man.

anthropotomy (an″thro-pot′o-me) [*anthropo-* + Gr. *tomē* cut]. Human anatomy.

anthropotoxin (an″thro-po-tok′sin) [*anthropo-* + *toxin*]. A poison said to be excreted by the human lungs.

anthropozoonosis (an″thro-po-zo″o-no′sis), pl. *anthropozoonoses* [*anthropo-* + *zoonosis*]. A disease of either animals or man that may be transmitted from one species to the other.

anthropozoophilic (an″thro-po-zo″o-fil′ik) [*anthropo-* + Gr. *zōon* animal + *philein* to love]. Attracted to both human beings and animals: said of certain mosquitoes. Cf. *anthropophilic* and *zoophilic.*

anthydropic (ant″hi-drop′ik). Antihydropic.

anthypnotic (ant″hip-not′ik). Antihypnotic.

anthysteric (ant″his-ter′ik). Antihysteric.

anti-, ant- [Gr. *anti* against]. A prefix signifying against or over against.

antiabortifacient (an″tĭ-ah-bor″ti-fa′shent). 1. Preventing abortion or promoting gestation. 2. An agent that prevents abortion or promotes successful gestation.

antiabortus (an″tĭ-ah-bor′tus). Neutralizing or destructive to *Brucella abortus.*

antiabric (an″tĭ-a′brik). Resisting the poisonous effects of abrin.

antiabrin (an″tĭ-a′brin). An antitoxin produced in response to the injection of abrin.

anti-achromotrichia (an″tĭ-ah-kro″mo-trik′e-ah). Opposed to the graying of hair; anticanitic.

antiaditis (an″tĭ-ah-di′tis) [Gr. *antias* tonsil + *-itis*]. Inflammation of the tonsils.

antiaerogenic (an″tĭ-a″er-o-jen′ik). Suppressing the production of gas, as by an aerogenic bacterium.

antiagglutinating (an″tĭ-ah-gloo′ti-nāt″ing). Preventing agglutination.

antiagglutinin (an″tĭ-ah-gloo′tĭ-nin). A substance that opposes the action of an agglutinin.

antiaggressin (an″tĭ-ah-gres′in). A substance formed in the body by repeated injection of an aggressin, and tending to oppose the action of the aggressin.

antialbumate (an″tĭ-al′bu-māt) [*anti-* + *albumin*]. Parapeptone; a product of the incomplete digestion of albumin. It resists digestion by pepsin, but is digested by trypsin, the pancreatic ferment changing it into antipeptone.

antialbumide (an″tĭ-al′bu-mid). Antialbumate.

antialbumin (an″tĭ-al-bu′min). 1. A precipitin for albumin. 2. A constituent of albumin which is changed by gastric digestion into antialbumose.

antialbuminate (an″tĭ-al-bu′mĭ-nāt). Antialbumate.

antialbumose (an″tĭ-al′bu-mōs). One of the albumoses formed by the action of gastric digestion on albumin. It is converted into antipeptone during digestion.

antialexic (an″tĭ-ah-lek′sik). Opposing or counteracting an alexin.

antialexin (an″tĭ-ah-lek′sin). A substance which opposes the action of alexin.

antiamboceptor (an″tĭ-am′bo-sep″tor). A substance which opposes the action of an amboceptor. Called also *anti-immune body.*

antiamebic (an″tĭ-ah-me′bik). 1. Destroying or suppressing the growth of amebas. 2. An agent that destroys or suppresses the growth of amebas.

antiamylase (an″tĭ-am′ĭ-lās). A substance counteracting the action of amylase.

antianaphylactin (an″tĭ-an-ah-fi-lak′tin). An antibody which counteracts an anaphylactin.

antianaphylaxis (an″tĭ-an-ah-fi-lak′sis). A condition in which the anaphylaxis reaction is not obtained because of the presence of free antibodies in the blood; the state of desensitization to antigens. Called *anergy* and *desensitization*.

antianemic (an″tĭ-ah-ne′mik). 1. Counteracting or preventing anemia. 2. An agent that counteracts or prevents anemia.

antianopheline (an″tĭ-ah-nof′ĕ-lin). Directed against anopheline mosquitoes or their larvae.

antiantibody (an″tĭ-an′tĭ-bod″e). A substance formed in the body after the injection of an antibody and supposed to counteract the latter.

antiantidote (an″tĭ-an′tĭ-dōt″). A substance that counteracts the action of an antidote.

antiantienzyme (an″tĭ-an″tĭ-en′zīm). A supposed substance formed in the body to prevent the undue accumulation of antienzyme.

antiantitoxin (an″tĭ-an″tĭ-tok′sin). An antibody, formed in immunization with an antitoxin, which counteracts the effect of the latter.

antiapoplectic (an″tĭ-ap″o-plek′tik). Affording relief in or preventing apoplexy.

antiarachnolysin (an″tĭ-ar″ak-nol′ĭ-sin). A substance counteracting the poison of the spider.

antiarin (an-te′ar-in). A poisonous principle, $C_{14}H_{20}O_5 + 2H_2O$ from upas poison, *Antiaris toxicaria:* a heart depressant.

Antiaris (an″tĭ-a′ris) [Javanese *antiar*]. A genus of artocarpous trees. *A. toxicaria* is the upas tree of Java: exceedingly poisonous.

antiarrhythmic (an″tĭ-ah-rith′mik). 1. Preventing or alleviating cardiac arrhythmia. 2. An agent that prevents or alleviates cardiac arrhythmia.

antiarsenin (an″tĭ-ar′sĕ-nin). A nonarsenical substance developed in the body by immunizing doses of arsenous acid.

antiarthritic (an″tĭ-ar-thrit′ik). Antarthritic.

antiasthmatic (an″tĭ-az-mat′ik). Antasthmatic.

antiatherogenic (an″tĭ-ath″er-o-jen′ik). Combatting the formation of atheromatous lesions in arterial walls.

antiautolysin (an″tĭ-aw-tol′ĭ-sin). A substance which opposes the action of autolysin.

antibacterial (an″tĭ-bak-te′re-al). 1. Destroying or suppressing the growth or reproduction of bacteria. 2. A substance which destroys bacteria or suppresses their growth or reproduction.

antibacteriolytic (an″tĭ-bak-te″re-o-lit′ik). Counteracting bacteriolytic action.

antibechic (an″tĭ-bek′ik) [*anti-* + Gr. *bēx* cough]. 1. Relieving a cough. 2. An agent that relieves cough.

antibilious (an″tĭ-bil′yus). 1. Counteracting or relieving disorder of the biliary tract. 2. An agent that counteracts or relieves disorder of the biliary tract.

antibiont (an″tĭ-bi′ont). An antibiotic organism.

antibiosis (an″tĭ-bi-o′sis) [*anti-* + Gr. *bios* life]. Bacterial antagonism; an association between different organisms which is detrimental to one or both of them.

antibiotic (an″tĭ-bi-ot′ik) [*anti-* + Gr. *bios* life]. 1. Destructive of life. 2. A chemical substance produced by microorganisms which has the capacity, in dilute solutions, to inhibit the growth of or to destroy bacteria and other microorganisms: used largely in the treatment of infectious diseases of man, animals, and plants. **bactericidal a.,** one which kills bacteria. **bacteriostatic a.,** one which suppresses the growth or reproduction of bacteria. **broad-spectrum a.,** one which is effective against a wide range of bacteria. **oral a.,** one that is effective when administered orally.

antibiotin (an″tĭ-bi′o-tin). A compound which is antagonistic to biotin.

antiblastic (an″tĭ-blas′tik) [*anti-* + Gr. *blastos* germ]. Retarding growth or multiplication, as of tumor or bacterial cells.

antiblennorrhagic (an″tĭ-blen-o-raj′ik). Preventing or relieving gonorrhea.

antibody (an′tĭ-bod″e). A modified type of serum globulin synthesized by lymphoid tissue in response to antigenic stimulus, each differing haptenic structure of one antigen molecule being capable of inciting a distinct response. By virtue of two specific combining sites, each of which is complementary in structure to the inciting haptenic grouping, antibody molecules combine with antigen in vivo and in vitro. Antibodies are classified according to their behavior on electrophoresis, ultracentrifugation, and immunoelectrophoresis. They are also classified according to the mode of their observed action, as agglutinins, amboceptors, antienzymes, antitoxins, bacteriolysins, blood group antibodies, cytotoxins, hemolysins, opsonins, and precipitins. **anaphylactic a.,** a substance formed as a result of the first injection of a foreign protein and responsible for the anaphylactic symptoms following the second injection of the same protein. See *sensibilisin*. **blocking a.,** an antibody which possesses the same specificity as one from another source but which interferes with the action of the other because of dissimilar associated properties in regard to the expected mode of that action. **complete a.,** Wiener's term for the Rh antibody that is capable of directly agglutinating Rh-positive erythrocytes in physiologic saline and implying that the antibody is multivalent, that is, possesses two or more reactive groups. The definition may be extended to include a number of other globulins with similar agglutinating, but not necessarily type-specific, features. **despeciated a.,** an antibody that has been deprived of its species characteristics. **heterogenetic a.,** an antibody capable of reacting with antigens phylogenetically unrelated to the antigen that stimulated its production as well as with the homologous antigen. **heterophile a.,** an accessory antibody produced by the injection of a heterogenetic or heterophilic antigen. **incomplete a.,** a gamma globulin, originally described as a univalent antibody combining specifically with Rh-positive erythrocytes without causing visible agglutination but which, in the presence of antihuman globulin (Coombs) serum or high molecular weight media, e.g., albumin, will cause red cell clumping. Other red cell coating proteins, not group specific, may demonstrate similar properties. **inhibiting a.,** blocking a. **lipoidotropic a.,** the substance in the blood serum of syphilitics which combines with the (lipoidal) antigen to produce a positive Wassermann test. **neutralizing a.,** antibody that, on mixture with the homologous infectious agent (usually viral), reduces or destroys infectivity by partial or complete destruction of the viable agent. **protective a.,** antibody responsible for immunity to an infectious agent observed in passive immunity. **Rh a., rhesus a.** See *blood type*. **sensitizing a.,** a loosely used term, applied to antibodies that are attached to body cells and that "sensitize" the cells or render them susceptible to destruction by body defenses. **Vi a.,** an antibody produced by immunizing rabbits with cultures of highly virulent typhoid bacilli. It will agglutinate the virulent strain which is resistant to ordinary O antibodies.

antibrachium (an″tĭ-bra′ke-um). [B N A] Antebrachium.

antibromic (an″tĭ-bro′mik) [*anti-* + Gr. *brōmos* smell]. Deodorant: overcoming bad smells.

antibubonic (an″tĭ-bu-bon′ik). Effective against bubonic plague.

anticachectic (an″tĭ-kah-kek′tik). 1. Preventing or relieving cachexia. 2. An agent that prevents or relieves cachexia.

anticalculous (an″tĭ-kal′ku-lus). Effective against calculus.

anticanitic (an″tĭ-kah-nit′ik). Counteracting graying of the hair.

anticarcinogen (an″tĭ-kar-sin′o-jen). An agent that counteracts the effect of a carcinogen.

anticarcinogenic (an″tĭ-kar-sin″o-jen′ik). Inhibiting or preventing the development of carcinoma.

anticardium (an″tĭ-kar′de-um) [*anti-* + Gr. *kardia* heart]. The epigastrium.

anticariogenic (an″tĭ-kār″e-o-jen′ik). Effective in suppressing caries production.

anticarious (an″tĭ-ka′re-us). Anticariogenic.

anticatalase (an″tĭ-kat′ah-lās). An antibody having an antagonistic action on catalase.

anticatalyst (an″tĭ-kat′ah-list). A substance that retards the action of a catalyzer by acting on the catalyzer itself.

anticatalyzer (an″tĭ-kat′ah-līz″er). Anticatalyst.

anticataphylactic (an″tĭ-kat″ah-fi-lak′tik). 1. Pertaining to, characterized by, or causing anticataphylaxis. 2. An agent which inhibits cataphylaxis.

anticataphylaxis (an″tĭ-kat″ah-fi-lak′sis). Inhibition of cataphylaxis.

anticatarrhal (an″tĭ-kah-tar′al). Curing or relieving catarrh.

anticathexis (an″tĭ-kah-thek′sis) [*anti-* + *cathexis*]. Expression of an emotional impulse as an emotion of opposite character.

anticathode (an″tĭ-kath′ōd). The part of a vacuum tube opposite the cathode; the target.

anticephalalgic (an″tĭ-sef-ah-lal′jik). Curing or preventing headache.

anticheirotonus (an″tĭ-ki-rot′o-nus) [Gr. *anticheir* thumb + *tonos* tension]. Spasmodic inflection of the thumb.

antichlorotic (an″tĭ-klo-rot′ik). Effective against chlorosis.

anticholagogic (an″tĭ-ko″lah-goj′ik). Inhibiting the production of bile by the liver.

anticholagogue (an″tĭ-ko′lah-gog). An agent which inhibits the production of bile by the liver.

anticholerin (an″tĭ-kol′er-in) [*anti-* + Gr. *cholera* cholera]. A substance from cultures of the cholera vibrio: used against cholera.

anticholinergic (an″tĭ-ko″lin-er′jik) [*anti-* + *cholinergic*]. Blocking the passage of impulses through the parasympathetic nerves; parasympatholytic.

anticholinesterase (an″tĭ-ko-lin-es′ter-ās) [*anti-* + *cholinesterase*]. A substance which inhibits the action of cholinesterase.

antichoromanic (an″tĭ-ko″ro-ma′nik). Effective against dancing mania and spasms.

antichymosin (an″tĭ-ki′mo-sin). An antibody which prevents the action of chymosin on milk.

anticipate (an-tis′ĭ-pāt) [*ante-* + L. *capere* to take]. To occur or recur before the regular time.

anticipation (an-tis″ĭ-pa′shun). The onset of a hereditary disease at a progressively earlier age in successive generations, presumably owing to progressive degeneration of the germ plasm.

anticlinal (an″tĭ-kli′nal) [*anti-* + Gr. *klinein* to slope]. Sloping in opposite directions.

anticnemion (an″tik-ne′me-on) [*anti-* + Gr. *knēmē* leg]. The shin.

anticoagulant (an″tĭ-ko-ag′u-lant). 1. Serving to prevent the coagulation of blood. Any substance that, *in vivo* or *in vitro*, suppresses, delays, or nullifies coagulation of the blood. **Bridge a.,** a hypothetical substance, of theoretical interest, postulated as being present in certain hemophiliacs, and opposing the action of intrinsic thromboplastin, thus explaining their resistance to transfusional therapy. **circulating a.,** a substance present in the blood which inhibits normal blood clotting and causes a hemorrhagic syndrome; it may be directed against a specific coagulation factor and may accompany various hematologic and non-hematologic diseases.

anticoagulative (an″tĭ-ko-ag′u-la″tiv). Preventing or opposing coagulation.

anticoagulin (an″tĭ-ko-ag′u-lin). A substance that suppresses, delays, or nullifies the coagulation of blood.

anticolibacillary (an″tĭ-ko-le-bas′e-la″re). Effective against *Escherichia coli* or against diseases caused by that organism.

anticollagenase (an″tĭ-ko-laj′ĭ-nās). An antienzyme which neutralizes the activity of collagenase.

anticolloidoclastic (an″tĭ-kŏ-loi″do-klas′tik). Combating hemoclastic crises.

anticomplement (an″tĭ-kom′ple-ment). A substance that opposes or counteracts the action of a complement.

anticomplementary (an″tĭ-kom″ple-men′ta-re). Capable of reducing or destroying the power of a complement.

anticonceptive (an″tĭ-kon-sep′tiv). Contraceptive.

anticoncipiens (an″tĭ-kon-sip′e-enz). A contraceptive agent.

anticonvulsant (an″tĭ-kon-vul′sant). 1. Preventing or relieving convulsions. 2. An agent that prevents or relieves convulsions.

anticonvulsive (an″tĭ-kon-vul′siv). Preventing or relieving convulsions.

anticor (an′tĭ-kor). A swelling or slough in the neck of a horse, caused by irritation of the harness.

anticreatinine (an″tĭ-kre-at′ĭ-nin). A leukomaine of the creatinine group, derived from creatinine.

anticrisis (an″tĭ-kri′sis). Anything that interferes with the occurrence of a crisis.

anticritical (an″tĭ-krit′e-kal). Relieving or preventing a crisis.

anticrotin (an″tĭ-kro′tin). The antitoxin of crotin.

anticurare (an″tĭ-koo-rah′re). An agent that counteracts the action of curare on skeletal muscle.

anticus (an-ti′kus) [L.]. Anterior.

anticutin (an″tĭ-ku′tin) [*anti-* + *cutaneous reaction*]. An antibody in the blood of certain tuberculous persons which, when added to tuberculin, neutralizes the latter so that it will not produce the cutaneous reaction.

anticytolysin (an″tĭ-si-tol′ĭ-sin). A substance opposing the action of cytolysin.

anticytotoxin (an″tĭ-si″to-tok′sin). A substance that opposes the action of a cytotoxin.

antideoxyribonuclease (an″tĭ-de-ok″se-ri″bo-nu′kle-ās) [*anti-* + *deoxyribonuclease*]. A substance which inhibits the action of deoxyribonuclease.

antidepressant (an″tĭ-de-pres′sant). 1. Preventing or relieving depression. 2. An agent which stimulates the mood of a depressed patient.

antidiabetic (an″tĭ-di″ah-bet′ik). 1. Preventing or alleviating diabetes 2. An agent that prevents or alleviates diabetes.

antidiabetogenic (an″tĭ-di-ah-be″to-jen′ik). 1. Preventing the development of diabetes. 2. An agent that prevents the development of diabetes.

antidiarrheal (an″tĭ-di″ah-re′al). 1. Counteracting diarrhea. 2. An agent which is effective in combating diarrhea.

antidiarrheic (an″tĭ-di″ah-re′ik). Antidiarrheal.

antidiastase (an″tĭ-di′as-tās). A substance formed in the blood serum on the injection of a diastase which opposes action of the diastase.

antidinic (an″tĭ-din′ik) [*anti-* + Gr. *dinos* whirl]. Effective against vertigo.

antidiphtherin (an″tĭ-dif′ther-in) [*anti-* + *diphtheria*]. A derivative from cultures of the diphtheria bacillus.

antidiphtheritic (an″tĭ-dif″thĕ-rit′ik). Counteracting diphtheria.

antidipsia (an″tĭ-dip′se-ah) [*anti-* + Gr. *dipsa* thirst + *-ia*]. Aversion to the ingestion of fluids.

antidipticum (an″tĭ-dip′te-kum). An agent that lessens thirst.

antidiuresis (an″tĭ-di″u-re′sis). Suppression of the urinary secretion.

antidiuretic (an″tĭ-di″u-ret′ik). 1. Suppressing the secretion of urine. 2. An agent which suppresses urinary secretion.

antidotal (an″tĭ-do′tal). Serving as an antidote.

antidote (an′tĭ-dōt) [L. *antidotum*, from Gr. *anti* against + *didonai* to give]. A remedy for counteracting a poison. **a. against arsenic,** hydrated oxide of iron with magnesia. **Bibron's a.,** an antidote against snake bite: potassium iodide 0.24, mercury bichloride 0.12, bromine 20. **chemical a.,** an antidote that reacts chemically with a poison to form a harmless compound. **Fantus' a.,** an antidote for mercury poisoning consisting of calcium sulfide solution: used by intravenous injection. **Hall a.,** a solution of 7.35 parts of potassium iodide and 4 parts of quinine hydrochloride in 480 parts of water: used as an antidote for mercuric chloride poisoning. **mechanical a.,** an antidote that prevents the absorption of a poison. **physiological a.,** an antidote that counteracts the effects of a poison by producing other effects. **universal a.,** a mixture of 2 parts activated charcoal, 1 part magnesium oxide, and 1 part tannic acid, given as ½ ounce in a half glass of warm water, to be followed, except after ingestion of a corrosive substance, by gastric lavage or an emetic. Useful in poisoning by acids, alkaloids, glycosides, and heavy metals.

antidotic (an″tĭ-dot′ik). Antidotal.

antidromic (an″tĭ-drom′ik) [Gr. *antidromein* to run in a contrary direction]. Conducting impulses in a direction opposite to the normal: said of nerve fibers. Cf. *orthodromic.*

antidynamic (an″tĭ-di-nam′ik) [*anti-* + Gr. *dynamis* might]. Reducing the strength.

antidyscratic (an″tĭ-dis-krat′ik) [*anti-* + Gr. *dyskrasia* bad temperament]. Effective against a dyscrasia.

antidysenteric (an″tĭ-dis″en-ter′ik). 1. Preventing, alleviating, or curing dysentery. 2. An agent that prevents, alleviates, or cures dysentery.

antidysentericum (an″tĭ-dis″en-ter′e-kum). A preparation of myrobalan, pelletierin, extract of rose, extract of pomegranate, and gum arabic: used in chronic diarrhea and in dysentery.

antiedematous (an″tĭ-e-dem′ah-tus). Antiedemic.

antiedemic (an″tĭ-e-dem′ik). 1. Preventing or alleviating edema. 2. An agent that prevents or alleviates edema.

antiemetic (an″tĭ-e-met′ik) [*anti-* + Gr. *emetikos* inclined to vomit]. 1. Preventing or alleviating nausea and vomiting. 2. An agent that prevents or alleviates nausea and vomiting.

antiemulsin (an″tĭ-e-mul′sin). An immune serum counteracting emulsin.

antiendotoxic (an″tĭ-en″do-tok′sik). Counteracting the effect of endotoxins.

antiendotoxin (an″tĭ-en″do-tok′sin). An antibody which counteracts the endotoxin of bacteria.

antienzyme (an″tĭ-en′zīm) [*anti-* + *enzyme*]. An agent that neutralizes the action of an enzyme.

antiepileptic (an″tĭ-ep″e-lep′tik). 1. Combating epilepsy. 2. An agent that combats epilepsy.

antiepithelial (an″tĭ-ep″e-the′le-al). Destructive to epithelial cells.

antierotica (an″tĭ-e-rot′e-kah). Agents which have an anaphrodisiac effect.

antiesterase (an″tĭ-es′ter-ās). An agent which inhibits or counteracts the activity of esterolytic enzymes.

antiestrogenic (an″tĭ-es″tro-jen′ik). Counteracting or suppressing estrogenic activity; blocking the effect of estrogen on the uterus.

antifebrile (an″tĭ-feb′ril). Antipyretic.

antifebrin (an″tĭ-feb′rin). Acetanilid.

antiferment (an″tĭ-fer′ment). An agent that hinders or prevents the action of a ferment.

antifermentative (an″tĭ-fer-men′tah-tiv). Checking a fermentation process.

antifertilizin (an″tĭ-fer′tĭ-li″zin). A substance, probably of protein nature, on the surface of the spermatozoon, which serves as the specific receptor that reacts with the fertilizin of the surface of the ovum, thus binding the spermatozoon to the ovum.

antifibrillatory (an″tĭ-fib′rĭ-lah-tor″e). 1. Preventing or stopping fibrillation of the heart. 2. An agent that prevents or stops fibrillation of the heart.

antifibrinolysin (an″tĭ-fi″brĭ-no-li′sin). An inhibitor of fibrinolysin. See also *antiplasmin.*

antifilarial (an″tĭ-fĭ-la′re-al). 1. Effective against filaria. 2. An agent that is effective against filaria.

antiflux (an′tĭ-fluks). A substance which prevents the attachment of solder.

antiformin (an″tĭ-for′min). A proprietary preparation of a strongly alkaline solution of sodium hypochlorite: used as a disinfectant and in the laboratory for concentrating and isolating tubercle bacilli from cultures.

antifungal (an″tĭ-fung′gal). Destructive to fungi, or suppressing their reproduction or growth; effective against fungus infections.

antifungoid (an″tĭ-fung′goid). Effective against fungoid organisms.

antigalactic (an″tĭ-gah-lak′tik) [*anti-* + Gr. *gala* milk]. 1. Diminishing the secretion of milk. 2. An agent that tends to suppress milk secretion.

antigametocyte (an″tĭ-gah-me′to-sīt). Effective against the gametocytes of malaria.

antigelatinase (an″tĭ-jeh-lat′ĭ-nās). A substance in the serum of animals infected with bacteria which prevents the digestion of gelatin.

antigen (an′tĭ-jen) [*antibody* + Gr. *gennan* to produce]. A high molecular weight substance or complex, usually protein or protein-polysaccharide complex in nature, which, when foreign to the blood stream of an animal, on gaining access to the tissues of such an animal stimulates the formation of specific antibody and reacts specifically in vivo or in vitro with its homologous antibody. In certain species (e.g., mouse and man), polysaccharides are antigenic. See also *haptene.* **acetone-insoluble a.,** an antigen for the Wassermann reaction consisting of the acetone-insoluble constituents of an alcoholic extract of beef heart. **beef heart a.,** an antigen for the Wassermann reaction made by extracting fresh normal beef heart tissue with absolute alcohol. The fresh normal hearts of guinea pigs, rabbits, and human beings are also used. **blood-group a's,** secreted soluble mucopolysaccharides possessing the H, A, and B haptenic structures that are characteristic of erythrocytes and some other tissues of the body. **carbohydrate a's,** numerous polysaccharides isolated from bacteria which function as specific haptenes and as more or less complete antigens. **chick embryo a.** See *Frei a.* **cholesterinized a.,** beef heart antigen to which has been added 0.4 per cent of cholesterol. **common a.,** an antigen which is found in two or more closely related animals. **F a.,** Forssman a. **febrile a's,** proprietary preparations consisting of suspensions of members of the typhoid-paratyphoid group for the performance of agglutination tests for enteric infections. **flagellar a.,** H antigen. **Forssman a.,** a heterogenetic antigen producing antisheep hemolysin, occurring in various unrelated animals, mainly in the organs but not in the erythrocytes (guinea pig, horse), but sometimes only in the erythrocytes (sheep), and occasionally in both (chicken). In the original and strict sense the antigen is typified by that found in the guinea pig kidney and characterized by heat stability and solubility in alcohol; the antigenic determinant is polysaccharide in nature. Its antibody is absorbed by tissues containing the antigen, contains no lysin for bovine cells and little or no agglutinin for sheep cells. The term is also used loosely to refer to any antigen producing sheep hemolysin, but antibodies to it are not identical, as they are in the case of the true Forssman, (or F) antigen. **Frei a.,** sterile pus from an unruptured bubo of suspected venereal lymphogranuloma for use in the intradermal Frei test. The virus of the disease is now propagated by inoculating it into the yolk sac of developing chick embryos (*yolk sac antigen, chick embryo antigen*), or by inoculating it into the brain tissue of mice (*mouse brain a.*). **H a.** (Ger. *Hauch*, film), the antigen which occurs in the flagella of motile bacteria. Cf. *O a.* **heterogenetic a.,** an antigen common to more than one species whose species distribution is unrelated to phylogeny (viz., Forssman's antigen, lens protein, certain caseins, etc.). **heterophile a.,** heterogenetic a. **Hitchens and Hansen's a.,** cultures of meningococcus are grown on salt-free agar, suspended in water, precipitated with alcohol, then with ether, dried, and rubbed up in a mortar with physiologic sodium chloride solution for use. **isophile a.,** one occurring within a species, but not in all individuals of the species, for example, human blood group antigens. **mouse brain a.** See *Frei a.* **Nègre a.,** an antigen prepared from dead, dried, and triturated tubercle bacilli by means of acetone and methyl alcohol: used in serum tests for tuberculosis. **O a.** (Ger. *ohne Hauch*, without film), the antigen which occurs in the bodies of bacteria. Cf. *H a.* **organ-specific a.,** a heterogenetic antigen or iso-antigen that is specific for an organ or tissue (e.g., kidney, central nervous system, etc.). **partial a.,** haptene. **pollen a.,** the essential protein of the pollen of plants extracted with a suitable menstruum: used in diagnosis, prophylaxis, and desensitization in hay fever. **residue a's,** naturally occurring haptene split from the antigenic complex by autolysis or methods of preparation of purified antigen. **Sachs's a.,** an antigen consisting of a cholesterinized alcoholic extract of beef heart. **shock a.,** the specific antigen which is capable of eliciting the characteristic anaphylactic or other reaction in a sensitized animal. **somatic a.,** O antigen. **species-specific a's,** specific antigens in the corresponding organs or fluids of different animals by means of which species can be distinguished, such as hemoglobins, egg whites, etc. **Stein's a.,** an antigen for the serologic diagnosis of relapsing fever. **therapeutic a.,** any substance which, on injection into the body, stimulates the formation of protective antibodies. **V a., Vi a.,** an antigen contained in the sheath of a bacterium, as the typhoid bacillus, and giving greater virulence to the strain containing it. **VDRL a.,** an alcohol solution containing 0.03 per cent cardiolipin, 0.99 per cent cholesterol, and enough lecithin to produce standard reactivity. **yolk sac a.** See *Frei a.*

antigenic (an-tĭ-jen′ik). Having the properties of an antigen.

antigenicity (an″tĭ-jĕ-nis′ĭ-te). Potency as an antigen.

antigenophil (an″tĭ-jen′o-fil). Antigentophil.

antigenotherapy (an″tĭ-jen″o-ther′ah-pe). The treatment of disease by the injection of an antigen to stimulate antibody formation.

antigentophil (an″tĭ-jen′to-fil) [*antigen* + Gr. *philein* to love]. Having an affinity for the antigen; said of that group of an amboceptor which attaches to the antigen or specific cell.

antigentotherapy (an″tĭ-jen″to-ther′ah-pe). Antigenotherapy.

antiglobulin (an″tĭ-glob′u-lin). A precipitin which precipitates globulin.

antiglyoxalase (an″tĭ-gli-ok′sah-lās). A pancreatic substance which antagonizes glyoxalase.

antigoitrogenic (an″tĭ-goi″tro-jen′ik) [*anti-* + *goiter* + Gr. *gennan* to produce]. Preventing or inhibiting the development of goiter.

antigonadotrophic (an″tĭ-go″nad-o-trof′ik). Inhibiting the gonadotrophic hormones.

antigonorrheic (an″tĭ-gon″o-re′ik). Effective against gonorrhea.

antigrowth (an′tĭ-grōth). Counteracting the growth hormone.

antihallucinatory (an″tĭ-hah-lu′sĭ-nah-to″re). Counteracting hallucinogenesis; suppressing hallucinations.

antihelix (an″tĭ-he′liks). Anthelix.

antihelmintic (an″tĭ-hel-min′tik). Anthelmintic.

antihemagglutinin (an″tĭ-hem-ah-gloo′tĭ-nin). A substance whose action is antagonistic to hemagglutinin.

antihemolysin (an″tĭ-he-mol′ĭ-sin). Any agent which opposes the action of a hemolysin.

antihemolytic (an″tĭ-he″mo-lit′ik). Preventing hemolysis.

antihemophilic (an″tĭ-he″mo-fil′ik). 1. Effective against the bleeding tendency in hemophilia. 2. An agent that counteracts the bleeding tendency in hemophilia.

antihemorrhagic (an″tĭ-hem″o-raj′ik). 1. Stopping hemorrhage. 2. An agent that prevents or stops hemorrhage.

antiheterolysin (an″tĭ-het″er-ol′ĭ-sin). A substance which counteracts heterolysin.

antihidrotic (an″tĭ-hi-drot′ik). Anhidrotic.

antihistamine (an″tĭ-his′tah-min). Antihistaminic.

antihistaminic (an″tĭ-his-tah-min′ik). 1. Counteracting the effect of histamine. 2. A drug which counteracts the action of histamine.

antihormone (an″tĭ-hor′mōn). A substance which neutralizes the action of a hormone; inhibitory hormone. Cf. *colyone*.

antihyaluronidase (an″tĭ-hi-ah-lu-ron′ĭ-dās). An antienzyme which opposes the action of hyaluronidase.

antihydrophobic (an″tĭ-hi-dro-fo′bik). Counteracting the development of hydrophobia (rabies).

antihydropic (an″tĭ-hi-drop′ik) [*anti-* + Gr. *hydrōpikos* dropsical]. 1. Preventing or relieving dropsical conditions. 2. An agent that prevents or relieves dropsical conditions (hydrops).

antihygienic (an″tĭ-hi″je-en′ik). Contrary to hygienic principles.

antihypercholesterolemic (an″tĭ-hi″per-koles″ter-ol-e′mik). Effective in decreasing or preventing an excessively high level of cholesterol in the blood. By extension, sometimes used to designate an agent which exerts that effect.

antihyperglycemic (an″tĭ-hi″per-gli-se′mik). 1. Counteracting high levels of glucose in the blood. 2. An agent that counteracts high levels of glucose in the blood.

antihypertensive (an″tĭ-hi″per-ten′siv). 1. Counteracting high blood pressure. 2. An agent that counteracts high blood pressure.

antihypnotic (an″tĭ-hip-not′ik). 1. Preventing or hindering sleep. 2. An agent that prevents or hinders sleep.

antihysteric (an″tĭ-his-ter′ik). 1. Preventing or relieving hysteria. 2. An agent that counteracts hysteria.

anti-icteric (an″tĭ-ik-ter′ik). Relieving icterus or jaundice.

anti-immune (an″tĭ-im-mūn′). Acting so as to prevent immunity.

anti-infectious (an″tĭ-in-fek′shus). Counteracting infection.

anti-infective (an″tĭ-in-fek′tiv). 1. Counteracting infection. 2. An agent that counteracts infection.

anti-inflammatory (an″tĭ-in-flam′ah-to″re). Counteracting or suppressing inflammation.

anti-insulin (an″tĭ-in′su-lin). A substance which counteracts the action of insulin.

anti-invasin (an″tĭ-in-va′sin). An enzyme which antagonizes hyaluronidase. **a. I,** an enzyme present in normal blood plasma which antagonizes hyaluronidase. **a. II,** an enzyme present in normal blood plasma which antagonizes pro-invasin I.

anti-isolysin (an″tĭ-i-sol′ĭ-sin). A substance which counteracts an isolysin.

antikataphylactic (an″tĭ-kat″ah-fi-lak′tik). Interfering with kataphylaxis.

antikenotoxin (an″tĭ-ke″no-tok′sin). A substance which inhibits the action of kenotoxin.

antiketogen (an″tĭ-ke′to-jen). A substance which inhibits the formation of ketone bodies.

antiketogenesis (an″tĭ-ke″to-jen′e-sis). The prevention of the development of ketones; reduction of ketones.

antiketogenetic (an″tĭ-ke″to-je-net′ik). Antiketogenic.

antiketogenic (an″tĭ-ke″to-jen′ik). Preventing or inhibiting the formation of ketone bodies.

antiketoplastic (an″tĭ-ke″to-plas′tik). Antiketogenic.

antikinase (an″tĭ-ki′nās). An antibody thought to inhibit the action of kinase.

antikinesis (an″tĭ-ki-ne′sis) [*anti-* + Gr. *kinēsis* movement]. The tendency of organisms to resist and lean in an opposite direction to a dragging rotary force, e.g., on a slowly revolving plane (Dubois, 1898).

antilactase (an″tĭ-lak′tās). An antienzyme that counteracts lactase.

antilactoserum (an″tĭ-lak″to-se′rum). A substance which inhibits the action of lactoserum.

antileishmanial (an″tĭ-lish-ma′ne-al). 1. Effective against leishmania. 2. An agent that is effective against leishmania.

antilemic (an″tĭ-le′mik) [*anti-* + Gr. *loimos* plague]. Effective against the plague.

antileprotic (an″tĭ-lep-rot′ik). 1. Therapeutically effective against leprosy. 2. An agent that is therapeutically effective against leprosy.

antilepsis (an″tĭ-lep′sis) [Gr. *antilēpsis* a receiving in return]. Revulsive or derivative treatment.

antileptic (an″tĭ-lep′tik). Pertaining to antilepsis; revulsive.

antilethargic (an″tĭ-lĕ-thar′jik). 1. Overcoming a tendency toward lethargy. 2. An agent that counteracts a tendency toward lethargy.

antileukocidin (an″tĭ-lu-ko′si-din). A substance that counteracts leukocidin.

antileukocytic (an″tĭ-lu″ko-sit′ik). Destructive to white blood corpuscles (leukocytes).

antileukoprotease (an″tĭ-lu″ko-pro′te-ās). An antienzyme of the blood plasma which inhibits the digestion of protein by leukoprotease.

antileukotoxin (an″tĭ-lu″ko-tok′sin). Antileukocidin.

anti-lewisite (an′tĭ-lu′ĭ-sīt). Dimercaprol. Also called *British anti-lewisite*, or *BAL*.

antilipase (an″tĭ-lip′ās). A substance counteracting a lipase.

antilipfanogen (an″tĭ-lip-fan′o-jen). A substance found in blood serum which inhibits the fat-depositing action of the lipfanogens that are present, by combining with them in part and forming a complex that is not converted into visible fat.

antilipoid (an″tĭ-lip′oid). An antibody having the power of reacting with a lipoid.

antilipotropic (an″tĭ-lip″o-trop′ik). Antagonistic to fat and consequently interfering with the removal of fat from the liver.

antilipotropism (an″tĭ-lip-ot′ro-pizm). The interference with the removal of fat from the liver.

antilithic (an″tĭ-lith′ik) [*anti-* + Gr. *lithos* stone]. 1. Preventing the formation of stone or calculus. 2. An agent that prevents the formation of stone or calculus.

antilobium (an″tĭ-lo′be-um) [L.; Gr. *antilobion*]. The tragus of the ear.

antilogia (an″tĭ-lo′je-ah) [Gr. "contradiction"]. A combination of contradictory symptoms rendering diagnosis uncertain.

antiluetic (an″tĭ-lu-et′ik). Antisyphilitic.

antilysin (an″tĭ-li′sin) [*anti-* + *lysin*]. An antibody that inactivates a lysin.

antilysis (an″tĭ-li′sis). The inhibition or suppression of lysis.

antilyssic (an″tĭ-lis′ik) [*anti-* + Gr. *lyssa* rabies]. Antirabic.

antilytic (an″tĭ-lit′ik). Pertaining to antilysis; inhibiting or suppressing lysis.

antimalarial (an″tĭ-mah-la′re-al). 1. Therapeutically effective against malaria. 2. An agent that is therapeutically effective against malaria.

antimaniacal (an″tĭ-mah-ni′ah-kal). 1. Preventing or diminishing mania. 2. An agent that prevents or diminishes mania.

antimedical (an″tĭ-med′ĭ-kal). Inconsistent with the principles of medical science.

antimephitic (an″tĭ-mĕ-fit′ik). Preventing or neutralizing mephitic substances.

antimere (an′tĭ-mēr) [*anti-* + Gr. *meros* a part]. One of the opposite corresponding parts of an organism which are symmetrical with respect to the longitudinal axis of its body. Cf. *metamere*.

antimeristem (an″tĭ-me-ris′tem). A preparation of a fungus, *Mucor racemus malignus*, grown on malignant tumors of animals.

antimesenteric (an″tĭ-mes′en-ter″ik). Designating that part of the intestine which is opposite to the site of attachment of the mesentery.

antimetabolite (an″tĭ-mĕ-tab′o-līt). A substance bearing a close structural resemblance to one required for normal physiological functioning, and exerting its desired effect perhaps by replacing or interfering with the utilization of the essential metabolite. Called also *metabolic antagonist, enzyme antagonist*, and *competitive antagonist*.

antimetropia (an″tĭ-mĕ-tro′pe-ah) [*anti-* + Gr. *metron* measure + *ōps* eye + *-ia*]. Hypermetropia in one eye with myopia in the other.

antimiasmatic (an″tĭ-mi″az-mat′ik) [*anti-* + Gr. *miasma* pollution]. Effective against noxious emanations or exhalations.

antimicrobial (an″tĭ-mi-kro′be-al). 1. Destroying microorganisms, or suppressing their multiplication or growth. 2. An agent which destroys microorganisms or suppresses their multiplication or growth.

antimicrobic (an″tĭ-mi-kro′bik). Antimicrobial.

antimicrophyte (an″tĭ-mi′kro-fīt). An agent that is effective against vegetable microorganisms.

antimitotic (an″tĭ-mi-tot′ik). Inhibiting or preventing mitosis.

antimongoloid (an″tĭ-mon′go-loid). Opposite to that characteristic of mongolism, as antimongoloid slant of the palpebral fissures.

antimonial (an″tĭ-mo′ne-al). Pertaining to or containing antimony.

antimonic (an″tĭ-mon′ik). Containing antimony in its pentad valency.

antimonid (an″tĭ-mo′nid). Any binary compound of antimony.

antimonious (an″tĭ-mo′ne-us). Containing antimony in its triad valency.

antimonium (an″tĭ-mo′ne-um), gen. *antimo′nii* [L.]. Antimony.

antimony (an′tĭ-mo″ne) [L. *antimonium* or *stibium*]. A crystalline metallic element with a bluish luster, symbol Sb, atomic number 51, atomic weight 121.75, forming various medicinal and poisonous salts. These salts are arterial and cardiac depressants, and have emetic and diaphoretic properties; in large doses they are gastro-intestinal irritants. **a. aniline-tartrate,** $SbO.C_6H_5-(NH_2)C_4H_4O_6$, a less toxic substitute for tartar emetic for intravenous chemotherapy. **a. chloride,** a deliquescent substance, $SbCl_3$, which is used as a caustic for small tumors and poisoned wounds; called also *butter of antimony.* **a. oxide,** antimonic oxide, Sb_2O_3, a white-gray powder. **a. pentachloride,** a reddish yellow, hygroscopic, caustic liquid, $SbCl_5$. **a. pentasulfide,** antimonic sulfide, Sb_2S_5, a golden-yellow compound. **a. potassium tartrate,** a colorless, crystalline compound, $SbOH(O.CH.COOK)_2.\frac{1}{2}H_2O$, soluble in water and having locally a marked irritant effect: used in treatment of parasitic infections, such as schistosomiasis or leishmaniasis; formerly used to induce vomiting. **a. sodium tartrate,** $Na(SbO)C_4H_4O_6.\frac{1}{2}H_2O$: used in trypanosomiasis and other tropical diseases. **a. sodium thioglycollate.** See under *sodium.* **tartrated a.,** a. potassium tartrate. **a. thioglycollamide,** an organic antimony compound, $Sb(S.CH_2.CO.-NH_2)_3$, the triamide of antimony thioglycollic acid, used in the treatment of granuloma inguinale, kala-azar, and filariasis.

antimonyl (an-tim′o-nil″). The univalent radical SbO—.

antimonyl-aniline tartrate. A yellow, crystalline substance, used in trypanosomiasis.

antimyasthenic (an″tĭ-mi″as-then′ik). 1. Counteracting or relieving muscular weakness in myasthenia gravis. 2. An agent that counteracts or relieves muscular weakness in myasthenia gravis.

antimycobacterial (an″tĭ-mi″ko-bak-te′re-al). Active against mycobacteria.

antimycotic (an″tĭ-mi-kot′ik). Counteracting the growth of fungi.

antinarcotic (an″tĭ-nar-kot′ik). Serviceable against narcotism; counteracting the effects of narcotics.

antinatriuresis (an″tĭ-na″tre-u-re′sis). Inhibition of the excretion of sodium in the urine.

antinauseant (an″tĭ-naw′se-ant). 1. Preventing or relieving nausea. 2. An agent that prevents or relieves nausea.

antineoplastic (an″tĭ-ne-o-plas′tik). Inhibiting or preventing the development of neoplasms; checking the maturation and proliferation of malignant cells.

antinephritic (an″tĭ-ne-frit′ik). Effective against nephritis.

antineuralgic (an″tĭ-nu-ral′jik). Relieving neuralgia.

antineuritic (an″tĭ-nu-rit′ik). Counteracting neuritis.

antineuronist (an″tĭ-nu′rōn-ist). An anatomist who is opposed to the neuron theory.

antineurotoxin (an″tĭ-nu″ro-tok′sin). A substance that counteracts a neurotoxin.

antiniad (an-tin′e-ad). Toward the antinion.

antinial (an-tin′e-al). Pertaining to the antinion.

antinion (an-tin′e-on) [*anti-* + Gr. *inion* occiput]. The frontal pole of the head; the median frontal point farthest from the inion.

antiodontalgic (an″tĭ-o″don-tal′jik). Relieving toothache.

antioncotic (an″tĭ-ong-kot′ik) [*anti-* + Gr. *onkos* bulk, mass]. 1. Tending to reduce swelling; effective against tumors. 2. An agent that reduces swelling or suppresses growth of tumors.

antiophidica (an″tĭ-o-fid′ĭ-kah) [*anti-* + Gr. *ophis* snake]. Remedies that combat the effects of snake bite.

antiophthalmic (an″tĭ-of-thal′mik). Counteracting ophthalmia.

antiopsonin (an″tĭ-op′so-nin). A substance that has an inhibitory influence on opsonins.

antiorgan (an″tĭ-or′gan). Directed against the tissues of an organ, as antiorgan ferment.

antiotomy (an″tĭ-ot′o-me) [Gr. *antias* tonsil + *temnein* to cut]. Excision of the tonsils.

antiovulatory (an″tĭ-ov′u-lah-to″re). Suppressing ovulation.

antioxidant (an″tĭ-ok′se-dant). Antioxygen.

antioxidase (an″tĭ-ok′se-dās). A substance which counteracts oxidase.

antioxidation (an″tĭ-ok-se-da′shun). The prevention of oxidation.

antioxygen (an″tĭ-ok′se-jen). A substance which hinders oxidation.

antipaludian (an″tĭ-pah-lu′de-an). Antimalarial.

antiparalytic (an″tĭ-par″ah-lit′ik) [*anti-* + *paralysis*]. Relieving paralytic conditions.

antiparasitic (an″tĭ-par″ah-sit′ik). 1. Destructive to parasites. 2. An agent destructive to parasites.

antiparastata (an″tĭ-pah-ras′tah-tah) [*anti-* + Gr. *parastatēs* testis]. Cowper's glands.

antiparastatitis (an″tĭ-par″ah-stah-ti′tis). Inflammation of Cowper's glands.

antiparasympathomimetic (an″tĭ-par″ah-sim″pah-tho-mĭ-met′ik). Producing effects which resemble those of interruption of the parasympathetic nerve supply.

antipathic (an″tĭ-path′ik) [*anti-* + Gr. *pathos* feeling]. Of diverse nature; antagonistic; marked by antipathy.

antipathogen (an″tĭ-path′o-jen). Any substance which acts against a pathogen or morbific agent.

antipathy (an-tip′ah-the) [*anti-* + Gr. *pathos* feeling]. An opposing quality or property; a feeling or attitude of strong aversion.

antipepsin (an″tĭ-pep′sin). An antienzyme that neutralizes the action of pepsin.

antipeptone (an″tĭ-pep′tōn). A peptone derived from antialbumose by digestion (Kühne).

antiperiodic (an″tĭ-pe″re-od′ik). Serviceable against malarial or periodic recurrence.

antiperistalsis (an″tĭ-per″ĭ-stal′sis). Peristaltic action proceeding from below upward. **esophageal a.,** regurgitation of food from the esophagus before it reaches the stomach.

antiperistaltic (an″tĭ-per″ĭ-stal′tik). 1. Pertaining to or causing antiperistalsis. 2. Diminishing peristaltic action.

antiperspirant (an″tĭ-per′spĭ-rant″). 1. Inhibiting or preventing perspiration. 2. An agent which inhibits or prevents perspiration.

antiphagin (an″tĭ-fa′jin). A specific component of virulent bacteria which renders them resistant to phagocytosis.

antiphagocytic (an″tĭ-fag-o-sit′ik). Counteracting or opposing phagocytosis.

antiphlogistic (an″tĭ-flo-jis′tik). 1. Counteracting inflammation and fever. 2. An agent which counteracts inflammation and fever.

antiphlogistine (an″tĭ-flo-jis′tin). A proprietary cataplasm of glycerin, kaolin, and aromatics: used as an anodyne, antiseptic, antiphlogistic, and as a surgical dressing.

antiphone (an′tĭ-fōn) [*anti-* + Gr. *phōnē* voice]. An instrument to be worn in the auditory meatus to protect the ear from noises.

antiphrynolysin (an″tĭ-frĭ-nol′ĭ-sin). The antivenene for the toxin of toad venom.

antiphthiriac (an″tĭ-ther′e-ak). Effective against lice.

antiphthisic (an″tĭ-tiz′ik). Checking or relieving phthisis.

antiphthisin (an-tif′the-sin). An extractive from cultures of tubercle bacilli, containing 0.5 per cent of cresol: used in treatment of phthisis. Called also *sozalbumin.*

antiplague (an″tĭ-plāg′). Preventing or curing the plague.

antiplasmin (an″tĭ-plaz′min). A principle in the blood that inhibits plasmin. Called also *antifibrinolysin, antiprotease, antiproteolysin, antitryptase,* and *serum inhibitor.*

antiplasmodial (an″tĭ-plaz-mo′de-al). Having a destructive action on plasmodia.

antiplastic (an″tĭ-plas′tik) [*anti-* + Gr. *plassein* to form]. 1. Unfavorable to the healing process. 2. An agent that impoverishes the blood.

antiplatelet (an″tĭ-plāt′let). Directed against or destructive to blood platelets.

antipnein (an″tĭ-ne′in). A substance which counteracts pnein.

antipneumococcic (an″tĭ-nu″mo-kok′sik). Destroying pneumococci.

antipneumotoxin (an″tĭ-nu″mo-tok′sin). An agent that antagonizes pneumotoxin.

antipodagric (an″tĭ-po-dag′rik). Effective against gout.

antiprecipitin (an″tĭ-pre-sip′ĭ-tin). A substance antagonistic in its action to precipitin.

antiprostate (an″tĭ-pros′tāt). Glandula bulbourethralis.

antiprostatitis (an″tĭ-pros″tah-ti′tis). Inflammation of Cowper's glands.

antiprotease (an″tĭ-pro′te-ās). A substance which checks the proteolytic action of enzymes. See *antiplasmin.*

antiprothrombin (an″tĭ-pro-throm′bin). Directed against prothrombin; a general term indicating a type of anticoagulant which acts by retarding the conversion of prothrombin to thrombin, without actually designating the specific means by which this occurs.

antiprotozoal (an″tĭ-pro-to-zo′al). 1. Destroying protozoa, or checking their growth or reproduction. 2. An agent that destroys protozoa, or checks their growth or reproduction.

antiprotozoan (an″tĭ-pro″to-zo′an). Antiprotozoal.

antipruriginous (an″tĭ-proo-rij′ĭ-nus). Therapeutically effective against prurigo.

antipruritic (an″tĭ-proo-rit′ik). Relieving or preventing itching.

antipsoric (an″tĭ-so′rik) [*anti-* + Gr. *psōra* itch]. Antipruritic.

antipsychomotor (an″tĭ-si′ko-mo″tor). Suppressing or inhibiting the motor effects of cerebral or psychic activity.

antipurpuric (an″tĭ-pur-pu′rik). Counteracting purpura.

antiputrefactive (an″tĭ-pu″tre-fak′tiv). Counteracting putrefaction.

antipyic (an″tĭ-pi′ik) [*anti-* + Gr. *pyon* pus]. Preventing or restraining suppuration.

antipyogenic (an″tĭ-pi″o-jen′ik) [*anti-* + Gr. *pyon* pus + *gennan* to produce]. Preventing or hindering the development of pus.

antipyresis (an″tĭ-pi-re′sis) [*anti-* + Gr. *pyressein* to have a fever]. The therapeutic use of antipyretics.

antipyretic (an″tĭ-pi-ret′ik) [*anti-* + Gr. *pyretos* fever]. 1. Relieving or reducing fever. 2. An agent which relieves or reduces fever.

antipyrine (an″tĭ-pi′rin) [*anti-* + Gr. *pyr* fire]. A grayish or reddish crystalline basic coal tar derivative, phenyldimethylpyrazolon, $C_{11}H_{12}N_2O$, soluble in water, chloroform, and alcohol: antipyretic, antirheumatic, and analgesic. **a. acetylsalicylate,** acetopyrine. **a. amygdalate,** a salt of antipyrine: used in treatment of whooping cough. **a. benzoate,** benzopyrine. **a. camphorate,** an antipyretic compound used in night sweats. **a. mandelate,** a salt of antipyrine: antipyretic. **a. metaoxybenzoate,** a liquid salt of antipyrine. **a. paraoxybenzoate,** a crystalline salt of antipyrine. **a. salicylate,** salipyrin. **a. tannate,** a yellowish, tasteless powder, insoluble in water, and containing 37 per cent of antipyrine.

antipyrinomania (an″tĭ-pi″rin-o-ma′ne-ah) [*antipyrine* + Gr. *mania* madness]. Insanity from excessive use of antipyrine, or a maniacal addiction to antipyrine.

antipyrotic (an″tĭ-pi-rot′ik) [*anti-* + Gr. *pyrōsis* a burning]. 1. Therapeutically effective against burns; 2. An agent that is effective in the treatment of burns.

antirabic (an″tĭ-ra′bik). Directed against or effective in preventing the development of rabies.

antirachitic (an″tĭ-rah-kit′ik). Therapeutically effective against rickets.

antiradiation (an″tĭ-ra″de-a′shun). Capable of counteracting the effects of radiation; effective against radiation injury.

antirennin (an″tĭ-ren′in). An antienzyme formed in the blood serum of animals injected with rennin. It conteracts the rennin and prevents coagulation of milk.

antirheumatic (an″tĭ-ru-mat′ik) [*anti-* + *rheumatic*]. Relieving or preventing rheumatism.

antiricin (an″tĭ-ri′sin). An antitoxin produced in the blood after the exhibition of ricin.

antirickettsial (an″tĭ-rik-et′se-al). 1. Effective against rickettsiae. 2. An agent that is effective against rickettsiae.

antirobin (an″tĭ-ro′bin). The antitoxin of robin, a poison of the locust tree.

antisaluresis (an″tĭ-sal″u-re′sis). Suppression of the excretion of salt in the urine.

antiscabious (an″tĭ-ska′be-us) [*anti-* + L. *scabies* itch]. Therapeutically effective against scabies.

antiscarlatinal (an″tĭ-skar-lah-ti′nal). Effective against scarlatina.

antischistosomal (an″tĭ-skis″to-so′mal). 1. Destructive to schistosomes. 2. An agent which is destructive to schistosomes.

antiscorbutic (an″tĭ-skor-bu′tik) [*anti-* + *scorbutus*]. Effective in the prevention or relief of scurvy.

antisensibilisin (an″tĭ-sen-sĭ-bil′ĭ-zin). An antibody in sensitized animals that unites with the antigen (sensibilisin) and thus induces anaphylactic shock.

antisensitization (an″tĭ-sen″sĭ-ti-za′shun). A condition produced in guinea pigs by a previous injection of normal rabbit serum, which makes it impossible to passively sensitize the guinea pig with rabbit's immune serum.

antisensitizer (an″tĭ-sen′sĭ-tiz″er). Antiamboceptor.

antisepsis (an″tĭ-sep′sis) [*anti-* + Gr. *sēpsis* putrefaction]. The prevention of sepsis by the inhibition or destruction of the causative organism. **physiologic a.,** the combination of methods by which the body excludes germs.

antiseptic (an″tĭ-sep′tik). 1. Preventing decay or putrefaction. 2. A substance that will inhibit the growth and development of microorganisms without necessarily destroying them. Cf. *disinfectant.* Some of the chief antiseptics are alcohol, boric acid, phenol, creosote, corrosive sublimate, sodium chloride, charcoal, chlorine, tannic acid, sugar, and vinegar. **Credé's a.,** silver citrate. **Dakin's a.** See *surgical solution of chlorinated soda,* under *solution.* **Lister's a.,** mercury-zinc cyanide.

antisepticism (an″tĭ-sep′tĭ-sizm). The systematic employment of antiseptic agents.

antisepticize (an″tĭ-sep′tĭ-sīz). To render antiseptic.

antiserotonin (an″tĭ-ser″o-to′nin). A substance capable of counteracting or inhibiting the action of serotonin. **benzyl a., Wooley's a.,** benanserin.

antiserum (an″tĭ-se′rum). A serum that contains antibody or antibodies. It may be obtained from an animal that has been subjected to the action of antigen either by injection into the tissues or blood or by infection. **Reenstierna a.,** a serum for the treatment of leprosy prepared by inoculating sheep with glycerin bouillon cultures of the mycobacterium of leprosy. **Rh a.** See under *Rh.*

antisialagogue (an″tĭ-si-al′ah-gog). 1. Counteracting any influence that promotes the flow of saliva. 2. An agent that counteracts any influence that promotes the flow of saliva.

antisialic (an″tĭ-si-al′ik) [*anti-* + Gr. *sialon* saliva]. 1. Checking the flow of saliva. 2. An agent that checks the secretion of saliva.

antisideric (an″tĭ-sĭ-der′ik) [*anti-* + Gr. *sidēros* iron]. Incompatible with iron.

antisocial (an″tĭ-so′shal). Characterized by antisocialism.

antisocialism (an″tĭ-so′shal-izm″). The manifestation of psychopathic personality with asocial or amoral trends.

antispasmodic (an″tĭ-spaz-mod′ik). 1. Relieving spasm. 2. An agent that relieves spasm. **biliary a.,** an agent that relieves spasm of the biliary duct and sphincter. **bronchial a.,** an agent that relieves bronchial spasm.

antispastic (an″tĭ-spas′tik). Antispasmodic.

antispermotoxin (an″tĭ-sper″mo-tok′sin). A substance that opposes the action of a spermotoxin.

antispirochetic (an″tĭ-spi″ro-ke′tik). Effective against spirochetes.

antisplenetic (an″tĭ-sple-net′ik). Therapeutically effective in diseases of the spleen.

antistalsis (an″tĭ-stal′sis). Reverse peristalsis.

antistaphylococcic (an″tĭ-staf″ĭ-lo-kok′sik). Destroying staphylococci.

antistaphylohemolysin (an″tĭ-staf″ĭ-lo-he-mol′ĭ-sin). Antistaphylolysin.

antistaphylolysin (an″tĭ-staf-ĭ-lol′ĭ-sin). A substance which opposes the action of staphylolysin.

antisteapsin (an″tĭ-ste-ap′sin). An antibody which counteracts steapsin.

antisterility (an″tĭ-ste-ril′ĭ-te). Combating sterility.

antistine (an-tis′tin). Trade mark for preparations of antazoline.

antistreptococcic (an″tĭ-strep″to-kok′sik). Antagonistic to streptococci.

antistreptococcin (an″tĭ-strep″to-kok′sin). A substance that opposes the action of streptococci.

antistreptokinase (an″tĭ-strep-to′kĭ-nās). A natural inhibitor of streptokinase.

antistreptolysin (an″tĭ-strep-tol′ĭ-sin). An inhibitor of streptolysin.

antistrumous (an″tĭ-stru′mus). Effective against struma and scrofula.

antisubstance (an″tĭ-sub′stans). Antibody.

antisudoral (an″tĭ-su′dor-al). Antisudorific.

antisudorific (an″tĭ-su″dor-if′ik) [*anti-* + L. *sudor* sweat]. 1. Preventing or relieving excessive perspiration. 2. An agent that prevents or relieves excessive perspiration.

antisympathetic (an″tĭ-sim″pah-thet′ik). 1. Producing effects which resemble those of interruption of the sympathetic nerve supply. 2. An agent that produces effects resembling those of interruption of the sympathetic nerve supply.

antisyphilitic (an″tĭ-sif″ĭ-lit′ik) [*anti-* + *syphilitic*]. 1. Effective against syphilis. 2. A remedy for syphilis.

antitabetic (an″tĭ-tah-bet′ik). 1. Effective against tabes dorsalis. 2. An agent that is effective against tabes dorsalis.

antitetanic (an″tĭ-tĕ-tan′ik). Preventing or curing tetanus.

antitetanolysin (an″tĭ-tet-ah-nol′ĭ-sin). The antibody to tetanolysin.

antithenar (an-tith′e-nar″) [*anti-* + Gr. *thenar* palm, sole]. Situated opposite to the palm or the sole.

antithermic (an″tĭ-ther′mik) [*anti-* + Gr. *thermē* heat]. Antipyretic.

antithrombin (an″tĭ-throm′bin) [*anti-* + *thrombin*]. A general term for a naturally occurring or therapeutically administered substance (e.g., heparin) that neutralizes the action of thrombin and thus limits or restricts blood coagulation.

antithromboplastin (an″tĭ-throm″bo-plas′tin). A naturally occurring, immunologically induced, or therapeutically administered material (e.g., heparin), having the property of interfering with intrinsic or extrinsic thromboplastin and therefore inhibiting the normal coagulation mechanism.

antithrombotic (an″tĭ-throm-bot′ik). Efficacious in preventing or relieving thrombosis.

antithyroid (an″tĭ-thi′roid). Counteracting the influence of thyroid.

antithyrotoxic (an″tĭ-thi″ro-tok′sik). Counteracting the toxic effect of thyroid and thyroid products.

antithyrotropic (an″tĭ-thi″ro-trop′ik). Inhibiting the action of the thyrotropic hormone.

antithyroxinogenesis (an″tĭ-thi-rok″sin-o-jen′e-sis) [*anti-* + *thyroxin* + *genesis*]. Production of antagonism to thyroxin, or interference with thyroxin production.

antitonic (an″tĭ-ton′ik). Reducing tone or tonicity.

antitoxic (an″tĭ-tok′sik). Good against a poison; pertaining to antitoxin.

antitoxigen (an″tĭ-tok′sĭ-jen) [*antitoxin* + Gr. *gennan* to produce]. Any substance that induces the formation of antitoxin in the animal body; antitoxinogen.

antitoxin (an″tĭ-tok′sin) [*anti-* + Gr. *toxicon* poison]. Antibody to the toxin of a microorganism, usually the bacterial exotoxins, that combines specifically with the toxin, in vivo and in vitro, with neutralization of toxicity. **botulinum a., botulinus a., botulism a.,** an antitoxin produced by immunizing horses against the toxins of both types of *Clostridium botulinium*. **bovine a.,** antitoxin containing antibodies derived from the cow instead of from the horse, for use on persons who are hypersensitive to horse serum. **diphtheria a.,** a sterile solution of refined and concentrated antibody globulins derived from the blood of horses immunized against diphtheria toxins. **gas gangrene a.,** a sterile solution of antibody globulins from the blood of horses immunized against the toxins of certain species of pathogenic clostridia. Bivalent antitoxin contains antibodies against *Clostridium welchii* and *Cl. septicum*, trivalent contains these plus antibodies against *Cl. novyi*. Antibodies against *Cl. histolyticum* and *Cl. bifermentans* are added to these in polyvalent antitoxins. **normal a.,** antitoxin capable of neutralizing an equal quantity of normal toxin solution. **tetanus a.,** a sterile solution of antibody globulins from the blood of horses or cattle ("bovine origin") immunized against tetanus toxin.

antitoxinogen (an″tĭ-tok-sin′o-jen) [*antitoxin* + Gr. *gennan* to produce]. An antigen which stimulates the production of antitoxin.

antitoxinum (an″tĭ-tok-si′num) [L.]. Antitoxin. **a. botulin′icum,** botulinum antitoxin. **a. diphther′icum,** diphtheria antitoxin. **a. gas-gangraeno′sum biva′lens,** bivalent gas gangrene antitoxin. **a. gas-gangraeno′sum pentava′lens,** polyvalent gas gangrene antitoxin. **a. gas-gangraeno′sum triva′lens,** trivalent gas gangrene antitoxin. **a. tetan′icum,** tetanus antitoxin.

antitragicus (an″tĭ-traj′e-kus). See *Table of Musculi*.

antitragus (an″tĭ-tra′gus) [*anti-* + *tragus*]. [N A, B N A]. A projection opposite the tragus, bounding the cavum conchae posteroinferiorly and continuous above with the anthelix.

antitreponemal (an″tĭ-trep″o-ne′mal). 1. Effective against Treponema. 2. An agent that is effective against Treponema.

antitrichomonal (an″tĭ-trich″o-mo′nal). 1. Destructive to Trichomonas. 2. An agent that is destructive to Trichomonas.

antitrismus (an″tĭ-triz′mus). A spasm which prevents the closure of the mouth.

antitrope (an′tĭ-trōp) [*anti-* + Gr. *trepein* to turn]. 1. Any organ which forms a symmetrical pair with another. 2. Antibody.

antitropic (an″tĭ-tro′pic). Similar, but oppositely oriented, as a right and a left glove.

antitropin (an″tĭ-tro′pin). Any substance that opposes the action of tropin; antiopsonin.

antitrypanosomal (an″tĭ-trĭ-pan″o-so′mal). 1. Destructive to trypanosomes. 2. A drug for combating trypanosomiasis.

antitrypsic (an″tĭ-trip′sik). Antitryptic.

antitrypsin (an″tĭ-trip′sin). A substance having an inhibitive action on trypsin.

antitryptase (an″tĭ-trip′tās). A substance which inhibits or counteracts the action of tryptase. See *antiplasmin*.

antitryptic (an″tĭ-trip′tik) [*anti-* + *tryptic*]. Counteracting the activity of trypsin.

antituberculin (an″tĭ-tu-ber′ku-lin). An antibody developed on the injection of tuberculin.

antituberculotic (an″tĭ-tu-ber″ku-lot′ik). 1. Therapeutically effective against tuberculosis. 2. An agent that is therapeutically effective against tuberculosis.

antituberculous (an″tĭ-tu-ber′ku-lus). Antituberculotic.

antitulase (an″tĭ-tu′lās). An immunizing serum for tuberculosis obtained from horses, cattle, and sheep.

antitumorigenic (an″tĭ-tu″mor-ĭ-jen′ik). Counteracting tumor formation.

antitussive (an″tĭ-tus′iv). 1. Relieving or preventing cough. 2. An agent that relieves or prevents cough.

antityphoid (an″tĭ-ti′foid). Counteracting or preventing typhoid.

antityrosinase (an″tĭ-ti-ro′sĭ-nās). An antienzyme that counteracts tyrosinase.

antiuratic (an″tĭ-u-rat′ik). Preventing the deposit of urates.

antiurease (an″tĭ-u′re-ās). An antibody which inhibits the activity of urease.

antivaccination (an″tĭ-vak″sĭ-na′shun). Opposition to vaccination.

antivaccinationist (an″tĭ-vak″sĭ-na′shun-ist). A person who is opposed to vaccination.

antivenene (an″tĭ-ven′ēn) [*anti-* + L. *venenum* poison]. Antivenin.

antivenereal (an″tĭ-vĕ-ne′re-al). Effective against venereal diseases.

antivenin (an″tĭ-ven′in). An antitoxic serum for venom, especially snake venom. **crotaline a., polyvalent,** a preparation containing globulins effective in neutralizing venoms of four species of pit vipers: used in immunization against snake bites.

antivenom (an″tĭ-ven′om). An antitoxin against snake venom.

antivenomous (an″tĭ-ven′o-mus). Counteracting venom.

antiviral (an″tĭ-vi′ral). Destroying viruses or suppressing their growth or multiplication.

antivirotic (an″tĭ-vi-rot′ik). 1. Antiviral. 2. An agent which destroys viruses or checks their growth or multiplication.

antivirulin (an″tĭ-vir′u-lin). Any substance that opposes the action of virulin; the substance in animals immunized against rabies, which neutralizes or inactivates the virus of rabies.

antivirus (an″tĭ-vi′rus). Besredka's name for the filtered and heated broth cultures of bacteria used by him to produce local immunity.

antivitamer (an″tĭ-vi′tah-mer). A substance which inactivates a vitamer.

antivitamin (an″tĭ-vi′tah-min). A substance which inactivates a vitamin.

antivivisection (an″tĭ-viv″ĭ-sek′shun). Opposition to vivisection.

antivivisectionist (an″tĭ-viv″ĭ-sek′shun-ist). An individual who is opposed to vivisection.

antixenic (an″tĭ-ze′nik) [*anti-* + Gr. *xenos* strange or foreign]. Pertaining to the reaction of living tissue to any foreign substance.

antixerophthalmic (an″tĭ-ze″rof-thal′mik). Counteracting xerophthalmia.

antixerotic (an″tĭ-ze-rot′ik). Counteracting or preventing xerosis.

antizymohexase (an″tĭ-zi″mo-hek′sās). An antienzyme which counteracts zymohexase.

antizymotic (an″tĭ-zĭ-mot′ik). Inhibiting or suppressing the action of enzymes.

antodontalgic (an″to-don-tal′jik). Antiodontalgic.

Anton's symptom, syndrome (an′tonz) [Gabriel *Anton*, German neuropsychiatrist, 1858–1933]. See under *symptom*.

antophthalmic (ant″of-thal′mik). Relieving ophthalmia.

antorphine (an-tor′fēn). Nalorphine.

antra (an′trah) [L.]. Plural of *antrum*.

antracele (an′trah-sēl). Antrocele.

antral (an′tral). Of or pertaining to an antrum.

antrectomy (an-trek′to-me) [*antrum* + Gr. *ektomē* excision]. Surgical excision of an antrum, as removal of the walls of the mastoid antrum, or resection of the pyloric antrum of the stomach.

antrenyl (an′trĕ-nil). Trade mark for a preparation of oxyphenonium.

Antricola (an-trik′ŏ-lah). A genus of soft ticks which infest bats.

antritis (an-tri′tis). Inflammation of an antrum, chiefly of the maxillary antrum.

antro- (an′tro) [L. *antrum;* Gr. *antron* cave]. Combining form denoting relationship to an antrum, or sinus; often used with specific reference to the maxillary antrum, or sinus.

antro-atticotomy (an″tro-at″ĭ-kot′o-me). The operation of opening the maxillary antrum and the attic of the tympanum.

antrobuccal (an″tro-buk′kal). Pertaining to or communicating with the maxillary antrum (sinus) and buccal cavity, as an antrobuccal fistula.

antrocele (an′tro-sēl) [*antro-* + Gr. *kēlē* tumor]. An accumulation of fluid in the maxillary antrum.

antroduodenectomy (an″tro-du″o-de-nek′to-me). Surgical removal of the antrum pyloricum and part of the duodenum, leaving a liberal portion of the stomach and maintaining passage through the duodenum: used in treatment of chronic duodenal ulcer.

antrodynia (an″tro-din′e-ah) [*antro-* + Gr. *odynē* pain]. Pain in an antrum.

antroidin (an-tro′ĭ-din). Antuitrin S.

antronalgia (an″tro-nal′je-ah) [*antro-* + *-algia*]. Pain in the maxillary antrum.

antronasal (an″tro-na′zal). Pertaining to the maxillary antrum and the nose.

antrophore (an′tro-fōr) [*antro-* + Gr. *pherein* to bear]. A form of soluble medicated bougie.

antrophose (an′tro-fōz) [*antro-* + *phose*]. A phose originating in the central ocular mechanism.

antropyloric (an″tro-pĭ-lor′ik). Pertaining to or affecting the antrum and the pylorus of the stomach.

antrorse (an-trors′). Directed forward or upward.

antroscope (an′tro-skōp″) [*antro-* + Gr. *skopein* to examine]. An instrument for illuminating and examining the maxillary antrum.

antroscopy (an-tros′ko-pe). The use of the antroscope; inspection of an antrum.

antrostomy (an-tros′to-me) [*antro-* + Gr. *stoma* mouth, opening]. The operation of making an opening into an antrum for purposes of drainage.

antrotome (an′tro-tōm). An instrument for performing antrotomy.

antrotomy (an-trot′o-me) [*antro-* + Gr. *tomē* cut]. The cutting open of an antrum.

antrotonia (an″tro-to′ne-ah). Tension in the pyloric antrum.

antrotympanic (an″tro-tim-pan′ik). Pertaining to the mastoid antrum and the tympanic cavity.

antrotympanitis (an″tro-tim″pah-ni′tis) [*antro-* + *tympanitis*]. Chronic purulent inflammation of the mastoid antrum and of the middle ear.

antrum (an′trum), pl. *an′trums* or *an′tra* [L.; Gr. *antron* cave]. A cavity or chamber; used as a general term in anatomical nomenclature, especially to designate a cavity or chamber within a bone. **a. au′ris,** meatus acusticus externus. **cardiac a., a. cardi′acum** [B N A], the short conical portion of the esophagus below the diaphragm, its base being continuous with the cardiac orifice of the stomach. **ethmoid a., a. ethmoida′le,** bulla ethmoidalis. **frontal a.,** sinus frontalis. **a. of Highmore, a. highmo′ri,** sinus maxillaris. **Malacarne's a.,** the posterior perforated space. **mastoid a., a. mastoi′deum** [N A], an air space in the mastoid portion of the temporal bone, communicating with the tympanic cavity and with the mastoid cells. **a. maxilla′re, maxillary a.,** sinus maxillaris. **a. pylo′ri, pyloric a., a. pylor′icum** [N A, B N A], the dilated part of the pyloric portion of the stomach, between the body of the stomach and the pyloric canal. **tympanic a., a. tympan′icum** [B N A], a. mastoideum. **a. of Willis,** a. pyloricum.

antrypol (an′trĭ-pol). The British name for naphuride.

ANTU. A powerful rat poison, alphanaphthyl thiourea.

antuitarism (an-tu′ĭ-tah-rizm) [*ante-* + *pituitarism*]. The condition produced by overactivity of the anterior lobe of the pituitary gland, marked by acromegaly or gigantism.

antuitary (an-tu′ĭ-ta-re). Pertaining to the anterior lobe of the pituitary gland.

anturane (an′tu-rān). Trade mark for a preparation of sulfinpyrazone.

Antyllus (an-til′lus) (2nd century A.D.). A noted Greek surgeon of antiquity, a Pneumatist, whose treatment of aneurysms by ligation above and below remained standard practice until the time of John Hunter (18th century). He also made contributions to plastic surgery, ophthalmology, and public health. His writings remain only in fragments, and in the works of others (particularly Oribasius).

anuclear (ah-nu′kle-ar). Having no nuclei: said of the noncellular tissue-products such as connective tissue, bone, cartilage, nervous white matter.

anulus (an′u-lus), pl. *an′uli* [L. dim. of *anus*]. N A term used to designate a ringlike anatomical structure; called *annulus* in B N A terminology. **a. of conjunctiva, a. conjuncti′vae** [N A], a ring at the junction of the conjunctiva and cornea. **a. femora′lis** [N A], the abdominal opening of the femoral canal, normally closed by the crural septum and peritoneum. Called also *femoral ring.* **a. fibrocartilagin′eus membra′nae tym′pani** [N A], the margin of attachment of the tympanic membrane. Called also *fibrocartilaginous ring of tympanic membrane.* **an′uli fibro′si cor′dis** [N A], dense fibrous rings, one of which surrounds each of the four major cardiac orifices: the right and left atrioventricular, the aortic, and the pulmonary trunk orifices. To these four rings, either directly or indirectly, are attached the atrial and ventricular muscle fibers. Called also *fibrous rings of heart.* **a. fibro′sus dis′ci intervertebra′lis** [N A], the circumferential ringlike portion of an intervertebral disc, composed of fibrocartilage and fibrous tissue. Called also *annulus fibrosus fibrocartilaginis intervertebralis* [B N A], and *fibrous ring of intervertebral disc.* **a. inguina′lis profun′dus** [N A], an aperture in the fascia transversalis for the spermatic cord or for the round ligament. Called also *annulus inguinalis abdominalis* [B N A], and *deep* or *internal abdominal ring.* **a. inguina′lis superficia′lis** [N A], an opening in the aponeurosis of the external oblique muscle for the spermatic cord or for the round ligament. Called also *annulus inguinalis subcutaneous* [B N A], and *superficial* or *external abdominal ring.* **a. i′ridis ma′jor** [N A], the less coarsely striated outer concentric circle on the anterior surface of the iris. Called also *greater circle of iris.* **a. i′ridis mi′nor** [N A], the more coarsely striated inner concentric circle on the anterior surface of the iris. Called also *lesser circle of iris.* **a. tendin′eus commu′nis** [N A], the anular ligament of origin common to the recti muscles of the eye, attached to the edge of the optic canal and the inner part of the superior orbital fissure. Called also *annulus tendineus communis* [*Zinni*] [B N A]. **a. tympan′icus** [N A], the bony ring forming part of the temporal bone at the time of birth and developing into the pars tympanica of the bone. Called also *tympanic ring.* **a. umbilica′lis** [N A], the aperture in the abdominal wall through which the umbilical cord communicates with the fetus. After birth it is felt for some time as a distinct fibrous ring surrounding the umbilicus; these fibers later shrink progressively. Called also *umbilical ring.*

anuresis (an-u-re′sis). 1. Retention of urine in the bladder. 2. Anuria.

anuretic (an-u-ret′ik). Pertaining to or characterized by anuresis.

anuria (ah-nu′re-ah) [*an* neg. + Gr. *ouron* urine + *-ia*]. Absence of excretion of urine from the body. **angioneurotic a.,** anuria occurring in cortical necrosis of the kidney and attributed to vasomotor disturbance. **calculous a.,** anuria caused by a renal calculus. **postrenal a.,** anuria resulting from obstruction of the ureters. **prerenal a.,** cessation of renal secretion of urine resulting from fall of blood pressure below the level necessary to maintain adequate filtration pressure in the glomeruli. **renal a.,** failure of urinary secretion by the kidney in the presence of adequate filtration pressure in the glomeruli and patency of the ureters.

anuric (ah-nu′rik). Pertaining to or characterized by anuria.

anurous (ah-nu′rus) [*an* neg. + Gr. *oura* tail]. Without a tail.

anus (a′nus), pl. *anus*, gen. *a′ni* [L.; said originally to have been derived from an Anglo-Saxon word meaning to sit]. The distal or terminal orifice of the alimentary canal. **artificial a.,** an opening from the bowel formed by an operation. **Bartholin's a., a. cer′ebri,** the anterior opening of the aqueduct of Sylvius. **entero-uterine a.,** a condition in which the intestine has herniated into the ruptured uterus, and fecal matter is discharged through the uterus and vagina. **imperforate a.,** an anus closed by a membrane or tissue so as to prevent the passage of the normal intestinal contents. **preternatural a.,** an anus situated at some unusual or abnormal place. **a. of Rusconi,** the blastopore. **a. vesica′lis,** anomalous opening of the rectum into the bladder, the anus being imperforate. **a. vestibula′ris,** anomalous opening of the rectum on the vulva, the anus being imperforate. **vulvovaginal a.,** a. vestibularis.

anusitis (a-nus-i′tis). Inflammation of the anus.

anvil (an′vil). Incus.

anxietas (ang-zi′ĕ-tas) [L.]. A nervous restlessness; anxiety. **a. preseni′lis,** a state of extreme anxiety preceding senility. **a. tibia′rum,** a painful condition of unrest leading to a continual change of the position of the limbs.

anxiety (ang-zi′ĕ-te). A feeling of apprehension, uncertainty and fear. **castration a.,** castration complex. **situation a.,** a feeling of apprehension coming on with the starting of some undertaking.

anydremia (an″ĭ-dre′me-ah) [*an* neg. + Gr. *hydōr* water + *haima* blood + *-ia*]. Anhydremia.

AO. Abbreviation for *anodal opening, axio-occlusal,* and *opening of the auriculoventricular valves.*

AOC. Abbreviation for *anodal opening contraction.*

AOCl. Abbreviation for *anodal opening clonus.*

A.O.M. Abbreviation for *Master of Obstetric Art.*

AOO. Abbreviation for *anodal opening odor.*

AOP. Abbreviation for *anodal opening picture.*

aorta (a-or′tah), pl. *aor′tas, aor′tae* [L.; Gr. *aortē*]. The main trunk from which the systemic arterial system proceeds [N A, B N A]. It arises from the left ventricle of the heart; passes upward (*a. ascen′dens*) bends over (*arcus aortae*), passes down through the thorax (*a. thoraca′lis*), and through the abdomen to the fourth lumbar vertebra (*a. abdomina′lis*) where it divides into the two common iliac arteries. See *Table of Arteriae.* **abdominal a., a. abdomina′lis** [N A, B N A], the continuation of the thoracic aorta, which gives rise to the inferior phrenic, lumbar, median sacral, superior mesenteric, inferior mesenteric, middle suprarenal, renal, and testicular or ovarian arteries, and the celiac trunk. **a. angus′ta,** an aorta of greatly reduced lumen. **a. ascen′dens** [N A, B N A], **ascending a.,** the proximal portion of the aorta, arising from the left ventricle, and giving origin to the right and left coronary arteries; it continues as the arcus aortae. **a. chlorot′ica,** a small aorta sometines seem in a patient with chlorosis. **a. descen′dens** [N A, B N A], **descending a.,** the continuation of the aorta from the arch of the aorta, in the thorax, to the point of its division into the common iliac arteries, in the abdomen. See also *abdominal a.* and *thoracic a.* **dynamic a.,** a condition in which the pulsations of the abdominal aorta are abnormally marked. **palpable a.,** one which, on account of a thin, retracted abdominal wall, is easily palpable. **primitive a.,** either of two main vascular trunks in the early embryo, appearing in the splanchnic mesoderm of the pericardial region and continuous with the vitelline veins. **a. sacrococcyg′ea,** arteria sacralis mediana. **a. thoraca′lis** [B N A], **thoracic a.,** a. thoracica. **a. thorac′ica** [N A], the proximal portion of the descending aorta, proceeding from the arch of the aorta, and giving rise to the bronchial, esophageal, pericardiac, and mediastinal branches, and the superior phrenic, posterior intercostal III to XI, and subcostal arteries; it is continuous through the diaphragm with the abdominal aorta. **throbbing a.,** abnormally strong pulsations of the aorta felt in the epigastric region in neurasthenia. **ventral a.,** a single short trunk which connects the heart with the aortic sac in the early embryo.

aortae (a-or′te). [L.]. Plural and genitive of *aorta.*

aortal (a-or′tal). Aortic.

aortalgia (a″or-tal′je-ah) [*aorta* + Gr. *algos* pain]. Pain in the region of the aorta.

aortarctia (a″or-tark′she-ah) [*aorta* + L. *arctare* to narrow]. Constriction or narrowing of the aorta.

aortectasia (a″or-tek-ta′ze-ah) [*aorta* + Gr. *ektasis* distention + *-ia*]. Dilatation of the aorta.

aortectasis (a″or-tek′tah-sis). Aortectasia.

aortectomy (a″or-tek′to-me) [*aorta* + Gr. *ektomē* excision]. Excision of part of the aorta.

aortic (a-or′tik). Of or pertaining to the aorta.

aorticorenal (a-or″te-ko-re′nal). Pertaining to the aorta and the kidneys.

aortism (a′or-tizm). A constitutional tendency toward aortic disease.

aortismus (a″or-tiz′mus). Aortic disease. **a. abdomina′lis,** phantom aneurysm.

aortitis (a″or-ti′tis) [*aorta* + *-itis*]. Inflammation of the aorta. **Döhle-Heller a.,** syphilitic a. **nummular a.,** aortitis with white, circular patches on the inner coat of the vessel. **syphilitic a., a. syphilit′ica,** aortitis associated with and caused by syphilis. **a. syphilit′ica oblit′erans,** syphilitic aortitis resulting in obliteration of the aorta or some of its branches.

aortoclasia (a″or-to-kla′ze-ah). Rupture of the aorta.

aortogram (a-or′to-gram″). The film produced by aortography.

aortography (a″or-tog′rah-fe) [*aorta* + Gr. *graphein* to write]. Roentgenography of the aorta after the intravascular injection of an opaque medium. **retrograde a.,** roentgenography of the aorta after forcible injection of a radiopaque substance into a peripheral artery counter to direction of the blood flow.

aortolith (a-or′to-lith) [*aorta* + Gr. *lithos* stone]. A calculus in the aorta.

aortomalacia (a-or″to-mah-la′she-ah) [*aorta* + Gr. *malakia* softness]. Abnormal softness of the aorta.

aortopathy (a″or-top′ah-the) [*aorta* + Gr. *pathos* disease]. Any disease of the aorta.

aortoptosia (a″or-top-to′se-ah) [*aorta* + Gr. *ptōsis* falling + *-ia*]. Downward displacement of the abdominal aorta.

aortoptosis (a″or-top-to′sis). Aortoptosia.

aortorrhaphy (a″or-tor′ah-fe) [*aorta* + Gr. *rhaphē* suture]. Suture of the aorta.

aortosclerosis (a-or″to-skle-ro′sis). Sclerosis of the aorta.

aortostenosis (a-or″to-ste-no′sis) [*aorta* + Gr. *stenōsis* narrowing]. Narrowing or stricture of the aorta.

aortotomy (a″or-tot′o-me) [*aorta* + Gr. *tomē* a cutting]. Incision of the aorta.

AOS. Abbreviation for *anodal opening sound.*

aosmic (a-oz′mik) Anosmic.

A.O.T.A. Abbreviation for *American Occupational Therapy Association.*

AOTe. Abbreviation for *anodal opening tetanus.*

A.P. Abbreviation for *Academy of Periodontology, anterior pituitary,* and *axiopulpal.*

ap-. See *apo-.*

A.P.A. Abbreviation for *American Physiotherapy Association.*

APA. Abbreviation for *antipernicious anemia factor.*

apaconitine (ap″ah-kon′ĭ-tin) [*ap-* + *aconitine*]. A poisonous base derived from aconitine.

apallesthesia (ah-pal″es-the′ze-ah). Pallanesthesia.

apamide (ap′ah-mīd). Trade mark for a preparation of acetaminophen.

apancrea (ah-pan′kre-ah). Absence of the pancreas.

apancreatic (ah-pan″kre-at′ik). 1. Not pertaining to the pancreas. 2. Due to absence of the pancreas.

apandria (ap-an′dre-ah) [*ap-* + Gr. *anēr* man). Morbid aversion to the male sex.

apanthropia (ap-an-thro′pe-ah) [*ap-* + Gr. *anthrōpos* man + *-ia*]. 1. Morbid fear of human companionship. 2. Apandria.

apanthropy (ap-an′thro-pe). Apanthropia.

aparalytic (ah-par″ah-lit′ik). Without paralysis.

aparathyreosis (ah-par″ah-thi-re-o′sis). Aparathyrosis.

aparathyroidism (ah-par″ah-thi′roid-izm). Aparathyrosis.

aparathyrosis (ah-par″ah-thi-ro′sis). Absence or deficiency of the parathyroid glands.

apareunia (ah″par-u′ne-ah). Absence of, or inability to perform, coitus.

aparthrosis (ap″ar-thro′sis) [Gr. *aparthrōsis*]. Diarthrosis.

apastia (ah-pas′te-ah) [Gr. "fasting"]. Abstention from food, as a neurologic symptom.

apastic (ah-pas′tik). Pertaining to or characterized by apastia.

apathetic (ap″ah-thet′ik). Indifferent; undemonstrative.

apathic (ah-path′ik). Without sensation or feeling.

apathism (ap′ah-thizm). The state of being slow in responding to stimuli.

apathy (ap′ah-the) [Gr. *apatheia*]. Lack of feeling or emotion; indifference.

apatite (ap′ah-tit) [Gr. *apate* deceit, because it has been mistaken for other minerals]. A series of minerals of the general formula $3Ca_3(PO_4)_2.CaF_2$.

APC. Abbreviation for *acetylsalicylic acid, phenacetin,* and *caffeine,* available in capsule or tablet form: used as an antipyretic and analgesic.

APE. Abbreviation for *anterior pituitary extract.*

apectomy (a-pek′to-me). Apicoectomy.

apeidosis (ap″i-do′sis) [*ap-* + Gr. *eidos* form]. Progressive disappearance of characteristic form in either the histologic or clinical aspect of a disease.

apellous (a-pel′us) [*a* neg. + L. *pellis* skin]. 1. Skinless; not covered with skin; not cicatrized: said of a wound. 2. Having no prepuce.

apenteric (ap″en-ter′ik) [*ap-* + Gr. *enteron* intestine]. Abenteric.

apepsia (ah-pep′se-ah) [*a* neg. + Gr. *peptein* to digest]. Cessation or failure of the digestive functions. **achlorhydria a.,** absence of the digestive secretions of the stomach. **hysteric a., a. nervo′sa,** anorexia nervosa.

apepsinia (ah″pep-sin′e-ah). Total absence or lack of secretion of pepsin or pepsinogen by the stomach.

aperient (ah-pe′re-ent) [L. *aperiens* opening]. 1. Mildly cathartic. 2. A gentle purgative.

aperiodic (ah″pe-rĭ-od′ik). Having no definite period: said of membranes which have no definite periods of vibration of their own, but are free to take up any vibrations imparted to them.

aperistalsis (ah″per-e-stal′sis) [*a* neg. + *peristalsis*]. Absence of peristaltic action.

aperitive (ah-per′ĭ-tiv). 1. Stimulating the appetite. 2. Aperient.

Apert's disease, syndrome (ah-parz′) [Eugène *Apert,* French pediatrician, 1868–1940]. Acrocephalosyndactylia.

apertometer (ap″er-tom′e-ter). An apparatus for measuring the angle of aperture of microscopical objectives.

apertura (ap″er-tu′rah), pl. *apertu′rae* [L.]. A general term used in anatomical nomenclature to designate an opening. **a. exter′na aqueduc′tus vestib′uli** [N A], the external opening for the aqueduct of the vestibule, located on the internal surface of the petrous part of the temporal bone, lateral to the opening for the internal acoustic meatus. Called also *external aperture of aqueduct of vestibule.* **a. exter′na canalic′uli coch′leae** [N A, B N A], the external opening of the cochlear canaliculus on the margin of the jugular foramen in the temporal bone. Called also *external aperture of canaliculus of cochlea.* **a. infe′rior canalic′uli tympan′ici** [B N A], the lower opening of the tympanic canaliculus on the inferior surface of the petrous portion of the temporal bone. Called also *inferior aperture of tympanic canaliculus.* **a. latera′lis ventric′uli quar′ti** [N A, B N A], a semilunar opening at the lateral angle of the fourth ventricle on either side. Called also *lateral aperture of fourth ventricle* and *Luschka's foramen.* **a. media′lis ventric′uli quar′ti** [B N A], a. mediana ventriculi quarti. **a. media′na ventric′uli quar′ti** [N A], a median aperture in the membranous roof of the fourth ventricle, connecting it with the subarachnoid space. Called also *apertura medialis ventriculi quarti* [B N A], *median aperture of fourth ventricle,* and *Magendie's foramen.* **a. pel′vis infe′rior** [N A], the inferior, very irregular aperture of the minor pelvis, bounded by the coccyx, the sacrotuberous ligaments, part of the ischium, the sides of the pubic arch, and the pubic symphysis. Called also *apertura pelvis [minoris] inferior* [B N A]. **a. pel′vis supe′rior** [N A], the superior aperture of the minor pelvis, bounded by the crest and pecten of the pubic bones, the arcuate lines of the ilia, and the anterior margin of the base of the sacrum. Called also *apertura pelvis [minoris] superior* [B N A]. **a. pirifor′mis** [N A, B N A], the anterior nasal opening in the skull. Called also *piriform aperture.* **a. si′nus fronta′lis** [N A], the external opening of the frontal sinus into the nasal cavity. Called also *aperture of frontal sinus.* **a. si′nus sphenoida′lis** [N A, B N A], a round opening just above the superior nasal concha, interconnecting the sphenoid sinus and nasal cavity. Called also *aperture of sphenoid sinus.* **a. supe′rior canalic′uli tympan′ici** [B N A], the upper opening of the tympanic canaliculus in the temporal bone, leading to the tympanum. Called also *superior aperture of tympanic canaliculus.* **a. thora′cis infe′rior** [N A, B N A], the irregular opening at the inferior part of the thorax bounded by the twelfth thoracic vertebra, the twelfth ribs, and the curving edge of the costal cartilages as they meet the sternum. Called also *inferior aperture of thorax.* **a. thora′cis supe′rior** [N A, B N A], the elliptical opening at the summit of the thorax, bounded by the first thoracic vertebra, the first ribs, and the upper margin of the manubrium sterni. Called also *superior aperture of thorax.* **a. tympan′ica canalic′uli chor′dae tympani** [N A], the opening through which the chorda tympani enters the tympanic cavity. Called also *tympanic aperture of canaliculus of chorda tympani.*

aperturae (ap″er-tu′re) [L.]. Plural of *apertura.*

aperture (ap′er-chŭr) [L. *apertura*]. An opening, or orifice. See also *apertura.* **angle of a., angular a.,** the angle formed at a luminous point between the most divergent rays that are capable of passing through the objective of a microscope. **external a. of aqueduct of vestibule,** apertura externa aqueductus vestibuli. **external a. of canaliculus of cochlea,** apertura externa canaliculi cochleae. **external a. of tympanic canaliculus,** apertura inferior canaliculi tympanici. **a. of frontal sinus,** apertura sinus frontalis. **a. of glottis,** rima glottidis. **inferior a. of minor pelvis,** apertura pelvis inferior. **inferior a. of thorax,** apertura thoracis inferior. **inferior a. of tympanic canaliculus,** apertura inferior canaliculi tympanici. **internal a. of femoral canal,** lacuna vasorum. **internal a. of tympanic canaliculus,** apertura superior canaliculi tympanici. **a. of larynx,** aditus laryngis. **lateral a. of fourth ventricle,** apertura lateralis ventriculi quarti. **a. of lens,** angle of a. **median a. of fourth ventricle,** apertura mediana ventriculi quarti. **nasal a., bony anterior,** apertura piriformis. **numerical a.,** a measure of the efficiency of a microscope objective, being the product of the sine of one-half the angle of the aperture times the lowest refractive index of any medium between the objective and specimen. Usually abbreviated N. A. **orbital a.,** aditus orbitae. **piriform a.,** apertura piriformis. **a. of sphenoid sinus,** apertura sinus sphenoidalis. **spinal a.,** foramen vertebrale. **spurious a. of facial canal,** hiatus canalis nervi petrosi majoris. **spurious a. of fallopian canal,** hiatus canalis nervi petrosi majoris. **superior a. of minor pelvis,** apertura pelvis superior. **superior a. of thorax,** apertura thoracis superior. **superior a. of tympanic canaliculus,** apertura superior canaliculi tympanici. **thoracic a., inferior,** apertura thoracis inferior. **thoracic a., superior,** apertura thoracis superior. **tympanic a. of canaliculus of chorda tympani,** apertura tympanica canaliculi chordae tympani.

apex (a'peks), pl. *apexes* or *a'pices* [L.]. 1. A general term used in anatomical nomenclature to designate the top of a body organ or part, or the pointed extremity of a conical structure. Called also *tip*. 2. The point of greatest activity, or the point of greatest response to any type of stimulation, such as electrical stimulation of a muscle. **a. of arytenoid cartilage,** a. cartilaginis arytenoideae. **a. auric'ulae** [N A, B N A], a pointed protrusion sometimes observed on the upper border of the ear. **a. of bladder,** a. vesicae urinariae. **a. cap'itis fib'ulae** [N A], a process pointing upward on the posterior surface of the head of the fibula, giving attachment to the arcuate popliteal ligament of the knee joint and part of the biceps tendon. Called also *a. capituli fibulae* [B N A], and *a. of head of fibula*. **a. capit'uli fib'ulae** [B N A], a. capitis fibulae. **a. cartilag'inis arytenoi'deae** [N A], the upper part of the arytenoid cartilage, which bends posteriorly and medially and connects with the corniculate cartilage. Called also *apex of arytenoid cartilage*. **a. colum'nae posterio'ris medul'lae spina'lis** [B N A], a. cornus posterioris medullae spinalis. **a. cor'dis** [N A, B N A], the blunt, rounded extremity of the heart formed by the left ventricle; it is directed ventrally, inferiorly, and to the left. **a. cor'nus posterio'ris medul'lae spina'lis** [N A], a rim of large neurons just dorsal to the gelatinous substance of the spinal cord; sometimes used to refer to the gelatinous substance. Called also *a. columnae posterioris medullae spinalis* [B N A], and *a. of posterior horn of spinal cord*. **Darwinian a.,** a. auriculae. **a. of head of fibula,** a. capitis fibulae. **a. of heart,** a. cordis. **a. lin'guae** [N A, B N A], the most distal portion of the tongue. **a. of lung,** a. pulmonis. **a. na'si** [N A, B N A], the most distal portion of the nose. **a. os'sis sa'cri** [N A, B N A], the caudal end of the body of the fifth sacral vertebra, which articulates with the coccyx. Called also *a. of sacrum*. **a. par'tis petro'sae os'sis tempora'lis** [N A], the truncated portion of the petrous part of the temporal bone that is directed anteriorly and medially and ends at the medial opening of the carotid canal. Called also *a. pyramidis ossis temporalis* [B N A]. **a. patel'lae** [N A, B N A], the inferiorly directed blunt point of the patella, to which the patellar ligament is attached. Called also *a. of patella*. **a. of petrous portion of temporal bone,** a. partis petrosae ossis temporalis. **a. of posterior horn of spinal cord,** a. cornus posterioris medullae spinalis. **a. prosta'tae** [N A, B N A], **a. of prostate gland,** the lower portion of the prostate, located just above the urogenital diaphragm. **a. pulmo'nis** [N A, B N A], the rounded upper extremity of either lung, extending upward as high as the first thoracic vertebra. Called also *a. of lung*. **a. pyram'idis os'sis tempora'lis** [B N A], a. partis petrosae ossis temporalis. **a. rad'icis den'tis** [N A, B N A], the terminal end of the root of a tooth. **a. of sacrum,** a. ossis sacri. **a. suprarena'lis [gl. dex'trae]** [B N A], the apex of the right suprarenal (adrenal) gland. **a. of tongue,** a. linguae. **a. vesi'cae urina'riae** [N A], the site of junction of the superior and inferolateral surfaces of the urinary bladder, from which the middle umbilical ligament (urachus) extends to the umbilicus. Called also *a. of bladder* and *vertex vesicae urinariae* [B N A].

A.P.F. Abbreviation for *animal protein factor*.

Apgar score (ap'gar) [Virginia *Apgar*, American anesthesiologist, born 1909]. See under *score*.

A.P.H.A. Abbreviation for *American Public Health Association* and for *American Protestant Hospital Association*.

aphacia (ah-fa'se-ah). Aphakia.

aphacic (ah-fa'sik). Aphakic.

aphagia (ah-fa'je-ah) [*a* neg. + Gr. *phagein* to eat + *-ia*]. Abstention from eating. **a. al'gera,** refusal of a person to take food because it gives pain.

aphagopraxia (ah-fa"go-prak'se-ah). Loss of the ability to swallow.

aphakia (ah-fa'ke-ah) [*a* neg. + Gr. *phakos* lentil + *-ia*]. Congenital absence of the lens of the eye.

aphakic (ah-fa'kik). Pertaining to aphakia; having no lens in the eye.

aphalangia (ah"fah-lan'je-ah). A developmental anomaly characterized by absence of a digit or of one or more phalanges of a finger or toe.

aphanisis (ah-fan'ĭ-sis). [Gr. "disappearance"]. The obliteration of sexuality.

Aphanocapsa, Aphanocapta (ah"fan-o-kap'sah, ah"fan-o-kap'tah) [Gr. *aphanēs* invisible + *kapsa* basket, case]. A genus of schizomycetes related to *Bacillus*, but having phycochrome in the cells.

Aphanozoa (af"ah-no-zo'ah) [Gr. *aphanēs* invisible + *zōon* animal]. Ultramicroscopic organisms.

aphantobiont (ah-fan"to-bi'ont) [Gr. *aphantos* invisible + *bioun* a living being]. One of the ultramicroscopic particles which make up a filtrable virus.

aphasia (ah-fa'ze-ah) [*a* neg. + Gr. *phasis* speech]. Defect or loss of the power of expression by speech, writing, or signs, or of comprehending spoken or written language, due to injury or disease of the brain centers. For types of aphasia not given below see *agrammatism, anomia, paragrammatism,* and *paraphasia*. **acoustic a.,** auditory a. **ageusic a.,** loss of power to express words relating to the sense of taste. **amnemonic a.,** forgetfulness of words, with consequent aphasia. **amnesic a., amnestic a.,** inability to remember words. **anosmic a.,** inability to express in words sensations of smell. **associative a.,** aphasia due to a disturbance of connection between the parts comprising the central structure. **ataxic a.,** aphasia in which the patient knows what he wishes to say, but cannot utter the words on account of inability to coordinate the muscles, because of disease of the speech center; called also *motor a*. **auditory a.,** aphasia due to disease of the hearing center of the brain; word deafness. **Broca's a.,** ataxic aphasia. **central a.,** aphasia due to lesion of the cerebral cortex; paraphasia. **combined a.,** aphasia of two or more forms occurring concomitantly in the same patient. **commissural a.,** aphasia due to a lesion in the insula interrupting the path between the motor and sensory speech centers. **complete a.,** aphasia due to lesion of all the speech centers, producing inability to communicate with others in any way. **cortical a., expressive-receptive a.,** global a. **frontocortical a.,** ataxic a. **frontolenticular a.,** commissural a. **functional a.,** aphasia resulting from hysteria or severe hysterical disorder. **gibberish a.,** aphasia with utterance of meaningless phrases. **global a.,** aphasia which involves all the functions which go to make up speech or communication. **graphomotor a.,** aphasia in which the patient cannot express himself in writing. **Grashey's a.,** aphasia due to lessened duration of sensory impressions, causing disturbance of perception and association, without lack of function of the centers or conductivity of the tracts. It is seen in acute diseases and concussion of the brain. **impressive a.,** sensory a. **intellectual a.,** true a. **jargon a.,** aphasia in which several words are run together as one. **Kussmaul's a.,** voluntary refraining from speech, as in the insane. **lenticular a.,** commissural a. **a. leth'ica,** amnemonic a. **Lichtheim's a.,** a form of aphasia in which spontaneous speech is lost but the ability to repeat words is retained. **mixed a.,** combined motor and sensory aphasia. **motor a.,** ataxic a. **nominal a.,** aphasia marked by the defective use of names of objects. Cf. *anomia* and *dysnomia*. **optic a.,** inability to name objects seen, due to interruption of the connection between the speech and visual centers. **parieto-occipital a.,** combined alexia and apraxia. **pathematic a.,** aphasia due to passion or fright. **pictorial a.,** cortical aphasia, so called because the cortex is the region containing the centers for images of words. **psychosensory a.,** inability to understand language, spoken, written, or expressed in any way. **puerperal a.,** aphasia occurring during pregnancy or the puerperium. **receptive a.,** sensory a. **semantic a.,** aphasia characterized by a lack of recognition of the full significance of words and phrases or by loss of memory for words. **sensory a.,** inability to understand the meaning of written, spoken or tactile speech symbols, due to disease of the auditory and visual word centers. **subcortical a.,** aphasia due to a lesion interrupting impulses toward the afferent tracts that proceed to the auditory speech center. **syntactical a.,** aphasia characterized by inability to arrange words properly, so that the patient talks jargon. **tactile a.,** inability to name objects which are felt. **temporoparietal a.,** cortical sensory aphasia. **total a.,** combined motor and sensory aphasia. **transcortical a.,** aphasia caused by a lesion of a pathway between the speech center and other cortical centers. **true a.,** aphasia due to lesion of any one of the speech centers; called also *intellectual a.* **verbal a.,** aphasia marked by a greatly restricted ability to form words for speech and thought. **visual a.,** inability to comprehend written words; word blindness; optical alexia. **Wernicke's a.,** cortical sensory aphasia.

aphasiac (ah-fa′ze-ak). Aphasic.

aphasic (ah-fa′zik). 1. Pertaining to, or affected with, aphasia. 2. A person affected with aphasia.

apheliotropism (ap″he-le-ot′ro-pizm). Negative heliotropism.

aphemesthesia (ah″fe-mes-the′ze-ah) [*a* neg. + Gr. *phēmē* voice + *aisthēsis* perception]. Failure of word perception; word blindness and word deafness.

aphemia (ah-fe′me-ah) [*a* neg. + Gr. *phēmē* voice]. Loss of the power of speech, due to a central lesion. See *ataxic aphasia,* under *aphasia.*

aphemic (ah-fem′ik). Pertaining to or characterized by aphemia.

aphephobia (af″e-fo′be-ah) [Gr. *haphē* touch + *phobia*]. A morbid dread of touching or of being touched.

apheter (af′ĕ-ter) [Gr. *aphienai* to dissolve]. A supposed material which gives to inogen the stimulus that decomposes it, and thus causes muscular contraction.

aphilopony (ah″fil-op′ŏ-ne) [*a* neg. + Gr. *philein* to love + *ponos* bodily exertion]. Fear of, or disinclination to, work.

Aphiochae′ta ferrugin′ea. A fly found in tropical America and in India which causes cutaneous myiasis in man.

Aphloi′a theafor′mis. A shrub of Madagascar; a decoction is used in hematuria.

aphonia (ah-fo′ne-ah) [*a* neg. + Gr. *phōnē* voice]. Loss of voice. **a. clerico′rum,** clergyman's sore throat. **hysteric a.,** loss of speech due to hysteria. **a. paralyt′ica,** aphonia due to paralysis or disease of the laryngeal nerves. **a. parano′ica,** stubborn and wilful silence. **spastic a.,** interference with speech caused by muscular spasm.

aphonic (ah-fon′ik). 1. Pertaining to or affected with aphonia. 2. Without audible sound.

aphonogelia (ah″fo-no-je′le-ah) [*a* neg. + Gr. *phōnē* voice + *gelōs* laughter]. Inability to laugh aloud.

aphoresis (af″o-re′sis). 1. Removal of a part. 2. Inability to endure, as of pain.

aphose (ah-fōz′) [*a* neg. + Gr. *phōs* light]. Any phose or subjective visual sensation due to absence or interruption of light.

aphosphagenic (ah-fos″fah-jen′ik). Due to deficiency of phosphorus.

aphosphorosis (ah-fos″fo-ro′sis). A morbid condition caused by a deficiency of phosphorus in the diet.

aphotesthesia (a″fot-es-the′ze-ah) [*a* neg. + Gr. *phōs* light + *aisthēsis* perception]. Reduced sensitivity of the retina to light resulting from excessive exposure to rays of the sun.

aphotic (ah-fot′ik). Without light; totally dark.

aphrasia (ah-fra′ze-ah) [*a* neg. + Gr. *phrasis* utterance]. Inability to speak or to understand words arranged as phrases. **a. parano′ica,** voluntary abstention from speech in the mentally ill.

aphrenia (ah-fre′ne-ah) [*a* neg. + Gr. *phrēn* mind]. Dementia.

aphrodisia (af″ro-diz′e-ah) [Gr. *aphrodisia* sexual pleasures]. 1. Sexual excitement, especially if morbid or excessive. 2. Venery or sexual congress.

aphrodisiac (af″ro-diz′e-ak). 1. Exciting the sexual impulse. 2. Any drug that arouses the sexual instinct.

aphrodisiomania (af″ro-diz″e-o-ma′ne-ah). Erotomania.

aphronesia (af″ro-ne′ze-ah) [*a* neg. + Gr. *phronēsis* good sense]. Dementia.

aphronia (ah-fro′ne-ah) [*a* neg. + Gr. *phronein* to understand]. Deficiency in mental discernment; defect in cerebration.

aphtha (af′thah), pl. *aph′thae* [L.; Gr. *aphtha*]. 1. A small ulcer. 2. [Usually plural.] Thrush; more correctly, the whitish spots in the mouth that characterize aphthous (maculofibrinous) stomatitis. **Bednar's a.,** an infected traumatic ulcer on the posterior portion of the hard palate in infants. **cachectic aphthae,** a fatal disease characterized by aphthous ulceration under the tongue, enlarged and degenerated liver and spleen, and skin pigmentation. **Cardarelli's aphthae,** cachectic aphthae. **chronic intermittent recurrent aphthae,** recurrent canker sores; a rare disease of the mouth marked by recurrent attacks of aphthae-like lesions of the mouth and tongue. **contagious aphthae, epizootic aphthae,** foot-and-mouth disease of cattle. **malignant aphthae,** contagious aphthae. **Mikulicz's aphthae,** chronic intermittent recurrent aphthae. **aphthae resisten′tiae,** periadenitis mucosa necrotica recurrens. **Riga's aphthae,** cachectic aphthae. **aphthae trop′icae,** an aphthous eruption with digestive disturbance occurring in the tropics.

aphthae (af′the) [L.]. Plural of *aphtha.*

aphthenxia (af-thenk′se-ah) [Gr. *aphthenktos* voiceless]. Impairment of the power to express articulate sounds.

aphthoid (af′thoid) [Gr. *aphtha* thrush + *eidos* form]. 1. Resembling thrush; thrushlike. 2. An exanthema resembling that of thrush.

aphthongia (af-thon′je-ah) [*a* neg. + Gr. *phthongos* sound]. Aphasia due to spasm of the speech muscles.

aphthosis (af-tho′sis). Any condition marked by aphthae.

aphthous (af′thus). Pertaining to, characterized by, or affected with, aphthae.

aphylactic (a″fi-lak′tik). Pertaining to or characterized by aphylaxis.

aphylaxis (a″fi-lak′sis). Absence of phylaxis.

apical (ap′e-kal). Pertaining to or located at the apex.

apicectomy (a″pe-sek′to-me). 1. Excision of the apex of the petrous portion of the temporal bone. 2. Apicoectomy.

apiceotomy (a-pis″e-ot′o-me). Apicoectomy.

apices (ap′ĭ-sēz) [L.]. Plural of *apex.*

apicitis (a″pe-si′tis). Inflammation of an apex, as the apex of a tooth, the apex of the lung, or the apex of the petrous portion of the temporal bone (petrositis).

apicoectomy (a″pe-ko-ek′to-me) [*apex* + Gr. *ektomē* excision]. Excision of the apical portion of a tooth root through an opening made in the overlying labial or buccal alveolar bone.

apicolocator (a″pe-ko-lo′ka-tor). An instrument for locating the apex of a tooth.

apicolysis (a″pe-kol′ĭ-sis) [*apex* + Gr. *lysis* dissolution]. The operation of causing the apex of the lung to collapse, thus obliterating the apical cavity.

apicostome (a′pe-ko-stōm). An instrument (trocar and cannula) for performing apicostomy.

apicostomy (a″pe-kos′to-me) [*apex* + Gr. *stoma* mouth or opening]. Surgical formation of an opening through the gum and bone to the apical end of a tooth.

apicotomy (a″pe-kot′o-me). 1. Puncture of the apex of the petrous portion of the temporal bone. 2. Apicoectomy.

apiectomy (a″pe-ek′to-me). Apicoectomy.

apii (a′pe-e). Genitive of *apium*. **a. fruc′tus.** See under *Apium*.

A.P.I.M. Abbreviation for *Association Professionnelle Internationale des Médicins*, an international body which deals with the conduct of medical practice from the economic point of view.

apinealism (ah-pi′ne-al-izm). The effects allegedly produced by removal of the pineal gland.

apinoid (ap′ĭ-noid) [*a* neg. + Gr. *pinos* dirt + *eidos* form]. Clean; free from filth.

apioectomy (a″pe-o-ek′to-me). Apicoectomy.

apiotherapy (a″pe-o-ther′ah-pe). Treatment with bee venom.

apiphobia (a″pe-fo′be-ah) [L. *apis* bee + *phobia*]. Morbid dread of bees and their sting.

apisination (a″pis-ĭ-na′shun) [L. *apis* bee]. Poisoning by the sting of bees.

apitoxin (a″pe-tok′sin). A sulfur-containing protein constituent of bee sting poison.

apituitarism (ah″pĭ-tu′ĭ-tar-izm). The condition in which the pituitary gland has been destroyed, resulting in a state of dwarfism or in Simmonds' disease.

Apium (a′pe-um) [L.]. A genus of umbelliferous plants, including celery. Celery seed (*apii fructus*), the ripe fruit of *A. graveolens*, is diuretic and antispasmodic.

A.P.L. 1. Abbreviation for *anterior pituitary-like*. 2. Trade mark for a preparation of human chorionic gonadotropin.

aplacental (a″plah-sen′tal) [*a* neg. + *placenta*]. Having no placenta.

aplanatic (ah″plah-nat′ik) [*a* neg. + Gr. *planan* to wander]. Correcting, or not affected by, spherical aberration.

aplanatism (ah-plan′ah-tizm). Freedom from spherical aberration.

aplasia (ah-pla′se-ah) [*a* neg. + Gr. *plassein* to form]. Lack of development of an organ; frequently used to designate complete suppression or failure of development of a structure from the embryonic primordium. Cf. *agenesis*. **a. axia′lis extracortica′lis congen′ita,** familial centrolobar sclerosis. **dental a.,** lack of formation or development of a tooth or teeth. **germinal a.,** gonadal a. **gonadal a.,** failure of development of gonadal tissue. **nuclear a.,** lack of formation or development of cranial nerve nuclei or of portions thereof. **a. pilo′rum intermit′tens,** spindle-shaped hairs (Virchow). **retinal a.,** failure of the retina to develop into functioning tissue, with subsequent secondary degenerative changes.

aplasmic (ah-plaz′mik). Containing no protoplasm or sarcoplasm.

aplastic (ah-plas′tik) [*a* neg. + Gr. *plassein* to form]. Pertaining to or characterized by aplasia; having no tendency to develop into new tissue.

Aplectana (ah-plek′tah-nah). A genus of parasitic nematodes.

apleuria (ah-plu′re-ah). Absence of ribs.

aplysiopurpurin (ah-pli″se-o-pur′pu-rin). A purple-red dye in the glands of *Aplysia*, marine gastropods.

apnea (ap-ne′ah) [*a* neg. + Gr. *pnoia* breath]. 1. The transient cessation of the breathing impulse that follows forced breathing. 2. Asphyxia. **deglutition a.,** a temporary arrest of the activity of the respiratory nerve center during an act of swallowing. **a. neonato′rum,** disturbance of the respiratory mechanism in an infant, occurring shortly after birth. **traumatic a.,** traumatic asphyxia.

apneumatic (ap″nu-mat′ik). 1. Free from air. 2. Done with the exclusion of air.

apneumatosis (ap″nu-mah-to′sis) [*a* neg. + Gr. *pneumatōsis* inflation]. Collapse of the air cells of the lungs; congenital atelectasis of the lungs.

apneumia (ap-nu′me-ah) [*a* neg. + Gr. *pneumōn* lung]. A developmental anomaly characterized by absence of the lungs.

apneusis (ap-nu′sis). A condition marked by maintained inspiratory activity unrelieved by expiration, each inspiration being long and cramplike. It follows excision of the upper portion of the pons (pneumotaxic center).

apneustic (ap-nu′stik). Pertaining to or characterized by apneusis.

apo-, ap- [Gr *apo* from]. A prefix implying separation or derivation from.

apobiosis (ap″o-bi-o′sis) [*apo-* + Gr. *bios* life]. Physiological death.

apobiotic (ap″o-bi-ot′ik). Pertaining to any change which decreases the vital energy of any tissue.

apocamnosis (ap″o-kam-no′sis). Intense and readily induced fatigue.

apocarteresis (ap″o-kar″ter-e′sis) [*apo-* + Gr. *karterein* to be steadfast]. Suicide by persistent refusal of food.

apocatastasis (ap″o-kah-tas′tah-sis). Restoration; especially subsidence of a tumor or abscess.

apocenosis (ap″o-se-no′sis). An increased flow of blood or other humor.

apochromat (ap″o-kro-mat′) [*apo-* + *chromatic* aberration]. An apochromatic objective.

apochromatic (ap″o-kro-mat′ik). Free from chromatic and spherical aberration. See under *objective*.

apocope (ah-pok′o-pe) [Gr. *apokopē*]. A cutting off; amputation.

apocoptic (ap″o-kop′tik). Resulting from, or pertaining to, an amputation.

apocrine (ap′o-krīn) [Gr. *apokrinesthai* to be secreted]. Denoting that type of glandular secretion in which the secretory products become concentrated at the free end of the secreting cell and are thrown off, along with the portion of the cell where they have accumulated, as in the mammary gland. Cf. *holocrine* and *merocrine*.

apocrustic (ap″o-krus′tik). 1. Astringent and repellent. 2. An astringent and repellent agent.

apodactylic (ap″o-dak-til′ik) [*apo-* + Gr. *daktylos* finger]. Without the use of, or the touch of, the human fingers.

apodal (ah-po′dal). Having no feet.

apodemialgia (ap″o-de″me-al′je-ah) [Gr. *apodēmia* journey + *algos* pain + *-ia*]. A morbid or insane longing to go away from home.

apodia (ah-po′de-ah) [*a* neg. + Gr. *pous* foot + *-ia*]. A developmental anomaly characterized by absence of one or both of the feet.

apoenzyme (ap″o-en′zīm). The portion of an enzyme which requires the presence of coenzyme to become a complete enzyme.

apoferment (ap-o-fer′ment). Apoenzyme.

apoferritin (ap-o-fer′ĭ-tin). A colorless protein, with a molecular weight of 460,000, occurring in the mucosal cells of the small intestine, forming a compound with iron called ferritin, which has been implicated in the regulation of iron absorption in the gastrointestinal tract.

apogamia (ap″o-gam′e-ah). Parthenogenesis.

apogee (ap′o-je). The state of greatest severity of a disease.

apokamnosis (ap″o-kam-no′sis). Abnormal liability to fatigue in myasthenia; a feeling of tiredness, numbness, and heaviness in a limb motion.

apolar (ah-po′lar) [*a* neg. + Gr. *polos* pole]. Not having poles or processes.

apolegamic (ap″o-leh-gam′ik) [Gr. *apolegein* to pick out + *gamos* marriage]. Pertaining to selection, especially sexual selection.

apolegamy (ap″o-leg′ah-me). Selection, especially sexual selection in breeding.

apolepsis (ap″o-lep′sis). The suppression of a natural secretion.

Apollonia (ap″o-lo′ne-ah). The patron saint of dentistry; a Christian martyr, who was first persecuted by having her teeth knocked out, and then burned at the stake in 249 A.D. Her feast is observed February 9.

Apollonius (ap″o-lo′ne-us). The name by which several physicians of classical antiquity were known. For example, (1) a Greek physician, also called "the Empiric," who lived c. 200 B.C.; (2) a physician of Citium in Cyprus, who lived in the first century B.C. and who wrote a commentary on Hippocrates' treatise on articulations.

apomixia (ap″o-mik′se-ah). Parthenogenesis.

apomorphine (ap″o-mor′fin) [*apo-* + *morphine*]. A crystalline alkaloid, $C_{17}H_{17}NO_2$, derived from morphine by the abstraction of a molecule of water: used to induce vomiting, to induce sleep, and as an expectorant. **a. hydrochloride,** a grayish, crystalline compound, $C_{17}H_{17}NO_2.HCl.\frac{1}{2}H_2O$, used as an emetic.

apomyelin (ap″o-mi′ĕ-lin) [*apo-* + *myelin*]. A principle derivable from brain substance.

apomyttosis (ap″o-mit-to′sis) [Gr. *apomyttein* to blow one's nose + *-osis*]. Any disease marked by stertor or sneezing.

aponea (ap″o-ne′ah). Aponoia.

aponeurectomy (ap″o-nu-rek′to-me) [*aponeurosis* + Gr. *ektomē* excision]. Excision of the aponeurosis of a muscle.

aponeurology (ap″o-nu-rol′o-je) [*aponeurosis* + *-logy*]. The sum of knowledge regarding aponeuroses and fasciae.

aponeurorrhaphy (ap″o-nu-ror′ah-fe) [*aponeurosis* + Gr. *rhaphē* suture]. Suture of an aponeurosis; fasciorrhaphy.

aponeuroses (ap″o-nu-ro′sēz). Plural of *aponeurosis*.

aponeurosis (ap″o-nu-ro′sis), pl. *aponeuro′ses* [Gr. *aponeurōsis*]. [N A, B N A] A white, flattened or ribbon-like tendinous expansion, serving mainly as an investment for muscle, or connecting a muscle with the parts that it moves. **abdominal a.,** the conjoined tendons of the oblique and transverse muscles on the abdomen. **a. of biceps muscle, bicipital a.,** a. musculi bicipitis brachii. **crural a.,** fascia cruris. **deep a. of leg,** fascia cruris. **Denonvilliers' a.,** Denonvilliers' fascia. **epicranial a.,** galea aponeurotica. **falciform a. of rectus abdominis muscle,** falx inguinalis. **femoral a.,** fascia lata femoris. **a. of insertion,** one which connects a muscle with the part or parts that it moves. **interchondral aponeuroses, internal.** See *membrana intercostalis interna.* **intercostal aponeuroses, external.** See *membrana intercostalis externa.* **intercostal aponeuroses, internal.** See *membrana intercostalis interna.* **a. of investment,** one that serves as an investment for a muscle. **ischioprostatic a.,** fascia diaphragmatis urogenitalis inferior. **ischiorectal a.,** fascia diaphragmatis pelvis inferior. **a. lin′guae** [N A], **lingual a.,** the connective tissue framework of the tongue, supporting and giving attachment to the intrinsic and extrinsic muscles; composed of the connective tissue layer of the tunica mucosa, the lingual septum, and the posterior transverse expansion of the septum which attaches to the hyoid bone. **a. mus′culi bicip′itis bra′chii** [N A], an expansion of the tendon of the biceps brachii muscle by which it is attached to the fascia of the forearm and to the ulna. Called also *a. of biceps muscle* and *lacertus fibrosus musculi bicipitis brachii* [B N A]. **a. of occipitofrontal muscle,** galea aponeurotica. **palatine a.,** a fibrous sheet in the anterior part of the soft palate, derived mainly from the tendons of the two tensor muscles, giving attachment to the musculus uvulae, and the palato-pharyngeus and levator palati muscles. **palmar a., a. palma′ris** [N A, B N A], bundles of fibrous tissue radiating toward the bases of the fingers from the tendon of the palmaris longus muscle. **perineal a.,** fascia diaphragmatis urogenitalis inferior. **perineal a., superficial,** fascia diaphragmatis pelvis inferior. **perineal a., superior,** fascia diaphragmatis pelvis superior. **pharyngeal a., a. pharyn′gis, pharyngobasilar a., a. pharyngobasila′ris,** fascia pharyngobasilaris. **plantar a., a. planta′ris** [N A, B N A], bands of fibrous tissue radiating toward the bases of the toes from the medial process of the tuberosity of the calcaneus. **prostatic a., lateral,** fascia diaphragmatis urogenitalis superior. **Sibson's a.,** membrana suprapleuralis. **subscapular a.,** a membrane attached to the circumference of the subscapular fossa. **a. of superior surface of levator ani muscle,** fascia diaphragmatis pelvis superior. **supraspinous a.,** a thick and dense membranous layer that partly envelops the supraspinatus muscle. **temporal a.,** fascia temporalis. **vertebral a.,** fascia thoracolumbalis. **a. of Zinn.** See *fibrae zonulares.*

aponeurositis (ap″o-nu-ro-si′tis) [*aponeurosis* + *-itis*]. Inflammation of an aponeurosis.

aponeurotic (ap″o-nu-rot′ik). Pertaining to or of the nature of an aponeurosis.

aponeurotome (ap″o-nu′ro-tōm). A knife for cutting aponeuroses.

aponeurotomy (ap″o-nu-rot′o-me) [*aponeurosis* + Gr. *tomē* a cut]. Surgical cutting of an aponeurosis.

aponia (ah-po′ne-ah) [Gr.]. Freedom from pain.

aponic (ah-po′nik). Relieving pain or fatigue.

aponoia (ap″o-noi′ah) [*apo-* + Gr. *nous* mind]. Amentia.

Aponomma (ap″o-nom′ah). A genus of ticks occurring on tropical reptiles of the Old World.

apopathetic (ap″o-pah-thet′ik). A term applied to behavior in which the individual adapts his actions to the presence of other persons.

apophlegmatic (ap″o-fleg-mat′ik). Causing a discharge of mucus; expectorant.

apophylactic (ap″o-fi-lak′tik). Pertaining to, or marked by, apophylaxis.

apophylaxis (ap″o-fi-lak′sis) [*apo-* + *phylaxis*]. Decrease of the phylactic power of the blood, as seen in the negative phase of vaccine therapy.

apophysary (ah-pof′i-za-re). Apophyseal.

apophyseal (ap″o-fiz′e-al). Pertaining to or of the nature of an apophysis.

apophyseopathy (ap″o-fiz-e-op′ah-the) [*apophysis* + Gr. *pathos* disease]. Disease of an apophysis, particularly Schlatter's disease.

apophyses (ah-pof′ĭ-sēz). Plural of *apophysis*.

apophysial (ap″o-fiz′e-al). Apophyseal.

apophysiary (ap″o-fiz′e-a″re). Apophyseal.

apophysis (ah-pof′ĭ-sis), pl. *apoph′yses* [Gr. "an offshoot"]. [N A, B N A] Any outgrowth or swelling, especially a bony outgrowth that has never been entirely separated from the bone of which it forms a part, such as a process, tubercle, or tuberosity. **basilar a.,** basilar process. **cerebral a., a. cer′ebri,** pineal body. **genial a.,** the four mental tubercles. **a. of Ingrassias,** ala minor ossis sphenoidalis. **a. lenticula′ris in′cudis,** processus lenticularis incudis. **odontoid a.,** dens of axis. **a. os′sium,** epiphysis. **pterygoid a.,** processus pterygoideus ossis sphenoidalis. **a. of Rau, a. ravia′na, a. raw′ii,** processus anterior mallei.

apophysitis (ah-pof″e-zi′tis). 1. Inflammation of an apophysis; especially a disorder of the foot caused by disease of the epiphysis of the os calcis (osteochondrosis of the calcaneus). 2. Appendicitis. **a. tibia′lis adolescen′tium,** Schlatter's disease.

apoplasmatic (ap″o-plaz-mat′ik). Pertaining to substances that are produced by cells and form a constituent part of the tissues of an organism, such as fibers of connective tissue or the matrix of bone and cartilage.

apoplasmia (ap″o-plaz′me-ah) [*apo-* + Gr. *plasma* anything formed]. Deficiency of the blood plasm.

apoplectic (ap″o-plek′tik) [Gr. *apoplēktikos*]. Pertaining to, caused by or affected with apoplexy.

apoplectiform (ap-o-plek′te-form). Resembling apoplexy.

apoplectoid (ap″o-plek′toid). Resembling apoplexy.

apoplexia (ap″o-plek′se-ah) [L.]. Apoplexy. **a. u′teri,** sudden uterine hemorrhage, due to arterial degeneration or hemorrhagic infarct.

apoplexy (ap′o-plek″se) [Gr. *apoplēxia*]. 1. Apoplectic stroke; a condition caused by acute vascular lesions of the brain, such as hemorrhage, thrombosis or embolism, and marked by coma followed by paralyses. 2. Copious extravasation of blood within any organ. **abdominal a.,** spontaneous intraperitoneal hemorrhage due to rupture of an intra-abdominal blood vessel, independent of any trauma to the abdomen. **adrenal a.,** a morbid condition resulting from massive hemorrhage into the adrenal gland. **asthenic a.,** apoplexy from debility. **Broadbent's a.,** cerebral hemorrhage beginning outside the ventricle, but progressing until it enters the ventricle. **bulbar a.,** effusion into the substance of the pons. **capillary a.,** apoplexy resulting from the rupture of capillary vessels. **cerebellar a.,** effusion into the substance of the cerebellum. **cerebral a.,** effusion into the cerebral substance. **congestive a.,** congestion without extravasation of blood, but followed by symptoms resembling those of true apoplexy. **cutaneous a.,** sudden effusion of blood to the skin and subcutaneous tissue. **delayed a.,** apoplexy which comes on several days after the receipt of the injury. **embolic a.,** apoplexy due to stopping of a cerebral artery by an embolus. **fulminating a.,** apoplexy in which the patient suddenly falls and quickly becomes unconscious. **functional a., nervous a.,** a condition simulating true apoplexy, but due to some functional disturbance of the nervous system. **heat a.,** heat stroke. **ingravescent a.,** progressive paralysis due to the slow leakage of blood from a ruptured vessel. **meningeal a.,** effusion occurring between the meninges. **multiple a.,** a succession of small cerebral effusions of blood, with slight attacks of paralysis. **neonatal a.,** apoplexy in newborn children. **ovarian a.,** extensive extravasation of blood into the ovary. **parturient a.,** parturient paralysis. **pituitary a.,** sudden massive degeneration with hemorrhagic necrosis of the pituitary body, associated with pituitary tumor, signaled by abrupt headache, followed by loss of sight, diplopia, drowsiness, and confusion, or coma. **placental a.,** hemorrhage into a centrally separated placenta with formation of a hematoma between the placenta and uterine wall. **pontile a.,** bulbar a. **pulmonary a.,** the escape of blood into the parenchyma of the lungs. **renal a.,** a morbid condition resulting from rupture of the renal artery. **sanguineous a.,** that which is caused by an effusion of blood. **serous a.,** the sudden effusion of a considerable quantity of serous fluid. **simple a.,** a fatal comatose state not due to a discoverable cerebral lesion. **spinal a.,** effusion into the substance of the spinal cord. **splenic a.,** malignant anthrax. **thrombotic a.,** apoplexy due to thrombosis of a cerebral artery. **traumatic late a.,** apoplexy following trauma and appearing several days or weeks after the accident. **uteroplacental a.,** Couvelaire's term for a severe uterine condition seen in some cases of separation of the placenta, in which the uterine musculature is disrupted and infiltrated with blood, especially at the placental site. **verminous a.,** coma due to the presence of worms in the intestine.

aporepressor (ap″o-re-pres′sor). A product of repressor genes, of unknown structure, which combines with low-molecular weight corepressor to form the complete repressor, which specifically represses the activity of certain structural genes.

aporinosis (ap″o-rĭ-no′sis). Gierke's term for deficiency disease.

aporioneurosis (ap-o″re-o″nu-ro′sis) [Gr. *aporia* doubt + *neurosis*]. Anxiety neurosis.

aporrhegma (ap″o-reg′mah) [*apo-* + Gr. *rhēgma* fracture]. Any one of the toxic substances split off from the amino acids of a protein by bacterial decomposition (Kutscher). Cf. *ptomaine.*

aposia (ah-po′ze-ah) [*a* neg. + Gr. *posis* drinking + *-ia*]. Absence of drinking, or reluctance to ingest fluids.

apositia (ap″o-sish′e-ah) [*apo-* + Gr. *sitos* food + *-ia*]. Aversion to food.

apositic (ap″o-sit′ik). Pertaining to, characterized by, or causing apositia.

aposome (ap′o-sōm) [*apo-* + Gr. *sōma* body]. An inclusion within the cytoplasm which has been made by the activity of the cell itself.

apospory (ah-pos′po-re) [*apo-* + Gr. *sporos* seed]. Lack of power of forming spores.

apostasis (ah-pos′tah-sis) [Gr.]. 1. An abscess. 2. The end or crisis of an attack of disease.

apostem (ap′os-tem). An abscess.

apostema (ap″os-te′mah) [Gr. *apostēma*]. An abscess.

aposthia (ah-pos′the-ah) [*a* neg. + Gr. *posthē* foreskin + *-ia*]. Congenital absence of the prepuce.

apothanasia (ap″o-thah-na′ze-ah) [*apo-* + Gr. *thanatos* death]. The postponing of death; the prolongation of life.

apothecary (ah-poth′e-ka″re) [Gr. *apothēke* storehouse]. A person who prepares and sells or dispenses drugs and compounds and makes up prescriptions. **surgeon a.,** in Great Britain, a practitioner who has passed the examinations required of a surgeon and of an apothecary.

apothem (ap′o-them) [*apo-* + Gr. *thema* deposit]. A dark deposit which sometimes appears in vegetable infusions and decoctions exposed to the air.

apotheme (ap′o-thēm). Apothem.

apotoxin (ap″o-tok′sin). Richet's term for the poison that produces the symptoms of anaphylaxis.

apotripsis (ap″o-trip′sis) [Gr. *apotribein* to abrade]. Removal of a corneal opacity (Hirschberg).

apotropaic (ap″o-tro-pa′ik) [Gr. *apotropaios* averting evil]. Prophylactic, in the sense of averting evil influence (in Greek medicine).

apotrophic (ap″o-trof′ik) [*apo-* + Gr. *trophē* nutrition]. Growing at the extremity of something else, as apotrophic cells.

apoxemena (ap″ok-sem′ĕ-nah). The material removed from a periodontal pocket in treatment of periodontitis.

apoxesis (ap″ok-se′sis) [Gr. *apoxein* to scrape off]. The removal of detritus from a periodontal pocket; called also *curettage,* or *scaling.*

apozem, apozema, apozeme (ap′o-zem, ap-oz′e-mah, ap′o-zēm) [Gr. *apozema* decoction, from *apo-* away + *zein* to boil]. A medicinal or medicated decoction.

apozymase (ap″o-zi′mās). The portion of a zymase which requires the presence of a cozymase to become a complete or holozymase.

apparatotherapy (ap″ah-rat″o-ther′ah-pe). Treatment by mechanic apparatus.

apparatus (ap″ah-ra′tus), pl. *apparatus* or *apparatuses* [L., from *ad* to + *parare* to make ready]. An arrangement of a number of parts acting together in the performance of some special function; used in anatomical nomenclature to designate a number of structures or organs which act together in serving some particular function. **absorption a.,** an apparatus used in gas analysis by means of which a portion of the substance to be examined is absorbed and its quantity thus estimated. **acoustic a.,** auditory a. **attachment a.,** the tissues by means of which a tooth is attached in the jaw, including fibers from the cementum, alveolar bone, periodontal membrane, and gingiva. **auditory a.,** the organ of hearing, including all its component parts. See *organum vestibulocochleare.* **Barcroft's a.,** a differential manometer for studying small samples of blood or other tissues. **Beckmann's a.,** an apparatus for determining molecular weight by lowering the freezing point or by raising the boiling point of a solution. **biliary a.,** the parts concerned in the formation, conduction, and storage of bile, including the secreting cells of the liver, bile ducts, and gallbladder. **central a.,** the dynamic organ of the cell which participates in mitosis. It consists of a centrosome, a centrosphere, and an astrosphere. **chromidial a.,** the chromatin staining material of the protoplasm of a cell, occurring in the form of granules, rods, strands, and networks. **ciliary a.,** the ciliary body. **a. derivato′rius,** the direct opening of small arteries into small veins without intervention of capillaries, as in phalanges and in erectile tissues. **Desault's a.,** Desault's bandage. **digestive a.,** a. digestorius. **a. digesto′rius** [N A, B N A], the organs associated with the ingestion and digestion of food, including the mouth and associated structures, pharynx, and components of the digestive tube, as well as the associated organs and glands. Called also *digestive system* and *systema digestorium.* **Fell-O'Dwyer a.,** a device used in performing artificial respiration and for preventing collapse of the lung in chest operations. **Finsen's a.,** an arrangement utilizing the principle of filtration as a means of increasing the efficiency of ultraviolet irradiation applied locally in the treatment of disease. **genitourinary a.,** a. urogenitalis. **Golgi a.,** a complex of membranes and vesicles in a cell, seen in stained preparations as an irregular network of blackened canals or solid strands; thought to play an important role in cellular activities, especially those dealing with secretion. **a. of Golgi-Rezzonico,** spiral filaments seen in the incisures of the neurilemma. **a. of Goormagtigh,** juxtaglomerular cells. **juxtaglomerular a.,** juxtaglomerular cells. **Kirschner's a.,** an apparatus for applying skeletal traction in leg fractures. **lacrimal a., a. lacrima′lis** [N A, B N A], the system concerned with the secretion and circulation of the tears and the normal fluid of the conjunctival sac; it consists of the lacrimal gland and ducts, and associated structures. **a. ligamento′sus col′li,** membrana tectoria. **masticatory a.** See under *system.* **mental a.,** the three different aspects or parts of the mind or psyche, i.e., the id, the ego, and the superego. **a. of Perroncito,** a mass of fibrils in the form of spirals and networks with newly formed axons which develop in the cut stump of a nerve during regeneration. **Potain's a.,** a kind of aspirating apparatus. **a. respirato′rius** [N A, B N A], **respiratory a.,** the tubular and cavernous organs that allow atmospheric air to reach the circulatory system. The chief organs involved are the nose, larynx, trachea, bronchi, and lungs. Called also *respiratory system* and *systema respiratorium.* **Sayre's a.,** an apparatus for suspending a patient during the application of a plaster-of-paris jacket. **segmental a.,** the brain stem. **sound-conducting a.,** those parts of the auditory apparatus that are essential for conduction of the impulses which are perceived as sound. **sound-perceiving a.,** those elements of the auditory apparatus that are essential for the perception of sounds. **Soxhlet's a.,** an apparatus by which constituents can be extracted from solutions. **steadiness a.,** ataxigraph. **sucker a.,** sucker foot. **a. suspenso′rius len′tis,** zonula ciliaris. **Tallerman's a.,** an apparatus for enclosing an extremity of the body for the purpose of applying to it dry hot air in the treatment of rheumatism, etc. **Taylor's a.,** a steel support for the spine, used in Pott's disease. **a. of Timofeew,** a terminal nervous globular network within a corpuscle of Pacini. **Tiselius a.,** an apparatus for the electrophoretic separation of the proteins of blood serum, plasma, and other body fluids. **Tobold's a.,** an illuminating apparatus for use with a laryngoscope. **urogenital a.,** a. urogenitalis. **a. urogenita′lis** [N A, B N A], the organs concerned in the production and excretion of urine, together with the organs of reproduction. Called also *genitourinary system, urogenital system,* and *systema urogenitale.* **vasomotor a.,** the neuromuscular mechanism controlling the constriction and dilation of blood vessels and thus the amount of blood supplied to a part. **vocal a.,** the various organs concerned in the production of voice sounds. **Waldenberg's a.,** an apparatus for exhausting or compressing air which is inhaled by the patient or into which the patient exhales. **Zander a.,** a machine designed to give exercise and to apply manipulations to the body. **Zünd-Burguet a.,** electrophonoide.

appearance (ah-pēr′ans) [L. *apparere* to be visible]. The visible manifestation of the characteristics of an object or entity. **ground-glass a.,** a filmy, hazy appearance, as of the lung in asbestosis, caused by the attendant fibrosis.

appendage (ah-pen′dij). A thing or part appended. See also *appendix.* **atrial a., auricular a.,** auricula atrii. **cecal a.,** appendix vermiformis. **cutaneous a's,** a's of the skin. **a. of epididymis,** appendix epididymidis. **epiploic a's,** appendices epiploicae. **a's of the eye,** the lashes, eyebrows, lacrimal apparatus, and conjunctiva. **a's of the fetus,** the umbilical cord, placenta, and membranes. **fibrous a. of liver,** appendix fibrosa hepatis. **ovarian a.,** the parovarium. **a's of the skin,** the hair, nails, sebaceous glands, sweat glands, and mammary glands. **testicular a., a. of the testis,** appendix testis. **uterine a's,** the ligaments of the uterus, the oviducts, and the ovaries. **a. of ventricle of larynx,** sacculus laryngis. **vermicular a.,** appendix vermiformis. **vesicular a's of epoophoron of Morgagni,** appendices vesiculosi epoophori.

appendalgia (ap″en-dal′je-ah) [*appendix* + *-algia*]. Pain in the region of the vermiform appendix.

appendectomy (ap″en-dek′to-me). 1. Surgical removal of the vermiform appendix. 2. Surgical excision of an appendage. **auricular a.,** excision of the auricular appendage (auricle) of the heart.

appendekthlipsia (ap″en-dek-thlip′se-ah) [*appendix* + Gr. *ekthlibein* to compress]. An operation for appendicitis with adhesions of the appendix done by closing the lumen by dividing the appendix with a thermocautery and leaving a clamp in place at that site.

appendical (ah-pen′de-kal). Appendiceal.

appendiceal (ap-en-dis′e-al). Pertaining to an appendix.

appendicealgia (ap″en-dis″e-al′je-ah) [*appendix* + *-algia*]. Appendalgia.

appendicectasis (ah-pen″dĭ-sek′tah-sis). A dilated condition of the vermiform appendix.

appendicectomy (ah-pen″dĭ-sek′to-me) [*appendix* + Gr. *ektomē* excision]. Appendectomy.

appendices (ah-pen′dĭ-sēz) [L.]. Plural of *appendix*.

appendicism (ah-pen′dĭ-sizm). A condition marked by symptoms in the region of the vermiform appendix.

appendicitis (ah-pen″dĭ-si′tis). Inflammation of the vermiform appendix. **concomitant a.,** appendicitis which occurs along with and is a partial manifestation of some other infectious disorder. **a. by contiguity,** appendicitis caused by infection from neighboring tissues. **foreign-body a.,** appendicitis due to a foreign body in the lumen. **fulminating a.,** appendicitis marked by sudden onset and rapid and fatal development. **gangrenous a.,** gangrene of the appendix due to interference with the circulation. **a. granulo′sa,** appendicitis developing on a disease of the mucous membrane which is marked by formation of granulation tissue between the gland tubules (Riedel). **helminthic a.,** verminous appendicitis. **a. larva′ta,** latent appendicitis in which the infection is in a quiescent state, but liable to break forth into activity at any time. **left-sided a.,** diverticulitis. So-called because the symptoms resemble those of appendicitis, and the descending (or left) colon is the usual site of involvement. **lumbar a.,** a type of appendicitis in which the appendix is posterior, lying against the peritoneum behind or below the cecum. **masked a.,** a. larvata. **myxoglobulosis a.,** myxoglobulosis. **a. oblit′erans,** appendicitis with sclerosis and shrinking of the submucous tissue and plastic peritonitis, causing obliteration of the lumen of the appendix. **obstructive a.,** appendicitis attended by obstruction of the lumen of the appendix. **perforating a., perforative a.,** appendicitis with perforation of the organ. **protective a.,** a. obliterans. **purulent a.,** suppurative appendicitis. **recurrent a.,** chronic appendicitis in which attacks recur after long intervals. **relapsing a.,** chronic appendicitis with frequently recurring attacks. **segmental a.,** inflammation confined to one section of the appendix: it may be proximal, central or distal. **skip a.,** appendicitis in which two or more areas of focal inflammation are separated by normal appendiceal tissue. **stercoral a.,** appendicitis in which a concretion is the assumed cause. **subperitoneal a.,** appendicitis in which the appendix is buried under the peritoneum instead of being free in the peritoneal cavity. **suppurative a.,** purulent infiltration of the walls of the appendix. **syncongestive a.,** noninfective appendicitis, marked by the presence of serous infiltrates and occurring synchronously with similar congestion of the neighboring tissues. **traumatic a.,** appendicitis caused by external traumatism. **verminous a.,** appendicitis due to the presence of a worm in the appendix.

appendiclausis (ap″en-dĭ-klaw′sis) [*appendix* + L. *clausus* closed]. Obstruction of the vermiform appendix producing symptoms simulating those of acute appendicitis.

appendicocecostomy (ah-pen″dĭ-ko-se-kos′to-me). The operation of draining the vermiform appendix into the cecum.

appendicocele (ah-pen′dĭ-ko-sēl″). Hernia of the vermiform appendix.

appendico-enterostomy (ah-pen″dĭ-ko″en-ter-os′to-me). 1. Appendicostomy. 2. The formation of an anastomosis between the vermiform appendix and the intestine.

appendicolithiasis (ah-pen″dĭ-ko″lĭ-thi′ah-sis) [*appendix* + *lithiasis*]. A condition marked by concretions in the vermiform appendix.

appendicolysis (ah-pen″dĭ-kol′ĭ-sis) [*appendix* + Gr. *lysis* dissolution]. An operation for appendicitis with adhesions.

appendicopathia (ah-pen″dĭ-ko-path′e-ah). Appendicopathy. **a. oxyu′rica,** disease of the vermiform appendix caused by oxyuris.

appendicopathy (ah-pen″dĭ-kop′ah-the) [*appendix* + Gr. *pathos* disease]. Any diseased condition of the vermiform appendix.

appendicosis (ah-pen″dĭ-ko′sis). Any degenerative (noninflammatory) lesion of the vermiform appendix.

appendicostomy (ah-pen″dĭ-kos′to-me) [*appendix* + Gr. *stomoun* to provide with an opening, or mouth]. Surgical creation of an opening into the vermiform appendix for the purpose of irrigating the lower bowel. Called also *Weir's operation.*

appendicular (ap″en-dik′u-lar). 1. Pertaining to the vermiform appendix. 2. Pertaining to an appendage.

appendiculoradiography (ap″en-dik″u-lo-ra″-de-og′rah-fe). Radiography of the vermiform appendix.

appendix (ah-pen′diks), pl. *appendixes, appen′dices* [L. from *appendere* to hang upon]. A general term used in anatomical nomenclature to designate a supplementary, accessory, or dependent part attached to a main structure. Called also *appendage.* Frequently used alone to refer to the *appendix vermiformis* [N A], or *vermiform appendix.* **auricular a.,** auricula atrii. **cecal a.,** a. vermiformis. **a. cer′ebri,** hypophysis cerebri. **ensiform a.,** processus xiphoideus. **a. epididymidis** [N A, B N A], **a. of epididymis,** a remnant of the mesonephros sometimes situated on the head of the epididymis. **epiploic appendices, appen′dices epiplo′icae** [N A, B N A], peritoneum-covered tabs of fat, 2 to 10 cm. long, attached in rows along the tenia of the colon. **a. fibro′sa hep′atis** [N A, B N A], **fibrous a. of liver,** a fibrous band at the left extremity of the liver, being the atrophied remnant of formerly more extensive liver tissue. **a. morgagn′ii.** See *appendix testis* and *appendices vesiculosi epoophori.* **a. tes′tis** [N A], the remnant of the müllerian duct on the upper end of the testis. Called also *hydatid of Morgagni.* **a. of ventricle of larynx, a. ventric′uli laryn′gis** [B N A], succulus laryngis. **a. vermic′ularis, vermiform a.,** a vermiformis. **a. vermifor′mis** [N A], a wormlike diverticulum of the cecum, varying in length from 3 to 6 inches, and measuring about ⅓ inch in diameter. Called also *processus vermiformis* [B N A]. **appen′dices vesiculo′si epooph′ori** [N A], small pedunculated structures attached to the uterine tubes near their fimbriated end, being remnants of the mesonephric ducts. Called also *vesicular appendages of epoophoron* and *hydatids of Morgagni.* **xiphoid a.,** processus xiphoideus.

appendolithiasis (ah-pen″do-lĭ-thi′ah-sis). Appendicolithiasis.

appendoroentgenography (ah-pen″do-rent″-gen-og′rah-fe). Roentgenographic examination of the vermiform appendix.

appendotome (ah-pen′do-tōm). An instrument for removal of the vermiform appendix.

apperception (ap″er-sep′shun) [L. *ad* to + *percipere* to perceive]. Conscious perception and appreciation; the power of receiving, appreciating, and interpreting sensory impressions.

apperceptive (ap″er-sep′tiv). Pertaining to apperception.

appersonification (ap″er-son″ĭ-fi-ka′shun). The identification of one's self with another person.

appestat (ap′pĕ-stat) [appetite + Gr. *histanai* to stand]. A center in the hypothalamus that reacts to a shortage of calories by promoting hunger and causing a desire for food, and reacts to food intake by inducing a feeling of satiety.

appet (ap′et). Dunlap's term for that which in connection with anticipatory thinking constitutes a desire.

appetite (ap′ĕ-tit) [L. *appetere* to desire]. A natural longing or desire, especially the natural and recurring desire for food. **excessive a.,** bulimia. **perverted a.,** the longing for unnatural and indigestible things as articles of food; pica.

appetition (ap″ĕ-tish′un) [L. *ad* toward + *petere* to seek]. The directing of desire toward a definite purpose or object.

applanation (ap″lah-na′shun) [L. *applanatio*]. Undue flatness, as of the cornea.

apple (ap′'l). The fruit of the rosaceous tree, *Pyrus malus;* also the tree itself. **Adam's a.,** prominentia laryngea. **balsam a.,** the cucurbitaceous plant, *Momordica balsamina,* which has purgative and vulnerary fruit. **bitter a.,** colocynth. **Indian a., May a.,** podophyllum. **thorn a.,** stramonium.

appliance (ah-pli′ans). A device used for performing or for facilitating the performance of a particular function. In orthodontics, a device used in the mouth to produce or prevent movement of teeth, so that malopposed teeth may be brought into proper alignment and occlusion. **prosthetic a.,** a device affixed to or implanted in the body, designed to take the place, or perform the function, of a missing body part, such as an artificial arm or leg, or a complete or partial denture.

applicator (ap′le-ka″tor). An instrument for making local applications.

appliqué form (ap″le-ka′). The early form of *Plasmodium falciparum* which appears as a fine blue line with a chromatin dot apparently applied to the margin of an erythrocyte. Called also *accolé form.*

apposition (ap″o-zish′un) [L. *appositio*]. The placement or position of adjacent structures or parts so that they oppose each other and can come into contact.

apprehension (ap″re-hen′shun). 1. Apperception. 2. Apprehensiveness; anticipatory fear.

approximal (ah-prok′sĭ-mal). Situated close together.

approximate (ah-prok′sĭ-māt″). 1. To bring close together, or into apposition. 2. Approximal.

apractic (ah-prak′tik). Pertaining to or characterized by apraxia.

apraxia (ah-prak′se-ah) [Gr. "a not acting," "want of success"]. Inability to carry out purposeful movements in the absence of paralysis or other motor or sensory impairment, especially inability to make proper use of an object. **akinetic a.,** loss of ability to carry out spontaneous movement. **a. al′gera,** akinesia algera. **amnestic a.,** loss of ability to carry out a movement on command as a result of inability to remember the command, although ability to perform the movement is present. **cortical a.,** motor a. **ideational a.,** sensory a. **ideokinetic a., ideomotor a.,** a form due to an interruption between the ideation center and the center for the limb. In it simple movements can be performed, but not complicated ones. **innervation a.,** motor a. **Liepmann's a.,** inability to perform coordinated movements of the limbs without actual paralysis. **limb-kinetic a.,** ideokinetic a. **motor a.,** loss of ability to make proper use of an object, although its proper nature is recognized. **sensory a.,** loss of ability to make proper use of an object, due to lack of perception of its proper nature and purpose. **transcortical a.,** ideokinetic a.

apraxic (ah-prak′sik). Apractic.

apresoline (ah-pres′o-lēn). Trade mark for preparations of hydralazine.

aprobarbital (ap″ro-bar′bĭ-tal). Chemical name: 5-allyl-5-isopropylbarbituric acid: used as a hypnotic and sedative.

Aprocta (ah-prok′tah). A genus of filarial organisms. *A. micro-analis* and *A. semenova* infest the eyes of birds.

aproctia (ah-prok′she-ah) [*a* neg. + Gr. *prōktos* anus]. Congenital absence or imperforation of the anus.

apron (a′prun). A piece of clothing worn as a protection for the body in front. **Hottentot a., pudendal a.,** artificially or abnormally elongated nymphae.

aprophoria (ap″ro-fo′re-ah) [*a* neg. + Gr. *propherein* to utter + *-ia*]. Inability to express articulated words in speech or writing (Heveroch, 1914).

aprosexia (ap″ro-sek′se-ah) [*a* neg. + Gr. *prosechein* to heed]. A condition in which there is inability to fix the attention; inattention due to mental weakness or to defective hearing, and often seen in chronic catarrh of the nose or of the nasopharynx (*aprosexia nasalis*).

aprosody (a-pros′o-de). Absence of the normal variations in stress, pitch, and rhythm of speech.

aprosopia (ap″ro-so′pe-ah) [*a* neg. + Gr. *prosōpon* face]. A developmental anomaly characterized by partial or complete absence of structures of the face.

aprosopus (ah-pro′so-pus). A fetal monster exhibiting aprosopia.

apselaphesia (ap″sel-ah-fe′ze-ah) [*a* neg. + Gr. *psēlaphēsis* touch]. Abnormal diminution of the sense of touch.

apsithyria (ap″sĭ-thi′re-ah) [*a* neg. + Gr. *psithyrizein* to whisper]. Hysterical loss of speech and even of the power of whispering (J. Solis-Cohen, 1883).

apsychia (ap-si′ke-ah) [*a* neg. + Gr. *psychē* soul + *-ia*]. 1. Loss or lack of consciousness. 2. A faint or swoon.

apsychical (ap-si′ke-kal). Not psychical or mental.

apsychosis (ah″si-ko′sis) [*a* neg. + Gr. *psychē* soul + *-osis*]. Absence or loss of the function of thought.

A.P.T. Abbreviation for *alum-precipitated toxoid.*

apterous (ap′ter-us) [*a* neg. + Gr. *pteron* wing]. Wingless.

aptitude (ap′tĭ-tūd). Natural ability and skill in certain lines of endeavor.

aptyalia, aptyalism (ap″ti-a′le-ah, ap-ti′ah-lizm) [*a* neg. + Gr. *ptyalizein* to spit]. Deficiency or absence of the saliva; xerostomia.

apulmonism (ah-pul′mo-nizm) [*a* priv. + L. *pulmo* lung]. A developmental anomaly characterized by partial or complete absence of a lung.

apus (a′pus) [*a* neg. + Gr. *pous* foot]. An individual exhibiting apodia.

apyetous (ah-pi′ĕ-tus) [*a* neg. + Gr. *pyon* pus]. Showing no pus; not suppurating.

apyknomorphous (ah-pik″no-mor′fus) [*a* neg. + Gr. *pyknos* compact + *morphē* form]. Not pyknomorphous; not having the stainable cell elements compactly placed: said of certain nerve cells.

apyogenous (ah″pi-oj′e-nus). Not caused by pus.

apyonin (ah-pi′o-nin) [*a* neg. + Gr. *pyon* pus]. Yellow pyoktanin.

apyous (ah-pi′us) [*a* neg. + Gr. *pyon* pus]. Having no pus; nonpurulent.

apyrene (ah′pi-rēn) [*a* neg. + Gr. *pyrēn* fruit stone, nucleus]. Having no nucleus or nuclear material.

apyretic (ah″pi-ret′ik) [*a* neg. + *pyretic*]. Having no fever; afebrile.

apyrexia (ah″pi-rek′se-ah) [*a* neg. + *pyrexia*]. The absence or intermission of fever.

apyrexial (ah″pi-rek′se-al). Pertaining to apyrexia, or to the stage of intermission of a fever.

apyrogenetic (ah-pi″ro-jĕ-net′ik). Apyrogenic.

apyrogenic (ah-pi-ro-jen′ik) [*a* neg. + Gr. *pyr* fever + *gennan* to produce]. Not producing fever.

A.Q. Abbreviation for *achievement quotient.*

Aq. Abbreviation for L. *a′qua,* water, **Aq. astr.** L. *a′qua astric′ta,* frozen water. **Aq. bull.** L. *a′qua bul′liens,* boiling water. **Aq. com.** L. *a′qua commu′nis,* common water. **Aq. dest.** L. *a′qua destilla′ta, distilled water.* **Aq. ferv.** L. *a′qua fer′vens,* hot water. **Aq. fluv.** L. *a′qua fluvia′lis,* river water. **Aq. font.** L. *a′qua fonta′na,* spring water. **Aq. mar.** L. *a′qua mari′na,* sea water. **Aq. niv.** L. *a′qua niva′lis,* snow water. **Aq.**

pluv. L. *a'qua pluvia'lis*, rain water. **Aq. pur.** L. *a'qua pu'ra*, pure water. **Aq. tep.** L. *a'qua tep'ida*, tepid water.

aqua (ah'kwah), gen. and pl. *a'quae* [L.]. Water. See *aromatic water* and various pharmaceutical preparations listed under *water*. **a. am'nii,** liquor amnii. **a. ani'si,** anise water. **a. aromat'ica,** aromatic water. **a. astric'ta,** frozen water. **a. auran'tii flo'rum,** orange flower water. **a. bul'liens,** boiling water. **a. cal'cis,** calcium hydroxide solution. **a. cam'phorae,** camphor water. **a. chlorofor'mi,** chloroform water. **a. cinnamo'mi,** cinnamon water. **a. commu'nis,** ordinary water. **a. destilla'ta,** distilled water. **a. destilla'ta steril'is,** sterile distilled water. **a. fer'vens,** hot water. **a. fluvia'lis,** river water. **a. foenic'uli,** fennel water. **a. fonta'na,** spring water. **a. for'tis,** an old name for reddish nitric acid containing more or less nitrogen dioxide (NO_2). **a. gaulthe'ria,** wintergreen water. **a. hamamel'idis,** hamamelis water. **a. labyrin'thi,** the clear fluid in the labyrinth of the ear. **a. mari'na,** sea water. **a. men'thae piperi'tae,** peppermint water. **a. men'thae vir'idis,** spearmint water. **a. niva'lis,** snow water. **a. oc'uli,** the aqueous humor or fluid of the eye. **a. pericar'dii,** the pericardial fluid. **a. pluvia'lis,** rain water. **a. pro injectio'ne,** water for injection. **a. pu'ra,** pure water. **a. re'gia,** nitrohydrochloric acid. **a. ro'sae,** rose water. **a. ro'sae for'tior,** stronger rose water. **a. sterilisa'ta,** sterilized water. **a. tep'ida,** warm water. **a. vi'tae,** brandy.

aquae (a'kwē) [L.]. Plural of *aqua*.

aquaeductus (ak″we-duk′tus), pl. *aquaeduc'tus* [L.]. [B N A] Aqueductus.

aquapuncture (ak″wah-pungk′tūr) [L. *aqua* water + *puncture*]. The subcutaneous injection of water.

aquatic (ah-kwat′ik). Inhabiting or frequenting water.

aqueduct (ak′we-dukt″). A passage or channel in a body structure or organ. See *aqueductus*. **cerebral a.,** aqueductus cerebri. **a. of cochlea,** canaliculus cochlea. **a. of Cotunnius.** 1. Aqueductus vestibuli. 2. Canaliculus cochleae. **fallopian a., a. of Fallopius,** canalis facialis. **a. of midbrain,** aqueductus cerebri. **a. of Sylvius,** aqueductus cerebri. **a. of the vestibule,** aqueductus vestibuli.

aqueductus (ak″we-duk′tus) [L., from *aqua* water + *ductus* canal]. [N A] A passage or channel in a body structure or organ, especially a channel for the conduction of fluid. **a. cer'ebri** [N A], a canal, about ¾ inch long, extending downward in the mesencephalon from the third to the fourth ventricle. Called also *cerebral aqueduct* and *aqueduct of Sylvius*. **a. endolymphat'icus,** ductus endolymphaticus. **a. vestib'uli** [N A], a small canal extending from the vestibule of the inner ear to open onto the posterior part of the internal surface of the petrous part of the temporal bone. It lodges the endolymphatic duct and an arteriole and a venule. Called also *aqueduct of vestibule*.

aqueous (a′kwe-us) [L. *aqua* water]. 1. Watery; prepared with water. 2. The aqueous humor of the eye. See under *humor*.

aquiparous (ak-wip′ah-rus) [L. *aqua* water + *parere* to produce]. Producing water or a watery secretion.

aquocapsulitis (a″kwo-kap″su-li′tis) [L. *aqua* water + *capsulitis*]. Serous iritis.

aquosity (ah-kwos′ĭ-te) [L. *aquositas*]. A watery state or condition.

aquula (ak′woo-lah) [L.]. A little stream. **a. auditi'va exter'na,** perilymph. **a. auditi'va inter'na,** endolymph. **a. cotun'nii, a. labyrin'thi exter'na,** perilymph. **a. labyrin'thi inter'na, a. labyrin'thi membrana'cei,** endolymph.

AR. Abbreviation for *alarm reaction*.

Ar. Chemical symbol for *argon*.

araban (ar′ah-ban). A pentosan $(C_5H_{10}O_5)_n$, which is found in various gums and pectins and which consists of a mixture of anhydrides of l-arabinose.

arabanase (ah-rab′ĭ-nās). An enzyme which catalyzes the hydrolysis of araban to arabinose.

arabate (ar′ah-bāt). A salt of arabic acid.

arabin (ar′ah-bin). An amorphous carbohydrate, $(C_5H_{10}O_5)_2 + H_2O$, from gum arabic, soluble in water. Called also *arabic acid*.

arabinose (ah-rab′ĭ-nōs). Gum sugar; a crystalline aldo-pentose, $CH_2OH(CHOH)_3CHO$, obtained from vegetable gums by acid hydrolysis. It is sometimes found in urine. d-Arabinose is a constituent of aloin; l-arabinose is the gum sugar.

arabinosis (ah-rab″ĭ-no′sis). Poisoning by arabinose, which may produce a nephrosis.

arabinosuria (ah-rab″ĭ-no-su′re-ah). The presence of arabinose in the urine.

arabinulose (ar″ah-bin′u-lōs). A ketopentose.

arabite (ar′ah-bit). A sweet crystalline principle, $C_5H_{12}O_5$, derivable from arabinose by the action of sodium amalgam.

arabitol (ah-rab′ĭ-tol). An alcohol, $CH_2OH-(CHOH)_3CH_2OH$, formed by the reduction of arabinose.

arabopyranose (ar″ah-bo-pi′rah-nōs). Arabinose.

arachanol (ah-rak′ah-nol). A solid, white alcohol, $C_{20}H_{41}OH$, from dermoid cysts.

arachidic (ar″ah-kid′ik) [L. *arachis* peanut]. Caused by peanut kernels; as arachidic bronchitis.

arachine (ar′ah-kin). An alkaloid, $C_5H_{14}N_2O$, isolated from peanuts.

arachnephobia (ah-rak″ne-fo′be-ah). Arachnophobia.

Arachnida (ah-rak′nĭ-dah) [Gr. *arachnē* spider]. A class of the Arthropoda, including the spiders, ticks, mites, and scorpions.

arachnidism (ah-rak′nĭ-dizm). The condition produced by the bite of a poisonous spider; spider poisoning.

arachnitis (ar″ak-ni′tis) [*arachno-* + *-itis*]. Inflammation of the arachnoid.

arachno- (ah-rak′no) [Gr. *arachnē* spider]. Combining form denoting relationship to the arachnoid membrane or to a spider.

arachnodactylia (ah-rak″no-dak-til′e-ah). Arachnodactyly.

arachnodactyly (ah-rak″no-dak′tĭ-le) [*arachno-* + Gr. *daktylos* finger]. A condition characterized by abnormal length and slenderness of the fingers and toes. Called also *dolichostenomelia*, *Marfan's syndrome* and *arachnodactylia*.

arachnogastria (ah-rak″no-gas′tre-ah) [*arachno-* + Gr. *gastēr* stomach + *-ia*]. Spider belly; the protuberant abdomen caused by ascites, especially in an emaciated person.

arachnoid (ah-rak′noid). 1. Resembling a spider's web. 2. Arachnoidea. **a. of brain, cranial a.,** arachnoidea encephali. **spinal a., a. of spinal cord,** arachnoidea spinalis.

arachnoidal (ar″ak-noi′dal). Or of pertaining to the arachnoid.

arachnoidea (ar″ak-noi′de-ah), pl. *arachnoi'deae* [Gr. *arachnoeidēs* like a cobweb]. [N A, B N A] A delicate membrane interposed between the dura mater and the pia mater, being separated from the pia mater by the subarachnoid space. **a. enceph'ali** [N A, B N A], the arachnoidea covering the brain. Called also *arachnoid of brain*. **a. spina'lis** [N A, B N A], the arachnoidea covering the spinal cord. Called also *arachnoid of spinal cord*.

arachnoideae (ar″ak-noi′de-e). Plural of *arachnoidea*.

arachnoidism (ah-rak′noi-dizm″). The condition produced by the bite of poisonous spiders.

arachnoiditis (ah-rak″noid-i′tis). Arachnitis.

arachnolysin (ar″ak-nol′ĭ-sin) [*arachno-* + *lysin*]. The active hemolytic principle of the poison of the garden spider.

arachnophobia (ah-rak″no-fo′be-ah) [*arachno-* + Gr. *phobos* fear + *-ia*]. Morbid fear of spiders.

arachnopia (ar″ak-no′pe-ah) [*arachno-* + *pia*]. The pia-arachnoid.

arachnorhinitis (ah-rak″no-ri-ni′tis) [*arachno-* + *rhinitis*]. Disease of the nasal passages caused by the presence of a spider.

arack, arrack (ah-rak′) [East Indian]. An alcoholic liquor distilled from fermented dates, rice, the sap of palms, mahua flowers, etc.

Aradidae (ah-rad′ĭ-de). A family of bugs, the fungus bugs.

araiocardia (ar″a-o-kar′de-ah) [Gr. *araios* thin + *kardia* heart]. Bradycardia.

aralen (ăr′ah-len). Trade mark for a preparation of chloroquine.

Aralia (ah-ra′le-ah) [L.]. A genus of aromatic and diaphoretic plants, including spikenard or pettymorrel (*A. racemosa*), dwarf elder (*A. hispida*), and other plants used in domestic medicine. **A. quinquefo′lia,** ginseng.

aralia (ah-ra′le-ah). The dried rhizome and roots of *Aralia racemosa.* Used as an ingredient of compound white pine syrup.

aralkyl (ah-ral′kil). An aryl derived from an alkyl radical.

aramine (ăr′ah-min). Trade mark for a preparation of metaraminol.

Aran's cancer, law (ar-ahnz′) [François Amilcar *Aran,* French physician, 1817–1861]. See under *cancer* and *law.*

Aran-Duchenne atrophy, disease, type (ar-ahn′doo-shen′) [François Amilcar *Aran;* Guillaume Benjamin Amand *Duchenne,* French neurologist, 1806–1875]. Myelopathic muscular atrophy.

araneism (ah-ra′ne-izm). Spider poisoning.

araneous (ah-ra′ne-us) [L. *araneum* cobweb]. Like a cobweb.

Arantius, bodies of, ventricle of (ah-ran′she-us) [Julius Caesar *Arantius* (Italian *Aranzio*), an Italian anatomist and physician, 1530–1589]. See *noduli valvularum aortae,* under *nodulus,* and under *ventricle.*

araphia (ah-ra′fe-ah) [*a* neg. + Gr. *rhaphē* seam]. Dysraphia.

araroba (ar″ah-ro′bah) [Brazilian]. 1. Andira. 2. Goa powder.

arbor (ar′bor), pl. *arbo′res* [L.]. A treelike structure or part; a structure or system resembling a tree with its branches. **a. alveola′ris,** the complicated terminal portion of an air passage of a lung, situated peripherally to a terminal bronchiole and varying widely in extent and arrangement. **a. medulla′ris ver′mis,** a. vitae cerebelli. **a. vi′tae,** the tree *Thuja occidentalis.* **a. vi′tae cerebel′li** [N A, B N A], the treelike outline of white substance seen on a sagittal section of the cerebellum. **a. vi′tae u′teri,** plicae palmatae. **a. vitae of vermis,** a. vitae cerebelli.

arboreal (ar-bo′re-al). Pertaining to trees; inhabiting or attached to trees.

arbores (ar-bo′rēz) [L.]. Plural of *arbor.*

arborescent (ar″bo-res′ent) [L. *arborescens*]. Branching like a tree.

arborization (ar″bor-ĭ-za′shun). 1. The branching termination of certain nerve cell processes. 2. A form of the termination of a nerve fiber when in contact with a muscle fiber. 3. The treelike appearance of capillary vessels in inflamed conditions.

arboroid (ar′bo-roid) [L. *arbor* a tree]. Branching like a tree.

arborvirus (ar″bor-vi′rus). See under *virus.*

arbovirus (ar″bo-vi′rus). Arbor virus. See under *virus.*

Arbutus (ar′bu-tus) [L.]. A genus of ericaceous trees and shrubs. **A. menzie′sii** is the madroño of the Pacific states, whose bark is astringent. **trailing a.** See *Epigaea.* **A. une′do,** the European arbutus, is astringent. **A. u′va-ur′si.** See *uva-ursi.*

A.R.C. Abbreviation for *anomalous retinal correspondence.*

arc (ark) [L. *arcus* bow]. Any part of the circumference of a circle. **auricular a., binauricular a.,** a measurement from the center of one auditory meatus to that of the other. **bregmatolambdoid a.,** extends along the course of the sagittal suture. **mercury a.,** an electric discharge through mercury vapor in a vacuum tube, giving off a light rich in ultraviolet and actinic rays. **nasobregmatic a.,** a line from the root of the nose to the bregma. **naso-occipital a.,** extends from the root of the nose to the lowest

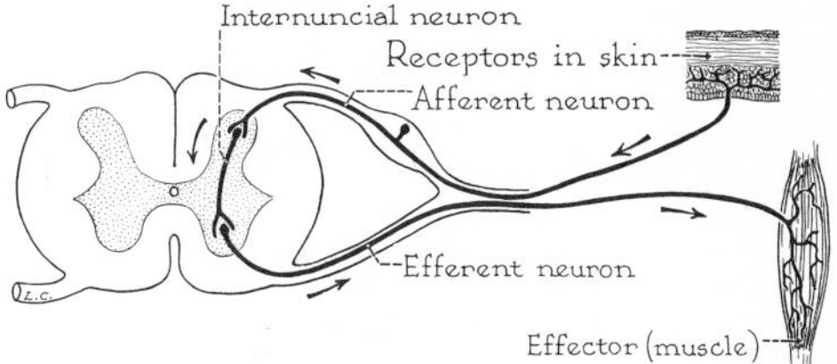

Reflex arc. (King and Showers.)

part of the occipital protuberance. **neural a.,** a series of four or more neurons forming a complete circuit between certain receptors and effectors of the body, and constituting the pathway for neural reactions. **nuclear a.,** vortex lentis. **reflex a.,** the nervous route utilized in a reflex act. An impulse travels inward over an afferent nerve to some nerve center, and the response outward to some peripheral organ or part over an efferent nerve. **sensorimotor a.,** neural a.

arcade (ar-kād′). An anatomical structure composed of a series of arches. **arterial a's,** a series of anastomosing arterial arches as in the intestinal branches of the superior mesenteric artery. **Flint's a.,** an arteriovenous arch at the base of the renal pyramids.

arcanum (ar-ka′num) [L. "secret"]. A secret medicine or nostrum.

arcate (ar′kāt) [L. *arcatus*]. Bow-shaped.

arcatura (ar-kah-tu′rah) [L. *arcus* bow]. Outward curvature of the fore legs of horses.

Arcella (ar-sel′ah). A genus of amebae which form a shell.

arch-. See *archi.*

arch (arch) [L. *arcus* bow]. A structure with a curved or bowlike outline. See also *arcus.* **abdominothoracic a.,** the lower boundary of the front of the thorax. **alveolar a.** See *arcus alveolaris mandibulae* and *arcus alveolaris maxillae.* **anterior a. of atlas,** arcus anterior atlantis. **a. of aorta,** arcus aortae. **aortic a's,** a series of five pairs of arterial arches of the embryo in the region of the neck. **arterial a's of kidney,** arteriae arcuatae renis. **branchial a's,** four pairs of mesenchymal and later cartilaginous arches of the embryo in the region of the neck. **carpal a., anterior,** an arch formed by anastomosis of the anterior branches of the radial and ulnar arteries, supplying ligaments and synovial membranes of radiocarpal and intercarpal joints. **carpal a., dorsal, carpal a., posterior,** rete carpi dorsale. **a. of colon,** colon transversum. **a's of Corti,** a series of arches made up of the rods of Corti. **costal a.,** arcus costalis. **a. of cricoid cartilage,** arcus cartilaginis cricoideae. **crural a.,** ligamentum inguinale. **crural a., deep,** a thickened band of fibers curving over the external iliac vessels at the site where they become femoral. **dental a.,** the curving structure formed by the crowns of the teeth in their normal position, or by the residual ridge after loss of the teeth. The *inferior dental* *arch*, or *arch of the mandible*, is formed by the lower teeth, and the *superior dental arch*, or *arch of the maxilla*, is formed by the upper teeth. **dental a., inferior.** See under *dental a.* **dental a., superior.** See under *dental a.* **diaphragmatic a., external,** ligamentum arcuatum laterale. **diaphragmatic a., internal,** ligamentum arcuatum mediale. **digital venous a's,** arcus venosi digitales. **dorsal venous a. of foot,** arcus venosus dorsalis pedis. **epiphyseal a.,** the embryonic structure in the roof of the third ventricle from which the pineal body develops. **expansion a.,** a wire appliance made to conform to the arch of the jaw, used in producing lateral movement of the teeth in orthodontic work. **fallopian a.,** ligamentum inguinale. **femoral a., superficial,** ligamentum inguinale. **fibrous a. of soleus muscle,** arcus tendineus musculi solei. **glossopalatine a.,** arcus palatoglossus. **Gothic a.,** a tracing made by the excursions to left and right and the protrusive movement of the mandible. **Haller's a's.** See *ligamentum arcuatum laterale* and *ligamentum arcuatum mediale.* **hemal a.,** the arch formed by the body and processes of a vertebra, a pair of ribs, and the sternum, or other like parts; also the sum of all such arches. **hyoid a.,** the second branchial arch, from which are developed the styloid process, the stylohyoid ligament, and lesser cornu of the hyoid bone. **jugular venous a.,** arcus venosis juguli. **Langer's axillary a.,** a thickened border of fascia forming a bridge across the occipital groove. **lingual a.,** a wire appliance made to conform to the lingual aspect of the dental arch: used to secure movement of the teeth in orthodontic work. **longitudinal a. of foot,** arcus pedis longitudinalis. **lumbocostal a., external, of diaphragm,** ligamentum arcuatum laterale. **lumbocostal a., internal, of diaphragm,** ligamentum arcuatum mediale. **lumbocostal a., lateral, of Haller,** ligamentum arcuatum laterale. **lumbocostal a., medial, of Haller,** ligamentum arcuatum mediale. **malar a.,** os zygomaticum. **mandibular a.** 1. The first branchial arch, from which are developed the jaw bones, with the malleus and incus. 2. The inferior dental arch. **maxillary a.** 1. The palatal arch. 2. The superior dental arch. **nasal a.,** the arch formed by the nasal bones and by the nasal processes of the maxilla. **neural a. of vertebra,** arcus vertebralis. **oral a.,** palatal a. **orbital a. of frontal bone,** margo supraorbitalis ossis frontalis. **palatal a.,** the arch formed by the roof of the mouth from the teeth on one side of the maxilla to the teeth on the other. **palatine a., anterior,** arcus palatoglossus. **palatine a., posterior,** arcus palatopharyngeus. **palatoglossal a.,** arcus palatoglossus. **palatomaxillary a.,** palatal a. **palatopharyngeal a.,** arcus palatopharyngeus. **palmar arterial a., deep,** arcus palmaris profundus. **palmar arterial a., superficial,** arcus palmaris superficialis. **palmar venous a., deep,** arcus venosus palmaris profundus. **palmar venous a., superficial,** arcus venosus palmaris superficialis. **palpebral a., inferior,** arcus palpebralis inferior. **palpebral a., superior,** arcus palpebralis superior. **paraphyseal a.,** the embryonic structure in the roof of the third ventricle of vertebrates from which the paraphysis develops. **a. of pelvis,** angulus subpubicus. **pharyngeal a's,** branchial a's. **pharyngoepiglottic a.,** arcus palatopharyngeus. **pharyngopalatine a.,** arcus palatopharyngeus. **plantar arterial a.,** arcus plantaris. **plantar venous a.,** arcus venosus plantaris. **popliteal a.,** ligamentum popliteum arcuatum. **postaural a's,** branchial a's. **posterior a. of atlas,** arcus posterior atlantis. **pubic a., a. of pubis,** arcus pubis. **pulmonary a's,** the most caudal of the aortic arches, which become the pulmonary arteries. **ribbon a.,** an appliance of flattened wire made to conform to the arch of the jaw and used in producing lateral movement of the teeth in orthodontic work. **a. of ribs,** arcus costalis. **Riolan's a.,** the arch formed by the mesentery of the transverse colon. **saddle a., saddle-shaped a.,** a palatal arch in which the lateral parts are contrasted. **Salus' a.,** the arching of a vein where it crosses an artery in the retina, seen in arteriosclerosis. **Shenton's a.,** Shenton's line. **subpubic a.,** angulus subpubicus. **superciliary a.,** arcus superciliaris. **supraorbital a. of frontal bone,** margo supraorbitalis ossis frontalis. **tarsal a's.** See *arcus palpebralis inferior*, and *arcus palpebralis superior*. **tendinous a.,** arcus tendineus. **tendinous a. of diaphragm, external,** ligamentum arcuatum laterale. **tendinous a. of diaphragm, internal,** ligamentum arcuatum mediale. **tendinous a. of levator ani muscle,** arcus tendineus musculi levatoris ani. **tendinous a. of lumbodorsal fascia,** ligamentum lumbocostale. **tendinous a. of pelvic fascia,** arcus tendineus fasciae pelvis. **tendinous a. of soleus muscle,** arcus tendineus musculi solei. **thyrohyoid a.,** the third fetal arch, which is represented by the greater cornu of the hyoid bone. **transpalatine a.,** transpalatine vault. **transverse a. of foot,** arcus pedis transversalis. **Treitz's a.,** an arch composed of the left superior colic artery and the mesenteric vein, and lying between the ascending portion of the duodenum and the inner edge of the left kidney. **venous a's of kidney,** venae arcuatae renis. **a. of vertebra, vertebral a.,** arcus vertebrae. **visceral a's,** branchial a's. **volar venous a., deep,** arcus venosus palmaris profundus. **volar venous a., superficial,** arcus venosus palmaris superficialis. **V-shaped a.,** a dental arch which comes to a point at the lingual junction of the upper medial incisors. **wire a.,** an arch or splint of wire adjusted to the dental arch, used in orthodontic work to produce movement of the teeth and achieve a normal contour of the dental arch. **Zimmermann's a.,** an inconstant, rudimentary arch of the embryo, supposed to explain the origin of certain occasionally occurring vessels between the fourth aortic and the pulmonary arch. **zygomatic a.,** arcus zygomaticus.

archaeus (ar-ke′us). Paracelsus's term for the vital principle, the living force in the body or the animate universe.

Archagathus (ark-ag′ah-thus). The first Greek physician to practice in Rome (219 B.C.), according to Pliny. At first known as "the wound-curer" (*Vulnerarius*), because of his surgical exploits he was later termed "the executioner" (*Carnifex*).

archaic (ar-ka′ik) [Gr. *archaios* ancient]. Very ancient; pertaining to early evolutionary stages.

archamphiaster (ark-am′fe-as″ter) [*arch-* + Gr. *amphi* around + *astēr* star]. The primitive amphiaster associated with the formation of polar bodies.

Archangelica (ar″kan-jel′e-kah) [L. from Gr. *archangelikos* archangelic]. A genus of umbelliferous plants.

Archangiaceae (ark-an″je-a′se-e). A systematic family of schizomycetes, order Myxobacterales, and made up of two genera, Archangium and Stelangium, of soil microorganisms.

Archangium (ark-an′je-um). A genus of schizomycetes of the family Archangiaceae, order Myxobacterales.

arche-. See *archi-*.

archebiosis (ar″ke-bi-o′sis) [*arche-* + Gr. *biōsis* way of life]. The supposed spontaneous generation of organisms.

archecentric (ar″ke-sen′trik) [*arche-* + *centric*]. Denoting a primitive type of structure from which the other types in the members of the group are derived.

archegenesis (ar″ke-jen′e-sis) [*arche-* + Gr. *genesis* reproduction]. Archebiosis.

archegonium (ar″ke-go′ne-um) [*arche-* + Gr. *gonos* offspring]. The female organ of a cryptogamic plant taking part in the formation of sexually produced spores. Cf. *antheridium*.

archegony (ar-keg′o-ne) [*arche-* + Gr. *gonē* seed]. Spontaneous generation.

archencephalon (ar″ken-sef′ah-lon) [*arche-* + Gr. *enkephalos* brain]. The primitive brain, anterior to the end of the notochord, from which the midbrain and the forebrain have developed.

archenteron (ar-ken′ter-on) [*arche-* + Gr. *enteron* intestine]. The primitive digestive cavity of the embryo, formed by the invagination of the blastodermic vesicle during the gastrula stage, and opening by the blastopore. Called also *coelenteron* or *gastrocoele*.

archeocinetic (ar″ke-o-si-net′ik). Archeokinetic.

archeocyte (ar′ke-o-sīt) [Gr. *archaios* ancient + *kytos* hollow vessel]. Any free or wandering ameboid cell.

archeokinetic (ar″ke-o-ki-net′ik) [Gr. *archaios* ancient + *kinēsis* motion]. A term applied to the primitive type of motor nerve mechanism, as seen in the peripheral and ganglionic nervous systems. Cf. *neokinetic* and *paleokinetic*.

archepyon (ar-kep′e-on) [*arche-* + Gr. *pyon* pus]. Very thick, cheesy pus.

archesperm (ar′ke-sperm). The fertilized contents of an archegonium.

archespore, (ar′ke-spōr) [*arche-* + Gr. *sporos* seed]. The mass of cells which give rise to spore mother cells.

archesporium (ar″ke-spo′re-um). Archespore.

archetype (ar″ke-tīp) [*arche-* + Gr. *typos* type]. An ideal, original, or standard type or form.

archi-, arch-, arche- [Gr. *archē* beginning]. Prefix, denoting first, beginning, or original.

archiblast (ar′ke-blast) [*archi-* + Gr. *blastos* germ]. 1. The formative material or protoplasm of an ovum. 2. His' term for the fundamental part of the blastodermic layers as distinguished from the parablast or peripheral portion of the mesoderm.

archiblastic (ar″ke-blas′tik). Derived from, or pertaining to, the archiblast.

archiblastoma (ar″ke-blas-to′mah). A tumor derived from archiblastic or parenchymatous material.

archicarp (ar′ke-karp). Ascogonium.

archicenter (ar″ke-sen′ter) [*archi-* + Gr. *kentron* sharp point]. An archetype; an organ or organism which is the primitive form from which another organ or organism is descended.

archicentric (ar-ke-sen′trik). Pertaining to an archicenter.

archicerebellum (ar″ke-ser″e-bel′um) [*archi-* + *cerebellum*]. A term once applied to the earliest developed portion of the cerebellum, namely, the flocculonodular lobe and areas predominantly supplied by vestibulocerebellar fibers.

archicortex (ar″ke-kor′teks). Archipallium.

archicyte (ar′ke-sīt) [*archi-* + Gr. *kytos* hollow vessel]. A fertilized ovum before cleavage has taken place.

archicytula (ar″ke-sit′u-lah) [*archi-* + Gr. *kytos* hollow vessel]. A fertilized ovum in the stage in which the nucleus is first discernible.

archigaster (ar′ke-gas″ter) [*archi-* + Gr. *gastēr* belly]. Archenteron.

archigastrula (ar″ke-gas′troo-lah) [*archi-* + *gastrula*]. The gastrula in its most primitive form of development.

Archigenes (ar-kij′ĕ-nēz) **of Apamea** (1st century A.D.). A celebrated Greek physician, a pupil of Agathinus (and a Pneumatist). He practiced in Rome and wrote several works, some portions of which are preserved; his surgical observations (e.g., on amputation and ligation) are noteworthy.

archigenesis (ar-ke-jen′e-sis). Archebiosis.

archigonocyte (ar″ke-gon′o-sīt) [*archi-* + *gonocyte*]. A primary germ cell formed by cleavage of the fertilized ovum.

archikaryon (ar″ke-kar′e-on) [*archi-* + Gr. *karyon* kernel]. The nucleus of a fertilized ovum.

archil (ar′kil). The lichen *Roccella tinctoria;* also, a violet coloring matter from this and other lichens.

archimonerula (ar″ke-mo-ner′u-lah) [*archi-* + *monerula*]. The monerula while undergoing a primitive and total cleavage.

archimorula (ar-ke-mor′u-lah) [*archi-* + *morula*]. A mass of cells arising from the division of the archicytula and preceding the archigastrula.

archinephron (ar″ke-nef′ron) [*archi-* + Gr. *nephros* kidney]. The pronephros.

archineuron (ar″ke-nu′ron) [*archi-* + Gr. *neuron* nerve]. The neuron at which an efferent impulse starts (Waldeyer).

archipallial (ar″ke-pal′e-al). Pertaining to the archipallium.

archipallium (ar″ke-pal′e-um) [*archi-* + L. *pallium* cloak]. That portion of the pallium which phylogenetically is the first to show the characteristic distinctive layering of the cellular elements, and possesses a simpler stratification and organization than the later differentiating mesopallium and neopallium. It corresponds in mammals to the cortex of the dentate gyrus and hippocampus (allocortex of Vogt and Brodmann).

archiplasm (ar′ke-plazm″) [*archi-* + Gr. *plasma* something formed]. 1. The most primitive living matter. 2. The substance of which the fertilized ovum consists. 3. Archoplasm.

archisome (ar′ke-sōm). Archiplasm.

archispore (ar′ke-spōr). Archespore.

archistome (ar′ke-stōm) [*archi-* + Gr. *stoma* mouth]. Blastopore.

archistriatum (ar″ke-stri-a′tum) [*archi-* + *striatum*]. The primitive striatum, represented in man by the corpus amygdaloideum.

architectonic (ar″ke-tek-ton′ik). 1. Pertaining to architectural pattern. 2. The structure or construction of, as architectonic of brain.

architis (ar-ki′tis) [*archo-* + *-itis*]. Inflammation of the lower rectum; proctitis.

archo- [Gr. *archos* rectum, from *archē* beginning, the rectum having been considered the first part of the bowel]. Combining form denoting relationship to the rectum or anus.

archocele (ar′ko-sēl) [*archo-* + Gr. *kēlē* hernia]. Hernia of the rectum.

archocystocolposyrinx (ar″ko-sis″to-kol″po-sir′inks) [*archo-* + Gr. *kystis* bladder + *kolpos* vagina + *syrinx* pipe]. Fistula of the anus, vagina, and bladder.

archocystosyrinx (ar″ko-sis″to-sir′inks) [*archo-* + Gr. *kystis* bladder + *syrinx* pipe]. Fistula of the anus and bladder.

archon (ar′kon). Vaughan's term for a poisonous radical common to all proteins.

archoplasm (ar′ko-plazm). Boveri's name for the substance composing the attraction sphere and the entire achromatic apparatus or spindle.

archoptoma (ar″ko-to′mah) [*archo-* + Gr. *ptōma* fall]. A prolapsed portion of the rectum.

archoptosis (ar″ko-to′sis) [*archo-* + Gr. *ptōsis* fall]. Prolapse of the lower rectum.

archorrhagia (ar″ko-ra′je-ah) [*archo-* + Gr. *rhēgnynai* to burst forth + *-ia*]. Hemorrhage from the rectum.

archorrhea (ar″ko-re′ah) [*archo-* + Gr. *rhoia* flow]. A liquid discharge from the rectum.

archosome (ar′ko-sōm). Archiplasm.

archostegnosis (ar″ko-steg-no′sis) [*archo-* + Gr. *stegnōsis* stoppage]. Archostenosis.

archostenosis (ar″ko-ste-no′sis) [*archo-* + Gr. *stenōsis* stricture]. Stricture of the rectum.

archosyrinx (ar″ko-sir′inks) [*archo-* + Gr. *syrinx* pipe]. 1. Fistula in ano. 2. A rectal syringe.

archusia (ar-ku′se-ah). A hypothetical substance necessary for cell growth.

archyl, archyle (ar′kil, ar-ki′le) [*arch-* + Gr. *hylē* matter]. Protyl.

arciform (ar′se-form) [L. *arcus* bow + *forma* shape]. Bow-shaped; arcuate.

arctation (ark-ta′shun) [L. *arctatio*]. Contracture or narrowing of any canal or opening.

arcual (ar′ku-al) [L. *arcualis*]. Pertaining to an arch.

arcuate (ar′ku-āt). Shaped like an arc; arranged in arches.

arcuation (ark-u-a′shun) [L. *arcuatio*]. Curvature; especially an abnormal curvature.

arcus (ar′kus), pl. *ar′cus* [L. "a bow"]. A general term used in anatomical nomenclature to designate any structure having a curved or bowlike outline. Called also *arch.* **a. adipo′sus,** a. senilis. **a. alveola′ris mandib′ulae** [N A], the superior free border of the alveolar process of the mandible. Called also *alveolar arch of mandible* and *limbus alveolaris mandibulae* [B N A]. **a. alveola′ris maxil′lae** [N A], the inferior free border of the alveolar process of the maxilla. Called also *alveolar arch of maxilla* and *limbus alveolaris maxillae* [B N A]. **a. ante′rior atlan′tis** [B N A], the more slender portion joining the lateral masses of the atlas ventrally, constituting about one-fifth of its entire circumference. Called also *anterior arch of atlas.* **a. aor′tae** [N A, B N A], the continuation of the ascending aorta, giving rise to the brachiocephalic trunk, and the left common carotid and left subclavian arteries; it continues as the thoracic aorta (aorta thoracica). **a. cartilag′inis cricoi′deae** [N A, B N A], the slender anterior portion of the cricoid cartilage. Called also *arch of cricoid cartilage.* **a. costa′lis** [N A], **a. costa′rum** [B N A], one of the two curving lateral borders of the inferior thoracic aperture, meeting at the infrasternal angle on the ventral aspect of the body. Each is formed by the seventh to tenth costal cartilages. Called also *costal arch.* **a. denta′lis** [N A, B N A], the curving structure formed by the crowns of the teeth in their normal position in the jaw. See *dental arch.* **a. denta′lis infe′rior** [N A, B N A], the curving structure formed by the crowns of the teeth of the lower jaw (mandible). **a. denta′lis supe′rior** [N A, B N A], the curving structure formed by the crowns of the teeth of the upper jaw (maxilla). **a. dorsa′lis pe′dis,** arteria arcuata pedis. **a. glossopalati′nus** [B N A], a. palatoglossus. **a. iliopectin′eus** [N A], the fascial partition that separates the lacuna musculorum and the lacuna vasorum. Called also *fascia iliopectinea* [B N A]. **a. juveni′lis,** a ring around the corneal margin of the iris, sometimes seen in young persons, but resembling arcus senilis. **a. lipoi′des cor′neae,** a crescentic deposit of fat and cholesterol crystals in the cornea. **a. lipoi′des myrin′gis,** a ring of degeneration in the drum membrane of old people. **a. lumbocosta′lis latera′lis** [B N A], ligamentum arcuatum laterale. **a. lumbocosta′lis media′lis** [B N A], ligamentum arcuatum mediale. **a. palati′ni** [B N A]. See *a. palatoglossus* and *a. palatopharyngeus.* **a. palatoglos′sus** [N A], the anterior one of the two folds of mucous membrane on either side of the oral pharynx, connected with the soft palate and enclosing the palatoglossal muscle. Called also *a. glossopalatinus* [B N A], and *palatoglossal arch.* **a. palatopharyn′geus** [N A], the posterior one of the two folds of mucous membrane on either side of the oral pharynx, connected with the soft palate and enclosing the palatopharyngeal muscle. Called also *a. pharyngopalatinus* [B N A], and *palatopharyngeal arch.* **a. palma′ris profun′dus** [N A], an arch formed by the terminal part of the radial artery and its anastomosis with the deep branch of the ulnar, and extending from the base of the metacarpal bone of the little finger to the proximal end of the first interosseous space; it gives off palmar metacarpal arteries and perforating branches. Called also *a. volaris profundus* [B N A], and *deep palmar arterial arch.* **a. palma′ris superficia′lis** [N A], an arch formed by the terminal part of the ulnar artery and its anastomosis with the superficial palmar branch of the radial, giving rise to the palmar digital arteries and supplying blood to the palmar aspect of the hands and fingers. Called also *a. volaris superficialis* [B N A], and *superficial palmar arterial arch.* **a. palpebra′les.** See *a. palpebralis inferior* and *a. palpebralis superior.* **a. palpebra′lis infe′rior** [N A], an arch derived from the medial palpebral artery, supplying the lower lid of the eye. Called also *a. tarseus inferior* [B N A], and *inferior palpebral arch.* **a. palpebra′lis supe′rior** [N A], an arch derived from the medial palpebral artery, supplying the upper lid of the eye. Called also *a. tarseus superior* [B N A], and *superior palpebral arch.* **a. parieto-occipita′lis,** the curved convolution formed by the backward continuation into the occipital lobe of the superior postcentral sulcus. **a. pe′dis longitudina′lis** [N A], the longitudinal arch of the foot, comprising the pars medialis and the pars lateralis. Called also *longitudinal arch of foot.* **a. pe′dis transversa′lis** [N A], the metatarsal arch of the foot, formed by the navicular, cuneiform, cuboid, and the five metatarsal bones, Called also *transverse arch of foot.* **a. pharyngopalati′nus** [B N A], a. palatopharyngeus. **a. pinguic′ulus,** a. senilis. **a. planta′ris** [N A, B N A], the deep arterial arch in the foot, formed by the anastomosis of the lateral plantar artery with the deep plantar branch of the dorsal artery of the foot, and giving off the plantar metatarsal arteries. Called also *plantar arterial arch.* **a. poste′rior atlan′tis** [N A, B N A], the slender portion joining the lateral masses of the atlas dorsally, constituting about two-fifths of its entire circumference. Called also *posterior arch of atlas.* **a. pu′bis** [N A, B N A], the arch formed by the conjoined rami of the ischial and pubic bones of the two sides of the body. Called also *pubic arch.* **a. senil′is,** a white ring around the margin of the cornea, produced by fatty degeneration of corneal tissue, especially in the aged. **a. supercilia′ris** [N A, B N A], a smooth elevation arching upward and laterally from the glabella, a little above the margin of the orbit. Called also *superciliary arch.* **a. tar′seus infe′rior** [B N A], a. palpebralis inferior. **a. tar′seus supe′rior** [B N A], a. palpebralis superior. **a. tendin′eus** [N A, B N A], a linear thickening of fascia over some part of a muscle, such as that over the soleus or the obturator internus. Called also *tendinous arch.* **a. tendin′eus fas′ciae pel′vis** [N A, B N A], a thickening of the superior fascia, extending from the ischial spine to the posterior part of the body of the pubic symphysis. Called also *tendinous arch of pelvic fascia.* **a. tendin′eus mus′culi levato′ris a′ni** [N A, B N A], a linear thickening of the fascia over the levator ani muscle. Called also *tendinous arch of levator ani muscle.* **a. tendin′eus mus′culi so′lei** [N A, B N A], an aponeurotic band in the front part of the soleus muscle, extending from the tubercle on the fibular neck to the soleal line of the tibia. Called also *tendinous arch of soleus muscle.* **a. ve′nosi digita′les** [B N A], communicating branches of veins across the backs of the fingers at their bases. Called also *digital venous arches.* **a. veno′sus dorsa′lis pe′dis** [N A, B N A], a transverse venous arch across the dorsum of the foot near the bases of the metatarsal bones. Called also *dorsal venous arch of foot.* **a. veno′sus jug′uli** [N A, B N A], a transverse connecting trunk between the anterior jugular veins of either side. Called also *jugular venous arch.* **a. veno′sus palma′ris profun′dus** [N A], a venous arch accompanying the deep palmar arterial arch. Called also *a. volaris venosus profundus* [B N A], and *deep palmar venous arch.* **a. veno′sus palma′ris superficia′lis** [N A], a venous arch accompanying the superficial palmar arterial arch. Called also *a. volaris venosus superficialis* [B N A], and *superficial palmar venous arch.* **a. veno′sus planta′ris** [N A, B N A], the deep venous arch that accompanies the arterial plantar arch. Called also *plantar venous* *arch.* **a. ver'tebrae** [N A, B N A], the bony arch composed of the laminae and pedicles of a vertebra. Called also *vertebral arch.* **a. vola'ris profun'dus** [B N A], a. palmaris profundus. **a. vola'ris superficia'lis** [B N A], a. palmaris superficialis. **a. vola'ris veno'sus profun'dus** [B N A], a. venosus palmaris profundus. **a. vola'ris veno'sus superficia'lis** [B N A], a. venosus palmaris superficialis. **a. zygomat'icus** [N A, B N A], the arch formed by the articulation of the broad temporal process of the zygomatic bone and the slender zygomatic process of the temporal bone, giving attachment to the masseter muscle. Called also *zygomatic arch.*

ARD. Abbreviation for *acute respiratory disease* (of any undefined form).

ardanesthesia (ar"dan-es-the'ze-ah) [L. *ardor* heat + *anesthesia*]. Thermanesthesia.

ardent (ar'dent) [L. *ardere* to glow]. 1. Hot or feverish. 2. Characterized by eager desire.

ardor (ar'dor) [L.]. 1. Intense heat. 2. Eager desire. **a. uri'nae,** a scalding sensation during the passage of urine. **a. ventric'uli,** pyrosis or heartburn.

Arduen'na (ar"du-en'nah). A genus of parasitic worms. **A. strongyli'na,** a small red blood-sucking worm found in the stomach of pigs.

area (a're-ah), pl. *a'reae* or *areas* [L.]. A limited space; a general term used in anatomical nomenclature to designate a specific plane surface or portion of an organ. **acoustic a., a. acus'tica** [B N A], a. vestibularis. **alisphenoid a.,** the surface of the great wing of the sphenoid bone. **aortic a.,** the area on the chest over the inner end of the right second costal cartilage. **apical a.,** the area about the apex of the root of a tooth. **association a's,** areas in the cerebral cortex whose function it is to correlate the impressions received and start motor impulses in harmony with them. **auditory a.,** a. vestibularis. **axial a.,** an area on a limb in which there is a hiatus in the numerical sequence of the spinal nerves in their cutaneous distribution. **Bamberger's a.,** an area of dulness in the left intercostal region, indicative of pericardial effusion. **bare a. of liver,** a. nuda hepatis. **basal seat a.,** that portion of the structures of the mouth that is available to support an artificial denture. **Betz cell a.,** psychomotor a. **Broca's a.,** a. subcallosa. **Brodmann's a's,** specific occipital and preoccipital areas of the cerebral cortex, identified by number, which are considered to be the seat of specific functions in the brain. **a. cel'si,** alopecia areata. **a. centra'lis,** a circular area of cells around the foveola in the ganglion cell layer of the retina. **a. coch'leae** [N A, B N A], the anterior part of the inferior portion of the fundus of the internal acoustic meatus, near the base of the cochlea. Called also *cochlear a. of internal acoustic meatus.* **cochlear a. of internal acoustic meatus,** a. cochleae. **Cohnheim's a's,** dark areas outlined by bright matter, seen on cross section of a muscle fiber. **contact a.,** the area at which two bodies or materials touch. In dentistry, the site on the proximal surfaces at which two adjacent teeth touch. **cribriform a. of renal papilla,** a. cribrosa papillae renalis. **a. cribro'sa me'dia,** a. vestibularis inferior. **a. cribro'sa papil'lae rena'lis** [N A, B N A], the tip of a pyramid of a kidney which is perforated by 10–25 openings for the papillary ducts. Called also *cribriform area of renal papilla.* **a. cribro'sa supe'rior,** a. vestibularis superior. **a. of critical definition,** that part of an optic image within which the detail is clear. **crural a.,** a space at the base of the brain between the chiasm and the pons. **denture-bearing a.,** denture foundation a. **denture foundation a.,** that portion of the basal seat area that, in occlusion, supports the complete or partial denture base. **denture-supporting a.,** denture foundation a. **dermatomic a.,** the area of skin supplied with afferent nerve fibers by a single posterior spinal root. Called also *dermatome.* **embryonic a.,** germinal a. **excitable a.,** the motor area in the cerebral cortex. **excitomotor a.,** that area of the cerebral cortex that gives rise to impulses which produce voluntary motion. **eye a.,** a nerve center in the frontal portion of the cortex. **a. of facial nerve,** a. nervi facialis. **Flechsig's a's,** three areas—anterior, lateral, and posterior—on each half of the medulla oblongata, marked out by the fibers of the vagus and hypoglossal nerves. **gastric a's, a'reae gas'tricae,** the several areas on organs adjacent to the stomach by which they make contact with the stomach. **genital a's,** areas on the inferior nasal concha and upper part of the nasal septum that may become engorged during menstruation **germinal a., a. germinati'va,** the disk on one side of the yolk membrane where the development of the embryo occurs. **glove a.,** that area —fingers, hand, and wrist—ordinarily covered by a glove, which sometimes coincides with the distribution of anesthesia in cases of multiple neuritis. **a. hypoglos'si,** the portion of the mouth beneath the tongue. **impression a.,** the surface of the oral structures that is recorded in an impression. **intercondylar a's of tibia.** See *a. intercondylaris anterior tibiae* and *a. intercondylaris posterior tibiae.* **a. intercondyla'ris ante'rior tib'iae** [N A], the broad area between the superior articular surfaces of the tibia. Called also *anterior intercondylar a.* and *fossa intercondyloidea anterior tibiae* [B N A]. **a. intercondyla'ris poste'rior tib'iae** [N A], a deep notch separating the condyles on the posterior surface of the tibia. Called also *posterior intercondylar a.* and *fossa intercondyloidea posterior tibiae* [B N A]. **interglobular a's,** the areas of dentin lying between the calcoglobules. **a. jonsto'ni,** alopecia areata. **Kiesselbach's a.,** an area on the anterior part of the nasal septum above the intermaxillary bone, which is richly supplied with capillaries and is a common site of nosebleed. **Krönig's a.,** Krönig's field. **Laimer-Haeckerman a.,** the region of the lower pharynx and upper esophagus, where diverticula most frequently develop. **a's of Langerhans,** islands of Langerhans. **lateral a.,** the part of the brain stem that is nourished by branches of the vertebral and basilar arteries which travel some distance from their point of origin before entering the substance of the brain. Cf. *paramedian a.* **Little's a.,** an area on the lower anterior part of the nasal septum: a frequent site of nosebleed. **a. luna'ta,** a cerebellar area situated cephalad of the postlunate fissure. **a. martegia'ni,** a slightly enlarged space at the optic disk, marking the beginning of the hyaloid canal. **a. medullo-vasculo'sa,** a median elongated area of vascular granulation-like tissue in rachischisis. **mesobranchial a.,** the pharyngeal floor, between the pharyngeal arches and pouches of each side. **mirror a.,** the reflecting surface of the cornea and lens when illuminated through the slit lamp. **motor a.,** the ascending frontal and ascending parietal convolutions where the nerve centers for motion are thought to be situated. **a. ner'vi facia'lis** [N A, B N A], the part of the fundus of the internal acoustic meatus where the facial nerve enters the facial canal. Called also *a. of facial nerve.* **a. nu'da hep'atis** [N A], the superior surface of the liver, adjacent to the diaphragm, that lacks a peritoneal covering. Its boundaries are formed by the hepatic coronary ligament proper and the triangular ligaments. Called also *bare area of liver.* **Obersteiner-Redlich a.,** the constricted area, devoid of myelin, at the point where a posterior nerve root enters the spinal cord. **olfactory a.,** the cerebral area, including the olfactory bulb, tract, and trigone, and the anterior portion of the callosal convolution and the uncus. **a. opa'ca,** the outer opaque part of the germinal area. **Panum's a's,** fusional areas on the retina. **paramedian a.,** that part of the brain stem which is nourished by short branches from the vertebral and basilar arteries. Cf. *lateral a.* **a. parapyramida'lis,** the area of the cerebellum lying caudad of the parapyramidal fissure. **a. parolfacto′ria [Brocae]** [B N A], **parolfactory a. of Broca,** a. subcallosa. **a. pellu′cida,** the central clear part of the germinal area. **a. perfora′ta,** perforated space. **postcentral a.,** the area of the cerebral cortex posterior to the central sulcus (fissure of Rolando). **post dam a.,** posterior palatal seal a. **posterior hypothalamic a.,** an extension of the periventricular cellular substance of the tuberal region of hypothalamus, laterally and caudally towards the mammillary region. **posterior palatal seal a.,** the soft tissues along the junction of the hard and soft palates on which pressure can be applied by a denture to aid in its retention. **a. postpterygoi′dea,** the area of the cerebellum situated caudad to the area pterygoidea. **a. postre′ma,** an area on the floor of the fourth ventricle bounded by the stria medullaris thalami and the funiculus separans. **postrolandic a.,** postcentral a. **precentral a.,** psychomotor a. **preoptic a.,** a diffuse collection of small cells which extends rostrally beyond the cephalic limits of the hypothalamus. **pressure a.,** an area which is subjected to excessive pressure, with consequent displacement of tissue. **projection a's,** Flechsig's name for the areas of the cerebral cortex that are concerned in the sensory and motor functions of the brain, being connected by projection fibers with the underlying parts of the central nervous system. **psychomotor a.,** the area of cerebral cortex which is concerned with integration and efferent transmission of the motor expression of the results of sensorial stimulation, situated just in front of the central fissure of Rolando and corresponding with the *precentral area* of Campbell. Also known as the *Betz cell area.* **a. pterygoi′dea,** the area of the cerebellum between the postlunate and the postpterygoid fissures. **pyriform a.,** pyriform lobe. **relief a.,** that portion of the surface of oral structures upon which pressures exerted by an artificial denture are reduced or eliminated. **rest a.,** that portion of a tooth or of a restoration in a tooth prepared to receive the incisal, lingual, or occlusal rest of a dental prosthesis. **rolandic a.,** excitomotor a. **sensation a., sense a.,** the area of distribution of a particular sensory nerve. **sensorial a.,** the general surface of the cerebrum, especially the part located between the interparietal, parietooccipital, and cingulate sulci. **septal a.,** the mesial surface of either half of the septum lucidum. **silent a.,** an area of the brain in which pathological conditions may occur without producing symptoms. **somesthetic a.,** the area for body feelings or for tactile sensation in the postcentral convolution. **Spencer's a.,** an area on the cortex of the frontal lobe of the brain just outside of the olfactory tract and anterior to the point where it joins the temporosphenoid lobe. Faradic stimulation of this area influences respiratory movements. **a. spongio′sa,** the peripheral part of the dorsal gray column of the spinal cord adjoining the substantia gelatinosa. **stress-bearing a.,** that portion of the surface of the oral structures upon which pressure is exerted in mastication. **a. stria′ta,** the part of the occipital lobe of the cerebral cortex containing the line of Gennari; it is the visual center. **a. subcallo′sa** [N A], **subcallosal a.,** a small gyrus on the medial surface of either cerebral hemisphere, immediately in front of the gyrus subcallosus. Called also *a. parolfactoria* [*Brocae*] [B N A]. **temporal a.,** an area above the temporal fossa, reaching to the outer canthus of the eye. **trigger a.,** an area, stimulation of which may cause physiological or pathological changes in another area. **vagus a.,** the area on the floor of the fourth ventricle in which the vagus nerve has its origin. **a. vasculo′sa,** that part of the area opaca where the blood vessels are first seen. **vestibular a.,** a. vestibularis. **vestibular a., inferior, of internal acoustic meatus,** a. vestibularis inferior. **vestibular a., superior, of internal acoustic meatus,** a. vestibularis superior. **a. vestibula′ris** [N A], the triangular lateral and median part of the floor of the fourth ventricle over which pass the striae medullares of the fourth ventricle. Called also *a. acustica* [B N A]. **a. vestibula′ris infe′rior** [N A, B N A], the lower portion of the fundus of the internal acoustic meatus. Called also *inferior vestibular a. of internal acoustic meatus.* **a. vestibula′ris supe′rior** [N A, B N A], the upper portion of the fundus of the internal acoustic meatus. Called also *superior vestibular a. of internal acoustic meatus.* **visual a.,** the angular gyrus and occipital lobe. **visuopsychic a.,** the area of the cerebral cortex concerned in the interpretation of visual sensations. **visuosensory a.,** the area of the cerebral cortex concerned in the reception of stimuli which give rise to visual sensations. **a. vitelli′na,** the yolk area in mesoblastic eggs beyond the area vasculosa. **Wernicke's a.,** a cerebral area composed of the supramarginal and angular gyri and portions of the superior and middle temporal gyri.

areatus (ar″e-a′tus). Occurring in patches.

Areca (ar′e-kah) [L.; East Indian]. A genus of palm trees, chiefly Asiatic. *A. catechu* affords betel nut and an inferior catechu.

areca (ar′e-kah). The dried ripe seed of *Areca catechu.* Use: veterinary anthelmintic.

arecoline (ah-rek′o-lin). Chemical name: methyl N-methyltetrahydronicotinite. Uses: 1. parasympathomimetic agent; 2. veterinary anthelmintic.

areflexia (ah″re-flek′se-ah) [*a* neg. + *reflex* + *-ia*]. Absence of the reflexes.

aregenerative (ah″re-jen′er-a″tiv). Characterized by absence of regeneration, applied especially to blood corpuscles in aplastic anemia.

arenaceous (ar″ĕ-na′se-us). Sandy; gritty.

arenation (ar″ĕ-na′shun) [L. *arena* sand]. Ammotherapy.

arenoid (ar′e-noid) [L. *arena* sand + Gr. *eidos* form]. Resembling sand.

areocardia (ar″e-o-kar′de-ah) [Gr. *areios* thin + *kardia* heart]. Bradycardia.

areola (ah-re′o-lah), pl. *are′olae* [L., dim. of *area* space]. 1. Any minute space or interstice in a tissue. 2. A circular area of a different color, surrounding a central point, as such an area surrounding a pustule or vesicle, or the part of the iris surrounding the pupil of the eye. **Chaussier's a.,** the areola of induration of a malignant pustule. **a. mam′mae** [N A, B N A], **a. of mammary gland,** the darkened ring surrounding the nipple of a breast. **a. of nipple,** a. mammae. **a. papilla′ris,** a. mammae. **second a.,** a ring which, during pregnancy, surrounds the areola papillaris. **umbilical a.,** a pigmented patch which sometimes surrounds the navel. **vaccinal a.,** the ring of redness that surrounds a vaccine pustule.

areolae (ah-re′o-le) [L.]. Plural of *areola.*

areolar (ah-re′o-lar). Pertaining to or containing areolae; containing minute interspaces.

areolitis (ar″e-o-li′tis). Inflammation of the areola of the breast.

areometer (ar″e-om′e-ter) [Gr. *araios* thin + *metron* measure]. A hydrometer.

areometric (ar″e-o-met′rik). Pertaining to hydrometry.

areometry (ar″e-om′e-tre). Hydrometry.

Aretaeus (ar-ĕ-te′us) **of Cappadocia** (2nd century A.D.). A famous Greek physician who wrote works on acute and chronic diseases. His clinical descriptions (e.g., of diabetes, pleurisy, tetanus) are outstanding, and in the best Hippocratic tradition.

arevareva (ah-ra″vah-ra′vah) [Tahitian]. A severe skin disease, with general decay of the vital powers, said to be due to excessive use of kava.

Arey's rule (ăr′ēz) [Leslie Brainerd *Arey,* American anatomist, born 1891]. See under *rule.*

arfonad (ar′fon-ad). Trade mark for a preparation of trimethaphan.

arg. Abbreviation for L. *argen'tum,* silver.

argamblyopia (ar″gam-ble-o′pe-ah) [Gr. *argos* idle + *amblyopia*]. Amblyopia due to long disuse of the eye.

Argand burner [Aimé *Argand,* Swiss physicist, 1755–1803]. See under *burner.*

Argas (ar′gas). A genus of ticks. **A. america′nus,** *A. persicus.* **A. minia′tus,** *A. persicus.* **A. per′sicus,** a cosmopolitan tick, one of the most important parasites of poultry, which sucks the blood of fowls, producing a weak and unthrifty condition of a flock. In Persia, India, Australia, and Brazil it acts as the carrier of fowl spirochetosis. **A. reflex′us,** a tick found on pigeons. Its bite causes local inflammation in man.

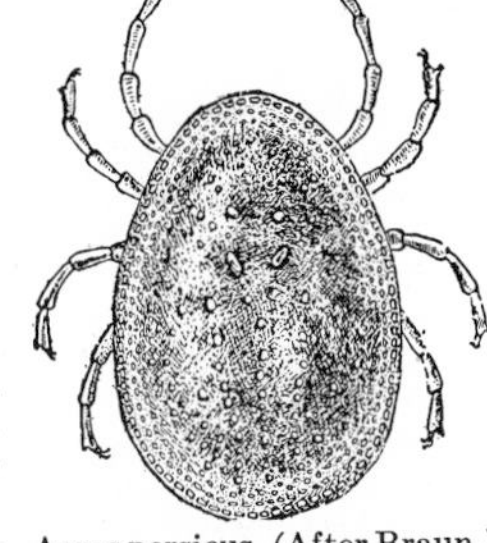

Argas persicus. (After Braun.)

Argasidae (ar-gas′ĭ-de). A family of the Ixodoidea, distinguished from the true ticks by absence of the scutum. The genera are: *Argas, Otobius, Antricola* and *Ornithodoros.*

Argasinae (ar-gas′ĭ-ne). A subfamily of the Arachnidae, including the ticks.

argema (ar′je-mah). A white ulcer of the cornea.

argentaffin, argentaffine (ar-jen′tah-fĭn) [L. *argentum* silver + *affinis* having affinity for]. Having affinity for silver or other metallic salts; staining with silver solutions.

argentaffinoma (ar″jen-taf″ĭ-no′mah). A tumor of the gastro-enteric tract (carcinoid) formed from the argentaffine cells (Kultschitzky's cells) found in the enteric canal. Cf. *enterochromaffine gland.*

argentation (ar″jen-ta′shun) [L. *argentum* silver]. Staining with a silver salt.

argenti (ar-jen′ti). Genitive of *argentum* [L. "silver"]. **a. io′didum colloida′le,** colloidal silver iodide. **a. ni′tras,** silver nitrate.

argentic (ar-jen′tik). Containing silver in its higher valency.

argentine (ar-jen′tīn) [L. *argentinus*]. Pertaining to or containing silver.

argentophil (ar-jen′to-fil) [L. *argentum* silver + Gr. *philein* to love]. Argyrophil.

argentoproteinum (ar-jen″to-pro″te-i′num). Silver protein.

argentous (ar-jen′tus). Containing silver in its lower valency.

argentum (ar-jen′tum), gen. *argen′ti* [L.]. Silver. **a. protein′icum for′te,** strong silver protein. **a. protein′icum mi′te,** mild silver protein.

argilla (ar-jil′lah). Kaolin.

argillaceous (ar″jĭ-la′shus). Composed of clay.

arginase (ar′jĭ-nās). An enzyme existing in the liver which splits arginine into urea and ornithine.

arginine (ar′jĭ-nin). An amino acid, amino-guanidine valerianic acid, $NH_2C(NH)_2(CH_2)_3CHNH_2$-$CO_2H$, produced by the hydrolysis or digestion of proteins. It is one of the hexone bases (Schulze and Steiger, 1886) and is found in invertebrate muscle where it functions as creatine does in vertebrate muscle. A preparation of this amino acid, in hydrochloride form, is injected intravenously in coma due to hepatic disease. **suberyl a.,** a compound that functions in the bufotoxins as glucose does in the glucosides: it is $COOH(CH_2)_6.CO.NH.$-$CO{:}NH(CH_2)_3.CH(NH_2).COOH$.

argininosuccinicaciduria (ar″jĭ-ne″no-suk-sin″ik-as″ĭ-du′re-ah). Presence in the urine of argininosuccinic acid, characteristic of a condition resulting from an inborn error of metabolism and accompanied by mental retardation.

argon (ar′gon) [Gr. *argos* inert]. A chemical element, at. no. 18, discovered in the atmosphere in 1895. It is one of the inert gases; its symbol is Ar; its atomic weight is 39.948.

Argyll Robertson pupil (ar-gil′ rob′ert-son) [Douglas Moray Cooper Lamb *Argyll Robertson,* Scotch physician, 1837–1909]. See under *pupil.*

argyremia (ar″jĭ-re′me-ah) [Gr. *argyros* silver + *haima* blood + *-ia*]. The presence of silver or silver salts in the blood.

argyria (ar-jir′e-ah). A permanent ashen-gray discoloration of the skin, conjunctiva and internal organs that results from the long continued use of silver salts. **a. nasa′lis,** argyria of the nasal mucosa.

argyriasis (ar″jĭ-ri′ah-sis). Argyria.

argyric (ar-ji′rik). Pertaining to, or caused by, silver.

argyrism (ar′jĭ-rizm). Argyria.

argyrophil (ar-ji′ro-fil) [Gr. *argyros* silver + *philein* to love]. Staining or easily impregnated with silver.

argyrosis (ar″jĭ-ro′sis) [Gr. *argyros* silver]. Argyria.

arhigosis (ah″rĭ-go′sis) [*a* neg. + Gr. *rhigos* cold]. Inability to perceive cold; absence of the cold sense.

arhinencephalia (ah″rin-en″se-fa′le-ah) [*a* neg. + *rhinencephalon*]. Congenital absence of the rhinencephalon.

arhinia (ah-rin′e-ah) [*a* neg. + Gr. *rhis* nose + *-ia*]. A developmental anomaly characterized by absence of the nose.

arhythmia (ah-rith′me-ah). Arrhythmia.

ariboflavinosis (a-ri″bo-fla-vĭ-no′sis). Deficiency of riboflavin in the diet, a condition marked by lesions in the angles of the mouth, on lips and around nose and eyes, by corneal or other eye changes and by seborrheic dermatitis.

aril (ar′il) [L. *arillus* dried grape]. An accessory covering or appendage of seeds.

arillode (ar′ĭ-lōd). An appendage of certain seeds attached to the micropyle or raphe.

aristin (ah-ris′tin). A crystalline principle from various species of *Aristolochia.*

aristocort (ah-ris′to-cort). Trade mark for a preparation of triamcinolone.

aristogenesis (ah-ris″to-jen′e-sis) [Gr. *aristos* best + *genesis* generation]. The gradual continuous adaptive genoplastic origin of new and better organic mechanisms.

aristogenics (ah-ris″to-jen′iks) [Gr. *aristos* best + *gennan* to produce]. Improvement of the race through promotion of optimal mating between individuals possessing superior characteristics.

Aristolochia (ah-ris″to-lo′ke-ah) [L.; Gr. *aristos* best + *lochia* lochia]. A genus of shrubs and herbs of many species: often actively medicinal. See *serpentaria* and *guaco.* **A. reticula′ta,** Texas snakeroot, and **A. serpenta′ria,** Virginia snakeroot, are the source (dried rhizome and roots) of serpentaria, an aromatic bitter.

Aristotle's anomaly (ar′ĭ-stot-elz) [A Greek philosopher, 384–322 B. C.] See under *anomaly.*

arithmomania (ah-rith″mo-ma′ne-ah) [Gr. *arithmos* number + *mania* madness]. A morbid impulse to count, with worriment about numbers.

arkyochrome (ar′ke-o-krōm) [Gr. *arkys* net + *chrōma* color]. Any nerve cell in which the chromatic substance arranges itself in the form of a network. Cf. *gyrochrome, perichrome,* and *stichochrome.*

arkyostichochrome (ar″ke-o-stik′o-krōm) [Gr. *arkys* net + *stichos* row + *chrōma* color]. Any nerve cell which is both an arkyochrome and a stichochrome.

arlidin (ar′lĭ-din). Trade mark for preparations of nylidrin.

Arloing-Courmont test (ahr-lyahn′ koor′mont) [Saturnin *Arloing,* French pathologist, 1846–1911]. Widal reaction in tuberculosis.

Arlt's operation, sinus, trachoma (arltz) [Carl Ferdinand Ritter von *Arlt*, oculist in Vienna, 1812–1887]. See under the nouns.

arm (arm) [L. *armus*]. 1. The upper extremity from the shoulder to the hand; also the part between the shoulder and the elbow as distinguished from the forearm. See also *brachium*. 2. An armlike appendage or extension; used in dentistry to designate a portion of the clasp by which a removable partial denture is retained in position in the mouth. **bar clasp a.,** an extension originating in the base or major connector of a denture, and consisting of the arm which traverses but does not contact the gingival structures, and a terminal end which approaches its contact with the tooth in a gingivo-occlusal direction. **bird a.,** reduction in size of the forearm from atrophy of the muscles. **brawny a.,** a hard swollen condition of the arm following breast amputation and caused by pressure on the axillary veins and lymphatics from scar tissue of malignant infiltrations. **circumferential clasp a.,** an extension originating in a minor connector of a removable partial denture, which follows the contour of the tooth approximately in a plane perpendicular to the path of insertion of the denture. **glass a.,** a condition of the arm due to an injury to the long tendon of the biceps muscle or to subdeltoid bursitis occurring in baseball pitchers, tennis players, and golfers. Called also *baseball shoulder, tennis shoulder,* and *golfer's shoulder*. **golf a.,** a form of neurosis seen in golf players after excessive exercise. **Krukenberg's a.** See under *hand*. **lawn tennis a.,** displacement of the pronator teres muscle due to excessive tennis playing. **reciprocal a.,** the arm of the clasp of a removable partial denture which stabilizes against lateral movement of the appliance and resists force generated by the retentive arm. **retentive a.,** the arm of the clasp of a removable partial denture which aids in resistance to displacement of the appliance. **stabilizing a.,** reciprocal a.

armadillo (ar″mah-dil′o). A lower mammal, one species of which in South America is a reservoir for *Trypanosoma cruzi*.

armamentarium (ar″mah-men-tā′re-um) [L.]. The equipment of a practitioner or institution, including books, instruments, medicines, and surgical appliances.

Armanni-Ebstein cells [Luciano *Armanni*, Italian pathologist, 1839–1903]. See under *cell*.

armarium (ar-ma′re-um) [L.]. Armamentarium.

armature (ar′mah-tūr) [L. *armatura* a defensive apparatus]. The iron bar or keeper across the open end of a horseshoe magnet.

Armenian bole (ar-me′ne-an). A pale, reddish clay used in tooth powders and sometimes for aphthae.

A.R.M.H. Abbreviation for *Academy of Religion and Mental Health*.

Armigeres (ar-mij′er-ēz). A genus of mosquitoes. **A. obtur′bans,** a mosquito which transmits dengue in Japan.

armilla (ar-mil′ah), pl. *armil′lae* [L. "bracelet"]. The annular enlargement of the wrist.

Armillifer (ar-mil′lĭ-fer). A name formerly given a genus of wormlike arthropods. **A. armilla′tus,** *Porocephalus armillatus*.

armpit (arm′pit). Fossa axillaris.

Arndt's law, Arndt-Schulz law [Rudolf *Arndt*, German psychiatrist, 1835–1900; Hugo *Schulz*, German pharmacologist, 1853–1932]. See under *law*.

Arneth's classification, count, formula, index (ar-nāts′) [Joseph *Arneth*, German physician, 1873–1955]. See under *formula*.

Arnica (ar′ne-kah) [L.]. A genus of composite-flowered plants. **A. monta′na,** a species whose flowerheads are sometimes used in medicine.

arnica (ar′nĭ-kah). The dried flowerheads of *Arnica montana*. Used in an alcoholic extract or tincture as a skin irritant.

Arnold (ar′nold) **of Villanova** (c. 1235 to c. 1312). A celebrated physician who wrote extensively on medicine, alchemy, and religion, and who translated Avicenna's writings on the heart from Arabic into Latin.

Arnold's bodies [Julius *Arnold*, German pathologist, 1835–1915]. See under *body*.

Arnold's canal, ganglion, etc. [Friedrich *Arnold*, German anatomist, 1803–1890]. See under the nouns.

Arnold's test [Vincenz *Arnold*, Austrian physician, born 1864]. See under *tests*.

Arnold-Chiari deformity, malformation or **syndrome.** See under *deformity*.

Arnott's bed (ar′nots) [Neil *Arnott*, Scotch physician, 1788–1874]. See under *bed*.

arnotto (ar-not′o). Annotto.

aroma (ah-ro′mah) [Gr. *arōma* spice]. Fragrance or odor, especially that of a spice or medicine or of articles of food or drink.

aromatic (ar-o-mat′ik) [L. *aromaticus;* Gr. *arōmatikos*]. 1. Having a spicy odor. 2. A medicinal substance with a spicy fragrance and stimulant qualities.

aromine (ah-ro′min). A fragrant alkaloid from urine containing benzene derivatives.

Aron's test (ar′onz) [Hans *Aron*, German pediatrician, born 1881]. See under *test*.

arrachement (ar″ash-mahw′) [Fr. "extraction"]. 1. Extraction of a tooth. 2. Extraction of a membranous cataract by pulling out the capsule through a corneal incision.

arrack (ar′ak). Arack.

arrector (ar-rek′tor), pl. *arrecto′res* [L.]. Raising, or that which raises. **a. pi′li,** pl. **arrecto′res pilo′rum** [L. "raisers of the hair"], minute involuntary muscles of the skin, attached to the connective tissue sheath of the hair follicles, the contraction of which causes the hair to stand erect and produces the appearance called cutis anserina, or goose flesh.

arrectores (ar″rek-to′rez) [L.]. Plural of *arrector*.

arrest (ah-rest′). Stoppage; the act of stopping. **cardiac a.,** cessation of cardiac function, with disappearance of arterial blood pressure. **developmental a.,** a temporary or permanent cessation of the process of development. **epiphyseal a.,** interruption of growth at the epiphysis of a bone by diaphyseal-epiphyseal fusion. **maturation a.,** interruption of the process of development before it is complete; applied especially to failure of maturation of granulocytes, with myeloblasts and promyelocytes constituting the dominant bone marrow elements.

arrested (ah-rest′ed). Detained; stopped. The head of the child is said to be arrested when it is *detained*, but not *impacted*, in the pelvic cavity.

arrhaphia (ah-ra′fe-ah). Dysrhaphia.

arrhenic (ah-ren′ik). Pertaining to arsenic.

Arrhenius' doctrine, formula, law, theory, (ah-re′ne-us) [Svante *Arrhenius*, Swedish chemist, 1859–1927]. See under *formula, law,* and *theory*.

arrheno- (ah-re′no) [Gr. *arrhēn* male]. Combining form meaning male.

arrhenoblastoma (ah-re″no-blas-to′mah) [*arrheno-* + Gr. *blastos* germ + *-oma*]. A malignant tumor of the ovary consisting of immature gonadal elements with male hormonal secretion and producing masculine secondary sex characteristics.

arrhenogenic (ar″e-no-jen′ik) [*arrheno* + Gr. *gennan* to produce]. Producing only male offspring.

arrhenokaryon (ar″e-no-kar′e-on). An organism which is produced by androgenesis.

arrhenoma (ar″e-no′mah). Arrhenoblastoma.

arrhenomimetic (ah-re″no-mĭ-met′ik) [*arrheno-* + Gr. *mimētikos* imitative]. Resembling the male: said of phenomena in the female which resemble those of the male, such as masculine hirsuties, deepened voice and hypertrophy of the clitoris. See *andromimetic*.

arrhenoplasm (ah-re′no-plazm) [*arrheno-* + *plasm*]. The male element of idioplasm.

arrhenotocia (ar″e-no-to′se-a). Arrhenotoky.

arrhenotoky (ar″e-not′o-ke) [*arrheno-* + Gr. *tokos* birth]. The production of males only by a virgin mother, as in the unfertilized queen bee.

arrhigosis (ah″rĭ-go′sis). Arhigosis.

arrhinencephalia (ah″rin-en″se-fa′le-ah). Arhinencephalia.

arrhinia (ah-rin′e-ah). Arhinia.

arrhythmia (ah-rith′me-ah) [*a* neg. + Gr. *rhythmos* rhythm]. Absence of rhythm, applied especially to any variation from the normal rhythm of the heart beat. The various forms of arrhythmia include sinus arrhythmia, extrasystole, heart block, atrial fibrillation, flutter, pulsus alternans, and paroxysmal tachycardia. **continuous a.,** irregularity in the force, quality, and sequence of the pulse beat, continuing as a permanent phenomenon: called also *perpetual a.* **inotropic a.,** disturbance of the cardiac rhythm due to disturbances of the contractility of the heart muscle. **juvenile a.,** the physiological sinus arrhythmia occurring normally in childhood and youth. **nodal a.** See *nodal rhythm*, under *rhythm*. **perpetual a.,** continuous a. **respiratory a.,** irregularity of the heart beat, the rate waxing and waning with inspiration and expiration. **sinus a.,** irregularity of the heart beat dependent on interference with the impulses originating at the sino-auricular node. **vagus a.,** arrhythmia dependent upon stimulation of the vagus nerve; the term embraces sinus arrhythmia, sino-auricular block, simple bradycardia, ventricular escape and wandering pacemaker.

arrhythmic (ah-rith′mik) [*a* neg. + Gr. *rhythmos* rhythm]. Characterized by absence of rhythm; recurring at irregular intervals.

arrhythmokinesis (ah-rith″mo-kĭ-ne′sis) [*a* neg. + Gr. *rhythmos* rhythm + *kinēsis* movement]. Defective ability to perform voluntary successive movement of a definite rhythm.

arrosion (ah-ro′zhun) [L. *ab* away + *rodere* to gnaw]. Erosion; the wasting away of a vessel wall under pressure.

arrow (ar′o). A sharply pointed instrument or tool. **caustic a.,** a sharply pointed bit of nitrate of silver or other caustic substance.

Arroyo's sign (ar-ro′yōz) [Carlos F. *Arroyo*, American physician, 1892–1928]. Asthenocoria.

arseniasis (ar″se-ni′ah-sis). Chronic arsenical poisoning.

arsenic[1] (ar′sĕ-nik) [L. *arsenicum*, *arsenium*, or *arsenum*; from Gr. *arsēn* strong]. 1. A medicinal and poisonous element; it is a brittle, lustrous, grayish solid, with a garlicky odor. Symbol, As; atomic number, 33; atomic weight, 74.922; specific gravity, 5.73. 2. Arsenic trioxide. **a. chloride,** a very poisonous liquid, $AsCl_3$. **a. disulfide,** As_2S_2: employed as a pigment, and sometimes as a medicine. **a. iodide,** a red, crystalline compound, AsI_3: used in coryza and skin diseases. **a. trichloride,** $AsCl_3$, one of the constituents of the lethal war gas vincennite. **a. trioxide,** white arsenic or arsenous acid, a white or glassy compound, As_2O_3, with a sweetish taste: formerly used in treatment of skin and lung diseases. **a. trisulfide,** orpiment, As_2S_3: employed as a pigment and sometimes as a medicine. **white a.,** a. trioxide.

arsenic[2] (ar-sen′ik). Pertaining to or containing arsenic in its pentad valency.

arsenical (ar-sen′ĭ-kal) [L. *arsenicalis*]. 1. Pertaining to or containing arsenic. 2. A drug containing arsenic.

arsenicalism (ar-sen′ĭ-kal″izm). Chronic arsenical poisoning.

arsenic-fast (ar′sen-ik-fast″). Resistant to treatment by arsenic.

arsenicophagy (ar″sen-ĭ-kof′ah-je) [*arsenic* + Gr. *phagein* to eat]. The eating of arsenic.

arsenicum (ar-sen′ĭ-kum) [L.]. Arsenic.

arsenide (ar′sĕ-nīd). Any compound of arsenic with another element, in which arsenic is the negative element.

arsenionization (ar″sen-i″on-i-za′shun). The electric administration of the ions of arsenic as a protozoacide.

arsenious (ar-sen′e-us). Arsenous.

arsenite (ar′sĕ-nīt). Any salt of arsenous acid.

arsenium (ar-se′ne-um) [L.]. The element arsenic.

arsenization (ar″sen-ĭ-za′shun). Treatment with arsenic.

arseno- (ar′sĕ-no). A prefix indicating the chemical group, —As:As—.

arseno-activation (ar″sĕ-no-ak″tĭ-va′shun). Increase of the manifestations of syphilis under treatment by arsenicals.

arseno-autohemotherapy (ar″sĕ-no-aw″to-he″mo-ther′ah-pe). Treatment of syphilis by injection of the arsenical drug mixed with some of the patient's own blood.

arsenobenzene (ar″sĕ-no-ben′zēn). A general term for the various arsphenamine compounds used in the treatment of spirochetal diseases.

arsenoblast (ar-sen′o-blast) [Gr. *arsēn* male + *blastos* germ]. The male element of a zygote; a male pronucleus.

arsenoceptor (ar-sen′o-sep″tor). A supposed chemical affinity in cells for arsenical preparations.

arsenophagy (ar″sĕ-nof′ah-je). Arsenicophagy.

arsenorelapsing (ar-sen″o-re-laps′ing). Relapsing after apparent cure by arsenical treatment: said of certain cases of syphilis.

arsenoresistant (ar-sen″o-re-zis′tant). Resistant to arsenicals such as arsphenamine: said of certain cases of syphilis.

arsenotherapy (ar″sĕ-no-ther′ah-pe) [*arsenic* + Gr. *therapeia* treatment]. Treatment of disease by the use of arsenic and arsenical preparations.

arsenous (ar′sĕ-nus). Containing arsenic in its lower or triad valency. **a. iodide,** an orange-red powder, soluble in water and alcohol, with an action similar to that of arsenic trioxide. **a. oxide,** arsenic trioxide.

arsenoxide (ar″sen-ok′sīd). Oxophenarsine.

arsenum (ar-se′num) [L.]. Arsenic.

arsine (ar′sin). Any member of a peculiar group of volatile arsenical bases, formed when arsenous acid is brought in contact with albuminous substances. The typical arsine is AsH_3, arsenous hydride or arseniuretted hydrogen, a very poisonous gas, and some of its compounds were once used in warfare. It causes hemolysis, jaundice, gastroenteritis, and nephritis.

arsonate (ar′so-nāt). A salt of arsonic acid.

arsonium (ar-so′ne-um). The univalent radical, AsH_4, which acts in combination like ammonium.

arsonvalization (ar″son-val″i-za′shun). D'arsonvalization.

arsphenamine (ars-fen′ah-min). Diaminodihydroxyarsenobenzene dihydrochloride, $[OH.C_6H_3(NH_2.HCl).As:]_2$: used in the treatment of syphilis, yaws, and other spirillum infections. It is a yellowish powder which rapidly oxidizes on exposure to air, and is, therefore, put up in hermetically sealed capsules. The substance is converted, immediately before injection, into an unstable sodium salt by the addition of sodium hydroxide solution. Called also *salvarsan* (Germany), *arsenobenzol* (France), *diarsenol* (Canada), *arsaminol* (Japan), 606, *Ehrlich-Hata preparation*. **silver a.,** sodium salt of silver diaminodihydroxyarsenobenzene: it contains about 19 per cent of arsenic and 12–14 per cent of silver; claimed to combine the therapeutic activities of silver and arsphenamine. Called also *argentum arsphenamina*. **sodium a.,** the sodium salt of arsphenamine, soluble in water without the addition of alkali. **a. sulfoxylate,** a condensation product of arsphenamine and sodium formaldehyde bisulfite, $[NaO.SO_2.CH.NH(OH)C_6H_4As]_2$.

arsphenamized (ars-fen′ah-mīzd). Treated with arsphenamine.

arsthinol (ars′thĭ-nol). Chemical name: 2-(3′-acetamido-4′-hydroxyphenyl)-1,3-dithia-2-arsacyclopentane-4-methanol. Uses: 1. arsenical preparation for treatment of intestinal amebiasis; 2. treatment of yaws.

artane (ar′tān). Trade mark for preparations of trihexyphenidyl hydrochloride.

artarine (ar′tah-rin). An alkaloid, $C_{21}H_{23}NO_4$, from the root of *Xanthoxylum senegalense*. It is a heart stimulant, resembling veratrine in its action.

artefact (ar′te-fakt). Artifact.

Artemisia (ar″tĕ-mis′e-ah) [L.; Gr. *artemisia* from *Artemis* Diana]. A genus of composite-flowered plants, including *A. abrot′anum*, or southernwood, *A. absin′thium*, and *A. marit′ima* (*A. pauciflora*), from which santonin is derived.

arterectomy (ar″tĕ-rek′to-me). Arteriectomy.

arterenol (ar″tĕ-re′nol). Norepinephrine.

arteria (ar-te′re-ah), pl. *arteriae* [L.; Gr. *artēria*]. A general term used in anatomical nomenclature to designate any vessel carrying blood away from the heart. For names and description of specific vessels, see *Table of Arteriae*. See also *artery*. **a. luso′ria,** an abnormally situated vessel in the region of the aortic arch, which may cause symptoms by compression of the esophagus, trachea, or a nerve.

arteriae (ar-te′re-e) [L.]. Plural of *arteria*.

arteriagra (ar″tĕ-re-ag′rah) [*artery* + Gr. *agra* seizure]. Any gouty affection of an artery.

TABLE OF ARTERIAE

Descriptions of vessels are given on N A terms, and include anglicized names of specific arteries. B N A terms, when different, are cross referred to names used in Nomina Anatomica.

a. aceta′buli [B N A], ramus acetabularis arteriae obturatoriae.

a. alveola′ris infe′rior [N A, B N A], inferior alveolar artery: *origin*, maxillary artery; *branches*, dental, mylohyoid rami, mental artery; *distribution*, lower teeth, gums, mandible, lower lip, and chin.

arte′riae alveola′res superio′res anterio′res [N A, B N A], anterior superior alveolar arteries: *origin*, infraorbital artery; *branches*, dental; *distribution*, incisors and canine teeth of upper jaw, and maxillary sinus.

a. alveola′ris supe′rior poste′rior [N A, B N A], posterior superior alveolar artery: *origin*, maxillary artery; *branches*, dental; *distribution*, molar and premolar teeth of upper jaw, maxillary sinus, and buccinator muscle.

a. angula′ris [N A, B N A], angular artery: *origin*, facial artery; *branches*, none; *distribution*, lacrimal sac, inferior portion of orbicularis oculi, and nose.

a. anon′yma [B N A], truncus brachiocephalicus.

a. aor′ta, aorta.

a. appendicula′ris [N A, B N A], appendicular artery: *origin*, ileocolic artery; *branches*, none; *distribution*, vermiform appendix.

arte′riae arcifor′mes re′nis [B N A], arteriae arcuatae renis.

a. arcua′ta pe′dis [N A, B N A], arcuate artery of foot: *origin*, dorsal artery of foot; *branches*, deep plantar branch and dorsal metatarsal artery; *distribution*, foot and toes.

arte′riae arcua′tae re′nis [N A], arcuate arteries of kidney: *origin*, interlobar artery; *branches*, interlobular artery and arteriolae rectae; *distribution*, parenchyma of kidney.

a. auditi′va inter′na [B N A], a. labyrinthi.

arte′riae auricula′res anterio′res, rami auriculares anteriores arteriae temporalis superficialis.

a. auricula′ris poste′rior [N A, B N A], posterior auricular artery: *origin*, external carotid; *branches*, auricular and occipital rami, stylomastoid artery; *distribution*, middle ear, mastoid cells, auricle, parotid gland, digastric and other muscles.

a. auricula′ris profun′da [N A, B N A], deep auricular artery: *origin*, maxillary artery; *branches*, none; *distribution*, skin of auditory canal, tympanic membrane, and temporomandibular joint.

a. axilla′ris [N A, B N A], axillary artery: *origin*, continuation of subclavian artery; *branches*, subscapular rami, and supreme thoracic, thoracoacromial, lateral thoracic, subscapular, and anterior and posterior circumflex humeral arteries; *distribution*, upper extremity, axilla, chest, and shoulder.

a. basila′ris [N A, B N A], basilar artery: *origin*, from junction of right and left vertebral arteries; *branches*, pontine branches, and anterior inferior cerebellar, labyrinthine, superior cerebellar, and posterior cerebral arteries; *distribution*, brain stem, internal ear, cerebellum, posterior cerebrum.

a. brachia′lis [N A, B N A], brachial artery: *origin*, continuation of axillary artery; *branches*, superficial brachial, deep brachial, nutrient of humerus, superior ulnar collateral, inferior ulnar collateral, radial, and ulnar arteries; *distribution*, shoulder, arm, forearm, and hand.

a. brachia′lis superficia′lis [N A], superficial brachial artery: a name given to a vessel that arises from high bifurcation of the brachial artery and assumes a more superficial course than usual.

arte′riae bronchia′les [B N A], rami bronchiales aortae thoracicae.

a. bucca′lis [N A], buccal artery: *origin*, maxillary artery; *branches*, none; *distribution*, buccinator muscle, mucous membrane of mouth.

a. buccinato′ria [B N A], a. buccalis.

a. bul′bi pe′nis [N A], artery of bulb of penis: *origin*, internal pudendal artery; *branches*, none; *distribution*, bulbourethral gland and bulb of penis.

a. bul′bi ure′thrae [B N A], a. bulbi penis.

a. bul′bi vestib′uli vagi′nae [N A, B N A], artery of bulb of vestibule of vagina: *origin*, internal pudendal artery; *branches*, none; *distribution*, vestibular bulb and greater vestibular glands.

a. cana′lis pterygoi′dei [N A], artery of pterygoid canal: *origin*, maxillary artery; *branches*, none; *distribution*, roof of pharynx, auditory tube.

a. carot′is commu′nis [N A, B N A], common carotid artery: *origin*, brachiocephalic trunk (right), aortic arch (left); *branches*, external and internal carotids; *distribution*, see *a. carotis externa* and *a. carotis interna*.

a. carot′is exter′na [N A, B N A], external carotid artery: *origin*, common carotid; *branches*, superior thyroid, ascending pharyngeal, lingual, facial, sternocleidomastoid, occipital, posterior auricular, superficial temporal, maxillary; *distribution*, neck, face, skull.

a. carot′is inter′na [N A, B N A], internal carotid artery: *origin*, common carotid; *branches*, caroticotympanic rami, and ophthalmic, posterior communicating, anterior choroid, anterior cerebral, and middle cerebral arteries; *distribution*, middle ear, brain, pituitary gland, orbit, choroid plexus of lateral ventricle.

a. centra′lis ret′inae [N A, B N A], central artery of retina: *origin*, ophthalmic artery; *branches*, none; *distribution*, retina.

a. cerebel′li infe′rior ante′rior [N A, B N A], anterior inferior cerebellar artery: *origin*, basilar artery; *branches*, labyrinthine artery; *distribution*, lower anterior cerebellar cortex, and inner ear.

a. cerebel′li infe′rior poste′rior [N A, B N A], posterior inferior cerebellar artery: *origin*, vertebral artery; *branches*, none; *distribution*, lower cerebellum, medulla, choroid plexus of fourth ventricle.

a. cerebel'li supe'rior [N A, B N A], superior cerebellar artery: *origin*, basilar artery; *branches*, none; *distribution*, upper cerebellum, midbrain, pineal body, choroid plexus of third ventricle.

arte'riae cer'ebri [N A, B N A], cerebral arteries: the arteries supplying the cerebral cortex, including *a. cerebri anterior*, *a. cerebri media*, and *a. cerebri posterior*.

a. cer'ebri ante'rior [N A, B N A], anterior cerebral artery: *origin*, internal carotid; *branches*, cortical (orbital, frontal, parietal), and central branches, and anterior communicating artery; *distribution*, orbital, frontal and parietal cortex, and corpus callosum.

a. cer'ebri me'dia [N A, B N A], middle cerebral artery: *origin*, internal carotid; *branches*, cortical (orbital, frontal, parietal, temporal), and central (striate) branches; *distribution*, orbital, frontal, parietal, and temporal cortex, and basal ganglia.

a. cer'ebri poste'rior [N A, B N A], posterior cerebral artery: *origin*, terminal bifurcation of basilar artery; *branches*, cortical (temporal, occipital, parietooccipital), central, and choroid branches; *distribution*, occipital and temporal lobes, basal ganglia, choroid plexus of lateral ventricle, thalamus, and midbrain.

a. cervica'lis ascen'dens [N A, B N A], ascending cervical artery: *origin*, inferior thyroid artery; *branches*, spinal rami; *distribution*, muscles of neck, vertebrae, and vertebral canal.

a. cervica'lis profun'da [N A, B N A], deep cervical artery: *origin*, costocervical trunk; *branches*, none; *distribution*, deep neck muscles.

a. cervica'lis superficia'lis, N A alternative for *ramus superficialis arteriae transversae colli*. The structure bearing this name in B N A is not included in N A.

a. chorioi'dea [B N A], a. choroidea anterior.

a. choroi'dea ante'rior [N A], anterior choroid artery: *origin*, internal carotid artery; *branches*, none; *distribution*, choroid plexus of lateral ventricle, hippocampus, fimbria.

arte'riae cilia'res anterio'res [N A, B N A], anterior ciliary arteries: *origin*, ophthalmic and lacrimal arteries; *branches*, episcleral and anterior conjunctival arteries; *distribution*, iris, conjunctiva.

arte'riae cilia'res posterio'res bre'ves [N A, B N A], short posterior ciliary arteries: *origin*, ophthalmic artery; *branches*, none; *distribution*, choroid coat of eye.

arte'riae cilia'res posterio'res lon'gae [N A, B N A], long posterior ciliary arteries: *origin*, ophthalmic artery; *branches*, none; *distribution*, iris and ciliary process.

a. circumflex'a fem'oris latera'lis [N A, B N A], lateral circumflex femoral artery: *origin*, deep femoral artery; *branches*, ascending, descending, and transverse branches; *distribution*, hip joint, thigh muscles.

a. circumflex'a fem'oris media'lis [N A, B N A], medial circumflex femoral artery: *origin*, deep femoral artery; *branches*, deep, ascending, transverse, and acetabular branches; *distribution*, hip joint, thigh muscles.

a. circumflex'a hu'meri ante'rior [N A, B N A], anterior circumflex humeral artery: *origin*, axillary artery; *branches*, none; *distribution*, shoulder joint and head of humerus, long tendon of biceps, and tendon of pectoralis major muscle.

a. circumflex'a hu'meri poste'rior [N A, B N A], posterior circumflex humeral artery: *origin*, axillary artery; *branches*, none; *distribution*, deltoideus, shoulder joint, teres minor and triceps muscles.

a. circumflex'a il'ium profun'da [N A, B N A], deep circumflex iliac artery: *origin*, external iliac artery; *branches*, ascending branches; *distribution*, psoas, iliacus, sartorius, tensor fasciae latae, oblique, and transverse abdominal muscles, and adjacent skin.

a. circumflex'a il'ium superficia'lis [N A, B N A], superficial circumflex iliac artery: *origin*, femoral artery; *branches*, none; *distribution*, inguinal glands, skin of thigh and abdomen.

a. circumflex'a scap'ulae [N A, B N A], circumflex artery of scapula: *origin*, subscapular artery; *branches*, none; *distribution*, subscapularis, scapula, shoulder joint, teres major and minor.

a. clitor'idis [B N A], artery of clitoris. Omitted in N A.

a. coelia'ca [B N A], truncus celiacus.

a. col'ica dex'tra [N A, B N A], right colic artery: *origin*, superior mesenteric artery; *branches*, none; *distribution*, ascending colon.

a. col'ica me'dia [N A, B N A], middle colic artery: *origin*, superior mesenteric artery; *branches*, none; *distribution*, transverse colon.

a. col'ica sinis'tra [N A, B N A], left colic artery: *origin*, inferior mesenteric; *branches*, none; *distribution*, descending colon.

a. collatera'lis me'dia [N A, B N A], middle collateral artery: *origin*, deep brachial artery; *branches*, none; *distribution*, triceps muscle and elbow joint.

a. collatera'lis radia'lis [N A, B N A], radial collateral artery: *origin*, deep brachial artery; *branches*, none; *distribution*, brachioradialis and brachialis muscles.

a. collatera'lis ulna'ris infe'rior [N A, B N A], inferior ulnar collateral artery: *origin*, brachial artery; *branches*, none; *distribution*, arm muscles at back of elbow.

a. collatera'lis ulna'ris supe'rior [N A, B N A], superior ulnar collateral artery: *origin*, brachial artery; *branches*, none; *distribution*, elbow joint and triceps muscle.

a. comitans' ner'vi ischia'dici [N A, B N A], sciatic artery: *origin*, inferior gluteal artery; *branches*, none; *distribution*, accompanies sciatic nerve.

a. commu'nicans ante'rior cer'ebri [N A, B N A], anterior communicating artery of cerebrum: *origin*, anterior cerebral artery; *branches*, none; *distribution*, establishes connection between the anterior cerebral arteries.

a. commu'nicans poste'rior cer'ebri [N A, B N A], posterior communicating artery of cerebrum: *origin*, internal carotid and posterior cerebral; *branches*, none; *distribution*, hippocampus, thalamus.

arte'riae conjunctiva'les anterio'res [N A, B N A], anterior conjunctival arteries: *origin*, anterior ciliary; *branches*, none; *distribution*, conjunctiva.

arte'riae conjunctiva'les posterio'res [N A, B N A], posterior conjunctival arteries: *origin*, medial palpebral artery; *branches*, none; *distribution*, caruncula lacrimalis and conjunctiva.

a. corona'ria dex'tra [N A], right coronary artery of heart: *origin*, right aortic sinus; *branches*, posterior interventricular; *distribution*, right ventricle and right atrium.

a. corona'ria sinis'tra [N A], left coronary artery of heart: *origin*, left aortic sinus; *branches*, anterior interventricular and circumflex rami; *distribution*, left ventricle and left atrium.

a. cremaster'ica [N A], cremasteric artery: *origin*, inferior epigastric; *branches*, none; *distribution*, cremaster muscle and coverings of spermatic cord.

a. cys'tica [N A, B N A], cystic artery: *origin*, right branch of proper hepatic artery; *branches*, none; *distribution*, gallbladder.

a. deferentia'lis [B N A], a. ductus deferentis.

arte'riae digita'les dorsa'les ma'nus [N A, B N A], dorsal digital arteries of hand: *origin*, dorsal metacarpal arteries; *branches*, none; *distribution*, dorsum of fingers.

arte'riae digita'les dorsa'les pe'dis [N A, B N A], dorsal digital arteries of foot: *origin*, dorsal metatarsal arteries; *branches*, none; *distribution*, dorsum of toes.

arte′riae digita′les palma′res commu′nes [N A], common palmar digital arteries: *origin*, superficial volar arch; *branches*, proper palmar digital arteries; *distribution*, fingers.

arte′riae digita′les palma′res pro′priae [N A], proper palmar digital arteries: *origin*, common palmar digital arteries; *branches*, none; *distribution*, fingers.

arte′riae digita′les planta′res commu′nes [N A], common plantar digital arteries: *origin*, plantar metatarsal arteries; *branches*, proper plantar digital arteries; *distribution*, toes.

arte′riae digita′les planta′res pro′priae [N A], proper plantar digital arteries: *origin*, common plantar digital arteries; *branches*, none; *distribution*, toes.

arte′riae digita′les vola′res commu′nes [B N A], arteriae digitales palmares communes.

arte′riae digita′les vola′res pro′priae [B N A], arteriae digitales palmares propriae.

a. dorsa′lis clitor′idis [N A, B N A], dorsal artery of clitoris: *origin*, internal pudendal artery; *branches*, none; *distribution*, clitoris.

a. dorsa′lis na′si [N A, B N A], dorsal artery of nose: *origin*, ophthalmic artery; *branches*, lacrimal; *distribution*, skin of dorsum of nose.

a. dorsa′lis pe′dis [N A, B N A], dorsal artery of foot: *origin*, continuation of anterior tibial; *branches*, lateral and medial tarsal and arcuate arteries; *distribution*, foot and toes.

a. dorsa′lis pe′nis [N A, B N A], dorsal artery of penis: *origin*, internal pudendal artery; *branches*, none; *distribution*, glans, corona, and prepuce of penis.

a. duc′tus deferen′tis [N A], artery of ductus deferens, deferential artery: *origin*, umbilical artery; *branches*, ureteral artery; *distribution*, ureter, ductus deferens, seminal vesicles, and testes.

a. epigas′trica infe′rior [N A], inferior epigastric artery: *origin*, external iliac; *branches*, pubic branch, cremasteric artery, a. of round ligament of uterus; *distribution*, cremaster and abdominal muscles, peritoneum.

a. epigas′trica superficia′lis [N A, B N A], superficial epigastric artery: *origin*, femoral; *branches*, none; *distribution*, skin of abdomen, superficial fascia, inguinal lymph nodes.

a. epigas′trica supe′rior [N A, B N A], superior epigastric artery: *origin*, internal thoracic artery; *branches*, none; *distribution*, abdominal muscles, diaphragm, skin, and peritoneum.

arte′riae episclera′les [N A, B N A], episcleral arteries: *origin*, anterior ciliary artery; *branches*, none; *distribution*, iris and ciliary process.

a. ethmoida′lis ante′rior [N A, B N A], anterior ethmoidal artery: *origin*, ophthalmic artery; *branches*, anterior meningeal; *distribution*, dura mater, nose, frontal sinus, skin, anterior ethmoidal cells.

a. ethmoida′lis poste′rior [N A, B N A], posterior ethmoidal artery: *origin*, ophthalmic artery; *branches*, none; *distribution*, posterior ethmoidal cells, dura mater, nose.

a. facia′lis [N A], facial artery: *origin*, external carotid; *branches*, ascending palatine, tonsillar, submental, inferior labial, superior labial, angular, glandular; *distribution*, face, tonsil, palate, submandibular gland.

a. femora′lis [N A, B N A], femoral artery: *origin*, continuation of external iliac; *branches*, superficial epigastric, superficial circumflex iliac, external pudendal, deep femoral, descending geniculate; *distribution*, lower abdominal wall, external genitalia, and lower extremity.

a. fibula′ris, N A alternative for *a. peronea*.

a. fronta′lis [B N A], a. supratrochlearis.

arte′riae gas′tricae bre′ves [N A, B N A], short gastric arteries: *origin*, splenic; *branches*, none; *distribution*, upper part of stomach.

a. gas′trica dex′tra [N A, B N A], right gastric artery: *origin*, common hepatic artery; *branches*, none; *distribution*, lesser curvature of stomach.

a. gas′trica sinis′tra [N A, B N A], left gastric artery: *origin*, celiac; *branches*, esophageal; *distribution*, esophagus, lesser curvature of stomach.

a. gastroduodena′lis [N A, B N A], gastroduodenal artery: *origin*, common hepatic artery; *branches*, superior pancreaticoduodenal and right gastroepiploic; *distribution*, stomach, duodenum, pancreas, and greater omentum.

a. gastroepiplo′ica dex′tra [N A, B N A], right gastroepiploic artery: *origin*, gastroduodenal artery; *branches*, epiploic branches; *distribution*, stomach, greater omentum.

a. gastroepiplo′ica sinis′tra [N A, B N A], left gastroepiploic artery: *origin*, splenic artery; *branches*, epiploic branches; *distribution*, stomach and greater omentum.

a. ge′nu infe′rior latera′lis [B N A], a. genus inferior lateralis.

a. ge′nu infe′rior media′lis [B N A], a. genus inferior medialis.

a. ge′nu me′dia [B N A], a. genus media.

a. ge′nu supe′rior latera′lis [B N A], a. genus superior lateralis.

a. ge′nu supe′rior media′lis [B N A], a. genus superior medialis.

a. ge′nu supre′ma [B N A], a. genus descendens.

a. ge′nus descen′dens [N A], descending genicular artery: *origin*, femoral artery; *branches*, saphenous, articular; *distribution*, knee joint, skin of upper and medial part of leg.

a. ge′nus infe′rior latera′lis [N A], lateral inferior genicular artery: *origin*, popliteal artery; *branches*, none; *distribution*, knee joint.

a. ge′nus infe′rior media′lis [N A], medial inferior genicular artery: *origin*, popliteal artery; *branches*, none; *distribution*, knee joint.

a. ge′nus me′dia [N A], middle genicular artery: *origin*, popliteal artery; *branches*, none; *distribution*, knee joint, cruciate ligaments, patellar synovial and alar folds.

a. ge′nus supe′rior latera′lis [N A], lateral superior genicular artery: *origin*, popliteal artery; *branches*, none; *distribution*, knee joint, femur, patella, contiguous muscles.

a. ge′nus supe′rior media′lis [N A], medial superior genicular artery: *origin*, popliteal artery; *branches*, none; *distribution*, knee joint, femur, patella, contiguous muscles.

a. glu′taea infe′rior [B N A], a. glutea inferior.

a. glu′taea supe′rior [B N A], a. glutea superior.

a. glu′tea infe′rior [N A], inferior gluteal artery: *origin*, internal iliac; *branches*, sciatic; *distribution*, buttock and back of thigh.

a. glu′tea supe′rior [N A], superior gluteal artery: *origin*, internal iliac artery; *branches*, superficial and deep branches; *distribution*, upper portion of gluteal muscles and overlying skin, obturator internus, piriformis, levator ani, and coccygeus muscles, hip joint.

a. haemorrhoida′lis infe′rior [B N A], a. rectalis inferior.

a. haemorrhoida′lis me′dia [B N A], a. rectalis media.

a. haemorrhoida′lis supe′rior [B N A], a. rectalis superior.

arte′riae helici′nae pe′nis [N A, B N A], helicine arteries of penis: helicine arteries arising from the vessels of the penis, whose engorgement causes erection of the organ.

a. hepat′ica [B N A], a. hepatica communis.

a. hepat′ica commu′nis [N A], common hepatic artery: *origin*, celiac artery; *branches*, right gastric, gastroduodenal, hepatic proper; *distribution*, stomach, pancreas, duodenum, liver, gallbladder, and greater omentum.

a. hepat′ica pro′pria [N A, B N A], proper hepatic artery: *origin*, common hepatic artery;

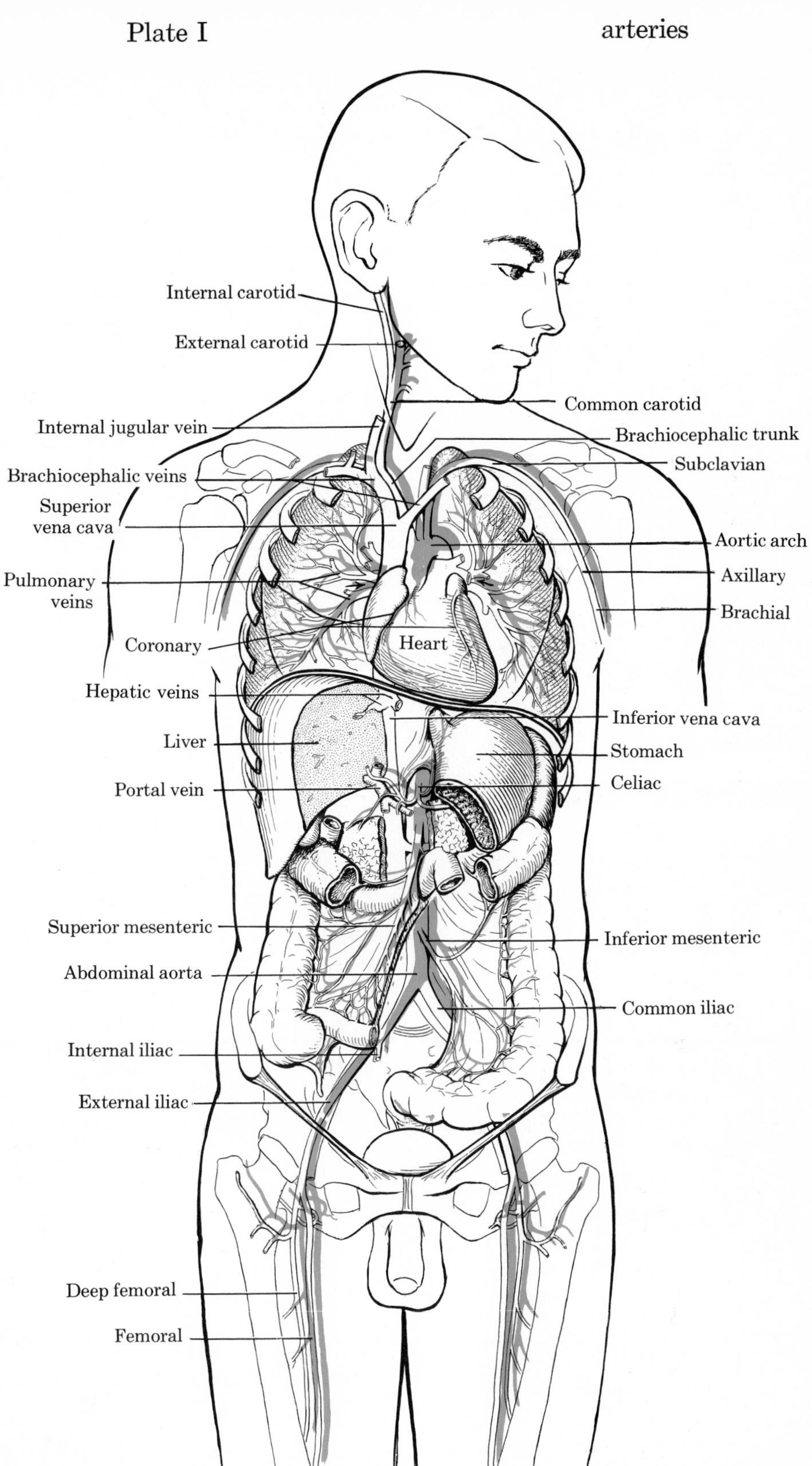

PRINCIPAL ARTERIES OF THE BODY AND PULMONARY VEINS

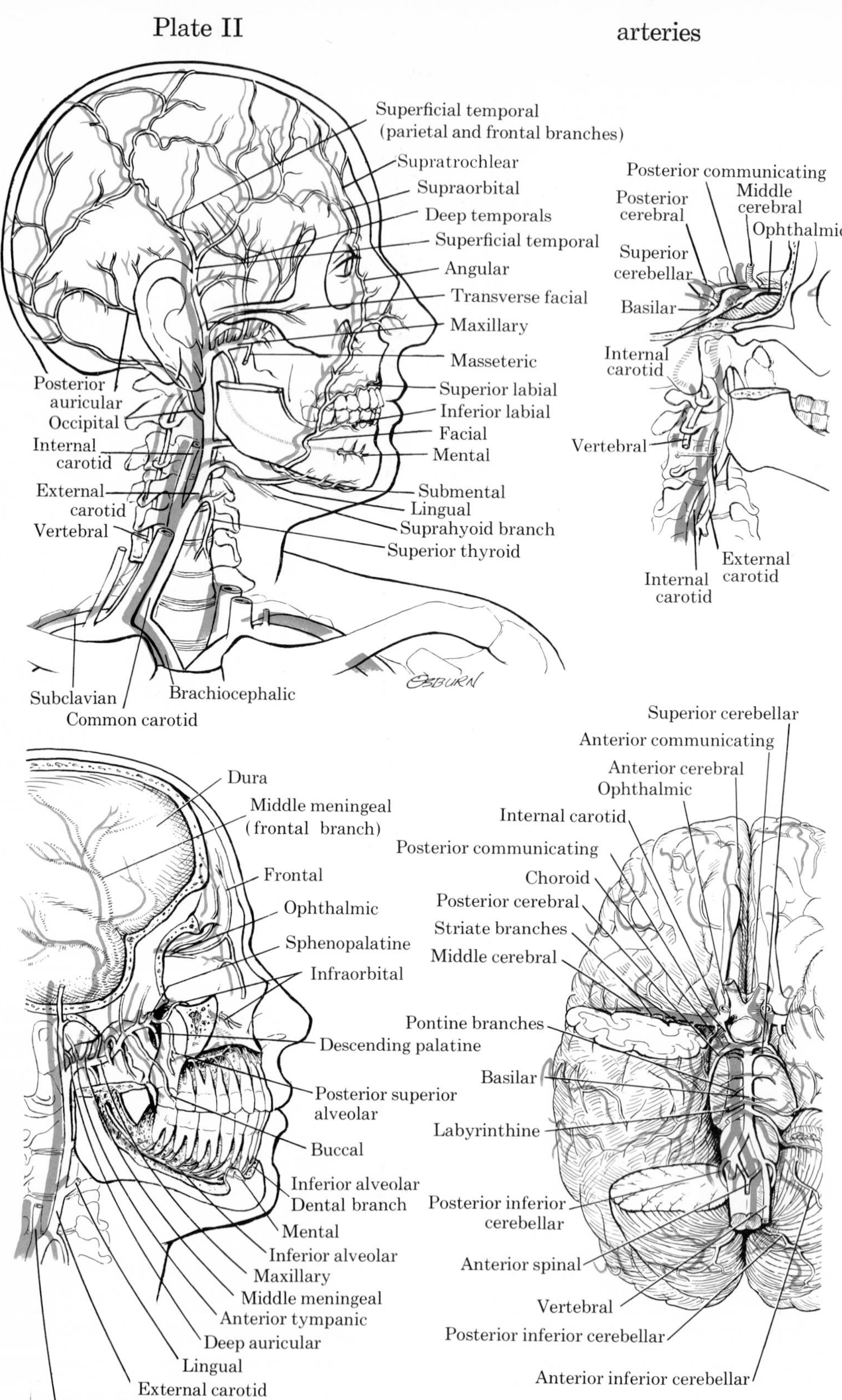

ARTERIES OF THE HEAD, NECK, AND BASE OF THE BRAIN

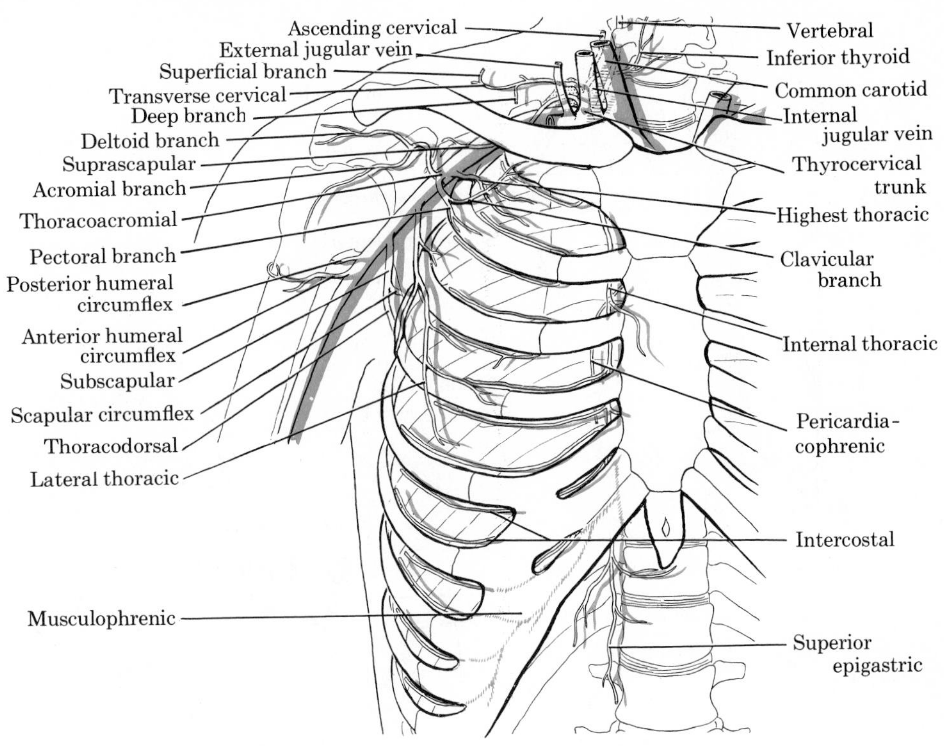

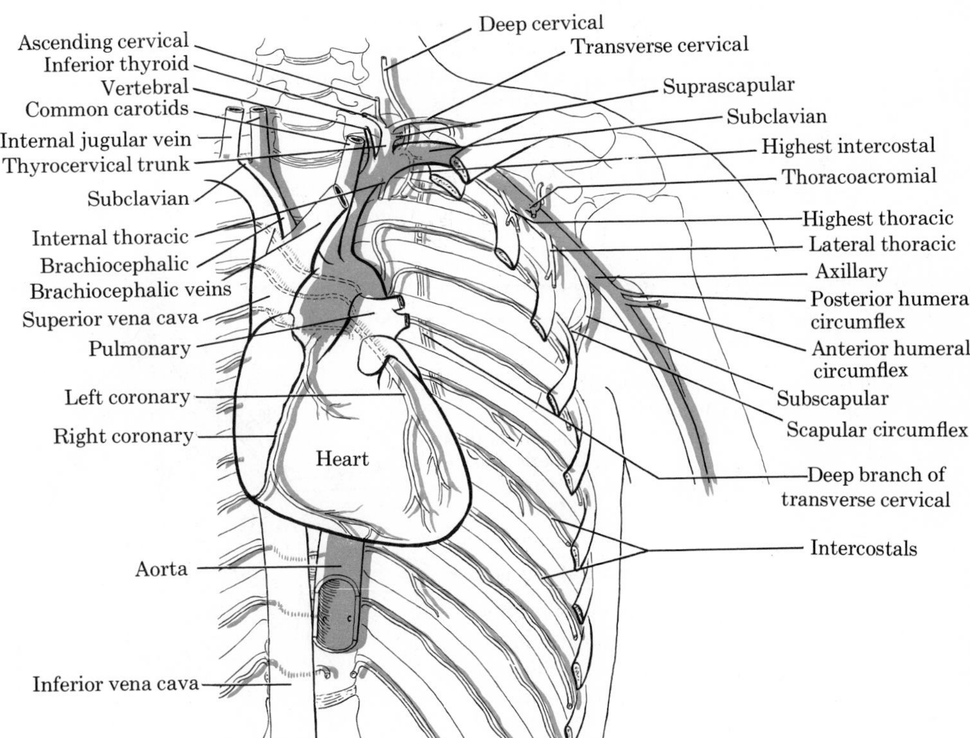

ARTERIES OF THE THORAX AND AXILLA

Plate IV

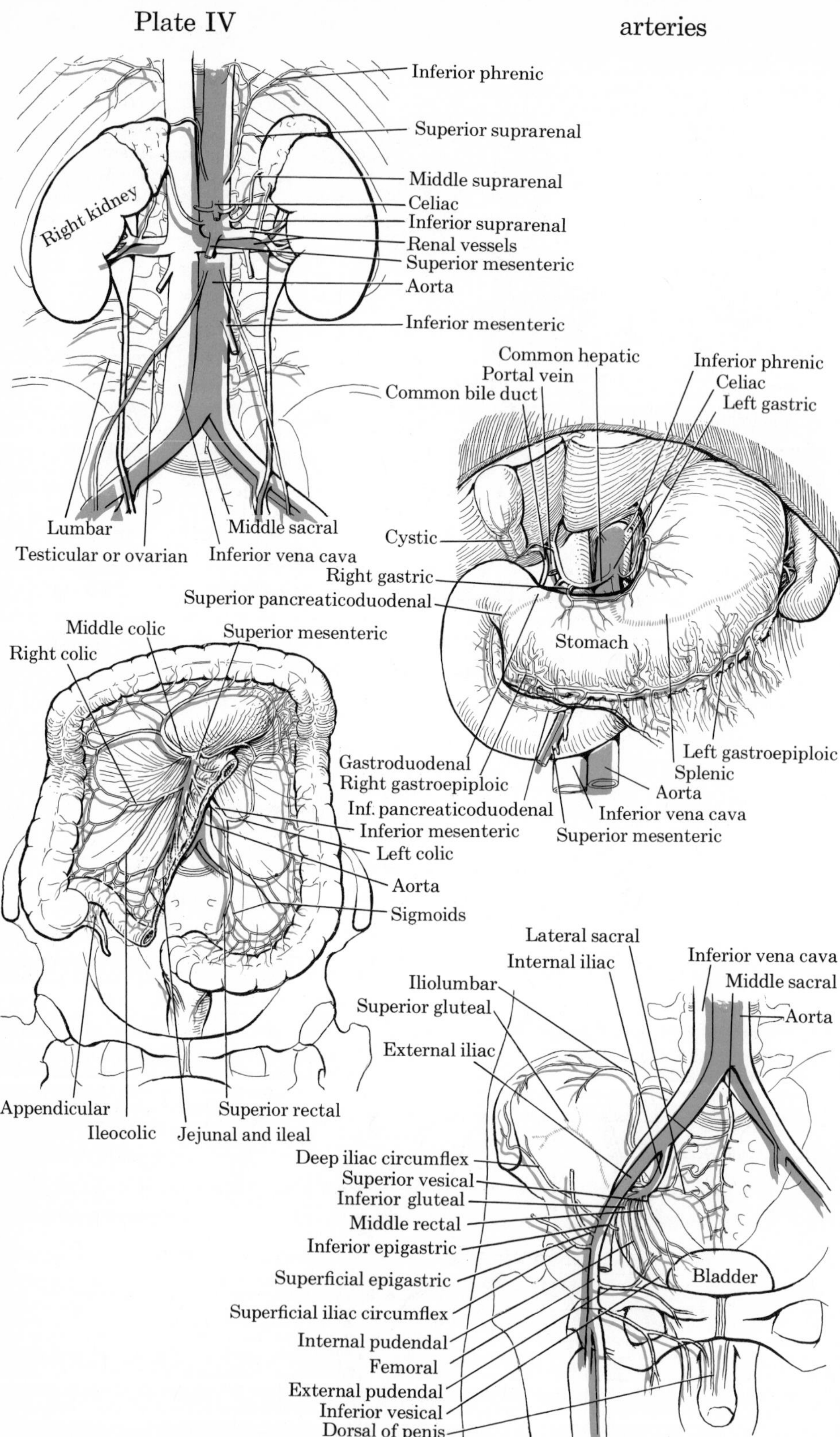

ARTERIES OF THE ABDOMEN AND PELVIS

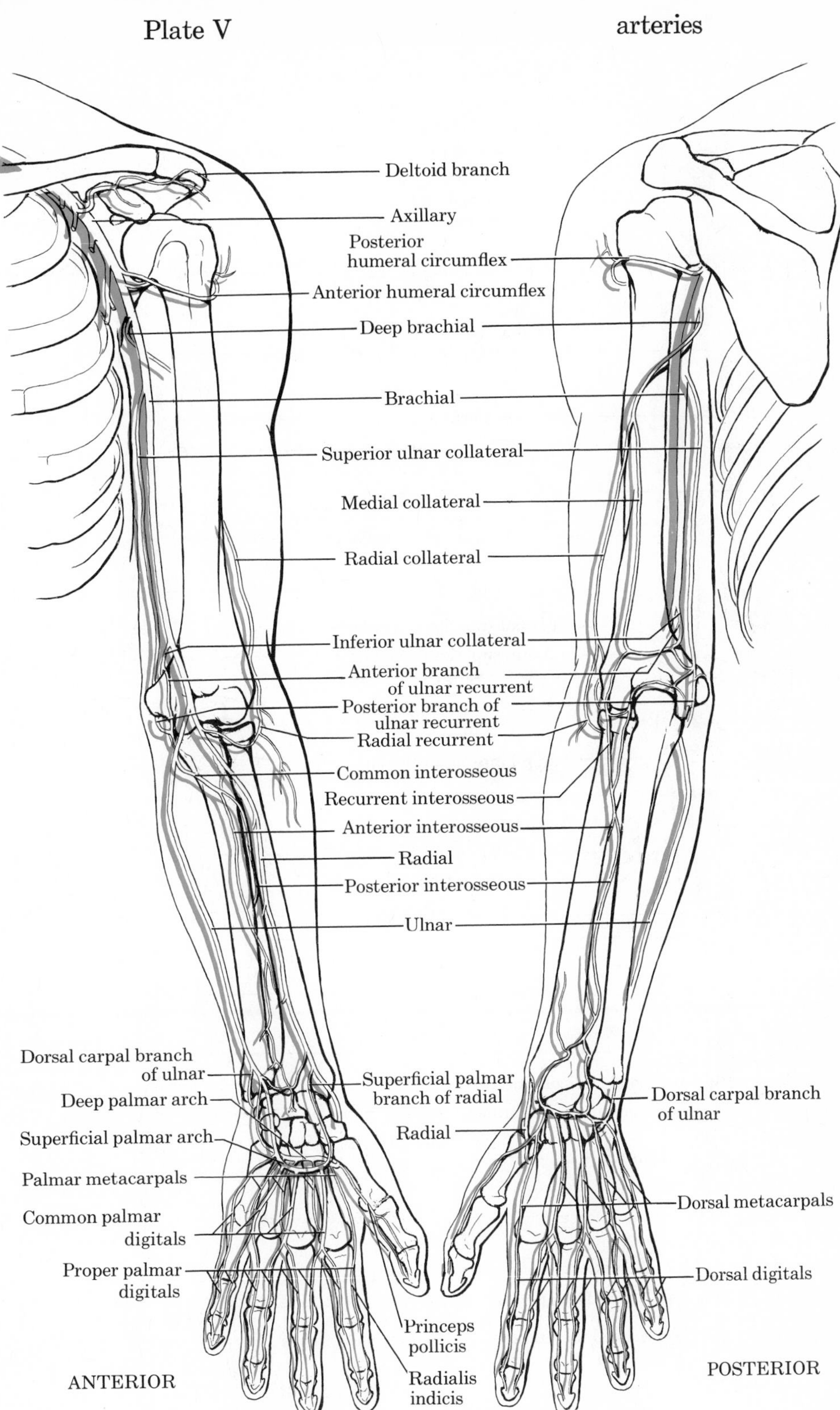

ARTERIES OF THE UPPER EXTREMITY

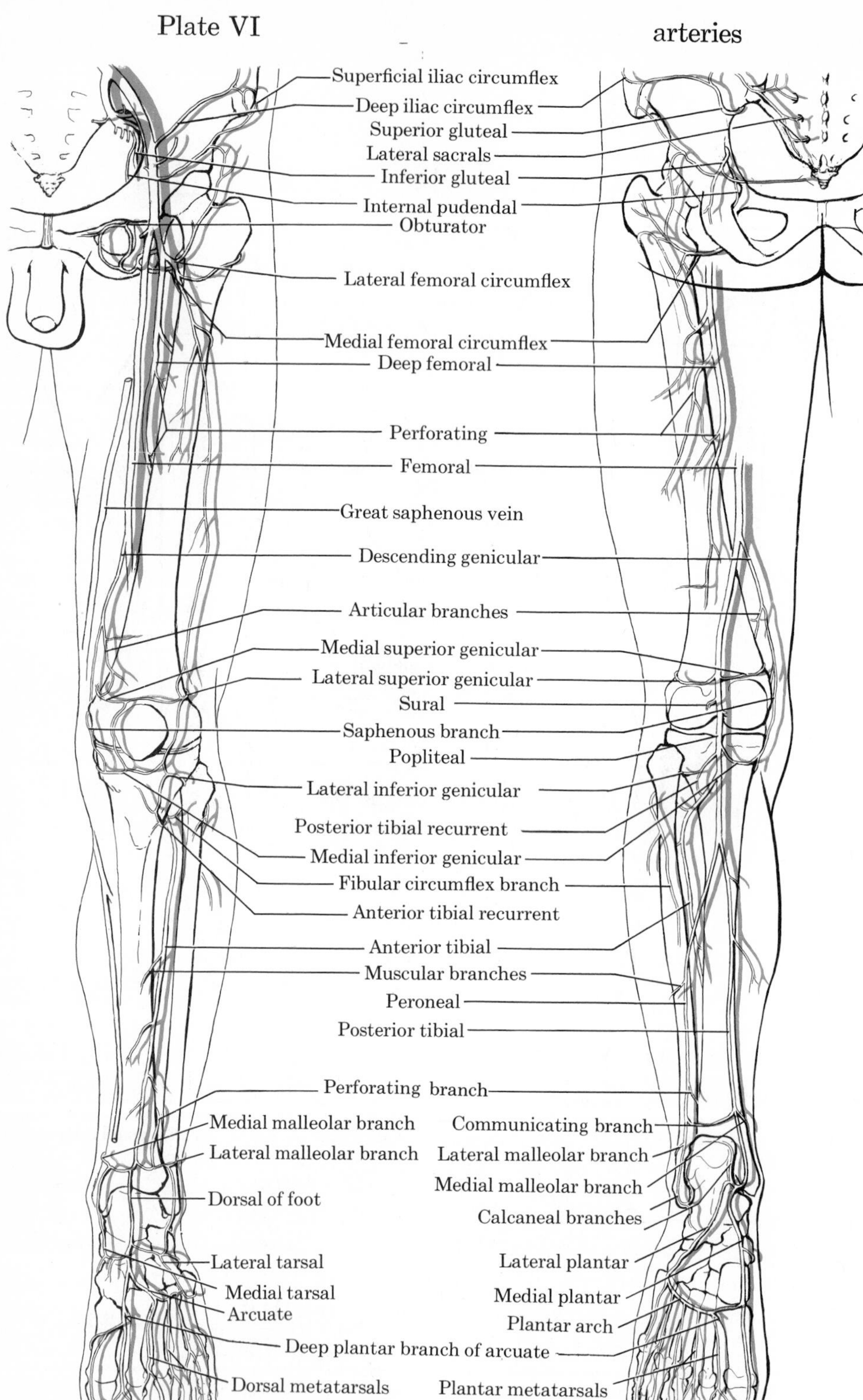

ARTERIES OF THE LOWER EXTREMITY

branches, right and left branches; *distribution*, liver and gallbladder.

a. hyaloi'dea [N A, B N A], hyaloid artery: a fetal vessel that continues forward from the central retinal artery through the vitreous body to supply the lens; it normally is not present after birth.

a. hypogas'trica [B N A], a. iliaca interna.

arte'riae il'eae [B N A], arteriae ilei.

arte'riae il'ei [N A], ileal arteries: *origin*, superior mesenteric; *branches*, none; *distribution*, ileum.

a. ileoco'lica [N A, B N A], ileocolic artery: *origin*, superior mesenteric; *branches*, appendicular; *distribution*, ileum, cecum, vermiform appendix, ascending colon.

a. ili'aca commu'nis [N A, B N A], common iliac artery: *origin*, abdominal aorta; *branches*, internal and external iliac; *distribution*, pelvis, abdominal wall, lower limb.

a. ili'aca exter'na [N A, B N A], external iliac artery: *origin*, common iliac; *branches*, inferior epigastric, deep circumflex iliac; *distribution*, abdominal wall, external genitalia, lower limb.

a. ili'aca inter'na [N A], internal iliac artery: *origin*, continuation of common iliac; *branches*, iliolumbar, obturator, superior gluteal, inferior gluteal, umbilical, inferior vesical, uterine, middle rectal, and internal pudendal arteries; *distribution*, wall and viscera of pelvis, buttock, reproductive organs, medial aspect of thigh.

a. iliolumba'lis [N A, B N A], iliolumbar artery: *origin*, internal iliac; *branches*, iliac and lumbar branches, lateral sacral arteries; *distribution*, pelvic muscles and bones, fifth lumbar segment, sacrum.

a. infraorbita'lis [N A, B N A], infraorbital artery: *origin*, maxillary artery; *branches*, anterior superior alveolar; *distribution*, maxilla, maxillary sinus, upper teeth, lower lid, cheek, side of nose.

a. innomina'ta, truncus brachiocephalicus.

arte'riae intercosta'les posterio'res I et II [N A], posterior intercostal arteries I and II: *origin*, highest intercostal artery; *branches*, dorsal and spinal rami; *distribution*, first and second intercostal spaces, back muscles, vertebral column.

arte'riae intercosta'les posterio'res III–XI [N A], posterior intercostal arteries III–XI: *origin*, thoracic aorta; *branches*, dorsal, lateral, and lateral cutaneous; *distribution*, thoracic wall.

a. intercosta'lis supre'ma [N A, B N A], highest intercostal artery: *origin*, costocervical trunk; *branches*, posterior intercostal arteries I and II; *distribution*, intercostal spaces, vertebral column, and back muscles.

arte'riae interloba'res re'nis [N A, B N A], interlobar arteries of kidney: *origin*, renal artery; *branches*, arcuate arteries of kidney; *distribution*, to lobes of kidney.

arte'riae interlobula'res hep'atis [N A], interlobular arteries of liver: arteries originating from the right or left branch of the proper hepatic artery, and passing between the lobules of the liver.

arte'riae interlobula'res re'nis [N A, B N A], interlobular arteries of kidney: arteries originating from the arcuate arteries of the kidney and distributed to the renal glomeruli.

a. interos'sea ante'rior [N A], anterior interosseous artery: *origin*, posterior or common interosseous artery; *branches*, median artery; *distribution*, flexor digitorum profundus, flexor pollicis longus, radius, and ulna.

a. interos'sea commu'nis [N A, B N A], common interosseous artery: *origin*, ulnar artery; *branches*, anterior and posterior interosseous arteries; *distribution*, deep structures of forearm.

a. interos'sea dorsa'lis [B N A], a. interossea posterior.

a. interos'sea poste'rior [N A], posterior interosseous artery: *origin*, common interosseous artery; *branches*, recurrent interosseous; *distribution*, superficial and deep muscles on back of forearm.

a. interos'sea recur'rens [N A, B N A], recurrent interosseous artery: *origin*, posterior interosseous or common interosseous artery; *branches*, none; *distribution*, back of elbow joint.

a. interos'sea vola'ris [B N A], a. interossea anterior.

arte'riae intestina'les [B N A], intestinal arteries: the arteries arising from the superior mesenteric, and supplying the intestines, including the pancreaticoduodenal, jejunal, iliac, ileocolic, and colic arteries.

arte'riae jejuna'les [N A, B N A], jejunal arteries: *origin*, superior mesenteric; *branches*, none; *distribution*, jejunum.

arte'riae labia'les anterio'res vul'vae [B N A], rami labiales anteriores arteriae femoralis.

a. labia'lis infe'rior [N A, B N A], inferior labial artery: *origin*, facial artery; *branches*, none; *distribution*, lower lip.

arte'riae labia'les posterio'res vul'vae [B N A], rami labiales posteriores arteriae pudendae internae.

a. labia'lis supe'rior [N A, B N A], superior labial artery: *origin*, facial artery, *branches*, septal and alar; *distribution*, upper lip and nose.

a. labyrin'thi [N A], artery of labyrinth, labyrinthine artery: *origin*, basilar or anterior inferior cerebellar artery; *branches*, vestibular and cochlear rami; *distribution*, internal ear.

a. lacrima'lis [N A, B N A], lacrimal artery: *origin*, ophthalmic artery; *branches*, lateral palpebral artery; *distribution*, lacrimal gland, upper and lower eyelids, and conjunctiva.

a. laryn'gea infe'rior [N A, B N A], inferior laryngeal artery: *origin*, inferior thyroid artery; *branches*, none; *distribution*, larynx, upper trachea, esophagus.

a. laryn'gea supe'rior [N A, B N A], superior laryngeal artery: *origin*, superior thyroid; *branches*, none; *distribution*, larynx.

a. liena'lis [N A, B N A], splenic artery: *origin*, celiac trunk; *branches*, pancreatic and splenic branches, left gastroepiploic, and short gastric arteries; *distribution*, spleen, pancreas, stomach, greater omentum.

a. ligamen'ti tere'tis u'teri [N A, B N A], artery of round ligament of uterus: *origin*, inferior epigastric artery; *branches*, none; *distribution*, round ligament of uterus.

a. lingua'lis [N A, B N A], lingual artery: *origin*, external carotid; *branches*, suprahyoid, sublingual, dorsal lingual, deep lingual; *distribution*, tongue, sublingual gland, tonsil, epiglottis.

arte'riae lumba'les [N A, N B A], lumbar arteries: *origin*, abdominal aorta; *branches*, dorsal and spinal branches; *distribution*, abdominal wall, vertebrae, lumbar muscles, renal capsule.

a. lumba'lis i'ma [N A, B N A], lowest lumbar artery: *origin*, middle sacral; *branches*, none; *distribution*, sacrum and gluteus maximus muscle.

a. malleola'ris ante'rior latera'lis [N A, B N A], lateral anterior malleolar artery: *origin*, anterior tibial artery; *branches*, none; *distribution*, ankle joint.

a. malleola'ris ante'rior media'lis [N A, B N A], medial anterior malleolar artery: *origin*, anterior tibial artery; *branches*, none; *distribution*, ankle joint.

a. malleola'ris poste'rior latera'lis [B N A]. See *rami malleolares laterales arteriae.*

a. malleola'ris poste'rior media'lis [B N A]. See *rami malleolares mediales.*

a. mammar'ia inter'na [B N A], a. thoracica interna.

a. masseter'ica [N A, B N A], masseteric artery: *origin*, maxillary artery; *branches*, none; *distribution*, masseter muscle.

a. maxilla'ris [N A], maxillary artery: *origin*, external carotid artery; *branches*, pterygoid rami, and deep auricular, anterior tympanic, inferior alveolar, middle meningeal, masseteric, deep temporal, buccal, posterior superior alveolar, infraorbital, descending palatine, sphenopalatine, and the artery of the pterygoid canal; *distribution*, both jaws, teeth, muscles of mastication, ear, meninges, nose, nasal sinus, palate.

a. maxilla′ris exter′na [B N A], a. facialis.

a. maxilla′ris inter′na [B N A], a. maxillaris.

a. max′ima Gale′ni, aorta.

a. media′na [N A, B N A], median artery: *origin*, anterior interosseous artery; *branches*, none; *distribution*, median nerve, muscles of front forearm.

arte′riae mediastina′les anterio′res [B N A], rami mediastinales arteriae thoracicae internae.

a. menin′gea ante′rior [N A, B N A], anterior meningeal artery: *origin*, anterior ethmoidal artery; *branches*, none; *distribution*, dura mater of anterior cranial fossa.

a. menin′gea me′dia [N A, B N A], middle meningeal artery: *origin*, maxillary artery; *branches*, frontal, parietal, and lacrimal anastomotic, accessory meningeal, and petrosal rami, and the superior tympanic artery; *distribution*, cranial bones and dura mater.

a. menin′gea poste′rior [N A, B N A], posterior meningeal artery: *origin*, ascending pharyngeal; *branches*, none; *distribution*, bones, dura mater of posterior cranial fossa.

a. menta′lis [N A, B N A], mental artery: *origin*, inferior alveolar; *branches*, none; *distribution*, skin and muscles of chin.

a. mesenter′ica infe′rior [N A, B N A], inferior mesenteric artery: *origin*, abdominal aorta; *branches*, left colic, sigmoid, and superior rectal arteries; *distribution*, descending colon and rectum.

a. mesenter′ica supe′rior [N A, B N A], superior mesenteric artery: *origin*, abdominal aorta; *branches*, inferior pancreaticoduodenal, jejunal, ileal, ileocolic, right colic, and middle colic arteries; *distribution*, small intestine, proximal half of colon.

arte′riae metacar′peae dorsa′les [N A, B N A], dorsal metacarpal arteries: *origin*, dorsal carpal rete and radial artery; *branches*, dorsal digital arteries; *distribution*, dorsum of fingers.

arte′riae metacar′peae palma′res [N A], palmar metacarpal arteries: *origin*, deep palmar arch; *branches*, none; *distribution*, interosseous muscles, and bones, second, third, and fourth lumbricales.

arte′riae metacar′peae vola′res [B N A], arteriae metacarpeae palmares.

arte′riae metatar′seae dorsa′les [N A, B N A], dorsal metatarsal arteries: *origin*, arcuate artery of foot; *branches*, dorsal digital arteries; *distribution*, foot and toes.

arte′riae metatar′seae planta′res [N A, B N A], plantar metatarsal arteries: *origin*, plantar arch; *branches*, perforating branches, and common and proper plantar digital arteries; *distribution*, toes.

a. musculophren′ica [N A, B N A], musculophrenic artery: *origin*, internal thoracic artery; *branches*, none; *distribution*, diaphragm, abdominal and thoracic walls.

arte′riae nasa′les posterio′res, latera′les et sep′ti [N A, B N A], lateral and septal posterior nasal arteries: *origin*, sphenopalatine artery; *branches*, none; *distribution*, structures bounding nasal cavity, nasal septum, and adjacent sinuses.

a. nutri′cia fem′oris infe′rior [B N A], omitted from N A.

a. nutri′cia fem′oris supe′rior [B N A], omitted from N A.

a. nutri′cia fi′bulae [B N A], omitted from N A.

arte′riae nutri′ciae hu′meri [N A, B N A], nutrient arteries of humerus: *origin*, brachial and deep brachial arteries; *branches*, none; *distribution*, humerus.

arte′riae nutri′ciae pel′vis rena′lis [B N A], omitted from N A.

a. nutri′cia ti′biae [B N A], omitted from N A.

a. obturato′ria [N A, B N A], obturator artery: *origin*, internal iliac; *branches*, pubic, acetabular, anterior, and posterior branches; *distribution*, pelvic muscles, hip joint.

a. obturato′ria accesso′ria [N A], accessory obturator artery: a name given to the obturator artery when it arises from the inferior epigastric instead of the internal iliac artery.

a. occipita′lis [N A, B N A], occipital artery: *origin*, external carotid; *branches*, auricular, meningeal, mastoid, descending, occipital, and sternocleidomastoid rami; *distribution*, muscles of neck and scalp, meninges, mastoid cells.

arte′riae oesophage′ae [B N A], rami esophagei aortae thoracicae.

a. ophthal′mica [N A, B N A], ophthalmic artery: *origin*, internal carotid; *branches*, lacrimal, supraorbital, central artery of retina, ciliary, posterior and anterior ethmoidal, palpebral, supratrochlear, dorsal nasal; *distribution*, eye, orbit, adjacent facial structures.

a. ova′rica [N A, B N A], ovarian artery: *origin*, abdominal aorta; *branches*, ureteral branch; *distribution*, ureter, ovary, uterine tube.

a. palati′na ascen′dens [N A, B N A], ascending palatine artery: *origin*, facial artery; *branches*, none; *distribution*, soft palate, portions of wall of pharynx, tonsil, auditory tube.

a. palati′na descen′dens [N A, B N A], descending palatine artery: *origin*, maxillary artery; *branches*, greater and lesser palatine arteries; *distribution*, soft palate, hard palate, tonsil.

a. palati′na ma′jor [N A, B N A], greater palatine artery: *origin*, descending palatine; *branches*, none; *distribution*, hard palate.

arte′riae palati′nae mino′res [N A, B N A], lesser palatine arteries: *origin*, descending palatine; *branches*, none; *distribution*, soft palate and tonsil.

arte′riae palpebra′les latera′les [N A, B N A], lateral palpebral arteries: *origin*, lacrimal artery; *branches*, none; *distribution*, eyelids and conjunctiva.

arte′riae palpebra′les media′les [N A, B N A], medial palpebral arteries: *origin*, ophthalmic artery; *branches*, posterior conjunctival; *distribution*, upper and lower eyelids.

a. pancreaticoduodena′lis infe′rior [N A, B N A], inferior pancreaticoduodenal artery: *origin*, superior mesenteric artery; *branches*, none; *distribution*, pancreas, duodenum.

a. pancreaticoduodena′lis supe′rior [N A, B N A], superior pancreaticoduodenal artery: *origin*, gastroduodenal artery; *branches*, none; *distribution*, pancreas, duodenum.

a. pe′nis [B N A], omitted from N A.

arte′riae perforan′tes [N A], perforating arteries: *origin*, deep femoral artery; *branches*, none; *distribution*, adductor, hamstring, and gluteal muscles, and femur. Called also *a. perforans prima*, *a. perforans secunda*, and *a. perforans tertia* [B N A].

a. perforans′ pri′ma fem′oris [B N A]. See *arteriae perforantes*.

a. perforans′ secun′da fem′oris [B N A]. See *arteriae perforantes*.

a. perforans′ ter′tia fem′oris [B N A]. See *arteriae perforantes*.

a. pericardiacophren′ica [N A, B N A], pericardiacophrenic artery: *origin*, internal thoracic artery; *branches*, none; *distribution*, pericardium, diaphragm, pleura.

a. perinea′lis [N A], perineal artery: *origin*, internal pudendal artery; *branches*, none; *distribution*, perineum, skin of external genitalia.

a. perine′i [B N A], a. perinealis.

a. pero′nea [N A], peroneal artery: *origin*, posterior tibial artery; *branches*, perforating, communicating, calcaneal, and lateral and medial malleolar branches, and the calcaneal rete; *distribution*, outside and back of ankle, deep calf muscles.

a. pharyn′gea ascen′dens [N A, B N A], ascending pharyngeal artery: *origin*, external carotid; *branches*, posterior meningeal, pharyngeal, and inferior tympanic; *distribution*, pharynx, soft palate, ear, meninges, cranial nerves, capitis muscles.

a. phren'ica infe'rior [N A, B N A], inferior phrenic artery: *origin*, abdominal aorta; *branches*, superior suprarenal; *distribution*, diaphragm and suprarenal gland.

arte'riae phren'icae superio'res [N A, B N A], superior phrenic arteries: *origin*, thoracic aorta; *branches*, none; *distribution*, upper surface of vertebral portion of diaphragm.

a. planta'ris latera'lis [N A, B N A], lateral plantar artery: *origin*, posterior tibial artery; *branches*, plantar arch, and plantar metatarsal arteries; *distribution*, sole of foot and toes.

a. planta'ris media'lis [N A, B N A], medial plantar artery: *origin*, posterior tibial artery; *branches*, deep and superficial branches; *distribution*, muscles, articulations, and skin of the medial aspect of the sole of the foot and toes.

a. poplit'ea [N A, B N A], popliteal artery: *origin*, continuation of femoral artery; *branches*, lateral and medial superior genicular, middle genicular, sural, lateral and medial inferior genicular, anterior and posterior tibial arteries, and the genicular articular and the patellar rete; *distribution*, knee and calf.

a. prin'ceps pol'licis [N A, B N A], principal artery of thumb: *origin*, radial artery; *branches*, radial of index finger; *distribution*, each side and palmar aspect of thumb.

a. profun'da bra'chii [N A, B N A], deep brachial artery: *origin*, brachial artery; *branches*, deltoid ramus, nutrient artery, and medial and radial collateral arteries; *distribution*, humerus, muscles and skin of arm.

a. profun'da clitor'idis [N A, B N A], deep artery of clitoris: *origin*, internal pudendal artery; *branches*, none; *distribution*, clitoris.

a. profun'da fem'oris [N A, B N A], deep femoral artery: *origin*, femoral artery; *branches*, medial and lateral circumflex arteries of thigh, and perforating arteries; *distribution*, thigh muscles, hip joint, gluteal muscles, femur.

a. profun'da lin'guae [N A, B N A], deep lingual artery: *origin*, lingual artery; *branches*, none; *distribution*, side and tip of tongue.

a. profun'da pe'nis [N A, B N A], deep artery of penis: *origin*, internal pudendal artery; *branches*, none; *distribution*, corpus cavernosum penis.

arte'riae puden'dae exter'nae [N A, B N A], external pudendal arteries: *origin*, femoral artery; *branches*, anterior scrotal or anterior labial and inguinal branches; *distribution*, external genitalia, medial thigh muscles.

a. puden'da inter'na [N A, B N A], internal pudendal artery: *origin*, internal iliac artery; *branches*, posterior scrotal or posterior labial branches and inferior rectal, perineal, urethral arteries, artery of bulb of penis or vestibule, deep artery of penis or clitoris, and dorsal artery of penis or clitoris; *distribution*, external genitalia, anal canal.

a. pulmona'lis [B N A], truncus pulmonalis.

a. pulmona'lis dex'tra [N A], right pulmonary artery: *origin*, pulmonary trunk; *branches*, numerous branches named according to the part of the lung to which they distribute unaerated blood; *distribution*, right lung.

a. pulmona'lis sinis'tra [N A], left pulmonary artery: *origin*, pulmonary trunk; *branches*, numerous branches named according to the part of the lung to which they distribute unaerated blood; *distribution*, left lung.

a. radia'lis [N A, B N A], radial artery: *origin*, brachial artery; *branches*, palmar carpal, superficial palmar and dorsal carpal rami, recurrent radial artery, principal artery of thumb, and deep palmar arch; *distribution*, forearm, wrist, hand.

a. radia'lis in'dicis [N A], radial artery of index finger: *origin*, principal artery of thumb; *branches*, none; *distribution*, index finger.

a. recta'lis infe'rior [N A], inferior rectal artery: *origin*, internal pudendal artery; *branches*, none; *distribution*, rectum, levator ani and external sphincter muscles, and overlying skin.

a. recta'lis me'dia [N A], middle rectal artery: *origin*, internal iliac artery; *branches*, none; *distribution*, rectum and vagina.

a. recta'lis supe'rior [N A], superior rectal artery: *origin*, inferior mesenteric artery; *branches*, none; *distribution*, rectum.

a. recur'rens radia'lis [N A, B N A], radial recurrent artery: *origin*, radial artery; *branches*, none; *distribution*, brachioradialis, brachialis, elbow joint.

a. recur'rens tibia'lis ante'rior [N A, B N A], anterior tibial recurrent artery: *origin*, anterior tibial artery; *branches*, none; *distribution*, tibialis anterior, extensor digitorum longus, knee joint, contiguous fascia and skin.

a. recur'rens tibia'lis poste'rior [N A, B N A], posterior tibial recurrent artery: *origin*, anterior tibial artery; *branches*, none; *distribution*, knee joint, tibiofibular joint.

a. recur'rens ulna'ris [N A], ulnar recurrent artery: *origin*, ulnar artery; *branches*, anterior and posterior; *distribution*, elbow joint, and adjacent skin and muscles.

a. rena'lis [N A, B N A], renal artery: *origin*, abdominal aorta; *branches*, ureteral branches, and inferior suprarenal artery; *distribution*, kidney, suprarenal gland and ureter.

arte'riae re'nis [N A, B N A], the arteries of the kidney, including the interlobar, arcuate, and interlobular arteries, and arteriolae rectae.

a. sacra'lis latera'lis [B N A]. See *rami spinales arteriae sacralium lateralium.*

arte'riae sacra'les latera'les [N A], lateral sacral arteries: *origin*, iliolumbar artery; *branches*, spinal branches; *distribution*, structures about coccyx and sacrum.

a. sacra'lis me'dia [B N A], a. sacralis mediana.

a. sacra'lis media'na [N A], median sacral artery: *origin*, continuation of abdominal aorta; *branches*, lowest lumbar artery; *distribution*, sacrum, coccyx, and rectum.

a. scapula'ris descen'dens, N A alternative for *ramus profundus arteriae transversae colli.*

arte'riae scrota'les anterio'res [B N A], rami scrotales anteriores arteriae femoralis.

arte'riae scrota'les posterio'res [B N A], rami scrotales posteriores arteriae pudendae internae.

arte'riae sigmoi'deae [N A, B N A], sigmoid arteries: *origin*, inferior mesenteric artery; *branches*, none; *distribution*, sigmoid colon.

a. spermat'ica exter'na [B N A], a. cremasterica.

a. spermat'ica inter'na [B N A], omitted from N A.

a. sphenopalati'na [N A, B N A], sphenopalatine artery: *origin*, maxillary artery; *branches*, lateral and septal posterior nasal arteries; *distribution*, structures adjoining the nasal cavity, and the nasopharynx.

a. spina'lis ante'rior [N A, B N A], anterior spinal artery: *origin*, vertebral artery; *branches*, none; *distribution*, anterior spinal cord.

a. spina'lis poste'rior [N A, B N A], posterior spinal artery: *origin*, vertebral artery; *branches*, none; *distribution*, posterior spinal cord.

a. sternocleidomastoi'dea [B N A]. See *rami sternocleidomastoidei arteriae occipitalis.*

a. stylomastoi'dea [N A, B N A], stylomastoid artery: *origin*, posterior auricular; *branches*, mastoid and stapedial rami, posterior tympanic artery; *distribution*, tympanic cavity walls, mastoid cells, stapedius muscle.

a. subcla'via [N A, B N A], subclavian artery: *origin*, brachiocephalic trunk (right); arch of aorta (left); *branches*, vertebral, internal thoracic arteries, thyrocervical and costocervical trunks; *distribution*, neck, thoracic walls, spinal cord, brain, meninges, upper limbs.

a. subcosta'lis [N A], subcostal artery: *origin*, thoracic aorta; *branches*, dorsal and spinal branches; *distribution*, upper abdominal wall.

a. sublingua'lis [N A, B N A], sublingual artery: *origin*, lingual artery; *branches*, none; *distribution*, sublingual gland, side of tongue, floor of mouth.

a. submenta'lis [N A, B N A], submental artery: *origin*, facial artery; *branches*, none; *distribution*, tissues under chin.

a. subscapula'ris [N A, B N A], subscapular artery: *origin*, axillary artery; *branches*, thoracodorsal and circumflex scapular arteries; *distribution*, scapular and shoulder region.

a. supraorbita'lis [N A, B N A], supraorbital artery: *origin*, ophthalmic artery; *branches*, none; *distribution*, forehead, upper muscles of orbit, upper eyelid, frontal sinus.

a. suprarena'lis infe'rior [N A, B N A], inferior suprarenal artery: *origin*, renal artery; *branches*, none; *distribution*, suprarenal gland.

a. suprarena'lis me'dia [N A, B N A], middle suprarenal artery: *origin*, abdominal aorta; *branches*, none; *distribution*, suprarenal gland.

arte'riae suprarena'les superio'res [N A], superior suprarenal arteries: *origin*, inferior phrenic artery; *branches*, none; *distribution*, suprarenal gland.

a. suprascapula'ris [N A], suprascapular artery: *origin*, thyrocervical trunk; *branches*, acromial branch; *distribution*, bone and periosteum of clavicle and scapula, shoulder joint, muscles.

a. supratrochlea'ris [N A], supratrochlear artery: *origin*, ophthalmic artery; *branches*, none; *distribution*, anterior scalp.

arte'riae sura'les [N A, B N A], sural arteries: *origin*, popliteal artery; *branches*, none; *distribution*, muscles of popliteal space and calf and adjacent skin.

a. tar'sea latera'lis [N A, B N A], lateral tarsal artery: *origin*, dorsal artery of foot; *branches*, none; *distribution*, muscles and joints of tarsus.

arte'riae tar'seae media'les [N A, B N A], medial tarsal arteries: *origin*, dorsal artery of foot; *branches*, none; *distribution*, skin and articulation of medial aspect of foot.

a. tempora'lis me'dia [N A, B N A], middle temporal artery: *origin*, superficial temporal artery; *branches*, none; *distribution*, temporal muscle.

arte'riae tempora'les profun'dae [N A], deep temporal arteries: *origin*, maxillary artery; *branches*, none; *distribution*, temporal muscle, pericranium, subjacent bone.

a. tempora'lis profun'da ante'rior [B N A]. See *arteriae temporales profundae*.

a. tempora'lis profun'da poste'rior [B N A]. See *arteriae temporales profundae*.

a. tempora'lis superficia'lis [N A, B N A], superficial temporal artery: *origin*, external carotid; *branches*, parotid, anterior auricular, frontal, and parietal rami, transverse facial, zygomaticoorbital, and middle temporal arteries; *distribution*, parotid gland, auricle, scalp, skin of face, and masseter muscle.

a. testicula'ris [N A, B N A], testicular artery: *origin*, abdominal aorta; *branches*, ureteral branches; *distribution*, ureter, epididymis, and testis.

a. thoraca'lis latera'lis [B N A], a. thoracica lateralis.

a. thoraca'lis supre'ma [B N A], a. thoracica suprema.

a. thora'cica inter'na [N A], internal thoracic artery: *origin*, subclavian artery; *branches*, mediastinal, thymic, bronchial, sternal, perforating, lateral costal, and anterior intercostal branches, pericardiacophrenic, musculophrenic, and superior epigastric arteries; *distribution*, anterior thoracic wall, mediastinal structures, diaphragm.

a. thora'cica latera'lis [N A], lateral thoracic artery: *origin*, axillary artery; *branches*, mammary branches; *distribution*, pectoral muscles, mammary gland.

a. thora'cica supre'ma [N A], highest thoracic artery: *origin*, axillary artery; *branches*, none; *distribution*, intercostal, serratus anterior, and pectoralis major and minor muscles.

a. thoracoacromia'lis [N A, B N A], thoracoacromial artery: *origin*, axillary artery; *branches*, clavicular, pectoral, deltoid, acromial rami; *distribution*, pectoral, deltoid, subclavian muscles, and acromion process.

a. thoracodorsa'lis [N A, B N A], thoracodorsal artery: *origin*, subscapular artery; *branches*, none; *distribution*, subscapular and terete muscles.

arte'riae thy'micae [B N A], rami thymici arteriae thoracicae internae.

a. thyreoi'dea i'ma [B N A], a. thyroidea ima.

a. thyreoi'dea infe'rior [B N A], a. thyroidea inferior.

a. thyreoi'dea supe'rior [B N A], a. thyroidea superior.

a. thyroi'dea i'ma [N A], lowest thyroid artery: *origin*, arch of aorta, brachiocephalic trunk, or right common carotid; *branches*, none; *distribution*, thyroid gland.

a. thyroi'dea infe'rior [N A], inferior thyroid artery: *origin*, thyrocervical trunk; *branches*, pharyngeal, esophageal, and tracheal rami, and inferior laryngeal and ascending cervical arteries; *distribution*, larynx, esophagus, trachea, neck muscles, thyroid gland.

a. thyroi'dea supe'rior [N A], superior thyroid artery: *origin*, external carotid artery; *branches*, hyoid, sternocleidomastoid, superior laryngeal, cricothyroid, muscular, and glandular branches; *distribution*, hyoid muscles, larynx, thyroid gland, pharynx.

a. tibia'lis ante'rior [N A, B N A], anterior tibial artery: *origin*, popliteal artery; *branches*, posterior and anterior tibial recurrent, and lateral and medial anterior malleolar arteries, and lateral and medial malleolar retes; *distribution*, leg, ankle, foot.

a. tibia'lis poste'rior [N A, B N A], posterior tibial artery: *origin*, popliteal artery; *branches*, fibular circumflex branch, peroneal, medial plantar, and lateral plantar arteries; *distribution*, leg, foot, heel.

a. transver'sa col'li [N A, B N A], transverse cervical artery: *origin*, subclavian artery; *branches*, deep and superficial rami; *distribution*, trapezius, muscles and lymph glands of neck, rhomboidei and latissimus dorsi.

a. transver'sa facie'i [N A, B N A], transverse facial artery: *origin*, superficial temporal artery; *branches*, none; *distribution*, parotid gland, masseter muscle, skin of face.

a. transver'sa scap'ulae [B N A], a. suprascapularis.

a. tympan'ica ante'rior [N A, B N A], anterior tympanic artery: *origin*, maxillary artery; *branches*, none; *distribution*, lining membrane of tympanic cavity.

a. tympan'ica infe'rior [N A, B N A], inferior tympanic artery: *origin*, ascending pharyngeal; *branches*, none; *distribution*, medial wall of tympanic cavity.

a. tympan'ica poste'rior [N A, B N A], posterior tympanic artery: *origin*, stylomastoid artery; *branches*, none; *distribution*, posterior part of tympanic membrane, secondary tympanic membrane.

a. tympan'ica supe'rior [N A, B N A], superior tympanic artery: *origin*, middle meningeal artery; *branches*, none; *distribution*, tensor tympani muscle and membrane of canal.

a. ulna'ris [N A, B N A], ulnar artery: *origin*, brachial artery; *branches*, palmar carpal, dorsal carpal, and deep palmar rami, ulnar recurrent and common interosseous arteries, and superficial palmar arch; *distribution*, forearm, wrist, hand.

a. umbilica'lis [N A, B N A], umbilical artery: *origin*, internal iliac artery; *branches*, deferential, superior vesical arteries; *distribution*, ductus deferens, seminal vesicles, testes, urinary bladder, and ureter.

a. urethra'lis [N A, B N A], urethral artery: *origin*, internal pudendal artery; *branches*, none; *distribution*, urethra.

a. uteri'na [N A, B N A], uterine artery: *origin*,

internal iliac artery; *branches*, ovarian and tubal rami and vaginal artery; *distribution*, uterus, vagina, round ligament of uterus, uterine tube, and ovary.

a. vagina'lis [N A, B N A], vaginal artery: *origin*, uterine artery; *branches*, none; *distribution*, vagina, fundus of bladder.

a. vertebra'lis [N A, B N A], vertebral artery: *origin*, subclavian artery; *branches*, spinal and meningeal branches, and posterior inferior cerebellar, basilar, and anterior and posterior spinal arteries; *distribution*, muscles of neck, vertebrae, spinal cord, cerebellum, interior of cerebrum.

a. vesica'lis infe'rior [N A, B N A], inferior vesical arteries: *origin*, internal iliac; *branches*, none; *distribution*, bladder, prostate, seminal vesicles.

arte'riae vesica'les superio'res [N A, B N A], superior vesical arteries: *origin*, umbilical artery; *branches*, none named in N A; *distribution*, bladder, urachus, ureter.

a. vola'ris indi'cis radia'lis [B N A], a. radialis indicis.

a. zygomaticoorbita'lis [N A, B N A], zygomaticoorbital artery: *origin*, superficial temporal; *branches*, none; *distribution*, orbicularis oculi muscle.

---

arterial (ar-te're-al). Pertaining to an artery or to the arteries.

arterialization (ar-te"re-al-i-za'shun). The change of venous into arterial blood; the provision or supplying of oxygenated instead of venous blood.

arteriarctia (ar"tĕ-re-ark'she-ah) [*artery* + L. *arctare* to contract]. Contraction of an artery; narrowing of the caliber of an artery.

arteriasis (ar"tĕ-ri'ah-sis). Degeneration of the walls of arteries.

arteriectasia (ar"tĕ-re-ek-ta'ze-ah). Arteriectasis.

arteriectasis (ar"tĕ-re-ek'tah-sis) [*artery* + Gr. *ektasis* dilatation]. Dilatation of an artery.

arteriectomy (ar"tĕ-re-ek'to-me) [*artery* + Gr. *ektomē* excision]. Excision of a portion of an artery.

arteriectopia (ar"tĕ-re-ek-to'pe-ah) [*artery* + Gr. *ektopos* out of place]. Displacement of an artery from its normal location.

arterin (ar'tĕ-rin). Oxyhemoglobin.

arterio- (ar-te're-o) [L. *arteria*, Gr. *artēria*]. Combining form denoting relationship to an artery, or arteries.

arterio-atony (ar-te"re-o-at'o-ne). Atony or relaxed condition of the walls of arteries.

arteriocapillary (ar-te"re-o-kap'ĭ-la"re). Pertaining to the arteries and the capillaries.

arteriochalasis (ar-te"re-o-kah-la'sis). Relaxation or atony of an arterial wall.

arteriodilating (ar-te"re-o-di'lāt-ing). Increasing the caliber of the arteries, particularly of arterioles.

arteriofibrosis (ar-te"re-o-fi-bro'sis) [*artery* + *fibrosis*]. The narrowing of the arteries and capillaries by an inflammatory internal fibrosis; arteriocapillary fibrosis.

arteriogenesis (ar-te"re-o-jen'e-sis) [*artery* + Gr. *genesis* production]. The formation of arteries.

arteriogram (ar-te're-o-gram) [*artery* + Gr. *gramma* a writing]. 1. A sphygmographic tracing of the arterial pulse. 2. A roentgenogram of an artery.

arteriograph (ar-te're-o-graf). An instrument for recording the arterial pulse.

arteriography (ar"te-re-og'rah-fe) [*artery* + Gr. *graphein* to write]. 1. A description of the arteries. 2. The sphygmographic recording of the arterial pulse. 3. Roentgenography of arteries after injection of radiopaque material into the blood stream.

arteriola (ar-te"re-o'lah), pl. *arterio'lae* [L., dim. of *arteria*]. A minute arterial branch, especially one just proximal to a capillary. Called also *arteriole*. **a. macula'ris infe'rior** [N A, B N A], the superior arteriole supplying the macula retinae. **a. macula'ris supe'rior** [N A, B N A], the superior arteriole supplying the macula retinae. **a. media'lis ret'inae** [N A, B N A], the small branch supplying blood to the central region of the retina. **a. nasa'lis ret'inae infe'rior** [N A, B N A], a small branch of the central artery of the retina supplying the inferior nasal region of the retina. **a. nasa'lis ret'inae supe'rior** [N A, B N A], a small branch of the central artery of the retina, supplying the superior nasal region of the retina. **arterio'lae rec'tae re'nis** [N A, B N A], branches of the arcuate arteries of the kidney that pass down to supply the pyramids. **a. tempora'lis ret'inae infe'rior** [N A, B N A], a small branch of the central artery of the retina, supplying the inferior temporal region of the retina. **a. tempora'lis ret'inae supe'rior** [N A, B N A], a small branch of the central artery of the retina, supplying the superior temporal region of the retina.

arteriolae (ar-te"re-o'le) [L.]. Plural of arteriola.

arteriolar (ar"te-ri'o-lar). Pertaining to or resembling arterioles.

arteriole (ar-te're-ōl) [L. *arteriola*]. A minute arterial branch, especially one just proximal to a capillary. Called also *arteriola* [N A, B N A]. **glomerular a., afferent,** preglomerular a. **glomerular a., efferent,** postglomerular a. **Isaacs-Ludwig a.,** an arteriolar twig which sometimes branches from the afferent glomerular arteriole of the kidney to communicate directly with the tubular capillary plexus. **macular a., inferior,** arteriola macularis inferior. **macular a., superior,** arteriola macularis superior. **medial a. of retina,** arteriola medialis retinae. **nasal a. of retina, inferior,** arteriola nasalis retinae inferior. **nasal a. of retina, superior,** arteriola nasalis retinae superior. **postglomerular a.,** the arteriole that carries blood away from a renal glomerulus. Called also *efferent glomerular arteriole*. **precapillary a's,** those terminal arterioles with incomplete investing coats that end in capillaries. **preglomerular a.,** a branch of the renal vascular system just as it enters a glomerulus. Called also *afferent glomerular arteriole*. **straight a's of kidney,** arteriolae rectae renis. **temporal a. of retina, inferior,** arteriola temporalis retinae inferior. **temporal a. of retina, superior,** arteriola temporalis retinae superior.

arteriolith (ar-te're-o-lith) [*artery* + Gr. *lithos* stone]. A chalky concretion in an artery.

arteriology (ar-te"re-ol'o-je) [*artery* + *-logy*]. The sum of what is known regarding the arteries; the science or study of the arteries.

arteriolonecrosis (ar-te"re-o"lo-ne-kro'sis). Necrosis of arterioles, such as is seen in nephrosclerosis.

arteriolosclerosis (ar-te"re-o"lo-skle-ro'sis). Sclerosis and thickening of all the coats of the smaller arteries (arterioles).

arteriolosclerotic (ar-te"re-o"lo-skle-rot'ik). Pertaining to or characterized by arteriolosclerosis.

arteriomalacia (ar-te"re-o-mah-la'she-ah) [*artery* + Gr. *malakia* softness]. Abnormal softness of the arterial coats.

arteriomalacosis (ar-te"re-o-mal"ah-ko'sis). Arteriomalacia.

arteriometer (ar"te-re-om'e-ter) [*artery* + Gr. *metron* measure]. An apparatus used for measuring any changes in the caliber of a pulsating artery.

arteriomotor (ar-te"re-o-mo'tor). Pertaining to or causing change in the caliber of an artery.

arteriomyomatosis (ar-te"re-o-mi"o-mah-to'sis]. A growth of irregular muscular fibers in the walls of an artery causing thickening of the walls.

arterionecrosis (ar-te"re-o-ne-kro'sis). Necrosis of an artery or of arteries.

arteriopalmus (ar-te"re-o-pal'mus). Palpitation or throbbing of an artery.

arteriopathy (ar″te-re-op′ah-the) [*artery* + Gr. *pathos* disease]. Any arterial disease. **hypertensive a.,** widespread involvement, chiefly of arterioles and small arteries, associated with arterial hypertension and characterized primarily by hypertrophy and thickening of the medial coat.

arterioperissia (ar-te″re-o-pĕ-ris′e-ah) [*artery* + Gr. *perissos* excessive]. Excessive arterial development.

arteriophlebotomy (ar-te″re-o-flĕ-bot′o-me) [*artery* + *phlebotomy*]. Bloodletting by scarification of the integument.

arterioplania (ar-te″re-o-pla′ne-ah) [*artery* + Gr. *planan* to wander + *-ia*]. The condition in which an artery takes an unusual course.

arterioplasty (ar-te″re-o-plas′te) [*artery* + Gr. *plassein* to form]. Surgical repair or reconstruction of an artery; applied to Matas' operation for aneurysm, restoring the continuity of the parent artery by making a new channel out of the sac walls.

arterioplegmus (ar-te″re-o-pleg′mus). Perplication.

arterioploce (ar-te″re-o-plo′se). Perplication.

arteriopressor (ar-te″re-o-pres′or). Producing increased blood pressure in the arteries.

arteriorenal (ar-te″re-o-re′nal). Pertaining to the arteries of the kidney.

arteriorrhagia (ar-te″re-o-ra′je-ah). Arterial hemorrhage.

arteriorrhaphy (ar-te″re-or′ah-fe) [*artery* + Gr. *rhaphē* suture]. Suture of an artery.

arteriorrhexis (ar-te″re-o-rek′sis) [*artery* + Gr. *rhēxis* rupture]. Rupture of an artery.

arteriosclerosis (ar-te″re-o-skle-ro′sis) [*artery* + Gr. *sklēros* hard]. A condition marked by loss of elasticity, thickening and hardening of the arteries. **cerebral a.,** arteriosclerosis of the arteries of the brain. **coronary a.,** arteriosclerosis of the coronary arteries. **decrescent a.,** senile arteriosclerosis. **diffuse a.,** general thickening of the walls of arteries and capillaries. It is most commonly seen in association with chronic nephritis and essential hypertension, the essential lesion being a thickening of the intima of the smaller vessels. Called also *diffuse hyperplastic sclerosis* and *arteriocapillary fibrosis*. **infantile a.,** diffuse hyperplastic sclerosis of arteries in infants and children, due to chronic nephritis or congenital syphilis. **intimal a.,** arteriosclerosis in which the major changes are in the intima of the arteries. **medial a.,** a condition of large and medium-sized arteries, with primary and rather widespread destruction of the muscle and elastic fibers of the medial coat, which are replaced by fibrous tissue; sometimes there are deposits of calcium. **Mönckeberg's a.,** medial arteriosclerosis with extensive deposits of calcium in the medial coat of the artery. **nodose a., nodular a.,** disease of the arteries marked by the formation of fibrous nodes or plaques in the lining membrane of the arteries. **a. oblit′erans,** arteriosclerosis in which proliferation of the intima has caused complete obliteration of the lumen of the artery. **peripheral a.,** arteriosclerosis of the extremities. **senile a.,** arteriosclerosis which is the natural concomitant of old age.

arteriosclerotic (ar-te″re-o-skle-rot′ik). Pertaining to, or affected with, arteriosclerosis.

arteriosity (ar-te″re-os′ĭ-te). The condition or quality of being arterial.

arteriospasm (ar-te′re-o-spazm″). Spasm of an artery.

arteriospastic (ar-te″re-o-spas′tik). Pertaining to, characterized by, or causing arteriospasm.

arteriostenosis (ar-te″re-o-ste-no′sis) [*artery* + Gr. *stenos* narrow]. The narrowing or diminution of the caliber of an artery.

arteriosteogenesis (ar-te″re-os″te-o-jen′e-sis) [*artery* + Gr. *osteon* bone + *gennan* to produce]. Calcification of an artery.

arteriostosis (ar-te″re-os-to′sis) [*artery* + Gr. *osteon* bone + *-osis*]. Ossification of an artery.

arteriostrepsis (ar-te″re-o-strep′sis) [*artery* + Gr. *streptos* twisted]. The twisting of an artery for the arrest of hemorrhage.

arteriosympathectomy (ar-te″re-o-sim″pah-thek′to-me). Periarterial sympathectomy.

arteriotome (ar-te′re-o-tōm). An instrument for performing arteriotomy.

arteriotomy (ar″te-re-ot′o-me) [*artery* + Gr. *tomē* cut]. Incision of an artery.

arteriotony (ar-te″re-ot′o-ne) [*artery* + Gr. *tonos* tension]. The intra-arterial tension of the blood; blood pressure.

arteriotrepsis (ar-te″re-o-trep′sis). Arteriostrepsis.

arterious (ar-te′re-us). Pertaining to the arteries; arterial.

arteriovenous (ar-te″re-o-ve′nus). Both arterial and venous; pertaining to or affecting an artery and a vein.

arterioversion (ar-te″re-o-ver′shun) [*artery* + L. *versio* a turning]. Surgical eversion of the coats of a bleeding artery for the purpose of arresting hemorrhage.

arterioverter (ar-te″re-o-ver′ter). An instrument for performing arterioversion.

arteritis (ar″tĕ-ri′tis) [*artery* + *-itis*]. Inflammation of an artery. Compare *endarteritis* and *periarteritis*. **a. defor′mans,** chronic endarteritis with calcareous infiltration. **a. hyperplas′tica,** arteritis with the formation of new connective tissue. **necrosing a.,** periarteritis nodosa. **a. nodo′sa,** periarteritis nodosa. **a. oblit′erans,** endarteritis resulting in the obliteration or closure of the lumen of the vessel. **temporal a.,** a vascular disease of unknown origin, marked by inflammation of the temporal artery, and characterized by loss of weight, diffuse rheumatic pain, and fever, with leukocytosis, increased erythrocyte sedimentation rate, and increased plasma fibrinogen. **a. umbilica′lis,** septic inflammation of the umbilical artery in newborn infants. **a. verruco′sa,** arteritis marked by fingerlike projections from the wall into the lumen of the blood vessel.

artery (ar′ter-e) [L. *arteria;* Gr. *artēria*, from *aēr* air + *tērein* to keep, because the arteries were supposed by the ancients to contain air, or from Gr. *aeirein* to lift or attach]. A vessel through which the blood passes away from the heart to the various parts of the body. Called also *arteria* [N A, B N A]. The wall of an artery consists typically of an outer coat (tunica adventitia), a middle coat (tunica media), and an inner coat (tunica intima). **accompanying a. of ischiadic nerve,** arteria comitans nervi ischiadici. **acetabular a.** 1. Ramus acetabularis arteriae circumflexae femoris medialis. 2. Ramus acetabularis arteriae obturatoriae. **adipose a's of kidney,** rami capsulares arteriae renis. **afferent a. of glomerulus,** vas afferens glomeruli. **alveolar a., inferior,** arteria alveolaris inferior. **alveolar a's, superior,**

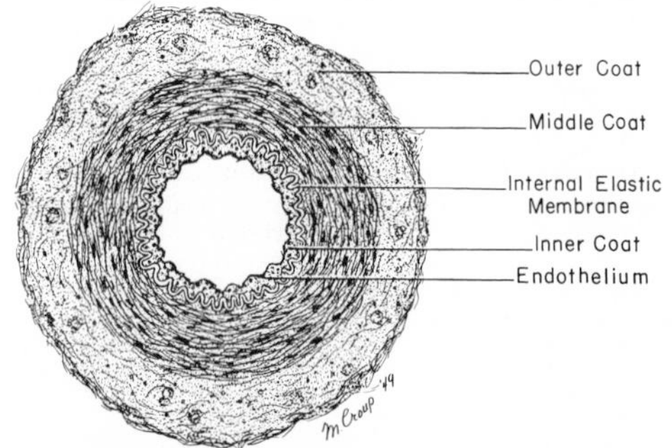

Cross section of artery. (Villee.)

anterior, arteriae alveolares superiores anteriores. **alveolar a., superior, posterior,** arteria alveolaris superior posterior. **angular a.,** arteria angularis. **appendicular a.,** arteria appendicularis. **arcuate a. of foot,** arteria arcuata pedis. **arcuate a's of kidney,** arteriae arcuatae renis. **articular a., proper, of little head of fibula,** ramus circumflexus fibulae arteriae tibialis posterioris. **auditory a., internal,** arteria labyrinthi. **auricular a's, anterior,** rami auriculares anteriores arteriae temporalis superficialis. **auricular a., deep,** arteria auricularis profunda. **auricular a., left,** arteria coronaria sinistra. **auricular a., posterior,** arteria auricularis posterior. **auricular a., right,** arteria coronaria dextra. **axillary a.,** arteria axillaris. **basilar a.,** arteria basilaris. **brachial a.,** arteria brachialis. **brachial a., deep,** arteria profunda brachii. **brachial a., superficial,** arteria brachialis superficialis. **brachiocephalic a.,** truncus brachiocephalicus. **bronchial a's,** rami bronchiales aortae thoracicae. **bronchial a's, anterior,** rami bronchiales arteriae thoracicae internae. **buccal a.,** arteria buccalis. **buccinator a.,** arteria buccalis. **bulbourethral a.,** arteria bulbi penis. **a. of bulb of penis,** arteria bulbi penis. **a. of bulb of vestibule of vagina,** arteria bulbi vestibuli vaginae. **capsular a., inferior,** arteria suprarenalis inferior. **capsular a., middle,** arteria suprarenalis media. **caroticotympanic a.** See *rami caroticotympanici.* **carotid a., common,** arteria carotis communis. **carotid a., external,** arteria carotis externa. **carotid a., internal,** arteria carotis interna. **caudal a.,** arteria sacralis mediana. **celiac a.,** truncus celiacus. **central a. of retina,** arteria centralis retinae. **cephalic a.,** arteria carotis communis. **cerebellar a., inferior, anterior,** arteria cerebelli inferior anterior. **cerebellar a., inferior, posterior,** arteria cerebelli inferior posterior. **cerebellar a., superior,** arteria cerebelli superior. **cerebral a's,** arteriae cerebri. **cerebral a., anterior,** arteria cerebri anterior. **cerebral a., middle,** arteria cerebri media. **cerebral a., posterior,** arteria cerebri posterior. **a's of cerebrum,** arteriae cerebri. **cervical a., ascending,** arteria cervicalis ascendens. **cervical a., deep,** a. cervicalis profunda. **cervical a., descending, deep.** See *rami occipitales arteriae occipitalis.* **cervical a., superficial,** ramus superficialis arteriae transversae colli. **cervical a., transverse,** arteria transversa colli. **choroidal a., anterior,** arteria choroidea anterior. **ciliary a's, anterior,** arteriae ciliares anteriores. **ciliary a's, long,** arteriae ciliares posteriores longae. **ciliary a's, posterior, long,** arteriae ciliares posteriores longae. **ciliary a's, posterior, short,** arteriae ciliares posteriores breves. **ciliary a's, short,** arteriae ciliares posteriores breves. **circumflex a., deep, internal,** ramus profundus arteriae circumflexae femoris medialis. **circumflex a., femoral, lateral,** arteria circumflexa femoris lateralis. **circumflex a., femoral, medial,** arteria circumflexa femoris medialis. **circumflex a., humeral, anterior,** arteria circumflexa humeri anterior. **circumflex a., humeral, posterior,** arteria circumflexa humeri posterior. **circumflex a., iliac, deep,** arteria circumflexa ilium profunda. **circumflex a., iliac, superficial,** arteria circumflexa ilium superficialis. **circumflex a. of scapula,** arteria circumflexa scapulae. **a. of clitoris,** arteria clitoridis [B N A], omitted from N A. **a. of clitoris, deep,** arteria profunda clitoridis. **a. of clitoris, dorsal,** arteria dorsalis clitoridis. **coccygeal a.,** arteria sacralis mediana. **Cohnheim's a.,** terminal a. **colic a., left,** arteria colica sinistra. **colic a., middle,** arteria colica media. **colic a., right,** arteria colica dextra. **colic a., right, inferior,** arteria ileocolica. **colic a., superior, accessory,** arteria colica media. **collateral a., middle,** arteria collateralis media. **collateral a., radial,** arteria collateralis radialis. **collateral a., ulnar, inferior,** arteria collateralis ulnaris inferior. **collateral a., ulnar, superior,** arteria collateralis ulnaris superior. **communicating a., anterior, of cerebrum,** arteria communicans anterior cerebri. **communicating a., posterior, of cerebrum,** arteria communicans posterior cerebri. **conducting a's,** large arterial trunks, characterized by their large size and elasticity, such as the aorta, subclavian, and common carotid, and the brachiocephalic and pulmonary trunks. **conjunctival a's, anterior,** arteriae conjunctivales anteriores. **conjunctival a's, posterior,** arteriae conjunctivales posteriores. **copper-wire a's,** retinal arteries on which the bright line of reflex is exaggerated: seen in arteriosclerosis. **corkscrew a's,** small arteries in the macular region of the eye which appear markedly tortuous. **coronary a., descending, posterior,** ramus interventricularis posterior. **coronary a., left, of heart,** arteria coronaria sinistra. **coronary a., left, of stomach,** arteria gastrica sinistra. **coronary a., right, of heart,** arteria coronaria dextra. **coronary a., right, of stomach,** arteria gastrica dextra. **cremasteric a.,** arteria cremasterica. **cricothyroid a.,** ramus cricothyroideus ateriae thyroideae superioris. **cystic a.,** arteria cystica. **deferential a.,** arteria ductus deferentis. **deltoid a.,** ramus deltoideus arteriae thoracoacromialis. **dental a's, anterior,** arteriae alveolares superiores anteriores. **dental a., inferior,** arteria alveolaris inferior. **dental a., posterior,** arteria alveolaris superior posterior. **diaphragmatic a.,** arteria phrenica inferior. **diaphragmatic a's, superior,** arteriae phrenicae superiores. **digital a's, collateral,** arteriae digitales palmares propriae. **digital a's of foot, common,** arteriae metatarseae plantares. **digital a's of foot, dorsal,** arteriae digitales dorsales pedis. **digital a's of hand, dorsal,** arteriae digitales dorsales manus. **digital a's, palmar, common,** arteriae digitales palmares communes. **digital a's, palmar, proper,** arteriae digitales palmares propriae. **digital a's, plantar, common,** arteriae digitales plantares communes. **digital a's, plantar, proper,** arteriae digitales plantares propriae. **digital a's, volar, common,** arteriae digitales palmares communes. **digital a's, volar, proper,** arteriae digitales palmares propriae. **distributing a's,** most of the arteries except the conducting arteries; of muscular type, they extend from the large vessels to the arterioles. **dorsal a. of clitoris,** arteria dorsalis clitoridis. **dorsal a. of foot,** arteria dorsalis pedis. **dorsal a. of nose,** arteria dorsalis nasi. **dorsal a. of penis,** arteria dorsalis penis. **duodenal a.,** arteria pancreaticoduodenalis inferior. **efferent a. of glomerulus,** vas efferens glomeruli. **emulgent a.,** arteria renalis. **epigastric a., external,** arteria circumflexa ilium profunda. **epigastric a., inferior,** arteria epigastrica inferior. **epigastric a., superficial,** arteria epigastrica superficialis. **epigastric a., superior,** arteria epigastrica superior. **episcleral a's,** arteriae episclerales. **esophageal a's,** rami esophagei aortae thoracicae. **esophageal a's, inferior,** rami esophagei gastricae sinistrae. **ethmoidal a., anterior,** arteria ethmoidalis anterior. **ethmoidal a., posterior,** arteria ethmoidalis posterior. **facial a.** 1. Arteria facialis. 2. Arteria carotis externa. **facial a., deep,** arteria maxillaris. **facial a., transverse,** arteria transversa faciei. **fallopian a.,** arteria uterina. **femoral a.,** arteria femoralis. **femoral a., deep,** arteria profunda femoris. **fibular a.,** arteria peronea. **a. of foot, dorsal,** arteria dorsalis pedis. **frontal a.,** arteria supratrochlearis. **funicular a.,** arteria testicularis. **gastric a., left,** arteria gastrica sinistra. **gastric a., left inferior,** arteria gastroepiploica sinistra. **gastric a., right,** arteria gastrica dextra. **gastric a., right inferior,** arteria gastroepiploica dextra. **gastric a's, short,** arteriae gastricae breves. **gastroduodenal a.,** arteria gastroduodenalis. **gastroepiploic a., left,** arteria gastroepiploica sinistra. **gastroepiploic a., right,** arteria gastroepiploica dextra. **genicular a., descending,** arteria genus descendens. **genicular a., inferior, lateral,** arteria genus inferior lateralis. **genicular a., inferior, medial,** arteria genus inferior mediales. **genicular a., middle,** arteria genus media. **genicular a., superior, lateral,** arteria genus superior lateralis. **genicular a., superior, medial,** arteria genus superior medialis. **a. of glomerulus,** vas afferens glomeruli. **gluteal a., inferior,** arteria glutea inferior. **gluteal a., superior,** arteria glutea superior. **helicine a's,** small arteries that possess on one side, throughout their length, a band of thickened intima in which longitudinal muscle fibers are embedded. They follow a convoluted or curled course and open directly into the cavernous sinuses instead of capillaries; they play a dominant role in erection of erectile tissue. **helicine a's of penis,** arteriae helicinae penis. **hemorrhoidal a., inferior,** arteria rectalis inferior. **hemorrhoidal a., middle,** arteria rectalis media. **hemorrhoidal a., superior,** arteria rectalis superior. **hepatic a., common,** arteria hepatica communis. **hepatic a., proper,** arteria hepatica propria. **hyaloid a.,** arteria hyaloidea. **hyoid a.,** ramus suprahyoideus arteriae lingualis. **hypogastric a.,** arteria iliaca interna. **hypogastric a., obliterated,** ligamentum umbilicale laterale. **ileal a's,** arteriae ilei. **ileocolic a.,** arteria ileocolica. **iliac a., anterior,** arteria iliaca externa. **iliac a., common,** arteria iliaca communis. **iliac a., external,** arteria iliaca externa. **iliac a., internal,** arteria iliaca interna. **iliac a., small,** arteria iliolumbalis. **iliolumbar a.,** arteria iliolumbalis. **infracostal a.,** ramus costalis lateralis arteriae thoracicae internae. **infraorbital a.,** arteria infraorbitalis. **inguinal a's,** rami inguinales arteriae femoralis. **innominate a.,** truncus brachiocephalicus. **intercostal a's, anterior,** rami intercostales anteriores arteriae thoracicae internae. **intercostal a., highest,** arteria intercostalis suprema. **intercostal a's, posterior, I and II,** arteriae intercostales posteriores I et II. **intercostal a's, posterior, III–XI,** arteriae intercostales posteriores III–XI. **interlobar a's of kidney,** arteriae interlobares renis. **interlobular a's of kidney,** arteriae interlobulares renis. **interlobular a's of liver,** arteriae interlobulares hepatis. **intermetacarpal a's, palmar,** arteriae metacarpeae palmares. **interosseous a., common,** arteria interossea communis. **interosseous a., dorsal, of forearm,** arteria interossea posterior. **interosseous a., posterior, of forearm,** arteria interossea posterior. **interosseous a., recurrent,** arteria interossea recurrens. **interosseous a., volar,** arteria interossea anterior. **intersegmental a's,** paired dorsal branches of the embryonic aorta that transform into the arteries of the neck, back, and body wall. **interventricular a., anterior,** ramus interventricularis anterior. **intestinal a's,** arteriae intestinales. **jejunal a's,** arteriae jejunales. **Kugel's a.,** an anastomotic artery in the heart. **labial a's, anterior, of vulva,** rami labiales anteriores arteriae femoralis. **labial a., inferior,** arteria labialis inferior. **labial a's, posterior, of vulva,** rami labiales posteriores arteriae pudendae internae. **labial a., superior,** arteria labialis superior. **a. of labyrinth, labyrinthine a.,** arteria labyrinthi. **lacrimal a.,** arteria lacrimalis. **laryngeal a., inferior,** arteria laryngea inferior. **laryngeal a., superior,** arteria laryngea superior. **lingual a.,** arteria lingualis. **lingual a., deep,** arteria profunda linguae. **lumbar a's,** arteriae lumbales. **lumbar a., fifth, lumbar a., lowest,** arteria lumbalis ima. **malleolar a., anterior, lateral,** arteria malleolaris anterior lateralis. **malleolar a., anterior, medial,** arteria malleolaris anterior medialis. **malleolar a., posterior, lateral.** See *rami malleolares laterales arteriae peroneae.* **malleolar a., posterior, medial.** See *rami malleolares mediales arteriae peroneae.* **mammary a., external.** 1. Arteria thoracica lateralis. 2. See *rami mammarii laterales arteriae thoracicae lateralis.* **mammary a., internal,** arteria thoracica interna. **mandibular a.,** arteria alveolaris inferior. **masseteric a.,** arteria masseterica. **mastoid a's,** rami mastoidei arteriae auricularis posterioris. **maxillary a.,** arteria maxillaris. **maxillary a., external,** arteria facialis. **maxillary a., internal,** arteria maxillaris. **medial a. of foot, superficial,** ramus superficialis arteriae plantaris medialis. **median a.,** arteria mediana. **mediastinal a's, anterior,** rami mediastinales arteriae thoracicae internae. **mediastinal a's, posterior,** rami mediastinales aortae thoracicae. **meningeal a., accessory,** ramus meningeus accessorius arteriae meningeae mediae. **meningeal a., anterior,** arteria meningea anterior. **meningeal a., middle,** arteria meningea media. **meningeal a., posterior.** 1. Arteria meningea posteria. 2. Ramus meningeus arteriae vertebralis. **mental a.,** arteria mentalis. **mesenteric a., inferior,** arteria mesenterica inferior. **mesenteric a., superior,** arteria mesenterica superior. **metacarpal a's, dorsal.** 1. Arteriae metacarpeae dorsales. 2. See *ramus carpeus dorsalis arteriae ulnaris.* **metacarpal a's, ulnar,** arteriae digitales palmares communes. **metacarpal a's, volar,** arteriae metacarpeae palmares. **metacarpal a., volar, deep,** ramus palmaris profundus arteriae ulnaris. **metatarsal a's, dorsal,** arteriae metatarseae dorsales. **metatarsal a's, plantar,** arteriae metatarseae plantraes. **a's of Mueller,** arteriae helicinae penis. **musculophrenic a.,** arteria musculophrenica. **mylohyoid a.,** ramus mylohyoideus arteriae alveolaris inferioris. **myomastoid a.,** ramus occipitalis arteriae auricularis posterioris. **nasal a's, posterior, lateral and septal,** arteriae nasales posteriores, laterale et septi. **nasopalatine a.,** arteria sphenopalatina. **Neubauer's a.,** arteria thyroidea. **a., of nose, dorsal,** arteria dorsalis nasi. **nutrient a.,** an artery which carries blood to the interior of a bone, passing through a nutrient foramen. **nutrient a. of femur, inferior,** arteria nutricia femoris inferior [B N A]; omitted from N A. **nutrient a. of femur, superior,** arteria nutricia femoris superior [B N A]; omitted from N A. **nutrient a. of fibula,** arteria nutricia fibulae [B N A]; omitted from N A. **nutrient a's of humerus,** arteriae nutriciae humeri. **nutrient a's of kidney,** rami capsulares arteriae renis. **nutrient a. of tibia,** arteria nutricia tibiae [B N A]; omitted from N A. **obturator a.,** arteria obturatoria. **obturator a., accessory,** arteria obturatoria accessoria. **occipital a.,** arteria occipitalis. **ophthalmic a.,** arteria ophthalmica. **ovarian a.,** arteria ovarica. **palatine a., ascending,** arteria palatina ascendens. **palatine a., descending,** arteria palatina descendens. **palatine a., greater,** arteria palatina major. **palatine a's, lesser,** arteriae palatinae minores. **palpebral a's, lateral,** arteriae palpebrales laterales. **palpebral a's, medial,** arteriae palpebrales mediales. **pancreaticoduodenal a., inferior,** arteria pancreaticoduodenalis inferior. **pancreaticoduodenal a., superior,** arteria pancreaticoduodenalis superior. **pelvic a., posterior,** arteria iliaca interna. **a. of penis,** arteria penis [B N A]; omitted from N A. **a. of penis, deep,** arteria profunda penis. **a. of penis, dorsal,** arteria dorsalis penis. **perforating a's,** arteriae perforantes. **pericardiac a's, posterior,** rami pericardiaci aortae thoracicae. **pericardiacophrenic a.,** arteria pericardiacophrenica. **perineal a.,** arteria perinealis. **peroneal a.,** arteria peronea. **peroneal a., perforating,** ramus perforans arteriae peroneae. **pharyngeal a., ascending,** arteria pharyngea ascendens. **phrenic a., great,** arteria phrenica inferior. **phrenic a., inferior,** arteria phrenica inferior. **phrenic a., superior.** 1. Arteria pericardiacophrenica. 2. See *arteriae phrenicae superiores.* **plantar a., external,** arteria plantaris lateralis. **plantar a., lateral,** arteria plantaris lateralis. **plantar a., medial,** arteria plantaris medialis. **popliteal a.,** arteria poplitea. **principal a. of thumb,** arteria princeps pollicis. **pterygoid a's,** rami pterygoidei. **a. of pterygoid canal,** arteria canalis pterygoidei. **pubic a.,** ramus pubicus arteriae epigastricae inferioris. **pudendal a's, external,** arteriae pudendae externae. **pudendal a., internal,** arteria pudenda interna. **pulmonary a.,** truncus pulmonalis. **pulmonary a., left,** arteria pulmonalis sinistra. **pulmonary a., right,** arteria pulmonalis dextra. **a. of the pulp,** a name given the first portion of a brushlike group of blood vessels in the spleen. **pyloric a.,** arteria gastrica dextra. **quadriceps a. of femur,** ramus descendens arteriae circumflexae femoris lateralis. **radial a.,** arteria radialis. **radial a., collateral,** arteria collateralis radialis. **radial a. of index finger,** arteria radialis indicis. **radial a., volar, of index finger,** arteria radialis indicis. **radiate a's of kidney,** arteriae interlobulares renis. **radicular a's,** a name applied to arteries that enter the spinal canal along with the anterior and posterior nerve roots. **ranine a.,** arteria profunda linguae. **rectal a., inferior,** arteria rectalis inferior. **rectal a., middle,** arteria rectalis media. **rectal a., superior,** arteria rectalis superior. **recurrent a., radial,** arteria recurrens radialis. **recurrent a., tibial, anterior,** arteria recurrens tibialis anterior. **recurrent a., tibial, posterior,** arteria recurrens tibialis posterior. **recurrent a., ulnar,** arteria recurrens ulnaris. **renal a.,** arteria renalis. **renal a's,** arteriae renis. **retrocostal a.,** ramus costalis lateralis arteriae thoracicae internae. **revehent a.,** vas efferens glomeruli. **a. of round ligament of uterus,** arteria ligamenti teretis uteri. **sacral a's, lateral,** arteriae sacrales laterales. **sacral a., median,** arteria sacralis mediana. **sacrococcygeal a.,** arteria sacralis mediana. **scapular a., dorsal,** ramus profundus arteriae transversae colli. **scapular a., posterior,** ramus profundus arteriae transversae colli. **scapular a., transverse,** arteria suprascapularis. **sciatic a.,** arteria comitans nervi ischiadici. **scrotal a's, anterior,** rami scrotales anteriores arteriae femoralis. **scrotal a's, posterior,** rami scrotales posteriores arteriae pudendae internae. **sigmoid a's,** arteriae sigmoideae. **spermatic a., external,** arteria cremasterica. **spermatic a., internal,** arteria spermatica interna. **sphenopalatine a.,** arteria sphenopalatina. **spinal a's,** rami spinales arteriae vertebralis. **spinal a., anterior,** arteria spinalis anterior. **spinal a., posterior,** arteria spinalis posterior. **splenic a.,** arteria lienalis. **sternal a's, posterior,** rami sternales arteriae thoracicae internae. **sternocleidomastoid a.** See *rami sternocleidomastoidei arteriae occipitalis.* **sternocleidomastoid a., superior,** ramus sternocleidomastoideus arteriae thyroideae superioris. **straight a's of kidney,** arteriolae rectae renis. **stylomastoid a.,** arteria stylomastoidea. **subclavian a.,** arteria subclavia. **subcostal a.** 1. Arteria subcostalis. 2. Ramus costalis lateralis arteriae thoracicae internae. **sublingual a.,** arteria sublingualis. **submental a.,** arteria submentalis. **subscapular a.,** arteria subscapularis. **supraorbital a.,** arteria supraorbitalis. **suprarenal a., aortic,** arteria suprarenalis media. **suprarenal a., inferior,** arteria suprarenalis inferior. **suprarenal a., middle,** arteria suprarenalis media. **suprarenal a's, superior,** arteriae suprarenales superiores. **suprascapular a.,** arteria suprascapularis. **supratrochlear a.,** arteria supratrochlearis. **sural a's,** arteriae surales. **sylvian a.,** arteria cerebri media. **tarsal a., lateral,** arteria tarsea lateralis. **tarsal a's, medial,** arteriae tarseae mediales. **temporal a., deep, anterior.** See *arteriae temporales profundae.* **temporal a., deep, posterior.** See *arteriae temporales profundae.* **temporal a., middle,** arteria temporalis media. **temporal a., superficial,** arteria temporalis superficialis. **terminal a.,** an artery that does not divide into branches, but is directly continuous with capillaries. **testicular a.,** arteria testicularis. **thoracic a., highest,** arteria thoracica suprema. **thoracic a., internal,** arteria thoracica interna. **thoracic a., lateral,** arteria thoracica lateralis. **thoracicoacromial a.,** arteria thoracoacromialis. **thoracodorsal a.,** arteria thoracodorsalis. **thymic a's,** rami thymici arteriae thoracicae internae. **thyroid a., inferior,** arteria thyroidea. **thyroid a., inferior, of Cruveilhier,** ramus cricothyroideus arteriae thyroideae superioris. **thyroid a., lowest,** arteria thyroidea ima. **thyroid a., superior,** arteria thyroidea superior. **tibial a., anterior,** arteria tibialis anterior. **tibial a., posterior,** arteria tibialis posterior. **a. of tongue, dorsal.** See *rami dorsales linguae arteriae lingualis.* **tonsillar a.,** ramus tonsillaris arteria facialis. **transverse a. of face,** arteria transversa faciei. **transverse a. of neck,** ramus superficialis arteriae transversae colli. **tuboovarian a.,** arteria ovarica. **tympanic a., anterior,** arteria tympanica anterior. **tympanic a., inferior,** arteria tympanica inferior. **tympanic a., posterior,** arteria tympanica posterior. **tympanic a., superior,** arteria tympanica superior. **ulnar a.,** arteria ulnaris. **ulnar collateral a., inferior,** arteria collateralis ulnaris inferior. **ulnar collateral a., superior,** arteria collateralis ulnaris superior. **umbilical a.,** arteria umbilicilis. **urethral a.,** arteria urethralis. **uterine a.,** arteria uterina. **uterine a., aortic,** arteria ovarica. **vaginal a.,** arteria vaginalis. **venous a's,** venae pulmonales. **vermiform a.,** arteria appendicularis. **vertebral a.,** arteria ventralis. **vesical a., inferior,** arteria vesicalis inferior. **vesical a's, superior,** arteriae vesicales superiores. **vidian a.,** arteria canalis pterygoidei. **a. of Zinn,** arteria centralis retinae. **zygomaticoorbital a.,** arteria zygomaticoorbitalis.

arthr-. See *arthro-.*

arthragra (ar-thrag′rah) [*arthr-* + Gr. *agra* seizure]. A gouty seizure in a joint or in the joints.

arthral (ar′thral). Pertaining to a joint.

arthralgia (ar-thral′je-ah) [*arthr-* + *-algia*]. Neuralgia or pain in a joint. **a. saturni′na,** arthralgia of lead poisoning.

arthralgic (ar-thral′jik). Pertaining to arthralgia; affected with arthralgia.

arthrectomy (ar-threk′to-me) [*arthr-* + Gr. *ektomē* excision]. The excision of a joint.

arthrempyesis (ar″threm-pi-e′sis) [*arthr-* + Gr. *empyēsis* suppuration]. Suppuration in a joint.

arthresthesia (ar″thres-the′ze-ah) [*arthr-* + Gr. *aisthēsis* perception]. Joint sensibility; the perception of joint motions.

arthrifuge (ar′thrĭ-fūj) [*arthritis* + L. *fugare* to put to flight]. A cure for gout.

arthritic (ar-thrit′ik). 1. Pertaining to or affected with gout or arthritis. 2. A person affected with arthritis.

arthritide (ar′thrĭ-tīd). Any skin eruption of arthritic or gouty origin.

arthritides (ar-thrit′ĭ-dēz). Plural of *arthritis.*

arthritis (ar-thri′tis), pl. *arthrit′ides* [Gr. *arthron* joint + *-itis*]. Inflammation of a joint. **acute a.,**

arthritis marked by pain, heat, redness, and swelling, due to gout, rheumatism, gonorrhea, or traumatism. **acute gouty a.,** acute arthritis associated with gout. **acute rheumatic a.,** rheumatic fever. **atrophic a.,** rheumatoid a. **Bechterew's a.,** arthritis of the spine in which only the intervertebral disks are affected. **blennorrhagic a.,** gonorrheal arthritis. **Charcot's a.,** tabetic arthropathy. **chronic infectious a.,** rheumatoid a. **chronic villous a.,** a form of arthritis deformans due to villous outgrowths from the synovial membranes, which cause impairment of function and crepitation: called also *dry joint.* **climactic a.,** menopausal a. **a. defor'mans,** rheumatoid a. **a. defor'mans neoplas'tica,** osteitis fibrosa. **degenerative a.,** hypertrophic a. **dental a.,** inflammation of the periodontal membrane. **diaphragmatic a.,** angina pectoris. **dysenteric a.,** arthritis due to the absorption of specific dysenteric toxins into a joint. **exudative a.,** arthritis with exudate into or about the joint. **a. fungo'sa,** white swelling; tuberculosis of a joint. **gonococcal a., gonorrheal a.,** acute arthritis due to gonococcus. **gouty a.,** arthritis due to gout. **hemophilic a.,** bleeding into the joint cavities occurring in arthritis. **a. hiema'lis,** special forms of arthritis occurring in winter. **hypertrophic a.,** a form of chronic arthritis occurring chiefly in elderly people, and marked by degeneration and hypertrophy of the bone and cartilage and thickening of the synovial membrane: called also *osteoarthritis* and *degenerative a.* **infectional a.,** arthritis due to infection (gonococcal, tuberculous, etc.). **a. inter'na,** gout of an internal organ. **menopausal a.,** a condition sometimes seen in women at the menopause, due to ovarian hormonal deficiency and marked by pain in the small joints, shoulders, elbows, or knees: called also *arthropathia ovaripriva.* **navicular a.,** inflammation of the cartilage covering the navicular bone of the hoof of a horse. **neuropathic a.,** neurogenic arthropathy. **a. nodo'sa.** 1. Arthritis deformans. 2. Gout. **a. pau'perum,** rheumatoid arthritis; also called *poor man's gout.* **proliferative a.,** rheumatoid a. **rheumatoid a.,** a chronic disease of the joints, usually polyarticular, marked by inflammatory changes in the synovial membranes and articular structures and by atrophy and rarefaction of the bones. In late stages deformity and ankylosis develop. Called also *atrophic arthritis, arthritis deformans, chronic infectious arthritis* and *proliferative a.* **Schüller's a.,** inflammatory hyperplasia of the synovial villi. **a. sic'ca,** arthritis without exudation into a joint cavity. **suppurative a.,** a form marked by purulent joint infiltration, often due to traumatism or to pyemia. **syphilitic a.,** a form associated with or due to syphilis. **tuberculous a.,** arthritis due to tuberculous infection. **uratic a.,** gouty a. **urethral a.,** gonorrheal arthritis. **vertebral a.,** inflammation involving the intervertebral disks. **visceral a.,** gout affecting an internal organ.

arthritism (ar'thrĭ-tizm) [*arthritis* + *-ism*]. The gouty diathesis; the peculiar diathesis or disposition of body that predisposes to joint disease.

arthro-, arthr- [Gr. *arthron* joint]. Combining form denoting some relationship to a joint or joints.

arthrobacter (ar″thro-bak'ter) [Gr. *arthron* a joint + *baktron* a rod]. A genus of microorganisms of the family Corynebacteriaceae, order Eubacteriales, consisting of pleomorphic, gram-variable soil bacteria.

arthrobacterium (ar″thro-bak-te're-um) [*arthro-* + *bacterium*]. A bacterium that reproduces by separation into joints or arthrospores.

Arthrobotrys (ar″thro-bo'tris). A genus of fungi some of which infect and destroy nematodes.

arthrocace (ar-throk'ah-se) [*arthro-* + Gr. *kakōs* bad]. Caries of a joint.

arthrocele (ar'thro-sel) [*arthro-* + Gr. *kēlē* tumor]. A swollen joint.

arthrocentesis (ar″thro-sen-te'sis). Puncture and aspiration of a joint.

arthrochalasis (ar″thro-kal'ah-sis) [*arthro-* + Gr. *chalasis* relaxation]. Abnormal relaxation or flaccidity of a joint. **a. mul'tiplex congen'ita,** overflaccidity of multiple joints, not associated with hyperelasticity of the skin.

arthrochondritis (ar″thro-kon-dri'tis) [*arthro-* + *chrondritis*]. The inflammation of the cartilages of a joint.

arthroclasia (ar″thro-kla'ze-ah) [*arthro-* + Gr. *klaein* to break]. The breaking down of an ankylosis in order to secure free movement in a joint.

arthroclisis (ar″thro-kli'sis). Arthrokleisis.

arthrodesia (ar″thro-de'se-ah). Arthrodesis.

arthrodesis (ar″thro-de'sis) [*arthro-* + Gr. *desis* binding]. The surgical fixation of a joint by fusion of the joint surfaces; artificial ankylosis.

arthrodia (ar-thro'de-ah) [Gr. *arthrōdia* a particular kind of articulation] [B N A]. Articulatio plana [N A].

arthrodial (ar-thro'de-al). Of the nature of an arthrodia.

arthrodynia (ar″thro-din'e-ah) [*arthro-* + *odynē* pain]. Pain in a joint.

arthrodysplasia (ar″thro-dis-pla'ze-ah) [*arthro-* + *dysplasia*]. A hereditary condition marked by deformity of various joints.

arthro-empyesis (ar″thro-em″pi-e'sis) [*arthro-* + Gr. *empyēsis* suppuration]. Suppuration within a joint.

arthro-endoscopy (ar″thro-en-dos'ko-pe). Arthroscopy.

arthroereisis (ar″thro-ĕ-ri'sis) [*arthro-* + Gr. *ereisis* a raising up]. Operative limiting of the motion in a joint which is abnormally mobile from paralysis.

arthrogenous (ar-throj'ĕ-nus) [*arthro-* + Gr. *gennan* to produce]. Formed as a separate joint; as, *arthrogenous* spore.

arthrogram (ar'thro-gram). A roentgenogram of a joint.

Arthrographis (ar-throg'rah-fis). A genus of fungi. **A. langero'ni,** a species of fungi which produces an onychomycosis in man and a benign dermatomycosis in animals.

arthrography (ar-throg'rah-fe) [*arthro-* + Gr. *graphein* to write]. 1. Roentgenography of a joint. 2. A description of the joints.

arthrogryposis (ar″thro-grĭ-po'sis) [*arthro-* + Gr. *grypōsis* a crooking]. 1. Persistent flexure or contracture of a joint. 2. Tetanoid spasm. **congenital multiple a., a. mul'tiplex congen'ita,** amyoplasia congenita.

arthrokatadysis (ar″thro-kah-tad'ĭ-sis) [*arthro-* + Gr. *katadysis* a falling down]. A sinking in or subsidence of the floor of the acetabulum with protrusion of the femoral head through it (intrapelvic protrusion) resulting in limitation of movement of the hip joint.

arthrokleisis (ar″thro-kli'sis) [*arthro-* + Gr. *kleisis* closure]. Ankylosis of a joint, or the production of such ankylosis.

arthrolith (ar'thro-lith) [*arthro-* + Gr. *lithos* stone]. A calculous deposit in a joint.

arthrolithiasis (ar″thro-lĭ-thi'ah-sis). Gout.

arthrology (ar-throl'o-je) [*arthro-* + *-logy*]. The sum of what is known regarding the joints.

arthrolysis (ar-throl'ĭ-sis) [*arthro-* + Gr. *lysis* dissolution]. The operative loosening of adhesions in an ankylosed joint.

arthromeningitis (ar″thro-men″in-ji'tis) [*arthro-* + Gr. *mēninx* membrane + *-itis*]. Synovitis.

arthrometer (ar-throm'e-ter) [*arthro-* + Gr. *metron* measure]. An instrument for measuring the angles of movements of joints as an indication of the range of mobility.

arthrometry (ar-throm'e-tre). The measurement of the range of mobility of joints.

Arthromitaceae (ar″thro-mi-ta′se-e). A family of Schizomycetes (order Caryophanales), made up of parasitic microorganisms found in the intestinal tracts of insects and crustaceans. It includes two genera, *Arthromitus* and *Coleomitus*.

Arthromitus (ar-throm′e-tus). A genus of bacteria, species of which occur in the intestinal walls of insects, tadpoles, and crustaceans.

arthroncus (ar-throng′kus) [*arthro-* + Gr. *onkos* mass]. Swelling of a joint.

arthroneuralgia (ar″thro-nu-ral′je-ah) [*arthro-* + *neuralgia*]. Neuralgia of a joint.

arthronosos (ar″thro-no′sos) [*arthro-* + Gr. *nosos* disease]. A disease of the joints. **a. defor′mans,** arthritis deformans.

arthro-onychodysplasia (ar″thro-on″e-ko-dis-pla′ze-ah) [*arthro-* + Gr. *onyx* nail + *dysplasia*]. A hereditary syndrome with involvement of the head of the radius, hypoplasia or absence of the patellae, posterior iliac spurs, and dystrophy of the nails.

arthropathia (ar″thro-path′e-ah) [L.]. Arthropathy. **a. ovaripri′va,** menopausal arthritis. **a. psoriat′ica,** a disease of the small joints seen in persons suffering from psoriasis.

arthropathology (ar″thro-pah-thol′o-je) [*arthro-* + *pathology*]. The study of the structural and functional changes produced in the joints by disease.

arthropathy (ar-throp′ah-the) [*arthro-* + Gr. *pathos* disease]. Any joint disease. **Charcot's a.,** neurogenic a. **inflammatory a.,** a disease of a joint of inflammatory origin. **neurogenic a.,** a condition of osteoarthritis with joint enlargement, affecting the hand, knee, hip, ankle, and spine, and resulting from trophic disturbance. **neuropathic a.,** neurogenic a. **osteopulmonary a.,** clubbing of the fingers and toes, enlargement and swelling of the ends of the long bones associated with cardiac and pulmonary disease. **static a.,** a disturbance in a joint of the extremity secondary to a disturbance in some other joint of the same extremity as one in the knee joint secondary to one in the hip joint. **tabetic a.,** a form of arthropathy occurring in patients with tabes dorsalis.

arthrophyma (ar″thro-fi′mah) [*arthro-* + Gr. *phyma* swelling]. The swelling of a joint.

arthrophyte (ar′thro-fit) [*arthro-* + Gr. *phyton* plant]. An abnormal growth in a joint cavity. Cf. *arthrolith* and *joint mouse*.

arthroplastic (ar″thro-plas′tik). Pertaining to arthroplasty.

arthroplasty (ar′thro-plas″te) [*arthro-* + Gr. *plassein* to form]. Plastic surgery of a joint or of joints; formation of movable joints.

arthropneumography (ar″thro-nu-mog′rah-fe). Arthropneumoroentgenography.

arthropneumoroentgenography (ar″thro-nu″mo-rent-gen-og′rah-fe) [*arthro-* + Gr. *pneuma* air + *roentgenography*]. Roentgenography of a joint after injection into it of air, oxygen, or carbon dioxide.

arthropod (ar′thro-pod). An animal belonging to the Arthropoda.

Arthropoda (ar-throp′o-dah) [*arthro-* + Gr. *pous* foot]. A phylum of the animal kingdom composed of organisms having a hard jointed exoskeleton and paired, jointed legs, and including, among other classes, the Arachnida and Insecta, many species of which are important medically as parasites or as vectors of organisms capable of causing disease in man.

arthropodan (ar′thro-po″dan). Arthropodous.

arthropodic (ar″thro-po′dic). Arthropodous.

arthropodous (ar-throp′o-dus). Pertaining to or caused by arthropods.

arthropyosis (ar″thro-pi-o′sis) [*arthro-* + Gr. *pyōsis* suppuration]. The formation of pus in a joint cavity.

arthrorheumatism (ar″thro-roo′mah-tizm) [*arthro-* + *rheumatism*]. Articular rheumatism.

arthrorisis (ar″thro-ri′sis). Arthroereisis.

arthrosclerosis (ar″thro-skle-ro′sis) [*arthro-* + *sklērōsis* hardening]. Stiffening or hardening of the joints.

arthroscope (ar″thro-skōp) [*arthro-* + Gr. *skopein* to examine]. An endoscope for examining the interior of a joint.

arthroscopy (ar-thros′ko-pe). Examination of the interior of a joint with an arthroscope.

arthrosis (ar-thro′sis). 1. [Gr. *arthrōsis* a jointing]. A joint or articulation. 2. [*arthro-* + *-osis*]. A disease of a joint. **Charcot's a.,** tabetic arthropathy. **a. defor′mans,** arthritis deformans.

arthrospore (ar′thro-spōr) [*arthro-* + Gr. *sporos* seed]. 1. Modified forms of bacteria at one time thought to be more resistant than the usual forms. 2. A spore formed by fragmentation from hyphae.

arthrosteitis (ar″thros-te-i′tis) [*arthro-* + Gr. *osteon* bone + *-itis*]. Inflammation of the bony structures of a joint.

arthrosteopedic (ar-thros″te-o-pe′dik). Pertaining to the extremities and skeleton.

arthrostomy (ar-thros′to-me) [*arthro-* + Gr. *stomoun* to provide with a mouth, or opening]. The surgical creation of an opening into a joint, as for the purpose of drainage.

arthrosynovitis (ar″thro-sin″o-vi′tis) [*arthro-* + *synovitis*]. Inflammation of the synovial membrane of a joint.

arthrotome (ar′thro-tōm) [*arthro-* + Gr. *tomē* cut]. A knife for incising a joint.

arthrotomy (ar-throt′o-me) [*arthro-* + Gr. *tomē* cut]. Surgical incision of a joint.

arthrotropic (ar″thro-trop′ik) [*arthro-* + Gr. *tropos* a turning]. Having an affinity for or tending to settle in the joints.

arthrotyphoid (ar″thro-ti′foid) [*arthro-* + *typhoid*]. Typhoid fever beginning with symptoms resembling those of rheumatic fever.

arthroxerosis (ar″thro-ze-ro′sis) [*arthro-* + Gr. *xēros* dry + *-osis*]. Chronic osteo-arthritis.

arthroxesis (ar-throk′se-sis) [*arthro-* + Gr. *xesis* scraping]. The scraping of an articular surface.

Arthus's phenomenon (ar-toos′ez) [Maurice *Arthus*, French physiologist, 1862–1945]. See under *phenomenon*.

artiad (ar′te-ad) [Gr. *artios* even]. Any element or radical with an even-numbered valence.

article (ar′te-kl) [L. *articulus* a little joint]. An interarticular segment; one of the portions or segments forming a jointed series.

articular (ar-tik′u-lar) [L. *articularis*]. Of or pertaining to a joint.

articulare (ar-tik″u-la′re). A cephalometric landmark, being the point of intersection of the dorsal contours of the articular process of the mandible and the temporal bone.

articulate (ar-tik′u-lāt) [L. *articulatus* jointed]. 1. Divided into or united by joints. 2. Enunciated in words and sentences. 3. To divide into or to unite so as to form a joint. 4. In dentistry, to adjust or place the teeth in their proper relation to each other in making an artificial denture.

articulated (ar-tik′u-lāt″ed). Connected by movable joints; consisting of separate segments joined in such fashion as to be movable on each other.

articulatio (ar-tik″u-la′she-o), pl. *articulationes* [L.]. A place of junction between two discrete objects; used in anatomical nomenclature to designate the place of union or junction between two or more bones of the skeleton, indicated by the modifying term. Also used in the plural as a general term to indicate such joints (*juncturae ossium*). Called also *articulation* and *joint*. **a. acromioclavicula′ris** [N A, B N A], the joint formed by the acromion of the scapula and the acromial extremity of the clavicle. Called also *acromioclavicular articulation*. **a. atlantoaxia′lis latera′lis** [N A], one of a pair of joints, one on either side of the body, formed by the inferior articular surface of the atlas and the superior surface of the axis. Called also *lateral atlantoaxial articulation.* **a. atlantoaxia'lis media'na** [N A], a single joint formed by the two articular facets of the dens of the axis, one in relation with the articular facet on the anterior arch of the atlas, the other in relation with the transverse ligament of the atlas. Called also *medial atlantoaxial articulation.* **a. atlantoepistroph'ica** [B N A]. See *a. atlantoaxialis lateralis* and *a. atlantoaxialis mediana.* **a. atlantooccipita'lis** [N A, B N A], one of two joints, each formed by a superior articular pit of the atlas and a condyle of the occipital bone. Called also *atlantooccipital articulation.* **a. calcaneocuboi'dea** [N A, B N A], one formed between the cuboidal articular surface of the calcaneus and the cuboid bone. Called also *calcaneocuboid articulation.* **a. cap'itis cos'tae** [N A], one of the two types of articulations between ribs and vertebrae: the articulation of the head of the rib with the bodies of two vertebrae. Called also *articulation of head of rib.* **articulatio'nes capitulo'rum costa'rum** [B N A]. See *a. capitis costae.* **articulatio'nes carpometacar'peae** [N A, B N A], joints formed by the trapezial, trapezoid, capitate, and hamate bones together with the bases of the four medial metacarpal bones. Called also *carpometacarpal articulations.* **a. carpometacar'pea pol'licis** [N A, B N A], the joint formed by the first metacarpal and the trapezial bones. Called also *carpometacarpal articulation of thumb.* **a. cochlea'ris** [B N A], a form of hinge joint that permits of some lateral motion. Omitted from N A. **a. compos'ita** [N A, B N A], a type of synovial joint in which more than two bones are involved. Called also *composite articulation.* **a. condyla'ris** [N A], a modification of the ball-and-socket type of synovial joint in which, due to the arrangement of the muscles and ligaments around the joint, all movements are permitted except rotation about a vertical axis. Called also *condylar articulation.* **a. costotransversa'ria** [N A], one of the two types of articulations between ribs and vertebrae: the articulation of the tubercle of the rib with the transverse process of a vertebra. This is lacking for the eleventh and twelfth ribs. Called also *costotransverse articulation.* **articulatio'nes costovertebra'les** [N A, B N A], the articulations between the ribs and vertebrae, of which there are two types: a. capitis costae and a. costotransversaria. Called also *costovertebral articulations.* **a. cotyl'ica,** N A alternative for *a. spheroidea.* **a. cox'ae** [N A, B N A], the joint formed between the head of the femur and the acetabulum of the hip bone. Called also *articulation of hip.* **a. cricoarytenoi'dea** [N A], the synovial joint between the upper border of the cricoid cartilage and the base of the arytenoid cartilage. Called also *a. cricoarytaenoidea* [B N A]. **a. cricothyroi'dea** [N A], the articulation between the lateral aspect of the cricoid cartilage and the inferior horn of the thyroid cartilage. Called also *a. cricothyreoidea* [B N A]. **a. cu'biti** [N A, B N A], the joint between the arm and forearm, comprising the humeroulnar, humeroradial, and proximal radioulnar articulations. Called also *cubital articulation* and *elbow joint.* **a. cuneonavicula'ris** [N A, B N A], the joint between the anterior surface of the navicular bone and the proximal ends of the three cuneiform bones. Called also *cuneonavicular articulation.* **articulatio'nes digito'rum ma'nus** [B N A], articulationes interphalangeae manus. **articulatio'nes digito'rum pe'dis** [B N A], articulationes interphalangeae pedis. **a. ellipsoi'dea** [N A, B N A], a modification of the ball-and-socket form of synovial joint in which the articular surfaces are ellipsoid rather than spheroid. Called also *ellipsoidal articulation.* **a. ge'nu** [B N A], a. genus. **a. ge'nus** [N A], the compound joint formed between the articular surface of the patella, the condyles and patellar surface of the femur, and the superior articular surface of the tibia. Called also *articulation of knee* and *knee joint.* **a. hu'meri** [N A, B N A], the joint formed by the head of the humerus and the glenoid cavity of the scapula. Called also *articulation of shoulder* and *shoulder joint.* **a. humeroradia'lis** [N A, B N A], the joint between the humerus and the radius. Called also *humeroradial articulation.* **a. humeroulna'ris** [N A, B N A], the joint between the humerus and the ulna. Called also *humeroulnar articulation.* **a. incudomallea'ris** [N A], the junction of the incus and the malleus. Called also *a. incudomalleolaris* [B N A] and *incudomalleolar articulation.* **a. incudomalleola'ris** [B N A], a. incudomallearis. **a. incudostape'dia** [N A, B N A], the junction of the incus and the stapes. Called also *incudostapedial articulation.* **articulatio'nes intercar'peae** [N A], articulations between the various carpal bones themselves. Called also *intercarpal articulations.* **articulatio'nes interchondra'les** [N A], the unions, on either side, between the costal cartilages of the upper false ribs, usually ribs seven through ten. Called also *articulationes interchondrales costarum* [B N A] and *interchondral articulations.* **articulatio'nes interchondra'les costa'rum** [B N A], articulationes interchondrales. **articulatio'nes intermetacar'peae** [N A, B N A], joints formed between the adjoining bases of the second, third, fourth, and fifth metacarpal bones. Called also *intermetacarpal articulations.* **articulatio'nes intermetatar'seae** [N A, B N A], the joints formed between the adjoining bases of the five metatarsal bones. Called also *intermetatarsal articulations.* **articulatio'nes interphalan'geae ma'nus** [N A], the joints between the phalanges of the fingers. Called also *articulationes digitorum manus* [B N A] and *interphalangeal articulations of hand.* **articulatio'nes interphalan'geae pe'dis** [N A], the joints between the phalanges of the toes. Called also *articulationes digitorum pedis* [B N A] and *interphalangeal articulations of foot.* **articulatio'nes intertar'seae** [N A, B N A], the articulations between the various tarsal bones. Called also *intertarsal articulations.* **a. mandibula'ris** [B N A], a. temporomandibularis. **articulatio'nes ma'nus** [N A], the joints of the hand. **a. mediocar'pea** [N A], the joint between the two rows of carpal bones. Called also *mediocarpal articulation.* **articulatio'nes metacarpophalan'geae** [N A, B N A], joints formed between the heads of the five metacarpal bones and the bases of the corresponding proximal phalanges. Called also *metacarpophalangeal articulations.* **articulatio'nes metatarsophalan'geae** [N A, B N A], the joints formed between the heads of the five metatarsal bones and the bases of the corresponding proximal phalanges. Called also *metatarsophalangeal articulations.* **articulatio'nes ossiculo'rum audi'tus** [N A, B N A], the articulations between the auditory ossicles themselves and between the stapes and the secondary tympanic membrane, including *a. incudomallearis, a. incudostapedia,* and *syndesmosis tympanostapedia.* Called also *articulations of auditory ossicles.* **a. os'sis pisifor'mis** [N A, B N A], the joint formed by the pisiform and triquetral bones. Called also *articulation of pisiform bone.* **articulatio'nes pe'dis** [N A, B N A], the joints of the foot, including those of the ankle, the tarsus, the metatarsus, and the phalanges. **a. pla'na** [N A], a type of synovial joint in which the opposed surfaces are flat or only slightly curved; it permits only simple gliding movement, in any direction, within narrow limits imposed by ligaments. Called also *arthrodia* [B N A] and *plane articulation.* **a. radiocar'pea** [N A, B N A], a joint formed by the radius and the articular disc with the scaphoid, lunate, and triquetral bones. Called also *radiocarpal articulation.* **a. radioulna'ris dista'lis** [N A, B N A], the joint formed by the head of the ulna and the ulnar notch of the radius. Called also *distal radioulnar articulation.* **a. radioulna'ris proxima'lis** [N A, B N A], the proximal of the two joints between the radius and the ulna; it enters into pronation and supination of the forearm. Called also *proximal radioulnar articulation.* **a. sacroili'aca** [N A, B N A], the joint formed between the auricular surfaces of the sacrum and ilium. Called also *sacroiliac articulation.* **a. sella'ris** [N A, B N A], a type of synovial joint in which the articular surface of one bone is concave in one direction and convex in the direction at right angles to the first (concavoconvex), and the articular surface of the second bone is reciprocally convexoconcave; movement is permitted along two main axes at right angles to each other. Called also *saddle articulation.* **a. sim'plex** [N A, B N A], a type of synovial joint in which only two bones are involved. Called also *simple articulation.* **a. sphaeroi'dea** [B N A], a. spheroidea. **a. spheroi'dea** [N A], a type of synovial joint in which a spheroidal surface on one bone ("ball") moves within a concavity ("socket") on the other bone. It is the most moveable type of joint. Called also *a. cotylica, a. sphaeroidea* [B N A], and *ball-and-socket articulation.* **a. sternoclavicula'ris** [N A, B N A], the joint formed by the sternal extremity of the clavicle, the clavicular notch of the manubrium of the sternum, and the first costal cartilage. Called also *sternoclavicular articulation.* **articulatio'nes sternocosta'les** [N A, B N A], the joints between the costal notches of the sternum and the medial ends of the costal cartilages of the upper seven ribs. Called also *sternocostal articulations.* **a. subtala'ris** [N A], the joint formed between the posterior calcaneal articular surface of the talus and the posterior articular surface of the calcaneus. Called also *a. talocalcanea* [B N A] and *subtalar articulation.* **a. talocalca'nea** [B N A], a. subtalaris. **a. talocalcaneonavicula'ris** [N A, B N A], a joint formed by the head of the talus, the anterior articular surface of the calcaneus, the plantar calcaneonavicular ligament, and the posterior surface of the navicular bone. Called also *talocalcaneonavicular articulation.* **a. talocrura'lis** [N A, B N A], the ankle joint, formed by the inferior articular and malleolar articular surfaces of the tibia, the malleolar articular surface of the fibula, and the medial malleolar, lateral malleolar, and superior surfaces of the talus. Called also *talocrural articulation.* **a. talonavicula'ris** [B N A], the junction between the talus and navicular bone; omitted from N A. **a. tar'si transver'sa** [N A], a joint comprising the articulation of the calcaneus and the cuboid bone and the articulation of the talus and the navicular bone. Called also *a. tarsi transversa* [*Choparti*] [B N A] and *transverse tarsal articulation.* **articulatio'nes tarsometatar'seae** [N A, B N A], joints formed by the cuneiform and cuboid bones together with the bases of the metatarsal bones. Called also *tarsometatarsal articulations.* **a. temporomandibula'ris** [N A], the joint formed by the head of the mandible and the mandibular fossa, and the articular tubercle of the temporal bone. Called also *a. mandibularis* [B N A] and *temporomandibular articulation.* **a. tibiofibula'ris** [N A, B N A]. 1. The joint formed at the proximal end of the tibia and fibula between the articular surface of the head of the fibula and the fibular articular surface of the tibia. Called also *tibiofibular articulation.* 2. N A alternative for *syndesmosis tibiofibularis* when it contains a prolongation of the cavity of the talocrural articulation. **a. trochoi'dea** [N A, B N A], a type of synovial joint that allows a rotary motion in but one plane; a pivot-like process turns within a ring, or a ring turns on a pivot. Called also *pivot articulation.*

articulation (ar-tik-u-la'shun) [L. *articulatio*]. 1. The place of union or junction between two or more bones of the skeleton. See also *articulatio, junctura,* and *joint.* 2. The enunciation of words and sentences. 3. In dentistry: (*a*) the contact relationship of the occlusal surfaces of the teeth while in action; (*b*) the arrangement of artificial teeth so as to accommodate the various positions of the mouth and to serve the purpose of the natural teeth which they are to replace. **acromioclavicular a.,** articulatio acromioclavicularis. **ambomalleolar a.,** articulatio incudomallearis. **articulator a.,** in dentistry, the use of a mechanical device by which movements of the temporomandibular joint or mandible can be simulated, to facilitate the arrangement of teeth in artificial dentures so that they articulate properly. **atlantoaxial a., lateral,** articulatio atlantoaxialis lateralis. **atlantoaxial a., medial,** articulatio atlantoaxialis mediana. **atlantoepistrophic a.** See *articulatio atlantoaxialis lateralis* and *articulatio atlantoaxialis mediana.* **atlantooccipital a.,** articulatio atlantooccipitalis. **a's of auditory ossicles,** articulationes ossiculorum auditus. **balanced a.,** in dentistry, a continuous change from one balanced occlusion into another for all occluded mandibular excursions. **ball-and-socket a.,** articulatio spheroidea. **brachiocarpal a.,** articulatio radiocarpea. **brachioradial a.,** articulatio humeroradialis. **brachioulnar a.,** articulatio humeroulnaris. **calcaneocuboid a.,** articulatio calcaneocuboidea. **capitular a.,** articulatio capitis costae. **carpal a's,** the junctions between the various carpal bones and between them and the bones of the forearm and hand. **carpometacarpal a's,** articulationes carpometacarpeae. **carpometacarpal a., first,** articulatio carpometacarpea pollicis. **carpometacarpal a. of thumb,** articulatio carpometacarpea pollicis. **chondrosternal a's,** articulationes sternocostales. **Chopart's a.,** articulatio tarsi transversa. **composite a.,** articulatio composita. **compound a.,** articulatio composita. **condylar a.,** articulatio condylaris. **confluent a.,** a manner of speaking in which the syllables are run together. **costocentral a.,** articulatio capitis costae. **costosternal a's,** articulationes sternocostales. **costotransverse a.,** articulatio costotransversaria. **costovertebral a's,** articulationes costovertebrales. **coxofemoral a. of Buisson,** articulatio coxae. **craniovertebral a.,** articulatio atlantooccipitalis. **cricoarytenoid a.,** articulatio cricoarytenoidea. **cricothyroid a.,** articulatio cricothyroidea. **cubital a.,** articulatio cubiti. **cubitoradial a., inferior,** articulatio radioulnaris distalis. **cubitoradial a., superior,** articulatio radioulnaris proximalis. **cuneonavicular a.,** articulatio cuneonavicularis. **a's of digits of foot,** articulationes interphalangeae pedis. **a's of digits of hand,** articulationes interphalangeae manus. **a. of elbow,** articulatio cubiti. **ellipsoid a.,** articulatio ellipsoidea. **ephippial a.,** articulatio sellaris. **femoral a.,** articulatio coxae. **a's of fingers,** articulationes interphalangeae manus. **a's of foot,** articulationes pedis. **gliding a.,** articulatio plana. **a's of hand,** articulationes manus. **a. of head of rib,** articulatio capitis costae. **a. of hip,** articulatio coxae. **humeroradial a.,** articulatio humeroradialis. **humeroulnar a.,** articulatio humeroulnaris. **a. of humerus,** articulatio humeri. **ileosacral a.,** articulatio sacroiliaca. **incudomalleolar a.,** articulatio incudomallearis. **incudostapedial a.,** articulatio incudostapedia. **intercarpal a's,** articulationes intercarpeae. **interchondral a's of ribs,** articulationes interchondrales. **intercostal a's,** articulationes interchondrales. **intermetacarpal a's,** articulationes intermetacarpeae. **intermetatarsal a's,** articulationes intermetatarseae. **interphalangeal a's of fingers,** articulationes interphalangeae manus. **interphalangeal a's of toes,** articulationes interphalangeae pedis. **intertarsal a's,** articulationes intertarseae. **a. of knee,** articulatio genus. **mandibular a.,** articulatio temporomandibularis. **maxillary a.,** articulatio temporomandibularis. **mediocarpal a.,** articulatio mediocarpea. **a's of metacarpal bones,** articulationes intermetacarpeae. **metacarpocarpal a's,** articulationes carpometacarpeae. **metacarpophalangeal**

a's, articulationes metacarpophalangeae. **a's of metatarsal bones,** articulationes intermetatarseae. **metatarsophalangeal a's,** articulationes metatarsophalangeae. **occipital a.,** articulatio atlantooccipitalis. **occipito-atlantal a.,** articulatio atlantooccipitalis. **petrooccipital a.,** synchondrosis petrooccipitalis. **phalangeal a's.** See *articulationes interphalangeae manus* and *articulationes interphalangeae pedis.* **a. of pisiform bone,** articulatio ossis pisiformis. **pisocuneiform a.,** articulatio ossis pisiformis. **pivot a.,** articulatio trochoidea. **plane a.,** articulatio plana. **a. of pubis,** symphysis pubica. **radiocarpal a.,** articulatio radiocarpea. **radioulnar a., distal, radioulnar a., inferior,** articulatio radioulnaris distalis. **radioulnar a., proximal, radioulnar a., superior,** articulatio radioulnaris proximalis. **sacrococcygeal a.,** junctura sacrococcygea. **sacroiliac a.,** articulatio sacroiliaca. **saddle a.,** articulatio sellaris. **scapuloclavicular a.,** articulatio acromioclavicularis. **a. of shoulder,** articulatio humeri. **simple a.,** articulatio simplex. **spheroidal a.,** articulatio spheroidea. **sternoclavicular a.,** articulatio sternoclavicularis. **sternocostal a's,** articulationes sternocostales. **subtalar a.,** articulatio subtalaris. **talocalcaneonavicular a.,** articulatio talocalcaneonavicularis. **talocrural a.,** articulatio talocruralis. **talonavicular a.,** articulatio talonavicularis. **tarsometatarsal a's,** articulationes tarsometatarseae. **temporomandibular a.,** articulatio temporomandibularis. **temporomaxillary a.,** articulatio temporomandibularis. **tibiofibular a.** 1. Articulatio tibiofibularis. 2. Syndesmosis tibiofibularis. **a's of toes,** articulationes interphalangeae pedis. **transverse tarsal a.,** articulatio tarsi transversa. **trochoidal a.,** articulatio trochoidea. **a. of tubercle of rib,** articulatio costotransversaria.

articulationes (ar-tik″u-la″she-o′nēz) [L.]. Plural of *articulatio.*

articulator (ar-tik′u-la″tor). A device for effecting a jointlike union. See also *dental articulator.* **adjustable a.,** a dental articulator which may be adjusted so that all its movements conform with the mandibular movements of the patient. **arbitrary-movement a.,** a dental articulator which permits movements in arbitrarily selected directions. **average-movement a.,** a dental articulator which permits movements generally accepted as average. **crown a.,** a small articulator used in formation of a single crown. **dental a.,** a mechanical device by which movements of the temporomandibular joints or mandible can be simulated, used in matching upper and lower dentures, and for mounting artificial teeth in order to obtain proper relations of occlusion and articulation. **hinge a., plain-line a.,** a dental articulator with only a hinge joint, permitting no lateral motion. **semiadjustable a.,** a dental articulator which may be adjusted so that at least one movement conforms with a mandibular movement of the patient.

articulatory (ar-tik′u-la″to-re). Pertaining to utterance.

articulo (ar-tik′u-lo) [L.]. Moment; crisis. **a. mor′tis,** at the moment, or point, of death.

articulus (ar-tik′u-lus), pl. *articuli* [L.]. A joint.

artifact (ar′tĭ-fakt) [L. *ars* art + *factum* made]. Any artificial product; any structure or feature that is not natural, but has been altered by processing. The term is used in histology and microscopy for a tissue that has been mechanically altered from its natural state.

artifactitious (ar′tĭ-fak-tish′us). Having the character of an artifact.

artificial (ar″tĭ-fish′al) [L. *ars* art + *facere* to make]. Made by art; not natural or pathological.

Artiodactyla (ar″te-o-dak′tĭ-lah) [Gr. *artios* even + *daktylos* finger]. An order of ungulates, having an even number of toes, including ruminants, pigs, deer, and antelopes. Cf. Perissodactyla.

artiodactylous (ar″te-o-dak′tĭ-lus). Having an even number of digits on a hand or foot; pertaining to Artiodactyla.

Artyfechinostomum (ar″te-fek″ĭ-nos′to-mum). A genus of flukes. **A. sufrar′tyfex,** an intestinal fluke reported from Assam.

Arum (a′rum). A genus of plants. *A. dracontium* is highly poisonous. *A. maculatum* furnishes sago.

aryepiglottic (ar″e-ep″ĭ-glot′ik). Arytenoepiglottic.

aryepiglotticus (ar″e-ep″ĭ-glot′ĭ-kus). See *Table of Musculi.*

aryepiglottidean (ar″e-ep″ĭ-glo-tid′e-an). Arytenoepiglottic.

aryl- (ar′il). A chemical prefix indicating a radical belonging to the aromatic series.

arytenectomy (ar″e-te-nek′to-me) [*arytenoid* + Gr. *ektomē* excision]. Excision of an arytenoid cartilage in the horse.

arytenoepiglottic (ar-it″e-no-ep″ĭ-glot′ik) [Gr. *arytaina* ladle + *epiglottis*]. Pertaining to the arytenoid cartilage and to the epiglottis.

arytenoid (ar″e-te′noid) [Gr. *arytaina* ladle + *eidos* form]. Shaped like a jug or pitcher.

arytenoidectomy (ar″e-te-noid-ek′to-me) [*arytenoid* + Gr. *ektomē* excision]. Surgical removal of an arytenoid cartilage.

arytenoideus (ar″e-te-noi′de-us) [L.]. See *Table of Musculi.*

arytenoiditis (ar-it″ĕ-noi-di′tis). Inflammation of the arytenoid cartilage or muscles.

arytenoidopexy (ar″ĭ-tĕ-noi′do-pek″se) [*arytenoid* + Gr. *pēxis* fixation]. Surgical fixation of arytenoid cartilage or muscle.

Arzberger's pear (arz′ber-gerz) [Friedrich *Arzberger*, Austrian physicist, 1833–1905]. An elliptical ball for insertion into the rectum where it is cooled by passing water through it.

As. 1. Chemical symbol for *arsenic.* 2. Abbreviation for *astigmatism.*

A.S. Abbreviation for L. *au′ris sinis′tra,* left ear.

A.S.A. (a′es-a). Trade mark for a preparation of acetylsalicylic acid, acetophenetidin, and caffeine. Use: analgesic and antipyretic.

asab (as′ab). An African venereal disease, said to differ from syphilis.

asacria (ah-sa′kre-ah). A developmental anomaly characterized by absence of the sacrum.

A.S.A.I.O. Abbreviation for *American Society for Artificial Internal Organs.*

asaphia (ah-sa′fe-ah) [Gr. *asapheia*]. Indistinctness of utterance.

asbestiform (as-bes′tĭ-form). Having a fibrous structure like asbestos.

asbestos (as-bes′tos) [Gr. *asbestos* unquenchable]. A fibrous magnesium and calcium silicate. It is incombustible.

asbestosis (as″bes-to′sis) [*asbestos* + *-osis*]. Lung disease (pneumoconiosis) caused by inhaling particles of asbestos.

ascariasis (as″kah-ri′ah-sis) [*ascaris* + *-iasis*]. The state of being infected with worms of the genus Ascaris.

ascaricidal (as-kar″ĭ-si′dal). Destructive to intestinal parasites of the genus Ascaris.

ascaricide (as-kar′ĭ-sīd) [Gr. *askaris* ascaris + L. *caedere* to kill]. An agent that destroys worms of the genus Ascaris.

ascarides (as-kar′ĭ-dēz). Plural of *ascaris.*

Ascaridia (as″kah-rid′e-ah). A genus of nematode parasites. **A. linea′ta,** a nematode parasite in the small intestine of fowls, the common roundworm of chickens in the United States.

ascaridiasis (as″kar-ĭ-di′ah-sis). Ascariasis.

ascaridosis (as-kar-ĭ-do′sis). Ascariasis.

ascariosis (as-kar-e-o′sis). Ascariasis.

Ascaris (as′kah-ris) [L.; Gr. *askaris*]. A genus of intestinal lumbricoid parasites of the order *Nematoda*. **A. ala′ta, A. ca′nis.** See *Toxascaris canis*. **A. e′qui, A. equo′rum,** a species found in horses. **A. lumbricoi′des,** the eelworm or roundworm, a common worm resembling the earthworm; it is found in the small intestine, especially in children, causing colicky pains and diarrhea. **A. margina′ta.** See *Toxascaris canis*. **A. megaloceph′ala,** a species found in horses. **A. mys′tax.** See *Belascaris mystax*. **A. o′vis,** a species found in sheep. **A. su′is, A. suil′la, A. su′um,** a name given to *A. lumbricoides* found in swine. **A. texa′na,** a species which was found in Texas. **A. vermicula′ris.** See *Enterobius vermicularis*. **A. vitulo′rum,** a species which is found in calves.

Ascaris lumbricoides (after Brumpt).

ascaris (as-kah-ris), pl. *ascar′ides*. A worm of the genus Ascaris.

ascending (ah-send′ing). Having an upward course.

ascensus (ah-sen′sus) [L.]. A going up; ascent. **a. u′teri,** an abnormally high position of the uterus.

Asch's operation, splint [Morris J. *Asch*, American laryngologist, 1833–1902]. See under *operation* and *splint*.

Ascher's glass-rod phenomenon, syndrome [K. W. *Ascher*, Cincinnati ophthalmologist, born in Prague, 1887]. See *aqueous-influx phenomenon*, under *phenomenon*, and under *syndrome*.

Ascherson's membrane, vesicles (ash′ersunz) [Ferdinand Moritz *Ascherson*, German physician, 1798–1879]. See under *membrane* and *vesicle*.

Aschheim-Zondek test (ash′hīm-tson′dek) [Selmar *Aschheim*, German gynecologist, born 1878; Bernhardt *Zondek*, German gynecologist, born 1891]. See under *test*.

aschistodactylia (ah-skis′to-dak-til′e-ah) [*a* neg. + Gr. *schistos* cleft + *daktylos* finger + *-ia*]. Syndactyly.

Aschner's phenomenon (ash′nerz) [Bernhard *Aschner*, Austrian gynecologist, 1883–1960]. See under *phenomenon*.

Aschoff's bodies or **nodules, node** (ash′ofs) [Ludwig *Aschoff*, German pathologist, 1866–1942]. See under *body* and *node*.

Aschoff-Tawara node [Ludwig *Aschoff;* Sunao *Tawara*, Japanese pathologist, born 1873]. See under *node*.

ascia (as′e-ah) [L. "ax," from the shape of its folds]. A form of spiral bandage.

ascites (ah-si′tēz) [L.; Gr. *askitēs*, from *askos* bag]. Effusion of serous fluid into the abdominal cavity. **a. adipo′sus,** a variety characterized by a milky appearance of the contained fluid, due to the presence of cells that have undergone a fatty degeneration. **bloody a.,** hemorrhagic a. **chyliform a., a. chylo′sus, chylous a.,** the presence of chyle in the peritoneal cavity, as a result of anomalies, injuries, or obstruction of the thoracic duct. **fatty a.,** a. adiposus. **hemorrhagic a.,** that in which the fluid is mixed with blood. **hydremic a.,** that which is associated with, or due to, a watery state of the blood. **milky a.,** a. adiposus. **a. prae′cox,** ascites which develops prior to edema in constrictive pericarditis. **preagonal a.,** a flow of serum into the peritoneal cavity just before death. **pseudochylous a.,** ascites in which the contained fluid resembles chyle in appearance, but does not contain fatty matter.

ascitic (ah-sit′ik). Pertaining to or characterized by ascites.

ascitogenous (as″e-toj′e-nus). Causing ascites.

asclepia (as-kle′pe-ah). Plural of *asclepion*.

Asclepiad (as-kle′pe-ad) [Gr. *Asklēpiadēs*]. A member of an organized guild of physicians, followers of Æsculapius, who were the priests in the early Greek temples of healing (see *asclepion*). The name is also applied to any devoted, high-minded physician.

Asclepiades (as″kle-pi′ah-dēz). Born in Bithynia (Asia Minor), in 124 B.C., this celebrated physician studied in Alexandria, and later popularized Greek medicine in Rome. Opposed to Hippocratic humoralism, he taught that disease resulted from a mechanical disturbance of the passage of atoms through the pores of the body. His followers, the Methodists, further simplified this concept.

Asclepias (as-kle′pe-as) [L.]. A genus of asclepiadaceous plants. The root of *A. tuberosa*, or pleurisy root, was formerly used in the fevers of rheumatism, pleurisy, and bronchitis.

Asclepios (as-klep′e-os). Æsculapius.

asclepion (as-kle′pe-on), pl. *asclepia* [Gr. *Asklēpieion* temple of Asklepios (Æsculapius)]. One of the early Greek temples of healing, the most celebrated of which were at Cos, Epidaurus, Cnidus, and Pergamos. Greek temple medicine flourished during the time of Hippocrates (late 5th century B.C.), but was quite independent of his school.

ascocarp (as′ko-karp) [Gr. *askos* bag + *karpos* fruit]. The developed fructification in ascomycetes, including asci and ascospores.

Ascococcus (as-ko-kok′us). An obsolete name for a genus of bacteria.

Ascocotyle (as″ko-ko′tĭ-le). A genus of nematode parasites. **A. pithecophagic′ola,** a nematode parasite in the monkey-eating eagle in the Philippines.

ascogonium (as″ko-go′ne-um). The female organ in some of the cryptogamous plants which, after fertilization, develops into asci. Called also *archicarp* and *carpogonium*.

Ascoli's reaction, test (as-ko′lēz) [Maurizio *Ascoli*, Italian pathologist, 1876–1958]. Miostagmin reaction.

Ascoli's test, treatment (as-ko′lēz) [Alberto *Ascoli*, Italian serologist, 1877–1957]. See under *test* (def. 1) and under *treatment*.

Ascomycetes (as″ko-mi-se′tēz) [Gr. *askos* bag + *mykēs* fungus]. A group of fungi which form ascospores. It includes the yeasts, Penicillium, Aspergillus, Trichophyton, and Achorion.

ascorbate (as′kor-bāt). A compound or derivative of ascorbic acid.

ascorbemia (as″kor-be′me-ah). The presence of ascorbic acid in the blood.

ascorburia (as-kor-bu′re-ah). The presence of ascorbic acid in the urine.

ascospore (as′ko-spōr) [Gr. *askos* bag + *sporos* seed]. One of a set of spores contained in a special spore case, or ascus.

ascotrophosome (as″ko-trof′o-sōm). A trophosome in the body of a bacterium.

ascus (as′kus), pl. *as′ci* [Gr. *askos* a bag]. The sporangium or spore case of certain lichens and fungi, consisting of a single terminal cell.

ase (ās). An enzyme; used as a word termination in forming names of enzymes, ordinarily affixed to a stem indicating the general nature of the substrate, the actual name of the substrate, the type of reaction catalyzed, or a combination of these factors.

asecretory (ah-se′kre-to″re). Without secretion.

Aselli's glands, pancreas (ah-sel′ēz) [Gasparo *Aselli*, Italian anatomist, 1581–1626]. See under *pancreas*.

asemasia (as″e-ma′ze-ah) [*a* neg. + Gr. *sēmasia* the giving of a signal]. Lack or loss of the power of communication by words or by signals.

asemia (ah-se′me-ah) [*a* neg. + Gr. *sēma* sign + *-ia*]. Inability to employ or to understand either speech or signs, due to a central lesion. **a. graph′ica,** inability either to write or to understand writing, due to a central lesion. **a. mim'ica,** inability to understand or to perform any action expressive of thought or emotion. **a. verba'lis,** inability to make use of or to understand words.

asepsis (ah-sep'sis) [*a* neg. + Gr. *sēpesthai* to decay]. 1. Absence of septic matter, or freedom from infection. 2. The prevention of the access of microorganisms. **integral a.,** an aseptic technique in which not only the instruments, the hands of the surgeon, etc., are sterile but also the entire operating room and the air are completely free of living germs.

aseptic (ah-sep'tik) [*a* neg. + Gr. *sēpsis* decay]. Not septic; free from septic material. **a.-antiseptic,** both aseptic and antiseptic.

asepticism (ah-sep'tĭ-sizm). The principles and practice of aseptic surgery.

asepticize (ah-sep'tĭ-sīz). To render aseptic; to free from pathogenic materials.

aseptule (ah-sep'tūl). A capsule that will preserve its contents from decomposition.

asequence (ah-se'kwens). Lack of the normal sequence between the auricular and ventricular contractions of the heart.

asetake (as"e-tak'e). A poisonous Japanese fungus of the genus *Hebeloma*.

asexual (a-seks'u-al). Having no sex; not sexual; not pertaining to sex.

asexuality (a"seks-u-al'ĭ-te). The state of being asexual; absence of sexual interests.

asexualization (a-seks"u-al-ĭ-za'shun). Sterilization of an individual, as by castration or vasectomy.

ASF. A synthetic resin composed of aniline, formaldehyde, and sulfur: used for mounting microscopic objects.

As. H. Abbreviation for *hypermetropic astigmatism*.

ash. 1. The incombustible residue remaining after any process of incineration. 2. Any tree or species of the genus *Fraxinus*. *F. ornus* and others afford manna. The bark of many species is astringent and antiperiodic. **bone a.,** tribasic calcium phosphate.

Ashby's agar (ash'bēz) [Sir Eric *Ashby*, English botanist, born 1904]. See under *agar*.

Ashhurst's splint (ash'hursts) [John *Ashhurst*, Philadelphia surgeon, 1839–1900]. See under *splint*.

asialia (ah"si-a'le-ah) [*a* neg. + Gr. *sialon* spittle]. Absence or deficiency of the secretion of the saliva; aptyalism.

asiderosis (ah"sid-er-o'sis) [*a* neg. + Gr. *sidēros* iron]. Abnormal decrease of the iron reserve of the body.

Asimina (ah-sim'ĭ-nah) [L., from its Algonkian name]. A genus of North American trees and shrubs. *A. triloba*, the papaw or pawpaw, has an edible fruit and medicinal properties.

asiminine (ah-sim'ĭ-nin). A narcotic alkaloid from the seeds of *Asimina triloba*.

-asis. Word termination denoting state or condition. See *-sis*.

asitia (ah-sish'e-ah) [*a* neg. + Gr. *sitos* food]. A loathing for food.

asjike (ahs-ji'ke). Beriberi.

Asklepios (as-klep'e-os) [Gr. *Asklēpios* son of Apollo and Coronis, tutelary god of medicine]. See *Æsculapius*.

As. M. Abbreviation for *myopic astigmatism*.

A.S.O. Abbreviation for *American Society of Orthodontists*.

As_2O_3. Arsenic trioxide.

asoma (a-so'mah), pl. *aso'mata* [*a* neg. + Gr. *sōma* body]. A fetal monster with an imperfect head and the merest rudiments of a trunk.

asomatophyte (a-so'mah-to-fīt") [*a* neg. + Gr. *sōma* body + *phyton* plant]. A plant in which there is no distinction between body and reproductive cells. Bacteria belong to this class.

asomnia (a-som'ne-ah). Insomnia.

Asopia (ah-so'pe-ah). A genus of pyralid moths. *A. farinalis*, the meal moth, acts as the intermediate host of *Hymenolepis diminuta*.

aspalasoma (as"pal-ah-so'mah) [Gr. *aspalax* the mole + *sōma* body]. A variety of monster fetus with lateral or median abdominal eventration and with other deformities.

asparaginase (as-par'ah-jin-ās"). An enzyme which catalyzes the hydrolysis of asparagin to aspartic acid and ammonia.

Asparagus (ah-spar'ah-gus) [L.; Gr. *asparagos*]. A genus of liliaceous plants. The root of *A. officinalis* is a mild diuretic.

aspartase (as'par-tās). An enzyme that splits aspartic acid into fumaric acid and ammonia.

asparthione (as-par'thi-ōn"). A tripeptide analogous to glutathione but containing aspartic acid in place of glutamic acid.

aspecific (ah"spe-sif'ik). Nonspecific; not caused by a specific organism.

aspect (as'pekt) [L. *aspectus*, from *aspicere* to look toward]. 1. That part of a surface viewed from any particular direction. 2. The look or appearance. **dorsal a.,** the surface of a body viewed from the back or from above. **ventral a.,** the surface of a body viewed from the front or from below.

aspergillar (as"per-jil'ar). Pertaining to or caused by Aspergillus.

aspergilli (as"per-jil'i). Plural of *aspergillus*.

aspergillin (as"per-jil'in). A black antibiotic substance, from the spore of various species of *Aspergillus;* called also *vegetable hematin*.

aspergillomycosis (as"per-jil"o-mi-ko'sis). Aspergillosis.

aspergillosis (as"per-jil-o'sis). A diseased condition caused by species of *Aspergillus* and marked by inflammatory granulomatous lesions in the skin, ear, orbit, nasal sinuses, lungs and sometimes in the bones and meninges. **aural a.** See *otomycosis*. **pulmonary a.,** infection of the lungs with *Aspergillus*, producing symptoms and lesions resembling those of pulmonary tuberculosis.

Aspergillus (as"per-jil'us) [L. *aspergere* to scatter]. A genus of ascomycetous fungi. It includes several of the common molds and some that are pathogenic. It is characterized by rounded conidiospores thickly set with chains of black conidia. **A. auricula'ris,** a mold found in the cerumen of the ear: pathogenic. **A. bar'bae** has been found in mycosis of the head. **A. bouffar'di** has been found in black mycetoma. **A. clava'tus,** a species occurring in soils, manure: its cultures produce an antibacterial substance clavacin. **A. concen'tricus,** a species formerly considered to be the cause of tinea imbricata. **A. fla'vus,** a mold found on corn and grain and believed to be concerned in the causation of blind staggers in horses. **A. fumiga'tus,** a fungus growing in soils and manure. It has been found in the ear, nose, and lungs. Its cultures produce an antibacterial substance fumigacin. **A. gigan'teus,** a species from which gigantic acid is obtained. **A. glau'cus,** a bluish mold found on dried fruit, occurring also in the ear. **A. gliocla'dium,** a species which furnishes the antibiotic gliotoxin. **A. mucoroi'des,** a species found in tuberculous or gangrenous lung tissue. **A. nid'ulans,** a species causing white mycetoma. **A. ni'ger,** a species found in the external ear causing otomycosis. It also causes diseases in animals that consume grain infected with it. **A. ochra'ceus,** the species which ferments the coffee berry and produces the characteristic and desirable odor. **A.**

Aspergillus (de Rivas).

pic′tor, a species found in the white patches of pinta. **A. re′pens,** a species found in the external auditory canal, where it may produce a false membrane.

aspergillus (as″per-jil′us), pl. *aspergil′li.* An individual of the genus Aspergillus.

aspermatism (ah-sper′mah-tizm). Aspermia.

aspermatogenesis (ah-sper″mah-to-jen′e-sis). Absence of development of spermatozoa.

aspermia (ah-sper′me-ah) [*a* neg. + Gr. *sperma* seed + *-ia*]. Failure of formation or emission of semen.

aspersion (as-per′shun) [L. *aspersio*]. The act of sprinkling the body with a therapeutic agent.

asphalgesia (as″fal-je′ze-ah) [Gr. *asphe-* self + *algos* pain]. A sensation of burning felt on touching certain articles: occurring during hypnosis.

aspherinia (as″fĕ-rin′e-ah) [*a* neg. + Gr. *sphaira* ball]. Aglobulia.

asphyctic (as-fik′tik). Pertaining to, or affected with, asphyxia.

asphyctous (as-fik′tus). Asphyctic.

asphygmia (as-fig′me-ah). Temporary disappearance of the pulse.

asphyxia (as-fik′se-ah) [*a* neg. + Gr. *sphyxis* pulse]. Suffocation; also suspended animation from suffocation. It is a condition in which there is anoxia and increased carbon dioxide tension in the blood and tissues. It is attended by a feeling of suffocation and by coma. **blue a.,** a. livida. **a. carbon′ica,** suffocation from the inhalation of coal gas, water gas, or carbon monoxide. **a. cyanot′ica,** a. livida. **fetal a.,** asphyxia of the fetus in utero from interference with the circulation as by premature placental separation. **a. liv′ida,** asphyxia in which the skin is cyanotic from the lack of oxygen in the blood. **local a.** See *Raynaud's disease,* under *disease.* **a. neonato′rum,** imperfect breathing in newborn infants. **a. pal′lida,** asphyxia attended with paleness of the skin, weak pulse, and abolition of the reflexes. **a. reticula′ris,** livedo reticularis. **secondary a.,** asphyxia recurring after apparent recovery from suffocation. **traumatic a.,** asphyxia occurring as a result of sudden or severe compression of the thorax or upper abdomen, or both. **white a.,** a. pallida.

asphyxial (as-fik′se-al). Characterized by or pertaining to asphyxia.

asphyxiant (as-fik′se-ant). Producing asphyxia.

asphyxiate (as-fik′se-āt). To put into a state of more or less complete asphyxia.

asphyxiation (as-fik″se-a′shun). Suffocation.

Aspidium (as-pid′e-um) [L.; Gr. *aspidion* little shield]. A genus of ferns called shield ferns.

aspidium (as-pid′e-um). The rhizome and stipes of *Dryopteris filix-mas,* yielding not less than 1.5 per cent of crude filicin.

aspirate (as′pĭ-rāt). 1. To treat by aspiration. 2. The substance or material obtained by aspiration. 3. A consonantal sound in which some part of the respiratory tract is constricted, the nasal cavity shut off, and the breath makes a whistling noise.

aspiration (as″pĭ-ra′shun) [L. *ad* to + *spirare* to breathe]. 1. The act of breathing or drawing in. 2. The removal of fluids or gases from a cavity by means of the aspirator.

aspirator (as′pĭ-ra″tor). An apparatus used for removing by suction the fluids or gases from a cavity. **Dieulafoy's a.,** an apparatus consisting of a glass cylinder with a piston, and having two openings, one for a trocar and cannula, the other for a discharge tube.

aspirin (as′pĭ-rin). Acetylsalicylic acid.

asplenia (ah-sple′ne-ah). Absence of the spleen.

asplenic (ah-splen′ik). Pertaining to asplenia; caused by absence of the spleen.

asporogenic (as″po-ro-jen′ik) [*a* neg. + *sporogenic*]. Not producing spores; not reproduced by spores.

asporogenous (as″po-roj′e-nus). Asporogenic.

asporous (ah-spo′rus) [*a* neg. + Gr. *sporos* seed]. Having no true spores: applied to microorganisms.

asporulate (ah-spor′u-lāt). Not producing spores.

A.S.S. Abbreviation for *anterior superior spine.*

assanation (as″ah-na′shun) [L. *ad* to + *sanus* sound]. Sanitation; the improvement of sanitary conditions.

assay (ah-sa′). Determination of the purity of a substance or the amount of any particular constituent of a mixture. **biological a.,** bio-assay. **microbiological a.,** assay by the use of microorganisms.

Assézat's triangle (ah-se-zahz′) [Jules *Assézat,* French anthropologist, 1832–1876]. See under *triangle.*

assident (as′ĭ-dent). Generally but not always accompanying a disease.

assimilable (ah-sim′ĭ-lah-bl). Susceptible of being assimilated.

assimilation (ah-sim″ĭ-la′shun) [L. *assimilatio,* from *ad* to + *similare* to make like]. The transformation of food into living tissue; constructive metabolism. **mental a.,** the reception and correct appreciation of sensory impressions. **primary a.,** chylification. **secondary a.,** the preparation of food elements for normal assimilation by the hematopoietic apparatus.

Assmann's focus, infiltrate [Herbert *Assmann,* German internist, 1882–1950]. See under *focus.*

associable (ah-so′se-ah-bl″). Easily affected by sympathy with other parts.

association (ah-so″se-a′shun) [L. *associatio,* from *ad* to + *socius* a fellow]. The coordination of the functions of similar parts. In neurology, correlation involving a high degree of modificability and also consciousness. See *association center,* under *center.* **clang a.,** a psychic association resulting from sounds. **controlled a's,** ideas called up into the consciousness in response to words spoken by the examiner. **dream a's,** emotions or thoughts associated with previous dreams, as developed by the patient in psychoanalysis. **free a.,** a psychoanalytical method in which the patient is allowed to describe the association of thoughts and emotions as they arise spontaneously during the analysis. **a. of ideas,** the mental operation by which a mental impression calls up the memory of other impressions that at some earlier time have been associated with the former.

assonance (as′o-nans). A morbid tendency to alliteration in speaking.

assuetude (as′we-tūd). The state of being habituated to disturbing influences.

assurin (as′u-rin). A diaminodiphosphatide $C_{46}H_{94}N_2P_2O_9$, said to occur in the brain substance.

Ast. Abbreviation for *astigmatism.*

astacene (as′tah-sēn). Astacin.

astacin (as′tah-sin). A carotenoid, $C_{40}H_{48}O_4$, obtained from the shells of various crustaceans.

astasia (as-ta′zhe-ah) [*a* neg. + Gr. *stasis* stand]. Motor incoordination with inability to stand. **a.-abasia,** inability to stand or to walk although the legs are otherwise under control.

astatic (as-tat′ik). Pertaining to astasia.

astatine (as′tah-tin) [Gr. *astatos* unstable]. The radioactive element of atomic number 85, atomic weight 210, symbol At. It is prepared by alpha particle bombardment of bismuth on the cyclotron. It has a half-life of 75 hours and may be of use in the treatment of hyperthyroidism.

astaxanthin (as″tah-zan′thin). A red carotenoid pigment, $C_{40}H_{52}O_4$, constituent of the green chromoprotein from the eggs of crayfish.

asteatodes (as″te-ah-to′dēz). Asteatosis.

asteatosis (as″te-ah-to′sis) [*a* neg. + Gr. *stear* tallow + *-osis*]. Any disease condition characterized by scantiness or absence of the sebaceous secretion. **a. cu′tis,** a dry, scaly, or fissured state of the skin, attended with a deficient secretion of sebaceous matter.

aster (as'ter) [L.; Gr. *astēr* star]. The group of radiations which extend from the centrosphere of a cell in mitosis. Called also *astrosphere*. **sperm a.,** the centriole, with astral rays, that precedes the male pronucleus during fertilization.

astereocognosy (ah-ste″re-o-kog'nŏ-se). Astereognosis.

astereognosis (ah-ste″re-og-no'sis) [*a* neg. + Gr. *stereos* solid + *gnōsis* recognition]. Loss of power to recognize objects or to appreciate their form by touching or feeling them.

asteriasterol (as-te″re-as'ter-ol). A sterol obtained from the starfish, *Asterias forbesi*.

asterion (as-te're-on), pl. *aste'ria* [Gr. "starred"]. The point on the surface of the skull where the lambdoid, parietomastoid and occipitomastoid sutures meet.

Asterionella (as-te″re-o-nel'ah). A genus of diatoms which sometimes impart an aromatic odor to a water supply.

asterixis (as″ter-ik'sis) [*a* neg. + Gr. *stērixis* a fixed position]. A motor disturbance marked by intermittent lapse of an assumed posture, as a result of intermittency of the sustained contraction of groups of muscles, a characteristic of hepatic coma but observed also in numerous other conditions.

asternal (a-ster'nal). 1. Not joined to the sternum. 2. Pertaining to asternia; lacking a sternum.

asternia (ah-ster'ne-ah) [*a* neg. + Gr. *sternon* sternum + *-ia*]. A developmental anomaly characterized by absence of the sternum.

Asterococcus (as″ter-o-kok'us). A genus of bacteria resembling filtrable viruses, which cause bovine pleuropneumonia and other diseases. **A. ca'nis,** a microorganism found in a form of dog distemper. **A. mycoi'des,** the minute organism which causes pleuropneumonia of cattle. It can be grown in various culture mediums and the bacteria-free filtrate will reproduce the disease.

asteroid (as'ter-oid) [Gr. *astēr* star + *eidos* form]. Star-shaped; resembling the aster.

asterol (as'ter-ol). Trade mark for preparations of diamthazole.

asterubin (as″te-roo'bin). A basic substance, $NH{:}C(NH.CH_2.SO_2OH).N(CH_3)_2$, which has been isolated from the starfish.

Asth. Abbreviation for *asthenopia*.

asthenia (as-the'ne-ah) [Gr. *asthenēs* without strength + *-ia*]. Lack or loss of strength and energy; weakness. **a. gra'vis hypophyseogen'ea,** a pituitary cachexia marked by emaciation, anorexia, constipation, amenorrhea, hypothermia, hypotonia, and hypoglycemia. **myalgic a.,** a condition in which the general symptoms are a sensation of general fatigue and muscular pains. **neurocirculatory a.,** a symptom-complex characterized by the occurrence of breathlessness, giddiness, a sense of fatigue, pain in the chest in the region of the precordium, and palpitation. It occurs chiefly in soldiers in active war service, though it is seen in civilians also. Called also *soldier's heart, irritable heart, effort syndrome, cardiac neurosis, DaCosta's syndrome, anxiety neurosis, neurasthenia,* and *disordered action of the heart* (D. A. H.). **periodic a.,** a condition marked by periodically returning attacks of marked asthenia. **a. pigmento'sa,** Addison's disease. **tropical anhidrotic a.,** a condition resulting from generalized, sometimes almost complete, anhidrosis in conditions of high temperature, characterized by a tendency to overfatigability, irritability, anorexia, inability to concentrate, and drowsiness, with headache and vertigo. **a. universa'lis,** constitutional visceroptosis with its attendant neurasthenic tendency, vasomotor weakness, and gastrointestinal atony (Stiller's theory).

asthenic (as-then'ik). Pertaining to or characterized by asthenia.

asthenobiosis (as-the″no-bi-o'sis) [*asthenia* + Gr. *bios* life + *-osis*]. A condition of reduced biologic activity resembling hibernation or estivation but not directly related to or dependent on temperature or humidity.

asthenocoria (as-the″no-ko're-ah) [*asthenia* + Gr. *korē* pupil + *-ia*]. A condition in which the pupillary light reflex is sluggish: seen in hypoadrenia.

asthenometer (as″thĕ-nom'e-ter) [*asthenia* + Gr. *metron* measure]. An instrument for measuring the degree of muscular asthenia or of asthenopia.

asthenope (as'then-ōp). A person affected with asthenopia.

asthenophobia (as″thĕ-no-fo'be-ah) [*asthenia* + *phobia*]. Morbid fear of being weak.

asthenopia (as″thĕ-no'pe-ah) [*asthenia* + Gr. *ōpē* sight + *-ia*]. Weakness or speedy tiring of the visual organs, attended by pain in the eyes, headache, dimness of vision, etc. **accommodative a.,** asthenopia due to strain of the ciliary muscle. **muscular a.,** that which is due to weakness of the external ocular muscles. **nervous a.,** asthenopia occurring as one of the symptoms of neurosis and marked by fatigue and contraction of the visual field: called also *retinal a.* and *asthenia of the retina*. **retinal a.,** that which is due to retinal disease. **tarsal a.,** asthenopia due to irregular astigmatism produced by the pressure of the lids on the cornea.

asthenopic (as″thĕ-nop'ik). Characterized by asthenopia.

asthenospermia (as″thĕ-no-sper'me-ah) [*asthenia* + Gr. *sperma* seed + *-ia*]. Reduction in the vitality of spermatozoa.

asthenoxia (as″then-ok'se-ah) [*asthenia* + *oxygen*]. Lack of power to oxidize waste products.

asthma (az'mah) [Gr. *asthma* panting]. A disease marked by recurrent attacks of paroxysmal dyspnea, with wheezing, cough, and a sense of constriction, due to spasmodic contraction of the bronchi. The paroxysms last from a few minutes to several days, and they may result from direct irritation of the bronchial mucous membrane or from reflex irritation. Many cases of asthma are allergic manifestations in sensitized persons. **abdominal a.,** asthma due to upward pressure on the diaphragm. **allergic a.,** bronchial asthma due to allergy. **alveolar a.,** that which is characterized by dilatation of the alveoli of the lungs. **amygdaline a.,** reflex asthma caused by a disease of the tonsils. **atopic a.,** allergic asthma. **bacterial a.,** asthma due to bacterial infection. **bronchial a.,** a recurring paroxysmal dyspnea, particularly evident in the expiratory phase, due to an allergic reaction in the bronchioles from the absorption of some substance to which the patient is hypersensitive. **bronchitic a.,** asthmatic disorder accompanying catarrhal bronchitis. **cardiac a.,** paroxysmal dyspnea which occurs in association with heart disease, such as left ventricular failure. **cat a.,** asthma brought on by cat dander. **catarrhal a.,** bronchitic a. **Cheyne-Stokes a.,** cardiac asthma. **a. convulsi'vum,** bronchial a. **cotton-dust a.,** attacks of cough and breathlessness due to inhalation of cotton dust by workers in the cotton industry. **cutaneous a.,** reflex asthma caused by some irritation of the skin. **dust a.,** a form of asthma caused by the dust encountered in houses, in the streets, or in trades. **a. dyspep'ticum,** reflex asthma dependent upon a dyspeptic disorder. **Elsner's a.,** angina pectoris. **emphysematous a.,** emphysema of the lungs attended with asthmatic paroxysms. **essential a.,** nervous asthma, true asthma, that due to nervous impulses solely, and not accompanied by any structural change in the bronchi. **extrinsic a.,** asthma caused by some factor in the environment. **food a.,** asthma brought on by ingestion of certain foods. **gastric a.,** asthma which is a symptom of some gastric disease. **grinders' a.,** an interstitial pneumonia due to the inhalation of fine particles set free in grinding steel, etc. **hay a.,** hay fever. **Heberden's a.,** angina pectoris. **horse a.,** a form of allergic asthma in which the attacks are brought on by the presence of horses or of horse products. **humid a.,** asthma with profuse expectoration. **infective a.,** asthma due to bacterial infection. **intrinsic a.,** asthma caused by some condition of the body. **Kopp's a.,** laryngismus stridulus. **Millar's a.,** laryngismus stridulus. **millers' a.,** a condition of the lungs found in millers; caused by the inhalation of flour. **miners' a.,** anthracosis. **nasal a.,** asthma caused by a disease of the nose. **nervous a.,** essential asthma. **pollen a.,** hay fever. **Pott's a.,** thymic asthma. **potters' a.,** pneumoconiosis. **reflex a.,** asthma due to some reflex action. **renal a.,** reflex asthma due to disease of the kidney. **sexual a.,** asthma due to sexual disturbance, such as excessive venery or genito-urinary catarrh. **spasmodic a.,** bronchial a. **steam-fitters' a.,** asbestosis. **stone a.,** pressure and pain in the chest due to the presence of a calculus in the bronchi. **stripper's a.,** byssinosis. **symptomatic a.,** asthma that is secondary to some other physical condition. **thymic a.,** an alleged condition occurring usually in children, but occasionally in adults, marked by enlargement of the thymus, paroxysmal attacks of asthma, and a tendency to sudden death. **true a.,** essential asthma. **Wichmann's a.,** laryngismus stridulus.

asthmatic (az-mat′ik) [L. *asthmaticus*]. Pertaining to, or affected with, asthma.

asthmogenic (az″mo-jen′ik). Causing asthma.

astigmagraph (ah-stig′mah-graf). An instrument for showing the astigmatism of the eye.

astigmatic (as″tig-mat′ik). Pertaining to, or affected with, astigmatism.

astigmatism (ah-stig′mah-tizm) [*a* neg. + Gr. *stigma* point]. Defective curvature of the refractive surfaces of the eye as a result of which a ray of light is not sharply focused on the retina but is spread over a more or less diffuse area. This results from the radius of curvature in one plane being longer or shorter than that of the radius at right angles to it (Airy, 1827). **acquired a.,** that due to some disease or injury of the eye. **a. against the rule,** that in which the meridian along which the greatest refraction takes place is horizontal. **compound a.,** that which is complicated with hypermetropia or with myopia in all meridians. **congenital a.,** that which exists at birth. **corneal a.,** that due to irregularity in the curvature or refracting power of the cornea. **direct a.** See *a. with the rule*. **hypermetropic a., hyperopic a.,** that which complicates hyperopia. **hyperopic a., compound,** astigmatism in which all meridians are hyperopic, the focus of each principal meridian being back of the retina: horizontal lines are usually more distinct. **hyperopic a., simple,** astigmatism in which one meridian, usually the vertical, is emmetropic and the horizontal meridian is hyperopic. The focus of the vertical meridian is not in the retina; that of the horizontal is behind the retina: horizontal lines appear distinct. **inverse a.** See *a. against the rule*. **irregular a.,** astigmatism in which the curvature in different parts of the same meridian of the eye varies or in which successive meridians differ irregularly in refraction, the image produced being an irregular area. **lenticular a.,** that which is due to some imperfection of the lens. **mixed a.,** that in which one principal meridian is myopic and the other hypermetropic. **myopic a.,** that which complicates myopia. **myopic a., compound,** astigmatism in which all meridians are myopic, both principal meridians having their foci in front of the retina; vertical lines are usually more distinct. **myopic a., simple,** astigmatism in which the focus of one meridian is situated on the retina, while that of the other lies in front of the retina: vertical lines appear distinct. **oblique a.,** astigmatism in which the direction of the principal meridians approaches 45° and 135°. **physiological a.,** the slight astigmatism possessed by nearly all eyes and causing the twinkling sensation when distant points of light are viewed. **regular a.,** astigmatism in which the refractive power of the eye shows a uniform increase or decrease from one meridian to the other, being practically constant in each meridian: the image produced is regular in shape, either a line, an oval, or a circle. **a. with the rule,** that wherein the meridian in which the greatest refraction takes place is vertical or nearly so.

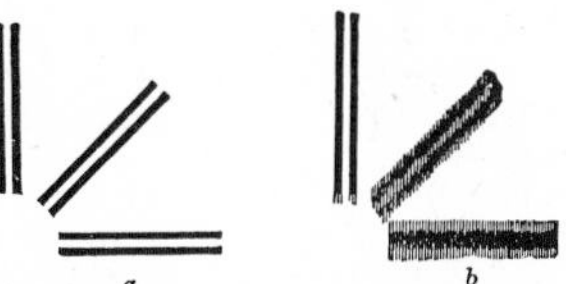

Astigmatism: Showing the appearance of lines as seen by *a*, the normal eye, and *b*, the astigmatic eye (Jackson).

astigmatometer (as″tig-mah-tom′e-ter) [*astigmatism* + Gr. *metron* measure]. An instrument used in measuring astigmatism.

astigmatoscope (as″tig-mat′o-skōp) [*astigmatism* + Gr. *skopein* to inspect]. An instrument for discovering and measuring astigmatism.

astigmatoscopy (ah-stig″mah-tos′ko-pe). The use of the astigmatoscope.

astigmia (as-tig′me-ah). Astigmatism.

astigmic (as-tig′mik). Astigmatic.

astigmometer (as″tig-mom′e-ter). Astigmatometer.

astigmometry (as″tig-mom′e-tre) [*astigmatism* + Gr. *metron* measure]. The measurement of astigmatism, the use of the astigmatometer.

astigmoscope (as-tig′mo-skōp). Astigmatoscope.

astomatous (as-tom′ah-tus) [*a* neg. + Gr. *stoma* mouth]. Having no mouth.

astomia (ah-sto′me-ah) [*a* neg. + Gr. *stoma* mouth]. A developmental defect in which the mouth opening is absent.

astomus (ah-sto′mus). A malformed fetus in which the mouth opening is absent.

astragalar (as-trag′ah-lar). Pertaining to the astragalus.

astragalectomy (as″trag-ah-lek′to-me) [*astragalus* + Gr. *ektomē* excision]. Excision of the astragalus.

astragalocalcanean (as-trag″ah-lo-kal-ka′ne-an). Pertaining to the astragalus and the calcaneus.

astragalocrural (as-trag″ah-lo-kroo′ral). Relating to the astragalus and the leg.

astragaloscaphoid (as-trag″ah-lo-skaf′oid). Pertaining to the astragalus and the scaphoid bone.

astragalotibial (as-trag″ah-lo-tib′e-al). Pertaining to the astragalus and the tibia.

Astragalus (as-trag′ah-lus). A genus of leguminous plants or many species. *A. gummifer* and other oriental species afford tragacanth: others are poisonous. *A. mollissimus*, of the United States (one of the plants called loco), is poisonous, and its active principle is mydriatic.

astragalus (as-trag′ah-lus) [L.; Gr. *astragalos* ball of the ankle joint or dice]. The talus (def. 1).

astral (as′tral). Of, or relating to, an aster.

astraphobia (as″tra-fo′be-ah). 1. Astrophobia. 2. Astrapophobia.

astrapophobia (as″trah-po-fo′be-ah) [Gr. *astrapē* lightning + *phobia*]. Morbid fear of lightning.

astriction (as-trik′shun) [L. *astringere* to constrict]. 1. The action of an astringent. 2. Constipation.

astringe (as-trinj′). To act as an astringent.

astringent (as-trin′jent) [L. *astringens*, from *ad* to + *stringere* to bind]. 1. Causing contraction and arresting discharges. 2. An agent which has an astringent action.

astro- (as′tro) [Gr. *astron* star]. A combining form indicating some relation to a star, as star-shaped.

astroblast (as′tro-blast) [*astro-* + Gr. *blastos* germ.] A cell that develops into an astrocyte.

astroblastoma (as″tro-blas-to′mah). A tumor made up of astroblasts.

astrocele (as′tro-sēl). Astrocoele.

astrocinetic (as″tro-si-net′ik). Astrokinetic.

astrocoele (as′tro-sēl) [*astro-* + Gr. *koilos* hollow]. The clear space within the astrosphere in which the centrosome lies.

astrocyte (as′tro-sīt) [*astro-* + Gr. *kytos* hollow vessel]. A star-shaped cell; especially such a cell of the neuroglia. **fibrillary a.,** fibrous a. **fibrous a.,** an adult astrocyte of the neuroglia, with long, relatively smooth, little-branched expansions, and with fibrillar structures embedded in the cytoplasm and the expansions. **plasmatofibrous a.,** an adult astrocyte of the neuroglia with processes of both the protoplasmic and the fibrous type. **protoplasmic a.,** an adult astrocyte of the neuroglia, with a large nucleus, abundant granular cytoplasm, and numerous, rather thick plasmatic expansions.

astrocytoma (as″tro-si-to′mah). A tumor composed of astrocytes; a typical adult glioma. **a. fibrilla′re,** astrocytoma composed of fibrillary astrocytes. **gemistocytic a.,** a. protoplasmaticum. **pilocytic a.,** a. fibrillare. **a. protoplasmat′icum,** one composed of protoplasmic astrocytes.

astroglia (as-trog′le-ah) [*astro-* + *neuroglia*]. Neuroglia tissue composed of astrocytes. Called also *macroglia.*

astroid (as′troid) [*astro-* + Gr. *eidos* form]. 1. Star-shaped. 2. A structure of the neuroglia formed by a felted mass of fibers.

astrokinetic (as″tro-ki-net′ik) [*astro-* + Gr. *kinēsis* motion]. Pertaining to the movements of the centrosome.

astroma (as-tro′mah). Astrocytoma.

astronaut (as′tro-naut″) [*astro-* + Gr. *nautēs* sailor, from *naus* ship]. A traveler in outer space; the occupant of a manned space rocket.

astrophobia (as″tro-fo′be-ah) [*astro-* + *phobia*]. Fear of the stars and celestial space.

astrophorous (as-trof′o-rus) [*astro-* + Gr. *phoros* bearing]. Having star-shaped processes.

astrosphere (as′tro-sfēr) [*astro-* + Gr. *sphaira* sphere]. 1. The central mass of an aster, exclusive of the rays. 2. Aster.

astrostatic (as-tro-stat′ik) [*astro-* + Gr. *statikos* standing]. Pertaining to the centrosome in its resting condition.

astyclinic (as″te-klin′ik) [Gr. *asty* city + *klinē* bed]. A city or municipal hospital, dispensary, or clinic.

asuerotherapy (as″oo-ār′o-ther″ah-pe). A system of healing exploited in 1929 by Fernando Asuero, a Spanish physician, and consisting of cauterization of the sphenopalatine ganglion combined with suggestion.

asulfurosis (ah-sul-fu-ro′sis). A condition due to lack of sulfur in the body.

asuprarenalism (ah″su-prah-re′nal-izm). Asurrenalism.

asurrenalism (ah-sur-re′nal-izm). Absence or deficiency of adrenal function.

asyllabia (ah″sil-la′be-ah). A condition in which letters are recognized by the patient, but he is unable to form them into syllables.

asylum (ah-si′lum) [L.]. A place of refuge and shelter, as an institution of the past for the support and care of helpless and deprived individuals, such as the mentally deficient, emotionally disturbed, or the blind.

asymbolia (ah-sim-bo′le-ah) [*a* neg. + Gr. *symbolon* symbol + *-ia*]. Loss of power to comprehend symbolic things, as words, figures, gestures, signs, etc. (Wernicke). **pain a.,** loss of power to make or to understand pain symbolism.

asymboly (ah-sim′bo-le). Asymbolia.

asymmetrical (a″sim-met′re-kal). Not symmetrical; pertaining to asymmetry.

asymmetry (a-sim′e-tre) [*a* neg. + Gr. *symmetria* symmetry]. Lack or absence of symmetry; dissimilarity in corresponding parts or organs on opposite sides of the body which are normally alike. In chemistry, lack of symmetry in the special arrangements of the atoms and radicals within the molecule. **chromatic a.,** difference in color in the irides of the two eyes. **encephalic a.,** a condition in which the two sides of the brain are not the same size.

asymphytous (ah-sim′fe-tus). Separate or distinct; not grown together.

asymptomatic (ah″simp-to-mat′ik). Showing or causing no symptoms.

asynchronism (ah-sin′kro-nizm) [*a* neg. + *synchronism*]. The occurrence at distinct times of events normally synchronous; disturbance of coordination.

asynchrony (ah-sin′kro-ne). Asynchronism.

asynclitism (ah-sin′klĭ-tizm) [*a* neg. + *synclitism*]. Oblique presentation of the head in parturition. **anterior a.,** Nägele's obliquity. **posterior a.,** Litzmann's obliquity.

asyndesis (ah-sin′dĕ-sis) [*a* neg. + Gr. *syn* together + *desis* binding]. Disorder of the thinking process in which related elements of a thought cannot be welded together as a whole.

asynechia (ah″sin-e′ke-ah) [*a* neg. + Gr. *synecheia* continuity]. Absence of continuity of structure.

asynergia (ah″sin-er′je-ah). Asynergy.

asynergic (ah″sin-er′jik). Marked by asynergy.

asynergy (ah-sin′er-je) [*a* neg. + Gr. *synergia* cooperation]. Lack of coordination among parts or organs normally acting in harmony. In neurology, disturbance of that proper association in the contraction of muscles which assures that the different components of an act follow in proper sequence, at the proper moment, and are of the proper degree, so that the act is executed accurately. **appendicular a.,** asynergy confined to the extremities. **axial a.,** asynergy affecting the axial musculature. **axio-appendicular a.,** asynergy affecting both the trunk and extremities. **a. ma′jor,** marked incoordination as indicated by staggering gait. **a. mi′nor,** mild incoordination as indicated by pointing tests. **trunkal a.,** asynergy affecting the muscles of the trunk.

asynesia (ah″sĭ-ne′ze-ah) [Gr. "want of understanding"]. Dulness of intellect.

asynodia (ah″sĭ-no′de-ah) [*a* neg. + Gr. *synodia* a journeying together]. Sexual impotence.

asynovia (ah-sĭ-no′ve-ah). Deficiency of the synovial secretion.

asyntaxia (ah″sin-tak′se-ah) [Gr. "want of arrangement"]. Lack of proper and orderly embryonic development. **a. dorsa′lis,** failure of the neural groove to close in the developing embryo.

asyntrophy (ah-sin′tro-fe) [*a* neg. + *syn* together + trophē growth]. Lack of symmetry in development.

asystematic (ah″sis-te-mat′ik). 1. Without system, or orderly arrangement. 2. Not confined to a single system, as to one system of nerve fibers or to a particular organ system.

asystole (ah-sis′to-le) [*a* neg. + *systole*]. Imperfect or incomplete systole; inability of the heart to perform a complete systole.

asystolia (ah″sis-to′le-ah). Asystole.

asystolic (ah″sis-tol′ik). Characterized by asystole.

asystolizm (ah-sis′to-lizm). Asystole.

A. T. German abbreviation for *old tuberculin* (Alt Tuberculin).

A. T. 10. Dihydrotachysterol.

At. Chemical symbol for *astatine.*

atabrine (at′ah-brin). Trade mark for a preparation of quinacrine.

atactic (ah-tak′tik) [Gr. *ataktos* irregular]. Lacking coordination; irregular; pertaining to or characterized by ataxia.

atactiform (ah-tak′tĭ-form). Resembling ataxia.

atactilia (ah″tak-til′e-ah). Loss of tactile sensibility.

ataractic (at″ah-rak′tik) [Gr. *ataraktos* without disturbance; quiet]. 1. Pertaining to or capable of producing ataraxia. 2. An agent capable of inducing ataraxia.

ataralgesia (at″ar-al-je′ze-ah) [Gr. *ataraktos* without trouble + *-algesia*]. A method of combined sedation and analgesia designed to abolish the mental distress and pain attendant on surgical procedures, with the patient remaining conscious and alert.

atarax (at′ah-raks). Trade mark for preparations of hydroxyzine hydrochloride.

ataraxia (at″ah-rak′se-ah) [Gr. "impassiveness," "calmness"]. Perfect peace or calmness of mind: used especially to designate a detached serenity without depression of mental faculties or clouding of consciousness.

ataraxic (at″ah-rak′sik). Ataractic.

ataraxy (at″ah-rak′se). Ataraxia.

atavic (at′ah-vik). Atavistic.

atavism (at′ah-vizm) [L. *atavus* grandfather]. The apparent inheritance of a characteristic from remote rather than from immediate ancestors, due to a chance recombination of genes or to unusual environmental conditions favorable to their expression in the embryo. Called also *reversion.*

atavistic (at-ah-vis′tik). Characterized by atavism.

ataxaphasia (ah-tak″sah-fa′ze-ah). Ataxiaphasia.

ataxia (ah-tak′se-ah) [Gr. *ataxia* lack of order]. Failure of muscular coordination; irregularity of muscular action. **acute a.,** an ataxic condition due to a general myelitis characterized by minute foci throughout all the nerve centers from the pons downward. It follows measles, smallpox, and other infectious diseases. **alcoholic a.,** a condition resembling locomotor ataxia, due to chronic alcoholism. **autonomic a.,** defective coordination between the sympathetic and parasympathetic nervous systems. **Briquet's a.,** a hysteric condition with anesthesia of the skin and leg muscles. **Broca's a.,** hysteric a. **central a.,** ataxia due to lesion of the centers controlling coordination. **cerebellar a.,** ataxia due to disease of the cerebellum. **cerebral a.,** ataxia due to disease of the cerebrum. **a. cor′dis,** auricular fibrillation. **enzootic a.** See *swayback*, 2nd def. **family a.,** Friedreich's a. **Fergusson and Critchley's a.,** a hereditary ataxia resembling multiple sclerosis, appearing between the ages of 30 and 45. **Friedreich's a.,** Friedreich's disease: an inherited disease, usually beginning in childhood or youth, with sclerosis of the dorsal and lateral columns of the spinal cord. It is attended by ataxia, speech impairment, lateral curvature of the spinal column, and peculiar swaying and irregular movements, with paralysis of the muscles, especially of the lower extremities (Friedreich, 1863–76). **frontal a.,** disturbance of equilibrium occurring in tumor of the frontal lobe. **hereditary a.,** Friedreich's a. **hereditary cerebellar a.,** a disease of early adult life, due to atrophy of the cerebellum, and marked by ataxia, increased knee jerk, speech defects, and nystagmus. **hysteric a.,** hysteria simulating ataxia. **intrapsychic a.,** an apparent lack of unity of ideation and emotional reaction, as in a patient who weeps at a funny occurrence or laughs outright at the death of a close relative: called also *noothymopsychic a.* **kinetic a.,** motor a. **labyrinthic a.,** vestibular a. **Leyden's a.,** pseudotabes. **locomotor a.,** tabes dorsalis. **Marie's a.,** hereditary cerebellar a. **motor a.,** inability to control the coordinate movements of the muscles. **noothymopsychic a.,** intrapsychic a. **ocular a.,** nystagmus. **professional a.,** occupation neurosis. **Sanger-Brown's a.,** spinocerebellar a. **spinal a.,** that which is due to disease of the spinal cord. **spinocerebellar a.,** hereditary cerebellar ataxia marked by degeneration of the spinocerebellar tracts. **static a.,** lack of muscular coordination during states of rest. **superior a.,** that which affects principally the face and upper extremities. **a.-telangiectasia,** a heredofamilial, progressive ataxia, associated with oculocutaneous telangiectasia, sinopulmonary disease with frequent respiratory infections, and abnormal eye movements. **thermal a.,** a condition characterized by great and paradoxic fluctuations of the temperature of the body. **vasomotor a.,** paralysis or spasm of blood vessels due to some derangement of vasomotor nerves or centers. **vestibular a.,** incoordination due to vestibular disease.

ataxiadynamia (ah-tak″se-ah-di-na′me-ah). Ataxo-adynamia.

ataxiagram (ah-tak′se-ah-gram″) [*ataxia* + Gr. *gramma* a writing]. A tracing drawn by an ataxic patient; also the record made by an ataxiagraph.

ataxiagraph (ah-tak′se-ah-graf″) [*ataxia* + Gr. *graphein* to write]. An apparatus used in ascertaining the extent of ataxia by measuring the amount of swaying of the body when standing erect and with the eyes closed.

ataxiameter (ah-tak″se-am′e-ter) [*ataxia* + Gr. *metron* measure]. An apparatus for measuring ataxia.

ataxiamnesic (ah-tak″se-am-ne′sik). Characterized by both ataxia and amnesia.

ataxiaphasia (ah-tak″se-ah-fa′ze-ah) [*ataxia* + Gr. *aphasia*]. A condition characterized by inability to arrange words into sentences.

ataxic (ah-tak′sik). Atactic.

ataxiophemia (ah-tak″se-o-fe′me-ah). Ataxophemia.

ataxiophobia (ah-tak″se-o-fo′be-ah). Ataxophobia.

ataxo-adynamia (ah-tak″so-ad″e-na′me-ah). Ataxia associated with marked weakness.

ataxophemia (ah-tak″so-fe′me-ah) [Gr. *ataxia* disorder + *phēmē* speech]. Lack of coordination of the speech muscles.

ataxophobia (ah-tak″so-fo′be-ah) [Gr. *ataxia* disorder + *phobia*]. Morbid or insane dread of disorder.

ataxy (ah-tak′se). Ataxia.

-ate (āt). Word termination forming a participial noun, as the object of the process indicated by the root to which it is affixed: e.g., *hemolysate*, something hemolyzed; *homogenate*, something homogenized; *injectate*, something injected.

atelectasis (at″e-lek′tah-sis) [Gr. *atelēs* imperfect + *ektasis* expansion]. 1. Incomplete expansion of the lungs at birth. 2. Collapse of the adult lung. **compression a.,** collapse of lung tissue caused by pressure from without, as from exudates, tumors, and the like.

atelectatic (at″e-lek-tat′ik). Pertaining to or characterized by atelectasis.

ateleiosis (ah-te″le-o′sis) [*a* neg. + Gr. *teleios* complete]. Hypophyseal infantilism.

atelencephalia (ah-tel″en-se-fa′le-ah) [Gr. *ateleia* incompleteness + *enkephalos* brain + *-ia*]. A developmental anomaly characterized by imperfect development of the brain.

atelia (ah-te′le-ah) [Gr. *ateleia* incompleteness]. Imperfect or incomplete development.

ateliosis (ah-te″le-o′sis). Ateleiosis.

ateliotic (ah-te″le-ot′ik). Pertaining to or characterized by atelia.

atelo- (at′e-lo) [Gr. *atelēs* incomplete]. Combining form meaning imperfect or incomplete.

atelocardia (at″e-lo-kar′de-ah) [*atelo-* + Gr. *kardia* heart]. A developmental anomaly characterized by incomplete development of the heart.

atelocephalous (at″e-lo-sef′ah-lus) [*atelo-* + Gr. *kephalē* head]. Having an incomplete head.

atelocheilia (at″e-lo-ki′le-ah) [*atelo-* + Gr. *cheilos* lip + *-ia*]. A developmental anomaly characterized by incomplete development of a lip.

atelocheiria (at″e-lo-ki′re-ah) [*atelo-* + Gr. *cheir* hand + *-ia*]. A developmental anomaly characterized by incomplete development of the hand.

atelo-encephalia (at″e-lo-en″se-fa′le-ah). Atelencephalia.

ateloglossia (at″e-lo-glos′e-ah) [*atelo-* + Gr. *glōssa* tongue + *-ia*]. A developmental anomaly characterized by incomplete development of the tongue.

atelognathia (at″e-log-na′the-ah) [*atelo-* + Gr. *gnathos* jaw + *-ia*]. A developmental anomaly characterized by incomplete development of the jaw.

atelomyelia (at″e-lo-mi-e′le-ah) [*atelo-* + Gr. *myelos* marrow + *-ia*]. A developmental anomaly characterized by incomplete development of the spinal cord.

atelopodia (at″e-lo-po′de-ah) [*atelo-* + Gr. *pous* foot + *-ia*]. A developmental anomaly characterized by incomplete development of the foot.

ateloprosopia (at″e-lo-pro-so′pe-ah) [*atelo-* + Gr. *prosōpon* face + *-ia*]. A developmental anomaly characterized by incomplete development of the face.

atelorachidia (at″e-lo-rah-kid′e-ah) [*atelo-* + Gr. *rhachis* spine + *-ia*]. A developmental anomaly characterized by incomplete development of the spinal column.

Atelosaccharomyces (at″e-lo-sak″ah-ro-mi′sēz). A genus of yeastlike fungi, many species of which have been isolated from blastomycotic lesions of man.

atelostomia (at″e-lo-sto′me-ah) [*atelo-* + Gr. *stoma* mouth + *-ia*]. A developmental anomaly characterized by incomplete development of the mouth.

athalposis (ah″thal-po′sis) [*a* neg. + Gr. *thalpos* warmth + *-osis*]. Inability to perceive warmth.

athelia (ah-the′le-ah) [*a* neg. + Gr. *thēlē* nipple + *-ia*]. A developmental anomaly characterized by absence of the nipples.

Athenaeus (ath″e-ne′us) **of Attalia** (1st century A.D.). A celebrated physician, latterly of Rome, and founder of the Pneumatist school of medicine. Only fragments of his many writings remain.

Atherix (ath′e-riks). A genus of flies. *A. longipes* of Mexico and *A. variegata* of North America and Europe are annoying to man.

athermal (ah-ther′mal) [*a* neg. + Gr. *thermē* heat]. Not warm: said of springs the water of which is below 15°C.

athermancy (ah-ther′man-se). The state of being athermanous.

athermanous (ah-ther′mah-nus) [*a* neg. + Gr. *thermē* heat]. Absorbing heat rays and not permitting them to pass.

athermic (ah-ther′mik) [*a* neg. + Gr. *thermē* heat]. Without fever or rise of temperature.

athermosystaltic (ah-ther″mo-sis-tal′tik) [*a* neg. + Gr. *thermē* heat + Gr. *systaltikos* drawing together]. Not contracting under the action of cold or heat: said of striated muscle.

atherocheuma (ath″er-o-ku′mah) [Gr. *athērē* gruel + *cheuma* stream]. Atheromatous abscess.

atherogenesis (ath″er-o-jen′e-sis). The formation of atheromatous lesions in arterial walls.

atherogenic (ath″er-o-jen′ik). Conducive to or causing atherogenesis.

atheroma (ath″er-o′mah) [Gr. *athērē* gruel + *-oma*]. 1. A sebaceous cyst. 2. Arteriosclerosis with marked degenerative changes. **a. cu′tis,** sebaceous cyst.

atheromasia (ath″er-o-ma′ze-ah). Atheromatous degeneration.

atheromatosis (ath″er-o″mah-to′sis). An atheromatous condition. **a. cu′tis,** sebaceous cyst.

atheromatous (ath″er-o′mah-tus). Affected with, or of the nature of, atheroma.

atheronecrosis (ath″er-o″ne-kro′sis). The necrosis or degeneration accompanying atherosclerosis.

atherosclerosis (ath″er-o″skle-ro′sis). A lesion of large and medium-sized arteries, with deposits in the intima of yellowish plaques containing cholesterol, lipoid material, and lipophages.

atherosis (ath″er-o′sis). Atherosclerosis.

Atherosperma (ath″er-o-sper′mah) [Gr. *athēr* spike + *sperma* seed]. A genus of monimiaceous trees: the bark of *A. moschatum*, sassafras tree of Australasia, is diaphoretic, diuretic, and sedative.

athetoid (ath′ĕ-toid) [Gr. *athetos* not fixed + *eidos* form]. 1. Resembling athetosis. 2. Affected with athetosis.

athetosic (ath″ĕ-to′sik). Pertaining to athetosis.

athetosis (ath″ĕ-to′sis) [Gr. *athetos* not fixed + *-osis*]. A derangement marked by ceaseless occurrence of slow, sinuous, writhing movements, especially severe in the hands, and performed involuntarily. **double a.,** Vogt's syndrome. **double congenital a.,** infantile spasmodic paraplegia. **pupillary a.,** hippus.

Position of fingers in movements of athetosis.

athetotic (ath″e-tot′ik). Athetosic.

athiaminosis (ah-thi″ah-mĭ-no′sis). Thiamine deficiency.

Athiorhodaceae (a″thi-o-ro-da′se-e). A family of Schizomycetes (order Pseudomonadales, suborder Rhodobacteriineae), made up of non-sulfur photosynthetic microorganisms which characteristically produce a pigment composed of bacteriochlorophyll and one or more carotenoids. It includes two genera, *Rhodopseudomonas* and *Rhodospirillum*.

athrepsia (ah-threp′se-ah) [*a* neg. + Gr. *threpsis* nutrition]. 1. Marasmus. 2. Ehrlich's term for immunity to tumor inoculation due to a supposed lack of the special nutritive material necessary for tumor growth.

athrepsy (ath′rep-se). Athrepsia.

athreptic (ah-threp′tik). Pertaining to or characterized by athrepsia.

athrocytosis (ath″ro-si-to′sis). Absorption of electronegative colloid by the apical surfaces of the cells of the proximal tubules of the kidney.

athrombia (ah-throm′be-ah). Defective clotting of blood.

athrophagocytosis (ath″ro-fag″o-si-to′sis). Nonnutritive phagocytosis.

athymia (ah-thim′e-ah) [*a* neg. + Gr. *thymos* mind]. 1. Dementia. 2. Loss of consciousness. 3. Absence of the thymus gland.

athymism (ah-thi′mizm). Absence of the thymus or the condition induced by removal of the thymus.

athymismus (ah″thi-mis′mus). Athymism.

athyrea (ah-thi′re-ah). Athyreosis.

athyreosis (ah-thi″re-o′sis) [*a* neg. + *thyreoid* (thyroid) + *-osis*]. The pathological condition produced by absence or inadequate functioning of the thyroid gland. If congenital, cretinism results; if acquired in adult life, myxedema.

athyria (ah-thi′re-ah). 1. A developmental anomaly characterized by absence of the thyroid gland. 2. Athyreosis.

athyroidation (ah-thi″roi-da′shun). Athyreosis.

athyroidemia (ah-thi″roi-de′me-ah) [*a* neg. + *thyroid* + Gr. *haima* blood + *-ia*]. Abnormal state of the blood due to athyreosis.

athyroidism (ah-thi′roid-izm). Athyreosis.

athyroidosis (ah-thi″roi-do′sis). Athyreosis.

athyrosis (ah″thi-ro′sis). Athyreosis.

athyrotic (ah″thi-rot′ik). Pertaining to or characterized by athyreosis.

Athysanus (ah-this′ah-nus). A genus of blood-sucking flies of Algeria.

atite (at′it). A substance in milk which reduces nitrate to nitrite.

atlantad (at-lan′tad). Toward the atlas.

atlantal (at-lan′tal). Pertaining to the atlas.

atlantoaxial (at-lan″to-ak′se-al). Pertaining to the atlas and the axis.

atlantodidymus (at-lan″to-did′ĭ-mus). Atlodidymus.

atlantomastoid (at-lan″to-mas′toid). Pertaining to the atlas and the mastoid process.

atlantoodontoid (at-lan″to-o-don′toid). Pertaining to the atlas and the odontoid process of the axis.

atlas (at′las) [Gr. *Atlas* the Greek god who bears up the pillars of Heaven]. 1. [N A, B N A]. The first cervical vertebra, which articulates above with the occipital bone and below with the axis. 2. A collection of illustrations on one subject, such as anatomy, blood and bone marrow, brain, cardiac disease.

atloaxoid (at″lo-ak′soid). Pertaining to the atlas and the axis.

atlodidymus (at″lo-did′ĭ-mus) [*atlas* + Gr. *didymos* twin]. A fetal monster with one body and two heads.

atlodymus (at-lod′ĭ-mus). Atlodidymus.

atloidooccipital (at-loi″do-ok-sip′ĭ-tal). Pertaining to the atlas and the occiput.

atmiatrics (at″me-at′riks) [*atmo-* + Gr. *iatrikos* healing]. Treatment by medicated vapors (P. Niemeyer).

atmiatry (at-mi′ah-tre). Atmiatrics.

atmidalbumin (at″mid-al′bu-min) [*atmo-* + *albumin*]. A protein formed by the action of superheated steam upon a protein.

atmidalbumose (at″mid-al′bu-mōs). An albumose derived from atmidalbumin by dehydration.

atmo- (at′mo) [Gr. *atmos* steam or vapor]. Combining form denoting relationship to steam or vapor.

atmocausis (at″mo-kaw′sis) [*atmo-* + Gr. *kausis* burning]. Treatment by the direct application of superheated steam: used chiefly in nonmalignant uterine affections and to arrest bleeding (*a. u′teri*).

atmocautery (at″mo-kaw′ter-e). An instrument for performing atmocausis.

atmograph (at′mo-graf) [*atmo-* + Gr. *graphein* to record]. An instrument for recording respiratory movements.

atmokausis (at″mo-kaw′sis). Atmocausis.

atmolysis (at-mol′ĭ-sis) [*atmo-* + Gr. *lysis* loosing]. 1. The separation of mixed gases by passing through a porous plate, the more diffusible passing through first. 2. The disintegration of organic tissue by the fumes of volatile fluids, such as benzine, ether, alcohol, etc.

atmometer (at-mom′e-ter) [*atmo-* + Gr. *metron* measure]. An instrument for measuring exhaled vapors, or the amount of water exhaled by evaporation in a given time, in order to ascertain the humidity of the atmosphere.

atmos (at′mos) [Gr. *atmos* steam or vapor]. A unit of air pressure, being a pressure of one degree per square centimeter: called also *aer*.

atmosphere (at′mos-fēr) [*atmo-* + Gr. *sphaira* sphere]. 1. The air encircling the earth. See *air*. 2. The pressure of the air upon the earth at the sea level (about 15 pounds to the square inch).

atmospheric (at″mos-fer′ik). Of, or pertaining to, the atmosphere.

atmospherization (at-mos″fer-ĭ-za′shun). The transformation of venous blood into arterial blood.

atmotherapy (at″mo-ther′ah-pe) [*atmo-* + Gr. *therapeia* treatment]. 1. Treatment by medicated vapors. 2. Treatment by methodic reduction of respiration.

atocia (ah-to′se-ah) [*a* neg. + Gr. *tokos* birth]. 1. Sterility in the female. 2. Nulliparity.

atom (at′om) [Gr. *atomos* indivisible]. Any one of the ultimate particles of a molecule or of any matter. An atom is the smallest quantity of an element that can exist and still retain the chemical properties of the element. The atom consists of a minute central nucleus, in which practically all of the mass of the atom is concentrated, and of surrounding electrons. The nucleus is positively charged; the amount of the charge corresponds to the atomic number of the atom. In a neutral atom the surrounding negative electrons are equal in number to the positive charges on the nucleus. The number and arrangement of these electrons determine all the properties of the atom except its atomic weight and its radioactivity. **activated a.** 1. An ionized atom. 2. An atom in which some of the orbital electrons have been driven out into larger and less stable orbits. The atom is thus prepared to release its stored energy as these electrons return to their normal and stable orbits. **Bohr a.,** the conception of a nuclear atom in which the orbital electrons are able to occupy only certain orbits, these orbits being determined by quantum limitations. **excited a.,** activated atom. **ionized a.,** an atom from which one or more of the outer or valence electrons have been removed. **nuclear a.,** the conception or theory of the atom as composed of a small central nucleus surrounded by orbital electrons. For table of the atoms see under *element*. **recoil a., rest a.,** the portion of an atom from which an alpha particle has been given off. This remaining part recoils with a velocity inversely proportional to its mass. **Rutherford a.,** nuclear a. **stripped a.,** an atom from which the orbital electrons have been more or less completely removed. **tagged a.,** one which has been made radioactive, so that its course in the body may be checked. See *radioactive tracer*, under *tracer*.

atomerg (at′om-erg). A hypothetical tiny particle of energy smaller than the neutron.

atomic (ah-tom′ik). Of or pertaining to an atom.

atomicity (at″o-mis′ĭ-te). Chemical valence or quantivalence.

atomism (at′om-izm). The hypothesis that the universe is composed of atoms.

atomitsuwari (at″um-it-su-war′e). A disease of infants in Japan caused by breast feeding while the mother is pregnant.

atomization (at″om-ĭ-za′shun). The act or process of breaking a liquid up into spray.

atomizer (at′om-iz″er). An instrument for throwing a jet of spray.

atonia (ah-to′ne-ah). Atony. **choreatic a.,** deficient muscular tonicity often seen in chorea.

atonic (ah-ton′ik). Lacking normal tone or strength; pertaining to or characterized by atony.

atonicity (at″o-nis′ĭ-te). The quality or condition of being without normal tone or strength.

atony (at′o-ne) [L. *atonia*, from *a* neg. + Gr. *tonos* tension]. Lack of normal tone or strength.

atopen (at′o-pen). The antigen responsible for atopy. Cf. *reagin*.

atopic (ah-top′ik) [*a* neg. + Gr. *topos* place]. 1. Out of place; displaced. 2. Pertaining to an atopen or to atopy.

atopognosia (ah-top″og-no′se-ah) [*a* neg. + Gr. *topos* place + *gnōsis* knowledge + *-ia*]. Loss of power of correctly locating a sensation.

atopognosis (ah-top″og-no′sis). Atopognosia.

atopomenorrhea (at″o-po-men-o-re′ah) [*a* neg. + Gr. *topos* place + *men* month + *rhoia* flow]. Vicarious menstruation.

atopy (at′o-pe). A clinical hypersensitivity state which is subject to hereditary influences; included are hay fever, asthma, and eczema.

atoxic (ah-tok′sik) [*a* neg. + Gr. *toxikon* poison]. Not poisonous; not due to a poison.

ATP. Abbreviation for *adenosine triphosphate*.

atrabiliary (at″rah-bil′e-a-re) [L. *atra* black + *bilis* bile]. Pertaining to black bile, one of the four humors, according to the humoral theory; by extension, characterized by melancholy or gloom, melancholic or gloomy.

atraumatic (a″traw-mat′ik) [*a* neg. + Gr. *traumatikos* of or for wounds]. Not inflicting or causing damage or injury.

atremia (ah-tre′me-ah) [*a* neg. + Gr. *tremein* to tremble]. 1. Absence of tremor. 2. Hysterical inability to walk.

atrepsy (at′rep-se) [*a* neg. + Gr. *threpsis* nutrition]. Athrepsia.

atreptic (ah-trep′tik). Athreptic.

atresia (ah-tre′ze-ah) [*a* neg. + Gr. *trēsis* a hole + *-ia*]. Absence or closure of a normal body orifice or passage. **a. a′ni,** imperforation of the anus. **aortic a.,** absence or closure of the aortic orifice; a rare congenital anomaly in which the left ventricle is hypoplastic or nonfunctioning, oxygenated blood passing from the left into the right atrium through a septal defect, and the mixed venous and arterial blood passing from the pulmonary artery to the aorta by way of a patent ductus. **follicle a., a. follic′uli,** blighting and death of an ovarian follicle. **a. i′ridis,** closure of the pupillary opening. **tricuspid a.,** absence of the orifice between the right atrium and ventricle, circulation being made possible by the presence of an atrial septal defect, blood passing from the right to the left atrium and thence to the left ventricle and aorta. It may or may not be associated with transposition of the great vessels, the prognosis being better when it is.

atresic (ah-tre′zik). Atretic.

atretic (ah-tret′ik) [Gr. *atrētos* not perforated]. Without an opening; pertaining to or characterized by atresia.

atreto- (ah-tre′to) [Gr. *atrētos* not perforated]. A combining form denoting absence of a normal opening; imperforate, or closed.

atretoblepharia (ah-tre″to-blĕ-fa′re-ah) [*atreto-* + Gr. *blepharon* eyelid + *-ia*]. Symblepharon.

atretocephalus (ah-tre″to-sef′ah-lus) [*atreto-* + Gr. *kephalē* head]. A fetal monster lacking the orifices normally present in the head.

atretocormus (ah-tre″to-kor′mus) [*atreto-* + Gr. *kormos* trunk]. A fetus having one of the body openings imperforate.

atretocystia (ah-tre″to-sis′te-ah) [*atreto-* + Gr. *kystis* bladder + *-ia*]. Lack of the normal opening from the bladder.

atretogastria (ah-tre″to-gas′tre-ah) [*atreto-* + Gr. *gastēr* stomach + *-ia*]. Lack of the normal opening into the stomach.

atretolemia (ah-tre″to-le′me-ah) [*atreto-* + Gr. *laimos* gullet + *-ia*]. Lack of the normal opening into the larynx or the esophagus.

atretometria (ah-tre″to-me′tre-ah) [*atreto-* + Gr. *mētra* uterus + *-ia*]. Lack of the normal opening into the uterus.

atretopsia (ah″tre-top′se-ah) [*atreto-* + Gr. *ōps* eye + *-ia*]. Lack of the normal opening in the iris of the eye.

atretorrhinia (ah-tre″to-rin′e-ah) [*atreto-* + Gr. *rhis* nose + *-ia*]. Absence of the normal opening into the nose.

atretostomia (ah-tre″to-sto′me-ah) [*atreto-* + Gr. *stoma* mouth + *-ia*]. Lack of the normal opening into the oral cavity.

atreturethria (ah-tre″tu-re′thre-ah) [*atreto-* + Gr. *ourēthra* urethra + *-ia*]. Lack of the normal urethral opening.

atria (a′tre-ah) [L.]. Plural of *atrium*.

atrial (a′tre-al). Pertaining to an atrium.

atrichia (ah-trik′e-ah) [*a* neg. + Gr. *thrix* hair + *-ia*]. 1. Absence of the hair. 2. Absence of flagella or cilia.

atrichosis (at″rĭ-ko′sis). Absence of the hair. See also *alopecia*. **a. congenita′lis,** partial or complete absence of the hair at birth, sometimes associated with deformities of the nails and teeth, and with other congenital anomalies.

atrichous (ah-trik′us) [*a* neg. + Gr. *thrix* hair]. 1. Having no flagella; said of bacteria. 2. Having no hair.

atrio- (a′tre-o) [L. *atrium* hall]. Combining form denoting relationship to an atrium of the heart.

atriocommissuropexy (a″tre-o-kom″ĭ-su′ro-pek″se) [*atrio-* + *commissure* + *-pexy*]. Fixation of the mitral valve with sutures passed from the ventricle through the valve leaflets and the atrial wall, for correction of mitral insufficiency.

atriomegaly (a″tre-o-meg′ah-le) [*atrio-* + Gr. *megaleios* magnitude]. Abnormal dilatation or enlargement of an atrium of the heart.

atrionector (at″re-o-nek′tor) [*atrio-* + L. *nector* connector]. The sino-auricular node.

atrioseptopexy (a″tre-o-sep″to-pek′se) [*atrio-* + *septum* + Gr. *pēxis* a fixing, putting together]. Surgical repair of a defect in the interatrial septum.

atriotome (at′re-o-tōm) [*atrio-* + Gr. *tomē* cut]. An instrument for incising the atrium.

atriotomy (a″tre-ot′o-me) [*atrio-* + Gr. *tomē* a cutting]. Surgical incision of an atrium of the heart, for repair of a cardiac defect.

atrioventricular (a″tre-o-ven-trik′u-lar). Pertaining to an atrium of the heart and to a ventricle.

atriplicism (ah-trip′lĭ-sizm). Poisoning produced by eating a kind of spinach, *Atriplex littoralis*.

atrium (a′tre-um), pl. *a′tria* [L.; Gr. *atrion* hall]. A chamber; used in anatomical nomenclature to designate such a chamber affording entrance to another structure or organ. Usually used alone to designate an atrium of the heart (a. cordis). **a. cor′dis** [N A, B N A], one of the pair of smaller cavities of the heart, with thin muscular walls, from which the blood passes to the ventricles. See *a. dextrum* and *a. sinistrum*. **a. dex′trum** [N A, B N A], the atrium of the right side of the heart, which receives blood from the superior and the inferior vena cava, and from which it passes to the right ventricle. **a. glot′tidis, a. of glottis,** vestibulum laryngis. **a. laryn′gis, a. of larynx,** vestibulum laryngis. **left a.,** a. sinistrum. **a. mea′tus me′dii** [N A, B N A], a depression in front of the middle nasal meatus, between the agger nasi and the middle nasal concha. Called also *a. of middle meatus of nose*. **a. pulmona′le, pulmonary a.** 1. Atrium sinistrum. 2. Respiratory atrium. **respiratory a.,** the expanded cavity at the end of an alveolar duct, into which the alveolar sacs open. **right a.,** a. dextrum. **a. sinis′trum** [N A, B N A], the atrium of the left side of the heart, which receives blood from the pulmonary veins, and from which it passes to the left ventricle. **a. vagi′nae,** vestibulum vaginae.

Atropa (at′ro-pah) [Gr. *Atropos* "undeviating," one of the Fates]. A genus of solanaceous plants, from which various alkaloids are derived. The species include *A. acuminata* and *A. belladonna.*

atrophedema (ah-trof″e-de′mah) [*atrophy* + *edema*]. A chronic hereditary disease probably of angioneurotic origin.

atrophia (ah-tro′fe-ah) [L.; Gr. *atrophia*, from *a* neg. + Gr. *trophē* nourishment]. Atrophy. **a. choroi′deae et ret′inae,** atrophy of the choroid and retina, associated with night blindness. **a. cu′tis, a. cu′tis idiopath′ica,** atrophoderma. **a. cu′tis seni′lis,** senile atrophy of the skin. **a. doloro′sa,** atrophy of the eyeball accompanied by violent attacks of pain. **a. infan′tum,** tabes mesenterica. **a. maculo′sa cu′tis** (Jadassohn), anetoderma. **a. mesenter′ica,** tabes mesenterica. **a. musculo′rum lipomato′sa,** pseudohypertrophic muscular paralysis. **a. pilo′rum pro′pria,** atrophy of the hair. **a. seni′lis,** atrophy accompanying old age. **a. stria′ta et maculo′sa,** cutaneous atrophy occurring in white, shining depressed lines or spots. **a. testic′uli,** wasting of the testicle. **a. un′guium,** atrophy of the nails.

atrophic (ah-trof′ik). Pertaining to or characterized by atrophy.

atrophie (at″ro-fe) [Fr.]. Atrophy. **a. blanche en plaque,** a condition marked by areas of atrophy, sometimes with painful and tender ulceration, and vesicular, bullous, or hemorrhagic lesions, eventuating in the characteristic whitened plaques, usually on legs and ankles, of middle-aged or older women, with varicosities and associated cutaneous changes.

atrophied (at′ro-fēd). Marked by atrophy; shrunken.

atrophoderma (at″ro-fo-der′mah) [Gr. *atrophia* want of nourishment + *derma* skin]. Atrophy of the skin or of any part of it. **a. biotrip′ticum,** senile atrophy of the skin. **a. diffu′sum,** acrodermatitis chronica atrophicans. **idiopathic a. of Pasini and Pierini,** a condition observed in youths and young adults, affecting chiefly the trunk and back, with variously sized bluish violaceous or brownish blue lesions. Histologically there is edema of collagen bundles of the deep part of the cutis, with loss of elastic tissue in this area. **a. macula′tum,** a condition characterized by atrophic changes in the skin and the formation of macules which gradually fade, leaving shiny white depressed spots; it may occur as a primary condition or be secondary to syphilis. **a. neurit′icum,** a painful condition of the skin resulting from injury to the nerves, characterized by profuse perspiration and smooth, glossy, pink, ruddy, or blotched appearance. **a. pigmento′sum,** xeroderma pigmentosum. **a. reticula′tum symmet′ricum facie′i,** folliculitis ulerythematosa reticulata. **a. seni′le,** a weather-beaten condition of the skin common in the aged, with dyspigmentation, telangiectasia, loss of elasticity, and dryness with fine scaling. **a. stria′tum et macula′tum,** atrophy of the skin with the changes presenting as linear lesions and spots. **a. vermicula′tum,** folliculitis ulerythematosa reticulata.

atrophodermatosis (at-ro″fo-der-mah-to′sis). Any skin disease having cutaneous atrophy as a prominent symptom.

atrophy (at′ro-fe) [L., Gr. *atrophia*]. A defect or failure of nutrition manifested as a wasting away or diminution in the size of cell, tissue, organ or part. **acute yellow a.,** a toxic necrosis and atrophy with yellow discoloration of the liver and jaundice. The disease is attended by delirium, coma, and convulsions, and is usually fatal. **adipose a.,** emaciation due to lack of adipose tissue. **Aran-Duchenne muscular a.,** myelopathic muscular a. **arthritic a.,** wasting of the muscles that surround a joint, due to injury or to constitutional disease. **blue a.,** a blue pigmentation which sometimes follows self-injection of drugs by individuals addicted to their use. **bone a.,** resorption of bone evident both in external form and in internal density. **brown a.,** atrophy in which the affected viscus assumes a brownish hue. It is seen chiefly in the heart, liver, and spleen. **Buchwald's a.,** progressive atrophy of the skin. **Charcot-Marie-Tooth a.,** progressive neuropathic (peroneal) muscular a. **circumscribed a. of brain,** lobar a. **compression a.,** atrophy of a part due to constant pressure. **concentric a.,** atrophy of a hollow organ in which its cavity is contracted. **convolutional a.,** lobar a. **correlated a.,** the wasting of a part following the destruction or removal of a correlated part. **Cruveilhier's a.,** progressive muscular atrophy. **degenerative a.,** the wasting of a part due to a degeneration of its cells. **Dejerine-Sottas type of a.,** hypertrophic interstitial neuropathy of infancy. **denervated muscle a.,** muscular atrophy resulting from severance of the motor nerve supplying the muscle. **dental a.,** erosion of the teeth. **a. of disuse,** wasting caused by lack of normal exercise of a part. **Duchenne-Aran muscular a.,** myelopathic muscular a. **eccentric a.,** atrophy of a hollow organ in which the size of the cavity is increased. **Erb's a.,** pseudohypertrophic muscular dystrophy. **facial a.,** progressive facial a. **facioscapulohumeral a.,** Landouzy-Dejerine dystrophy. **familial spinal muscular a.,** Werdnig-Hoffmann paralysis. **fatty a.,** fatty infiltration following atrophy of the tissue elements of a part. **Fazio-Londe a.,** progressive bulbar palsy in children. **granular a. of kidney,** chronic interstitial inflammation of the kidney producing compression and atrophy of the parenchyma. **gray a.,** a degeneration of the optic disk in which it becomes gray. **hemifacial a.,** atrophy of one side of the face. **hemilingual a.,** atrophy of one side of the tongue. **Hoffmann's a.,** a variety of progressive muscular atrophy affecting the legs below the knees, and the forearms and hand. **Hunt's a.,** neuropathic atrophy of the small muscles of the hand unattended by sensory disturbance. **hypoglossal a.,** atrophy of the tongue due to lesion of the hypoglossal nerve. **idiopathic muscular a.,** progressive muscular dystrophy. **infantile a.,** marasmus. **inflammatory a.,** atrophy of the functioning part of an organ caused by hypertrophy of the fibrous elements from inflammation. **interstitial a.,** absorption of the mineral matter of bones, so that only the reticulated portion remains. **ischemic muscular a.,** Volkmann's contracture. **juvenile muscular a.,** pseudohypertrophic muscular paralysis. **Kienböck's a.,** acute atrophy of bone occurring in inflammatory conditions of the extremities. **lactation a.,** hyperinvolution of the uterus which may follow prolonged lactation. **Landouzy-Dejerine a.,** Landouzy-Dejerine dystrophy. **leaping a.,** progressive muscular atrophy beginning in the hand and extending to the shoulder without affecting the muscles of the arm. **Leber's optic a.,** Leber's disease. **linear a.,** atrophy of the papillary layer of the skin, causing the appearance of blue and white lines. **lobar a.,** progressive atrophy of the cerebral convolutions in a limited area (lobe) of the brain, marked by progressive degeneration of the higher faculties and by the gradual development of aphasia. **macular a., Schweninger-Buzzi type,** anetoderma. **muscular a.,** a wasting of muscle tissue: of this condition there are many kinds and causes. **myelopathic muscular a.,** a progressive muscular wasting due to degeneration of the cells of the anterior horns of the spinal cord. Beginning usually in the small muscles of the hands, but in some cases (scapulohumeral type) in those of the upper arm and shoulder, the atrophy progresses slowly to the muscles of the lower extremity. Called also *progressive spinal muscular a., Aran-Duchenne muscular a.,* and *Duchenne-Aran muscular a.* **myopathic a.,** muscular atrophy due to disease of the muscle tissue. **neural a.,** neuropathic a. **neuritic muscular a.,** a degeneration of the nerve trunks, often involving the spinal cord and causing a wasting of the muscles, beginning with the feet. It is hereditary, usually begins in early life, and is never cured. **neuropathic a.,** atrophy of muscular tissue due to disease of the nervous system. **neurotic a.,** atrophy due to disease of the nervous system. **neurotrophic a.,** atrophy attributed to destruction of the peripheral neurons which maintain the nutrition of a tissue. **numeric a.,** atrophy due to diminution in the number of the constituent elements, as well as shrinkage of those which remain. **olivopontocerebellar a.,** atrophy affecting the cerebellar cortex, the middle peduncles and the inferior olivary bodies. **Parrot's a. of the newborn,** primary infantile atrophy or marasmus. **peroneal a.,** progressive neuropathic (peroneal) muscular a. **Pick's convolutional a.,** lobar sclerosis. **pigmentary a.,** wasting marked by the deposit of pigment in the atrophied cells. **postmenopausal a.,** atrophy of various tissues, such as oral or genital mucosa, occurring after the menopause. **pressure a.,** decrease in the size of a tissue cell caused by excessive pressure. **progressive muscular a.,** a chronic disease marked by progressive wasting of the muscles with paralysis, due to degeneration of the ventral gray horns of the spinal cord, followed by degeneration of anterior nerve roots and muscles. Called also *chronic anterior poliomyelitis* and *wasting palsy.* **progressive neuromuscular a., progressive neuropathic (peroneal) muscular a.,** a form of muscular atrophy due to degeneration of the cells of the posterior columns of the spinal cord and of the peripheral motor nerves. It begins in the muscles supplied by the peroneal nerves, progressing slowly to involve the muscles of the hands and arms. Called also *peroneal a., Charcot-Marie-Tooth type disease, progressive neural muscular a.* **progressive unilateral facial a.,** an affection attended by progressive wasting of the skin, tissues, and bone, often of the muscles of one side of the face. **pseudohypertrophic muscular a.,** pseudohypertrophic muscular dystrophy. **receptoric a.,** a condition assumed to be due to atrophy of the cell receptors. Animals kept immune by repeated injections of an antigen sometimes cease to respond by the formation of antibodies. **red a.,** atrophy, mainly of the liver, due to chronic congestion from valvular heart disease. **reversionary a.,** anaplasia. **rheumatic a.,** atrophy of muscles after an attack of rheumatism. **senile a.,** the normal atrophy of old age. **serous a.,** atrophy with the effusion of a serous fluid into the wasted tissues. **simple a.,** atrophy due to a shrinkage in size of individual cells. **spinoneural a.,** atrophic muscular paralysis resulting from some lesion of the lower portion of the motor tract of the cord. Called also *degenerative atrophy* or *paralysis.* **Sudeck's a.,** post-traumatic osteoporosis. **toxic a.,** atrophy of an organ due to poisons, as in the course of infectious diseases. **trophoneurotic a.,** atrophy due to disease of the nerves or of a center supplying a part. **unilateral facial a.,** progressive wasting of the tissues of one side of the face. **von Leber's a.,** Leber's disease. **Vulpian's a.,** scapulohumeral type of progressive spinal muscular atrophy. **Werdnig-Hoffmann a.,** progressive myelopathic muscular atrophy of childhood of familial or hereditary character. **white a.,** atrophy of a nerve, leaving only white connective tissue.

atropine (at′ro-pin). An alkaloid derived from *Atropa belladonna, Datura stramonium,* and other Solanaceae. Uses: 1. parasympatholytic agent for relaxation of smooth muscles in various organs; 2. increase heart rate by blocking the vagus nerve; 3. treat parkinsonism; 4. applied locally to the eye to dilate the pupil and paralyze ciliary muscle for accommodation. **a. methyl nitrate,** a white, soluble powder, used as a mydriatic and as an antispasmodic in asthma, biliary and intestinal colic, congenital pyloric stenosis, and nocturnal enuresis. **a. sulfate,** a highly poisonous compound, $(C_{17}H_{23}NO_3)_2.H_2SO_4.H_2O$, occurring as colorless crystals or a white crystalline powder.

atropinism (at′ro-pin-izm). Poisoning due to misuse of atropine or of belladonna.

atropinization (at-ro″pin-i-za′shun). 1. Subjection to influence of atropine. 2. Atropinism.

atropism (at′ro-pizm). Atropinism.

A. T. S. Abbreviation for *antitetanic serum* and *anxiety tension state.*

attachment (ah-tach′ment). 1. The state of being fixed or attached. 2. The means or device by which something is fixed or stabilized. In dentistry, anything, such as a clasp, retainer, or cap, which is used to stabilize or to attach a partial denture to a natural tooth in the mouth. **epithelial a. of Gottlieb,** the area of fusion between the enamel epithelium and the oral epithelium, forming a collar around the crown of a tooth. **frictional a., internal a., key-and-keyway a., parallel a.,** precision a. **precision a.,** an attachment used in fixed and removable partial dentures, consisting of closely fitting male and female parts, the latter usually inserted in the crown of the abutment tooth; the denture is maintained precisely because of the friction or resistance between the parallel surfaces of the two parts forming the attachment. **slotted a.,** precision a.

attar (at′ar) [Persian "essence"]. Any essential or volatile oil of vegetable origin. **a. of roses,** a volatile oil derived from rose petals.

attendant (ah-ten′dant) [L. *attendere,* to wait upon]. A nonprofessional person attached to a hospital or asylum.

attenuant (ah-ten′u-ant). 1. Causing thinness, as of the blood. 2. A medicine that thins the blood.

attenuate (ah-ten′u-āt) [L. *attenuare* to thin]. 1. To render thin. 2. To render less virulent.

attenuation (ah-ten″u-a′shun) [L. *attenuatio,* from *ad* to + *tenuis* thin]. 1. The act of thinning or weakening. 2. The alteration of the virulence of a pathogenic microorganism by passage through another host species, decreasing virulence of the organism for the native host and increasing it for the new host.

attic (at′ik) [L. *atticus*]. A cavity situated on the tegmental wall of the tympanic cavity, just above the facial canal. Called also *recessus epitympanicus* [N A], and *attic of middle ear.*

atticitis (at″e-ki′tis). Inflammation of the attic of the middle ear.

attico-antrotomy (at″e-ko-an-trot′o-me). The surgical opening of the attic and the antrum of the middle ear.

atticomastoid (at″e-ko-mas′toid). Pertaining to the attic and the mastoid process of the temporal bone.

atticotomy (at″e-kot′o-me) [*attic* + Gr. *temnein* to cut]. The surgical opening of the attic of the middle ear. **transmeatal a.,** removal through the external auditory meatus of the outer wall of the attic of the middle ear.

attitude (at′ĭ-tūd) [L. *attitudo* posture]. 1. A posture or position of the body. In obstetrics, the relation of the various parts of the fetal body to one another, the normal attitude being one of moderate flexion of all the joints, with the back curved forward, the head slightly bent on the chest, and the arms and legs free to move in all natural directions. 2. A disposition to act or react in a certain direction. **a. of combat** [Fr. *attitude de combat*], the stiff defensive position of the corpse of one burned to death in a conflagration. **crucifixion a.,** rigidity of the body, with the arms extended at right angles: seen in hystero-epilepsy. **discobolus a.,** a position resembling that of a discus thrower that is caused by stimulation of the semicircular canals. **Duvergie's a.,** the posture of a dead body marked by flexed elbows and knees and with closed fingers and extended ankles. **forced a.,** an abnormal position or attitude due to some disease, such as is seen in meningitis or as the result of contractures. **frozen a.,** a peculiar stiffness of the gait, especially seen in amyotrophic lateral sclerosis. **illogical a's,** the strange and grotesque attitudes assumed by those suffering from hystero-epilepsy. **a. passionnelle, passionate a.,** the dramatic or theatrical expression or gesture often assumed by hysterical patients. **stereotyped a.,** an attitude assumed and maintained for a long time, a phenomenon often seen in mental disease.

attollens (ah-tol′enz) [L.]. Lifting up. **a. aurem,** musculus auricularis superior.

attractant (ah-trak′tant) [L. *attrahere* to draw toward]. A substance which exerts an attracting influence, such as one used to attract insect or animal pests to traps or to poisons.

attraction (ah-trak′shun) [L. *attractio*]. 1. The force, act, or process that draws one body toward another. 2. In dentistry, malocclusion in which the occlusal plane is closer than normal to the eye-ear plane. It causes shortening of the face. Cf. *abstraction.* **a. of affinity,** chemical a. **capillary**

a., the force that attracts the particles of a fluid into and along the caliber of a tube. **chemical a.,** the tendency of atoms of one element to unite with those of another. **electric a.,** the tendency of bodies bearing opposite electric charges to move toward each other. **magnetic a.,** the influence of a magnet upon iron and certain other elements.

attrahens (at′rah-henz) [L.]. Drawing toward. **a. au′rem,** musculus auricularis anterior.

attraxin (ah-trak′sin). Fischer's name for supposed specific bodies existing in solutions which, when the solution is injected into the tissues, exert a chemotactic influence on the epithelial cells.

attrition (ah-trish′un) [L. *attritio* a rubbing against]. The physiologic wearing away of a substance or structure (such as the teeth) in the course of normal use.

At. wt. Abbreviation for *atomic weight.*

atylosis (ah″ti-lo′sis). Atypical tuberculosis.

atypia (a-tip′e-ah). The condition of being irregular or not conformed to type.

atypical (a-tip′e-kal) [*a* neg. + Gr. *typos* type or model]. Irregular; not conformable to the type; in microbiology, applied specifically to strains of *Mycobacterium tuberculosis* of unusual type.

A. U. Abbreviation for *Angström unit,* and for *au′res u′nitas,* both ears together, or *au′ris uter′que,* each ear.

Au. Chemical symbol for *gold* (L. *au′rum*).

auantic (aw-an′tik) [Gr. *auainein* to wither away]. Characterized by wasting; atrophic.

Aub-Dubois table (awb-doo-bois′) [Joseph C. *Aub,* Boston physician, born 1890; Eugene F. *Dubois,* New York physician, born 1882]. A table of normal basal metabolic rates for persons of various ages.

Aubert's phenomenon (o-bārz′) [Herman *Aubert,* German physiologist, 1866–1892]. See under *phenomenon.*

Auchmeromyia (awk″mer-o-mi′yah). A genus of flies. **A. lute′ola,** a fly of Congo and Nigeria having a blood-sucking larva known as the Congo floor maggot.

$AuCl_3$. Gold chloride.

audiclave (aw′de-klāv). An instrument which aids hearing.

audile (aw′dil). Pertaining to hearing; a term applied to that type of mentality which recalls most easily that which has been heard. Cf. *motile* and *visile.*

audimutitas (aw″de-mu′tĭ-tas). Dumbness without deafness.

audioanalgesia (aw″de-o-an″al-je′ze-ah). Reduction or abolition of pain accomplished electronically, by listening, through a stereophonic head set, to recorded music to which has been added a background sound, so-called white sound.

audiogenic (aw″de-o-jen′ik). Produced by sound.

audiogram (aw′de-o-gram″) [L. *audire* to hear + Gr. *gramma* a writing]. A chart of the variations of the acuteness of hearing of an individual.

audiologist (aw″de-ol′o-jist). A person skilled in audiology.

audiology (aw″de-ol′o-je) [L. *audire* to hear + *-logy*]. The study of hearing, including the treatment of patients with impaired hearing.

audiometer (aw″de-om′e-ter) [L. *audire* to hear + Gr. *metron* measure]. A device to test the power of hearing.

audiometrician (aw″de-o-mĕ-trish′an). A specialist in the measurement of hearing ability (audiometry).

audiometry (aw″de-om′e-tre). The testing of the sense of hearing.

audiosurgery (aw″de-o-sur′jer-e). Surgery of the ear.

audiovisual (aw″de-o-vizh′u-al). Simultaneously stimulating, or pertaining to simultaneous stimulation of, the senses of both hearing and sight.

audiphone (aw′dĭ-fōn) [L. *audire* to hear + Gr. *phōnē* voice]. A device for aiding the deaf to hear.

audition (aw-dish′un) [L. *auditio*]. The act of hearing; ability to hear. **chromatic a., a. colorée,** a sensation of color produced by sound; a variety of chromesthesia. **gustatory a.,** a condition in which certain sounds call up a sensation of taste.

auditive (aw′dĭ-tiv). A person in whom the prime sense is hearing.

auditognosis (aw″dĭ-tog-no′sis) [L. *auditio* hearing + Gr. *gnōsis* knowledge]. The sense by which sounds are understood and interpreted.

auditory (aw′dĭ-to-re) [L. *auditorius*]. Pertaining to the sense of hearing.

Audouin's microsporon (ow-doo-anz′) [Jean Victor *Audouin,* Parisian physician, 1797–1838]. *Microsporum audouini.*

Auenbrugger's sign (ow-en-broog′erz) [Leopold Joseph *Auenbrugger,* Austrian physician, 1722–1809]. See under *sign.*

Auer's bodies (ow′erz) [John *Auer,* American physician, 1875–1948]. See under *body.*

Auerbach's ganglion, plexus, etc. (ow′er-bahks) [Leopold *Auerbach,* German anatomist, 1828–1897]. See under *ganglion, plexus,* etc.

Aufrecht's sign (owf′rekhts) [Emanual *Aufrecht,* German physician, 1844–1933]. See under *sign.*

augmentor (awg-men′tor). 1. Increasing: applied to nerves or nerve cells concerned in increasing the size and force of heart contractions. 2. A substance supposed to increase the action of an auxetic.

augnathus (awg-na′thus) [Gr. *au* again + *gnathos* jaw]. A fetal monster with a double lower jaw.

Aujeszky's disease (aw-jes′kēz) [Aladár *Aujeszky,* Hungarian physician 1869–1933]. See under *disease.*

aula (aw′lah) [L.; Gr. *aulē* hall]. 1. The anterior end of the third ventricle of the cerebrum where it communicates with the lateral ventricles through the intraventricular foramina. 2. The red erythematous areola formed about the periphery of the vesicle of the vaccination lesion.

aulatela (aw-lah-te′lah) [L. *aula* hall + *tela* web]. The membranous covering of the aula.

aulic (aw′lik) [L. *aulicus*]. Pertaining to the aula.

auliplex (aw′le-pleks). Auliplexus.

auliplexus (aw-le-plek′sus) [*aula* + *plexus*]. A part of the choroid plexus within the aula.

aulix (aw′liks) [L. "furrow"]. Sulcus hypothalamicus.

aura (aw′rah), pl. *au′rae* [L. "breath"]. A subjective sensation or phenomenon that precedes and marks the onset of a paroxysmal attack, such as an epileptic attack (Galen). **a. asthmat′ica,** premonitory attacks of oppression of the chest, flatulence, etc., preceding an attack of bronchial asthma. **auditory a.,** an auditory sensation which sometimes precedes an attack of epilepsy. **electric a.,** a breezy sensation experienced on the receipt of a discharge of static electricity. **epigastric a.,** a painful sensation in the epigastrium which sometimes precedes an epileptic attack. **epileptic a.,** a peculiar sensation which sometimes gives warning of an approaching attack of epilepsy. **a. hyster′ica,** an aura like that preceding an epileptic attack sometimes experienced by hysterical patients. **intellectual a.,** a dreamy condition that sometimes precedes an attack of epilepsy. **kinesthetic a.,** a sensation of movement of some part of the body, with or without such actual movement. **motor a.,** some special movement which precedes an epileptic attack. **a. procursi′va,** a spell of running which precedes an epileptic attack. **reminiscent a.,** intellectual a. **a. vertigino′sa,** a sudden attack of vertigo occurring in certain neuroses.

aural (aw′ral) [L. *auralis*]. 1. Pertaining to the ear. 2. Pertaining to, or of the nature of, an aura.

aurantia (aw-ran′she-ah). An orange coal tar stain, the ammonium salt of hexanitrodiphenylamine, $C_6H_2(NO_2)_3.N:C_6H_2(NO_2)_2.N.O.O.NH_4$: used in staining mitochondria.

aurantiamarin (aw-ran″te-am′ah-rin). A glycoside from orange peel.

aurantiasis (aw″ran-ti′ah-sis) [L. *aurantium* orange + *-iasis*]. A golden yellow discoloration, as of the skin (*a. cu′tis*), caused by eating large quantities of carrots, oranges, etc. Called also *carotinosis cutis* and *carotinoid pigmentation.*

aureolin (aw-re′o-lin). A yellow dye.

aureomycin (aw″re-o-mi′sin). Trade mark for preparations of crystalline chlortetracycline hydrochloride.

aures (aw′rēz) [L.]. Plural of *auris.*

auriasis (aw-ri′ah-sis). Chrysiasis.

auric (aw′rik). Pertaining to or containing gold.

auricle (aw′re-kl) [L. *auricula* a little ear]. 1. The portion of the external ear not contained within the head; the pinna, or flap of the ear. Called also *auricula.* 2. Auricula atrii cordis. The term is sometimes mistakenly used to designate an atrium of the heart. **cervical a.,** a flap of skin and yellow cartilage sometimes seen on the side of the neck at the external opening of a persistent branchial cleft. **left a. of heart,** auricula atrii sinistri. **right a. of heart,** auricula atrii dextri.

auricula (aw-rik′u-lah), pl. *auric′ulae* [L., dim. of *auris*]. A little ear; the N A and B N A term for the portion of the external ear not contained within the head; the pinna, or flap of the ear. Applied also to the ear-shaped appendage of either atrium of the heart (*auricula atrii*), and sometimes mistakenly used as a synonym for the atrium (*atrium cordis*). **a. a′trii** [N A], the ear-shaped appendage of either atrium of the heart. **a. a′trii dex′tri** [N A], the ear-shaped appendage of the right atrium of the heart. **a. a′trii sinis′tri** [N A], the ear-shaped appendage of the left atrium of the heart. **a. cor′dis** [B N A], a. atrii. **a. dex′tra cor′dis** [B N A], a. atrii dextri. **a. sinis′tra cor′dis** [B N A], a. atrii sinistri.

auriculae (aw-rik′u-le) [L.]. Plural of *auricula.*

auricular (aw-rik′u-lar) [L. *auricularis*]. Pertaining to an auricle, or to the ear.

auriculare (aw-rik″u-la′re) [L. *auricularis* pertaining to the ear]. A craniometric point at the top of the opening of the external auditory meatus.

auricularis (aw″rik-u-la′ris) [L.]. Pertaining to the ear; auricular.

auriculocranial (aw-rik″u-lo-kra′ne-al). Pertaining to an ear and the cranium.

auriculotemporal (aw-rik″u-lo-tem′pŏ-ral). Pertaining to an ear and the temporal region.

auriculoventricular (aw-rik″u-lo-ven-trik′u-lar). Pertaining to an auricle (atrium) and a ventricle.

aurid (aw′rid) [L. *aurum* gold]. A skin eruption produced by the use of gold salts.

auriform (aw′re-form). Ear-shaped.

auriginous (aw-rij′ĭ-nus) [L. *aurigineus, auriginosus*]. Jaundiced; icteric.

aurilave (aw′re-lāv) [L. *auris* ear + *lavare* to wash]. An apparatus for washing out or cleaning the ear.

aurin (aw′rin). Rosolic acid (def. 2). **a. R,** peonin.

aurinarium (aw″re-na′re-um). A medicated suppository for insertion into the external auditory meatus.

aurinasal (aw″re-na′zal). Pertaining to the ear and the nose.

auriphone (aw′re-fōn) [L. *auris* ear + Gr. *phōnē* voice]. A form of ear trumpet in which the sound conveyed is amplified.

auripuncture (aw′re-punk″tūr) [L. *auris* ear + *punctu′ra* puncture]. Surgical puncture of the membrana tympani.

auris (aw′ris), pl. *au′res* [L.]. [N A, B N A] The ear; the organ concerned with hearing. **a. exter′na** [N A], the portion of the auditory organ comprising the auricle and the external acoustic meatus. Called also *external ear.* **a. inter′na** [N A, B N A], the labyrinth, comprising the vestibule, cochlea and semicircular canals. Called also *internal ear.* **a. me′dia** [N A], the space immediately medial to the membrana tympani; it contains the auditory ossicles and connects with the mastoid cells and auditory tube. Called also *cavum tympani* [B N A] and *middle ear.*

auriscalpium (aw″re-skal′pe-um) [L. *auris* ear + *scalpere* to scrape]. An instrument for scooping or scraping foreign matter from the ear.

auriscope (aw′re-skōp) [L. *auris* ear + Gr. *skopein* to examine]. A form of otoscope.

aurist (aw′rist). A specialist in ear diseases.

auristics (aw-ris′tiks) [L. *auris* ear]. The art of treating diseases of the ear.

auristilla (aw″ris-til′ah) [L.]. Singular of *auristillae.*

auristillae (aw″ris-til′e) [L., pl.]. Ear drops.

aurochromoderma (aw″ro-kro″mo-der′mah) [L. *aurum* gold + Gr. *chrōma* color + Gr. *derma* skin]. A permanent greenish-blue staining of the skin due to injection of certain gold compounds.

aurococcus (aw″ro-kok′us). *Staphylococcus pyogenes* var. *aureus.*

aurogauge (aw′ro-gāj). An apparatus for determining the value of hearing aids to individual patients.

aurometer (aw-rom′e-ter) [L. *auris* ear + Gr. *metron* measure]. An apparatus for measuring the sense of hearing of each ear by means of an arrangement for suspending a watch opposite the external canal on a bar fitted so that watch may be slid toward and away from the ear.

aurotherapy (aw″ro-ther′ah-pe) [L. *aurum* gold + *therapy*]. The use of gold in the treatment of disease; chrysotherapy.

aurothioglucose (aw″ro-thi″o-gloo′kōs). A gold preparation used in treating rheumatoid arthritis.

aurothioglycanide (aw″ro-thi″o-gli′kah-nīd). Chemical name: α-auromercaptoacetanilid. Use: to treat rheumatoid arthritis.

aurothioglycolanilide (aw″ro-thi″o-gli″kol-an′ĭ-līd). Aurothioglycanide.

aurum (aw′rum) [L.]. Gold. **a. vegeta′bile** [L. "vegetable gold"], pipitzahoic acid.

auscult (aws-kult′). Auscultate.

auscultate (aws′kul-tāt) [L. *auscultare* to listen to]. To perform or practice auscultation; to examine by listening.

auscultation (aws″kul-ta′shun). The act of listening for sounds within the body, chiefly for ascertaining the condition of the lungs, heart, pleura, abdomen and other organs, and for the detection of pregnancy. **direct a., immediate a.,** auscultation performed without the stethoscope. **Korányi's a.,** auscultatory percussion done by tapping with one forefinger the second joint of the other forefinger applied perpendicularly to the part. **mediate a.** (Laennec, 1819), auscultation performed by the aid of an instrument (stethoscope) interposed between the ear and the part being examined. **obstetric a.,** auscultation in pregnancy for the study of the sounds of the fetal heart, etc. **oral a.,** listening to the breathing sounds by placing the stethoscope in front of the open mouth. **parallel a.,** simultaneous auscultation of corresponding spots on each side of the chest. **rod a.,** auscultatory percussion performed by rubbing the fingers up and down a grooved wooden stick applied perpendicularly to the surface. **stroke a.,** auscultatory percussion performed by stroking of the surface with the fingertips. **transmanual a.,** auscultation through the hand laid over the part. **vibratory a.,** auscultation of a tuning fork through the chest.

auscultatory (aws-kul′tah-to″re). Of, or pertaining to, auscultation.

auscultoplectrum (aws-kul″to-plek′trum). An instrument for use both in auscultation and percussion.

auscultoscope (aws-kul′to-skōp). Phonendoscope.

Auspitz's dermatosis (ow′spitzes) [Heinrich *Auspitz*, German physician, 1835–1886]. Mycosis fungoides.

aut-. See *auto-*.

autacoid (aw′tah-koid) [*aut-* + Gr. *akos* remedy]. "A specific organic substance formed by the cells of one organ and passed from them into the circulatory fluid to produce effects upon other organs similar to those produced by drugs" (Schäfer). **chalonic a.,** a colyone. **duodenal a.,** secretin. **excitatory a.,** a hormone. **hormonic a.,** a hormone. **inhibitory a., restraining a.,** a colyone.

autarcesiology (awt″ar-se″se-ol′o-je) [*autarcesis* + *-logy*]. The branch of immunology which has to do with autarcesis.

autarcesis (awt-ar′se-sis) [*aut-* + Gr. *arkein* to ward off]. The power to resist infection by the normal activity of the body cells as distinguished from immunity of the antibody type.

autarcetic (awt-ar-set′ik). Pertaining to autarcesis.

autechoscope (aw-tek′o-skōp) [*aut-* + Gr. *ēchos* sound + Gr. *skopein* to examine]. An instrument for auscultating one's own body.

autecic (aw-te′sik). Autoecic.

autecology (aw″te-kol′o-je) [*aut-* + *ecology*]. The ecology of an organism as an individual. Cf. *synecology*.

autemesia (aw″tĕ-me′se-ah) [*aut-* + Gr. *emesis* vomiting]. Functional or idiopathic vomiting.

autism (aw′tizm) [Gr. *autos* self + *-ism*]. The condition of being dominated by subjective, self-centered trends of thought or behavior.

autistic (aw-tis′tik). Self-centered; sufficient unto itself.

auto-, aut- [Gr. *autos* self]. A prefix denoting relationship to self.

auto-activation (aw″to-ak″te-va′shun). The activation of a gland by its own secretion.

autoagglutination (aw″to-ah-gloo″ti-na′shun). Clumping or agglutination of an individual's cells by his own serum; autohemagglutination.

autoagglutinin (aw″to-ah-gloo″tĭ-nin). An autologous serum factor with the property of agglutinating the individual's own cellular elements: e.g., the red cells (red cell autoagglutinin), platelets (platelet autoagglutinin), etc.; autohemagglutinin.

auto-amputation (aw″to-am″pu-ta′shun). The spontaneous detachment from the body and elimination of an appendage or of an abnormal growth, such as a polyp.

auto-analysis (aw″to-ah-nal′ĭ-sis). The analysis and interpretation, on the part of a nervous patient, of the state of mind underlying his disorder: employed as a means of treatment.

auto-anamnesis (aw″to-an″am-ne′sis). A history obtained from the patient himself.

auto-anaphylaxis (aw″to-an″ah-fi-lak′sis). Anaphylaxis from reactions within the body independent of the introduction of substances from without and induced by substances derived from the individual himself. Anaphylaxis induced by serum or other substances from the individual himself.

autoantibody (aw″to-an′tĭ-bod″e). An antibody or antibody-like factor demonstrable by a number of laboratory methods, supposedly directed against tissue components of the same organism; its precise function in the pathogenesis of any clinical syndrome remains undefined.

auto-anticomplement (aw″to-an″te-kom′plement). An anticomplement formed in the body against its own complement.

autoantigen (aw″to-an′tĭ-jen). An antigen present in the tissues of the antibody-producer.

auto-antisepsis (aw″to-an″te-sep′sis). Physiological antisepsis.

auto-antitoxin (aw″to-an″te-tok′sin) [*auto-* + *antitoxin*]. Antitoxin produced by the organs of the body and serving to protect the body from disease.

auto-audible (aw″to-aw′dĭ-bl). Audible to one's self: said of heart sounds.

autobacteriophage (aw″to-bak-te′re-o-fāj). Bacteriophage derived from the patient under treatment.

autoblast (aw′to-blast). An independent, solitary bioblast; a microorganism.

autoblood (aw′to-blud). Blood from a patient's own body.

autocatalysis (aw″to-kah-tal′ĭ-sis). A catalytic reaction which gradually accelerates in velocity, because of participation of some of the products of the reaction themselves as catalytic agents.

autocatalyst (aw″to-kat′ah-list). One of the elements participating in autocatalysis.

autocatalytic (aw″to-kat-ah-lit′ik). Pertaining to, characterized by, or producing autocatalysis.

autocatharsis (aw″to-kah-thar′sis). Psychiatric treatment by encouraging the patient to write out his troubles and thus rid himself of his mental complexes.

autocatheterism (aw″to-kath′e-ter-izm) [*auto-* + *catheterism*]. The passage of the catheter by the patient himself.

autocerebrospinal (aw″to-ser″e-bro-spi′nal). The patient's own cerebrospinal fluid used in treating epidemic meningitis.

autocholecystectomy (aw″to-ko″le-sis·tek″tome) [*auto-* + *cholecystectomy*]. Invagination of the gallbladder into the intestine, with final separation and expulsion of the organ.

autochthonous (aw-tok′tho-nus) [Gr. *autochthōn* sprung from the land itself]. Found in the place of formation; not removed to a new site.

autocinesis (aw″to-si-ne′sis) [*auto-* + Gr. *kinēsis* motion]. Voluntary motion.

autoclasis (aw-tok′lah-sis) [*auto-* + Gr. *klasis* breaking]. Destruction of a part by influences developed within itself.

autoclave (aw′to-klāv) [*auto-* + L. *clavis* key]. An apparatus for effecting sterilization by steam under pressure. It is fitted with a gauge that automatically regulates the pressure, and therefore the degree of heat to which the contents are subjected.

autocondensation (aw″to-kon-den-sa′shun). A method of applying high-frequency currents for therapeutic purposes in which the patient constitutes one plate of a capacitor.

autoconduction (aw″to-kon-duk′shun). A method of applying high-frequency currents for therapeutic purposes by electromagnetic induction, the patient being placed inside a large solenoid and constituting the secondary of a transformer.

autocystoplasty (aw″to-sis′to-plas″te). A plastic operation on the bladder with grafts from the patient's body.

autocytolysin (aw″to-si-tol′ĭ-sin). Autolysin.

autocytolysis (aw″to-si-tol′ĭ-sis). Autolysis.

autocytolytic (aw″to-si″to-lit′ik). Autolytic.

autocytotoxin (aw″to-si″to-tok′sin). A cytotoxin for the cells of the body in which it is formed.

autodermic (aw″to-der′mik) [*auto-* + Gr. *derma* skin]. Made of the patient's own skin; a term applied to skin grafts. See *dermato-autoplasty*.

autodesensitization (aw″to-de-sen″sĭ-ti-za′shun). Desensitization of a patient by withdrawing blood from his vein and then injecting it intramuscularly.

autodestruction (aw″to-de-struk′shun). Self-destruction; specifically the self-destruction that certain enzymes undergo in solution.

autodiagnosis (aw″to-di-ag-no′sis). Diagnosis of one's own disease.

autodiagnostic (aw″to-di-ag-nos′tik). Pertaining to or causing autodiagnosis.

autodidact (aw′to-de-dakt″) [*auto-* + Gr. *didaktos* taught]. One who is self-taught in his profession.

autodigestion (aw″to-di-jes′chun). Self-digestion, autolysis; applied especially to the digestion of the walls of the stomach and contiguous structures after death.

autodiploid (aw″to-dip′loid) [*auto-* + *diploid*]. 1. Having two sets of chromosomes as a result of redoubling of the chromosomes of a haploid individual or cell. 2. An individual or cell having two sets of chromosomes as a result of redoubling of the haploid set.

autodiploidy (aw″to-dip′loi-de). The state of having two sets of chromosomes as a result of redoubling of the haploid set.

autodrainage (aw″to-drān′ij). Drainage of a cavity by diverting the fluid into a new channel made in the patient's own tissues.

autodyne (aw′to-dīn). A white, crystalline compound, the monophenyl ester of glycerin, C_6H_5-$OCH_2CHOH.CH_2OH$.

auto-echolalia (aw″to-ek″o-la′le-ah) [*auto-* + *echolalia*]. Repetition of one's own words.

autoecic (aw-te′sik) [*auto-* + Gr. *oikos* house]. Always living upon the same organism.

autoeczematization (aw″to-ek-zem″ah-tĭ-za′-shun). The spread, at first locally, and later more generally, of lesions from an originally circumscribed focus of eczema.

auto-epilation (aw″to-ep″e-la′shun) [*auto-* + *epilation*]. Spontaneous falling out of hair.

auto-erastic (aw″to-e-ras′tik). Auto-erotic.

auto-erotic (aw″to-e-rot′ik). Marked by auto-erotism.

auto-eroticism (aw″to-e-rot′ĭ-sizm). Auto-erotism.

auto-erotism (aw″to-er′o-tizm). Erotic behavior directed toward one's self.

auto-erythrophagocytosis (aw″to-e-rith″ro-fag″o-si-to′sis) [*auto-* + *erythro*cyte + *phagocytosis*]. Phagocytosis of red blood corpuscles by autologous phagocytic cells (e.g., neutrophils, monocytes).

autofundoscope (aw″to-fun′do-skōp). An instrument which makes use of the fact that by observing an illuminated blank space through a pin-perforated card one can see faint images of the retinal vessels of his own eyes.

autofundoscopy (aw″to-fun-dos′ko-pe). Examination with the autofundoscope.

autogamous (aw-tog′ah-mus). Characterized by self-fertilization.

autogamy (aw-tog′ah-me) [*auto-* + Gr. *gamos* marriage]. 1. Self-fertilization; fertilization within a cell itself by union of two chromatin masses derived from the same primary nucleus. Called also *automixis* and *syngamic nuclear union*. Cf. *endogamy* and *exogamy*. 2. Conjugation of closely related cells.

autogenesis (aw″to-jen′e-sis) [*auto-* + Gr. *genesis* production]. Self-generation; origination within the organism.

autogenetic (aw″to-je-net′ik). Pertaining to autogenesis.

autogenous (aw-toj′e-nus) [*auto-* + *genesis*]. Self-generated; originated within the body. As applied to bacterial vaccines, the term denotes those vaccines which are made from the patient's own bacteria, as opposed to stock vaccines which are made from standard cultures.

autognosis (aw″tog-no′sis) [*auto-* + Gr. *gnōsis* knowledge]. Self-diagnosis; a form of psychoanalysis consisting of giving the patient self-knowledge by revealing to him through his own confessions the course of mental change leading to his symptoms.

autognostic (aw″tog-nos′tik). Characterized by self-diagnosis; a term applied to the psychoanalytical method.

autograft (aw′to-graft). A graft of tissue derived from another site in or on the body of the organism receiving it.

autografting (aw″to-graft′ing). Autotransplantation.

autogram (aw′to-gram) [*auto-* + Gr. *gramma* mark]. A mark forming on the skin following pressure by a blunt instrument.

autographism (aw-tog′rah-fizm) [*auto-* + Gr. *graphein* to write]. Dermographism.

autohemagglutination (aw″to-hem″ah-gloo″-tĭ-na′shun). Agglutination of erythrocytes by a hemagglutinin produced by the same individual.

autohemagglutinin (aw″to-hem-ah-gloo′tĭ-nin). A hemagglutinin that causes the clumping or agglutination of autologous erythrocytes.

autohemic (aw″to-he′mik) [*auto-* + Gr. *haima* blood]. Done with the patient's own blood.

autohemolysin (aw″to-he-mol′ĭ-sin). A type of antibody or related factor having the ability to lyse autologous erythrocytes.

autohemolysis (aw″to-he-mol′ĭ-sis). Hemolysis of the blood corpuscles of a person by his own serum.

autohemolytic (aw″to-he″mo-lit′ik). Pertaining to autohemolysis.

autohemopsonin (aw″to-hem″op-so′nin). An opsonin which renders the red cells susceptible of destruction by the other cells of the patient's body.

autohemotherapy (aw″to-he″mo-ther′ah-pe) [*auto-* + Gr. *haima* blood + *therapeia* treatment]. Treatment by reinjection of the individual's own blood.

autohemotransfusion (aw″to-he″mo-trans-fu′-zhun]. The withdrawal of a small amount of venous blood and reinjection directly into the same individual.

autohistoradiograph (aw″to-his″to-ra′de-o-graf). Autoradiograph.

autohormonoclasis (aw″to-hor″mōn-ok′lah-sis) [*auto-* + *hormone* + Gr. *klasis* destruction]. The inactivation of the hormone of a given gland in the presence of activity of the gland.

autohydrolysis (aw″to-hi-drol′ĭ-sis). Spontaneous hydrolysis, such as proteins undergo in neutral solutions.

autohypnosis (aw″to-hip-no′sis). Self-induced hypnotism.

autohypnotic (aw″to-hip-not′ik). 1. Pertaining to self-induced hypnotism. 2. One who can put himself into a hypnotic state.

auto-immunization (aw″to-im″mu-ni-za′shun). The production in an organism of reactivity to its own tissues, with appearance of certain clinical and laboratory manifestations as a result of the altered immunological response.

auto-infection (aw″to-in-fek′shun) [*auto-* + *infection*]. Infection by an agent already present in the body.

auto-infusion (aw″to-in-fu′zhun) [*auto-* + *infusion*]. The forcing of the blood toward the heart by bandaging the extremities, compression of the abdominal aorta, etc.

auto-inoculable (aw″to-in-ok′u-lah-bl) [*auto-* + *inoculable*]. Susceptible of being inoculated with virus from one's own body.

auto-inoculation (aw″to-in-ok′u-la″shun) [*auto-* + *inoculation*]. Inoculation with a virus from one's own body.

auto-intoxicant (aw″to-in-tok′se-kant). A poison generated within the system.

auto-intoxication (aw″to-in-tok″se-ka′shun) [*auto-* + *intoxication*]. Poisoning by some uneliminated toxin generated within the body. **dyscratic a.,** an abnormal condition of the body fluids from nutritional disturbance. **intestinal a.,** a disordered state due to the accumulation of intestinal poisons in the blood; called also *alimentary toxemia*.

auto-isolysin (aw″to-i-sol′ĭ-sin). A lysin which destroys the corpuscles of the subject from which it was obtained as well as those of other animals of the same species.

autokeratoplasty (aw″to-ker′ah-to-plas″te) [*auto-* + *keratoplasty*]. Corneal grafting with tissue from the patient's other eye.

autokinesis (aw″to-ki-ne′sis) [*auto-* + Gr. *kinēsis* motion]. Voluntary motion. **visible light a.** See *autokinetic visible light phenomenon,* under *phenomenon.*

autokinetic (aw″to-ki-net′ik). Having the power of voluntary motion.

autolaryngoscopy (aw″to-lar″in-gos′ko-pe). Observation of one's own larynx.

autolavage (aw″to-lah-vahzh′) [*auto-* + *lavage*]. Lavage performed on one's self or on one's own stomach.

autolesion (aw′to-le″zhun). A self-inflicted injury.

autolesionism (aw′to-le″zhun-izm). The infliction of injury upon one's self.

autolesionist (aw′to-le″zhun-ist). One who inflicts injury upon himself.

autoleukocytotherapy (aw″to-lu″ko-si″to-ther′ah-pe). Treatment by administration of the patient's own, previously withdrawn leukocytes.

autologous (aw-tol′o-gus) [*auto-* + Gr. *logos* relation]. Related to self; designating products or components of the same individual organism.

autology (aw-tol′o-je). The science of one's own self.

autolysate (aw-tol′ĭ-sāt). A substance or substances produced by autolysis. Autolysates of cancer tissue have been used subcutaneously in the treatment of cancer.

autolysin (aw-tol′ĭ-sin). A lysin present in an organism and capable of destroying the cells or tissues of that organism.

autolysis (aw-tol′ĭ-sis) [*auto-* + Gr. *lysis* dissolution]. 1. The spontaneous disintegration of tissues or of cells by the action of their own autogenous enzymes, such as occurs after death and in some pathological conditions; autodigestion. 2. The destruction of cells of the body by its own serum. **hereditary transmissible a.,** bacteriophage. **postmortem a.,** a change much like cloudy swelling which occurs in many tissues shortly after death.

autolytic (aw-to-lit′ik). Pertaining to or causing autolysis.

autolyze (aw′to-līz). To undergo or to cause to undergo autolysis.

automatic (aw″to-mat′ik) [Gr. *automatos* self-acting]. Spontaneous or involuntary; done by no act of the will.

automatin (aw-tom′ah-tin). 1. A hypothetical substance in the heart which is the natural excitant of the heart beat. 2. An extract of bovine heart muscle used in circulatory disorders.

automatinogen (aw-tom″ah-tin′o-jen) [*automatin* + Gr. *gennan* to produce]. A substance in the heart and muscles which is activated into automatin by the radiations from the potassium in the heart.

automatism (aw-tom′ah-tizm) [Gr. *automatismos* self-action]. 1. The performance of non-reflex acts without conscious volition. 2. The doctrine that the brain causes, manufactures, or calls into action mental processes and that all mental processes are dependent on brain activity. Cf. *parallelism.* **ambulatory a.,** a condition in which the patient walks about and performs acts mechanically and without consciousness of what he is doing. **command a.,** an abnormal responsiveness to commands, the subject performing suggested acts without exercising any critical judgment, as observed in hypnosis and certain mental states.

automatogen (aw″to-mat′o-jen) [*automatin* + Gr. *gennan* to produce]. The mother substance or precursor of automatin.

automatograph (aw″to-mat′o-graf) [Gr. *automatismos* self-action + *graphein* to write]. An instrument for recording involuntary movements.

Autom′eris i′o. The io moth that produces a dermatitis by means of irritant hairs on its larva.

automixis (aw″to-mik′sis) [*auto-* + Gr. *mixis* mixture]. Autogamy.

automnesia (aw″tom-ne′ze-ah) [*auto-* + Gr. *mnēsis* memory]. Spontaneous recall to memory of past conditions of one's life.

automonosexualism (aw″to-mon″o-seks′u-al-izm). Narcissism.

automysophobia (aw″to-mis″o-fo′be-ah) [*auto-* + *mysophobia*]. Abnormally exaggerated dread of personal uncleanness.

autonarcosis (aw″to-nar-ko′sis). Insensibility due to autosuggestion.

autonephrectomy (aw″to-ne-frek′to-me) [*auto-* + Gr. *nephros* kidney + Gr. *ektomē* excision]. Obliteration of a kidney as the result of disease.

autonephrotoxin (aw″to-nef″ro-tok′sin). A toxic substance for the cells of the kidney of the body in which it is formed.

autonomic (aw″to-nom′ik). Self-controlling; functionally independent.

autonomin (aw-ton′o-min). A hypothetical hormone secreted by the pancreas under the influence of the vagal autonomic system which is supposed to antagonize epinephrine.

autonomotropic (aw″to-nom-o-trop′ik) [*autonomic* + Gr. *tropos* a turning]. Having an affinity for the autonomic nervous system.

autonomous (aw-ton′o-mus). Pertaining to or characterized by autonomy.

autonomy (aw-ton′o-me) [*auto-* + Gr. *nomos* law]. The state of functioning independently, without extraneous influence.

auto-ophthalmoscope (aw″to-of-thal′mo-skōp) [*auto-* + *ophthalmoscope*]. An ophthalmoscope for examining one's own eyes.

auto-ophthalmoscopy (aw″to-of-thal-mos′ko-pe). The use of the auto-ophthalmoscope.

auto-oxidation (aw″to-ok″se-da′shun). Spontaneous oxidation.

autopath (aw′to-path). A person who has allergic symptoms, because of a sensitive autonomic nervous system.

autopathography (aw″to-pah-thog′rah-fe) [*auto-* + Gr. *pathos* disease + *graphein* to write]. A written description of one's own disease.

autopathy (aw-top′ah-the) [*auto-* + Gr. *pathos* disease]. A disease without apparent external causation.

autopepsia (aw″to-pep′se-ah) [*auto-* + Gr. *peptein* to digest]. Self-digestion; autolysis.

autophagia (aw″to-fa′je-ah). Autophagy.

autophagy (aw-tof′ah-je) [*auto-* + Gr. *phagein* to eat]. 1. The eating of one's own flesh. 2. Nutrition of the body by the consumption of its own tissues.

autopharmacology (aw″to-far″mah-kol′o-je). The chemical regulation of bodily function by the natural constituents of the body tissues.

autophil (aw′to-fil). A person with a tendency to allergic manifestations because of a sensitive autonomic nervous system.

autophilia (aw″to-fil′e-ah) [*auto-* + Gr. *philein* to love]. Pathological self-esteem.

autophobia (aw″to-fo′be-ah) [*auto-* + Gr. *phobos* fear]. Abnormal dread of being alone.

autophonia (aw″to-fo′ne-ah). Autophony.

autophonomania (aw″to-fo″no-ma′ne-ah) [*auto-* + Gr. *phonos* murder + *mania* madness]. Suicidal mania.

autophonometry (aw″to-fo-nom′e-tre) [*auto-* + Gr. *phōne* voice + *metron* measure]. The application of a vibrating tuning fork to the body of a patient for the purpose of having him describe the sensations which it produces.

autophony (aw-tof′o-ne) [*auto-* + Gr. *phōne* voice]. 1. Observation of one's own voice as transmitted through a patient's chest. 2. A condition in which a patient's voice seems to himself abnormal.

autophthalmoscope (aw″tof-thal′mo-skōp). Auto-ophthalmoscope.

autophthysmotherapy (aw″to-tiz-mo-ther′ah-pe). Autoptysomtherapy.

autophyte (aw′to-fīt) [*auto-* + Gr. *phyton* plant]. A plant which does not depend on organized food material, but derives its nourishment directly from inorganic matter. Cf. *saprophyte.*

autoplasmotherapy (aw″to-plaz″mo-ther′ah-pe) [*auto-* + L. *plasma* + Gr. *therapeia* treatment]. Treatment of disease by injections of the patient's own blood plasma.

autoplast (aw′to-plast). An autograft.

autoplastic (aw″to-plas′tik). Pertaining to autoplasty.

autoplasty (aw′to-plas″te) [*auto-* + Gr. *plassein* to form]. 1. The replacement or reconstruction of diseased or injured parts by tissue taken from another part of the patient's own body. 2. In psychoanalysis, instinctive modification within the psychic systems in adaptation to reality. **peritoneal a.,** peritonization.

autoploid (aw′to-ploid) [*auto-* + *-ploid*]. 1. Having any number (two or many) of chromosome sets as a result of redoubling of the chromosomes of a haploid individual or cell. 2. An individual or cell having any number (two or many) of chromosome sets as a result of redoubling of the haploid set.

autoploidy (aw″to-ploi′de). The state of having any number (two or many) of chromosome sets as a result of redoubling of chromosomes of a haploid individual or cell. See *autodiploidy* and *autopolyploidy.*

autoplugger (aw″to-plug′er). A mechanical instrument used for condensing a gold filling in a tooth cavity.

autopoisonous (aw″to-poi′zun-us). Poisonous to the organism by which it is formed.

autopolymer (aw″to-pol′ĭ-mer). A material which polymerizes without the use of heat, but on the addition of an activator and a catalyst.

autopolymerization (aw″to-pol″ĭ-mer″i-za′shun). Polymerization occurring without the use of heat but as a chemical reaction following the addition of an activator and a catalyst.

autopolyploid (aw″to-pol′e-ploid) [*auto-* + *polyploid*]. 1. Having more than two chromosome sets as a result of redoubling of the chromosomes of a haploid individual or cell. 2. An individual or cell having more than two chromosome sets as a result of redoubling of the haploid set.

autopolyploidy (aw″to-pol′e-ploi″de). The state of having more than two chromosome sets as a result of redoubling of the haploid set.

autoprecipitin (aw″to-pre-sip′ĭ-tin). An autoantibody with the characteristics of a precipitin.

autoprotection (aw″to-pro-tek′shun). Self-protection; particularly the protection of the body from disease by the formation of auto-antitoxins.

autoproteolysis (aw″to-pro-te-ol′ĭ-sis). Autolysis.

autoprothrombin (aw″to-pro-throm′bin). Seegers' term for an activation product of prothrombin. **a. I, factor VII.** See under *coagulation factors.* **a. II, factor IX.** See under *coagulation factors.*

autopsia (aw-top′se-ah). Autopsy. **a. in vi′vo** [L. "autopsy on the living"], examination of an organ by means of an exploratory incision.

autopsy (aw′top-se) [*auto-* + Gr. *opsis* view]. The postmortem examination of a body.

autopsychic (aw″to-si′kik) [*auto-* + Gr. *psychē* soul]. Pertaining to self-consciousness.

autopsychorhythmia (aw″to-si-ko-rith′me-ah) [*auto-* + Gr. *psychē* soul + Gr. *rhythmos* rhythm]. Pathological rhythmic activity of the brain.

autopsychosis (aw″to-si-ko′sis). A psychosis or mental disease marked by derangement of ideas relating to the patient's self.

autopsychotherapy (aw″to-si″ko-ther′ah-pe). Psychotherapy administered by a patient on himself, such as by the exercise of self-control and will power.

autoptysmotherapy (aw″to-tis″mo-ther′ah-pe) [*auto-* + Gr. *ptysma* spittle + *therapy*]. Treatment by subcutaneous injection of the patient's own sputum.

autopunition (aw″to-pu-nish′un) [*auto-* + L. *punire* to punish]. Self-punishment.

autopyotherapy (aw″to-pi″o-ther′ah-pe) [*auto-* + Gr. *pyon* pus + *therapeia* treatment]. Treatment of suppuration by the subcutaneous injection of pus aspirated from the patient's abscess.

autoradiogram (aw″to-ra′de-o-gram). An autoradiograph.

autoradiograph (aw″to-ra′de-o-graf). A radiograph of an object or tissue made by its own radioactivity, especially after the purposeful introduction into it of radioactive material.

autoradiography (aw″to-ra″de-og′rah-fe). The making of a radiograph of an object or tissue by means of its own radioactivity.

autoreinfusion (aw″to-re″in-fu′zhun). Intravenous infusion into a patient of his own blood or serum which has been effused in his body cavities.

autorrhaphy (aw-tor′ah-fe) [*auto-* + Gr. *rhaphē* suture]. Closure of a wound by the use of strands of tissue taken from the flaps of the wound.

autoscope (aw″to-skōp). An instrument for the examination of one's own organs.

autoscopy (aw″tos′ko-pe) [*auto-* + Gr. *skopein* to examine]. 1. The examination of one's own organs by means of an autoscope. 2. The visual hallucination of one's self.

autosensitization (aw″to-sen″sĭ-ti-za′shun). Sensitization toward one's own tissues. See *autoimmunization.*

autosensitized (aw″to-sen′sĭ-tīzd). Rendered sensitive to one's own serum or tissues. See *autoimmunization.*

autosepticemia (aw″to-sep″tĭ-se′me-ah). Septicemia due to poisons developed within the body.

autoserobacterin (aw″to-se″ro-bak′ter-in). An autosensitized vaccine; a vaccine sensitized by the patient's own serum.

autoserodiagnosis (aw″to-se″ro-di-ag-no′sis). Diagnostic use of a serum from the patient's own blood.

autoserosalvarsan (aw″to-se-ro-sal′var-san). See *Swift-Ellis treatment,* under *treatment.*

autoserotherapy (aw″to-se″ro-ther′ah-pe) [*auto-* + *serum* + Gr. *therapeia* treatment]. Treatment of disease by injections of serum derived from the patient's own blood.

autoserous (aw″to-se′rus). Accomplished by means of one's own serum.

autoserum (aw″to-se′rum) [*auto-* + *serum*]. A serum which is used on the patient from which it is derived.

autosexualism (aw″to-seks′u-al-izm). Narcissism.

autosite (aw′to-sīt) [*auto-* + Gr. *sitos* food]. The larger, more nearly normal component of asymmetrical conjoined twins, to which the parasite is attached as a dependent growth.

autositic (aw″to-sit′ik). Pertaining to or of the nature of an autosite.

autosmia (aw-tos′me-ah) [*auto-* + Gr. *osmē* smell]. The smelling of one's own bodily odor.

autosomal (aw″to-so′mal). Pertaining to an autosome.

autosomatognosis (aw″to-so″mah-tog-no′sis) [*auto-* + Gr. *sōma* body + *gnosis* recognition]. The feeling that a part of the body that has been removed, as by amputation, is still present.

autosomatognostic (aw″to-so″mah-tog-nos′tik). Pertaining to autosomatognosis.

autosome (aw′to-sōm) [*auto-* + Gr. *sōma* body]. Any ordinary paired chromosome as distinguished from a sex chromosome.

autospermotoxin (aw″to-sper″mo-tok′sin). A substance capable of agglutinating the spermatozoa of the animal in which they are formed.

autosplenectomy (aw″to-sple-nek′to-me). The almost complete disappearance of the spleen through progressive fibrosis and shrinkage, such as may occur in sickle cell anemia.

autospray (aw′to-spra). An apparatus for spraying, to be used by the patient himself.

autosterilization (aw″to-ster″ĭ-li-za′shun). A tendency of certain viruses (e.g., that of poliomyelitis) to disappear from the tissues after a short time.

autostethoscope (aw″to-steth′o-skōp) [*auto-* + *stethoscope*]. A stethoscope for use upon one's own chest.

autostimulation (aw″to-stim″u-la′shun). Stimulation of an animal with antigenic material originating from its own tissues.

autosuggestibility (aw″to-sug-jes″tĭ-bil′ĭ-te). A peculiar mental state with loss of will, in which suggestions become easy.

autosuggestion (aw″to-sug-jes′chun) [*auto-* + *suggestion*]. The spontaneous occurrence to the mind of ideas produced in the individual himself. Also the peculiar mental state often occurring after accidents, in which suggestions are easily received, so that the slightest injury to a part induces an hysterical paralysis or other disability. This latter state is also called *traumatic suggestion.*

autosynnoia (aw″to-sin-noi′ah) [*auto-* + Gr. *synnoia* meditation]. A mental condition in which the patient is so concentrated in his thoughts and hallucinations that he loses all interest in the outside world.

autosynthesis (aw″to-sin′the-sis). Self-reproduction.

autotemnous (aw″to-tem′nus) [*auto-* + Gr. *temnein* to cut]. Capable of spontaneous division.

autotherapy (aw″to-ther′ah-pe) [*auto-* + Gr. *therapeia* treatment]. 1. The spontaneous cure of disease. 2. Self-cure. 3. Treatment of disease by filtrates from the patient's own secretions.

autotomy (aw-tot′o-me) [*auto-* + Gr. *tomē* cut]. 1. Self-division; fission. 2. A surgical operation performed on one's self. 3. The spontaneous shedding of an appendage, as in some invertebrates.

autotopagnosia (aw″to-top″ag-no′se-ah) [*auto-* + Gr. *topos* place + *a* neg. + *gnōsis* knowledge]. Inability to localize or orient correctly different parts of the body; body-image agnosia.

autotoxemia (aw″to-tok-se′me-ah). Autotoxicosis.

autotoxic (aw″to-tok′sik) [*auto-* + Gr. *toxikon* poison]. Pertaining to auto-intoxication.

autotoxicosis (aw″to-tok″se-ko′sis) [*auto-* + Gr. *toxikon* poison + *-osis*]. Poisoning by material generated within the body.

autotoxin (aw″to-tok′sin). Any pathogenic principle developed within the body from tissue metamorphosis.

autotoxis (aw″to-tok′sis). Autotoxicosis.

autotransformer (aw″to-trans-for′mer). A transformer which has part of its turns common to both primary and secondary circuits.

autotransfusion (aw″to-trans-fu′zhun). 1. The forcing of the blood into vital parts by bandaging or elevating the limb. 2. Reinfusion of the patient's own blood.

autotransplant (aw″to-trans′plant). A piece of tissue taken from one part of a subject and transplanted to another part of the same subject.

autotransplantation (aw″to-trans″plan-ta′shun). The operation of taking a piece of tissue from one part of a subject and inserting it in another part.

autotrepanation (aw″to-trep″ah-na′shun). Erosion of the skull by a brain tumor.

autotroph (aw′to-trōf). An autotrophic organism.

autotrophic (aw″to-trof′ik) [*auto-* + Gr. *trophē* nutrition]. Self-nourishing: said of organisms which are able to build up carbohydrates and protein out of carbon dioxide and inorganic salts; ordinarily requiring no growth factors, or only small amounts. Cf. *heterotrophic.*

autotrophy (aw-tot′ro-fe). The state of being autotrophic; autotrophic nutrition.

autotuberculin (aw″to-tu-ber′ku-lin). Tuberculin made from cultures obtained from a patient's own sputum.

autotuberculinization (aw″to-tu-ber″ku-lin-i-za′shun). Absorption of tuberculin or similar products from a patient's own foci of disease.

autotyphization (aw″to-ti″fi-za′shun). The production of a state like typhoid fever from accumulation of waste matters in the system.

auto-urotherapy (aw″to-u″ro-ther′ah-pe) [*auto-* + *urine* + *therapy*]. Treatment of disease by injections of the patient's own urine.

autovaccination (aw″to-vak″sĭ-na′shun). 1. Treatment of a patient with autovaccine. 2. Treatment of a patient by causing liberation of antigenic products from some invading microorganism or diseased tissue and thus bringing about the formation of antibodies.

autovaccine (aw″to-vak′sēn). A bacterial vaccine prepared from cultures of organisms isolated from the patient's own secretions or tissues.

autovaccinotherapy (aw″to-vak″sĭ-no-ther′ah-pe). Autovaccination.

autoxemia (aw″tok-se′me-ah). Autotoxemia.

autoxidation (aw″tok-se-da′shun). Spontaneous oxidation of a substance which is in direct contact with oxygen.

autoxidator (aw-tok′se-da″tor). A substance in any active cell which can be oxidized by water, producing hydrogen dioxide.

autoxidizable (aw-tok″se-dīz′ah-bl). Spontaneously oxidizable.

auxanogram (awks-an′o-gram). The plate culture in auxanography.

auxanographic (awks″an-o-graf′ik). Pertaining to auxanography.

auxanography (awks″an-og′rah-fe) [Gr. *auxanein* to increase + *graphein* to write]. Determination of the most suitable medium for a microbe by placing drops of various solutions on a plate containing a poor medium. The microbe will develop the strongest colonies on the spot that contains the best medium.

auxanology (awks″an-ol′o-je) [Gr. *auxanein* to increase + *-logy*]. The science of growth; applied especially to the study or science of the growth of microorganisms.

auxesis (awk-se′sis) [Gr. *auxēsis*]. Increase in the size of an organism; often used specifically to designate increase in volume of an organism as a result of growth of its individual cells, without increase in their number.

auxetic (awk-set′ik) [Gr. *auxētikos* growing]. 1. Pertaining to auxesis. 2. A substance which stimulates auxesis.

auxiliary (awk-sil′e-a″re) [L. *auxiliaris*]. 1. Affording aid. 2. That which affords aid.

auxiliomotor (awk-sil″e-o-mo′tor). Aiding or stimulating motion.

auxilysin (awk-sil′ĭ-zin). Manwaring's term for the factor in heated goat's serum that increases the action of goat antisheep hemolysin.

auxilytic (awk-sĭ-lit′ik) [Gr. *auxein* to increase + *lysis*]. Increasing the lytic or destructive power.

auximone (awk′se-mōn) [Gr. *auxein* to increase + *hormone*]. A hypothetical substance, akin to vitamin, which favors growth in plants.

auxin (awk′sin) [Gr. *auxē* increase]. A hormone-like substance from sprouts of plants and from human urine which promotes growth in plant cells and tissues by elongation rather than by multiplication of cells. There are two forms, *auxin A*, a cyclopentene derivative of trihydroxy valeric acid, $C_{18}H_{32}O_5$, and *auxin B*, which is heteroauxin.

auxiometer (awk″se-om′e-ter) [Gr. *auxein* to increase + *metron* measure]. 1. An apparatus for measuring the magnifying powers of lenses. 2. A dynamometer.

auxo- [Gr. *auxē* increase]. A combining form denoting relationship to growth, or to stimulation or to acceleration.

auxo-action (awk″so-ak′shun). The accelerating or stimulating action of a substance.

auxo-amylase (awk″so-am′ĭ-lās). A substance which accelerates the action of amylase.

auxocardia (awk″so-kar′de-ah) [*auxo-* + Gr. *kardia* heart]. 1. Diastole. 2. Enlargement of the heart.

auxochrome (awk′so-krōm) [*auxo-* + Gr. *chrōma* color]. A chemical group which, if introduced into a chromogen, will convert the latter into a dye.

auxochromous (awk″so-kro′mus). Increasing or developing color; pertaining to an auxochrome.

auxocyte (awk′so-sīt) [*auxo-* + Gr. *kytos* hollow vessel]. An oocyte, spermatocyte, or sporocyte in the early stages of its development.

auxodrome (awk′so-drōm) [Gr. *auxē* growth + *dromos* a course]. The course of growth as plotted on a Wetzel grid.

auxoflore (awk′so-flōr). A substance which increases the intensity of fluorescence of a compound. Cf. *bathoflore*.

auxoflur (awk′so-floor). Auxoflore.

auxogluc (awk′so-glook) [*auxo-* + Gr. *glykys* sweet]. A tasteless atom with which a gluciphore combines to form a compound which has a sweet taste.

auxohormone (awk″so-hor′mōn) [*auxo-* + *hormone*]. A vitamin.

auxology (awk-sol′o-je). Auxanology.

auxometer (awks-om′e-ter). Auxiometer.

auxoneurotropic (awk″so-nu″ro-trop′ik) [*auxo-* + *neurotropic*]. Increasing or strengthening the neurotropic properties of any substance.

auxospireme (awk″so-spi′rēm). The postsynaptic spireme.

auxotherapy (awk″so-ther′ah-pe) [*auxo-* + *therapy*]. Substitution therapy, as by hormonotherapy or organotherapy.

auxotonic (awk″so-ton′ik) [*auxo-* + Gr. *tonos* tension]. Contracting against increasing resistance.

auxotox (awk′so-toks). A chemical group which causes a compound to become toxic.

auxotroph (awk′so-trōf). An auxotrophic organism.

auxotrophic (awk″so-trof′ik) [*auxo-* + Gr. *trophē* nutrition]. Having growth factor requirements differing from those of the ancestral or prototype strain: said of microbial mutants.

A. V. Abbreviation for *atrioventricular*.

Av. Abbreviation for *average* and *avoirdupois*.

avalvular (ah-val′vu-lar). Having no valves.

avantin (av′an-tin). Isopropyl alcohol.

avariosis (ah-var″e-o′sis) [Fr. *avarie* damage]. Syphilis.

avascular (ah-vas′ku-lar) [*a* neg. + *vascular*]. Not supplied with blood vessels.

avascularization (ah-vas″ku-lar-i-za′shun). The expulsion of blood from a part, as by elastic bandages.

Aveling's repositor (av′el-ingz) [James Hobson *Aveling*, British obstetrician, 1828–1892]. An apparatus for exerting continuous pressure on the fundus of the inverted uterus in order to secure replacement.

Avellis's paralysis, syndrome (av-el′ēz) [Georg *Avellis*, German laryngologist, 1864–1916]. See under *syndrome*.

Avena (ah-ve′nah) [L.]. A genus of grasses. **A. sati′va,** the common oat. The seeds are nutritious and stimulant.

avenin (ah-ve′nin). 1. A stimulant and tonic preparation from oats. 2. A principle like casein, obtainable from oats.

avenolith (ah-ve′no-lith) [L. *avena* oats + Gr. *lithos* stone]. An intestinal calculus or enterolith formed around a grain of oats.

Avenzoar (av″en-zo′ar) (1113–1162). A renowned Arabian physician, born in Seville, Spain, whose principal writing was a compendium of practice, *al-Teïsir*, which contains many interesting clinical reports. Also in his writings he described the itch-mite (*Acarus scabiei*), and did not hesitate to criticize Galen.

Averroes (av-er′ro-ēz) (1126–1198). A distinguished Spanish-Arabian philosopher and physician, born at Cordova. Better known as a philosopher, his chief philosophical work is his commentary on Aristotle; his chief medical work is the *Colliget*, a predominantly philosophical approach to a system of medicine.

avertin (ah-ver′tin). Trade mark for a preparation of tribromoethanol.

Avery's sodium oleate agar (a′vur-ēz) [Oswald Theodore *Avery*, American bacteriologist, 1877–1955]. See *sodium oleate agar*, under *agar*.

avian (a′ve-an) [L. *avis* bird]. Of or pertaining to birds.

Avicenna (av″ĭ-sen′nah) (980–1037). A celebrated Iranian (Persian) physician and philosopher, surnamed the "Prince of Physicians." His great encyclopedia, the *Canon*, written in Arabic, influenced medical thought and teaching for hundreds of years, its dogmatic, pontifical style having particular appeal for the medieval physician.

avidin (av′ĭ-din). A specific protein in egg albumin which interacts with biotin to render it unavailable to an animal, thus producing the syndrome known as egg-white injury. See also *biotin* and *egg-white injury*.

avirulence (a-vir′u-lens). The lack of strength or virulence; the lack of competence of an infectious agent to produce pathologic effects.

avirulent (ah-vir′u-lent). Not virulent.

avitaminosis (a-vi″tah-mĭ-no′sis). A condition due to a deficiency of vitamins in the diet.

avitaminotic (a-vi″tah-mĭ-not′ik). Pertaining to or characterized by avitaminosis.

avivement (ah-vēv-mon′) [Fr.]. The operative refreshing of the edges of a wound.

Avogadro's constant, law (av-o-gad′rōz) [Amadeo *Avogadro*, Italian physicist, 1776–1856]. See under *constant* and *law*.

avulsion (ah-vul′shun) [L. *avulsio*, from *a-* away + *vellere* to pull]. The tearing away of a part of structure. **nerve a.,** the operation of tearing a nerve from its central origin by traction. **phrenic a.,** extraction of a piece of the phrenic nerve through an incision at the base of the neck; done in pulmonary tuberculosis to paralyze the corresponding side of the diaphragm in order to secure rest of the lung.

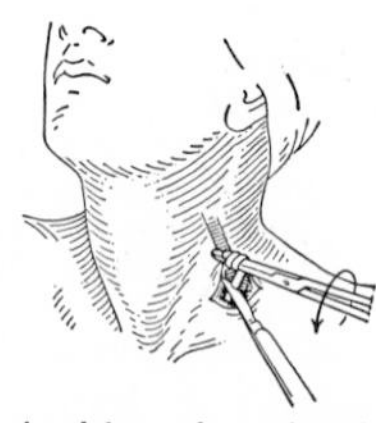
Avulsion of a phrenic nerve.

ax. Abbreviation for *axis*.

axanthopsia (ak″san-thop′se-ah) [*a* neg. + Gr. *xanthos* yellow + *opsis* vision + *-ia*]. Yellow blindness.

Axenfeld's test (ak′sen-felts) [David *Axenfeld*, German physiologist, 1848–1912]. See under *tests*.

Axenfeld-Morax. See *Morax-Axenfeld*.

axenic (a-zen′ik) [*a* neg. + Gr. *xenos* a guest-friend, stranger]. Not contaminated by or associated with any foreign organisms; used in reference to pure cultures of microorganisms or to germ-free animals.

axerophthol (ak″ser-of′thol). Vitamin A.

axes (ak′sēz) [L.]. Plural of *axis*.

axial (ak′se-al). Of, or pertaining to, the axis of a structure or part. In dentistry, pertaining to the long axis of a tooth.

axiation (ak″se-a′shun). The establishment of an axis, or the development of polarity in an organ or other body structure.

axifugal (ak-sif′u-gal) [L. *axis* axis + *fugere* to flee]. Directed away from an axon or axis.

axile (ak′sil). Axial.

axilemma (ak″si-lem′ah) [*axis* + Gr. *lemma* husk]. Axolemma.

axilla (ak-sil′ah), pl. *axil′lae* [L.]. [N A, B N A] The small hollow beneath the arm, where it joins the body at the shoulder. Called also *armpit, axillary cavity* or *fossa*, and *fossa axillaris*.

axillae (ak-sil′e) [L.]. Plural of *axilla*.

axillary (ak′si-lar″e). Pertaining to the axilla.

axin (ak′sin). A varnish-like fat from an insect, *Laccus axinus*: vulnerary and resolvent.

axio- (ak′se-o) [L. *axis;* Gr. *axōn* axle]. A combining form denoting relationship to an axis. In dentistry it is used in special reference to the long axis of a tooth, as in the names of cavity angles. See specific terms.

axiobuccal (ak″se-o-buk′kal). Pertaining to or formed by the axial and buccal walls of a tooth cavity.

axiobuccocervical (ak-se-o-buk″ko-ser′vĭ-kal). Pertaining to or formed by the axial, buccal, and cervical walls of a tooth cavity.

axiobuccogingival (ak″se-o-buk″ko-jin′jĭ-val). Pertaining to or formed by the axial, buccal, and gingival walls of a tooth cavity.

axiobuccolingual (ak″se-o-buk″ko-ling′gwal). Pertaining to the long axis and the buccal and lingual surfaces of a posterior tooth.

axiocervical (ak″se-o-ser′vĭ-kal). Pertaining to or formed by the axial and cervical walls of a tooth cavity.

axiodistal (ak″se-o-dis′tal). Pertaining to or formed by the axial and distal walls of a tooth cavity.

axiodistocervical (ak″se-o-dis″to-ser′vĭ-kal). Pertaining to or formed by the axial, distal, and cervical walls of a tooth cavity.

axiodistogingival (ak″se-o-dis″to-jin′jĭ-val). Pertaining to or formed by the axial, distal, and gingival walls of a tooth cavity.

axiodistoincisal (ak″se-o-dis″to-in-si′zal). Pertaining to or formed by the axial, distal, and incisal walls of a tooth cavity.

axiodisto-occlusal (ak″se-o-dis″to-ŏ-kloo′zal). Pertaining to or formed by the axial, distal, and occlusal walls of a tooth cavity.

axiogingival (ak″se-o-jin′jĭ-val). Pertaining to or formed by the axial and gingival walls of a tooth cavity.

axioincisal (ak″se-o-in-si′zal). Pertaining to or formed by the axial and incisal walls of a tooth cavity.

axiolabial (ak″se-o-la′be-al). Pertaining to or formed by the axial and labial walls of a tooth cavity.

axiolabiogingival (ak″se-o-la″be-o-jin′jĭ-val). Pertaining to or formed by the axial, labial, and gingival walls of a tooth cavity.

axiolabiolingual (ak″se-o-la″be-o-ling′gwal). Pertaining to the long axis and the labial and lingual surfaces of an anterior tooth.

axiolemma (ak″se-o-lem′ah). Axolemma.

axiolingual (ak″se-o-ling′gwal). Pertaining to or formed by the axial and lingual walls of a tooth cavity.

axiolinguocervical (ak″se-o-ling″gwo-ser′vĭ-kal). Pertaining to or formed by the axial, lingual, and cervical walls of a tooth cavity.

axiolinguogingival (ak″se-o-ling″gwo-jin′jĭ-val). Pertaining to or formed by the axial, lingual, and gingival walls of a tooth cavity.

axiolinguo-occlusal (ak″se-o-ling″gwo-ŏ-kloo′-sal). Pertaining to or formed by the axial, lingual, and occlusal walls of a tooth cavity.

axiomesial (ak″se-o-me′ze-al). Pertaining to or formed by the axial and mesial walls of a tooth cavity.

axiomesiocervical (ak″se-o-me″ze-o-ser′vĭ-kal). Pertaining to or formed by the axial, mesial, and cervical walls of a tooth cavity.

axiomesiodistal (ak″se-o-me″ze-o-dis′tal). Pertaining to the long axis and the mesial and distal surfaces of a tooth.

axiomesiogingival (ak″se-o-me″ze-o-jin′jĭ-val). Pertaining to or formed by the axial, mesial, and gingival walls of a tooth cavity.

axiomesio-incisal (ak″se-o-me″ze-o-in-si′zal). Pertaining to or formed by the axial, mesial, and incisal walls of a tooth cavity.

axiomesio-occlusal (ak″se-o-me″ze-o-ŏ-kloo′-zal). Pertaining to or formed by the axial, mesial, and occlusal walls of a tooth cavity.

axion (ak-se′on). The brain and spinal cord.

axio-occlusal (ak″se-o-ŏ-kloo′zal). Pertaining to or formed by the axial and occlusal walls of a tooth cavity.

axioplasm (ak′se-o-plazm″). The protoplasm of an axis-cylinder.

axiopodium (ak″se-o-po′de-um), pl. *axiopo′dia* [*axio-* + Gr. *pous* foot]. A pseudopodium which is ray-shaped, with a central axial rod. Cf. *lobopodium*.

axiopulpal (ak″se-o-pul′pal. Pertaining to or formed by the axial and pulpal walls of a tooth cavity.

axipetal (ak-sip′e-tal) [L. *axis* axis + *petere* to seek]. Directed toward an axon or axis.

axis (ak′sis), pl. *axes* [L.; Gr. *axōn* axle]. 1. A line about which a revolving body turns or about which a structure would turn if it did revolve; used as a general term in N A terminology. 2. [N A] The second cervical vertebra. **arterial a., costocervical,** truncus costocervicalis. **basi-bregmatic a.,** a vertical line from the basion to the bregma; the maximum height of the cranium. **basicranial a.,** a line from the basion to the gonion. **basifacial a.,** a line joining the gonion and the subnasal point. **binauricular a.,** a line joining the two auricular points. **brain a.,** the brain stem. **a. bul′bi exter′nus** [N A], an imaginary line that passes from the anterior to the posterior pole of the eyeball. Called also *external axis of eye* and *axis oculi externa* [B N A]. **a. bul′bi inter′nus** [N A], an imaginary line in the eyeball, passing from the anterior pole to a point on the anterior surface of the retina just deep to the posterior pole. Called also *internal axis of eye* and *axis oculi interna* [B N A]. **celiac a.,** truncus celiacus. **cell a.,** a line connecting the proximal and distal sides of a cell or passing through the centrosome and nucleus of a cell. **cephalocaudal a.,** the long axis of the body. **cerebrospinal a.,** the central nervous system. **condylar a.,** a line through the two mandibular condyles around which the mandible may rotate during a part of the opening movement of the jaw. **conjugate a.,** the conjugate diameter of the pelvis. **craniofacial a.,** the axis of the bones at the base of the skull, including the mesethmoid, presphenoid, basisphenoid, and basioccipital. **dorsoventral a.,** any line in the median plane at right angles to the long axis of the body. **electrical a. of heart,** the resultant of the electromotive forces within the heart at any instant. **embryonic a.,** a line traversing the anterior and posterior regions of an embryonic area or embryo. **encephalomyelonic a., encephalospinal a.,** the central nervous system. **external a. of eye,** a. bulbi externus. **facial a.,** basifacial a. **frontal a.,** an imaginary line running from right to left through the center of the eyeball. **a. of heart,** a line passing through the center of the base of the heart and the apex. **hinge a.,** the imaginary line connecting the mandibular condyles around which the mandible can rotate without translatory movement. **internal a. of eye,** a. bulbi internus.

a. of lens, a. lentis. **a. len'tis** [N A, B N A], an imaginary line joining the anterior and posterior poles of the lens of the eye. **long a. of body,** the imaginary straight line through the neck, thorax, abdomen, and pelvis about which the weights of the torso are most symmetrically distributed. **mandibular a.,** hinge a. **neural a.,** the central nervous system. **a. oc'uli exter'na** [B N A], a. bulbi externus. **a. oc'uli inter'na** [B N A], axis bulbi internus. **opening a.,** an imaginary line around which the condyles may rotate during opening and closing movements of the mandible. **optic a.** 1. Axis opticus. 2. Optical axis. 3. The direction, or directions, in a crystal, or other refracting media, along which light is not doubly refracted. **a. op'tica** [B N A], a. opticus. **optical a.,** the line formed by the coinciding principal axes of elements composing an optical system, being the continuous line passing through the centers of curvature of the optical surfaces of those elements. **a. op'ticus** [N A], an imaginary line passing from the midpoint of the visual field to the fovea centralis of the macula. Called also *a. optica* [B N A], and *optic a.* **a. pel'vis** [N A, B N A], **a. of pelvis,** an imaginary curved line drawn through the minor pelvis at right angles to the planes of the superior aperture, of the cavity, and of the inferior aperture at their central points. **principal a.,** optical a. **pupillary a.,** the line perpendicular to the cornea which passes through the center of the pupil of entrance. **sagittal a. of eye,** a. opticus. **secondary a.,** an imaginary line passing through the optical center of a lens. **thoracic a.,** arteria thoracoacromialis. **thyroid a.,** truncus thyrocervicalis. **vertical a. of eye,** an imaginary line connecting the extreme upper and lower points of the eyeball. **visual a.,** a. opticus.

axis-cylinder (ak″sis-sil′in-der) [*axis* + *cylinder*]. Axon.

axite (ak′sīt). Any one of the terminal filaments of an axon.

axodendrite (ak″so-den′drīt). One of the nonmedullated side fibrils given off from an axon: used in distinction from *cytodendrite.*

axofugal (ak-sof′u-gal). Axifugal.

axograph (ak′so-graf). An apparatus for recording axes in kymographic tracings.

axoid (ak′soid). Pertaining to the axis or second cervical vertebra.

axoidean (ak-soi′de-an). Axoid.

axolemma (ak-so-lem′ah). The thin membrane enclosing the centrally placed bundle of neurofibrils and the matrix of cytoplasm of which a nerve fiber is composed.

axolotl (ak′so-lotl). A larval salamander of the genus *Ambystoma:* used in experiments with thyroid feeding.

axolysis (ak-sol′ĭ-sis) [*axon* + Gr. *lysis* dissolution]. Degeneration and breaking up of the axis-cylinder of a nerve cell.

axometer (ak-som′e-ter) [*axis* + Gr. *metron* measure]. An instrument for measuring an axis; especially an instrument for adjusting a pair of spectacles with respect to the optic axes of the eyes.

axon (ak′son) [Gr. *axōn* axle, axis]. 1. The axis of the body; the spine. 2. The central core which forms the essential conducting part of a nerve fiber. It is an extension from and a part of the cytoplasm of some nerve cell. Called also *axis-cylinder, axis-cylinder process, neurite, neuraxis,* and *neuraxon.* **naked a.,** an axon which has no inclosing medullary sheath.

axonal (ak′so-nal). Pertaining to or affecting an axon.

axone (ak′son). Axon.

axoneme (ak′so-nēm) [*axon* + Gr. *nēma* thread]. 1. The axial thread of the chromosome in which is located the axial combination of genes. Called also *genoneme.* 2. An axial filament which extends forward from the blepharoplast as the edge of an undulating membrane and becomes free anteriorly to form a single flagellum.

axoneure (ak′so-nūr). Axoneuron.

axoneuron (ak″so-nu′ron) [*axis* + Gr. *neuron* nerve]. Any cell of the cerebrospinal axis.

axonometer (ak″so-nom′e-ter) [*axon* + Gr. *metron* measure]. An apparatus for the rapid determination of the cylindrical axis of a lens.

axonotmesis (ak″son-ot-me′sis) [*axon* + Gr. *tmēsis* a cutting apart]. Damage to nerve fibers of such severity that complete peripheral degeneration follows; the internal architecture, however, is fairly well preserved, so that recovery is spontaneous and of good quality. Cf. *neurapraxia* and *neurotmesis.*

axopetal (ak-sop′e-tal). Axipetal.

axophage (ak′so-fāj). A glia cell occurring in excavations in the myelin in myelitis.

axoplasm (ak′so-plazm) [*axon* + Gr. *plasma* plasma]. The matrix of protoplasm containing a centrally placed bundle of neurofibrils, and constituting an individual nerve fiber.

axopodium (ak-so-po′de-um). Axiopodium.

axospongium (ak″so-spun′je-um) [*axon* + Gr. *spongos* sponge]. The meshwork structure making up the substance of the axis-cylinder of a nerve cell.

axostyle (ak′so-stīl). The central supporting structure of an axiopodium.

axungia (ak-sun′je-ah) [L. *axis* axle + *unguere* grease]. Grease. **a. por′ci,** lard.

Ayala's equation, index, quotient [A. G. *Ayala,* Italian neurologist]. See under *quotient.*

ayapana (ah″yah-pah′nah). The leaves of *Eupato′rium tripliner′ve,* a plant growing in many hot countries. It is aromatic, stomachic, diaphoretic, and stimulant: used like tea and coffee, and also as a household polychrest remedy in various hot regions.

Ayer's test (ārz) [James B. *Ayer,* Boston neurologist, born 1882]. See under *test.*

Ayerza's disease, syndrome (ah-yer′thaz) [Abel *Ayerza,* Buenos Aires physician, 1861–1918]. See under *disease* and *syndrome.*

ayfivin (a-fi′vin). An impure polypeptide mixture derived from a strain of *Bacillus licheniformis:* said to possess powerful antibacterial properties and to have low toxicity for mice.

ayurvedism (ah″yoor-va′dism). Native Indian treatment by plants and drugs.

Az. Abbreviation for *azote* or *nitrogen.*

azacyclonol (a″zah-si′klo-nol). Chemical name: α,α-diphenyl-4-piperidinemethanol: used as a tranquilizer.

azaleine (ah-za′le-in) [L. *azalea* a plant name]. Fuchsin.

azamethonium (a″zah-mĕ-tho′ne-um). Chemical name: [(methylimino)diethylene]bis-ethyldimethylammonium. Uses: 1. ganglionic blockade; 2. reduce blood pressure.

azapetine (a″zah-pet′ēn). Chemical name: 6-allyl-6,7-dihydro-5H-benz[c,e]azepine. Uses: 1. sympathetic blockade; 2. dilate peripheral blood vessels.

azarin (az′ah-rin). A nonpoisonous yellow coloring matter from coal tar.

azaserine (a″zah-ser′ēn). Chemical name: O-diazoacetyl-1-serine: used in treatment of acute leukemia.

azeotropic (a″ze-o-trop′ik). Pertaining to or characterized by azeotropy.

azeotropy (a″ze-ot′ro-pe) [*a* neg. + Gr. *zein* to boil + *tropē* a turn, or turning]. The absence of any change in the composition of a mixture of substances when it is boiled under a given pressure.

azerin (az′er-in). An enzyme from *Drosera, Nepenthes,* and various other insectivorous plants.

azid, azide (az′id). A compound which contains the group —CO.N_3.

azo-. A prefix indicating presence of the group —N:N—.

azoamyly (a-zo-am′ĭ-le) [*a* neg. + Gr. *zōon* animal + *amylon* starch]. Inability of the hepatic cells to store up a normal amount of glycogen.

Azobacter (a-zo-bak′ter). Azotobacter.

azobenzene (az″o-ben′zēn) [*azote* + *benzene*]. An orange-red, crystalline derivative, $C_6H_5.N:N.C_6H_5$, from nitrobenzene, soluble in alcohol and ether, but only sparingly so in water.

azo-bordeaux (az″o-bor-do′). Cerasin.

azocarmine (az″o-kar′min). A series of azo dyes used in preparing tissue stains.

azoic (ah-zo′ik) [*a* neg. + Gr. *zōe* life]. Destitute of living organisms.

azoimide (az″o-im′id). 1. The group $-N\langle{N \atop N}$ (N=N, double bond). 2. A protoplasmic poison, hydrazoic acid, N_3H, resembling hydrocyanic acid in its action, made by heating hydrogen chloride with sodium nitrate. It is highly explosive. Called also *triazoic acid* and *hydronitric acid.*

azole (az′ōl). 1. A derivative of a five-membered ring containing nitrogen and either oxygen, sulfur, or an additional nitrogen atom, as well as carbon atoms. 2. Pyrrole.

azolesterase (az″ol-es′ter-ās). An enzyme which hydrolyzes nitrogen-alcohol esters.

azolitmin (az″o-lit′min). A coloring principle, $C_7H_7NO_4$, from litmus. It is used as an indicator and has a pH range of 4.5 to 8.3, being red at 4.5 and blue at 8.3.

azoospermatism (ah-zo″o-sper′mah-tizm). Azoospermia.

azoospermia (ah-zo″o-sper′me-ah) [*a* neg. + *zoosperm*]. Lack of spermatozoa in the semen.

azoprotein (az″o-pro′te-in). A protein some constituents of which have been diazotized.

azosulfamide (az″o-sul′fah-mid). Chemical name: disodium 2-(4′-sulfamylphenylazo)-7-acetamido-1-hydroxynaphthalene-3,6-disulfonate: used to treat infection.

azotase (az′o-tās). An enzyme in Azotobacter which catalyzes the fixation of nitrogen.

azotation (az″o-ta′shun). The absorption of nitrogen from the air.

azote (az′ōt) [*a* neg. + Gr. *zōe* life]. Nitrogen.

azotemia (az″o-te′me-ah) [*azote* + Gr. *haima* blood + *-ia*]. 1. The presence of urea or other nitrogenous bodies in the blood. 2. A disease of horses due to urea in the blood. It is caused by overfeeding and insufficient exercise, and is marked by a sudden attack of perspiration, paralysis of the hind quarters, and blood in the urine. **chloropenic a.,** hypochloremic a. **extrarenal a.,** excess of nonprotein nitrogen in the blood in the absence of renal disease sufficient to account for it. **hypochloremic a.,** a condition characterized by deficiency of sodium chloride, fixation of chlorine in the tissues and azoturia. **prerenal a.,** extrarenal a.

azotemic (az″o-te′mik). Pertaining to or characterized by azotemia.

azotenesis (az″o-tĕ-ne′sis). Any disease due to an excess of nitrogenous substances in the system.

azothermia (az″o-ther′me-ah) [*azote* + Gr. *thermē* heat]. Temperature increase produced by nitrogenous matter in the blood.

azotification (az-o″tĭ-fi-ka′shun). The fixation of atmospheric nitrogen.

azotize (az′o-tīz). To combine or charge with nitrogen.

Azotobacter (ah-zo″to-bak′ter). A genus of microorganisms of the family Azotobacteraceae, order Eubacteriales. It includes three species, *A. a′gilis, A. chroococ′cum,* and *A. in′dicus.*

Azotobacteraceae (ah-zo″to-bak″tĕ-ra′se-e). A family of Schizomycetes (order Eubacteriales), occurring as relatively large rods and even cocci. They are free-living nitrogen-fixing bacteria widely distributed in soil, which are capable of fixing atmospheric nitrogen in the presence of carbohydrate or other source of energy, and grow best on media deficient in nitrogen. It includes a single genus, *Azotobacter.*

azotometer (az″o-tom′e-ter) [*azote* + Gr. *metron* measure]. An instrument for measuring the proportion of nitrogen compounds in a solution.

Azotomonas (ah-zo″to-mo′nas). A genus of microorganisms of the family Pseudomonadaceae, suborder Pseudomonadineae, order Pseudomonadales, occurring as rod-shaped to coccoid cells found in the soil and active in fixation of atmospheric nitrogen. It includes two species, *A. fluores′cens* and *A. inso′lita.*

azotorrhea (az″o-to-re′ah) [*azote* + Gr. *rhoia* flow]. Excessive loss of nitrogen in the feces.

azoturia (az″o-tu′re-ah) [*azote* + Gr. *ouron* urine]. Excess of urea or other nitrogen compounds in the urine.

azoturic (az″o-tu′rik). Pertaining to azoturia or the urinary excretion of nitrogen.

azoxybenzene (az″ok-se-ben-zēn′). A product, $C_6H_5.N.(.O.)N.C_6H_5$, of the reduction of nitrobenzene.

azoxy compound (az-ok′se). A compound which contains the group $O\langle{N- \atop N-}$ (N–N single bond).

AZT. Abbreviation for *Aschheim-Zondek test.*

Aztec type (az′tek) [*Aztec,* a tribe of aboriginal Mexicans]. See under *idiocy.*

azul (az′ool). Pinta.

azulene (az′u-lēn). A liquid hydrocarbon, $C_{15}H_{18}$, from certain volatile oils, such as oil of cubebs.

azulfidine (a-zul′fĭ-dēn). Trade mark for a preparation of salicylazosulfapyridine.

azulin (az′u-lin). A blue aniline color or dye.

azulmin (ah-zul′min). A black compound, $C_4H_5N_5O$, formed during decomposition of prussic acid.

azure (az′ūr). A methyl thionine dye. **a. A,** asymmetrical dimethyl thionine, $(CH_3)_2N.C_6H_3(SN)C_6H_3.NH.HCl$. **a. B,** tri-methyl thionine, $(CH_3)_2N.C_6H_3(SN)C_6H_3.N(CH_3).HCl$. **a. I,** a trade name for a mixture of azure A and azure B. **a. II,** a mixture of equal parts of azure I and methylthionine chloride. **methylene a.,** any one of several azures present in polychrome methyl-thionine chloride.

azuresin (az″u-rez′in). A complex combination of azure A dye and carbacrylic cationic exchange resin: used as a diagnostic aid in detection of gastric secretion.

azurophil (az-u′ro-fil) [*azure* + Gr. *philein* to love]. An element or cell that stains well with blue aniline dyes.

azurophile (az″u-ro-fīl). 1. Azurophil. 2. Azurophilic.

azurophilia (az″u-ro-fil′e-ah). A condition in which the blood contains cells having azurophil granulations.

azurophilic (az″u-ro-fil′ik). Staining well with blue aniline dyes; pertaining to or characterized by azurophilia.

azygogram (az′ĭ-go-gram). The roentgenogram obtained by azygography.

azygography (az″ĭ-gog′rah-fe). Roentgenography of the azygous venous system, usually employed for evaluation of abnormal tumor masses in the mediastinum, as evidenced by extrinsic pressure upon or complete obstruction of the visualized azygous vein.

azygos (az′ĭ-gos) [*a* neg. + Gr. *zygon* yoke or pair]. 1. Unpaired. 2. Any unpaired part.

azygosperm (ah-zi′go-sperm″) [*a* neg. + Gr. *zygon* yoke or pair + *sperma* seed]. Azygospore.

azygospore (ah-zi′go-spōr″) [*a* neg. + Gr. *zygon* yoke or pair + *sporos* seed]. A spore developed directly from a gamete without conjugation.

azygous (az′ĭ-gus). Having no fellow; unpaired.

azymia (ah-zim′e-ah) [*a* neg. + Gr. *zymē* ferment]. Absence of an enzyme.

azymic (ah-zim′ik). Not causing fermentation; not arising from fermentation.

azymous (ah-zi′mus). Azymic.

B

B. Chemical symbol for *boron;* also the symbol of *gauss* and an abbreviation for *Bacillus,* L. *bal′neum* (bath), *Baumé scale, Benoist scale,* and *buccal.*

β. The second letter of the Greek alphabet. See *beta-.*

Ba. The chemical symbol for *barium.*

B.A. Abbreviation for L. *bal′neum are′nae* (sand bath), *Bachelor of Arts,* and *buccoaxial.*

B. and M. 693. Sulfapyridine.

Babbitt metal (bab′it) [Isaac *Babbitt,* American inventor, 1799–1862]. See under *metal.*

Babcock's operation (bab′koks) [William Wayne *Babcock,* Philadelphia surgeon, born 1872]. See under *operation.*

Babcock's test (bab′koks) [Stephen Moulton *Babcock,* American agricultural chemist, 1843–1931]. See under *tests.*

Babes' treatment, tubercle (bah′bāz) [Victor *Babes,* Roumanian bacteriologist, 1854–1926]. See under *treatment* and *tubercle.*

Babes-Ernst bodies (bah′bāz-ernst) [Victor *Babes;* Paul *Ernst,* German pathologist, 1859–1937]. Metachromatic granules.

Babesia (ba-be′ze-ah) [Victor *Babes*]. A genus of protozoan parasites found in red blood corpuscles of various animals, including cattle, dogs, sheep, goats, swine, and horses, and transmitted by ticks. Formerly called *Piroplasma.* **B. bigemina,** the causative organism of Texas fever, is transmitted by *Margaropus annulatus.* **B. bovis,** the cause of hemoglobinuria, fever, and anemia in cattle in Europe, is transmitted by *Ixodes ricinus.* **B. canis,** the cause of malignant jaundice in dogs, is transmitted by *Haemaphysalis leachi, Rhipicephalus sanguineus,* and *Dermacentor reticulatus.*

babesiasis, babesiosis (ba-be-si′ah-sis, ba-be″se-o′sis). Infection with Babesia.

Babesiella (ba-be″se-el′ah). Babesia.

Babinski's law, reflex, sign, syndrome (bah-bin′skēz) [Josef François Felix *Babinski,* physician in Paris, 1857–1932]. See under the nouns.

baby (ba′be). An infant; a child not yet able to walk. **blue b.,** an infant born with cyanosis due to a congenital heart lesion or to congenital atelectasis. **"cloud b.,"** an apparently well infant who, because of the interaction of viruses and bacteria present in the respiratory tract or elsewhere, is able to contaminate the surrounding atmosphere with clouds of bacteria, and is thus responsible for nursery epidemics of staphylococcal infection.

B.A.C. Abbreviation for *buccoaxiocervical.*

bacca (bak′ah), pl. *bac′cae* [L.]. A berry.

baccate (bak′āt). Resembling a berry.

Baccelli's method, sign (bak-chel′ēz) [Guido *Baccelli,* Italian physician, 1832–1916]. See under *method* and *sign.*

bacciform (bak′sĭ-form) [L. *bacca* berry + *forma* shape]. Berry-shaped.

Bachman reaction, test [George William *Bachman,* American parasitologist, born 1890]. See under *tests.*

Bachmann's bundle [Jean George *Bachmann,* American physiologist, born 1877]. See under *bundle.*

Bacillaceae (bas″ĭ-la′se-e). A systematic family of schizomycetes, order Eubacteriales, made up of rod-shaped cells capable of producing cylindrical, ellipsoidal, or spherical endospores which are located terminally, subterminally, or centrally. They are mostly saprophytic, commonly found in the soil, but a few are parasitic on insects or animals, and may produce disease. It includes two genera, *Bacillus* and *Clostridium,* the former aerobic, and the latter obligate anaerobes.

bacillar (bas′ĭ-lar). Bacillary.

bacillary (bas′ĭ-la″re). Pertaining to bacilli or to rodlike forms.

bacillemia (bas″ĭ-le′me-ah) [*bacillus* + Gr. *haima* blood]. The presence of bacilli in the blood.

bacilli (bah-sil′i) [L.]. Plural of *bacillus.*

bacillicidal (bas″ĭ-lĭ-si′dal). Destructive to bacilli.

bacillicide (bah-sil′ĭ-sīd) [*bacillus* + L. *caedere* to kill]. An agent that is destructive to bacilli.

bacilliculture (bah-sil′ĭ-kul-chur). The artificial propagation of bacilli.

bacilliform (bah-sil′ĭ-form) [*bacillus* + L. *forma* form]. Having the appearance of a bacillus.

bacilligenic (bah-sil″ĭ-jen′ik). Bacillogenic.

bacilliparous (bas-ĭ-lip′ah-rus) [*bacillus* + L. *parere* to produce]. Producing bacilli.

bacillogenic (bah-sil″o-jen′ik). 1. Caused by bacilli. 2. Producing bacilli.

bacillogenous (bas″ĭ-loj′e-nus). Caused by bacilli.

bacillophobia (bas″ĭ-lo-fo′be-ah) [*bacillus* + Gr. *phobos* fear + *-ia*]. A morbid fear of disease-producing microorganisms.

bacilloscopy (bas″ĭ-los′ko-pe) [*bacillus* + Gr *skopein* to examine]. Examination to detect bacilli.

bacillosis (bas″ĭ-lo′sis) [L. *bacillum* a rod]. The state of bacillary infection.

bacillotherapy (bah-sil′o-ther″ah-pe). Bacteriotherapy.

bacilluria (bas″e-lu′re-ah) [*bacillus* + Gr. *ouron* urine + *-ia*]. The presence of bacilli in the urine.

Bacillus (bah-sil′lus) [L. "little rod"]. A genus of microorganisms of the family Bacillaceae, order Eubacteriales, including large gram-positive, aerobic, spore-forming bacteria separated into 25 species, of which 3 are pathogenic, or potentially pathogenic, and the remainder are saprophytic soil forms. Many organisms historically called Bacillus are now classified in other genera. **B. ac′idi lac′tici,** *Escherichia coli* var. *acidilactici.* **B. aerog′enes capsula′tus,** *Clostridium perfringens.* **B. al′vei,** the etiologic agent of European foulbrood of honey bees. **B. an′thracis,** the causative agent of anthrax in lower animals and man. **B. botuli′nus,** *Clostridium botulinum.* **B. bre′vis,** an organism which is the source of the antibiotics gramicidin and tyrocidin. **B. bronchisep′ticus,** *Bordetella bronchiseptica.* **B. co′li,** *Escherichia coli.* **B. dysente′riae,** *Shigella dysenteriae.* **B. enterit′idis,** *Salmonella enteritidis.* **B. faeca′lis alcalig′enes,** *Alcaligenes faecalis.* **B. lar′vae,** the specific etiologic agent of American foulbrood of honeybees, not pathogenic for man. **B. lep′rae,** *Mycobacterium leprae.* **B. mal′lei,** *Actinobacillus mallei.* **B. oedem′atis malig′ni No. II,** *Clostridium novyi.* **B. pneumo′niae,** *Klebsiella pneumoniae.* **B. polymyx′a,** a saprophytic soil and water microorganism which produces the antibiotic polymyxin. **B. pseudomal′lei,** *Pseudomonas pseudomallei.* **B. pyocya′neus,** *Pseudomonas aeruginosa.* **B. sub′tilis,** a common saprophytic soil and water form, often occurring as a laboratory contaminant, and in rare instances found in apparently causal relation to pathologic processes, such as conjunctivitis. **B. tet′ani,** *Clostridium tetani.* **B. ty′phi, B. typho′sus,** *Salmonella typhosa.* **B. welch′ii,** *Clostridium perfringens.* **B. whit′mori,** *Pseudomonas pseudomallei.*

Bacillus anthracis.

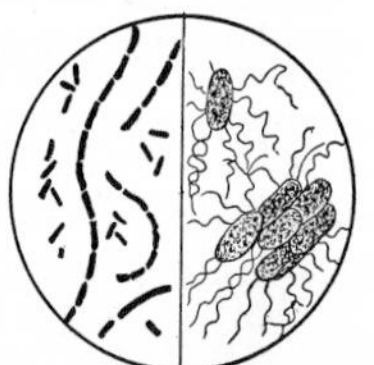

Bacillus subtilis.

bacillus (bah-sil′us), pl. *bacilli* [L.]. 1. In general, any rod-shaped bacterium; any spore-forming, rod-shaped microorganism of the order Eubacteriales. 2. An organism of the genus *Bacillus*. **b. aborti′vus equi′nus,** *Salmonella abortivo-equina*. **Bang's b.,** *Brucella abortus*. **Battey bacilli,** unclassified mycobacteria of Group III (nonphotochromogens), which may produce tuberculosis-like disease in man. **Boas-Oppler b.,** an organism first found in gastric juice of patients with stomach carcinoma, similar to if not identical with *Lactobacillus bulgaricus*. **Bordet-Gengou b.,** *Bordetella pertussis*. **Calmette-Guerin b.,** an organism of the strain *Mycobacterium tuberculosis* var. *bovis*, rendered completely avirulent by cultivation for many years on bile-glycero-potato medium. **colon b.,** *Escherichia coli*. **Döderlein's b.,** a large, gram-positive microorganism commonly found in the vagina, said to be identical with *Lactobacillus acidophilus;* a preparation of a lyophilized strain of the true Döderlein bacillus is available for the treatment of vaginitis. **Ducrey's b.,** *Haemophilus ducreyi*. **dysentery bacilli,** gram-negative, non–spore-forming rods related to other enteric bacteria, and causing dysentery in man. See *Shigella*. **Fick's b.,** *Proteus vulgaris*. **Flexner's b.,** *Shigella flexneri*. **Friedländer's b.,** *Klebsiella pneumoniae*. **Gärtner's b.,** *Salmonella enteritidis*. **Ghon-Sachs b.,** *Clostridium septicum*. **glanders b.,** *Pseudomonas mallei*. **Hansen's b.,** *Mycobacterium leprae*. **Hofmann's b.,** *Corynebacterium pseudodiphtheriticum*. **Johne's b.,** *Mycobacterium paratuberculosis*. **Klebs-Löffler b.,** *Corynebacterium diphtheriae*. **Koch-Weeks b.,** *Haemophilus aegyptius*. **Morax-Axenfeld b.,** *Haemophilus duplex*. **Morgan's b.,** *Proteus morgani*. **Newcastle-Manchester b.,** *Shigella flexneri* type 6, Boyd 88. **Nocard's b.,** *Salmonella typhimurium*. **paracolon bacilli,** microorganisms commonly found in the intestinal flora, distinguished by delayed (5–21 days) fermentation of lactose. See *Paracolobactrum*. **Pfeiffer's b.,** *Haemophilus influenzae*. **Preisz-Nocard b.,** *Corynebacterium pseudotuberculosis*. **rhinoscleroma b.,** a microorganism closely resembling *Klebsiella pneumoniae*, isolated from granulomatous lesions in rhinoscleroma. **Schmitz's b.,** *Shigella ambigua*. **Schmorl's b.,** *Bacteroides funduliformis*. **smegma b.,** an acid-fast microorganism found in both male and female smegma, closely resembling the tubercle bacillus. **Sonne-Duval b.,** *Shigella sonnei*. **swine rotlauf b.,** *Erysipelothrix rhusiopathiae*. **timothy b.,** *Mycobacterium phlei*. **tubercle b.,** *Mycobacterium tuberculosis*. **typhoid b.,** *Salmonella typhi*. **vole b.,** *Mycobacterium microti*. **Whitmore's b.,** *Pseudomonas pseudomallei*.

bacitracin (bas″ĭ-tra′sin). A substance produced by the growth of a gram-positive, spore-forming organism belonging to the licheniformis group of *Bacillus subtilis:* used as an antibiotic for topical application or intramuscular injection; effective against susceptible gram-positive bacteria, gonococci, meningococci, and *Entamoeba histolytica*.

back (bak). The posterior part of the trunk from the neck to the pelvis. **bent b.,** camptocormia. **flat b.,** a back which appears flat as a result of decrease of normal lumbar lordosis and normal thoracic kyphosis. **functional b.,** a condition of fatigue and defective balance marked by more or less continuous lumbar pain. **hollow b.,** lordosis. **hump b., hunch b.,** kyphosis. **poker b.,** spondylitis deformans. **saddle b.,** lordosis.

backalgia (bak-al′je-ah). Traumatic back pain.

backbone (back′bōn). The vertebral column, forming a continuous, comparatively rigid structure in the midline of the back. Called also *Columna vertebralis* [N A].

back-cross (bak′kros). The mating of an offspring of the first generation of a hybrid mating with one of the parents.

backflow (bak′flo). The flowing of a current in a direction the reverse of that normally taken; regurgitation. **pyelovenous b.,** the drainage of fluid from the pelvis of the kidney into the venous system under certain conditions of back pressure.

backing (bak′ing). In dentistry, the piece of metal which supports the porcelain facing, and to which the pins of the tooth are soldered. **alloy b.,** one made of an alloy instead of pure platinum or gold.

backknee (bak′ne). Genu recurvatum.

back-raking (bak-rāk′ing). Extraction of impacted feces from the rectum of an animal.

back-up (bak′up). The distance through which a high voltage current passes in the atmosphere.

$BaCl_2$. Barium chloride.

Bacon's anoscope (ba′kunz) [Harry E. *Bacon*, American proctologist, born 1900]. See under *anoscope*.

Bact. Abbreviation for *Bacterium*.

bacteremia (bak″ter-e′me-ah) [Gr. *baktērion* little rod + *haima* blood]. The presence of bacteria in the blood.

bacteria (bak-te′re-ah) [L.]. Plural of *bacterium*.

Bacteriaceae (bak″te-re-a′se-e). A name formerly given a family of schizomycetes.

bacterial (bak-te′re-al). Pertaining to, or caused by, bacteria.

bactericholia (bak″ter-e-ko′le-ah). Bacteriocholia.

bactericidal (bak″ter-ĭ-si′dal) [*bacterium* + L. *caedere* to kill]. Capable of destroying bacteria.

bactericide (bak-ter′ĭ-sīd). An agent that destroys bacteria. **specific b.,** bacteriolysin.

bactericidin (bak-ter″ĭ-si′din). A substance which kills bacteria.

bacterid (bak′ter-id). A skin eruption caused by bacteria or bacterial infection. **pustular b.,** a pustular disease of the skin of the palms or soles having some relationship to focal infection (Andrews).

bacteride (bak″ter-īd). Bacterid.

bacteridia (bak″ter-id′e-ah). Plural of *bacteridium*.

bacteridium (bak″ter-id′e-um), pl. *bacterid′ia*. A term formerly used as a generic name for certain bacilli.

Bacterieae (bak-te′re-e-e). A name formerly given a tribe of schizomycetes.

bacteriemia (bak″ter-e-e′me-ah). Bacteremia.

bacteriform (bak-ter′e-form). Resembling a bacterium in form.

bacterin (bak′ter-in). A bacterial vaccine.

bacterination (bak-ter-ĭ-na′shun). 1. Inoculation with bacteria; microbination. 2. Treatment with a bacterial vaccine.

bacterinia (bak-tĕ-rin′e-ah). The condition of unfavorable action which sometimes follows inoculation with bacterial vaccines.

bacterio-agglutinin (bak-te″re-o-ah-gloo′tĭ-nin). An agglutinin which causes the clumping of bacteria.

bacteriochlorin (bak-te″re-o-klo′rin). A pyrrol compound structurally similar to, but not identical with, chlorophyll, found in photosynthetic bacteria and catalyzing the photoreduction of CO_2.

bacteriochlorophyll (bak-te″re-o-klo′ro-fil). A green pigment, related to chlorophyll, produced by certain bacteria and capable of causing photosynthesis.

bacteriocholia (bak-te″re-o-ko′le-ah). The presence of bacteria in the biliary tract.

bacteriocidin (bak-te″re-o-si′din). An antibacterial antibody which causes death of the bacteria.

bacterioclasis (bak-te″re-ok′lah-sis) [*bacteria* + Gr. *klasis* breaking]. The breaking up or fragmentation of bacteria.

bacteriodiagnosis (bak-te″re-o-di″ag-no′sis). Diagnosis by bacteriological examination of body tissues and fluids.

bacterio-erythrin (bak-te″re-o-er′ĭ-thrin). A red pigment obtained from bacteriopurpurin.

bacteriofluorescein (bak-te″re-o-floo-o-res′e-in). A fluorescent coloring matter produced by bacteria.

bacteriogenic (bak-te″re-o-jen′ik). 1. Bacterial in origin. 2. Producing bacteria.

bacteriogenous (bak-te″re-oj′e-nus). Bacteriogenic.

bacteriohemagglutinin (bak-te″re-o-hem″ah-gloo′tĭ-nin). A hemagglutinin formed in the body by the action of bacteria.

bacteriohemolysin (bak-te″re-o-he-mol′ĭ-sin). A hemolysin produced in the body by the action of bacteria.

bacterioid (bak-te′re-oid) [Gr. *baktērion* little rod + *eidos* form]. 1. Resembling the bacteria. 2. A structure resembling a bacterium.

bacteriologic (bak-te″re-o-loj′ik). Bacteriological.

bacteriological (bak-te″re-o-loj′e-kl). Pertaining to bacteriology.

bacteriologist (bak-te″re-ol′o-jist). An expert in bacteriology.

bacteriology (bak-te″re-ol′o-je) [*bacteria* + *-logy*]. The science which treats of bacteria. Cf. *microbiology*. **hygienic b.,** sanitary b. **medical b.,** that branch of bacteriology which treats of the microorganisms that cause disease in the animal body. **pathological b.,** that branch of bacteriology which treats chiefly of the effects produced upon the animal body by the presence of bacteria and their toxins. **sanitary b.,** bacteriology which deals chiefly with methods of disease prevention based upon the knowledge of the organisms causing disease and the manner in which they spread. **systematic b.,** that branch of bacteriology which studies the classification and relationship of bacteria.

bacteriolysant (bak-te″re-ol′ĭ-sant). An agent which causes bacteriolysis.

bacteriolysin (bak-te″re-ol′ĭ-sin). An antibacterial antibody which produces lysis of bacterial cells.

bacteriolysis (bak-te″re-ol′ĭ-sis) [*bacteria* + Gr. *lysis* dissolution]. The destruction or solution of bacteria within or without the living organism (Pfeiffer, 1894).

bacteriolytic (bak-te″re-o-lit′ik). Pertaining to, characterized by, or promoting the solution or destruction of bacteria.

bacteriolyze (bak-te′re-o-līz″). To produce or cause bacteriolysis.

bacterio-opsonin (bak-te″re-o-op-so′nin). An opsonin that acts on bacteria.

bacteriopathology (bak-te″re-o-pah-thol′o-je). The study of science of microorganisms in their relations to pathology.

bacteriopexia (bak-te″re-o-pek′se-ah]. Bacteriopexy.

bacteriopexy (bak-te″re-o-pek′se) [*bacteria* + Gr. *pēxis* fixation]. The fixing of bacteria by histiocytes.

bacteriophage (bak-te′re-o-fāj″) [*bacteria* + Gr. *phagein* to eat]. A bacterial virus.

bacteriophagia (bak-te″re-o-fa′je-ah). The destruction of bacteria by a lytic agent; bacteriolysis.

bacteriophagic (bak-te″re-o-faj′ik) [*bacteria* + Gr. *phagein* to eat]. Pertaining to, characterized by, or producing bacteriophagia.

bacteriophagology (bak-te″re-o-fah-gol′o-je). The study of the bacteriophage.

bacterioph′agum intestina′le. Bacteriophage.

bacteriophagy (bak-te″re-of′ah-je). Bacteriophagia.

bacteriophobia (bak-te″re-o-fo′be-ah). A morbid fear of bacteria, or disease-producing microorganisms.

bacteriophytoma (bak-te″re-o-fi-to′mah). A tumor caused by bacteria.

bacterioplasmin (bak-te″re-o-plaz′min). Any one of a class of unchanged albuminous poisons existing in the expressed juice of certain bacteria.

bacterioprecipitin (bak-te″re-o-pre-sip′ĭ-tin). A precipitin produced in the body by the action of bacteria.

bacterioprotein (bak-te″re-o-pro′te-in). Any one of a class of poisonous albuminous (protein) bodies, unaltered by heat, derivable from certain bacteria. The bacterioproteins produce fever, inflammation, and suppuration, but are not thought to be specific.

bacteriopsonic (bak-te″re-op-son′ik). Exerting an opsonic effect on bacteria.

bacteriopsonin (bak-te″re-op′so-nin). Bacterio-opsonin.

bacteriopurpurin (bak-te″re-o-pur′pu-rin) [*bacteria* + L. *pur′pur* purple]. A light purple pigment produced by certain bacteria.

bacterioscopic (bak-te″re-o-skop′ik). Pertaining to bacterioscopy.

bacterioscopy (bak″te-re-os′ko-pe) [*bacteria* + Gr. *skopein* to examine]. The microscopic study of bacteria.

bacteriosis (bak-te″re-o′sis). Any bacterial disease.

bacteriosolvent (bak-te″re-o-sol′vent). 1. Causing lysis or dissolution of bacteria. 2. An agent which causes lysis or dissolution of bacteria.

bacteriostasis (bak-te″re-os′tah-sis) [*bacteria* + Gr. *stasis* stoppage]. The inhibition of growth, but not killing, of bacteria, usually by means of chemical compounds such as triphenylmethane or acridine, or by other dyes, sulfonamides, and antibiotics.

bacteriostat (bak-te′re-o-stat″). An agent which inhibits the growth of bacteria.

bacteriostatic (bak-te″re-o-stat′ik). 1. Inhibiting the growth or multiplication of bacteria. 2. An agent which inhibits the growth or multiplication of bacteria.

bacteriotherapy (bak-te″re-o-ther′ah-pe) [*bacteria* + *therapy*]. Treatment of disease by the introduction of bacteria into the system.

bacteriotoxemia (bak-te″re-o-tok-se′me-ah). The presence of bacterial toxins in the blood.

bacteriotoxic (bak-te″re-o-tok′sik). 1. Toxic to bacteria. 2. Caused by bacterial toxins.

bacteriotoxin (bak-te″re-o-tok′sin) [*bacteria* + *toxin*]. Any toxin produced by or toxic to bacteria.

bacteriotropic (bak-te″re-o-trop′ik) [*bacteria* + Gr. *tropos* a turning]. Turning toward or changing bacteria; opsonic.

bacteriotropin (bak-te″re-ot′ro-pin). Immune opsonin.

bacteriotrypsin (bak-te″re-o-trip′sin). A proteolytic.

bacteritic (bak″ter-it′ik). Caused by or characterized by bacteria.

Bacterium (bak-te′re-um) [L.; Gr. *baktērion* little rod]. A name formerly given a genus of schizomycetes, order Eubacteriales, made up of non–spore-forming, rod-shaped bacteria, not necessarily closely related, that were not fitted into other formally defined genera. **B. aerog′enes,** *Aerobacter aerogenes*. **B. aerugino′sum,** *Pseudomonas aeruginosa*. **B. chol′erae su′is,** *Salmonella choleraesuis*. **B. cloa′cae,** *Aerobacter cloacae*. **B. co′li, B. co′li commu′ne,** *Escherichia coli*. **B. dysente′riae,** *Shigella dysenteriae*, strain *Shigae*. **B. pes′tis bubon′icae,** *Pasteurella pestis*. **B. son′nei,** *Shigella sonnei*. **B. tularen′se,** *Pasteurella tularensis*. **B. typho′sum,** *Salmonella typhosa*.

bacterium (bak-te′re-um), pl. *bacteria* [L.; Gr. *baktērion* little rod]. In general, any microorganism of the order Eubacteriales; a non–spore-forming, rod-shaped or non-motile, rod-shaped microorganism. A loosely used generic name for any rod-shaped microorganism, especially enteric bacilli and morphologically similar forms. **acid-fast**

Plate VII

bacteria

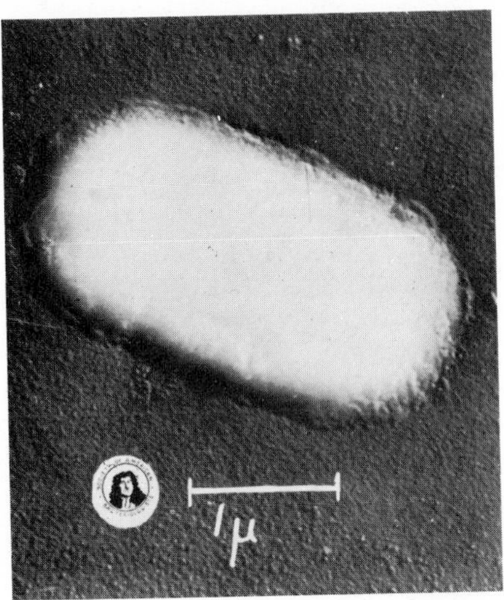

Escherichia coli. (Hedén and Wyckoff, S.A.B. LS-290.)

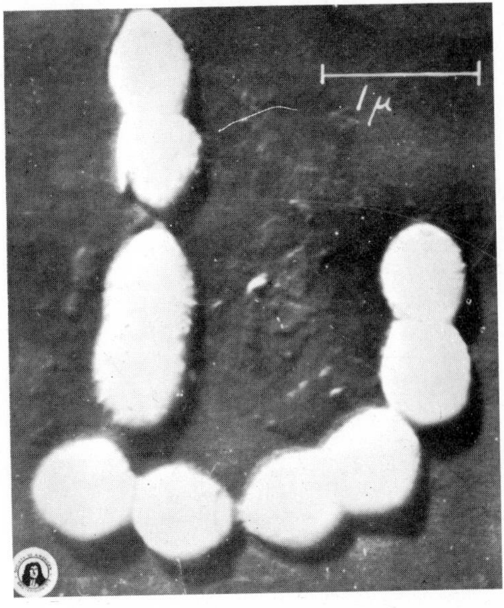

Diplococcus pneumoniae, type 2. (Williams, S.A.B. LS-162.)

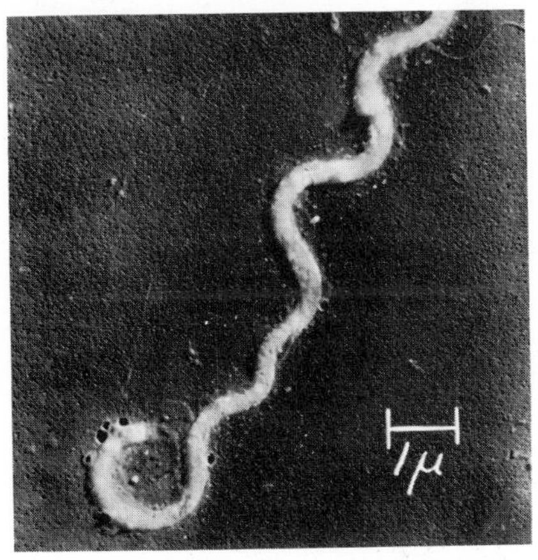

Borrelia vincentii. (Hampp, Scott, and Wyckoff, S.A.B. LS-248.)

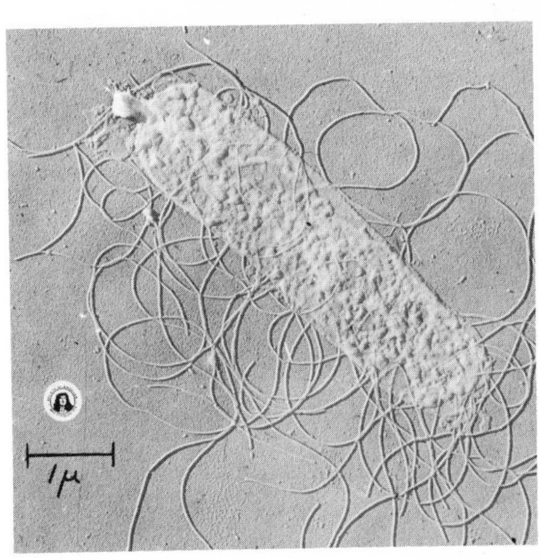

Proteus vulgaris. (Robinow and van Iterson, S.A.B. LS-260.)

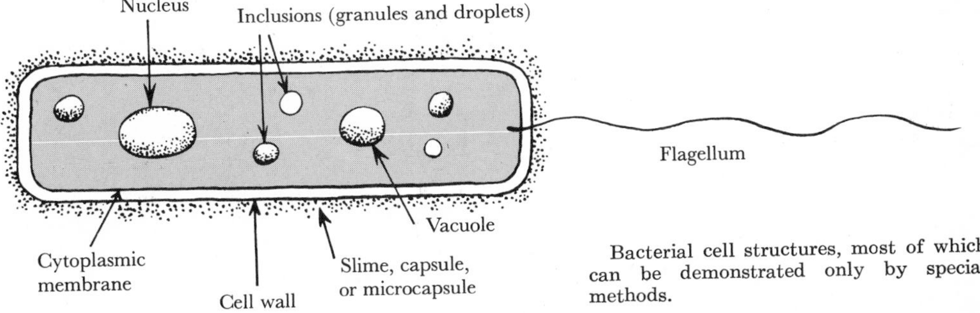

Bacterial cell structures, most of which can be demonstrated only by special methods.

ELECTRON MICROGRAPHS OF VARIOUS MICROORGANISMS, AND DIAGRAM SHOWING VARIOUS STRUCTURES OF TYPICAL BACTERIAL CELL

b., one which retains aniline stains so tenaciously that it is not decolorized by 5 per cent mineral acids. **autotrophic b.**, one which has no organic nutritional requirements. None are pathogenic. **beaded b.**, one having deeply staining granules equally spaced along the rod. **Binn's b.**, an organism of the typhoid-paratyphoid group. **chemoautotrophic b.**, an autotrophic microorganism that obtains energy by the oxidation of inorganic compounds of iron, nitrogen, sulfur, or hydrogen. None are pathogenic. **chemoheterotrophic b.**, a heterotrophic microorganism that obtains energy through the oxidation of organic compounds by mechanisms closely similar to those existing in higher animals. **chromo b., chromogenic b.**, a microorganism which produces pigment. **coliform bacteria.** See *Escherichia, Aerobacter*, and *Paracolobactrum*. **Dar es Salaam b.**, a microorganism identified as a Salmonella serotype. **denitrifying b.**, a microorganism that is able to reduce nitrates to nitrites and even to ammonia and nitrogen gas. **heterotrophic b.**, a microorganism which requires organic compounds of carbon and nitrogen as sources of energy or as essential parts of the cell. **higher bacteria,** microorganisms, mostly filamentous in form, which seem to be intermediate between Schizomycetes and the fungi (Hyphomycetes). **hydrogen b.**, a facultative autotrophic microorganism that respires by the oxidation of hydrogen to end-products such as H_2O, H_2S, and CH_4 (*Hydrogenomonas, Sporovibrio, Methanobacterium*). **iron b.**, an autotrophic microorganism that oxidizes iron from the ferrous to the ferric state (*Gallionella, Leptothrix*). **mantle b.** See *Chlamydozoa*. **mesophilic b.**, a microorganism whose optimum temperature for growth is about the same as the temperature of the human body. **nitrifying b.**, a microorganism in the soil that oxidizes ammonia to nitrite (*Nitrosomonas, Nitrosococcus*), and nitrite to nitrate (*Nitrobacter*). **nodule bacteria,** bacteria which by their growth in specific nodules on the roots of plants (legumes) tend to bring about fixation of atmospheric nitrogen. **parasitic b.**, a microorganism that is dependent on a living host for its nutrition. **pathogenic b.**, a microorganism capable of causing disease. **photoautotrophic b.**, an autotrophic microorganism which is capable of deriving energy from light. **photoheterotrophic b.**, a heterotrophic microorganism which is capable of deriving energy from light. **photosynthetic b.**, an anaerobic microorganism using radiant light for the assimilation of CO_2 as its carbon source. **psychrophilic b.**, a microorganism whose optimum temperature for growth is 15 to 20°C. **pyrogenetic b.**, a microorganism, infection with which produces fever. **rough b.**, a variant form of a bacterium which grows in rough colonies in solid media. **saprophytic b.**, a microorganism which lives in decaying organic matter. **sulfur b.**, an obligate and facultative chemoautotrophic microorganism that respires by the oxidation of sulfur and its compounds, belonging predominantly to the genera *Beggiatoa* and *Thiobacillus*. **sulfur b., purple,** a photosynthetic anaerobic microorganism whose photoreduction of CO_2 and oxidation of H_2S is catalyzed by the pigment bacteriochlorin (*Thiorhodaceae*). **thermophilic b.**, a microorganism whose optimum temperature for growth lies between 55 and 65°C. **toxigenic b.**, a microorganism which produces poison or toxin. **virulent bacteria,** bacteria which cause a high incidence of morbidity or mortality.

bacteriuria (bak-te″re-u′re-ah) [*bacteria* + Gr. *ouron* urine + *-ia*]. The presence of bacteria in the urine.

bacteroid (bak′tĕ-roid) [*bacteria* + Gr. *eidos* form]. 1. Resembling a bacterium. 2. A structurally modified bacterium.

Bacteroidaceae (bak″tĕ-roi-da′se-e) [Gr. *baktērion* rod + *eidos* form]. A family of Schizomycetes (order Eubacteriales), occurring as nonsporulating obligate anaerobic rods with rounded or pointed ends, and varying in size from minute filterable forms to long, branching, filamentous forms. It includes five genera.

Bacteroideae (bak″tĕ-roi′de-e). A name formerly given a tribe of schizomycetes.

Bacteroides (bak″tĕ-roi′dēz). A genus of nonsporulating obligate anaerobic filamentous bacteria occurring as normal flora in the mouth and large bowel; often found in necrotic tissue, probably as secondary invaders. Thirty species have been described, the type species being *B. fragilis*.

bacteroides (bak″tĕ-roi′dēz). 1. A general term for highly pleomorphic rod-shaped bacteria. 2. A microorganism of the genus Bacteroides.

bacteroidosis (bak″te-roi-do′sis). Infection with organisms of the genus Bacteroides.

bacteruria (bak″te-ru′re-ah). Bacteriuria.

baculiform (bah-ku′le-form) [L. *baculum* rod + *forma* shape]. Rod-shaped.

baculum (bak′u-lum) [L. "a stick, staff"]. A heterotopic bone developed in the fibrous septum between the corpora cavernosa and above the urethra, forming the skeleton of the penis in all insectivores, bats, rodents, and carnivores, and in primates except man.

Badal's operation (bad-alz′) [Antoine Jules *Badal*, French ophthalmologist, 1840–1929]. See under *operation*.

Baelz's disease (bāltz′es) [Erwin von *Baelz*, German physician, 1845–1913]. See under *disease*.

Baer's cavity, law, vesicle (bārz) [Karl Ernst von *Baer*, Russian anatomist, 1792–1876]. See under *cavity, law*, and *vesicle*.

Baer's method (bārz) [William Stevenson *Baer*, American orthopedic surgeon, 1872–1931]. See under *method*.

Baerensprung's erythrasma (bār′en-sproongs) [Friedrich Wilhelm Felix von *Baerensprung*, German physician, 1822–1864]. See under *erythrasma*.

Baeyer's test (ba′erz) [Adolf von *Baeyer*, German chemist, 1835–1917]. See under *test*.

B.A.G. Abbreviation for *buccoaxiogingival*.

bag (bag). A sac or pouch. **Barnes's b.**, a rubber bag for dilating the cervix uteri. **Bunyan b.**, a bag of light water-proof material to be applied over wet dressings. **Champetier de Ribes' b.**, a conic bag of silk or rubber for dilating the cervix uteri. **Chapman's b.**, a long, narrow ice-bag for application to the spine. **Hagner b.**, an inflatable rubber bag to be used by traction through the urethra to prevent hemorrhage following prostatectomy. **ice-b.**, a bag filled with ice, for applying cold to the body. **Lyster b.**, a rubber-lined bag with faucets and with straps for slinging: used for the water supply in temporary camps. **Petersen's b.**, an inflatable rubber bag inserted into the rectum so as to elevate the bladder in the operation of suprapubic cystotomy. **Pilcher b.**, a modification of the Hagner bag which provides urethral drainage as well as hemostasis. **Politzer's b.**, a soft bag of rubber for inflating the middle ear. **sarcolemmal b.**, one of the large masses of phagocytic cells, being reactive cells and nuclei of sarcolemma, seen in necrotic foci of degenerating muscle. **testicular b.**, scrotum. **Voorhees' b.**, a rubber bag which can be inflated with water: used for dilating the cervix uteri. **b. of waters,** the membranes which enclose the liquor amnii of the fetus.

bagasscosis (bag″as-ko′sis). Bagassosis.

bagassosis (bag″ah-so′sis). A respiratory disorder due to the inhalation of the dust of bagasse, the waste of sugar cane after the sugar has been extracted.

bahnung (bahn′ung) [Ger.]. Facilitation.

Baillarger's band, layer, line, sign (bi-yar-zhāz′) [Jules Gabriel François *Baillarger*, French psychiatrist, 1809–1890]. See under *line* and *sign*.

bake (bāk). To expose to high temperature at low humidity, as in the hardening of porcelain.

Baker's cyst (ba′kerz) [William Morrant *Baker*, British surgeon, 1839–1896]. See under *cyst.*

bakkola (bak′o-lah). A fungus obtained from birch trees in Finland, used in the form of a decoction in the treatment of cancer.

BAL [*British anti-lewisite*]. Dimercaprol.

balance (bal′ans) [L. *bilanx*]. 1. An instrument for weighing. 2. The harmonious adjustment of parts; the harmonious performance of functions. **acid-base b.** See under *equilibrium.* **calcium b.,** the balance between the calcium intake and its output through the body excretions. **enzyme b.** (in bacteria), a postulated steady state in relative enzyme and substrate concentrations in a bacterial culture that is altered in a different environment, thus accounting for bacterial adaptation. **fluid b.,** the state of the body in relation to ingestion and excretion of water, electrolytes, and colloids. **genic b.,** the ratio of male- to female-sex producers in the chromosome assortment as the determiner of sex. **hemogenic-hemolytic b.,** the normal balance between formation and destruction of erythrocytes, by which the number of erythrocytes and the hemoglobin level of the blood are maintained at a constant value. **nitrogen b.,** the state of the body in regard to ingestion and excretion of nitrogen. In *negative nitrogen balance* the amount of nitrogen excreted is greater than the quantity ingested; in *positive nitrogen balance* the amount excreted is smaller than the amount ingested. **occlusal b.** See *balanced occlusion.* **torsion b.** 1. A weighing balance in which the scale beam is supported by metallic ribbons which act by torsion. 2. An electrometer which acts by the twisting of a single fiber of the web of a silkworm. **water b.,** fluid b.

balaneutics (bal-ah-nu′tiks). The science of giving baths.

balanic (bah-lan′ik). Pertaining to the glans penis or glans clitoridis.

balanine (bal′ah-nin). A nitrogenous compound, balanyl histidine, occurring in muscle extract.

balanism (bal′ah-nizm) [L. *balanismus*]. Treatment with pessaries or suppositories.

balanitis (bal″ah-ni′tis) [*balano-* + *-itis*]. Inflammation of the glans penis. It is usually associated with phimosis. **b. circina′ta,** a variety attributed to the presence of *Spirochaeta balanitidis.* **b. diabet′ica,** a variety caused by the irritation of the urine in diabetes. **Follmann's b.,** a serous balanitis and posthitis without induration. **b. gangraeno′sa, gangrenous b.,** a rapidly destructive infection producing erosion of the glans penis and often destruction of the entire external genitals. The infection is believed to be due to a spirochete. **b. xerot′ica oblit′erans,** kraurosis penis; a condition in which the glans penis is shriveled, white and glossy and the meatus is stenosed. Called also *Stühmer's disease.*

balano- (bal′ah-no) [Gr. *balanos* an acorn]. A combining form indicating relationship to the glans penis or to the glans clitoridis.

balanoblennorrhea (bal″ah-no-blen″o-re′ah) [*balano-* + Gr. *blennos* mucus + *rhoia* flow]. Gonorrheal inflammation of the glans penis.

balanocele (bal′ah-no-sēl″) [*balano-* + Gr. *kēlē* hernia]. Protrusion of the glans penis through a rupture of the prepuce.

balanochlamyditis (bal″ah-no-klam″e-di′tis) [*balano-* + Gr. *chlamys* hood + *-itis*]. Inflammation of the glans clitoridis and hood.

balanoplasty (bal′ah-no-plas″te) [*balano-* + Gr. *plassein* to form]. Plastic surgery of the glans penis.

balanoposthitis (bal″ah-no-pos-thi′tis) [*balano-* + Gr. *posthē* prepuce + *-itis*]. Inflammation of the glans penis and prepuce. **specific gangrenous and ulcerative b.,** an acute inflammatory disease of the glans penis and opposed surface of the prepuce, marked by ulcerations and sometimes by gangrene, with a flow of odorous pus, and caused by a spirochete. Called also *fourth venereal disease.*

balanoposthomycosis (bal″ah-no-pos″tho-mi-ko′sis). Gangrenous balanitis.

balanopreputial (bal″ah-no-pre-pu′she-al). Pertaining to the glans penis and the prepuce.

balanorrhagia (bal″ah-no-ra′je-ah) [*balano-* + Gr. *rhēgnynai* to break]. Balanitis with free discharge of pus.

balantidiasis (bal″an-tĭ-di′ah-sis). Infestation by parasites of the genus *Balantidium.*

balantidicidal (bal-an″tĭ-dĭ-si′dal) [*Balantidium* + L. *caedere* to kill]. Destructive to Balantidium.

balantidiosis (bal″an-tid-e-o′sis). Balantidiasis.

Balantidium (bal″an-tid′e-um) [Gr. *balantidion* little bag]. A genus of Protozoa of the subclass Ciliata. **B. co′li** (Malmsten, 1857), the largest protozoal parasite of man, being 50 to 100 μ in length and 40 to 70 μ in width. It is commonly found in the intestines of swine, has been found in orangutans and monkeys, and is rarely found in man, where it may cause a balantidial dysentery. It is oval in form, actively motile, and may be found free in the contents of the cecum if they are fluid or buried in the walls. It has been called *Holophrya coli, Leucophrya coli, Paramecium coli,* and *Plagiotoma coli.* **B. minu′tum,** a species resembling *Balantidium coli,* but smaller.

balantidosis (bal″an-tĭ-do′sis). Balantidiasis.

balanus (bal′ah-nus). The glans penis.

balarsen (bah-lar′sen). Trade mark for preparations of arsthinol.

balata (bal′ah-tah). The inspissated juice or latex of *Mimusops globosa,* a tree of tropical America: used much like India rubber and gutta-percha.

Balbiana (bal″be-a′nah). A genus of Sarcosporidia. *B. gigantea* is sometimes found in the esophagus of sheep; *B. rileyi,* in the muscles of ducks.

Balbiani's body, nucleus (bahl-be-ah′nēz) [Edouard Gérard *Balbiani,* French embryologist, 1823–1899]. Yolk nucleus.

balbuties (bal-bu′she-ēz) [L.]. Stammering.

baldness (bawld′nes). Alopecia. The term is usually used to denote specifically the loss of hair on the head. **common female b.,** female pattern alopecia. **common male b.,** male pattern alopecia.

Baldy's operation (bawl′dēz) [John Montgomery *Baldy,* American gynecologist, 1860–1934]. See under *operation.*

baleri (bah-le′ri). A form of trypanosomiasis of horses, sheep, goats, and cattle in the French Sudan, caused by *Trypansoma pecaudi.* The disease is marked by severe fever, swellings over the body, injection of the conjunctiva, and considerable emaciation.

Balfour's disease (bal′forz) [George William *Balfour,* British physician, 1822–1903]. Chloroma.

Balfour's granule (bal′forz) [Sir Andrew *Balfour,* physician in Khartoum, 1873–1931]. See under *granule.*

Balkan frame, splint (bawl′kan). See under *splint.*

ball (bawl). A more or less spherical mass. **chondrin b.,** one of the ball-like masses in hyaline cartilage, consisting of cells surrounded by a capsule and basophilic matrix. **fatty b. of Bichat,** sucking pad. **food b.,** phytobezoar. **hair b.,** trichobezoar. **Marchi b's,** ellipsoid or ovoid segments of myelin produced by degeneration, staining brown by Marchi methods. **oat hair b.,** a trichobezoar formed in the stomach of the horse from the fine hairs within the outer husk of the oat grain and other materials. **wool b.,** a trichobezoar containing wool fibers and other substances.

Ball's operation, valve (bawlz) [Sir Charles Bent *Ball,* Irish surgeon, 1851–1916]. See under *operation,* and *plicae transversales recti.*

Ballance's sign (bal′an-siz) [Sir Charles *Ballance,* British surgeon, 1856–1936]. See under *sign.*

Ballet's disease, sign (bal-āz′) [Gilbert *Ballet*, French neurologist, 1853–1916]. See under *disease* and *sign*.

Ballingall's disease (bal′ing-gawlz) [Sir George *Ballingall*, British surgeon, 1780–1855]. Mycetoma.

ballism (bal′izm). Ballismus.

ballismus (bah-liz′mus) [Gr. *ballismos* a jumping about, dancing]. Violent flinging movements caused by contractions of the proximal limb muscles as a result of destruction of the subthalamic nucleus of Luysii or its fiber connections, sometimes affecting only one side of the body (hemiballismus).

ballistic (bah-lis′tik). 1. Jerking or twitching; pertaining to or characterized by ballismus. 2. Pertaining to or caused by projectiles.

ballistics (bah-lis′tiks) [Gr. *ballein* to throw]. The scientific study of the motion of projectiles. **wound b.,** the scientific study of the motion (speed and direction) of missiles (bullets and other projectiles) in relation to the injuries produced by them.

ballistocardiogram (bah-lis″to-kar′de-o-gram). The tracing made by a ballistocardiograph.

ballistocardiograph (bah-lis″to-kar′de-o-graf). An apparatus for recording the stroke volume of the heart as a means of calculating the cardiac output. The heart beat of the subject causes movement of the supporting structure, usually a table on which he lies, and these movements are recorded photographically as a series of waves.

ballistocardiography (bah-lis″to-kar″de-og′rah-fe). The recording, by means of a ballistocardiograph, of the recoil movements of an animal body which result from motion of its heart and blood.

ballistophobia (bah-lis″to-fo′be-ah) [Gr. *ballein* to throw + *phobia*]. A morbid dread of missiles.

ballonnement (bah-lōn-mon′) [Fr.]. Ballooning.

balloon (bah-lo͞on′). To distend with air or gas.

ballooning (bah-lo͞on′ing). The operation of distending any cavity of the body with air for therapeutic purposes.

ballotable (bah-lot′ah-bl). Capable of showing ballottement.

ballottement (bah-lot-mon′) [Fr. "a tossing about"]. A palpatory maneuver to test for a floating object. The term is applied especially to a maneuver for detecting the existence of pregnancy by pushing up the uterus by a finger inserted into the vagina, so as to cause the fetus to rise and fall again like a heavy body in water. **abdominal b., indirect b.,** that which is effected by the finger applied to the abdominal wall. **direct b., vaginal b.,** that done by the finger in the vagina. **b. of the eye, ocular b.,** the falling of opaque masses in a fluid vitreous after movements of the eyeball. **renal b.,** palpation of the kidney by pressing one hand into the abdominal wall while the other hand makes quick thrusts forward from behind so as to throw the kidney against the anterior hand.

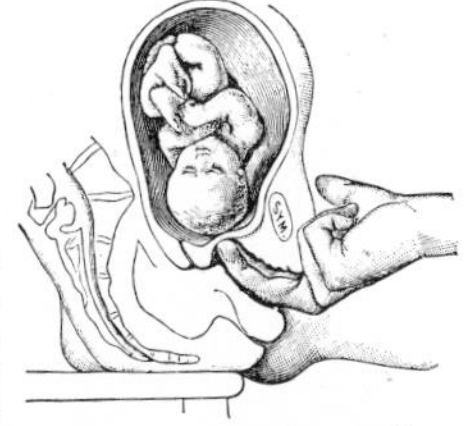

Ballottement (Jewett).

balm (bahm) [Fr. *baume*]. 1. A healing or soothing medicine. 2. A plant of the genus *Melis′sa*, especially *M. officina′lis:* carminative and aromatic. 3. Balsam. **blue b.,** Melissa. **b. of Gilead,** balsam of Gilead. **lemon b.,** Melissa. **mountain b.,** Eriodictyon. **sweet b.,** Melissa.

Balme's cough (bahlmz) [Paul Jean *Balme*, French physician, born 1857]. See under *cough*.

balmony (bal′mo-ne). The scrophulariaceous herb, *Chelone glabra*, of North America.

balneary (bal′ne-a″re) [L. *balnearium*]. An institution or department of an institution where therapeutic baths are administered.

balneation (bal″ne-a′shun). Balneotherapy.

balneography (bal″ne-og′rah-fe) [L. *balneum* bath + Gr. *graphein* to write]. A treatise on baths.

balneology (bal″ne-ol′o-je) [L. *balneum* bath + *-logy*]. The science of baths and their therapeutic uses.

balneotechnics (bal″ne-o-tek′niks). The art of preparing and administering baths.

balneotherapeutics (bal″ne-o-ther-ah-pu′tiks). Balneotherapy.

balneotherapy (bal″ne-o-ther′ah-pe) [L. *balneum* bath + Gr. *therapeia* treatment]. The treatment of disease by baths.

balneum (bal′ne-um), pl. *bal′nea* [L.]. A bath. **b. are′nae,** a sand bath; also *ammotherapy* and *psammotherapy*. **b. coeno′sum,** mud bath. **b. lac′teum,** milk bath. **b. lu′teum,** mud bath. **b. pneumat′icum,** air bath.

balopticon (bal-op′te-kon) [Gr. *ballein* to throw + *optikos* pertaining to sight]. Trade mark of a projection apparatus for throwing an enlarged image on a screen.

Bals. Abbreviation for *balsam*.

balsam (bawl′sam) [L. *balsamum;* Gr. *balsamon*]. A semifluid, resinous, and fragrant juice of vegetable origin. The balsams are resins combined with oils. **Canada b.,** a turpentine procured from *Abies balsamea*, the balsam fir of North America. **b. of copai′ba,** copaiba. **friars' b.,** compound benzoin tincture. **b. of Gilead,** the resinous juice of *Commiphora opobalsamum*, a small evergreen tree growing in the region of the Red Sea, still used as a medicine and cosmetic in eastern countries. **gurjun b.,** an oleoresin from *Dipterocarpus turbinatus* and other species of Dipterocarpus growing in East India. **Holland b.,** juniper tar. **Mecca b.,** b. of Gilead. **b. of Peru, peruvian b.,** a dark brown viscid liquid obtained from *Myroxylon pereirae*, used as a local irritant. **St. Thomas' b.,** a resinous juice obtained from the tree, *Santiriopsis balsamifera*, grown on the island of St. Thomas. **silver b.,** juniper tar. **b. of sulfur,** a preparation made by boiling sulfur in linseed or olive oil. **tolu b.,** a balsam obtained from *Myroxylon balsamum*, used as an ingredient of compound benzoin tincture. **Turlington's b., Wade's b.,** compound benzoin tincture.

balsamic (bawl-sam′ik) [L. *balsamicus*]. Of the nature of a balsam.

balsamo (bal′sah-mo) [Sp.]. Balsam. **b. de tolu′,** tolu balsam. **b. del Peru′,** balsam of Peru.

Balsamodendron (bal″sah-mo-den′dron) [L.; Gr. *balsamon* balsam + *dendron* tree]. A genus of old world amyridaceous trees of many species, producing bdellium myrrh, and other balsamic drugs.

balsamum (bal′sah-mum) [L.]. Balsam. **b. peruvia′num,** balsam of Peru.

Balser's necrosis (bahl′zerz) [W. *Balser*, German physician]. See under *necrosis*.

balteum (bal′te-um) [L.]. Belt, or girdle. **b. vene′reum,** Venus' girdle.

Bamberger's albuminuria, disease, fluid, pulse, sign, etc. (bahm′ber-gerz) [Heinrich von *Bamberger*, Austrian physician, 1822–1888]. See under the nouns.

Bamberger-Marie disease [Eugen *Bamberger*, Austrian physician, 1858–1921; Pierre *Marie*, French physician, 1853–1940]. Hypertrophic pulmonary osteoarthropathy.

Bancroft's filariasis (ban′krofts) [Joseph *Bancroft*, English physician in Australia, 1836–1894]. See under *filariasis*.

bancroftosis (ban″krof-to′sis). Infestation with *Wuchereria bancrofti*.

band (band). A part, structure, or appliance that binds. In dentistry, a thin strip of metal formed to encircle horizontally the crown of a natural tooth or its root. See *anchor b.* and *matrix b.* **absorption b's,** dark bands in the spectrum due to absorption of light by the medium (a solid, a liquid, or a gas) through which the light has passed. Cf. *absorption lines*, under *line.* **adjustable b.,** a dental band provided with an adjusting screw. **all-closing b.,** a dental band, which encircles the entire tooth. **amniotic b.,** a fibrous band passing from the fetus to its amnion. **anchor b.,** a band which is applied to a tooth in order to secure anchorage for tooth movement. **angiomesenteric b.,** Harris's b. **Angle b.,** a clamp band used in orthodontics which clamps on the lingual side. **anogenital b.,** a fetal fillet which is the rudiment of the perineum. **anterior b. of colon,** tenia libera. **atrioventricular b., auriculoventricular b.,** bundle of His. **axis b.,** the primitive streak. **belly b.,** a flannel strip worn around the abdomen. **Biets's b's,** bands of linear ichthyosis. **b. of Broca,** a part of the primordial rhinencephalon close to the anterior perforated space. **Büngner's b's,** bands of syncytium formed by the union of sheath cells during the regeneration of peripheral nerves: called also *Ledbänder*. **Clado's b.,** the suspensory ligament of the ovary covered with peritoneum. **clamp b.,** a dental band held in place with a screw nut. **coagulation b.,** the band formed in Weltmann's coagulation test. **b's of colon, longitudinal,** teniae coli. They are the *mesocolic b.*, the *free b.*, and the *omental b.* **contoured b.,** a dental band which is shaped to the contour of the tooth. **coronary b.** See *coronary cushion*, under *cushion.* **dentale b.** See *fascia dentata.* **free b. of colon,** tenia libera. **Giacomini's b.,** the grayish band constituting the anterior end of the gyrus dentatus of the hippocampus. **H. b.,** Hensen's disk. **Harris's b.,** a fold of peritoneum extending from the gallbladder and cystic duct across the transverse colon or transverse mesocolon, forming a distinct fold across the ventral surface of the duodenum at the hepatic flexure. It produces compression of the duodenum. Called also *hepatoduodenal band* or *membrane.* **head b.,** a strap that fastens a mirror to the forehead. **Henle's b.,** fibers from the anterior aponeurosis of the transversus abdominis muscle extending behind the rectus below the arcuate line. **horny b.,** the anterior part of the tenia semicircularis. **I b.,** the light disk or band within a striated muscle fibril; isotropic disk, intermediate disk. **iliotibial b.,** tractus iliotibialis. **Johnson b.,** a form of dental band to be adjusted to the tooth by pliers. **Lane's b.,** a congenital anomalous band or membrane in the small intestine which helps the mesentery and ileum to hold up the loaded cecum; its kinking produces obstruction of the terminal ileum, which is called *Lane's kink, ileal kink,* or *angulation of the ileum.* **Leonardo's b.,** a term proposed by Sudhoff for the moderator band of Reil, first delineated by Leonardo da Vinci. **limbic b's,** a superior and an inferior muscular band developed in the right atrium of the fetal heart which become the basis of Lower's tubercle and the sinus septum. **lip furrow b.,** labiodental sulcus. **Luken's b.,** a clamp band used in orthodontics which clamps on the buccal side. **Magill b.,** a plain anchor band used in orthodontics. **Maissiat's b.,** tractus iliotibialis. **Matas's b.,** an aluminum band for temporarily occluding large blood vessels in order to test the condition of the collateral circulation. **matrix b.,** a thin piece of metal that is fitted around a tooth to supply a missing wall of a multisurface cavity or to support the tooth as amalgam is packed into the cavity. **Meckel's b.,** a part of the anterior ligament fastening the malleus to the wall of the tympanum. **mesocolic b.,** tenia mesocolica. **moderator b.,** trabecula septomarginalis. **omental b.,** tenia omentalis. **Parham b.,** a metallic ribbon used to fix a fractured long bone by encircling the bone at the site of the fracture. **pecten b.,** a name given a band of fibrous tissue thought to form beneath the pecten. **perioplic b.,** the band of secretor cells at the upper border of the hoof of animals. It secretes the periople. **phonatory b's,** the vocal cords, or an artificial substitute for them. **primitive b.,** the transparent material in the axis of a nerve tube. **Q b.,** the dark disk or band of a striated muscle fibril: called also *anisotropic disk, Brucker's line,* and *transverse disk.* **b. of Reil.** 1. A muscular fillet extending across the right ventricle of the heart, now regarded as forming one of the terminal parts of the bundle of His. See *bundle of His.* 2. Lemniscus medialis. **b. of Remak,** axon. **retention b.,** muscle of Treitz. **b's of Schreger,** a series of bands, visible by reflected light, in the enamel of longitudinal sections of human teeth. **Sebileau's b's,** three thickenings in Sibson's fascia. **Simonart's b's,** bands formed by adhesions between the amnion and the fetus, which have been drawn out by distention of the amniotic cavity with fluid. **sinoventricular b.,** bundle of His. **Soret's b.,** a band in the violet end of the spectrum of hemoglobin. **b. of Tarinus,** horny b. **Vicq d'Azyr's b.,** Baillarger's line. **Z b.,** Krause's membrane. **zonular b.,** zona orbicularis articulationis coxae.

bandage (ban′dij). 1. A strip or piece of gauze or other material for wrapping or applying over any body part or member. 2. To apply a strip of gauze or other material around any body part. **abdominal b.,** a wide support worn about the hips, during pregnancy, after an abdominal operation, or for obesity. **ace b.,** trade mark for a bandage of woven elastic material. **adaptic b.,** trade mark for various dressing materials. **adhesive absorbent b.,** a sterile individual dressing consisting of a plain absorbent compress affixed to a film or fabric coated with a pressure-sensitive adhesive substance. **A-S-E b.,** the third roller of Desault's bandage which forms a triangle, the angles of which are located at the axilla, shoulder, and elbow. **Barton's b.,** a figure-of-8 bandage supporting the lower jaw below and in front. **Baynton's b.,** adhesive plaster strapping of the leg for indolent ulcer. **binocle b.,** a bandage covering both eyes. **Borsch's b.,** an eye bandage covering both the diseased and the healthy eye. **capeline b.,** a bandage applied like a cap or hood to the head or shoulder or to a stump. **circular b.,** a bandage applied in circular turns about a part. **compression b.,** a bandage by which pressure is applied to a part or area. **crucial b.,** T bandage. **demigauntlet b.,** a bandage that covers the hand, but leaves the fingers uncovered. **Desault's b.,** a bandage binding the elbow to the side, with a pad in the axilla: for fractured clavicle. **elastic b.,** a bandage of India rubber for exerting continuous pressure upon a part. **Esmarch's b.,** an India rubber bandage applied to a limb from the distal part proximally, so as to expel blood from the portion to be operated on. **figure-of-8 b.,** a bandage in which the turns cross each other like the figure eight (8). **Fricke's b.,** strapping of the scrotum for orchitis and epididymitis. **Galen's b.,** a bandage with each end split into three pieces: the middle is placed on the crown of the head; the two anterior strips are fastened at the back of the neck; the two posterior ones, on the forehead; and the two middle ones are tied under the chin. **Garretson's b.,** a bandage for the lower jaw, running above the forehead and back again to cross under the occiput, and ending under the chin. **gauntlet b.,** a bandage which covers the hand and fingers like a glove. **gauze b.,** a sterilized continuous strip of absorbent gauze, in various widths and lengths, substantially free from loose threads and ravelings and tightly rolled. **Genga's b.,** Theden's b. **Gibney b.,** a bandage created by overlapping strips of ½-inch adhesive, applied over the sides and back of the foot and leg, holding the foot in slight varus and leaving the dorsum of the foot and anterior aspect of the leg uncovered. **Gibson's b.,** a bandage for retaining the bone in fracture of lower jaw. **Hamilton's b.,** a compound bandage for the lower jaw, composed of a

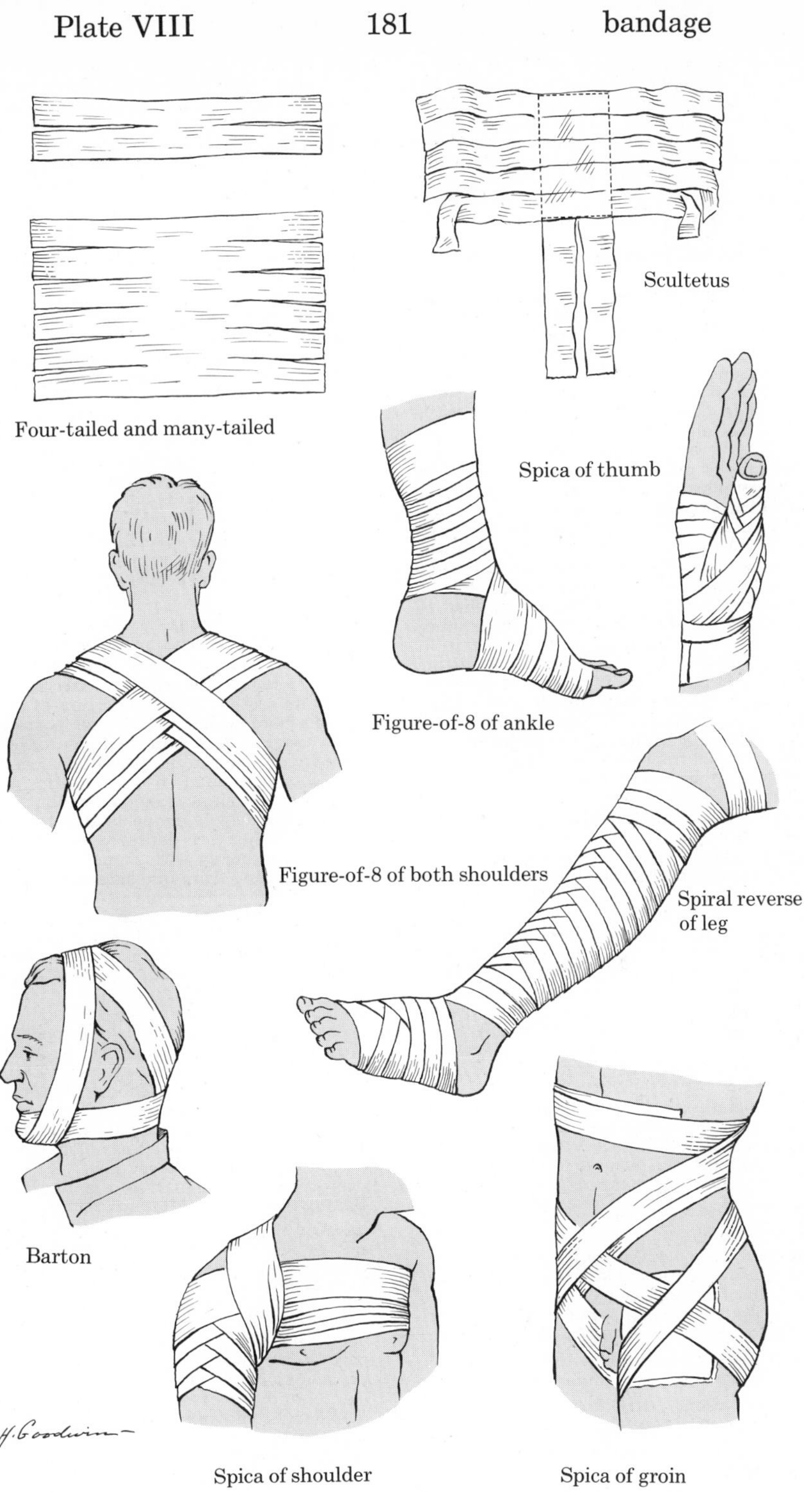

VARIOUS TYPES OF BANDAGE

leather string with straps of linen webbing. **hammock b.,** a bandage for retaining dressings on the head, consisting of a broad strip over the dressing and brought down over the ears. This strip is then held in place by a circular bandage around the head. **Heliodorus' b.,** a T bandage. **Hippocrates' b.,** capeline b. **Hueter's b.,** a spica bandage for the perineum. **immobilizing b., immovable b.,** a bandage for immobilizing a part. **Kiwisch's b.,** a form of figure-of-8 bandage of both breasts to support and firmly compress them. **Langier's b.,** a many-tailed paper bandage. **Larrey's b.,** a many-tailed bandage with the edges glued together. **Maisonneuve's b.,** a plaster-of-paris bandage made of folded cloth held in place by other bandages. **many-tailed b.,** a wide bandage so made that each end consists of many different strips. **Martin's b.,** a roller bandage of thin elastic rubber. **oblique b.,** a bandage applied obliquely up a limb without reverses. **plaster b.,** a bandage stiffened with a paste of plaster of paris, which sets and becomes very hard. **pressure b.,** a bandage for applying pressure. **Priessnitz's b.,** a cold, wet compress. **protective b.,** a bandage for covering a part or for keeping dressings in place. **recurrent b.,** a bandage of overlapping strips carried forward and backward, each turn retained by a circular bandage. **reversed b.,** one applied to a limb in such a way that the roller is inverted or half-twisted at each turn, so as to make it fit smoothly. **Ribble's b.,** the spica of the instep. **Richet's b.,** a bandage of plaster of paris to which a little gelatin has been added. **roller b.,** a simple continuous strip, to be applied spirally or circularly. **Sayre's b.,** an adhesive plaster bandage used in cases of fracture of the clavicle. **scultetus b.,** one applied in strips overlapping each other in shingle fashion. **Seutin's b.,** a starch and plaster bandage. **spica b.,** a spiral bandage folded regularly on itself like the letter V. **spiral b.,** a roller bandage applied spirally around a limb. **spiral reverse b.,** a spiral bandage applied with reverses, in order better to adapt it to the part. **starch b.,** a bandage which has been impregnated with a solution of starch which hardens after the bandage is applied. **suspensory b.,** a bandage for supporting the scrotum. **T b.,** a bandage shaped like the letter T. **Theden's b.,** a roller bandage applied from below upward over a graduated compress to control hemorrhage. **Thillaye's b.,** an arrangement of bandages for approximating the edges of the wound in the operation for harelip. **triangular b.,** a triangle of cloth used as a sling. **Tuffnell's b.,** a roller bandage of cheesecloth impregnated with a mixture of white of egg and flour. **Velpeau's b.,** a bandage to support the arm in fracture of the clavicle. **Y b.,** a bandage shaped like the letter Y.

bandager (ban′dij-er). A person who is skilled in applying bandages.

bandicoot (ban′de-ko͞ot). An Indian rodent, *Nesokia bengalensis*, which is a reservoir of *Spirillum minus*, the causative organism of rat-bite fever. It also harbors *Coxiella burneti*, which is transmitted by the bandicoot tick, *Haemaphysalis humerosa*.

Bandl's ring (ban′dl) [Ludwig *Bandl*, German obstetrician, 1842–1892]. See under *ring*.

bane (bān). A poison. **dog b.** See *Apocynum*. **leopard's b., wolf's b.** See *arnica*.

banewort (bān′wort). Belladonna leaf.

bang (bang). Bhang.

Bang's bacillus (bangz) [Bernhard L. F. *Bang*, Danish physician, 1848–1932]. *Brucella abortus*.

Bang's method (bangz) [Ivar *Bang*, Swedish physiological chemist, 1869–1918]. See under *method*.

banian (ban′yan). The *Ficus bengalensis*, an East Indian fig tree: its seeds and bark are tonic, antifebrile, and diuretic.

banisterine (ban-is′ter-in). An alkaloid from *Banisteria caapi*.

bank (bangk). A stored supply of human material or tissues for future use by other individuals, as *blood b., bone b., eye b., human-milk b., skin b.,* etc.

Bannister's disease (ban′nis-terz) [Henry Martyn *Bannister*, Chicago physician, 1844–1920]. Angioneurotic edema.

banthine (ban′thīn). Trade mark for preparations of methantheline bromide.

Banti's disease, syndrome (ban′tēz) [Guido *Banti*, Italian pathologist, 1852–1925]. See under *syndrome*.

Banting, Sir Frederick Grant (ban′ting). A Canadian physician, 1891–1941; co-discoverer of insulin, in 1922, with Charles Herbert Best and John James Rickard Macleod; co-winner, with Macleod, of the Nobel prize for medicine in 1923.

bantingism (ban′ting-izm) [William *Banting*, English coffin-maker, 1797–1878, who devised the method in 1863]. The treatment of corpulence by a restricted diet, especially by the avoidance of food containing much saccharine, farinaceous, or oily matter.

Baptisia (bap-tiz′e-ah) [L.; Gr. *baptizein* to dip in or under water]. A genus of leguminous plants. **B. tincto′ria,** a species of herbs of North America.

baptisin (bap′tĭ-zin). A glycoside from *Baptisia tinctoria:* a brownish powder, soluble in alcohol.

bar (bahr). 1. The upper part of the gums of a horse, between the grinders and the tusks, which bears no teeth. 2. That portion of the wall of a horse's hoof which is reflected posteriorly at an acute angle. 3. A unit of pressure, being a pressure by one megadyne per square centimeter. 4. A heavy wire used in orthodontics or in dental prostheses, such as a metal segment, longer than it is wide, which connects different parts of a removable partial denture. See also *connector*. **arch b.,** a heavy wire shaped to the dental arch and extending from one side to the other so that intervening teeth may be attached to it. **articulomachelian b.,** the cartilaginous structure of the embryo from which the lower jaw is developed. **b. of bladder,** Mercier's b. **clasp b.** See *clasp*. **connector b.,** a minor connector. See under *connector*. **hyoid b's,** a pair of cartilaginous plates forming the second visceral arch: a part of the hyoid bone is developed from them. **Kennedy b.,** continuous bar retainer. **labial b.,** a major connector located labial to the dental arch, and joining two or more bilateral parts of a mandibular removable partial denture. **lingual b.** 1. A heavy wire, usually of gold or stainless steel, placed along the gums on the lingual surface of the teeth of the lower jaw. 2. A major connector located lingual to the dental arch, and joining two or more bilateral parts of a mandibular removable partial denture. **median b.,** a fibrotic formation across the neck of the prostate gland, causing obstruction of the urethra. **Mercier's b.,** a ridge forming the posterior boundary of the trigone of the bladder (*plica interureterica* [N A]). **occlusal rest b.,** a minor connector used to attach an occlusal rest to a major part of a removable partial denture. **palatal b.,** a major connector which extends across the palate, and joins two or more bilateral parts of a maxillary removable partial denture. **Passavant's b.,** a "cross-roll" which appears on the posterior wall of the pharynx during speech in a person with cleft palate. It is caused by contraction of muscle fibers (palatopharyngeal sphincter). **sternal b.,** one of the paired cartilaginous bars in the embryo which unite to form the sternum. **T b.,** an orthodontic appliance that is shaped like the letter T. **terminal b's,** rods of solid cement substance which solder the edges of the free surfaces of epithelial cells.

Bar's incision (bahrz) [Paul *Bar*, French obstetrician, 1853–1945]. See under *incision*.

Barach's index (bar′aks) [Alvan Leroy *Barach*, New York physician, born 1895]. See under *index*.

baragnosis (bar″ag-no′sis) [Gr. *baros* weight + *a* neg. + *gnōsis* knowledge]. Absence of the power to recognize weight.

Bárány's sign, symptom, test (bah′rah-nēz) [Robert *Bárány*, Austrian otologist, 1876–1936; winner of the Nobel prize for medicine in 1914]. See under *symptom.*

barba (bar′bah) [L. "the beard"]. [N A, B N A] The heavy hair which grows on the lower part of a man's face, usually appearing after puberty as a secondary sex character.

barbaralalia (bar″bar-ah-la′le-ah). A form of dyslalia that is shown when speaking a foreign language.

barbasco (bar-bas′ko). Tropical plants, *Jacquinia paramensis* and *Paullinia pinnata:* used as fish poisons.

Barberio's test (bar-be′re-ōz) [Michele *Barberio*, physician in Naples, born 1872]. See under *test.*

barberry (bar′bār-e). The shrub *Berberis vulgaris* and its fruit.

barbital (bar′bĭ-tal). A white powder, 5,5-diethylbarbituric acid. Used as a central nervous system depressant. **b. sodium, b. soluble,** the monosodium salt of barbital, which is soluble.

barbitalism (bar′bĭ-tal-izm). Barbituism.

barbitone (bar′bĭ-tōn). A British name for barbital.

barbituism (bar′bĭ-tu-izm). A condition caused by the use of barbital or its derivatives and marked by chill, headache, fever, and cutaneous eruptions.

barbiturate (bar-bit′u-rāt). A salt of barbituric acid.

barbiturism (bar′bĭ-tu-rizm). Barbituism.

barbone (bar-bo′na) [It. "bearded"]. Pasteurellosis in buffalo.

barbotage (bar″bo-tahzh′) [Fr. *barboter* to dabble]. Fillestre's method of spinal anesthesia by injection of a portion of the anesthetic into the spinal fluid, followed by partial withdrawal of the fluid and then by repeated partial reinjection and withdrawal until the entire amount of anesthetic has been administered.

barbula (bar′bu-lah) [L.]. A little beard. **b. hir′ci,** hirci.

Barcoo disease, rot (bar-koo′) [*Barcoo*, a river in South Australia]. See *desert sore*, under *sore.*

Barcroft's apparatus (bar′krofts) [Sir Joseph *Barcroft*, British physiologist, 1872–1947]. See under *apparatus.*

Bard's sign (bardz′) [Louis *Bard*, French physician, 1857–1930]. See under *sign.*

Bard-Pic syndrome [Louis *Bard;* Adrien *Pic*, French physician, 1863–1944]. See under *syndrome.*

Bardach's test (bar′dakz) [Bruno *Bardach*, Vienna chemist]. See under *tests.*

Bardenheuer's extension (bar′den-hoi″erz) [Bernhard *Bardenheuer*, Cologne surgeon, 1839–1913]. See under *extension.*

Bardet-Biedl syndrome (bar-da′ be′del) [Georges *Bardet*, French physician, born 1885]. Laurence-Biedl syndrome.

Bardinet's ligament (bar″de-nāz′) [Barthélemy Alphonse *Bardinet*, French physician, 1819–1874]. See under *ligament.*

baregin (bah-re′jin). Glairin.

baresthesia (bar″es-the′ze-ah) [Gr. *baros* weight + *aisthēsis* perception + *-ia*]. Sensibility for weight or pressure; pressure sense.

baresthesiometer (bar″es-the″ze-om′e-ter) [Gr. *baros* weight + *aisthēsis* perception + *metron* measure]. An instrument for determining sensitiveness as to weight or pressure.

Barety's method (bar″a-tēz′) [Jean Paul *Barety*, French surgeon, 1887–1912]. See under *method.*

Barfoed's test (bahr′fedz) [Christen Thomsen *Barfoed*, Swedish physician, 1815–1899]. See under *tests.*

Bargen's serum, streptococcus, treatment (bar′genz) [J. Arnold *Bargen*, American physician, born 1894]. See under the nouns.

baric (ba′rik). Pertaining to barium.

barite (ba′rīt). Native barium sulfite ($BaSO_3$), occurring as a mineral.

baritosis (bar″ĭ-to′sis). Pneumoconiosis due to inhalation of barite or barium dust.

barium (ba′re-um), gen. *ba′rii* [L.; Gr. *baros* weight]. A pale yellowish, metallic element belonging to the alkaline earths, whose acid soluble salts are poisonous. Its atomic number is 56; atomic weight 137.34; symbol, Ba. **b. arsenate,** a salt, $Ba_3(AsO_4)_2$, used in phthisis and in skin diseases. **b. bromide,** a compound, $BaBr_2 + 2H_2O$, used as a heart tonic and in aneurysm and scrofula. **b. carbonate,** a poisonous salt, $BaCO_3$, formerly used in medicine; now employed in preparing the chloride, etc. **b. chloride,** a compound, $BaCl_2 + 2H_2O$, a cardiac stimulant; has been used in sclerosis of the nervous tissues and in heart block and aneurysm. **b. dioxide,** a salt, BaO_2, used in pharmacy. **b. hydrate, b. hydroxide,** $Ba(OH)_2$, a crystalline salt employed as a test for sulfates. **b. oxide,** baryta. **b. platinocyanide,** a substance, $BaPt(CN)_4.4H_2O$, used for coating the screen of the fluoroscope. **b. sulfate,** a bulky, fine, white powder without odor or taste, and free from grittiness, $BaSO_4$: used as a contrast medium in roentgenography of the digestive tract.

bariumize (bār′e-um-īz). To treat with barium.

bark (bark) [L. *cortex*]. The rind or outer cortical cover of the woody parts of a plant, tree, or shrub. **bearberry b.,** cascara sagrada. **bitter b.,** the dried bark of *Alstonia constricta*, a tree of New South Wales and Queensland. **buckthorn b.,** the dried bark of *Rhamnus frangula.* **butternut b.,** the dried inner bark of the root of *Juglans cinerea.* **calisaya b.,** cinchona. **casca b.,** the bark of *Erythrophloeum guineense.* **chittem b.,** cascara sagrada. **cinchona b.,** cinchona. **cotton root b.,** the air dried bark of roots of various species of Gossypium. **cramp b.,** the dried bark of *Viburnum opulus.* **cuprea b.,** the bark of *Remijia purdieana* or *Remijia pedunculata.* **dita b.,** the dried bark of *Alstonia scholaris*, a tree of India and the Philippines. **dogwood b.** 1. Cascara sagrada. 2. See *Cornus.* **elm b.,** the dried inner bark of *Ulmus fulva.* **fringe tree b.,** the dried bark of the root of *Chionanthus virginicus.* **Jesuit's b.,** cinchona. **Mancona b.,** casca b. **Persian b.,** cascara sagrada. **Peruvian b.,** cinchona. **Purshiana b.,** cascara sagrada. **quebracho b.,** bark that is derived from a large evergreen tree of the genus Aspidosperma, indigenous to various parts of South America. **sacred b.,** cascara sagrada. **seven b's,** Hydrangea. **soap b., soap tree b.,** quillaja. **wahoo b.,** the dried bark of the root of *Euonymus atropurpureus.* **white ash b.,** the dried bark of *Fraxinus americana.* **white oak b.,** the dried inner bark of *Quercus alba.* **wild black cherry b.,** the dried stem bark of *Prunus serotina.*

barley (bar′le). The annual grasses, *Hordeum vulgare, H. distichon*, etc.; also their seed, a cereal grain: used for malting and distillation, and to some extent as a food substance. **pearl b.,** decorticated polished barley grain.

Barlow's disease (bar′lōz) [Sir Thomas *Barlow*, physician in London, 1845–1945]. Infantile scurvy.

barn (barn). A unit of nuclear cross-section, being 10^{-24} square centimeter.

Barnes's bag, curve, dilator, etc. (barn′zez) [Robert *Barnes*, English obstetrician, 1817–1907]. See under the nouns.

baro- (bar′o) [Gr. *baros* weight]. Combining form denoting relationship to weight or pressure.

baroagnosis (bar″o-ag-no′sis). Baragnosis.

baroceptor (bar″o-sep′tor). Baroreceptor.

barodontalgia (bar″o-don-tal′je-ah). Aerodontalgia.

baroelectroesthesiometer (bar″o-e-lek″tro-es-the″ze-om′e-ter) [*baro-* + *electric* + Gr. *aisthēsis* perception + *metron* measure]. An instrument to measure the amount of pressure at the time electric sensibility to tingling or pain is felt.

barognosis (bar″og-no′sis) [*baro-* + Gr. *gnōsis* knowledge]. The faculty by which weight is recognized; weight knowledge.

barograph (bar′o-graf) [*baro-* + Gr. *graphein* to record]. A form of self-registering barometer.

baromacrometer (bar″o-mah-krom′e-ter) [*baro-* + Gr. *makros* long + *metron* measure]. An instrument for measuring and weighing newborn infants.

barometer (bah-rom′e-ter) [*baro-* + Gr. *metron* measure]. An instrument for determining the atmospheric pressure. **aneroid b.,** one which contains no mercury or other liquid.

barometrograph (bar″o-met′ro-graf) [*baro-* + Gr. *metron* measure + *graphein* to record]. A self-registering barometer.

baro-otitis (bar″o-o-ti′tis). Barotitis. **b. me′dia,** barotitis media.

barophilic (bar″o-fil′ik) [*baro-* + Gr. *philein* to love]. Growing best under high atmospheric pressure: applied to bacterial cells.

baroreceptor (bar″o-re-sep′tor). A sensory nerve terminal which is stimulated by changes in pressure.

baroscope (bar′o-skōp) [*baro-* + Gr. *skopein* to examine]. 1. A delicate form of barometer. 2. An instrument used in the quantitative determination of urea.

barosinusitis (bar″o-si″nus-i′tis). A symptom complex produced by a difference between the atmospheric pressure of the environment and the air pressure in the paranasal sinuses.

barospirator (bar″o-spi′ra-tor) [*baro-* + L. *spirare* to breathe]. A machine for producing artificial respiration by means of variations in the air pressure in a closed chamber.

barotaxis (bar″o-tak′sis) [*baro-* + Gr. *taxis* arrangement]. Stimulation of living matter by change of the pressure relations under which it exists.

barotitis (bar″o-ti′tis). A morbid condition of the ear produced by exposure to differing atmospheric pressures. **b. me′dia,** a symptom complex produced by a difference between the atmospheric pressure of the environment and the air pressure in the middle ear.

barotrauma (bar″o-traw′mah) [*baro-* + Gr. *trauma* wound]. Injury caused by pressure: specifically injury of the cartilaginous walls of the eustachian tube and the ear drum in aviators, due to the difference between atmospheric and intratympanic pressures. **otitic b.,** aero-otitis media. **sinus b.,** aerosinusitis.

barotropism (bar-ot′ro-prizm) [*baro-* + Gr. *tropos* a turning]. Barotaxis.

Barr body (bahr) [Murray Llewellyn *Barr*, Canadian anatomist, born 1908]. Sex chromatin.

Barraquer's disease (bar-rak-erz′) [Roviralta Jose Antonio *Barraquer*, Spanish physician]. Lipodystrophia progressiva.

Barraquer's method, operation (bar-rak-erz′) [Ignacio *Barraquer*, Spanish ophthalmologist]. Phacoerysis.

Barré-Guillain syndrome (bar-ra′ ge-yan′) See *Guillain-Barré syndrome*, and under *syndrome*.

barren (bar′en). Sterile; unfruitful.

barrier (bār′e-er). An obstruction. **blood-brain b., blood-cerebral b.,** the barrier separating the blood from the parenchyma of the central nervous system (including the cerebrospinal fluid). Presumably it consists of the walls of the blood vessels of the central nervous system and the surrounding glial membranes. **placental b.,** the semipermeable barrier interposed between the maternal and the fetal blood by the placental membrane.

Barry's retinacula (bar′ēz) [Martin *Barry*, English biologist, 1802–1855]. See under *retinaculum*.

barsati (bar-sat-e′). Leeches.

Barth's hernia (barths) [Jean Baptiste Philippe *Barth*, German physician, 1806–1877]. See under *hernia*.

Barthélemy's disease (bar-tāl′mez) [P. Toussaint *Barthélemy*, French dermatologist, 1850–1906]. Tuberculosis papulonecrotica.

Bartholin's anus (bar′to-linz) [Thomas *Bartholin*, Danish anatomist, 1616–1680]. See under *anus*.

Bartholin's duct, gland (bar′to-linz) [Casper *Bartholin*, Jr., Danish anatomist, 1655–1738]. See under *duct* and *gland*.

bartholinitis (bar″to-lin-i′tis). Inflammation of Bartholin's glands.

Barton's bandage, fracture (bar′tunz) [John Rhea *Barton*, Philadelphia surgeon, 1794–1871]. See under *bandage* and *fracture*.

Bartonella (bar″to-nel′lah) [A. L. *Barton*, Peruvian physician, who described the organisms in 1909]. A genus of the family Bartonellaceae, order Rickettsiales, occurring as a single species. **B. bacillifor′mis,** the etiologic agent of the anemic (Oroya fever) and eruptive (verruga peruana) types of human bartonellosis.

Bartonellaceae (bar″to-nel-la′se-e). A family of the order Rickettsiales, class Microtatobiotes, made up of small rod-shaped, coccoid, or ring- or disk-shaped, filamentous and beaded organisms, usually measuring less than 3 μ, occurring as pathogenic parasites in the erythrocytes of man and other animals. It includes four genera, *Bartonella*, *Eperythrozoon*, *Grahamella*, and *Haemobartonella*.

bartonellemia (bar″to-nel-e′me-ah). Presence in the blood of organisms of the genus *Bartonella*.

bartonelliasis (bar″to-nel-li′ah-sis). Bartonellosis.

bartonellosis (bar″to-nel-lo′sis). Infection with *Bartonella bacilliformis;* Carrion's disease.

Baruch's law, sign (bar′ooks) [Simon *Baruch*, physician in New York, 1840–1921]. See under *law* and *sign*.

baruria (bah-roo′re-ah) [Gr. *baros* weight + *ouron* urine + *-ia*]. The passage of urine of a high specific gravity.

bary- [Gr. *barys* heavy]. A combining form meaning heavy or difficult.

barye (bar′e). Bar, def. 3.

baryecoia (bar″ĭ-e-koi′ah). Dulness of hearing.

baryencephalia (bar″ĭ-en-se-fa′le-ah) [*bary-* + Gr. *enkephalos* brain]. Dulness of the intellect.

baryesthesia (bar″ĭ-es-the′ze-ah). Baresthesia.

baryglossia (bar″ĭ-glos′e-ah) [*bary-* + Gr. *glōssa* tongue + *-ia*]. Thick, slow utterance of speech.

barylalia (bar″ĭ-la′le-ah) [*bary-* + Gr. *lalia* speech]. Thick, indistinct speech due to imperfect articulation.

baryphonia (bar″ĭ-fo′ne-ah) [*bary-* + Gr. *phōnē* voice + *-ia*]. A thick, heavy quality of voice.

barytes (bar′ĭ-tēz). Barium oxide, BaO; a poisonous alkaline earth. **synthetic b.,** barium sulfate.

barythymia (bar″ĭ-thim′e-ah) [*bary-* + Gr. *thymos* mind]. Melancholia.

barytic (bar′ĭ-tic). Pertaining to or containing baryta.

barytosis (bar″ĭ-to′sis). Baritosis.

barytron (bar′ĭ-tron) [*bary-* + elec*tron*]. An electrical particle lighter than a proton but heavier than an electron, and charged both positively and negatively: called also *yukon*.

basad (ba′sad). Toward a base or basal aspect.

basal (ba′sal). 1. Pertaining to or situated near a base. 2. Fundamental.

basaljel (ba′sal-jel). Trade mark for basic aluminum carbonate gel.

basaloma (ba″sah-lo′mah). A basal cell carcinoma.

basculation (bas″ku-la′shun) [Fr. *basculer* to swing]. Replacement of a retroverted uterus by simultaneously elevating the corpus and depressing the cervix.

base (bās) [L., Gr., *basis*]. 1. The lowest part or foundation of anything. See also *basis*. 2. The main ingredient of a compound. 3. In chemistry, the nonacid part of a salt: a substance which combines with acids to form salts. **acidifiable b.,** a chemical substance which will unite with water to form an acid. **acrylic resin b.,** a denture base made of an acrylic resin. **aldehyde b.,** a chemical substance derived from an ammonia compound of aldehyde. **alloxur b's, alloxuric b's,** purine b's. **animal b.,** a ptomaine or leukomaine. **cheoplastic b.,** a denture base produced by casting molten metal in a mold. **denture b.,** the material in which the teeth of a denture are set, and which rests on the supporting tissues when the denture is in place in the mouth. **b. of heart,** basis cordis. **hexone b's,** diaminomonocarboxylic acids formed by the hydrolysis of proteins, and containing six atoms of carbon. They include arginine, lysine, and histidine. Called also *histone b's* and *diamino-acids*. **histone b's,** hexone b's. **b. of lung,** basis pulmonis. **neulein b's, nucleinic b's,** purine b's. **pressor b.,** pressor substance. **b. of prostate,** basis prostatae. **purine b's,** a group of chemical compounds of which purine is the base, including 6-oxypurine (hypoxanthine); 2,6-dioxypurine (xanthine); 6-aminopurine (adenine); 2-amino-6-oxypurine (guanidine); 2,6,8-trioxypurine (uric acid); 3,7-dimethyl xanthine (theobromine). **pyramidin b.,** a base, such as cytosine, thymine, and uracil, formed from the splitting up of protein. **record b.,** baseplate. **Schreiner's b.,** spermine. **temporary b.,** baseplate. **tooth-borne b.,** the base of a partial denture which is supported by the abutment teeth and not by the tissues beneath it. **trial b.,** baseplate. **xanthine b's,** purine b's.

basedoid (bas′e-doid). A condition resembling Basedow's disease, but without thyrotoxicosis.

Basedow's disease (bas′e-dōz) [Carl A. von *Basedow*, German physician, 1799–1854]. Exophthalmic goiter.

basedowian (bas″e-do′e-an). A person affected with Basedow's disease.

basedowiform (bas″e-do′ĭ-form). Resembling Basedow's disease (exophthalmic goiter).

baseosis (ba″se-o′sis). Alkalosis.

baseplate (bās′plāt). A sheet of wax, gutta-percha, or other plastic material used as a temporary base in the construction and fitting of artificial dentures. **stabilized b.,** a baseplate lined with a plastic material to improve its fit and stability in the mouth.

bases (ba′sēz) [L.]. Plural of *basis*.

bas-fond (bah-fon′) [Fr.]. A fundus, especially that of the urinary bladder.

basi-, basio- (ba′se, ba′se-o) [L., Gr. *basis*]. Combining form denoting relationship to a base or foundation.

basial (ba′se-al). Pertaining to the basion.

basialis (ba″se-a′lis) [L.]. Basial; used in the NK terminology and denoting relationship to a base or to the basion.

basialveolar (ba″se-al-ve′o-lar). Extending from the basion to the alveolar point.

basiarachnitis (ba″se-ar″ak-ni′tis). Inflammation of the basal part of the arachnoid.

basiarachnoiditis (ba″se-ah-rak″noi-di′tis). Basiarachnitis.

basic (ba′sik). 1. Pertaining to or having the properties of a base. 2. Capable of neutralizing acids.

basicaryoplastin (ba″se-kar″e-o-plas′tin) [*basi-* + Gr. *karyon* kernel + *plassein* to form]. The basophil paraplastin of the nucleus.

basichromatin (ba″se-kro′mah-tin). The basophil portion of the chromatin of a cell.

basichromiole (ba″se-kro′me-ōl) [*basophil* + *chromiole*]. One of the basophil particles forming the chromatin of the nucleus.

basicity (bah-sis′ĭ-te). 1. The quality of being a base, or basic. 2. The combining power of an acid. It is measured by the number of hydrogen atoms replaceable by a base.

basicranial (ba″se-kra′ne-al) [*basi-* + Gr. *kranion* cranium]. Pertaining to the base of the skull.

basicytoparaplastin (ba″se-si″to-par″ah-plas′-tin). The basophil paraplastin of the cytoplasm.

basidia (bah-sid′e-ah). Plural of *basidium*.

Basidiomycetes (bah-sid″e-o-mi-se′tēz). An order of true fungi in which the spores are borne on club-shaped organs (basidia).

basidiospore (bah-sid′e-o-spōr). A spore formed on a basidium.

basidium (bah-sid′e-um), pl. *basid′ia* [Gr. *basis* base]. The clublike spore-producing organ of certain of the higher fungi.

basifacial (ba-se-fa′shal) [L. *basis* base + *facies* face]. Pertaining to the lower part of the face.

basigenous (bah-sij′e-nus). Capable of forming a chemical base.

basihyal (ba″se-hi′al). Basihyoid.

basihyoid (ba″se-hi′oid). The body of the hyoid bone; in certain of the lower animals, either of the two lateral bones that are its homologues.

basil (ba′sil). An aromatic labiate plant, *Ocymum basilicum;* called also *sweet basil.*

basilad (bas′ĭ-lad). Toward the basilar aspect.

basilar (bas′ĭ-lar) [L. *basilaris*, from *basis* base]. Pertaining to a base or basal part.

basilaris (bas″ĭ-la′ris) [L.]. Situated at the base. **b. cra′nii,** a composite of the numerous bones which serve the brain as a supportive floor and form the axis of the whole skull.

basilateral (ba″se-lat′er-al). Both basilar and lateral.

basilemma (ba″se-lem′ah) [*basi-* + Gr. *lemma* husk]. Basement membrane.

basilic (bah-sil′ik) [L. *basilicus;* Gr. *basilikos* royal]. Important or prominent.

basilicon (bah-sil′ĭ-kon) [Gr. *basilikos* royal]. A popular name for various ointments, and especially for resin cerate.

basiloma (bas-e-lo′mah). A basal cell carcinoma.

basilysis (bah-sil′ĭ-sis) [*basi-* + Gr. *lysis* dissolution]. The crushing of the base of the fetal skull to facilitate delivery.

basilyst (bas′ĭ-list). An instrument for performing a basilysis.

basin (ba′sn). 1. The third ventricle of the brain. 2. The pelvis.

basinasial (ba″se-na′ze-al). Pertaining to the basion and the nasion.

basio-. See *basi-*.

basioccipital (ba″se-ok-sip′ĭ-tal). Pertaining to the basilar process of the occipital bone.

basioglossus (ba″se-o-glos′us) [*basio-* + Gr. *glōssa* tongue]. The part of the hyoglossus muscle which is attached to the base of the hyoid bone.

basion (ba′se-on) [Gr. *basis* base]. The midpoint of the anterior border of the foramen magnum.

basiotic (ba″se-ot′ik) [*basi-* + Gr. *ous* ear]. See under *bone*.

basiotribe (ba′se-o-trib″) [*basio-* + Gr. *tribein* to crush]. An instrument for crushing the fetal head in order to facilitate delivery.

basiotripsy (ba′se-o-trip″se). The crushing of the fetal head; cranioclasis.

basiotriptor (ba′se-o-trip″ter). Basiotribe.

basiparachromatin (ba″se-par″ah-kro′-mah-tin). The basophil paraplastin of the nucleus.

basiparaplastin (ba″-se-par″ah-plas′tin). The basophil portion of the paraplastin.

Basiotribe.

basiphilic (ba″se-fil′ik). Basophilic.

basiphobia (ba″se-fo′be-ah). Basophobia.

basirhinal (ba″se-ri′nal) [*basi-* + Gr. *rhis* nose]. Pertaining to the base of the brain and to the nose.

basis (ba′sis), pl. *bases* [L.; Gr.]. The lower, basic, or fundamental part of an object; used in anatomical nomenclature as a general term to designate the base of a structure or organ, or the part opposite to or distinguished from the apex. **b. cartilag′inis arytenoi′deae** [N A], the triangular inferior part of the arytenoid cartilage, which bears the articular surface. Called also *base of arytenoid cartilage.* **b. cer′ebri** [B N A], facies inferior cerebri. **b. coch′leae** [N A, B N A], the posterior of the cochlea, which rests upon the internal acoustic meatus. Called also *base of cochlea.* **b. cor′dis** [N A, B N A], a poorly delimited region of the heart, formed, in general, by the atria and the area occupied by the roots of the great vessels. It lies opposite the bodies of the fifth, sixth, seventh, and eighth thoracic vertebrae, and is directed superiorly, posteriorly, and to the right. Called also *base of heart.* **b. cra′nii exter′na** [N A, B N A], the outer surface of the inferior region of the skull. Called also *external base of cranium.* **b. cra′nii inter′na** [N A, B N A], the inner surface of the inferior region of the skull, constituting the floor of the cranial cavity. Called also *internal base of cranium.* **b. enceph′ali,** facies inferior cerebri. **b. mandib′ulae** [N A, B N A], the lower margin of the body of the mandible. Called also *base of mandible.* **b. modi′oli** [N A, B N A], the broad part of the modiolus situated near the lateral part of the internal acoustic meatus. Called also *base of modiolus.* **b. na′si** [B N A], the portion of the nose opposite to the apex: omitted in N A. **b. os′sis metacarpa′lis** [N A, B N A], the proximal end of a metacarpal bone, which articulates with bone(s) of the carpus and with adjacent metacarpal bones. Called also *base of metacarpal bone.* **b. os′sis metatarsa′lis** [N A, B N A], the wedge-shaped proximal end of a metatarsal bone, which articulates with bone(s) of the tarsus and with adjacent metatarsal bones. Called also *base of metatarsal bone.* **b. os′sis sa′cri** [N A, B N A], the cranial surface of the sacrum, part of which articulates with the fifth lumbar vertebra. Called also *base of sacral bone.* **b. patel′lae** [N A, B N A], the superior border of the patella, to which the tendon of the quadriceps femoris muscle is attached. Called also *base of patella.* **b. pedun′culi cer′ebri** [B N A], crus cerebri. **b. phalan′gis digito′rum ma′nus** [N A, B N A], the proximal extremity of each phalanx of the fingers. Called also *base of phalanx of fingers.* **b. phalan′gis digito′rum pe′dis** [N A, B N A], the proximal end of each phalanx of the toes. Called also *base of phalanx of toes.* **b. prosta′tae** [N A, B N A], the broad upper part of the prostate, in contact with the lower surface of the urinary bladder. Called also *base of prostate.* **b. pulmo′nis** [N A, B N A], the portion of each lung that is directed toward the diaphragm. **b. pyram′idis rena′lis** [N A, B N A], the part of a renal pyramid that is directed away from the renal sinus. Called also *base of renal pyramid.* **b. scap′ulae,** a name applied to both the vertebral and the axillary border of the scapula (margo medialis and margo lateralis). **b. sta′pedis** [N A, B N A], the oval plate of bone on the stapes that fits into the fenestra vestibuli. Called also *base of stapes.*

basisphenoid (ba″se-sfe′noid). An embryonic bone which becomes the back part of the body of the sphenoid.

basisylvian (ba″se-sil′ve-an) [*basi-* + *sylvian*]. Pertaining to the basilar part of the sylvian fissure.

basitemporal (ba″se-tem′po-ral) [*basi-* + *temporal*]. Pertaining to the lower part of the temporal bone.

basivertebral (ba″se-ver′te-bral) [*basi-* + L. *vertebra* joint]. Pertaining to the body of a vertebra.

basket (bas′ket). 1. Basket cell. 2. One of the condensations of intracellular neurofibrils in senile dementia, called also *Alzheimer's b.* **fiber b's,** fine fibers extending from the external limiting membrane of the retina to surround the adjacent portions of the rods and cones.

Basle nomina anatomica (bah′zl) [*Basle,* Switzerland, where it was presented for final criticism at the annual meeting of the German Anatomic Society in 1895]. See under *nomen.*

$BaSO_4$. Barium sulfate.

basocyte (ba′so-sīt). A basophilic cell or leukocyte.

basocytopenia (ba″so-si″to-pe′ne-ah) [*basocyte* + Gr. *penia* poverty]. Basophilic leukopenia.

basocytosis (ba″so-si-to′sis). 1. Abnormal increase in the proportion of basophilic leukocytes in the blood. 2. Basophilia.

baso-erythrocyte (ba″so-e-rith′ro-sīt). An erythrocyte containing basophilic granules.

baso-erythrocytosis (ba″so-e-rith″ro-si-to′sis). Basophilia, def. 1.

basograph (ba′so-graf) [Gr. *basis* a walking + *graphein* to write]. An instrument for recording abnormalities of gait.

basometachromophil (ba″so-met″ah-kro′mo-fil) [*basic* + Gr. *meta* beyond + *chrōma* color + *philein* to love]. Staining with basic dyes to a color different from that of surrounding substances.

basopenia (ba″so-pe′ne-ah). Basophilic leukopenia.

basophil (ba′so-fil) [Gr. *basis* base + *philein* to love]. 1. A structure cell, or other histological element staining readily with basic dyes. 2. A polymorphonuclear granulocyte distinguished by the presence of coarse, large, round bluish-black cytoplasmic granules of non-uniform size and a relatively lightly staining, slightly lobulated nucleus.

basophile (ba′so-fīl). 1. Basophil. 2. Basophilic.

basophilia (ba″so-fil′e-ah). 1. An abnormal increase in the blood of basophilic erythrocytes; the staining may be either punctate, when it is called stippling, or diffuse, when it is recognized as polychromasia. 2. Basocytosis.

basophilic (ba-so-fil′ik). Staining readily with basic dyes.

basophilism (ba-sof′ĭ-lizm). Abnormal increase of basophil cells. **Cushing's b., pituitary b.,** a syndrome due to overgrowth of the basophil cells of the anterior lobe of the pituitary (basophil adenoma) and marked by rapidly developing and painful adiposity of the face, neck and trunk, kyphosis from softening of the spinal bones, amenorrhea in females and impotence in males, hypertrichoses in females, dusky complexion with purple markings, hypertension, polycythemia, pains in abdomen and back and muscular weakness.

basophilous (ba-sof′ĭ-lus). Basophilic.

basophobia (ba″so-fo′be-ah) [Gr. *basis* a walking + *phobia*]. Morbid fear of walking, or fear of being unable to walk.

basophobiac (ba″so-fo′be-ak). A person affected with basophobia.

basophobic (ba″so-fo′bik). Pertaining to or characterized by basophobia.

basoplasm (ba′so-plazm″). Cytoplasm that stains with basic dyes.

Basset's operation (bas-sāz′) [Antoine *Basset*, French surgeon, 1882–1951]. See under *operation*.

Bassini's operation (bah-se′nēz) [Edoardo *Bassini*, surgeon in Padua, 1844–1924]. See under *operation*.

Bassler's sign (bas′lerz) [Anthony *Bassler*, physician in New York, 1874–1959]. See under *sign*.

bast (bast). The inner part of the bark of various trees: used to a very limited extent in surgery.

bastard (bas′tard) [Old Fr.]. 1. An illegitimate person; one born out of wedlock. 2. Illegitimate. 3. Of inferior quality; not genuine.

Bastedo's rule, sign (bas-te′dōz) [Walter Arthur *Bastedo*, physician in New York, 1873–1952]. See under *rule* and *sign*.

Bastian-Bruns law (bas′chan-broonz′) [Henry Charlton *Bastian*, British neurologist, 1837–1915; Ludwig *Bruns*, neurologist in Hanover, 1858–1916]. See under *law*.

Bastianelli's method (bast-yan-el′ēz) [Raffaele *Bastianelli*, Italian surgeon]. See under *method*.

basyl (ba′sil) [Gr. *basis* base + *hylē* substance]. The electropositive element of a compound.

basylous (bas′ĭ-lus). Acting as a base in chemical composition.

Bateman's disease, etc. (bāt′manz) [Thomas *Bateman*, English physician, 1778–1821]. See under the nouns.

bath (bath). 1. A conductive medium, as water, vapor, sand, or mud, with which the body is laved or in which the body is wholly or partly immersed for therapeutic or cleansing purposes. 2. The application of a conductive medium to the body for therapeutic or cleansing purposes. 3. A piece of equipment or scientific apparatus in which a body or object may be immersed. **acid b.,** one of water medicated with a mineral acid. **air b.,** the therapeutic exposure of the naked body to the air, which is usually warmed or charged with a vapor. **alcohol b.,** a term frequently applied to laving the body of a patient in dilute alcohol: it is defervescent and stimulant. **alkaline b.,** the washing of a patient in a weak solution of an alkaline carbonate: useful in skin diseases, etc. **alum b.,** the use of alum water as a bathing medium. **antipyretic b.,** a bath given to reduce fever. **antiseptic b.,** a bath containing an antiseptic such as carbolic acid. **aromatic b.,** a medicated bath in which the water is scented with a decoction of aromatic plants or volatile oils. **arsenical b.,** a warm bath in a weak arsenical solution. **astringent b.,** a bath in a liquid containing tannic acid, alum, or other astringent. **borax b.,** one in water medicated with glycerin and borax. **box b.,** one in which the patient is enclosed, except his head, in a box, into which hot-water pipes extend. **bran b.,** an emollient bath made of water in which bran has been boiled. **Brand b.** (1861), a cold bath in which the water is at 68°F., and in which the patient is gently massaged. **bubble b.,** a bath in which the water has been filled with bubbles produced by mechanical or chemical means. **cabinet b.,** a hot-air bath or an electric bath in which the patient is inclosed in a special cabinet. **camphor b.,** a bath given in an atmosphere charged with the vapor of camphor. **carbon dioxide b.,** a bath impregnated with carbon dioxide, such as the Nauheim bath. **Charcot's b.,** a bath taken by standing in ankle-deep hot water and sponging the body locally with cold water. **chemical b.,** an apparatus for regulating the temperature of various chemical processes by surrounding the substance to be heated with water, sand, or other material. **cold b.,** one in which cold water is used, the temperature of the latter varying from 32 to 70°F. **colloid b.,** a bath containing gelatin, bran, starch, or similar substances. **continuous b.,** a bath of flowing water. **contrast b.,** immersion of a part alternately in hot and in cold water. **cool b.,** one in water from 60 to 75°F. **creosote b.,** a bath containing creosote and glycerin: used in scaly skin diseases. **douche b.,** the application of water to the body in a jet. **Dowsing b.,** an electric light hot-air bath given at very high temperature. **drip-sheet b.** See *drip sheet*, under *sheet*. **earth b.,** the placing of a patient in a mass of earth or of sand, usually warmed. **electric-light b.,** application of rays from electric light bulbs lining a cabinet in which the patient's body is enclosed. **emollient b.,** a bath in an emollient liquid, like a decoction of bran. **Finnish b.,** a sweat bath given in an enclosed, steamy room. Hyperemia of the skin is produced by beating with twigs, and the bath is followed by a cold plunge. **Finsen b.,** a general irradiation of the patient's entire body with ultraviolet rays. **foam b.,** a bath of foam produced by blowing air or oxygen through the water to which a foam-forming substance (saponin) has been added. Called also *Schaum b.* and *Sandor foam b.* **fucus b.,** a bath containing seaweed or a decoction of it, imparting the effect of sodium chloride and iodine. **full b.,** one in which the patient's body is fully immersed in the water. **gas-bubble b.,** a bath of water containing gases in such quantities that gas bubbles are set free and ascend to the surface of the water, as in carbon dioxide and oxygen baths. **gelatin b.,** an emollient bath in a very thin hot solution of gelatin. **glycerin b.,** a warm emollient bath in water containing glycerin and gum acacia. **graduated b.,** one in which the temperature of the water is gradually modified. **grease b.,** a scrubbing of the body with some greasy preparation (petrolatum, lanolin). **Greville b.,** an electric hot-air bath. **hafussi b.,** a bath of hot water impregnated with carbon dioxide in which the hands and feet of the patient are immersed. **half b.,** a bath of the hips and lower part of the body. **herb b.,** one which contains a decoction of aromatic herbs. **hip b.,** sitz b. **hot b.,** one in water from 98 to 112°F. **hot-air b.,** one in air or vapor from 100 to 130°F. **hyperthermal b.,** a bath in which the water is from 105 to 120°F. **immersion b.,** one in which the body of the patient is immersed. **iron b.,** one in water which contains iron sulfate. **kinetotherapeutic b.,** a bath providing facilities for underwater exercise. **light b.,** exposure of the naked skin of all or part of the body to light rays, either of the sun or from an apparatus. **linseed b.,** a bath to which has been added the mucilage extracted from linseed. **lukewarm b.,** a bath in which the water is between 94 and 96°F. **medicated b.,** a bath variously charged with medicinal substances. **mercurial b.,** a bath in a weak solution of mercuric chloride. **milk b.,** one taken in milk. **moor b.,** a bath in water containing earth from a moor or from waste land. **mustard b.,** one taken in water containing pulverized mustard. **Nauheim b.,** a bath in which the patient is immersed in warm carbonated water. **needle b.,** a shower bath in which the water is projected in a fine, needle-like spray. **oil b.,** one taken in warm olive oil, sometimes variously medicated. **oxygen b.,** a bath impregnated with oxygen. See *gas-bubble b.* and *perogen*. **pack b.,** one in which the body is packed in wet cloths. **peat b.,** a bath in water (usually that of a mineral spring) containing peat. **Peng b.,** a variety of foam bath. **perogen b.** See *perogen*. **Russian b.,** a hot vapor bath followed by friction and a plunge in cold water. **sand b.** 1. The immersion of the body in dry, heated sand. 2. The covering of the body with the damp sand of the seashore. **Sandor b.,** a variety of foam bath. **Sarason's ozet b.,** a bath made by adding to the water sodium hyperborate and manganese borate, the latter being spread in powder form over the surface of the water, resulting in the liberation of oxygen. **Sauna b.** See *Finnish b.* **Schaum b.** See *foam b.* **Schott b.** See *Schott treatment*, under *treatment*. **sea b., sea-water b.,** a bath in water from the sea; usually warmed or heated. **sedative b.,** a warm bath in which the patient is immersed for a considerable time. **sheet b.,** the applications of wet sheets to the body. **sitz b.,** a bath in which the patient sits in the tub, the hips and buttocks being immersed. **sponge b.,** one in which the patient's body is not immersed in water but is rubbed with a wet cloth or sponge. **stimulating b.,** a bath containing tonic, astringent, or aromatic substances: used for stimulating the body. **sulfur b.,** a bath in which potassium sulfide or sublimed sulfur is added to the water. **sweat b.,** any bath given to promote sweating. **temperate b.,** one in water from 75 to 85°F. **tepid b.,** one in water from 85 to 92°F. **vapor b.,** exposure of the body to steam, vaporized alcohol, or other vapor. **warm b.,** one taken in water of from 90 to 104°F. **water b.,** a vessel containing water for immersing bodies or for immersing other liquid-containing vessels that are to be heated or cooled, or are to be held at a given temperature. **wax b.,** the application of liquid wax to part of the body, the wax being permitted to solidify: used to heat the part. **whirlpool b.,** a variously sized tank in which the body or an extremity can be submerged, the water being mechanically agitated to produce both thermic and kinetic effects. **Ziemssen b.,** a bath in which the temperature of the water is at first 88°F. and is then gradually reduced to 65°F. by the addition of cold water.

bathesthesia (bath″es-the′ze-ah). Bathyesthesia.

bathmic (bath′mik). Pertaining to bathmism.

bathmism (bath′mizm) [Gr. *bathmos* threshold]. The force which controls the processes of nutrition and growth.

bathmophobia (bath″mo-fo′be-ah) [Gr. *bathmos* threshold + *phobia*]. Morbid fear of stairways or steep slopes.

bathmotropic (bath″mo-trop′ik) [Gr. *bathmos* threshold + *tropos* a turning]. Influencing the response of tissue to stimuli. A term used to designate supposed fibers in the cardiac nerves which affect the excitability of cardiac muscles. **negatively b.,** lessening response to stimuli. **positively b.,** increasing response to stimuli.

bathmotropism (bath-mot′ro-pizm). Influence on the excitability of muscle tissue.

batho-. See *bathy-*.

bathoflore (bath′o-flōr) [*batho-* + *fluorescence*]. A substance which decreases the intensity of fluorescence of a compound. Cf. *auxoflore*.

bathomorphic (bath″o-mor′fik) [*batho-* + Gr. *morphē* form]. Having a deep or myopic eye.

bathophobia (bath″o-fo′be-ah) [*batho-* + *phobia*]. Morbid dread of depths or of looking down from a high place, with fear of falling.

bathrocephaly (bath′ro-sef′ah-le) [Gr. *bathron* a step + *kephalē* head]. A condition characterized by a steplike posterior projection of the skull, caused by external bulging of the squamous portion of the occipital bone.

bathy-, batho- (bath′e, bath′o) [Gr. *bathys* deep, *bathos* depth]. Combining form meaning deep, or denoting relationship to depth.

bathyanesthesia (bath″e-an″es-the′ze-ah) [*bathy-* + *anesthesia*]. Loss of deep sensibility.

bathycardia (bath″e-kar′de-ah) [*bathy-* + Gr. *kardia* heart]. A low position of the heart due to anatomical conditions and not to disease.

bathycentesis (bath″e-sen-te′sis) [*bathy-* + Gr. *kentēsis* puncture]. Deep surgical puncture.

bathyesthesia (bath″e-es-the′ze-ah) [*bathy-* + Gr. *aisthēsis* perception]. Deep sensibility; the sensibility in the parts of the body beneath the surface, such as muscle sensibility and joint sensibility.

bathygastria (bath″e-gas′tre-ah) [*bathy-* + Gr. *gastēr* stomach + *-ia*]. A low position of the stomach; gastroptosis.

bathygastry (bath″e-gas′tre). Bathygastria.

bathyhyperesthesia (bath″e-hi″per-es-the′ze-ah) [*bathy-* + *hyperesthesia*]. Increased sensitiveness of deep structures of the body.

bathyhypesthesia (bath″e-hīp″es-the′za-ah) [*bathy-* + *hypesthesia*]. Decreased sensitiveness of the deep structures of the body.

bathypnea (bath″e-ne′ah) [*bathy-* + Gr. *pnoia* breath]. Deep breathing.

batonet (ba-to-net′). Pseudochromosome.

batophobia (bat″o-fo′be-ah) [Gr. *batos* passable + *phobia*]. Morbid dread of passing near or among high objects, as buildings, mountains, etc.

batrachoplasty (bat′rah-ko-plas″te) [Gr. *batrachos* frog + *plassein* to form]. A plastic surgical operation for the cure of ranula.

battarism (bat′ah-rizm). Battarismus.

battarismus (bat′ah-riz-mus) [Gr. *battarizein* to stammer]. Stuttering or stammering.

battery (bat′er-e). A set or series of cells which afford an electric current. **caustic b.,** a battery employed in galvanocautery. **dynamo b.,** a dynamo electric generator; a machine for converting mechanical into electric force. **electric b.,** an apparatus consisting essentially of a set or series of cells for producing an electric current. **faradic b.,** one which produces an induced or faradic current. **galvanic b.,** one which affords a chemically produced current. **primary b.,** one in which a number of primary cells are combined, so as to act together. **secondary b.,** the combination of several storage cells. **storage b.,** an apparatus for storing energy which is regained in the form of electricity.

Battey bacilli (bat′e) [*Battey*, a tuberculosis hospital in Rome, Georgia, where many strains of these mycobacteria were first recognized]. See under *bacillus*.

batteyin (bat′e-in) [*Battey* bacillus]. A product prepared from Battey bacilli (Group III of the unclassified mycobacteria), comparable to tuberculin, used in a cutaneous test of hypersensitivity.

Battley's sedative (bat′lēz) [Richard *Battley*, English chemist, 1770–1856]. See under *sedative*.

Baudelocque's diameter (bo-dloks′) [Jean Louis *Baudelocque*, French obstetrician, 1746–1810]. See under *diameter*.

Bauhin's gland, valve (bo′anz) [Gaspard (Caspar) *Bauhin*, Swiss anatomist, 1560–1624]. See under *gland* and *valve*.

Bauman's diet (bow′manz) [Louis *Bauman*, New York physician, born 1880]. See under *diet*.

Baumé's scale (bo-māz′) [Antoine *Baumé*, French chemist, 1728–1805]. See under *scale*.

Baumès' law (bo-mez′) [Pierre Prosper François *Baumès*, French physician, 1791–1871]. See *Colles' law*, under *law*.

Baumès' sign, symptom (bo-mez′) [Jean Baptiste *Baumès*, French physician, 1777–1828]. See under *sign*.

baunscheidtism (bown′shīd-tizm) [from Karl *Baunscheidt*, the inventor]. Treatment of chronic rheumatism, etc., by acupuncture with the révulseur, an instrument furnished with many fine needle points, which are dipped into an irritant liquid, as oil of mustard.

bay (ba). A recess or inlet. **lacrimal b.,** the depression at the inner canthus of the eye in which the lacrimal canaliculi lie.

bayberry (ba′ber-e). 1. The fruit of *Laurus nobilis*, the European laurel. 2. The wax myrtle, *Myrica cerifera*, and its berry. 3. The tree, *Pimenta acris*, and its fruit: allspice or pimenta.

Bayer 205 (ba′er). Suramin sodium.

Bayle's disease (bālz) [Antoine L. J. *Bayle*, French physician, 1799–1858]. Progressive general paralysis of the insane.

Bayle's granulations (bālz) [Gaspard Laurent *Bayle*, French physician, 1774–1816]. See under *granulation*.

Baynton's bandage (bān′tonz) [Thomas *Bayn-*

ton, English surgeon, 1761–1820]. See under *bandage*.

baytinal (ba′tĭ-nal). Chemical name: 5-allyl-5 (2-methylpropyl)-2-thiobarbituric acid. Use: intravenous anesthetic agent.

bazin (ba′zin). Molluscum contagiosum.

Bazin's disease (bah-zaz′) [Antoine Pierre Ernest *Bazin*, French dermatologist, 1807–1878]. Tuberculosis cutis indurativa.

B.B.B. Abbreviation for *blood-brain barrier*. See under *barrier*.

BBT. Abbreviation for *basal body temperature*.

B.C. Abbreviation for *bone conduction* and *buccocervical*.

BCG. 1. Abbreviation for *bacille Calmette Guérin*. *See BCG vaccine*, under *vaccine*. 2. Abbreviation for *bicolor guaiac test*. See under *tests*.

B.D. Abbreviation for *base of prism down* and *buccodistal*.

b.d. Abbreviation for L. *bis di'e*, twice a day.

B.D.A. Abbreviation for *British Dental Association*.

Bdella (del′ah) [Gr. "leech"]. A genus of mites. **B. cardina′lis,** the snout mite, which is parasitic on other insects.

bdellepithecium (del″e-pĭ-the′se-um) [Gr. *bdella* leech + *epithesis* application]. A kind of artificial leech or tube used in leeching.

bdellium (del′le-um) [L.; Gr. *bdellion*]. The fragrant gum-resin of *Balsamodendron mukul*, a tree of India, and *B. africanum;* also a gum from *Borassus flabelliformis*, a palm of Africa.

bdellometer (del-lom′e-ter). A mechanical substitute for a leech.

bdellotomy (del-lot′o-me) [Gr. *bdella* leech + *tomē* cutting]. The act of cutting a sucking leech to increase the amount of blood it will take.

bdelygmia (del-ig′me-ah) [Gr.]. Loathing for food; nausea.

B.D.S. Abbreviation for *Bachelor of Dental Surgery*.

B.D.Sc. Abbreviation for *Bachelor of Dental Science*.

B.E. Abbreviation for *Bacillen emulsion*. See under *tuberculin*.

Be. Chemical symbol for *beryllium*.

bead (bēd). A small spherical structure or mass. **rachitic b's,** a series of palpable or visible prominences at the points where the ribs join their cartilages: seen in certain cases of rickets.

beaded (bēd′ed). Having the appearance of a string of beads.

Beadle (be′d′l), George Wells. United States biochemist, born 1903; co-winner, with Edward Lawrie Tatum and Joshua Lederberg, of the Nobel prize in medicine and physiology for 1958, for the discovery that genes act by regulating specific chemical processes.

beaker (bēk′er). A form of glass cup used by chemists and apothecaries.

Beale's cells (bēlz) [Lionel Smith *Beale*, British physician, 1828–1906]. See under *cell*.

beamtherapy (bēm-ther′ah-pe). See *beam therapy*, under *therapy*, and *chromotherapy*, def. 2.

beard (bērd). Barba.

Beard's disease (bērdz) [George Miller *Beard*, American physician, 1839–1883]. Neurasthenia.

bearing down (bār′ing down). 1. A feeling of weight in the pelvis occurring in certain diseases. 2. The expulsive effort of a woman in labor.

bearwood (bār′wood). Cascara sagrada.

beat (bēt). A throb or pulsation, as of the heart or of an artery. See also *pulse*. **apex b.,** the pulsation of the heart felt over its apex, usually in the fifth left intercostal space, 8 or 9 cm. from the midline. **dropped b.,** intermittent pulse. **ectopic b.,** a heart beat originating at some point other than the sino-auricular node. **forced b.,** an extrasystole produced by artificial stimulation of the heart. **premature b.,** extrasystole.

Beau's disease, lines, syndrome (bōz) [Joseph Honoré Simon *Beau*, French physician, 1806–1865]. See under the nouns.

Beauperthuy's treatment (bo″per-tēz′) [Louis Daniel *Beauperthuy*, physician in the West Indies, 1803–1871]. See under *treatment*.

Beccari process (bĕ-kah′re) [Giuseppe *Beccari*, physician in Florence]. See under *process*.

bechic (bek′ik) [L. *bechicus*, from Gr. *bēx* cough]. Pertaining to cough.

Bechterew's disease, method, nucleus, reflex, sign, symptom, test (bek-ter′yefs) [Vladimir Mikhailovich von *Bechterew*, Russian neurologist, 1857–1927]. See under the nouns.

Beck's gastrostomy (beks) [Carl *Beck*, American surgeon, 1856–1911]. See under *gastrostomy*.

Beck's triad (beks) [Claude S. *Beck*, Cleveland surgeon, born 1894]. See under *triad*.

Becker's phenomenon, test (bek′erz) [Otto Heinrich Enoch *Becker*, German oculist, 1828–1890]. See under *phenomenon* and *tests*.

Beckmann's apparatus (bek′manz) [Ernst *Beckmann*, Berlin chemist, 1853–1923]. See under *apparatus*.

Béclard's hernia, triangle (ba-klahrz′) [Pierre Augustin *Béclard*, French anatomist, 1785–1825]. See under the nouns.

Becquerel's rays (bek-relz′) [Antoine Henri *Becquerel*, French physicist, 1852–1908]. See under *ray*.

bed (bed). 1. A supporting structure or tissue. 2. A couch or support for the body during sleep. **air b.,** an air-tight, inflatable mattress. **Arnott's b.,** a rubber mattress filled with water employed to prevent bed sores. **Bandeloux's b.,** an air bed with a vessel beneath for the collection of urine, the whole being surmounted by a cradle covered with gauze. **capillary b.,** the total combined mass of capillaries forming a large reservoir which may be more or less completely filled with blood. **ether b.,** a bed made up for the proper care and protection of a patient returned from the operating room after general anesthesia. **Fisher b.,** a spinal suspension bed for the continuous treatment of spinal affections. **fracture b.,** a bed for the use of patients with broken bones. **Gatch b.,** a bed fitted with a jointed bed rest by which the patient can be raised into a half-sitting position and kept so. **hydrostatic b.,** a water bed. **Klondike b.,** a bed arranged for outdoor sleeping so that the patient is protected from draughts. **metabolic b.,** a bed so arranged that all the feces and urine of the patient are saved. The amount of excreta compared with the intake gives an indication of the metabolism in the body. **nail b.,** matrix unguis. **Sanders b.,** a bed for administering passive postural exercises in the treatment of chronic occlusive arterial disease. **water b.,** a rubber mattress filled with water: used to prevent bed sores.

bedbug (bed′bug). A bug of the family Cimicidae. *Cimex lectularius*, of temperate regions, and *Cimex hemipterus*, of the tropics, are flattened, oval, reddish insects which inhabit houses, furniture and neglected beds and feed on man, usually at night.

bedfast (bed′fast). Unable to leave the bed.

bedlam (bed′lam) [*Bedlam*, the Bethlehem Royal Hospital, London, a mental hospital established in 1547]. 1. An institution for patients with mental illness. 2. Bedlamism.

bedlamism (bed′lam-izm). A state of wild tumult.

Bednar's aphtha (bed′narz) [Alois *Bednar*, physician in Vienna, 1816–1888]. See under *aphtha*.

bedpan (bed′pan). A vessel for receiving the urinary and fecal discharges of a patient unable to leave his bed.

beef (bēf). The meat of the ox, used as an item of diet and in the preparation of beef extract. **b., iron, and wine,** a preparation of beef extract, ferric ammonium citrate, and other ingredients in sherry wine: used as a hematinic agent.

beer (bēr). The fermented infusion of malted barley and hops.

Beer's collyrium, knife, operation (ba′erz) [Georg Joseph *Beer*, German ophthalmologist, 1763–1821]. See under the nouns.

beerwort (bēr′wert). An infusion of malt in water intended to be converted into beer. It is sometimes used for the cultivation of yeasts and molds.

beeswax (bēz′waks). Wax derived from the honeycomb of *Apis mellifera*. See *yellow wax*, under *wax*. **bleached b.** See *white wax*, under *wax*.

Beevor's sign (be′vorz) [Charles Edward *Beevor*, British neurologist, 1854–1908]. See under *sign*.

Begbie's disease (beg′bēz) [James *Begbie*, Scottish physician, 1798–1869]. See under *disease*.

Beggiatoa (bej″je-ah-to′ah) [named for F. S. *Beggiato*]. A genus of microorganisms (order Beggiatoales, family Beggiatoaceae).

Beggiatoaceae (bej″je-ah-to-a′se-e). A systematic family of Schizomycetes (order Beggiatoales), made up of cells which are generally not visible without staining, arranged in chains within trichomes which show flexing motion and also show gliding movements when in contact with a substrate. It includes four genera, Beggiatoa, Thioploca, Thiospirillopsis, and Thiothrix. These are free-living sulfur bacteria, often found in association with blue-green algae.

Beggiatoales (bej″je-ah-to-a′lēz). A taxonomic order of class Schizomycetes, made up of cells which occur singly, or in motile or non-motile trichomes, and which multiply by transverse fission. They are found in fresh or salt water, and in soil and decomposing organic material, especially algae. It includes four families, Achromatiaceae, Beggiatoaceae, Leukotrichaceae, and Vitreoscillaceae.

begma (beg′mah) [Gr. *bēgma* phlegm]. 1. A cough. 2. The material evacuated from the lungs by coughing.

behavior (be-hāv′yor). The manner in which an individual acts or performs. **automatic b.,** automatism. **invariable b.,** activity whose character is determined by innate structure, such as reflex action. **variable b.,** behavior which is modifiable by individual experience.

behaviorism (be-hāv′yor-izm). A school of psychology based upon a purely objective observation and analysis of human and animal behavior without reference to the testimony of consciousness.

behaviorist (be-hāv′yor-ist). A psychologist who is a disciple of behaviorism.

Behçet's disease, syndrome (ba′sets) [Hulusi *Behçet*, dermatologist, Istanbul, Turkey, 1889–1948]. See under *syndrome*.

Béhier-Hardy sign (ba′he-a har′de) [Louis Jules *Béhier*, French physician, 1813–1875; Louis Phillipe Alfred *Hardy*, French physician, 1811–1893]. See under *sign*.

Behla's bodies (ba′lahs) [Robert Franz *Behla*, German physician, born 1850]. Plimmer's bodies.

Behring's law (ba′ringz) [Emil A. von *Behring*, German bacteriologist, 1854–1917; winner of the Nobel prize for medicine in 1901]. See under *law*.

Beigel's disease (bi′gelz) [Hermann *Beigel*, German physician, 1830–1879]. Piedra.

bejel (bej′el). A nonvenereal form of treponematosis (*Treponema pallidum*) occurring among children in the Middle East.

Bekesy (bek′ĕ-se), Georg von. Hungarian-born physicist, born 1899; winner of the Nobel prize in medicine and physiology for 1961, for his discoveries concerning the physical mechanisms of stimulation within the cochlea.

bel (bel). A unit of sound intensity, being the smallest increase in loudness which the ear can differentiate. Cf. *decibel*.

Belascaris (bĕ-las′kah-ris). A genus of ascarid worms. **B. ca′ti,** an ascarid worm from the intestine of cats. **B. mys′tax,** an ascarid worm common in the dog and cat, but sometimes found in the intestines of children.

belching (belch′ing). The eructation of gas.

belemnoid (be-lem′noid) [Gr. *belemnon* dart + *eidos* form]. 1. Dart-shaped. 2. The styloid process of the ulna or of the temporal bone.

Belfield's operation (bel′fēldz) [William Thomas *Belfield*, surgeon in Chicago, 1856–1929]. Vasotomy.

Bell's disease, mania [Luther V. *Bell*, American physician, 1806–1862]. See under *mania*.

Bell's law, nerve, palsy, phenomenon [Sir Charles *Bell*, Scottish physiologist in London, 1774–1842]. See under the nouns.

Bell's muscle [John *Bell*, Scottish surgeon and anatomist, 1763–1820]. See under *muscle*.

Bell's treatment [William Blair *Bell*, British gynecologist, 1871–1936]. See under *treatment*.

belladonna (bel″ah-don′ah) [Ital. "fair lady"]. The *Atropa belladonna*, or deadly nightshade, a plant of Europe and Asia. A preparation of the dried leaves and tops of *Atropa belladonna* (belladonna leaf) is used to produce parasympathetic blockade and to relieve gastrointestinal spasm.

bell-crowned (bel-krownd′). Having a crown shaped like a bell: said of a tooth which is largest at the occlusal surface, and tapers toward the neck.

Bellini's ducts, ligament (bel-e′nēz) [Lorenzo *Bellini*, Italian anatomist, 1643–1704]. See under *duct* and *ligament*.

Bellocq's cannula (bel-oks′) [Jean Jacques *Bellocq*, French surgeon, 1732–1807]. See under *cannula*.

bellond (bel′ond). Plumbism in cattle due to grazing in the neighborhood of lead smelters where the soil is impregnated with the lead that settles from the fumes of the foundry.

bellones (bel-lonz′). Polypoid tumors in the nostrils of horses, which interfere with their proper breathing.

belly (bel′e). 1. The abdomen. 2. The fleshy, contractile part of a muscle. Called also *venter musculi* [N A]. **big b.,** abdominal distention with gastric disturbance. **drum b.,** tympanites. **frog b.,** a semitympanic state of the abdomen such as sometimes occurs in rachitic children. **spider b.,** arachnogastria. **swollen b.,** tympanites in animals. **wooden b.,** abdominal rigidity.

belonephobia (bel″o-ne-fo′be-ah) [Gr. *belonē* needle + *phobia*]. Dread of needles and pins.

belonoid (bel′o-noid) [Gr. *belonē* needle + *eidos* form]. Needle-shaped; styloid.

belonoskiascopy (bel″o-no-ski-as′ko-pe) [Gr. *belonē* needle + *skia* shadow + *skopein* to examine]. A method of skiascopic retinoscopy.

belt (belt). An encircling band worn about the waist or abdomen. **Beck's b.,** a canvas abdominal binder used in postpartum hemorrhage. **Momburg's b.,** a rubber tube or band passed two or three times around the waist and then drawn tight to arrest the bleeding in postpartum hemorrhage.

Belyando spew (bel-yan′do) [*Belyando*, a district in Australia]. Grass sickness.

bemegride (bem′e-grīd). Chemical name: β-ethyl-β-methylglutarimide: used as a respiratory stimulant, and as an antagonist in treatment of barbiturate poisoning.

bemidone (bem′ĭ-dōn). Chemical name: ethyl 4-(m-hydroxyphenyl)-1-methylisonipecotate: used as a narcotic.

benactyzine (ben-ak′tĭ-zēn). Chemical name: 2-diethylaminoethyl benzilate: used in parasympathetic blockade, and as an ataractic.

benadryl (ben′ah-dril). Trade mark for preparations of diphenhydramine hydrochloride.

benanserin (ben-an′ser-in). Chemical name: 1-benzyl-2-methyl-3 (2-aminoethyl)-5methoxyindole: used as a serotonin antagonist.

Bence Jones albumin, albumosuria, bodies, cylinders, protein, reaction [Henry *Bence Jones*, English physician, 1813–1873]. See under the nouns.

bend (bend). A turn or curve; a curved part. **head b.,** a bend of the embryonic body in the region of the midbrain. **neck b.,** a bend of the embryo at the posterior limit of the hindbrain.

Bendien's test (ben'de-enz) [S. G. T. *Bendien*, physician of Zeist, Holland]. See under *tests*.

bendroflumethiazide (ben"dro-floo"mĕ-thi'ah-zid). Chemical name: 3-benzyl-3,4-dihydro-6-(trifluoromethyl)-2H-1,2,4-benzothiadiazine-7-sulfonamide 1,1-dioxide: used as a diuretic and antihypertensive.

bends (bendz). Pain in the limbs and abdomen occurring as a result of rapid reduction of air pressure. **diver's b., flier's b.** See *decompression sickness*.

bene (be'ne) [L.]. Well.

beneceptor (ben'e-sep-tor) [L. *bene* well + *ceptor*]. Crile's name for a nerveceptor which transmits stimuli of a beneficial character. Cf. *nociceptor* and *ceptor*, def. 2.

Beneckea (be-nek'e-ah). A genus of microorganisms of the family Achromobacteraceae, order Eubacteriales, made up of small to medium-sized rods, found in salt and fresh water and soil, which may or may not be chromogenic. It includes six species, *B. chitino'vora*, *B. hyperop'tica*, *B. indolthe'tica*, *B. la'bra*, *B. lipo'phaga*, and *B. ureaso'phora*.

Benedict's test (ben'e-dikts) [Stanley Rossiter *Benedict*, American physiological chemist, 1884–1936]. See under *tests*.

Benedikt's syndrome (ben'e-dikts) [Moritz *Benedikt*, Austrian physician, 1835–1920]. See under *syndrome*.

benemid (ben'ĕ-mid). Trade mark for probenecid.

benign (be-nīn') [L. *benignus*]. Not malignant; not recurrent; favorable for recovery.

benignant (be-nig'nant). Benign.

Béniqué's sound (ba-ne-kāz') [Pierre Jules *Béniqué*, French physician, 1806–1851]. See under *sound*.

benjamin (ben'jah-min). Benzoin.

Bennet's corpuscles (ben'ets) [James Henry *Bennet*, English obstetrician, 1816–1891]. See under *corpuscle*.

Bennett's disease (ben'ets) [John Hughes *Bennett*, English physician, 1812–1875]. Leukemia.

Bennett's fracture, operation (ben'ets) [Edward Hallaran *Bennett*, Irish surgeon, 1837–1907]. See under *fracture* and *operation*.

Benoist's scale (bĕ-nwahz') [Louis *Benoist*, French physicist, born 1856]. See under *scale*.

benoquin (ben'o-kwin). Trade mark for a preparation of monobenzone.

benoxinate (ben-ok'sĭ-nāt). Chemical name: 2-diethylaminoethyl 4-amino-3-butoxybenzoate: used as a surface anesthetic for the eye.

Benson's disease (ben'sunz) [A. H. *Benson*, British ophthalmologist]. Asteroid hyalitis.

benthos (ben'thos) [Gr. *benthos* bottom of the sea]. The flora and fauna of the bottom of oceans.

bentonite (ben'ton-īt). A native colloidal hydrated aluminum silicate, used as a bulk laxative and as a base for preparations which may be used on the skin.

benzaldehyde (ben-zal'de-hīd). Artificial essential oil of almond: used as a flavoring agent in orally administered medicaments.

benzalin (ben'zah-lin). Nigrosin.

benzalkonium (benz"al-ko'ne-um). A mixture of alkyldimethylbenzylammonium salt: used as a surface antiseptic in 1:1000 to 1:40,000 solution.

benzamidase (ben-zam'i-dās). An enzyme which catalyzes the change of benzoic acid into benzamide.

benzanthracene (ben-zan'thrah-sēn). One of a group of hydrocarbons some of which have carcinogenic properties.

benzcurine (benz'ku-rēn). Gallamine.

benzedrex (ben'zĕ-dreks). Trade mark for a propylhexedrine inhaler.

benzedrine (ben'zĕ-drēn). Trade mark for preparations of amphetamine.

benzene (ben'zēn). A colorless, volatile liquid hydrocarbon, C_6H_6, obtained mainly as a by-product in the destructive distillation of coal, along with coal tar, etc. It has an aromatic odor, and burns with a light-giving flame. It dissolves fats, resins, sulfur, phosphorus, iodine, and several alkaloids. Inhaling the fumes may cause fatal poisoning. It is used as a pulmonary antiseptic in influenza, etc., as a teniacide, externally as a parasiticide, and has been suggested in leukemias. Called also *benzol*. **acetyl b.,** acetophenone. **dimethyl b.,** xylene. **b. hexachloride,** C_6Cl_6, a powerful insecticide. **methyl b.,** toluene. **b. picrate,** fortoin.

benzenoid (ben'zĕ-noid). A compound having benzene linkage as distinguished from quinonoid linkages.

benzestrol (ben-zes'trol). Chemical name: 4,4'-(1,2-diethyl-3-methyltrimethylene) diphenol: used as an estrogenic compound.

benzethonium (ben"ze-tho'ne-um). Chemical name: benzyldimethyl{2[2-(p-1,1,3,3-tetramethylbutylphenoxy)ethoxy]ethyl}ammonium: used as a local anti-infective.

benzhexol (benz-hek'sol). Trihexyphenidyl.

benzhydramine (benz-hi'drah-mēn). Diphenhydramine.

benzidine (ben'zĭ-din). A colorless, crystalline compound, para-diamino-diphenyl, ($NH_2.C_6H_4.$-$C_6H_4.NH_2$), formed by the action of acids on hydrazobenzene: used as a test for blood.

benzimidazole (ben"zim-ĭ-da'zōl). A compound, $C_6H_4.NH.CH:N$ (with a bond linking C_6H_4 and N), which is toxic to yeast in the absence of its homologous compounds, adenine and guanine.

benzin, benzine (ben'zin) [L. *benzinum*]. A clear, volatile distillate from petroleum made up of hexane and heptane and distilling at 70 to 90°C. It is inflammable, and has a strong ethereal odor. It is used as a solvent for fats, resin, caoutchouc, and certain alkaloids. **petroleum b., purified b.,** a purified distillate from petroleum consisting of hydrocarbons chiefly of the methane series: used principally as a solvent.

benzmalecene (benz-mal'ĕ-sēn). Chemical name: N-[1-methyl-2,3-bis(p-chlorophenyl)-propyl] maleamic acid: used experimentally to reduce hypercholesterolemia.

benzoate (ben'zo-āt). A salt of benzoic acid.

benzoated (ben'zo-āt-ed). Containing or combined with benzoin or benzoic acid.

benzocaine (ben'zo-kān). Ethyl aminobenzoate.

benzoin (ben'zoin). A balsamic resin from *Styrax benzoin*: used as an expectorant, and as an antiseptic and protective for external use.

benzolism (ben'zo-lizm). Poisoning by benzene or its vapor.

benzomethamine (ben"zo-meth"ah-mēn). Chemical name: N-diethylaminoethyl-N'-methylbenzilamide: used to produce parasympathetic blockade and to reduce the secretion of hydrochloric acid in the stomach.

benzonatate (ben-zo'nah-tāt). Chemical name: ω-methoxypoly (ethyleneoxy) ethyl-p-butylaminobenzoate: used as an antitussive.

benzononatine (ben-zo"no-na'tin). Benzonatate.

benzopropyl (ben"zo-pro'pil). Alypin.

benzopurpurine (ben"zo-pur'pu-rin). Any one of a series of azo-dyes of a scarlet color, used especially as a contrast stain with hematoxylin and other blue stains, **b. B,** an indicator with a pH range of 2.0–4.0.

benzoquinonium (ben"zo-kwĭ-no'ne-um). Chemical name: [2,5-p-benzoquinonylenebis (iminotrimethylene)] bis-[benzyldiethylammonium]: used as a relaxant for skeletal muscle.

benzotherapy (ben″zo-ther′ah-pe). Treatment with benzoates; especially the treatment of pulmonary abscess by intravenous injection of sodium benzoate.

benzoyl (ben′zo-il). The radical, $C_6H_5.CO$, of benzoic acid and of an extensive series of compounds. **b. peroxide,** a crystalline substance formed by the action of sodium peroxide on benzoyl chloride.

benzpyrene (benz-pi′rēn). A carcinogenic polycyclic hydrocarbon, $C_{20}H_{12}$.

benzpyrinium (benz′pi-rin′e-um). Chemical name: 1-benzyl-3-(dimethylcarbamyloxy) pyridinium: used as a parasympathomimetic agent, and to relieve paralytic ileus.

benzpyrrole (benz-pir′ol). Indole.

benztropine (benz′tro-pēn). Chemical name: 3-diphenylmethoxytropane: used to produce parasympathetic blockade, as an antihistaminic, and to reduce tremors of parkinsonism.

benzyl (ben′zil). The hydrocarbon radical, C_7H_7 or $C_6H_5.CH_2$, of benzyl alcohol and various other bodies. **b. benzoate,** an aromatic, clear, colorless oily liquid with a sharp, burning taste, $C_{14}H_{12}O_2$, used externally as a scabicide. **b. bromide,** a war gas, $C_6H_5.CH_2Br$, causing lacrimation. **b. carbinol,** phenyl ethyl alcohol, a constituent of oil of rose, possessing anesthetic properties. **b. fumarate,** a white crystalline substance, $C_6H_5CH_2.OOC.CH{:}CH{:}COO.CH_2C_6H_5$, containing 63.6 per cent of benzyl. **b. glycocoll,** hippuric acid. **b. mandelate,** the benzyl ester of mandelic acid: used as an antispasmodic on smooth muscle fiber, as in high blood pressure. **b. succinate,** the dibenzyl ester of succinic acid, $(C_6H_5.CH_2.O.CO.CH_2)_2$: formerly used as an antispasmodic to nonstriated muscle.

benzylidene (ben-zil′ĭ-dēn). A hydrocarbon radical, $C_6H_5CH{:}$.

benzylpenicillin (ben″zil-pen-ĭ-sil′in). Penicillin G. See under *penicillin.* **b. benzhydrylamine,** penicillin G benzhydrylamine. **b. potassium,** penicillin G potassium. **b. procaine,** penicillin G procaine.

bepti. A word used in malaria epidemiology, composed from the initial letters of the five important factors: b—bionomics; e—environment; p—plasmodium; t—treatment; i—immunity. This, with X—human carrier, Y—mosquito vector, Z—human victim, gives: $(X + Y + Z)$ bepti = malaria incidence.

Béraneck's tuberculin (ba-ran-eks′) [Edmond *Béraneck,* Swiss bacteriologist, 1859–1920]. See under *tuberculin.*

Bérard's aneurysm, ligament (ba-rarz′) [Auguste *Bérard,* French surgeon, 1802–1846]. See under *aneurysm* and *ligament.*

Béraud's valve (ba-rōz′) [Bruno Jean Jacques *Béraud,* French surgeon, 1825–1865]. See under *valve.*

bergamot (ber′gah-mot) [L. *bergamium*]. 1. The tree, *Citrus bergamia;* also its orange-like fruit, whose rind affords the fragrant oil of bergamot. 2. A popular name for various fragrant labiate plants, such as *Mentha citrata* and *Monarda fistulosa.* **wild b.** See *Monarda.*

Bergenhem's operation (ber′gen-hemz) [B. *Bergenhem,* contemporary Swedish surgeon]. See under *operation.*

Berger's method, operation (bār-zhāz′) [Paul *Berger,* French surgeon, 1845–1908]. See under *method* and *operation.*

Berger's paresthesia (ber′gerz) [Oskar *Berger,* neurologist in Breslau, 1844–1885]. See under *paresthesia.*

Berger rhythm (ber′ger) [Hans *Berger,* Jena neurologist, 1873–1941]. See under *rhythm.*

Berger's sign, symptom (ber′gerz) [Emil *Berger,* Austrian ophthalmologist, 1855–1926]. See under *sign.*

Bergeron's disease (berzh′ronz) [Etienne Jules *Bergeron,* French physician, 1817–1900]. Hysterical chorea.

Bergmann's cords, fibers (berg′manz) [Gottlieb Heinrich *Bergmann,* German physician, died 1860]. See under *cord* and *fiber.*

Bergmann's incision (berg′manz) [Ernst von *Bergmann,* German surgeon, 1836–1907]. See under *incision.*

Bergonié method, treatment (bār-go-nya′) [Jean A. *Bergonié,* French physician, 1857–1925]. See under *treatment.*

beriberi (ber″e-ber′e) [Singhalese, "I cannot," signifying that the person is too ill to do anything]. An endemic form of polyneuritis prevalent chiefly in Japan, India, China, the Philippines, and the Malay Peninsula (Bontius, 1642). It is marked by spasmodic rigidity of the lower limbs, with muscular atrophy, paralysis, anemia, and neuralgic pains. The condition is due to a deficiency of vitamin B_1 (thiamine) and other vitamins, and is frequently caused by a diet consisting too exclusively of white (polished) rice. Called also *kakke, asjike, hinchavon, inchacao, perneiras, loempe, endemic multiple neuritis, panneuritis epidemica,* and *polyneuritis endemica.* **atrophic b., dry b.,** a form in which flaccid paralyses are the dominant feature. **infantile b.,** a disease of infants in the Philippines who are nursed by mothers affected with beriberi. **paralytic b.,** atrophic beriberi. **ship b.,** a disease resembling tropical beriberi, seen on Norwegian ships, but with edema a more prominent symptom than neuritis. **wet b.,** a form with anemia and edema, but without paralysis.

beriberic (ber″e-ber′ik). Pertaining to, or of the nature of, beriberi.

Berkefeld filter (ber′ke-feld) [Wilhelm *Berkefeld,* manufacturer, 1836–1897]. See under *filter.*

berkelium (berk′le-um) [named for *Berkeley,* California, where it was produced]. An element of atomic number 97, atomic weight 247, symbol Bk, produced by bombardment of the isotope of americium of atomic weight 241 by helium ions. Half-life $4\frac{1}{2}$ hours.

Berlin's disease, edema (ber′linz) [Rudolf *Berlin,* German oculist, 1833–1897]. See under *edema.*

berloque dermatitis (ber-lok′) [Fr. *breloque* charm (especially on a chain)]. See under *dermatitis.*

Bernard's canal, duct, layer, puncture, etc. (ber-narz′) [Claude *Bernard,* French physiologist, 1813–1878]. See under the nouns.

Bernay's sponge (ber′nāz) [Augustus Charles *Bernay,* American surgeon, 1854–1907]. See under *sponge.*

Bernhardt's disease, paresthesia (bern′harts) [Martin *Bernhardt,* German neurologist, 1844–1915]. Meralgia paresthetica.

Bernhardt-Roth disease, syndrome [Martin *Bernhardt;* Vladimir K. *Roth,* Russian neurologist, 1848–1916]. Meralgia paresthetica.

Bernheimer's fibers (bern′hi-merz) [Stephan *Bernheimer,* Austrian ophthalmologist, 1861–1918]. See under *fiber.*

berry (ber′e). A small fruit with a succulent pericarp. **bear b.,** *Uva ursi.* **buckthorn b.,** *Rhamnus cathartica.* **elder b.,** Sambucus. **fish b.,** Cocculus. **horse nettle b.,** Solanum. **horse savin b.,** Juniperus. **Indian b.,** Cocculus. **poke b.,** Phytolacca. **prickly ash b.,** Xanthoxylum. **saw palmetto b.,** Serenoa. **spice b.,** aralia. **sumac b.,** *Rhus glabra.*

Berry's ligaments (ber′ēz) [Sir James *Berry,* Canadian surgeon, born 1860]. See under *ligament.*

Berthollet's fluid, law (ber-to-lāz′) [Claude Louis *Berthollet,* French chemist, 1748–1822]. See under *fluid* and *law.*

Bertiella (ber″te-el′lah). A genus of tapeworms. **B. sat′yri, B. stu′deri,** a tapeworm found occasionally in man and in the higher apes in Mauritius, India, Cuba, and the Phillippines.

bertielliasis (ber″te-el-li′ah-sis). Infection with Bertiella.

bertillonage (bär-te-yon-nahzh′) [Alphonse *Bertillon*, French criminologist, 1853–1914]. The recorded measurement and description of criminals.

Bertin's bones, column, ligament (ber′tinz) [Exupère Joseph *Bertin*, French anatomist, 1712–1781]. See under the nouns.

Bertrand's test (bär-trahnz′) [Gabriel *Bertrand*, Paris chemist, born 1867]. See under *tests*.

berubigen (be-roo′bĭ-jen). Trade mark for preparations of vitamin B_{12}. See *cyanocobalamin*.

berylliosis (ber″il-le-o′sis). A morbid condition, usually of the lungs, more rarely of the skin, subcutaneous tissue, lymph nodes, liver, and other structures, characterized by formation of granulomas. Fumes of beryllium salts or finely divided dust may be inhaled or the substance may be accidentally implanted in the skin or subcutaneous tissue by laceration or puncture.

beryllium (ber-il′le-um) [Gr. *bēryllos* beryl]. A metallic element of atomic number 4, atomic weight 9.012, symbol Be.

Berzelius' test (bär-za′le-us) [Johann Jacob *Berzelius*, Swedish chemist, 1779–1848]. See under *tests*.

besiclometer (bes″ĭ-klom′e-ter). An instrument for measuring the forehead to ascertain the proper width of spectacle frames.

Besnier-Boeck disease [Ernest *Besnier*, Paris dermatologist, 1831–1909; Caesar *Boeck*, dermatologist in Christiana, 1845–1917]. Boeck's sarcoid.

besoin (bez-wan′) [Fr.]. Want; necessity. **b. de respirer** (bez-wan′ dĕ res″pe-ra′), the sensation which prompts the act of breathing.

Besredka's antivirus, reaction (bes-red′kahz) [Alexandre *Besredka*, Russian pathologist at Pasteur Institute, Paris, 1870–1940]. See under *antivirus* and *reaction*.

Best (best), Charles Herbert. A Canadian physiologist, born 1899; associated with Sir Frederick Banting and John James Macleod in the discovery of insulin in 1922.

Best's operation (bestz) [Van *Best*, Scottish surgeon, 1836–1875]. See under *operation*.

bestiality (bes-te-al′ĭ-te) [L. *bestia* beast]. Sexual connection with an animal.

Beta (be′tah) [L.]. A genus of plants to which the beet belongs. **B. vulga′ris,** the common beet.

beta (ba′tah). The second letter of the Greek alphabet, β; used as part of a chemical name to distinguish one of two or more isomers or to indicate the position of substituting atoms or groups in certain compounds. See *alpha*.

beta-albumosease (ba″tah-al-bu-mo′se-ās). Erepsin.

Betabacterium (ba″tah-bak-te′re-um). A subgenus of Lactobacillus.

beta-cholestanol (ba″tah-ko-les′tah-nol). See under *cholestanol*.

betacism (ba′tah-sizm) [Gr. *bēta* the second letter of the Greek alphabet]. The excessive use of the *b* sound in speaking.

betadine (ba′tah-din). Trade mark for preparations of povidone-iodine.

beta-hypophamine (ba″tah-hi-pof′ah-min). Vasopressin.

betaine (be′tah-in). Chemical name: trimethylglycocoll: used as a lipotropic agent, and in hydrochloride form as a substitute for HCl in achlorhydria.

beta-lactose (ba″tah-lak′tōs). A disaccharide isomeric with lactose, obtained by allowing a solution of lactose to crystallize above 93°C. It is more soluble and sweeter than lactose.

betalin (ba′tah-lin). Trade mark for preparations containing components of the vitamin B complex. *b. S* is synthetic thiamine chloride (vitamin B_1). *b. 12 crystalline* is a sterile, isotonic, stable solution of crystalline cyanocobalamine (vitamin B_{12}).

betalysin (ba-tal′ĭ-sin). A relatively thermostable lysin for gram-positive bacteria (Patterson).

betanaphthol (ba″tah-naf′thol). A form of naphthol, occurring as a colorless or pale-buff crystalline compound having the odor of carbolic acid. Uses: 1. locally as a counterirritant in alopecia; 2. anthelmintic; 3. antiseptic. **b. benzoate,** benzonaphthol. **b. benzylamine,** a reagent by which aldoses can be distinguished from ketoses. It combines with aldoses to produce crystalline products, but it does not combine with ketoses. **b. bismuth,** a brown, powdery mixture of bismuth oxide, 8 parts, with betanaphthol, 2 parts, insoluble in water: used as an intestinal antiseptic. **b. carbonate,** an ester in colorless, shining scales: used as an intestinal antiseptic. **b. diiodide,** a yellow-green powder, $C_{16}H_6I_2O_2$: used as an antiseptic wound dressing. **b. salicylate,** betol.

betanaphthyl (ba″tah-naf′thil). The combining group, $C_{10}H_8$, of betanaphthol. **b. benzoate,** benzonaphthol. **b. salicylate,** betol.

betanin (be′tah-nin). The red pigment of the root of the beet.

beta-oxybutyria (ba″tah-ok″se-bu-ti′re-ah). The presence of beta-oxybutyric acid in the urine. Cf. *ketonuria*.

betaprone (ba′tah-prōn). Trade mark for a preparation of betapropiolactone.

betapropiolactone (ba″tah-pro″pe-o-lak′tōn). Chemical name: hydracrylic acid β-lactone. Use: sterilization of human arterial grafts.

betaquinine (ba″tah-kwin′in). See *quinidine*.

beta-serolysin (ba″tah-se-rol′ĭ-sin). A relatively heat-resistant bactericidal substance present in the blood.

betatron (ba′tah-tron). An apparatus for accelerating electrons to millions of electron volts by means of magnetic induction.

betaxin (be-tak′sin). Trade mark for preparations of thiamine hydrochloride.

betazole (ba′tah-zōl). Chemical name: 3-(β-aminoethyl)pyrazole. Use: in place of histamine to stimulate gastric acid secretion.

bête (bet) [Fr.]. Beast. **b. rouge** (bet-ro͞ozh′) [Fr. "red beast"], the red mite of Martinique and Honduras which burrows into the skin. It is probably a species of *Trombicula*.

betel (be′t'l) [Tamil *vettilei*]. An East Indian masticatory, consisting of a piece of betel nut rolled up with lime in a betel leaf. It is tonic, astringent, and stimulant. **b. leaf,** the leaf of *Piper betle:* used as a masticatory. **b. nut,** the dried ripe seed of *Areca catechu*, a palm tree of South Asia: formerly used as an anthelmintic in veterinary medicine.

bethanechol (bĕ-tha′ne-kol). Chemical name: carbamylmethylcholine: used as a parasympathomimetic agent, and in treatment of abdominal distention or urinary retention.

Bethea's method, sign (bĕ-tha′ez) [Oscar Walter *Bethea*, New Orleans physician, born 1878]. See under *sign*.

Betonica (be-ton′ĭ-kah) [L.]. A genus of labiate plants. *B. officinalis,* wood betony, was formerly used in medicine: the tops are astringent and aromatic; the root, emetic and cathartic.

Bettendorff's test (bet′en-dorfz) [Anton Joseph Hubert Maria *Bettendorff*, German chemist, 1839–1902]. See under *tests*.

Betula (bet′u-lah) [L.]. A genus of trees: the birches. **B. al′ba** (white birch), the source of a bark from which rectified birch tar oil is derived. **B. len′ta** (black birch), a tree whose bark is an important commercial source of methyl salicylate.

betweenbrain (be-twēn′brān). The diencephalon.

Betz's cells (bet′zes) [Vladimir Aleksandrovich *Betz*, Russian anatomist, 1834–1894]. See under *cell*.

Beurmann's disease (bowr′manz) [Lucien de

Beurmann, French physician, 1851–1923]. Disseminated gummatous sporotrichosis.

Bev. Abbreviation for *billion electron volts;* the equivalent of 3.82 × 10^{-11} gram calorie, or 1.6 × 10^{-3} erg.

Bevan's incision (bev′anz) [Arthur Dean *Bevan*, American surgeon, 1861–1943]. See under *incision.*

Bevan-Lewis cells (bev′an loo′is) [William *Bevan-Lewis*, English physiologist, 1847–1929]. See under *cell.*

bevel (bev′el). 1. A slanting edge. 2. To produce a slanting of the enamel edges of a tooth cavity.

bevidox (bev′ĭ-doks). Trade mark for a solution of vitamin B_{12}. See *cyanocobalamin.*

Beyerinck's reaction (bi′er-inks) [M. W. *Beyerinck*, Dutch physician]. Cholera reaction.

beziehungswahn (ba-ze′hoongz-vahn″) [Ger.]. A form of guilt psychosis marked by morbid ideas of reference.

bezoar (be′zōr) [Persian]. A concretion of various character sometimes found in the stomach or intestines of man or other animals. They may belong to one of four types: trichobezoar (hair), phytobezoar (fruit and vegetable fibers), trichophytobezoar (a mixture of hair, and fruit and vegetable fibers), or concretions of shellac.

Bezold's abscess, mastoiditis, perforation, sign, triad, etc. (ba′zoltz) [Friedrich *Bezold*, aurist in Munich, 1842–1908]. See under the nouns.

Bezold's ganglion (ba′zoltz) [Albert von *Bezold*, German physiologist, 1838–1868]. See under *ganglion.*

B.F. Abbreviation for *bouillon filtré.* See *tuberculin bouillon filtrate.*

BFP. Abbreviation for *biologically false positivity* (*biologic false positive* reaction), the presence of positive findings in the serologic tests for syphilis when syphilis is known not to exist.

B.G. Abbreviation for *buccogingival.*

bhang (bang) [Hind.]. The Indian name for a dried mixture of the larger leaves and young twigs of *Cannabis sativa.* See *Cannabis.*

B.I. Abbreviation for *base of prism in.*

Bi. Chemical symbol for *bismuth.*

bi- [L. *bi* two]. Combining form meaning two or twice.

Bial's test (be′alz) [Manfred *Bial*, German physician, 1870–1908]. See under *tests.*

Bianchi's nodules, valve (be-ang′kēz) [Giovanni Battista *Bianchi*, Italian anatomist, 1681–1761]. See *corpora arantii*, and under *valve.*

Bianchi's syndrome (be-ang′kēz) [Leonardo *Bianchi*, Italian psychiatrist, 1848–1927]. See under *syndrome.*

biarticular (bi″ar-tik′u-lar). Pertaining to two joints.

biasteric (bi″as-ter′ik). Pertaining to the two asteria.

biauricular (bi″aw-rik′u-lar). Pertaining to the two auricles.

Bib. Abbreviation for L. *bi′be*, drink.

bib (bib). A fragment of a red blood cell often seen attached to the crescent bodies of the blood of estivo-autumnal fever.

bibasic (bi-ba′sik). Doubly basic; having two hydrogen atoms that may be replaced by bases.

bibeveled (bi′bev-eld). Having a slanting surface on two sides.

bibliofilm (bib′le-o-film). A negative microfilm of material for a library. It is a term trade-marked by Science Service with the idea that it would be applied only to the product of Bibliofilm Services, Incorporated, under the proposed Documentation Institute.

bibliomania (bib″le-o-ma′ne-ah) [Gr. *biblion* book + *mania* madness). Abnormally intense desire to collect books.

bibliotherapy (bib″le-o-ther′ah-pe) [Gr. *biblion* book + *therapeia* treatment]. The employment of books and reading of them in the treatment of nervous disorders.

Bibron's antidote (bib′ronz) [Gabriel *Bibron*, French naturalist, 1806–1848]. See under *antidote.*

bibulous (bib′u-lus) [L. *bibulus*, from *bibere* to drink]. Having the property of absorbing moisture.

bicameral (bi-kam′er-al) [*bi-* + L. *camera* chamber]. Having two chambers.

bicapsular (bi-kap′su-lar) [*bi-* + L. *capsula* a capsule]. Having two capsules.

bicarbonate (bi-kar′bo-nāt). Any salt having two equivalents of carbonic acid to one of a basic substance. **blood b.,** the bicarbonate of the blood, an index of the alkali reserve. **plasma b.,** blood bicarbonate.

bicarbonatemia (bi-kar″bo-nāt-e′me-ah). The presence of an excessive amount of bicarbonate in the blood.

bicardiogram (bi-kar′de-o-gram″). A curve in an electrocardiogram indicating the composite effect of the right and left atria.

bicaudal (bi-kaw′dal) [*bi-* + L. *cauda* tail]. Having two tails.

bicaudate (bi-kaw′dāt). Bicaudal.

bicellular (bi-sel′u-lar). Made up of two cells, or having two cells.

bicephalus (bi-sef′ah-lus). Dicephalus.

biceps (bi′seps) [*bi-* + L. *caput* head]. A muscle having two heads. **b. bra′chii, b. fem′oris.** See *Table of Musculi.*

biceptor (bi-sep′tor). An amboceptor which has two complementophil groups.

Bichat's canal, fissure, foramen (be-shaz′) [Marie François Xavier *Bichat*, an eminent French anatomist and physiologist, 1771–1802, founder of scientific histology and pathological anatomy]. See under the nouns.

bichloride (bi-klo′rīd). 1. Any chloride which contains two equivalents of chlorine. 2. Corrosive mercuric chloride.

bichromate (bi-kro′māt). Dichromate.

biciliate (bi-sil′e-āt). Possessing two cilia.

bicipital (bi-sip′ĭ-tal). 1. Having two heads. 2. Pertaining to a biceps muscle.

biconcave (bi-kon′kāv). Having two concave surfaces.

bicontaminated (bi″kon-tam′ĭ-nāt″ed). Infected by or associated with two different species of microorganisms, or by two different types of contaminating agents.

biconvex (bi-kon′veks). Having two convex surfaces.

bicornate (bi-kor′nāt). Bicornuate.

bicornuate (bi-kor′nu-āt) [*bi-* + L. *cornutus* horned]. Having two horns.

bicorporate (bi-kor′po-rāt) [*bi-* + L. *corpus* body]. Having two bodies.

bicoudate (bi′koo-dāt). Twice bent.

bicuspid (bi-kus′pid) [*bi-* + L. *cuspis* point]. 1. Having two cusps or points. 2. A bicuspid valve. 3. A premolar tooth.

bicuspidal (bi-kus′pĭ-dal). 1. Pertaining to a bicuspid tooth. 2. Having two cusps.

bicuspidate (bi-kus′pĭ-dāt). Having two cusps.

bicuspoid (bi-kus′poid). A figure in space resembling a bicuspid tooth and representing the space traversed in all its movements by a point in one jaw in relation to the other jaw.

b.i.d. Abbreviation for L. *bis in di′e*, twice a day.

Bidder's ganglion, organ (Heinrich Friedrich *Bidder*, German anatomist, 1810–1894]. See under *ganglion* and *organ.*

bidental (bi-den′tal) [*bi-* + L. *dens* tooth]. Having, pertaining to, or affecting two teeth.

bidentate (bi-den′tāt). Having two teeth.

bidermoma (bi″der-mo′mah) [*bi-* + Gr. *derma* skin + *-oma*]. A teratoid growth containing two germ layers.

biduotertian (bid″u-o-ter′shun). Noting malaria caused by *Plasmodium vivax*, in which two broods of parasites are segmenting on alternate days, so that febrile paroxysms occur daily.

biduous (bid′u-us). Lasting for two days.

Biederman's sign (be′der-manz) [J. B. *Biederman*, Cincinnati physician, born 1907]. See under *sign*.

Biedert's cream mixture (be′derts) [Philipp *Biedert*, pediatrist in Strasburg, 1847–1916]. See under *mixture*.

Biedl's disease, syndrome (be′dlz) [Artur *Biedl*, Austrian physician, 1869–1933]. Laurence-Moon-Biedl syndrome.

bielectrolysis (bi″e-lek-trol′ĭ-sis). Electrolysis in which decomposition takes place at both poles.

Bielschowsky's method (be″el-show′skēz) [Max *Bielschowsky*, German neuropathologist, 1869–1940]. See *table of stains and staining methods*.

Bielschowsky-Jansky disease (be″el-show′ske yan′ske). Late infantile form of amaurotic family idiocy.

Bier's anesthesia, hyperemia, etc. (bērz) [August Karl Gustav *Bier*, surgeon in Berlin, 1861–1949]. See under the nouns.

Biermer's anemia, sign (bēr′merz) [Anton *Biermer*, German physician, 1827–1892]. See under *anemia*, and *Gerhardt's sign*, def. 2, under *sign*.

Biernacki's sign (byēr-naht′skēz) [Edmund *Biernacki*, Polish physician in Lemberg, Austria, 1866–1911]. See under *sign*.

Biesiadecki's fossa (bya-syah-det′skēz) [Alfred von *Biesiadecki*, Polish physician, 1839–1888]. Iliacosubfascial fossa.

Biett's disease, solution (be-ets′) [Laurent Théodore *Biett*, Parisian dermatologist, 1781–1840]. See *lupus erythematosus*, and under *solution*.

bifid (bi′fid) [L. *bifidus*]. Cleft into two parts or branches.

bifocal (bi-fo′kal). 1. Having two foci. 2. Pertaining to the compound spectacle, which contains a smaller lens for near vision placed below the center of the larger lens, which is for distant vision.

biforate (bi-fo′rāt) [*bi-* + L. *fora* opening]. Having two foramina or openings.

bifurcate (bi-fur′kāt) [L. *bifurcatus*, from *bi* two + *furca* fork]. Forked; divided into two like a fork.

bifurcatio (bi″fur-ka′she-o), pl. *bifurcationes* [L.]. The site of division of a single structure into two. **b. tra′chea** [N A, B N A], the site of division of the trachea into the right and left main bronchi. Called also *bifurcation of trachea*.

bifurcation (bi″fur-ka′shun) [L. *bifurcatio*, from *bi* two + *furca* fork]. 1. Division into two branches. 2. The site where a single structure divides into two. **b. of trachea,** bifurcatio tracheae.

bifurcationes (bi″fur-ka″she-o′nēz) [L.]. Plural of *bifurcatio*.

Bigelovia (big″e-lo′ve-ah) [Jacob *Bigelow*, 1787–1879]. A genus of composite-flowered plants. *B. vene′ta*, of North America, is one of the species affording *damiana* (q.v.).

Bigelow's ligament, litholapaxy, septum (big′e-lōz) [Henry Jacob *Bigelow*, Boston surgeon, 1818–1890]. See under the nouns.

bigemina (bi-jem′ĭ-nah). A bigeminal pulse.

bigeminal (bi-jem′ĭ-nal). Occurring in twos; twin.

bigeminum (bi-jem′ĭ-num), pl. *bigem′ina* [L. "twin"]. Either one of the corpora bigemina of the fetus or of a bird; the fetal bigemina become the corpora quadrigemina.

bigeminy (bi-jem′ĭ-ne). The condition of occurring in pairs; especially the occurrence of two beats of the pulse in rapid succession. See *bigeminal pulse*, under *pulse*. **nodal b.,** a form of arrhythmia consisting of nodal extrasystoles followed by nodal automatic beats.

bigerminal (bi-jer′mĭ-nal). Pertaining to two germs or ova.

bighead (big′hed). 1. Bulging of the skull bones of an animal, due to osteomalacia. 2. A contagious pneumo-enteritis of young turkeys.

bigjaw (big′jaw). Actinomycosis in cattle.

bigleg (big′leg). Lymphangitis of a horse's leg.

bigonial (bi-go′ne-al). Connecting the two gonions.

bilabe (bi′lāb) [*bi-* + L. *labium* lip]. An instrument for taking small calculi from the bladder through the urethra.

bilaminar (bi-lam′ĭ-nar) [*bi-* + L. *lamina* layer]. Having or pertaining to two layers.

bilateral (bi-lat′er-al) [*bi-* + L. *latus* side]. Having two sides, or pertaining to both sides.

bilateralism (bi-lat′er-al-izm). Bilateral symmetry.

bile (bil) [L. *bilis*]. A fluid secreted by the liver and poured into the intestine. It varies in color from a golden brown to a greenish yellow; it has a bitter taste and it aids in the production of an alkaline reaction in the intestine, in the emulsification and absorption of fats, and in preventing putrefaction. Important constituents of bile are the bile acids and pigments, alkali carbonates, cholesterol, and mucin. Bile salts have been used in medicine to stimulate the secretory activity of the liver, as in obstructive jaundice and biliary fistula. **A b.,** bile from the common bile duct. **B b.,** bile from the gallbladder. **C b.,** bile from the hepatic duct. **cystic b.,** the bile which is held for some time in the gallbladder before moving into the intestine. **limy b.,** bile containing a milk-white fluid composed of calcium carbonate. **milk of calcium b.** See *limy b.* **ox b.,** fel bovis. **Platner's crystallized b.,** a crystalline substance obtained by the action of ether in an alcoholic extract of bile. **white b.,** the colorless liquid sometimes found in the gallbladder in obstructions above the entrance of the cystic duct; believed to be a secretion of the mucosa of the biliary passages.

Bilharzia (bil-har′ze-ah) [Theodor Maximilian *Bilharz*, German physician, 1825–1862]. A former name of a genus of flukes or trematodes, now known as *Schistosoma*.

bilharzial (bil-har′ze-al). Bilharzic.

bilharziasis (bil″har-zi′ah-sis). Schistosomiasis.

bilharzic (bil-har′zik). Pertaining to, or caused by, Bilharzia (Schistosoma).

bilharzioma (bil-har″ze-o′mah). A tumor in the skin or mucous membrane caused by Bilharzia (Schistosoma).

bilharziosis (bil-har″ze-o′sis). Schistosomiasis.

bili- (bil′e) [L. *bilis* bile]. A combining form denoting relationship to the bile.

biliary (bil′e-a-re). Pertaining to the bile, to the bile ducts, or to the gallbladder.

biliation (bil″e-a′shun). The secretion of bile.

bilicyanin (bil″e-si′ah-nin) [*bili-* + L. *cyaneus* blue]. A blue pigment derivable from biliverdin by oxidation.

bilidigestive (bil″e-di-jes′tiv). Pertaining to the gallbladder and digestive tract.

bilifaction (bil″e-fak′shun). Bilification.

bilifecia (bil″e-fe′se-ah). Bile in the feces.

bilification (bil″e-fi-ka′shun). The formation or secretion of bile.

biliflavin (bil″e-fla′vin) [*bili-* + L. *flavus* yellow]. A yellow pigment obtainable from biliverdin.

bilifulvin (bil″e-ful′vin) [*bili-* + L. *fulvus* tawny]. An impure bilirubin of a tawny color; also a tawny pigment from ox gall, not normally found in healthy human bile.

bilifuscin (bil″e-fus′in) [*bili-* + L. *fuscus* brown]. A pigment from human bile and gallstones.

biligenesis (bil″e-jen′e-sis). The production or formation of bile.

biligenetic (bil″e-je-net′ik). 1. Pertaining to biligenesis. 2. Biligenic.

biligenic (bil″e-jen′ik) [*bili-* + Gr. *gennan* to produce]. Producing bile.

biligulate (bi-lig′u-lāt) [*bi-* + L. *ligula* little tongue]. Having two tonguelike processes.

bilihumin (bil″e-hu′min) [*bili-* + L. *humus* earth]. An insoluble ingredient of gallstones.

bilin (bi′lin) [L. *bilis* bile]. The main constituent of the bile, composed chiefly of the sodium salts of the normal bile acids.

bilious (bil′yus) [L. *biliosus*]. Characterized by bile, by excess of bile, or by biliousness.

biliousness (bil′yus-nes). Malaise, with constipation, headache, and indigestion, attributed to an excessive secretion of bile.

biliphein (bil″e-fe′in) [*bili-* + Gr. *phaios* dusky, gray]. Bilirubin; also, a mixed pigment obtainable from the bile.

biliprasin (bil″e-pra′sin) [*bili-* + Gr. *prasinos* green]. A green pigment from gallstones.

bilipurpurin (bil″e-pur′pu-rin) [*bili-* + L. *purpur* purple]. A purple pigment, $C_{34}H_{36}O_6N_4$, from biliverdin.

bilipyrrhin (bil″e-pir′in) [*bili-* + Gr. *pyrrhos* red-yellow]. Biliphein.

bilirhachia (bil″ĭ-ra′ke-ah) [*bili-* + Gr. *rhachis* spine + *-ia*]. The presence of bile pigments in the spinal fluid.

bilirubin [bil″e-roo′bin) [*bili-* + L. *ruber* red]. A red bile pigment, $C_{33}H_{36}O_6N_4$, occurring in the bile as soluble sodium bilirubinate and in gallstones as a calcium salt. It is sometimes found in urine and occurs in the blood and tissues in jaundice. It is formed from the hemoglobin of erythrocytes by the reticuloendothelial cells.

bilirubinate (bil″e-roo′bĭ-nāt). A salt of bilirubin.

bilirubinemia (bil″e-roo-bĭ-ne′me-ah) [*bilirubin* + Gr. *haima* blood + *-ia*]. The presence of bilirubin in the blood.

bilirubinic (bil″e-roo-bin′ik). Pertaining to bilirubin.

bilirubinuria (bil″e-roo-bĭ-nu′re-ah). Presence of bilirubin in the urine.

bilis (bi′lis) [L.]. Bile. **b. bovi′na, b. buba′ta.** See *ox bile extract*, under *extract.*

bilitherapy (bil″e-ther′ah-pe). Treatment with bile or bile salts.

biliuria (bil″e-u′re-ah) [*bili-* + Gr. *ouron* urine + *-ia*]. The presence of bile pigments in the urine.

biliverdin (bil″e-ver′din) [*bili-* + L. *viridis* green]. A green pigment, $C_{33}H_{34}O_6N_4$, or dehydrobilirubin, formed from bilirubin by oxidation. It occurs in bile and in the urine in jaundice.

biliverdinate (bil″e-ver′dĭ-nāt). A salt of biliverdin.

bilixanthine (bil″e-zan′thin) [*bili-* + Gr. *xanthos* yellow]. Choletelin.

Billroth's disease, operation, strands, suture, etc. (bil′rōts) [Christian Albert Theodor *Billroth*, surgeon in Vienna, 1829–1894]. See under the nouns.

bilobate (bi-lo′bāt) [*bi-* + L. *lobus* lobe]. Having two lobes.

bilobular (bi-lob′u-lar). Having two lobules.

bilocular (bi-lok′u-lar) [*bi-* + L. *loculus* cell]. Having two compartments.

biloculate (bi-lok′u-lāt). Bilocular.

bilophodont (bi-lof′o-dont) [*bi-* + Gr. *lophos* ridge + *odous* tooth]. Having posterior teeth with two ridges on them; applied to certain animals, as the kangaroo.

Bimana (bim′ah-nah) [*bi-* + L. *manus* hand]. A name sometimes applied to a category of mammals distinguished by possessing hands of character differing from that of the feet, and made up of man alone.

bimanual (bi-man′u-al) [*bi-* + L. *manualis* of the hand]. With both hands; performed by both hands.

bimastic (bi-mas′tik). Having two mammae.

bimastism (bi-mas′tizm) [*bi-* + Gr. *mastos* breast]. The state of having two mammae.

bimastoid (bi-mas′toid). Pertaining to both mastoid processes.

bimaxillary (bi-mak′sĭ-ler″e). Pertaining to or affecting both sides of the upper jaw.

bimester (bi′mes-ter). A period of two months.

bimodal (bi-mo′dal). Having two modes or peaks: said of a graphic curve.

bimolecular (bi″mo-lek′u-lar). Relating to or formed from two molecules.

binangle (bin′ang-g'l). Having two angles; Black's term for a dental instrument having two angulations in the shank connecting the handle, or shaft, with the working portion of the instrument, known as the blade, or nib.

binary (bi′na-re) [L. *binarius* of two]. Made up of two elements or of two equal parts.

binaural (bin-aw′ral) [L. *bini* two + *auris* ear]. Pertaining to both ears.

binauricular (bin″aw-rik′u-lar) [L. *bini* two + *auricula* little ear]. Pertaining to both auricles.

binder (bīnd′er). An abdominal girdle or bandage, chiefly for women in childbed **(obstetric b.).**

bindweb (bīnd′web). 1. The neuroglia. 2. Any connective tissue or stroma.

binegative (bi-neg′ah-tiv). Having two negative balances.

Binet's test (be-nāz′) [Alfred *Binet*, French physiologist, 1857–1911]. See under *tests.*

Binet-Simon test (be-na′ se-mon′) [Alfred *Binet;* Theodore *Simon*, French physician, born 1873]. See under *tests.*

Bing's entotic test (bingz) [Albert *Bing*, German otologist, 1844–1922]. See under *tests.*

biniodide (bin-i′o-dīd). Any iodide that has two atoms of iodine in each molecule.

binocular (bin-ok′u-lar) [L. *bini* two + *oculus* eye]. 1. Pertaining to both eyes. 2. Having two eyepieces, as in a microscope.

binoculus (bin-ok′u-lus). The two eyes considered as one organ.

binomial (bi-no′me-al) [*bi-* + L. *nomen* name]. Composed of two names or terms, as the names of organisms formed by the combination of genus and species names.

binophthalmoscope (bin″of-thal′mo-skōp). An ophthalmoscope for examining both fundi of the patient at one time.

binoscope (bin′o-skōp) [L. *bini* two + Gr. *skopein* to examine]. An instrument for inducing binocular vision in squint by presenting one object in the central part of the field of vision, the lateral parts of the field being screened out.

binotic (bin-ot′ik) [L. *bini* two + Gr. *ous* ear]. Pertaining to both ears.

binovular (bin-ov′u-lar) [L. *bini* two + *ovum* an egg]. Pertaining to or derived from two different ova.

binoxide (bin-ok′sīd). Dioxide.

Binswanger dementia (bins′wang-er) [Otto *Binswanger*, German neurologist, 1852–1929]. Presenile dementia marked by loss of memory and mental hebetude.

binuclear (bi-nu′kle-ar) [*bi-* + L. *nucleus* nut]. Having two nuclei.

Binucleata (bi-nu″kle-a′tah) [*bi-* + L. *nucleus*]. A proposed new order of flagellate protozoa, including the Haemosporidia and the trypanosomes.

binucleate (bi-nu′kle-āt). Binuclear.

binucleation (bi″nu-kle-a′shun). The formation of two nuclei within a cell through division of the nucleus without division of the cytoplasm.

binucleolate (bi-nu-kle′o-lāt) [*bi-* + L. *nucleolus*]. Having two nucleoli.

Binz's test (bints′ez) [Karl *Binz*, German pharmacologist, 1832–1913]. See under *tests.*

bio- (bi′o) [Gr. *bios* life]. Combining form denoting relationship to life.

bio-aeration (bi″o-a″er-a′shun). A modification

of the activated sludge method of purifying sewage.

bio-assay (bi″o-as-sa′) [*bio-* + *assay*]. Determination of the active power of a sample of a drug by noting its effect on animals, as compared with the effect of a standard preparation.

bioastronautics (bi″o-as′tro-naw-tiks). The science concerned with study of the effects of space and interplanetary travel on living organisms.

bioblast (bi′o-blast) [*bio-* + Gr. *blastos* germ]. A fundamental element concerned with cell activity. See *micelle* and *mitochondria*.

biocatalyst (bi″o-kat′ah-list) [*bio-* + *catalyst*]. A name suggested by Bayliss for enzyme.

biocatalyzer (bi″o-kat′ah-līz″er). A substance (probably a vitamin) which when added to an inadequate bacterial cultural solution permits the growth of the bacterium. Called also *bacterial vitamin* and *growth hormone*.

biocenosis (bi″o-se-no′sis) [*bio-* + Gr. *koinos* common]. The relation of diverse organisms which live in association.

biocenotic (bi″o-se-not′ik). Characterized by biocenosis.

biochemics (bi″o-kem′iks) [*bio-* + Gr. *chēmeia* chemistry]. The chemistry of life.

biochemistry (bi″o-kem′is-tre) [*bio-* + *chemistry*]. The chemistry of living organisms and of vital processes; physiological chemistry.

biochemorphic (bi″o-ke-mor′fik). Pertaining to biochemorphology.

biochemorphology (bi″o-ke-mor-fol′o-je). The study of the relationship between chemical constitution and biological action.

biochemy (bi-ok′e-me) [*bio-* + Gr. *chēmeia* chemistry]. The chemical forces at work in living organisms.

biocidal (bi″o-si′dal). Destructive to living organisms.

bioclimatics (bi″o-kli-mat′iks). Bioclimatology.

bioclimatologist (bi″o-kli″mah-tol′o-jist). An individual skilled in bioclimatology.

bioclimatology (bi″o-kli″mah-tol′o-je) [*bio-* + *climatology*]. The science devoted to the study of effects on living organisms of conditions of the natural environment (rainfall, daylight, temperature, humidity, air movement) prevailing in specific regions of the earth. See also *biometeorology*.

$(BiO)_2CO_2$. Subcarbonate of bismuth.

biocoenosis (bi″o-se-no′sis). Biocenosis.

biocolloid (bi″o-kol′oid) [*bio-* + *colloid*]. A colloid from animal or vegetable tissue.

biocycle (bi″o-si′k'l) [*bio-* + Gr. *kyklos* cycle]. The rhythmic repetition of certain phenomena observed in living organisms.

bio-des (bi′o-des). Trade mark for a preparation of diethylstilbestrol.

biodetritus (bi″o-de-tri′tus). Detritus derived from the disintegration and decomposition of once-living organisms; further designated as phytodetritus or zoodetritus, depending on whether the original organism was vegetal or animal.

biodynamics (bi″o-di-nam′iks) [*bio-* + Gr. *dynamis* might]. The scientific study of the nature and determinants of all organismic (including human) behavior.

bioelectricity (bi″o-e″lek-tris′ĭ-te). The electrical phenomena which appear in living tissues.

bioelement (bi″o-el′e-ment). Any chemical element which is a component of living tissue.

bioenergetics (bi″o-en″er-jet′iks). The study of the energy transformations in living organisms.

bioflavonoid (bi″o-fla′vo-noid). A generic term for a group of compounds which are widely distributed in plants and which are concerned with maintenance of a normal state of the walls of small blood vessels.

biogen (bi′o-jen) [*bio-* + Gr. *gennan* to produce]. Micelle.

biogenesis (bi″o-jen′e-sis) [*bio-* + Gr. *genesis* origin]. 1. The origin of life, or of living organisms. 2. The theory that living organisms can originate only from organisms already living.

biogenetic (bi″o-je-net′ik). Pertaining to biogenesis.

biogenous (bi-oj′e-nus). Originating from life or producing life.

biogeochemistry (bi″o-je″o-kem′is-tre) [*bio-* + Gr. *gē* earth + *chemistry*]. The study of the effects of earth chemicals on animal and plant life.

biograph (bi′o-graf). 1. An instrument for analyzing and rendering visible the movements of animals: used in diagnosis of certain nervous diseases. 2. Pneumatograph.

biohydraulic (bi″o-hi-draw′lik) [*bio-* + Gr. *hydōr* water]. Pertaining to the action of water and solutions in living tissue.

biokinetics (bi″o-ki-net′iks) [*bio-* + Gr. *kinētikos* of or for putting in motion]. The science of the movements within developing organisms.

Biol. Abbreviation for *biology*.

biologic (bi″o-loj′ik). Biological.

biological (bi-o-loj′e-kal). Pertaining to biology.

biologicals (bi-o-loj′e-kalz). Medicinal preparations made from living organisms and their products: they include serums, vaccines, antigens and antitoxins.

biologist (bi-ol′o-jist). An expert in biology.

biologos (bi-ol′o-gos) [*bio-* + Gr. *logos* reason]. The intelligent power displayed in organic activities.

biology (bi-ol′o-je) [*bio-* + *-logy*]. The science which deals with the phenomena of life and living organisms in general.

bioluminescence (bi″o-loo″mĭ-nes′ens). Chemiluminescence occurring in living cells.

biolysis (bi-ol′ĭ-sis). Chemical decomposition of organic matter by the action of living organisms.

biolytic (bi-o-lit′ik) [*bio-* + Gr. *lytikos* loosening]. 1. Pertaining to or characterized by biolysis. 2. Destructive to life.

biomass (bi′o-mass). The entire assemblage of living organisms, both animal and vegetable, of a particular region, considered collectively.

biomathematics (bi″o-math″e-mat′iks) [*bio-* + *mathematics*]. Mathematics as applied to the phenomena of living things.

biome (bi′ōm) [Gr. *bios* life + *-ome* (-oma) mass]. The recognizable community unit of a given region, produced by interaction of climatic factors, biota, and substrate, usually designated according to the characteristic adult vegetation, as grassland, coniferous forest, deciduous forest, and the like.

biomechanics (bi″o-me-kan′iks) [*bio-* + *mechanics*]. The application of mechanical laws to living structures, specifically to the locomotor system of the human body.

biomedicine (bi″o-med′ĭ-sin). Clinical medicine based on the principles of physiology and biochemistry.

biometeorologist (bi″o-me″te-or-ol′o-jist). An individual skilled in biometeorology.

biometeorology (bi″o-me″te-or-ol′o-je) [*bio-* + Gr. *meteōros* raised from off the ground + *logos* treatise]. That branch of ecology which deals with the effects on living organisms of the extra-organic aspects of the physical environment (such as temperature, humidity, barometric pressure, rate of air flow, and air ionization). It considers not only the natural atmosphere but also artificially created atmospheres such as those to be found in buildings and shelters, and in closed ecological systems, such as satellites and submarines.

biometer (bi-om′e-ter) [*bio-* Gr. *metron* measure]. An apparatus by which extremely minute quantities of carbon dioxide can be measured: used in measuring the carbon dioxide given off from functioning tissue.

biometrician (bi″o-mĕ-trish′an). An individual skilled in biometry.

biometrics (bi-o-met′riks). Biometry.

biometry (bi-om′e-tre) [*bio-* + Gr. *metron* measure]. 1. The science of the application of statistical methods to biological facts; mathematical analysis of biological data. 2. In life insurance, the calculation of the expectation of life.

biomicroscope (bi″o-mi′kro-skōp). A microscope for examining living tissue in the body.

biomicroscopy (bi″o-mi-kros′ko-pe). 1. Microscopic examination of living tissue in the body. 2. Examination of the cornea or the lens by a combination of slit lamp and corneal microscope.

biomolecule (bi″o-mol′e-kūl). A molecule of living substance.

biomonad (bi″o-mo′nad). One of the granules of protoplasm.

biomone (bi′o-mōn). A minute particle of living matter made up of biomolecules.

biomore (bi′o-mōr). A mass of biomolecules forming one of the organs of a cell.

biomotor (bi″o-mo′tor). An apparatus for producing artificial respiration.

biomutation (bi″o-mu-ta′shun). The acquirement of different characteristics produced in an organism when injected into the animal body.

bion (bi′on) [Gr. *bioun* a living being]. An individual living organism.

bionecrosis (bi″o-ne-kro′sis). Necrobiosis.

bionergy (bi-on′er-je) [*bion* + Gr. *ergon* work]. Life force; the force exercised in the living organism.

bionics (bi-on′iks). The science concerned with study of the functions, characteristics and phenomena found in the living world and application of the knowledge gained to new devices and techniques in the world of machines.

bionomics (bi″o-nom′iks) [*bio-* + Gr. *nomos* law]. The study of the relations of organisms to their environment; ecology.

bionomy (bi-on′o-me) [*bio-* + Gr. *nomos* law]. The sum of knowledge regarding the laws of life.

bionosis (bi-o-no′sis) [*bio-* + Gr. *nosos* disease]. Any disease caused by living agencies, as bacteria or parasites.

bionucleonics (bi″o-nu″kle-on′iks). The study of the biological applications of radioactive and rare stable isotopes.

bio-occlusion (bi″o-ŏ-kloo′zhun). Normal occlusion of the teeth.

bio-osmotic (bi″o-oz-mot′ik) [*bio-* + *osmotic*]. A term applied to the osmotic pressure in living things.

biophagism (bi-of′ah-jizm) [*bio-* + Gr. *phagein* to eat]. The eating or absorption of living matter.

biophagous (bi-of′ah-gus). Feeding on living matter.

biophagy (bi-of′ah-je). Biophagism.

biophore (bi′o-fōr) [*bio-* + Gr. *phoros* bearing]. One of the hypothetical vital units which according to Weismann are aggregated into groups called *determinants*, these groups being gathered into larger ones called *ids*, which are the visible chromatin granules, and these in turn into larger groups called *idants*, which are the chromosomes.

biophoric (bi-o-for′ik). Relating to biophores.

biophotometer (bi″o-fo-tom′e-ter) [*bio-* + Gr. *phōs* light + *metron* measure]. An instrument for measuring the dark adaptation of the eye as an indication of vitamin A deficiency.

biophylactic (bi″o-fi-lak′tik) [*bio-* + Gr. *phylaktikos* preservative]. Guarding or preserving life.

biophylaxis (bi″o-fi-lak′sis) [*bio-* + Gr. *phylaxis* a guarding]. The defensive mechanism of the body against the invasion of noxious or infective principles.

biophysics (bi-o-fiz′iks) [*bio-* + *physics*]. The science dealing with the application of physical methods and theories to biological problems.

biophysiography (bi″o-fiz-e-og′rah-fe) [*bio-* + *physiography*]. Structural or descriptive biology.

biophysiology (bi″o-fiz-e-ol′o-je) [*bio-* + Gr. *physis* nature + *-logy*]. That part of biology which includes organogeny, morphology, and physiology.

bioplasia (bi-o-pla′ze-ah) [*bio-* + Gr. *plassein* to form]. The storing up of food energy in the form of growth.

bioplasm (bi′o-plazm) [*bio-* + Gr. *plasma* anything molded]. 1. The primitive matter out of which organized tissues are composed; protoplasm. 2. The more essential or vital part of protoplasm, contrasted with the *paraplasm*.

bioplasmic (bi-o-plaz′mik). Of or pertaining to bioplasm.

bioplasmin (bi-o-plaz′min). A substance supposed to exist in all living cells, which is essential to the functioning of the cell, but which gradually becomes exhausted, causing a diminution of metabolic activity.

bioplasminogen (bi″o-plaz-min′o-jen). The supposed substance from which bioplasmin is developed during embryonic growth, and which is itself formed by the junction of substances (called spermatoplasmon and ovoplasmon) in the elementary male and female cells.

bioplasson (bi-o-plas′on) [*bio-* + Gr. *plassōn* forming]. Protoplasm.

bioplast (bi′o-plast). 1. An independently existing mass of living matter. See *micelle*. 2. A cell.

bioplastic (bi″o-plas′tik). Aiding in growth: said of food energy. Cf. *catabiotic*, def. 2.

biopoiesis (bi″o-poi-e′sis) [*bio-* + Gr. *poiein* to make]. The origin of life from inorganic matter.

biopsy (bi′op-se) [*bio-* + Gr. *opsis* vision]. The removal and examination, usually microscopic, of tissue or other material from the living body for purposes of diagnosis. **aspiration b.,** needle b. **fractional b.,** histologic study of only fragments of a growth which have been removed for the purpose, before excision of the lesion in its entirety. **needle b.,** biopsy of material obtained by aspiration through a needle. **punch b.,** biopsy of material obtained from the body tissue by a punch. **sponge b.,** examination of material (cells, particles of tissue, and tissue juices) obtained by rubbing a sponge of suitable material over a lesion or over a mucous membrane; the entire sponge is then fixed and processed as a routine surgical specimen, being sectioned, stained, and examined in the usual manner. **sternal b.,** examination of a piece of the bone marrow of the sternum of a living patient removed by puncture or trephining. **surface b.,** the microscopic examination of cells scraped from the surface of suspected lesions, most commonly employed in examination for cancer of the cervic. **surgical b.,** examination of tissue removed from the body by surgical excision. **total b.,** histologic study of a growth which has been removed in its entirety for the specific purpose, having a therapeutic as well as a diagnostic value.

biopsychic (bi″o-si′kik). Pertaining to psychical phenomena in their relation to the living organism.

biopsychical (bi″o-si′kĭ-kal). Biopsychic.

biopsychology (bi″o-si-kol′o-je). Psychobiology.

bioptic (bi-op′tik). Pertaining to or based on biopsy.

biopyoculture (bi″o-pi′o-kul″tūr) [*bio-* + Gr. *pyon* pus + *culture*]. A culture made from pus whose cells are alive.

biorbital (bi-or′bĭ-tal) [*bi-* + L. *orbita* orbit]. Pertaining to both orbits.

biorgan (bi′or-gan). A physiological organ, as distinguished from a morphological organ, or *idorgan*.

biorheology (bi″o-re-ol′o-je). The study of the deformation and flow of matter in living systems and in materials directly derived from them.

bioroentgenography (bi″o-rent″gen-og′rah-fe) [*bio-* + *roentgenography*]. The making of kinematographic roentgen-ray pictures.

bios (bi′os) [Gr. "life"]. Any one of a group of growth factors for single celled organisms such as yeast. Bios occurs in yeast, leaves of plants, bran and the outer covering of seeds. **bios I,** inositol. **bios II,** biotin.

bioscope (bi′o-skōp). An instrument used in bioscopy.

bioscopy (bi-os′ko-pe) [*bio-* + Gr. *skopein* to examine]. The examination of the body to see whether or not life is extinct.

biose (bi′ōs). 1. A sugar containing two carbon atoms. 2. A disaccharide.

bioside (bi′o-sīd). A glycoside which contains a biose plus a noncarbohydrate group.

biosis (bi-o′sis) [Gr. *bios* life]. Vitality, or life.

biosmosis (bi″os-mo′sis). Osmosis through a living membrane.

biospectrometry (bi″o-spek-trom′e-tre) [*bio-* + *spectrometry*]. Measurement by a spectroscope of the quantity of a substance in living tissue.

biospectroscopy (bi″o-spek-tros′ko-pe) [*bio-* + *spectroscopy*]. Examination of living tissue with the spectroscope.

biosphere (bi′o-sfēr). 1. That part of the earth which is occupied by living matter. 2. The sphere of action between an organism and its environment.

biostatics (bi″o-stat′iks) [*bio-* + Gr. *statikos* causing to stand]. The science of the structure of organisms in relation to their function.

biostatistics (bi″o-stah-tis′tiks) [*bio-* + *statistics*]. Vital statistics. See under *statistics*.

biosynthesis (bi″o-sin′the-sis) [*bio-* + *synthesis*]. The building up of a chemical compound in the physiologic processes of a living organism.

Biot's breathing, respiration (be-ōz) [Camille *Biot*, French physician of 19th century]. See under *respiration*.

biota (bi-o′tah) [Gr. *bios* life]. All the living organisms of a particular area; the combined flora and fauna of a region.

biotaxis (bi″o-tak′sis) [*bio-* + Gr. *taxis* arrangement]. The selecting and arranging powers of living cells.

biotaxy (bi″o-tak′se). Taxonomy.

biotelemetry (bi″o-tel-em′e-tre). The recording and measuring of certain vital phenomena of living organisms, occurring at a distance from the measuring device.

biotherapy (bi″o-ther′ah-pe) [*bio-* + *therapy*]. Treatment by means of biologicals (serums, vaccines, etc.) or by living organisms such as kefir, lactobacilli, yeast or with vital products such as gastric juice, bile, etc.

biotic (bi-ot′ik). 1. Pertaining to life or living matter. 2. Pertaining to the biota.

biotics (bi-ot′iks) [Gr. *biōtikos* living]. The functions and qualities peculiar to living organisms, or the sum of knowledge regarding these qualities.

biotin (bi′o-tin). A colorless crystalline compound, 2′-keto-3,4-imidazolido-2-tetrahydrothiophene-δ-n-valeric acid, $CH_2.CH.NH.CO.NH.CH.(CH_2)_4.COOH$, identical with vitamin H and coenzyme R: most potent and ubiquitous member of the vitamine B complex known, and required by or occurring in all forms of life tested. Deficiency of biotin in the diet of experimental rats fed on uncooked egg white results in egg-white injury, the injury being due to the avidin present in the egg white which renders the biotin of the diet unavailable. *alpha b.* is the product isolated from egg yolk; *beta b.* is that isolated from liver. Cf. *avidin*.

biotomy (bi-ot′o-me) [*bio-* + Gr. *tomē* a cutting]. 1. The study of animal and plant structure by dissection. 2. Vivisection.

biotoxication (bi″o-tok″sĭ-ka′shun). An intoxication resulting from a plant or animal poison (biotoxin).

biotoxicology (bi″o-tok″sĭ-kol′o-je) [*bio-* + Gr. *toxikon* poison + *-logy*]. The science of poisons produced by living things, their cause, detection, and their effects, and of the treatment of conditions produced by them.

biotoxin (bi″o-tok′sin) [*bio-* + *toxin*]. Any poisonous substance produced by and derived from a living organism, either plant or animal.

biotrepy (bi-ot′rĕ-pe). The study of the body by means of its reactions to chemical substances.

biotripsis (bi″o-trip′sis) [*bio-* + Gr. *tripsis* rubbing]. Wearing away of the skin, seen in old people.

biotropic (bi″o-trop′ik). Exhibiting biotropism; tending to become active.

biotropism (bi-ot′ro-pizm) [*bio-* + Gr. *tropos* a turning]. 1. A reduction of resistance which allows a latent infection to become active or a saprophytic germ to become pathogenic. 2. An orientation response to stimulus afforded by a living organism or living tissue. **direct b.,** biotropism in which the organism for which the drug is being given is stimulated. **indirect b.,** biotropism in which another organism than that for which the drug is given is stimulated.

biotype (bi′o-tīp) [*bio-* + *type*]. A group of individuals possessing the same genotype.

biotypology (bi″o-ti-pol′o-je). The study of anthropological types with their constitutional variations, inadequacies, etc.

biovular (bi-ov′u-lar). Binovular.

B.I.P. Abbreviation for *bismuth iodoform paraffin*. See *Morison's method*, under *method*.

bipara (bip′ah-rah) [*bi-* + L. *parere* to bring forth, produce]. Secundipara.

biparasitic (bi″par-ah-sit′ik). Living parasitically upon a parasite.

biparental (bi″pah-ren′tal). Derived from two parents, male and female.

biparietal (bi″pah-ri′e-tal). Pertaining to the two parietal eminences.

biparous (bip′ah-rus) [*bi-* + L. *parere* to produce]. 1. Producing two ova or offspring at one time. 2. Secundiparous.

bipartite (bi-par′tīt) [L. *bipartitus*]. Having two parts or divisions.

biped (bi′ped) [*bi-* + L. *pes* foot]. 1. Having two feet. 2. An animal with two feet.

bipedal (bip′e-dal). With, or pertaining to, both feet.

bipenniform (bi-pen′ĭ-form). Doubly feather shaped: said of muscles whose fibers are arranged on each side of a tendon, like the barbs on the shaft of a feather.

bipeptide (bi-pep′tid). Dipeptide.

biperforate (bi-per′fo-rāt). Having two perforations.

biperiden (bi-per′ĭ-den). Chemical name: α-(bicyclo[2,2,1]hept-5-en-2-yl)-α-phenyl-1-piperidinepropanol: used to produce parasympathetic blockade, and to reduce tremors of parkinsonism.

bipolar (bi-po′lar). 1. Having two poles; having processes at both poles. 2. Pertaining to both poles; noting electrotherapeutic treatments in which two poles are used; also bacterial staining confined to the poles (ends) of the organism. 3. A two-poled nerve cell. **cone b.,** any one of those bipolar nerve cells of the inner muscular layer of the retina which are related to the terminations of the cone visual cells. **giant b's,** those cone bipolars which lie beneath the external plexiform layer of the retina. **rod b.,** any one of those bipolar nerve cells which are related to the terminations of the rod visual cells.

bipositive (bi-poz′ĭ-tiv). Having two positive valences.

bipotential (bi″po-ten′shal). Pertaining to or characterized by bipotentiality.

bipotentiality (bi″po-ten″she-al′ĭ-te) [*bi-* + L. *poten′tia* power]. Possession of the power of developing or acting in either of two possible ways. **b. of the gonad,** the double nature of the primitive gonad, which may develop into either an ovary or a testis.

bipp. A vernacular term in the British Isles for bismuth iodoform paraffin paste. See *Morison's method*, under *method*.

bipubiotomy (bi″pu-be-ot′o-me) [*bi-* + *pubiotomy*]. Ischiopubiotomy.

biramous (bi-ra′mus) [*bi-* + L. *ramus* branch]. Consisting of, or possessing, two branches.

Bircher's operation (bēr′kerz) [Heinrich *Bircher*, Swiss surgeon, 1850–1923]. See under *operation*.

Bird's formula, treatment (birdz) [Golding *Bird*, English physician, 1814–1854]. See under *formula* and *treatment*.

Bird's sign (birdz) [Samuel Dougan *Bird*, Australian physician, 1832–1904]. See under *sign*.

bird-arm (bird′arm). A forearm that is greatly reduced in size as the result of atrophy of the muscles.

bird-face (bird′fās). A form of dyscephaly in which the skull is small and the facial bones are large, giving a birdlike appearance. The appearance of the face in microcephaly, the skull small and the facial bones large.

bird-leg (bird′leg). A leg that is greatly reduced in size as the result of atrophy of the muscles.

bird-lime (bird′līm) [*bird* + L. *limus* slime]. A viscous or gummy substance of various origin, used for catching small birds; some kinds are employed to some extent in dressing wounds and sores.

birefractive (bi″re-frak′tiv). Doubly refractive.

birefringent (bi″re-frin′jent) [*bi-* + L. *refringere* to break up]. Doubly refractive.

birhinia (bi-rin′e-ah) [*bi-* + Gr. *rhis* nose]. Double nose.

Birkett's hernia (ber′kets) [John *Birkett*, English surgeon, 1815–1904]. See under *hernia*.

Birkhaug's test, toxin (birk′hawg) [Konrad Elias *Birkhaug*, Norwegian bacteriologist in America, born 1892]. See under *tests* and *toxin*.

birth (birth). The act or process of being born. **cross b.,** labor with the fetus lying in a transverse position in the uterus. **dead b.,** birth of a fetus which, during or before birth, has lost all signs of antenatal life, heart beat, pulsation, movement. **head b.,** a birth in which the head presents. **multiple b.,** the birth of two or more offspring produced in the same gestation period, the frequency of birth of viable offspring after such multiple pregnancy having been computed as follows: twins, 1 in 80; triplets, 1 in 6400 (80 × 80); quadruplets, 1 in 512,000 (80 × 80 × 80); etc. (Hellin's law). **post-term b.,** birth of a postmature, or post-term, infant. **premature b.,** birth of a premature infant.

birthmark (birth′mark). A circumscribed new growth of congenital origin, such as a vascular nevus (hemangioma). **physiologic b.,** a small nevus flammeus in the occipital region, frequently seen at birth and commonly persisting.

bis-. A prefix signifying two or twice.

bisacodyl (bis-ak′o-dil). Chemical name: 4,4′-(2-pyridylmethylene)diphenol diacetate: used as a laxative.

bisacromial (bis″ah-kro′me-al). Pertaining to the two acromial processes.

bisalbuminemia (bis″al-bu″mĭ-ne′me-ah). A congenital abnormality characterized by the presence of two distinct serum albumins which differ in their electrophoretic mobility at pH 8.6.

bisalt (bi′salt). An acid salt.

bisamylose (bis-am′ĭ-lōs). The ultimate structural element of starch; it is an anhydride of maltose, $C_{12}H_{20}O_{10}$; called also *diamylose*.

bisaxillary (bis-ak′sĭ-lar″e). Pertaining to both axillae.

Bischoff's corona, crown (bish′ofs) [Theodor Ludwig Wilhelm von *Bischoff*, German anatomist, 1807–1882]. See under *crown*.

Bischoff's test (bish′ofs) [Carl Adam *Bischoff*, German chemist, 1855–1908]. See under *tests*.

biscuit (bis′ket). Porcelain which has undergone the first baking, before it is subjected to the glazing or enameling. Called also *bisque*. **hard b.,** biscuit after shrinking but before vitrification has begun. **soft b.,** biscuit during the process of stiffening, before shrinkage has begun.

biscuiting (bis′ket-ing). The first baking of porcelain paste, by which biscuit is formed.

bisection (bi-sek′shun) [*bi-* + L. *sectio* a cut]. A cutting into two parts.

biseptate (bi-sep′tāt). Divided into two parts by a septum.

bisexual (bi-seks′u-al) [*bi-* + L. *sexus* sex]. 1. Having gonads of both sexes; hermaphrodite. 2. Having both active (male) and passive (female) sexual interests or characteristics.

bisferious (bis-fe′re-us) [L. *bis* twice + *ferire* to beat]. Having two beats.

Bishop's sphygmoscope (bish′ups) [Louis Faugères *Bishop*, American physician, 1864–1941]. See under *sphygmoscope*.

bishydroxycoumarin (bis″hi-drok″se-koo′mah-rin). A white or creamy white, crystalline powder, $C_{19}H_{12}O_6$: anticoagulant.

bisiliac (bi-sil′e-ak) [L. *bis* twice + *iliac*]. Pertaining to the two most remote points of the iliac crests.

bis in die (bis in de′a) [L.]. Twice a day; abbreviated b.d. or b.i.d.

bismuth (biz′muth) [L. *bismuthum*]. A silver-white metal; atomic number 83; atomic weight 208.980; symbol Bi: its salts have been used in inflammatory diseases of the stomach and intestine, and in the treatment of syphilis. **b. albuminate,** a white or grayish insoluble powder: used for intestinal and gastric cramps. **b. and ammonium citrate,** a white, crystalline compound: astringent in intestinal irritation. **b. arsanilate,** a preparation suggested for the treatment of syphilis. **b. benzoate,** a whitish, tasteless powder, $Bi(C_6H_5CO_2)_3Bi(OH)_3$: an external and internal antiseptic. **b. betanaphthol,** a light brown insoluble aromatic powder: used as an intestinal astringent and antiseptic. **b. borophenate,** a compound used as an antiseptic dusting powder. **b. carbolate,** b. phenylate. **b. carbonate, basic,** b. subcarbonate. **b. cerium salicylate,** a bismuth salt, in the form of a pinkish, insoluble powder: used in enteritis, diarrhea, etc. **b. chrysophanate,** an amorphous yellow powder, $(C_{15}H_9O_4)_3Bi_2O_3$, resulting from the mixture of chrysarobin and bismuth hydroxide: it is an antiseptic used in skin diseases. **b. citrate,** an amorphous powder, $BiC_6H_5O_7$, used in pharmacy and in the preparation of other bismuth remedies. **b. ethylcamphorate,** a bismuth preparation containing 23.5 per cent of bismuth: used as an antisyphilitic by intramuscular injection. **b. glycolylarsanilate,** glycobiarsol. **b. hydroxide,** a white amorphous powder, $Bi(OH)_3$. **b. magma,** an aqueous suspension of bismuth hydroxide and bismuth subcarbonate: used in digestive disturbances. **b. nitrate,** $Bi(NO_3)_3.5H_2O$: used as an astringent in diarrhea. **b. oxybromide,** an impalpable yellowish powder, BiOBr, to be given in a tragacanth emulsion: it is useful in nervous dyspepsia. **b. oxychloride,** a white powder, sometimes known as pearl white, BiOCl, used like bismuth subnitrate. **b. oxyiodide,** a brownish-red powder, BiOI, a local antiseptic: useful in certain stomach diseases. **b. oxyiodogallate,** airol. **b. oxyiodopyrogallate,** a fine, yellowish-red powder, $C_6H_2(OH)_2.O.Bi(OH)I$, recommended as a surgical antiseptic powder. **pancreatinized b.,** a proprietary remedy for dyspepsia. **b. permanganate,** a black, bulky powder, $Bi(MnO_4)_3$: used as an antiseptic dusting powder. **b. phosphate,** a white powder: used as an intestinal antiseptic and astringent. **b. and potassium tartrate,** a white, odorless powder, $C_4H_2O_9Bi_3K.4H_2O$: used intramuscularly in syphilis. **b. pyrogallate,** a yellow powder, $C_6H_3.OH.O.O.BiOH$: used as an internal and external antiseptic. **b. salicylate,** a white, tasteless, and insoluble powder for internal and external use. **b. sodium tartrate,** a compound sometimes used in the treatment of syphilis. **b. sodium triglycollamate,** double salt of sodium bismuthyl triglycollamate and disodium triglycollamate: used as a suppressant for lupus erythematosus, and in treatment of chronic syphilis. **b. subcarbonate,** an odorless, tasteless, white or pale yellowish white powder, yielding at least 90 per cent of Bi_2O_3: used as an astringent, antacid, and protective. **b. subgallate,** a basic salt which, on drying, yields 52 to 57 per cent of bismuth trioxide: used as an astringent, antacid, and protective. **b. subnitrate,** a basic salt which, on ignition, yields not less than 71 per cent of bismuth trioxide: used as an astringent, external antiseptic, and as a radiopaque medium. **b. subsalicylate,** a basic salt which, on ignition, yields 62 to 66 per cent bismuth trioxide: used as a suppressant for lupus erythematosus, and in treatment of syphilis and other spirochetal infections. **b. tannate,** a compound formed by the action of tannic acid on bismuth hydroxide: used as an astringent in diarrhea, dysentery, etc. **b. tribromphenate,** xeroform. **b. trioxide,** one of the oxides of bismuth, Bi_2O_3. **b. white,** b. subnitrate.

bismuthia (biz-mu′the-ah). Blue discoloration of the skin and mucous membranes as the result of the administration of bismuth compounds.

bismuthism (biz′muth-izm). Bismuthosis.

bismuthosis (biz″mu-tho′sis). A state of chronic poisoning from the misuse of bismuth; also, an alleged deposit of a bismuth salt in the gums.

bismuthotartrate (biz-mu″tho-tar′trāt). A complex organic radical (negative) containing bismuth. There are a number of sodium or potassium bismuthotartrates used in medicine.

bispherical (bi-sfer′e-kal). Spherical on both sides.

bisque (bisk) [Fr.]. Biscuit. **hard b., soft b.** See under *biscuit.*

bissa (bis′ah). A dropsical disease of lower Egypt affecting men and sheep, attributed to the feeding of the latter on a plant called bisse.

bistephanic (bi″ste-fan′ik). Pertaining to the two stephanions.

bistort (bis′tort) [L. *bis* twice + *tortus* twisted]. The plant, *Polygonum bistorta:* its root [L. *bistortae radix*) is a mild astringent.

bistoury (bis′too-re) [Fr. *bistouri*]. A long, narrow, surgical knife, straight or curved, used for incising abscesses, opening up sinuses, fistulas, etc.

bistratal (bi-stra′tal) [*bi-* + L. *stratum* layer]. Disposed in two layers.

bistrimate (bis′trĭ-māt). Trade mark for a preparation of bismuth sodium triglycollamate.

bistrimin (bis′trĭ-min) Phenyltoloxamine.

bisulfate (bi-sul′fāt). A salt having two equivalents of sulfate to one of a base. An acid sulfate.

bisulfide (bi-sul′fid). A compound of sulfur and an element containing two atoms of sulfur to one of the other element.

bisulfite (bi-sul′fit). An acid sulfite; a sulfite containing twice as much sulfurous acid as the ordinary sulfite in proportion to the base.

bit (bit). A rotary drill.

bita higoidea (bi′tah hi-goi′de-ah). Xanthoma.

bitartrate (bi-tar′trāt). Any tartrate with twice the amount of acid contained in a normal salt in proportion to the base.

bite (bit). 1. Seizure with the teeth. 2. A wound or puncture made by the teeth or other mouth parts of a living organism. 3. An impression made by closure of the teeth upon a thin sheet of some malleable material. **balanced b.,** balanced occlusion. **check b.,** a thin sheet of wax or paraffin placed between the teeth in the mouth and used as a check upon the teeth in the articulator. **close b., closed b.,** that condition in which the incisal edges of the mandibular anterior teeth extend lingually past the incisal edges of the maxillary, approaching the gingival margin, when the jaws are in centric occlusion. **cross b.,** crossbite. **edge-to-edge b., end-to-end b.,** occlusion in which the incisors of both jaws meet along the incisal edges when the jaws are in centric occlusion. **open b.,** a condition marked by failure of opposing teeth to establish occlusal contact when the jaws are closed. **over b.,** overbite. **stork b's,** capillary flames. **underhung b.,** that condition in which the incisal edges of the mandibular anterior teeth extend labially to the incisal edges of the maxillary anterior teeth when the jaws are in centric occlusion. **wax b.,** an impression, made simultaneously, of both the upper and the lower jaw, by having the subject bite on a double layer of soft baseplate wax.

bite-block (bīt′blok). Occlusion rim. See under *rim.*

bitegage (bīt′gāj). A device used in dentistry as an aid in securing proper occlusion of the maxillary and mandibular teeth.

bitelock (bīt′lok). A device used in dentistry for retaining the bite-rims in the same relation outside of the mouth which they occupied in the mouth.

bitemporal (bi-tem′po-ral). Pertaining to both temples or temporal bones.

biteplate (bīt′plāt). A tooth- and tissue-borne appliance, usually fabricated of plastic and worn in the palate; used as a diagnostic or therapeutic adjunct in orthodontics or prosthodontics. Sometimes used for temporomandibular joint disorders, or as a diagnostic splint in full mouth restorations.

bite-rim (bīt′rim). A rim of wax placed on the baseplate in an arch such as is described by the teeth as a guide for placing the artificial teeth.

biterminal (bi-ter′me-nal). Performed by using two terminals of an alternating current.

bite-wing (bīt′wing). A dental x-ray film with a wing or fin attached midway on the tooth side on which the patient can bite; used for taking roentgenograms showing simultaneously the coronal one-half of the teeth of both the upper and the lower arch, as well as the periodontal tissues.

bithionol (bi-thi′ō-nol). A white or grayish white crystalline powder, 2,2′-thiobis(4,6-dichlorophenol): used as a local anti-infective.

Bitot's patches, spots (be′tōz) [Pierre *Bitot,* Bordeaux physician, 1822–1888]. See under *spot.*

bitrochanteric (bi″tro-kan-ter′ik). Pertaining to both trochanters.

bitropic (bi′trop-ik) [*bi-* + Gr. *tropos* a turning]. Having affinity for two tissues or two organisms.

bitter (bit′er). 1. Having an austere and unpalatable taste, like that of quinine. 2. [Pl.] A medicinal agent that has a bitter taste: used as a tonic, alterative, or appetizer. **aromatic b's,** bitter vegetable drugs which have an aromatic quality. **simple b's,** any drug with a bitter taste, which has no general influence upon the system except through its action upon the stomach and intestine. **Stoughton b's,** the compound tincture of absinth. **styptic b's,** bitter drugs with a markedly astringent quality. **Swedish b's,** compound tincture of aloes.

bitterling (bit′er-ling). See *bitterling test,* under *tests.*

bitters (bit′erz). A popular name for various alcoholic medicines and drinks. See under *bitter.*

Bittorf's reaction (bit′orfs) [Alexander *Bittorf,* German physician, 1876–1949]. See under *reaction.*

bitumen (bĭ-tu′men) [L.]. Any one of various natural and artificial dry petroleum products. **sulfonated b.,** a preparation made by sulfonating bitumen and neutralizing the product with ammonia. It is a viscid brownish fluid with a strong odor, soluble in water and in glycerin. Used like ichthyol.

bituminosis (bit″u-mĭ-no′sis). A form of pneumoconiosis due to the dust from soft coal.

biurate (bi′u-rāt). An acid urate; a monobasic salt of uric acid.

biuret (bi′u-ret) [L. *bis* twice + *urea*]. A derivative of urea, $H_2NCO.NH.CO.NH_2$, equivalent to two molecules of urea less one of ammonia.

bivalence (biv′ah-lens) [*bi-* + L. *valens* powerful]. A chemical valence double that of the hydrogen atom.

bivalent (biv′ah-lent). 1. Having a valence of two. 2. Representing or composed of two homologous chromosomes joined end to end or associated in pairs.

bivalve (bi′valv) [*bi-* + L. *valva* valve]. Having two valves; applied to the shells of such mollusks as clams.

biventer (bi′ven-ter) [*bi-* + L. *venter* belly]. A part or organ (as a muscle) with two bellies. **b. cer′vicis,** musculus spinalis capitis.

biventral (bi-ven′tral). Having two bellies: digastric.

bivitelline (bi″vi-tel′in). Having two yolks.

bixin (bik′sin) [L. *Bixa* a plant genus]. An orange-red color or stain, $C_{25}H_{30}O_4$, from annotto.

bizygomatic (bi″zi-go-mat′ik) [*bi-* + Gr. *zygōma* zygoma]. Pertaining to the two most prominent points on the two zygomatic arches.

Bizzozero's cells, corpuscles, platelets (bit-sot′ser-ōz) [Giulio *Bizzozero,* Italian physician, 1846–1901]. See under *corpuscle.*

Bjerrum's screen (byer′oomz) [J. *Bjerrum,* Danish ophthalmologist, 1827–1892]. See under *screen.*

Bjerrum's sign (byer′oomz) [Jannik Petersen *Bjerrum,* Danish ophthalmologist, 1851–1920]. See under *sign.*

Bk. Chemical symbol for *berkelium.*

B.L. Abbreviation for *buccolingual.*

black (blak). Reflecting no light or true color; of the darkest hue. **animal b., bone-b.,** animal charcoal. **indulin b.,** nigrosin. **ivory b.,** animal charcoal. **lamp b.,** finely divided carbon deposited from the smoky flame of burning oils, rosin, etc. **Paris b.,** animal charcoal.

Black's crown, classification (blaks) [Greene Vardiman *Black,* Chicago dentist, 1836–1915]. See under *cavity* and *crown.*

Black's formula (blaks) [J. A. *Black,* English army surgeon]. See under *formula.*

Blackberg and Wanger's test (blak′berg wang′gerz) [S. N. *Blackberg,* American physician, born 1897; J. O. *Wanger*]. See under *tests.*

blackhead (blak′hed). 1. A comedo. 2. A disease of turkeys. See *enterohepatitis,* def. 2.

blackleg (blak′leg). Symptomatic anthrax.

blackout (blak′owt). A condition characterized by failure of vision and momentary unconsciousness, due to diminished circulation to the brain and the retina.

blackquarter (blak kwor′ter). Symptomatic anthrax.

blacktongue (blak-tung′). Pellagra in dogs.

bladder (blad′der) [L. *vesica, cystis;* Gr. *kystis*]. A membranous sac, such as one serving as receptacle for a secretion. Often used alone to designate the urinary bladder. **allantoic b.,** a type of bladder formed in amphibians as an outgrowth of the cloaca. **atonic b.,** a condition marked by paralysis of the motor nerves of the bladder without any evidence of central nervous lesion. **autonomic b.,** a form of cord bladder characterized by periodic reflex micturition. **brain b.,** any one of the embryonic cerebral vesicles. **cord b.,** defective bladder function from a lesion in the nervous system, as myelitis or tabes dorsalis. **fasciculated b.,** a bladder which, from hypertrophy of the muscular coat, is ridged on its inner surface. **gall b.** See *gallbladder.* **irritable b.,** a state of the bladder marked by a constant desire to urinate. **nervous b.,** a condition characterized by a constant desire to urinate without the power to do so completely. **neurogenic b.,** any vesical disturbance due to a lesion of the nervous system. **sacculated b.,** a bladder with pouches between the hypertrophied muscular fibers. **stammering b.,** a bladder which acts spasmodically, causing irregular urination. **string b.,** cord bladder. **urinary b.,** the musculomembranous sac, situated in the anterior part of the pelvic cavity, that serves as a reservoir for urine. Called also *vesica urinaria* [N A].

Blainville's ear (blah′vēlz) [Henri Marie Ducrotay de *Blainville,* French zoologist, 1778–1850]. See under *ear.*

Blake's disk (blākz) [Clarence John *Blake,* Boston otologist, 1843–1919]. See under *disk.*

Blalock-Taussig operation (bla′lok taw′sig) [Alfred *Blalock,* American surgeon, 1899–1964; Helen Brooke *Taussig,* American pediatrician, born 1898]. See under *operation.*

blanc (blaw) [Fr.]. White. **b. fixe,** barium sulfate.

Blanchard's method, treatment (blanch′ardz) [Wallace *Blanchard,* American surgeon, 1857–1922]. See under *treatment.*

bland (bland) [L. *blandus*]. Mild or soothing.

Blandin's gland (blah-daz′) [Philippe Frédéric *Blandin,* French surgeon, 1798–1849]. See under *gland.*

Blanfordia (blan-for′de-ah). A genus of mollusks, the intermediate host of *Schistosoma japonicum.*

blanquet (blaw-ka′) [Old Fr.]. Leper.

Blasius's duct (blah′se-ooz) [Gerhard *Blasius,* Dutch anatomist of the 17th century]. See under *duct.*

blast (blast) [Gr. *blastos* germ]. 1. An immature stage in cellular development before appearance of the definitive characteristics of the cell; used also as a word termination. See *blasto-*. 2. One of the small filamentous spindles formed by the splitting up of meres. See under *mere.* 3. [Anglo-Saxon *blæst* a puff of wind]. The wave of air pressure (*air concussion*) produced by the detonation of a high-explosive bomb, shell, or other explosion. A wave of high-pressure velocity (shock wave) is created and this is followed by one of negative decreased velocity, exerting a suction-like action. Blast causes pulmonary concussion and hemorrhage (*lung blast, blast chest*), laceration of other thoracic and abdominal viscera, ruptured ear drums, and minor effects in the central nervous system. **bechic b.,** the vigorous rush of air through the trachea and bronchi in coughing. **immersion b.,** internal injury to seamen in the water caused by explosion of a depth bomb near them.

blastation (blas-ta′shun). Any variation of the germ plasm which is inheritable.

blastema (blas-te′mah) [Gr. *blastēma* shoot]. 1. The primitive substance from which cells are formed. 2. A group of cells that will give rise to a new individual, in asexual reproduction, or to an organ or part, in either normal development or in regeneration.

blastemic (blas-tem′ik). Pertaining to the blastema.

blastid (blas′tid). The site indicative of an organizing nucleus in a fertilized ovum.

blastide (blas′tīd). Blastid.

blastin (blas′tin). A substance which stimulates or increases cell proliferation; a substance providing alimentation for cells.

blasto- (blas′to) [Gr. *blastos* germ]. A combining form denoting relationship to a bud or budding, particularly to an early embryonic stage, as to a primitive or formative element, cell, or layer.

Blastocaulis (blas″to-kaw′lis). A genus of microorganisms of the family Pasteuriaceae, order Hyphomicrobiales, made up of pear-shaped or globular cells with long slender stalks, attached to a firm substrate in fresh-water environments. The type species is *B. sphae′rica.*

blastocele (blas′to-sēl). Blastocoele.

blastocelic (blas-to-se′lik). Blastocoelic.

blastochyle (blas′to-kil) [*blasto-* + Gr. *chylos* juice]. The fluid contained in the blastocoele.

blastocoele (blas′to-sēl) [*blasto-* + Gr. *koilos* hollow]. The fluid-filled cavity of the mass of cells (blastula) produced by cleavage of a fertilized ovum.

blastocoelic (blas″to-se′lik). Pertaining to the blastocoele.

blastocyst (blas′to-sist) [*blasto-* + Gr. *kystis* bladder]. The modified blastula of mammals.

Blastocystis (blas″to-sis′tis). A genus of vegetable microorganisms related to yeast. **B. hom′inus,** a vegetable microorganism appearing as a spherical cystic structure, 5–15 μ in diameter, frequently found in the stools of patients who have lived in tropical climates.

blastocyte (blas′to-sīt) [*blasto-* + Gr. *kytos* hollow vessel]. An embryonic cell that has not yet become differentiated.

blastocytoma (blas″to-si-to′mah). A tumor composed of undifferentiated tissue.

Blastodendrion (blas″to-den′dre-on). A genus of yeastlike fungi, many species of which have been isolated from human lesions.

blastodendriosis (blas″to-den″dre-o′sis). Infection with Blastodendrion.

blastoderm (blas′to-derm) [*blasto-* + Gr. *derma* skin]. Collectively, the mass of cells produced by cleavage of a fertilized ovum, forming the hollow sphere of the blastula, or the cellular cap above a floor of segmented yolk in the discoblastula of telolecithal eggs. **bilaminar b.,** the stage of development in which the embryo is represented by two primary layers: ectoderm and entoderm. See *gastrula*. **embryonic b.,** the region of the blastoderm forming the embryo proper. **extraembryonic b.,** the region of the blastoderm forming membranes rather than the embryo proper. **trilaminar b.,** the stage of development in which the embryo is represented by the three primary layers: the ectoderm, the mesoderm, and the entoderm.

blastodermal (blas″to-der′mal). Pertaining to or derived from the blastoderm.

blastodermic (blas″to-der′mik). Blastodermal.

blastodisc (blas′to-disk) [*blasto-* + Gr. *diskos* disk]. The convex structure formed by the blastomeres at the animal pole of an ovum undergoing incomplete cleavage.

blastogenesis (blas″to-jen′e-sis). 1. The development of an individual from a blastema, that is, by asexual reproduction. 2. Transmission of inherited characters by the germ plasm.

blastogenetic (blas″to-jĕ-net′ik). Blastogenic.

blastogenic (blas″to-jen′ik). Originating in the germ or germ cell.

blastogeny (blas-toj′ĕ-ne) [*blasto-* + Gr. *genesis* production]. The germ history of an organism or species.

blastolysis (blas-tol′ĭ-sis) [*blasto-* + Gr. *lysis* dissolution]. Destruction or splitting up of germ substance.

blastolytic (blas″to-lit′ik). Pertaining to, characterized by, or producing blastolysis.

blastoma (blas-to′mah), pl. *blasto′mas* or *blasto′mata* [*blasto-* + *-oma*]. 1. A true tumor; a tumor, not teratogenous, which exhibits an independent localized growth. 2. Blastocytoma. **autochthonous b.,** a tumor which arises in a body by proliferation of cells belonging to that body. **heterochthonous b.** Same as *teratogenous b.* **pluricentric b.,** a neoplasm which arises from a number of scattered cells or groups of cells. **teratogenous b.,** a tumor formed of one order of cell, not from the tissues of the host, but from the tissues of another individual within the host. **unicentric b.,** a tumor arising from one cell or from a single group of cells.

blastomatoid (blas-to′mah-toid) [*blastoma* + Gr. *eidos* form]. Resembling blastomas.

blastomatosis (blas″to-mah-to′sis). The formation of blastomas; tumor formation.

blastomatous (blas-to′mah-tus). Pertaining to or of the nature of blastoma.

blastomere (blas′to-mēr) [*blasto-* + Gr. *meros* a part]. One of the cells produced by cleavage of a fertilized ovum, forming the blastoderm.

blastomerotomy (blas″to-mēr-ot′o-me) [*blastomere* + Gr. *tomē* a cut]. Destruction of a blastomere or of blastomeres.

blastomogenic (blas″to-mo-jen′ik). Producing or tending to produce new growths or tumors.

blastomogenous (blas″to-moj′e-nus). Blastomogenic.

Blastomyces (blas″to-mi′sēz) [*blasto-* + Gr. *mykēs* fungus]. A genus of yeastlike fungi, morphologically the same as *Saccharomyces*. The term is applied to the yeasts pathogenic for man and animals. **B. brasilien′sis,** the fungus which causes South American blastomycosis. **B. coccidioi′des,** *Coccidioides immitis*. **B. dermatit′idis,** a species causing North American blastomycosis. **B. farcimino′sus,** a species causing blastomycotic epizootic lymphangitis in horses.

blastomyces (blas″to-mi′sēz), pl. *blastomyce′tes*. A fungus of the genus Blastomyces.

blastomycetes (blas″to-mi-se′tēz). Plural of *blastomyces*.

blastomycin (blas″to-mi′sin). A sterile broth filtrate of a culture of *Blastomyces dermatitidis:* injected intracutaneously as a test for blastomycosis.

Blastomycoides immitis (blas″to-mi-koi′dēz im-mi′tis). *Coccidioides immitis*.

blastomycosis (blas″to-mi-ko′sis). Infection caused by organisms of the genus Blastomyces. **Brazilian b.,** South American b. **cutaneous b.** See *North American b.* **European b.,** cryptococcosis. **keloidal b.,** an infection characterized by the appearance of red, smooth, hard cutaneous nodules, mostly in the sacral region. **North American b.,** an infection caused by *Blastomyces dermatitidis*, marked by suppurating tumors in the skin (*cutaneous b.*) or by lesions in the lungs, bones, subcutaneous tissues, liver, spleen and kidneys (*systemic b.*). **South American b.,** an infection by *Blastomyces brasiliensis*. It begins as an ulcer on the buccal tissues and extends to the adjacent skin, the tonsils, the gastrointestinal lymphatics, the liver and spleen. **systemic b.** See *North American b.*

blastoneuropore (blas″to-nu′ro-pōr) [*blasto-* + Gr. *neuron* nerve + *poros* opening]. In certain embryos, a temporary aperture formed by the coalescence of the blastopore and neuropore.

blastophore (blas′to-fōr) [*blasto-* + Gr. *pherein* to bear]. That part of a sperm cell or spermatoblast that is not converted into spermatozoa.

blastophthoria (blas″tof-tho′re-ah) [*blasto-* + Gr. *phthora* corruption]. Degeneration of the germ cells.

blastophthoric (blas″tof-tho′rik). Pertaining to, characterized by, or producing blastophthoria.

blastophyllum (blas″to-fil′um) [*blasto-* + Gr. *phyllon* leaf]. A primitive germ layer.

blastophyly (blas-tof′ĭ-le) [*blasto-* + Gr. *phylē* tribe]. The tribal history, or arrangement, of organisms.

blastopore (blas′to-pōr) [*blasto-* + Gr. *poros* opening]. The opening of the archenteron to the exterior of the embryo, at the gastrula stage. Called also *protostoma* and *anus of Rusconi*.

blastosphere (blas′to-sfēr) [*blasto-* + Gr. *sphaira* sphere]. Blastula.

blastospore (blas′to-spōr) [*blasto-* + *spore*]. A spore formed by budding from a hypha.

blastostroma (blas″to-stro′mah). That part of the egg which takes an active part in the formation of the blastoderm.

blastotomy (blas-tot′o-me). Blastomerotomy.

blastotoxy (blas′to-tok″se). Toxic impregnation of the protoplasm of germ cells.

blastozooid (blas″to-zo′oid) [*blasto-* + Gr. *zōoeides* like an animal]. An organism that develops from a blastema, that is, by asexual reproduction.

blastula (blas′tu-lah), pl. *blas′tulae* [L.]. The usually spherical structure produced by cleavage of a fertilized ovum, consisting of a single layer of cells (blastoderm) surrounding a fluid-filled cavity (blastocoele). See also *discoblastula*.

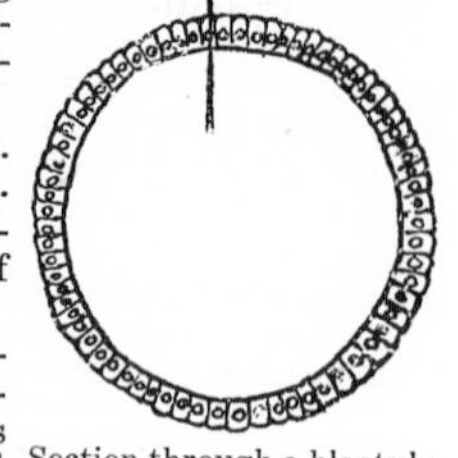

Section through a blastula (Hill).

blastular (blas′tu-lar). Pertaining to the blastula.

blastulation (blas″tu-la′shun). The formation of the blastula.

Blatta (blat′ah) [L.]. A genus of insects—the cockroaches. The dried insects are used as a diuretic, and afford antihydropin and blattic acid. They may act as the intermediate host of *Davainea madagascariensis* and *Gongylonema scutatum*. *B.* (*Blatella*) *germanica*, the German roach, now widely distributed, is called the Croton bug. It is light brown in color and small in size. *B. orientalis*, the black beetle, a common European species.

Blaud's pill (blōz) [Pierre *Blaud*, French physician, 1774–1858]. See under *pill*.

blaze (blāz). An electric current which passes through living tissue when a mechanical stimulus is applied.

bleb (bleb). A bulla or skin vesicle filled with fluid.

bleeder (blēd′er). 1. One who bleeds freely or is subject to the hemorrhagic diathesis. 2. One who lets blood; a phlebotomist.

bleeding (blēd′ing). 1. The escape of blood, as from an injured blood vessel. 2. The letting of blood; venesection. **functional b.,** bleeding from the uterus when no organic lesions are present. **implantation b.,** bleeding occurring at the time of implantation of the fertilized ovum in the uterine wall, being due to leakage of blood into the uterine lumen from dilated glands about the implantation site. Cf. *placentation b.* **occult b.,** escape of such a small amount of blood that it can be detected only by chemical test or by examination with the microscope or spectroscope. **placentation b.,** bleeding occurring from the uterus during the early weeks of pregnancy, when the maternal blood vessels are being eroded and tapped. Cf. *implantation b.*

blenn-. See *blenno-*.

blennadenitis (blen″ad-ĕ-ni′tis) [*blenn-* + Gr. *adēn* gland + *-itis*]. Inflammation of mucous glands.

blennaphrosin (blen-af′ro-sin). A preparation of a double salt of potassium nitrate and methenamine with extract of kava-kava: used in gonorrhea and cystitis.

blennemesis (blen-em′ĕ-sis) [*blenn-* + Gr. *emesis* vomiting]. The vomiting of mucus.

blenno-, blenn- (blen′no, blen′) [Gr. *blennos* mucus]. Combining form denoting a relationship to mucus.

blennogenic (blen″no-jen′ik) [*blenno-* + Gr. *gennan* to produce]. Producing mucus.

blennogenous (blen-noj′e-nus). Blennogenic.

blennoid (blen′noid) [*blenn-* + Gr. *eidos* form]. Resembling mucus.

blennorrhagia (blen″no-ra′je-ah) [*blenno-* + Gr. *rhēgnynai* to break forth]. 1. Any discharge of mucus. 2. Gonorrhea.

blennorrhagic (blen″no-raj′ik). Pertaining to or of the nature of blennorrhagia.

blennorrhea (blen″no-re′ah) [*blenno-* + Gr. *rhoia* flow]. A free discharge from the mucous surfaces, especially a gonorrheal discharge from the urethra or vagina; gonorrhea. **b. adulto′rum,** gonorrheal ophthalmia. **b. alveola′ris,** pyorrhoea alveolaris. **inclusion b.,** an inflammatory condition of the conjunctiva, urethra or cervix, caused by a filtrable virus and characterized by the presence of large basophilic inclusion bodies. **b. neonato′rum,** ophthalmia neonatorum. **Stoerk's b.,** blennorrhea with profuse chronic suppuration producing hypertrophy of the mucosa of the nose, pharynx and larynx.

blennorrheal (blen″no-re′al). Pertaining to, or of the nature of, blennorrhea.

blennostasis (blen-nos′tah-sis) [*blenno-* + Gr. *stasis* standing]. The suppression of an abnormal mucous discharge, or the correction of an excessive one.

blennostatic (blen″no-stat′ik) [*blenno-* + Gr. *histanai* to halt]. Correcting of excessive mucous secretion.

blennothorax (blen″no-tho′raks) [*blenno-* + Gr. *thōrax* chest]. An accumulation of mucus in the chest.

blennuria (blen-nu′re-ah) [*blenn-* + Gr. *ouron* urine]. The existence of mucus in the urine.

blephar-. See *blepharo-*.

blepharadenitis (blef″ar-ad″ĕ-ni′tis) [*blephar-* + Gr. *adēn* gland + *-itis*]. Inflammation of the meibomian glands.

blepharal (blef′ah-ral). Pertaining to the eyelids.

blepharectomy (blef″ah-rek′to-me) [*blephar-* + Gr. *ektomē* excision]. Excision of a lesion of the eyelids.

blepharelosis (blef″ah-rel-o′sis) [*blephar-* + Gr. *eilein* to roll]. Entropion.

blepharism (blef′ah-rizm) [L. *blepharismus;* Gr. *blepharizein* to wink]. Spasm of the eyelids; continuous blinking.

blepharitis (blef″ah-ri′tis) [*blephar-* + *-itis*]. Inflammation of the eyelids. **b. angula′ris,** blepharitis ulcerosa affecting the medial commissure (angle) and blocking the punctum lacrimalis. **b. cilia′ris, b. margina′lis,** a chronic inflammation of the hair follicles and sebaceous glands of the margins of the eyelids. **b. squamo′sa,** a marginal blephritis in which the edges of the lids become scaly. **b. ulcero′sa,** an ulcerous form of marginal blephritis.

blepharo-, blephar- (blef′ah-ro, blef′ahr) [Gr. *blepharon* eyelid; Gr. *blephrais* eyelash]. Combining form denoting a relationship to an eyelid or eyelash.

blepharo-adenitis (blef″ah-ro-ad″ĕ-ni′tis). Blepharadenitis.

blepharo-adenoma (blef″ah-ro-ad″ĕ-no′mah). Adenoma of the eyelid.

blepharo-atheroma (blef″ah-ro-ath″er-o′mah). An encysted tumor or sebaceous cyst of an eyelid.

blepharochalasis (blef″ah-ro-kal′ah-sis) [*blepharo-* + Gr. *chalasis* relaxation]. Relaxation of the skin of the eyelid, due to atrophy of the intercellular tissue. Called also *dermatolysis palpebrarum*.

blepharochromidrosis (blef″ah-ro-kro-mĭ-dro′sis) [*blepharo-* + Gr. *chrōma* color + Gr. *hidrōs* sweat + *-osis*]. Excretion of a colored sweat from the eyelids, usually of a bluish shade.

blepharoclonus (blef″ah-rok′lo-nus) [*blepharo-* + *clonus*]. Clonic spasm of orbicularis oculi muscle, appearing as an increased winking of the eye.

blepharoconjunctivitis (blef″ah-ro-kon-junk″tĭ-vi′tis). Inflammation of the eyelids and conjunctiva.

blepharodiastasis (blef″ah-ro-di-as′tah-sis) [*blepharo-* + Gr. *diastasis* separation]. Excessive separation of the eyelids, causing the eye to be open very wide.

blepharoncus (blef″ah-rong′kus) [*blepharo-* + Gr. *onkos* bulk, mass]. A tumor on the eyelid.

blepharopachynsis (blef″ah-ro-pak-in′sis) [*blepharo-* + Gr. *pachynsis* thickening]. The morbid thickening of an eyelid.

blepharophimosis (blef″ah-ro-fi-mo′sis) [*blepharo-* + Gr. *phimōsis* a muzzling]. A narrowing of the slit between the eyelids.

blepharophryplasty (blef″ah-rof′re-plas″te) [*blephar-* + Gr *ophrys* eyebrow + *plassein* to form]. Surgical restoration of eyelid and eyebrow.

blepharoplast (blef′ah-ro-plast) [*blepharo-* + Gr. *plassein* to form]. 1. A minute, oval or round granule, forming one part of the kinetoplast; from it arises the axoneme. 2. One of the tiny rods in the cytoplasm of ependymal cells in ependymoma.

blepharoplasty (blef′ah-ro-plas″te). The plastic surgery of the eyelids.

blepharoplegia (blef″ah-ro-ple′je-ah) [*blepharo-* + Gr. *plēgē* stroke]. Paralysis of an eyelid (Desmarres); paralysis of both muscles of the eyelid (Graefe-Saemisch).

blepharoptosis (blef″-ah-ro-to′sis) [*blepharo-* + Gr. *ptōsis* a fall]. Drooping of an upper eyelid from paralysis.

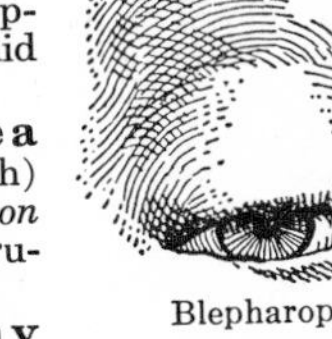
Blepharoptosis.

blepharopyorrhea (blef″ah-ro-pi-ŏ-re′ah) [*blepharo-* + Gr. *pyon* pus + *rhoia* flow]. Purulent ophthalmia.

blepharorrhaphy (blef″ah-ror′ah-fe) [*blepharo-* + Gr. *rhaphē* suture]. The operation of suturing an eyelid.

blepharospasm (blef′ah-ro-spazm) [*blepharo-* + Gr. *spasmos* spasm]. Tonic spasm of the orbicularis oculi muscle, producing more or less complete closure of the eyelids. **essential b.,** blepharospasm that is present when there is no abnormality or the eye or trigeminal (fifth cranial) nerve. **symptomatic b.,** blepharospasm occurring in association with a lesion of the eye or of the trigeminal (fifth cranial) nerve.

blepharosphincterectomy (blef″ah-ro-sfingk″-ter-ek′to-me) [*blepharo-* + Gr. *sphinktēr* sphincter + *ektomē* excision]. Excision of some of the fibers of the orbicularis muscle, together with overlying skin, to relieve pressure of the eyelid on the cornea in blepharospasm.

blepharostat (blef′ah-ro-stat″) [*blepharo-* + Gr. *histanai* to cause to stand]. An instrument for holding the eyelids and keeping them apart during surgical operations upon the eye.

blepharostenosis (blef″ah-ro-ste-no′sis) [*blepharo-* + Gr. *stenōsis* a narrowing]. An abnormal narrowing of the palpebral slit.

blepharosynechia (blef″ah-ro-sĭ-ne′ke-ah) [*blepharo-* + Gr. *synecheia* a holding together]. The growing together or adhesion of the eyelids.

blepharotomy (blef″ah-rot′o-me) [*blepharo-* + Gr. *tomē* a cut]. The surgical incision of an eyelid.

blepharoxysis (blef″ah-ro-zi′sis) [*blepharo-* + Gr. *xysis* a polishing]. Hippocrates' treatment for trachoma, consisting of rubbing the inner surface of the lid with wool wound round a core of wood, followed by cauterization and instillation of copper peroxide.

Blessig's cysts, groove, lacunae (bles′sigz) [Robert *Blessig*, German physician, 1830–1878]. See under *cyst* and *groove*.

blind (blīnd). Not having the sense of sight.

blindgut (blīnd′gut). The cecum.

blindness (blīnd′nes). Lack or loss of ability to see; lack of perception of visual stimuli, due to disorder of the organs of sight, or to lesions in certain areas of the brain. **amnesic color b.,** inability to recognize or to name a hue, although it is correctly perceived. **blue b.,** imperfect perception of blue tints. See *tritanopia*. **blue-yellow b.,** imperfect perception of blue and yellow tints. See *tetartanopia*. **Bright's b.,** dimness or complete loss of sight occurring in uremia, without lesion of the retina or optic disk. **color b.,** a term colloquially and incorrectly applied to any deviation from normal perception of hues. See *deuteranopia*, *protanopia*, etc. **concussion b.,** functional blindness due to violent explosions, as by high explosive shells, bombs, etc. **cortical b.,** blindness due to a lesion of the cortical visual center. **cortical psychic b.,** loss of optic memory image and of spatial orientation due to lesion of the optic lobe. **day b.,** hemeralopia. **flight b.,** amaurosis fugax caused by high centrifugal forces encountered in aviation. **functional b.,** inability to see occurring without disorder of the organs of sight. **green b.,** imperfect perception of green tints. See *deuteranopia*. **letter b.,** inability to recognize individual letters. **mind b.,** psychic b. **night b.,** nyctalopia. **note b.,** inability to read musical notes, due to a lesion of the central nervous system. **object b.,** inability to recognize the nature and purpose of objects seen. **psychic b.,** inability to recognize the nature of the source of visual stimuli, because of some lesion of the brain. **red b.,** imperfect perception of red tints. See *protanopia*. **red-green b.,** imperfect perception of red and green tints. **snow b.,** dimness of vision, usually temporary, due to the glare of the sun upon snow. **soul b.,** psychic b. **syllabic b.,** inability to recognize syllables. **taste b.,** inability to perceive certain gustatory stimuli, some substances producing no sensation of taste. **total b.,** complete absence of light perception. **twilight b.,** aknephascopia. **word b.,** inability to recognize written words as the symbols of ideas.

blister (blis′ter) [L. *vesicula*]. 1. A localized collection of fluid in the epidermis causing elevation of the horny upper layer and its separation from the underlying parts. See *bulla*. 2. An agent producing a vesication. **ambulant b.,** one that is shifted from place to place. **blood b.,** a blister having bloody contents. It may be caused by a bruise, but is often due to persistent friction. **fever b.,** herpes febrilis. **fly b.,** a blister of cantharides. **flying b.,** a blister applied long enough to produce redness, but not vesication. **Marochetti's b's,** small blisters seen under the tongue in hydrophobia.

Bloch (blok), Konrad. German biochemist in the United States, born 1912; co-winner, with Feodor Lynen, of the Nobel prize for medicine and physiology in 1964, for investigations in biosynthesis of cholesterol and fatty acids.

Bloch's reaction (bloks) [Bruno *Bloch*, Swiss dermatologist, 1878–1933]. See under *reaction*.

Bloch's scale (bloks) [Marcel *Bloch*, French pathologist, 1885–1925]. See under *scale*.

block (blok). 1. An obstruction or stoppage. 2. A term introduced by Romanes to express the obstruction of the passage of muscular or nervous impulses. 3. Regional anesthesia. See under *anesthesia*. **air b.,** interference with the normal inflation and deflation of the lungs and with the pulmonary blood flow, produced by the leakage of air from the pulmonary alveoli into the interstitial tissue of the lung and into the mediastinum. **arborization b.,** heart block in which the ventricular conduction is impaired. **bundle-branch b.** See under *heart-block*. **comparator b.** See *comparator*. **dynamic b.** Same as *spinal subarachnoid b.* **ear b.,** trauma of the middle ear and the resulting inflammation and pain in compressed air workers in which the eustachian tube is not patulous. **extrahepatic-bed b.,** the occlusion of the splenic vein occurring in Banti's syndrome. **field b.,** regional anesthesia obtained by creating walls of anesthesia encircling the operative field. **heart b.** See *heart-block*. **nerve b.,** regional anesthesia secured by making extraneural or paraneural injections in close proximity to the nerve whose conductivity is to be cut off. **paravertebral b.,** infiltration of the stellate ganglion with procaine hydrochloride: done for apoplexy, tachycardia, etc. **sino-auricular b.,** an interruption of impulses from the sinus node. **sinus b.,** pain in the sinuses due to air being trapped in them in compressed air illness. **spinal subarachnoid b.,** a condition in which the flow of cerebrospinal fluid is interfered with by an obstruction in the spinal canal. **stellate b.,** the analgesic blocking of the stellate ganglion. **sympathetic b.,** blocking of the sympathetic trunk by paravertebral infiltration with an anesthetic agent. **tubal b.,** ear block. **ventricular b.,** obstruction to the flow of cerebrospinal fluid caused by meningitic inflammatory exudate blocking the foramina of Magendie and Luschka by which the cerebral ventricles communicate with the subarachnoid space.

blockade (blok-ād′). The rendering of the reticuloendothelial cells of the body less capable of phagocytosis by the intravenous injection of harmless material, such as carmine, lampblack, etc. **renal b.,** anuria due to suppression of function of the renal tubules. **virus b.,** interference by a virus with the action of another virus. Attenuated virus of a disease has been used to inhibit the multiplication of an active virus. Called also *virus interference* and *cell blockade.*

blockain (blok′ān). Trade mark for a preparation of propoxycaine hydrochloride.

blocking (blok′ing). 1. The cutting off of an afferent nerve path, as by the injection of cocaine (*cocaine b.*). 2. The Freudian term for a sudden stop in an association produced when a complex is touched. 3. The fastening of a histological specimen impregnated with celloidin to a block of wood or other suitable material which may be clamped in the microtome. **b. of thought,** a mental condition in which the patient expresses himself with difficulty, because, as he claims, "the avenues of thought are obstructed."

Blocq's disease (bloks) [Paul Oscar *Blocq*, French physician, 1860–1896]. Astasia abasia.

Blondlot rays (blond-lo′) [Prosper René *Blondlot*, French physicist, 1849–1930]. See under *ray.*

blood (blud) [L. *sanguis, cruor;* Gr. *haima*]. The fluid that circulates through the heart, arteries, capillaries, and veins, carrying nutriment and oxygen to the body cells. Called also *sanguis* [N A, B N A]. The arterial blood in the systemic circulation is of a bright red color, but after passing to the veins it becomes very dark or brownish red. It consists of a pale yellow liquid, the *plasma,* containing the microscopically visible formed elements of the blood: the erythrocytes, or red blood corpuscles; the leukocytes, or white blood corpuscles; and the thrombocytes, or blood platelets. **central b.,** blood obtained from the pulmonary venous system; sometimes applied to splanchnic blood, or blood obtained from chambers of the heart or from bone marrow. **cord b.,** blood contained within the umbilical vessels, at time of delivery of the fetus. **defibrinated b.,** whole blood from which fibrin has been removed and which therefore does not clot. **laky b.,** blood that has become darkened and somewhat transparent through the solution or destruction of the red corpuscles. **occult b.,** blood present in such small quantities that it can be detected only by chemical tests of suspected material, or by microscopic or spectroscopic examination. **oxalated b.,** blood to which oxalate solution has been added to prevent coagulation. **peripheral b.,** blood obtained from acral areas, or from the circulation remote from the heart, as from ear lobe, finger tip, or heel pad (in a child), or from the antecubital vein. **sludged b.,** blood in which the red cells have become aggregated into masses: it occurs in the smaller blood vessels, where it slows the flow of the blood. **splanchnic b.,** a general term applied to blood in the thoracic, abdominal, and pelvic viscera; further distinguished, in case of blood from a specific organ, by the appropriate modifier, such as pulmonary, hepatic, or splenic blood. **whole b.,** blood from which none of the elements have been removed.

bloodless (blud′les). 1. Anemic or exsanguine. 2. Performed with little or no loss of blood.

blood plasma (blud plaz′mah). See under *plasma.*

bloodroot (blud′ro͝ot). Sanguinaria.

blood serum (blud se′rum). 1. The clear liquid which separates from the blood when it is allowed to clot. It is therefore blood plasma from which fibrinogen has been removed in the process of clotting. 2. A bacteriological culture medium composed largely of blood serum. See also under *culture medium.* **alkaline b. s.,** blood serum to which sodium hydroxide has been added, consisting mostly of alkali albuminate. **coagulated b. s.,** plain blood serum from the horse, cow, sheep, dog or other animal, coagulated and sterilized at a temperature not above 80°C. **Councilman and Mallory's b. s.,** blood serum coagulated in a hot-air sterilizer and sterilized with steam. **glycerin b. s.,** blood serum containing glycerin. **inspissated b.,** blood serum heated to coagulation, usually in test tubes and in an inclined position. **Löffler's b. s.,** nutrient bouillon containing dextrose and blood serum, mixed, and coagulated in an inclined position. **Lorrain Smith's b. s.,** blood serum containing sodium hydroxide.

blood type (blud′tīp). 1. The phenotype of erythrocytes defined by one or more antigenic determinants that are controlled by allelic genes, as in the Landsteiner classification shown in the accompanying table. In addition to the antigenic determinants establishing these types, a considerable number of other blood type antigens exist in man, such as MN, Rh (Dd, Cc, etc.), Kell (Kk), Duffy (Fy^{a+b}), Kidd (Jk^{a+b}), Lutheran (Lu^{a+b}), and Lewis (Le^{a+b}), to name a few examples. Available antigenic structural groupings permit red cells to be agglutinated by specific reagents which may be human antisera, animal antisera, or hemagglutinating substances (lectins) extracted from certain plant seeds. 2. Any characteristic, function, or trait of a cellular or fluid component of blood, considered as the expression (phenotype) of the actions and interactions of dominant genes, and useful in medicolegal and other studies of human inheritance. Such characteristics include the antigenic groupings of erythrocytes, leukocytes, platelets, and plasma proteins.

CLASSIFICATIONS OF BLOOD TYPES

Blood Type Designation			Agglutinogens in erythrocytes (Red cell antigens)	Agglutinins in serum (Serum antibodies)
International (Landsteiner)	Moss	Jansky		
O	IV	I	—	α, β
A	II	II	A	β
B	III	III	B	α
AB	I	IV	A, B	—

Bloor's test [Walter Ray *Bloor*, American bio: chemist, born 1877]. See under *tests.*

Blot's perforator (blōz) [Claude Philibert Hippolyte *Blot*, French obstetrician, 1822–1888]. See under *perforator.*

blotch (bloch). A blemish or spot. **palpebral b.,** pinguecula.

blowpipe. A tube through which a current of air or other gas is forced upon a flame to concentrate and intensify the heat.

blows (blōz). A noninfectious disease of hogs in northern Ireland, marked by a severe anemia of unknown causation.

blue (blu). 1. One of the principal colors of the spectrum, the color of the sky. 2. Having the color of the clear sky. 3. A dye which is blue in color. **afridol b.,** the sodium salt of orthodichlor-benzidine-diazo-bis-1-amino-8-naphthol-3,6-disulfonic acid, a trypanocidal agent resembling trypan blue. **alcian b.,** a copper-containing dye for staining acid mucopolysaccharides; it may be combined with periodic acid–Schiff reagent. **alizarin b.,** a blue dyestuff derived from anthracene. **alkali b.,** a dye, sodium triphenylrosaniline monosulfate. **aniline b.,** a mixture of the trisulfonates of tri-phenyl rosaniline and of di-phenyl rosaniline. **aniline**

b., W. S., a mixture of the sulfonation products of mixtures of phenylated rosaniline and pararosaniline, soluble in water. **anthracene b.,** alizarin blue. **azidine b., 3 B.,** trypan b. **benzamine b., 3 B.,** trypan b. **benzo b.,** trypan b. **Berlin b.,** Prussian b. **Borrel's b.,** a silver oxide stain for spirochetes. **brilliant b., C.,** brilliant cresyl b. **brilliant cresyl b.,** an oxazin dye, usually $C_{15}H_{16}N_3OCl$, used in staining blood. **bromchlorphenol b.,** an indicator, dibromdichlor-phenol-sulfonphthalein, $(C_6H_2ClBrOH)_2$-$C.C_6H_4.SO_2ONa$. **bromophenol b.,** a dye, tetrabromophenolsulfonphthalein, used as an indicator in determining hydrogen ion concentration, being yellow at pH 3 and blue at pH 4.6. **bromothymol b.,** a dye, dibromothymolsulfonphthalein, used as an indicator in determining hydrogen ion concentration. It has a pH range of 6 to 7.6, being yellow at 6 and blue at 7.6. **china b.,** aniline b. **chlorazol b., 3 B.,** trypan b. **Congo b., 3 B.,** trypan b. **coomassie b.,** trade mark for 8-(4-anilino-5-sulfo-1-naphthylazo) naphthol-3,6-disulfonic acid trisodium salt (sodium anazolene), an agent used in dye dilution studies of cardiac output or in determinations of blood volume. **cresyl b., 2 R. N.** or **B. B. S.,** brilliant cresyl b. **cyanol b.,** a bright blue acid coal tar color related to triphenylmethane. **diamine b.,** trypan b. **dianil b., H. 3 G.,** trypan b. **Evans b.,** an odorless, green, bluish green, or brown powder, $C_{34}H_{24}N_6Na_4O_{14}S_4$: injected intravenously in determining blood volume. **Helvetia b.,** methyl b. **indigo b.,** indigotin. **indigo b., soluble,** indigotindisulfonate. **indophenol b.,** the blue pigment produced in the Nadi reaction and in the indophenol test. It is $(CH_3)_2N.C_6H_4.N:C_{10}H_6:O$. **isamine b.,** alkali b. **Kühne's methylene b.,** a mixture of methylene blue and dehydrated alcohol in phenol solution. **Löffler's methylene b.,** a mixture of methylene blue and alcohol in aqueous solution of potassium hydroxide. **marine b.,** aniline b. **methyl b.,** a dark blue powder, sodium triphenyl-para-rosaniline sulfonate: used as an antiseptic. **methylene b.,** 3,7-bis(dimethylamino)phenazothionium chloride; used as a stain and as an indicator; also used as an antidote in cyanide poisoning, and in treatment of methemoglobinemia. **methylene b., N. N.,** new methylene blue, N. **methylene b., O.,** toluidine blue, O. **naphthamine b., 3 B. X.,** trypan blue. **new methylene b., N.,** $C_2H_5.NH(CH_3)C_6H_2(SN)C_6H_2(CH_3)N(C_2H_5)HCl$. **Niagara b., 3 B.,** trypan b. **Nile b., A., Nile b. sulfate,** an oxazin dye which stains fatty acids blue. It is $(C_2H_5)_2N.C_6H_3(ON)C_{10}H_5.NH_2.(SO_4)\frac{1}{2}$. **polychrome methylene b.,** a mixture of methylene green, methylene azure, methylene violet, and methylene blue. **Prussian b.,** an amorphous blue powder, $Fe_4[Fe(CN)_6]_3$. **pyrrole b.,** $C_4H_4N.C[C_6H_4.N(CH_3)_2]_2$. **soluble b., 3 M.** or **2 R.,** aniline b. **spirit b.,** a mixture of diphenylrosaniline, $C_6H_5.NHCl.C_6H_4.C[C_6H_3(CH_3)NH_2]C_6H_4.NH.C_6H_5$, and triphenylrosaniline, $C_6H_5.NHCl.C_6H_4C[C_6H_4(CH_3)NH.C_6H_5]C_6H_4.NH.C_6H_5$. **Swiss b.,** methylene b. **thymol b.,** an indicator, thymolsulfonphthalein, with an acid pH range of 1.2 to 2.8, being red at 1.2 and yellow at 2.8, and an alkaline pH range of 8 to 9.6, being yellow at 8 and blue at 9.6. **toluidine b., toluidine b., O,** the chloride salt or zinc chloride double salt of aminodimethylaminotoluphenazthionium chloride: useful as a stain for demonstrating basophilic and metachromatic substances. **trypan b.,** an acid, azo dye which has been used in vital staining and as a remedy in protozoan infections. It is the sodium salt of toluidin-diazo-diamino-naphthol-disulfonic acid, $[CH_3.C_6H_3.N:N.C_{10}H_3(NH_2)(SO_2.ONa)_2.OH]_2$. **Victoria b.,** a triphenylmethane dye with bacteriostatic properties. It is a phenyl-tetramethyl-triamino-triphenylmethane chloride, $C_6H_5.NH(Cl)$-$C_6H_4:C[C_6H_4.N(CH_3)_2]_2Cl$. **b. vitriol,** copper sulfate. **water b.,** aniline b.

bluecomb (bloo′kōm). A disease of turkeys marked by cyanosis and caused by *Erysipelothrix rhuziopathiae*.

blue-eye (bloo′i). See *bungeye*.

bluestone (blu′stōn). Cupric sulfate.

Blum's reagent test (bloomz) [Léon *Blum*, German physician, 1878–1930]. See under *tests*.

Blumberg's sign (blum′bergz) [Jacob Moritz *Blumberg*, surgeon and gynecologist in Berlin, and later in London, 1873–1955]. See under *sign*.

Blumenau's nucleus (bloo′men-owz) [Leonid Wassiljewitsch *Blumenau*, Russian neurologist, 1862–1932]. See under *nucleus*.

Blumenbach's clivus, process (bloo′men-bahks) [Johann Frederich *Blumenbach*, German physiologist, 1752–1840]. See under *clivus* and *process*.

Blumenthal's disease [Ferdinand *Blumenthal*, German physician, born 1870]. Erythroleukemia.

blunthook (blunt′hook). An instrument used mainly in embryotomy.

blutene (bloo′tēn). Trade mark for a preparation of tolonium.

Blyth's test [Alexander Wynter *Blyth*, English physician]. See under *tests*.

B.M. Abbreviation for L. *bal′neum ma′ris* (seawater bath), and *buccomesial*.

B.M.A. Abbreviation for *British Medical Association*.

B.M.R. Abbreviation for *basal metabolic rate*.

B.M.S. Abbreviation for *Bachelor of Medical Science*.

BNA. Abbreviation for *Basle Nomina Anatomica*, the anatomical terminology accepted at Basel, Switzerland, in 1895. See under *nomen*.

B.O. Abbreviation for *base of prism out*, and *bucco-occlusal*.

Boas' point, reagent, sign, test, etc. (bo′az) [Ismar *Boas*, physician in Berlin, 1858–1938]. See under the nouns.

Boas-Oppler bacillus (bo′az op′ler) [Ismar *Boas*, Bruno *Oppler*, German physician]. See under *bacillus*.

Bobbs's operation (bobz) [John Stough *Bobbs*, American surgeon, 1809–1870]. See under *operation*.

Bobroff's operation (bob′rofs) [V. F. *Bobroff*, Russian surgeon, born 1858]. See under *operation*.

Bochdalek's foramen, ganglion, valve (bok′dal-eks) [Vincent Alexander *Bochdalek*, anatomist in Prague, 1801–1883]. See under the nouns.

Bock's ganglion, nerve (boks) [August Carl *Bock*, German anatomist, 1782–1833]. See under *ganglion* and *nerve*.

Bockhart's impetigo (bok′harts) [Max *Bockhart*, German physician of the nineteenth century]. See under *impetigo*.

Bodansky unit (bo-dan′ske) [Aaron *Bodansky*, American biochemist, 1896–1941]. See under *unit*.

bodenplatte (bo″den-plaht′tĕ) [Ger.]. Floor plate

Bodo (bo′do). A genus of the Bodonidae, being small oval bodies with two anterior flagella, one of which projects forward and the other back. **B. cauda′tus,** a common coprozoic flagellate found in human feces. They are polymorphic and their motility is jerky. **B. sal′tans,** the "springing monad" which has been found in ulcers. **B. urina′ria** has been found in urine. Other species are: *Bodo asiatica*, *B. javanensis*, *B. parva*, and *B. weinbergi*.

Bodonidae (bo-don′ĭ-de). A family of flagellates sometimes found in human feces. They are spherical in form with one flagellum projecting forward and one backward. There is no undulating membrane and they are probably not pathogenic.

body (bod′e) [L. *corpus;* Gr. *sōma*]. 1. The trunk, or animal frame, with its organs. 2. The cadaver or corpse. 3. The largest and most important part of any organ. See also *corpus*. 4. Any mass or collection of material. **accessory b.,** a body of indefinite structure found in the protoplasm of a spermatid. **acetone b's,** acetone, aceto-acetic acid, and beta-oxybutyric acid, being intermediates in fat metabolism. Called also *ketone bodies.* **adipose b. of cheek,** corpus adiposum buccae. **adipose b. of ischiorectal fossa,** corpus adiposum fossae ischiorectalis. **adipose b. of orbit,** corpus adiposum orbitae. **adrenal b.,** adrenal gland. **alkapton b's,** a class of substances with an affinity for alkali, found in the urine and causing the condition known as alkaptonuria. The compound commonly found, and most commonly referred to by the term, is homogentisic acid. **alloxur b's,** purine bases. **Amato b's,** irregular, pale-staining, blue cytoplasmic clumps, occurring in neutrophils of patients with various infectious diseases, such as diphtheria, scarlet fever, and pneumonia, and probably identical with Döhle bodies. **amygdaloid b.,** corpus amygdaloideum. **amylaceous b's, amyloid b's,** corpora amylacea. **anaphylactic reaction b.,** sensibilin. **anococcygeal b.,** ligamentum anococcygeum. **anti-immune b., anti-intermediary b.,** antiamboceptor. **aortic b's,** small groups of chromophil cells on either side of the aorta in the region of the inferior mesenteric artery. **apical b.,** acrosome. **b's of Arantius,** noduli valvularum aortae. **Arnold's b's,** small pieces of erythrocytes in the blood or red cell shadows. **asbestosis b's,** golden yellow bodies of various shapes occurring in the sputum, lung secretion, and feces of patients with asbestosis. **Aschoff b's,** submiliary collections of cells and leukocytes in the interstitial tissues of the heart in rheumatic myocarditis. **asteroid b.,** an irregularly star-shaped inclusion body found in the giant cells in sarcoidosis and also found in numerous other diseases. **Auer b's,** elongated inclusions, thought to be nucleoprotein, found in the cytoplasm of myeloblasts, myelocytes, monoblasts, and granular histiocytes, rarely in plasma cells, absent in lymphoblasts or lymphocytes, and virtually pathognomonic of leukemia. **Babes-Ernst b's,** metachromatic granules. **Balbiani's b.,** yolk nucleus. **Balfour b's,** *Aegyptianella pullorum.* **Barr b.,** sex chromatin. **Bartonia b's,** *Bartonella bacilliformis.* **basal b.,** basal corpuscle. **Behla's b's,** Plimmer's b's. **Bence Jones b's.** See *Bence Jones protein,* under *protein.* **Bender's b's,** Cesaris-Demel b's. **between b.** See *complement.* **bigeminal b's,** corpora bigemina. **Bollinger b's,** inclusion bodies found in all tissue cells in fowl-pox. Cf. *Borrel b's.* **Borrel b's,** minute granules composing the Bollinger bodies of fowl-pox; regarded as the possible infective agent of the disease. **Bracht-Wächter b's,** necrotic areas in the myocardium containing polymorphonuclear leukocytes and a serous exudate: seen in bacterial endocarditis. **brassy b.,** a dark, shrunken blood corpuscle seen in malaria. **Buchner's b's,** defensive proteins. **Cabot's ring b's,** lines in the form of loops or figures of eight, seen in stained erythrocytes in severe anemias. They are stained red with the Wright-Leishman stain and blue with eosinate of methylthionine chlorides. **Call-Exner b's,** structures characteristic of granulosa-cell tumors, which are spaces in larger masses of granulosa cells produced by liquefaction. **cancer b's.** See *Plimmer's b's* and *Russell's b's.* **carotid b.,** glomus caroticum. **cavernous b.,** corpus cavernosum. **cell b.,** that portion of a cell which encloses the nucleus. **central b.,** the structures at the center of the aster during mitosis. **Cesaris-Demel b's,** degenerative bodies in leukocytes after severe anemia, appearing as light vacuoles by Wright's stain. **chromaffin b.,** paraganglion. **chromatinic b's,** aggregates of desoxyribonucleic acid found in bacterial cells, and demonstrable by staining with Giemsa following hydrolysis of cytoplasmic ribonucleic acid and osmic acid fixation. They are tentatively regarded as representing a morphologically discrete bacterial nucleus. **chromophilous b's,** Nissl b's. **ciliary b.,** corpus ciliare. **coccobacillary b's of Nelson,** small organisms from the nasal passages of fowls, mice, and rats, which are considered to have causal relationship with infectious catarrh. **coccoid x b's,** minute bodies found in the blood in psittacosis. **coccygeal b.,** glomus coccygeum. **colloid b's,** masses of an irregularly shaped, gluelike substance in the cerebrospinal axis. **colostrum b's,** colostrum corpuscles. **Councilman b's,** bodies formed by hyaline degeneration of parenchymal cells of the liver in yellow fever. **crescent b.,** achromocyte. **crystalloid b.,** a body seen near the nuclei of the cells of the seminiferous tubules. **Deetjen's b's,** blood platelets. **demilune b.,** achromocyte. **dentate b. of cerebellum,** nucleus dentatus cerebelli. **dentate b. of medulla oblongata,** nucleus olivaris. **denticulate b.,** gyrus dentatus. **Döhle's inclusion b's,** small coccus-shaped bodies occurring in the polynuclear leukocytes of the blood in several diseases, especially scarlet fever. **Donne's b's,** colostrum corpuscles. **Donovan's b's.** 1. *Donovania granulomatis.* 2. Leishman-Donovan bodies. **Ehrlich's hemoglobinemic b's,** dark bodies, occurring in the center of degenerated erythrocytes, which do not represent true red cell inclusions. **elementary b.** 1. A blood platelet. 2. An inclusion body. **Elschnig b's,** clear grapelike clusters formed by proliferation of the epithelial cells after extracapsular extraction of a cataractous lens. **Elzholz's b's,** bodies described by Elzholz in degenerated medullated nerve fibers. **end b.** See *complement.* **endoglobar b.,** archiplasm. **epithelial b.,** a parathyroid gland. **epithelioneural b.,** a structure characterized by an intimate or intricate association of epithelial cells and neural elements. **falciform b.,** sporozoite. **filling b's,** fullkörper. **fimbriated b., of uterine tube,** fimbriae tubae uterinae. **flagellated b.,** the gametocyte of the malarial parasite. **foreign b.,** a mass or particle of material which is not normal to the place where it is found. **b. of fornix,** corpus fornicis. **fuchsin b's,** Russell's b's. **gamma-Favre b's,** small intracytoplasmic inclusion bodies found in lymphogranuloma venereum. **geniculate b.,** See *corpus geniculatum laterale* and *corpus geniculatum mediale.* **Giannuzzi's b's,** Giannuzzi's crescents. **glass b.,** demilune b. **Golgi b.** See *Golgi apparatus.* **Gordon's elementary b.,** a particle originally thought to be the viral cause of Hodgkin's disease, but later shown to be obtainable from any tissue containing eosinophils or involved with this neoplasm. Called also *Gordon's encephalopathic agent.* **Guarnieri's b's,** inclusion bodies in the cells of the affected tissues in smallpox and vaccinia, regarded as caused by the reaction of the cell to the virus of the disease. **habenular b.,** nucleus habenulae. **Harting b's,** deposits of calcium (calcospherites) in the cerebral capillaries. **Hassall's b's,** Hassall's corpuscles. **Heinz b's,** Heinz-Ehrlich b's. **Heinz-Ehrlich b's,** intracorpuscular coccoid structures resulting from oxidative injury to and polymerization, of denatured hemoglobin; refractile in fresh blood smears, they are not visible when stained with Romanowsky dyes but they may be stained supravitally. **Hensen's b.,** a rounded modified Golgi net under the cuticle of an outer hair cell of the organ of Corti. **Herring b's,** hyaline or colloid masses scattered throughout the posterior lobe of the hypophysis. **b. of Highmore,** mediastinum testis. **Howell's b's,** Howell-Jolly b's. **Howell-Jolly b's,** small, round or oval structures, pinkish or bluish in color, observed in erythrocytes in various anemias and leukemias and after splenectomy; they probably represent unphysiologic red cell nuclear remnants. **hyaloid b.,** vitreous body. **immune b.** See *amboceptor.* **inclusion b's,** round, oval or irregular shaped bodies occurring in the protoplasm and nuclei of cells of the body, as in disease caused by filterable virus infection such as rabies, smallpox, herpes, etc. **infrapatellar fatty b.,** corpus adiposum infrapatellare. **infundibular b.,** lobus posterior hypophyseos. **in-**

ner b's, round bodies seen in erythrocytes after certain stainings, such as Ehrlich's bodies, Heinz bodies, and Schmauch's bodies. **intercarotid b.,** glomus caroticum. **intermediary b.** See *amboceptor*. **intermediate b. of Flemming,** a small bridge of acidophil material connecting the two daughter cells for a time at the end of mitosis. **interrenal b.,** an elongated organ which lies between the kidneys in elasmobranch fishes and which corresponds to the adrenal medulla in mammals. **intravertebral b.,** corpus vertebrae. **Joest's b's,** bodies found in the brain of animals with Borna disease. **Jolly's b's,** Howell-Jolly b's. **juxtarestiform b.,** a structure connecting the lateral vestibular nucleus with the nucleus fastigii and conveying vestibular impulses. **ketone b's,** acetone b's. **Kurloff's b's,** bodies seen in the large mononuclear leukocytes of guinea pigs and other animals; supposed by some to be a stage in the development of the granules of the eosinophilic leukocytes; by others to be a stage in the development of a protozoan organism. Called also *Lymphocytozoon cobayae*. **Lallemand-Trousseau b's,** Bence Jones cylinders. **Landolt's b's,** small elongate bodies between the rods and cones on the outer nuclear layer of the retina. **Langerhan's b's.** See *islands of Langerhans*. **Laveran's b's** (1880), the plasmodia of malarial disease. See *Laverania*. **L.C.L. b's,** minute coccoid bodies found in tissue infected with psittacosis. **Leishman-Donovan b's,** small round or oval bodies found in the spleen and liver of patients suffering with kala-azar, the intracellular forms of the protozoan *Leishmania donovani*, the parasite causing the disease. **lenticular b.,** nucleus dentatus cerebelli. **Levinthal-Coles-Lillie b's,** L.C.L. b's. **Lieutaud's b.,** trigonum vesicae. **Lindner's initial b's,** bodies resembling inclusion bodies found in epithelial cells in trachoma. **Lipschütz b's,** intranuclear inclusion bodies found in the lesions of herpes simplex, both in the epithelial cells of the primary skin lesion (skin or cornea) and in the affected nerve cells. **Lostorfer's b's,** Lostorfer's corpuscles. **Luschka's b.,** glomus coccygeum. **Luys' b.,** nucleus subthalamicus. **lyssa b's,** red staining masses somewhat resembling Negri bodies but less sharply defined and with less internal structure. **Mallory's b's,** bodies resembling protozoa, seen in the lymph spaces and epithelial cells of the skin in scarlet fever. **malpighian b's of kidney,** corpuscula renis. **mamillary b., mammillary b.,** corpus mamillare. **Maragliano b.,** a round or elliptical body found as an artifact in degenerated or degenerating erythrocytes; it resembles a vacuole, and is not to be considered a true red cell inclusion. **Marchal b's,** cell inclusion bodies observed in ectromelia. **medullary b. of cerebellum,** corpus medullare cerebelli. **medullary b. of vermis,** arbor vitae cerebelli. **melon-seed b.,** any of a class of small fibrous masses sometimes occurring in the joints and in cysts of the tendon sheaths. **metachromatic b's,** metachromatic granules. **Michaelis-Gutmann b's,** bodies found in the lesion of malacoplakia of the bladder. **molluscous b's,** peculiar round or oval microscopical bodies within the papules of molluscum epitheliale. **Mooser b's,** bodies resembling rickettsiae: seen in the epithelial cells of the tunica vaginalis exudate in some forms of typhus. **Morner's b.,** nucleoalbumin. **Mott b's,** clear globules present in the cytoplasm of plasma cells in multiple myeloma. **Müller's dust b's,** hemoconia. **muriform b.,** the morula. **Negri b's,** oval or round inclusion bodies, seen in the protoplasm and sometimes in the processes of nerve cells of animals dead of hydrophobia; their presence is considered conclusive proof of rabies. Called also *Neurorrhyctes hydrophobiae*. **Neill-Mooser b.** See *Neill-Mooser reaction* under *reaction*. **Nelson's b's,** coccobacillary b's. **nigroid b's,** black or brown outgrowths from the edge of the iris in horses. **Nissl b's,** large granular protein bodies which stain with basic dyes, forming the substance of the reticulum of the cytoplasm of a nerve cell. Ribonucleoprotein has been found to be one of the main constituents. **Nothnagel's b's,** oval or round bodies, plain or striated, from 15 to 60 μ in diameter, sometimes found in the stools of persons who eat meat. **no-threshold b's,** no-threshold substances. **nuclear b.,** the nuclear disk of a maturing ovum after it takes an ellipsoidal form. **Oken's b.,** mesonephros. **olivary b.,** oliva. **onion b's,** epidermic pearls. **oryzoid b's,** rice b's. **pacchionian b's,** granulationes arachnoideales. **pampiniform b.,** epoophoron. **Pappenheimer b's,** basophilic iron-containing granules observed in various types of erythrocytes. **paraaortic b's,** corpora paraaortica. **parabasal b.,** an oval or rodlike body, in the kinetoplast, larger than the blepharoplast, and connected therewith by a delicate fibril. **paranuclear b.,** centrosome. **paraterminal b.,** the cerebral area from the olfactory peduncle backward to the lamina terminalis and upward between the corpus callosum and the hippocampal fissure. **parathyroid b.,** parathyroid gland. **parolivary b's,** accessory olivary nuclei. **Paschen b's,** inclusion bodies in the cells of the tissues in variola and vaccinia: they are infective but whether they are the infective agents or mechanical carriers of the invisible virus is not known. **pearly b's,** epidermic pearls. **perineal b.,** centrum tendineum perinei. **Perls' anemia b's,** a name once given small, actively moving, club-shaped bodies described as being observed in the blood in certain cases of pernicious anemia. **pineal b.,** a small, flattened, cone-shaped body, an outgrowth from the epithalamus, resting upon the mesencephalon in the interval between the two halves of the thalamus. It is not composed of nervous elements and is a rudimentary glandular structure said to produce an internal secretion. Called also *corpus pineale* [N A], *conarium*, *epiphysis cerebri*, and *pineal gland*. **pituitary b.,** pituitary gland, or hypophysis cerebri. **Plimmer's b's,** small round capsulated bodies found in cancer, and thought by the discoverer to be the parasite causing the disease. **polar b's.** 1. The small impotent cells extruded during the maturation divisions of the oocyte, which form at and mark the animal pole of the mature ovum. 2. Metachromatic granules located at the ends of bacteria. **postbranchial b.,** ultimobranchial b. **presegmenting b's,** malarial parasites before they undergo segmentation. **Prowazek's b's.** 1. Trachoma bodies. 2. Extremely small inclusion bodies found in the material from smallpox pustules and in cowpox vaccine and regarded by Prowazek as the cause of the disease. **Prowazek-Greeff b's,** trachoma b's. **psammoma b.,** a spherical, concentrically laminated mass of calcareous material, usually of microscopic size; such bodies occur in both benign and malignant epithelial and connective-tissue tumors, and are sometimes associated with chronic inflammation. **pseudolutein b.,** corpus atretica. **purine b's,** purine bases. **pyknotic b's,** bodies in the mucus of the stools in amebiasis: they are the nuclear remains of tissue cells and leukocytes. **quadrigeminal b's,** corpora quadrigemina. **reaction b.,** sensibilisin. **Renaut's b's,** pale granules in the degenerating nerve fibers in muscular dystrophy. **restiform b.** See *pedunculus cerebellaris inferior*. **restiform b. of Clark,** fasciculus cuneatus medullae oblongatae. **b. of Retzius,** a protoplasmic mass containing pigment granules at the lower end of a hair cell of the organ of Corti. **rice b's,** small bodies resembling grains of rice which form in the tendons of joints and in the fluid of hygroma. **Rosenmüller's b.,** epoophoron. **Ross's b's,** spherical copper-colored bodies showing dark granulations and sometimes having ameboid movements: seen in the blood and tissue fluids in syphilis. **Russell b's,** globular plasma cell inclusions, mucoprotein in nature, containing surface gamma globulin, and probably resulting from condensation of internal cellular secretions. **sand b's,** corpora arenacea. **Schaumann's b's,** the red or brown nodular, shell-like lesions of sarcoidosis. **Schmauch's b's,** round bodies seen in the stained erythrocytes of cats. **Schmorl b.,** a portion of the nucleus pulposus which has protruded into an adjoining vertebra. **Seidelin b's,** a name once applied to structures observed in the red blood corpuscles in yellow fever, believed by the discoverer to be the cause of the disease. **selenoid b.,** achromocyte. **semilunar b's,** Giannuzzi's crescents. **Spengler's immune b's,** immune bodies extracted from the red blood corpuscles of animals immunized against tuberculosis: used in tuberculosis. Called also *I. K.* (*immunkörper*). **spherical b.,** the first stage of the sexual cycle of the malarial parasite, developing later into the gametocyte. **spiculated b's,** a name once applied to spiny-looking bodies occurring enclosed in leukocytes or giant cells in the spleen in certain conditions. **spongy b. of male urethra,** corpus spongiosum penis. **spongy b. of penis,** corpus cavernosum penis. **striate b.,** corpus striatum. **supracardial b's,** aortic paraganglia. **suprarenal b.,** adrenal gland. **Symington's b.,** ligamentum anococcygeum. **telobranchial b.,** ultimobranchial b. **thermostabile b.,** amboceptor. **threshold b's,** threshold substances. **thyroid b.,** thyroid gland. **tigroid b's,** Nissl b's. **Todd b's,** eosinophilic structures formed in the cytoplasm of the red blood cells of certain amphibians. **Torres-Teixeira b's,** inclusion bodies found in the cells in alastrim and variola minor. **trachoma b's,** inclusion bodies found in clusters in the protoplasm of the epithelial cells from the conjunctiva of trachomatous eye. **trapezoid b.,** corpus trapezoideum. **Trousseau-Lallemand b's,** Bence Jones cylinders. **ultimobranchial b.,** an embryonic derivative from a bud in the pharyngeal wall which migrates along with the parathyroid and fuses with the thyroid: called also *postbranchial b.* and *telobranchial b.* **Verocay b's,** whorls of cells found in neurinoma. **b. of Vicq d'Azyr,** substantia nigra. **vitelline b.,** yolk nucleus. **vitreous b.,** the transparent substance that fills the part of the eyeball between the lens and the retina. Called also *corpus vitreum* [N A]. **Winkler's b.,** spherical bodies seen in the lesions of syphilis. **wolffian b.,** mesonephros. **xanthine b's,** purine bases. **yellow b. of ovary,** corpus luteum. **Zuckerkandl's b's,** paraganglia found along the course of the aorta near its bifurcation.

body rocking (bod′e rok′ing). A rhythmic backward and forward motion in a sitting position.

body snatching (bod′e snach′ing). The illegal procural of dead bodies, especially the robbing of a grave of a recently buried corpse.

B.O.E.A. Ethyl biscoumacetate.

Boeck's disease, sarcoid (beks) [Caesar P. M. *Boeck*, Norwegian dermatologist and syphilologist, 1845–1917]. See under *sarcoid.*

Boeck's itch, scabies (beks) [Carl William *Boeck*, Norwegian dermatologist, 1808–1875]. Norwegian scabies.

Boedeker's test (ba′dek-erz) [Carl Heinrich Detlef *Boedeker*, German chemist, 1815–1895]. See under *tests.*

Boerhaave's glands (boor′hahv-ez) [Hermann *Boerhaave*, Dutch physician, 1668–1738]. The sweat glands.

Boerhaavia (boor-hah′ve-ah) [Hermann *Boerhaave*]. A large genus of East India plants. **B. diffusa,** a species which contains a diuretic alkaloid.

Boettcher (bet′sher). See *Böttcher.*

Boettger. See *Böttger.*

Bogomolets' serum (Aleksandr Alexsandrovich *Bogomolets*, Russian biologist, 1881–1946]. Antireticular cytotoxic serum.

Bogros' space (bōg-rōz′) [Annet Jean *Bogros*, French anatomist, 1786–1823]. See under *space.*

Bogue's symptom (bōgz) [A. E. *Bogue*, American dentist, 1838–1921]. See under *symptom.*

boguskinin (bo″gus-ki′nin). A synthetic compound resembling bradykinin, but lacking one of the proline molecules and therefore inactive.

bohemium (bo-he′me-um). Rhenium.

Böhler splint (bāl′er) [Lorenz *Böhler*, Vienna surgeon, born 1885]. See under *splint.*

Bohun upas (bo′hun u′pas). The poison tree of Java, *Antiaris toxicaria.*

boil (boil). Furuncle. **Aleppo b., Bagdad b., Biskra b.,** cutaneous leishmaniasis. **blind b.,** a boil of brief duration which does not form a core. **Bulama b.** [from *Bulama*, an island of West Africa], a chronic sore of West Africa, said to be due to a burrowing insect larva. **Delhi b.,** cutaneous leishmaniasis. **Gafsa b.** [from *Gafsa*, in Tunis], a variety of oriental furunculus. **godovnik b.,** cutaneous leishmaniasis. **gum b.,** parulis. **Jerico b.,** cutaneous leishmaniasis. **madura b.,** mycetoma. **Natal b., oriental b., Penjdeh b.,** cutaneous leishmaniasis. **salt water b.,** a papular and pustular condition on the wrists and forearms of salt-water fishermen. **Scinde b.,** cutaneous leishmaniasis. **shoe b.,** capped elbow. **tropical b.,** cutaneous leishmaniasis.

Bol. Abbreviation for L. *bo′lus*, pill.

boldo (bol′do) [L. *boldus, boldoa*]. The leaves and stems of *Baldu* (*Peumus*) *boldus*, a tree of Chili.

boldoa (bol′do-ah) [L.]. Boldo.

boldoin (bol′do-in). A glycoside obtainable from boldo.

bole (bōl) [L. *bolus;* Gr. *bōlos* lump of earth]. A name of various earths, mostly clayey and of a dark color; usually astringent and absorbent iron tonics: used somewhat in veterinary surgery and externally in skin diseases. **Armenian b.,** a pale reddish bole from a native ferric oxide. **white b.,** kaolin.

Boletus (bo-le′tus) [L.; Gr. *bōlitēs*]. A genus of fungi or mushrooms, some of which are edible and others poisonous.

Bolk's retardation theory [Louis *Bolk*, Dutch anatomist, 1866–1930]. See under *theory.*

Bollinger's bodies, granules (bol′in-gerz) [Otto von *Bollinger*, German pathologist, 1843–1909]. See under *body* and *granule.*

bolometer (bo-lom′e-ter) [Gr. *bolē* a throw, a ray + *metron* measure]. 1. An instrument for measuring the force of the heart beat. 2. An instrument for measuring minute degrees of radiant heat.

boloscope (bo′lo-skōp) [Gr. *bolē* a ray + *skopein* to examine]. An apparatus for detecting and locating metallic foreign bodies in the tissues.

Boltz reaction, test [Oswald Herman *Boltz*, American neurologist, born 1895]. See under *tests.*

bolus (bo′lus) [L.; Gr. *bōlos* lump]. 1. A mass of food ready to be swallowed or a mass passing along the intestines. 2. In pharmacy a rounded mass larger than a pill. 3. In veterinary medicine a rounded mass for administration to an animal. 4. Bole. **b. al′ba,** kaolin. **alimentary b.,** the portion of food that is swallowed at one time.

bomb (bom). An apparatus containing a large quantity of radium or other radioactive element and so arranged as to permit the application of rays to any desired part of the body.

bombard (bom-bard′). To subject a body to the impingement of small particles or rays.

bombicesterol (bom″be-ses′ter-ol). A sterol obtained from the chrysalis of the silkworm and from sponges.

bond (bond). 1. The linkage between different atoms or radicals of a chemical compound. 2. A mark used to indicate the number and attachment of the valencies of an atom in constitutional formulas. It is represented by a dot or a line between the atoms, as H.O.H or H—O—H, Ca:O or

Ca=O, HC⋮CH or HC≡CH. **high energy phosphate b.,** an energy-rich phosphate linkage present in adenosine triphosphate, phosphocreatine, and certain other intermediates of carbohydrate metabolism. On hydrolysis it yields about 11,000 calories per mole, in contrast to the 3,000 calories of the ester phosphate bond. This energy can be transferred, stored, or used in metabolic processes, such as the synthesis of glycogen from glucose, or in the supply of energy for muscle activity. **hydrogen b.,** the weaker of the two bonds which function when a hydrogen atom joins two other atoms. **peptide b.,** a .CO.NH. group which forms the bond linking amino acids into peptides.

Bond's splint [Thomas *Bond*, Philadelphia physician and surgeon, 1712–1784]. See under *splint.*

bone (bōn) [L. *os;* Gr. *osteon*]. 1. The material of the skeleton of most vertebrate animals. It consists of connective tissue, the substratum of which is collagen, and which yields gelatin on boiling, impregnated with $Ca_{10}(PO_4)_6(OH)_2$. 2. Any distinct piece of the osseous framework or skeleton of the body. Called also *os.* **accessory b.,** an occasionally occurring bone or ossicle adjoining one of the bones of the carpus or of the tarsus: recognized in the roentgenogram. **acetabular b.,** acetabulum. **acromial b.,** acromion scapulae. **alar b.,** os sphenoidale. **Albers-Schönberg marble b's,** osteopetrosis. **Albrecht's b.,** basiotic b. **alisphenoid b.,** ala minor ossis sphenoidalis. **alveolar b.,** the bone forming the inner wall of the dental alveoli, in the form of a thin plate pierced by many small openings which transmit blood and lymph vessels and nerves. **ankle b.,** talus. **astragaloid b.,** talus. **astragaloscaphoid b.,** Pirie's b. **back b.,** the vertebral column. **basal b.,** the relatively fixed and unchangeable framework of the mandible and maxilla, which limits the extent to which teeth can be moved if the occlusion is to remain stable. **basihyal b.,** the body of the hyoid bone. **basilar b.,** basioccipital b. **basioccipital b.,** a bone developing from a separate ossification center in the fetus, which becomes the basilar process of the occipital bone. **basiotic b.,** a small bone of the fetus between the basisphenoid and the basioccipital bones. Called also *Albrecht's b.* **basisphenoid b.,** an embryonic bone which becomes the back part of the body of the sphenoid. **Bertin's b.,** concha sphenoidalis. **breast b.,** corpus sterni. **bregmatic b.,** os parietale. **brittle b's,** osteogenesis imperfecta. **bundle b.,** one of the two types of bone comprising the alveolar bone, so called because of the continuation into it of the principal fibers of the periodontal membrane. Cf. *lamellated b.* **calcaneal b.,** calcaneus. **calf b.,** fibula. **cancellated b.,** substantia spongiosa ossium. **cannon b.,** a bone in the limb of hoofed animals, extending from the fetlock to the knee or hock joint. **capitate b.,** os capitatum. **carpal b's,** the eight bones of the wrist. See *ossa carpi.* **carpal b., central,** os centrale. **carpal b., first,** os trapezium. **carpal b., fourth,** os hamatum. **carpal b., great,** os capitatum. **carpal b., intermediate,** os lunatum. **carpal b., radial,** os scaphoideum. **carpal b., second,** os trapezoideum. **carpal b., third,** os capitatum. **carpal b., ulnar,** os triquetrum. **cartilage b.,** any bone which develops within cartilage, in contrast to membrane bone, ossification taking place within a cartilage model. **cavalry b.,** rider's b. **central b.,** os centrale. **chalky b's,** osteopetrosis. **cheek b.,** os zygomaticum. **chevron b.,** the V-shaped hemal arches of the third, fourth, and fifth coccygeal vertebrae of a dog. **coccygeal b.,** coccyx. Also called *os coccygis.* **coffin b.,** the third or distal phalanx of the foot of a horse. **collar b.,** clavicula. **compact b.,** substantia compacta ossium. **coronary b.,** the small pastern bone of the horse. **cortical b.,** the solid portion of the shaft of a bone which surrounds the medullary cavity. **costal b.,** os costale. **cranial b's, b's of cranium,** the bones that constitute the cranial part of the skull, including the occipital, sphenoid, temporal, parietal, frontal, ethmoid, lacrimal and nasal bones, the inferior nasal concha, and vomer. Called also *ossa cranii.* **cribriform b.,** os ethmoidale. **cuboid b.,** os cuboideum. **cuckoo b.,** os coccygis. **cuneiform b. of carpus,** os triquetrum. **cuneiform b., external,** os cuneiforme laterale. **cuneiform b., first,** os cuneiforme mediale. **cuneiform b., intermediate,** os cuneiforme intermedium. **cuneiform b., internal,** os cuneiforme mediale. **cuneiform b., lateral,** os cuneiforme laterale. **cuneiform b., middle, cuneiform b., second,** os cuneiforme intermedium. **cuneiform b., third, dermal b.,** a bone developed by ossification in the skin. **ear b's,** auditory ossicles. **ectethmoid b's,** the lateral masses of the ethmoid bone. **ectocuneiform b.,** os cuneiforme laterale. **endochondral b.,** cartilage b. **entocuneiform b.,** os cuneiforme mediale. **epactal b's,** ossa suturarum. **epactal b., proper,** os interparietale. **ethmoid b.,** the sievelike bone that forms a roof for the nasal fossae and part of the floor of the anterior fossa of the skull. Called also *os ethmoidale.* **exercise b.,** a bone developed in a muscle, tendon, or fascia, as a result of excessive exercise. **exoccipital b.,** one of the two lateral portions of the occipital bone, developing, from separate centers of ossification, into the portions which bear the condyles. **b's of face, facial b's,** the bones that constitute the facial part of the skull, including the hyoid, palatine, and zygomatic bones, the mandible, and the maxilla. Called also *ossa faciei.* **femoral b.,** femur. **fibular b.,** fibula. **b's of fingers,** ossa digitorum manus. **flank b.,** os ilium. **flat b.,** one whose thickness is slight, sometimes consisting of only a thin layer of compact bone, or of two layers with intervening spongy bone and marrow; usually bent or curved, rather than flat. Called also *os plana.* **frontal b.,** a single bone that closes the front part of the cranial cavity and forms the skeleton of the forehead; it is developed from two halves, the line of separation sometimes persisting in adult life. Called also *os frontale.* **funny b.,** the region of the median condyle of the humerus, where it is crossed by the ulnar nerve. **hamate b.,** os hamatum. **haunch b.,** os coxae. **heel b.,** calcaneus. **hip b.,** os coxae. **humeral b.,** humerus. **hyoid b.,** a horseshoe-shaped bone situated at the base of the tongue, just above the thyroid cartilage. Called also *os hyoideum.* **iliac b.,** os ilium. **incarial b.,** os interparietale. **incisive b.,** os incisivum. **innominate b.,** os coxae. **intermaxillary b.,** os incisivum. **intermediate b.,** os lunatum. **interparietal b.,** os interparietale. **intrachondrial b.,** osseous tissue occurring in the lacunae of cartilage matrix which has undergone calcification; consistently found in patches within the middle layer of the otic capsule. **ischial b.,** os ischii. **jaw b., lower,** mandibula. **jaw b., upper,** maxilla. **jugal b.,** os zygomaticum. **lacrimal b.,** a thin scalelike bone at the anterior part of the medial wall of the orbit, articulating with the frontal and ethmoidal bones and the maxilla and inferior nasal concha. Called also *os lacrimale.* **lamellated b.,** one of the two types of bone comprising the alveolar bone, with some lamellae roughly parallel with the marrow spaces, and others forming haversian systems. Cf. *bundle b.* **lenticular b. of hand, lentiform b.,** os pisiforme. **lingual b.,** os hyoideum. **long b.,** a bone whose length exceeds its breadth and thickness. Called also *os longa.* **lunate b.,** os lunatum. **malar b.,** os zygomaticum. **marble b's,** osteopetrosis. **mastoid b.,** pars mastoidea ossis temporalis. **maxillary b.,** maxilla. **maxillary b., inferior,** mandible. **maxillary b., superior,** maxilla. **maxilloturbinal b.,** concha nasalis inferior ossea. **membrane b.,** any bone which develops within membrane, in contrast to cartilage bone. **mesocuneiform b.,** os cuneiforme intermedium.

metacarpal b's I-V, the five cylindrical bones of the hand. See *ossa metacarpalia.* **metatarsal b's,** the five bones extending from the tarsus to the phalanges of the toes, forming the skeleton of the metatarsus. Called also *ossa metatarsalia I-V.* **multangular b., accessory,** os centrale. **multangular b., larger,** os trapezium. **multangular b., smaller,** os trapezoideum. **nasal b.,** either of the two small oblong bones that together form the bridge of the nose. Called also *os nasale.* **navicular b. of foot,** os naviculare. **navicular b. of hand,** os scaphoideum. **occipital b.,** a single trapezoidal-shaped bone situated at the posterior and inferior part of the cranium. See *os occipitale.* **odontoid b.,** dens axis. **orbital b.,** os zygomaticum. **orbitosphenoidal b.,** ala minor ossis sphenoidalis. **palate b.,** palatine b. **palatine b.,** the irregularly shaped bone forming the posterior part of the hard palate, the lateral wall of the nasal fossa between the medial pterygoid plate and the maxilla, and the posterior part of the floor of the orbit. Called also *os palatinum.* **parietal b.,** one of the two quadrilateral bones forming part of the superior and lateral surfaces of the skull, and joining each other in the midline at the sagittal suture. Called also *os parietale.* **pastern b.,** either of two bones of the horse's foot: *large pastern b.,* the first phalanx of a horse's foot; *small pastern b.,* the second phalanx of a horse's foot. **pedal b.,** coffin b. **pelvic b.,** os coxae. **periosteal b.,** bone which is developed directly from and beneath the periosteum. **petrosal b., petrous b.,** pars petrosa ossis temporalis. **phalangeal b's of foot,** ossa digitorum pedis. **phalangeal b's of hand,** ossa digitorum manus. **Pirie's b.,** an occasionally occurring ossicle found above the head of the talus. **pisiform b.,** os pisiforme. **pneumatic b.,** one that contains air-filled cavities or sinuses. Called also *os pneumaticum.* **postulnar b.,** os pisiforme. **prefrontal b.,** pars nasalis ossis frontalis. **prefrontal b. of von Bardeleben,** processus frontalis maxillae. **preinterparietal b.,** a wormian bone which is sometimes observed, detached from the anterior part of the interparietal bone. **premaxillary b.,** os incisivum. **presphenoidal b.,** os sphenoidale. **pterygoid b.,** processus pterygoideus ossis sphenoidalis. **pubic b.,** the anterior inferior part of the hip bone on either side. See *os pubis.* **pyramidal b.,** os triquetrum. **radial b.,** radius. **replacement b.,** cartilage b. **resurrection b.,** sacrum. **rider's b.,** an ossification sometimes seen in the tendon of the adductor muscle of the thigh in those who ride on horseback. **Riolan's b's,** small bones resembling wormian bones, sometimes found in the suture between the occipital bone and the petrous portion of the temporal bone. **rudimentary b.,** a bone that has only partially developed. **sacral b.,** os sacrum. **scaphoid b.,** os scaphoideum. **scaphoid b. of foot,** os naviculare. **scaphoid b. of hand,** os scaphoideum. **scapular b.,** scapula. **semilunar b.,** os lunatum. **sesamoid b's,** a type of short bone occurring mainly in the hands and feet, and found embedded in tendons or joint capsules. Called also *ossa sesamoidea.* **sesamoid b's of foot,** ossa sesamoidea pedis. **sesamoid b's of hand,** ossa sesamoidea manus. **shin b.,** tibia. **short b.,** one whose main dimensions are approximately equal. Called also *os breve.* **b's of skull,** ossa cranii. **sphenoid b.,** a single, irregular, wedge-shaped bone at the base of the skull, which forms a part of the floor of the anterior, middle, and posterior cranial fossae. Called also *os sphenoidale.* **sphenoturbinal b.,** concha sphenoidalis. **splint b's,** the reduced second and fourth metacarpal and metatarsal bones of the Equidae. **spoke b.,** radius. **spongy b.,** substantia spongiosa ossium. **spongy b., inferior,** concha nasalis inferior ossea. **spongy b., superior,** concha nasalis superior ossea. **squamooccipital b.,** the squamous portion of the fetal occipital bone, including the supraoccipital and interparietal bones. **squamous b.,** pars squamosa ossis temporalis. **stifle b.,** the patella of the horse. **stirrup b.,** stapes. **substitution b.,** cartilage b. **supernumerary b.,** a bone occurring in addition to the normal one, as a vertebra or a rib (cervical rib). **suprainterparietal b.,** a wormian bone sometimes occurring at the posterior part of the sagittal suture. **supraoccipital b.,** a bone developing from a separate ossification center in the fetus, which becomes the squamous part of the temporal bone below the superior nuchal line. **suprapharyngeal b.,** os sphenoidale. **suprasternal b's,** ossa suprasternalia. **sutural b's,** ossa suturarum. **tarsal b's,** the seven bones of the ankle. See *ossa tarsi.* **tarsal b., first,** os cuneiforme mediale. **tarsal b., second,** os cuneiforme intermedium. **tarsal b., third,** os cuneiforme laterale. **temporal b.,** one of the two irregular bones forming part of the lateral surfaces and base of the skull, and containing the organs of hearing. Called also *os temporale.* **thigh b.,** femur. **b's of toes,** ossa digitorum pedis. **tongue b.,** os hyoideum. **trapezium b.,** os trapezium. **trapezium b., lesser,** os trapezoideum. **trapezium b. of Lyser,** os trapezoideum. **trapezoid b.,** os trapezoideum. **trapezoid b. of Henle,** processus pterygoideus ossis sphenoidalis. **trapezoid b., of Lyser,** os trapezium. **triangular b.,** os triquetrum. **triangular b. of tarsus,** os trigonum tarsi. **triquetral b.,** os triquetrum. **turbinate b., highest,** concha nasalis suprema ossea. **turbinate, inferior b.,** concha nasalis inferior ossea. **turbinate b., middle,** concha nasalis media ossea. **turbinate b., superior,** concha nasalis superior ossea. **turbinate b., supreme,** concha nasalis suprema ossea. **tympanic b.,** pars tympanica ossis temporalis. **ulnar b.,** ulna. **unciform b., uncinate b.,** os hamatum. **vesalian b.,** os vesalianum. **vomer b.,** vomer. **whettle b's,** thoracic vertebrae. **whirl b.** 1. The patella. 2. The head of the femur. **wormian b's,** ossa suturarum. **xiphoid b.,** sternum. **zygomatic b.,** the triangular bone of the cheek. See *os zygomaticum.*

bonelet (bōn′let). A small bone, or ossicle.

boneplasty (bōn′plas-te). Plastic surgery on bone.

Bonfils' disease (bawn-fēs′) [Emile Adolphe *Bonfils,* French physician of the 19th century]. Hodgkin's disease.

Bonhoeffer's symptom (bon′hef-erz) [Karl *Bonhoeffer,* psychiatrist in Berlin, 1868–1948]. See under *symptom.*

bonine (bo′nēn). Trade mark for preparations of meclizine hydrochloride.

Bonnaire's method (bon-ārz′) [Erasme *Bonnaire,* French obstetrician, 1858–1918]. See under *method.*

Bonnet's capsule (bo-nāz′) [Amédée *Bonnet,* French surgeon, 1802–1858]. The capsule enclosing the posterior part of the eyeball. See *vaginae bulbi.*

Bonnier's syndrome (bon-e-āz) [Pierre *Bonnier,* French physician, 1861–1918]. See under *syndrome.*

Bonwill triangle (bon′wil) [William Gibson Arlington *Bonwill,* American dentist, 1833–1899]. See under *triangle.*

Boophilus (bo-of′ĭ-lus) [Gr. *bous* ox + *philein* to love]. A genus of cattle ticks. **B. annula′tus, B. bo′vis,** the southern cattle tick which transmits *Babesia bigemina.* **B. decolora′tus,** a tick of South Africa which serves as the means of transmitting the anaplasma of galziekte. **B. microplus,** the common cattle tick in Panama: it transmits Texas fever.

boopia (bo-o′pe-ah) [Gr. *bous* ox + ōps eye]. The languishing oxlike eyes of hysterical patients.

Booponus (bo-op′o-nus) [Gr. *bous* ox + *ponos* pain]. A fly of the Philippines whose larvae (foot maggots) cause lameness in cattle and goats.

booster (bo͞ost′er). An agent or means by which energy or an effect may be increased, such as a device for increasing the electromotive force in an alternating current circuit or a device such as a dynamo in series to increase the voltage in a direct current circuit. See also under *dose*.

boot (bo͞ot). An encasement for the foot. **Junod's b.,** an air-tight boot to which is fitted an air pump. A partial vacuum causes a flow of blood to the parts inclosed in the boot, producing the effect of bloodletting by causing a fainting spell. **Unna's paste b.,** a dressing for varicose ulcers, consisting of a paste made from gelatin, zinc oxide and glycerin, which is applied to the entire leg, then covered with a spiral bandage, this in turn being given a coat of the paste: the process is repeated until satisfactory rigidity is attained.

borate (bo′rāt). Any salt or boric acid.

borated (bo′rāt-ed). Combined with or containing borax or boric acid.

borax (bo′raks), gen. *bora′cis* [L. from Arabic; Persian *būrah*]. Sodium borate.

borborygmus (bor″bo-rig′mus), pl. *borboryg′mi* [L.]. The rumbling noises caused by the propulsion of flatus through the intestines.

Borchardt's test (bor′chartz) [Leo *Borchardt*, German chemist, born 1879]. See under *tests*.

border (bor′der). A bounding line, or edge borders of various anatomical structures not included here, see entries under *margo*. **b. of acetabulum,** labrum acetabulare. **alveolar b. of mandible,** arcus alveolaris mandibulae. **alveolar b. of maxilla,** arcus alveolaris maxillae. **brush b.,** a specialization of the free surface of a cell, consisting of minute cylindrical processes which greatly increase the surface area; noted especially on the cells of the proximal convolution in a renal tubule. **external b. of tibia,** facies lateralis tibiae. **inferior b. of mandible,** basis mandibulae. **orbital b. of sphenoid bone,** facies orbitalis alae majoris. **b. of oval fossa,** limbus fossae ovalis. **posterior b. of petrous portion of temporal bone,** angulus posterior pyramidis ossis temporalis. **posterointernal b. of fibula,** crista medialis fibulae. **striated b.,** a specialization of the free surface of a cell, consisting of rodlike structures which greatly increase the surface area; noted especially on the intestinal epithelium of all vertebrates. **superior b. of patella,** basis patellae. **superior b. of petrous portion of temporal bone,** angulus superior pyramidis ossis temporalis. **vermilion b.,** the exposed red portion of the upper or lower lip.

Bordet's phenomenon (bor-dāz′) [Jules Jean Baptiste Vincent *Bordet*, Belgian bacteriologist, 1870–1961; winner of Nobel prize in medicine and physiology for 1919]. See under *phenomenon*.

Bordetella (bor″dě-tel′lah) [Jules Jean Baptiste Vincent *Bordet*]. A genus of microorganisms of the family Brucellaceae, order Eubacteriales, made up of minute motile or non-motile gram-negative coccobacilli which are parasitic and produce a dermonecrotic toxin. **B. pertus′sis,** the causative agent of whooping cough in man. **B. parapertus′sis,** a microorganism occasionally found in whooping cough in man. **B. bronchisep′tica,** the causative agent of bronchopneumonia of guinea pigs and other rodents.

borism (bo′rizm). Poisoning by a boron compound.

borjom (bor′jom). A natural mineral water from Caucasia.

Borna disease [*Borna*, a district in Saxony where an epidemic occurred]. See under *disease*.

Bornholm disease (born′hōm) [named from the Danish island, *Bornholm*]. Epidemic pleurodynia.

boroglyceride (bo″ro-glis′er-id). Boroglycerin.

boroglycerin (bo″ro-glis′er-in). A compound ($C_3H_5BO_3$) prepared by heating 2 parts of boric acid and 3 parts of glycerin. **b. glycerite,** a preparation of boric acid and glycerin, containing between 47.5 and 52.5 per cent of boroglycerin: used as an antibacterial.

boroglycerol (bo″ro-glis′er-ol). Boroglycerin.

boron (bo′ron) [L. *borium*]. A nonmetallic element occurring in the form of crystals and as a powder. It is the base of borax and boric acid: symbol, B; atomic number 5; specific gravity, 2.54; atomic weight, 10.811. **b. carbide,** a substance, BoC, obtained by heating boron at an extremely high temperature to effect its union with carbon, used in dentistry as an abrasive agent.

Borrelia (bor-re′le-ah) [Amédée *Borrel*, French bacteriologist in Strasbourg, 1867–1936]. A genus of microorganisms of the family Treponemataceae, order Spirochaetales, made up of cells 8 to 16 μ long, with coarse, shallow, irregular spirals, generally tapering into fine filaments at the ends; parasitic in many animals, some of them causing relapsing fever in birds and in man and other mammals. Twenty-eight different species have been described. **B. anseri′na,** the etiologic agent of fowl spirochetosis, transmitted by species of Argas ticks, nonpathogenic for man. **B. ber′bera,** the causative agent of relapsing fever in North Africa, thought to be transmitted by the human body louse. **B. bucca′lis,** a parasite of the human oral cavity which has slight pathogenicity. **B. car′teri,** the etiologic agent of Indian relapsing fever, transmitted by the human body louse. **B. caucas′ica,** an etiologic agent of relapsing fever in the Caucasus, transmitted by *Ornithodoros verrucosus* from a reservoir of infection in field mice. **B. dutto′nii,** an etiologic agent of relapsing fever in central and south Africa, transmitted by *Ornithodoros moubata*. **B. herm′sii,** an etiologic agent of relapsing fever in western United States and Canada, transmitted by *Ornithodoros hermsi* but not by other species of ticks. **B. hispan′ica,** the etiologic agent of relapsing fever in the Iberian peninsula and northwest Africa, transmitted by Ornithodoros ticks. **B. ko′chii,** an etiologic agent of African relapsing fever, considered to be identical with *B. duttonii*. **B. par′keri,** an etiologic agent of relapsing fever in western United States, transmitted by *Ornithodoros parkeri* but not by other species of Ornithodoros. **B. per′sica,** an etiologic agent of relapsing fever in Iran, transmitted by *Ornithodoros tholozani*. **B. recurren′tis,** the causative agent of relapsing fever transmitted by the human body louse; considered by some to include all relapsing fever spirochetes, other named species being regarded as serotypes or serological variants of a single species of organisms. **B. turica′tae,** an etiologic agent of relapsing fever in southwestern United States, transmitted by *Ornithodoros turicata* but not by other species of Ornithodoros. **B. venezuelen′sis,** an etiologic agent of relapsing fever in northern South America and Central America, transmitted by *Ornithodoros rudis*. **B. vincen′tii,** a parasite of the human oral cavity, occurring in large numbers with a fusiform bacillus in Vincent's angina.

Borsieri's line (bor″se-er′ēz) [Giovanni Battista *Borsieri*, French physician, 1725–1785]. See under *line*.

borsten (bor′sten) [Fin. "bristles"]. A cutaneous disease of new-born infants in Finland, due to irritation of the sebaceous glands, producing goose flesh with fever.

Borthen's operation (bor′tenz) [Johan *Borthen*, Norwegian oculist]. Iridotasis.

bos (bos) [L.]. Cow. **b. sin′icus,** schistosoma infection in cattle.

Bose's hooks (bo′sez) [Heinrich *Bose*, German surgeon, 1840–1900]. See under *hook*.

boss (bos). A rounded eminence, as on the surface of a bone or of a tumor.

bosselated (bos′e-lāt-ed) [Fr. *bosseler*]. Marked or covered with small bosses.

bosselation (bos″e-la′shun). 1. A small eminence; one of a set of small bosses. 2. The condition or fact of being bosselated; the process of becoming bosselated.

Bossi's dilator (bos'ēz) [Luigi Maria *Bossi*, gynecologist in Genoa, 1859–1919]. See under *dilator*.

Bostock's catarrh (bos'toks) [John *Bostock*, English physician, 1773–1846]. See under *catarrh*.

Boston's sign (bos'tonz) [L. Napoleon *Boston*, American physician, 1871–1931]. See under *sign*.

bot (bot). The larva of botflies, which may be parasitic in the stomach of animals and sometimes in that of man. **sheep nose b.,** the larva of *Oestrus ovis*, which is frequently found in the nasal passages of sheep.

Botallo's duct, foramen, etc. [Leonardo *Botallo*, Italian surgeon in Paris, born 1530]. See under the nouns.

botanic (bo-tan'ik). 1. Pertaining to or derived from plants; of the vegetable kingdom. 2. Pertaining to botany.

botany (bot'ah-ne) [L. *botanica* from Gr. *botanē* herb]. The science of plants or of the vegetable kingdom. **medical b.,** the botany of plants used in medicine.

Botelho's test (bo-tel'yōz) [Dr. *Botelho*, physician in Paris]. See under *tests*.

botfly (bot'fli). An insect of the order Diptera, family Oestridae, whose larvae are parasitic in animals, especially horses and sheep. The genera include Oestrus, Gasterophilus, Dermatobia, and Cuterebra.

bothridium (both-rid'e-um). Bothrium.

bothriocephaliasis (both″re-o-sef″ah-li'ah-sis). Diphyllobothriasis.

Bothriocephalus (both″re-o-sef'ah-lus) [Gr. *bothrion* pit + *kephalē* head]. Diphyllobothrium.

bothrium (both're-um) [Gr. *bothrion* pit]. A sucker in the form of a groove such as is seen on the head of *Dibothriocephalus latus*.

bothropik (both-rop'ik). Pertaining to, characteristic of, or derived from snakes of the genus *Bothrops*.

Bothrops (both-rops) [Gr. *bothros* pit + *ōps* eye]. A genus of South American serpents. *B. atrox* is the fer-de-lance. *B. jararaca*. See *jararaca*.

botogenin (bot-o-je'nin). A substance derived from *Dioscorea mexicana*, which may prove a source for the extraction of cortisone.

botryoid (bot're-oid) [Gr. *botrys* bunch of grapes + *eidos* form]. Resembling a bunch of grapes.

botryomycosis (bot″re-o-mi-ko'sis). A purulent granulomatous infection in horses and camels and sometimes in cattle, caused by *Micrococcus ascoformans:* called also *staphylococcal actinophytosis* and *scirrhus cord* (Bollinger, 1869). **b. hom'inis,** granuloma pyogenicum.

botryomycotic (bot″re-o-mi-kot'ik). Pertaining to or affected with botryomycosis.

botryotherapy (bot-re-o-ther'ah-pe) [Gr. *botrys* cluster of grapes + *therapeia* therapy]. The grape cure.

botrytimycosis (bo-tri″te-mi-ko'sis). Infection with fungi of the genus Botrytis.

Botrytis (bo-tri'tis). A genus of fungi. **B. bassia'na,** causes the disease muscardine in silkworms. **B. tenel'la,** causes a disease of the larvae of May beetles.

bots (bots). A name given the diseased condition in horses and other animals, attributed to the presence of larvae of botflies of various genera.

Böttcher's cells, crystals, etc. (bet'sherz) [Arthur *Böttcher*, German anatomist, 1831–1889]. See under the nouns.

Böttger's test (bet'gerz). 1. [Rudolf *Böttger*, German chemist, 1806–1881]. See under *tests*, def. 1. 2. [Wilhelm Carl *Böttger*, German chemist, 1871–1949]. See under *tests*, def. 2.

Bottini's operation (bo-te'nēz) [Enrico *Bottini*, Italian surgeon, 1837–1903]. See under *operation*.

bottle (bot″l). A hollow, narrow-necked vessel of glass or other material, used in laboratory procedures or for other purposes. **Senoran's b.,** a bottle used in withdrawing stomach contents after a test meal. **Spritz b.,** a wash bottle for laboratory use. **wash b.** 1. A bottle having two tubes through the cork, and so arranged that blowing into one will force a stream of water from the other: used in washing chemical materials. 2. A bottle containing some washing fluid, through which gases are passed for the purpose of freeing them from impurities. **Woulfe's b.,** a three-necked bottle used for washing gases or for saturating liquids with a gas.

botuliform (bot-u'lĭ-form) [L. *botulus* sausage + *forma* shape]. Sausage-shaped.

botulin (bot'u-lin) [L. *botulus* sausage]. A highly active neurotoxin sometimes found in imperfectly preserved or canned meats and vegetables: it is produced by *Clostridium botulinum* and is peculiar in that it resists the action of the gastric juice.

botulinogenic (bot″u-lin″o-jen'ik) [*botulin* + Gr. *gennan* to produce]. Producing or containing botulin.

botulism (bot'u-lizm) [L. *botulus* sausage]. A type of food poisoning caused by a toxin which is produced by the growth of *Clostridium botulinum* in improperly canned or preserved foods. It is characterized by vomiting, abdominal pain, difficulty of vision, nervous symptoms of central origin, disturbances of secretion, motor disturbances, dryness of the mouth and pharynx, dyspepsia, a barking cough, mydriasis, ptosis, etc.

botulismotoxin (bot″u-liz″mo-tok'sin). Botulin.

bouba (boo'bah). A form of oriental sore (leishmaniasis) endemic in Brazil and Paraguay. See *leishmaniasis americana*.

Bouchard's coefficient, disease, nodes, sign (boo-sharz') [Charles Jacques *Bouchard*, French physician, 1837–1915]. See under the nouns.

Bouchardat's test (boo-shar-dahz') [Apollinaire *Bouchardat*, French chemist, 1806–1886]. See under *tests*.

bouche (boosh') [Fr.]. Mouth. **b. de tapir** (de tah-pēr'), tapir mouth.

bouchon (boo-shaw') [Fr.]. An internal clot.

Bouchut's respiration, tube (boo-shooz') [Jean Antoine Eugéne *Bouchut*, French physician, 1818–1891]. See under *respiration* and *tube*.

Boudin's law (boo-dahz') [Jean Christian Marie François Joseph *Boudin*, French physician, 1806–1867]. See under *law*.

Bougard's paste (boo-garz') [Jean Joseph *Bougard*, French physician, 1815–1884]. See under *paste*.

bougie (boo-zhe') [Fr. "wax candle"]. 1. A slender cylinder for introduction into the urethra, or a large one for the rectum or some other orifice. 2. A taper-shaped medicinal preparation for introduction into the urethra, rectum, or other orifice. **b. à boule** (ah-bool') [Fr.], a bulbous bougie. **acorn-tipped b.,** one of the forms of bulbous bougies. **armed b.,** caustic b. **bellied b.,** fusiform b. **bulbous b.,** one with a bulb-shaped tip. **caustic b.,** one which has a piece of silver nitrate or other caustic attached to its end: a form of portcaustic. **conic b.,** a form with a cone-shaped tip. **cylindrical b.,** one with a round or circular section. **dilatable b.,** one whose diameter can be increased by turning a screw, or which swells in its place like a surgeon's tent. **dilating b.,** one which is designed to effect the dilatation of a stricture. **ear b.,** one for use in aural surgery. **elastic b.,** one made of India rubber or other elastic material. **elbowed b.,** one shaped like a *sonde coudé*. **exploring b.,** one designed to be used like a probe. **filiform b.,** one of very slender and almost hair-like caliber. **fusiform b.,** one with a belly or expansion in its shaft. **Gruber's b's,** bougies

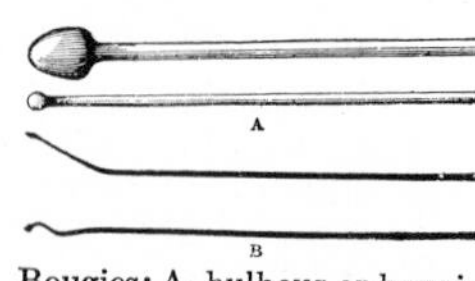

Bougies: A, bulbous or bougie à boule; B, filiform.

of medicated gelatin for insertion into the auditory meatus. **medicated b.,** one which is charged with a medicinal substance. **olive-tipped b.,** a form of bulbous bougie. **rosary b.,** a beaded bougie for use in a strictured urethra. **soluble b.,** one composed of a material that will melt or dissolve in situ. **wax b.,** one made of linen, gauze, or silk dipped in melted wax and then rolled. **whip b.,** one with a filiform point and a stem of gradually increasing caliber.

bougienage (boo-zhe-nahzh′). The passage of a bougie through a body orifice or through a tubular organ, as a means of increasing its caliber, as in treatment of stricture of the esophagus.

bouginage (boo-zhe-nahzh′). Bougienage.

Bouillaud's disease, tinkle (boo-e-yōz′) [Jean Baptiste *Bouillaud,* French physician, 1796–1881]. See under *disease* and *tinkle.*

bouillon (boo-e-yaw′) [Fr.]. A broth or soup prepared from the flesh of animals: used in food preparations and as a bacteriological culture medium. See also *culture medium.* **ascitic b.,** a mixture of ascitic, pleuritic, or hydrocele fluid with nutrient bouillon. **calcium carbonate b.,** nutritive bouillon containing dextrose and calcium carbonate: used for obtaining mass cultures of the pneumococcus or of the streptococcus. The calcium carbonate neutralizes acids formed during the growth of the bacteria. **carbolized b.,** nutrient bouillon containing phenol. **dextrose b.,** nutrient bouillon containing dextrose. **Durham's inosite-free b.** See *inosite-free b.* **egg-albumen b.,** a bacteriological culture medium containing dried egg-albumen, tenth-normal sodium hydroxide, water, and nutrient bouillon. **b. filtre,** 5 per cent glycerin bouillon in which tubercle germs have grown. For use it is sterilized by filtration through porcelain, but it is not concentrated or heated. **fish b.,** a nutritive bouillon in which fish water is used in place of meat extract. **Gasperini's wheat b.** See *wheat b.* **glucose-formate b.,** nutrient bouillon containing glucose and sodium formate. **glycerin b.,** nutrient bouillon containing glycerin. **glycerin-potato b.,** a cold water extract of grated potatoes containing glycerin. **haricot b.,** an extract of haricot beans with salt and cane sugar. **hydrocele b.** See *ascitic b.* **inosite-free b.,** nutrient bouillon in which *Bacillus coli* or some other sugar-fermenting organism has grown and thus removed all sugars. It is then clarified and sterilized. **iron b.,** nutrient bouillon containing ferric tartrate or ferric lactate. **Kitasato's glucose-formate b.** See *glucose-formate b.* **lactose-litmus b.,** nutrient bouillon containing lactose and sufficient litmus to color it a deep purple. **lead b.,** nutrient bouillon containing lead acetate. **litmus b.,** nutrient bouillon containing enough litmus solution to give it a dark lavender color. **MacConkey's b.,** bouillon containing bile salts and sugars. **malachite green b.,** nutrient bouillon with malachite green. **malt extract b.,** a nutritive medium made by dissolving powdered malt extract in water; adjusting the reaction to plus 1.5 to phenolphthalein and heating in the autoclave for fifteen minutes, filtering through paper and sterilizing. **Martin's b.,** a preparation of peptone from digested pig's stomach and cattle or rabbit's serum. **meat extract b.,** one prepared with commercial meat extract. **meat infusion b.** See *nutrient b.* **nitrate b.,** nutrient bouillon containing potassium nitrate. **nutrient b.,** meat infusion with added peptone and salt. The reaction is usually set at a desired point and then the whole is sterilized. **Parietti's b.,** nutrient bouillon containing small amounts of a mixture of hydrochloric acid and phenol solution. **pleuritic b.** See *ascitic b.* **Reddish's malt extract b.** See *malt extract b.* **serum b.,** a mixture of horse serum and nutrient bouillon. **sugar b.** See *dextrose b.* **sulfindigotate b.,** nutrient bouillon containing glucose and sodium sulfindigotate. **Weyl's sulfindigotate b.** See *sulfindigotate b.* **wheat b.,** a nutritive medium made from wheat flour, magnesium sulfate, potassium nitrate, and glucose, in water.

Bouin's fluid (bwahz′) [Paul *Bouin,* French anatomist, born 1870]. See under *fluid.*

boulimia (boo-lim′e-ah). Bulimia.

bound (bownd). 1. Restrained or confined; not free. 2. Held in chemical combination.

bouquet (boo-ka′) [Fr.]. 1. A structure suggesting resemblance to a bunch of flowers, as a cluster of vessels, nerves, or fibers, or the polarized stage of synapsis at the start of meiosis. 2. Dengue.

bourbonal (bo͝or′bo-nal). Ethyl vanillin.

Bourdin's paste (boor-dahz′) [Claude Étienne *Bourdin,* French physician, born 1815]. See under *paste.*

bourdonnement (boor-don-maw′) [Fr.]. A humming or buzzing sound.

Bourgery's ligament (boor′jer-ēz) [Marc-Jean *Bourgery,* French anatomist and surgeon, 1797–1849]. Ligamentum popliteum obliquum.

Bourget's test (boor-zhāz′) [Louis *Bourget,* Swiss physician, 1856–1913]. See under *tests.*

Bourneville's disease (boor′ne-vēz) [Désiré-Magloire *Bourneville,* neurologist in Paris, 1840–1909]. See under *disease.*

bout (bout). An attack.

bouton (boo-taw′) [Fr.]. Button. **b. de Biskra, b. d'orient,** cutaneous leishmaniasis. **b's terminaux′,** end-feet.

boutonneuse (boo-ton-ez′). Boutonneuse fever.

boutonnière (boo-ton-yār′). An incision made into the urethra in order to extract an impacted calculus.

Bouveret's disease, sign, ulcer (boo-ver-āz′) [Léon *Bouveret,* French physician, 1850–1929]. See under *disease, sign,* and *ulcer.*

Boveri's test (bo′va-rēz) [Piero *Boveri,* Italian neurologist, 1879–1932]. See under *tests.*

Bovet (bo′vet), Daniel. Italian pharmacologist, born 1907; winner of the Nobel prize in medicine and physiology for 1957, for work that led to development of antihistamines and muscle relaxants.

Bovimyces pleuropneumoniae (bo″ve-mi′sēz ploor″o-nu-mo′ne-e). *Asterococcus mycoides.*

bovine (bo′vīn) [L. *bovinus*]. Pertaining to, characteristic of, or derived from the ox (cattle).

bovinoid (bo′vĭ-noid) [*bovine* + Gr. *eidos* form]. Resembling that of the ox; a term applied to a form of tubercle bacillus found in man and resembling true bovine tubercle bacilli.

bovovaccination (bo″vo-vak″sĭ-na′shun). Vaccination with bovovaccine.

bovovaccine (bo-vo-vak′sēn). An attenuated and ground human tubercle bacillus used by von Behring for protective inoculation against bovine tuberculosis.

Bowditch's law (bow′dich) [Henry Pickering *Bowditch,* Boston physiologist, 1840–1911]. See under *law.* See also *treppe.*

bowel (bow′el) [Fr. *boyau*]. The intestine. **greedy b.,** a condition marked by abnormally copious intestinal absorption of alimentary material.

Bowen's disease (bo′enz) [John T. *Bowen,* American dermatologist, 1857–1941]. See under *disease.*

bowleg (bo′leg). An outward curve of one or both legs at or below the knee: genu varum.

Bowman's capsule, membrane, theory, etc. (bo′manz) [Sir William *Bowman,* an English physician, 1816–1892]. See under the nouns.

box (boks). A rectangular structure. **fracture b.,** a long box, without cover or ends, to support a broken limb.

boxing (boks′ing). In dentistry, the building up of vertical walls, usually in wax, around the impression to produce the desired size and form of the base of the cast, and to preserve certain landmarks of the impression.

box-note (boks′nōt). A hollow sound heard in percussing the chest in emphysema.

Boyer's bursa, cyst (bwah-yāz′) [Alexis, Baron, *de Boyer*, French surgeon, 1757–1833]. See under *bursa* and *cyst*.

Boyle's law (boilz) [Robert *Boyle*, British physicist, 1627–1691]. See under *law*.

Bozeman's catheter, position, etc. (bōz′manz) [Nathan *Bozeman*, American surgeon, 1825–1905]. See under the nouns.

Bozeman-Fritsch catheter (bōz′man-fritsh) [Nathan *Bozeman;* Heinrich *Fritsch*, German gynecologist, 1844–1915]. See under *catheter*.

Bozzolo's sign (bot′tso-lōz) [Camillo *Bozzolo*, Italian physician, 1845–1920]. See under *sign*.

B. P. Abbreviation for *blood pressure, British Pharmacopocia*, and *buccopulpal*.

b.p. Abbreviation for *boiling point*.

B. Ph. Abbreviation for *British Pharmacopoeia*.

Br. Chemical symbol for *bromine*.

bracelet (brās′let). A small encircling band, applied, in the plural, to transverse markings across the palmar surface of the skin of the wrists. **Nageotte's b's,** bands covered with circular spines on the axons at the level of the nodes of Ranvier. **Nussbaum's b.,** a device for assisting a person with writers' cramp.

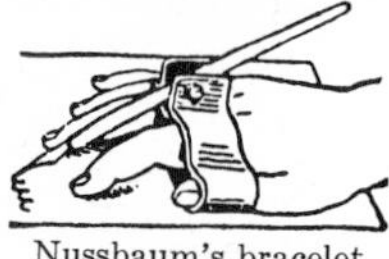

Nussbaum's bracelet (Guttmann).

brachia (bra′ke-ah) [L.]. Plural of *brachium*.

brachial (bra′ke-al) [L. *brachialis*, from *brachium* arm]. Pertaining to the arm.

brachialgia (bra″ke-al′je-ah) [Gr. *brachiōn* arm + *-algia*]. Pain in the arm or arms. **b. stat′ica paraesthet′ica,** painful paresthesias in arm and hand during sleep.

brachiation (bra″ke-a′shun) [L. *brachium* + *-ation* suffix implying action]. Locomotion in a position of suspension by means of the hands and arms, as exhibited by monkeys when swinging from branch to branch.

brachiocephalic (brak″e-o-se-fal′ik) [Gr. *brachiōn* arm + *kephalē* head]. Pertaining to the arm and head.

brachiocrural (brak″e-o-kroo′ral). Pertaining to the arm and thigh.

brachiocubital (brak″e-o-ku′bĭ-tal) [Gr. *brachiōn* arm + L. *cubitus* forearm]. Pertaining to the arm and forearm.

brachiocyllosis (brak″e-o-sĭ-lo′sis) [Gr. *brachiōn* arm + *kyllōsis* a crooking]. Crookedness of the arm.

brachiocyrtosis (brak″e-o-ser-to′sis) [Gr. *brachiōn* arm + *kyrtos* bent]. Crookedness of the arm.

brachiofaciolingual (brak″e-o-fa″she-o-ling′gwal). Pertaining to or affecting the arm, the face, and the tongue.

brachiogram (brak′e-o-gram). A tracing of the pulse beat at the brachial artery.

brachiotomy (bra″ke-ot′o-me) [Gr. *brachiōn* arm + *tomē* a cut]. The surgical or obstetrical cutting or removal of an arm.

brachiplex (bra′ke-pleks). The brachial plexus.

brachium (bra′ke-um), pl. *bra′chia* [L.; Gr. *brachiōn*]. [N A, B N A] 1. The arm; specifically the arm from shoulder to elbow. 2. A general term used to designate an armlike process or structure. **b. cerebel′li,** pedunculus cerebellaris superior. **b. cer′ebri,** b. colliculi superioris. **b. collic′uli inferio′ris** [N A], fibers from the lateral lemniscus that pass deep to the inferior colliculus and run forward to terminate in the medial geniculate body. Called also *b. quadrigeminum inferius* [B N A], and *b. of inferior colliculus.* **b. collic′uli superio′ris** [N A], fibers from the optic tract that pass dorsal to the medial geniculate body to enter the superior colliculus. Called also *b. quadrigeminum superius* [B N A], and *b. of superior colliculus.* **conjunctival b., anterior,** b. colliculi superioris. **conjunctival b., posterior,** b. colliculi inferioris. **b. conjuncti′vum ante′rius,** b. colliculi superioris. **b. conjuncti′vum cerebel′li** [B N A], pedunculus cerebellaris superior. **b. conjuncti′vum poste′rius,** b. colliculi inferioris. **b. copulati′vum,** pedunculus cerebellaris superior. **b. of inferior colliculus,** b. colliculi inferioris. **b. of mesencephalon, inferior,** b. colliculi inferioris. **b. of mesencephalon, superior,** b. colliculi superioris. **b. pon′tis** [B N A], pedunculus cerebellaris medius. **b. quadrigem′inum infe′rius** [B N A], b. colliculi inferioris. **b. quadrigem′inum supe′rius** [B N A], b. colliculi superius. **b. of superior colliculus,** b. colliculi superioris.

brachy- (brak′e) [Gr. *brachys* short]. A combining form meaning short.

brachybasia (brak″e-ba′se-ah) [*brachy-* + Gr. *basis* walking]. A slow, shuffling, short stepped gait, such as seen in double hemiplegia.

brachycardia (brak″e-kar′de-ah). Bradycardia.

brachycephalia (brak″e-se-fa′le-ah). Brachycephaly.

brachycephalic (brak″e-se-fal′ik) [*brachy-* + Gr. *kephalē* head]. Having a cephalic index of 81.0–85.4.

brachycephalism (brak″e-sef′ah-lizm). Brachycephaly.

brachycephalous (brak″e-sef′ah-lus). Brachycephalic.

brachycephaly (brak″e-sef′ah-le). The fact or quality of being brachycephalic.

brachycheilia (brak″e-ki′le-ah) [*brachy-* + Gr. *cheilos* lip + *-ia*]. Shortness of the lip.

brachychily (brak-ik′ĭ-le). Brachycheilia.

brachychronic (brak″e-kron′ik) [Gr. *brachychronios* of short duration]. Acute: said of a disease (Rabagliati).

brachycranic (brak″e-kra′nik). Having a cranial index of 80.0–84.9.

brachydactylia (brak″e-dak-til′e-ah) [*brachy-* + Gr. *daktylos* finger + *-ia*]. Abnormal shortness of the fingers and toes.

brachyesophagus (brak″e-e-sof′ah-gus) [*brachy-* + *esophagus*]. Abnormal shortness of the esophagus.

brachyfacial (brak″e-fa′shal). Having a low broad face, with a facial index of 90 or less.

brachygnathia (brak-ig-na′the-ah) [*brachy-* + Gr. *gnathos* jaw + *-ia*]. Abnormal shortness of the under jaw.

brachygnathous (brah-kig′nah-thus) [*brachy-* + Gr. *gnathos* jaw]. Having an unusually short jaw.

brachykerkic (brak″e-ker′kik). Having a radiohumeral index less than 75.

brachyknemic (brak″e-ne′mik). Having a tibiofemoral index of 82 or less.

brachymetacarpalism (brak″e-met″ah-kar′pal-izm). Brachymetacarpia.

brachymetacarpia (brak″e-met″ah-kar′pe-ah). Abnormal shortness of the metacarpal bones.

brachymetapody (brak″e-mĕ-tap′o-de). Abnormal shortness of some of the metacarpal or metatarsal bones.

brachymetatarsia (brak″e-met″ah-tar′se-ah). Abnormal shortness of the metatarsal bones.

brachymetropia (brak″e-mĕ-tro′pe-ah) [*brachy-* + Gr. *metron* measure + *opsis* sight]. Myopia, or near-sightedness.

brachymetropic (brak″e-mĕ-trop′ik). Near-sighted, or myopic.

brachymorphic (brak″e-mor′fik) [*brachy-* + Gr. *morphē* form]. Built along lines that are shorter and broader than those of the normal figure.

brachyphalangia (brak″e-fah-lan′je-ah) [*brachy-* + *phalanx*]. Abnormal shortness of one or more of the phalanges of a finger or toe.

brachyskelous (brak″e-ske′lus). Having short legs.

brachystaphyline (brak″e-staf′ĭ-lin) [*brachy-* + Gr. *staphylē* uvula]. Having a palatal index of 85.0 or more.

brachystasis (brah-kis′tah-sis) [*brachy-* + *stasis*]. A state in which a muscle fiber is relatively decreased in length, and resists stretch, contracts and relaxes, and manifests the same tension as before shortening.

brachytypical (brak″e-tip′e-kl). Brachymorphic.

brachyuranic (brak″e-u-ran′ik). Having a maxillo-alveolar index of 115.0 or more.

bract (brakt). A small modified leaf in a flower cluster.

Bradford frame (brad′ford) [Edward Hickling *Bradford*, Boston orthopedic surgeon, 1848–1926]. See under *frame*.

brady- [Gr. *bradys* slow]. A combining form meaning slow.

bradyacusia (brad″e-ah-ku′se-ah) [*brady-* + Gr. *akouein* to hear]. Dullness of hearing.

bradyarthria (brad″e-ar′thre-ah) [*brady-* + Gr. *arthroun* to utter distinctly]. Bradylalia.

bradyauxesis (brad″e-awk-se′sis) [*brady-* + Gr. *auxēsis* increase]. A form of heterauxesis in which the part grows more slowly than the whole.

bradycardia (brad″e-kar′de-ah) [*brady-* + Gr. *kardia* heart]. Abnormal slowness of the heart beat, as evidenced by slowing of the pulse rate to 60 or less. **Branham's b.** See under *sign*. **cardiomuscular b.,** that caused by disease of the muscle of the heart. **central b.,** bradycardia dependent on disease of the central nervous system. **clinostatic b.,** a condition marked by bradycardia, lessened blood pressure, and acrocyanosis when the patient lies down (Vincent). **essential b.,** bradycardia occurring without discoverable cause. **nodal b.,** bradycardia in which the venous tracings show no wave due to the contraction of the auricle and in which the stimulus of the heart's contraction arises in the auriculoventricular node. **postinfective b.,** bradycardia occurring after infectious disease. **sinus b.,** a slow sinus rhythm with a rate below 60 due to disturbance of the sinus node. **vagal b.,** bradycardia due to disturbed vagal tone.

bradycardiac (brad″e-kar′de-ak). 1. Pertaining to, characterized by, or causing bradycardia. 2. An agent that acts to slow the pulse.

bradycardic (brad″e-kar′dik). Bradycardiac.

bradycinesia (brad″e-sĭ-ne′ze-ah). Bradykinesia.

bradycrotic (brad″e-krot′ik) [*brady-* + Gr. *krotos* pulsation]. Pertaining to, characterized by, or inducing slowness of pulse.

bradydiastalsis (brad″e-di″ah-stal′sis). Slow or delayed bowel movement.

bradydiastole (brad″e-di-as′to-le) [*brady-* + *diastole*]. Abnormal prolongation of the diastole.

bradydiastolia (brad″e-di″as-to′le-ah). Bradydiastole.

bradyecoia (brad″e-e-koi′ah) [Gr. *bradyēkoos* slow of hearing]. Partial deafness.

bradyesthesia (brad″e-es-the′ze-ah) [*brady-* + Gr. *aisthēsis* perception]. Slowness or dullness of perception.

bradygenesis (brad″e-jen′e-sis) [*brady-* + *genesis*]. The lengthening of certain stages in embryonic development.

bradyglossia (brad″e-glos′e-ah) [Gr. *bradyglōssos* slow of speech]. Abnormal slowness of utterance.

bradykinesia (brad″e-kĭ-ne′se-ah) [*brady-* + Gr. *kinēsis* movement]. Abnormal slowness of movement; sluggishness of physical and mental responses.

bradykinetic (brad″e-kĭ-net′ik) [*brady-* + Gr. *kinēsis* motion]. Characterized by or performed by slow movement; a term applied to a method of showing the details of motor action by motion pictures taken very rapidly and shown very slowly.

bradykinin (brad″e-ki′nin) [*brady-* + Gr. *kinein* to move]. A kinin composed of a chain of nine amino acids (arginine, proline, proline, glycine, phenylalanine, serine, proline, phenylalanine, and arginine), liberated by the action of trypsin or of certain snake venoms on a globulin of blood plasma.

bradylalia (brad″e-la′le-ah) [*brady-* + Gr. *lalein* to talk]. Abnormally slow utterance of words due to a brain lesion.

bradylexia (brad″e-lek′se-ah) [*brady-* + Gr. *lexis* word]. Abnormal slowness in reading, due neither to defect of intelligence or of vision nor to ignorance of the alphabet.

bradylogia (brad″e-lo′je-ah) [Gr.]. Abnormal slowness of speech due to slowness of thinking, as in a mental disorder.

bradymenorrhea (brad″e-men″o-re′ah) [*brady-* + *menorrhea*]. Menstruation marked by a long duration.

bradypepsia (brad″e-pep′se-ah) [Gr.]. Abnormally slow digestion.

bradypeptic (brad″e-pep′tik). Pertaining to or characterized by slow digestion.

bradyphagia (brad″e-fa′je-ah) [*brady-* + Gr. *phagein* to eat]. Abnormalness of eating.

bradyphasia (brad″e-fa′ze-ah) [*brady-* + Gr. *phasis* speech]. Slow utterance due to a central lesion.

bradyphemia (brad″e-fe′me-ah) [*brady-* + Gr. *phēmē* speech]. Slowness of speech.

bradyphrasia (brad″e-fra′ze-ah) [*brady-* + Gr. *phrasis* utterance]. Slowness of speech due to mental disorder.

bradyphrenia (brad″e-fre′ne-ah) [*brady-* + Gr. *phrēn* mind]. A condition marked by extreme fatigability of initiative, interest, and psychomotor activity resulting from epidemic encephalitis.

bradypnea (brad″e-ne′ah) [*brady-* + Gr. *pnoia* breath]. Abnormal slowness of breathing.

bradypragia (brad″e-pra′je-ah) [*brady-* + Gr. *prattein* to act]. Slowness of action.

bradypsychia (brad″e-si′ke-ah) [*brady-* + Gr. *psychē* soul]. Slowness in psychic or mental reactions.

bradyrhythmia (brad″e-rith′me-ah) [*brady-* + Gr. *rhythmos* rhythm]. Bradycardia.

bradyspermatism (brad″e-sper′mah-tizm) [*brady-* + Gr. *sperma* semen]. Abnormally slow ejaculation of semen.

bradysphygmia (brad″e-sfig′me-ah) [*brady-* + Gr. *sphygmos* pulse]. Bradycardia.

bradystalsis (brad″e-stal′sis) [*brady-* + (*peri*)-*stalsis*]. Abnormal slowness of peristalsis.

bradyteleocinesia (brad″e-tel″e-o-si-ne′ze-ah). Bradyteleokinesis.

bradyteleokinesis (brad″e-tel″e-o-kĭ-ne′sis) [*brady-* + Gr. *telein* to complete + *kinēsis* movement]. A defect of motor coordination in which a movement is slowed or stopped prior to reaching its goal.

bradytocia (brad″e-to′se-ah) [*brady-* + Gr. *tokos* birth]. Lingering or slow parturition.

bradytrophia (brad″e-tro′fe-ah). A condition characterized by slow-acting nutritive processes.

bradytrophic (brad″e-trof′ik) [*brady-* + Gr. *trophē* nutrition]. Having slow-acting nutritive processes.

bradyuria (brad″e-u′re-ah) [*brady-* + Gr. *ouron* urine]. Abnormally slow passage of urine.

Bragada (brah-ga′dah). A genus of blood-sucking insects. **B. pic′ta,** a species which attacks man in India.

Bragg-Paul pulsator (brag′paul). An apparatus for maintaining respiration, consisting of an air bag placed around the patient's chest and abdomen and rhythmically inflated and deflated by an electric pump.

Brahmachari's test (brah″mah-kah′rez) [Upendranath *Brahmachari*, Indian physician, 1870–1946]. See under *tests.*

braidism (brād′izm) [after James *Braid*, English surgeon, 1795–1860]. Hypnotism.

Brailey's operation (bra′lēz) [William Arthur *Brailey*, English ophthalmologist, 1845–1915]. See under *operation.*

braille (brāl) [Louis *Braille*, a French teacher of the blind, 1809–1852]. A system of writing and printing for the blind by means of tangible points or dots.

brain (brān) [L. *encephalon;* Gr. *enkephalos*]. The mass of nerve tissue contained within the cranium, including the cerebrum, cerebellum, pons, and medulla oblongata. Called also *encephalon.* **abdominal b.,** plexus celiacus. **eye b.,** ophthalmencephalon. **little b.,** cerebellum. **new b.,** neencephalon. **old b.,** paleencephalon. **olfactory b., smell b.,** rhinencephalon. **'tween b.,** diencephalon. **water b.,** a disease of sheep marked by a staggering gait. **wet b.,** an edematous condition of the brain due to alcoholism.

Brain's reflex (brānz) [W. Russell *Brain*, British physician, born 1895]. See under *reflex.*

bran (bran). The meal derived from the epidermis or outer covering of a cereal grain.

branch (branch). A division or offshoot from the main stem of blood vessels, nerves, or lymphatics. For specific anatomical structures, see under *ramus.*

branchia (brang′ke-ah) [Gr. *branchia* gills]. The gills of fishes and of others of the lower vertebrates: represented in the human fetus by the branchial arches, separated by clefts.

branchial (brang′ke-al). Pertaining to or resembling the gills of a fish.

branchiogenic (brang″ke-o-jen′ik). Branchiogenous.

branchiogenous (brang″ke-oj′ĕ-nus) [*branchia* + Gr. *gennan* to produce]. Formed from a branchial cleft or arch.

branchioma (brang″ke-o′mah). A tumor connected with a branchial arch, or derived from an epithelial rest of the branchial apparatus.

branchiomere (brang′ke-o-mēr″). A segment of the splanchnic mesoderm from which the visceral arches are developed.

branchiomeric (brang″ke-o-mer′ik). Pertaining to the branchiomeres or visceral arches.

branchiomerism (brang″ke-om′er-izm) [*branchia-* + Gr. *meros* part]. Metamerism based on the serial repetition of the branchial arches.

Brand bath (brahnt) [Ernst *Brand*, German physician, 1827–1897]. See under *bath.*

Brande's test (brands) [William Thomas *Brande*, English chemist, 1788–1866]. See under *tests.*

Brandt's method (brahnts) [Thure *Brandt*, Swedish physician, 1819–1895]. See under *method.*

Branham's bradycardia, sign (bran′hamz) [H. H. *Branham*, American surgeon of 19th century]. See under *sign.*

Brasdor's operation (brah-dōrz′) [Pierre *Brasdor*, French surgeon, 1721–1798]. See under *operation.*

brash (brash). A burning sensation of the stomach; pyrosis. **weaning b.,** diarrhea in a nursling when put on food other than its mother's milk.

brassard (bras-ar′) [Fr.]. A band worn on the left arm and bearing a distinguishing mark or insigne of military authority.

Brauer's method (brow′erz) [Ludolph *Brauer*, German physician, 1865–1951]. See under *method.*

Braun's anastomosis (brawnz) [Heinrich *Braun*, German surgeon, 1847–1911]. See under *anastomosis.*

Braun's canal (brawnz) [Carl von *Braun*, Viennese obstetrician, 1822–1891]. See under *canal.*

Braun's hook (brawnz) [Gustav von *Braun*, Austrian gynecologist, 1829–1911]. See under *hook.*

Braun's test (brawnz) [Christopher Heinrich *Braun*, German physician, born 1847]. See under *tests.*

Braun-Fernwald's sign (brawn-fārn′valts) [Richard *Braun* von *Fernwald*, Viennese obstetrician, born 1866]. See under *sign.*

Braun-Husler reaction, test (brawn hoos′ler) [Ludwig *Braun*, German physician, born 1881]. See under *tests.*

Braune's canal (brawn′ez) [Christian Wilhelm *Braune*, German anatomist, 1831–1892]. See under *canal.*

Braxton Hicks sign. See *Hicks sign*, and under *sign.*

braxy (brak′se). The symptomatic anthrax of sheep caused by *Clostridium septique.* **German b.,** black disease. **water b.,** an intestinal inflammation of sheep with hemorrhage into the peritoneal cavity.

brazilin (brah-zil′in). A yellow crystalline substance obtained from the bark of *Biancea sappan* and other red wood trees. It is very similar to hematoxylin and oxidizes to a bright red dye, brazilein.

breadth (bredth). The distance measured horizontally from side to side. See also under *diameter.* **bizygomatic b.,** the distance between the most laterally situated points (zygia) on the zygomatic arches.

break (brāk). 1. To interrupt the continuity, or an interruption in the continuity of a structure, especially a bone. See *fracture.* 2. The interruption of an electric circuit, as distinguished from the make. **chromatid b.,** interruption of the continuity of a chromatid, the portions immediately proximal and distal to the site being out of alignment.

breast (brest). The anterior aspect of the chest, often applied especially to the modified cutaneous glandular structure it bears. See *mamma* [N A]. **broken b.,** mammary abscess. **caked b.** See *stagnation mastitis*, under *mastitis.* **chicken b.,** pigeon b. **Cooper's irritable b.,** neuralgia of the breast. **funnel b.** See *funnel chest*, under *chest.* **gathered b.,** mammary abscess. **hysterical b.,** painful swelling of the breast due to hysteria. **pigeon b.,** a condition of the chest in which the sternum is prominent: due to obstruction to infantile respiration or to rickets. **proemial b.,** the condition of the female breast which is a prelude to pathologic changes. **shoe-makers' b.,** sinking in of the sternum in shoe-makers, produced by the pressure of tools against the lower part of the sternum and the xiphoid cartilage. **shotty b.,** Schimmelbusch's disease. **thrush b.,** the speckled appearance of the muscle tissue under the endocardium in fatty degeneration of the heart.

breast-feeding (brest′ fēd′ing). The nursing of an infant at the mother's breast, instead of with a formula given by bottle.

breath (breth) [L. *spiritus halitus*]. The air taken in and expelled by the expansion and contraction of the thorax. **lead b.,** the metallic odor of the breath in lead poisoning. **liver b.,** hepatic fetor.

breathing (brēth′ing). The alternate inspiration and expiration of air into and out of the lungs. See *respiration.* **glossopharyngeal b.,** respiration unaided by the primary or ordinary accessory muscles of respiration, the air being "swallowed" rapidly into the lungs, by use of the tongue and muscles of the pharynx.

breathometer (breth-om′e-ter). An apparatus for testing and recording the breathing of a patient.

Breda's disease (bra′dahz) [Achille *Breda*, Italian dermatologist, 1850–1933]. Yaws.

bredouillement (bra-dwe-maw′). A speech defect in which only part of the word is pronounced, due to extreme rapidity of utterance.

breech (brēch). The lower part of the body posteriorly. **frank b.** See under *presentation.*

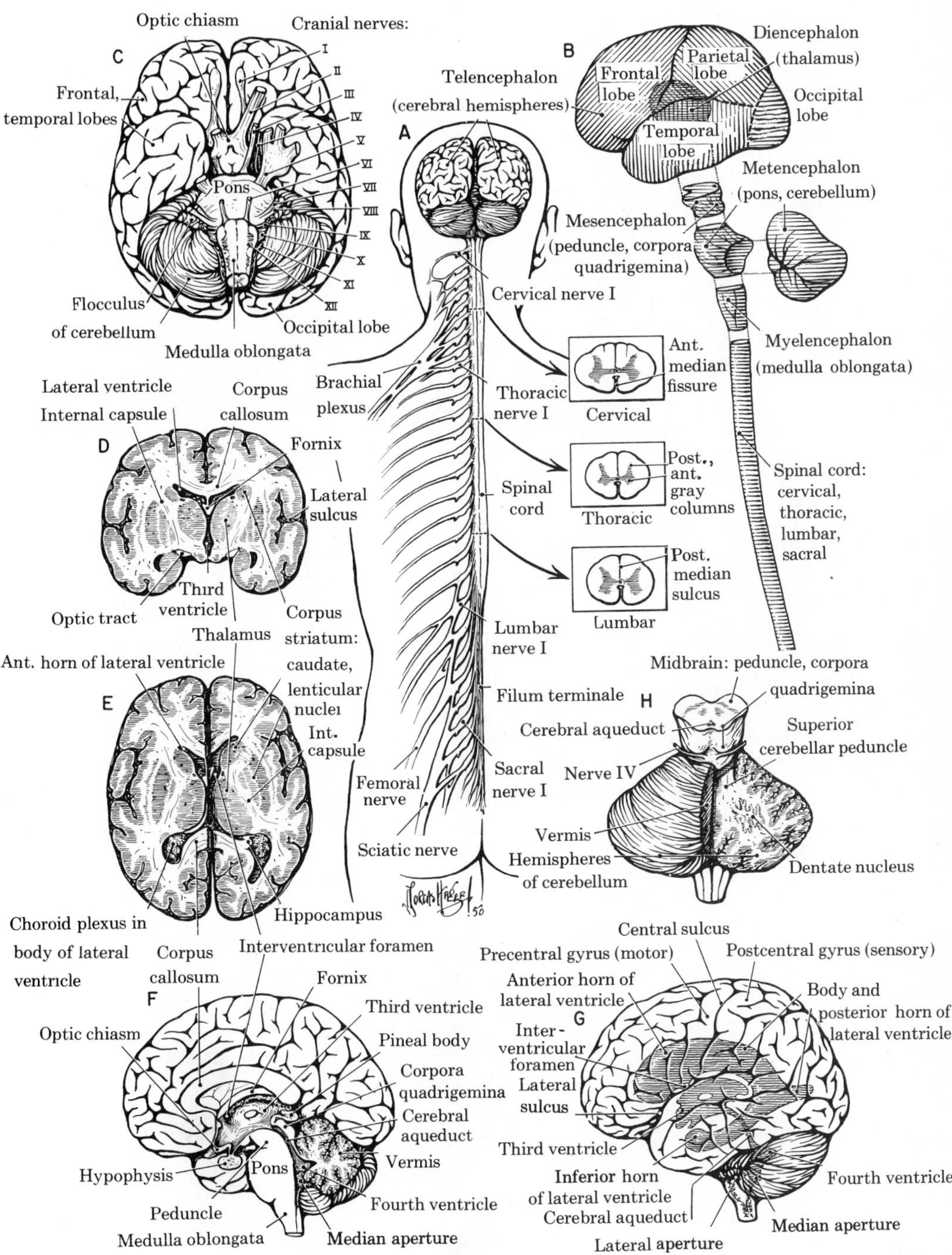

VARIOUS ASPECTS AND SECTIONS OF BRAIN AND SPINAL CORD

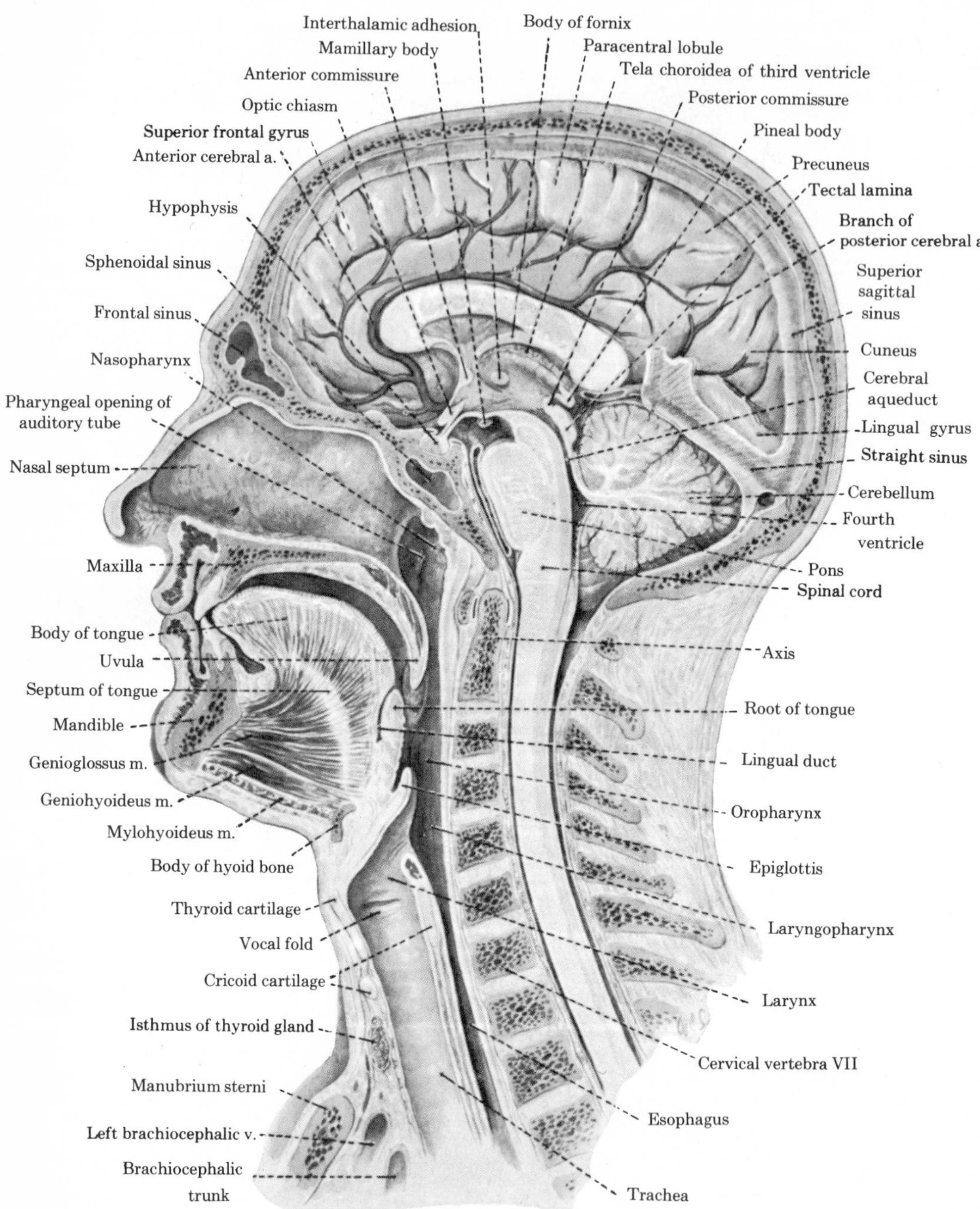

HEMISECTION OF HEAD AND NECK, SHOWING VARIOUS PARTS OF BRAIN AND OTHER STRUCTURES

(Anson)

breeze (brēz). A mild flow of air; applied also to electric energy. **electric b.,** static b. **head b.,** electricity applied to the head by a plate with pencils for subdividing the current. **static b.,** the convection discharge from a static machine used therapeutically, the electrified air current being directed to the desired area.

bregenin (breg′ĕ-nin) [A.S. *bregen* brain]. An aminolipin, $C_{40}H_{81}NO_5$, obtained from brain substance.

bregma (breg′mah) [L.; Gr.]. The point on the surface of the skull at the junction of the coronal and sagittal sutures.

bregmatic (breg-mat′ik). Pertaining to the bregma.

bregmatodymia (breg″mah-to-dim′e-ah) [*bregma* + Gr. *didymos* twin + *-ia*]. The state of conjoined twins fused at the bregmas.

Brehmer's method, treatment (bra′merz) [Herman *Brehmer*, German physician, 1826–1889]. See under *treatment.*

brei (bri) [Ger. "pulp"]. Tissue which has been ground to a pulp.

brein (bre′in). A glycoside derived from *Bryonia alba;* said to be a stimulant to the arterioles.

Breisky's disease (bri′skēz) [August *Breisky*, German gynecologist, 1832–1889]. Kraurosis vulvae.

Bremer's test (brem′erz) [Ludwig *Bremer*, American physician, 1844–1914]. See under *tests.*

Brennemann's syndrome (bren′e-manz) [Joseph *Brennemann*, Chicago pediatrician, 1872–1944]. See under *syndrome.*

Brenner's formula, test (bren′erz) [Rudolf *Brenner*, German physician, 1821–1884]. See under *formula.*

Brenner operation [Alexander *Brenner*, Austrian surgeon, 1859–1936]. See under *operation.*

Brenner tumor [Fritz *Brenner*, German pathologist, born 1877]. See under *tumor.*

brenz- (brents). A pure German prefix, meaning burnt. For words beginning thus, see those beginning *pyro-*.

brephic (bref′ik) [Gr. *brephos* embryo]. Pertaining to an early stage of development.

brepho- (bref′o) [Gr. *brephos* embryo or newborn infant]. A combining form denoting relationship to the embryo or fetus, or to the newborn infant.

brephoplastic (bref″o-plas′tik) [*brepho-* + Gr. *plassein* to form]. Formed from embryonic tissue or during embryonic life.

brephopolysarcia (bref″o-pol″e-sar′se-ah) [*brepho-* + *polysarcia*]. Excessive fleshiness in an infant.

brephotrophic (bref″o-trof′ik) [*brepho-* + Gr. *trophē* nutrition]. Pertaining to the nourishment of infants.

Breschet's canals, veins, etc. (brĕ-shāz′) [Gilbert *Breschet*, French anatomist, 1784–1845]. See under the nouns.

Bretonneau's angina, disease (bret-o-nōz′) [Pierre *Bretonneau*, French physician, 1778–1862]. Diphtheria of the pharynx.

bretylium (bre-til′e-um). Chemical name: (o-Bromobenzyl)-ethyldimethylammonium. Uses: 1. sympathetic nerve blockade; 2. antihypertensive.

Breus's mole (broys′ez) [Carl *Breus*, Austrian obstetrician, 1852–1914]. See under *mole.*

brevi- (brev′e) [L. *brevis* short]. Combining form meaning short.

Brevibacteriaceae (brev″e-bak-te″re-a′se-e). A family of Schizomycetes (order Eubacteriales), occurring as motile or non-motile cells without endospores. It includes two genera, *Brevibacterium* and *Kurthia.*

Brevibacterium (brev″e-bak-te′re-um). A genus of microorganisms of the family Brevibacteriaceae, order Eubacteriales, made up of generally non-motile, short, unbranched rods. Found in soil, salt and fresh water, dairy products, and decomposing material of many types. It includes 23 species.

brevicollis (brev″e-kol′is) [*brevi-* + L. *collum* neck]. Shortness of the neck. See *dystrophia brevicollis.*

breviductor (brev″e-duk′tor) [*brevi-* + L. *ductor* leader]. Musculus adductor brevis.

breviflexor (brev″e-flek′sor) [*brevi-* + L. *flexor* bender]. A short flexor muscle.

brevilineal (brev″e-lin′e-al). Brachymorphic.

breviradiate (brev″e-ra′de-āt). Having short processes: a term applied to one type of neuroglia cells.

brevital (brev′ĭ-tal). Trade mark for a preparation of methohexital.

brevium (bre′ve-um). A name formerly given to a supposed isotope of tantalum now known to be the element protactinium.

Brewer's infarcts, operation, point (broo′-erz) [George Emerson *Brewer*, New York surgeon, 1861–1939]. See under the nouns.

brickpox (brik′poks). A form of swine erysipelas (Ger. *Backsteinblattern*) due to a specific organism.

bridge (brij). 1. A form of dental prosthesis which replaces one or more lost or missing teeth, being supported and held in position by attachments to adjacent teeth. See *partial denture*, under *denture.* 2. See *pons.* 3. A protoplasmic structure which unites adjacent elements of a cell, similar in plants and animals. **arch b.,** span b. **arteriolovenular b.,** the main and largest capillary connecting an arteriole and a venule. It retains some muscle elements and is rarely completely collapsed. **cantilever b.,** a fixed partial denture which is attached at one end to one or more natural teeth or roots, the other end not being rigidly attached. **cell b's,** intercellular b's. **cytoplasmic b.,** a band of protoplasm joining two adjacent blastomeres. **fixed b.,** a fixed partial denture. **Gaskell's b.,** bundle of His. **intercellular b's,** processes of cell substance connecting adjoining cells. **b. of the nose,** the upper portion of the external nose formed by the junction of the nasal bones. **removable b.,** a removable partial denture. **span b.,** a fixed partial denture which is attached at each end to one or more abutment teeth. **stationary b.,** a fixed partial denture. **b. of Varolius,** pons. **Wheatstone's b.,** an instrument for measuring electric resistance.

bridle (bri′dl). 1. A frenum. 2. A loop or filament which crosses the lumen of a passage on the surface of an ulcer.

bridou (bre-doo′). Perleche.

Brieger's test (bre′gerz) [Ludwig *Brieger*, physician in Berlin, 1849–1919]. See under *tests.*

brier, bamboo (bri′er). The root of *Smilax rotunifolia*, of the United States.

Bright's disease (brīts) [Richard *Bright*, English physician, 1789–1858]. See *nephritis* and under *disease.*

brightic (bri′tik). 1. Affected with Bright's disease. 2. A patient ill of Bright's disease.

brightism (brīt′izm). Chronic nephritis.

Brill's disease (brilz) [Nathan E. *Brill*, New York physician, 1860–1925]. See under *disease.*

Brill-Symmers disease [Nathan E. *Brill;* Douglas *Symmers*, New York pathologist, born 1879]. Giant follicular lymphadenopathy.

Brinton's disease (brin′tonz) [William *Brinton*, English physician, 1823–1867]. Linitis plastica.

Brion-Kayser disease (bre-on′ ki′zer) [Albert *Brion*, physician in Strasburg; Heinrich *Kayser*, German physician]. Paratyphus.

Briquet's ataxia, syndrome (bre-kāz′) [Paul *Briquet*, French physician, 1796–1881]. See under *ataxia* and *syndrome.*

brisement (brēz-maw′) [Fr. "crushing"]. The breaking up of anything, as of an ankylosis. **b. forcé,** the forcible breaking up of a bony ankylosis.

brise-pierre (brēs-pe-är′) [Fr. "stone-breaker"]. A form of lithotrite.

Brissaud's disease, infantilism, reflex, scoliosis (bre-sōz′) [Edouard *Brissaud*, French physician, 1852–1909]. See under the nouns.

bristamin (bris′tah-min). Trade mark for a preparation of phenyltoloxamine.

Brittain's sign [Robert *Brittain*, American physician]. See under *sign*.

broach (brōch). A fine instrument used by dentists for assisting in the instrumental cleansing of a root canal or for extirpating the pulp. **barbed b.,** one whose surface is covered with barbs. **root-canal b.,** a broach for use in removing the contents of a root canal of a tooth. **smooth b.,** one without barbs, used for exploring fine and tortuous root canals.

Broadbent's apoplexy, sign (brod′bentz) [Sir William *Broadbent*, English physician, 1835–1907]. See under *apoplexy* and *sign*.

Broca's aphasia, area, center, convolution, fissure, formula, plane, pouch, space, etc. (bro′kahz) [Pierre Paul *Broca*, a French surgeon, 1824–1880]. See under the nouns.

Brock syndrome (brok) [Russell Claude *Brock*, British surgeon, born 1903]. Middle lobe syndrome.

Brocq's disease (broks) [Anne Jean Louis *Brocq*, French dermatologist, 1856–1928]. Parakeratosis psoriasiformis.

Broders' classification, index (bro′derz) [Albert C. *Broders*, American pathologist, born 1885]. See under *index*.

Brodie's abscess, disease, knee, etc. (bro′-dēz) [Sir Benjamin Collins *Brodie*, English surgeon, 1783–1862]. See under the nouns.

Brodie's ligament (bro′dēz) [Charles Gordon *Brodie*, London surgeon, d. 1929]. See under *ligament*.

Brodmann's area [Korbinian *Brodmann*, German neurologist, 1868–1918]. See under *area*.

Broesike's fossa (bre′ze-kēz) [Gustav *Broesike*, German anatomist, born 1853]. See *parajejunal fossa*, under *fossa*.

brom-. For words beginning thus, see also words beginning *bromo-*.

bromate (bro′māt). Any salt of bromic acid.

bromated (bro′māt-ed). Combined with or containing bromine.

bromatherapy (bro″mah-ther′ah-pe). Bromatotherapy.

bromatology (bro″mah-tol′o-je) [Gr. *brōma* food + *-logy*]. The science of foods and dietetics.

bromatotherapy (bro″mah-to-ther′ah-pe) [Gr. *brōma* food + *therapeia* treatment]. The use of food in treating disease.

bromatotoxin (bro″mah-to-tok′sin) [Gr. *brōma* food + *toxin*]. The poison formed in food by fermentation, etc.

bromatotoxismus (bro″mah-to-tok-siz′mus). Bromatoxism.

bromatoxism (bro-mah-tok′sizm) [Gr. *brōma* food + *toxikon* poison]. Poisoning by food.

bromelin (bro-mel′in) [L. *bromelia* pineapple]. A proteolytic enzyme derived from pineapples, used in certain blood typing procedures.

bromethol (bro-meth′ol). Tribromoethanol solution.

bromhidrosis (brōm″hid-ro′sis) [Gr. *brōmos* stench + *hidrōs* sweat]. Fetid perspiration.

bromic (bro′mik). Pertaining to or containing bromine.

bromide (bro′mīd). Any binary compound of bromine in which the bromine carries a negative charge (Br^-); specifically a salt (or organic ester) of hydrobromic acid (H^+Br^-); many of them are useful in epilepsy, being cardiac and cerebral depressants.

bromidrosiphobia (brōm″id-ro-se-fo′be-ah) [Gr. *brōmos* stench + *hidrōs* sweat + *phobia*]. Morbid dread of bodily odors, with delusions as to their perception.

bromidrosis (brōm-id-ro′sis). Bromhidrosis.

bromine (bro′min) [L. *bromium, brominium, bromum;* Gr. *brōmos* stench]. A reddish-brown liquid element, symbol Br, giving off suffocating vapors. Its atomic number is 35; atomic weight, 79.909. Its compounds (bromides) are used in medicine as sedatives.

brominism (bro′min-izm). A condition of poisoning produced by the excessive use of bromine or a bromine compound. The symptoms produced are an eruption of acne upon the face and body, headache, coldness of the extremities, fetor of breath, sleepiness, and loss of strength and sexual power.

brominized (bro′min-īzd). Treated with or containing bromine.

bromism (bro′mizm). Brominism.

bromisovalum (brōm″i-so-val′um). Chemical name: (α-bromoisovaleryl) urea: used as a sedative and hypnotic.

bromization (bro″mi-za′shun). Impregnation with bromides or bromine; the administration of large doses of bromides.

bromized (bro′mīzd). Under the influence of bromides.

bromochlorotrifluoroethane (bro″mo-klo″ro-tri-floo-o″ro-eth′ān). Halothane.

bromoderma (bro″mo-der′mah) [*bromine* + Gr. *derma* skin]. A skin eruption due to the use of bromine or bromides.

bromodiphenhydramine (bro″mo-di″fen-hi′-drah-min). Chemical name: β-(p-bromobenzhydryloxy) ethyldimethylamine: used as an antihistaminic.

bromoformin (bro″mo-for′min). Bromalin.

bromoformism (bro″mo-for′mizm). Poisoning with bromoform.

bromohyperhidrosis (bro″mo-hi″per-hid-ro′sis) [Gr. *brōmos* stench + *hyper* over, excessive + *hidrōsis* perspiration]. Excessive and foul smelling perspiration.

bromoiodism (bro″mo-i′o-dizm). Poisoning with bromine and iodine or their compounds.

bromomania (bro″mo-ma′ne-ah) [*bromin* + *mania*]. Mental disorder induced by the injudicious use of the bromine compounds.

bromomenorrhea (bro″mo-men-o-re′ah) [Gr. *brōmos* stench + *mēn* month + *rhoia* flow]. The discharge of menses characterized by an offensive odor.

bromophenol (bro″mo-fe′nol). A violet-colored, strong-smelling liquid, C_6H_4BrOH.

bromopnea (brōm″op-ne′ah) [Gr. *brōmos* stench + *pnoia* breath]. Fetid breath.

brompheniramine (brōm″fen-ir′ah-mēn). Chemical name: 2-[p-bromo-α-(2-dimethylamino-ethyl) benzyl] pyridine: used as an antihistaminic.

bromphenol (brōm-fe′nol). One of a series of brominized phenols, sometimes found in the precipitates of tested urine.

bromphenyl-acetyl-cysteine (brōm-fen″il-as″e-til-sis′te-in). Bromphenylmercapturic acid.

bromsaligenin (brōm″sal-ĭ-jen′in). Chemical name: 5-bromo-2-hydroxy-benzylalcohol: used as an antispasmodic.

bromsulphalein (brom-sul′fah-lin). Trade mark for a preparation of sulfobromophthalein.

bromum (brō′mum) [L.]. Bromine.

bromural (brōm-u′ral). Trade mark for preparations of bromisovalum.

bromurated (brōm′u-rāt″ed). Containing bromine or bromine salts.

bromuret (brōm′u-ret). A bromide.

bronchadenitis (brong″kad-e-ni′tis) [Gr. *bronchia* bronchia + *adēn* gland + *-itis*]. Inflammation of the bronchial glands.

bronchi (brong′ki) [L.]. Plural of *bronchus*.

bronchia (brong′ke-ah) [L.; Gr.]. Plural of *bronchium.*

bronchial (brong′ke-al) [L. *bronchialis*]. Pertaining to the bronchi or bronchia.

bronchiarctia (brong″ke-ark′she-ah) [*bronchus* + L. *arctare* to constrict]. Bronchostenosis.

bronchiectasia (brong″ke-ek-ta′ze-ah). Bronchiectasis.

bronchiectasic (brong″ke-ek-ta′zik). Bronchiectatic.

bronchiectasis (brong″ke-ek′tah-sis) [*bronchus* + Gr. *ektasis* dilatation]. A chronic dilatation of the bronchi or bronchioles marked by fetid breath and paroxysmal coughing, with the expectoration of mucopurulent matter. It may affect the tube uniformly (*cylindric b.*), or may occur in irregular pockets (*sacculated b.*), or the dilated tubes may have terminal bulbous enlargements (*fusiform b.*). **capillary b.,** dilatation of the bronchioles.

bronchiectatic (brong″ke-ek-tat′ik). Pertaining to or characterized by bronchiectasis.

bronchiloquy (brong-kil′o-kwe) [*bronchus* + L. *loqui* to speak]. A high-pitched pectoriloquy due to a consolidated lung.

bronchiocele (brong′ke-o-sēl) [*bronchiole* + Gr. *kēlē* tumor]. A dilatation or swelling of a branch smaller than a bronchus.

bronchiocrisis (brong″ke-o-kri′sis). Bronchial crisis.

bronchiogenic (brong″ke-o-jen′ik). Bronchogenic.

bronchiole (brong′ke-ōl) [L. *bronchiolus*]. One of the finer subdivisions of the branched bronchial tree. Called also *bronchiolus.* **alveolar b's, respiratory b's, terminal b's,** bronchioli respiratorii.

bronchiolectasis (brong″ke-o-lek′tah-sis) [*bronchiole* + Gr. *ektasis* dilatation]. Dilatation of the bronchioles.

bronchioli (brong-ki′o-li) [L.]. Plural of *bronchiolus.*

bronchiolitis (brong″ke-o-li′tis). Bronchopneumonia. **acute obliterating b.,** cirrhosis of the lung due to induration of the walls of the bronchioles. **b. exudati′va** (Curschmann), inflammation of the bronchioles, with exudation of Curschmann's spirals and grayish, tenacious sputum; often merging into asthma. **b. fibro′sa oblit′erans,** bronchiolitis marked by ingrowth of connective tissue from the wall of the terminal bronchi with occlusion of their lumina. **vesicular b.,** bronchopneumonia.

bronchiolus (brong-ki′o-lus), pl. *bronchi′oli* [L.]. [N A, B N A]. One of the finer subdivisions of the branched bronchial tree. Called also *bronchiole.* **bronchi′oli respirato′rii** [N A, B N A], the final branches of the bronchioles, into which the alveolar ducts open.

bronchiospasm (brong′ke-o-spazm″). Spasmodic bronchostenosis.

bronchiostenosis (brong″ke-o-stĕ-no′sis). Bronchostenosis.

bronchiotetany (brong″ke-o-tet′ah-ne). Bronchotetany.

bronchisepticin (brong″ke-sep′tĭ-sin). An antigen prepared from *Bacillus bronchisepticus:* used in the skin test for canine distemper.

bronchismus (brong-kis′mus). Bronchiospasm.

bronchitic (brong-kit′ik) [L. *bronchiticus*]. Pertaining to, affected with, or of the nature of, bronchitis.

bronchitis (brong-ki′tis) [*bronchus* + *-itis*]. Inflammation of the bronchial tubes. **acute b.,** a bronchitic attack with a short and more or less severe course. It is due to exposure to cold, to the breathing of irritant substances, and to acute general diseases. It is marked by fever, pain in the chest, especially on coughing, dyspnea, and cough. **arachidic b.,** bronchitis caused by the aspiration of peanut kernels into the bronchi. **capillary b.,** bronchopneumonia. **Castellani's b.,** bronchospirochetosis. **catarrhal b.,** a form of acute bronchitis with a profuse mucopurulent discharge. **cheesy b.,** a form accompanying some cases of tuberculosis of the lung, in which the alveoli are filled with cells that undergo a cheesy degeneration. **chronic b.,** a long-continued form, often with a more or less marked tendency to recurrence after stages of quiescence. It is due to repeated attacks of acute bronchitis or to chronic general diseases; characterized by attacks of coughing, by expectoration, either scanty or profuse, and secondary changes in the lung tissue. **croupous b.,** bronchitis characterized by violent cough and paroxysms of dyspnea, in which casts of the bronchial tubes are expectorated with Charcot-Leyden crystals and eosinophil cells. **dry b.,** a form with a scanty secretion of tough sputum. **epidemic b.,** influenza. **epidemic capillary b.,** a dangerous form which sometimes accompanies an epidemic of measles. **ether b.,** that due to the irritation of ether. **exudative b.,** croupous b. **fibrinous b.,** croupous b. **hemorrhagic b.,** bronchospirochetosis. **mechanic b.,** a variety caused by the inhalation of dust or of solid particles. **membranous b.,** croupous b. **b. oblit′erans,** a form in which the smaller bronchi become filled with nodules made up of fibrinous exudate. **phthinoid b.,** tuberculous bronchitis with purulent expectoration. **plastic b.,** croupous b. **polypoid b.,** croupous b. **productive b.,** bronchitis with the development of fibrous tissue in and around the bronchi. **pseudomembranous b.,** croupous b. **putrid b.,** a form of chronic bronchitis in which the sputum is very offensive. **secondary b.,** that which occurs either as a complication of some acute disease, such as a fever, or as a local expression of some constitutional disorder. **staphylococcus b.,** bronchitis caused by staphylococci. **streptococcus b.,** bronchitis due to streptococci. **suffocative b.,** capillary b. **summer b.,** hay fever. **verminous b.,** bronchitis in sheep and cattle, due to the presence of a worm, *Strongylus filaria.* **vesicular b.,** that in which the inflammation extends into the alveoli, which are sometimes visible under the pleura as whitish-yellow granulations like millet seeds.

bronchium (brong′ke-um), pl. *bron′chia* [L.]. One of the subdivisions of a bronchus, smaller than the bronchus and larger than the bronchioles.

broncho-adenitis (brong″ko-ad″e-ni′tis). Bronchadenitis.

broncho-alveolar (brong″ko-al-ve′o-lar). Bronchovesicular.

broncho-alveolitis (brong″ko-al″ve-o-li′tis). Bronchopneumonia.

broncho-aspergillosis (brong″ko-as″per-jil-lo′sis). Bronchial disease from infection with *Aspergillus.*

bronchobiliary (brong″ko-bil′e-a-re). Pertaining to or communicating with a bronchus and the biliary tract, as a bronchobiliary fistula.

bronchoblastomycosis (brong″ko-blas″to-mi-ko′sis). Pulmonary blastomycosis.

bronchoblennorrhea (brong″ko-blen″o-re′ah). Chronic bronchitis in which the sputum is copious, thin, and mucopurulent.

bronchocandidiasis (brong″ko-kan″dĭ-di′ah-sis). Infection of the bronchi caused by fungi of the genus Candida.

bronchocavernous (brong″ko-kav′er-nus). Both bronchial and cavernous.

bronchocele (brong′ko-sēl) [*bronchus* + Gr. *kēlē* tumor]. 1. A localized dilatation of a bronchus. 2. Goiter. **cystic b.,** goiter containing cysts.

bronchocephalitis (brong″ko-sef″ah-li′tis). Whooping cough.

bronchoclysis (brong-kok′lĭ-sis) [*bronchus* + Gr. *klysis* injection]. An injection into the bronchial tubes; particularly the slow instillation by gravity of remedial solutions into the bronchial tubes.

bronchoconstriction (brong″ko-kon-strik′shun). Bronchostenosis.

bronchoconstrictor (brong″ko-kon-strik′tor). 1. Constricting or narrowing the lumina of the air passages of the lungs. 2. An agent that causes narrowing of the lumina of the air passages of the lungs.

bronchodilatation (brong″ko-dil-ah-ta′shun). A dilated state of a bronchus, or the site at which a bronchus is dilated.

bronchodilation (brong″ko-di-la′shun). The act or process of increasing the caliber of a bronchus.

bronchodilator (brong″ko-di-la′tor). 1. Dilating or expanding the lumina of air passages of the lungs. 2. An agent that causes expansion of the lumina of the air passages of the lungs.

broncho-egophony (brong″ko-e-gof′o-ne). Egobronchophony.

bronchoesophageal (brong″ko-e-sof″ah-je′al). Pertaining to or communicating with a bronchus and the esophagus, as a bronchoesophageal fistula.

bronchoesophagology (brong″ko-e-sof-ah-gol′o-je). That branch of medicine which deals with the bronchial tree and the esophagus.

bronchoesophagoscopy (brong″ko-e-sof-ah-gos′ko-pe). The instrumental examination of the bronchi and esophagus.

bronchogenic (brong-ko-jen′ik). Originating in a bronchus.

bronchogram (brong′ko-gram). The roentgenogram obtained by bronchography.

bronchography (brong-kog′rah-fe) [*bronchus* + Gr. *graphein* to write]. Roentgenography of the lung after the instillation of an opaque medium in a bronchus.

broncholith (brong′ko-lith [*bronchus* + Gr. *lithos* stone]. A bronchial calculus.

broncholithiasis (brong″ko-lĭ-thi′ah-sis). A condition in which calculi are formed in the bronchi.

bronchologic (brong″ko-loj′ik). Pertaining to bronchology.

bronchology (brong-kol′o-je). The study and treatment of diseases of the bronchial tree.

bronchomoniliasis (brong″ko-mo-nĭ-li′ah-sis). Bronchocandidiasis.

bronchomotor (brong″ko-mo′tor). Affecting the caliber of the bronchi.

bronchomycosis (brong″ko-mi-ko′sis) [*bronchus* + Gr. *mykēs* fungus]. Any bronchial disorder due to fungi, particularly infection of the lungs caused by *Candida albicans*.

bronchonocardiosis (brong″ko-no-kar″de-o′sis). Nocardial infection of the bronchi.

broncho-oidiosis (brong″ko-o-id″e-o′sis). Infection of the bronchi by fungi of the genus Oidium.

bronchopathy (brong-kop′ah-the) [*bronchus* + Gr. *pathos* disease]. Any disease of the air passages of the lungs.

bronchophony (brong-kof′o-ne) [*bronchus* + Gr. *phōnē* voice]. The sound of the voice as heard through the stethoscope applied over a healthy bronchus. Heard elsewhere, it indicates solidification of the lung tissue. **pectoriloquous b.,** a bronchophony with an accompaniment of pectoriloquy. **sniffling b.,** that which is accompanied with a sniffing sound, as of air drawn through the nose. **whispered b.,** that which is heard while the patient is whispering.

bronchoplasty (brong′ko-plas″te) [*bronchus* + Gr. *plassein* to mold]. Plastic surgery of the bronchus; surgical closure of a fistula in the bronchus.

bronchoplegia (brong″ko-ple′je-ah). Paralysis of the bronchial tubes.

bronchopleural (brong″ko-ploor′al). Pertaining to a bronchus and the pleura, or communicating with a bronchus and the pleural cavity, as a bronchopleural fistula.

bronchopleuropneumonia (brong″ko-plu″ro-nu-mo′ne-ah). Pneumonia complicated by bronchitis and pleurisy.

bronchopneumonia (brong″ko-nu-mo′ne-ah) [*bronchus* + *pneumonia*]. A name given to an inflammation of the lungs which usually begins in the terminal bronchioles. These become clogged with a mucopurulent exudate forming consolidated patches in adjacent lobules. The disease is essentially secondary in character, following infections of the upper respiratory tract, specific infectious fevers, and debilitating diseases. In infants and debilitated persons of any age it may occur as a primary affection. Called also *catarrhal pneumonia, lobular pneumonia,* and *capillary bronchitis.* **hiberno-vernal b.,** an epidemic disease occurring in the Mediterranean area, which is identical with Q fever. **subacute b.,** peribronchitis. **virus b.,** virus pneumonia.

bronchopneumonic (brong″ko-nu-mon′ik). Pertaining to, affected with, or caused by bronchopneumonia.

bronchopneumonitis (brong″ko-nu″mo-ni′tis). Bronchopneumonia.

bronchopneumopathy (brong″ko-nu-mop′ah-the). Disease of the bronchi and lung tissue.

bronchopulmonary (brong″ko-pul′mo-ner″e). Pertaining to the lungs and their air passages; both bronchial and pulmonary.

bronchoradiography (brong″ko-ra-de-og′rah-fe). Radiographic visualization of the bronchial tree.

bronchorrhagia (brong″ko-ra′je-ah) [*bronchus* + Gr. *rhēgnynai* to burst forth]. Hemorrhage from the bronchi.

bronchorrhaphy (brong-kor′ah-fe) [*bronchus* + Gr. *rhaphē* suture]. The suturing of an incised or wounded bronchus.

bronchorrhea (brong-ko-re′ah) [*bronchus* + Gr. *rhoia* flow]. Excessive discharge of mucus from the air passages of the lungs.

bronchoscope (brong′ko-skōp). An instrument for inspecting the interior of the bronchi.

bronchoscopic (brong″ko-skop′ik). Pertaining to bronchoscopy or to the bronchoscope.

bronchoscopy (brong-kos′ko-pe) [*bronchus* + Gr. *skopein* to examine]. Examination of the bronchi through a tracheal wound or through a bronchoscope (Killian, 1898).

bronchosinusitis (brong″ko-si″nus-i′tis). Coexisting infection of the paranasal sinuses and the lower respiratory passages.

bronchospasm (brong′ko-spazm). Spasmodic bronchostenosis.

bronchospirochetosis (brong″ko-spi″ro-ke-to′sis). An infectious disease caused by the presence in the bronchi of the *Spirochaeta bronchialis* and marked by chronic bronchitis attended by the spitting of blood; called also *Castellani's bronchitis* and *hemorrhagic bronchitis.*

bronchospirography (brong″ko-spi-rog′rah-fe). A form of spirography in which measurement is made of the airflow in one lung only, or even in one lobe.

bronchospirometer (brong″ko-spi-rom′e-ter). An instrument used in bronchospirometry.

bronchospirometry (brong″ko-spi-rom′e-tre). Determination of the vital capacity, oxygen intake, and carbon dioxide excretion of a single lung.

bronchostaxis (brong″ko-stak′sis). Bleeding from the bronchial wall.

bronchostenosis (brong″ko-ste-no′sis) [*bronchus* + Gr. *stenōsis* a narrowing]. Stricture or abnormal diminution of the caliber of a bronchial tube. **spasmodic b.,** spasmodic contraction of the walls of the bronchi.

bronchostomy (brong-kos′to-me) [*bronchus* + Gr. *stomoun* to provide with a mouth, or opening]. The surgical creation of an opening through the chest wall into a bronchus.

bronchotetany (brong″ko-tet′ah-ne). Extreme dyspnea caused by spasm of the bronchial musculature, preventing access of air.

bronchotome (brong′ko-tōm). A cutting instrument used in performing bronchotomy.

bronchotomy (brong-kot′o-me) [*bronchus* + Gr. *tomē* cut]. Surgical incision of a bronchus.

bronchotracheal (brong″ko-tra′ke-al). Pertaining to the bronchi and trachea.

bronchotyphoid (brong″ko-ti′foid). Typhoid fever beginning with severe bronchitis.

bronchotyphus (brong″ko-ti′fus). Typhus complicated with bronchial catarrh.

bronchovesicular (brong″ko-ve-sik′u-lar). Both bronchial and vesicular.

bronchus (brong′kus), pl. *bron′chi* [L.; Gr. *bronchos* windpipe]. One of the larger air passages within the lungs. **apical b.,** a branch which arises from the left bronchus and passes upward into the apex of the left lung. **cardiac b.,** a branch of the right bronchus which is homologous with the branch in some mammals which supplies the infracardiac lobe. **eparterial b.,** ramus bronchialis eparterialis. **hyparterial bronchi,** rami bronchiales hyparteriales. **lobar bronchi, bron′chi loba′res** [N A], passages arising from the principal bronchi and passing to the lobes of the right and left lungs, being the *right superior, right middle,* and *right inferior,* and the *left superior* and *left inferior lobar bronchi.* **primary b., b. principa′lis** [N A], one of the two main branches, right [**dex′ter**] and left [**sinis′ter**], into which the trachea divides, each passing to the respective lung. **segmental bronchi, bronchi segmenta′les** [N A], air passages arising from the lobar bronchi and passing to the different segments of the two lungs, where they further subdivide into smaller and smaller passages (bronchioles). **stem b.,** the continuation of the primary bronchus of the embryo, from which branches are given off to the lobes of the lungs. **tracheal b.,** an ectopic or supernumerary bronchus, extending directly from the trachea to the apical segment of the upper lobe of the right lung, occurring normally in some animals but as a congenital anomaly in man.

brontophobia (bron″to-fo′be-ah) [Gr. *brontē* thunder + *phobos* fear + *-ia*]. Abnormal fear of thunder and thunder storms.

Brooke's disease (brooks) [Henry Ambrose Grundy *Brooke,* English (Manchester) dermatologist, 1854–1919]. 1. Psorospermosis. 2. Epithelioma adenoides cysticum. 3. Keratosis follicularis contagiosa. **B's tumor,** epithelioma adenoides cysticum.

Brophy's operation (bro′fēz) [Truman William *Brophy,* American oral surgeon, 1848–1928]. See under *operation.*

brossage (bro-sahzh′) [Fr. "brushing"]. The operation of removing granulations by a stiff brush, as in trachoma.

broth (broth). 1. A thin soup prepared by boiling meat or vegetables. 2. A liquid culture medium for the cultivation of microorganisms. See under *bouillon* and *culture medium.* **bile salt b.** See *bile salt medium,* under *culture medium.* **carbohydrate b.,** a plain broth or a peptone solution which contains only one carbohydrate. **Lipschutz's egg-albumen b.** See *egg-albumen bouillon,* under *bouillon.* **MacConkey's bile salt b.** See *bile salt medium,* under *culture medium.* **nitrate b.,** a 1 per cent peptone solution containing 0.1 per cent of potassium nitrate free of nitrite. **Rosenow's veal-brain b.,** a mixture of nutrient bouillon, glucose, and Andrade's indicator, with a few small pieces of crushed calf brain and a few small pieces of crushed marble, autoclaved at 10 pounds.

Brouha test (broo′hah) [L. *Brouha;* Adèle *Brouha,* French physicians]. See under *tests.*

broussaisism (broo-sa′izm) [after F. J. V. *Broussais,* 1772–1838]. The obsolete opinion taught by Broussais, that irritability of the mucous membrane of the alimentary canal was a point of primary importance in the causation of disease.

brow (brow). The forehead, or either lateral half thereof. **olympic b.,** the overdeveloped forehead seen in congenital syphilis.

brown (brown). A dusky, reddish-yellow color. **aniline b., Bismarck b.,** a basic aniline dye, phenylene-diazo-metaphenylene-diamine, C_6H_4-$[N_2C_6H_3(NH)_2]_2$, much used as a stain and counterstain in histology. **Manchester b., phenylene b.,** Bismarck brown.

Brown's reaction, test [Thomas Kenneth *Brown,* American gynecologist, 1898–1951]. See under *tests.*

Brown-Séquard's disease, sign, syndrome, etc. (brown′ sa-karz′) [Charles Edouard *Brown-Séquard,* French physiologist, 1818–1894]. See under the nouns.

brownian movement (brow′ne-an) [Robert *Brown,* English botanist, 1773–1858]. See under *movement.*

Browning's vein (brown′ingz) [William *Browning,* Brooklyn anatomist, 1855–1941]. See under *vein.*

brownism (brown′izm). Brunonianism.

broxolin (brok′so-lin). Trade mark for a preparation of glycobiarsol.

Bruce's septicemia (brōōs′ez) [Sir David *Bruce,* surgeon in British army, 1855–1931]. Brucellosis.

Bruce's tract (brōōs′ez) [Alexander *Bruce,* Edinburgh anatomist, 1854–1911]. The septomarginal tract. See under *tract.*

Brucella (broo-sel′lah) [Sir David *Bruce*]. A genus of microorganisms of the family Brucellaceae, order Eubacteriales, made up of non-motile short, rod-shaped to coccoid, gram-negative encapsulated cells. It includes three species which may be differentiated on the basis of (1) the relative content of two antigens, A and M, (2) sensitivity to thionine and basic fuchsin, (3) production of hydrogen sulfide, and (4) the requirement for carbon dioxide on primary isolation. **B. abor′tus,** the commonest cause of brucellosis (undulant fever) in man; it is the causative agent of contagious abortion of cattle, which constitute the animal reservoir of infection. **B. bronchisep′tica,** *Bordetella bronchiseptica.* **B. meliten′sis,** the causative agent of classic Malta fever (undulant fever); occurring primarily, although not exclusively, in goats as the reservoir of infection. **B. su′is,** a species found primarily in swine, and which is capable of producing severe disease in man.

Brucellaceae (broo″sel-la′se-e). A family of Schizomycetes (order Eubacteriales), occurring as small coccoid to rod-shaped cells, singly or in pairs, chains, or groups. It includes eight genera, *Actinobacillus, Bordetella, Brucella, Calymmatobacterium, Haemophilus, Moraxella, Noguchia,* and *Pasteurella,* some of which are parasitic on and pathogenic for warm-blooded animals, including man and birds.

brucellar (broo-sel′ar). Pertaining to or caused by Brucella.

brucellemia (broo″sel-le′me-ah). The presence in the blood of microorganisms of the genus Brucella; brucellosis.

brucellergen (broo-sel′er-jin). Trade mark for a suspensoid of protein nucleate derived from Brucella cells: used in a skin test for brucellosis.

brucelliasis (broo″sel-li′ah-sis). Brucellosis.

brucellin (broo-sel′in). A preparation from pooled cultures of the three species of *Brucella,* used in the diagnosis and treatment of undulant fever.

brucellosis (broo″sel-lo′sis). A generalized infection caused by one of the species of *Brucella,* namely *Br. melitensis* of goats, *Br. abortus* of cattle, and *Br. suis* of hogs. In man the disease is marked by remittent undulatory fever, malaise, cervical pain, headache, sweating, constipation, weakness and anemia. Called also *undulant fever, Malta fever, Mediterranean fever, Cyprus fever, goat fever, Gibraltar fever, mountain fever, Neapolitan* *fever, rock fever, febris melitensis, febris undulans, Bruce's septicemia, melitensis septicemia,* and *melitococcosis.*

Bruch's glands, etc. (brooks) [Karl Wilhelm Ludwig *Bruch*, German anatomist, 1819–1884]. See under *gland*, etc.

Bruck's disease (brooks) [Alfred *Bruck*, German physician, born 1865]. See under *disease.*

Bruck's test (brooks) [Carl *Bruck*, German dermatologist, 1879–1944]. See under *tests.*

Brücke's muscle, etc. (bre′kez) [Ernst Wilhelm Ritter von *Brücke*, Austrian physiologist, 1819–1892]. See under *muscle*, etc.

Brudzinski's sign (brōōd-zin′skēz) [Josef von *Brudzinski*, Polish physician, 1874–1917]. See under *sign.*

Brugsch's disease (brōōg′shez) [Theodor *Brugsch*, German internist, born 1878]. Akromikrie.

bruise (brōōz). A superficial injury produced by impact without laceration; a contusion. **stone b.,** a painful bruise, especially of the bare feet of children.

bruissement (brwēs-maw′) [Fr.]. A purring tremor.

bruit (brwe) [Fr.]. A sound or murmur heard in auscultation, especially an abnormal one. **aneurysmal b.,** a blowing sound heard over an aneurysm. **b. d'airain** (brwe da-rā′) [Fr. "sound of brass"], a clear ringing musical note sometimes heard on percussion over a pneumothorax cavity. **b. de bois** (brwe duh bwah′) [Fr. "sound of wood"], a dull wooden nonmusical note sometimes heard on percussion over a pneumothorax cavity. **b. de canon** (brwe duh kahnaw′) [Fr. "sound of cannon"], an abnormally loud first heart sound: heard in complete heart block. **b. de choc** (brwe duh shawk′) [Fr. "sound of impact"], the second cardiac sound, accompanied by a sound of impact, such as is heard over an aneurysm of the aorta. **b. de clapotement** (brwe duh klah-pōt-maw′) [Fr. "sound of rippling"] a splashing sound indicative of dilatation of the stomach when pressure is made on the wall of the abdomen. **b. de claquement** (brwe duh klak′maw) [Fr. "sound of clapping"], a snapping sound caused by the sudden contact of parts. **b. de craquement** (brwe duh krak-maw′) [Fr. "a sound of crackling"], a crackling pericardial or pleural bruit. **b. de cuir neuf** (brwe duh kwēr nuf) [Fr. "sound of new leather"], a creaking noise; usually a sign of pericarditis or pleurisy. Called also *Bright's murmur.* **b. de diable** (brwe duh de-ahbl′) [Fr. "humming top"], a buzzing venous murmur in anemia. See *hum, venous.* **b. de drapeau** (brwe duh drah-po′) [Fr. "sound of a flag"], a flapping rustle heard in croup and laryngitis, and sometimes in nasal polyp. **b. de froissement** (brwe duh frwahs-maw′) [Fr. "sound of clashing"], a clashing noise of various origin. **b. de frolement** (brwe duh frol-maw′) [Fr. "sound of rustling"], a rustling murmur from pericardial or pleural friction. **b. de frottement** (brwe duh frot-maw′) [Fr. "sound of friction"], a rubbing sound of various origin. **b. de galop** (brwe duh gah-lo′) [Fr. "sound of galloping"], cantering rhythm. **b. de grelot** (brwe duh gruh-lo′) [Fr. "sound of a rattle"], a rattling sound usually caused by the presence of a foreign body in the respiratory passages. **b. de Leudet** (brwe duh led-a′), Leudet's tinnitus. **b. de lime** (brwe duh lēm) [Fr. "sound of a file"], a filing cardiac sound. **b. de moulin** (brwe duh moo-lă′) [Fr. "sound of a mill"], a splashing or waterwheel sound synchronous with systole, sometimes audible at some distance from the patient, variously attributed to cardiac, pericardiac, or mediastinal causes. **b. de parchemin** (brwe duh parshmaw′) [Fr. "sound of parchment"], a sound as of two pieces of parchment rubbed together: of valvular cardiac origin. **b. de piaulement** (brwe duh pyōl-maw′) [Fr. "sound of whining"], a cardiac murmur like the mewing of a cat. **b. de pot fêlé** (brwe duh po fĕ-la′) [Fr. "cracked-pot sound"], a sound heard in percussion over cavities of the chest. **b. de rape** (brwe duh rahp) [Fr. "sound of a grater"], a rasping, cardiac, valvular murmur. **b. de rappel** (brwe duh rah-pel′) [Fr. "sound of drum beating to arms"], a sound as of a drum; a delayed mitral murmur. **b. de Roger** (brwe duh ro-zha′), a loud, continuous murmur with no interval between the systolic and diastolic periods, heard in the third interspace to the left of the sternum in perforation of the interventricular septum. Called also *Roger's murmur.* **b. de scie** (brwe duh se) [Fr. "sound of a saw"], a cardiac murmur resembling the sound of a saw. **b. de soufflet** (brwe duh soofla′) [Fr. "sound of a bellows"]. See *souffle.* **b. de tabourka** (brwe duh tah-bōōr′kah), timbre métallique. **false b.,** one due to pressure by the stethoscope, or derived from the circulation in the ear of the auscultator. **Leudet's b.** See under *tinnitus.* **b. placentaire** (brwe pla″-sawn-tār′) [Fr. "placental sound"], a blowing sound heard over the pregnant uterus, and caused by the fetal circulation. **Roger's b.,** b. de Roger. **b. skodique** (brwe skaw-dēk′), skodaic resonance. **systolic b.,** a pathologic heart sound heard, on auscultation, with the systole of the heart. **Verstraeten's b.,** an abnormal sound heard in auscultation over the lower border of the liver in cachectic patients.

Brunn's membrane, nests (brōōnz) [Albert von *Brunn*, German anatomist, 1849–1895]. See under *membrane* and *nest.*

Brunner's glands (brun′erz) [Johann Conrad *Brunner*, Swiss anatomist, 1653–1727]. See under *gland.*

Brünninghausen's method (brin′ing-how″-senz) [Hermann J. *Brünninghausen*, German physician, 1761–1834]. Dilatation of the cervix for the induction of premature labor.

brunonianism (broo-no′ne-an-izm″) [John *Brown*, Scottish physician, 1735–1788]. The obsolete doctrine that all disease is due to either excess or lack of stimulus.

Bruns's disease (brunz′ez) [John Dickson *Bruns*, New Orleans physician, 1836–1883]. Pneumopaludism.

Bruns's sign, syndrome (brōōnz) [Ludwig *Bruns*, neurologist in Hanover, 1858–1916]. See under *syndrome.*

Brunschwig's operation (brōōn′swigz) [Alexander *Brunschwig*, American surgeon, born 1901]. Pancreatoduodenectomy.

brush (brush). A tuft of flexible materials fastened to a handle: varieties used in medical practice are the acid brush, made of glass; the electric brush, a form of electrode; also, laryngeal, nasal, pharyngeal, stomach, and other brushes. **faradic b.,** a brushlike wire electrode used in applying electricity to the body. **Haidinger's b.,** a brushlike image seen on looking toward a source of polarized light. **Kruse's b.,** a brush made of fine platinum wires for spreading bacterial material over the surface of a culture medium. **b's of Ruffini,** a form of nerve ending occurring in the papillae of the skin in the form of densely interlaced branches: called also *terminal cylinders* and *organ of Ruffini.* **stomach b.,** a brush used to cleanse and stimulate the mucous lining of the stomach.

brushing (brush′ing). 1. The operation of searing the surface of a lesion by the electric current. 2. Interfering.

bruxism (bruk′sizm) [Gr. *brychein* to gnash the teeth]. Grinding of the teeth in other than chewing movements of the mandible, especially such movements performed during sleep.

bruxomania (bruk″so-ma′ne-ah). Grinding of the teeth occurring as a neurotic habit in the waking state.

Bryant's line (bri′ants) [Thomas *Bryant*, English surgeon, 1828–1914]. See under *line.*

Bryce's test (brīs′ez) [James *Bryce*, Scottish physician of the 19th century]. See under *tests*.

Bryce-Teacher ovum [Thomas Hastie *Bryce*, Scottish anatomist, 1862–1946; John Hammond *Teacher*, Scottish pathologist, 1869–1930]. See under *ovum*.

brychomania (bri″ko-ma′ne-ah) [Gr. *brychē* a gnashing of teeth + *mania*]. Bruxomania.

Bryobia (bri-o′be-a). A genus of insects. **B. praetio′sa,** a red spider or spinning mite, found on clover, which may greatly annoy man.

Bryonia (bri-o′ne-ah) [L.; Gr. *bryōnia*]. A genus of cucurbitaceous plants, source of a substance formerly used as an active hydragogue cathartic.

Bryson's sign (bri′sonz) [Alexander *Bryson*, English physician, 1802–1860]. See under *sign*.

B.S. Abbreviation for *Bachelor of Surgery*, *Bachelor of Science*, *breath sounds*, and *blood sugar*.

BSA. Abbreviation for body surface area.

BSP. Abbreviation for bromsulphalein.

B.T.U., B.Th.U. Abbreviation for *British thermal unit*.

B.U. Abbreviation for *base of prism up*.

buba (boo′bah). The native name in South American countries for mucocutaneous leishmaniasis.

bubo (bu′bo) [L. from Gr. *boubōn* groin]. The inflammatory swelling of a lymphatic gland, particularly in the axilla or groin. Buboes are due to absorption of infective material, and are seen after gonorrhea or syphilis. **bullet b.,** the characteristic hard bubo of primary syphilis. **chancroidal b.,** a suppurating form accompanying or following chancroid. **climatic b.,** lymphogranuloma venereum. **gonorrheal b.,** a bubo following or accompanying gonorrhea. **indolent b.,** one which is hard and nearly painless, and shows little tendency to suppurate. **inguinal b.,** bubo in the groin. **malignant b.,** the bubo of bubonic plague. **nonvenereal b.,** climatic b. **parotid b.,** parotitis. **pestilential b.,** that which is associated with oriental plague. **primary b.,** a bubo which is due to venereal exposure but which is not preceded by any visible lesion. **strumous b.,** lymphogranuloma venereum. **sympathetic b.,** one due to friction or injury. **syphilitic b.,** an indolent bubo following a true or hard chancre. **tropical b.,** lymphogranuloma venereum. **venereal b.,** one due to venereal disease. **virulent b.,** chancroidal b.

bubon (bu-baw′) [Fr.]. Bubo. **b. d'emblée** (bu-baw″dah-bla′) [Fr. "at the first onset"], primary bubo.

bubonalgia (bu″bo-nal′je-ah) [Gr. *boubōn* groin + *-algia*]. Pain in the groin.

bubonic (bu-bon′ik) [L. *bubonicus*]. Characterized by or pertaining to buboes.

bubonocele (bu-bon′o-sēl) [Gr. *boubōn* groin + *kēlē* tumor]. Incomplete inguinal hernia forming a swelling in the groin.

bubonulus (bu-bon′u-lus) [L. "a small bubo"). A nodule or abscess along a lymphatic vessel; especially one on the dorsum of the penis.

bucardia (bu-kar′de-ah) [Gr. *bous* ox + *kardia* heart]. Cor bovinum.

bucca (buk′ah) [L.]. [N A, B N A] The fleshy portion of the side of the face; the cheek. **b. ca′vi o′ris** [N A, N B A], the fleshy portion of the side of the oral cavity, which is continuous with the commissure of the lips.

buccal (buk′al) [L. *buccalis*, from *bucca* cheek]. Pertaining to or directed toward the cheek.

buccally (buk′al-le). Toward the cheek.

buccellation (buk″sel-la′shun) [L. *buccellatio*, from *buccella* morsel]. The arrest of hemorrhage by a pad of lint.

buccilingual (buk″sĭ-ling′gwal). Buccolingual.

buccinator (buk′sĭ-na″tor) [L. "trumpeter"]. See *Table of Musculi*.

bucco- (buk′ko) [L. *bucca* cheek]. A combining form denoting relationship to the cheek.

buccoaxial (buk″ko-ak′se-al). Pertaining to or formed by the buccal and axial walls of a tooth cavity.

buccoaxiocervical (buk″ko-ak″se-o-ser′vĭ-kal). Buccoaxiogingival.

buccoaxiogingival (buk″ko-ak″se-o-jin′jĭ-val). Pertaining to or formed by the buccal, axial, and gingival walls of a tooth cavity.

buccocervical (buk″ko-ser′vĭ-kal). 1. Pertaining to the cheek and neck. 2. Pertaining to the buccal surface of the neck of a posterior tooth. 3. Buccogingival.

buccoclination (buk″ko-kli-na′shun). Deviation of a posterior tooth from the vertical, in the direction of the cheek.

buccoclusal (buk″ko-kloo′sal). 1. Pertaining to buccoclusion. 2. Bucco-occlusal.

buccoclusion (buk″ko-kloo′zhun). Malocclusion in which the dental arch or a quadrant or group of teeth is buccal to the normal.

buccodistal (buk″ko-dis′tal). Pertaining to or formed by the buccal and distal surfaces of a tooth, or the buccal and distal walls of a tooth cavity.

buccogingival (buk″ko-jin′jĭ-val). 1. Pertaining to the cheek and gingiva. 2. Pertaining to or formed by the buccal and gingival walls of a tooth cavity.

buccoglossopharyngitis (buk″ko-glos′o-far″-in-ji′tis). Inflammation involving the cheek, tongue, and pharynx. **b. sicca,** inflammation and dryness of the buccal mucosa, tongue and pharynx. Cf. *Sjögren's syndrome* under *syndrome*.

buccolabial (buk″ko-la′be-al). Pertaining to the cheek and lip.

buccolingual (buk″ko-ling′gwal). 1. Pertaining to the cheek and tongue. 2. Pertaining to the buccal and lingual surfaces of a posterior tooth.

buccolingually (buk″ko-ling′gwal-le). From the cheek toward the tongue.

buccomaxillary (buk″ko-mak′sĭ-ler″e). 1. Pertaining to the cheek and maxilla. 2. Communicating with the buccal cavity and the maxillary sinus, as a buccomaxillary fistula.

buccomesial (buk″ko-me′ze-al). Pertaining to or formed by the buccal and mesial surfaces of a tooth, or the buccal and mesial walls of a tooth cavity.

bucco-occlusal (buk″ko-ŏ-kloo′zal). Pertaining to or formed by the buccal and occlusal surfaces of a tooth.

buccopharyngeal (buk″ko-fah-rin′je-al). Pertaining to the mouth and pharynx.

buccoplacement (buk′ko-plās″ment). Displacement of a tooth toward the cheek.

buccopulpal (buk″ko-pul′pal). Pertaining to or formed by the buccal and pulpal walls of a tooth cavity.

buccoversion (buk″ko-ver′zhun). The position of a tooth which lies buccally to the line of occlusion.

buccula (buk′u-lah) [L.]. A redundant fleshy or fatty fold under the chin.

Bucephalus (bu-sef′ah-lus). A genus of trematodes. **B. papillo′sus,** a trematode parasitic in the stomach and intestines of fresh water fish.

Buchner's stain, theory, tuberculin, etc. (book′nerz) [Hans *Buchner*, German bacteriologist, 1850–1892]. See under the nouns.

Buck's extension, fascia, operation (buks) [Gurdon *Buck*, American surgeon, 1807–1877]. See under the nouns.

buckeye (buk′i). A popular designation for *Aesculus glabra*, and of other trees and shrubs of the same genus: tonic and astringent.

buckhorn (buk′horn). The royal (or so-called flowering) fern, *Osmunda regalis*.

Bucky diaphragm, rays (buk′e) [Gustav P. *Bucky*, German roentgenologist in America, 1880–

1963]. See under *diaphragm*, and *grenz rays*, under *ray*.

buclizine (bu'klĭ-zēn). Chemical name: 1(p-chlorobenzhydryl)-4(p-tert-butylbenzyl) diethylene diamine. Used as an antihistaminic.

bucnemia (buk-ne'me-ah) [L., from Gr. *bous* ox + *knēmē* leg]. A diffuse, tense, and inflammatory swelling of the leg.

bud (bud). Any small part of the embryo or adult metazoan more or less resembling the bud of a plant. **bronchial b.,** an outgrowth from the stem bronchus giving rise to the air passages of its respective pulmonary lobe. **cassia b.,** the unripe fruit of several species of Cinnamomum. **end b.,** the remnant of the primitive knot, from which arises the caudal portion of the trunk. **gustatory b.,** taste b. **limb b.,** a swelling on the trunk of the embryo that becomes a limb. **liver b.,** a diverticulum from the foregut that gives rise to the liver and its ducts. **lung b.,** an outgrowth from the primitive trachea that gives rise to a primary bronchus and all of its branchings that form a respiratory tree. **metanephric b.,** ureteric b. **tail b.** 1. The primordium of the caudal appendage. 2. End bud. **taste b.,** one of the minute terminal organs of the gustatory nerve. See *caliculus gustatorius*. **tooth b.,** the knoblike primordium of a tooth. **ureteric b.,** an outgrowth of the mesonephric duct that gives rise to all but the nephrons of the permanent kidney. **vascular b.,** an outgrowth from an existing vessel from which a new blood vessel arises. **wing b.,** a swelling on the trunk of an avian embryo that gives rise to a wing.

Budd's cirrhosis, jaundice (budz) [George *Budd*, London physician, 1808–1882]. See under *cirrhosis* and *jaundice*.

buddeized milk (boo'de-īzd) [E. *Budde*, Danish sanitary engineer]. See under *milk*.

budding (bud'ing). 1. Gemmation; a form of asexual reproduction in which the body divides into two unequal parts, the larger part being considered the parent and the smaller one the bud. 2. The process by which a new blood vessel arises from a preexisting vessel.

Budge's center (bood'gēz) [Julius Ludwig *Budge*, German physiologist, 1811–1888]. 1. The ciliospinal center. 2. The genital center.

budgerigar (buj"er-e-gar') [Australian name]. A species of parakeet used for experimental work with psittacosis.

Budin's joint, rule (boo-daz') [Pierre-Constant *Budin*, Paris gynecologist, 1846–1907]. See under *joint* and *rule*.

Büdinger-Ludloff-Laewen disease [Konrad *Büdinger*, surgeon in Vienna, born 1867; Karl *Ludloff*, orthopedic surgeon in Frankfort, born 1864; Arthur *Laewen*, Königsberg surgeon, born 1876]. See under *disease*.

Buerger's disease (ber'gerz) [Leo *Buerger*, physician in New York, 1879–1943]. Thrombo-angiitis obliterans.

büffelseuche (bif'el-zoi"kĕ) [Ger.]. Pasteurellosis of the buffalo.

buffer (buf'er). 1. Any substance in a fluid which tends to lessen the change in hydrogen ion concentration (reaction), which otherwise would be produced by adding acids or alkalis. 2. Any substance which decreases or prevents the reaction that a chemotherapeutic agent would produce if administered alone.

buffering (buf'er-ing). The action produced by a buffer.

bufin (bu'fin). A white secretion obtained by stimulating the parotid gland of the toad by electricity. It has a physiologic action similar to that of digitalis.

bufotenin (bu-fo'tĕ-nin). A specific basic pressor principle, 5-hydroxy indole ethyl dimethyl amine, $OH.C_8H_5N.CH_2.CH_2.N(CH_3)_2$, from the skin glands of the toad, *Bufo bufo bufo*.

bufotherapy (bu"fo-ther'ah-pe) [L. *bufo* toad + *therapy*]. The use of toad toxins in the treatment of disease.

bug (bug). An insect of the order Hemiptera. **assassin b.** See *Reduviidae*. **barley b.** See *Acarus*. **blister b.** See *Cantharis*. **blue b.,** *Argas persicus*. **cone-nose b.** See *Reduviidae*. **croton b.,** *Blatta germanica*. **harvest b.** See *Leptus*. **hemophagous b.,** a bug which lives on blood, such as the bedbug. **kissing b.** See *Reduviidae*. **Malay b.** See *Lamus*. **miana b.,** *Argas persicus*. **red b.** See *Leptus*. **wheat b.** See *Pediculoides*.

Buhl's disease (būlz) [Ludwig von *Buhl*, German pathologist, 1816–1880]. See under *disease*.

Buist's method (būsts) [Robert C. *Buist*, Scotch obstetrician, 1860–1939]. See *artificial respiration*, under *respiration*.

Bülau's method, treatment (be'lowz) [Gotthard *Bülau*, physician in Hamburg, 1835–1900]. See under *method*.

bulb (bulb) [L. *bul'bus;* Gr. *bolbos*]. A rounded mass, or enlargement, such as a globular subterranean part of a plant, or an anatomical structure of similar shape. **b. of aorta,** bulbus aortae. **auditory b.,** the membranous labyrinth and cochlea. **b. of corpus cavernosum,** bulbus penis. **duodenal b.,** pileus ventriculi. **b. of eye,** bulbus oculi. **gustatory b.,** caliculus gustatorius. **b. of hair,** bulbus pili. **b. of heart,** bulbus cordis. **b. of jugular vein, inferior,** bulbus venae jugularis inferior. **b. of jugular vein, superior,** bulbus venae jugularis superior. **b's of Krause,** corpuscula bulboidea. **medullary b.,** medulla oblongata. **olfactory b.,** bulbus olfactorius. **b. of ovary,** a plexus of veins and arteries of the ovary. **b. of penis,** bulbus penis. **b. of posterior horn,** bulbus cornus posterioris. **Rouget's b.,** b. of ovary. **sino-vaginal b.,** one of paired sacculations of the urogenital sinus, forming the lowermost part of the vagina. **spinal b., b. of spinal cord,** medulla oblongata. **taste b.,** caliculus gustatorius. **b. of urethra,** bulbus penis. **vaginal b.** 1. A solid end of a müllerian duct in the embryo, helping to form the lower vagina. 2. Bulbus vestibuli vaginae. **b. of vestibule of vagina, vestibulovaginal b.,** bulbus vestibuli vaginae.

bulbar (bul'bar). Pertaining to a bulb, often used alone with particular reference to the medulla oblongata.

bulbi (bul'bi) [L.]. Plural of *bulbus*.

bulbiform (bul'bĭ-form). Bulb-shaped.

bulbitis (bul-bi'tis). Inflammation of the bulbous portion of the urethra.

bulbo-atrial (bul"bo-a'tre-al). Pertaining to the bulbus cordis and atrium.

bulbocavernosus (bul"bo-kav"er-no'sus). Musculus bulbospongiosus.

bulboid (bul'boid). Bulb-shaped.

bulbonuclear (bul"bo-nu'kle-ar). Pertaining to the medulla oblongata and its nerve nuclei.

bulbopontine (bul"bo-pon'tin). A term applied to that portion of the brain made up of the pons and the region of the medulla oblongata situated dorsad to it.

bulbospongiosus (bul"bo-spon"je-o'sus). See *Table of Musculi*.

bulbo-urethral (bul"bo-u-re'thral). Pertaining to the bulb of the urethra (bulbus penis [N A]).

bulbous (bul'bus). Having the form or nature of a bulb; bearing or arising from a bulb.

bulbus (bul'bus), pl. *bul'bi* [L.]. A rounded mass, or enlargement. **b. aor'tae** [N A, B N A], the enlargement of the aorta at its point of origin from the heart, where the bulges of the aortic sinuses occur. Called also *bulb of aorta*. **b. arterio'sus,** b. cordis. **b. carot'icus,** carotid sinus. **b. cor'dis,** the foremost of the three parts of the primitive heart of the embryo. **b. cor'nu posterio'ris ventric'uli latera'lis** [B N A], b. cornus posterioris. **b. cor'nus posterio'ris** [N A], an eminence produced in the posterior horn of the lateral ventricle by the splenial fibers of the corpus callosum as they pass posteriorly into the occipital lobe. Called also *b. cornu posterioris ventriculi lateralis* [B N A], and *bulb of posterior horn.* **b. medul'lae,** medulla oblongata. **b. oc'uli** [N A, B N A], the bulb, or globe, of the eye. See *eye.* **b. olfacto'rius** [N A, B N A], the bulblike expansion of the olfactory tract on the under surface of the frontal lobe of each cerebral hemisphere. The olfactory nerves enter it. Called also *olfactory bulb.* **b. pe'nis** [N A], the enlarged proximal part of the corpus spongiosum found between the two crura of the penis. Called also *b. urethrae* [B N A], and *bulb of penis.* **b. pi'li** [N A, B N A], the bulbous expansion at the proximal end of a hair. Called also *bulb of hair.* **b. ure'thrae** [B N A], b. penis. **b. ve'nae jugula'ris infe'rior** [N A, B N A], a dilatation of the internal jugular vein just before it joins the brachiocephalic vein. Called also *inferior bulb of jugular vein.* **b. ve'nae jugula'ris supe'rior** [N A, B N A], a dilatation at the beginning of the internal jugular vein. Called also *superior bulb of jugular vein.* **b. vestib'uli vagi'nae** [N A, B N A], a body consisting of paired elongated masses of erectile tissue, one on either side of the vaginal opening, united anteriorly in a thin strand that passes along the lower surface of the clitoris. Called also *bulb of vestibule of vagina.*

bulesis (bu-le'sis) [Gr. *boulēsis*]. The will, or an act of the will.

bulimia (bu-lim'e-ah) [L.; Gr. *bous* ox + *limos* hunger]. Abnormal increase in the sensation of hunger.

bulimiac (bu-lim'e-ak). Bulimic.

bulimic (bu-lim'ik). Pertaining to or affected with bulimia.

Bulinus (bu-li'nus). A genus of snails, several species of which are the intermediate hosts of *Schistosoma haematobium* and *Clonorchis.*

bulkage (bulk'ij). Material which will increase the bulk of the intestinal contents and consequently will stimulate peristalsis.

Bulkley diet (bulk'le) [L. D. *Bulkley*, New York dermatologist, 1843–1928]. See under *diet.*

Bull. Abbreviation for L. *bul'liat*, let it boil.

bulla (bul'ah), pl. *bul'lae* [L.]. A bladder, or bubble, especially a large blister or cutaneous vesicle filled with serous fluid. **ethmoid b.** See *b. ethmoidalis cavi nasi* and *b. ethmoidalis ossis ethmoidalis.* **b. ethmoida'lis ca'vi na'si** [N A, B N A], the large ethmoid air cell lodged in the bulla ethmoidalis ossis ethmoidalis. Called also *ethmoidal b. of nasal cavity.* **b. ethmoida'lis os'sis ethmoida'lis** [N A, B N A], a rounded projection of the ethmoid bone into the lateral wall of the middle nasal meatus just below the middle nasal concha, enclosing a large ethmoid air cell. Called also *ethmoidal b. of ethmoidal bone.* **b. for'nicis, b. of fornix,** corpus mamillare. **b. os'sea,** the dilated part of the bony external meatus of the ear.

bullate (bul'āt) [L. *bullatus*]. 1. Characterized by the presence of bullae. 2. Inflated.

bullation (bul-la'shun) [L. *bullatio*]. 1. The condition characterized by the presence of bullae. 2. The state of being inflated.

Buller's bandage, shield (bul'erz) [Frank *Buller*, Canadian ophthalmic surgeon, 1844–1905]. See under *shield.*

bullous (bul'us). Pertaining to or characterized by bullae.

bumblefoot (bum'bel-foot). Inflammation of the ball of the foot of fowls.

Bumke's pupil (bo͝om'kez) [Oswald Conrad Edward *Bumke*, German neurologist, 1877–1950]. See under *pupil.*

bumps (bumpz). Coccidioidomycosis.

BUN. Abbreviation for *blood urea nitrogen.*

bunamiodyl (bu″nah-mi'o-dil). Chemical name: 3-(3-butyryl-amino-2,4,6-triiodophenyl)-2-ethylacrylate: used as a radiopaque medium in roentgenography of the biliary tract.

bunch (bunch). Traumatic swelling of a bone in horses.

bundle (bun'd'l). A collection of fibers or strands, as of muscle fibers, or a fasciculus or band of nerve fibers. **aberrant b's,** collections of pyramidal fibers leaving the corticonuclear tract at successive levels of the brain stem, and giving off fibers to the motor nuclei of the cranial nerves. **atrioventricular b., a-v. b.,** b. of His. **Bachmann's b.,** a transverse band of muscle fibers extending between the bases of the right and left auricles of the heart. **basis b's,** fasciculi proprii. **Bruce's b.,** cornucommissural b. **cornucommissural b.,** a name once given the fasciculus proprius on the surface of the posterior column and posterior commissure of the spinal cord. **fundamental b's, ground b's,** fasciculi proprii. **b. of Helweg,** olivospinal tract. **b. of His,** a small band of atypical cardiac muscle fibers that originates in the atrioventricular node in the right atrium, passes through the atrioventricular junction, and then runs beneath the endocardium of the right ventricle on the membranous part of the interventricular septum. It finally divides at the upper end of the muscular part of the interventricular septum into right and left branches which descend in the septal wall of the right and left ventricle, respectively, to be distributed to those two chambers. This bundle propagates the atrial contraction rhythm to the ventricles, and its interruption produces heart block. Called also *fasciculus atrioventricularis* [N A] and *atrioventricular bundle.* **Keith's b.,** a bundle of fibers in the wall of the left atrium, between the openings of the venae cavae. Called also *sino-atrial b.* **Kent's b.,** a muscular bundle in the heart of animals (sometimes in man) below the node of Tawara. **Kent-His b.,** b. of His. **longitudinal medial b.,** fasciculus longitudinalis medialis. **main b.,** the portion of the bundle of His between the atrioventricular node and the right and left septal divisions. See *b. of His.* **Meynert's b.,** fasciculus retroflexus. **Monakow's b.,** rubrospinal tract. **muscle b.,** one of the primary longitudinal subdivisions of a muscle, made up of muscle fibers and separated from other bundles by fascial septa or perimysium. **oval b.,** a projection marking the outer surface of the dorsal zone of the human embryo. **posterior longitudinal b.,** fasciculus longitudinalis medialis. **predorsal b.,** tectospinal tract. **Schultze's b.,** interfascicular fasciculus. **sino-atrial b.,** Keith's b. **solitary b.,** tractus solitarius medullae oblongatae. **b. of Stanley-Kent,** b. of His. **thalamomamillary b.,** fasciculus mamillothalamicus. **Thorel's b.,** a bundle of muscle fibers in the heart, connecting the sinoatrial and atrioventricular nodes, and passing around the mouth of the inferior vena cava. **transverse b's of palmar aponeurosis,** fasciculi transversi aponeurosis palmaris. **Türck's b.,** temporopontile tract. **b. of Vicq d'Azyr,** fasciculus mamillothalamicus. **Weissmann's b.,** the bundle of striated muscle fibers of a neuromuscular spindle.

Bungarus (bung'gah-rus). A genus of poisonous snakes found in India; the krait.

Bunge's amputation (bo͝ong'gez) [Richard *Bunge*, German surgeon, born 1870]. Aperiosteal amputation.

Bunge's law (bo͝ong'gez) [Gustav von *Bunge*, physiologist at Basel, 1844–1920]. See under *law.*

Bunge's spoon (bo͝ong'gez) [Paul *Bunge*, German ophthalmologist, 1853–1926]. An instrument for eviscerating the eyeball.

bungeye (bung'i). A condition seen in Australia, caused by infestation of the eye with *Habronema*, and marked by small worm-containing granulomas in the conjunctiva. Called also *blue-eye.*

Büngner's bands, cell cordons (bing′nerz) [Otto von *Büngner*, German neurologist, 1858–1905]. See under *band.*

bungpagga (bung-pag′gah). An epidemic disease of West Africa characterized by fever and the development of suppurating tumors in the muscles. It is probably caused by a yeast fungus.

buninoid (boo′ne-noid) [Gr. *bounos* hill + *eidos* form]. Having a rounded form: said of tumors.

bunion (bun′yun) [L. *bunio;* Gr. *bounion* turnip]. A swelling of the bursa mucosa of the ball of the great toe, with thickening of the overlying skin and forcing of the toe outward (toward the little toe). **tailor's b.,** bunionette.

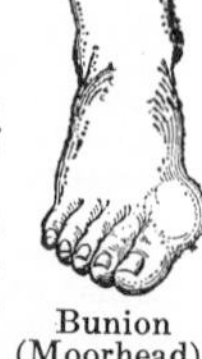
Bunion (Moorhead).

bunionectomy (bun-yun-ek′to-me) [*bunion* + Gr. *ektomē* excision]. Excision of a bunion by arthroplasty of the metatarsophalangeal joint.

bunionette (bun-yun-et′). A bunion-like enlargement of the joint of the little toe due to pressure over the lateral surface of the foot. Called also *tailor's bunion.*

bunodont (bu′no-dont) [Gr. *bounos* hill + *odous* tooth]. Having cheek teeth with low rounded cusps, forming small hillocks on the occlusal surface of the crown, as in mammals with mixed diet, such as swine and man.

bunolophodont (bu″no-lo′fo-dont) [Gr. *bounos* hill + *lophos* ridge + *odous* tooth]. Having cheek teeth with both rounded cusps and transverse ridges on the occlusal surface of the crown.

bunoselenodont (bu″no-se-le′no-dont) [Gr. *bounos* hill + *selēnē* moon + *odous* tooth]. Having cheek teeth with both rounded cusps and crescentic ridges on the occlusal surface of the crown.

Bunsen burner, coefficient, etc. (bun′sen) [Robert Wilhelm Eberhard von *Bunsen*, German chemist, 1811–1899]. See under the nouns.

Bunyan-Stannard envelope (bun′yan stan′-nard). A waterproof airtight envelope of oiled silk which is sealed to the skin of a burned area, providing for irrigation with 5 per cent sodium hypochloride solution through openings in the envelope for entrance and exit of fluid.

buphthalmia (būf-thal′me-ah). Buphthalmos.

buphthalmos (būf-thal′mos) [Gr. *bous* ox + *ophthalmos* eye]. The first stage of hydrophthalmos; keratoglobus, or enlargement of the eye.

buphthalmus (būf-thal′mus). Buphthalmos.

bur (bur). A form of drill used for creating openings in bone or similar hard substances. Such an instrument is used in dentistry, in the hand piece of a dental engine, for opening and preparing tooth cavities. **carbide b.,** one in which the steel is alloyed with tungsten carbide, to increase its hardness and cutting ability.

Burdach's columns, etc. (boor′daks) [Karl Friedrich *Burdach*, German physiologist, 1776–1847]. See under the nouns.

buret (bu-ret′). A graduated glass used in volumetric chemistry.

burette (bu-ret′) [Fr.]. Buret.

Burghart's symptom (bo͝org′harts) [Hans Gerny *Burghart*, German physician, 1862–1932]. See under *symptom.*

burn (burn). A lesion caused by the contact of heat. Burns of the first degree show redness, of the second degree, vesication, of the third degree, necrosis through the entire skin and fourth degree, more or less charring. **brush b.,** a wound caused by violent rubbing or friction, as by a rope pulled through the hands. **cement b., concrete b.,** a corrosive destruction of tissue caused by contact with cement or concrete. **cosmetic b.,** a burn of the scalp due to the inept use of permanent-wave machines. **flash b.,** a thermal lesion produced by a very brief exposure to radiant heat of high intensity, as in an explosion or a sudden discharge of electricity. **friction b.,** brush b. **Kangri b.,** a burn on the abdomen caused by the portable stove (Kangri) carried by natives of Kashmir. Such a burn may be followed by cancer. **Kromayer b.,** a burn made with a Kromayer lamp. **radiation b.,** a burn caused by exposure to the x-ray, radium, sunlight or any other type of radiant energy. **thermal b.,** injury due to contact with flame, hot objects or hot liquids, as distinguished from chemical and electric burns. **x-ray b.,** a lesion caused by exposure to x-rays.

Burnam's test (bur′namz) [Curtis Field *Burnam*, Baltimore surgeon, 1877–1947]. See under *tests.*

burner (burn′er). The part of a lamp from which the flame issues. **Argand b.,** a burner for oil or gas, with an inner tube for supplying air to the flame. **Bunsen b.,** a gas burner in which the gas is mixed with air before ignition, in order to give complete oxidation.

Burnet (bur-net′), Macfarlane. Australian physician-virologist, born 1899; co-winner, with Peter B. Medawar, of the Nobel prize in medicine and physiology for 1960, for the theoretical solution to the problem of transplanting tissues and vital organs from one animal to another.

Burnett's solution (bur′nets) [Sir W. *Burnett*, English surgeon, 1779–1861]. See under *solution.*

burnisher (bur′nish-er). A dental instrument for finishing and polishing dental fillings, crowns, and dentures.

burnishing (bur′nish-ing). A dental procedure somewhat related to polishing and abrading, the height or thickness of the surface being purposefully reduced by the process.

Burns' amaurosis (burnz) [John *Burns*, Scottish physician, 1774–1850]. See under *amaurosis.*

Burns' ligament, space [Allan *Burns*, Scottish anatomist, 1781–1813]. See under *ligament* and *space.*

Burow's operation, solution, vein, etc. (bo͞or′ovz) [Karl August von *Burow*, surgeon in Königsberg, 1809–1874]. See under nouns.

burquism (burk′izm) [V. B. *Burq*, French neurologist, 1823–1884]. A system of metallotherapy.

burr (bur). Bur.

bursa (bur′sah), pl. *bur′sae* [L.; Gr. "a wine skin"]. A sac or saclike cavity filled with a viscid fluid and situated at places in the tissues at which friction would otherwise develop. Certain bursa are so consistently recognized as to be given official names in anatomical nomenclature. **b. of Achilles,** b. tendinis calcanei [Achillis]. **acromial b.,** b. subdeltoidea. **adventitious b.,** an abnormal cyst due to friction or some other mechanical cause, and containing synovial fluid. **anconeal b.,** b. subcutanea olecrani. **anconeal b. of triceps muscle,** b. subtendinea musculi tricipitis brachii. **b. anseri′na** [N A, B N A], **anserine b.,** a bursa between the tendons of the sartorius, gracilis, and semitendinosus muscles, and the tibial collateral ligament. **bicipital b., bicipitofibular b.,** b. subtendinea musculi bicipitis femoris inferior. **b. bicipitogastrocnemia′lis** [B N A], omitted in N A. **bicipitoradial b., b. bicipitoradia′lis** [N A, B N A], a bursa between the ventral part of the radial tuberosity and the biceps tendon. **Boyer's b.,** one situated beneath the hyoid bone. **Brodie's b.,** b. subtendinea musculi gastrocnemii lateralis. **calcaneal b.,** b. tendinis calcanei [Achillis]. **calcaneal subcutaneous b.,** b. subcutanea calcanea. **b. of calcaneal tendon,** b. tendinis calcanei [Achillis]. **Calori's b.,** a bursa situated between the trachea and the arch of the aorta. **b. coccy′gea** [B N A], omitted from N A. **b. copula′trix,** an appendage at the posterior end of the male of certain nematodes. **coracobrachial b.,** b. musculi coracobrachialis. **coracoid b.,** b. subtendinea musculi subscapularis. **b. cubita′lis interos′sea** [N A, N B A], **cubitoradial b.,** a bursa between the ulna, the biceps tendon, and nearby muscles. Called also *interosseous cubital b.* **deltoid b.,** b. subacromialis. **b. of Fabricius,** an epithelial outgrowth of the cloaca in chick embryos, which develops in a manner similar to that of the thymus in mammals, atrophying after 5 or 6 months and persisting as a fibrous remnant in sexually mature birds. **fibular b.,** b. subtendinea musculi bicipitis femoris inferior. **b. of flexor carpi radialis muscle,** vagina synovialis tendinis musculi flexoris carpi radialis. **gastrocnemiosemimembranous b.,** b. musculi semimembranosi. **genual b., anterior,** b. anserina. **genual b., external inferior,** b. subtendinea musculi bicipitis femoris inferior. **genual bursae, internal superior,** bursae subtendineae musculi sartorii. **genual b., posterior,** b. musculi semimembranosi. **bur′sae glutaeofemora′les** [B N A], bursae intermusculares musculorum gluteorum. **gluteal b.,** one situated beneath the gluteus maximus muscle. **gluteal intermuscular bursae,** bursae intermusculares musculorum gluteorum. **gluteofascial bursae,** bursae intermusculares musculorum gluteorum. **gluteofemoral bursae,** bursae intermusculares musculorum gluteorum. **gluteotuberosal b.,** b. ischiadica musculi glutei maximi. **His's b.,** the dilatation at the end of the archenteron. **humeral b.** 1. Bursa subacromialis. 2. Bursa subtendinea musculi gastrocnemii lateralis. **hyoid b.,** b. subcutanea prominentiae laryngeae. **iliac b., subtendinous, b. ili′aca subtendin′ea** [B N A], b. subtendinea iliaca. **b. iliopectine′a** [N A, B N A], **iliopectineal b.,** a bursa between the iliopsoas tendon and the iliopectineal eminence. **b. of iliopsoas muscle,** b. subtendinea iliaca. **inferior b. of biceps femoris muscle,** b. subtendinea musculi bicipitis femoris inferior. **infracardiac b.,** the cranial end of a celomic recess of the embryo, extending upward between the esophagus and right lung bud; frequently persisting in the adult. **infracondyloid b., external,** recessus subpopliteus. **infragenual b.,** b. infrapatellaris profunda. **infrahyoid b., b. infrahyoi′dea** [N A], a bursa sometimes present below the hyoid bone at the attachment of the sternohyoid muscle. **infrapatellar b.,** b. subtendinea prepatellaris. **infrapatellar b., deep,** b. infrapatellaris profunda. **infrapatellar b., subcutaneous,** b. subcutanea infrapatellaris. **infrapatellar b., superficial inferior,** b. subcutanea tuberositatis tibiae. **b. infrapatella′ris profun′da** [N A, B N A], a bursa between the patellar ligament and the tibia. Called also *deep infrapatellar b.* **b. infrapatella′ris subcuta′nea** [B N A], b. subcutanea infrapatellaris. **bur′sae intermetacarpophalan′geae** [B N A], omitted in N A. **bur′sae intermetatarsophalan′geae** [B N A], omitted in N A. **bur′sae intermuscula′res musculo′rum gluteo′rum** [N A], several sacs that surround the tendon attaching the gluteus maximus to the femur. Called also *bursae glutaeo femorales* [B N A] and *intermuscular gluteal bursae.* **intertubercular b.,** vagina synovialis intertubercularis. **b. intratendin′ea olecra′ni** [N A, B N A], a bursa within the triceps tendon near its insertion. Called also *intratendinous b. of olecranon.* **ischiadic b.,** b. ischiadica musculi obturatorii interni. **b. ischiad′ica mus′culi glu′tei max′imi** [N A], a bursa between the ischial tuberosity and the gluteus maximus. Called also *ischial b. of gluteus maximus muscle.* **b. ischiad′ica mus′culi obturato′rii inter′ni** [N A], a bursa between the tendon of the obturator internus muscle and the lesser sciatic notch. Called also *ischial b. of internal obturator muscle.* **ischial b. of gluteus maximus muscle,** b. ischiadica musculi glutei maximi. **ischial b. of internal obturator muscle,** b. ischiadica musculi obturatorii interni. **lateral b. of gastrocnemius muscle,** b. subtendinea musculi gastrocnemii lateralis. **Luschka's b.,** b. pharyngea. **medial b. of gastrocnemius muscle,** b. subtendinea musculi gastrocnemii medialis. **Monro's b.,** b. intratendinea olecrani. **b. muco′sa** [B N A], b. synovialis. **b. muco′sa patella′ris profun′da,** b. subtendinea prepatellaris. **b. muco′sa radia′lis,** b. bicipitoradialis. **b. muco′sa radia′lis inter′ni,** vagina synovialis tendinis musculi flexoris carpi radialis. **b. muco′sa subcuta′nea** [B N A], b. synovialis subcutanea. **b. muco′sa subfascia′lis** [B N A], b. synovialis subfascialis. **b. muco′sa submuscula′ris** [B N A], b. synovialis submuscularis. **b. muco′sa subtendin′ea** [B N A], b. synovialis subtendinea. **b. muco′sa superficia′lis ge′nu, Loder,** b. subtendinea prepatellaris. **mucous b.,** b. synovialis. **mucous b., subpatellar,** b. infrapatellaris profunda. **mucous b., supracondyloid, medial,** b. subtendinea musculi gastrocnemii medialis. **mucous b. of knee, superficial,** b. subtendinea prepatellaris. **multilocular b.,** one which is subdivided into several compartments. **b. mus′culi bicip′itis fem′oris infe′rior** [B N A], b. subtendinea musculi bicipitis femoris inferior. **b. mus′culi bicip′itis fem′oris supe′rior** [N A, B N A], a bursa between the long head of the biceps, the semitendinosus, the tendon of the semimembranosus, and the ischial tuberosity. **b. mus′culi coracobrachia′lis** [N A, B N A], a bursa between the coracobrachialis and subscapularis muscles and the coracoid process. Called also *coracobrachial b.* **b. mus′culi extenso′ris car′pi radia′lis bre′vis** [N A, B N A], a bursa between the tendon and the base of the third metacarpal bone. **b. mus′culi flexo′ris car′pi radia′lis** [B N A], vagina synovialis tendinis musculi flexoris carpi radialis. **b. mus′culi flexo′ris car′pi ulna′ris** [B N A], omitted in N A. **b. mus′culi gastrocne′mii latera′lis** [B N A], b. subtendinea musculi gastrocnemii lateralis. **b. mus′culi gastrocne′mii media′lis** [B N A], b. subtendinea musculi gastrocnemii medialis. **b. mus′culi infraspina′ti** [B N A], b. subtendinea musculi infraspinati. **b. mus′culi latis′simi dor′si** [B N A], b. subtendinea musculi latissimi dorsi. **bur′sae musculo′rum lumbrica′lium pe′dis** [B N A], omitted in N A. **b. mus′culi obturato′ris inter′ni** [B N A]. See *b. ischiadica musculi obturatorii interni* and *b. subtendinea musculi obturatorii interni.* **b. mus′culi pectine′i** [B N A], omitted in N A. **b. mus′culi pirifor′mis** [N A, B N A], a bursa between the piriformis tendons, the superior gemellus muscles, and the femur. Called also *b. of piriform muscle.* **b. mus′culi poplite′i** [B N A], recessus subpopliteus. **b. mus′culi rec′ti fem′oris** [B N A], omitted in N A. **b. mus′culi sarto′rii pro′pria** [B N A]. See *bursae subtendineae musculi sartorii.* **b. mus′culi semimembrano′si** [N A, B N A], a bursa between the semimembranosus muscle and the medial head of the gastrocnemius. Called also *b. of semimembranosus muscle.* **b. mus′culi sternohyoi′dei** [B N A]. See *b. intrahyoidea* and *b. retrohyoidea.* **b. mus′culi tenso′ris ve′li palati′ni** [N A, B N A], a bursa between the hamular process of the sphenoid bone and the tendon of the tensor veli palatini. Called also *b. of tensor veli palatini muscle.* **b. mus′culi tere′tis majo′ris** [B N A], b. subtendinea musculi teretis majoris. **b. mus′culi thyreohyoi′dei** [B N A], a bursa under the thyrohyoid muscle. **b. mus′culi trochlea′ris** [B N A], vagina synovialis musculi obliqui superioris. **omental b., b. omenta′lis** [N A, B N A], a serous cavity situated behind the stomach, the lesser omentum, and part of the liver and in front of the pancreas and duodenum. It communicates with the general peritoneal cavity through the epiploic foramen and sometimes is continuous with the cavity of the greater omentum. **ovarian b., b. ova′rica** [B N A], omitted in N A. **patellar b., deep,** b. subtendinea prepatellaris. **patellar b., middle,** b. subfascialis prepatellaris. **patellar b., prespinous,** b. subcutanea tuberositatis tibiae. **patellar b., subcutaneous,** b. subcutanea prepatellaris. **peroneal b., common,** vagina synovialis tendinum musculorum peroneorum communis. **b. pharyn'gea** [N A, B N A], **pharyngeal b.,** an inconstant blind sac found on the caudal part of the pharyngeal tonsil. **b. of piriform muscle,** b. musculi piriformis. **popliteal b., b. of popliteal muscle,** recessus subpopliteus. **postcalcaneal b.,** b. subcutanea calcanea. **postcalcaneal b., deep,** b. tendinis calcanei [Achillis]. **postgenual b., external,** b. subtendinea musculi gastrocnemii lateralis. **b. praepatella'ris subcuta'nea** [B N A], b. subcutanea prepatellaris. **b. praepatella'ris subfascia'lis** [B N A], b. subfascialis prepatellaris. **b. praepatella'ris subtendin'ea** [B N A], b. subtendinea prepatellaris. **prepatellar b., middle,** b. subfascialis prepatellaris. **prepatellar b., subcutaneous,** b. subcutanea prepatellaris. **prepatellar b., subfascial,** b. subfascialis prepatellaris. **prepatellar b., subtendinous,** b. subtendinea prepatellaris. **bur'sae prepatella'res.** See *b. subcutanea prepatellaris, b. subfascialis prepatellaris,* and *b. subtendinea prepatellaris.* **b. prepatella'ris profun'da, b. prepatella'ris subaponeurot'ica,** b. subtendinea prepatellaris. **pretibial b.,** b. subcutanea tuberositatis tibiae. **bur'sae pro'priae mus'culi sarto'rii,** bursae subtendineae musculi sartorii. **pyriform b.,** b. musculi piriformis. **b. of quadratus femoris muscle,** b. subtendinea iliaca. **retrocondyloid b.,** b. musculi semimembranosi. **retroepicondyloid b., lateral, deep,** b. subtendinea musculi gastrocnemii lateralis. **retrohyoid b., b. retrohyoi'dea** [N A], a bursa sometimes present behind the hyoid bone at the attachment of the sternohyoid muscle. **retromammary b.,** a well defined space, containing loose areolar tissue, between the deep layer of superficial fascia on the posterior aspect of the breast, and the deep fascia covering the pectoralis major and other muscles of the chest wall. **sciatic b. of internal obturator muscle,** b. ischiadica musculi obturatorii interni. **semimembranosogastrocnemial b., semimembranous b.,** b. musculi semimembranosi. **semitendinous b.,** b. musculi bicipitis femoris superior. **b. si'nus tar'si** [B N A], omitted in N A. **sternohyoid b., b. sternohyoi'dea.** See *b. infrahyoidea* and *b. retrohyoidea.* **subachilleal b.,** b. tendinis calcanei [Achillis]. **subacromial b., b. subacromia'lis** [N A, B N A], a large sac between the acromion and the insertion of the supraspinatus muscle, extending between the deltoid and the greater tubercle of the humerus. **subcalcaneal b.,** b. subcutanea calcanea. **subclavian b.,** an inconstant bursa between the fibers of the rhomboid ligament. **subcoracoid b.** 1. Bursa musculi coracobrachialis. 2. Bursa musculi subscapularis subtendinea. **subcrural b.,** b. suprapatellaris. **b. subcuta'nea acromia'lis** [N A, B N A], a bursa between the acromion and the overlying skin. Called also *subcutaneous acromial b.* **b. subcuta'nea calca'nea** [N A, B N A], a bursa between the calcaneum and the skin on the sole of the foot. Called also *subcutaneous calcaneal b.* **bur'sae subcuta'neae digitor'um dorsa'les** [B N A], omitted from N A. **b. subcuta'nea epicon'dyli [hu'meri] latera'lis** [B N A], omitted from N A. **b. subcuta'nea epicon'dyli [hu'meri] media'lis** [B N A], omitted from N A. **b. subcuta'nea infrapatella'ris** [N A], a bursa between the upper end of the patellar ligament and the skin. Called also *b. infrapatellaris subcutanea* [B N A] and *subcutaneous infrapatellar b.* **b. subcuta'nea malle'oli latera'lis** [N A, B N A], a bursa between the lateral malleolus and the skin. Called also *subcutaneous b. of lateral malleolus.* **b. subcuta'nea malle'oli media'lis** [N A, B N A], a bursa between the medial malleolus and the skin. Called also *subcutaneous b. of medial malleolus.* **bur'sae subcuta'neae metacarpophalan'geae dorsa'les** [B N A], omitted in N A. **b. subcuta'nea olecra'ni** [N A, B N A], a bursa between the olecranon process and the skin. Called also *subcutaneous b. of olecranon.* **b. subcuta'nea praementa'lis** [B N A], omitted in N A. **b. subcuta'nea prepatella'ris** [N A], a bursa between the patella and the skin. Called also *b. praepatellaris subcutanea* [B N A] and *subcutaneous prepatellar b.* **b. subcuta'nea prominen'tiae laryn'geae** [N A, B N A], a bursa over the anterior prominence of the thyroid cartilage of the larynx, under the skin. Called also *subcutaneous b. of prominence of larynx.* **b. subcuta'nea sacra'lis** [B N A], omitted in N A. **b. subcuta'nea tuberosita'tis tib'iae** [N A, B N A], a bursa between the tibial tuberosity and the skin. Called also *subcutaneous b. of tuberosity of tibia.* **subcutaneous b. of lateral malleolus,** b. subcutanea malleoli lateralis. **subcutaneous b. of medial malleolus,** b. subcutanea malleoli medialis. **subcutaneous b. of tuberosity of tibia,** b. subcutanea tuberositatis tibiae. **subdeltoid b., b. subdeltoi'dea** [N A, B N A], a bursa between the deltoid and the shoulder joint capsule, usually connected to the subacromial bursa. **b. subfascia'lis prepatella'ris** [N A], a bursa between the front of the patella and the investing fascia of the knee. Called also *b. praepatellaris subfascialis* [B N A]. **subhyoid b.,** b. subcutanea prominentiae laryngeae. **subiliac b.** 1. Bursa iliopectinea. 2. Bursa subtendinea iliaca. **subligamentous b.,** b. infrapatellaris profunda. **subpatellar b.** 1. Bursa infrapatellaris profunda. 2. Bursa subcutanea infrapatellaris. **b. subtendin'ea ili'aca** [N A], a bursa between the iliopsoas tendon and the lesser trochanter. Called also *b. iliaca subtendinea* [B N A] and *subtendinous iliac b.* **b. subtendin'ea mus'culi bicip'itis fem'oris infe'rior** [N A], a bursa between the tendon of the biceps femoris muscle and the fibular collateral ligament of the knee joint. Called also *inferior subtendinous b. of bicipitis femoris muscle.* **b. subtendin'ea mus'culi gastrocne'mii latera'lis** [N A], a bursa between the tendon of the lateral head of the gastrocnemius muscle and the joint capsule. Called also *b. musculi gastrocnemii lateralis* [B N A] and *subtendinous b. of lateral head of gastrocnemius muscle.* **b. subtendin'ea mus'culi gastrocne'mii media'lis** [N A], a bursa between the tendon of the medial head of the gastrocnemius, the condyle of the femur, and the joint capsule. Called also *b. musculi gastrocnemii medialis* [B N A] and *subtendinous b. of medial head of gastrocnemius muscle.* **b. subtendin'ea mus'culi infraspina'ti** [N A], a bursa between the tendon of the infraspinatus and the joint capsule or the greater tubercle. Called also *b. musculi infraspinati* [B N A] and *subtendinous b. of infraspinatus muscle.* **b. subtendin'ea mus'culi latis'simi dor'si** [N A], a bursa between the tendons of the latissimus dorsi and teres major muscles. Called also *b. musculi latissimi dorsi* [B N A] and *b. of latissimus dorsi muscle.* **b. subtendin'ea mus'culi obtura'to'rii inter'ni** [N A], a bursa beneath the tendon of the obturator internus muscle. Called also *subtendinous b. of internal obturator muscle.* **bur'sae subtendin'eae mus'culi sarto'rii** [N A], bursae between the tendons of the sartorius, semitendinosus, and gracilis muscles. Called also *subtendinous bursae of sartorius muscle.* **b. subtendin'ea mus'culi subscapula'ris** [N A], a bursa between the tendon of the subscapularis muscle and the glenoid border of the scapula. Called also *b. musculi subscapularis* [B N A] and *subtendinous b. of subscapularis muscle.* **b. subtendin'ea mus'culi tere'tis majo'ris** [N A], a bursa deep to the tendon of insertion of the teres major muscle. Called also *b. musculi teretis majoris* [B N A] and *subtendinous b. of teres major muscle.* **b. subtendin'ea mus'culi tibia'lis anterio'ris** [N A, B N A], a bursa between the tibialis anterior and the medial surface of the medial cuneiform bone. Called also *subtendinous b. of anterior tibial muscle.*

b. subtendin'ea mus'culi tibia'lis posterio'ris [N A, B N A], a bursa between the tibialis posterior and the navicular fibrocartilage. Called also *subtendinous b. of posterior tibial muscle.* **b. subtendin'ea mus'culi trape'zii** [N A], a bursa between the trapezius and the medial end of the spine of the scapula. **b. subtendin'ea mus'culi tricip'itis bra'chii** [N A], **b. subtendin'ea olecra'ni** [B N A], an inconstant sac between the triceps tendon, the olecranon, and the dorsal ligament of the elbow. **b. subtendin'ea prepatella'ris** [N A], a bursa sometimes present between the quadriceps tendon and the patellar periosteum. Called also *b. praepatellaris subtendinea* [B N A] and *subtendinous prepatellar b.* **subtendinous b. of anterior tibial muscle,** b. subtendinea musculi tibialis anterioris. **subtendinous b. of biceps femoris muscle, inferior,** b. subtendinea musculi bicipitis femoris inferior. **subtendinous b. of internal obturator muscle,** b. subtendinea musculi obturatorii interni. **subtendinous b. of medial head of gastrocnemius muscle,** b. subtendinea musculi gastrocnemii medialis. **subtendinous b. of posterior tibial muscle,** b. subtendinea musculi tibialis posterioris. **subtendinous bursae of sartorius muscle,** bursae subtendineae musculi sartorii. **superficial b. of knee,** b. subcutanea infrapatellaris. **superficial b. of olecranon,** b. subcutanea olecrani. **superior b. of biceps femoris muscle,** b. musculi bicipitis femoris superior. **supernumerary b.,** adventitious b. **supraanconeal b., intratendinous,** b. intratendinea olecrani. **supracondyloid b., internal, supracondyloid b., medial,** b. subtendinea musculi gastrocnemii medialis. **supragenual b., suprapatellar b.,** b. suprapatellaris. **b. suprapatella'ris** [N A, B N A], a bursa between the distal end of the femur and the quadriceps tendon. Called also *suprapatellar b.* **synovial b.,** b. synovialis. **synovial b., subcutaneous,** b. synovialis subcutanea. **synovial b. of trochlea,** b. synovialis trochlearis. **b. synovia'lis** [N A], a closed synovial sac interposed between surfaces which glide upon each other; it may be simple or multilocular in structure, and subcutaneous, submuscular, subfascial, or subtendinous in location. Called also *b. mucosa* [B N A], *mucous b.*, and *synovial b.* **b. synovia'lis subcuta'nea** [N A], a synovial sac found beneath the skin. Called also *b. mucosa subcutanea* [B N A]. **b. synovia'lis subfascia'lis** [N A], a synovial sac found beneath a fascial layer. Called also *b. mucosa subfascialis* [B N A]. **b. synovia'lis submuscula'ris** [N A], a synovial sac found beneath a muscle. Called also *b. mucosa submuscularis* [B N A]. **b. synovia'lis subtendin'ea** [N A], a synovial sac found beneath a tendon. Called also *b. mucosa subtendinea* [B N A]. **b. synovia'lis trochlea'ris** [N A], the synovial bursa that encloses the tendon of the superior oblique muscle as it passes through the trochlea. Called also *synovial bursa of trochlea.* **b. ten'dinis calca'nei [Achil'lis]** [N A, B N A], **b. of tendon of Achilles,** a bursa between the calcaneal tendon and the back of the calcaneus. Called also *b. of Achilles tendon* and *b. of calcaneal tendon.* **b. of testes,** scrotum. **thyrohyoid b.,** b. subcutanea prominentiae laryngeae. **thyrohyoid b., anterior.** See *b. infrahyoidea* and *b. retrohyoidea.* **trochanteric b., subcutaneous,** b. trochanterica subcutanea. **trochanteric b. of gluteus maximus muscle,** b. trochanterica musculi glutei maximi. **trochanteric bursae of gluteus medius muscle,** bursae trochantericae musculi glutei medii. **trochanteric b. of gluteus minimus muscle,** b. trochanterica musculi glutei minimi. **b. trochanter'ica mus'culi glu'taei me'dii ante'rior** [B N A]. See *bursae trochantericae musculi glutei medii.* **b. trochanter'ica mus'culi glu'taei me'dii poste'rior** [B N A]. See *bursae trochantericae musculi glutei medii.* **b. trochanter'ica mus'culi glu'tei max'imi** [N A], a bursa between the fascial tendon of the gluteus maximus, the posterolateral surface of the greater trochanter, and the vastus lateralis muscle. Called also *trochanteric b. of gluteus maximus muscle.* **bur'sae trochanter'icae mus'culi glu'tei me'dii** [N A], bursae between the gluteus medius and the lateral surface of the greater trochanter, and sometimes between the tendons of the gluteus medius and the piriformis. Called also *trochanteric bursae of gluteus medius muscle.* **b. trochanter'ica mus'culi glu'tei min'imi** [N A], a bursa between the edge of the gluteus minimus and the greater trochanter. Called also *trochanteric b. of gluteus minimus muscle.* **b. trochanter'ica subcuta'nea** [N A, B N A], a bursa between the greater trochanter of the femur and the skin. Called also *subcutaneous trochanteric b.* **tuberoischiadic b.,** b. ischiadica musculi obturatorii interni. **ulnoradial b.,** b. cubitalis interossea. **vesicular b., ileopubic,** b. iliopectinea. **vesicular b. of sternohyoideus muscle.** See *b. infrahyoidea* and *b. retrohyoidea.*

bursae (bur'se) [L.]. Plural of *bursa.*

bursal (bur'sal) [L. *bursalis*]. Of, or pertaining to, a bursa.

bursalogy (bur-sal'o-je) [*bursa* + *-logy*]. The sum of knowledge regarding the bursae.

Bursata (bur-sa'tah). A division of Nematoda comprising forms which have a bursa copulatrix.

bursatti, bursautee (bur-sat'e, bur-sawt'e). See *leeches.*

bursectomy (bur-sek'to-me) [*bursa* + Gr. *ektomē* excision]. Excision of a bursa.

bursitis (bur-si'tis). Inflammation of a bursa. **Achilles b.,** achillobursitis. **Duplay's b.,** subacromial or subdeltoid bursitis. **omental b.,** seropurulent inflammation of the omental bursa. **pharyngeal b.,** Thornwaldt's b. **radiohumeral b.,** tennis elbow. **retrocalcaneal b.,** achillodynia. **Thornwaldt's b., Tornwaldt's b.,** chronic inflammation of the pharyngeal bursa, attended with formation of a pus-containing cyst, and nasopharyngeal stenosis.

bursolith (bur'so-lith) [*bursa* + Gr. *lithos* stone]. A calculus or concretion in a bursa.

bursopathy (bur-sop'ah-the) [*bursa* + Gr. *pathos* disease]. Any disease of a bursa.

bursotomy (bur-sot'o-me) [*bursa* + Gr. *tomē* a cutting]. Incision of a bursa.

bursula (bur'su-lah) [L.]. A small bag or pouch. **b. tes'tium,** the scrotum.

Burton's line (bur'tunz) [Henry *Burton*, British physician, 1799–1849]. See *blue line*, under *line.*

Bury's disease [Judson S. *Bury*, English physician, 1852–1944]. Erythema elevatum diutinum.

Busacca's gelatin test (bus-ah'kaz) [Attilio *Busacca*]. See under *tests.*

Buscaino's reaction, test (bus-ki'nōz) [Vito Maria *Buscaino*, Italian neurologist, born 1887]. See under *tests.*

Buschke's disease (bo͝osh'kez) [Abraham *Buschke*, German dermatologist, 1868–1943]. Blastomycosis.

bushmaster (bush'mas-ter). A large venomous snake, *Lachesis muta*, of the Amazon region of South America.

Busquet's disease (bo͞os-kāz') [P. *Busquet*, French physician]. See under *disease.*

Busse-Buschke disease [Otto *Busse*, German physician, 1867–1922; Abraham *Buschke*], German dermatologist, 1868–1943]. Cryptococcosis.

busulfan (bu-sul'fan). Chemical name: tetramethylene dimethanesulfonate: used to suppress chronic myelogenous leukemia.

But. Abbreviation for L. *bu'tyrum*, butter.

butabarbital sodium (bu-tah-bar′bĭ-tal so′de-um). A barbituric acid derivative, sodium 5-*sec*-butyl-5-ethylbarbiturate: a sedative and hypnotic.

butacaine sulfate (bu″tah-kān′ sul′fāt). An anesthetic compound, $(C_{18}H_{30}N_2O_2)_2H_2SO_4$, used for surface anesthesia in the eye and on mucous membranes, in 2 per cent solution or as a 2 per cent ointment.

butalanine (bu-tal′ah-nin). An amino acid, alpha-amino-valerianic acid, $CH_3(CH_2)_2CHNH_2CO.H$, produced by the hydrolysis or digestion of proteins.

butamben (bu-tam′ben). Butylaminobenzoate.

butane (bu′tān). A normal hydrocarbon, CH_3-$(CH_2)_2.CH_3$, from petroleum. It is the fourth member of the paraffin series. **normal b.,** CH_3-$(CH_2)_2CH_3$.

butazolidin (bu″tah-zol′ĭ-din). Trade mark for preparations of phenylbutazone.

Butcher's saw (booch′erz) [Richard George Herbert *Butcher*, Irish surgeon, 1819–1891]. See under *saw*.

Butea (bu′te-ah) [for John Stuart, Earl of *Bute*, 1713–1792]. A genus of tropical leguminous trees. *B. frondosa*, a tree of South Asia, is one of the species that afford kino. The seeds yield an anthelmintic oil, moodooga oil.

butesin (bu-te′sin). Trade mark for a preparation of butyl aminobenzoate.

butethal (bu′tĕ-thal). An odorless, bitter compound, 5-ethyl-5-*n*-butylbarbituric acid, with sedative and hypnotic action resembling but more powerful than that of barbital.

butethamine (bu-teth′ah-mēn). Chemical name: 2-isobutylaminoethyl p-aminobenzoate: used as a local anesthetic.

Buthus (bu′thus). A genus of scorpions. **B. carolinianus,** a species occurring in the southern United States. **B. quinquestria′tus,** a dangerous species occurring in Egypt.

butisol (bu′tĭ-sol). Trade mark for preparations of butabarbital.

butment (but′ment). Abutment.

butopyronoxyl (bu″to-pi″ro-nok′sil). An aromatic yellow to pale reddish brown liquid, C_{12}-$H_{18}O_4$: used as an insect repellent.

Bütschli's nuclear spindle (bitsh′lēz) [Otto *Bütschli*, German zoologist, 1848–1920]. See *spindle*, def. 1.

Bütschlia (bitsh′le-ah). A genus of ciliates, species of which have been found in the stomachs of cattle.

butt (but). To bring the surfaces of two distinct objects squarely or directly into contact with each other.

butter (but′er) [L. *butyrum;* Gr. *boutyron*]. The oily mass procured by churning cream. **b. of antimony,** a concentrated acid solution of antimony trichloride, $SbCl_3$: used as a caustic application to tumors or ulcers. **cacao b., cocoa b.,** theobroma oil. **b. of tin,** stannic chloride. **b. of zinc,** zinc chloride.

butterfly (but′er-fli). 1. A mass of absorbent cotton with wing-shaped appendages: used mainly in uterine surgery. 2. A form of doubly wing-shaped skin flaps. 3. In anesthesia, a piece of paper arranged over the nostrils and mouth of a patient to indicate whether he is breathing.

buttock (but′ok). One of the gluteal prominences.

button (but′n). 1. A knoblike elevation or structure. 2. A knoblike device used in surgery. **Aleppo b.,** cutaneous leishmaniasis. **Bagdad b., Biskra b.,** cutaneous leishmaniasis. **Boari b.,** a device analogous to the Murphy button for use in ureterocystostomy. **bromide b.,** a verrucous cutaneous lesion occurring as a result of sensitivity to bromides. **Chlumsky's b.,** a button for intestinal suture made of pure magnesium on the pattern of the Murphy button. **dog b.,** nux vomica. **iodide b.,** a verrucous cutaneous lesion occurring as a result of sensitivity to iodides. **Jaboulay b.,** a device for lateral intestinal anastomosis, consisting of two button-like cylinders of metal which fit together on the screw and key-ring principle through a small intestinal opening and without the aid of sutures. **Lardennois's b.,** a modified form of Murphy button for intestinal anastomosis. **mescal b.** See *mescal.* **Murphy's b.,** a device for joining the ends of a divided intestine, consisting of two button-like plates of metal, each fitted with a collar having a hollow stem fastened to the center, one stem being smaller than the other, so as to fit into it. **oriental b.,** cutaneous leishmaniasis. **peritoneal b.,** a flanged glass tube for insertion between the peritoneal cavity and a subcutaneous pocket, to drain away by absorption a peritoneal transudate. **quaker b.,** nux vomica. **terminal b's.** See *end-feet.* **Villard's b.,** a modified form of Murphy button.

buttonhole (but′n-hōl). A small straight incision into a cavity or organ. **mitral b.,** an advanced state of stenosis of the mitral orifice of the heart.

butyl (bu′til). A hydrocarbon radical, C_4H_9 or $CH_3.CH_2.CH_2.CH_2^-$. **b. aminobenzoate,** chemical name, n-butyl p-aminobenzoate: used for topical anesthesia. **b. chloride,** chemical name, 1-chlorobutane: used as a veterinary anthelmintic. **b. formate,** an industrial solvent, $CH_3(CH_2)_3COOH$, the vapors of which are powerfully lacrimatory and suffocating. **b. hydride,** a hydrocarbon, C_4H_{10}, from petroleum: its vapor is an unsafe anesthetic.

butylmercaptan (bu″til-mer-kap′tan). A thioalcohol, thiobutyl alcohol, $CH_3.CH_2.CH_2CH_2SH$, the active principle of the odoriferous secretion of the skunk.

butyr- (bu′tir) [L. *butyrum;* Gr. *boutyron* butter]. A combining form denoting a relationship to butter.

butyraceous (bu″tĭ-ra′she-us). Of a buttery consistency.

butyrase (bu′tĭ-rās). Butyrinase.

butyrate (bu′tĭ-rāt). A salt of butyric acid.

Butyribacterium (bu-ti″re-bak-te′re-um) [Gr. *boutyron* butter + *baktērion* little rod]. A genus of microorganisms of the family Propionibacteriaceae, order Eubacteriales, made up of non-spore-forming, anaerobic or microaerophilic gram-positive bacilli, nonpathogenic but occurring as parasites in the intestinal tract.

butyric (bu-tir′ik). Derived from butter.

butyrin (bu′tĭ-rin). A glyceride existing in butter, $C_3H_5(C_4H_7O_2)_3$: a liquid fat with an acrid, bitter taste.

butyrinase (bu′tĭ-rin-ās). An enzyme of the blood serum which is capable of catalyzing the hydrolysis of butyrin.

butyrine (bu′tĭ-rin). An amino acid derivative of butyric acid: it is α-amino butyric acid.

butyroid (bu′tĭ-roid) [*butyr-* + Gr. *eidos* form]. Resembling or having the consistency of butter.

butyromel (bu-tir′o-mel). Fresh, unsalted butter, 2 parts, and honey, 1 part: a substitute for cod liver oil.

butyrometer (bu″tĭ-rom′e-ter) [*butyr-* + Gr. *metron* measure]. An apparatus for estimating the proportion of butter fat in milk.

butyroscope (bu-ti′ro-skōp) [*butyr-* + Gr. *skopein* to examine]. Butyrometer.

butyrous (bu′tĭ-rus). Like butter; having a butter-like appearance.

B.V. Abbreviation for L. *bal′neum vapo′ris*, vapor bath.

by-product (bi-prod′ukt). A secondary product obtained during the manufacture of a primary product.

Byrd-Dew method [Harvey Leonidas *Byrd*,

American physician, 1820–1884; James Harvie *Dew*, American physician, 1843–1914]. See under *method*.

bysma (bis′mah). A tampon or plug.

byssaceous (bis-sa′she-us) [Gr. *byssos* flax]. Composed of fine flaxlike threads.

byssinosis (bis″ĭ-no′sis) [Gr. *byssos* flax + *-osis*]. A form of pneumoconiosis due to the inhalation of cotton dust in factories.

byssocausis (bis″o-kaw′sis) [Gr. *byssos* flax + *kausis* burning]. Moxibustion, or cauterization by the moxa.

byssoid (bis′oid) [Gr. *byssos* flax + *eidos* form]. Made up of a fringe, the filaments of which are unequal in length.

byssophthisis (bis″o-thi′sis) [Gr. *byssos* flax + *phthisis* consumption]. Phthisis due to the inhalation of the dust of cotton mills.

byssus (bis′us) [L.; Gr. *byssos*]. Lint, charpie, or cotton.

Bythnia (bith′ne-ah). A genus of snails. **B. longicor′nus,** *Alocimua longicornis.*

bythus (bith′us) [Gr. *bythos* depth]. The lower portion of the abdomen.

C

C. 1. Chemical symbol for *carbon*. 2. Abbreviation for *cathode* or *cathodal, Celsius* or *centigrade* (thermometer), *congius* (gallon), *closure, contraction, color sense, cylinder, cervical* (in vertebral formulas), *clonus*, and *clearance* (in kidney function tests). 3. In the electrocardiogram, C stands for chest (precordial) lead: CR for chest and right arm, CL for chest and left arm, CF for chest and left leg. See *precordial leads*, under *lead*.

c. Abbreviation for *contact* and *curie*.

C′. Symbol for *complement*.

c′. Symbol for *coefficient of partage*.

C_{alb}. Abbreviation for *albumin clearance*.

C_{cr}. Abbreviation for *creatinine clearance*.

C_{in}. Abbreviation for *inulin clearance*.

$C_{T\text{-}1824}$. Abbreviation for *clearance of Evans blue*, or T-1824.

CA. Abbreviation for *chronological age*.

C.A. Abbreviation for *cervicoaxial*.

Ca. 1. Chemical symbol for *calcium*. 2. Abbreviation for *cathode* or *cathodal*.

cabinet (kab′ĭ-net). A small closet, or place of enclosure. **Sauerbruch's c.,** a cabinet within which the air pressure can be increased or diminished. It is used in operations on the chest, the patient's head being outside the cabinet, and his body and the surgeon within it.

Cabot's ring bodies (kab′ots) [Richard C. *Cabot*, Boston physician, 1868–1939]. See under *body*.

Cabot's splint (kab′ots) [Arthur Tracy *Cabot*, Boston surgeon, 1852–1912]. See under *splint*.

CaC_2. Calcium carbide.

cac-. See *caco-*.

cacaerometer (kak″a-er-om′e-ter) [*cac-* + Gr. *aēr* air + *metron* measure]. An instrument for measuring the impurity of air.

cacanthrax (kak-an′thraks). Contagious anthrax.

cacao (kah-ka′o). A powder prepared from the roasted, cured kernels of the ripe seed of *Theobroma cacao:* used as a flavoring agent.

cacation (kak-a′shun). Defecation.

cacatory (kak′ah-to″re). Marked by severe diarrhea.

CaCC. Abbreviation for *cathodal closure contraction*.

cacergasia (kak″er-gas′e-ah) [*cac-* + Gr. *ergon* work]. Poor functioning, bodily or mental.

cacesthenic (kak″es-then′ik). Having defective sense organs.

cacesthesia (kak″es-the′ze-ah) [*cac-* + Gr. *aisthēsis* perception]. Any morbid sensation or any disorder of sensibility.

caché (kah-sha′) [Fr.]. An apparatus for making applications of radium, consisting of a cone of lead covered with paper and having a mica-covered window at the bottom.

cachectic (kah-kek′tik). Pertaining to or characterized by cachexia.

cachet (kah-sha′) [Fr.]. A lenticular capsule for enclosing a dose of unpleasant medicine.

cachexia (kah-kek′se-ah) [*cac-* + Gr. *hexis* habit + *-ia*]. A profound and marked state of constitutional disorder; general ill health and malnutrition. **African c.** 1. Ancylostomiasis. 2. Geophagia, or earth eating. **c. aquo′sa,** ancylostomiasis. **cancerous c.,** the weak, emaciated condition seen in cases of malignant tumor. **c. exophthal′mica,** exophthalmic goiter. **fluoric c.,** fluorosis. **Grawitz's c.,** a condition resembling pernicious anemia, but without degeneration of the red blood corpuscles, seen in old persons. **hypophysial c.,** Simmonds' disease. **c. hypophysiopri′va,** the train of symptoms resulting from total deprivation of function of the pituitary gland, including fibrillary twitchings, opisthotonos, bradycardia, hypothermia, apathy, and coma. **lymphatic c.,** pseudoleukemia. **malarial c.,** a condition of physical and mental retardation caused by repeated malarial infection: seen in natives in regions where malaria is endemic. **c. mercuria′lis,** chronic mercurial poisoning. **Negro c.,** African c. **c. ovariopri′va,** cachexia due to loss of the ovaries. **pachyder′mic c.,** myxedema. **pituitary c.,** Simmonds' disease. **saturnine c.,** chronic lead poisoning. **splenic c., c. splen′ica,** progressive anemia associated with enlargement of the spleen. **c. strumipri′va,** the train of symptoms resulting from deprivation of the function of the thyroid gland. **strumous c.,** scrofula. **c. suprarena′lis,** Addison's disease. **c. thymopri′va,** cachexia due to loss of the thymus gland. **c. thyreoidectom′ica, c. thyreopri′va,** c. strumipriva. **thyroid c.,** exophthalmic goiter. **tropical c.,** a general condition of ill health affecting residents in the tropics, frequently associated with disease of the liver or spleen. **urinary c.,** the cachectic condition seen in chronic suppurative disease of the kidney. It is marked by dyspepsia, loss of appetite, flatulence, tympanites, diarrhea, weakness, and mental depression. **verminous c.,** the condition of anemia and debility which accompanies infection with worms, especially ancylostoma.

cachexy (kah-kek′se). Cachexia.

cachinnation (kak″ĭ-na′shun) [L. *cachinnare* to laugh aloud]. Excessive, hysterical laughter.

cacidrosis (kak-e-dro′sis) [*cac-* + Gr. *hidrōs* sweat]. Abnormal or malodorous sweating.

$CaCl_2$. Calcium chloride.

$Ca(ClO_3)_2$. Calcium chlorate.

$CaCl(OCl)$. Chlorinated lime.

$CaCO_3$. Calcium carbonate.

CaC_2O_4. Calcium oxalate.

caco- [Gr. *kakos* bad]. A combining form meaning bad, or ill.

cacodemonomania (kak″o-de″mon-o-ma′ne-ah). A condition marked by delusions of being possessed by evil spirits.

cacodontia (kak″o-don′she-ah) [*cac-* + Gr. *odous* tooth]. The condition characterized by the presence of bad teeth.

cacodyl (kak′o-dil) [*caco-* + Gr. *ozein* to smell + *hylē* matter]. Dimethylarsine; a colorless liquid, $(CH_3)_2As—As(CH_3)_2$, with an offensive odor. It gives off a poisonous vapor and is inflammable when exposed to air. **c. cyanide,** a white powder, $(CH_3)_2As.CN$, which, when exposed to the air, gives off an extremely poisonous vapor.

cacodylate (kak′o-dil-āt). A salt of cacodylic acid. The cacodylates are used in skin diseases, tuberculosis, malaria, and other conditions where arsenic is indicated.

cacoethes (kak″o-e′thēz) [Gr. *kakoēthēs* an ill habit or itch for doing a thing]. A bad habit. **c. operan′di,** undue eagerness to perform surgical operations; tomomania.

cacoethic (kak″o-e′thik). Ill-conditioned; malignant.

cacogenesis (kak″o-jen′e-sis) [*caco-* + Gr. *genesis* production]. Defective development.

cacogenic (kak″o-jen′ik). 1. Having a tendency toward race degeneracy. 2. Pertaining to cacogenesis.

cacogenics (kak″o-jen′iks) [*caco-* + Gr. *gennan* to generate]. Deterioration of the physical and moral properties of a race resulting from the mating and propagation of inferior individuals.

cacogeusia (kak″o-gu′se-ah) [*caco-* + Gr. *geusis* taste]. A bad taste.

cacomelia (kak″o-me′le-ah) [*caco-* + Gr. *melos* limb]. Congenital deformity of a limb.

cacomorphosis (kak″o-mor-fo′sis) [*caco-* + Gr. *morphē* form]. Malformation.

Caconema (kak″o-ne′mah). A genus of nematodes resembling *Heterodera*.

cacoplastic (kak″o-plas′tik) [*caco-* + Gr. *plastikos* forming]. Susceptible of only an imperfect organization.

cacorhythmic (kak″o-rith′mik) [*caco-* + Gr. *rhythmos* rhythm]. Marked by irregularity of rhythm.

cacosmia (kak-oz′me-ah) [*caco-* + Gr. *osmē* smell]. 1. A bad odor; stench. 2. A hallucination of unpleasant odor.

cacostomia (kak″o-sto′me-ah) [*caco-* + Gr. *stoma* mouth]. A foul or gangrenous state of the mouth.

cacothenic (kak″o-then′ik). Pertaining to cacothenics.

cacothenics (kak″o-then′iks) [Gr. *kakothēneein* to be in a bad state]. Deterioration of a race resulting from deleterious influences in the environment.

cacothymia (kak″o-thi′me-ah). A morbid condition caused by derangement of the thymus gland.

cacotrophy (kak-ot′ro-fe) [*caco-* + Gr. *trophē* nourishment]. Malnutrition; impaired or disordered nourishment.

cacumen (kak-u′men), pl. *cacu′mina* [L.]. 1. The top or apex of an organ. 2. The top and uppermost branchlets of a plant. 3. Culmen.

cacuminal (kak-u′mĭ-nal). Pertaining to the cacumen.

cadaver (kah-dav′er) [L., from *cadere,* to fall, to perish]. A dead body; generally applied to a human body long after death, such as one preserved for anatomical study.

cadaveric (kah-dav′er-ik). Of, or pertaining to, a cadaver.

cadaverine (kah-dav′er-in) [L. *cadaver* corpse]. A nitrogenous base, pentamethylenediamine, $NH_2.CH_2(CH_2)_3CH_2.NH_2$: a thick liquid having a foul odor. It is sometimes one of the products of *Vibrio proteus* and of *Vibrio comma.* It occasionally occurs in the urine in cystinuria.

cadaverous (kah-dav′er-us). Resembling a cadaver.

caddis (kad′is). A fly of the order Trichoptera. Hairs and scales from these flies are an exciting cause of allergic coryza and asthma.

caderas (kad-e′ras). Mal de caderas.

cadmium (kad′me-um) [Gr. *kadmia* earth]. A bivalent metal, not unlike tin in appearance and properties; symbol, Cd; atomic number, 48; atomic weight, 112.40: its salts are poisonous. **c. bromide,** a poisonous substance, $CdBr_2$. **c. iodide,** a compound, CdI_2. **c. oleate,** a preparation used in various skin diseases. **c. salicylate,** a salt, $(C_6H_4(OH)CO_2)_2Cd + H_2O$, in fine, white, tabular crystals, or in an amorphous powder: antiseptic. **c. sulfate,** a salt, $CdSO_4$, weak solutions of which are used as astringents in eye, ear, and urethral inflammations. **c. sulfide,** a light yellow or orange powder, CdS: used in 1 per cent suspension in treatment of seborrheic dermatitis of the scalp.

Ca.D.Te. Abbreviation for *cathodal duration tetanus.*

caduca (kah-du′kah). The decidua.

caduceus (kah-du′se-us). The wand of Hermes or Mercury, the messenger of the gods: used as a medical symbol and as the emblem of the Medical Corps, U.S. Army. The official symbol of the medical profession is the staff of Æsculapius.

caducous (kah-du′kus) [L. *cadere* to fall]. Falling off; deciduous.

cae-. For words beginning thus, see also those beginning *ce-*.

caecitas (ses′ĭ-tas) [L.]. Blindness.

caecus (se′kus) [L.]. A blind pouch. **c. mi′nor ventric′uli,** the cardiac part of the stomach (pars cardiaca ventriculi [N A]).

Caelius Aurelianus (se′le-us aw-re″le-a′nus) (5th century A.D.). An outstanding physician and medical writer, whose most famous work, *De morbis acutis et chronicis,* although clearly influenced by Soranus, contains much fresh material and "conforms to the modern standard of what a medical work should be" (Major).

caelotherapy (se″lo-ther′ah-pe) [L. *caelum* heaven + *therapy*]. The use of religion and religious symbols for therapeutic purposes.

caeno-. For words beginning thus, see those beginning *ceno-*.

caesarean (se-za′re-an). Cesarean.

caesium (se′ze-um). Cesium.

CaF_2. Calcium fluoride.

cafard (kah-far′) [Fr.]. A severe form of mental depression.

caffea (kaf′e-ah) [L.]. Coffee.

caffeine (kaf′fe-in) [L. *caffeina*]. An odorless, bitter, white powder, $C_8H_{10}N_4O_2$, soluble in water and alcohol, and obtainable from coffee, tea, guarana, and maté: used as a central nervous system stimulant, cardiac stimulant, and in treatment of migraine. **c. borocitrate,** a white, soluble powder that has been used for its sedative and antiseptic effect. **c. chloral,** a soluble crystalline combination of caffeine and chloral, $C_8H_{10}N_4O_2—CCl_3COH$: analgesic and sedative. **c. citrate, citrated c.,** a preparation of equal parts of caffeine and citric acid: used as a central nervous system stimulant. **c. hydrobromide,** a diuretic: used subcutaneously. **c. nitrate,** a salt, in yellowish, needle-like crystals. **c. phthalate,** a sedative and antiseptic: used subcutaneously. **c. sodium benzoate,** an odorless white powder with a slightly bitter taste, consisting of equal parts of anhydrous caffeine and sodium benzoate: used as a central nervous system stimulant. **c. triiodide,** a compound in dark-green prisms, $(C_8H_{10}N_4O_2I_2.HI)_2 + 3H_2O$, used as an iodine substitute. **c. valerianate,** a compound used in whooping cough and hysteric vomiting.

caffeinism (kaf′e-in-izm″). A morbid condition resulting from ingestion of excessive amounts of caffeine.

caffeone (kaf′e-ōn). An aromatic principle from

roasted coffee: it is said to have hypnotic properties.

Caffey's disease (kaf′fēz) [John *Caffey*, American pediatrician, born 1895]. Infantile cortical hyperostosis.

CaH_2O_2. Calcium hydroxide.

cainotophobia (ki-no″to-fo′be-ah) [Gr. *kainotēs* novelty + *phobia*]. Cenotophobia.

Cajal's cells, stain (ka-halz′) [Santiago Ramón y *Cajal*, Spanish histologist, 1852–1934; co-winner, with Camillo Golgi, of the Nobel prize in medicine for 1906]. See under *cell*, and *Table of Stains*.

cajeputol (kaj′e-pu-tol). Eucalyptol.

Cal. Abbreviation for *large calorie*.

cal. Abbreviation for *small calorie*.

calage (kah-lahzh′) [Fr.]. Propping with pillows to immobilize the viscera and thus relieve seasickness.

calamine (kal′ah-mīn). A preparation of zinc oxide with about 0.5 per cent ferric oxide. Uses: 1. astringent; 2. antiseptic for inflammatory skin conditions.

calamus (kal′ah-mus) [L.]. 1. A reedlike structure. 2. The plant *Acorus calamus* and its aromatic rhizone. It is a carminative and stimulant tonic. **c. scripto′rius** [B N A], a name given a space at the lower part or floor of the fourth ventricle, between the restiform bodies; omitted in N A.

calcaneal (kal-ka′ne-al). Pertaining to the calcaneus.

calcanean (kal-ka′ne-an). Calcaneal.

calcaneitis (kal-ka″ne-i′tis). Inflammation of the calcaneus.

calcaneo-apophysitis (kal-ka′ne-o-ah-pof″e-zi′tis). An affection of the posterior part of the calcaneus marked by pain at the point of insertion of the Achilles tendon, with swelling of the soft parts.

calcaneo-astragaloid (kal-ka″ne-o-ah-strag′-ah-loid). Pertaining to the calcaneus and astragalus.

calcaneocavus (kal-ka″ne-o-ka′vus). Clubfoot in which talipes calcaneus is combined with talipes cavus.

calcaneocuboid (kal-ka″ne-o-ku′boid). Pertaining to the calcaneus and cuboid bone.

calcaneodynia (kal-ka″ne-o-din′e-ah). Pain in the heel, or calcaneus.

calcaneofibular (kal-ka″ne-o-fib′u-lar). Pertaining to the calcaneus and the fibula.

calcaneonavicular (kal-ka″ne-o-nah-vik′u-lar). Pertaining to the calcaneus and navicular bone.

calcaneoplantar (kal-ka″ne-o-plan′tar). Pertaining to the calcaneus and the sole of the foot.

calcaneoscaphoid (kal-ka″ne-o-ska′foid). Calcaneonavicular.

calcaneotibial (kal-ka″ne-o-tib′e-al). Pertaining to the calcaneus and tibia.

calcaneovalgocavus (kal-ka″ne-o-val″go-ka′-vus). Clubfoot in which talipes calcaneus, talipes valgus, and talipes cavus are combined.

calcaneum (kal-ka′ne-um), pl. *calca′nea* [L.]. Calcaneus.

calcaneus (kal-ka′ne-us) [L.]. [N A, B N A] The irregular quadrangular bone at the back of the tarsus. Called also *heel bone*, and *os calcis*.

calcanodynia (kal″kah-no-din′e-ah). Calcaneodynia.

calcar (kal′kar) [L.]. A spur, or structure resembling a spur. **c. a′vis** [N A, B N A], a white elevation on the floor of the posterior horn of the lateral ventricle. Called also *hippocampus minor*. **c. pe′dis,** the heel.

calcarea (kal-ka′re-ah) [L.]. Lime; calcium oxide or hydroxide. **c. carbon′ica,** a homeopathic preparation made from the middle layer of the oyster shell: used in rickets, scrofula, acid dyspepsia, etc. **c. chlora′ta,** chlorinated lime: a disinfectant and bleaching agent. **c. fluor′ica,** a homeopathic preparation of fluorspar, given in tumors of bone, varicose veins, and cataract. **c. hy′drica,** a solution of calcium hydroxide; liquor calcis, or lime water. **c. phosphor′ica,** precipitated calcium phosphate. **c. us′ta,** quicklime or caustic lime; calcium oxide or unslaked lime.

calcareous (kal-ka′re-us) [L. *calcarius*]. Pertaining to or containing lime or calcium; chalky.

calcarine (kal′kar-in) [L. *calcarinus* spur-shaped]. 1. Spur-shaped. 2. Pertaining to the calcar.

calcariuria (kal-ka″re-u′re-ah) [L. *calcarius* containing lime + Gr. *ouron* urine + *-ia*]. The presence of lime salts in the urine.

calcaroid (kal′kar-oid). Resembling calcium; a term given to certain deposits in cerebral tissue which resemble calcification but do not give a specific reaction for calcium.

calcemia (kal-se′me-ah) [*calcium* + Gr. *haima* blood + *-ia*]. The presence of an abnormally large amount of calcium in the blood.

calcibilia (kal″sĭ-bil′e-ah). The presence of calcium in the bile.

calcic (kal′sik). Of, or pertaining to, lime or to calcium.

calcicosilicosis (kal″sĭ-ko-sil″ĭ-ko′sis). A variety of pneumoconiosis due to the inhalation of mineral dust containing silica and lime.

calcicosis (kal″sĭ-ko′sis) [L. *calx* lime]. A morbid condition of the lung resulting from the inhalation of marble dust.

calcifames (kal-sif′ah-mēz). Calcium hunger.

calciferol (kal-sif′er-ol). An activation product of ergosterol, produced by ultraviolet irradiation or electronic bombardment, $C_{28}H_{44}O$, occurring in white odorless crystals, insoluble in water but soluble in alcohol, chloroform, ether, and fatty oils: used in the prophylaxis and treatment of vitamin D deficiency.

calcific (kal-sif′ik). Forming lime.

calcification (kal″sĭ-fĭ-ka′shun) [*calcium* + L. *facere* to make]. The process by which organic tissue becomes hardened by a deposit of calcium salts within its substance. **metastatic c.,** the anomalous deposition of lime salts in a tissue or part at the same time that marked decalcification of the bones is taking place, as in osteomalacia. **Mönckeberg's c.** See under *sclerosis*.

calcigerous (kal-sij′er-us) [*calcium* + L. *gerere* to bear]. Producing or carrying calcium salts.

calcimeter (kal-sim′e-ter) [*calcium* + Gr. *metron* measure]. An instrument for estimating the amount of calcium present, as in the blood.

calcination (kal″sĭ-na′shun) [L. *calcinare* to char]. The process of roasting or reducing to a powder or of drying by heat.

calcine (kal′sīn). To roast or reduce to a powder or dry thoroughly by heat.

calcinosis (kal″sĭ-no′sis). A condition marked by the deposition of calcium salts in various tissues of the body. **c. circumscrip′ta,** a condition marked by calcifications occurring only in subcutaneous fat. **c. cu′tis,** a condition marked by deposits of calcium salts in the skin in the form of nodules or plaques. **c. interstitia′lis,** a disorder of calcium metabolism marked by abnormal deposits of calcium in the connective tissues. **c. intervertebra′lis,** deposit of calcium in one or more intervertebral disks. **c. universa′lis,** calcinosis in which calcifications appear in other connective tissues, such as muscles, ligaments, and tendons, as well as in subcutaneous fat.

calciokinesis (kal″se-o-ki-ne′sis). Mobilization of calcium stored in the body.

calciokinetic (kal″se-o-ki-net′ik). Pertaining to or causing calciokinesis.

calciorrhachia (kal″se-o-ra′ke-ah) [*calcium* + Gr. *rhachis* spine + *-ia*]. The presence of calcium in the spinal fluid.

calciotropism (kal″se-ot′ro-pizm). An exaggerated reaction of cells to the administration of calcium.

calcipectic (kal″sĭ-pek′tik). Pertaining to, characterized by, or causing calcipexy.

calcipenia (kal″sĭ-pe′ne-ah) [*calcium* + Gr. *penia* poverty]. Deficiency of calcium.

calcipenic (kal″sĭ-pe′nik). Pertaining to or characterized by calcipenia.

calcipexic (kal″sĭ-pek′sik). Calcipectic.

calcipexis (kal″sĭ-pek′sis). Calcipexy.

calcipexy (kal′sĭ-pek-se) [*calcium* + Gr. *pēxis* fixation]. Fixation of calcium in the tissues of the organism.

calciphylactic (kal″sĭ-fi-lak′tik). Pertaining to or characterized by calciphylaxis.

calciphylaxis (kal″sĭ-fi-lak′sis). The formation of calcified tissue in response to administration of a challenging agent subsequent to induction of a hypersensitive state. **systemic c.,** the generalized appearance of calcifications in internal organs or tissues, occurring in response to intravenous or intraperitoneal injection of the challenging agent. **topical s.,** the formation of a circumscribed area of calcification in response to subcutaneous injection of the challenging agent.

calciphilia (kal″sĭ-fil′e-ah) [*calcium* + Gr. *philein* to love]. A tendency to absorb lime salts from the blood and thus to become calcified.

calciprivia (kal″sĭ-priv′e-ah) [*calcium* + L. *privus* without + *-ia*]. Deprivation or loss of calcium.

calciprivic (kal′sĭ-priv″ik). Pertaining to or characterized by calciprivia.

calcipyelitis (kal″sĭ-pi-ĕ-li′tis). Calculous pyelitis.

calcium (kal′se-um), gen. *cal′cii* [L. *calx* lime]. A yellow metal, the basic element of lime. Symbol, Ca; atomic number, 20; atomic weight, 40.08. It is found in nearly all organized tissues, and has been called *coagulation factor IV* because of its role in the first, second, and probably the third stage of blood coagulation. **c. acetate,** a resolvent, $Ca(C_2H_3O_2)_2$. **c. aminosalicylate,** odorless, white to cream colored crystals or powder, with an alkaline, slightly bittersweet taste, $C_{14}H_{12}CaN_2O_6$: used as an antibacterial in tuberculosis. **c. aurothiomalate,** a gold- and sulfur-containing compound, used in arthritis. **c. benzoate,** a compound, $Ca(C_6H_5CO_2)_2 + 3H_2O$, employed in nephritis and albuminuria of pregnancy. **c. bisulfite,** a colorless, strong-smelling fluid, $Ca(HSO_3)_2$. **c. borate,** an antiseptic agent, $Ca_3(BO_3)_2$. **c. bromide,** an odorless, white, deliquescent granular salt, $CaBr_2.xH_2O$: central nervous system depressant. **c. carbonate,** a compound, $CaCO_3$, occurring naturally in bones, shells, etc., and prepared artificially: astringent and antacid, used in dyspepsia, colic, diarrhea, and locally as a dusting powder. **c. carbonate, precipitated,** an odorless, tasteless, fine white crystalline powder: used as an antacid and to reduce intestinal peristalsis. **c. caseinate,** casein from cow's milk rendered partially soluble by combination with calcium. **c. chloride,** an odorless compound, $CaCl_2.2H_2O$, occurring as hard white fragments or granules: used in solution to restore electrolyte balance or as an antidote for magnesium poisoning. **c. creosotate,** a mixture of the calcium constituents of creosote. **c. cresylate,** a syrupy preparation of calcium hydroxide and cresol. **c. cyclamate,** a white, crystalline, practically odorless powder with a very sweet taste, practically insoluble in alcohol but freely soluble in water: used as a non-nutritive sweetening agent. **c. disodium edathamil, c. disodium edetate,** chemical name, calcium disodium(ethylenedinitrilo)tetraacetate: used as an antidote in cases of poisoning by lead and other metals. **c. disodium versenate,** trade mark for *calcium disodium edathamil.* **c. dithiocarbonate,** an orange-red crystalline powder, $CaCOS_2$. **c. ethylisopropylbarbiturate.** See *ipral.* **c. fluoride,** a compound, CaF_2, occurring in the bones and teeth. **c. gluconate,** a calcium salt of gluconic acid, $C_{12}H_{22}CaO_{14}$, occurring as odorless, tasteless, white crystalline granules or powder: used in tablets or solution to restore electrolyte balance. **c. glycerophosphate,** an odorless, almost tasteless, fine white powder, $C_3H_7CaO_6P$. **c. hydroxide,** a white powder with an alkaline, slightly bitter taste, $Ca(OH)_2$: used as an astringent or antiemetic. **c. hypophosphite,** an odorless, bitter compound, $Ca(PH_2O_2)_2$, occurring in colorless, transparent, monoclinic prisms, as small, lustrous scales, or as a white, crystalline powder. **c. iodate,** an antipyretic and antiseptic salt, $Ca(IO_3)_2 + 6H_2O$. **c. iodide,** CaI_2, an irritant antiseptic. **c. iodobehenate,** a white or yellowish powder, $(C_{21}H_{42}ICOO)_2Ca$, containing at least 23.5 per cent of iodine: antigoitrogenic. **c. iodostearate,** stearodine. **c. lactate,** an efflorescent compound, $C_6H_{10}CaO_6.5H_2O$, occurring as white, almost odorless granules or powder: used orally as a source of calcium ion in the treatment of hypocalcemic tetany, or as an antidote for a variety of ingested poisons. **c. lactophosphate,** a mixture of calcium lactate, calcium acid lactate, and calcium acid phosphate. **c. levulinate,** a compound, $C_{10}H_{14}CaO_6.2H_2O$, occurring as a white, crystalline or amorphous powder, with a faint odor of burnt sugar and a bitter, salty taste. **c. mandelate,** an odorless, white powder, $C_{16}H_{44}CaO_6$: used in infections of the urinary tract. **c. ortho-iodoxybenzoate,** the calcium salt of iodoxybenzoic acid. **c. oxalate,** a compound, CaC_2O_4, occurring in the urine in crystals and in certain calculi. **c. oxide,** a corrosively alkaline and caustic earth, CaO. **c. pantothenate,** an odorless, bitter white powder, the calcium salt of the dextrorotatory isomer of pantothenic acid $(C_{18}H_{32}CaN_2O_{10})$: a vitamin of the B complex. **c. pantothenate, racemic,** a mixture of the calcium salts of the dextrorotatory and levorotatory isomers of pantothenic acid, with a physiological activity about half of that of calcium pantothenate. **c. permanganate,** a crystalline salt, $Ca(MnO_4)_2 + 5H_2O$. **c. phenolsulfonate,** c. sulfocarbolate. **c. phosphate,** a compound containing calcium and the phosphate radical (PO_4). **c. phosphate, dibasic,** an odorless, tasteless, white powder, $CaHPO_4.2H_2O$: used as a dietary supplement of calcium and phosphorus. **c. phosphate, tribasic,** an odorless, tasteless, white powder, $Ca_3(PO_4)_2$, insoluble in alcohol and almost insoluble in water, but readily soluble in diluted hydrochloric and nitric acids: used as an antacid and a dietary supplement of calcium and phosphorus. **c. salicylate,** a white, tasteless, crystalline powder, $Ca(OH.C_6H_4.CO.O)_2 + 2H_2O$. **c. sulfate,** a compound occurring in the form of gypsum, $2CaSO_4 + H_2O$, and as burnt gypsum or plaster of paris, $CaSO_4$. See *plaster of paris* and *gypsum.* **c. sulfhydrate,** a preparation of sulfuretted calcium: used as a depilatory. **c. sulfide,** a compound, CaS. **c. sulfite,** a compound, $CaSO_3$. **c. sulfocarbolate,** a white, crystalline substance, $Ca(C_6H_5SO_4)_2 + 6H_2O$, soluble in water.

calciuria (kal″sĭ-u′re-ah). The presence of calcium in the urine.

calcoglobule (kal″ko-glob′ūl). One of the irregular shaped globules of calcium salts deposited in developing dentin and constituting the spherical type of calcification.

calcoglobulin (kal″ko-glob′u-lin). The form of globulin which occurs in calcifying tissue.

calcoid (kal″koid). A tumor or new growth of the tooth pulp.

calcospherite (kal″ko-sfēr′it). One of the small globular bodies formed during the process of calcification, by chemical union between the calcium particles and the albuminous organic matter of the intercellular substance. These cells coalesce to form calcoglobulin.

calculary (kal′ku-la-re). Pertaining to calculus.

calculifragous (kal″ku-lif′rah-gus) [*calculus* + L. *frangere* to break]. Breaking a bladder stone; lithotritic.

calculogenesis (kal″ku-lo-jen′e-sis). The formation of calculi.

calculosis (kal″ku-lo′sis). Lithiasis.

calculous (kal′ku-lus). Pertaining to, of the nature of, or affected with, calculus.

calculus (kal′ku-lus), pl. *cal′culi* [L. "pebble"]. An abnormal concretion occurring within the animal body, and usually composed of mineral salts. **alternating c.,** a urinary calculus made up of successive layers of different composition. **alvine c.,** a concretion in the intestine formed by hardening of portions of the fecal contents. **arthritic c., articular c.,** a deposit in or near a joint in gout. It is usually composed of sodium urate; sometimes of calcium urate. Called also *chalk stone*. **aural c.,** a lump of hardened cerumen in the external meatus of the ear. **biliary c.,** a gallstone. **blood c.,** a phlebolith, or concretion of coagulated blood. **bronchial c.,** a concretion in an air passage. **calcium oxalate c.,** a hard, rough calculus composed of calcium oxalate. **cardiac c.,** cardiolith. **cholesterol c.,** a calculus formed of cholesterol. **combination c.,** alternating calculus. **coral c.,** a branched, coral-like calculus found in the pelvis of the kidney. **cutaneous c.,** milium. **cystine c.,** a soft variety of urinary calculus composed of cystine. **decubitus c.,** a calculus formed in the urinary tract as a result of long immobilization. **dendritic c.,** coral c. **dental c.,** calcium phosphate and carbonate, with organic matter, deposited upon the surfaces of the teeth. See *subgingival c.* and *supragingival c.* **encysted c.,** a urinary calculus inclosed in a sac developed from the wall of the bladder. **fibrin c.,** urinary calculi formed from blood clots. **fusible c.,** a calculus formed of a mixture of calcium phosphate and triple phosphates which fuses to a black, enamel-like mass under the blowpipe. **gastric c.,** gastrolith. **gonecystic c.,** calculus of a seminal vesicle. **hematogenic c.,** subgingival c. **hemic c.,** a calculus developed from a blood clot. **hemp seed c.,** a small, smooth, pale urinary calculus of calcium oxalate of the size and shape of a hemp seed. **hepatic c.,** a gallstone formed and remaining in the substance of the liver. **indigo c.,** calculus formed by oxidation of the indican of the urine. **intestinal c.,** enterolith. **joint c.,** articular calculus. **lacteal c.,** mammary calculus. **lung c.,** concretions formed in the bronchi by accretion about an inorganic nucleus, or from calcified portions of lung tissue. Called also *lung stones*. **mammary c.,** a concretion in one of the lactiferous ducts. **metabolic c.,** cholesterol calculus. **mulberry c.,** a urinary calculus of calcium oxalate, so called from its shape. **nasal c.,** rhinolith. **nephritic c.** renal calculus. **ovarian c.,** an enlarged and calcified corpus luteum. **oxalate c.,** mulberry calculus. **pancreatic c.,** a concretion formed in the pancreatic duct from calcium carbonate with other salts and organic materials. **phosphate c., phosphatic c.,** calculus composed of calcium oxalate and ammonium urate. **pocketed c.,** encysted c. **preputial c.,** postholith. **prostatic c.,** a concretion formed in the prostate, chiefly of calcium carbonate and phosphate. **renal c.,** a calculus occurring in the kidney. **salivary c.** 1. A concretion occurring in a salivary gland or duct. 2. Supragingival calculus. **serumal c.,** subgingival c.; so called because it is supposed to result from exudation of serum. **shellac c.,** a gastrolith caused by drinking shellac varnish. **spermatic c.,** a concretion in a seminal vesicle. **stag-horn c.,** a many-branched calculus occurring in the pelvis of a kidney. **stomachic c.,** a bezoar or other concretion in the stomach: a gastrolith. **struvit c.,** a urinary calculus composed of very pure ammoniomagnesium phosphate, forming the hard crystals known to mineralogists as struvit. **subgingival c.,** calculus on the concealed surface of a tooth, that is, apical to the crest of the gingival margin. **submorphous c.,** a calculus made up of molecules of a crystalline salt, together with molecules of the colloid matter in which the salt is contained. **supragingival c.,** dental calculus on the exposed surface of a tooth, that is, coronal to the crest of the gingival margin. **tonsillar c.,** a calcareous concretion in a tonsil. **urate c.,** calculus composed of urates, occurring chiefly in newborn or young infants. **uric acid c.,** hard, yellow or reddish-yellow calculi formed from uric acid. **urinary c.,** a calculus in any part of the urinary tract. It is *vesical* when lodged in the bladder (stone, gravel), and *renal* when in the pelvis of the kidney. **urostealith c.,** urinary calculus formed of fatty matter. **uterine c.,** an intra-uterine concretion formed mainly by the calcareous degeneration of a tumor; a womb stone. **vesical c.,** a form found in the urinary bladder. **vesicoprostatic c.,** a prostatic calculus, extending into the bladder. **xanthic c.** a urinary calculus composed mainly of xanthine.

Caldani's ligament (kal-dah′nēz) [Leopoldo Marco Antonio *Caldani*, Italian anatomist, 1725–1813]. See under *ligament*.

Caldwell-Luc operation (kald′wel-luk′) [George W. *Caldwell*, American physician, 1834–1918; Henry *Luc*, French laryngologist, 1855–1925]. See under *operation*.

Caldwell-Moloy classification [William E. *Caldwell*, American obstetrician, 1880–1943; H. C. *Moloy*, American obstetrician, 1903–1953]. Classification of female pelves as gynecoid, android, anthropoid and platypelloid. See under *pelvis*.

Calef. Abbreviation for L. *calefactus*, warmed, or for L. *calefac*, make warm.

calefacient (kal″e-fa′shent) [L. *calidus* warm + *facere* to make]. Warming; causing a sensation of warmth.

Calendula (kah-len′du-lah) [L.]. A genus of composite-flowered plants. *C. officinalis*, pot marigold, is stimulant and resolvent, and is used externally as a vulnerary.

calentura (kal-en-too′rah) [Sp. "fever"]. Calenture.

calenture (kal′en-tūr) [Sp. *calentura*]. Sun-stroke, or thermic fever: the name is applied also to various tropical fevers.

calf (kaf) [L. *sura*]. The fleshy mass formed by the gastrocnemius muscle at the back of the leg below the knee.

caliber (kal′ĭ-ber) [Fr. *calibre* the bore of a gun]. The diameter of a canal or tube.

calibrator (kal′ĭ-bra-tor). An instrument for dilating a tubular structure, such as the urethra, or for determining the inner or outer diameter of such a passage.

caliceal (kal″ĭ-se′al). Pertaining to or affecting a calix.

calicectasis (kal″ĭ-sek′tah-sis). Dilatation of a calix of a kidney

calicectomy (kal″ĭ-sek′to-me). Excision of a calix of a kidney.

calices (kal′ĭ-sēz). Plural of *calix*.

calicine (kal′ĭ-sēn). Related to or resembling a calix.

caliculus (kah-lik′u-lus) [L., dim. of *calix*]. A small cup, or cup-shaped structure. **c. gustato′rius** [N A], one of the minute, barrel-shaped terminal organs of the gustatory nerve, situated around the bases of the circumvallate papillae of the tongue, each consisting of a group of spindle-shaped cells made up of outer supporting cells and inner sense cells. Called also *taste bud*. **c. ophthal′micus** [N A, B N A], an indentation of the distal wall of the optic vesicle, brought about by rapid marginal growth and producing a double-layered cup, attached to the diencephalon by a tubular stalk. Called also *optic cup*.

caliectasis (ka″lĭ-ek′tah-sis) [*calix* + Gr. *ektasis* dilatation]. Calicectasis.

caliectomy (ka″lĭ-ek′to-me) [*calix* + Gr. *ektomē* excision]. Calicectomy.

californium (kal″ĭ-for′ne-um) [named from *California* (University and state), where it was produced]. Chemical element of atomic number 98, atomic weight 249, symbol Cf, produced by irradiation of the isotope of curium of atomic weight 242 with helium ions. Half-life 45 minutes.

caligation (kal″ĭ-ga′shun). Caligo.

caligo (kah-li′go) [L. "fog"]. Dimness of vision. **c. cor′neae,** obscurity of vision due to an opacity of the cornea. **c. len′tis,** obscurity of vision due to cataract. **c. pupil′lae,** dimness of vision due to contraction of the pupil.

calipers (kal′ĭ-perz) [from *caliber*]. Compasses with bent or curved legs used for measuring diameters.

calisthenics (kal″is-then′iks) [Gr. *kalos* beautiful + *sthenos* strength]. A system of light gymnastics for promoting strength and grace of carriage.

calix (ka′liks), pl. *cal′ices* [L.]. A cup-shaped organ or cavity. **renal calices,** calices renales. **renal calices, greater,** calices renales majores. **renal calices, minor,** calices renales minores. **cal′ices rena′les** [N A], any one of the recesses of the pelvis of the kidney which enclose the pyramids. Called also *calyces renales* [B N A], and *renal calices.* **cal′ices rena′les majo′res** [N A], the two or more larger subdivisions of the renal pelvis, into which the minor calices open. Called also *calyces renales majores* [B N A], and *major renal calices.* **cal′ices rena′les mino′res** [N A], a varying number of smaller subdivisions of the renal pelvis which enclose the pyramids, and open into the major calices. Called also *calyces renales minores* [B N A], and *minor renal calices.*

Callander's amputation (kal′an-derz) [C. Latimer *Callander*, San Francisco surgeon, 1892–1947]. See under *amputation.*

Callaway's test (kal′ah-wāz) [Thomas *Callaway*, English physician, 1791–1848]. See under *tests.*

Calleja's islands, islets (kal-ya′hahz) [Camilo *Calleja* y Sanchez, Spanish anatomist, died 1913]. See under *islet.*

callenders (kal′en-ders). Malanders.

callicrein (kal″ik-re′in). Kallikrein.

Calliphora (kah-lif′o-rah) [Gr. *kallos* beauty + *phoros* bearing]. A genus of scavenger flies which deposit their eggs in decaying matter, on wounds, or in the openings of the body. **C. vomito′ria,** the common blowfly or bluebottle fly, whose larvae may invade the nasal fossae and produce intestinal myiasis. Other species are *C. azurea, C. erythrocephala,* and *C. lionensis.*

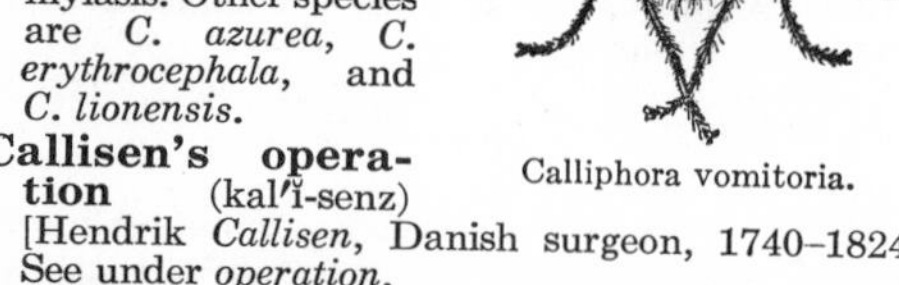

Calliphora vomitoria.

Callisen's operation (kal′ĭ-senz) [Hendrik *Callisen*, Danish surgeon, 1740–1824]. See under *operation.*

Callison's fluid (kal′ĭ-sunz) [James S. *Callison*, American physician, born 1873]. See under *fluid.*

callomania (kal″o-ma′ne-ah) [Gr. *kallos* beauty + *mania* madness]. A condition marked by delusions of personal beauty.

callosal (kah-lo′sal). Pertaining to the corpus callosum.

callositas (kah-los′ĭ-tas) [L.]. Callosity.

callosity (kah-los′ĭ-te) [L. *callositas*, from *callus*]. A circumscribed thickening of the skin, and hypertrophy of the horny layer, due to friction, pressure, or other irritation.

callosomarginal (kah-lo″so-mar′jĭ-nal). Pertaining to the callosal and marginal gyri.

callosum (kah-lo′sum). Corpus callosum.

callous (kal′us). Hard; like callus.

callus (kal′us) [L.]. 1. A callosity. 2. An unorganized meshwork of woven bone developed on the pattern of the original fibrin clot, which is formed following fracture of a bone and is normally ultimately replaced by hard adult bone. **central c.,** provisional callus formed within the medullary cavity of a fractured bone. **definitive c.,** the exudate formed between the fractured ends of the bone, which is permanent and becomes changed into true bone. **ensheathing c.,** provisional callus forming a sheath about the ends of the fragments of a fractured bone. **inner c.,** central c. **intermediate c.,** definitive c. **medullary c., myelogenous c.,** central c. **permanent c.,** definitive c. **pin c.,** central c. **provisional c.,** callus which is formed within the medullary cavity and about the ends of a broken bone, and which is absorbed after the repair is completed.

calmative (kahm′ah-tiv). 1. Sedative; allaying excitement. 2. An agent that allays excitement or has a sedative effect.

Calmette's reaction, serum, test (kal-metz′) [Albert Léon Charles *Calmette*, French bacteriologist, 1863–1933]. See under *reaction* and *serum.*

Calobata (kah-lo′bah-tah). A genus of South American flies whose larvae occur in the human intestine.

calomel (kal′o-mel) [L. *calomelas;* Gr. *kalos* fair + *melas* black]. Mercurous chloride. **vegetable c.,** podophyllum.

calor (ka′lor) [L.]. Heat; one of the cardinal signs of inflammation. **c. febri′lis,** the heat of fever. **c. fer′vens,** a boiling heat. **c. inna′tus,** the normal or natural heat of the body. **c. inter′nus,** the heat of the interior of the body. **c. mor′dax, c. mordi′cans,** biting or stinging heat; also the hot, burning, reddish-colored skin occurring in scarlet fever.

caloradiance (kal″o-ra′de-ans). The radiation or rays which lie between 250 and 55,000 millimicrons, such as the rays from the sun, carbon arcs, incandescent rods and filaments, and hot black bodies.

calorescence (kal″o-res′ens). The conversion of nonluminous into luminous heat rays.

Calori's bursa (kah-lo′rēz) [Luigi *Calori*, Italian anatomist, 1807–1896]. See under *bursa.*

caloric (kah-lo′rik). Pertaining to heat.

caloricity (kal″o-ris′ĭ-te). The power of the animal body of developing and maintaining heat.

calorie (kal′o-re) [Fr.; L. *calor* heat]. A unit of heat. The term is commonly used alone to designate the *small calorie.* The calorie used in the study of metabolism is the *large calorie*, or *kilocalorie.* **15° c.,** the amount of heat required to raise the temperature of 1 gram of water from 14.5°C. to 15.5°C. **gram c.,** small c. **I.T. c., International Table c.,** a unit of heat, equivalent to 4.1868 joules. **large c.,** the calorie used in metabolic studies, being the amount of heat required to raise the temperature of 1 kilogram of water 1 degree Celsius (centigrade). Called also *kilocalorie.* **mean c.,** one one-hundredth of the amount of heat required to raise the temperature of 1 gram of water from 0 to 100°C. **small c.,** the amount of heat required to raise the temperature of 1 gram of water 1 degree Celsius (centigrade). Called also *gram c.* and *standard c.* **standard c.,** small c. **thermochemical c.,** a unit of heat, equivalent to 4.184 joules.

calorifacient (kah-lor″ĭ-fa′shent) [L. *calor* heat + *facere* to make]. Producing heat: used of certain foods.

calorific (kal″o-rif′ik) [L. *calor* heat + *facere* to make]. Producing heat.

calorigenetic (kah-lor″ĭ-je-net′ik). Calorigenic.

calorigenic (kah-lor″ĭ-jen′ik) [L. *calor* heat + Gr. *gennan* to produce]. Producing heat or energy; increasing heat or energy production.

calorimeter (kal″o-rim′e-ter) [L. *calor* heat + Gr. *metron* measure]. An instrument for measuring the amount of heat exchanged in any system. In physiology it is an apparatus for measuring the amount of heat produced by an individual. **bomb c.,** an apparatus for measuring the potential energy of food, a weighed amount of the food being placed on a platinum dish inside a hollow steel container (bomb) filled with pure oxygen. The heat produced by its combustion is absorbed by a known quantity of water in which the container is immersed, permitting its measurement. **compensating c.,** an apparatus in which the object to be tested, such as a developing chick in an egg, is placed at one junction of a thermocouple and an electrical resistance at the other. From the amount of current which must pass through the resistance to keep both junctions at the same temperature (as shown by lack of current in the thermocouple circuit) it is possible to calculate the amount of heat generated in the object being tested. **respiration c.,** an apparatus for the measurement of the gaseous exchange between a living organism and the atmosphere surrounding it and the simultaneous measurement of the amount of heat produced by that organism.

calorimetric (kah-lor″ĭ-met′rik). Pertaining to or performed by calorimetry.

calorimetry (kal″o-rim′e-tre) [L. *calor* heat + Gr. *metron* measure]. Measurement of the amounts of heat absorbed or given out. **direct c.,** measurement of the amount of heat produced by a subject enclosed within a small chamber. **indirect c.,** measurement of the amount of heat produced by a subject by determination of the amount of oxygen consumed and the quantity of nitrogen and carbon dioxide eliminated.

caloripuncture (kal″o-rĭ-punk′tūr) [L. *calor* heat + *puncture*]. Ignipuncture.

caloriscope (kah-lor′ĭ-skōp). An instrument for showing the caloric values of mixtures for infant feeding.

caloritropic (kah-lor″ĭ-trop′ik) [L. *calor* heat + Gr. *tropos* a turning]. Thermotropic.

calorization (kah-lor″ĭ-za′shun). The application of heat.

calory (kal′o-re), pl. *calories*. Calorie.

Calot's operation, solution, treatment triangle (kal-ōz′) [Jean-François *Calot*, French surgeon, 1861–1944]. See under the nouns.

calotte (kah-lot′) [Fr. "cap"]. 1. A part shaped like a skull cap. 2. The calva.

calutron (kal′u-tron). An apparatus for separating the isotopes of uranium.

calva (kal′va) [L.]. The bald scalp of the head.

calvaria (kal-va′re-ah) [L.]. [N A, B N A] The domelike superior portion of the cranium, composed of the superior portions of the frontal, parietal, and occipital bones. Called also *skullcap*.

calvarial (kal-va′re-al). Pertaining to the calvaria.

calvarium (kal-va′re-um). The calvaria.

Calvé-Perthes disease (kal-va′per-tās) [Jacques *Calvé*, French orthopedist, 1875–1954]. Georg Clemens *Perthes*, German surgeon, 1869–1927]. See under *disease*.

Calvert's test (kal′vertz) [E. G. B. *Calvert*, British physician]. See under *tests*.

calvities (kal-vish′e-ēz) [L.]. Baldness. See *alopecia*.

calvitium (kal-vish′e-um). Baldness.

calx (kalks) [L.]. 1. Lime or chalk. 2. [N A, B N A] The hindmost part of the foot; the heel. 3. Any residue obtained by calcination. 4. Lime or calcium oxide, CaO; quick-lime: alkaline, caustic, and escharotic. **c. chlora′ta, c. chlorina′ta,** chlorinated lime; a white, pasty substance: used as a bleaching agent and disinfectant; also an alterative, antiseptic, and stimulant. **c. sulfura′ta,** a mixture of at least 60 per cent of calcium sulfide with a variable proportion of calcium sulfate and carbon. It is useful in skin and pustular diseases, and as a depilatory.

calyceal (kal″ĭ-se′al). Caliceal.

calycectasis (kal″ĭ-sek′tah-sis). Calicectasis.

calycectomy (kal″ĭ-sek′to-me). Calicectomy.

calyces (kal′ĭ-sēz). Plural of *calyx*.

calycine (kal′ĭ-sin). Calicine.

calycle (kal′ĭ-kl). A caliculus.

calyculi (kah-lik′u-li) [L.]. Caliculi.

calyculus (kah-lik′u-lus), pl. *calyc′uli* [L. "a little cup," from Gr. *kalyx* cup of a flower]. Caliculus. **c. gustato′rius** [B N A], caliculus gustatorius. **c. ophthal′micus** [B N A], caliculus ophthalmicus.

Calymmatobacterium (kah-lim″mah-to-bak-te′re-um) [Gr. *kalymma* a hood or veil + *baktērion* a little staff]. A genus of microorganisms of the family Brucellaceae, order Eubacteriales, made up of pleomorphic non-motile, gram-negative rods, which may or may not be encapsulated. **C. granulo′matis,** the type species of Calymmatobacterium, isolated from granulomatous lesions in man and causally related to granuloma inguinale.

calyx (ka′liks), pl. *cal′yces* [Gr. *kalyx* cup of a flower]. Calix. **cal′yces rena′les** [B N A], calices renales. **cal′yces rena′les majo′res** [B N A], calices renales majores. **cal′yces rena′les mino′res** [B N A], calices renales minores.

Camallanus (kam″ah-la′nus). A genus of Filaroidea, species of which are parasites in the intestines of fishes, reptiles and amphibians.

Cambaroides (kam″bah-roi′dēz). A genus of crayfish which harbor the cercaria of Paragonimus.

cambium (kam′be-um) [L. "exchange"]. 1. The loose cellular inner layer of the periosteal tissue in the intramembranous ossification of bone. 2. A layer of cells beneath the bark of woody plants.

cambogia (kam-bo′je-ah) [L.]. Gamboge; a yellow gum-resin from *Garcinia hanburyi* and other guttiferous East Indian trees. It is a drastic hydragogue cathartic.

cameloid (kam′ĕ-loid). Possessing characteristics similar to those observed in a camel.

camera (kam′er-ah), pl. *cameras* or *cam′erae* [L. "chamber"]. 1. A box, chamber, or compartment. 2. Any open space or ventricle. **c. ante′rior bul′bi** [N A], that portion of the aqueous-containing space between the cornea and the lens which is bounded in front by the cornea and part of the sclera, and behind by the iris, part of the ciliary body, and that part of the lens which presents through the pupil. Called also *c. oc′uli ante′rior* [B N A], and *anterior chamber of eye*. **c. lu′cida,** an optical device utilizing a prism, so arranged as to throw the reflected image of an object upon paper, thus permitting its outlines to be traced with a pencil. **c. obscu′ra,** a combined box, lens, and screen, used for viewing, tracing, or making photographs. **c. oc′uli,** either one of the chambers of the eye. **c. oc′uli ante′rior** [B N A], c. anterior bulbi. **c. oc′uli poste′rior** [B N A], c. posterior bulbi. **c. poste′rior bul′bi** [N A], that portion of the aqueous-containing space between the cornea and the lens which is bounded in front by the iris, and behind by the lens and suspensory ligament. Called also *c. oculi posterior* [B N A], and *posterior chamber of the eye*. **c. pul′pi,** the pulp cavity of a tooth. **recording c.,** photokymograph. **c. sep′ti pellu′cidi,** cavum septi pellucidi.

camerae (kam′er-e) [L.]. Plural of *camera*.

Camerer's law (kam′er-erz) [Johann Friedrich Wilhelm *Camerer*, German pediatrician, 1842–1910]. See under *law*.

camisole (kam′ĭ-sōl) [Fr.]. A strait-jacket, sometimes used for the restraint of violently disturbed persons.

Cammann's stethoscope (kam′anz) [George Philip *Cammann*, American physician, 1804–1863]. A binaural stethoscope.

Cammidge reaction (kam′ij) [P. J. *Cammidge*, English physician]. See *pancreatic reaction*, under *reaction*.

camoquin (kam′o-kwin). Trade mark for a preparation of amodiaquine.

campanula (kam-pan′u-lah) [L. *campana* a bell]. A bell-shaped organ or part. **c. hal′leri,** the swollen end of the falciform process in the eye of fish.

Campbell's ligament (kam′belz) [William Francis *Campbell*, American surgeon, 1867–1926]. The suspensory ligament of the axilla.

campeachy, campechy (kam-pe′che). Hematoxylon.

Camper's fascia, ligament, line, etc. (kam′-perz) [Pieter *Camper*, Dutch physician, 1722–1789]. See under the nouns.

campesterol (kam-pes′ter-ol). A sterol, $C_{28}H_{48}O$, from rape seed oil, soy bean oil and wheat germ oil.

camphor (kam′for) [L. *camphora;* Gr. *kamphora*]. 1. A colorless or white compound, $C_{10}H_{16}O$, occurring as crystals, granules, or crystalline masses, or as translucent, tough masses, with a penetrating, characteristic odor, and a pungent, aromatic taste, obtained from *Cinnamomum camphora* and used locally as an antipruritic. 2. A general term applied to other compounds possessing characteristics similar to those of camphor. **anise c.,** anethole. **artificial c.,** a compound, pinene chloride, $C_{10}H_{16}Cl$, prepared from oil of turpentine by the action of hydrochloric acid. **blumea c.,** a good and abundant camphor produced in Indo-China by the shrub *Blu′mea balsamif′era.* **Borneo c.,** a peculiar stearopten from *Dryobal′-anops aromat′ica,* a tree of Borneo and Sumatra. **carbolated c.,** a mixture of camphor, $1\frac{1}{2}$ parts, with phenol and alcohol, each 1 part: an antiseptic dressing for wounds. **chloral c.,** equal parts of camphor and chloral hydrate: a sedative for external use. **mace c.,** a camphor, $C_{16}H_{32}O_5$, derivable from oil of mace. **mentholated c.,** a liquid mixture of equal parts of camphor and menthol. It is used as a counterirritant locally and as a spray. **monobromated c.,** camphor in which one atom of hydrogen is replaced by one atom of bromine, $C_{10}H_{15}OBr$. **naphthol c.,** betanaphthol, 1 part, fused with camphor, 2 parts; a syrupy fluid: used externally as an antiseptic. **orris c.,** a fragrant, crystalline body from orris. **peppermint c.,** menthol. **phenol c.,** a clear, oily solution of camphor in phenol in various proportions: a germicide and toothache remedy. **resorcinated c.,** a mixture of resorcinol and camphor: used in pediculosis and in pruritus. **c. salicylate,** a crystalline product of the fusion of camphor, 84 parts, with salicylic acid, 65 parts: used externally in ointments for various skin affections, and internally, as in diarrheas. **salol c.,** a clear, oily preparation of camphor, 2 parts, and salol, 3 parts: a local antiseptic. **thyme c.,** thymol. **turpentine c.,** terpin.

camphora (kam-fo′rah) [L.]. Camphor.

camphoraceous (kam″fo-ra′shus). Having characteristics resembling those of camphor.

camphorated (kam′fo-rāt″ed) [L. *camphoratus*]. Containing or tinctured with camphor.

camphorism (kam′for-izm). Poisoning by camphor; the condition is marked by convulsions, coma, and gastritis.

campimeter (kam-pim′e-ter) [L. *campus* field + *metrum* measure]. An apparatus for mapping the central portion of the visual field on a flat surface.

campimetry (kam-pim′e-tre). The determination of the presence of defects in the central portion of the visual field by use of the campimeter.

campospasm (kam′po-spazm) [Gr. *kampē* a bending + *spasm*]. Camptocormia.

camptocormia (kamp″to-kor′me-ah) [Gr. *kamptos* bent + *kormos* trunk + *-ia*]. A static deformity consisting of forward flexion of the trunk.

camptocormy (kamp″to-kor′me). Camptocormia.

camptodactylia (kamp″to-dak-til′e-ah) [Gr. *kamptos* bent + *daktylos* finger + *-ia*]. Permanent and irreducible flexion of one or more fingers (Landouzy).

camptodactylism (kamp″to-dak′til-izm). Camptodactylia.

camptodactyly (kamp″to-dak′tĭ-le). Camptodactylia.

camptospasm (kamp′to-spazm). Camptocormia.

campylognathia (kam″pĭ-lo-na′the-ah) [Gr. *kampylos* curved + *gnathos* jaw + *-ia*]. A deformity of the lip or jaw producing a resemblance to that of a hare or rabbit.

canal (kah-nal′). A relatively narrow tubular passage or channel. See also *canalis.* **abdominal c.,** canalis inguinalis. **accessory palatine c's,** canales palatini minores. **adductor c. of Hunter,** canalis adductorius. **Alcock's c.,** canalis pudendalis. **alimentary c.,** canalis alimentarius. **alisphenoid c.,** a canal in the alisphenoid bone which in many animals transmits the external carotid artery. **alveolar c's.** See *canalis mandibulae* and *canales alveolares maxillae.* **alveolar c., anterior, alveolar c., posterior.** See *canales alveolares maxillae.* **anal c.** 1. The terminal portion of the alimentary canal, extending from the rectum to its distal opening. Called also *canalis analis* [N A]. 2. A transient lumen in the distal portion of the alimentary canal occurring during embryonic development. **arachnoid c.,** cisterna venae magnae cerebri. **c. of Arantius,** ductus venosus. **archenteric c.,** neurenteric c. **archinephric c.,** archinephric duct. **Arnold's c.,** a channel in the petrous portion of the temporal bone for passage of the auricular branch of the vagus nerve. **arterial c.,** ductus arteriosus. **atrioventricular c.,** the common canal connecting the primitive atrium and ventricle. It sometimes persists as a congenital anomaly, as a result of failure of closure of the gap between the interatrial and interventricular septa due to arrest in development of the endocardial cushions. **auditory c., external,** meatus acusticus externus. **auditory c., internal,** meatus acusticus internus. **basipharyngeal c.,** canalis vomerovaginalis. **Bernard's c.,** ductus pancreaticus accessorius. **Bichat's c.,** canalis venae magnae cerebri. **biliary c's, interlobular,** ductuli interlobulares. **biliary c's, intralobular,** smaller passages for conducting the bile within the substance of the lobules of the liver. **birth c.,** the canal through which the child passes in birth, comprising the cervix uteri, vagina, and vulva. **blastoporic c.,** neurenteric c. **bony c's of ear.** See entries beginning *canalis semicircularis.* **Braun's c.,** neurenteric c. **Braune's c.,** the uterine cavity and vagina, after complete dilation of the os of the cervix in labor. **Breschet's c's,** canales diploici. **bullular c's,** spatia zonularia. **calciferous c's,** canals containing lime salts in cartilage that is undergoing calcification. **caroticotympanic c's,** canaliculi caroticotympanici. **carotid c.,** canalis caroticus. **carpal c., c. of carpus,** canalis carpi. **c's of cartilage,** canals in an ossifying cartilage during its stage of vascularization. **central c. of modiolus.** See *canales longitudinales modioli.* **central c. of myelon, central c. of spinal cord,** canalis centralis medullae spinalis. **central c. of Stilling, central c. of vitreous,** canalis hyaloideus. **cerebrospinal c.** 1. The space that contains the brain and spinal cord, considered as a continuous unit. 2. The primitive cavity of the brain and spinal cord. **cervical c. of uterus,** canalis cervicis uteri. **c. of chorda tympani,** canaliculus chordae tympani. **chordal c.,** notochordal c. **ciliary c's,** spatia anguli iridocornealis. **Civinini's c.,** canaliculus chordae tympani. **Cloquet's c.,** canalis hyaloideus. **cochlear c.,** ductus cochlearis. **condylar c., condyloid c.,** canalis condylaris. **condyloid c., anterior,** canalis hypoglossi. **connecting c.,** the arched or coiled part of a uriniferous tubule, joining it to a collecting tubule. **c. of Corti,** a space between the outer and inner rods of Corti. **c. of Cotunnius,** the aqueductus vestibuli and canaliculus cochlea considered as a continuous passage. **craniopharyngeal c.,** an occasional passage through the sphenoid bone, opening into the sella turcica. **craniovertebral c.,** cerebrospinal c. **crural c.,** canalis femoralis. **crural c. of Henle,** canalis adductorius. **c. of Cuvier,** ductus venosus. **dental c., inferior,** canalis mandibulae. **dental c's, posterior.** 1. See *canales alveolares maxillae.* 2. Foramina alveolaria maxillae. **dentinal c's,** canaliculi dentales. **digestive c.,** alimentary tract. **diploic c's,** canales diploici. **Dorello's c.,** an opening in the temporal bone through which the abducens nerve and inferior petrosal sinus together enter the cavernous sinus. **entodermal c.,** the primitive digestive tube. **c. of epididymis,** ductus epididymidis. **ethmoid c., anterior,** a passage in the frontal and ethmoid bones for the nasal branch of the ophthalmic nerve and anterior ethmoid vessels. **ethmoid c., posterior,** foramen ethmoidale posterius. **eustachian c.,** tuba auditiva. **eustachian c., osseous,** canalis musculotubarius. **facial c., c. for facial nerve,** canalis facialis. **fallopian c.,** canalis facialis. **femoral c.,** canalis femoralis. **Ferrein's c.,** a canal said to be formed by the edges of the closed eyelids, which conducts the tears during sleep to the puncta lacrimalia. **flexor c.,** canalis carpi. **Fontana's c's,** spatia anguli iridocornealis. **ganglionic c.,** canalis spiralis modioli. **Gartner's c.,** Gartner's duct. **genital c.,** any canal for the passage of ova or for copulatory service. **gubernacular c's,** four small openings in young crania, one behind each incisor tooth. **c. of Guidi,** canalis pterygoideus. **gynecophorous c.,** the ventral slot in which the male schistosome carries the female. **hair c.,** an epidermal canal through which a hair grows in order to erupt. **Hannover's c.,** a potential space existing between the anterior and posterior portions of the suspensory ligament. **haversian c.,** one of the freely anastomosing channels of the haversian system in compact bone. Called also *canalis nutricius ossis* [N A]. **hemal c.,** the space within the hemal arch. **Henle's c's,** the looped uriniferous tubules. **Hensen's c.,** ductus reuniens. **hepatic c.** 1. The hepatic duct, or any of its smaller branches. 2. Any one of the canals in the liver for passage of the veins of that organ. **c's of Hering,** openings through which the bile canaliculi communicate with the terminal branches of the bile duct system, the cholangiole; characterized by their walls, which consist of parenchymal liver cells on one side and cells of the ductules (cholangioles) on the other. **hernial c.,** the passage which transmits the herniated portion of an organ. **Hirschfeld's c's,** interdental c's. **His's c.,** ductus thyroglossus. **Holmgren-Golgi c's,** minute canals in the cytoplasm of cells, particularly of nerve cells, forming a complex apparatus throughout the cytoplasm. Called also *intracytoplasmic c's.* **c. of Hovius,** one of a series of connections between the venae vorticosae in certain mammals. **Huguier's c.,** canaliculus chordae tympani. **Hunter's c.,** canalis adductorius. **Huschke's c.,** a passage formed by union of the tubercles of the tympanic ring: it commonly disappears during the years of childhood. **hyaloid c.,** canalis hyaloideus. **hypoglossal c.,** canalis hypoglossi. **iliac c.,** lacuna musculorum. **incisive c.,** canalis incisivus. **infraorbital c.,** canalis infraorbitalis. **inguinal c.,** canalis inguinalis. **interdental c's,** channels in the alveolar process of the mandible, between the roots of the medial and lateral incisors, for the passage of anastomosing blood vessels between the sublingual and inferior dental arteries. **intersacral c's,** foramina intervertebralia ossis sacri. **intestinal c.,** the intestines; that part of the alimentary canal which lies between the pylorus and the anus. **intracytoplasmic c's,** Holmgren-Golgi c's. **Jacobson's c., c. for Jacobson's nerve,** canaliculus tympani. **Kovalevsky's c.,** neurenteric c. **lacrimal c.** 1. Canalis nasolacrimalis. 2. Any passage for transmission of the secretion of the lacrimal glands. **Laurer's c.,** a passage in trematode worms extending from the ovarian duct to the dorsal surface of the body. **Löwenberg's c.,** the part of the ductus cochlearis above the membrane of Corti. **mandibular c.,** canalis mandibulae. **maxillary c., superior,** foramen rotundum ossis sphenoidalis. **medullary c.** 1. Canalis vertebralis. 2. Cavum medullare. **c's of modiolus.** See *canalis spiralis modioli* and *canales longitudinales modioli.* **Müller's c.,** ductus paramesonephricus. **musculotubal c.,** canalis musculotubarius. **nasal c.,** canalis nasolacrimalis. **nasolacrimal c.,** canalis nasolacrimalis. **nasopalatine c.,** canalis incisivus. **neural c.,** canalis vertebralis. **neurenteric c. (of Kovalevsky),** a passage, in the embryo, from the posterior part of the neural tube into the archenteron. **notochordal c.,** a tunnel extending from the primitive pit into the head process of the embryo. **c. of Nuck,** a small diverticulum of peritoneum accompanying the round ligament of the uterus through the inguinal canal. **nutrient c. of bone,** haversian c., or canalis nutricius ossis. **obstetric c.,** birth c. **obturator c.,** canalis obturatorius. **obturator c. of pubic bone,** sulcus obturatorius ossis pubis. **c. of Oken,** ductus mesonephricus. **olfactory c.,** the nasal fossae at an early stage of their embryonic development. **omphalomesenteric c.,** omphalomesenteric duct. **optic c.,** canalis opticus. **orbital c's,** foramina ethmoidalia. **orbital c., anterior internal,** foramen ethmoidale anterius. **orbital c., posterior internal,** foramen ethmoidale posterius. **palatine c's, accessory,** canales palatini minores. **palatine c., anterior.** 1. Canalis incisivus. 2. Foramen incisivum. **palatine c's, lesser, palatine c's, posterior,** canales palatini minores. **palatinovaginal c.,** canalis palatinovaginalis. **palatomaxillary c.** 1. Canalis palatinus major. 2. See *foramina palatina minora.* **parturient c.,** birth c. **pelvic c.,** the passage from the superior to the inferior strait of the pelvis. **perivascular c.,** a lymph space about a blood vessel. **Petit's c.** See *spatia zonularia.* **pharyngeal c.,** canalis palatinovaginalis. **plasmatic c.,** haversian c. **pleural c's,** a pair of passages in the embryo, connecting the primitive pericardial and peritoneal cavities. **portal c.,** a space within the capsule of Glisson and liver substance, containing the portal veins, branches of the hepatic vessels and also of the hepatic duct. **pterygoid c.,** canalis pterygoideus. **pterygopalatine c.** 1. Canalis palatinus major. 2. Canalis palatinovaginalis. **pudendal c.,** canalis pudendalis. **pulmoaortic c.,** ductus arteriosus. **pulp c.,** root c. **pyloric c.,** canalis pyloricus. **c's of Recklinghausen,** small lymph channels in the connective tissue which are regarded as the ultimate branches of the lymphatic vascular system. **recurrent c.,** canalis pterygoideus. **c's of Rivinus,** ductus sublinguales minores. **root c.,** that portion of the pulp cavity in the root of a tooth extending from the pulp chamber to the apical foramen; more than one canal may be present in a root, two commonly being present in the mesial root of the mandibular first molar. Called also *canalis radicis dentis* [N A]. **root c., accessory,** a lateral branching of the main root canal, usually occurring in the apical third of the root. **Rosenthal's c.,** canalis spiralis modioli. **ruffed c.** See *spatia zonularia.* **sacculocochlear c.,** a passage connecting the sacculus and the cochlea.

sacculo-utricular c., ductus utriculosaccularis. **sacral c.,** canalis sacralis. **Santorini's c.,** ductus pancreaticus accessorius. **Saviotti's c's,** artificially formed spaces between the cells of the injected pancreas. **Schlemm's c.,** a circular channel at the junction of the sclera and cornea. Called also *sinus venosus sclerae* [N A]. **scleral c., scleroticochoroidal c.,** canalis opticus. **semicircular c's.** See *canalis semicircularis anterior, canalis semicircularis lateralis,* and *canalis semicircularis posterior.* **semicircular c's, membranous.** See *ductus semicircularis anterior, ductus semicircularis lateralis,* and *ductus semicircularis posterior.* **seminal c.,** a passage for the transmission of semen, or of spermatozoa. **serous c.,** a minute lymph vessel. **sheathing c.,** the passage from the peritoneal cavity to the tunica vaginalis testis. **Sondermann's c's,** conical extensions of the lumen of Schlemm's canal sometimes observed in the inner wall of the canal. **spermatic c.,** the canalis inguinalis in the male, providing for passage of the spermatic cord. **sphenopalatine c.** 1. Canalis palatinovaginalis. 2. Canalis palatinus major. **sphenopharyngeal c.,** canalis palatinovaginalis. **spinal c.,** canalis vertebralis. **spinal medullary c.,** canalis centralis medullae spinalis. **spiral c. of cochlea,** canalis spiralis cochleae. **spiral c. of modiolus,** canalis spiralis modioli. **spiroid c.,** canalis facialis. **c. of Steno, Stensen's c.,** ductus parotideus. **c. of Stilling,** canalis hyaloideus. **subsartorial c.,** canalis adductorius. **Sucquet-Hoyer c.,** Sucquet-Hoyer anastomosis. **supraciliary c.,** a small opening sometimes present near the supraorbital notch, which transmits a nutrient artery and a branch of the supraorbital nerve to the frontal sinus. **supraoptic c.,** a minute canal above the optic chiasm and connected with the third ventricle. **supraorbital c.,** incisura frontale. **tarsal c.,** sinus tarsi. **c. for tensor tympani muscle,** semicanalis musculi tensoris tympani. **Theile's c.,** a space formed by reflection of the pericardium on the aorta and the pulmonary artery. **Tourtual's c.,** canalis palatinus major. **tubal c.,** semicanalis tubae auditivae. **tubotympanal c.,** the inner division of the first branchial cleft in the fetus, from which the internal auditory passages are derived. **tympanic c. of cochlea,** scala tympani. **umbilical c.,** anulus umbilicalis. **urogenital c's,** that portion of the urogenital sinus used jointly by the müllerian and mesonephric ducts. **uterine c.,** the cavity of the uterus. **uterocervical c.,** canalis cervicis uteri. **utriculosaccular c.,** ductus utriculosaccularis. **vaginal c.,** the space within the vagina. **vector c.,** a channel for the passage of ova; an oviduct. **ventricular c.,** canalis ventriculi. **Verneuil's c's,** collateral vessels of a venous trunk. **vertebral c.,** canalis vertebralis. **vestibular c.,** scala vestibuli. **vidian c.,** canalis pterygoideus. **Volkmann's c's,** passages other than haversian canals, for the passage of blood vessels through bone. **vomerine c.,** canalis vomerovaginalis. **vomerobasilar c., lateral inferior,** canalis palatinovaginalis. **vomerobasilar c., lateral superior,** canalis palatinovaginalis. **vomerovaginal c.,** canalis vomerovaginalis. **vulvar c.,** vestibulum vaginae. **vulvo-uterine c.,** vaginal c. **c. of Wirsung,** ductus pancreaticus. **zygomaticofacial c.,** foramen zygomaticofaciale. **zygomaticotemporal c.,** foramen zygomaticotemporale.

canales (kah-na'lēz) [L.]. Plural of *canalis.*

canalicular (kan″ah-lik'u-lar). Resembling or pertaining to a canaliculus.

canaliculi (kan″ah-lik'u-li) [L.]. Plural of *canaliculus.*

canaliculization (kan″ah-lik″u-li-za'shun). The development of canaliculi, as in bone.

canaliculus (kan″ah-lik'u-lus), pl. *canalic'uli* [L., dim. of *canalis*]. An extremely narrow tubular passage or channel; used as a general term in anatomical nomenclature for various small channels. **bile canaliculi, biliary canaliculi,** fine tubular canals running between liver cells, throughout the parenchyma, usually occurring singly between each adjacent pair of cells, and forming a three-dimensional network of polygonal meshes, with a single cell in each mesh. **caroticotympanic canaliculi, canalic'uli caroticotympan'ici** [N A, B N A], tiny passages in the temporal bone interconnecting the carotid canal and the tympanic cavity, and carrying communicating twigs between the internal carotid and tympanic plexuses. **c. of chorda tympani, c. chor'dae tym'pani** [N A, B N A], a small canal that opens off the facial canal just before its termination, transmitting the chorda tympani nerve into the tympanic cavity. **c. of cochlea, c. coch'leae** [N A, B N A], a small canal in the petrous part of the temporal bone that interconnects the scala tympani of the inner ear with the subarachnoid cavity; it lodges the perilymphatic duct and a small vein. **dental canaliculi, canalic'uli denta'les** [N A, B N A], minute channels in dentin, extending from the pulp cavity to the cement and enamel. Called also *dental tubules.* **haversian c.,** any one of a system of minute channels in compact bone connected with each haversian canal. **incisor c.,** ductus incisivus. **innominate c., c. innomina'tus,** sulcus nervi petrosi minoris. **c. lacrima'lis** [N A], the short passage in an eyelid, beginning at the punctum, that leads from the lacrimal lake to the lacrimal sac. Called also *lacrimal duct.* **c. laqueifor'mis,** Henle's canal. **mastoid c., mastoid c. for Arnold's nerve,** c. mastoideus. **c. mastoi'deus** [N A, B N A], a minute passage beginning in the lateral wall of the jugular fossa of the temporal bone and passing into the temporal bone. The tympanic branch of the vagus nerve passes through it to exit via the tympanomastoid fissure. **c. petro'sus, petrous c.,** sulcus nervi petrosi minoris. **pseudobile c.,** one of the dark-staining columns of cells from the bile ducts seen in the portal area of the liver in cirrhosis. **Thiersch's c.,** one of the small channels in newly formed repair tissue through which the nutritive fluids circulate. **tympanic c., tympanic c. for Jacobson's nerve,** c. tympanicus. **c. tympan'icus** [N A, B N A], a small opening on the inferior surface of the petrous part of the temporal bone in the floor of the petrosal fossa; it transmits the tympanic branch of the glossopharyngeal nerve and a small artery.

canalis (kah-na'lis), pl. *cana'les* [L.]. [N A, B N A], a general term for a relatively narrow tubular passage or channel. Called also *canal.* **c. adducto'rius** [N A], an intramuscular space on the medial aspect of the middle third of the thigh, which contains the femoral vessels and the saphenous nerve. The lateral wall is formed by the vastus medialis, the posterior wall by the adductor longus and adductor magnus, the roof by a layer of deep fascia, and it is covered by the sartorius. Called also *canalis adductorius [Hunteri]* [B N A] and *adductor canal.* **c. alimenta'rius** [N A], that part of the digestive tract formed by the esophagus, stomach, and small and large intestines. Called also *alimentary canal* and *tubus digestorius* [B N A]. **cana'les alveola'res.** See *canales alveolares maxillae* and *c. mandibulae.* **cana'les alveola'res maxil'lae** [N A, B N A], several canals in the maxilla for the passage of the posterior superior alveolar vessels and nerves, each canal beginning on the infratemporal surface of the maxilla at an alveolar foramen. Called also *alveolar canals of maxilla.* **c. ana'lis** [N A], the terminal portion of the alimentary canal, extending from the rectum to the anus. Called also *anal canal,* and *pars analis recti* [B N A]. **c. basipharyn'geus** [B N A], canalis vomerovaginalis. **c. carot'icus** [N A, B N A], a passage in the petrous portion of the temporal bone, beginning on the inferior surface just anterior to the jugular foramen, and running anteromedially for about 2 cm.; it is seen interiorly in the floor of the middle cranial fossa, where it meets the carotid sulcus on the body of the sphenoid bone. It lodges the internal carotid artery. Called also *carotid canal.* **c. car'pi** [N A, B N A], a tunnel for the tendons of the flexor muscles of the hand and digits, formed by the flexor retinaculum as it roofs over the concavity of the carpus on the palmar surface. Called also *carpal canal.* **c. centra'lis medul'lae spina'lis** [N A, B N A], a small canal extending throughout the length of the spinal cord, lined by ependymal cells. Above, it continues into the medulla oblongata, where it opens into the fourth ventricle. Called also *central canal of spinal cord.* **c. cerv'icis u'teri** [N A, B N A], the part of the uterine cavity that lies within the cervix. Called also *cervical canal of uterus.* **c. chor'dae tym'pani,** canaliculus chordae tympani. **c. condyla'ris** [N A], an opening sometimes present in the floor of the condylar fossa for the transmission of a vein from the transverse sinus. Called also *c. condyloideus* [B N A], and *condylar canal.* **c. condyloi'deus** [B N A], canalis condylaris. **cana'les diplo'ici** [N A], bony canals in the cranial bones, located in the spongy bone between the compact tables and providing for passage of the veins of the diploë. Called also *canales diploici* [*Brescheti*] [B N A] and *diploic canals.* **c. facia'lis** [N A], **c. fascia'lis [fallo'pii]** [B N A], a canal in the temporal bone for the facial nerve, beginning in the internal acoustic meatus and passing anterolaterally dorsal to the vestibule of the inner ear for about 2 mm. Turning sharply backward at the genu of the facial canal, it runs along the medial wall of the tympanic cavity, then turns inferiorly and reaches the exterior of the petrous part of the bone at the stylomastoid foramen. Called also *facial canal.* **c. femora'lis** [N A, B N A], the cone-shaped medial part of the femoral sheath lateral to the base of the lacunar ligament. Called also *femoral canal.* **c. hyaloi'deus** [N A, B N A], a passage running from in front of the optic disc to the lens of the eye; in the fetus it transmits the *hyaloid artery.* Called also *hyaloid canal.* **c. hypoglos'si** [N A, B N A], an opening in the lateral part of the occipital bone at the base of the condyle, which transmits the hypoglossal nerve and a branch of the posterior meningeal artery. Called also *hypoglossal canal.* **c. incisi'vus** [N A, B N A], one of the small canals opening into the incisive fossa of the hard palate, and transmitting small vessels and nerves from the floor of the nose into the front part of the roof of the mouth. Called also *incisive canal.* **c. infraorbita'lis** [N A, B N A], a passage beneath the orbital surface of the maxilla, continuous posteriorly with the infraorbital sulcus, and opening anteriorly on the anterior surface of the body of the maxilla in the infraorbital foramen. It contains the infraorbital vessels and nerve. Called also *infraorbital canal.* **c. inguina'lis** [N A, B N A], the passage superficial to the deep inguinal ring for transmission of the spermatic cord in the male and the round ligament in the female. Called also *inguinal canal.* **cana'les longitudina'les modi'oli** [N A, B N A], short tunnels in the modiolus that transmit blood vessels and nerves. Called also *longitudinal canals of modiolus.* **c. mandib'ulae** [N A, B N A], a canal that traverses the ramus and body of the mandible between the mandibular and mental foramina, transmitting the inferior alveolar vessels and nerve. Called also *mandibular canal.* **c. musculotuba'rius** [N A, B N A], the combined canals of the auditory tube and the tensor tympani muscle in the temporal bone. Called also *musculotubal canal.* **c. nasolacrima'lis** [N A, B N A], a canal formed by the lacrimal sulcus of the maxilla, lacrimal bone, and inferior nasal concha; it contains the nasolacrimal duct. Called also *nasolacrimal canal.* **c. nutri'cius os'sis** [N A, B N A], one of the freely anastomosing channels of the haversian system of compact bone, which contain blood vessels, lymph vessels, nerves, and marrow. Called also *haversian canal.* **c. obturato'rius** [N A, B N A], an opening within the obturator membrane for the passage of the obturator vessels and nerve; its boundaries are the edge of the obturator membrane, together with the obturator groove of the pubic bone. Called also *obturator canal.* **c. op'ticus** [N A], one of the paired openings in the sphenoid bone where the small wings are attached to the body of the bone at the apex of the orbit; each canal transmits one of the optic nerves and the ophthalmic artery of that side. Called also *optic canal* and *foramen opticum ossis sphenoidalis* [B N A]. **c. palati'novagina'lis** [N A], a narrow canal located in the roof of the nasal cavity between the inferior surface of the body of the sphenoid bone and the sphenoidal process of the palatine bone. It opens posteriorly into the nasal cavity and anteriorly into the pterygopalatine fossa. Called also *c. pharyngeus* [B N A], and *palatovaginal canal.* **cana'les palati'ni** [B N A], canales palatini minores. **c. palati'nus ma'jor** [N A], a passage in the sphenoid and palatine bones for the pterygopalatine vessels and pharyngeal nerve. Called also *c. pterygopalatinus* [B N A]. **cana'les palati'ni mino'res** [N A], openings in the palatine bone that branch off the great palatine canal to carry the lesser and middle palatine nerves and vessels to the roof of the mouth. Called also *canales palatini* [B N A], and *lesser palatine canals.* **c. pharyn'geus** [B N A], canalis palatinovaginalis. **c. pterygoi'deus** [N A], a horizontally running canal that passes forward through the base of the medial pterygoid plate of the sphenoid bone to open into the posterior wall of the pterygopalatine fossa just medial and inferior to the foramen rotundum; it transmits the pterygoid vessels and nerves. Called also *c. pterygoideus* [*Vidii*] [B N A] and *pterygoid canal.* **c. pterygopalati'nus** [B N A], c. palatinus major. **c. pudenda'lis** [N A], the tunnel in the special fascial sheath through which the pudendal vessels and nerve pass. It is intimately related to the obturator fascia. Called also *pudendal canal.* **c. pylor'icus** [N A], the short constricted part of the pyloric portion of the stomach, between the pyloric antrum and the pylorus. Called also *pyloric canal.* **c. rad'icis den'tis** [N A, B N A], that portion of the pulp cavity in the root of a tooth, extending from the pulp chamber to the apical foramen. Called also *root canal of tooth.* **c. reu'niens,** ductus reuniens. **c. sacra'lis** [N A, B N A], the continuation of the vertebral canal through the sacrum. Called also *sacral canal.* **c. semicircula'ris ante'rior** [N A], the anterior of the osseous semicircular canals, lodging the ductus semicircularis anterior. Called also *c. semicircularis superior* [B N A] and *anterior semicircular canal.* See *canales semicirculares ossei.* **c. semicircula'ris latera'lis** [N A, B N A], the lateral of the semicircular canals, lodging the ductus semicircularis lateralis. Called also *lateral semicircular canal.* See *canales semicirculares ossei.* **cana'les semicircular'es os'sei** [N A, B N A], three long canals of the bony labyrinth of the ear (lateral, anterior, and posterior), forming loops and opening into the vestibule by five openings. They lodge the semicircular ducts (ductus semicirculares [N A]) of the membranous labyrinth. Called also *semicircular canals.* **c. semicircula'ris poste'rior** [N A, B N A], the posterior of the semicircular canals, lodging the ductus semicircularis posterior. Called also *posterior semicircular canal.* See *canales semicirculares ossei.* **c. spina'lis** [B N A], c. vertebralis [N A]. **c. spira'lis coch'leae** [N A, B N A], a winding tube that makes two and one-half turns about the modiolus of the cochlea; it is divided into two compartments, scala tympani and scala vestibuli, by the lamina spiralis. Called also *spiral canal of cochlea.* **c. spira'lis modio'li** [N A, B N A], a canal following the course of the bony spiral lamina of the cochlea and containing the spiral ganglion of the cochlear division of the vestibulocochlear nerve. Called also *spiral canal of modiolus.* **c. subsartoria'lis,** c. adductorius. **c. ventric'uli** [N A], the longitudinal grooved channel formed by the more or less regular ridges along the lesser curvature of the stomach. Called also *ventricular canal.* **c. vertebra'lis** [N A, B N A], the canal formed by the foramina in the successive vertebrae, which encloses the spinal cord and meninges. Called also *vertebral canal.* **c. vomerovagina'lis** [N A], an inconstant opening formed by the articulating margins of the ala of the vomer and the body of the sphenoid bone. Called also *c. basipharyngeus* [B N A], and *vomerovaginal canal.*

canalization (kan″al-i-za′shun). 1. The formation of canals, natural or morbid. 2. The surgical formation of holes or canals without tubes for wound drainage. 3. The formation of new canals or paths, especially blood vessels, through an obstruction, such as a clot. 4. In psychology, the formation in the central nervous system of new pathways by the repeated passage of nerve impulses.

canavalin (kan″ah-val′in). An antibacterial substance isolated from the flour of soy beans.

canavanase (kan-av′ah-nās). An enzyme from human liver which catalyzes the hydrolysis of canavanine into caveline and urea.

canavanine (kan-av′ĭ-nin). A diamino acid isolated from soy bean meal: it is $NH_2.C(:NH).NH.O.CH_2.CH_2.CH(NH_2).COOH$.

cancellated (kan′sel-lāt-ed). Having a lattice-like structure.

cancelli (kan-sel′i) [L.]. Plural of *cancellus.*

cancellous (kan′sĕ-lus). Of a reticular, spongy, or lattice-like structure: used mainly of bony tissue.

cancellus (kan-sel′us), pl. *cancel′li* [L. "a lattice"]. A lattice-like bony structure.

cancer (kan′ser) [L. "crab"]. A cellular tumor the natural course of which is fatal and usually associated with formation of secondary tumors. See *carcinoma* and *sarcoma.* **acinous c.,** acinous carcinoma. **adenoid c.,** a malignant tumor made up of or containing cylindrical tubes lined with epithelium. **c. a deux** [Fr. "cancer in two"], cancer attacking simultaneously or consecutively two persons who live together. **alveolar c.,** colloma. **aniline c.,** cancer due to aniline dyes, occurring among those who work in dye factories and dyeing establishments. **c. aquat′icus,** cancrum oris, or gangrenous stomatitis. **Aran's green c.,** malignant lymphoma of the orbit, with severe leukemia and a tendency to form metastases by the lymphatics. **areolar c.,** colloid carcinoma. **c. atroph′icans,** scirrhous cancer which is surrounded by sclerosed and atrophied tissue. **betel c.,** buyo cheek c. **black c.,** melanotic c. **boring c.,** epithelioma of the skin of the face. **branchiogenous c.,** a cancer originating in the superior cervical triangle, and supposed to be derived from a relic of an embryonal branchial cleft. **Butter's c.,** cancer of the hepatic flexure of the colon. **buyo cheek c.,** cancer of the cheek seen in natives of the Philippine Islands from chewing buyo leaf or betel. **cellular c.,** encephaloid c. **cerebriform c.,** encephaloid c. **chimney-sweeps' c.,** cancer of the scrotum due to soot poisoning. **chondroid c.,** scirrhous cancer with a cartilage-like texture. **claypipe c.,** epithelioma of the lip due to irritation caused by a pipe stem. **colloid c.,** colloma. **conjugal c.,** cancer attacking nearly simultaneously a man and his wife. **contact c.,** cancer developing in a part of the body in contact with a previously existing cancer. **corset c.,** cancer en cuirasse. **cystic c.,** carcinoma that has undergone cystic degeneration. **dendritic c.,** papilloma. **dermoid c.,** a cancer containing nests and pegs of flat epithelium with colloid masses. **duct c.,** cancer of the epithelium of the mammary ducts. **dye workers' c.,** cancer of the urinary bladder frequently observed among workers in aniline dyes. **encephaloid c.,** a soft cancer of brainlike consistency; encephaloma. **c. en cuirasse,** a cancer about the skin of the thorax. **endothelial c.,** endothelioma. **epidermal c.,** epithelioma. **epithelial c.,** epithelioma. **fungous c.,** fungus haematodes. **glandular c.,** adenocarcinoma and adenosarcoma. **green c.,** chloroma. **hard c.,** one containing an excess of fibrous tissue. **hematoid c.,** fungus haematodes. **c. in situ,** carcinoma in situ. **jacket c.,** c. en cuirasse. **kang c., kangri c.,** epithelioma in the thigh or abdomen affecting Indian and Chinese natives, and attributed to irritation from the kang or heated brick oven or from the kangri or fire basket. **Lobstein's c.,** retroperitoneal sarcoma. **medullary c.,** one made up largely of soft, marrow-like cellular material. **melanotic c.,** a malignant growth of a black or deeply pigmented color. **mule-spinners' c.,** a form of epithelioma affecting mule spinners in the cotton-spinning industry. **paraffin c.,** a malignant growth occurring in those who work in paraffin. **pitch-workers' c.,** epithelioma of the face, neck, and scrotum seen in those who work in pitch. **retrograde c.,** a dormant atrophied malignant growth. **rodent c.,** rodent ulcer. **roentgenologist's c.,** cancer affecting the hands of those who work with roentgen rays. **scirrhous c.,** a hard or fibroid malignant growth; scirrhus. **smokers' c.,** epithelioma of the lip due to irritation by the pipe stem; also cancer of the throat, ascribed to excessive smoking. **soft c.,** an encephaloid or colloid cancer. **solanoid c.,** one which resembles a potato in its texture. **soot c.,** chimney-sweeps' c. **spider c.,** naevus araneosus. **tar c.,** carcinoma caused by inflammatory irritation of fumes of tar. **tubular c.,** a form of mammary cancer believed to arise from the mammary ducts. **villous duct c.,** cancer developed from a cyst with villous malignant growth. **water c.,** noma. **withering c.,** scirrhous carcinoma.

canceration (kan-ser-a′shun). The appearance of malignant change in a previously benign lesion.

canceremia (kan″ser-e′me-ah). The presence of cancer cells in the blood.

cancericidal (kan″ser-ĭ-si′dal) [*cancer* + L. *caedere* to kill]. Destructive to cancer or malignant cells.

cancerigenic (kan″ser-ĭ-jen′ik). Carcinogenic.

cancerin (kan′ser-in). A white, crystalline ptomaine, $C_8H_5NO_3$, from the urine in carcinoma.

cancerism (kan′ser-izm). The cancerous diathesis; a tendency to the development of malignant disease.

cancerocidal (kan″ser-o-si′dal). Cancericidal.

canceroderm (kan′ser-o-derm″). Numerous angiomas of large size seen on the chest and abdomen of certain patients and thought to be connected with malignant growths. Called also *de Morgan spots.*

cancerogenic (kan″ser-o-jen′ik). Carcinogenic.

cancerology (kan″ser-ol′o-je). Cancrology.

cancerophobia (kan″ser-o-fo′be-ah). Carcinophobia.

cancerous (kan′ser-us). Of the nature of or pertaining to cancer.

cancerphobia (kan″ser-fo′be-ah). Carcinophobia.

cancriform (kang′krĭ-form). Resembling a cancer.

cancrocirrhosis (kang″kro-sĭ-ro′sis). Cancer of the lung associated with cirrhosis of the parenchyma.

cancroid (kang′kroid) [*cancer* + Gr. *eidos* form]. 1. Resembling cancer. 2. A skin cancer of a moderate degree of malignancy.

cancrology (kang-krol′o-je) [*cancer* + *-logy*]. The science and study of cancer.

cancrum (kang′krum) [L.]. Canker. **c. na′si,** gangrenous rhinitis of children. **c. o′ris,** gangrenous stomatitis. **c. puden′di,** ulceration of the pudenda.

candicidin (kan″dĭ-si′din). A substance produced by species of Streptomyces which is actively fungicidal in vitro.

Candida (kan′dĭ-dah) [L. *candidus* glowing white]. A genus of yeastlike fungi, characterized by producing mycelia but not ascospores. **C. al′bicans,** the species which may cause human infection. Other species are *C. tropicalis, C. krusei, C. parakrusei, C. stellatoidea* and *C. guilliermondi.*

Candida (de Rivas).

candidemia (kan″dĭ-de′me-ah). Presence in the blood of fungi of the genus Candida.

candidiasis (kan″dĭ-di′ah-sis). Infection with fungi of the genus Candida.

candidid (kan′dĭ-did). Moniliid.

candiru (kan-dĭ-roo′). Any of certain small catfishes of the Amazon River which are said to enter the urethra of men and the vulva of women who bathe in the river.

candle (kan′d'l). 1. A mass of wax or similar substance, usually cylindrical in shape, with a wick for burning, to furnish illumination or heat. 2. A cylindrical mass of material used as a filter. **foot c.,** a common unit of illumination, being 1 lumen per foot or equivalent to 1.0764 milliphots. **international c.,** the unit of luminous intensity. This unit, established in 1909, is maintained by electric incandescent lamps in the national laboratories of France, Great Britain, and the United States. **meter c.** See *lux.*

candle-fish (kan′d'l fish). A fish yielding a fixed oil, eulachon oil, with properties similar to cod liver oil.

candol (kan′dol). A dry malt extract.

cane (kān). A simple stick used for support in walking. **English c.,** a supporting device consisting of a single upright with a hand rest at right angles to it; an extension piece above the hand rest, attached at an angle of about 125 degrees to the upright and bent away from the body, has a holder at the top which fits around the forearm, permitting the weight of the body to be supported on the hand and back of the forearms. **Jamaica c.,** the bark of *Cinnamodendron corticosum* and *C. macranthum,* which is often substituted for canella bark.

canescent (kah-nes′ent) [L. *canus* gray]. Grayish.

canine (ka′nīn) [L. *caninus*]. Of, pertaining to, or like that which belongs to a dog. See under *tooth.*

caniniform (ka-nīn′ĭ-form). Resembling a canine tooth.

caninus (ka-ni′nus). Musculus levator anguli oris.

canities (kah-nish′e-ēz) [L.]. Grayness or whiteness of the hair.

canker (kang′ker). 1. Ulceration, chiefly of the mouth and lips; aphthous stomatitis. 2. Disease of the keratogenous membrane in horses, beginning at the frog and extending to the sole and wall, marked by a loss of function of the horn-secreting cells and the discharge of a serous exudate in place of normal horn. 3. Inflammation of the lining of the external ear in dogs and cats.

canna (kan′ah) [L.]. A reed, or cane. **c. ma′jor,** the tibia. **c. mi′nor,** the fibula.

cannabis (kan′ah-bis) [Gr. *kannabis* hemp]. The dried flowering tops of hemp plants, *Cannabis sativa,* known popularly as *marihuana, hashish* and *bhang.*

cannabism (kan′ah-bizm). A morbid state produced by misuse of cannabis.

Cannizzaro's reaction (kan″e-zah′rōz) [Stanislao *Cannizzaro,* chemist in Rome, 1826–1910]. See under *reaction.*

cannon (kan′un). Canon.

Cannon's ring (kan′unz) [Walter Bradford *Cannon,* Boston physiologist, 1871–1945]. See under *ring.*

cannula (kan′u-lah) [L., dim. of *canna* "reed"]. A tube for insertion into the body, its lumen being usually occupied by a trocar during the act of insertion. **Bellocq's c.,** a curved cannula for plugging the posterior nares for nosebleed. **Dupuis's c.,** a T-shaped tracheal cannula. **Hahn's c.,** a cannula surrounded by compressed sponge by the swelling of which the trachea is closed. **Lindemann's c.,** a form of needle cannula for use with a syringe in the transfusion of unmodified blood. **perfusion c.,** a double tube for running a continuous flow of liquid into and out of a cavity of the body. **Soresi c.,** a double-cylindered instrument for vein-to-vein or artery-to-vein anastomosis. **Strauss' c.** See *Strauss needle,* under *needle.* **Trendelenburg's c.,** a cannula covered with a dilatable rubber bag: used for closing the trachea to prevent the entrance of blood after tracheotomy. **washout c.,** a cannula attached to a manometer and inserted into a blood vessel so that the connection between the artery and the manometer can be washed out in long observations.

cannulate (kan′u-lāt). To penetrate with a cannula, which may be left in place.

cannulation (kan″u-la′shun). The insertion of a cannula into a hollow organ or body cavity.

cannulization (kan″u-li-za′shun). Cannulation.

Canomyces (ka″no-mi′sēz). A microorganism of the pleuropneumonia group found in dog distemper.

canon (kan′un). A working rule or formula for use in scientific procedure.

Cantani's diet, serum, treatment (kahn-tah′nēz) [Arnoldo *Cantani,* Italian physician, 1837–1893]. See under the nouns.

canthal (kan′thal). Pertaining to a canthus.

canthariasis (kan″thah-ri′ah-sis) [Gr. *kantharos* beetle]. Infection of the body by beetles or by their eggs or larvae.

cantharidal (kan-thar′ĭ-dal). Containing or pertaining to cantharides.

cantharidate (kan-thar′ĭ-dāt). Any salt of cantharidic acid.

cantharides (kan-thar′ĭ-dēz) [L.]. The dried Spanish fly, *Cantharis* (*Meloe*) *vesicatoria,* sometimes called "blister bug." Cantharides are applied externally as powerful rubefacient and blistering agents. Taken internally in moderate doses, they are diuretic and stimulant to the urinary and reproductive organs; in large doses they are highly poisonous.

cantharidin (kan-thar′ĭ-din). The most important active principle of cantharides; it is the lactone of cantharidic acid, $C_{10}H_{12}O_4$. It occurs in crystalline form, has a bitter taste, and produces blistering of the skin.

cantharidism (kan-thar′ĭ-dizm). A morbid condition resulting from the misuse of cantharides.

Cantharis (kan′thah-ris) [L.; Gr. *kantharos* beetle]. A genus of beetles. **C. vesicato′ria,** a species of beetles known as Spanish fly, or blister bug: the source of cantharides.

canthectomy (kan-thek′to-me) [Gr. *kanthos* canthus + *ektomē* excision]. Surgical removal of a canthus.

canthi (kan′thi) [L.]. Plural of *canthus.*

canthitis (kan-thi′tis). Inflammation of a canthus or of the canthi.

cantho- (kan′tho) [Gr. *kanthos*]. Combining form denoting relationship to the canthus.

cantholysis (kan-thol′ĭ-sis) [*cantho-* + *lysis* dissolution]. Surgical division of the canthus of an eye or of a canthal ligament.

canthoplasty (kan′tho-plas″te) [*cantho-* + *plassein* to form]. Plastic surgery of the palpebral fissure, especially the section of a canthus to lengthen said fissure; also the surgical restoration of a defective canthus (Ammon). **provisional c.,** canthotomy when performed as a temporary expedient or for the relief of blepharospasm.

canthorrhaphy (kan-thor′ah-fe) [*cantho-* + Gr. *rhaphē* suture]. The suturation of the palpebral fissure at either canthus.

canthotomy (kan-thot′o-me) [*cantho-* + Gr. *temnein* to cut]. Surgical division of the outer canthus.

canthus (kan′thus), pl. *can′thi* [L.; Gr. *kanthos*]. The angle at either end of the slit between the eyelids: the canthi are distinguished as an outer or temporal and inner or nasal.

cantil (kan′til). Trade mark for a preparation of mepenzolate bromide.

Cantlie's foot tetter [Sir James *Cantlie*, British physician, 1851–1926]. Epidermophytosis of the toes.

Cantor tube (kan′tor). [Meyer *Cantor*, American physician, born 1907]. See under *tube*.

cantus (kan′tus) [L.]. Song, or melody. **c. gal′li** [L. "cock-crowing"], laryngismus stridulus.

canula (kan′u-lah). Cannula.

CaO. Calcium oxide.

CaOC. Abbreviation for *cathodal opening contraction.*

$Ca(OH)_2$. Calcium hydroxide.

caoutchouc (koo′cho͝ok) [Fr.]. Gum-elastic or india rubber; the concrete juice of various trees and plants, such as *Siphonia elastica*, etc. It is a hydrocarbon, $C_{20}H_{32}$, soluble in chloroform, ether, and carbon disulfide.

Cap. Abbreviation for L. *ca′piat*, let him take.

cap (kap). A protective covering for the head, or similar structure. **bishop's c.,** pileus ventriculi. **cradle c.,** crusta lactea. **duodenal c.,** pileus ventriculi. **dutch c.,** a contraceptive vaginal diaphragm. **enamel c.,** the enamel organ after it covers the top of the growing tooth papilla. **head c., anterior,** acrosome. **head c., posterior,** postnuclear c. **knee c.,** patella. **metanephric c's,** masses of metanephric blastema that adhere to the primordial pelvis of the kidney and to its ampullar dilatations. **petroleum c.,** an application of coal oil (or equal parts of coal oil and olive oil) to the scalp for 12–24 hours to kill lice. **phrygian c.,** the cholecystographic appearance of the gallbladder showing kinking between the body and the fundus, in which the fundus is fixed and folded. **postnuclear c.,** a caplike investment of the posterior half of the head of a spermatozoon. **pyloric c.,** pileus ventriculi. **skull c.,** calvaria. **c. of Zinn,** a prominence of the pulmonary arc in the left upper portion of the cardiac silhouette, usually seen in posteroanterior roentgenograms in cases of patent ductus arteriosus, and representing the dilated pulmonary artery.

capacitance (kah-pas′ĭ-tans). Electric capacity.

capacitor (kah-pas′ĭ-tor). A device for holding and storing charges of electricity.

capacity (kah-pas′i-te) [L. *capacitas*, from *capere* to take]. 1. Power or ability to hold, retain, or contain, or the ability to absorb. 2. An expression of the measurement of material that may be held or contained. 3. In electricity, the property by which a given body will take and hold an electric charge. 4. Mental ability to receive, accomplish, endure, or understand. **cranial c.,** an expression of the amount of space within the cranium. **functional residual c.,** the amount of gas remaining in the lung at the resting expiratory level. Abbreviated FRC. **heat c.,** thermal c. **inspiratory c.,** the maximal amount of gas that can be inspired from the resting expiratory level. Abbreviated IC. **maximal tubular excretory c.** See *tubular maximum*, under *maximum*. **respiratory c.** 1. The ability of the blood to absorb oxygen from the lungs and carbon dioxide from the tissues. 2. The space within the lungs normally occupied by the inspired gas (air). **thermal c.,** the amount of heat absorbed by a body in being raised from 15 to 16°C. in temperature. **total lung c.,** the amount of gas that is contained in the lung at the end of a maximal inspiration. Abbreviated TLC. **vital c.,** the maximal amount of gas that can be expelled from the lung by forceful effort after a maximal inspiration. Abbreviated VC.

capelet (kap′e-let) [L. *capelletum*]. A swelling on the point of a horse's hock or on its elbow.

capeline (kap′e-lin) [Fr.]. A cap-shaped bandage for the head or for the stump of an amputated limb.

capiat (ka′pe-at) [L. "let it take"]. An instrument for removing foreign bodies from a cavity, as of the uterus.

capillarectasia (kap″ĭ-lăr″ek-ta′se-ah) [*capillary* + Gr. *ektasis* distention]. Dilatation of capillaries.

Capillaria (kap″ĭ-la′re-ah). A genus of nematodes parasitic in birds and mammals.

capillariomotor (kap″ĭ-lăr″e-o-mo′tor). Pertaining to the functional activity of the capillaries.

capillarioscopy (kap″ĭ-lăr″e-os′ko-pe). Capillaroscopy.

capillaritis (kap″ĭ-lăr-i′tis). Inflammation of the capillaries.

capillarity (kap″ĭ-lăr′ĭ-te). The action by which the surface of a liquid where it is in contact with a solid, as in capillary tubes, is elevated or depressed.

capillaropathy (kap″ĭ-lăr-op′ah-the) [*capillary* + Gr. *pathos* disease]. Any disease of the capillaries.

capillaroscopy (kap″ĭ-lăr-os′ko-pe) [*capillary* + Gr. *skopein* to examine]. Diagnostic examination of the capillaries of the skin with the microscope.

capillary (kap′ĭ-lăr″e) [L. *capillaris* hair-like]. 1. Pertaining to or resembling a hair. 2. Any one of the minute vessels that connect the arterioles and venules, forming a network in nearly all parts of the body. Called also *vas capilla′re* [N A, B N A]. Their walls act as semipermeable membranes for the interchange of various substances between the blood and tissue fluid. **arterial c's,** the minute channels distal to the arterioles, which carry arterial (oxygenated) blood. **bile c's.** 1. Bile canaliculi. 2. A term sometimes used to designate the cholangioles. **erythrocytic c's,** capillaries of the bone marrow of early life which seem to produce erythrocytes. **lymph c., lymphatic c.,** one of the most minute vessels of the lymphatic system, having a caliber slightly greater than that of a capillary of the circulatory system. **Meigs's c's,** capillaries in the myocardium. **secretory c's,** extremely fine canals situated between adjacent gland cells, being formed by the apposition of grooves in the surfaces of the cells. **sinusoidal c's.** See *sinusoid*. **venous c's,** minute channels proximal to the venules, which carry venous blood.

capilli (kah-pil′li) [L.]. Plural of *capillus*.

capilliculture (kah-pil′ĭ-kul″tūr) [L. *capillus* hair + *cultu′ra* culture]. Treatment for the cure of baldness or the preservation of the hair.

capillitium (kap″ĭ-lish′e-um) [L. "head of hair"]. The interlacing, filamentous structure which, with the spores, fills the spore case of myxomycetes.

capillomotor (kap″ĭ-lo-mo′tor). Capillariomotor.

capillus (kah-pil′lus), pl. *capil′li* [L.]. A hair. Used in the plural, in anatomical terminology, especially to designate the aggregate of hair on the scalp.

capistration (kap″ĭ-stra′shun) [L. *capistratus* masked]. Phimosis.

capita (kap′ĭ-tah) [L.]. Plural of *caput*.

capital (kap′ĭ-tal). Of the highest importance; involving danger to life.

capitate (kap′ĭ-tāt) [L. *caput* head]. Head-shaped.

capitatum (kap″ĭ-ta′tum) [L. "having a head"]. The os magnum of the carpus, the os capitatum.

capitellum (kap″ĭ-tel′um) [L., dim. of *caput* head]. Capitulum humeri.

capitonnage (kap″ĭ-to-nahzh′) [Fr.]. The surgical closure of a cyst cavity by applying sutures in such a way as to cause approximation of the opposing surfaces of the cavity.

capitopedal (kap″ĭ-to-ped′al). Pertaining to the head and foot.

capitula (kah-pit′u-lah) [L.]. Plural of *capitulum.*

capitular (kah-pit′u-lar). Pertaining to a capitulum or head of a bone.

capitulum (kah-pit′u-lum), pl. *capit′ula* [L., dim. of *caput*]. [N A, B N A] A general term for a little head, or a small eminence on a bone by which it articulates with another bone; in N A applied only to the distal end of the humerus, since that bone already possesses a head (caput). **c. cos′tae** [B N A], caput costae. **c. fib′ulae** [B N A], caput fibulae. **c. hu′meri** [N A, B N A], **c. of humerus,** an eminence on the distal end of the lateral epicondyle of the humerus for articulation with the head of the radius. **c. mal′lei** [B N A], caput mallei. **c. os′sis metacarpa′lis** [B N A], caput ossis metacarpalis. **c. os′sis metatarsa′lis** [B N A], caput ossis metatarsalis. **c. proces′sus condyloi′dei mandib′ulae** [B N A], caput mandibulae. **c. ra′dii** [B N A], caput radii. **c. sta′pedis** [B N A], caput stapedis. **c. ul′nae** [B N A], caput ulnae.

capla (kap′lah). Trade mark for a preparation of mebutamate.

capnophilic (kap-no-fil′ik) [Gr. *kapnos* smoke + *philein* to love]. Growing best in the presence of carbon dioxide: said of bacteria.

$Ca_3(PO_4)_2$. Tribasic calcium phosphate.

capotement (kah-pōt-maw′) [Fr.]. A splashing sound heard in the dilated stomach.

cappa (kap′ah). A superficial layer of gray matter of the quadrigeminal body, situated just beneath the expansion of the optic tracts.

capping (kap′ing). The provision of a protective or obstructive covering. **pulp c.,** the covering of an exposed dental pulp with some material, medicated or non-medicated, to provide protection against external influences.

Capps' reflex, sign (kap′zes) [Joseph A. *Capps,* American physician, born 1872]. See under *reflex.*

caprate (kap′rāt). Any salt of capric acid.

capreolary (kap′re-o-la″re). Capreolate.

capreolate (kap′re-o-lāt). Tendril shaped, like the spermatic vessels.

caprillic (kah-pril′ik) [L. *caper* goat]. Goatlike.

capriloquism (kah-pril′o-kwizm) [L. *caper* goat + *loqui* to speak]. Egophony.

caprin (kap′rin). Any one of the caprates of glyceryl, especially the glyceryl tricaprate, or tricaprin, $C_3H_5[CH_3(CH_2)_8COO]_3$, from ordinary butter.

caprine (kap′rīn) [L. *caper* goat]. 1. Pertaining to or derived from a goat. 2. Norleucine.

caprizant (kap′rĭ-zant) [L. *caprizans,* from *caper* a goat]. Leaping or bounding like a goat.

caproate (kap′ro-āt). Any salt of caproic acid.

caproin (kah-pro′in). Any caproate of glyceryl, especially the tricaproate, $C_3H_5(O_6H_{13}O_2)_3$; called also *tricaproin:* it occurs in butter.

caprone (kap′rōn). A volatile oil, di-*n*-amylketone, $CH_3(CH_2)_4.CO(CH_2)_4.CH_3$, from butter.

caproyl (kap-ro′il). The hydrocarbon radical, C_6H_{13}; hexyl.

caproylamine (kap″ro-il-am′in). A poisonous ptomaine, $CH_3(CH_2)_5NH_2$, or hexylamine, from spoiled yeast and rancid cod liver oil.

caprylate (kap′rĭ-lāt). Any salt of caprylic acid.

caprylin (kap′rĭ-lin). Any caprylate of glyceryl, especially the tricaprylate: called also *tricaprylin,* $C_3H_5(C_7H_{15}CO_2)_3$.

capsebon (kap′se-bon). Trade mark for a suspension of cadmium sulfide.

capsicum (kap′sĭ-kum). The dried fruit of *Capsicum frutescens:* used as an irritant and carminative.

capsitis (kap-si′tis). Inflammation of the capsule of the crystalline lens.

capsorubin (kap″so-ru′bin). A carotinoid, $C_{40}H_{60}O_4$, closely associated with capsanthin.

capsotomy (kap-sot′o-me). Capsulotomy.

Capsul. Abbreviation for L. *cap′sula,* capsule.

capsula (kap′su-lah), pl. *cap′sulae* [L.]. [N A, B N A] A general term for a cartilaginous, fatty, fibrous, or membranous structure enveloping another structure, organ, or part. Called also *capsule.* **c. adipo′sa,** a capsule consisting principally of fat. **c. adipo′sa re′nis** [N A, B N A], the investment of perirenal fat surrounding the fibrous capsule of the kidney and continuous at the hilus with the fat in the renal sinus. Called also *adipose capsule of kidney.* **c. articula′ris** [N A, B N A], the sac-like envelope which encloses the cavity of a synovial joint by attaching to the circumference of the articular end of each involved bone; it consists of a fibrous membrane and a synovial membrane. Called also *articular capsule.* **c. articula′ris acro′mioclavicula′ris** [N A, B N A], a ligamentous sac surrounding the acromioclavicular joint. Called also *acromioclavicular articular capsule.* **c. articula′ris articulatio′nis tar′si transver′sae** [N A], a ligamentous sac surrounding the transverse tarsal joint. **c. articula′ris articulatio′nis temporomandibula′ris** [N A], a ligamentous sac surrounding the temporomandibular joint. Called also *c. articularis mandibulae* [B N A] and *capsule of temporomandibular joint.* **c. articula′ris articulatio′num vertebra′rum** [N A], one of the bands of tissue, partly white fibrous and partly yellow elastic, that unite the articular processes of adjacent vertebrae. Called also *capsule of vertebral articulations.* **c. articula′ris atlantoaxia′lis latera′lis** [N A], a ligamentous sac surrounding the lateral atlantoaxial joint. Called also (pl.) *capsulae articulares atlantoepistrophicae* [B N A] and *atlantoaxial articular capsule.* **cap′sulae articula′res atlantoepistro′phicae** [B N A]. See *c. articularis atlantoaxialis lateralis.* **c. articula′ris atlantooccipita′lis** [N A], one of a pair of distinct ligamentous bands, each of which is attached at one end to the lateral mass of the atlas and at the other end to the margins of an occipital condyle. Called also *capsule of atlantooccipital articulation.* **c. articula′ris calcaneocuboi′dea** [N A, B N A], a ligamentous sac surrounding the calcaneocuboidal joint. Called also *capsule of calcaneocuboidal joint.* **c. articula′ris capi′tis cos′tae** [N A], a ligamentous sac surrounding the articulation of the head of a rib. Called also *capsulae articulares capituli costae* [B N A], and *articular capsule of head of rib.* **cap′sulae articula′res capit′uli cos′tae** [B N A]. See *c. articularis capitis costae.* **cap′sulae articula′res carpometacar′peae** [N A, B N A], ligamentous sacs surrounding the carpometacarpal joints; they are continuous with the capsules of the intercarpal joints. Called also *capsules of carpometacarpal joints.* **c. articula′ris carpometacar′pea pol′licis** [N A, B N A], a ligamentous sac surrounding the carpometacarpal joint of the thumb. Called also *capsule of carpometacarpal articulation of thumb.* **c. articula′ris costotransversa′ria** [N A], a ligamentous sac surrounding the costotransverse articulation. Called also *capsule of costotransverse joint.* **c. articula′ris cox′ae** [N A, B N A], a large, strong ligamentous sac surrounding the hip joint. Called also *capsule of hip joint.* **c. articula′ris cricoarytenoi′dea** [N A], the fibrous and synovial layers enclosing the cricoarytenoid joint. Called also *c. articularis cricoarytaenoidea* [B N A], and *cricoarytenoid articular capsule.* **c. articula′ris criocothyroi′dea** [N A], the capsule of the cricothyroid joint. Called also *c. articularis cricothyreoidea* [B N A]. **c. articula′ris cu′biti** [N A, B N A], the capsule formed around the cubital articulation by its various ligaments. Called also *articular capsule of elbow.*

cap'sulae articula'res digito'rum man'us [B N A], capsulae articulares interphalangearum manus. **cap'sulae articula'res digito'rum pe'dis** [B N A], capsulae articulares interphalangearum pedis. **c. articula'ris ge'nus** [N A], the loose, thin, but strong sac enclosing the knee joint. Called also *c. articularis genu* [B N A], and *capsule of knee joint.* **c. articula'ris hu'meri** [N A, B N A], a ligamentous sac surrounding the shoulder joint. Called also *articular capsule of humerus.* **cap'sulae articula'res intermetacar'peae** [N A, B N A], ligamentous sacs that surround the intermetacarpal joints; they are continuous with the capsules of the carpometacarpal joints. Called also *capsules of intermetacarpal joints.* **cap'sulae articula'res intermetatar'seae** [N A, B N A], the capsules around the four joints between the bases of the metatarsal bones. Called also *capsules of intermetatarsal joints.* **cap'sulae articula'res interphalangea'rum man'us** [N A], incomplete ligamentous sacs surrounding the interphalangeal joints of the hand. Called also *capsulae articulares digitorum manus* [B N A], and *capsules of interphalangeal joints of hand.* **cap'sulae articula'res interphalangea'rum pe'dis** [N A], the capsules surrounding the interphalangeal articulations of the toes. Called also *capsulae articulares digitorum pedis* [B N A], and *capsules of interphalangeal joints of foot.* **c. articula'ris mandib'ulae** [B N A], c. articularis articulationis temporomandibularis. **c. articula'ris man'us** [N A, B N A], a loose ligamentous sac surrounding the radiocarpal joint and the intercarpal joints together. Called also *capsule of radiocarpal joint.* **cap'sulae articula'res metacarpophalan'geae** [N A, B N A], ligamentous sacs that surround the metacarpophalangeal joints. Called also *capsules of metacarpophalangeal joints.* **cap'sulae articula'res metatarsophalan'geae** [N A, B N A], the five capsules surrounding the metatarsophalangeal articulations. Called also *capsules of metatarsophalangeal joints.* **c. articula'ris os'sis pisifor'mis** [N A, B N A], a thin, loose ligamentous sac surrounding the joint of the pisiform bone. Called also *articular capsule of pisiform bone.* **c. articula'ris radioulna'ris dista'lis** [N A, B N A], a loose ligamentous sac surrounding the distal radioulnar joint. Called also *distal radioulnar articular capsule.* **c. articula'ris sternoclavicula'ris** [N A, B N A], a ligamentous sac surrounding the sternoclavicular joint. Called also *capsule of sternoclavicular joint.* **c. articula'ris sternocosta'lis** [N A], the ligamentous sac that surrounds a sternocostal joint. Called also *sternocostal articular capsule.* **c. articula'ris talocalca'nea** [N A, B N A], a loose ligamentous sac surrounding the subtalar joint. Called also *capsule of subtalar joint.* **c. articula'ris talocrura'lis** [N A, B N A], a thin ligamentous sac surrounding the ankle joint. Called also *capsule of ankle joint.* **c. articula'ris talonavicula'ris** [B N A], a capsule surrounding the talonavicular joint; omitted in N A. **cap'sulae articula'res tarsometatar'seae** [N A, B N A], the three capsules that surround the joints between the metatarsal and cuneiform bones. Called also *capsules of tarsometatarsal joints.* **c. articula'ris tibiofibula'ris** [N A, B N A], a fibrous sac enclosing the tibiofibular articulation. Called also *capsule of tibiofibular joint.* **c. bul'bi.** See *vaginae bulbi.* **c. cor'dis,** pericardium. **c. exter'na** [N A, B N A], the layer of white fibers forming the outer border of the corpus striatum. **c. exter'na nu'clei lentifor'mis,** c. externa. **c. fibro'sa,** a capsule consisting largely of fibrous elements. **c. fibro'sa glan'dulae thyroi'deae** [N A], a connective tissue coat intimately adherent to the underlying gland. Called also *fibrous capsule of thyroid gland.* **c. fibro'sa [Glisso'ni]** [B N A], **c. fibro'sa hep'atis,** c. fibrosa perivascularis. **c. fibro'sa perivascula'ris** [N A], the connective tissue sheath that accompanies the vessels and ducts through the hepatic portal. It is continuous with the tunica fibrosa. Called also *c. fibrosa [Glissoni]* [B N A], and *perivascular fibrous capsule.* **c. fibro'sa re'nis** [N A], the connective tissue investment of the kidney, which continues through the hilus to line the renal sinus. Called also *fibrous capsule of kidney* and *tunica fibrosa renis* [B N A]. **c. glan'dulae thyroi'deae,** c. fibrosa glandulae thyroideae. **c. glomeru'li** [N A, B N A], the globular dilatation that forms the beginning of a uriniferous tubule within the kidney, and surrounds the glomerulus. Called also *capsule of glomerulus.* **c. inter'na** [N A, B N A], a broad band of white substance that separates the lentiform nucleus from the caudate nucleus and thalamus. It consists of a genu, an anterior limb, and a posterior limb, and carries both afferent and efferent fibers of the cerebral cortex. Called also *internal capsule.* **c. inter'na nu'clei lentifor'mis,** c. interna. **c. len'tis** [N A, B N A], the elastic envelope covering the lens of the eye and fusing with the fibers of the ciliary zonule. Called also *capsule of lens.* **c. li'enis,** noduli lymphatici lienales. **c. nu'clei denta'ti** [B N A], a layer of gray substance surrounding the white substance of the dentate nucleus; omitted in N A. **cap'sulae nu'clei lentifor'mis.** See *c. externa* and *c. interna.* **cap'sulae re'nis.** See *c. adiposa renis* and *c. fibrosa renis.* **c. sero'sa lie'nis,** tunica serosa lienis.

capsulae (kap'su-le) [L.]. Plural of *capsula.*

capsular (kap'su-lar). Pertaining to a capsule.

capsulation (kap"su-la'shun). The inclosure of a medicine in a capsule.

capsule (kap'sūl) [L. *capsula* a little box]. 1. A structure in which something is enclosed, such as a hard or a soft, soluble container of a suitable substance, for enclosing a dose of medicine. 2. An anatomical structure enclosing an organ or body part. See *capsula.* **adherent c.,** an enveloping structure which is not readily separated from the organ or substance contained within it. **adipose c.,** one consisting largely of fat. **adrenal c.,** adrenal gland (glandula suprarenalis [N A]). **adrenal c's, accessory,** glandulae suprarenales accessoriae. **articular c.,** the sac-like envelope which encloses the cavity of a synovial joint. See *capsula articularis,* and for names of capsules of particular joints see other entries beginning *capsula articularis,* under *capsula.* **articular c., fibrous,** membrana fibrosa capsulae articularis. **auditory c.,** the cartilaginous capsule of the embryo which develops into the external ear. **bacterial c.,** an envelope of gelatinous material surrounding a bacterial cell, usually polysaccharide but sometimes polypeptide in nature, which is associated with the virulence of pathogenic bacteria. **Bonnet's c.** See *vaginae bulbi.* **Bowman's c.,** capsula glomeruli. **c's of the brain,** layers of white matter in the cerebrum. See *capsula externa* and *capsula interna.* **brood c's,** capsular projections from the internal membrane of hydatid cysts, from which the scolices arise. **cartilage c.,** a basophilic zone of cartilage matrix bordering on a lacuna and its enclosed cartilage cell. **crystalline c.,** capsula lentis. **decavitamin c.,** a capsule containing a mixture of 10 vitamins: vitamins A and D, ascorbic acid, calcium pentothenate, cyanocobalamin, folic acid, nicotinamide, pyridoxine hydrochloride, riboflavin, and thiamine hydrochloride or thiamine mononitrate. **dental c.,** periodontium. **external c.,** capsula externa. **fatty c. of kidney,** capsula adiposa renis. **fibrous c.,** one composed chiefly of fibrous elements. **fibrous c. of corpora cavernosa penis,** tunica albuginea corporum cavernosorum penis. **fibrous c. of graafian follicle,** theca folliculi. **fibrous c. of kidney,** capsula fibrosa renis. **fibrous c. of liver,** capsula fibrosa perivascularis. **fibrous c. of spleen,** tunica fibrosa lienis. **fibrous c. of testis,** tunica albuginea testis. **fibrous c. of thyroid gland,**

capsula fibrosa glandulae thyroideae. **Gerota's c.,** the fascia surrounding the kidney. **Glisson's c.,** capsula fibrosa perivascularis. **glomerular c., c. of glomerulus,** capsula glomeruli. **Hearson's c.,** a thermostatic chamber for regulating the temperature in incubators. **c. of heart,** pericardium. **hepatobiliary c.,** capsula fibrosa perivascularis. **hexavitamin c.,** a capsule containing vitamins A, D, C, B_1, B_2, and B_3: used as a dietary supplement. **internal c.,** capsula interna. **joint c.,** articular c. See also under *capsula articularis*. **c. of lens,** capsula lentis. **malpighian c.,** capsula glomeruli. **müllerian c.,** capsula glomeruli. **nasal c.,** a cartilaginous embryonic pouch from which the nose is developed. **ocular c.** See *vaginae bulbi*. **optic c.,** the embryonic structure from which the sclera is developed. **pelvioprostatic c.,** fascia prostatae. **perinephric c.** See *capsula adiposa renis* and *capsula fibrosa renis*. **periotic c.,** the tissue surrounding the auditory sac in the embryo. **renal c.** See *capsula adiposa renis* and *capsula fibrosa renis*. **serous c. of spleen,** tunica serosa lienis. **suprarenal c.,** adrenal gland (glandula suprarenalis [N A]). **synovial c.,** articular c. **Tenon's c.** See *vaginae bulbi*. **triasyn B c's,** capsules containing thiamine, riboflavin, and nicotinamide, used as a vitamin supplement.

capsulectomy (kap″su-lek′to-me) [L. *capsula* capsule + Gr. *ektomē* excision]. Excision of a capsule, especially a joint capsule or the capsule of the lens. **renal c.,** excision of the capsule of the kidney.

capsulitis (kap″su-li′tis). The inflammation of a capsule, as that of the lens. **hepatic c.,** perihepatitis. **c. of the labyrinth,** otosclerosis.

capsulolenticular (kap″su-lo-len-tik′u-lar). Pertaining to the lens of the eye and its capsule.

capsuloma (kap″su-lo′mah). A capsular or subcapsular tumor of the kidney.

capsuloplasty (kap′su-lo-plas″te) [*capsule* + Gr. *plassein* to form]. A plastic operation on a joint capsule.

capsulorrhaphy (kap″su-lor′ah-fe) [*capsule* + Gr. *rhaphē* suture]. Suture of a capsule, especially a joint capsule.

capsulotome (kap-su′lo-tōm). A cutting instrument used for incising the capsules of the lens.

capsulotomy (kap″su-lot′o-me) [*capsule* + Gr. *temnein* to cut]. The incision of a capsule, especially of that of the eye, as in cataract operation; or that of a joint. **renal c.,** incision of a renal capsule.

captation (kap-ta′shun) [L. *captatio* seizure]. The first stage of hypnotism.

captodiamine (kap″to-di′ah-mēn). Chemical name: 2[p(butylthio)-α-phenylbenzylthio]-N,N-dimethylethylamine: used as an antihistaminic and sedative.

captodramin (kap″to-dram′in). Captodiamine.

capulet (kap′u-let). Capelet.

caput (kap′ut), pl. *cap′ita* [L. "head"] [N A, B N A]. 1. The superior extremity of the body, comprising the cranium and face, and containing the brain, the organs of special sense, and the first organs of the digestive system. 2. A general term applied to the proximal, anterior, or superior extremity of an organ or part. **c. angula′re mus′culi quadra′ti la′bii superio′ris** [B N A], musculus levator labii superioris alaeque nasi. **c. bre′ve mus′culi bicip′itis bra′chii** [N A, B N A], the short head of the biceps brachii muscle, originating from the apex of the coracoid process. **c. bre′ve mus′culi bicip′itis fem′oris** [N A, B N A], the short head of the biceps femoris muscle, originating from the linea aspera femoris. **c. co′li,** cecum. **c. cos′tae** [N A], the posterior end of a rib, which articulates with the body of a vertebra. Called also *capitulum costae* [B N A], and *head of rib*. **c. distor′tum,** torticollis. **c. epididym′idis** [N A, B N A], the upper part of the epididymis, in which are found the straight and coiled portions of the efferent ductules of the testis. Called also *head of epididymis*. **c. fem′oris** [N A, B N A], the proximal end of the femur, articulating with the hip bone. Called also *head of femur*. **c. fib′ulae** [N A], the proximal extremity of the fibula. Called also *capitulum fibulae* [B N A], and *head of fibula*. **c. gallinag′inis** [L., "woodcock's head"], colliculus seminalis. **c. humera′le mus′culi flexo′ris car′pi ulna′ris** [N A, B N A], the humeral head of the flexor carpi ulnaris muscle, originating from the medial epicondyle of the humerus. **c. humera′le mus′culi flexo′ris digito′rum subli′mis** [B N A], c. humeroulnare musculi flexoris digitorum superficialis. **c. humera′le mus′culi pronato′ris tere′tis** [N A, B N A], the humeral head of the pronator teres muscle originating from the medial epicondyle of the humerus. **c. humera′lis,** c. humeri. **c. hu′meri** [N A, B N A], the proximal end of the humerus, which articulates with the glenoid cavity of the scapula. Called also *head of humerus*. **c. humeroulna′re mus′culi flexo′ris digito′rum superficia′lis** [N A], the humeroulnar head of the superficial flexor digitorum muscle, originating from the medial epicondyle of the humerus, coronoid process of ulna. **c. incunea′tum,** impaction of the fetal head during labor. **c. infraorbita′le mus′culi quadra′ti la′bii superio′ris** [B N A], musculus levator labii superioris. **c. latera′le mus′culi gastrocne′mii** [N A, B N A], the lateral head of the gastrocnemius muscle, originating from the lateral condyle and posterior surface of the femur, and the capsule of the knee joint. **c. latera′le mus′culi tricip′itis bra′chii** [N A, B N A], the lateral head of the triceps brachii muscle, originating from the posterior surface of the humerus, the lateral border of the humerus, and the lateral intermuscular septum. **c. lie′nis,** extremitas posterior lienis. **c. lon′gum mus′culi bicip′itis bra′chii** [N A, B N A], the long head of the biceps brachii muscle, originating from the upper border of the glenoid cavity. **c. lon′gum mus′culi bicip′itis fem′oris** [N A, B N A], the long head of the biceps femoris muscle, originating from the ischial tuberosity. **c. lon′gum mus′culi tricip′itis bra′chii** [N A, B N A], the long head of the triceps brachii muscle, originating from the infraglenoid tuberosity of the scapula. **c. mal′lei** [N A], the upper portion of the malleus, which articulates with the incus. Called also *capitulum mallei* [B N A], and *head of malleus*. **c. mandib′ulae** [N A], the articular surface of the condyloid process of the mandible. Called also *capitulum [processus condyloidei] mandibulae* [B N A] and *head of mandible*. **c. media′le mus′culi gastrocne′mii** [N A, B N A], the medial head of the gastrocnemius muscle, originating from the upper back part of the median condyle and of the femur, and the capsule of the knee joint. **c. media′le mus′culi tricip′itis bra′chii** [N A, B N A], the medial head of the triceps brachii muscle, originating from the posterior surface of the humerus below the radial groove, the medial border of the humerus, and the medial intermuscular septa. **c. medu′sae,** a peculiar appearance due to dilatation from stasis of the cutaneous veins around the navel: seen mainly in the newborn and in patients suffering with cirrhosis of the liver. Called also *cirsomphalos*. **c. mus′culi** [N A, B N A], the end of a muscle at the site of its attachment to a bone or other fixed structure (origin). Called also *head of muscle*. **c. natifor′me,** a head in rickets in which the eminences of the frontal and parietal bones form elevations separated by depressions which mark the lines of the cranial sutures. **c. nu′clei cauda′ti** [N A, B N A], the largest and most anterior part of the caudate nucleus, which bulges into the anterior horn of the lateral ventricle. **c. obli′quum mus′culi adducto′ris hal′lucis** [N A, B N A], the oblique head of the adductor hallucis muscle, originating from the bases of the second, third, and fourth metatarsal bones, and the sheath of the peroneus longus muscle. **c. obli'quum mus'culi adducto'ris pol'licis** [N A], the oblique head of the adductor pollicis muscle, originating from the sheath of the flexor carpi radialis muscle, the anterior carpal ligament, capitate bone, and the bases of second and third metacarpals. **c. ob'stipum,** torticollis. **c. os'sis metacarpa'lis** [N A], the distal extremity of each metacarpal bone, which articulates with the base of a proximal phalanx. Called also *capitulum ossis metacarpalis* [B N A], and *head of metacarpal bone.* **c. os'sis metatarsa'lis** [N A], the distal part of each metatarsal bone, which articulates with the base of a proximal phalanx. Called also *capitulum ossis metatarsalis* [B N A], and *head of metatarsal bone.* **c. pancre'atis** [N A, B N A], the discoidal mass forming the enlarged right extremity of the pancreas, lying in a flexure of the duodenum. Called also *head of pancreas.* **c. pe'nis,** glans penis. **c. phalan'gis digito'rum ma'nus** [N A], the distal articular surface of each of the proximal and middle phalanges of the fingers. Called also *head of phalanx of fingers,* and *trochlea phalangis digitorum manus* [B N A]. **c. phalan'gis digito'rum pe'dis** [N A], the distal articular extremity of each of the proximal and middle phalanges of the toes. Called also *head of phalanx of toes,* and *trochlea phalangis digitorum pedis* [B N A]. **c. pla'num,** a flattened head occurring with osteochondritis deformans juvenilis. **c. proge'neum,** forward projection of the jaw. **c. quadra'tum,** an abnormally shaped head, sometimes occurring with rickets. **c. radia'le mus'culi flexo'ris digito'rum superficia'lis** [N A, B N A], the radial head of the superficial flexor digitorum muscle, originating from the oblique line of the radius, anterior border. **c. ra'dii** [N A], the disk on the proximal end of the radius that articulates with the capitulum of the humerus. Called also *capitulum radii* [B N A], and *head of radius.* **c. stape'dis** [N A], the head of the stapes, which articulates with the incus. Called also *capitulum stapedis* [B N A]. **c. succeda'neum,** edema sometimes occurring in and under the fetal scalp during labor. **c. ta'li** [N A, B N A], the rounded anterior end of the talus. Called also *head of talus.* **c. transver'sum mus'culi adducto'ris hal'lucis** [N A, B N A], the transverse head of the adductor hallucis muscle, originating from the capsules of the metatarsophalangeal joints of the third, fourth, and fifth toes. **c. transver'sum mus'culi adducto'ris pol'licis** [N A], the transverse head of the adductor pollicis muscle originating from the lower two thirds of the anterior surface of the third metacarpal. **c. ul'nae** [N A], the articular surface of the distal extremity of the ulna. Called also *capitulum ulnae* [B N A], and *head of ulna.* **c. ulna're mus'culi flexo'ris car'pi ulna'ris** [N A, B N A], the ulnar head of the flexor carpi ulnaris muscle, originating from the olecranon, ulna, and intermuscular septum. **c. ulna're mus'culi pronato'ris tere'tis** [N A, B N A], the ulnar head of the pronator teres muscle, originating from the coronoid process of the ulna. **c. zygomat'icum mus'culi quadra'ti labii superio'ris** [B N A], musculus zygomaticus minor.

caraate (kah″rah-ah′ta). Pinta.

Carabelli cusp, tubercle (kah-rah-bel′e) [Georg C. *Carabelli,* dentist in Vienna, 1787–1842]. See under *cusp.*

caramel (kar′ah-mel). A concentrated solution of the product obtained by heating sugar or glucose until the sweet taste is destroyed and a uniform dark brown mass results. Used as a coloring agent for pharmaceuticals.

caramiphen (kah-ram′ĭ-fen). Chemical name: 2-diethyl-aminoethyl 1-phenylcyclopentanecarboxylate. Used in parasympathetic blockade, as an antispasmodic agent, and in treatment of parkinsonism.

carapatos (kar″ah-pat′os). *Ornithodoros moubata.*

Carassini's spool (kar-ah-se′nēz). A sectional spool made of aluminum for use in end-to-end intestinal anastomosis.

carat (kar′at). 1. A measure of the fineness of gold, pure gold being 24 carats. 2. A unit of weight of precious stones, being 205.5 milligrams or $3\frac{1}{6}$ grains troy.

carate (kah-rah′ta). Pinta.

caraway (kar′ah-way). The dried ripe fruit of *Carum carvi:* used as a flavoring agent for pharmaceuticals.

carbachol (kar′bah-kol). An odorless, hygroscopic compound, $C_6H_{15}ClN_2O_2$, occurring as white or faintly yellow crystals or as a crystalline powder: used as a parasympathomimetic and applied topically to the conjunctiva to constrict the pupil.

carbamate (kar′bah-māt). Any ester of carbamic acid. **ethyl c.,** urethan.

carbamide (kar-bam′īd). Urea in anhydrous, lyophilized, sterile powder form: injected intravenously in dextrose or invert sugar solution to induce diuresis.

carbaminohemoglobin (kar-bam″ĭ-no-he″mo-glo′bin). A chemical combination of carbon dioxide with hemoglobin, CO_2HHb, being one of the forms in which carbon dioxide exists in the blood.

carbamylcholine chloride (kar″bah-mil-ko′lēn klo′rīd). Carbachol.

carbarsone (kar′bar-sōn). A white crystalline compound, $C_7H_9AsN_2O_4$: used as an antiamebic.

carbasus (kar′bah-sus) [L.; Gr. *karpasos* cotton]. 1. An old name for lint, charpie, or cotton. 2. Canvas or surgical gauze. **c. absor'bens,** absorbent gauze. **c. absor'bens adhesivus,** adhesive absorbent gauze. **c. absor'bens steri'lis,** sterile absorbent gauze. **c. carbola'ta,** carbolized gauze. **c. iodoforma'ta,** iodoform gauze.

carbazide (kar′bah-zīd). A urea derivative, carbodiazide, $CO(N_3)_2$, in which both the amide groups of urea have been replaced by hydrazine residues.

carbazochrome salicylate (kar-baz′o-krōm sal′ĭ-sil″āt). Chemical name: adrenochrome monosemicarbazone sodium salicylate complex. Used as a hemostatic agent for capillary bleeding.

carbazotate (kar-baz′o-tāt). Any salt of picric acid: a picrate.

carbetapentane (kar-ba″tah-pen′tān). Chemical name: 2-(diethylaminoethoxy) ethyl 1-phenylcyclopentyl-1-carboxylate. Used as an antitussive agent.

carbethyl salicylate (kar-beth′il sal′ĭ-sil″āt). Chemical name: salicylic ethyl ester carbonate. Used as an analgesic and antiarthritic agent.

carbhemoglobin (karb″he-mo-glo′bin). Carbohemoglobin.

carbide (kar′bīd). A compound of carbon with an element or radical. **metallic c.,** a compound of carbon with a metal.

carbinol (kar′bĭ-nol). 1. Methyl alcohol. 2. Any aromatic or fatty alcohol formed by substituting one, two, or three hydrocarbon groups for hydrogen in the methyl radical. **acetylmethyl c.,** a keto-isomer of aldol, $CH_3.CHOH.CO.CH_3$, which is formed from glucose by certain bacteria and which is detected in a broth culture of bacteria by the Voges-Proskauer reaction. **dimethyl c.,** isopropyl alcohol.

carbinoxamine (kar″bin-ok′sah-mēn). Chemical name: 2[p-chloro-α-(2-dimethylaminoethoxy)-benzyl]pyridine. Used as an antihistaminic.

carbo (kar′bo) [L.]. Charcoal. **c. activa'tus,** activated charcoal. **c. anima'lis,** a variety prepared from bones and other animal matter: a decolorizing agent. **c. anima'lis purifica'tus,** purified animal charcoal. **c. lig'ni,** wood charcoal: deodorant, adsorbent, and disinfectant.

carbocaine (kar′bo-kān). Trade mark for preparations of mepivacaine hydrochloride.

carbocholine (kar″bo-ko′lēn). Carbachol.

carbocyclic (kar″bo-si′klik). Having or pertaining to a closed chain or ring formation which includes only carbon atoms: applied to chemical compounds.

carbodiimide (kar″bo-di-im′id). A derivative of urea, NH:C:NH.

carbogaseous (kar″bo-gas′e-us). Charged with carbon dioxide gas.

carbogen (kar′bo-jen). A mixture of oxygen with 5 per cent carbon dioxide.

carbohemia (kar″bo-he′me-ah) [*carbon* dioxide + Gr. *haima* blood + *-ia*]. Presence of carbon monoxide in the blood.

carbohemoglobin (kar″bo-he-mo-glo′bin). Hemoglobin compounded with carbon dioxide, constituting 8 to 10 per cent of the total CO_2 component of the blood.

carbohydrase (kar″bo-hi′drās). Any one of a group of enzymes which catalyze the hydrolysis of higher carbohydrates to lower forms, each enzyme being usually specific for one substrate only.

carbohydrate (kar″bo-hi′drāt). An aldehyde or ketone derivative of a polyhydric alcohol, particularly of the pentahydric and hexahydric alcohols. They are so named because the hydrogen and oxygen are usually in the proportion to form water, $(CH_2O)_n$. The most important carbohydrates are the starches, sugars, celluloses, and gums. They are classified into mono-, di-, tri-, poly- and heterosaccharides. **reserve c's,** carbohydrates which can be stored in the plant or animal in the form of high molecular weight, hydrolyzable compounds such as starch or glycogen.

carbohydraturia (kar″bo-hi″drah-tu′re-ah). Excess of carbohydrates in the urine.

carbohydrogenic (kar″bo-hi″dro-jen′ik). Producing carbohydrates.

carbolate (kar′bo-lāt). 1. Phenate. 2. To charge with carbolic acid.

carbolfuchsin (kar″bol-fo͝ok′sin). A histologic staining fluid made up of fuchsin, alcohol, and phenol solution.

carboligase (kar″bol-i′gās). An enzyme found in both plant and animal tissues that catalyzes the linking up of carbon atoms and thus changes pyruvic acid to acetyl-methyl-carbinol.

carbolism (kar′bol-izm). Phenol poisoning.

carbolize (kar′bol-īz). To treat with phenol.

carboluria (kar″bo-lu′re-ah) [*carbolic* + Gr. *ouron* urine + *-ia*]. The presence of phenol in the urine.

carbolxylene (kar″bol-zi′lēn). A mixture of 1 part of carbolic acid and 3 parts of xylene: used for clearing microscopical sections.

carbometer (kar-bom′e-ter). Carbonometer.

carbometry (kar-bom′e-tre). Carbonometry.

carbomycin (kar″bo-mi′sin). A crystalline, monobasic substance isolated from the elaborated products of *Streptomyces halstedii*, and bacteriostatic for gram-positive organisms.

carbon (kar′bon) [L. *carbo*, coal, charcoal]. 1. A nonmetallic tetrad element, found nearly pure in the diamond, and approximately pure in charcoal, graphite, and anthracite; symbol, C; atomic number, 6; atomic weight, 12.011. 2. An electrode made of carbon shell in which medicaments may be enclosed. **C^{13},** a natural isotope of carbon, of atomic weight 13: used as a tracer in chemical reactions in living tissue. **C^{14},** a radioactive isotope of carbon, of atomic weight 14: used in cancer and metabolic research. **c. dioxide,** an odorless, colorless gas, CO_2, resulting from the oxidation of carbon. It is formed in the tissues and excreted by the lungs. CO_2 and the carbonates assist in maintaining the neutrality of the tissues and fluids of the body. It is used, in a 5 to 7 per cent mixture with oxygen, to stimulate respiration, and, in solid form (carbon dioxide snow), in the treatment of certain skin lesions. **c. disulfide,** a poisonous liquid, CS_2, a counterirritant and local anesthetic: valuable as a solvent. **c. monoxide,** a colorless, poisonous gas, CO, formed by burning carbon with a scanty supply of oxygen. It causes asphyxiation by combining irreversibly with the blood hemoglobin. **c. oxysulfide,** a colorless gas, COS, uniting with air to form an explosive mixture. **radioactive c.,** an unstable isotope of carbon which decays with the emission of radiation from the nucleus. **c. tetrachloride,** a clear, colorless, mobile liquid, CCl_4: anthelmintic. **c. trichloride,** a white solid, hexachlorethane, C_2Cl_6: a stimulant and local anesthetic.

carbonate (kar′bon-āt). Any salt of carbonic acid.

carbonemia (kar″bon-e′me-ah). Carbohemia.

carboneol (kar-bo′ne-ol). A black liquid obtained by dissolving coal tar in carbon tetrachloride: used in skin diseases.

carbonize (kar′bon-īz). To char, or convert into charcoal.

carbonometer (kar″bo-nom′e-ter). An apparatus for performing carbonometry.

carbonometry (kar″bo-nom′e-tre) [*carbon* + Gr. *metron* measure]. Measurement of the amount of carbon dioxide exhaled with the breath.

carbonuria (kar″bo-nu′re-ah) [*carbon* + Gr. *ouron* urine + *-ia*]. The presence of carbon dioxide or other carbon compounds in the urine. **dysoxidative c.,** pathologic increase of carbon compounds in the urine due to deficient oxidation.

carbonyl (kar′bo-nil) [*carbon* + Gr. *hylē* matter]. The hypothetical organic radical: C:O. **c. chloride,** phosgene.

carbophilic (kar-bo-fil′ik). Tending to grow best in the presence of carbon dioxide.

carbo-resin (kar′bo-rez″in). Trade mark for a mixture of carbacrylamine resins.

carborundum (kar″bo-run′dum). A compound of carbon and silicon, silicon carbide, SiC, a substance which ranks next to the diamond in hardness.

carbowax (kar′bo-waks). Proprietary name for a series of polyethylene glycols: used in compounding water-soluble ointment vehicles.

Carboxydomonas (kar-bok″se-do-mo′nas). A genus of microorganisms of the family Methanomonadaceae, suborder Pseudomonadineae, order Pseudomonadales, occurring as chemoautotrophic rod-shaped cells capable of securing growth energy by oxidizing CO to CO_2. The type species is *C. oligocarbophi′la.*

carboxyhemoglobin (kar-bok″se-he″mo-glo′bin). A compound formed from hemoglobin on exposure to carbon monoxide, with formation of a covalent bond with oxygen and without change of the charge of the ferrous state.

carboxyhemoglobinemia (kar-bok″se-he″mo-glo″bin-e′me-ah). The presence of carboxyhemoglobin in the blood.

carboxyl (kar-bok′sil). The radical, or group, —COOH, occurring in nearly all organic acids.

carboxylase (kar-bok′sĭ-lās). An enzyme which catalyzes the removal of carbon dioxide from the carboxyl group of alpha keto acids. Decarboxylation of pyruvic acid is the essential step in alcoholic fermentation by which pyruvic acid is converted into acetaldehyde and carbon dioxide. **amino acid c.,** an enzyme in many bacteria which catalyzes the removal of CO_2 from amino acids, thus producing amines.

carboxylesterase (kar-bok″sil-es′ter-ās). An enzyme that catalyzes the hydrolysis of the esters of carboxylic acids.

carboxymyoglobin (kar-bok″se-mi″o-glo′bin). A compound formed from myoglobin on exposure to carbon monoxide, with formation of a covalent bond with oxygen and without change of the charge of the ferrous state.

carboxypeptidase (kar-bok″se-pep′tĭ-dās). An exopeptidase that acts on the peptide bond of terminal amino acids possessing a free carboxyl group.

carbromal (kar-bro′mal). Bromdiethylacetylurea, $(C_2H_5)_2C(Br).CO.NH.CO.NH_2$: used as a central nervous system depressant.

carbuncle (kar′bung-kl) [L. *carbunculus* little coal]. A necrotizing infection of skin and subcutaneous tissue, usually due to *Staphylococcus aureus hemolyticus*, with multiple formed or incipient drainage sinuses and an indurated border around the lesion. **malignant c.**, malignant anthrax in man. **renal c.**, a massive localized parenchymal suppuration consequent to bacterial metastasis, following localized vascular thrombosis or infarction of the kidney.

carbuncular (kar-bung′ku-lar). Resembling or of the nature of a carbuncle.

carbunculosis (kar-bung″ku-lo′sis). A condition marked by the development of carbuncles.

carbylamine (kar″bil-am′in). Isocyanide.

carcass (kar′kas) [Fr. *carcasse*]. A dead body; generally applied to other than a human body. Sometimes used to designate the framework of a living body.

Carcassonne's ligament (kar-kah-sonz′) [Bernard Gauderic *Carcassonne*, French surgeon, born 1728]. See under *ligament*.

carcholin (kar′ko-lin). Trade mark for a preparation of carbachol.

carciag (kar′se-ag). A disease of sheep in the Balkan States caused by *Babesia* (*Piroplasma*) *ovis* and transmitted by the tick *Rhipicephalus bursa*.

carcinectomy (kar″sin-ek′to-me) [*carcinoma* + Gr. *ektomē* excision]. Excision of carcinoma.

carcinelcosis (kar″sin-el-ko′sis) [Gr. *karkinos* cancer + *helkōsis* ulceration]. Malignant or cancerous ulceration.

carcinemia (kar″sin-e′me-ah) [*carcinoma* + Gr. *haima* blood + *-ia*]. Cancerous cachexia.

carcinogen (kar′sĭ-no-jen). Any cancer-producing substance.

carcinogenesis (kar″sĭ-no-jen′e-sis) [Gr. *karkinos* cancer + *genesis* production]. The production of cancer.

carcinogenic (kar″sĭ-no-jen′ik). Producing cancer.

carcinogenicity (kar″sĭ-no-jĕ-nis′ĭ-te). The power, ability or tendency to produce cancer.

carcinoid (kar′sĭ-noid). A yellow circumscribed tumor occurring in the small intestine, appendix, stomach or colon.

carcinology (kar″sĭ-nol′o-je). The study of cancer.

carcinolysin (kar″sĭ-nol′ĭ-sĭn) [*carcinoma* + Gr. *lysis* dissolution]. A ferment derived from a Chinese variety of pine called "haisung." It has been given subcutaneously or intramuscularly for cancer.

carcinolysis (kar″sĭ-nol′ĭ-sis). Destruction of cancer cells, as by perfusion of an antineoplastic agent through the vessels of the body segment in which the growth occurs.

carcinolytic (kar″sĭ-no-lit′ik) [*carcinoma* + Gr. *lytikos* destroying]. Pertaining to, characterized by, or causing carcinolysis.

carcinoma (kar″sĭ-no′mah) pl. *carcinomas* or *carcino′mata* [Gr. *karkinōma* from *karkinos* crab, cancer]. A malignant new growth made up of epithelial cells tending to infiltrate the surrounding tissues and give rise to metastases. **acinous c.**, carcinoma having an acinous structure, and including encephaloid and scirrhus. **acute c.**, soft cancer. **c. adenomato′sum**, a cancer with a disposition to form glandlike acini. **alveolar c.**, carcinoma in which the cells appear in groups, either small or large, enclosed in a moderate amount of connective tissue. **basal cell c.**, **c. basocellula′re**, an epidermal tumor with potentialities for local invasion and destruction. **bronchogenic c.**, carcinoma of the lung, so called because it arises in a bronchus. **chorionic c.**, carcinoma of the chorion. **chronic c.**, scirrhous cancer. **colloid c.**, carcinoma in which the cells have undergone colloid degeneration. Called also *gelatiniform c.* **comedo c.** See *comedocarcinoma*. **corpus c.**, carcinoma of the body of the uterus. **c. cuta′neum**, epithelioma. **cylindrical c., cylindrical cell c.**, carcinoma in which the cells are cylindrical or nearly so. **duct c.**, carcinoma of a mammary duct. **c. du′rum**, scirrhous c. **embryonal c.**, seminoma. **encephaloid c.**, cancer of a soft, brainlike structure, resembling scirrhous carcinoma, but having less connective tissue, larger alveoli, and more cells. **epibulbar c.**, a carcinoma which starts at the edge of the cornea and spreads over the cornea and conjunctiva. **epidermoid c.**, carcinoma in which the cells tend to differentiate in the same way that the cells of the epidermis do, that is, they tend to form prickle cells and undergo cornification. **epithelial c.**, epithelioma. **c. epithelia′le adenoi′des**, carcinoma forming in epithelial surfaces, but made up of adenoid or glandlike forms. **erectile c.**, an encephaloid containing many blood vessels: called also *hematoid c.* **c. ex ul′cere**, carcinoma of the stomach developed from simple ulcer. **c. fibro′sum**, scirrhous carcinoma. **gelatiniform c.**, colloid c. **c. gigantocellula′re**, carcinoma containing many giant cells. **glandular c.**, carcinoma in which the cells are of the glandular or secreting type; adenocarcinoma. **granulosa cell c.**, folliculoma. **hair-matrix c.**, basal cell c. **hematoid c.**, erectile c. **hyaline c.**, colloid c. **c. in situ**, a neoplastic entity wherein the tumor cells still lie within the epithelium of origin, without invasion of the basement membrane; popularly applied to such cells in the uterine cervix. **lenticular c., c. lenticula′re**, scirrhous carcinoma of the skin with the formation of flattened papules and nodules which run together, forming fungoid masses. **lipomatous c.**, carcinoma containing much fat. **c. mastitoi′des**, a rapidly growing variety of breast cancer which, by setting up violent irritation, produces a round cell infiltration resembling mastitis; called also *mastitis carcinosa*. **c. medulla′re**, medullary cancer. **melanotic c., c. melano′des**, encephaloid carcinoma which is blackened with melanin. **c. mol′le**, medullary cancer. **mucinous c.**, a rare malignant tumor of the epithelium in which the cells retain the power to secrete mucin. Sometimes erroneously called colloid or gelatinous c. **c. mucip′arum**, colloid c. **c. mucocellula′re**, Krukenberg's tumor. **c. muco′sum, mucous c.**, colloid c. **c. myxomato′des**, a form of colloid cancer in which the stroma has undergone myxomatous degeneration. **c. ni′grum**, melanotic c. **c. ossif′icans, osteoid c.**, carcinoma in which there is deposit of bone. **periportal c.**, cancer of the liver, extending along and around the portal vessels. **preinvasive c.**, c. in situ. **pultaceous c.**, encephaloid carcinoma whose alveoli have thick walls and a pulpy juice. **c. sarcomato′des**, carcinoma showing transformation toward sarcoma. **schneiderian c.**, a neoplasm of the mucosa of the nose and the paranasal sinuses. **scirrhous c.**, carcinoma with a hard structure composed of connective tissue alveoli filled with masses of cells which have no vessels or interstitial substance; called also *chronic c.* and *hard c.* **c. scro′ti**, cancer of the scrotum. **c. sim′plex**, carcinoma in which the relative proportion between the stroma and the cells is normal. **solanoid c.**, one having the consistency of raw potato. **c. spongio′sum**, medullary cancer. **squamous c., squamous cell c.**, carcinoma developed from squamous epithelium, and having cuboid cells. **c. telangiectat′icum, c. telangiecto′des**, a carcinoma involving the cutaneous capillaries and producing telangiectatic changes. **c. tubero′sum, tuberous c.**, scirrhous carcinoma of the skin with the formation of nodular projections. **c. villo′sum**, malignant papilloma.

carcinomatoid (kar″sĭ-nom′ah-toid). Resembling carcinoma.

carcinomatophobia (kar″sĭ-no″mah-to-fo′be-ah). Carcinophobia.

carcinomatosis (kar″sĭ-no-mah-to′sis). Carcinosis; the condition of widespread dissemination of cancer throughout the body.

carcinomatous (kar″sĭ-nom′ah-tus). Pertaining to, or of the nature of, cancer; malignant.

carcinomectomy (kar″sĭ-no-mek′to-me). Carcinectomy.

carcinomelcosis (kar″sĭ-no-mel-ko′sis) [*carcinoma* + Gr. *helkōsis* ulceration]. A malignant or cancerous ulceration.

carcinophilia (kar″sĭ-no-fil′e-ah) [*carcinoma* + Gr. *philein* to love]. Special affinity for cancerous tissue.

carcinophilic (kar″sĭ-no-fil′ik). Having an affinity for cancerous tissue.

carcinophobia (kar″sĭ-no-fo′be-ah) [*carcinoma* + *phobia*]. 1. Morbid dread of becoming affected with cancer. 2. Delusion of being affected with cancer.

carcinosarcoma (kar″sĭ-no-sar-ko′mah). A mixed tumor combining the elements of carcinoma and sarcoma. **embryonal c.,** a rapidly developing sarcoma of the kidneys, made up of embryonal elements, and occurring chiefly in children before the fifth year. Called also *Wilms' tumor*, *embryonal sarcoma*, *embryoma*, *embryonal adenomyosarcoma* and *embryonal nephroma*.

carcinosectomy (kar″sĭ-no-sek′to-me). Carcinectomy.

carcinosis (kar″sĭ-no′sis). 1. Widespread dissemination of cancer throughout the body; carcinomatosis. 2. A cancer or malignant tumor. **miliary c.,** carcinosis marked by development of numerous nodules resembling miliary tubercles. **c. pleu′rae,** secondary cancer of the pleura in which the membrane is studded with nodules. **pulmonary c.,** a diffuse and fatal non-metastasizing epithelial hyperplasia of the alveolar and bronchiolar cells of the lungs in man and various animals.

carcinostatic (kar″sĭ-no-stat′ik). Tending to check the growth of carcinoma.

carcinous (kar′sĭ-nus). Cancerous.

carcoma (kar-ko′mah) [Spanish, for the wood dust formed under the bark of trees]. Dark reddish-brown, granular matter occurring in the feces in tropical countries.

cardamom (kar′dah-mom) [L. *cardamomum;* Gr. *kardamōmon*]. The seeds of *Elettaria cardamo′mum*, a plant of tropical Asia; aromatic and carminative.

Cardarelli's sign, symptom (kar-dar-el′ēz) [Antonio *Cardarelli*, Italian physician, 1831–1926]. See under *sign*.

Carden's amputation (kar′denz) [Henry Douglas *Carden*, English surgeon, 19th century]. See under *amputation*.

cardia (kar′de-ah) [Gr. *kardia* heart]. 1. Cardia ventriculi. 2. Formerly a vague term for the heart, or for the region of the heart. **c. of stomach, c. ventric′uli** [B N A]. See *ostium cardiacum* [N A].

cardia- (kar′de-ah). See *cardio-*.

cardiac (kar′de-ak) [L. *cardiacus*, from Gr. *kardiakos*]. 1. Pertaining to the heart. 2. A cordial, or restorative medicine. 3. A person with heart disorder.

cardiagra (kar-de-ag′rah) [*cardia-* + Gr. *agra* seizure]. Gout or pain of the heart.

cardial (kar′de-al). Pertaining to the cardia.

cardialgia (kar″de-al′je-ah) [*cardia-* + *-algia*]. 1. An uneasy or painful sensation in the stomach; heart burn. 2. Cardiodynia.

cardialgic (kar″de-al′jik). Pertaining to or characterized by cardialgia:

cardianastrophe (kar″de-ah-nas′tro-fe) [*cardia-* + Gr. *anastrophē* a turning upside down]. Congenital dislocation of the heart to the right side.

cardianesthesia (kar″de-an″es-the′ze-ah) [*cardia-* + *anesthesia*]. Absence of sensation in the heart.

cardianeuria (kar″de-ah-nu′re-ah) [*cardia-* + Gr. *aneuros* without nerves + *-ia*]. Deficiency of tone in the heart.

cardiant (kar′de-ant). A drug or agent stimulating the heart.

cardiasthenia (kar″de-as-the′ne-ah) [*cardia-* + Gr. *astheneia* weakness]. Neurasthenic weakness of the heart.

cardiasthma (kar-de-as′mah). Cardiac asthma.

cardiataxia (kar″de-ah-tak′se-ah) [*cardia-* + *ataxia*]. Incoordination in the movements of the heart.

cardicentesis (kar″dĭ-sen-te′sis). Cardiocentesis.

cardiectasis (kar″de-ek′tah-sis) [*cardia-* + Gr. *ektasis* dilatation]. Dilatation of the heart.

cardiectomized (kar″de-ek′to-mīzd). Having the heart removed.

cardiectomy (kar″de-ek′to-me) [*cardia-* + Gr. *ektomē* excision]. Excision of the cardiac portion of the stomach.

cardinal (kar′dĭ-nal) [L., *cardinalis*, from *cardo* a hinge]. Of primary or preeminent importance.

cardio- (kar′de-o) [Gr. *kardia* heart]. A combining form denoting relationship to the heart.

cardio-accelerator (kar″de-o-ak-sel′er-a-tor). 1. Quickening the heart action. 2. An agent that accelerates the heart action.

cardio-active (kar″de-o-ak′tiv). Having an effect upon the heart.

cardio-angiography (kar″de-o-an″je-og′rah-fe). Angiocardiography.

cardio-angiology (kar″de-o-an″je-ol′o-je) [*cardio-* + Gr. *angeion* vessel + *-logy*]. The medical specialty which deals with the heart and blood vessels.

cardio-aortic (kar″de-o-a-or′tik). Pertaining to the heart and the aorta.

cardio-arterial (kar″de-o-ar-te′re-al). Pertaining to the heart and the arteries.

cardiocairograph (kar″de-o-ki′ro-graf) [*cardio-* + Gr. *kairos* time + *graphein* to write]. A technique by means of which roentgenograms of the heart can be made at any chosen phase of its cycle.

cardiocele (kar′de-o-sēl) [*cardio-* + Gr. *kēlē* tumor]. Protrusion of the heart through a fissure of the diaphragm or through a wound.

cardiocentesis (kar″de-o-sen-te′sis) [*cardio-* + Gr. *kentēsis* puncture]. Surgical puncture or incision of the heart.

cardiocinetic (kar″de-o-sĭ-net′ik). Cardiokinetic.

cardiocirrhosis (kar″de-o-sir-ro′sis) [*cardio-* + *cirrhosis*]. Cirrhosis of the liver associated with heart disease. See *Hutinel's disease*, under *disease*.

cardioclasis (kar″de-ok′lah-sis) [*cardio-* + Gr. *klasis* break]. Rupture of the heart.

cardiodiaphragmatic (kar″de-o-di″ah-frag-mat′ik). Pertaining to the heart and diaphragm.

cardiodilator (kar″de-o-di′la-tor). An instrument for dilating the cardia in cardiospasm or stricture.

cardiodiosis (kar″de-o-di-o′sis). The operation of dilating the cardiac end of the stomach.

cardiodynamics (kar″de-o-di-nam′iks) [*cardio-* + *dynamics*]. The science of the motions and forces involved in the heart's action.

cardiodynia (kar″de-o-din′e-ah) [*cardio-* + Gr. *odynē* pain]. Pain in the heart.

cardiogenesis (kar″de-o-jen′e-sis) [*cardio-* + Gr. *gennan* to produce]. The development of the heart in the embryo.

cardiogenic (kar″de-o-jen′ik) [*cardio-* + Gr. *gennan* to produce]. 1. Originating in the heart; caused by a condition affecting the heart. 2. Pertaining to cardiogenesis.

cardiografin (kar″de-o-gra′fin). Trade mark for a solution of methylglucamine diatrizoate.

cardiogram (kar′de-o-gram) [*cardio-* + Gr. *gramma* a writing]. A tracing which is made by means of the cardiograph. **esophageal c.,** a tracing of the contractions of the left auricle of the heart made by registering the pulsations of a column of air in a stomach tube. **negative c.,** a cardiogram in which the curve falls below the abscissa instead of rising above it. **vector c.** See *vectorcardiogram.*

cardiograph (kar′de-o-graf) [*cardio-* + Gr. *graphein* to write]. An instrument placed over the heart to indicate the force and form of the heart's movements.

cardiographic (kar″de-o-graf′ik). Pertaining to cardiography.

cardiography (kar″de-og′rah-fe). The recording of the heart's movements.

cardio-green (kar′de-o-grēn). Trade mark for a preparation of indocyanine green.

cardiohepatic (kar″de-o-hĕ-pat′ik). Pertaining to the heart and the liver.

cardiohepatomegaly (kar″de-o-hep″ah-to-meg′ah-le). Enlargement of the heart and liver.

cardioid (kar′de-oid). Heartlike; resembling a heart.

cardio-inhibitory (kar″de-o-in-hib′ĭ-to-re). Restraining or inhibiting the movements of the heart.

cardiokinetic (kar″de-o-ki-net′ik). 1. Stimulating the action of the heart. 2. An agent that stimulates action of the heart.

cardiolipin (kar″de-o-lip′in) [*cardio-* + Gr. *lipos* fat]. A substance extracted from fresh beef hearts which, when combined with lecithin and cholesterol, forms an antigen for use in flocculation and precipitation tests for syphilis.

cardiolith (kar′de-o-lith) [*cardio-* + Gr. *lithos* stone]. A concretion or calculus within the heart.

cardiologist (kar-de-ol′o-jist). An individual skilled in the diagnosis and treatment of heart disease.

cardiology (kar-de-ol′o-je) [*cardio-* + *-logy*]. The study of the heart and its functions.

cardiolysin (kar″de-ol′ĭ-sin). A lysin which acts on heart muscle.

cardiolysis (kar″de-ol′ĭ-sis) [*cardio-* + Gr. *lysis* loosening]. 1. Destruction of the heart. 2. An operation of freeing the heart and its adherent pericardium from its adhesion to the sternal periosteum in adhesive mediastinopericarditis. It is done by resecting the ribs and the sternum over the pericardium. Called also *thoracolysis praecordiaca.*

cardiomalacia (kar″de-o-mah-la′she-ah) [*cardio-* + Gr. *malakia* softness]. Morbid softening of the muscular substance of the heart.

cardiomegalia (kar″de-o-mĕ-ga′le-ah). Cardiomegaly. **c. glycogen′ica circumscrip′ta,** glycogenic cardiomegaly.

cardiomegaly (kar″de-o-meg′ah-le) [*cardio-* + Gr. *megas* large]. Cardiac hypertrophy. **glycogenic c.,** a morbid condition characterized by enlargement of the heart, with localized deposits of glycogen in the heart muscle.

cardiomelanosis (kar″de-o-mel″ah-no′sis). Melanosis of the heart.

cardiometer (kar″de-om′e-ter) [*cardio-* + Gr. *metron* measure]. An instrument used in estimating the power of the heart's action.

cardiometry (kar″de-om′e-tre). The estimation of the force of the heart's action.

cardiomotility (kar″de-o-mo-til′ĭ-te). The movements of the heart; the motility of the heart.

cardiomyoliposis (kar″de-o-mi″o-li-po′sis) [*cardio-* + Gr. *mys* muscle + *lipos* fat]. Fatty degeneration of the heart muscle.

cardiomyopathy (kar″de-o-mi-op′ah-the) [*cardio-* + Gr. *mys* muscle + *pathos* disease]. A subacute or chronic disorder of heart muscle of unknown or obscure etiology, often with associated endocardial, and sometimes with pericardial, involvement, but not atherosclerotic in origin.

cardiomyopexy (kar″de-o-mi′o-pek″se) [*cardio-* + Gr. *mys* muscle + *pēxis* fixation]. Surgical removal of the epicardium and application of a partially resected portion of the pectoralis muscle to the denuded myocardium and pericardium, as a means of supplying collateral circulation to the heart.

cardiomyotomy (kar″de-o-mi-ot′o-me) [*cardio-* + Gr. *mys* muscle + *tomē* incision]. Incision of the esophagogastric junction, the incision extending equal distances in the muscular coat of the esophagus and that of the stomach.

cardionecrosis (kar″de-o-nĕ-kro′sis). Necrosis or gangrene of the heart.

cardionector (kar″de-o-nek′ter) [*cardio-* + L. *nector* joiner]. The structures which regulate the heart beat, comprising the sino-auricular node (atrionector) and the bundle of His (ventriculonector).

cardionephric (kar″de-o-nef′rik). Pertaining to the heart and the kidney.

cardioneural (kar″de-o-nu′ral). Pertaining to the heart and nervous system.

cardioneurosis (kar″de-o-nu-ro′sis) [*cardio-* + *neurosis*]. A functional nervous disorder marked by attacks of deranged cardiac action, such as palpitation and irregularity, a feeling of suffocation, hot flushes, and a sensation of impending trouble; called also *pseudo-angina pectoris* and *cardiac neurasthenia.*

cardio-omentopexy (kar″de-o-o-men″to-pek″-se). The operation of suturing a portion of the omentum to the heart, the omentum having been drawn through an incision in the diaphragm.

cardiopalmus (kar″de-o-pal′mus) [*cardio-* + Gr. *palmos* palpitation]. Palpitation of the heart.

cardiopaludism (kar″de-o-pal′u-dizm). Heart disease due to malaria, marked by gallop rhythm in the tricuspid area, intermittent heart action, dilatation of the right heart, and reduplication of the diastolic sound.

cardiopath (kar′de-o-path). A person with heart disease.

cardiopathia (kar″de-o-path′e-ah). Cardiopathy.

cardiopathic (kar″de-o-path′ik). Pertaining to or marked by disease of the heart.

cardiopathy (kar″de-op′ah-the) [*cardio-* + Gr. *pathos* disease]. Any disorder or disease of the heart. In addition to heart disease of inflammatory origin there are *arteriosclerotic cardiopathy,* due to arterial sclerosis; *fatty cardiopathy,* due to growth of fatty tissue; *hypertensive cardiopathy,* due to high blood pressure; *nephropathic cardiopathy,* due to kidney disease; *thyreotoxic cardiopathy,* due to thyroid intoxication; *toxic cardiopathy,* due to the effect of some toxin; *valvular cardiopathy,* due to faulty valve action. **gastric c.** See *gastrocardiac syndrome,* under *syndrome.* **infarctoid c.,** a heart condition with symptoms resembling those of myocardial infarction.

cardiopericardiopexy (kar″de-o-per″ĭ-kar′de-o-pek-se) [*cardio-* + *pericardium* + Gr. *pēxis* fixation]. The operative establishment of adhesive pericarditis: for the relief of coronary disease.

cardiopericarditis (kar″de-o-per″ĭ-kar-di′tis) [*cardio-* + *pericarditis*]. Inflammation of both the heart and the pericardium.

cardiophobia (kar″de-o-fo′be-ah) [*cardio-* + *phobia*]. Morbid dread of heart disease.

cardiophone (kar′de-o-fōn) [*cardio-* + Gr. *phōnē* voice]. An instrument for recording the heart sounds in connection with the electrocardiograph.

cardiophrenia (kar″de-o-fre′ne-ah). Phrenocardia.

cardioplasty (kar′de-o-plas″te) [*cardio-* + Gr. *plassein* to form]. Esophagogastroplasty.

cardioplegia (kar″de-o-ple′je-ah) [*cardio-* + Gr. *plēgē* stroke + *-ia*]. Interruption of contraction of the myocardium, as may be induced by the use of chemical compounds or of cold (cryocardioplegia) in the performance of surgery upon the heart.

cardiopneumatic (kar″de-o-nu-mat′ik) [*cardio-* + Gr. *pneuma* breath]. Of or pertaining to the heart and respiration.

cardiopneumograph (kar″de-o-nu′mo-graf) [*cardio-* + Gr. *pneuma* breath + *graphein* to record]. A machine which registers the cardiopneumatic movements.

cardiopneumonopexy (kar″de-o-nu-mon′o-pek″se). An operation designed to provide collateral blood supply to the heart muscle by various methods of connecting the heart with the left lung, including production of vascular adhesions through the use of mechanical abrasion or chemical irritants.

cardioptosia (kar″de-o-to′se-ah). Cardioptosis.

cardioptosis (kar″de-o-to′sis) [*cardio-* + Gr. *ptōsis* falling]. Downward displacement of the heart. Called also *Rummo's disease.*

cardiopulmonary (kar″de-o-pul′mo-ner-e). Pertaining to the heart and lungs.

cardiopuncture (kar″de-o-punk′tūr). Cardiocentesis.

cardiopyloric (kar″de-o-pĭ-lor′ik). Pertaining to the cardia and the pylorus.

cardiorenal (kar″de-o-re′nal). Pertaining to the heart and the kidney.

cardiorrhaphy (kar″de-or′ah-fe) [*cardio-* + Gr. *rhaphē* suture]. The operation of suturing the heart muscle.

cardiorrhexis (kar″de-o-rek′sis) [*cardio-* + Gr. *rhēxis* rupture]. Rupture of the heart.

cardioschisis (kar″de-os′kĭ-sis). The breaking up of adhesions between the heart and the chest wall in adhesive pericarditis.

cardiosclerosis (kar″de-o-skle-ro′sis) [*cardio-* + Gr. *sklēros* hard]. Fibroid induration of the heart.

cardioscope (kar′de-o-skōp) [*cardio-* + Gr. *skopein* to examine]. An instrument for inspecting the interior of the heart and for manipulation within the heart.

cardiospasm (kar′de-o-spazm). Spasm of the cardiac sphincter of the stomach. Cardiospasm should not be confused with achalasia of the esophagus. **tropical c.,** entalação.

cardiosphygmogram (kar″de-o-sfig′mo-gram). A tracing made by the cardiosphygmograph.

cardiosphygmograph (kar″de-o-sfig′mo-graf). A combination of the cardiograph and sphygmograph for recording the movements of the heart and radial pulse.

cardiosplenopexy (kar″de-o-splen′o-pek″se). Suture of splenic parenchyma to the denuded surface of the heart, as a method of revascularization of the myocardium.

cardiosurgery (kar″de-o-sur′jer-e). Surgery of the heart.

cardiosymphysis (kar″de-o-sim′fĭ-sis) [*cardio-* + Gr. *symphysis* growing together]. A condition in which the heart has become fixed to the chest by combined adhesion of the visceral and parietal pericardia to each other and by adhesion of the parietal pericardium to the mediastinal structures.

cardiotachometer (kar″de-o-tah-kom′e-ter) [*cardio-* + Gr. *tachos* speed + *metron* measure]. An instrument for counting the total number of heart beats over long periods of time.

cardiotherapy (kar″de-o-ther′ah-pe) [*cardio-* + Gr. *therapeia* treatment]. The treatment of heart diseases.

cardiothyrotoxicosis (kar″de-o-thi″ro-tok″se-ko′sis). Toxic hyperthyroidism with cardiac involvement.

cardiotomy (kar″de-ot′o-me) [*cardio-* + Gr. *tomē* cut]. 1. Surgical incision of the heart for repair of cardiac defects. 2. The operation of cutting the cardia for stricture of the esophagus.

cardiotonic (kar″de-o-ton′ik). Having a tonic effect on the heart.

cardiotopometry (kar″de-o-to-pom′e-tre) [*cardio-* + Gr. *topos* place + *metron* measure]. Measurement of the area of cardiac dulness.

cardiotoxic (kar″de-o-tok′sik). Having a poisonous or deleterious effect upon the heart.

cardiotrophotherapy (kar″de-o-trof″o-ther′ah-pe) [*cardio-* + Gr. *trophē* nutrition + *therapeia* treatment]. Metabolic treatment of heart disorders.

cardiovalvular (kar″de-o-val′vu-lar). Pertaining to the valves of the heart.

cardiovalvulitis (kar″de-o-val″vu-li′tis). Inflammation of the valves of the heart.

cardiovalvulotome (kar″de-o-val′vu-lo-tōm″) [*cardio-* + L. *valvula* valve + Gr. *tomē* cut]. An instrument for performing cardiovalvulotomy.

cardiovalvulotomy (kar″de-o-val″vu-lot′o-me). The operation of incising the mitral valve, or of excising a portion of it, done for the relief of mitral stenosis.

cardiovascular (kar″de-o-vas′ku-lar). Pertaining to the heart and blood vessels.

cardiovascular-renal (kar″de-o-vas″ku-lar-re′nal). Pertaining to the heart, blood vessels, and kidney.

cardiovasology (kar″de-o-vas-ol′o-je). Cardioangiology.

carditis (kar-di′tis) [*cardio-* + *-itis*]. Inflammation of the heart. **Sterges' c.,** a combination of endocarditis and pericarditis.

cardrase (kar′drās). Trade mark for a preparation of ethoxzolamide.

careotrypanosis (ka″re-o-trip-ah-no′sis). Chagas' disease.

Cargile membrane (kar′gil) [Charles H. *Cargile*, American surgeon, 1853–1930]. See under *membrane.*

caribi (kah-re′be). Epidemic gangrenous rectitis.

caricous (kar′ĭ-kus) [L. *carica* fig]. Shaped like or resembling a fig.

caries (ka′re-ēz) [L. "rottenness"]. The molecular decay or death of a bone, in which it becomes softened, discolored, and porous. It produces a chronic inflammation of the periosteum and surrounding tissues, and forms a cold abscess filled with a cheesy, fetid, puslike liquid, which generally burrows through the soft parts until it opens externally by a sinus or fistula. **backward c.,** dental caries which progresses backward from the dentino-enamel junction into the enamel. **central c.,** a chronic abscess in the interior of a bone. **dental c.,** a disease of the calcified tissues of the teeth resulting from the action of microorganisms on carbohydrates, characterized by a decalcification of the inorganic portions of the tooth and accompanied or followed by disintegration of the organic portion. It is of four degrees of severity: *c. of first degree,* in which the enamel alone has become decalcified; *c. of second degree,* in which the enamel and dentin are affected; *c. of third degree,* in which the pulp is exposed; *c. of fourth degree,* in which the pulp has undergone putrefactive decomposition. **dry c.,** a form of tuberculous caries of the joints and ends of bones. **c. fungo′sa,** a form of tuberculosis of a bone. **lateral c.,** dental caries which extends laterally at the dentino-enamel junction. **necrotic c.,** a disease in which pieces of bone lie in a suppurating cavity. **primary c.,** dental caries which attacks either the pits and fissures, or the smooth surfaces of a tooth. **secondary c.,** dental caries recurring after the placement of a dental restoration. **c. sic′ca,** dry c. **spinal c.,** tuberculotic osteitis of the vertebrae and of the intervertebral cartilages.

carina (kah-ri′nah), pl. *cari′nae* [L. "keel"]. A ridgelike structure. **c. for′nicis,** a mesial ridge on the under surface of the fornix. **c. of trachea, c. tra′cheae** [N A, B N A], a projection of the lowest tracheal cartilage, forming a prominent semilunar ridge running anteroposteriorly between the orifices of the two bronchi. **urethral c. of vagina, c. urethra′lis vagi′nae** [N A, B N A], the column of rugae in the lower part of the anterior wall of the vagina, immediately beneath the urethra.

carinae (kah-ri′ne) [L.]. Plural of *carina*.

carinate (kar′ĭ-nāt) [L. *carina* a keel]. Keel shaped; having a keel-like process.

carination (kar″ĭ-na′shun). A ridged condition of a part.

cariogenic (kār″e-o-jen′ik) [*caries* + Gr. *gennan* to produce]. Conducive to caries.

cariogenicity (kār″e-o-jĕ-nis′ĭ-te). The quality of being conducive to the production of caries.

cariosity (kar″e-os′ĭ-te). The quality of being carious.

carious (ka′re-us) [L. *cariosus*]. Affected with or of the nature of caries.

carisoprodol (kar″i-so′pro-dol). Chemical name: N-isopropyl-2-methyl-2-propyl-1,3-propanediol dicarbamate. Used as an analgesic, and skeletal muscle relaxant.

Carleton's spots (karl′tonz) [Bukk G. *Carleton*, American physician, 1856–1914]. See under *spot*.

carmalum (kar-mal′um). A stain composed of carmine, alum, and water.

Carmichael crown (kar′mi-kel) [J. P. *Carmichael*, American dentist, 1856–1946]. See under *crown*.

carminative (kar-min′ah-tiv) [L. *carminare* to card, to cleanse, from *carmen*, a card for wool]. 1. Relieving flatulence. 2. A medicine which relieves flatulence and assuages pain.

carmine (kar′min). A red coloring matter derived from cochineal by the addition of alum: used as a histologic stain. **alizarin c.,** alizarin red. **indigo c.,** indigotindisulfonate. **lithium c.,** a vital stain for macrophages. **Schneider's c.,** a saturated solution of carmine in concentrated acetic acid.

carminophil (kar-min′o-fil) [*carmine* + Gr. *philein* to love]. 1. Easily stainable with carmine. 2. A cell or other element that readily takes a stain from carmine.

carminum (kar-mi′num). Carmine.

carnaubon (kar″nah-oo′bon). A phospholipin occurring in the kidney.

carneous (kar′ne-us) [L. *carneus*, from *caro* flesh]. Fleshy.

carniferrin (kar″nĭ-fer′in) [L. *caro*, *carnis* flesh + *ferrum* iron]. A complex body isolated from milk that yields carnic, lactic, succinic, and oxylic acids on decomposition.

carnification (kar″nĭ-fi-ka′shun) [L. *caro* flesh + *facere* to make]. The change of any other structure into flesh or a substance resembling it.

carnine (kar′nin) [L. *caro* flesh]. A leukomaine, inosine, $C_7H_8N_4O + H_2O$, derivable from meat extract and from yeast. It is said to be poisonous.

carnitine (kar′nĭ-tin). A betaine derivative found in the skeletal muscle of horses, hogs, and calves. It causes vomiting, purging, salivation, and mydriasis when injected into animals. Called also *novain*.

Carnivora (kar-niv′o-rah) [L. *caro* flesh + *vorare* to devour]. An order of mammals which are carnivorous in habit, with teeth adapted for flesh eating, a simple stomach, and a short intestine.

carnivore (kar′nĭ-vōr). An animal which eats flesh; especially an animal of the order Carnivora.

carnivorous (kar-niv′o-rus). Eating or subsisting on flesh.

Carnochan's operation (kar′nok-anz) [John M. *Carnochan*, American surgeon, 1817–1887]. See under *operation*.

carnophobia (kar″no-fo′be-ah) [L. *caro* flesh + *phobia*]. Abnormal aversion to meat diet.

carnosine (kar′no-sin). A dipeptide made up of histidine and alanine, found in skeletal muscle of vertebrates.

carnosity (kar-nos′ĭ-te) [L. *carnositas* fleshiness]. Any abnormal fleshy excrescence.

Carnot's test (kar′nōz) [Paul *Carnot*, French physician, 1869–1957]. See under *tests*.

carnutine (kar-nu′tin). A ptomaine found in muscle tissue.

caro (ka′ro), pl. *car′nes* [L.]. Flesh or muscular tissue. **c. quadra′ta ma′nus,** musculus palmaris brevis. **c. quadra′ta syl′vii,** musculus quadratus plantae.

carota (kah-ro′tah), pl. *caro′tae* [L.]. Carrot.

carotenase (kar-ot′ĕ-nās). An enzyme capable of converting carotene into vitamin A.

carotene (kar′o-tēn). A yellow or red pigment that is found in carrots, sweet potatoes, leafy vegetables, milk fat, body fat, egg yolk, etc. It is a chromolipoid hydrocarbon and exists in several forms; alpha, beta, and gamma carotene are provitamins and may be converted into vitamin A in the body. The formula of β-carotene is $[(CH_3)_3.C_6H_6.CH:CH:C(CH_3):CH.CH:CH.C(CH_3):CH.CH]_2$.

carotenemia (kar″o-te-ne′me-ah) [*carotene* + Gr. *haima* blood + *-ia*]. Presence of carotene in the blood; it sometimes occurs in sufficient quantities to produce pigmentation of the skin resembling jaundice.

carotenodermia (kah-rot″ĕ-no-der′me-ah). Yellowness of the skin due to carotene in the blood. Cf. *carotenemia*.

carotenoid (kah-rot′ĕ-noid). 1. Marked by a yellow color resembling that of carotene. 2. A lipochrome.

carotenosis (kar″o-te-no′sis). Aurantiasis.

carotic (kah-rot′ik) [Gr. *karos* deep sleep]. Pertaining to or of the nature of carus, or stupor.

caroticotympanic (kah-rot″ĭ-ko-tim-pan′ik). Pertaining to the carotid canal and the tympanum.

carotid (kah-rot′id) [Gr. *karōtis* from *karos* deep sleep]. Relating to the principal artery of the neck (arteria carotis communis). See also under *body*, *sinus*, etc.

carotidynia (kah-rot″ĭ-din′e-ah). Carotodynia.

carotin (kar′o-tin). Carotene.

carotinase (kar′o-tĭ-nās). Carotenase.

carotinemia (kar″o-tin-e′me-ah). Carotenemia.

carotinosis (kar″o-tĭ-no′sis). Aurantiasis.

carotodynia (kah-rot″o-din′e-ah) [*carotid* + Gr. *odynē* pain]. Tenderness along the course of the common carotid artery.

carpal (kar′pal) [L. *carpalis*]. Of or pertaining to the carpus, or wrist.

carpale (kar-pa′le). A carpal bone.

carpectomy (kar-pek′to-me) [*carpus* + Gr. *ektomē* excision]. Excision of one or more of the carpal bones.

carpel (kar′pel). A one-celled pistil, or one of the members composing a compound pistil or seed vessel.

carphologia (kar″fo-lo′je-ah). Carphology.

carphology (kar-fol′o-je) [Gr. *karphologein* to pick bits of wool off a person's coat]. The involuntary picking at the bedclothes seen in grave fevers and in conditions of great exhaustion.

carpitis (kar-pi′tis). Inflammation of the synovial membranes of the bones of the carpal joint of domestic animals, producing swelling, pain, and lameness.

carpocarpal (kar″po-kar′pal). Pertaining to two parts of the carpus.

Carpoglyphus (kar″po-gli′fus). A genus of mites. **C. passula′rum,** a tyroglyphid mite which infests dried fruit, causing dermatitis in those who handle the infested fruit.

carpogonium (kar″po-go′ne-um). Ascogonium.

carpometacarpal (kar″po-met″ah-kar′pal). Pertaining to the carpus and metacarpus.

carpopedal (kar″po-pe′dal) [*carpus* + L. *pes*, *pedalis* foot]. Pertaining to the carpus and the foot.

carpophalangeal (kar″po-fah-lan′je-al). Pertaining to the carpus and the phalanges.

carpoptosis (kar″pop-to′sis) [*carpus* + *ptosis*]. Wristdrop.

carppox (karp′poks). An infectious disease of carp and other fish, producing whitish spots on the skin.

Carpue's operation (kar′pūz) [Joseph C. *Carpue*, English surgeon, 1764–1846]. See under *operation*.

carpus (kar′pus) [L.; Gr. *karpos*]. [N A, B N A], The joint between the arm and hand, the wrist, made up of eight bones. See *ossa carpi*, and names of specific bones. The term is also applied to the corresponding joint in quadrupeds. **c. cur′vus,** Madelung's deformity.

Carr-Price test [Francis Howard *Carr*, British chemist, born 1874; E. A. *Price*]. See under *tests*.

carrageen, carragheen (kar′ah-gēn). Irish moss. See *Chondrus*.

carreau (kar-ro′) [Fr.]. Enlargement and hardening of the abdomen caused by disease of the peritoneum and abdominal walls.

carrefour (kahr″uh-fo͞or′) [Fr.]. Crossway; decussation. **c. sensitif** (kahr″uh-fo͞or′ saw″se-tēf′), the last third of the posterior limbs of the internal capsule in the lowest part of the optostriate region.

Carrel's method, mixture, treatment (kar-elz′) [Alexis *Carrel*, French surgeon, 1873–1944; winner of the Nobel prize for physiology and medicine in 1912]. See under the nouns.

Carrel-Dakin fluid [Alexis *Carrel;* Henry Drysdale *Dakin*, American chemist, 1880–1952]. See *Dakin f.*, under *fluid*.

carrier (kar′e-er). 1. An individual who harbors in his body the specific organisms of a disease without manifest symptoms and thus acts as a carrier or distributor of the infection. The condition of such an individual is known as *carrier state*. 2. A substance in a cell which can accept hydrogen and so be reduced and can then be re-oxidized. 3. An instrument or apparatus for carrying or transporting something. **active c.,** a carrier who has not yet recovered completely from the disease. **amalgam c.,** a dental instrument for transporting portions of mixed amalgam, used as a restorative material, to a prepared tooth cavity. **bacilli c.,** typhoid carrier. **chronic c.,** a person in whom the organism of a disease persists for a considerable time, say a year, after clinical recovery. **closed c.,** a carrier who does not excrete and distribute the causative organism. **contact c.,** a person who has been exposed to an infection and, although healthy, may act as a carrier of the infection. **convalescent c.,** a person convalescent from a disease who may act as a carrier of infection. **foil c.,** a dental instrument for transporting foil, used as a restorative material, from the annealor to a prepared tooth cavity. **gamete c., gametocyte c.,** in malaria, a person who has gametocytes in his blood stream and so can infect Anopheles mosquitoes that feed on him. **healthy c.,** a person who has no clinical symptoms but harbors within his body microorganisms which are capable of causing disease. **hemophiliac c.,** the female transmitter of classical sex-linked, recessive hemophilia who generally, but not always, demonstrates no overt manifestations of a hemorrhagic diathesis but in whom a coagulation factor deficiency may be detected by quantitative assay. **incubatory c.,** an individual who is in the incubation period of an infectious disease and will soon manifest the symptoms. **intermittent c.,** a carrier who discharges the pathogenic organisms from time to time. **intestinal c.,** a carrier who harbors the infective bacteria in the feces. **passive c.,** a carrier who harbors a pathogenic organism without having had the disease. **temporary c., transitory c.,** a carrier who harbors a pathogenic organism for brief periods of time. **typhoid c.,** a carrier or distributor of live typhoid germs. The organisms frequently grow in the gallbladder and are eliminated in the feces. **urinary c.,** a carrier who discharges infective organisms in his urine.

Carrión's disease (kar-e-onz′) [Daniel A. *Carrión*, (1850–1886), a student in Peru who inoculated himself and died of the disease]. See under *disease*.

carrot (kar′ut) [L. *carota*]. The umbelliferous plant, *Daucus carota:* its seed is diuretic and stimulant.

carrotene (kar′o-tēn). Carotene.

Carswell's grapes (karz′welz) [Sir Robert *Carswell*, English physician, 1793–1857]. See under *grapes*.

Carter's fever (kar′terz) [Henry Vandyke *Carter*, Anglo-Indian physician, 1831–1907]. See under *fever*.

Carter's operation, splint (kar′terz) [William Wesley *Carter*, New York rhinologist, born 1869]. See under *operation* (2d def.) and *splint*.

cartilage (kar′tĭ-lij) [L. *cartilago*]. A specialized, fibrous connective tissue, forming most of the temporary skeleton of the embryo, providing a model in which most of the bones develop, and constituting an important part of the growth mechanism of the organism. It exists in several types, the most important of which are hyaline cartilage, elastic cartilage, and fibrocartilage. Also used as a general term to designate a mass of such tissue in a particular site in the body. See *cartilago*. **accessory c's of nose,** cartilagines alares minores. **c. of acoustic meatus,** cartilago meatus acustici. **alar c., greater,** cartilago alaris major. **alar c's, lesser,** cartilagines alares minores. **annular c.,** cartilago cricoidea. **aortic c.,** the second costal cartilage on the right side. **arthrodial c.,** articular c. **articular c.,** a thin layer of cartilage, usually hyaline, on the articular surface of bones in synovial joints. Called also *cartilago articularis*. **arytenoid c.,** cartilago arytenoidea. **c. of auditory tube,** cartilago tubae auditivae. **auricular c.,** cartilago auriculae. **branchial c.,** one of the rods of cartilage in the branchial arches of the embryo. **calcified c.,** cartilage in which granules of calcium phosphate and calcium carbonate have been deposited in the interstitial substance. **cariniform c.,** the cartilaginous prolongation at the anterior end of the sternum of a horse. **cellular c.,** a variety composed almost entirely of cells, with little interstitial substance. **central c.,** an opacity in the center of the crystalline lens. **ciliary c's.** See *tarsus inferior palpebrae* and *tarsus superior palpebrae*. **circumferential c.,** labrum glenoidale. **conchal c.,** cartilago auriculae. **connecting c.,** cartilage connecting the surfaces of an immovable joint. **corniculate c.,** cartilago corniculata. **costal c.,** cartilago costalis. **costal c., interarticular,** ligamentum sternocostale intraarticulare. **cricoid c.,** cartilago cricoidea. **cuneiform c.,** cartilago cuneiformis. **dentinal c.,** the substance remaining after the lime salts of dentin have been dissolved in an acid. **diarthrodial c.,** articular c. **elastic c.,** a substance that is more opaque, flexible, and elastic than hyaline cartilage, and is further distinguished by its yellow color. The interstitial substance is penetrated in all directions by frequently branching fibers which give all of the reactions for elastin. **ensiform c.,** processus xiphoideus. **epactal c's,** cartilagines sesamoideae nasi. **epiglottic c.,** cartilago epiglottica. **epiphyseal c.,** cartilago epiphysialis. **eustachian c.,** cartilago tubae auditivae. **falciform c's.** See *meniscus lateralis articulationis genus* and *meniscus medialis articulationis genus*. **floating c.,** a detached piece of articular cartilage, particularly a portion of the medial meniscus loose in the knee joint cavity. **gingival c.,** the tissue covering the loculus which contains an unerupted tooth. **guttural c.,** cartilago arytenoidea. **hyaline c.,** a flexible, somewhat elastic, semitransparent substance with an opal-

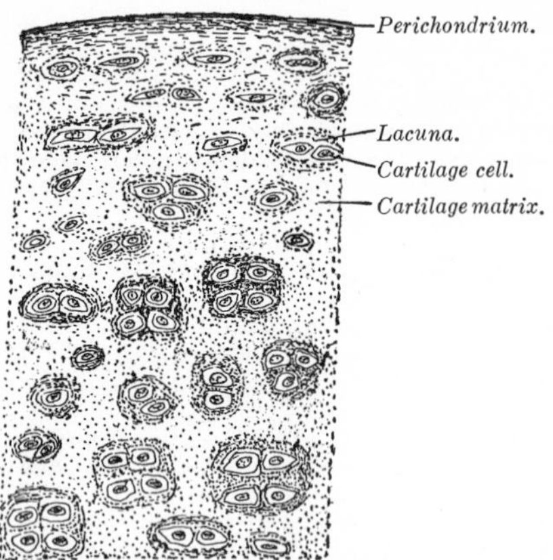

Section of hyaline cartilage from the trachea (Hill).

escent bluish tint, composed of a basophilic, fibril-containing interstitial substance with cavities in which the chondrocytes occur. **inferior c. of nose,** cartilago alaris major. **innominate c.,** cartilago cricoidea. **interarticular c.,** ligamentum longitudinale posterius. **interarticular c. of little head of rib,** ligamentum capitis costae intraarticulare. **interosseous c.,** connecting c. **intervertebral c's,** disci intervertebrales. **intrathyroid c.,** a cartilage connecting the alae of the thyroid cartilage in early life. **investing c.,** articular c. **Jacobson's c.,** cartilago vomeronasalis. **laryngeal c's,** cartilagines laryngis. **laryngeal c. of Luschka,** cartilago sesamoidea ligamenti vocalis. **lateral c's,** in the horse, the cartilages from the end of the third phalanx to the heel of the hoof. **lateral c. of nose,** cartilago nasi lateralis. **Luschka's c.,** cartilago sesamoidea ligamenti vocalis. **mandibular c.,** Meckel's c. **meatal c.,** cartilago meatus acustici. **Meckel's c.,** the cartilage of the first branchial arch. **minor c's,** cartilagines sesamoideae. **mucronate c.,** processus xiphoideus. **nasal c's,** cartilagines nasi. **nasal c's, accessory,** cartilagines nasales accessoriae. **nasal c., lateral,** cartilago nasi lateralis. **c. of nasal septum,** cartilago septi nasi. **c's of nose,** cartilagines nasi. **obducent c.,** articular c. **ossifying c.,** temporary c. **palpebral c's.** See *tarsus inferior palpebrae* and *tarsus superior palpebrae.* **parachordal c's,** the two cartilages at the sides of the occipital part of the notochord of the fetus. **parenchymatous c.,** cellular c. **periotic c.,** an oval mass on each side of the upper surface of the fetal chondrocranium. **permanent c.,** cartilage which does not normally become ossified. **precursory c.,** temporary c. **pulmonary c.,** the third costal cartilage on the left side. **pyramidal c.,** cartilago arytenoidea. **Reichert's c.,** the cartilage of the hyoid arch of the embryo from which the styloid process and adjacent structures are developed. **reticular c.,** elastic c. **Santorini's c.,** cartilago corniculata. **scutiform c.,** cartilago thyroidea. **semilunar c., external, of knee joint,** meniscus lateralis articulationis genus. **semilunar c., internal, of knee joint,** meniscus medialis articulationis genus. **septal c. of nose,** cartilago septi nasi. **sesamoid c.,** cartilago triticea. **sesamoid c's of nose,** cartilagines nasales accessoriae. **sesamoid c. of vocal ligament,** cartilago sesamoidea ligamenti vocalis. **sigmoid c's.** See *meniscus lateralis articulationis genus* and *meniscus medialis articulationis genus.* **slipping rib c.,** loosening and deformity of the costal cartilages, producing a group of painful symptoms. **sternal c.,** cartilago costalis. **stratified c.,** fibrocartilage. **subvomerine c's,** vomeronasal c's. **supra-arytenoid c.,** cartilago corniculata. **tarsal c's.** See *tarsus inferior palpebrae* and *tarsus superior palpebrae.* **temporary c.,** any cartilage which is normally destined to become changed into bone. **tendon c.,** a form of embryonic cartilage by which tendons and bones are united. **thyroid c.,** cartilago thyroidea. **tracheal c's,** cartilagines tracheales. **triangular c. of nose,** cartilago nasi lateralis. **triquetral c., triquetrous c.** 1. Cartilago arytenoidea. 2. Discus articularis articulationis radioulnaris distalis. **triticeal c., triticeous c.,** cartilago triticea. **tubal c.,** cartilago tubae auditivae. **tympanomandibular c.,** Meckel's c. **vomeronasal c.,** cartilago vomeronasalis. **Wrisberg's c.,** cartilago cuneiformis. **xiphoid c.,** processus xiphoideus. **Y c.,** a Y-shaped cartilage in the acetabulum, joining the ilium, ischium, and pubes. **yellow c.,** elastic c.

cartilagin (kar′tĭ-laj″in). A principle found in cartilage, which is changed by boiling into chondrin.

cartilagines (kar″tĭ-laj′ĭ-nēz) [L.]. Plural of *cartilago.*

cartilaginification (kar″tĭ-lah-jin″ĭ-fi-ka′shun). Conversion into cartilage.

cartilaginiform (kar″tĭ-lah-jin′ĭ-form). Resembling cartilage.

cartilaginoid (kar″tĭ-laj′ĭ-noid). Cartilaginiform.

cartilaginous (kar″tĭ-laj′ĭ-nus). Consisting of or of the nature of cartilage.

cartilago (kar-tĭ-lah′go), pl. *cartilag′ines* [L.]. A specialized, fibrous connective tissue. See *cartilage.* Used in anatomical nomenclature to designate a mass of such tissue in a particular site in the body. **c. ala′ris ma′jor** [N A, B N A], either of two thin, curved cartilages, one on either side at the apex of the nose, each of which possesses a lateral and a medial crus. Called also *greater alar cartilage.* **cartilag′ines ala′res mino′res** [N A, B N A], various small cartilages located in the fibrous tissue of the alae nasi. Called also *lesser alar cartilages.* **c. articula′ris** [N A, B N A], a thin layer of cartilage, usually hyaline, on the articular surface of bones in synovial joints. Called also *articular cartilage.* **c. arytenoi′dea** [N A], one of the paired, pitcher-shaped cartilages of the back of the larynx at the upper border of the cricoid cartilage. Called also *c. arytaenoidea* [B N A] and *arytenoid cartilage.* **c. auric′ulae** [N A, B N A], the internal plate of elastic cartilage which is found in the external ear. Called also *cartilage of auricle.* **c. cornicula′ta** [N A], a small nodule of cartilage at the apex of each arytenoid cartilage. Called also *c. corniculata* [*Santorini*] [B N A], and *corniculate cartilage.* **c. cornicula′ta [Santori′ni]** [B N A], c. corniculata. **c. costa′lis** [N A, B N A], a bar of hyaline cartilage by which the ventral extremity of a rib is attached to the sternum in the case of the true ribs, or to the superiorly adjacent ribs in the case of the upper false ribs. Called also *costal cartilage.* **c. cricoi′dea** [N A, B N A], a ringlike cartilage forming the lower and back part of the larynx. Called also *cricoid cartilage.* **c. cuneifor′mis** [N A], either of the paired cartilages, one on either side in the aryepiglottic fold. Called also *c. cuneiformis* [*Wrisbergi*] [B N A], and *cuneiform cartilage.* **c. cuneifor′mis [Wrisber′gi]** [B N A], c. cuneiformis. **c. ensifor′mis,** processus xiphoideus. **c. epiglot′tica** [N A, B N A], the plate of cartilage that constitutes the central part of the epiglottis. Called also *epiglottic cartilage.* **c. epiphysia′lis** [N A], cartilage interposed between the epiphysis and the shaft of the bone during the period of growth; by its growth the bone increases in length. Called also *synchondrosis epiphyseos* [B N A]. **cartilag′ines falca′tae.** See *meniscus lateralis articulationis genus* and *meniscus medialis articulationis genus.* **c. jacobso′ni,** c. vomeronasalis. **cartilag′ines laryn′gis** [N A, B N A], cartilages of the larynx, including the cricoid, thyroid, and epiglottic, and two each of arytenoid, corniculate, and cuneiform cartilages. Called also *laryngeal cartilages.* **c. mea′tus acus′tici** [N A, B N A], the trough-shaped cartilage of the cartilaginous part of the external acoustic meatus. Called also *cartilage of acoustic meatus.* **cartilag'ines nasa'les accesso'riae** [N A], one or more small cartilages on either side of the nose between the greater alar and lateral nasal cartilages. Called also *accessory nasal cartilages* and *cartilagines sesamoideae nasi* [B N A]. **cartilag'ines na'si** [N A, B N A], the cartilages of the nose, including the lateral nasal, greater and lesser alar, nasal septal, vomeronasal, and the accessory nasal cartilages. **c. na'si latera'lis** [N A, B N A], a lateral expansion of the septal cartilage on either side of the nose just inferior to the nasal bone. Called also *lateral nasal cartilage.* **c. santori'ni,** c. corniculata. **c. sep'ti na'si** [N A, B N A], the hyaline cartilage forming the framework of the cartilaginous part of the nasal septum, and including the lateral nasal cartilages. Called also *cartilage of nasal septum.* **c. sesamoi'dea laryn'gis, Luschka,** c. sesamoidea ligamenti vocalis. **c. sesamoi'dea ligamen'ti voca'lis** [N A, B N A], a small cartilage occasionally found within the vocal ligaments. Called also *sesamoid cartilage of vocal ligament.* **cartilag'ines sesamoi'deae na'si** [B N A], cartilagines nasales accessoriae. **c. thyroi'dea** [N A], the largest cartilage of the larynx, with two broad, posteriorly diverging laminae and two pairs of horns, superior and inferior, that extend from the posterior borders of the laminae. Called also *c. thyreoidea* [B N A], and *thyroid cartilage.* **cartilag'ines trachea'les** [N A, B N A], the 16 to 20 incomplete rings which, held together and enclosed by a strong, elastic, fibrous membrane, constitute the wall of the trachea. Called also *tracheal cartilages.* **c. triquet'ra.** 1. Cartilago arytenoidea. 2. Discus articularis articulationis radioulnaris distalis. **c. tritic'ea** [N A, B N A], a small cartilage in the thyrohyoid ligament. Called also *triticeal cartilage.* **c. tu'bae auditi'vae** [N A, B N A], the cartilage on the inferomedial surface of the temporal bone that supports the walls of the cartilaginous portion of the auditory tube. Called also *cartilage of auditory tube* and *tubal cartilage.* **c. vomeronasa'lis** [N A], either of the two narrow, longitudinal strips of cartilage, one lying on either side of the anterior portion of the lower margin of the septal cartilage. Called also *c. vomeronasalis* [*Jacobsoni*] [B N A], and *vomeronasal cartilage.* **c. vomeronasa'lis [Jacobso'ni]** [B N A], c. vomeronasalis. **c. wrisber'gi,** c. cuneiformis.

cartilagotropic (kar″tĭ-lag-o-trop'ik) [L. *cartilago* cartilage + Gr. *tropos* a turning]. Having affinity for cartilage.

caruncle (kar'ung-kl). A small fleshy eminence, whether normal or abnormal. **hymenal c's,** carunculae hymenales. **lacrimal c.,** caruncula lacrimalis. **major c. of Santorini,** papilla duodeni major. **morgagnian c.,** lobus medius prostatae. **sublingual c.,** caruncula sublingualis. **urethral c.,** a small red eminence on the mucous membrane of the urinary meatus in women.

caruncula (kah-rung'ku-lah), pl. *carun'culae* [L., dim. of *caro* flesh]. [N A, B N A] A small fleshy eminence. Called also *caruncle.* **carun'culae hymena'les** [N A, B N A], small elevations of the mucous membrane encircling the vaginal orifice, being relics of the torn hymen. **c. lacrima'lis** [N A, B N A], the red eminence at the medial angle of the eye. Called also *lacrimal caruncle.* **c. mammilla'ris,** trigonum olfactorium. **carun'culae myrtifor'mes,** carunculae hymenales. **c. saliva'ris,** c. sublingualis. **c. sublingua'lis** [N A, B N A], an eminence on each side of the frenulum of the tongue, at the apex of which are the openings of the major sublingual duct and the submandibular duct. Called also *sublingual caruncle.*

carunculae (kah-rung'ku-le) [L.]. Plural of *caruncula.*

Carus circle, curve (kah'rus) [Karl Gustav *Carus,* German obstetrician, 1789–1868]. See under *curve.*

carver (kar'ver). An instrument for producing and perfecting anatomical forms in artificial teeth and dental restorations.

carvone (kar'vōn). An essential oil from *Anethum graveolens.* It is a terpene ketone, $C_3H_5.C_6H_6O.CH_3$.

caryo- (kar'e-o) [Gr. *karyon* nucleus, or nut]. Combining form denoting relationship to a nucleus. See also words beginning *karyo-*

Caryococcus (kar″e-o-kok'kus) [*caryo-* + Gr. *kokkos* berry]. A genus of microorganisms of uncertain affinities which are parasitic on protozoa.

Caryophanaceae (kar″e-o-fah-na'se-e). A family of Schizomycetes (order Caryophanales), made up of large motile or non-motile trichomes and bacillary structures which do not form spores. It includes three genera, *Caryophanon, Lineola,* and *Simonsiella,* comprising non-pathogenic parasitic forms found in the oral cavity and in the intestinal content of ruminants.

Caryophanales (kar″e-o-fah-na'lēz). An order of class Schizomycetes, made up of microorganisms which occur as cylindrical or discoidal cells enclosed in a continuous wall, forming long filaments (trichomes) or shorter structures which function as hormogonia. Found in water and in decomposing organic materials, and in the intestines of arthropods and vertebrates. It includes three families, *Arthromitaceae, Caryophanaceae,* and *Oscillospiraceae.*

caryophil (kar'e-o-fil). Staining easily with thiazinammonium stains.

Carysomyia (kar″ĭ-so-mi'yah). A genus of flies. **C. bezzia'na,** a myiasis-producing fly of India and Africa, the larvae of which can develop only in living tissues.

Casal's necklace (kah-salz') [Gaspar *Casal,* Spanish physician, 1691–1759]. An area of erythema and pigmentation around the neck in pellagra.

cascara (kas-kăr'ah) [Sp.]. Bark. **c. amar'ga** [Sp. "bitter bark"], the bark of *Picramnia antidesma,* a tree of tropical America: alterative and tonic. **c. sagra'da** [Sp. "sacred bark"], the dried bark of *Rhamnus purshiana,* a shrub of the Pacific states of the United States: used as a cathartic.

case (kās). 1. A particular instance of disease; as a *case* of leukemia; sometimes used incorrectly to designate the patient with the disease. 2. A term sometimes used incorrectly in dentistry to designate a flask, denture, casting, or the like. **basket c.,** that of a patient in whom all four limbs are amputated. **borderline c.,** an instance of a disease in which the symptoms resemble those of a recognized condition but are not typical of it. **custodial c.,** the case of an individual who requires supervision or removal from society because of mental disease, criminality, etc. **index c.,** the case of the original patient (propositus, or proband), which provides the stimulus for study of other members of the family, to ascertain a possible genetic factor in causation of the presenting condition. **trial c.,** a box containing + and — spherical and + and — cylindrical lenses, arranged in pairs, a trial spectacle frame, and various other devices used in testing vision.

casease (ka'se-ās) [L. *caseus* cheese]. An enzyme derived from bacterial cultures, capable of dissolving albumin and the casein of milk and cheese.

caseation (ka″se-a'shun) [L. *caseus* cheese]. 1. The precipitation of casein. 2. A form of necrosis in which the tissue is changed into a dry, amorphous mass resembling cheese.

casebook (kās-book). A book in which a physician enters the records of his cases.

caseification (ka″se-ĭ-fi-ka'shun). Caseation.

casein (ka'se-in) [L. *caseus* cheese]. A phosphoprotein, the principal protein of milk, the basis of curd and of cheese. It is precipitated from milk as a white amorphous substance by dilute acids and redissolves on the addition of alkalis or an excess of acid. Rennet and calcium change it to an insoluble curd. Casein is used as a food, being added to other ingredients of the diet, when it is desired to increase the protein content of the diet. **c. dyspepton,** a substance formed when milk is digested with pepsin and hydrochloric acid. **gluten c.,** a form of casein from the seeds of various cereal plants; glutin. **c. iodine,** iodocasein. **c.-mercury,** a preparation of casein and mercuric chloride, soluble in water: antiseptic. **Panum's c.,** serum globulin. **c. saccharide,** a preparation of casein and sugar: used in making emulsions. **serum c.,** paraglobulin. **c.-sodium,** a nutrient preparation of casein and sodium hydroxide. **vegetable c.,** a protein contained in gluten and resembling casein.

caseinogen (ka″se-in′o-jen) [*casein* + Gr. *gennan* to produce]. A protein of milk producing casein when acted upon by rennin.

caseinogenate (ka″se-in′o-jĕ-nāt). A salt of caseinogen.

caseogenous (ka″se-oj′ĕ-nus). Producing caseation.

caseose (ka′se-ōs). A proteose produced during the digestion of casein (Chittenden).

caseoserum (ka″se-o-se′rum). An antiserum produced by immunization with casein.

caseous (ka′se-us). Resembling cheese or curd.

caseum (ka′se-um) [L. "cheese"]. Cellular debris of a cheeselike consistency, produced as a result of caseation.

caseworm (kās′werm). Echinococcus.

$CaSO_4$. Calcium sulfate.

Casoni's intradermal test, reaction (kah-so′nēz) [Tommaso *Casoni*, Italian physician, 1880–1933]. See under *tests.*

cassava (kah-sah′vah) [Sp. *casabe*]. The plants *Manihot utilissima* and *M. aipi;* also the starch from their roots, which furnishes tapioca.

Casselberry position (kas′el-ber-e) [William Evans *Casselberry*, American laryngologist, 1858–1916]. See under *position.*

casserian fontanelle, ganglion, etc. (kah-se′re-an) [Giulio *Casserio*, Italian anatomist, 1556–1616]. See under the nouns.

cassette (kah-set′) [Fr. "a little box"]. A lightproof housing for x-ray film, containing front and back intensifying screens between which the film is placed.

cassiopeium (kas″e-o-pe′um). Lutetium.

cast (kast). 1. A positive copy or likeness of an object, such as a mold of a hollow organ, as a renal tubule or bronchiole, formed of effused plastic matter and extruded from the body, or a reproduction of a body part, such as teeth or other oral structures, made by pouring plaster or other plastic material into an impression or mold. 2. To form an object in a mold. 3. A stiff dressing made of bandage impregnated with plaster of paris or other hardening material; used for immobilization of various parts of the body, in cases of fractures, dislocations and infected wounds. 4. Strabismus. **bacterial c.,** a tube cast made up of bacteria or containing a large number of bacteria. **blood c.,** a renal cast that bears blood cells on its surface. **coma c.,** a renal cast containing strongly refracting granules: said to indicate oncoming coma in diabetes. Called also *Külz's cylinder.* **decidual c.,** the fleshy mass discharged from the uterus at the time of rupture of an ectopic pregnancy. **dental c.,** the facsimile of oral structures obtained by pouring plaster into an impression made of the mouth. **diagnostic c.,** a facsimile of oral structures made for the specific purpose of study as a means of determining the proper method of treatment. **epithelial c.,** a urinary cast made up of columnar renal epithelium or of round cells. **false c.,** pseudocast. **fatty c.,** any cast made up of material loaded with fat globules. **fibrinous c.,** a cast resembling a waxy cast, but having a distinctly yellow color like beeswax, often seen in acute nephritis. **granular c.,** a dark colored renal cast of granular or cell-like substance, it being a degenerated form of a hyaline or waxy cast. **hair c.,** trichobezoar. **hemoglobin c.,** an irregular, dark, granular cast composed of disintegrated red blood corpuscles. **hyaline c.,** a nearly transparent urinary cast made up of homogeneous protein, but slightly refractive. **investment c.,** refractory c. **Külz's c.,** coma c. **master c.,** a facsimile of oral structures, including the prepared tooth surfaces, residual ridge areas, and/or other parts of the dental arch, reproduced from an impression. **mucus c.,** cylindroid. **pre-extraction c., preoperative c.,** diagnostic c. **pus c.,** a urinary cast made up of pus cells. **quarter c.,** a cut in the quarter of a horse's hoof. **refractory c.,** one made of a material that will withstand high temperatures without disintegrating. **renal c.,** urinary c. **spiral c.,** a urinary cast having a spiral or twisted shape. **spurious c., spurious tube c.,** cylindroid. **study c.,** diagnostic c. **tube c.,** urinary c. **urate c.,** an agglomeration of urates on a shred of fibrin or other substance. **urinary c.,** a mold of a renal tubule, of variable composition, discharged in the urine. **waxy c.,** a urinary cast made up of a highly refractive, translucent, amyloid substance.

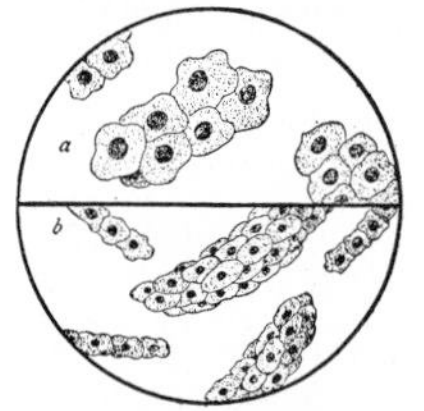

a, Squamous epithelium from urine; *b*, epithelial casts.

Hyaline casts.

Granular casts.

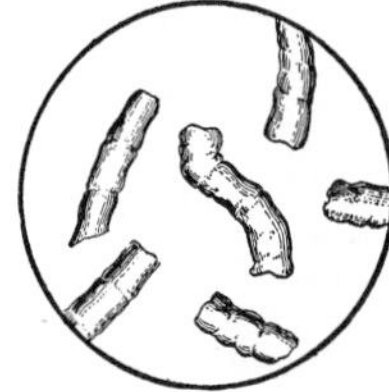

Waxy casts.

Castanea (kas-ta′ne-ah) [L.; Gr. *kastanea*]. A genus of trees, the chestnuts.

Castellanella (kas″tel-ah-nel′ah) [Aldo *Castellani*]. A genus of trypanosomes to which some of the old species of Trypanosoma are now referred. **C. castellan′i,** a trypanosome causing the more acute and violent form of sleeping sickness. **C. gambien′se,** *Trypanosoma gambiense.*

Castellani's bronchitis, mixture, paint, test (kas-tel-an′ēz) [Aldo *Castellani*, Italian physician, born 1877]. See under the nouns.

Castellani-Low symptom [Aldo *Castellani*; George Carmichael *Low*, English physician, 1872–1952]. See under *symptom.*

Castellania (kas-tel-a′ne-ah) [Aldo *Castellani*]. A genus of yeastlike fungi, numerous species of which have been isolated from various lesions of man.

casting (kast′ing). An object formed by the solidification of plastic material, such as molten metal, poured into an impression or mold, or the act of formation of such an object. **vacuum c.,** the pouring of plastic material into an impression or mold, under conditions of lowered atmospheric pressure.

Castle's intrinsic factor (kas′elz) [William Bosworth *Castle*, American physician, born 1897]. See under *factor.*

castrate (kas′trāt). 1. To deprive of the gonads, rendering the individual incapable of reproduction. 2. An individual that has been rendered incapable of reproduction by removal of the gonads.

castration (kas-tra′shun) [L. *castratio*]. Removal of gonads. **female c.,** bilateral complete ovariectomy, or spaying. **parasitic c.,** defective sexual development due to infestation with parasites in early life.

castroid (kas′troid). Eunuchoid.

casual (kaz′u-al) [L. *casualis*]. 1. Pertaining to accidental injuries or to accidents. 2. An occupant of a casual bed in a hospital.

casualty (kaz′u-al-te). An accident; an accidental wound; death or disablement from an accident; also the person so injured.

casuistics (kaz″u-is′tiks). The recording and study of cases of disease.

cata- [Gr. *kata* down]. A prefix signifying down, lower, under, against, along with, very. See also words beginning *kata-*.

catabasial (kat-ah-ba′ze-al) [*cata-* + *basion*]. Having the basion lower than the opisthion: used of certain skulls.

catabasis (kah-tab′ah-sis) [*cata-* + Gr. *bainein* to go]. The stage of decline of a disease.

catabatic (kat-ah-bat′ik). Pertaining to the decline of a disease; abating.

catabiosis (kat″ah-bi-o′sis) [Gr. *katabiōsis* a passing life]. The normal senescence of cells.

catabiotic (kat″ah-bi-ot′ik). 1. Pertaining to or characterized by catabiosis. 2. Dissipated or used up in the performance of function: said of the energy obtained from food. Cf. *bioplastic*.

catabolergy (kat″ah-bol′er-je) [*catabolic* + Gr. *ergon* work]. The energy consumed in a catabolic process.

catabolic (kat″ah-bol′ik). Pertaining to or of the nature of catabolism; retrograde or destructive.

catabolin (kah-tab′o-lin). Catabolite.

catabolism (kah-tab′o-lizm) [Gr. *katabolē* a throwing down]. Any destructive process by which complex substances are converted by living cells into more simple compounds; destructive metabolism.

catabolite (kah-tab′o-līt). Any product of catabolism, or of a destructive metabolic process.

catabythismus (kat″ah-bi-thiz′mus) [Gr. *katabythizein* to make to sink]. Suicide by drowning.

catacausis (kat″ah-kaw′sis) [*cata-* + Gr. *kausis* burning]. Spontaneous combustion.

catachronobiology (kat″ah-kron″o-bi-ol′o-je). A term suggested to denote the study of the deleterious effects of time on a living system. Cf. *anachronobiology*.

catacrotic (kat″ah-krot′ik). Pertaining to or characterized by catacrotism.

catacrotism (kah-tak′ro-tizm) [*cata-* + Gr. *krotos* beat]. An anomaly of the pulse evidenced by appearance of a small additional wave or notch in the descending limb of the pulse tracing.

catadicrotic (kat″ah-di-krot′ik). Pertaining to or characterized by catadicrotism.

catadicrotism (kat″ah-di′kro-tizm) [*cata-* + Gr. *dis* twice + *krotos* beat]. An anomaly of the pulse evidenced by appearance of two small additional waves or notches in the descending limb of the pulse tracing.

catadidymus (kat″ah-did′ĭ-mus). Katadidymus.

catadioptric (kat″ah-di-op′trik). Deflecting and reflecting light at the same time.

catagen (kat′ah-jen). The transitional phase of the hair cycle, between anagen and telogen, beginning with cessation of active proliferation of the cells of the hair matrix, and marked by diminution in size of the follicle, and the formation, by partially keratinized cells, of a bulbous enlargement at the base of the hair.

catagenesis (kat″ah-jen′e-sis) [*cata-* + Gr. *genesis* production]. Involution or retrogression.

catagenetic (kat″ah-je-net′ik). Pertaining to catagenesis.

catagmatic (kat″ag-mat′ik) [Gr. *katagma* fracture]. Having the power of consolidating a broken bone.

catalase (kat′ah-lās). A crystalline enzyme which specifically catalyzes the decomposition of hydrogen peroxide and which is found in practically all cells except certain anaerobic bacteria.

catalatic (kat″ah-lat′ik). Pertaining to catalase.

catalepsy (kat′ah-lep″se) [Gr. *katalēpsis*]. A condition characterized by a waxy rigidity (flexibilitas cerea) of the muscles so that the patient tends to remain in any position in which he is placed.

cataleptic (kat″ah-lep′tik). 1. Pertaining to, characterized by, or inducing catalepsy. 2. A person affected with catalepsy.

cataleptiform (kat″ah-lep′tĭ-form). Cataleptoid.

cataleptoid (kat″ah-lep′toid). Resembling catalepsy.

catalogia (kat″ah-lo′je-ah). Verbigeration.

Catalpa (kah-tal′pah). A genus of bignoniaceous trees. *C. bignonioides*, of the United States, affords seeds used in asthma.

catalysis (kah-tal′ĭ-sis) [Gr. *katalysis* dissolution]. Change in the velocity of a reaction produced by the presence of a substance which does not form part of the final product. **contact c.,** catalysis produced by the adsorbing power of contact surfaces; e.g., catalysis caused by colloidal platinum. **negative c.,** catalysis in which the velocity of the reaction is retarded. **positive c.,** catalysis in which the velocity of the reaction is accelerated. **surface c.,** catalysis in which the reacting substances are adsorbed onto the surface of the catalyst and there react.

catalyst (kat′ah-list). Any substance which brings about catalysis. **negative c.,** a catalyst which retards the velocity of a reaction. **positive c.,** a catalyst which accelerates the velocity of a reaction.

catalytic (kat″ah-lit′ik) [Gr. *katalyein* to dissolve]. 1. Causing or pertaining to an alterative effect; causing catalysis. 2. An alterative or specific medicine.

catalyzator (kat″ah-lĭ-za′tor). Catalyst.

catalyze (kat′ah-līz). To cause or produce catalysis.

catalyzer (kat′ah-līz″er). Catalyst.

catamenia (kat″ah-me′ne-ah) [Gr. *katamēnia*]. The monthly uterine discharge; menstruation, or the menses.

catamenial (kat″ah-me′ne-al). Pertaining to the menses or to menstruation.

catamenogenic (kat″ah-men″o-jen′ik). Inducing menstruation.

catamnesis (kat″am-ne′sis). The history of a patient from the time he is discharged from treatment or from a hospital to the time of his death.

catamnestic (kat″am-nes′tik). Pertaining to catamnesis.

catapasm (kat′ah-pazm) [Gr. *katapasma*]. A powder to be applied to the surface.

cataphasia (kat″ah-fa′ze-ah) [*cata-* + Gr. *phasis* speech]. A speech disorder in which the patient constantly or repeatedly utters the same word or phrase.

cataphora (kah-taf′o-rah) [Gr. *kataphora*]. Lethargy with intervals of imperfect waking.

cataphoresis (kat″ah-fo-re′sis) [*cata-* + Gr. *phorēsis* bearing]. The introduction of charged particles or ions into the tissues by means of an electric field. **anemic c.,** that in which the drug is confined in any particular part, as by compression with an Esmarch bandage.

cataphoretic (kat″ah-fo-ret′ik). Of, or pertaining to, cataphoresis.

cataphoria (kat″ah-fo′re-ah) [*cata-* + Gr. *pherein* to bear]. A downward turning of the visual axes of both eyes; double hypophoria.

cataphoric (kat″ah-for′ik). Pertaining to cataphoresis or to cataphora.

cataphrenia (kat″ah-fre′ne-ah) [*cata-* + Gr. *phrēn* mind]. A state of mental debility of the dementia type which tends to eventuate in recovery.

cataphylaxis (kat″ah-fi-lak′sis) [*cata-* + Gr. *phylaxis* a guarding]. 1. The movement of leukocytes and antibodies to the locality of an infection (Wright). 2. A breaking down of the body's natural defense to infection (Bullock and Cranmer).

cataplasia (kat″ah-pla′se-ah) [*cata-* + Gr. *plassein* to form]. Retrograde metamorphosis; a form of atrophy in which the tissues revert to earlier and more embryonic conditions.

cataplasis (kat-ap′lah-sis). Cataplasia.

cataplasm (kat′ah-plazm) [L. *cataplasma;* Gr. *kataplasma*]. A poultice or soft external application, often medicated. **kaolin c.,** a poultice prepared with kaolin, boric acid, and glycerin.

cataplasma (kat″ah-plaz′mah) [L.; Gr. *kataplasma*]. Cataplasm. **c. fermen′ti,** a poultice containing yeast. **c. kaoli′ni,** kaolin cataplasm.

cataplectic (kat″ah-plek′tik). 1. Pertaining to or characterized by cataplexy. 2. Coming on suddenly and overwhelmingly.

cataplexie (kat′ah-plek″se) [Fr.]. Cataplexy. **c. du réveil,** awakening of the psyche occurring before physical awakening.

cataplexis (kat′ah-plek″sis) [Gr.]. Cataplexy.

cataplexy (kat′ah-plek-se). A state of immobility and rigidity seen in some animals as a result of certain forms of stimulation. It may occur in man as a sudden loss of muscular tonus causing him to sink to the ground.

catapophysis (kat″ah-pof′ĭ-sis). A process of bone or of brain matter.

cataract (kat′ah-rakt) [L. *cataracta,* from Gr. *katarrhēgnynai* to break down]. An opacity of the crystalline eye lens or of its capsule. **adherent c.,** a cataract with adhesions between the iris and the lens capsule. **adolescent c.,** cataract developing in youth. **after-c.,** a recurrent capsular cataract; any membrane in the pupillary area after removal or absorption of the lens. **arborescent c.,** one in which the opacity has a branched appearance. **aridosiliculose c., aridosiliquate c.,** siliculose c. **axial c.,** nuclear c. **axillary c.,** spindle c. **black c.,** a nuclear cataract with a dark colored opacity. **blood c.,** blocking of the lens by a blood clot. **blue c., blue dot c.,** a condition characterized by the presence of small punctate opacities of a delicate bluish tint, scattered throughout the nucleus and cortex of the lens; vision is not interfered with, nor does the condition progress. **bony c.,** cataracta ossea. **bottlemakers' c.,** glassblowers' c. **calcareous c.,** one containing a chalky deposit. **capsular c.,** one which consists of an opacity in the capsule. **capsulolenticular c.,** that which is seated partly in the capsule and partly in the lens. **caseous c., cheesy c.,** a hypermature cataract which has undergone a cheesy degeneration. **central c.,** opacity of the center of the eye lens. **cerulean c.,** blue c. **choroidal c.,** a brownish diffuse opacity of the lens nucleus associated with chronic choroidal disease. **complete c.,** one which involves the whole lens. **complicated c.,** cataract due to disease of other parts of the eye. **congenital c.,** one which originates before birth. **contusion c.,** one which is due to shock or to injury of the eyeball. **coralliform c.,** a cataract having the shape of coral. **coronary c.,** a congenital condition in which club-shaped opacities are arranged in a ring or crown around the lens, the center of the lens and the extreme periphery remaining clear. **cortical c.,** a stellate opacity in the cortical layers of the lens. **cystic c.,** a cataract showing cystic degeneration. **diabetic c.,** one which occurs as a complication of diabetes. **discission of c.,** the rupturing of the capsule, so that the aqueous humor may gain access to the lens. **dry-shelled c.,** siliculose c. **electric c.,** cataract attributed to the light formed in electric welding or to a flash of lightning. **embryonal nuclear c.,** an opacity confined to the embryonal nucleus of the lens. **fibroid c.,** a variety of capsular cataract which does not affect the lens. **floriform c.,** a cataract having the form of a rayed flower (sunflower). **fluid c.,** a hypermature cataract in which the lens has become a milky fluid. **fusiform c.,** a spindle-shaped opacity extending from the anterior to the posterior pole of the lens. **general c.,** a cataract in which the opacity affects both the cortex and nucleus of the lens. **glassblowers' c.,** cataract in glassblowers, due to exposure to intense heat and light. **glaucomatous c.,** opacity which is dependent upon an attack of glaucoma. **gray c.,** senile cortical cataract. **green c.,** a greenish opacity, sometimes glaucomatous, and sometimes due to a slight lack of transparency in the mediums. **hard c.,** one with a hard nucleus. **heat-ray c.,** cataract due to long-continued exposure to high temperatures: e.g., glassblowers' c. **hedger's c.,** perforation of the cornea by a thorn, occurring in persons who trim hedges. **heterochromic c.,** cataract associated with heterochromia of the iris. **hypermature c.,** one in which the lens has passed maturity and become either solid and shrunken or soft and liquid. **immature c.,** includes the incipient and intercurrent varieties, or any cataract which affects only a part of the lens or capsule. **incipient c.,** any cataract in its early stages, or one which has sectors of opacity with clear spaces intervening. **infantile c.,** a lamellar cataract of early childhood, commonly associated with rickets or convulsions. **intumescent c.,** one with an opaque and swollen lens. **irradiation c.,** cataract caused by large doses of radium and roentgen rays. **juvenile c.,** a soft cataract in a young person. **lacteal c.** Same as *fluid c.* **lamellar c.,** opacity which affects certain layers only between the cortex and nucleus of the lens. **lenticular c.,** opacity of the lens not affecting the capsule. **lightning c.,** cataract caused by a stroke of lightning passing through the body. **mature c.,** one in which the lens is completely opaque, is separable from its capsule and is ready for operation. **membranous c.,** a condition in which the lens substance has shrunk, leaving remnants of the capsule and fibrous tissue formation. Called also *pseudoaphakia.* **milky c.,** fluid c. **mixed c.,** general c. **morgagnian c.,** a fluid cataract with a hard nucleus. **naphthalinic c.,** cataract caused by the injection of naphthalene. **nuclear c.,** one in which the opacity is seated in the central nucleus of the lens. **overripe c.,** hypermature c. **partial c.,** any cataract which affects only a part of the lens: it may be central or fusiform. **perinuclear c.,** a disklike opacity around the central nucleus of the lens. **peripheral c.,** a cataract in the periphery of the lens. **polar c., anterior,** one seated at the center of the anterior capsule of the lens. **polar c., posterior,** one seated at the center of the posterior capsule of the lens. **primary c.,** a cataract developing independently of any other disease. **progressive c.,** one which, if not removed, passes through three stages—the immature, the mature, and the hypermature—and becomes total. **puddler's c.,** cataract in iron puddlers due to intense radiation from open-hearth furnaces. **punctate c.,** one made up of a collection of dotlike opacities. **pyramidal c.,** a conoid anterior polar cataract with its apex pointing forward. **reduplication c.,** a series of similar opacities situated at various levels in the lens, usually connected by opaque lines. **ripe c.,** mature cataract. **sanguineous c.,** a blood clot in the prepupillary opening. **secondary c.** 1. A cataract that returns after it has once been removed by operation. 2. Complicated cataract. **sedimentary c.,** a soft cataract in which the denser parts have gravitated downward. **senile c.,** a hard opacity of the nucleus of the lens of the eye, occurring in the aged. **siliculose c., siliquose c.,** a cataract in which there is absorption of the lens, with calcareous deposit in the capsule, so that the atrophied lens resembles a silique. Called also *dry-shelled c., aridosiliculose c.* and *cataracta aridosiliquata.* **snowflake c., snowstorm c.,** cataract which has the appearance of numerous grayish or bluish-white flaky opacities. **soft c.,** one with no hard nucleus. **spindle c.,** a cataract characterized by a spindle-shaped opacity reaching through the capsule in an anteroposterior direction. **stationary c.,** opacity of the lens which does not increase in extent. **stellate c.,** cortical c. **subcapsular c.,** an opacity situated beneath the anterior or posterior capsule of the lens. **sunflower c.,** chalcosis lentis; a sunflower-shaped cataract caused by the presence of a spicule of copper in the eye. **sutural c.,** a congenital opacity of the lens affecting the Y-shaped sutures of the fetal membrane. **total c.,** opacity of all the fibers of the lens. **traumatic c.,** cataract following an injury. **tremulous c.,** one attended by a tremulous movement of the pupil and iris. **unripe c.,** immature c. **zonular c.** 1. Lamellar cataract. 2. One which involves the zonula.

cataracta (kat″ah-rak′tah) [L.]. Cataract. **c. accre′ta,** a condition in which the lens and the iris are fastened together as a result of iritis. **c. brunes′cens,** black cataract. **c. ceru′lea,** blue cataract. **c. complica′ta,** complicated cataract. **c. congen′ita membrana′cea,** congenital membranaceous cataract. **c. corona′ria,** a crown-shaped cataract. **c. elec′trica,** electric cataract. **c. membrana′cea accre′ta,** an after-cataract due to adhesions of the remains of the anterior capsule to the posterior capsule. **c. neurodermat′ica,** a type of cataract occurring as a complication of generalized dermatitis. **c. ni′gra,** black cataract. **c. os′sea,** a condition in which lens tissue is invaded by scar tissue which has become ossified. **c. syndermot′ica,** cataract occurring as an accompaniment of a skin disease.

cataractopiesis (kat″ah-rak″to-pi-e′sis). Couching.

cataractous (kat″ah-rak′tus). Of the nature of or affected with cataract.

cataria (kah-ta′re-ah) [L. "catnip"]. The leaves and tops of *Nepeta cataria,* or catnip, a labiate plant: a carminative and mild nerve stimulant.

catarrh (kah-tahr′) [L. *catarrhus,* from Gr. *katarrhein* to flow down]. Inflammation of a mucous membrane, with a free discharge (Hippocrates); especially such inflammation of the air passages of the head and throat. This word has been practically eliminated from the scientific vocabulary. **atrophic c.,** chronic rhinitis with wasting of mucous and submucous tissues. **autumnal c.,** hay fever. **Bostock's c.,** hay fever. **contagious c. of fowls,** roup. **epidemic c.,** influenza or grip. **Fruehjahr c.,** vernal conjunctivitis. **hypertrophic c.,** chronic catarrh which results in irregular, and sometimes papillary, thickening of the mucous and the submucous tissues. **Laennec's c.,** a kind of asthmatic bronchitis, with viscous, pearly expectoration. **malignant c. of cattle,** a virus disease of cattle characterized by inflammation of the mucous membranes and enlargement of the lymphatic glands. **postnasal c.,** chronic rhinopharyngitis. **Russian c.,** influenza. **spring c.,** vernal conjunctivitis. **suffocative c.,** asthma. **vernal c.,** vernal conjunctivitis.

catarrhal (kah-tahr′al). Of the nature of or pertaining to catarrh.

Catarrhina (kat″ah-ri′nah) [*cata-* + Gr. *rhis* nose]. A superfamily of the order Primates (suborder Anthropoidea), characterized by nostrils which are close together and directed downward, and including the Old World apes and monkeys, and man.

catarrhine (kat′ah-rīn). 1. Pertaining to the superfamily Catarrhina. 2. Characterized by nostrils which are close together and directed downward.

catastalsis (kat″ah-stal′sis) [*cata-* + Gr. *stalsis* contraction]. A downward moving wave of contraction without a preceding wave of inhibition occurring in the digestive tube in addition to the peristaltic wave. Cf. *anastalsis* and *diastalsis.*

catastaltic (kat″ah-stal′tik) [Gr. *katastaltikos*]. 1. Inhibitory; restraining. 2. An agent which tends to restrain or check any process.

catastate (kat′ah-stāt) [*cata-* + Gr. *histanai* to stand]. A result of catabolism; any substance or condition resulting from a catabolic process.

catastatic (kat″ah-stat′ik). Of the nature of or pertaining to a catastate.

catatasis (kah-tat′ah-sis) [Gr. *katatasis* a stretching]. Extension applied for the reduction of a dislocation or fracture.

catathermometer (kat″ah-ther-mom′e-ter). Katathermometer.

catathymic (kat″ah-thi′mik). Meyer's term for psychic disorders marked by perseveration, in the course of which a single depressive topic tends to be complex-determined.

catatonia (kat-ah-to′ne-ah) [*cata-* + Gr. *tonos* tension + *-ia*]. A form of schizophrenia characterized by negativistic reactions, phases of stupor or excitement, and impulsive or stereotype behavior.

catatoniac (kat″ah-to′ne-ak). Catatonic.

catatonic (kat″ah-ton′ik). 1. Pertaining to catatonia. 2. A person affected with catatonia.

catatony (kah-tat′o-ne). Catatonia.

catatricrotic (kat″ah-tri-krot′ik). Pertaining to or characterized by catatricrotism.

catatricrotism (kat″ah-tri′kro-tizm) [*cata-* + Gr. *treis* three + *krotos* beat]. An anomaly of the pulse evidenced by appearance of three small additional waves or notches in the descending limb of the pulse tracing.

catatropia (kat″ah-tro′pe-ah) [*cata-* + Gr. *trepein* to turn]. Cataphoria.

cataxia (kah-tak′se-ah) [Gr. *katagnymai* to break in pieces]. The separation or breaking up of bacterial associations; especially in those cases in which the association is pathogenic, but individual bacterial species are not.

catechin (kat′e-kin). 1. A crystalline principle, $C_{19}H_{18}O_8 + 5H_2O$, from catechu. 2. [Gr. *katechein* to restrain]. A substance in the blood which has a restraining effect on the action of a hormone.

catechol (kat′e-kol). A compound, 1,2-dihydroxybenzene, $C_6H_6O_2$.

catecholamine (kat″e-kol-am′in). One of a group of similar compounds having a sympathomimetic action, the aromatic portion of whose molecule is catechol, and the aliphatic portion an amine. Such compounds include dopamine, norepinephrine, and epinephrine.

catechu (kat′e-ku). A powerfully astringent extract from the leaves and twigs of the rubiaceous plant, *Ourouparia gambir:* formerly used in diarrhea, and locally for sore throat, etc.

catelectrotonus (kat″e-lek-trot′o-nus) [*cata-* + *electrotonus*]. Increase of irritability of a nerve or muscle when near the cathode.

Catenabacterium (kat″e-nah-bak-te′re-um) [L. *catena* chain + *bacterium*]. A genus of microorganisms of the tribe Lactobacilleae, family Lactobacillaceae, order Eubacteriales, made up of non-sporulating, anaerobic, gram-positive bacilli, found in the intestinal tract and occasionally associated with purulent infections.

catenating (kat′e-nāt″ing) [L. *catena* a chain]. Forming part of a chain or complex of symptoms.

catenoid (kat′e-noid) [L. *catena* chain]. Arranged like a chain; resembling a chain.

catenulate (kah-ten′u-lāt). Catenoid.

catgut (kat′gut). Sheep's intestine prepared as a cord, asepticized, and used as a ligature and in drainage. **chromic c., chromicized c.,** catgut sterilized and impregnated with chromium trioxide. **formaldehyde c.,** catgut impregnated with a solution of formaldehyde by boiling in an alcohol-formaldehyde solution. **I.K.I. c.,** catgut treated with a solution of 1 part of iodine in 100 parts of a potassium iodide solution. **iodine c.,** catgut that has been immersed in a solution of iodine and iodide of potassium. **iodochromic c.,** catgut treated with a solution of iodine, potassium iodide, and potassium dichromate. **silverized c.,** catgut impregnated with silver to give it increased strength and resisting qualities.

Cath. Abbreviation for L. *cathar'ticus*, cathartic.

Catha (kath'ah). A genus of plants. **C. ed'ulis,** a plant of Arabia and Abyssinia whose leaves and twigs are employed in preparing a stimulating beverage called khat.

cathaeresis (kah-thĕr'ĕ-sis). Catheresis.

catharma (kah-thar'mah) [Gr. *katharma*]. The refuse of sacrifice: used as remedies in Greek medicine.

catharmos (kah-thar'mos) [Gr. *katharmos* a cleansing]. Incantations (hymns) against disease.

catharometer (kath"ah-rom'e-ter). An instrument for measuring the thermal conductivity of air by the rate of heat loss from a heated platinum wire.

catharsis (kah-thar'sis) [Gr. *katharsis* a cleansing]. 1. A cleansing or purgation. 2. Freud's treatment of psychoneuroses by encouraging the patient to tell everything that happens to be associated with a given train of thought, thus "purging" the mind of the repressed material which is the cause of the symptoms. Called also *psychocatharsis* and *abreaction*.

cathartic (kah-thar'tik) [Gr. *kathartikos*]. 1. Purgative or causing purgation. 2. A medicine that quickens and increases the evacuation from the bowels and produces purgation. See *purgative*. **bulk c.,** one which stimulates evacuation of the bowel by increasing the bulk of the feces.

cathectic (kah-thek'tik). Pertaining to cathexis.

Cathelin's segregator (kat-laz') [Fernand *Cathelin*, Paris urologist, born 1873]. See under *segregator*.

cathemoglobin (kath"em-o-glo'bin). A substance produced by oxidizing hemochromogen. It consists of oxidized heme and denatured globin.

cathepsin (kah-thep'sin). A proteinase found in most cells, which takes part in cell autolysis and in the self-digestion of tissues.

catheresis (kah-thĕr'ĕ-sis) [Gr. *kathairesis* a reduction]. 1. Weakness caused by medicine. 2. A mild action.

catheretic (kath"ĕ-ret'ik). 1. Mildly caustic. 2. Weakening or prostrating.

catheter (kath'ĕ-ter) [Gr. *kathetēr*]. A tubular surgical instrument for withdrawing fluids from a cavity of the body, especially one for introduction into the bladder through the urethra for the withdrawal of urine. **bicoudate c., c. bicoudé,** a twice-bent Mercier catheter. **Bozeman's c., Bozeman-Fritsch c.,** a double-current uterine catheter. **c. coudé,** an elbowed c. **c. à demeure,** a catheter that is held in position in the urethra. **de Pezzer c.,** a self-retaining catheter having a bulbous extremity. **elbowed c.,** one with a sharp bend near the beak: used principally in cases of enlarged prostate. **eustachian c.,** an instrument for extending the eustachian tube and for treating diseases of the middle ear. **faucial c.,** a eustachian catheter to be used through the fauces. **female c.,** a short catheter for passage through the female urethra. **flexible c.,** Nélaton's c. **Fritsch's c.,** Bozeman-Fritsch c. **Gouley's c.,** a solid, curved steel instrument, grooved on its inferior surface so that it can be passed over a guide through a urethral stricture. **indwelling c.,** a catheter that is held in position in the urethra. **Itard's c.,** a variety of eustachian catheter. **lobster-tail c.,** one with three joints at the tip. **Mercier's c.,** a flexible catheter elbowed at the end: used in hypertrophied prostate. **Nélaton's c.,** a catheter of soft India rubber. **Pezzer's c.** See *de Pezzer c.* **Phillips' c.,** a urethral catheter with a woven filiform guide. **prostatic c.,** a catheter having a short angular tip for passing an enlarged prostate. **railway c.,** a straight elastic catheter with an open end to be introduced with a filiform guide in cases of stricture. **Schrötter's c.,** a hard-rubber catheter of varying caliber, used for dilating laryngeal strictures. **self-retaining c.,** a catheter so constructed as to be retained at will and effect a drainage of the bladder. **Skene's c.,** a strong glass self-retaining catheter for the female bladder. **soft c.,** Nélaton's c. **Squire's c.,** a vertebrated catheter. **two-way c.,** a form used in irrigation. **vertebrated c.,** a catheter made in small sections fitted together so as to be flexible. **whistle-tip c.,** a catheter with a terminal opening as well as a lateral one. **winged c.,** a catheter with two projections on the end to retain it in the bladder.

catheterism (kath'ĕ-ter-izm). The habit of using a catheter.

catheterization (kath"ĕ-ter-i-za'shun). The employment or passage of a catheter. **cardiac c.,** passage of a small catheter into a vein in the arm and through the blood vessels into the heart, permitting the securing of blood samples, determination of intracardiac pressure, and detection of cardiac anomalies. **hepatic vein c.,** passage of a cardiac catheter through an arm vein, right atrium, inferior vena cava, and hepatic vein, into a small hepatic venule, for recording of intrahepatic venous pressures. **laryngeal c.,** insertion of a catheter into the larynx, for the evacuation of secretions or introduction of a gas. **retrourethral c.,** passage through the urethra of a catheter first introduced through an incision into the bladder, and then passed through the internal urethral orifice.

catheterize (kath'ĕ-ter-īz). To introduce a catheter within a body cavity; usually used to designate the passage of a catheter into the bladder for the withdrawal of urine.

catheterostat (kath-e'ter-o-stat). A holder for containing and sterilizing catheters.

cathetometer (kath"e-tom'e-ter). An instrument for aiding in the reading of thermometers, burets, etc.

cathexis (kah-thek'sis) [Gr. *kathexis*]. Concentration of mental or emotional energy upon an idea or object.

cathisophobia (kath"ĭ-so-fo'be-ah) [Gr. *kathizein* to sit down + *phobia*]. Akathisia.

cathodal (kath'o-dal). Of or pertaining to the cathode.

cathode (kath'ōd) [Gr. *kata* down + *hodos* way]. The negative electrode or pole of a galvanic circuit; the electrode through which a current leaves a nerve or other substance.

cathodic (kah-thod'ik). 1. Pertaining to or emanating from a cathode. 2. Efferent or centrifugal, as applied to the course of nervous influence.

catholicon (kah-thol'ĭ-kon) [Gr. *katholikos* general]. A panacea or universal medicine.

catholyte (kath'o-lit). That portion of an electrolyte that adjoins the cathode.

cathomycin (kath'o-mi"sin). Trade mark for preparations of novobiocin.

cation (kat'i-on) [Gr. *kata* down + *iōn* going]. The element or elements of an electrolyte which in electrochemical decomposition appear at the negative pole or cathode; an electropositive element (opposed to *anion*). Cations include all the metals and hydrogen. In reactions cations are indicated by a dot or a plus sign, as $H^{\cdot}$ or H^{+}.

cationic (kat"ĭ-on'ik). Pertaining to or containing a cation.

cationogen (kat″ĭ-on′o-jen). A compound which may become or liberate a cation in the body.

cativi (kah-te′ve). A parasitic skin disease of Central America, resembling pinta.

catlin (kat′lin). A long, straight, sharp-pointed, doubled-edged knife used in amputations.

catling (kat′ling). Catlin.

catoptric (kah-top′trik) [Gr. *katoptrikos* in a mirror]. Pertaining to a reflected image, or to reflected light.

catoptrics (kah-top′triks). That branch of physics which treats of reflected light.

catoptrophobia (kat″op-tro-fo′be-ah) [Gr. *katoptron* mirror + *phobia*]. Morbid dread of mirrors.

catoptroscope (kah-top′tro-skōp) [Gr. *katoptron* mirror + *skopein* to examine]. An instrument for examining objects by reflected light.

catotropia (kat″o-tro′pe-ah). Katotropia.

Cattani's serum (kah-tan′ez) [Giuseppina *Cattani*, Italian pathologist, 1859–1914]. See under *serum*.

cauda (kaw′dah), pl. *cau′dae* [L.]. A tail, or taillike appendage; in anatomical nomenclature, a general term for a structure resembling such an appendage. **c. cerebel′li,** vermis. **c. cor′poris stria′ti,** c. nuclei caudati. **c. epididym′idis** [N A, B N A], the lower part of the epididymis, where the ductus epididymidis is continuous with the ductus deferens. Called also *tail of epididymis.* **c. equi′na** [N A, B N A], the sheaf of roots of the lower spinal nerves descending in the spinal canal from their point of attachment to the spinal cord to the site of their emergence between the vertebrae. **c. he′licis** [N A, B N A], the termination of the posterior margin of the cartilage of the helix. **c. lie′nis,** extremitas anterior lienis. **c. nu′clei cauda′ti** [N A, B N A], the part of the caudate nucleus that tapers off from the body, curves around in the roof of the inferior horn of the lateral ventricle, and extends rostrally as far as the amygdaloid nucleus. Called also *tail of caudate nucleus.* **c. pancre′atis** [N A, B N A], the left extremity of the pancreas, usually in contact with the medial aspect of the spleen and the junction of the transverse and descending colon. Called also *tail of pancreas.*

caudad (kaw′dad). Directed toward a cauda or tail; opposite to cephalad.

caudae (kaw′de) [L.]. Plural of *cauda.*

caudal (kaw′dal). 1. Pertaining to a cauda. 2. Denoting a position more toward the cauda, or tail, than some specified point of reference; same as inferior, in human anatomy. See *caudalis.*

caudalis (kaw-da′lis). Pertaining to the cauda (tail), or to the inferior end of the body; in official anatomical terminology, used to designate relationship to the distal, posterior, or inferior extremity of an organ or part.

caudalward (kaw′dal-ward). Toward the caudal or posterior end.

Caudamoeba (kaw″dah-me′bah). A genus of ameba. **C. sinen′sis,** a species of ameba, found in dysentery stools in China, characterized by its attenuate posterior end drawn out in a taillike caudostyle.

caudate (kaw′dāt) [L. *caudatus*]. Having a tail.

caudatolenticular (kaw-da″to-len-tik′u-lar). Pertaining to the caudate and lenticular nuclei of the striatum.

caudatum (kaw-da′tum) [L.]. The nucleus caudatus.

caudex (kaw′deks), pl. *cau′dices* or *caudexes* [L.]. A stem or stemlike part. **c. cere′bri,** pedunculus cerebri.

caudiduct (kaw′de-dukt) [L. *cauda* tail + *ducere* to draw]. To draw in a caudal direction.

caudocephalad (kaw-do-sef′ah-lad) [L. *cauda* tail + Gr. *kephalē* head + L. *ad* toward]. 1. Proceeding in a direction from the tail toward the head; cephalad. 2. In both a caudal and a cephalic direction.

caul (kawl). 1. A piece of amnion which sometimes envelops a child's head at birth. 2. The omentum, usually used to designate the greater omentum. **pseudoperitoneal c.,** a pseudomembrane formed about the colon.

Caulk punch [John R. *Caulk*, St. Louis urologist, 1881–1938]. See under *punch.*

Caulobacter (kaw″lo-bak′ter) [Gr. *kaulos* stalk + *baktron* a staff]. A genus of microorganisms of the family Caulobacteraceae, suborder Pseudomonadineae, order Pseudomonadales, occurring as stalked, curved, rod-shaped cells, the long axis of the cell coinciding with the long axis of the stalk. The type species is *C. vibrioi′des.*

Caulobacteraceae (kaw″lo-bak″ter-a′se-e). A family of Schizomycetes (order Pseudomonadales, suborder Pseudomonadineae), occurring as nonfilamentous rod-shaped bacteria singly or in pairs or short chains, in fresh or salt water. It includes five genera, *Caulobacter, Gallionella, Nevskia,* and *Siderophacus.*

Caulobacteriineae (kaw″lo-bak-te-re-in′e-e). A name formerly given a suborder of microorganisms now considered to constitute a family (Caulobacteraceae) of the suborder Pseudomonadineae, order Pseudomonadales.

caumesthesia (kaw″mes-the′ze-ah) [Gr. *kauma* burn + *aisthēsis* perception]. A condition in which, with a low temperature, the patient experiences a sense of burning heat.

causal (kaw′zal). Pertaining to a cause; directed against a cause.

causalgia (kaw-zal′je-ah) [Gr. *kausos* heat + *-algia*]. A burning pain, often accompanied by trophic skin changes, due to a wound or other injury of a peripheral nerve.

causative (kawz′ah-tiv). Effective as a cause or agent.

cause (kawz) [L. *causa*]. That which brings about any condition or produces any effect. **constitutional c.,** one within the body which is not restricted to a specific site. **exciting c.,** one which leads directly to a specific condition. **immediate c.,** a cause which is operative at the beginning of the specific effect. **local c.,** one which is not general or constitutional, but is confined to the site where the effect is produced. **predisposing c.,** anything which renders a person more liable to a specific condition without actually producing it. **primary c.,** the principal factor contributing to the production of a specific result. **proximate c.,** that which immediately precedes and produces an effect. **remote c.,** any cause which does not immediately precede and produce a specific condition; a predisposing, secondary, or ultimate cause. **secondary c.,** one which is supplemental to the primary cause. **specific c.,** one which produces a special or specific effect. **ultimate c.,** the earliest factor, in point of time, that has contributed to production of a specific result.

caustic (kaws′tik) [L. *causticus;* Gr. *kaustikos*]. 1. Burning or corrosive; destructive to living tissues. 2. Having a burning taste. 3. An escharotic or corrosive agent. **Churchill's iodine c.,** a caustic solution of iodine and potassium iodide in water. **Filhos's c.,** 5 parts of potassium hydroxide and 1 part of quicklime. **Landolfi's c.,** a compound containing chlorides of antimony, bromine, gold, and zinc. **Lugol's c.,** 1 part each of iodine and potassium iodide dissolved in 2 parts of water. **lunar c.,** silver nitrate. **mitigated c.,** silver nitrate diluted with potassium nitrate. **Plunket's c.,** a caustic paste made of 60 parts of arsenic, 100 of sulfur, and 480 each of *Ranunculus acris* and *Ranunculus flammula.* **Rousselot's c.,** a caustic containing red mercuric sulfide, burnt sponge, and arsenous acid. **Vienna c.,** caustic potash with lime. **zinc c.,** a mixture of 1 part of zinc chloride and 3 parts of flour.

causticize (kaws′tĭ-sīz). To render caustic.

cauter (kaw′ter) [Gr. *kauter*]. A metallic instrument to be heated and used in actual cautery.

cauterant (kaw′ter-ant). 1. Any caustic material or application. 2. Caustic.

cauterization (kaw″ter-i-za′shun). The application of a cautery or caustic.

cautery (kaw′ter-e) [L. *cauterium;* Gr. *kautērion*]. 1. The application of a caustic substance, a hot iron, an electric current, or other means of killing tissue. 2. A substance or hot iron used in cauterization. **actual c.** 1. Fire, a lens, a red-hot iron, or the moxa, used as a cauterizing agent. 2. The application of an agent that actually burns the flesh. **button c.,** an iron disk with a handle, to be used as a cautery. **chemical c.,** chemicocautery. **cold c.,** cautery produced by the application of carbon dioxide. **Corrigan's c.,** a form of button cautery. **dento-electric c.,** a form of galvanocautery for dental use. **electric c., galvanic c.** See *galvanocautery.* **gas c.,** cauterization by means of a specially arranged jet of burning gas. **Paquelin's c.,** a platinum point for use in cauterizing: hollow and filled with platinum sponge, through which a heated hydrocarbon vapor is blown. **Percy c.,** an electric cautery introduced into the uterus and maintained at a temperature not sufficient to cause any charring of the tissues, but merely to cook the whole area, the heat being sufficient to destroy malignant cells without devitalizing healthy tissue: used in inoperable carcinoma of the cervix. Called also *cold iron method.* **potential c.,** cauterization by an escharotic without applying heat. **solar c.,** cauterization by means of the rays of the sun concentrated with a lens or mirror. **Souttar's c.,** a steam-heated cautery producing a constant temperature of about 100°C. used to produce coagulation. **steam c.,** atmocausis. **sun c.,** cauterization by the rays of the sun concentrated by a lens. **virtual c.,** potential c.

cava (ka′vah) [L.]. 1. Plural of *cavum.* 2. A vena cava.

caval (ka′val). Pertaining to a vena cava.

cavascope (kav′ah-skōp) [L. *cavum* hollow + Gr. *skopein* to examine]. An instrument for illuminating and examining a cavity.

cave (kāv) [L. *cavum*]. A small enclosed space within the body or an organ. See under *cavity* and *cavum.*

cavern (kav′ern). A pathologic cavity, such as occurs in the lung in tuberculosis. **c's of corpora cavernosa of penis,** cavernae corporum cavernosorum penis. **c's of corpus spongiosum,** cavernae corporis spongiosi.

caverna (ka-ver′nah), pl. *caver′nae* [L.]. A general term used in B N A terminology to designate a cavity. **caver′nae corpo′ris spongio′si** [N A], the dilatable spaces within the corpus spongiosum of the penis, which fill with blood and become distended with erection. Called also *caverns of corpus spongiosum.* **caver′nae corpo′rum cavernoso′rum pe′nis** [N A, B N A], the dilatable spaces within the corpora cavernosa of the penis, which fill with blood and become distended with erection. Called also *caverns of corpora cavernosa of penis.*

caverniloquy (kav″er-nil′o-kwe) [L. *caverna* cavity + *loqui* to speak]. The low-pitched pectoriloquy indicative of a cavity.

cavernitis (kav″er-ni′tis). Inflammation of the corpora cavernosa or corpus spongiosum of the penis. **fibrous c.,** Peyronie's disease.

cavernoma (kav″er-no′mah), pl. *caverno′mas, cavernoma′ta.* Angioma cavernosum. **c. lymphat′icum,** lymphangioma cavernosum.

cavernoscope (kav′er-no-skōp″). An instrument for viewing pulmonary cavities. It is pushed through an intercostal space and on into the cavity.

cavernoscopy (kav″er-nos′ko-pe). The inspection of pulmonary cavities by the aid of a cavernoscope.

cavernositis (kav″er-no-si′tis). Cavernitis.

cavernostomy (kav″er-nos′to-me). Operative drainage of a pulmonary abscess cavity.

cavernous (kav′er-nus) [L. *cavernosus*]. Containing caverns or hollow spaces.

Cavia (ka′ve-ah). A genus of small rodents. **C. coba′ya,** the guinea pig.

cavilla (kah-vil′ah). Os sphenoidale.

cavitary (kav′ĭ-ta″re). 1. Characterized by the presence of a cavity or cavities. 2. Any entozoon with a body space or alimentary canal.

cavitas (kav′ĭ-tas), pl. *cavita′tes* [L., from *cavus* hollow]. A hollow space or depression. Called also *cavity.* **c. den′tis,** cavum dentis. **c. glenoida′lis** [N A, B N A], a depression in the lateral angle of the scapula for articulation with the humerus. Called also *glenoid cavity.*

cavitates (kav″ĭ-tah′tēz) [L.]. Plural of *cavitas.*

cavitation (kav″ĭ-ta′shun). The formation of cavities, as in pulmonary tuberculosis.

Cavite fever (kah-ve′tah) [*Cavite,* a town in the Philippine Islands]. See under *fever.*

cavitis (ka-vi′tis). Inflammation of a vena cava.

cavity (kav′ĭ-te) [L. *cavitas*]. 1. A hollow place or space; especially a space within the body or in one of its organs. See also *cavitas* and *cavum.* 2. In dentistry, the lesion, or area of destruction of elements of a tooth, produced by dental caries; classified as simple, compound, or complex, according to the number of surfaces involved. Also classified by Greene Vardiman Black into five groups on the basis of similarity of treatment required. (See table for Black's Classification of Tooth Cavities, to which a sixth group is sometimes

BLACK'S CLASSIFICATION OF TOOTH CAVITIES

Class I. Cavities beginning as structural defects in pits and fissures.
Class II. Cavities in the proximal surfaces of bicuspids and molars.
Class III. Cavities in the proximal surfaces of incisors and cuspids not requiring the removal of the incisal angle.
Class IV. Cavities in the proximal surfaces of incisors and cuspids which require the removal of the incisal angle.
Class V. Cavities in the gingival third of the labial, or lingual or buccal surfaces.
[Class VI. Cavities in the incisal edge or occlusal cusps due to either abrasion, erosion, or attrition.]

added.) **abdominal c.,** the cavity of the body, located between the diaphragm above and the pelvis below, which contains all the abdominal organs. Called also *cavum abdominis* [N A]. **alveolar c.** See *alveoli dentales mandibulae* and *alveoli dentales maxillae.* **amniotic c.,** the closed sac between the embryo and the amnion, containing the liquor amnii. **arachnoid c.,** cavum subdurale. **articular c.,** cavum articulare. **axial c.,** a carious lesion beginning on any axial surface of a tooth, as buccal, distal, labial, lingual, or mesial. **Baer's c.,** the cleavage cavity beneath the blastoderm. **body c.,** any natural cavity of the body, such as the thoracic, abdominal, or pelvic cavity. **bony c. of nose,** cavum nasi osseum. **buccal c.** 1. Vestibulum oris. 2. A carious lesion beginning on the buccal surface of a posterior tooth. **cleavage c.,** the cavity of the blastula; blastocoele. **complex c.,** a carious lesion which involves three or more surfaces of a tooth in its prepared state. **compound c.,** a carious lesion which involves two surfaces of a tooth in its prepared state. **c. of concha,** cavum conchae. **cotyloid c.,** acetabulum. **cranial c.,** the space enclosed by the bones of the cranium. **cutigeral c.,** the depression in the inner upper edge of a horse's hoof. **distal c.,** a carious lesion beginning on the distal surface of a tooth. **dorsal c.,** the space enclosed by the bones of the cranium and the vertebrae, considered as a unit. **epidural c.,** cavum epidurale. **faucial c.,** cavum pharyngis. **fissure c.,** a carious lesion beginning in a fissure of a tooth. **glandular c.,** a hollow sac formed by invagination of the epithelial sheath in the developing multicellular gland. **glenoid c.,** cavitas glenoidalis. **head c.,** modified somites that in lower vertebrates give rise to eye muscles. **hemal c.,** coelom. **incisal c.,** a carious lesion beginning on the incisal surface of an anterior tooth. **infraglottic c.,** cavum infraglotticum. **ischiorectal c.,** fossa ischiorectalis. **labial c.,** a carious lesion beginning on the labial surface of an anterior tooth. **laryngeal c.,** cavum laryngis. **laryngopharyngeal c.,** pars laryngea pharyngis. **lingual c.,** a carious lesion beginning on the lingual surface of a tooth. **lymph c's,** the larger lymph spaces and cisterns of the body. **marrow c.,** cavum medullare ossium. **mastoid c.,** antrum mastoideum. **Meckel's c.,** cavum trigeminale. **mediastinal c., anterior,** mediastinum anterius. **mediastinal c., posterior,** mediastinum posterius. **medullary c. of bones,** cavum medullare ossium. **mesial c.,** a carious lesion beginning on the mesial surface of a tooth. **nasal c.,** cavum nasi. **nasal c., bony,** cavum nasi osseum. **nerve c.,** pulp c. **occlusal c.,** a carious lesion beginning on the occlusal surface of a posterior tooth. **oral c.,** the cavity of the mouth. See *cavum oris* [N A]. **oral c., external,** vestibulum oris. **oral c., proper,** cavum oris proprium. **orbital c.,** orbita. **pectoral c.,** thoracic c. **pelvic c.,** the space within the walls of the pelvis. Called also *cavum pelvis.* **pericardial c.,** cavum pericardii. **peritoneal c., peritoneal c., greater,** cavum peritonei. **peritoneal c., lesser,** bursa omentalis. **pharyngeal c.,** cavum pharyngis. **pharyngolaryngeal c.,** pars laryngea pharyngis. **pharyngonasal c.,** pars nasalis pharyngis. **pharyngo-oral c.,** pars oralis pharyngis. **c. of pharynx,** cavum pharyngis. **pit c.,** a carious lesion beginning in a pit of a tooth. **pleural c.,** cavum pleurae. **pleuroperitoneal c.,** the temporarily continuous coelomic cavity in the embryo that will later be partitioned by the developing diaphragm. **popliteal c.,** fossa poplitea. **prepared c.,** one that is produced in a tooth to support and retain the filling material and still protect the tooth structure remaining after removal of all carious tissue. **proximal c.,** a carious lesion beginning on a proximal (the mesial or distal) surface of a tooth. **pulp c.,** the pulp-filled central chamber in the crown of a tooth. Called also *cavum dentis* [N A]. **rectoischiadic c.,** fossa ischiorectalis. **Retzius's c.,** spatium retropubicum. **Rosenmüller's c.,** recessus pharyngeus. **segmentation c.,** cleavage c. **c. of septum pellucidum,** cavum septi pellucidi. **serous c.,** any cavity, like that enclosed by the peritoneum or pleura, not communicating with the outside of the body, and whose lining membrane secretes serum. **sigmoid c. of radius,** incisura ulnaris radii. **sigmoid c. of ulna, greater,** incisura trochlearis ulnae. **sigmoid c. of ulna, lesser,** incisura radialis ulnae. **simple c.,** a carious lesion which involves only one surface of a tooth in its preparation, designated according to the surface involved as buccal, distal, incisal, labial, lingual, mesial, or occlusal. **somatic c.,** coelom. **somite c.,** myocoele. **splanchnic c.,** visceral c. **subarachnoid c.,** cavum subarachnoideale. **subdural c.,** cavum subdurale. **subgerminal c.** 1. Yolk cavity. 2. Cleavage cavity. **thoracic c.,** the portion of the ventral body cavity situated between the neck and the respiratory diaphragm. Called also *cavum thoracis* [N A]. **trigeminal c.,** cavum trigeminale. **tympanic c.,** auris media. **ventral c.,** the body cavity lying in front of the spinal column, composed of the mouth, throat, thorax, abdomen, and pelvis. **visceral c.,** one of the cavities of the body containing important organs, such as the cranial, thoracic, abdominal, or pelvic cavity. **yolk c.,** the open space found within the yolk of the developing ovum of some animals.

cavovalgus (ka″vo-val′gus). See *talipes cavovalgus.*

cavum (ka′vum), pl. *ca′va* [L.]. [N A, B N A] A general term used to designate a cavity or space. See also *cavitas.* **c. abdom′inis** [N A, B N A], the cavity of the body, located between the diaphragm above and the pelvis below. Called also *abdominal cavity.* **c. articula′re** [N A, B N A], the minute space of a synovial joint, enclosed by the synovial membrane and articular cartilages. Called also *articular cavity.* **c. con′chae** [N A, B N A], the inferior part of the concha of the auricle, which leads into the external acoustic meatus. **c. den′tis** [N A, B N A], the pulp-filled central cavity of a tooth. **c. doug′lasi,** excavatio rectouterina. **c. epidura′le** [N A, B N A], the space between the dura mater and the walls of the vertebral canal, containing venous plexuses and fibrous and alveolar tissue. Called also *epidural space.* **c. infraglot′ticum** [N A], the most inferior part of the laryngeal cavity, extending from the rima glottidis above to the cavity of the trachea below. Called also *infraglottic cavity.* **c. laryn′gis** [N A, B N A], the space enclosed by the walls of the larynx. Called also *laryngeal cavity.* **c. meck′lii,** c. trigeminale. **c. mediastina′le ante′rius** [B N A], mediastinum anterius. **c. mediastina′le poste′rius** [B N A], mediastinum posterius. **c. medulla′re os′sium** [N A, B N A], the spacious cavity, containing marrow, in the diaphysis of a long bone. Called also *medullary,* or *marrow, cavity.* **c. na′si** [N A, B N A], the proximal portion of the passages of the respiratory system, extending from the nares to the pharynx. Called also *nasal cavity.* **c. na′si os′seum** [N A, B N A], the space between the floor of the cranium and the roof of the mouth, extending between the pharynx posteriorly and the external nose anteriorly, and divided by a median septum. Called also *bony nasal cavity.* **c. o′ris** [N A, B N A], the cavity of the mouth and the associated structures, including the cheek, palate, oral mucosa, the glands whose ducts open into the cavity, the teeth, and the tongue. Called also *oral cavity.* **c. o′ris exter′num,** vestibulum oris. **c. o′ris pro′prium** [N A, B N A], the part of the oral cavity internal to the teeth. Called also *oral cavity proper.* **c. pec′toris,** c. thoracis. **c. pel′vis** [N A, B N A], the space within the walls of the pelvis. Called also *pelvic cavity.* **c. pericar′dii** [N A], a potential space between the visceral portion (epicardium) and the parietal portion of the serous pericardium. Called also *pericardial cavity.* **c. peritonae′i** [B N A], **c. peritone′i** [N A], the potential space between the parietal and visceral layers of the peritoneum. Called also *peritoneal cavity.* **c. pharyn′gis** [N A, B N A], the space enclosed by the walls of the pharynx. Called also *pharyngeal cavity.* **c. pleu′rae** [N A, B N A], the potential space between the parietal and visceral pleurae. Called also *pleural cavity.* **c. pul′pae,** c. dentis. **c. rectoischiad′icum,** fossa ischiorectalis. **c. ret′zii,** spatium retropubicum. **c. sep′ti pellu′cidi** [N A, B N A], the median cleft between the two laminae of the septum pellucidum; called also *cavity of septum pellucidum, fifth ventricle,* and *pseudocele.* **c. subarachnoidea′le** [N A, B N A], the space between the arachnoidea and the pia mater, containing cerebrospinal fluid and bridged by delicate trabeculae. Called also *subarachnoid space.* **c. subdura′le** [B N A], a narrow, fluid-containing space between the dura mater and arachnoid. Called also *subdural space.* **c. thora′cis** [N A, B N A], the portion of the ventral body cavity situated between the neck and the respiratory diaphragm. Called also *thoracic cavity.* **c. trigemina′le** [N A], a cavity between the two layers of the dura mater at the end of the petrous portion of the temporal bone, which contains the trigeminal ganglion. Called also *trigeminal cavity.* **c. tym′pani,** B N A term and N A alternative for *auris media.* **c. u′teri** [N A, B N A], the anteroposteriorly flattened space within the uterus, communicating on either side with the uterine tubes and below with the vagina. Called also *cavity of uterus.* **c. ver′gae,** Verga's ventricle.

cavus (kav′us) [L. "hollow"]. See *talipes cavus.*

cavy (ka′ve). A small rodent of the family Caviidae, the best known representative of which is the guinea pig.

Cazenave's disease (kahz-nahvz′) [P. L. Alphée *Cazenave*, French dermatologist, 1795–1877]. 1. Lupus erythematosus. 2. Pemphigus foliaceus. **C's lupus,** lupus erythematosus. **C's vitiligo,** alopecia areata.

Cb. Chemical symbol for *columbium*.

C.B. Abbreviation for L. *Chirurgiae Baccalaureus*, Bachelor of Surgery.

c.b.c. Abbreviation for *complete blood count*.

C. C. Abbreviation for *chief complaint*.

cc. Abbreviation for *cubic centimeter*.

CCA. Abbreviation for *chimpanzee coryza agent* (respiratory syncytial virus).

C. C. 914. A thioarsenite, *p*-carbamido-phenyl-bis (carboxymethyl-mercapto) arsine: used in treatment of intestinal amebiasis.

C. C. 1037. A thioarsenite, *p*-carbamido-phenyl-bis (2-carboxyphenyl-mercapto) arsine: used in intestinal amebiasis.

CCAT. The conglutinating complement absorption test, used in the serodiagnosis of glanders.

CCC. Abbreviation for *cathodal closure contraction*.

CCCl. Abbreviation for *cathodal closure clonus*.

CCK. Abbreviation for *cholecystokinin*.

CCl_4. Carbon tetrachloride.

$CCl_3.CHO$. Chloral.

$CCl_3.CH(OH)_2$. Chloral hydrate.

C.C.S. Abbreviation for *casualty clearing station*.

CCTe. Abbreviation for *cathodal closure tetanus*.

C.D. Abbreviation for L. *conjugata diagonalis*, the diagonal conjugate diameter of the pelvic inlet.

$C.D._{50}$. Median curative dose; a dose that abolishes symptoms in 50 per cent of the test subjects.

Cd. 1. Chemical symbol for *cadmium*. 2. Abbreviation for *caudal* or *coccygeal:* used in vertebral formulas.

Ce. Chemical symbol for *cerium*.

ceasmic (se-as′mik) [Gr. *keasma* chip]. Characterized by the persistence after birth of embryonic fissures.

cebocephalia (se″bo-se-fa′le-ah) [Gr. *kebos* monkey + *kephalē* head + *-ia*]. A developmental anomaly characterized by a monkey-like head, the nose being defective and the eyes close together.

cebocephalus (se″bo-sef′ah-lus). A fetal monster exhibiting cebocephalia.

cecal (se′kal) [L. *caecalis*]. 1. Ending in a blind passage. 2. Pertaining to the cecum. 3. Pertaining to the blind spot in the field of vision.

cecectomy (se-sek′to-me) [*cecum* + Gr. *ektomē* excision]. Surgical removal of a part of the cecum.

cecitis (se-si′tis). Inflammation of the cecum.

cecocele (se′ko-sēl). A hernia containing part of the cecum.

cecocentral (se″ko-sen′tral). Centrocecal.

cecocolic (se″ko-kol′ik). Pertaining to the cecum and the colon.

cecocolon (se″ko-ko′lon). The cecum and colon considered as a unit.

cecocoloplicopexy (se″ko-ko″lo-pli′ko-pek-se). An operation for fixing the cecum and ascending colon.

cecocolostomy (se″ko-ko-los′to-me). The surgical creation of an anastomosis between the cecum and the colon.

cecofixation (se″ko-fik-sa′shun). Cecopexy.

ceco-ileostomy (se″ko-il″e-os′to-me) [*cecum* + *ileum* + Gr. *stomoun* to provide with a mouth, or opening]. Ileocecostomy.

cecon (se′kon). Trade mark for preparations of ascorbic acid.

cecopexy (se′ko-pek″se) [*cecum* + Gr. *pēxis* fixation]. The operation of fixing the cecum to the abdominal wall to correct excessive mobility of the part.

cecoplication (se″ko-pli-ka′shun) [*cecum* + L. *plica* fold]. The operation of taking a fold in the cecum to correct ptosis of the part.

cecoptosis (se″kop-to′sis) [*cecum* + Gr. *ptōsis* falling]. Ptosis or downward displacement of the cecum.

cecorectal (se″ko-rek′tal). Pertaining to cecum and rectum.

cecorrhaphy (se-kor′ah-fe) [*cecum* + Gr. *rhaphē* suture]. Suture of the cecum.

cecosigmoidostomy (se″ko-sig″moi-dos′to-me). The surgical formation of an anastomosis between the cecum and the sigmoid.

cecostomy (se-kos′to-me) [*cecum* + Gr. *stomoun* to provide with a mouth, or opening]. The surgical creation of an artificial opening or fistula into the cecum.

cecotomy (se-kot′o-me) [*cecum* + Gr. *tomē* cut]. The operation of cutting into the cecum.

cecum (se′kum) [L. *caecum* blind, blind gut]. 1. [N A] The dilated intestinal pouch into which open the ileum, the colon, and the appendix vermiformis. 2. Any blind pouch or cul-de-sac. **cupular c. of cochlear duct, c. cupula′re duc′tus cochlea′ris** [N A], the closed blind upper end of the cochlear duct. Called also *caecum cupulare ductus cochlearis* [B N A], and *lagena*. **hepatic c.,** a pouching of the embryonic intestine which develops into the liver. **high c.,** a cecum situated higher up in the abdomen than normal. **c. mo′bile,** abnormal mobility of the cecum and lower portion of the ascending colon. **vestibular c. of cochlear duct, c. vestibula′re duc′tus cochlea′ris** [N A]. A small blind outpouching at the lower vestibular end of the cochlear duct. Called also *caecum vestibulare ductus cochlearis* [B N A].

cedilanid (se″dĭ-lan′id). Trade mark for a preparation of a crystalline digitalis glycoside (lanatoside C) in tablet form. **c.-D,** a preparation of a derivative of lanatoside C (deslanoside) in ampule form. Uses: 1. congestive heart failure; 2. auricular fibrillation; 3. paroxysmal supraventricular tachycardia.

Cediopsylla (se″de-o-sil′ah). A genus of fleas, including some of the rabbit fleas.

Cel. Abbreviation for *Celsius* (thermometric scale).

cel (sel). A unit of velocity, being the velocity of 1 cm. per second.

celarium (sĕ-la′re-um). Coelarium.

celation (se-la′shun) [L. *celare* to conceal]. The concealing of pregnancy or of the birth of a child.

-cele- (sēl). 1. [Gr. *kēlē* hernia]. A combining form signifying relationship to a tumor or swelling. 2. [Gr. *koilia* cavity]. A combining form signifying a relationship to a cavity. See also words spelled *coel-* or *-coele*.

celectome (se′lek-tōm) [Gr. *kēlē* tumor + *ektomē* excision]. An instrument for removing a piece of tissue from a tumor for examination.

celenteron (se-len′ter-on). Archenteron.

celiac (se′le-ak) [Gr. *koilia* belly]. Pertaining to the abdomen.

celiaca (se-li′ah-kah). Disease of the abdominal organs, especially celiac disease in children, which is probably identical with sprue.

celialgia (se″le-al′je-ah) [*celio-* + *-algia*]. Pain in the abdomen.

celiectasia (se″le-ek-ta′ze-ah) [*celio-* + Gr. *ektasis* distention]. Excessive size of the abdominal cavity.

celiectomy (se″le-ek′to-me) [*celio-* + Gr. *ektomē* excision]. 1. Surgical removal of any abdominal organ. 2. Excision of the celiac branches of the vagus nerve for the relief of essential hypertension.

celio- (se′le-o) [Gr. *koilia* belly]. A combining form denoting relationship to the abdomen. For words beginning thus see also words beginning *celo-* and *coelo-*.

celiocentesis (se″le-o-sen-te′sis) [*celio-* + Gr. *kentēsis* puncture]. Puncture of the abdomen.

celiocolpotomy (se″le-o-kol-pot′o-me) [*celio-* + Gr. *kolpos* vagina + *tomē* cut]. Incision into the vagina through the abdomen.

celiodynia (se″le-o-din′e-ah). Celialgia.

celio-elytrotomy (se″le-o-el″e-trot′o-me) [*celio-* + Gr. *elytron* sheath + *tomē* cut]. Celiocolpotomy.

celio-enterotomy (se″le-o-en″ter-ot′o-me) [*celio-* + *enterotomy*]. Incision through the abdominal wall into the intestine.

celiogastrotomy (se″le-o-gas-trot′o-me) [*celio-* + *gastrotomy*]. Incision through the abdominal wall into the stomach.

celiohysterectomy (se″le-o-his″ter-ek′to-me) [*celio-* + *hysterectomy*]. 1. Excision of the uterus by an abdominal incision. 2. Cesarean hysterectomy.

celiohysterotomy (se″le-o-his″ter-ot′o-me) [*celio-* + *hysterotomy*]. Opening of the uterus by an abdominal incision; cesarean section.

celioma (se-le-o′mah) [*celio-* + *-oma*]. A tumor of the abdomen.

celiomyalgia (se″le-o-mi-al′je-ah). Myocelialgia.

celiomyomectomy (se″le-o-mi″o-mek′to-me) [*celio-* + *myomectomy*]. Myomectomy by an abdominal incision.

celiomyomotomy (se″le-o-mi″o-mot′o-me) [*celio-* + *myomotomy*]. Celiomyomectomy.

celiomyositis (se″le-o-mi″o-si′tis) [*celio-* + *myositis*]. Inflammation of the abdominal muscles.

celioncus (se″le-on′kus). A tumor of the abdomen.

celioparacentesis (se″le-o-par″ah-sen-te′sis) [*celio-* + *paracentesis*]. Paracentesis of the abdomen.

celiopathy (se″le-op′ah-the) [*celio-* + Gr. *pathos* disease]. Any abdominal disease.

celiophyma (se″le-o-fi′mah). Celioncus.

celiopyosis (se″le-o-pi-o′sis) [*celio-* + *pyosis*]. Suppuration in the abdominal cavity.

celiorrhaphy (se″le-or′ah-fe) [*celio-* + Gr. *rhaphē* suture]. Suture of the abdominal wall.

celiosalpingectomy (se″le-o-sal″pin-jek′to-me) [*celio-* + *salpingectomy*]. Excision of a uterine tube through an abdominal incision.

celiosalpingotomy (se″le-o-sal″pin-got′o-me). Incision of a uterine tube through an incision in the abdominal wall.

celioscope (se′le-o-skōp) [*celio-* + Gr. *skopein* to examine]. An endoscope for examining a body cavity, especially the abdominal cavity.

celioscopy (se″le-os′ko-pe). Examination of a body cavity, especially the abdominal cavity, through a celioscope.

celiosite (se′le-o-sīt″) [*celio-* + para*site*]. An abdominal parasite.

celiothelioma (se″le-o-the″le-o′mah). Mesothelioma.

celiotomy (se″le-ot′o-me) [*celio-* + Gr. *tomē* a cut]. Surgical incision into the abdominal cavity. **vaginal c.,** the operation of entering the abdominal cavity by an incision through the vagina. **ventral c.,** the operation of entering the abdominal cavity through the abdominal wall.

celitis (se-li′tis). Any abdominal inflammation.

cell (sel) [L. *cella* compartment]. 1. Any one of the minute protoplasmic masses which make up organized tissue, consisting of a circumscribed mass of protoplasm containing a nucleus. In some of the low forms of life, as bacteria and viruses, a morphological nucleus is absent, although nucleoproteins (and genes) are present. 2. A small, more or less closed space. **A c.,** alpha c. **Abbe-Zeiss counting c.** See under *chamber.* **acid c.,** a large cell of the stomach glands of a kind believed to secrete the acid of the gastric juice. **acidophilic c.,** a cell having an affinity for acid dyes. **acoustic hair c.,** any one of the cells provided with bristles that serve as sensory receptors in the organ of Corti. **adelomorphous c.,** a variety of columnar cells forming the greater part of the tubules of the gastric glands, the other cells of the tubules being the delomorphous cells. They are believed to secrete pepsinogen. Called also *chief c's, principal c's, zymogenic c's,* and *peptic c's* **adipose c.,** a fat cell. **adventitial c's,** Marchand's name for the phagocytic cells, especially those close to the blood vessels; called also *perithelial c's* and *perithelium.* **agger nasi c's,** the cells of the anterior part of the ethmoid crest. **air c.,** one containing air, such as an alveolus of the lungs (alveolus pulmonis) or one of the air-containing cells of the auditory tube (cellulae pneumaticae tubae auditivae). **albuminous c.** See *serous c.* **algoid c's,** cells resembling algae, seen in cases of chronic diarrhea. **alpha c's.** 1. Cells in the islands of the pancreas containing large granules which stain a brilliant red with azocarmine or pale red with eosin, and are insoluble in alcohol. 2. The so-called acidophil cells of the anterior lobe of the hypophysis. **alveolar c.,** pneumonocyte. **Alzheimer's c's.** 1. Giant glia cells with large prominent nuclei found in the brain in pseudosclerosis. 2. Degenerated astrocytes. **amacrine c.** See *amacrine,* def. 2. **ameboid c.,** any cell which is able to change its form and move about. **Anitschkow's c.** See *Anitschkow's myocyte* under *myocyte.* **antipodal c's,** a group of four cells in the early embryo. **apocrine c's.** See *apocrine.* **apolar c.,** a nerve cell with no processes or poles. **apoplectic c.,** a cavity in the brain formed by effusion of blood in apoplexy. **apotrophic c's,** hypothetical cells in the peripheral stump of a divided nerve, which attract young axons from the proximal stump to aid in regeneration. **argentaffine c's,** cells with granules which stain with silver salts, found among the crypts of intestinal epithelium and of the gastric mucosa: called also *chromaffine c's.* **arkyochrome c.,** a nerve cell in which the Nissl bodies are arranged in a network. **Armanni-Ebstein c's,** epithelial cells in the terminal part of the first convoluted renal tubule containing deposits of glycogen: a lesion characteristic of diabetes. **Aschoff's c's,** a type of giant cell as seen in the rheumatic nodule. **auditory c's,** cells in the internal ear bearing the auditory hairs. **B c's.** See *beta c's.* **balloon c's,** peculiar degenerated cells in the vesicles of herpes zoster. **banana c's,** cells of banana frequently found in feces and which may be mistaken for cestodes. **band c.** See *staff c.* **basal c.,** the name applied to the early keratinocyte, present in the basal layer of the epidermis. **basket c.** 1. A cell of the cerebellar cortex whose axon gives off brushes of fibrils, forming a basket-like nest in which the body of each Purkinje cell rests. 2. Long spindle-shaped elements with a fibrillary protoplasm between the glandular cells and the basement membrane of the sweat glands and glands of the oral cavity. **basophilic c.,** a cell staining readily with basic dyes. **battery c.,** one of the chambers of a galvanic battery, containing its fluids and essential elements. **beaker c.,** goblet c. **Beale's ganglion c's,** bipolar cells with one process coiled around the other. **Bergmann's c's,** peculiar glial cells in the molecular layer of the cerebellar cortex having dendrites which extend outward through that layer. **berry c.,** a term applied to plasma cells and plasmacytoid reticulum cells whose cytoplasm contains numerous transparent bluish vesicles, most probably protein in nature; found in disorders associated with pronounced hypergammaglobulinemia. Called also *grape c.* and *morular c.* **beta c's,** cells in the pancreas which make up most of the bulk of the islands of Langerhans: they contain granules which are soluble in alcohol. **Betz's c's,** large pyramidal ganglion cells forming one of the layers of the motor area of the gray matter of the brain; called also *giant pyramids* and *giant pyramidal c's.* **Bevan-Lewis c's,** certain pyramidal cells in the motor cortex of the brain. **bichromate c., dichromate c.** See *Grenet c.* **bipolar c.,** a nerve cell with two processes. **bladder c's,** Zander's cells; swollen cells of Rauber's layer of the epidermis of the tips of the fingers and toes of the embryo. **blast c.,** the least differentiated blood cell type without commitment as to its particular series. **bloated c.,** a swollen fattened astrocyte. **blood c's.** See under *corpuscle.* **bone c.,** a nucleated cell occupying each a separate lacuna of bone. **border c's.** See *delomorphous c's.* **Böttcher's c's,** cells of the cochlea, occurring in a single layer on the basilar membrane. **breviradiate c's,** neuroglia cells which have short prolongations. **bristle c's,** the hair cells associated with the auditory and cochlear nerves. **bronchic c.,** an air cell of the lungs. **brood c.,** mother cell. **C c's,** cells in the islands of Langerhans, especially in the guinea pig, which contain no granules. **Cajal c.** 1. An astrocyte. 2. One of the neuroglia cells arranged horizontally in the stratum zonale of the cerebral cortex. **caliciform c.,** goblet c. **cameloid c.,** an elliptocyte. **capsule c.,** amphicyte. **cartilage c's,** cells embedded in the lacunae of the cartilages. **caryochrome c's.** See *karyochrome c's.* **castration c's,** peculiar cells observed in the anterior pituitary in gonadal insufficiency. **caudate c's,** neuroglia cells of the gray matter having several streaming prolongations like the tail of a comet; called also *cometal c's.* **central c.** See *adelomorphous c.* **centro-acinar c's,** the intra-acinar beginnings of the intralobular duct system of the pancreas. **chalice c.,** goblet c. **chief c's.** 1. See *adelomorphous c's.* 2. The chromophobe cells of the pars distalis of the hypophysis: called also *principal cells* or *reserve cells.* 3. The epithelial cells of the parathyroid glands which have a clear, pale cytoplasm and a large vesicular nucleus: called also *principal cells.* **chromaffin c's.** See *argentaffine c's* and *chromaffin.* **ciliated c.,** any cell with movable cilia. **Clarke's c's,** pigmented cells in the dorsal nucleus of the spinal cord. **Claudius' c's,** large nucleated cells on each side of the arches of Corti. **clear c's,** water-clear cells. **cleavage c.,** any one of the cells derived from the fertilized ovum by mitosis; a blastomere. **clump c's,** round, thick, pigmented cells seen in the sphincter muscle of the iris. **cochlear c's,** specialized cells of the cochlea, some of which are percipient elements connected with the auditory nerve; others, hair cells associated with the cochlear nerve. **columnar c.,** an epithelial cell which is taller than it is broad. **cometal c's,** caudate c's. **commissural c's,** heteromeral c's. **compound granule c.,** a macrophage developed from microglia or from an adventitial histiocyte: called also *gitter c.* **cone c's,** retinal cone c's. **connective tissue c's,** a general name for the cellular elements of the various forms of connective tissue. See *fibroblast.* **contractile fiber c's,** the spindle-shaped and nucleated cells which, collected into bundles, make up unstriped muscular fiber. **corneal c.,** a modified connective tissue cell occupying each corneal space. **c's of Corti,** the hair cells on the outer surface of the organ of Corti. **counting c.** See under *chamber.* **cover c.,** any cell which covers and protects other cells; especially any long epithelial cell of the outer layer of the taste buds. **crescent c's,** demilune c's. **cribrose c.,** a cell whose walls are perforated with numerous sievelike pores. **cuboid c.,** an epithelial cell of which the transverse and vertical diameters are equal. **Custer c's,** cells with long delicate protoplasmic processes replacing the lymphoid tissue of lymph nodes in reticuloendothelial disease. **cylindric c.,** columnar c. **D c's,** cells in the islands of Langerhans of the pancreas which are filled with small granules staining with aniline blue. **Daniell c.,** a form of two-fluid cell for the galvanic battery: the collecting plate is of copper, and the fluids (dilute sulfuric acid and copper sulfate solution) are separated by a porous diaphragm. **daughter c.,** any cell formed by the division of a mother cell. **Davidoff's c's,** Paneth's c's. **decidual c's,** connective-tissue cells of the uterine mucous membrane, enlarged and specialized during pregnancy. **Deiters' c's.** 1. The outer phalangeal cells of the organ of Corti. See under *supporting c's.* 2. Neuroglia cells. **delomorphous c's,** the supposed acid-secreting cells of the stomach. They are large cells lying between the basement membrane of the tubules of the fundic glands and the adelomorphous cells. Called also *acid c's, oxyntic c's,* and *parietal c's.* **demilune c's,** crescents of Giannuzzi. **dentin c.,** odontoblast. **dome c's,** the large cells which compose the epitrichium of the fetus. **Dorothy Reed c's,** Sternberg-Reed c's. **dust c's,** macrophages containing carbon or dust particles found in the alveoli of the lungs. **Edelmann's c.,** kinetocyte. **egg c.,** the immature ovum when it is embedded within the ovary. **elementary c's, embryonal c's,** small round cells produced by cleavage of the ovum. **emigrated c.,** a leukocyte which has passed through the wall of a blood vessel into the neighboring tissue. **enamel c.,** ameloblast. **encasing c.,** cover c. **endothelioid c's,** large protoplasmic cells frequently seen in disease of the blood-making organs and believed by some to be derived from the endothelial lining of the blood vessels and lymph vessels. **entoplastic c's,** those in which the processes of metamorphosis take place within their substance and not on their surface. **ependymal c's,** the cells of the ependyma. **epidermic c's,** the cells of the epidermis. **epithelial c's,** cells which cover the surface of the body and line its cavities. **epithelioid c's.** 1. Cells of connective tissue arranged so as to simulate epithelium. 2. Large phagocytes with prominent, pale-staining nuclei, characteristic of leprosy, tuberculosis, etc. **erythroid c's,** blood cells of the erythrocytic series. **ethmoidal c's, bony,** cellulae ethmoidales osseae. **fat c.,** a connective tissue cell bloated with stored fat. **fatty granule c.,** microglia containing fat. **ferment c.,** a cell which secretes a ferment. **Ferrata's c.** See *hemohistioblast.* **fiber c.,** any elongated and linear cell. **flagellate c.,** any motile cell having long cilia for propulsion. **floor c's,** the cells of the floor of the arch of Corti. **Foà-Kurloff c.,** inclusion-containing non-granular leukocytes of guinea pigs: the inclusions may be arranged in granulations and rods of varying size. **foam c's.** 1. Cells with a peculiar vacuolated appearance due to the presence of complex lipoids. Such cells are seen notably in xanthoma and have, therefore, been termed *xanthoma c's.* 2. Same as *Mikulicz's c's.* **follicle c.,** one of the cells which make up a follicle. **follicle c's of ovarian follicle,** modified epithelial cells that surround the ovum in a primary follicle and, in a vesicular follicle, form the stratum granulosum and cumulus oophorus and secrete the follicular fluid; after ovulation they are transformed into glandular cells of the corpus luteum. **follicular lutein c's,** lutein c's. **foot c's.** 1. Basal cells. 2. Sertoli's cells. **formative c.,** an embryonal cell. **Foulis' c's,** large nucleated epithelial cells seen in fluids from malignant ovarian cysts. **Fuller c.,** a battery cell resembling the Grenet cell, but employing a mixture of mercury and water as an amalgamating agent. **fusiform c.** Same as *spindle c.* **gametoid c's,** cancer cells resembling reproductive cells. **ganglion c.,** a form of large nerve cell characteristic of ganglia. **Gaucher's c.,** a large and distinctive cell characteristic of Gaucher's disease, with one or more eccentrically placed nuclei and with fine wavy fibrils running parallel to the long axis of the cell, imparting a wrinkled, tissue-paper appearance to the gray or bluish opaque cytoplasm. **Gegenbaur's c.,** osteoblast. **genitaloid c's,** primary germ c's. **germ c's,** the cells of an organism whose function it is to reproduce the kind. **germinal c.,** dividing cells of the embryonic brain or spinal cord; neuroblasts. **ghost c.,** one which appears only as a shadowy outline. **c's of Giannuzzi.** See under *crescent.* **giant c.,** a very large cell

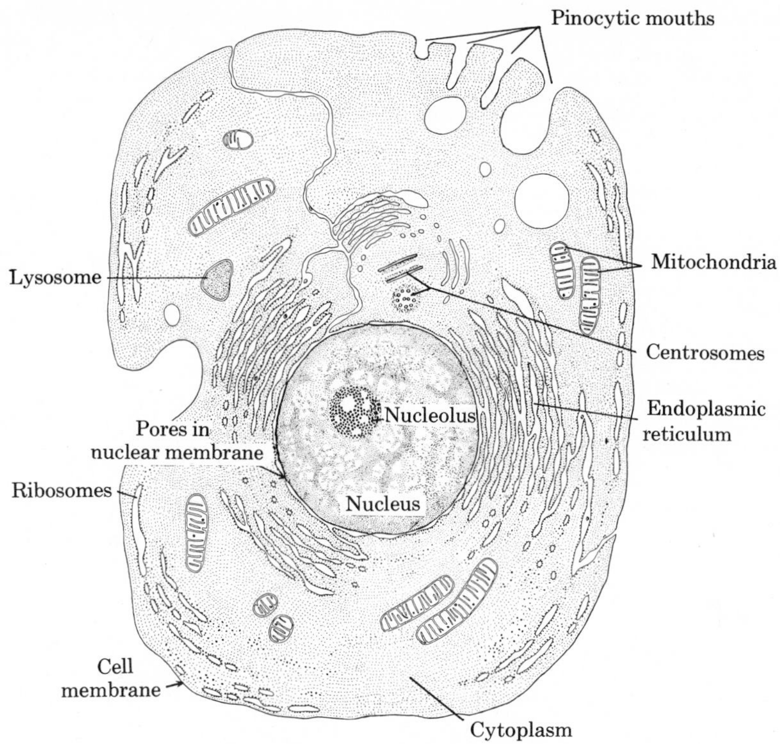

TYPICAL ANIMAL CELL
(Modified from Scientific American)

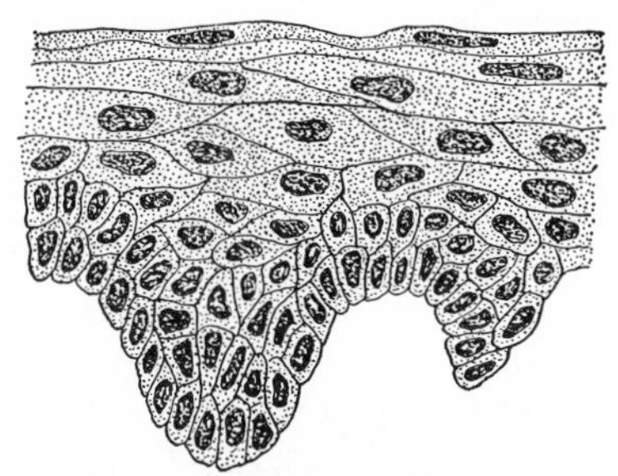

Stratified squamous, esophagus

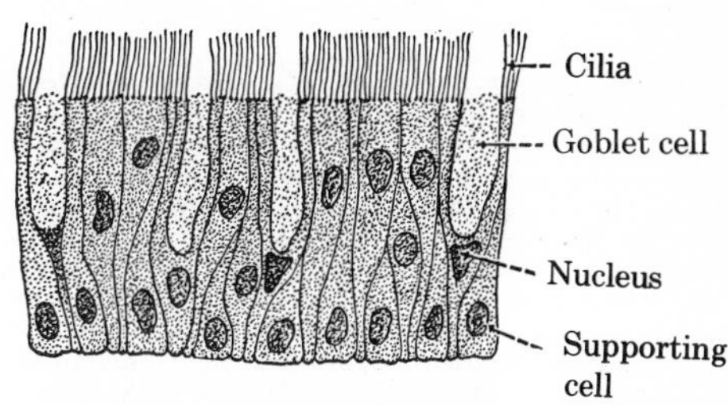

Pseudostratified ciliated columnar, trachea

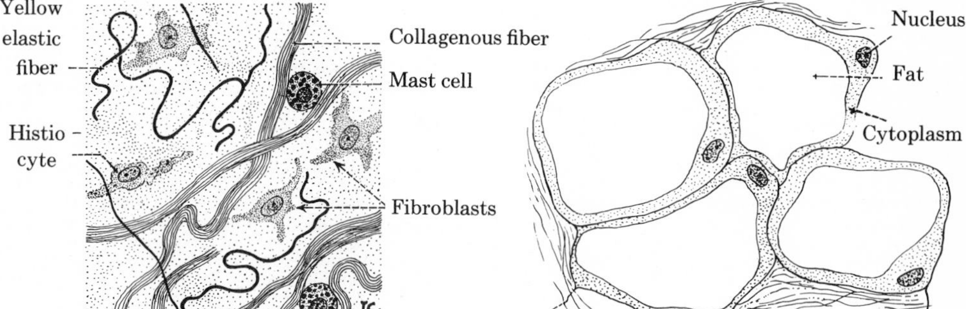

Fibroelastic, fascia

Adipose

VARIOUS TYPES OF EPITHELIAL CELL
(King and Showers)

frequently having several nuclei. The name is applied to the megakaryocytes of bone marrow and also to the giant cells which occur in the lesion of tuberculosis and other infectious granulomas and about foreign bodies. **giant pyramidal c's.** See *Betz's c's.* **Gierke's c's,** small, deeply staining nerve cells which constitute the chief cells of the substantia gelatinosa. **gitter c.,** microglia. **Gley's c's,** cells in the interstitial tissue of the testicle. **glia c.,** a cell of the neuroglia. **globuliferous c's,** leukocytes that have taken up red corpuscles. **goblet c.,** a form of epithelial cell containing mucin and bulged out like a goblet. Cf. *ptyocrinous.* **Golgi's c's,** astrocytes; nerve cells with very short processes in the posterior horns of the spinal cord. In Golgi cells of *type I* the axons pass out of the gray matter, in those of *type II* the axons do not pass out of the gray matter. **Goormaghtigh c's,** juxtaglomerular c's. **granular c.,** the name applied to a keratinocyte in the stratum granulosum of the epidermis, when it has become flattened and rhomboidal in shape, and contains a dense collection of variously sized darkly staining granules, before it dies and desquamates. **granule c's,** phagocytic microglia. **granulosa c.,** a cell of the membrana granulosa of the ovary. An ovarian tumor originating in such cells is called granulosa tumor, folliculoma, or oophoroma. **granulosa-lutein c's,** lutein cells of follicular origin. **grape c.,** berry c. **gravity c.,** a battery cell like the Sieman and Halske, but the fluids are superimposed upon each other with no intervening diaphragm, being kept partly separate by the force of gravity. **Grenet c.,** a battery cell with a carbon-collecting plate, the fluid and depolarizer being a solution of potassium dichromate. **Grove c.,** a two-fluid galvanic cell charged with dilute sulfuric and nitric acids, containing respectively an element of zinc and of platinum. **guanine c.,** a small oval variety of cell filled with white, refracting granules of guanine. **gustatory c's,** the taste cells. **gyrochrome c.** See *gyrochrome.* **hair c's,** epithelial cells with hairlike processes. **Hargraves' c.,** L.E. c. **heart-disease c's, heart-failure c's, heart-lesion c's,** macrophages containing granules of iron: found in the sputum in chronic bronchitis from heart disease. **hecatomeral c's,** cells of gray matter of the spinal cord whose axis cylinder processes divide, send one branch into the white substance of the same side of the cord, and another into the anterolateral columns of the other side. **heckle c.,** prickle c. **Heidenhain's c's,** the adelomorphous and delomorphous cells of the gastric glands. **HeLa c's,** cells of the first continuously cultured carcinoma strain, descended from a human cervical carcinoma: used in the study of life processes, including viruses, at the cell level. **Henle's c's,** large granular nucleated cells in the seminiferous tubules. **Hensen's c's,** the outermost supporting cells covering the organ of Corti. See under *supporting c's.* **hepatic c's,** the polygonal epithelial cells that constitute the substance of an acinus of the liver. **heteromeral c's,** nerve cells of the gray matter of the spinal cord whose axis-cylinder processes pass to the white matter of the opposite side. **Hill's c.,** gravity c. **Hodgkin's c's,** Sternberg-Reed c's. **Hofbauer c's,** large chromophilic cells in the chorionic villi which are probably macrophages. **horn c's.** 1. Epithelial cells that have lost their protoplasm, have sharp edges and look horny. 2. Any ganglion cell of the horns of the spinal cord. **Hortega c.,** microglia. **Hürthle c's,** large eosinophilic cells sometimes found in the thyroid gland. They seem to be parathyroid rests included by chance in thyroid tissue. **hyperchromatic c.,** one that stains more intensely than is typical of its cell type. **ichthyoid c's.** See *megaloblast.* **incasing c's,** a single layer of fusiform cells around the gustatory cells of the tongue. **indifferent c.,** a cell which has no characteristic structure, or which is not an essential part of the tissue in which it is found. **initial c's,** germ c's. **intercalary c's,** dark, rod-like structures between the other (secretory and nonsecretory) cells of the endosalpinx, which may be emptied secretory cells. **interstitial c's of Leydig.** See *Leydig's c's,* def. 1. **islet c's,** cells composing the islands of Langerhans. See *islands of Langerhans.* **juvenile c.,** Schilling's name for a polymorphonuclear leukocyte in which the nuclear element is a single fragment no longer containing a definite nucleolus: called also *young form* and *metamyelocyte.* **juxtaglomerular c's,** specialized cells, containing secretory granules, located in the tunica media of the afferent glomerular arterioles. Called also *apparatus of Goormagtigh, juxtaglomerular apparatus, sentinel cells, periarterial pad,* and *polkissen.* **karyochrome c's,** cells of the chromatophil substance of nerve cells which contain much chromatin in the nucleus and a small amount of cytoplasm. **Kulchitsky's c's,** argentaffine cells situated between the cells which line the glands of Lieberkühn of the intestine. **Kupffer's c's,** large star-shaped or pyramidal cells which are attached to the walls of the sinusoids of the liver. They form a part of the reticulo-endothelial system (q.v.). Called also *stellate c's.* **lacrimoethmoid c's,** the ethmoid cells situated under the lacrimal bone. **Langerhans' c's.** 1. Star-shaped cells in the deeper portions of the germinative layer of the epidermis. 2. Irregular wandering cells in the intercellular spaces of the cornea. **Langhans' c's.** 1. Polygonal epithelial cells constituting Langhans' layer. 2. The giant cells of tubercle. **L.E. c.,** a mature neutrophilic polymorphonuclear leukocyte, containing a large phagocytic vacuole containing partially digested and lysed nuclear material; a characteristic of lupus erythematosus, and to be distinguished from a tart cell. **Leclanché c.,** a battery cell having a carbon collecting plate and employing as a fluid a solution of ammonium chloride, and as a depolarizer manganese dioxide. **Leishman's chrome c's,** basophil granular leukocytes occurring in black-water fever. **lepra c.,** a cell in a leprous nodule which has been converted by the action of lepra bacilli into a sac containing degenerated protoplasm and bacilli. **Leydig's c's.** 1. The interstitial cells of the seminiferous tubules and of the mediastinum and connective tissue septa of the testes, believed to furnish the internal secretion of the testicle. 2. Mucous cells which do not pour their secretion out over the surface of the epithelium. **Lipschütz c.** See *centrocyte.* **littoral c's,** flattened cells lining the walls of lymph or blood sinuses. **liver c's,** hepatic c's. **longiradiate c's,** neuroglia cells having long prolongations. **lutein c's,** cells of the corpus luteum. **lymphadenoma c's,** Sternberg-Reed c's. **lymphoid c.,** a mononuclear cell found in lymphoid tissue, such as the lymph node, spleen, and tonsil, which ultimately is concerned with humoral or cellular immunologic reactivity. **malpighian c.,** keratinocyte. **Marchand's c.,** adventitial c. **marginal c's,** demilune c's. **Marié-Davy c.,** a battery cell with a carbon collecting plate, the fluid, depolarizer, and amalgamator being a paste of mercuric or mercurous sulfate and water. **marrow c.,** any one of the immature blood cells which develop in the bone marrow. **Martinotti's c's,** fusiform cells with ascending axis-cylinder processes in the polymorphic layer of the cerebral cortex. **mast c.,** a connective tissue cell whose specific physiologic function remains unknown; capable of elaborating basophilic, metachromatic cytoplasmic granules which contain histamine, heparin, and, in certain species such as the rat and mouse, serotonin. **mastoid c's,** cellulae mastoideae. **Mauthner's c.,** a large cell in the metencephalon of fishes and amphibians that gives rise to Mauthner's fiber. **Merkel-Ranvier c's,** melanoblasts of the skin. **mesothelial c's,** flattened epithelial cells of mesenchymal origin which line the serous cavities. **Meynert's c's,** solitary pyramidal cells in cerebral cortex about the calcarine fissure. **migratory c's,** cells in blood and tissue spaces: so called from their ameboid movements. **Mikulicz's c's,** the cells in rhinoscleroma which contain the bacillus of the disease. **mitral c's,** the pyramidal cells forming one of the layers of the olfactory bulb. **Mooser c.,** a large mononuclear (serosal) cell with numerous rickettsiae in the cytoplasm, observed in inflammatory exudate in murine typhus. **morular c.,** berry c. **mossy c.,** a neuroglia cell having a large body and many short processes. **mother c.,** a cell that divides so as to form new or daughter cells. **motor c.,** an efferent neuron, especially one of the cells of the spinal cord which has its neuraxon continued into a motor nerve fiber. **mucoalbuminous c's, mucoserous c's.** Same as *trophochrome c's.* **mucous c's,** cells which secrete mucus or mucin. **mucous neck c's,** cells found in the necks of gastric glands. They fill the spaces between the parietal cells and are filled with pale transparent granules. **mulberry c.** 1. A vacuolated plasma cell. See also *berry c.* 2. A rounded cell, with centrally placed nuclei and coarse cytoplasmic vacuoles all around the outside, developing at the periphery of a retrogressing corpus luteum. **muscle c.,** an elongated and nucleated contractile fiber cell peculiar to muscle. **myeloid c.,** marrow c. **myeloma c.,** a cell found in bone marrow and occasionally in peripheral blood of patients with multiple myeloma. In the more anaplastic forms the cell is large, has abundant blue-staining cytoplasm with no perinuclear pallor, and has one or more moderately large and vesicular nuclei that may be centrally or eccentrically placed and may contain nucleoli. In better differentiated tumors the cell is smaller and, except for the finer chromatic structure, greatly resembles a plasmacyte. **myoepithelial c's,** smooth muscle cells of epithelial origin occurring in certain glands such as the mammary gland, glands of the skin, glands of the eyelid and salivary glands, which provide a muscular mechanism that may serve to narrow and empty the ducts. **myoid c's,** cells resembling striated muscle fibers, found in the thymus. **Nageotte's c's,** cells of the cerebrospinal fluid which become greatly increased in number in disease. **nerve c.,** any cell of the nervous system, especially a ganglion cell or one of the special cells of nerve centers; a neuron or neurodendron. A nerve cell is an ovoid, pear-shaped, or polygonal mass of protoplasm, containing a spherical nucleus, and giving off one process (the *axon, Deiters' process, neuraxon, axis-cylinder, neurite,* etc.) and several branching protoplasmic processes (*dendrites* or *cytodendrites*). According to the number of protoplasmic processes given off, cells are distinguished as *unipolar, bipolar,* or *multipolar.* Nerve cells are of two types. Those of the first type have an axis-cylinder which is continuous with the axis-cylinder of a nerve fiber. In cells of the second type the axis-cylinder process (*dendraxon*) does not extend into the gray matter, but, remaining in the white substance, eventually undergoes division into a mass of delicate fibrillae (*neuropodia* or *telodendrons*). In both types delicate *collateral branches* (*axodendrites*) are given off from the axis-cylinder processes. The protoplasmic processes, or dendrites, end in arborizations of treelike, branching terminations, known as *end-branches,* or *telodendrons.* **Neumann's c's,** nucleated red cells in the bone marrow developing into erythrocytes. **neuroepithelial c's,** neuroglia c's. **neuroglia c's,** the cells of the neuroglia. They are of two kinds, the spider cells and the mossy cells. **neuromuscular c.,** a form of cell chiefly or always seen in the lower animals, of which the outer part receives stimuli and the inner part is contractile. **neurosensory c.,** the primitive cell which is the first type of nervous cell to form in the embryo. **niche c.,** pneumonocyte. **Niemann-Pick c's,** Pick's c's. **noble c's,** the differentiated cells of the organs and tissues of the body. **normal c.,** any cell found naturally in any part or organ free from disease. **nucleated c.,** any cell having a nucleus. **nurse c's, nursing c's,** Sertoli's c's. **oat c's, oat-shaped c's,** cells shaped like oat grains, seen in some kinds of sarcoma. **olfactory c's,** a set of specialized and nucleated fusiform cells of the mucous membrane of the nose embedded among the epithelial cells. **one-fluid c.,** any battery cell which makes use of but one kind of fluid. **osseous c.,** a bone cell. **oxyntic c's,** delomorphous c's. **oxyphil c's,** the large cells of the parathyroid glands which stain with acid dyes. **Paget's c's,** degenerating cells, swollen, rounded and pigmented, found in the epidermis in Paget's disease of the nipple. **palatine c's,** those parts of the ethmoid cells which are extended into the palatine bone. **Paneth's c's,** cells in the fundus of the crypts of Lieberkühn, containing eosinophil granules, and probably concerned in the elaboration of an enzyme. **paraluteal c's, paralutein c's,** theca lutein c's. **parent c.,** mother c. **parietal c's,** delomorphous c's. **pathologic c.,** any cell which results from a disease process or which belongs to or arises from a pathogenic microorganism. **pavement c's,** the flat cells composing pavement epithelium. **pediculated c's,** neuroglia cells which possess a pedicle implanted into a capillary wall. **peg c's,** intercalary c's. **peptic c's,** a name sometimes given to the adelomorphous cells of the stomach. **pericapillary c's,** perithelium. **pericellular c's,** neuroglia cells which surround a neuron. **perithelial c.,** adventitial c. **perithral c's,** plasma cells surrounding the walls of blood vessels. **perivascular c's,** cells accumulated around the outside of small blood vessels. **persensitized c.,** a cell which has been sensitized by union with the midpiece of complement so that it will be dissolved when the endpiece is added. **pessary c.,** a markedly hypochromic erythrocyte in which the hemoglobin is present merely as a narrow circumferential rim. **phalangeal c's.** See under *supporting c's.* **pheochrome c's,** cells of the medulla of the adrenal gland which stain dark with chromium salts. **physaliferous c's,** spheroidal nucleated cells, containing glycogen or mucin, characteristic of chordoma. **Pick's c's,** round, oval, or polyhedral cells present in the bone marrow and spleen of patients with Niemann-Pick disease, with foamy, lipid-containing cytoplasm, in the form of sphingomyelin, giving a positive reaction with Sudan III and other fat stains. **pigment c.,** any cell containing pigment granules. **pillar c's,** elongated cells in the organ of Corti, forming, by articulation of the heads of the *outer and inner pillar cells,* the triangular canal known as the inner tunnel or Corti's tunnel: called also *pillar of Corti's organ.* **plasma c.,** a spherical or ellipsoidal cell, with a single, eccentrically placed nucleus containing clumped, radially arranged chromatin, an area of perinuclear clearing (hof), a generally abundant, sometimes vacuolated cytoplasm; functionally involved, under varying circumstances, in the synthesis of several forms of gamma globulin. **pneumatic c's,** the cell-like structures of the petrous bone. **polar c's,** polar bodies. **polychromatic c's, polychromatophil c's,** immature erythrocytes staining with both acid and basic stains so that their color is a diffuse mixture of blue-gray and pink. **polyhedral c's,** cells having a polyhedral shape. **polyplastic c.,** a cell made up of various structural elements; also one which passes through various modifications of form. **pregnancy c.,** altered chromophobe cell observed in the anterior pituitary in pregnant women. **prickle c.,** a cell provided with delicate radiating processes which connect with similar cells; the name applied to one of the dividing keratinocytes present in the stratum germinativum of the epidermis. **primary c.,** a device consisting of a container, two solid conducting elements and an electrolyte, for the production of electric current by chemical energy. **primitive wandering c.,** a small mononuclear cell of the embryo which arises from the mesoderm and subsequently by differentiation gives rise to wandering cells of the body (Saxer, Maximow). **primordial c's,** embryonal cells. **primordial germ c's,** the earliest germ cells, at first located outside the gonad. **principal c's,** chief c's. **prop c's,** Purkinje c's. **psychic c's,** the cells of the cerebral cortex. **pulpar c.,** the typical cell of the spleen substance. **Purkinje's c's,** large branching neurons in the middle layer of the cortex cerebelli. **pyramidal c.,** one of the large multipolar pyramid-shaped ganglion cells of the cerebral cortex which, with their attached fibers, constitute the pyramidal neurons. **Reed c's,** Sternberg-Reed c's. **residential c.,** a cell which does not wander, especially one of the cells of the substantia propria of the cornea. **resting c.,** a cell that is not undergoing karyokinesis. **resting wandering c.** See *clasmatocyte.* **reticular c.,** reticulum c. **reticuloendothelial c.** See *reticuloendothelial system,* under *system.* **reticulum c.,** a primitive mesenchymal cell, forming the framework of lymph glands, bone marrow, and spleen, which, according to the complete polyphyletic school of hematopoiesis (Wiseman), remains multipotential and, under appropriate stimuli and conditions, may differentiate into a myeloblast, lymphoblast, or monoblast. **retinal c's,** specialized cells of various kinds, found especially in the ganglionic, molecular, nuclear, and pigmentary layers of the retina. **rhagiocrine c.,** a histiocyte. **Rieder c.,** an immature leukocyte observed in leukemia, having a nucleus with several wide and deep indentations suggesting lobulation, which may represent asynchronism of nuclear and cytoplasmic maturation. **Rindfleisch's c's,** granular eosinophil leukocytes. **rod c's,** retinal rods. **Rohon-Beard c's,** giant ganglion cells in the spinal cord of some vertebrates. **Rolando's c's,** the ganglion cells of Rolando's gelatinous substance. **root c's,** cells of the nerve roots. **Rouget c's,** contractile cells found upon the walls of capillaries. See *pericyte.* **round c.,** any cell having a spherical shape, especially a lymphocyte. **Salla's c's,** star-shaped cells of connective tissue in the fibers which form the sensory nerve endings that are situated in the pericardium. **sarcogenic c's,** the cells which are developed into muscle fiber. **satellite c's.** 1. Neurilemmal elements encapsulating a ganglion cell. 2. Free nuclei which accumulate around cells in certain diseases. **sauroid c.,** normoblast. **Schwann's c.,** one of the large nucleated masses of protoplasm lining the inner surface of the sheath of Schwann or neurilemma. **segmented c.,** a polymorphonuclear leukocyte in which the nucleus is divided into definite lobes. **seminal c's,** epithelial cells within the tubuli seminiferi. **sensory c.,** one of the nerve cells of the peripheral sense organs. **sentinel c's,** juxtaglomerular c's. **septal c.,** pneumonocyte. **serous c.,** a cell concerned in the secretion of an albuminous fluid, like the secretory cells of the parotid gland. **Sertoli's c's,** elongated cells in the tubules of the testes to the ends of which the spermatids become attached apparently for the purpose of nutrition until they become transformed into mature spermatozoa; called also *sustentacular c's, nurse c's, foot c's,* and *trophocytes.* **sexual c's,** the immature cells in the testis and ovary which give rise to the mature sex cells. **Sézary c.,** a reticular lymphocyte characterized by a large convoluted or folded nucleus with a narrow rim of cytoplasm which may contain vacuoles; seen in many proliferative states of the reticuloendothelial system, and massively present in the skin and blood in the Sézary syndrome. **shadow c.,** ghost c. **sickle c.,** an erythrocyte shaped like a sickle or crescent, the abnormal shape caused by the presence of varying proportions of hemoglobin S. **Siemens and Halske c.,** a battery cell with a copper collecting plate: the fluids are water and solution of copper sulfate, separated by a porous diaphragm with a papier-mâché packing. **signet-ring c.,** a cell in which the nucleus has been pressed to one side. See *Krukenberg's tumor* under *tumor.* **silver c's,** argentaffine c's. **skein c.,** a reticulocyte. **skeletogenous c.,** an osteoblast. **Smee c.,** an electric battery cell consisting of a plate of zinc and one of platinized silver in a dilute solution of sulfuric acid. **smudge c's,** a name applied to disrupted leukocytes appearing during the course of preparation of peripheral blood smears. **Snell c.,** a one-fluid battery cell having a collecting plate of platinized silver; its fluid is dilute sulfuric acid. **somatic c's,** the cells of the somatoplasm; undifferentiated body cells. **sperm c.,** a spermatozoon. **spermatogenic c's,** cells that produce sperm. **spermatogonial c.,** spermatogonium. **sphenoid c's,** two large cavities or sinuses of the sphenoid bone. **spider c.** 1. Astrocyte. 2. A cell occurring in rhabdomyosarcoma, the nucleus, with a narrow rim of cytoplasm, being located in what appears to be a large vacuole, with thread-like processes radiating to the outer cell wall. **spindle c.,** a fusiform or spindle-shaped cell. **squamous c.,** a flat, scalelike epithelial cell. **stab c.,** staff c. **staff c.,** a polymorphonuclear leukocyte in which the nucleus is not lobulated but is in the form of a continuous band, horseshoe shaped, twisted, or coiled: called also *band form.* **star c's,** cells with large vacuoles in the cytoplasm and cytoplasmic bridges, in adamantinoma. **stellate c.,** a star-shaped cell, particularly a neuroglia cell having a large number of filaments extending from it in all directions. **stellate c's of liver,** Kupffer's c's. **stem c.,** a generalized mother cell whose descendants specialize, often in different directions, such as an undifferentiated mesenchymal cell which may be considered to be a progenitor of the blood and fixed-tissue cells of the bone marrow. **Sternberg's giant c's,** Sternberg-Reed c's. **Sternberg-Reed c's,** giant, polyploid mesenchymal cells with hyperlobulated nuclei and multiple large nucleoli, considered a characteristic histologic feature of Hodgkin's disease. **stipple c.,** a red blood cell containing granules of varying size and shape, taking a basic or bluish stain with Wright's stain. **supporting c's,** the cells which form a framework for supporting the organ of Corti. They include (1) the outer and inner pillars or rods, (2) the inner and outer phalangeal cells (cells of Deiters), (3) the border cells and (4) the cells of Hensen. **sustentacular c's,** Sertoli's c's. **sympathicotrophic c's,** large epithelioid cells occurring in groups and connected with bundles of nonmyelinated nerve fibers in the hilus of the ovary. **sympathochromaffin c's,** small round cells in the fetal suprarenal gland, the forerunners of the sympathetic and medullary cells. **syncytial c.,** a syncytium or a component of it. **tactile c.** See under *corpuscle.* **target c.,** an abnormally thin erythrocyte which, when stained, shows a dark center and a peripheral ring of hemoglobin, separated by a pale unstained ring containing less hemoglobin; occurring in various chronic anemias. **tart c.,** a histiocyte or monocytoid reticuloendothelial cell that contains a second, characteristic nucleus, usually placed in the hof of the primary nucleus and showing a nuclear membrane and definitely visible chromatin in thick structural arrangement, with relatively sharp differentiation between chromatin and parachromatin. **taste c's,** the interior cells of a taste bud hidden by the cover cells. **tautomeral c's,** cells of the gray matter of the spinal cord whose axis cylinders pass into the white substance of the same side of the cord. **tegmental c's,** cells which cover any delicate structure. **tendon c's,** flattened tissue cells of connective tissue occurring in rows between the primary bundles of the tendons. **theca-lutein c's,** epithelioid cells of the theca interna of the ovary which come to resemble lutein cells. **Thoma-Zeiss counting c.** See under *chamber.*

totipotential c., a cell which is capable of developing into any variety of body cell. **touch c.**, tactile corpuscle. **Touton giant c's**, large multinucleated cells containing lipoid material found in the lesions of xanthoma. **trophochrome c's**, serous cells whose secretory granules give a staining reaction for mucus with mucicarmine. **tubal air c's**, cellulae pneumaticae tubae auditivae. **Türk c.**, a nongranular, mononuclear cell displaying morphologic characteristics of both an atypical lymphocyte and a plasma cell, observed in the peripheral blood during severe anemias, chronic infections, and leukemoid reactions. Called also *Türk's irritation leukocyte.* **tympanic c's**, cellulae tympanicae. **Tzanck c.**, a degenerated epithelial cell caused by acantholysis, and found especially in pemphigus. **Unna's plasma c.**, a term mainly of historical interest, arising from the erroneous concept that Unna-Lappenheim stain, which is taken up by several bone marrow elements, is specific for the recognition of plasma cells. **vacuolated c.**, a cell whose protoplasm contains vacuoles. **c's of van Gehuchten**, Golgi cells of type II, i.e., neurons with short branching processes. **vasofactive c's, vasoformative c's**, cells which join with other cells to form blood vessels. **Vignal's c's**, embryonal connective tissue cells secreting myelin and associated with the formation of the axis-cylinders of nerves in the fetus. **Vimtrump's c's**, Rouget c's. **Virchow's c.**, lepra c. **visual c's**, the neuroepithelial elements of the retina, the outer specialized segments of which are the rods and cones. **von Kupffer's c's.** See *Kupffer's c's.* **wandering c.**, a name applied to mononuclear, phagocytic cells that are components of the reticuloendothelial system. **wasserhelle c's** [Ger.], water-clear c. **water-clear c.**, a large clear cell found in the parathyroid gland. They have a ballooned appearance and are especially numerous in adenoma of the gland. **wing c's**, cells in the corneal epithelium with convex anterior surfaces and concave posterior surfaces. **xanthoma c.**, foam c. **Zander's c's**, bladder c's. **zymogenic c's**, cells at the bottom of gastric glands that contain secretory granules.

cella (sel′ah), pl. *cel′lae* [L.]. An enclosure, or compartment. **c. latera′lis ventric′uli latera′lis**, the lateral part of the lateral ventricle of the brain. **c. me′dia ventric′uli latera′lis**, the central part of the lateral ventricle of the brain: called also *pars centralis.*

cellae (sel′le) [L.]. Plural of *cella.*

Cellano (seh-lan′o). A hereditary factor in human blood. Its antibody is called *anti-Cellano*, from the name of the patient in whose blood the antibody was discovered.

cellase (sel′ās). An enzyme which acts upon cellose.

Cellfalcicula (sel″fal-sik′u-lah). A genus of microorganisms of the family Spirillaceae, suborder Pseudomonadineae, order Pseudomonadales, made up of short rod- or spindle-shaped cells with pointed ends, containing metachromatic granules. It includes three species, *C. fus′ca, C. muco′sa*, and *C. vi′ridis.*

Cellia (sel′e-ah) [Angelo *Celli*, Italian physician, 1857–1914]. A genus of anopheline mosquitoes, several species of which act as malaria carriers.

cellicolous (sel-lik′o-lus) [L. *cella* cell + *colere* to dwell]. Inhabiting cells.

celliferous (sel-lif′er-us). Producing or bearing cells.

celliform (sel′ĭ-form). Cell-like.

cellifugal (sel-lif′u-gal). Cellulifugal.

cellipetal (sel-lip′e-tal). Cellulipetal.

cellobiase (sel″lo-bi′ās). An enzyme which breaks down cellobiose into glucose.

cellobiose (sel″lo-bi′ōs). A disaccharide, $C_{12}H_{22}O_{11}$, formed from cellulose by the action of cellulase.

cellohexose (sel″o-hek′sōs). A crystalline hexasaccharide, $C_{36}H_{62}O_{31}$, obtained by the hydrolysis of cellulose.

celloidin (sel-loi′din). A concentrated preparation of pyroxylin, employed in microscopy for embedding specimens for section cutting.

cellon (sel′on). Acetylene tetrachloride, $CHCl_2.CHCl_2$, or tetrachlorethane.

cellophane (sel′o-fān). A cellulose product: used as a filtering medium, and for bandages, compresses, etc.

cellose (sel′ōs). Cellobiose.

cellotetrose (sel″o-tet′rōs). A crystalline tetrasaccharide, $C_{24}H_{42}O_{21}$, obtained by the hydrolysis of cellulose.

cellotriose (sel″o-tri′ōs). A crystalline trisaccharide, $C_{18}H_{32}O_{16}$, obtained by the hydrolysis of cellulose.

cellula (sel′lu-lah), pl. *cel′lulae* [L.]. A small cell; in anatomical nomenclature, used to designate a small, more or less enclosed space. **cel′lulae ethmoida′les** [B N A]. See *sinus ethmoidalis.* **cel′lulae ethmoida′les os′seae** [N A, B N A], numerous irregularly shaped air spaces in the labyrinths of the ethmoid bone. Called also *bony ethmoid cells.* **cel′lulae mastoi′deae** [N A, B N A], the air spaces of the mastoid process of the temporal bone. Called also *mastoid cells.* **cel′lulae pneumat′icae tu′bae auditi′vae** [N A], air cells in the floor of the auditory tube close to the carotid canal, being extensions from the air cells of the mastoid part of the temporal bone. Called also *air cells of auditory tube* and *cellulae pneumaticae tubariae* [B N A]. **cel′lulae pneumat′icae tuba′riae** [B N A], cellulae pneumaticae tubae auditivae. **cel′lulae tympan′icae** [N A, B N A], spaces in the tympanic cavity between the bony projections from the floor, or jugular wall. Called also *tympanic cells.*

cellulae (sel′u-le) [L.]. Plural of *cellula.*

cellular (sel′u-lar). Pertaining to, or made up of, cells.

cellularity (sel″u-lăr′ĭ-te). The state of a tissue or other mass as regards the number of constituent cells.

cellulase (sel′u-lās). An enzyme that hydrolyzes cellulose to cellobiose. It is secreted by certain bacteria and by fungi which destroy wood.

cellule (sel′ūl) [L. *cellula*]. A small cell.

cellulicidal (sel″u-lis′ĭ-dal) [L. *cellula* cellule + *caedere* to kill]. Destroying cells.

cellulifugal (sel″u-lif′u-gal) [L. *cellula* cellule + *fugere* to flee]. Directed away from a cell body.

cellulin (sel′u-lin). A principle of animal origin much resembling cellulose.

cellulipetal (sel″u-lip′e-tal) [L. *cellula* cellule + *petere* to seek]. Directed toward a cell body.

cellulitis (sel″u-li′tis). Inflammation of cellular tissue; especially purulent inflammation of the loose subcutaneous tissue. **orbital c.**, inflammation of the cellular tissue within the orbit. **pelvic c.**, parametritis. **phlegmonous c.**, phlegmona diffusa. **streptococcus c.**, cellulitis due to streptococcus infection and frequently associated with erysipelas.

cellulocutaneous (sel″u-lo-ku-ta′ne-us). Composed of loose connective tissue and skin.

cellulofibrous (sel″u-lo-fi′brus). Partly cellular and partly fibrous.

celluloid (sel′u-loid). A substance composed largely of pyroxylin and camphor: used in the arts and to some extent in dentistry and surgery.

Cellulomonas (sel″lu-lo-mo′nas) [*cellulo*se + Gr. *monas* a unit]. A genus of microorganisms of the family Corynebacteriaceae, order Eubacteriales, made up of pleomorphic, gram-variable microorganisms found in soil.

celluloneuritis (sel″u-lo-nu-ri′tis). Inflammation of nerve cells. **acute anterior c.**, Raymond's name for acute anterior poliomyelitis, polyneuritis, and Landry's paralysis, which he considered one disease.

cellulose (sel′u-lōs). A carbohydrate, $(C_6H_{10}O_5)_n$, forming the skeleton of most plant structures and of plant cells. It is a colorless, transparent solid, insoluble in water, alcohol, etc., but soluble in Schweitzer's reagent. **absorbable c.,** oxidized c. **acid c.,** any combination of cellulose with carboxyl groups, such as pectinic acid. They are mostly gelatinous bodies. **oxidized c.,** cellulose dried in vacuum over phosphorus pentoxide: used as a local hemostatic. **recessive c.,** lichenin. **starch c.,** the outer portion of the starch grain. See *amylopectin.*

cellulosity (sel″u-los′ĭ-te). The condition of being composed of cells.

cellulotoxic (sel″u-lo-tok′sik). 1. Toxic to cells. 2. Produced by cell toxins.

cellulous (sel′u-lus). Made up of cells.

Cellvibrio (sel-vib′re-o). A genus of microorganisms of the family Spirillaceae, suborder Pseudomonadineae, order Pseudomonadales, made up of straight or slightly curved rods sometimes joined in long chains or bundles. It includes four species, *C. flaves′cens, C. ful′vus, C. ochra′ceus,* and *C. vulga′ris.*

celo- (se′lo). 1. [Gr. *kēlē* hernia]. Combining form denoting relationship to a tumor or swelling. 2. [Gr. *koilia* cavity]. Combining form denoting relationship to a cavity. See also words beginning *celio-* and *coelo-.*

celology (se-lol′o-je) [*celo-* (1) + *-logy*]. The science or study of hernia.

celom (se′lom). Coelom.

celomic (se-lom′ik). Coelomic.

celontin (se-lon′tin). Trade mark for a preparation of methsuximide.

celonychia (se″lo-nik′e-ah). Koilonychia.

celophlebitis (se″lo-fle-bi′tis) [*celo-* (2) + *phlebitis*]. Inflammation of a vena cava.

celoschisis (se-los′kĭ-sis) [*celo-* (2) + *schisis* cleft]. Fissure of the abdominal wall.

celoscope (sel′o-skōp″). Celioscope.

celoscopy (se-los′ko-pe). Celioscopy.

celosomia (se-lo-so′me-ah) [*celo-* (1) + Gr. *sōma* body]. A developmental anomaly characterized by eventration, fissure, or absence of the sternum, with hernial protrusion of the viscera.

celosomus (se″lo-so′mus). A fetal monster exhibiting celosomia.

celothel (se′lo-thel). Mesothelium.

celothelioma (se″lo-the-le-o′mah). Mesothelioma.

celothelium (se″lo-the′le-um). Mesothelium.

celotomy (se-lot′o-me). Kelotomy.

celozoic (se″lo-zo′ik) [*celo-* (2) + *zōon* animal]. Inhabiting the intestinal cavities of the body; said of parasites.

Celsius scale, thermometer (sel′se-us) [Anders *Celsius,* Swedish astronomer, 1701–1744]. See under *scale.*

Celsus (sel′sus), Aurelius Cornelius (1st century A.D.). A celebrated Roman medical encyclopedist—"the Cicero of medicine." Of his many writings, only his *De re medicina* (in eight books) survives; the four classical signs of inflammation—*calor* (heat), *dolor* (pain), *rubor* (redness) and *tumor* (swelling)—are mentioned in the third book of this work.

celtium (sel′she-um). Hafnium.

cement (se-ment′) [L. *cemen′tum*]. 1. A substance that serves to produce solid union between two surfaces. 2. An adhesive filling material, such as zinc oxyphosphate, used in dentistry to retain gold castings in prepared teeth and to insulate the tooth pulp from metallic fillings. 3. Cementum. **intercellular c.,** a plastic material that holds cells, and especially epithelial cells, together. **interprismatic c.,** the material that binds together the enamel prisms. **muscle c.,** the myoglia. **nerve c.,** the neuroglia. **silicate c.,** a material containing magnesium phosphate and calcium phosphate, carbonate, and fluoride, used for filling anterior tooth cavities. **tooth c.,** cementum.

cementation (se″men-ta′shun). The attachment of anything by the means of cement, such as the use of cement in attaching restorative material to a natural tooth.

cementicle (se-men′tĭ-kel). A small, discrete globular mass of dentin in the region of a tooth root. **adherent c., attached c.,** one that is firmly connected with the cementum. **free c.,** one that is completely surrounded by connective tissue of the periodontal membrane. **interstitial c.,** one that is completely enveloped by cementum.

cementification (se-men″tĭ-fĭ-ka′shun). Cementogenesis.

cementin (se-men′tin). The material that sometimes unites the margins of squamous endothelial cells.

cementitis (se″men-ti′tis). Inflammation of the cementum of a tooth.

cementoblast (se-men′to-blast) [*cementum* + Gr. *blastos* germ]. A large cuboidal cell with spheroid or ovoid nucleus, found on the surface of cementum, between the fibers, which is active in the formation of cementum.

cementoblastoma (se-men″to-blas-to′mah). An odontogenic fibroma in which the cells are developing into cementoblasts, and there is only a small proportion of calcified tissue.

cementoclasia (se-men″to-kla′se-ah) [*cementum* + Gr. *klasis* breaking]. Disintegration of the cementum of a tooth.

cementocyte (se-men′to-sīt). A cell found in lacunae of cellular cementum, frequently having long processes radiating from the cell body toward the periodontal surface of the cementum.

cemento-exostosis (se-men″to-ek″sos-to′sis). Cementicle.

cementogenesis (se-men″to-jen′e-sis) [*cementum* + Gr. *genesis* formation]. The development of the cementum on the root dentin of a tooth.

cementoma (se″men-to′mah). An odontogenic fibroma in which the cells have developed into cementoblasts, and which consists largely of cementum.

cementoperiostitis (se-men″to-per″e-os-ti′tis). Periodontal disease.

cementosis (se″men-to′sis). A condition characterized by proliferation of cementum.

cementum (se-men′tum) [L.]. [N A] The bony material covering the root of a tooth, differing in structure from ordinary bone in containing a greater number of Sharpey's fibers. Called also *substantia ossea dentis* [B N A].

cenadelphus (se″nah-del′fus) [Gr. *koinos* common + *adelphos* brother]. A double fetal monster in which the two components are equally developed.

cenencephalocele (se″nen-sef′ah-lo-sēl). An encephalocele or protrusion of the brain without cystic condition.

cenesthesia (se″nes-the′ze-ah) [Gr. *koinos* common + *aisthēsis* perception]. The general feeling or sense of conscious existence; the sense of normal functioning of the organs of the body.

cenesthesic (se″nes-the′sik). Pertaining to cenesthesia.

cenesthesiopathy (se″nes-the″ze-op′ah-the) [*cenesthesia* + Gr. *pathos* disease + *-ia*]. Any disturbance of cenesthesia.

cenesthetic (se″nes-thet′ik). Cenesthesic.

cenesthopathia (se″nes-tho-path′e-ah). Cenesthesiopathy.

ceno- (se′no). 1. [Gr. *kainos* new, fresh]. Combining form meaning new. 2. [Gr. *kenos* empty]. Combining form meaning empty. 3. [Gr. *koinos* shared in common]. Combining form denoting relationship to a common feature or characteristic. See also words beginning *keno-.*

cenobium (se-no′be-um) [Gr. *koinobios* living in communion with others]. A colony of independent cells or organisms held together by a common investment.

cenogenesis (se″no-jen′e-sis) [*ceno-* (1) + Gr. *genesis* production]. The appearance of new features in development, in adaptive response to environmental conditions. Cf. *palingenesis*, def. 2.

cenophobia (se″no-fo′be-ah) [*ceno-* (2) + *phobia*]. 1. Morbid dread of large open spaces. 2. Cenotophobia.

cenopsychic (se″no-si′kik) [*ceno-* (1) + Gr. *psychē* soul]. Of recent appearance in mental development.

cenosis (se-no′sis) [Gr. *kenōsis* an emptying, or emptiness]. A morbid discharge.

cenosite (se′no-sīt). Coinosite.

cenotic (se-not′ik). Pertaining to or characterized by cenosis.

cenotophobia (se″no-to-fo′be-ah) [Gr. *kainotēs* novelty + *phobia*]. Fear of novelty; neophobia.

cenotoxin (se″no-tok′sin). Kenotoxin.

cenotype (se′no-tīp) [*ceno-* (3) + *type*]. The original type from which all forms have arisen.

censor (sen′sor). 1. A member of a committee on ethics or for critical examination and supervision of a medical or other society. 2. In freudian terminology, the psychic influence which prevents certain unconscious thoughts and wishes coming into consciousness unless they are disguised so as to be unrecognizable. Called also *freudian c.* and *psychic c.*

censorship (sen′sor-ship). The operation of the censor.

censur (sen′shur). Censor.

Cent. Abbreviation for *centigrade* and *centimeter*.

center (sen′ter) [Gr. *kentron;* L. *centrum*]. 1. The middle point of a body. 2. A collection of nerve cells which is concerned with performance of a particular function. **abdominal c.,** a cutaneous reflex center in the gray matter of the cord: said to be between the sixth and eleventh dorsal vertebrae. **accelerating c.,** a center in the oblongata which sends accelerating fibers to the heart. **acoustic c.,** auditory c. **ankle clonus c.,** a cutaneous reflex center in the gray matter of the cord: said to be between the fifth lumbar and first sacral vertebrae. **anospinal c's,** the centers for contracting the sphincter ani, that for relaxing it (defecation center), and that for the anal reflex: all are in the lumbar enlargement. **apneustic c.,** a nerve center controlling normal respiration. **arm c.,** a cortical center at the middle third of the fissure of Rolando, controlling the arm movements. **association c.,** any portion of the cerebral cortex which, though not itself functionally differentiated, is connected with the cortical centers by association fibers. **auditopsychic c.,** a center dealing with the interpretation of sounds, in the superior temporal gyrus. **auditory c.,** the center for hearing, in the more anterior of the transverse temporal gyri. **automatic c.,** a group of cells in the spinal cord producing motion independently of volition or reflection. **brain c.** 1. An area of the cerebral cortex having a specialized structure or function. 2. A group of cells in the brain having a special function. **Broca's c.,** the speech center. **Budge's c.** 1. Ciliospinal center. 2. Genital center. **calorific c.,** a center in the caudate nucleus of the spinal cord which controls heat production. **cardio-accelerating c.** See *accelerating c.* **cardio-inhibitory c.,** a center in the oblongata which sends inhibitions to the heart by way of the vagus. **cardiomotor c.,** Tawara's name for the auriculoventricular node, on the theory that the heart's impulse arises there. **cerebrospinal c.,** the brain and spinal cord. **cheirokinesthetic c.,** the center in the posterior part of the left second frontal gyrus, controlling movements concerned in writing. **ciliospinal c.,** a center in the lower cervical and upper dorsal portions of the spinal cord, connected with the dilatation of the pupil. **color c.,** the center for the perception of color: said to be situated in the occipital cortex. **convulsion c.,** a center in the oblongata, at the floor of the fourth ventricle: its stimulation causes convulsions. **coordination c.,** a nerve center serving the function of coordination. **correlation c.,** a nerve center serving the function of correlation. **cortical c.,** any portion of the cerebral cortex which can be differentiated functionally from its neighbors. Such a center is sometimes called area, field, or zone. **coughing c.,** a center in the oblongata, situated above the respiratory center, which presides over the act of coughing. **cremasteric c.,** a cutaneous reflex center in the cord: said to be above the level of the second lumbar vertebra. **cutaneous reflex c's,** a set of centers in the gray matter of the spinal cord: these, with the musculotendinous centers, embrace nearly all the reflex centers of the cord. **defecation c.,** the anospinal center. **deglutition c.,** a nerve center in the oblongata which controls the function of swallowing. **dentary c.,** an ossification center of the mandible, giving origin to the lower border and outer plate. **deputy c.,** any secondary or association center; also any center of origin for a spinal nerve. **diabetic c.,** a center situated in the posterior part of the floor of the fourth ventricle: if tampered with, diabetes mellitus follows. **dominating c.,** the principal or controlling center of a group having a common function. **ejaculation c.,** the center which controls the erection of the penis and the normal discharge of semen: it is in the lumbar region of the spinal cord, and is itself regulated from the oblongata. **epigastric c.,** abdominal c. **epiotic c.,** a center of ossification which forms the lower part of the mastoid bone. **erection c.,** ejaculation c. **eupraxic c.,** any cerebral center which controls the proper performance of any action or set of actions. **facial c.,** a center for face movements: in the lower part of the ascending frontal convolution. **foot clonus c.,** a musculotendinous reflex center of the cord, situated between the fifth lumbar and first sacral vertebrae. **ganglionic c.,** any mass of gray matter between the lateral ventricles and the decussation of the anterior pyramids, including the thalami, striati, and other basal ganglia. **genital c., genitospinal c.,** the ejaculation center of the male or the parturition center of the female; said to be in the cord, near the second lumbar vertebra. **germinal c.,** the area in lymphoid tissue in which mitotic figures are observed frequently, differentiation and formation of lymphocytes occur, and elements related to antibody synthesis are found. **glossokinesthetic c.,** the center in the posterior part of the left second frontal gyrus which controls movements concerned in articulate speech. **gluteal c.,** a cutaneous reflex center of the cord: said to be at the level of the fourth lumbar vertebra. **glycogenic c.,** diabetic c. **gustatory c.,** the cerebral center supposed to control taste: situated in the cortex of the uncinate convolution. **health c.,** a community health organization for creating health work and coordinating the efforts of all health agencies. **heat c's,** centers in the brain which regulate heat production and heat elimination. **heat-regulating c's,** thermotaxic c's. **high-level c.,** a center controlling thought, reason, etc. **idea c.,** the name center. **ideomotor c's,** brain centers that preside over ideomotion. **independent c.,** parenchymatous c. **inhibitory c.,** any nerve center which restrains any function or process or controls other centers. **kinetic c.,** the centrospheres of a fertilized ovum. **knee jerk c.,** a musculotendinous reflex center in the cord, at the level of the third and fourth lumbar vertebrae. **Kronecker's c.,** the inhibitory center of the heart. **Kupressoff's c.,** the spinal center for the sphincter of the bladder. **language c.,** any center controlling the understanding or use of language. **leg c.,** a motor center for the legs, in the ascending frontal convolution. **low-level c.,** a center concerned in any sort of automatic action. **Lumsden's c.,** pneumotaxic c. **mastication c.,** a part of the facial center. **medullary c. of cerebellum,** corpus medullare cerebelli. **micturition c.,** a center controlling the bladder and inhibiting the tension of the vesical sphincter: situated in the lumbar enlargement. **mid-level c.,** any center which acts as an association center or in controlling muscular movement or storing up memories. **motor c.,** any center which originates, controls, inhibits, or maintains a motor impulse. **musculotendinous c's,** the centers for foot clonus and ankle clonus, the knee jerk, and for the reflexes of the flexors and extensors of the upper extremity: they are all situated in the cord. **name c.,** an area in the upper temporal lobe which controls the remembrance of names. **nerve c.,** a collection of nerve cells in the central nervous system which are associated together in the performance of some particular function. **olfactory c.,** the center for smell, probably in the hippocampal gyrus. **optic c.,** that point in a lens, or combination of lenses, where all rays that help to form a clear image cross the principal axis: in the eye, about 2 mm. back of the cornea (Fording). **ossification c.,** any point at which the process of ossification begins in a bone. **oval c., greater,** centrum semiovale. **panting c.,** a center in the tuber cinereum which accelerates the rate of breathing. **parenchymatous c.,** a nerve center situated in the substance of a viscus. **parturition c.,** the center for the contraction of the uterus and fetal expulsion: it corresponds with the ejaculation center of the male. **phrenic c.,** centrum tendineum. **plantar reflex c.,** a cutaneous reflex center in the gray matter of the cord: said to be at the level of the second sacral vertebra. **pneumotaxic c.,** a center in the upper part of the pons which rhythmically inhibits inspiration independently of the vagi. **polypneic c.,** panting c. **projection c.,** any center in the cerebral cortex which gives rise to projection fibers. **proportionizing c.,** a center in the cortex, on the motor side, corresponding to the name center. **psychocortical c.,** the center in the cerebral cortex concerned in voluntary muscular movement. It is located around the central fissure. **psychomotor c.,** psychocortical c. **pteriotic c.,** a center of ossification from which are developed the tegmen tympani and the covering of the semicircular canals. **pupillary c's,** the ciliospinal center, which dilates the pupil; also one in the corpus quadrigeminum for contracting the pupil. **rectovesical c.,** a cord reflex center for the rectum and bladder. **reflex c.,** any center in the brain or cord in which a sensory impression is changed into a motor impulse: the reflex centers already discovered are numerous. **reserve c.,** a nerve center which is normally unused, but which can come into action in an emergency. **respiration c.,** that which coordinates the respiratory movements: it is situated in the oblongata. **rotation c.,** the point or axis about which a body rotates. **salivary c., salivation c.,** the center, situated in the floor of the fourth ventricle, which controls salivary secretion. **scapular c.,** a cutaneous reflex center of the spinal cord: said to be located between the fifth cervical and the first thoracic vertebra. **Setchenow's c's,** reflex inhibitory centers in the cord and oblongata. **semioval c.,** centrum semiovale. **sensory c.,** a center that receives or appreciates a sensory impulse. **smell c.,** the olfactory center. **sneezing c.,** the respiration center or a portion of it. **somatic c.,** the pituitary body: so called from the belief that it influences the growth of the whole body. **spasm c.,** a center in the oblongata, at its junction with the pons. **speech c.,** a center in the left (or right) inferior frontal gyrus. **sphenotic c.,** a center of ossification in the sphenoid bone for the lingula. **spinal c.,** a group of nerve cells in the spinal cord which serves as center of integration for a specific sensorimotor function. **splenial c.,** one of the ossification centers of the mandibles, forming a part of its inner plate. **spoken-word c.,** a center in the left inferior frontal gyrus. **sudorific c's, sweat c's,** centers in the spinal cord controlling diaphoresis, with a dominant center in the oblongata. **suprasegmental c.,** one of the centers of the prosencephalon controlling the correlation of the higher functions. **swallowing c.,** a center that controls the act of swallowing, on the floor of the fourth ventricle. **tactile c.,** one for the sense of touch: situated in the hippocampal region. **taste c.,** the gustatory center. **tendinous c.,** centrum tendineum. **thermogenic c.** 1. Calorific center. 2. A center for the physiologic production of heat: in the hypothalamus, with lower ones probably in the striatum and cord. **thermo-inhibitory c's,** those for inhibiting the production of heat: probably in the tuber cinereum and in the gray matter near the fissure of Sylvius. **thermolytic c's,** those for the dissipation of heat: thought to be in the oblongata and tuber cinereum. **thermotaxic c's,** the cerebral centers which maintain a balance between the production and dissipation of heat. **thumb c.,** a center in the cerebral cortex controlling movements of the thumbs. It is situated in the lowest part of the center for movements of the upper limbs. **trophic c.,** any nerve center which regulates or influences nutrition. **vasoconstrictor c.,** a center which controls contraction of the blood vessels. **vasodilator c.,** one for dilating the blood vessels: supposed to be in the oblongata, with dependent centers in the spinal cord. **vasomotor c's,** centers in the tuber cinereum, oblongata, and cord: believed to regulate the caliber of the blood vessels, and to cause their contraction and dilatation. **vasotonic c.,** any vasomotor center: there is said to exist also a higher center in the thalami, regulating vascular tension. **vesical c., vesicospinal c.,** the micturition center or rectovesical center. **visual c's,** centers which regulate the power of vision: probably situated in the cuneus of the occipital lobes. **vomiting c.,** a center in the lower central region of the medulla oblongata: its stimulation causes vomiting. **Wernicke's c.,** the chief speech center. See under *area.* **winking c.,** a reflex center in the oblongata which controls winking. **word c., auditory,** a center in the left superior temporosphenoid convolution which controls the perception of words that are heard. **word c., visual,** one in the posterior part of the left parietal lobe: it appears to govern the perception of printed or written words. **written-word c.,** a center in the second left frontal convolution.

centesimal (sen-tes′ĭ-mal) [L. *centesimus* hundredth]. Divided into hundredths or based upon divisions into hundredths.

centesis (sen-te′sis) [Gr. *kentēsis*]. Perforation or tapping, as with an aspirator, trocar, or needle. Used also as a word termination, affixed to a root indicating the part on which the operation is performed, as *abdominocentesis, thoracocentesis,* and the like.

centi- (sen′tĭ) [L. *centrum* a hundred]. Combining form denoting relationship to 100; usually used in naming units of measurement to indicate one-hundredth (10^{-2}) of the unit designated by the root with which it is combined.

centibar (sen′tĭ-bar). A unit of atmospheric pressure, being one-hundredth part of a bar, or 10^{-2} bar.

centigrade (sen′tĭ-grād) [L. *centum* hundred + *gradus* a step]. Consisting of or having 100 gradations (steps or degrees). See *Celsius* (*centigrade*) *scale.*

centigram (sen′tĭ-gram). One hundredth part of a gram (10^{-2} gram), or the equivalent of 0.1543 grain (Troy). Abbreviated cg. or cgm.

centiliter (sen′tĭ-le″ter). One hundredth part of a

liter (10^{-2} l.), or the equivalent of 0.33815 of a fluid ounce. Abbreviated cl.

centimeter (sen′tĭ-me″ter) [Fr. *centimètre*]. A unit of linear measure of the metric system, being one hundredth part of a meter (10^{-2} m.), or approximately 0.3937 inch. Abbreviated cm. **cubic c.,** a unit of mass, being that of a cube each side of which measures 1 cm. Abbreviated cm.^{3}, cu. cm., or cc.

centinem (sen′tĭ-nem). Pirquet's term for one one-hundredth of a nem.

centinormal (sen″tĭ-nor′mal) [L. *centum* hundred + *norma* rule]. Having a hundredth part of the standard strength.

centipede (sen′tĭ-pēd). An arthropod of the order Chilopoda characterized by having one pair of legs to each body segment. The bite of some large tropical centipedes frequently produces a severe local inflammation which is often attended with vomiting, headache, and fever. See *Scolopendra.*

centipoise (sen′tĭ-poiz). One one-hundredth of a poise.

centiunit (sen″te-u′nit). One one-hundredth of the conventional unit.

centra (sen′trah) [L.]. Plural of *centrum.*

centrad (sen′trad). 1. Toward the center or a center; especially toward the center of the body. 2. A measure of the angle of deviation, being 0.57 degree, or one one-hundredth part of a portion of the arc of a circle equal in length to the radius of the circle.

centrage (sen′trāj). The condition in which the centers of the various refracting surfaces of the eye are in the same straight line.

central (sen′tral). Situated at or pertaining to a center; not peripheral.

centraphose (sen′trah-fōz). Any aphose, or sensation of darkness, originating in the optic or visual centers.

centraxonial (sen″trak-so′ne-al). Having the axis in a median line.

centre (sen′ter). Center.

centrencephalic (sen″tren-se-fal′ik). Pertaining to the center of the encephalon. See under *system.*

centric (sen′trik). Pertaining to a center; not acentric or peripheral.

centriciput (sen-tris′ĭ-put) [*center* + L. *caput* head]. That part of the head which is situated between the occiput and sinciput; the midhead.

centrifugal (sen-trif′u-gal) [*center* + L. *fugere* to flee]. Moving away from a center; moving away from the cerebral cortex; efferent or exodic.

centrifugalization (sen-trif″u-gal-ĭ-za′shun). Centrifugation.

centrifugation (sen-trif″u-ga′shun). The process of separating the lighter portions of a solution, mixture or suspension from the heavier portions by centrifugal force.

centrifuge (sen′trĭ-fūj) [*center* + L. *fugere* to flee]. 1. A machine by which centrifugation is effected. 2. To subject to centrifugation. **microscope c.,** a high-speed centrifuge with a built-in microscope, permitting a specimen to be viewed under centrifugal force.

centrilobular (sen″trĭ-lob′u-lar). Pertaining to the central portion of a lobule.

centriole (sen′trĭ-ōl). A minute cell organoid within the centrosome. Mammalian cells contain two (or more) centrioles which are called the *diplosome.* **anterior c.,** that one in a spermatid from which extends the axial filament of a spermatozoon. **posterior c.,** that one in the spermatid which becomes the annulus in the body of a spermatozoon.

centripetal (sen-trip′e-tal) [*center* + L. *petere* to seek]. Moving toward a center; moving toward the cerebral cortex; afferent or esodic.

centro- (sen′tro) [Gr. *kentron;* L. *centrum*]. Combining form indicating relationship to a center, or to a central location.

centrocecal (sen″tro-se′kal). Pertaining to the central macular area and the blind spot.

Centrocestus (sen″tro-ses′tus). A genus of flukes. **C. cuspida′tus,** a fluke occurring in Formosa.

centrocinesia (sen″tro-si-ne′se-ah). Centrokinesia.

centrocinetic (sen″tro-si-net′ik). Centrokinetic.

centrocyte (sen′tro-sīt). A cell, seen in the lesions of lichen ruber, whose protoplasm contains single or double granules, staining with hematoxylin. Called also *Lipschütz cell.*

centrodesmose (sen″tro-des′mōs). Centrodesmus.

centrodesmus (sen″tro-des′mus) [*centro-* + Gr. *desmos* a band]. The matter connecting the centrosomes of a cell and forming the beginning of the central spindle.

centrokinesia (sen″tro-ki-ne′se-ah) [*center* + Gr. *kinēsis* movement]. Movement originating from central stimulation.

centrokinetic (sen″tro-ki-net′ik). Pertaining to, characterized by, or promoting centrokinesia.

centrolecithal (sen″tro-les′ĭ-thal) [*centro-* + Gr. *lekithos* yolk]. Having the yolk centrally located. See under *ovum.*

centrolobular (sen″tro-lob′u-lar). Centrilobular.

centromere (sen′tro-mēr). Kinetochore.

centronucleus (sen″tro-nu′kle-us). Amphinucleus.

centro-osteosclerosis (sen″tro-os″te-o-skle-ro′-sis). Centrosclerosis.

centrophose (sen′tro-fōz). Any phose, or sensation of light, originating in the visual centers.

centroplasm (sen′tro-plazm). The protoplasm of the centrosome.

centrosclerosis (sen″tro-skle-ro′sis) [*center* + *osteosclerosis*]. The filling of the marrow cavity of a bone with osseous material.

centrosome (sen′tro-sōm) [*centro-* + Gr. *sōma* body]. A specialized area of condensed cytoplasm which contains the centrioles and plays an important part in mitosis. Called also *centrosphere, cytocentrum, microcentrum,* and *attraction sphere.*

centrosphere (sen′tro-sfēr) [*centro-* + Gr. *sphaira* sphere]. Centrosome.

centrostaltic (sen″tro-stal′tik) [*centro-* + Gr. *stellein* to send]. Pertaining to a center of motion.

centrotaxis (sen″tro-tak′sis) [*centro-* + Gr. *taxis* arrangement]. A one-sided orientation of the chromatin thread of the spermatogonial nucleus toward the centrosome.

centrotherapy (sen″tro-ther′ah-pe). Externally applied treatment designed to act upon the nerve centers.

centrum (sen′trum), pl. *cen′tra* [L.; Gr. *kentron*]. An anatomical or other center. **c. commu′ne** ["common center"], the solar plexus. **c. media′-num,** a cluster of cells in the nucleus medialis of the thalamus. **c. ova′le ma′jus,** c. semiovale. **c. semiova′le** [B N A], a mass of white matter seen on removing the upper portion of the cerebrum at the level of the corpus callosum. Omitted in N A. **c. tendine′um** [N A, B N A], **c. tendine′um [diaphrag′matis],** the trefoil-shaped aponeurosis, immediately below the pericardium, onto which the diaphragmatic fibers converge to insert. Called also *central tendon of diaphragm.* **c. tendine′um perine′i** [N A], the fibromuscular mass in the median plane of the perineum where converge and attach the bulbospongiosus and external anal sphincter muscles, the two levatores ani, and the two deep and the two superficial transverse perineal muscles. Often referred to as the *perineal body,* and called also *central tendon of perineum.* **c. ver′tebrae,** corpus vertebrae.

Centruroides (sen″troo-roi′dēz). A genus of scorpions. **C. suffu′sus,** a scorpion of Mexico, having a poisonous sting.

Cenurus (sen-u′rus). Coenurus. **C. cerebra′lis,** *Coenurus cerebralis.*

Cephaelis (sef″a-e′lis). A genus of plants. See *ipecac.*

cephal- (sef′al). See *cephalo-.*

cephalad (sef′ah-lad) [Gr. *kephalē* head]. Toward the head; opposite to caudad.

cephalalgia (sef″ah-lal′je-ah) [Gr. *kephalalgia*]. Pain in the head; headache. **histamine c.,** recurring headaches over the region of the external carotid artery, with local temperature elevation, lacrimation, and rhinorrhea, caused by the administration of histamine or by the release of histamine in the body. **pharyngotympanic c.,** Legal's disease. **quadrantal c.,** headache affecting one quadrant of the head.

cephaledema (sef″al-e-de′mah) [*cephal-* + Gr. *oidēma* swelling]. Edema of the head.

cephalematocele (sef″al-e-mat′o-sēl). Cephalhematocele.

cephalematoma (sef″al-em″ah-to′mah). Cephalhematoma.

cephalemia (sef″ah-le′me-ah). Congestion of the brain, or in the head.

cephalgia (sĕ-fal′je-ah). Cephalalgia.

cephalhematocele (sef″al-he-mat′o-sēl) [*cephal-* + Gr. *haima* blood + *kēlē* tumor]. A bloody tumor under the pericranium, communicating with one or more sinuses of the dura through the cranial bones. **Stromeyer's c.,** a subperiosteal cephalhematocele which communicates with veins and becomes filled with blood during strong expiratory efforts.

cephalhematoma (sef″al-he″mah-to′mah) [*cephal-* + *hematoma*]. A tumor or swelling filled with blood beneath the pericranium. **c. defor′mans,** a bulging of the anterior part of the skull due to hyperostosis, osteoporosis and cavity formation in the bone.

cephalhydrocele (sef″al-hi′dro-sēl) [*cephal-* + *hydrocele*]. A serous or watery accumulation under the pericranium.

cephalic (sĕ-fal′ik) [L. *cephalicus;* Gr. *kephalikos*]. Pertaining to the head, or to the head end of the body.

cephalin (sef′ah-lin) [Gr. *kephalē* head]. 1. A mon-amino-monophosphatide existing in brain tissue, nerve tissue and yolk of egg. 2. A general term indicating a fraction of crude phospholipid, usually extracted from brain tissue, which is soluble in petroleum and ethyl ethers and precipitated by ethyl alcohol, and is used as a clotting agent in blood coagulation work.

cephalitis (sef″ah-li′tis). Encephalitis.

cephalization (sef″al-i-za′shun) [Gr. *kephalē* head]. The concentration or initiation of the growth tendency at the head end of the embryo.

cephalo- (sef″ah-lo) [Gr. *kephalē* head]. A combining form denoting relationship to the head.

cephalocathartic (sef″ah-lo-kah-thar′tik) [*cephalo-* + Gr. *kathartikos* purgative]. Cleansing or clearing the head.

cephalocaudad (sef″ah-lo-kaw′dad). 1. Proceeding in a direction from the head toward the tail; caudad. 2. In both a cephalic and caudal direction.

cephalocaudal (sef″ah-lo-kaw′dal) [*cephalo-* + L. *cauda* tail]. Pertaining to the long axis of the body, in a direction from head to tail.

cephalocele (se-fal′o-sēl) [*cephalo-* + Gr. *kēlē* hernia]. A protrusion of a part of the cranial contents.

cephalocentesis (sef″ah-lo-sen-te′sis) [*cephalo-* + Gr. *kentēsis* puncture]. The surgical puncture of the head.

cephalocercal (sef″ah-lo-ser′kal) [*cephalo-* + Gr. *kerkos* tail]. Cephalocaudal.

cephalochord (sef′ah-lo-kord″) [*cephalo-* + Gr. *chordē* cord]. The intracranial portion of the embryonic chorda dorsalis.

cephalocyst (sef′ah-lo-sist″). A cestode worm.

cephalodiprosopus (sef″ah-lo-di-pros′o-pus) [*cephalo-* + Gr. *di-* twice + *prosopus* face]. A fetal monster with a partially incomplete head attached to the head proper.

cephalodymia (sef″ah-lo-dim′e-ah). The condition of a cephalodymus.

cephalodymus (sef″ah-lod′ĭ-mus) [*cephalo-* + Gr. *didymos* twin]. A twin monstrosity with a single or united head.

cephalodynia (sef″ah-lo-din′e-ah) [*cephalo-* + Gr. *odynē* pain]. Pain in the head; headache.

cephalogaster (sef″ah-lo-gas′ter) [*cephalo-* + Gr. *gastēr* belly]. The anterior portion of the enteric canal of the embryo.

cephalogenesis (sef″ah-lo-jen′e-sis) [*cephalo-* + Gr. *gennan* to produce]. The development of the head in the embryo.

cephalogyric (sef″ah-lo-ji′rik) [*cephalo-* + Gr. *gyros* a turn]. Pertaining to turning motions of the head.

cephalohematocele (sef″ah-lo-he-mat′o-sēl). Cephalhematocele.

cephalohematoma (sef″ah-lo-he″mah-to′mah). Cephalhematoma.

cephalohemometer (sef″ah-lo-he-mom′e-ter) [*cephalo-* + Gr. *haima* blood + *metron* measure]. An instrument for ascertaining changes in the intracranial blood pressure.

cephaloma (sef-ah-lo′mah). An encephaloid or soft cancer.

cephalomelus (sef″ah-lom′e-lus) [*cephalo-* + Gr. *melos* limb]. A fetal monster with an accessory limb growing from the head.

cephalomenia (sef″ah-lo-me′ne-ah) [*cephalo-* + Gr. *mēn* month]. Vicarious menstruation from the head, as in a nasal discharge at the menstrual period.

cephalomeningitis (sef″ah-lo-men″in-ji′tis) [*cephalo-* + *meningitis*]. Inflammation of the membranes of the brain.

cephalometer (sef″ah-lom′e-ter) [*cephalo-* + Gr. *metron* measure]. An instrument for measuring the head; an orienting device for positioning the head for radiographic examination and measurement.

cephalometry (sef″ah-lom′e-tre). Scientific measurement of the dimensions of the head.

cephalomotor (sef″ah-lo-mo′tor) [*cephalo-* + L. *motus* motion]. Moving the head; pertaining to motions of the head.

Cephalomyia (sef″ah-lo-mi′yah). Oestrus.

cephalone (sef′ah-lōn). A large-headed idiot.

cephalonia (sef″ah-lo′ne-ah). A condition in which the head is abnormally large and the brain hypertrophied.

cephalont (sef′ah-lont) [*cephalo-* + Gr. *ōn* being]. That stage of a developing gregarine protozoan in which it is attached to the epithelial host cell.

cephalopagus (sef″ah-lop′ah-gus). Craniopagus.

cephalopathy (sef″ah-lop′ah-the) [*cephalo-* + Gr. *pathos* disease]. Any disease of the head.

cephalopelvic (sef″ah-lo-pel′vik). Pertaining to the relationship of the fetal head to the maternal pelvis.

cephalopharyngeus (sef″ah-lo-fah-rin′je-us). Musculus constrictor pharyngis superior. See *Table of Musculi.*

cephalopin (sef′ah-lo″pin). An oily substance extracted from brain tissue.

cephaloplegia (sef″ah-lo-ple′je-ah) [*cephalo-* + Gr. *plēgē* stroke]. Paralysis of the muscles about the head and face.

Cephalopoda (sef″ah-lop′o-dah) [*cephalo-* + Gr. *pous* foot]. The highest class of mollusks, embracing the octopus, squid, nautilus and cuttlefish.

cephalorhachidian (sef″ah-lo-rah-kid′e-an). Pertaining to the head and the spinal column.

cephalosporiosis (sef″ah-lo-spo″re-o′sis). Infection with Cephalosporium.

Cephalosporium (sef″ah-lo-spo′re-um). A genus of fungi. **C. granulo′matis,** a sporotrichum-like fungus causing gumma-like lesions in man.

cephalostyle (sef′ah-lo-stīl″). The cranial end of the notochord.

cephalotetanus (sef″ah-lo-tet′ah-nus). Kopf-tetanus.

cephalothoracic (sef″ah-lo-tho-ras′ik). Pertaining to the head and thorax.

cephalothoracopagus (sef″ah-lo-tho″rah-kop′-ah-gus). A double monster consisting of two similar components united in the frontal plane, the fusion extending from the crown of the head to the middle abdominal region. **c. disym′metros,** a cephalothoracopagus fused squarely in the frontal plane and presenting two broad anterior surfaces and two narrow posterior ones, with a common head bearing two faces, each being formed by the right and left halves of the different components. **c. monosym′metros,** a cephalothoracopagus with one complete face formed by a right and a left half of the two components, the other face being only rudimentary.

Cephalothoracopagus (Abt's Pediatrics).

cephalotome (sef′ah-lo-tōm). An instrument for cutting the fetal head.

cephalotomy (sef-ah-lot′o-me) [*cephalo-* + Gr. *temnein* to cut]. 1. The cutting up of the fetal head to facilitate delivery. 2. Dissection of the fetal head.

cephalotractor (sef″ah-lo-trak′tor) [*cephalo-* + *tractor*]. An obstetric forceps.

cephalotribe (sef′ah-lo-trīb″) [*cephalo-* + Gr. *tribein* to crush]. An instrument for use in cephalotripsy.

cephalotripsy (sef′ah-lo-trip″se) [*cephalo-* + Gr. *tripsis* a rubbing]. The crushing of the fetal head in order to facilitate delivery.

cephalotropic (sef″ah-lo-trop′ik) [*cephalo-* + Gr. *tropos* a turning]. Having an affinity for brain tissue.

cephalotrypesis (sef″ah-lo-tri-pe′sis) [*cephalo-* + Gr. *trypēsis* a boring]. The trephination of the cranium.

cepharanthine (sef″ar-an′thin). A yellow alkaloid, $C_{37}H_{38}O_6N_2$, from *Stephania cepharantha.* It has been suggested for use as a tuberculosis remedy.

ceptor (sep′tor). 1. See *Ehrlich's side-chain theory,* under *theory.* 2. Any one of the nervous apparatus for, or organs which, receive external stimuli or impressions and transfer them to the nerve centers. Cf. *beneceptor* and *nociceptor.* **chemical c.,** a ceptor which transforms proper stimuli into chemical reactions in the body. **contact c.,** a ceptor which receives stimuli of direct physical contact. **distance c.,** the nervous apparatus through which an individual perceives or is affected by his distant environment. **effector c.,** a ceptor in the brain which receives impulses of special actions and becomes so trained for them that subsequent similar impulses are much facilitated. **nerve c.** See *ceptor,* def. 2.

cera (se′rah) [L.]. Wax. **c. al′ba,** white wax. **c. fla′va,** yellow wax.

ceraceous (se-ra′shus) [L. *cera* wax]. Waxlike in appearance.

ceramics (sĕ-ram′iks) [Gr. *keramos* potters' clay]. The modeling and processing of objects made of clay or similar material. **dental c.,** the employment of porcelain and similar materials in restorative dentistry.

ceramodontics (se-ram″o-don′tiks). Dental ceramics.

cerasin (ser′ah-sin). 1. A substance from the gum of cherry, plum, and other trees: said to be a carbohydrate charged with a lime salt. 2. Kerasin.

cerasine (ser′ah-sīn). A red azo dye, $C_{10}H_7.N{:}N.C_{10}H_4(SO_2ONa)_2.OH$: used as a cytoplasmic stain.

cerasinose (sĕ-ras′ĭ-nōs). A carbohydrate from cherry gum.

cerasus (ser′ah-sus) [L.]. Cherry, or cherry tree. See *Prunus.*

cerate (se′rāt) [L. *ceratum,* from *cera* wax]. A medicinal preparation for external application, made with a basis of fat or wax, or both, intermediate in consistency between an ointment and a plaster. **simple c.,** a mixture of benzoinated lard and white wax, melted together.

ceratectomy (ser-ah-tek′to-me). Keratectomy.

ceratiasis (ser-ah-ti′ah-sis). Keratiasis.

ceratin (ser′ah-tin). Keratin.

ceratitis (ser″ah-ti′tis). Keratitis.

cerato-. For words beginning thus, see also those beginning *kerato-.*

ceratocricoid (ser″ah-to-kri′koid). Pertaining to the posterior horn of the thyroid cartilage and the cricoid cartilage.

ceratohyal (ser″ah-to-hi′al). Pertaining to a cornu minus of the hyoid bone.

ceratonosus (ser″ah-ton′o-sus) [Gr. *keras* cornea + *nosos* disease]. Any disease of the cornea.

Ceratophyllus (ser″ah-tof′ĭ-lus) [Gr. *keras* horn + *phyllon* leaf]. A genus of fleas, now including only bird fleas, but formerly including those of birds and small mammals. **C. acu′tus,** *Diamanus montanus.* **C. fascia′tus,** *Nosopsyllus fasciatus.* **C. galli′nae,** a species which attacks chickens and man. **C. idahoen′sis,** *Oropsylla idahoensis.* **C. monta′nus,** *Diamanus montanus.* **C. punjaben′sis,** a rat flea of India. **C. silantiew′i,** *Oropsylla silantiewi.* **C. tesquo′rum,** a plague-transmitting flea of ground squirrels in the Russian steppes.

Ceratopogonidae (ser″ah-to-po-gon′ĭ-de). Heleidae.

ceratum (se-ra′tum) [L.]. Cerate.

cerberine (ser′bĕ-rin). A poisonous alkaloid, $C_{27}H_{40}O_8$, from *Cerebera odallam,* a tree of Asia.

cercaria (ser-ka′re-ah), pl. *cerca′riae* [Gr. *kerkos* tail]. The final free-swimming larval stage of a trematode parasite, consisting of a body and tail. Cercariae encyst on aquatic vegetation or on the surface film of water; if they penetrate the skin of a fish or if the larvae become encysted in the tissues of an aquatic arthropod, metacercariae may be formed.

cercaricidal (ser-ka″re-si′dal). Destructive to cercariae.

cerclage (sār-klahzh′) [Fr. "an encircling"]. Encircling of a part with a ring or loop, such as encirclement of the incompetent cervix uteri, or the binding together of the ends of a fractured bone with a metal ring or wire loop.

cercocystis (ser″ko-sis′tis). A form of larval tapeworm resembling cysticercus, but provided with a caudal appendage.

cercomonad (ser-kom′ŏ-nad). Any monad or protozoan of the genus Cercomonas.

Cercomonas (ser-kom′ŏ-nas) [Gr. *kerkos* tail + *monas* monad]. A genus of flagellate protozoa found in the stools of man and other animals. **C. hom′inis,** the name formerly given to the organisms now known as *Trichomonas hominis* and *Chilomastix mesnili.* **C. intestina′lis,** *Giardia intestinalis.* **C. longicau′da,** a species found in human feces, probably coprozoic.

cercomoniasis (ser″ko-mo-ni′ah-sis). Infestation with Cercomonas.

Cercosphae′ra addiso′ni. *Microsporon audouini.*

Cercosporal′la vex′ans. A mold that has been known to cause skin eruptions.

cercus (ser′kus), pl. *cer′ci* [L.; Gr. *kerkos* tail]. A bristle-like structure.

cereal (se′re-al) [L. *cerealis*]. 1. Pertaining to edible grain. 2. Any graminaceous plant bearing an edible seed; also the seed or grain of such a plant.

cerealin (se-re′ah-lin). A ferment contained in grain extract and capable of converting starch into dextrose.

cerealose (se′re-ah-lōs). A substance containing maltose and glucose, obtained by the action of enzymes on grains.

cerebellar (ser″e-bel′ar). Pertaining to the cerebellum.

cerebellifugal (ser″e-bel-lif′u-gal) [*cerebellum* + L. *fugere* to flee]. Tending or proceeding from the cerebellum.

cerebellipetal (ser″e-bel-lip′e-tal) [*cerebellum* + L. *petere* to seek]. Tending or moving toward the cerebellum.

cerebellitis (ser″e-bel-li′tis). Inflammation of the cerebellum.

cerebellofugal (ser″e-bel-lof′u-gal). Cerebellifugal.

cerebello-olivary (ser″e-bel″o-ol′ĭ-va-re). Connecting the cerebellum and olivary body.

cerebellopontile (ser″e-bel″o-pon′tēl). Pertaining to the cerebellum and the pons varolii.

cerebellopontine (ser″e-bel″o-pon′tēn). Cerebellopontile.

cerebellorubral (ser″e-bel″o-ru′bral). Pertaining to the cerebellum and the red nucleus.

cerebellorubrospinal (ser″e-bel″o-roo″bro-spi′nal). Pertaining to the cerebellum, the red nucleus, and the spine.

cerebellospinal (ser″e-bel″o-spi′nal). Pertaining to the cerebellum and spinal cord.

cerebellum (ser″e-bel′um) [L., dim. of *cerebrum* brain]. [N A, B N A] That division of the central nervous system posteroinferior to the cerebrum and above the pons and fourth ventricle. It consists of a median lobe (vermis) and two lateral lobes (the hemispheres) connected with the other portions of the brain by three pairs of peduncles, the superior connecting it with the cerebrum, the middle with the pons, and the inferior with the medulla oblongata. The cerebellum is concerned in the coordination of movements.

cerebral (ser′e-bral). Pertaining to the cerebrum.

cerebralgia (ser″e-bral′je-ah) [*cerebrum* + *-algia*]. Headache.

cerebrasthenia (ser″e-bras-the′ne-ah) [*cerebrum* + *asthenia*]. Debility, mental or other, associated with brain lesions.

cerebration (ser″e-bra′shun) [L. *cerebratio*]. Functional activity of the cerebrum. **unconscious c.,** mental action of which the subject has no consciousness.

cerebriform (sĕ-reb′rĭ-form) [L. *cerebrum* brain + *forma* form]. Resembling the brain or brain substance.

cerebrifugal (ser″e-brif′u-gal) [*cerebrum* + L. *fugere* to flee]. Conducting or proceeding away from the brain, or cerebrum.

cerebripetal (ser″e-brip′e-tal) [*cerebrum* + L. *petere* to seek]. Conducting or proceeding toward the brain, or cerebrum.

cerebritis (ser″e-bri′tis). Inflammation of the cerebrum. **saturnine c.,** brain inflammation due to lead poisoning.

cerebrocardiac (ser″e-bro-kar′de-ak) [*cerebrum* + L. *cardia* heart]. Pertaining to the brain and heart.

cerebrocentric (ser″e-bro-sen′trik) [*cerebro-* + Gr. *kentrikos* of or from the center]. Relating to the concept, or designating, that control of the personality centers in the physical brain, as distinguished from the mind or the psychical system of the individual. Cf. *psychocentric.*

cerebrogalactose (ser″e-bro-gah-lak′tos). Cerebrose.

cerebrogalactoside (ser″e-bro-gah-lak′to-sīd). Cerebroside.

cerebrohyphoid (ser″e-bro-hi′foid) [*cerebrum* + Gr. *hyphē* web + *eidos* form]. Resembling brain tissue.

cerebroid (ser′e-broid). Resembling the brain substance.

cerebrol (ser′e-brol). An oily substance from the brain.

cerebrolein (ser″e-bro′le-in). An olein obtainable from the brain.

cerebrology (ser″e-brol′o-je) [*cerebrum* + *-logy*]. The sum of knowledge regarding the brain.

cerebroma (ser″e-bro′mah). Any abnormal mass of brain substance.

cerebromalacia (ser″e-bro-mah-la′she-ah) [*cerebrum* + Gr. *malakos* soft]. Abnormal softening of the substance of the cerebrum.

cerebromedullary (ser″e-bro-med′u-la-re). Cerebrospinal.

cerebromeningeal (ser″e-bro-mĕ-nin′je-al). Pertaining to the brain and its membranes.

cerebromeningitis (ser″e-bro-men″in-ji′tis). Inflammation of the brain and its membranes.

cerebrometer (ser″e-brom′e-ter). An instrument for registering the pulsatory movements of the brain.

cerebron (ser′e-bron). A crystalline cerebroside from brain tissue; probably a mixture of phrenosin and kerasin.

cerebro-ocular (ser″e-bro-ok′u-lar). Pertaining to the brain and the eye.

cerebropathia (ser″e-bro-path′e-ah) [L.]. Cerebropathy. **c. psy′chica toxe′mica,** Korsakoff's psychosis.

cerebropathy (ser″e-brop′ah-the) [*cerebrum* + Gr. *pathos* disease]. Any disorder of the brain.

cerebrophysiology (ser″e-bro″fiz-e-ol′o-je). The physiology of the cerebrum.

cerebropontile (ser″e-bro-pon′til). Pertaining to the cerebrum and pons.

cerebropsychosis (ser″e-bro″si-ko′sis) [*cerebrum* + *psychosis*]. Any mental disorder due to disease of the cerebrum.

cerebrorachidian (ser″e-bro″rah-kid′e-an). Cerebrospinal.

cerebrosclerosis (ser″e-bro″skle-ro′sis) [*cerebrum* + *sclerosis*]. Morbid hardening of the substance of the cerebrum.

cerebroscope (sĕ-re′bro-skōp). An ophthalmoscope used in examination for the detection of brain disease.

cerebroscopy (ser″e-bros′ko-pe) [*cerebrum* + Gr. *skopein* to examine]. 1. Examination of the eye with an ophthalmoscope, for the detection of disease of the brain. 2. Postmortem examination of the brain.

cerebrose (ser′e-brōs). Brain sugar, $C_6H_{12}O_6$; a principle derivable from the brain substance, and sometimes found in diabetic sugar: called also *cerebrogalactose.*

cerebroside (ser′e-bro-sīd″). A general designation of an acid amide of a fatty acid with sphingosine or dihydrosphingosine in glycosidic linkage with galactose or glucose. Kerasin and phrenosin are typical members of this class.

cerebrosidosis (ser″e-bro″si-do′sis). A lipoidosis in which the fatty accumulation in the body consists largely of kerasin: e.g., Gaucher's disease.

cerebrosis (ser″e-bro′sis). Any disease of the cerebrum.

cerebrospinal (ser″e-bro-spi′nal). Pertaining to the brain and spinal cord.

cerebrospinant (ser″e-bro-spi′nant). Any medicine or agent that affects the brain and spinal cord.

cerebrospinase (ser″e-bro-spi′nās). An oxidizing ferment occurring in the cerebrospinal fluid.

cerebrostimulin (ser″e-bro-stim′u-lin). A component of the cerebrospinal fluid which has a stimulating action on the brain.

cerebrostomy (ser″e-bros′to-me) [*cerebrum* + Gr. *stoma* opening]. The making of an artificial opening into the cerebrum.

cerebrosuria (ser″e-bro-su′re-ah) [*cerebrose* + Gr. *ouron* urine + *-ia*]. The occurrence of cerebrose in the urine; cerebral diabetes.

cerebrotomy (ser″e-brot′o-me) [*cerebrum* + Gr. *temnein* to cut]. The anatomy or dissection of the brain.

cerebrotonia (ser″e-bro-to′ne-ah) [*cerebro-* + Gr. *tonos* tension + *-ia*]. A psychic type characterized by predominance of restraint, inhibition, and desire for concealment.

cerebrovascular (ser″e-bro-vas′ku-lar). Pertaining to the blood vessels of the cerebrum, or brain.

cerebrum (ser′e-brum) [L.]. [N A, B N A] The main portion of the brain occupying the upper part of the cranium, the two cerebral hemispheres, united by the corpus callosum, forming the largest part of the central nervous system in man. It consists of derivatives of the mesencephalon, diencephalon, and telencephalon. **c. abdomina′le,** plexus celiacus. **c. exsicca′tum,** the gray substance of the brain of calves, freed from fats, dried, and pulverized: used therapeutically in brain and nervous diseases.

cerecloth (sēr′kloth). Cloth impregnated with wax and made antiseptic: used in dressings.

Cerenkov radiation (ka′ren-kof) [P. A. *Cerenkov*, Russian physicist]. See under *radiation*.

cereoli (se-re′o-li). Plural of *cereolus*.

cereolus (se-re′o-lus), pl. *cere′oli* [L., dim. of *cereus* wax taper]. A medicated bougie.

cerevisia (ser″e-viz′e-ah), pl. and gen., *cerevis′iae* [L.]. Beer, ale, porter, or other brewed malt liquor. **cerevis′iae fermen′tum,** brewer's yeast. **cerevis′iae fermen′tum compres′sum,** compressed yeast.

cerevisiae (ser″e-viz′e-e) [L.]. Plural and genitive singular of *cerevisia*.

cerin (se′rin). Cerotic acid.

cerium (se′re-um) [L.]. A metallic element: symbol, Ce; atomic number, 58; atomic weight, 140.12. **c. oxalate,** a white, insoluble powder, a mixture of the oxalates of cerium, didymium, lanthanum, and other elements; sedative, tonic, and nervine; used in gastric irritability, vomiting of pregnancy, and reflex cough.

cer-o-cillin (ser′o-sil″lin). Trade mark for preparations of penicillin O for parenteral administration.

ceroid (se′roid). An insoluble pigment found in the fibrous tissue of cirrhotic livers.

cerolipoid (se″ro-li′poid). A waxy substance existing in plants.

cerolysin (se-rol′ĭ-sin) [L. *cera* wax + *lysin*]. A lysin which decomposes wax.

ceroma (se-ro′mah) [Gr. *kērōma* waxy mass]. A tumor of tissue which has undergone a waxy degeneration.

ceroplasty (se′ro-plas″te) [L. *cera* wax + Gr. *plassein* to mold]. The making of anatomical models in wax.

cerotin (ser′o-tin). Ceryl alcohol.

certifiable (ser″tĭ-fi′ah-b'l). Capable of being certified: said of infectious diseases, cases of which must by law be reported to the health officers.

ceruloplasmin (sĕ-roo″lo-plaz′min). An alpha$_2$-globulin of the blood, being the form in which 96 per cent of the plasma copper is transported.

cerumen (sĕ-roo′men) [L., from *cera* wax]. The waxlike secretion found within the external meatus of the ear. Called also *earwax*. Official in B N A, but omitted in N A. **inspissated c.,** dried earwax in the external canal of the ear.

ceruminal (sĕ-roo′mĭ-nal). Of or pertaining to the cerumen.

ceruminolysis (sĕ-roo″mĭ-nol′ĭ-sis). The solution or disintegration of cerumen in the external auditory meatus.

ceruminolytic (sĕ-roo″mĭ-no-lit′ik). 1. Pertaining to, characterized by, or promoting ceruminolysis. 2. An agent that dissolves cerumen in the external auditory canal.

ceruminosis (sĕ-roo″mĭ-no′sis). Excessive or disordered secretion of cerumen.

ceruminous (sĕ-roo′mĭ-nus). Ceruminal.

ceruse (se′ro͞os) [L. *cerussa*]. The basic carbonate of lead; white lead.

cervanthropy (ser-van′thro-pe) [L. *cervus* deer + Gr. *anthrōpos* man]. Delusion that one has turned into a deer.

cervical (ser′vĭ-kal) [L. *cervicalis*, from *cervix* neck]. Pertaining to the neck or to any cervix.

cervicalis (ser″vĭ-ka′lis) [L.]. Cervical.

cervicectomy (ser″vĭ-sek′to-me). Trachelectomy.

cerviciplex (ser-vis′ĭ-pleks). The cervical plexus of nerves.

cervicitis (ser″vĭ-si′tis). Inflammation of the cervix uteri.

cervico-axillary (ser″vĭ-ko-ak′sĭ-lār-e). Pertaining to the neck and axilla.

cervicobrachial (ser″vĭ-ko-bra′ke-al). Pertaining to the neck and arm.

cervicobuccal (ser″vĭ-ko-buk′al). Buccocervical.

cervicocolpitis (ser″vĭ-ko-kol-pi′tis). Inflammation of the cervix uteri and vagina. **c. emphysemato′sa,** colpitis emphysematosa with similar lesions occurring beneath the squamous mucosa of the cervix uteri.

cervicodorsal (ser″vĭ-ko-dor′sal). Pertaining to the neck and the back.

cervicodynia (ser″vĭ-ko-din′e-ah) [*cervix* + Gr. *odynē* pain]. Pain in the neck.

cervicofacial (ser″vĭ-ko-fa′she-al). Pertaining to the neck and face.

cervicolabial (ser″vĭ-ko-la′be-al). Labiocervical.

cervicolingual (ser″vĭ-ko-ling′gwal). Linguocervical.

cervico-occipital (ser″vĭ-ko-ok-sip′ĭ-tal). Pertaining to the neck and occiput.

cervicoplasty (ser″vĭ-ko-plas′te) [*cervix* + Gr. *plassein* to form]. Plastic surgery on the neck.

cervicoscapular (ser″vĭ-ko-skap′u-lar). Pertaining to the neck and scapula.

cervicothoracic (ser″vĭ-ko-tho-ras′ik). Pertaining to the neck and thorax.

cervicovaginitis (ser″vĭ-ko-vaj″ĭ-ni′tis). Inflammation involving both the cervix uteri and vagina.

cervicovesical (ser″vĭ-ko-ves′e-kal). Pertaining to the cervix uteri and urinary bladder.

cervilaxin (ser″vĭ-lak′sin). Trade mark for a preparation of relaxin.

cervimeter (ser-vim′e-ter) [*cervix* + Gr. *metron* measure]. An apparatus for measuring the cervix uteri.

cervix (ser′viks), pl. *cer′vices* [L.]. Neck; used in anatomical nomenclature to designate the lower front portion of the part connecting the head and trunk (collum), or a constricted part of an organ (e.g., cervix uteri). **c. of axon,** a constricted part of an axon, before the myelin sheath is added. **c. colum′nae posterio′ris** [B N A], **c. cor′nu,** the constricted part of the dorsal horn of gray matter in the spinal cord. Omitted in N A. **c. den′tis,** collum dentis. **c. glan′dis,** collum glandis. **c. mal′lei,** collum mallei. **tapiroid c.,** a uterine cervix with a peculiarly elongated anterior lip. **c. u′teri,** the lower and narrow end of the uterus, between the isthmus and the ostium uteri. **c. vesi′cae** [N A], a constricted portion of the urinary bladder, formed by the meeting of its inferolateral surfaces proximal to the opening of the urethra.

Cervus (ser′vus) [L. "a stag"]. A genus of deer.

C. brasilien′sis, a Brazilian deer, whose skin and hair afforded a substance once used as a homeopathic remedy.

ceryl (se′ril). A univalent hydrocarbon radical of the fatty series, having the formula $C_{27}H_{55}$.

c.e.s. Abbreviation for *central excitatory state.*

cesarean (se-sa′re-an) [L. *caesarea,* from *caedere* to cut]. See under *section.*

Cesaris-Demel bodies (cha′sar-is da′mel) [Antonio *Cesaris-Demel,* Italian pathologist, born 1866]. See under *body.*

cesarotomy (se″zar-ot′o-me). Cesarean section.

cesium (se′ze-um) [L. *caesium,* from *caesius* blue]. A rare univalent metallic element with an alkaline oxide; atomic number, 55; atomic weight, 132.905; symbol, Cs. Some of its salts and binary compounds are used like those of potassium. **c. bitartrate,** a salt, $Cs_2C_4H_4O_6$, in colorless, soluble prismatic crystals: recommended for nervous heart palpitation. **c. bromide,** a white, soluble, granular powder, CsBr: used in nervous heart palpitation. **c. carbonate,** a white, granular, hygroscopical salt, Cs_2CO_3: used as a nervine. **c. eosinate** has been used to protect against shock in the arsphenamine treatment of syphilis. **c. hydroxide,** a grayish, hygroscopical substance, CsOH: antiepileptic and nervine. **c. sulfate,** a colorless, soluble salt, Cs_2SO_4, in stable prisms: antiepileptic.

Cestan-Chenais syndrome (ses-tan′ shen-āz′) [Raymond *Cestan,* French neurologist, 1872–1933]. See under *syndrome.*

cesticidal (ses″tĭ-si′dal). Destructive to platyhelminths, or cestodes.

Cestoda (ses-to′dah). An order of Platyhelminthes which includes the tapeworms, which have a head or scolex and segments of proglottides. There are five families: Trypanorhynchidae or Tetrarhynchidae, Tetraphyllidae, Diphyllidae, Pseudophyllidae or Bothriocephalidae, and Cyclophyllidae or Taeniidae.

cestode (ses′tōd). 1. Any tapeworm or platyhelminth of the order to which the tapeworms belong. 2. Cestoid.

cestodiasis (ses″to-di′ah-sis). Infestation by cestodes.

cestoid (ses′toid) [Gr. *kestos* girdle + *eidos* form]. Resembling a tapeworm.

cestus (ses′tus) [L. "a belt"]. A fold of the metatela surrounding the dorsal portion of the brain tube.

cetaceum (sĕ-ta′se-um). See *spermaceti.*

cetanol (se′tah-nol). A solid white alcohol, $C_{16}H_{33}OH$, from sperm oil.

Ceterach (set′er-ak) [Arabic]. A genus of ferns. *C. officinarum* was formerly much used as a mucilaginous astringent.

Cetraria (sĕ-tra′re-ah). 1. A genus of lichens. 2. The official name of *C. islandica,* the so-called Iceland moss. It is nutritious and useful in lung and bowel affections.

cetyl (se′til). A univalent alcohol radical, $C_{16}H_{33}$.

cetylid (set′ĭ-lid). A compound formed by boiling cerebrin with water.

cetylpyridinium (se″til-pi″rĭ-din′e-um). Chemical name: 1-hexadecylpyridinium: used as a local anti-infective. **c. chloride,** the monohydrate of the quarternary salt of pyridine and cetyl chloride: used in tincture or aqueous solution as a detergent antiseptic for skin disinfection and in treatment of minor wounds.

cevalin (se′vah-lin). Trade mark for preparations of ascorbic acid (vitamin C).

cevex (se′veks). Trade mark for a liquid preparation of ascorbic acid (vitamin C).

ce-vi-sol (se′vi-sol). Trade mark for a preparation of ascorbic acid for calibrated dropper dosage.

Ceylancyclostoma (se″lan-si-klos′to-mah). *Ancylostoma ceylanicum.*

ceyssatite (sēs′ah-tit) [*Ceyssat,* a village of France]. A white earth from France: useful as an adsorbent powder in eczema and hyperidrosis, and in preparing ointments and medicated pastes.

C.F. Abbreviation for *carbolfuchsin.*

Cf. Chemical symbol for *californium.*

cf. Abbreviation L. *confero* bring together, compare.

C.F.T. Abbreviation for *complement-fixation test.*

CG. Abbreviation for *phosgene.*

cg. Abbreviation for *centigram.*

cgm. Abbreviation for *centigram.*

C.G.S. Abbreviation for *centimeter-gram-second* system, a system of measurements in which the units are based on the centimeter as the unit of length, the gram as the unit of mass, and the second as the unit of time.

C.H. Abbreviation for *crown-heel* (length of fetus).

$(CH_2)_2$. Ethylene.

CH_4. Methane.

C_2H_2. Acetylene.

C_6H_6. Benzene.

Chabert's disease (shah-bārz′) [Philebert *Chabert,* French veterinarian, 1737–1814]. Symptomatic anthrax.

Chabertia (shah-ber′te-ah). A genus of worms parasitic in animals. **C. ovi′na,** a species of worms, the large-mouth bowel worm, parasitic in the colon of cattle.

Chaddock's sign (chad′oks) [Charles Gilbert *Chaddock,* St. Louis neurologist, 1861–1936]. See under *sign.*

Chadwick's sign (chad′wiks) [James Read *Chadwick,* American gynecologist, 1844–1905]. Jacquemier's sign. See under *sign.*

Chagas' disease (chag′as) [Carlos *Chagas,* physician in Brazil, 1879–1934]. See under *disease.*

Chagasia (chah-gas′e-ah) [Carlos *Chagas*]. A genus of South American mosquitoes.

Chagres fever (chag′res) [named from a river in Panama]. See under *fever.*

Chailletia (ka-il-e′she-ah). A genus of trees and shrubs, nearly all tropical. *C. toxicaria,* of West Africa, bears poisonous fruit and seeds.

Chain (chān), Ernst Boris. A German pathologist, born 1906; co-winner, with Sir Alexander Fleming and Sir Howard Walter Florey, of the Nobel prize for medicine in 1945.

chain (chān). A collection of objects linked together in linear fashion, or end to end, as the assemblage of atoms or radicals in a chemical compound, or an assemblage of individual bacterial cells. **closed c.,** several atoms linked together so as to form a ring. Such compounds are derived from benzene, C_6H_6, and are known as *aromatic, cyclic, carbocyclic,* or *coal tar* compounds. **open c.,** several atoms united to form an open chain. Compounds of this series are related to methane and are also called *fatty, aliphatic, acyclic,* or *paraffin* compounds. **sympathetic c.,** the sympathetic trunk.

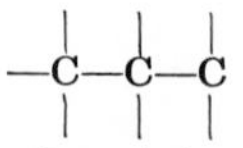

Open chain.

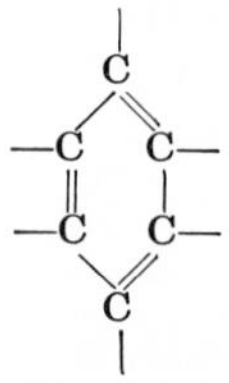

Closed chain.

Chalara (kah-lar′ah). A genus of fungi which produce the infection chalarosis.

chalarosis (kal″ah-ro′sis). The state of being infected by the fungus *Chalara.* It is attended by the development of nodules beneath the skin which degenerate into ulcers.

chalasia (kah-la′ze-ah) [Gr. *chalasis* relaxation]. Relaxation of a bodily opening, such as the cardiac sphincter, which is a cause of vomiting in infants.

chalastodermia (kah-las″to-der′me-ah). Dermatolysis.

chalaza (kah-la′zah) [Gr. "lump"]. A spiral band of albumin extending from either end of the yolk of a bird's egg to the shell.

chalazia (kah-la′ze-ah) [Gr.]. Plural of *chalazion.*

chalazion (kah-la′ze-on), pl. *chala′zia* or *chalazions* [Gr. "small lump"]. A small tumor of the eyelid, formed by the distention of a meibomian gland with secretion.

chalazodermia (kah-laz″o-der′me-ah). Dermatolysis.

chalcitis (kal-si′tis). Chalkitis.

chalcone (kal′kōn) [Gr. *chalkos* copper or brass]. Any one of a group of yellow pigments which are substituted benzalacetophenone derivatives.

chalcosis (kal-ko′sis) [Gr. *chalkos* copper]. The presence of copper deposits in the tissues. **c. len′tis,** sunflower cataract.

chalicosis (kal-ĭ-ko′sis) [Gr. *chalix* gravel]. A disorder of the lungs or bronchioles (chiefly among stone-cutters), due to the inhalation of fine particles of stones; a form of pneumoconiosis.

chalinoplasty (kal′ĭ-no-plas″te) [Gr. *chalinos* a corner of the mouth + *plassein* to mold]. Plastic surgery of the angle of the mouth.

chalk (chawk) [L. *calx* or *creta*]. Amorphous calcium carbonate; a white, lusterless, slightly alkaline, insoluble earth: used as a polishing agent in dentistry, and frequently as an ingredient in dentifrices. **French c.,** talc. **prepared c.,** precipitated calcium carbonate.

chalkitis (kal-ki′tis) [Gr. *chalkos* brass]. Inflammation of the eyes caused by rubbing the eyes after the hands have been used on brass. Called also *brassy eye.*

chalone (kal′ōn) [Gr. *chalan* to relax]. Colyone.

chalonic (kah-lon′ik). Colyonic.

chaluni (chal-oo′ne). Keratodermia plantare sulcatum.

chalybeate (kah-lib′e-āt) [L. *chalybs;* Gr. *chalyps* steel]. Containing or charged with iron: ferruginous or martial.

chamaecephalic (kam″e-se-fal′ik). Pertaining to or characterized by chamaecephaly.

chamaecephaly (kam″e-sef′ah-le) [Gr. *chamai* low + *kephalē* head]. The condition of having a low flat head, that is, a cephalic index of 70 or less.

Chamaelirium (kam-ĕ-lir′e-um) [Gr. *chamai* low + *leirion* lily]. See *helonin.*

chamaeprosopic (kam″e-pro-sop′ik). Pertaining to or characterized by chamaeprosopy.

chamaeprosopy (kam″e-pros′o-pe) [Gr. *chamai* low + *prosōpon* face]. The condition of having a low, broad face, i.e., a facial index of 90 or less.

chamber (chām′ber) [L. *camera;* Gr. *kamara*]. An enclosed space or antrum. **Abbe-Zeiss counting c.,** Thoma-Zeiss counting c. **air c.,** in dentistry, a recess in the palatal surface of the base of an upper denture to assist in retaining the denture by creating a partial vacuum. **anterior c. of eye,** that portion of the aqueous-containing space between the cornea and the lens which is bounded in front by the cornea and part of the sclera, and behind by the iris, part of the ciliary body, and that part of the lens which presents through the pupil. Called also *camera anterior bulbi* [N A]. **aqueous c.,** that part of the eyeball which is filled with aqueous humor. See *anterior c. of eye* and *posterior c. of eye.* **counting c.,** a space of definite thickness provided with a ruled base, into which blood samples of specific dilutions may be placed, for counting and quantitating the formed elements. **detonating c.,** a muffler surrounding the discharging balls of a static machine or resonator for deadening the sound of a spark discharge. **c's of eye,** the various spaces in the eyeball. See *anterior c. of eye, posterior c. of eye,* and *vitreous c.* **Haldane c.,** an air-tight chamber in which animals may be confined for the performance of metabolic studies. **c's of the heart,** the cavities of the atria and ventricles. **hyperbaric c.,** a compartment in which the air pressure may be raised to more than normal atmospheric pressure: used in treatment of gas gangrene and other anaerobic infections, or other conditions in which a high concentration of oxygen is desirable. **ionization c.,** an enclosure containing two or more electrodes between which an electric current may be passed when the enclosed gas is ionized by any radiation: used for determining the intensity of roentgen and other rays. **lethal c.,** a chamber which may be filled with gas, for killing small animals. **posterior c. of eye,** that portion of the aqueous-containing space between the cornea and the lens which is bounded in front by the iris, and behind by the lens and suspensory ligament. Called also *camera posterior bulbi* [N A]. **pulp c.,** the natural cavity in the central portion of the tooth crown occupied by the dental pulp. **relief c.,** a recess in the surface of a denture which rests on the oral structures, to reduce or eliminate pressure on the tissues at that particular site in the mouth. **Storm Van Leeuwen c.,** a room that can be kept free of airborne antigens for allergic patients. **suction c.,** air c. **Thoma-Zeiss counting c.,** a device consisting of a receptacle in the bottom of a slide for a microscope, with ruled lines dividing the area into minute squares, to facilitate the counting of blood corpuscles or other cells. **vacuum c.,** air c. **vitreous c.,** the space in the eyeball enclosing the vitreous humor, bounded anteriorly by the lens and ciliary body, and posteriorly by the posterior wall of the eyeball. **Zappert's c.,** a form of counting chamber.

Chamberland filter (shahm-ber-lah′) [Charles Edouard *Chamberland,* French bacteriologist, 1851–1908]. See under *filter.*

Chamberlen forceps [Peter (Pierre) *Chamberlen,* English accoucheur, 1560–1631]. See under *forceps.*

chamecephalic (kam″e-se-fal′ik). Chamaecephalic.

chamecephaly (kam″e-sef′ah-le). Chamaecephaly.

chameprosopic (kam″e-pro-sop′ik). Chamaeprosopic.

chameprosopy (kam″e-pros′o-pe). Chamaeprosopy.

Champetier de Ribes' bag (shahmp-te-a′ de rēbz′) [Camille Louis Antoine *Champetier de Ribes,* French obstetrician, 1848–1935]. See under *bag.*

champignon (sham″pēn-yaw′) [Fr. "mushroom"]. Suppurative inflammation of the spermatic cord of a horse sometimes following castration.

Ch'an su (chan soo). The dried venom of the Chinese toad.

chancre (shang′ker) [Fr. "canker," from L. *cancer* crab]. The primary lesion of syphilis developing at the site of entrance of the syphilitic infection and appearing as a small papule which erodes into a reddish ulcer covered with a yellowish exudation. **fungating c.,** soft chancre, characterized by fungoid granulations. **hard c., hunterian c., indurated c.,** a constitutional venereal sore, followed by true syphilis. Its base and sides are distinctly hard, and it gives off a thin secretion that produces syphilis when inoculated upon another person. **mixed c.,** a lesion due to infection with *Treponema pallidum* and *Haemophilus ducreyi.* **Nisbet's c.,** nodular abscesses in the penis after acute lymphangitis from soft chancre. **non-infecting c.,** chancroid. **c. re′dux,** chancre developing on the scar of a healed primary chancre, caused by organisms which remain in the scar. **Ricord's c.,** the parchment-like initial lesion of syphilis. **Rollet's c.,** mixed c. **simple c., soft c.,** chancroid. **sporotrichotic c.,** the first developing sore at the site of sporotrichic infection. **sulcus c., true c.,** hard c.

chancriform (shang′kre-form). Resembling a chancre.

chancroid (shang′kroid). An infection caused by *Haemophilus ducreyi.* It begins as a pustule on the genitals, forming soon after inoculation: it grows rapidly, and finally breaks down into a virulent ulcer, discharging pus. **phagedenic c.,** a variety attended by sloughing of the tissues. **serpiginous c.,** a variety which tends to spread in curved lines.

chancroidal (shang-kroi′dal). Pertaining to chancroid.

chancrous (shang′krus). Of the nature of chancre.

Ch'ang Shan (chang′shan). The Chinese name for the root of *Dichroa febrifuga,* which has an antiparasitic and antipyretic effect in malaria.

change (chānj). An alteration. **Biermer's c., Gerhardt's c. of sound,** alteration of percussion note according to the patient's position: an indication of pneumothorax, etc.

channel (chan′el) [L. *canalis* a water pipe]. That through which anything flows; a cut or groove. **blood c's,** narrow passages with no distinct walls, but containing blood: they are found in fresh granulation tissue. **central c.,** a long straight capillary which connects an arteriole to a venule. **lymph c's,** the smaller lymph sinuses; irregular spaces in and about the lymphatic glands and around lymphatic vessels. **perineural c.,** a lymph channel which surrounds a nerve trunk. **thoroughfare c.,** a channel between terminal arterioles and venules, larger than a capillary.

Chantemesse' reaction (shant-mes′) [André *Chantemesse,* French bacteriologist, 1851–1919]. See under *reaction.*

Chaoul therapy, tube (showl) [Henri *Chaoul,* Berlin radiologist, born 1887]. See under *therapy* and *tube.*

Chapman's bag [John *Chapman,* English physician in Paris, died 1894]. See under *bag.*

chappa (chap′ah). A disease of West Africa some what resembling syphilis or yaws. It is characterized by the formation of marble-sized nodules beneath the skin which degenerate and give off scaly material.

chapped (chapt). Cracked or slit open by the cold, as chapped hands.

Chaput's method, operation (shap-o͞oz′) [Henri *Chaput,* French surgeon, 1857–1919]. See under *method* and *operation.*

character (kar′ak-ter). A quality or attribute indicative of the nature of an object or an organism. **acquired c.,** a modification produced in an animal as a result of its own activities or environment. **compound c.,** a character which is dependent on two or more genes for its production. **dominant c.,** a mendelian character which develops when it is transmitted by a single gene. **imvic c's,** four important characters in the classification of the coliform organisms: they are indole, methyl-red, Voges-Proskauer reaction and sodium citrate. **mendelian c's,** in genetics, the separate and distinct traits that are exhibited by an animal or plant, and are dependent on the genetic constitution of the organism; they may be recessive or dominant. See *Mendel's law,* under *law.* **primary sex c's,** those characters that are concerned directly in reproduction. **recessive c.,** a mendelian character which develops only when it is transmitted by both genes determining the trait. **secondary sex c's,** those specific to the male or female organism but not directly concerned in reproduction. **sex-linked c.,** one transmitted consistently to individuals of one sex only, being carried in the sex chromosome. **unit c.,** a trait which is transmitted from parent to offspring intact, that is, without blending or mixing, though it may be either dominant or recessive.

characteristic (kar″ak-ter-is′tik). 1. Character. 2. Typical of an individual or other entity.

characterology (kar″ak-ter-ol′o-je). The study of character and personality.

charbon (shar-baw′) [Fr. "coal"]. Anthrax. **c. symptomatique′,** symptomatic anthrax.

charcoal (char′kōl). Carbon prepared by charring organic material. **activated c.,** the residue from the destructive distillation of various organic materials, treated to increase its absorptive powers: used as an adsorbent. **animal c.,** charcoal prepared from bone.

Charcot's bath, disease, joint, syndrome, etc. (shar-kōz′) [Jean Martin *Charcot,* French neurologist, 1825–1893]. See under the nouns.

Charcot-Leyden crystals (shar-ko′ li′den) [J. M. *Charcot;* Ernest Victor von *Leyden,* German physician, 1832–1910]. See under *crystal.*

Charcot-Marie type, Charcot-Marie-Tooth type (shar-ko′ mah-re′ to͞oth) [J. M. *Charcot;* Pierre *Marie,* French physician, 1853–1940; Howard Henry *Tooth,* English physician, 1856–1926]. See *progressive neuropathic (peroneal) muscular atrophy,* under *atrophy.*

Charcot-Neumann crystals (shar-ko′ noy′-mahn). See under *crystal.*

Charcot-Vigouroux sign (shar-ko′ ve-goo-roo′) [J. M. *Charcot;* Romain *Vigouroux,* French physician of 19th century]. See under *sign.*

charlatan (shar′lah-tan) [Fr.]. A pretender to knowledge or skills that he does not possess; in medicine, a quack.

charlatanism (shar′lah-tan-izm). The pretension of knowledge and skills that one does not possess. In medicine, quackery.

charlatanry (shar′lah-tan-re). Charlatanism.

Charles' law (sharlz) [Jacques Alexandre César *Charles,* French physicist, 1746–1823]. See under *law.*

charleyhorse (char′le-hors). Soreness and stiffness in a muscle caused by overstrain. The term is usually restricted to injuries of the quadriceps muscle.

Charlouis's disease (shar″loo-ēz′) [M. *Charlouis,* Dutch physician in Java]. Yaws.

Charrière scale (shar″e-ār′) [Joseph Frédéric Benoit *Charrière,* French instrument maker, 1803–1876]. See under *scale.*

Charrin's disease (shar-raz′) [Albert *Charrin,* pathologist in Paris, 1857–1907]. Pyocyanic infection.

charring (char′ing). Carbonization; in surgical diathermy, the reduction of tissue into a residue of carbon.

Chart. Abbreviation for L. *char′ta,* paper.

chart (chart). 1. A simplified graphic representation of the fluctuation of some variable, as of pulse, temperature, and respiration, or a record of all the clinical data of a particular case. 2. To record graphically the fluctuation of some variable, or to record the clinical data of a particular case. **Gibson's c.,** a graphic representation of the total increase of leukocytes and the increase in neutrophil percentages, for comparison as a means of testing a patient's resistance to infection. **Guibor's c.,** a chart containing outline pictures for orthoptic training. **reading c.,** a chart bearing material printed in type of gradually increasing sizes; used in testing acuity of near vision. **Snellen's c.,** a chart imprinted with block letters (Snellen's test type) in gradually decreasing sizes, identified according to distances at which they are ordinarily visible; used in testing distance vision.

charta (kar′tah). pl. *char′tae* [L.; Gr. *chartēs*]. 1. Paper. 2. A piece of paper, medicated or otherwise. **c. explorato′ria coeru′lea,** blue litmus paper. **c. explorato′ria lu′tea,** turmeric paper; paper stained with turmeric for use as a test paper. **c. explorato′ria ru′bra,** red litmus paper.

chartula (kar′tu-lah), pl. *char′tulae* [L. dim. of *charta* paper]. A small piece of paper, as for containing a dose of a medicinal powder.

Chase's sign [Ira C. *Chase*, American physician, 1868–1933]. See under *sign*.

chasma (kaz′mah) [Gr. *chasma* a cleft]. A yawning; an opening.

chasmatoplasson (kaz-mat′o-plas″on). Plasson in an expanded condition.

chasmus (kas′mus). Chasma.

Chassaignac's tubercle (shas″ăn-yahks′) [Charles Marie E. *Chassaignac*, French surgeon, 1805–1879]. See under *tubercle*.

chaude-pisse (shōd-pēs) [Fr.]. A burning sensation experienced during micturition.

chauffage (sho-fahzh′) [Fr. *chauffer* to heat]. Treatment with a cautery at a low heat which is passed to and fro across the tissue about ¼ inch away from it.

Chauffard's syndrome (sho-farz′) [Anatole-Marie-Emile *Chauffard*, French physician, 1855–1932]. See under *syndrome*.

Chauliac (sho″le-ahk′), Guy de (1300–1368). An eminent French surgeon who practiced in Avignon. His treatise on surgery (*Chirurgia magna*) was regarded as a standard work until Paré's time.

Chaussier's areola, line, sign, tube (sho″se-āz′) [François *Chaussier*, Parisian surgeon and anatomist, 1746–1828]. See under the nouns.

Chauveau's bacillus, bacterium (sho-vōz′) [Auguste *Chauveau*, Paris veterinarian, 1827–1917]. *Clostridium chauvoei*.

Ch.B. Abbreviation for L. *Chirur′giae Baccalau′reus*, Bachelor of Surgery.

C_2H_5Br. Ethyl bromide.

$CHCl_3$. Chloroform.

$C_2H_4Cl_2$. Ethylene chloride.

C_2H_5Cl. Ethyl chloride.

$C_2HCl_3(OH)_2$. Chloral hydrate.

$C_2H_5CO_2NH_2$. Ethyl carbamate.

$(CH_3.CO)_2O$. Acetic anhydride.

$CH_3.COOH$. Acetic acid.

$C_4H_9.COOH$. Valerianic acid.

Ch.D. Abbreviation for L. *Chirur′giae Doc′tor*, Doctor of Surgery.

ChE. Cholinesterase.

Cheadle's disease (che′delz) [Walter Butler *Cheadle*, London pediatrician, 1835–1910]. Infantile scurvy.

check-bite (chek′bīt). A sheet of hard wax or modeling compound placed between the teeth in centric, eccentric, lateral, or protrusive occlusion, to be used as a check on the occlusion of the teeth in those positions in the articulator.

Chediak reaction, test [Alejandro *Chediak*, Cuban physician]. See under *test*.

cheek (chēk). A fleshy protuberance, especially the fleshy portion of the side of the face. Called also *bucca* [N A]. Also applied to the fleshy mucous-membrane covered side of the oral cavity (bucca cavum oris [N A]). **cleft c.,** a developmental anomaly characterized by an abnormal fissure, caused by failure of union of some of the facial processes.

cheesy (che′ze). Caseous, resembling cheese.

cheil-. See *cheilo-*.

cheilectomy (ki-lek′to-me) [*cheil-* + Gr. *ektomē* excision]. 1. Excision of a lip. 2. The operation of chiseling off the irregular bony edges of a joint cavity which interfere with motion.

cheilectropion (ki″lek-tro′pe-on) [*cheil-* + *ectropion*]. Eversion of the lip.

cheilitis (ki-li′tis) [*cheil-* + *-itis*]. Inflammation affecting the lips. **actinic c., c. actin′ica,** involvement of the lips after exposure to actinic rays, with pain and swelling and development of a scaly crust on the vermilion border. **acute c.,** eczema of the lips. **apostematous c.,** c. glandularis apostematosa. **commissural c.,** cheilitis affecting principally the angles (commissures) of the mouth. **c. exfoliati′va,** seborrheic dermatitis affecting the vermilion border of the lips. **c. glandula′ris apostemato′sa,** a condition in which the lower lip becomes enlarged, firm, and finally everted, exposing the openings of the accessory salivary glands which are inflamed and dilated, appearing as small red macules on the mucosa; the glands themselves are enlarged and sometimes nodular. Called also *Puente's disease* and *myxadenitis labialis*. **impetiginous c.,** impetigo of the lips. **migrating c.,** perlèche. **c. venena′ta,** inflammation of the lips caused by a chemical irritant.

cheilo-, cheil- (ki′lo, kil′) [Gr. *cheilos* lip; an edge, or brim]. Combining form denoting relationship to the lip, or to an edge or brim.

cheiloangioscopy (ki″lo-an″je-os′ko-pe) [*cheilo-* + Gr. *angeion* vessel + *skopein* to examine]. Microscopical observation of the circulation in the blood vessels of the lip.

cheilocarcinoma (ki″lo-kar″sĭ-no′mah). Cancer of the lip.

cheilognathopalatoschisis (ki″lo-na″tho-pal″ah-tos′kĭ-sis). Cheilognathouranoschisis.

cheilognathoprosoposchisis (ki″lo-na″tho-pros″o-pos′kĭ-sis) [*cheilo-* + Gr. *gnathos* jaw + *prosōpon* face + *schisis* cleft]. A developmental anomaly characterized by presence of an oblique facial cleft continuing into the lip and upper jaw.

cheilognathoschisis (ki″lo-na-thos′kĭ-sis) [*cheilo-* + Gr. *gnathos* jaw + *schisis* cleft]. A developmental anomaly characterized by the presence of a cleft in the lip and jaw.

cheilognathouranoschisis (ki″lo-na″tho-u-rah-nos′kĭ-sis) [*cheilo-* + Gr. *gnathos* jaw + *ouranos* palate + *schisis* cleft]. A developmental anomaly characterized by the presence of a cleft in the lip, upper jaw, and palate.

cheiloncus (ki-long′kus). A tumor of the lip.

cheilophagia (ki″lo-fa′je-ah) [*cheilo-* + Gr. *phagein* to eat]. Biting of the lips.

cheiloplasty (ki′lo-plas″te) [*cheilo-* + Gr. *plassein* to form]. Surgical repair of a defect of the lip.

Cheilopoda (ki-lop′o-dah). Chilopoda.

cheilopodiasis (ki″lo-po-di′ah-sis). Chilopodiasis.

cheilorrhaphy (ki-lor′ah-fe) [*cheilo-* + Gr. *rhaphē* suture]. The operation of suturing the lip.

cheiloschisis (ki-los′kĭ-sis) [*cheilo-* + Gr. *schisis* cleft]. Harelip.

cheilosis (ki-lo′sis) [*cheilo-* + *-osis*]. A condition marked by fissuring and dry scaling of the vermilion surface of the lips and angles of the mouth. It is characteristic of riboflavin deficiency.

cheilostomatoplasty (ki″lo-sto-mat′o-plas″te) [*cheilo-* + Gr. *stoma* mouth + *plassein* to form]. Plastic surgery or restoration of the lips and mouth, as after the removal of a cancer.

cheilotomy (ki-lot′o-me) [*cheilo-* + Gr. *tomē* cut]. Cheilectomy.

cheimaphobia (ki″mah-fo′be-ah) [Gr. *cheima* winter + *phobia*]. Morbid fear of cold.

cheir-. See *cheiro-*.

Cheiracanthus (ki″rah-kan′thus). Gnathostoma

cheiragra (ki-rag′rah) [*cheir-* + Gr. *agra* seizure]. Gout of the hand, especially tophaceous gout with torsion of the fingers.

cheiralgia (ki-ral′je-ah). Pain in the hand. **c. paresthet′ica,** isolated neuritis of the superficial ramus of the radial nerve.

cheirapsia (ki-rap′se-ah) [Gr. "a touching with the hands"]. Massage; gentle hand friction.

cheirarthritis (ki″rar-thri′tis) [*cheir-* + *arthritis*]. Inflammation of the joints of the hand and fingers.

cheiro-, cheir- [Gr. *cheir* hand]. Combining form denoting relationship to the hand. For words beginning with this root see also those beginning with *chir-* and *chiro-*.

cheirobrachialgia (ki″ro-bra″ke-al′je-ah). A syndrome of paresthesia and pain in the arm, hand and fingers. Called also *cheirobrachialgia paresthetica*.

cheirocinesthesia (ki″ro-sin″es-the′ze-ah). Cheirokinesthesia.

cheirognomy (ki-rog′no-me) [*cheiro-* + Gr. *gnomōn* judge]. The study of the hand as a guide to characteristics of the individual.

cheirognostic (ki″rog-nos′tik) [*cheiro-* + Gr. *gnostikos* knowing]. Pertaining to or characterized by the ability to distinguish stimuli as originating on the right or the left side of the body.

cheirokinesthesia (ki″ro-kin″es-the′ze-ah). The subjective perception of the movements of the hand, especially in writing.

cheirokinesthetic (ki″ro-kin″es-thet′ik). Pertaining to or characterized by cheirokinesthesia.

cheirology (ki-rol′o-je). Dactylology.

cheiromegaly (ki-ro-meg′ah-le). Abnormal enlargement of the hands.

cheiroplasty (ki′ro-plas″te) [*cheiro-* + Gr. *plassein* to form]. Plastic surgery on the hand.

cheiropodalgia (ki″ro-po-dal′je-ah) [*cheiro-* + Gr. *pous* foot + *algos* pain]. Pain in the hands and feet.

cheiropompholyx (ki″ro-pom′fo-liks) [*cheiro-* + Gr. *pompholyx* a bubble]. A skin disease with peculiar vesicles on the palms and soles.

cheiroscope (ki′ro-skōp) [*cheiro-* + Gr. *skopein* to view]. An instrument used in the training of binocular vision, by which the image of a test object seen reflected in a mirror by the sound eye is projected by the other eye to a drawing board where it is traced with a pencil guided by the hand of the subject.

cheirospasm (ki′ro-spazm) [*cheiro-* + Gr. *spasmos* spasm]. Spasm of the muscles of the hand.

chelate (ke′lāt) [Gr. *chēlē* claw]. To combine with a metal in weakly dissociated complexes in which the metal is part of a ring. By extension, applied to a chemical compound in which a metallic ion is sequestered and firmly bound into a ring within the chelating molecule.

chelen (ke′len). Ethyl chloride.

chel-iron (kēl′i-ron). Trade mark for preparations of ferrocholinate.

cheloid (ke′loid). Keloid.

cheloma (ke-lo′mah). Keloid.

chelonian (ke-lo′ne-an) [Gr. *chelōnē* tortoise]. Pertaining to the tortoise.

chemasthenia (kem″as-the′ne-ah). An asthenic condition of the chemical processes of the body.

chemesthesis (kem″es-the′sis). The sensation of matter.

chemiatric (kem″e-at′rik). Pertaining to chemiatry.

chemiatry (kem′e-ah-tre) [Gr. *chēmeia* chemistry + *iatreia* treatment]. Iatrochemistry.

chemical (kem′ĭ-kal). 1. Of, or pertaining to, chemistry. 2. A substance composed of chemical elements, or obtained by chemical processes.

chemicobiological (kem″ĭ-ko-bi″o-loj′e-kal). Pertaining to the chemistry of living matter.

chemicocautery (kem″ĭ-ko-kaw′ter-e). Destruction of tissue by application of a caustic chemical substance.

chemicogenesis (kem″ĭ-ko-jen′e-sis) [*chemistry* + Gr. *genesis* production]. Stimulation of the development of an ovum by chemical action.

chemicophysical (kem″ĭ-ko-fiz′e-kal). Pertaining to chemistry and physics; pertaining to physical chemistry.

chemicophysiologic (kem″ĭ-ko-fiz″e-o-loj′ik). Pertaining to physiology and chemistry.

chemicovital (kem″ĭ-ko-vi′tal). Pertaining to the chemistry of living things.

chemiluminescence (kem″ĭ-loo″mĭ-nes′ens). Chemoluminescence.

cheminosis (kem″ĭ-no′sis) [*chemistry* + Gr. *nosos* disease]. Any disease due to chemical agents.

chemiotaxis (kem″e-o-tak′sis). Chemotaxis.

chemiotherapy (kem″e-o-ther′ah-pe). Chemotherapy.

chemism (kem′izm). Chemical activity; chemical property or relationship.

chemist (kem′ist). An individual skilled in chemistry.

chemistry (kem′is-tre) [Gr. *chēmeia*]. The science which treats of the elements and atomic relations of matter, and of the various compounds of the elements. **analytical c.,** chemistry which deals with analysis of different elements in a compound. **applied c.,** the application of chemistry to industry and the arts. **biological c.,** physiologic c. **colloid c.,** chemistry dealing with the nature and composition of colloids. **dental c.,** the chemistry of materials which are used in dental procedures and the processes to which they are subjected. **forensic c.,** use of chemical knowledge in the solution of legal problems. **gross c.,** macrochemistry. **industrial c.,** applied c. **inorganic c.,** that branch of the science of chemistry which deals with compounds that do not contain carbon. **medical c.,** chemistry as it relates to medicine. **metabolic c.,** physiologic c. **mineral c.,** inorganic chemistry. **organic c.,** that branch of chemistry which deals with compounds that contain carbon. **pharmaceutical c.,** chemistry which deals with the composition and preparation of substances used in treatment of patients or diagnostic studies. **physical c.,** that branch of chemistry which deals with the relationship of chemical and physical properties and relationships. **physiologic c.,** that branch of chemistry which deals with chemical processes that take place in animals and plants. **structural c.,** chemical study of the structure of molecules. **synthetic c.,** that branch of chemistry which deals with the building up of chemical compounds from simpler substances or from the elements.

chemo- (ke′mo, kem′o) [Gr. *chēmeia* chemistry]. A combining form denoting a relationship to chemistry, or to a chemical.

chemoantigen (kem″o-an′tĭ-jen). A chemical compound having antigenic properties.

chemoautotroph (ke″mo-aw′to-trōf). A chemoautotrophic microorganism.

chemoautotrophic (kem″o-aw″to-trof′ik). Capable of synthesizing cell constituents from carbon dioxide by means of the energy derived from inorganic reactions.

chemobiotic (ke″mo-bi-ot′ik). The combination of a chemotherapeutic agent and an antibiotic, as of one or more of the sulfonamide compounds with penicillin.

chemocephalia (ke″mo-sĕ-fa′le-ah). Chamaecephaly.

chemocephaly (ke″mo-sef′ah-le). Chamaecephaly.

chemoceptor (ke′mo-sep-tor). Chemoreceptor.

chemocoagulation (ke″mo-ko-ag″u-la′shun). Coagulation or destruction of growths by the application of chemicals.

chemodectoma (ke″mo-dek-to′mah) [*chemo-* + *dektos* to be received or accepted + *-oma*]. Any tumor of the chemoreceptor system, such as a carotid body tumor.

chemodifferentiation (ke″mo-dif″er-en-she-a′-shun). A term proposed by Huxley for the invisible point of decision which foreruns and controls the actual differentiation of cells into the rudimentary organs of the embryo.

chemoimmunity (ke″mo-ĭ-mu′nĭ-te). Immunity to disease produced by use of chemicals.

chemoimmunology (ke″mo-im-u-nol′o-je). The study of the chemical processes involved in immunity.

chemokinesis (ke″mo-ki-ne′sis) [*chemo-* + Gr. *kinēsis* motion]. Increased activity of an organism due to the presence of a chemical substance.

chemokinetic (ke″mo-ki-net′ik). Pertaining to or exhibiting chemokinesis.

chemoluminescence (ke″mo-loo″mĭ-nes′ens). 1. Radiation which produces chemical action. 2. Luminescence produced by the direct transformation of chemical energy.

chemolysis (ke-mol′ĭ-sis) [*chemo-* + Gr. *lysis* solution]. Chemical decomposition.

chemomorphosis (ke″mo-mor-fo′sis) [*chemo-* + Gr. *morphē* form]. Change of form due to chemical action.

chemopallidectomy (ke″mo-pal″ĭ-dek′to-me) [*chemo-* + *pallidum* + *ektomē* excision]. Creation of a lesion of the globus pallidus by destruction of tissue by a chemical agent.

chemopallidothalamectomy (ke″mo-pal″ĭ-do-thal″ah-mek′to-me). Creation of a lesion of the globus pallidus and thalamus by a chemical agent.

chemopharmacodynamic (ke″mo-far″mah-ko-di-nam′ik). Denoting the relationship between chemical constitution and biologic or pharmacologic activity.

chemophysiology (ke″mo-fiz-ĭ-ol′o-je). Physiologic chemistry.

chemoprophylaxis (ke″mo-pro″fi-lak′sis) [*chemo-* + Gr. *prophylax* an advanced guard]. Use of a chemotherapeutic agent as a means of preventing development of a specific disease. **primary c.,** prophylactic use of a chemotherapeutic agent before infection has occurred in an individual. **secondary c.,** prophylactic use of a chemotherapeutic agent in an individual after infection has occurred (with *Mycobacterium tuberculosis,* for example) but before disease has become manifest.

chemopsychiatry (ke″mo-si-ki′ah-tre). The use of drugs in the treatment of mental and emotional disorders.

chemoreception (ke″mo-re-sep′shun) [*chemo-* + L. *receptio,* from *recipere* to receive]. The process of being sensitive to or perceiving chemical stimuli in the surrounding medium.

chemoreceptor (ke″mo-re-sep′tor). 1. A receptor adapted for excitation by chemical substances, e.g., olfactory and gustatory receptors, or a sense organ, as the carotid body or the aortic (supracardial) bodies, which is sensitive to chemical changes in the blood stream, especially reduced oxygen content, and reflexly increases both respiration and blood pressure. See *receptor.* 2. A supposed group of atoms in cell protoplasm having the power of fixing chemicals, in the same way as bacterial poisons are fixed.

chemoreflex (ke″mo-re′fleks). Reflex resulting from chemical action.

chemoresistance (ke″mo-re-zis′tans). Specific resistance acquired by cells to the action of chemicals.

chemosensitive (ke″mo-sen′sĭ-tiv). Sensitive to changes in chemical composition.

chemoserotherapy (ke″mo-se″ro-ther′ah-pe). The treatment of disease with both drugs and serum.

chemosis (ke-mo′sis) [Gr. *chēmōsis*]. Excessive edema of the ocular conjunctiva.

chemosmosis (ke″mos-mo′sis). Chemical action taking place through an intervening membrane.

chemosterilant (ke″mo-ster′ĭ-lant). A chemical compound the ingestion of which causes sterility of an organism; such compounds have been used as a means of controlling various insect and other pests by inducing sterility in the male.

chemosurgery (ke″mo-sur′jer-e). The destruction of tissue by chemical agents; originally applied to chemical fixation of malignant, gangrenous, or infected tissue, with use of frozen sections to facilitate systematic microscopic control of its excision.

chemosynthesis (ke″mo-sin′the-sis) [*chemo-* + Gr. *synthesis* putting together]. The synthesis of carbohydrate from carbon dioxide and water as a result of the energy derived from chemical reactions, rather than from absorbed light. Such synthesis is carried out by certain bacteria and algae. Cf. *photosynthesis.*

chemotactic (ke″mo-tak′tik). Of or pertaining to chemotaxis.

chemotaxis (ke″mo-tak′sis) [*chemo-* + Gr. *taxis* arrangement]. The movement of an organism in response to a chemical concentration gradient. **negative c.,** movement of an organism from a region of high to a region of low concentration of a specific chemical compound or element. **positive c.,** movement of an organism from a region of low to a region of high concentration of a specific chemical compound or element.

chemotherapeutical (ke″mo-ther-ah-pu′te-kal). Pertaining to chemotherapy.

chemotherapeutics (ke″mo-ther-ah-pu′tiks). Chemotherapy.

chemotherapy (ke″mo-ther′ah-pe). The treatment of disease by chemical agents; first applied to use of chemicals that affect the causative organism unfavorably but do not harm the patient.

chemotic (ke-mot′ik). Pertaining to, or affected with, chemosis.

chemotrophy (ke-mot′ro-fe) [*chemo-* + Gr. *trophē* nutrition]. That type of bacterial nutrition in which the source of energy is chemical oxidation (Van Niel).

chemotropic (ke″mo-trop′ik). Of or pertaining to chemotropism.

chemotropism (ke-mot′ro-pizm) [*chemo-* + Gr. *tropos* a turning]. An orienting response to a chemical stimulus, as in a plant root.

chemurgy (kem′er-ge) [*chemo-* + Gr. *ergon* work]. The practical application of chemistry to the arts.

cheoplastic (ke″o-plas′tik). Pertaining to cheoplasty.

cheoplasty (ke′o-plas″te). [Gr. *chein* to pour + *plassein* to form]. A method once used of molding artificial teeth with an alloy of tin, silver, and bismuth.

Cherchevski's (Cherchewski's) disease (sher-shev′skēz) [Michael *Cherchevski,* Russian physician]. See under *disease.*

cheromania (ke″ro-ma′ne-ah) [Gr. *chairein* to rejoice + *mania* madness]. Mania characterized by exaltation and cheerfulness.

Cheron's serum (sha-rawz′) [Jules *Cheron,* French gynecologist, 1837–1900]. See under *serum.*

cherophobia (ke″ro-fo′be-ah) [Gr. *chairein* to rejoice + Gr. *phobos* fear + *-ia*]. Morbid dislike or fear of gaiety.

cherry (cher′e) [L. *cerasus*]. The name of various rosaceous trees and species of the genus *Prunus.* See *Prunus virginiana.* **choke c.,** *Prunus virginiana.* **c. laurel,** an old world evergreen cherry tree, *Prunus laurocerasus.* **rum c.,** *Prunus serotina.* **wild c.,** the carefully dried stem bark of *Prunus serotina,* used in a syrup as a flavored vehicle for drugs.

cherubism (cher′u-bizm) [*cherub* + *-ism*]. The facial condition produced by fibrous dysplasia of the jaws.

Chervin's method, treatment (sher-vaz′) [Claudius *Chervin,* French teacher, 1824–1896]. A method of treatment for stuttering.

chest (chest). The thorax. **alar c.,** phthinoid chest. **barrel c.,** a rounded, bulging chest, showing little movement on respiration: seen in emphysema. **blast c.,** pulmonary concussion and hemorrhage occurring as the result of injury by a blast. **cobbler's c.,** a chest showing a sinking in at the lower end of the sternum. **flat c.,** deformity of the chest in which it is flattened from before back. **foveated c.,** funnel chest. **funnel c.,** a chest in which there is funnel-shaped depression in the middle of the anterior thoracic wall, the deepest part being in the sternum: called also *funnel breast, pectus excavatum, koilosternia,* *chonechondrosternon*, and *trichterbrust*. **keeled c.,** pigeon breast. **paralytic c.,** a long and narrow chest with emaciation so that the ribs stand out sharply under the skin. **phthinoid c.,** the same as *flat chest;* so called as indicating a tubercular diathesis. **pterygoid c.,** phthinoid chest. **tetrahedron c.,** a chest which suggests a solid with four sides, each an equilateral triangle, the chest projecting in a peak between the nipples.

chestnut (chest′nut). 1. Castanea. 2. One of the masses of horn on the medial surface of the forearm and on the distal part of the medial surface of the tarsus of horses. **horse c.,** Aesculus.

chétivism (sha′tĭ-vizm) [Fr. *chétive* puny + *-ism*]. A form of infantilism in which the arrest of development affects the mass of the individual rather than any special organ or part.

Cheyletiella (sha″lĕ-te-el′lah). A genus of arachnids. **c. parasitov′orax,** an acarine living on the cat, which may cause a dermatosis in human beings.

Cheyne's operation (chānz) [Sir William Watson *Cheyne*, British surgeon, 1852–1932]. See under *operation*.

Cheyne-Stokes nystagmus, respiration, etc. (chān′stōks) [John *Cheyne*, Scottish physician, 1777–1836; William *Stokes*, Irish physician, 1804–1878]. See under the nouns.

CHI_3. Iodoform.

C_2H_5I. Ethyl iodide.

Chiari's disease, network (ke-ar′ēz) [Hans *Chiari*, German pathologist, 1851–1916]. See under *disease* and *network*.

chiasm (ki′azm) [L., Gr. *chiasma*]. A decussation or X-shaped crossing. See *chiasma*. **c. of digits of hand,** chiasma tendinum digitorum manus. **optic c.,** chiasma opticum. **tendinous c. of flexor sublimis digitorum muscle,** chiasma tendinum digitorum manus.

chiasma (ki-as′mah) [L.; Gr.]. A decussation or X-shaped crossing, such as the crossing of the members of a chromosome pair or tetrad in the prophase of the first maturation division of germ cells; used in official anatomical nomenclature to designate the crossing of two elements or structures. Called also *chiasm*. **c. op′ticum** [N A, B N A], the decussation, or crossing, of the fibers of the optic nerve from the medial half of the retina, on the ventral surface of the brain. Called also *optic chiasm*. **c. ten′dinum digito′rum ma′nus** [N A, B N A], the crossing of the tendons of the flexor digitorum profundus through the tendons of the flexor digitorum sublimis.

chiasmal (ki-az′mal). Chiasmatic.

chiasmatic (ki-az-mat′ik). Resembling a chiasm; crosswise.

chiasmatypy (ki-az′mah-ti″pe) [Gr. *chiasma* a crossing + *type*]. Crossing over.

chiasmic (ki-az′mik). Chiasmatic.

chiastometer (ki″as-tom′e-ter) [Gr. *chiastos* crossed + *metron* measure]. An apparatus for measuring any deviation of the optic axes from their normal parallelism.

chickenpest (chik′en-pest). Fowl plague.

chickenpox (chik′en-poks). An acute communicable disease, principally of young children, caused by a virus, and marked by slight fever and an eruption of macular vesicles, which appear in crops, and are superficial and rarely umbilicated. They rarely become pustular, but dry up, and are only occasionally followed by scars. The duration of the disease is about a week, during which time it runs a very mild course.

chick-pea (chik′pe). The plant *Cicer arietinum* of Southern Europe whose seeds are used as food and may cause poisoning.

Chiene's operation (shēnz) [John *Chiene*, Scottish surgeon, 1843–1923]. See under *operation*.

Chievitz's layer, organ (che′wits-ez) [Johan Henrik *Chievitz*, Danish anatomist, 1850–1901]. See under *layer* and *organ*.

chigger (chig′er). The six-legged red larva of the mite *Eutrombicula alfreddugési* (*Trombicula irritans*), known as harvest mite and red bug. The bites of chiggers produce a wheal on the skin which is accompanied by intense itching. The habitat of this mite is tall grass and underbrush. The chigger of Europe is *Trombicula* (*Leptus*) *autumnalis*. Chiggers are to be distinguished from jiggers or chigoes. Cf. *chigoe*.

chigo (chig′o). Chigoe.

chigoe (chig′o). The sand flea, *Tunga penetrans*, of tropical America and the southern United States. The pregnant female flea burrows into the skin of the feet and legs of man, causing intense irritation and resulting in ulceration if untreated.

chilblain (chil′blān) [L. *pernio*]. Pernio; a localized itching and painful erythema on the fingers, toes or ears, produced by cold damp weather. **chronic c.** is a disease of the small blood vessels of the skin and may result in ulceration and necrosis. **necrotized c.,** lupus pernio.

child (chīld). The human young, from infancy to puberty. **preschool c.,** a child between 2 and 6 years old. **school c.,** a child between 6 and 10–12 years old.

childhood (chīld′hood). The period of life of the human young generally considered to extend from infancy to puberty.

chilitis (ki-li′tis). Cheilitis.

chill (chil). A shivering or shaking; an attack of involuntary contractions of the voluntary muscles, accompanied by a sense of cold and pallor of the skin. **brass c., brazier's c.,** metal fume fever caused by fumes in brass foundries. **congestive c.,** pernicious malaria with gastrointestinal congestion and diarrhea, preceded by a chill. **creeping c.,** a chilly sensation, without any definite tremor or chattering of the teeth. **nervous c.,** a tremor due to some form of excitement and unaccompanied by alteration of temperature. **shaking c.,** a chill in which there is a definite tremor. **spelter c's,** metal fume fever. **urethral c.,** a chilly sensation, with or without tremor, sometimes following the passage of a catheter. **zinc c.,** metal fume fever caused by fumes in zinc smelters.

chilo-. For words thus beginning, see also words beginning *cheilo-*.

Chilodon (ki′lo-don). A genus of ciliates. *C. dentatus* has been found in the feces in a case of dysentery. *C. uncinatus* was found in the feces in a case of schistosomiasis.

Chilognatha (ki-log′nah-thah). An order of the class Myriapoda embracing the millipedes.

chilomastigiasis (ki″lo-mas″tĭ-gi′ah-sis). Infection with *Chilomastix*.

Chilomastix (ki″lo-mas′tiks). A genus of protozoa. **C. mesnil′i,** a minute flagellate protozoan, with a cytostome and three anterior flagellae, frequently parasitic in the human intestine.

chilomastixiasis (ki″lo-mas″tik-si′ah-sis). Chilomastigiasis.

chilomastosis (ki″lo-mas-to′sis). Chilomastigiasis.

Chilopoda (ki-lop′o-dah) [Gr. *cheilos* lip + *pous* foot]. A class of the phylum Arthropoda embracing the centipedes.

chilopodiasis (ki″lo-po-di′ah-sis) [*Chilopoda* + *-iasis*]. The presence of a centipede of the class Chilopoda in a body cavity.

chimaera (ki-me′rah). Chimera.

chimatlon (ki-mat′lon) [Gr. *cheima* winter]. An injury by frost. **mild c.,** chilblain. **severe c.,** frost-bite.

chimera (ki-me′rah) [Gr. *chimaira* a mythological fire-spouting monster with a lion's head, goat's body, and serpent's tail]. An individual organism whose body contains cell populations derived from different zygotes, of the same or of different species, occurring spontaneously, as in twins (blood group chimeras), or produced artificially, as an organism which develops from combined portions of different embryos, or one in which tissues or cells of another organism have been introduced. **heterologous c.,** a chimera in which the foreign cells or tissues are derived from an organism of a different species. **homologous c.,** a chimera in which the foreign cells or tissues are derived from an organism of the same species but of a different genotype. **isologous c.,** a chimera in which the foreign cells or tissues are derived from a different organism of the same genotype, such as an identical twin.

chimerism (ki-mēr′izm). The quality of being a chimera; in genetics, the presence in an individual of cells of different origin, as of blood cells derived from a heterozygous twin.

chimpanzee (chim-pan′ze). One of the anthropoid apes, *Anthropopithecus troglodytes*, used for experimental purposes because of its susceptibility to some of the diseases of man.

chin (chin). The anterior prominence of the lower jaw; the mentum. **galoche c.** (gah-losh′) [Fr. "galosh"], a long pointed chin.

china (ki′nah). Cinchona, or Peruvian bark.

chinacrine (kin′ah-krin). Quinacrine.

chiniofon (kin′ĭ-o-fon). A canary yellow powder, containing 26.5–29.0 per cent of iodine: used as an antiprotozoan.

chionablepsia (ki″o-nah-blep′se-ah) [Gr. *chiōn* snow + *ablepsia* blindness]. Snow blindness.

chip-blower (chip-blo′er). Chip syringe. See under *syringe*.

chir-. See *chiro*. For words beginning thus, see also those beginning *cheir-* and *cheiro-*.

chirality (ki-ral′ĭ-te). The power of turning the plane of polarization of light to the right or left.

chirapsia (ki-rap′se-ah). Cheirapsia.

chiro-, chir- (ki′ro, kir′) [Gr. *cheir* hand]. Combining form denoting relationship to the hand. For words beginning with this root see also those beginning with *cheir-* and *cheiro-*.

chirobrachialgia (ki″ro-bra″ke-al′je-ah). Cheirobrachialgia.

chirognostic (ki″rog-nos′tik). Cheirognostic.

chirology (ki-rol′o-je). Dactylology.

chiromegaly (ki″ro-meg′ah-le). Cheiromegaly.

Chironomidae (ki″ro-nom′ĭ-de). A family of Diptera which comprises the true midges.

chiropodalgia (ki″ro-po-dal′je-ah). Cheiropodalgia.

chiropodist (ki-rop′o-dist). Podiatrist.

chiropody (ki-rop′o-de). Podiatry.

chiropractic (ki″ro-prak′tik) [*chiro-* + Gr. *prattein* to do]. A system of therapeutics based upon the claim that disease is caused by abnormal function of the nerve system. It attempts to restore normal function of the nerve system by manipulation and treatment of the structures of the human body, especially those of the spinal column.

chiropractor (ki″ro-prak′tor). A practitioner of chiropractic.

chiropraxis (ki″ro-prak′sis). Chiropractic.

chiroscope (ki′ro-skōp). Cheiroscope.

chirospasm (ki′ro-spazm). Cheirospasm.

chirurgenic (ki″rōōr-jen′ik) [L. *chirur*gia surgery + Gr. *gennan* to produce]. Induced by or occurring as a result of a surgical procedure.

chirurgeon (ki-rur′jun). A surgeon.

chirurgery (ki-rur′jer-e) [L. *chirurgia*, from Gr. *cheir* hand + *ergon* work]. Surgery.

chirurgic (ki-rur′jik). Pertaining to surgery.

chitin (ki′tin) [Gr. *chitōn* tunic]. A white, insoluble, horny polysaccharide, $C_{30}H_{50}O_{19}N_4$, which is the principal constituent of the shells of crabs and lobsters and the shards of beetles. It is found also in certain fungi, and yields an acetyl glucosamine on hydrolysis.

chitinase (ki′tĭ-nās). An enzyme which catalyzes the hydrolysis of chitin to acetyl glucosamine.

chitinous (kit′ĭ-nus). Composed of or of the nature of chitin.

chitobiose (ki″to-bi′ōs). A disaccharide-like constituent of chitin, composed of two glucosamine units.

chitoneure (ki′to-nūr) [Gr. *chitōn* tunic + *neuron* nerve]. A general term for the sheaths of nervous structure including the perineurium, endoneurium, and neurilemma.

chitonitis (ki″to-ni′tis). Inflammation of any investing membrane.

chitosan (ki′to-san). A product, probably an acetyl glucosamine, obtained from chitin.

chitose (ki′tōs). A sugar, $C_6H_{12}O$, formed by the reduction of chitonic acid.

chitotriose (ki″to-tri′ōs). A trisaccharide-like substance of chitin, composed of three glucosamine units.

Chittenden's diet (chit′en-denz) [Russell Henry *Chittenden*, American physiologic chemist, 1856–1943]. See under *diet*.

chiufa (che-oo′fah). A gangrenous inflammation of the colon and rectum occurring in mountain regions of South America and South Africa.

Chlamydia (klah-mid′e-ah) [Gr. *chlamys* cloak]. A genus of the family Chlamydiaceae, order Rickettsiales, occurring as two species, both pathogenic for man. **C. oculogenita′lis,** the agent causing inclusion conjunctivitis (inclusion blennorrhea), commonly acquired in swimming pools, and persisting as a urogenital infection, symptomless in the female but producing a nonspecific urethritis in the male. **C. tracho′matis,** the etiological agent of trachoma.

Chlamydiaceae (klah-mid″e-a′se-e). A family of the order Rickettsiales, class Microtatobiotes, made up of small, coccoid microorganisms with a characteristic developmental cycle, occurring as saprophytes or obligate intracytoplasmic parasites in various warm-blooded animals, in which they usually cause disease. It includes five genera, *Chlamydia, Colesiota, Colettsia, Miyagawanella,* and *Ricolesia.*

Chlamydobacteriaceae (klah-mi″do-bak-te″re-a′se-e). A family of Schizomycetes (order Chlamydobacteriales), made up of filamentous, alga-like cells, frequently showing false branching. It includes three genera, *Leptothrix, Sphaerotilus,* and *Toxothrix.*

Chlamydobacteriales (klah-mi″do-bak-te″re-a′lēz). An order of Schizomycetes, made up of non-pigmented alga-like bacteria occurring in filaments which may or may not be ensheathed, and which frequently show false branching as a result of lateral displacement of cells within a sheath. It includes three families, *Chlamydobacteriaceae, Crenotrichaceae,* and *Peloplocaceae.*

Chlamydophrys (klah-mid′o-fris). A genus of protozoa. **C. anchel′ys, C. sterco′rea,** species of protozoa found in the feces of man and various animals.

chlamydospore (klam′ĭ-do-spōr″) [Gr. *chlamys* cloak + *spore*]. 1. The reproductive organ of certain fungi; so named because of its being inclosed by two envelopes. 2. A spore that is covered.

Chlamydozoaceae (klam″ĭ-do″zo-a′se-e). A name formerly given the family Chlamydiaceae.

Chlamydozoon (klam″ĭ-do-zo′on). A name formerly given a genus of gram-negative microorganisms. See *Chlamydia.*

chloasma (klo-az′mah) [Gr. *chloazein* to be green]. A cutaneous discoloration occurring in yellowish-brown patches and spots. The term is applied vaguely to various pigmentary skin discolorations. **bronze c., c. bronzi′num,** bronze-colored pigmentation of the face, neck, and chest from constant exposure to the sun in the tropics. Called also *tropical mask.* **c. gravida′rum,** discoloration of the skin occurring in pregnancy, with brownish areas usually on the upper part of the face—forehead and cheeks. **c. hepat'icum,** discoloration of the skin allegedly resulting from disorder of the liver. **c. periora'le virgin'ium,** brownish or blackish pigmentation, associated with macular seborrhea, situated chiefly around the mouth but involving other parts of the face, and occurring in normal young girls at the time of the first menstrual period. **c. phthisico'rum,** brown patches on the cheeks and forehead of tuberculous patients. **c. traumat'icum,** discoloration of the skin from pressure, friction, or other traumatic agencies. **c. uteri'num,** c. gravidarum.

chlophedianol (klo″fĕ-di′ah-nol). Chemical name: α(2-dimethylaminoethyl)-o-chlorobenzhydrol: used as an antitussive.

chloracetization (klor-as″e-tĭ-za′shun). The production of local anesthesia by application of equal parts of chloroform and glacial acetic acid.

chloracne (klor-ak′ne). An acneiform eruption caused by exposure to chlorine and chlorine compounds.

chloral (klo′ral) [*chlor*ine + *-al*]. 1. A colorless, oily liquid, trichloracetic aldehyde, $Cl_3C.CHO$, prepared by the mutual action of alcohol and chlorine. 2. Chloral hydrate. **butyl c.,** an oily, pungent liquid, $CH_3CHCl.CCl_2CHO$, whose hydrate, *butyl c. hydrate,* a crystalline compound, is used like chloral hydrate. **c. carmine,** a staining fluid made of carmine, 0.05 Gm.; hydrochloric acid, 30 minims; alcohol, 20 cc.; and chloral hydrate, 25 Gm. **c. hydrate,** $CCl_3CH(OH)_2$, a deliquescent, crystalline substance with an aromatic, penetrating odor and a bitter, caustic taste: used as a sedative, hypnotic, and anticonvulsant.

chloralism (klo′ral-izm). A morbid condition caused by excessive use of chloral.

chloralization (klo″ral-ĭ-za′shun). 1. Chloralism. 2. Anesthesia by the use of chloral.

chloralomania (klo″ral-o-ma′ne-ah). An insane addiction to chloral.

chloralose (klo′rah-lōs). A crystalline hypnotic substance, $C_8H_{11}Cl_3O_6$, a compound of chloral and dextrose. Soluble in alcohol and hot water; sparingly soluble in cold water.

chloramphenicol (klo″ram-fen′ĭ-kol). An antibiotic substance originally derived from cultures of *Streptomyces venezuelae,* and later produced synthetically: effective against certain gram-negative organisms and against Rickettsia.

chloranemia (klo″rah-ne′me-ah). Idiopathic hypochromic anemia.

chloranemic (klo″rah-ne′mik). Pertaining to or characterized by chloranemia.

chlorate (klo′rāt). Any salt of chloric acid.

chlorazol (klo′rah-zol). A highly poisonous oily liquid obtained by treating albumin, glutin, or dried muscle with nitric and hydrochloric acids. **fast pink BKS c.,** an anticoagulant dye for use in animal experiments.

chlorbutol (klōr-bu′tol). Chlorobutanol.

chlorcyclizine (klōr-si′klĭ-zēn). A white, odorless, or almost odorless powder, 1(p-chloro-α-phenylbenzyl)-4-methylpiperazine: antihistaminic.

chlordiazepoxide (klōr″di-a″ze-pok′sīd). Chemical name: 7-chloro-2-methylamino-5-phenyl-3H-1,4-benzodiazepine 4-oxide hydrochloride: used as a tranquilizer.

chlorellin (klo-rel′in). A bacteriostatic substance derived from fresh water algae of the genus *Chlorella.*

chloremia (klo-re′me-ah) [Gr. *chlōros* green + *haima* blood + *-ia*]. 1. Chlorosis. 2. The presence of excessive chlorides in the blood.

chlorenchyma (klo-ren′kĭ-mah). The chlorophyll-bearing tissue of plants.

chlorephidrosis (klo″ref-e-dro′sis) [Gr. *chlōros* green + *ephidrōsis* perspiration]. Green perspiration.

chloretone (klo′re-tōn). Trade mark for a preparation of chlorobutanol.

chlorguanide (klōr-gwan′id). Proguanil.

chlorhistechia (klōr″his-tek′e-ah) [*chloride* + Gr. *histos* tissue + *echein* to hold + *-ia*]. The presence of an abnormally large amount of chloride in a tissue.

chlorhydria (klōr-hi′dre-ah). An excess of free hydrochloric acid in the stomach.

chloric (klo′rik) [L. *chloricus*]. Derived from or containing pentavalent chlorine; a term used to distinguish those compounds which contain a smaller proportion of chlorine than the chlorous compounds, and forming salts known as chlorates.

chloride (klo′rīd). A salt of hydrochloric acid; any binary compound of chlorine in which the latter carries a negative charge of electricity (Cl^-). **acid c.,** a substance formed by substituting chlorine for hydroxyl in an acid molecule.

chloridemia (klo″rĭ-de′me-ah) [*chloride* + Gr. *haima* blood + *-ia*]. The retention of chlorides in the blood.

chloridimeter (klo″rĭ-dim′e-ter) [*chloride* + Gr. *metron* measure]. An instrument for measuring the chloride content of the urine or other fluid.

chloridimetry (klo″rĭ-dim′e-tre). The determination of the chloride content of fluids.

chloridion (klo″rid-i′on). Negatively ionic chlorine, the anion of hydrochloric acid and the chlorides.

chloridometer (klo″rĭ-dom′e-ter). Chloridimeter.

chloriduria (klo″rĭ-du′re-ah) [*chloride* + Gr. *ouron* urine + *-ia*]. Excess of chlorides in the urine.

chlorinated (klo′rĭ-nāt″ed). Charged with chlorine.

chlorine (klo′rin) [L. *chlorum* or *chlorinum,* from Gr. *chlōros* green]. A yellowish-green, gaseous element, of suffocating odor; symbol, Cl; atomic number, 17; atomic weight, 35.453; specific gravity, 1.56. It is disinfectant, decolorant, and an irritant poison. It is used for disinfecting, fumigating, and bleaching, either in an aqueous solution or in the form of chlorinated lime. **c. dioxide,** an oxidizing and germicidal agent, ClO_2, used in the purification of water.

chlorinum (klo-ri′num) [L.]. Chlorine.

chloriodized (klōr-i′o-dīzd). Containing chlorine and iodine.

chlorisondamine (klōr″i-son′dah-mēn). Chemical name: 4,5,6,7-tetrachloro-2-(2-dimethylaminoethyl) isoindoline: used to produce ganglionic blockade, and to reduce blood pressure.

chlorite (klo′rīt). Any salt of chlorous acid.

chlormerodrin (klōr-mer′o-drin). Chemical name: 1-[3-(chloromercuri)-2-methoxypropyl]-urea: used as a diuretic.

chlormethyl (klōr-meth′il). Methyl chloride.

chlormezanone (klōr-mez′ah-nōn). Chemical name: 2-(4-chorophenyl)-3-methyl-4-metathiazanone-1,1-dioxide: used as a muscle relaxant and tranquilizer.

chloro- (klo′ro) [Gr. *chlōros* green]. Combining form meaning green.

chloro-anemia (klo″ro-ah-ne′me-ah). 1. Chlorosis. 2. Anemia associated with rickets, tuberculosis, cancer, syphilis, etc.

Chlorobacteriaceae (klo″ro-bak-te″re-a′se-e). A family of Schizomycetes (order Pseudomonadales, suborder Rhodobacteriineae), composed of microorganisms developing in environments containing considerable hydrogen sulfide and exposed to light, and containing green pigments resembling but not identical with chlorophylls. It includes six genera, *Chlorobacterium, Chlorobium, Chlorochromatium, Clathrochloris, Cylindrogloea,* and *Pelodictyon.*

Chlorobacterium (klo″ro-bak-te′re-um). A genus of microorganisms of the family Chlorobacteriaceae, suborder Rhodobacteriineae, order Pseudomonadales, occurring as non-motile, often slightly curved rod-shaped cells growing symbiotically on the outside of protozoa. The type species is *C. symbiot'icum.*

Chlorobium (klo-ro'be-um). A genus of microorganisms of the family Chlorobacteriaceae, suborder Rhodobacteriineae, order Pseudomonadales, occurring as spherical to rod-shaped cells, singly or in chains. It includes two species, *C. limi'cola* and *C. thiosulfato'philum.*

chloroblast (klo'ro-blast) [*chloro-* + Gr. *blastos* germ]. An erythroblast.

chlorobrightism (klo″ro-brīt'izm). Chlorosis with albuminuria.

chlorobutanol (klo″ro-bu'tah-nol). A white crystalline compound, 1,1,1-trichloro-2-methyl-2-propanol: used as a preservative for various solutions, and as a hypnotic.

Chlorochromatium (klo″ro-kro-ma'te-um). A genus of microorganisms of the family Chlorobacteriaceae, suborder Rhodobacteriineae, order Pseudomonadales, occurring as ovoid to rod-shaped cells with rounded ends, forming barrel-shaped aggregates about a large, colorless bacterium. The type species is *C. aggregat'um.*

chlorocruorin (klo″ro-kroo'o-rin). A green respiratory pigment occurring in certain marine worms.

chloro-erythroblastoma (klo″ro-e-rith″ro-blas-to'mah). A new growth containing the elements of chloroma and erythroblastoma.

chloroform (klo'ro-form) [L. *chloroformum;* from *chlorine* + *formyl*]. A clear, colorless, volatile liquid, $CHCl_3$, with a strong ethereal smell and a sweetish, burning taste: used to induce general anesthesia by inhalation of its vapor. **acetone c.,** chlorobutanol. **alcoholized c.,** a mixture of chloroform and alcohol. **Anschütz's c.,** a crystalline substance; called also *salicylide chloroform,* gentle heat liberates a vapor of pure chloroform from it. **colloidal c.,** desalgin. **methyl c.,** an anesthetic, CH_3CCl_3, said to be safer than ordinary chloroform. **Pictet's c.,** chloroform purified by congelation at a very low temperature.

chloroformin (klo″ro-for'min). A poison (like etherin, benzenin, and xylenin) extractable by chloroform from tubercle bacilli; called also *chloroformobacillin.*

chloroformism (klo'ro-form″izm). 1. The habitual use of chloroform for its narcotic effect. 2. The anesthetic effect of the vapor of chloroform.

chloroformization (klo″ro-form″i-za'shun). The administration of chloroform.

chloroglobin (klo″ro-glo'bin) [*chloro-* + L. *globus* globe]. A protein substance in the form of green, oily globules, derived from plant leaves by the action of resorcinol.

chloroleukemia (klo″ro-lu-ke'me-ah). Myelogenous leukemia in which no specific tumor masses are present at autopsy but the body organs and fluids show a definite green color.

chlorolymphosarcoma (klo″ro-lim″fo-sar-ko'mah). Chloroma; so called because mononuclear cells in the peripheral blood were thought to be lymphocytes rather than myeloblasts.

chloroma (klo-ro'mah) [*chloro-* + *-oma*]. A malignant green-colored tumor arising from myeloid tissue, associated with myelogenous leukemia and occurring anywhere in the body. Besides containing green pigment, which has no clear metabolic role and is principally myeloperoxidase (verdoperoxidase), chloroma tissue demonstrates a bright red fluorescence under ultraviolet light.

chlorometry (klo-rom'e-tre). The quantitative determination of chlorine.

chloromycetin (klo″ro-mi-se'tin). Trade mark for preparations of chloramphenicol.

chloromyeloma (klo″ro-mi-ĕ-lo'mah). Chloroma attended with growths in the bone marrow.

chloropenia (klo″ro-pe'ne-ah) [*chlorine* + Gr. *penia* poverty]. Deficiency in chlorine.

chloropenic (klo″ro-pe'nik). Pertaining to or characterized by chloropenia.

chloropexia (klo″ro-pek'se-ah). The fixation of chlorine in the body.

chlorophane (klo'ro-fān) [*chloro-* + Gr. *phainein* to show]. A greenish-yellow pigment obtainable from the retina.

chlorophenol (klo″ro-fe'nol). A substance, $C_6H_4Cl.OH$, prepared by the action of chlorine on phenol.

chlorophenothane (klo″ro-fen'o-thān). Chemical name: 1,1,1-trichloro-2-2-bis (p-chlorophenyl) ethane: used as a contact insecticide.

chlorophyl (klo'ro-fil). Chlorophyll.

chlorophylase (klo'ro-fil-ās). An esterase which occurs in green leaves and hydrolyzes chlorophyll.

chlorophyll (klo'ro-fil) [*chloro-* + Gr. *phyllon* leaf]. The green coloring matter of plants by which photosynthesis is accomplished. **c. A,** $C_{55}H_{72}O_5N_4Mg$, is bluish green in color and more abundant in plants than **c. B,** $C_{55}H_{70}O_6N_4Mg$, which is yellowish green in color. Chlorophyll derivatives are sometimes used to promote healing of wounds, ulcers, etc.

chloropia (klo-ro'pe-ah). Chloropsia.

chloroplast (klo'ro-plast) [*chloro-* + Gr. *plastos* formed]. Any one of the chlorophyll-bearing bodies of plant and animal cells.

chloroplastid (klo″ro-plas'tid). Chloroplast.

chloroprivic (klo″ro-pri'vik) [*chlorine* + L. *privare* to deprive]. Deprived of chlorides; due to loss of chlorides.

chloroprocaine (klo″ro-pro'kān). Chemical name: β-diethylaminoethyl 2-chloro-4-aminobenzoate: used as a local or an epidural anesthetic.

chloropsia (klo-rop'se-ah) [*chloro-* + Gr. *opsis* vision + *-ia*]. Green vision; a visual defect in which all objects seen appear to have a greenish tinge.

chloroquine (klo'ro-kwin). A compound, 7-chloro-4(4-diethylamino-1-methylbutyl-amino) quinoline: used in treatment of malaria, hepatic amebiasis, and certain cardiac arrhythmias.

chlorosarcolymphadeny (klo″ro-sar″ko-lim-fad'ĕ-ne). Chlorolymphosarcoma.

chlorosarcoma (klo″ro-sar-ko'mah). Chloroma.

chlorosarcomyeloma (klo″ro-sar″ko-mi″ĕ-lo'mah). Chloromyeloma containing sarcomatous elements.

chlorosis (klo-ro'sis). A disorder, generally of pubescent females, characterized by greenish-yellow color of the skin and hypochromic red cells. The abnormality is apparently related mainly to iron lack, although the precise basis for this deficiency may be multifold. **achylic c.,** idiopathic hypochromic anemia. **Egyptian c.,** ancylostomiasis. **c. gigan'tea,** congenital chlorosis with obesity (Schönlein). **late c.,** idiopathic hypochromic anemia. **c. ru'bra,** a name applied to anemia without apparent pallor. **tropical c.,** ancylostomiasis.

Chlorostigma (klo″ro-stig'mah). A genus of plants. **C. stuckertia'num,** a plant of the Argentine: used as a galactogogue.

chlorothen (klo'ro-then). Chemical name: 2-[(5-chloro-2-thenyl) (2-dimethylaminoethyl) amino] pyridine: antihistaminic.

chlorothiazide (klo″ro-thi'ah-zīd). Chemical name: 6-chloro-7-sulfamyl-2H-1,2,4-benzothiadiazine-1,1-dioxide: used as a diuretic and antihypertensive.

chlorothymol (klo″ro-thi'mol). Chemical name: 6-chloro-4-isopropyl-1-methyl-3-phenol: used as an antibacterial.

chlorotic (klo-rot'ik). Pertaining to, or affected with chlorosis.

chlorotrianisene (klo″ro-tri-an'ĭ-sēn). An estrogenic compound, chlorotris (p-methoxyphenyl) ethylene.

chlorous (klo'rus). Derived from or containing trivalent chlorine; a term used to distinguish those compounds which contain a larger proportion of chlorine than the chloric compounds, and forming salts known as chlorites.

chlorovinyldichloroarsine (klo″ro-vin″il-di-klo″ro-ar′sin). Lewisite.

chlorpheniramine (klōr″fen-ir′ah-mēn). Chemical name: 2-[p-chloro-α-(2-dimethylaminoethyl) benzyl] pyridine: antihistaminic.

chlorphenoxamine (klōr″fen-ok′sah-mēn). Chemical name: 2-(p-chloro-α-methyl-α-phenylbenzyloxy)-N, N-dimethylamine. Uses: 1. antihistaminic; 2. reduce muscular rigidity.

chlorpromazine (klōr-pro′mah-zēn). A phenothiazine derivative, 2-chloro-10-(3-dimethylaminopropyl) phenothiazine: used as a tranquilizer, and an antiemetic, and to potentiate analgesics.

chlorpropamide (klōr-pro′pah-mīd). Chemical name: 1-propyl-3(p-chlorophenyl) sulfonylurea: an orally effective antidiabetic agent.

chlorprophenpyridamine (klōr″pro-fen-pi-rid′ah-mēn). Chlorpheniramine.

chlorquinaldol (klōr-kwin′al-dol). Chemical name: 5,7-dichloro-8-hydroxyquinaldine: a bactericide and fungicide for application to the skin.

chlorzoxazone (klōr-sok′sah-zōn). Chemical name: 5-chloro-2-benzoxazolamine: used as a skeletal muscle relaxant.

chlortetracycline (klōr″tet-rah-si′klēn). An antibiotic substance, 7-chloro-4-dimethylamino-1,4,-4α,5,5α,6,11,12α-octahydro-3,6,10,12,12α-pentahydroxy-6-methyl-1,11-dioxo-2-naphthacenecarboxamide, obtained from *Streptomyces aureofaciens.*

chlorthalidone (klōr-thal′ĭ-dōn). Chemical name: 3-hydroxy-3-(4-chloro-3-sulfamylphenyl) phthalimidine: used as a diuretic and antihypertensive.

chlor-trimeton (klōr-tri′mĕ-ton). Trade mark for preparations of chlorpheniramine.

chlorum (klo′rum) [L.]. Chlorine.

chloruremia (klo″roo-re′me-ah) [*chloride* + Gr. *ouron* urine + *haima* blood + *-ia*]. Presence of urinary chlorides in the blood; chloridemia.

chloruremic (klo″roo-re′mik). Pertaining to or marked by chloruremia.

chloruresis (klōr″u-re′sis) [*chloride* + Gr. *ourein* to urinate]. The excretion of chlorides in the urine.

chloruretic (klōr″u-ret′ik). 1. Promoting the excretion of chlorides in the urine. 2. An agent which promotes the excretion of chlorides in the urine.

chloruria (klo-roo′re-ah) [*chloride* + Gr. *ouron* urine + *-ia*]. Presence of chlorides in the urine.

Chlumsky's button (klum′skēz) [Vitezslav *Chlumsky*, Czech surgeon, 1867–1943]. See under *button.*

Ch.M. Abbreviation for L. *Chirurgiae Magister*, Master of Surgery.

$C_6H_5NH_2$. Aniline.

$C_3H_5(NO_3)_3$. Glyceryl trinitrate (nitroglycerin).

$C_5H_4N_4O_3$. Uric acid.

$C_5H_{11}NO_2$. Amyl nitrite.

C_8H_9NO. Acetanilid.

$C_9H_9NO_3$. Hippuric acid.

$C_6H_2(NO_2)_3OH$. Trinitrophenol (picric acid).

CH_2O. Formaldehyde.

CH_2O_2. Formic acid.

CH_4O. Methyl alcohol.

$C_2H_2O_4$. Oxalic acid.

$C_2H_4O_2$. Acetic acid.

C_2H_6O. Ethyl alcohol.

C_3H_6O. Acetone.

$C_3H_6O_3$. Lactic acid.

$C_3H_8O_3$. Glycerin.

$C_4H_6O_2$. Crotonic acid.

$C_4H_6O_5$. Malic acid.

$C_4H_6O_6$. Tartaric acid.

$C_4H_8O_2$. Butyric acid; isobutyric acid.

$C_4H_{10}O$. Ether (ethyl ether).

$C_5H_{10}O_2$. Valerianic acid.

$C_5H_{12}O$. Amyl alcohol.

C_6H_6O. Phenol.

$C_6H_8O_7$. Citric acid.

$(C_6H_{10}O_5)_n$. Starch.

$C_6H_{12}O_6$. Dextrose (*d*-glucose).

$C_7H_4O_7$. Meconic acid.

$C_7H_6O_2$. Benzoic acid.

$C_7H_6O_3$. Salicylic acid.

$C_7H_6O_5$. Gallic acid.

$C_{12}H_{22}O_{11}$. Cane sugar.

$C_{14}H_{10}O_9$. Tannic acid.

$C_{15}H_{10}O_4$. Chrysophanic acid.

$C_{18}H_{34}O_2$. Oleic acid.

$C_{18}H_{36}O_2$. Stearic acid.

choana (ko′a-nah), pl. *choa′nae* [L.; Gr. *choanē* funnel]. 1. Any funnel-shaped cavity or infundibulum. 2. [Pl.] [N A, B N A] The paired openings between the nasal cavity and the nasopharynx. Called also *choanae osseae* and *posterior nares.* **bony choanae, choa′nae os′seae.** See *choana*, def. 2. **primary c.,** the opening of the embryonic olfactory sac into the mouth. **secondary c.,** the definitive choana after the formation of the palate.

choanae (ko-a′ne) [L.]. Plural of *choana.*

choanal (ko′ah-nal). Pertaining to a choana.

choanoid (ko′ah-noid) [Gr. *choanē* funnel + *eidos* form]. Funnel-shaped.

Choanotaenia (ko-a″no-te′ne-ah). A genus of tapeworms. **C. infundib′ulum,** an important tapeworm which is found as a parasite in both chickens and turkeys.

choc (shok) [Fr.]. Shock. **c. en dome** (shok an dom), the domelike, heaving impulse of the heart in aortic insufficiency. **c. en retour** (shok an reh-toor′) ["return-shock"]. 1. The impulse of the descending fetus against the finger in ballottement. 2. The alleged infection of a pregnant woman with syphilis derived through the fetus.

chocolate (chok′o-lat) [L. *chocolata*, from Mexican *chocolatl*]. A dried paste prepared from the kernels of the cacao, *Theobroma cacao*, with sugar and flavoring substances.

$C_2H_5.OH$. Ethyl alcohol.

C_6H_5OH. Phenol.

$C_6H_4.OH.COOH$. Salicylic acid.

choke (chōk). 1. To interrupt respiration by obstruction or compression, or the condition resulting from such interruption. 2. [Pl.] A burning sensation beginning in the substernal region, with increasing uncontrollable urge to cough, and great apprehension and anxiety, leading to vasodepressor syncope, experienced during decompression. **ophthalmovascular c.,** interference with the blood supply of the retina due to pressure of the retinal vessels against one another. **thoracic c.,** obstruction of the thoracic part of the esophagus with a foreign body. **water c.,** laryngeal spasm caused by fluid entering the larynx and especially by getting between the true and false vocal cords.

chol-. See *chole-.*

cholagogic (ko″lah-goj′ik). Stimulating the flow of bile from the liver.

cholagogue (ko′lah-gog) [*chol-* + Gr. *agōgos* leading]. An agent which stimulates flow of bile from the liver.

cholaligenic (ko-lal″ĭ-jen′ik) [*cholalic* acid + Gr. *gennan* to produce]. Forming cholalic acid from cholesterol—one of the functions of the liver.

cholan (ko′lan). Trade mark for preparations of dehydrocholic acid.

cholaneresis (ko″lah-ner′e-sis). Increase in the output or elimination of cholic acid, its conjugates, or its salts.

cholangeitis (ko″lan-ji′tis). Cholangitis.

cholangia (ko-lan′je-ah). Cholangie.

cholangie (ko-lan′je). Naunyn's term for noninflammatory morbid processes of the bile passages.

cholangiectasis (ko-lan″je-ek′tah-sis). Dilatation of a bile duct.

cholangiocholecystocholedochectomy (ko-lan″ge-o-ko″le-sis″to-ko″le-do-kek′to-me). Excision of hepatic duct, common bile duct and gallbladder.

cholangio-enterostomy (ko-lan″je-o-en″ter-os′to-me) [*chol-* + Gr. *angeion* vessel + *enteron* intestine + *stomoun* to provide with an opening, or mouth]. Surgical anastomosis of a bile duct to the intestine.

cholangiogastrostomy (ko-lan″je-o-gas-tros′-to-me) [*chol-* + Gr. *angeion* vessel + *gastēr* stomach + *stomoun* to provide with an opening, or mouth]. Surgical anastomosis of a bile duct to the stomach.

cholangiogram (ko-lan′je-o-gram″). A roentgenogram of the gallbladder and bile ducts.

cholangiography (ko-lan″je-og′rah-fe) [*chol-* + Gr. *angeion* vessel + *graphein* to write]. Roentgenography of the biliary ducts after administration or injection of a contrast medium. **operative c.,** cholangiography performed during a surgical procedure on the gallbladder.

cholangiohepatoma (ko-lan″je-o-hep″ah-to′-mah). A tumor consisting of abnormally mixed masses of liver cord cells and bile ducts.

cholangiojejunostomy (ko-lan″je-o-jĕ-ju-nos′-to-me). Surgical anastomosis of a bile duct to the jejunum. **intrahepatic c.,** surgical creation of an anastomosis between an intrahepatic bile duct and the jejunum.

cholangiolar (ko″lan-je′o-lar). Pertaining to a cholangiole.

cholangiole (ko-lan′je-ōl) [*chol-* + Gr. *angeion* vessel + *-ole* diminutive suffix]. One of the fine terminal elements of the bile duct system, leaving the portal canal, and pursuing a course at the periphery of a lobule of the liver. Called also *bile ductule*.

cholangiolitis (ko-lan″je-o-li′tis). Inflammation of the cholangioles.

cholangioma (ko-lan″je-o′mah) [*chol-* + Gr. *angeion* vessel + *-oma*]. A tumor of the bile ducts.

cholangiostomy (ko″lan-je-os′to-me) [*chol-* + Gr. *angeion* vessel + *stomoun* to provide with an opening, or mouth]. Fistulization of a bile duct.

cholangiotomy (ko″lan-je-ot′o-me) [*chol-* + Gr. *angeion* vessel + *tomē* a cutting]. Incision of a bile duct.

cholangitis (ko″lan-ji′tis) [*chol-* + Gr. *angeion* vessel + *-itis*]. Inflammation of a bile duct. **catarrhal c.,** catarrhal jaundice. **c. len′ta,** chronic infectious cholangitis without stones.

cholanopoiesis (ko″lah-no-poi-e′sis). The synthesis of cholic acid or of its conjugates and salts or of natural bile salts by the liver.

cholanopoietic (ko″lah-no″poi-et′ik). 1. Pertaining to or promoting cholanopoiesis. 2. An agent that promotes cholanopoiesis.

cholanthrene (ko-lan′thrēn). A pentacyclic hydrocarbon, $C_{20}H_{14}$, of great carcinogenicity.

cholascos (ko-las′kos) [*chol-* + Gr. *askos* bag]. Effusion of bile into the peritoneal cavity (Ponfick).

cholate (ko′lāt). A salt or ester of cholic acid.

chole-, chol-, cholo- (ko′le, kōl, ko′lo) [Gr. *cholē* bile]. Combining form denoting relationship to the bile.

cholebilirubin (ko″le-bil″e-ru′bin). A pigment, $C_{32}H_{50}O_{11}N_2$, differing from bilirubin, occurring in gallbladder bile.

cholecalciferol (ko″le-kal-sif′er-ol). Activated 7-dehydrocholesterol.

cholechromeresis (ko″le-kro-mer′ĕ-sis). Increase in the output or elimination of bile pigments.

cholechromopoiesis (ko″le-kro″mo-poi-e′sis). The synthesis of bile pigments by the liver.

cholecyanin (ko″le-si′ah-nin). Bilicyanin.

cholecyst (ko′le-sist) [*chole-* + Gr. *kystis* bladder]. The gallbladder.

cholecystagogic (ko″le-sis″tah-goj′ik). Pertaining to or promoting evacuation of bile from the gallbladder.

cholecystagogue (ko″le-sis′tah-gog). An agent that promotes evacuation of the gallbladder.

cholecystalgia (ko″le-sis-tal′je-ah) [*cholecyst* + *-algia*]. Biliary colic.

cholecystatony (ko″le-sis-tat′o-ne). Atony of the gallbladder.

cholecystectasia (ko″le-sis″tek-ta′ze-ah) [*cholecyst* + Gr. *ektasis* distention]. Distention of the gallbladder.

cholecystectomy (ko″le-sis-tek′to-me) [*cholecyst* + Gr. *ektomē* excision]. Surgical removal of the gallbladder.

cholecystelectrocoagulectomy (ko″le-sist-e-lek″tro-ko-ag″u-lek′to-me). Removal of the gallbladder by electric coagulation.

cholecystendysis (ko″le-sis-ten′dĭ-sis) [*cholecyst* + Gr. *endysis* entrance]. Excision of a gallstone from the gallbladder, followed by suturing the opening in the gallbladder and anchoring it to the abdominal incision, which is closed over it.

cholecystenteric (ko″le-sis″ten-ter′ik). Pertaining to or communicating with the gallbladder and intestine.

cholecystentero-anastomosis (ko″le-sis-ten″-ter-o-ah-nas″to-mo′sis). Cholecystenterostomy.

cholecystenterorrhaphy (ko″le-sis-ten″ter-or′-ah-fe). Suture of the gallbladder to the small intestine.

cholecystenterostomy (ko″le-sis-ten″ter-os′to-me). Cholecystoenterostomy.

cholecystgastrostomy (ko″le-sist-gas-tros′to-me). Cholecystogastrostomy.

cholecystic (ko″le-sis′tik). Pertaining to the gallbladder.

cholecystis (ko″le-sis′tis) [Gr. *chole* bile, gall + *kystis* bladder]. The gallbladder.

cholecystitis (ko″le-sis-ti′tis) [*cholecyst* + *-itis*]. Inflammation of the gallbladder. **c. emphysemato′sa,** emphysematous c. **emphysematous c.,** inflammation of the gallbladder caused by a gas-producing organism, characterized by gas in the gallbladder lumen and frequently infiltrating into the wall of the gallbladder and surrounding tissues. **gaseous c.,** emphysematous c. **c. glandula′ris prolif′erans,** a thickening of the wall of the chronically inflamed gallbladder, with formation of crypts which may develop into cysts.

cholecystnephrostomy (ko″le-sist″ne-fros′to-me). Cholecystopyelostomy.

cholecystocholangiogram (ko″le-sis″to-ko-lan′je-o-gram). Roentgenogram of the gallbladder and bile ducts.

cholecystocolonic (ko″le-sis″to-ko-lon′ik). Pertaining to or communicating with the gallbladder and colon, as cholecystocolonic fistula.

cholecystocolostomy (ko″le-sis″to-ko-los′to-me). Surgical anastomosis of the gallbladder to the colon.

cholecystocolotomy (ko″le-sis″to-ko-lot′o-me). Surgical incision of the gallbladder and colon.

cholecystoduodenostomy (ko″le-sis″to-du″o-dĕ-nos′to-me). Surgical anastomosis of the gallbladder and the duodenum.

cholecysto-enterostomy (ko″le-sis″to-en″ter-os′to-me) [*cholecyst* + Gr. *enteron* bowel + *stomoun* to provide with an opening, or mouth]. Surgical anastomosis of the gallbladder to the intestine.

cholecystogastric (ko″le-sis″to-gas′trik). Pertaining to or communicating with the gallbladder and stomach, as a cholecystogastric fistula.

cholecystogastrostomy (ko″le-sis″to-gas-tros′-

to-me). Surgical anastomosis of the gallbladder and the stomach.

cholecystogram (ko″le-sis′to-gram). A roentgenogram of the gallbladder.

cholecystography (ko″le-sis-tog′rah-fe) [*cholecyst* + Gr. *graphein* to write]. Roentgenography of the gallbladder.

cholecystoileostomy (ko″le-sis″to-il″e-os′to-me). Surgical anastomosis of the gallbladder and the ileum.

cholecystointestinal (ko″le-sis″to-in-tes′tĭ-nal). Cholecystenteric.

cholecystojejunostomy (ko″le-sis″to-jĕ-ju-nos′to-me). Surgical anastomosis of the gallbladder and the jejunum.

cholecystokinase (ko″le-sis″to-ki′nās). An enzyme in the blood which catalyzes the decomposition of cholecystokinin.

cholecystokinetic (ko″le-sis″to-ki-net′ik). Causing or promoting contraction of the gallbladder.

cholecystokinin (ko″le-sis″to-kin′in) [*cholecyst* + Gr. *kinein* to move]. A hormone secreted by the mucosa of the upper intestine which increases the motility of the gallbladder.

cholecystolithiasis (ko″le-sis″to-lĭ-thi′ah-sis) [*cholecyst* + *lithiasis*]. Presence of gallstones in the gallbladder.

cholecystolithotripsy (ko″le-sis″to-lith′o-trip″-se) [*cholecyst* + *lithotripsy*]. The crushing of gallstones in the gallbladder.

cholecystonephrostomy (ko″le-sis″to-ne-fros′-to-me). Cholecystopyelostomy.

cholecystopathy (ko″le-sis-top′ah-the) [*cholecyst* + Gr. *pathos* disease]. Any gallbladder disease.

cholecystopexy (ko″le-sis′to-pek″se) [*cholecyst* + Gr. *pēxis* fixation]. The operation of suturing the gallbladder to the abdominal wall.

cholecystoptosis (ko″le-sis″to-to′sis) [*cholecyst* + Gr. *ptōsis* fall]. Downward displacement of the gallbladder.

cholecystopyelostomy (ko″le-sis″to-pi″ĕ-los′-to-me). Surgical anastomosis of the gallbladder to the pelvis of the kidney.

cholecystorrhaphy (ko″le-sis-tor′ah-fe) [*cholecyst* + Gr. *rhaphē* suture]. The suturation of the gallbladder.

cholecystostomy (ko″le-sis-tos′to-me) [*cholecyst* + Gr. *stomoun* to provide with an opening, or mouth]. The surgical incision into the gallbladder with drainage.

cholecystotomy (ko″le-sis-tot′o-me) [*cholecyst* + Gr. *tomē* a cutting]. Surgical incision of the gallbladder.

cholecystotyphoid (ko″le-sis″to-ti′foid). Typhoid fever complicated by acute cholecystitis.

choledochal (kol′e-dok-al). Pertaining to the common bile duct.

choledochectomy (kol″e-do-kek′to-me) [*choledochus* + Gr. *ektomē* excision]. Excision of a portion of the common bile duct.

choledochendysis (kol″e-do-ken′dĭ-sis) [*choledochus* + Gr. *endysis* entrance]. Choledochotomy.

choledochitis (kol″e-do-ki′tis). Inflammation of the common bile duct, or ductus choledochus.

choledochocholedochorrhaphy (ko-led″ŏ-ko-ko-led″ŏ-kor′ah-fe). The suturing together of the ends of a divided common bile duct.

choledochocholedochostomy (ko-led″ŏ-ko-ko-led″ŏ-kos′to-me). Surgical formation of an anastomosis between two portions of the common bile duct.

choledochoduodenostomy (ko-led″ŏ-ko-du″o-dĕ-nos′to-me). Surgical anastomosis of the common bile duct to the duodenum.

choledocho-enterostomy (ko-led″ŏ-ko-en″ter-os′to-me). Surgical anastomosis of the common bile duct to the intestine.

choledochogastrostomy (ko-led″ŏ-ko-gas-tros′-to-me]. Surgical anastomosis of the common bile duct to the stomach.

choledochogram (ko-led′ŏ-ko-gram″). A roentgenogram of the common bile duct.

choledochography (ko-led″o-kog′rah-fe) [*choledochus* + Gr. *graphein* to write]. Roentgenography of the common bile duct after the administration of opaque material.

choledochohepatostomy (ko-led″ŏ-ko-hep″ah-tos′to-me). Surgical anastomosis of the common bile duct to the hepatic duct.

choledochoileostomy (ko-led″ŏ-ko-il-e-os′to-me). Surgical anastomosis of the common bile duct to the ileum.

choledochojejunostomy (ko-led″ŏ-ko-jĕ-ju-nos′to-me). Surgical anastomosis of the common bile duct to the jejunum.

choledocholith (ko-led′ŏ-ko-lith″). A calculus in the common bile duct.

choledocholithiasis (ko-led″ŏ-ko-lĭ-thi′ah-sis). The occurrence of calculi in the common bile duct.

choledocholithotomy (ko-led″ŏ-ko-lĭ-thot′o-me). Incision of the common bile duct for the removal of stone.

choledocholithotripsy (ko-led″ŏ-ko-lith′o-trip″-se). The crushing of a gallstone within the common bile duct.

choledochoplasty (ko-led′ŏ-ko-plas″te). The performance of a plastic operation on the common bile duct.

choledochorrhaphy (ko″led-o-kor′ah-fe) [*choledochus* + Gr. *rhaphē* suture]. Suturing of the common bile duct.

choledochostomy (ko″led-o-kos′to-me) [*choledochus* + Gr. *stomoun* to provide with an opening, or mouth]. Surgical formation of an opening into the common bile duct.

choledochotomy (ko″led-o-kot′o-me) [*choledochus* + Gr. *tomē* a cutting]. Surgical incision of the common bile duct.

choledochus (ko-led′o-kus) [*chole-* + Gr. *dochos* receptacle]. The ductus choledochus, or common bile duct.

choledyl (kōl′ĕ-dil). Trade mark for a preparation of oxtriphylline.

choleglobin (ko″le-glo′bin). A compound of globin and an open-ring iron porphyrin, being an intermediate in the formation of bile pigment.

cholehematin (ko″le-hem′ah-tin). A red pigment found in the bile of herbivorous animals. It is derived from chlorophyll and is the same as phylloerythrin and bilipurpurine.

cholehemia (ko″le-he′me-ah). Cholemia.

choleic (ko-le′ik). Pertaining to, or derived from, the bile.

cholelith (ko′le-lith) [*chole-* + Gr. *lithos* stone]. A gallstone.

cholelithiasis (ko″le-lĭ-thi′ah-sis) [*chole-* + *lithiasis*]. The presence or formation of gallstones.

cholelithic (ko″le-lith′ik). Pertaining to or caused by gallstones.

cholelithotomy (ko″le-lĭ-thot′o-me). Removal of gallstones by means of an incision.

cholelithotripsy (ko″le-lith′o-trip-se). Cholelithotrity.

cholelithotrity (ko″le-lĭ-thot′rĭ-te) [*cholelith* + Gr. *tribein* to crush]. The crushing of gallstones.

cholemesis (ko-lem′e-sis) [*chole-* + Gr. *emein* to vomit]. Vomiting of bile.

cholemia (ko-le′me-ah) [*chole-* + Gr. *haima* blood + *-ia*]. The presence of bile or bile pigments in the blood. **familial c., Gilbert's c.,** the congenital form of hemolytic jaundice.

cholemic (ko-le′mik). Pertaining to, marked by, or due to cholemia.

cholemimetry (ko″le-mim′e-tre). Determination of the amount of bile pigment in the blood.

choleophosphatase (ko″le-o-fos′fah-tās). An enzyme in the pancreas and in the intestinal juice which liberates choline from lecithin.

cholepathia (ko″le-path′e-ah) [*chole-* + Gr. *pathos*

disease + *-ia*]. A morbid condition of the biliary tract. **c. spas′tica,** a morbid condition of the biliary tract, characterized by spasm of the bile ducts.

choleperitoneum (ko″le-per″ĭ-to-ne′um) [*chole-* + *peritoneum*]. The presence of bile in the peritoneum resulting from rupture of the bile passages. Called also *biliary peritonitis.*

choleperitonitis (ko″le-per″ĭ-to-ni′tis). Choleperitoneum.

cholepoiesis (ko″le-poi-e′sis). The formation of bile by the liver.

cholepoietic (ko″le-poi-et′ik) [*chole-* + Gr. *poiein* to make]. 1. Forming or secreting bile. 2. Choleretic.

choleprasin (ko″le-pra′sin). One of the pigments of bile.

cholepyrrhin (ko″le-pir′in) [*chole-* + Gr. *pyrrhos* yellowish red]. Biliphein.

cholera (kol′er-ah) [Gr., from *cholē* bile]. A name applied to a condition marked by diarrhea and vomiting, specific entities usually being indicated by a modifying term or phrase. Frequently used alone to designate Asiatic cholera. **algid c.,** Asiatic c. **Asiatic c.,** an acute infectious disease, chiefly epidemic, marked by severe diarrhea, vomiting, dehydration, cramps, prostration, and suppression of the urine. The disease is due to the *Vibrio cholerae*, which is contained in the discharges from the bowels, and becomes disseminated by means of drinking water. The disease has a high mortality, death resulting from convulsions and exhaustion or from congestion of the lungs. Called also *algid c., asphyctic c., epidemic c., Indian c., malignant c.,* and *pestilential c.* **asphyctic c.,** Asiatic c. **automatic c.,** cholera characterized by movements which appear to be intentional, but which are entirely independent of the patient's volition. **bilious c.,** a less dangerous infection of the gastrointestinal tract, characterized by violent and painful vomiting and by copious bilious stools. Called also *c. nostras, simple c., sporadic c.,* etc. **chicken c.,** pasteurellosis in chickens. See *fowl c.* **dry c.,** c. sicca. **English c.,** c. morbus. **epidemic c.,** Asiatic c. **European c.,** bilious c. **fowl c.,** an infectious disease, caused by *Pasteurella multicida*, and occurring in all species of domestic poultry, canaries, waterfowl, seagulls, game birds, and birds of prey, all over the world. **c. ful′minans,** c. sicca. **hog c.,** an infectious communicable disease of swine occurring in epizootics and caused by a filterable virus; marked by fever, loss of appetite, emaciation, ulceration of the intestines, diarrhea, and ecchymoses in the kidney and on the skin of the ventral surface of the body. Called also *swine fever.* **c. infan′tum,** a common, noncontagious diarrhea of young children prevailing in the summer months. **malignant c.,** Asiatic c. **c. mor′bus,** a popular name for an acute gastroenteritis, with diarrhea, cramps, and vomiting, occurring in summer or autumn. **c. nos′tras,** bilious c. **c. nos′tras paratypho′sa,** gastroenteritis paratyphosa. **pandemic c.,** Asiatic c. **c. of sheep,** an epizootic and enzootic disease of sheep of Scotland, occurring in August and September and affecting lambs of that year; marked by swelling of the head in the parotid region and sometimes by jaundice. Called also *jaundice, yellows, headgrit,* and *plocach.* **c. sic′ca, c. sid′erans,** cholera in which death takes place before diarrhea has occurred. **simple c.,** bilious c. **spasmodic c.,** Asiatic c. **sporadic c.,** bilious c. **summer c.,** c. morbus. **typhoid c.,** a malignant form of Asiatic cholera, marked by extreme depression. **winter c.,** a mild diarrheal disease of unknown cause, occurring in the winter months.

choleraic (kol″er-a′ik). Of, pertaining to, or of the nature of, cholera.

choleraphage (kol′er-ah-fāj). A bacteriophage which destroys cholera bacilli.

cholerase (kol′er-ās). An enzyme developed by the spirillum of cholera and capable of destroying it.

choleresis (ko-ler′ĕ-sis) [*chole-* + Gr. *hairesis* a taking]. The excretion of bile by the liver.

choleretic (ko″ler-et′ik). 1. Stimulating the production of bile by the liver. 2. An agent which stimulates excretion of bile by the liver.

choleric (kol′er-ik). Hot-tempered; irascible.

choleriform (ko-ler′ĭ-form). Choleroid.

cholerigenous (kol-er-ij′e-nus). Causing cholera.

cholerine (kol′er-in). 1. The earliest stage of Asiatic cholera. 2. A comparatively mild form of bilious cholera, sometimes closely simulating Asiatic cholera, but not often of a fatal issue.

cholerization (kol″er-i-za′shun). Protective inoculation with cholera.

choleroid (kol′er-oid) [Gr. *cholera* + *eidos* form]. Resembling cholera.

choleromania (kol″er-o-ma′ne-ah) [*cholera* + Gr. *mania* madness]. Mania sometimes seen in cholera.

cholerophobia (kol″er-o-fo′be-ah) [*cholera* + *phobia*]. An abnormal dread of cholera.

cholerrhagia (kol-er-a′je-ah) [*chole-* + Gr. *rhēgnynai* to burst forth]. An excessive flow of bile.

cholerythrin (kol-er′ĭ-thrin) [*chole-* + Gr. *erythros* red]. Bilirubin.

cholerythrogen (kol-er-ith′ro-jen). A precursor of cholerythrin (bilirubin).

cholestane (ko′les-tān). A saturated hydrocarbon, $C_{27}H_{48}$, from cholesterol.

cholestanol (ko-les′tah-nol). A compound, $C_{27}H_{47}OH$, formed by the reduction of cholesterol. **beta-c.,** an isomer of coprosterol derived from cholesterol and found in the feces.

cholestasia (ko″le-sta′se-ah). Cholestasis.

cholestasis (ko″le-sta′sis) [*chole-* + Gr. *stasis* stoppage]. Stoppage or suppression of the flow of bile.

cholestatic (ko″le-stat′ik). Pertaining to or characterized by cholestasis.

cholesteatoma (ko″le-ste″ah-to′mah) [*chole-* + *steatoma*]. A cystic mass, with a lining of stratified squamous epithelium, usually of keratinizing type, filled with desquamating debris frequently including cholesterol. Steatomas occur in the meninges, central nervous system, and bones of the skull, but are most common in the middle ear and mastoid region. **congenital c.,** epidermoidoma. **c. tym′pani,** cholesteatoma associated with chronic infection of the middle ear, formed of the outer desquamating layers of stratified squamous epithelium which has extended inward and upward to line the tympanum, epitympanum, and antrum.

cholesteatomatous (ko″le-ste″ah-to′mah-tus). Relating to or of the nature of cholesteatoma.

cholesteatosis (ko″le-ste-ah-to′sis). Fatty degeneration due to cholesterol esters; cholesterol steatosis.

cholestene (ko′les-tēn). The hydrocarbon, $C_{27}H_{46}$, formed by the oxidation of cholestane.

cholesterase (ko-les′ter-ās). An enzyme which splits up cholesterol.

cholesteremia (ko-les″ter-e′me-ah) [*cholesterol* + Gr. *haima* blood + *-ia*]. Excess of cholesterol in the blood.

cholesterin (ko-les′ter-in). Cholesterol.

cholesterinemia (ko-les″ter-in-e′me-ah). Cholesteremia.

cholesterinosis (ko-les″ter-ĭ-no′sis). Cholesterosis.

cholesterinuria (ko-les″ter-ĭ-nu′re-ah). Cholesteroluria.

cholesteroderma (ko-les″ter-o-der′mah). Xanthoderma.

cholesterohistechia (ko-les″ter-o-his-tek′e-ah) [*cholesterol* + Gr. *histos* tissue + *echein* to hold + *-ia*]. The presence of an abnormally large amount of cholesterol in a tissue.

cholesterohydrothorax (ko-les″ter-o-hi″dro-tho′raks). Presence in the thoracic cavity of watery fluid which contains cholesterol crystals.

cholesterol (ko-les′ter-ol) [*chole-* + Gr. *stereos* solid]. A fatlike, pearly substance, a monatomical alcohol, $C_{27}H_{45}OH$, crystallizing in the form of acicular crystals, and found in all animal fats and oils, in bile, blood, brain tissue, milk, yolk of egg, the medullated sheaths of nerve fibers, the liver, kidneys, and adrenal glands. It constitutes a large part of the most frequently occurring type of gallstones and occurs in atheroma of the arteries, in various cysts, and in carcinomatous tissue.

cholesterolemia (ko-les″ter-ol-e′me-ah) [*cholesterol* + Gr. *haima* blood + *-ia*]. Cholesteremia.

cholesteroleresis (ko-les″ter-ol-er′e-sis). Increased elimination of cholesterol in the bile.

cholesterolestersturz (ko-les″ter-ol-es′ter-stoorts) [Ger.]. Decrease in the proportion of esters in the blood cholesterol.

cholesterolopoiesis (ko-les″ter-ol″o-poi-e′sis). The synthesis of cholesterol by the liver.

cholesterolosis (ko-les″ter-ol-o′sis). Cholesterosis.

cholesteroluria (ko-les″ter-ol-u′re-ah) [*cholesterol* + Gr. *ouron* urine + *-ia*]. The presence of cholesterol in the urine.

cholesterone (ko-les′ter-ōn). A ketone produced by the oxidation of cholesterol.

cholesterosis (ko-les″ter-o′sis). A condition in which cholesterol is deposited in abnormal quantities. **c. cu′tis,** xanthomatosis.

choletelin (ko-let′ĕ-lin) [*chole-* + Gr. *telos* end]. A yellow pigment, $C_{16}H_{18}N_2O_6$, the final result of the oxidation of bilirubin; bilixanthine.

choletherapy (ko″le-ther′ah-pe) [*chole-* + *therapy*]. Treatment by the administration of bile salts.

choleuria (ko″le-u′re-ah) [*chole-* + Gr. *ouron* urine + *-ia*]. Choluria.

choleverdin (ko″le-ver′din). Bilicyanin.

choline (ko′lin). A vitamin, hydroxyethyl trimethyl ammonium hydroxide, $CH_2OH.CH_2.N(CH_3)_3.OH$, derivable from many animal and some vegetable tissues. It prevents the deposition of fat in the liver. **c. chloride,** a preparation, $C_5H_{11}ClNO$, used in the treatment of fatty infiltration of the liver. **c. dihydrogen citrate,** a compound, $C_{11}H_{21}NO_3$, which has been used in fatty degeneration and cirrhosis of the liver.

choline-acetylase (ko″lin-ah-set′ĭ-lās). An enzyme which brings about the synthesis of acetylcholine.

cholinergic (ko″lin-er′jik). Stimulated, activated or transmitted by choline (acetylcholine): a term applied to those nerve fibers which liberate acetylcholine at a synapse when a nerve impulse passes, i.e., the parasympathetic nerve endings. Cf. *adrenergic.*

cholinesterase (ko″lin-es′ter-ās). An esterase present in all body tissues which hydrolyzes acetylcholine into choline and acetic acid.

cholinolytic (ko″lin-o-lit′ik). 1. Blocking the action of acetylcholine, or of cholinergic agents. 2. An agent that blocks the action of acetylcholine in cholinergic areas, that is, organs supplied by parasympathetic nerves, and voluntary muscles.

cholinomimetic (ko″lĭ-no-mi-met′ik). Having an action similar to that of choline.

cholo-. See *chole-.*

cholochrome (kol′o-krōm) [*cholo-* + Gr. *chrōma* color]. Any biliary pigment.

cholocyanin (kol″o-si′ah-nin) [*cholo-* + Gr. *kyanos* blue]. Bilicyanin.

chologenetic (kol″o-je-net′ik) [*cholo-* + Gr. *gennan* to produce]. Producing bile; cholepoietic.

cholografin (ko″lo-gra′fin). Trade mark for preparations of iodipamide.

cholohematin (kol-o-hem′ah-tin). Cholehematin.

cholohemothorax (ko″lo-he″mo-tho′raks) [*cholo-* + Gr. *haima* blood + *thōrax* chest]. Presence of bile and blood in the thorax.

chololith (kol′o-lith). Cholelith.

chololithiasis (kol′o-lĭ-thi′ah-sis). Cholelithiasis.

chololithic (kol″o-lith′ik). Cholelithic.

choloplania (kol″o-pla′ne-ah) [*cholo-* + Gr. *planē* wandering]. Bile in the blood and tissues; jaundice.

cholopoiesis (kol″o-poi-e′sis). Cholepoiesis.

cholorrhagia (kol″o-ra′je-ah). Cholerrhagia.

cholorrhea (kol″o-re′ah). Cholerrhagia.

choloscopy (ko-los′ko-pe) [*cholo-* + Gr. *skopein* to examine]. Examination of the biliary system or testing of the biliary function.

cholothorax (ko″lo-tho′raks) [*cholo-* + Gr. *thōrax* chest]. Presence of bile in the thorax.

choluria (ko-lu′re-ah) [*chol-* + Gr. *ouron* urine + *-ia*]. The presence of bile in the urine; discoloration of the urine with bile pigments.

choluric (ko-lur′ik). Pertaining to or marked by choluria.

Chondodendron (kon″do-den′dron). A genus of climbing menispermaceous shrubs. **C. tomento′sum,** a shrub that affords pareira.

chondr-. See *chondro-.*

chondral (kon′dral). Pertaining to cartilage.

chondralgia (kon-dral′je-ah). Chondrodynia.

chondralloplasia (kon″dral-lo-pla′se-ah) [*chondr-* + Gr. *allos* other + *plassein* to form]. Chondrodysplasia.

chondrectomy (kon-drek′to-me) [*chondr-* + Gr. *ektomē* excision]. Surgical removal of a cartilage.

chondri-. See *chondrio-.*

chondric (kon′drik). Cartilaginous; of or relating to cartilage.

chondrification (kon″drĭ-fĭ-ka′shun) [*chondri-* + L. *facere* to make]. The formation of cartilage; transformation into cartilage.

chondrigen (kon′drĭ-jen). Chondrogen.

chondriglucose (kon″drĭ-gloo′kōs) [*chondri-* + *glucose*]. A glucose prepared from cartilage by boiling in acidulated water.

chondrin (kon′drin). A protein, resembling gelatin, from cartilage (Johannes Müller, 1837). It is considered to be a mixture of gelatin and mucin.

chondrio- (kon′dre-o) [Gr. *chondrion,* diminutive of *chondros* (1) a groat, grit, or lump of salt, or (2) gristle or cartilage]. Combining form denoting relationship (1) to a granule, or (2) to cartilage. See also words beginning *chondro-.*

chondriocont (kon′dre-o-kont″). A rod-shaped chondriosome.

chondriokont (kon′dre-o-kont″). Chondriocont.

chondriome (kon′dre-ōm). The total chondriosome content of a cell.

chondriomere (kon′dre-o-mēr). Cytomere.

chondriomite (kon′dre-o-mīt). A thread-shaped chondriosome.

chondriosome (kon′dre-o-sōm) [*chondrio-* + Gr. *sōma* body]. Any one of the structures occurring in the cytoplasm of cells in the form of minute granules, rods, and threads, and regarded as important organs of the cell. Cf. *mitrochondria.*

chondriosphere (kon′dre-o-sfēr). A spherical chondriosome.

chondritis (kon-dri′tis) [*chondr-* + *-itis*]. Inflammation of cartilage. **c. intervertebra′lis calca′nea,** calcinosis intervertebralis.

chondro-, chondr- (kon′dro, kon′dr) [Gr. *chondros* cartilage]. Combining form denoting a relationship to cartilage. See also words beginning *chondri-* and *chondrio-.*

chondro-adenoma (kon″dro-ad″e-no′mah). An adenoma containing cartilaginous elements.

chondro-angioma (kon″dro-an″je-o′mah). An angioma containing cartilaginous elements.

chondroblast (kon′dro-blast) [*chondro-* + Gr. *blastos* germ]. A cell which arises from a fibroblast and which, as it matures, is associated with the production of cartilage.

chondroblastoma (kon″dro-blas-to′mah) [*chondroblast* + *-oma*]. A tumor, the cells of which tend to differentiate into cartilage cells. The term includes chondroma and chondrosarcoma.

chondrocalcinosis (kon″dro-kal″sĭ-no′sis). Pseudogout.

chondrocarcinoma (kon″dro-kar-sĭ-no′mah). A carcinoma containing cartilaginous elements in its stroma.

chondroclast (kon′dro-klast) [*chondro-* + Gr. *klan* to break]. A giant cell of the class that is believed associated with the absorption of cartilage.

Chondrococcus (kon″dro-kok′us). A genus of microorganisms of the family Myxococcaceae, found on dung of various animals.

chondroconia (kon″dro-ko′ne-ah) [*chondro-* + Gr. *konis* dust]. Schridde's granules.

chondrocostal (kon″dro-kos′tal) [*chondro-* + L. *costa* rib]. Of or pertaining to the ribs and costal cartilages.

chondrocranium (kon″dro-kra′ne-um) [*chondro-* + Gr. *kranion* head]. The cartilaginous cranial structure of the embryo.

chondrocyte (kon′dro-sīt) [*chondro-* + Gr. *kytos* hollow vessel]. A cartilage cell. **isogenous c's,** cartilage cells that make up a single group.

chondrodermatitis (kon″dro-der″mah-ti′tis). An inflammatory process involving cartilage and skin. **c. nodula′ris chron′ica hel′icis,** a condition marked by the presence of round nodules and painful growths occurring on the helix of the ear.

chondrodynia (kon″dro-din′e-ah) [*chondro-* + Gr. *odynē* pain]. Pain in a cartilage.

chondrodysplasia (kon″dro-dis-pla′ze-ah) [*chondro-* + *dysplasia*]. Dyschondroplasia. **hereditary deforming c.,** dyschondroplasia.

chondrodystrophia (kon″dro-dis-tro′fe-ah) [*chondro-* + *dys-* + Gr. *trophē* nutrition]. Chondrodystrophy. **c. feta′lis,** achondroplasia. **c. feta′lis calcif′icans,** a rare condition characterized by the roentgenological appearance of multiple punctate opacities in the unossified epiphyseal cartilages, usually present at birth. The infants frequently are stillborn or die of associated anomalies in the first year.

chondrodystrophy (kon″dro-dis′tro-fe). A morbid condition characterized by abnormal development of cartilage. **hereditary deforming c.,** dyschondroplasia. **hyperplastic c.,** chondrodystrophy with excessive growth of the epiphyses. **hypoplastic c.,** chondrodystrophy in which the bone is spongy and the epiphyses are irregularly developed. **c. mala′cia,** a form marked by softening of the epiphyseal cartilage.

chondroendothelioma (kon″dro-en″do-the″le-o-mah). An endothelioma containing cartilaginous elements.

chondroepiphyseal (kon″dro-ep″ĭ-fiz′e-al). Pertaining to the epiphyseal cartilages.

chondroepiphysitis (kon″dro-ep″ĭ-fiz-i′tis). Inflammation involving the epiphyseal cartilages.

chondrofibroma (kon″dro-fi-bro′mah) [*chondroma* + *fibroma*]. A fibroma with cartilaginous elements.

chondrogen (kon′dro-jen) [*chondro-* + Gr. *gennan* to produce]. A substance regarded as the basis of cartilage and of the corneal tissue: boiling turns it into chondrin.

chondrogenesis (kon″dro-jen′e-sis) [*chondro-* + Gr. *genesis* production]. The formation of cartilage.

chondrogenic (kon″dro-jen′ik). Giving rise to or forming cartilage.

chondroglossus (kon″dro-glos′us). See *Table of Musculi*.

chondroglucose (kon″dro-glu′kōs). A sugar formed by the action of hydrochloric acid on chondrin.

chondrography (kon-drog′rah-fe) [*chondro-* + Gr. *graphein* to write]. A description or account of the cartilages.

chondroitic (kon″dro-it′ik). Pertaining to, derived from, or resembling cartilage.

chondroituria (kon″dro-ĭ-tu′re-ah). The presence of chondroitic acid in the urine.

chondrolipoma (kon″dro-lĭ-po′mah). A lipoma containing cartilaginous elements.

chondrology (kon-drol′o-je) [*chondro-* + *-logy*]. The sum of knowledge in regard to the cartilages.

chondrolysis (kon-drol′ĭ-sis) [*chondro-* + Gr. *lysis* dissolution]. The degeneration of cartilage cells that occurs in the process of intracartilaginous ossification.

chondroma (kon-dro′mah) [*chondro-* + *-oma*]. A hyperplastic growth of cartilage tissue. It may remain in the interior or substance of a cartilage or bone (*true chondroma*, or *enchondroma*), or may develop on the surface of a cartilage and project under the periosteum of the bone (*ecchondroma*, or *ecchondrosis*). **joint c.,** a mass of cartilage in the synovial membrane of a joint. See *synovial chondromatosis*. **c. sarcomato′sum,** chondrosarcoma. **synovial c.,** a cartilaginous body formed in a synovial membrane. See *synovial chondromatosis*. **true c.,** one remaining in the interior or substance of the cartilage or bone, enchondroma.

chondromalacia (kon″dro-mah-la′she-ah) [*chondro-* + Gr. *malakia* softness]. Preternatural softness of the cartilages. **c. feta′lis,** a condition in which the limbs of the fetus are soft and pliable due to softening of the epiphyseal cartilage.

chondromatosis (kon″dro-mah-to′sis). Multiple formation of chondromas. **Reichel's c.,** the presence of cartilaginous tumors within the capsule of the knee joint. **synovial c.,** a rare condition in which cartilage is formed in the synovial membranes of joints, tendon sheaths, or bursa, by metaplasia of the connective tissue beneath the surface of the membrane. Some metaplastic foci on the surface of the membrane may become sessile, and then pedunculated, and finally become detached, producing a number of loose bodies.

chondromatous (kon-drom′ah-tus). Pertaining to or of the nature of cartilage.

chondromere (kon′dro-mēr) [*chondro-* + Gr. *meros* part]. A cartilaginous vertebra of the fetal vertebral column.

chondrometaplasia (kon″dro-met″ah-pla′ze-ah). A condition characterized by metaplastic activity of the chondroblasts. **tenosynovial c.,** synovial chondromatosis affecting the sheath of a tendon.

chondromitome (kon″dro-mi′tōm) [*chondro-* + Gr. *mitos* thread]. The paranucleus.

chondromucin (kon″dro-mu′sin). A dense homogeneous intercellular substance in cartilage, being a compound of a protein with chondroitic acid.

chondromucoid (kon″dro-mu′coid). Chondromucin.

Chondromyces (kon″dro-mi′sēz) [*chondro-* + Gr. *mykēs* fungus]. A genus of bacteria of the family Polyangiaceae, found on animal manure and decaying fungi.

chondromyoma (kon″dro-mi-o′mah). Myoma with cartilaginous elements.

chondromyxoma (kon″dro-mik-so′mah). Myxoma containing cartilaginous elements.

chondromyxosarcoma (kon″dro-mik″so-sar-ko′mah). A sarcoma containing cartilaginous and mucous elements.

chondronecrosis (kon″dro-ne-kro′sis). Necrosis of cartilage.

chondro-osseous (kon″dro-os′e-us). Composed of cartilage and bone.

chondro-osteodystrophy (kon″dro-os″te-o-dis′tro-fe) [*chondro-* + Gr. *osteon* bone + *dys-*

trophy]. See *eccentro-osteochondrodysplasia* and *lipochondrodystrophy*.

chondropathology (kon″dro-pah-thol′o-je). The pathology of disease of cartilage.

chondropathy (kon-drop′ah-the) [*chondro-* + Gr. *pathos* disease]. Disease of a cartilage.

chondrophyte (kon′dro-fit) [*chondro-* + Gr. *phyton* a growth]. A cartilaginous growth at the articular extremity of a bone.

chondroplast (kon′dro-plast) [*chondro-* + Gr. *plassein* to form]. Chondroblast.

chondroplastic (kon″dro-plas′tik). Pertaining to plastic operations on cartilage.

chondroplasty (kon′dro-plas″te) [*chondro-* + Gr. *plassein* to form]. Plastic surgery on cartilage; repair of lacerated or displaced cartilage.

chondroporosis (kon″dro-po-ro′sis) [*chondro-* + Gr. *poros* a passage]. The formation of spaces or sinuses in the cartilages: it occurs normally during ossification.

chondroproteid (kon″dro-pro′te-id). Chondroprotein.

chondroprotein (kon″dro-pro′te-in). One of a series of glucoproteins occurring in cartilage, comprising lardacein and chondromucoid. They furnish chondroitic acid on decomposition.

chondrosamine (kon-dro′sam-in). A galactosamine, $CH_2OH(CHOH)_3CH(NH_2)CHO$, which results from splitting chondrosin.

chondrosarcoma (kon″dro-sar-ko′mah) [*chondro-* + *sarcoma*]. Sarcoma with cartilaginous elements; a cartilaginous tumor characterized by rapidity of growth.

chondrosarcomatosis (kon″dro-sar″ko-mah-to′sis). The formation of multiple chondrosarcomas.

chondrosarcomatous (kon″dro-sar-ko′mah-tus). Pertaining to or of the nature of chondrosarcoma.

chondroseptum (kon″dro-sep′tum) [*chondro-* + *septum*]. The cartilaginous part of the nasal septum.

chondrosin (kon′dro-sin). A gummy substance with reducing properties, $C_{12}H_{21}NO_{11}$, formed by the hydrolysis of chondroitin.

chondrosis (kon-dro′sis) [Gr. *chondros* cartilage]. The formation of cartilaginous tissue.

chondroskeleton (kon″dro-skel′ĕ-ton). A cartilaginous skeleton.

chondrosome (kon′dro-sōm) [*chondro-* + Gr. *sōma* body]. Mitochondria.

chondrosteoma (kon″dros-te-o′mah). A tumor composed of osseous and cartilaginous tissue.

chondrosternal (kon″dro-ster′nal). Pertaining to the costal cartilage and the sternum.

chondrosternoplasty (kon″dro-ster′no-plas″te). Surgical correction of funnel chest.

chondrotome (kon′dro-tōm). An instrument for cutting the cartilages.

chondrotomy (kon-drot′o-me) [*chondro-* + Gr. *temnein* to cut]. The dissection or surgical division of cartilage.

chondrotrophic (kon″dro-trof′ik) [*chondro-* + Gr. *trophē* nutrition]. Having an influence on the formation or growth of cartilage.

chondroxiphoid (kon″dro-zi′foid) [*chondro-* + *xiphoid*]. Pertaining to the xiphoid process.

Chondrus (kon′drus) [L.; Gr. *chondros* cartilage]. A genus of seaweeds. **C. cris′pus,** a species which is one of the sources of chondrus.

chondrus (kon′drus). The dried, sun-bleached plant of *Chondrus crispus* or of *Gigartina mamillosa:* used as a protective agent for the skin.

chonechondrosternon (ko″ne-kon″dro-ster′non). Funnel chest.

Chopart's amputation, etc. (sho-parz′) [François *Chopart*, French surgeon, 1743–1795]. See under the nouns.

chorangioma (ko-ran″je-o′mah). Chorioangioma.

chord (kord). Cord. **condyle c.,** condylar axis.

chorda (kor′dah), pl. *chor′dae* [L.; Gr. *chordē* cord]. Any cord or sinew. **c. chirurgica′lis,** catgut suture. **c. dorsa′lis,** notochord. **c. guberna′culum,** a portion of the gubernaculum testis or of the round ligament of the uterus that develops in the inguinal crest and adjoining body wall. **c. mag′na,** tendo calcaneus. **c. obli′qua membra′nae interos′seae antebra′chii** [N A], a small ligamentous band extending from the lateral face of the tuberosity of the ulna to the radius a little distal to its tuberosity. **c. sperma′tica,** funiculus spermaticus. **c. spina′lis,** medulla spinalis. **c. tendin′eae cor′dis** [N A, B N A], the tendinous cords that connect each cusp of the two atrioventricular valves to appropriate papillary muscles in the heart ventricles. **c. tym′pani** [N A, B N A], a nerve originating from the facial nerve (nervus intermedius) and distributed to the submandibular and sublingual glands and the anterior two-thirds of the tongue: parasympathetic and special sensory. **c. umbilica′lis,** funiculus umbilicalis. **c. voca′lis,** ligamentum vocale. **chor′dae willis′ii.** See *adhesio interthalamica*.

chordae (kor′de) [L.]. Plural of *chorda*.

chordal (kor′dal). Pertaining to any chorda (chiefly used of the notochord).

chorda-mesoderm (kor″dah-mez′o-derm). Tissue of the dorsal lip of the blastopore, which gives rise to both notochord and mesoderm.

Chordata (kor-da′tah). A phylum which includes the vertebrates and the animals which have a notochord.

chordate (kor′dāt). An animal belonging to the phylum Chordata.

chordectomy (kor-dek′to-me) [*chordo-* + Gr. *ektomē* excision]. Excision of a vocal cord.

chordee (kor-de′) [Fr. *cordée* corded]. Downward bowing of the penis as a result of a congenital anomaly (hypospadias) or a urethral infection (gonorrhea).

chorditis (kor-di′tis). Inflammation of a vocal or spermatic cord. **c. canto′rum,** inflammation of the vocal cords in professional singers. **c. fibrino′sa,** acute laryngitis marked by the deposition of fibrin and the formation of erosions on the vocal cords. **c. nodo′sa,** c. tuberosa. **c. tubero′sa,** a condition marked by the formation of a small whitish nodule on one or both vocal cords; occurring in persons who use their voice excessively. **c. voca′lis,** inflammation of the vocal cords. **c. voca′lis infe′rior,** chronic subglottic laryngitis.

chordo- (kor′do) [Gr. *chordē* cord]. Combining form denoting relationship to a cord.

chordoblastoma (kor″do-blas-to′mah) [*chordo-* + Gr. *blastos* germ + *-oma*]. A tumor, the cells of which tend to differentiate into cells like those of the notochord.

chordocarcinoma (kor″do-kar″sĭ-no′mah). Chordoma.

chordo-epithelioma (kor″do-ep″ĭ-the″le-o′mah). Chordoma.

chordoid (kor′doid). Resembling the notochord.

chordoma (kor-do′mah) [*chordo-* + *-oma*]. A malignant tumor arising from the embryonic remains of the notochord.

chordopexy (kor′do-pek″se). Cordopexy.

chordoskeleton (kor″do-skel′ĕ-ton) [*chordo-* + *skeleton*]. That portion of the bony skeleton which is formed around the notochord.

chordotomy (kor-dot′o-me) [*chordo-* + Gr. *tomē* a cutting]. Surgical division of the anterolateral tracts of the spinal cord: for intractable pain.

chorea (ko-re′ah) [L.; Gr. *choreia* dance]. The ceaseless occurrence of a wide variety of rapid, jerky but well coordinated movements, performed involuntarily. **automatic c.,** a disease characterized by the performance of actions which seem to be intentional, but which are really performed independently of the will in response to some impulse or external stimulus. **Bergeron's c.,** a disease characterized by violent rhythmic spasms, but running a benign course. **button-makers' c.,** an occupation neurosis observed in buttonmakers. **chronic c.,** a hereditary affection of adults marked by irregular movements, speech disturbances, and dementia; called also *Huntington's c.* **c. cor'dis,** chorea with great irregularity of the heart's action. **dancing c.,** saltatory chorea. **degenerative c.,** chronic c. **diaphragmatic c.,** the utterance of a peculiar cry in cases of painless tic. **c. dimidia'ta,** hemichorea. **Dubini's c., electric c.,** a variety with violent and sudden movements, progressing, as a rule, from bad to worse, and often characterized by atrophy and muscular paralysis. Called also *Dubini's disease.* **epidemic c.,** dancing mania. **c. fes'tinans,** old name for ataxia with festination; paralysis agitans. **fibrillary c.,** fibrillary contractions of various muscles; paramyoclonus. **c. gravida'rum,** chorea with symptoms similar to those of the ordinary form seen in pregnancy. **habit c.,** tic. **hemilateral c.,** hemichorea. **Henoch's c.,** spasmodic tic. **hereditary c.,** chronic c. **Huntington's c.,** chronic c. **hyoscine c.,** chorea-like movements occurring in acute hyoscine intoxication. **hysterical c.,** c. major. **imitative c.,** a pseudochorea, or hysterical affection; a kind of habit spasm due to imitation. **c. insa'niens,** chorea with symptoms of insanity; chiefly seen in pregnant women. **juvenile c.,** c. minor. **laryngeal c.,** diaphragmatic c. **limp c.,** a condition in which chorea is associated with paralysis; called also *c. mollis.* **local c.,** occupation neurosis. **c. ma'jor,** hysteria with continuous and somewhat regular oscillatory movements. **malleatory c.,** rhythmic chorea in which the patient performs persistent movements of hammering. **maniacal c.,** chorea insaniens. **methodic c.,** a variety in which the movements take place at regular intervals: called also *rhythmic c.* **mimetic c.,** that which is caused by imitation. **c. mi'nor,** the ordinary chorea with comparatively moderate convulsive movements (Sydenham, 1686). **c. mol'lis,** limp c. **Morvan's c.,** fibrillary contractions of the muscles of the calves and posterior part of the thighs, sometimes extending to the trunk, but never affecting the neck and face. **c. noctur'na,** chorea in which the movements continue during sleep. **c. nu'tans,** nodding spasm, or chorea with nodding head movements. **one-sided c.,** hemichorea. **paralytic c.,** chorea in which immobility replaces movement. **posthemiplegic c.,** a form which affects the partially paralyzed muscles after hemiplegia; athetosis. **prehemiplegic c.,** choreic movements which may precede an attack of hemiplegia. **procursive c.,** paralysis agitans. **rhythmic c.,** hysterical chorea in which the patient performs persistent rhythmic movements. **rotary c.,** hysterical chorea marked by rhythmic movements of the head or body. **saltatory c.,** rhythmic chorea with dancing movements. **school-made c.,** chorea from overstimulation at school. **Schrötter's c.,** diaphragmatic c. **c. scripto'rum,** writers' cramp. **senile c.** 1. An affection resembling chorea, coming on in old age. 2. Paralysis agitans. **simple c.,** c. minor. **Sydenham's c.,** c. minor. **tetanoid c.,** progressive lenticular degeneration. **tic c.,** tic.

choreal (ko're-al). Pertaining to, of the nature of, or characterized by chorea.

choreatic (ko"re-at'ik). Choreal.

choreic (kŏ-re'ik). Choreal.

choreiform (kŏ-re'ĭ-form) [*chorea* + L. *forma* form]. Resembling chorea.

choreo-athetoid (ko"re-o-ath'ĕ-toid). Pertaining to or characterized by choreo-athetosis.

choreo-athetosis (ko"re-o-ath"ĕ-to'sis). A condition marked by choreic and athetoid movements.

choreoid (ko're-oid). Resembling chorea.

choreomania (ko"re-o-ma'ne-ah) [Gr. *choreia* dance + *mania* madness]. Dancing mania.

choreophrasia (ko-re"o-fra'ze-ah). A condition in which the patient repeats phrases without regard to form or meaning.

chorial (ko're-al). Of, or relating to, the chorion.

chorioadenoma (ko"re-o-ad"e-no'mah). Adenomatous tumor of the chorion; destructive placental mole: called also *c. destruens, invasive mole,* and *malignant mole.*

chorioallantoic (ko"re-o-al"an-to'ik). Pertaining to the chorioallantois.

chorioallantois (ko"re-o-ah-lan'to-is). An extra-embryonic sac of some vertebrate embryos, formed by fusion of the chorion and allantois.

chorioamnionitis (ko"re-o-am"ne-o-ni'tis). Inflammation of fetal membranes caused by bacterial infection.

chorioangiofibroma (ko"re-o-an"je-o-fi-bro'mah). Angiofibroma of the chorion.

chorioangioma (ko"re-o-an"je-o'mah). An angiomatous tumor of the chorion.

chorioblastoma (ko"re-o-blas-to'mah). Chorioma.

chorioblastosis (ko"re-o-blas-to'sis). Overgrowth of the chorion.

choriocapillaris (ko"re-o-kap"ĭ-la'ris) [*chorioid* + L. *capillaris* capillary]. The capillary or second layer of the choroid coat of the eye.

choriocarcinoma (ko"re-o-kar"sĭ-no'mah). Carcinoma developed from the chorionic epithelium. See *syncytioma malignum.*

choriocele (ko're-o-sēl) [*chorion* + Gr. *kēlē* hernia]. Protrusion of the eye through an aperture in the choroid.

chorioepithelioma (ko"re-o-ep"ĭ-the"le-o'mah). Chorionic carcinoma; a tumor formed by malignant proliferation of the epithelium of the chorionic villi and including chorio-adenoma, choriosarcoma, choriocarcinoma and syncytioma. Called also *chorioma, chorionic epithelioma.* **c. malig'num,** syncytioma malignum.

choriogenesis (ko"re-o-jen'e-sis) [*chorio-* + Gr. *genesis* origin]. The development of the chorion.

chorioid (ko're-oid). Choroidea.

chorioidea (ko"re-oi'de-ah). [B N A] Choroidea.

chorioido-. For words beginning thus, see those beginning *choroido-.*

chorioma (ko"re-o'mah) [*chorion* + *-oma*]. Chorioepithelioma.

choriomeningitis (ko"re-o-men"in-ji'tis). Cerebral meningitis with lymphocytic infiltration of the choroid plexuses. **lymphocytic c.,** an acute virus disease characterized by a lymphocytic reaction in the meninges and marked by malaise, headache, vomiting, fever, stiffness of the neck and slow pulse. **pseudolymphocytic c.,** a benign, aseptic lymphocytic meningitis, with virus in the cerebrospinal fluid, and characterized by severe frontal headache, drowsiness, irritability, and vomiting.

chorion (ko're-on) [Gr.]. The outermost envelope of the growing zygote or fertilized ovum which serves as a protective and nutritive covering. It consists of two layers, an outer ectoderm, or trophoderm, and an inner mesoderm. **c. frondo'sum,** the external surface of the chorion which develops vascular processes (chorionic villi) and later forms the embryonic portion of the placenta. **c. lae've,** the smooth and membranous part of the chorion. **primitive c.,** that stage of the late blastocyst during which it develops many small villi. **shaggy c.,** c. frondosum.

chorionepithelioma (ko"re-on-ep"ĭ-the"le-o'mah). Chorioepithelioma.

chorionic (ko"re-on'ik). Pertaining to the chorion.

chorionitis (ko"re-o-ni'tis) [*chorion* + *-itis*]. Inflammation of the corium of the skin, which becomes hard and thick; scleroderma.

chorioplacental (ko″re-o-plah-sen′tal). Pertaining to the chorion and the placenta.

chorioplaque (ko′re-o-plak″). A form of multinucleated giant cell occurring in cellular infiltrations of the skin.

Chorioptes (ko″re-op′tēz). A genus of parasitic mites infesting the skin and hair of domestic animals and causing a sort of mange (*chorioptic acariasis* or *itch*).

chorioretinal (ko″re-o-ret′ĭ-nal). Pertaining to the choroid and retina.

chorioretinitis (ko″re-o-ret″ĭ-ni′tis). Inflammation of the choroid and retina.

chorioretinopathy (ko″re-o-ret″ĭ-nop′ah-the). A noninflammatory process involving both chorion and retina.

chorista (ko-ris′tah) [Gr. *chōristos* separated]. Defective development due to, or characterized by, displacement of the anlage.

choristoblastoma (ko-ris″to-blas-to′mah) [Gr. *chōristos* separated + *blastos* germ + *-oma*]. Choristoma.

choristoma (ko″ris-to′mah) [Gr. *chōristos* separated + *-oma*]. A mass of tissue histologically normal for an organ or part of the body other than the site at which it is located.

choroid (ko′roid) [*chorion* + Gr. *eidos* form]. 1. Resembling the chorion or the corium. 2. Choroidea.

choroidal (ko-roi′dal). Pertaining to the choroid.

choroidea (ko-roi′de-ah). [N A] The thin, dark brown, vascular coat investing the posterior five-sixths of the eyeball. Called also *chorioidea* [B N A], and *choroid*.

choroidectomy (ko″roi-dek′to-me). Surgical removal or destruction of the choroid plexus of the lateral ventricles of the brain.

choroideremia (ko″roi-der-e′me-ah) [*choroid* + Gr. *erēmia* destitution]. Absence of the choroid.

choroiditis (ko″roid-i′tis) [*choroid* + *-itis*]. Inflammation of the choroid. **anterior c.,** that in which there are points of exudation at the periphery. **areolar c.,** that which starts around or near the macula lutea and progresses toward the periphery. **areolar central c.,** Förster's c. **central c.,** a variety in which the exudation is in the region of the macula lutea. **diffuse c., disseminated c.,** that which is characterized by spots scattered over the fundus. **Doyne's familial honeycombed c.,** a hereditary degenerative choroiditis marked by light-colored patches in the neighborhood of the optic disk and macula. **exudative c.,** that which is characterized by scattered patches of an exudate. **Förster's c.,** a form of central choroiditis in which the spots are black at first, but later enlarge and become white. **c. gutta′ta seni′lis,** Tay's c. **metastatic c.,** a form due to metastasis in pyemia, meningitis, etc. **c. myop′ica,** choroiditis due to eyestrain from defective vision. **c. sero′sa,** glaucoma. **suppurative c.,** that which leads to the formation of pus. **Tay's c.,** degeneration of the choroid, marked by irregular yellow spots around the macula lutea, and believed to be due to an atheromatous state of the arteries; seen in advanced life. Called also *choroiditis guttata senilis*.

choroidocyclitis (ko-roi″do-sik-li′tis). Inflammation of the choroid and ciliary processes.

choroido-iritis (ko-roi″do-i-ri′tis). Inflammation of the choroid coat and the iris.

choroidopathy (ko″roi-dop′ah-the) [*choroid* + Gr. *pathos* disease]. Any morbid process affecting the choroid.

choroidoretinitis (ko-roi″do-ret″ĭ-ni′tis). Inflammation of the choroid and retina.

chorology (ko-rol′o-je) [Gr. *chōros* place + *-logy*]. The science of geographic distribution.

choromania (ko″ro-ma′ne-ah) [Gr. *choros* dance + *mania* madness]. A morbid desire to dance.

chortosterol (kor-tos′ter-ol) [Gr. *chortis* grass]. The sterol of grass.

Chr. Abbreviation for *Chromobacterium*.

chrematophobia (kre″mat-o-fo′be-ah) [Gr. *chrema* money + *phobia*]. Morbid dread of money.

Christian's disease, syndrome (kris′chanz) [Henry Asbury *Christian*, American physician, 1876–1951]. Hand-Schüller-Christian disease.

Christison's formula (kris′tĭ-sonz) [Sir Robert *Christison*, Scotch physician, 1797–1882]. See under *formula*.

Christmas disease, factor [*Christmas*, for the name of the first patient with the disease who was studied in detail]. See under *disease* and *factor*.

chrom-. See *chromo-*.

chromaffin (kro-maf′in) [*chrom-* + L. *affinis* having affinity for]. Taking up and staining strongly with chromium salts: said of certain cells occurring in the adrenal, coccygeal, and carotid glands, along the sympathetic nerves, and in various organs.

chromaffinoblastoma (kro-maf″ĭ-no-blas-to′mah). A tumor in which the cells are an early form of chromaffin-reacting cell.

chromaffinoma (kro″maf-ĭ-no′mah). Any tumor containing chromaffin cells. **medullary c.,** pheochromocytoma.

chromaffinopathy (kro″maf-ĭ-nop′ah-the) [*chromaffin* + Gr. *pathos* disease]. Any disease of the chromaffin system.

chromagogue (kro′mah-gog) [*chrom-* + Gr. *agōgos* leading]. Tending to eliminate pigments.

chromaphil (kro′mah-fil) [*chrom-* + Gr. *philein* to love]. Chromaffin.

chromargentaffin (krōm″ar-jen′tah-fin) [*chrom-* + L. *argentum* silver + L. *affinis* having affinity for]. Staining with chromium salts and impregnable with silver: said of certain cells of the mucous membrane of the intestinal tract. Cf. *enterochromaffin gland* and *argentaffinoma*.

chromate (kro′māt). 1. Any salt of chromic acid. 2. To subject to the action of a salt of chromic acid.

chromatelopsia (kro″mat-el-op′se-ah) [*chrom-* + Gr. *atelēs* imperfect + *opsis* sight + *-ia*]. Imperfect perception of colors.

chromatic (kro-mat′ik). 1. Pertaining to color; stainable with dyes. 2. Pertaining to chromatin.

chromatid (kro′mah-tid). One of the two spiral filaments making up a chromosome, which separate in cell division, each going to a different pole of the dividing cell.

chromatin (kro′mah-tin) [Gr. *chrōma* color]. The more readily stainable portion of the cell nucleus, forming a network of nuclear fibrils within the achromatin of a cell. It is a desoxyribose nucleic acid attached to a protein structure base and is the carrier of the genes in inheritance. Called also *chromoplasm*. **distributed c., extranuclear c.,** chromidia. **sex c.,** a mass of chromatin, situated at the periphery of the nucleus, which is present in normal females but not in normal males.

chromatinic (kro″mah-tin′ik). Of or pertaining to the chromatin.

chromatin-negative (kro″mah-tin-neg′ah-tiv). Lacking sex chromatin; characteristic of the nuclei of cells in a normal male.

chromatinolysis (kro″mah-tĭ-nol′ĭ-sis) [*chromatin* + Gr. *lysis* dissolution]. Chromatolysis.

chromatinorrhexis (kro″mat-ĭ-no-rek′sis) [*chromatin* + Gr. *rhēxis* rupture]. Splitting up of the chromatin.

chromatin-positive (kro″mah-tin-poz′ĭ-tiv). Containing sex chromatin; characteristic of the nuclei of cells in a normal female.

chromatism (kro′mah-tizm). 1. Abnormal pigmentation. 2. A hallucinatory perception of colored light.

Chromatium (kro-ma′te-um). A genus of microorganisms of the family Thiorhodaceae, suborder Rhodobacteriineae, order Pseudomonadales, made up of more or less ovoid, bean-shaped, or vibrio-shaped cells, or short rods, occurring singly. It includes 12 species.

chromatize (kro′mah-tīz). To charge with some chromium compound.

chromato- (kro′mah-to). 1. Combining form denoting relationship to chromatin. 2. See *chromo-*.

chromatoblast (kro-mat′o-blast) [*chromato-* + Gr. *blastos* germ]. A cell that can become a chromatophore, or bearer of pigment.

chromatocinesis (kro″mah-to-si-ne′sis). Chromatokinesis.

chromatodermatosis (kro″mah-to-der″mah-to′sis) [*chromato-* + *dermatosis*]. Any skin disease with pigmentation.

chromatodysopia (kro″mah-to-dis-o′pe-ah). Chromatelopsia.

chromatogenous (kro″mah-toj′e-nus) [*chromato-* + Gr. *gennan* to produce]. Producing color or coloring matter.

chromatogram (kro-mat′o-gram). The record produced by the bands of color in an adsorption column after a solution for analysis has been poured into an adsorbent-containing vertical glass tube, or that produced in paper chromatography.

chromatography (kro″mah-tog′rah-fe) [*chromato-* + Gr. *graphein* to write]. A method of chemical analysis in which the solution to be analyzed is poured into an adsorbent-containing vertical glass tube, the different solutes moving through the adsorption column at different velocities, and producing bands of color at different levels of the column. The term has been extended to include other methods utilizing the same principle, although no colors are produced in the column. Kaolin, alumina, silica, and activated charcoal have been used as adsorbing substances. **electric c.,** electrochromatography. **filter paper c.,** paper c. **paper c.,** a form of chromatography in which a sheet of blotting paper, usually filter paper, is substituted for the adsorption column. After appropriate treatment, colored areas are produced at specific sites on the paper, depending on the velocity of the solute, the capillary action of the paper, and the solvent. Called also *filter paper chromatography*. **partition c.** 1. A form of separation of solutes utilizing the partition of the solutes between two liquid phases, namely, the original solvent and the film of solvent on the adsorption column. 2. A form of separation of solutes utilizing the principle of the adsorption column, the different solutes traveling through the column at different velocities.

chromatoid (kro′mah-toid). Staining deeply with dye. Chromatoid bodies are deeply staining rods in the cytoplasm of certain amebae.

chromatokinesis (kro″mah-to-ki-ne′sis) [*chromatin* + Gr. *kinēsis* movement]. Movement of chromatin during the life and division of a cell.

chromatology (kro″mah-tol′o-je) [*chromato-* + *-logy*]. The science of colors.

chromatolysis (kro″mah-tol′ĭ-sis) [*chromato-* + Gr. *lysis* dissolution]. 1. The solution and disintegration of the chromatin of cell nuclei. 2. Disintegration of the Nissl (chromophil) bodies of a nerve cell as the result of injury, or of fatigue or exhaustion; a part of the so-called axon reaction.

chromatolysm (kro-mat′o-lizm). Chromatolysis.

chromatolytic (kro″mah-to-lit′ik). Pertaining to chromatolysis.

chromatometer (kro″mah-tom′e-ter) [*chromato-* + Gr. *metron* measure]. An instrument for measuring color or color perception.

chromatopathy (kro″mah-top′ah-the) [*chromato-* + Gr. *pathos* disease]. Any skin disease characterized by a disorder of pigmentation.

chromatopectic (kro″mah-to-pek′tik). Chromopectic.

chromatopexis (kro″mah-to-pek′sis). Chromopexis.

chromatophagus (kro″mah-tof′ah-gus) [*chromato-* + Gr. *phagein* to devour]. Destroying pigments.

chromatophil (kro′mah-to-fil″). A cell or element which stains easily.

chromatophile (kro′mah-to-fil″). 1. Chromatophil. 2. Chromatophilic.

chromatophilia (kro″mah-to-fil′e-ah) [*chromato-* + Gr. *philein* to love + *-ia*]. The condition of staining easily.

chromatophilic (kro″mah-to-fil′ik). Staining easily.

chromatophilous (kro″mah-tof′ĭ-lus). Chromatophilic.

chromatophobia (kro″mah-to-fo′be-ah) [*chromato-* + Gr. *phobos* fear + *-ia*]. Morbid aversion to certain colors.

chromatophore (kro′mah-to-fōr″) [*chromato-* + Gr. *pherein* to bear]. Any pigmentary cell or color-producing plastid, such as those of the cutis or deep layers of the epidermis. Cf. *melanophore*.

chromatophoroma (kro″mah-to-fo-ro′mah). A tumor made up of chromatophores. Cf. *melanoma*.

chromatophoromatosis (kro″mah-to-fo″ro-mah-to′sis). Melanomatosis.

chromatophorotropic (kro″mah-to-fo″ro-trop′-ik). Having an influence or effect on chromatophores: applied to a principle of the pars intermedia of the pituitary.

chromatoplasm (kro′mah-to-plazm). The colored portions of the protoplasm of a pigmented cell.

chromatopseudopsis (kro″mah-to-su-dop′sis) [*chromato-* + Gr. *pseudēs* false + *opsis* vision]. Abnormal perception of color.

chromatopsia (kro″mah-top′se-ah) [*chromato-* + Gr. *opsis* vision + *-ia*]. 1. A visual defect in which colorless objects appear to be tinged with color. 2. A visual defect in which various colors are imperfectly perceived; anomalous color vision.

chromatoptometer (kro″mah-top-tom′e-ter) [*chromato-* + Gr. *op-* to see + *metron* measure]. A device used in measuring color perception.

chromatoptometry (kro″mah-top-tom′e-tre). The testing of the power of discriminating colors.

chromatosis (kro″mah-to′sis). Pigmentation; especially abnormal pigmentation of the skin.

chromatoskiameter (kro″mah-to-ski-am′e-ter). An instrument for measuring the color sense.

chromatosome (kro-mat′o-sōm) [*chromato-* + Gr. *sōma* body]. Chromosome.

chromatotaxis (kro″mah-to-tak′sis) [*chromatin* + Gr. *taxis* arrangement]. The attraction or influence of certain substances on the chromatin of a cell nucleus, causing destruction of the chromatin, while the cell body remains intact.

chromatotropism (kro″mah-tot′ro-pizm) [*chromato-* + Gr. *tropos* a turning]. An orienting response to a color.

chromaturia (kro″mah-tu′re-ah) [*chromato-* + Gr. *ouron* urine + *-ia*]. Abnormal coloration of the urine.

chromesthesia (kro″mes-the′ze-ah) [*chrom-* + Gr. *aisthēsis* perception]. The association of imaginary sensations of color with actual sensations of hearing, taste, or smell. See *photism*.

chromhidrosis (krom″hid-ro′sis) [*chrom-* + Gr. *hidrōs* sweat]. The secretion of colored sweat.

chromicize (kro′mĭ-sīz). To treat with a chromium compound.

chromidia (kro-mid′e-ah). Plural of *chromidium*.

chromidial (kro-mid′e-al). Pertaining to, or composed of, chromidia.

chromidiation (kro″mid-e-a′shun). Chromidiosis.

chromidien (kro-mid′e-en) [Ger.]. That part of the extranuclear chromatin not concerned in the reproduction of the cell.

chromidiosis (kro-mid-e-o′sis). The outpouring of nuclear substance and chromatin from the nucleus into the cytoplasm of a cell.

chromidium (kro-mid′e-um), pl. *chromid′ia.* Any one of the granules of extranuclear chromatin seen in the cytoplasm of a cell, and staining deeply with basic stains.

chromidrosis (kro″mid-ro′sis). Chromhidrosis.

chromiole (kro′me-ōl). One of the minute granules of chromatin composing the chromosomes (Eisen, 1899).

chromium (kro′me-um) [L.; Gr. *chrōma* color]. A whitish, brittle metal: atomic number, 24; atomic weight, 51.996; specific gravity, 7.1; symbol, Cr; several of its compounds are pigments. **c. oxide,** a substance used in dentistry as a polishing agent, especially for stainless steel. **c. trioxide,** chromic acid.

chromo-, chrom-, chromato- [Gr. *chrōma, chrōmatos* color]. Combining form denoting relationship to color.

Chromobacterium (kro″mo-bak-te′re-um). A genus of microorganisms of the family Rhizobiaceae, order Eubacteriales, made up of small flagellated rods which characteristically produce a violet pigment which is soluble in alcohol but not in water or chloroform. It includes four species, *C. amythis′tinum, C. jan′thinum, C. marismor′tui,* and *C. viola′ceum.*

chromoblast (kro′mo-blast) [*chromo-* + Gr. *blastos* germ]. An embryonic cell which develops into a pigment cell.

chromoblastomycosis (kro″mo-blas″to-mi-ko′sis). A chronic fungus infection of the skin, producing wartlike nodules or papillomas which may or may not ulcerate. It occurs sporadically in many areas of the world, and may be caused by *Phialophora verrucosa, Hormodendron pedrosoi, H. compactum,* or *H. carrionii.*

chromocenter (kro′mo-sen″ter). 1. Karyosome. 2. A fused mass of heterochromatin with spokelike extensions of euchromatin, representing the chromosomes in the salivary glands of some insects.

chromocholoscopy (kro″mo-ko-los′ko-pe) [*chromo-* + Gr. *cholē* bile + Gr. *skopein* to examine]. Testing the biliary function by a pigment excretion test (methylthionine chloride).

chromocrater (kro″mo-kra′ter). A blood corpuscle shaped like a crater.

chromocrinia (kro″mo-krin′e-ah) [*chromo-* + Gr. *krinein* to separate]. The secretion or excretion of coloring matter.

chromocystoscopy (kro″mo-sis-tos′ko-pe) [*chromo-* + *cystoscopy*]. Examination of the interior of the bladder after administration of indigo carmine or other dye which is excreted in the urine, for identification and study of the activity of the ureteral orifices.

chromocyte (kro′mo-sīt) [*chromo-* + Gr. *kytos* hollow vessel]. Any colored cell or pigmented corpuscle.

chromocytometer (kro″mo-si-tom′e-ter) [*chromo-* + Gr. *kytos* hollow vessel + *metron* measure]. An instrument for measuring the amount of hemoglobin in the red corpuscles of the blood.

chromocytometry (kro″mo-si-tom′e-tre). Measurement of the hemoglobin or counting of the red corpuscles of blood.

chromodacryorrhea (kro″mo-dak″re-o-re′ah) [*chromo-* + Gr. *dacryon* tear + *rhoia* flow]. The shedding of bloody tears.

chromodermatosis (kro″mo-der-mah-to′sis). Chromatodermatosis.

chromodiagnosis (kro″mo-di-ag-no′sis) [*chromo-* + *diagnosis*]. 1. Diagnosis by change of color. 2. Diagnosis of functional derangements by observing the rate at which coloring matters, such as methylthionine chloride, are excreted. 3. Diagnostic examination made through colored glass or sheets of colored gelatin.

chromoflavine (kro″mo-fla′vin). Acriflavine.

chromogen (kro′mo-jen). Any substance which may give origin to a coloring matter.

chromogene (kro′mo-jēn) [*chromosome* + *gene*]. A gene that is located on a chromosome. Cf. *plasmagene.*

chromogenesis (kro″mo-jen′e-sis) [*chromo-* + *genesis*]. The formation of pigments or colors, as by bacterial action.

chromogenic (kro″mo-jen′ik). 1. Producing a pigment or coloring matter. 2. Pertaining to chromogenes.

chromo-isomerism (kro″mo-i-som′er-izm) [*chromo-* + *isomerism*]. Isomerism in which the isomers have different colors.

chromolipoid (kro″mo-li′poid). Lipochrome.

chromolume (kro′mo-lo͞om) [*chromo-* + L. *lumen* light]. An apparatus for producing colored light rays for therapeutic purposes.

chromolysis (kro-mol′ĭ-sis). Chromatolysis.

chromoma (kro-mo′mah). An ulcerous malignant tumor supposed to be derived from chromatophore cells.

chromomere (kro′mo-mēr) [*chromo-* + Gr. *meros* part]. 1. Any one of the beadlike granules of chromatin composing a chromosome. 2. Granulomere.

chromometer (kro-mom′e-ter) [*chromo-* + Gr. *metron* measure]. Colorimeter.

chromomycosis (kro″mo-mi-ko′sis). Chromoblastomycosis.

chromone (kro′mōn) [Gr. *chrōma* color]. A colorless ketone, $C_9H_6O_2$, from the hypothetical compound benzopyran, C_9H_8O.

chromonema (kro″mo-ne′mah), pl. *chromonemata* [*chromo-* + Gr. *nēma* thread]. A twisted chromatic thread forming a kind of structural member of the chromosome.

chromonemata (kro″mo-ne′mah-tah). Plural of *chromonema.*

chromoneme (kro′mo-nēm). Chromonema.

chromoparic (kro-mo-par′ik) [*chromo-* + L. *parere* to produce]. Producing or giving rise to color: said of chromogenic bacteria, which secrete a coloring matter but which themselves remain colorless. Cf. *chromophoric* and *parachromophoric.*

chromopathy (kro-mop′ah-the). Chromatopathy.

chromopectic (kro″mo-pek′tik). Pertaining to, characterized by, or promoting chromopexy.

chromopexic (kro″mo-pek′sik). Chromopectic.

chromopexy (kro′mo-pek″se) [*chromo-* + Gr. *pēxis* fixation]. The fixation of pigment, a term applied especially to the function of the liver in forming bilirubin.

chromophage (kro′mo-fāj) [*chromo-* + Gr. *phagein* to eat]. Pigmentophage.

chromophane (kro′mo-fān) [*chromo-* + Gr. *phainein* to show]. A retinal pigment.

chromophil (kro′mo-fil) [*chromo-* + Gr. *philein* to love]. Any easily stainable cell, structure, or tissue.

chromophile (kro′mo-fīl). 1. Chromophil. 2. Chromophilic.

chromophilic (kro-mo-fil′ik). Readily or easily stained: used especially of certain leukocytes and other histologic elements.

chromophilous (kro-mof′ĭ-lus). Chromophilic.

chromophobe (kro′mo-fōb) [*chromo-* + *phobia*]. Any cell, structure or tissue which does not stain readily; applied especially to the non-staining cells of the anterior hypophysis.

chromophobia (kro″mo-fo′be-ah). 1. The quality of staining poorly with dyes. 2. A morbid aversion to colors.

chromophobic (kro″mo-fo′bik). Pertaining to or characterized by chromophobia.

chromophore (kro′mo-fōr). Any chemical group whose presence gives a decided color to a compound and which unites with certain other groups (auxochromes) to form dyes. Called also *color radical.*

chromophoric (kro″mo-fōr′ik) [*chromo-* + Gr. *pherein* to bear]. 1. Bearing color: said of chromogenic bacteria when the pigment is a component of the bacterial cell itself. Cf. *parachromophoric*. 2. Pertaining to a chromophore.

chromophorous (kro-mof′o-rus). Chromophoric.

chromophose (kro′mo-fōs) [*chromo-* + *phose*]. A subjective sensation of color.

chromophototherapy (kro″mo-fo″to-ther′ah-pe) [*chromo-* + Gr. *phōs* light + *therapeia* treatment]. Treatment with colored light.

chromophytosis (kro″mo-fi-to′sis) [*chromo-* + Gr. *phyton* plant + *-osis*]. Skin discoloration due to the presence of a vegetable parasite; tinea versicolor.

chromoplasm (kro′mo-plazm) [*chromo-* + Gr. *plasma* something formed]. The easily staining network of a cell nucleus.

chromoplast (kro′mo-plast). Chromoplastid.

chromoplastid (kro″mo-plas′tid) [*chromo-* + *plastid*]. Any pigment-producing plastid other than a chloroplast.

chromoprotein (kro″mo-pro′te-in) [*chromo-* + *protein*]. A colored conjugated protein. Examples are: the red hemoglobin of the higher animals, the blue hemocyanin of many lower animals, and the red and blue pigments of seaweeds. Chromoproteins have respiratory functions and are closely related to the green chlorophyll of the higher plants.

chromopsia (kro-mop′se-ah). Chromatopsia.

chromoptometer (kro″mop-tom′e-ter) [*chromo-* + Gr. *op-* to see + *metron* measure]. Chromatoptometer.

chromoradiometer (kro″mo-ra″de-om′e-ter) [*chromo-* + L. *radius* ray + Gr. *metron* measure]. An apparatus for measuring roentgen-ray dosage by means of the color changes produced in slides placed next to the skin. **Holzknecht's c.,** an apparatus for measuring the roentgen-ray dosage, consisting of a capsule which contains a substance color sensitive to the roentgen ray. This capsule is placed near the part treated by the rays, and its color is then compared with a color scale whose colors are numbered from 3 to 24. The quantities indicated by these numbers are known as *Holzknecht's units*.

chromoretinography (kro″mo-ret″ĭ-nog′rah-fe) [*chromo-* + *retina* + Gr. *graphein* to write]. Color photography of the retina.

chromorhinorrhea (kro″mo-ri″no-re′ah) [*chromo-* + Gr. *rhis* nose + Gr. *rhoia* a flow]. The discharge of a pigmented secretion from the nose.

chromosantonin (kro″mo-san′to-nin). Yellow santonin; an isomeric form produced when santonin is exposed to sunlight.

chromoscope (kro′mo-skōp) [*chromo-* + Gr. *skopein* to examine]. An instrument for testing color perception.

chromoscopy (kro-mos′ko-pe) [*chromo-* + Gr. *skopein* to examine]. 1. The testing of color vision. 2. Diagnosis of renal function by the color of the urine following the administration of dyes. **gastric c.,** diagnosis of gastric function by the color of the gastric contents: a test for achylia gastrica.

chromosin (kro′mo-sin). A deoxyribose nucleoprotein complex in the cell nucleus.

chromosomal (kro″mo-so′mal). Pertaining to chromosomes.

chromosome (kro′mo-sōm) [*chromo-* + Gr. *sōma* body]. One of several small dark-staining and more or less rod-shaped bodies which appear in the nucleus of a cell at the time of cell division. They contain the genes, or hereditary factors, and are constant in number in each species. The normal number in man is 46, with 22 pairs of autosomes and 2 sex chromosomes (XX or XY). Many chromosomal aberrations may occur, some of them being typically associated with various abnormalities. **accessory c.** See *sex c's*. **bivalent c.,** a pair of chromosomes temporarily united during the division of sex cells. **giant c's.** 1. Polytene c's. 2. Lampbrush c's. **heterotypical c's.** See *sex c's*. **homologous c.,** one of a pair of chromosomes as found in somatic cells. **lampbrush c's,** giant chromosomes of the oocytes of many lower animals arranged like a cylindrical brush. **m-c.,** a small chromosome which conjugates only in the first spermatocyte division. **nucleolar c's,** those in relation to which the nucleoli reorganize during the telophase of mitosis. **odd c's.** See *sex c's*. **Ph′ c., Philadelphia c.,** an abnormally small acrocentric chromosome, one of the four small acrocentric chromosomes, pairs 21 and 22, the abnormality apparently resulting from loss of chromosome material from the long arm of the chromosome; a characteristic abnormality observed in the leukemic leukocytes derived both from blood and from marrow of patients with chronic granulocytic leukemia. **polytene c's,** giant bundles of unseparated chromonemata occurring especially in the salivary glands of some insects. **sex c's,** chromosomes that are associated with the determination of sex, in mammals constituting an unequal pair, called the X and the Y chromosome. **small c.,** m-c. **X c.,** the differential sex chromosome carried by half the

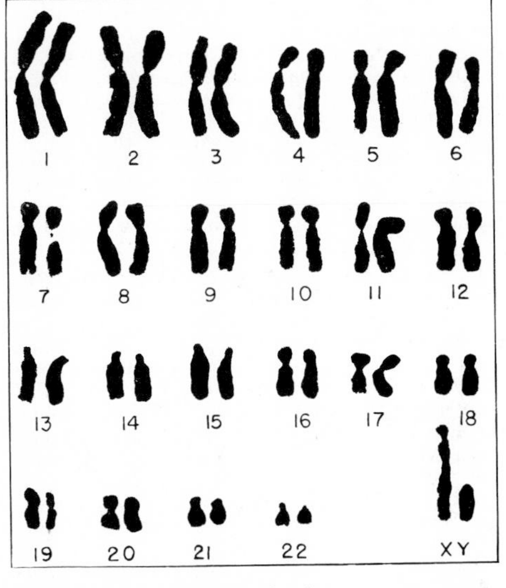

Normal male

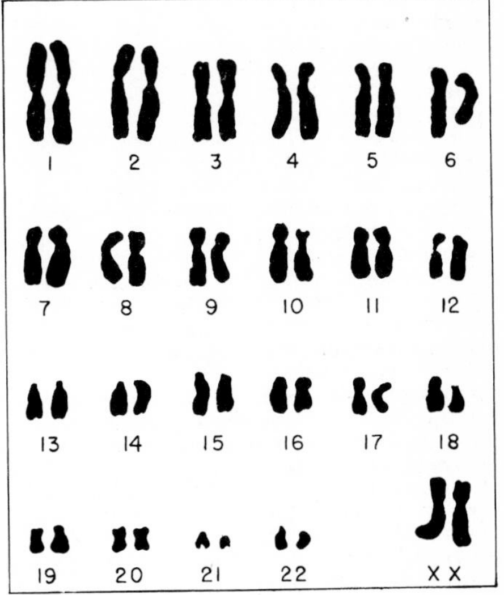

Normal female

Human chromosomes. (Grumbach.)

male and all female gametes in man and other male-heterogametic species. **Y c.,** the differential sex chromosome carried by half the male gametes in man and some other male-heterogametic species in which the homologue of the X chromosome has been retained.

chromospermism (kro″mo-sper′mizm) [*chromo-* + *sperm*]. A colored condition of the sperm.

chromotherapy (kro″mo-ther′ah-pe) [*chromo-* + Gr. *therapeia* treatment]. 1. Treatment of disease by variously colored lights. 2. The therapeutic use of restricted areas of the spectrum: called also *beamtherapy.*

chromotoxic (kro″mo-tok′sik) [*chromo-* + Gr. *toxikon* poison]. Destructive to hemoglobin or due to the destruction of hemoglobin.

chromotrichia (kro″mo-trik′e-ah) [*chromo-* + Gr. *thrix* hair + *-ia*]. Coloration of the hair.

chromotrichial (kro″mo-trik′e-al). Pertaining to the coloration of the hair.

chromotropic (kro″mo-trop′ik) [*chromo-* + Gr. *tropikos* turning]. Turning to or attracting color or pigment.

chromo-ureteroscopy (kro″mo-u-re″ter-os′ko-pe). Chromocystoscopy.

chromo-urinography (kro″mo-u″rĭ-nog′rah-fe). Diagnosis by measuring the intensity of color and the time of appearance in the urine after injection of a dye.

chron-. See *chrono-.*

chronaxia (kro-nak′se-ah). Chronaxy.

chronaxie (kro′nak-se). Chronaxy.

chronaximeter (kron″ak-sim′e-ter). Lapicque's instrument for measuring chronaxy in nerve lesions.

chronaximetric (kron″ak-sĭ-met′rik). Pertaining to chronaximetry.

chronaximetry (kron″ak-sim′e-tre). The measurement of chronaxy.

chronaxy (kro′nak-se) [*chron-* + Gr. *axios* fit]. The time required for the excitation of a nervous element by a definite stimulus; the minimum time at which a current just double the rheobase will excite contraction.

chronic (kron′ik) [L. *chronicus,* from Gr. *chronos* time]. Persisting over a long period of time.

chronicity (kro-nis′ĭ-te). The quality of being chronic.

chroniosepsis (kron″e-o-sep′sis). A chronic form of sepsis.

chrono- (kron′o) [Gr. *chronos* time]. A combining form denoting relationship to time.

chronobiology (kron″o-bi-ol′o-je) [*chrono-* + Gr. *bios* life + *-logy*]. The scientific study of the effect of time on living systems. See *anachronobiology* and *catachronobiology.*

chronognosis (kron″og-no′sis) [*chrono-* + Gr. *gnōsis* knowledge]. The subjective appreciation of the passage of time.

chronograph (kron′o-graf) [*chrono-* + Gr. *graphein* to write]. An instrument for recording small intervals of time.

chronometry (kro-nom′e-tre) [*chrono-* + Gr. *metrein* to measure]. The measurement of time or intervals of time. **mental c.,** the measurement and study of the duration of mental processes.

chronomyometer (kron″o-mi-om′e-ter). Malone's apparatus for measuring chronaxy.

chronophobia (kron″o-fo′be-ah) [*chrono-* + Gr. *phobos* fear + *-ia*]. A morbid fear of time: a common psychoneurosis in prison inmates.

chronophotograph (kron″o-fo′to-graf) [*chrono-* + *photograph*]. One of a series of photographs of a moving object taken for the purpose of showing successive phases of the motion.

chronoscope (kron′o-skōp) [*chrono-* + Gr. *skopein* to examine]. An instrument for measuring minute intervals of time.

chronosphygmograph (kron″o-sfig′mo-graf). Jaquet's instrument for observing the rhythm as well as the character of the pulse.

chronotaraxis (kro-no-tar-ak′sis) [*chrono-* + Gr. *taraxis* confusion]. Disorientation for time; observed as a transient symptom following thalamic or frontal lobe lesions.

chronotropic (kron″o-trop′ik) [*chrono-* + Gr. *tropikos* turning]. Affecting the time or rate, applied especially to nerves whose stimulation or agents whose administration affects the rate of contraction of the heart. **negatively c.,** decreasing the rate of contraction, as of the cardiac muscle fibers. **positively c.,** increasing the rate of contraction, as of the cardiac muscle fibers.

chronotropism (kro-not′ro-pizm). Interference with the regularity of a periodical movement, such as the heart beat.

chrotoplast (kro′to-plast) [Gr. *chrōs* skin + *plassein* to form]. A dermal cell: a skin cell.

chrysalis (kris′ah-lis) [L.]. The pupa of an insect, especially of a moth or butterfly.

chrysarobin (kris″ah-ro′bin) [L. *chrysarobinum,* from Gr. *chrysos* gold + *araroba*]. A mixture of neutral principles obtained from Goa powder: used as a local antipsoriatic.

chrysiasis (krĭ-si′ah-sis) [Gr. *chrysos* gold]. The deposition of gold in the tissues.

Chrysippus (kri-sip′us) **of Cnidos** (4th century B.C.). A Greek physician who was a teacher of Erasistratus.

chryso- (kris′o) [Gr. *chrysos* gold]. A combining form indicating relationship to gold.

chrysocreatinine (kris″o-kre-at′ĭ-nin) [*chryso-* + *creatinine*]. A yellow, crystalline leukomaine, $C_5H_8N_4O$, from muscle tissue.

chrysocyanosis (kris″o-si″ah-no′sis). Cutaneous pigmentation following the injection of gold salts.

chrysoderma (kris″o-der′mah) [*chryso-* + Gr. *derma* skin]. A permanent pigmentation of the skin due to gold deposit.

Chrysomyia (kris″o-mi′yah) [*chryso-* + Gr. *myia* fly]. A genus of flies of the family Calliphoridae, of Africa, Australia and parts of Asia. **C. al′biceps,** an Australian species whose larvae (wool maggots) live in the soiled wool of sheep. **C. bezzia′na,** a species widely distributed in Asia and frequently found in wounds of man and animals. **C. dux** causes myiasis in man and animals in India and Australia. **C. macella′ria,** *Cochliomyia macellaria.*

chrysophoresis (kris″o-fo-re′sis). Diffusion of gold particles to various organs of the body after therapeutic administration of preparations of gold, by macrophages and polymorphonuclear leukocytes.

Chrysops (kris′ops) [*chryso-* + Gr. *ōps* eye]. A genus of tropical tabanid flies. *C. cecutiens* inflicts bites about the eyes on men and animals. *C. dimidiata,* or mango fly, is believed to be the intermediate host of *Loa loa. C. discalis* is the deer fly which probably is one of the transmitters of tularemia. *C. silacea* is an intermediate host of *Loa loa.*

chrysosis (kris-o′sis). Chrysiasis.

chrysotherapy (kris″o-ther′ah-pe) [*chryso-* + *therapy*]. Treatment with gold salts.

Chrysozona (kris″o-zo′nah) [*chryso-* + Gr. *zōne* girdle]. A genus of tabanid flies. *C. ital′ica* and *C. pluvia′lis* are common in Europe.

chthonophagia (thon″o-fa′je-ah) [Gr. *chthōn* earth + *phagein* to eat]. The morbid habit of eating clay or other earth; geophagy.

chthonophagy (thon-of′ah-je). Chthonophagia.

Chutro's stirrup (choo′trōz) [Pedro *Chutro,* South American surgeon, 1880–1937]. See under *stirrup.*

Chvostek's anemia, sign, symptom (vos′teks) [Franz *Chvostek,* Austrian surgeon, 1835–1884]. See under *anemia* and *sign.*

chylangioma (ki″lan-je-o′mah) [*chyle* + *angioma*]. A tumor made up of intestinal lymph vessels.

chylaqueous (ki-la′kwe-us) [*chyle* + L. *aqua* water]. Both chylous and watery.

chyle (kīl) [L. *chylus* juice]. The milky fluid taken up by the lacteals from the food in the intestine after digestion. It consists of lymph and emulsified fat. It passes into the veins by the thoracic duct, becoming mixed with the blood.

chylectasia (ki″lek-ta′se-ah) [*chyle* + Gr. *ektasis* dilatation]. Dilatation of a chylous vessel.

chylemia (ki-le′me-ah) [*chyle* + Gr. *haima* blood + *-ia*]. The presence of chyle in the blood.

chylidrosis (ki″lid-ro′sis) [*chyle* + Gr. *hidrōs* sweat + *-osis*]. Chylous perspiration.

chylifacient (ki″lĭ-fa′shent). Forming chyle.

chylifaction (ki″lĭ-fak′shun) [*chyle* + L. *facere* to make]. The formation of chyle.

chylifactive (ki″lĭ-fak′tiv) [*chyle* + L. *facere* to make]. Forming or making chyle.

chyliferous (ki-lif′er-us) [*chyle* + L. *ferre* to bear]. 1. Forming chyle. 2. Conveying chyle.

chylification (ki″lĭ-fĭ-ka′shun) [*chyle* + L. *facere* to make]. The formation of chyle.

chyliform (ki′lĭ-form). Resembling chyle.

chylocele (ki′lo-sēl) [*chyle* + Gr. *kēlē* tumor]. A chylous effusion into the tunica vaginalis of the testis. **parasitic c.,** lymph scrotum.

chylocyst (ki′lo-sist) [*chyle* + Gr. *kystis* bladder]. The receptaculum chyli.

chyloderma (ki″lo-der′mah) [*chyle* + Gr. *derma* skin]. Lymph scrotum.

chyloid (ki′loid). Resembling chyle.

chylology (ki-lol′o-je). The study of chyle.

chylomediastinum (ki″lo-me″de-as-ti′num). The presence of chyle in the mediastinum.

chylomicrograph (ki″lo-mi′kro-graf). A curve plotted from counts of chylomicrons.

chylomicron (ki″lo-mi′kron). A particle of emulsified fat, about 1 μ in diameter, found in the blood during the digestion of fat.

chylomicronemia (ki″lo-mi″kron-e′me-ah) [*chylomicron* + Gr. *haima* blood + *-ia*]. The presence of chylomicrons in the blood.

chylopericarditis (ki″lo-per″ĭ-kar-di′tis). Pericarditis with effusion of chyle into the pericardial sac.

chylopericardium (ki″lo-per″ĭ-kar′de-um) [*chyle* + *pericardium*]. The presence of effused chyle in the pericardium.

chyloperitoneum (ki″lo-per″ĭ-to-ne′um). The presence of effused chyle in the peritoneal cavity.

chylophoric (ki″lo-for′ik) [*chyle* + Gr. *phoros* bearing]. Conveying chyle.

chylopleura (ki″lo-ploo′rah). The presence of effused chyle within the pleural cavity.

chylopneumothorax (ki″lo-nu″mo-tho′raks). The presence of chyle and air in the pleural cavity.

chylopoiesis (ki″lo-poi-e′sis) [*chyle* + Gr. *poiēsis* formation]. Chylification.

chylopoietic (ki″lo-poi-et′ik). Concerned in the formation of chyle.

chylorrhea (ki″lo-re′ah). 1. Discharge of chyle due to rupture of or injury to the thoracic duct. 2. Chylous diarrhea, due to rupture of lymphatics in the small intestine.

chylosis (ki-lo′sis). The process of conversion of food into chyle and of absorption of the latter into the tissues.

chylothorax (ki″lo-tho′raks) [*chyle* + Gr. *thōrax* chest]. The presence of effused chyle in the thoracic cavity.

chylous (ki′lus). Pertaining to, mingled with, or of the nature of, chyle.

chyluria (ki-lu′re-ah) [*chyle* + Gr. *ouron* urine + *-ia*]. The presence of chyle in the urine, giving it a milky appearance. **c. trop′ica,** chyluria caused by the presence of a nematode parasite, *Wuchereria bancrofti*.

chylus (ki′lus). [B N A] Chyle. Omitted in N A.

chymar (ki′mar). Trade mark for preparations of chymotrypsin.

chymase (ki′mās). An enzyme of the gastric juice, which accelerates the action of the pancreatic juice.

chyme (kīm) [Gr. *chymos* juice]. The semifluid, homogeneous, creamy or gruel-like material produced by gastric digestion of food.

chymification (ki″mĭ-fĭ-ka′shun) [*chyme* + L. *facere* to make]. The formation of chyme; gastric digestion.

chymopapain (ki″mo-pah-pa′in). An enzyme from the latex of *Carica papaya* which curdles milk.

chymorrhea (ki″mo-re′ah) [*chyme* + Gr. *rhoia* flow]. A discharge or flow of chyme.

chymosin (ki-mo′sin). Rennin.

chymosinogen (ki″mo-sin′o-jen). Renninogen.

chymotrypsin (ki″mo-trip′sin). 1. One of the proteolytic and milk-curdling enzymes of the pancreatic secretion. It is a protein endopeptidase which catalyzes the hydrolysis of native food proteins to peptones, polypeptides, and amino acids, by breaking the peptide linkages of the carboxyl groups of tyrosine and phenylalanine. 2. A pharmaceutical preparation containing a number of proteolytic enzymes of the pancreatic juice: used to reduce and prevent local inflammation, edema, and pain.

chymotrypsinogen (ki″mo-trip-sin′o-jen). A crystallizable enzyme occurring in the pancreas and giving rise to chymotrypsin.

chymous (ki′mus). Pertaining to chyme.

chymus (ki′mus). [B N A] Chyme. Omitted in N A.

Chytridium (ki-trid′e-um). A genus of fungi parasitic on plants.

C.I. Abbreviation for *color index*.

Ciaccio's glands (chah′chōz) [Giuseppe Vincenzo *Ciaccio*, Italian anatomist, 1824–1901]. Glandulae lacrimales accessoriae.

Ciarrocchi's disease (char-ro′kēz) [Gaetano *Ciarrocchi*, Italian dermatologist, 1857–1924]. See under *disease*.

Cib. Abbreviation for L. *ci′bus*, food.

cibarian (sĭ-ba′re-an) [L. *cibus* food]. Pertaining to food.

cibisotome (sĭ-bis′o-tōm) [Gr. *kibisis* pouch + *tomē* cut]. An instrument for opening the capsule of the lens in removing cataract.

cibophobia (si″bo-fo′be-ah) [L. *cibus* food + *phobia*]. Abnormal loathing of food.

cicatrectomy (sik″ah-trek′to-me). Excision of a cicatrix.

cicatricial (sik″ah-trish′al). Pertaining to or of the nature of a cicatrix.

cicatricotomy (sik″ah-tri-kot′o-me) [*cicatrix* + Gr. *tomē* cut]. Incision of or surgical removal of a cicatrix.

cicatrisotomy (sik″ah-tri-sot′o-me). Cicatricotomy.

cicatrix (sik-a′triks, or sik′ah-triks), pl. *cica′trices* [L.]. The new tissue which is formed in the healing of a wound. **filtering c.,** a cicatrix following glaucoma operation through which the aqueous humor escapes. **hypertrophic c.,** a hard, rigid tumor formed by hypertrophy of the tissue of a cicatrix. **manometric c.,** a cicatrix of the drum membrane of the ear that moves in and out with variations of the intratympanic pressure. **vibratory c.,** a cicatrix which moves with the pulse, the respiration, or the voice. **vicious c.,** a cicatrix which causes deformity or impairs the function of a part.

cicatrizant (sik-at′rĭ-zant). 1. Causing or promoting cicatrization. 2. An agent which promotes cicatrization.

cicatrization (sik″ah-trĭ-za′shun). A healing process which leaves a scar or cicatrix.

cicatrize (sik′ah-trīz). To heal over so as to leave a scar.

cicutism (sik′u-tizm). Poisoning with *Cicuta virosa*.

ciguatera (se″gwah-ta′rah) [Sp. (orig. Taino) *cigua* a poisonous snail + *-era*, Sp. noun suffix]. A form of ichthyosarcotoxism, the mildest type produced by marine fishes. The term was formerly applied to all types of fish poisoning in the West Indies, where the name originated.

cilia (sil′e-ah) [L.]. Plural of *cilium*.

ciliaris (sil″e-a′ris) [L., from *cilium*]. See *Table of Musculi*.

ciliariscope (sil″e-ar′ĭ-skōp) [*ciliary* + Gr. *skopein* to examine]. An instrument for examining the ciliary region of the eye.

ciliarotomy (sil″e-ar-ot′o-me). Surgical division of the ciliary zone for glaucoma.

ciliary (sil′e-er″e) [L. *ciliaris*, from *cilium*]. Pertaining to or resembling the eyelashes or cilia; used particularly in reference to certain structures in the eye, as the ciliary (ciliaris) muscle, ciliary process, and ciliary ring.

Ciliata (sil″e-a′tah). A class of infusoria characterized by the presence of cilia. Three species are parasitic in man: *Balantidium coli*, *B. minutum*, and *Nyctotherus faba*.

ciliated (sil′e-āt″ed). Provided with cilia or with a fringe of hairs.

ciliectomy (sil″e-ek′to-me) [*cilia* + Gr. *ektomē* excision]. 1. Excision of a portion of the ciliary body. 2. Excision of a portion of the ciliary margin of the eyelid with the roots of the lashes.

ciliogenesis (sil″e-o-jen′e-sis). The formation or development of cilia.

cilioretinal (sil″e-o-ret′ĭ-nal). Pertaining to the retina and the ciliary body.

cilioscleral (sil″e-o-skle′ral). Pertaining to the ciliary apparatus and to the sclera.

ciliospinal (sil″e-o-spi′nal). Pertaining to the ciliary body and the spinal cord.

ciliotomy (sil″e-ot′o-me). Surgical division of the ciliary nerves.

cilium (sil′e-um) pl. *cilia* [L.]. 1. An eyelid or its outer edge. 2. [pl.] [N A, B N A] The hairs growing on the edges of the eyelids. Called also *eyelashes*. 3. A minute vibratile, hairlike process attached to a free surface of a cell.

cillo (sil′lo). Cillosis.

Cillobacterium (sil″lo-bak-te′re-um). A genus of microorganisms of the tribe Lactobacilleae, family Lactobacillaceae, order Eubacteriales, made up of non-sporulating, anaerobic, gram-positive bacilli found in the intestinal tract and occasionally associated with purulent infections.

cillosis (sil-lo′sis) [L.]. A spasmodic quivering of the eyelid.

cimbia (sim′be-ah) [L.]. A white band running across the ventral surface of the crus cerebri.

Cimex (si′meks) [L. "bug"]. A genus of insects; the bedbugs. **C. boue′ti,** the tropical bedbug of Africa and South America. **C. hemip′terus,** a species which infests man in the tropics. **C. lectula′rius,** the common bedbug which infests man. **C. pilosel′lus,** an American species found in bats. **C. pipistrel′la,** a species which transmits a trypanosome disease of bats.

cimex (si′meks), pl. *cim′ices* [L.]. An individual of the genus Cimex; a bedbug.

cimices (sim′ĭ-sēz). Plural of *cimex*.

cimicosis (sim″ĭ-ko′sis). Itching of the skin due to the bites of *Cimex lectularius* (bedbug).

cinching (sinch′ing). Operative shortening of an ocular muscle by plicating.

Cinchona (sin-ko′nah) [named from a countess of *Chinchon*]. A genus of rubiaceous trees, all natives of South America.

cinchonine (sin′ko-nin) [L. *cinchonina*]. A white, crystalline alkaloid, $C_{19}H_{22}N_2O$, with a bitter taste, from cinchona bark. It is used like quinine and in the same dose. **c. sulfate,** a white crystalline salt, $(C_{19}H_{22}N_2O)_2.H_2SO_4 + 2H_2O$, with properties like quinine sulfate.

cinchonism (sin′ko-nizm). The morbid or injurious effect of the injudicious use of cinchona bark or its alkaloids. It is attended by headache, tinnitus aurium, deafness, and symptoms of cerebral congestion.

cinchonize (sin′ko-nīz). To bring under the influence of cinchona or of any of its alkaloids.

cinchonology (sin-ko-nol′o-je) [*cinchona* + *-logy*]. The sum of what is known regarding the botany and culture of cinchona and regarding its alkaloids and their effects.

cinclisis (sin′klĭ-sis) [Gr. *kinklisis* a wagging]. A rapidly repeated movement, such as rapid breathing, or rapid winking.

cineangiocardiography (sin″e-an″je-o-kar″de-og′rah-fe). The photographic recording of fluoroscopic images of the heart and great vessels by motion picture techniques.

cineangiography (sin″e-an″je-og′rah-fe). The photographic recording of fluoroscopic images of the blood vessels by motion picture techniques.

cinedensigraphy (sin″e-den-sig′rah-fe). The recording of movements of internal body structures by means of x-rays and radiosensitive cells.

cinefluorography (sin″e-floo″or-og′rah-fe). Cineradiography.

cinemascopia (sin″e-mah-sko′pe-ah). The use of motion picture records for the study of movements of the body.

cinemascopy (sin″e-mas′ko-pe). Cinemascopia.

cinematics (sin″e-mat′iks). Kinematics.

cinematization (sin″e-mat-ĭ-za′shun). Kineplasty.

cinematography (sin″e-mah-tog′rah-fe). Cineradiography.

cinematoradiography (sin″e-mah-to-ra″de-og′rah-fe). Cineradiography.

cinemicrography (sin″e-mi-krog′rah-fe). The making of moving pictures of a small object through the lens system of a microscope. **time-lapse c.,** the taking of motion pictures of a minute object through a microscope at a slower than normal speed, so that with projection at normal speed the movements of the object appear to occur more rapidly.

cineol (sin′e-ol). Eucalyptol.

cineplastics (sin″e-plas′tiks). Kineplasty.

cineplasty (sin′e-plas″te). Kineplasty.

cineradiography (sin″e-ra″de-og′rah-fe). The making of a motion picture record of the successive images appearing on a fluoroscopic screen.

cinerea (sĭ-ne′re-ah) [L. *cinereus* ashen hued]. The gray matter of the nervous system.

cinereal (sĭ-ne′re-al). Pertaining to the gray matter of the brain or nervous system.

cineritious (sin″er-ish′us) [L. *cineritius*]. Ashen gray; of the color of ashes.

cineroentgenofluorography (sin″e-rent″gen-o-floo″or-og′rah-fe). Cineradiography.

cineroentgenography (sin″e-rent″gen-og′rah-fe). Cineradiography.

cinesalgia (sin″es-al′je-ah) [Gr. *kinēsis* motion + *-algia*]. Pain in a muscle when it is brought into action.

cinesi-. For words beginning thus, see those beginning *kinesi-*.

cineto-. For words beginning thus, see those beginning *kineto-*.

cingule (sin′gūl). Cingulum.

cingulectomy (sin″gu-lek′to-me). Bilateral extirpation of the anterior half of the gyrus cinguli.

cingulum (sin′gu-lum), pl. *cin′gula* [L. "girdle"]. 1. [N A, B N A] A bundle of association fibers which partly encircles the corpus callosum not far from the median plane, the fibers of which interrelate the cingulate and hippocampal gyri. 2. The lingual lobe of an anterior tooth, making up the bulk of the cervical third of its lingual surface. **c. extremita'tis inferio'ris** [B N A], c. membri inferioris. **c. extremita'tis superio'ris** [B N A], c. membri superioris. **c. hemisphe'rii,** gyrus cinguli. **c. mem'bri inferio'ris** [N A], the encircling bony structure supporting the lower limbs, comprising the two ossa coxae, articulating with each other and with the sacrum, to complete the essentially rigid bony ring. Called also *c. extremitatis inferioris* [B N A], and *pelvic girdle.* **c. mem'bri superio'ris** [N A], the encircling bony structure supporting the upper limbs, comprising the clavicles and scapulae, articulating with each other and with the sternum and vertebral column, respectively. Called also *c. extremitatis superioris* [B N A], and *shoulder girdle.*

cingulumotomy (sing″gu-lum-ot′o-me). The creation of precisely placed lesions in the cingulum of the frontal lobe, for relief of intractable pain.

Ciniselli's method (che″ne-sel′lēz) [Luigi *Ciniselli,* Italian surgeon, 1803–1878]. See under *method.*

cinnamon (sin′ah-mon) [L.; Gr. *kinnamon*]. The dried inner bark of various species of *Cinnamomum:* an agreeable aromatic and cordial, carminative, and astringent.

cinology (sĭ-nol′o-je). Kinesiology.

cinometer (sĭ-nom′e-ter). Kinesimeter.

cinoplasm (sin′o-plazm). Kinoplasm.

cionectomy (si″o-nek′to-me) [Gr. *kiōn* uvula + *ektomē* excision]. Excision of the uvula or of a part of it.

cionitis (si″o-ni′tis) [Gr. *kiōn* uvula + *-itis*]. Inflammation of the uvula.

cionoptosis (si″on-op-to′sis) [Gr. *kiōn* uvula + Gr. *ptōsis* a falling]. Undue elongation of the uvula.

cionorrhaphy (si″ŏ-nor′ah-fe). Plastic repair of the uvula.

cionotome (si-on′o-tōm) [Gr. *kiōn* uvula + *tomē* cut]. A cutting instrument for amputating the uvula.

cionotomy (si″o-not′o-me) [Gr. *kiōn* uvula + *temnein* to cut]. Surgical removal of part of the uvula.

circadian (ser″kah-de′an) [L. *circa* about + *dies* a day]. Pertaining to a period of about 24 hours. Applied especially to the rhythmic repetition of certain phenomena in living organisms at about the same time each day.

circellus (ser-sel′lus). A small ring, or circle. **c. veno'sus hypoglos'si,** plexus venosus canalis hypoglossi.

circinate (ser′sĭ-nāt). Resembling a ring, or circle.

circle (ser′k′l) [L. *circulus*]. A round figure structure, or part. **arterial c. of iris, greater,** circulus arteriosus iridis major. **arterial c. of iris, lesser,** circulus arteriosus iridis minor. **arterial c. of Willis,** circulus arteriosus cerebri. **Berry's c's,** charts with circles on them for testing stereoscopic vision. **c. of confusion,** a disk representing the image of a theoretical point made by a lens. **defensive c.,** the coexistence of two conditions which tend to have an antagonistic or inhibitory effect on each other. **diffusion c.,** a confused image formed on the retina when the latter is not at the focus of the eye. **c. of dispersion, c. of dissipation,** the circular space on the retina within which the image of a luminous point is formed. **c. of Haller.** 1. Circulus vasculosus nervi optici. 2. Valvula pylori. **c. of Hovius,** an intrascleral circular arrangement of anastomosing ciliary veins anterior to the vorticose veins, not far from the corneoscleral margin, occurring in mammals other than man. **Huguier's c.,** the circle formed about the junction of the cervix with the body of the uterus by the uterine arteries. **c. of iris, greater,** anulus iridis major. **c. of iris, lesser,** anulus iridis minor. **Latham's c.,** a circle 2 inches in diameter covering the area of pericardial dulness and situated midway between the left nipple and the lower end of the sternum. **Minsky's c's,** a device used for the graphic recording of eye lesions. **Pagenstecher's c.,** the circle formed on the abdominal wall by joining the points marking the positions occupied by a movable abdominal tumor which has been moved over its entire range. The center of such a circle indicates the point of attachment of the tumor. **Robinson's c.,** an arterial circle formed by anastomoses between the abdominal aorta, common iliac, hypogastric, uterine, and ovarian arteries. **sensory c.,** an area on the body within which it is impossible to distinguish separately the impressions arising from two sites of stimulation. **vascular c. of optic nerve,** circulus vasculosus nervi optici. **vicious c.,** a concatenation of conditions which have a deleterious effect upon each other, leading progressively to a worsening of the situation. **c's of Weber,** circles of points on the skin marking the points of tactile sense discrimination. **c. of Willis,** circulus arteriosus cerebri. **Zinn's c.,** circulus vasculosus nervi optici.

circlet (ser′klet). A small circular structure. **Zinn's c.,** circulus vasculosus nervi optici.

circling (ser′kling). Movement in a circle; a name formerly applied to listeriosis in sheep, because of the tendency of affected animals to move in a circle.

circuit (ser′kit) [L. *circuitus*]. The round or course traversed by an electrical current. The circuit is said to be *closed* when it is continuous, so that the current may pass through it; it is *open, broken,* or *interrupted* when it is not continuous and the current cannot pass through it. **magnetic c.,** the closed path of magnetic lines. **open c.,** a circuit having some break in it so that current is not passing or cannot pass. **organic c.,** reflex c. **reflex c.,** a chain of neurons which function in a reflex act. **short c.** 1. A current developed between two branches of another circuit at a point short of the terminals, so that the current does not reach the latter. 2. A communication between two portions of intestine, one above and the other below an obstruction.

circular (ser′ku-lar) [L. *circularis*]. Shaped like a circle; occurring in a circle.

circulation (ser″ku-la′shun) [L. *circulatio*]. Movement in a regular or circutious course, as the movement of the blood through the heart and blood vessels. **allantoic c.,** circulation in the fetus through the umbilical vessels. **collateral c.,** that which is carried on through secondary channels after obstruction of the principal vessel supplying the part. **compensatory c.,** collateral c. **coronary c.,** that within the muscular tissue of the heart. **cross c.,** the circulation in a portion of the body of one animal of blood supplied from another animal. **derivative c.,** the passage of blood from arteries to the veins without going through capillaries. **enterohepatic c.,** the reabsorption of bile salts from the intestine and their re-excretion by the liver. **extracorporeal c.,** the circulation of blood outside of the body, as through an artificial kidney for removal of substances usually excreted in the urine, or through a heart-lung apparatus for carbon dioxide–oxygen exchange. **fetal c.,** that which is carried on in the fetus, umbilical cord, and placenta. **first c.,** primitive c. **greater c.,** systemic c. **hypophyseoportal c.,** that passing through the venules from the capillaries of the median eminence of the hypothalamus into the sinusoidal capillaries of the hypophysis. **intervillous c.,** the flow of maternal blood through the intervillous space. **lesser c.,** pulmonary c. **lymph c.,** the passage of the lymph through lymph vessels and glands. **omphalomesenteric c.,** vitelline c. **placental c.,** fetal c. **portal c.,** the circulation of blood through larger vessels from the capillaries of one organ to the capillaries of another, before returning through larger veins back to the heart, especially the passage of the blood from capillaries of the gastrointestinal tract and spleen through capillaries of the liver before entering the hepatic vein. See also *hypophyseoportal c.* **primitive c.,** that by which the earliest nutriment and oxygen is conveyed to the embryo. **pulmonary c.,** that carrying the venous blood from the right ventricle to the lungs, and returning oxygenated blood to the left atrium of the heart. **sinusoidal c.,** that occurring through the sinusoids of various organs. **systemic c.,** the general circulation, carrying oxygenated blood from the left ventricle to various tissues of the body, and returning the venous blood to the right atrium of the heart. **thebesian c.,** the circulation of blood through the thebesian veins. **umbilical c.,** allantoic c. **vitelline c.,** the circulation through the blood vessels ramifying upon the yolk.

circulatory (ser′ku-lah-to″re). Pertaining to the circulation.

circulus (ser′ku-lus), pl. *cir′culi* [L. "a ring"]. A circle or circuit, used in anatomical nomenclature to designate such an arrangement, usually of arteries or veins. **c. arterio′sus cer′ebri** [N A], the circular system formed by the internal carotid, the anterior and posterior cerebral arteries, the anterior communicating artery, and the posterior communicating arteries. Called also *c. arteriosus* [*Willisi*] [B N A], and *arterial circle of Willis.* **c. arterio′sus hal′leri** [B N A], c. vasculosus nervi optici. **c. arterio′sus i′ridis ma′jor** [N A, B N A], a circle of anastomosing arteries situated in the ciliary body along the ciliary margin of the iris. Called also *greater arterial circle of iris.* **c. arterio′sus i′ridis mi′nor** [N A, B N A], a circle of anastomosing arteries in the iris near the pupillary margin. Called also *lesser arterial circle of iris.* **c. arterio′sus [Willis′i]** [B N A], c. arteriosus cerebri. **c. artic′uli vasculo′sus,** an arrangement of anastomosing vessels encircling a joint. **c. umbilica′lis,** an arterial plexus in the subperitoneal tissue surrounding the navel. **c. vasculo′sus ner′vi op′tici** [N A], a circle of arteries in the sclera surrounding the site of entrance of the optic nerve. Called also *c. vasculosus nervi optici* [*Halleri*] [B N A], and *vascular circle of optic nerve.* **c. veno′sus hal′leri,** plexus venosus areolaris. **c. veno′sus ho′vii,** circle of Hovius. **c. veno′sus rid′leyi,** sinus circularis. **c. willis′ii,** c. arteriosus cerebri. **c. zinn′ii,** c. vasculosus nervi optici.

circum- (ser′kum) [L.]. A prefix signifying around.

circumanal (ser″kum-a′nal). Surrounding the anus.

circumarticular (ser″kum-ar-tik′u-lar). Around a joint.

circumaxillary (ser″kum-ak′sĭ-lār″e). Around the axilla.

circumbulbar (ser″kum-bul′bar). Surrounding the eyeball.

circumcallosal (ser″kum-kah-lo′sal). Surrounding the corpus callosum.

circumcision (ser″kum-sizh′un) [L. *circumcisio* a cutting around]. The removal of all or a part of the prepuce, or foreskin. **pharaonic c.,** infibulation.

circumclusion (ser″kum-kloo′zhun) [L. *circumcludere* to shut in]. The compression of an artery by a wire and pin.

circumcorneal (ser″kum-kor′ne-al). Around the cornea.

circumcrescent (ser″kum-kres′ent) [*circum-* + L. *crescere* to grow]. Growing around and over.

circumduction (ser″kum-duk′shun) [L. *circumducere* to draw around]. The active or passive circular movement of a limb or of the eye.

circumference (ser-kum′fer-ens) [*circum-* + L. *ferre* to bear]. The outer limit or margin of a rounded body. **articular c.,** circumferentia articularis. See specific names under *circumferentia.*

circumferentia (ser-kum″fer-en′she-ah) [L.]. Circumference. **c. articula′ris,** the rounded surface of a bone which is received into a depression of another bone with which it articulates. **c. articula′ris cap′itis ul′nae** [N A], the semilunar surface of the head of the ulna which articulates with the ulnar notch of the radius. Called also *c. articularis capituli ulnae* [B N A], and *articular circumference of head of ulna.* **c. articula′ris capit′uli ul′nae** [B N A], c. articularis capiti ulnae. **c. articula′ris ra′dii** [N A, B N A], the rounded surface of the radius which articulates with the radial notch of the ulna. Called also *articular circumference of head of radius.*

circumferential (ser″kum-fer-en′shal). Pertaining to forming a circumference.

circumflex (ser′kum-fleks) [L. *circumflexus* bent about]. Curved like a bow.

circumflexus (ser″kum-flek′sus) [L.]. Bent about; circumflex.

circumgemmal (ser″kum-jem′al) [*circum-* + L. *gemma* bud]. Surrounding a bud; a term applied to that form of nerve ending in which an end-bud is surrounded by fibrils.

circuminsular (ser″kum-in′su-lar) [*circum-* + L. *insula* island]. Surrounding, situated, or occurring about the island of Reil.

circumintestinal (ser″kum-in-tes′tĭ-nal). Surrounding the intestine.

circumlental (ser″kum-len′tal) [*circum-* + L. *lens* lens]. Situated or occurring around the lens.

circumnuclear (ser″kum-nu′kle-ar). Surrounding or occurring near the nucleus.

circumocular (ser″kum-ok′u-lar) [*circum-* + L. *oculus* eye]. Surrounding or occurring around the eye.

circumoral (ser″kum-o′ral) [*circum-* + L. *os, oris* mouth]. Around or near the mouth.

circumorbital (ser″kum-or′bĭ-tal) [*circum-* + L. *orbita* orbit]. Situated around or occurring near an orbit.

circumpolarization (ser″kum-po″lar-i-za′shun) [*circum-* + *polarization*]. The rotation of a ray of polarized light to the right or left.

circumrenal (ser″kum-re′nal) [*circum-* + L. *ren* kidney]. Situated or occurring near a kidney.

circumscribed (ser′kum-skrībd) [*circum-* + L. *scribere* to write]. Bounded or limited; confined to a limited space.

circumscriptus (ser″kum-skrip′tus) [L.]. Circumscribed.

circumstantiality (ser″kum-stan″she-al′ĭ-te). A mental symptom marked by the introduction into the conversation of details only distantly related or entirely unrelated to the main subject of conversation.

circumtractor (ser′kum-trak″tor). A self-retaining circular retractor (H. R. Arnold).

circumvallate (ser″kum-val′āt) [*circum-* + L. *vallare* to wall]. Surrounded by a trench or by a ridge. See under *papilla.*

circumvascular (ser″kum-vas′ku-lar) [*circum-* + L. *vasculum* vessel]. Situated or occurring about the vessels.

circumvolute (ser″kum-vo′lūt) [*circum-* + L. *volutus* rolled]. Twisted about.

circumvolutio (ser″kum-vo-lu′she-o). A convolution, or the folding of some object about another. **c. crista′ta,** gyrus fornicatus.

cirrhogenous (sir-roj′e-nus). Producing cirrhosis or hardening.

cirrhonosus (sir-ron′o-sus) [Gr. *kirrhos* orange yellow + *nosos* disease]. A fetal disease characterized by a golden-yellow appearance of the pleura and peritoneum.

cirrhosis (sir-ro′sis) [Gr. *kirrhos* orange yellow]. 1. A disease of the liver, marked by progressive destruction of liver cells, accompanied by regeneration of the liver substance and increase of connective tissue. 2. Chronic interstitial inflammation of any organ. **alcoholic c.,** a cirrhosis due to an inadequate diet in heavy drinkers. **atrophic c.,** a form characterized by shrinkage in size and shriveling. It is frequently seen in heavy drinkers and in a late stage of subacute yellow atrophy of the liver. Cf. *Laennec's c.* **bacterial c.,** a variety said to be of microbic origin. **biliary c.,** that which is caused by chronic retention of bile from obstruction of the bile ducts (*obstructive biliary c.*) or chronic cholangitis (*hypertrophic biliary c.*). It is marked by jaundice, pain in the abdomen, and enlargement of the liver and spleen. **biliary c. of children,** a disease of children in India consisting of a fibrous connective tissue growth within the lobules of the liver: called also *infantile liver.* **Budd's c.,** chronic hepatic enlargement caused by intestinal intoxication. **calculus c.,** cirrhosis due to the presence of gallstones. **capsular c.,** cirrhosis due to lesions of Glisson's capsules, especially chronic perihepatitis; called also *Glisson's c.* and *lymphatic c.* **cardiac c.,** fibrosis of the liver associated with cardiac disease. **cardiotuberculous c.,** Hutinel's disease. **Charcot's c.,** hypertrophic cirrhosis of the liver. **Cruveilhier-Baumgarten c.,** congenital cirrhosis of the liver. **fatty c.,** a form in which the liver cells become infiltrated with fat. **Glisson's c.** See *capsular c.* **Hanot's c.,** hypertrophic cirrhosis. **hypertrophic c.,** a variety in which the liver becomes enlarged by overgrowth of the connective tissue. **c. of kidney,** granular kidney. **Laennec's c.,** atrophic cirrhosis of the liver, a form of portal cirrhosis, in which the liver is fibrotic, tawny in color, and smaller than normal: use of alcohol is the chief etiologic factor. **c. of liver,** biliary c. **c. of lung,** interstitial pneumonia. **malarial c.,** a form due to malaria, with lesions similar to those of alcoholic cirrhosis. **c. mam'mae,** chronic interstitial mastitis. **multilobular c.,** atrophic c. **periportal c.,** atrophic c. **pigmentary c.,** pigmentation of the liver seen in bronze diabetes. **pipe stem c.,** cirrhosis of the liver characterized by fibrotic scars around the large portal vessels. **portal c.,** a chronic degenerative and inflammatory disease of the liver marked by recurring degeneration and regeneration of the parenchyma of the liver and by fibrosis in and about the interlobar and portal spaces, leading eventually to obstruction of the portal circulation. **pulmonary c.,** interstitial pneumonia. **stasis c.,** cirrhosis due to obstruction of the outflow of the hepatic vein. The condition produced is called *cyanotic induration of the liver* and *cardiac liver.* **c. of stomach,** sclerotic gastritis. **syphilitic c.,** cirrhosis due to syphilis. **Todd's c.,** hypertrophic cirrhosis of the liver. **toxic c.,** cirrhosis of the liver from chronic poisoning. **unilobular c.,** hypertrophic c. **vascular c.,** cirrhosis following upon obstruction of the hepatic vein, portal vein, or general hepatic circulation.

cirrhotic (sir-rot'ik). Pertaining to or characterized by cirrhosis.

cirrus (sir'rus). The sexual orifice of a segment of tapeworms and flukes.

cirsectomy (ser-sek'to-me) [Gr. *kirsos* varix + *ektomē* excision]. Excision of a portion of a varicose vein.

cirsenchysis (ser-sen'kĭ-sis) [Gr. *kirsos* varix + *enchysis* injection]. Treatment of varicose veins by injection of a sclerosing solution.

cirso- (ser'so) [Gr. *kirsos* varix]. Combining form denoting relationship to a varix.

cirsocele (ser'so-sēl) [*cirso-* + Gr. *kēlē* tumor]. Varicocele.

cirsodesis (ser-sod'ĕ-sis) [*cirso-* + Gr. *desis* ligation]. The ligation of varicose veins.

cirsoid (ser'soid) [*cirso-* + Gr. *eidos* form]. Resembling a varix.

cirsomphalos (ser-som'fah-los) [*cirso-* + *omphalos* navel]. A varicose state of the navel.

cirsophthalmia (ser"sof-thal'me-ah) [*cirso-* + Gr. *ophthalmos* eye]. A varicose state of the conjunctival vessels.

cirsotome (ser'so-tōm) [*cirso-* + Gr. *tomē* cut]. A cutting instrument for use in operating on varicosities.

cirsotomy (ser-sot'o-me) [*cirso-* + Gr. *temnein* to cut]. Incision of varicose veins.

cismatan (sis'mah-tan). The seeds of *Cassia absus:* used in Egypt as a cure for ophthalmia.

cissa (sis'ah) [Gr. *kissa* longing for strange food]. Pica.

Cissampelos (sis-am'pĕ-los) [Gr. *kissos* ivy + *ampelos* vine]. A genus of menispermaceous climbing plants. *C. capensis,* of Africa, is emetic and purgative. *C. pareira,* of tropical America, is a spurious variety of pareira.

cistern (sis'tern). A closed space serving as a reservoir for fluid. See *cisterna.* **basal c.,** cisterna interpeduncularis. **cerebellomedullary c.,** cisterna cerebellomedullaris. **c. of chiasma, chiasmatic c.,** cisterna chiasmatis. **c. of fossa of Sylvius,** cisterna fossae lateralis cerebri. **great c.,** cisterna cerebellomedullaris. **interpeduncular c.,** cisterna interpeduncularis. **c. of lateral fossa of cerebrum,** cisterna fossae lateralis cerebri. **c. of Pecquet,** cisterna chyli. **posterior c.,** cisterna cerebellomedullaris. **subarachnoidal c's,** cisternae subarachnoideales. **c. of Sylvius,** cisterna fossae lateralis cerebri.

cisterna (sis-ter'nah), pl. *cister'nae* [L.]. [N A, B N A] A closed space serving as a reservoir for lymph or other body fluid, especially one of the enlarged subarachnoid spaces containing cerebrospinal fluid. Called also *cistern.* **c. am'biens,** c. venae magnae cerebri. **c. basa'lis,** c. interpeduncularis. **c. cerebellomedulla'ris** [N A, B N A], the enlarged subarachnoid space between the under surface of the cerebellum and the posterior surface of the medulla oblongata. Called also *cerebellomedullary cistern.* **c. chiasmat'ica,** c. chiasmatis. **c. chias'matis** [N A, B N A], a subarachnoid space between the optic chiasm and the rostrum of the corpus callosum. **c. chy'li** [N A, B N A], a dilated portion of the thoracic duct at its origin in the lumbar region; it receives several lymph-collecting vessels, including the intestinal, lumbar, and descending intercostal trunks. **c. fos'sae latera'lis cer'ebri** [N A, B N A], the space between the arachnoid and the lateral cerebral fossa. Called also *c. fossae lateralis cerebri* [*Sylvii*] and *cistern of lateral fossa of cerebrum.* **c. fos'sae Syl'vii,** c. fossae lateralis cerebri. **c. intercrura'lis profun'da,** c. interpeduncularis. **c. interpeduncula'ris** [N A, B N A], a dilatation of the subarachnoid space between the cerebral peduncles. Called also *interpeduncular cistern.* **c. mag'na,** c. cerebellomedullaris. **cister'nae subarachnoida'les** [B N A], cisternae subarachnoideales. **cister'nae subarachnoidea'les** [N A], localized enlargements of the subarachnoid space, occurring in areas where the dura mater and arachnoid do not closely follow the contour of the brain with its covering pia mater, and serving as reservoirs of cerebrospinal fluid. Called also *cisternae subarachnoidales* [B N A], and *subarachnoidal cisterns.* **c. sul'ci latera'lis, c. Sylvii,** c. fossae lateralis cerebri. **c. ve'nae mag'nae cer'ebri** [B N A], an enlarged space lying in the angle between the splenium of the corpus callosum and the superior surfaces of the cerebellum and mesencephalon, which contains the great vein of the cerebrum. Omitted in N A.

cisternae (sis-ter'ne) [L.]. Plural of *cisterna.*

cisternal (sis-ter'nal). Pertaining to a cistern, especially the cisterna cerebellomedullaris.

cistron (sis'tron) [L. *cis* on this side + *trans* on the other side + Gr. *on* neuter ending]. A term used to designate a gene, when specified as a hereditary unit of function (identified by an experimental method called the *cis-trans test*). Cf. *muton* and *recon.*

cisvestitism (sis-ves'tĭ-tizm) [L. *cis* on this side of + *vestitus* dressed]. Dressing in clothes that are proper for one's sex but are not appropriate to one's situation in life, as a citizen in army or navy uniform.

Citelli's syndrome (che-tel′ēz) [Salvatore *Citelli*, Italian laryngologist, 1875–1947]. See under *syndrome.*

Citellus (si-tel′us). A genus of rodents which may harbor organisms transmissible to man. *C. beecheyi*, the ground squirrel of California, one of the natural reservoirs of *Pasteurella tularensis*, which is also extensively infected with plague. *C. mollis*, the ground squirrel of Utah, and *C. oregonus* of Oregon are also natural reservoirs of *Pasteurella tularensis.*

citrate (sit′rāt). Any salt of citric acid.

citrated (sit′rāt-ed). Containing a citrate, especially potassium citrate.

citrinin (sit′rĭ-nin). A yellow pigment, $C_{13}H_{14}O_5$, from *Penicillium citrinum*, which is somewhat bacteriostatic.

Citromyces (sit″ro-mi′sēz) [*citric acid* + Gr. *mykes* fungus]. A genus of fungi, species of which change sugar into citric acid.

citron (sit′ron) [L. *citrus*]. 1. The orange-like tree, *Citrus medica*, and its fruit. 2. In bacteriology, shaped like a lemon.

citrophosphate (sit″ro-fos′fāt). A compound of a citrate and a phosphate.

citrulline (sit-rul′līn). An alpha-amino acid, alpha-amino delta-carbamido normal valeric acid, $NH_2.CO.NH.(CH_2)_3.CH(NH_2).COOH$.

citrullinuria (sit-rul″lĭ-nu′re-ah). Presence of large amounts of citrulline in the urine, with increased levels of citrulline in both plasma and spinal fluid.

Citrus (sit′rus) [L.]. A genus of rutaceous trees: *C. acida*, the lime; *C. aurantium*, the orange; *C. bergamia*, the bergamot; *C. limonum*, the lemon; *C. medica*, the citron.

citta (sit′ah) [Gr. *kitta* longing for strange food]. Pica.

cittosis (sit-to′sis). Pica.

Civatte's disease, poikiloderma (siv-ats′) [Achille *Civatte*, French dermatologist, 1877–1956]. See under *poikiloderma.*

Civiale's operation (se″ve-alz′) [Jean *Civiale*, French physician, 1792–1867]. See under *operation.*

Civinini's process, spine (che″ve-ne′nēz) [Filippo *Civinini*, Italian anatomist, 1805–1844]. Processus pterygospinosus.

Cl. 1. Chemical symbol for *chlorine.* 2. Abbreviation for *closure* of an electric circuit and for *Clostridium.*

cl. Abbreviation for *centiliter.*

cladiosis (klad″e-o′sis). A fungus disease found in a butcher, marked by chains of subcutaneous nodules along the forearm and caused by *Scopulariopsis blochii.*

Clado's anastomosis, band, ligament, point (klah′dōz) [Spiro *Clado*, French gynecologist, born 1856]. See under the nouns.

Cladonia (klah-do′ne-ah) [Gr. *klados* branch]. A genus of lichens. *C. rangiferina*, reindeer moss, was formerly used as a stomachic and pectoral.

Cladorchis watsoni (kla-dor′kis wat-so′ni). *Watsonius watsoni.*

cladosporiosis (klad″o-spo″re-o′sis). Infection with *Cladosporium.*

Cladosporium (klad″o-spo′re-um). A genus of fungi. *C. cancrogenes.* Same as *Canceromyces. C. herbarum* produces "black spot" on meat in cold storage. It will grow at a temperature of 18°F. (−8°C.). *C. madagascariense* causes a condition marked by gummatous nodules. *C. mansoni* causes tinea nigra.

cladothricosis (klad″o-thrĭ-ko′sis). Infection with Cladothrix (Nocardia).

Cladothrix (klad′o-thriks) [Gr. *klados* branch + *thrix* hair]. A former name of a genus of bacteria, now discarded.

clairaudience (klār-aw′de-ens) [Fr. *clair* clear + *audience* a hearing]. The subjective impression of sound. See *clairvoyance.*

clairsentience (klār-sen′she-ens) [Fr. *clair* clear + *sentience* perception]. Clairvoyance.

clairvoyance (klār-voi′ans) [Fr.]. A form of extrasensory perception in which knowledge of objective events is acquired without the use of the senses. Cf. *telepathy.*

clamp (klamp). A surgical device for effecting compression. **Cope's c.**, a crushing clamp made up of several hinged segments for use in surgery of the colon and excision of the rectum. **Crile's c.**, a rubber-shod clamp for temporary hemostasis in suture of blood vessels. **Doyen's c.**, a forceps for clamping the tissues in operations on the stomach. **Gant's c.**, a right-angled clamp used in operating for piles. **Goldblatt's c.**, a clamp for the renal artery to produce experimental hypertension. **Gussenbauer's c.**, a bar of metal for joining the fragments in ununited fracture. **Martel's c.**, a crushing clamp used in resection of the colon. **Michel's c's**, metallic clips used for fastening together the edges of a wound. **Mikulicz's c.**, a clamp (kentotribe) used in crushing the septum between the proximal and distal segments of the colon in exteriorization. **Payr c.**, a crushing clamp used in colonic resection. **pedicle c.** See *clamp forceps*, under *forceps.* **Rankin c.**, a three-bladed clamp for crushing the colon in resection operations. **rubber dam c's**, metallic rings that fit snugly about the teeth and secure the rubber dam in the mouth. **Willet's c.**, a special scalp clamp by which traction can be exerted on the presenting head in labor. **Yellen c.**, a special clamp used in circumcision.

clams (klamz). Actinomycosis in cattle.

clang (klang). A harsh quality of a sound or of the voice.

clapotage (klap″o-tahzh′). Clapotement.

clapotement (klah-pawt-maw′) [Fr.]. A splashing sound heard on succussion.

clappa (klap′ah). A Cuban term applied to a combination of leprosy and sporotrichosis.

clarificant (klar-if′ĭ-kant). An agent which clears liquids of turbidity.

clarification (klar″ĭ-fĭ-ka′shun) [L. *clarus* clear + *facere* to make]. The clearing of a liquid from turbidity.

clarify (klar′ĭ-fi) [L. *clarificare* to render clear]. To clear of turbidity or of suspended matter.

Clark II. A war gas, diphenylcyanoarsine, $(C_6H_5)_2$-AsCN.

Clark's sign [Alonzo *Clark*, American physician, 1807–1887]. See under *sign.*

Clarke's cells, column, nucleus (klarks) [Jacob Augustus Lockhart *Clarke*, English anatomist and physician, 1817–1880]. See under the nouns.

Clarke's ulcer (klarks) [Sir Charles Mansfield *Clarke*, English physician, 1782–1857]. See under *ulcer.*

clasmatocyte (klaz-mat′o-sīt) [Gr. *klasma* a piece broken off + *kytos* hollow vessel]. Ranvier's name (1900) for certain branched cells in connective tissue that allegedly detach portions of their processes as a means of discharging their secretions. As now used the term is equivalent to the cell described under macrophage.

clasmatocytosis (klaz-mat″o-si-to′sis). An excess of clasmatocytes.

clasmatodendrosis (klaz-mat″o-den-dro′sis) [Gr. *klasma* a piece broken off + *dendron*]. A breaking up of the protoplasmic expansions of astrocytes.

clasmatosis (klaz″mah-to′sis) [Gr. *klasma* a piece broken off]. The breaking off of parts of a cell.

clasp (klasp). A device by which something is held, such as a part of a removable partial denture which retains and stabilizes the denture by contacting or partially surrounding an abutment tooth. **bar c.**, one with two or more separate arms located opposite to each other on the tooth, one acting as a retentive and the other as a reciprocal arm. **circumferential c.,** one which encircles more than half of the circumference of the abutment tooth.

class (klas). 1. A taxonomic category subordinate to a phylum (or subphylum) and superior to an order. 2. In statistics, a group of variables all of which show a particular value or a value falling between certain limits. The *frequency of class* is the number of variables which it contains.

classic (klas′ik). Of first class or rank; standard.

clastic (klas′tik) [Gr. *klastos* broken]. 1. Causing or undergoing a division into parts. 2. Separable into parts.

clastothrix (klas′to-thriks) [Gr. *klastos* broken + *thrix* hair]. *Trichorrhexis nodosa.*

Clathrochloris (klath″ro-klo′ris). A genus of microorganisms of the family Chlorobacteriaceae, suborder Rhodobacteriineae, order Pseudomonadales, occurring usually as spherical cells arranged in chains and joined in trellis-like aggregates. The type species is *C. sulphu′rica.*

Clathrocystis (klath″ro-sis′tis). A genus name formerly given microorganisms, some of which are now classified in the genus Lamprocystis.

Clauberg's culture medium, test (klaw′-bergz) [Karl Wm. *Clauberg*, German bacteriologist, born 1893]. See under *culture medium* and *test.*

Claude's hyperkinesis sign, syndrome (klawdz) [Henri *Claude*, French psychiatrist, 1869–1945]. See under *sign* and *syndrome.*

claudicant (klaw′dĭ-kant). Pertaining to or affected by claudication; by extension, sometimes used to denote a patient with intermittent claudication.

claudication (klaw″dĭ-ka′shun) [L. *claudicatio*]. Limping or lameness. **intermittent c.,** a complex of symptoms characterized by absence of pain or discomfort in a limb when at rest, the commencement of pain, tension, and weakness, after walking is begun, intensification of the condition until walking becomes impossible, and the disappearance of the symptoms after a period of rest. The condition is seen in occlusive arterial diseases of the limbs, such as thrombo-angiitis obliterans. Called also *dysbasia, angiosclerotica intermittens* and *angina cruris.* **venous c.,** intermittent claudication caused by venous stasis.

claudicatory (klaw′dĭ-kah-tor″e). Pertaining to or marked by claudication.

Claudius' cell, fossa (klaw′de-us) [Friedrich Matthias *Claudius*, Austrian anatomist, 1822–1869]. See under *cell* and *fossa.*

claustra (klaws′trah) [L.]. Plural of *claustrum.*

claustral (klaws′tral). Pertaining to or of the nature of a claustrum.

claustrophilia (klaws″tro-fil′e-ah). A morbid desire to be shut in, to close all doors, windows, etc.

claustrophobia (klaws″tro-fo′be-ah) [L. *claudere* to shut + *phobia*]. Morbid dread of being shut up in a confined space.

claustrum (klaws′trum), pl. *claus′tra* [L. "a barrier"]. [N A, B N A] The thin layer of gray matter outside the external capsule of the brain, dividing it from the white matter of the insula. It is mainly composed of spindle cells. Called also *claustrum of insula.* **c. gut′turis, c. o′ris,** velum palatinum. **c. virgina′le,** hymen.

clausura (klaw-su′rah) [L. "closure"]. Atresia.

clava (kla′vah) [L. "stick"]. [B N A] Tuberculum nuclei gracilis medullae oblongata.

clavacin (kla′vah-sin). An antibiotic substance, anhydro 3-hydroxymethylene tetrahydro gamma-pyrone 2-carboxylic acid, $C_7H_6O_4$, from cultures of *Aspergillus clavatus:* it is bacteriostatic and bactericidal for gram-positive microorganisms and is apparently chemically identical with patulin, but as a protoplasmic poison it is too poisonous for therapeutic use.

claval (kla′val). Pertaining to the clava.

clavate (kla′vāt) [L. *clavatus* club]. Pertaining to the clava; club-shaped.

clavelization (klav″ĕ-li-za′shun) [Fr. *clavelée* sheep pox]. Inoculation with the virus of sheep pox.

Claviceps (klav′ĭ-seps) [L. *clava* club + *caput* head]. A genus of parasitic fungi which infest the seeds of various plants. *C. purpurea* is the source of the common ergot.

clavicle (klav′ĭ-k′l). The bone articulating with sternum and scapula. See *clavicula.*

clavicotomy (klav″ĭ-kot′o-me) [*clavicle* + Gr. *tomē* a cutting]. The operation of cutting or dividing the clavicle.

clavicula (klah-vik′u-lah) [L. dim. of *clavis* key]. [N A, B N A] A bone, curved like the letter *f*, that articulates with the sternum and scapula, forming either anterior half of the shoulder girdle. Called also *clavicle* and *collar bone.*

clavicular (klah-vik′u-lar). Pertaining to the clavicle.

claviculus (klah-vik′u-lus), pl. *clavic′uli* [L. dim. of *clavus* nail]. Any one of Sharpey's fibers (a set of fibers which hold together the laminae of a bone).

claviformin (klav″ĭ-for′min). An antibiotic substance obtained from cultures of *Penicillium claviforme.*

clavin (kla′vin). A physiologically inert mixture of leucine and aspartic acid.

clavipectoral (klav″ĭ-pek′to-ral) [L. *clavis* clavicle + *pectus* breast]. Pertaining to the clavicle and thorax.

clavus (kla′vus) [L. "nail"]. A corn, or horny tubercle of the skin. **c. hyster′icus,** a sensation as if a nail were being driven into the head. **c. secali′nus,** ergot of rye. **c. syphilit′icus,** a flat, horny growth on the hand or the foot, believed to be due to syphilis.

clawfoot (klaw-fut′). Atrophy and distortion of the foot.

clawhand (klaw-hand′). Flexion and atrophy of the hand and fingers. It occurs in lesions of the ulnar nerve, in leprosy, and in syringomyelia. Called also *main en griffe.*

Clawhand.

clay (kla). A native hydrated aluminum silicate, resulting from the decomposition of rocks caused by weathering; various forms of clays have been used in medicine, both externally and internally, since earliest times. **China c.,** kaolin.

$Cl_3C.CHO$. Chloral.

clear (klēr). To remove cloudiness from microscopical specimens by the use of a clearing agent.

clearance (klēr′ans). 1. The act of clearing; specifically removal from the blood by an excretory organ of a particular substance, as removal of albumin, urea, or certain dyes by the kidneys, or of rose bengal dye by the liver. 2. The space existing between opposed structures. **blood-urea c.,** the volume of the blood which is cleared of urea per minute by renal elimination. **creatinine c.,** the volume of plasma cleared of creatinine after the ingestion of a specified amount of the substance. **interocclusal c.,** the space between the upper and lower teeth when the mandible is at physiologic rest. **inulin c.,** an expression of the renal efficiency in eliminating inulin from the blood. **urea c.,** blood-urea c.

clearer (klēr′er). A clearing agent; an agent used in microscopy to remove the cloudiness from a specimen.

cleavage (klēv′ij). The mitotic segmentation of the fertilized ovum, the size of the zygote remaining unchanged and the cleavage cells, or blastomeres, becoming smaller and smaller with each division. **accessory c.,** peripheral cleavage in telolecithal eggs due to polyspermy. **adequal**

c., a form in which the blastomeres are practically equal in size. **complete c.,** holoblastic c. **determinate c.,** a form in which the fates of the blastomeres are already fixed. **discoidal c.,** cleavage which is limited to the animal pole of highly telolecithal eggs. **equal c.,** a form in which the blastomeres are equal in size. **equatorial c.,** cleavage which occurs in a plane passing through the equator of the egg. **holoblastic c.,** a form in which the entire egg participates in cell division. **incomplete c.,** meroblastic c. **indeterminate c.,** a form in which the determination of the fates of the blastomeres enters late. **latitudinal c.,** cleavage in planes passing at right angles to the egg axis. **meridional c.,** cleavage in planes passing through the egg axis. **meroblastic c.,** a form in which only the protoplasmic portions of the egg participate. **partial c.,** meroblastic c. **superficial c.,** a form in which only the surface region of centrolecithal eggs participates. **total c.,** holoblastic c. **unequal c.,** a form in which the blastomeres about the vegetal pole remain larger in size than those nearer the animal pole.

cleavers (kle′verz). The *Galium aparine*, a rubiaceous herb: diuretic.

cleft (kleft). A longitudinal opening or fissure, especially one occurring in the embryo. **anal c.,** rima ani. **branchial c.,** the clefts between the branchial arches of the embryo, formed by rupture of the membrane separating corresponding entodermal pouch and ectodermal groove. **cholesterol c.,** a cleft in a section of tissue embedded in paraffin, due to the dissolving of cholesterol crystals. **clunial c.,** rima ani. **corneal c.,** rima cornealis. **facial c.,** the clefts between the embryonic processes which normally unite to form the face. Failure of such union, depending on its site, causes such developmental defects as cleft lip (harelip); cleft mandible; oblique facial cleft; and transverse facial cleft. **facial c., oblique,** a fissure extending from the ala nasi to the outer canthus of the eye, caused by failure of union of the maxillary and lateral nasal processes in the embryo. **facial c., transverse,** macrostomia. **genital c.,** a depression of the external genital regions of the fetus which develops into the urethra or vestibule. **hyobranchial c.,** the cleft between the hyoid and the next succeeding arch in the developing embryo. **hyoid c.,** hyomandibular c. **hyomandibular c.,** the cleft between the mandibular and hyoid arches in the developing embryo. **Larrey's c.,** the sternocostal triangle. **Maurer's c's,** Maurer's dots. **posthyoidean c.,** hyobranchial c. **visceral c's,** branchial c's. **vulval c.,** rima pudendi.

clegs (klegz). A common name for certain tabanid flies, the horseflies or gadflies.

cleid-. See *cleido-*.

cleidagra (kli-dag′rah) [*cleid-* + Gr. *agra* seizure]. Gouty pain in the clavicle.

cleidal (kli′dal). Pertaining to or affecting the clavicle.

cleidarthritis (kli″dar-thri′tis) [*cleid-* + Gr. *arthron* joint]. Gout in the clavicular region.

cleido-, cleid- (kli′do, klīd) [Gr. *kleis* that which serves for closing; the collar bone (clavicle), so called because it locks the neck and breast together]. Combining form denoting relationship to the clavicle, or to something barred.

cleidocostal (kli″do-kos′tal). Pertaining to the clavicle and the ribs.

cleidocranial (kli″do-kra′ne-al) [*cleido-* + Gr. *kranion* head]. Pertaining to the clavicles and the head.

cleidocranialiasis (kli″do-kra″ne-al-i′ah-sis). Cleidocranial dysostosis.

cleidoic (kli-do′ik) [Gr. *kleidouchos* holding the keys]. Isolated from the environment, as the ova (eggs) of birds, which are self-sufficient, having become a closed system, and, except for oxygen intake, developing at the expense of the substances stored inside the egg itself.

cleidomastoid (kli″do-mas′toid). Pertaining to the clavicle and the mastoid process.

cleidorrhexis (kli″do-rek′sis) [*cleido-* + Gr. *rhēxis* rupture]. Cleidotomy.

cleidotomy (kli-dot′o-me) [*cleido-* + Gr. *tomē* a cutting]. Surgical division of the clavicle of the infant in difficult labor, to facilitate passage of the shoulders through the birth canal.

cleidotripsy (kli′do-trip″se) [*cleido-* + Gr. *tribein* to rub]. Crushing of the fetal clavicle to facilitate delivery.

cleisagra (kli-sag′rah). Cleidagra.

cleisiophobia (kli″se-o-fo′be-ah) [Gr. *kleisis* closure + *phobia*]. Claustrophobia.

cleithrophobia (kli″thro-fo′be-ah). Claustrophobia.

Clematis (klem′ah-tis) [Gr. *klēmatis*]. A genus of ranunculaceous plants, many of them active poisons.

clemizole (klem′ĭ-zōl). Chemical name: 1-p-chlorobenzyl-2-pyrrolidylmethyl benzimidazole. Uses: 1. antiallergic; 2. antihistaminic.

cleoid (kle′oid) [Anglo-Saxon *cle*, claw + Gr. *eidos* form]. A dental instrument, shaped like a claw, used for excavating cavities and carving dental restorations.

cleptomania (klep″to-ma′ne-ah). Kleptomania.

cleptophobia (klep″to-fo′be-ah). Kleptophobia.

Clérambault-Kandinsky complex or **syndrome** (kla″rah-bo′ kan-din′ske) [Gatian de *Clérambault*, French psychiatrist, 1872–1934]. See under *complex*.

Clevenger's fissure (klev′en-jerz) [Shobal Vail *Clevenger*, American neurologist, 1843–1920]. Sulcus temporalis inferior.

clid-. For words beginning thus, see those beginning *cleid-*.

clier (kli′er). A glandular swelling or tumor of the skin occurring in cattle.

climacophobia (kli″mah-ko-fo′be-ah) [Gr. *klimax* a ladder, staircase + *phobia*]. Morbid fear of stairs or of climbing.

climacteric (kli″mak-ter′ik) [Gr. *klimaktēr* rung of ladder, critical point in human life]. The syndrome of endocrine, somatic, and psychic changes occurring at the termination of the reproductive period in the female, or accompanying the normal diminution of sexual activity in the male.

climacterium (kli″mak-te′re-um). Climacteric. **c. prae′cox,** premature menopause.

climatology (kli″mah-tol′o-je) [Gr. *klima* the supposed slope of the earth from the equator to the pole + *logos* treatise]. The science devoted to the study of the conditions of the natural environment (rainfall, daylight, temperature, humidity, air movement) prevailing in specific regions of the earth.

climatotherapeutics (kli″mah-to-ther″ah-pu′tiks). Climatotherapy.

climatotherapy (kli″mah-to-ther′ah-pe) [*climate* + Gr. *therapeia* treatment]. The treatment of disease by means of a favorable climate.

climax (kli′maks) [Gr. *klimax* a ladder, staircase]. The acme, or period of greatest intensity, as in the course of a disease (crisis), or in sexual excitement (orgasm).

climograph (kli′mo-graf) [*climate* + Gr. *graphein* to write]. A diagram representing the effect of climate on man.

clinarthrosis (klin″ar-thro′sis) [Gr. *klinein* to bend + *arthrōsis* a jointing]. Abnormal deviation in the alignment of the bones at a joint.

clinic (klin′ik) [Gr. *klinikos* pertaining to a bed]. 1. A clinical lecture; examination of patients before a class of students; instruction at the bedside. 2. An establishment where patients are admitted for special study and treatment by a group of physicians practicing medicine together. **ambulant c.,** one for patients not confined to the bed. **dry c.,** a clinical lecture with the presentation of case histories but without the presence of the patients described.

clinical (klin′e-k'l). Pertaining to a clinic or to the bedside; pertaining to or founded on actual observation and treatment of patients, as distinguished from theoretical or experimental.

clinician (klĭ-nish′an). An expert clinical physician and teacher.

clinicopathologic (klin″e-ko-path″o-loj′ik). Pertaining both to the symptoms of disease and to its pathology.

clinocephalism (kli-no-sef′ah-lizm) [Gr. *klinein* to bend + *kephalē* head]. Congenital flatness or concavity of the vertex of the head.

clinocephaly (kli″no-sef′ah-le). Clinocephalism.

Clinocoris (kli-nok′o-ris) [Gr. *klinē* bed + *koris* bug]. Cimex.

clinodactylism (kli″no-dak′tĭ-lizm). Clinodactyly.

clinodactyly (kli″no-dak′tĭ-le) [Gr. *klinein* to bend + *daktylos* finger]. Permanent lateral or medial deviation or deflection of one or more fingers.

clinography (kli-nog′rah-fe) [Gr. *klinē* bed + *graphein* to write]. A system of graphic representations of the temperature, symptoms, and pathologic manifestations exhibited by a patient.

clinoid (kli′noid) [Gr. *klinē* bed + *eidos* form]. Resembling a bed; bed-shaped.

clinology (kli-nol′o-je) [Gr. *klinein* to recline + *-logy*]. The science of the retrogression of an animal organism.

clinomania (kli″no-ma′ne-ah) [Gr. *klinein* to recline + *mania* madness]. A morbid desire to lie in bed or at least in a horizontal position.

clinometer (kli-nom′e-ter) [Gr. *klinein* to recline + *metron* measure]. Clinoscope.

Clinophilus (kli-nof′ĭ-lus). Cimex.

clinoscope (kli′no-skōp) [Gr. *klinein* to recline + *skopein* to examine]. An instrument for measuring an angle of deviation, as the torsion of the eyes when gazing at a fixed object. It is used for measuring paralysis of the ocular muscles.

clinostatic (kli″no-stat′ik). Occurring when the patient lies down.

clinostatism (kli′no-stat″izm) [Gr. *klinē* bed + *stasis* position]. A lying-down position of the body.

clinotherapy (kli″no-ther′ah-pe). Treatment by keeping the patient in bed.

cliseometer (klis″e-om′e-ter) [Gr. *klisis* inclination + *metron* measure]. An instrument for measuring the angle which the pelvic axis makes with the spinal column.

clisis (kli′sis) [Gr. *klisis* inclination]. Attraction or inclination.

clistin (klis′tin). Trade mark for preparations of carbinoxamine maleate.

clithridium (klith-rid′e-um) [Gr. *kleithria* a keyhole]. Any bacterium having a shape like a keyhole or figure of 8.

clithrophobia (klith″ro-fo′be-ah). Claustrophobia.

clition (klit′ĭ-on) [Gr. *kleitys* slope, clivus]. The midpoint of the anterior border of the clivus.

clitocybine (klit″o-si′bin). An antibiotic substance obtained from a mushroom, *Clitocybe gigantea*, of the Agaricus family.

clitoral (kli′to-ral). Pertaining to the clitoris.

clitoridauxe (kli′to-rid-awk′se) [*clitoris* + Gr. *auxe* increase]. Enlargement of the clitoris.

clitoridean (kli″to-rid-e′an). Pertaining to the clitoris.

clitoridectomy (kli″to-rid-ek′to-me) [*clitoris* + Gr. *ektomē* excision]. Excision of the clitoris.

clitoriditis (kli″to-rid-i′tis). Inflammation of the clitoris.

clitoridotomy (kli″to-rid-ot′o-me) [*clitoris* + Gr. *tomē* cut]. Female circumcision.

clitoris (kli′to-ris) [Gr. *kleitoris*]. A small, elongated, erectile body, situated at the anterior angle of the rima pudendi; homologous with the penis in the male.

clitorism (kli′to-rism). 1. Hypertrophy of the clitoris. 2. Persistent erection of the clitoris.

clitoritis (kli″to-ri′tis). Inflammation of the clitoris.

clitoromania (kli″to-ro-ma′ne-ah). Nymphomania.

clitorotomy (kli″to-rot′o-me) [*clitoris* + Gr. *tomē* a cut]. Surgical incision of the clitoris.

clival (kli′val). Pertaining to the clivus.

clivus (kli′vus) [L. "slope"]. [N A] A bony surface, in the posterior cranial fossa, sloping upward from the foramen magnum to the dorsum sellae, the lower part being formed by a portion of the basilar part of the occipital bone (c. ossis occipitalis [B N A]), and the upper part by a surface of the body of the sphenoid bone (c. ossis sphenoidalis [B N A]). **basilar c., c. basila′ris,** c. ossis occipitalis. **c. blumenbach′ii,** clivus. **c. montic′uli,** declive. **c. os′sis occipita′lis,** B N A term for the lower part of the clivus, formed by the basilar portion of the occipital bone. **c. os′sis sphenoida′lis,** B N A term for the upper part of the clivus, formed by a surface of the body of the sphenoid bone.

clo (klo). A unit of measurement, being the insulation provided by man's normal everyday clothing and representing approximately the insulation provided by $\frac{1}{4}$ in. thickness of wool.

cloaca (klo-a′kah) [L. "drain"]. 1. An opening or cavity at the posterior end of the body of a vertebrate, into which the intestinal, urinary, and reproductive ducts open; in most mammals it is only a transient structure in embryonic development. 2. An opening in the involucrum of a necrosed bone. **congenital c.,** persistent c. **ectodermal c.,** that portion of the embryonic cloaca originally external to the cloacal membrane. **entodermal c.,** that portion of the embryonic cloaca originally internal to the cloacal membrane. **persistent c.,** the congenital persistence of a common cavity into which the intestinal, urinary, and reproductive ducts open.

cloacal (klo-a′kal). Pertaining to the cloaca.

cloacitis (klo″ah-si′tis). An infectious disease of fowls, marked by ulceration of the cloaca and a chronic discharge.

clock (klok). A device by which time may be measured. **biological c.,** the physiologic mechanism which governs the rhythmic occurrence of certain biochemical, physiological, and behavioral phenomena in plants and animals.

clone (klōn) [Gr. *klōn* young shoot or twig]. 1. In microbiology, the asexual progeny of a single cell. 2. A group of plants which have been propagated vegetatively (i.e., by cutting or budding) from one single seedling or stock. The members of a clone are identical in character with one another, but they will not come true from seed. Called also *clonal variety*. 3. A strain of cells descended in culture from a single cell. Used also as a verb to denote the establishment or initiation of such a strain.

clonic (klon′ik) [Gr. *klonos* turmoil]. Pertaining to, or of the nature of, clonus.

clonicity (klo-nis′ĭ-te). The condition of being clonic.

clonicotonic (klon″e-ko-ton′ik). Both clonic and tonic.

clonism (klon′izm) [Gr. *klonos* turmoil]. A succession of clonic spasms.

clonismus (klo-niz′mus). Clonism.

clonograph (klon′o-graf) [*clonus* + Gr. *graphein* to write]. An instrument for recording spasmodic movements of parts and tendon reflexes.

clonorchiasis (klo″nor-ki′ah-sis). The state of being infected with flukes of the genus Clonorchis.

clonorchiosis (klo-nor″ke-o′sis). Clonorchiasis.

Clonorchis (klo-nor′kis) [Gr. *klōn* branch + *orchis* testicle]. A genus of liver flukes of Asia. **C. en-**

dem′icus, C. sinen′sis, one of the most common parasitic trematodes infesting the liver of man, especially in China and Japan. They have two intermediate hosts; the first is a molluscan (*Bythnia striatula*) and the second is some edible fish from which man becomes infected. Called also *Distoma sinensis, D. japonicum, Opisthorchis sinensis.*

clonospasm (klon′o-spazm) [Gr. *klonos* turmoil + *spasmos* spasm]. Clonic spasm.

Clonothrix (klo′no-thriks) [Gr. *klōn* branch + *thrix* hair]. A genus of microorganisms of the family Crenotrichaceae, order Chlamydobacteriales, made up of colorless cylindrical cells occurring in attached trichomes which show false branching and are enclosed in sheaths encrusted with iron or manganese compounds. The type species is *C. putea′lis.*

clonus (klo′nus) [Gr. *klonos* turmoil]. Spasm in which rigidity and relaxation alternate in rapid succession. **ankle c.,** a series of convulsive movements of the ankle, induced by suddenly pushing up the foot while the leg is extended. **anodal closure c.** (ACC), clonic muscular contraction occurring at the anode when the electrical circuit is closed. **anodal opening c.** (AOC), clonic muscular contraction occurring at the anode when the electrical circuit is opened or broken. **cathodal closure c.** (CCCl), clonic muscular contraction occurring at the cathode when the electrical circuit is closed. **cathodal opening c.** (COCl), clonic muscular contraction occurring at the cathode when the electrical circuit is opened or broken. **foot c.,** ankle c. **patellar c.,** rhythmic jerking up and down of the patella produced by grasping the patella between the thumb and forefinger and pushing it forcibly down one or more times. **toe c.,** rhythmic contraction of the great toe, induced by suddenly extending the first phalanx. **wrist c.,** spasmodic contraction of the muscles of the hand, which is induced by forcibly bending the hand backward.

clopane (klo′pān). Trade mark for preparations of cyclopentamine.

Cloquet's canal, hernia, etc. (klo-kāz′) [Jules Germain *Cloquet,* French surgeon, 1790–1883]. See under the nouns.

Cloquet's ganglion (klo-kāz′) [Hippolyte *Cloquet,* anatomist in Paris, 1787–1840]. See under *ganglion.*

clostridia (klos-trid′e-ah). Plural of *clostridium.*

clostridial (klos-trid′e-al). Pertaining to or caused by clostridia.

Clostridium (klos-trid′e-um) [Gr. *klōstēr* spindle]. A genus of Schizomycetes, family Bacillaceae, order Eubacteriales, made up of obligate anaerobic or microaerophilic, gram-positive, spore-forming, rod-shaped bacteria, with spores of greater diameter than the vegetative cells. The spores may be central, terminal, or subterminal. Ninety-three species have been differentiated on the basis of physiology, morphology, and toxin formation. **C. acetobutyl′icum,** a species found widely distributed in agricultural soils but not found to be pathogenic. **C. ag′ni,** a name once given type B of *C. perfringens,* which causes dysentery in lambs. **C. bifermen′tans,** a species found widely distributed in nature, occurring commonly in feces, sewage, and soil; variously reported as being associated with 4 to 54 per cent of cases of gas gangrene. **C. botuli′num,** the agent causing botulism in man, limberneck of chickens, botulism of wild ducks, and forage poisoning of cattle; it produces a powerful exotoxin that is resistant to proteolytic digestion, and is divided into types A, B, C alpha and beta, D, and E on the basis of the immunological specificity of the toxin. **C. butyl′icum,** a species isolated from the soil. **C. chauvoe′i,** the etiologic agent of symptomatic anthrax, or blackleg, in cattle. **C. fe′seri,** *C. chauvoei.* **C. haemolyt′icum,** a species isolated from the blood and other tissues of cattle dying with icterohemoglobinuria, thought by some to be a type of *C. novyi.* **C. histolyt′icum,** a species found occasionally in feces and soil, originally isolated from necrotic war wounds; according to one report found in 6 per cent of cases of gangrene. **C. kluy′veri,** a species thought to be widely distributed in nature, which has been used in study of both microbial synthesis and microbial oxidation of fatty acids. **C. no′vyi,** a species which is an important cause of gaseous gangrene, being reported in 32 to 48 per cent of cases; three immunological types have been identified, designated A, B, and C. **C. oedemat′iens,** *C. novyi.* **C. ovitox′icus,** a name once given type D of *C. perfringens,* which causes enterotoxemia of sheep. **C. pal′udis,** a name once given type C of *C. perfringens,* which causes struck in sheep. **C. paraboturli′num,** a species which is widely dispersed in soil and is pathogenic for animals, producing a powerful neurotoxin. **C. parabotuli′num e′qui,** *C. botulinum* type D. **C. pasteuria′num,** an anaerobic microorganism occurring in soil, which was the first nitrogen-fixing bacteria to be studied in pure culture. **C. pastoria′num,** *C. pasteurianum.* **C. perfrin′gens,** the most common etiological agent of gas gangrene, variously reported as occurring in 39 to 83 per cent of cases; differentiable, on the basis of the distribution of nine different toxins and three other substances, which are enzymes, into several different types: type A (the cause of classic gas gangrene in man), B (lamb dysentery), C (struck in sheep), D (enterotoxemia in sheep), E (enterotoxemia in lambs and calves), F (enteritis necroticans in man). **C. sep′ticum,** a species commonly occurring in animal intestines and soil, strikingly pathogenic for various animals but reportedly associated with gaseous infections in man in only 4 to 24 per cent of cases. Six groups have been distinguished. **C. sordel′lii,** a name commonly given more toxic and virulent strains of *C. bifermentans.* **C. sporog′enes,** a species widely distributed in nature; a harmless saprophyte in pure culture, it is reportedly associated with pathogenic anaerobes in 37 to 72 per cent of gangrenous infections. **C. ter′tium,** a species found widely distributed in feces, sewage, and soil, and variously reported as present in 3 to 59 per cent of gangrenous infections. **C. tet′ani,** a common inhabitant of soil and human and horse intestines, and the cause of tetanus in man and domestic animals; its potent exotoxin is made up of two components, a neurotoxin, or tetanospasmin, and a hemolytic toxin, or tetanolysin. It is variously reported as associated with gangrene in 4 to 13 per cent of cases. **C. welch′ii,** *C. perfringens.*

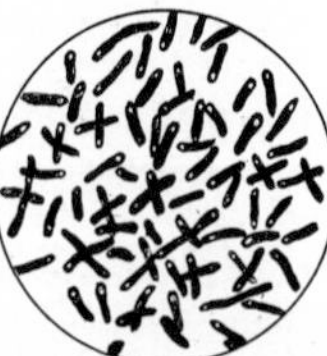
Clostridium botulinum.

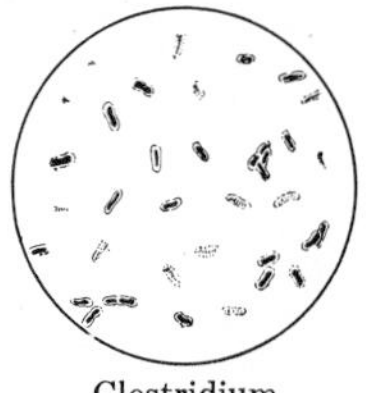
Clostridium perfringens.

Clostridium tetani.

clostridium (klos-trid′e-um), pl. *clostrid′ia.* A microorganism belonging to the genus Clostridium.

closure (klo′shur). The act of shutting, or of bringing together two parts, one or both of which may be movable. **flask c.,** the bringing together of the two halves or parts of a flask in which a denture base is formed. **flask c., final,** the last closure of a flask before curing the denture-base material packed in the mold. **flask c., trial,** preliminary closure of the flask, to eliminate excess material and to ensure that the mold is completely filled.

clot (klot). A semisolidified mass, as of blood or lymph. **agony c.,** a blood clot formed in the heart during the death agony. **antemortem c.,** a blood clot formed in the heart or in a large vessel before death. **blood c.,** a coagulum formed of blood, either in or out of the body. **chicken fat c.,** a blood clot that appears yellow because of the settling out of the erythrocytes before clotting occurred. **currant jelly c.,** a clot of reddish color because of the presence of erythrocytes enmeshed in it. **distal c.,** a clot formed in a blood vessel distal to a ligature. **external c.,** a clot formed outside a blood vessel. **heart c.,** a thrombus formed within the heart. **internal c.,** a blood clot formed within a blood vessel. **laminated c.,** a blood clot formed by successive deposits, giving it a layered appearance. **marantic c.,** a blood clot formed because of enfeebled circulation and general malnutrition. **muscle c.,** a clot formed by coagulation of muscle plasm. **passive c.,** a clot formed in the sac of an aneurysm through which the blood has stopped circulating. **plastic c.,** a clot formed from the intima of an artery at the point of ligation, permanently obstructing the artery. **postmortem c.,** a blood clot formed in the heart or in a large blood vessel after death. **proximal c.,** a clot formed in a blood vessel proximal to a ligature. **Schede's c.** See under *treatment*. **stratified c.,** laminated c. **washed c., white c.,** a blood clot composed of fibrin and colorless corpuscles.

clouding (klowd′ing). Loss of clarity. **c. of consciousness,** loss of perception or comprehension of the environment, with loss of ability to respond properly to external stimuli.

clove (klōv) [L. *clavus* a nail or spike]. An aromatic spice, the dried flower bud of *Eugenia aromatica* (*Jambosa caryophyllus*): sometimes used as a carminative and for the relief of nausea; also externally as an anodyne in toothache and colic.

clownism (klown′izm). The hysterical performance of grotesque actions.

clubbing (klub′ing). A proliferative change in the soft tissues about the terminal phalanges of the fingers or toes, with no constant osseous changes.

clubfoot (klub′foot). A congenitally deformed foot. See *talipes*.

clubhand (klub′hand). A hand deformity analogous to clubfoot.

clump (klump). An aggregation as of bacteria caused by the action of agglutinins (agglutination).

clumping (klump′ing). The aggregation of bacteria into irregular masses. See *agglutination*, def. 3, and *Gruber-Widal reaction*, under *reaction*.

cluneal (kloo′ne-al). Pertaining to the buttocks.

clunis (kloo′nis), pl. *clu′nes* [L.]. The buttock.

clupeine (kloo′pe-in) [L. *clupea* herring]. A protamine obtainable from the spermatozoa of the herring.

cluttering (klut′er-ing). Hurried nervous speech, marked by the dropping of syllables.

Clutton's joints (klut′unz) [Henry Hugh *Clutton*, London surgeon, 1850–1909]. See under *joint*.

clyer (kli′er). A scrofulous tumor in the ox due to tuberculous infection.

clyers (kli′erz). Actinomycosis in cattle.

clysis (kli′sis) [Gr. *klysis*]. The washing out of a cavity.

clysma (kliz′mah), pl. *clys′mata* [Gr. *klysma*]. A clyster, or enema.

clyster (klis′ter) [Gr. *klystēr* a syringe]. An injection into the rectum; an enema.

clysterize (klis′ter-īz) [L. *clysterizare;* Gr. *klystēr*]. To treat with enemas, or with injections into the rectum.

clytocybine (kli″to-si′bēn). A substance extracted from a mold, *Clytocybe gigantea* and its culture mycelium, which has a bacteriolytic effect on *Mycobacterium tuberculosis*.

C.M. Abbreviation for L. *Chirur′giae Magis′ter*, Master in Surgery, and for L. *cras ma′ne*, tomorrow morning.

Cm. Chemical symbol for *curium*.

cm. Abbreviation for *centimeter*.

cm.³. Symbol for *cubic centimeter*.

C.M.A. Abbreviation for *Canadian Medical Association*.

C.M.B. Abbreviation for *carbolic methylene blue*.

c./min. Abbreviation for *cycles per minute*.

c.mm. Abbreviation for *cubic millimeter*.

C.M.R. Abbreviation for *cerebral metabolic rate*.

c.m.s. Abbreviation for L. *cras ma′ne sumen′dus*, to be taken tomorrow morning.

CN. Cyanogen.

C.N. Abbreviation for L. *cras noc′te*, tomorrow night.

cnemial (ne′me-al). Pertaining to the shin.

Cnemidocoptes (ne″mĭ-do-kop′tēz). A genus of sarcoptid mites. *C. gallinae* causes the depluming of fowls. *C. mutans* causes scaly legs in fowls and cage birds.

cnemis (ne′mis). The lower leg, shin, or tibia.

cnemitis (ne-mi′tis). Inflammation of the tibia.

cnemoscoliosis (ne″mo-sko″le-o′sis) [Gr. *knēmē* leg + *skoliōsis* crookedness]. A lateral bending of the leg.

cnida (ni′dah), pl. *cni′dae* [Gr. *knidē* a nettle]. Nematocyst.

cnidae (ni′de). Plural of *cnida*.

Cnidian (ni′de-an) [*Cnidos*, site of one of the early Greek temples of medicine]. 1. An early school of medicine in Greece that stressed the diagnosis and classification of disease. 2. A believer in or practitioner of the Cnidian theory of medicine.

cnidoblast (ni′do-blast). One of the interstitial cells in the epidermis of coelenterates, and especially numerous in the tentacles, which contain the nematocysts.

cnidocil (ni′do-sil) [Gr. *knidē* nettle + L. *cilium* hair]. A bristle-like process at one end of a cnidoblast, which, when stimulated, triggers the discharge of the nematocyst.

cnidocyst (ni′do-sist). Nematocyst.

cnidom (ni′dom). The nematocyst pattern or spectrum of a particular coelenterate, which is believed to be sufficiently specific and consistent to be of taxonomic significance.

cnidosis (ni-do′sis) [Gr. *knidōsis* an itching, such as is caused by a nettle]. Urticaria.

CNOH. Cyanic acid.

CNS. Chemical symbol for *sulfocyanate*.

C.N.S. Abbreviation for *central nervous system*.

c.n.s. Abbreviation for L. *cras noc′te sumen′dus*, to be taken tomorrow night.

CO. Carbon monoxide.

CO_2. Carbon dioxide.

Co. Chemical symbol for *cobalt*.

co-. A prefix signifying with, together.

coacervate (ko-as′er-vāt) [L. *coacervatus* heaped up]. The viscous phase separating from a colloid-containing system in the phenomenon of coacervation.

coacervation (ko-as″er-va′shun). A phenomenon which involves both lyophilic and hydrophilic colloids, but particularly the latter, being the separation of microscopic liquid droplets when sols of two hydrophilic colloids of opposite electric charge are mixed. These droplets may later unite to form a viscous layer at the bottom of the container, constituting a new phase.

coadaptation (co″ad-ap-ta′shun) [*co-* + L. *adapta′re* to adapt]. The mutual, correlated, adaptive changes in two interdependent organs.

coadunation (ko″ad-u-na′shun) [L. *co-* together + *ad* to + *u′nus* one]. Union of dissimilar substances in one mass.

coadunition (ko″ad-u-nish′un). Coadunation.

coagglutination (ko″ah-gloo″tĭ-na′shun). Group agglutination.

coagglutinin (ko″ah-gloo′tĭ-nin). Partial agglutinin.

coagula (ko-ag′u-lah) [L.]. Plural of *coagulum.*

coagulability (ko-ag″u-lah-bil′ĭ-te). The state of being capable of forming or of being formed into clots.

coagulable (ko-ag′u-lah-b'l). Susceptible of being coagulated.

coagulant (ko-ag′u-lant) [L. *coagulans*]. 1. Promoting, accelerating, or making possible the coagulation of blood. 2. An agent which promotes or accelerates the coagulation of blood.

coagulase (ko-ag′u-lās). An enzyme which accelerates the formation of blood clots, but is not involved in *in vivo* coagulation of human blood.

coagulate (ko-ag′u-lāt) [L. *coagulare*]. 1. To cause to clot. 2. To become clotted.

coagulation (ko-ag″u-la′shun) [L. *coagulatio.*] 1. The process of clot formation. See *blood coagulation.* 2. In colloid chemistry, the solidification of a sol into a gelatinous mass; the degree of dispersion of the disperse phase from the continuous phase is lessened, thus resulting in the complete or partial separation of this phase which appears as a nonrigid, insoluble, continuous mass, called the clot or curd. Coagulation is usually irreversible. **blood c.,** the process by which a blood clot is formed, in whole blood or plasma, generally considered divisible into three stages: stage 1, the formation of intrinsic and extrinsic thromboplastin; stage 2, the formation of thrombin; stage 3, the formation of fibrin. **electric c.,** the effect produced on tissues by the application of a bipolar current delivered by a needle point: the tissue is broken down and condensed into a necrotic mass. **massive c.,** coagulation of the spinal fluid so as to form an almost solid clot; a condition seen in some cases of *Froin's syndrome* in meningomyelitis or tumor of the cord.

coagulative (ko-ag′u-la″tiv). Associated with coagulation or promoting a process of coagulation; of the nature of coagulation.

coagulin (ko-ag′u-lin). 1. Thromboplastin. 2. An antibody (precipitin) that coagulates its antigen.

coagulinoid (ko-ag′u-lĭ-noid). A coagulin, the active coagulating portion of which has been destroyed by heating.

coagulogram (ko-ag′u-lo-gram″). The graphic record of a series of tests measuring the various parameters of hemostasis.

coagulometer (ko-ag″u-lom′e-ter) [*coagulation* + Gr. *metron* measure]. An apparatus for determining the coagulability of the blood.

coagulotomy (ko-ag″u-lot′o-me). Diathermic excision with a low frequency and strong current in which the raw surfaces are coagulated and bleeding arrested.

coaguloviscosimeter (ko-ag″u-lo-vis″ko-sim′e-ter). An instrument for determining the coagulation time of the blood.

coagulum (ko-ag′u-lum), pl. *coag′ula* [L.]. A clot or curd. **closing c.,** the clot which closes the gap made in the uterine lining by the implanting blastocyst.

Coakley's operation (kōk′lēz) [Cornelius G. *Coakley,* laryngologist in New York, 1862–1934]. See under *operation.*

coalescence (ko-ah-les′ens) [L. *coalescere* to grow together]. The fusion or blending of parts.

coapt (ko′apt) [L. *coaptare*]. To fit closely together, as the edges of a wound or the ends of a fractured bone.

coarctate (ko-ark′tāt) [L. *coarctare* to straighten or tighten]. To press close together; contract.

coarctation (ko″ark-ta′shun) [L. *coarctatio,* from *cum* together + *arctare* to make tight]. A straightening or pressing together; a condition of stricture or contraction. **c. of the aorta,** a malformation characterized by deformity of the aortic media, causing narrowing, usually severe, of the lumen of the vessel.

coarctotomy (ko″ark-tot′o-me) [L. *coarctus* pressed together + Gr. *tomē* a cut]. The cutting of a stricture.

coarse (kōrs). Not fine; not microscopical.

coarticulation (ko″ar-tik″u-la′shun) [L. *con* together + *articulare* to join]. A synarthrosis.

coat (kōt) [L. *cot'ta* a tunic]. A membrane or other structure covering or lining a part or organ. See also *tunic* and *tunica.* **adventitious c.,** tunica adventitia. See terms beginning thus under *tunica.* **adventitious c. of uterine tube,** tela subserosa. **albugineous c.,** tunica albuginea. See terms beginning thus under *tunica.* **buffy c.,** the reddish gray layer observed above packed red cells in centrifuged blood. Called also *leukocytic cream.* **cremasteric c. of testis,** musculus cremaster. **dartos c.,** tunica dartos. **external c. of capsule of graafian follicle,** tunica externa thecae folliculi. **external c. of esophagus,** tunica adventitia esophagi. **external c. of ureter,** tunica adventitia ureteris. **external c. of vessels,** tunica externa vasorum. **external c. of viscera,** tunica adventitia. **fibrous c.,** tunica fibrosa. **fibrous c. of corpus cavernosum of penis,** tunica albuginea corporum cavernosorum. **fibrous c. of eye,** tunica fibrosa bulbi. **fibrous c. of ovary,** theca folliculi. **fibrous c. of testis,** tunica albuginea testis. **internal c. of capsule of graafian follicle,** tunica interna thecae folliculi. **internal c. of pharynx of Luschka,** tela submucosa pharyngis. **mucous c.,** tunica mucosa. For various specific structures see terms beginning thus under *tunica.* **muscular c.,** tunica muscularis. See terms beginning thus under *tunica.* **pharyngobasilar c.,** fascia pharyngobasilaris. **proper c.,** tunica propria. **proper c. of corium,** tunica propria corii. **proper c. of pharynx,** tela submucosa pharyngis. **proper c. of small intestine,** tela submucosa intestini tenuis. **proper c. of testis,** tunica albuginea testis. **serous c.,** tunica serosa. See terms beginning thus under *tunica.* **submucous c.,** tela submucosa. See terms beginning thus under *tela.* **subserous c.,** tela subserosa. See terms beginning thus under *tela.* **vaginal c. of testis,** tunica vaginalis testis. **vascular c. of pharynx,** tela submucosa pharyngis. **vascular c. of stomach,** tela submucosa ventriculi. **vascular c. of viscera,** tela submucosa. **villous c. of small intestine,** tunica mucosa intestini tenuis. **white c.,** tunica albuginea.

Coats's disease, retinitis (kōts) [George *Coats,* London ophthalmologist, 1876–1915]. Exudative retinopathy.

cobalamin (ko-bal′ah-min). The cobalt-containing complex common to all members of the vitamin B_{12} group; frequently used generically to designate any substituted derivative, even cyanocobalamin. **c. concentrate,** a dried, partially purified product resulting from the growth of selected Streptomyces cultures: used as a vitamin supplement.

cobalt (ko′bawlt) [L. *cobaltum*]. A metal, atomic number, 27; atomic weight 58.9332; symbol Co; whose compounds afford pigments. In animals, a deficiency of this element leads to anemia; an excess of normal dietary requirements leads to polycythemia. In the human, although cobalt has been used with limited transient effectiveness to treat the anemia of infection, renal disease, and cancer, its sole physiological function, most probably, is as a constituent of vitamin B_{12}. **c. salipyrine,** a salicylate of cobalt and antipyrine, forming a pale red powder.

cobra (ko′brah). A poisonous snake, cobra dicapello, *Naja tripudians,* of India. By inoculating animals with the cobra venom a serum is obtained which is used in counteracting the effect of bites by the snake. See also *Ophiophagus.*

cobraism (ko′brah-izm). Poisoning by cobra venom.

cobralysin (ko-bral′ĭ-sin). A hemolytic substance derived from the poison of the cobra.

COBS. Abbreviation for *cesarean-obtained barrier-sustained*, a term applied to animals delivered by cesarean section into a germ-free environment and maintained under the same conditions.

cobweb (kob′web) [A.S. Abbreviation of *attercop*, poison head, and *web*, from *wefan*]. The web of various kinds of spider; sometimes used as a styptic, in the moxa, and as a domestic remedy: a febrifuge and antispasmodic.

COC. Abbreviation for *cathodal opening contraction*.

coca (ko′kah). The leaves of *Erythroxylon coca*, a South American plant from which cocaine is obtained: nervine and stimulant.

cocaine (ko′kān). A crystalline alkaloid, methyl benzoyl ecgonine, $CH_3.N:C_6H_9(CO.O.CH_3).CH.O$, from coca leaves: used as a surface anesthetic. **c. hydrochloride,** the hydrochloride of cocaine, $C_{17}H_{21}NO_4.HCl$, occurring as colorless crystals or a white crystalline powder.

cocainism (ko′kān-izm). The morbid condition resulting from prolonged misuse of cocaine as a stimulant or a narcotic.

cocainist (ko′kān-ist). A person addicted to the habitual use of cocaine.

cocainization (ko″kān-ĭ-za′shun). The act of putting under the influence of cocaine. **spinal c.,** the injection of cocaine into the subdural space at the base of the spinal cord by a puncture through the fourth or fifth lumbar interspace.

cocainize (ko′kān-īz). To put under the influence of cocaine.

cocarboxylase (ko″kar-bok′si-lās). The coenzyme of carboxylase necessary for the activity of the latter. It is a crystalline diphosphoric acid ester of thiamine (vitamin B_1).

cocarcinogen (ko″kar-sin′o-jen). An agent which increases the effect of a carcinogen by direct concurrent local effect on the tissue.

cocarcinogenesis (ko-kar″sĭ-no-jen′e-sis). The development, according to one theory, of cancer only in preconditioned cells and as a result of conditions favorable to its growth.

coccal (kok′al). Resembling or pertaining to cocci.

coccerin (kok′sĕ-rin). A wax from the cochineal insect: it is an ester of cocceryl alcohol and two acids, 13-keto-n-dotriacontanoic acid and n-triacontanoic acid.

cocci (kok′si). Plural of *coccus*.

coccidia (kok-sid′e-ah). Plural of *coccidium*.

coccidial (kok-sid′e-al). Pertaining to Coccidium.

coccidioidal (kok-sid″e-oi′dal). Caused by Coccidioides.

Coccidioides (kok-sid″e-oi′dēz). A genus of pathogenic fungi of the family Endomycetales. *C. im′mitis* causes coccidioidomycosis.

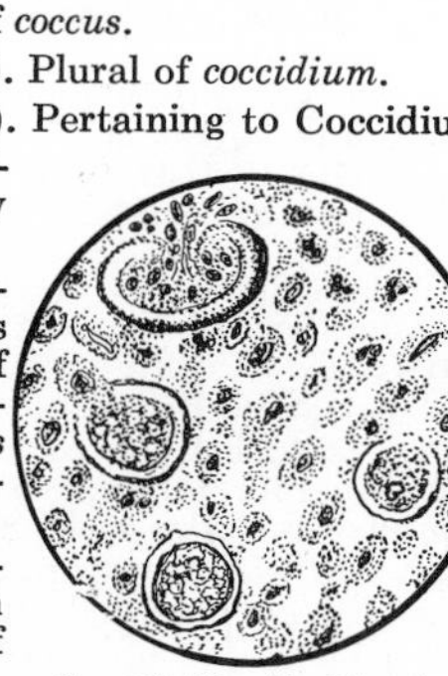

coccidioidin (kok″sid-e-oi′din). A sterile broth filtrate of a culture of *Coccidioides immitis*, injected intracutaneously as a test for coccidioidomycosis.

Coccidioides (de Rivas).

coccidioidomycosis (kok-sid″e-oi″do-mi-ko′sis). A disease caused by infection of the lungs with *Coccidioides immitis*. It is marked in initial stages by symptoms resembling those of pulmonary tuberculosis, with erythema nodosum (primary coccidioidomycosis, valley fever, San Joaquin Valley fever). The disease may progress to a generalized form (progressive coccidioidomycosis, coccidioidal granuloma).

coccidioidosis (kok-sid″e-oi-do′sis). Coccidioidomycosis.

coccidiosis (kok″sid-e-o′sis). A morbid state caused by the presence of coccidia. In man the term is applied to an infection caused by *Isospora hominis*, a rare condition marked by severe watery mucous diarrhea.

Coccidium (kok-sid′e-um) [L.; dim. of Gr. *kokkos* berry]. A name formerly given to a group of organisms of the order of the Sporozoa. They go through a complicated life history both in schizogony and in sporogony resembling that of the malarial parasites. **C. bigem′inum,** *Isospora bigemina*. **C. cunic′uli,** *Eimeria stiedae*. **C. hom′inis,** *Isospora hominis*. **C. ovifor′me,** *Eimeria stiedae*. **C. syphil′idis,** *Leukocytozoon syphilidis*. **C. tenel′lum,** *Eimeria tenella*.

coccidium (kok-sid′e-um), pl. *coccid′ia*. An individual organism of the Coccidium group.

coccigenic (kok″sĭ-jen′ik). Caused by a micrococcus.

coccillana (kok″sĭ-yah′nah). Cocillana.

coccinella (kok″sĭ-nel′ah). Cochineal.

coccinellin (kok″sĭ-nel′in) [L. *coccinellinum*]. Carmine; the coloring principle of cochineal.

coccobacillary (kok″o-bas′ĭ-ler″e). Pertaining to or resembling a coccobacillus.

coccobacilli (kok″o-bah-sil′li). Plural of *coccobacillus*.

Coccobacillus (kok″o-bah-sil′us). Asterococcus.

coccobacillus (kok″o-bah-sil′us), pl. *coccobacilli*. An oval bacterial cell intermediate between the coccus and bacillus forms.

coccobacteria (kok″o-bak-te′re-ah) [Gr. *kokkos* berry + *baktērion* rod]. A common name for the spheroid bacteria, or for the various bacterial cocci.

coccode (kok′ōd). A globular granule.

coccogenic (kok″o-jen′ik). Coccogenous.

coccogenous (kok-oj′e-nus) [*coccus* + Gr. *gennan* to produce]. Caused by cocci.

coccoid (kok′oid). Resembling a coccus; globose.

Coccoloba (kok-ol′o-bah) [L. *coccolobis*]. A genus of polygonaceous trees and shrubs. *C. uvifera*, the seaside grape of tropical America, has an edible fruit, and affords an astringent extract called Jamaica kino.

coccomelasma (kok″o-me-las′mah) [Gr. *kokkos* berry + *melas* black]. Granular melanosis of the skin.

cocculin (kok′u-lin). Picrotoxin.

cocculus (kok′u-lus) [L. dim. of *coccus*]. A small berry. **c. in′dicus,** the dried berry or fruit of *Anamirta cocculus*, from which picrotoxin is derived.

Coccus (kok′us) [L.; Gr. *kokkos* berry]. A genus of hemipterous insects, which are the source of cochineal, kermes, and lac.

coccus (kok′us), pl. *coc′ci* [L.]. A spherical bacterial cell, usually slightly less than 1 μ in diameter.

coccyalgia (kok″se-al′je-ah). Coccygodynia.

coccycephalus (kok″se-sef′ah-lus) [Gr. *kokkyx* cuckoo + *kephalē* head]. A fetal monster whose head is beak shaped.

coccydynia (kok″se-din′e-ah). Coccygodynia.

coccygalgia (kok″se-gal′je-ah). Coccygodynia.

coccygeal (kok-sij′e-al). Pertaining to or located in the region of the coccyx.

coccygectomy (kok″se-jek′to-me) [*coccyx* + Gr. *ektomē* excision]. Excision of the coccyx.

coccygerector (kok″se-je-rek′tor). The ventral sacrococcygeal muscle.

coccygeus (kok-sij′e-us) [L.]. Pertaining to the coccyx.

coccygodynia (kok″se-go-din′e-ah) [*coccyx* + Gr. *odynē* pain]. Pain in the coccyx and neighboring region.

coccygotomy (kok″se-got′o-me) [*coccyx* + Gr. *tomē* a cut]. Incision of the coccyx.

coccyodynia (kok″se-o-din′e-ah). Coccygodynia.

coccyx (kok′siks) [Gr. *kokkyx* cuckoo, whose bill it

is said to resemble]. The small bone caudad to the sacrum in man, formed by union of four (sometimes five or three) rudimentary vertebrae, and forming the caudal extremity of the vertebral column. Also called *os coccygis* [N A].

cochineal (koch″ĭ-nēl′). The dried female insects, *Coccus cacti,* enclosing the young larvae: used as a coloring agent for pharmaceutical preparations.

cochl. Abbreviation for L. *cochlea're,* a spoonful. **cochl. amp.,** L. *cochlea're am'plum,* heaping spoonful. **cochl. mag.,** L. *cochlea're mag'num,* tablespoonful. **cochl. med.,** L. *cochlea're me'dium,* dessertspoonful. **cochl. parv.,** L. *cochlea're par'vum,* teaspoonful.

cochlea (kok′le-ah) [L. "snail shell"]. 1. Anything of a spiral form. 2. [N A, B N A] The essential organ of hearing: a spirally wound tube, resembling a snail shell, which forms part of the inner ear. Its base lies against the lateral end of the internal acoustic meatus and its apex is directed anterolaterally. **membranous c.,** ductus cochlearis.

cochlear (kok′le-ar). Of or pertaining to the cochlea.

cochleare (kok″le-a′re) [L.]. Spoon or spoonful. **c. am′plum** [L. "large spoon"], a heaping spoonful. **c. mag′num,** a tablespoon or tablespoonful. **c. me′dium,** a dessertspoon or dessertspoonful. **c. par′vum,** a teaspoon or teaspoonful.

Cochlearia (kok″le-a′re-ah) [L.]. A genus of cruciferous plants. **C. armora′cia** is the horseradish; its root is a stimulant condiment and a stomachic. **C. officina′lis,** scurvy grass, is diuretic, antiscorbutic, and stimulant.

cochleariform (kok″le-ar′ĭ-form) [L. *cochleare* spoon + *forma* form]. Shaped like a spoon.

cochleate (kok′le-āt) [L. *cochlea* snail]. Shaped like a snail shell: said of bacterial cultures.

cochleitis (kok″le-i′tis). Inflammation of the cochlea.

cochleovestibular (kok″le-o-ves-tib′u-lar). Pertaining to the cochlea and vestibule of the ear.

Cochliomyia (kok″le-o-mi′yah) [Gr. *kochlias* snail with a spiral shell + *myia* fly]. A genus of flies of the family Calliphoridae. **C. hominivor′ax,** the American screwworm fly, a bluish-green fly that deposits its eggs during the warmest hours of the day on wounds of animals; the larvae, known as screwworms, after hatching, burrow into the wound and feed on living tissue. **C. macella′ria,** a species closely resembling *C. hominivorax,* the larvae of which feed on dead tissues or carcasses.

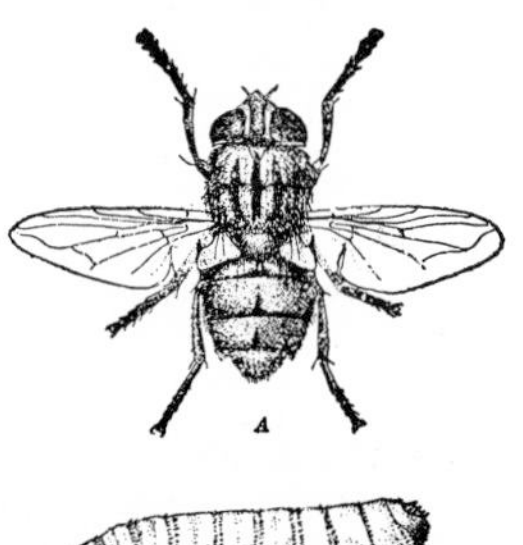

Cochliomyia hominivorax: *A,* adult; *B,* maggot. (× 3).

cochlitis (kok-li′tis). Cochleitis.

cocillana (ko″se-yah′nah). The bark of *Guarea swartvii* (*rusbyi*), once used as an emetic, expectorant, and cathartic. Sometimes used in veterinary medicine.

Cock's operation (koks) [Edward *Cock,* English surgeon, 1805–1892]. See under *operation.*

cocktail (kok′tāl). A beverage concocted of various ingredients. **frostbite c.,** a solution of alcohol, procaine, and heparin, in 5 per cent glucose, once recommended in treatment of frostbite. **lytic c.,** a concoction of various drugs used to block the function of the autonomic nervous system at every level, thus inhibiting the homeostatic defense reactions of the organism and producing the state known as artificial hibernation. **McConckey c.,** an emulsion of cod liver oil and tomato juice. **Philadelphia c.,** Rivers' c. **Rivers' c.,** a solution of dextrose in isotonic saline solution, with thiamine chloride and insulin added, given by intravenous drip for detoxification in acute alcoholism.

COCl. Abbreviation for *cathodal opening clonus.*

cocoa (ko′ko). See *cacao* and *chocolate.*

coconscious (ko-kon′shus). Not in the field of the conscious yet capable under favorable circumstances of being remembered.

coconsciousness (ko-kon′shus-nes). Consciousness which is secondary to the main stream of consciousness, being made up of processes outside that stream.

cocontraction (ko″kon-trak′shun). The mutual coordination of antagonist muscles as of flexors and extensors in maintaining a straight limb.

coconut (ko′ko-nut). The fruit of *Cocos nucifera,* a palm tree whose sap affords palm wine or toddy, while the nut is an important article of food, and supplies great quantities of a valuable oil.

Coct. Abbreviation for L. *coc'tio,* boiling.

coction (kok′shun) [L. *coctio,* a cooking]. 1. The process of boiling. 2. Digestion.

cocto-immunogen (kok″to-ĭ-mu′no-jen). An immunogen which has been heated.

coctolabile (kok″to-la′bil) [L. *coctus* cooked + *labilis* perishable]. Destroyed or altered by heating to the boiling point of water.

coctoprecipitin (kok″to-pre-sip′ĭ-tin) [L. *coctus* cooked + *precipitin*]. A precipitin produced by injection of a heated serum or other antigen (thermoprecipitinogen). It reacts not only with the heated antigen, but with the unheated one also.

coctostabile (kok″to-sta′bil) [L. *coctus* cooked + *stabilis* resisting]. Not altered by heating to the temperature of boiling water.

coctostable (kok″to-sta′b'l). Coctostabile.

code (kōd) [L. *codex* something written]. 1. A set of rules governing one's conduct. 2. A system by which information can be communicated. **genetic c.,** the mathematical aspect of the system by which information is transferred from genetic material to proteins, the pattern of the nucleotides in the nucleic acids being thought to determine each amino acid in the chain making up each protein. **c. of medical ethics.** See *principles of medical ethics,* under *principle.*

codehydrogenase I (ko″de-hi′dro-jen-ās″). Diphosphopyridine nucleotide. **c. II,** triphosphopyridine nucleotide.

codeine (ko′dēn) [L. *codeina*]. A white or whitish, crystalline alkaloid, morphine-3-methyl ether, $C_{18}H_{21}NO_3 + H_2O$, from opium: used as an analgesic and antitussive. **c. phosphate,** a salt, $C_{18}H_{21}NO_3.H_3PO_4 + 1\frac{1}{2}H_2O$, occurring as fine white, needle-shaped crystals or a white crystalline powder: used as an analgesic and antitussive. **c. sulfate,** a white crystalline powder $(C_{18}H_{21}O_2N)_2.H_2SO_4.5H_2O$.

codex (ko′deks), pl. *cod'ices* [L.]. An authorized medicinal formulary; especially the French Pharmacopoeia, *Codex medicamentarium.*

Codivilla's extension, operation (ko″di-vil′ahz) [Alessandro *Codivilla,* surgeon in Bologna, 1861–1912]. See under *extension* and *operation.*

Codman's sign, triangle (kod′manz) [Ernest Amory *Codman,* Boston surgeon, 1869–1940]. See under *sign* and *triangle.*

codon (ko′don). The specific pattern of nucleotides (perhaps three) in the genetic material which corresponds to a particular amino acid in the genetic code. It is thought some amino acids may have more than one codon.

coe-. For words beginning thus, see also words beginning *ce-.*

coefficient (ko″ĕ-fish′ent). 1. An expression of the change or effect produced by the variation in certain factors, or of the ratio between two different quantities. 2. In chemistry, a number or figure put before a chemical formula to indicate how many times the formula is to be multiplied. **absorption c.** 1. The ratio of the linear rate of change of roentgen rays in a homogeneous material to the intensity at a given point (A. M. A.). 2. A number indicating the volume of a gas absorbed by a unit volume of a liquid at 0°C. and a pressure of 760 mm. Hg; called also *Bunsen c.* **Amann's c.,** the normal proportion between the quantities of ethereal sulfates and the total nitrogen in the urine. It is expressed as follows: (Eth. S. × 100)/Urea in Urine. **Ambard's c.,** Ambard's formula. **Baumann's c.,** the ratio of the ethereal to the total sulfates in the urine. **biological c.,** the amount of potential energy consumed by the body when at rest. **Bouchard's c.** 1. The ratio between the amount of urine and the total solids of the urine. 2. Urotoxic coefficient. **Bunsen c.,** absorption c., def. 2. **c. of conductivity,** a number indicating the quantity of heat that passes in a unit of time through a unit thickness of a substance when the difference in temperature is 1°C. **creatinine c.,** the figure obtained by dividing the total of milligrams of creatinine in the day's urine by the body weight expressed in kilograms. **c. of demineralization,** the proportion of mineral matter to the total dry residue of the urine. It averages 30 per cent. **distribution c.,** partition c. **c. of expansion,** a number indicating the amount a substance expands when heated 1°C. **c. of extinction,** that dilution of an antibody at which the specific activity is no longer manifest. **Falta's c.,** the percentage of ingested sugar eliminated from the system. **Haines' c.** See under *formula.* **Häser's c.** See under *formula.* **hemoglobin c.,** the number of grams of hemoglobin per 100 cc. of blood calculated for red cell count of 5 million per cu. mm. **hygienic laboratory c.,** a number representing the disinfecting value of a substance obtained by dividing the weakest solution of the disinfectant that will kill typhoid bacilli by the weakest solution of carbolic acid that will kill the bacilli in the same length of time. **isometric c. of lactic acid,** the ratio of the total isometric tension a muscle can produce before fatigue to the milligrams of lactic acid it produced. **isotonic c.,** a number showing the quantity of salt which should be added to distilled water to prevent its destroying the erythrocytes when added to blood. **Lancet c.,** a number representing the disinfecting value of a substance as compared with carbolic acid. **lethal c.,** that concentration of a disinfectant that will kill sporeless bacteria (*inferior lethal c.*) or bacterial spores (*superior lethal c.*) in water at a temperature of 20–25°C. in the shortest time. **Loebisch's c.** See under *formula.* **Long's c.** See under *formula.* **Maillard's c.,** a coefficient expressing the relationship between the urea and the total nitrogen of the urine. **c. of partage,** a number indicating the ratio between the amount of an acid absorbed by ether from an aqueous solution of the acid and the amount remaining in solution. **partition c.,** the ratio in which a given substance distributes itself between two or more different solvents. Called also *distribution c.* **phenol c.,** a measure of the bactericidal activity of a chemical compound in relation to phenol. The test and test microorganisms are standardized (Rideal-Walker method, U. S. Department of Agriculture method), and the activity of the unknown is expressed as the ratio of dilution in which it kills in 10 minutes but not in 5 minutes, to the dilution of phenol (ca. 1:90) which kills in 10 minutes but not in 5 minutes under the specified conditions. It can be determined in the absence of organic matter, or in presence of a standard amount of added organic matter. **respiratory c.,** respiratory quotient. See *quotient.* **Rideal-Walker c.** See *phenol c.* **temperature c.,** the effect of temperature upon chemical reactions; a number indicating the change of the reaction velocity constant with the temperature. Cf. *van Hoff's law,* under *law.* **Trapp's c.** See under *formula.* **urohemolytic c.,** the smallest degree of dilution necessary to render a specimen of urine hemolytic. **urotoxic c.,** a number expressing the toxicity of the urine: it is the quantity of urotoxic units produced per unit weight and eliminated in unit time (Bouchard). **c. of variability,** the ratio of the standard deviation to the mean. **velocity c.,** a number expressing the rate of a reaction; the rate of transformation of a unit mass of a substance in a chemical reaction. **c. of viscosity,** the force necessary to slide tangentially a unit of area of smooth surface at unit velocity on another parallel surface separated from the first surface by a unit layer of viscous substance. **volume c.,** the average number of cc. of packed red cells per 100 cc. of blood. **Yvon's c.,** the ratio between the quantity of urea and the phosphates of the urine.

coel- (sēl) [Gr. *koilia* cavity]. Combining form denoting relationship to a cavity or space. Sometimes spelled *cel-*.

coelarium (se-la′re-um) [L., from Gr. *koilos* a hollow]. The membrane that lines the body cavity, or coelom: it consists of a parietal layer, the *exocoelarium,* and a visceral layer, the *endocoelarium.* Called also *mesothelium* or *coelom epithelium.*

-coele (sēl) [Gr. *koilia* cavity]. Combining form denoting relationship to a cavity or space. Sometimes spelled *-cele.*

coelectron (ko″e-lek′tron) [L. *con* together + *electron*]. The atomic core; the core which, with the electron attached, forms an atom of matter.

Coelenterata (se-len″ter-a′tah) [Gr. *koilos* hollow + *enteron* intestine]. A phylum of invertebrates which includes the hydras, jellyfish, sea anemones, and corals.

coelenterate (se-len′ter-āt). 1. Pertaining or belonging to the Coelenterata. 2. An individual of the phylum Coelenterata.

coelenteron (se-len′ter-on). Archenteron.

coeliac (se′le-ak). Celiac.

coeloblastula (se-lo-blas′tu-lah) [*coelo-* + Gr. *blastos* germ]. The common type of blastula, consisting of a hollow sphere composed of blastomeres.

coelom (se′lom) [Gr. *koilōma*]. The body cavity of the embryo, situated between the somatopleure and the splanchnopleure. It is both extraembryonic and intraembryonic. From the intraembryonic portion arise the principal cavities of the trunk. **extraembryonic c.,** the cavity bordered by chorionic mesoderm and the mesoderm of the amnion and yolk sac; it communicates temporarily at the umbilicus with the intraembryonic coelom.

coeloma (se-lo′mah). Coelom.

coelomic (se-lom′ik). Pertaining to the coelom.

coelomyarian (se″lo-mi-a′re-an). Designating a type of nematode musculature in which the muscle fibers are next to the hypodermis and perpendicular to it; myofibrils extend varying distances up the side of the muscle cell, partially enclosing the sarcoplasm.

coelosomy (se″lo-so′me). A developmental anomaly characterized by protrusion of the viscera from and their presence outside the body cavity.

coelothel (se′lo-thel) [Gr. *koilos* hollow + *thēlē* nipple]. Mesothelium.

Coenogonimus (se″no-gon′ĭ-mus). A name formerly given a genus of minute trematode worms. **C. heteroph′yes,** *Heterophyes heterophyes.*

coenurosis (se″nu-ro′sis). Infection of sheep with the *Coenurus cerebralis.* See *staggers.*

Coenurus (se-nu′rus) [Gr. *koinos* common + *oura* tail]. A genus name formerly given certain tapeworm larvae. **C. cerebra′lis,** the larva of the *Multiceps multiceps,* found in the brain of sheep, goats, and other ruminants.

coenzyme (ko-en′zim). An organic, dialyzable, thermostable compound with which an apoenzyme must unite in order to function. **c. A,** pantothenic acid. **c. I,** diphosphopyridine nucleotide. **c. II,** triphosphopyridine nucleotide. **c. R.,** biotin. **Warburg's c.,** triphosphopyridine nucleotide.

coetaneous (ko″e-ta′ne-us) [L. *co* with + *aetas* age]. Having the same age.

coeur (ker) [Fr.]. Heart. **c. en sabot** (ker-on-să-bo′), a heart visible roentgenographically as having an increased transverse diameter, a convexity in the inferior line, and an elevation and rounded shape of the apex, so that its form suggests vaguely that of a wooden shoe: noted in tetralogy of Fallot.

coexcitation (ko-ek-si-ta′shun). Simultaneous excitation.

cofactor (ko′fak-tor). An element or principle with which another must unite in order to function. **platelet c. I,** factor VIII. See under *coagulation factors*. **platelet c. II,** factor IX. See under *coagulation factors*.

coferment (co-fer′ment). Coenzyme.

coffee (kof′e) [L. *coffea, caffea*]. The dried seeds of *Coffea arabica*, a tree believed to have originated in Africa, but now growing in nearly all tropical regions: the infusion is invigorating, tonic, and conservant; useful in chronic asthma, headache, and opium poisoning.

coffeinism (kof′e-in-izm). A morbid condition resulting from excessive use of coffee.

coffeurin (kof-e-u′rin). A substance said to be present in the urine after the free use of coffee.

Coffey-Humber treatment [Walter B. *Coffey*, American surgeon, 1868–1944; John D. *Humber*, American surgeon, born 1895]. See under *treatment*.

cogentin (ko-jen′tin). Trade mark for preparations of benztropine.

cognition (kog-nish′un) [L. *cognitio*, from *cognoscere* to know]. That operation of the mind by which we become aware of objects of thought or perception, including understanding and reasoning.

cohesion (ko-he′zhun) [L. *cohaesio*, from *con* together + *haerere* to stick]. The force which causes various particles to unite.

cohesive (ko-he′siv). Uniting together, or characterized by cohesion.

Cohn's test (kōnz) [Hermann Ludwig *Cohn*, German oculist, 1838–1936]. See under *tests*.

$C_4O_6H_4NaK$. Potassium and sodium tartrate.

Cohnheim's areas, field, frog, theory, etc. (kōn′hīmz) [Julius Friedrich *Cohnheim*, German pathologist, 1839–1884]. See under the nouns.

cohobation (ko″ho-ba′shun). The repeated distilling of a liquid from the same material; redistillation.

cohosh (ko-hosh′). A North American (Algonkin) name for various medicinal plants, as *Actaea spicata*, or red cohosh; *Caulophyllum thalictroides*, or blue cohosh; and *Cimicifuga racemosa*, or black cohosh.

cohydrogenase (ko″hi-dro′jen-ās). Coenzyme.

CoI. Abbreviation for *coenzyme I* (diphosphopyridine nucleotide).

CoII. Abbreviation for *coenzyme II* (triphosphopyridine nucleotide).

coil (koil). Anything wound in a spiral. **choke c.,** a coil of wire which may or may not be provided with a movable laminated iron core, used to limit the flow of current in a.c. circuits. An electrical device using the inductive properties of the alternating current to limit or retard the current entering an apparatus. **induction c.,** an apparatus for inducing an electric current. It consists of a coil of coarse wire (*primary coil*), which contains an iron core and is surrounded by a long coil of fine wire (*secondary coil*). When a galvanic current is passed through the primary coil, a faradic current is induced in the secondary coil. **Leiter's c.,** a coil of thin metal tubing wound round a part of the body, through which hot or cold water is passed for the purpose of varying the temperature of the part. **primary c.** See *induction c.* **resistance c.,** a coil of wire placed in an electrical circuit to increase the resistance. **Ruhmkorff c.,** an induction coil in which the secondary coil is not movable. **secondary c.** See *induction c.* **spark c.,** induction c. **Tesla c.,** an induction coil without an iron core: used for the production of a Tesla discharge.

coilonychia (koi″lo-nik′e-ah). Koilonychia.

coinosite (koi′no-sīt) [Gr. *koinos* common + *sitos* food]. A free or unfixed commensal organism.

coition (ko-ish′un) [L. *coitio* a going together]. Coitus.

coitophobia (ko″ĭ-to-fo′be-ah) [*coitus* + *phobia* fear]. Morbid dread of coitus.

coitus (ko′ĭ-tus) [L.]. Sexual union between individuals of opposite sex. **c. incomple′tus, c. interrup′tus,** coitus in which the penis is withdrawn from the vagina before ejaculation. **c. reserva′tus,** coitus in which ejaculation is intentionally suppressed: called also *karezza*. **c. à la vache,** coitus from behind, with the woman in the knee-chest position.

Coix (ko′iks) [L.; Gr. *koix* a palm]. A genus of grasses. *C. lacryma*, an Asiatic species, bears large seeds called *Job's tears*, which are often strung as beads for infants' use in teething: said to be anodyne and diuretic.

Col. Abbreviation for L. *co′la*, strain.

colalgia (ko-lal′je-ah) [Gr. *kolon* colon + *-algia*]. Pain in the colon.

colamine (ko′lah-min). Amino-ethanol, $NH_2.CH_2.$-CH_2OH, contained in cephalins.

Colat. Abbreviation for L. *cola′tus*, strained.

colation (ko-la′shun) [L. *colatio*]. 1. The process of straining or filtration. 2. The product of such a process.

colatorium (kol″ah-to′re-um), pl. *colato′ria* [L., from *colare* to strain]. 1. A strainer or colander; a sieve. 2. The pituitary body.

colature (ko′lah-tūr) [L. *colatura*, from *colare* to strain]. A liquid obtained by straining.

colauxe (ko-lawk′se) [Gr. *kolon* colon + *auxē* increase]. Dilatation of the colon.

colchicine (kol′chĭ-sin). An alkaloid obtained from *Colchicum autumnale*, occurring as pale yellow amorphous scales or powder: used in the treatment of gout.

cold (kōld). 1. Privation or relatively low degree of heat. 2. Common cold; a catarrhal disorder of the upper respiratory tract, sometimes following exposure to cold and wet, which may be viral, a mixed infection, or an allergic reaction. It is marked by acute coryza, slight rise in temperature, chilly sensations and general indisposition. **allergic c.,** hay fever. **June c.,** hay fever. **rose c.,** a form of hay fever caused by the pollen of roses.

coldsore (kōld′sōr). Herpes simplex of lip (herpes labialis).

cole-. See *coleo-*.

Cole's sign (kōlz) [Lewis Gregory *Cole*, American roentgenologist, 1874–1954]. See under *sign*.

colectasia (ko″lek-ta′se-ah). Dilatation of the colon.

colectomy (ko-lek′to-me) [*colon* + Gr. *ektomē* excision]. Excision of a portion of the colon (*partial c.*) or of the whole colon (*complete* or *total c.*).

coleitis (kol″e-i′tis) [*cole-* + *-itis*]. Vaginitis.

Coleman-Shaffer diet [Warren *Coleman*, New York physician, 1869–1948; P. A. *Shaffer*, American biochemist, born 1881]. See under *diet*.

coleo-, cole- (kol′e-o, kol′e) [Gr. *koleos* sheath]. Combining form denoting relationship to the vagina, or to a sheath.

coleocele (kol′e-o-sēl″) [*coleo-* + Gr. *kēlē* hernia]. Vaginal hernia.

coleocystitis (kol″e-o-sis-ti′tis) [*coleo-* + *cystitis*]. Inflammation of the vagina and bladder.

Coleoptera (kol″e-op′ter-ah) [*coleo-* + Gr. *pteron* wing]. An order of insects comprising the beetles.

coleoptosis (kol″e-op-to′sis) [*coleo-* + Gr. *ptōsis* falling]. Prolapse of the vagina.

coleospastia (kol″e-o-spas′te-ah) [*coleo-* + Gr. *span* to contract]. Vaginismus.

coleotomy (kol″e-ot′o-me). Colpotomy.

coles (ko′lēz) [Gr. *kōlē*]. The penis. **c. femini′nus,** the clitoris.

Colesiota (ko-le″se-o′tah) [J. D. W. A. *Coles*]. A genus of the family Chlamydiaceae, order Rickettsiales, occurring as a single species, *C. conjuncti′vae,* the agent causing infectious ophthalmia of sheep.

Colet. Abbreviation for L. *cole′tur,* let it be strained.

Colettsia (ko-let′se-ah) [J. D. W. A. *Coles*]. A genus of the family Chlamydiaceae, order Rickettsiales, occurring as a single species, *C. pe′coris,* a parasitic microorganism found in the conjunctiva of domestic animals.

Coley's fluid, toxin (ko′lēz) [William B. *Coley* surgeon in New York, 1862–1936]. See under *fluid* and *toxin.*

colibacillary (ko″lĭ-bas′ĭ-ler-e). Produced by *Escherichia coli.*

colibacillemia (ko″lĭ-bas-ĭ-le′me-ah). The presence of *Escherichia coli* in the blood.

colibacillosis (ko″lĭ-bas-ĭ-lo′sis). Infection with *Escherichia coli.* **c. gravida′rum,** severe infection with *Escherichia coli* during pregnancy.

colibacilluria (ko″lĭ-bas″ĭ-lu′re-ah). Presence of *Escherichia coli* in the urine.

colibacillus (ko″lĭ-bah-sil′us). *Escherichia coli.*

colic (kol′ik) [Gr. *kōlikos*]. 1. Pertaining to the colon. 2. Acute abdominal pain. **appendicular c.,** vermicular c. **biliary c.,** paroxysms of pain and other severe symptoms due to the passage of gallstones along the bile duct. Called also *hepatic c.* **bilious c.,** abdominal pain accompanied by the vomiting of bile and the passage of bilious stools. **copper c.,** a severe colic common among workers in copper. **crapulent c.,** that which is due to excess in eating and drinking. **Devonshire c.,** lead colic. **endemic c.,** a dangerous form of colic peculiar to hot countries. **flatulent c.,** tympanites. **gallstone c.,** biliary c. **gastric c.,** gastralgia. **hepatic c.,** biliary c. **hill c.,** a febrile diarrhea prevalent in the hill tracts of India. **intestinal c.,** acute abdominal pain. **lead c.,** that which is due to lead poisoning. **meconial c.,** colic of newborn infants. **menstrual c.,** severe abdominal pain at the menstrual period; dysmenorrhea. **mucous c.,** mucous colitis. **nephritic c.,** pain in the kidney from either stone or acute inflammation. **ovarian c.,** ovarian pain from disease of the organ. **painters' c.,** lead c. **pancreatic c.,** abdominal pain caused by obstruction of the excretory duct of the pancreas. **Poitou c.,** lead c. **pseudomembranous c.,** pseudomembranous enteritis. **renal c.,** pain produced by the passage of stone along the ureter. **saburral c.,** colic from intestinal indigestion. **salivary c.,** pain in the region of the salivary gland occurring in cases of salivary calculus. **sand c.,** chronic indigestion in horses and cattle due to the presence in the stomach or intestine of sand taken in with food or drink. **saturnine c.,** lead c. **stercoral c.,** intestinal colic due to accumulation of feces. **tubal c.,** painful spasmodic contraction of the fallopian tube. **ureteral c.,** colicky pains due to obstruction of the ureter. **uterine c.,** severe abdominal pain from some uterine disease or at the menstrual epoch. **vermicular c.,** a condition of colic in the vermiform appendix occasioned by a catarrhal inflammation resulting from blocking of the outlet of the appendix. **verminous c.,** colic due to the presence of intestinal worms. **wind c.,** pain in the bowels due to their distention with air or gas. **worm c.,** verminous c. **zinc c.,** colic resulting from chronic zinc poisoning.

colica (kol′ĭ-kah) [L.]. Colic. **c. muco′sa,** mucous colitis. **c. pas′sio,** colic. **c. pic′tonum,** lead colic. **c. scorto′rum,** severe colicky pain in the region of the fallopian tubes: seen in salpingitis.

colicin (kol′ĭ-sin) [*coli* (from *Escherichia coli*) + *-cin* (adapted from L. *caedere* to kill)]. An antibiotic produced from *Escherichia coli* and affecting other strains of the same species.

colicolitis (ko′lĭ-ko-li′tis). Colitis caused by *Escherichia coli.*

colicoplegia (kol″ĭ-ko-ple′je-ah) [Gr. *kōlikos* colic + *plēgē* stroke]. Lead colic and lead paralysis together.

colicystitis (ko″lĭ-sis-ti′tis). Cystitis dependent upon the presence of *Escherichia coli.*

colicystopyelitis (ko-lĭ-sis″to-pi″e-li′tis) [*colon* + Gr. *kystis* bladder + *pyelos* pelvis]. Inflammation of bladder and kidney pelvis due to *Escherichia coli.*

coliform (ko′lĭ-form) [L. *colum* a sieve]. 1. Cribriform. 2. Resembling the *Escherichia coli.*

colilysin (ko-lil′ĭ-sin). A lysin formed by *Escherichia coli.*

colinephritis (ko″lĭ-ne-fri′tis). Nephritis due to the presence of *Escherichia coli.*

coliplication (ko″lĭ-pli-ka′shun). Coloplication.

colipuncture (ko′lĭ-punk″tūr). Colocentesis.

colipyelitis (ko″lĭ-pi″ĕ-li′tis). Pyelitis due to the *Escherichia coli.*

colipyuria (ko″lĭ-pi-u′re-ah) [*colon* bacillus + Gr. *pyon* pus + *ouron* urine + *-ia*]. Pus in the urine due to infection with *Escherichia coli.*

colisepsis (ko″lĭ-sep′sis). Infection with *Escherichia coli.*

colistatin (ko″lĭ-sta′tin). An antibiotic substance from an aerobic sporulating bacillus, which is bacteriolytic for *Escherichia coli, Proteus vulgaris, Salmonella typhosa,* as well as for certain gram-positive organisms.

colistimethate (ko-lis″tĭ-meth′at). A methane sulfonate derivative of colistin: used in the treatment of urinary tract infections.

colistin (ko-lis′tin). An antibiotic substance produced by a microorganism found in the soil, related chemically to polymyxin. **c. sulfate,** a water-soluble salt of colistin, effective against several gram-negative bacilli but not against Proteus.

colitis (ko-li′tis). Inflammation of the colon. **amebic c.,** colitis due to *Entamoeba histolytica;* amebic dysentery. **balantidial c.,** colitis due to infestation with *Balantidium coli.* **c. gra′vis,** ulcerative c. **mucous c.,** a chronic disease, affecting chiefly neurotic subjects, characterized by the excessive secretion of mucus in the colon and marked by colic, constipation, or diarrhea, and the passage of mucus and membranous shreds. Called also *mucous colic, myxomembranous colitis, mucocolitis, membranous enteritis, colic* or *intestinal myxoneurosis, spastic irritable colon,* and *tubular diarrhea.* **myxomembranous c.,** mucous c. **c. polypo′sa,** colitis in which the swollen mucosa projects from the surface in polypoid masses. **c. ulcerati′va, ulcerative c.,** chronic ulceration in the colon.

colitoxemia (ko″lĭ-tok-se′me-ah). Toxemia due to infection with *Escherichia coli.*

colitoxicosis (ko″lĭ-tok″sĭ-ko′sis). Intoxication caused by *Escherichia coli.*

colitoxin (ko″lĭ-tok′sin). A substance contained in *Escherichia coli* which is the cause of colitoxicosis.

coliuria (ko″lĭ-u′re-ah). Presence of *Escherichia coli* in the urine.

colla (kol′lah) [L.]. Plural of *collum.*

collagen (kol′ah-jen) [Gr. *kolla* glue + Gr. *gennan* to produce]. An albuminoid, the main supportive protein of skin, tendon, bone, cartilage, and connective tissue. It is converted into gelatin by boiling.

collagenase (kol-laj′e-nās). An enzyme which catalyzes the destruction of collagen.

collagenation (kol-laj″ĕ-na′shun). The appearance of collagen in developing cartilage.

collagenic (kol″ah-jen′ik). 1. Collagenous. 2. Collagenogenic.

collagenoblast (kol-laj′ĕ-no-blast). A cell which arises from a fibroblast and which, as it matures, is associated with the production of collagen; it may also, at times, form cartilage and bone by metaplasia.

collagenogenic (kol″lah-jen-o-jen′ik). Pertaining to or characterized by the production of collagen.

collagenolytic (kol-laj″ĕ-no-lit′ik). Effecting the digestion of collagen.

collagenosis (kol-laj″ĕ-no′sis). A disease characterized by the presence of areas of collagenous degeneration, such as lupus erythematosus, dermatomyositis, sclerosis of the legs, etc.

collagenous (kol-laj′e-nus). Pertaining to collagen; forming or producing collagen.

collapse (kŏ-laps′) [L. *collapsus*]. 1. A state of extreme prostration and depression, with failure of circulation. 2. Abnormal falling in of the walls of any part or organ. **circulatory c.,** shock; circulatory insufficiency without congestive heart failure. **c. of the lung,** an airless or fetal state of all or a part of a lung. **massive c.,** a condition in which the lung becomes airless without the existence of any lesion interfering with the free entry of air.

collapsotherapy (kŏ-lap″so-ther′ah-pe). Collapse therapy; artificial pneumothorax to collapse and immobilize a lung.

collar (kol′er). An encircling band, generally around the neck. **Biett's c.,** a ring of epidermis around a papulolenticular syphilid. **Casal's c.,** a bandlike arc of pellagrous eruption about the neck. **periosteal bone c.,** a band of spongy bone which forms around the middle of the diaphysis of early bones. **c. of Stokes,** an edematous thickening of the neck and soft parts of the thorax associated with dilatation of the veins from the neck to the diaphragm, seen in cases of obstruction of the superior vena cava. **venereal c., c. of Venus,** melanoleukoderma colli.

collarette (kol″er-et′). 1. A small collar; especially a collar-like area of dermatitis seen in pellagra. 2. Ciliary zone.

collastin (kŏ-las′tin). Degenerate collagenous tissue which stains like normal elastic tissue.

collateral (kŏ-lat′er-al) [L. *con* together + *la′tus* side]. 1. Secondary or accessory; not direct or immediate. 2. A small side branch, as of a blood vessel or nerve.

collemia (kŏ-le′me-ah) [Gr. *kolla* glue + *haima* blood + *-ia*]. A glutinous or viscid condition of the blood.

Colles' fascia, fracture, law, etc. (kol′ēz) [Abraham *Colles*, an Irish surgeon, 1773–1843]. See under the nouns.

Colles-Baumès law (kol′ēz-bo-māz′) [Abraham *Colles;* Pierre Prosper François *Baumès*, French physician, 1791–1871]. See *Colles' law*, under *law*.

Collet's syndrome (kol-lāz′) [Frédéric-Justin *Collet*, Lyons laryngologist, born 1870]. Villaret's syndrome.

colliculectomy (kŏ-lik″u-lek′to-me) [*colliculus* + Gr. *ektomē* excision]. Excision of the colliculus seminalis.

colliculi (kŏ-lik′u-li). Plural of *colliculus*.

colliculitis (kŏ-lik″u-li′tis). Inflammation about the colliculus seminalis.

colliculus (kŏ-lik′u-lus) [L.]. A small elevation, or mound. **c. of arytenoid cartilage,** c. cartilaginis arytenoideae. **bulbar c.,** corpus spongiosum penis. **c. cartilag′inis arytenoi′deae** [N A], a small eminence on the anterior margin and anterolateral surface of the arytenoid cartilage. Called also *c. of arytenoid cartilage* and *c. cartilaginis arytaenoideae* [B N A]. **c. cauda′lis,** c. inferior laminae tecti. **c. cauda′tus,** nucleus caudatus. **cervical c. of female urethra, of Barkow,** crista urethralis femininae. **c. crania′lis,** c. superior laminae tecti. **facial c., c. facia′lis** [N A, B N A], a thickening of the medial eminence above the medullary striae in the rhomboid fossa, caused by the internal genu of the facial nerve. **inferior c., c. infe′rior lam′inae quadrigem′inae** [B N A], c. inferior laminae tecti. **c. infe′rior lam′inae tec′ti** [N A], the caudal of the two pairs of rounded eminences in the tectum of the mesencephalon. It is primarily concerned with auditory reflexes. Called also *inferior c.* and *c. inferior laminae quadrigeminae* [B N A]. **seminal c., c. semina′lis** [N A, B N A], a prominent portion of the urethral crest on which are the opening of the prostatic utricle and, on either side of it, the orifices of the ejaculatory ducts. **superior c., c. supe′rior lam′inae quadrigem′inae** [B N A], c. superior laminae tecti. **c. supe′rior lam′inae tec′ti** [N A], the rostral of the two pairs of rounded eminences in the tectum of the mesencephalon. It is primarily concerned with visual reflexes. Called also *superior c.* and *c. superior laminae quadrigeminae* [B N A].

collifixation (kol″ĭ-fik-sa′shun). Collopexia.

colligation (kol″ĭ-ga′shun). 1. A form of mental composition in which the units maintain their own distinction. 2. The bringing together of isolated elements in a composite experience.

colligative (kol′ĭ-ga″tiv). In physical chemistry, depending on the number of molecules present in a given space, rather than on their size, molecular weight or chemical constitution.

collimation (kol″lĭ-ma′shun). In microscopy, the process of making light rays parallel; the process of aligning the optical axis of the optical system to the reference mechanical axes or surfaces of the instrument, or the adjustment of two or more optical axes with respect to each other.

Collin's osteoclast (kol′inz) [Anatole *Collin*, Parisian instrument maker, 1831–1923]. See under *osteoclast.*

Collinsonia (kol″in-so′ne-ah) [after Peter *Collinson*, 1694–1768]. A genus of labiate herbs. *C. canadensis*, stoneroot or richweed, is tonic and diuretic.

Collip unit (kol′ip) [James Bertram *Collip*, Canadian biochemist, born 1892]. See under *unit.*

colliquation (kol″ĭ-kwa′shun) [L. *con* together + *liquare* to melt]. Liquefactive degeneration. **ballooning c.,** liquefaction of cell protoplasm attended by edematous swelling. **reticulating c.,** liquefaction of cell protoplasm with the formation of reticulations.

colliquative (kŏ-lik′wah-tiv) [L. *con* together + *liquare* to melt]. 1. Characterized by an excessive fluid discharge. 2. Marked by liquefaction of tissues.

collochemistry (kol″o-kem′is-tre). The chemistry of colloids.

collodiaphysial (kol″o-di″ah-fiz′e-al) [L. *collum* neck + *diaphysis*]. Pertaining to the neck and shaft of a long bone, especially the femur.

collodion (ko-lo′de-on) [L. *collodium*, from Gr. *kollōdēs* glutinous]. A clear or slightly opalescent, syrupy liquid compounded of pyroxylin, ether, and alcohol, which dries to a transparent, tenacious film. **c. elastique′,** flexible c. **flexible c.,** a preparation of camphor, castor oil, and collodion: used topically as a skin protective. **salicylic acid c.,** a preparation of salicylic acid in flexible collodion: used topically as a keratolytic.

colloid (kol′oid) [Gr. *kollōdēs* glutinous]. 1. Glutinous or resembling glue. 2. A state of matter in which the matter is dispersed in or distributed throughout some medium called the dispersion medium. The matter thus dispersed is called the disperse phase of the colloid system. The particles of the disperse phase are larger than an ordinary crystalloid molecule, but are not large enough to settle out under the influence of gravity; they range in size from $\frac{1}{10}$ micron to 1 micromicron. There are two kinds of colloids: first, the *suspension colloids*, in which the disperse phase consists of particles of any insoluble substance, as a metal, and the dispersion medium may be gaseous, liquid, or solid; and second, the *emulsion colloids*, in which the dispersion medium is usually water and the disperse phase consists of highly complex organic substances, such as starch or glue, which absorb much water, swell, and become uniformly distributed throughout the dispersion medium in a manner not well understood. The former tend to be less stable than the latter. 3. The translucent, yellowish, gelatinous substance resulting from colloid degeneration. **amyl c., anodyne c.,** a local anodyne preparation containing ½ ounce each of amyl hydride and absolute alcohol, 1 grain aconitine, 6 grains veratrine, and 2 oz. of collodion. **association c.,** a colloid in which the dispersed particles are each made up of many molecules. **bovine c.** See *conglutinin.* **dispersion c.** See *colloid,* 2nd def. **emulsion c.** See *colloid,* 2nd def. **hydrophilic c.,** emulsion colloid. **hydrophobic c.,** suspension colloid. **irreversible c.,** a colloid which is not reversible. **lyophilic c.,** emulsion colloid. **lyophobic c.,** suspension colloid. **lyotropic c.,** emulsion colloid. **protective c.,** one which is able to prevent the precipitation of another colloid. **reversible c.,** a colloid which can be dispersed after having been precipitated or a gel which can be converted into a sol. **stable c.,** a reversible colloid. **suspension c.** See *colloid,* 2nd def. **thyroid c.,** the colloid found in the acini of the thyroid gland, consisting essentially of thyroglobulin.

colloidal (kŏ-loi′dal). Of the nature of a colloid. **c.-S,** an iron-oxide preparation used intravenously in severe infections.

colloidin (ko-loi′din). A jelly-like substance, $C_9H_{15}NO_6$, one of the products of colloid degeneration.

colloidoclasia (ko-loi″do-kla′se-ah) [*colloid* + Gr. *klasis* breaking up]. A breaking up of the physical equilibrium of the colloids of the body, producing an anaphylactoid crisis (colloidoclastic shock) attributed to absorption into the blood of unchanged colloids: called also *colloidoclastic crisis.*

colloidoclasis (kŏ-loi″do-kla′sis). Colloidoclasia.

colloidogen (kŏ-loi′do-jen). A substance assumed to be present in the body for the purpose of keeping the inorganic elements of the body in a colloid solution.

colloidopexic (kŏ-loi″do-pek′sik). Fixing or holding colloids.

colloidopexy (kŏ-loi′do-pek″se) [Gr. *kollōdēs* glutinous + *pēxis* fixing]. Metabolic fixation of colloids within the organism, a function ascribed to the liver.

colloidophagy (kol″oi-dof′ah-je) [*colloid* + Gr. *phagein* to eat]. Resorption of colloid by macrophages under the influence of the thyroid-stimulating hormone.

colloidoplasmatic (kŏ-loi″do-plaz-mat′ik). Pertaining to colloids and plasma.

colloma (kŏ-lo′mah) [Gr. *kolla* glue + *-oma*]. A colloid cancer; carcinoma whose degenerated substance has assumed a gluelike character.

collonema (kol″o-ne′mah) [Gr. *kolla* glue]. A tumor produced by the diffuse mucinous degeneration of a lipoma (Müller).

collopexia (kol″o-pek′se-ah) [L. *collum* neck + Gr. *pēxis* fixing]. The surgical fixation of the uterine neck.

colloxylin (kŏ-lok′sĭ-lin) [Gr. *kolla* glue + *xylinos* woody]. Pyroxylin.

collum (kol′lum), pl. *col′la* [L.] [N A, B N A]. 1. The portion of the body connecting the head and trunk. Called also *cervix* and *neck.* 2. A general term applied to any necklike part of a body structure or organ. **c. anatom′icum hu′meri** [N A, B N A], the somewhat constricted zone on the humerus just distal to the head, separating the articular surface from the tubercles. Called also *anatomical neck of humerus.* **c. chirur′gicum hu′meri** [N A, B N A], the region on the humerus just below the tubercles, where the bone becomes constricted. Called also *surgical neck of humerus.* **c. cos′tae** [N A, B N A], the part of a rib extending from the head to the tubercle. Called also *neck of rib.* **c. den′tis** [N A, B N A], the slightly constricted region of union of the crown and the root or roots of a tooth. Called also *neck of a tooth.* **c. distor′tum,** torticollis. **c. fem′oris** [N A, B N A], the heavy column of bone connecting the head of the femur and the shaft. Called also *neck of femur.* **c. follic′uli pi′li** [B N A], the narrow portion of a hair follicle between the hair bulb and the opening on the surface of the skin. Omitted in N A. **c. glan′dis pe′nis** [N A, B N A], the constricted portion between the corona of the glans penis and the corpora cavernosa. Called also *neck of glans penis.* **c. mal′lei** [N A, B N A], the constricted portion of the malleus below the head. Called also *neck of malleus.* **c. mandib′ulae** [N A], the narrow portion supporting the head of the mandible. Called also *c. processus condyloidei mandibulae* [B N A], and *neck of mandible.* **c. proces′sus condyloi′dei mandib′ulae** [B N A], c. mandibulae. **c. ra′dii** [N A, B N A], the somewhat constricted portion of the radius just distal to the head. Called also *neck of radius.* **c. scap′ulae** [N A, B N A], the somewhat constricted part of the scapula that surrounds the lateral angle. Called also *neck of scapula.* **c. ta′li** [N A, B N A], the constriction between the head and body of the talus. Called also *neck of talus.* **c. val′gum,** coxa valga. **c. vesi′cae fel′leae** [N A, B N A], the upper, constricted part of the gallbladder, between the body and the cystic duct. Called also *neck of gallbladder.*

collunaria (kol″u-na′re-ah). Plural of *collunarium.*

collunarium (kol″u-na′re-um), pl. *colluna′ria* [L.]. A nasal douche.

Collut. Abbreviation for L. *collutorium* (mouth wash).

collutoria (kol″u-to′re-ah) [L.]. Plural of *collutorium.*

collutorium (kol″u-to′re-um), pl. *colluto′ria* [L.]. Collutory.

collutory (kol′u-to″re) [L. *collutorium*]. A mouth wash or gargle. **Miller's c.,** a mouth wash containing benzoic acid, tincture of krameria, oil of peppermint.

Collyr. Abbreviation for L. *collyr′ium,* an eye wash.

collyria (ko-lir′e-ah) [L.]. Plural of *collyrium.*

Collyriculum (kol″le-rik′u-lum). A genus of trematode parasites. **C. fa′ba,** a trematode parasite forming subcutaneous cysts in chickens, turkeys, and sparrows.

collyrium (ko-lir′e-um), pl. *collyr′ia* [L.; Gr. *kollyrion* eye salve]. A lotion for the eyes; an eye wash. **Beer's c.,** lead acetate, rose water, and spirit of rosemary.

coloboma (kol″o-bo′mah), pl. *colobomas* or *colobo′mata* [L.; Gr. *kolobōma*]. A mutilation or defect; especially a congenital fissure of any part of the eye. **bridge c.,** a variety of coloboma of the iris in which a strip of iris tissue bridges over the fissure. **c. of choroid,** fissure in the choroid coat due to persistence of a fetal fissure and causing a scotoma on the retina. **Fuchs's c.,** a small, crescent-shaped defect of the choroid, at the lower edge of the optic disk. **c. i′ridis, c. of iris,** a fissure of the iris, usually of the lower portion. **c. len′tis,** a defect in the lens of the eye in which the periphery is incomplete or indented. **c. lob′uli,** fissure of the ear lobe, which may occur as a congenital defect, or be acquired. **c. of optic nerve,** a defect attributed to the incomplete closure of the fetal fissure of the optic stalk. **c. palpebra′le,** a vertical fissure of an eyelid. **c. of retina, c. ret′inae,** a congenital fissure of the retina attributed to incomplete closure of the fetal fissure in the optic cup. **c. of vitreous,** a notch in the lower border of the vitreous.

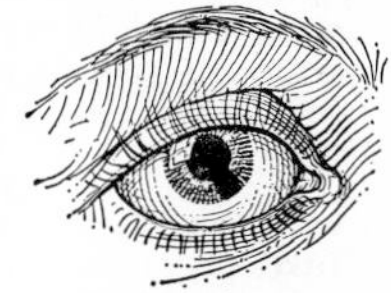
Coloboma of iris (Arey).

colocecostomy (ko″lo-se-kos′to-me) [*colon* + *cecum* + Gr. *stoma* opening]. Cecocolostomy.

colocentesis (ko″lo-sen-te′sis) [*colon* + Gr. *kentēsis* puncture]. Surgical perforation of the colon.

colocholecystostomy (ko″lo-ko″le-sis-tos′to-me). Cholecystocolostomy.

coloclysis (ko-lok′lĭ-sis) [*colon* + Gr. *klysis* a drenching]. Irrigation of the colon.

coloclyster (ko″lo-klis′ter). An enema injected into the rectum.

colocolic (ko″lo-kol′ik). Relating to two portions of the colon.

colocolostomy (ko″lo-ko-los′to-me) [*colon* + *colostomy*]. The operation of forming an anastomosis between two portions of the colon.

colocutaneous (ko″lo-ku-ta′ne-us). Pertaining to the colon and skin, or communicating with the colon and the cutaneous surface of the body, as colocutaneous fistula.

colocynth (kol′o-sinth) [L. *colocynthis;* Gr. *kolokynthē*]. The dried pulp of the unripe but full-grown fruit of *Citrullus colocynthus:* used as a cathartic.

colocynthidism (kol″o-sin′thĭ-dizm). Poisoning by colocynth.

colocynthin (kol″o-sin′thin). A bitter, purgative glycoside, $C_{56}H_{84}O_{23}$, from colocynth.

colocynthis (kol″o-sin′this), gen. *colocyn′thidis* [L.]. Colocynth.

colodyspepsia (ko″lo-dis-pep′se-ah). Dyspepsia due to reflex disturbance set up by the constipated colon.

coloenteritis (ko″lo-en″ter-i′tis) [*colon* + *enteritis*]. Inflammation of the small intestine and colon.

colofixation (ko″lo-fik-sa′shun). The operation of fixing or suspending the colon in cases of ptosis.

cologel (kol′o-jel). Trade mark for a preparation of methylcellulose.

colohepatopexy (ko″lo-hep′ah-to-pek″se) [*colon* + Gr. *hēpar* liver + *pēxis* fixation]. The suturing of the colon to the liver to take the place of adhesions between the liver and the stomach which form after gallstone operations.

coloileal (ko″lo-il′e-al). Pertaining to or communicating with the colon and ileum, as a coloileal fistula.

cololysis (ko-lol′ĭ-sis) [*colon* + Gr. *lysis* dissolution]. The operation of freeing the colon from adhesions.

colomba (ko-lom′bah). Calumba.

colometrometer (ko″lo-mĕ-trom′e-ter). An apparatus for measuring the activity of the colon.

colon (ko′lon) [L.; Gr. *kolon*]. [N A, B N A] That part of the large intestine which extends from the cecum to the rectum. Sometimes used also as a synonym for the entire large intestine. **c. ascen′dens** [N A, B N A], **ascending c.,** the portion of the colon which passes cephalad between the cecum and the right colic flexure. **c. descen′dens** [N A, B N A], **descending c.,** the portion of the colon which passes caudad between the left colic flexure and the sigmoid colon. **giant c.,** an abnormally large colon. **irritable c.,** a condition marked by abdominal pain or distress, gas, and tenderness along the colon. **lead-pipe c.,** a condition in which the colon has become a rigid tube incapable of functioning: sometimes seen in ulcerative colitis. **left c.,** the distal portion of the large intestine, developing embryonically from the hind gut and functioning in the storage and elimination from the body of non-absorbed residue. **pelvic c. of Waldeyer,** flexura sacralis recti. **right c.,** the proximal portion of the large intestine, extending from the ileocecal valve usually to a point proximal to the left colic flexure, developing embryonically from the terminal portion of the midgut and functioning in absorption. **sigmoid c., c. sigmoi′deum** [N A, B N A], the part of the colon in the pelvis that extends from the descending colon to the rectum. **thrifty c.,** a colon which absorbs so much fluid from the colonic contents that the fecal masses become small and dry and insufficient in amount to stimulate peristalsis. **transverse c., c. transver′sum** [N A, B N A], the portion of the colon that runs transversely across the upper part of the abdomen, from the right to the left colic flexure.

colonalgia (ko″lon-al′je-ah) [*colon* + *-algia*]. Pain in the colon.

colonic (ko-lon′ik). Pertaining to the colon.

colonitis (ko″lo-ni′tis). Colitis.

colonization (kol″ŏ-nĭ-za′shun). 1. Innidiation. 2. The care of mental patients in community groups.

Colonna's operation (kŏ-lōn′ah) [Paul *Colonna,* American orthopedic surgeon, born 1892]. See under *operation.*

colonometer (kol″o-nom′e-ter) [*colony* + Gr. *metron* measure]. An apparatus for counting the colonies of bacteria on a culture plate.

colonopathy (ko″lo-nop′ah-the) [*colon* + Gr. *pathos* disease]. Any disease or disorder of the colon.

colonopexy (ko-lon′o-pek″se). Colopexy.

colonorrhagia (ko″lon-o-ra′je-ah). Hemorrhage from the colon.

colonorrhea (ko″lon-o-re′ah) [*colon* + Gr. *rhoia* flow]. Mucous colitis.

colonoscope (ko-lon′o-skōp) [*colon* + Gr. *skopein* to examine]. A speculum for examining the lower part of the bowel.

colonoscopy (ko″lon-os′ko-pe). Examination of the lower part of the bowel with a colonoscope.

colony (kol′o-ne) [L. *colonia*]. A collection or group of bacteria in a culture derived from the increase of an isolated single organism or group of organisms. **beaten-copper c.,** a bacterial culture on the surface of which there are numerous small depressions. **bitten c.,** a colony from the edge of which a portion has been removed as though bitten out but has really been lysed out by the action of bacteriophage. **butyrous c.,** a colony of butter-like consistency. **D. c.,** dwarf c. **daughter c.,** a small bacterial colony formed as a papilla on the surface or in the margin of a normal colony. **dysgonic c.,** a bacterial colony that grows feebly and slowly. **dwarf c.,** a bacterial colony smaller than normal and containing poorly developed forms. **effuse c.,** one that is very thin and flat. **G. c., gonidial c.,** a bacterial colony averaging about 0.5 mm. in diameter and composed of minute coccoid and bacillary forms, originally thought to represent the gonidial stage in the life cycle of bacteria. **H c.** (Ger. *Hauch* film), a type of bacterial colony which spreads in a thin film over the culture medium. **M. c.,** mucoid c. **matte c.** (Ger. "mat"), a variant of the R. colony in beta-hemolytic streptococci, indicating virulence. **mucoid c.,** a colony that is large, dome-shaped, and shiny, and may be drawn out in viscid strings by a needle. **nibbled c.,** bitten c. **O. c.,** (Ger. *ohne Hauch* without film), a bacterial colony which is compact as contrasted with an H colony. **psakadic c's,** small dustlike colonies. **R. c., rough c.,** a bacterial colony showing a rough, wrinkled, granular, flattened surface; known as R-type. **S. c., smooth c.,** a bacterial colony showing the smooth, glistening, rounded, regular surface, normally shown by colonies of organisms; known as S-type.

colopathy (ko-lop′ah-the). Colonopathy.

colopexia (ko″lo-pek′se-ah). Colopexy.

colopexostomy (ko″lo-pek-sos′to-me) [*colon* + Gr. *pēxis* fixation + *stoma* mouth]. Resection of the colon with cecostomy or appendicostomy.

colopexotomy (ko″lo-pek-sot′o-me) [*colon* + Gr. *pēxis* fixation + *tomē* a cutting]. Fixation and incision of the colon.

colopexy (ko′lo-pek″se) [*colon* + Gr. *pēxis* fixation]. Fixation of the sigmoid flexure to the abdominal wall by suturation.

colophene (kol′o-fēn). A colorless hydrocarbon, $C_{20}H_{32}$, derivable from turpentine.

colophony (ko-lof′o-ne) [L. *colophonia;* Gr. *Kolophōn* (Colophon) a city of Asia Minor]. Common resin, or rosin, derived from various species of pine.

coloplication (ko″lo-pli-ka′shun) [*colon* + L. *plica* fold]. The operation of unfolding or taking a reef in the colon in cases of dilatation.

coloproctectomy (ko″lo-prok-tek′to-me). Surgical removal of the colon and rectum.

coloproctia (ko″lo-prok′she-ah) [*colon* + Gr. *prōktos* anus]. Colostomy.

coloproctitis (ko″lo-prok-ti′tis). Inflammation of the colon and rectum.

coloproctostomy (ko″lo-prok-tos′to-me) [*colon* + Gr. *prōktos* anus + *stoma* mouth]. Colorectostomy.

coloptosis (ko″lop-to′sis) [*colon* + Gr. *ptōsis* fall]. Prolapse or falling of the colon. Cf. *enteroptosis.*

colopuncture (ko′lo-punk″tūr). Colocentesis.

Color. Abbreviation for L. *colore′tur,* let it be colored.

color (kul′or) [L. *color, colos*]. 1. A property of a surface or substance resulting from absorption of certain of the incident light rays and reflection of others falling within the range of wavelengths (roughly 370–760 mμ) adequate to excite the retinal receptors. 2. Radiant energy within the range of adequate chromatic stimuli of the retina, that is, between the infrared and ultraviolet. 3. A sensory impression of one of the rainbow hues, excited by stimulation of the retinal receptors, notably the cones, by radiant energy of the appropriate wavelength. **complementary c's,** a pair of colors the sensory mechanisms for which are so linked that when they are mixed on the color wheel they cancel each other out, leaving neutral gray. Complementary colors are also associated with each other in after-image and contrast. **confusion c's,** different colors which are likely to be mistakenly matched by individuals with defective color vision (e.g., violet and blue with defect of vision for red); for this reason they are combined in the design on charts used for detecting different types of color vision defects. **contrast c.,** an illusory tinge of complementary hue or brightness induced by a vivid hue or luminance on the area surrounding it in the visual field. **incidental c.,** that seen as an after-image. **metameric c's,** colors which appear identical to the normal eye, but which are the resultants of different combinations of chromatic stimuli or wavelengths. **Munsell's c's,** a set of standardized colors, representing 40 hues in varying degrees of brightness and saturation, identifiable by a simple letter-number formula. **primary c's,** a small number of fundamental colors, usually referred to the retinal receptor cones, mixture of varying proportions of the approximate stimuli of which will yield the 150 discriminable hues of normal human vision. According to (*a*) the Newton theory, the seven rainbow hues: violet, indigo, blue, green, yellow, orange, red; (*b*) the painter and printer: blue (cyan), yellow, red (or magenta); (*c*) the Helmholtzian theory (old school): red, green, blue (or violet); (*d*) the Hering theory: four paired complementary hues, red-green and blue-yellow, plus a black-white pair. (*e*) Other theories list five to seven colors as primaries. **pseudo-isochromatic c's,** colors which appear the same to an individual with defective color vision. See *confusion c's.* **pure c.,** a color whose stimulus consists of homogeneous wavelengths, with little or no admixture of other hues. **saturation c.,** one which is high on the chroma or vividness scale, the farthest possible removed from gray.

colorectitis (ko″lo-rek-ti′tis). Inflammation of the colon and rectum.

colorectostomy (ko″lo-rek-tos′to-me) [*colon* + *rectum* + Gr. *stomoun* to provide with an opening, or mouth]. Surgical creation of a new opening between the colon and rectum.

colorimeter (kul″or-im′e-ter) [*color* + Gr. *metron* measure]. An instrument for measuring color differences; especially one for measuring the color of the blood in order to determine the proportion of hemoglobin.

colorrhaphy (ko-lor′ah-fe) [*colon* + Gr. *rhaphē* suture]. Suture of the colon.

colorrhea (ko″lo-re′ah). A discharge of mucus from the colon.

colosigmoidostomy (ko″lo-sig″moi-dos′to-me). The surgical creation of a new opening between the colon and sigmoid.

colostomy (ko-los′to-me) [*colon* + Gr. *stomoun* to provide with an opening, or mouth]. The surgical creation of a new opening of the colon on the surface of the body. Sometimes incorrectly used to refer to the opening, or stoma. **dry c.,** colostomy performed in the left half of the colon, the discharge from the stoma consisting of soft or formed fecal residue. **ileotransverse c.,** anastomosis of the ileum to the transverse colon, with exclusion of the cecum and ascending colon from the gastrointestinal tract. **wet c.** 1. Colostomy performed in the right half of the colon, the discharges from the stoma being liquid. 2. An intestinal stoma from which urine is also discharged, that is, following ureterocolostomy, as well as colostomy.

colostration (ko″los-tra′shun) [L. *colostratio*]. Illness of a newborn infant caused by the colostrum.

colostric (ko-los′trik). Pertaining to or occurring in colostrum.

colostrorrhea (ko-los″tro-re′ah) [L. *colostrum* + Gr. *rhoia* flow]. Spontaneous discharge of colostrum.

colostrous (ko-los′trus) [L. *colostrosus*]. Containing or filled with colostrum.

colostrum (ko-los′trum) [L.]. The thin, milky fluid secreted by the mammary gland a few days before or after parturition. It is characterized by containing many colostrum corpuscles and usually will coagulate on boiling due to a large amount of lactalbumin. The term, included in B N A, was omitted in N A. **c. gravida′rum,** the colostrum secreted before parturition. **c. puerpera′rum,** the colostrum secreted after parturition.

colotomy (ko-lot′o-me) [*colo-* + Gr. *tomē* a cutting]. Incision of the colon through the abdominal wall, for removal of a foreign body or excision of a polyp or other benign tumor, the wound subsequently being closed.

colotyphoid (ko″lo-ti′foid). Typhoid in which there is follicular ulceration of the colon, with extensive lesions in the small intestine.

colovaginal (ko″lo-vaj′ĕ-nal). Pertaining to or communicating with the colon and vagina, as a colovaginal fistula.

colovesical (ko″lo-ves′ĭ-kal). Pertaining to or communicating with the colon and urinary bladder, as a colovesical fistula.

colp-. See *colpo-.*

colpalgia (kol-pal′je-ah) [*colp-* + *-algia*]. Pain in the vagina.

colpatresia (kol″pah-tre′ze-ah) [*colp-* + *atresia*]. Atresia or occlusion of the vagina.

colpectasia (kol-pek-ta′se-ah) [*colp-* + Gr. *ektasis* distention + *-ia*]. Distention or dilatation of the vagina.

colpectasis (kol-pek′tah-sis). Colpectasia.

colpectomy (kol-pek′to-me) [*colp-* + Gr. *ektomē* excision]. Excision or surgical obliteration of the vagina.

colpeurynter (kol′pu-rin″ter) [*colp-* + Gr. *eurynein* to dilate]. Metreurynter.

colpeurysis (kol-pu′rĭ-sis) [*colp-* + Gr. *eurynein* to dilate]. Operative dilatation of the vagina.

colpismus (kol-piz′mus) [Gr. *kolpos* vagina]. Vaginismus.

colpitic (kol-pit′ik). Pertaining to colpitis.

colpitis (kol-pi′tis) [*colpo-* + *-itis*]. Inflammation of the vagina. See also *vaginitis.* **c. emphysemato′sa, emphysematous c.,** inflammation of the vagina characterized by the presence of small gas-filled spaces in the lamina propria mucosae. **c. granulo'sa,** vaginitis verrucosa. **c. mycot'ica,** inflammation of the vagina due to the presence of fungi.

colpo-, colp- (kol'po, kolp) [Gr. *kolpos* a fold, or bosom-like hollow]. Combining form denoting relationship to the vagina.

colpocele (kol'po-sēl) [*colpo-* + Gr. *kēlē* hernia]. 1. Hernia into the vagina. 2. Colpoptosis.

colpoceliocentesis (kol″po-se″le-o-sen-te'sis). Puncture of the abdominal cavity through the vagina.

colpoceliotomy (kol″po-se″le-ot'o-me) [*colpo-* + Gr. *koilia* belly + *tomē* a cutting]. Incision into the abdomen through the vagina.

colpocleisis (kol″po-kli'sis) [*colpo-* + Gr. *kleisis* closure]. Surgical closure of the vaginal canal.

colpocystitis (kol″po-sis-ti'tis) [*colpo-* + Gr. *kystis* bladder]. Inflammation of the vagina and of the bladder.

colpocystocele (kol″po-sis'to-sēl) [*colpo-* + Gr. *kystis* bladder + *kēlē* hernia]. Hernia of the bladder into the vagina, of which the anterior wall becomes prolapsed.

colpocystoplasty (kol″po-sis'to-plas″te) [*colpo-* + Gr. *kystis* bladder + *plassein* to form]. Plastic operation for the repair of the vesicovaginal wall.

colpocystotomy (kol″po-sis-tot'o-me) [*colpo-* + Gr. *kystis* bladder + *tomē* cutting]. Incision of the bladder through the vaginal wall.

colpocysto-ureterocystotomy (kol″po-sis″to-u-re″ter-o-sis-tot'o-me) [*colpo-* + Gr. *kystis* bladder + *ourētēr* ureter + *cystotomy*]. The operation of exposing the ureteral orifices by incising the walls of the bladder and vagina.

colpocytogram (kol″po-si'to-gram). A tabulation of the various types of cells observed in smears taken from the mucous membrane of the vagina.

colpocytology (kol″po-si-tol'o-je). The quantitative and differential study of cells exfoliated from the epithelium of the vagina.

colpodynia (kol″po-din'e-ah) [*colpo-* + Gr. *odynē* pain]. Pain in the vagina.

colpoepisiorrhaphy (kol″po-e-piz″e-or'ah-fe) [*colpo-* + Gr. *episeion* pubes + *rhaphē* stitch]. The operation of suturing the vagina and vulva.

colpohyperplasia (kol″po-hi-per-pla'ze-ah) [*colpo-* + *hyperplasia*]. Excessive growth of the mucous membrane and wall of the vagina. **c. cys'tica,** a variety characterized by the presence of cysts in the mucous membrane. **c. emphysemato'sa,** a variety characterized by the presence of small gas-filled spaces in the mucous membrane.

colpohysterectomy (kol″po-his″ter-ek'to-me) [*colpo-* + *hysterectomy*]. Surgical removal of the uterus by a vaginal operation.

colpohysteropexy (kol″po-his'ter-o-pek″se) [*colpo-* + Gr. *hystera* uterus + *pēxis* fixation]. Vaginal hysteropexy.

colpohysterorrhaphy (kol″po-his″ter-or'ah-fe) [*colpo-* + Gr. *hystera* uterus + *rhaphē* suture]. Vaginal hysteropexy.

colpohysterotomy (kol″po-his-ter-ot'o-me) [*colpo-* + *hysterotomy*]. Surgical incision of the vagina and uterus.

colpolaparotomy (kol″po-lap″ah-rot'o-me). Incision into the abdominal cavity through the vagina.

colpomicroscope (kol″po-mi'kro-skōp). An instrument especially designed for insertion in the vagina, for the microscopic examination of stained tissues of the cervix in situ.

colpomicroscopic (kol″po-mi″kro-skop'ik). Performed with the colpomicroscope, or pertaining to colpomicroscopy.

colpomicroscopy (kol″po-mi-kros'ko-pe). Examination of stained tissues of the cervix in situ with the colpomicroscope.

colpomycosis (kol″po-mi-ko'sis) [*colpo-* + Gr. *mykēs* fungus]. Colpitis mycotica.

colpomyomectomy (kol″po-mi″o-mek'to-me) [*colpo-* + *myomectomy*]. Myomectomy performed by vaginal incision.

colpoperineoplasty (kol″po-per″ĭ-ne'o-plas″te) [*colpo-* + Gr. *perinaion* perineum + *plassein* to form]. Plastic surgery of the vagina and perineum.

colpoperineorrhaphy (kol″po-per″ĭ-ne-or'ah-fe) [*colpo-* + Gr. *perinaion* perineum + *rhaphē* suture]. Suturation of the ruptured vagina and perineum.

colpopexy (kol'po-pek″se) [*colpo-* + Gr. *pēxis* fixation]. Suture of a relaxed vagina to the abdominal wall.

colpoplasty (kol'po-plas″te) [*colpo-* + Gr. *plassein* to shape]. Plastic surgery involving the vagina.

colpopoiesis (kol″po-poi-e'sis) [*colpo-* + Gr. *poiein* to make]. The formation of a vagina by plastic operation.

colpopolypus (kol″po-pol'e-pus) [*colpo-* + *polypus*]. Polypus of the vagina.

colpoptosis (kol″po-to'sis) [*colpo-* + Gr. *ptōsis* prolapse]. Prolapse or falling of the vagina.

colporectopexy (kol″po-rek'to-pek″se) [*colpo-* + *rectum* + Gr. *pēxis* fixation]. The operation of suturing a prolapsed rectum to the vaginal wall.

colporrhagia (kol″po-ra'je-ah) [*colpo-* + Gr. *rhēgnynai* to burst out]. Vaginal hemorrhage.

colporrhaphy (kol-por'ah-fe) [*colpo-* + Gr. *rhaphē* suture]. 1. The operation of suturing the vagina. 2. The operation of denuding and suturing the vaginal wall for the purpose of narrowing the vagina.

colporrhexis (kol″po-rek'sis) [*colpo-* + Gr. *rhēxis* rupture]. Laceration of the vagina.

colposcope (kol'po-skōp) [*colpo-* + Gr. *skopein* to examine]. 1. A speculum for examining the vagina. 2. Colpomicroscope.

colposcopy (kol-pos'ko-pe). Examination of the vagina and cervix by means of the colposcope.

colpospasm (kol'po-spazm) [*colpo-* + Gr. *spasmos* spasm]. Vaginal spasm.

colpostat (kol'po-stat) [*colpo-* + Gr. *statos* standing]. An appliance for retaining something, such as a radium applicator, in the vagina.

colpostenosis (kol″po-ste-no'sis) [*colpo-* + Gr. *stenōsis* stricture]. Contraction or narrowing of the vagina.

colpostenotomy (kol″po-ste-not'o-me) [*colpo-* + Gr. *stenōsis* stricture + *tomē* a cutting]. A cutting operation for stricture or atresia of the vagina.

colpotherm (kol'po-therm) [*colpo-* + Gr. *thermē* heat]. An electrical apparatus for applying heat within the vagina.

colpotomy (kol-pot'o-me) [*colpo-* + Gr. *tomē* a cutting]. Incision of the vagina.

colpo-ureterocystotomy (kol″po-u-re″ter-o-sis-tot'o-me) [*colpo-* + *ureter* + *cystotomy*]. The exposure of the orifices of the ureters by cutting through the walls of the vagina and bladder.

colpo-ureterotomy (kol″po-u-re″ter-ot'o-me). Incision of the ureter through the vagina, performed for the relief of ureteral stricture.

colpoxerosis (kol″po-ze-ro'sis) [*colpo-* + Gr. *xēros* dry]. Abnormal dryness of the vulva and vagina.

colt-ill (kōlt-il). An infectious catarrhal fever of young horses. See *strangles*.

Colubridae (kol-u'brĭ-de) [L. *coluber* serpent]. A family of snakes having rear, immovable, grooved teeth. Most of the species are harmless though the boomslang of South Africa is poisonous.

columbium (ko-lum'be-um). A former name of the element *niobium*.

columbo (ko-lum'bo). Calumba.

columella (kol″u-mel'lah), pl. *columel'lae* [L.]. 1. A little column. 2. In molds, the central axis of the spore case, around which the spores are arranged. **c. coch'leae,** modiolus. **c. for'nicis,**

columna fornicis. **c. na′si,** the fleshy distal margin of the nasal septum.

columellae (kol″u-mel′le) [L.]. Plural of *columella.*

column (kol′um) [L. *colum′na*]. An anatomical part in the form of a pillar-like structure, sometimes used specifically for the gray column of the spinal cord. See also *columna.* **c's of abdominal ring,** thickened fibers of the aponeurosis of the external oblique muscle around the external abdominal ring. **anal c's,** columnae anales. **anterior c. of fauces,** arcus palatoglossus. **anterior c. of spinal cord,** columna anterior medullae spinalis. **anterolateral c.,** funiculus lateralis medullae spinalis. **c's of Bertin,** columnae renales. **c. of Burdach of medulla oblongata,** fasciculus cuneatus medullae oblongatae. **c. of Burdach of spinal cord,** fasciculus cuneatus medullae spinalis. **cerebellar c., direct,** tractus spinocerebellaris posterior. **Clarke's c. of spinal cord,** nucleus thoracicus. **dorsal c.,** columna vertebralis. **enamel c's,** prismata adamantina. **fat c's,** columns of fatty tissue extending from the cutaneous connective tissue to the hair follicles and sweat glands. **Flechsig's c.** See *fasciculi proprii.* **fleshy c's of heart,** trabeculae carneae cordis. **c's of folds of tongue,** papillae foliatae. **fornix c., c. of fornix,** columna fornicis. **fundamental c.** See *fasciculi proprii.* **c. of Goll of medulla oblongata,** fasciculus gracilis medullae oblongatae. **c. of Goll of spinal cord,** fasciculus gracilis medullae spinalis. **c. of Gowers,** tractus spinocerebellaris anterior. **gray c's of spinal cord,** columnae griseae. **gray c. of spinal cord, anterior,** columna anterior medullae spinalis. **gray c. of spinal cord, lateral,** columna lateralis medullae spinalis. **gray c. of spinal cord, posterior,** columna posterior medullae spinalis. **c. of Koelliker,** sarcostyle. **lateral c. of spinal cord,** columna lateralis medullae spinalis. **c. of Lissauer,** tractus dorsolateralis. **c's of Morgagni,** columnae anales. **muscle c.,** sarcostyle. **c. of nose,** septum nasi. **positive c.,** a pinkish stream of light seen when a current of high potential is passed through a tube from which the air has been partly exhausted. **posterior c. of fauces,** arcus palatopharyngeus. **posterior c. of spinal cord,** columna posterior medullae spinalis. **posteromedian c. of medulla oblongata,** fasciculus gracilis medullae oblongatae. **posteromedian c. of spinal cord,** fasciculus gracilis medullae spinalis. **posterovesicular c.,** nucleus thoracicus. **Rathke's c's,** two cartilages at the anterior end of the notochord. **rectal c's,** columnae anales. **renal c's of Bertin,** columnae renales. **respiratory c.,** tractus solitarius. **c. of Rolando,** a name once given an eminence on the lateral edge of the oblongata. **c's of rugae of vagina,** columnae rugarum vaginae. **c. of Sertoli,** an elongated sustentacular cell in the parietal layer of the seminiferous tubules, holding together the spermatogenic cells. **spinal c.,** columna vertebralis. **c. of Spitzka-Lissauer,** a name given a group of nerve fibers of the cord in front of and behind the posterior columns. **Stilling's c.,** nucleus thoracicus. **Türck's c.,** tractus corticospinalis [pyramidalis] anterior. **c's of vagina,** columnae rugarum vaginae. **vertebral c.,** the columnar assemblage of the vertebrae from the cranium through the coccyx. Called also *columna vertebralis* [N A] and *backbone.* **vesicular c.,** nucleus thoracicus.

columna (ko-lum′nah), pl. *colum′nae* [L.]. A pillar-like structure; in anatomical nomenclature, used to designate a pillar-like structure or part. **colum′nae adipo′sae,** fat columns. **colum′nae ana′les** [N A], **colum′nae a′ni,** vertical ridges or folds of mucous membrane at the upper half of the anal canal. Called also *columnae rectales* [*Morgagnii*] [B N A], and *anal columns.* **c. ante′rior medul′lae spina′lis** [N A, B N A], the ventral portion of the gray substance of the spinal cord. In transverse section it is seen as a horn. Called also *anterior column of spinal cord.* **colum′nae berti′ni,** columnae renales. **colum′nae car′neae cor′dis,** trabeculae carneae cordis. **c. for′nicis** [N A, B N A], either of the two columnar masses of fibers diverging from the anterior end of the body of the fornix to descend into the diencephalon. Called also *fornix column* and *anterior pillar of fornix.* **colum′nae gris′eae** [N A, B N A], the longitudinally oriented parts of the spinal cord in which the nerve cell bodies are found, comprising the gray substance of the spinal cord. Called also *gray columns of spinal cord.* **c. latera′lis medul′lae spina′lis** [N A, B N A], the lateral portion of the gray matter of the spinal cord, in transverse section seen as a horn. It is present only in the thoracic and upper lumbar regions. Called also *lateral column of spinal cord.* **c. na′si,** septum nasi. **c. poste′rior medul′lae spina′lis** [N A, B N A], the dorsal portion of the gray substance of the spinal cord, in transverse section seen as a horn. Called also *posterior column of spinal cord.* **colum′nae recta′les [Morgagnii]** [B N A], columnae anales. **colum′nae rena′les** [N A], inward extensions of the cortical structure of the kidney, between the renal pyramids. Called also *columnae renales* [*Bertini*] [B N A], and *renal columns.* **colum′nae rena′les [Berti′ni]** [B N A], columnae renales. **c. ruga′rum ante′rior vagi′nae** [N A, B N A], a well-marked longitudinal ridge on the anterior wall of the vagina. **c. ruga′rum poste′rior vagi′nae** [N A, B N A], a well-marked longitudinal ridge on the posterior wall of the vagina. **colum′nae ruga′rum vagi′nae** [N A, B N A], well-marked longitudinal ridges on either the anterior (c. rugarum anterior vaginae) or posterior (c. rugarum posterior vaginae) wall of the vagina. Called also *columns of rugae of vagina.* **c. vertebra′lis** [N A, B N A], the columnar assemblage of the vertebrae from the cranium through the coccyx. Called also *vertebral column* and *backbone.*

columnae (ko-lum′ne) [L.]. Plural of *columna.*

columnella (kol″um-nel′ah) [L.]. Columella.

columning (kol′um-ing). Columnization.

columnization (kol″um-nĭ-za′shun). The supporting of the prolapsed uterus with tampons.

coly-mycin (kol′e-mi″sin). Trade mark for preparations of colistimethate.

colyone (ko′le-ōn) [Gr. *kōlyein* to hinder]. A substance produced in an organ which, being carried to other organs by the blood stream, produces in such organs a diminution or inhibition of function. Cf. *hormone.*

colyonic (ko″le-on′ik). Having the inhibitory effect of a colyone.

colypeptic (ko″le-pep′tik). Kolypeptic.

colyphrenia (ko″le-fre′ne-ah). Kolyphrenia.

colyseptic (ko″le-sep′tik). Kolyseptic.

colytic (ko-lit′ik) [Gr. *kōlyein* to hinder]. Inhibitory.

coma (ko′mah) [L.; Gr. *kōma*]. 1. A state of unconsciousness from which the patient cannot be aroused, even by powerful stimulation. 2. The optical aberration produced when an image is received upon a screen which is not exactly at right angles to the line of propagation of the incident light. **agrypnodal c.,** c. vigil. **alcoholic c.,** stupor following an alcoholic debauch. **apoplectic c.,** the stupor which accompanies apoplexy. **diabetic c.,** the coma of severe diabetic acidosis. **hepatic c., c. hepat′icum,** coma secondary to disease of the liver. **c. hypochlorae′micum,** coma occurring in disorders associated with sodium chloride loss. **Kussmaul's c.,** the coma and air hunger of diabetic acetonuria. **c. somnolen′tium,** cataphora. **uremic c.,** lethargic state due to uremia. **c. vigil,** stupor with delirium, wakefulness, and semiconsciousness.

comatose (ko′mah-tōs). Pertaining to or affected with coma.

combing (kōm′ing). Hersage.

Combretum (kom-bre′tum). A genus of tropical plants. **C. pilo′sum,** a shrub from the plains district of Cachar: a decoction of the leaves is used as an anthelmintic. **C. sundi′acum,** the jungle plant, a shrub of the Malay States: said to be useful as a cure for the opium habit.

combustion (kom-bust′yun) [L. *combustio*]. Rapid oxidation with emission of heat.

Comby's sign (kom′bēz) [Jules *Comby*, pediatrician in Paris, 1853–1947]. See under *sign*.

comedo (kŏ-me′do), pl. *comedo′nes*. A plug of dried sebum in an excretory duct of the skin, sometimes containing *Demodex folliculorum*.

comedocarcinoma (kŏ-me″do-kar-sĭ-no′mah). A carcinoma of the breast composed of ductlike acini which are filled with hardened secretion.

comedomastitis (kŏ-me″do-mas-ti′tis). Mammary duct ectasia.

comes (ko′mēz), pl. *com′ites* [L. "*companion*"]. An artery or vein which accompanies a nerve trunk.

cometophobia (kom″ĕ-to-fo′be-ah). Morbid fear of comets.

comfimeter (kum-fim′e-ter). An apparatus devised by Leonard Hill to measure the cooling power of the atmosphere at body temperature. It is used as a guide to keeping comfortable conditions in rooms.

comfortization (kum″fort-i-za′shun). The scientific application of physiological principles for the promotion of comfort in potentially stressful situations.

comites (kom′ĭ-tēz). Plural of *comes*.

commasculation (kom-mas″ku-la′shun). Masculine homosexuality.

commensal (kŏ-men′sal) [L. *com-* together + *mensa* table]. 1. Living on or within another organism, and deriving benefit without injuring or benefiting the other individual. 2. An organism living on or within another, but not causing injury to the host.

commensalism (kŏ-men′sal-izm″). Symbiosis in which one population (or individual) gains from the association and the other is neither harmed nor benefited.

comminuted (kom′ĭ-nūt″ed) [L. *comminutus*, from *com-* together + *minuere* to diminish]. Broken or crushed into small pieces.

comminution (kom″ĭ-nu′shun) [L. *comminutio*]. The act of breaking, or condition of being broken, into small fragments.

commissura (kom″mĭ-su′rah), pl. *commissurae* [L. "a joining together"]. A site of union of corresponding parts; a general term used to designate such a junction of corresponding anatomical structures, frequently, but not always, across the midline of the body. **c. al′ba medul′lae spina′lis** [N A], the structure formed by fibers crossing from one side of the spinal cord to the other, anterior and posterior to the central canal. Called also *white commissure of spinal cord*. **c. ante′rior al′ba medul′lae spina′lis** [B N A], the aggregate of fibers crossing from one side of the spinal cord to the other, anterior to the central canal. See *c. alba medullae spinalis* [N A]. **c. ante′rior cer′ebri** [N A, B N A], the band of fibers passing transversely through the lamina terminalis and connecting the parts of the two cerebral hemispheres, and consisting of a pars anterior and a pars posterior. Called also *anterior commissure of cerebrum*. **c. ante′rior gris′ea medul′lae spina′lis** [B N A], a network of gray matter anterior to the central canal of the spinal cord. Omitted in N A. **c. bre′vis lobo′rum posterio′rum inferio′rum cerebel′li,** tuber vermis. **c. cerebel′li,** pons. **c. for′nicis** [N A], a band of fibers connecting the hippocampi of the two sides through the body of the fornix. Called also *c. hippocampi* [B N A], and *commissure of fornix*. **c. habenula′rum** [N A, B N A], a band of fibers of the stria medullaris that pass through the habenula of each side to decussate and terminate in the habenula of the other side. Called also *commissure of habenulae*. **c. hippocam′pi** [B N A], c. fornicis. **c. infe′rior [Guddeni]** [B N A]. See *commissurae supraopticae*. **c. labio′rum ante′rior** [N A, B N A], the junction of the two labia majora anteriorly, at the lower border of the pubic symphysis. Called also *anterior commissure of labia*. **c. labio′rum o′ris** [N A, B N A], the junction of the upper and lower lips at either side of the mouth. Called also *commissure of lips of mouth*. **c. labio′rum poste′rior** [N A, B N A], the apparent junction of the labia majora posteriorly, formed by the forward projection of the tendinous center of the perineum into the pudendal cleft. Called also *posterior commissure of labia*. **c. labio′rum puden′di.** See *c. labiorum anterior* and *c. labiorum posterior*. **c. mag′na cer′ebri,** corpus callosum. **c. me′dia cer′ebri, c. mol′lis,** adhesio interthalamica. **c. oliva′rum.** See *fibrae arcuatae internae*. **c. palpebra′rum latera′lis** [N A, B N A], the lateral junction of the superior and inferior eyelids. **c. palpebra′rum media′lis** [N A, B N A], the medial junction of the superior and inferior eyelids. **c. palpebra′rum nasa′lis,** c. palpebrarum medialis. **c. palpebra′rum tempora′lis,** c. palpebrarum lateralis. **c. poste′rior cer′ebri** [N A, B N A], a large fiber bundle that crosses from one side of the cerebrum to the other just dorsal to the point where the aqueduct opens into the third ventricle. Called also *posterior commissure of cerebrum*. **c. poste′rior medul′lae spina′lis** [B N A], a transverse bar of gray substance connecting the lateral crescents of gray matter and lying posterior to the central canal of the spinal cord. Omitted in N A. **c. supe′rior [Meynerti]** [B N A]. See *commissurae supraopticae*. **commissu′rae supraop′ticae** [N A], fibers that cross the midline dorsal to the caudal border of the optic chiasm; although lying in the hypothalamus, they make no connection with the hypothalamic nuclei. Called also *supraoptic commissures*.

commissurae (kom″mĭ-su′re) [L.]. Plural of *commissura*.

commissural (kom-mis′u-ral). Pertaining to or acting as a commissure.

commissure (kom′mĭ-sūr). A site of union of corresponding parts. See *commissura*. Used also with specific reference to the sites of junction between adjacent cusps of the valves of the heart. **anterior c. of cerebrum,** commissura anterior cerebri. **anterior c. of labia,** commissura labiorum anterior. **arcuate c., arcuate c., posterior.** See *commissurae supraopticae*. **basal c.** See *commissurae supraopticae*. **Forel's c.,** a name applied to a band extending across the posterior prefrontal space and joining the body of Luys of each side. **c. of fornix,** commissura fornicis. **Gudden's c.** See *commissurae supraopticae*. **c. of habenulae,** commissura habenularum. **hippocampal c.,** commissura fornicis. **inferior c.** See *commissurae supraopticae*. **interthalamic c.,** adhesio interthalamica. **laryngeal c.,** the region of junction (anterior or posterior) of the two sides of the larynx. **lateral c. of eyelids,** commissura palpebrarum lateralis. **c. of lips of mouth,** commissura labiorum oris. **medial c. of eyelids,** commissura palpebrarum medialis. **Meynert's c.** See *commissurae supraopticae*. **middle c. of cerebrum,** adhesio interthalamica. **optic c.,** chiasma opticum. **posterior c.,** commissura posterior cerebri. **posterior c., chiasmatic.** See *commissurae supraopticae*. **posterior c. of labia,** commissura labiorum posterior. **soft c.,** adhesio interthalamica. **superior c.** See *commissurae supraopticae*. **supraoptic c's,** commissurae supraopticae. **white c. of spinal cord,** commissura alba medullae spinalis. **white c. of spinal cord, lateral,** funiculus lateralis medullae spinalis.

commissurorrhaphy (kom″ĭ-sūr-or′ah-fe) [*commissure* + Gr. *rhaphē* a seam]. Suture of connecting bands of a commissure, to lessen the size of the orifice.

commissurotomy (kom″ĭ-sūr-ot′o-me) [*commissure* + Gr. *tomē* cutting]. Surgical incision of the connecting bands of a commissure, to increase the size of the orifice, as at the angles of the mouth or the commissure of a cardiac valve.

commitment (kŏ-mit′ment). The legal consignment of a mental patient to an institution for treatment.

commotio (kŏ-mo′she-o) [L. "disturbance"]. A concussion; a violent shaking, or the shock which results from it. **c. cer′ebri,** concussion of the brain. **c. ret′inae,** impairment of vision following a blow on or near the eye. **c. spina′lis,** concussion of the spine.

communicable (kŏ-mu′nĭ-kah-b′l). Capable of being transmitted from one person to another.

communicans (kŏ-mu′ne-kanz) [L.]. Communicating.

communis (kŏ-mu′nis) [L.]. Common; belonging to several, or not rare.

commutator (kom′u-ta″tor). A device for reversing or interrupting electric currents.

Comp. Abbreviation for L. *compos′itus*, compound.

compact (kom-pakt′). Dense; having a dense structure.

comparascope (kom-par′ah-skōp″). A device attached to a microscope for the purpose of comparing two slides.

comparator (kom′pah-ra″tor). A simple colorimeter consisting of a block of wood with holes in which to place the test tubes which are to be compared, and transverse holes through which to view the colors.

compartment (com-part′ment). A small enclosure within a larger space. **muscular c.,** lacuna musculorum. **vascular c.,** lacuna vasorum.

compatibility (kom-pat″ĭ-bil′ĭ-te) [L. *compatibilis* accordant]. The quality of being compatible.

compatible (kom-pat′ĭ-b′l). Capable of harmonious coexistence; of medications, suitable for simultaneous administration without nullification or aggravation of the effects of either.

compazine (kom′pah-zēn). Trade mark for preparations of prochlorperazine.

compensation (kom″pen-sa′shun) [L. *compensatio*, from *cum* together + *pensare* to weigh]. The counterbalancing of any defect of structure or function. In psychoanalysis, the mechanism by which an approved character trait is put forward to conceal from the ego the existence of an opposite trait. In cardiology, the maintenance of an adequate blood flow without distressing symptoms, accomplished by such cardiac and circulatory adjustments as tachycardia or cardiac hypertrophy, or increase of blood volume by sodium and water retention. **broken c.,** inability of the heart to maintain sufficient velocity of the blood through the arteries, so that stagnation ensues and symptoms of stasis are produced.

compensator (kom′pen-sa″tor). An appliance for regulating compensating currents.

compensatory (kom-pen′sah-to″re). Making good a defect or loss; restoring a lost balance.

competence (kom′pĕ-tens). The ability of an organ or part to perform adequately any function required of it. **embryonic c.,** the ability of embryonic tissue to respond normally to the influence of an inductor.

complaint (kom-plānt′). A disease or disorder. **chief c.,** the symptom or group of symptoms about which the patient first consults the doctor; the presenting symptom. **summer c.,** cholera morbus.

complement (kom′ple-ment). A lytic substance in normal serum that combines with antigen-antibody complex, producing lysis when the antigen is an intact cell. Symbol C′. It is differentiated into four components: C'_1, a euglobulin containing carbohydrate that is the mid-piece of complement, precipitated by passing CO_2 through serum diluted 1:10 or by dialysis of serum against distilled water. C'_2, a mucoglobulin which is the end-piece of complement, remaining in solution after C'_1 is precipitated. C'_3, a heat-stable component of complement that is inactivated by treatment with yeast, zymin, or cobra venom. C'_4, a heat-stable component of complement that is inactivated by treatment with ammonia or hydrazine, or by shaking with chloroform or ether. It is the carbohydrate portion of C'_2 containing labile carbonyl groups. **dominant c.,** that one of several complements which exerts the specific action. **endocellular c.,** endocomplement. **insulin c.,** the unknown substance in muscle tissue which together with insulin is able to transform ordinary alpha-beta-glucose into new glucose.

complemental (kom″ple-men′tal). Complementary.

complementary (kom″ple-men′tă-re) [L. *complere* to fill]. Supplying a defect, or helping to do so; making complete; accessory.

complemented (kom′ple-ment″ed). Joined with complement so as to be active.

complementoid (kom″ple-men′toid). A complement that has lost its activity, the zymotoxic group being destroyed, without affecting its binding property with amboceptors. A complementoid, produced by heating a complement, is capable of producing an anticomplement when injected.

complementophil (kom″ple-men′to-fil) [L. *complement* + Gr. *philein* to love]. Possessing an affinity for a complement, a term applied to that element of the amboceptor to which the complement becomes attached. See *Ehrlich's side-chain theory*, under *theory*.

complex (kom′pleks) [L. *complexus* woven together]. 1. Complicated; not simple. 2. The sum or combination of various things, like or unlike, as, a *complex* of symptoms. See *syndrome*. 3. The Freudian term for a series of emotionally accentuated ideas in a repressed state (Brill). 4. That portion of an electrocardiographic tracing which represents the systole of an auricle or ventricle. **anomalous c.,** an electrocardiographic complex which varies from the normal type. **auricular c.,** the P wave of the electrocardiogram. See *electrocardiogram*. **Cain c.,** the rivalry between siblings. **calcarine c.,** the hippocampus minor. **castration c.,** an unconscious dread of castration. **Clerambaut-Kandinsky c.,** a mental state in which the patient thinks his mind is controlled by some outside influence or by another person. **Diana c.,** masculine psychic tendencies in a female. **EAHF c.,** the symptom complex of eczema, asthma, and hay fever. **Eisenmenger c.,** defects of the interventricular septum with dilatation of the pulmonary artery, hypertrophy of right ventricle, and dextrolocation of the aorta. **Electra c.,** libidinous fixation of a daughter toward her father. Cf. *Oedipus c.* **father c.,** Electra c. **Friedmann's c.** See *Friedmann's syndrome*, under *syndrome*. **inferiority c.,** a combination of emotionally charged inferiority feelings which operate in the unconscious to produce timidity or, as a compensation, exaggerated aggressiveness and expression of superiority. **Jocasta c.,** libidinous fixation of a mother toward a son. **Lear c.,** libidinous fixation of a father toward his daughter. **Lutembacher's c.,** mitral stenosis with defect of the interauricular septum. **mother c.,** Oedipus c. **Oedipus c.,** libidinous fixation of a son toward his mother. **sex c.,** the correlation between the internal secretions and the sex functions. **superiority c.** See *inferiority c.* **symptom c.,** a set of symptoms which occur together, the sum of signs of any morbid state, a syndrome. **urobilin c.,** a hypothetical substance consisting of a number of urobilinogen molecules linked together, which is the form in which urobilinogen exist in the blood and tissues. **ventricular c.,** the Q, R, S, T waves, of the electrocardiogram.

See *electrocardiogram.* **zymase c.,** the enzyme system of systems which function in alcoholic fermentation.

complexion (kom-plek'shun) [L. *complexio* combination]. 1. Physical constitution or bodily habit [old]. 2. The color and appearance of the skin of the face.

complexus (kom-plek'sus) [L. "encompassing"]. Musculus semispinalis capitis.

complicated (kom'plĭ-kāt'ed) [L. *complicare* to infold]. Involved; associated with other injuries, lesions, or diseases.

complication (kom"plĭ-ka'shun) [L. *complicatio,* from *cum* together + *plicare* to fold]. 1. A disease or diseases concurrent with another disease. 2. The concurrence of two or more diseases in the same patient.

component (kom-po'nent). A constituent element or part; specifically in neurology, a series of neurons forming a functional system for conducting the afferent and efferent impulses in the somatic and splanchnic mechanisms of the body. **active c.,** the component of an alternating current which is in phase with the electromotive force. **anterior c.,** Angle's term for "a forward propelling force which is the result of meshing and pounding of the occlusal inclined planes of the teeth and the mesial inclination of the teeth." **plasma thromboplastin c.,** factor IX. See under *coagulation factors.* **somatic motor c.,** the system of neurons which conduct impulses to the somatic effectors of the body. **somatic sensory c.,** the system of neurons conducting impulses from the somatic receptors. **splanchnic motor c.,** the system of neurons conducting impulses to the splanchnic receptors. **splanchnic sensory c.,** the system of neurons conducting impulses from the splanchnic receptors.

compos mentis (kom'pos men'tis) [L.]. Of sound mind.

compound (kom-pownd) [L. *componere* to place together]. 1. Made of two or more parts or ingredients. 2. Any substance made up of two or more kinds of materials. 3. In chemistry, a substance which consists of two or more chemical elements in union. **c. A,** 11-dehydrocorticosterone. **acyclic c.,** an open-chain compound. See under *chain.* **addition c.,** a compound formed by the immediate union of two or more elements. **aliphatic c.,** an open-chain compound. See under *chain.* **APC c.,** trade mark for a preparation of acetylsalicylic acid, phenacetin, and caffeine citrate. **aromatic c.,** a closed-chain compound. See under *chain.* **c. B,** corticosterone. **benzene c's,** aromatic compounds. **benzoin tincture c.,** a preparation of benzoin, aloe, storax, and tolu balsam: used as a protective. **binary c.,** a compound whose molecule is composed of two elements or atoms. **closed-chain c.** See under *chain.* **coal-tar c.,** a closed-chain compound. See under *chain.* **condensation c.,** a compound which is formed by union of substances with the loss of one or more molecules. **cyclic c.,** a closed-chain compound. **diazo c.,** a compound containing the group $—N_2—$. **c. E,** cortisone. **endothermic c.,** one whose formation is attended with absorption of heat. **exothermic c.,** a compound which is formed from its elements with evolution of heat. **c. F,** cortisol. **fatty c.,** an open-chain compound. **heterocyclic c.,** a chemical substance which contains a ring-shaped nucleus composed of dissimilar elements. **inorganic c.,** a compound which contains no carbon. **isocyclic c.,** a chemical substance which contains a ring-shaped nucleus composed of the same elements throughout. **isopropyl alcohol rubbing c.,** a solution containing 70 per cent isopropyl alcohol in water. Use: rubefacient. **Kendall's c. E,** cortisone. **Kendall's c. F,** cortisol. **nonpolar c.,** a compound that ionizes in solution. **open-chain c.** See under *chain.* **paraffin c.,** an open-chain compound. See under *chain.* **quaternary c.,** one which is composed of four elements. **quaternary ammonium c.** See *tetraethylammonium.* **ring c.** See *closed chain,* under *chain.* **saturated c.,** a compound in which the combining capacities of all the elements are satisfied. **substitution c.,** a compound formed by replacement of elements of a molecule by other the elements. **ternary c., tertiary c.,** a compound composed of three elements. **unsaturated c.,** a compound in which the combining capacities of all the elements are not satisfied. See *unsaturated,* 2nd def. **Wintersteiner's c. F,** cortisone.

compress (kom'pres) [L. *compressus*]. A pad or bolster of folded linen or other material, applied so as to make pressure upon any particular part: it is sometimes medicated. **cribriform c.,** one perforated with holes, like a sieve, for the escape of fluids from a wound. **fenestrated c.,** one pierced with a hole for the discharge of matter or to admit of inspection of a sore or wound. **graduated c.,** one made up of layers of gradually decreasing size. **Priessnitz c.,** a cold wet compress.

compression (kom-presh'un) [L. *compressio* from *comprimere* to squeeze together]. 1. The act of pressing together; an action exerted upon a body by an external force which tends to diminish its volume and augment its density. 2. The shortening or omission of certain stages during development. **c. of the brain,** a condition in which the brain is compressed by fractures, tumors, blood clots, abscesses, etc. **digital c.,** compression of a blood vessel by the fingers for the purpose of checking hemorrhage or of curing aneurysm. **instrumental c.,** compression of a blood vessel by instruments. **Leriche's c.,** scalenus anticus syndrome.

compressor (kom-pres'or) [L.]. That which compresses, such as a muscle or instrument by which a part may be compressed. **Deschamps' c.,** an instrument for the direct compression of an artery. **c. na'ris,** pars transversa musculi nasalis. **shot c.,** a sort of forceps for compressing split shot on sutures. **c. ure'thrae,** musculus sphincter urethrae. **c. vagi'nae,** the bulbospongiosus muscle in the female.

compressorium (kom"pres-o're-um), pl. *compressoria* [L.]. A device for making graduated pressure upon objects under microscopical examination.

Compsomyia (komp"so-mi'yah). A name formerly given a genus of flies. **C. macella'ria,** *Cochliomyia hominovorax.*

Compton effect (komp'ton) [Arthur Holly *Compton,* American physicist, born 1892; winner of the Nobel prize in physics for 1927]. See under *effect.*

compulsion (kom-pul'shun). An irresistible impulse to perform some act contrary to one's better judgment or will.

compulsive (kom-pul'siv). Pertaining to or characterized by compulsion.

con- [L.]. A prefix signifying with.

conalbumin (kon"al-bu'min). A glucoprotein, formed by the acidification of egg white to pH 3.9, containing 2.1 per cent of mannose and 0.7 per cent of galactose.

conamen (ko-na'men) [L., "an effort"]. Attempted suicide.

conarial (ko-na're-al). Pertaining to the conarium.

conarium (ko-na're-um) [L.; Gr. *kōnarion* a cone]. The pineal body; so called from its conical shape.

conation (ko-na'shun). In psychology, the power which impels to effort of any kind; the conscious tendency to act.

conative (kon'ah-tiv). Pertaining to the will power.

conavanine (kon-ah-van'in). A basic amino acid from soy bean meal.

concameration (kon-kam"er-a'shun). An arrangement of connecting cavities or chambers.

concanavallin (kon"ka-nav'ah-lin). A globulin derived from Jack bean, which agglutinates the red blood cells of animals.

concassation (kon″kah-sa′shun). The act of breaking up roots or woods into small pieces in order that their active principles may be more easily extracted by solvents.

concatenate (kon-kat′e-nāt) [L. *con* together + *catena* chain]. To fasten or link together, as in a chain.

concatenation (kon-kat″e-na′shun). A series of events or objects occurring together or in sequence.

Concato's disease (kon-kah′tōz) [Luigi Maria *Concato*, Italian physician, 1825–1882]. See under *disease*.

concave (kon′kāv) [L. *concavus*]. Having a rounded, somewhat depressed surface, resembling the hollowed inner surface of a segment of a sphere.

concavity (kon-kav′ĭ-te) [L. *concavitas*, from *con* together + *cavus* hollow]. A hollowed-out space on the surface of an organ or other structure; a hollow, depressed area on a curved surface, organ, or line.

concavoconcave (kon-ka″vo-kon′kāv). Concave on each of two opposite surfaces.

concavoconvex (kon-ka″vo-kon′veks). Concave on one surface and convex on the opposite one.

concentrate (kon′sen-trāt) [L. *con* together + *centrum* center]. 1. To bring to a common center; to gather together at one point. 2. To increase the strength by diminishing the bulk of, as of a liquid; to condense. 3. A drug or other preparation which has been strengthened by the evaporation of its nonactive parts. **liver c.,** a dried, unfractionated product produced from a water extract derived from mammalian liver: used as a hematopoietic. **plant protease c.,** a concentrate of bromelains, proteolytic enzymes derived from pineapple plants: used to reduce inflammation and edema, and to accelerate tissue repair. **vitamin c.,** a concentrated medicinal preparation of a vitamin or vitamins.

concentration (kon″sen-tra′shun) [L. *concentratio*]. 1. Increase in strength by evaporation. 2. The ratio of the mass or volume of a solute to the mass or volume of the solution. **hydrogen ion c.,** the degree of concentration of hydrogen ions (the acid element) in a solution, used to indicate or express the reaction of that solution. Its symbol is pH but it is often expressed in terms of the logarithm of the figure giving the concentration, which logarithm is known as the *hydrogen exponent*, pH. **ionic c.,** the number of gram atoms or gram equivalents of an ion which are contained in the unit volume of a solution. **MC c.,** the limiting living population density of microorganisms which is possible in any fluid culture medium.

concentric (kon-sen′trik) [L. *concentricus*, from *con* together + *centrum* center]. Having a common center; extending out equally in all directions from a common center.

concept (kon′sept). The image of a thing as held in the mind.

conception (kon-sep′shun) [L. *conceptio*]. 1. The fecundation of the ovum. 2. Concept.

conceptive (kon-sep′tiv). Able to conceive.

conceptus (kon-sep′tus) [L.]. The whole product of conception at any stage of development, from fertilization of the ovum to birth.

concha (kong′kah), pl. *con′chae* [L.; Gr. *konchē*]. A shell. Used in anatomical nomenclature to designate a structure or part that resembles a shell in shape. **c. of auricle, c. auric′ulae** [N A, B N A], the hollow of the auricle of the external ear, bounded anteriorly by the tragus and posteriorly by the anthelix. **bony inferior nasal c.,** c. nasalis inferior ossea. **bony middle nasal c.,** c. nasalis media ossea. **bony superior nasal c.,** c. nasalis superior ossea. **bony supreme nasal c.,** c. nasalis suprema ossea. **c. bullosa,** a cystic distention of the middle nasal concha, sometimes seen in chronic rhinitis. **c. of cranium,** calvaria. **ethmoidal c., inferior,** c. nasalis media ossea. **ethmoidal c., superior,** c. nasalis superior ossea. **ethmoidal c., supreme,** c. nasalis suprema ossea. **c. of eye,** orbita. **c. nasa′lis infe′rior** [N A, B N A], the bony inferior nasal concha and its covering mucous membrane. Called also *inferior nasal c.* **c. nasa′lis infe′rior os′sea** [N A, B N A], a thin bony plate with curved margins, articulating with the ethmoid, maxilla, and lacrimal and palatine bones, and forming the lower part of the lateral wall of the nasal cavity. Called also *bony inferior nasal concha*, or *inferior turbinate bone*. **c. nasa′lis me′dia** [N A, B N A], the bony middle nasal concha and its covering mucous membrane. Called also *middle nasal c.* **c. nasa′lis me′dia os′sea** [N A, B N A], the lower of two bony plates projecting from the inner wall of the ethmoid labyrinth and separating the superior from the middle meatus of the nose. Called also *bony middle nasal c., inferior ethmoidal c.*, and *inferior turbinate bone*. **c. nasa′lis supe′rior** [N A, B N A], the bony superior nasal concha and its covering mucous membrane. Called also *superior nasal c.* **c. nasa′lis supe′rior os′sea** [N A, B N A], the upper of two bony plates projecting from the inner wall of the ethmoid labyrinth and forming the upper boundary of the superior meatus of the nose. Called also *bony superior nasal c., superior ethmoidal c.*, and *superior turbinate bone*. **c. nasa′lis supre′ma os′sea** [N A, B N A], a thin bony plate occasionally found projecting from the inner wall of the ethmoid labyrinth, above the bony superior nasal concha. Called also *bony supreme nasal c.*, and *highest turbinate bone*. **c. nasa′lis supre′ma [Santori′ni].** B N A term omitted in N A. See *c. nasalis suprema ossea*. **nasoturbinal c.,** agger nasi. **sphenoidal c.** 1. Concha sphenoidalis. 2. Ala minor ossis sphenoidalis. **c. sphenoida′lis** [N A], a thin curved plate of bone at the anterior and lower part of the body of the sphenoid bone, on either side, forming part of the roof of the nasal cavity. Called also *sphenoturbinal bone*.

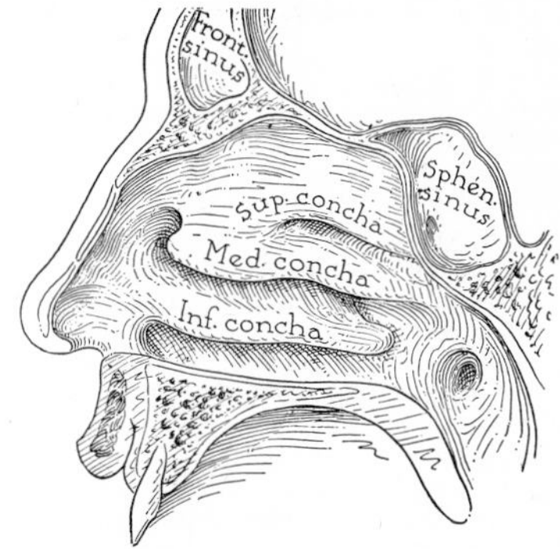

Nasal conchae (Anson).

conchae (kong′ke) [L.]. Plural of *concha*.

conchiform (kong′kĭ-form) [L. *concha* shell + *forma* shape]. Shaped like one half of a bivalve shell.

conchiolin (kong-ki′o-lin) [Gr. *konchē* shell]. A substance, isomeric with ossein, from the shells of certain mollusks.

conchiolinosteomyelitis (kong-ki″o-lin-os″te-o-mi″ĕ-li′tis). A form of osteomyelitis occurring in pearl workers.

conchitis (kong-ki′tis). An inflammation of the concha.

conchoidal (kong-koi′dal). Like a shell.

conchoscope (kong′ko-skōp) [Gr. *konchē* shell + Gr. *skopein* to examine]. A speculum for examining the walls of the nasal cavity.

conchotome (kong′ko-tōm) [Gr. *konchē* shell + *tomē* a cutting]. An instrument for the surgical removal of the nasal conchae.

conchotomy (kong-kot′o-me). Incision of a nasal concha.

Concis. Abbreviation for L. *conci'sus,* cut.

conclination (kon"klĭ-na'shun) [L. *con* together + *clinatus* leaning]. Inward rotation of the upper pole of the vertical meridian of each eye. Cf. *disclination.*

concoction (kon-kok'shun) [L. *concoctio*]. 1. A mixture of medicinal substances usually prepared by the aid of heat. 2. The digestive process.

concomitant (kon-kom'ĭ-tant) [L. *concomitans,* from *cum* together + *comes* companion]. Accompanying; accessory; joined with another.

conconscious (kon-kon'shus). Prince's term used to denote associated mental processes of which the subject is not aware.

concrement (kon'kre-ment) [L. *concrementum*]. A concretion, especially a calcified tubercle or similar mass.

concrescence (kon-kres'ens) [L. *con* together + *crescere* to grow]. A growing together; a union of parts originally separate. In embryology, the flowing together and piling up of cells. In dentistry, the union of the roots of two approximating teeth by a deposit of cementum.

concrete (kon-krēt') [L. *concretus*]. 1. Solid; tangible. 2. A mass of coalesced particles, solidified or hardened after having been more or less fluid.

concretio (kon-kre'she-o) [L.]. Concretion. **c. cor'dis,** a form of adherent pericardium in which the pericardial cavity is obliterated.

concretion (kon-kre'shun) [L. *concretio,* from *cum* together + *crescere* to grow]. 1. A calculus or inorganic mass in a natural cavity or in the tissues of an organism. 2. Abnormal union of adjacent parts. 3. A process of becoming harder or more solid. **alvine c.,** a bezoar, or calculus, in the stomach or intestine. **calculous c.,** arthritic calculus. **cutaneous c.,** a concretion in the subcutaneous tissue. **preputial c.,** a concretion formed beneath a tight foreskin through deposit of urinary salts on the accumulated smegma. **prostatic c's,** rounded and often lamellated masses of amyloid material present in many prostatic alveoli. **tophic c.,** tophus.

concretism (kon-krēt'izm). Thinking and behaving at simple and concrete (as contrasted with abstract) levels which are related to sensation.

concussion (kon-kush'un) [L. *concussio*]. A violent jar or shock, or the condition which results from such an injury. **abdominal c., hydraulic,** abdominal injury produced in persons in the water by violent underwater explosions. **air c.** See under *blast,* 3rd def. **c. of the brain,** vertigo, loss of consciousness, nausea, weak pulse, and slow respiration as the result of brain injury caused by violent blows to the head. **c. of the labyrinth,** deafness with tinnitus, resulting from a blow on or explosion near the ear. **pulmonary c.,** damage to the lungs by the explosion of a high power bomb. **c. of the retina,** commotio retinae. **c. of the spine,** muscular weakness and atrophy, pains in limbs and back, anesthesia, and mental and physical deterioration, as a result of injury to the spinal cord caused by blows or shocks to the vertebral column.

concussor (kon-kus'or) [L.]. An instrument for applying gentle strokes in massage and vibratory therapeutics.

condensation (kon"den-sa'shun) [L. *condensatio,* from *con* together + *densare* to make thick]. 1. The act of rendering, or process of becoming, more compact; in dentistry, the packing of filling materials into tooth cavities. 2. A Freudian term for a fusion of events, thoughts or concepts to produce a new and simpler concept.

condenser (kon-den'ser) [L. *condensare* to make thick, press close together]. 1. A vessel or apparatus for condensing gases or vapors. 2. A device on a microscope used to supply illumination of the degree necessary for the specimen under study to be easily visible, and under the conditions necessary for the full resolving power of the instrument to be realized. 3. An apparatus by which charges of electricity can be accumulated, consisting of two conducting surfaces separated by a nonconductor. 4. In dentistry, an instrument used to pack a plastic filling material into the prepared cavity of a tooth. **Abbe's c.,** as originally designed, a two-lens condenser combination placed below the stage of a microscope. **cardioid c.,** a special type of condenser for illuminating a specimen in darkfield microscopy. **darkfield c.,** one with a central stop, permitting production of a hollow cone of light having its apex in the plane of the specimen. **paraboloid c.,** a special type of condenser for illuminating a specimen in darkfield microscopy.

condom (kon'dum) [L. *condus* a receptacle; according to some authorities a corruption of *Condon,* the inventor]. A sheath or cover for the penis, worn during coitus to prevent impregnation or infection.

conductance (kon-duk'tans). Capacity for conducting or ability to convey. The unit of electrical conductance is the mho.

conduction (kon-duk'shun) [L. *conductio*]. The transfer of sound waves, heat, nerve influences, or electricity. **aerial c.,** the passing of sound waves to the ear through the air. **aerotympanal c.,** the conduction of sound to the sensorium through the air and tympanum. **antidromic c.,** the conduction of a nerve impulse in a direction contrary to the normal direction. **avalanche c.,** the conduction of nerve currents which takes place when the terminals of one neuron come in contact with the bodies of several neurons. **bone c.,** the conduction of sound to the sensorium through the bones of the skull. **cranial c.,** bone conduction. **delayed c.,** a mild degree of heart block in the main bundle of His producing an increase above the normal 0.2 second in the time interval between the auricular and ventricular contractions. **osteotympanic c.,** bone c. **synaptic c.,** the conduction of a nerve impulse across a synapse. **tissue c.,** bone conduction.

conductivity (kon"duk-tiv'ĭ-te). The capacity of a body to conduct a current. When expressed in figures conductivity is the reciprocal of resistance. Gold, silver, and copper are good conductors.

conductor (kon-duk'tor) [L.]. 1. A substance or part that possesses conductivity; a substance which transmits electricity. 2. A grooved director for surgeons' use. 3. A healthy transmitter of a hereditary condition, as the daughter of a hemophiliac.

conduplicato (kon-du"plĭ-kah'to) [L. *conduplicare* to double up]. Doubled up. **c. cor'pore,** a doubled-up attitude of a fetus in transverse presentation.

condurangin (kon"du-rang'gin). Either of two poisonous glycosides from condurango.

Condy's fluid (kon'dēz) [Henry Bollmann *Condy,* English physician of the 19th century]. See under *fluid.*

condylar (kon'dĭ-lar). Pertaining to a condyle.

condylarthrosis (kon"dil-ar-thro'sis) [*condyle* + Gr. *arthrōsis* joint]. Articulatio ellipsoidea.

condyle (kon'dīl) [L. *condylus;* Gr. *kondylos* knuckle]. A rounded projection on a bone. See *condylus.* **extensor c. of humerus,** epicondylus lateralis humeri. **external c. of femur,** condylus lateralis femoris. **external c. of humerus,** epicondylus lateralis humeri. **external c. of tibia,** condylus lateralis tibiae. **fibular c. of femur,** condylus lateralis femoris. **flexor c. of humerus,** epicondylus medialis humeri. **c. of humerus,** condylus humeri. **internal c. of femur,** condylus medialis femoris. **internal c. of humerus,** epicondylus medialis humeri. **internal c. of tibia,** condylus medialis tibiae. **lateral c. of femur,** condylus lateralis femoris. **lateral c. of humerus,** epicondylus lateralis humeri. **lateral c. of tibia,** condylus lateralis tibiae. **c. of mandible,** processus condylaris mandibulae. **medial c. of femur,** condylus medialis femoris. **medial c. of humerus,** epicondylus medialis humeri. **medial c. of tibia,** condylus medialis tibiae. **c. of metacarpal bone,** caput ossis metacarpalis. **occipital c.,** condylus occipitalis. **radial c. of humerus,** epicondylus lateralis humeri. **c. of scapula,** angulus lateralis scapulae. **tibial c. of femur,** condylus medialis femoris. **ulnar c. of humerus,** epicondylus medialis humeri.

condylectomy (kon″dil-ek′to-me) [*condyle* + Gr. *ektomē* excision]. Excision of a condyle.

condylicus (kon-dil′ĭ-kus). Pertaining to a condyle; condylar.

condylion (kon-dil′ĭ-on) [Gr. *kondylion* knob]. The most lateral point on the surface of the caput mandibulae.

condyloid (kon′dĭ-loid) [*condyle* + Gr. *eidos* form]. Resembling a condyle or knuckle.

condyloma (kon″dĭ-lo′mah), pl. *condylomas* or *condylo′mata* [Gr. *kondylōma* wart]. 1. A wartlike excrescence near the anus or vulva; especially the flat, moist papule of secondary syphilis. 2. In veterinary medicine, a hyperplasia of the papillary layer of the skin in cloven-hoofed animals, forming in the interdigital spaces and resulting from chronic inflammation. **c. acumina′tum,** a papilloma with a central core of connective tissue in a treelike structure covered with epithelium. Caused by a filterable virus, it is infectious and autoinoculable. **flat c.,** c. latum. **c. la′tum,** a broad and flat syphilitic condyloma, often with a yellowish discharge, occurring about the genitals and the anus. **pointed c.,** c. acuminatum. **c. subcuta′neum,** molluscum epitheliale.

condylomatoid (kon″dĭ-lo′mah-toid). Resembling a condyloma.

condylomatosis (kon″dĭ-lo″mah-to′sis). The presence of numerous condylomas.

condylomatous (kon″dĭ-lo′mah-tus). Of the nature of a condyloma.

condylotomy (kon″dĭ-lot′o-me) [Gr. *kondylos* condyle + *temnein* to cut]. Surgical incision or division of a condyle or of condyles.

condylus (kon′dĭ-lus), pl. *con′dyli* [L.; Gr. *kondylos* knuckle]. [N A, B N A] A rounded projection on a bone, usually for articulation with another. Called also *condyle.* **c. hu′meri** [N A], the distal end of the humerus, including the various fossae as well as the trochlea and capitulum. Called also *condyle of humerus.* **c. latera′lis fem′oris** [N A, B N A], the lateral of the two surfaces at the distal end of the femur that articulate with the superior surfaces of the head of the tibia. Called also *lateral condyle of femur.* **c. latera′lis hu′meri,** epicondylus lateralis humeri. **c. latera′lis tib′iae** [N A, B N A], the lateral articular eminence on the proximal end of the tibia. Called also *lateral condyle of tibia.* **c. media′lis fem′oris** [N A, B N A], the medial of the two surfaces at the distal end of the femur that articulate with the superior surfaces of the head of the tibia. Called also *medial condyle of femur.* **c. media′lis hu′meri,** epicondylus medialis humeri. **c. media′lis tib′iae** [N A, B N A], the medial articular eminence on the proximal end of the tibia. Called also *medial condyle of tibia.* **c. occipita′lis** [N A, B N A], one of two oval processes on the lateral portions of the occipital bone, on either side of the foramen magnum, for articulation with the atlas. Called also *occipital condyle.* **c. tibia′lis fem′oris,** c. medialis femoris.

cone (kōn) [Gr. *kōnos;* L. *conus*]. A solid figure or body with a circular base tapering to a point: specifically one of the conelike bodies of the retina. See *retinal* c's. **adjusting c's,** a pair of hollow cones used in measuring the distance between the axes of the eyes when they are parallel. **antipodal c.,** the cone of rays opposite the spindle fibers of the amphiaster. **arterial c.,** conus arteriosus. **attraction c.,** fertilization c. **bifurcation c.,** the cone-shaped structure at the bifurcation of a dendrite. **cerebellar pressure c.,** a deformity of the brain caused by increased intracranial pressure which forces the cerebellum downward into the spinal canal. **ectoplacental c.,** the thickened trophoblast of the blastocyst in rodents which becomes the fetal portion of the placenta. **elastic c. of larynx,** conus elasticus laryngis. **ether c.,** an apparatus to be placed over the face for the administration of ether by inhalation. **fertilization c.,** a bulging of the cytoplasm in the ovum at the site of contact of a spermatozoon, which gradually engulfs the spermatozoon and then retracts, carrying the spermatozoon inward. **growth c.,** a bulbous enlargement of the growing tip of a nerve axon. **Haller's c's,** lobuli epididymidis. **implantation c.,** the cone-shaped insertion of a neuraxon in its neuron. **keratosic c's,** horny elevations on the hands and feet in gonorrheal rheumatism. **c. of light,** the triangular reflection of light seen on the membrana tympani. Called also *Politzer's c.* **medullary c.,** conus medullaris. **ocular c.,** a cone of light in the eye, the base being on the cornea, the apex on the retina. **Politzer's c.,** c. of light. **primitive c.,** the conelike arrangement of the collecting tubules in the kidney. **retinal c's,** the specialized outer ends of the visual cells; these with the rods form the second of the ten layers of the retina. **sarcoplasmic c.,** the conical mass of sarcoplasm at each end of the nucleus of a smooth or cardiac muscle fiber. **terminal c. of spinal cord,** conus medullaris. **theca interna c.,** a wedgelike structure on the theca interna with its point toward the ovarian surface, found only in growing follicles. **twin c's,** cone cells of the retina in which two cells are blended. **visual c.** 1. Ocular cone. 2. Retinal cone.

cone-nose (kōn′nōs). See *Reduviidae.*

confabulation (kon″fab-u-la′shun). A symptom of certain forms of mental disorder consisting in making ready answers and reciting experiences without regard to truth.

confectio (kon-fek′she-o) [L.]. Confection.

confection (kon-fek′shun) [L. *confectio*]. A medicated conserve, sweetmeat, or electuary. **Damocrates' c.,** a confection of some thirty ingredients, the chief of which were agaric, frankincense, galbanum, cinnamon, garlic, gentian, ginger, opium, etc.

confertus (kon-fer′tus) [L.]. Close together; confluent.

configuration (kon-fig″u-ra′shun). The general form of a body. In chemistry, the arrangement in space of the atoms of a molecule. In gestalt psychology an organized whole with interdependent parts so that the whole is more than the sum of its parts.

confinement (kon-fīn′ment). Restraint within a specific area; used especially to designate the termination of pregnancy with delivery of the infant.

conflict (kon′flikt). A painful state of consciousness due to clash between opposing trends found to a certain extent in every person.

confluence (kon′floo-ens) [L. *confluens* running together]. The meeting of streams; in embryology the flowing of cells, a component process of gastrulation. **c. of sinuses,** confluens sinuum.

confluens (kon′floo-ens) [L.]. A place of running together; the meeting of streams. **c. sin′uum** [N A, B N A], the dilated point of confluence of the superior sagittal, straight, occipital, and two transverse sinuses of the dura mater, lodged in a depression at one side of the internal occipital protuberance. Called also *confluence of sinuses* and *torcular herophili.*

confluent (kon′floo-ent) [L. *confluens* running together]. Becoming merged; not discrete.

confocal (kon-fo′kal). Having the same focus.

confrication (kon″frĭ-ka′shun) [L. *confricatio*]. The rubbing of a drug to the condition of a powder.

confrontation (kon″frun-ta′shun) [L. *con* together + *frons* face]. The bringing of two patients together for diagnostic purposes.

confusion (kon-fu′zhun). A mental state marked by the mingling of ideas with consequent disturbance of comprehension and understanding and leading to bewilderment.

confusional (kon-fu′zhun-al). Pertaining to, characterized by, or resulting in confusion.

cong. Abbreviation for L. *con′gius*, gallon.

congelation (kon″jĕ-la′shun) [L. *congelatio*]. Frost-bite or freezing.

congener (kon′jĕ-ner). A congenerous muscle.

congenerous (kon-jen′er-us) [L. *con* together + *genus* race]. Having a common action or function; applied mainly to certain muscles.

congenital (kon-jen′ĭ-tal) [L. *congenitus* born together]. Existing at, and usually before, birth; referring to conditions that are present at birth, regardless of their causation.

congested (kon-jest′ed). Overloaded, as with blood; in a state of congestion.

congestin (kon-jes′tin). A toxic substance derived from the tentacles of sea anemones which, when injected into dogs, causes intense congestion of the splanchnic vessels, and hemorrhage. Originally called *actinocongestin*.

congestion (kon-jest′yun) [L. *congestio*, from *congerere* to heap together]. Excessive or abnormal accumulation of blood in a part. **active c.,** accumulation of blood in a part on account of the dilatation of the lumen of its blood vessels. **functional c.,** increased flow of blood to an organ during the performance of its function. **hypostatic c.,** congestion of the lowest part of an organ by reason of the action of gravity when the circulation is much enfeebled. **neuroparalytic c.,** that which results from paralysis of the constrictor fibers of the vasomotor nerves. **neurotonic c.,** that which is due to irritation of the vasodilator nerves. **passive c.,** the congestion of a part due to the obstruction to the escape of blood from the part. **physiologic c.,** the congestion that occurs during functional activity. **pleuropulmonary c.,** Woillez' disease. **venous c.,** passive c.

congestive (kon-jes′tiv). Pertaining to, characterized by, or resulting in congestion.

congius (kon′je-us) [L.]. A gallon: abbreviated *cong.*

conglobate (kon′glo-bāt) [L. *conglobatus*]. Forming a rounded mass or clump: used of certain glands.

conglobation (kon″glo-ba′shun). The act of forming, or the state of being formed, into a rounded mass.

conglomerate (kon-glom′er-āt) [L. *con* together + *glomerare* to heap]. Heaped together.

conglutin (kon-gloo′tin). A protein from almonds and from seeds of various leguminous plants.

conglutinant (kon-gloo′tĭ-nant) [L. *conglutinare* to glue together]. Promoting union, as of the lips of a wound.

conglutinatio (kon-gloo″tĭ-na′she-o) [L.]. Conglutination. **c. orific′ii exter′ni,** a condition in labor in which the circular fibers around the cervical os will not relax, and the cervix remains closed.

conglutination (kon-gloo″tĭ-na′shun). 1. Agglutination of erythrocytes that is dependent upon complement as well as antibodies. See *conglutinin*. 2. The abnormal adherence of parts to each other.

conglutinin (kon-gloo′tĭ-nin). A factor present in fresh bovine and certain other sera that agglutinates erythrocytes in the presence of complement. It has been used as the indicator system in the conglutinating complement absorption test (CCAT) in the serodiagnosis of glanders, Q fever, and infection with viruses of the psittacosis-lymphogranuloma group.

congressus (kon-gres′us) [L. "a coming together"]. Coitus.

$CO(NH_2)_2$. Urea.

coni (ko′ni) [L.]. Plural of *conus*.

coniasis (ko-ni′ah-sis) [Gr. *konis* dust]. Dust in the gallbladder or bile ducts, in contradistinction to calculus (Merle).

conic (kon′ik). Conical.

conical (kon′e-kal). Cone-shaped.

conidia (ko-nid′e-ah). Plural of *conidium*.

conidial (ko-nid′e-al). Pertaining to, or of the nature of, conidia; bearing conidia.

conidiophore (ko-nid′e-o-fōr) [L. *conidium* + Gr. *phoros* bearing]. The branch of the mycelium of a fungus which bears conidia.

Conidiosporales (ko-nid″e-o-spo-ra′lēz). An order of fungi.

conidiospore (ko-nid′e-o-spōr) [Gr. *konidion* a particle of dust + *spore*]. Conidium.

conidium (ko-nid′e-um), pl. *conid′ia*. An asexual spore formed by splitting off from the summit of a conidiophore. See *spore*.

coniferase (ko-nif′er-ās). An enzyme which catalyzes the hydrolysis of coniferin.

coniism (ko′ne-izm). Poisoning by conium.

coniofibrosis (ko″ne-o-fi-bro′sis) [Gr. *konis* dust + *fibrosis*]. A form of pneumoconiosis marked by an exuberant growth of connective tissue caused by a specific irritant. It includes asbestosis, silicosis, and silicotuberculosis.

coniology (ko-ne-ol′o-je) [Gr. *konis* dust + *-logy*]. The scientific study of dust, its influence, and its effects.

coniolymphstasis (ko″ne-o-limf′stah-sis). A form of pneumoconiosis caused by dusts that act by blocking the lymphatics, such as anthracosis and siderosis.

coniometer (ko″ne-om′e-ter). Konometer.

coniophage (ko′ne-o-fāj″) [Gr. *konis* dust + *phagein* to eat]. A macrophage cell which ingests dust particles.

coniosis (ko″ne-o′sis) [Gr. *konis* dust]. A disease state caused by the inhalation of dust. See *pneumoconiosis*.

coniotomy (ko″ne-ot′o-me). Incision through the conus elasticus laryngis in the creation of an artificial opening into the trachea (tracheostomy).

coniotoxicosis (ko″ne-o-tok″sĭ-ko′sis). A form of pneumoconiosis in which the irritants affect the tissues directly.

conization (kon″ĭ-za′shun). The removal of a cone of tissue, as in partial excision of the cervix uteri.

conjugal (kon′ju-gal) [L. *con* together + *jugum* a yoke]. Pertaining to marriage; pertaining to husband and wife.

conjugata (kon″ju-ga′tah). [N A, B N A] The anteroposterior diameter of the superior aperture of the minor pelvis. See also *true conjugate diameter*. **c. anatom′ica,** true conjugate diameter. **c. diagona′lis,** diagonal conjugate diameter. **c. ve′ra,** true conjugate diameter. **c. ve′ra obstet′rica,** obstetric conjugate diameter.

conjugate (kon′ju-gāt) [L. *conjugatus* yoked together]. 1. Paired, or equally coupled; working in unison. 2. A conjugate diameter of the pelvic inlet. Used alone usually to note the true conjugate diameter. See under *diameter*. **anatomic c., diagonal c., external c., obstetric c., true c.** See under *diameter*.

conjugation (kon″ju-ga′shun) [L. *conjugatio* a blending]. The act of joining together. In biology, the union of one organism with another for the exchange of nuclear material. In chemistry, the joining together of two compounds to produce another compound, such as the combination of a toxic product with some substance in the body to form a detoxified product which is then eliminated.

conjunctiva (kon″junk-ti′vah) [L.]. The delicate membrane that lines the eyelids (*palpebral conjunctiva*) and covers the exposed surface of the eyeball (*bulbar* or *ocular conjunctiva*). Called also *tunica conjunctiva.*

conjunctival (kon″junk-ti′val). Pertaining to the conjunctiva.

conjunctiviplasty (kon-junk′tĭ-vĭ-plas″te). Conjunctivoplasty.

conjunctivitis (kon-junk″tĭ-vi′tis). Inflammation of the conjunctiva. **actinic c.,** conjunctivitis produced by invisible ultraviolet (actinic) rays, as that of Klieg lights, therapeutic lamps, or acetylene torches. **acute contagious c.,** a mucopurulent inflammation of the conjunctiva occurring in epidemic form. **allergic c., anaphylactic c.,** hay fever. **angular c.,** conjunctivitis with characteristic reddening at the canthi. **arc-flash c.,** actinic conjunctivitis from electric welding. **atropine c.,** follicular conjunctivitis from continued use of atropine. **blennorrheal c.,** gonorrheal c. **calcareous c.,** c. petrificans. **catarrhal c.,** a mild form due to cold or irritation. **croupous c.,** a variety associated with the formation of a whitish-gray membrane. **diphtheritic c.,** a purulent form due to the Klebs-Löffler bacillus; diphtheria of the conjunctiva. **diplobacillary c.,** Morax-Axenfeld's c. **eczematous c.,** phlyctenular c. **Egyptian c.** (Larrey, 1802), trachoma. **epidemic c.,** acute contagious c. **follicular c.,** a form characterized by the round or pinkish bodies in the fornix conjunctivae. **gonorrheal c.,** a severe form caused by infection with gonococci. **granular c.,** trachoma. **inclusion c.,** an inflammatory condition of the conjunctiva, caused by a filterable virus and characterized by the presence of large basophilic inclusion bodies. **larval c.,** myiasis of the conjunctiva. **c. medicamento′sa,** conjunctivitis due to medication. **membranous c.,** croupous c. **meningococcus c.,** conjunctivitis occurring as a complication of epidemic cerebrospinal meningitis. **molluscum c.,** conjunctivitis occurring as a complication of molluscum contagiosum. **Morax-Axenfeld's c.,** a form of conjunctivitis due to *Haemophilus duplex.* **c. necrot′icans infectio′sus,** an infectious conjunctivitis characterized by unilateral swelling of the parotid and submaxillary glands. **Parinaud's c.,** infectious conjunctivitis of animal origin, attributed to a leptothrix; leptothricosis of the conjunctiva. **Pascheff's c.,** c. necroticans infectiosus. **c. petrif′icans,** a variety of conjunctivitis marked by the formation of deposits of chalky concretions in the conjunctiva and attended with necrosis. **phlyctenular c.,** a variety marked by small vesicles or ulcers, each surrounded by a reddened zone. **prairie c.,** chronic conjunctivitis marked by white spots on the conjunctiva of the lids. **pseudomembranous c.,** diphtheritic c. **purulent c.,** a variety characterized by a discharge of pus. **Samoan c.,** acute infectious conjunctivitis caused by *Diplococcus samoensis.* **scrofular c.,** phlyctenular c. **shipyard c.,** epidemic keratoconjunctivitis. **spring c.,** vernal c. **squirrel plague c.,** c. tularensis. **swimming pool c.,** inclusion c. **trachomatous c.,** trachoma. **c. tularen′sis,** a severe form of conjunctivitis ascribed to *Pasteurella tularensis.* **uratic c.,** conjunctivitis marked by the deposit of crystals of uric acid or sodium urate in the conjunctiva. **vernal c.,** conjunctivitis characteristically occurring in the spring. **welder's c.,** conjunctivitis occurring in welders, caused by the glare from electric or acetylene torches. **Widmark's c.,** congestion of the inferior tarsal conjunctiva, with occasionally slight stippling of the cornea.

conjunctivoma (kon-junk″tĭ-vo′mah). A tumor of the eyelid made up of conjunctival tissue.

conjunctivoplasty (kon″junk-ti′vo-plas″te) [*conjunctiva* + Gr. *plassein* to form]. Repair of a defect of the conjunctiva by plastic operation.

Conn's syndrome (konz) [Jerome W. *Conn,* American internist, born 1907]. Primary aldosteronism.

connatal (kon-na′tal) [L. *con* along with + *natus* birth]. Occurring at the time of birth; acquired at birth.

connate (kon′nāt). Connatal.

connectivum (kon″ek-ti′vum) [L.]. Connective tissue.

connector (kŏ-nek′tor). Anything serving as a link between two separate objects or units, such as the portion of a neural arc between the receptor and the effector. In dentistry, the portion of a partial denture that unites its components. **major c.,** a plate or bar, such as a labial, lingual, or palatal bar, which unites two or more bilateral parts of a removable partial denture. **minor c.,** a connecting link between the major connector or base of a partial denture and other units of the prosthesis, such as clasps, indirect retainers, and occlusal rests.

Connell's suture (kŏn′elz) [F. Gregory *Connell,* American surgeon, born 1875]. See under *suture.*

connexus (kŏ-nek′sus) [L. *con* together + *nectere* to bind]. A connecting structure. **c. intertendin′eus** [N A], narrow bands extending obliquely between the tendons of insertion of the extensor digitorum muscles on the back of the hand. Called also *juncturae tendinum* [B N A]. **c. interthalam′icus,** adhesio interthalamica.

conoid (ko′noid) [Gr. *kōnoeidēs*]. Resembling, or shaped like a cone. **Sturm's c.,** the changing shapes of the diffusion images of a point in various forms of astigmatism. The image may be an ellipse, a circle, or a sharp line.

Conolly's system (kon′ŏ-lēz) [John *Conolly,* English alienist, 1795–1866]. The system of nonrestraint for treating the mentally and emotionally disturbed.

conomyoidin (ko″no-mi-oi′din) [Gr. *kōnos* cone + *mys* muscle + *eidos* form]. A protoplasmic material within the cones of some retinas which expands and contracts under the influence of light, causing the cones to shift.

conophthalmus (kōn″of-thal′mus) [Gr. *kōnos* cone + *ophthalmos* eye]. Staphyloma of the cornea.

Conorhinus (ko″no-ri′nus) [Gr. *kōnos* cone + *rhis* nose]. A genus name formerly applied to insects of the family Reduviidae, now placed in the genera *Panstrongylus* and *Triatoma.*

conquinine (kon-kwin′in). Quinidine.

Conradi's line (kon-rah′dez) [Andrew Christian *Conradi,* Norwegian physician, 1809–1869]. See under *line.*

Conradi-Drigalski medium. See *Drigalski-Conradi,* and under *medium.*

Cons. Abbreviation for L. *conser′va,* keep.

consanguinity (kon″san-gwin′ĭ-te) [L. *consanguinitas*]. Kinship: relationship by blood.

conscious (kon′shus) [L. *conscius* aware]. Capable of responding to sensory stimuli and having subjective experiences.

consciousness (kon′shus-nes). The state of being conscious; responsiveness of the mind to the impressions made by the senses. **collective c.,** the aggregation of the conscious processes of all the individuals in a group. **colon c.,** a condition in which the patient is aware of the colon and its activities, because of disturbance of the normal defecation reflex; embracing chronic constipation, visceroptosis, etc. **double c.,** an abnormal condition in which the patient seems to lead two lives, completely forgetting in one state the experiences of the other. **noetic c.,** consciousness in which the experiences are largely cognitive.

consensual (kon-sen′shu-al) [L. *consensus* agreement]. Excited by reflex stimulation; used especially to designate the similar reaction of both pupils to a stimulus applied to only one.

conservative (kon-ser′vah-tiv) [L. *conservare* to preserve]. Aiming at the preservation of health or at the restoration and repair of parts and function.

conserve (kon′serv) [L. *conserva*]. A confection, electuary, or medicated sweetmeat.

consilia (kon-sil′e-ah) [L., pl. of *consilium* a deliberation, consultation]. Letters published by physicians of the 13th to 17th centuries, outlining the symptomatology and treatment of diseases under their observation.

consolidant (kon-sol′ĭ-dant) [L. *consolidare* to make firm]. 1. Promoting the healing or union of parts. 2. An agent which promotes the healing or union of parts.

consolidation (kon-sol″ĭ-da′shun) [L. *consolidatio*]. Solidification, as of a lung in pneumonia.

consolute (kon′so-lūte). Perfectly miscible.

consonation (kon″so-na′shun). The presence of consonating rales.

constant (kon′stant) [L. *constans* standing together]. 1. Not failing; remaining unaltered. 2. A datum, fact, or principle that is not subject to change. **Ambard's c.** See *Ambard's formula*, under *formula*. **Avogadro's c.,** the number of particles, real or imaginary, of the type specified by the chemical formula in one gram mole of any substance having a chemical formula; assigned different values by different investigators, but often stated to be 6.02246×10^{23}. **dielectric c.,** the dielectric value of any substance compared with air, which is taken as 1. **dissociation c.,** a constant which expresses the degree of ionization of an acid. It is the product of the concentrations of both component ions, divided by the concentration of the molecules of the acid. **Faraday's c.,** the quantity of electricity which is necessary to liberate a gram atom of a univalent element in electrolysis. **Lapicque's c.,** the figure 0.37, used for converting noninductive resistance into direct current equivalents. **Planck's c.,** a constant, h, which represents the ratio of the energy of any quantum of radiation to its frequency. The value of h is 6.55×10^{-27} erg seconds. Called also *quantum constant*. **urea c.** See *Ambard's formula*, under *formula*.

constellation (kon″stĕ-la′shun). 1. A term used by Prof. Tendeloo, of Leiden, to indicate all the factors, with their mutual influences on one another, which determine any particular action or effect. 2. In psychoanalysis, a group of emotional ideas which have not become repressed.

constipated (kon′stĭ-pāt″ed). Affected with constipation.

constipation (kon″stĭ-pa′shun) [L. *constipatio* a crowding together]. Infrequent, or difficult evacuation of the feces. **atonic c.,** constipation due to intestinal atony. **gastrojejunal c.,** constipation due to reflex inhibition from some disease of the gastrointestinal tract. **proctogenous c.,** constipation due to some abnormality of the defecation reflex resulting in failure of fecal masses in the rectum to excite impulses leading to their evacuation. **spastic c.,** constipation marked by spasmodic constriction of a portion of the intestine: seen in neurasthenia and lead poisoning.

constitution (kon″stĭ-tu′shun) [L. *constitutio*]. 1. The make-up or functional habit of the body, determined by the genetic, biochemical, and physiologic endowment of the individual, and modified in great measure by environmental factors. See *type*. 2. In chemistry, the arrangement of atoms in a molecule. Cf. *configuration*. **arterial c.,** that bodily constitution in which the blood contains much fibrin and a large proportion of red corpuscles. **carbonitrogen c.,** in homeopathy, a constitution which is characterized by the slow oxidation of the blood. **hydrogenoid c.,** a temperament in which the subject cannot tolerate moisture. **ideo-obsessional c.,** a peculiar psychic constitution marked by a tendency to worrying, fretting, exaggerated doubts, and excessive introspection. **lymphatic c.,** a condition of hyperplasia of the lymphatic system. **neuropathic c.,** that quality of mind and body which predisposes to nervous disease. **psychopathic c.,** a tendency toward mental imbalance. **vasoneurotic c.,** a constitution characterized by instability of the vasomotor mechanism.

constitutional (kon″stĭ-tu′shun-al). 1. Affecting the whole constitution of the body; not local. 2. Pertaining to the constitution.

constriction (kon-strik′shun) [L. *con* together + *stringere* to draw]. 1. A constricted part or place; a stricture. 2. A morbid sensation, as of tightness. **duodenopyloric c.,** the constriction marking the junction of the stomach and duodenum. **Ranvier's c's,** Ranvier's nodes.

constrictive (kon-strik′tiv). Causing constriction or having a tendency to constriction.

constrictor (kon-strik′tor) [L.]. That which constricts, such as a muscle or an instrument by which a part may be constricted. See *Table of Musculi*. **c. isth′mi fau′cium,** musculus palatoglossus. **c. na′ris,** pars transversa musculi nasalis. **c. ure′thrae,** musculus sphincter urethrae. **c. vagi′nae,** the musculus bulbospongiosus in the female.

constructive (kon-struk′tiv). Pertaining to any process of construction; anabolic.

consult (kon-sult′) [L. *consultus*]. To confer with another physician about a case.

consultant (kon-sul′tant) [L. *consultare* to counsel]. A physician called in for advice and counsel.

consultation (kon″sul-ta′shun) [L. *consultatio*]. A deliberation of two or more physicians with respect to the diagnosis or treatment in any particular case.

consumption (kon-sump′shun) [L. *consumptio* a wasting]. A wasting away of the body, applied especially to pulmonary tuberculosis. **cell c.,** the physiologic degeneration of the blood cells. **galloping c.,** pulmonary consumption which runs an exceptionally rapid course. **luxus c.,** the metabolism of excess protein which does not form part of the tissues but remains in the body as a reserve supply.

consumptive (kon-sump′tiv). 1. Of the nature of consumption. 2. Affected with consumption. 3. A person who is affected with tuberculosis of the lungs.

Cont. Abbreviation for L. *contu′sus*, bruised.

contact (kon′takt) [L. *contactus* a touching together]. 1. A mutual touching of two bodies or persons. 2. The completing of an electrical circuit. 3. An individual who is known to have been sufficiently near to an infected individual to have been exposed to the transfer of infectious material. **balancing c.,** the contact between the upper and lower teeth (of the natural or artificial dentition) on the side opposite the working contact. **complete c.,** contact of the entire proximal surface of one tooth with the entire proximal surface of the adjacent tooth. **direct c., immediate c.,** the touching by a healthy person of a person having a communicable disease, the disease being transmitted as a result. **indirect c.,** that achieved through some intervening medium, as the propagation of a communicable disease through the air or by means of fomites. **initial c.,** the first meeting of the upper and lower teeth when the jaws are brought together. **mediate c.,** indirect c. **occlusal c.,** the contact between the upper and lower teeth when the jaws are closed. **occlusal c., deflective,** a condition in which the mandible is diverted from a normal path of closure to centric jaw relation by abnormal contact between upper and lower teeth. **occlusal c., interceptive,** a condition in which the normal movement of the mandible is stopped or deviated by an initial contact of the teeth. **proximal c., proximate c.,** touching of the proximal surfaces of two adjoining teeth. **weak c.,** contact in which the proximal surface of one tooth barely touches that of the adjacent tooth. **working c.,** the contact between the upper and lower teeth (of the natural or artificial dentition) on the side toward which the mandible has been moved.

contactant (kon-tak′tant). A substance which touches or may touch the surface of the body.

contactologist (kon″tak-tol′o-jist). An individual skilled in contactology.

contactology (kon″tak-tol′o-je). The specialized field of knowledge related to the use and prescription of contact lenses.

contagion (kon-ta′jun) [L. *contagio* contact, infection]. 1. The communication of disease from one person to another. 2. A contagious disease. 3. A contagium.

contagiosity (kon-ta″je-os′ĭ-te). The quality of being contagious.

contagious (kon-ta′jus) [L. *contagiosus*]. Capable of being transmitted from one person to another.

contagium (kon-ta′je-um), pl. *conta′gia* [L.]. Any virus or morbific matter which may transmit a disease. **c. anima′tum, c. vi′vum,** a living organism transmissible from one person to another.

contaminant (kon-tam′ĭ-nant). Something that causes contamination, such as a foreign organism developing accidentally in a pure culture.

contamination (kon-tam″ĭ-na′shun) [L. *contaminatio*, from *con* together + *tangere* to touch]. 1. The soiling or making inferior by contact or mixture. 2. The freudian term for a fusion of words.

content (kon′tent). That which is contained within a thing. **latent c.,** the hidden part of a dream or thought which can be discovered only by free association or by some other appropriate technic. **manifest c.,** the outward form of a dream as remembered by the dreamer.

contiguity (kon″tĭ-gu′ĭ-te) [L. *contiguus* in contact]. Contact or close proximity; the quality of being contiguous.

contiguous (kon-tig′u-us) [L. *contiguus*]. In contact or nearly so.

Contin. Abbreviation for L. *continue′tur*, let it be continued.

continence (kon′tĭ-nens) [L. *continentia*]. The ability to refrain from yielding to desire, as self-restraint with respect to sexual indulgence. **fecal c.,** the ability to retain the contents of the colon until conditions are proper for defecation. **urinary c.,** the ability to retain the contents of the bladder until conditions are proper for urination.

continent (kon′tĭ-nent). Able to refrain from yielding to normal impulses, as sexual desire, or the urge to defecate or urinate.

continued (kon-tin′ūd). Having no remission, intermission, or interruption.

continuity (kon″tĭ-nu′ĭ-te) [L. *continuitas*, uninterrupted succession]. The quality of being without interruption or separation.

continuous (kon-tin′u-us) [L. *continuus*]. Not interrupted; having no interruption.

contologist (kon-tol′o-jist). Contactologist.

contology (kon-tol′o-je). Contactology.

contour (kon′toor) [Fr.]. 1. The normal outline or configuration of the body or of a part. 2. To shape a solid along certain desired lines. **flange c.,** the form of the flange of a denture. **gingival c.,** the form of the base or of other material surrounding the necks of the teeth in an artificial denture. **gum c.,** gingival c.

contoured (kon′toord). 1. Having an irregularly undulating outline or surface: said of bacterial colonies. 2. Shaped along certain desired lines, as a dental or other prosthesis or plastic restoration.

contra- (kon′trah) [L. *contra* against]. A prefix signifying against, opposed.

contra-angle (kon″trah-ang′g'l). An angulation by which the working point of an instrument is which the working point of an instrument is brought close to the long axis of its shaft; it may involve two, three, or four bends, or angles, in its shank.

contra-aperture (kon″trah-ap′er-tūr) [*contra-* + L. *apertura* opening]. A second opening made in an abscess to facilitate the discharge of matter.

contraception (kon″trah-sep′shun). The prevention of conception or impregnation.

contraceptive (kon″trah-sep′tiv). 1. Diminishing the likelihood of or preventing conception. 2. An agent that diminishes the likelihood of or prevents conception.

contract (kon-tract′) [L. *contractus*, from *contrahere* to draw together]. 1. To shorten. 2. To acquire or incur.

contractile (kon-trak′til) [L. *con* together + *trahere* to draw]. Having the power or tendency to contract in response to a suitable stimulus.

contractility (kon″trak-til′ĭ-te). Capacity for becoming short in response to a suitable stimulus. **galvanic c.,** galvanocontractility. **idiomuscular c.,** a contractility peculiar to wasted or degenerated muscles. **neuromuscular c.,** normal, as distinguished from idiomuscular, contractility.

contractinogen (kon″trak-tin′o-jen). A fibrinogen fraction which accelerates the rate of erythrocyte sedimentation.

contraction (kon-trak′shun) [L. *contractus* drawn together]. A shortening; in connection with muscles contraction implies shortening and/or development of tension. 2. A morbid or pathologic shortening or shrinkage. 3. In orthodontics, unusual narrowness of the dental arch. **anodal closure c.,** contraction of the muscles at the anode when the electrical circuit is closed. **anodal opening c.,** contraction of the muscles at the anode when the electrical circuit is broken. **automatic ventricular c.,** a ventricular contraction caused by an impulse arising in the atrioventricular node. **carpopedal c.,** a kind of tetany of infants, with flexing of the fingers, toes, elbows, and knees, and a general tendency to convulsions. **cathodal closure c.,** contraction of muscles at the cathode when the electrical circuit is closed. **cathodal opening c.,** contraction of the muscles at the cathode when the electrical circuit is opened. **cicatricial c.,** the drawing together of the tissues in the healing of a wound with formation of a cicatrix. **clonic c.,** contraction of a muscle alternating with periods of relaxation. **closing c.,** contraction occurring at the point of application of the stimulus when the electrical circuit is closed. **Dupuytren's c.,** Dupuytren's contracture. **Dupuytren's c., false,** a contracted state of the palm and fingers due to injury of the palmar fascia. **escaped ventricular c.,** automatic ventricular c. **fibrillary c's,** abnormal spontaneous contractions occurring successively in different bundles of the fibers of a diseased muscle. **fixation c.,** Westphal's c. **front tap c.,** a contraction of the gastrocnemius on tapping the muscles of the leg. **galvanotonic c.,** a tonic muscular contraction produced by a continuous electrical current. **Gowers's c.,** front tap c. **hourglass c.,** contraction of an organ (as the stomach or uterus) at or near the middle. **idiomuscular c.,** a contraction produced by direct stimulation of a wasted muscle. **isometric c.,** change in the tension of a muscle without approximation of its extremities. **isotonic c.,** approximation of the extremities of a muscle without change in its tension. **myotatic c.,** contraction or irritability of a muscle brought into play by sudden passive stretching or by tapping on its tendon. **opening c.,** contraction occurring at the point of application of the stimulus when the electrical circuit is opened. **palmar c.,** Dupuytren's contracture. **paradoxical c.,** the contraction of a muscle caused by the passive approximation of its extremities. **postural c.,** that state of muscular tension and contraction which just suffices to maintain the posture of the body. **rheumatic c.,** tetany. **tetanic c.,** sustained contraction of a muscle without alternating intervals of relaxation. **tone c.,** a muscular contraction developing slowly and showing a prolonged phase of relaxation. **tonic c.,** tetanic c. **Westphal's c.,** involuntary (reflex) contraction of a muscle caused by approximating its extremities; observed in paralysis agitans and in various spinal affections.

contracture (kon-trak′tūr) [L. *contractura*]. A condition of fixed high resistance to passive stretch of a muscle, resulting from fibrosis of the tissues supporting the muscles or the joints, or from disorders of the muscle fibers. **Dupuytren's c.,** shortening, thickening, and fibrosis of the palmar fascia, producing a flexion deformity of a finger. Applied also to flexion deformity of a toe caused by involvement of the plantar fascia. **ischemic c.,** contracture and degeneration of a muscle due to interference with the circulation from pressure, as by a tight bandage, or from injury or cold. **organic c.,** one that is permanent and continuous. **postpoliomyelitic c.,** any distortion of a joint following an attack of poliomyelitis. **veratrin c.,** a peculiar type of muscular contraction produced by injecting a muscle with veratrin. **Volkmann's c.,** a contraction of the fingers and sometimes of the wrist, with loss of power, developing rapidly after a severe injury in the region of the elbow joint or improper use of a tourniquet.

contraextension (kon″trah-eks-ten′shun). Counterextension.

contrafissura (kon-trah-fis-su′rah). Contrafissure.

contrafissure (kon″trah-fish′ur). A fracture in a part opposite the site of a blow.

contraincision (kon″trah-in-sizh′un). Counteropening.

contraindicant (kon″trah-in′dĭ-kant). Rendering any particular line of treatment undesirable or improper.

contraindication (kon″trah-in″dĭ-ka′shun). Any condition, especially any condition of disease, which renders some particular line of treatment improper or undesirable.

contrainsular (kon″trah-in′su-lar). Having an inhibiting influence on insular secretion.

contralateral (kon″trah-lat′er-al) [*contra-* + L. *latus* side]. Situated on or pertaining to the opposite side.

contraparetic (kon″trah-pah-ret′ik). 1. Counteracting paresis. 2. A preparation useful in the treatment of paresis.

contrasexual (kon″trah-seks′u-al). Pertaining to or characteristic of the opposite sex.

contrastimulant (kon″trah-stim′u-lant) [*contra-* + *stimulant*]. 1. Counteracting or opposing stimulation. 2. A depressant medicine.

contrastimulism (kon″trah-stim′u-lizm). The systematic use of contrastimulant medicines or appliances.

contrastimulus (kon″trah-stim′u-lus) [*contra-* + *stimulus*]. A remedy, force, or agent which opposes stimulation.

contravolitional (kon″trah-vo-lish′un-al). Done in opposition to the will; involuntary.

contrecoup (kon-tr-koo′) [Fr. "counterblow"]. Injury resulting from a blow on another site, such as a fracture of the skull caused by a blow on the opposite side.

contrectation (kon″trek-ta′shun) [L. *contrectare* to handle]. The fondling of a person of the opposite sex.

Cont. rem. Abbreviation for L. *continue′tur reme′dium*, let the medicine be continued.

control (kon-trōl′) [Fr. *contrôle* a register]. 1. The governing or limitation of certain objects or events. 2. A standard against which experimental observations may be evaluated, as a procedure identical in all respects to the experimental procedure except for absence of the one factor that is being studied. **associative automatic c.,** nerve impulses which arise in the corpus striatum and act upon the final common pathway, and thus upon the muscles. **birth c.,** the regulation of childbearing by measures designed to prevent conception. **idiodynamic c.,** nerve impulses from the cells of the ventral gray column and the motor nuclei of the brain which maintain the muscles in their normal trophic condition. **reflex c.,** control of muscular activity by nerve impulses transmitted to the muscles by one of the reflex arcs by which reflex action is maintained. **sex c.,** the attempted determination of the sex of future offspring by artificial means. **synergic c.,** nerve impulses transmitted to the common pathway from the cerebellum for the regulation of the muscular activity of the synergic units of the body. **tonic c.,** nerve impulses transmitted to the final common pathway through the reflex arc for the maintenance of the muscle tone. **vestibulo-equilibratory c.,** nerve impulses from the semicircular canals, saccule, and utricle for the maintenance of body equilibrium. **volitional c., voluntary c.,** impulses from the motor area of the cerebral cortex which direct muscular action under the influence of the will.

contrude (kon-trood′). To crowd or push together; said of teeth.

contrusion (kon-troo′zhun). A condition in which teeth are crowded and pushed together.

contund (kon-tund′) [L. *contundere*]. To bruise.

contuse (kon-tūz′). To bruise.

contusion (kon-tu′zhun) [L. *contusio*, from *contundere* to bruise]. A bruise.

contusive (kon-tu′siv). Producing a bruise.

conular (kon′u-lar). Cone-shaped.

Conus (ko′nus). A genus of mollusks, some species of which are able to inflict severe wounds.

conus (ko′nus), pl. *co′ni* [L.; Gr. *kōnos*]. 1. A cone; used in anatomical nomenclature to designate a structure resembling a cone in shape. 2. Posterior staphyloma of the myopic eye. **c. arterio′sus** [N A, B N A], the anterosuperior portion of the right ventricle of the heart which is delimited from the rest of the ventricle by the supraventricular crest and which joins the pulmonary trunk. Called also *infundibulum*. **distraction c.,** a crescentic white area at the temporal edge of the papilla of the optic nerve sometimes seen with the ophthalmoscope in myopic eyes. **c. elas′ticus laryn′gis** [N A, B N A], the lower part of the fibroelastic membrane of the larynx. Called also *elastic cone of larynx*. **co′ni epididym′idis,** N A alternative for *lobuli epididymidis*. **c. medulla′ris** [N A, B N A], the conical extremity of the spinal cord, at the level of the upper lumbar vertebrae. **myopic c.,** posterior staphyloma of the myopic eye. **supertraction c.,** a gray or yellowish ring on the nasal side of the optic papilla sometimes seen with the ophthalmoscope, especially in myopic eyes. **c. termina′lis,** c. medullaris. **co′ni vasculo′si,** lobuli epididymidis.

convalescence (kon″vah-les′ens) [L. *convalescere* to become strong]. The stage of recovery following an attack of disease, a surgical operation, or accidental injury.

convalescent (kon″vah-les′ent). Pertaining to or characterized by convalescence. By extension, applied to a patient who is recovering from a disease, surgical operation, or accidental injury.

convection (kon-vek′shun) [L. *convectio*, from *convehere* to convey]. Transmission of heat in liquids or gases by a circulation carried on by the heated particles.

convergence (kon-ver′jens). 1. Inclination toward a common point. In embryology, the movement of cells from the periphery toward the midline during gastrulation. In physiology the coordinated movement of the two eyes toward fixation of the same near point. 2. The point of meeting of convergent lines. **negative c.,** outward deviation of the visual axes. **positive c.,** inward deviation of the visual axes.

convergent (kon-ver′jent) [L. *con* together + *vergere* to incline]. Meeting at or tending toward a common point.

convergiometer (kon-ver″je-om′e-ter). An instrument for measuring latent strabismus.

conversion (kon-ver′zhun) [L. *con* with + *versio* turning]. 1. A freudian term for the process by which emotions become transformed into physical (motor or sensory) manifestations. 2. Manipulative correction of any malposition of a fetal part during the course of labor. **Mantoux c.,** a term suggested to designate the change from a tuberculin-negative to a tuberculin-positive state.

convex (kon′veks) [L. *convexus*]. Having a rounded, somewhat elevated surface, resembling a segment of the external surface of a sphere. **low c.,** having a rounded, slightly elevated surface, resembling a segment of the external surface of a sphere of long radius.

convexity (kon-vek′sĭ-te) [L. *convexitas*]. 1. The condition of being convex. 2. A rounded, somewhat elevated space on the surface of an organ or other structure; the protruding side of a curved surface, organ, or line.

convexobasia (kon-vek″so-ba′se-ah) [*convex* + *base* of the skull]. A deformity of the occipital bone, which is bent forward by the spine; seen in osteitis deformans.

convexoconcave (kon-vek″so-kon′kāv). Convex on one surface and concave on the other.

convexoconvex (kon-vek″so-kon′veks). Convex on each of two opposite surfaces.

convoluted (kon′vo-lūt-ed) [L. *convolutus*]. Rolled together or coiled.

convolution (kon-vo-lu′shun) [L. *convolutus* rolled together]. A tortuous irregularity or elevation caused by a structure being infolded upon itself, as the convolutions of the intestines. See also *gyrus*. **Broca's c.,** the inferior frontal gyrus of the left hemisphere of the cerebrum. **c's of cerebrum,** gyri cerebri. **Heschl's c.,** the anterior transverse temporal gyrus. **occipitotemporal c.,** gyrus occipitotemporalis lateralis. **Zuckerkandl's c.,** gyrus paraterminalis.

convolutional (kon″vo-lu′shun-al). Of or pertaining to a convolution or convolutions.

convolutionary (kon″vo-lu′shun-a-re). Convolutional.

convulsant (kon-vul′sant). 1. Producing or causing convulsions. 2. A drug or agent that causes convulsions.

convulsibility (kon-vul″sĭ-bil′ĭ-te). Capability of being convulsed.

convulsion (kon-vul′shun) [L. *convulsio*, from *convellere* to pull together]. A violent involuntary contraction or series of contractions of the voluntary muscles. **central c.,** a convulsion not excited by any external cause, but due to a lesion of the central nervous system. **choreic c.,** any convulsion or spasm of the kind characteristic of chorea. **clonic c.,** a convulsion marked by alternating contracting and relaxing of the muscles. **coordinate c.,** a convulsion marked by clonic movements similar to natural, purposeful movements. **crowing c.,** laryngismus stridulus. **epileptiform c.,** any convulsion attended with loss of consciousness. **essential c.,** central c. **external c.,** spasmodic contraction of the voluntary muscles. **hysterical c.,** any spasmodic movement attendant upon a hysterical disorder. **hysteroid c.,** hysteroepilepsy. **internal c.,** a slight involuntary spasmodic movement with no loss of consciousness. **local c.,** any minor spasm affecting but one muscle or only one part or member. **mimetic c., mimic c.,** facial spasm or tic. **puerperal c.,** spasm or eclampsia occurring just before, or just after, childbirth. **salaam c.,** nodding spasm. **spontaneous c.,** central c. **static c.,** saltatory spasm. **tetanic c.,** any form of spasm characteristic of tetanus; a tonic convulsion without loss of consciousness. **tonic c.,** persistent contraction of a muscle or set of muscles, not atrophic or due to muscular shrinkage. **uremic c.,** one due to uremia, or retention in the blood of material that should have been expelled by the kidneys.

convulsivant (kon-vul′sĭ-vant). Convulsant.

convulsive (kon-vul′siv). Pertaining to, characterized by, or of the nature of, convulsion.

Cooke's count, criterion, formula, index [William Edmond *Cooke*, 1881–1939]. A modification of Arneth's formula based on the statement that "if there is any band of nuclear material except the chromatin filament connecting the different parts of a nucleus of a leukocyte, such a nucleus is classed as undivided."

Cooley's anemia, disease [Thomas Benton *Cooley*, American pediatrician, 1871–1945]. Thalassemia.

Coolidge tube (koo′lij) [William David *Coolidge*, American physicist, born 1863]. See under *tube*.

cooling (kōōl′ing). The process of reducing the temperature of a substance or object; especially the reduction of body temperature in experimental animals or patients. **peritoneal c.,** reduction of body temperature achieved experimentally by circulation of a cooled irrigation fluid through the peritoneal cavity. **pleural c.,** reduction of body temperature accomplished experimentally by circulation of a cooled irrigation fluid through the pleural cavity.

Coombs' test (kōōmz) [R. R. A. *Coombs*, British immunologist]. See under *tests*.

Cooper's disease, fascia, hernia, ligament, etc. [Sir Astley Paston *Cooper*, English surgeon, 1768–1841]. See under the nouns.

Cooperia (koo-pe′re-ah). A genus of parasitic worms. **C. oncoph′ora, C. pectina′ta, C. puncta′ta,** species of parasitic worms sometimes occurring in the small intestine of cattle.

cooperid (koo′per-id). A parasitic worm of the genus Cooperia.

Coopernail's sign (koo′per-nālz) [George P. *Coopernail*, American physician, born 1876]. See under *sign*.

coordination (ko-or″dĭ-na′shun). The harmonious functioning of interrelated organs and parts. Applied especially to the process of the motor apparatus of the brain which provides for the coworking of particular groups of muscles for the performance of definite adaptive useful responses.

coossification (ko-os″ĭ-fĭ-ka′shun). The action, or state, of being joined together by ossification.

coossify (ko-os′ĭ-fi). To grow together by ossification.

copaiba (ko-pi′bah). The resinous juice (balsam) of various leguminous trees of tropical America, especially *Copaifera officinalis* and *C. langsdorffii*; it was formerly used for gonorrhea and chronic disease of mucous membranes.

copal (ko-pal′) [Mex.]. The commercial name of many resinous substances of extremely varied origin and character; the original copals came from trees of tropical America, chiefly of the leguminous genus *Hymenaea*.

copalchi (ko-pal′che). The febrifugal bark of *Strychnos pseudoquina*, of South America, and also of *Croton niveus*, of Mexico.

coparaffinate (ko-par′ah-fin-āt). A mixture of water-insoluble isoparaffinic acids partially neutralized with isoctyl hydroxybenzyldialkyl amines: used as an anti-infective for the skin.

cope (kōp). 1. The upper half of a flask used in the casting art; applied in prosthetic dentistry to the upper or cavity side of a denture flask. 2. Coping.

copepod (ko′pe-pod) [Gr. *kōpē* oar + *pous* foot]. A minute crustacean animal which is an intermediate host of *Diphyllobothrium* and *Dracunculus*.

coping (kōp′ing). A thin metal covering or cap, such as the plate of metal applied over the root of a tooth preparatory to attaching an artificial crown. **transfer c.,** a covering or cap of metal, acrylic resin, or other material, used to position a die in an impression.

copiopia (kop-e-o′pe-ah) [Gr. *kopos* fatigue + *opsis* sight]. Eyestrain from overwork or improper use of the eyes.

copodyskinesia (kop″o-dis″ki-ne′ze-ah) [Gr. *kopos* fatigue + *dys-* + *kinēsis* motion]. Any difficulty of movement due to fatigue from the habitual performance of some particular action; occupation neurosis.

copper (kop′er) [L. *cuprum;* Gr. *Kypros*]. A reddish, malleable metal; atomic number, 29; atomic weight, 63.54; symbol Cu, with poisonous salts. **c. abietinate,** a copper salt in green scales, soluble in oil: used as an anthelmintic and vermifuge in veterinary practice. **c. citrate,** a bluish-green crystalline powder, $Cu_3(C_6H_5O_7)_2$, astringent and antiseptic. **c. iodide,** cuprous iodide, Cu_2I_2. **c. oxyphosphate,** a salt of copper, zinc phosphate, and glacial acetic acid, used as a temporary filling material for tooth cavities. **c. phenolsulfonate,** green prismatic crystals, $(OH.C_6H_4.SO_2O)_2Cu.6H_2O$. **c. sulfate,** cupric sulfate.

copperas (kop′er-as). Commercial ferrous sulfate, $FeSO_4.7H_2O$: disinfectant and deodorizer.

copracrasia (kop″rah-kra′se-ah) [Gr. *kopros* dung + *akrasia* want of self control]. Loss of ability to retain the feces.

copragogue (kop′rah-gog) [Gr. *kopros* dung + *agōgos* leading]. Cathartic.

coprecipitin (ko″pre-sip′ĭ-tin). A precipitin in the same serum with one or more other precipitins.

copremesis (kop-rem′e-sis) [Gr. *kopros* dung + *emesis* vomiting]. The vomiting of fecal material.

copremia (kop-re′me-ah) [Gr. *kopros* dung + Gr. *haima* blood + *-ia*]. Blood poisoning from the retention of fecal matters in the blood or from the absorption of fecal matter from the intestine.

copro- (kop′ro) [Gr. *kopros* dung]. Combining form denoting relationship to feces.

coprodaeum (kop″ro-de′um) [*copro-* + Gr. *hodiaos* on the way]. The large dorsal passage in the proximal part of the cloaca in monotremes, into which the intestine opens.

coprodeum (kop″ro-de′um). Coprodaeum.

coprohematology (kop″ro-hem″ah-tol′o-je) [*copro-* + *hematology*]. The hematology of the feces.

coprolagnia (kop″ro-lag′ne-ah) [*copro-* + Gr. *lagneia* lust]. A form of paraphilia in which sexual excitement is associated with feces or defecation.

coprolalia (kop″ro-la′le-ah) [*copro-* + Gr. *lalia* babble]. The use of foul language, particularly of words relating to the feces.

coprolalomania (kop″ro-lal″o-ma′ne-ah). A morbid tendency to use foul or obscene language.

coprolith (kop′ro-lith) [*copro-* + Gr. *lithos* a stone]. A hard fecal concretion.

coprology (kop-rol′o-je) [*copro-* + *-logy*]. The study of the feces.

coproma (kop-ro′mah) [*copro-* + *-oma*]. Stercoroma.

Copromastix (kop″ro-mas′tiks). A genus of flagellate organisms. **C. prowazek′i,** a minute flagellate organism with four anterior flagella, found in feces in Brazil.

Copromonas (kop-rom′o-nas). A genus of flagellate organisms. **C. subti′lis,** an oval coprozoic flagellate found in the feces of frogs and sometimes in the human stool.

coprophagous (kop-rof′ah-gus). Feeding on dung, or feces.

coprophagy (kop-rof′ah-je) [*copro-* + Gr. *phagein* to eat]. The ingestion of dung, or feces.

coprophil (kop′ro-fil). A coprophilic microorganism.

coprophile (kop′ro-fil). 1. Coprophil. 2. Coprophilic.

coprophilia (kop″ro-fil′e-ah) [*copro-* + Gr. *philia* affection]. A psychopathologic interest in filth, especially in feces and in defecation.

coprophiliac (kop″ro-fil′e-ak). An individual exhibiting coprophilia.

coprophilic (kop″ro-fil′ik). 1. Pertaining to or characterized by coprophilia. 2. Inhabiting dung, or feces: said of bacteria.

coprophilous (kop-rof′ĭ-lus). Coprophilic.

coprophobia (kop″ro-fo′be-ah) [*copro-* + *phobia*]. Abnormal repugnance to defecation and to feces.

coprophrasia (kop″ro-fra′ze-ah). Coprolalia.

coproplanesis (kop″ro-plah-ne′sis) [*copro-* + Gr. *planēsis* wandering]. Escape of feces from the bowel through a wound or fistula.

coproporphyria (kop″ro-por-fir′e-ah). A state of increased formation and excretion of coproporphyrin without increase of uroporphyrin or porphobilinogen; at times familial, it is probably a variant of genetic porphyria.

coproporphyrin (kop′ro-por′fir-in) [*copro-* + *porphyrin*]. A porphyrin, $C_{36}H_{38}O_8N_4$, formed in the intestine from bilirubin and found in the feces and in the urine in coproporphyrinuria. Called also *stercoporphyrin.*

coproporphyrinogen (kop″ro-por″fĭ-rin′o-jin). The fully reduced, colorless compound, readily giving rise to coproporphyrin by oxidation.

coproporphyrinuria (kop″ro-por″fir-in-u′re-ah). The presence of coproporphyrin in the urine.

coprostanol (kop″ro-sta′nol). A saturated sterol, $C_{27}H_{48}O$, found in feces, probably as a reduced form of cholesterol.

coprostasis (kop-ros′tah-sis) [*copro-* + Gr. *stasis* stoppage]. Impaction of the feces in the intestine.

coprostasophobia (kop″ro-sta″so-fo′be-ah) [*coprostasis* + *phobia*]. Morbid dread of fecal stasis.

coprosterin (kop″ro-ste′rin) [*copro-* + *sterin*]. Coprostanol.

coprosterol (kop″ro-ste′rol). Coprostanol.

coprozoa (kop″ro-zo′ah) [*copro-* + Gr. *zōon* animal]. Protozoa which are found in fecal matter outside the body, but which do not inhabit the intestine.

coprozoic (kop″ro-zo′ik). Living in fecal material; found in fecal material.

Coptis (kop′tis) [L.]. A genus of ranunculaceous plants. *C. tee′ta,* an Asiatic species: tonic. *C. trifo′lia* (goldthread), of North America: tonic and astringent.

coptosystole (kop″to-sis′to-le) [Gr. *koptein* to cut + *systole*]. The cutting off of a ventricular systole.

copula (kop′u-lah) [L.]. 1. Any connecting part or structure. 2. Copula linguae. 3. A name for *amboceptor.* **c. lin′guae,** a median ventral elevation on the embryonic tongue formed by union of the second branchial arches. It represents the future root of the tongue.

copulation (kop″u-la′shun) [L. *copulatio*]. Sexual congress; coitus.

Coq. Abbreviation for L. *co′que,* boil.

Coq. in s. a. Abbreviation for L. *co′que in sufficien′te a′qua,* boil in sufficient water.

Coq. s. a. Abbreviation for L. *co′que secun′dum ar′tem,* boil properly.

coquille (ko-kēl′) [Fr.]. A glass or lens shaped like a watch crystal.

cor (kor), gen. *cor′dis* [L.]. [N A, B N A] The muscular organ that maintains the circulation of the blood. See *heart.* **c. adipo′sum,** a heart which has undergone fatty degeneration or which has an accumulation of fat around it. **c. arterio′sum,** the left side of the heart, so called because it contains oxygenated (arterial) blood. **c. bilocula′re,** a congenital anomaly caused by failure of formation of the atrial and ventricular septums, the heart having only two chambers, a single atrium and a single ventricle, and a common atrioventricular valve. **c. bovi′num** [L. "ox heart"], a greatly enlarged heart. **c. dex′trum** [L. "right heart"], the right atrium and ventricle. **c. hirsu′tum,** c. villosum. **c. ju′venum,** a condition of arrhythmia, palpitation, tachycardia, and systolic murmur seen in orthostatic albuminuria. **c. mo′bile,** an abnormally movable heart. **c. pen′dulum,** a heart so movable that it seems to be hanging by the great blood vessels. **c. pseudotrilocula′re biatria′tum,** a congenital cardiac anomaly in which the heart functions as a three-chambered heart, because of tricuspid atresia, the right ventricle being extremely small or rudimentary and the right atrium greatly dilated. Blood passes from the right to the left atrium and thence to the left ventricle and aorta. **c. pulmona'le,** heart disease secondary to disease of the lungs or of their blood vessels. **c. sinis'trum** [L. "left heart"], the left atrium and ventricle. **c. tauri'num,** c. bovinum. **c. tomento'sum,** c. villosum. **c. triatria'tum,** a congenital anomaly caused by failure of incorporation of the embryonic common pulmonary vein into the left atrium, the pulmonary veins emptying into an accessory chamber superior to the true left atrium and communicating with it by a small opening, which obstructs pulmonary venous flow. **c. trilocular'e biatria'tum,** a congenital anomaly caused by failure of formation of the ventricular septum, the heart having two atria, communicating, by the tricuspid and mitral valves, with a single ventricle. **c. trilocula're biventricula're,** a three-chambered heart with one atrium and two ventricles. **c. veno'sum,** the right side of the heart, so called because it contains unaerated blood. **c. villo'sum** [L. "hairy heart"], a roughened state of the pericardium caused by exudate on its surface, occurring in pericarditis.

coracidium (kor'ah-sid'e-um). Miracidium.

coraco-acromial (kor"ah-ko-ah-kro'me-al). Pertaining to the coracoid and acromion processes.

coracoclavicular (kor"ah-ko-klah-vik'u-lar). Pertaining to the coracoid process and the clavicle.

coracohumeral (kor"ah-ko-hu'mer-al). Pertaining to the coracoid process and the humerus.

coracoid (kor'ah-koid) [Gr. *korakoeidēs* crowlike]. 1. Like a raven's beak. 2. The coracoid process.

coracoiditis (kor"ah-koi-di'tis). A painful condition in the region of the scapula and of the coracoid process, with deltoid atrophy: attributed to injury of the coracoid process.

coracoradialis (kor"ah-ko-ra"de-a'lis). Caput breve musculi bicipitis brachii.

coraco-ulnaris (kor"ah-ko-ul-na'ris). The fibers of the biceps muscle attached to the fascia of the forearm.

coralliform (ko-ral'ĭ-form) [L. *corallum* coral + *forma* shape]. Having the form of a coral; branching like a coral.

corallin (kor'ah-lin). A lipochrome pigment found in *Streptothrix corallinus*. **red c.,** peonin. **yellow c.,** the sodium salt of rosolic acid.

coralloid (kor'ah-loid). Coralliform.

Corallorhiza (kor"al-lo-ri'zah) [Gr. *korallion* coral + *rhiza* root]. A genus of orchidaceous plants. The root of *C. odontorhiza*, coralroot or crawley, is antipyretic and diaphoretic.

coramine (ko'rah-min). Trade mark for preparations of nikethamide.

corasthma (kor-az'mah). Hay fever.

Corbus' disease (kor'bus) [Budd C. *Corbus*, Chicago urologist, born 1876]. See under *disease*.

cord (kord) [L. *chorda;* Gr. *chordē*]. Any long, rounded, flexible body or organ. **Bergmann's c's,** striae acusticae. **Billroth's c's,** red pulp c's. **Braun's c's,** strings of cells which have been observed in the kidney of the early embryo. **dental c.,** a cord-like mass of cells from which the enamel organ develops. **enamel c.,** a vertical extension of the enamel knot in a developing tooth, connecting the enamel knot with the outer dental epithelium, a temporary structure which disappears before enamel formation begins. **Ferrein's c's,** the inferior, or true, vocal cords. **ganglionated c.,** truncus sympatheticus. **genital c.,** a structure in the embryo formed by the union of the two mesonephric and the two müllerian ducts. **gubernacular c.,** gubernaculum testis. **hepatic c's,** anastomosing plates of hepatic cells radiating outward from the central vein and composing an hepatic lobule. Called also *hepatic cell c's.* **lumbosacral c.,** a cord arising from the branches of the fourth and the fifth lumbar nerves (truncus lumbosacralis [N A]). **medullary c's,** thin, irregular strands of epithelial tissues in the early ovary. **nephrogenic c.,** a longitudinal cord, formed by fusion of the nephrotome plates, that gives rise to the mesonephric and metanephric tubules. **nerve c.,** any nerve trunk or bundle of nerve fibers. **oblique c. of elbow joint,** chorda obliqua membranae interosseae antebrachii. **ovigerous c's,** sex cords of the primitive ovary which resolve into eggs and their follicles. **psalterial c.,** stria vascularis ductus cochlearis. **red pulp c's,** the masses of red pulp of the spleen. **rete c's,** the strands that become the rete testis and rete ovarii. **sex c's,** extensions from the germinal epithelium that give rise to most of the gonad. **sexual c's,** the seminiferous tubules during the early fetal stage. **spermatic c.,** the structure that extends from the abdominal inguinal ring to the testis, comprising the ductus deferens, testicular artery, pampiniform plexus, and nerves, as well as various other vessels, enclosed by its various coverings (tunicae funiculi spermatici et testis). Called also *funiculus spermaticus* [N A, B N A]. **spinal c.,** that part of the central nervous system which is lodged in the vertebral canal; it extends from the foramen magnum to about the level of the third lumbar vertebra. Called also *medulla spinalis* [N A]. **splenic c's,** red pulp c's. **umbilical c.,** the flexible structure connecting the umbilicus with the placenta and giving passage to the umbilical arteries and vein. In the newborn it measures about 2 feet in length and ½ inch in diameter. First formed during the fifth embryonic week, it contains the yolk sac and the body stalk, with the enclosed allantois. Called also *funiculus umbilicalis* [N A, B N A]. **vocal c., false,** a fold of mucous membrane in the larynx separating the ventricle from the vestibule. Called also *plica vestibularis* [N A], and *false vocal fold.* **vocal c., true,** a fold of mucous membrane in the larynx forming the inferior boundary of the ventricle. The vocalis muscle is deep to it. Called also *plica vocalis* [N A], and *true vocal fold.* **Weitbrecht's c.,** chorda obliqua membranae interosseae antebrachii. **Wilde's c's,** the transverse striae of the corpus callosum. **Willis' c's,** strands of tissue composing the adhesio interthalamica.

cordal (kor'dal). Pertaining to a cord; used specifically in referring to the vocal cord, or the plica vocalis.

cordate (kor'dāt) [L. *cor* heart]. Heart-shaped.

cordectomy (kor-dek'to-me) [*cord* + Gr. *ektomē* excision]. Excision of a cord, as a vocal cord.

cordial (kord'yal) [L. *cordialis*]. 1. Stimulating the heart; invigorating. 2. An aromatized alcoholic liqueur.

cordiale (kor-de-a'le) [L.]. Cordial.

Cordiceps (kor'dĭ-seps). A genus of fungi; certain species produce fatal disease of caterpillars.

cordiform (kor'dĭ-form) [L. *cor* heart + *forma* form]. Heart-shaped.

corditis (kor-di'tis). Inflammation of the spermatic cord.

cordopexy (kor'do-pek"se) [*cord* + Gr. *pēxis* fixation]. The operation of displacing outward the vocal cord for laryngeal stenosis.

cordotomy (kor-dot'o-me). 1. Section of a vocal cord. 2. Chordotomy.

cordran (kor'dran). Trade mark for preparations of flurandrenolone.

Cordylobia (kor"dĭ-lo'be-ah). A genus of flies. **C. anthropoph'aga,** a species of flies of Africa the larvae of which burrow under the skin of man and animals, causing a myiasis.

core (kōr). 1. The central part of anything; such as the central mass of necrotic matter in a boil. 2. A bar of iron around which a wire is wound to form an induction coil or electromagnet. 3. A disease of sheep caused by worms in the liver. 4. A disease of cows marked by the formation of lumps in the udder. 5. In dentistry, a metallic foundation inserted in a tooth to support a cast gold restoration.

core-, coro- (kōr′e, kōr′o) [Gr. *korē* pupil]. Combining form denoting relationship to the pupil of the eye. See also words beginning *irid-* and *irido-*.

coreclisis (kōr″e-kli′sis) [*core-* + Gr. *kleisis* closure]. Iridencleisis.

corectasis (kōr-ek′tah-sis) [*core-* + Gr. *ektasis* a dilatation]. Morbid dilatation of the pupil.

corectome (kōr-ek′tōm) [*core-* + Gr. *tomē* a cutting]. A cutting instrument used in performing iridotomy (corectomy).

corectomedialysis (ko-rek″to-me″de-al′ĭ-sis) [*core-* + Gr. *ektemnein* to excise + *dialysis* separating]. The operation of forming an artificial pupil by detaching the iris from the ciliary ligament.

corectomy (ko-rek′to-me) [*core-* + Gr. *ektomē* excision]. Iridectomy.

corectopia (kōr-ek-to′pe-ah) [*core-* + Gr. *ek* out + *topos* place]. Abnormal situation of the pupil.

coredialysis (ko″re-di-al′ĭ-sis) [*core-* + Gr. *dialysis* separating]. The separation of the external margin of the iris from the ciliary body.

corediastasis (ko″re-di-as′tah-sis) [*core-* + Gr. *diastasis* distention]. The dilatation or a dilated state of the pupil.

coregonin (ko-reg′o-nin). A protamine obtained from the sperm of the white fish.

corelysis (ko-rel′ĭ-sis) [*core-* + Gr. *lysis* dissolution]. Operative destruction of the pupil; especially the surgical detachment of adhesions of the pupillary margin of the iris from the lens.

coremorphosis (kōr″e-mor-fo′sis) [*core-* + Gr. *morphōsis* formation]. The formation of an artificial pupil.

corenclisis (kōr″en-kli′sis) [*core-* + Gr. *enkleiein* to inclose]. Iridencleisis.

coreometer (ko″re-om′e-ter) [*core-* + Gr. *metron* measure]. Pupillometer.

coreometry (ko″re-om′e-tre). Pupillometry.

coreoplasty (ko′re-o-plas″te) [*core-* + Gr. *plassein* to form]. Any plastic operation on the iris.

corepressor (ko″re-pres′sor). A small molecule which combines with an aporepressor to form the substance that controls the synthesis of an enzyme.

corestenoma (ko″re-ste-no′mah) [*core-* + Gr. *stenōma* contraction]. An abnormally contracted state of the pupil. **c. congen′itum,** a congenital condition in which the pupil is partially occluded by excrescences which meet, leaving small openings here and there.

Corethra (ko-re′thrah). A genus of short-beaked, non–blood-sucking mosquitoes.

coretomedialysis (ko″re-to-me-dĭ-al′ĭ-sis) [*core-* + Gr. *temnein* to cut + *dialysis* separation]. The formation of an artificial pupil by a combined cutting and tearing operation upon the iris.

coretomy (ko-ret′o-me) [*core-* + Gr. *temnein* to cut]. Iridotomy.

Cori cycle, ester (ko′re) [Carl Ferdinand *Cori*, born 1896, and Gerty Theresa *Cori*, 1896–1955: American biochemists; co-winners, with Bernardo Alberto Houssay, of the Nobel prize for medicine and physiology in 1947]. See under *cycle* and *ester*.

coriaceous (ko-re-a′shus) [L. *corium* leather]. Resembling leather; leathery, tough: said of bacterial cultures.

coriander (ko″re-an′der) [L. *coriandrum*]. The umbelliferous plant, *Coriandrum sativum;* also its aromatic carminative fruit.

coriin (ko′re-in). A substance formed by treating fibrous connective tissue with alkalis.

corium (ko′re-um) [L. "hide"]. [N A, B N A] The layer of the skin deep to the epidermis, consisting of a dense bed of vascular connective tissue. Called also *dermis*. **c. phlogis′ticum,** crusta phlogistica.

Corlett's pyosis (kor′lets) [William Thomas *Corlett*, American dermatologist, 1854–1948]. Impetigo contagiosa bullosa.

corm (korm) [L. *cormus*]. A solid bulblike expansion of a plant stem below the surface of the ground.

corn (korn) [L. *cornu* horn]. 1. A horny induration and thickening of the skin, produced by friction and pressure. It forms a conical mass extending down into the derma and producing pain and irritation. 2. A swelling on the bottom of a horse's foot between the wall of the heel and the bar. **soft c.,** a soft thickening of the epidermis between the toes, which is kept softened by moisture, and often leads to painful inflammation beneath the corn.

cornage (kor-nahzh′) [Fr.]. Roaring in horses.

cornea (kor′ne-ah) [L. *corneus* horny]. [N A, B N A] The transparent structure forming the anterior part of the fibrous tunic of the eye. It consists of five layers: (1) the anterior corneal epithelium, continuous with that of the conjunctiva; (2) the anterior limiting layer; (3) the substantia propria; (4) the posterior limiting layer; and (5) the endothelium of the anterior chamber. **conical c.,** keratoconus. **c. farina′ta,** degeneration of the cornea marked by fine dustlike stippling. **flat c.,** atrophy of the eyeball resulting in a shallow ocular chamber. **c. globo′sa,** buphthalmia. **c. gutta′ta,** a spotted condition of the cornea due to dystrophy of the endothelial cells. **c. opa′ca,** the sclerotic coat of the eye. **c. pla′na,** congenital flatness of the cornea. **sugar-loaf c.,** keratoconus.

corneal (kor′ne-al) [L. *cornealis*]. Pertaining to the cornea.

corneitis (kor″ne-i′tis). Inflammation of the cornea.

corneoblepharon (kor″ne-o-blef′ah-ron) [*cornea* + Gr. *blepharon* eyelid]. Adhesion between the eyelid and cornea.

corneo-iritis (kor″ne-o-i-ri′tis). Inflammation of the cornea and iris.

corneosclera (kor″ne-o-skle′rah). The cornea and sclera regarded as forming one organ.

corneoscleral (kor″ne-o-skle′ral). Affecting, or pertaining to, both the cornea and the sclera.

corneous (kor′ne-us) [L. *corneus*]. Hornlike, or horny.

corner (kor′ner). The third incisor on either side of each jaw in the horse.

Corner's tampon [Edred Moss *Corner*, British surgeon, 1873–1950]. See under *tampon*.

Corner-Allen test (George Washington *Corner*, American anatomist, born 1889; Willard Myron *Allen*, American gynecologist, born 1904]. See under *tests*.

Cornet's forceps (kor′nets) [George *Cornet*, German bacteriologist, 1858–1915]. A cover glass forceps.

corneum (kor′ne-um) [L. "horny"]. The stratum corneum of the skin.

corniculate (kor-nik′u-lāt). Shaped like a small horn.

corniculum (kor-nik′u-lum) [L. dim. of *cornu*]. Cartilago corniculata.

cornification (kor″nĭ-fĭ-ka′shun) [L. *cornu* horn + *facere* to make]. 1. Conversion into horn. 2. Conversion of epithelium to the stratified squamous type.

cornified (kor′nĭ-fīd). Converted into horny tissue.

Corning's anesthesia, method (kor′nings) [James Leonard *Corning*, New York neurologist, 1855–1923]. See under *anesthesia*.

cornu (kor′nu), pl. *cor′nua* [L. "horn"]. A hornlike excrescence or projection. Used in anatomical nomenclature to designate a structure resembling a horn in shape, especially in section. Called also *horn*. **c. Ammo′nis** [L. "horn of Ammon"], hippocampus. **c. ante′rius medul′lae spina′lis** [N A], the horn-shaped structure seen in transverse section of the spinal cord, formed by the anterior column of the cord (columna anterior medullae spinalis). **c. ante′rius ventric′uli latera′lis** [N A, B N A], the part of the lateral ventricle that extends forward from the pars centralis into the frontal lobe. Called also *anterior horn of lateral ventricle.* **cor′nua cartilag′inis thyroi′deae,** the horns of the thyroid cartilage. See *c. inferius cartilaginis thyroideae* and *c. superius cartilaginis thyroideae.* **c. cer′vi,** the horn of a stag or deer; hart's horn. **coccygeal c., c. coccy′geum** [N A], **c. of coccyx,** either of the cranial pair of rudimentary articular processes of the coccyx that articulate with the cornua of the sacrum. **c. cuta′neum,** a horny excrescence of the skin, mostly seen on the scalp and face. Called also *c. humanum.* **ethmoid c.,** concha nasalis medialis. **c. huma′num,** c. cutaneum. **c. infe′rius cartilag′inis thyroi′deae** [N A], the inferior extension of the posterior border of the thyroid cartilage. Called also *inferior horn of thyroid cartilage.* **c. infe′rius mar′ginis falcifor′mis** [N A, B N A], the distal edge of the falciform margin of the saphenous hiatus, deep to the great saphenous vein. **c. infe′rius ventric′uli latera′lis** [N A, B N A], the part of the lateral ventricle that extends forward from the pars centralis and the posterior horn into the temporal lobe. Called also *inferior horn of cerebrum.* **c. latera′le medul′lae spina′lis** [N A], the horn-shaped structure seen in transverse section of the spinal cord, formed by the lateral column of the cord (columna lateralis medullae spinalis). **c. ma′jus os′sis hyoi′dei** [N A, B N A], a bony projection passing backward and upward from either side of the body of the hyoid bone. Called also *greater horn of hyoid bone.* **c. mi′nus os′sis hyoi′dei** [N A, B N A], a small conical eminence projecting upward on either side of the hyoid bone at the angle of junction between the body and the greater horns. Called also *lesser horn of hyoid bone.* **c. occipita′le,** c. posterius ventriculi lateralis. **cor′nua os′sis hyoi′dei,** the horns of the hyoid bone. See *c. majus ossis hyoidei* and *c. minus ossis hyoidei.* **c. poste′rius medul′lae spina′lis** [N A], the horn-shaped structure seen in transverse section of the spinal cord, formed by the posterior column of the cord (columna posterior medullae spinalis). **c. poste′rius ventric′uli latera′lis** [N A, B N A], the part of the lateral ventricle that extends posteriorly from the pars centralis into the occipital lobe. Called also *posterior horn of lateral ventricle.* **sacral c., c. sacra′le** [N A], either of the two hook-shaped processes extending downward from the arch of the last sacral vertebra. **cor′nua of spinal cord,** the horn-shaped structures seen in transverse section of the spinal cord. See *columna anterior medullae spinalis, columna lateralis medullae spinalis,* and *columna posterior medullae spinalis.* **c. supe′rius cartilag′inis thyreoi′deae,** [N A] the superior extension of the posterior border of the thyroid cartilage. Called also *superior horn of thyroid cartilage.* **c. supe′rius mar′ginis falcifor′mis** [N A, B N A], the proximal extremity of the falciform margin of the saphenous hiatus. **c. us′tum** [L. "burnt horn"], the burnt or charred horn of the deer or stag, formerly used in medicine as an antacid.

cornua (kor′nu-ah) [L.]. Plural of *cornu.*

cornual (kor′nu-al). Pertaining to a cornu or to cornua.

cornucommissural (kor″nu-kŏ-mis′u-ral). Pertaining to a cornu and to a commissure.

cornucopia (kor″nu-ko′pe-ah) [L. *cornu copiae* "horn of plenty"]. An extension of the choroid plexus into each of the lateral recesses of the fourth ventricle.

Cornus (kor′nus) [L.]. A genus of cornaceous trees and shrubs of both hemispheres; the cornels or dogwoods. The root bark of many, especially that of *C. florida,* the common dogwood of North America, is astringent, tonic, and antiperiodic.

coro-. See *core-.*

corodiastasis (ko″ro-di-as′tah-sis). Corediastasis.

corolla (ko-rol′ah) [L. "little crown"]. The inner set of leaves of a floral envelope, the individual portions of which are called *petals.*

corometer (ko-rom′e-ter). Coreometer.

corona (ko-ro′nah), pl. *coronas,* or *coro′nae* [L.; Gr. *korōnē*]. A crown; used in anatomical nomenclature to designate a crownlike eminence or encircling structure. **c. cilia′ris** [N A, B N A], the region on the anterior inner surface of the ciliary body from which radiate the ciliary processes. Called also *ciliary crown.* **dental c., c. den′tis** [N A, B N A], the portion of a tooth that is covered by enamel, and is separated from the root or roots by a slightly constricted region, known as the neck, Called also *anatomical crown.* **c. glan′dis pe′nis** [N A, B N A], **c. of glans penis,** the rounded proximal border of the glans penis, separated from the corpora cavernosa penis by the neck of the glans. **c. radia′ta.** 1. [N A, B N A] The radiating crown of projection fibers which pass from the internal capsule to every part of the cerebral cortex. 2. An investing layer of radially elongated follicle cells surrounding the zona pellucida of an ovum. **c. seborrhe′ica,** a red line or band along the upper border of the forehead and temples sometimes seen in severe cases of dermatitis seborrheica or pityriasis capitis. **c. ven′eris,** a ring of syphilitic sores around the forehead, sometimes deeply affecting the bones of the head. **Zinn's c.,** circulus vasculosus nervi optici.

coronad (kor′o-nad). Toward the crown of the head or any corona.

coronae (ko-ro′ne) [L.]. Plural of *corona.*

coronal (ko-ro′nal) [L. *coronalis*]. 1. Pertaining to the crown of the head or to any corona. 2. Situated in the direction of the coronal suture: said of a transverse plane or section parallel to the long axis of the body.

coronale (kor-o-na′le). 1. The point of the coronal suture at the end of the maximum frontal diameter. 2. The frontal bone (os frontale [NA]).

coronalis (kor″o-na′lis) [L.]. [N A] Coronal, or situated in the direction of the coronal suture.

coronamen (kor″o-na′men). The coronet of a horse.

coronarism (kor′o-nar-izm). A condition marked by attacks of spasm of the coronary arteries.

coronaritis (kor″o-nah-ri′tis). Inflammation of the coronary arteries.

coronary (kor′o-na-re) [L. *corona;* Gr. *korōnē*]. Encircling in the manner of a crown: a term applied to vessels, nerves, ligaments, etc.

corone (kŏ-ro′ne) [L.; Gr. *korōnē* anything hooked or curved]. The coronoid process of the lower jawbone.

coroner (kor′o-ner). An officer who holds inquests in regard to violent, sudden, or unexplained deaths.

coronet (kor′o-net). The lower part of the pastern of a horse, where the horn joins the skin.

coronion (ko-ro′ne-on). The tip of the coronoid process of the jaw.

coronitis (kor-o-ni′tis). Inflammation of the coronary cushion of the horse.

coronoid (kor′o-noid) [Gr. *korōnē* anything hooked or curved]. 1. Shaped like a crow's beak. 2. Crown-shaped.

coroparelcysis (ko″ro-par-el′sĭ-sis) [*coro-* + Gr. *parelkein* to draw aside]. The drawing aside of the pupil in partial corneal opacity in order to bring it under a transparent portion.

coroplasty (ko′ro-plas″te). Coreoplasty.

coroscopy (ko-ros′ko-pe) [*coro-* + Gr. *skopein* to examine]. The shadow test for determining the refractive powers of the eye.

corotomy (ko-rot′o-me) [*coro-* + Gr. *temnein* to cut]. Any cutting operation upon the iris at the pupil; coretomy.

corpora (kor'po-rah) [L.]. Plural of *corpus.*

corporal (kor'po-ral). Corporeal.

corporeal (kor-po're-al). Pertaining to the body.

corporic (kor-po'rik) [L. *corpus* body]. Affecting the body or corpus of an organ.

corps (kōr) [Fr., from L. *corpus*]. 1. An organized body, or group of individuals. 2. Corpus. **medical c.,** the surgeon officers of the army or navy, comprising a surgeon general, medical directors, medical inspectors, surgeons, passed assistant surgeons, and assistant surgeons. **c. ronds,** Darier's name for round, double contoured cells seen in keratosis follicularis.

corpse (korps) [L. *corpus* body]. A dead body; used to refer specifically to a human body in the early period after death.

corpulency (kor'pu-len″se) [L. *corpulentia*]. Undue fatness or obesity.

corpus (kor'pus), pl. *cor'pora,* gen. *cor'poris* [L. "body"]. A discrete mass of material, as of specialized tissue. Used in anatomical nomenclature to designate the entire organism, and applied also to the main portion of an anatomical part, structure, or organ. **c. adipo'sum buc'cae** [N A, B N A], a thick layer of fat external to the buccinator muscle, containing the buccal glands. Called also *adipose body of cheek.* **c. adipo'sum fos'sae ischiorecta'lis** [N A], a pad of fat found in the ischiorectal fossa. **c. adipo'sum infrapatella're** [N A], a mass of fibrous fatty tissue inferior to the patella, in the angle between the deep surface of the patellar ligament and the tibia. Called also *infrapatellar fatty body.* **c. adipo'sum or'bitae** [N A, B N A], a mass of fatty tissue in the posterior part of the orbit, around the optic nerve, extraocular muscles, and vessels. Called also *adipose body of orbit.* **c. albi'cans** (pl. *cor'pora albican'tia*). 1. [N A, B N A] The mass of fibrous scar tissue replacing the corpus luteum. 2. Corpus mamillare. **c. albi'cans, Quain,** c. mamillare. **c. alie'num,** a foreign body. **c. amygdaloi'deum** [NA], a small mass of subcortical gray matter within the tip of the temporal lobe, anterior to the inferior horn of the lateral ventricle of the brain. Called also *nucleus amygdalae* [B N A], and *amygdaloid body.* **cor'pora amyla'cea** [L. "starchy bodies"], small hyaline masses of degenerate cells found in the prostate, neuroglia, etc. **cor'pora aran'tii** [L. "bodies of Arantius"], noduli valvularum aortae. **cor'pora arena'cea,** acervulus. **cor'pora atret'ica,** ovarian follicles which never mature, but undergo degeneration. **cor'pora bigem'ina** (sing. *cor'pus bigem'inum*), corpora quadrigemina. **c. calca'nei** [B N A], the body of the calcaneus. Omitted in N A. **c. callo'sum** [N A, B N A], an arched mass of white matter, situated at the bottom of the longitudinal fissure, and made up of transverse fibers connecting the cerebral hemispheres. **c. can'dicans,** c. mamillare. **c. caverno'sum clitor'idis** [N A, B N A], a column of erectile tissue on either side [dextrum et sinistrum], the two fusing to form the body of the clitoris (c. clitoridis). **c. caverno'sum pe'nis** [N A, B N A], one of the columns of erectile tissue forming the dorsum and sides of the penis. **c. caverno'sum ure'thrae vir'ilis** [B N A], c. spongiosum penis. **c. cilia're** [N A], **c. cilia'ris** [B N A], the thickened part of the vascular tunic of the eye anterior to the ora serrata, connecting the choroid with the iris. It comprises the ciliary crown, ciliary processes and folds, ciliary orbiculus, the ciliary muscle, and a basal lamina. Called also *ciliary body.* **c. clitor'idis** [N A, B N A], the main part of the clitoris, formed by the two fused corpora cavernosa, which are embedded anteriorly in the floor of the vestibule of the vagina. **c. cos'tae** [N A, B N A], the part of a rib extending between its dorsally placed tubercle and its ventral extremity. **c. denta'tum cerebel'li,** nucleus dentatus cerebelli. **c. denta'tum oli'vae,** nucleus olivaris. **c. epididym'idis** [N A, B N A], the middle part of the epididymis, which is formed by the convolutions of the single ductus epididymidis. **c. fem'oris** [N A, B N A], the main part or shaft of the femur. **c. fibro'sum,** c. albicans, def. 1. **c. fib'ulae** [N A, B N A], the main part or shaft of the fibula. **c. fimbria'tum** [L. "fringed body"], a narrow band of white substance bordering the lateral edge of the lower cornu of the lateral ventricle. **c. fimbria'tum hippocam'pi,** fimbria hippocampi. **cor'pora fla'va** [L. "yellow bodies"], waxy bodies found in the central nervous system and elsewhere, thought to be formed by the transformation of nerve cells. **c. for'nicis** [N A, B N A], the middle part of the fornix, formed by fusion of the two lateral halves under the corpus callosum. **c. genicula'tum latera'le** [N A, B N A], an eminence produced by the underlying lateral geniculate nucleus, just lateral to the medial geniculate body. It is related to the central visual pathway. Called also *lateral geniculate body.* **c. genicula'tum media'le** [N A, B N A], an eminence produced by the underlying medial geniculate nucleus, just lateral to the superior colliculus. It is related to the central auditory pathway. Called also *medial geniculate body.* **c. glan'dulae bulbourethra'lis** [B N A], the body of the bulbourethral gland. Omitted in N A. **c. glan'dulae sudorif'erae** [N A, B N A], the coiled secretory part of a sweat gland, found in the deep part of the corium. **c. glandula're prosta'tae** [B N A], substantia glandularis prostatae. **c. glandulo'sum,** a spongy eminence surrounding the orifice of the female urethra. **c. hemorrhag'icum.** 1. A blood clot in a corpus luteum. 2. The stage of a corpus luteum when it contains clotted blood. **c. Highmo'ri, c. highmoria'num** [L. "body of Highmore"], mediastinum testis. **c. hu'meri** [N A, B N A], the main part or shaft of the humerus. **c. hypothalam'icum,** nucleus subthalamicus. **c. in'cudis** [N A, B N A], the central part of the incus, which contains an excavation in which the head of the malleus articulates. **c. interpeduncula're,** nucleus interpeduncularis. **c. li'berum pericar'dii,** a free fatty or fibrous mass in the pericardial cavity, occurring in lipomatosis pericardii. **c. lin'guae** [N A, B N A], the larger anterior part of the tongue, in the floor of the mouth. **c. lu'teum** (pl. *cor'pora lu'tea*) [L. "yellow body"] [N A, B N A], a yellow glandular mass in the ovary formed by an ovarian follicle that has matured and discharged its ovum; if the ovum has been impregnated, the corpus luteum increases in size and persists for several months (*true c. luteum, c. luteum of pregnancy, c. luteum graviditatis*); if impregnation has not taken place, the corpus luteum degenerates and shrinks (*false c. luteum, c. luteum of menstruation, c. luteum menstruationis*). The corpus luteum secretes progesterone. **cor'pora lu'tea atret'ica,** corpora lutea in which regressive changes have occurred. **c. Luy'sii,** nucleus subthalamicus. **c. Malpig'hii,** stratum papillare corii. **c. mamilla're** [N A, B N A], either one of the pair of small spherical masses of gray substance situated close together in the interpeduncular space rostral to the posterior perforated substance. Called also *mamillary body.* **c. mam'mae** [N A, B N A], the essential mass of the mammary gland, which is thickest beneath the nipple and thinner toward the periphery. **c. mandib'ulae** [N A, B N A], the horizontal horseshoe-shaped portion of the mandible. **c. maxil'lae** [N A, B N A], the large central portion of the maxilla, roughly pyramidal in shape, to which four major processes are connected. It contains the maxillary sinus. **c. medulla're cerebel'li** [N A, B N A], the white substance of the cerebellum. **c. medulla're ver'mis,** arbor vitae cerebelli. **c. muco'sum,** stratum germinativum epidermidis (Malpighii). **c. nu'clei cauda'ti** [N A], the part of the caudate nucleus lying in the floor of the pars centralis of the lateral ventricle, extending posteriorly from the head and continuous with the tail. **c. of Oken,** mesonephros. **cor'pora oryzoi'dea** (sing. *cor'pus oryzoi'deum*), rice bodies. **c. os'sis hyoi'dei** [N A, B N A], the central portion of the hyoid bone to which the large and small horns are attached. **c. os'sis il'ii** [N A], **c. os'sis il'ium** [B N A], the inferior portion of the ilium, which forms roughly the superior two-fifths of the acetabulum. **c. os'sis isch'ii** [N A, B N A], the thick, irregular, prismatic part of the ischium. Its superior end participates in the acetabulum, and from its inferior end the ramus of the ischium projects. It incorporates what was formerly called the superior ramus. **c. os'sis metacarpa'lis** [N A, B N A], the main part or shaft of a metacarpal bone. **c. os'sis metatarsa'lis** [N A, B N A], the main part or shaft of a metatarsal bone. **c. os'sis pu'bis** [N A, B N A], the irregular mass of the pubic bone that lies alongside the median plane, articulating with the similar portion of the opposite pubic bone. From it extend the superior and inferior rami of the pubic bone. **c. os'sis sphenoida'lis** [N A, B N A], the central, cuboidal part of the sphenoid bone to which the great wings, small wings, and pterygoid processes are attached. **c. pampinifor'me,** epoophoron. **c. pancrea'tis** [N A, B N A], the triangularly prismatic portion of the pancreas, extending from the neck on the right to the tail on the left. **c. papilla're cor'ii** [B N A], stratum papillare corii. **cor'pora paraaor'tica** [N A], exclaves of sympathetic ganglion cells found near the sympathetic ganglia along the aorta in the abdominal cavity. Called also *para-aortic bodies*. **c. pe'nis** [N A, B N A], the free part of the penis between the root and the glans, consisting chiefly of the paired corpora cavernosa and the unpaired corpus spongiosum penis. **c. phalan'gis digito'rum ma'nus** [N A, B N A], the main part or shaft of each phalanx of the fingers. **c. phalan'gis digito'rum pe'dis** [N A, B N A], the main part or shaft of each phalanx of the toes. **c. pinea'le** [N A, B N A], a small, flattened, cone-shaped body resting upon the mesencephalon in the interval between the two halves of the thalamus. See *pineal body*. **c. pontobulba're,** a ridge running obliquely across the restiform body just caudal to the ridge formed by the cochlear nuclei. **c. pyramida'le medul'lae,** pyramis medullae oblongatae. **cor'pora quadrigem'ina** [B N A] (sing. *cor'pus quadrigem'inum*), four rounded eminences, on the posterior surface of the mesencephalon. Omitted from N A. **c. ra'dii** [N A, B N A], the main part or shaft of the radius. **cor'pora restifor'mia** [B N A] (sing. *cor'pus restifor'mis*). See *pedunculus cerebellaris inferior*. **c. rhomboida'le,** nucleus dentatus cerebelli. **cor'pora santoria'na,** cornicula laryngis. **c. spongio'sum pe'nis** [N A], the column of erectile tissue that forms the urethral surface of the penis, and in which the urethra is found; its distal expansion forms the glans penis. **c. spongio'sum pi'li,** the modified inner connective tissue sheath of the highly specialized follicles of certain active tactile hairs. **c. spongio'sum ure'thrae mulie'bris** [B N A], the submucous layer of the female urethra. Omitted in N A. **c. ster'ni** [N A, B N A], the second or principal portion of the sternum, located between the manubrium above and the xiphoid process below. Called also *gladiolus*. **c. stria'tum** (pl. *cor'pora stria'ta*) [N A, B N A], a subcortical mass of gray and white substance in front of and lateral to the thalamus in each cerebral hemisphere. The gray substance of this structure is arranged in two principal masses, the caudate nucleus and the lentiform nucleus; the striate appearance on section of the area being produced by connecting bands of gray substance passing from one of these nuclei to the other through the white substance of the internal capsule. **c. subthalam'icum, Henle,** nucleus subthalamicus. **c. ta'li** [N A, B N A], the roughly quadrilateral portion of the talus, which presents several surfaces. **c. tib'iae** [N A, B N A], the main part or shaft of the tibia. **c. trapezoi'deum** [N A, B N A], a mass of transverse fibers extending through the central part of the pons and forming a part of the path of the cochlear nerve. **c. tritic'eum,** cartilago triticea. **c. ul'nae** [N A, B N A], the main part or shaft of the ulna. **c. un'guis** [N A, B N A], the large distal, exposed portion of the nail of a digit. **c. u'teri** [N A, B N A], that part of the uterus above the isthmus and below the orifices of the uterine tubes. **c. ventric'uli** [N A, B N A], that part of the stomach between the fundus and the pyloric portion. **cor'pora versicolora'ta,** corpora amylacea. **c. ver'tebrae** [N A, B N A], the main part of a vertebra, including the centrum and part of the neural arch. **c. vesi'cae fel'leae** [N A, B N A], that part of the gallbladder between the fundus and the neck. **c. vesi'cae urina'riae** [N A, B N A], that part of the urinary bladder between the apex and the fundus. **c. vesic'ulae semina'lis** [B N A], the main portion of the seminal vesicle. Omitted in N A. **c. vit'reum** [N A, B N A], the transparent substance that fills the part of the eyeball between the lens and the retina. Called also *vitreous body* and *vitreous humor*. **c. Wolf'fi** [B N A], mesonephros.

corpuscle (kor'pus'l). Any small mass or body. See also *corpusculum*. **Alzheimer's c's,** compound granular corpuscles in the oligodendroglia of the brain. **amylaceous c's, amyloid c's,** corpora amylacea. **articular c's,** corpuscula articularia. **axile c., axis c.,** the central part of a tactile corpuscle. **Babes-Ernst c's,** metachromatic granules. **basal c.,** a small thickening at the base of each cilium of ciliated cells. **Bennett's large c's,** Nunn's gorged c's. **Bennett's small c's,** Drysdale's c's. **Bizzozero's c's,** blood platelets. **blood c's,** formed elements found in the blood. **blood c., red.** See *erythrocyte*. **blood c., white.** See *leukocyte*. **bone c.,** bone cell. **bridge c.,** desmosome. **bulboid c's,** corpuscula bulboidea. **Burckhardt's c's,** peculiar yellowish bodies found in trachoma secretion. **cancroid c's,** small nodules occurring in epithelioma of the skin. **cartilage c.,** cartilage cell. **cement c.,** cementocyte. **chorea c's,** a name given peculiar round hyaline bodies, concentrically laminated and strongly refractile, found in the perivascular sheaths of the vessels of the corpora striata and internal capsule in chorea. **chromophil c.,** Nissl's body. **chyle c.,** a lymphocyte found in chyle. **colloid c's,** corpora amylacea. **colostrum c's,** large rounded bodies in colostrum, containing droplets of fat and sometimes a nucleus. **concentric c's,** Hassall's c's. **corneal c's,** star-shaped connective tissue cells within the corneal spaces. **Dogiel's c.,** a sensory end-organ found in the mucous membrane of the eyes, nose, mouth, and genitals. **Donné's c's,** colostrum c's. **Drysdale's c's,** transparent microscopical cells seen in the fluid of ovarian cysts. **dust c's,** hemokonia. **Eichhorst's c's,** a name once given a peculiar variety of microcytes seen in pernicious anemia. **genital c's,** corpuscula genitalia. **ghost c.,** phantom c. **Gierke's c's,** roundish bodies found in the nervous system, probably identical with Hassall's corpuscles. **Gluge's c's,** granular corpuscles occurring in diseased nerve tissue. **Golgi's c's,** small, spindle-shaped corpuscles found in tendons at the junction of the tendon with the muscular fibers. **Golgi-Mazzoni c's,** tactile corpuscles found in the subcutaneous tissue of the fingertips, resembling pacinian corpuscles, but possessing fewer lamellae and a relatively larger cone, and having the contained nerve fibers more extensively branched. **Grandry's c's, Grandry-Merkel c's,** Merkel's c's. **Hassall's c's,** small concentrically striated bodies in the thymus, being the remains of epithelial tissue found in early stages of development of the gland. **Hayem's elementary c's,** blood

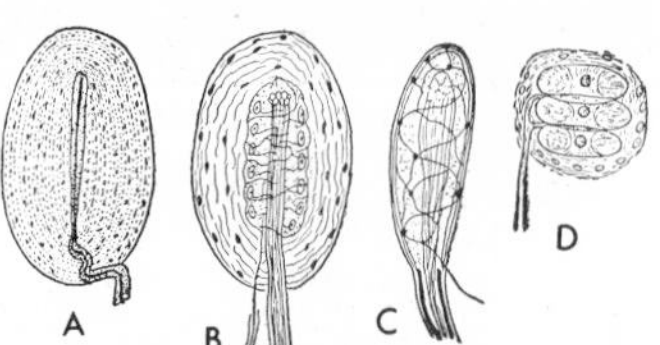

Sense corpuscles. A, Herbst's corpuscle from the tongue of a duck. B, Pacinian corpuscle from the mesentery of a cat. C, Krause's corpuscle. D, Merkel's corpuscle.

platelets. **Herbst's c's,** peculiar sensory end-organs in the skin of the bill and in the mucous membrane of the tongue of the duck. **Jaworski's c's,** spiral mucous bodies seen in the secretion of the stomach in hyperchlorhydria. **Krause's c's,** corpuscula bulboidea. **lamellar c's, lamellated c's,** corpuscula lamellosa. **Langerhans's stellate c's,** terminations of nerve fibers seen in the rete mucosum of the epidermis. **Leber's c's,** Hassall's c's. **Lostorfer's c's,** granular bodies observed in the blood in syphilis. **lymph c's,** lymphocytes observed in lymph. **lymphoid c's,** lymphocytes observed in tissues. **malpighian c.** See *folliculi lymphatici lienales.* **malpighian c's of kidney,** corpuscula renis. **marginal c.,** a small peripheral granule, single or multiple, seen in intensive staining, in the erythrocytes in the course of certain anemias. **Mazzoni's c's,** sensory nerve endings resembling Krause's corpuscles. **meconium c's,** epithelial cells containing many coarse yellow granules, observed in the lower part of the small intestine in a fetus. **Meissner's c's,** corpuscula tactus. **Merkel's c's,** tactile corpuscles in the submucosa of the tongue and mouth, each consisting of a sheath which is continuous with the sheath of Henle of the nerve. Enclosed within the sheath are two flattened epithelial cells between the opposed surfaces of which is a biconvex disk continuous with the end of the neurofibrils. **Miescher's c's,** Rainey's c's. **milk c's,** delicate particles of fat suspended in the serum of the milk. **molluscous c's,** molluscous bodies. **mucous c's,** bodies resembling leukocytes occurring in mucus. **muscle c.,** a muscle nucleus, especially of striated muscle. **nerve c's,** the sheath cells lying between the neurilemma and the medullary sheath. **Norris' c's,** colorless, transparent, disks in the blood serum. **Nunn's gorged c's,** epithelial cells found in ovarian cysts which have undergone a high degree of fatty degeneration. Called also *Bennett's large corpuscles.* **oval c's,** corpuscula tactus. **Pacini's c's, pacinian c's,** corpuscula lamellosa; applied particularly to certain endings which are concerned in the perception of pressure. **Patterson's c's,** molluscous bodies. **pessary c.** See under *cell.* **phantom c.,** an artifactual red cell from which the hemoglobin has been dissolved; an achromocyte. **Purkinje's c's,** large branched nerve cells composing the middle layer of the cortex of the cerebellum. **pus c.,** one of the cells of pus, chiefly neutrophilic leukocytes. **Rainey's c's,** encapsulated, ovoid, sporiferous bodies found in the muscles of various animals. **red c.,** erythrocyte. **renal c's,** corpuscula renis. **reticulated c's,** erythrocytes which on proper staining show filamentous reticulations filling a greater part of the cell. **Röhl's marginal c's,** small bodies seen in the margins of erythrocytes of animals after the administration of chemotherapeutic drugs. **Ruffini's c's,** corpuscula lamellosa; applied particularly to certain endings which are concerned in the perception of pressure and of warmth. **salivary c's,** swollen spherical lymphocytes found in the saliva. **Schwalbe's c.,** caliculus gustatorius. **sensitized c.,** a given kind of erythrocyte laden with an amboceptor specific for that variety of corpuscle. If such corpuscles are brought into contact with complement, hemolysis takes place. **shadow c.,** phantom c. **splenic c's,** folliculi lymphatici lienales. **tactile c's,** corpuscula tactus. **taste c's,** taste cells. **tendon c's,** flattened cells of connective tissue occurring in rows between the primary bundles of the tendons. **terminal nerve c's,** corpuscula nervosa terminalia. **thymus c's,** Hassall's c's. **Timofeew's c's,** a specialized form of pacinian corpuscle found in the submucosa of the membranous and prostatic portions of the urethra. **touch c's,** corpuscula tactus. **Toynbee's c's,** corneal c's. **Traube's c.,** phantom c. **typhic c's,** epithelial cells of Peyer's patches which have undergone degeneration in typhoid fever. **Valentin's c's,** small amyloid bodies found in nerve tissue. **Vater's c's,** corpuscula lamellosa. **Virchow's c's,** corneal c's. **von Tröltsch's c's,** connective tissue spaces lined with flattened endothelial cells, and appearing like corpuscular bodies among the radial fibers of the membrana tympani. **Wagner's c's,** corpuscula tactus. **washed c's,** isolated erythrocytes which have been suspended in saline solution and separated by centrifugation to free them from serum or plasma constituents. **Weber's c.,** utriculus prostaticus. **white c.,** leukocyte. **Zimmermann's c.** 1. A blood platelet. 2. A phantom corpuscle.

corpuscula (kor-pus′ku-lah) [L.]. Plural of *corpusculum.*

corpuscular (kor-pus′ku-lar). Pertaining to, or of the nature of, corpuscles.

corpusculum (kor-pus′ku-lum), pl. *corpus′cula* [L., dim. of *corpus*]. A small mass or body. Used as a general term in anatomical nomenclature to designate certain small discrete masses of specialized tissue, especially of nerve tissue. **corpus′cula articula′ria** [N A], encapsulated nerve endings found within joints. Called also *articular corpuscles* and *corpuscula nervorum articularia.* **corpus′cula bulbifor′mia,** corpuscula bulboidea. **corpus′cula bulboi′dea** [N A, B N A], small encapsulated nerve endings found in the skin, mucous membranes, conjunctiva, and heart, at varying levels. Called also *bulboid corpuscles.* **corpus′cula genita′lia** [N A], small encapsulated nerve endings occurring in the mucous membrane in the genital region. Called also *genital corpuscles* and *corpuscula nervorum genitalia.* **corpus′cula lamello′sa** [N A, B N A], large encapsulated nerve endings, which are the most complicated of the nerve endings and are found throughout the body. Called also *lamellar corpuscles.* Concerned with the perception of different sensations, various such endings are named for the men who originally described them. **corpus′cula nervo′rum articula′ria** [B N A], corpuscula articularia. **corpus′cula nervo′rum genita′lia** [B N A], corpuscula genitalia. **corpus′cula nervo′sa termina′lia** [N A], nerve endings characterized by a fibrous capsule of varying thickness which is continuous with the endoneurium. For different named varieties, see under *corpuscle.* Called also *corpuscula nervorum terminalia* and *encapsulated nerve endings.* **corpus′cula re′nis** [N A, B N A], bodies forming the beginnings of the nephrons, each consisting of a tuft of blood vessels, the glomerulus, surrounded by an expanded portion of the renal tubule, the glomerular capsule. Called also *renal corpuscles* and *malpighian corpuscles.* **corpus′cula tac′tus** [N A, B N A], medium-sized encapsulated nerve endings found in the skin, most commonly in the palms and soles. Called also *tactile corpuscles.* **c. tritic′eum,** cartilago triticea.

correction (kor-rek′shun) [L. *correctio* straightening out; amendment]. A setting right, as the provision of specific lenses for the improvement of vision, or an arbitrary adjustment made in values or devices in performance of experimental procedures.

correlation (kor″e-la′shun). In neurology, those combinations of the afferent impulses within the sensory centers which provide for the integration of the impulses into appropriate responses (Herrick).

correspondence (kor″e-spon′dens). The condition of being in agreement, or conformity. **anomalous retinal c.,** a condition in which disparate points on the retinas of the two eyes come to be associated sensorially. Abbreviated A.R.C. **harmonious retinal c.,** the condition in which corresponding points on the retinas of the two eyes are associated sensorially. **retinal c.,** the state regarding the impingement of images on the retinas of the two eyes.

Corrigan's button, cautery, disease, pulse, respiration, sign (kor′e-ganz) [Sir Dominic John *Corrigan*, physician in Dublin, 1802–1880]. See under the nouns.

corrigent (kor′ĕ-jent) [L. *corrigens* correcting]. 1. Amending or rendering milder. 2. Any agent which favorably modifies the action of a drug which is too powerful or harsh or which improves its taste.

corrosion (kŏ-ro′zhun) [L. *corrosio*]. The slow destruction of the texture or substance of a tissue, as a tissue by the action of a corrosive substance.

corrosive (kŏ-ro′siv) [L. *con* with + *rodere* to gnaw]. 1. Destructive to the texture or substance of the tissues. 2. A substance which destroys the texture or substance of the tissues.

corrugator (cor′u-ga″tor) [L. *con* together + *ruga* wrinkle]. That which wrinkles; a muscle which wrinkles.

Cort. Abbreviation for L. *cor′tex*, bark.

cortate (kor′tāt). Trade mark for preparations of desoxycorticosterone acetate.

cort-dome (kort′dōm). Trade mark for preparations of hydrocortisone.

cortef (kor′tef). Trade mark for preparations of hydrocortisone.

cortex (kor′teks), gen. *cor′ticis*, pl. *cor′tices*, [L. "bark, rind, shell"]. 1. An external layer, as the bark of a tree, or the rind of a fruit. 2. [N A] The outer layer of an organ or other body structure, as distinguished from the underlying substance. **adrenal c.,** the outer firm, yellowish layer that comprises the larger part of the adrenal (suprarenal) gland. Called also *cortex glandulae suprarenalis* [N A] and *substantia corticalis glandulae suprarenalis* [B N A]. **cerebellar c., c. cerebel′li** [N A], **c. of cerebellum,** the superficial gray matter of the cerebellum. Called also *substantia corticalis cerebelli* [B N A]. **cerebral c., c. cer′ebri** [N A], **c. of cerebrum,** the convoluted layer of gray substance that covers each cerebral hemisphere, about half of it hidden within the walls of the sulci. The cells and fibers are arranged in fairly definite layers, which can be differentiated microscopically and vary in structure and relative proportion from area to area of the cortex. Called also *substantia corticalis palli* [B N A], and *pallium*. **c. glan′dulae suprarena′lis** [N A], the outer, firm yellowish layer that comprises the larger part of the suprarenal gland. Called also *adrenal cortex*. **c. len′tis** [N A], the softer, external part of the lens of the eye. Called also *substantia corticalis lentis* [B N A]. **c. no′di lympha′tici** [N A], the outer portion of a lymph node, consisting mainly of lymph follicles. Called also *substantia corticalis lymphoglandulae* [B N A]. **provisional c.,** the cortex of the fetal adrenal gland that undergoes involution in early fetal life. **renal c., c. re′nis** [N A], the outer part of the substance of the kidney, composed mainly of glomeruli and secretory ducts. Called also *c. of kidney* and *substantia corticalis renis* [B N A].

cortexone (kor-tek′sōn). Desoxycorticosterone.

Corti's arch, canal, organ [Alfonso *Corti*, Italian anatomist, 1822–1888]. See under the nouns.

cortiadrenal (kor″te-ad-re′nal). Pertaining to the cortex of the adrenal gland.

cortical (kor′tĭ-kal) [L. *corticalis*]. Pertaining to or of the nature of a cortex or bark.

corticate (kor′tĭ-kāt). Possessing a cortex or bark.

corticectomy (kor″tĭ-sek′to-me). Excision of an area of cerebral cortex (scar or microgyrus) in the treatment of focal epilepsy.

cortices (kor′tĭ-sēz) [L.]. Plural of *cortex*.

corticifugal (kor″tĭ-sif′u-gal) [*cortex* + L. *fugere* to flee]. Proceeding, conducting, or moving away from the cortex.

corticipetal (kor″tĭ-sip′e-tal) [*cortex* + L. *petere* to seek]. Proceeding, conducting, or moving toward the cortex.

cortico-adrenal (kor″tĭ-ko-ad-re′nal). Pertaining to the adrenal cortex.

cortico-afferent (kor″tĭ-ko-af′fer-ent). Conveying impressions from the lower levels inward and upward to the cerebral cortex: said of certain nerve fibers.

cortico-autonomic (kor″tĭ-ko-aw″to-nom′ik). Noting the relationship of autonomic function to definite areas in the cerebral cortex.

corticobulbar (kor″tĭ-ko-bul′bar). Pertaining to the cerebral cortex and the medulla oblongata.

corticocerebral (kor″tĭ-ko-ser′e-bral). Pertaining to the cerebral cortex.

corticodiencephalic (kor″tĭ-ko-di″en-se-fal′ik). Pertaining to the cerebral cortex and the diencephalon.

cortico-efferent (kor″tĭ-ko-ef′er-ent). Carrying impressions outward and downward from the cerebral cortex: said of certain nerve fibers.

corticofugal (kor″tĭ-kof′u-gal). Corticifugal.

corticoid (kor′tĭ-koid). A term applied to hormones of the adrenal cortex or to any other natural or synthetic compound having a similar activity.

corticomesencephalic (kor″tĭ-ko-mes″en-se-fal′ik). Pertaining to the cerebral cortex and the mesencephalon.

corticopeduncular (kor″tĭ-ko-pe-dung′ku-lar). Pertaining to the cortex and the peduncles of the brain.

corticopetal (kor″tĭ-kop′e-tal). Corticipetal.

corticopleuritis (kor″tĭ-ko-ploo-ri′tis). Inflammation of the cortical pleura.

corticopontine (kor″tĭ-ko-pon′tīn). Noting tracts connecting the cerebral cortex with the pons.

corticospinal (kor″tĭ-ko-spi′nal). Pertaining to the cortex of the brain and the spinal cord.

corticosterone (kor″tĭ-ko-stēr′ōn). A crystalline steroid, $\triangle^4$-pregnene-11,21-diol-3,20-dione, found in the adrenal cortex. It possesses life-maintaining properties in adrenalectomized animals and several other activities ascribed to the adrenal cortex. See *desoxycorticosterone*. Also known as compound B (Kendall).

corticosuprarenaloma (kor″tĭ-ko-su″prah-re″-nal-o′mah). Corticosuprarenoma.

corticosuprarenoma (kor″tĭ-ko-su″prah-re-no′mah). A tumor derived from the adrenal cortex.

corticothalamic (kor″tĭ-ko-thah-lam′ik). Noting tracts between the cerebral cortex and the thalamus.

corticotrophic (kor″tĭ-ko-trof′ik). Corticotropic.

corticotrophin (kor′tĭ-ko-tro′fin). Corticotropin.

corticotropic (kor″tĭ-ko-trop′ik). Exerting a specific effect upon the cortex of the adrenal gland.

corticotropin (kor″tĭ-ko-tro′pin). 1. A hormone of the anterior pituitary that has an affinity for or that specifically stimulates the adrenal cortex. 2. A pharmaceutical preparation derived from the anterior pituitary of mammals: used to stimulate adrenal cortical activity.

cortisol (kor′tĭ-sol). An adrenal cortical hormone, 17-hydroxycorticosterone, or hydrocortisone, as it is usually referred to pharmaceutically. Its physiological effects closely simulate those of cortisone.

cortisone (kor′tĭ-sōn). A carbohydrate-regulating hormone from the adrenal cortex, which is concerned in glyconeogenesis. Chemical name: 4-pregnene-17α,21-diol-3,11,20-trione.

cortogen (kor′to-jen). Trade mark for preparations of cortisone.

cortone (kor′tōn). Trade mark for preparations of cortisone.

cortrophin (kor-tro′fin). Trade mark for preparations of corticotropin.

corundum (ko-run′dum). Native aluminum oxide, Al_2O_3: used in dentistry as an abrasive and polishing agent.

coruscation (kor″us-ka′shun). A glittering sensation, as of flashes of light before the eyes.

Corvisart's disease, facies (kor″ve-sarz′) [Jean Nicolas *Corvisart* Des Marest, French physician, 1755–1821]. See under *disease* and *facies*.

corybantiasm (kor″e-ban′te-azm). Corybantism.

corybantism (kor″e-ban′tizm) [Gr. *Korybas* a reveller]. Wild, frenzied, and sleepless delirium.

Corydalis (kŏ-rid′ah-lis) [L., from Gr. *korys* helmet]. A genus of fumariaceous herbs, of which various species are actively medicinal. *C. bulbo′sa* and *C. tubero′sa* are emmenagogic and anthelmintic. *C. formo′sa* is antiperiodic and diuretic.

Corynebacteriaceae (ko-ri″ne-bak-te″re-a′se-e). A family of Schizomycetes (order Eubacteriales), made up of usually non-motile rods, sometimes showing marked variation in form, and sometimes beaded or banded with metachromatic granules. It includes six genera, *Arthrobacter*, *Cellulomonas*, *Corynebacterium*, *Erysipelothrix*, *Listeria*, and *Microbacterium*.

Corynebacterium (ko-ri″ne-bak-te′re-um) [Gr. *korynē* club + *baktērion* little rod]. A genus of microorganisms of the family Corynebacteriaceae, order Eubacteriales, made up of straight to slightly curved rods, which are generally aerobic but may be microaerophilic or even anaerobic. Thirty-three species have been described. **C. ac′nes,** a non-pathogenic diphtheroid bacillus found on the skin but unrelated to acne; it differs from the diphtheria bacillus in being non-toxigenic and microaerophilic, and in producing a pink pigment in culture. **C. diphthe′riae,** the specific etiologic agent of diphtheria, producing a potent exotoxin, and separable into three types—mitis,

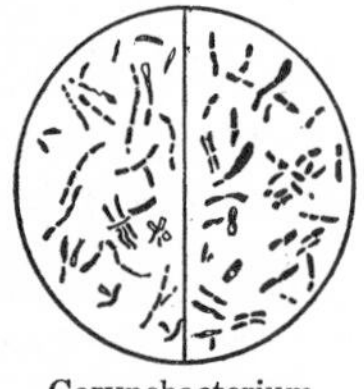
Corynebacterium diphtheriae.

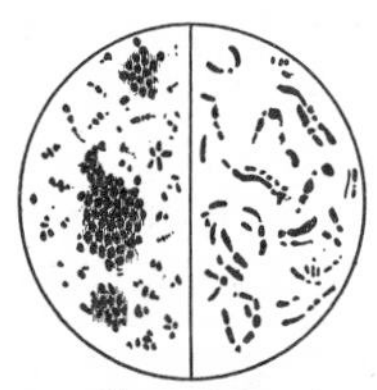
Corynebacterium pseudodiphtheriticum.

gravis, and intermedius, which are now thought to be without pathological significance. **C. enzy′micum,** a diphtheria-like bacillus found largely in and of uncertain pathogenicity for man, but the etiological agent of an epidemic ophthalmia of sheep. **C. e′qui,** an etiological agent of pneumonia in foals, occurring as coccoid and bacillary forms, the former being acid-fast. **C. murisep′ticum,** a diphtheria-like bacillus producing septicemic disease in mice and apparently non-pathogenic for other animals. **C. o′vis,** *C. pseudotuberculosis.* **C. pseudodiphtherit′icum,** a microorganism present in the upper respiratory tract, morphologically indistinguishable from the diphtheria bacillus but non-pathogenic and non-toxigenic. **C. pseudotuberculo′sis,** a weakly toxigenic diphtheria-like bacillus whose toxin is unrelated to diphtheria toxin; non-pathogenic for man, but pathogenic for domestic animals, in which it produces a caseous lymphadenitis and ulcerative lymphangitis, referred to as pseudotuberculosis. **C. pyog′enes,** a diphtheria-like bacillus producing an exotoxin less potent than the diphtheria toxin and differing from it immunologically; a common cause of purulent infections in lower animals, but non-pathogenic for man. **C. rena′le,** a diphtheria-like bacillus closely related to *C. pseudotuberculosis*, and pathogenic for lower animals, in which it produces purulent infections of the urinary tract.

coryza (kŏ-ri′zah) [L.; Gr. *koryza*]. An acute catarrhal condition of the nasal mucous membrane, with a profuse discharge from the nostrils. **allergic c.,** hay fever. **c. foe′tida,** ozena. **c. of horses,** strangles. **c. oedemato′sa,** a serous inflammation of the inferior and middle turbinate bones.

coryzavirus (kŏ-ri″zah-vi′rus). One of a group of viral agents isolated from patients with the common cold.

Coschwitz' duct (kosh′vits) [Georgius Daniel *Coschwitz*, German physician, 1679–1729]. See under *duct*.

cosensitize (ko-sen′sĭ-tiz). To sensitize to two or more sensitizing agents.

cosmesis (koz-me′sis) [Gr. *kosmēsis*]. The art of increasing and preserving beauty.

cosmetic (koz-met′ik) [Gr. *kosmētikos*]. 1. Beautifying; tending to preserve or restore comeliness. 2. A beautifying substance or preparation.

cosmetology (koz″mĕ-tol′o-je). The study of the proper care of the body from the point of view of cleanliness and comeliness.

cosmic (koz′mik) [Gr. *kosmikos* pertaining to the world]. Pertaining to the universe; expansive and vast.

costa (kos′tah) [L. "rib"], pl. **costae** [N A, B N A] The paired bones, 12 on each side, that extend from the thoracic vertebrae toward the median line on the ventral aspect of the trunk; the ribs. **c. fluc′tuans,** one of the lowest two ribs on either side, whose ventral tips ordinarily have no attachment. **c. fluc′tuans dec′ima,** Stiller's sign. **cos′tae spu′riae** [N A, B N A], the lower five ribs on either side. The ventral tips of the upper three of the five pairs connect with the costal cartilages of the superiorly adjacent ribs. The ventral tips of the lower two pairs ordinarily have no attachment. Called also *false ribs.* **cos′tae ve′rae** [N A, B N A], the upper seven ribs on either side, which are connected to the sides of the sternum by their costal cartilages. Called also *true ribs.*

costae (kos′te) [L.]. Plural of *costa* (q. v.).

costal (kos′tal) [L. *costalis*]. Pertaining to a rib or ribs.

costalis (kos-ta′lis) [L.]. Costal; used in anatomical nomenclature to denote relationship to a rib.

costalgia (kos-tal′je-ah) [*costa* + *-algia*]. Pain in the ribs.

costatectomy (kos″tah-tek′to-me). Costectomy.

costectomy (kos-tek′to-me) [*costa* + Gr. *ektomē* excision]. The operation of excising or resecting a rib.

Costen's syndrome (kos′tenz) [James Bray *Costen*, American otolaryngologist, born 1895]. Temporomandibular joint syndrome.

costicartilage (kos″tĭ-kar′tĭ-lij) [*costa* + *cartilage*]. The cartilage of a rib.

costicervical (kos″tĭ-ser′ve-kal). Pertaining to or connecting the ribs and the neck.

costiferous (kos-tif′er-us) [*costa* + L. *ferre* to carry]. Bearing a rib, as the thoracic vertebrae of man.

costiform (kos′tĭ-form). Shaped like a rib.

costispinal (kos-tĭ-spi′nal). Pertaining to or connecting the ribs and spine.

costive (kos′tiv). 1. Pertaining to, characterized by, or producing constipation. 2. An agent that depresses intestinal motility.

costiveness (kos′tiv-nes). Constipation.

costo- (kos′to) [L. *costa* rib]. A combining form denoting relationship to the ribs.

costrocentral (kos″to-sen′tral). Pertaining to a rib and the centrum (body) of a vertebra.

costocervicalis (kos″to-ser″vĭ-ka′lis) [*costo-* + *cervicalis*]. Musculus iliocostalis cervicis. See *Table of Musculi.*

costochondral (kos″to-kon′dral). Pertaining to a rib and its cartilage.

costoclavicular (kos″to-klah-vik′u-lar). Pertaining to the ribs and clavicle.

costocolic (kos″to-kol′ik). Pertaining to or joining the ribs and the colon.

costocoracoid (kos″to-kor′ah-koid). Pertaining to the ribs and coracoid process.

costogenic (kos″to-jen′ik) [*costo-* + Gr. *gennan* to produce]. Arising from a rib, especially from defect of the bone marrow of the ribs.

costo-inferior (kos″to-in-fe′re-or). Pertaining to the lower ribs.

costophrenic (kos″to-fren′ik). Pertaining to the costal and diaphragmatic pleurae; phrenicocostal.

costopleural (kos″to-plu′ral). Pertaining to the ribs and the pleura.

costopneumopexy (kos″to-nu′mo-pek″se) [*costo-* + Gr. *pneumōn* lung + *pēxis* fixing]. The operation of anchoring the lung to a rib.

costoscapular (kos″to-skap′u-lar). Pertaining to the ribs and the scapula.

costoscapularis (kos″to-skap″u-la′ris). Musculus serratus anterior. See *Table of Musculi.*

costosternal (kos″to-ster′nal). Pertaining to a rib and to the sternum.

costosternoplasty (kos″to-ster′no-plas″te). Surgical repair of funnel chest, a segment of rib being used to support the sternum.

costosuperior (kos″to-su-pe′re-or). Pertaining to the upper ribs.

costotome (kos′to-tōm) [*costo-* + Gr. *temnein* to cut]. A knife for dividing the costal cartilages.

costotomy (kos-tot′o-me) [*costo-* + Gr. *tomē* a cut]. Incision or division of a rib or costal cartilage.

costotransverse (kos″to-trans-vers′). Lying between the ribs and transverse processes of the vertebrae.

costotransversectomy (kos″to-trans″ver-sek′to-me). Excision of a part of a rib with the transverse process of a vertebra.

costovertebral (kos″to-ver′te-bral). Pertaining to a rib and a vertebra.

costoxiphoid (kos″to-zi′foid). Connecting the ribs and the xiphoid cartilage.

Cotard's syndrome (ko-tarz′) [Jules *Cotard*, French neurologist, 1840–1887]. See under *syndrome.*

COTe. Abbreviation for *cathodal opening tetanus.*

cothera (ko-ther′ah). Trade mark for preparations of dimethoxanate hydrochloride.

Cotte's operation (kots) [Gaston *Cotte*, Lyons surgeon, 1879–1951]. Removal of the presacral nerve.

Cotting's operation (kot′ingz) [Benjamin E. *Cotting*, American surgeon, 1812–1898]. See under *operation.*

cotton (kot′n). [L. *gossypium*]. A textile material derived from the seeds of one or more of the cultivated varieties of *Gossypium.* **absorbent c.,** purified c. **collodion c.,** pyroxylin. **gun c.,** pyroxylin. **gun c., soluble,** pyroxylin. **purified c.,** the hair of the seed of cultivated varieties of *Gossypium hirsutum* Linné, freed from impurities, deprived of fatty matter, bleached and sterilized. **salicylated c.,** purified cotton charged with salicylic acid: an antiseptic dressing. **styptic c.,** cotton impregnated in a styptic solution and dried.

cottonpox (kot′n-poks). The benign type of smallpox; alastrim.

Cotugno (ko-toon′yo). See *Cotunnius.*

Co-Tui treatment (ko-twe′) [Frank Wang *Co-Tui*, New York surgeon, born 1896]. See under *treatment.*

Cotunnius' aqueduct, nerve (ko-tun′e-us) [Domenico *Cotugno*, Italian anatomist, 1736–1822]. See under the nouns.

cotwin (ko′twin). One of two individuals produced at the same birth; a twin.

cotyledon (kot″ĭ-le′don) [Gr. *kotylēdōn*]. 1. The seed leaf of the embryo of a plant. 2. Any one of the subdivisions of the uterine surface of a discoidal placenta. 3. One of the tufted areas of a ruminant's placenta.

Cotylogonimus (kot″ĭ-lo-gon′ĭ-mus) [Gr. *kotylē* cup + *gonimos* productive]. Heterophyes.

cotyloid (kot′ĭ-loid) [Gr. *kotyloeides* cup shaped]. 1. Cup-shaped. 2. Pertaining to the cotyloid cavity or acetabulum.

cotylopubic (kot″ĭ-lo-pu′bik). Relating to the acetabulum and the os pubis.

cotylosacral (kot″ĭ-lo-sa′kral). Relating to the acetabulum and the sacrum.

couchgrass (kowch′gras). The perennial grass, *Agropyrum (Triticum) repens.* Its long roots are diuretic and have been used in cystitis.

couching (kowch′ing). Displacement of the lens in cataract.

cough (kawf) [L. *tussis*]. A sudden noisy expulsion of air from the lungs. **aneurysmal c.,** a variety of cough commonly associated with aneurysm, and often with paralysis of one vocal cord. **Balme's c.,** cough on lying down, seen in obstruction of the nasopharynx. **barking c.,** the barklike cough of early youth. **compression c.,** a deep resonant cough caused by compression of the bronchi. It resembles in character the cough of a dog and is sometimes called *dog c.* **dog c.** See *compression c.* **dry c.,** one which is not accompanied with expectoration. **ear c.,** a reflex cough caused by disease of the ear. **extrapulmonary c.,** a cough due to causes outside the lungs. **hacking c.,** a short, frequent, and feeble cough. **hebetic c.,** the dry barking of puberty: cynobex hebetica. **mechanical c.,** expulsion of air from the lungs produced by use of an exsufflator, with effects similar to those of a natural cough. **minute gun c.,** whooping cough with the paroxysms occurring close together. **Morton's c.,** a persistent cough in pulmonary tuberculosis which brings on vomiting and thus causes loss of nourishment. **privet c.,** an allergic cough noted in China and attributed to the pollen of privet. **productive c.,** a cough which is effective in removing material from the respiratory tract. **reflex c.,** a cough due to the irritation of some remote organ. **stomach c.,** a cough caused by reflex irritation from stomach disorder. **Sydenham's c.,** hysterical spasm of the respiratory muscles. **tea taster's c.,** cough in tasters of tea, due to inhaling fungi, such as *Monilia, Aspergillus,* etc., from tea leaves. **trigeminal c.,** a cough due to irritation of the fibers of the trigeminal nerve distributed to the throat, nose, and external meatus of the ear. **wet c.,** one which is attended with expectoration. **whooping c.** See *whooping cough.* **winter c.,** chronic bronchitis recurring in the winter.

coulomb (koo′lom) [after C. A. de *Coulomb*, French physicist, 1736–1806]. The unit of quantity in current electricity; the quantity afforded by an ampere of current in one second flowing against one ohm of resistance with a force of one volt.

coumadin (koo-mah-din). Trade mark for preparations of warfarin sodium.

coumarin (koo′mah-rin). Fragrant colorless crystals, the lactone of ortho-oxycinnamic acid, from tonka bean, sweet clover, other plants, and also prepared synthetically.

Councilman bodies, lesions (kown′sil-man) [William Thomas *Councilman*, American pathologist, 1854–1933]. See under *body.*

Councilmania (kown″sil-ma′ne-ah) [William Thomas *Councilman*]. A genus of amebas. **C.**

dissim'ilis, a species resembling *Entamoeba histolytica.* **C. lafleu'ri,** a species of ameba resembling *Entamoeba coli,* but distinguished by multiplying during its encystment.

count (kownt) [L. *computare* to reckon]. A numerical computation. **Addis c.,** a count of the cells in 10 cc. of urinary sediment for the purpose of calculating the total urinary sediment of the twelve-hour specimen. **blood c.,** determination of the number of formed elements in a measured volume of blood, usually a cubic millimeter (as red blood cell, white blood cell, or platelet count.) **differential c.,** a count made by observation, on the stained blood smear, of the proportion of the different types of leukocytes (or other cells), expressed in percentages. **direct platelet c.,** determination of the total number of platelets per cubic millimeter of blood, in a counting chamber, with the use of conventional light or phase microscopy. **filament-nonfilament c.,** determination of the number of filamentous and nonfilamentous leukocytes in a measured quantity of blood. **indirect platelet c.,** calculation of the total number of platelets per cubic millimeter of blood by determining, in a peripheral blood smear, the ratio of platelets to erythrocytes, and computing the number of platelets from the total red cell count. **parasite c.,** determination of the number of parasites per unit volume of infected fluid, as, in malaria, the number of plasmodia per cubic millimeter of blood. **Schilling blood c.,** a differential blood count in which the neutrophilic leukocytes are divided into four groups: myelocytes, juvenile cells, or young forms, staff cells, and segmented forms. **staff c.,** Schilling blood c.

counter (kown'ter). An instrument or apparatus by which something is counted. **Coulter c.,** an automatic photoelectric instrument used in the enumeration of formed peripheral blood elements, based on the principle that cells are poor electrical conductors compared with saline solution. **Geiger c., Geiger-Müller c.,** an amplifying device which indicates the presence of ionizing particles. **scintillation c.,** an instrument for indicating the emission of ionizing particles, making possible determination of the concentration of radioactive isotopes in the body.

counterdie (kown'ter-di). The reverse image of a die, usually made of a softer and lower fusing metal than the die.

counterextension (kown"ter-eks-ten'shun). Traction in a proximal direction coincident with traction in the opposite direction.

counterincision (kown"ter-in-sizh'un). Counteropening.

counterinvestment (kown"ter-in-vest'ment). Anticathexis.

counterirritant (kown"ter-ir'ĭ-tant). 1. Producing a counterirritation. 2. Any agent which causes counterirritation.

counterirritation (kown"ter-ir"ĭ-ta'shun). A superficial irritation; an irritation which is intended to relieve some other irritation.

counteropening (kown"ter-o'pen-ing). A second incision made opposite to another, as in an abscess, to promote drainage.

counterpoison (kown'ter-poi"zn). A poison given to counteract another poison.

counterpuncture (kown'ter-punk"tūr). A second opening made opposite to another.

counterstain (kown'ter-stān). A stain which is applied to render the effects of another stain more discernible.

countersuggestion (kown"ter-sug-jes'chun). A suggestion which is opposed to another suggestion.

countertraction (kown'ter-trak"shun). Traction which is opposed to another traction: employed in the reduction of fractures.

countertransference (kown"ter-trans-fer'ens). In the course of psychoanalysis, the transference to the patient by the physician of his suppressed desires.

coup (koo) [Fr.]. Stroke. **c. de fouet** (koo-duh-fwa') [Fr. "stroke of the whip"], rupture of the plantaris muscle accompanied by a sharp disabling pain. **c. de sabre** (koo-duh-sahb') [Fr. "saber stroke"], a linear, circumscribed lesion of scleroderma on the forehead or scalp; so called because of its resemblance to the scar of a saber wound. **c. de sang** (koo-duh-sang'), congestion of the brain. **c. de soleil** (koo-duh-sŏ-la'), a sunstroke. **c. sur coup** (koo-ser-koo') ["blow on blow"], the administration of a drug in small doses at short intervals, to secure rapid, complete or continuous action: abbreviated C.S.C.

courap (koo-rap'). A disease of the skin occurring in India, with eruption and itching of the armpits, groin, breast, and face.

courbature (koor'bah-tūr) [Fr.]. 1. Aching of the muscles. 2. Caisson disease.

Cournand (ko͝or'nand), André F. United States physiologist, born 1895; co-winner, with Werner T. O. Forssmann and Dickinson W. Richards, of the Nobel prize in medicine and physiology for 1956, for the development of new techniques to measure more precisely lung and heart function.

courses (kor'sez). Menses.

Courvoisier's law, sign (koor-vwah"ze-āz') [Ludwig J. *Courvoisier,* a French surgeon, 1843–1918]. See under *law.*

Courvoisier-Terrier syndrome (koor-vwah"-ze-a'ter-ya') [L. J. *Courvoisier;* Louis-Félix *Terrier,* Paris surgeon, 1837–1908]. See under *syndrome.*

Coutard's method (koo-tarz') [Henri *Coutard,* French radiologist in United States, 1876–1950]. A method of x-ray irradiation by protracted and fractional dosage.

couvade (koo-vad'). An ethnic custom, in which the husband feigns illness during his wife's parturient and puerperal periods.

Couvelaire uterus (koo"vel-ār') [Alexandre *Couvelaire,* Parisian obstetrician, 1873–1948]. See *uteroplacental apoplexy,* under *apoplexy.*

couvercle (koo'ver-kl) [Fr.]. A blood clot formed outside a vessel.

couveuse (koo-vuz') [Fr.]. Incubator.

coverglass (kov'er-glas). A thin glass plate which covers a mounted microscopical object or a culture.

Cowdria (kow'dre-ah) [Edmund V. *Cowdry,* American anatomist and zoologist, born 1888]. A genus of the tribe Ehrlichieae, family Rickettsiaceae, order Rickettsiales, containing a single species. **C. ruminan'tium,** the etiologic agent of heartwater disease of sheep, goats, and cattle; non-pathogenic for man.

cowl (kowl). See *pileus.*

Cowper's cyst, gland (kow'perz) [William *Cowper,* English surgeon, 1666–1709]. See under *cyst* and *gland.*

cowperian (kow-pe're-an). Described by or named in honor of William Cowper.

cowperitis (kow"per-i'tis). Inflammation of Cowper's glands.

coxa (kok'sah) [L.]. [N A, B N A] The hip or hip joint. **c. adduc'ta, c. flex'a,** c. vara. **c. mag'na,** a condition marked by broadening of the head and neck of the femur. **c. pla'na,** osteochondrosis of the capitular epiphysis. **c. val'ga,** deformity of the hip in which the angle formed by the axis of the head and the neck of the femur and the axis of its shaft is materially increased. **c. va'ra,** deformity of the hip in which the angle formed by the axis of the head and neck of the femur and the axis of its shaft is materially decreased. **c. va'ra lux'ans,** fissure of the neck of the femur with dislocation of the head developing from coxa vara.

coxalgia (kok-sal'je-ah) [L. *coxa* hip + *-algia*].

1. Hip joint disease; tuberculosis of the hip joint. 2. Pain in the hip.

coxankylometer (kok-sang″kil-om′e-ter) [L. *coxa* hip + Gr. *ankylos* bent + *metron* measure]. An instrument for measuring the deformity in hip disease.

coxarthria (koks-ar′thre-ah). Coxitis.

coxarthritis (koks″ar-thri′tis). Coxitis.

coxarthrocace (koks″ar-throk′ah-se). Fungus disease of the hip joint.

coxarthropathy (koks″ar-throp′ah-the) [L. *coxa* hip + Gr. *arthron* joint + *pathos* disease]. Hip joint disease.

Coxiella (kok″se-el′lah) [Herald Rae *Cox*, American bacteriologist, born 1907]. A genus of microorganisms of the tribe Rickettsieae, family Rickettsiaceae, order Rickettsiales, occurring as a single species. **C. burnet′ii,** the etiological agent of Q fever, transmitted by Haemaphysalis, Ixodes, Dermacentor, and Amblyomma ticks, and also acquired by inhalation of infectious dust and other materials from animal reservoirs of infection.

coxitis (kok-si′tis). Inflammation of the hip joint. **c. fu′gax,** a transient benign coxitis. **senile c.,** rheumatoid arthritis of the hip joint.

coxodynia (kok″so-din′e-ah). Coxalgia.

coxofemoral (kok″so-fem′o-ral) [L. *coxa* hip + *femur* thigh]. Pertaining to the hip and thigh.

coxotomy (kok-sot′o-me). The operation of opening the hip joint.

coxotuberculosis (kok″so-tu-ber″ku-lo′sis) [L. *coxa* hip + *tuberculosis*]. Tuberculous disease of the hip joint.

Coxsackie virus (kok-sak′e) [*Coxsackie*, N. Y., where it was first identified]. See under *virus*.

cozymase (ko-zi′mās). Diphosphopyridine nucleotide.

C.P. Abbreviation for *chemically pure* and *candle power*.

C.P.H. Abbreviation for *Certificate in Public Health*.

c.p.m. Abbreviation for *counts per minute*.

C.P.P. Abbreviation for *cyclopentenophenanthrene*.

c.p.s. Abbreviation for *cycles per second*.

C.R. Abbreviation for *crown-rump* length.

Cr. Chemical symbol for *chromium*.

crackle (krak′l). A small sharp sound. **pleural c's,** superficial crepitation heard in the early stages of acute fibrinous pleurisy.

cradle (kra′dl). A frame for keeping bed clothes from a wounded limb. **electric c., heat c.,** a frame with wiring for electric light bulbs, for application of heat to the body of a patient. **ice c.,** a device for refrigerating fever patients.

Crafts' test (krafts) [Leo M. *Crafts*, American neurologist, 1863–1938]. See under *tests*.

Craigia (kra′ge-ah) [Charles F. *Craig*, U. S. Army surgeon, 1872–1950]. A genus of flagellate protozoans, two species of which, *C. hom′inis* and *C. mi′grans*, inhabit the intestine and cause dysentery-like symptoms. This genus was originally named *Paramoeba* by Craig.

craigiasis (kra-gi′ah-sis). A condition produced by infection of the intestine with *Craigia*, marked by lassitude, mild headache, abdominal discomfort, and moderate diarrhea.

Cramer's splint (krah′merz) [Friedrich *Cramer*, German surgeon, 1847–1903]. See under *splint*.

cramp (kramp). A painful spasmodic muscular contraction, especially a tonic spasm. **accessory c.,** spastic torticollis due to a lesion of the accessory nerve. **heat c.,** muscular spasm attended by pains, dilated pupils, and weak pulse: seen in those who labor in intense heat (stokers, miners, cane-cutters) and lose much water and salt. **intermittent c.,** tetany. **writers' c.,** an occupation neurosis which is characterized by spasmodic contraction of the muscles of the fingers, hand, and forearm, together with neuralgic pain therein. It comes on whenever an attempt is made to write.

Crampton's line, muscle (kramp′tonz) [Sir Philip *Crampton*, Irish surgeon, 1777–1858]. See under *line* and *muscle*.

Crampton's test (kramp′tonz) [C. Ward *Crampton*, American physician, born 1877]. See under *tests*.

craniad (kra′ne-ad) [L. *cranium* head + *ad* toward]. In a cranial direction; toward the anterior (front) or superior end of the body.

cranial (kra′ne-al) [L. *cranialis*]. Pertaining to the cranium, or to the anterior (front) or superior end of the body.

cranialis (kra″ne-a′lis) [L.]. Pertaining to the cranium, or to the superior end of the body; in official anatomical terminology, used to designate relationship to the superior extremity of the body.

craniamphitomy (kra″ne-am-fit′o-me) [*cranium* + Gr. *amphi* around + *tomē* cutting]. Division of the entire circumference of the skull for securing decompression.

craniectomy (kra″ne-ek′to-me) [*cranium* + Gr. *ektomē* excision]. Excision of a part of the skull. **linear c.,** excision of a strip of the skull, done for the relief of microcephalus.

cranio- (kra′ne-o) [L. *cranium;* Gr. *kranion* skull]. A combining form denoting relationship to the cranium or skull.

cranioacromial (kra″ne-o-ah-kro′me-al). Pertaining to the cranium and acromion.

cranioaural (kra″ne-o-aw′ral). Pertaining to the cranium and the ear.

craniobuccal (kra′ne-o-buk′al). Pertaining to the head and mouth.

craniocele (kra′ne-o-sēl) [*cranio-* + Gr. *kēlē* hernia]. A protrusion of any part of the cranial contents through a defect in the skull.

craniocerebral (kra″ne-o-ser′e-bral). Pertaining to the cranium and the cerebrum.

cranioclasis (kra″ne-ok′lah-sis) [*cranio-* + Gr. *klasis* fracture]. The operation of crushing of the fetal head.

cranioclast (kra′ne-o-klast) [*cranio* + Gr. *klan* to break]. An instrument for performing cranioclasis.

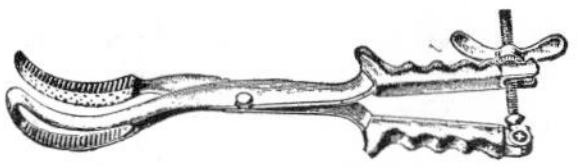

A cranioclast.

cranioclasty (kra′ne-o-klas″te). Cranioclasis.

craniocleidodysostosis (kra″ne-o-kli″do-dis″-os-to′sis) [*cranio-* + Gr. *kleis* clavicle + *dys-* bad + *osteon* bone]. Cleidocranial dysostosis.

craniodidymus (kra″ne-o-did′ĭ-mus) [*cranio-* + Gr. *didymos* twin]. A fetal monster with two heads.

craniofacial (kra″ne-o-fa′shal). Pertaining to the cranium and the face.

craniofenestria (kra″ne-o-fĕ-nes′tre-ah) [*cranio-* + L. *fenestra* an opening]. Defective development of the bones of the vault of the fetal skull, marked by areas in which no bone is formed.

craniognomy (kra-ne-og′no-me) [*cranio-* + Gr. *gnōmōn* an interpreter or judge]. The study of the shape of the head.

craniograph (kra′ne-o-graf) [*cranio-* + Gr. *graphein* to write]. An instrument for outlining the skull.

craniography (kra″ne-og′rah-fe). The study of the skull by means of photographs, charts, etc.

craniolacunia (kra″ne-o-lah-ku′ne-ah) [*cranio-* + L. *lacuna* a hollow + *-ia*]. Defective development of the bones of the vault of the fetal skull marked by depressed areas on the inner surfaces of the bones.

craniology (kra″ne-ol′o-je) [*cranio-* + *-logy*]. The scientific study of skulls.

craniomalacia (kra″ne-o-mah-la′she-ah) [*cranio-* + Gr. *malakia* softness]. Abnormal softness of the skull.

craniomeningocele (kra″ne-o-mĕ-nin′go-sēl) [*cranio-* + Gr. *mēninx* membrane + *kēlē* hernia]. Protrusion of cerebral membranes through a defect in the skull.

craniometer (kra″ne-om′e-ter) [*cranio-* + Gr. *metron* measure]. An instrument for use in craniometry.

craniometric (kra″ne-o-met′rik). Pertaining to craniometry.

craniometry (kra″ne-om′e-tre) [*cranio-* + Gr. *metrein* to measure]. The scientific measurement of the dimensions of the bones of the skull and face.

craniopagus (kra″ne-op′ah-gus) [*cranio-* + Gr. *pagos* a thing fixed]. A double monster united by the heads. **c. occipita′lis,** a craniopagus in which fusion is in the occipital region. **c. parasit′icus,** a craniopagus in which a parasitic head is attached to the head of the autosite. **c. parieta′lis,** a craniopagus in which fusion is in the parietal region.

craniopathy (kra″ne-op′ah-the) [*cranio-* + Gr. *pathos* disease]. Any disease of the skull. **metabolic c.,** a condition characterized by lesions of the calvarium with multiple metabolic changes and marked by headache, obesity and visual disturbances.

craniopharyngeal (kra″ne-o-fah-rin′je-al). Pertaining to the cranium and the pharynx.

craniopharyngioma (kra″ne-o-fah-rin″je-o′mah). A tumor arising from cell rests derived from the hypophyseal stalk or Rathke's pouch, frequently associated with increased intracranial pressure, and showing calcium deposits in the capsule or in the tumor proper. Called also *craniopharyngeal duct tumor*, *Rathke's pouch tumor*, *suprasella cyst*, and *pituitary adamantinoma* or *ameloblastoma*.

craniophore (kra′ne-o-fōr) [*cranio-* + Gr. *phoros* bearing]. A device for holding a skull during measurement of its diameters and angles.

cranioplasty (kra′ne-o-plas″te) [*cranio-* + Gr. *plassein* to mold]. Any plastic operation on the skull; surgical correction of defects of the skull.

craniopuncture (kra′ne-o-punk″tūr). Puncture of the brain for exploratory purposes in cranial disease.

craniorachischisis (kra″ne-o-rah-kis′kĭ-sis) [*cranio-* + Gr. *rhachis* spine + *schisis* fissure]. Congenital fissure of the skull and spinal column.

craniosacral (kra″ne-o-sa′kral). Pertaining to the skull and the sacrum.

cranioschisis (kra″ne-os′kĭ-sis) [*cranio-* + Gr. *schisis* fissure]. Congenital fissure of the cranium.

craniosclerosis (kra″ne-o-skle-ro′sis) [*cranio-* + Gr. *sklēros* hard]. Thickening of the bones of the skull.

cranioscopy (kra″ne-os′ko-pe) [*cranio-* + Gr. *skopein* to examine]. Diagnostic examination of the head.

craniospinal (kra″ne-o-spi′nal). Pertaining to the cranium and spine.

craniostenosis (kra″ne-o-ste-no′sis) [*cranio-* + Gr. *stenōsis* narrowing]. Deformity of the skull caused by premature fusion of the cranial sutures, with consequent cessation of growth, the nature of the deformity depending on the sutures involved in the process.

craniostosis (kra″ne-os-to′sis) [*cranio-* + Gr. *osteon* bone]. Congenital ossification of the cranial sutures.

craniosynostosis (kra″ne-o-sin″os-to′sis). Premature closure of the sutures of the skull.

craniotabes (kra″ne-o-ta′bēz) [*cranio-* + L. *tabes* a wasting]. Reduction in the mineralization of the skull, with abnormal softness of the bone, and widening of the sutures and fontanelles, occurring chiefly in rickets.

craniotome (kra′ne-o-tōm) [*cranio-* + Gr. *tomē* a cut]. An instrument for use in performing craniotomy.

craniotomy (kra″ne-ot′o-me) [*cranio-* + Gr. *tomē* a cut]. 1. Any operation on the cranium. 2. The cutting in pieces of the fetal head to facilitate delivery (*fetal c.*).

craniotonoscopy (kra″ne-o-to-nos′ko-pe) [*cranio-* + Gr. *tonos* tone + Gr. *skopein* to examine]. The auscultatory percussion of the head.

craniotopography (kra″ne-o-to-pog′rah-fe) [*cranio-* + *topography*]. The study of the relations of the surface of the skull to the various parts of the brain beneath.

craniotrypesis (kra″ne-o-trĭ-pe′sis) [*cranio-* + Gr. *trypēsis* a piercing]. The trephination of the skull.

craniotympanic (kra″ne-o-tim-pan′ik). Pertaining to the skull and the tympanum.

cranitis (kra-ni′tis). Inflammation of the cranial bones.

cranium (kra′ne-um), pl. *crania* [L.; Gr. *kranion* the upper part of the head]. The skeleton of the head, variously construed as including all of the bones of the head, all of them except the mandible, or all of them except the mandible and those forming the skeleton of the face. **c. bif′idum,** congenital cleft of the cranium. **c. bif′idum occul′tum,** congenital cleft of the cranium without associated abnormality of the brain or meninges, detectable only roentgenographically. **cerebral c., c. cerebra′le** [B N A], those portions of the bones of the head which contribute to the brain case. **visceral c., c. viscera′le** [B N A], those portions of the bones of the head which form the skeleton of the face. This includes the mandible and hyoid bone.

cranter (kran′ter). A third molar tooth.

crapulent, crapulous (krap′u-lent, krap′u-lus) [L. *crapulentus*, *crapulosus* drunken]. Due to excess in eating or drinking.

crasis (kra′sis) [L.; Gr. *krasis* mixture]. The individual temperament or constitution. **parasitic c.,** a weakened state due to the presence of parasites or favorable to infestation by them.

crassamentum (kras″ah-men′tum) [L.]. A clot, as of blood.

Crast. Abbreviation for L. *cras′tinus*, for tomorrow.

crataegin (krah-te′jin). A bitter crystalline compound from the bark of the twigs of *Crataegus*.

crater (kra′ter). A circular area of depression surrounded by an elevated margin.

crateriform (kra-ter′ĭ-form) [L. *crater* bowl + *forma* shape]. Depressed or hollowed, like a bowl.

craterization (kra″ter-i-za′shun). The operation of excising a craterlike piece from a bone.

craunology (kraw-nol′o-je). Crenology.

craunotherapy (kraw″no-ther′ah-pe). Crenotherapy.

cravat (krah-vat′) [Fr. *cravate*]. A form of bandage made by folding a triangular piece of cloth from its apex toward the base.

craw-craw (kraw′kraw). An obstinate form of skin disease occurring in West Africa, and affecting chiefly the thighs and genitals, though it may spread over the whole body. It is caused by *Onchocerca volvulus*.

cream (krēm) [L. *cremor*]. The oily or fatty part of milk from which butter is prepared, or a fluid mixture of similar consistency. **leukocytic c.,** the reddish gray layer observed above the packed red cells in centrifuged blood. **Moynihan's c.,** a mixture consisting of as much bismuth carbonate in 1:1000 aqueous solution of HgI_2 as will make a thick paste: used as a wound dressing. **c. of tartar,** potassium bitartrate.

creamalin (krem′ah-lin). Trade mark for preparations of aluminum hydroxide gel.

creamometer (kre-mom′e-ter) [*cream* + Gr. *metron* measure]. An instrument for the determination of the percentage of cream in milk.

crease (krēs). A longitudinal line or slight depression.

creasote (kre′ah-sōt). Creosote.

creatinase (kre-at′ĭ-nās). An enzyme which catalyzes the transformation of creatine into urea and ammonia.

creatine (kre′ah-tin) [Gr. *kreas* flesh]. A crystallizable nitrogenous compound synthesized in the body, phosphorylated creatine being an important storage form of high-energy phosphate.

creatinemia (kre″ah-tĭ-ne′me-ah) [*creatin* + Gr. *haima* blood + *-ia*]. Excess of creatine in the blood.

creatininase (kre″ah-tin′ĭ-nās). An enzyme which decomposes creatinine into urea and methyl glycocoll.

creatinine (kre-at′ĭ-nin). A basic substance, $NH.C(:NH).N(CH_3).CH_2$, creatine anhydride,
|————CO————|
procurable from creatine and from urine.

creatinuria (kre-at″ĭ-nu′re-ah). Increased concentration of creatine in the urine.

creaton (kre′ah-ton). Oxalyl-methyl-guanidine, a compound isolated from muscle.

creatorrhea (kre″ah-to-re′ah) [Gr. *kreas* flesh + *rhoia* flow]. The presence of undigested muscle fibers in the feces.

creatotoxism (kre″ah-to-tok′sism). Meat poisoning.

creatoxicon (kre″ah-tok′se-kŏn). Kreotoxicon.

creatoxin (kre″ah-tok′sin). Kreotoxin.

crèche (kresh) [Fr.]. A day nursery for infants.

Credé's antiseptic, ointment (kra-dāz′) [Benno C. *Credé*, German surgeon, 1847–1929]. See under *antiseptic* and *ointment.*

Credé's method, etc. (kra-dāz′) [Karl Sigmund Franz *Credé*, German gynecologist, 1819–1892]. See under *method.*

cremaster (kre-mas′ter) [L.; Gr. *kremasthai* to suspend]. See *Table of Musculi.* **internal c. of Henle,** fibers of the gubernaculum testis, inserted in elements of the fetal spermatic cord.

cremasteric (kre″mas-ter′ik). Pertaining to the cremaster.

cremation (kre-ma′shun) [L. *crematio* a burning]. The burning or incineration of dead bodies.

crematorium (kre″mah-to′re-um). An establishment for the burning of dead bodies.

cremnocele (krem′no-sēl). Labial hernia.

cremnophobia (krem″no-fo′be-ah) [Gr. *krēmnos* cliff + *phobia*]. Insane dread of precipices.

cremor (kre′mor) [L.]. Cream. **c. tar′tari** ["cream of tartar"], potassium bitartrate.

crena (kre′nah), pl. *cre′nae* [L.]. A notch or cleft. **c. a′ni** [N A, B N A], the cleft between the buttocks on which the anus opens. **c. clu′nium,** c. ani. **c. cor′dis,** sulcus interventricularis anterior.

crenae (kre′ne) [L.]. Plural of *crena.*

crenate, crenated (kre′nāt, kre′nāt-ed) [L. *crena′tus*]. Scalloped or notched.

crenation (kre-na′shun). The creation of abnormal notching in the edge of an erythrocyte, or the appearance caused by its creation.

Crenated erythrocytes (Hill).

crenilabrin (kren-il-a′-brin). A protamine obtained from the sperm of the cunner (fish).

crenocyte (kre′no-sīt). A crenated erythrocyte.

crenocytosis (kre″no-si-to′sis). The presence of crenated erythrocytes in the blood.

crenology (kre-nol′o-je) [Gr. *krēnē* spring + *-logy*]. The science of therapeutic springs.

crenotherapy (kren″o-ther′ah-pe) [Gr. *krēnē* spring + *therapeia* treatment]. Treatment by water from mineral springs.

Crenothrix (kre′no-thriks) [Gr. *krēnē* spring + *thrix* hair]. A genus of microorganisms of the family Crenotrichaceae, order Chlamydobacteriales, made up of disc-shaped to cylindrical cells occurring in attached trichomes which are unbranched or show false branching, and are enclosed in plainly visible sheaths, encrusted at the base with iron or manganese oxides. The type species is *C. poly′spora.*

Crenotrichaceae (kre″no-trĭ-ka′se-e). A family of Schizomycetes, order Chlamydobacteriales, made up of firmly attached trichomes, showing differentiation of base and tip, enclosed in sheaths that may be encrusted with oxides of iron or manganese. It includes three genera, *Clonothrix, Crenothrix,* and *Phragmidiothrix.*

crenulation (kren″u-la′shun). Crenation.

creophagism, creophagy (kre-of′ah-jism, kre-of′ah-je) [Gr. *kreas* flesh + *phagein* to eat]. The use of flesh as food.

creosol (kre′o-sol) [*creosote* + L. *oleum* oil]. A colorless, oily liquid, the methyl ether of methyl catechol, $CH_3.O.C_6H_3(OH)CH_3$, from potassium creosotate: antiseptic.

creosote (kre′o-sōt). A mixture of phenols obtained from wood tar: used as a disinfectant.

creotoxin (kre″o-tok′sin). Kreotoxin.

creotoxism (kre″o-tok′sizm). Kreotoxism.

crepitant (krep′ĭ-tant) [L. *crepitare* to rattle]. Rattling or crackling.

crepitation (krep″ĭ-ta′shun) [L. *crepitare* to crackle]. 1. A sound like that made by rubbing the hair between the fingers, or like that made by throwing fine salt into a fire. 2. The noise made by rubbing together the ends of a fractured bone.

crepitus (krep′ĭ-tus) [L.]. 1. The discharge of flatus from the bowels. 2. Crepitation. 3. A crepitant rale. **articular c.,** false crepitus. **bony c.,** the crackling sound produced by the rubbing together of fragments of fractured bone. **false c.,** joint c. **c. in′dux,** a crepitant rale, or crackling sound, heard in pneumonia at the beginning of the process of solidification of the lung. **joint c.,** the grating sensation caused by the rubbing together of the dry synovial surfaces of joints. **c. re′dux,** crepitus heard in the resolving stage of pneumonia. **silken c.,** a sensation as of two pieces of silk rubbed between the fingers, felt on moving a joint affected with hydrarthrosis.

crepuscular (kre-pus′ku-lar) [L. *crepusculum* twilight]. Referring to twilight, as a twilight state; also imperfectly luminous or glimmering.

crescent (kres′ent) [L. *crescens*]. 1. Shaped like a new moon. 2. A crescent-shaped structure. **articular c.,** a crescent-shaped articular fibrocartilage. **epithelial c.,** a more or less crescentic mass of epithelial cells between the glomerular tuft and the inside of Bowman's capsule in glomerulonephritis. **c's of Giannuzzi,** darkly staining crescents surrounding the mucous tubules, appearing in sections of mixed (mucous and albuminous) glands, and formed by the outnumbered albuminous cells pushed to the blind ends of the terminal portions or into saccular outpocketings. Called also *demilunes of Heidenhain.* **gray c.,** an area on some eggs which gives rise to mesoderm. **malarial c's,** the gametocytes of *Plasmodium falciparum.* They may be male (microgametocytes) or female (macrogametocytes). **myopic c.,** a crescentic posterior staphyloma in the fundus of the eye in myopia. **c's of the spinal cord,** either of the two lateral bands of gray substance in the spinal cord, each made up of the anterior and posterior horn of the respective side. **sublingual c.,** the crescent-shaped area on the floor of the mouth, formed by the lingual wall of the mandible and the adjacent part of the floor of the mouth.

crescentic (krĕ-sen′tik). Shaped like a new moon.

crescograph (kres′ko-graf) [L. *crescere* to grow + Gr. *graphein* to write]. An instrument which magnifies movements and shows the growth of plants.

cresol (kre′sol). A phenol from coal tar or wood tar. A pharmaceutical preparation consisting of a mixture of isomeric cresols obtained from coal tar or from petroleum is used as a disinfectant. **c. naphthol,** a viscous brown liquid: a germicide.

cresolphthalein (kre″sol-thal′e-in). An indicator which is colorless at 7.2 and red at 8.8.

cresomania (kre″so-ma′ne-ah) [*Croesus*, king of Lydia in 6th century B. C., renowned for his great wealth]. Hallucinations consisting in the imagination of the possession of great wealth.

cresorcin (kre-sor′sin). A crystalline derivative from cresol, $C_7H_8O_2$.

cresotate (kres′o-tāt). Cresylate.

cresoxydiol (kres-ok″se-di′ol). Mephenesin.

cresoxypropanediol (kres-ok″se-pro-pān′de-ol). Mephenesin.

crest (krest) [L. *crista*]. A projection or projecting structure, or ridge, especially one surmounting a bone or its border. See also *crista* and *ridge*. **acoustic c.,** crista ampullaris. **acusticofacial c.,** the embryonic cell mass from which develop the ganglia of the seventh and eighth nerves. **ampullar c., ampullary c.,** crista ampullaris. **anterior c. of fibula,** margo anterior fibulae. **anterior c. of tibia,** margo anterior tibiae. **arcuate c. of arytenoid cartilage,** crista arcuata cartilaginis arytenoideae. **basilar c.,** crista basilaris ductus cochlearis. **basilar c. of occipital bone,** tuberculum pharyngeum. **buccinator c.,** crista buccinatoria. **cerebral c's of cranial bone,** juga cerebralis ossis cranii. **c. of cochlear window,** crista fenestrae cochleae. **conchal c. of maxilla,** crista conchalis maxillae. **conchal c. of palatine bone,** crista conchalis ossis palatini. **cross c.,** a ridge of enamel extending across the face of a tooth. **deltoid c.,** tuberositas deltoidea humeri. **dental c.,** the maxillary ridge passing along the alveolar processes of the fetal maxillary bones. **ethmoid c. of maxilla,** crista ethmoidalis maxillae. **ethmoid c. of palatine bone,** crista ethmoidalis ossis palatini. **femoral c.,** linea aspera femoris. **fimbriated c.,** plica fimbriata. **frontal c.,** crista frontalis. **frontal c., external,** linea temporalis ossis frontalis. **frontal c., internal,** crista frontalis. **glandular c. of larynx,** ligamentum vestibulare. **gluteal c.,** tuberositas glutea femoris. **c. of greater tubercle of humerus,** crista tuberculi majoris. **c. of hypotrochanteric fossa,** tuberositas glutea femoris. **iliac c.,** crista iliaca. **iliopectineal c. of iliac bone,** linea arcuata. **iliopectineal c. of pelvis,** linea terminalis pelvis. **iliopectineal c. of pubis,** eminentia iliopubica. **c. of ilium,** crista iliaca. **infratemporal c.,** crista infratemporalis. **infundibuloventricular c.,** crista supraventricularis. **inguinal c.,** a prominence on the inguinal body wall in the embryo, participating in the formation of the gubernaculum testis. **interosseous c. of fibula,** margo interosseus fibulae. **interosseous c. of radius,** margo interosseus radii. **interosseous c. of tibia,** margo interosseus tibiae. **interosseous c. of ulna,** margo interosseus ulnae. **intertrochanteric c.,** crista intertrochanterica. **intertrochanteric c., anterior,** linea intertrochanterica. **jugular c. of great wing of sphenoid bone,** margo zygomaticus alae majoris. **lacrimal c., anterior,** crista lacrimalis anterior. **lacrimal c., posterior,** crista lacrimalis posterior. **c. of larger tubercle,** crista tuberculi majoris. **lateral c. of fibula,** margo posterior fibulae. **c. of lesser tubercle,** crista tuberculi minoris. **c. of little head of rib,** crista capitis costae. **malar c. of great wing of sphenoid bone,** margo zygomaticus alae majoris. **c. of matrix of nail,** cristae matricis unguis. **medial c. of fibula,** crista medialis fibulae. **mental c., external,** protuberantia mentalis. **nasal c. of maxilla,** crista nasalis maxillae. **nasal c. of palatine bone,** crista nasalis ossis palatini. **c. of neck of rib,** crista colli costae. **neural c.,** a cellular band dorsolateral to the neural tube that gives origin to the cerebrospinal ganglia. **obturator c., anterior,** crista obturatoria. **occipital c., external,** crista occipitalis externa. **occipital c., internal,** eminentia cruciformis. **orbital c.,** margo supraorbitalis ossis frontalis. **palatine c. of palatine bone,** crista palatina ossis palatini. **pectineal c. of femur,** linea pectinea. **pharyngeal c. of occipital bone,** tuberculum pharyngeum. **pubic c., c. of pubis,** crista pubica. **radial c.,** margo interosseus radii. **c. of ridge,** the highest continuous surface of the ridge, but not necessarily the center of the ridge. The top of a residual or alveolar ridge. **rough c. of femur,** linea aspera femoris. **sacral c.,** crista sacralis mediana. **sacral c., articular,** crista sacralis intermedia. **sacral c., external,** crista sacralis lateralis. **sacral c., lateral,** crista sacralis lateralis. **sacral c., medial,** crista sacralis mediana. **seminal c.,** colliculus seminalis. **c. of smaller tubercle,** crista tuberculi minoris. **sphenoidal c.,** crista sphenoidalis. **spinal c. of Rauber,** processus spinosus vertebrarum. **c. of spinous processes of sacrum,** crista sacralis mediana. **supinator c., c. of supinator muscle,** crista musculi supinatoris. **supramastoid c.,** linea temporalis ossis frontalis. **supraventricular c.,** crista supraventricularis. **temporal c. of frontal bone,** linea temporalis ossis frontalis. **terminal c. of right atrium,** crista terminalis atrii dextri. **tibial c.,** margo anterior tibiae. **transverse c. of internal auditory meatus,** crista transversa. **trigeminal c.,** the embryonic cell mass from which the trigeminal ganglion develops. **turbinal c. of maxilla, inferior,** crista conchalis maxillae. **turbinal c. of maxilla, superior,** crista ethmoidalis maxillae. **turbinal c. of palatine bone, inferior,** crista conchalis ossis palatini. **turbinal c. of palatine bone, superior,** crista ethmoidalis ossis palatini. **ulnar c.,** margo interosseus ulnae. **urethral c., female,** crista urethralis femininae. **urethral c., male,** crista urethralis masculini. **c. of vestibule,** crista vestibuli. **zygomatic c. of great wing of sphenoid bone,** margo zygomaticus alae majoris.

cretin (kre′tin) [Fr.]. A person affected with cretinism.

cretinine (kre′tĭ-nin). A compound found in the thyroid gland.

cretinism (kre′tin-izm). A chronic condition due to congenital lack of thyroid secretion. It is marked by arrested physical and mental development with dystrophy of the bones and soft parts and lowered basal metabolism. It is the juvenile or congenital form of this deficiency while myxedema is the adult or acquired form. **fetal c.,** achondroplasia. **spontaneous c., sporadic c.,** cretinism in a person not descended from cretins, and who has not lived in a region where cretinism prevails.

cretinistic (kre″tin-is′tik). Pertaining to cretinism.

cretinoid (kre′tin-oid). Resembling a cretin; resembling cretinism.

cretinous (kre′tin-us). Affected with cretinism.

crevice (krev′is) [Fr. *crever* to split]. A longitudinal fissure. **gingival c.,** the space between the surface of the cervical enamel of a tooth and the overlying unattached gingiva; called also *subgingival space*.

crevicular (kre-vik′u-lar). Pertaining to a crevice, especially the gingival crevice.

crib (krib). In dentistry, a removable anchorage for orthodontic appliances. **clinical c.,** a crib in which an infant is placed for observation.

cribbing (krib′ing). A bad habit of some horses in which the animal grasps the manger or other object with the incisor teeth, arches the neck, makes peculiar movements with the head, and swallows quantities of air. Called also *crib-biting* and *wind-sucking*.

cribra (kri′brah) [L.]. Plural of *cribrum*.

cribral (krib′ral). Pertaining to a cribrum, or sieve-like structure.

cribrate (krib′rāt) [L. *cribratus*]. Pitted with depressions like the holes in a sieve.

cribration (krib-ra′shun). 1. The quality of being cribrate. 2. The process or act of sifting or passing through a sieve.

cribriform (krib′rĭ-form) [*cribrum* + L. *forma* form]. Perforated with small apertures like a sieve.

cribrum (kri′brum), pl. *cri′bra* [L. "sieve"]. Lamina cribrosa ossis ethmoidalis. **cri′bra orbita′lia of Welcker,** the small apertures in the lamina cribrosa, which give the bone a porous appearance and are thought to transmit veins from the diplöe to the orbit.

Cricetus (kri-se′tus). A genus of rodents. See *hamster.*

Crichton-Browne's sign (kri′ton-brownz) [Sir James *Crichton-Browne,* English physician, 1842–1938]. See under *sign.*

Crick (krik), Francis. English biochemist, born 1916; co-winner, with Maurice Wilkins and James Dewey Watson, of the Nobel prize in medicine and physiology for 1962, for the discovery of the molecular structure of deoxyribonucleic acid.

cricoarytenoid (kri″ko-ar″ĭ-te′noid). Pertaining to or extending between the cricoid and arytenoid cartilages.

cricoid (kri′koid) [Gr. *krikos* ring + *eidos* form]. 1. Resembling a ring; ring shaped. 2. The cricoid cartilage (cartilago cricoidea [N A]).

cricoidectomy (kri″koi-dek′to-me). Excision of the cricoid cartilage.

cricoidynia (kri″koi-din′e-ah) [Gr. *krikos* ring + *odynē* pain]. Pain in the cricoid cartilage.

cricopharyngeal (kri″ko-fah-rin′je-al). Pertaining to the cricoid cartilage and the pharynx.

cricothyreotomy (kri″ko-thi″re-ot′o-me) [Gr. *krikos* ring + *thyreos* shield + *tomē* a cut]. Incision through the cricoid and thyroid cartilages.

cricothyroid (kri-ko-thi′roid). Pertaining to or connecting the cricoid and thyroid cartilages.

cricothyroidotomy (kri″ko-thi″roi-dot′o-me). Cricothyreotomy.

cricotomy (kri-kot′o-me) [Gr. *krikos* ring + *tomē* a cut]. Incision of the cricoid cartilage.

cricotracheotomy (kri″ko-tra″ke-ot′o-me). Incision of the cricoid cartilage and trachea.

criminaloid (krim′ĭ-nal-oid). Resembling a criminal. By extension, sometimes used to designate an individual with characteristics resembling those of a criminal.

criminology (krim″ĭ-nol′o-je) [L. *crimen* crime + *-logy*]. The scientific study of crime and criminals.

criminosis (krim-ĭ-no′sis). A neurosis marked by criminal behavior.

crines (kri′nēz) [L.]. Plural of *crinis.*

crinin (krin′in) [Gr. *krinein* to separate]. A substance which stimulates glandular secretion.

crinis (kri′nis), pl. *cri′nes* [L.]. Hair. **c. cap′itis,** the hair of the head. **c. pu′bis,** the pubic hair.

crinogenic (krin″o-jen′ik) [Gr. *krinein* to separate + *gennan* to produce]. Stimulating secretion.

crinosin (kri′no-sin) [L. *crinis* hair]. A substance occurring in hairlike filaments, derivable from brain tissue.

Crinum (kri′num). A genus of amaryllidaceous plants; the root of *C. asiaticum,* of India, has properties like those of squill.

Cripps's obturator, operation (krips) [William Harrison *Cripps,* 1850–1923]. See under *obturator* and *operation.*

crise (krēz) [Fr.]. Crisis. **c. de deglobuliza′tion,** deglobulinization crisis.

crisis (kri′sis), pl. *cri′ses* [L.; Gr. *krisis*]. 1. The turning point of a disease for good or evil; especially, a sudden change, usually for the better, in the course of an acute disease. A disease terminates by crisis when recovery is indicated by a sudden and definite decrease in the intensity of the symptoms. Cf. *lysis.* 2. A sudden paroxysmal intensification of symptoms in the course of a disease. **addisonian c.,** the symptoms accompanying an acute onset of Addison's disease, viz., fatigue, nausea and vomiting, loss of weight. **anaphylactoid c.,** symptoms resembling those of anaphylaxis due to colloidoclasia. **aplastic c.,** a transient condition, marked by sudden disappearance of erythroblasts from the bone marrow, developing in certain hemolytic states and, rarely, during infections in children. **asthmatic c.,** status asthmaticus. **blood c.,** a sudden temporary appearance of great numbers of nucleated red cells (erythroblasts) in the blood. **bronchial c.,** a paroxysm of dyspnea in the course of a case of tabes dorsalis. **cardiac c.,** a severe paroxysm of palpitation of the heart occurring in tabes dorsalis. **celiac c.,** an attack of severe watery diarrhea and vomiting producing dehydration and acidosis which sometimes occurs in celiac disease. **cerebral c.,** a severe and sudden attack of hemiplegia, apoplexy, or other cerebral disorder. **clitoris c.,** an attack of sexual excitement occurring in women with tabes dorsalis. **colloidoclastic c.,** colloidoclasia. **deglobulinization c.,** a condition observed in congenital spherocytic anemia, characterized clinically by the acute onset of fever, abdominal pain, and vomiting, associated with reticulocytopenia, leukopenia, thrombocytopenia, erythroblastopenia, and return of the serum bilirubin to normal. **Dietl's c.,** sudden severe attack of nephralgia or gastric pain, chills, fever, nausea and vomiting, and general collapse: said to be due to partial turning of the kidney upon its pedicle. **febrile c.,** an attack of chilliness, fever, and sweating. **gastric c.,** a paroxysm of intense abdominal pain in a case of tabes dorsalis. **genital c. of newborn,** a condition characterized by estrinization of the vaginal mucosa and hyperplasia of the breasts, under the influence of transplacentally acquired estrogens. **hematic c.,** a term previously used to indicate a sudden increase in blood platelets during fever. **hemoclastic c.,** a temporary leukopenia, with a relative lymphocytosis, associated with a lowered blood pressure and changes in blood coagulability: due to the presence of toxic protein-split products in the blood stream. It occurs in anaphylactic shock after a meal of albuminoids in persons whose liver function is disordered. **hepatic c.,** an attack of intense pain in the region of the liver. **intestinal c.,** a sharp attack of pain in the intestine in a case of tabes dorsalis. **laryngeal c.,** paroxysmal spasm of the larynx in the earlier course of tabes dorsalis. **Lundvall's blood c.,** a term used by Lundvall to designate a shift from leukopenia to leukocytosis in patients with dementia praecox. **myelocytic c.,** a sudden appearance of myelocytes in the blood. **nefast c.,** a peculiar onset of severe and unaccountable symptoms in experimental icterogenous spirochetosis. **nephralgic c.,** a paroxysm of pain in the course of the ureter in a case of tabes dorsalis. **nitritoid c.,** a group of symptoms sometimes following the injection of arsphenamine, consisting of redness of the face, dyspnea, a feeling of distress, cough, and precordial pain. The condition is named from its resemblance to the symptoms of amyl nitrite poisoning. **ocular c.,** a sudden attack of intense pain in the eyes, with lacrimation, photophobia, etc. **oculogyric c.,** a crisis occurring in epidemic encephalitis in which the eyeballs become fixed in one position for minutes or hours. **Pel's c's,** ocular crises in tabes dorsalis. **pharyngeal c.,** a sudden attack occurring in tabes dorsalis, marked by peculiar sensations in the pharynx and involuntary swallowing movements. **rectal c.,** a severe seizure of rectal pain in tabes dorsalis. **renal c.,** an attack of pain resembling renal colic, occurring in tabes. **tabetic c.,** a painful paroxysm with functional disturbance occurring in the course of tabes dorsalis. **thoracic c.,** an attack of pain resembling angina pectoris, but with spasmodic contracture of the muscles of the chest and arms in tabes dorsalis. **thrombocytic c.,** a spontaneous and more or less permanent increase of blood platelets in the blood. **thyroid c., thyrotoxic c.,** a sudden and dangerous increase of the symptoms of thyrotoxicosis. **vesical c.,** a severe seizure of pain in the bladder in cases of tabes dorsalis. **visceral c.,** a paroxysm of shooting pain in any viscus occurring in a case of tabes dorsalis.

Crismer's test (kris'merz) [Leon *Crismer*, Belgian chemist, born 1858]. See under *tests.*

crispation (kris-pa'shun) [L. *crispare* to curl]. Slight convulsive or spasmodic muscular contractions producing a creeping sensation.

crista (kris'ta), pl. *cris'tae* [L.]. [N A, B N A] A projection or projecting structure, or ridge, especially one surmounting a bone or its border. Called also *crest* and *ridge.* **c. acus'tica,** c. ampullaris. **c. ampulla'ris** [N A, B N A], the most prominent part of a localized thickening of the membrane that lines the ampullae of the semicircular ducts, covered with neuroepithelium containing endings of the vestibular nerve. Called also *ampullary crest.* **c. ante'rior fib'ulae** [B N A], margo anterior fibulae. **c. ante'rior tib'iae** [B N A], margo anterior tibiae. **c. arcua'ta cartilag'inis arytenoi'deae** [N A], a ridge on the external surface of the arytenoid cartilage between the triangular pit and the oblong pit. Called also *arcuate crest of arytenoid cartilage.* **c. basila'ris duc'tus cochlea'ris** [N A], the triangular eminence on the spiral ligament to which the basilar membrane is attached. Called also *basilar crest.* **c. buccinato'ria** [B N A], a ridge running from the base of the coronoid process of the mandible to a point near the last molar tooth, giving attachment to the buccinator muscle. Omitted in N A. **c. cap'itis cos'tae** [N A], **c. capit'uli cos'tae** [B N A], a horizontal crest dividing the articular surface of the head of the rib into two facets, for articulation with the depression on the bodies of two adjacent vertebrae. Called also *crest of head of rib.* **c. col'li cos'tae** [N A, B N A], a crest on the superior border of the neck of a rib, giving attachment to the anterior costotransverse ligament. Called also *crest of neck of rib.* **c. concha'lis maxil'lae** [N A, B N A], an oblique ridge on the nasal surface of the body of the maxilla, just anterior to the lacrimal sulcus, which articulates with the inferior nasal concha. Called also *conchal crest of maxilla.* **c. concha'lis os'sis palati'ni** [N A, B N A], a sharp transverse ridge, near the posterior edge of the palatine bone, which articulates with the inferior concha. Called also *conchal crest of palatine bone.* **cris'tae cu'tis** [N A, B N A], ridges of the skin produced by the projecting papillae of the corium on the palm of the hand or sole of the foot, producing a finger- or foot-print that is characteristic of the individual. Called also *dermal ridges.* **c. ethmoida'lis maxil'lae** [N A, B N A], a low, oblique ridge on the medial surface of the frontal process of the maxilla, which articulates with the middle nasal concha. Called also *ethmoidal crest of maxilla.* **c. ethmoida'lis os'sis palati'ni** [N A, B N A], a ridge near the upper end of the medial surface of the palatine bone, which articulates with the middle concha. Called also *ethmoidal crest of palatine bone.* **c. falcifor'mis,** c. transversa. **c. fem'oris,** linea aspera femoris. **c. fenes'trae coch'leae** [N A, B N A], the ledge of bone that overhangs the cochlear window of the middle ear. Called also *crest of cochlear window.* **c. fronta'lis** [N A, B N A], a median ridge on the internal surface of the frontal bone, extending upward from the foramen cecum to unite with the sulcus for the superior sagittal sinus. Called also *frontal crest.* **c. gal'li** [N A, B N A], a thick triangular process projecting upward from the cribriform plate of the ethmoid bone. The falx cerebri attaches to it. **c. hel'icis,** crus helicis. **c. ili'aca** [N A, B N A], **c. il'ii,** the thickened, expanded upper border of the ilium. Called also *iliac crest.* **c. infratempora'lis** [N A, B N A], a crest separating the temporal surface of the great wing of the sphenoid bone into a temporal portion above and an infratemporal portion below. Called also *infratemporal crest.* **c. interos'sea fib'ulae,** margo interosseus fibulae. **c. interos'sea ra'dii** [B N A], margo interosseus radii. **c. interos'sea tib'iae** [B N A], margo interosseus tibiae. **c. interos'sea ul'nae** [B N A], margo interosseus ulnae. **c. intertrochanter'ica** [N A, B N A], a prominent ridge running obliquely downward and medialward from the summit of the greater trochanter on the posterior surface of the neck to the lesser trochanter. Called also *intertrochanteric crest.* **c. lacrima'lis ante'rior** [N A, B N A], the lateral margin of the groove on the posterior border of the frontal process of the maxilla. Called also *anterior lacrimal crest.* **c. lacrima'lis poste'rior** [N A, B N A], a vertical ridge dividing the lateral or orbital surface of the lacrimal bone into two parts, and forming one margin of the fossa for the lacrimal gland. Called also *posterior lacrimal crest.* **c. latera'lis fib'ulae** [B N A], margo posterior fibulae. **cris'tae ma'tricis un'guis** [N A, B N A], vascular longitudinal ridges in the nail matrix. Called also *crests of matrix of nail.* **c. media'lis fib'ulae** [N A, B N A], the long crest on the posterior surface of the body of the fibula, which separates the origin of the tibialis posterior muscle from that of the flexor hallucis longus muscle. Called also *medial crest of fibula.* **c. mus'culi supinato'ris** [N A, B N A], a strong ridge forming the posterior margin of the supinator fossa below the radial notch of the ulna, and with it giving attachment to the supinator muscle. Called also *crest of supinator muscle.* **c. nasa'lis maxil'lae** [N A, B N A], a ridge, raised along the medial border of the palatine process of the maxilla, with which the vomer articulates. Called also *nasal crest of maxilla.* **c. nasa'lis os'sis palati'ni** [N A, B N A], a thick ridge projecting upward from the medial part of the horizontal plate of the palatine bone. Called also *nasal crest of palatine bone.* **c. obturato'ria** [N A, B N A], the inferior border of the superior ramus of the os pubis, a strong ridge of bone beginning near the pubic tubercle and extending to the anterior part of the gap in the rim of the acetabulum, giving attachment to the obturator membrane. Called also *obturator crest.* **c. occipita'lis exter'na** [N A, B N A], a variable crest of bone that sometimes extends from the external occipital protuberance toward the foramen magnum. Called also *external occipital crest.* **c. occipita'lis inter'na** [N A], a median ridge on the internal surface of the occipital bone extending from the midpoint of the cruciform eminence toward the foramen magnum, being a variant form of the internal occipital protuberance. Called also *internal occipital crest.* **c. palati'na** [N A], a transverse crest often seen on the inferior surface of the horizontal plate of the palatine bone a short distance anterior to the posterior border. Called also *palatine crest.* **c. pu'bica** [N A, B N A], the thick, rough, anterior border of the body of the pubic bone. Called also *pubic crest.* **cris'tae sacra'les articula'res** [B N A]. See *crista sacralis intermedia.* **c. sacra'lis interme'dia** [N A], either of two indefinite crests just medial to the dorsal sacral foramina, formed by fusion of the articular processes of the sacral vertebrae. Called also *intermediate sacral crest.* **c. sacra'lis latera'lis** [N A], either of two series of tubercles lateral to the dorsal sacral foramina, representing the transverse processes of the sacral vertebrae. Called also *lateral sacral crest.* **c. sacra'lis me'dia** [B N A], **c. sacra'lis media'na** [N A], a median ridge on the dorsal surface of the sacrum, formed by the remnants of the spinous processes of the upper four sacral vertebrae. Called also *medial sacral crest.* **c. sphenoida'lis** [N A, B N A], a median ridge on the anterior surface of the body of the sphenoid bone, articulating with the perpendicular plate of the ethmoid. Called also *sphenoidal crest.* **c. spira'lis,** labium limbi vestibulare laminae spirales. **c. supraventricula'ris** [N A, B N A], a ridge on the inner wall of the right ventricle, marking off the conus arteriosus. Called also *infundibuloventricular* or *supraventricular crest.* **c. tempora'lis,** linea temporalis ossis frontalis. **c. termina'lis a'trii dex'tri** [N A, B N A], a ridge on the posterior internal surface of the right atrium of the heart, located to the right of the orifices of the superior and inferior venae cavae. The pectinate muscles of the right atrium end at this crest. It corresponds to a groove on the external surface, the sulcus terminalis. Called also *terminal crest of right atrium.* **c. transver'sa** [N A, B N A], a ridge of bone that divides the fundus of the internal acoustic meatus into a superior and an inferior fossa. Called also *transverse crest of internal acoustic meatus.* **c. tuber'culi majo'ris** [N A, B N A], a projection on the greater tubercle of the humerus, forming one lip of the intertubercular groove. **c. tuber'culi mino'ris** [N A, B N A], a projection on the lesser tubercle of the humerus, forming one lip of the intertubercular groove. **c. tympan'ica,** a ridge on the tympanic ring. **c. ul'nae,** margo interosseus ulnae. **c. urethra'lis femini'nae** [N A], a prominent longitudinal fold of the mucosa along the posterior wall of the female urethra. Called also *c. urethralis muliebris* [B N A], and *female urethral crest.* **c. urethra'lis masculi'nae** [N A], a median elevation along the posterior wall of the urethra in the male, lying between the prostatic sinuses. Called also *c. urethralis virilis* [B N A], and *male urethral crest.* **c. urethra'lis mulie'bris** [B N A], crista urethralis femininae. **c. urethra'lis vir'ilis** [B N A], c. urethralis masculinae. **c. vestib'uli** [N A, B N A], a ridge between the spherical and elliptical recesses of the vestibule, dividing posteriorly to bound the cochlear recess. Called also *crest of vestibule.*

cristae (kris'te) [L.]. Plural of *crista.*

cristal (kris'tal). Pertaining to a crest or ridge.

Cristispira (kris"tĭ-spi'rah) [L. *crista* crest + Gr. *speira* coil]. A genus of microorganisms of the family Spirochaetaceae, order Spirochaetales, made up of coarse, flexuous, spiral cells with cross striations and a thin membrane on one side, extending the whole length of the body; found in the intestinal tracts of molluscs. It contains three species, *C. anodon'tae, C. balbia'nii,* and *C. pin'nae.*

Critchett's operation (krich'ets) [George *Critchett,* oculist in London, 1817–1882]. See under *operation.*

criterion (kri-te're-on) [Gr. *kritērion* a means for judging]. A standard by which something may be judged. **Koeppe's c.,** translucency of the column of packed red cells when little or no plasma is present between them in the hematocrit tube.

crith (krith) [Gr. *krithē* barleycorn, the smallest weight]. The unit of weight for gases, being the weight of a liter of hydrogen gas at 0°C. and pressure equivalent to that of a column of mercury 760 mm. high.

Crithidia (krĭ-thid'e-ah). 1. A genus of protozoan organisms resembling Trypanosoma: found as parasites in the intestines of certain insects. 2. One of the developmental forms assumed by a trypanosome during its life in its insect host. **C. cunninghami,** *Leishmania tropica.*

critical (krit'ĭ-kl). Pertaining to or of the nature of a crisis.

crocated (kro'kāt-ed) [L. *crocatus*]. Tinctured with or containing saffron.

crocein (kro'se-in). Any one of a series of bright red stains.

crocidismus (kro"se-diz'mus) [Gr. *krokē* a tuft of wool]. Carphology.

crocose (kro'kōs). A white, crystalline sugar, $C_6H_{12}O_6$, formed by the decomposition of crocin.

Crocq's disease (kroks) [Jean B. *Crocq,* Belgian physician, 1868–1925]. Acrocyanosis.

Crohn's disease (krōnz) [Burrill B. *Crohn,* New York physician, born 1884]. Regional ileitis.

Cronin Lowe reaction or **test** [E. *Cronin Lowe,* British physician]. See under *tests.*

Crooke's changes [Arthur Carleton *Crooke,* British pathologist]. Hyalinization of the cytoplasm of the basophilic cells of the anterior lobe of the hypophysis, disappearance of their basophilic granules, ballooning of their nuclei, enlargement and multinucleation of the cells.

Crookes's space, tube [Sir William *Crookes,* English physicist, 1832–1919]. See under *space* and *tube.*

cross (kros). Any figure or structure in the shape of a cross. **clavicular c.,** a figure-of-8 bandage on both shoulders, crossing over a pad placed in the interscapular space. **green c.,** phenylcarbylamine chloride. **Ranvier's c's,** dark, cross-shaped markings at the nodes of Ranvier, seen on longitudinal section after staining with silver nitrate. **silver c.,** a crosslike marking seen at the nodes of certain bundles of medullated nerve fibers. **yellow c.,** dichlorodiethyl sulfide.

crossbite (kros'bīt). A condition in which mandibular teeth are in buccal version to the maxillary teeth, bilaterally, unilaterally, or involving only a pair of opposing teeth.

crossed (krost). Shaped or arranged like a cross: decussating.

cross-eye (kros'i). Esotropia.

crossfoot (kros'foot). Talipes varus.

crossing over (kros'ing o'ver). Exchange of genes between homologous chromosomes of a hybrid.

crossmatching (kros-mach'ing). See under *matching.*

crossway (kros'wā). The path by which something crosses. **sensory c.,** posterior part of the internal capsule of the brain.

crotalin (kro'tah-lin). A protein found in the venom of rattlesnakes and certain other serpents. It has been used hypodermically in the treatment of epilepsy.

crotalism (kro'tal-izm). A disease of horses caused by eating rattlebox, *Crotalaria sagittalis.*

crotalotoxin (kro"tah-lo-tok'sin). A poisonous substance from rattlesnake venom.

Crotalus (krot'ah-lus) [L., from Gr. *krotalon* rattle]. A genus of rattlesnakes of the family Crotalidae. *C. hor'ridus* is the common rattlesnake of the eastern United States; *C. adaman'teus* is the diamond-back rattlesnake of Georgia, Alabama and Florida; *C. vir'idis* is the prairie rattler.

crotamiton (kro"tah-mi'ton). A compound, N-ethyl-o-crotonotoluide, used in the treatment of scabies.

crotaphion (kro-taf'e-on) [Gr. *krotaphos* the temple]. A craniometric point at the tip of the great wing of the sphenoid.

crotchet (kroch'et) [Fr. *crochet*]. A hook used in delivering the fetus after craniotomy.

crotin (kro'tin). A poisonous substance derived from the seeds of *Croton tiglium.*

Croton (kro'ton) [L.; Gr. *krotōn* tick]. A large genus of euphorbiaceous trees, shrubs, and herbs, many of them poisonous and medicinal. See *Cascarilla. C. tig'lium* furnishes croton oil bean.

crotonism (kro'ton-izm). Poisoning by croton oil.

crotoxin (kro-tok'sin). A crystalline neurotoxic principle from the venom of the rattlesnake, *Crotalus terrificus.*

crounotherapy (kroo"no-ther'ah-pe) [Gr. *krounos* spring + *therapeia* treatment]. Crenotherapy.

croup (kro͞op). A condition resulting from acute obstruction of the larynx caused by allergy, foreign body, infection, or new growth, occurring chiefly in infants and children, and characterized by resonant barking cough, hoarseness, and persistent stridor. **catarrhal c.,** croup accompanied with a catarrhal discharge. **diphtheritic c.,** croup associated with infection by *Corynebacterium diphtheriae.* **false c.,** laryngismus stridulus. **membranous c., pseudomembranous c.,** croup associated with a fibrinous exudate forming a membrane-like deposit. **spasmodic c.,** laryngismus stridulus.

croupous (kroo′pus). Of the nature of croup, or attended with an exudation like that of croup.

croupy (kro͞op′e). Affected with or resembling croup.

Crouzon's disease (kroo-zonz′) [O. *Crouzon*, French neurologist, 1874–1938]. Craniofacial dysostosis.

crown (krown) [L. *corona*]. The topmost part of an organ or other structure, such as the top of the head, or the upper part of a tooth (corona dentis [N A]). See also *anatomical c.* and *physiological c.* **anatomical c.,** the portion of a tooth that is covered by enamel. See *corona dentis.* **artificial c.,** a restoration of metal, porcelain, or plastic which reproduces the entire surface anatomy of the clinical crown of a tooth and which is affixed to the remains of the natural tooth structure. **Beer's c.,** a gold-banded crown for a tooth, with swaged occlusal carvings, introduced in the early 1870's. **bell c.,** a tooth crown which is largest at the occlusal surface and tapers toward the neck. **Bischoff's c.,** the inner layer formed from the duplication of the epithelial capsule of the ovum. **Black's c.,** a porcelain-faced crown for an anterior tooth fastened by a screw passing into a gold-lined root canal. **cap c.,** an artificial crown that is applied like a cap over the remaining natural crown of a tooth. **Carmichael c.,** partial veneer c. **ciliary c.,** corona ciliaris. **clinical c.,** that portion of a tooth which is exposed beyond the gingiva. **collar c.,** an artificial crown attached by a metal ferrule to a natural tooth root. **Davis c.,** an artificial crown attached by a pin which is inserted into both the crown and the natural root of the tooth. **extra-alveolar c.,** that portion of a tooth which is distal to the attachment of the tooth in the alveolus. **full c.,** a dental restoration that completely reproduces the clinical crown of a natural tooth. **half-cap c.,** an artificial crown attached by a metal band which covers only the lingual surface of the tooth that supports it. **jacket c.,** a resin or porcelain restoration that is applied over the clinical crown of a tooth and terminates at or under the gingiva. **Morrison c.,** a cap crown of gold made in two pieces, a band and a swaged occlusal surface. **open-face c.,** half-cap c. **partial veneer c.,** a restoration applied to the proximal and lingual surfaces and the occlusal surface or incisal edge of a tooth, used as a retainer for a bridge or as a single-unit restoration on a fractured tooth. **physiological c.,** the portion of a tooth that is exposed distal to the gingival crevice or to the margin of the gum; it may or may not coincide with the anatomical crown, which is the portion covered by enamel. **pivot c.,** an artificial crown attached by a post in the root canal of the tooth. **post c.,** an artificial crown secured to the root of the tooth by a post or dowel. **Richmond c.,** a factory-made porcelain tooth with a gold post and soldered back, introduced in the late 1870's. **shell c.,** cap c. **three-quarter c.,** partial veneer c. **veneer c.,** an artificial crown which bears a thin layer of resin or porcelain on the buccal or labial surface, attached to or bonded to the metal casting. **window c.,** veneer c. **Wood c.,** an artificial crown consisting of porcelain baked to a platinum cap.

crowning (krown′ing). That stage in childbirth when the top of the infant's head becomes visible at the vaginal orifice.

cruces (kroo′sēz) [L.]. Plural of *crux*.

Cruchet's disease (kroo-shāz′) [René *Cruchet*, Bordeaux physician, born 1875]. Epidemic encephalomyelitis.

crucial (kroo′shal) [L. *crucialis*]. 1. Shaped like a cross. 2. Severe, searching, and decisive.

cruciate (kroo′she-āt). Shaped like a cross.

crucible (kroo′sĭ-bl) [L. *crucibulum*]. A vessel for melting refractory substances.

cruciform (kroo′sĭ-form) [*crux* + L. *forma* form]. Shaped like a cross.

crude (kro͞od) [L. *crudus* raw]. Raw or unrefined.

cruentation (kroo″en-ta′shun) [L. *cruor* blood]. In medieval jurisprudence, the supposed bleeding of the corpse in the presence of the murderer.

cruor (kroo′or), pl. *cruo′res* [L.]. A blood clot that contains red corpuscles.

crupper (krup′er). The rump of a horse, or the part behind the saddle.

crura (kroo′rah) [L.]. Plural of *crus.*

crural (kro͞or′al). Pertaining to the leg or to a leglike structure (crus).

crureus (kroo-re′us). Musculus vastus intermedius. See *Table of Musculi.*

crus (krus), pl. *cru′ra* [L.] [N A, N B A]. 1. The leg, from knee to foot. 2. A general term used to designate a leglike part. **anterior c. of anterior inguinal ring,** c. mediale anuli inguinalis superficialis. **anterior c. of internal capsule,** c. anterius capsulae internae. **anterior c. of stapes,** c. anterius stapedis. **c. ante′rius cap′sulae inter′nae** [N A], the part of the internal capsule that separates the caudate and the lentiform nuclei. Called also *anterior limb of internal capsule* and *pars frontalis capsulae internae* [B N A]. **c. ante′rius stape′dis** [N A, B N A], the anterior of the two bony limbs that connect the base and head of the stapes. Called also *anterior crus of stapes.* **cru′ra anthel′icis** [N A, B N A], **crura of anthelix,** the two ridges marking the superior termination of the anthelix and bounding the triangular fossa. **c. bre′ve in′cudis** [N A, B N A], the backward-projecting process on the incus that is connected to the posterior wall of the tympanic cavity. Called also *short crus of incus.* **c. cerebel′li ad pon′tem,** pedunculus cerebellaris medius. **c. cer′ebri** [N A], the ventral part of the cerebral peduncle, composed of descending fiber tracts that pass from the cerebral cortex to form the longitudinal fascicles of the pons, including the corticospinal, corticopontine, and corticobulbar tracts. Called also *basis pedunculi cerebri* [B N A]. **c. clitor′idis** [N A, B N A], **c. of clitoris,** the continuation of each corpus cavernosum clitoridis, diverging posteriorly to be attached to the pubic arch. **c. commu′ne cana′lis semicircula′ris** [B N A], c. osseum commune. **crura of diaphragm, cru′ra diaphrag′matis.** See *pars lumbalis diaphragmatis.* **external c. of anterior inguinal ring,** c. laterale anuli inguinalis superficialis. **c. fascic′uli atrioventricula′ris [dex′trum et sinis′trum]** [N A], either branch (right or left) of the atrioventricular bundle, arising from the main trunk of the bundle at the superior end of the muscular part of the interventricular septum and descending on either side to be distributed to the respective ventricle. **c. for′nicis** [N A, B N A], **c. of fornix,** either of the two flattened bands of white substance that are in close contact with the splenium and that unite under the posterior part of the body of the corpus callosum to form the body of the fornix. **c. glan′dis clitor′idis,** frenulum clitoridis. **c. hel′icis** [N A, B N A], **c. of helix,** the anterior termination of the helix, located above the entrance to the external acoustic meatus. **c. infe′rior an′nuli inguina′lis subcuta′nei** [B N A], c. laterale anuli inguinalis superficialis. **c. interme′dium par′tis lumba′lis diaphrag′matis** [B N A], omitted in N A. **internal c. of anterior inguinal ring,** c. mediale anuli inguinalis superficialis. **internal c. of greater alar cartilage of nose,** c. mediale cartilaginis alaris majoris. **lateral c. of greater alar cartilage,** c. laterale cartilaginis alaris majoris. **c. latera′le an′uli inguina′lis superficia′lis** [N A], the part of the superficial inguinal ring that blends with the inguinal ligament as it goes to the pubic tubercle. Called also *c. inferius annuli inguinalis subcutanei* [B N A], and *lateral c. of superficial inguinal ring.* **c. latera′le cartilag′inis**

ala'ris majo'ris [N A, B N A], the part of the greater alar cartilage that curves laterally around the nostril and helps maintain its contour. Called also *lateral c. of greater alar cartilage*. **c. latera'le par'tis lumba'lis diaphrag'matis** [B N A], omitted in N A. **c. lon'gum in'cudis** [N A, B N A], a process on the incus directed downward and inward, parallel with the manubrium of the malleus. Called also *long crus of incus*. **medial c. of external inguinal ring,** ligamentum inguinale reflexum. **medial c. of greater alar cartilage,** c. mediale cartilaginis alaris majoris. **medial c. of superficial inguinal ring,** c. mediale anuli inguinalis superficialis. **c. media'le an'uli inguina'lis superficia'lis** [N A], the part of the superficial inguinal ring that is attached to the symphysis and that blends with the fundiform ligament of the penis. Called also *medial c. of superficial inguinal ring* and *c. superius annuli inguinalis subcutanei* [B N A]. **c. media'le cartilag'inis ala'ris majo'ris** [N A, B N A], the part of the greater alar cartilage, loosely attached to its fellow of the opposite side, and helping to form the mobile septum of the nose. Called also *medial c. of greater alar cartilage*. **c. media'le par'tis lumba'lis diaphrag'matis** [B N A], omitted in N A. **cru'ra membrana'cea** [N A], the two ends of each semicircular duct, both opening into the utricle. See *crura membranacea ampullaria ductus semicircularis*, *c. membranaceum commune ductus semicircularis*, and *c. membranaceum simplex ductus semicircularis*. **cru'ra membrana'cea ampulla'ria duc'tus semicircula'ris** [N A], the end of each semicircular duct in which the membranous ampulla is situated. Called also *ampullary membranous crura of semicircular ducts*. **c. membrana'ceum commu'ne duc'tus semicircula'ris** [N A], the joined non-ampullary ends of the anterior and posterior semicircular ducts. Called also *common membranous crus of semicircular ducts*. **c. membrana'ceum sim'plex duc'tus semicircula'ris** [N A], the non-ampullary end of the lateral semicircular duct, opening into the utricle. Called also *simple membranous crus of semicircular duct*. **membranous crura,** crura membranacea. **cru'ra os'sea** [N A], those parts of the bony semicircular canals that lodge the correspondingly named parts of the membranous crura of the semicircular ducts. See *crura ossea ampullaria*, *c. osseum commune*, and *c. osseum simplex*. **cru'ra os'sea ampulla'ria** [N A], the parts of the bony semicircular canals that lodge the crura membranacea ampullaria ductus semicircularis. Called also *ampullary osseous crura*. **osseous crura,** crura ossea. **c. os'seum commu'ne** [N A], the part of the bony semicircular canals that lodges the crus membranaceum commune ductus semicircularis. Called also *common osseous crus*. **c. os'seum sim'plex** [N A], that part of the bony semicircular canals that lodges the crus membranaceum simplex ductus semicircularis. Called also *simple osseous crus*. **c. pe'nis** [N A, B N A], **c. of penis,** the continuation of each corpus cavernosum penis, diverging posteriorly to be attached to the pubic arch. **posterior c. of anterior inguinal ring,** c. laterale anuli inguinalis superficialis. **posterior c. of internal capsule,** c. posterius capsulae internae. **posterior c. of stapes,** c. posterius stapedis. **c. poste'rius cap'sulae inter'nae** [N A], the part of the internal capsule that separates the thalamus from the lentiform nucleus. It includes a pars sublentiformis and a pars retrolentiformis. Called also *posterior limb of internal capsule* and *pars occipitalis capsulae internae* [B N A]. **c. poste'rius stape'dis** [N A, B N A], the posterior of the two bony limbs that connect the base and head of the stapes. Called also *posterior c. of stapes*. **short c. of incus,** c. breve incudis. **c. sim'plex cana'lis semicircula'ris** [B N A], c. osseum simplex. **superior c. of cerebellum,** pedunculus cerebellaris superior. **superior c. of subcutaneous inguinal ring,** c. mediale anuli inguinalis superficialis. **c. supe'rius an'nuli inguina'lis subcuta'nei** [B N A], c. mediale anuli inguinalis superficialis.

crust (krust) [L. *crusta*]. A formed outer layer, especially an outer layer of solid matter formed by the drying of a bodily exudate or secretion. **buffy c.,** buffy coat. **milk c.,** crusta lactea.

crusta (krus'tah), pl. *crus'tae* [L.]. 1. A crust. 2. Basis pedunculi. **c. lac'tea,** seborrhea of the scalp of nursing infants. **c. petro'sa den'tis,** the cement of a tooth. **c. phlogis'tica,** buffy coat.

Crustacea (krus-ta'she-ah) [L. from *crusta* shell]. A large class of animals, including the lobsters, crabs, shrimps, wood lice, water fleas, barnacles, etc.

crustaceorubin (krus-ta″se-o-roo'bin). A brown-black pigment (chromoprotein) found in lobster shells and eggs and in certain crabs. Called also *zoonerythrin*, *tetra-erythrin*, and *vitellorubin*.

crustae (krus'te) [L.]. Plural of *crusta*.

crustal (krus'tal). Pertaining to the crusta.

crustosus (krus-to'sus) [L.]. Crusted: said of certain lesions of the skin.

crutch (kruch). A device of wood or metal, ordinarily long enough to reach from the armpit to the ground, with a concave surface fitting under the arm and a cross bar for the hand, used for supporting the weight of the body. **California c.,** Canadian c. **Canadian c.,** a variation of the English cane consisting of two uprights extending halfway between the elbow and shoulder, with a cross piece for the hand and a curved upper arm part against which the subject leans his upper arm.

Cruveilhier's atrophy, disease (kroo-vāl-yāz') [Jean *Cruveilhier*, French pathologist, 1791–1874. He held the first chair of pathology in the Paris faculty]. See under the nouns.

crux (kruks), pl. *cru'ces* [L.]. Cross. **c. of heart,** the intersection of the walls separating the right and left sides and the upper and lower chambers of the heart. **cru'ces pilo'rum** [N A], crosslike figures formed by the pattern of hair growth, the hairs lying in opposite directions.

Cruz trypanosomiasis (kruz) [Oswaldo *Cruz*, Brazilian physician, 1871–1917]. Chagas' disease.

cry (kri). A sudden loud, involuntary vocal sound. **arthritic c., articular c.,** night c. **Douglas c.,** a sharp, prolonged cry by a patient when, during laparotomy, the cul-de-sac of Douglas is touched. **epileptic c.,** a loud scream that often occurs at the onset of an epileptic attack. **hydrocephalic c.,** the loud cry of a patient with acute tuberculous meningitis. **joint c.,** night c. **night c.,** a shrill cry uttered by a child in sleep, often heard in beginning joint disease.

cryalgesia (kri″al-je'ze-ah) [*cryo-* + Gr. *algēsis* pain]. Pain due to the application of cold.

cryanesthesia (kri″an-es-the'ze-ah) [*cryo-* + *anesthesia*]. Loss of the power of perceiving cold.

Cryer's elevator (kri'erz) [Matthew H. *Cryer*, American surgeon, 1840–1921]. See under *elevator*.

cryesthesia (kri″es-the'ze-ah) [*cryo-* + Gr. *aisthēsis* perception]. Abnormal sensitiveness to cold.

crymo- (kri'mo) [Gr. *krymos* frost]. Combining form denoting relationship to cold.

crymoanesthesia (kri″mo-an-es-the'ze-ah) [*crymo-* + *anesthesia*]. Refrigeration anesthesia.

crymodynia (kri″mo-din'e-ah) [*crymo-* + Gr. *odynē* pain]. Rheumatic pain coming on in cold or damp weather.

crymophilia (kri″mo-fil'e-ah) [*crymo-* + Gr. *philein* to love]. Cryophilia.

crymophilic (kri″mo-fil'ik). Cryophilic.

crymophylactic (kri″mo-fi-lak'tik). Cryophylactic.

crymotherapeutics (kri″mo-ther″ah-pu'tiks). Cryotherapy.

crymotherapy (kri″mo-ther′ah-pe). Cryotherapy.

cryo- (kri′o) [Gr. *kryos* cold]. A combining form denoting relationship to cold.

cryoaerotherapy (kri″o-a″er-o-ther′ah-pe) [*cryo-* + Gr. *aēr* air + *therapy*]. Cold air treatment.

cryobiology (kri″o-bi-ol′o-je) [*cryo-* + Gr. *bios* life + *-logy*]. The science dealing with the effect of low temperatures on biological systems.

cryocardioplegia (kri″o-kar″de-o-ple′je-ah). Cessation of contraction of the myocardium produced by application of cold during cardiac surgery.

cryocautery (kri″o-kaw′ter-e) [*cryo-* + *cautery*]. Cold cautery.

cryocrit (kri′o-krit) [*cryo-* + Gr. *krinein* to separate]. The percentage of the total volume of blood serum or plasma which is occupied by cryoprecipitates after separation by centrifugation.

cryoextraction (kri″o-eks-trak′shun). The application of low temperature in the removal of a cataractous lens.

cryoextractor (kri″o-eks-trak′tor). A pencil-shaped instrument made of copper and provided with a small ball at its end, to be chilled in a freezing mixture and used in cryoextraction.

cryofibrinogen (kri″o-fi-brin′o-jen) [*cryo-* + *fibrinogen*]. A blood protein resembling fibrinogen which precipitates from plasma on cooling.

cryofibrinogenemia (kri″o-fi-brin″o-jen-e′me-ah). The presence of cryofibrinogens in the blood.

cryogammaglobulin (kri″o-gam″ah-glob′u-lin). A gamma globulin that is readily precipitated by reduced temperature (cold).

cryogen (kri′o-jen) [*cryo-* + Gr. *gennan* to produce]. A substance used for lowering temperatures.

cryogenic (kri″o-jen′ik). Pertaining to or causing the production of low temperatures.

cryoglobulin (kri″o-glob′u-lin). A serum globulin which precipitates, gels, or crystallizes spontaneously at low temperatures.

cryoglobulinemia (kri″o-glob″u-lin-e′me-ah). Presence in the serum of cryoglobulins.

cryohydrate (kri″o-hi′drāt) [*cryo-* + *hydrate*]. A eutectic mixture, especially one having water as one of its constituents.

cryometer (kri-om′e-ter) [*cryo-* + Gr. *metron* measure]. A thermometer for measuring very low temperatures.

cryopathy (kri-op′ah-the) [*cryo-* + Gr. *pathos* disease]. Any morbid condition caused by cold.

cryophilia (kri″o-fil′e-ah) [*cryo-* + Gr. *philein* to love]. The condition of growing best at low temperatures: said of bacteria.

cryophilic (kri″o-fil′ik) [*cryo-* + Gr. *philein* to love]. Growing best at low temperatures.

cryophylactic (kri″o-fi-lak′tik) [*cryo-* + Gr. *phylaxis* a guarding]. Resistant to very low temperatures: said of bacteria.

cryoprecipitability (kri″o-pre-sip″ĭ-tah-bil′ĭ-te). The quality of being readily precipitated by reduced temperature (cold).

cryoprecipitate (kri″o-pre-sip′ĭ-tāt) [*cryo-* + *precipitate*]. Any precipitate which results from cooling.

cryoprecipitation (kri″o-pre-sip″ĭ-ta′shun). The precipitation of a substance in solution on exposure to lowered temperature.

cryoprotein (kri″o-pro′te-in) [*cryo-* + *protein*]. Any blood protein which precipitates on cooling.

cryoscope (kri′o-skōp). An apparatus for performing cryoscopy.

cryoscopical (kri″o-skop′e-kl). Pertaining to cryoscopy.

cryoscopy (kri-os′ko-pe) [*cryo-* + Gr. *skopein* to examine]. Examination of liquids, based on the principle that the freezing point of solutions varies according to the amount and the nature of the substance contained in them in solution.

cryostat (kri′o-stat) [*cryo-* + Gr. *histanai* to halt]. A device interposed in a refrigerating system by which the temperature can be automatically maintained between certain levels.

cryosurgery (kri″o-sur′jer-e). The destruction of tissue by application of extreme cold, as in production of lesions in the thalamus for the treatment of parkinsonism, or in the treatment of malignant lesions of the skin.

cryotherapy (kri″o-ther′ah-pe) [*cryo-* + Gr. *therapeia* treatment]. The therapeutic use of cold.

cryotolerant (kri″o-tol′er-ant). Able to withstand unusually low temperatures.

crypt (kript) [L. *crypta*, from Gr. *kryptos* hidden]. A minute, tubelike depression opening on a free surface. **alveolar c.,** the bony compartment surrounding a developing tooth. **anal c's,** sinus anales. **dental c.,** the space occupied by a developing tooth. **enamel c.,** a space bounded by the dental ledges on either side and usually by the enamel organ. It is filled with mesenchyma. **c's of Fuchs,** c's of iris. **c's of Haller,** glandulae preputiales. **c's of iris,** pitlike depressions which are found in the iris, in the region of the circulus arteriosus minor. **c's of Lieberkühn of large intestine,** glandulae intestinales intestini crassi. **c's of Lieberkühn of rectum,** glandulae intestinales intestini recti. **c's of Lieberkühn of small intestine,** glandulae intestinales intestini tenuis. **c's of Littre,** glandulae preputiales. **Luschka's c's,** peculiar outpouchings of the mucosa of the gallbladder. **c. of Morgagni.** 1. Fossa navicularis urethrae. 2. See *sinus anales*. **mucous c.,** glandula mucosa. **mucous c's of duodenum,** glandulae duodenales. **odoriferous c's of prepuce,** glandulae preputiales. **c's of palatine tonsil,** fossulae tonsillares. **c's of pharyngeal tonsil,** fossulae tonsillares tonsillae pharyngeae. **synovial c.,** a pouch in the synovial membrane of a joint. **c's of tongue,** deep, irregular invaginations from the surface of the lingual tonsil. **tonsillar c's,** cryptae tonsillares tonsillae pharyngeae. **c's of Tyson,** glandulae preputiales.

crypt- (kript). See *crypto-*.

crypta (krip′tah), pl. *cryp′tae* [L.]. [N A, B N A] A minute tubelike depression opening on a free surface. **cryp′tae min′imae intesti′ni ten′uis,** glandulae intestinales intestini tenuis. **cryp′tae muco′sae.** See *glandula mucosa*. **cryp′tae muco′sae duode′ni,** glandulae duodenales. **cryp′tae odorif′erae, cryp′tae praeputia′les,** glandulae preputiales. **cryp′tae tonsilla′res tonsil′lae palati′nae** [N A], the blind ends of the tonsillar fossulae on the palatine tonsils. Called also *tonsillar crypts of palatine tonsils*. **cryp′tae tonsilla′res tonsil′lae pharyn′geae** [N A], the blind ends of the tonsillar fossulae of the pharyngeal tonsils. Called also *tonsillar crypts of pharyngeal tonsils*. **cryp′tae ure′thrae mulie′bris,** glandulae urethrales urethrae femininae.

cryptae (krip′te) [L.]. Plural of *crypta*.

cryptal (krip′tal). A terpene aldehyde, $(CH_3)_2CH.$-$C_6H_8.CHO$, from *Eucalyptus hemiphloia*.

cryptanamnesia (kript″an-am-ne′ze-ah). Cryptomnesia.

cryptectomy (krip-tek′to-me) [*crypt-* + Gr. *ektomē* excision]. Excision or obliteration of a crypt.

cryptenamine (krip-ten′ah-mīn). A mixture of alkaloids derived from an extract of *Veratrum viride;* used to lower blood pressure.

cryptesthesia (krip″tes-the′ze-ah) [*crypt-* + Gr. *aisthēsis* perception]. Subconscious appreciation or perception of occurrences not ordinarily perceptible to the senses.

cryptic (krip′tik) [Gr. *kryptikos* hidden]. Concealed, hidden, larval.

cryptitis (krip-ti′tis). Inflammation of a crypt.

crypto- (krip′to) [Gr. *kryptos* hidden]. A combining form meaning hidden or concealed, or denoting relationship to a crypt.

cryptocephalus (krip″to-sef′ah-lus) [*crypto-* + Gr. *kephalē* head]. A fetal monster with an inconspicuous head.

cryptococcosis (krip″to-kok-o′sis). An infection by *Cryptococcus neoformans* which may involve the skin, lungs or other parts, but has a predilection for the brain and meninges. The cutaneous form is marked by acneiform lesions. The generalized form invades the central nervous system; less often the lungs, liver, spleen and joints. Called also *European blastomycosis, torulosis* and *Busse-Buschke disease.*

Cryptococcus (krip″to-kok′us) [*crypto-* + Gr. *kokkos* berry]. A genus of yeastlike organisms. **C. capsula′tus,** *Histoplasma capsulatum.* **C. gilchris′ti,** *Blastomyces dermatitidis.* **C. histolyt′icus,** *C. neoformans.* **C. hom′inis,** *C. neoformans.* **C. meningit′idis,** *C. neoformans.* **C. neofor′mans,** a species causing an infection in humans. See *cryptococcosis.*

cryptocrystalline (krip″to-kris′tah-līn) [*crypto-* + *crystalline*]. Composed of crystals of microscopic size.

Cryptocys′tis trichodec′tis. The cysticercoid larval form of *Dipylidium caninum.*

cryptodidymus (krip″to-did′ĭ-mus) [*crypto-* + Gr. *didymos* twin]. A teratism in which one twin is concealed within the body of the other.

crypto-empyema (krip″to-em″pi-e′mah) [*crypto-* + *empyema*]. Empyema that cannot be diagnosed by puncture.

cryptogam (krip′to-gam) [*crypto-* + Gr. *gamos* marriage]. Any one of the lower plants that have no true flowers, but propagate by spores.

cryptogenetic (krip″to-je-net′ik) [*crypto-* + Gr. *gennan* to produce]. Of obscure, doubtful, or unascertainable origin.

cryptogenic (krip″to-jen′ik). Cryptogenetic.

cryptoglioma (krip″to-gli-o′mah) [*crypto-* + *glioma*]. One of the stages in the development of glioma of the retina, marked by shrinking of the eyeball due to cyclitis, which masks the presence of the growth.

cryptolepine (krip-tol′e-pin). An alkaloid, $C_{17}H_{16}ON_2$, from *Cryptolepsis sanguinolenta.*

cryptoleukemia (krip″to-lu-ke′me-ah) [*crypto-* + *leukemia*]. An archaic term previously applied to a hyperplastic blood process in which there were no abnormal cells in the blood stream.

cryptolith (krip′to-lith) [*crypto-* + Gr. *lithos* stone]. A calculus or concretion in a crypt.

cryptolithiasis (krip″to-lĭ-thi′ah-sis). Calcification of tumors of the skin.

Cryptolucil′ia caesa′rion. A bright green fly which breeds in cow manure.

cryptomenorrhea (krip″to-men″o-re′ah) [*crypto-* + *menorrhea*]. A condition in which the symptoms of the monthly molimina are experienced but no external bleeding occurs, as in cases of imperforate hymen.

cryptomere (krip′to-mēr) [*crypto-* + Gr. *meros* part]. A cystic or saclike condition.

cryptomerorachischisis (krip″to-me″ro-rah-kis′kĭ-sis) [*crypto-* + Gr. *meros* part + *rhachis* spine + *schisis* cleavage]. Spina bifida occulta.

cryptomnesia (krip″tom-ne′ze-ah) [*crypto-* + Gr. *mnasthai* to be mindful]. The recall of events not recognized as part of one's conscious experience.

cryptomnesic (krip″tom-ne′sik). Hidden in the memory; pertaining to or characterized by cryptomnesia.

cryptoneurous (krip″to-nu′rus) [*crypto-* + Gr. *neuron* nerve]. Having no definite or distinct nervous system.

cryptophthalmia (krip″tof-thal′me-ah). Cryptophthalmos.

cryptophthalmos (krip″tof-thal′mos) [*crypto-* + Gr. *ophthalmos* eye]. A developmental anomaly in which the skin is continuous over the eyeballs without any indication of the formation of eyelids.

cryptophthalmus (krip″tof-thal′mus). Cryptophthalmos.

Cryptophyceae (krip″to-fi′se-e) [*crypto-* + Gr. *phykos* seaweed]. An order of algae.

cryptopine (krip′to-pin) [*crypto-* + Gr. *opion* opium]. A hypnotic, anodyne, and poisonous alkaloid, $C_{21}H_{23}NO_5$, from opium and various species of *Dicentra.*

cryptoplasmic (krip″to-plaz′mik). Occurring in a concealed form: said of an infection in which the infecting organism has concealed itself.

cryptopodia (krip″to-po′de-ah) [*crypto-* + Gr. *pous* foot]. A condition characterized by swelling of the lower part of the leg and dorsum of the foot so as to cover all but the soles of the feet.

cryptopsychic (krip″to-si′kik). Of concealed or vague psychic significance.

cryptopsychism (krip″to-si′kizm). Parapsychology.

cryptopyic (krip″to-pi′ik) [*crypto-* + Gr. *pyon* pus]. Attended by concealed suppuration.

cryptoradiometer (krip″to-ra″de-om′e-ter) [*crypto-* + L. *radius* ray + Gr. *metron* measure]. An apparatus for measuring the penetrative power of roentgen rays.

cryptorchid (krip-tor′kid) [*crypto-* + Gr. *orchis* testis]. Pertaining to or characterized by cryptorchidism. By extension, sometimes used to designate an individual exhibiting cryptorchidism.

cryptorchidectomy (krip″tor-kĭ-dek′to-me) [*cryptorchid* + Gr. *ektomē* excision]. Excision of an undescended testis.

cryptorchidism (krip-tor′kĭ-dizm). A developmental defect characterized by failure of the testes to descend into the scrotum.

cryptorchidopexy (krip-tor″kĭ-do-pek′se). Orchiopexy.

cryptorchidy (krip-tor′kĭ-de). Cryptorchidism.

cryptorchism (krip-tor′kizm). Cryptorchidism.

cryptorrhea (krip″to-re′ah) [*crypto-* + Gr. *rhoia* flow]. Abnormal activity of an endocrine organ.

cryptorrheic (krip″to-re′ik). Cryptorrhetic.

cryptorrhetic (krip″to-ret′ik). 1. Pertaining to the internal secretions. 2. Pertaining to cryptorrhea.

cryptoscope (krip′to-skōp) [*crypto-* + Gr. *skopein* to examine]. A fluoroscope. **Satvioni's c.,** one of the early forms of fluoroscope.

cryptoscopy (krip-tos′ko-pe). Fluoroscopy.

cryptosterol (krip-tos′ter-ol). A triterpenic sterol, $C_{30}H_{50}O$, from yeast.

cryptotoxic (krip″to-tok′sik) [*crypto-* + *toxic*]. Having hidden toxic properties: said of a solution normally nontoxic, but which may become toxic when the colloidal balance is disturbed.

cryptoxanthin (krip″to-zan′thin). A yellow carotenoid from yellow corn, which can be converted into vitamin A in the body.

cryptozoite (krip″to-zo′īt) [*crypto-* + Gr. *zōon* animal]. A sporozoite in the exo-erythrocytic stage as it lives in the tissues before entering the blood to attack a blood corpuscle.

cryptozygous (krip-toz′ĭ-gus) [*crypto-* + Gr. *zygon* yoke]. Having the face no wider than the cranium, so that the zygomatic arches are concealed by the bulging of the cranium when the skull is viewed from above. Cf. *phenozygous.*

Crys. Abbreviation for *crystal.*

crystal (kris′tal) [Gr. *krystallos* ice]. A naturally produced angular solid of definite form in which the ultimate units from which it is built up are systematically arranged; they are usually evenly spaced on a regular space lattice. **asthma c's,** Charcot-Leyden c's. **blood c's,** hematoidin crystals in the blood. **Böttcher's c's,** microscopic crystals seen on adding a drop of solution of ammonium phosphate to a drop of prostatic fluid. **Charcot-Leyden c's,** crystalline structures found wherever eosinophilic leukocytes are undergoing fragmentation. **Charcot-Neumann c's,** minute crystals of spermine phosphate found in semen and various animal tissues. **Charcot-**

Robin c's, minute crystals occurring in the blood of leukemic patients. **coffin lid c's,** peculiar indented crystals of ammoniomagnesium phosphate from alkaline urine. **Dubos crude c's,** tyrothricin. **dumbbell c's,** crystals of calcium oxalate occurring in the urine. **ear c.,** otolith. **Florence c's,** crystals formed by the action of iodine on any liquid containing lecithin, as in semen. **hedgehog c's,** a spiny form of uric acid concretions. **knife rest c's,** coffin lid c's. **leukocytic c's, Leyden's c's,** Charcot-Leyden c's. **liquid c's,** certain solutions which manifest some of the optical properties of crystals. **Lubarsch's c's,** crystals in the testis resembling sperm crystals. **Platner's c's,** crystals of the salts of the bile acids. **rock c.,** a transparent form of quartz, silicon dioxide, SiO_2: used for lenses. **sperm c's, spermin c's,** crystals of spermine phosphate in the semen. **Teichmann's c's,** crystals of hemin. **thorn-apple c's,** yellow or reddish-brown spheres of ammonium urate which are covered with sharp spicules or prisms, as found in the urine. **Virchow's c's,** yellow or orange-colored crystals of hematoidin sometimes seen in extravasated blood. **whetstone c's,** crystals of xanthine sometimes seen in urine. **Zenker's c's,** Charcot-Leyden c's.

crystalbumin (kris″tal-bu′min). 1. An albuminous substance found in an aqueous extract of the crystalline lens. 2. A general term for crystallizable albumins of the type of egg albumin and serum albumin.

crystalfibrin (kris″tal-fi′brin). A substance extracted from the crystalline lens by the action of hydrochloric acid.

crystalli (kris-tal′e). Chickenpox.

crystallin (kris-tal′lin). A protein belonging to the class of vitellins and existing in the crystalline lens of the eye. *Alpha c.* is precipitated by dilute acetic acid; *beta c.* is not.

crystalline (kris′tal-līn). Resembling a crystal in nature or clearness.

crystallitis (kris-tal-li′tis). Phakitis.

crystallization (kris″tal-li-za′shun). The formation of crystals. **fern-leaf c.,** crystallization of cervical mucus in a fernlike pattern, observable during the first half of the menstrual cycle and said to be most conspicuous at the time of ovulation.

crystallography (kris″tal-log′rah-fe) [*crystal* + Gr. *graphein* to write]. The science dealing with the study of crystals.

crystalloid (kris′tal-loid) [*crystal* + Gr. *eidos* form]. 1. Resembling a crystal. 2. A noncolloid substance; a substance which, in solution, passes readily through animal membranes, lowers the freezing point of the solvent containing it, and is generally capable of being crystallized. Cf. *colloid.*

crystalloiditis (kris-tal-loi-di′tis). Phakitis.

crystallophobia (kris″tal-lo-fo′be-ah) [*crystal* + *phobia*]. Morbid fear of glass or of objects made of glass.

crystalluria (kris-tal-lu′re-ah). The excretion of crystals in the urine, producing renal irritation.

crystalluridrosis (kris″tal-lu-rĭ-dro′sis) [*crystal* + Gr. *ouron* urine + *hidrōs* sweat + *-osis*]. A condition in which urinary elements from the sweat crystallize on the skin.

crysticillin (kris″tĭ-sil′lin). Trade mark for aqueous preparations of penicillin G procaine.

crystodigin (kris″to-dig′in). Trade mark for preparations of crystalline digitoxin.

crystoids (kris′toidz). Trade mark for anthelmintic pills of hexylresorcinol.

C.S. Abbreviation for *current strength.*

Cs. Chemical symbol for *cesium;* also abbreviation for *conscious* or *consciousness.*

CS_2. Carbon disulfide.

C.S.C. Abbreviation for *coup sur coup.*

C.S.F. Abbreviation for *cerebrospinal fluid.*

C.S.M. Abbreviation for *cerebrospinal meningitis.*

C.S.M.M.G. Abbreviation for *Chartered Society of Massage and Medical Gymnastics* (British).

CST. Abbreviation for *convulsive shock therapy.*

cteinophyte (ti′no-fīt) [Gr. *kteinein* to kill + *phyton* plant]. A parasitic fungus which has a destructive action upon its host.

Ctenocephalides (te″no-se-fal′ĭ-dēz). A genus of small wingless insects (fleas) subsisting on the blood of animals on which they occur as external parasites. **C. ca′nis,** a species frequently found on dogs, which may transmit the dog tapeworm to man. **C. fe′lis,** a species commonly found parasitic on cats.

Ctenophthalmus (te″nof-thal′mus). A genus of fleas. **C. agry′tes,** the European mouse flea.

Ctenopsyllus (te″no-sil′us). A genus of fleas found on rats and mice. **C. seg′nis,** the common flea of the house mouse and rat.

Ctesias (te′se-as) (5th century B.C.). A Greek physician who was a contemporary of Hippocrates, and who was said by Galen to have written the Cnidian aphorisms.

ctetology (te-tol′o-je) [Gr. *ktētos* acquired + *-logy*]. That branch of biology which treats of acquired characters.

ctetosome (tet′o-sōm) [Gr. *ktētos* acquired + Gr. *sōma* body]. A supernumerary chromosome; a heterochromosome.

Cu. Chemical symbol for *copper* (L. *cuprum*).

cuajani (kwah-hah′ne). An expectorant preparation from *Prunus occidentalis.*

cubeb (ku′beb) [L. *cubeba;* Arabic *kabāba*]. The dried unripe fruit of *Piper cubeba,* a piperaceous plant of Java: stimulant and diuretic.

cubebene (ku′beb-ēn). An eleopten from oil of cubeb, $C_{15}H_{24}$.

cubebin (ku-be′bin). An inactive crystalline principle, $C_{10}H_{10}O_3$, from cubeb.

cubebism (ku′beb-izm). Poisoning by cubeb.

cubicle (ku′bĭ-k'l). A compartment in a larger area, such as a dormitory or a ward, separated from similar adjoining compartments and from the rest of the room by low partitions.

cubilose (ku′bĭ-lōs) [L. *cubile* nest]. A mucilaginous and nutritious principle from the edible nest of the swiftlet, *Collocalia esculenta,* of southern Asia. It is an excretion from the stomach of the bird.

cubit (ku′bit) [L. *cubitus*]. A unit of measure, being the distance from the joint between the arm and forearm (elbow) to the tip of the middle finger; ranging, according to various systems of measurement, between 46 and 53 cm.

cubital (ku′bĭ-tal). Pertaining to the ulna or to the forearm.

cubitalis (ku-bĭ-ta′lis) [L.]. Cubital.

cubitocarpal (ku″bĭ-to-kar′pal). Pertaining to the ulna and the carpus.

cubitoradial (ku″bĭ-to-ra′de-al). Pertaining to the ulna and the radius.

cubitus (ku′bĭ-tus) [L.]. 1. [N A, B N A] The bend of the arm; the joint between the arm and forearm. 2. The upper limb distal to the humerus: the elbow, forearm, and hand. 3. Cubit. 4. Ulna. **c. val′gus,** deformity of the forearm (judged with the palm facing forward), in which it deviates away from the midline of the body when extended. **c. va′rus,** a rare deformity (judged with the palm facing forward), in which the forearm deviates toward the midline of the body when extended.

cuboid (ku′boid) [Gr. *kyboeidēs*]. 1. Resembling a cube. 2. The cuboid bone (os cuboideum [N A]).

cuboidal (ku-boi′dal). Resembling a cube.

cu. cm. Abbreviation for *cubic centimeter.*

cucullaris (ku-ku-la′ris) [L. *cucullus* hood]. Musculus trapezius. See *Table of Musculi.*

cucumber (ku′kum-ber) [L. *cucumis*]. The fruit of various species of *Cucumis*, chiefly *C. sativus*. The seeds are diuretic. **bitter c.**, colocynth.

Cucurbita (ku-ker′bĭ-tah). A genus of vines. *C. pe′po* is the pumpkin. *C. citrul′lus* is the watermelon. *C. lagena′ria* is the poisonous tula de mate.

cucurbitol (ku-ker′bĭ-tol). A sterol, $C_{24}H_{40}O_4$, obtained from watermelon seeds.

cucurbitula (ku″ker-bit′u-lah) [L., dim. of *cucurbita*, a gourd]. A cupping glass. **c. cruen′ta** [L. "bloody cup"], a cupping glass applied to draw blood. **c. sic′ca** [L. "dry cup"], a cupping glass that does not draw blood.

cucurbocitrin (ku″ker-bo-sit′rin). An extract from watermelon seeds: has been tried in the treatment of hypertension.

cudbear (kud′bār). A red-brown powder, obtained from lichens, such as *Lecanora tartarea:* used as a coloring matter in pharmacy.

cuff (kuf). A small bandlike structure encircling a part. **musculotendinous c.**, one formed by intermingled muscle and tendon fibers. See *rotator c.* **rotator c.**, a musculotendinous structure about the capsule of the shoulder joint, formed by the inserting fibers of the supraspinatus, infraspinatus, teres minor, and subscapularis muscles, blending with the capsule, and providing strength to the shoulder joint.

cuffing (kuf′ing). The formation of a cufflike surrounding border, such as collections of leukocytes surrounding blood vessels, noted in certain virus diseases.

cuichunchuli (kwe-chun-choo′ye) [Spanish American]. A violaceous plant, *Ionidium parviflorum*, of South America: emetic, cathartic, and diuretic.

Cuignet's method (ke-ēn-yāz′) [Ferdinand Louis Joseph *Cuignet*, French ophthalmologist, born 1823]. Retinoscopy.

cuirass (kwe-ras′) [Fr. *cuirasse* breastplate]. A covering for the chest. **tabetic c.**, an area of diminished sense of touch encircling the chest of a patient with tabes dorsalis.

Cuj., cuj. Abbreviation for L. *cu′jus*, of which.

cul-de-sac (kul′dĕ-sahk′) [Fr.]. A blind pouch or cecum; a cavity closed at one end. **conjunctival c.**, the fold formed by the junction of the palpebral and the ocular conjunctiva. **Douglas' c.**, excavatio rectouterina. **dural c.**, the terminal portion of the dural sac.

culdocentesis (kul″do-sen-te′sis) [*cul*-de-sac + *centesis*]. Aspiration of fluid from the recto-uterine excavation by puncture of the vaginal wall.

culdoscope (kul′do-skōp). An endoscope for performing culdoscopy.

culdoscopy (kul-dos′ko-pe). Visual examination of the female pelvic viscera by means of an endoscope introduced into the pelvic cavity through the posterior vaginal fornix.

Culex (ku′leks) [L. "gnat"]. A genus of culicine mosquitoes characterized by short palpi and by holding the body parallel to the surface on which it rests while the head and beak are bent at an angle to the body. Many species occurring throughout the world are vectors of various disease-producing agents. Species include *C. annuliros′tris*, *C. fat′igans*, *C. moles′tus*, *C. pi′piens*, *C. quinquefascia′tus*, *C. tarsa′lis*, and *C. tritaeniorhyn′cus*.

culicicide (ku-lis′ĭ-sīd). Culicide.

Culicidae (ku-lis′ĭ-de). A family of insects of the order Diptera, including the mosquitoes. There are ten tribes, of which three are of particular medical interest: Anophelini, Culicini, and Megarhinini.

culicidal (ku-lĭ-si′dal). Destructive to gnats and mosquitoes.

culicide (ku′lĭ-sīd) [L. *culex* gnat + *caedere* to kill]. An agent destructive to gnats and mosquitoes. **Mimm's c.**, phenol camphor volatilized by heat and allowed to diffuse through a room.

culicifuge (ku-lis′ĭ-fūj) [L. *culex* gnat + *fugare* to put to flight]. A preparation that repels gnats and mosquitoes.

Culicinae (ku-lĭ-si′ne). A subfamily of the Culicidae, the true mosquitoes, containing the tribes Anophelini, Culicini and Megarhinini.

Culicini (ku-lĭ-si′ni). A tribe of the subfamily Culicinae containing many genera, the most important of which are *Aedes*, *Culex*, *Mansonia*, *Psorophora*, *Theobaldia*, and *Wyeomyia*.

Culicoides (ku-lĭ-koi′dēz). A genus of biting flies of the family Heleidae. *C. aus′teni* and *C. gra′hami* are intermediate hosts of *Acanthocheilonema perstans*.

Cullen's sign (kul′enz) [Thomas S. *Cullen*, Baltimore surgeon, 1868–1953]. See under *sign*.

culling (kul′ing). The process of selective removal. The term is applied to the removal from the circulation, by the spleen, of abnormal erythrocytes, such as those occurring in congenital spherocytosis, or to the selective separation of other elements or organisms.

culmen (kul′men), pl. *cul′mina* [L. "ridge"]. [N A] The part of the vermis of the cerebellum between the lobulus centralis and the primary fissure. Called also *culmen monticuli* [B N A].

culmina (kul′mĭ-nah) [L.]. Plural of *culmen*.

cult (kult). A system of treating disease based on some special and unscientific theory of disease causation.

cultivation (kul″tĭ-va′shun) [L. *cultivatio*]. The propagation of living organisms, applied especially to the propagation of cells in artificial media. **fractional c.**, cultivation in which a small portion of a culture containing several species of microorganisms is used to form a new culture, and a small portion of this culture to form another, and so on until practically a pure culture is obtained.

cultural (kul′tu-ral). Pertaining to a culture.

culture (kul′tūr) [L. *cultura*]. 1. The propagation of microorganisms or of living tissue cells in special media conducive to their growth. 2. A growth of microorganisms or other living cells. **attenuated c.**, a culture of microorganisms that have become less virulent. **chorio-allantoic c.**, the cultivation of microorganisms, cells, or tissues on the chorio-allantois of the developing chick. **direct c.**, one made by direct transfer from a natural source to an artificial medium. **flask c.**, one grown on a medium contained in a flask. **hanging-block c.**, one grown on a block of agar medium fastened to a coverglass, which is then inverted over a hollow slide. **hanging-drop c.**, a culture in which the material to be cultivated is inoculated into a drop of fluid attached to a coverglass, which is inverted over a hollow slide. **needle c.**, stab c. **plate c.**, one grown on a

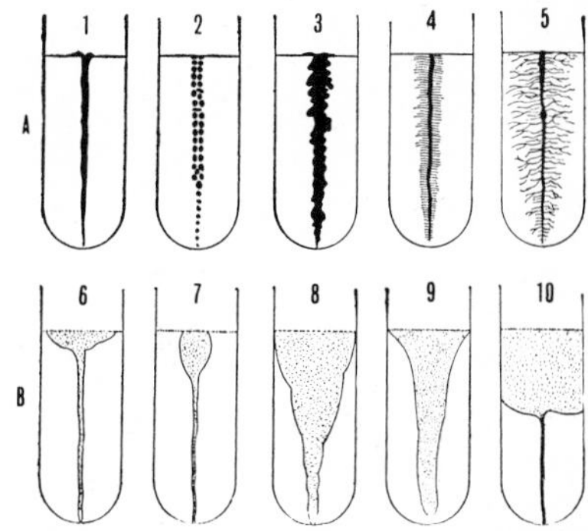

Types of growth in stab cultures. A, Nonliquefying: 1, filiform (B. coli); 2, beaded (Str. pyogenes); 3, echinate (Bact. acidi-lactici); 4, villous (Bact. murisepticum); 5, arborescent (B. mycoides). B, Liquefying: 6, crateriform (B. vulgare, 24 hours); 7, napiform (B. subtilis, 48 hours); 8, infundibuliform (B. prodigiosus); 9, saccate (Msp. Finkleri); 10, stratiform (Ps. fluorescens). (Frost.)

medium, usually agar or gelatin, spread on a sterilized glass plate, usually a Petri dish. **pure c.,** a culture of a single species of cell, without presence of any contaminants. **sensitized c.,** a bacterial culture to which has been added its specific antiserum. **shake c.,** a culture made by inoculating the medium and distributing the organism through it by shaking. **slant c.,** one made on a slanting surface of a solidified medium. **smear c.,** one made by smearing the inoculating material on the surface of the medium. **stab c.,** one in which the medium is inoculated by a needle thrust deeply into its substance. **stock c.,** a permanent culture from which transfers may be made. **streak c., stroke c.,** one in which the medium is inoculated by drawing an infected wire across it. **thrust c.,** stab c. **tissue c.,** the cultivation of tissue cells in vitro. **tube c.,** one made in a test tube. **type c.,** a culture generally agreed to represent a particular species of microorganism.

culture medium (kul′tūr me′de-um). Any substance or preparation used for the cultivation of living cells. **Abe's c.,** one for the growth of gonococci. **agar c.,** one in which agar is used as the solidifying agent. See under *agar* and also *agar gelatin*, under *gelatin*. **Aronson's c.,** an alkaline medium for the isolation of the cholera spirillum, consisting of agar, meat extract, peptone, sodium chloride, sodium carbonate, cane sugar, dextrin, basic fuchsin, sodium sulfite, and water. **ascitic fluid c.** See *ascitic fluid agar* and *ascitic fluid bouillon*. **Ashby's c.,** Ashby's agar. **asparagin c.** 1. (Fraenkel and Voges). A synthetic medium containing asparagin, disodium acid phosphate, ammonium lactate, and sodium chloride. 2. (Uschinsky). A synthetic medium containing asparagin, ammonium lactate, sodium chloride, magnesium sulfate, calcium chloride, monopotassium acid phosphate, and glycerin. **Avery's c.,** a glucose meat infusion broth containing 5 per cent of sterile defibrinated rabbit blood. **Avery's sodium oleate c.** See *sodium oleate agar*. **Bariekow's c.,** to a 1 per cent solution of nutrose add ½ per cent of sodium chloride, 1 per cent of lactose, and sufficient litmus to color it a pale blue. **beer wort c.,** crushed malt macerated in water, then filtered and sterilized. **Besredka and Jufille's c.,** one made up of incoagulable egg albumin, incoagulable egg yolk, and beef broth. **Beyerinck's c.** See under *solution*. **bile c.,** a mixture of ox bile, glycerin, and peptone. **bile salt c.,** nutrient bouillon containing dextrose and sodium taurocholate and sufficient litmus solution to color it a deep purple. See *bile salt agar*. **Blaxall's c.,** English proof agar. **blood serum c.,** one composed largely of blood serum. **Boeck and Drbohlav's c.,** a culture for amoeba containing sodium chloride, calcium chloride, potassium chloride, sodium bicarbonate, and glucose. **Bordet-Gengou c.** See under *agar*. **bouillon c.,** bouillon, plain or modified, used as a culture medium. **Braun's c.,** fuchsin agar. **brilliant green-bile salt c.,** brilliant green–bile salt agar. **brilliant green-eosin c.,** brilliant green–eosin agar. **calcium carbonate c.,** calcium carbonate bouillon. **Capaldi-Proskauer c.** 1. A synthetic medium containing sodium chloride, magnesium sulfate, calcium chloride, monopotassium acid phosphate, asparagin, mannite, and litmus solution. 2. A medium containing peptone, mannite, and litmus solution. **carbolized c.** See under *agar*, *bouillon*, and *gelatin*. **China green c.,** China green agar. **chocolate c.,** nutrient bouillon or agar to which fresh blood has been added and which is then heated, the red blood changing to a chocolate brown color: used for growing the influenza organism. **Clark and Lubs c.,** a buffered peptone solution containing dextrose. **Clauberg's c.,** a culture medium consisting of ox or sheep serum (coagulated) with glycerol and potassium tellurite. **Cohn's c.,** Cohn's solution. **Conradi's c.,** brilliant green agar, def. 1. **Conradi-Drigalski's c.,** litmus nutrose agar. **Corper's c.,** a culture medium for tubercle bacilli consisting of glycerolated pieces of potato that have been soaked in crystal violet solution. **Councilman and Mallory's c.** See *blood serum*. **Craig's c.** (for intestinal protozoa), a mixture of sterile human or rabbit serum and Locke's solution. **Czapek-Dox c.,** a glucose nitrate culture medium. **dextrose c.** See under *agar*, *bouillon*, and *gelatin*. **Dieudonné's c.,** Dieudonné's alkaline blood agar. **Dorset's egg c.** See *egg c.*, def. 1. **Drigalski-Conradi c.,** litmus nutrose agar. **Dubos' c.,** a medium containing hydrolized casein and a proprietary detergent, Tween 80: for culturing tubercle bacilli in test tubes. **Dunham's c.** See *peptone water c.* **Durham's c.,** inosite-free bouillon. **egg c.** 1. (Dorset). A bacteriological medium prepared by mixing whole eggs and physiologic sodium chloride solution. It is usually coagulated in test tubes in an inclined position and used for the cultivation of *Mycobacterium tuberculosis*. 2. (Lubenau). Dorset's egg medium with added glycerin. 3. (Petroff). A meat juice prepared by extracting chopped beef with glycerin solution and filtering, to which is added whole eggs, well mixed, and gentian violet. **egg albumin c.** (See also under *agar* and *bouillon*.) 1. (Inspissated). A mixture of egg white, distilled water, sodium hydroxide, and glucose; filtered and coagulated in an inclined position. 2. (Tarchanoff and Kolesnikoff). Unbroken eggs are placed in dekanormal sodium hydroxide for ten days, the shell removed and the contents cut into slices, washed in running water two hours, placed in Petri dishes, and sterilized. **egg meat c.** (Rettger), a medium prepared from ground lean meat and egg whites, heated separately, but mixed before tubing, with calcium carbonate added to stabilize the reaction. Anaerobes may be grown in this mixture without anaerobic precautions. **egg yolk c.,** egg yolk agar. **Eisenberg's milk-rice c.** See *milk-rice c.* **Elsner's c.,** potato gelatin. **Endo's c.,** fuchsin sulfite agar. **English proof c.,** English proof agar. **eosin-methylthionine chloride c.,** eosin–methylene blue agar. **esculin c.,** a medium containing esculin and iron citrate on which the colon bacillus produces a black colony. **Eyre's nutrose c.,** nutrose agar. **Fawcus's c.,** brilliant green–bile salt agar. **Fildes c.,** a peptic digest of blood for the growth of *Haemophilus influenzae*. **fish c.** See under *agar*, *bouillon*, *gelatin*, and *water*. **Fleming's c.,** oleic acid agar. **Fränkel and Voges' asparagin c.** See *asparagin c.*, def. 1. **French mannite c., French proof c.,** French proof agar. **fuchsin c., fuchsin sulfite c.,** fuchsin agar. **Gasperini's c.,** wheat bouillon. **gelatin c.,** one in which gelatin is used as the solidifying agent. **gelatin agar c.,** gelatin agar. **glucose formate c.** See under *agar*, *bouillon*, and *gelatin*. **glycerin c.** See under *agar*, *blood serum*, and *bouillon*. **glycerinated potato c.,** potato culture medium in which the wedges of potato have been soaked, and in which the cotton pads at the bottom are moistened with a 25 per cent solution of glycerin. **Goadsby's c.,** potato gelatin. **Guarniari's c.,** agar gelatin. **Guy's c.,** blood agar. **haricot c.** See under *agar* and *bouillon*. **Heiman's c.,** serum agar, def. 1. **Heller's c.,** urine gelatin. **Hershell's c.,** malt extract solution. **Hiss's c.** See *semisolid c.* and *serum-dextrose water*. **Hitchen's c.,** Hitchen's agar. **Holt-Harris and Teague's c.,** Holt-Harris and Teague's E.-M. B. agar. **Holz's c.,** potato gelatin. **hormone c.,** a bacteriological culture medium made without filtration. It is thought that the filter material removes by adsorption or by some other process constituents which enhance the nutritive value of the medium. **hydrocele c.** See *serum agar* and *ascitic bouillon*. **indicator c.,** one so prepared that it changes in appearance when certain bacteria grow in or on it; as Endo or tellurite plates. **inosite-free c.,** inosite-free bouillon. **iron c.,** iron bouillon. **Kanthack and Stephens' c.,** serum agar, def. 2. **Kendall's c.,** a culture medium prepared from animal or human small intestine, previously extracted with alcohol and benzol, and therefore relatively protein-rich and peptone-free. **Kitasato's c.** See *glucose formate agar*, and under *bouillon* and *gelatin*. **Krumwiede's c.,** brilliant green agar, def. 2. **lactose bile c.,** a mixture of fresh ox bile, peptone, and lactose. **lactose litmus c.** See under *agar*, *bouillon*, and *gelatin*. **lead c.,** lead bouillon. **lead acetate c.,** lead acetate agar. **Les c.,** Boeck and Drbohlav's c. **Libman's c.,** serum agar, def. 3. **Lipschuetz's c.,** egg albumin bouillon. **Li-Rivers c.,** Tyrode's solution containing minced chick embryo for the cultivation of filtrable viruses and toxoplasmata. **litmus c.** See under *bouillon* and *gelatin*. **litmus milk c.,** milk culture medium containing sufficient litmus solution to give it a deep lavender color. **litmus nutrose c.,** litmus nutrose agar. **litmus whey c.,** litmus whey gelatin. **Löffler's c.** 1. Malachite green agar. 2. Löffler's blood serum. **Löwenstein's c.,** a culture medium containing monopotassium phosphate, sodium citrate, magnesium sulfate, asparagin, glycerin, starch, egg yolk, and Congo red or malachite green, for culturing tubercle bacilli in blood. **Lubenau's egg c.,** egg c., def. 2. **MacConkey's bile salt c.** See *bile salt c.* and *bile salt agar*. **malachite green c.** See under *agar* and *bouillon*. **malt extract c.,** malt extract bouillon. **meat extract c.** See under *agar*, *bouillon*, and *gelatin*. **meat infusion c.** See under *agar*, *bouillon*, and *gelatin*. **milk c.,** milk, usually in test tubes, free from cream, and sterilized for use as a culture medium. **milk-rice c.,** a mixture of nutrient bouillon and milk solidified with rice powder: used for growing chromogenic bacteria. **Moor's c.,** nitrogen-free agar. **Naegeli's c.,** Naegeli's solution. **neutral red c.,** glucose agar containing neutral red. **nitrate c.** See under *bouillon* and *solution*. **nitrogen-free c.,** nitrogen-free agar. **N. N. N. c.,** a medium containing agar, salt, and rabbit blood, for growing *Leishmania donovani*. **Noguchi's tissue c.** See *tissue culture medium*. **nutrient c.** See under *agar*, *bouillon*, and *gelatin*. **nutrose c.,** nutrose agar. **Omeliansky's nutritive c.,** a synthetic medium containing potassium phosphate, magnesium sulfate, ammonium sulfate, sodium chloride, and precipitated chalk: for growing cellulose-fermenting organisms. **Pai's c.,** a medium for the cultivation of diphtheria bacilli. **Parietti's c.,** Parietti's bouillon. **Park and Williams' chocolate c.,** chocolate culture medium. **Pasteur's c.** See under *solution*. **peptone water c.,** a salt solution containing peptone. **Petroff's egg c.,** egg c., def. 3. **Petroff's synthetic c.,** a synthetic medium for growing the tubercle bacillus. **Petruschky's c.,** litmus whey. **Piorkowski's c.,** a medium consisting of urine that has undergone ammoniacal fermentation, peptone, and gelatin. **pleuritic c.** See *serum agar*, and under *bouillon*. **potato c.,** cylindric or wedge-shaped pieces of potatoes in test tubes or flat pieces in Petri dishes sterilized and used as a bacteriologic culture medium, especially for the chromogenic germs and for the sporogenic aerobes. **protein-free c.,** a synthetic medium containing calcium chloride, magnesium sulfate, monopotassium acid phosphate, potassium aspartate, sodium chloride, ammonium lactate, and glycerin. **rabbit's blood c.,** sterile rabbit's blood allowed to clot in a test tube and inactivated at 56°C. for 30 minutes. **Reddish's c.,** malt extract bouillon. **Rettger's egg-meat c.** See *egg-meat c.* **Robertson's c.,** a beef heart infusion medium. **rosolic acid-peptone c.,** Dunham's peptone water containing alcoholic solution of rosolic acid. **Russell's double sugar c.,** Russell's double sugar agar. **Sabouraud's c.,** French proof agar. **Sabouraud's conservation c.,** a culture medium containing peptone and agar, of pH 5–6. **Sabouraud's maltose c.,** French proof agar. **saccharose-mannitol c.,** saccharose-mannitol agar. **selective c.,** one that stimulates the growth of certain bacteria and inhibits that of others. **semisolid c.,** a medium containing agar, gelatin, peptone, meat extract, sodium chloride, and glucose or some other sugar. **serum c.** See under *agar*, *bouillon*, and *water*. **silicate jelly c.,** a synthetic medium containing ammonium sulfate, ammonium phosphate, calcium chloride, potassium phosphate, and sodium carbonate, solidified with silicic acid: for the growth of nitrogen-fixing bacteria. **sodium oleate c.,** sodium oleate agar. **Soyka's milk-rice c.** See *milk-rice c.* **starch c.,** starch agar. **sugar c.,** sugar bouillon. **sugar-free c.,** a medium in which *Escherichia coli* has grown and thus removed all sugars by decomposition. After clarification it is used as a basis for fermentation tests with the various sugars. **sulfindigotate c.** See under *agar*, *bouillon*, and *gelatin*. **Tarchanoff and Kolesnikoff's egg albumin c.,** egg albumin c., def. 2. **Teague and Travis's c.,** a sugar-free nutrient agar to which is added nutrose, saccharose, bluish eosin, and Bismarck brown. **tellurite c.,** Clauberg's c. **tissue c.,** nutrient agar to which is added ascitic or hydrocele fluid and a piece of fresh animal tissue. Paraffin oil is also placed on the surface to favor anaerobic conditions. **trypagar c.** See *tryp agar*. **urine c.,** freshly passed urine is heated, filtered, tubed, and sterilized for use as a culture medium. See also under *agar* and *gelatin*. **Uschinsky's c.** See *asparagin c.*, def. 2, and *protein-free bouillon*. **Vedder's c.,** starch agar. **Washbourn's c.,** blood agar, def. 2. **Wassermann's c.** See *ascitic fluid agar* and under *bouillon*. **Werbitski's c.,** China green agar. **Wertheimer's c.,** serum agar, def. 4. **Weyl's c.** See *sulfindigotate bouillon* and under *gelatin*. **wheat c.,** wheat bouillon. **whey c.** See under *agar* and *gelatin*. **Winogradsky's c.** See *silicate jelly culture medium*, and under *solution*. **wort c.** See under *agar* and *gelatin*. **Wurtz's c.** See *lactose litmus agar*, and under *gelatin*. **yeast autolysate c.,** a solution prepared by incubating yeast in water, kept sterile with chloroform, filtered, and solidified with agar. **yeast water c.,** yeast water.

cumidin (ku′mĭ-din). A liquid base, $C_3H_7.C_6H_4.NH_2$, derived from cumic acid.

cu. mm. Abbreviation for *cubic millimeter*.

cumulative (ku′mu-la″tiv) [L. *cumulus* heap]. Increasing by successive additions, the total being greater than the expected sum of its parts.

cumuli (ku′mu-li) [L.]. Plural of *cumulus*.

cumulus (ku′mu-lus), pl. *cu′muli* [L.]. A little mound. **c. ooph′orus** [N A, B N A], **ovarian c., c. ova′ricus,** a solid mass of follicular cells surrounding the ovum in the side of a developing vesicular ovarian follicle: called also *discus proligerus* and *germ hillock*.

cuneate (ku′ne-āt) [L. *cuneus* wedge]. Wedge-shaped.

cunei (ku′ne-i) [L.]. Plural of *cuneus*.

cuneiform (ku-ne′ĭ-form) [L. *cuneus* wedge + *forma* form]. Shaped like a wedge.

cuneihysterectomy (ku″ne-i-his″ter-ek′to-me) [L. *cuneus* wedge + *hysterectomy*]. The excision of a wedge-shaped piece from the uterine tissue for the correction of anteflexion.

cuneocuboid (ku″ne-o-ku′boid). Pertaining to the cuneiform and cuboid bones.

cuneonavicular (ku″ne-o-nah-vik′u-lar). Pertaining to the cuneiform and navicular bones.

cuneoscaphoid (ku″ne-o-skaf′oid). Cuneonavicular.

cuneus (ku′ne-us), pl. *cu′nei* [L. "wedge"]. A wedge-shaped lobule of the occipital lobe of the cerebrum on its medial aspect, between the parietooccipital and calcarine sulci.

cuniculi (ku-nik′u-li) [L.]. Plural of *cuniculus*.

cuniculus (ku-nik′u-lus), pl. *cunic′uli* [L. "rabbit," "rabbit-burrow"]. The burrow of an itch mite, *Sarcoptes hominis*, in the skin.

Cunila (ku-ni′lah). A genus of labiate plants. *C.*

maria'na, of North America (dittany), is diuretic and diaphoretic.

cunnus (kun'us) [L.]. Pudendum femininum.

CuO. Cupric oxide.

CuO_2. Cuprous oxide.

cuorin (ku'o-rin). A mono-amino-diphosphatide lipoid compound occurring in the heart muscle.

cup (kup). 1. A cupping glass. 2. A cup-shaped part or structure. **Diogenes c.**, poculum Diogenis. **dry c.**, a cupping glass applied to the intact skin in order to induce a flow of blood to the part. **glaucomatous c.**, a form of ocular disk depression which is peculiar to glaucoma. **impression c.**, impression tray. **Montgomery's c's**, the dilated canals of the tubular glands of the uterus. **ocular c.**, caliculus ophthalmicus. **ophthalmic c.**, caliculus ophthalmicus. **optic c.** 1. Excavatio papillae nervi optici. 2. Caliculus ophthalmicus. **physiological c.**, a depression in the center of the optic disk. Called also *excavatio papillae nervi optici* [N A]. **wet c.**, a cupping glass applied to the incised skin in order to abstract blood.

cupola (ku'po-lah). Cupula.

cupped (kupt). Hollowed out like a cup.

cupping (kup'ing). 1. The application of a cupping glass. 2. The formation of a cup-shaped depression.

cuprammonia (ku″prah-mo'ne-ah). A solution of cupric hydroxide in ammonia: used as a reagent and as a solvent for cellulose.

cupremia (ku-pre'me-ah) [L. *cuprum* copper + Gr. *haima* blood + *-ia*]. The presence of copper in the blood.

cupric (ku'prik). Containing copper in its divalent form (>Cu), and yielding divalent ions (Cu^{++}) in aqueous solution.

cupriuria (ku″pre-u're-ah). The presence of copper in the urine.

cuprous (ku'prus). Containing copper in its monovalent form (Cu^{-}).

cupruresis (ku″proo-re'sis) [L. *cuprum* copper + Gr. *ourēsis* a making water]. The urinary excretion of copper.

cupruretic (ku″proo-ret'ik) [L. *cuprum* copper + Gr. *ourētikos* promoting urine]. Pertaining to or promoting the urinary excretion of copper.

cupula (ku'pu-lah), pl. *cu'pulae* [L.]. A small inverted cup or dome-shaped cap over some structure. **c. of cochlea, c. coch'leae** [N A, B N A], the rounded or dome-shaped apex of the spiral cochlear duct. **c. cris'tae ampulla'ris** [N A], a cap of viscid, gelatinous fluid over the crista of the ampulla; in fixed material this cap stains slightly and is thus differentiated from the rest of the ampullar fluid. Called also *c. of ampullary crest.* **c. of pleura, c. pleu'rae** [N A, B N A], the domelike roof of the pleural cavity on either side, extending up through the superior aperture of the thorax.

cupulae (ku'pu-le) [L.]. Plural of *cupula.*

curage (ku-rahzh') [Fr.]. Curettage.

curare (koo-rah're) [South American]. A highly toxic dried extract of various species of *Strychnos* used originally in South America as an arrow poison and now used in pharmacological research and in anesthesia. It paralyzes the motor end plates of nerves. It is used for the reduction of spasm in tetanus and in shock treatments, plastic muscular rigidity, spastic paralysis, and similar conditions; also as an adjunct to general anesthesia. Cf. *intocostrin* and *tubocurarine.*

curaremimetic (koo-rah″re-mi-met'ik). Having an action similar to that of curare, or producing similar effects.

curari (koo-rah're). Curare.

curariform (ku-ra'rĭ-form). Resembling curare.

curarization (ku″rar-i-za'shun). Administration of curare until the physiologic effect of the drug is produced.

curative (kūr'ah-tiv) [L. *curare* to take care of]. Tending to overcome disease and promote recovery.

curb (kurb). A thickening of the metatarsocalcaneal ligament of the horse, causing a swelling at the back of the hock joint and resulting in lameness.

curd (kurd). The coagulum of milk, consisting mainly of casein. **alum c.**, a coagulum formed by agitating milk containing a piece of alum. **alum c. of Riverius**, a coagulum prepared with white of an egg and a drachm of alum.

cure (kūr) [L. *curatio*, from *cura* care]. 1. The course of treatment of any disease, or of a special case. 2. The successful treatment of a disease or wound. 3. A system of treating diseases. 4. A medicine effective in treating a disease. **Banting c.**, bantingism. **diet c.**, treatment by the systematic regulation of the diet. **dew c.**, kneippism. **economic c.**, cure of a disease which, while not complete, is sufficient to restore the patient to his wage-earning capacity. **faith c.**, a form of psychotherapy. **gold c.**, Keeley c. **grape c.**, the use of an exclusive diet of grapes. **hunger c.**, the treatment of disease by severe fasting. **Karell's c.** See under *treatment.* **Keeley c.**, a proprietary method of treatment for the alcohol and opium habits. **liman c.**, a method of treatment that was practiced at Odessa, consisting of bathing in the water of "limans," or sheets of water that have been isolated from the sea and converted into salt lakes: used in cases of scrofula, rickets, chronic rheumatism, and chronic skin diseases. **milk c.**, an exclusive diet of milk as a means of treatment. **mind c.**, psychotherapy. **movement c.**, kinesitherapy. **potato c.**, treatment of foreign bodies in the alimentary canal by ingesting mashed potatoes. **radical c.**, a complete and permanent cure. **rest c.**, Weir Mitchell treatment. **starvation c.**, the treatment of a disease by a restricted diet. **terrain c.**, a method of treatment for a weak heart, neurasthenia, corpulence, etc., consisting of systematic exercise, mountain climbing, and regulation of diet. **thirst c.**, treatment by restricting the intake of fluids. **water c.**, hydrotherapy. **whey c.**, treatment by drinking whey. **work c.**, the treatment of neurasthenia by systematically arranged work.

curet (ku-ret') [Fr. *curette* scraper]. 1. An instrument for removing growths or other material from the walls of cavities. 2. To remove growths or other material from the wall of a cavity or other surface with a spoon-shaped instrument. **Hartmann's c.**, an instrument for removing adenoids.

curettage (ku″rĕ-tahzh') [Fr.]. The removal of growths or other material from the wall of a cavity or other surface, as with a curet. **medical c.**, the induction of regression of and flow from the endometrium by administration and withdrawal of any progestational agent. **periapical c.**, removal with a curet of diseased periapical tissue without excision of the root tip.

curette (ku-ret') [Fr.]. Curet.

curettement (ku-ret'ment). Curettage.

curie (ku're) [Marie Sklodowska *Curie*, Polish chemist in Paris, 1867–1934, the discoverer of radium, and Pierre *Curie*, 1859–1906, co-winners, with H. A. Becquerel, of the Nobel prize in physics for 1903, for studies on spontaneous radioactivity; Mme. Curie also received the Nobel prize in chemistry in 1911 for discovery and isolation of radium]. A unit of radioactivity, defined as the quantity of any radioactive nuclide in which the number of disintegrations per second is 3.700×10^{10}.

curiegram (ku're-gram). A print made by radium emanation on a sensitized plate.

curie-hour (ku're-our″). A unit of dose equivalent to that obtained by exposure for one hour to radioactive material disintegrating at the rate of 3.7×10^{10} atoms per second. Abbreviated c-hr.

curietherapy (ku″re-ther'ah-pe). Radium therapy.

curioscopy (ku″re-os′ko-pe). The detection and mapping of objects by means of the nuclear radiations coming from them.

curium (ku′re-um) [Pierre and Marie *Curie*]. The chemical element of atomic number 96, atomic weight 247, symbol Cm, obtained by cyclotron bombardment of uranium and plutonium.

Curling's ulcer (kur′lingz) [Thomas Blizard *Curling*, English physician, 1811–1888]. See under *ulcer*.

current (kur′ent) [L. *currens* running]. 1. Anything which flows. 2. The stream of electricity which moves along a conductor. An electric current is due to a difference of potential between two points, this difference being measured in volts. The volume of flow depends on the difference of potential and the resistance to be overcome and is measured in amperes. The quantity of current is measured in coulombs. **abnerval c.,** an electric current passing from a nerve to and through a muscle. **action c.,** an electric current occurring during the action of a muscle or nerve. **alternating c.,** a current which periodically flows in opposite directions. Alternating current waves may be either sinusoidal or nonsinusoidal. The alternating current wave used most commonly therapeutically is the sinusoidal. Its variations in strength in either direction are the same, i.e., starting from zero it rises with a gradual increase in voltage and amperage until a certain maximum is reached, when without any pause or break it decreases in the same gradual manner until the zero line is again attained; then, still without pause, the same process is repeated with equal intensity but in the opposite direction. Furthermore, the variations follow a definite law, being proportional to the sine of the angular displacement. **anionic c.,** that part of the electric current which is carried by the anion. **ascending c.,** centripetal c. **axial c.,** the central colored part of the blood current. **battery c.,** a galvanic current. **blaze c.,** an electric current produced in living tissue by mechanical stimulation. **centrifugal c.,** an electric current in the body with the positive pole near the nerve center and the negative at the periphery; called also *descending c.* **centripetal c.,** an electric current passing through the body with the positive electrode on the nerve or at the periphery and the negative near the nerve center: called also *ascending c.* **compensating c.,** an electric current used to neutralize the intensity of a muscle current. **constant c., continuous c.,** an uninterrupted direct galvanic current. **damped c.** See *oscillating c.* **d'Arsonval c.,** a high-frequency, low-voltage current of comparatively high amperage. Such currents are used therapeutically to stimulate metabolism. **demarcation c.,** the electrical current which flows from uninjured surface of a muscle to the injured end of the muscle, called also *current of injury.* **descending c.,** centrifugal c. **De Watteville c.,** a combined galvanic and faradic current. **direct c.,** a current which flows in one direction only. When used medically it is called the galvanic current. This current has distinct and important polarity and marked secondary chemical effects. **direct vacuum tube c.,** a current administered from one pole of a static machine, the other pole of which is grounded, and regulated by the discharging spark gap with which vacuum electrodes are used instead of the metal electrodes employed with the static wave current. **electric c.,** the flow of electricity through a conductor. **electrostatic c.** See *static c.* **electrotonic c.,** a current induced in the sheath of a nerve by a current passing through the conducting part of that nerve. **electrovital c's,** two electric currents supposed to exist in animal bodies; called also *neuro-electric c's.* **extra c.,** an induced current produced in a faradic battery in addition to the regular primary and induced currents. **eye c.,** an electric current passing from the cornea to the optic nerve under the influence of light. **faradic c.,** an intermittent alternating current obtained from the secondary winding of an induction coil. **fulguration c.,** high-frequency current. **galvanic c.,** a steady direct current. See *direct current.* This current was first produced chemically from batteries. At present its sources are: (1) A direct current lighting or power circuit ("Main"). (2) Alternating current circuit with introduction of: (*a*) Motor generator; (*b*) rectifier; (*c*) "B-battery" eliminator. (3) Battery of cells, dry or wet. The galvanic and static currents are the only unidirectional currents and the only ones possessing constant polarity. **high-frequency c.,** an alternating current having a frequency of interruption or change of direction sufficiently high so that tetanic contractions are not set up when it is passed through living contractile tissues. See *d'Arsonval c.* **high potential c., high tension c.,** a current having a high electromotive force. **induced c.,** electricity in a circuit generated by proximity to another current. **inducing c.,** the current which induces a secondary current. **c. of injury,** demarcation c. **interrupted c.,** a current which is frequently opened and closed. **inverse c.,** a current flowing through a tube in the wrong direction as a result of imperfect rectification of an alternating current or of a current from an induction coil. **ionization c.,** the movement of an electric charge produced by the action of an electric field on an ionized gas. **labile c.,** a current applied to the body with electrodes moving over the surface. **Leduc c.,** an interrupted direct current, each pulse of which is approximately of the same current strength and same duration. It produces unconsciousness similar to that of ether or chloroform, from which the subject emerges as soon as the current is removed. **Morton's c.,** a series of electric charges from a Leyden jar, the jar being constantly recharged from a static machine. **nerve-action c.,** action c. **oscillating c.,** a current alternating in direction and of either constant or gradually decreasing amplitude: when of constant amplitude it is called *undamped current;* when of gradually decreasing amplitude it is called *damped current.* **Oudin c.,** a high-frequency current of higher voltage than the high-frequency currents used for ordinary diathermy treatment. **pulsating c.,** a current pulsating regularly in magnitude. **reversed c.,** a current which is frequently made to reverse its direction. **secondary c.,** induced c. **sine wave c.,** sinusoidal c. **sinusoidal c.,** an electric current in which the potential rises gradually from zero to a maximum, then gradually returns to zero or to a minimum, and then reversingly repeats this action. Cf. *alternating c.* **spark gap c.,** static c. **stabile c.,** a current applied to the body with both electrodes stationary. **static c.,** an electric current derived from a static apparatus. **static induced c.,** the charging and discharging current of a pair of Leyden jars or other condensers, which current is passed through a patient. **static wave c.,** the current resulting from the sudden periodic discharging of a patient who has been raised to a high potential by means of an electrostatic generator. **surgical c.,** an electric current used in surgical dissecting. **swelling c.,** a current which is alternately weak and strong. **Tesla's c.,** a high-frequency current of higher voltage than that of the high-frequency currents used for ordinary diathermy treatment, but not so high as that of the Oudin current. **undamped c.** See *oscillating c.* **voltaic c.,** galvanic c.

curricula (kur-rik′u-lah) [L.]. Plural of *curriculum.*

curriculum (kur-rik′u-lum), pl. *curric′ula* [L.]. A regular and established course of study.

Curschmann's disease, mask, spirals, trocar (koorsh′manz) [Heinrich *Curschmann*, physician in Leipzig, 1846–1910]. See under the nouns.

curtometer (kur-tom′e-ter). Cyrtometer.

curvatura (kur″vah-tu′rah), pl. *curvatu′rae* [L.]. A nonangular deviation from a straight course in a line or surface. **c. ventric′uli ma′jor** [N A, B N A], the left or lateral and inferior border of the stomach, marking the inferior junction of the anterior and posterior surfaces. Called also *greater curvature of stomach*. **c. ventric′uli mi′nor** [N A, B N A], the right or medial border of the stomach, marking the superior junction of the anterior and posterior surfaces. Called also *lesser curvature of stomach*.

curvature (kur′vah-tūr) [L. *curvatura*]. Deviation from a rectilinear direction. **gingival c.,** the line of the gingiva where it is attached to the neck of a tooth. **greater c. of stomach,** curvatura ventriculi major. **lesser c. of stomach,** curvatura ventriculi minor. **occlusal c.,** curve of occlusion. See under *curve*. **Pott's c.,** abnormal curvature of the vertebral column caused by tuberculous caries. **spinal c.,** deviation of the spine from its normal direction or position. See *kyphosis, lordosis, scoliosis*.

curve (kurv) [L. *curvum*]. A nonangular deviation from a straight course in a line or surface. **alignment c.,** the dental curve determined by a line passing through the center of the teeth paralleling the dental arch. **anti-Monson c.,** reverse c. **Barnes's c.,** the segment of a circle whose center is the promontory of the sacrum, the concavity being directed dorsally. **buccal c.,** the portion of the dental curve from the mesial surface of the first premolar to the distal surface of the third molar. **c. of Carus,** the normal axis of the pelvic outlet. **compensating c.,** the anteroposterior and lateral curvature in the alignment of the occlusal surfaces and incisal edges of artificial teeth, which is used to develop balanced occlusion. **Damoiseau's c.,** Ellis's line. **dental c.,** the curve of the dental arch as viewed from the occlusal aspect. **dromedary c.,** a temperature or other curve showing two phases of elevation separated by a phase of depression. **c. of Ellis and Garland,** Ellis's line. **frequency c.,** a curve representing graphically the probabilities of different numbers of recurrences of an event. **gaussian c.,** normal curve of distribution. **growth c.,** the curve obtained by plotting increase in size or numbers against the elapsed time, as a measure of the growth of a child, or the multiplication of microorganisms. **Harrison's c.,** Harrison's groove. **labial c.,** that portion of the dental curve between the distal surfaces of the two canine teeth in the dental arch. **logistic c.,** in biometry, an S-shaped curve to describe the growth of a population in an area of fixed limits. **milled-in c's.** See under *path*. **Monson c.,** a curve of occlusion conforming to a segment of the surface of a sphere 8 inches in diameter, with its center in the region of the glabella. **normal c. of distribution,** the symmetrical bell-shaped curve that is usually produced by plotting a single variable. **c. of occlusion,** a curved line determined by the occlusal surfaces and incisal edges of the existing teeth, when viewed from the lateral aspect. **Pleasure c.,** reverse c. **Price-Jones c.,** a graphic curve representing the variation in the size of the red blood corpuscles. **probability c.,** frequency c. **pulse c.,** sphygmogram. **reverse c.,** a curve of occlusion which is convex upward. Described by Pleasure, and sometimes called *Pleasure curve*. **Spee's c.,** a curved line touching the tops of the buccal cusps of the teeth from the first premolar to the third molar, when viewed from the lateral aspect. **temperature c.,** a graphic tracing showing variations in temperature. **tension c's,** lines observed in the arrangement of the cancellous tissue of bones, depending on the directions of tension exerted on the bones. **Traube's c's, Traube-Hering c's,** high bold curves seen in the tracings of the sphygmograph when respiration has been completely arrested. **Wunderlich's c.,** the typical variation shown by the temperature in a patient with typhoid fever.

cuscamidine (kus-kam′ĭ-din). A cinchona alkaloid.

cuscamine (kus-kam′in). A cinchona alkaloid.

Cusco's speculum (koos′kōz) [Edouard Gabriel *Cusco*, French surgeon, 1819–1894]. See under *speculum*.

cuscohygrine (kus-ko-hi′grin). An alkaloid, $C_{13}H_{24}ON_2$, from cusco leaves.

cusconidine (kus-kon′ĭ-din). A cinchona alkaloid, $C_{23}H_{23}N_2O_4$.

cusconine (kus′ko-nin). An alkaloid of cinchona, $C_{23}H_{26}O_4N_2.2H_2O$.

Cushing's disease, law, reaction, syndrome (koosh′ingz) [Harvey *Cushing*, Boston surgeon, 1869–1939]. See under the nouns.

Cushing's suture (koosh′ingz) [Hayward W. *Cushing*, Boston surgeon, 1854–1934]. See under *suture*.

cushion (koosh′un). A fleshy, padlike anatomical structure. **coronary c.,** a band of vascular tissue at the upper edge of the wall of the hoof of the horse, which is concerned in the secretion of the horny wall. Called also *coronary band, coronary ring, cutidure*, or *cutiduris*. **endocardial c's,** elevations on the atrioventricular canal of the embryonic heart, which later fuse with the free edge of the septum primum to separate the right and left atria. **c. of epiglottis.** 1. Petiolus epiglottidis. 2. Tuberculum epiglotticum. **eustachian c., c. of eustachian orifice,** torus tubarius. **Passavant's c.** See under *bar*. **plantar c.,** a wedge-shaped mass of elastic tissue overlying the frog of a horse's foot. **sucking c.,** corpus adiposum buccae.

cusp (kusp) [L. *cuspis* point]. A tapering projection; especially (*a*) one of the triangular segments of a cardiac valve (see under *cuspis*), or (*b*) a notably pointed or rounded eminence on or near the masticating surface of a tooth, usually designated according to its position in relation to the axial surfaces of the tooth. Called also *tuberculum* (pl. *tubercula*) *coronae dentis* [N A]. Those of the maxillary first molar are: distobuccal, distolingual, mesiobuccal, and mesiolingual. **Carabelli c.,** a fifth, or supplemental, cusp, sometimes found lingual to the mesiolingual cusp of the maxillary first molar tooth.

cuspad (kus′pad). Directed toward a cusp, as toward the cusp of a tooth.

cusparine (kus′pah-rin). A crystalline alkaloid, $C_{19}H_{17}NO_3$, from the bark of *Galipea cusparia*.

cuspid (kus′pid). 1. Having one cusp or point. 2. A canine tooth.

cuspidate (kus′pĭ-dāt) [L. *cuspidatus*]. Having a cusp or cusps.

cuspides (kus′pĭ-dēz) [L.]. Plural of *cuspis*.

cuspis (kus′pis), pl. *cus′pides* [L.]. 1. A tapering projection or structure, applied especially to one of the triangular segments of a cardiac valve. 2. A cusp of a tooth. **c. ante′rior val′vae atrioventricula′ris dex′trae** [N A], the anterior of the three cusps of the right atrioventricular valve. **c. ante′rior val′vae atrioventricula′ris sinis′trae** [N A], the anterior of the two cusps of the left atrioventricular valve. **c. ante′rior val′vulae bicuspida′lis** [B N A], c. anterior valvae atrioventricularis sinistrae. **c. ante′rior val′vulae tricuspida′lis** [B N A], c. anterior valvae atrioventricularis dextrae. **c. media′lis val′vulae tricuspida′lis** [B N A], c. septalis valvae atrioventricularis dextrae. **c. poste′rior val′vae atrioventricula′ris dex′trae** [N A], the posterior of the three cusps of the right atrioventricular valve. **c. poste′rior val′vae atrioventricula′ris sinis′trae** [N A], the posterior of the two cusps of the left atrioventricular valve. **c. poste′rior val′vulae bicuspida′lis** [B N A], c. posterior valvae atrioventricularis sinistrae. **c. poste′rior val′vulae tricuspida′lis** [B N A], c. posterior valvae atrioventricularis dextrae. **c. septa′lis val′vae atrioventricula′ris dex′trae** [N A], the cusp of the right atrioventricular valve which is attached to the membranous interventricular septum.

cutaneous (ku-ta′ne-us) [L. *cutis* skin]. Pertaining to the skin.

cute (kūt). The local name in Venezuela for a skin disease marked by the presence of bright yellow patches. It is probably tinea flava.

Cuterebra (ku-ter-e′brah). A genus of botflies whose larvae commonly infest rodents.

cuticle (ku′te-kl) [L. *cuticula*, from *cutis* skin]. 1. The epidermis. 2. A layer of more or less solid substance which covers the free surface of an epithelial cell. 3. Eponychium. **dental c.,** a membrane covering the surface of the crown of a tooth at the time of eruption; formed by fusion of a thin hornified oral and a reduced enamel epithelium (cuticula dentis). **enamel c.** 1. Dental cuticle. 2. Nasmyth's membrane. **keratose c.,** the outer surface layer of the pigment cells of the eye. **c. of root sheath,** a layer of cells lining the hair follicles.

cuticolor (ku-tik′o-lor) [L. *cutis* skin + *color* color]. Having the color of the skin.

cuticula (ku-tik′u-lah), pl. *cutic′ulae* [L. "little skin"]. A covering membrane. **c. den′tis** [N A, B N A], keratinized epithelial remnants on the enamel of a tooth.

cuticulae (ku-tik′u-le) [L.]. Plural of *cuticula.*

cuticularization (ku-tik″u-lar-i-za′shun). The formation of skin upon a sore or wound.

cuticulum (ku-tik′u-lum). A thin covering layer. **Flechsig's c.,** a layer of flat cells on the external surface of the neuroglia.

cutidure (ku′tĭ-dūr). Coronary cushion.

cutiduris (ku″tĭ-du′ris). Coronary cushion.

cutin (ku′tin) [L. *cutis* skin]. 1. A waxy substance which, combined with cellulose, forms the cuticle of plants. 2. A preparation of the gut of the ox, used as a substitute for catgut and silk and as a dressing for wounds.

cutinization (ku″tin-i-za′shun). The operation of lining a cavity, such as a fistulous cavity in bone, with skin.

cutireaction (ku″te-re-ak′shun) [L. *cutis* skin + *reaction*]. An inflammatory or irritative reaction on the skin, occurring in certain infectious diseases, on the application to or injection into the skin of a preparation of the organism causing the disease. Such reactions occur in glanders, leprosy, syphilis, tinea, tuberculosis, typhoid fever, etc. See the following reactions or tests: *Deehan's typhoid reaction, Dick test, Lautier's test, Lignière's test, Moro's reaction, Noguchi's luetin reaction, pallidin reaction, Pirquet's reaction, Schick test, typhoidin test.* **differential c.,** inoculation at one and the same time of old tuberculin, a filtrate of human tubercle bacilli, and a filtrate of bovine tubercle bacilli in order to determine whether the patient is tuberculous or not, and if he is, whether the infection is human or bovine.

cutis (ku′tis) [L.]. [N A, B N A] The outer protective covering of the body, or skin, consisting of the epidermis and the corium, or dermis, and resting upon the subcutaneous tissues. **c. anseri′na** ["goose skin"], erection of the papillae of the skin, as from cold or shock. **c. elas′tica,** c. hyperelastica. **c. hyperelas′tica,** a condition in which the skin is loosely attached to the underlying tissue and has the property of great elasticity and distensibility. The skin capillaries are fragile and there may be bleeding into the skin (dermatorrhexis); subcutaneous fatty nodules are often present; called also *elastic skin* and *cutis elastica.* **c. lax′a,** dermatolysis. **c. marmora′ta,** a transitory mottling of the skin sometimes occurring on exposure of the skin to cold. **c. pen′dula** ["hanging skin"], abnormal flabbiness of the skin. **c. pen′silis,** dermatolysis. **c. rhomboida′lis nu′chae,** a thickened and furrowed condition of the skin exposed to the sun, especially that of the back of the neck. **c. testa′cea** ["shelly skin"], general seborrhea. **c. unctuo′sa** ["greasy skin"], seborrhea. **c. ve′ra** ["true skin"], corium. **c. ver′ticis gyra′ta,** thickening of the skin of the scalp, which lies in folds resembling gyri and sulci of the brain. The condition may be related to acromegaly, neurofibromatosis, leukemic or leproid infiltration, or chronic hyperplastic dermatitis of the scalp.

cutisector (ku′te-sek-tor) [L. *cutis* skin + *sector* cutter]. An instrument for removing bits of the skin.

cutitis (ku-ti′tis). Inflammation of the skin.

cutization (ku-ti-za′shun). The change of exposed mucous membrane into true skin.

cuvette (ku-vet′) [Fr., dim. of *cuve* vat or tub]. A glass container, generally possessing well-defined characteristics with regard to dimensions (particularly thickness) and optical properties, and generally used to examine colored and colorless solutions free of turbidity, but also used to examine the light scattering of turbid suspensions, such as bacterial suspensions. Its area of usefulness is determined to a large extent by the chemical composition of the glass: a *silica cuvette* is used for examination of materials in the ultraviolet region of the spectrum; a *Pyrex cuvette* is used for examination of materials in the visible range.

Cuvier's duct (koo′ve-āz) [Georges Léopold Chrétien Frédéric Dagobert, Baron de la *Cuvier*, French naturalist, 1769–1832]. See under *duct.*

C.V. Abbreviation for L. *cras ves′pere*, tomorrow evening, and L. *conjuga′ta ve′ra*, true conjugate diameter of the pelvic inlet.

C.V.A. Abbreviation for *costovertebral angle.*

C.V.D. Abbreviation for *color-vision-deviant* (showing anomalies of color vision) or *color vision deviate* (an individual showing anomalies of color vision).

C.V.O. Abbreviation for L. *conjuga′ta ve′ra obstet′rica*, obstetric conjugate diameter of the pelvic inlet.

Cwt. Abbreviation for *hundredweight.*

Cx. Abbreviation for *convex.*

Cy. Symbol for *cyanogen.*

cyan-. See *cyano-.*

cyanalcohol (si″an-al′ko-hol). Cyanhydrin.

cyanamide (si-an′ah-mīd). Carbamic acid nitril, $CN.NH_2$ or NH.C.NH, the anhydride of urea.

cyanate (si′ah-nāt). A salt of cyanic acid which contains the radical CNO.

cyanein (si-an′e-in). The blue coloring matter from Medusa.

cyanemia (si″ah-ne′me-ah) [*cyan-* + Gr. *haima* blood + *-ia*]. Bluishness of the blood, as in cyanosis.

cyanephidrosis (si″an-ef″ĭ-dro′sis) [*cyan-* + Gr. *ephidrōsis* superficial perspiration]. The excretion of bluish sweat.

cyanhematin (si″an-hem′ah-tin). A compound of cyanogen and hematin.

cyanhemoglobin (si″an-he″mo-glo′bin). A compound formed in the blood by the action of hydrocyanic acid on hemoglobin. It gives the blood a bright red color.

cyanhidrosis (si″an-hĭ-dro′sis). Cyanephridrosis.

cyanhydrin (si″an-hi′drin). A compound formed by the addition of HCN to the aldehyde or ketone group.

cyanide (si′ah-nīd). Any binary compound of cyanogen.

cyanin (si′ah-nin). A coumarin glycoside, $C_{27}H_{30}O_{16}$. Its aglycon is cyanidin, and it is used as an indicator with a pH of 7 to 8.

cyanmethemoglobin (si″an-met″he-mo-glo′bin). A crystalline substance formed by the action of hydrocyanic acid on methemoglobin in the cold or on oxyhemoglobin at the body temperature: the pigment most widely employed in clinical hemoglobinometry.

cyanmetmyoglobin (si″an-met-mi″o-glo′bin). A compound formed from metmyoglobin by addition of the cyanide ion to yield reduction to the ferrous state.

cyano- (si′ah-no) [Gr. *kyanos* blue]. A combining form denoting blue.

cyanochroia (si″ah-no-kroi′ah) [*cyano-* + Gr. *chroia* color]. Bluishness of the skin; cyanosis.

cyanocobalamin (si″ah-no-ko-bal′ah-min). A substance possessing hematopoietic activity apparently identical with that of the antianemia factor of liver: used in prophylaxis and treatment of pernicious anemia and other macrocytic anemias. Called also *vitamin* B_{12}.

cyanocrystallin (si″ah-no-kris′tal-lin). A blue coloring matter from the integument of decapods.

cyanoderma (si″ah-no-der′mah) [*cyano-* + Gr. *derma* skin]. Blue discoloration of the skin.

cyanoform (si-an′o-form). A crystalline substance, $CH(CN)_3$, formed by the action of potassium cyanide on chloroform.

cyanogen (si-an′o-jen) [*cyano-* + Gr. *gennan* to produce]. The radical CN; also CN.CN (dicyanogen), the latter an exceedingly poisonous gas. **c. bromide,** a lacrimatory war gas, BrCN. **c. chloride,** a gas, ClCN, used for fumigating houses, ships, etc. It is as lethal for rats and other vermin as HCN, but less dangerous to man, as it causes lacrimation.

cyanogenesis (si″ah-no-jen′e-sis) [*cyano-* + Gr. *genesis* production]. The formation or production of cyanogen or hydrocyanic acid.

cyanogenetic (si″ah-no-je-net′ik). Producing cyanogen or hydrocyanic acid.

cyanolophia (si″ah-no-lo′fe-ah) [*cyano-* + Gr. *lophia* crest]. A specific infectious disease of fowls known as avian pest.

cyanomycosis (si″ah-no-mi-ko′sis) [*cyano-* + Gr. *mykēs* fungus]. Infection by *Micrococcus pyocyaneus.*

cyanopathy (si″ah-nop′ah-the) [*cyano-* + Gr. *pathos* disease]. Cyanosis.

cyanophil (si-an′o-fil). 1. Cyanophilous. 2. A cell or other histologic element readily stainable with blue.

cyanophilous (si″ah-nof′ĭ-lus) [*cyano-* + Gr. *philein* to love]. Stainable with blue dyes.

cyanophoric (si″ah-no-fōr′ik). Bearing hydrocyanic acid: said of glycosides that yield hydrocyanic acid on hydrolysis.

cyanophose (si′ah-no-fōz) [*cyano-* + Gr. *phōs* light]. A blue phose.

cyanopia (si″ah-no′pe-ah). Cyanopsia.

cyanopsia (si″ah-nop′se-ah) [*cyano-* + Gr. *opsis* vision + *-ia*]. A visual defect in which all objects appear to have a blue tinge.

cyanopsin (si″ah-nop′sin) [*cyano-* + Gr. *opsis* vision]. A visual pigment of bluish tint found in the retinal cones of some animals and important for vision.

cyanose (si′ah-nōs″) [Fr.]. Cyanosis. **c. tardive′,** tardive cyanosis.

cyanosed (si′ah-nōsd). Cyanotic.

cyanosis (si″ah-no′sis) [Gr. *kyanos* blue]. A bluish discoloration, applied especially to such discoloration of skin and mucous membranes due to excessive concentration of reduced hemoglobin in the blood. **c. bul′bi.** 1. Congenital violet flecks in the sclera (Liebisich). 2. Bluish discoloration of the white of the eye in cyanosis (Hirschfeld). **central c.,** cyanosis produced as a result of arterial unsaturation, the aortic blood carrying reduced hemoglobin. **enterogenous c.,** a syndrome characterized by cyanosis, severe enteritis, and clubbing of the fingers. It is due to the presence of sulfhemoglobin in the blood, the H_2S being absorbed from the intestine. **false c.,** cyanosis due to the presence of pigment and not to deficient oxygenation of the blood. **hereditary methemoglobinemic c.,** a condition present at birth and occurring predominantly in males, characterized by methemoglobin in the blood. **c. lie′nis,** passive congestion of the spleen. **peripheral c.,** cyanosis produced as a result of an excessive amount of reduced hemoglobin in the venous blood, caused by extensive oxygen extraction at the capillary level. **pulmonary c.,** central cyanosis caused by poor oxygenation of the blood in the lungs. **c. ret′inae,** distinct cyanosis of the retina, observable in reversed patent ductus arteriosus and other congenital cardiac anomalies. **shunt c.,** central cyanosis caused by mixing of unoxygenated blood with the arterial blood in the heart or great vessels. **tardive c.,** cyanosis in congenital interauricular septal defect which appears only after cardiac failure has developed.

cyanotic (si-ah-not′ik). Pertaining to or characterized by cyanosis.

Cyanthomastix hominis (si″an-tho-mas′tiks hom′ĭ-nis). *Chilomastix hominis.*

cyanuria (si″ah-nu′re-ah). The passage of blue-colored urine.

cyanurin (si″ah-nu′rin) [*cyan-* + Gr. *ouron* urine]. Indigo blue found in the urine on the addition of a mineral acid to it.

cyasma (si-az′mah). Pigmentation of the skin in pregnancy.

Cyath. Abbreviation for L. *cy′athus*, a glassful. **Cyath. vin.,** L. *cy′athus vina′rius*, a wineglass.

cyathus (si′ah-thus) [L.; Gr. *kyathos* cup]. The canal of the infundibulum cerebri.

cybernetics (si″ber-net′iks) [Gr. *kybernētēs* helmsman]. The science of communication and control in the animal and in the machine.

cyclaine (si′klān). Trade mark for preparations of hexylcaine hydrochloride.

Cyclamen (sik′lah-men) [L.]. A genus of primulaceous plants. *C. europaeum* has an acrid, cathartic root.

cyclamin (sik′lah-min). A glycoside, $C_{20}H_{34}O_{10}$, from *Cyclamen europaeum:* strongly purgative and emetic.

cyclamycin (si′klah-mi″sin). Trade mark for preparations of triacetyloleandomycin.

cyclandelate (si-klan′dĕ-lāt). Chemical name: 3,3,5-trimethylcyclohexyl mandelate. Use: vasodilator for peripheral vascular disease.

cyclarthrodial (sik″lar-thro′de-al). Pertaining to a cyclarthrosis.

cyclarthrosis (sik″lar-thro′sis) [Gr. *kyklos* circle + *arthrosis*]. A joint which permits rotation.

cycle (si′kl) [Gr. *kyklos* circle]. A round or succession of observable phenomena, recurring usually at regular intervals and in the same sequence. **aberrant c.,** one which shows variation in the interval or the sequence of events. **anovulatory c.,** a sexual cycle in which no ovum is discharged. **asexual c.,** generation by budding or division of the parent organism. **biliary c.** See *Schiff's biliary c.* **cardiac c.,** a complete cardiac movement or heart beat. The period from the beginning of one heart beat to the beginning of the next; the systolic and diastolic movement, with the interval between them. **chewing c.,** masticating c. **citric acid c.,** tricarboxylic acid c. **Cori c.,** glucose-lactate c. **cytoplasmic c.,** that stage in the life of a parasite during which it lives in cytoplasm of the cells of the host. **endogenous c.,** that portion of the life of a protozoan parasite which is spent within the body of its vertebrate host. **estrous c.,** the progressive accomplishment of the alterations characteristic of estrus, metestrus, diestrus, and proestrus, which occurs in females of the lower mammals. **exogenous c.,** that part of the life of a protozoan parasite which is spent in the body of its invertebrate host. **forced c.,** a cardiac cycle which is interrupted by a forced beat. **gastric c.,** rhythmical alterations in the shape of the stomach due to peristaltic waves. **genesial c.,** the reproductive period of a woman's life. **glucose-lactate c.,** the cycle in carbohydrate metabolism in which muscle glycogen becomes lactic acid, liver glycogen, blood glucose and muscle glycogen: called also *Cori cycle.* **Golgi's c.,** that cycle in the life of the *Plasmodium malariae*

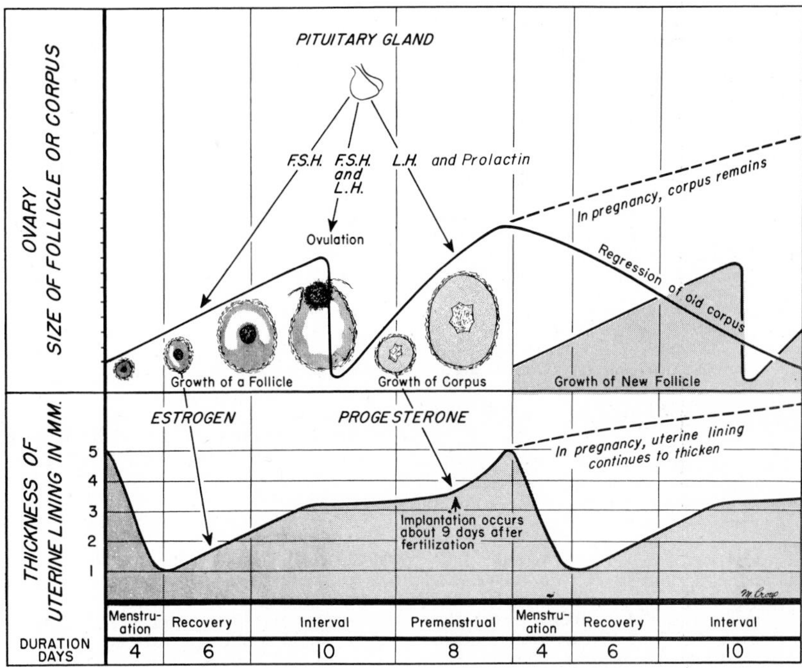

CHANGES IN MENSTRUAL CYCLE IN HUMAN FEMALE

Solid lines indicate course of events when ovum is not fertilized; dotted lines indicate course of events when fertilization occurs. Actions of hormones of pituitary and ovary in regulating the cycle are indicated by arrows. (Villee.)

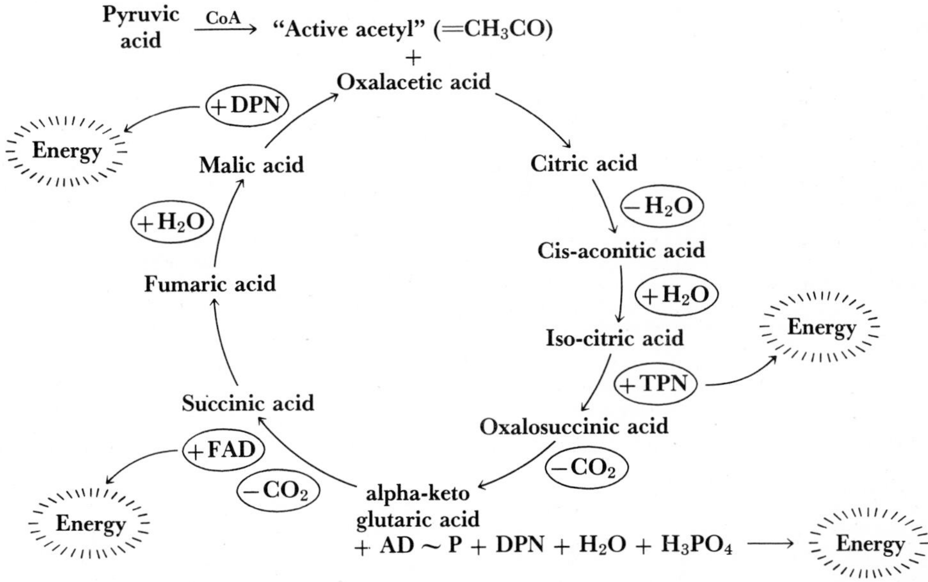

TRICARBOXYLIC ACID (KREBS) CYCLE

Diagrammatic representation of reactions by which the carbon chains of sugars, fatty acids, and amino acids are metabolized to yield carbon dioxide, water, and energy. (Frobisher.)

which is passed in human blood. Cf. *Ross's c.* **gonotrophic c.,** the interval in the life of an insect between the time of feeding to deposit of the ova. **hair c.,** the successive phases in the production of hair, from initiation of its growth to its loss from the follicle, consisting of anagen, catagen, and telogen. **human c.,** the schizogenic stage of a protozoan parasite when it passes that stage in the human body. **intranuclear c.,** that stage in the life of a microorganism during which it lives in the nuclei of the cells of the host. **Krebs' c.,** tricarboxylic acid c. **life c.,** the successive events in the life history of an organism; for example, the entire life of a protozoan blood parasite, including the endogenous and exogenous cycles. **masticating c.,** a complete course of movement of the mandible performed in mastication of food, from midline position back to the midline. **menstrual c.,** the period of the regularly recurring physiologic changes in the endometrium which culminate in its shedding (menstruation). **mosquito c.,** that period of the life of a malarial parasite that is spent in the body of the mosquito host. **oogenetic c.,** ovarian c. **ovarian c.,** the sequence of physiologic changes in the ovary, including development and rupture of the follicle, discharge of the ovum, and corpus luteum formation and regression. **reproductive c.,** the cycle of physiologic changes occurring in the reproductive organs, from the time of fertilization of the ovum through gestation and parturition. **restored c.,** a cardiac cycle following a returning cycle and taking up the normal rhythm. **returning c.,** a cardiac cycle which begins with an extrasystole. **Ross's c.,** that cycle in the development of *Plasmodium malariae* which is passed in the mosquito. Cf. *Golgi's c.* **Schiff's biliary c.,** bile salts secreted along with the bile are absorbed by the intestinal villi and are then conveyed back to the liver, where they are used over again. **schizogenic c., schizogenous c.,** the asexual cycle in protozoa during which growth and segmentation occur. **sex c., sexual c.** 1. The physiologic changes recurring regularly in the genital organs of female mammals when pregnancy does not supervene. 2. The period of sexual reproduction in an organism which also reproduces asexually. **sporogenic c., sporogenous c.,** the sexual cycle in protozoa which is usually passed in another host, often an insect. **tricarboxylic acid c.,** the cyclic metabolic mechanism by which the complete oxidation of the acetyl moiety of acetyl-coenzyme A is effected.

cyclectomy (sik-lek'to-me) [Gr. *kyklos* circle, ciliary body + *ektomē* excision]. 1. Excision of a piece of the ciliary body. 2. Excision of a portion of the ciliary border of the eyelid.

cyclencephalus (sik"len-sef'ah-lus) [Gr. *kyklos* circle + *enkephalos* brain]. A fetal monster with the cerebral hemispheres blended into one.

cyclic (sik'lik) [Gr. *kyklikos*]. Pertaining to or occurring in a cycle or cycles. The term is applied to chemical compounds which contain a ring of atoms in the nucleus. See *closed chain,* under *chain.*

cyclicotomy (sik"le-kot'o-me). Cyclotomy.

cyclitis (sik-li'tis) [Gr. *kyklos* ciliary body + *-itis*]. Inflammation of the ciliary body. **heterochromic c.,** chronic cyclitis producing difference in the color of the two irides. **plastic c.,** cyclitis with exudation of fibrinous matter into the anterior chamber. **pure c.,** inflammation of the ciliary body without involvement of the iris. **purulent c.,** suppuration in the ciliary body. **serous c.,** simple inflammation of the ciliary body; serous iritis.

cyclizine (si'klĭ-zēn). Chemical name: 1-diphenylmethyl-4-methylpiperazine: used as an antihistaminic and antinauseant, to prevent motion sickness.

cyclo- (si'klo) [Gr. *kyklos* circle]. A combining form denoting round or recurring; see *cyclic.* Often used with particular reference to the eye, or to the ciliary body of the eye.

cycloanemization (si"klo-an"ĕ-mi-za'shun). Kettesy's name for his procedure of obstructing the long ciliary arteries in the surgical treatment of glaucoma.

cyclobarbital (si"klo-bar'bĭ-tal). A white, odorless powder, 5-(1-cyclohexenyl)-5-ethylbarbituric acid: used as an intravenous anesthetic and hypnotic.

cyclocephalus (si"klo-sef'ah-lus) [*cyclo-* + Gr. *kephalē* head]. A cyclops.

cycloceratitis (si"klo-ser"ah-ti'tis). Cyclokeratitis.

cyclochoroiditis (si"klo-ko"roid-i'tis) [*cyclo-* + *choroid*]. Inflammation of the choroid and of the ciliary body.

cyclodamia (si"klo-da'me-ah) [*cyclo-* + Gr. *damnao* I subdue]. Subdued or suppressed accommodation.

cyclodialysis (si"klo-di-al'ĭ-sis) [*cyclo-* + Gr. *dialysis* dissolution]. The operative formation of a communication between the anterior chamber of the eye and the suprachoroidal space: done for glaucoma.

cyclodiathermy (si"klo-di'ah-ther"me). Destruction of a portion of the ciliary body by diathermy in cases of glaucoma.

cycloduction (si"klo-duk'shun) [*cyclo-* + *duction*]. The duction of the eyeball produced by the oblique muscle.

cyclogeny (si-kloj'ĕ-ne) [*cyclo-* + Gr. *gennan* to produce]. The developmental cycle of a microorganism.

cyclogram (si'klo-gram). 1. A graph or chart of the visual field made with the cycloscope, 1st def. 2. A graph recording observations by the cycloscope, 2nd def.: used in determining ovulation time, pregnancy, etc.

cyclogyl (si'klo-jil). Trade mark for a preparation of cyclopentolate.

cyclohexanol (si"klo-hek'sah-nol). Cyclose.

cycloid (si'kloid). 1. Containing a ring of atoms: said of organic chemical compounds. 2. Tending toward the cyclic or circular form of psychosis or toward the manic-depressive type; also applied to a physical type of the jolly, care-free individual. Cf. *schizoid.*

cyclokeratitis (si"klo-ker-ah-ti'tis) [*cyclo-* + *keratitis*]. Inflammation of the cornea and ciliary body.

cyclomastopathy (si"klo-mas-top'ah-the) [*cyclo-* + Gr. *mastos* breast + *pathos* disease]. An affection of the mammae, presenting excessive connective tissue overgrowth or epithelial proliferation or both in response to growth stimuli or as a manifestation of abnormal involution following normal response. Cf. *eccyclomastoma.*

cyclomethycaine (si"klo-meth'ĭ-kān). Chemical name: 3-(2-methylpiperidino)-propyl p-cyclohexyloxybenzoate: used as a surface anesthetic.

cyclopentamine (si"klo-pen'tah-mēn). Chemical name: Nα-dimethylcyclopentaneethylamine: used as a sympathomimetic, nasal decongestant, and hypertensive.

cyclopentane (si"klo-pen'tān). A hydrocarbon, C_5H_{10}, isomeric with pentane.

cyclopentenophenanthrene (si"klo-pen-tēn"o-fĕ-nan'thrēn). A polycyclic nucleus present in sterols, bile acids, sex hormones, cardiac poisons, and saponins.

cyclopentolate (si"klo-pen'to-lāt). Chemical name: 2-dimethylaminoethyl-1-hydroxy-α-phenylcyclopentaneacetate: used to produce parasympathetic blockade, and topically to the conjunctiva to dilate the pupil and paralyze accommodation.

cyclophoria (si"klo-fo're-ah) [*cyclo-* + Gr. *phoros* bearing]. Deviation of an eye around the anteroposterior axis only when fusion is prevented. See *excyclophoria* and *incyclophoria.* **accommodative c.,** cyclophoria due to oblique astigmatism. **minus c., negative c.,** incyclophoria. **plus c., positive c.,** excyclophoria.

cyclophorometer (si″klo-fo-rom′e-ter). An instrument for measuring cyclophoria.

cyclophosphamide (si″klo-fos′fah-mīd). Chemical name: 1-bis[2-chloroethyl]-amino-1-oxo-2-aza-5-oxaphosphoridin: used as an anti-neoplastic agent.

cyclophrenia (si″klo-fre′ne-ah). Cyclothymia.

cyclopia (si-klo′pe-ah) [Gr. *kyklos* circle + *ōpo* eye + *-ia*]. A developmental anomaly characterized by a single orbital fossa, with the globe absent or rudimentary, apparently normal or duplicated, and the nose absent or present as a tubular appendage located above the orbit.

cycloplegia (si″klo-ple′je-ah) [*cyclo-* + Gr. *plēgē* stroke]. Paralysis of the ciliary muscle; paralysis of accommodation.

cycloplegic (si″klo-ple′jik). 1. Pertaining to, characterized by, or causing cycloplegia. 2. An agent that causes cycloplegia.

cyclopropane (si″klo-pro′pān). A colorless, inflammable and explosive gas, C_3H_6, with characteristic odor and pungent taste: used by inhalation as a general anesthetic.

Cyclops (si′klops). A genus of minute crustaceans species of which are hosts to *Dracunculus* and others transmit *Diphyllobothrium*.

cyclops (si′klops) [Gr. *kyklōps* one of a race of one-eyed giants]. A fetal monster exhibiting cyclopia. **c. hypogna′thus,** a modified cyclops, lacking the typical proboscis, with ears abnormally low, rudimentary mandible, and extremely small orifice of the buccal cavity.

cyclopterin (si-klop′ter-in). A protamine derived from the spermatozoa of the lump-sucker, *Cyclopterus lumpus*.

cycloscope (si′klo-skōp) [*cyclo-* + Gr. *skopein* to examine]. 1. Donders' apparatus for measuring the field of vision. 2. A form of spectroscope for observing oxygen metabolism in the web of the thumb. The observation recorded on a chart constitutes a cyclogram or endocrinogram.

cyclose (si′klōs). Any one of a class of carbohydrates which are polyhydroxy cyclohexanes. They include inositol and phytol.

cycloserine (si″klo-ser′ēn). An antibiotic substance elaborated by *Streptomyces orchidaceus* or *S. garyphalus:* used in treatment of urinary tract infections.

cyclosis (si-klo′sis) [Gr. *kyklōsis* a surrounding, enclosing]. Movement of the protoplasm within a cell, without deformation of the cell wall. Called also *cytoplasmic* or *protoplasmic streaming*.

cyclospasm (si′klo-spazm). Spasm of accommodation.

cyclospasmol (si″klo-spaz′mol). Trade mark for preparations of cyclandelate.

cyclostat (si′klo-stat). A cylinder of glass in which an experimental animal is rotated about its vertical axis.

cyclotherapy (si″klo-ther′ah-pe) [*cyclo-* + Gr. *therapeia* treatment]. Use of the bicycle in treatment of disease.

cyclothymia (si″klo-thim′e-ah) [*cyclo-* + Gr. *thymos* spirit]. A temperament characterized by cyclic alternations of mood between elation and depression, often associated with the pyknic type of body build.

cyclothymiac (si″klo-thim′e-ak). An individual exhibiting cyclothymia.

cyclothymic (si″klo-thi′mik). Pertaining to, characterized by, or causing cyclothymia.

cyclothymosis (si″klo-thi-mo′sis). Any mental disease of the cyclothymic and manic-depressive group (Southard).

cyclotol (si′klo-tol). A polyhydroxy cyclohexane, such as inositol.

cyclotome (si′klo-tōm). A cutting instrument for use in cyclotomy or other operations upon the eye.

cyclotomy (si-klot′o-me) [*cyclo-* + Gr. *temnein* to cut]. Division of or incision of the ciliary muscle.

cyclotron (si′klo-tron). An apparatus for accelerating protons or deuterons to high energies by a combination of a constant magnet and an oscillating electric field.

cyclotropia (si″klo-tro′pe-ah) [*cyclo-* + Gr. *tropos* a turning]. Deviation of an eye around the anteroposterior axis when fusion is a possibility. See *excyclotropia* and *incyclotropia*. **minus c., negative c.,** incyclotropia. **plus c., positive c.,** excyclotropia.

cycrimine (si′krĭ-mīn). Chemical name: α-cyclopentyl-α-phenyl-l-piperidinepropanol: used to produce parasympathetic blockade, and in treatment of parkinsonism.

cyema (si-e′mah) [Gr. *kyēma* embryo]. The product of conception during all its stages.

cyemology (si″e-mol′o-je). Embryology.

cyesedema (si″e-se-de′mah) [Gr. *kyēsis* conception + *edema*]. A peculiar bloating of the body, especially of the face, sometimes seen in pregnant women.

cyesiognosis (si-e″se-og-no′sis) [Gr. *kyēsis* conception + *gnōsis* knowledge]. Diagnosis of pregnancy.

cyesiology (si-e″se-ol′o-je) [Gr. *kyēsis* conception + *-logy*]. The sum of knowledge regarding pregnancy.

cyesis (si-e′sis) [Gr. *kyēsis*]. Pregnancy.

cyestein (si-es′te-in). A skinlike formation sometimes seen on the surface of urine of a pregnant woman.

cyesthein (si-es′the-in). Cyestein.

cygnine (sig′nin). An alkaloid, $C_{19}H_{22}N_2O_3$, from *Gastrolobium colycinum*. It is a convulsant poison.

cyl. Abbreviation for *cylinder* or *cylindrical lens*.

cylicotomy (sil″e-kot′o-me) [Gr. *kylix* cup + *tomē* cut]. Surgical division of the ciliary muscle.

cylinder (sil′in-der) [Gr. *kylindros* a roller]. A solid body shaped like a column; especially a cylindrical cast or cylindrical lens. **Bence Jones c's,** cylindrical gelatinous bodies forming the contents of the seminal vesicles. **crossed c's,** two cylindrical lenses at right angles to each other. **Külz's c.,** coma cast. **Leydig's c's,** bundles of muscular fibers separated by partitions of protoplasm. **Ruffini's c's,** Ruffini's corpuscles. **terminal c's,** brushes of Ruffini. **urinary c.,** a urinary cast.

cylindrarthrosis (sil″in-drar-thro′sis) [*cylinder* + Gr. *arthrōsis* joint]. A joint in which the articular surfaces are cylindrical.

cylindraxile (sil″in-drak′sil). An axon.

cylindrical (sĭ-lin′drĭ-k′l). Pertaining to or shaped like a cylinder.

cylindriform (sĭ-lin′drĭ-form). Cylindrical.

cylindro-adenoma (sĭ-lin″dro-ad″e-no′mah). A tumor formed by hyaline degeneration of an adenoma and containing cylindrical masses of hyaline matter.

cylindrocellular (sil″in-dro-sel′u-lar). Composed of or containing cylindrical cells.

cylindrodendrite (sil″in-dro-den′drīt). Paraxon.

Cylindrogloea (sĭ-lin″dro-gle′ah). A genus of microorganisms of the family Chlorobacteriaceae, suborder Rhodobacteriineae, order Pseudomonadales, occurring as small ovoid to rod-shaped cells, forming cylindrical aggregates about a filamentous, colorless bacterium. The type species is *C. bacterif′era*.

cylindroid (sĭ-lin′droid) [Gr. *kylindroeidēs* cylindrical]. 1. Resembling, or shaped like a cylinder. 2. A spurious or mucous cast in the urine, of various origins and of various forms, generally resembling hyaline casts, but differing from the latter in that they taper to a slender tail which is often twisted or curled upon itself.

Cylindroids.

cylindroma (sil″in-dro′mah). 1. A tumor in which

the stroma has the form of elongated, twisted cords of hyaline material. 2. Billroth's name for epithelioma composed of translucent cylinders of hyaline connective tissue with a network of tumor cells between them.

cylindromatous (sil″in-drom′ah-tus). Pertaining to or of the nature of cylindroma.

cylindrosarcoma (sĭ-lin″dro-sar-ko′mah). A tumor containing both cylindromatous and sarcomatous elements.

cylindruria (sil″in-droo′re-ah) [Gr. *kylindros* cylinder + *ouron* urine + *-ia*]. The presence of tube casts in the urine.

cylite (si′līt). Benzyl bromide.

cyllosis (sil-lo′sis) [Gr. *kyllōsis*]. Clubfoot or similar deformity of the foot or leg.

cyllosoma (sil″lo-so′mah) [Gr. *kyllos* lame + *sōma* body]. A fetal monster with lower lateral abdominal eventration and absence or imperfect development of the lower extremity on the side having the eventration.

cyllosomus (sil″lo-so′mus). Cyllosoma.

cymarose (si′mah-rōs). A desoxyhexomethyl sugar, $CH_3(CHOH)_2CHO(CH_3)CH_2.CHO$, derived from various strophanthin glycosides.

cymba (sim′bah), pl. *cym′bae* [L.; Gr. *kymbē*]. A boat-shaped structure. **c. con′chae auric′ulae** [N A, B N A], the upper part of the concha of the auricle.

cymbiform (sim′bĭ-form) [L. *cymba* boat + L. *forma* form]. Boat-shaped; scaphoid.

cymbo- (sim′bo) [L. *cymba*, Gr. *kymbē*, boat]. Combining form meaning boat-shaped.

cymbocephalia (sim″bo-se-fa′le-ah). Scaphocephaly.

cymbocephalic (sim″bo-se-fal′ik) [*cymbo-* + *kephalē* head]. Scaphocephalic.

cymbocephalous (sim″bo-sef′ah-lus). Scaphocephalic.

cymbocephaly (sim″bo-sef′ah-le). Scaphocephaly.

cyme (sīm). A form of inflorescence composed of a flat-topped cluster of blossoms.

cymograph (si′mo-graf). Kymograph.

cyn- (sin). See *cyno-*.

cynanche (sĭ-nan′ke) [*cyn-* + Gr. *anchein* to choke]. Severe sore throat with threatened suffocation. **c. malig′na,** a gangrenous or putrid sore throat, often diphtheritic or scarlatinal. **c. sublingua′lis,** inflammation of the submaxillary connective tissue. **c. tonsilla′ris,** quinsy.

cynanthropy (sĭ-nan′thro-pe) [*cyn-* + Gr. *anthrōpos* man]. Delusion in which the patient considers himself a dog or behaves like a dog.

cynarase (si′nar-ās). A ferment derived from the plant *Cynara*.

cyniatria (sin″e-at′re-ah). Cyniatrics.

cyniatrics (sin″e-at′riks) [*cyn-* + Gr. *iatreia* cure]. That branch of veterinary medicine which treats of diseases of dogs.

cynic (sin′ik) [Gr. *kynikos*]. Doglike.

cyno- (si′no) [Gr. *kyōn* dog]. A combining form denoting relationship to a dog, or meaning doglike.

cynobex (si′no-beks) [*cyno-* + Gr. *bēx* cough]. The barking cough of early youth.

cynocephalic (si″no-se-fal′ik) [*cyno-* + Gr. *kephalē* head]. Having a head shaped like that of a dog.

cynodont (si′no-dont) [*cyno-* + Gr. *odous* tooth]. A canine tooth.

Cynomyia (si″no-mi′yah). A genus of blue-bottle flies which deposit their ova in decaying meat and in wounds.

Cynomys (si′no-mis). A genus of prairie dogs species of which harbor plague-transmitting fleas.

cynophobia (si″no-fo′be-ah) [*cyno-* + *phobia*]. 1. Morbid fear of dogs. 2. Pseudorabies.

cynorexia (si″no-rek′se-ah) [*cyno-* + Gr. *orexis* appetite]. Morbidly excessive hunger; bulimia.

cynothyrotoxin (si″no-thi″ro-tok′sin) [*cyno-* + *thyrotoxin*]. A hypothetical substance assumed to occur normally in the thyroid of dogs and to be toxic for man.

cyogenic (si″o-jen′ik) [Gr. *kyos* fetus + *gennan* to produce]. Producing pregnancy.

Cyon's experiment, nerve (se′onz) [Elie de *Cyon*, a Russian physiologist, 1843–1912]. See under *experiment* and *nerve*.

cyonin (si′o-nin) [Gr. *kyos* fetus]. A general term for gonad-stimulating hormones of placental origin.

cyophoria (si″o-fo′re-ah) [Gr. *kyos* fetus + *phoros* bearing]. Pregnancy.

cyophoric (si″o-for′ik). Pertaining to pregnancy.

cyophorin (si-of′o-rin). Gravidin.

cyopin (si′o-pin) [Gr. *kyanos* blue + *pyon* pus]. The substance responsible for the color of blue pus.

cyotrophy (si-ot′ro-fe) [Gr. *kyos* fetus + *trophē* nutrition]. Nutrition of the fetus.

Cyperus (si-pe′rus) [L.; Gr. *kypeiros* rush]. A genus of grasslike sedges or rushes. See *adrue*.

cypho- (si′fo). For words beginning thus, see those beginning *kypho-*.

cypridology (sip″re-dol′o-je) [Gr. *Kypris* Venus + *-logy*]. Venereology.

cypridopathy (sip″re-dop′ah-the) [Gr. *Kypris* Venus + *pathos* disease]. A venereal disease.

cypridophobia (sip″re-do-fo′be-ah) [Gr. *Kypris* Venus + *phobia*]. 1. A morbid fear of becoming infected with venereal disease. 2. Morbid dread of sexual intercourse.

cyprinin (sip′rĭ-nin). A toxic substance derived from the milt of the carp, *Cyprinus carpio*.

cypriphobia (sip″re-fo′be-ah). Cypridophobia.

cyproheptadine (si″pro-hep′tah-dēn). Chemical name: 1-methyl-4-(5-dibenzo-[α-e]-cycloheptatrienylidene)-piperidine: used as an antihistaminic and antiserotonin.

cyrtograph (sir′to-graf) [Gr. *kyrtos* bent + *graphein* to write]. A cyrtometer which registers the movements of the chest wall.

cyrtometer (sir-tom′e-ter) [Gr. *kyrtos* bent + *metron* measure]. A device for use in measuring the curves and curved surfaces of the body.

cyrtosis (sir-to′sis) [Gr. *kyrtōsis*]. 1. Kyphosis. 2. Distortion of the bones.

cyst (sist) [Gr. *kystis* sac, bladder]. Any sac, normal or abnormal, especially one which contains a liquid or semisolid material. **adventitious c.,** a cyst formed about a foreign body or an exudate. **allantoic c.,** urachal c. **apoplectic c.,** a cyst formed in a part by extravasation of blood. **atheromatous c.,** a sebaceous tumor of the skin having pultaceous contents. **Baker's c.,** a swelling behind the knee, caused by escape of synovial fluid which has become enclosed in a sac of membrane; popliteal bursitis; synovial cyst of the popliteal space. **bile c.,** the gallbladder. **Blessig's c's,** cystic spaces which frequently appear at the periphery of the retina close to the ora serrata: called also *cystoid degeneration* and *Iwanoff's retinal edema*. **blood c.,** a cyst containing extravasated blood. **blue dome c.,** a benign retention cyst of the breast containing straw-colored fluid that shows a blue color when viewed from above. **bone c., aneurysmal,** a solitary lesion of bone which typically causes a bulging of the overlying cortex bearing some resemblance to the saccular protrusion of the aortic wall in aortic aneurysm. **Boyer's c.,** a painless and gradual enlargement of the subhyoid bursa. **branchial c., branchial cleft c., branchiogenetic c., branchiogenous c.,** a cyst arising from epithelial remnants of a branchial cleft, usually located between the second and third branchial arches. **bursal c.,** a cyst derived from a serous bursa. **butter c.** 1. A necrotic mass in a lipoma. 2. A retention cyst of the mammary gland filled with the products of the alteration of milk, such as butyric acid. **cervical c.,**

a branchial or thyroglossal cyst. **chocolate c.,** one having dark, syrupy contents, resulting from collection of brownish serum, such as sometimes occurs after mastectomy or in the ovary in ovarian endometriosis. **choledochus c.,** a cyst of the common bile duct. **chyle c.,** an abnormal sac of the mesentery containing chyle. **ciliated epithelial c.,** a cyst lined with ciliated epithelium. They occur in the gastro-intestinal tract (enterocystoma), in the hair, thorax, lung, and genital organs. **colloid c.,** a cyst which contains jelly-like material. **compound c.,** multilocular c. **coronodental c.,** odontoma. **corpus luteum c.,** a cyst of the ovary formed by a serous accumulation developed from a corpus luteum. **craniobuccal c.,** a cyst of Rathke's pouch. **cutaneous c., cuticular c.,** a dermoid cyst. **daughter c.,** a small cyst developed from the wall of a larger one. **degeneration c.,** evolution cyst. **dental c.,** one occurring adjacent to a tooth. **dentigerous c.,** a cyst containing one or more fairly well formed teeth. **dermoid c.,** a cyst of developmental origin consisting of a fibrous wall lined with stratified epithelium and containing hair follicles, sweat glands, and sebaceous glands. **dilatation c.,** a cyst formed by dilation of a previously existing cavity. **distention c.,** a collection of watery fluid in a normal, but distended cavity. **echinococcus c.,** hydatid c. **endometrial c.,** chocolate c. **endothelial c.,** a cyst whose sac has an endothelial lining. **enteric c., enterogenous c.,** a cyst of the intestine arising or developing from some fold or pouch along the intestinal tract. **ependymal c.,** a circumscribed dilatation of some part of the ependyma. **epidermoid c.,** a cyst with an epidermal lining but with definite dermal structures lacking. **epithelial c.,** a dermoid cyst. **extravasation c.,** a cyst formed by hemorrhage into the tissues. **exudation c.,** a cyst formed by an exudate collected in a closed cavity. **false c.,** an adventitious cyst. **fissural c.,** one arising along a line of fusion of the various embryonic processes. According to location, those of the oral region are classified as median palatal, median anterior maxillary, globulomaxillary, and nasoalveolar. **follicular c.,** one due to the occlusion of the duct of a follicle or small gland; especially a cyst formed by the enlargement of a graafian follicle as a result of accumulated transudate. **gartnerian c.,** a cystic tumor developed from Gartner's duct. **gas c.,** a small cyst filled with gas, of bacterial origin. **globulomaxillary c.,** a bony cyst of the maxilla at the junction of the globular portion of the medial nasal process and the maxillary process, usually between the lateral incisor and the canine tooth. **granddaughter c.,** a cyst sometimes seen within a daughter cyst. **hemorrhagic c.,** an encapsulated mass of extravasated blood. **hydatid c.** echinococcus cyst; the cyst stage of an embryonic tapeworm in which the cyst contains daughter cysts, each of which contains many scolices. **I-c.** See *Iodamoeba buetschlii.* **implantation c.,** a cyst formed from a piece of skin that has become implanted into the deep tissues. **incisive canal c.,** median anterior maxillary c. **inclusion c.,** one formed by the inclusion of a small portion of the epiblast within the mesoblast. **intra-epithelial c's,** round or oval cavities which develop in the epithelium of the ureter, bladder and urethra and contain a peculiar colloid substance. **involution c.,** a multiple cystic dilatation of the milk ducts after the menopause. It is not always malignant, but may result in cancer. **iodine c.** See *Iodamoeba buetschlii.* **lacteal c.,** a cyst of the breast due to obstruction of a lactiferous duct. **lutein c.,** a cyst of the ovary developed from a corpus luteum. **median anterior maxillary c.,** a cyst in or near the incisive canal, arising from proliferation of epithelial remnants of the nasopalatine duct, or arising from remnants of the dental lamina anterior to the incisive canal. **median palatal c.,** one located in the midline of the hard palate, between the lateral palatal processes. **meibomian c.** See *chalazion.* **milk c.,** lacteal c. **morgagnian c.,** a hydatid of Morgagni. **mother c.,** a cyst enclosing other cysts. **mucous c.,** a retention cyst which contains mucus. **multilocular c.,** a cyst containing many loculi or spaces, which usually are endogenous daughter cysts. **nabothian c's,** nabothian follicles. **nasoalveolar c.,** a fissural cyst arising at the junction of the globular portion of the medial nasal process, the lateral nasal process, and the maxillary process, sometimes secondarily involving the maxilla. **nasolabial c.,** nasoalveolar c. **nasopalatine duct c.,** median anterior maxillary c. **necrotic c.,** a cyst containing necrotic matter. **neural c.,** a cystlike dilatation of a ventricle or lymph space of the brain or spinal cord. **nevoid c.,** an abnormal cyst with vascular walls. **oil c.,** a cyst containing oily matter, due to fatty degeneration of the epithelial lining. **oophoritic c.,** a cyst of the ovary proper. **pancreatic c.,** a retention cyst of the pancreatic duct. **paradental c.,** a lateral radicular cyst. **paranephric c.,** a cyst of the fatty tissue surrounding the kidney. **parasitic c.,** a cyst formed by the larva of a parasite, such as a hydatid cyst. **parent c.,** a mother cyst. **paroophoritic c., parovarian c.,** a cyst of the parovarium. **pearl c.,** a cyst or a solid mass of epithelial cells in the iris caused by implantation of an eyelash. **periodontal c.,** a cyst occurring adjacent to a tooth. **periodontal c., apical,** radicular c. **piliferous c., pilonidal c.,** a hair-containing sacrococcygeal dermoid cyst or sinus which often opens at a postanal dimple. Cf. *coccygeal sinus,* under *sinus.* **porencephalic c.,** a cyst occurring in the brain substance in porencephaly. **preauricular c., congenital,** a cyst resulting from imperfect fusion of the first and second branchial arches in formation of the auricle, communicating with a pitlike depression just in front of the helix and above the tragus (ear pit). **proliferous c.,** a cyst which produces multiple daughter cysts: often malignant. **proligerous c.,** adenocarcinoma. **psorospermal c.,** a cyst containing psorosperms. **pyelogenic renal c.,** calyceal diverticulum. **radicular c.,** an epithelium-lined sac, which may contain cholesterol, at the apex of a tooth. **radiculodental c.,** radicular c. **Rathke's c's,** groups of epithelial cells forming small colloid-filled cysts in the pars intermedia of the hypophysis. **retention c.,** one caused by retention of glandular secretion. **root c.,** radicular c. **Sampson's c.,** chocolate c. **sanguineous c.,** a cyst containing blood. **sebaceous c.,** the retention cyst of a sebaceous gland. **secondary c.,** a daughter cyst. **secretory c.,** a cyst produced by retention of the normal secretion of a gland. **seminal c.,** a cyst containing semen. **sequestration c.,** a dermoid cyst separated from the skin, due to embryonic displacement of a piece of skin. **serous c.,** a cyst containing a thin liquid or serum. **soap c.,** a collection of yellow fatty matter encysted in the breast. **soapsuds c's,** cysts which stud the cerebral cortex in torulosis. **sterile c.,** a true hydatid cyst which fails to produce brood capsules. **sublingual c.,** ranula. **subsynovial c.,** one caused by the distention of a synovial follicle. **suprasellar c.,** craniopharyngioma. **synovial c.,** a distended synovial bursa or tendon sheath. **tarry c.,** a corpus luteum cyst resulting from hemorrhage into a corpus luteum. **tarsal c.,** chalazion. **thecal c.,** distention of a sheath of a tendon. **theca-lutein c.,** a cyst of the ovary in which the lutein cells lining the cystic cavity are theca interna cells. **thyroglossal c., thyrolingual c.,** a cyst in the neck caused by persistence of portions of or by lack of closure of the primitive thyroglossal duct. **true c.,** any cyst not normal and not formed by the dilatation of a passage or cavity. **tubular c.,** tubulocyst. **umbilical c.,** vitello-intestinal c. **unilocular c.,** a cyst containing but one cavity. **urachal** c., a form of cystic dilatation of the urachus. **urinary c.,** a cyst containing urine. **vitello-intestinal c.,** a cystlike tumor at the umbilicus, caused by persistence of a portion of the umbilical duct. **wolffian c.,** a cyst of the broad ligaments of the uterus, regarded as developed from vestiges of the wolffian body.

cyst- (sist). See *cysto-*.

cystadenocarcinoma (sis-tad″e-no-kar″si-no′mah). Carcinoma and cystadenoma.

cystadenolymphoma (sis-tad″e-no-lim-fo′mah). Papillary cystadenoma lymphomatosum.

cystadenoma (sis″tad-e-no′mah) [*cyst-* + *adenoma*]. Adenoma which is associated with cystoma. **c. adamanti′num,** adamantinoma. **mucinous c.,** a multilocular tumor of the ovary, the cavities of which are filled with a stringy, sticky mucoid secretion known to be true mucus, the changes being due to staleness. **c. par′tim sim′plex par′tim papillif′erum,** a combination of simple and papillary cystadenoma. **pseudomucinous c.,** mucinous c.; so called because the cavity contents were thought to be pseudomucin. **serous c.,** a cystic tumor of the ovary, containing thin, clear, yellow serous fluid and varying amounts of solid tissue, with a malignant potential several times greater than that of mucinous cystadenoma.

cystadenosarcoma (sis-tad″e-no-sar-ko′mah). Cystadenoma blended with sarcoma.

cystalgia (sis-tal′je-ah) [*cyst-* + *-algia*]. Pain in the bladder.

cystathionine (sis″tah-thi′o-nin). An unsymmetrical thio-ether of cysteine and methionine, $COOH.CH(NH_2).CH_2.CH_2.S.CH_2.CH(NH_2).$-COOH, which occurs as an intermediate in cystine synthesis.

cystathioninuria (sis″tah-thi″o-nin-u′re-ah). The excretion of cystathionine in the urine.

cystatrophia (sis″tah-tro′fe-ah) [*cyst-* + Gr. *atrophia* atrophy]. Atrophy of the bladder.

cystauchenitis (sis″taw-kĕ-ni′tis) [*cyst* + Gr. *auchēn* neck + *-itis*]. Inflammation of the neck of the bladder.

cystauchenotomy (sis″taw-kĕ-not′o-me) [*cyst-* + Gr. *auchēn* neck + *tomē* cut]. Surgical incision of the neck of the bladder.

cystauxe (sis′tauk-se). Enlargement of the bladder.

cystduodenostomy (sist″du-od″e-nos′to-me). Internal drainage of a pseudocyst of the pancreas into the duodenum.

cystectasia, cystectasy (sis-tek-ta′ze-ah, sis-tek′tah-se) [*cyst-* + Gr. *ektasis* dilatation]. Slitting of the membranous portion of the urethra and dilatation of the neck of the bladder for the extraction of stone.

cystectomy (sis-tek′to-me) [*cyst-* + Gr. *ektomē* excision]. 1. Excision of a cyst. 2. Excision of the bladder (*complete* or *total c.*) or resection of the bladder (*partial c.*).

cysteine (sis-te′in). An amino acid produced by the digestion or by the acid hydrolysis of proteins. It is alpha-amino-beta-thio-lactic acid, $SH.CH_2.$-$CH(NH_2).COOH$. It is easily oxidized to cystine and is sometimes found in the urine. **c. hydrochloride** has been suggested for the treatment of cutaneous ulcers.

cystelcosis (sis″tel-ko′sis) [*cyst-* + Gr. *helkōsis* ulceration]. Ulceration of the bladder.

cystencephalus (sis″ten-sef′ah-lus) [*cyst-* + Gr. *enkephalos* brain]. A fetal monster with a membranous sac in place of a brain.

cystendesis (sis″ten-de′sis) [*cyst-* + Gr. *endesis* suturation]. Suturation of a wound of the gallbladder or of the urinary bladder.

cysterethism (sis-ter′e-thizm) [*cyst-* + Gr. *erethismos* irritation]. Irritability of the bladder.

cystgastrostomy (sist″gas-tros′to-me) [*cyst* + Gr. *gastēr* stomach + *stomoun* to provide with an opening, or mouth]. Internal drainage of a pseudocyst of the pancreas into the stomach.

cysthypersarcosis (sist-hi″per-sar-ko′sis) [*cyst-* + Gr. *hyper* over + *sarkōsis* growth of flesh]. A thickening of the muscular coat of the bladder.

cysti- (sis′te). See *cysto-*.

cystic (sis′tik) [Gr. *kystis* bladder]. 1. Pertaining to a cyst. 2. Pertaining to the urinary bladder or to the gallbladder.

cysticerci (sis″tĭ-ser′si). Plural of *cysticercus*.

cysticercoid (sis″tĭ-ser′koid). A form of larval tapeworm resembling Cysticercus, but having the cyst small and almost devoid of fluid.

cysticercosis (sis″tĭ-ser-ko′sis). The condition of being infested with cysticerci.

Cysticercus (sis″tĭ-ser′kus) [Gr. *kystis* bladder + *kerkos* tail]. A genus name once given to larval forms of tapeworms, with such species names as *C. acanthro′trias*, *C. bo′vis* (beef tapeworm), *C. cellulo′sae* (pork tapeworm), *T. fasciola′ris*, *C. o′vis*, and *C. tenuicollis*.

cysticercus (sis″tĭ-ser′kus), pl *cysticer′ci*. A larval form of tapeworm, consisting of a single scolex enclosed in a bladder-like cyst. See *hydatid*.

cysticolithectomy (sis″tĭ-ko″lĭ-thek′to-me) [Gr. *kystis* bladder + *lithos* stone + *ektomē* excision]. Removal of stone from the gallbladder by an incision through the cystic duct.

cysticolithotripsy (sis″tĭ-ko-lith′o-trip-se). Crushing of a calculus in the cystic duct.

cysticorrhaphy (sis″tĭ-kor′ah-fe) [*cystic duct* + *rhaphē* suture]. Suture of the cystic duct.

cysticotomy (sis″tĭ-kot′o-me) [*cystic duct* + Gr. *tomē* a cut]. Incision into the cystic duct.

cystides (sis′tĭ-dēz). Plural of *cystis*.

cystido- (sis′tĭ-do). See *cysto-*.

cystidoceliotomy (sis″tĭ-do-se″le-ot′o-me). Cystidolaparotomy.

cystidolaparotomy (sis″tĭ-do-lap″ah-rot′o-me) [*cystido-* + *laparotomy*]. Incision of the bladder through the abdominal wall.

cystidotrachelotomy (sis″tĭ-do-tra-kel-ot′o-me) [*cystido-* + Gr. *trachēlos* neck + *tomē* a cut]. Incision of the neck of the bladder.

cystifellotomy (sis″tĭ-fel-lot′o-me) [*cysti-* + L. *fel* bile + Gr. *tomē* a cut]. Cholecystotomy.

cystiferous (sis-tif′er-us). Cystigerous.

cystiform (sis′tĭ-form) [*cysti-* + L. *forma* form]. Having the form or appearance of a cyst.

cystigerous (sis-tij′er-us) [*cysti-* + L. *gerere* to bear]. Containing cysts.

cystine (sis′tin). Dicysteine, $[S.CH_2.CH(NH_2).$-$COOH]_2$, an amino acid produced by the digestion or acid hydrolysis of proteins. It is sometimes found in the urine and in the kidneys in the form of minute hexagonal crystals, frequently forming cystine calculus in the bladder. Cystine is the chief sulfur-containing compound of the protein molecule.

cystinemia (sis″tĭ-ne′me-ah) [*cystine* + Gr. *haima* blood + *-ia*]. Presence of cystine in the blood.

cystinosis (sis″tĭ-no′sis) [*cystine* + *-osis*]. A congenital metabolic disturbance characterized by deposition of cystine throughout the reticuloendothelial system and in various organs, notably the kidneys. Renal insufficiency, renal rickets, and dwarfism result.

cystinuria (sis″tĭ-nu′re-ah) [*cystine* + *urine*]. The occurrence of cystine in the urine.

cystinuric (sis″tĭ-nu′rik). Pertaining to or affected with cystinuria.

cystirrhagia (sis″te-ra′je-ah). Cystorrhagia.

cystirrhea (sis″te-re′ah). Cystorrhea.

cystis (sis′tis), pl. *cys′tides* [Gr. *kystis*]. A pouch or sac; a cyst. **c. fel′lea,** gallbladder.

cystistaxis (sis″te-stak′sis) [*cysti-* + Gr. *staxis* dripping]. Oozing of blood from the mucous membrane into the bladder.

cystitis (sis-ti′tis). Inflammation of the urinary

bladder. **allergic c.,** cystitis resulting from some unusual hypersensitivity, characterized by a large number of mononuclear leukocytes and eosinophils in the bladder mucosa and musculature, and in the urinary sediment. **bacterial c.,** cystitis occurring as a complication of bacterial infection elsewhere in the body. **catarrhal c., acute,** cystitis resulting from injury, irritation by foreign bodies, gonorrhea, etc., and marked by burning in the bladder, pain in the urethra, and painful micturition. **c. col'li,** inflammation involving the neck of the bladder. **croupous c.,** diphtheritic c. **cystic c., c. cys'tica,** cystitis with the formation of multiple submucosal cysts in the bladder wall. **diphtheritic c.,** cystitis due to infection by *Corynebacterium diphtheriae*, and characterized by the formation of a false membrane. **c. emphysemato'sa,** an unusual inflammation of the bladder, characterized by the presence of gas-filled vesicles and cysts in the bladder mucosa and musculature. **eosinophilic c.,** cystitis characterized by the presence of large numbers of eosinophils in the urinary sediment. **exfoliative c.,** cystitis with sloughing of the bladder mucosa. **c. follicula'ris,** cystitis in which the mucosa of the bladder is studded with nodules containing lymph follicles. **c. glandula'ris,** cystitis in which the mucosa contains mucin-secreting glands, observed more frequently in cases of exstrophy of the bladder, and sometimes leading to malignant degeneration. **incrusted c.,** an intense cystitis characterized by deposition of phosphatic or other inorganic salts on the chronically inflamed bladder wall, generally at the site of ulcerations, granulations, or tumors. **interstitial c., chronic,** a condition of the bladder occurring predominantly in women, with an inflammatory lesion, usually in the vertex, and involving the entire thickness of the wall, appearing as a small patch of brownish red mucosa, surrounded by a network of radiating vessels. The lesions, known as Fenwick-Hunner or Hunner ulcers, may heal superficially, and are notoriously difficult to detect. **mechanical c.,** cystitis resulting from irritation by a vesical calculus or a foreign body in the bladder. **panmural c.,** interstitial c., chronic. **c. papillomato'sa,** cystitis characterized by the presence of papillomatous growths on the inflamed mucous membrane. **c. seni'lis femina'rum,** a chronic cystitis occurring in elderly women, marked by abnormal frequency of micturition, with tenesmus and burning. **submucous c.,** interstitial c., chronic.

cystitome (sis'tĭ-tōm) [*cysti-* + Gr. *temnein* to cut]. An instrument for opening the sac of the lens of the eye.

cystitomy (sis-tit'o-me) [*cysti-* + Gr. *tomē* a cut]. The surgical division of the capsule of the lens; capsulotomy.

cystjejunostomy (sist″je-ju-nos'to-me). Internal drainage of a pseudocyst of the pancreas into the jejunum.

cysto- (sis'to) [Gr. *kystis, kystides* a sac or bladder]. A combining form denoting a relationship to a sac, cyst, or bladder, most frequently used in reference to the urinary bladder.

cystoadenoma (sis″to-ad″e-no'mah). A tumor containing cystic and adenomatous elements.

cystoblast (sis'to-blast) [*cysto-* + Gr. *blastos* germ]. The layer of cells that lines the amniotic cavity of the early embryo on the side of the enveloping layer.

cystocarcinoma (sis″to-kar″sĭ-no'mah). Carcinoma associated with cysts.

cystocele (sis'to-sēl) [*cysto-* + Gr. *kēlē* hernia]. Hernial protrusion of the urinary bladder through the vaginal wall.

cystochrome (sis'to-krōm) [*cysto-* + Gr. *chrōma* color]. A mixture of indigo carmine and methenemine: used by intramuscular or intravenous injection for the indigo carmine test of renal function.

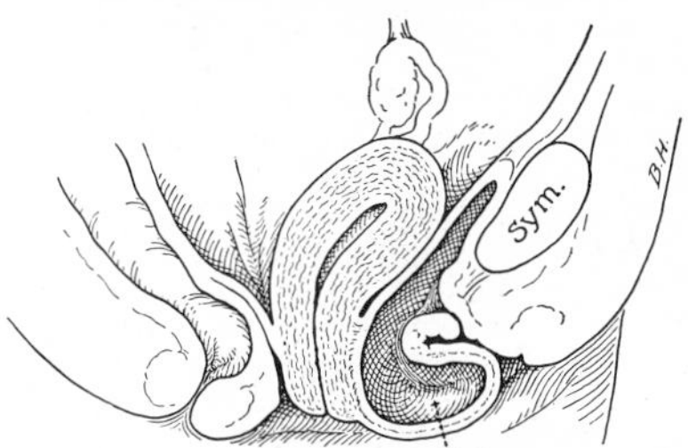

Cystocele (after Curtis).

cystochromoscopy (sis″to-kro-mos'ko-pe). Chromocystoscopy.

cystocolostomy (sis″to-ko-los'to-me) [*cysto-* + *colostomy*]. The surgical creation of a permanent passage from the bladder to the colon.

cystodiaphanoscopy (sis″to-di″ah-fah-nos'ko-pe) [*cysto-* + *diaphanoscopy*]. Diaphanoscopy of abdominal viscera.

cystodynia (sis″to-din'e-ah) [*cysto-* + Gr. *odynē* pain]. Pain in the urinary bladder.

cystoelytroplasty (sis″to-e-lit'ro-plas″te) [*cysto-* + Gr. *elytron* sheath + *plassein* to form]. Surgical repair of vesicovaginal injuries.

cystoenterocele (sis″to-en'ter-o-sēl). Hernia of a portion of the bladder and of the intestine.

cystoepiplocele (sis″to-e-pip'lo-sēl). Hernia of a portion of the bladder and of the omentum.

cystoepithelioma (sis″to-ep″ĭ-the″le-o'mah). A tumor containing cystic and epitheliomatous elements.

cystofibroma (sis″to-fi-bro'mah) [L.]. Fibroma containing cysts.

cystogastrostomy (sis″to-gas-tros'to-me). Surgical anastomosis of a pancreatic cyst to the stomach.

cystogram (sis'to-gram). A roentgenogram of the bladder.

cystography (sis-tog'rah-fe) [*cysto-* + Gr. *graphein* to write]. Roentgenography of the bladder after injection of the organ with opaque solution.

cystoid (sis'toid) [*cysto-* + Gr. *eidos* form]. 1. Resembling a cyst. 2. A cystlike, circumscribed collection of softened material, differing from a true cyst in having no enclosing capsule.

cystojejunostomy (sis″to-je-ju-nos'to-me). Surgical anastomosis of a pancreatic cyst to the jejunum.

cystolith (sis'to-lith) [*cysto-* + Gr. *lithos* stone]. A vesical calculus.

cystolithectomy (sis″to-lĭ-thek'to-me) [*cysto-* + Gr. *lithos* stone + *ektomē* excision]. The removal of a calculus by cutting into the bladder. The term has been used erroneously for excision of a gallstone from the gallbladder.

cystolithiasis (sis″to-lĭ-thi'ah-sis) [*cysto-* + Gr. *lithos* stone]. The development of calculi in the bladder.

cystolithic (sis″to-lith'ik). Pertaining to vesical calculi.

cystolithotomy (sis″to-lĭ-thot'o-me). Cystolithectomy.

cystolutein (sis″to-lu'te-in) [*cysto-* + L. *luteus* yellow]. A yellow pigment from certain ovarian cysts.

cystoma (sis-to'mah) [*cysto-* + *-oma*]. A tumor containing cysts of neoplastic origin; a cystic tumor. **myxoid c.,** a proliferating cyst of the ovary, so called because its inner surface resembles mucous membrane. **c. sero'sum sim'plex,** simple cyst of the ovary.

cystomatitis (sis″to-mah-ti'tis). Inflammation of one or more of the cysts of a cystoma.

cystomatous (sis-to'mah-tus). Relating to or containing cystoma.

cystometer (sis-tom'e-ter) [*cysto-* + Gr. *metron*

measure]. An instrument for studying the neuromuscular mechanism of the bladder by means of measurements of pressure and capacity.

cystometrogram (sis″to-met′ro-gram). The tracing recorded by cystometrography.

cystometrography (sis″to-mĕ-trog′rah-fe). The graphic recording of the pressure exerted at varying degrees of filling of the urinary bladder.

cystometry (sis-tom′e-tre). The study of bladder efficiency by means of the cystometer.

Cystomonas (sis-tom′o-nas). Bodo.

cystomorphous (sis″to-mor′fus) [*cysto-* + Gr. *morphē* form]. Resembling a cyst or bladder.

cystomyoma (sis″to-mi-o′mah). Cystoma blended with myoma.

cystomyxo-adenoma (sis″to-mik″so-ad″e-no′-mah). Cystomyxoma blended with adenoma.

cystomyxoma (sis″to-mik-so′mah). Myxoma which is associated with cysts.

cystonephrosis (sis″to-ne-fro′sis) [*cysto-* + Gr. *nephros* kidney]. Cystiform dilatation or enlargement of the kidney.

cystoneuralgia (sis″to-nu-ral′je-ah) [*cysto-* + *neuralgia*]. Neuralgia of the bladder.

cystoparalysis (sis″to-pah-ral-ĭ-sis). Paralysis of the bladder.

cystopexy (sis′to-pek″se) [*cysto-* + Gr. *pēxis* fixation]. Fixation of the bladder to the abdominal wall in the treatment of cystocele.

cystophorous (sis-tof′o-rus) [*cysto-* + Gr. *phoros* bearing]. Containing cysts.

cystophotography (sis″to-fo-tog′rah-fe). The photographing of the inside of the bladder.

cystophthisis (sis-tof′thĭ-sis) [*cysto-* + Gr. *phthisis* consumption]. Tuberculosis of the bladder.

cystoplasty (sis′to-plas″te) [*cysto-* + Gr. *plassein* to mold]. Any plastic or reconstructive operation on the bladder.

cystoplegia (sis″to-ple′je-ah) [*cysto-* + Gr. *plēgē* stroke]. Paralysis of the bladder.

cystoproctostomy (sis″to-prok-tos′to-me) [*cysto-* + Gr. *proktos* rectum + *stomoun* to provide with an opening, or mouth]. The surgical creation of a communication between the urinary bladder and rectum.

cystoptosis (sis″top-to′sis) [*cysto-* + Gr. *ptōsis* a falling]. Prolapse of a part of the inner coat of the bladder into the urethra.

cystopyelitis (sis″to-pi-e-li′tis). Inflammation involving both the urinary bladder and the pelvis of the kidney.

cystopyelography (sis″to-pi″e-log′rah-fe). Roentgenography of the urinary bladder and the pelvis of the kidney.

cystopyelonephritis (sis″to-pi″e-lo-ne-fri′tis) [*cysto-* + Gr. *pyelos* pelvis + *nephros* kidney + *-itis*]. Combined cystitis and pyelonephritis.

cystoradiography (sis″to-ra″de-og′rah-fe) [*cysto-* + *radiography*]. Radiography of the bladder.

cystorectostomy (sis″to-rek-tos′to-me). Cystoproctostomy.

cystorrhagia (sis″to-ra′je-ah) [*cysto-* + Gr. *rhēgnynai* to burst forth]. Hemorrhage from the bladder.

cystorrhaphy (sis-tor′ah-fe) [*cysto-* + Gr. *rhaphē* suture]. The operation of suturing the bladder.

cystorrhea (sis″to-re′ah) [*cysto-* + Gr. *rhoia* flow]. Catarrh of the bladder.

cystosarcoma (sis″to-sar-ko′mah). Sarcoma with cysts. **c. phylloi′des (phyllo′des),** cystadenoma in which the cavity is filled with cauliflower-like masses of connective tissue.

cystoschisis (sis-tos′kĭ-sis) [*cysto-* + Gr. *schisis* fissure]. Fissure of the bladder.

cystoscirrhus (sis″to-skir′us) [*cysto-* + Gr. *skirrhos* scirrhus]. Hard cancer of the bladder.

cystosclerosis (sis″to-skle-ro′sis). A cyst which has undergone sclerosis or fibrosis.

cystoscope (sis′to-skōp″) [*cysto-* + Gr. *skopein* to examine]. An endoscope for examining the urinary tract.

cystoscopic (sis″to-skop′ik). Pertaining to cystoscopy, or performed with the cystoscope.

cystoscopy (sis-tos′ko-pe). Direct visual examination of the urinary tract with a cystoscope. **air c.,** cystoscopy in which the bladder is distended with air. **water c.,** cystoscopy in which the bladder is distended with water.

cystose (sis′tōs). Resembling or containing a cyst or cysts.

cystospasm (sis′to-spazm) [*cysto-* + Gr. *spasmos* spasm]. Spasm of the bladder.

cystospermitis (sis″to-sper-mi′tis) [*cysto-* + Gr. *sperma* semen]. Inflammation of a seminal vesicle.

cystostaxis (sis″to-stak′sis). Cystistaxis.

cystostomy (sis-tos′to-me) [*cysto-* + Gr. *stoma* opening]. The formation of an opening into the bladder.

cystotome (sis′to-tōm) [*cysto-* + Gr. *tomē* a cut]. 1. An instrument for incising the bladder. 2. Cystitome.

cystotomy (sis-tot′o-me). Surgical incision of the urinary bladder. **suprapubic c.,** the operation of cutting into the bladder by an incision just above the pubic symphysis.

cystotrachelotomy (sis″to-tra″kel-ot′o-me) [*cysto-* + Gr. *trachēlos* neck + *tomē* a cut]. Surgical incision of the neck of the bladder.

cystoureteritis (sis″to-u-re″ter-i′tis). Inflammation involving the urinary bladder and ureters.

cystoureterogram (sis″to-u-re′ter-o-gram). A roentgenogram of the urinary bladder and ureters.

cystoureteropyelitis (sis″to-u-re″ter-o-pi″e-li′-tis). Inflammation involving the urinary bladder, ureter, and pelvis of the kidney.

cystoureteropyelonephritis (sis″to-u-re″ter-o-pi″e-lo-ne-fri′tis). Combined inflammation of the bladder, ureter, and pelvis and pyramids of the kidney.

cystourethritis (sis″to-u″re-thri′tis). Inflammation of the bladder and urethra.

cystourethrocele (sis″to-u-re′thro-sēl). Prolapse of the female urethra and bladder.

cystourethrogram (sis″to-u-re′thro-gram). A roentgenogram of the urinary bladder and urethra.

cystourethroscope (sis″to-u-re′thro-skōp). An instrument for examining the bladder and posterior urethra.

cystous (sis′tus). Cystose.

cytagenin (si-taj′ĕ-nin). An antianemic substance occurring in the blood.

cytarme (sit-ar′me) [Gr. *kytos* cell + *armē* union]. The flattening of rounded blastomeres at the conclusion of cleavage.

cytase (si′tās) [Gr. *kytos* hollow vessel + *-ase*]. 1. Metchnikoff's term for the complement regarded as an enzyme. 2. An enzyme occurring in the seeds of various plants, having the power of making soluble the material of the cell wall.

cytaster (si′tas-ter) [Gr. *kytos* hollow vessel + *astēr* star]. Aster.

cytax (si′taks) [Gr. *kytos* hollow vessel + L. *taxare* to estimate]. An instrument for automatically estimating and registering the proportions of the various cells of the blood.

-cyte (sīt) [Gr. *kytos* hollow vessel, anything that contains or covers]. Word termination denoting a cell, the type of which is designated by the root to which it is affixed, as *elliptocyte*, *erythrocyte*, *leukocyte*, etc.

cytemia (si-te′me-ah) [Gr. *kytos* hollow vessel + *haima* blood + *-ia*]. The presence of extraneous cells in the blood.

cythemolysis (si″thĕ-mol′ĭ-sis). Hemocytolysis.

cythemolytic (si″them-o-lit′ik). Pertaining to destruction of blood corpuscles.

cytheromania (sith″er-o-ma′ne-ah) [Gr. *Kythereia* Venus + *mania* madness]. Nymphomania.

cytidin (si′tĭ-din). A pentoside from nucleic acid. On hydrolysis it yields cytosine and ribose.

cytisine (sit′ĭ-sin) [Gr. *kytisos* laburnum]. A white, crystalline base, $C_{11}H_{14}N_2O$, from *Cytisus laburnum*, the laburnum tree of Europe, and others of the same genus.

cytisism (sit′ĭ-sizm). Poisoning by *Cytisus laburnum*.

cyto- (si′to) [Gr. *kytos* hollow vessel; anything that contains or covers]. A combining form denoting relationship to a cell.

cytoarchitectonic (si″to-ar″kĭ-tek-ton′ik). Pertaining to cellular structure or the arrangement of cells in a tissue.

cytoarchitectural (si″to-ar″kĭ-tek′tu-ral). Cytoarchitectonic.

cytoarchitecture (si″to-ar′kĭ-tek″tūr). The organization of cells in the structure of an organ or tissue, especially that in the cerebral cortex.

cytobiology (si″to-bi-ol′o-je) [*cyto-* + *biology*]. The biology of cells.

cytobiotaxis (si″to-bi-o-tak′sis) [*cyto-* + Gr. *bios* life + *taxis* arrangement]. Cytoclesis.

cytoblast (si′to-blast) [*cyto-* + Gr. *blastos* germ]. 1. Mitochondrium. 2. The cell nucleus.

cytoblastema (si″to-blas-te′mah) [*cyto-* + *blastema*]. Schleiden's name for the mother liquid from which cells were held to form.

cytocannibalism (si″to-kan′ĭ-bal-izm). The destruction and absorption of one cell by another.

cytocentrum (si″to-sen′trum) [*cyto-* + Gr. *kentron* center]. Centrosome.

cytocerastic (si″to-se-ras′tik). Cytokerastic.

cytochemism (si″to-kem′izm) [*cyto-* + *chemism*]. Chemical activity of cells.

cytochemistry (si″to-kem″is-tre) [*cyto-* + *chemistry*]. The scientific study of the chemical organization and activity of the cell in general.

cytochrome (si′to-krōm) [*cyto-* + Gr. *chrōma* color]. 1. Any one of a class of hemochromogens which are widely distributed in animal and plant tissues where they play a highly important role in oxidation processes. Cytochrome A, B, and C are distinguished by their absorption spectra. 2. A nerve cell having an ill-developed cell body, in which the stained nucleus appears to be completely surrounded, and does not exceed in size the nucleus of a leukocyte.

cytochylema (si″to-ki-le′mah) [*cyto-* + Gr. *chylos* juice]. Hyaloplasm.

cytocidal (si″to-si′dal). Destructive to cells.

cytocide (si′to-sīd) [*cyto-* + L. *caedere* to kill]. An agent which destroys cells.

cytocinesis (si″to-si-ne′sis). Cytokinesis.

cytoclasis (si-tok′lah-sis) [*cyto-* + Gr. *klasis* a breaking]. The destruction of cells.

cytoclastic (si″to-klas′tik). Pertaining to, characterized by, or causing cytoclasis.

cytoclesis (si″to-kle′sis) [*cyto-* + Gr. *klēsis* a call]. A form of energy, totally unrelated to electricity, light, heat, or sound, which is generated by living tissues; the vital principle in all living tissues (M. Kelly). The term was first introduced in 1923 by Frederic Wood Jones, who defined it as the influence of body cells on other body cells; the "call of cell to cell."

cytocletic (si″to-klet′ik). Pertaining to cytoclesis.

cytocyst (si′to-sist) [*cyto-* + Gr. *kystis* sac]. A cyst-like structure enclosing a mass of merozoites, being the remains of the host cell in which the merozoites were formed.

cytode (si′tōd) [*cyto-* + Gr. *eidos* form]. A non-nucleated cell or cell element.

cytodendrite (si″to-den′drīt) [*cyto-* + *dendrite*]. Any dendrite other than an axodendrite; a dendrite given off from the cell itself, as distinguished from an *axodendrite*.

cytodesma (si″to-dez′mah) [*cyto-* + Gr. *desma* band]. The lamellar or bridgelike tissues binding animal cells together (Studnicka).

cytodiagnosis (si″to-di″ag-no′sis) [*cyto-* + *diagnosis*]. Diagnosis of disease based on the examination of cells. **exfoliative c.,** the examination of cells which have desquamated from the external or internal surfaces of the body as a means of detecting cancer.

cytodieresis (si″to-di-er′ĕ-sis) [*cyto-* + Gr. *diairesis* division]. Indirect cell division.

cytodistal (si″to-dis′tal) [*cyto-* + *distal*]. Denoting that part of an axon remote from the cell of origin.

cytofin (si′to-fin). One of the alloxur bases allied to thymin.

cytoflav (si′to-flav). A phosphoric acid ester of riboflavin, found in the liver and in the heart.

cytoflavin (si″to-fla′vin). A flavin that was first isolated from heart muscle. It is the phosphoric acid ester of lactoflavin.

cytogene (si′to-jēn) [*cyto-* + *gene*]. A self-perpetuating cytoplasmic particle that traces origin to the genes of the nucleus.

cytogenesis (si″to-jen′e-sis) [*cyto-* + Gr. *genesis* origin]. The origin and development of cells.

cytogenetical (si″to-je-net′e-kal). Pertaining to cytogenetics.

cytogeneticist (si″to-je-net′ĭ-sist). A specialist in cytogenetics.

cytogenetics (si″to-je-net′iks). The branch of genetics devoted to study of the cellular constituents which are concerned in heredity, that is, the chromosomes and genes. **clinical c.,** the scientific study of the relationship between chromosomal aberrations and pathological conditions.

cytogenic (si-to-jen′ik). 1. Pertaining to cytogenesis. 2. Forming or producing cells.

cytogenous (si-toj′e-nus) [*cyto-* + Gr. *gennan* to produce]. Producing cells.

cytogeny (si-toj′e-ne). 1. Cytogenesis. 2. Cell lineage.

cytoglobin (si″to-glo′bin) [*cyto-* + *globin*]. A name formerly given a protein substance from white blood corpuscles; obtainable also from lymph nodes (Schmidt).

cytoglucopenia (si″to-gloo″ko-pe′ne-ah). Cytoglycopenia.

cytoglycopenia (si″to-gli″ko-pe′ne-ah) [*cyto-* + *glucose* + Gr. *penia* poverty]. Deficient glucose content of body or blood cells.

cytogony (si-tog′o-ne) [*cyto-* + Gr. *gonos* seed]. Cytogenic reproduction.

cytohistogenesis (si″to-his″to-jen′e-sis) [*cyto-* + Gr. *histos* web + *genesis* formation]. The development of the structure of cells.

cytohormone (si″to-hor′mōn) [*cyto-* + *hormone*]. A cell hormone.

cytohyaloplasm (si″to-hi′ah-lo-plazm″) [*cyto-* + Gr. *hyalos* crystal + *plasma* plasm]. The clear substance of cell protoplasm.

cytohydrolist (si″to-hi′dro-list) [*cyto-* + *hydrolist*]. An enzyme which breaks up the cell wall by hydrolysis.

cytoid (si′toid) [*cyto-* + Gr. *eidos* form]. Resembling a cell.

cyto-inhibition (si″to-in″hĭ-bish′un) [*cyto-* + L. *inhibere* to restrain]. The action of phagocytic cells in protecting bacteria or viruses which they have absorbed from lysis or chemical destruction.

cytokalipenia (si″to-kal″ĭ-pe′ne-ah) [*cyto-* + L. *kalium* potassium + Gr. *penia* poverty]. Deficient potassium content of body or blood cells.

cytokerastic (si″to-kĕ-ras′tik) [*cyto-* + Gr. *kerastos* mixed]. Pertaining to the development of cells from a lower to a higher order.

cytokinesis (si″to-ki-ne′sis) [*cyto-* + Gr. *kinēsis* motion]. The changes that take place in the cytoplasm during mitosis, miosis, and fertilization.

cytolergy (si″to-ler′je) [*cyto-* + Gr. *ergon* work]. Cell activity.

cytolist (si′to-list). Cytolysin.

cytologic (si″to-loj′ik). Pertaining to cytology.

cytologist (si-tol′o-jist). A specialist in cytology.

cytology (si-tol′o-je) [*cyto-* + *-logy*]. The scientific study of cells, their origin, structure, and functions.

cytolymph (si′to-limf) [*cyto-* + *lymph*]. Hyaloplasm.

cytolysate (si-tol′ĭ-sāt). A preparation of lyzed cells. **blood c.,** a solution of hemolyzed erythrocytes prepared by washing the red cells in physiologic saline and hemolyzing them by adding distilled water to make a solution of the same volume as the original quantity of blood from which the cells were obtained.

cytolysin (si-tol′ĭ-sin). A substance or antibody which produces dissolution of cells. Cytolysins which have a specific action for certain cells are named accordingly, as *hemolysins*, etc.

cytolysis (si-tol′ĭ-sis) [*cyto-* + Gr. *lysis* dissolution]. The dissolution or destruction of cells.

cytolytic (si″to-lit′ik). Pertaining to, characterized by, or causing cytolysis.

cytoma (si-to′mah) [*cyto-* + *-oma*]. A cell tumor, as a sarcoma.

cytomachia (si″to-mak′e-ah) [*cyto-* + Gr. *machē* fight]. The struggle between bacteria and the protective cells of the body.

cytomegaloviruria (si″to-meg″ah-lo-vi-roo′re-ah). Presence in the urine of cytomegaloviruses.

cytomegalovirus (si″to-meg″ah-lo-vi′rus). One of a group of highly host-specific viruses that infect man, monkeys, or rodents, with the production of unique large cells bearing intranuclear inclusions. Also termed *salivary gland virus.* The virus specific for man causes cytomegalic inclusion disease.

cytomel (si′to-mel). Trade mark for a preparation of the sodium salt of liothyronine.

cytomere (si′to-mēr) [*cyto-* + Gr. *meros* part]. 1. One of the bodies formed in coccidian reproduction by division of the trophozoite, each cytomere becoming the center of merozoite formation. 2. That part of the sperm which is composed of cytoplasm.

cytometaplasia (si″to-met″ah-pla′ze-ah) [*cyto-* + Gr. *metaplasis* change]. Alteration in the form or function of a cell.

cytometer (si-tom′e-ter) [*cyto-* + Gr. *metron* measure]. A device for counting and measuring blood cells.

cytometry (si-tom′e-tre). The counting of blood cells; blood counting.

cytomitome (si″to-mi′tōm) [*cyto-* + Gr. *mitos* thread]. A fibril or fibrillary structure of the spongioplasm.

cytomorphology (si″to-mor-fol′o-je). The morphology of cells.

cytomorphosis (si″to-mor-fo′sis) [*cyto-* + Gr. *morphōsis* a shaping]. The series of changes through which cells go in the process of formation, development, senescence, etc.

cytomycosis (si″to-mi-ko′sis) [*cyto-* + Gr. *mykēs* fungus]. A fatal disease marked by splenomegaly, irregular fever and leukopenia, caused by a fungus which attacks the phagocytic cells of the blood (the reticuloendothelial system). Cf. *histoplasmosis.*

cyton (si′ton). The cell body of a neuron.

cytopathic (si″to-path′ik). Pertaining to or characterized by pathological changes in cells.

cytopathogenesis (si″to-path″o-jen′e-sis). The production of pathological changes in cells.

cytopathogenetic (si″to-path″o-je-net′ik). Pertaining to or characterized by cytopathogenesis.

cytopathogenic (si″to-path″o-jen′ik). Capable of producing pathological changes in cells.

cytopathogenicity (si″to-path″o-je-nis′ĭ-te). The quality of being capable of producing pathological changes in cells.

cytopathology (si″to-pah-thol′o-je) [*cyto-* + Gr. *pathos* disease + *-logy*]. The study of cells in disease; cellular pathology.

cytopenia (si″to-pe′ne-ah) [*cyto-* + Gr. *penia* poverty]. Deficiency in the cellular elements of the blood.

Cytophaga (si-tof′ah-gah) [*cyto-* + Gr. *phagein* to eat]. A genus of schizomycetes (family Cytophagaceae), species of which dissolve vegetable fiber and hydrolyze cellulose.

Cytophagaceae (si″to-fah-ga′se-e). A family of Schizomycetes, order Myxobacterales, made up of saprophytic soil microorganisms, many of which decompose cellulose. It includes a single genus, *Cytophaga.*

cytophagocytosis (si″to-fag″o-si-to′sis). Cytophagy.

cytophagous (si-tof′ah-gus) [*cyto-* + Gr. *phagein* to eat]. Devouring or consuming cells.

cytophagy (si-tof′ah-je). The absorption of cells by other cells.

cytopharynx (si″to-far′inks). The depression in the body of infusoria through which food matter is received.

cytophil (si′to-fil). An element or substance that has an affinity for cells.

cytophilic (si-to-fil′ik) [*cyto-* + Gr. *philein* to love]. Having an affinity for cells, as, the *cytophilic* group of molecules of an amboceptor.

cytophylactic (si″to-fi-lak′tik). Pertaining to cytophylaxis.

cytophylaxis (si″to-fi-lak′sis) [*cyto-* + Gr. *phylaxis* a guarding]. 1. The protection of cells. 2. Increase of cellular activity.

cytophyletic (si″to-fi-let′ik) [*cyto-* + Gr. *phylē* a tribe]. Pertaining to the genealogy of cells.

cytophysics (si″to-fiz′iks). The physics of cell activity.

cytophysiology (si″to-fiz-e-ol′o-je) [*cyto-* + *physiology*]. The physiology of the cell.

cytopigment (si′to-pig″ment). Any pigment found in cells.

cytoplasm (si′to-plazm″) [*cyto-* + Gr. *plasma* plasm]. The protoplasm of a cell exclusive of that of the nucleus. Cf. *nucleoplasm.*

cytoplasmic (si″to-plaz′mik). Pertaining to or contained in the cytoplasm.

cytoplast (si′to-plast″). The contents of the cell body as distinguished from the nuclear contents.

cytoplastin (si″to-plas′tin). The plastin of cell cytoplasm.

cytoproximal (si″to-prok′sĭ-mal) [*cyto-* + *proximal*]. Denoting that part of an axon nearer to the cell of origin.

cytoreticulum (si″to-rĕ-tik′u-lum) [*cyto-* + L. *retic′ulum* network]. A fibrillar network of spongioplasm.

cytorrhyctes (si″to-rik′tēz) [*cyto-* + Gr. *oryssein* to dig]. Cell inclusions, found in various diseases, which may be specific protozoal pathogens, or they may be manifestations of cell reactions to the parasite of the disease, or they may be degeneration caused by the disease.

cytoscopy (si-tos′ko-pe) [*cyto-* + Gr. *skopein* to examine]. Examination of cells.

cytosiderin (si″to-sid′er-in). Intracellular pigment due probably to derangement of iron metabolism.

cytosine (si′to-sin). A base, oxyaminopyrimidine, $C_4H_5N_3O$, one of the disintegration products of nucleic acid.

cytosis (si-to′sis) [Gr. *kytos* hollow vessel]. A term used by Arneth to denote the condition of the nucleus of a leukocyte. According to the condition or characteristics of the nucleus there are distinguished *isocytosis, anisocytosis, hypercytosis, hypocytosis,* and *normocytosis.*

cytosome (si′to-sōm) [*cyto-* + Gr. *sōma* body]. The body of a cell apart from its nucleus.

cytospongium (si″to-spon′je-um) [*cyto-* + Gr. *spongos* sponge]. The cell network or spongioplasm.

cytost (si′tost) [Gr. *kytos* hollow vessel]. A specific toxin given off from a cell as a result of injury to it; a specific agent given off from broken-down tissue.

cytostasis (si-tos′tah-sis) [*cyto-* + Gr. *stasis* halt]. The closure of capillaries by white blood corpuscles in the early stages of inflammation.

cytostatic (si″to-stat′ik) [*cyto-* + Gr. *statikos* bringing to a stand-still]. Checking the growth and multiplication of cells.

cytostome (si′to-stōm) [*cyto-* + Gr. *stoma* mouth]. The cell mouth; the mouth aperture of certain protozoa.

cytostromatic (si″to-stro-mat′ik) [*cyto-* + *stroma*]. Pertaining to the stroma of a cell.

cytotactic (si″to-tak′tik). Pertaining to cytotaxis.

cytotaxis (si-to-tak′sis) [*cyto-* + Gr. *taxis* arrangement]. The movement and arrangement of cells with respect to a specific source of stimulation.

cytotherapy (si″to-ther′ah-pe) [*cyto-* + Gr. *therapeia* treatment]. 1. Treatment by the administration of animal cells. 2. The therapeutic use of a cytolytic or cytotoxic serum.

cytothesis (si-toth′ĕ-sis) [*cyto-* + Gr. *thesis* placing]. The restitution of injured cells to their normal condition.

cytotoxic (si″to-tok′sik). Pertaining to, resulting from, or having the action of a cytotoxin.

cytotoxicosis (si″to-tok″se-ko′sis). A condition produced by a cytotoxin or by poisoning cells.

cytotoxin (si″to-tok′sin) [*cyto-* + *toxin*]. A toxin or antibody which has a specific toxic action upon cells of special organs. Cytotoxins are named according to the special variety of cell for which they are specific, as, *nephrotoxin*.

cytotrochin (si″to-tro′kin) [*cyto-* + Gr. *trochia* track]. That element of a toxin which carries the active element to the cell.

cytotrophoblast (si″to-trof′o-blast) [*cyto-* + Gr. *trophē* nutrition + *blastos* germ]. The cellular (inner) layer of the trophoblast.

cytotropic (si″to-trop′ik) [*cyto-* + Gr. *tropos* a turning]. Attracting cells; possessing an affinity for cells.

cytotropism (si-tot′ro-pizm). 1. Cell movement in response to external stimulation. 2. The tendency of viruses, bacteria, drugs, etc. to exert their effect upon certain cells of the body.

cytoxan (si-tok′san). Trade mark for preparations of cyclophosphamide.

cytozoic (si″to-zo′ik). Living within or attached to cells: said of parasites.

cytozoon (si″to-zo′on), pl. *cytozo′a* [*cyto-* + Gr. *zōon* animal]. A protozoan parasite inhabiting a cell or having the structure of a simple cell.

cytozyme (si′to-zīm) [*cyto-* + Gr. *zymē* ferment]. Bordet's term for the substance liberated from the corpuscular elements of the blood, which combines with serozyme to form thrombin; thrombokinase. Cf. *serozyme*.

cyttarrhagia (sit″ah-ra′je-ah) [Gr. *kyttaros* cell of a honey-comb + *rhēgnynai* to burst forth]. Alveolar hemorrhage.

cytula (sit′u-lah). The impregnated ovum.

cytuloplasm (sit′u-lo-plazm″). The combined ovoplasm and spermoplasm in a cytula.

cyturia (sĭ-tu′re-ah) [Gr. *kytos* hollow vessel + *ouron* urine + *-ia*]. Presence of cells of any sort in the urine.

Czermak's lines, spaces (chăr′mahks) [Johann Nepomuk *Czermak*, Bohemian physician, 1828–1873]. See under *line* and *space*.

Czerny's anemia, diathesis (chăr′nēz) [Adalbert *Czerny*, German pediatrician, 1863–1941]. See under *anemia* and *diathesis*.

Czerny's operation, suture (chăr′nēz) [Vincenz *Czerny*, surgeon in Heidelberg, 1842–1916]. See under *operation* and *suture*.

D

D. 1. Abbreviation for L., *dosis*, dose; *da*, give; *detur*, let it be given; *dexter*, right; also for *deciduous*, *density*, *died*, *didymium*, *diopter*, *distal*, *dorsal* (in vertebral formulas), and *duration*. A symbol for the unit of vitamin D potency. It is the potency of cod liver oil. 2. The chemical symbol for *deuterium*.

D- (de). Chemical prefix (small capital) which specifies that the substance corresponds in configuration to the standard substance D-glyceraldehyde, that is, belongs to the same configurational family. In carbohydrate nomenclature, the symbol refers to the configurational family of the *highest numbered* asymmetric carbon atom, as in D-glucose. In amino acid nomenclature, under rules adopted in 1947, the symbol refers to the configurational family to which the *lowest numbered* asymmetric carbon atom, i.e., the 2-carbon atom or α-carbon atom, belongs, as in D-threonine. Opposed to L-.

D_g- (de-sub-je). See D-; this chemical prefix (with the subscript *g*) is occasionally used to emphasize that the rules of carbohydrate nomenclature are being employed, as in D_g-glucosaminic acid. The subscript refers to the standard substance glyceraldehyde. Opposed to L_g-.

D_s- (de-sub-es). See D-; this chemical prefix (with the subscript *s*) is used where needed in amino acid nomenclature to avoid possible confusion with carbohydrate nomenclature, as in D_s-threonine. The subscript refers to the standard substance serine. Opposed to L_s-.

d- (de-). 1. Chemical abbreviation for *dextro-* (i.e., right or clockwise), with reference to the direction in which the plane of polarized light is rotated when passed through a solution of the substance or through the substance itself if a liquid: opposed to *l-* (levo-). 2. A prefix used with one of the additional symbols (+) or (−), especially in amino acid nomenclature in the literature from 1923 until 1947 or a little later, with reference to the configurational family to which the 2-carbon or α-carbon atom of the amino acid belongs, the actual direction of the rotation in a specified solvent being indicated by the plus or minus sign, as in *d*(−)-alanine; opposed to *l*(+)- or *l*(−)-, as in *l*(+)-alanine or *l*(−)-cystine.

Dabney's grip (dab′nēz) [William Cecil *Dabney*, American physician, 1849–1894]. Epidemic pleurodynia.

Daboia (dah-boi′ah). A genus of snakes. **D. russel′li,** a very poisonous Indian snake. See *Russell's viper*, under *viper*.

D. and C. Abbreviation for *dilation and curettement* (dilation of the cervix and curettement of the uterus).

dacnomania (dak-no-ma′ne-ah). A morbid impulse to kill.

DaCosta's disease, syndrome [Jacob Mendes *DaCosta*, American physician, 1833–1900]. See *misplaced gout* and *neurocirculatory asthenia*.

dacry- (dak′re). See *dacryo-*.

dacryadenalgia (dak″re-ad-ĕ-nal′je-ah). Dacryoadenalgia.

dacryadenitis (dak″re-ad-ĕ-ni′tis). Dacryoadenitis.

dacryadenoscirrhus (dak″re-ad″ĕ-no-skir′us)

[*dacry-* + Gr. *adēn* gland + *skirrhos* scirrhus]. Scirrhus of a lacrimal gland.

dacryagogatresia (dak″re-ah-gog″ah-tre′ze-ah) [*dacry-* + Gr. *agōgos* leading + *atresia*]. Atresia, imperforation, or closure of a lacrimal duct.

dacryagogic (dak″re-ah-goj′ik). 1. Inducing a flow of tears. 2. Serving as a channel for discharge of the secretion of the lacrimal glands.

dacryagogue (dak′re-ah-gog) [*dacry-* + Gr. *agōgos* leading]. An agent that induces a flow of tears.

dacrycystalgia (dak″re-sis-tal′je-ah). Dacryocystalgia.

dacrycystitis (dak″re-sis-ti′tis). Dacryocystitis.

dacryelcosis (dak″re-el-ko′sis). Dacryohelcosis.

dacryo- (dak′re-o) [Gr. *dakryon* tear]. A combining form denoting relationship to tears.

dacryoadenalgia (dak″re-o-ad″ĕ-nal′je-ah) [*dacryo-* + Gr. *adēn* gland + *algos* pain + *-ia*]. Pain in a lacrimal gland.

dacryoadenectomy (dak″re-o-ad″ĕ-nek′to-me). Excision of a lacrimal gland.

dacryoadenitis (dak″re-o-ad″ĕ-ni′tis). Inflammation of a lacrimal gland.

dacryoblennorrhea (dak″re-o-blen″o-re′ah) [*dacryo-* + Gr. *blennos* mucus + *rhein* to flow]. Mucous discharge from the lacrimal ducts, as in chronic dacryocystitis.

dacryocanaliculitis (dak″re-o-kan″ah-lik″u-li′-tis). Inflammation of the lacrimal ducts.

dacryocele (dak′re-o-sēl). Dacryocystocele.

dacryocyst (dak′re-o-sist) [*dacryo-* + Gr. *kystis* sac]. The lacrimal sac.

dacryocystalgia (dak″re-o-sis-tal′je-ah). Pain in a lacrimal sac.

dacryocystectasia (dak″re-o-sis″tek-ta′ze-ah) [*dacryocyst* + Gr. *ektasis* dilatation + *-ia*]. Dilatation of the lacrimal sac.

dacryocystectomy (dak″re-o-sis-tek′to-me) [*dacryocyst* + Gr. *ektomē* excision]. Excision of the wall of the lacrimal sac.

dacryocystis (dak″re-o-sis′tis). The lacrimal sac.

dacryocystitis (dak″re-o-sis-ti′tis). Inflammation of the lacrimal sac.

dacryocystitome (dak″re-o-sis′tĭ-tōm) [*dacryocyst* + Gr. *temnein* to cut]. An instrument for incising strictures of the lacrimal duct.

dacryocystoblennorrhea (dak″re-o-sis″to-blen″o-re′ah). A chronic catarrhal inflammation of the lacrimal sac, with constriction of the lacrimal duct.

dacryocystocele (dak″re-o-sis′to-sēl) [*dacryocyst* + Gr. *kēlē* hernia]. Hernial protrusion of the lacrimal sac.

dacryocystoptosis (dak″re-o-sis″top-to′sis) [*dacryocyst* + Gr. *ptōsis* fall]. Prolapse or downward displacement of the lacrimal sac.

dacryocystorhinostenosis (dak″re-o-sis″to-ri″no-ste-no′sis). Narrowing of the duct leading from the lacrimal sac to the nasal cavity.

dacryocystorhinostomy (dak″re-o-sis″to-ri-nos′to me) [*dacryocyst* + Gr. *rhis* nose + *stomoun* to provide with an opening, or mouth]. Surgical creation of a communication between the lacrimal sac and the nasal cavity.

dacryocystorhinotomy (dak″re-o-sis″to-ri-not′o-me). Passage of a probe through the lacrimal sac into the nasal cavity.

dacryocystostenosis (dak″re-o-sis″to-ste-no′-sis). Narrowing of the lacrimal sac.

dacryocystostomy (dak″re-o-sis-tos′to-me) [*dacryocyst* + Gr. *stomoun* to provide with an opening, or mouth]. Surgical creation of a new opening into the lacrimal sac.

dacryocystosyringotomy (dak″re-o-sis″to-sir″-in-got′o-me) [*dacryocyst* + Gr. *syrinx* tube + *tomē* a cutting]. Incision of the lacrimal sac and duct.

dacryocystotome (dak″re-o-sis′to-tōm). An instrument for incising the lacrimal sac.

dacryocystotomy (dak″re-o-sis-tot′o-me). Incision of the lacrimal sac.

dacryogenic (dak″re-o-jen′ik). Promoting the secretion of tears.

dacryohelcosis (dak″re-o-hel-ko′sis) [*dacryo-* + Gr. *helkōsis* ulceration]. Ulceration of the lacrimal sac or lacrimal duct.

dacryohemorrhea (dak″re-o-hem″o-re′ah) [*dacryo-* + Gr. *haima* blood + *rhein* to flow]. The discharge of tears mixed with blood.

dacryolin (dak′re-o-lin). An albuminous substance found in tears.

dacryolith (dak′re-o-lith) [*dacryo-* + Gr. *lithos* stone]. A concretion in the lacrimal sac or duct. **Desmarres' d's**, masses of *Nocardia foersteri* in the lacrimal sac or duct.

dacryolithiasis (dak″re-o-lĭ-thi′ah-sis) [*dacryo-* + *lithiasis*]. The presence of calculi in the lacrimal sac or duct.

dacryoma (dak″re-o′mah). A tumor-like swelling caused by obstruction of the lacrimal duct.

dacryon (dak′re-on) [Gr. *dakryon* tear]. A cranial point at the juncture of the lacrimal and frontal bones, and the maxilla.

dacryops (dak′re-ops) [*dacry-* + Gr. *ōps* eye]. 1. A watery state of the eye. 2. Distention of a lacrimal duct by contained fluid.

dacryopyorrhea (dak″re-o-pi″o-re′ah) [*dacryo-* + Gr. *pyon* pus + *rhein* to flow]. The discharge of tears mixed with pus.

dacryopyosis (dak″re-o-pi-o′sis) [*dacryo-* + Gr. *pyōsis* suppuration]. Suppuration of the lacrimal sac and duct.

dacryorhinocystotomy (dak″re-o-ri″no-sis-tot′o-me). Dacryocystorhinotomy.

dacryorrhea (dak″re-o-re′ah) [*dacryo-* + Gr. *rhein* to flow]. A profuse flow of tears.

dacryosinusitis (dak″re-o-si″nus-i′tis). Inflammation of the lacrimal duct and ethmoid sinus.

dacryosolenitis (dak″re-o-so-lĕ-ni′tis) [*dacryo-* + Gr. *sōlēn* duct + *-itis*]. Inflammation of a lacrimal duct.

dacryostenosis (dak″re-o-ste-no′sis) [*dacryo-* + Gr. *stenōsis* a narrowing]. Stricture or narrowing of a lacrimal duct.

dacryosyrinx (dak″re-o-si′rinks) [*dacryo-* + Gr. *syrinx* tube]. 1. A lacrimal duct. 2. A lacrimal fistula. 3. A syringe for irrigating the lacrimal ducts.

dactil (dak′til). Trade mark for preparations of piperidolate hydrochloride.

dactyl (dak′til) [Gr. *daktylos* a finger]. 1. A digit; a finger or toe. 2. The fruit of the date.

dactylate (dak′tĭ-lāt). Possessing finger-like processes.

dactyledema (dak″til-e-de′mah). Edema of the fingers or toes.

dactylion (dak-til′e-on). Webbing together or union of fingers.

dactylitis (dak″tĭ-li′tis) [*dactyl-* + *-itis*]. Inflammation of a finger or toe. **d. strumo′sa**, d. tuberculosa. **d. syphilit′ica**, syphilitic inflammation of a finger or toe. **d. tuberculo′sa**, tuberculous inflammation of a finger or toe.

dactylium (dak-til′e-um). Dactylion.

dactylo- (dak′tĭ-lo) [Gr. *daktylos* a finger]. A combining form denoting relationship to a digit, usually referring to a finger but sometimes to the toes.

dactylocampsodynia (dak″tĭ-lo-kamp″so-din′e-ah) [*dactylo-* + Gr. *kampsis* bend + *odynē* pain]. Painful flexure of the fingers.

dactylogram (dak-til′o-gram) [*dactylo-* + Gr. *gramma* mark]. A finger print taken for purposes of identification.

dactylography (dak″tĭ-log′rah-fe) [*dactylo-* + Gr. *graphein* to write]. The study of finger prints.

dactylogryposis (dak″tĭ-lo-grĭ-po′sis) [*dactylo-* + Gr. *grypōsis* a hooking]. A permanent bending of the fingers.

dactylology (dak″til-ol′o-je) [*dactylo-* + Gr. *logos* discourse]. Use of movements of the hands and fingers as a means of communication between individuals.

dactylolysis (dak″tĭ-lol′ĭ-sis) [*dactylo-* + Gr. *lysis* a loosening]. 1. Surgical correction of syndactylia. 2. Loss or amputation of a digit. **d. spontane′a,** the spontaneous loss of fingers and toes, as in ainhum or in leprosy.

dactylomegaly (dak″tĭ-lo-meg′ah-le) [*dactylo-* + Gr. *megaleia* largeness]. Abnormally large size of the fingers or toes.

Dactylomyia (dak″tĭ-lo-mi′yah). A genus of anopheline mosquitoes, some species of which act as carriers of the malarial parasite.

dactylophasia (dak″tĭ-lo-fa′ze-ah) [*dactylo-* + Gr. *phasis* speech]. Dactylology.

dactyloscopy (dak″tĭ-los′ko-pe) [*dactylo-* + Gr. *skopein* to examine]. Examination of finger prints for purposes of identification.

dactylospasm (dak′tĭ-lo-spazm) [*dactylo-* + Gr. *spasmos* spasm]. Spasm or cramp of a finger or toe.

dactylosymphysis (dak″tĭ-lo-sim′fĭ-sis) [*dactylo-* + *symphysis*]. A growing together of fingers or toes; syndactylism.

dactylus (dak′tĭ-lus) [Gr. *daktylos* finger]. A finger or toe.

daes (da′ēz). Stilbestrol.

Daffy's elixir (daf′ēz) [Thomas *Daffy*, an English clergyman of the 17th century]. Compound tincture of senna.

dagenan (dag′ĕ-nan). Sulfapyridine.

dagga (dag′ah). The leaves of African plants of the genus *Leonotis:* used by the natives for colds, snakebites, and as a purgative and emmenagogue.

D.A.H. Abbreviation for *disordered action of the heart.* See *neurocirculatory asthenia,* under *asthenia.*

dahlia (dahl′yah). A violet dye, methyl-triethyl-amino-triphenyl-carbinol chloride, $C_2H_5.NH-(CH_3).C_6H_3.C(C_6H_4:NH.C_2H_5)_2Cl$. Called also *Hoffmann's violet.* **d. B.** See *gentian violet,* under *violet.*

dahlin (dah′lin). 1. A reddish-purple aniline dye, formed by treating mauvein with ethyl iodide. It has been used as an antiseptic in streptococcic throat infections. 2. Inulin.

dahllite (dahl′īt). A complex salt, $CaCO_3.2Ca_3(PO_4)_2$, formerly believed to be the principal inorganic constituent of bone and teeth.

Dakin's fluid, solution (da′kinz) [Henry Drysdale *Dakin,* New York chemist, 1880–1952]. See under *fluid.*

dakinization (da″kin-i-za′shun). Treatment with Dakin's fluid.

dakryon (dak′re-on). Dacryon.

Dale reaction (dāl) [Sir Henry Hallett *Dale,* British physiologist and pharmacologist, born 1875; co-winner in 1936, with Otto Loewi, of the Nobel prize for medicine and physiology, for their work on the chemical transmission of nerve impulses]. See under *reaction.*

Dalrymple's disease, sign (dal′rim-pelz) [John *Dalrymple,* an English oculist, 1804–1852]. See under *disease* and *sign.*

dalton (dawl′ton) [John *Dalton,* English chemist and physicist, 1766–1844: the founder of the atomic theory]. A unit of mass, being one sixteenth of the mass of the oxygen atom, or approximately 1.65×10^{-24} gm.

Dalton's law (dawl′tonz) [John *Dalton*]. See under *law.*

Dalton-Henry law (dawl′ton hen′re) [John *Dalton;* Joseph *Henry,* American physicist, 1797–1878]. See under *law.*

daltonism (dawl′ton-izm) [John *Dalton*]. A name applied to defective perception of red and green.

Dam (dam), Carl Peter Henrik. A Danish biochemist, born 1895; co-winner in 1943, with Edward Adelbert Doisy, of the Nobel prize for medicine and physiology, for the discovery of vitamin K.

dam (dam). A sheet of latex rubber used to isolate teeth from the fluids of the mouth during dental treatments; used also in surgical procedures to isolate certain tissues or structures.

damiana (dah″me-ah′nah). The leaves of *Turnera aphrodisiaca* (*T. diffusa*) and *Haplopappus discoideus,* Mexican plants: said to be tonic, analeptic, diuretic, and aphrodisiac.

Dammann's bacillus (dam′anz) [Karl *Dammann,* Berlin veterinarian, 1839–1914]. *Sphérophorus necrophorus.*

dammar (dam′ar). A transparent resin of *Dammara orientalis, D. alba, Hopea micrantha, H. splendida,* and other trees: used in plasters, in varnishing and in microscopy.

dämmerschlaf (dem′er-shlaf) [Ger.]. Twilight sleep.

Damoiseau's curve, sign (dam-wah-zōz′) [Louis Hyacinthe Céleste *Damoiseau,* French physician, 1815–1890]. See *Ellis's line,* under *line.*

damp (damp). A noxious gas in a mine. **after-d.,** a gaseous mixture formed in a mine by the explosion of fire damp or dust. It contains nitrogen, carbon dioxide, and usually carbon monoxide. **black d., choke d.,** a nonrespirable atmosphere sometimes formed in a mine by the gradual absorption of the oxygen and the giving off of carbon dioxide by the coal. **cold d.,** foggy vapor charged with carbon dioxide. **fire d.,** light explosive hydrocarbon gases, chiefly methane, CH_4, found in coal mines. **stink d.,** hydrogen sulfide. **white d.,** carbon monoxide.

damping (damp′ing). The steady diminution of the amplitude of vibration of a specific form of energy, as of electricity or sound waves.

Dana's operation (da′nahz) [Charles Loomis *Dana,* neurologist in New York, 1852–1935]. See under *operation.*

dance (dans). Movement of a rhythmic, or of an unusual or exaggerated type. **d. of the arteries,** exaggerated pulsation in the arteries as seen in aortic regurgitation. **hilus d.,** marked pulsations of the hilus shadows of both lungs on roentgen examination: seen in pulmonic regurgitation. **St. Anthony's d., St. Guy's d., St. John's d., St. Vitus' d.,** chorea. **St. Vitus' d. of the voice,** stammering.

Dance's sign (dan′sez) [Jean Baptiste Hippolyte *Dance,* a French physician, 1797–1832]. See under *sign.*

dander (dan′der). Small scales from the hair or feathers of animals, which may be the cause of allergy in sensitive persons.

dandruff (dan′druf). Scaly material desquamated from the scalp.

dandy (dan′de). A litter for the wounded, used to some extent in armies.

daniell (dan′yel) [John Frederick *Daniell,* English physicist, 1790–1845]. A unit of electromotive force equal to 1.124 volts.

Daniell's cell (dan′yelz) [J. F. *Daniell*]. See under *cell.*

Danielssen's disease (dan′yel-senz) [Daniel Cornelius *Danielssen,* Norwegian physician, 1815–1894]. Anesthetic leprosy.

danilone (dan′ĭ-lōn). Trade mark for a preparation of phenindione.

Danlos' disease, syndrome (dan′los) [Henri-Alexandre *Danlos,* French dermatologist, 1844–1912]. See under *syndrome.*

danthron (dan′thron). Chemical name: 1,8-dihydroxyanthraquinone: used as a laxative.

Danysz's phenomenon (dan′ēz) [Jean *Danysz,* Polish pathologist in Paris, 1860–1928]. See under *phenomenon.*

DAP. Abbreviation for *dihydroxy acetone phosphate.*

Daphne (daf′ne) [Gr. *daphnē* bay tree]. A genus of trees and shrubs, *D. gnidium* and *D. mezereum,* the principal medicinal species, are stimulant, vesicatory, and purgative. See *mezereon.*

daphnetin (daf-ne′tin). The aglycon of daphnin, $C_9H_6O_4$.

Daphnia (daf′ne-ah). A genus of fresh water crustaceans, called water fleas. The best known species, *D. pu′lex*, is used in biological research.

daphnin (daf′nin). A volatile, acrid glycoside, $C_{15}H_{16}O_9 + 2H_2O$, from *Daphne mezereum*. It has vesicating properties.

daphnism (daf′nizm). Poisoning by species of *Daphne*.

daranide (dar′ah-nīd). Trade mark for a preparation of dichlorphenamide.

Darányi's test (dar′ahn-yēz) [Julius von *Darányi*, Budapest bacteriologist, born 1888]. See under *tests*.

daraprim (dar′ah-prim). Trade mark for a preparation of pyrimethamine.

darbid (dar′bid). Trade mark for a preparation of isopropamide iodide.

Dar es Salaam bacterium (dahr es sah-lahm′) [*Dar es Salaam*, East Africa, where it was isolated in 1922]. See under *bacterium*.

daricon (dar′ĭ-kon). Trade mark for a preparation of oxyphencyclimine hydrochloride.

Darier's disease (dar′e-āz) [Jean *Darier*, French dermatologist, 1856–1938]. Keratosis follicularis.

Darkschewitsch's fibers, nucleus (dark-sha′vich-ez) [Liverij Osipovich *Darkschewitsch*, Russian neurologist, 1858–1925]. See under the nouns.

Darling's disease (dar′lingz) [Samuel Taylor *Darling*, American physician, 1872–1925]. Histoplasmosis.

darmous (dahr′moos). Fluorine poisoning in North Africa.

Darrow's solution (dar′ōz) [Daniel Cady *Darrow*, American pediatrician, born 1895]. See under *solution*.

d'arsonvalism, d'arsonvalization (dar′son-val″izm, dar″son-val″i-za′shun) [A. *d'Arsonval*, French physicist, 1851–1940]. High-frequency treatment: the therapeutic use of very high-frequency intermittent isolated trains of heavily damped oscillations of very high voltage and very low current.

dartal (dar′tal). Trade mark for a preparation of thiopropazate dihydrochloride.

dartoic (dar-to′ik). Of the nature of a dartos; having a slow, involuntary contractility like that of the dartos.

dartoid (dar′toid). Resembling the dartos.

dartos (dar′tos) [Gr. "flayed"]. Tunica dartos.

dartre (dartr) [Fr.]. Herpes, or any skin disease resembling it.

dartrous (dar′trus). 1. Of, pertaining to, or resembling, the dartos. 2. Pertaining to herpes.

darvon (dar′von). Trade mark for a preparation of dextro propoxyphene hydrochloride.

darwinism (dar′win-izm) [Charles Robert *Darwin*, English naturalist, 1809–1882]. The theory of evolution according to which higher organisms have been developed from lower ones through the influence of natural selection.

dasetherapy (das″e-ther′ah-pe) [Gr. *dasos* thicket, copse + *therapeia* treatment]. Treatment by living in a region surrounded by pine or spruce trees.

Dastre-Morat's law (dastr-mo-rahz′) [Albert *Dastre*, Paris biologist, 1844–1917; Jean-Pierre *Morat*, French physiologist, 1846–1920]. See under *law*.

dasymeter (das-im′e-ter). An instrument for measuring the density of a gas.

Dasypus (das′e-pus) [Gr. *dasypous* a rough foot]. A genus of tropical armadillos, species of which are reservoirs of *Trypanosoma cruzi*.

data (da′tah) [L., plural of *datum*]. The material, or collection of facts on which a discussion or an inference is based.

date (dāt). Fruit of the date palm, *Phoenix dactylifera*.

Datura (da-tu′rah). A genus of solanaceous plants. See *stramonium*.

daturine (da-tu′rin). Hyoscyamine.

daturism (da-tu′rizm). Poisoning by stramonium.

Daubenton's angle, line, plane (do-bon-tonz′) [Louis Jean Marie *Daubenton*, French physician and naturalist, 1716–1800]. See under the nouns.

dauernarkose (dow′er-nar-kōs) [Ger.]. Dauerschlaf.

dauerschlaf (dow′er-shlaf) [Ger.]. Prolonged sleep.

Davainea (da-va′ne-ah) [Casimir Joseph *Davaine*, French physician, 1812–1882]. A genus of tapeworms. See *Raillietina*. **D. proglotti′na,** a species found in fowls.

David's disease (dah-vidz′). 1. [Jean Pierre *David*, French surgeon, 1738–1784]. Pott's disease. 2. [W. *David*, German physician, born 1890]. See under *disease*, def. 2.

Davidoff's cells (da′vid-ofs) [M. von *Davidoff*, histologist in Munich, d. 1904]. See under *cell*.

Davidsohn's sign (da′vid-sōnz) [Hermann *Davidsohn*, Prussian physician, 1842–1911]. See under *sign*.

Daviel's operation, spoon (dav-e-elz′) [Jacques *Daviel*, French oculist, 1696–1762: the originator of the modern treatment of cataract by extraction of the lens]. See under *operation* and *spoon*.

Davis graft (da′vis) [John Staige *Davis*, American surgeon, 1872–1946]. A pinch graft.

Davy's test (da′vēz) [Edmund William *Davy*, Irish physician, 1826–1899]. See under *tests*.

Dawbarn's sign [Robert Hugh Mackay *Dawbarn*, New York surgeon, 1860–1915]. See under *sign*.

day (day). A unit of time; 24 hours. **green d.,** a day, during the diet for diabetes, on which the patient is permitted to take green vegetables, butter, eggs, and bacon. **hunger d.,** a day, during the diet for diabetes, on which the patient is permitted to take nothing but broth.

Day's test (dāz) [Richard Hance *Day*, American physician, 1813–1892]. See under *tests*.

D.B. Abbreviation for *distobuccal*.

Db. Chemical symbol for *dubhium* (ytterbium).

DBA. Dibenzanthracene.

DBE. A synthetic estrogen, $(C_2H_5.O.C_6H_4)_2C{:}C(Br).C_6H_5$.

DBI (de′be-i). Trade mark for preparations of phenformin hydrochloride.

D.B.O. Abbreviation for *distobucco-occlusal*.

D.B.P. Abbreviation for *distobuccopulpal*.

DC. Abbreviation for *diphenylarsine cyanide*.

D.C. Abbreviation for *direct current, distocervical*, and *Doctor of Chiropractic*.

DCA. Abbreviation for desoxycorticosterone acetate.

D.Cc. Abbreviation for *double concave*.

DCF. Abbreviation for *direct centrifugal flotation*. See *Lane method*, under *method*.

D.C.H. Abbreviation for *Diploma in Child Health*.

D.C.O.G. Abbreviation for *Diploma of the College of Obstetricians and Gynaecologists* (British).

D.Cx. Abbreviation for *double convex*.

D.D. Abbreviation for L. *de′tur ad*, "let it be given to."

D.D.S. Abbreviation for *Doctor of Dental Surgery*.

D.D.Sc. Abbreviation for *Doctor of Dental Science*.

DDT (de′de-te). Chlorophenothane.

de-. Latin prefix often signifying down or from: it is sometimes negative or privative, and is frequently intensive.

deacidification (de″ah-sid″ĭ-fĭ-ka′shun). The act

or art of correcting or destroying acidity or of neutralizing an acid.

deactivation (de″ak-tĭ-va′shun). The process of making or becoming inactive, such as removal or loss of radioactivity from a previously radioactive material.

dead (ded). 1. Destitute of life. 2. Numb.

deadlimb (ded′lim). Numbness in a limb.

deaf (def). Lacking the sense of hearing or not having the full power of hearing.

deafferentate (de-af′er-en-tāt″). To suppress afferent nerve impulses, as by removal of part of the pathway.

deafferentation (de-af″er-en-ta′shun). The suppression of afferent nerve impulses, as by removal of part of the pathway.

deaf-mute (def-mūt′). An individual who is unable to hear or speak; it has been demonstrated that many deaf children thought to be mute can be trained to speak.

deaf-mutism (def-mūt′izm). The absence both of the sense of hearing and of the faculty of speech.

deafness (def′nes). Lack or loss, complete or partial, of the sense of hearing. **apoplectiform d.,** Meniere's syndrome. **bass d.,** deafness to certain low tones. **boilermakers' d.,** that which is caused by working in places where the sound is very deafening. **central d.,** deafness due to causes in the auditory pathways or in the auditory center. **cerebral d.,** that which is due to brain lesion. **ceruminous d.,** that which is due to plugs of earwax. **clang d.,** the inability to perceive the more delicate qualities of tone. **conduction d.,** deafness due to defect of the sound-conducting apparatus, i.e., the auditory meatus, ear drum, or ossicles. **cortical d.,** deafness due to a lesion of cortical brain substance. **functional d.,** deafness due to defective functioning of the auditory apparatus without organic lesion. **hysterical d.,** that which may appear or disappear in a hysterical patient without discoverable cause. **labyrinthine d.,** that which is due to disease of the labyrinth. **malarial d.,** that which occurs as a result of malarial poisoning. **mental d., mind d.,** a condition in which auditory sensations persist, but, owing to some lesion of the auditory center of the brain, they convey no meaning to the mind. **midbrain d.,** deafness dependent on injury of the fillet tract of the tegmentum. **music d.,** inability to recognize musical notes; amusia. **nerve d., nervous d.,** that which is due to a lesion of the auditory nerve. **organic d.,** deafness due to defect in the ear or auditory apparatus. **paradoxic d.,** deafness in which the hearing is best during the continuance of a loud noise; paracusis willisiana. **perceptive d.,** deafness due to dysfunction of the end-organ of Corti or to dysfunction of the ganglion cells of the spiral ganglion of the auditory division of the eighth cranial nerve. **pocket handkerchief d.,** deafness due to excessive pressure on the eustachian tubes from blowing the nose. **psychic d., sensory d., soul d.,** mental d. **throat d.,** that due to enlarged tonsils or to closure of the eustachian tube. **tone d.,** sensory amusia. **toxic d.,** deafness caused by the effect of poisons on the auditory nerve. **transmission d.,** conduction d. **vascular d.,** that due to disease of blood vessels of the ear. **word d.,** disease of the auditory center in which sounds are heard, but convey no meaning to the mind.

dealbation (de″al-ba′shun). Bleaching.

dealcoholization (de-al″ko-hol-i-za′shun). The removal of alcohol from an object or substance.

deallergization (de-al″er-ji-za′shun). The desensitization of an allergic person.

deamidase (de-am′ĭ-dās). An enzyme which splits adenine and guanine.

deamidation (de-am″ĭ-da′shun). Deamidization.

deamidization (de-am″ĭ-di-za′shun). Liberation of the ammonia from an amide.

deaminase (de-am′ĭ-nās). An enzyme which causes deamination, or the removal of the amino group from organic compounds. **adenosine d.,** an enzyme that catalyzes the change of adenosine into hypoxanthine and ammonia. **adenylic acid d.,** an enzyme which catalyzes the change of adenylic acid into inosine 5-phosphoric acid and ammonia. **cytidine d.,** an enzyme which catalyzes the change of cytidine into uridine and ammonia. **guanosine d.,** an enzyme which catalyzes the change of guanosine into xanthosine and ammonia. **guanylic acid d.,** an enzyme which catalyzes the change of guanylic acid into xanthylic acid and ammonia.

deamination (de-am″ĭ-na′shun). Removal of the amino group, $—NH_2$, from an amino body.

deaminization (de-am″ĭ-ni-za′shun). Deamination.

deaner (de′ner). Trade mark for a preparation of deanol.

deanesthesiant (de″an-es-the′ze-ant). An agent or measure that will arouse a patient from anesthesia.

deanol acetaminobenzoate (de′ah-nol as″et-am″ĭ-no-ben′zo-āt). Chemical name: p-acetamidobenzoic acid salt of 2-dimethylaminoethanol: used as a cerebral stimulant.

deaquation (de″ak-wa′shun) [L. *de* from + *aqua* water]. Removal of water from anything; dehydration.

Dearg. pil. Abbreviation for L. *deargen′tur pil′-ulae,* let the pills be silvered.

dearterialization (de″ar-te″re-al-i-za′shun). 1. The conversion of arterial into venous blood. 2. Interruption of the supply of oxygenated blood to a part or organ.

dearticulation (de″ar-tik″u-la′shun). Abarticulation.

death (deth). Suspension or cessation of vital processes of the body, as heart beat and respiration. **black d.,** old name for an epidemic plague which occurred in Europe in the 14th century. **cell d.,** complete degeneration or necrosis of cells. **cot d.,** the death, in its sleeping quarters, of an infant who had previously been apparently well. **fetal d.,** death of a fetus in utero; failure of the product of conception to show evidence of respiration, heart beat, or definite movement of a voluntary muscle after expulsion from the uterus. **fetal d., early,** fetal death occurring during the first 20 weeks of gestation. **fetal d., intermediate,** fetal death occurring during the twenty-first to twenty-eighth week of gestation. **fetal d., late,** fetal death occurring after 28 weeks of gestation. **liver d.,** sudden death following surgical procedures on the gallbladder and bile tracts. **local d.,** death of a part of the body. **molecular d.,** caries, catastasis, or the last stage of a catabolic process. **somatic d.,** cessation of vital activity in all the cells of the body.

Deaur. pil. Abbreviation for L. *deauren′tur pil′-ulae,* let the pills be gilded.

Deaver's incision (de′verz) [John B. *Deaver,* American surgeon, 1855–1931]. See under *incision.*

deba (de′bah). Diethylbarbituric acid.

Debaryomy′ces neofor′mans, D. hom′inis. *Cryptococcus neoformans.*

debilitant (de-bil′ĭ-tant) [L. *debilis* weak]. 1. Causing debility. 2. A remedy for too great excitement.

debility (de-bil′ĭ-te). Lack or loss of strength.

débouchement (da-boosh-maw′) [Fr.]. An opening out.

Debout's pill (dĕ-bo͞oz′) [Emile *Debout,* French physician, 1811–1865]. See under *pill.*

Debove's disease, membrane, tube (dĕ-bōvz′) [Maurice Georges *Debove,* French physician, 1845–1920]. See under the nouns.

debride (de-brīd′). To subject to removal of foreign matter and devitalized tissue.

débridement (da-brēd-maw′) [Fr.]. The removal

of all foreign matter and devitalized tissue in or about a traumatic or other lesion. Cf. *épluchage.* **enzymatic d.,** removal of fibrinous or purulent exudation with an enzyme which is capable of lysing fibrin, denatured collagen, elastin, and exudate, but which is nontoxic and nonirritating, and does not destroy normal tissue. **surgical d.,** removal of foreign material and devitalized tissue by mechanical methods.

debris (dĕ-bre′) [Fr.]. Accumulated fragments; rubbish. In dentistry, soft foreign matter loosely attached to the surface of a tooth. **word d.,** sounds made by an aphasic patient in attempting to talk.

Deb. spis. Abbreviation for L. *deb′ita spissitu′dine,* of the proper consistency.

Dec. Abbreviation for L. *decan′ta,* pour off.

deca- (dek′ah) [Gr. *deka* ten]. Combining form designating ten; used in naming units of measurement to indicate a quantity 10 times the unit designated by the root with which it is combined.

decacurie (dek″ah-ku′re). A unit of radioactivity, being ten (10) curies.

decadron (dek′ah-dron). Trade mark for preparations of dexamethasone.

decagram (dek′ah-gram) [*deca-* + *gram*]. Ten grams, or 154.32 grains troy.

decalcification (de″kal-sĭ-fi-ka′shun). 1. The process of removing calcareous matter. 2. The loss of calcium salts from a bone or tooth.

decalcify (de-kal′sĭ-fi) [L. *de* priv. + *calx* lime]. To deprive of calcium salts.

decaliter (dek′ah-le″ter) [*deca-* + *liter*]. Ten liters, or 610.28 cubic inches.

decalvant (de-kal′vant). Removing or destroying hair.

decameter (dek′ah-me″ter) [*deca-* + *meter*]. Ten meters.

decamethonium bromide (dek″ah-mĕ-tho′ne-um). A muscle relaxant with properties resembling those of curare, decamethylene-1,10-bistrimethylammonium dibromide: used as a muscle relaxant. **d. iodide,** bistrimethylammonium decane diiodide; a muscle relaxant for use in anesthesia and in electroshock treatment.

decane (dek′ān). A hydrocarbon, $C_{10}H_{22}$, from paraffin.

decannulation (de-kan″u-la′shun). Removal of a cannula, especially of a tracheostomy cannula.

decanormal (dek″ah-nor′mal) [*deca-* + *normal*]. Having ten times the strength of normal: said of solutions.

decantation (de″kan-ta′shun) [*de-* + L. *canthus* tire of a wheel]. The pouring of a clear supernatant liquid from a sediment.

decapeptide (dek″ah-pep′tīd). A peptide containing ten amino acids.

decapitation (de-kap″ĭ-ta′shun) [*de-* + L. *caput* head]. The removal of the head as of a person, a fetus, or a bone.

decapitator (de-kap′ĭ-ta″tor). An instrument for removing the head of a fetus in embryotomy.

Decapoda (de-kap′o-dah) [Gr. *deka* ten + *pous* foot]. An order of *Crustacea,* including the crabs, lobsters, shrimps, etc. They have five pairs of legs upon the thorax.

decapsulation (de-kap″su-la′shun). Removal of the capsule; especially removal of the renal capsule.

decarbonization (de-kar″bon-i-za′shun). The removal of carbon from the blood in the lungs by the substitution of oxygen for carbon dioxide.

decarboxylase (de″kar-bok′sĭ-lās). Carboxylase.

decarboxylation (de″kar-bok″sĭ-la′shun). Removal of the carboxyl group.

decarboxylization (de″kar-bok″sil-i-za′shun). Decarboxylation.

decay (de-ka′) [*de-* + L. *cadere* to fall]. 1. The gradual decomposition of dead organic matter. 2. The process or stage of decline; old age and its effects on mind and body.

deceleration (de-sel″er-a′shun). Decrease in speed or rate.

decentered (de-sen′terd). Said of a lens in which the visual axis does not pass through the axis of the lens.

decentration (de″sen-tra′shun) [*de-* + L. *centrum* center]. The act or process of removing from a center.

deceration (de″se-ra′shun) [*de-* + L. *cera* wax]. The removal of paraffin from a section prepared for the microscope.

decerebellation (de-ser″ĕ-bel-la′shun). Removal of the cerebellum.

decerebrate (de-ser′ĕ-brāt). Having the brain removed.

decerebration (de″ser-ĕ-bra′shun) [*de-* + *cerebrum*]. 1. Removal of the brain. 2. Interruption of the nervous system just below the level of the brain.

decerebrize (de-ser′ĕ-brīz). 1. To remove the brain. 2. To section the nervous system just below the level of the brain.

dechloridation (de-klo″rĭ-da′shun). The removal of chloride, or salt.

dechlorination (de-klo″rĭ-na′shun). Dechloridation.

dechlorurant (de-klo′roo-rant). An agent which causes dechloruration.

dechloruration (de-klo″roo-ra′shun). Diminution of excretion of chlorates in the urine.

decholesterinization (de″ko-les″ter-in-i-za′-shun). Decholesterolization.

decholesterolization (de″ko-les″ter-ol-i-za′-shun). Extraction of cholesterol from the blood.

decholin (de′ko-lin). Trade mark for preparations of dehydrocholic acid.

deci- (des′ĭ) [L. *decem* ten]. Combining form designating one-tenth; used in naming units of measurement to indicate one-tenth of the unit designated by the root with which it is combined (10^{-1}).

decibel (des′ĭ-bel). A unit of hearing or audition. One decibel is the least intensity of sound at which any given note can be heard, and a scale is constructed of so many decibels to describe the intensity above this for any sound of the same pitch. Abbreviated db.

decidua (de-sid′u-ah) [L. from *decid′uus* falling off]. A term applied to the mucous lining of the uterus which is thrown off after parturition. Called also *membranae deciduae.* **basal d., d. basa′lis** [N A, B N A], the portion of the decidua directly underlying the chorionic vesicle. **capsular d., d. capsula′ris** [N A, B N A], the portion of the decidua directly overlying the chorionic vesicle. **menstrual d., d. menstrua′lis,** the hyperemic mucosa of the uterus during the menstrual period. **parietal d., d. parieta′lis** [N A], the portion of the decidua lining the uterus elsewhere than at the site of attachment of the chorionic vesicle and in the cervix. Called also *d. vera.* **reflex d., d. reflex′a,** d. capsularis. **d. seroti′na,** d. basalis. **d. ve′ra** [B N A], d. parietalis.

decidual (de-sid′u-al). Pertaining to the decidua.

decidualitis (de-sid″u-ah-li′tis). A bacterial disease leading to alterations in the decidua.

deciduate (de-sid′u-āt). Characterized by shedding.

deciduation (de-sid″u-a′shun). The shedding of the decidua menstrualis during menstruation.

deciduitis (de-sid″u-i′tis). Decidual endometritis.

deciduoma (de-sid″u-o′mah) [*decidua* + *-oma*]. An intra-uterine neoplasm containing decidual cells; probably derived from portions of retained decidua after abortion. The tumor may be malignant and is then called *d. malignum* and also *chorio-epithelioma*, on the theory that it is derived from the epithelial structures. **Loeb's d.,** maternal placenta produced in guinea pigs by the action of progesterone. **d. malig'num,** syncytioma malignum.

deciduomatosis (de-sid″u-o-mah-to′sis). The excessive and irregular formation of decidual tissue in the nonpregnant state.

deciduosarcoma (de-sid″u-o-sar-ko′mah). Syncytioma malignum.

deciduous (de-sid′u-us) [L. *deciduus*, from *decidere* to fall off]. Not permanent, but cast off at maturity. The term is used to designate the teeth of the first dentition.

decigram (des′ĭ-gram). The tenth part of a gram; 1.544 grains.

deciliter (des′ĭ-le″ter). One tenth of a liter, equal to 6.1028 cubic inches.

decimeter (des′ĭ-me″ter). One tenth of a meter; 3.937 linear inches.

decinem (des′ĭ-nem). Pirquet's term for one tenth of a nem or the nutritive value of 1 decigram of milk. It is abbreviated dn.

decinormal (des″ĭ-nor′mal) [L. *decimus* tenth + *norma* rule]. Having one tenth of the normal strength.

decipara (des-ĭ-par′ah) [L. *decem* ten + *parere* to produce]. A woman who has had ten pregnancies which resulted in viable offspring. Also written Para X.

decitellization (de-si″tel-i-za′shun) [*de-* + L. *citellus* ground squirrel]. The destruction of ground squirrels, which are carriers of plague.

deckplatte (dek′plaht-tĕ) [Ger.]. Roof plate.

declination (dek″lĭ-na′shun) [L. *declinare* to decline]. Deviation from a normally vertical position, as rotation of the eye about its anteroposterior axis so that its vertical meridian lies to the temporal (*positive d.*) or to the nasal side (*negative d.*) of its proper position.

declinator (dek′lĭ-na″tor). An instrument by which parts (as the meninges of the brain) are held aside during an operation.

decline (de-klīn′). 1. The period or stage of the abatement of a disease or paroxysm. 2. Any wasting disease, especially pulmonary tuberculosis.

declive (de-klīv′) [Fr. *déclive;* L. *declivis*]. [N A] The part of the vermis of the cerebellum just caudal to the primary fissure. Called also *d. monticuli cerebelli* [B N A].

declivis (de-kli′vis) [L.]. Declive.

declomycin (dek′lo-mi″sin). Trade mark for preparations of demethylchlortetracycline.

decoagulant (de″ko-ag′u-lant). 1. Reducing the amount of existing coagulants or procoagulants in the blood. 2. A substance which inhibits coagulation of blood by reducing the amount of existing coagulants or procoagulants.

Decoct. Abbreviation for L. *decoc′tum*, a decoction.

decoction (de-kok′shun) [L. *decoctum*, from *de* down + *coquere* to boil]. 1. The act or process of boiling. 2. A medicine or other substance prepared by boiling. **d. of the woods,** Zittmann's decoction. **Zimmermann's d.,** a cathartic decoction of rhubarb, potassium bitartrate, barley, water, and syrup. **Zittmann's d.,** a decoction of sarsaparilla, calomel, cinnabar, alum, senna, licorice, anise seed, and fennel.

decoctum (de-kok′tum) [L.]. A decoction.

decollation (de″kol-la′shun) [*de-* + L. *collum* neck]. Decapitation, or beheadal; removal of the head, chiefly of the fetus in difficult labor.

décollement (da″kol-maw′) [Fr. "ungluing"]. The operation of separating an organ from the adjoining tissue to which it normally adheres, as of the parietal pleura from the chest wall.

decoloration (de-kul″or-a′shun). 1. Removal of color; bleaching. 2. Lack or loss of color.

decolorize (de-kul′or-īz). To free from color; to bleach.

decompensation (de″kom-pen-sa′shun). Inability of the heart to maintain adequate circulation. It is marked by dyspnea, venous engorgement, cyanosis and edema.

decomplementize (de-kom′ple-men″tīz). To remove complement from.

decomposition (de″kom-po-zish′un) [*de-* + L. *componere* to put together]. 1. The separation of compound bodies into their constituent principles. The decomposition of proteins is termed putrefaction, that of carbohydrates is called fermentation, and fats are said to rancidify. 2. Finkelstein's name for marasmus. **d. of movement,** lack of coordination characterized by irregularity in the successive flexion and extension of joints in performing a movement with the limb.

decompression (de″kom-presh′un). The removal of pressure, particularly the slow lessening of pressure on deep-sea divers and caisson workers to prevent the onset of bends, and the reduction of pressure on aviators as they ascend to great heights. **cerebral d.,** removal of a flap of the skull and incision of the dura mater for the purpose of relieving intracranial pressure. **explosive d.,** decompression more rapid than that corresponding to a rate of ascent greater than 5000 feet per minute. **d. of heart,** pericardiotomy with evacuation of a hematoma. **d. of pericardium,** d. of heart. **d. of rectum,** proctotomy for imperforate anus. **d. of spinal cord,** incision of spinal cord with removal of hematoma, bone fragments, etc.

decongestant (de″kon-jes′tant). 1. Tending to reduce congestion or swelling. 2. An agent that reduces congestion or swelling.

decongestive (de″kon-jes′tiv). Reducing congestion.

decontamination (de″kon-tam-ĭ-na′shun). The freeing of a person or an object of some contaminating substance such as war gas, radioactive material, etc.

decortication (de″kor-tĭ-ka′shun) [*de-* + L. *cortex* bark]. 1. The removal of bark, hull, husk, or shell from a plant, seed, or root, as in pharmacy. 2. Removal of portions of the cortical substance of a structure or organ, as of the brain, kidney, lung, etc. **arterial d.,** periarterial sympathectomy. **chemical d., enzymatic d.,** removal of cortical substance by chemical agents or enzymes. **d. of lung,** removal of the pleura for the relief of empyema. **renal d.,** removal of the capsule of the kidney; decapsulation of the kidney.

decrement (dek′re-ment) [L. *decrementum*]. 1. Subtraction, or decrease; the amount by which a quantity or value is decreased. 2. The stage of decline of a disease. See *stadium decrementi.*

decrepitate (de-krep′ĭ-tāt). To explode with a crackling noise.

decrepitation (de-krep″ĭ-ta′shun) [L. *decrepitare* to crackle]. A crackling noise, such as that made by throwing certain bodies, as salt, on the fire.

decrudescence (de″kroo-des′ens). Diminution of the intensity of symptoms.

decrustation (de″krus-ta′shun). The detachment of a crust.

Decub. Abbreviation for L. *decu′bitus*, lying down.

decubation (de″ku-ba′shun) [*de-* + L. *cubare* to lie down]. The period in the course of an infectious disease from the disappearance of the symptoms to complete recovery and the end of the infectious period. Cf. *incubation.*

decubital (de-ku′bĭ-tal). Pertaining to decubitus, or to a decubitus ulcer.

decubitus (de-ku′bĭ-tus) [L. "a lying down"]. 1. An act of lying down; also the position assumed in lying down. 2. Decubitus ulcer. See under *ulcer.* **d. acu′tus,** a severe and fatal form of decubitus ulcer on a paralyzed side in hemiplegia. **Andral's d.,** decubitus on the sound side; a position assumed in the early stages of pleurisy. **d.**

chron'icus, ordinary decubitus ulcer due to recumbent position. **dorsal d.,** recumbency in the supine position. **ventral d.,** lying on the stomach.

decurrent (de-kur'ent) [L. *decurrere* to run down]. Extending or moving from above downward.

decursus (de-kur'sus) [L.]. A running down. **d. fibra'rum cerebra'lium** [B N A], the running down of the cerebral fibers, indicating the course of fiber tracts of the brain. Omitted in N A.

decurtate (de-kur'tāt) [L. *decurtatus* cut short]. Abridged, or cut short.

decussate (de-kus'āt) [L. *decussare* to cross in the form of an X]. 1. To cross or intersect in the form of the letter X. 2. Crossing in the form of the letter X.

decussatio (de"kus-sa'she-o), pl. *decussationes* [L.]. [N A, B N A] A general term for the crossing over of two fellow parts or structures. Called also *decussation.* See also *chiasma* and *commissura.* **d. bra'chii conjuncti'vi** [B N A], d. pedunculorum cerebellarium superiorum. **d. lemnis'ci, d. lemnisco'rum** [N A, B N A], the region at the caudal end of the medulla oblongata in which the fibers from the nucleus cuneatus and the nucleus gracilis cross from one side to the other, before they form the medial lemniscus. Called also *decussation of lemniscus.* **d. nervo'rum trochlea'rium** [N A, B N A], the crossing of the fibers of the trochlear nerves on the upper surface of the superior medullary velum. Called also *decussation of trochlear nerves.* **d. pedunculo'rum cerebella'rium superio'rum** [N A], the crossing of the fibers of the superior cerebellar peduncle within the tegmentum of the mesencephalon. Called also *d. brachii conjunctivi* [B N A], and *decussation of superior cerebellar peduncles.* **d. pyram'idum** [N A, B N A], the region of the anterocaudal medulla oblongata in which most of the fibers of the pyramids cross from one side to the other to form the lateral corticospinal tracts. Called also *pyramidal decussation.* **decussatio'nes tegmen'ti** [N A], **decussatio'nes tegmento'rum** [B N A], crossing fibers in the mesencephalon, including the ventral tegmental decussation of the rubrospinal and rubroreticular tracts, and the dorsal tegmental decussation of the tectospinal tract. Called also *decussations of tegmentum.* **d. trac'tuum optico'rum,** chiasma opticum.

decussation (de"kus-sa'shun). A crossing over. See *decussatio.* **d. of fillet,** decussatio lemniscorum. **Forel's d.,** the ventral tegmental decussation of the rubrospinal and rubroreticular tracts in the mesencephalon. **fountain d. of Meynert,** the dorsal tegmental decussation of the tectospinal tract in the mesencephalon. **d. of lemnicus,** decussatio lemniscorum. **motor d.,** decussatio pyramidum. **optic d., d. of optic nerves,** chiasma opticum. **pyramidal d., d. of pyramids,** decussatio pyramidum. **pyramidal d., superior,** decussatio lemniscorum. **d. of superior cerebellar peduncles,** decussatio pedunculorum cerebellarium superiorum. **tegmental d's, d's of tegmentum,** decussationes tegmenti. **d. of trochlear nerves,** decussatio nervorum trochlearium.

decussationes (de"kus-sa"she-o'nēz) [L.]. Plural of *decussatio.*

decussorium (de"kus-so're-um). An instrument for depressing the dura mater in trephining.

dedentition (de"den-tish'un) [*de-* + L. *dens* tooth]. The shedding or loss of teeth.

dedifferentiation (de-dif"er-en"she-a'shun). Reverse differentiation of a tissue to a more primitive tissue in which it passes through the stages of its development but in reverse order.

de d. in d. Abbreviation for L. *de di'e in di'em,* from day to day.

dedolation (ded"o-la'shun). 1. A sensation as if the limbs had been bruised. 2. The shaving off of a piece of skin by an oblique cut.

deelectronation (de"e-lek"tro-na'shun). The removal of an electron or electrons from an element; a term proposed as a substitute for oxidation.

deemanate (de-em'ah-nāt). To deprive of the property of giving off radioactive emanations.

Deen's test (dēnz) [Izaak Abrahamszoon van *Deen,* Dutch physiologist, 1804–1869]. See under *tests.*

deep (dēp). Situated far beneath the surface; not superficial.

Deetjen's bodies (dāt'yenz) [Hermann *Deetjen,* German physician, 1867–1915]. Blood platelets.

def (de'e-ef). An expression of dental caries experience in deciduous teeth, *d* representing the number of teeth indicated for filling; *e* the number indicated for extraction; *f* the number of filled teeth.

defatigation (de-fat"ĭ-ga'shun). Overstrain or fatigue of muscular or nervous tissue.

defatted (de-fat'ed). Deprived of fat.

defaunate (de-fawn'āt) [*de-* + L. *fauna* animal life]. To remove or destroy an animal population, such as hookworms from the intestinal tract, delousing, etc.

defecalgesiophobia (def"e-kal-je"se-o-fo'be-ah) [*defecation* + Gr. *algēsis* pain + *phobia*]. Fear of defecation because of pain it causes.

defecation (def"e-ka'shun) [L. *defaecare* to deprive of dregs]. 1. The removal of impurities. 2. The evacuation of fecal material from the rectum. **chemical d.,** the process of freeing a solution of impurities as by adding a reagent that will cause them to separate. **fragmentary d.,** the evacuation of a small amount of feces at frequent intervals.

defect (de'fekt). An imperfection, failure, or absence. **acquired d.,** an imperfection gained secondarily, after birth. **congenital d.,** an imperfection present at birth, because of abnormal embryonic development. **ectodermal d., congenital,** hereditary ectodermal dysplasia. **filling d.,** any localized defect in the contour of the stomach, duodenum, or intestine, as seen in the roentgenogram after a barium enema, due to a lesion of the wall projecting into the lumen or to an object in the lumen. **retention d.,** a defect in the power of recalling or remembering names or numbers. **septal d.,** a defect in the cardiac septum, resulting in an abnormal communication between the opposite chambers of the heart.

defective (de-fek'tiv). 1. Imperfect. 2. A person lacking in some physical, mental, or moral quality.

defeminization (de-fem"ĭ-ni-za'shun). Loss of female sexual characteristics.

defense (de-fens'). Behavior directed to the protection of the individual from injury. **muscular d.,** the muscular tension and rigidity which accompanies a localized inflammation, as in appendicitis. **ur d.** See *ur-defense.*

deferens (def'er-enz) [L.]. Deferent. See *ductus deferens.*

deferent (def'er-ent) [L. *deferens* carrying away]. Conveying anything away, as from a center.

deferentectomy (def"er-en-tek'to-me). Surgical removal of a ductus deferens.

deferential (def"er-en'shal). Pertaining to the ductus deferens.

deferentitis (def"er-en-ti'tis). Inflammation of the ductus deferens.

defervescence (def"er-ves'ens) [L. *defervescere* to cease boiling]. The period of disappearance of fever.

defervescent (def"er-ves'ent). 1. Causing reduction of fever. 2. An agent that acts to reduce fever.

defibrillation (de-fib"rĭ-la'shun). 1. The stoppage of fibrillation of the heart. 2. The separation of the fibers of a tissue by blunt dissection.

defibrillator (de-fib"rĭ-la'tor) [*de-* + *fibrillation*]. An apparatus used to counteract fibrillation by application of electric impulses to the heart.

defibrinated (de-fi′brĭ-nāt″ed). Deprived of fibrin.

defibrination (de-fi″brĭ-na′shun). Deprival of fibrin.

deficiency (de-fish′en-se). A lack or defect. **mental d.,** feeblemindedness. **taste d.,** taste blindness.

deficit (def′ĭ-sit). A lack or deficiency. **oxygen d.** See *anoxia* and *anoxemia*. **pulse d.,** the difference between the heart rate and the pulse rate, resulting from failure of some of the ventricular contractions to produce peripheral pulse waves.

definition (def″ĭ-nish′un). The clear determination of the limits of anything, as of a disease process or a microscopical image.

definitive (de-fin′ĭ-tiv). Established with certainty. In embryology, denoting acquisition of final differentiation or character.

deflagration (def″lah-gra′shun) [L. *deflagrare* to be consumed by fire]. A rapid, violent combustion with flame and explosion.

deflection (de-flek′shun). A turning aside; in psychoanalysis, an unconscious diversion of ideas from conscious attention. **d. of the complement,** deviation of the complement.

defloration (def″lo-ra′shun) [L. *deflora′tio*]. The rupturing of the hymen, either in sexual intercourse or in vaginal examination.

deflorescence (def″lo-res′ens). The disappearance of the eruption in any exanthematous disease.

defluvium (de-floo′ve-um) [L.]. Defluxio. **d. capillo′rum,** defluxio capillorum.

defluxio (de-fluk′se-o) [L.]. 1. A flowing down. 2. A disappearance. **d. capillo′rum,** sudden loss of the hair. **d. cilio′rum,** sudden loss of the eyelashes.

defluxion (de-fluk′shun) [L. *defluxio*]. 1. A sudden disappearance. 2. A copious discharge.

deformation (de″for-ma′shun). Deformity.

deforming (de-form′ing). Causing or producing deformity.

deformity (de-for′mĭ-te). Distortion of any part or general disfigurement of the body. **Akerlund d.,** a deformity of the duodenal cap in the radiogram in duodenal ulcer consisting of an indentation (incisura) in addition to the niche. **anterior d.,** lordosis. **Arnold-Chiari d.,** elongation of the cerebellar tonsils, smallness and deformity of the medulla, smallness of the pons with degeneration of its transverse fibers and herniation of the cerebellum into the spinal canal; caudal displacement of brain stem. **gun stock d.,** cubitus varus. **Ilfeld-Holder d.,** prominent scapula with difficulty in raising the arm. **lobster-claw d.,** a developmental anomaly characterized by an abnormal cleft between the central metacarpal bones, the soft tissues of the digits being fused into two masses, one on either side of the cleft. **Madelung's d.,** distortion of the radius at its lower end, with ulnar displacement backward. **reduction d.,** congenital absence of a portion or all of a body part, especially the limbs. **seal fin d.,** outward deflection of the fingers in rheumatoid arthritis. **silver fork d.,** the peculiar deformity seen in Colles' fracture. See illustration under *fracture*. **Sprengel's d.,** congenital upward displacement of the scapula. **Velpeau's d.,** silver fork deformity. **Volkmann's d.,** congenital tibio-tarsal dislocation.

defunctionalization (de-funk″shun-al-i-za′-shun). Loss or deprival of a function.

defundation (de″fun-da′shun) [*de-* + L. *fundus*]. Excision of the fundus of the uterus along with the uterine tubes.

defundectomy (de″fun-dek′to-me). Defundation.

defurfuration (de-fur″fu-ra′shun) [*de-* + L. *furfur* bran]. The formation and shedding of fine, branlike scales from the skin.

Deg. Abbreviation for *degeneration* and *degree*.

deganglionate (de-gang′gle-on-āt″). To deprive of a ganglion; to remove a ganglion or ganglia from.

degassing (de-gas′ing). Treatment of men who have been subjected to the fumes of gas.

degeneracy (de-jen′er-ah-se). A state characterized by deterioration of the powers of body and mind. **inferior d.,** degeneracy marked by deformity or by weakened mentality. **superior d.,** degeneracy with brilliant mental powers.

degenerate (de-jen′er-āt). 1. To change from a higher to a lower type or form. 2. A person of a perverted mental or physical constitution.

degeneratio (de-jen″er-a′she-o) [L.]. Degeneration. **d. mi′cans,** glistening degeneration.

degeneration (de-jen″er-a′shun) [L. *degeneratio*]. Deterioration; change from a higher to a lower form; especially change of tissue to a lower or less functionally active form. When there is chemical change of the tissue itself, it is *true* degeneration; when the change consists in the deposit of abnormal matter in the tissues, it is *infiltration*. **Abercrombie's d.,** amyloid d. **abiotrophic d.,** primary d. **adipose d.,** fatty d. **adiposogenital d.,** dystrophia adiposogenitalis. **albuminoid d., albuminous d.,** cloudy swelling. **amyloid d.,** degeneration with the deposit of lardacein in the tissues. It indicates impairment of nutritive function, and is seen in wasting diseases. **anemic d.,** polychromatophilia. **angiolithic d.,** one characterized by mineral deposits and hyaline changes in the coats of the vessels. **Armanni-Ehrlich's d.,** hyaline degeneration of the epithelial cells of Henle's loops: seen in diabetes. **ascending d.,** wallerian degeneration affecting centripetal nerve fibers and progressing toward the brain or spinal cord. **atheromatous d.,** the change in the arterial coats which occurs in arteritis deformans; atheroma. **axonal d.,** the reaction of a nerve cell to injury to its axon. It consists of central chromatolysis and eccentricity of the nucleus. **bacillary d.,** a condition characterized by occurrence, in degenerating red cells, of rodlike hyaline areas that appear to show motion. **bacony d.,** amyloid d. **basic d., basophilic d.,** basophilia. **Biber-Haab-Dimmer d.,** reticular d. **blastophthoric d.,** blastophthoria. **calcareous d.,** degeneration with infiltration of calcareous materials into the tissues. **caseous d., cheesy d.,** caseation. **cellulose d.,** amyloid d. **cerebromacular d., cerebroretinal d.,** any one of a group of hereditary or familial disorders characterized by progressive mental degeneration and loss of vision. This group includes amaurotic family idiocy, Bielschowsky-Jansky disease, Spielmeyer-Vogt disease and Kufs' disease. **chitinous d.,** amyloid d. **colloid d.,** the assumption by the tissues of a gumlike or gelatinous character. **combined d.,** degeneration of both the posterior and the lateral columns of the spinal cord; a progressive disease of middle life which occurs in severe anemias and cachexias. It is marked by paresthesias, ataxia, unsteadiness of gait, and sometimes by mental deterioration. Called also *subacute* or *combined sclerosis* and *ataxic paraplegia*. **comma d.,** progressive degeneration of the nervous matter of the comma tract. **congenital macular d.,** Best's disease; the infantile type of retinal atrophy. **crenation d.,** a condition in which the cells of the corium become irregular and toothed: seen in granuloma fungoides. **cystic d.,** degeneration with the formation of cysts. **cystoid d.,** Blessig's cysts. **descending d.,** wallerian degeneration extending peripherally along nerve fibers. **earthy d.,** calcareous d. **Ehrlich's hemoglobinemic d.,** a condition characterized by the appearance, in the center of degenerating red cells, of dark bodies that are not actually specific inclusions. **elastoid d.,** amyloid degeneration of the elastic tissue of arteries. **endoglobular d.,** a condition sometimes seen in large red blood corpuscles (megalocytes) in which they exhibit irregularly shaped colorless areas. **fascic-**

ular d., degeneration of paralyzed muscles due to lesion in the motor ganglion cells of the central tube of gray matter of the cord. **fatty d.,** deposit of fat globules in a tissue. **fibrinous d.,** necrosis with deposit of fibrin within the cells of the tissue. **fibroid d.,** degeneration into fibrous tissue. **fibrous d.,** fibrosis. **gelatiniform d.,** colloid d. **glassy d.,** a peculiar change occurring in the heart muscle and other muscles in fevers. **glistening d.,** degeneration of glia tissue characterized by the formation of glistening masses. **glycogenic d.,** a form of degeneration in which abnormal amounts of glycogen accumulate in the cells, as in glycogenosis. **Gombault's d.,** segmental periaxial neuritis. **granular d.,** basophilia. **granulovascular d.,** a condition in which the ganglion cells become filled with vacuoles containing condensed granules of protoplasm. **Grawitz's d.,** basophilia. **gray d.,** degeneration of the white substance of the spinal cord, in which it loses myelin and assumes a gray color. **Haab's d.,** reticular degeneration of the cornea. **hematohyaloid d.,** a form of hyaline degeneration of thrombi due to conglutination of the red cells or blood platelets. **hemoglobinemic d.,** an archaic term applied to accumulation of hemoglobin in the center of the erythrocyte. **hepatolenticular d.,** a group of disorders characterized by degeneration of the liver and of the lenticular nucleus. The term includes progressive lenticular degeneration (Wilson's disease), pseudosclerosis of Westphal, dystonia musculorum deformans, acquired bilateral athetosis, and intermittent spasmodic torticollis. **Holmes's d.,** primary progressive cerebellar d. **Horn's d.,** degeneration with nuclear proliferation in striated muscles. **hyaline d.,** abnormal transformation of a tissue into a translucent glassy material which stains brightly with fuchsin. **hyaloid d.,** amyloid d. **hydropic d.,** a variety in which the epithelial cells absorb much water. **keratoid d.,** change of the plasma of a cell into keratin. **lardaceous d.,** amyloid d. **lattice d. of cornea,** lattice keratitis. **lenticular d.** See *progressive lenticular d.* **lipoidal d.,** a condition somewhat resembling fatty degeneration or infiltration but in which the extraneous material is lipoid. **macular d.,** degenerative changes in the macula lutea of the retina. **Maragliano's d.,** a condition of erythrocytes characterized by presence of Maragliano bodies. **Mönkeberg's d.,** medial arteriosclerosis. **mucinoid d.,** a term used to include both mucoid and colloid degeneration. **mucinous d.,** mucous d. **mucoid d.,** degeneration accompanied by deposit of myelin and lecithin in the cells. **mucous d.,** a form in which mucus accumulates in epithelial tissues. **myelinic d.,** mucoid d. **myxomatous d.,** degeneration in which mucus accumulates in connective tissues. **neurosomatic d.,** a condition resulting from prolonged duration of the convulsive state, consisting of parkinsonism, dementia, and flexion contractures of the cerebral type. **Nissl d.,** degeneration of a nerve cell after division of the nerve fiber supplying it. **pallidal d.,** degeneration of the globus pallidus. **parenchymatous d.,** cloudy swelling. **Paschulin's d.,** the degeneration peculiar to diabetes. **pigmental d., pigmentary d.,** in which cells of affected tissue become abnormally pigmented. **polychromatophilic d.,** polychromatophilia. **polypoid d.,** the development, on a mucous membrane, of polypoid growths. **primary progressive cerebellar d.,** a familial disease marked by motor disorders and due to cerebellar degeneration, occurring in adults between the ages of thirty and forty and progressing slowly to a fatal termination (Holmes). **progressive lenticular d.,** a rare disease characterized by bilateral degeneration of the basal ganglia and cirrhosis of the liver, and marked by tremor, spastic contractures, psychic disturbance, and increasing weakness and emaciation. **Quain's d.,** the fibrous degeneration of the muscles of the heart. **red d.,** degeneration of a uterine fibroid during pregnancy, marked by the formation of soft red areas. **reticular d.,** a lattice-like degeneration of the corneal epithelium (Haab, Biber, Dimmer). **rim d.,** degeneration of the spinal cord affecting the periphery only. **Rosenthal's d.,** glistening d. **sclerotic d.,** a variety of hyaline degeneration affecting connective tissue, especially the intima of arteries. **secondary d.,** wallerian d. **senile d.,** the widespread degenerative changes, principally fibroid and atheromatous, that occur in old age. **theroid d.,** acquirement of beastlike qualities by the insane. **trabecular d.,** a change in the walls of the bronchi, which become thin and wasted in respect to the muscular and mucous elements, while the stroma is increased in volume. **traumatic d.,** degeneration of a divided nerve up to the nearest node of Ranvier. **Türck's d.,** secondary parenchymatous degeneration of nerve tracts of the cord. **uratic d.,** degeneration marked by the deposit of urates or uric acid. **vacuolar d.,** the formation of vacuoles in the cells of a tissue. **Virchow's d.,** amyloid d. **vitreous d.,** hyaline d. **wallerian d.,** fatty degeneration of a nerve fiber which has been severed from its nutritive centers. **waxy d.,** amyloid d. **Wilson's d.,** progressive lenticular d. **Zenker's d.,** necrosis and hyaline degeneration of striated muscle.

degenerative (de-jen′er-a-tiv). Of or pertaining to degeneration.

dégénéré (da-zha″na-ra′) [Fr.]. A person of a perverted mental or physical constitution. **d. supe′rior** (da-zha″na-ra′ soo-pa″re-er′), a person of superior mind, but of morbid or degenerate tendencies.

degenerescence (de-jen″er-es′ens). Incipient degeneration.

degenitalize (de-gen′ĭ-tal-īz). In psychiatry, to remove the genital aspects of an affect.

degerm (de-germ′). To remove or destroy the microorganisms on or in an object.

Deglut. Abbreviation for L. *deglutia′tur*, let it be swallowed.

deglutible (de-gloo′tĭ-bl). Capable of being swallowed.

deglutition (deg″loo-tish′un) [L. *deglutitio*]. The act of swallowing.

deglutitive (de-gloo′tĭ-tiv). Deglutitory.

deglutitory (de-gloo′tĭ-to″re). Pertaining to or promoting deglutition.

degradation (deg-rah-da′shun). The reduction of a chemical compound to one less complex, as by splitting off one or more groups.

degranulation (de-gran″u-la′shun). The process of losing granules: said of certain granular cells.

degrease (de-grēs′). To remove grease or fat from.

degree (de-gre′). 1. A grade or rank awarded scholars by a college or university. 2. A unit of measure of temperature. 3. A unit of measure of arcs and angles. **prism d.,** centrad, def. 2.

degrowth (de′grōth). Decrease in the mass of living matter because of use of the proteins of the protoplasm to produce energy by the organism.

degustation (de″gus-ta′shun) [L. *degustatio*]. The act or function of tasting.

dehab (de′hahb). Surra.

dehematize (de-hem′ah-tīz) [*de-* + Gr. *haima* blood]. To deprive of blood.

dehemoglobinize (de″hem-o-glo′bĭ-nīz). To remove hemoglobin from the red blood corpuscles.

dehepatized (de-hep′ah-tīzd). Having the liver removed.

Dehio's test (da′he-ōz) [Karl Konstantinovitch *Dehio*, Russian physician, 1851–1927]. See under *tests*.

dehiscence (de-his′ens) [L. *dehiscere* to gape]. The act or process of splitting. **iris d.,** the presence of accessory slits in the iris. **wound d.,** separation of all the layers of an incision or wound. **Zuckerkandl's d's,** small gaps occasionally seen in the papyraceous layer of the ethmoid bone.

dehumanization (de-hu″man-i-za′shun) [*de-* + L. *humanus* human]. Loss of the qualities of humanity, as in some deep psychosis.

dehumidifier (de″hu-mid′ĭ-fi″er). An apparatus by which the content of moisture in the air is reduced.

dehydrant (de-hi′drant). 1. Reducing hydration. 2. An agent that reduces body water.

dehydrase (de-hi′drās). Dehydrogenase.

dehydrate (de-hi′drāt). To remove water from.

dehydration (de″hi-dra′shun) [L. *de* away + Gr. *hydōr* water]. Removal of water from the body or a tissue; or the condition which results from undue loss of water.

dehydroandrosterone (de-hi″dro-an-dros′ter-ōn). An androgen, $C_{19}H_{28}O_2$, 3-trans-hydroxy-17-keto-$\triangle^5$-androstene, occurring in human urine and synthesized from cholesterol.

dehydrobilirubin (de-hi″dro-bil-ĭ-ru′bin). Biliverdin.

dehydrocholaneresis (de-hi″dro-ko″lan-er′ĕ-sis). Increase in the output of dehydrocholic acid in the bile.

dehydrocholate (de-hi″dro-ko′lāt). A salt of dehydrocholic acid.

dehydrocholesterol (de-hi″dro-ko-les′ter-ol). A sterol found in the skin which, when properly irradiated, forms vitamin D. **7-d., activated,** a compound used in prophylaxis and treatment of vitamin D deficiency.

11-dehydrocorticosterone (de-hi″dro-kor-te-ko′ster-ōn). A steroid from the adrenal cortex, which has a slight effect on protein and carbohydrate metabolism. Called also *Kendall's compound A.*

dehydrocorydaline (de-hi″dro-kŏ-rid′ah-lin). A yellowish crystalline alkaloid, $C_{22}H_{23}O_4N$, from the roots of species of *Corydalis.*

dehydrogenase (de-hi′dro-jen-ās). An enzyme which mobilizes the hydrogen of a substrate so that it can pass to a hydrogen acceptor. Cf. *coenzyme.* Dehydrogenases are variously designated according to their specific activity, or the substrate acted upon. **acetaldehyde d.,** oxidizes acetaldehyde to acetic acid and H_2O_2. **aerobic d.,** one that transfers hydrogen directly to oxygen. **alcohol d.,** catalyzes the oxidation of ethyl alcohol to acetaldehyde and H_2O. **anaerobic d.,** one that is linked with a carrier. **beta hydroxybutyric d.,** catalyzes the oxidation of beta hydroxybutyric acid to acetoacetic acid. **fatty acid d.,** catalyzes the removal of hydrogen from higher fatty acids. **formic d.,** catalyzes the change of formic acid into carbon dioxide and hydrogen. **glucose d.,** catalyzes the oxidation of glucose to gluconic acid. **glutamic acid d.,** catalyzes the change of glutamic acid into ketoglutaric acid. **glycerolphosphate d.,** catalyzes the oxidation of glycerolphosphate into phosphoglyceric acid. **hexose d.,** catalyzes the oxidation of hexose to hexonic acid. **lactate d.,** catalyzes the oxidation of alpha hydroxy acids to alpha keto acids. **malate d.,** catalyzes the oxidation of malic acid to oxaloacetic acid. **pyruvic d.,** catalyzes the complicated oxidation of pyruvic acid. **Robison ester d.,** catalyzes the transformation of the Robison ester into phosphohexonic acid. **succinic d.,** catalyzes the change of succinic acid into fumaric acid provided a hydrogen acceptor is present. **xanthine d.,** catalyzes the oxidation of xanthine to uric acid.

dehydrogenate (de-hi′dro-jen-āt). 1. To remove hydrogen from. 2. A compound from which hydrogen has been removed.

dehydrogenation (de-hi″dro-jen-a′shun). Indirect oxidation due to removal of hydrogen by the reaction of a hydrogen acceptor.

dehydrogenize (de-hi′dro-jen-iz). To remove hydrogen from.

dehydroisoandrosterone (de-hi″dro-i″so-an-dro′ster-ōn). A ketosteroid occurring in normal human urine.

dehydromorphine (de-hi″dro-mor′fin). A compound, $C_{34}H_{36}N_2O_6.3H_2O$, occurring in opium and prepared by the oxidation of morphine. Called also *pseudomorphine* and *oxymorphine.*

dehydropeptidase (de-hi″dro-pep′tĭ-dās). An enzyme which catalyzes the hydrolysis of glycyl dehydrophenylalanine to glycine, ammonia, and phenylpyruvic acid.

dehypnotize (de-hip′no-tīz). To arouse from the hypnotic state.

de-inebriating (de″in-e′bre-āt″ing). Counteracting alcoholic intoxication.

deinsectization (de″in-sek″ti-za′shun). The destruction of infesting insects.

de-ionization (de-i″on-i-za′shun). The production of a mineral-free state by the removal of ions.

deiteral (di′ter-al). Pertaining to Deiters' nucleus.

Deiters' cells, nucleus, process, etc. (di′terz) [Otto Friedrich Carl *Deiters,* German anatomist, 1834–1863]. See under the nouns.

déjà entendu (da-zhah′ on″ton-doo′) [Fr. "already heard"]. The feeling that one has heard or perceived something previously.

déjà éprouvé (da-zhah′ a″proo-va′) [Fr. "already tested"]. A feeling that something a person has never engaged in has been carried out.

déjà fait (da-zhah′ fa) [Fr. "already done"]. A feeling that what is happening has happened before.

déjà pensé (da-zhah′ pon-sa′) [Fr. "already thought"]. A feeling that one has thought the same thoughts before.

déjà raconté (da-zhah′ rak″on-ta′) [Fr. "already told"]. A feeling that a forgotten experience has been told to the patient by someone else.

déjà vécu (da-zhah′ va-koo′) [Fr. "already lived"]. An illusory feeling that a new experience has been previously encountered.

déjà voulu (da-zhah′ voo-loo′) [Fr. "already desired"]. A feeling that one has entertained the same desires before.

déjà vu (da-zhah′ voo′) [Fr. "already seen"]. An illusion in which a new situation is incorrectly viewed as a repetition of a previous situation.

dejecta (de-jek′tah). Excrementitious substances.

dejection (de-jek′shun) [L. *dejectio*]. 1. Discharge of excrementitious material. 2. Excrementitious material which has been discharged by the organism. 3. A mental state marked by depression and melancholy.

Dejerine's disease, sign, syndrome (deh″-zher-ēnz′) [Joseph Jules *Dejerine,* French neurologist, 1849–1917]. See under the nouns.

Dejerine-Klumpke paralysis (deh″zher-ēn′ klump′ke) [Auguste *Dejerine Klumpke,* French neurologist, 1859–1927]. Klumpke's paralysis.

Dejerine-Landouzy type (deh″zher-ēn′ lan-doo′ze) [J. J. *Dejerine;* Louis Théophile Joseph *Landouzy,* French physician, 1845–1917]. See *Landouzy-Dejerine dystrophy,* under *dystrophy.*

Dejerine-Lichtheim phenomenon (deh″zher-en′ lict′hīm) [J. J. *Dejerine;* Ludwig *Lichtheim,* German physician, 1845–1928]. Lichtheim sign.

Dejerine-Roussy syndrome (deh″zher-ēn′ roo-se′) [J. J. *Dejerine;* Gustav *Roussy,* French pathologist, 1874–1948]. Thalamic syndrome.

Dejerine-Sottas disease (deh″zher-ēn′ sot′-tahz) [J. J. *Dejerine;* Jules *Sottas,* French neurologist, born 1866]. Progressive hypertrophic interstitial neuropathy.

deka- (dek′ah) [Gr. *deka* ten]. Combining form meaning ten. For words beginning thus, see also those beginning *deca-.*

dekanem (dek′ah-nem). Ten nems.

delacrimation (de-lak″rĭ-ma′shun) [L. *de* from + *lacrima* tear]. Excessive and abnormal flow of tears.

delactation (de″lak-ta′shun). 1. Weaning. 2. The cessation of lactation.

Delafield's hematoxylin (del′ah-fēldz) [Francis *Delafield*, pathologist in New York, 1841–1915]. See *stains, table of*.

delalutin (del″ah-lu′tin). Trade mark for a preparation of hydroxyprogesterone caproate.

delamination (de″lam-ĭ-na′shun) [L. *de* apart + *lamina* plate]. Separation of the blastoderm into the epiblast and hypoblast.

delatestryl (del″ah-tes′tril). Trade mark for a preparation of testosterone enanthate.

Delbet's sign (del-bāz′) [Paul *Delbet*, French surgeon, 1866–1924]. See under *sign*.

de-lead (de-led′). To remove lead from a tissue, as from the bones in lead poisoning by the administration of potassium iodide.

deleterious (del″ĕ-te′re-us) [Gr. *dēlētērios*]. Hurtful; injurious.

deletion (de-le′shun). Removal or banishment; applied in genetics to loss from a chromosome of genetic material.

deligation (del″ĭ-ga′shun) [*de-* + L. *ligere* to bind]. The application of a ligature or bandage.

delimitation (de-lim″ĭ-ta′shun) [*de-* + L. *limitare* to limit]. 1. The process of limiting or of becoming limited. 2. Ascertainment of the limits and extent of some diseased tissue or process.

delineascope (de-lin′e-ah-skōp). A form of lantern for the projection of slides on to a screen.

delinquency (de-lin′kwen-se). Antisocial, illegal or criminal conduct.

delinquent (de-lin′kwent). 1. Characterized by antisocial, illegal, or criminal conduct. 2. An individual whose conduct is antisocial, illegal, or criminal; applied especially to a minor exhibiting such behavior **(juvenile d.)**.

deliquescence (del″e-kwes′ens) [L. *deliquescere* to grow moist]. The condition of becoming liquefied as a result of the absorption of water from the air.

deliquescent (del″e-kwes′ent). Having a tendency to melt or become liquid by the absorption of moisture from the air.

deliquium (de-lik′we-um) [L. "failure"]. Impairment of mental faculties. **d. an′imi**, syncope.

délire (da-lēr′) [Fr.]. Delirium; frenzy. **d. de toucher** (da-lēr′ duh too-sha′), an unreasonable and irresistible impulse to handle or to feel various objects.

deliria (de-lir′ĭ-ah). Plural of *delirium*.

deliriant (de-lir′ĭ-ant). 1. Capable of producing delirium. 2. A drug which may produce delirium. 3. A delirious person.

delirifacient (de-lir″ĭ-fa′she-ent) [L. *delirium* + *facere* to make]. 1. Capable of causing delirium. 2. A drug which may produce delirium.

delirious (de-lir′ĭ-us). Suffering from delirium.

delirium (de-lir′ĭ-um), pl. *delir′ia* [*de-* + L. *lira* furrow or track; i.e., "off the track"]. A mental disturbance marked by illusions, hallucinations, short unsystematized delusions, cerebral excitement, physical restlessness and incoherence, and having a comparatively short course. Delirium may occur in the course of a more prolonged mental disorder or as a result of fever, disease, or injury. **active d.**, delirium accompanied by maniacal movements. **acute d.**, a suddenly appearing and severe delirium lasting only a short time. **afebrile d.**, delirium not attended by, nor occurring in the course of, fever. **d. alcohol′icum**, d. tremens. **anxious d.**, a condition of excitement marked by an undefined feeling of anxiety. **Bell's d.**, acute d. **chronic alcoholic d.**, Korsakoff's psychosis. **d. cor′dis**, auricular fibrillation. **d. ebriosita′tis**, d. tremens. **exhaustion d.**, delirium due to strain or exhaustion from metabolic or nutritional disturbance. **febrile d.**, the delirium of fever. **grave d.**, acute d. **lingual d.**, the utterance of meaningless words and sentences. **low d.**, delirium marked by confusion of ideas and slowness of mental action rather than by excitement. **macromaniacal d.**, macroptic d. **macroptic d.**, a psychosensory disturbance in which the patient believes that his body or limbs, or both, have assumed enormous proportions. **micromaniacal d.**, microptic d. **microptic d.**, a psychosensory disturbance in which the patient believes that his body or limbs, or both, have assumed minute proportions. **d. mus′sitans**, delirium in which the patient murmurs to himself. **oneiric d.**, oneirism. **d. schizophrenoi′des**, delirium accompanied by reactions typical of dementia praecox. **senile d.**, dotage: the imbecility of old age. **d. si′ne delir′io** [L. "delirium without delirium"], delirium tremens without hallucinations and mental distress, but with all the physical symptoms present. **specific febrile d.**, acute d. **toxic d.**, delirium caused by poisons. **traumatic d.**, that which follows severe head injury. Superficially the patient is alert, but there is marked disorientation, memory defect and confabulation. **d. tre′mens**, a variety of acute mental disturbance marked by delirium with trembling and great excitement, and attended by anxiety, mental distress, sweating, and precordial pain. It is one of the forms of alcoholic psychosis, but is also seen in opium addiction.

delitescence (del″ĭ-tes′ens) [L. *delitescere* to lie hidden]. 1. Sudden disappearance of symptoms or of objective signs of a disease or of a lesion. 2. The period of latency or incubation of a poison or morbific agent.

deliver (de-liv′er). 1. To aid in the process of childbirth. 2. To remove, as the fetus, placenta, or the lens of the eye.

delivery (de-liv′er-e). 1. Expulsion or extraction of the child at birth. 2. Removal of a part, as the placenta or lens. **abdominal d.**, delivery of an infant through an incision made into the uterus through the abdominal wall. **breech d.**, delivery of an infant in breech presentation. See *breech extraction*. **forceps d.**, extraction of the child from the maternal passages by application of forceps to the child's head, without injury to the child or to the mother. **forceps d., high**, forceps delivery in which the forceps is applied to the head before engagement has taken place. **forceps d., low**, forceps delivery in which the forceps is applied when the sagittal suture of the fetal head is in the anteroposterior diameter of the pelvis and the bony portion of the head reaches the perineal floor with pains. **midforceps d.**, forceps delivery in which the forceps is applied after engagement has taken place but before the criteria of low forceps delivery have been met. **postmature d.**, delivery of a postmature infant. **postmortem d.**, birth of a child after the death of the mother. **premature d.**, delivery of a premature infant.

dell (del′). A slight depression or dimple.

delle (del′eh). The clear area in the center of a stained erythrocyte.

delling (del′ing). The formation of a slight depression; dimpling.

delomorphic (del″o-mor′fik). Delomorphous.

delomorphous (del″o-mor′fus) [Gr. *dēlos* evident + *morphē* form]. Having definitely formed and well-defined limits.

Delore's method (da-lorz′) [Xavier *Delore*, French physician, 1828–1916]. Forcible manual correction of genu valgum.

Délorme's operation (da-lormz) [Edmond *Délorme*, Paris surgeon, 1847–1929]. See under *operation*.

delousing (de-lows′ing). The freeing from lice; destruction of lice.

Delpech's abscess, operation (del-pesh′ez) [Jacques Mathieu *Delpech*, French surgeon, 1777–1832]. See under *abscess* and *operation*.

Delphian node [*Delphi*, a town of ancient Greece, the location of the sanctuary and (Delphian) oracle of Apollo]. See under *node*.

delphine (del′fin). Delphinine.

delphinine (del′fĭ-nin). A poisonous alkaloid, $C_{34}H_{47}NO_9$, from the seeds of *Delphinium staphisagria:* used for the most part externally to relieve pain in neuralgia, rheumatism, and paralysis.

Delphinium (del-fin′e-um) [L.]. A genus of ranunculaceous plants, including *D. consolida,* or larkspur, the seeds of which are diuretic, emmenagogue, and poisonous. The seeds of *D. staphisagria,* or stavesacre, are used for destroying lice.

delphinoidine (del″fĭ-noid′in). An alkaloid from the seeds of *Delphinium staphisagria.*

delphisine (del′fĭ-sin). An alkaloid, isomeric with delphinine, from seeds of *Delphinium staphisagria.*

delta (del′tah) [Gr. letter *delta* δ, △]. 1. A triangular space. 2. The fourth letter of the Greek alphabet. See *alpha.* **Galton's d.,** a triangular arrangement of the lines of a fingerprint near the base. **d. mesoscap′ulae,** the triangular area at the root of the spine of the scapula.

delta-cortef (del′tah kor″tef). Trade mark for a preparation of prednisolone.

deltacortisone (del″tah-kor′tĭ-sōn). Prednisone.

deltalin (del′tah-lin). Trade mark for a preparation of synthetic vitamin D_2.

deltasone (del′tah-sōn). Trade mark for a preparation of prednisone.

deltoid (del′toid) [L. *deltoides* triangular]. Of a triangular outline.

deltoiditis (del″toi-di′tis). Inflammation of the deltoid muscle.

deltra (del′trah). Trade mark for a tablet containing prednisone.

de lunatico inquirendo (de lu-nat′ĭ-ko in-kwĭ-ren′do) [L.]. A commission, board, inquisition, or jury appointed by a court for the investigation of the mental condition of a person whose sanity has been disputed.

delusion (de-lu′zhun) [L. *delusio,* from *de* from + *ludus* a game]. A false belief which cannot be corrected by reason. It is logically founded and cannot be corrected by argument or persuasion or even by the evidence of the patient's own senses. Cf. *illusion.* **depressive d.,** delusion in which the patient experiences feelings of uneasiness, unworthiness, and futility. **expansive d.,** a pathologically unreasonable belief in one's own greatness, goodness, or power, encountered in the manic form of manic-depressive psychosis. **d. of grandeur,** delusional conviction of one's own importance, power, wealth, etc., such as is seen in general paresis. **d. of negation,** the delusion that some part of the body is missing or that the world has ceased to exist. **nihilistic d.,** a delusion which denies the existence of something or everything. **d. of persecution,** a morbid belief on the part of a patient that he is being mistreated, slandered, and injured by secret enemies. **d. of reference,** idea of reference. **somatic d.,** a delusion of the patient that there is some alteration in a bodily organ or its function. **systematized d.,** a delusion which is formulated by the patient in a logical manner; a delusion which has a logical structure, especially characteristic of true paranoia. **unsystematized d.,** a delusion made up of disconnected parts.

delusional (de-lu′zhun-al). Pertaining to or characterized by delusions.

delvinal (del′vĭ-nal). Trade mark for preparations of vinbarbital.

demagnetize (de-mag′nĕ-tīz). To deprive of magnetic properties.

demarcation (de″mar-ka′shun) [L. *demarcare* to limit]. The marking off or ascertainment of boundaries. **surface d.,** any dividing line apparent on the surface of a solid body, such as the boundary between living and necrotic tissue.

Demarquay's sign (dem-ar-kāz′) [Jean Nicholas *Demarquay,* a French surgeon, 1811–1875]. See under *sign.*

demasculinization (de-mas″ku-lin-i-za′shun). The loss of normal male characters, with testicular atrophy and involution of the prostate.

Dematium (de-ma′she-um). A genus of fungi, several species of which have been isolated from human lesions.

demecarium (dem″e-ka′re-um). Chemical name: diester of (m-hydroxyphenyl) trimethyammonium: used as a parasympathomimetic, and to reduce intraocular pressure in glaucoma.

demedication (de-med″ĭ-ka′shun). The removal of drugs from the system. **catalytic d., cataphoretic d.,** the removal of foreign matter from the tissues by cataphoresis.

dement (de-ment′). A person affected with dementia (used often in contrast with *ament*).

demented (de-ment′ed). Deprived of reason, mentally deteriorated.

dementia (de-men′she-ah) [*de-* + L. *mens* mind]. A general designation for mental deterioration. **Alzheimer's d.** See under *disease.* **Binswanger d.,** a form of presenile dementia marked by loss of memory and mental hebetude. **chronic d.,** dementia praecox, or schizophrenia. **epileptic d.** See under *psychosis.* **d. myoclon′ica,** mental deterioration occurring in paramyoclonus multiplex. **paralytic d., d. paralyt′ica,** a chronic syphilitic meningoencephalitis, characterized by progressive dementia and a generalized paralysis which is ultimately fatal. Called also *general paresis, general paralysis of the insane, paretic dementia, cerebral tabes,* and *syphilitic meningoencephalitis.* **d. paranoi′des,** the paranoid type of dementia praecox. **paretic d.,** dementia paralytica. **d. prae′cox,** term for a large group of psychoses of psychogenic origin, often recognized during or shortly after adolescence but not infrequently in later maturity. The chief characteristics are disorientation, loss of contact with reality, splitting of the personality (schizophrenia, Bleuler). The types include the simple and the paranoid, and the forms known as *hebephrenia* and *catatonia.* See also *schizophrenia.* **d. praeseni′lis,** dementia beginning at middle age and becoming resolved into one of the senile psychoses. It is due to cerebral arteriosclerosis. **primary d.,** dementia occurring independently of any other form of psychosis. **d. pugilis′tica,** cerebral concussion in a boxer caused by repeated blows to the head. **secondary d.,** dementia following and due to some other form of psychosis. **semantic d.,** inability to experience values and meaning in life. **senile d.,** senile psychosis. **tabetic d.,** that which sometimes follows tabes dorsalis. **terminal d.,** dementia coming on as a final result of nervous or mental disease. **toxic d.,** that which is due to the excessive use of some poisonous drug.

demerol (dem′er-ol). Trade mark for preparations of meperidine.

demethylation (de″meth-ĭ-la′shun). The removal of a methyl group, $—CH_3$, from a compound.

demethylchlortetracycline (de-meth″il-klōr″-tet-rah-si′klēn). A broad-spectrum antibiotic produced by a mutant strain of *Streptomyces aureofaciens;* it is closely related to the other tetracyclines, and differs from chlortetracycline only in the absence of the methyl group in position 6 of the polycyclic nucleus.

demi- [Fr. *demi;* L. *dimidius* half]. A prefix signifying half.

demibain (dem′e-bān) [Fr.]. A half bath, sitz bath, or hip bath.

demic (dem′ik) [Gr. *demas* the living body of man]. Pertaining to the human body; human, as contrasted with *zootic* or pertaining to lower animals.

demifacet (dem″e-fas′et). A small plane surface on either of two bones which both articulate with a third bone. **inferior d. for head of rib,** fovea costalis inferior. **superior d. for head of rib,** fovea costalis superior.

demigauntlet (dem-e-gawnt′let). A form of bandage for the hand and fingers.

demilune (dem′e-lūn). 1. A half moon, or crescent. 2. Crescentic; crescent shaped. **d's of Adamkiewicz,** crescent-shaped cells beneath the neurilemma of medullated nerve fibers. **d's of Giannuzzi, d's of Heidenhain,** crescents of Giannuzzi.

demimonstrosity (dem″e-mon-stros′ĭ-te). Malformation of a part which does not prevent the exercise of its function.

demineralization (de-min″er-al-i-za′shun). Excessive elimination of mineral or inorganic salts, such as is seen in pulmonary tuberculosis and cancer.

demipenniform (dem″e-pen′ĭ-form). Feather-shaped or wing-shaped as to one of the two margins: used of certain muscles.

Democritus (de-mok′rĭ-tus) of Abdera (5th century B.C.). A Greek philosopher who was the first to state that everything in nature, including the body and the soul, is made up of atoms of different sizes and shapes, the movements of which are the cause of life and mental activity.

demodectic (dem-o-dek′tik). Pertaining to, or caused by, Demodex.

Demodex (dem′o-deks) [Gr. *dēmos* fat + *dēx* worm]. A genus of mites or acarids. **D. ca′nis** causes follicular mange in dogs. **D. e′qui,** a species causing a sarcoptic mange in horses. **D. fol-liculo′rum,** a species found in hair follicles and in sebaceous secretions, especially of the face and nose.

Demodex folliculorum (× 100). (Brumpt.)

demodicidosis (dem″o-dis″e-do′sis). Infestation with Demodex.

demogram (de′mo-gram). A graphic representation, in grid form, of the population of a given area according to the time period and the age and sex of the individuals comprising it.

demography (de-mog′rah-fe) [Gr. *dēmos* people + *graphein* to write]. The study of mankind collectively; especially of their geographical distribution and physical environment. **dynamic d.,** collective physiology of communities, with statistics of births, marriages, deaths, etc. **static d.,** collective anatomy of communities and study of their environment.

demoniac (de-mo′ne-ak). 1. Possessed by a demon; frenzied. 2. A lunatic.

demonology (de″mon-ol′o-je) [*demon* + *-logy*]. The earlier approach to problems of mental disorder, by which evil spirits were believed to possess the patient and exorcisms constituted the treatment.

demonomania (de″mon-o-ma′ne-ah) [Gr. *daimōn* demon + *mania* madness]. Monomania in which the patient considers himself possessed of devils.

demonopathy (de″mon-op′ah-the) [Gr. *daimōn* demon + *pathos* disease]. Demonomania.

demonophobia (de″mon-o-fo′be-ah) [Gr. *daimōn* demon + *phobia*]. Morbid fear of demons.

demonstrator (dem′on-stra″tor) [L.]. 1. An instructor who teaches individuals or small groups by using dissections or other aids. 2. The fore-finger.

De Morgan's spots (de-mor′ganz) [Campbell *De Morgan*, English physician, 1811–1876]. See under *spot*.

demorphinization (de-mor″fin-i-za′shun). The gradual depriving of one addicted to the morphine habit of the drug until the habit is cured.

Demours' membrane (da-moorz′) [Pierre *Demours*, French ophthalmologist, 1702–1795]. Lamina limitans posterior corneae.

demucosatio (de″mu-ko-sa′she-o) [L.]. Demucosation. **d. intesti′ni,** demucosation of the intestine.

demucosation (de″mu-ko-sa′shun). Removal of mucous membrane from a part.

demulcent (de-mul′sent). 1. Soothing; bland; allaying the irritation of inflamed or abraded surfaces. 2. A soothing, mucilaginous or oily medicine or application.

demustardization (de-mus″tard-i-za′shun). Treatment of men who have been subjected to the fumes of mustard gas.

demutization (de″mu-ti-za′shun) [*de-* + L. *mutus* mute]. The teaching of deaf children to communicate by lip language or by dactylology.

demyelinate (de-mi′ĕ-lin-āt). To destroy or remove the myelin sheath of a nerve or nerves.

denarcotize (de-nar′ko-tīz). To deprive of narcotine, or of a narcotic.

denatality (de″na-tal′ĭ-te). Decrease in the number of births in proportion to the population.

denaturation (de-na-tūr-a′shun). The destruction of the usual nature of a substance, as the addition of methanol or acetone to alcohol to render it unfit for drinking. **protein d.,** any non-proteolytic change in the chemistry, composition or structure of a native protein which causes it to lose some or all of its unique or specific characteristics.

denatured (de-na′tūrd). Having its nature changed; rendered unfit for human consumption.

dendraxon (den-drak′son) [Gr. *dendron* tree + *axon*]. A nerve cell whose axon breaks up into terminal filaments almost immediately after leaving the cell. Cf. *inaxon*.

dendric (den′drik). Having a dendron or dendrons.

dendriceptor (den′drĭ-sep″tor). One of the sensitive points at the ends of the branching processes of a dendrite, capable of being stimulated by the mittors of other neurons.

dendriform (den′drĭ-form). Branched, or tree-shaped.

dendrite (den′drīt) [Gr. *dendron* tree]. A branched and tree-shaped protoplasmic process from a nerve cell which conducts impulses toward the cell body. Cf. *axon*.

dendritic (den-drit′ik). 1. Branched like a tree. 2. Pertaining to or possessing dendrons.

dendroid (den′droid) [Gr. *dendron* tree + *eidos* form]. Branching like a tree or shrub.

dendron (den′dron) [Gr.]. A dendrite.

dendrophagocytosis (den″dro-fag″o-si-to′sis). The absorption by microglia cells of broken portions of degenerating astrocytes.

dendrophilia (den″dro-fil′e-ah) [Gr. *dendron* tree + *philein* to love]. Erotic love for trees.

denebium (dĕ-ne′be-um). Thulium.

denematize (de-nem′ah-tīz). To remove nematode worms from the infested individual.

denervate (de-ner′vāt). To deprive of a nerve supply.

denervation (de″ner-va′shun). Resection of or removal of the nerves to an organ or part.

dengue (deng′e; Spanish, dān-ga) [Sp.]. An infectious, eruptive, febrile disease, coming on suddenly, and marked by severe pains in the head, eyes, muscles, and joints, sore throat, catarrhal symptoms, and sometimes a cutaneous eruption and painful swellings of the parts. The disease comes on suddenly after an incubation period of from three to six days. The symptoms increase in severity for two or three days, then decrease somewhat, only to increase again on the fourth or fifth day, at which time the eruption appears. It occurs epidemically and sporadically in India, Egypt, Persia, the West Indies, and the South Pacific, and epidemics have occurred in Greece. It is caused by a virus, and is transmitted by the bite of the mosquitoes *Aedes aegypti* and *Aedes albopictus*.

denicotinized (de-nik′o-tin-īzd). Deprived of nicotine.

denidation (den″ĭ-da′shun) [*de-* + L. *nidus* nest]. Degeneration and expulsion of the uterine mucous membrane.

Deniges's test (den-ĭ-zhāz′) [Georges *Denigès*, French chemist, 1859–1951]. See under *tests.*

Denis' method (den′is) [Wiley Glover *Denis*, American biochemist, born 1879]. See under *method.*

denitrification (de-ni″trĭ-fi-ka′shun). The setting free of gaseous nitrogen from nitrites and nitrates.

denitrifier (de-ni′trĭ-fi″er). A bacterium which causes denitrification.

denitrogenation (de-ni″tro-jĕ-na′shun). Removal of the dissolved nitrogen from the body, as a preventive of caisson disease, aero-embolism, etc.

Denman's evolution, version (den′manz) [Thomas *Denman*, English obstetrician, 1733–1815]. See under *evolution.*

Dennett's diet (den′itz) [Roger H. *Dennett*, American pediatrician, 1876–1935]. See under *diet.*

Denonvilliers' aponeurosis, fascia, operation (den-aw-vēl-yāz′) [Charles Pierre *Denonvilliers*, surgeon in Paris, 1808–1872]. See under *fascia* and *operation.*

dens (dens), pl. *den′tes* [L.]. A tooth or toothlike structure; used in official anatomical nomenclature, in the plural, to designate the small bonelike structures of the jaws, serving in the mastication of food and the production of certain sounds in speech. See also *tooth.* **den′tes acus′tici** [N A], elevations along the free surface and margin of the labium limbi vestibulare. **d. acu′tus,** incisor tooth. **d. ax′is** [N A], the toothlike process that projects from the superior surface of the body of the axis, ascending to articulate with the atlas. Called also *d. epistrophei* [B N A], and *odontoid process of axis.* **den′tes cani′ni** [N A, B N A], the four teeth, one on either side in each jaw, immediately lateral to the lateral incisors. Called also *canine teeth.* **den′tes decid′ui** [N A, B N A], the teeth of the first dentition. Called also *deciduous teeth.* **d. epistro′phei** [B N A], d. axis. **den′tes incisi′vi** [N A, B N A], the four front teeth of each jaw. Called also *incisor teeth.* **d. in den′te,** a malformed tooth resulting from invagination of the crown before it is calcified; so named because severe invagination of enamel and dentin gives the appearance of a "tooth within a tooth." **den′tes mola′res** [N A, B N A], the grinders, or double teeth, situated in the back part of either jaw. Called also *molar teeth.* **den′tes permanen′tes** [N A, B N A], the teeth of the second dentition. Called also *permanent teeth.* **den′tes premola′res** [N A], the two permanent teeth on either side of each jaw, between the canine teeth and the molars. Called also *premolar teeth.* **d. sapien′tia,** d. serotinus. **d. seroti′nus** [N A, B N A], the aftermost tooth on each side of each jaw, being the last of the molar teeth to appear. Called also *wisdom tooth.*

densimeter (den-sim′e-ter) [L. *densus* dense + *metrum* measure]. Densitometer.

densitometer (den″sĭ-tom′e-ter). An apparatus for determining the density of a liquid.

densitometry (den″sĭ-tom′e-tre). Determination of variations in density by comparison with that of another material, or with a certain standard.

density (den′sĭ-te) [L. *densitas*]. 1. The quality of being compact or dense. 2. The quantity of matter in a given space. 3. The quantity of electricity in a given area or in a given volume or in a given time. **mosquito d.,** the average number of mosquitoes per person, per room, per house, etc. **parasite d.,** the average parasite count in any particular community, age group, or area.

densography (den-sog′rah-fe). The exact determination of the contrast densities in a roentgen negative by a photo-electric cell.

dent-, denta-. See *dento-.*

dentagra (den-tag′rah, den′tah-grah) [*dent-* + Gr. *agra* seizure]. 1. A forceps or key for extracting teeth. 2. Odontalgia.

dental (den′tal) [L. *dentalis*]. 1. Pertaining to a tooth or teeth. 2. A letter or sound made by or in part by the front teeth.

dentalgia (den-tal′je-ah). Odontalgia.

dentaphone (den′tah-fōn) [*denta-* + Gr. *phōne* sound]. An instrument by means of which deaf persons are enabled to hear sounds propagated through the medium of the teeth.

dentata (den-ta′tah). The second vertebra or axis, so called from its toothlike process.

dentate (den′tāt) [L. *dentatus*]. Having teeth or projections like saw teeth on the edges.

dentatum (den-ta′tum) [L. "toothed"]. The nucleus dentatus.

dentes (den′tēz) [L.]. Plural of *dens.*

denti-, dentia-. See *dento-.*

dentia (den′she-ah) [L.]. A condition relating to development or eruption of the teeth. Used also as a combining form, denoting relationship to the teeth. **d. prae′cox,** premature eruption of the teeth; the presence of teeth in the mouth at birth. **d. tar′da,** delayed eruption of the teeth, beyond the usual time for their appearance.

dentibuccal (den-tĭ-buk′al). Pertaining to the teeth and cheek.

denticle (den′tĭ-kl) [L. *denticulus* a little tooth]. 1. A small toothlike process. 2. A relatively large body of calcified substance in the pulp chamber of a tooth. **adherent d., attached d.,** a calcified formation in a pulp chamber partially fused with the dentin. **embedded d.,** interstitial d. **false d.,** a calcified formation in the pulp chamber of a tooth that does not show the structure of true dentin. **free d.,** a calcified formation in a tooth completely surrounded by the dental pulp. **interstitial d.,** a calcified formation within a tooth, completely surrounded by dentin. **true d.,** a calcified formation in the pulp chamber of a tooth that consists of dentin and shows traces of dentinal tubules and odontoblasts.

denticulated (den-tik′u-lāt″ed) [L. *denticulatus*]. Provided with minute teeth.

dentification (den″tĭ-fi-ka′shun). The formation of dentin or tooth substance.

dentiform (den′tĭ-form). Shaped like a tooth.

dentifrice (den′tĭ-fris) [L. *dentifricium*]. A preparation composed of an inorganic abrasive, detergent, humectant, binder, and flavoring agent, intended to clean and polish the teeth.

dentigerous (den-tij′er-us) [*denti-* + L. *gerere* to carry]. Bearing teeth.

dentilabial (den″tĭ-la′be-al) [*denti-* + L. *labium* lip]. Pertaining to the teeth and lips.

dentilingual (den″tĭ-ling′gwal) [*denti-* + L. *lingua* tongue]. Pertaining to the teeth and tongue.

dentimeter (den-tim′e-ter) [*denti-* + Gr. *metron* measure]. An instrument for measuring teeth.

dentin (den′tin) [L. *dens* tooth]. The chief substance or tissue of the teeth, which surrounds the tooth pulp and is covered by enamel on the crown and by cementum on the roots of the teeth. Called also *dentinum* [N A] and *substantia eburnea dentis* [B N A]. Similar to bone, but harder and denser, it consists of a solid organic substratum, infiltrated with lime salts. Dentin is permeated by numerous branching spiral canaliculi or tubules which contain processes of the connective tissue cells (odontoblasts) that line the pulp cavity. **adventitious d.,** secondary d. **circumpulpar d.,** the inner portion of the dentin, adjacent to the pulp chamber, consisting of thinner fibrils. **cover d.,** the peripheral portion of the dentin, adjacent to the enamel or cementum, consisting of coarser fibers than the circumpulpar dentin. **hereditary opalescent d.,** the brown opalescent-appearing dentin observed in dentinogenesis imperfecta. **interglobular d.,** imperfectly calcified dentinal matrix situated between the calcified globules near the periphery of the dentin. **intermediate d.,** the soft matrix of the predentin. **irregular d.,** secondary d. **mantle d.,** cover d. **primary d.,** the dentin formed before the eruption of a tooth. **sclerotic d.,** transparent d. **secondary d.,** new dentin formed in response to stimuli associated with the normal aging process or with pathological conditions such as caries or injury, or cavity preparation; such dentin is highly irregular in nature. **sensitive d.,** dentin which is highly sensitive owing to distal irritation of the dentinal tubules. **transparent d.,** dentin in which some dentinal tubules have become sclerotic or calcified (dental sclerosis), producing the appearance of translucency.

dentinal (den′tĭ-nal). Pertaining to dentin.

dentinalgia (den″tĭ-nal′je-ah). Pain in the dentin.

dentine (den′tēn). Dentin.

dentinification (den-tin″ĭ-fi-ka′shun). The formation of dentin.

dentinoblast (den′tĭ-no-blast) [*dentin* + Gr. *blastos* germ]. A cell that forms dentin.

dentinoblastoma (den″tĭ-no-blas-to′mah). A tumor of odontogenic origin composed of connective tissue cells of round or spindle shape, among which are islands of irregularly shaped masses of dentin.

dentinogenesis (den″tĭ-no-jen′e-sis) [*dentin* + Gr. *genesis* formation]. The formation of dentin. **d. imperfec′ta,** a hereditary condition characterized by defective formation and calcification of the dentin, giving the teeth a brown opalescent appearance.

dentinogenic (den″tĭ-no-jen′ik). Forming or producing dentin.

dentinoid (den′tĭ-noid). 1. Resembling dentin. 2. A tumor composed of dentin. 3. Predentin.

dentinoma (den″tĭ-no′mah). A tumor of odontogenic origin, consisting mainly of dentin.

dentinosteoid (den″tin-os′te-oid). A tumor composed of or containing dentin and bone.

dentinum (den-ti′num). [N A] The chief substance or tissue of the teeth. See *dentin.* Called also *substantia eburnea dentis* [B N A].

dentiparous (den-tip′ah-rus). Bearing teeth.

dentist (den′tist). A person authorized to practice dentistry. **surgeon d.,** a practitioner of dentistry who has been authorized to surgically excise or remove tooth tissue.

dentistry (den′tis-tre). 1. That department of the healing arts which is concerned with the teeth, oral cavity, and associated structures, including the diagnosis and treatment of their diseases and the restoration of defective and missing tissue. 2. The work done by dentists, such as the creation of restorations, crowns, and bridges, and surgical procedures performed in and about the oral cavity. 3. The practice of the dental profession collectively. **cosmetic d., esthetic d.,** that aspect of dental practice concerned with the repair and restoration of carious, broken, or defective teeth in such a manner as to improve on their original appearance. **forensic d.,** dental jurisprudence. **geriatric d.,** gerodontics. **operative d.,** that phase of dentistry concerned with restoration of parts of the teeth that are defective through disease, trauma, or abnormal development to a state of normal function, health, and esthetics. **pediatric d.,** pedodontics. **preventive d.,** that phase of dentistry concerned with maintenance of a normal masticating mechanism by fortifying the oral cavity against damage and disease. **prosthetic d.,** prosthodontics. **psychosomatic d.,** that phase of dentistry which considers the mind-body relationship.

dentition (den-tish′un) [L. *dentitio*]. The teeth in the dental arch; ordinarily used to designate the natural teeth in position in their alveoli. **artificial d.,** an artificial substitute for the natural teeth. See *denture.* **deciduous d.,** the teeth which erupt first and are later replaced by the permanent teeth. **mixed d.,** the complement of teeth in the jaws after eruption of some of the permanent teeth, before all of the deciduous teeth are shed. **natural d.,** the natural teeth in the dental arch, considered collectively; it may comprise deciduous or permanent teeth, or a mixture of the two, present at one time. **permanent d.,** the teeth which erupt after the deciduous teeth are lost. **primary d.,** deciduous d. **secondary d.,** permanent d. **transitional d.,** mixed d.

dento-, dent-, denta-, denti-, dentia- [L. *dens* tooth]. Combining form denoting relationship to a tooth or to the teeth. Cf. *odonto-.*

dento-alveolar (den″to-al-ve′o-lar). Pertaining to a tooth and its alveolus.

dento-alveolitis (den″to-al″ve-o-li′tis). Periodontal disease.

dentography (den-tog′rah-fe). Odontography.

dentoid (den′toid). Odontoid.

dentoidin (den-toi′din). The organic or albuminous ground substance of a tooth.

dentolegal (den″to-le′gal). Pertaining to dental jurisprudence.

dentoliva (den″to-li′vah) [*dento-* + L. *oliva* olive]. The olivary nucleus.

dentology (den-tol′o-je). Odontology.

dentoma (den-to′mah). Dentinoma.

dentomechanical (den″to-mĕ-kan′i-k′l). Pertaining to the mechanics of dentistry.

dentonomy (den-ton′o-me). Odontonomy.

dentosurgical (den″to-sur′jĭ-k′l). Pertaining to or used in dentistry and surgery.

dentotropic (den″to-trop′ik). Turning toward or having an affinity for tissues composing the teeth.

dentulous (den′tu-lus). Possessing natural teeth.

dentural (den′tu-ral). Pertaining to a denture.

denture (den′tūr) [Fr.; L. *dens* tooth]. An entire set of natural or artificial teeth; ordinarily used to designate an artificial replacement for the natural teeth. **acrylic resin d.,** an artificial denture made of acrylic resin. **artificial d.,** a structure for the replacement of missing natural teeth. **clasp d.,** a partial denture which is retained and stabilized by means of clasps. **complete d.,** an appliance worn in the mouth to replace all the teeth of one jaw, as well as associated structures of the jaw. **continuous gum d.,** a dental substitute in which the teeth are implanted in tinted base material fused to a platinum base. **duplicate d.,** a second denture which is identical with the first. **esthetic d.,** one which is designed to improve the appearance of the patient. **full d.,** complete d. **immediate d., immediate-insertion d.,** an artificial denture made before all the teeth are extracted, and placed immediately after the final extraction. **implant d.,** a denture constructed with a metal framework (substructure) which is embedded within the underlying soft tissues, in contact with the bone, giving stability to and retaining the teeth and overlying material (superstructure) of the appliance. **partial d.,** a prosthetic appliance replacing one or more missing teeth in one jaw, and receiving its support and retention from both the underlying tissues and some or all of the remaining teeth. **partial d., distal extension,** a removable partial denture that is retained by natural teeth at one end of the base segments only, a portion of the functional load being carried by the residual ridge. **partial d., fixed,** an appliance for replacement of one or more natural teeth, primarily supported by natural teeth or roots to which it is permanently attached, so that it is not readily removed by patient or dentist. **partial d., removable,** an appliance for the replacement of one or more natural teeth, so constructed that it may readily be removed and replaced in the mouth. **partial d., unilateral,** an appliance for the replacement of one or more natural teeth on the same side of the jaw. **permanent d.,** a term applied to an artificial denture that is constructed and inserted after the oral tissues have healed and the condition of the alveolar ridges has become fairly stabilized. **trial d.,** an artificial denture fabricated for placement in the patient's mouth for verification of its esthetic qualities, the making of records, or other procedures before the final denture is completed. **wax model d.,** one fabricated in wax for use as a trial denture.

Denucé's ligament (den-u-sāz') [Jean Henri Maurice *Denucé,* French surgeon, 1859–1924]. See under *ligament.*

denucleated (de-nu'kle-āt"ed). Deprived of the nucleus.

denudation (den"u-da'shun) [L. *denudare* to make bare]. The act of laying bare; the deprival of a surface of its epithelial covering, by surgery, trauma, or pathologic change.

denutrition (de"nu-trish'un). A withdrawal or failure of the nutritive processes, with consequent atrophy and degeneration.

Denys' tuberculin (den-ēs') [Joseph *Denys,* Belgian bacteriologist (Louvain), died 1932]. See under *tuberculin.*

deobstruent (de-ob'stroo-ent) [L. *de* priv. + *obstruere* to block up]. 1. Removing obstructions or obstructive material. 2. An agent that removes obstructions.

deodorant (de-o'der-ant) [L. *de* from + *odorare* to perfume]. 1. Removing undesirable or offensive odors. 2. A substance that destroys offensive odors.

deodorize (de-o'der-īz) [L. *de* from + *odor* odor]. To deprive of odor.

deodorizer (de-o'der-īz-er). A deodorizing agent.

deolepsy (de'o-lep"se) [L. *deus* god + Gr. *lēpsis* seizure]. Belief that one is possessed by a god.

deontology (de"on-tol'o-je) [Gr. *deonta* things that ought to be done + *-logy*]. The science of professional duties and etiquette.

deoppilant (de-op'ĭ-lant). Removing obstructions.

deoppilation (de-op"ĭ-la'shun) [L. *de* away + *oppilatio* obstruction]. The removal of obstructions.

deorsum (de-or'sum) [L.]. Downward.

deorsumduction (de-or"sum-duk'shun) [L. *deorsum* downward + *ducere* to lead]. The turning down of a part, as of the eyes.

deorsumvergence (de-or"sum-ver'jens). A downward movement, especially of the eyes.

deorsumversion (de-or"sum-ver'zhun) [L. *deorsum* downward + *vertere* to turn]. An act of turning or directing downward; especially the simultaneous and equal downward turning of both eyes.

deossification (de-os"ĭ-fi-ka'shun) [L. *de* from + *os* bone + *facere* to make]. Loss of or removal of the mineral elements of bone.

deoxidation (de-ok"sĭ-da'shun) [L. *de* from + *oxygen*]. The removal of oxygen from a chemical compound.

deoxidize (de-ok'sĭ-dīz). To deprive of chemically combined oxygen.

deoxy- (de-ok'se). A prefix used in naming chemical compounds, to designate a compound containing one less atom of oxygen than the reference substance. For words beginning thus see also those beginning *desoxy-.*

deoxygenation (de-ok"sĭ-jen-a'shun). The act of depriving of oxygen.

deoxyribonuclease (de-ok"se-ri"bo-nu'kle-ās) [*deoxyribonucleic* acid + *-ase*]. An enzyme which catalyzes the depolymerization of deoxyribonucleic acid. See also *dornase.*

deoxyribose (de-ok"se-ri'bōs). An aldopentose, $CH_2.OH.(CHOH)_2.CH_2.CHO$, found in thymus nucleic acid.

Dep. Abbreviation for L. *depura'tus,* purified.

depancreatize (de-pan'kre-ah-tīz). To deprive of the pancreas, as by operation.

dependence (de-pend'ens). The total psychophysical state of an addict in which the usual or increasing doses of the drug are required to prevent the onset of abstinence symptoms.

dependency (de-pen'den-se). The quality of being dependent. **cortical d.,** that part of the brain stem which is developed as a subsidiary of the cerebral cortex.

depepsinized (de-pep'sin-īzd). Deprived of pepsin; peptically inactivated: said of gastric juice.

depersonalization (de-per"sun-al-i-za'shun). Loss of the sense of personal identity, or of personal ownership of the parts of one's body.

dephlogisticate (de"flo-jis'tĭ-kāt). To reduce inflammation in.

dephosphorylation (de-fos"for-i-la'shun) [*de-* + *phosphorylation*]. Removal of the trivalent PO group from organic molecules.

depigmentation (de"pig-men-ta'shun). The removal of pigment.

depilate (dep'ĭ-lāt) [L. *de* away + *pilus* hair]. To remove the hair from.

depilation (dep"ĭ-la'shun). The process of removing hair; epilation.

depilatory (de-pil'ah-to-re) [L. *de* from + *pilus* hair]. 1. Having the power to remove the hair. 2. An agent for removing or destroying the hair. **Atkinson's d.,** 6 parts of quicklime, 1 part of orpiment mixed with flour and colored yellow.

deplasmolysis (de"plaz-mol'ĭ-sis). Return to the initial volume, after plasmolysis, of the protoplasm of a cell in hypertonic solution.

deplete (de-plēt') [L. *deplere* to empty]. To empty; to unload; to cause depletion.

depletion (de-ple'shun) [L. *deplere* to empty]. 1. The act or process of emptying; removal of a fluid, as the blood. 2. Exhausted state which results from excessive loss of blood. **plasma d.,** plasmapheresis.

deplumation (dep"loo-ma'shun) [L. *de* from + *pluma* down]. Loss of the eyelashes by disease.

depolarization (de-po"lar-i-za'shun). The process or act of neutralizing polarity.

depolarize (de-po'lar-īz) [L. *de* from + *polus* pole]. To reduce to a nonpolarized condition; to deprive of polarity.

depolarizer (de-po'lar-īz"er). A chemical agent placed in a galvanic cell for preventing the accumulation of gas upon either of the plates.

depolymerization (de-pol"e-mer-i-za'shun). The conversion of a compound into one of smaller molecular weight and different physical properties without changing the percentage relationships of the elements composing it.

depolymerize (de-pol'e-mer-īz). To cause to undergo depolymerization.

deposit (de-poz'it) [L. *de* down + *ponere* to place]. 1. Sediment or dregs. 2. Extraneous inorganic matter collected in the tissues or in a viscus or cavity. 3. In dentistry, hard or soft material adherent to the surface of a tooth.

depositive (de-poz'ĭ-tiv). Depositing: said of the condition in which lymph is exuded into the derma, forming papules.

depo-testosterone (de"po-tes-tos'ter-ōn). Trade mark for a sustained-action preparation of testosterone.

depravation (dep"rah-va'shun) [L. *depravare* to vitiate; *de* down + *pravus* bad]. Deterioration; a change for the worse.

depraved (de-prāvd'). Vitiated or perverted.

deprementia (dep"re-men'she-ah). A psychosis marked by depression, impairment of memory, etc.

depressant (de-pres'ant). 1. Diminishing functional activity. 2. An agent that reduces functional activity and the vital energies in general by producing muscular relaxation and diaphoresis. **cardiac d.,** an agent that depresses the rate and force of contraction of the heart.

depressed (de-prest'). Carried below the normal level; associated with depression.

depressing (de-pres'ing). Couching.

depression (de-presh'un) [L. *depressio; de* down

+ *premere* to press]. 1. A hollow or depressed area. 2. Downward or inward displacement. 3. A lowering or decrease of functional activity. 4. Absence of cheerfulness or hope: emotional dejection. **auricular d.,** great lowering in the sphygmographic tracing of the venous pulse, representing the diastole of the right auricle. **averse d.,** depression tending to rut formation with evidence of judgment defect. **aversion d.,** depression characterized by aversion to the facts of the illness and to the medical attention which it involves. **d. of cataract,** couching. **otic d.,** auditory pit. **pacchionian d's,** foveolae granulares. **postdormital d.,** mental depression following awakening from sleep. **precordial d.** See *scrobiculus cordis.* **pterygoid d.,** pterygoid pit. **radial d.,** a fossa on the anterior surface of the humerus, just above the radial head. **reactive d.,** depression which is caused by some external situation and is relieved when that situation is removed. **retarded d.,** the depressive phase of manic-depressive psychosis. **supratrochlear d.,** a slight depression on the anterior surface of the femur, above the trochlea. **systolic d.,** a falling of the precordial region of the chest observed during the systole. **ventricular d.,** that part of the venous pulse tracing which lies between the ventricular and auricular waves.

depressive (de-pres′iv). Causing depression.

depressomotor (de-pres″o-mo′tor) [L. *deprimere* to press down + *motor* mover]. 1. Retarding or abating motion. 2. An agent which lessens or depresses motor activity.

depressor (de-pres′or) [L.]. That which depresses, as a muscle, agent, instrument, or apparatus which depresses, or afferent nerve whose stimulation causes a fall of blood pressure. **d. an′guli o′ris.** See *Table of Musculi.* **d. epiglot′tidis,** a portion of the thyroepiglotticus muscle which depresses the epiglottis. **d. la′bii inferio′ris.** See *Table of Musculi.* **Sims's d.,** a loop of stout wire used in depressing the anterior vaginal wall in examinations. **tongue d.,** an instrument for pressing the tongue against the floor of the mouth.

deprimens oculi (dep′re-menz ok′u-le) [L.]. Musculus rectus inferior bulbi.

deprivation (dep-rĭ-va′shun) [L. *de* from + *priva′re* to remove]. Loss or absence of parts, organs, powers, or things that are needed.

deproteinization (de-pro″te-in-i-za′shun). Removal of protein.

depside (dep′sīd). One of a class of compounds which are products of the condensation of two or more molecules of the oxyacids of benzene, e.g., digallic acid.

depth (depth). An expression of the distance separating the upper and lower surfaces of an object. **focal d.,** the measure of the power of a lens to yield clear images of objects at different distances from it.

depula (dep′u-lah) [L., from Gr. *depas* goblet]. The developing egg in the stage succeeding the blastula and preceding the gastrula.

depulization (de″pu-lĭ-za′shun) [L. *de* away + *pulex* flea]. The destruction of fleas in infested dwellings.

depurant (dep′u-rant). 1. Cleansing or purifying. 2. An agent that cleanses or purifies.

depurate (dep′u-rāt) [L. *depurare* to purify]. To cleanse, refine, or purify.

depurative (dep′u-ra″tiv). Tending to purify or cleanse.

depurator (dep′u-ra″tor). 1. An agent that cleanses or purifies. 2. A vacuum-producing apparatus for stimulating the excretory function of the skin.

De R. Symbol for *reaction of degeneration.*

der- (der) [Gr. *derē* neck]. Combining form denoting relationship to the neck.

deradelphus (der-ah-del′fus) [*der-* + Gr. *adelphos* brother]. A fetal monster made up of twins fused at or near the navel, and having only one head.

deradenitis (der″ad-ĕ-ni′tis) [*der-* + Gr. *adēn* gland]. Inflammation of the glands of the neck.

deradenoncus (der″ad-ĕ-nong′kus) [*der-* + Gr. *adēn* gland + *onkos* bulk]. A swelling of a gland of the neck.

deranencephalia (der-an″en-se-fa′le-ah) [*der-* + *an* neg. + Gr. *enkephalos* brain]. Monstrosity marked by defect of the brain and upper part of the spinal cord.

derangement (de-rānj′ment). 1. Mental disorder. 2. Disarrangement of a part or organ. **Hey's internal d.,** partial dislocation of the knee, marked by great pain and spasm of the muscles.

Dercum's disease (der′kumz) [Francis Xavier *Dercum,* American physician, 1856–1931]. Adiposis dolorosa.

dereism (de′re-izm) [L. *de* away + *res* thing]. Mental activity in which fantasy runs on unhampered by reality.

dereistic (de″re-is′tik). Pertaining to or characterized by dereism.

derencephalocele (der″en-se-fal′o-sēl) [*der-* + Gr. *enkephalos* brain + *kēlē* hernia]. Protrusion of the brain substance through a slit in one or more of the cervical vertebrae.

derencephalus (der″en-sef′ah-lus) [*der-* + Gr. *enkephalos* brain]. A fetal monster with rudimentary skull bones and bifid cervical vertebrae, the brain resting in the bifurcation.

derepression (de″re-presh′un). Elevation of the level of an enzyme above the normal, either by lowering of the corepressor concentration or by a mutation that decreases the formation of aporepressor or the response to the complete repressor.

deric (der′ik) [Gr. *deros* skin]. Pertaining to the ectoderm; dermic.

dericin (der′ĭ-sin). A light-colored oil derived from castor oil.

derism (de′rizm). Dereism.

derivant (der′ĭ-vant). Derivative.

derivation (der″ĭ-va′shun) [L. *derivatio,* from *derivare* to draw off]. 1. The process or act of drawing off, as the withdrawal of blood, or the removal of a disease process to another part. 2. The origination of a substance from its source. 3. A lead in electrocardiography.

derivative (de-riv′ah-tiv). 1. Producing or causing a derivation. 2. A chemical substance derived from another substance either directly or by modification or partial substitution. 3. An agent which withdraws blood from the seat of a disease.

derma (der′mah) [Gr.]. The skin, sometimes used with special reference to the corium.

derma-. See *dermato-.*

Dermacentor (der″mah-sen′tor) [*derma-* + Gr. *kentein* to prick, stab]. A genus of ticks which are important as the transmitters of disease. **D. albipic′tus,** a species of brown ticks widely distributed in the United States, parasitic in cattle, horses, deer, elk, and moose, in which it may cause severe anemia and sometimes death. Called also *winter tick.* **D. anderso′ni,** a reddish-brown tick which is responsible for transmitting Rocky Mountain spotted fever to man and for causing tick paralysis and tularemia. Its hosts include deer, elk, antelope, grizzly bear, porcupine, prairie dog, and various species of rabbits. Called also *Rocky Mountain wood tick.* **D. hal′li,** a yellow-brown tick found on peccaries in Texas. **D. hun′teri,** a brown tick found on Rocky Mountain sheep in southwestern United States, particularly in southwestern

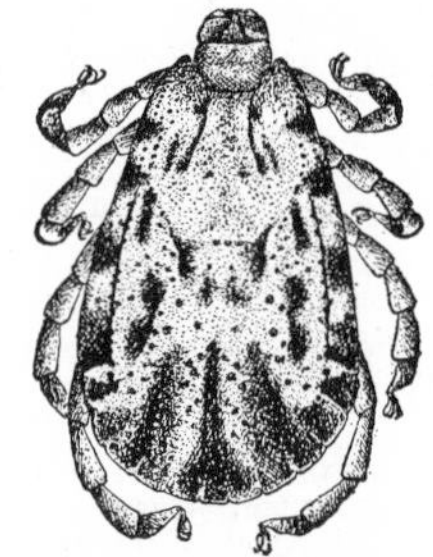

Dermacentor andersoni (Chandler).

Arizona. **D. margina'tus, D. modes'tus,** *D. parumapertus.* **D. ni'tens,** *Otocentor nitens.* **D. occidenta'lis,** a brown tick found widely distributed along the west coast of the United States, from southwestern Oregon to southern California, the principal hosts being the cow, horse, deer, dog, and man. Called also *Pacific coast tick.* **D. parumaper'tus,** a reddish brown tick which is found widely distributed in the southwestern United States, found on deer and coyotes, and abundant on various species of rabbits. **D. reticula'tus,** a tick which attacks sheep and oxen, occurring in Europe, Asia, and America. **D. varia'bilis,** a dark brown tick found along the California coast and widely distributed east of the Rocky Mountains, the dog being the principal host of the adults, which are found also on cattle, horses, rabbits, and man. Called also *American dog tick.* **D. venus'tus,** *D. andersoni.*

Dermacentroxenus (der″mah-sen″trok-se'nus) [*Dermacentor* + Gr. *xenos* a guest-friend]. A genus name formerly given microorganisms parasitic in ticks, now included in the genus Rickettsia; later used as the name of a subgenus including the species *R. a'kari, R. austra'lis, R. cono'rii,* and *R. rickett'sii.* **D. a'kari,** *Rickettsia akari.* **D. austra'lis,** *Rickettsia australis.* **D. cono'ri,** *Rickettsia conorii.* **D. orienta'lis,** *Rickettsia tsutsugamushi.* **D. pijpe'ri,** *Rickettsia conorii.* **D. rickett'si,** *Rickettsia rickettsii.* **D. siber'icus,** a name proposed for the tick-borne agent causing tick typhus in Siberia, thought to be identical with *Rickettsia conorii.* **D. ty'phi,** *Rickettsia typhi.*

dermad (der'mad). Toward the integument.

dermadrome (der'mah-drōm) [*derma-* + Gr. *dromos* a running]. Wiener's name for any skin manifestation of internal disorder; the cutaneous part of a syndrome.

dermagen (der'mah-jen). A reagin or antibody circulating in the blood responsible for specific skin reactions.

dermagraph (der'mah-graf). 1. Dermatograph. 2. Dermograph.

dermagraphy (der-mag'rah-fe). Dermatography.

dermahemia (der″mah-he'me-ah). Dermathemia.

dermal (der'mal). Of or pertaining to the skin.

dermalaxia (der″mah-lak'se-ah) [*derma-* + Gr. *malaxis* softening]. Softening of the skin.

dermalgia (der-mal'je-ah). Dermatalgia.

dermametropathism (der″mah-me-trop'ah-thizm). The diagnosis of disease by observing the character of the markings that result from pressure on the skin with some blunt instrument.

dermamyiasis (der″mah-mi-i'ah-sis) [*derma-* + Gr. *myia* fly]. Disease of the skin caused by flies. **d. linea'ris mi'grans oestro'sa,** larva migrans.

dermanaplasty (der-man'ah-plas″te) [*derma-* + Gr. *anaplassein* to form again]. Skin grafting.

Dermanyssus (der″mah-nis'sus) [*derma-* + Gr. *nyssein* to prick]. A genus of mites. **D. a'vium et galli'nae,** the bird mite, poultry mite, or chicken louse, which sometimes infests man.

dermapostasis (der″mah-pos'tah-sis) [*derma-* + Gr. *apostasis* a falling away]. A skin disease with abscess formation.

dermaskeleton (der″mah-skel'ĕ-ton). Exoskeleton.

dermat-. See *dermato-.*

dermatalgia (der″mah-tal'je-ah) [*dermat-* + *-algia*]. Pain in the skin with no local lesion: of reflex origin or due to a nervous disease.

dermataneuria (der″mat-ah-nu're-ah) [*dermat-* + Gr. *neuron* nerve]. Disorder of the nerve supply of the skin.

dermatatrophia (der″mat-ah-tro'fe-ah). Dermatrophia.

dermatauxe (der″mah-tawk'se) [*dermat-* + Gr. *auxē* increase]. Hyperemia of the skin.

dermatergosis (der″mat-er-go'sis) [*dermat-* + Gr. *ergon* work]. Any occupational affection of the skin.

dermathemia (der″mat-he'me-ah) [*dermat-* + Gr. *haima* blood + *-ia*]. Hyperemia of the skin.

dermatic (der-mat'ik). Dermal.

dermatitides (der″mah-tit'ĭ-dēz). Plural of *dermatitis.*

dermatitis (der″mah-ti'tis), pl. *dermatit'ides* [*dermato-* + *-itis*]. Inflammation of the skin. **actinic d.,** dermatitis resulting from exposure to actinic radiation, such as that from the sun, or ultraviolet waves. **d. aestiva'lis,** a dermatitis coming on in hot weather. **allergic d.,** any inflammation of the skin believed to be due to allergy. If the allergen is contacted externally it may be termed *extrinsic;* if the allergen is carried to the skin through the blood or lymph, it is *intrinsic.* **d. ambustio'nis,** dermatitis due to a burn, scald, or sunburn. **ancylostome d.,** ground itch. **arsphenamine d.,** dermatitis resulting from use of arsphenamine. **d. artefac'ta,** a condition of the skin characterized by the presence of lesions that are self-inflicted by the patient, as by heat, chemicals, or other physical or mechanical means. **atopic d.,** allergic eczema. **d. atroph'icans,** diffuse atrophy of the skin. **berlock d.,** berloque d. **berloque d.,** pigmentation and erythema of the skin, principally of the face and neck, occurring in drop-shaped or quadrilateral patches or streaks, as a result of sensitization caused by eau de cologne or other toilet articles containing ethereal oils. **bhiwanol d.,** dhobie itch. **blastomycetic d.,** a morbid condition of the skin caused by *Blastomycetes dermatitidis* and characterized by the presence of suppurating tumors. **brown-tail moth d.,** a cutaneous irritation produced by the hairs of the brown-tail moth, *Euproctis chrysorrhoea.* **brucella d.,** dermatitis occurring in veterinarians and stockmen who come in contact with cows affected with infectious abortion (brucellosis). **d. bullo'sa,** a vesicobullous eruption on the skin. **d. calor'ica,** inflammation of the skin due to heat or cold. **caterpillar d.,** a transient but sometimes painful dermatitis caused by contact with caterpillars. **d. combustio'nis,** d. ambustionis. **d. congelatio'nis,** dermatitis due to cold or frostbite; chilblain. **contact d.,** d. venenata. **d. contusifor'mis,** erythema nodosum. **cosmetic d.,** dermatitis caused by some ingredient in a cosmetic preparation. **dhobie mark d.,** dhobie itch. **diaper d.,** napkin area d. **d. dysmenorrhoe'ica,** a rosacea-like eruption on the cheeks of women, recurring during menstrual periods. **d. epidem'ica,** an epidemic disease marked by blotches or patches which become confluent and form a red, desquamating patch. It is attended with itching and burning. **d. erythemato'sa,** erythema. **d. escharot'ica,** severe and destructive dermatitis caused by contact with acids, alkalies and metallic salts. **d. excoriati'va infan'tum,** inflammatory excoriation of the skin in infants. **d. exfoliati'va,** a skin disease characterized by very extensive scaling, itching, abnormal redness, and loss of hair. **d. exfoliati'va epidem'ica,** d. epidemica. **d. exfoliati'va neonátorum,** a rare severe exfoliative skin inflammation affecting infants. **exfoliative d.,** d. exfoliativa. **exudative discoid and lichenoid d.,** a disease seen in older men, characterized by the development of an itching oval or disk-shaped plaque, which later becomes a widespread dermatitis, followed by oozing and lichenification. **d. facti'tia, factitial d., d. fic'ta,** d. artefacta. **flannel moth d.,** dermatitis caused by contact with the so-called flannel moth *Megalopyge.* **d. gangreno'sa,** gangrene of the skin. **d. gangreno'sa infan'tum,** disseminated gangrene of the skin of infants. **glue d.,** dermatitis in workers in plywood and wood laminating plants, caused by the irritation of glue. **guayule d.,** a dermatitis produced by contact with the leaves of the Mexican rubber plant or guayule (*Parthenium argentatum*).

halowax d., chloracne. **d. hemostat'ica,** d. hypostatica. **d. herpetifor'mis,** dermatitis marked by grouped, erythematous, papular, vesicular, pustular, or bullous lesions occurring in varied combinations, accompanied by burning and itching. **d. hiema'lis,** a dermatitis coming on with cold weather. **d. hypostat'ica,** a blotchy mottling and pigmentation of the skin due to passive congestion. **industrial d.,** a dermatitis caused by the material used in the industry in which the patient is employed. **d. infectio'sa eczematoi'des,** a pustular eczematoid eruption frequently following or occurring coincidentally with some pyogenic process. **insect d.,** dermatitis caused by the irritant hairs of certain insects, especially moths and caterpillars. **io-moth d.,** dermatitis caused by the irritant hairs of the larva of *Automeris io*. **Jacquet's d.,** an eruption of papules and vesicles formed by erosions on the diaper region of infants. **d. lichenoi'des chron'ica atroph'icans,** lichen sclerosus et atrophicus. **livedoid d.,** a condition marked by painful swelling of the buttocks with a reddish or bluish coloration, caused by gluteal injection of a drug. **malignant d., malignant papillary d.,** Paget's disease of the nipple. **d. medicamento'sa,** dermatitis caused by the action of drugs. **d. micropapulo'sa erythemato'sa hyperidrot'ica na'si,** granulosis rubra nasi. **d. multifor'mis,** dermatitis herpetiformis. **mycotic d.,** dermatitis caused by yeast infections. **napkin area d.,** d. of the gluteal region of infants due to ammonia formed in the wet diaper. **d. nodo'sa,** a papular dermatitis with abundant lesions on the legs and arms: it is related to craw-craw. **d. nodula'ris necrot'ica,** a chronic recurrent dermatitis with hemorrhagic lesions, sometimes attended by mild constitutional symptoms. **occupational d.,** a dermatitis caused by the material employed in the patient's occupation. **onion mite d.,** a dermatitis affecting handlers of decaying onions, caused by the onion mite, *Acarus rhyzoglypticus hyacinthi*. **d. papilla'ris capilli'tii,** keloidal folliculitis. **d. pediculoi'des ventrico'sus,** straw itch. **perfume d.,** berloque d. **pigmented purpuric lichenoid d.,** a dermatitis of the extremities, especially the lower ones, characterized by papules which become purpuric or pigmented. **precancerous d.,** Bowen's disease. **d. psoriasifor'mis nodula'ris,** the guttate variety of parapsoriasis. **purpuric pigmented lichenoid d.,** a chronic superficial dermatosis marked by tiny rust colored papules which fuse into plaques. **radiation d.,** radiodermatitis. **rat-mite d.,** dermatitis resulting from the bite of *Liponyssus bacoti*. **d. re'pens,** acrodermatitis continua. **roentgen-ray d.,** radiodermatitis resulting from exposure to the roentgen rays. **satinwood d.,** dermatitis occurring among workers in satinwood, a fine-grained wood used in cabinet-making. **d. schamber'gi,** grain itch. **schistosome d.,** an itching dermatitis caused by penetration into the skin of larval forms (cercaria) of schistosomes. It occurs in bathers and waders in waters infested with these organisms. **seborrheic d., d. seborrhe'ica,** an inflammatory disease of the skin characterized by yellowish, greasy scaling of the skin of the scalp, mid-parts of the face, ears, and supra-orbital regions, and usually accompanied by itching. **d. sim'plex,** erythema. **d. skiagraph'ica,** roentgen-ray d. **d. sola'ris,** inflammation of the skin resulting from excessive exposure to rays of the sun. **straw-mat d.,** grain itch. **swimmer d.,** schistosome d. **tetryl d.,** an occupational eruption which results from working with tetryl. **d. traumat'ica,** a form due to local injury or bruising. **uncinarial d.,** an irritation of the skin due to the entrance of the larvae of hookworm. **vanilla d.,** dermatitis from handling vanilla beans. **d. veg'etans,** a condition characterized by the growth of red fungous masses on eczematous areas, as a result of superimposed staphylococcal infection. **d. venena'ta,** an acute allergic inflammation of the skin caused by contact with various substances of a chemical, animal, or vegetable nature. **d. verruco'sa,** chromoblastomycosis. **weeping d.,** an oozing inflammation of the skin produced by scratching to relieve intense itching. **x-ray d.,** radiodermatitis resulting from exposure to x-rays (roentgen radiation).

dermato-, derma-, dermat-, dermo- [Gr. *derma, dermatos* skin]. Combining forms denoting relationship to the skin.

dermato-autoplasty (der″mah-to-aw′to-plas″te) [*dermato-* + Gr. *autos* self + *plassein* to mold]. The grafting on denuded areas of skin taken from some other portion of the patient's own body.

Dermatobia (der″mah-to′be-ah) [*dermato-* + Gr. *bios* life]. A genus of warble flies of the family Oestridae. **D. hom'inis,** the human botfly of South America whose larvae (called ver macaque or ver moyocuil) are parasitic in the skin of man, mammals and birds. The eggs are deposited by the female on the bodies of mosquitoes, flies or ticks and by them transported to the host.

Dermatobia.

dermatobiasis (der″mah-to-bi′ah-sis). The presence of Dermatobia in the body.

dermatocele (der′mah-to-sēl″) [*dermato-* + Gr. *kēlē* hernia]. Dermatolysis. **d. lipomato'sa,** lipoma showing cystic degeneration.

dermatocelidosis (der″mah-to-sel″ĭ-do′sis). Dermatokelidosis.

dermatocellulitis (der″mah-to-sel″u-li′tis) [*dermato-* + *cellulitis*]. Inflammation of the skin and subcutaneous cellular tissue.

Dermatocentor (der″mah-to-sen′tor). Dermacentor.

dermatochalasis (der″mah-to-kal′ah-sis) [*dermato-* + Gr. *chalasthai* to become slack]. Abnormal relaxation or looseness of the skin.

dermatoconiosis (der″mah-to-ko″ne-o′sis) [*dermato-* + Gr. *konis* dust]. Any skin affection caused by dust.

dermatoconjunctivitis (der″mah-to-kon-junk″tĭ-vi′tis). Inflammation of the conjunctiva and of the skin around the eyes.

dermatocyst (der′mah-to-sist) [*dermato-* + *cyst*]. A cyst of the skin.

dermatodynia (der″mah-to-din′e-ah) [*dermato-* + Gr. *odynē* pain]. Dermatalgia.

dermatodysplasia (der″mah-to-dis-pla′ze-ah). A condition characterized by abnormal development of the skin. **d. verrucifor'mis,** a generalized eruption of warts.

dermatofibroma (der″mah-to-fi-bro′mah). A fibroma of the skin. **d. protu'berans,** a large-sized molluscum growth that tends to recur after incision.

dermatofibrosarcoma (der″mah-to-fi″bro-sar-ko′mah). A fibrosarcoma of the skin. **d. protu'berans,** dermatofibroma protuberans.

dermatofibrosis (der″mah-to-fi-bro′sis). A condition characterized by fibrotic changes in the skin. **d. lenticula'ris dissemina'ta,** a hereditary condition of the skin associated with osteopoikilosis and marked by the presence of papular fibromas over the back, arms, and thighs.

dermatogen (der-mat′o-jen). An antigen of any skin disease.

dermatogenic (der″mah-to-jen′ik). Dermatogenous.

dermatogenous (der″mah-toj′e-nus). Producing skin; producing a skin disease.

dermatoglyphics (der″mah-to-glif′iks) [*dermato-* + Gr. *glyphein* to carve]. The study of the patterns of ridges of the skin of the fingers, palms, toes, and soles; successively of anatomical and anthropological interest, an instrument for establishment of identification, and later assuming importance as a tool in medicine, both clinically and as a genetic indicator.

dermatograph (der-mat′o-graf) [*dermato-* + Gr. *graphein* to write]. 1. An instrument for marking or writing on the skin as in marking the boundaries of the body. 2. Dermograph.

dermatographia (der″mah-to-graf′e-ah). Dermographia.

dermatographism (der-mah-tog′rah-fizm). Dermographia.

dermatography (der-mah-tog′rah-fe) [*dermato-* + Gr. *graphein* to write]. 1. A description of the skin. 2. Dermographia.

dermatoheteroplasty (der″mah-to-het′er-o-plas″te) [*dermato-* + Gr. *heteros* other + *plassein* to form]. The grafting of skin derived from the body of another individual.

dermatoid (der′mah-toid) [*dermato-* + Gr. *eidos* form]. Skinlike.

dermatokelidosis (der″mah-to-kel″ĭ-do′sis) [*dermato-* + Gr. *kēlidoun* to stain]. A spotted condition of the skin.

dermatokoniosis (der″mah-to-ko″ne-o′sis). Dermatoconiosis.

dermatologist (der″mah-tol′o-jist). An individual skilled in dermatology.

dermatology (der″mah-tol′o-je). The branch of medicine concerned with the diagnosis and treatment of diseases of the skin.

dermatolysis (der″mah-tol′ĭ-sis) [*dermato-* + Gr. *lysis* loosening]. Hypertrophy of the skin and subcutaneous tissues, with a tendency of the skin to hang in folds. **d. palpebra′rum,** blepharochalasis.

dermatoma (der″mah-to′mah) [*dermat-* + *-oma*]. An abnormal or perverted growth of skin tissue. **corneal d.,** a tumorous growth upon the cornea of animals: its surface contains hair.

dermatome (der′mah-tōm) [*derma-* + Gr. *temnein* to cut]. 1. An instrument for incising the skin, or for cutting thin skin transplants. 2. A sensory root field on the skin; the area of skin supplied with afferent nerve fibers by a single posterior spinal root. 3. The lateral portion of a mesodermal somite; the cutis plate. **Padgett d.,** an instrument for cutting thick-split skin grafts which enables the surgeon to cut a sheet of skin of any size up to 4 × 7½ inches and of any desired thickness. **Reese d.,** an instrument for cutting split skin grafts of 0.008 to 0.034 inch in thickness.

dermatomegaly (der″mah-to-meg′ah-le). A condition in which the skin is larger than is necessary to cover the body, so that it hangs in folds; it may occur as a rare congenital anomaly or physiologically with old age.

dermatomere (der′mah-to-mēr) [*dermato-* + Gr. *meros* part]. Any segment or metamere of the embryonic integument.

dermatomic (der″mah-tom′ik). Pertaining to a dermatome.

dermatomucosomyositis (der″mah-to-mu-ko″-so-mi″o-si′tis). Inflammation involving the skin, the mucous membrane of the mouth, throat and nose, and the muscles.

dermatomyces (der″mah-to-mi′sēz). Dermatophyte.

dermatomycin (der″mah-to-mi′sin). An antigen used in the diagnosis, prophylaxis, and treatment of dermatomycosis.

dermatomycosis (der″mah-to-mi-ko′sis) [*dermato-* + Gr. *mykes* fungus]. A superficial infection of the skin or its appendages by fungi of the genera *Trichophyton, Microsporum* and *Epidermophyton.* The term includes dermatophytosis and the various clinical forms of tinea. **blastomycetic d.,** blastomycosis of the skin. **d. furfura′cea,** pityriasis versicolor. **d. microspori′na,** tinea versicolor. **d. trichophy′tina,** tinea trichophytina.

dermatomyiasis (der″mah-to-mi-i′ah-sis). Dermamyiasis.

dermatomyoma (der″mah-to-mi-o′mah) [*dermato-* + *myoma*]. A myoma of the skin.

dermatomyositis (der″mah-to-mi″o-si′tis) [*dermato-* + Gr. *mys* muscle + *-itis*]. A non-suppurative inflammation of the skin, subcutaneous tissue, and underlying muscle.

dermatonecrotic (der″mah-to-ne-krot′ik). Dermonecrotic.

dermatoneurology (der″mah-to-nu-rol′o-je) [*dermato-* + Gr. *neuron* nerve + *-logy*]. The study of the nerves of the skin in health and disease.

dermatoneurosis (der″mah-to-nu-ro′sis) [*dermato-* + *neurosis*]. Any neurosis of the skin.

dermatonosis (der″mah-to-no′sis). Dermatopathy.

dermato-ophthalmitis (der″mah-to-of″thal-mi′tis). Inflammation of the skin and of the eye, including the conjunctiva, cornea, etc.

dermatopathia (der″mah-to-path′e-ah). Dermatopathy.

dermatopathology (der″mah-to-pah-thol′o-je). Pathology of the skin.

dermatopathophobia (der″mah-to-path″o-fo′-be-ah) [*dermato-* + Gr. *pathos* disease + *phobia*]. Morbid anxiety with regard to the skin, its diseases, etc.

dermatopathy (der″mah-top′ah-the) [*dermato-* + Gr. *pathos* disease]. Any disease of the skin.

dermatophiliasis (der″mah-to-fĭ-li′ah-sis). Invasion of the skin by Dermatophilus.

Dermatophilus (der″mah-tof′ĭ-lus). A genus of mites. **D. pen′etrans.** See *chigger.*

dermatophobe (der-mat′o-fōb). A person affected with dermatophobia.

dermatophobia (der″mah-to-fo′be-ah) [*dermato-* + *phobia*]. A morbid dread of having some cutaneous lesion.

dermatophone (der′mah-to-fōn) [*dermato-* + Gr. *phōnē* sound]. An instrument for auscultating the sounds of the blood current of the skin.

dermatophylaxis (der″mah-to-fi-lak′sis) [*dermato-* + Gr. *phylaxis* a guarding]. Protection against skin infection; protection of the skin against infection.

dermatophyte (der′mah-to-fīt) [*dermato-* + Gr. *phyton* plant]. A fungus parasite upon the skin. The term embraces *Achorion, Microsporum, Epidermophyton, Trichophyton* and other species.

dermatophytid (der″mah-tof′ĭ-tid). A secondary or allergic skin rash associated with a dermatophytosis.

dermatophytosis (der″mah-to-fi-to′sis). A fungal infection of the skin, or infection caused by a dermatophyte; often used specifically to designate such an infection of the skin of the feet (tinea pedis). **d. furfuracea,** tinea versicolor.

dermatoplastic (der″mah-to-plas′tik). Pertaining to dermatoplasty.

dermatoplasty (der′mah-to-plas″te) [*dermato-* + Gr. *plassein* to form]. Any plastic operation on the skin; operative replacement of destroyed or lost skin.

dermatopolyneuritis (der″mah-to-pol″e-nu-ri′-tis). Erythredema polyneuropathy.

dermatoptic (der″mah-top′tik) [*dermato-* + Gr. *optikos* optic]. Seeing with the integument; a power alleged to be possessed by the mollusk *Pholas dactylus.*

dermatorrhagia (der″mah-to-ra′je-ah). Discharge of blood from the skin. **d. parasit′ica,** a disease of the skin of horses in Europe and Asia, marked by hard elevations formed by accumulations of blood between the layers of the skin, and caused by the presence of a parasitic worm.

dermatorrhea (der″mah-to-re′ah) [*dermato-* + Gr. *rhoia* flow]. A morbid excess of sweat.

dermatorrhexis (der″mah-to-rek′sis) [*dermato-* + Gr. *rhēxis* a breaking]. Rupture of the skin capillaries; cutis hyperelastica.

dermatosclerosis (der″mah-to-skle-ro′sis) [*dermato-* + Gr. *sklērōsis* hardening]. Scleroderma.

dermatoscopy (der″mah-tos′ko-pe) [*dermato-* + Gr. *skopein* to examine]. Examination of the skin; especially microscopical examination of the superficial capillaries of the skin.

dermatoses (der″mah-to′sēz). Plural of *dermatosis*.

dermatosiophobe (der″mah-to′se-o-fōb). Dermatophobe.

dermatosiophobia (der″mah-to″se-o-fo′be-ah) [*dermatosis* + *phobia*]. Dermatophobia.

dermatosis (der″mah-to′sis), pl. *dermato′ses* [*dermat-* + *-osis*]. Any skin disease. **acarine d.,** a dermatosis produced by a mite. **angioneurotic d.,** a skin disease in which the manifestations are due to disturbance of the vasomotor innervation to the vessels in the skin. **Bowen's precancerous d.,** Bowen's disease. **chick nutritional d.,** a disease of chicks marked by eruptions on the head and feet and due to deficiency of the filtrate factor of vitamin B. **industrial d.,** occupational dermatitis. **lichenoid d.,** a skin disease characterized by the appearance of lichen-like lesions in wide red patches. **d. papulo′sa ni′gra,** a variety of seborrheic keratosis that is observed principally in Negroes, with multiple miliary pigmented papules usually on the upper lateral aspect of the cheek, but sometimes occurring more widely on the face and neck. **precancerous d.,** any skin condition in which the lesions, such as warts, moles, or other excrescences, are likely to undergo malignant degeneration. **progressive pigmentary d.,** a slowly progressive pigmentary disease of the skin affecting chiefly the shins, ankles and dorsums of the feet. **Schamberg's d.,** progressive pigmentary d. **stasis d.,** skin disease marked by disturbances of the circulation and of lymphatic absorption. **subcorneal pustular d.,** a bullous dermatosis resembling dermatitis herpetiformis, with single and grouped vesicles and pustules occurring beneath the horny layer of the skin. **Unna's d.,** seborrheic eczema.

dermatosome (der′mah-to-sōm) [*dermato-* + Gr. *sōma* body]. A thickening on each spindle fiber in the equatorial region during mitosis.

dermatostomatitis (der″mah-to-sto″mah-ti′tis). Ectodermosis erosiva pluriorificialis.

dermatotherapy (der″mah-to-ther′ah-pe) [*dermato-* + Gr. *therapeia* treatment]. Treatment of the skin and its diseases.

dermatothlasia (der″mah-to-thla′ze-ah) [*dermato-* + Gr. *thlasis* bruising]. A morbid tendency to injure determinate areas of the skin by pinching and bruising (H. Fournier, 1898).

dermatotome (der′mah-to-tōm) [*dermato-* + Gr. *temnein* to cut]. 1. A knife for cutting the skin. 2. One of the skin segments of the embryo.

dermatotropic (der″mah-to-trop′ik). Dermotropic.

dermatoxerasia (der″mah-to-ze-ra′ze-ah) [*dermato-* + Gr. *xērasia* dryness]. Xeroderma.

dermatozoiasis (der″mah-to-zo-i′ah-sis). Dermatozoonosus.

dermatozoon (der″mah-to-zo′on) [*dermato-* + Gr. *zōon* animal]. Any animal parasite of the skin; an ectozoon.

dermatozoonosus (der″mah-to-zo″o-no′sus) [*dermato-* + Gr. *zōon* animal + *nosos* disease]. A skin disease caused by a dermatozoon.

dermatrophia (der″mah-tro′fe-ah) [*derma-* + Gr. *atrophia* atrophy]. Atrophy of the skin.

dermatrophy (der-mat′ro-fe). Dermatrophia.

dermenchysis (der-men′kĭ-sis) [*derma-* + Gr. *enchysis* pouring in]. The hypodermic administration of medicines.

dermepenthesis (der″me-pen′thĕ-sis) [*derma-* + Gr. *epenthesis* insertion]. Skin grafting.

dermiatrics (der″me-at′riks) [Gr. *derma* skin + *iatreia* cure]. The science of healing skin diseases.

dermic (der′mik). Pertaining to the skin or dermis.

dermis (der′mis). The skin; sometimes used with special reference to the corium, or true skin.

dermitis (der-mi′tis) [*derma-* + *-itis*]. Inflammation of the skin.

dermo-. See *dermato-*.

dermo-anergy (der″mo-an′er-je). Lack of response by skin to antigen; absence of reactivity in skin.

dermoblast (der′mo-blast) [*dermo-* + Gr. *blastos* germ]. That part of the mesoblast which develops into the true skin or corium.

dermochrome (der′mo-krōm) [*dermo-* + Gr. *chrōma* color]. A colored illustration of the skin or of a skin disease.

dermocyma (der″mo-si′mah) [*dermo-* + Gr. *kyma* fetus]. A monstrosity in which one fetus is inclosed within another.

dermocymus (der″mo-si′mus). Dermocyma.

dermofluorometer (der″mo-floo-o-rom′e-ter). An instrument for measuring capillary permeability.

dermoglyphics (der″mo-glif′iks). Dermatoglyphics.

dermograph (der′mo-graf). The elevated mark or wheal which appears on the skin in dermographia.

dermographia (der″mo-graf′e-ah) [*dermo-* + Gr. *graphein* to write]. A condition in which scratching the skin with a dull instrument provokes a linear, raised, pale streak, bordered on each side by a hyperemic line.

dermographic (der″mo-graf′ik). Pertaining to or characterized by dermographia.

dermohemia (der″mo-he′me-ah) [*dermo-* + Gr. *haima* blood + *-ia*]. Hyperemia of the skin.

dermoid (der′moid) [*derma-* + Gr. *eidos* form]. 1. Resembling the skin. 2. A dermoid cyst. **implantation d.,** a dermoid cyst resulting from an injury by which a portion of the epiblastic structure is driven into the body. **inclusion d.,** a dermoid cyst due to the inclusion of foreign tissue in the closure of a developmental cleft. **sequestration d.,** a dermoid cyst formed along the line of coalescence of the opposite halves of the body of the embryo. **thyroid d.,** a tumor formed from a retention cyst of the persistent thyroid duct or of the thyrolingual duct. **tubal d.,** tubulodermoid.

dermoidectomy (der″moid-ek′to-me) [*dermoid* + Gr. *ektomē* excision]. Excision of a dermoid cyst.

dermolipoma (der″mo-lĭ-po′mah). A congenital yellow growth beneath the bulbar conjunctiva.

dermolysin (der-mol′ĭ-sin). A substance, circulating in the blood, capable of dissolving the skin.

dermolysis (der-mol′ĭ-sis). Dissolution or destruction of the skin.

dermometer (der-mom′e-ter). The instrument used in dermometry.

dermometry (der-mom′e-tre) [*dermo-* + Gr. *metron* measure]. The measurement of areas of skin resistance to a passage of direct electric current: these areas will correspond to the areas of sensory loss.

dermomycosis (der″mo-mi-ko′sis) [*dermo-* + Gr. *mykēs* fungus]. Any skin disease caused by a fungus.

dermomyotome (der″mo-mi′o-tōm) [*dermo-* + *myo-* + *-tome*]. All but the sclerotome of a mesodermal somite; the primordium of skeletal muscle and, perhaps, of corium.

dermonecrotic (der″mo-ne-krot′ik). Causing necrosis of the skin.

dermoneurosis (der″mo-nu-ro′sis) [*dermo-* + Gr. *neuron* nerve]. Any neurosis of the skin.

dermonosology (der″mo-no-sol′o-je) [*dermo-* + *nosology*]. The nosology or classification of skin diseases.

dermopathic (der″mo-path′ik). Pertaining to disease of the skin.

dermopathy (der-mop′ah-the) [*dermo-* + Gr. *pathos* disease]. Any skin disease.

dermophlebitis (der″mo-fle-bi′tis) [*dermo-* + Gr. *phleps* a vein + *-itis*]. Inflammation of the veins of the skin.

dermophobe (der′mo-fōb). Dermatophobe.

dermophylaxis (der″mo-fi-lak′sis). Dermatophylaxis.

dermophyte (der′mo-fīt). Dermatophyte.

dermoplasty (der′mo-plas″te). Dermatoplasty.

dermoreaction (der″mo-re-ak′shun). Cutireaction.

dermoskeleton (der″mo-skel′ĕ-ton). Exoskeleton.

dermostenosis (der″mo-ste-no′sis) [*dermo-* + Gr. *stenōsis* contraction]. Contraction of the skin.

dermostosis (der″mos-to′sis) [*dermo-* + Gr. *osteon* bone]. Ossification in the skin.

dermosynovitis (der″mo-sin-o-vi′tis) [*dermo-* + *synovitis*]. A malignant inflammation of the sole of the foot with a tendency to involve the synovial sheaths.

dermosyphilography (der″mo-sif″ĭ-log′rah-fe). That department of medicine which deals with the skin and with syphilis.

dermosyphilopathy (der″mo-sif″ĭ-lop′ah-the) [*dermo-* + *syphilopathy*]. Any syphilitic skin disease.

dermotactile (der-mo-tak′til) [*dermo-* + L. *tactus* touch]. Pertaining to the tactile sensibility of the skin.

dermotoxin (der″mo-tok′sin). A toxin of staphylococci which produces a necrotic area in the skin when injected.

dermotropic (der″mo-trop′ik) [*dermo-* + Gr. *tropos* a turning]. Having a selective affinity for the skin and mucous membranes: exerting its principal effect on the skin.

dermovaccine (der″mo-vak′sin) [*dermo-* + *vaccine*]. Vaccine virus prepared from dermal inoculations.

dermovascular (der″mo-vas′ku-lar) [*dermo-* + *vas* vessel]. Pertaining to the blood vessels of the skin.

dermovirus (der′mo-vi″rus). Dermovaccine.

derodidymus (der″o-did′ĭ-mus). Dicephalus.

deronil (der′o-nil). Trade mark for a preparation of dexamethasone.

derrengadera (der″en-gah-da′rah) [Sp. "*crooked*"]. Murrina.

Derrien's test (dār″e-anz′) [Eugène *Derrien*, French chemist, 1879–1931]. See under *tests*.

derriengue (der″e-eng′geh) [Sp.]. A highly fatal disease of cattle in western Mexico, caused by an organism closely related to the rabies virus and transmitted by vampire bats.

derris (der′is). A plant of the South Sea Islands. Extracts of the leaves and dried root are used as insecticides. Cf. *rotenone*.

desalination (de″sal-ĭ-na′shun) [L. *de* from + *sal* salt]. The removal of salt from a substance.

desalivation (de″sal-ĭ-va′shun). The depriving of saliva.

desamidase (des-am′ĭ-dās). Deamidase.

desamidization (des″am-ĭ-di-za′shun). Deamidization.

desaminase (des-am′ĭ-nās). Deaminase.

desanimania (des″an-ĭ-ma′ne-ah) [L. *dis-* neg. + *animus* mind + *mania* madness]. Amentia, or mindless insanity.

Desault's bandage, ligature, sign (dĕ-sōz′) [Pierre Joseph *Desault*, French surgeon, 1744–1795]. See under the nouns.

Descartes's body (da-kartz′) [René *Descartes*, famous French natural philosopher, 1596–1650]. The pineal body.

Descemet's membrane (des-ĕ-māz′) [Jean *Descemet*, French anatomist, 1732–1810]. Lamina limitans posterior corneae.

descemetitis (des″ĕ-mĕ-ti′tis). Inflammation of Descemet's membrane; cyclitis or serous iritis.

descemetocele (des″ĕ-met′o-sēl) [*Descemet's membrane* + Gr. *kēlē* hernia]. Herniation of Descemet's membrane.

descendens (de-sen′denz) [L.]. A descending structure or part. **d. cer′vicis, d. hypoglos′si, d. no′ni,** nerve fibers to the sternohyoid, omohyoid, etc., formerly thought to originate from the hypoglossal nerve.

descending (de-send′ing) [L. *descendere* to go down]. Extending downward or distad.

descensus (de-sen′sus), pl. *descen′sus* [L.]. The process of descending or falling. **d. tes′tis** [N A, B N A], the descent of the testis from its fetal position in the abdominal cavity to the scrotum. It normally occurs during the last three months of fetal life and is essential to spermatogenesis. **d. u′teri,** prolapse of the uterus. **d. ventric′uli,** gastroptosis.

Deschamps' needle (da-shawz′) [Joseph François Louis *Deschamps*, French surgeon, 1740–1824]. See under *needle*.

desensin (de-sen′sin). A hypothetical hormone from the corpus luteum.

desensitization (de-sen″sĭ-ti-za′shun). 1. A condition in which the organism does not react to a specific antigen; also the process by which this is brought about. See *antianaphylaxis*. 2. In psychiatry, the removal of a mental complex.

desensitize (de-sen′sĭ-tīz). 1. To deprive of sensation; paralysis of a sensory nerve by section or blocking. 2. To remove antibody from sensitized cells for the purpose of preventing allergy or anaphylaxis.

desequestration (de″se-kwes-tra′shun). The release of sequestered material, such as release into the general circulation of blood formerly withheld from it, by either physiological or mechanical means.

deserpidine (de-ser′pĭ-dēn). Chemical name: 11-desmethoxyreserpine: used as a tranquilizer.

desexualize (de-seks′u-al-īz). To deprive of sexual characters; to castrate.

deshydremia (des″hi-dre′me-ah) [L. *de* from + Gr. *hydōr* water + *haima* blood + *-ia*]. Deficiency of the watery element of the blood.

desiccant (des′ĭ-kant). 1. Promoting dryness; causing to dry up. 2. An agent which promotes dryness.

desiccate (des′ĭ-kāt) [L. *desiccare* to dry up]. To render thoroughly dry.

desiccation (des″ĭ-ka′shun). The act of drying up. **electric d.,** the treatment of a tumor or other disease by drying up the part by the application of a monopolar electric current (short spark) of high frequency and high tension.

desiccative (des′ĭ-ka″tiv). Causing to dry up.

desiccator (des′ĭ-ka″tor). A closed vessel for containing apparatus or chemicals that are to be kept free from moisture.

Desjardins' point (da″zhar-danz′) [Abel *Desjardins*, French surgeon]. See under *point*.

deslanoside (des-lan′o-sīd). Chemical name: desacetyl lanatoside C. Use: for improving function of a failing heart.

desmalgia (des-mal′je-ah) [*desmo-* + *-algia*]. Pain in a ligament.

Desmarres' dacryoliths (da-marz′) [Louis Augusta *Desmarres*, French oculist, 1810–1882]. See under *dacryolith*.

desmectasis (des-mek′tah-sis) [*desmo-* + Gr. *ektasis* stretching]. The stretching of a ligament.

desmepithelium (des″mep-ĭ-the′le-um) [*desmo-* + *epithelium*]. The endothelial lining of blood vessels, lymphatics, and synovial membranes.

desmiognathus (des″me-o-nath′us) [Gr. *desmios* binding + *gnathos* jaw]. A fetal monster with a parasitic head attached to the jaw or neck.

desmitis (des-mi′tis) [*desmo-* + *-itis*]. Inflammation of a ligament.

desmo- (des′mo) [Gr. *desmos* band, ligament]. A combining form denoting relationship to a band, bond, or ligament.

Desmobacteriaceae (des″mo-bak-te″re-a′se-e). A family of Schizomycetes in the Lehmann and Newmann outline classification of bacteria.

desmocranium (des″mo-kra′ne-um) [*desmo-* + *cranium*]. The mass of mesoderm at the cranial end of the notochord in the early embryo, forming the earliest stage of the skull.

desmocyte (des′mo-sīt) [*desmo-* + Gr. *kytos* hollow vessel]. Fibroblast.

desmocytoma (des″mo-si-to′mah). A tumor of desmocytes; a sarcoma.

desmodynia (des″mo-din′e-ah) [*desmo-* + Gr. *odynē* pain]. Pain in a ligament.

desmo-enzyme (des″mo-en′zīm). An enzyme which is bound to the protoplasm of the secreting cell and therefore not easily extractable.

desmogenous (des-moj′e-nus) [*desmo-* + Gr. *gennan* to produce]. Of ligamentous origin.

desmography (des-mog′rah-fe) [*desmo-* + Gr. *graphein* to write]. A description of the ligaments.

desmohemoblast (des″mo-hem′o-blast) [*desmo-* + Gr. *haima* blood + *blastos* germ]. Mesenchyme.

desmoid (des′moid) [*desmo-* + Gr. *eidos* form]. 1. Fibrous or fibroid. 2. A lesion produced by progressive fibroblastic proliferation in striated muscle and sometimes in periosteum.

desmolase (des′mo-lās). An enzyme that catalyzes the addition or removal of some chemical group to or from a substrate without hydrolysis, oxidation, or reduction, the group being taken up from or liberated in the free state.

desmology (des-mol′o-je) [*desmo-* + *-logy*]. 1. The anatomy of the ligaments. 2. The art of bandaging.

desmoma (des-mo′mah) [*desmo-* + *-oma*]. A fibroma, or connective tissue tumor.

desmon (des′mon) [Gr. *desmos* band]. 1. Amboceptor. 2. A term for hypothetical substances which circulate in protoplasm from cell to cell through fine anastomoses and control the growth and proliferation of tissue cells.

desmone (des′mōn). Desmon.

desmoneoplasm (des″mo-ne′o-plazm) [*desmo-* + *neoplasm*]. A neoplasm formed of connective tissue.

desmopathy (des-mop′ah-the) [*desmo-* + Gr. *pathos* disease]. Any disease of the ligaments.

desmopexia (des″mo-pek′se-ah) [*desmo-* + Gr. *pēxis* fixation]. The operation of suturing the round ligaments to the abdominal wall or to the vaginal wall for the correction of uterine displacement.

desmoplasia (des″mo-pla′ze-ah). The formation and development of fibrous tissue.

desmoplastic (des″mo-plas′tik) [*desmo-* + Gr. *plassein* to form]. Characterized by or causing the growth of fibrous tissue; producing or forming adhesions.

desmopyknosis (des″mo-pik-no′sis) [*desmo-* + Gr. *pyknōsis* condensation]. Dudley's operation of shortening the round ligaments by fastening them to an oval denuded area on the anterior vaginal wall.

desmorrhexis (des″mo-rek′sis) [*desmo-* + Gr. *rhēxis* rupture]. Rupture of a ligament.

desmosis (des-mo′sis) [*desmo-* + *-osis*]. A disease of the connective tissue.

desmosome (des′mo-sōm) [*desmo-* + Gr. *sōma* body]. A bridge corpuscle; a small thickening at the middle of an intercellular bridge.

desmosterol (des-mos′ter-ol). The immediate precursor of cholesterol in the biosynthetic pathway, 24-dehydrocholesterol; normally not present in the blood in amounts that can be detected by ordinary means.

desmotomy (des-mot′o-me) [*desmo-* + Gr. *tomē* a cutting]. The cutting or division of ligaments.

desmotropism (des-mot′ro-pizm). Tautomerism.

desmotrypsin (des″mo-trip′sin). An inactive trypsin material left in the pancreas after extraction with glycerol.

Desnos' disease (da-nōz′) [Louis Joseph *Desnos*, French physician, 1828–1893]. Splenopneumonia.

desoleolecithin (des-o″le-o-les′ĭ-thin). One of the components, the other being oleic acid, into which lecithin is split by the action of cobra venom.

desomorphine (des″o-mor′fin). Dihydroxydesoxymorphine.

desoxy-. A prefix used in names of chemical compounds. See also words beginning *deoxy-*.

desoxycholaneresis (des-ok″se-ko″lan-er′e-sis). Increase in the output of desoxycholic acid in the bile.

desoxycorticosterone (des-ok″se-kor″te-ko′ster-ōn). A crystalline steroid, Δ^4-pregnene-21-ol-3,20-dione, identical with corticosterone except for having a hydrogen atom in place of the hydroxyl group in position 11. It has a marked effect on the metabolism of water and electrolytes but does not influence carbohydrate metabolism and cannot be used as a complete substitute for the secretion of the adrenal cortex. **d. acetate,** a white crystalline powder, $C_{23}H_{32}O_4$, used in the treatment of Addison's disease.

desoxycortone (des″ok-se-kōr′tōn). Desoxycorticosterone. **d. acetate,** desoxycorticosterone acetate.

desoxyephedrine (des″ok-se-ef′ĕ-drin). Methamphetamine.

desoxymorphine (des″ok-se-mor′fin). A product of the reduction of morphine.

desoxyn (des-ok′sin). Trade mark for preparations of methamphetamine hydrochloride.

desoxyphenobarbital (des-ok″se-fe″no-bar′bĭ-tol). Primidone.

desoxyribonuclease (des-ok″se-ri″bo-nu′kle-ās). Deoxyribonuclease.

desoxyribose (des″ok-se-ri′bōs). Deoxyribose.

desoxy-sugar (des-ok′se-shoog″ar). A sugar having one oxygen atom less than the parent monosaccharide.

despeciation (de-spe″se-a′shun). Deviation from or loss of species characteristics.

d'Espine's sign (des-pēnz′) [Jean Henri Adolphe *d'Espine*, French physician, 1844–1931]. See under *sign*.

despumation (des″pu-ma′shun) [L. *de* away + *spuma* froth]. The removal of froth or scum from the surface of a liquid.

desquamation (des″kwah-ma′shun) [L. *de* from + *squama* scale]. The shedding of epithelial elements, chiefly of the skin, in scales or sheets. **furfuraceous d.,** desquamation in branlike scales. **membranous d.,** desquamation in large sheets. **siliquose d.,** the shedding from the skin of dried vesicles resembling siliques.

desquamative (des-kwam′ah-tiv). Pertaining to or characterized by desquamation.

desquamatory (des-kwam′ah-to-re). Desquamative.

dest. Abbreviation for L. *destil′la* distil, and *destilla′tus* distilled.

desternalization (de-ster″nal-i-za′shun) [L. *de* from + *sternum*]. Separation from the sternum.

desthiobiotin (des″thi-o-bi′o-tin). Biotin in which the sulfur has been replaced by two atoms of hydrogen. It is an analogue, $CH_2.CH.NH.CO.NH.$-$CH.CH_2.(CH_2)_4.COOH$, of ascorbic acid which competitively inhibits the activity of the latter.

destil. Abbreviation for L. *destil′la,* distil.

destructive (de-struk′tiv). Characterized by or causing destruction.

Desulfovibrio (de-sul″fo-vib′re-o). A genus of microorganisms of the family Spirillaceae, suborder Pseudomonadineae, order Pseudomonadales, made up of actively motile, slightly curved rods of variable length, usually occurring singly but sometimes in short chains. It includes three species, *D. aestua'rii*, *D. desulfur'icans*, and *D. rubentschi'kii.*

Desvoidea (des-voi'de-ah). A genus of mosquitoes. **D. obtur'bans,** a mosquito which transmits dengue.

Det. Abbreviation for L. *de'tur*, let it be given.

detachment (de-tach'ment) [Fr. *détacher* to unfasten; to separate]. The condition of being unfastened, or separated. **d. of retina, retinal d.,** a condition in which the inner layers of the retina are separated from the pigment layer.

detector (de-tek'tor). A device by which the presence of something, or the existence of a certain condition, is discovered. **sterility d.,** a device for indicating whether the desired temperature has been attained in sterilizing by heat: often shown by change of color in the detector.

detelectasis (de"tel-ek'tah-sis) [*de* negative + Gr. *telos* end + *ektasis* dilatation]. Loss of normal inflation; collapse.

detergent (de-ter'jent) [L. *detergere* to cleanse]. 1. Purifying, cleansing. 2. An agent which purifies or cleanses.

deterioration (de-tēr"e-o-ra'shun) [L. *deterior* worse, poorer]. The process of becoming or the state of being worse. **emotional d.,** a condition in which the emotional response is not appropriate to or commensurate with the stimuli which arouse it. **mental d.,** a condition of progressive impairment of the mental faculties.

deteriorative (de-tēr'e-o-ra"tiv). Pertaining to or characterized by deterioration.

determinant (de-ter'mĭ-nant) [L. *determinare* to bound, limit, or fix]. A factor that establishes the nature of an entity or event. **antigenic d.,** haptene. **germ-cell d.,** oosome.

determination (de-ter"mĭ-na'shun). Establishment of the exact nature of an entity or event. **embryonic d.,** the loss of pluripotency in any part of an embryo and its start on the way toward an unalterable fate. **sex d.,** the process by which the sex of an organism is fixed, associated, in man, with the presence or absence of the Y chromosome.

determiner (de-ter'min-er). Determinant.

determinism (de-ter'min-izm). The doctrine that the will is not free but is absolutely determined by psychical and physical conditions. **psychic d.,** the theory that mental processes are always determined by motives.

dethyroidism (de-thi'roid-izm). A condition produced by abolition of the function of the thyroid gland.

dethyroidize (de-thi'roid-iz). To deprive of the function of the thyroid gland by chemical or surgical means.

Det. in dup., Det. in 2 plo. Abbreviations for L. *de'tur in du'plo*, let twice as much be given.

detonation (de"to-na'shun) [L. *de* intensive + *tonare* to thunder]. Loudly explosive combustion.

detorsion (de-tor'shun). 1. The correction of a curvature or deformity; as the reduction of torsion of the testis. 2. A deficiency in a normal twisting as may occur in the early development of the heart.

detoxicate (de-tok'sĭ-kāt). To remove the toxic quality of a substance.

detoxication (de-tok"sĭ-ka'shun). Detoxification.

detoxification (de-tok"sĭ-fi-ka'shun). Reduction of the toxic properties of poisons. **metabolic d.,** reduction of the toxic properties of a substance by chemical changes induced in the body, producing a compound which is less poisonous or is more readily eliminated.

Detre's reaction (det'erz) [Ladislaus *Detre*, Hungarian physician, 1875–1939]. See under *reaction.*

detrition (de-trish'un) [L. *de* away + *terere* to wear]. A wearing away, as of the teeth, by friction.

detritivorous (de"tri-tiv'o-rus). Subsisting on particulate matter (detritus), a mode of existence important in certain, such as aquatic, ecosystems.

detritus (de-tri'tus) [L., from *deterere* to rub away]. Particulate matter produced by or remaining after the wearing away or disintegration of a substance or tissue; designated as organic or nonorganic, depending on the nature of the original material. See also *biodetritus.*

detruncation (de"trun-ka'shun) [L. *de* off + *truncus* trunk]. Decapitation, or decollation; beheadal, chiefly of the fetus.

detrusor (de-tru'sor) [L. *detrudere* to push down]. That which pushes down. **d. uri'nae,** musculus pubovesicalis.

D. et s. Abbreviation for L. *de'tur et signe'tur*, let it be given and labeled.

detubation (de"tu-ba'shun). Removal or extraction of a tube.

detuberculization (de"tu-ber"ku-li-za'shun). Systematic effort toward the eradication of tuberculosis.

detumescence (de"tu-mes'ens) [L. *de* down + *tumescere* to swell]. The subsidence of swelling, or turgor.

deutan (du'tan). An individual exhibiting deuteranomalopia or deuteranopia, marked by derangement or loss of the red-green sensory mechanism but without noticeable shift or shortening of the spectrum or luminancy loss in the long-wave (red) end; includes those with the commoner and less severe types of color vision defect. Cf. *protan.*

deutencephalon (du"ten-sef'ah-lon) [Gr. *deuteros* second + *enkephalos* brain]. Diencephalon.

deuteranomalopia (du"ter-ah-nom"ah-lo'pe-ah) [Gr. *deuteros* second + *anōmalos* irregular + *ōpē* sight + *-ia*]. A problematic variant of normal color vision, in which none of the constituents for complete chromatic perception are lacking, but a greater than usual proportion of thallium green light to lithium red is required to match a fixed sodium yellow. The defect may be congenital or acquired, and occurs in different degrees of severity. Sometimes called "green weakness," and viewed as a transitional stage to "green blindness."

deuteranomalopsia (du"ter-ah-nom"ah-lop'se-ah). Deuteranomalopia.

deuteranomalous (du"ter-ah-nom'ah-lus). Pertaining to or characterized by deuteranomaly (deuteranomalopia).

deuteranomaly (du"ter-ah-nom'ah-le). Deuteranomalopia.

deuteranope (du'ter-ah-nōp). An individual exhibiting deuteranopia.

deuteranopia (du"ter-ah-no'pe-ah) [Gr. *deuteros* second + *an-* neg. + *ōpē* sight + *-ia*]. Defective color vision of the dichromatic type, characterized by retention of the sensory mechanism for two hues only (blue and yellow) of the normal 4-primary quota, and lacking that for red and green and their derivatives, without loss of luminance or shift or shortening of the spectrum. Coined by von Kries (1897) to replace "green blindness." Cf. the correlative terms *protanopia*, *tritanopia*, and *tetartanopia*, in which the color vision deficiency is in the first, third, and fourth primary, respectively.

deuteranopic (du"ter-ah-nop'ik). Pertaining to or characterized by deuteranopia.

deuteranopsia (du"ter-ah-nop'se-ah). Deuteranopia.

deuterate (du'ter-āt). To treat (combine) with deuterium.

deuterion (du-te're-on). Deuteron.

deuterium (du-te're-um) [Gr. *deuteros* second]. The mass two isotope of hydrogen, symbol ^2H, or D. It is available as a gas or as heavy water and is used as a tracer or indicator in studying fat and amino acid metabolism. **d. oxide,** heavy water.

deutero-, deuto- [Gr. *deuteros* second]. Combining form meaning second.

deutero-albumose (du″ter-o-al′bu-mōs). Deuteroproteose.

deuteroconidium (du″ter-o-ko-nid′e-um) [*deutero-* + *conidium*]. A reproductive element derived from a protoconidium.

deutero-elastose (du″ter-o-e-las′tōs). A product of the digestion of elastin; elastin peptone.

deuterofat (du′ter-o-fat). A fat containing deuterium.

deuterofibrinose (du″ter-o-fi′brin-ōs). A proteolyte formed from blood fibrin by digestion.

deuteroglobulose (du″ter-o-glob′u-lōs). One of the proteolytes formed in the digestion of paraglobulin.

deuterohemin (du″ter-o-hem′in). A derivative of hemin, $C_{30}H_{28}O_4N_4FeCl$.

deuterohemophilia (du″ter-o-he″mo-fil′e-ah). A condition resembling classical hemophilia; a hemophilioid state.

deuterohydrogen (du″ter-o-hi′dro-jen). Deuterium.

Deuteromyces (du″ter-o-mi′zēz). Fungi Imperfecti.

deuteromyosinose (du″ter-o-mi-os′ĭ-nōs). An albumose derived from the digestion of myosin.

deuteron (du′ter-on). The nucleus of deuterium, or heavy hydrogen. Deuterons are used as bombing particles for nuclear disintegration.

deuteropathic (du″ter-o-path′ik). Occurring secondarily to some other disease.

deuteropathy (du″ter-op′ah-the) [*deutero-* + Gr. *pathos* disease]. A disease that is secondary to another disease.

deuteropine (du″ter-o′pin). An alkaloid, $C_{20}H_{21}O_3N$, from opium.

deuteroplasm (du′ter-o-plazm″) [*deutero-* + Gr. *plasma* something formed]. Deutoplasm.

deuteroporphyrin (du″ter-o-por′fĭ-rin). A hemin-porphyrin derivative, $C_{30}H_{30}O_4N_4$.

deuteroproteose (du″ter-o-pro′te-ōs). One of the hydrolytic cleavage products of a protein which is precipitated by complete saturation with ammonium sulfate. Called also *secondary proteose* and *deutero-albumose*.

deuterotocia (du″ter-o-to′se-ah) [*deutero-* + Gr. *tokos* birth]. Asexual reproduction in which the female produces offspring of both sexes.

deuterotoxin (du″ter-o-tok′sin). The second of the three groups into which toxins may be divided on the basis of their affinity for antitoxin. It has less affinity for antitoxin than has prototoxin and more than has tritotoxin.

deuthyalosome (du″thi-al′o-sōm) [Gr. *deuteros* second + *hyalos* glass + *sōma* body]. The matured nucleus of an ovum.

deutiodide (du-ti′o-dīd). An iodide which contains twice the normal proportion of iodine.

deutipara (du-tip′ah-rah). Secundipara.

deuto-. See *deutero-*.

deutobromide (du″to-bro′mīd). That one of two bromides of the same base which contains twice the amount of bromine that is contained in the other.

deutochloride (du″to-klo′rīd). Any chloride which contains twice the normal proportion of chlorine.

deutohydrogen (du″to-hi′dro-jen). Deuterium.

deutomerite (du″to-me′rīt) [*deuto-* + Gr. *meros* portion]. The posterior portion of certain gregarine protozoa.

deuton (du′ton). Deuteron.

deutonephron (du″to-nef′ron) [*deuto-* + Gr. *nephros* kidney]. Mesonephros.

deutoplasm (du′to-plazm). The passive or inactive materials in protoplasm, especially reserve foodstuffs, such as yolk.

deutoplasmolysis (du″to-plaz-mol′ĭ-sis). Destruction or disintegration of deutoplasm.

deutoscolex (du″to-sko′leks) [*deuto-* + *scolex*]. A secondary scolex; the hydatid form of a tapeworm.

Deutschländer's disease (doich′len-derz) [Karl Ernst Wilhelm *Deutschländer*, surgeon in Hamburg, 1872–1942]. 1. Tumor of a metatarsal bone. 2. March foot.

devasation (de″vas-a′shun) [L. *de* away + *vas* vessel]. Devascularization. **senile cortical d.,** interruption of the circulation to the cerebral cortex as a result of arteriosclerosis of the blood vessels.

devascularization (de-vas″ku-lar-i-za′shun). Interruption of the circulation of blood to a part caused by obstruction or destruction of the blood vessels supplying it.

devegan (dev′e-gan). Trade mark for a preparation of acetarsone.

development (de-vel′op-ment). Gradual growth or expansion, especially from a lower to a higher stage of complexity. **arrested d.,** cessation of the development process at some stage prior to its normal completion. **mosaic d.,** the development of an embryo in a fixed, unalterable way, local regions being independent portions of a mosaic whole. **postnatal d.,** that which occurs after birth. **prenatal d.,** that which occurs before birth. **psychosexual d.,** the development of the personality through the infantile and adolescent stages on to maturity. **regulative d.,** the development of an embryo, the determination of the various organs and parts being gradually attained through the action of inductors.

developmental (de-vel″op-men′tal). Pertaining to development.

Deventer's diameter, pelvis (de-ven′terz) [Hendrik van *Deventer*, Dutch obstetrician, 1651–1724]. See under *diameter* and *pelvis*.

Devergie's attitude, disease (dev-er-zhēz′) [Marie Guillaume *Devergie*, French physician, 1798–1879]. See under *attitude* and *disease*.

deviant (de′ve-ant) [L. *deviare* to turn aside]. 1. Varying from a determinable standard. 2. An individual with characteristics varying from what is considered normal, or standard. **color d.,** an individual whose color perception varies from the norm, usually lacking discrimination of a pair of primaries (red-green or blue-yellow). See *deuteranope*, *protanope*, and *tritanope*. **sex d.,** an individual exhibiting paraphilia.

deviation (de″ve-a′shun) [L. *deviare* to turn aside]. A turning away from the regular standard or course. In ophthalmology, a tendency for the visual axes of the eye to fall out of alignment due to muscular imbalance. **animal d.,** the attracting of zoophilous mosquitos from human beings by the proximity of animals preferred by the insects. **axis d.,** a change in direction of the Q R S complex in the electrocardiogram. This change may be due to alteration in the anatomical position of the heart (axis shift) or to hypertrophy of a ventricle (ventricular preponderance). **d. of complement,** when more amboceptors are introduced into the mixture than can be taken up by the bacteria, those that remain free are capable of combining with the complement that is present and thus prevent a portion or all of the complement from acting on the amboceptor attached to the bacteria—i.e., the complement has been deviated or deflected from its natural course. (This phenomenon is not to be confounded with fixation of the complement and may be simply a zone phenomenon, q.v.) **conjugate d.,** the deflection of two similar parts, as the eyes, in the same direction at the same time. **Hering-Hellebrand d.,** any deviation of the horopter from the circle. **latent d.** See *heterophoria*. **manifest d.** See *heterotropia*. **minimum d.,** the smallest deflection of a ray of light that can be produced by a given prism. **primary d.,** deviation of the visual axis of the squinting eye in strabismus when the sound eye fixates. **secondary d.,** deviation of the visual axis of the sound eye in strabismus when the squinting eye fixates. **skew d.,** downward and inward rotation of the eye on the side of the cerebellar lesion and upward and outward deviation on the opposite side. **squint d.,** squint angle. See under *angle*. **standard d.,** the measure of variability of any frequency curve. It is found by multiplying the square of the deviation of each class from the mean by the frequency of the class, adding together the products so obtained, dividing the number by the total number of variables, and extracting the square root of the result. **strabismic d.,** deviation of the visual axis of an eye in strabismus. **d. to the left,** shift to the left. **d. to the right,** shift to the right.

deviometer (de″ve-om′e-ter) [*deviation* + Gr. *metron* measure]. An instrument for measuring the amount of deviation in strabismus.

devisceration (de-vis″er-a′shun) [L. *de* away + *viscus* viscus]. The removal of viscera.

devitalization (de-vi″tal-i-za′shun). The deprivation of vitality or life. **pulp d.,** the destruction of vitality of the pulp of a tooth.

devitalize (de-vi′tal-iz) [L. *de* from + *vita* life]. To deprive of vitality or of life.

devolution (dev″o-lu′shun) [L. *de* down + *volvere* to roll]. 1. The reverse of evolution. 2. Catabolic change.

devolutive (dev′o-lu″tiv). Characterized by devolution; specifically applied to a type of mental defect due to intercurrent destructive factors. Cf. *evolutive*.

devorative (dev′o-ra″tiv) [L. *devorare* to devour]. Intended to be swallowed without chewing.

De Vries' theory (de-vrēz′) [Hugo *de Vries*, botanist in Amsterdam, 1848–1935]. See *theory of mutations*.

dewatered (de-wah′terd). Having the water removed: a term applied to sludge from which the water has been removed by drying or pressing.

Dewees' sign (de-wēz′) [William Potts *Dewees*, American obstetrician, 1768–1841]. See under *sign*.

deworming (de-werm′ing). The destruction and removal of worms from an infected individual.

dexamethasone (dek″sah-meth′ah-sōn). Chemical name: 9α-fluoro-16α-methylprednisolone: used as an anti-inflammatory steroid with little salt-retaining action.

dexbrompheniramine (deks″brōm-fen-i′rah-mēn). Chemical name: d-2-[p-bromo-α-(2-dimethylaminoethyl) benzyl] pyridine: used as an antihistaminic.

dexchlorpheniramine (deks″klōr-fen-i′rah-mēn). Chemical name: d-2-[p-chloro-α-(2-dimethylaminoethyl) benzyl] pyridine: used as an antihistaminic.

dexedrine (dek′sĕ-drēn). Trade mark for preparations of dextroamphetamine.

dexiocardia (dek″se-o-kar′de-ah). Dextrocardia.

dexiotropic (dek″se-o-trop′ik) [Gr. *dexios* on the right + *tropos* a turning]. Wound in a spiral from left to right.

dexoval (dek′so-val). Trade mark for a preparation of methamphetamine.

dexter (deks′ter) [L.]. Right; in official anatomical nomenclature, used to designate the right hand one of two similar structures, or the one situated on the right side of the body.

dextrad (deks′trad). Toward the right side or right hand.

dextral (deks′tral). 1. Right as opposed to left. 2. A right-handed person.

dextrality (deks-tral′ĭ-te) [L. *dexter* right]. The preferential use, in voluntary motor acts, of the right member of the major paired organs of the body, as the right eye, hand, or foot.

dextran (dek′stran). A water-soluble, high-glucose polymer produced by the action of *Leuconostoc mesenteroides* on sucrose: used as a plasma substitute.

dextransucrase (deks″tran-soo′krās). An enzyme which synthesizes dextran from sucrose.

dextrase (deks′trās). An enzyme which catalyzes the conversion of dextrose into lactic acid.

dextraural (deks-traw′ral) [L. *dexter* right + *auris* ear]. Hearing better with the right ear than with the left.

dextren (deks′tren). Belonging to the right side.

dextrin (deks′trin) [L. *dexter* right]. Any one, or the mixture, of the intermediate products $(C_6H_{10}O_5)_n$, formed during the hydrolysis of starch, which are dextrorotatory, soluble in water, and precipitable by alcohol. Commercial dextrin or starch sugar is a white or yellowish powder, in aqueous solution forming mucilage. See *achroodextrin* and *erythrodextrin*. **animal d.,** glycogen. **liver d.,** glycogen.

dextrinase (deks′trin-ās). An enzyme which catalyzes the conversion of starch into isomaltose.

dextrinate, dextrinize (deks′trin-āt, deks′trin-iz). To convert into dextrin.

dextrinose (deks′trin-ōs). Isomaltose.

dextrinosis (deks″trĭ-no′sis). Accumulation in the tissues of an abnormal polysaccharide. **limit d.,** a form of hepatic and muscle glycogen disease resulting from deficiency of debranching enzyme (amylo-1,6-glucosidase); during the fasting state the glycogen has shortened outer chains and is a highly branched polysaccharide.

dextrinuria (deks″trin-u′re-ah) [*dextrin* + Gr. *ouron* urine + *-ia*]. The presence of dextrin in the urine.

dextro- [L. *dexter* right]. 1. Combining form denoting relationship to the right. 2. Chemical prefix, for which the symbol (+)- is frequently substituted, used to emphasize that the substance is the dextrorotatory enantiomorph, whether the configurational family is known or not. This practice avoids possible confusion with the occasional erroneous use of *d-* standing alone to designate the configurational family to which the substance belongs. Opposed to *levo-*.

dextroamphetamine (dek″stro-am-fet′ah-mēn). The dextrorotatory isomer of amphetamine, an isomer having a more conspicuous stimulant effect on the central nervous system than the equivalent dose of racemic amphetamine.

dextrocardia (deks″tro-kar′de-ah). Location of the heart in the right hemithorax, with the apex pointing to the right, occurring with accompanying transposition (situs inversus) of the abdominal viscera, or without such transposition (*isolated d.*). **mirror-image d.,** location of the heart in the right side of the chest, the atria being transposed and the right ventricle lying anteriorly and to the left of the left ventricle.

dextrocardiogram (deks″tro-kar′de-o-gram) [L. *dexter* right + *cardiogram*]. That part of the normal cardiogram which represents the action of the right side of the heart.

dextrocerebral (deks″tro-ser′e-bral) [L. *dexter* right + *cerebrum*]. Having the right hemisphere of the brain more active than the left.

dextroclination (deks″tro-klĭ-na′shun) [L. *dexter* right + L. *clinatus* leaning]. Rotation of the upper poles of the vertical meridians of the two eyes to the right. Cf. *levoclination*.

dextrococaine (deks″tro-ko′kān). Isococaine.

dextrocompound (deks″tro-kom′pound). A dextrorotatory compound.

dextrocular (deks-trok′u-lar). Right eyed; affected with dextrocularity.

dextrocularity (deks″trok-u-lar′ĭ-te) [L. *dexter* right + *oculus* eye]. The condition of having greater visual power in the right eye and, therefore, using it more than the left.

dextrocycloduction (deks″tro-si″klo-duk′shun). Dextroclination.

dextroduction (deks″tro-duk′shun) [L. *dexter*

right + *ducere* to draw]. Movement of either eye to the right.

dextrogastria (deks′tro-gas′tre-ah) [L. *dexter* right + Gr. *gastēr* stomach]. Displacement of the stomach to the right.

dextroglucose (deks″tro-glu′kōs). Dextrose.

dextrogram (deks′tro-gram) [*dextro-* + Gr. *graphein* to record]. An electrocardiographic tracing showing right axis deviation, indicative of right ventricular hypertrophy.

dextrogyral (deks″tro-ji′ral) [L. *dexter* right + *gyrare* to turn]. Dextrorotatory.

dextrogyration (deks″tro-ji-ra′shun). A turning to the right; motion to the right: said of movements of the eye and of the plane of polarization.

dextromanual (deks″tro-man′u-al) [L. *dexter* right + *manus* hand]. Right handed.

dextromenthol (deks″tro-men′thol). An oxidation product of menthol.

dextromethorphan (dek″stro-meth′or-fan). Chemical name: d-3-methoxy-N-methylmorphinan: used as an antitussive.

dextropedal (deks-trop′e-dal) [L. *dexter* right + *pes* foot]. Using the right leg in preference to the left.

dextrophobia (deks″tro-fo′be-ah) [L. *dexter* right + Gr. *phobos* fear]. Morbid dread of objects on the right side of the body.

dextroposition (deks″tro-po-zish′un). Displacement to the right.

dextropropoxyphene (dek″stro-pro-pok′se-fēn). Chemical name: α-d-4-dimethylamino-1,2-diphenyl-3-methyl-2-butanol propionate: used as an analgesic.

dextrorotatory (deks″tro-ro′tah-to-re) [L. *dexter* right + *rotare* to turn]. Turning the plane of polarization, or rays of light, to the right.

dextrose (deks′trōs). A white crystalline powder, $C_6H_{12}O_6.H_2O$. The official preparation, usually obtained by the hydrolysis of starch, occurs as colorless crystals or as a white crystalline or granular powder, without odor and with a sweetish taste: used intravenously as a nutrient in various conditions.

dextrosinistral (deks″tro-sin′is-tral) [L. *dexter* right + *sinister* left]. Extending from right to left. The term is also applied to a person naturally left-handed but trained to use the right hand in certain performances.

dextrosozone (deks″tro-so′zōn). Glucosozone.

dextrosuria (deks″tro-su′re-ah) [*dextrose* + Gr. *ouron* urine + *-ia*]. The presence of dextrose in the urine.

dextrotorsion (deks″tro-tor′shun). Dextroclination.

dextrotropic (deks″tro-trop′ik) [L. *dexter* right + Gr. *tropos* a turning]. Turning to the right.

dextroversion (deks″tro-ver′zhun) [L. *dexter* right + *vertere* to turn]. 1. Version to the right side; especially movement of the eyes to the right. 2. Location of the heart in the right hemithorax, the left ventricle remaining on the left as in the normal position, but lying anterior to the right ventricle.

dextroverted (deks″tro-vert′ed). Turned to the right.

dezymotize (de-zīm′o-tīz) [L. *de* priv. + Gr. *zymē* leaven]. To deprive of ferments or of enzymes.

DFDT. A powerful insecticide, difluoro-diphenyl-trichloro-ethane.

DFP. A gas, diisopropyl fluorophosphate, $[(CH_3)_2.CHO]_2PO.F$, which inhibits the action of cholinesterase. It has been used in treating glaucoma and myasthenia gravis. A radioactive form, containing P^{32}, has been used in measuring the life span of erythrocytes and platelets, and in studies of the rates of formation and destruction of leukocytes.

D.G. Abbreviation for *distogingival.*

dg. Abbreviation for *decigram.*

DHE45. Dihydroergotamine.

d'Herelle phenomenon (dĕ-rel′) [Felix Hubert *d'Herelle* of the Pasteur Institute, Paris, 1873–1949]. See *Twort-d'Herelle phenomenon,* under *phenomenon.*

D.Hg., D.Hy. Abbreviations for *Doctor of Hygiene.*

dhobie itch (do′be) [Hindoo "laundryman"]. See under *itch.*

dhurrin (du′rin). A cyanogenetic glycoside, $C_{14}H_{17}NO_7$, from sorghum which hydrolyzes into parahydroxy benzaldehyde, glucose, and hydrocyanic acid.

di- [Gr. *dis* twice, double]. A prefix meaning twice.

dia- [Gr. *dia* through]. A prefix meaning through, apart, across, or between.

diabetes (di″ah-be′tēz) [Gr. *diabētēs* a syphon, from *dia* through + *bainein* to go]. A deficiency condition marked by habitual discharge of an excessive quantity of urine; particularly diabetes mellitus, q. v. **achrestic d.,** a condition characterized by inability of the tissues to utilize sugar despite the availability of biologically active insulin. **d. albumin′icus,** a profuse discharge of albuminous urine. **d. albuminurin′icus,** lipoid nephrosis. **alimentary d.,** diabetes due to defective metabolism of the carbohydrates of the food. **alloxan d.,** a condition resembling diabetes, produced by the injection of 100–200 mg. of alloxan per kilogram of body weight. **d. alter′nans,** diabetes in which albuminuria alternates with glycosuria. **artificial d.,** puncture, or experimental, diabetes. **azotic d., azoturic d.,** diabetes with increase of urea in the urine. **biliary d.,** Hanot's disease. **bronze d., bronzed d.,** hemochromatosis. **cerebral d.,** a form in which brain sugar, or cerebrose, appears in the urine in place of glucose; cerebrosuria. **composite d.,** that which is at first lipogenous, but afterward is marked by emaciation. **conjugal d.,** diabetes affecting both husband and wife. **d. decip′iens,** glycosuria with no excess in amount of urine or in the drinking of water. **fat d.,** a variety in which the patient becomes fat. **gouty d.,** diabetes associated with the gouty diathesis. **hydruric d.,** diabetes with excess of water in the urine, but no increase in the solid elements. **d. in′nocens,** a condition marked by the presence of glycosuria which is not associated with pancreatic disease. **d. inosi′tus,** diabetes in which the sugar of the urine is inosite; inosituria. **d. insip′idus,** a metabolic disorder, marked by great thirst and the passage of a large amount of urine with no excess of sugar. It is often attended by voracious appetite, loss of strength, and emaciation. **d. insip′idus, nephrogenic,** diabetes insipidus resulting from congenital failure of renal tubules to reabsorb water, and characterized by failure to respond to administration of antidiuretic hormone. **d. intermit′tens,** diabetes mellitus in which sugar is absent during certain periods. **Lancereaux's d.,** diabetes mellitus with marked emaciation and frequently associated with disease of the pancreas. **latent d.,** the state following derangement of glucose tolerance, when the glucose tolerance test is normal. **lean d.,** a variety with marked emaciation. **d. le′vis,** diabetes in a mild form. **lipoatrophic d.,** diabetes characterized by deficiency or absence of fat storage in the body. **lipoplethoric d.,** diabetes characterized by excessive storage of fat in the body. **lipuric d.,** diabetes marked by the presence of fat in the urine. **masked d.,** obesity without glycosuria: at a later stage it passes into diabetes mellitus. **d. melli′tus,** a metabolic disorder in which the ability to oxidize carbohydrates is more or less completely lost, usually due to faulty pancreatic activity, especially of the islets of Langerhans, and consequent disturbance of normal insulin mechanism. This produces hyperglycemia with resulting glycosuria and polyuria giving symptoms of thirst, hunger, emaciation and weakness and also imperfect combustion of fats with resulting acidosis, sometimes leading to dyspnea, lipemia, ketonuria, and finally coma. There may also be pruritus and lowered resistance to pyogenic infections. **Mosler's d.,** inosituria with polyuria. **neurogenous d.,** a form which is due to disease of a nerve center. **overflow d.,** the loss of sugar into the urine when it is steadily administered intravenously in amounts greater than can be utilized by the body. Dogs can thus utilize about 7 Gm. per kilogram of body weight per hour. All above this passes into the urine. **pancreatic d.,** that which is associated with disease of the pancreas. **phlorhizin d.,** a form produced by administering phlorhizin. **phosphatic d.,** polyuria and polydipsia in which the urine is loaded with phosphates. **puncture d.,** a form produced by puncturing the oblongata near the diabetic center. **renal d.,** diabetes thought to be dependent on defective renal function; renal glycosuria. **skin d.,** Urbach's term for the "syndrome of therapy-resistant, recurrent or chronic dermatosis, a high fasting skin sugar level together with a normal blood sugar curve, and pronounced improvement of the skin disease, as well as a drop in the high skin sugar level, on a low carbohydrate diet, sometimes combined with insulin." **steroid d.,** experimental diabetes produced in rats by the administration of a 17-ketosteroid. **subclinical d.,** a state characterized by an abnormal glucose-tolerance test but without any clinical signs of diabetes. **temporary d.,** a temporary state characterized by an abnormality shown on the glucose-tolerance test, which later becomes normal. **toxic d.,** diabetes due to a poison which prevents the liver from responding normally to hyperglycemia. **true d.,** diabetes due to insufficiency of insulin secretion.

diabetic (di″ah-bet′ik). 1. Pertaining to or affected with diabetes. 2. A person affected with diabetes. **brittle d.,** a person affected with diabetes who spontaneously shows considerable oscillation between high and low levels of sugar in the blood.

diabetid (di″ah-be′tid). A cutaneous manifestation of diabetes.

diabetogenic (di″ah-bet″o-jen′ik) [*diabetes* + Gr. *gennan* to produce]. Producing diabetes.

diabetogenous (di″ah-be-toj′e-nus). Produced by diabetes.

diabetograph (di″ah-be′to-graf) [*diabetes* + Gr. *graphein* to write]. An instrument used in urinalysis, with a graduated scale to show the proportion of glucose present.

diabetometer (di″ah-be-tom′e-ter) [*diabetes* + Gr. *metron* measure]. A polariscope for use in estimating the percentage of sugar in urine.

diabetophobia (di″ah-be″to-fo′be-ah) [*diabetes* + *phobia*]. An abnormal fear of diabetes.

diabetotherapy (di″ah-be″to-ther′ah-pe). The treatment of diabetes.

diabinese (di-ab′ĭ-nēs). Trade mark for chlorpropamide.

diabolepsy (di-ab′o-lep″se) [L. *diab′olus* devil + Gr. *lēpsis* a taking hold, a seizure]. A state in which the subject believes he is possessed by a devil, or that he is endowed with supernatural powers.

diabrosis (di″ah-bro′sis) [*dia-* + Gr. *brōsis* eating]. Perforation resulting from a corrosive process; perforating ulceration.

diabrotic (di″ah-brot′ik) [Gr. *diabrōtikos*]. 1. Ulcerative; caustic. 2. A corrosive or escharotic agent.

diacele (di′ah-sēl). Diacoele.

diacetate (di-as′ĕ-tāt). Any salt of diacetic acid.

diacetemia (di″as-ĕ-te′me-ah) [*diacetic acid* + Gr. *haima* blood + *-ia*]. The presence of aceto-acetic acid (diacetic acid) in the blood.

diaceticaciduria (di″ah-set″ik-as″ĭ-du′re-ah). Diaceturia.

diacetin (di-as′ĕ-tin). Glyceryl diacetate.

diacetonuria (di-as″ĕ-to-nu′re-ah). Diaceturia.

diaceturia (di″as-ĕ-tu′re-ah) [*diacetic acid* + Gr. *ouron* urine + *-ia*]. The excretion of aceto-acetic acid (diacetic acid) in the urine.

diacetyl (di-as′ĕ-til). A yellow liquid, diketobutane, $CH_3COCOCH_3$, having the odor of butter. **d. peroxide,** a compound, $CH_3CO.O.O.CO.CH_3$: used in solution as an antiseptic.

diacetylmorphine (di″ah-se″til-mor′fin). Heroin; a white, bitterish, crystalline powder, $C_{17}H_{17}(O.OC.CH_3)_2.NO$, the diacetic acid ester of morphine. An anodyne and sedative, it has been used in irritative coughs of phthisis and bronchitis, and in dyspnea. The importation of heroin and its salts into the United States is now illegal. **d. hydrochloride,** a white, crystalline powder, $C_{17}H_{17}(O.CO.CH_3)_2ON.HCl.H_2O$: used like heroin.

diachesis (di-ak′ĕ-sis) [Gr.]. A confused state.

diachorema (di″ah-ko-re′mah) [Gr. *diachōrēma*]. Excrement; feces.

diachoresis (di-ah-ko-re′sis). Defecation.

diachylon (di-ak′ĭ-lon) [*dia-* + Gr. *chylos* juice]. Lead plaster.

diacid (di-as′id) [Gr. *dis* twice + *acid*]. Having two replaceable hydrogen atoms; also, capable of saturating a dibasic acid, or two molecules of a monobasic acid.

diaclasis (di-ak′lah-sis) [*dia-* + Gr. *klasis* fracture]. A fracture, especially one made for a surgical purpose.

diaclast (di′ah-klast). An instrument for perforating the fetal skull in craniectomy.

diacoele (di″ah-se′le). The third ventricle.

diacoelia (di-ah-se′le-ah) [*dia-* + Gr. *koilia* a hollow]. The third ventricle.

diacrinous (di-ak′rĭ-nus) [Gr. *diakrinein* to separate]. Giving off secretion directly, as from a filter: said of gland cells, as those of the kidney. Opposed to *ptyocrinous*.

diacrisis (di-ak′rĭ-sis) [Gr. *diakrisis* separation]. 1. Diagnosis. 2. A disease marked by a morbid state of the secretions. 3. A critical discharge or excretion.

diacritic (di-ah-krit′ik) [*dia-* + Gr. *krinein* to judge]. Diagnostic.

diactinic (di″ak-tin′ik). Transmitting chemically active rays.

diactinism (di-ak′tin-izm) [*dia-* + Gr. *aktis* ray]. The property of transmitting chemically active rays.

diad (di′ad). 1. Having a valency or combining power of two. 2. Dyad.

diaderm (di′ah-derm) [*dia-* + Gr. *derma* skin]. The blastoderm during that stage in which it consists of an ectoderm and an entoderm.

diadermic (di-ah-der′mik). 1. Pertaining to the diaderm. 2. Through the skin.

diadochocinesia (di-ad″ŏ-ko-si-ne′se-ah). Diadochokinesia.

diadochocinetic (di-ad″ŏ-ko-si-net′ik). Diadochokinetic.

diadochokinesia (di-ad″ŏ-ko-ki-ne′se-ah) [Gr. *diadochos* succeeding + *kinēsis* motion]. The function of arresting one motor impulse and substituting for it one that is diametrically opposite.

diadochokinesis (di-ad″ŏ-ko-ki-ne′sis). Diadochokinesia.

diadochokinetic (di-ad″ŏ-ko-ki-net′ik). Pertaining to diadochokinesia.

diadol (di′ah-dol). Trade mark for a preparation of diallyl barbituric acid.

diafen (di′ah-fen). Trade mark for a preparation of diphenylpyraline hydrochloride.

diagnose (di′ag-nōs). To make a diagnosis of; to recognize the nature of an attack of disease.

diagnosis (di″ag-no′sis) [*dia-* + Gr. *gnōsis* knowledge]. 1. The art of distinguishing one disease from another. 2. The determination of the nature of a case of disease. **biological d.,** diagnosis by tests performed on animals, as by the Aschheim-Zondek test. **clinical d.,** diagnosis based on the symptoms shown during life, irrespective of the morbid changes producing them. **cytohistologic d.,** cytologic diagnosis. **cytologic d.,** diagnosis of malignant conditions based on discovery in body transudates or exudates of neoplastic cells, which are exfoliated from many types of malignant epithelial tumors. **differential d.,** the determination of which one of two or more diseases or conditions a patient is suffering from, by systematically comparing and contrasting their symptoms. **direct d.,** pathologic diagnosis by observing structural lesions or pathognomonic symptoms. **d. ex juvan′tibus,** a diagnosis based on the results of treatment. **d. by exclusion,** recognition of a disease by excluding all other known diseases. **laboratory d.,** diagnosis based on the findings of various laboratory examinations or tests. **niveau d.** [Fr. "level diagnosis"], localization of the exact level of a lesion; as, for instance, of an intervertebral tumor. **pathologic d.,** diagnosis by observing the structural lesions present. **physical d.,** determination of disease by inspection, palpation, percussion, or auscultation. **provocative d.,** the induction of a condition for the purpose of diagnosis; as the induction of a fit in a doubtful case of epilepsy. **roentgen d.,** diagnosis made by means of roentgen rays. **serum d.,** diagnosis by means of serums.

diagnostic (di″ag-nos′tik). Pertaining to or subserving diagnosis.

diagnosticate (di″ag-nos′te-kāt). Diagnose.

diagnostician (di″ag-nos-tish′an). An expert in diagnosis.

diagnostics (di″ag-nos′tiks). The science and practice of diagnosis of disease.

diagnosticum, Ficker's (di″ag-nos′te-kum). An emulsion of killed typhoid bacilli for use in the Gruber-Widal reaction.

diagram (di′ah-gram). A graphic representation, in simplest form, of an object or concept, made up of lines and lacking entirely any pictorial elements.

diagrammatic (di″ah-grah-mat′ik). Pertaining to or of the nature of a diagram.

diagraph (di′ah-graf) [*dia-* + Gr. *graphein* to write]. An instrument for recording outlines: used in craniometry, etc.

diakinesis (di″ah-ki-ne′sis) [*dia-* + Gr. *kinēsis* motion]. The stage in the maturation of a sex cell in which double chromosome threads fuse to form the haploid number.

dial (di′al) [L. *dialis* daily, from *dies* day]. 1. A circular area with graduations around the circumference and a centrally fixed pointer for indicating values of time, pressure, etc. 2. A proprietary brand of allobarbital. **astigmatic d.,** a diagram like the face of a watch used in testing for astigmatism.

dialectrolysis (di″ah-lek-trol′ĭ-sis). Bourguignon's term for ionization treatment.

Dialister (di″ah-lis′ter). A genus of minute gram-negative rod-shaped bacteria found in the respiratory tract. They pass some bacteria-proof filters, and at one time *D. pneumosintes* was thought to be etiologically related to epidemic influenza.

diallyl (di-al′il). 1. Any compound containing two allyl molecules. 2. A liquid unsaturated hydrocarbon, $CH_2.CH.CH_2.CH_2.CH{:}CH_2$, having the odor of radishes. **d. disulfide,** an odorous principle, $(C_3H_5)_2S_2$, found in oil of garlic.

dialurate (di-al′u-rāt). A salt of dialuric acid.

dialysance (di″ah-li′sans) [*dialysis* + *-ance* suffix denoting action or process]. The minute rate of net exchange of a substance between blood and bath fluid, per unit blood-bath concentration gradient; a parameter in artificial kidney kinetics (non-filtration) functionally equivalent to the clearance of the natural kidney.

dialysate (di-al′ĭ-sāt). The material which passes through the membrane in dialysis.

dialysis (di-al′ĭ-sis) [*dia-* + Gr. *lysis* dissolution]. 1. The process of separating crystalloids and colloids in solution by the difference in their rates of diffusion through a semipermeable membrane: crystalloids pass through readily, colloids very slowly or not at all. 2. Solution of continuity. **Abderhalden's d.,** Abderhalden's reaction. **cross d.,** dialytic parabiosis. **d. ret′inae,** rupture of the retina at the ora serrata.

dialyzable (di-ah-līz′ah-b'l). Capable of dialysis or of passing through a membrane.

dialyzed (di′ah-līzd). Separated or prepared by dialysis.

dialyzer (di′ah-līz″er). An apparatus for effecting dialysis.

diamagnetic (di″ah-mag-net′ik) [*dia-* + Gr. *magnēs* magnet]. Taking a position at right angles with the lines of magnetic influence.

Diamanus (di″ah-ma′nus). A genus of fleas. **D. monta′nus,** a flea of rodents in the Western United States which has been implicated in the transmission of sylvatic plague.

diameter (di-am′e-ter). The length of a straight line passing through the center of a circle and connecting opposite points on its circumference; hence the distance between two specified opposite points on the periphery of a structure such as the cranium or pelvis. **anteroposterior d.,** the distance between two points located on the anterior and posterior aspects, respectively, of the structure being measured; such as the true conjugate diameter of the pelvis, or the occipitofrontal diameter of the skull. **anterotransverse d.** (of the cranium), temporal d. **Baudelocque's d.,** the external conjugate diameter of the pelvic inlet. **biischial d.,** the distance between the two ischial tuberosities. **biparietal d.,** the distance between the two parietal eminences. **bispinous d.,** the distance between the opposite spines of the ischia. **bitemporal d.,** the distance between the two extremities of the coronal suture. **buccolingual d.,** the distance from the buccal to the lingual surface of a tooth crown. **cervicobregmatic d.,** the distance between the center of the anterior fontanel and the junction of the neck with the floor of the mouth. **coccygeopubic d.,** the distance from the tip of the coccyx to the under margin of the symphysis pubis. **conjugate d.,** the distance between two specified opposite points on the periphery of the pelvic inlet, usually used in reference to the true conjugate diameter. **conjugate d., anatomic,** the true conjugate diameter. **conjugate d., diagonal,** the distance from the under margin of the pubis to the tip of the sacral promontory. **conjugate d., external,** the distance from the depression under the last lumbar spine to the upper margin of the pubis. **conjugate d., internal,** true conjugate d. **conjugate d., obstetric,** the shortest anteroposterior diameter of the pelvic inlet; the distance from a point 1 cm. below the top of the pubis to the tip of the sacral promontory, measuring about 11 cm. in the normal pelvis. So called because it is intimately concerned in the process of labor. **conjugate d., true,** the anteroposterior diameter of the superior aperture of the minor pelvis, measured from the superior margin of the symphysis pubis to the sacrovertebral angle. Called also *conjugata* [N A]. In practice, the measurement is obtained by subtracting 8 cm. from the value for the external conjugate. **cranial d's,** distances measured between certain landmarks of the skull, such as the *biparietal d., bitemporal d., cervicobregmatic d., frontomental d., occipitofrontal d., occipitomental d.,* and *suboccipitobregmatic d.* **craniometric d.,** any line connecting two craniometric points of the same name. **Deventer's d.,** d. obliqua pelvis. **extracanthic d.,** the distance between the lateral points of junction of the upper and lower eyelids of the two eyes. **frontomental d.,** the distance from the forehead to the chin.

fronto-occipital d., occipitofrontal d. **intercanthic d.,** the distance between the medial points of junction of the upper and lower eyelids of the two eyes. **intercristal d.,** the distance between the middle points of the iliac crests. **intertuberal d.,** the distance between the sciatic notches. **Löhlein's d.,** the distance between the center of the subpubic ligament and the superior-interior angle of the great sacrosciatic foramen. **median d., d. media'nus,** true conjugate d. **longitudinal d., inferior,** the distance from the foramen cecum to the internal occipital protuberances. **mento-occipital d.,** occipitomental d. **mentoparietal d.,** the distance from the chin to the vertex of the skull. **d. obli'qua pel'vis** [N A, B N A], the oblique diameter of the superior aperture of the minor pelvis, measured from one sacroiliac articulation to the iliopubic eminence of the other side. **oblique d. of pelvis,** d. obliqua pelvis; designated right or left depending on the sacroiliac joint used for reference; the left is uniformly 0.5 cm. shorter than the right. **occipitofrontal d.,** the distance from the external occipital protuberance to the most prominent midpoint of the frontal bone. **occipitomental d.,** the distance from the external occipital protuberance to the most prominent midpoint of the chin. **parietal d.,** the distance between tuberosities of parietal bones. **pelvic d.,** any diameter of the pelvis. **posterotransverse d.,** parietal d. **pubosacral d.,** true conjugate d. **pubotuberous d.,** the distance from the tuberosity of the ischium to a point on the superior ramus of the pubis which is located directly perpendicular to the tuberosity. **sacropubic d.,** the distance from the end of the sacrum to the ligamentum pubicum superius. **sagittal d.,** the distance from the glabella to the external occipital protuberance. **suboccipitobregmatic d.,** the distance from the lowest posterior point of the occiput to the center of the anterior fontanel. **temporal d.,** the distance between the tips of the alae magnae. **d. transver'sa pel'vis** [N A, B N A], the greatest distance from side to side of the superior aperture of the minor pelvis. Called also *transverse d. of pelvis.* **transverse d.,** the distance between two points located on the opposite sides of the body part being measured, such as the biparietal diameter of the head. **true d. of pelvis,** d. transversa pelvis. **vertical d.,** the distance between two points situated on the upper and lower aspects of the structure being measured, such as the distance between the occipital foramen and the vertex of the skull.

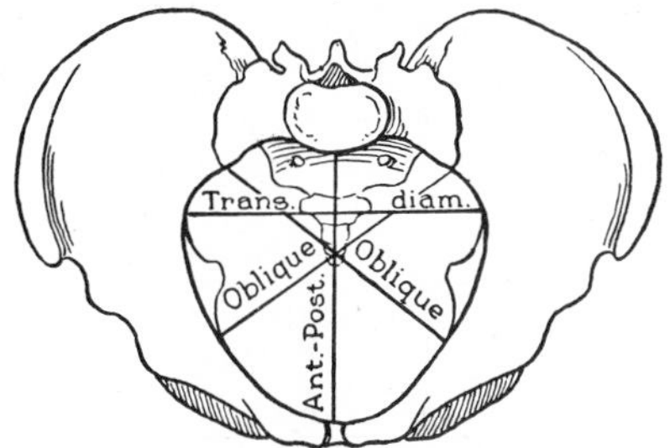

Diameters of pelvic inlet. (See also pelvic planes.) (Moloy.)

diamide (di-am'id) [L. *di* two + *amide*]. 1. A compound which contains two amido groups. 2. Hydrazine.

diamidine (di-am'ĭ-dēn). A compound that contains two amidine groups.

diamido-. A prefix indicating the possession of two amido groups.

diamine (di-am'in) [L. *di* two + *amine*]. 1. A compound which contains two amino groups. 2. Hydrazine sulfate, $H_2SO_4.H_2N.H_2N.NH_2.NH_2.H_2SO_4$; a poisonous germicide in colorless crystals. **diethylene d.,** piperazine.

diamino-acridine (di-am"ĭ-no-ak'rĭ-din). Proflavine.

diaminodiphosphatide (di-am"ĭ-no-di-fos'fah-tīd"). A phosphatide containing two atoms of nitrogen and two of phosphorus to the molecule.

diaminomonophosphatide (di-am"ĭ-no-mon"-o-fos'fah-tīd"). A phosphatide containing two atoms of nitrogen and one of phosphorus to the molecule.

diaminuria (di-am"ĭ-nu're-ah). The presence of diamines in the urine.

diamonds (di'ah-munz). An urticarial form of swine erysipelas characterized by well-defined quadrangular or rhombic patches on the skin.

diamorphine (di-ah-mor'fin). Diacetylmorphine.

diamorphosis (di"ah-mor-fo'sis). Growth into normal shape.

diamox (di'ah-moks). Trade mark for preparations of acetazolamide.

diamthazole (di-am'thah-zōl). Chemical name: 6-(2-diethylaminoethoxy)-2-dimethylaminobenzothiazole: used as an antifungal agent.

diamylene (di-am'ĭ-lēn). Dipentene.

diamylose (di-am'ĭ-lōs). Bisamylose.

dianabol (di-an'ah-bol). Trade mark for methandrostenolone.

dianhydro-antiarigenin (di"an-hi"dro-an"te-ar'ĭ-jen"in). An aglycone, $C_{23}H_{28}O_5$, from antiarin.

dianhydro-gitoxigenin (di"an-hi"dro-jĭ-tok'sĭ-jen"in). An aglycone, $C_{23}H_{30}O_3$, from digitalin and oleandrin.

dianoetic (di-ah-ne'tik) [*dia-* + Gr. *nous* mind]. Pertaining to the intellectual functions, especially to reasoning.

diantebrachia (di"an-te-bra'ke-ah). A developmental anomaly characterized by duplication of a forearm.

diaparene (di-ap'ah-rēn). Trade mark for preparations of methylbenzethonium chloride.

diapason (di"ah-pa'son) [*dia-* + Gr. *pasōn* all]. A tuning-fork: used in the diagnosis of ear troubles.

diapedesis (di"ah-pĕ-de'sis) [*dia-* + Gr. *pēdan* to leap]. The outward passage through intact vessel walls of corpuscular elements of the blood.

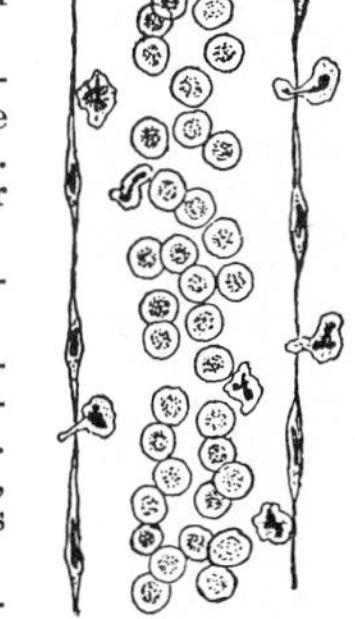
Diapedesis of leukocytes. (Williams.)

diapedetic (di"ah-pĕ-det'ik). Pertaining to or characterized by diapedesis.

diaphane (di'ah-fān) [Gr. *diaphanēs* transparent]. 1. The investing membrane of a cell. 2. A minute electric lamp for use in transillumination.

diaphaneity (di"ah-fah-ne'ĭ-te). Transparency.

diaphanometer (di-af"ah-nom'e-ter) [Gr. *diaphanēs* transparent + Gr. *metron* measure]. An instrument for testing milk, urine, and other fluids by means of transmitted light.

diaphanometry (di-af"ah-nom'e-tre). The measurement of the transparency of a fluid.

diaphanoscope (di-af'ah-no-skōp") [Gr. *diaphanēs* transparent + *skopein* to examine]. An instrument for illuminating a body cavity and rendering it visible.

diaphanoscopy (di-af"ah-nos'ko-pe). Examination with the diaphanoscope; transillumination.

diaphemetric (di"ah-fĕ-met'rik) [*dia-* + Gr. *haphē* touch + *metron* measure]. Pertaining to the measurement of tactile sensibility.

diaphorase (di-af'o-rās). A flavoprotein which catalyzes the oxidation of coenzyme I.

diaphoresis (di"ah-fo-re'sis) [Gr. *diaphorēsis*]. Perspiration, especially profuse perspiration.

diaphoretic (di"ah-fo-ret'ik) [Gr. *diaphorētikos*]. 1. Pertaining to, characterized by, or promoting diaphoresis. 2. An agent that promotes diaphoresis.

diaphragm (di′ah-fram). 1. The musculomembranous partition separating the abdominal and thoracic cavities. Called also *diaphragma* [N A]. 2. Any separating membrane or structure. 3. A disk with one or more openings in it, or with an adjustable opening, mounted in relation to a lens, by which part of the light may be excluded from the area. **accessory d.,** diaphragma urogenitale. **Akerlund d.,** a spiral type of diaphragm used in roentgenography. **Bucky d., Bucky-Potter d.,** a diaphragm used in roentgenography to prevent the secondary rays from reaching the plate, thereby securing better contrast and definition. **contraceptive d.,** a device of molded rubber or other soft plastic material, fitted over the cervix uteri to prevent entrance of spermatozoa. **d. of mouth, oral d.,** musculus mylohyoideus. **pelvic d., d. of pelvis,** diaphragma pelvis. **Potter-Bucky d.,** Bucky d. **secondary d.,** diaphragma urogenitale. **d. of sella turcica,** diaphragma sellae. **urogenital d.,** diaphragma urogenitale.

diaphragma (di″ah-frag′mah), pl. *diaphragmata* [Gr. "a partition-wall, barrier"]. [N A, B N A] The musculomembranous partition separating the abdominal and thoracic cavities. Called also *diaphragm.* Also used in anatomical nomenclature in the names of other separating structures. **d. o′ris,** musculus mylohyoideus. **d. pel′vis** [N A, B N A], the portion of the floor of the pelvis formed by the coccygei and levatores ani muscles and their fasciae. Called also *pelvic diaphragm.* **d. sel′lae** [N A, B N A], a ring-shaped fold of dura mater covering the sella turcica, and containing an aperture for passage of the infundibulum of the hypophysis. Called also *diaphragm of sella turcica.* **d. urogenita′le** [N A, B N A], the musculomembranous layer superficial to the pelvic diaphragm, extending between the ischiopubic rami and surrounding the urogenital ducts. Called also *urogenital diaphragm.*

diaphragmalgia (di″ah-frag-mal′je-ah) [*diaphragm* + Gr. *algos* pain + *-ia*]. Pain in the diaphragm.

diaphragmata (di″ah-frag′mah-tah) [Gr.]. Plural of *diaphragma.*

diaphragmatic (di″ah-frag-mat′ik). Pertaining to or of the nature of a diaphragm.

diaphragmatitis (di″ah-frag″mah-ti′tis). Diaphragmitis.

diaphragmatocele (di″ah-frag-mat′o-sēl) [*diaphragm* + Gr. *kēlē* hernia]. Diaphragmatic hernia.

diaphragmitis (di″ah-frag-mi′tis). Inflammation of the diaphragm.

diaphragmodynia (di″ah-frag″mo-din′e-ah) [*diaphragm* + Gr. *odynē* pain]. Diaphragmalgia.

diaphysary (di-af′ĭ-zār-e). Diaphyseal.

diaphyseal (di″ah-fiz′e-al). Pertaining to or affecting the shaft of a long bone (diaphysis).

diaphysectomy (di″ah-fiz-ek′to-me) [*diaphysis* + Gr. *ektomē* excision]. Excision of a portion of the shaft of a long bone.

diaphyses (di-af′ĭ-sēz). Plural of *diaphysis.*

diaphysial (di″ah-fiz′e-al). Diaphyseal.

diaphysis (di-af′ĭ-sis), pl. *diaph′yses* [Gr. "the point of separation between stalk and branch"]. 1. [N A, B N A] The portion of a long bone between the ends or extremities, which are usually articular, and wider than the shaft; it consists of a tube of compact bone, enclosing the medullary cavity. Called also *shaft.* 2. The portion of a bone formed from a primary center of ossification.

diaphysitis (di″ah-fiz-i′tis). Inflammation of a diaphysis. **tuberculous d.,** inflammation involving intermediate segments of the shafts of long bones, caused by the tubercle bacillus.

diapiresis (di″ah-pi-re′sis) [Gr. *diapeirein* to drive through]. Diapedesis.

diaplacental (di″ah-plah-sen′tal). Through the placenta.

diaplasis (di-ap′lah-sis) [Gr.]. The setting of a fracture or the reduction of a dislocation.

diaplastic (di″ah-plas′tik). Pertaining to the setting of a fracture or the reduction of a dislocation.

diaplex (di′ah-pleks). Diaplexus.

diaplexal (di-ah-plek′sal). Pertaining to the diaplexus.

diaplexus (di″ah-plek′sus). Plexus choroideus ventriculi tertii.

diapnoic (di-ap-no′ik) [Gr. *diapnein* to perspire]. Pertaining to or causing mild perspiration.

diapophysis (di-ah-pof′ĭ-sis) [*dia-* + Gr. *apophysis* outgrowth]. The superior or articular part of a transverse process of a vertebra.

Diaptomus (di-ap′to-mus). A genus of crustaceans species of which act as hosts of the larvae of *Diphyllobothrium latum.*

diapyesis (di″ah-pi-e′sis). Suppuration.

diapyetic (di″ah-pi-et′ik). Promoting suppuration.

diarhemia (di-ah-re′me-ah). Diarrhemia.

diarrhea (di″ah-re′ah) [*dia-* + Gr. *rhein* to flow]. Abnormal frequency and liquidity of fecal discharges (Hippocrates). **d. ablactato′rum,** a diarrhea of infants at the time they are weaned. **d. al′ba,** a disease of hot countries, affecting children especially. It is thought to be of filarial origin. **cachectic d.,** that which is due to some constitutional disease. **choleraic d.,** acute diarrhea with serous stools, accompanied by vomiting and collapse. **d. chylo′sa,** diarrhea in which the discharge consists of a yellowish-white, mucopurulent substance. **Cochin-China d.** 1. Sprue. 2. Anguilluliasis. **colliquative d.,** profuse diarrhea, producing a state of dehydration, sometimes seen in the late stages of pulmonary tuberculosis. **crapulous d.,** that due to excess in eating or drinking. **critical d.,** diarrhea occurring at the crisis of a disease or producing a crisis. **dissecting room d.,** severe diarrhea caused by exposure to the effluvia of a dissecting room. **dysenteric d.,** diarrhea with mucous and bloody stools. **enteral d.,** diarrhea due to infection within the gastrointestinal tract. **epidemic d.** See *Reimann's epidemic d.* **epidemic d. of newborn,** a contagious diarrhea occurring in epidemics among newborn infants in hospitals. **fermental d., fermentative d.,** diarrhea caused by fermentation due to microorganisms. **flagellate d.,** diarrhea marked by the presence of flagellate organisms (*Giardia*) in the stools. **gastrogenic d.,** diarrhea due to gastric disorder. **hill d.,** a severe type of chronic intestinal catarrh peculiar to hot climates and occurring only at elevations of several thousand feet: named from the hill districts of India. By some it is considered to be identical with sprue. **infantile d.,** summer diarrhea. **inflammatory d.,** diarrhea in which there is an inflammation of the intestine due to bacterial action. **irritative d.,** diarrhea due to irritation of the intestine by improper food, poisons, purgatives, etc. **lienteric d.,** diarrhea with fluid stools containing undigested food. **mechanical d.,** diarrhea due to mechanical obstruction to the portal circulation, producing gastro-intestinal hyperemia. **morning d.,** a condition marked by diarrhea in the morning only. **mucous d.,** a kind characterized by the presence of mucus in stools. **neonatal d.,** epidemic diarrhea of the newborn. **d. pancreat′ica,** the diarrhea that accompanies parenchymatous degeneration or cystic disease of the pancreas. **pancreatogenous fatty d.,** a diarrhea in which the stools contain an excessive amount of fat due to dysfunction of the pancreas. **paradoxical d.,** stercoral d. **parenteral d.,** diarrhea due to infections outside the gastrointestinal tract, such as tuberculosis, syphilis, etc. **putrefactive d.,** diarrhea due to putrefaction of the intestinal contents. **serous d.,** discharge of feces softened by copious serous fluid. **stercoral d.,** diarrhea accompanied by colic and following two or three days of constipation. **summer d.,** acute diarrhea in children during great heat of summer. **trench d.,** a form of diarrhea and dysentery occurring in troops in the trenches. **tropical d.** See *sprue* (1st def.). **tubercular d.,** a variety of diarrhea peculiar to cases of tuberculosis. **tubular d.,** mucous colitis. **d. urino′sa,** polyuria. **vicarious d.,** that which is due to the impairment or suppression of some function. **virus d.,** a specific infectious condition manifested by diarrhea in infants and by stomatitis and diarrhea in older children. **watery d.,** serous d. **white d.** 1. A form in which the stools contain a thin, white mucus. 2. An infectious disease of young chickens marked by loss of appetite, dulness, and diarrhea, the discharges of which leave white lumps around the cloaca. It is caused by *Salmonella pullorum* (bacillary variety) or by *Eimeria avium* (coccidial variety).

diarrheal (di″ah-re′al). Pertaining to, or marked by, diarrhea.

diarrheic (di″ah-re′ik). Diarrheal.

diarrhemia (di″ah-re′me-ah) [Gr. *diarrhein* to flow through + *haima* blood + *-ia*]. A watery condition of the blood occurring in sheep infested with parasites.

diarthric (di-ar′thrik) [*di-* + Gr. *arthron* a joint]. Pertaining to or affecting two different joints.

diarthroses (di″ar-thro′sēz). Plural of *diarthrosis*.

diarthrosis (di″ar-thro′sis) [Gr. *diarthrōsis* a movable articulation], pl. *diarthroses* [B N A]. Junctura synovialis.

diarticular (di″ar-tik′u-lar). Diarthric.

diaschisis (di-as′kĭ-sis) [*dia-* + Gr. *schizein* to split]. Monakow's term for a loss of functional continuity between the various centers or neuron tracts, constituting one of the cerebral mechanisms.

diascope (di′ah-skōp) [*dia-* + Gr. *skopein* to examine]. A glass plate pressed against the skin to permit observation of changes produced in the underlying area by the pressure.

diascopy (di-as′ko-pe). 1. Examination with the diascope. 2. Transillumination.

diasone (di′ah-sōn). Trade mark for a preparation of sulfoxone.

diasostic (di″ah-sos′tik). Hygienic.

diaspironecrobiosis (di-as″pi-ro-nek″ro-bi-o′sis) [*dia-* + Gr. *speirein* to sow + *necrobiosis*]. Disseminated necrobiosis.

diaspironecrosis (di-as″pi-ro-ne-kro′sis). Disseminated necrosis.

diastalsis (di″ah-stal′sis) [*dia-* + Gr. *stalsis* contraction]. A downward moving wave of contraction with a preceding wave of inhibition occurring in the digestive tube, in addition to the peristaltic wave. Cf. *anastalsis* and *catastalsis*.

diastaltic (di″ah-stal′tik). 1. Pertaining to diastalsis. 2. Performed reflexly; reflex.

diastase (di′ah-stās) [Gr. *diastasis* separation]. 1. A white, amorphous, soluble enzyme produced during the germination of seeds, and contained in malt. It converts starch into maltose and then into dextrose. 2. Any enzyme (in French usage). **pancreatic d.,** an enzyme obtained from the pancreatic secretions and given for indigestion. **taka d.** See *taka diastase*. **d. ve′ra,** pancreatin.

diastasemia (di″as-tah-se′me-ah) [Gr. *diastasis* separation + Gr. *haima* blood + *-ia*]. The dissociation of the elements of the red blood corpuscles.

diastasic (di″as-ta′sik). Diastatic.

diastasimetry (di″as-tah-sim′e-tre). The estimation of the diastatic power of a substance.

diastasis (di-as′tah-sis) [Gr.]. 1. A form of dislocation in which there is separation of two bones normally attached to each other without the existence of a true joint; as in separation of the epiphysis of a bone. 2. Diastasis cordis. **d. cor′dis,** the rest period of the cardiac cycle, which occurs just before systole. **iris d.,** iridodiastasis. **d. rec′ti abdom′inis,** separation of the rectus muscle of the abdomen away from the median line, sometimes occurring in pregnancy and after abdominal operations.

diastasum (di″ah-sta′sum). Diastase.

diastasuria (di″ah-stās-u′re-ah). The presence of diastase in the urine.

diastatic (di″ah-stat′ik). 1. Pertaining to diastase. 2. Pertaining to diastasis.

diastem (di′ah-stem). Diastema.

diastema (di″ah-ste′mah), pl. *diastem′ata* [Gr. *diastēma* an interval]. A space or cleft. In dentistry, a space between the two adjacent teeth in the same dental arch. In cytology, a narrow zone in the equatorial plane through which the cytosome divides in mitosis.

diastematocrania (di″ah-stem″ah-to-kra′ne-ah) [Gr. *diastēma* an interval + *kranion* cranium]. Congenital longitudinal fissure of the cranium.

diastematomyelia (di″ah-stem″ah-to-mi-e′le-ah) [Gr. *diastēma* an interval + *myelos* marrow]. Congenital longitudinal fissure of the spinal cord, separating the lateral halves.

diastematopyelia (di″ah-stem″ah-to-pi-e′le-ah) [Gr. *diastēma* an interval + *pyelos* pelvis]. Congenital median fissure of the pelvis.

diaster (di′as-ter) [*di-* two + Gr. *astēr* star]. Amphiaster.

diastereoisomer (di″ah-ster″e-o-i′so-mer). A compound exhibiting, or capable of exhibiting, diastereoisomerism.

diastereoisomeric (di″ah-ster″e-o-i″so-mer′ik). Exhibiting diastereoisomerism.

diastereoisomerism (di″ah-ster″e-o″i-som′er-izm). A special type of optical isomerism in which the respective molecules of the compounds do not, at any time, exhibit a mirror-image, or enantiomorphic, relationship to one another. For example, the relationship between either *dextro-* or *laevo-*tartaric acid and *meso*-tartaric acid is called diastereoisomeric. Diastereoisomers, in contrast to enantiomorphs, differ in both physical and chemical properties.

diastin (di-as′tin). A form of diastase.

diastole (di-as′to-le) [Gr. *diastolē* a drawing asunder; expansion]. The dilatation, or period of dilatation, of the heart, especially that of the ventricles. It coincides with the interval between the second and the first heart sound.

diastolic (di″ah-stol′ik). Of or pertaining to the diastole.

diastolization (di-as″tol-i-za′shun). 1. Dilatation. 2. The treatment of hypertrophic rhinitis by gentle dilation of the nasal passages combined with massage of the mucosa by means of hollow rubber bougies which are alternately inflated and deflated by pressure on a rubber bulb.

diastomyelia (di-as″to-mi-e′le-ah). Diastematomyelia.

diataxia (di″ah-tak′se-ah) [*di-* two + *ataxia*]. Ataxia affecting both sides of the body. **cerebral d., d. cerebra′lis infanti′lis,** the ataxic form of cerebral birth palsy.

diatela, diatele (di-ah-te′lah, di′ah-tēl). The roof of the third ventricle.

diaterma (di″ah-ter′mah) [*dia-* + Gr. *terma* end]. A portion of the floor of the third ventricle.

diathermacy (di″ah-ther′mah-se). The state of being diathermanous.

diathermal (di″ah-ther′mal). Diathermanous.

diathermanous (di″ah-ther′mah-nus) [*dia-* + Gr. *thermainein* to warm]. Admitting the passage of heat rays.

diathermia (di″ah-ther′me-ah). Diathermy.

diathermic (di″ah-ther′mik). Pertaining to diathermy; permeable by heat rays.

diathermocoagulation (di″ah-ther″mo-ko-ag″u-la′shun). Surgical diathermy.

diathermy (di′ah-ther″me) [*dia-* + Gr. *thermē* heat]. The generation of heat in the body tissues due to the resistance offered by the tissues to the passage of high frequency electric currents. In *medical d.* (thermopenetration) the tissues are warmed to a point short of tissue destruction; in *surgical d.* (electrocoagulation) the heat generated is sufficient to coagulate tissue cells and destroy tissue. **short wave d.,** the therapeutic heating of the body tissues or parts by means of an oscillating electric current of high frequency. The frequency varies from 10 million to 100 million cycles per second and the wavelength from 30 to 3 meters. **ultrashort wave d.,** a short wave diathermy in which the wavelength used is less than 10 meters.

diathesis (di-ath'ĕ-sis) [Gr. "arrangement, disposition"]. A constitution or condition of the body which makes the tissues react in special ways to certain extrinsic stimuli and thus tends to make the person more than usually susceptible to certain diseases. Cf. *constitution.* **aneurysmal d.,** liability to formation of multiple aneurysms. **asthenic d.,** a low state of general vitality. **bilious d.,** a tendency toward imperfect elimination of bile. **catarrhal d.,** special liability to catarrhal diseases. **contractural d.,** a hysterical tendency to contractures. **cystic d.,** a tendency to the development of multiple cysts in an organ. **Czerny's d.,** exudative d. **dartrous d.,** a constitutional tendency to eczema, herpes, and other skin diseases. **eosinophil d.,** a condition marked by permanent or prolonged eosinophilia. **exudative d.,** a diathesis marked by thickening of the lingual mucous membrane, seborrhea of the scalp, prurigo, intertrigo, severe itching, glandular enlargement, and edema. **fibroplastic d.,** a tendency of the body to develop connective tissue in excess in response to trauma. **furuncular d.,** furunculosis. **gouty d.,** predisposition to gout. **hemorrhagic d.,** a predisposition to abnormal hemostasis. **inopectic d.,** a bodily predisposition to embolism and thrombosis. **insane d.,** a natural predisposition to insanity. **neuropathic d.,** a congenital predisposition to nervous instability. **ossifying d.,** a tendency to the formation of bony deposits in the muscles. **oxalic d.,** one characterized by unusual amounts of oxalic acid in the urine. **psychopathic d.,** neuropathic diathesis. **rheumatic d.,** predisposition to rheumatism. **spasmodic d., spasmophilic d.,** spasmophilia; a condition of abnormal excitability of the peripheral motor nerves, tending to tetany and general convulsions. **strumous d.,** predisposition to scrofulous or tuberculous disease. **tuberculous d.,** special liability to the acquisition of tuberculosis. **uric acid d.,** a tendency to the collection of uric acid and urates in the tissues, resulting in gout, diabetes, etc. **varicose d.,** a tendency to the formation of varicose veins.

diathetic (di″ah-thet'ik). Of or pertaining to a diathesis.

diatom (di'ah-tom). Any unicellular microscopical form of alga having a wall of silica.

diatomic (di″ah-tom'ik) [*di-* + *atom*]. 1. Made up of two atoms. 2. Dibasic. 3. Composed of diatoms: said of earth composed of the shells of diatoms.

diauchenos (di-awk'ĕ-nos). A dicephalic monster with two necks also.

diauxic (di-awk'sik). Pertaining to or characterized by diauxie; implying two periods of growth separated by a lag period.

diauxie (di-awk'se) [*di-* + Gr. *auxein* to increase in size]. A phenomenon of bacterial growth in which an organism given a mixture of organic compounds first grows exclusively on one until that compound is exhausted, and then, after a lag during which it forms induced enzymes for utilizing the second compound, resumes growth on the latter.

diaxon (di-ak'son) [*di-* + *axon*]. A nerve cell having two axons or axis-cylinder processes.

diaxone (di-ak'sōn). Diaxon.

diazine (di-az'in). A compound containing a ring of four carbon and two nitrogen atoms.

diazo- (di-az'o). Prefix indicating possession of the group $—N_2—$.

diazobenzene (di-az″o-ben'zēn). A univalent organic radical, $C_6H_5N_2$.

diazoma (di″ah-zo'mah) [Gr. *diazōma* that which is put round]. The diaphragm.

diazomethane (di-az″o-meth'ān). An extremely poisonous yellow gas, $N_2.CH_2$, used in organic synthesis.

diazonal (di″ah-zo'nal). 1. Situated across or bridging two zones. 2. Pertaining to a diazone.

diazone (di'ah-zōn). One of the dark bands, alternating with white bands (*parazones*), formed by the layers of enamel prisms and seen in cross section of a tooth.

diazosulfobenzol (di-az″o-sul″fo-ben'zol). A substance which acts upon certain principles in the urine to form aniline colors.

diazotization (di-az″o-ti-za'shun). Conversion into a diazo compound.

diazotize (di-az'o-tīz). To introduce the diazo group into a compound.

diazouracil (di-az″o-u'rah-sil). A compound used as a test medium for sucrose.

dibasic (di-ba'sik) [*di-* + Gr. *basis* base]. Containing two hydrogen atoms replaceable by bases, and thus yielding two series of salts, as H_2SO_4.

dibenzanthracene (di-benz-an'thrah-sēn). An aromatic polycyclic hydrocarbon, $C_{22}H_{14}$, capable, when injected into the body, of producing epithelial tumors.

dibenz-dibutyl anthraquinol (di-benz″di-bu'til an″thrah-kwin'ol). A carcinogenic and estrogenic substance, 1,2,5,6-dibenz-9,10,di-n-butyl anthraquinol.

dibenzothiazine (di-ben″zo-thi'ah-zēn). Phenothiazine.

dibenzyline (di-ben'zĭ-lēn). Trade mark for a preparation of phenoxybenzamine hydrochloride.

diblastula (di-blas'tu-lah) [*di-* + *blastula*]. A blastula in which the ectoderm and entoderm are both present.

dibothriocephaliasis (di-both″re-o-sef″ah-li'ah-sis). Diphyllobothriasis.

Dibothriocephalus (di-both″re-o-sef'ah-lus) [*di-* + Gr. *bothrion* pit + *kephalē* head]. Diphyllobothrium.

dibrachia (di-bra'ke-ah) [*di-* + Gr. *brachion* arm]. A developmental anomaly characterized by duplication of an arm.

dibrachius (di-bra'ke-us). A twin monster having only two arms.

dibromide (di-bro'mīd). Any bromide which combines two atoms of bromine with one of another element or radical.

dibromoketone (di-bro″mo-ke'tōn). $CH_3.CO.-CHBr.CH_2Br$, a war gas.

dibucaine (di-bu'kān). Chemical name: 2-n-butoxy-N-(2-diethylaminoethyl) cinchoninamide. Used as a surface and spinal anesthetic.

dibuline (di'bu-lēn). Trade mark for a preparation of dibutoline sulfate.

dibutoline (di-bu'to-lēn). Chemical name: bis-[dibutylcarbamate of ethyl-(2-hydroxyethyl) dimethylammonium]: used in parasympathetic blockade, and as an antispasmodic.

dibutyl (di-būt'il). A hydrocarbon, C_8H_{18}, occurring in mineral oil.

dicacodyl (di-kak'o-dīl). A colorless, poisonous compound, $(CH_3)_2AsAs(CH_3)_2$, formed by the action of zinc on cacodyl chloride.

dicalcic (di-kal'sik). Having in each molecule two atoms of calcium.

dicalcium phosphate (di-kal'se-um fos'fāt). A compound, $CaHPO.2H_2O$, used in calcium therapy.

dicamphendion (di″kam-fen′de-on). A substance $(C_{10}H_{14}O)_2$, obtained by the action of metallic sodium upon bromocamphor, dicamphor being produced at the same time.

dicamphor (di-kam′for). A principle in colorless needles, $(C_{10}H_{15}O)_2$, produced at the same time and from the same materials as dicamphendion.

dicarbonate (di-kar′bon-āt). Bicarbonate.

dicelous (di-se′lus) [*di-* + Gr. *koilos* hollow]. 1. Hollowed on both sides. 2. Having two cavities.

dicephalous (di-sef′ah-lus). Having two heads.

dicephalus (di-sef′ah-lus) [*di-* + Gr. *kephalē* head]. A fetal monster with two heads. **d. di′pus dibra′chius,** a fetal monster with two heads but only two feet and two arms. **d. di′pus tetrabra′chius,** a fetal monster with only two legs, but with varying degrees of fusion of the upper trunk, each component having a head and pair of arms. **d. di′pus tribra′chius,** a fetal monster with two heads, two feet, but with a median third arm or arm rudiment. **d. dipy′gus,** anakatadidymus. **d. parasit′icus,** desmiognathus. **d. tri′pus tribra′chius,** a fetal monster with a common trunk, but with two heads, three arms, and three legs, the third limbs being either rudimentary or complete.

dicephaly (di-sef′ah-le). A developmental anomaly characterized by the presence of two heads.

dicheilia (di-ki′le-ah). The appearance of a double lip, owing to folding of the oral mucosa.

dicheiria (di-ki′re-ah) [*di-* + Gr. *cheir* hand]. A developmental anomaly characterized by duplication of a hand.

dicheirus (di-ki′rus). An individual exhibiting dicheiria.

dichlordioxydiamido-arsenobenzol (di-klor″di-ok″se-di-am″ĭ-do-ar″sĕ-no-ben′zol). Arsphenamine.

dichlorhydrin (di″klor-hi′drin). A colorless fluid, $CH_2Cl.CHOH.CH_2Cl$: used as a solvent for resins and prepared by heating anhydrous glycerin with sulfur monochloride.

dichloride (di-klo′rīd). A combination of a base with two atoms of chlorine.

dichlorisone (di-klōr′ĭ-sōn). Chemical name: $9\alpha,11\beta$-dichloro-1,4-pregnadiene-17α,21-diol-3,20 dione: a steroid used for topical anti-inflammatory action.

dichlorodiethyl sulfide (di-klo″ro-di-eth″il sul′fīd). Mustard gas, $(CH_2ClCH_2)_2S$; a vesicant gas employed in war. It produces blistering and subsequent sloughing of the skin with involvement of the eyes and respiratory tract. Death results from bronchopneumonia. Called also *yperite* and *lost.*

dichloroformoxime (di-klo″ro-for-mok′sim). A suffocating war gas, CCl_2:N.OH.

dichlorphenamide (di″klōr-fen′ah-mīd). Chemical name: 1,2-dichloro-3,5-disulfamylbenzene: used as a carbonic anhydrase inhibitor, and to reduce intraocular pressure in glaucoma.

dichogeny (di-koj′e-ne) [Gr. *dicha* in two + *gennan* to produce]. Development of tissues in different ways in accordance with changes in conditions affecting them.

dichorial (di-ko′re-al). Dichorionic.

dichorionic (di″ko-re-on′ik). Having two distinct chorions.

dichotomization (di-kot″ŏ-mi-za′shun). Dichotomy.

dichotomy (di-kot′o-me) [Gr. *dicha* in two + *temnein* to cut]. A process of division into two parts.

dichroic (di-kro′ik). Exhibiting dichroism.

dichroism (di′kro-izm) [*di-* + Gr. *chroa* color]. The quality or condition of presenting one color in reflected and another in transmitted light.

dichromasy (di-kro′mah-se). Dichromatism.

dichromat (di′kro-mat). An individual exhibiting dichromatopsia.

dichromate (di-kro′māt). Any salt containing the bivalent Cr_2O_7 radical.

dichromatic (di-kro-mat′ik). Pertaining to or characterized by dichromatism.

dichromatism (di-kro′mah-tism). 1. The quality of existing in or exhibiting two different colors. 2. Dichromatopsia.

dichromatopsia (di″kro-mah-top′se-ah) [*di-* + Gr. *chrōma* color + *opsis* vision + *-ia*]. A condition characterized by ability to perceive only 2 of the 160 colors discriminable by the normal eye; usually a complementary blue and yellow or, rarely, a red and green.

dichromic (di-kro′mik). Pertaining to two colors.

dichromophil (di-kro′mo-fil). An element that stains with both acid and basic dyes.

dichromophilism (di″kro-mof′ĭ-lizm). Capacity for double staining, that is, with both acid and basic dyes.

dick (dik). A war gas, ethyldichlorarsine, C_6H_5.-$AsCl_2$.

Dick test, toxin (dik) [George F. *Dick* and Gladys H. *Dick,* American physicians, born 1881]. See under *tests* and *toxin.*

dicliditis (dik″lid-i′tis) [Gr. *diklis* double door + *-itis*]. Inflammation of a valve, especially of one of the heart valves.

diclidostosis (dik″lid-os-to′sis) [Gr. *diklis* double door + *osteon* bone + *-osis*]. Ossification of the valves of the veins.

diclidotomy (dik″lid-ot′o-me) [Gr. *diklis* double door + *tomē* a cut]. The cutting of a valve, especially of the rectal valve or fold.

dicodid (di-ko′did). Trade mark for preparations of dihydrocodeinone.

dicoelous (di-se′lus) [*di-* + Gr. *koilos* hollow]. 1. Hollowed on each of two sides. 2. Having two cavities.

diconchinine (di-kon′kĭ-nin). An amorphous alkaloid, $C_{40}H_{46}O_3N_4$, from quinoidine.

dicophane (di′ko-fān). Chlorophenothane.

dicoria (di-ko′re-ah) [*di-* + Gr. *korē* pupil]. Doubleness of the pupil.

dicoumarin (di-koo′mah-rin). Dicumarol.

dicroceliasis (dik″ro-se-li′ah-sis). Infection with Dicrocoelium.

Dicrocoelium (dik″ro-se′le-um) [Gr. *dikroos* forked + *koilia* bowel]. A genus of trematodes. **D. dendrit′icum,** a lancet-shaped fluke infesting the liver of cattle and sheep in Europe, North and South America, and northern Africa. It has been found in the human biliary passages. **D. hos′pes** is found in the gallbladder of cattle in the Soudan. **D. lancea′tum,** *D. dendriticum.* **D. macrosto′mum,** a species found in the gallbladder of guinea fowl in Egypt.

dicrotic (di-krot′ik) [Gr. *dikrotos* double beating]. Pertaining to or characterized by dicrotism.

dicrotism (di′kro-tizm). The quality of having two sphygmographic waves or elevations to one beat of the pulse.

Dictyocaulus (dik″te-o-kaw′lus). A genus of nematode lung parasites of horses, sheep, and cattle.

dictyokinesis (dik″te-o-ki-ne′sis) [Gr. *diktyon* net + *kinēsis* movement]. The migration and distribution of the dictyosomes to the daughter cells in mitosis.

dictyoma (dik″te-o′mah) [Gr. *diktyon* net (retina) + *-oma*]. Diktyoma.

dictyosome (dik′te-o-sōm) [Gr. *diktyon* net + *sōma* body]. One of the fragments into which the Golgi body breaks up in mitosis.

dicumarol (di-koo′mah-rol). Registered name of a coumarin derivative, 3,3′-methylenebis(4-hydroxycoumarin), isolated originally from spoiled sweet clover and later made synthetically. It is used clinically as an anticoagulant in thrombotic states, and acts by depressing the factors concerned with the formation of thrombin (factors II, VII, IX, and X).

dicurin (di-kur′in). Trade mark for a preparation of merethoxylline.

dicyclic (di-si′klik). Pertaining to or having two cycles. In chemistry, having an atomic structure containing two rings.

dicyclomine (di-si′klo-mēn). Chemical name: 2-diethylaminoethyl bicyclohexyl-1-carboxylate: used in parasympathetic blockade, and as an antispasmodic.

dicysteine (di″sis-te′in). Cystine.

dicytosis (di″si-to′sis) [*di-* + Gr. *kytos* hollow vessel + *-osis*]. The condition of the blood with regard to the number of both mononuclear and polynuclear leukocytes.

didactic (di-dak′tik) [Gr. *didaktikos*]. Conveying instruction by lectures and books rather than by practice.

didactylism (di-dak′til-izm) [*di-* + Gr. *daktylos* finger]. The condition of having only two digits on one hand or foot.

didactylous (di-dak′tĭ-lus). Having only two digits on one hand or foot.

didelphia (di-del′fe-ah) [*di-* + Gr. *delphys* uterus]. The condition characterized by presence of a double uterus.

didelphic (di-del′fik). Pertaining to or possessing a double uterus.

Didelphis (di-del′fis). See *opossum.*

didermoma (di″der-mo′mah). Bidermoma.

didymalgia (did″ĭ-mal′je-ah). Orchialgia.

didymitis (did″ĭ-mi′tis). Orchitis.

didymodynia (did″ĭ-mo-din′e-ah). Orchialgia.

didymus (did′ĭ-mus) [Gr. *didymos* double, twofold, twain]. A testis. Sometimes used as a word termination to designate a fetal monster with a duplication of parts or one consisting of conjoined symmetrical twins. See also *-pagus.*

die (di). A form to be used in the construction of something, such as a positive reproduction of the form of a prepared tooth in a suitable hard substance, such as metal or a specially prepared artificial stone. See *counterdie.* **amalgam d.,** a model of a tooth in amalgam, used for preparing an inlay or crown. **stone d.,** a positive reproduction of a tooth or other structure, created in artificial stone, for use in making a dental prosthesis.

Dieb. alt. Abbreviation for L. *die′bus alter′nis,* on alternate days.

Dieb. tert. Abbreviation for L. *die′bus ter′tiis,* every third day.

diechoscope (di-ek′o-skōp) [*di-* + Gr. *ēchō* echo + *skopein* to examine]. An instrument for the simultaneous perception of two different sounds in auscultation.

diecious (di-e′shus) [*di-* + Gr. *oikos* house]. Sexually distinct: having two sexes in separate individuals.

Dieffenbach's operation (de′fen-bahks) [Johann Friedrich *Dieffenbach,* Prussian surgeon, 1792–1847]. See under *operation.*

dielectric (di″e-lek′trik). Transmitting electric effects by induction, but not by conduction. The term is applied to an insulating substance through or across which electric force is acting or may act, by induction without conduction—as the walls of a Leyden jar, the insulating cushion of an autocondensation couch, or an air space.

dielectrography (di″e-lek-trog′rah-fe). Rheocardiography.

dielectrolysis (di″e-lek-trol′ĭ-sis) [Gr. *dia* through + *electrolysis*]. Electrolysis of a drug, the current being passed through a diseased portion of the body, so that the drug passes through the part.

diembryony (di-em′bre-on-e) [*di-* + *embryon* embryo]. The production of two embryos from a single egg.

diencephalic (di″en-se-fal′ik). Pertaining to the diencephalon.

diencephalohypophysial (di″en-sef″ah-lo-hi″po-fiz′e-al). Pertaining to the diencephalon and the pituitary body.

diencephalon (di″en-sef′ah-lon) [*dia-* + Gr. *enkephalos* brain]. 1. [N A, B N A] The posterior part of the prosencephalon, consisting of the hypothalamus, thalamus, metathalamus, and epithalamus. 2. The posterior of the two brain vesicles formed by specialization of the prosencephalon in the developing embryo.

-diene. A suffix used in chemistry to denote an unsaturated hydrocarbon containing two double bonds.

diener (de′ner) [Ger. "man-servant"]. A man-of-all-work in a laboratory.

dienestrol (di″ēn-es′trol). Chemical name: 4,4′-(diethylidineethylene) diphenol: used as an estrogenic substance.

Dienst's test (dēnsts) [Arthur *Dienst,* Breslau gynecologist, born 1871]. See under *test.*

Dientamoeba (di″ent-ah-me′bah). A genus of protozoa. **D. frag′ilis,** a pathogenic species which has been associated with acute dysentery.

dieresis (di-er′ĕ-sis) [Gr. *diairesis* a taking]. 1. The division or separation of parts normally united, as by a wound or burn. 2. In surgery, the operative separation of parts, as by incision, diathermy, or cautery.

Dierk's layer, zone (dērks). See under *layer.*

diesophagus (di-e-sof′ah-gus). Doubling of the esophagus.

diestrum (di-es′trum). Diestrus.

diestrus (di-es′trus). A short period of sexual quiescence occurring between metestrus and proestrus in female mammals. **gestational d.,** the period of sexual inactivity occurring during gestation in female mammals. **lactational d.,** the period of sexual inactivity occurring during lactation in female mammals.

diet (di′et) [Gr. *diaita* way of living]. The customary allowance of food and drink taken by any person from day to day, particularly one especially planned to meet specific requirements of the individual, and including or excluding certain items of food. **absolute d.,** fasting. **acid-ash d.,** a diet of meat, fish, eggs and cereals; little fruit and vegetables; no cheese or milk. **adequate d.,** one which enables an animal to grow, mature, and reproduce in a normal manner. **alkali-ash d.,** a diet of fruit, vegetables, and milk with as little as possible of meat, fish, eggs, and cereals: for urinary calculus. **Andresen d.,** a diet for peptic ulcer. **antiretentional d.,** a diet for epilepsy designed to prevent accumulation of liquids in the tissues and spaces within the brain. **balanced d.,** one containing all the nutritive factors in proper proportion for adequate nutrition. **Banting d.,** one designed to reduce fatness. **basal d.,** one which is just sufficient to meet the caloric requirements of basal metabolism. **basic d.,** a diet which contains a preponderant proportion of alkaline ash. **Bauman's d.,** an obesity diet supplying 70 Gm. protein, 60 Gm. fat and 100 Gm. carbohydrate, giving 1220 calories. **bland d.,** one that is free from any irritating or stimulating foods. **Caesar's d.,** diet of milk and barley water, used in the early stages of gout. **Cantani's d.,** an exclusive meat diet for diabetics. **Chittenden's d.,** one containing 47 to 55 Gm. of protein. **Coleman-Shaffer d.,** a typhoid fever diet, composed of eggs, cream, cocoa, milk sugar, and bread and butter. It has a high carbohydrate ratio and is rich in protein. The food is administered in small quantities, but frequently. **Dennett's d.,** a diet of fat-free buttermilk, baked potatoes, and large quantities of arrowroot: used in diarrheal disease in infants. **diabetic d.,** one in which ordinary sugar, starchy food, fruits, and ordinary bread are prohibited. **dissociate d., dissociated d.,** a diet in which nitrogenous foods and carbohydrates are given at different meals instead of at the same meal. **Du Bois d.,** one consisting of varying amounts of milk. The time limitation is not definite and the transition to light diet is abrupt. **Ebstein's d.,** an obesity diet containing very little carbohydrate, a moderate amount of albumin, and large quantities of fat. **elimination d.,** a diet for food allergy based on the omission of foods that cause symptoms. **eucaloric d.,** one containing the optimum number of calories. **fever d.,** one especially designed for the requirements of fever patients. **Garton d.,** a milkless diet for typhoid fever patients. **Gerson d., Gerson-Herrmannsdorfer d.,** a diet for lupus vulgaris and tuberculosis: it is salt-free, low in fat and protein, and very rich in carbohydrates, vitamins and minerals. **Goldberger's d.,** a diet for pellagra in which 30 Gm. of dried brewers' yeast is added to a mixed diet. **gouty d.,** one devised for the mitigation of gout, and restricting the use of nitrogenous foods and prohibiting sweet wines and fermented liquors. **Guelpa d.,** a diet for diabetics: three days of fasting with purgation; then a milk day, a vegetable day, and gradual resumption of normal diet. **Harrop d.,** an obesity diet which consists of milk and bananas. **high fat d.,** ketogenic d. **Jarotsky d.,** a diet for gastric ulcer consisting of white of egg and olive oil, given separately, several hours apart, in increasing daily amounts. **Karell d.,** one for nephritis and cardiac conditions, consists of 26 ounces of milk per day. The milk diet, running from six days to a week, is amplified gradually by the use of eggs, dry toast, meat, rice, and vegetables. **Keith's low ionic d.,** a diet for chronic nephritis based on decrease in the water content, reduction of the amount of sodium, and the minimum water content kept constant from day to day. **Kempner's d.,** a diet consisting of only rice, fruit juices, and sugar, supplemented with vitamins and iron: for hypertension and chronic renal disease. **ketogenic d.,** one containing a large amount of fat with minimal amounts of protein and carbohydrate, the object of such a diet being to produce ketosis. **Lenhartz d.** See under *treatment.* **light d.,** a simple mixed diet suitable for convalescents. **low-oxalate d.,** no potatoes, beans, or fiber vegetables, no sweet fruit, tea, chocolate or sweets. **low residue d.,** a diet which gives the least possible fecal residue: such as gelatin, sucrose, dextrose, broth, hard boiled egg, meat, liver, rice, and cottage cheese. **Meulengracht d.,** a full-feeding diet for peptic ulcer. **Minot-Murphy d.,** a diet containing large amounts of liver given in pernicious anemia. **Moro-Heisler d.,** a diet of grated apple for diarrheal conditions in infants. **optimal d.,** a diet which produces the most rapid growth and the most successful reproduction. Cf. *adequate d.* **Petrén's d.,** a diabetic diet consisting of extremely small amounts of protein and carbohydrate and very large amounts of fat, chiefly butter. **Prochownick d.,** a diet for the last eight weeks of pregnancy, which should limit the size and weight of the child, while strengthening the mother. The essential features of the diet are the withholding of carbohydrates and fluids and the giving of sufficient amounts of proteins. **protective d.,** an extremely light diet employed for the purpose of lessening the work of the digestive apparatus as much as possible. **provocative d.,** a diet designed to include the most common allergenic foods, from which they are eliminated one by one, as a means of determining the offending substances in cases of food allergy. **purine-free d.,** a diet omitting meat, fowl and fish, but using milk, eggs, cheese, and vegetable proteins. **rachitic d.,** an inadequate diet which will bring about rickets in an experimental animal. **rheumatic d.,** a diet devised to meet the requirements of rheumatic patients. **salt-free d.,** a diet which contains very little sodium chloride. **Sauerbruch-Herrmannsdorfer d.,** Gerson d. **Schemm d.,** a low-sodium, neutral and acid ash diet for patients with congestive heart failure. **Schmidt d.,** a daily diet consisting of 1.5 liters of milk, 100 Gm. of zwieback, 2 eggs, 50 Gm. of butter, 125 Gm. of beef, 190 Gm. of boiled potato, and gruel made from 80 Gm. of oatmeal. It contains 102 Gm. of protein, 111 Gm. of fat, and 191 Gm. of carbohydrate, giving 2234 calories. **Schmidt-Strassburger d.,** Schmidt d. **Sippy d.,** for gastric ulcer and in conditions in which the patient is emaciated and is unable to take bulky foods. It consists of nothing but milk for the first few days, with the addition of crackers, cereals, and eggs on the third day; the amounts increasing gradually until during the later days of the diet puréed vegetables are included. On the twenty-eighth day the patient is placed on the regular ward diet. **smooth d.,** one which avoids the use of roughage foods. **subsistence d.,** a diet on which one can just live. **Taylor's d.,** a preparation of white of egg, olive oil, and sugar, given when the urine is to be tested for chlorides. **Tufnell's d.,** a rich diet (with small allowance of liquids) sometimes prescribed in treatment of aneurysm. **Wilder's d.,** a low-potassium diet for Addison's disease.

dietary (di'ĕ-ta"re). A regular or systematic scheme of diet.

dietetic (di"ĕ-tet'ik) [Gr. *diaitētikos*]. Pertaining to diet or proper food.

dietetics (di"ĕ-tet'iks). The science or study and regulation of the diet.

diethylamine (di"eth-il-am'in). A nonpoisonous liquid ptomaine, $NH(C_2H_5)_2$, from decaying fish and putrid sausages.

diethylcarbamazine (di-eth"il-kar-bam'ah-zēn). Chemical name: N,N-diethyl-4-methyl-1-piperazinecarboxamide: used as an antifilarial agent.

diethylene diamine (di-eth"il-ēn di-am'in). Piperazine.

diethylmalonylurea (di-eth"il-mal"o-nil-u-re'-ah). Barbital.

diethyloxyacetylurea (di-eth"il-ok-se-as"ĕ-til-u-re'ah). A condensation product of urea and oxyacetic acid, a clear, transparent fluid, proposed as a hypnotic.

diethylpropion (di-eth'il-pro'pe-on). Chemical name: α-diethylaminopropiophenone: used as an anorectic.

diethylstilbestrol (di-eth"il-stil-bes'trol). An estrogenic compound, $C_{18}H_{20}O_2$, which is not related to the natural estrogens containing the phenanthrene nucleus, but which has estrogenic activity similar to but greater than that of estrone. It is used in treating menopausal symptoms, vaginitis and suppressed lactation. Called also *stilbestrol.* **s. dipropionate,** an ester of diethylstilbestrol having a prolonged activity.

diethyltoluamide (di-eth"il-tol-u'ah-mīd). Chemical name: N,N-diethyl-m-toluamide: used as an insect repellant.

dietitian (di-ĕ-tish'an). A person trained in the scientific use of diet in health and disease.

Dietl's crisis (de'tlz) [Joseph *Dietl*, physician in Cracow, 1804–1878]. See under *crisis.*

dietotherapy (di"ĕ-to-ther'ah-pe). Dietetic treatment.

dietotoxic (di"ĕ-to-tok'sik). Having the quality of dietotoxicity.

dietotoxicity (di"ĕ-to-tok-sis'ĭ-te). A quality in certain food substances which renders them toxic when used in an unbalanced diet.

Dieudonné's medium (dyuh-don-āz') [Adolf *Dieudonne*, serologist in Munich, 1864–1945]. See under *culture medium.*

Dieulafoy's aspirator, erosion, theory, triad (dyuh-lah-fwahz') [Georges *Dieulafoy*, physician in Paris, 1839–1911]. See under the nouns.

differential (dif"er-en'shal) [L. *differre* to carry apart]. Pertaining to a difference or differences.

differentiate (dif"er-en'she-āt). 1. To distinguish, on the bases of differences. 2. To develop specialized form, character, or function differing from that of surrounding cytoplasm, cells, or tissue.

differentiation (dif″er-en″she-a′shun). 1. The distinguishing of one thing or disease from another. 2. The act or process of acquiring completely individual characters, such as occurs in the progressive diversification of cells and tissues of the embryo. 3. Increase in morphological or chemical heterogeneity. **correlative d.,** differentiation caused by factors outside of the tissue itself, as by an inductor. **dependent d.,** correlative d. **functional d.,** differentiation which results from the functioning of the tissue of a part. **invisible d.,** the development toward a fixed fate, through chemodifferentiation, by cells that show no visible signs of this determination. **regional d.,** the appearance of regional differences within a field of development. **self d.,** differentiation produced by factors solely within the tissue or part.

diffluence (dif′loo-ens). The act of becoming fluid or of flowing readily.

diffluent (dif′loo-ent) [L. *diffluere* to flow off]. Easily flowing away or dissolving; deliquescent; temporary.

diffraction (dĭ-frak′shun) [L. *dis-* apart + *frangere* to break]. The bending or breaking up into its component parts of a ray of light. **d. grating,** a strip of glass ruled closely with fine lines for use in the spectroscope.

diffusate (dif′u-sāt). Material that has passed through a membrane.

diffuse (dif-fūs′) [L. *dis-* apart + *fundere* to pour]. 1. Not definitely limited or localized; widely distributed. 2. (dif-fūz′) To pass through, or to spread widely through a tissue or structure.

diffusible (dif-fūz′ĭ-b′l). Susceptible of becoming widely spread.

diffusiometer (dĭ-fu″ze-om′e-ter). An apparatus for measuring the speed of diffusion.

diffusion (dĭ-fu′zhun). 1. The process of becoming diffused, or widely spread. 2. Dialysis through a membrane. **free d.,** diffusion in which there is no obstacle such as a membrane. **impeded d.,** diffusion in which the rate is slowed down by the difficulty of passing through a membrane.

Dig. Abbreviation for L. *digera′tur*, let it be digested.

digametic (di″gah-met′ik). 1. Pertaining to or producing gametes or sex cells of two different types, female (ova) and male (spermatozoa). 2. Heterogametic.

digastric (di-gas′trik) [*di-* + Gr. *gastēr* belly]. 1. Having two bellies. 2. Musculus digastricus.

digenesis (di-jen′e-sis). Alternation of generation.

digenetic (di″je-net′ik) [*di-* + Gr. *genesis* generation]. Having two stages of multiplication, one sexual in the mature forms, the other asexual in the larval stages: said of flukes and many other parasites.

digestant (di-jes′tant). 1. Assisting or stimulating digestion. 2. An agent which assists or stimulates digestion.

digestion (di-jest′yun) [L. *digestio*, from *dis-* apart + *gerere* to carry]. 1. The process or act of converting food into materials fit to be absorbed and assimilated. 2. The subjection of a body to prolonged heat and moisture, so as to disintegrate and soften it. **artificial d.,** that which is performed outside the body. **biliary d.,** the digestive effect of the bile upon food. **gastric d.,** that which is carried on in the stomach by aid of the gastric juice. **gastrointestinal d.,** the gastric and intestinal digestions together. **intercellular d.,** digestion carried on within an organ by secretions from the cells of the organ. **intestinal d.,** that which is carried on in the intestine. **intracellular d.,** digestion carried on within a single cell. **pancreatic d.,** that which is performed by the pancreatic secretion. **parenteral d.,** digestion taking place somewhere else in the body than in the alimentary canal, as in the blood or under the skin. **peptic d.,** gastric d. **primary d.,** gastrointestinal d. **salivary d.,** the change of starch into maltose by the saliva. **secondary d.,** the final preparation of food for assimilation by aid of closed glands, lymphatics, marrow, and body cells in general. **sludge d.,** the biochemical process by which organic matter in sludge is gasified, liquefied, mineralized, or converted into more stable organic matter.

digestive (di-jes′tiv). 1. Pertaining to digestion. 2. Digestant.

digit (dij′it). A finger or toe.

digital (dij′ĭ-tal). 1. Of, pertaining to, or performed with, a finger. 2. Resembling the imprint of a finger.

digitaline nativelle (dij″ĭ-tal′ēn na″tĭ-vel′). Trade mark for preparations of the crystalline pure glycoside of *Digitalis purpurea*. See *digitoxin*.

Digitalis (dij″ĭ-ta′lis) [L., from *digitus* finger, because of the finger-like leaves of the corolla of its flowers]. A genus of herbs. *D. purpu′rea* is the foxglove whose leaves furnish digitalis. *D. lana′ta* is a Balkan species which yields digoxin and lanatoside.

digitalis (dij″ĭ-tal′is). The dried leaf of *Digitalis purpurea:* used as a cardiotonic agent.

digitalism (dij′ĭ-tal-izm). The effect produced on the body by the administration of digitalis.

digitalization (dij″ĭ-tal-i-za′shun). Administration of digitalis until the physiologic effect of the drug is produced.

digitaloid (dij′ĭ-tal-oid). Resembling or related to digitalis.

digitalose (dij′ĭ-tal-ōs). A hexose sugar, 6-desoxy-*d*-allose, $CH_3(CHOH_3)CH(O.CH_3).CHO$, from digitalin.

digitate (dij′ĭ-tāt). Having several finger-like processes.

digitatio (dij″ĭ-ta′she-o), pl. *digitatio′nes* [L.]. A finger-like process. **digitatio′nes hippocam′pi.** See *pes hippocampi*.

digitation (dij″ĭ-ta′shun). 1. A finger-like process, as of a muscle. 2. Surgical creation of a functioning digit by making a cleft between two adjacent metacarpal bones, after amputation of the hand.

digitationes (dij″ĭ-ta″she-o′nez) [L.]. Plural of *digitatio*.

digiti (dij′ĭ-ti) [L.]. Plural of *digitus*.

digitigrade (dij′ĭ-tĭ-grād″) [L. *digitus* finger or toe + *gradi* to walk]. Characterized by walking on the toes; applied to animals whose digits only touch the ground, the posterior part of the foot being more or less raised, such as horses and cattle.

digitogenin (dij″ĭ-toj′ĕ-nin). A sapogenin, $C_{27}H_{44}O_5$, from digitonin.

digitonin (dij″ĭ-to′nin). Saponin, $C_{55}H_{29}O_{29}$, from *Digitalis purpurea*.

digitoplantar (dij″ĭ-to-plan′tar) [L. *digitus* finger or toe + *planta* sole]. Pertaining to the toes and the sole of the foot.

digitoxin (dij″ĭ-tok′sin). A cardiotonic glycoside obtained from *Digitalis purpurea* and other species of *Digitalis:* used in treatment of congestive heart failure.

digitoxose (dij″ĭ-tok′sōs). A hexose sugar, $CH_3(CHOH)_3CH_2.CHO$, derived from several of the digitalis glycosides.

digitus (dij′ĭ-tus), pl. *dig′iti* [L.]. A finger or a toe. **d. anula′ris** [N A], the fourth digit, or ring finger, of the hand. **d. hippocrat′icus,** clubbed finger. **d. I,** the first digit; N A alternative for *hallux* and *pollex*. **d. II.** 1. The second digit of the foot. 2. N A alternative for *index* (finger). **d. III.** 1. The third digit of the foot. 2. N A alternative for *d. medius*. **d. IV.** 1. The fourth digit of the foot. 2. N A alternative for *d. anularis*. **d. mal′leus,** mallet finger. **dig′iti ma′nus** [N A, B N A], the digits of the hand, or the fingers. **d. me′dius** [N A], the middle, or third, finger of the hand. **d. min′imus** [N A, B N A], the fifth digit of the hand or foot; the little finger (*d. minimus manus*) or toe (*d. minimus* *pedis*). **d. mor'tuus** [L. "dead finger"]. See *acrocyanosis*. and *pneumatic hammer disease*, under *disease*. **dig'iti pe'dis** [N A, B N A], the digits of the foot, or the toes. **d. postmin'imus,** an appendage ranging from a small round mass of fat and connective tissue to a longer mass containing bones and with a nail at its distal end, attached by a small pedicle to the soft tissue covering the lateral surface of the little finger or toe. **d. recel'lens,** trigger finger. **d. V,** the fifth digit of the hand or foot; N A alternative for *d. minimus*. **d. val'gus,** deviation of a digit in the medial direction, or toward the digit of next lower number. **d. va'rus,** deviation of a digit in the lateral direction, or toward the digit of next higher number.

diglossia (di-glos'e-ah) [*di-* + Gr. *glōssa* tongue]. Double tongue, or bifid tongue.

diglutathione (di-glu"tah-thi'ōn). An oxidized form of glutathione.

diglyceride (di-glis'er-id). A glyceride containing two fatty acid molecules.

dignathus (dig-na'thus) [*di-* + Gr. *gnathos* jaw]. A fetal monster with two lower jaws.

digoxin (dij-ok'sin). A cardiotonic glycoside obtained from the leaves of *Digitalis lanata:* used in the treatment of congestive heart failure.

diheterozygote (di-het"er-o-zi'gōt). An individual heterozygous for two pairs of genes.

dihexose (di-hek'sōs). Disaccharide.

dihomocinchonine (di-ho"mo-sin'ko-nin). An alkaloid, $C_{38}H_{44}O_2N_4$, from cinchona.

dihybrid (di-hi'brid). The offspring of parents who differ in two characters.

dihydrate (di-hi'drāt) [*di-* + Gr. *hydōr* water]. 1. Any compound containing two hydroxyl groups. 2. Any compound containing two molecules of water.

dihydrated (di-hi'drāt-ed). Compounded with two molecules of water.

dihydric (di-hi'drik). Having two hydrogen atoms in each molecule.

dihydrocholesterol (di-hi"dro-ko-les'ter-ol). A sterol, $C_{27}H_{48}O$, found in most tissues.

dihydrocodeinone (di-hi"dro-ko'de-ĭ-nōn). A synthetic analgesic, $C_{18}H_{21}NO_3$. **d. bitartrate,** a compound used as an antitussive.

dihydrocoenzyme I. Diphosphopyridine nucleotide.

dihydrocollidine (di-hi"dro-kol'ĭ-din). An oily base, $C_8H_{11}N.H_2$, from decaying flesh and fish; regarded as a ptomaine.

dihydrocoridine (di-hi"dro-kor'ĭ-din). The base, $C_8H_{13}N$, supposed to be identical with a ptomaine derived from *Bacillus allii*.

dihydrodiethylstilbestrol (di-hi"dro-di-eth"il-stil-bes'trol). Hexestrol.

dihydroergocornine (di-hi"dro-er"go-kor'nin). An ergot derivative which has sympatholytic and adrenolytic properties.

dihydroergotamine (di-hi"dro-er-got'ah-mēn). A product of the catalytic hydrogenation of ergotamine: used to treat migraine headache.

dihydroestrin (di-hi"dro-es'trin). Estradiol.

dihydrofolliculin (di-hi"dro-fol-lik'u-lin). Estradiol.

dihydrol (di-hi'drol). The associated water molecule, $(H_2O)_2$.

dihydrolutidine (di-hi"dro-lu'tĭ-din). An oily, poisonous, caustic base, $C_7H_{11}N$, from rancid cod liver oil.

dihydromorphinone (di-hi"dro-mor'fĭ-nōn). A fine, white, odorless, crystalline powder, $C_{17}H_{19}NO_3.HCl$ used as a narcotic analgesic.

dihydrostreptomycin (di-hi"dro-strep"to-mi'sin). A substance produced by the hydrogenation of streptomycin: used as an antibiotic.

dihydrotachysterol (di-hi"dro-tak-is'tĕ-rol). A steroid, 9,10-seco-5,7,22-ergostratrien-3β-ol: used to increase the blood calcium level.

dihydrotestosterone (di-hi"dro-tes-tos'ter-ōn). An active synthetic male hormone.

dihydrotheelin (di-hi"dro-the'ĕ-lin). Estradiol.

dihydroxodeinone (di"hi-drok"so-de'ĭ-nōn). An antitussive compound.

dihydroxyacetone (di"hi-drok"se-as'e-tōn). One of the trioses, the ketotriose, $CH_2OH.CO.CH_2OH$. **d. phosphate,** a triosephosphate, $CH_2OH.CO.CH_2O.PO(OH)_2$, which is produced in the splitting of fructose-1,6-diphosphate in muscle metabolism.

dihydroxyaluminum aminoacetate (di-hi-drok"se-ah-lu'mĭ-num am"ĭ-no-as'e-tāt). An antacid compound.

dihydroxyfluorane (di"hi-drok"se-floo'o-rān). Fluorescein.

dihypercytosis (di-hi"per-si-to'sis). Hyperhypercytosis.

dihyprylone (di-hi'prĭ-lōn). Chemical name: 3,3-diethyl-2,4-dioxopiperidine: used as an antitussive.

dihysteria (di"his-te're-ah) [*di-* + Gr. *hystera* uterus + *-ia*]. The condition of having a double uterus.

diiodide (di-i'o-dīd). An iodide containing two atoms of iodine in the molecule to one of the base.

diiodocarbazol (di-i"o-do-kar'bah-zol). An antiseptic agent, $(C_6H_3I)_2NH$, in yellow scales.

diiodofluorescein (di"i-o"do-floo"o-res'in). A radioactive compound of iodine and fluorescein.

diiodoform (di"i-o'do-form). An iodide of carbon, ethylene tetraiodide or periodide, C_2I_4: a strong cicatrizant.

diiodohydroxyquin (di"i-o"do-hi-drok'se-kwin). Chemical name: 5,7-diiodo-8-quinolinol: used as an anti-amebic.

diiodothyronine (di"i-o"do-thi'ro-nēn). An organic, iodine-containing compound formed by the conjugation of two molecules of monoiodothyronine.

diiodotyrosine (di"i-o"do-ti'ro-sēn). One of the thyroid hormones: an organic iodine-containing compound liberated from thyroglobulin by hydrolysis, and thought to be formed by the iodination of monoiodotyrosine.

dikaryon (di-ka're-on) [*di-* + Gr. *karyon* kernel]. A growth stage in the mycelium of fungi in which each cell has two haploid nuclei.

dikephobia (di"ke-fo'be-ah) [Gr. *dikē* right, justice + *phobia*]. Morbid fear of justice.

diketone (di-ke'tōn). A ketone containing two carbonyl groups.

diketopiperazine (di-ke"to-pi-per'ah-zin). A closed-ring compound produced by the condensation of two amino acids, the carboxyl group of each combining with the amino group of the other.

diktyoma (dik"te-o'mah) [Gr. *diktyon* net + *-oma*]. A tumor of the ciliary epithelium derived from embryonic retinal tissue.

dikwakwadi (dik"wak-wad'e). Witkop.

dil. Abbreviation for L. *dil'ue*, dilute or dissolve.

dilaceration (di"las-er-a'shun) [L. *dilaceratio*]. A tearing asunder, as of a cataract. See *discission*. In dentistry, a condition due to injury to a tooth during its developmental period and characterized by a crease or band at the junction of the crown and root, or by tortuous roots with abnormal curvatures.

dilantin (di-lan'tin). Trade mark for preparations of diphenylhydantoin.

dilatation (dil-ah-ta'shun). 1. The condition of being dilated or stretched beyond the normal dimensions. 2. Dilation. **digital d.,** digital dilation. **gastric d.,** d. of the stomach. **d. of the heart,** enlargement of the cavities of the heart, with thinning of its walls and diminution of the force of its beatings. **idiopathic d.,** dilatation of a vessel or other channel, especially of the pulmonary artery, not associated with any causative abnormality. **post-stenotic d.,** dilatation of a vessel distal to a stenosed segment, often seen in the pulmonary artery distal to the site of pulmonary stenosis. **prognathic d., prognathion d.,** dilatation of the pyloric end of the stomach greater than that of the fundus, giving a protruding appearance in the roentgen-ray picture. **d. of the stomach,** enlargement of the stomach from weakening of its walls and distention with gas in chronic gastritis.

dilatator (dil″ah-ta′tor) [L.]. That which dilates. See *Table of Musculi.*

dilation (di-la′shun). 1. The action of dilating or stretching. 2. Dilatation. **digital d.,** the expansion or stretching of a cavity or orifice by means of a finger.

dilator (di-la′tor). An appliance used in enlarging an orifice or canal by stretching. **anal d.,** an instrument for dilating or stretching the anal sphincter. **Arnott's d.,** a distensible cylinder of oiled silk for urethral strictures. **Bailey d.,** an instrument designed especially for use in dilating the aortic valve in cardiac surgery. **Barnes's d.,** a rubber bag used in dilating the cervix uteri. **Bossi's d.,** an instrument for dilating the cervix uteri. **De Seigneux's d.,** one for dilating the cervix uteri. **Frommer's d.,** a modified Bossi dilator for the cervix uteri. **Hegar's d's,** a series of bougies of varying sizes for dilating the os uteri. **laryngeal d.,** an instrument with two or more blades which is used for distending a stenosed larynx.

dilaudid (di-law′did). Trade mark for preparations of dihydromorphinone.

dilecanus (di″lĕ-ka′nus) [*di-* + Gr. *lekanē* a dish]. Dipygus.

dilipoxanthine (di-lip″o-zan′thin) [*di-* + Gr. *lipos* fat + *xanthos* yellow]. A yellow lipochrome produced by various bacteria.

diloderm (di′lo-derm). Trade mark for preparations of dichlorisone acetate.

Diluc. Abbreviation for L. *dilu′culo,* at daybreak.

diluent (dil′u-ent) [L. *diluere* to wash]. 1. Diluting. 2. An agent that dilutes or renders less potent or irritant.

dilut. Abbreviation for L. *dilu′tus,* dilute.

dilution (di-lu′shun). 1. The art or process of diluting or the state of being diluted. 2. A diluted or attenuated medicine. 3. In homeopathy, the diffusion of a given quantity of a medicinal agent in ten or one hundred times the same quantity of water.

dim. Abbreviation for L. *dimid′ius,* one half.

dimargarin (di-mar′gar-in). A glyceride having two molecules of margaric acid combined with a molecule of glycerin.

Dimastigamoeba (di-mas″tig-ah-me′bah). A genus of coprozoic amebae which has both an ameboid and a flagellate stage in its life history. In the latter stage it has two flagella and has been called also *Amoeba gruberi, A. tachypodia, Naegleria gruberi, N. punctata, Vahlkampfia punctata,* and *Wasielewskia gruberi.*

dimelia (di-me′le-ah) [*di-* + Gr. *melos* limb]. A developmental anomaly characterized by duplication of a limb.

dimelus (di-me′lus). A fetal monster exhibiting dimelia.

dimenhydrinate (di″men-hi′drĭ-nāt). Chemical name: 2-(benzohydryloxy)-N,N-dimethylethylamine 8-chlorotheophyllinate: used as an antihistaminic, and in prevention and treatment of motion sickness.

dimension (dĭ-men′shun). A numerical expression, in appropriate units, of a linear measurement of an object, such as an organ, or body part. **vertical d.,** the distance between two points, measured perpendicular to the horizontal. In prosthodontics, the distance between two arbitrarily selected points on the face, one above and one below the mouth, usually in the midline, measured with the jaws in centric occlusion (*occlusal vertical d.*) or in rest position (*rest vertical d.*).

dimercaprol (di″mer-kap′rol). Chemical name: 2,3-dimercapto-1-propanol: used as an antidote against poisoning with arsenic, gold, and mercury.

dimerous (dim′er-us) [*di-* + Gr. *meros* part]. Made up of two parts.

dimetallic (di″me-tal′ik). Containing two atoms or equivalents of a metallic element in the molecule.

dimetane (di′mĕ-tān). Trade mark for preparations of brompheniramine.

dimethicone (di-meth′ĭ-kōn). A silicone oil consisting of dimethylsiloxane polymers, and technically designated as dimethylpolysiloxane of the D. C. 200 series of fluids: used as an ingredient in a base for ointments.

dimethisoquin (di″mĕ-thi′so-kwin). Chemical name: 3-butyl-1-(2-dimethylaminoethoxy) isoquinoline: used as a local anesthetic.

dimethoxanate (di-mĕ-thok′sĭ-nāt). Chemical name: β-dimethylaminoethyl-phenothiazine-10-carboxylate: used as an antitussive.

dimethylacetal (di″meth-il-as′ĕ-tal). A colorless, volatile, anesthetic liquid, ethylidene dimethyl ether, $CH_3.CH(OCH_3)_2$: it may be used like chloroform, by inhalation.

dimethylamine (di″meth-il-am′in). A gaseous and liquid ptomaine, $(CH_3)_2NH$, from decaying gelatin, decomposing yeast, rotten fish, etc.

dimethyl-amino-azobenzene (di-meth″il-am″ĭ-no-az″o-ben′zēn). A carcinogenic dye, C_6H_5-$N_2C_6H_4.N(CH_3)_2$: used as an indicator in Toepfer's test for free hydrochloric acid in gastric juice. It has a pH range of 2.9 to 4, being red at 2.9 and yellow at 4.

dimethylane (di-meth′ĭ-lān). Trade mark for a preparation of promoxolane.

dimethylarsine (di-meth″il-ar′sin). Cacodyl.

dimethylbenzene (di-meth″il-ben′zēn). Xylene.

dimethylcarbinol (di-meth″il-kar′bĭ-nol). Isopropyl alcohol.

dimethyl-ethyl-pyrrol (di-meth″il-eth″il-pir′-ol). A substituted pyrrol which is obtained from bilirubin.

dimethyl-guanidine (di-meth″il-guan′ĭ-din). A ptomaine, $CH_3.NH.C(:NH).NH.CH_3$, found in small amounts in the urine.

dimethylketone (di-meth″il-ke′ton). Acetone.

dimethylphenanthrene (di-meth″il-fe-nan′-thrēn). A carcinogenic and weakly estrogenic hydrocarbon.

dimethylphosphine (di-meth″il-fos′fēn). A phosphine extremely destructive to infusorial life, $(CH_3)_2PH$.

dimethylphthalate (di-meth″il-thal′āt). A clear, colorless, oily liquid, $C_6H_4(COO.CH_3)_2$: used as an insect repellent.

dimethyl sulfate (di-meth′il sul′fāt). An industrial poison and war gas, $(CH_3)_2SO_4$, causing nystagmus, convulsions, and death from pulmonary complications.

dimetria (di-me′tre-ah) [*di-* + Gr. *mētra* womb]. Uterus duplex.

diminution (dim″ĭ-nu′shun). Reduction, or decrease, in size or substance.

Dimmer's keratitis (dim″erz) [Friedrich *Dimmer,* Austrian ophthalmologist, 1855–1926]. Keratitis nummularis.

dimorphic (di-mor′fik). Dimorphous.

dimorphism (di-mor′fizm) [*di-* + Gr. *morphē* form]. The property of having or existing under two forms. **physical d.,** the property of certain solids of existing in two crystalline or allotropic forms. **sexual d.** 1. The property of existing in two different forms, depending on the sex. 2. The condition of having some of the properties of both sexes, as in the early embryo and in some hermaphrodites.

dimorphobiotic (di-mor″fo-bi-ot′ik) [*di-* + Gr. *morphē* form + *biōsis* life]. Showing alternation of generations and having a parasitic and a nonparasitic stage in the complete life history.

dimorphous (di-mor′fus) [*di-* + Gr. *morphē* form]. Occurring in two distinct forms; having the property of dimorphism.

dimple (dim′pl). A slight depression. **Fuchs' d's,** transient dimple-like elevations seen on the cornea near the limbus in elderly persons. **postanal d.,** foveola coccygea.

dimpling (dim′pling). The formation of slight depressions or dimples.

dineric (di-ner′ik) [*di-* + Gr. *nēros* liquid]. Noting a solution made up of two immiscible solvents with a single solute soluble in each.

dineuric (di-nu′rik). Having two neurons or axis-cylinder processes: said of nerve cells.

dinical (din′ĭ-kl) [Gr. *dinos* whirl, giddiness]. Pertaining to dizziness; relieving dizziness.

dinitrate (di-ni′trāt). A compound of a base with two molecules of nitric acid.

dinitrated (di-ni′trāt-ed). Compounded with or having two molecules of nitric acid, or of nitroxyl.

dinitrobenzene (di-ni″tro-ben′zēn). A poisonous substance, $C_6H_4(NO_2)_2$. Its fumes may cause breathlessness and final asphyxia.

dinitrocellulose (di-ni″tro-sel′u-lōs). Pyroxylin.

dinitrocresol (di-ni″tro-kre′sol). A poisonous cresol compound, $CH_3.C_6H_2(NO_2)_2OH$. Also known as *saffron substitute.* Dinitro-*o*-cresol has a similar effect to α-dinitrophenol.

dinitrophenol (di-ni″tro-fe′nol). Any one of six isomeric compounds, $C_6H_3(OH)(NO_2)_2$: used in making dyes. Alpha-dinitrophenol has the power of stimulating metabolism, thus producing pyrexia: it has been suggested for administration in the treatment of myxedema and obesity. It has been reported as a cause of agranulocytosis.

dinitroresorcin (di-ni″tro-re-sor′sin). A green coal tar derivative, $C_6H_2(NO_2)_2(OH)_2$, used in preparing degenerated nerve tissue for study.

dinomania (din″o-ma′ne-ah) [Gr. *dinos* whirl, giddiness + *mania* madness]. Dancing mania.

dinophobia (din″o-fo′be-ah) [Gr. *dinos* whirl, giddiness + *phobia*]. A morbid fear of becoming dizzy.

dinormocytosis (di-nor″mo-si-to′sis) [*di-* + L. *norma* rule + Gr. *kytos* hollow vessel]. Isonormocytosis.

D. in p. aeq. Abbreviation for L. *div′ide in par′tes aequa′les,* divide into equal parts.

dinucleotide (di-nu′kle-o-tīd). One of the two cleavage products into which a tetranucleotide (nucleic acid) is split. A dinucleotide itself may be split into two mononucleotides.

Diocles (di′ŏ-klēz) **of Carystus** (4th century B.C.). An eminent Greek physician and able anatomist, who belonged to the Dogmatist school.

diocoele (di′o-sēl) [*di-* + Gr. *koilos* hollow]. The cavity of the diencephalon; the third ventricle.

Dioctophyma (di-ok″to-fi′mah). A genus of nematodes. **D. rena′le,** the kidney worm, the largest nematode known, found commonly in dogs, cattle, horses, and other animals, but rarely in man; red in color, 1 to 3 feet in length, and found usually in the pelvis of the kidney or free in the peritoneal cavity.

dioctyl calcium sulfosuccinate (di-ok′til kal′se-um sul″fo-suk′sĭ-nāt). Chemical name: bis-2-ethylhexyl calcium sulfosuccinate: used as a fecal softener.

dioctyl sodium sulfosuccinate (di-ok′til so′-de-um sul″fo-suk′sĭ-nāt). Chemical name: bis-2-ethylhexyl sodium sulfosuccinate: used as a fecal softener, and as a wetting agent.

Diodon (di′o-don). A genus of fishes, some species of which are poisonous.

diodoquin (di″o-do′kwin). Trade mark for a preparation of diiodohydroxyquin.

diodrast (di′o-drast). Trade mark for a preparation of iodopyracet for injection.

diogenism (di-oj′ĕ-nizm) [from *Diogenes,* a Greek philosopher of the 5th century B.C. noted for his contempt of the common aims and conditions of life]. An effort or tendency to get rid of the refinements of civilization and to lead a life closer to nature.

dioloxol (di″o-lok′sol). Trade mark for a preparation of mephenesin.

diopsimeter (di″op-sim′e-ter) [Gr. *diopsis* vision + *metron* measure]. A device for measuring the field of vision.

diopter (di-op′ter) [Gr. *dioptra* optical instrument for measuring angles]. The refractive power of a lens with a focal distance of one meter: assumed as a unit of measurement for refractive power (Monoyer, Donders). **prism d.,** a unit of prismatic deviation; deflection of one centimeter at a distance of one meter.

dioptometer (di″op-tom′e-ter) [*dioptric* + Gr. *metron* measure]. An instrument for use in testing ocular refraction.

dioptometry (di″op-tom′e-tre). The measurement of refraction and accommodation of the eye.

dioptoscopy (di″op-tos′ko-pe) [*dioptric* + Gr. *skopein* to examine]. Measurement of ocular refraction by means of the ophthalmoscope.

dioptre (di-op′ter). Diopter.

dioptric (di-op′trik) [Gr. *dioptrikos* belonging to the use of the *dioptra*]. Pertaining to refraction or to transmitted and refracted light; refracting.

dioptrics (di-op′triks). The science of refracted light.

dioptrometer (di″op-trom′e-ter). Dioptometer.

dioptrometry (di″op-trom′e-tre). Dioptometry.

dioptroscopy (di″op-tros′ko-pe). Dioptoscopy.

dioptry (di′op-tre). Diopter.

Dioscorea (di″os-ko′re-ah). A genus of plants, the yams. **D. hirsu′ta,** the source of dioscorine. **D. mexica′na,** the source of botogenin. **D. villo′sa,** the source of a substance formerly used in medicine.

Dioscorides (di″ŏ-skōr′ĭ-dēz) **of Anazarbos** (1st century A.D.). Noted botanist and pharmacologist whose encyclopedia of materia medica was widely used for centuries after his death.

diose (di′ōs). The simplest sugar, a monosaccharide containing two carbon atoms in the molecule: $CH_2OH—COH$.

diospyrobezoar (di″os-pi″ro-be′zōr). A bezoar made up of persimmon fibers.

diovulatory (di-ov′u-lah-to″re). Ordinarily discharging two ova in one ovarian cycle.

dioxane (di-ok′sān). Diethylene dioxide, a clear fluid, used for dehydrating and clearing tissues preparatory to paraffin embedding. It is an industrial poison.

dioxide (di-ok′sīd) [*di-* + Gr. *oxys* sharp]. A molecule having two atoms of oxygen.

dioxyacetone (di-ok″se-as′e-tōn). A compound, $HOCH_2.CO.CH_2OH$, one of the constituents of glycerose, the ketotriose. It is formed by the oxidation of glycerin with nitric acid. It has been used in the treatment of diabetes.

dioxyline (di-ok′sĭ-līn). Chemical name: 1-(4-ethoxy-3-methoxybenzyl)-6,7-dimethoxy-3-methylisoquinoline: used as a vasodilator.

dioxynaphthalene (di-ok″se-naf′thah-len). A poisonous compound, $C_{16}H_6(OH)_2$, said to build up the strength of asthenic patients.

dioxytoluene (di″ok-se-tol′u-ēn). Orcin.

dipaxin (di-pak′sin). Trade mark for a preparation of diphenadione.

dipentene (di-pen′tēn). A terpene, $C_{10}H_{16}$, found in many volatile oils.

dipeptidase (di-pep′tĭ-dās). An exopeptidase which hydrolyzes only peptide linkages, the amino acids of which bear both free amino and carboxyl groups.

dipeptide (di-pep′tīd). A peptide which, on hydrolysis, yields two amino acids.

diperodon (di-per′o-don). Chemical name: 3-(1-piperidyl)-1,2-propanediol dicarbanilate: used as a surface anesthetic.

Dipetalonema perstans (di-pet″ah-lo-ne′mah per′stans). *Acanthocheilonema perstans.*

dipetalonemiasis (di-pet″ah-lo-ne-mi′ah-sis). Infestation with *Acanthocheilonema perstans.*

diphallia (di-fal′e-ah) [*di-* + Gr. *phallos* penis]. Duplication of the penis.

diphallus (di′fal-lus). A double penis.

diphasic (di-fa′zik) [*di-* + Gr. *phasis* phase]. Occurring in two phases or stages.

diphebuzol (di-feb′u-zol). Phenylbutazone.

diphemanil (di-fe′mah-nil). Chemical name: 4-diphenylmethylene-1,1-dimethylpiperidinium: used to produce parasympathetic blockade, and as a relaxant for gastrointestinal spasm.

diphenadione (di-fen″ah-di′ōn). Chemical name: 2-diphenylacetyl-1,3-indandione: used as an anticoagulant.

diphenhydramine (di″fen-hi′drah-min). Chemical name: 2-(benzhydryloxy)-N,N-dimethylethylamine: used as an antihistaminic.

diphenoxylate (di″fen-ok′sĭ-lāt). Chemical name: 2,2-diphenyl-4-(4-carbethoxy-4-phenyl-1-piperidino)butyronitrile: used to reduce intestinal motility.

diphenyl (di-fe′nil). A colorless compound, $C_6H_5C_6H_5$, found in coal tar.

diphenylamine (di-fen″il-am′in). A compound, phenyl-aniline, $(C_6H_5)_2NH$; used as a test for nitric acid and chlorine.

diphenylaminearsine chloride (di-fen″il-am″-in-ar′sin klo′rīd). A toxic smoke for war use, $NH(C_6H_5)_2AsCl$.

diphenylamino-azo-benzene (di-fen″il-am″ĭ-no-az″o-ben′zēn). An indicator with a pH range of 1.2–2.1.

diphenylchlorarsine (di-fen″il-klor-ar′sin). Sneezing gas, $(C_6H_5)_2AsCl$, a toxic smoke, used in war, causing sneezing, coughing, headache, salivation, and vomiting. Called also *Clark I* and *AD.*

diphenyl-cyanarsine (di-fen″il-si″an-ar′sin). A lethal war gas, $(C_6H_5)_2.AsCN$: called also *Clark II.*

diphenylhydantoin (di-fen″il-hi-dan′to-in). Chemical name: 5-5-diphenyl-2,4-imidazolidinedione: used as an anticonvulsant in grand mal epilepsy.

diphenylpyraline (di-fen″il-pi′rah-lēn). Chemical name: 4-diphenylmethoxy-1-methylpiperidine. Use: antihistaminic.

diphonia (di-fo′ne-ah) [*di-* + Gr. *phōnē* voice]. A condition in which two different tones are produced in speaking; double voice.

diphosgene (di-fos′jēn). A gas, $ClCO.COCl_3$, which is intensely irritating to the lungs, producing pulmonary edema.

diphtheria (dif-the′re-ah) [Gr. *diphthera* membrane + *-ia*]. An acute infectious disease or toxicosis due to the presence of *Corynebacterium diphtheriae,* with swelling of the larynx and pharynx, and consequent dyspnea, aphonia, and dysphagia. The general symptoms are fever, heart weakness, anemia, and great prostration. The disease may be attended with patches of false membrane in the throat or on other mucous surfaces and the resulting absorption of diphtheria toxin. **avian d.** See *roup.* **Bretonneau's d.,** true diphtheria of the pharynx. **calf d.,** a contagious disease of young calves in which grayish patches form in the mouth and throat: caused by *Sphaerophorus necrophorus.* **cutaneous d.,** diphtheria with skin lesions occurring primarily, or secondarily to lesions of the mucous membranes. **false d.,** diphtheroid, def. 2. **faucial d.,** a mild form of infection by the diphtheria bacillus, with or without soreness of the throat. **gangrenous d.,** diphtheria attended with gangrene of the skin or mucous membrane, or both. **d. gra′vis,** malignant d. **laryngeal d.,** inflammation of the larynx caused by *Corynebacterium diphtheriae.* **laryngotracheal d.,** diphtheria in which the infection invades the larynx and trachea, with edema, congestion, and development of a pseudomembrane. **latent d.,** diphtheritic infection without membranous exudation. **malignant d.,** a form beginning with rigors and vomiting, and marked with typhoid symptoms; often fatal. **nasal d.,** diphtheria in which the infection is mainly in the nasal passages. **nonmembranous d.,** löffleria. **pharyngeal d.,** that which is especially manifested on the mucous membrane of the pharynx. **scarlatinal d.,** a sort of membranous tonsillitis occurring in scarlet fever, and caused by streptococci. **septic d.,** diphtheria rendered especially severe by secondary infection with pyogenic cocci. **swine d.,** hog cholera. **umbilical d.,** diphtherial infection of the umbilical cord in the newborn. **wound d.,** the formation of false membrane on the surface of a wound.

diphtherial (dif-the′re-al). Pertaining to or derived from diphtheria.

diphtheric (dif-the′rik). Diphtheritic.

diphtherin (dif′the-rin). 1. The poison developed and evolved by the *Corynebacterium diphtheriae.* 2. A polyvalent diphtheritic antigen for use in anaphylactic skin test.

diphtheriolysin (dif-the″re-ol′ĭ-sin). A lysin having a specific affinity for diphtheria bacillus.

diphtheritic (dif″the-rit′ik). Pertaining to diphtheria.

diphtheritis (dif″the-ri′tis). Diphtheria.

diphtheroid (dif′ther-oid). 1. Resembling diphtheria. 2. A disease resembling diphtheria, but not due to *Corynebacterium diphtheriae.* 3. A microorganism closely resembling the diphtheria bacillus in morphology, but not producing toxin.

diphtherotoxin (dif″thĕ-ro-tok′sin). Toxin from cultures of diphtheria bacillus.

diphthongia (dif-thon′je-ah) [*di-* + Gr. *phthongos* sound]. The production of double vocal sounds.

diphyllobothriasis (di-fil″o-both-ri′ah-sis). The state of being infected with tapeworms of the genus *Diphyllobothrium.*

Diphyllobothrium (di-fil″o-both′re-um) [*di-* + Gr. *phyllon* leaf + *bothrion* pit]. A genus of tape-

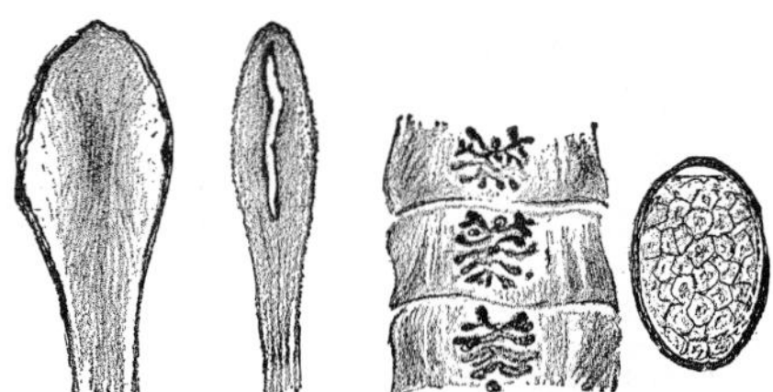

Diphyllobothrium latum: head, segments, and egg (de Rivas).

worms, formerly called *Bothriocephalus* and *Dibothriocephalus.* **D. corda′tum,** the heart-headed tapeworm. A small species found in dogs and in seals in Greenland and only occasionally in man; the plerocercoids are found in man. **D. erina′cei,** a species found in the adult form in the dog and other carnivores. **D. la′tum,** the broad tapeworm or fish tapeworm; a very large tapeworm found in the intestines of man and (somewhat smaller) in cats and dogs. It may be ¾ inch wide and 20 feet long. The head is marked with two grooves or suckers (bothridia). It has two hosts: the first a crustacean, the second a fish. Infection with this parasite in man, acquired by eating inadequately cooked fish, may result in a clinical and blood picture resembling that of addisonian pernicious anemia. **D. manso′ni,** *D. erinacei.* **D. mansonoi′des,** a species whose migrating larvae cause sparganosis. **D. par′vum,** a species found in man in Tasmania, Japan, Rumania, Persia, and Minnesota. **D. taenioi′des,** *D. latum.*

diphyodont (dif′ĭ-o-dont) [*di-* + Gr. *phyein* to produce + *odous* tooth]. Having two dentitions, a deciduous and a permanent.

Diplacanthus nanus (dip″lah-kan′thus na′nus). *Hymenolepis nana.*

diplacusia (dip″lah-ku′ze-ah). Diplacusis.

diplacusis (dip″lah-ku′sis) [Gr. *diplous* double + *akousis* hearing]. The perception of a single auditory stimulus as two sounds, as a result of a pathologic condition involving the vibrating structure in the cochlea. **binaural d.,** different perception of a single auditory stimulus by the two ears. The difference may be in tone (disharmonic d.) or timing (echo d.). **d. binaura′lis dysharmon′ica,** disharmonic d. **d. binaura′lis echo′ica,** echo d. **disharmonic d.,** a form of diplacusis in which a given pure tone is heard differently in the two ears. **echo d.,** a form of diplacusis in which a sound of brief duration is heard in the one ear a fraction of a second later than in the other ear. **monaural d.,** a form of diplacusis in which a pure tone is heard in the same ear as a split tone of two frequencies. **d. monaura′lis,** monaural d.

diplasmatic (di″plaz-mat′ik) [*di-* + Gr. *plasma* something formed]. Containing substances besides protoplasm: said of cells.

diplegia (di-ple′je-ah) [*di-* + Gr. *plēgē* stroke]. Paralysis affecting like parts on both sides of the body; bilateral paralysis. **atonic-astatic d.,** diplegia characterized by hypotonia instead of spasticity. **facial d.,** facial paralysis affecting both sides of the face. **infantile d.,** birth palsy. **masticatory d.,** paralysis of all the muscles which take part in mastication. **spastic d.,** Little's disease.

diplegic (di-ple′jik). Pertaining to or marked by diplegia.

diplo- (dip′lo) [Gr. *diplous* double]. Combining form meaning *double, twin, twofold,* or *twice.*

diplo-albuminuria (dip″lo-al-bu″mĭ-nu′re-ah) [*diplo-* + *albuminuria*]. The presence of both physiologic and pathologic albuminuria.

diplobacillary (dip″lo-bas′e-lār″e). Caused by diplobacilli.

diplobacilli (dip″lo-bah-sil′i). Plural of *diplobacillus.*

diplobacillus (dip″lo-bah-sil′us), pl. *diplobacil′li* [*diplo-* + *bacillus*]. A short, rod-shaped organism occurring in pairs; diplobacterium. **Morax's d.,** *Moraxella lacunata.*

diplobacterium (dip″lo-bak-te′re-um), pl. *diplobacteria* [*diplo-* + *bacterium*]. A short, rod-shaped organism occurring in pairs.

diploblastic (dip″lo-blas′tik) [*diplo-* + Gr. *blastos* germ]. Made up of two germ layers.

diplocardia (dip″lo-kar′de-ah) [*diplo-* + Gr. *kardia* heart]. A condition in which the right and left heart are somewhat separated by a fissure.

diplocephalus (dip″lo-sef′ah-lus). Dicephalous.

diplocephaly (dip″lo-sef′ah-le). Dicephaly.

diplococcal (dip″lo-kok′al). Pertaining to or caused by diplococci.

diplococcemia (dip″lo-kok-se′me-ah) [*diplococcus* + Gr. *haima* blood + *-ia*]. The presence of diplococci in the blood.

diplococci (dip″lo-kok′si). Plural of *diplococcus.*

diplococcoid (dip″lo-kok′oid). 1. Resembling diplococci. 2. An organism that resembles a diplococcus.

Diplococcus (dip″lo-kok′kus). A genus of microorganisms of the tribe Streptococceae, family Lactobacillaceae, order Eubacteriales, made up of spherical or elongate cells dividing in one plane and occurring in pairs or chains. The single species is *D. pneumo′niae,* the pneumococcus, the commonest cause of lobar pneumonia. The lanceolate-shaped bacteria occur in pairs, virulent forms are heavily encapsulated, and are gram-positive. They occur as 80 differentiable serotypes, or fewer if some are condensed as subtypes, on the basis of the specificity of the polysaccharide hapten making up the capsular substance.

diplococcus (dip″lo-kok′us), pl. *diplococci.* 1. A spherical bacterium occurring predominantly in pairs as a consequence of incomplete cell division in a single plane. The organism may also be lanceolate (Pneumococcus) or coffee-bean-shaped (Gonococcus). 2. An organism of the genus *Diplococcus.* **d. of Morax-Axenfeld,** *Moraxella lacunata.* **d. of Neisser,** *Neisseria gonorrhoeae.* **Weichselbaum's d.,** *Neisseria meningitidis.*

diplocoria (dip″lo-ko′re-ah) [*diplo-* + Gr. *korē* pupil]. Double pupil.

Diplodia (dĭ-plo′de-ah). A genus of fungi producing the dry-rot or corn-stalk disease of corn.

Diplodinium (dip″lo-din′e-um). A genus of ciliate protozoa species of which are parasitic in the stomachs of cattle.

diploë (dip′lo-e) [Gr. *diploē* fold]. [N A, B N A] The loose osseous tissue between the two tables of the cranial bones.

diploetic (dip″lo-et′ik). Of or pertaining to the diploë.

Diplogaster (dip′lo-gas″ter) [*diplo-* + Gr. *gastēr* stomach]. A genus of free-living coprozoic nematodes which may, in fecal examination, be confused with hookworms or Strongyloides.

diplogen (dip′lo-jen). Deuterium.

diplogenesis (dip″lo-jen′e-sis) [*diplo-* + Gr. *genesis* production]. The production of a double monster.

Diplogonoporus (dip″lo-go-nop′o-rus) [*diplo-* + Gr. *gonos* seed + *poros* passage]. A genus of tapeworms. **D. brau′ni, D. gran′dis,** species which are a common parasite in whales and have been found in man in Japan.

diplogram (dip′lo-gram) [*diplo-* + Gr. *gramma* a writing]. A roentgenogram containing two exposures.

diplohydrogen (dip″lo-hi′dro-jen). Deuterium.

diploic (dip-lo′ik). 1. Double. 2. Diploetic.

diploid (dip′loid) [Gr. *diploos* twofold]. 1. Having two sets of chromosomes, as normally found in the somatic cells of higher organisms. Cf. *haploid.* 2. An individual or cell having two full sets of homologous chromosomes.

diploidy (dip′loi-de). The state of having two full sets of homologous chromosomes.

diplokaryon (dip″lo-kar′e-on) [*diplo-* + Gr. *karyon* nucleus]. A nucleus which has twice the diploid number of chromosomes.

diplomate (dip′lo-māt). A person who has received a diploma or certificate. In medicine the term refers particularly to a holder of a certificate of the National Board of Medical Examiners or of one of the American Boards in the Specialties.

diplomellituria (dip″lo-mel″ĭ-tu′re-ah). Contemporaneous or alternate occurrence of diabetic and nondiabetic glycosuria in the same individual.

diplomyelia (dip″lo-mi-e′le-ah) [*diplo-* + Gr. *myelos* marrow + *-ia*]. Lengthwise fissure and seeming doubleness of spinal cord.

diplon (dip′lon) [Gr. *diploos* double]. Deuteron.

diplonema (dip″lo-ne′mah) [*diplo-* + Gr. *nema* thread]. The double chromosomes in the diplotene stage.

diploneural (dip″lo-nu′ral) [*diplo-* + Gr. *neuron* nerve]. Having a double nerve supply.

diplont (dip′lont) [Gr. *diploō* to double + *ōn* being]. A diploid individual.

diplopagus (dip-lop′ah-gus) [Gr. *diploos* double + *pagos* a thing fixed]. A double monster in which the component parts are equal to and the symmetrical equivalents of one another.

diplophase (dip′lo-fāz). That phase in the life history of certain organisms in which the nuclei are diploid.

diplophonia (dip″lo-fo′ne-ah) [*diplo-* + Gr. *phōnē* voice]. Diphthongia.

diplopia (dĭ-plo′pe-ah) [*diplo-* + Gr. *ōpē* sight + *-ia*]. The perception of two images of a single object. **binocular d.,** the perception of a separate image of a single object by each of the two eyes. **crossed d.,** double vision in which the image belonging to the right eye is displaced to the left of the image belonging to the left eye. **direct d.,** double vision in which the image belonging to the right eye appears to the right of the image belonging to the left eye. **heteronymous d.,** crossed d. **homonymous d.,** direct d. **horizontal d.,** diplopia in which the images lie in the same horizontal plane, being either crossed or direct. **monocular d.,** the perception by the same eye of two images of a single object, due to double pupil, early cataract, or irregular astigmatism. **paradoxical d.,** crossed d. **torsional d.,** double vision in which the upper pole of the vertical axis of one image is inclined toward or away from that of the other. **vertical d.** double vision in which one image appears to be above the other.

diplopiaphobia (dĭ-plo″pe-ah-fo′be-ah) [*diplopia* + *phobia*]. Horror fusionis.

diplopiometer (dĭ-plo″pe-om′e-ter) [*diplopia* + Gr. *metron* measure]. An instrument for measuring diplopia.

Diplopylidium (dip″lo-pi-lid′e-um). Dipylidium.

diploscope (dip′lo-skōp) [*diplo-* + Gr. *skopein* to examine]. An apparatus for the study of binocular vision.

diplosomatia, diplosomia (dip″lo-so-ma′she-ah, dip″lo-so′me-ah) [*diplo-* + Gr. *sōma* body]. A condition in which complete twins are joined at some part of their bodies.

diplosome (dip′lo-sōm) [*diplo-* + Gr. *sōma* body]. The two centrioles of mammalian cells.

diplostreptococcus (dip″lo-strep″to-kok′us). A streptococcus with many pairs.

diplotene (dip′lo-tēn). In miosis, the stage in which the apparently single chromosomes of the pachytene become visibly and distinctly double.

diploteratology (dip″lo-ter″ah-tol′o-je) [*diplo-* + *teratology*]. The sum of what is known regarding joined twin monstrosities.

Diplozoa (dip″lo-zo′ah) [*diplo-* + Gr. *zōon* animal]. A suborder of protozoa embracing the genus *Giardia.*

dipodia (di-po′de-ah) [*di-* + Gr. *pous* foot]. A developmental anomaly characterized by duplication of a foot.

dipotassium phosphate (di″po-tas′e-um fos′fāt). Potassium phosphate.

dipping (dip′ing). Palpation of the liver by a quick depressing movement of the fingers with the hand flat across the abdomen.

dippoldism (dip′ol-dizm) [Dippold, a German school teacher]. Flagellation.

diprosopus (di-pros′o-pus) [*di-* + Gr. *prosōpon* face]. A fetal monster with a single trunk and normal limbs, but with varying degrees of duplication of the face. **d. tetrophthal′mus,** a monster having two fused faces, the median eye of each being fused into a common orbit.

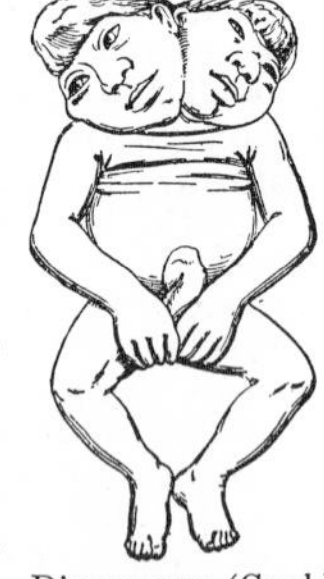
Diprosopus (Gould and Pyle).

diprotrizoate (di″pro-tri′zo-āt). Chemical name: 3,5-dipropionamido-2,4,6-triiodobenzoate: used as a contrast medium in roentgenography of the urinary tract.

dipsesis (dip-se′sis) [Gr. *dipsēsis* a thirst, longing]. Thirst.

dipsetic (dip-set′ik) [Gr. *dipsētikos* thirsty; provoking thirst]. Pertaining to, characterized by, or producing dipsesis.

dipsia (dip′se-ah) [Gr. *dipsa* thirst + *-ia*]. Thirst. Often used as a word termination, denoting a condition relative to thirst, or the physiological state of the body leading to the ingestion of fluids.

dipsogen (dip′so-jen) [Gr. *dipsa* thirst + *gennan* to produce]. An agent or measure which induces thirst and promotes the ingestion of fluids.

dipsomania (dip″so-ma′ne-ah) [Gr. *dipsa* thirst + *mania* madness]. Uncontrollable desire for spirituous liquor.

dipsopathy (dip-sop′ah-the) [Gr. *dipsa* thirst + *pathos* disease]. The nervous condition characterized by dipsomania.

dipsosis (dip-so′sis) [Gr. *dipsa* thirst + *-osis*]. Morbid thirst.

dipsotherapy (dip″so-ther′ah-pe) [Gr. *dipsa* thirst + *therapeia* treatment]. Treatment by strict limitation of the amount of water to be ingested.

Diptera (dip′ter-ah) [Gr. *dipteros* two winged]. An order of insects including the flies, gnats, and mosquitoes.

Dipterocarpus (dip″ter-o-kar′pus) [Gr. *dipteros* two winged + *karpos* fruit]. A genus of trees from southern Asia, affording gurjun balsam.

dipterous (dip′ter-us). 1. Having two wings. 2. Pertaining to insects of the order Diptera.

dipus (di′pus) [*di-* + Gr. *pous* foot]. A conjoined twin monster with only two feet.

dipygus (di-pi′gus) [*di-* + Gr. *pygē* rump]. A fetal monster with double pelvis. **d. parasit′icus,** gastrothoracopagus dipygus.

dipylidiasis (dip″ĭ-lĭ-di′ah-sis). Infestation with *Dipylidium caninum.*

Dipylidium (dip″ĭ-lid′e-um) [Gr. *dipylos* having two entrances]. A genus of tapeworms found in cats and other small carnivorae. **D. cani′num,** a common tapeworm of dogs and cats, the larval stage living in fleas (*Ctenocephalus canis*) and lice (*Trichodectes canis*) of cats and dogs, as well as in *Pulex irritans,* which thus act as vectors. It has been found in man.

dipyridamole (di″pi-rid′ah-mōl). Chemical name: 2,6-bis-(diethanolamino)-4,8-dipiperidinopyrimido(5,4-d)pyrimidine: used to improve coronary circulation.

dipyrone (di′pi-rōn). Chemical name: sodium (antipyrinylmethylamino) methanesulfonate hydrate, or 1-phenyl-2,3-dimethyl-5-pyrazolone-4-methylaminomethanesulfonate sodium: used as an analgesic and antipyretic.

direct (di-rekt′) [L. *directus*]. 1. Straight; in a straight line. 2. Performed immediately and without the intervention of subsidiary means.

director (di-rek′tor) [L. *dirigere* to direct]. Any thing or device which guides or directs. **grooved d.,** an instrument grooved to guide the knife in surgery.

directoscope (di-rek′to-skōp). An instrument for the direct examination of the larynx.

dirhinic (di-ri′nik). Pertaining to both nasal cavities.

dirigation (dir″ĭ-ga′shun) [L. *dis-* apart + *rigare* to turn]. The exercise of voluntary control over ordinarily involuntary bodily functions such as pulse, temperature, digestion, through concentration of the attention upon a particular function or organ.

dirigomotor (dir″ĭ-go-mo′tor) [L. *dirigere* to direct + *motor* mover]. Controlling muscular activity.

Dirofilaria (di″ro-fĭ-la′re-ah). A genus of filarial worms with very long filiform bodies and a striated cuticle. **D. immit′is,** the heartworms; a species found in the right heart and veins of the dog, wolf, and fox in China, Japan, and the southern United States. **D. magalhae′si,** found in the heart of a child in Brazil. **D. re′pens** is found in the subcutaneous connective tissues.

dirofilariasis (di″ro-fil″ah-ri′ah-sis). Human infection with a parasite of the genus Dirofilaria, thought to be the dog heartworm, *Dirofilaria immitis.*

Dir. prop. Abbreviation for L. *directio′ne pro′pria,* with a proper direction.

dis-. A prefix denoting (1) reversal or separation [L. *dis-* apart], or (2) duplication [Gr. *dis* twice, doubly].

disaccharidase (di-sak′ah-rĭ-dās). An enzyme which hydrolyzes disaccharides.

disaccharide (di-sak′ah-rid). Any one of a class of sugars which yield two monosaccharides on hydrolysis and having the general formula $C_n(H_2O)_{n-1}$ or $C_{12}H_{22}O_{11}$. They include sucrose, lactose, and maltose. **reducing d's,** disaccharides which can reduce Fehling's solution, owing to the presence of a functional aldehyde group.

disacchariduria (di-sak″ah-ri-du′re-ah). Presence of a disaccharide (lactose or sucrose) in the urine.

disaccharose (di-sak′ah-rōs). Disaccharide.

disacidify (dis-ah-sid′ĭ-fi). To remove an acid from, or to neutralize an acid in, a mixture.

disaggregation (dis″ag-re-ga′shun). Failure of the hysterical mind to connect new sensations with each other and to bring them into relation with the eye; it often results in double consciousness.

disallergization (dis-al″er-ji-za′shun). The destruction or neutralization of allergic activity.

disamidize (dis-am′ĭ-dīz). Deamidize.

disarticulation (dis″ar-tik″u-la′shun) [L. *dis-* apart + *articulus* joint]. Amputation or separation at a joint.

disassimilate (dis″ah-sim′ĭ-lāt). Dissimilate.

disassimilation (dis″ah-sim″ĭ-la′shun) [*dis-* + *assimilation*]. Dissimilation.

disazo (dis-az′o). Diazo-.

disc (disk) [L. *discus*]. Disk.

discharge (dis-charj′). 1. A setting free, or liberation. 2. Matter or force set free. 3. An excretion or substance evacuated. **brush d.,** in electrotherapeutics, the discharge from a static machine (less commonly from a high frequency apparatus), having a disruptoconvective character. **convective d.,** a discharge from a high potential source in the form of visible or invisible streams of electrical energy passing through the air to the patient. **disruptive d.,** the passing of a current through an insulating medium due to the breakdown of the medium under the electrostatic stress. **disrupto-convective d.,** the static brush discharge which stimulates both the convective effluve and the disruptive or spark discharge. **nervous d., neural d.,** the propagated excitation produced by stimulation of a center in the nervous system. **systolic d.** See *stroke volume,* under *volume.*

discharger (dis-charj′er). An instrument for setting free electricity, as from a Leyden jar.

dischronation (dis″kro-na′shun) [L. *dis-* apart + Gr. *chronos* time]. A dislocation in the consciousness of time.

disci (dis′i) [L.]. Plural of *discus.*

disciform (dis′ĭ-form) [L. *discus* disk + *forma* shape]. In the form of a disk.

discission (dis-sizh′un) [L. *discissio; dis-* apart + *scindere* to cut]. A cutting in two, or division, as of a soft cataract. **d. of cervix uteri,** incisions on each side of the cervix uteri for the relief of stenosis of the cervix. **d. of pleura,** cruciform sections into the pleura for empyema. **posterior d.,** incision of the capsule of a cataract from behind.

discitis (dis-ki′tis). Diskitis.

disclination (dis″klĭ-na′shun) [L. *dis-* apart + *clinatus* leaning]. Outward rotation of the upper pole of the vertical meridian of each eye. Cf. *conclination.*

disco- (dis′ko) [L. *discus*; Gr. *diskos*]. Combining form denoting relationship to a disk, or disk-shaped. See also words beginning *disko-.*

discoblastic (dis″ko-blas′tik) [*disco-* + Gr. *blastos* germ]. Pertaining to a discoblastula or to discoidal cleavage.

discoblastula (dis″ko-blas′tu-lah). The specialized blastula formed by cleavage of a fertilized telolecithal ovum, consisting of a cellular cap—the germinal disk, or blastoderm—separated by the blastocoele from a floor of uncleaved yolk.

discogastrula (dis″ko-gas′troo-lah). A modified, flattened gastrula formed by discoidal cleavage of a highly telolecithal ovum.

discogenic (dis″ko-jen′ik) [*disco-* + Gr. *gennan* to produce]. Caused by derangement of an intervertebral disk.

discogenetic (dis″ko-je-net′ik) Discogenic.

discogram (dis′ko-gram). Diskogram.

discography (dis-kog′rah-fe). Diskography.

discoid (dis′koid) [Gr. *diskos* disk + *eidos* form]. 1. Shaped like a disk. 2. A disklike medicated tablet. 3. A dental instrument with a disklike or circular blade, used for excavating cavities and carving dental restorations.

discoidectomy (dis″koid-ek′to-me). Excision of an intervertebral disk.

Discomyces (dis″ko-mi′sēz) [*disco-* + Gr. *mykēs* fungus]. A name formerly given to certain organisms now included under *Streptomyces.*

discomycosis (dis″ko-mi-kos′sis). Infestation with *Discomyces.*

discopathy (dis-kop′ah-the) [*disco-* + Gr. *pathos* disease]. Disease of an intervertebral cartilage (disk).

discophorous (dis-kof′ŏ-rus) [*disco-* + Gr. *phoros* bearing]. Possessing a disklike organ or part.

discoplacenta (dis″ko-plah-sen′tah). A discoid placenta.

discoplasm (dis′ko-plazm). The spongelike colorless framework or stroma of a red blood corpuscle.

discord (dis′kord) [L. *discordia*]. A simultaneous assemblage of two or more inharmonious sounds.

discoria (dis-ko′re-ah). Dyscoria.

discrete (dis-krēt′) [L. *discretus; discernere* to separate]. Made up of separated parts or characterized by lesions which do not become blended.

discus (dis′kus), pl. *disci* [L.; Gr. *diskos*]. A circular or rounded flat plate or organ; used as a general term in anatomical nomenclature to designate such a structure. Called also *disc* or *disk.* **d. articula ris** [N A, B N A], a pad composed of fibrocartilage or dense fibrous tissue found in some synovial joints; it extends into the joint from a marginal attachment at the articular capsule and in some cases completely divides the joint cavity into two separate compartments. Called also *articular disk.* **d. articula′ris articulatio′nis acromioclavicula′ris** [N A, B N A], a pad of fibrocartilage, sometimes present, commonly imperfect, within the articular cavity of the acromioclavicular joint. Called also *articular disk of acromioclavicular articulation.* **d. articula′ris articulatio′nis mandibula′ris** [B N A], discus articularis articulationis temporomandibularis. **d. articula′ris articulatio′nis radioulna′ris dista′lis** [N A, B N A], a triangular pad of fibrocartilage, attached at its base to the radius and at its apex, to the base of the stylid process of the ulna. It separates the articular cavity of the distal radioulnar joint from that of the radiocarpal joint. Called also *articular disk of distal radioulnar articulation.* **d. articula′ris articulatio′nis sternoclavicula′ris** [N A, B N A], a pad of fibrocartilage, the circumference of which is connected to the articular capsule of the sternoclavicular joint. It is attached superiorly to the clavicle and inferiorly to the first costal cartilage near its union with the sternum, and divides the joint cavity into two parts. Called also *articular disk of sternoclavicular articulation.* **d. articula′ris articulatio′nis temporomandibula′ris** [N A], a plate of fibrocartilage or fibrous tissue that divides the temporomandibular joint into two separate cavities. Its circumference is connected to the articular capsule. Called also *d. articularis articulationis mandibularis* [B N A], and *articular disk of temporomandibular joint.* **d. interpu′bicus** [N A], a midline plate of fibrocartilage interposed between the symphysial surfaces of the pubic bones, these surfaces being covered by a thin layer of hyaline cartilage. Called also *interpubic disk* and *lamina fibrocartilaginea interpubica* [B N A]. **dis′ci intervertebra′les** [N A], the 23 plates of fibrocartilage found, from the axis to the sacrum, between the bodies of adjacent vertebrae, each consisting of a fibrous ring (anulus fibrosus) enclosing a pulpy center (nucleus pulposus). Called also *intervertebral disks* and *fibrocartilagines intervertebrales* [B N A]. **d. lentifor′mis,** nucleus subthalamicus. **d. ner′vi op′tici** [N A], a round white disk in the back of the eyeball, medial to the posterior pole of the eye, at the site of entrance of the optic nerve and the retinal blood vessels. Only the ganglionic layer of the optic nerve is present, and the area is insensitive to light. Called also *optic disk* and *papilla nervi optici* [B N A]. **d. ooph′orus,** cumulus oophorus. **d. op′ticus,** d. nervi optici. **d. ovig′erus, d. prolig′erus,** cumulus oophorus.

discussive (dis-kus′iv). Discutient.

discutient (dis-ku′she-ent) [L. *discutere* to dissipate]. 1. Scattering; causing a disappearance. 2. A remedy which so acts.

disdiaclast (dis-di′ah-klast) [Gr. *dis* twice + *diaklan* to break through]. Any one of the doubly refracting elements of the contractile substance of muscle.

disease (dĭ-sēz′) [Fr. *dès* from + *aise* ease]. A definite morbid process having a characteristic train of symptoms; it may affect the whole body or any of its parts, and its etiology, pathology, and prognosis may be known or unknown. **A A A d.,** ancylostomiasis. **Abrami's d.,** acquired hemolytic icterus. **accumulation d.,** thesaurismosis. **Acosta's d.,** mountain sickness. **acute d.,** a disease characterized by a swift onset and short course. **acute demyelinating d.,** postinfection encephalitis. **Adams' d., Adams-Stokes d.,** a condition characterized by sudden attacks of unconsciousness, with or without convulsions, which frequently accompanies heart block: called also *Adams-Stokes symptom* or *syndrome,* and *Stokes-Adams d.* **Addison's d.,** a disease characterized by a bronzelike pigmentation of the skin, severe prostration, progressive anemia, low blood pressure, diarrhea, and digestive disturbance; it is due to disease (hypofunction) of the adrenal glands and is usually fatal. Called also *melasma suprarenale* and *bronzed skin.* **akamushi d.,** scrub typhus. **Albarran's d.,** colibacilluria. **Albers-Schönberg d.,** osteopetrosis. **Albert's d.,** achillobursitis. **Albright's d.,** osteitis fibrosa cystica. **Alibert's d.,** mycosis fungoides. **Alibert-Bazin d.,** psoriasis with arthritis. **alkali d.** 1. Tularemia. 2. A disease of live stock, prevalent in the North Central Great Plains of the United States, due to feeding on selenium-bearing vegetation. **alligator-skin d.,** ichthyosis. **Almeida's d.,** South American blastomycosis. **altitude d.,** mountain sickness. **Alzheimer's d.,** presenile dementia. **Anders' d.,** adiposis tuberosa simplex. **Andes d.,** a condition marked by erythremic symptoms which sometimes affects people crossing the Andes Mountains. **Andrews' d.,** pustular bacterid. **angiospasmodic d.,** a disease marked by spasms of the various vessels of the body. **anserine d.,** a disease marked by emaciation of the extremities, causing the hands and feet to resemble a goose's feet. **Apert's d.,** acrocephalosyndactylia. **Aran-Duchenne d.,** myelopathic muscular atrophy. **atopic d.,** atopy. **attic d.,** chronic suppurative inflammation of the attic. **Aufrecht's d.,** parenchymatous alterations in the liver and kidney in infectious jaundice. **Aujeszky's d.,** pseudohydrophobia; pseudorabies, an infectious (virus) bulbar paralysis of cattle, horses, and other domestic animals, first observed in Hungary and Brazil, where it is called the "scratching pest" (*peste de cocar*). **Australian X d.,** an acute encephalitis of viral origin observed in Australia during the summer months between 1917 and 1926. See *Murray Valley encephalitis.* **autoimmune d.,** disease resulting from the immunological action of cells or antibodies on components of the body. **aviators' d.,** a term formerly applied to acute altitude anoxia in aviators. **Ayerza's d.,** a form of erythremia marked by chronic cyanosis, chronic dyspnea, chronic bronchitis, bronchiectasis, enlargement of liver and spleen, hyperplasia of bone marrow, and associated with sclerosis of the pulmonary artery. **Baelz's d.,** a disease characterized by painless papules on the mucous membrane of the lips. **Balfour's d.,** chloroma or chlorosarcoma. **Ballet's d.,** ophthalmoplegia externa. **Ballingall's d.,** mycetoma. **Balo's d.,** a form of infantile demyelinating encephalopathy. **Bamberger's d.** 1. Saltatory spasm. 2. Chronic polyserositis (1872). **Bamberger-Marie d.,** hypertrophic pulmonary osteoarthropathy. **Bamle d.,** epidemic diaphragmatic pleurodynia. **Bang's d.,** infectious abortion in cattle caused by *Brucella abortus.* **Bannister's d.,** angioneurotic edema. **Banti's d.,** originally described as a primary disease of the spleen associated with splenomegaly and pancytopenia, but later considered secondary to portal hypertension; better called Banti's syndrome or congestive splenomegaly. **barbed-wire d.,** the condition seen in prisoners of war who fall victims of the monotony and boredom of confinement in prison camps. **Barcoo d.,** desert sore. **Barlow's d.,** infantile scurvy. **barometer-makers' d.,** chronic mercurial poisoning in makers of barometers, due to the inhalation of the fumes of mercury. **Barraquer's d.,** lipodystrophia progressiva. **Barthélemy's d.,** tuberculosis papulonecrotica. **Basedow's d.,** exophthalmic goiter. **Basel d.,** an epidemic form of keratosis follicularis occurring in Switzerland. **Bateman's d.,** molluscum contagiosum. **Batten-Mayou d.,** a juvenile form of amaurotic family idiocy with pigmentation of the macula and pallor of the optic disk. **Bayle's d.,** progressive general paralysis of the insane. **Bazin's d.,** tuberculosis cutio indurativa. **Beard's d.,** neurasthenia. **Beau's d.,** cardiac insufficiency. **Beauvais' d.,** chronic articular rheumatism. **Bechterew's d.,** rheumatoid spondylitis. **Beck's d.,** a disease affecting young people in Siberia and marked by fatigue and swelling of the phalanges; later all the joints of the body become enlarged and normal growth is retarded. **Begbie's d.** 1. Exophthalmic goiter. 2. Hysterical or localized chorea. **Behr's d.,** degeneration of the macula lutea in adult life. **Beigel's d.,** piedra. **Bell's d.** See under *mania.* **Bennett's d.,** leukemia. **Benson's d.,** asteroid hyalitis. **Bergeron's d.,** hysterical chorea. **Berlin's d.,** Berlin's edema. See under *edema.* **Bernhardt's d.,** meralgia paraesthetica. **Besnier-Boeck d.,** sarcoid of Boeck. **Best's d.,** congenital macular degeneration. **Beurmann's d.,** disseminated gummatous sporotrichosis. **Biedl's d.** See *Laurence-Moon-Biedl syndrome,* under *syndrome.* **Bielschowsky-Jansky d.,** the late infantile form of amaurotic family idiocy. **Biermer's d.,** pernicious anemia. **Biett's d.,** lupus erythematosus. **Billroth's d.** 1. Spurious meningocele. 2. Malignant lymphoma. **Bird's d.,** oxalic diathesis. **black d.,** infectious necrotic hepatitis of sheep; a fatal disease of sheep, and occasionally of man, in New South Wales, Victoria and Tasmania, marked by necrotic areas in the liver. **bleeder's d.,** hemophilia. **Blocq's d.,** astasia-abasia. **Blount's d.,** aseptic necrosis of the medial condyle of the tibia, sometimes producing lateral bowing of the leg (tibia vara). **blue d.** 1. An old term for congenital heart disease. See *morbus caeruleus.* 2. Rocky Mountain spotted fever. **Blumenthal's d.,** erythroleukemia. **Boeck's d.** See under *sarcoid.* **Bonfils' d.,** Hodgkin's disease. **Borna d.,** a fatal enzootic encephalitis of horses, cattle, and sheep, caused by a virus. **Bornholm d.,** epidemic pleurodynia. **Bostock's d.,** hay fever. **bottom d.,** a condition in horses that results from their eating rattlebox weed, *Crotalaria sagittalis.* It occurs in low bottom land. **Bouchard's d.,** dilatation of the stomach from inefficiency of the gastric muscles. **Bouchet's d.,** swineherds' d. **Bouillaud's d.,** rheumatic endocarditis. **Bourneville's d.,** tuberous sclerosis of the brain. **Bouveret's d.,**

paroxysmal tachycardia. **Bowen's d.,** a precancerous condition characterized by scaly lesions resembling psoriasis, with disorganization of the epidermal cells, clumping of the nuclei, and other histologic changes. **Bozzolo's d.,** multiple myeloma. **Bradley's d.,** epidemic nausea and vomiting. **Breda's d.,** yaws. **Breisky's d.,** kraurosis vulvae. **Bretonneau's d.,** diphtheria of the pharynx. **bridegrooms' d.,** thrombosis of the pampiniform plexus from sexual excesses. **Bright's d.,** any one of a group of kidney diseases attended with albuminuria and edema. See *nephritis.* **Brill's d.,** recrudescent louse-borne typhus. **Brill-Symmers d.,** giant follicular lymphoma, one of the group of malignant lymphoproliferative disorders. **Brill-Zinsser d.,** recrudescent louse-borne typhus. **Brinton's d.,** linitis plastica. **Brion-Kayser d.,** paratyphus. **Brissaud's d.,** habit spasm. **Brocq's d.,** parakeratosis psoriasiformis. **Brodie's d.** 1. Chronic synovitis, especially of the knee, with a pulpy degeneration of the parts affected. 2. Hysterical pseudofracture of the spine. **bronzed d.,** Addison's d. **Brooke's d.** 1. Psorospermosis. 2. Epithelioma adenoides cysticum. 3. Keratosis follicularis contagiosa. **Brown-Séquard d.** See under *syndrome.* **Brown-Symmers d.,** acute serous encephalitis in children. **Bruck's d.,** a condition marked by deformity of bones, multiple fractures, ankylosis of joints, and atrophy of muscles. **Brugsch's d.,** akromikrie. **Bruhl's d.,** splenic anemia with fever. **Bruns's d.,** pneumopaludism. **Brushfield-Wyatt d.,** nevoid amentia. **Budd's d.,** Budd's cirrhosis. **Büdinger-Ludloff-Laewen d.,** spontaneous fracture of the cartilage of the patella. **Buerger's d.,** thromboangiitis obliterans. **Buerger-Grütz d.,** idiopathic hyperlipemia. **buffalo d.** 1. Barbone. 2. Buffalo encephalitis. **Buhl's d.,** a condition affecting newborn infants, marked by hemorrhages into the skin, mucous membranes, and navel attended with cyanosis and jaundice; there are also hemorrhages in the intestinal organs. **Bury's d.,** erythema elevatum diutinum. **Buschke's d.,** blastomycosis. **bush d.,** a disease of sheep and cattle in certain parts of New Zealand, marked by progressive anemia. **Busquet's d.,** exostoses on the dorsum of the foot due to osteoperiostitis of the metatarsal bones. **Busse-Buschke d.,** cryptococcosis. **button d.,** a parasitic disease of young chickens in the tropics, marked by the formation of tubercles at the angles of the mouth. **Caffey's d.,** infantile cortical hyperostosis. **caisson d.,** decompression sickness. **California d.,** coccidioidomycosis. **caloric d.,** any disease due to exposure to high temperature. **Calvé-Perthes d.,** osteochondrosis of capitular epiphysis of femur. **carapato d.,** a disease of tropical Africa, believed to be caused by a protozoan blood parasite. **Carrión's d.,** bartonellosis, an infectious disease occurring in the valleys of the Andes Mountains in Peru, Chile, Bolivia and Colombia. It appears in an acute febrile anemic stage (*Oroya fever*) followed in several weeks by a nodular skin eruption (*verruga peruana*). It is caused by *Bartonella bacilliformis*, which is transmitted by the sandfly, *Phlebotomus verrucarum.* **Castellani's d.,** spirochetal hemorrhagic bronchitis. **cat-scratch d.** See under *fever.* **Cavare's d.,** familial periodic paralysis. **celiac d.,** Gee's name for a diarrhea condition in children: probably identical with sprue. **Chabert's d.,** symptomatic anthrax. **Chagas' d.,** a form of trypanosomiasis found in man and in the armadillo (*Dasypus novemcintus*) in the interior of Brazil. It is produced by *Trypanosoma cruzi* which is transmitted by the *Panstrongylus megistus, P. infestans* and other reduviid bugs. It runs an acute course in children and a chronic course in adults, but is regularly fatal. Called also *Brazilian trypanosomiasis, thyroiditis parasitaria,* and *careotrypanosis.* **Chagas-Cruz d.,** Chagas' d. **Charcot's d.,** neurogenic arthropathy. **Charcot-Marie-Tooth d.,** progressive neuropathic (peroneal) muscular atrophy. **Charlouis' d.,** yaws. **Charrin's d.,** pyocyaneus infection. **Cheadle's d.,** infantile scurvy. **Cherchevski's d.,** ileus of nervous origin. **Chester's d.,** xanthomatosis of the long bones with spontaneous fractures. **Chiari's d.,** endophlebitis obliterans hepatica. **Chiari-Frommel d.,** Frommel's d. **Chicago d.,** American blastomycosis. **Chiffonnier's d.,** anthrax. **chignon d.,** piedra. **Christian's d.,** Schüller-Christian d. **Christian-Weber d.,** nonsuppurative nodular panniculitis. **Christmas d.,** a congenital hemorrhagic diathesis clinically similar to classical hemophilia A, transmitted as a sex-linked recessive, and characterized by a deficiency of factor IX (also called *Christmas factor*), which results in impaired formation of intrinsic thromboplastin. Called also *hemophilia B.* **chronic d.,** one which is slow in its progress and of long continuance. **chylopoietic d.,** one which affects the digestive organs. **Ciarrocchi's d.,** dermatitis in the third interdigital space. **Civatte's d.** See under *poikiloderma.* **climatic d.,** any disease thought to be produced by a change of climate. **coast d.,** bush sickness. **Coats's d.,** exudative retinopathy. **Cogan's d.,** nonluetic interstitial keratitis with vestibuloauditory symptoms. **Cohnorl's d.,** necrobacillosis of rabbits. **collagen d.,** one of the conditions in which collagen tissue is involved, such as rheumatic fever, acute systemic lupus erythematosus, scleroderma, and dermatomyositis. **comb d.,** a kind of favus which affects the combs of fowls, and is caused by a fungus, *Lophophyton gallinarum.* **combined system d.,** an older designation of subacute combined degeneration of the spinal cord, as it occurs with pernicious anemia. Also called funicular degeneration of the spinal cord. **communicable d.,** a disease the causative agent of which may pass or be carried from one person to another directly or indirectly. **complicating d.,** one which occurs in the course of some other disease as a complication. **compressed-air d.,** compressed air illness. **Concato's d.,** progressive malignant inflammation of the serous membranes, especially of the pleura. **conditional d.,** a latent infectious disease which requires some additional factor for it to become manifest. **Conor and Bruch's d.,** boutonneuse fever. **constitutional d.,** one which involves a system of organs or the whole body. **contagious d.,** a disease that is communicable by contact with an individual suffering from it or with some secretion of such an individual, or with an object touched by him. Cf. *infectious d.* **Cooley's d.,** Cooley's anemia. **Cooper's d.,** chronic cystic disease of the breast. **Corbus' d.,** corrosive or gangrenous balanitis. **cornstalk d.,** staggers. **Corrigan's d.,** aortic incompetency. **Corvisart's d.** 1. Chronic hypertrophic myocarditis. 2. Tetralogy of Fallot associated with right aortic arch. **Cotugno's d.,** sciatica. **Couton's d.,** tuberculous spondylosis. **covering d.,** dourine. **crazy d.,** Borna disease. **creeping d.,** creeping eruption. **Crocq's d.,** acrocyanosis. **Crohn's d.,** regional ileitis. **Crouzon's d.,** craniofacial dysostosis. **Cruchet's d.,** epidemic encephalomyelitis. **Cruveilhier's d.** 1. Progressive myelopathic muscular atrophy. 2. Ulceration of the stomach due to excess of acids and local anemia. **Cruz-Chagas d.,** Chagas' d. **Csillag's d.,** chronic atrophic lichenoid dermatitis. **Curschmann's d.,** frosted liver. **Curtis' d.,** a condition characterized by the presence of pseudo-myxomatous tumors in the skin that contain *Saccharomyces subcutaneus tumefaciens.* **Cushing's d.** 1. Pituitary basophilism. 2. Adrenal cortical hyperfunction. **cysticercus d.,** an affection due to the presence of the larva forms of the *Taenia solium* (the pork tapeworm). **cytomegalic inclusion d.,** a disease, particularly of the neonatal period, characterized by hepatosplenomegaly and often by microcephaly and mental or motor retardation; due to infection with a cytomegalovirus, often congenitally acquired. **Czerny's d.,** periodic hydrarthrosis of the knee. **Daae's d., Daae-Finsen d.,** epidemic pleurodynia. **DaCosta's d.** 1. Misplaced gout. 2. Neurocirculatory asthenia. **Dalrymple's d.,** cyclokeratitis. **dancing d.,** tarantism. **Danielssen's d.,** anesthetic leprosy. **Danlos' d.** See under *syndrome*. **Darier's d.,** keratosis follicularis. **Darling's d.,** histoplasmosis. **David's d.** 1. [J. P. David.] Pott's d. 2. [W. David.] An unexplained form of hemorrhagic disease in women, marked by severe bleeding from the gums and mucous membranes, attributed, without definite basis, to deficiency of ovarian hormone. **de aar d.,** a pasteurellosis among veldt rodents of South Africa. **Debove's d.,** splenomegaly. **de Bruns' d.,** pneumopaludism. **deer fly d.,** tularemia. **deficiency d.,** avitaminosis or other condition produced by other dietary or metabolic deficiency. The term includes beriberi, scurvy, pellagra, etc. Cf. *avitaminosis*. **Dejerine's d.,** hypertrophic interstitial neuritis in infants. **Dejerine-Sottas d.,** progressive hypertrophic interstitial neuropathy. **demyelinating d.,** a condition characterized by destruction of myelin. **deprivation d.,** deficiency d. **de Quervain's d.** See *Quervain's d.* **Dercum's d.,** adiposis dolorosa. **Desnos' d.,** splenopneumonia. **Deutschländer's d.** 1. Tumor of the metatarsal bones. 2. March foot. **Devergie's d.,** pityriasis rubra pilaris. **Devic's d.,** optic neuro-encephalomyelopathy. **diamond-skin d.,** the urticarial and mildest form of swine erysipelas. **Dieulafoy's d.,** exulceratio simplex. **diffuse d.,** a disease involving several tracts of the spinal cord. **Dimitri's d.,** nevoid amentia. **displaced persons' d.,** a form of atrophic gastritis with vitamin B deficiency. **Ditmarsch d.,** a syphilitic disease of Ditmarsch (Holstein). **Döhle d.,** syphilitic aortitis. **Down's d.,** mongolism. **Dressler's d.,** intermittent hemoglobinuria. **drug d.** 1. A morbid condition due to long-continued use of a drug. 2. In homeopathy, the group of symptoms seen after the administration of a drug for the purpose of proving. **Dubin-Sprinz d.,** Dubin-Johnson syndrome. **Dubini's d.,** electric chorea. **Dubois' d.,** the development of multiple abscesses in the thymus gland in congenital syphilis. **Duchenne's d.** 1. Duchenne-Aran d. 2. Bulbar paralysis. 3. Locomotor ataxia. **Duchenne-Aran d.,** myelopathic muscular atrophy. **Duchenne-Griesinger d.,** infantile muscular atrophy with pseudohypertrophy. **Duhring's d.,** dermatitis herpetiformis. **Dukes' d.,** exanthema subitum. **Duplay's d.,** subdeltoid or subacromial bursitis. **Durand's d.,** a virus disease, characterized by headache and by upper respiratory, meningeal, and gastrointestinal symptoms. **Durand-Nicolas-Favre d.,** venereal lymphogranuloma. **Durante's d.,** fragilitas ossium. **Duroziez's d.,** congenital mitral stenosis. **Dutton's d.,** trypanosomiasis. **Eales's d.,** a condition marked by recurrent hemorrhages into the retina and vitreous. **Ebstein's d.** 1. Hyaline degeneration and necrosis of the epithelial cells of the renal tubules: seen in diabetes. 2. See under *anomaly*. **echinococcus d.,** unilocular hydatid d. **Economo's d.,** epidemic encephalitis. **Eddowes' d.** See under *syndrome*. **Edsall's d.,** heat cramp. **Ehlers-Danlos d.,** Danlos' syndrome. **Eichhorst's d.,** neuritis fascians. **Eichstedt's d.,** pityriasis versicolor. **elevator d.,** pneumoconiosis affecting persons who work in grain elevators. **endemic d.,** a disease which is at all times present in a small number of persons in a particular region. **Engel-Recklinghausen d.,** osteitis fibrosa cystica. **English d.,** rickets. **Engman's d.,** dermatitis infectiosa eczematoides. **enzootic d.,** a disease which is at all times present in a small number of animals in a particular region. **epidemic d.,** a disease which affects a large number of people in some particular region within a short period of time. **epizootic d.,** a disease which affects a large number of animals in some particular region within a short period of time. **Epstein's d.,** pseudodiphtheria. **Epstein-Pel d.,** a relapsing type of pseudoleukemia. **Erb's d.,** progressive muscular dystrophy. **Erb-Charcot d.,** spasmodic ataxia. **Erb-Goldflam d.,** myasthenia gravis pseudoparalytica. **Erb-Landouzy d.,** progressive muscular dystrophy. **Erichsen's d.,** railway spine. **Eulenburg's d.,** paramyotonia congenita. **Fahr-Volhard d.,** malignant nephrosclerosis. **Fallot's d.,** tetralogy of Fallot. **Fanconi's d.,** congenital aplastic anemia of childhood, associated with musculoskeletal defects. **fat-deficiency d.,** a condition characterized by cessation of growth and skin lesions that result when fats are absent from the diet. Various unsaturated fatty acids especially arachidonic acid and linoleic acid relieve the condition. **fatigue d.** 1. Febrile attack due to over-exercise and the absorption of waste products. 2. Occupation neurosis. **Fauchard's d.,** periodontal d. **Favre-Durand-Nicolas d.,** venereal lymphogranuloma. **Fede's d.,** sublingual fibroma. **Feer's d.,** erythredema polyneuropathy. **Fenwick's d.,** primary atrophy of the stomach. **Fernels' d.,** aortic aneurysm. **fibrocystic d. of the pancreas,** cystic fibrosis of the pancreas (q.v. under *fibrosis*). **Fiedler's d.,** leptospiral jaundice. **fifth d.,** erythema infectiosum. **fifth venereal d.,** lymphogranuloma venereum. **Filatow-Dukes d.,** fourth d. **file-cutters' d.,** lead poisoning from inhaling particles of lead which arise from the bed of lead used in file cutting. **filth d.,** one due to dirt and unclean habits. **finger and toe d.,** a disease of cruciferous plants caused by *Plasmodiophora brassicae*. **fish-handler's d.,** erysipeloid. **fish skin d.,** ichthyosis. **fish slime d.,** septicemia following a punctured wound made by the spine of a fish. **Flajani's d.,** exophthalmic goiter. **Flatau-Schilder d.,** progressive subcortical encephalopathy. **flax-dressers' d.,** a kind of pneumonia seen in flax-dressers, and caused by inhaling particles of flax. **Fleischner's d.,** osteochondritis affecting the middle phalanges of the hand. **flint d.,** chalicosis. **fluke d.,** infestation with flukes. **focal d.,** one which is localized at one or more foci. **Fölling's d.,** phenylpyruvic oligophrenia. **foot-and-mouth d.,** an acute febrile disease marked by the formation of an eruption of vesicles in the mucous membrane of the cheeks and the skin of the digits. Caused by a virus, it is very contagious among ruminant animals and pigs, and is often transmitted from the animal to man and other domestic animals. **Fordyce's d.** 1. Enlarged sebaceous glands in the mucosa of the lips, cheeks and gums, marked by the formation of yellowish milium-like bodies. 2. Fox-Fordyce d. **Förster's d.** See under *choroiditis*. **Fothergill's d.** 1. [John Fothergill]. Scarlatina anginosa. 2. [Samuel Fothergill]. Trigeminal neuralgia. **Fournier's d.,** fulminating gangrene of the genitals. **fourth d.,** exanthema subitum. **fourth venereal d.** 1. See *specific ulcerative* and *gangrenous balanoposthitis*, under *balanoposthitis*. 2. Granuloma inguinale. **Fox's d.,** Fox-Fordyce d. **Fox-Fordyce d.,** a papular itchy eruption, limited chiefly to the axillae and the pubes, due to chronic inflammation of the apocrine sweat glands probably under gonadal influence. **Francis' d.,** tularemia. **Frankl-Hochwart's d.,** polyneuritis cerebralis menieriformis. **Frei's d.,** lymphogranuloma venereum. **Freiberg's d.,** Köhler's bone disease, def. 2. **Friedländer's d.,** obliterative arteritis. **Friedreich's d.** 1. Paramyoclonus multiplex. 2. Friedreich's ataxia. **frien d.,** friente. **fright d.,** canine hysteria; psychic disturbance in dogs marked by symptoms of fright and by hysterical barking and running. **Frommel's d.,** a condition marked by prolonged lactation and atrophy of the uterus. **functional d.,** any disease without discoverable lesion. **Fürstner's d.,** pseudospastic paralysis with tremor. **Gaisböck's d.,** polycythemia hypertonica. **gambian horse d.,** a disease of horses in Senegambia caused by the *Trypanosoma dimorpha*. **Gamna's d.,** a form of splenomegaly, with thickening of the splenic capsule and the presence of small brownish areas (Gamna nodules) which are usually surrounded by a hematogenous zone. Ferruginous pigment is deposited in the splenic pulp. **Gandy-Nanta d.,** siderotic splenomegaly. **gannister d.,** pneumoconiosis due to the inhalation of dust by workers in gannister. **Garré's d.,** sclerotic nonsuppurative osteitis. **Gaucher's d.,** a familial disorder characterized by splenomegaly, skin pigmentation, scleral pingueculae, and the presence of distinctive kerasin-containing cells in the liver, spleen, and bone marrow. **Gayet's d.,** a rare form of fatal lethargic sleep resembling nelavan. **Gee's d., Gee-Herter d., Gee-Herter-Heubner d.,** intestinal infantilism. **Gee-Thaysen d.,** idiopathic steatorrhea of adults and adolescents in nontropical countries, probably identical with sprue. **genetotrophic d.,** a metabolic disease resulting from a genetically transmitted enzyme defect; called also *inborn error of metabolism.* **Gensoul's d.,** Ludwig's angina. **Gerhardt's d.,** erythromelalgia. **Gerlier's d.,** paralytic vertigo; a disease of the nerves and nerve centers attacking farm laborers and stablemen, and characterized by pain, paresis, vertigo, ptosis, and muscular contractions. **Gibert's d.,** pityriasis rosea. **Gibney's d.,** perispondylitis. **Gierke's d.,** glycogenosis. **Gilbert's d.,** the congenital forms of hemolytic jaundice. **Gilchrist's d.,** blastomycosis. **Gilles de la Tourette's d.,** motor incoordination associated with echolalia and coprolalia. **Giovannini's d.,** a rare nodular disease of the hair produced by a fungus. **Glanzmann's d.,** Glanzmann's thrombasthenia. **glass-blowers' d.,** a disturbance with enlargement of the parotid gland occurring in glass-blowers. **Glénard's d.,** splanchnoptosis. **Glisson's d.,** rickets. **glycogen d.,** glycogenosis. **glycogen-storage d.,** glycogenosis. **Goldflam's d., Goldflam-Erb d.,** myasthenia gravis pseudoparalytica. **Goldscheider's d.,** hereditary epidermolysis bullosa. **Goldstein's d.,** hereditary telangiectasia with hereditary (familial) epistaxis. **Gougerot's d.** See under *syndrome.* **Gowers' d.,** saltatory spasm. **Graefe's d.,** progressive ophthalmoplegia. **Grancher's d.,** splenopneumonia. **Graves' d.,** exophthalmic goiter. **Greenfield's d.,** a form of infantile demyelinating encephalopathy. **Greenhow's d.,** vagabonds' d. **Griesinger's d.,** ancylostomiasis. **grinders' d.,** silicosis. **Gross's d.,** encysted rectum. **Gruby's d.,** a form of tinea tonsurans seen in children, and due to the fungus *Trichophyton microsporon.* **di Guglielmo's d.,** a condition originally described as acute erythremic myelosis, but later grouped with the myeloproliferative disorders. See also *di Guglielmo's syndrome.* **guinea worm d.,** dracontiasis. **Guinon's d.,** Gilles de la Tourette's d. **Guiteras' d.,** a condition resembling blastomycosis. **Gull's d.,** atrophy of the thyroid with myxedema. **Gull and Sutton's d.,** arteriosclerosis. **Habermann's d.,** pityriasis lichenoides et varioliformis acuta. **Haff d.,** a condition which affects fishermen of the Koenigsberg Haff. The men are suddenly seized with severe pain in the limbs, great weariness, and myoglobinuria. The disease is said to be the result of poisoning by arsine introduced into the Haff through the waste water of cellulose factories. **Haglund's d.,** bursitis in the region of the Achilles tendon. **Hagner's d.,** an obscure bone disease somewhat resembling acromegaly (Pierre Marie described this obscure bone disease in the two Hagner brothers). **Hailey and Hailey d.,** familial benign chronic pemphigus. **Hall's d.,** spurious hydrocephalus. **Hallervorden-Spatz d.** See under *syndrome.* **Hallopeau's d.,** lichen sclerosus et atrophicus. **Halstern's d.,** endemic syphilis. **Hamman's d.,** spontaneous interstitial emphysema of the lungs, a condition that may simulate acute coronary thrombosis. See under *sign.* **Hammond's d.** Same as *athetosis.* **Hand's d.,** Hand-Schüller-Christian d. **hand-foot-and-mouth d.,** a mild, highly infectious virus disease of children, characterized by vesicular lesions in the mouth and on the hands and feet. **Hand-Schüller-Christian d.,** a type of cholesterol lipoidosis characterized clinically by the triad of defects in the membranous bones, exophthalmos, and diabetes insipidus. Called also *chronic idiopathic xanthomatosis.* **Hanot's d.,** biliary cirrhosis. **Hansen's d.,** leprosy. **Harley's d.,** recurrent hemoglobinuria. **Hartnup d.,** a condition characterized by hereditary pellagra-like skin rash, with transient cerebellar ataxia, constant renal aminoaciduria, and other bizarre biochemical abnormalities. **Hashimoto's d.,** struma lymphomatosa. **heart d.,** any organic, mechanical or functional condition of the heart that causes trouble. It may be valvular, myocardial or neurogenic. **heartwater d.** See *heartwater.* **Heberden's d.** 1. Rheumatism of the smaller joints, accompanied by nodosities. 2. Angina pectoris. **Hebra's d.,** erythema multiforme exudativum. **Heerfordt's d.,** uveoparotid fever. **Heine-Medin d.,** the major form of poliomyelitis, with involvement of the central nervous system and perhaps paralysis. **Heller-Döhle d.,** syphilitic aortitis. **helminthic d.,** a disease caused by worms. **hematopoietic d.,** disease affecting the blood-making organs. **hemolytic d. of newborn,** erythroblastosis fetalis. **hemorrhagic d.,** any one of a group of diseases marked by a tendency to hemorrhage from the membranes and into the tissues, and including purpura haemorrhagica, hemophilia, and melena neonatorum. **hemorrhagic d., epidemic,** epidemic hemorrhagic fever. **hemorrhagic d. of the newborn,** a self-limited hemorrhagic disorder of the first days of life, caused by a marked deficiency of blood coagulation factors II and VII, and most probably involving also factors IX and X. **Henderson-Jones d.,** osteochondromatosis characterized by the presence of numerous cartilaginous foreign bodies in the joint cavity or in the bursa of a tendon sheath. **Henoch's d.,** Henoch's purpura. **hepatolenticular d.,** progressive lenticular degeneration. **hereditary d.,** one that is transmitted from parents to children. **heredoconstitutional d.,** an inherited pathologic condition which does not progress. **heredodegenerative d.,** a disease of the central nervous system characterized by specific loss of neural tissue due to hereditary influence. **Herter's d., Herter-Heubner d.,** intestinal infantilism. **Heubner's d.,** syphilitic endarteritis of the cerebral vessels. **Hildenbrand's d.,** typhus. **hip-joint d.,** tuberculosis of the hip joint. **Hippel's d.,** angioma confined principally to the retina. See also *Lindau-von Hippel d.* **Hirschfeld's d.,** acute diabetes mellitus. **Hirschsprung's d.,** massive enlargement of the colon, resulting from obstruction caused by an aganglionic segment of bowel. **His's d., His-Werner d.,** trench fever. **hock d.,** perosis. **Hodara's d.,** a kind of trichorrhexis nodosa seen in women in Constantinople. **Hodgkin's d.,** a painless, progressive, and fatal enlargement of the lymph nodes, spleen, and general lymphoid tissues, which often begins in the neck and spreads over the body. Called also *infectious granuloma, malignant granuloma, malignant lymphoma, lymphomatosis granulomatosa, lymphadenoma, lymphogranulomatosis, granulomatosis maligna, lymphosarcoma, anemia lymphatica,* and *pseudoleukemia.* **Hodgson's d.,** an aneurysmal dilatation of the proximal part of the aorta, often accompanied by dilatation or hypertrophy of the heart. **Hoffa's d.,** traumatic proliferation of fatty tissue (solitary lipoma) in the knee joint (Albert Hoffa, 1904). **Holla d.** (*Holla,* a Norwegian town), recurring anemic crises in hemolytic jaundice, occurring endemically. **hoof-and-mouth d.,** foot-and-mouth d. **hookworm d.** See *uncinariasis* and *ancylostomiasis.* **Huchard's d.,** continued arterial hypertension, thought to be a cause of arteriosclerosis. **Hueppe's d.,** hemorrhagic septicemia of animals.

Huguier's d., fibromyoma uteri. **hunger d., hungry d.,** excessive hunger accompanied by weakness and nervousness due to hyperinsulism. **Hunt's d.,** dyssynergia cerebellaris myoclonica. **Huntington's d.** See under *chorea.* **Huppert's d.,** multiple myeloma. **Hurler's d.,** gargoylism. **Hutchinson's d.** 1. Summer prurigo. 2. Infectious angioma. 3. Cheiropompholyx. 4. Tay's choroiditis. **Hutchinson-Boeck d.,** generalized sarcoidosis. **Hutchinson-Gilford d.,** progeria. **Hutinel's d.,** cardiotuberculous cirrhosis of the liver in childhood; marked by cirrhosis of the liver, ascites, cyanosis, and swelling of the extremities. **hyaline membrane d.,** idiopathic respiratory distress of newborn. **hydatid d.,** an infection caused by larval forms of certain cestodes (Echinococcus), and characterized by the development of expanding cysts. **hydatid d., alveolar,** an infection caused by the larval form of *Echinococcus multilocularis* and marked by invasion and destruction of the host's tissues, the early lesion breakdown in the center, forming an abscess-like cavity, while the peripheral cysts continue to multiply. **hydatid d., unilocular,** an infection caused by the larval form of *Echinococcus granulosus* and marked by the formation of single or multiple cysts which are unilocular in character. **Hyde's d.,** prurigo nodularis. **hydrocephaloid d.,** a condition which is similar to hydrocephalus, but marked by depression of the fontanels, due to diarrhea or some other wasting disease. **idiopathic d.,** one not consequent upon any other disease, or upon any known lesion or injury. **inclusion d.,** any disease in which cell inclusions are found. **infectious d.,** a disease due to an infection. **inherited d.,** a disease that came from one's ancestors. **insect-borne d's,** diseases caused by microorganisms which are transmitted by insects, the principal ones being dengue, encephalitis lethargica, filariasis, infantile paralysis, Japanese river fever, kala-azar, leishmaniasis, malaria, nagana, pappataci fever, plague, relapsing fever, Rocky Mountain spotted fever, surra, Texas fever, trypanosomiasis, tularemia, typhus fever, and yellow fever. **insufficiency d.,** deficiency d. **intercurrent d.,** a disease occurring during the course of another disease with which it has no connection. **interstitial d.,** one in which the stroma of an organ is mainly affected. **Isambert's d.,** acute miliary tuberculosis of larynx and pharynx. **island d.,** scrub typhus. **Isle of Wight d.,** paralysis of the muscles of flight in honey bees caused by the presence of *Acarapis woodi* in the tracheae of the bees. **itch d.,** a form of dermatitis in horses due to the presence of *Fusarium equinum.* **Jaffe-Lichtenstein d.,** cystic osteofibromatosis; a form of polyostotic fibrous dysplasia characterized by an enlarged medullary cavity with a thin cortex, which is filled with fibrous tissue (fibroma). **Jakob's d., Jakob-Creutzfeldt d.,** spastic pseudosclerosis. **Jaksch's d.,** anemia pseudoleukemica infantum. **Janet's d.,** psychasthenia. **jeep d.,** pilonidal sinus activated by riding in a jeep, truck, or tank. **Jensen's d.,** retinochoroiditis juxtapapillaris. **Johne's d.,** chronic dysentery in cattle; a pseudo-tuberculous enteritis caused by *Mycobacterium paratuberculosis.* **Johnson-Stevens d.,** ectodermosis erosiva pluriorificialis. **Jourdain's d.,** suppurative inflammation of the gums and alveolar processes. **jumping d.,** Gilles de la Tourette's d. **Jüngling's d.,** osteitis tuberculosa multiplex cystoides. **Kahler's d.,** multiple myeloma. **Kaiserstuhl d.,** a form of chronic arsenic poisoning in the Kaiserstuhl wine district of Germany. **Kalischer's d.,** nevoid amentia. **Kaposi's d.** 1. Xeroderma pigmentosum. 2. Kaposi's varicelliform eruption. 3. Idiopathic hemorrhagic sarcoma (Kaposi). **Kaposi's varicelliform d.** See under *eruption.* **Kaschin-Beck d.,** an endemic disease of Manchukuo, Korea, and Siberia marked by shortness of the long bones with swelling of the joints, especially those of the phalanges. **Katayama d.,** schistosomiasis japonica. **Kayser's d.,** a condition characterized by pigmentation of the body, greenish discoloration of the cornea, and intention tremor, and attended by diabetes, enlargement of the spleen, and hepatic cirrhosis. **Kedani d.,** scrub typhus. **Kienböck's d.** 1. Chronic slowly progressive osteochondrosis of the semilunar (carpal lunate) bone. It may affect other bones of the wrist. Called also *lunatomalacia.* 2. Traumatic cavity formation in the spinal cord. **Kimmelstiel's d.,** intercapillary nephrosclerosis. **Kirkland's d.,** an acute infection of the throat with regional lymphadenitis. **Klebs' d.,** glomerulonephritis. **Klein's d.,** fowl typhoid. **Klemperer's d.,** Banti's d. **Klippel-Feil d.,** arthritic general pseudoparalysis. **knight's d.,** infection of the perianal region following a minute abrasion of the skin, so called historically because of the frequency of its occurrence in horsemen. **Köbner's d.,** epidermolysis bullosa. **Koenig-Wichman d.,** chronic bullous disease (pemphigus). **Köhler's bone d.** 1. Disease or malformation of the navicular bone of the foot in children, of obscure pathology, due to traumatism and developmental defect conditioned by traumatism. The symptoms are: limping and pain on walking, usually tenderness over the navicular bone, sometimes redness and swelling. Called also *tarsal scaphoiditis, epiphysitis juvenilis, osteoarthrosis juvenilis,* and *os naviculare pedis retardatum.* 2. A disease of the second metatarsal bone, with thickening of its shaft and changes about its articular head, characterized by pain in the second metatarsophalangeal joint on walking or standing. Called also *Kohler's second d., Panner's d., Freiberg's infraction of metatarsal head,* and *juvenile deforming metatarsophalangeal osteochondritis.* **Köhler-Pellegrini-Stieda d.,** Pellegrini-Stieda d. **Kokka d.,** epidemic hemorrhagic fever. **Korsakoff's d.,** Korsakoff's psychosis. **Krabbe's d.,** diffuse infantile familial cerebral sclerosis. **Krishaber's d.,** a neuropathy affecting the nerves of sensation and the heart, and marked by tachycardia, vertigo, hyperesthesia, and sense illusions. **Kufs's d.,** the late juvenile form of cerebromacular degeneration, occurring after the age of fifteen. **Kümmell's d.,** compression fracture of vertebra; a complex of symptoms coming on in a few weeks after spinal injury, and consisting of pain in the spine, intercostal neuralgia, motor disturbances of the legs, and a gibbosity of the spine which is painful on pressure and easily reduced by extension; post-traumatic spondylitis. **Kümmell-Verneuil d.,** Kümmell's d. **Kussmaul's d., Kussmaul-Maier d.,** periarteritis nodosa. **Kyasanur Forest d.,** a highly fatal viral disease of monkeys in the Kyasanur Forest in India, communicable to man, in whom it produces hemorrhagic symptoms. **Laennec's d.** 1. Alcoholic cirrhosis of the liver. 2. Dissecting aneurysm. **Lagleyze-von Hippel d.,** angiomatosis of the retina. **Lain's d.,** burning and erosion of the mouth and tongue resulting from electrogalvanism caused by presence in the mouth of dental restorations of dissimilar metals. **Lancereaux-Mathieu d.,** Weil's d. **Landry's d.,** acute ascending spinal paralysis. **Lane's d.,** chronic intestinal stasis. **Langdon-Down's d.,** mongolism. **Larrey-Weil d.,** leptospiral jaundice. **Larsen's d., Larsen-Johansson d.,** a disease of the patella in which the x-ray shows an accessory center of ossification in the lower pole of the patella. **Lasègue's d.,** mania of persecution. **Leber's d.,** a hereditary form of optic or retrobulbar neuritis which is often sex-linked. **Lederer's d.** See under *anemia.* **Legal's d.,** a disease affecting the pharyngotympanic region, and marked by headache and local inflammatory changes. **Legg's d., Legg-Calvé d., Legg-Calvé-Waldenström d.,** osteochondrosis of capitular epiphysis. **Leiner's d.,** desquamative erythroderma in infants. **Leloir's d.,** lupus vulgaris erythematodes. **Leriche's d.,** Sudeck's atrophy. **Letterer-Siwe d.,** a non-familial, non-lipid reticuloendotheliosis of early childhood, characterized by a hemorrhagic tendency, eczematoid skin eruption, hepatosplenomegaly with lymph node enlargement, and progressive anemia. **Lewandowsky's d.**, rosacea-like tuberculid. **Lewandowsky-Lutz d.**, epidermodysplasia verruciformis. **Leyden's d.**, a form of periodic vomiting. **Libman-Sacks d.**, verrucous endocarditis complicated with lupus erythematosus disseminatus. **Lichtheim's d.**, subacute combined degeneration of the spinal cord. **Lindau's d.**, angioma in the central nervous system, particularly in the cerebellum. See also *Lindau-von Hippel d.* **Lindau-von Hippel d.**, angioma of the cerebellum, usually cystic, associated with hemangioma of the retina, polycystic pancreas, and polycystic kidneys. **Lipschütz's d.**, ulcus vulvae acutum. **Little's d.**, congenital spastic stiffness of the limbs, a form of cerebral spastic paralysis dating from birth and due to lack of development of the pyramidal tracts. **Lobo's d.**, keloidal blastomycosis. **Lobstein's d.**, osteogenesis imperfecta. **local d.**, a condition which originates in and remains confined to one part. **loco d.**, locoism. **Lorain's d.**, ateleiosis. **Loriga's d.**, pneumatic hammer d. **Lowe's d.**, oculocerebrorenal syndrome. **Lucas-Championniére d.**, chronic pseudomembranous bronchitis. **Lutembacher's d.**, a combination of mitral stenosis and interauricular septal defect, producing first a right-sided hypertrophy and later a reversal of the blood flow and cyanosis. **Lutz-Splendore-Almeida d.**, South American blastomycosis. **lymphocystic d. of fish**, a disease of fish marked by the formation on the skin of spherical nodules: caused by a filtrable virus. **Mackenzie's d.**, x disease. **MacLean-Maxwell d.**, a chronic condition of the os calcis marked by enlargement of its posterior third and attended by pain on pressure. **Madelung's d.** 1. Congenital dislocation of the wrists. 2. Multiple symmetrical lipomatosis on the neck, shoulders, and back. **Magitot's d.**, osteoperiostitis of the alveoli of the teeth. **Mahler's d.**, paracolpitis. **Majocchi's d.**, purpura annularis telangiectodes. **Malassez's d.**, cyst of the testis. **Manson's d.**, schistosomiasis. **maple bark d.**, a granulomatous interstitial pneumonitis caused by a rare mold, *Cryptostroma corticale*, so called because spores of the mold were found beneath the bark of maple logs. **maple syrup urine d.**, a genetotrophic disease involving an enzyme defect in the metabolism of the branched chain amino acids, the plasma and urinary levels of valine, leucine, and isoleucine being greatly increased. The name derives from the characteristic odor of the urine. **March's d.**, exophthalmic goiter. **Marchiafava-Bignami d.**, degeneration of the corpus callosum. **Marchiafava-Micheli d.** See under *syndrome*. **Marek's d.**, avian lymphomatosis. **Marfan's d.**, progressive spastic paraplegia in children with hereditary syphilis, due to myelitis. **Marie's d.** 1. Acromegaly. 2. Hypertrophic pulmonary osteoarthropathy. **Marie-Bamberger d.**, hypertrophic pulmonary osteoarthropathy. **Marie-Strümpell d.**, rheumatoid spondylitis. **Marie-Tooth d.**, progressive neuropathic (peroneal) muscular atrophy. **Marsh's d.**, exophthalmic goiter. **Martin's d.**, periosteoarthritis of the foot from excessive walking. **Massai d.**, a disease of East Africa, marked by fever, vomiting, and abdominal tenderness: it is thought to be filarial in nature. **Mathieu's d.**, Weil's disease. **Mauriac's d.**, erythema nodosum syphiliticum. **Maxcy's d.**, a form of typhus fever endemic in the southeastern part of the United States. **Medin's d.**, anterior poliomyelitis. **Mediterranean d.**, Cooley's anemia. **Meige's d.**, Milroy's d. **Meleda d.**, familial hyperkeratosis palmaris et plantaris. **Menetrier's d.**, diffuse thickening of the wall of the stomach, caused by excessive proliferation of the mucosa. **Meniere's d.** See under *syndrome*. **Merzbacher-Pelizaeus d.**, familial centrolobar sclerosis. **metazoal d.**, a disease caused by metazoal parasites, such as nematodes, cestodes, trematodes and arthropods. **Meyer's d.**, adenoid vegetations of the pharynx. **miasmatic d.**, one due to malarial poisoning. **Mibelli's d.**, porokeratosis. **microdrepanocytic d.**, a form of hemoglobinopathy, in which thalassemia is associated with the sickling trait. **Mikulicz's d.**, a chronic lymphocytic infiltration and enlargement of the lacrimal and salivary glands of unknown etiology; associated with sarcoidosis, malignant lymphoma or collagen disease, the similar clinical picture is called *Mikulicz's syndrome*. **milk-borne d's**, diseases caused by organisms transmitted in milk; the principal ones are Asiatic cholera, diphtheria, dysentery, food infections, foot-and-mouth disease, infantile diarrhea, Malta fever, scarlatina, septic sore throat, tuberculosis, and typhoid fever. **Miller's d.**, osteomalacia. **Mills's d.**, progressive ascending hemiplegia. **Milroy's d.**, a form of hereditary edema of the legs. **Minamata d.**, a severe neurological disorder usually characterized by peripheral and circumoral paresthesia, ataxia, dysarthria, and loss of peripheral vision, resulting from poisoning by organic mercury, and leading to severe permanent neurological and mental disabilities or death. **Minor's d.**, central hematomyelia. **Minot's d.**, a self-limiting hemorrhagic disease of the newborn. **mish d.**, a dysentery in Syria caused by eating apricots. **Mitchell's d.**, erythromelalgia. **Moebius' d.**, periodic migraine with paralysis of the oculomotor muscles. **Moeller-Barlow d.**, subperiosteal hematoma in rickets. **Molten's d.**, Pictow d. **Mondor's d.**, phlebitis affecting the large subcutaneous veins normally crossing the lateral chest region and breast from the epigastric or hypochondriac region to the axilla, occurring in both males and females. **Monge's d.**, Andes d. **Morand's d.**, paresis of the extremities. **Morel-Kraepelin d.**, dementia praecox. **Morgagni's d.**, endocranial hyperostosis. **Morquio's d.**, eccentro-osteochondrodysplasia. **Mortimer's d.**, lupus vulgaris multiplex nonulcerans et nonserpiginosus. **Morton's d.**, metatarsalgia. **Morvan's d.**, a form of syringomyelia marked by painless ulceration of the tips of the fingers (panaris) and analgesic paralysis and atrophy of the forearms and hands. **mosaic d's**, infectious diseases of plants caused by viruses. **Moschcowitz's d.** 1. Thrombotic thrombocytopenic purpura. 2. Febrile pleiochromic anemia. **motor neuron d.**, any disease of a motor neuron, including progressive muscular atrophy, progressive bulbar paralysis, amyotrophic lateral sclerosis and lateral sclerosis. **mountain d.**, mountain sickness. **Mozer's d.**, myelosclerosis in adults. **Mucha's d.**, pityriasis lichenoides et varioliformis acuta. **mule spinner's d.**, warts or ulcers of the skin, especially of the scrotum, which tend to become malignant. They are so called because found chiefly among the operators of spinning mules in cotton mills. **multiglandular d.**, a condition in which several of the glands of internal secretion are involved. **Münchmeyer's d.**, a diffuse progressive ossifying polymyositis. **Munk's d.**, lipoid nephrosis. **Murri's d.**, paroxysmal hemoglobinuria. **Myâ's d.**, congenital dilatation of the colon. **Nairobi d.**, an infectious disease of sheep and goats in Nairobi, marked by acute hemorrhagic gastroenteritis and caused by a virus from the brown tick, *Rhipicephalus appendiculatus* and *Amblyomma variegatum*. **nanukayami d.**, nanukayami. **naronian d.**, an endemic intermittent fever once prevalent at Narenta (Bosnia). **navicular d.**, necrotic inflammation of the navicular bone in horses, causing intermittent lameness. **nervous d.**, any disease involving or affecting the nervous system. **Nettleship's d.**, urticaria pigmentosa. **Neumann's d.**, pemphigus vegetans. **Newcastle d.**, a viral disease of birds, including domestic fowl, characterized by respiratory and gastrointestinal or pneumonic and encephalitic symptoms.

The infection is also transmissible to man. **Nicolas-Favre d.,** lymphogranuloma venereum. **Nidoko d.,** epidemic hemorrhagic fever. **Niemann's d.,** Niemann-Pick d. **Niemann-Pick d.,** a heredofamilial disease characterized by massive hepatosplenomegaly, brownish-yellow discoloration of the skin, nervous system involvement, and presence in the liver, spleen, lungs, lymph nodes, and bone marrow of foamy reticular cells or histiocytes which store phospholipids, chiefly lecithin and sphingomyelin. Called also *lipid histiocytosis.* **nodule d.,** a disease of sheep, caused by a minute worm, *Oesophagostoma columbianum,* which infests the intestines, becoming embedded in the mucous membrane, where it forms small nodules. **Nordau's d.,** degeneracy. **nutritional d.,** disturbance of nutrition and function without visible lesion. **occupation d.,** one due to one's employment. **Oguchi's d.,** a form of congenital night blindness occurring in Japan. **Ohara's d.,** a disease observed in Japan, probably identical with tularemia. **Ollier's d.,** dyschondroplasia. **Olmer's d.,** Mediterranean exanthematous fever. **Opitz's d.,** thrombophlebitic splenomegaly. **Oppenheim's d.,** amyotonia congenita. **Oppenheim-Urbach d.,** necrobiosis lipoidica diabeticorum. **organic d.,** one due to or accompanied by structural changes in the body. **Osgood-Schlatter d.,** osteochondrosis of the tuberosity of the tibia. **Osler's d.** 1. Polycythemia vera. 2. Hereditary hemorrhagic telangiectasia. **Osler-Vaquez d.,** polycythemia vera. **Otto's d.,** osteo-arthritic protrusion of the acetabulum. **Owren's d.,** parahemophilia. **Paas's d.,** a familial disorder marked by skeletal deformities such as coxa valga, shortening of phalanges, scoliosis, spondylitis, etc. **Page's d.,** railway spine. **Paget's d.** 1. Osteitis deformans. 2. An inflammatory cancerous affection of the areola and nipple. **Paltauf-Sternberg d.,** Hodgkin's disease. **pandemic d.,** one which occurs over an entire country, or even more or less over the world. **Panner's d.,** Köhler's d., def. 2. **parasitic d.,** one caused by vegetable or animal parasites. **parenchymatous d.,** one which attacks the parenchyma of an organ. **Parkinson's d.,** paralysis agitans. **paroxysmal d.,** one occurring in sudden seizures. **Parrot's d.,** syphilitic pseudoparalysis. **Parry's d.,** exophthalmic goiter. **Parson's d.,** exophthalmic goiter. **Pavy's d.,** recurrent physiologic albuminuria. **Paxton's d.,** tinea nodosa or trichorrhexis nodosa. **Payr's d.,** a kinking of an adhesion between the transverse and the descending colon producing chronic intestinal stenosis. **pearl d.,** tuberculosis of the peritoneum and mesentery of cattle. **pearl-workers' d.,** recurrent inflammation of bone with hypertrophy, seen in persons who work in pearl dust. **Pel-Ebstein d.,** Hodgkin's d. **Pelizaeus-Merzbacher d.,** familial centrolobar sclerosis. **Pellegrini's d., Pellegrini-Stieda d.,** a condition characterized by a semilunar bony formation in the upper portion of the medial lateral ligament of the knee, due to traumatism. **periodic d.,** a condition characterized by regularly recurring and intermittent episodes of fever, edema, arthralgia, or gastric pain and vomiting, continuing for years without further development in otherwise healthy individuals. **periodontal d.,** a disease or disorder of the tissues surrounding the root of a tooth. **Perrin-Ferraton d.,** snapping hip. **Perthes' d.,** osteochondrosis of capitular epiphysis. **Petit's d.,** eventration of the diaphragm. **Peyronie's d.,** induration of the corpora cavernosa of the penis, producing a fibrous chordee: called also *fibrous cavernitis, penis plasticus, penile induration,* and *strabismus of the penis.* **Pfeiffer's d.,** infectious mononucleosis. **Philippine fowl d.,** Newcastle d. **Phoca's d.,** chronic glandular mastitis with the formation of numerous small nodules. **Pick's d.** 1. (Arnold Pick) Lobar atrophy. 2. (F. J. Pick) Erythromelia. 3. (Friedel Pick) A condition marked by enlargement of the liver with peritonitis and obstinately recurring ascites, but without jaundice, occurring in patients with a previous history of pericarditis. It is a form of multiple serositis and has been called *pericardial pseudocirrhosis of the liver.* 4. Niemann-Pick d. **Pictow d.,** a cirrhosis of the liver in horses and cattle in Nova Scotia due to eating certain species of Senecio. **pink d.,** erythredema polyneuropathy. **Pinkus' d.,** lichen nitidus. **plaster-of-paris d.,** atrophy of a limb which has been enclosed in a plaster-of-paris splint. **Plummer's d.,** the development of toxicity (hyperthyroidism) in simple adenoma of the thyroid. **pneumatic hammer d.,** acrocyanosis resulting from use of a pneumatic hammer. **policeman's d.,** tarsalgia. **Politzer's d.,** hidrosadenitis destruens suppurativa. **polyhedral d.,** a group of virus diseases of caterpillars. **Pompe's d.,** generalized glycogenosis. **Poncet's d.,** tuberculous rheumatism. **porcupine d.,** ichthyosis. **Posada-Wernicke's d.,** coccidioidomycosis. **Potain's d.,** pulmonary and pleural edema. **Pott's d.,** osteitis or caries of the vertebrae, usually of tuberculous origin; it is marked by stiffness of the vertebral column, pain on motion, tenderness on pressure, prominence of certain of the vertebral spines, and occasionally abdominal pain, abscess formation, and paralysis. **Poulet's d.,** rheumatic osteoperiostitis. **Preiser's d.,** osteoporosis and atrophy of the carpal scaphoid due to trauma or to fracture which has not been kept immobilized. **Pringle's d.,** adenoma sebaceum. **Proficbet's d.** See under *syndrome.* **Puente's d.,** simple glandular cheilitis. **pullorum d.,** white diarrhea. **puppy d.,** a destructive disease of puppies, marked by digestive, respiratory, and nervous disturbances. **Purtscher's d.,** traumatic angiopathy in the retina with lymphorrhagia. **pyramidal d.,** buttress foot. **Quervain's d.,** painful tenosynovitis due to relative narrowness of the common tendon sheath of the abductor pollicis longus and the extensor pollicis brevis. **Quincke's d.,** angioneurotic edema. **Quinquaud's d.,** a purulent folliculitis of the scalp, causing irregular bald patches; called also *acne decalvans.* **rag-sorter's d.,** anthrax. **rat-bite d.** See under *fever.* **Rauzier's d.,** blue edema. **Rayer's d.,** xanthoma. **Raynaud's d.** 1. A primary or idiopathic vascular disorder characterized by bilateral attacks of Raynaud's phenomenon. The criteria for making a diagnosis of Raynaud's disease are the continuation of the attacks for two years or more, and a minimum amount of cutaneous gangrene. The disease affects females more frequently than males. Cf. *Raynaud's phenomenon,* under *phenomenon.* 2. Paralysis of the throat muscles following parotiditis. **Recklinghausen's d.** 1. Multiple neurofibromas. 2. Osteitis fibrosa cystica. 3. Neoplastic arthritis deformans. **Recklinghausen-Applebaum d.,** hemochromatosis. **Reclus' d.** 1. A painless cystic enlargement of the mammae, marked by multiple dilatations of the acini and ducts. 2. Ligneous phlegmon. **Reed-Hodgkin d.,** Hodgkin's disease. **Refsum's d.,** a familial disease marked by hemeralopia, polyneuritis, ataxia, and paresthesias: called also *heredopathia atactica polyneuritiformis.* **Reichmann's d.,** continuous secretion of gastric juice; gastrosuccorrhea. **Reiter's d.,** a disease of males marked by initial diarrhea which is followed by urethritis, conjunctivitis and migratory polyarthritis and frequently accompanied by keratotic lesions of the skin. **Rendu-Osler-Weber d.,** hereditary hemorrhagic telangiectasia. **Renikhet d.,** Newcastle d. **rheumatic heart d.,** the most important and constant manifestation of rheumatic fever. It consists of the inflammatory changes, including valvular deformations and various other residua. **rheumatoid d.,** a systemic condition which is best known by its articular manifestations. **Ribas-Torres d.,** alastrim. **rice d.,** beriberi. **Riedel's d.,** ligneous thyroiditis. **Riga's d.,** cachectic aphthae. **Riga-Fede d.,** granuloma of the frenum linguae in children, occurring after abrasion by the lower central incisors. **Rigg's d.**, periodontal d. **Ritter's d.**, dermatitis exfoliativa infantum. **Rivalta's d.**, actinomycosis. **Robinson's d.**, hydrocystoma. **Robles' d.**, ocular onchocerciasis. **Roger's d.**, the presence of an abnormal congenital communication between the ventricles of the heart. **Rokitansky's d.**, acute yellow atrophy of the liver. **rolling d.**, a disease of laboratory mice characterized by lateral rolling movements, by neurolysis and by a polymorphonuclear leukocytic reaction in the brain. It is caused by a pleuropneumonia-like organism. **Romberg's d.**, facial hemiatrophy. **Rose d.**, swine erysipelas. **Rosenbach's d.** 1. (A. J. F. Rosenbach) Erysipeloid. 2. (O. Rosenbach) Heberden's nodes. **Rossbach's d.**, hyperchlorhydria. **Roth's d.** 1. Septic retinitis. 2. Meralgia paraesthetica. **Roth-Bernhardt d.**, meralgia paraesthetica. **Roussy-Levy's d.**, a type of familial ataxia marked by disorders of gait, clubfoot, and lack of tendon reflexes. **Rowland's d.**, xanthomatosis. **Rummo's d.**, downward displacement of the heart. **Runneberg's d.**, the remittent type of pernicious anemia. **runt d.**, a syndrome produced experimentally by injecting immunologically competent cells into genetically foreign hosts that are unable to reject these elements, resulting in gross retardation of host development and fatal consequences. Called also *graft vs. host reaction.* **Rust's d.**, tuberculous spondylitis of the cervical vertebrae. **Ruysch's d.**, megacolon. **Sachs' d.**, amaurotic family idiocy. **sacroiliac d.**, chronic tuberculous inflammation of the sacroiliac joint. **St. Agatha's d.**, mammitis. **St. Aignon's d.**, tinea favosa. **St. Aman's d.**, pellagra. **St. Anthony's d.** 1. Chorea. 2. Epidemic gangrene. **St. Appolonia's d.**, toothache. **St. Avertin's d.**, epilepsy. **St. Avidus' d.**, deafness. **St. Blasius' d.**, quinsy. **St. Clair's d.**, ophthalmia. **St. Dymphna's d.**, insanity. **St. Erasmus' d.**, colic. **St. Fiacre's d.**, hemorrhoids. **St. Francis' d.**, erysipelas. **St. Gervasius' d.**, rheumatism. **St. Gete's d.**, carcinoma. **St. Giles' d.** 1. Leprosy. 2. Carcinoma. **St. Gotthard's tunnel d.**, ancylostomiasis. **St. Hubert's d.**, hydrophobia. **St. Job's d.**, syphilis. **St. Main's d.**, scabies. **St. Mathurin's d.**, idiocy. **St. Modestus' d.**, chorea. **St. Roch's d.**, plague. **St. Sement's d.**, syphilis. **St. Valentine's d.**, epilepsy. **St. Zachary's d.**, dumbness. **salivary gland d.**, cytomegalic inclusion d. **San Joaquin Valley d.**, coccidioidal granuloma. **Sander's d.** 1. A form of paranoia. 2. Epidemic keratoconjunctivitis. **sandworm d.**, larva migrans. **sartian d.**, a facial skin disease endemic in Asiatic Russia: probably furunculus orientalis. **Saunders' d.**, a dangerous condition seen in infants having digestive disturbances to whom is given a large percentage of carbohydrates. It is marked by vomiting, cerebral symptoms, and depression of circulation. **Savill's d.**, dermatitis epidemica. **Schamberg's d.**, progressive pigmentary dermatosis. **Schanz's d.**, traumatic inflammation of the tendo achillis. **Schaumann's d.**, Boeck's sarcoid. **Schenck's d.**, sporotrichosis. **Scheuermann's d.**, necrosis of the epiphyses of the vertebrae; osteochondrosis of the vertebrae. **Schilder's d.**, progressive subcortical encephalopathy. **Schimmelbusch's d.**, a form of productive mastitis marked by the production of many small cysts. **Schlatter's d.**, a condition marked by pain in the region of the tuberosity of the tibia at the point of insertion of the ligamentum patellae: it is seen chiefly in young persons and is an osteochondrosis of the tuberosity of the tibia. **Schlatter-Osgood d.**, Schlatter's d. **Schmorl's d.** 1. Herniation of the nucleus pulposus. 2. Necrobacillosis of rabbits. **Scholz's d.**, the familial juvenile form of diffuse cerebral sclerosis (demyelinating encephalopathy). **Schönlein's d.**, **Schönlein-Henoch d.** Schönlein-Henoch purpura. **Schottmüller's d.**, paratyphoid. **Schriddes' d.**, congenital generalized dropsy. **Schroeder's d.**, a condition characterized by hypertrophic endometrium and excessive uterine bleeding, probably due to deficiency of the gonadotropic hormone. **Schüller's d.** 1. Hand-Schüller-Christian disease. 2. Osteoporosis circumscripta cranii. **Schüller-Christian d.**, Hand-Schüller-Christian d. **Schultz's d.**, agranulocytosis. **secondary d.**, disease resulting from the introduction of mature, immunologically competent cells in a patient or animal rendered capable of accepting them by heavy exposure to ionizing radiation. **Secretan's d.**, severe traumatic edema. **Senear-Usher d.**, pemphigus erythematosus. **senecio d.**, cirrhosis of the liver occurring as the result of senecio poisoning. **septic d.**, one which arises from the development of pyogenic or putrefactive organisms. **serum d.** See under *sickness.* **Sever's d.**, epiphysitis of the os calcis. **shimamushi d.**, scrub typhus. **shipyard d.**, epidemic keratoconjunctivitis. **Shishito d.**, scrub typhus. **shuttlemaker's d.**, a condition in shuttlemakers, marked by faintness, shortness of breath, headache, nausea, etc., attributed to inhaling the dust of poisonous wood from which the shuttles are made. **silage d.**, staggers. **silk stocking d.**, erythrocyanosis crurum. **silo-filler's d.**, a granulomatous type of chronic inflammatory reaction, principally in interstitial tissues of the lung, caused by exposure to dusty, moldy plant materials, such as hay, mushrooms, or organic fertilizers. **Simmonds' d.**, a condition of premature senility accompanied by psychic symptoms due to total atrophy of the pituitary body. It occurs chiefly in women and is marked by progressive emaciation, premature ageing, wrinkling of the skin, loss of pubic and axillary hair, loss of sexual desire, and depression of the basal metabolic rate. Called also *hypophysial cachexia* and *pituitary cachexia.* **Simons' d.**, lipodystrophia progressiva. **sixth d.**, exanthema subitum. **sixth venereal d.**, lymphogranuloma venereum. **Sjögren's d.**, the association of lacrimal deficiency and corneal inflammation; keratoconjunctivitis sicca. **Skevas-Zerfus d.**, sponge-divers' d. **sleeping d.**, narcolepsy. **Smith's d.**, mucous colitis. **specific d.**, any disease, such as syphilis, due to a characteristic morbific agency. **Spencer's d.**, polytropous enteronitis. **Spielmeyer-Stock d.**, retinal atrophy in juvenile amaurotic familial idiocy. **Spielmeyer-Vogt d.**, juvenile amaurotic familial idiocy. **sponge-divers' d.**, a condition caused by contact with the venom of the actinia which lives in sponges, marked by the formation of ulcers, chills, fever and pain. **sporadic d.**, a disease occurring in single cases. **stalk d.**, an eruptive disease of cattle. **Stargardt's d.**, degeneration of the macula lutea occurring before puberty. **Steinert's d.**, myotonia atrophica. **Sterbe d.**, a disease of horses in South Africa. A serum prepared from horses affected with this disease is said to be curative of malarial poisoning. **sterility d.**, a deficiency disease due to a lack of vitamin E in the diet. **Sternberg's d.**, Hodgkin's d. **Stieda's d.**, Pellegrini-Stieda d. **Still's d.**, a variety of chronic polyarthritis affecting children and marked by enlargement of lymph nodes, generally of the spleen, and irregular fever. **Stiller's d.**, asthenia universalis. **Stokes' d.**, exophthalmic goiter. **Stokes-Adams d.**, Adams-Stokes d. **Stokvis' d.**, enterogenous cyanosis; intense cyanosis with marked intestinal disturbances of long duration; methemoglobin or sulfhemoglobin in the blood, dizziness and weakness. **storage d.**, thesaurismosis. **Strachan's d.**, a form of multiple neuritis described by Strachan in patients in Kingston, Jamaica: now believed to be pellagra. **straw mattress d.**, straw itch. **structural d.**, any disease in which there are microscopical changes. **Strümpell's d.** 1. Hereditary spastic spinal paralysis. 2. Polioencephalomyelitis. **Strümpell-Leichtenstern d.**, hemorrhagic encephalitis. **Strüm-**

pell-Marie d., rheumatoid spondylitis. **Stühmer's d.**, balanitis xerotica obliterans. **Sturge's d., Sturge-Weber-Dimitri d.**, nevoid amentia. **Stuttgart d.**, a non-jaundice type of leptospirosis. **subacute d.**, a disease more protracted and less active than an acute disease. **subchronic d.**, one more protracted than an acute disease, but less so than a chronic one. **Sudeck's d.**, post-traumatic osteoporosis. **Sutton's d.** 1. [R. L. Sutton. Sr.]. Leukoderma acquisitum centrifugum. 2. [R. L. Sutton, Jr.]. Granuloma fissuratum. **Sutton and Gull's d.**, arteriosclerosis. **Swediaur's d.**, inflammation of the calcaneal bursa. **sweet clover d.**, hemorrhagic disease of cattle caused by ingestion of spoiled sweet clover, with a hemostatic defect resembling that produced in humans by clinical administration of coumarin-like anticoagulants. **Swift's d.**, erythredema polyneuropathy. **Swift-Feer d.**, erythredema. **swineherd's d.**, a benign meningitis seen in those who work with swine or pork. **Sylvest d.**, epidemic pleurodynia. **Symmers' d.**, giant follicular lymphoma, one of the group of malignant lymphoproliferative disorders. **Taenzer's d.**, ulerythema ophryogenes. **Talfan d.**, Teschen d. **Talma's d.**, myotonia acquisita. **Tangier d.**, a familial disorder characterized by a deficiency of high-density lipoproteins in the blood serum, with storage of cholesterol esters in the tonsils and other tissues. **tarabagan d.**, an epizootic disease affecting marmots (*tarabagans*) in Mongolia. The disease resembles bubonic plague, and is highly infective to man. **tartaric d.**, gout and calculus (Paracelsus). **Tay's d.** See under *choroiditis*. **Tay-Sachs d.**, amaurotic familial idiocy. **Taylor's d.**, diffuse idiopathic atrophy of the skin. **teart d. in cattle**, a diarrhea that affects cattle that graze on certain pastures in England, due to the presence of molybdenum in the herbage. **Teschen d.**, a highly fatal encephalomyelitis of swine, caused by a virus and characterized by a flaccid ascending paralysis, similar in character to the paralysis of human poliomyelitis. **Theiler's d.**, spontaneous encephalomyelitis of mice, caused by invasion of the nervous system by a common virus infection of the intestinal tract; mouse poliomyelitis. **Thomsen's d.**, myotonia congenita. **Thomson's d.**, a congenital condition characterized by developmental hyperkeratotic lesions and xerodermatous changes. **Thornwaldt's d.** See *bursitis*. **Tietze's d.**, costal chondritis. **Tillaux's d.**, mammitis with the formation of multiple tumors in the breast. **Tommaselli's d.**, pyrexia and hematuria due to excessive use of quinine. **Tourette's d.**, Gilles de la Tourette's d. **Traum's d.**, infectious abortion (brucellosis) in swine. **Trevor's d.**, dysplasia epiphysealis hemimelica. **Trousseau's d.**, stomachal vertigo. **tsetse fly d.**, infection of animals in South Africa with trypanosomes which are inoculated into them by means of the tsetse fly. **tsutsugamushi d.**, scrub typhus. **tunnel d.** 1. Ancylostomiasis. 2. Decompression sickness. **Tyzzer's d.**, a disease of Japanese waltzing mice characterized by inflammatory lesions of the liver. **Underwood's d.**, sclerema neonatorum. **Unna's d.**, seborrheic eczema. **Unverricht's d.**, myoclonus epilepsy. **Urbach-Oppenheim d.**, necrobiosis lipoidica diabeticorum. **Urbach-Wiethe's d.**, lipid proteinosis. **vagabonds' d., vagrants' d.**, parasitic melanoderma: discoloration of the skin in persons of filthy habits, caused by the irritation of lice. **Vallee's d.**, equine infectious anemia. **Valsuani's d.**, progressive pernicious anemia in puerperal and lactating women. **Vaquez' d., Vaquez-Osler d.**, polycythemia vera. **veldt d.**, heartwater. **venereal d.**, a contagious disease, most commonly acquired in sexual intercourse. The venereal diseases include syphilis, gonorrhea, chancroid, granuloma inguinale, lymphogranuloma venereum, and balanitis gangraenosa. **veno-occlusive d. of the liver**, a morbid condition encountered predominantly in children, the chief signs being stunting of growth, ascites, and hepatomegaly, and the essential pathological finding being blockage of the smaller hepatic veins. **vent d.**, a disease of rabbits caused by *Treponema cuniculi*. **Verneuil's d.**, syphilitic disease of the bursae. **Verse's d.**, calcinosis intervertebralis. **Vidal's d.**, neurodermatitis. **Vincent's d.**, ulceromembranous stomatitis. **Virchow's d.**, leontiasis ossium. **Vogt's d.**, cerebral spastic diplegia. **Vogt-Spielmeyer d.**, juvenile familial amaurotic idiocy. **Volkmann's d.**, a congenital deformity of the foot due to a tibiotarsal dislocation. **Voltolini's d.**, an acute purulent inflammation of the internal ear, with violent pain, followed by fever, delirium, and unconsciousness. **von Economo's d.**, epidemic encephalitis. **von Gierke's d.**, glycogenosis. **von Hippel's d.** See *Hippel's d.* **von Jaksch's d.**, anemia pseudoleukemica infantum. **von Recklinghausen's d.** See *Recklinghausen's d.* **von Willebrand's d.**, angiohemophilia. **Wagner's d.**, colloid milium. **Waldenström's d.**, osteochondrosis of the capitular epiphysis. **Wardrop's d.**, onychia maligna. **Wartenberg's d.** 1. Cheiralgia paraesthetica. 2. Brachial paresthesia during sleep. 3. Partial thenar atrophy. **Wassilieff's d.**, Weil's disease. **Weber's d.** 1. Localized epidermolysis bullosa. 2. Nevoid amentia. **Weber-Christian d.**, nodular, nonsuppurative panniculitis. **Weber-Dimitri d.**, nevoid amentia. **Wegner's d.**, osteochondritic separation of the epiphyses in hereditary syphilis. **Weil's d.**, leptospiral jaundice. **Weingarten's d.**, tropical eosinophilia. **Weir Mitchell's d.**, erythromelalgia. **Wenckebach's d.**, cardioptosis. **Werdnig-Hoffmann d.**, a form of hereditary muscular atrophy, in which muscular weakness affects particularly the proximal muscles and begins in the first year of life; appearing usually in siblings rather than in successive generations. **Werlhof's d.**, idiopathic thrombocytopenic purpura. **Werner-His d.**, trench fever. **Werner-Schultz d.**, agranulocytosis. **Wernicke's d.**, acute hemorrhagic polioencephalitis. **Westberg's d.**, a condition marked by the formation of white spots upon the skin. **Westphal-Strümpell d.** See under *pseudosclerosis*. **Whipple's d.**, intestinal lipodystrophy. **White's d.**, keratosis follicularis. **white-spot d.**, degeneration of the papillary and reticular layers of the skin, marked by the formation of white, beadlike spots; morphea guttata. **Whitmore's d.**, melioidosis. **Whytt's d.**, tuberculous meningitis causing acute hydrocephalus. **Widal-Abrami d.**, acquired hemolytic jaundice. **Wilks' d.**, chronic parenchymatous nephritis. **Willis' d.**, diabetes. **Wilson's d.** 1. Dermatitis exfoliativa. 2. Progressive lenticular degeneration. **Wilson-Bracq d.**, Wilson's disease, def. 1. **Winckel's d.**, a fatal disease of newborn infants characterized by icterus, hemorrhage, bloody urine and cyanosis. **Windscheid's d.**, the series of nervous symptoms associated with arteriosclerosis. **Winkelman's d.**, progressive pallidal degeneration. **Winkler's d.**, chondrodermatitis nodularis chronica helicis. **winter vomiting d.**, outbreaks of vomiting which have been observed in various countries. **Winton d.**, Pictow d. **Woillez's d.**, acute idiopathic congestion of the lungs. **woolsorters' d.**, a form of pulmonary anthrax attacking those who handle wool. **x d.** 1. Mackenzie's name for a series of morbid symptoms of unknown origin, consisting of a feeling of general ill health with sensitiveness to cold, dyspepsia, intestinal disorder, and disturbance of respiration and of the action of the heart. 2. A virus disease of cattle, characterized by inflammation and thickening of the horny layer of the skin: called also *hyperkeratosis* and *perkeratosis*. **Zagari's d.**, xerostomia. **Zahorsky's d.**, exanthem subitum. **Ziehen-Oppenheim d.**, dystonia musculorum deformans. **zymotic d.**, a disease due to the action of an enzyme, as of a morbific germ or a ptomaine.

disequilibrium (dis-e″kwĭ-lib′re-um). A disturbed state of equilibrium, either physical or mental.

disesthesia (dis″es-the′ze-ah). Feeling of discomfort.

disgerminoma (dis-jer″mĭ-no′mah). Dysgerminoma.

dish (dish). A shallow vessel of glass or other material for laboratory work. **culture d.,** a shallow glass vessel for making bacterial cultures. **Petri d.,** a shallow glass receptacle for growing bacterial cultures. **Stender d.,** a vessel of various forms and sizes, used in preparing and staining histologic specimens.

disharmonious (dis″har-mo′ne-us). Out of harmony: a term applied by Abderhalden to substances foreign to the body and thus out of harmony with the body cells.

disimmune (dis″ĭ-mūn′). Deprived of immunity.

disimmunity (dis″ĭ-mu′nĭ-te). The state that results from the loss of immunity.

disimmunize (dis-im′u-nīz). To deprive of immunity.

disimpaction (dis″im-pak′shun). The relief or removal of an impaction.

disinfect (dis″in-fekt′) [*dis-* + L. *inficere* to corrupt]. To free from pathogenic substances or organisms, or to render them inert.

disinfectant (dis″in-fek′tant). 1. Freeing from infection. 2. An agent that disinfects chiefly by destroying infective agents (pathogenic microorganisms) or rendering ferments inactive. **coal-tar d.,** creosote. **complete d.,** a disinfectant which destroys spores as well as vegetative forms of microorganisms. **incomplete d.,** a disinfectant which destroys vegetative forms of organisms, but does not injure spores.

disinfection (dis″in-fek′shun). The destruction of pathogenic germs or agents; a vague term usually taken to imply the killing, by means of bactericidal chemical compounds, of vegetative cells but not of spores of microorganisms. **concomitant d., concurrent d.,** immediate disinfection and disposal of discharges and infective matter all through the course of a disease. **terminal d.,** disinfection and destruction of infectious material after the recovery of a patient from an infectious disease or after his death.

disinfestation (dis″in-fes-ta′shun). The extermination or destruction of insects, rodents or other animal forms which might transmit infection and which are present on the person or clothing of an individual or in his surroundings; defaunation.

disinhibition (dis″in-hĭ-bish′un). The abolition of inhibition; in an experimental animal, the revival of an extinguished conditioned reflex or response by a stimulus to which the animal is unaccustomed.

disinomenine (di″sĭ-nom′ĕ-nin). An alkaloid $(C_{19}H_{22}O_4N)_2.2CH_2OH$, formed by the oxidation of sinomenine.

disinsected (dis″in-sekt′ed). Freed from insects or vermin.

disinsection (dis″in-sek′shun). Disinsectization.

disinsectization (dis″in-sek″ti-za′shun). Removal of insects from; extermination of insects or vermin.

disinsector (dis″in-sek′tor). An apparatus for the removal of insects or vermin from patients or their clothing.

disinsertion (dis″in-ser′shun). 1. Rupture of a tendon from its insertion into a bone. 2. Detachment of the retina at its periphery; retinodialysis.

disintegration (dis″in-te-gra′shun) [*dis-* + L. *integer* entire]. 1. The process of breaking up or decomposing. 2. Disassimilation or catabolism.

disintegrator (dis-in″tĕ-gra′tor). An agent or device that produces disintegration of material, such as an apparatus that converts plant or animal tissues or other solid material into a homogeneous pulplike or semiliquid mass.

disintoxication (dis″in-tok-sĭ-ka′shun). 1. Detoxification. 2. Treatment designed to free an addict from his drug habit.

disinvagination (dis″in-vaj″ĭ-na′shun). Reduction of an invagination.

disipal (dis′ĭ-pal). Trade mark for a preparation of orphenadrine hydrochloride.

disjoint (dis-joint′). To disarticulate.

disjugate (dis′ju-gāt). Not joined together in position or action; not acting in common: the opposite of conjugate.

disjunction (dis-junk′shun). The moving apart of chromosomes at anaphase of meiosis.

disk (disk) [L. *discus;* Gr. *diskos*]. A circular or rounded flat plate or organ. **A d.,** Q d. **Amici's d.,** Krause's membrane. **anangioid d.,** a retinal disk without blood vessels. **anisotropic d., anisotropous d.,** Q d. **articular d.** 1. A pad of fibrocartilage or dense fibrous tissue found in some synovial joints. See *discus articularis,* and for names of articular disks of particular joints see entries beginning *discus articularis,* under *discus.* 2. Meniscus articularis. **Bardeen's primitive d.,** the embryonic structure which develops into the intervertebral ligament. **Blake's d's,** disks of paper for pasting over the drum after operation for otitis. **blastodermic d.,** the early germinal disk during the period of cleavage. **blood d.,** a blood platelet. **Bowman's d's,** flat, disklike plates which make up striated muscle fibers. **carborundum d.,** a dental disk charged with carborundum. **choked d.,** papilledema. **ciliary d.,** orbiculus ciliaris. **cloth d.,** a dental disk made of one or more round pieces of cloth. **cutting d.,** a dental disk charged with an abrasive material and used for grinding or reducing teeth. **cuttle fish d.,** a dental disk charged with powdered cuttle-fish bone. **dental d.,** a thin, circular piece of paper or other material, usually operated by a dental engine, and used in procedures on the teeth or dental restorations. It may be used for carrying polishing powders, such as chalk, pumice, rouge, or whiting, or be specially treated with such substances as cuttlefish bone, emery, garnet, or sand, for fine cutting or polishing. **diamond d.,** a dental disk charged with small diamond particles. **embryonic d.,** a flattish area in a cleaved ovum in which the first traces of the embryo are seen. **emery d.,** a dental disk charged with emery powder. **Engelmann's d.,** Hensen's d. **gelatin d.,** a disk or lamella of gelatin, variously medicated: used chiefly in eye diseases. **germinal d.,** embyronic d. **Hensen's d.,** the pale, thin disk dividing a muscle case into two portions. **I d.,** the light disk or band of a striated muscle fiber: called also *isotropic disk* or *J disk.* **interarticular d.,** articular d. **intercalated d.,** short lines or V-shaped stripes extending across the fibers of heart muscle. **intermediate d.,** Krause's membrane. **interpubic d.,** discus interpubicus. **intervertebral d's,** layers of fibrocartilage between the bodies of adjacent vertebrae, consisting of a fibrous ring enclosing a pulpy center. Called also *disci intervertebrales* [N A]. **isotropic d., J d.,** I d. **M d.,** a thin stripe in the middle of Hensen's disk. **Merkel's d's,** Merkel's corpuscles. **micrometer d.,** a glass disk, engraved with a scale, used in an ocular in making microscopical measurements. **Newton's d.,** a disk which is divided into seven sectors that are colored the seven primary colors of the spectrum and which, when rotated rapidly, appears to be white. **optic d.,** discus nervi optici. **Placido's d.,** a disk having concentric circles marked on it: used in examining the cornea. **polishing d.,** a dental disk charged with a polishing agent rather than an abrasive material, and used for polishing teeth or fillings. **proligerous d.,** cumulus oophorus. **Q d.,** the dark disk or band of a striated muscle fiber; called also *anisotropic disk* and *transverse disk.* **Ranvier's tactile d's,** terminations of nerve fibers in cup-shaped bodies in the transparent substance between Grandry's corpuscles. **Rekoss d.,** the rotating device for quickly changing the lenses in the ophthalmoscope. **sandpaper d.,** a dental disk charged with pulverized silica. **Schiefferdecker's d's,** a substance staining black with silver nitrate, assumed to occupy the space in Ranvier's nodes between Schwann's sheath and the axon. **stenopeic d.,** an opaque disk having a narrow slit: used for testing for astigmatism. **stroboscopic d.,** a disk used in eye examinations to produce distortion of objects seen. **tactile d.,** a disklike nerve termination in a tactile cell, as in an end-organ of a nerve of special sense. **transverse d.,** Q d. **Z d.,** Krause's membrane.

diskectomy (disk-ek′to-me). Excision of an intervertebral disk.

diskiform (dis′kĭ-form). In the shape of a disk.

diskitis (dis-ki′tis). Inflammation of a disk, particularly of an interarticular disk.

diskogram (dis′ko-gram). A roentgenogram of an intervertebral disk.

diskography (dis-kog′rah-fe). Roentgenography of the spine, for visualization of an intervertebral disk, after injection into the disk itself of an absorbable contrast medium.

dislocatio (dis″lo-ka′she-o) [L.]. Dislocation. **d. erec′ta,** subglenoid dislocation of the shoulder with the arm in a vertical position and the hand on top of the head.

dislocation (dis″lo-ka′shun) [*dis-* + L. *locare* to place]. The displacement of any part, more especially of a bone. See Plate XIII. **Bell-Dally d.,** nontraumatic dislocation of the atlas. **closed d.,** simple d. **complete d.,** one which completely separates the surfaces of a joint. **complicated d.,** one which is associated with other important injuries. **compound d.,** one in which the joint communicates with the external air. **congenital d.,** one which exists from or before birth. **consecutive d.,** one in which the luxated bone has changed its position since its first displacement. **divergent d.,** one in which the ulna and radius are dislocated separately. **habitual d.,** one which often recurs after replacement. **incomplete d.,** a subluxation; a slight displacement. **intra-uterine d.,** one which occurs to the fetus in utero. **Kienböck's d.,** isolated dislocation of the semilunar bone. **d. of the lens,** displacement of the crystalline lens of the eye. **Monteggia's d.,** dislocation of the hip joint in which the head of the femur is near the anterosuperior spine of the ilium. **Nélaton's d.,** dislocation of the ankle in which the talus is forced up between the end of the tibia and the fibula. **old d.,** a dislocation in which inflammatory changes have occurred. **partial d.,** incomplete d. **pathologic d.,** one which results from paralysis, or from a local or other disease. **primitive d.,** one in which the bones remain as originally displaced. **recent d.,** one in which there is no complicating inflammation. **simple d.,** one in which the joint is not penetrated by a wound. **Smith's d.,** upward and backward dislocation of the metatarsals and the medial cuneiform bone. **subastragalar d.,** separation of the calcaneus and the navicular bone from the talus. **thyroid d.,** displacement of the head of the femur into the thyroid foramen. **traumatic d.,** one due to an injury or to violence.

dismemberment (dis-mem′ber-ment). Amputation of an extremity or a portion of it.

dismutation (dis″mu-ta′shun). A complex vital enzymic process that results simultaneously in oxidation and reduction or also in decarboxylation, as in staphylococci.

disobliteration (dis″ob-lit″er-a′shun). The restoration of the lumen of a stenosed vessel or of other anatomical space which had previously been obliterated.

disocclude (dis″ŏ-kl o͞od′). To grind a tooth so that it does not touch its antagonist in the other jaw in any of the movements of mastication.

disodic (di-so′dik). Having two atoms of sodium in each molecule.

disome (di′sōm) [*di-* + Gr. *sōma* body]. A chromosome set having paired members.

disomer (di′so-mer). Trade mark for preparations of dexbrompheniramine maleate.

disomus (di-so′mus) [*di-* + Gr. *sōma* body]. A double-bodied fetal monster.

disorder (dis-or′der). A derangement or abnormality of function; a morbid physical or mental state. **affective d.,** manic-depressive psychosis. **sleep d.,** somnipathy. **vegetative d.,** a condition of disturbed nutrition.

disorganization (dis-or″gan-i-za′shun). The process of destruction of any organic tissue; any profound change in the tissues of an organ or structure which causes the loss of most or all of its proper characters.

disorientation (dis-o″re-en-ta′shun). The loss of proper bearings, or a state of mental confusion as to time, place, or identity.

disoxidation (dis″ok-se-da′shun). Deoxidation.

Disp. Abbreviation for *dispensatory.*

dispar (dis′par) [L.]. Unequal.

disparasitized (dis-par′ah-si-tīzd). Freed from parasites.

disparate (dis′pah-rāt) [L. *disparatus, dispar* unequal]. Not situated alike; not exactly paired; dissimilar in kind.

dispensary (dis-pen′sah-re) [L. *dispensarium,* from *dispensare* to dispense]. 1. A place where medical or dental skill, treatment and remedies are provided for the indigent, ambulant sick at little or no cost to them. 2. Any place where drugs and medicines are actually dispensed.

dispensatory (dis-pen′sah-to-re) [L. *dispensatorium*]. A treatise on the qualities and composition of medicines.

dispense (dis-pens′) [L. *dispensare, dis-* out + *pensare* to weigh]. To prepare and distribute medicines to those who are to use them.

dispermine (di-sper′min). Piperazine.

dispermy (di′sper-me). The penetration of two spermatozoa into one ovum.

dispersate (dis′pur-sāt). A suspension of finely divided particles of a substance.

disperse (dis-pers′) [L. *dis-* apart + *spargere* to scatter]. To scatter the component parts, as of a tumor or the fine particles in a colloid system; also the particles so dispersed.

dispersible (dis-per′sĭ-b′l). Capable of being dispersed.

dispersidology (dis-per″sĭ-dol′o-je). Colloid chemistry; the chemistry of colloids.

dispersion (dis-per′shun) [L. *dispersio*]. 1. The act of scattering or separating; the condition of being scattered. 2. The incorporation of the particles of one substance into the body of another, comprising solutions, suspensions, and colloid solutions. 3. A colloid solution. **coarse d.,** a mechanical suspension. **colloid d.,** a colloid solution. **insect d.,** the distance that insects may spread from their breeding place. It may be *active,* as by flying, or *passive,* as when carried by some conveyance. **molecular d.,** a true solution.

dispersity (dis-per′sĭ-te). The degree of dispersion of a colloid, i.e., the degree to which the dimensions of the disperse particles have been reduced.

dispersoid (dis-per′soid). A colloid in which the dispersity is relatively great.

dispersonalization (dis-per″son-al-i-za′shun). A mental condition in which a person denies the existence of his personality or believes that certain parts of his body are lacking or that they belong to other persons or animals.

dispert (dis′pert). A medicinal preparation obtained from a vegetable drug or endocrine gland by extracting its therapeutical constituents in the cold and then reducing the product to a dry concentrated form.

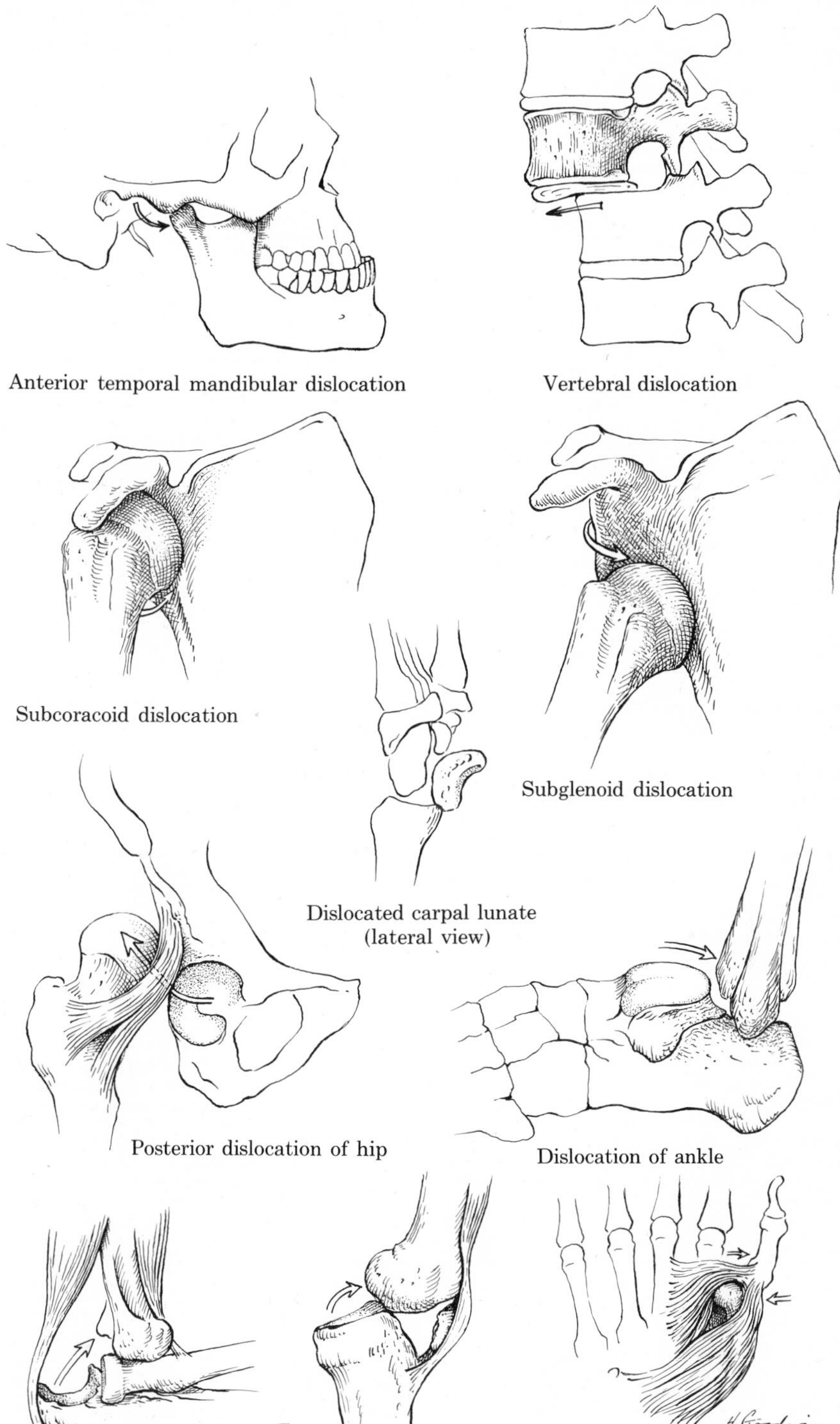

Posterior dislocation of elbow   Posterior dislocation of knee   Dislocation of thumb

VARIOUS TYPES OF DISLOCATION

dispira (di-spi′rah) [*di-* + Gr. *speira* coil]. Dispireme.

dispireme (di-spi′rem, di-spi′rēm) [*di-* + Gr. *speirēma* coil]. The stage of cell division which follows the diaster; so called because the protoplasm is divided into two parts, in each of which the chromatin appears to assume the form of a coil. See *mitosis*.

displaceability (dis-plās″ah-bil′ĭ-te). The quality of being susceptible to movement from an initial position, or the degree to which such movement is possible.

displacement (dis-plās′ment). 1. Removal from the normal position or place; ectopia. 2. Percolation. 3. A mental mechanism of the unconscious in which emotionally charged material is suppressed and replaced by symptoms made up of symbols. 4. In dentistry, the malposition of the crown and root of an individual tooth to an equal degree and in the same direction. **fetal d.,** a group of cells which, during fetal development, has become displaced from its normal relations. **fish-hook d.,** a form of displacement of the stomach in which the orifice of the pylorus faces directly upward, and the duodenum runs upward and to the right to join the pylorus at an angle, producing a constricting hook. **tissue d.,** change in the position of tissues as the result of pressure or other force.

disporous (di′spo-rus). Having two spores.

disposition (dis″po-zish′un). A tendency either physical or mental toward certain diseases.

disproportion (dis″pro-por′shun). A lack of the proper relationship between two elements or factors. **cephalopelvic d.,** a condition in which the head of the fetus is larger than normal in relation to the pelvis of the mother.

disruptive (dis-rup′tiv). Bursting apart; rending.

Disse's spaces (dis′ēz) [Josef *Disse*, German anatomist, 1852–1912]. See under *space*.

dissect (dis-sekt′) [L. *dissecare* to cut up]. To cut apart, or separate; applied especially to the exposure of body structures of a cadaver, for anatomical study.

dissection (dis-sek′shun) [L. *dissectio*]. 1. The act of dissecting. 2. A part or whole of an organism prepared by dissecting. **blunt d.,** the separation of tissues along natural cleavage lines, without cutting. **sharp d.,** that accomplished by incising tissues with a sharp edge.

dissector (dis-sek′tor). 1. One who dissects. 2. A handbook used as a guide for the act of dissecting.

disseminated (dis-sem′ĭ-nāt″ed) [L. *dis-* apart + *seminare* to sow]. Scattered; distributed over a considerable area.

dissepiment (dis-sep′ĭ-ment). Partition; separation.

dissimilate (dis-sim′ĭ-lāt) [L. *dis-* neg. + *similare* to make alike]. To decompose a substance into simpler compounds, for the production of energy or of materials that can be eliminated.

dissimilation (dis″sim-ĭ-la′shun). The act or process of dissimilating; the reverse of assimilation.

dissociable (dis-so′shĕ-b'l). Easily separable into component parts; separable from associations.

dissociant (dis-so′she-ant). A strain of microorganisms derived by bacterial dissociation.

dissociated (dis-so′she-āt″ed). Split off from consciousness. Cf. *dissociation* (3d def.).

dissociation (dis-so″she-a′shun) [L. *dis-* neg. + *sociatio* union]. 1. The act of separating or state of being separated. 2. Resolution by heat of a molecule into two or more simpler molecules. 3. A defect of mental integration in which one or more groups of mental processes become separated off from normal consciousness and, thus separated, function as a unitary whole. Cf. *unconscious*. **albuminocytologic d.,** increase of protein with normal cell count in the spinal fluid. **auriculoventricular d.,** heart block. **bacterial d.,** the apparently spontaneous change in colonial morphology of bacteria in culture on laboratory media; the predominant colonial types are mucoid, smooth, and rough. Most pathogenic bacteria are virulent in the smooth or mucoid state, but occasional species (viz., *Bacillus anthracis*) are virulent in the rough form. **d. by interference.** See under *interference*. **microbic d.,** bacterial d. **peripheral d.,** sensory disturbance in which touch, superficial pain, and temperature sensibility are diminished in the hands and feet: seen in polyneuritis. **syringomyelic d.,** loss of pain and temperature sense due to a lesion in the region of the central canal of the cord implicating the spinothalamic fibers. **tabetic d.,** disturbance of the vibratory and muscle-tendon sensibility due to lesion of the dorsal columns.

dissogeny (dis-soj′ĕ-ne) [Gr. *dissos* twofold + *gennan* to produce]. The state of having sexual maturity in both a larval and an adult stage.

dissolecule (dis-ol′ĕ-kūl). The apparent molecular weight of a substance in solution at the boiling point of the solution.

dissolution (dis″so-lu′shun) [L. *dissolutio*, *dissolvere* to dissolve]. 1. Separation of a compound into its elements or simpler compounds by chemical action. 2. Liquefaction. 3. The process of loosening, or of relaxing. 4. Death.

dissolve (diz-zolv′). 1. To cause a substance to melt away in a liquid. 2. To melt away in a liquid.

dissolvent (diz-zol′vent). 1. A solvent medium. 2. A medicine capable of dissolving concretions within the body. 3. Solvent; capable of dissolving substances.

dissonance (dis′so-nans). A combination of tones which produce discords.

Dist. Abbreviation for L. *distil′la*, distil.

distad (dis′tad). In a distal direction.

distal (dis′tal) [L. *distans* distant]. Remote; farther from any point of reference; opposed to proximal. In dentistry, used to designate a position on the dental arch farther from the median line of the jaw.

distalis (dis-ta′lis). Distal; in official anatomical nomenclature, used to designate remoteness from the point of origin or attachment of an organ or part.

distally (dis′tal-le). In a distal direction.

distance (dis′tans). The measure of space intervening between two objects or two points of reference. **angular d.,** the aperture of the angle made at the eye by lines drawn from the eye to two objects. **focal d.,** the distance from the focal point to the optical center of a lens or the surface of a concave mirror. **infinite d.,** in ophthalmology, a distance of 20 feet or more: so called because rays entering the eye from an object at that distance are practically as parallel as if they came from a point at an infinite distance. **interarch d.,** the vertical distance between the maxillary and mandibular arches (alveolar or residual) under certain conditions that must be specified. **interocclusal d.,** the distance between the occluding surfaces of the maxillary and mandibular teeth when the mandible is in physiologic rest position. **interocular d.,** the distance between the two eyes, usually used in reference to the interpupillary distance. **interpediculate d.,** the distance between the vertebral pedicles as measured on the roentgenogram. **interpupillary d.,** the distance between the centers of the pupils of the two eyes when the visual axes are parallel; in practice usually measured from the lateral margin of one pupil to the medial margin of the other. **interridge d.,** interarch d. **target-skin d.,** the distance intervening between the anode from which roentgen rays are deflected and the skin of the body surface interposed in their path. **working d.,** the distance between the front lens of a microscope and the object when the instrument is correctly focused.

distemper (dis-tem′per). A name of several infectious diseases of animals: especially **canine d.,** a specific infectious catarrhal disease of dogs characterized by fever, dulness, loss of appetite, and a discharge from the eyes and nose. It is caused by a filterable virus, and it is also infectious for foxes and ferrets. Called also *maladie de Carré*. **cat d.,** panleukopenia. **colt d.,** strangles.

distemperoid (dis-tem′per-oid). A term that has been applied to an attenuated virus.

distensibility (dis-ten″sĭ-bil′ĭ-te). Capability of being distended.

distention (dis-ten′shun). The state of being distended or enlarged; the act of distending.

distichia (dis-tik′e-ah) [Gr. "a double line"]. The presence of a double row of eyelashes on an eyelid, one or both of which are turned in against the eyeball.

distichiasis (dis″tĭ-ki′ah-sis). Distichia.

distil (dis-til′) [L. *destillare; de* from + *stillare* to drop]. To volatilize by heat and then cool and re-collect the evaporated matter.

distillate (dis′til-lāt). The material which has been obtained by distillation.

distillation (dis-til-la′shun). Vaporization; the process of distilling and condensing vapor. **destructive d.,** that which is attended with chemical decomposition and formation of new compounds in the distillate. **dry d.,** distillation of solids without the addition of liquids. **fractional d.,** that which is attended by the successive separation of volatilizable substances in the order of their respective volatility. **molecular d.,** a process of purification applied to drugs and pharmaceuticals during which the crude material is evaporated under high vacuum of about one millionth of an atmosphere, and the condensate is caught on a cooled surface held close in front of the evaporating layer. The process is applied currently to vitamins A, D, and E, to animal and vegetable sterols and hormones, and to drugs and intermediates.

distinctometer (dis″tink-tom′e-ter). An instrument by which one can palpate the abdomen, differentiate the boundaries of the abdominal organs and measure the pressure that the instrument exerts over them.

distinctor (dis-tink′tor). Palpatorium.

distobuccal (dis″to-buk′kal). Pertaining to or formed by the distal and buccal surfaces of a tooth, or by the distal and buccal walls of a tooth cavity.

distobucco-occlusal (dis″to-buk″ko-ŏ-kloo′zal). Pertaining to or formed by the distal, buccal, and occlusal surfaces of a tooth.

distobuccopulpal (dis″to-buk″ko-pul′pal). Pertaining to or formed by the distal, buccal, and pulpal walls of a tooth cavity.

distocervical (dis″to-ser′vĭ-kal). 1. Pertaining to the distal surface of the neck of a tooth. 2. Distogingival.

distoclination (dis″to-kli-na′shun). Deviation of a tooth from the vertical, in the direction of the tooth next distal to it in the dental arch.

distoclusal (dis″to-kloo′zal). Disto-occlusal.

distoclusion (dis″to-kloo′zhun). Posteroclusion, the teeth of the mandibular arch being distal to their opposite numbers in the maxillary arch.

distogingival (dis″to-jin-jĭ-val). Pertaining to or formed by the distal and gingival walls of a tooth cavity.

distolabial (dis″to-la′be-al). Pertaining to or formed by the distal and labial surfaces of a tooth, or the distal and labial walls of a tooth cavity.

distolabioincisal (dis″to-la″be-o-in-si′zal). Pertaining to or formed by the distal, labial, and incisal surfaces of a tooth.

distolingual (dis″to-ling′gwal). Pertaining to or formed by the distal and lingual surfaces of a tooth, or the distal and lingual walls of a tooth cavity.

distolinguoincisal (dis″to-ling″gwo-in-si′zal). Pertaining to or formed by the distal, lingual, and incisal surfaces of a tooth.

distolinguo-occlusal (dis″to-ling″gwo-ŏ-kloo′zal). Pertaining to or formed by the distal, lingual, and occlusal surfaces of a tooth.

distolinguopulpal (dis″to-ling″gwo-pul′pal). Pertaining to or formed by the distal, lingual, and pulpal walls of a tooth cavity.

Distoma (dis′to-mah) [*di-* + Gr. *stoma* mouth]. The former name of a genus of trematode worms: but as now used, a general term including the various genera of trematodes or flukes, such as *Paragonimus*, *Fasciola*, etc. **D. bus′ki,** *Fasciolopsis buski*. **D. capen′ee,** *Schistosoma haematobium*. **D. conjunc′tum,** *Opisthorchis noverca*. **D. co′nus,** *Opisthorchis felineus*. **D. cras′sum,** *Fasciolopsis buski*. **D. feli′neum,** *Opisthorchis felineus*. **D. haemato′bium,** *Schistosoma haematobium*. **D. hepat′icum,** *Fasciola hepatica*. **D. heteroph′yes,** *Heterophyes heterophyes*. **D. japon′icum,** *Clonorchis sinensis*. **D. lanceola′tum,** *Dicrocoelium dendriticum*. **D. pulmona′le, D. rin′geri,** *Paragonimus westermani*. **D. sinen′sis,** *Clonorchis sinensis*. **D. wester-man′i,** *Paragonimus westermani*.

distomatosis (dis″to-mah-to′sis). Distomiasis.

distomiasis (dis″to-mi′ah-sis). Infection by trematodes or flukes. **hemic d.,** schistosomiasis. **hepatic d.,** infection by *Clonorchis sinensis*, *Fasciola hepatica*, or *Dicrocoelium*. **intestinal d.,** infection by *Fasciolopsis buski*. **pulmonary d.,** infection by *Paragonimus westermani*.

distomolar (dis″to-mo′lar). A supernumerary molar.

Distomum (dis′to-mum). Distoma.

distomus (di-sto′mus) [*di-* + Gr. *stoma* mouth]. A fetal monster with more or less of a double mouth.

disto-occlusal (dis″to-ŏ-kloo′zal). Pertaining to or formed by the distal and occlusal surfaces of a tooth, or the distal and occlusal walls of a tooth cavity.

disto-occlusion (dis″to-ŏ-kloo′zhun). Distoclusion.

distoplacement (dis-to-plās′ment). Displacement of a tooth distally.

distopulpal (dis″to-pul′pal). Pertaining to or formed by the distal and pulpal walls of a tooth cavity.

distopulpolabial (dis″to-pul″po-la′be-al). Pertaining to or formed by the distal, pulpal, and labial walls of a tooth cavity.

distopulpolingual (dis″to-pul″po-ling′gwal). Pertaining to or formed by the distal, pulpal, and lingual walls of a tooth cavity.

distortion (dis-tor′shun) [L. *dis-* apart + *torsio* a twisting]. The state of being twisted out of a natural or normal shape or position. In psychiatry a dream mechanism through which material offensive to the superego is replaced by indefinite objects.

distortor (dis-tor′tor) [L.]. That which distorts. **d. o′ris,** musculus zygomaticus minor. See *Table of Musculi*.

distoversion (dis″to-ver′zhun). The position of a tooth which is farther than normal from the median line of the face along the dental arch.

distractibility (dis″trak-tĭ-bil′ĭ-te). A morbid or abnormal variation of attention; inability to fix attention on any subject.

distraction (dis-trak′shun) [L. *dis-* apart + *tractio* a drawing]. 1. A state in which the attention is diverted from the main portion of an experience or is divided among various portions of it. 2. A form of dislocation in which the joint surfaces have been separated without rupture of their binding ligaments and without displacement. 3. In orthodontics, unusual width of the dental arch.

distress (dis-tres′) [L. *distringere* to draw apart]. Physical or mental anguish or suffering. **idiopathic respiratory d. of newborn,** a condition of the newborn characterized by difficulty in breathing, heralded by such prodromal signs as dilatation of the alae nasi, expiratory grunt, and retraction of the suprasternal notch or costal margins; occurring in premature infants, children of diabetic mothers, and infants delivered by cesarean section. Presence of an eosinophilic hyaline material lining the alveoli, alveolar ducts, and bronchioles is an important autopsy finding.

distribution (dis″trĭ-bu′shun) [L. *distributio*]. The specific location or arrangement of continuing or successive objects or events in space or time.

districhiasis (dis″trĭ-ki′ah-sis) [Gr. *dis* double + Gr. *thrix* hair + *-iasis*]. A condition in which two hairs grow from a single follicle.

distrix (dis′triks) [Gr. *dis* double + Gr. *thrix* hair]. The splitting of hairs at their distal ends.

disubstituted (di-sub′stĭ-tūt-ed). Having two atoms in each molecule replaced by other atoms or radicals.

disulfanilamide (di-sul″fah-nil′ah-mid). Sulfanilylsulfanilamide.

disulfate (di-sul′fāt). A sulfate having a replaceable hydrogen atom.

disulfide (di-sul′fīd). A compound of a base with two atoms of sulfur.

disulfiram (di-sul′fi-ram). Chemical name: bis-(diethylthiocarbamyl)disulfide: used to treat chronic alcoholism.

disulfurase (di-sul′fu-rās). An enzyme which splits cystine into hydrogen sulfide, ammonia, and pyruvic acid.

disvolution (dis″vo-lu′shun) [L. *dis-* neg. + *volvere* to roll]. Retrogradation; extreme catabolism; degeneration.

dithiazanine (di″thi-az′ah-nēn). Chemical name: 3-ethyl-2-[5-(3-ethyl-2-benzothiozolinylidene)-1,-3-pentadienyl]benzothiazolium: used as an anthelmintic.

dithio (di-thi′o). The chemical group —S_2—.

dithiol (di-thi′ol). A chemical compound containing two sulfhydryl (thiol) radicals.

dithymoldiiodide (di-thi″mol-di-i′o-dīd). Thymol iodide.

Ditropenotus aureoviridis (di″tro-pĕ-no′tus aw″re-o-vir′ĭ-dis). *Pediculoides ventricosus.*

Dittel's operation (dit′elz) [Leopold Ritter von *Dittel*, Vienna urologist, 1815–1898]. See under *operation.*

Dittrich's plugs (dit′riks) [Franz *Dittrich*, German pathologist, 1815–1859]. See under *plug.*

diurate (di-u′rāt). Biurate.

diureide (di-u′re-id). See *ureide.*

diureses (di″u-re′sēz). Plural of *diuresis.*

diuresis (di″u-re′sis), pl. *diure′ses* [Gr. *diourein* to urinate, to pass in urine]. Increased secretion of urine. **tubular d.,** diuresis resulting from the presence of low threshold substances (urea, uric acid, creatinine, etc.) in the renal tubules.

diuretic (di″u-ret′ik) [Gr. *diourētikos* promoting urine]. 1. Increasing the secretion of urine. 2. An agent that promotes the secretion of urine. **A.B.C. d.,** a diuretic mixture of potassium acetate, bicarbonate, and urate. **alterative d.,** any drug eliminated by the kidney and having a salutary effect on the diseased surfaces of the urinary tract. **cardiac d.,** a drug which causes diuresis by increasing the force of the heart beat. **direct d.,** stimulant d. **hemopiesic d.,** one that acts by raising the blood pressure. **hydragogue d.,** one which promotes a copious discharge of water from the kidneys. **indirect d.,** any diuretic which acts by relieving renal congestion or compression. **mechanical d.,** any agent which acts favorably by washing out the urinary tubules. **refrigerant d.,** one which renders the urine less irritating. **saline d.,** any saline agent which, being absorbed, carries water into the blood. **stimulant d.,** any agent which acts by irritating the parenchyma of the kidney.

diuria (di-u′re-ah) [L. *dies* day + *urine*]. Frequency of urination during the day.

diuril (di′u-ril). Trade mark for preparations of chlorothiazide.

diurnal (di-er′nal) [L. *dies* day]. Occurring during the day.

diurnule (di-ern′ūl) [L. *diurnus* daily]. A pill or other preparation containing the complete allowance of a medicine for one day.

Div. Abbreviation for L. *div′ide*, divide.

divagation (di″vah-ga′shun). Incoherent speech.

divalent (di-va-lent) [Gr. *dis* twice + *valent*]. Bivalent.

divarication (di-var″ĭ-ka′shun). Separation; divergence; diastasis.

divergence (di-ver′jens). A spreading or tending apart. In ophthalmology, the simultaneous abduction of both eyes. **negative vertical d.** (−V.D.), the condition in which the visual line of the left eye deviates upward or the visual line of the right eye deviates downward (Hering). **positive vertical d.** (+V.D.), the condition in which the visual line of the right eye deviates up, or the visual line of the left eye deviates downward (Hering).

divergent (di-ver′jent) [L. *divergens; dis-* apart + *vergere* to tend]. Tending apart; deviating or radiating away from a common point.

diversine (di-ver′sin). An amorphous sinomenine alkaloid, $C_{20}H_{27}O_5N$.

diverticula (di″ver-tik′u-lah) [L.]. Plural of *diverticulum.*

diverticular (di″ver-tik′u-lar). Pertaining to or resembling a diverticulum.

diverticularization (di″ver-tik″u-lar-i-za′shun). The act of forming diverticula, pockets, etc., during development.

diverticulectomy (di″ver-tik″u-lek′to-me) [*diverticulum* + Gr. *ektomē* excision]. Excision of a diverticulum.

diverticuleve (di″ver-tik′u-lēv). An instrument for lifting up a bladder diverticulum so that the subjacent bladder wall may be separated.

diverticulitis (di″ver-tik-u-li′tis). Inflammation of a diverticulum; a condition marked by the formation of small pouches along the border of the colon, which become filled with feces which sometimes set up irritation and give rise to inflammation and abscess.

diverticulogram (di″ver-tik′u-lo-gram) [*diverticulum* + Gr. *gramma* mark]. A roentgenogram of a diverticulum.

diverticulopexy (di″ver-tik″u-lo-pek′se). Surgical fixation of a diverticulum, after it has been separated from surrounding tissue, to some other tissue.

diverticulosis (di″ver-tik″u-lo′sis). The presence of diverticula, particularly of intestinal diverticula.

diverticulum (di″ver-tik′u-lum), pl. *divertic′ula* [L. *divertere* to turn aside]. A circumscribed pouch or sac of variable size created by herniation of the lining mucous membrane through a defect in the muscular coat of a tubular organ. **acquired d.,** any diverticulum produced secondarily, mechanically or by disease. **allantoic d.,** the entodermal sacculation from the primitive cloaca that becomes the allantois. **divertic′ula ampul′lae duc′tus deferen′tis** [N A, B N A], sacculations in the wall of the ampulla of the ductus deferens. **calyceal d.,** an epithelial-lined cavity in the kidney, situated peripherally to a calyx and connected to it by a narrow isthmus, the lining of the cavity being continuous with that of the calyx. **cervical d.,** one related to an embryonic branchial groove or pouch. **congenital d.,** one present at birth, as opposed to one which may be acquired after birth. **false d.,** an intestinal diverticulum due to the protrusion of the mucous membrane through a tear in the muscular coat. **ganglion d.,** a hernial protrusion of the synovial membrane through a tendon sheath. **Ganser's d.,** multiple pulsion diverticula of the sigmoid flexure. **Heister's d.,** bulbus venae jugularis superior. **hepatic d.,** one arising from the embryonic duodenum and forming the liver, gallbladder, and bile ducts. **d. il′ei ve′rum,** Meckel's d. **intestinal d.,** a pouch or sac formed by hernial protrusion of the mucous membrane through a defect in the muscular coat of the intestine. **Kirchner's d.,** a diverticulum of the eustachian tube. **laryngeal d.,** a diverticulum of the laryngeal mucous membrane. **Meckel's d.,** an occasional sacculation or appendage of the ileum, derived from an unobliterated yolk stalk. **Nuck's d.,** processus vaginalis peritonei. **pancreatic diverticula,** two outpocketings from the embryonic duodenum, later forming the pancreas and its ducts. **Pertik's d.,** an unusually deep fossa of Rosenmüller. **pharyngo-esophageal d.,** a diverticulum at the junction of the pharynx and esophagus. **pituitary d.,** Rathke's pouch. **pressure d., pulsion d.,** a sac or pouch formed by hernial protrusion of the mucous membrane through the muscular coat of the esophagus as a result of pressure from within. **Rokitansky's d.,** a traction diverticulum of the esophagus. **supradiaphragmatic d.,** a diverticulum of the esophagus situated just above the diaphragm. **synovial d.,** a hernial protrusion of the synovial membrane of a joint or a tendon sheath. **thyroid d.,** an outpouching of the ventral floor of the embryonic pharynx, at the site of the permanent foramen cecum linguae, that becomes the thyroid gland. **traction d.,** a localized distortion, angulation, or funnel-shaped bulging of the full thickness of the wall of the esophagus, caused by adhesions resulting from some external lesion. **true d.,** a pouch or sac formed by hernial protrusion of the mucous membrane and the submucous layers through a defect in the muscular coat of the organ. **vesical d.,** diverticulum of the bladder. **Zenker's d.,** a pulsion diverticulum of the esophagus.

divi-divi (div″e-div′e). The pods of *Caesalpinia,* plants of South America. They contain tannin and are used as astringents.

divinyl (di-vi′nil). A gaseous hydrocarbon, vinyl ethylene, CH_2:CH.CH:CH_2. **d. oxide,** vinyl ether.

division (dĭ-vizh′un) [L. *divisio*]. The act of separating into two or more parts. **cell d.,** the fission of a cell. **cell d., direct.** See *amitosis.* **cell d., indirect.** See *meiosis* and *mitosis.* **maturation d.,** meiosis.

divulse (dĭ-vuls′). To pull apart forcibly.

divulsion (dĭ-vul′shun) [L. *dis-* apart + *vellere* to pluck]. The act of separating or pulling apart.

divulsor (dĭ-vul′sor). An instrument for dilating the urethra.

dixenic (di-zen′ik) [*di-* + Gr. *xenos* a guest-friend, stranger]. Associated with two species of microorganisms.

dizygotic (di″zi-got′ik). Pertaining to or derived from two separate zygotes.

dizziness (diz′ĭ-nes). A disturbed sense of relationship to space; a sensation of unsteadiness with a feeling of movement within the head, giddiness. Cf. *vertigo.*

D.L. Abbreviation for *distolingual.*

DL- (de-el). Chemical prefix denoting that the substance is an equimolecular mixture of two enantiomorphs, one of which corresponds in configuration to D-glyceraldehyde, the other to L-glyceraldehyde.

dl- (de-el). Chemical prefix denoting that the substance is an equimolecular mixture of the dextrorotatory and levorotatory enantiomorphs, such as is produced by chemical synthesis without resolution or by the process of racemization.

D.La. Abbreviation for *distolabial.*

D.La.I. Abbreviation for *distolabioincisal.*

D.L.I. Abbreviation for *distolinguoincisal.*

D.L.O. Abbreviation for *distolinguo-occlusal.*

D.L.P. Abbreviation for *distolinguopulpal.*

D.M. See *diphenylamine-arsine chloride.*

D.M.D. Abbreviation for *Doctor of Dental Medicine.*

dmelcos (dmel′kos). A culture of Ducrey's bacillus, grown on gelose and sterilized: it is used as a test for chancroid, and is injected into patients with paresis to induce high temperature.

DMF. An expression of the accumulated dental caries experience in permanant teeth, *D* representing the number of carious teeth; *M* the number of missing teeth; and *F* the number of filled teeth.

Dn. Abbreviation for *dekanem.*

dn. Abbreviation for *decinem.*

DNA. Deoxyribonucleic acid (q. v. under *acid*).

D.N.B. 1. Abbreviation for *dinitrobenzene.* 2. Abbreviation for *Diplomate of the National Board* of Medical Examiners.

D.N.P.M. Abbreviation for *dinitrophenylmorphine.*

D.O. Abbreviation for *Doctor of Osteopathy, diamine oxidase,* and *disto-occlusal.*

D_2O. The symbol for deuterium oxide or heavy water.

D.O.A. Abbreviation for *dead on arrival.*

Dobell's solution (do-belz′) [Horace Benge *Dobell,* English physician, 1828–1917]. See under *solution.*

Dobie's globule, layer, line (do′bēz) [William Murray *Dobie,* English physician, 1828–1915]. See under *globule* and *line.*

DOCA (do′kah). Trade mark for desoxycorticosterone.

dochmiasis (dok-mi′ah-sis). Ancylostomiasis.

Dochmius duodenalis (dok′me-us du″o-dĕ-na′lis). *Ancylostoma duodenale.*

docibin (do′si-bin). Trade mark for a crystalline preparation of vitamin B_{12}. See *cyanocobalamin.*

docimasia (do″se-ma′ze-ah) [Gr. *dokimazein* to examine]. An assay or examination; an official test. **auricular d.,** Wreden's sign. **hepatic d.,** the search for glycogen or glucose in the liver. **pulmonary d.,** determination as to whether air has entered the lungs of a dead infant, as an indication whether it was born dead or alive.

docimastic (do″se-mas′tik). Pertaining to docimasia; of the nature of an assay or test.

Dock's test breakfast (doks) [George *Dock,* American physician, born 1860]. See under *test meal.*

doctor (dok′tor) [L. "teacher"]. 1. A practitioner of medicine or surgery, especially one who has received the degree of M.D. from a medical school. 2. A person who, having received a diploma of the highest degree from one of the faculties of a university, qualifies as a specialist in some field of learning.

dodecadactylitis (do″dek-ah-dak″tĭ-li′tis) [*dodecadactylon* + *-itis*]. Duodenitis.

dodecadactylon (do″dek-ah-dak′tĭ-lon) [Gr. *dōdeka* twelve + *daktylos* finger, from its length]. The duodenum. Cf. *zwölffingerdarm.*

Döderlein's bacillus (ded′er-līnz) [Albert *Döderlein,* German obstetrician and gynecologist, 1860–1941]. See under *bacillus.*

doegling (deg′ling) [Norwegian]. The *Balaena rostrata,* or lesser rorqual; a whale whose oil (really a wax) has been used in ointment bases.

Dogiel's corpuscles (do-zhe-elz′) [Jean von *Dogiel,* Russian physiologist, 1830–1905]. See under *corpuscle.*

Dogmatist (dog′mah-tist). 1. The first of the post-hippocratic schools of medicine, in which the open-minded spirit of Hippocrates' teaching became merged with strict formalism which cared more for rigid doctrine than for investigation. The most important members of this school—Diocles of Carystus and Praxagoras of Cos—were, however, far more enlightened than the label "Dogmatist" would seem to imply. 2. A believer in or practitioner of the Dogmatist theory of medicine.

Döhle's inclusion bodies (de'lēz) [Paul *Döhle*, German pathologist, 1855–1928]. See under *body*.

doigt (dwa) [Fr.]. Finger or toe. **d. mort** [Fr. "dead finger"]. See *acroasphyxia*.

Doisy, Edward Adelbert (doi'se). An American biochemist, born 1893; co-winner, with Carl Peter Henrik Dam, of the Nobel prize for medicine and physiology in 1945, for the isolation and synthesis of vitamin K.

dol (dōl) [L. *do'lór* pain]. A unit of pain intensity.

dolabrate (do-lab'rāt) [L. *dolabra* ax]. Ax-shaped.

dolabriform (do-lab'rĭ-form). Dolabrate.

Dold's reaction, test (dolts) [Herman *Dold*, German bacteriologist, born 1882]. See under *test*.

Doléris' operation (dol-a-rēz') [Jacques Amédée *Doléris*, French gynecologist, 1852–1938]. See under *operation*.

dolicho- (dol'ĭ-ko) [Gr. *dolichos* long]. A combining form meaning long.

dolichocephalia (dol"ĭ-ko-se-fa'le-ah). Dolichocephaly.

dolichocephalic, dolichocephalous (dol"ĭ-ko-se-fal'ik, dol"ĭ-ko-sef'ah-lus) [*dolicho-* + Gr. *kephalē* head]. Long headed; having a cephalic index of 75.9 or less.

dolichocephalism, dolichocephaly (dol"ĭ-ko-sef'ah-lizm, dol"ĭ-ko-sef'ah-le). The quality of being dolichocephalic.

dolichocolon (dol"ĭ-ko-ko'lon) [*dolicho-* + *colon*]. An abnormally long colon.

dolichocranial (dol"ĭ-ko-kra'ne-al). Having a cranial index of 74.9 or less.

dolichoderus (dol"ĭ-ko-dēr'us) [*dolicho-* + Gr. *dere* neck]. An individual with a long neck.

dolichofacial (dol"ĭ-ko-fa'shal). Having a long face.

dolichogastry (dol"ĭ-ko-gas'tre) [*dolicho-* + Gr. *gastēr* stomach]. A term proposed to replace gastroptosis, because the condition is one of stretching of the center of the stomach.

dolichohieric (dol"ĭ-ko-hi-er'ik). Having a sacral index below 100.

dolichokerkic (dol"ĭ-ko-ker'kik). Having a radiohumeral index above 80.

dolichoknemic (dol"ĭ-ko-ne'mik). Having a tibiofemoral index of 83 or above.

dolichomorphic (dol"ĭ-ko-mor'fik) [*dolicho-* + Gr. *morphē* form]. Built along lines that tend toward the slender or longer type.

dolichopellic, dolichopelvic (dol"ĭ-ko-pel'ik, dol"ĭ-ko-pel'vik) [*dolicho-* + Gr. *pella* bowl]. Having a pelvic index above 95.

dolichoprosopic (dol"ĭ-ko-pro-sop'ik). Dolichofacial.

dolichosigmoid (dol"ĭ-ko-sig'moid) [*dolicho-* + *sigmoid*]. An abnormally long sigmoid flexure.

dolichostenomelia (dol"ĭ-ko-ste"no-me'le-ah) [*dolicho-* + Gr. *stenos* narrow + *melos* limb]. Arachnodactyly.

dolichuranic (dol"ik-u-ran'ik) [*dolicho-* + Gr. *ouranos* palate]. Having a maxillo-alveolar index of 109.9 or less.

Döllinger's ring (del'ing-erz) [Johann Ignaz Josef *Döllinger*, German physiologist, 1770–1841]. See under *ring*.

dolophine (do'lo-fēn). Trade mark for preparations of methadone.

dolor (do'lor), pl. *dolo'res* [L.]. Pain: one of the cardinal signs of inflammation. **d. cap'itis,** pain in the head. **d. cox'ae,** sciatica. **dolo'res va'gi,** wandering pains.

dolorific (do"lor-if'ik). Producing or causing pain.

dolorimetry (do"lor-im'e-tre) [L. *dolor* pain + Gr. *metrein* to measure]. The measurement of pain.

dolorogenic (do-lor"o-jen'ik). Dolorific.

Domagk (do'mak), Gerhard. A German physician and biochemist, 1895–1964; winner of the Nobel prize for medicine in 1939, for his work on the chemotherapy of infectious diseases.

domatophobia (do"mah-to-fo'be-ah) [Gr. *dōma* house + *phobia*]. Abnormal or morbid dread of being in a house.

domiciliary (dom"ĭ-sil'e-ār"e) [L. *domus* house]. Pertaining to or carried on in the house, as domiciliary treatment.

domicilium (dom"ĭ-sil'e-um) [L. "a little house"]. A pneumatic chamber for the application of rarefied or compressed air.

dominance (dom'ĭ-nans). 1. The supremacy, or superior manifestation, in a specific situation of one of two or more competitive or mutually antagonistic factors. 2. The appearance, in a heterozygote, of one of two mutually antagonistic parental characters. See *Mendel's law*, under *law*. **cerebral d.,** the dominance of one cerebral hemisphere over the other, in cerebral functions, demonstrated by laterality in voluntary motor acts. **lateral d.,** the preferential use, in voluntary motor acts, of ipsilateral members of the major paired organs of the body (arm, ear, eye, and leg). **ocular d.,** the preferential use of one eye over the other, in vision. **one-sided d.,** lateral d.

dominant (dom'ĭ-nant). Exerting a ruling or controlling influence. In genetics, capable of expression when carried by only one of a set of homologous chromosomes.

Dominici's tube (dom"ĭ-ne'sēz) [Henri *Dominici*, French physician, 1867–1919]. See under *tube*.

Donath-Landsteiner test (do'nath-land'stiner) [Julius *Donath*, German physician, 1870–1950; Karl *Landsteiner*, German physician in New York, 1868–1943]. See under *test*.

donator (do'na-tor). A thing which gives something. **hydrogen d.,** a substance or compound which gives up hydrogen to another substance called *hydrogen acceptor*.

donda ndugu (don'dah ndoo'goo) [African for "brother ulcer" or "clinging ulcer"]. A disease occurring in Africa, in which the legs swell and slough.

Donders' glaucoma, law, etc. (don'derz) [Franz Cornelius *Donders*, Dutch physician and ophthalmologist, 1818–1889]. See under the nouns.

Donec alv. sol. fuerit. Abbreviation for L. *do'nec al'vus solu'ta fu'erit*, until the bowels are opened.

donee (do-ne'). The person who receives something, as the transfused blood from the donor.

Don Juan (don-joo'an, or don-hwan). Sexual promiscuousness in the male.

Donnan's equilibrium (don'anz) [Frederick George *Donnan*, English chemist, 1870–1956]. See under *equilibrium*.

Donné's corpuscles, test (don-āz') [Alfred *Donné*, French physician, 1801–1878]. See under *corpuscle* and *tests*.

donor (do'nor). An individual organism which supplies living tissue or material to be used in another body, such as a person who furnishes blood for transfusion. **general d., universal d.,** a person with group O blood (International Classification): such blood is sometimes used in emergency transfusion. **skin d.,** one who supplies his skin for skin grafting.

Donovan bodies (don'o-van) [Charles *Donovan*, Irish physician, formerly in Sanitary Service in India, born 1863]. 1. *Donovania granulomatis*. 2. Leishman-Donovan bodies.

Donovan's solution (don'o-vanz) [Michael *Donovan*, Irish pharmacist, died 1876]. See under *solution*.

Donovania (don-o-va'ne-ah) [Charles *Donovan*]. A proposed genus of schizomycetes, included in the order Eubacteriales, suborder Eubacteriineae, family Parvobacteriaceae, tribe Pasteurelleae. **D. granulo'matis,** a gram-negative, pleomorphic, rod-shaped microorganism which is not cultivable on non-viable media but grows in the yolk, yolk sac, and amniotic fluid of the chick embryo. It is serologically related to *Klebsiella pneumoniae* and coliform bacilli, and is grouped with Pasteurella, Malleomyces, and Actinobacillus by some workers. It is the causative agent of granuloma inguinale in man. Called also *Donovan body* or *organism.*

donovanosis (don″o-van-o′sis). Granuloma inguinale.

dopa (do′pah). A compound, 3,4-dihydroxyphenylalanine, produced by oxidation of tyrosine by tyrosinase, an intermediate product in the synthesis of both epinephrine and melanin.

dopamine (do′pah-mēn). A compound, hydroxytyramine, produced by the decarboxylation of dopa, an intermediate product in the synthesis of norepinephrine.

dopa-oxidase (do″pah-ok′sĭ-dās). An enzyme which oxidizes dihydroxyphenylalanine to melanin in the skin, producing pigmentation.

dopase (do′pās). Dopa-oxidase.

Doppler's operation (dop′lerz) [Karl *Doppler,* Vienna surgeon]. See under *operation.*

Doppler's phenomenon (dop′lerz) [Christian *Doppler,* American mathematician, 1803–1853]. See under *phenomenon.*

doraphobia (do″rah-fo′be-ah) [Gr. *dora* hide + *phobia*]. A morbid dread of the skin or fur of animals.

dorbane (dor′bān). Trade mark for a preparation of danthron.

Dorendorf's sign (dor′en-dorfs) [Hans *Dorendorf,* German physician, born 1866]. See under *sign.*

doriden (dor′ĭ-den). Trade mark for preparations of glutethimide.

dormancy (dor′man-se). The state of being dormant; in bacteriology, the property exhibited by some bacteria of lying dormant for a time before starting growth.

dormant (dor′mant) [L. *dormire* to sleep]. Sleeping, inactive, quiescent.

dormifacient (dor″mĭ-fa′shent) [L. *dormire* to sleep + *facere* to make]. Producing sleep; counteracting the conditions which tend to prevent sleep.

dormison (dor′mĭ-son). Trade mark for a preparation of methylparafynol.

dormoron (dor′mo-ron) [L. *dormire* to sleep + *moron*]. A person with an inert stupid mental disposition like a person in a trance.

Dorn and Sugarman test [John H. *Dorn,* American obstetrician; Edward J. *Sugarman,* American chemist]. See under *tests.*

dorna (dor′nah). Acronym for *deoxyribonucleic acid.*

dornase (dor′nās). A shortened term for *deoxyribonuclease.* Used also as a word termination, as in *streptodornase.* **pancreatic d.,** a stabilized preparation of deoxyribonuclease, prepared from beef pancreas: used as an aerosol to reduce tenacity of pulmonary secretions.

dornavac (dor′nah-vak). Trade mark for a preparation of pancreatic dornase.

Dorno rays (dor′no) [Carl *Dorno,* Swiss climatologist, 1865–1942]. See under *ray.*

doromania (do″ro-ma′ne-ah) [Gr. *dōron* a gift + *mania* madness]. A morbid desire to give presents.

dorsa (dor′sah) [L.]. Plural of *dorsum.*

dorsacaine (dor′sah-kān). Trade mark for a preparation of benoxinate hydrochloride.

dorsad (dor′sad). Toward the back or dorsal aspect.

dorsal (dor′sal) [L. *dorsalis;* from *dorsum* back]. 1. Pertaining to the back or to any dorsum. 2. Denoting a position more toward the back surface than some other object of reference; same as posterior in human anatomy.

dorsalgia (dor-sal′je-ah) [*dorsum* + *-algia*]. Pain in the back.

dorsalis (dor-sa′lis) [L.]. Dorsal; in official anatomical nomenclature, used to designate a position closer to the back surface. Cf. *posterior.*

dorsi- (dor′si). See *dorso-.*

dorsiduct (dor′sĭ-dukt) [*dorsi* + L. *ducere* to draw]. To draw toward the back or dorsum.

dorsiflexion (dor″sĭ-flek′shun) [*dorsi-* + *flexion*]. Backward flexion or bending, as of the hand or foot.

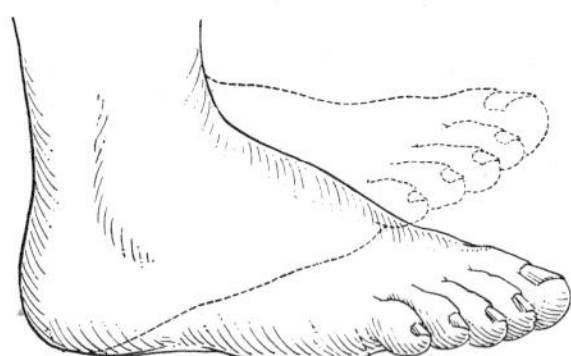

Dorsiflexion of foot. (Hauser.)

dorsimesad (dor″sĭ-mes′ad). Toward the dorsimeson.

dorsimesal (dor″sĭ-mes′al). Dorsomesial.

dorsimeson (dor″sĭ-mes′on) [*dorsi-* + Gr. *meson* middle]. The median longitudinal line of the back.

dorsispinal (dor″sĭ-spi′nal). Pertaining to the back and vertebral column.

dorso-, dorsi- [L. *dorsum* back]. Combining form denoting relationship to a dorsum or to the back (posterior) aspect of the body.

dorsoanterior (dor″so-an-te′re-or). Having the back directed forward; designating the position of the fetus in utero in relation to the body of the mother.

dorsocephalad (dor″so-sef′ah-lad) [*dorso-* + Gr. *kephalē* head]. Directed toward the back of the head.

dorsodynia (dor″so-din′e-ah). Dorsalgia.

dorsointercostal (dor″so-in″ter-kos′tal). Situated in the back and between the ribs.

dorsolateral (dor″so-lat′er-al). Pertaining to the back and to the side.

dorsolumbar (dor″so-lum′bar). Pertaining to the back and the loins.

dorsomedian (dor″so-me′de-an). Dorsomesial.

dorsomesial (dor″so-me′se-al). Pertaining to the median line of the back.

dorsonasal (dor″so-na′sal). Pertaining to the bridge of the nose.

dorsonuchal (dor″so-nu′kal). Pertaining to the back of the neck.

dorso-occipital (dor″so-ok-sip′ĭ-tal). Pertaining to the back and the posterior part of the head.

dorsoposterior (dor″so-pos-te′re-or). Having the back directed backward; designating the position of the fetus in utero in relation to the body of the mother.

dorsoradial (dor″so-ra′de-al). Pertaining to the radial or outer side of the back of the forearm or hand.

dorsoscapular (dor″so-skap′u-lar). Pertaining to the posterior surface of the scapula.

dorsoventrad (dor″so-ven′trad) [*dorso-* + *venter* belly]. Directed from the dorsal toward the ventral aspect.

dorsum (dor′sum), pl. *dor′sa* [L.] [N A, B N A]. 1. The vertebral aspect of the body; the back. 2. The aspect of an anatomical part or structure corresponding in position to the back; posterior, in the human. **d. of foot,** d. pedis. **d. of hand,** d. manus. **d. lin′guae** [N A, B N A], the superior surface of the tongue. **d. ma′nus** [N A, B N A], the back of the hand; the surface opposite the palm. **d. na′si** [N A, B N A], **d. of nose,** that part of the external surface of the nose formed by junction of the lateral surfaces. **d. pe′dis** [N A, B N A], the upper surface of the foot; the surface opposite the sole.

d. pe'nis [N A, B N A], **d. of penis,** the anterior, more extensive surface of the dependent penis, opposite the urethral surface. **d. of scapula,** facies dorsalis scapulae. **d. sel'lae** [N A, B N A], the quadrilateral plate on the sphenoid bone that forms the posterior boundary of the sella turcica; the posterior clinoid processes project from its superior extremity, and it is continuous inferiorly with the clivus. **d. of testis,** margo posterior testis. **d. of tongue,** d. linguae.

dosage (do'sij). The determination and regulation of doses.

dose (dōs) [Gr. *dosis* a giving]. A quantity to be administered at one time, such as a specified amount of medication, or a given quantity of roentgen-ray or other radiation. **air d.,** the intensity of a roentgen-ray or gamma-ray beam in air. **amitogenic d.,** the amount of radiation required to arrest mitosis. **average d.,** the quantity of an agent which will usually produce the therapeutic effect for which it is administered. **booster d.,** an amount of vaccine or toxoid, usually smaller than the amount given originally, injected at an interval after primary immunization to maintain protection of the individual. **daily d.,** the total amount of an agent to be administered in a 24-hour period. **depth d.,** the intensity of radiation received by tissues below the skin, expressed in percentage of that received at the surface of the body. **divided d.,** a fraction of the total quantity of the therapeutic agent prescribed, to be given at short intervals. **effective d.,** that quantity of an agent which will produce the effects for which it is administered. **effective d., median,** the amount of pathogenic bacteria, bacterial toxin, or other poisonous substance, required to kill or produce some characteristic symptom or lesion in 50 per cent of uniformly susceptible animals inoculated with it. Abbreviated ED_{50}. **emergency d.,** an immunizing injection of toxoid or vaccine given immediately after an injury. **epilating d.,** the quantity of x-ray or radium necessary to cause a temporary loss of hair. **erythema d.,** that amount of radiant energy which, when applied to the skin, will, after a few days, cause a slight reddening. **exit d.,** the amount of radiation emerging from the body on the surface opposite the portal of entry. **fatal d.,** lethal d. **fractional d's,** amounts of an agent less than that usually administered, given at shorter intervals than usual. **intoxicating d.,** the dose of sensitinogen required to bring on an allergic reaction. **L+ d.,** the smallest amount of diphtheria toxin which will kill a 250-Gm. guinea pig within four days when mixed with one unit of diphtheria antitoxin before being injected subcutaneously. **lethal d.,** the amount of an agent which will cause death. **lethal d., median,** the amount of pathogenic bacteria, bacterial toxin, or other poisonous substance, required to kill 50 per cent of uniformly susceptible animals inoculated with it. Abbreviated LD_{50}. **lethal d., minimum.** 1. The amount of toxin which will just kill the experimental animal: abbreviated MLD. 2. The smallest quantity of diphtheria toxin which will kill a guinea pig of 250-Gm. weight in four to five days when injected subcutaneously. **Lf d.,** the amount of diphtheria toxin which in the shortest time produces precipitation when mixed with one standard unit of antitoxin. **limes nul d., Lo d.,** the amount of diphtheria toxin which is exactly neutralized by one standard unit of antitoxin. **Lr d.,** the amount of diphtheria toxin which, when mixed with one standard unit of antitoxin, will produce a minimal skin reaction in a guinea pig. **maintenance d.,** a quantity sufficient to maintain at the desired level the influence of a drug achieved by earlier administration of larger amounts. **maximum d.,** the largest quantity of an agent that may be safely administered. **minimal d., minimum d.,** the smallest quantity of an agent that is likely to produce an appreciable effect. **optimum d.,** the quantity of an agent which will produce the effect desired without unfavorable side effects. **organ tolerance d.,** that amount of radiation which can be administered without damage to the tissues of a normal organ. **reacting d.,** the second dose of protein or other sensitizing antigen in anaphylaxis. Cf. *sensitizing d.* **sensitizing d.,** the first dose of protein or other sensitizing antigen in anaphylaxis. Cf. *reacting d.* **skin d.,** that amount of roentgen radiation which is received on the surface of the skin, being the sum of primary radiation and the back-scatter. **tissue d.,** depth d. **tolerance d.,** the largest quantity of an agent, such as x-ray energy, that may be administered without harm. **toxic d.,** the amount of a therapeutic agent which will cause toxic symptoms.

dosimeter (do-sim'e-ter). A dosage meter for measuring x-ray output.

dosimetric (do″se-met'rik). Of or pertaining to dosimetry.

dosimetry (do-sim'e-tre) [Gr. *dosis* dose + *metron* measure]. The accurate and systematic determination of doses.

dosis (do'sis) [L., Gr. "a giving"]. Dose. **d. curati'va,** the minimum amount of a therapeutic agent that will effect a cure. **d. ef'ficax,** d. curativa. **d. refrac'ta,** fractional dose. **d. tolera'ta,** the largest amount of a therapeutic agent that can be given with safety.

dossier (dos'e-a) [Fr.]. The accumulated records of a patient's case history.

dot (dot). A small spot or speck. **Gunn's d's,** white dots seen about the macula lutea on oblique illumination. **Maurer's d's,** irregular dots, staining red with Leishman's stain, seen in erythrocytes infected with *Plasmodium falciparum*. **Schüffner's d's,** minute granules observed in erythrocytes infected with *Plasmodium vivax* when stained by certain methods, such as Romanowsky's or Wright's stain. **Trantas' d's,** small, white calcareous looking dots in the limbus of the conjunctiva in vernal conjunctivitis.

dotage (do'tij). Feebleness of mind in old age; senility.

dotard (do'tard). A person who is weak minded from old age.

dothienenteria, dothienenteritis (do″the-en″en-te're-ah, do″the-en″en-ter-i'tis) [Gr. *dothiēn* a boil + *enteron* intestine]. Bretonneau's name for typhoid fever (1823).

dothienesia (do″the-ĕ-ne'se-ah) [Gr. *dothiēn* boil]. Furunculosis.

doublet (dub'let). A combination of two similar or complementary entities, as a combination of two components into a single lens, or of two nucleotides in a genetic codon. **Wollaston's d.,** a microscopical lens consisting of a combination of two planoconvex lenses for correcting chromatic abberation.

douche (dōōsh) [Fr.]. A stream of water, gas or vapor directed against a part or into a cavity. **air d.,** a current of air blown into a cavity, particularly into the tympanum, for opening the eustachian tube. **alternating d.,** transition douche. **fan d.,** water applied to the body in a fan-shaped spray. **jet d.,** water applied to the body in a single stream. **Scotch d.,** transition d. **Tivoli d.,** a reclining bath in which the patient lies covered with warm mineral water while a hot wave douche is played upon his abdomen: used for constipation. **transition d.,** a douche of alternating hot and cold water. **Weber's d.,** a nasal douche.

Douglas' cul-de-sac, fold, line, pouch [James *Douglas*, Scottish anatomist in London, 1675–1742]. See *excavatio rectouterina, plica rectouterina,* and *linea arcuata* (def. 2).

douglascele (dug'lah-sēl). Posterior vaginal hernia.

douglasitis (dug-lah-si'tis). Inflammation of Douglas' pouch.

doundaké (doon-dak′a). The bark of *Sarcocephalus esculentus:* tonic, febrifuge, and astringent.

dourine (doo-rēn′). A contagious disease of donkeys and horses, characterized by swelling of lymph glands, genital inflammation, and paralysis of hind limbs. It is caused by *Trypanosoma equiperdum* and spread by sexual contact. Called also *mal de coit.*

Dover's powder (do′verz) [Thomas *Dover*, English physician, 1660–1743]. Ipecac and opium powder.

dowel (dow″l). A peg or pin, generally of metal, for fastening an artificial crown or core to the root of a natural tooth, or for fastening a die into a working model for the construction of a crown, inlay, or partial denture.

Dowell's test (dow′elz) [Donald M. *Dowell*, American physician, born 1904]. See under *tests.*

Down's disease, syndrome (downz) [John Langdon Haydon *Down*, English physician, 1828–1896]. Mongolism.

doxinate (dok′sĭ-nāt). Trade mark for a preparation of dioctyl sodium sulfosuccinate.

doxogenic (dok″so-jen′ik) [Gr. *doxe* opinion + *gennan* to produce]. Caused by one's own mental conceptions, as doxogenic disease.

doxylamine (dok″sĭl-am′en). Chemical name: 2-[α-(2-dimethylaminoethyoxy)-α-methylbenzyl]-pyridine: used as an antihistaminic.

doxylamine succinate [dok″sĭl-am′en suk′sĭ-nāt). A white or creamy white powder, $C_{17}H_{22}N_2O.$-$C_4H_6O_4$: antihistaminic.

Doyen's clamp, operation (dwah-yahz′) [Eugene Louis *Doyen*, surgeon in Paris, 1859–1916]. See under *clamp* and *operation.*

Doyère's eminence (dwa-yārz′) [Louis *Doyère*, French physiologist, 1811–1863]. See under *eminence.*

Doyne's choroiditis (doinz) [Robert Walter *Doyne*, Oxford ophthalmologist, 1857–1896]. See under *choroiditis.*

D.P. Abbreviation for L. *directio′ne prop′ria* ["with proper direction"], *distopulpal*, and *Doctor of Pharmacy.*

D.P.H. Abbreviation for *Diploma in Public Health.*

D.P.L. Abbreviation for *distopulpolingual.*

D.P.La. Abbreviation for *distopulpolabial.*

D.P.M. Abbreviation for *Diploma in Psychological Medicine.*

DPN. Abbreviation for *diphosphopyridine nucleotide.*

DR. Abbreviation for *reaction of degeneration.*

dr. Abbreviation for *dram.*

drachm (dram) [Gr. *drachmē*]. Dram.

dracontiasis (drak″on-ti′ah-sis) [Gr. *drakontion* (little dragon) tapeworm]. Dracunculiasis.

dracuncular (drah-kung′ku-lar). Pertaining to or caused by nematodes of the genus Dracunculus.

dracunculiasis (drah-kung″ku-li′ah-sis). The state of being infected with nematodes of the genus Dracunculus.

dracunculosis (drah-kung″ku-lo′sis). Dracunculiasis.

Dracunculus (drah-kung′ku-lus) [L. "little dragon"]. A genus of nematode filarial parasites. **D. medinen′sis** is the guinea worm or Medina worm, a threadlike worm, 20–30 inches long, which inhabits the subcutaneous and intermuscular tissues of man and several domestic animals in India, Africa, and Arabia. Its embryos are discharged through an opening in the skin upon contact with water, in which they enter the bodies of a small crustacean, *Cyclops*, where they pass their embryonic life. Formerly called *Filaria medinensis.*

draft (draft). A potion; a large dose of medicine to be taken at once. **black d.,** the compound infusion of senna. **effervescing d.,** one which contains an acid and sodium or potassium bicarbonate. **mustard d.,** a mild rubefacient paste of mustard and flour. **Riverius' d.,** Rivière's potion.

drag (drag). The lower or cast side of a denture flask.

dragée (drah-zha′) [Fr. "sugar-plum"]. A sugar-coated pill, or medicated confection.

Dragendorff's test (drag′en-dorfs) [Johann Georg Noël *Dragendorff*, German physician, 1836–1898]. See under *tests.*

drain (drān). An appliance or substance that affords a channel of exit or discharge from a wound. **cigarette d.,** a drain made by surrounding a strip of gauze with a protective covering of rubber, gutta-percha, etc. Larger drains of this character, i.e., those as thick as a cigar, are called cigar d's. **controlled d.,** a drain made by pressing a square of gauze into the wound and packing the inside of the former with gauze strips, the ends of which, together with the corners of the square, are left projecting from the wound. **Mikulicz's d.,** a drain formed by pushing a single layer of gauze into a wound cavity, the layer of gauze being packed with several thick wicks of gauze as it is pushed into the cavity. **Mosher d.,** a truncated cone of copper mesh: used in the drainage of brain wounds. **Penrose d.,** a cigarette drain consisting of a piece of rubber tubing through which gauze has been pulled. **quarantine d.,** a drain left in place after a laparotomy to drain the peritoneal cavity and prevent infection. **stab wound d.,** drainage accomplished by making a small puncture wound at some distance from the operative incision and bringing out the drain through this wound; it is done to prevent infection of the operation wound. **Wylie d.,** a stem pessary of hard rubber having a groove along the stem.

drainage (drān′ij). 1. The systematic withdrawal of fluids and discharges from a wound, sore, or cavity. 2. The drawing off of a nerve impulse from a nervous arc. **basal d.,** withdrawal of the cerebrospinal fluid from the basal subarachnoid space for the relief of intracranial pressure. **button d.,** drainage of a peritoneal transudate by means of a peritoneal button. **capillary d.,** drainage effected by strands of hair, catgut, spun glass, or other material which acts by capillary attraction. **closed d.,** drainage of an empyema cavity carried out with protection against the entrance of outside air into the pleural cavity. **continuous suction d.** See *Wangensteen d.* **funnel d.,** drainage by glass funnels inserted into edematous tissues. **Monaldi's d.,** a method of suction drainage of tuberculous cavities of the lungs. **open d.,** drainage of an empyema cavity through an opening in the chest wall into which a rubber drainage tube is inserted, the opening not being sealed against the entrance of outside air. **postural d.,** therapeutic drainage in bronchiectasis and lung abscess by placing the patient with the head downward so that the trachea will be inclined downward and below the affected area. **suction d.,** closed drainage of a cavity, with a suction apparatus attached to the drainage tube. **through d.,** drainage affected by passing a perforated tube through the cavity, so that irrigation may be effected by injecting fluid into one aperture and letting it escape out of another. **tidal d.,** drainage of the urinary bladder by an apparatus which alternately fills the bladder to a predetermined extent and then empties it by a combination of siphonage and gravity flow. **Wangensteen d.,** continuous suction drainage through an indwelling duodenal tube: for treatment of intestinal obstruction, paralytic ileus, etc.

dram (dram). A unit of weight which, in the apothecaries' system, equals 60 grains, or $\frac{1}{8}$ ounce; in the avoirdupois system it equals 27.34 grains, or $\frac{1}{16}$ ounce. Symbol ʒ. **fluid d.,** a unit of capacity (liquid measure) of the apothecaries' system, being 60 minims, or the equivalent of 3.697 ml.

dramamine (dram′ah-mēn). Trade mark for preparations of dimenhydrinate.

dramatism (dram′ah-tizm). Pompous and dramatic speech and behavior in mental disorder.

dramatization (dram″ah-ti-za′shun). That part of the dream-work in which the manifest content of the dream is an action or situation.

drapetomania (drap″e-to-ma′ne-ah) [Gr. *drapetēs* runaway + *mania* madness]. The insane desire to wander away from home.

drastic (dras′tik) [Gr. *drastikos* effective]. 1. Acting powerfully or thoroughly. 2. A violent purgative.

draught (draft). Draft.

dream (drēm). A conscious series of imagery that occurs during sleep. **clairvoyant d.,** one that seems to reveal a real event to the sleeper. **day d.,** an indulgence in wishful, purposeless reveries, without regard to reality. **veridical d.,** one that depicts events unknown to the sleeper.

Drechsel's test (drek′selz) [Edmund *Drechsel*, Swiss chemist, 1843–1897]. See under *tests*.

drench (drench). A draft of medicine given to an animal by pouring it into its mouth.

Drepanidium (drep″ah-nid′e-um) [Gr. *drepanē* sickle]. A genus or larval stage of certain protozoa; certain species are entozoan and parasitic, but probably not in man. **D. rano′rum,** a cytozoon of frog's blood, probably parasitic.

drepanocyte (drep′ah-no-sīt) [Gr. *drepanē* sickle + *kytos* cell]. A sickle-shaped erythrocyte.

drepanocytemia (drep″ah-no-si-te′me-ah). Sickle cell anemia.

drepanocytic (drep″ah-no-si′tik). Pertaining to drepanocytes; having sickle-shaped cells.

Drepanospira (drep″ah-no-spi′rah) [Gr. *drepanē* sickle + *speira* coil]. A genus of microorganisms of uncertain affinities which are parasitic on protozoa.

Dresbach's anemia, syndrome (dres′bahks) [Melvin *Dresbach*, American physician, 1874–1946]. Sickle cell anemia.

dresser (dres′er). A surgical assistant who dresses wounds, etc.

dressing (dres′ing). 1. The application of various materials for protecting a wound. 2. Material applied for the protection of a body wound. **antiseptic d.,** a dressing of gauze impregnated with an antiseptic solution. **Bavarian d., bran d.,** a fracture box filled with bran, sometimes used for a compound fracture of the leg. **cocoon d.,** a wound dressing consisting of a layer of gauze and collodion. **cross d.,** eonism. **dry d.,** the application to a wound of dry gauze, absorbent cotton, etc. **fixed d.,** a dressing impregnated with plaster of paris, starch, or silicate of soda so as to secure fixation of the part when it dries. **Lister's d.,** a covering of a wound with gauze impregnated with phenol. **occlusive d.,** a dressing which completely closes a wound or covers a body area, preventing all contact of air or moisture. **paraffin d.,** a dressing of gauze impregnated with paraffin. **pressure d.,** one which exerts pressure on the area covered, preventing collection of fluids in the part, and, after skin grafting, maintaining contact between the graft and the host bed. **protective d.,** a dressing to shield a part from injury or from septic infection. **Scott's d.,** compound mercury ointment. **stent d.,** a dressing incorporating a mold of stent, such as is used to maintain position of a graft.

Dressler's disease (dres′lerz) [*Dressler*, physician in Wurzburg]. Intermittent hemoglobinuria.

Dreyer formula (dri′er) [Georges *Dreyer*, English physician, 1873–1934]. See under *formula*.

Drigalski-Conradi medium [Wilhelm *von Drigalski*, German bacteriologist, 1871–1950; Heinrich *Conradi*, German bacteriologist, born 1876]. See under *culture medium*.

drill (dril). A rotating instrument for making holes in hard substances, such as bones or teeth. **bur d.** See *bur*. **cannulate d.,** a tubular drill. **dental d.,** a rotatory cutting instrument of various forms for use in dentistry.

drinalfa (drin-al′fah). Trade mark for preparations of methamphetamine hydrochloride.

Drinker respirator (drink′er) [Philip *Drinker*, American public health engineer, born 1894]. See under *respirator*.

drip (drip). The slow, drop by drop, infusion of a liquid. **intravenous d.,** continuous intravenous instillation, drop by drop, of saline or other solution. **Murphy d.** See *Murphy method*, 2d def., under *method*. **nasal d.,** a method of giving fluid slowly to dehydrated infants through a catheter inserted into the nose and pushed down into the esophagus. **postnasal d.,** the dripping of irritating discharges from the postnasal region into the pharynx in chronic sinusitis.

drisdol (driz′dol). Trade mark for preparations of crystalline vitamin D. See *calciferol*.

drive (drīv). The force which activates human impulses.

drocarbil (dro-kar′bil). Chemical name: arecolinium 3-acetamido-4-hydroxybenzene-arsonate: used as an anthelmintic in veterinary medicine.

drolban (drol′ban). Trade mark for a preparation of dromostanolone propionate.

dromo- (drom′o) [Gr. *dromos* a course]. Combining form denoting relation to conduction, or to running.

dromograph (drom′o-graf) [*dromo-* + Gr. *graphein* to record]. A recording hemodromometer.

dromomania (drom″o-ma′ne-ah) [*dromo-* + Gr. *mania* madness]. A mania for roaming.

dromophobia (drom″o-fo′be-ah) [*dromo-* + Gr. *phobos* fear + *-ia*]. Morbid fear of running.

dromostanolone (dro″mo-stan′o-lōn). Chemical name: 17β-hydroxy-2α-methyl-5α-androstan-3-one, a steroid compound related to testosterone but with less virilizing effect: used as a palliative in advanced or metastatic carcinoma of the breast.

dromotropic (drom″o-trop′ik). Affecting the conductivity of a nerve fiber.

dromotropism (dro-mot′ro-pizm) [Gr. *dromos* a course + *tropē* a turn, turning]. The quality or property of affecting the conductivity of a nerve fiber. **negative d.,** the property of diminishing the conductivity of a nerve. **positive d.,** the property of increasing the conductivity of a nerve.

drop (drop) [L. *gutta*]. A minute sphere of liquid as it hangs or falls. **ear d's,** medicated oil or water to be dropped into the external auditory meatus. **enamel d.,** enameloma. **eye d's,** a medicated solution to be dropped into the conjunctival sac. **head d.,** a malarial disease of Japan characterized by dropping of the head. **Hoffmann's d's,** ether spirit. **nose d's,** a medicated solution to be dropped into the nostrils. **d. phalangette′,** a condition in which the terminal phalanx of a finger or toe is permanently flexed.

dropacism (drop′ah-sizm) [Gr. *drōpax* plaster]. The removal of hairs by means of a plaster.

droplet (drop′let). A diminutive drop, such as the particles of moisture expelled from the mouth in coughing, sneezing, or speaking, which may carry infection to others through the air.

dropping (drop′ing). The limping gait of a horse affected with elbow disease.

dropsical (drop′sĭ-kal). Affected with or pertaining to dropsy.

dropsy (drop′se) [L. *hydrops*, from Gr. *hydōr* water]. The abnormal accumulation of serous fluid in the cellular tissue or in a body cavity. **abdominal d.,** ascites. **acute anemic d.,** epidemic d. **d. of amnion,** hydramnion. **articular d.,** hydrarthrosis. **d. of belly,** ascites. **d. of brain,** hydrocephalus. **cardiac d.,** that which is due to failure of compensation in cardiac disease. **d. of chest,** hydrothorax. **cutaneous d.,** edema. **epidemic d.,** a disease epidemic in India among the natives only, characterized by fever, anemia, diarrhea, paresthesia, and followed by sudden edema. **famine d.,** nutritional edema. **d. of head,** hydrocephalus. **hepatic d.,** that which is due to disease of the liver. **nutritional d.,** nutritional edema. **ovarian d.,** ovarian cystoma. **d. of pericardium,** hydropericardium. **peritoneal d.,** ascites. **renal d.** 1. Anasarca due to kidney disease. 2. Hydronephrosis. **salpingian d.,** hydrosalpinx. **subchoroid d.,** an accumulation of fluid between the choroid and the retina. **subsclerotic d.,** an accumulation of fluid between the choroid and sclerotic coat of the eye. **tubal d.,** hydrosalpinx. **uterine d.,** hydrometra. **war d.,** nutritional edema. **wet d.,** beriberi.

Drosera (dros′ĕ-rah) [Gr. *droseros* dewy]. A genus of plants; sundew.

Drosophila (dro-sof′ĭ-lah) [Gr. *drosos* dew + *philein* to love]. A genus of flies; the fruit flies. **D. melanogas′ter,** a small fly often seen about decaying fruit; used extensively in experimental genetics.

Drouot's plaster (droo-ōz′) [Théophile *Drouot*, Parisian oculist, born 1803]. See under *plaster.*

drug (drug). Any chemical compound or any noninfectious biological substance, not used for its mechanical properties, which may be administered to or used on or for patients, either human or animal, as an aid in the diagnosis, treatment or prevention of disease or other abnormal condition, for the relief of pain or suffering, or to control or improve any physiological or pathological condition. **antagonistic d.,** one that tends to counteract or neutralize the effect of another. **crude d.,** the whole drug with all its ingredients. **habit-forming d's,** drugs which tend to addiction, such as alcohol, tobacco, morphine, cocaine, opium.

drug-fast (drug′fast). Resistant to the action of drugs: said of microorganisms.

drum (drum). The membrana tympani. Called also *ear drum.*

drumine (droo′min). An alkaloid from *Euphorbia drummondii;* said to be a local anesthetic.

Drummond's sign (drum′unds) [Sir David *Drummond*, English physician, 1852–1932]. See under *sign.*

Drummond-Morison operation [David *Drummond;* James Rutherford *Morison*, British surgeon, 1853–1939]. See under *operation.*

drumstick (drum′stik). A nuclear lobule attached by a slender strand to the nucleus of a neutrophilic leukocyte; found in a small proportion (2–3 per cent) of neutrophils of normal females but lacking in neutrophils of normal males.

drusen (droo′sen) [Ger., pl. of *druse* stony nodule, geode]. 1. Hyaline excrescences in Bruch's membrane (lamina basalis choroidea); comparable to the so-called Hassall-Henle warts in the periphery of Descemet's membrane. 2. Rosettes of granules occurring in the lesions of actinomycosis.

Drysdale's corpuscles (drīz′dālz) [Thomas Murray *Drysdale*, American gynecologist, 1831–1904]. See under *corpuscle.*

D.S.C. Abbreviation for *Doctor of Surgical Chiropody.*

D.T. Abbreviation for *distance test.*

Dt. Abbreviation for *duration tetany.*

D.T.D. Abbreviation for L. *da′tur ta′lis do′sis*, give of such a dose.

D.T.N. Abbreviation for *diphtheria toxin normal.*

D.T.P. Abbreviation for *distal tingling on percussion.* See *Tinel's sign,* under *sign.*

D.T.V.M. Abbreviation for *Diploma in Tropical Veterinary Medicine.*

D.U. Abbreviation for *dog unit.*

dualism (du′al-izm) [L. *duo* two]. 1. The theory that there are two distinct stem cells for blood corpuscle formation; one for the lymphatic cells and the other for the myeloid cells. 2. The theory that human beings are made up of two independent systems, mind and body, and that psychic and physical phenomena are fundamentally independent and different in nature.

dualist (du′al-ist). An adherent of the dualistic theory.

dualistic (du″al-is′tik). 1. Twofold. 2. Pertaining to dualism.

Duane's syndrome, test (du-ānz′) [Alexander *Duane*, ophthalmologist in New York, 1858–1926]. See under the nouns.

dubhium (dub′e-um). Ytterbium.

dubi (doo′be). The native name on the Gold Coast for frambesia.

Dubini's disease (du-be′nēz) [Angelo *Dubini*, Italian physician, 1813–1902]. Electric chorea.

dubo (du′bo). Pirquet's term for double strength nutrition (lac *du*plex *bo*vinum, double cow's milk).

Dubois's abscess, disease (du-bwahz′) [Paul *Dubois*, French obstetrician, 1795–1871]. See under *abscess* and *disease.*

DuBois diet (doo-boyz′) [Eugene Floyd *DuBois*, New York physician, 1882–1959]. See under *diet.*

Dubois's method, treatment (du-bwahz′) [Paul-Charles *Dubois*, Swiss psychiatrist, 1848–1918]. See under *method.*

Duboisia (du-boi′se-ah). A genus of medicinal plants. *D. hopwoodii* yields piturine. *D. myoporoides*, a tree of Australia which yields duboisine.

DuBois-Reymond's key, law (dŭ-bwah″ri-maw′) [Emil Heinrich *DuBois-Reymond*, German physiologist, 1818–1896]. See under *key* and *law.*

Dubos enzyme, lysin, medium (doo-bos′) [René J. *Dubos*, French biochemist in America, born 1901]. See *tyrothricin,* and under *culture medium.*

Duboscq colorimeter (du-bosk′) [Jules *Duboscq*, French optician]. A form of colorimeter.

Duchenne's disease, paralysis, trocar (du-shenz′) [Guillaume Benjamin Amand *Duchenne*, French neurologist, 1806–1875]. See under the nouns.

Duchenne-Aran disease, type (du-shen′ar-an′) [G. B. A. *Duchenne;* F. A. *Aran*]. Myelopathic muscular atrophy.

Duchenne-Erb paralysis (du-shen′airb) [G. B. A. *Duchenne;* W. H. *Erb*]. See under *paralysis.*

Duchenne-Landouzy type [G. B. A. *Duchenne;* L. T. J. *Landouzy*]. See *Landouzy-Dejerine dystrophy,* under *dystrophy.*

Duckworth's phenomenon (duk′worths) [Sir Dyce *Duckworth*, British physician, 1840–1928]. See under *phenomenon.*

ducobee (doo′ko-be). Trade mark for preparations of vitamin B_{12}. See *cyanocobalamin.*

Ducrey's bacillus (doo-krāz′) [Augosto *Ducrey*, Italian dermatologist, 1860–1940]. *Hemophilus ducreyi.*

duct (dukt) [L. *ductus*, from *ducere* to draw or lead]. A passage with well-defined walls, especially a tube for the passage of excretions or secretions. Called also *ductus* [N A]. **aberrant d.,** any duct that is not usually present or that takes an unusual course or direction, such as the ductulus aberrans superior. **acoustic d.,** meatus acusticus externus. **adipose d.,** an elongated sac in the cellular tissue filled with fat. **alimentary d.,** ductus thoracicus. **allantoic d.,** allantoic stalk. **alveolar d's,** ductuli alveolares. **d. of Arantius,** ductus venosus. **archinephric d.,** pronephric d. **arterial d.,** ductus arteriosus. **auditory d.,** a space in the cochlea, between the membrana tectoria and the membrana cochlearis. **Bartholin's d.,** ductus sublingualis major. **Bellini's d's,** tubuli renales recti. **Bernard's d.,** ductus pancreaticus accessorius. **bile d., common,** ductus choledochus. **bile d's, interlobular,** ductuli interlobulares. **biliary d's, biliferous d's,** the passages for the conveyance of bile in and from the liver. **Blasius' d.,** ductus parotideus. **Bochdalek's d.,** ductus thyroglossus. **d. of Botallo,** ductus arteriosus. **branchial d's,** drawn-out branchial grooves 2, 3, and 4, which open into the temporary cervical sinus of the embryo. **canalicular d's,** ductus lactiferi. **cervical d.,** the opening from the exterior into the temporary cervical sinus of the embryo. **choledochous d.,** ductus choledochus. **chyliferous d.,** ductus thoracicus. **cloacal d.,** Reichel's cloacal d. **cochlear d.** 1. A spirally arranged membranous tube in the bony canal of the cochlea. See *ductus cochlearis* [N A]. 2. Canalis spiralis cochleae. **common bile d.,** the duct formed by union of the cystic duct and the hepatic duct. Called also *ductus choledochus* [N A]. **Coschwitz' d.,** a supposed salivary duct forming an arch over the dorsum of the tongue, proved by von Haller to be a vein. **cowperian d.,** d. glandulae bulbourethralis. **craniopharyngeal d.,** hypophyseal d. **d's of Cuvier,** two short venous trunks in the fetus opening into the auricle of the heart; the right one becomes the superior vena cava. **cystic d.,** ductus cysticus. **deferent d.,** ductus deferens. **efferent d.,** the duct which gives outlet to a glandular secretion. **ejaculatory d.,** ductus ejaculatorius. **endolymphatic d.,** ductus endolymphaticus. **d. of epididymis,** ductus epididymidis. **d. of epoophoron,** ductus epoophori longitudinalis. **excretory d.,** one which is merely conductive and not secretory. **excretory d. of bulbourethral gland,** ductus glandulae bulbourethralis. **excretory d. of seminal vesicle,** ductus excretorius vesiculae seminalis. **excretory d. of testis,** ductus deferens. **frontonasal d.,** a duct in the lateral wall of the nasal cavity extending from the infundibulum of the ethmoid bone to the frontal air cells. **galactophorous d's,** ductus lactiferi. **gall d's,** biliary d's. **d. of gallbladder,** ductus cysticus. **Gartner's d.,** ductus epoophori longitudinalis. **gasserian d.,** ductus paramesonephricus. **genital d.,** genital canal. **gutteral d.,** tuba auditiva. **Haller's aberrant d.,** a small coiled tube extending from the lower part of the canal of the epididymis. **Hensen's d.,** ductus reuniens. **hepatic d., common,** ductus hepaticus communis. **hepatic d., left,** ductus hepaticus sinister. **hepatic d., right,** ductus hepaticus dexter. **hepaticopancreatic d.,** ductus pancreaticus. **hepatocystic d.,** ductus choledochus. **d. of His,** ductus thyroglossus. **Hoffmann's d.,** ductus pancreaticus. **hypophyseal d.,** an embryonic structure composed of the elongated Rathke's pouch joining the infundibulum of the embryonic hypophysis: called also *craniopharyngeal duct.* **incisive d., incisor d.,** ductus incisivus. **intercalated d.,** a slender terminal portion of the duct system interposed between an acinus of a gland and a secretory duct. **interlobular d's,** channels located between different lobules of a glandular organ. See *ductuli interlobulares.* **lacrimal d.,** canaliculus lacrimalis. **lacrimonasal d.,** ductus nasolacrimalis. **lactiferous d's,** ductus lactiferi. **Leydig's d.,** d. mesonephricus. **lingual d.,** a depression on the dorsum of the tongue at the apex of the terminal sulcus. **longitudinal d. of epoophoron,** ductus epoophori longitudinalis. **Luschka's d's,** tubular structures in the wall of the gallbladder. Some are connected with bile ducts but none is connected with the lumen of the gallbladder. They may be aberrant bile ducts. **lymphatic d.,** channels for conducting lymph. **lymphatic d., left,** ductus thoracicus. **lymphatic d., right,** ductus lymphaticus dexter. **mammary d's, mammillary d's,** ductus lactiferi. **mesonephric d.,** ductus mesonephricus. **metanephric d.,** ureter. **milk d's,** ductus lactiferi. **mucous d.,** any duct lined with mucous membrane. **d. of Müller, müllerian d.,** ductus paramesonephricus. **nasal d., nasolacrimal d.,** ductus nasolacrimalis. **nasopharyngeal d.,** meatus nasopharyngeus. **nephric d.,** ureter. **omphalomesenteric d.,** the narrow tube connecting the umbilical vesicle (yolk sac) with the midgut of the embryo. Called also *umbilical duct, vitelline duct, vitello-intestinal duct,* and *yolk stalk.* **ovarian d.,** tuba uterina. **pancreatic d.,** ductus pancreaticus. **pancreatic d., accessory, pancreatic d., minor,** ductus pancreaticus accessorius. **papillary d's,** tubuli renales recti. **paramesonephric d.,** ductus paramesonephricus. **paraurethral d's,** ductus paraurethrales. **parotid d.,** ductus parotideus. **d. of Pecquet,** ductus thoracicus. **perilymphatic d's,** ductus perilymphatici. **primordial d.,** ductus paramesonephricus. **pronephric d.,** the duct of the pronephros, which later serves as the mesonephric duct (ductus mesonephricus). **d's of prostate gland, prostatic d's,** ductuli prostatici. **Rathke's d.,** that part of the ductus paramesonephricus lying between its main part and the sinus pocularis. **Reichel's cloacal d.,** the cleft between Douglas' septum and the cloaca in the embryo. **renal d.,** ureter. **d's of Rivinus,** ductus sublinguales minores. **Rokitansky-Aschoff d's.** See under *sinus.* **sacculoutricular d.,** ductus utriculosaccularis. **salivary d's,** the ducts that convey the saliva: they are the ductus parotideus, ductus submandibularis, ductus sublingualis major, and ductus sublinguales minores. **d. of Santorini,** ductus pancreaticus accessorius. **Schüller's d's,** ductus paraurethrales. **secretory d.,** any one of the smaller ducts that are tributary to the excretory ducts of a gland and also have a secretory function. **segmental d.,** ductus mesonephricus. **semicircular d's,** the long ducts of the membranous labyrinth of the ear. Called also *ductus semicirculares* [N A]. **semicircular d., anterior,** ductus semicircularis anterior. **semicircular d., lateral,** ductus semicircularis lateralis. **semicircular d., posterior,** ductus semicircularis posterior. **semicircular d., superior,** ductus semicircularis anterior. **seminal d's,** the passages for the conveyance of spermatozoa and semen, including the ductus deferens, ductus excretorius vesiculae seminalis, and ductus ejaculatorius. **d. of seminal vesicle,** ductus excretorius vesiculae seminalis. **Skene's d's,** ductus paraurethrales. **spermatic d.,** ductus deferens. **d. of Steno, Stensen's d.,** ductus parotideus. **sublingual d's,** the ducts of the sublingual salivary glands, including the ductus sublingualis major and ductus sublinguales minores. **sublingual d., major,** ductus sublingualis major. **sublingual d's, minor,** ductus sublinguales minores. **submandibular d., submaxillary d. of Wharton,** ductus submandibularis. **sweat d.,** ductus sudoriferus. **tear d's,** the ducts conveying the secretion of the lacrimal glands. **testicular d.,** ductus deferens. **thoracic d.,** the canal that ascends from the cisterna chyli to the junction of the left subclavian and left internal jugular vein. Called also *ductus thoracicus* [N A]. **thoracic d., right,** ductus thoracicus dexter. **thyroglossal d., thyrolingual d.,** ductus thyroglossus. **umbilical d.,** omphalomesenteric d. **urogenital d's,** the ductus paramesonephricus and ductus mesonephricus. **utriculosaccular d.,** ductus utriculosaccularis. **d. of Vater,** ductus thyroglossus. **vitelline d., vitello-intestinal d.,** omphalomesenteric d. **Walther's d's,** ductus sublinguales minores. **Wharton's d.,** ductus submandibularis. **d. of Wirsung,** ductus pancreaticus. **d. of Wolff, wolffian d.,** ductus mesonephricus.

ductal (duk′tal). Pertaining to a duct.

ductile (duk′til) [L. *ductilis,* from *ducere* to draw, to lead]. Susceptible of being drawn out, as into a wire.

ductless (dukt′les). Having no excretory duct.

ductule (dukt′ūl). A minute duct, especially that part or branch of a duct which is nearest the alveolus of a gland. Called also *ductulus* [N A]. **aberrant d's,** ductules that are not usually present, or that follow an unusual course or direction. See *ductuli aberrantes* [N A]. **aberrant**

d., superior, ductulus aberrans superior. **alveolar d's,** ductuli alveolares. **bile d's, biliary d's.** 1. Ductuli biliferi [N A]. 2. Cholangioles. **efferent d's of testis,** ductuli efferentes testis. **excretory d's of lacrimal gland,** ductuli excretorii glandulae lacrimales. **d's of prostate,** ductuli prostatici. **transverse d's of epoophoron,** ductuli transversi epoophori.

ductuli (duk′tu-li) [L.]. Plural of *ductulus*.

ductulus (duk′tu-lus), pl. *duc′tuli* [L.]. [N A, B N A] A general term for a minute duct. Applied especially to branches of ducts nearest to the alveoli of a gland, or the smallest beginnings of the duct system of an organ. Called also *ductule*. **duc′tuli aberran′tes** [N A, B N A], blind vestiges of mesonephric tubules standing in relation to the epididymis. Called also *aberrant ductules*. **d. aber′rans supe′rior** [N A, B N A], a narrow tube of variable length that lies in the epididymis and is connected with the rete testis. Called also *superior aberrant ductule of epididymis*. **duc′tuli alveola′res** [N A, B N A], small passages connecting the respiratory bronchioles and the alveolar sacs. Called also *alveolar ductules*. **duc′tuli bilif′eri** [N A], the small channels that connect the interlobular ductules with the right and left hepatic ducts. Called also *ductus biliferi* [B N A]. **duc′tuli efferen′tes tes′tis** [N A, B N A], ductules entering the head of the epididymis from the rete testis. Called also *efferent ductules of testis*. **duc′tuli excreto′rii glan′dulae lacrima′lis** [N A, B N A], numerous ductules that traverse the palpebral part of the lacrimal gland and open into the superior fornix of the conjunctiva. Called also *excretory ductules of lacrimal gland*. **duc′tuli interlobula′res** [N A], small channels between the hepatic lobules, draining into the bile ductules. Called also *ductus interlobulares* [B N A], and *interlobular ductules*. **duc′tuli prostat′ici** [N A], minute ducts from the prostate gland that open on either side into or near the prostatic sinuses on the posterior wall of the urethra. Called also *ductus prostatici* [B N A], and *ductules of prostate gland*. **duc′tuli transver′si epooph′ori** [N A, B N A], the remains of the mesonephric ducts, opening into the longitudinal duct of the epoophoron. Called also *transverse ductules of epoophoron*.

ductus (duk′tus), pl. *duc′tus* [L.]. [N A, B N A] A general term for a passage with well defined walls, especially such a channel for the passage of excretions or secretions. Called also *duct*. **d. aber′rans,** ductulus aberrans superior. **d. aber′rans hal′leri,** Haller's aberrant duct. **d. Aran′tii,** d. venosus. **d. arterio′sus** [N A], a fetal blood vessel connecting the pulmonary artery directly to the descending aorta. Called also *Botallo's duct*. **d. arteriosus, patent,** a congenital anomaly consisting of persistence of an open lumen in the ductus arteriosus after birth, the direction of flow being from the aorta to the pulmonary artery, resulting in recirculation of arterial blood through the lungs. **d. arteriosus, reversed,** a congenital anomaly consisting of persistence of an open lumen in the ductus arteriosus after birth, the direction of flow being from the pulmonary artery to the aorta, resulting in return of venous blood to the systemic circulation. **d. bilif′eri,** ductuli biliferi. **d. choled′ochus** [N A, B N A], the duct formed by union of the common hepatic and the cystic duct which empties into the duodenum at the major duodenal papilla, along with the pancreatic duct. Called also *common bile duct*. **d. cochlea′ris** [N A, B N A], a spirally arranged membranous tube in the bony canal of the cochlea along its outer wall, lying between the scala tympani below and the scala vestibuli above. Called also *cochlear duct*. **d. cow′peri,** d. glandulae bulbourethralis. **d. cuvi′eri,** ducts of Cuvier. **d. cys′ticus** [N A, B N A], the passage connecting the neck of the gallbladder and the common bile duct. Called also *cystic duct*. **d. def′erens** [N A, B N A], the excretory duct of the testis, which unites with the excretory duct of the seminal vesicle to form the ejaculatory duct. Called also *vas deferens*. **d. ejaculato′rius** [N A, B N A], the canal formed by union of the ductus deferens and the excretory duct of the seminal vesicle. It enters the prostatic part of the urethra on the colliculus seminalis. Called also *ejaculatory duct*. **d. endolymphat′icus** [N A, B N A], a canal connecting the membranous labyrinth with the endolymphatic sac. Called also *endolymphatic duct*. **d. epididym′idis** [N A, B N A], the single tube into which the coiled ends of the efferent ductules of the testis open, the convolutions of which make up the greater part of the epididymis. **d. epooph′ori longitudina′lis** [N A], a closed rudimentary duct lying parallel to the uterine tube, into which 10 to 15 transverse ducts of the epoophoron open. It is a remnant of the part of the mesonephros which participates in formation of the reproductive organs. Called also *Gartner's duct*, and *longitudinal duct of epoophoron*. **d. excreto′rius glan′dulae bulbourethra′les** [B N A], ductus glandulae bulbourethralis. **d. excreto′rius vesic′ulae semina′lis** [N A, B N A], the duct that drains the seminal vesicle and unites with the ductus deferens to form the ejaculatory duct. Called also *excretory duct of seminal vesicle*. **d. glan′dulae bulbourethra′lis** [N A], a duct passing from the bulbourethral gland through the urogenital diaphragm into the bulb of the penis and entering the spongy part of the urethra. Called also *d. excretorius glandulae bulbourethralis* [B N A], and *duct of bulbourethral gland*. **d. hepat′icus commu′nis** [N A, B N A], the duct which is formed by union of the right and left hepatic ducts, and in turn joins the cystic duct to form the common bile duct. Called also *common hepatic duct*. **d. hepat′icus dex′ter** [N A], the duct that drains the right lobe and part of the caudate lobe of the liver. Called also *right hepatic duct*. **d. hepat′icus sin′ister** [N A], the duct that drains the left and the quadrate lobe and part of the caudate lobe of the liver. Called also *left hepatic duct*. **d. inci′sivus** [N A, B N A], a passage sometimes found in the incisive canal that interconnects the nasal and oral cavities during embryonic development. It occasionally remains open in the adult. Called also *incisor duct*. **d. interlobula′res** [B N A], ductuli interlobulares. **d. lacrima′les,** B N A term for ducts conveying the secretion of the lacrimal glands. Called *canaliculus lacrimalis* [N A]. **d. lactif′eri** [N A, B N A], channels conveying the milk secreted by the lobes of the breast to and through the nipples. Called also *lactiferous ducts*. **d. lingua′lis** [B N A], a depression on the dorsum of the tongue, at the apex of the terminal sulcus. Omitted in N A. **d. lymphat′icus dex′ter** [N A, B N A], a vessel draining the lymph from the upper right side of the body, receiving lymph from the right subclavian, jugular, and mediastinal trunks when those vessels do not open independently into the right brachiocephalic vein. Called also *right lymphatic duct*. **d. mesoneph′ricus** [N A], an embryonic duct of the mesonephros which in development of the male forms various ducts of the urogenital system and in the female is largely obliterated. Called also *d. Wolffi* [B N A], *mesonephric duct*, and *wolffian duct*. **d. Muel′leri** [B N A], ductus paramesonephricus. **d. nasolacrima′lis** [N A, B N A], the passage that conveys the tears from the lacrimal sac into the inferior nasal meatus. Called also *nasolacrimal duct*. **d. pancrea′ticus** [N A], the main excretory duct of the pancreas, which usually unites with the common bile duct before entering the duodenum at the major duodenal papilla. Called also *duct of Wirsung* and *pancreatic duct*. **d. pancrea′ticus accesso′rius** [N A], a small inconstant duct draining a part of the head of the pancreas into the minor duodenal papilla. Called also *accessory pancreatic duct* and *duct of Santorini*. **d. paramesoneph′ricus** [N A], either of two ducts of the embryo that empty into the cloaca, in the female developing into the vagina, uterus, and uterine tubes. Called also *d. Muelleri* [B N A], and *paramesonephric duct*. **d. paraurethra'les** [N A, B N A], inconstantly present ducts that drain a group of the urethral glands into the vestibule. Called also *paraurethral ducts* and *Skene's glands*. **d. paroti'deus** [N A], the duct that drains the parotid gland and empties into the oral cavity opposite the second superior molar. Called also *parotid duct* and *Stensen's duct*. **d. perilymphat'ici** [N A, B N A], small canals that connect the scala tympani with the subarachnoid space. Called *perilymphatic ducts*. **d. prostat'ici** [B N A], ductuli prostatici. **d. reu'niens** [N A], a small canal leading from the saccule to the cochlear duct. Called also *Hensen's duct*. **d. semicircula'res** [N A, B N A], the long ducts of the membranous labyrinth of the ear, corresponding to the semicircular canals of the bony labyrinth and designated anterior, posterior, and lateral, according to the canal they occupy. Their diameter is only one-fourth that of the bony canals containing them, and each is affixed by one wall to the endosteal lining of the canal. They give information about the movement of the head. Called also *semicircular ducts*. **d. semicircula'ris ante'rior** [N A], the semicircular duct occupying the anterior semicircular canal. Called also *d. semicircularis superior* [B N A]. See *ductus semicirculares*. **d. semicircula'ris latera'lis** [N A, B N A], the semicircular duct occupying the lateral semicircular canal. See *ductus semicirculares*. **d. semicircula'ris poste'rior** [N A, B N A], the semicircular duct occupying the posterior semicircular canal. See *ductus semicirculares*. **d. semicircula'ris supe'rior** [B N A], d. semicircularis anterior. **d. spermat'icus,** d. deferens. **d. sublingua'lis ma'jor** [N A, B N A], the duct that drains the sublingual gland and opens alongside the submandibular duct on the sublingual caruncle. Called also *major sublingual duct*. **d. sublingua'les mino'res** [N A, B N A], the ducts that drain the sublingual gland and open along the crest of the sublingual fold. Called also *minor sublingual ducts*. **d. submandibula'ris** [N A], **d. submaxilla'ris [Wharto'ni]** [B N A], the duct that drains the submandibular gland and opens at the sublingual caruncle. Called also *submandibular duct*. **d. sudorif'erus** [N A, B N A], the duct that leads from the body of a sweat gland to the surface of the skin. Called also *sudoriferous duct*. **d. thora'cicus** [N A, B N A], the vessel that ascends from the cisterna chyli to the junction of the left subclavian and left internal jugular veins. It acts as a channel for the collection of the lymph from the portions of the body below the diaphragm and from the left side of the body above the diaphragm. **d. thora'cicus dex'ter** [N A], a lymphatic channel formed by union of the right jugular, subclavian, and bronchomediastinal trunks and opening into the right brachiocephalic vein. **d. thyroglos'sus** [N A], a duct in the embryo extending between the thyroid primordium and the posterior part of the tongue. Called also *thyroglossal duct*. **d. utriculosaccula'ris** [N A, B N A], a narrow duct uniting the utricle and saccule of the membranous labyrinth. Called also *utriculosaccular duct*. **d. veno'sus** [N A], a fetal blood vessel connecting the umbilical vein directly to the inferior vena cava, thus bypassing the liver. Called also *duct of Arantius*. **d. wolf'fi** [B N A], ductus mesonephricus.

Duddell's membrane (dud'elz) [Benedict *Duddell*, English physician of the 18th century]. Lamina limitans posterior corneae.

Dugas' test (doo'gahz) [Louis Alexander *Dugas*, American physician, 1806–1884]. See under *tests*.

Duhot's line (dŭ-hōz') [Robert *Duhot*, urologist and dermatologist in Brussels, born 1867]. See *line*.

Duhring's disease (du'rings) [Louis Adolphus *Duhring*, dermatologist in Philadelphia, 1845–1913]. Dermatitis herpetiformis.

Dührssen's operation, tampon, etc. (dēr'senz) [Alfred *Dührssen*, German gynecologist, 1862–1933]. See under the nouns.

duipara (du-ip'ah-rah). Secundipara.

Dujarier's clasp. A metal device for use in fractures of the calcaneum.

Dukes' disease (dūks) [Clement *Dukes*, English physician, 1845–1925]. Exanthema subitum.

dulcite, dulcitol (dul'sīt, dul'sĭ-tol) [L. *dulcis* sweet]. A polyhydric alcohol, $CH_2OH(CHOH)_4$-CH_2OH, occurring in various plants.

dulcolax (dul'ko-laks). Trade mark for preparations of bisacodyl.

dulcose (dul'kōs). Dulcite.

dull (dul). Not resonant on percussion.

dulness (dul'nes). Diminished resonance on percussion; also a peculiar percussion sound which lacks the normal resonance. **Grocco's triangular d.,** Grocco's sign. **post-cardial d.,** dulness on percussion on the back over the site of the heart. **shifting d.,** dulness on abdominal percussion, the level of which shifts as the patient is rolled from side to side: indicative of free fluid in the abdominal cavity. **tympanitic d.,** resonance of a dull and diminished quality.

dulse (duls). A coarse red seaweed used as a food in Scotland and other northern countries.

dumbbell (dum'bel). A dumbbell-shaped body; a mass consisting of two spherical portions connected by a narrow isthmus. **d's of Schäfer,** microscopic bodies found in striated muscular tissue.

dumbness (dum'nes) [L. *surditas*]. Muteness, or aphasia.

Dumontpallier's test (du"maw-pal-yāz') [Alphonse *Dumontpallier*, French physician, 1826–1898]. See under *tests*.

dumping (dump'ing). Sudden, massive emptying. **jejunal d.,** the rapid emptying of the stomach contents into the jejunum which sometimes follows gastrojejunostomy. See *dumping syndrome*, under *syndrome*.

Duncan's folds, position, ventricle (dun'kanz) [James Matthews *Duncan*, British gynecologist, 1826–1890]. See under the nouns.

Duncan's method (dun'kanz) [Charles H. *Duncan*, American physician, born 1880]. See under *method*.

Dunfermline scale (dun-ferm'lin) [*Dunfermline*, a city in Scotland where the scheme was devised]. See under *scale*.

Dungern's test (dōōn'gărnz) [Emil Freiherr von *Dungern*, German bacteriologist, born 1867]. See *von Dungern's test*, under *tests*.

Dunham's fans, cones, triangles. Pyramidal formations, seen in the roentgenogram in silicosis, made up of nodules connected by fine lines in a pyramidal arrangement.

Dunham's solution (dun'amz) [Edward Kellogg *Dunham*, New York pathologist, 1860–1922]. See under *solution*.

duodenal (du"o-de'nal). Of, pertaining to, or situated in, the duodenum.

duodenectomy (du"o-dĕ-nek'to-me) [*duodenum* + Gr. *ektomē* excision]. Excision of the duodenum, total or partial.

duodenin (du"o-de'nin). A substance in extracts of the duodenum which is said to stimulate the islands of Langerhans in the pancreas to produce insulin. Called also *incretin*. 2. A proprietary preparation of desiccated duodenal mucosa.

duodenitis (du"od-ĕ-ni'tis). Inflammation of the duodenum.

duodeno- (du"o-de'no) [L. *duodeni* twelve]. Combining form denoting relationship to the duodenum.

duodenocholangeitis (du"o-de"no-ko-lan"je-i'tis). Inflammation of the duodenum and common bile duct.

duodenocholecystostomy (du"o-de"no-ko"le-sis-tos′to-me). Surgical creation of a communication between the gallbladder and the duodenum.

duodenocholedochotomy (du″o-de″no-ko″led-o-kot′o-me). Surgical incision of the duodenum and common bile duct.

duodenocolic (du″o-de″no-kol′ik). Pertaining to the duodenum and colon.

duodenocystostomy (du″o-de″no-sis-tos′to-me) [*duodeno-* + Gr. *kystis* bladder + *stomoun* to provide with an opening or mouth]. Surgical formation of a communication between the duodenum and the gallbladder.

duodenoduodenostomy (du″o-de″no-du″o-de-nos′to-me). Anastomosis of the two portions of a divided duodenum.

duodeno-enterostomy (du″o-de″no-en″ter-os′-to-me). Surgical formation of a communication from the duodenum to another part of the small intestine.

duodenogram (du-od′ĕ-no-gram″). A roentgenogram of the duodenum.

duodenohepatic (du-od″e-no″he-pat′ik). Pertaining to the duodenum and the liver.

duodeno-ileostomy (du″o-de″no-il″e-os′to-me). Surgical formation of a communication between the duodenum and the ileum.

duodenojejunostomy (du″o-de″no-jĕ-joo-nos′-to-me). Surgical formation of a communication between the duodenum and the jejunum.

duodenolysis (du″o-dĕ-nol′ĭ-sis). The operation of loosening the duodenum from adhesions.

duodenopancreatectomy (du″o-de″no-pan″-kre-ah-tek′to-me). Pancreatoduodenectomy.

duodenorrhaphy (du″o-de-nor′ah-fe) [*duodeno-* + Gr. *rhaphē* suture]. The operation of suturing the duodenum.

duodenoscopy (du″od-e-nos′ko-pe) [*duodeno-* + Gr. *skopein* to examine]. Endoscopic examination of the duodenum.

duodenostomy (du″od-e-nos′to-me) [*duodeno-* + Gr. *stomoun* to provide with an opening or mouth]. Surgical formation of a permanent orifice into the duodenum.

duodenotomy (du″od-e-not′o-me) [*duodeno-* + Gr. *tomē* a cut]. Incision of the duodenum.

duodenum (du″o-de′num) [L. *duode′ni* twelve at a time]. [N A, B N A] The first or proximal portion of the small intestine, extending from the pylorus to the jejunum: so called because it is about 12 fingerbreadths in length.

duoparental (du″o-pah-ren′tal) [L. *duo* two + *parens* parent]. Pertaining to or derived from two parents or sexual elements.

duphaston (du-fas′ton). Trade mark for a preparation of isopregnenone.

Duplay's bursitis, disease (doo-plāz′) [Simon *Duplay*, French surgeon, 1836–1924]. See under *bursitis*.

duplicitas (du-plis′ĭ-tas) [L.]. A doubling, or duplication. **d. ante′rior,** katadidymus. **d. asym′metros,** heteropagus. **d. comple′ta,** a double fetal monster in which each component is completely or almost completely developed. **d. crucia′ta,** conjoined twins with fused heads, each face being a joint product whose midplane forms a right angle with that of the body. **d. incomple′ta,** a double fetal monster in which the two components are not completely developed. **d. infe′rior,** anadidymus. **d. me′dia,** a double monster in which the duplication is restricted to the middle region of the body. **d. paral′lela,** a double monster consisting of two components united in the sagittal plane. **d. poste′rior,** anadidymus. **d. supe′rior,** katadidymus. **d. sym′metros,** diplopagus.

duplitized (du′plĭ-tīzd). Double coated; a term applied to x-ray films.

dupp. A syllable used to represent the second sound heard at the apex of the heart in auscultation: it is shorter and higher pitched than the first sound. See *lubb* and *lubb-dupp*.

Dupré's disease, syndrome (du-prāz′) [Ernest Pierre *Dupré*, French physician, 1862–1921]. Meningism, def. 1.

Dupuis's cannula (du-pwēz′) [Edmund *Dupuis*, physician, 1839–1892]. See under *cannula*.

Dupuytren's contracture, splint (du-pwe-trahnz′) [Baron Guillaume *Dupuytren*, a celebrated French surgeon, 1777–1835]. See under *contracture* and *splint*.

dura (du′rah) [L. "hard"]. Dura mater.

durabolin (dur-ab′o-lin). Trade mark for a preparation of nandrolone phenpropionate.

duracillin (du″rah-sil′lin). Trade mark for preparations of crystalline procaine penicillin G.

dural (du′ral). Pertaining to the dura mater.

dura mater (du′rah ma′ter) [L. "hard mother"]. The outermost, toughest, and most fibrous of the three membranes (meninges) covering the brain and spinal cord. **d. m. of brain, d. m. enceph′ali** [N A, B N A], the dura mater covering the brain, composed of two partially fused layers, the outer being the periosteum; venous sinuses and the trigeminal ganglion are located between the layers. **d. m. of spinal cord, d. m. spina′lis** [N A, B N A], the dura mater covering the spinal cord. It is separated from the periosteum of the enclosing vertebrae by a space containing blood vessels and fibrous and areolar tissue.

duramatral (du-rah-ma′tral). Dural.

Duran-Reynals factor [Francisco *Duran-Reynals*, American bacteriologist, 1899–1958]. Hyaluronidase.

Durand's disease (du-ranz′) [P. *Durand*, French physician, born 1895]. See under *disease*.

Durand-Nicolas-Favre disease [J. *Durand*, Joseph *Nicolas*, M. *Favre*, French physicians]. Venereal lymphogranuloma.

Durande's remedy (du-rahndz′) [Jean François *Durande*, French physician, died 1794]. See under *remedy*.

Durante's treatment (doo-ran′tēz) [Francesco *Durante*, surgeon in Rome, 1845–1934]. See under *treatment*.

duraplasty (du′rah-plas-te) [*dura mater* + Gr. *plassein* to form]. A plastic operation on the dura mater; graft of the dura.

Dürck's nodes (derks) [Hermann *Dürck*, Munich pathologist, born 1869]. See under *node*.

Dur. dolor. Abbreviation for L. *duran′te dolo′re*, while the pain lasts.

durematoma (du″rem-ah-to′mah). Hematoma of the dura mater.

Duret's lesion (du-rāz) [Henri *Duret*, French neurological surgeon, 1849–1921]. See under *lesion*.

Durham's tube (dur′hamz). [1. Arthur Edward *Durham*, English surgeon, 1834–1895. 2. Herbert Edward *Durham*, English bacteriologist, 1866–1945]. See under *tube*.

duritis (du′ri-tis). Pachymeningitis.

duro-arachnitis (du″ro-ar″ak-ni′tis). Inflammation of the dura mater and arachnoid.

durosarcoma (du″ro-sar-ko′mah). Meningioma.

Duroziez' disease, murmur, sign (du-ro″-ze-ez′) [Paul Louis *Duroziez*, French physician, 1826–1897]. See under *disease* and *murmur*.

dust (dust). Fine, dry particles of earth or any other substance small enough to be blown by the wind. **blood d.,** hemoconia. **chromatin d.,** small red granules, smaller than Howell's bodies, sometimes seen at the periphery of stained erythrocytes. **ear d.,** statoconia.

Dutton's disease (dut′unz) [J. Everett *Dutton*, English physician, 1876–1905]. Trypanosomiasis. **D.'s fever.** See under *fever*. **D.'s spirochete,** *Borrelia duttonii*.

Duttonella (dut-o-nel′ah) [J. Everett *Dutton*]. A genus of trypanosomes.

Duval's nucleus (du-valz′) [Mathias Marie *Du-*

val, French anatomist, 1844–1915]. See under *nucleus.*

Duverney's gland (du-ver-nāz′) [Joseph Guichard *Duverney,* French anatomist, 1648–1730]. Glandula bulbourethralis.

d.v. Abbreviation for *double vibrations,* a unit for the measurement of sound waves.

D.V.H. Abbreviation for *Diploma in Veterinary Hygiene.*

D.V.M. Abbreviation for *Doctor of Veterinary Medicine.*

D.V.M.S. Abbreviation for *Doctor of Veterinary Medicine and Surgery.*

D.V.S. Abbreviation for *Doctor of Veterinary Science* or *Doctor of Veterinary Surgery.*

D.V.S.M. Abbreviation for *Diploma in Veterinary State Medicine.*

dwale (dwāl). Belladonna leaf.

dwarf (dwarf). An abnormally undersized person. **achondroplastic d.,** the commonest type of dwarf, showing relatively large head with saddle nose and brachycephaly, short extremities, and usually lordosis. See also *achondroplasia.* **aortic d.,** an individual showing distinct underdevelopment occurring as a result of severe aortic stenosis. **asexual d.,** an adult dwarf with deficient sexual development. **ateliotic d.,** a dwarf whose skeleton is infantile in condition with persistent nonunion between epiphyses and diaphyses. **Brissaud's d.,** one with infantile myxedema. **cretin d.,** a thyroid-deficient dwarf. **deformed d.,** a person who is both abnormally undersized and deformed. **hypophysial d.,** pituitary d. **hypothyroid d.,** cretin d. **infantile d.,** a person with marked retardation of mental and physical development. **Levi-Lorain d.,** pituitary d. **micromelic d.,** a dwarf with very small limbs. **normal d.,** a person who is abnormally undersized, but is perfectly formed. **Paltauf's d.,** pituitary d. **phocomelic d.,** a dwarf in whom the diaphyses of the long bones are abnormally short. **physiologic d.,** normal d. **pituitary d.,** a dwarf whose retarded development is due to hypofunction of the anterior pituitary. **primordial d., pure d.,** normal d. **rachitic d.,** a person dwarfed by rickets, having a high forehead with prominent bosses, bent long bones, and Harrison's sulcus. **renal d.,** a dwarf whose condition is due to renal osteodystrophy. **sexual d.,** a dwarf with normal sexual development. **true d.,** normal d.

dwarfism (dwarf′izm). The state of being a dwarf; under-development of body.

Dy. Chemical symbol for *dysprosium.*

dyad (di′ad). 1. Any element or radical capable of replacing or combining with two hydrogen atoms. 2. A double chromosome resulting from the halving of a tetrad.

dyaster (di′as-ter). Amphiaster.

dyclone (di′klōn). Trade mark for preparations of dyclonine.

dyclonine (di′klo-nēn). Chemical name: 4′-butoxy-3-piperidinopropiophenone: used as a topical anesthetic.

dye (di). A material used for staining or coloring. The dyes used in medicine may be divided into the following classes: 1, **acridine d's,** such as acriflavine and proflavine; 2, **azo d's,** such as scarlet red and dimazon; 3, **fluorescein's d's,** fluorescein, flumerin, and mercurochrome; 4, **phenolphthalein d's;** 5, **triphenylmethane** or **rosaniline d's,** such as gentian violet, crystal violet, methyl violet, and fuchsin; 6, **pyronidine d's,** fluorescein dyes; 7, miscellaneous dyes. **triple d's,** a mixture of 1 per cent each of gentian violet, brilliant green, and acriflavine: used as an antiseptic.

dynamic (di-nam′ik) [Gr. *dynamis* power]. Pertaining to or manifesting force.

dynamics (di-nam′iks). That phase of mechanics which deals with the motions of material bodies taking place under different specific conditions.

dynamization (di″nam-i-za′shun). The hypothetical increase of medicinal effectiveness by dilution and trituration.

dynamo (di′nah-mo). A machine for converting mechanical force directly into electric current.

dynamo- (di′nah-mo) [Gr. *dynamis* power]. Combining form denoting relationship to power or strength.

dynamogenesis (di″nah-mo-jen′e-sis) [*dynamo-* + Gr. *genesis* production]. The development of energy or force.

dynamogenic (di″nah-mo-jen′ik) [*dynamo-* + Gr. *gennan* to produce]. Producing or favoring the development of power; pertaining to the development of power.

dynamogeny (di-nah-moj′e-ne). Dynamogenesis.

dynamograph (di-nam′o-graf) [*dynamo-* + Gr. *graphein* to write]. A self-registering dynamometer.

dynamometer (di″nah-mom′e-ter) [*dynamo-* + Gr. *metron* measure]. An instrument for measuring the force of muscular contraction. **squeeze d.,** one by which the grip of the hand is measured.

dynamoneure (di-nam′o-nūr) [*dynamo-* + Gr. *neuron* nerve]. A spinal neuron which is connected with the muscles.

dynamopathic (di-nam″o-path′ik) [*dynamo-* + Gr. *pathos* disease]. Affecting function; functional.

dynamophore (di-nam′o-fōr) [*dynamo-* + Gr. *phoros* carrying]. Food or any substance that supplies energy to the body.

dynamoscope (di-nam′o-skop) [*dynamo-* + Gr. *skopein* to examine]. A device for performing dynamoscopy.

dynamoscopy (di″nah-mos′ko-pe). The observation of the performance of function by an organ or structure, as of muscle action or of kidney function by ureteral catheterization.

dyne (dīn). The C.G.S. unit of force, being that amount of force which, when acting continuously upon a mass of 1 gram, will impart to it an acceleration of 1 cm. per second per second.

dyphylline (di-fil′lin). Chemical name: 7-(2,3-dihydroxypropyl)theophylline: used as a diuretic, and as a bronchodilator and peripheral vasodilator.

dys- [Gr. *dys-*]. Combining form signifying difficult, painful, bad, disordered, etc.; the opposite of *eu-.*

dysacousia (dis″ah-koo′ze-ah) [*dys-* + Gr. *akousis* hearing + *-ia*]. A condition in which certain sounds produce discomfort.

dysacousis (dis″ah-koo′sis). Dysacousia.

dysacousma (dis″ah-kōōs′mah). Dysacousia.

dysadaptation (dis″ad-ap-ta′shun). Dysaptation.

dysadrenia (dis″ad-re′ne-ah). Disorder of adrenal function.

dysalbumose (dis-al′bu-mōs). A variety of albumose characterized by insolubility in water and hydrochloric acid.

dysallilognathia (dis-al″il-lo-na′the-ah). A condition characterized by disproportion of the maxilla and mandible.

dysanagnosia (dis″an-ag-no′se-ah). A form of dyslexia in which certain words cannot be recognized.

dysantigraphia (dis″an-te-gra′fe-ah). Loss of power to copy writing. It is due to a lesion of the association path between the word-seeing center and the word-writing center.

dysaphia (dis-a′fe-ah) [*dys-* + Gr. *haphē* touch]. Impairment of the sense of touch.

dysaptation (dis″ap-ta′shun). Defective power of accommodation of the iris and retina to light variations.

dysarteriotony (dis″ar-te″re-ot′o-ne) [*dys-* + Gr. *artēria* artery + *tonos* tension]. Abnormality of blood pressure.

dysarthria (dis-ar′thre-ah) [*dys-* + Gr. *arthroun* to utter distinctly + *-ia*]. Imperfect articulation in speech. **d. litera'lis,** stammering. **d. syllaba'ris spasmod'ica,** stuttering.

dysarthric (dis-ar'thrik). Characterized by or pertaining to dysarthria.

dysarthrosis (dis"ar-thro'sis) [*dys-* + Gr. *arthrōsis* joint]. 1. Deformity or malformation of a joint. 2. Dysarthria.

dysaudia (dis-aw'de-ah) [*dys-* + L. *audire* to hear]. Defective hearing.

dysautonomia (dis"aw-to-no'me-ah) [*dys-* + Gr. *autonomia* freedom to use its own laws]. A familial condition characterized by defective lacrimation, skin blotching, emotional instability, motor incoordination, and hyporeflexia. Called also *familial autonomic dysfunction.*

dysbarism (dis'bar-iz'm). A general term applied to any clinical syndrome caused by difference between the surrounding atmospheric pressure and the total gas pressure in the various tissues, fluids, and cavities of the body, including such conditions as barotitis media, barosinusitis, or expansion of gases in the hollow viscera.

dysbasia (dis-ba'ze-ah) [*dys-* + Gr. *basis* step]. Difficulty in walking, especially that due to nervous lesion. **d. angiosclerot'ica, d. angiospas'tica, d. intermit'tens angiosclerot'ica,** intermittent claudication. **d. lordot'ica progressi'va,** dystonia musculorium deformans. **d. neurasthen'ica intermit'tens,** intermittent limping of neurasthenic origin.

dysbolism (dis'bo-lizm) [*dys-* + *metabolism*]. A condition of disturbed metabolism not necessarily of a disease nature.

dysboulia (dis-bu'le-ah). Dysbulia.

dysboulic (dis-bu'lik). Dysbulic.

dysbulia (dis-bu'le-ah) [*dys-* + Gr. *boulē* will + *-ia*]. Abnormal weakness or perversion of the will.

dysbulic (dis-bu'lik). Pertaining to or characterized by dysbulia.

dyscephaly (dis-sef'ah-le). Malformation of the cranium and bones of the face.

dyschesia (dis-ke'se-ah). Dyschezia.

dyschezia (dis-ke'ze-ah) [*dys-* + Gr. *chezein* to go to stool + *-ia*]. Difficult or painful evacuation of feces from the rectum.

dyschiasia (dis-ki-a'se-ah). Any disorder of sense localization.

dyschiria (dis-ki're-ah) [*dys-* + Gr. *cheir* hand + *-ia*]. Derangement of the power to tell which side of the body has been touched. See *acheiria, allochiria,* and *synchiria.*

dyscholia (dis-ko'le-ah) [*dys-* + Gr. *cholē* bile + *-ia*]. A disordered condition of the bile.

dyschondroplasia (dis"kon-dro-pla'ze-ah) [*dys-* + Gr. *chondros* cartilage + *plassein* to form + *-ia*]. A condition of abnormal growth of cartilage at the diaphysial end of long bones with the formation of cartilaginous and bony tumors on the shafts of the bones near the epiphyses. Called also *multiple cartilaginous exostoses, Ollier's disease, skeletal enchondromatosis, diaphysial aclasia,* and *hereditary deforming chondrodysplasia.*

dyschondrosteosis (dis"kon-dros"te-o'sis). A form of chondrodysplasia that may produce micromelia.

dyschromasia (dis"kro-ma'ze-ah). 1. Dyschromia. 2. Dyschromatopsia.

dyschromatopsia (dis"kro-mah-top'se-ah) [*dys-* + Gr. *chrōma* color + *opsis* vision + *-ia*]. Disorder of color vision.

dyschromia (dis-kro'me-ah) [*dys-* + Gr. *chrōma* color]. Any disorder of pigmentation of the skin or hair.

dyschronism (dis-kro'nizm). Separate in time; disturbance of any time relation.

dyschylia (dis-ki'le-ah). Disorder of the chyle.

dyscinesia (dis-si-ne'se-ah). Dyskinesia.

dyscoimesis (dis"koi-me'sis). Dyskoimesis.

dyscoria (dis-ko're-ah) [*dys-* + Gr. *korē* pupil]. Abnormality of the form or shape of the pupil or in the reaction of the two pupils.

dyscorticism (dis-kor'tĭ-sizm). Disordered functioning of the adrenal cortex.

dyscrasia (dis-kra'ze-ah) [Gr. *dyskrasia* bad temperament]. A term formerly used to indicate a depraved state of the humors, now used generally to indicate a morbid condition, especially one which involves an imbalance of component elements. **blood d.,** an abnormal or pathological condition of the blood. **lymphatic d.** 1. Status lymphaticus. 2. Hodgkin's disease.

dyscrasic (dis-kra'sik). Dyscratic.

dyscratic (dis-krat'ik) [Gr. *dyskratos*]. Pertaining to or characterized by dyscrasia.

dyscrinism (dis-kri'nizm) [*dys-* + Gr. *krinein* to separate]. Endocrine disorder; perversion of the secretion of any endocrine gland or the state resulting from such perversion.

dysdiadochocinesia (dis"di-ad"ŏ-ko"si-ne'se-ah). Dysdiadochokinesia.

dysdiadochocinetic (dis"di-ad"ŏ-ko-si-net'ik). Dysdiadochokinetic.

dysdiadochokinesia (dis"di-ad"ŏ-ko-ki-ne'se-ah). Derangement of the function of diadochokinesia.

dysdiadochokinetic (dis"di-ad"ŏ-ko-ki-net'ik). Pertaining to or characterized by dysdiadochokinesia.

dysdiemorrhysis (dis"di-e-mor'ĭ-sis) [*dys-* + Gr. *dia* through + *haima* blood + *rhysis* flow]. Retardation of the capillary circulation.

dysdipsia (dis-dip'se-ah) [*dys-* + Gr. *dipsa* thirst]. Difficulty in drinking.

dysecoia (dis"ĕ-koi'ah). Dysacousia.

dysembryoma (dis-em"bre-o'mah). A tumor formed by maldevelopment of embryonic sex cells.

dysembryoplasia (dis-em"bre-o-pla'se-ah) [*dys-* + Gr. *embryon* embryo + *plasis* formation + *-ia*]. Malformation occurring during embryonic life.

dysemia (dis-e'me-ah) [*dys-* + Gr. *haima* blood + *-ia*]. Deterioration of the blood.

dysendocrinia (dis-en"do-krin'e-ah). Dysendocrisiasis.

dysendocriniasis (dis-en"do-krĭ-ni'ah-sis). Dysendocrisiasis.

dysendocrinism (dis"en-dok'rĭ-nizm). Dysendocrisiasis.

dysendocrisiasis (dis-en"do-kris-i'ah-sis) [*dys-* + Gr. *endon* within + *krinein* to separate]. Disorder of the internal secretions.

dysenteric (dis"en-ter'ik). Pertaining to or of the nature of dysentery.

dysenteriform (dis"en-ter'ĭ-form). Resembling dysentery.

dysentery (dis'en-ter"e) [L. *dysenteria,* from Gr. *dys-* + *enteron* intestine]. A term given to a number of disorders marked by inflammation of the intestines, especially of the colon, and attended by pain in the abdomen, tenesmus, and frequent stools containing blood and mucus. The causative agent may be chemical irritants, bacteria, protozoa, or parasitic worms. There are two specific varieties, the *amebic* and the *bacillary.* **amebic d.,** a form of dysentery caused by *Entamoeba histolytica* and known also as *intestinal amebiasis.* **asylum d.,** dysentery occurring in a closed community. **bacillary d.,** an infectious disease caused by bacteria of the genus *Shigella,* and marked by intestinal pain, tenesmus, diarrhea with mucus and blood in the stools, and more or less toxemia. It is especially prevalent in tropical countries, but it frequently occurs elsewhere. **balantidial d.,** dysentery caused by *Balantidium coli.* **bilharzial d.,** dysentery caused by the parasitic worm *Bilharzia haematobia.* **catarrhal d.,** sprue. **chronic d. of cattle,** a chronic form of dysentery in cattle, with emaciation and anemia, finally ending in death. It is caused by the bacillus of Johne. **ciliary d., ciliate d.,** dysentery due to ciliate organisms, such as *Balantidium coli.* **epi-**

demic d., a variety that becomes epidemic and is often fatal. **flagellate d.**, dysentery due to a flagellate organism, such as *Lamblia intestinalis* or *Trichomonas*. **Flexner's d.**, bacillary d. **fulminant d.**, bacillary dysentery marked by collapse and toxemia and followed by death. **institutional d.**, bacillary dysentery affecting patients in an institution, especially in hospitals for the insane. **Japanese d.**, bacillary d. **malarial d.**, that which is complicated with intermittent febrile attacks. **malignant d.**, a form in which the symptoms are all very intense and progress rapidly to a fatal ending. **protozoal d.**, amebic and balantidial dysentery. **scorbutic d.**, that which is an accompaniment of scurvy. **Sonne d.**, a form of dysentery caused by the Sonne strain of *Shigella dysenteriae*, *Shigella sonnei*. **spirillar d.**, dysentery caused by spirilla in the intestines. **sporadic d.**, dysentery occurring in scattered cases that have apparently no connection. **viral d.**, a virus-caused dysentery occurring in epidemics and marked by acute watery diarrhea.

dysepulotic (dis″ep-u-lot′ik) [*dys-* + Gr. *epoulōtikos* promoting cicatrization]. Cicatrizing slowly and imperfectly.

dysequilibrium (dis″e-kwĭ-lib′re-um). Any derangement of proper balance.

dyserethesia (dis″er-e-the′ze-ah) [*dys-* + Gr. *erethizein* to irritate]. Impairment of sensibility to stimuli.

dyserethism (dis-er′e-thizm). Dyserethesia.

dysergasia (dis″er-ga′ze-ah) [*dys-* + Gr. *ergon* work]. Meyer's term for a behavior disorder due to defective brain support and including disorientative and hallucinatory states and delirious reactions.

dysergastic (dis″er-gas′tik). Meyer's term for psychic disorders due to inadequate support or metabolism of the brain (disorientation, hallucination, fears, dreamy states, etc.).

dysergia (dis-er′je-ah) [*dys-* + Gr. *ergon* work]. Motor incoordination due to defect of efferent nerve impulse.

dysesthesia (dis″es-the′ze-ah) [*dys-* + Gr. *aisthēsis* perception]. 1. Impairment of any sense, especially of that of touch. 2. A painful and persistent sensation induced by a gentle touch of the skin. **auditory d.**, dysacousia.

dysesthetic (dis″es-thet′ik). Pertaining to or characterized by dysesthesia.

dysfunction (dis-funk′shun). Disturbance, impairment, or abnormality of the functioning of an organ.

dysgalactia (dis″gah-lak′te-ah) [*dys-* + Gr. *gala* milk]. Disordered milk secretion.

dysgammaglobulinemia (dis-gam″mah-glob″-u-lĭ-ne′me-ah). An abnormality of the gamma globulins in the blood serum, such as disproportion of the various types, or presence of abnormal compounds.

dysgenesia (dis″jĕ-ne′ze-ah) [*dys-* + Gr. *gennan* to generate + *-ia*]. Impairment of the powers of procreation.

dysgenesis (dis-jen′e-sis). Defective development. **gonadal d.**, a condition characterized by the presence of gonads which contain germinal cells but which have not developed properly.

dysgenic (dis-jen′ik). Detrimental to the race or tending to counteract race improvement.

dysgenics (dis-jen′iks) [*dys-* + Gr. *gennan* to produce]. The study of racial deterioration. Cf. *eugenics*.

dysgenitalism (dis-jen′ĭ-tal-izm). An abnormality of genital development, as eunuchism.

dysgenopathy (dis″jen-op′ah-the) [*dys-* + Gr. *gennan* to produce + *pathos* disease]. A disorder of bodily development.

dysgerminoma (dis″jer-mĭ-no′mah) [*dys-* + *germ* + *-oma*]. A solid ovarian or testicular tumor derived from germinal epithelium which has not been differentiated to cells of either male or female type.

dysgeusia (dis-gu′ze-ah) [*dys-* + Gr. *geusis* taste]. Perversion of the sense of taste.

dysglandular (dis-glan′du-lar). Due to or marked by disordered functioning of glands, particularly the glands of internal secretion.

dysglobulinemia (dis-glob″u-lin-e′me-ah) [*dys-* + *globulin* + Gr. *haima* blood + *-ia*]. A condition characterized by abnormality of the serum globulins.

dysglycemia (dis″gli-se′me-ah) [*dys-* + Gr. *glykys* sweet + *haima* blood + *-ia*]. Any derangement of the sugar content of the blood.

dysgnathic (dis-nath′ik) [*dys-* + Gr. *gnathos* jaw]. Pertaining to or characterized by abnormality of the maxilla and mandible.

dysgnosia (dis-no′se-ah) [Gr. *dysgnōsia* difficulty of knowing]. Any disorder of intellectual function.

dysgonesis (dis″go-ne′sis) [*dys-* + Gr. *gonē* seed]. A functional disorder of the genital organs.

dysgonic (dis-gon′ik). Seeding badly: said of bacterial cultures that grow poorly on culture media.

dysgrammatism (dis-gram′ah-tizm). Partial impairment of the ability to speak grammatically because of brain injury or disease.

dysgraphia (dis-gra′fe-ah) [*dys-* + Gr. *graphein* to write]. Inability to write properly because of ataxia, tremor, or motor neurosis.

dyshematopoiesis (dis-hem″ah-to″poi-e′sis). Defective blood formation.

dyshematopoietic (dis-hem″ah-to-poi-et′ik). Pertaining to or characterized by dyshematopoiesis.

dyshemopoiesis (dis-he″mo-poi-e′sis). Dyshematopoiesis.

dyshemopoietic (dis-he″mo-poi-et′ik). Dyshematopoietic.

dyshepatia (dis-hĕ-pa′she-ah) [*dys-* + Gr. *hēpar* liver]. Disordered liver function. **lipogenic d.**, a liver disorder of children due to excessive fats in the diet.

dyshidria (dis-hid′re-ah). Dyshidrosis.

dyshidrosis (dis-hid-ro′sis) [*dys-* + Gr. *hidrōsis* a sweating]. 1. Any disorder of the perspiratory apparatus. 2. Pompholyx or cheiropompholyx. **trichophytic d.**, athlete's foot.

dyshormonal (dis-hōr′mo-nal). Due to hormone or endocrine disturbance.

dyshormonic (dis-hōr-mon′ik). Dyshormonal.

dyshormonism (dis-hōr′mōn-izm). Disturbance of the hormone secretions.

dyshydrosis (dis-hid-ro′sis). Dyshidrosis.

dyshypophysia (dis″hi-po-fiz′e-ah). Dyspituitarism.

dyshypophysism (dis″hi-pof′ĭ-sizm). Dyspituitarism.

dysidrosis (dis-id-ro′sis). Dyshidrosis.

dysimmunity (dis-ĭ-mu′nĭ-te). Disordered or misdirected immunity.

dysinsulinism (dis-in′su-lin-izm). A condition caused by disordered secretion of insulin.

dysinsulinosis (dis-in″su-lĭ-no′sis). Dysinsulinism.

dyskaryosis (dis-kar″e-o′sis). Abnormal changes in cell nuclei, such as those observed in epithelial cells of the cervix during pregnancy.

dyskaryotic (dis″kar-e-ot′ik) [*dys-* + Gr. *karyon* nucleus]. Pertaining to, characterized by, or promoting dyskaryosis.

dyskeratosis (dis″ker-ah-to′sis). A condition characterized by abnormal, premature, or imperfect keratinization of the keratinocytes. **d. congen′ita**, a rare hereditary syndrome consisting of widespread poikiloderma-like changes in the skin, associated with oral leukoplakia and dystrophy of the nails. **d. follicula′ris**, keratosis follicularis.

dyskinesia (dis″ki-ne′ze-ah) [Gr. *dyskinēsia* difficulty of moving]. Impairment of the power of voluntary movement, resulting in fragmentary or incomplete movements. **d. al'gera,** a condition in which movement is painful: seen in hysteria. **biliary d.,** derangement of the filling and emptying mechanism of the gallbladder. **d. intermit'tens,** disability of the limbs, coming on intermittently, and due to impairment of the circulation. **occupational d.,** occupation neurosis. **uterine d.,** pain in the uterus on movement: a sign of displacement of the uterus.

dyskinetic (dis″ki-net′ik). Pertaining to or characterized by dyskinesia.

dyskoimesis (dis″koi-me′sis) [*dys-* + Gr. *koimēsis* sleeping]. Difficulty in getting to sleep.

dyslalia (dis-la′le-ah) [*dys-* + Gr. *lalein* to talk + *-ia*]. Impairment of utterance with abnormality of the external speech organs (Kussmaul).

dyslexia (dis-lek′se-ah) [*dys-* + Gr. *lexis* diction]. 1. An inability to read understandingly, due to a central lesion. 2. A condition in which reading is possible, but is attended with fatigue and disagreeable sensations.

dyslipidoses (dis″lip-ĭ-do′sēz). Plural of *dyslipidosis.*

dyslipidosis (dis″lip-ĭ-do′sis), pl. *dyslipido′ses.* A general designation applied to a localized or systemic disturbance of fat metabolism.

dyslipoidosis (dis-lip″oi-do′sis), pl. *dyslipoido′ses.* Dyslipidosis.

dyslochia (dis-lo′ke-ah) [*dys-* + Gr. *lochia* lochia]. Disordered lochial discharge.

dyslogia (dis-lo′je-ah) [*dys-* + Gr. *logos* understanding]. Impairment of the reasoning power; also impairment of the speech, due to mental disorders.

dysmasesia (dis″mah-se′ze-ah). Dysmasesis.

dysmasesis (dis″mah-se′sis) [*dys-* + Gr. *masēsis* mastication]. Difficult mastication.

dysmegalopsia (dis″meg-ah-lop′se-ah) [*dys-* + Gr. *megas* big + *opsis* vision]. A disturbance of the visual appreciation of the size of objects, in which they appear larger than they are.

dysmelia (dis-me′le-ah) [*dys-* + Gr. *melos* limb + *-ia*]. Malformation of a limb or limbs as a result of a disturbance in embryonic development. The term includes defects of excessive development as well as reduction deformities.

dysmenorrhea (dis″men-o-re′ah) [*dys-* + Gr. *mēn* month + *rhein* to flow]. Painful menstruation. **acquired d.,** secondary dysmenorrhea. **congestive d.,** that which is accompanied by great congestion of the uterus. **essential d.,** painful menstruation for which there is no demonstrable cause. **inflammatory d.,** that which comes from or is due to inflammation. **d. intermenstrua′lis,** intermenstrual pain. **mechanical d.,** that which is due to mechanical interference with the flow, as from clots or flexion of the uterus. **membranous d.,** that which is characterized by membranous exfoliations derived from the uterus. **obstructive d.,** that which is due to mechanical obstruction to the discharge of the menstrual fluid. **ovarian d.,** neuralgic pain which is due to ovarian disease. **plethoric d.,** congestive d. **primary d.,** essential dysmenorrhea. **psychogenic d.,** dysmenorrhea due to disturbance of psychic control. **secondary d.,** dysmenorrhea due to definite pelvic lesion. **spasmodic d.,** that form which is due to spasmodic uterine contraction. **tubal d.,** that which is due to disease of the oviduct, such as chronic salpingitis. **uterine d.,** that which arises from a uterine lesion.

dysmetria (dis-me′tre-ah) [*dys-* + Gr. *metron* measure]. A condition in which there is improper measuring of distance in muscular acts; disturbance of the power to control the range of movement in muscular action.

dysmetropsia (dis″mĕ-trop′se-ah) [*dys-* + Gr. *metron* measure + *opsis* vision]. Defect in the visual appreciation of the measure or size of objects.

dysmicrobialism (dis″mi-kro′be-al-izm). Disturbance of the normal balance of microorganisms, especially in the intestines.

dysmimia (dis-mim′e-ah) [*dys-* + Gr. *mimia* imitation]. Impairment of the power of expressing thought by gestures.

dysmnesia (dis-ne′se-ah) [*dys-* + Gr. *mnēmē* memory]. Impaired memory.

dysmnesic (dis-ne′zik). Characterized by impairment or disorder of memory.

dysmorphism (dis-mor′fizm) [*dys-* + Gr. *morphē* form]. 1. Allomorphism. 2. The condition of appearing under different forms; for example, some fungi grow differently under parasitic and under saprophytic conditions.

dysmorphophobia (dis″mor-fo-fo′be-ah) [Gr. *dysmorphos* deformed + *phobia*]. Morbid fear of bodily deformity or of becoming deformed.

dysmorphopsia (dis″mor-fop′se-ah) [Gr. *dysmorphos* deformed + *opsis* vision + *-ia*]. Defective vision, with distortion of the shape of objects perceived.

dysmorphosis (dis″mor-fo′sis) [Gr. *dysmorphos* deformed]. Malformation.

dysmyotonia (dis″mi-o-to′ne-ah) [*dys-* + Gr. *mys* muscle + *tonos* tension]. Muscular dystonia; abnormal tonicity of muscle.

dysneuria (dis-nu′re-ah) [*dys-* + Gr. *neuron* nerve]. Impairment of the nerve function.

dysnomia (dis-no′me-ah) [*dys-* + Gr. *onoma* name]. Partial nominal aphasia.

dysodontiasis (dis″o-don-ti′ah-sis) [*dys-* + Gr. *odous* tooth + *-iasis*]. Defective, delayed, or difficult eruption of the teeth.

dysoemia (dis-e′me-ah) [*dys-* + Gr. *oimos* road, path]. A medicolegal term for death from obscure causes, traceable to chronic mineral poisoning.

dysontogenesis (dis″on-to-jen′e-sis) [*dys-* + *ontogenesis*]. Defective embryonic development.

dysontogenetic (dis″on-to-je-net′ik). Pertaining to or characterized by dysontogenesis.

dysopia (dis-o′pe-ah) [*dys-* + Gr. *ōpē* sight + *-ia*]. Defective vision. **d. al′gera,** disturbances of vision due to pains in the eyes and head on looking at objects.

dysopsia (dis-op′se-ah). Dysopia.

dysorexia (dis″o-rek′se-ah) [*dys-* + Gr. *orexis* appetite]. Impaired or deranged appetite.

dysorganoplasia (dis-or″gan-o-pla′se-ah) [*dys-* + Gr. *organon* organ + *plasis* formation]. Disordered development of an organ.

dysosmia (dis-oz′me-ah) [*dys-* + Gr. *osmē* smell]. Defect or impairment of the sense of smell.

dysosteogenesis (dis-os″te-o-jen′e-sis). Defective bone formation; dysostosis.

dysostosis (dis″os-to′sis) [*dys-* + Gr. *osteon* bone]. Defective ossification; defect in the normal ossification of fetal cartilages. **cleidocranial d.** (Marie), a rare congenital condition in which there are defective ossification of the cranial bones and complete or partial absence of the clavicles, so that the shoulders may be brought together in front. **d. cleidocrania′lis congen′ita,** cleidocranial d. **craniofacial d.,** deformity of the bones of the face and skull, attributed to premature fusion of the bones of the skull, a condition often having familial incidence. **d. enchondra′lis epiphysa′ria,** dysplasia epiphysealis multiplex. **mandibulofacial d.,** a congenital condition characterized by antimongoloid slant of palpebral fissures, hypoplasia of facial bones, deformity of the ears, macrostomia, and other abnormalities of the face and jaw. **metaphyseal d.,** a skeletal abnormality in which the epiphyses

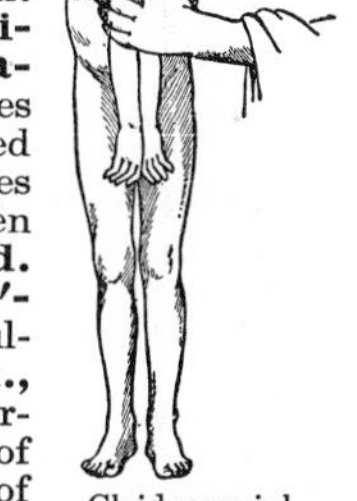

Cleidocranial dysostosis.

are normal, or nearly so, and the metaphyseal tissues are replaced by masses of cartilage, producing interference with enchondral bone formation, and expansion and thinning of the metaphyseal cortices. **d. mul'tiplex,** lipochondrodystrophy. **orodigitofacial d.,** a condition occurring only in females, characterized by anomalies of the mouth and tongue, of the fingers, and frequently of the face, and accompanied by anomaly of chromosome No. 1. (Denver nomenclature).

dysoxidative (dis-ok'sĭ-da"tiv). Due to deficient oxidation.

dysoxidizable (dis-ok'sĭ-dīz"ah-b'l) [*dys-* + *oxidizable*]. Not easily oxidizable.

dyspancreatism (dis-pan'kre-ah-tizm). Disorder of the function of the pancreas.

dysparathyroidism (dis"par-ah-thi'roid-izm). Disorder of parathyroid function.

dyspareunia (dis"pah-roo'ne-ah) [Gr. *dyspareunos* badly mated]. Difficult or painful coitus in women.

dyspepsia (dis-pep'se-ah) [*dys-* + Gr. *peptein* to digest]. Impairment of the power or function of digestion. **acid d.,** a variety associated with excessive acidity of the stomach. **appendicular d., appendix d.,** dyspeptic symptoms occurring in chronic appendicitis. **atonic d.,** a form ascribed to a lack of tone in the digestive organs. **catarrhal d.,** a variety accompanied by gastric inflammation. **chichiko d.,** a condition of farinaceous malnutrition found in badly nourished infants of the poor in Japan, who are fed mostly on solutions of polished rice powder. **cholelithic d.,** the sudden dyspeptic attacks characteristic of gallbladder disturbance. **colon d.,** functional disturbance of the large intestine, giving rise to the symptoms of dyspepsia. **fermentative d.,** that characterized by the fermentation of ingested food. **flatulent d.,** that which is associated with the formation of gas in the stomach. **functional d.,** that which is either atonic or of reflex or nervous origin. **gastric d.,** that which originates within the stomach. **intestinal d.,** that which arises in the intestines. **nervous d.,** that due to some disease of the nerves of the stomach. **ovarian d.,** a form of reflex indigestion due to ovarian disease. **reflex d.,** that which is due to reflex influence from some disease of an organ not directly concerned in digestion. **salivary d.,** dyspepsia due to defective or deficient saliva.

dyspeptic (dis-pep'tik). Pertaining to or affected with dyspepsia.

dyspeptone (dis-pep'tōn). A variety of insoluble peptone produced during digestion.

dysperistalsis (dis"per-ĭ-stal'sis) [*dys-* + *peristalsis*]. Painful or abnormal peristalsis.

dysphagia (dis-fa'je-ah) [*dys-* + Gr. *phagein* to eat]. Difficulty in swallowing. **d. inflammato'ria,** dysphagia due to inflammation of the esophagus. **d. luso'ria,** dysphagia resulting from compression of the esophagus caused by some developmental anomaly (lusus naturae). **d. nervo'sa,** esophagism. **d. paralyt'ica,** dysphagia due to paralysis of the esophageal muscles. **sideropenic d.,** Plummer-Vinson syndrome. **d. spas'tica,** esophagism. **tropical d.,** entalação. **vallecular d.,** dysphagia caused by the lodgment of food above or at the sides of the epiglottis. **d. valsalvia'na,** dysphagia due to subluxation of the major cornu of the hyoid bone.

dysphagy (dis'fah-je). Dysphagia.

dysphasia (dis-fa'ze-ah) [*dys-* + Gr. *phasis* speech]. Impairment of speech, consisting in lack of coordination and failure to arrange words in their proper order. It is due to a central lesion.

dysphemia (dis-fe'me-ah). Stammering or other speech disorder due to psychoneurosis.

dysphonia (dis-fo'ne-ah) [*dys-* + Gr. *phōnē* voice]. Any impairment of voice: a difficulty in speaking. **d. clerico'rum,** impairment of voice due to much public speaking. **d. pli'cae ventricula'ris,** a condition in which phonation is performed by the false vocal cords (ventricular bands). **d. pu'berum,** the harsh, irregular utterance of puberty, and of the change of voice in youth. **d. spas'tica,** difficulty in speaking caused by spasm of the muscles of phonation.

dysphonic (dis-fon'ik). Pertaining to or characterized by dysphonia.

dysphoretic (dis"fo-ret'ik). 1. Dysphoric. 2. Dysphoriant.

dysphoria (dis-fo're-ah) [Gr. "excessive pain, anguish, agitation"]. Disquiet; restlessness; malaise.

dysphoriant (dis-fo're-ant). 1. Producing a condition of dysphoria. 2. An agent that produces dysphoria.

dysphoric (dis-for'ik). Pertaining to or characterized by dysphoria.

dysphrasia (dis-fra'ze-ah) [*dys-* + Gr. *phrasis* speech + *-ia*]. Imperfection of utterance due to a central or cerebral defect.

dysphrenia (dis-fre'ne-ah) [*dys-* + Gr. *phrēn* mind + *-ia*]. Any secondary (functional) psychosis as distinguished from an idiopathic (organic) brain disease (Kahlbaum).

dysphylaxia (dis"fi-lak'se-ah) [*dys-* + Gr. *phylaxis* watching]. A condition marked by too early waking.

dyspigmentation (dis"pig-men-ta'shun). A disorder of pigmentation of the skin or hair or of other specialized structures of the skin.

dyspinealism (dis-pin'e-al-izm). Disordered function of the pineal gland.

dyspituitarism (dis"pĭ-tu'ĭ-tar-izm). A condition due to disordered activity of the pituitary body. Cf. *hyperpituitarism* and *hypopituitarism*.

dysplasia (dis-pla'se-ah) [*dys-* + Gr. *plassein* to form]. Abnormality of development. **anteroposterior facial d.,** defective development resulting in abnormal anteroposterior relationship of the maxilla and mandible to each other or to the cranial base. **cardiovascular d., hereditary,** a condition characterized by hypertrophy of the cephalic portion of the interventricular septum, disorganization of the myocardium, and hypoplasia of the large arteries. **chondroectodermal d.,** achondroplasia occurring in association with defective development of skin, hair, and teeth, polydactyly, and defect of the cardiac septum. **congenital alveolar d.,** idiopathic respiratory distress of newborn. **cretinoid d.,** abnormality of development characteristic of cretinism, consisting of retarded ossification, and smallness of the internal and sex organs. **dental d.,** abnormality of development producing abnormal relationship of a varying number of teeth with their opposing members. **diaphyseal d.,** a condition characterized by thickening of the cortex of the mid-shaft area of the long bones, progressing toward the epiphyses, the thickening sometimes occurring also in the flat bones; excessive growth in length of bones of the extremities usually results in abnormal stature. **ectodermal d.,** a rare hereditary condition marked by a smooth glossy skin, total absence of sweat glands, abnormality of the teeth, and defective hair formation. There may also be atrophic rhinitis, saddle nose, prominent eyebrows, large chin, thick lips, and mental impairment. **encephalo-ophthalmic d.,** a developmental structural defect of the eye due to faulty development of the brain. **epiphyseal d.,** faulty growth and ossification of the epiphyses, with roentgenographically apparent stippling and decreased stature, not associated with thyroid disease. **d. epiphysea'lis hemimel'ica,** a rare condition characterized by swellings in the extremities, usually on the inner and outer aspects of the ankles and knees, made up of bone covered with epiphyseal cartilage, and leading to limitation of motion of the joints. **d. epiphysea'lis mul'tiplex,** a developmental abnormality of various epiphyses, which appear late and are mottled, flattened, fragmented, and usually hypoplastic; the digits are short and thick, with blunt ends, and stature may be diminished owing to flattening deformities at the hips, knees, and ankles. **d. epiphysea'lis puncta'ta,** chondrodystrophia fetalis calcificans. **fibrous d.,** a disease of bone marked by thinning of the cortex and replacement of bone marrow by gritty fibrous tissue containing bony spicules, producing pain, disability, and gradually increasing deformity. Only one bone may be involved (*monostotic fibrous d.*), with the process later affecting several or many bones (*polyostotic fibrous d.*). **metaphyseal d.,** a disturbance in enchondral bone growth, failure of modeling causing the ends of the shafts to remain larger than normal in circumference. **d. pilo'rum thysanofor'mis,** trichostasis spinulosa. **skeletodental d.,** abnormality of development producing not only abnormal relationship of varying numbers of apposing teeth, but also abnormal relationship of the maxilla and mandible to each other or to the base of the skull.

dysplastic (dis-plas'tik). 1. Marked by dysplasia. 2. Having a body form which does not belong to one of the three main classes, athletic, asthenic or pyknic.

dyspnea (disp'ne-ah) [Gr. *dyspnoia* difficulty of breathing]. Difficult or labored breathing. **cardiac d.,** difficult breathing caused by heart disease. **exertional d.,** dyspnea provoked by physical effort or exertion. **expiratory d.,** difficulty in breathing caused by hindrance to the free egress of air from the lungs. **inspiratory d.,** difficulty in breathing caused by hindrance to the free ingress of air into the lungs. **nonexpansional d.,** difficulty in breathing caused by failure of expansion of the chest. **orthostatic d.,** difficulty in breathing experienced when in the erect position. **paroxysmal d.,** respiratory distress occurring in attacks without apparent cause, usually during sleep at night, but also in the daytime, in patients who also have exertional dyspnea and orthopnea. **renal d.,** difficulty in breathing attributable to kidney disease. **sighing d.,** a syndrome characterized by deep sighing respirations, the depth of inspiration being greatly increased, without significant alteration in the respiratory rate and without wheezing. **Traube's d.,** difficult breathing marked by slow respiratory movements and expansion and collapse of the thorax during inspiration and expiration.

dyspneic (disp-ne'ik). Pertaining to or characterized by dyspnea.

dyspneoneurosis (disp-ne"o-nu-ro'sis). Dyspnea of nervous origin.

dyspoiesis (dis"poi-e'sis). A disorder of formation, as of blood cells.

dysponderal (dis-pon'der-al) [*dys-* + L. *pondus* weight]. Pertaining to disorder of weight, either obesity or underweight.

dyspragia (dis-pra'je-ah) [Gr. *dyspragia* ill success]. Painful performance of any function. **d. intermit'tens angiosclerot'ica intestina'lis,** a painful intestinal spasmodic affection, due to derangement of the intestinal blood supply.

dyspraxia (dis-prak'se-ah) [Gr. *dyspraxia* ill success]. Partial loss of ability to perform coordinated movements.

dysprosium (dis-pro'se-um). A rare chemical element, atomic number 66, atomic weight 162.50, symbol Dy.

dysprosody (dis-pros'o-de). Disturbance of stress, pitch, and rhythm of speech.

dysproteinemia (dis-pro"te-in-e'me-ah) [*dys-* + *protein* + Gr. *haima* blood + *-ia*]. Derangement of the protein content of the blood.

dysproteose (dis-pro'te-ōs). Heteroproteose modified by treatment with water.

dysrhaphia (dis-ra'fe-ah) [*dys-* + Gr. *rhaphē* seam + *-ia*]. Incomplete closure of the primary neural tube; status dysraphicus.

dysrhythmia (dis-rith'me-ah) [*dys-* + Gr. *rhythmos* any regularly recurring motion + *-ia*]. 1. Disturbance of rhythm. 2. Abnormality of rhythm in speech: *d. pneumophra'sia* is defective breath grouping; *d. proso'dia* is defective placement of stress; *d. to'nia* is defective inflection. **cerebral d.,** disturbance or irregularity in the rhythm of the brain waves as recorded by electroencephalography. **electroencephalographic d.,** cerebral d.

dyssebacea (dis"se-ba'she-ah) [*dys-* + *sebum*]. Disorder of sebaceous follicles; specifically a condition seen in riboflavin deficiency, marked by greasy, branny seborrhea on the midface, with erythema in the nasal folds, canthi, and other folds of the skin.

dyssomnia (dis-som'ne-ah) [*dys-* + L. *somnus* sleep]. Any disorder of sleep.

dysspermia (dis-sper'me-ah) [*dys-* + Gr. *sperma* seed + *-ia*]. Impairment of the spermatozoa, or of the semen.

dysstasia (dis-sta'se-ah) [*dys-* + Gr. *stasis* standing]. Difficulty in standing.

dysstatic (dis-stat'ik). Pertaining to or characterized by dysstasia.

dyssymbolia (dis"sim-bo'le-ah). Failure of conceptual thinking so that thoughts can not be intelligently formulated in language.

dyssymboly (dis-sim'bo-le). Dyssymbolia.

dyssymmetry (dis-sim'e-tre). A condition characterized by absence of symmetry.

dyssynergia (dis"sin-er'je-ah) [*dys-* + Gr. *synergia* cooperation]. Disturbance of muscular coordination. **biliary d.,** failure of coordinated action of the different parts of the biliary system. **d. cerebella'ris myoclon'ica,** a condition characterized by cerebellar dyssynergia, myoclonus, and epilepsy; called also *Hunt's disease.* **d. cerebella'ris progres'siva,** a condition marked by generalized tremors associated with disturbance of muscle tone and of muscular coordination; due to disorder of cerebellar function.

dyssystole (dis-sis'to-le) [*dys-* + *systole*]. Abnormal cardiac systole, especially asystole.

dystaxia (dis-tak'se-ah) [*dys-* + Gr. *taxis* arrangement]. Difficulty in controlling voluntary movements; partial ataxia. **d. ag'itans,** a tremor from irritation of the spinal cord resembling paralysis agitans, but without paralysis (Sanders, 1868).

dystectia (dis-tek'she-ah) [*dys-* + L. *tectum* roof]. Defective closure of the neural tube, resulting in such malformations as anencephaly, porencephaly, meningocele, spina bifida, etc.

dysteleology (dis"te-le-ol'o-je). 1. The study of apparently useless organs or parts. 2. Lack of purposefulness, or of contribution to the final result.

dysthermosia (dis"ther-mo'se-ah) [*dys-* + Gr. *thermē* heat]. Disturbance of heat production.

dysthymia (dis-thim'e-ah). 1. [*dys-* + Gr. *thymos* mind]. Mental depression; also, any intellectual anomaly. 2. [*dys-* + Gr. *thymos* thymus]. The condition produced by disordered thymus secretion in childhood.

dysthymiac (dis-thi'me-ak). An individual exhibiting dysthymia.

dysthyreosis (dis"thi-re-o'sis). Dysthyroidism.

dysthyroidea (dis"thi-roi'de-ah). Dysthyroidism.

dysthyroidism (dis-thi'roid-izm). Imperfect development and function of the thyroid gland.

dystimbria (dis-tim'bre-ah). Defect in quality or resonance of the voice.

dystithia (dis-tith'e-ah) [*dys-* + Gr. *tithēnē* a nurse + *-ia*]. Difficulty in breast feeding.

dystocia (dis-to'se-ah) [*dys-* + Gr. *tokos* birth]. Abnormal labor or childbirth. **constriction ring d., contraction ring d. (of White),** difficult labor caused by contraction of an area of circular muscle fibers, which may occur at various levels of the parturient uterus. **fetal d.,** that which is due to the shape, size, or position of the fetus. **maternal d.,** that which is due to some condition inherent in the mother. **placental d.,** difficulty in delivering the placenta.

dystonia (dis-to′ne-ah) [*dys-* + Gr. *tonos*]. Disordered tonicity of muscle. **d. defor′mans progres′siva,** d. musculorum deformans. **d. lenticula′ris,** dystonia due to a lesion of the lenticular nucleus. **d. musculo′rum defor′mans** (Oppenheim), a rare chronic disease marked by involuntary, irregular, clonic contortions of the muscles of the trunk and extremities. The symptoms appear chiefly on walking, at which time the contortions twist the body forward and sideways in a grotesque fashion (tortipelvis). Called also *Ziehen-Oppenheim disease, dystonia deformans progressiva,* and *dysbasia lordotica progressiva.*

dystonic (dis-ton′ik). Pertaining to or characterized by dystonia.

dystopia (dis-to′pe-ah) [*dys-* + Gr. *topos* place]. Malposition; faulty placement of an organ.

dystopic (dis-top′ik). Misplaced; out of its normal place.

dystopy (dis′to-pe). Dystopia.

dystrophia (dis-tro′fe-ah) [L.]. Dystrophy. **d. adipo′sa cor′neae,** primary fatty degeneration of the cornea. **d. adiposogenita′lis,** adiposogenital dystrophy. **d. brevicol′lis,** a condition of dwarfism characterized especially by shortness of the neck. **d. diffu′sa,** diffuse atrophy, as of the alveolar bone, in advanced periodontal disease. **d. endothelia′lis cor′neae,** cornea guttata. **d. epithelia′lis cor′neae,** a dystrophia of the epithelium of the cornea marked by erosions: called also *Fuchs' dystrophy.* **d. hypophyso-pri′va chron′ica,** the condition produced by partial removal of the hypophysis cerebri and marked by obesity, increased carbohydrate tolerance, hypothermia, hypoplasia of the sex glands, retardation of skeletal growth, and mental dullness. **d. myoton′ica,** myotonia atrophica. **d. periosta′lis hyperplas′tica familia′ris,** a familial condition marked by acrocephaly and with thickening of the bones. **d. un′guium,** dystrophy of the nails; changes in the texture and color of the nails due to systemic or other disease. **d. un′guium media′na canalifor′mis,** solenonychia.

dystrophic (dis-trof′ik). Pertaining to or characterized by dystrophy.

dystrophodextrin (dis″trof-o-deks′trin) [*dys-* + Gr. *trophē* nutrition + *dextrin*]. A starchlike material said to exist in normal blood.

dystrophoneurosis (dis-trof″o-nu-ro′sis) [*dys-* + Gr. *trophē* nutrition + *neurosis*]. 1. Any nervous disorder due to poor nutrition. 2. Impairment of nutrition which is caused by nervous disorder.

dystrophy (dis′tro-fe) [L. *dystrophia,* from *dys-* + Gr. *trephein* to nourish]. A disorder arising from defective or faulty nutrition. **adiposogenital d.,** a condition characterized by adiposity of the feminine type, genital hypoplasia, changes in secondary sex characters, and metabolic disturbances; seen with lesions of the hypophysis and hypothalamus. **elastic d.,** disorder of the elastic components of the skin, such as occurs in pseudoxanthoma elasticum, senile elastosis, and colloid milium. **Erb's d.,** pseudohypertrophic muscular dystrophy. **Fuchs' d.,** dystrophia epithelialis corneae. **hypophyseal d.,** hypopituitarism. **Landouzy-Dejerine d.,** a type of dystrophy in which there is marked atrophy of the muscles of the face, shoulder girdle and arm, producing a facial expression called myopathic face. **Leyden-Moebius d.,** progressive muscular dystrophy. **median canaliform d. of the nail,** solenonychia. **papillary and pigmentary d.** (Darier), acanthosis nigricans. **progressive muscular d.,** progressive atrophy of the muscles with no discoverable lesion of the spinal cord. **pseudohypertrophic muscular d.,** a dystrophy of the muscles of the shoulder girdle and sometimes of the pelvic girdle, commencing in childhood with hypertrophy and followed later by atrophy. Sometimes called *Erb's paralysis.* **reflex sympathetic d.,** a disturbance of the sympathetic nervous system marked by pallor or rubor, pain, sweating, edema, or skin atrophy following sprain, fracture or injury to nerves or blood vessels. **Salzmann's nodular corneal d.,** a progressive hypertrophic degeneration of the epithelial layer, Bowman's membrane and the outer portion of the corneal stroma. **thyroneural d.,** a condition marked by chorea, athetosis, rigidity, ataxia, and other indications of disturbed function of the vegetative nervous system with mental and thyroid defects. **wound d.,** a syndrome of defective protein metabolism (hypoproteinemia) that sometimes develops after severe injury.

dystropic (dis-tro′pik) [*dys-* + Gr. *tropos* a turning]. Characterized by abnormal behavior.

dystropy (dis′tro-pe). Abnormal behavior.

dystrypsia (dis-trip′se-ah) [*dys-* + *trypsin* + *-ia*]. Derangement of intestinal or pancreatic digestion due to lack of trypsin.

dysuresia (dis-u-re′se-ah). Dysuria.

dysuria (dis-u′re-ah) [*dys-* + Gr. *ouron* urine + *-ia*]. Painful or difficult urination. **psychic d.,** difficulty in passing the urine in the presence of other persons. **spastic d.,** difficult urination due to spasm of the bladder.

dysuriac (dis-u′re-ak). An individual exhibiting dysuria.

dysuric (dis-u′rik). Pertaining to dysuria.

dysury (dis′u-re). Dysuria.

dysvitaminosis (dis″vi-tah-min-o′sis). A disorder due to an excess or deficiency of a vitamin.

dyszooamylia (dis-zo″o-ah-mi′le-ah) [*dys-* + *zooamylon*]. Failure of the liver to store up glucose in the form of glycogen (zooamylon).

dyszoospermia (dis-zo-o-sper′me-ah) [*dys-* + *zoospermia*]. A disorder of spermatozoon formation.

E

E. Abbreviation for *emmetropia, eye, electromotive force* and *experimenter.*

e. Abbreviation for *electron,* or for the amount of charge on an electron.

Ea. A god of the Babylonians and Assyrians, said to be the earliest deity associated with the art of healing.

ead. Abbreviation for L. *ea′dem,* the same.

Eagle test (e′gl) [Harry *Eagle,* American physician, born 1905]. See under *test.*

EAHF. Abbreviation for *eczema, asthma, hay fever.* See *EAHF complex,* under *complex.*

Eales' disease (ēlz) [Henry *Eales,* British physician, 1852–1913]. See under *disease.*

EAP. Abbreviation for *epiallopregnanolone.*

Ea. R. Abbreviation for Ger. *Entartungs-Reaktion,* reaction of degeneration.

ear (ēr) [L. *auris;* Gr. *ous*]. The organ of hearing. **acute e.,** acute middle ear catarrh, otitis media acuta. **aviator's e.,** aero-otitis media. **Aztec e.,** an ear in which the lobule is wanting, the whole ear looking as if it were pushed forward and downward. **bat e.,** lop e. **beach e.,** maceration and inflammation of the auditory canal as a result of ocean bathing. **Blainville e's,** asymmetry of the two ears. **bleeding e.,** nambi-uvu. **Cagot e.,** an ear in which the lobule is wanting. **cat's e.,** an ear that is folded over on itself. **cauliflower e.,** a crumpled ear following the absorption of effusion after an injury. **Darwin's e.,** an ear having an eminence on the edge of the helix. **diabetic e.,** mastoiditis complicating diabetes. **external e.,** the pinna and external meatus together (auris externa [N A]). **hairy e's,** hypertrichosis pinnae auris. **Hong Kong e.,** aural aspergillosis. **hot weather e.,** an otitis externa, especially of the meatus, which is rather common in the hot and humid tropics and is often caused by *Pseudomonas aeruginosa.* **inner e.,** the labyrinth, comprising the vestibule, cochlea and semicircular canals (auris interna [N A]). **insane e.,** hematoma of the ear. **lop e.,** deformity of the external ear in which the conchal portion grows at a right angle to the head. **middle e.,** the space immediately medial to the membrana tympani (auris media [N A]). It consists of the tympanic cavity, which is crossed by the auditory ossicles, and connects with the mastoid cells and auditory tube. **Morel e.,** a deformed ear marked by abnormal development of the helix, anthelix, and scaphoid fossa, so that the folds of the ear seem obliterated, and the ear is smooth, large, and often prominent, with a thin edge. **satyr e.,** one with a pointed pinna. **scroll e.,** one in which the pinna is rolled up. **Singapore e.,** otomycosis, **Stahl e., No. 1,** a deformed ear in which the helix is broad and coalesces with the anthelix; the fossa ovalis and fossa scaphoidea are scarcely to be seen, and the lower portion of the helix is obliterated. **Stahl e., No. 2,** a deformed ear in which there are three instead of two crura anthelicis. **tank e.,** a condition like beach ear from bathing in swimming pools. **tropical e.,** a local infection of the external auditory meatus prevalent in tropical and semitropical countries. **Wildermuth's e.,** a deformed ear with prominent anthelix and poorly developed helix.

ear-minded (ēr-mind′ed). Remembering chiefly the impressions made on the sense of hearing. Cf. *audile.*

earth (erth). 1. The soil and other pulverulent substances forming the ground. 2. Any amorphous, easily pulverizable mineral. **alkaline e.,** any oxide of a metal of the group to which calcium and magnesium belong. **fullers' e.,** an impure aluminum silicate used as dressing for sores. **infusorial e.,** a silicious earth composed mostly of the frustules and fragments of diatoms. By boiling with dilute hydrochloric acid, washing, and calcining it can be so purified as to be a very pure form of silica, SiO_2 (terra silicea purificata). **silicious e.** See *infusorial e.*

earwax (ēr′waks). Cerumen.

E.B. Abbreviation for *elementary body.*

Ebbinghaus test (eb′ing-hows) [Hermann *Ebbinghaus,* psychologist in Halle, 1850–1909]. See under *tests.*

Eberth's lines (ā′berts) [Karl Joseph *Eberth,* pathologist in Halle, 1835–1926]. See under *line.*

Eberthella (e″ber-thel′ah) [K. J. *Eberth*]. A former genus name applied to bacteria now included in the genus *Salmonella.*

eberthian (e-ber′the-an). Pertaining to or caused by the bacillus of typhoid fever.

Ebner's fibrils, glands, reticulum (eb′nerz) [Victor *Ebner,* histologist in Vienna, 1842–1925]. See under the nouns.

ebonation (e″bo-na′shun) [L. *e* out + *bone*]. The removal of fragments of bone after injury.

ébranlement (a-brahnl-maw′) [Fr.]. Removal of a polypus by revolving the tumor on its base.

ebrietas (e-bri′ĕ-tas) [L.]. Drunkenness; alcoholic intoxication.

ebriety (e-bri′ĕ-te). Drunkenness.

Ebstein's diet, disease, treatment, etc. (eb′stīnz) [Wilhelm *Ebstein,* physician in Göttingen, 1836–1912]. See under the nouns.

ebullition (eb-u-lish′un) [L. *ebullire* to boil]. 1. The process or condition of boiling. 2. The motion of a boiling liquid.

ebur (e′bur) [L.]. Ivory. **e. den′tis,** dentin.

eburnation (e″bur-na′shun) [L. *ebur* ivory]. The conversion of a bone into an ivory-like mass. In dentistry, a condition of exposed dentin which is hard, and yellow, brown or black in color, with a polished look.

eburneous (e-bur′ne-us). Resembling ivory.

eburnitis (e″bur-ni′tis) [L. *eburnus* of ivory + *-itis*]. Increased hardness and density of the tooth enamel.

écarteur (a-kar-ter′) [Fr.]. A retractor.

ecaudate (e-kaw′dāt) [L. *e* without + *cauda* tail]. Without a tail.

Ecballium (ek-bal′e-um) [Gr. *ekballein* to cast out]. A genus of cucurbitaceous plants. *E. elaterium* affords the drug elaterium.

ecbolic (ek-bol′ik) [Gr. *ekbolikos* throwing out]. Oxytocic.

eccentric (ek-sen′trik). 1. Situated or occurring away from a center. 2. Proceeding from a center.

eccentrochondroplasia (ek-sen″tro-kon″dro-pla′se-ah). Eccentro-osteochondrodysplasia.

eccentro-osteochondrodysplasia (ek-sen″tro-os″te-o-kon″dro-dis-pla′se-ah) [Gr. *ekkentros* from the center + *osteon* bone + *chondros* cartilage + *dys-* + *plassein* to form]. A peculiar type of ossification in which there are multiple discrete centers of ossification instead of a single center. It is apparently a familial condition marked by dwarfing and bodily deformities.

eccentropiesis (ek-sen″tro-pi-e′sis) [Gr. *ekkentros* from the center + *piesis* pressure]. Pressure from within outward.

eccephalosis (ek″sef-ah-lo′sis) [Gr. *ek* out + *kephalē* head]. Craniotomy.

ecchondroma (ek″kon-dro′mah) [Gr. *ek* out + *chondros* cartilage + *-oma*]. A hyperplastic growth of cartilage tissue developing on the surface of a cartilage or projecting under the periosteum of a bone. Called also *ecchondrosis.*

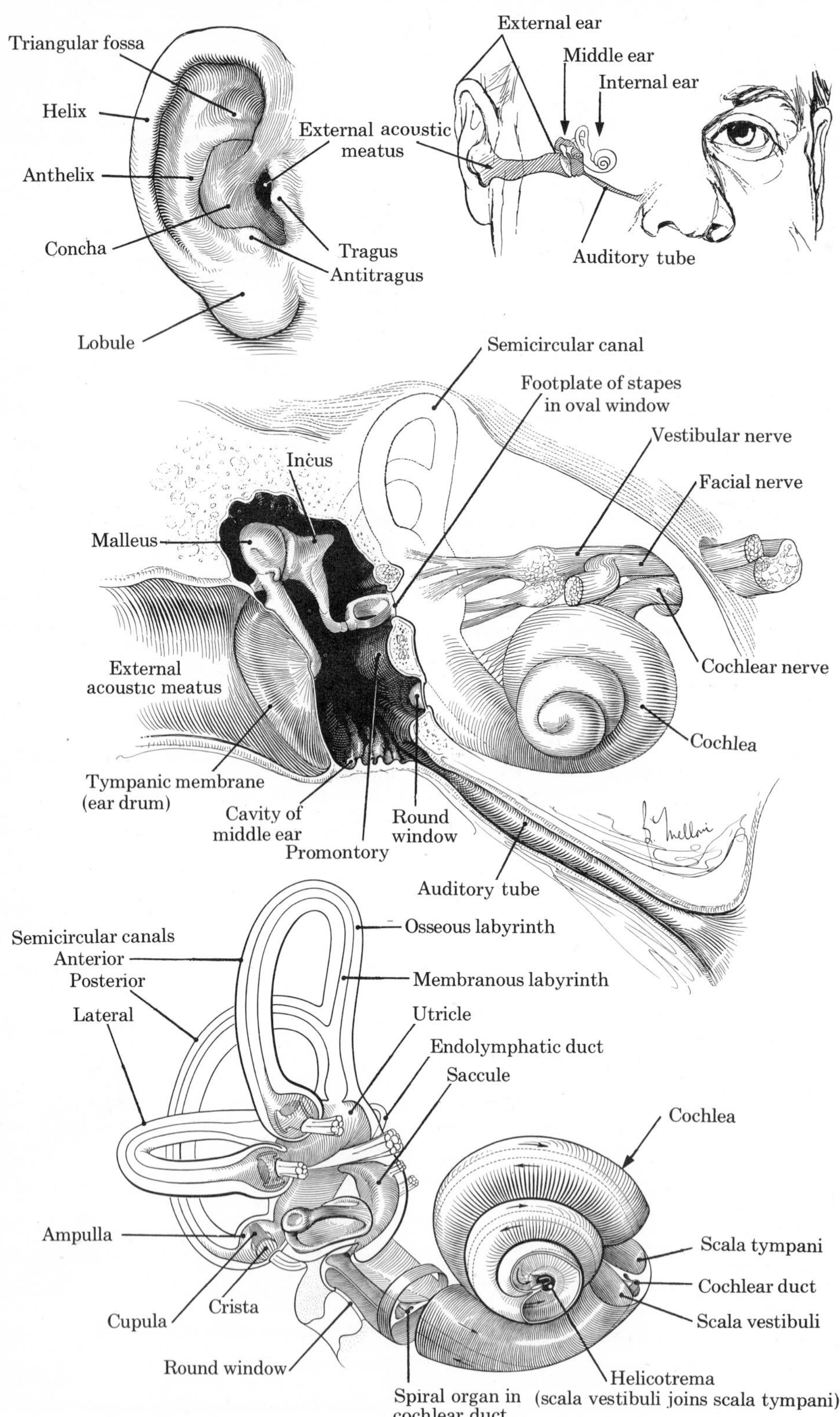

EXTERNAL AND INTERNAL STRUCTURES OF EAR

ecchondrosis (ek″kon-dro′sis). Ecchondroma.

ecchondrotome (ek-kon′dro-tōm) [Gr. *ek* out + *chondros* cartilage + *tomē* cut]. A knife for excising cartilaginous tissue.

ecchordosis physaliphora (ek″kor-do′sis fis″-ah-lif′o-rah). Jelly-like notochordal projections from the middle of the clivus blumenbachii into the interior of the cranium. Cf. *chordoma.*

ecchymoma (ek-ĭ-mo′mah). A swelling due to a bruise and formed by subcutaneous extravasation of blood.

ecchymosed (ek′ĭ-mōsd). Characterized by ecchymosis.

ecchymoses (ek″ĭ-mo′sēz). Plural of *ecchymosis.*

ecchymosis (ek″ĭ-mo′sis), pl. *ecchymo′ses* [Gr. *ekchymōsis*]. An extravasation of blood under the skin. **cadaveric e's,** stains seen on the more dependent portions of the body after death, giving the appearance of bruises.

ecchymotic (ek-ĭ-mot′ik). Pertaining to or of the nature of an ecchymosis.

Eccles (ek′k'lz), John Carew. Australian physiologist, born 1903; co-winner, with Alan Lloyd Hodgkin and Andrew Fielding Huxley, of the Nobel prize in medicine and physiology for 1963, for discoveries concerning the ionic mechanisms involved in excitation and inhibition in the peripheral and central portions of the nerve cell membrane.

eccoprotic (ek″o-prot′ik) [Gr. *ek* out + *kopros* dung]. Cathartic.

eccrine (ek′rin). Exocrine.

eccrinology (ek-rĭ-nol′o-je) [Gr. *ekkrinein* to secrete + *-logy*]. The study or science of secretions and excretions.

eccrisiology (ek-kris″e-ol′o-je). Eccrinology.

eccrisis (ek′rĭ-sis) [Gr. *ek* out + *krisis* separation]. The excretion or expulsion of waste products.

eccritic (ek-krit′ik) [Gr. *ekkritikos*]. 1. Promoting excretion. 2. An agent that promotes excretion.

eccyclomastoma (ek-si″klo-mas-to′mah) [Gr. *ek* out + *kyklos* circle + *mastos* breast + *-oma*]. A breast lesion which is a localized area of cyclomastopathy giving rise to a palpable mass.

eccyclomastopathy (ek-si″klo-mas-top′ah-the). Eccyclomastoma.

eccyesis (ek″si-e′sis) [Gr. *ek* out + *kyēsis* pregnancy]. Extra-uterine pregnancy.

ecdemic (ek-dem′ik) [Gr. *ekdēmos* gone on a journey]. Not endemic; applied to a disease caused by a factor originating far from the place in which the disease is observed.

ecdemomania (ek″de-mo-ma′ne-ah) [Gr. *ekdēmos* away from home + *mania* madness]. An insane desire to wander away from home.

ecdemonosus (ek″de-mon′o-sus) [Gr. *ekdēmos* away from home + *nosos* illness]. Ecdemomania.

ecderon (ek′der-on) [Gr. *ek* out + *deros* skin]. The outer layer of the skin and the mucous membrane.

ecdysiasm (ek-di′sĭ-azm) [Gr. *ekdyein* to strip off]. An abnormal tendency to take off one's clothes.

ecdysis (ek′dĭ-sis) [Gr. *ekdysis* a way out]. Desquamation or sloughing; especially the shedding of an outer covering and the development of a new one such as occurs in certain arthropods, crustaceans and snakes. Also called *molting.*

ECG. Abbreviation for *electrocardiogram.*

echeosis (ek″e-o′sis) [Gr. *ēchē* loud sound]. A neurosis produced by continuous loud or harassing noises.

echidnase (e-kid′nās) [Gr. *echidna* viper + *-ase*]. A phlogogenic ferment found in the venom of vipers.

echidnin (e-kid′nin) [Gr. *echidna* viper]. Serpent poison, or a nitrogenous poisonous principle from serpent poisoning.

Echidnophaga (ek″id-nof′ah-gah). A genus of fleas. **E. gallina′cea,** the sticktight flea. It collects in dense masses on the heads of chickens, in the ears of other animals, and on man.

echidnotoxin (e-kid″no-tok′sin). A poisonous principle existing in the venom of vipers.

echidnovaccine (e-kid″no-vak′sēn) [Gr. *echidna* viper + *vaccine*]. Viper venom that has been deprived of its poisonous power by heating. It is used as a vaccine against venom.

Echinacea (ek″ĭ-na′se-ah) [Gr. *echinos* hedgehog]. A genus of composite plants. *E. angustifo′lia* and *E. purpu′rea* have tonic properties.

echinate (ek′ĭ-nāt). Echinulate.

echinenone (e-kin′ĕ-nōn). A carotenoid provitamin which is prepared from the sex glands of sea urchins and which in the body becomes vitamin A.

echino- (e-ki′no) [Gr. *echinos* a prickly husk; hedgehog]. Combining form denoting relationship to spines, or spiny.

echinochrome (e-ki′no-krōm). A brown respiratory pigment found in sea urchins. **e. A.,** a naphthoquinone, $C_2H_5.C_{10}HO_2(OH)_5$, from *Arbacia,* which helps to bring egg and sperm together in reproduction.

echinococciasis (e-ki″no-kok-ki′ah-sis). Echinococcosis.

echinococcosis (e-ki″no-kok-ko′sis). A morbid condition produced by infection with the larval form of *Echinococcus granulosus.* See *hydatid disease.*

echinococcotomy (e-ki″no-kok-kot′o-me) [*echinococcus* + Gr. *tomē* a cut]. Excision or evacuation of an echinococcus cyst.

Echinococcus (e-ki″no-kok′us) [*echino-* + Gr. *kokkos* berry]. A genus of tapeworms. **E. granulo′sus,** a small tapeworm parasitic in dogs and wolves and occasionally in cats. Its larva, known as the hydatid, may develop in nearly all mammals, forming hydatid tumors or cysts in the liver, lungs, kidneys, and other organs.

echinoderm (e-kin′o-derm). One of the Echinodermata.

Echinodermata (e-ki″no-der′mah-tah) [*echino-* + Gr. *derma* skin]. A phylum of the animal kingdom, including starfishes, sea urchins, etc.

echinophthalmia (e-kin″of-thal′me-ah) [*echino-* + *ophthalmia*]. Inflammation of the eyelids marked by projection of the lashes.

Echinorhynchus (e-ki″no-ring′kus) [*echino-* + Gr. *rhynchos* beak]. A genus of parasitic worms occasionally found in man. **E. gi′gas,** *Gigantorhynchus gigas.* **E. hom′inis,** a species once found in a boy. **E. monilifor′mis** is parasitic in rats and mice.

echinosis (ek″ĭ-no′sis) [Gr. *echinos* hedgehog + *-osis*]. Irregularity in the form of an erythrocyte, giving it a spiny appearance. Cf. *crenation.*

Echinostoma (ek″ĭ-nos′to-mah) [*echino-* + Gr. *stoma* mouth]. A genus of parasitic flukes. *E. echina′tum* is found in the intestines of ducks and geese and occasionally in man in the Philippine Islands. *E. iloca′num* has been found in the feces of natives of Java and the Philippine Islands. *E. lindoen′sis* occurs in Celebes; *E. perfobia′tus* in Japan. *E. revolu′tum* occurs in the rectum and cecum of aquatic birds in Formosa.

echinostomiasis (e-kin″o-sto-mi′ah-sis). Infection by flukes of the genus *Echinostoma.*

echinulate (e-kin′u-lāt) [L. *echinus* hedgehog]. Having small prickles or spines; applied in bacteriology to cultures showing toothed or pointed outgrowths.

Echis (e′kis). A genus of small poisonous vipers of India.

echitamine (e-kit′ah-min). Ditaine.

echo (ek′o) [Gr. *ēchō* a returned sound]. Repetition of a sound; sometimes used also to refer to repetition of movement. **amphoric e.,** a resonant repetition of a sound heard on auscultation of the chest, occurring at an appreciable interval after the vocal sound. **metallic e.,** a peculiar ringing repetition of the heart sounds sometimes heard in patients with pneumopericardium and pneumothorax.

echo-acousia (ek″o-ah-koo′ze-ah) [*echo* + Gr. *akousis* hearing + *-ia*]. The subjective experience of hearing echoes after normally heard sounds.

echographia (ek-o-gra′fe-ah) [*echo* + Gr. *graphein* to write + *-ia*]. An aphasic condition in which the patient can copy writing, but cannot write to express ideas.

echokinesis (ek″o-ki-ne′sis) [*echo* + Gr. *kinesis* motion]. The spasmodic and involuntary imitation of movements seen.

echolalia (ek″o-la′le-ah) [*echo* + Gr. *lalia* speech, babble]. The meaningless repetition by a patient of words addressed to him.

echolalus (ek″o-la′lus), pl. *echola′li* [L.]. A person who in a hypnotized state repeats meaninglessly the words he hears.

echomimia (ek″o-mim′e-ah) [*echo* + Gr. *mimia* imitation]. The purposeless repetition of the words of others.

echomotism (ek″o-mo′tizm) [*echo* + L. *motio* movement]. A condition characterized by the purposeless repetition of the movements of others.

echopathy (ek-op′ah-the) [*echo* + Gr. *pathos* disease]. A neurosis marked by the senseless repetition of words or actions.

echophony (ek-of′o-ne) [*echo* + Gr. *phōne* voice]. An echo-like sound heard immediately after a vocal sound on auscultation of the chest.

echophotony (ek″o-fot′o-ne) [*echo* + Gr. *phōs* light + *tonos* tone]. The association of certain colors with certain sounds.

echophrasia (ek″o-fra′se-ah). Echolalia.

echopraxia (ek″o-prak′se-ah). Echopraxis.

echopraxis (ek″o-prak′sis) [*echo* + Gr. *prassein* to perform]. 1. The meaningless and purposeless repetition, on the part of a patient, of motions which have been started by the examining physicians. 2. Echomotism.

echothiophate (ek″o-thi′o-fāt). Chemical name: O,O-diethyl-S-(2-dimethylaminoethyl) phosphorothiolate: used as a cholinesterase inhibitor, and to reduce intraocular pressure in glaucoma.

Eck's fistula (eks) [Nicolai Vladimirovich *Eck*, Russian physiologist, 1847–1908]. See under *fistula.*

Ecker's convolution, fissure (ek′erz) [Alexander *Ecker*, German anatomist, 1816–1887]. See under *convolution* and *fissure.*

Ecker's fluid (ek′erz) [Enrique E. *Ecker*, American bacteriologist, born 1859]. A diluting fluid for counting blood platelets.

eclabium (ek-la′be-um) [Gr. *ek* out + L. *labium* lip]. Eversion of the lips or of a lip.

eclampsia (ek-lamp′se-ah) [Gr. *eklampein* to shine forth]. Convulsions and coma, rarely coma alone, occurring in a pregnant or puerperal woman, associated with hypertension, edema, or proteinuria.

eclampsism (ek-lamp′sizm). Bar's term for puerperal eclampsia without convulsive seizures, but with other signs of intoxication.

eclamptic (ek-lamp′tik). Pertaining to or of the nature of eclampsia.

eclamptism (ek-lamp′tizm). The condition due to the autointoxication incident to pregnancy, and marked by headache, visual impairment, and sometimes by convulsions.

eclamptogenic (ek-lamp″to-jen′ik). Causing convulsions.

Eclec. Abbreviation for *eclectic.*

eclectic (ek-lek′tik) [Gr. *eklektikos* selecting]. Designating a sect or school which professes to select what is best from all other systems of medicine. See *eclecticism.*

eclecticism (ek-lek′tĭ-sizm) [Gr. *eklegein* to pick out]. A system of medicine which treats diseases by the application of single remedies to known pathologic conditions, without reference to nosology, special attention being given to developing indigenous plant remedies.

eclysis (ek′lĭ-sis). Mild syncope.

ecmnesia (ek-mne′ze-ah) [Gr. *ek* out of + *mnēmē* memory]. Forgetfulness of recent events with normal memory for more remote ones.

ecochleation (e-kok″le-a′shun). 1. Excision of the cochlea. 2. Enucleation.

ecoid (e′koid). The colorless framework of a red blood corpuscle.

ecolid (e′ko-lid). Trade mark for a preparation of chlorisondamine.

ecologist (e-kol′o-jist). An individual skilled in ecology.

ecology (e-kol′o-je) [Gr. *oikos* house + *-logy*]. The science of organisms as affected by the factors of their environments; study of the environment and life history of organisms.

ecomania (e″ko-ma′ne-ah) [Gr. *oikos* house + *mania* madness]. An attitude of mind that is dominating toward members of the family but humble toward those in authority.

Economo's disease (a-kon′o-mōz) [Constantin von *Economo*, Austrian neurologist, 1876–1931]. Encephalitis lethargica.

economy (e-kon′o-me) [Gr. *oikos* house + *nomos* law]. The management of domestic affairs. **animal e.,** the system of operation of the bodily processes in organic bodies; also the body as an organized whole.

ecoparasite (e″ko-par′ah-sīt). Ecosite.

ecophobia (e″ko-fo′be-ah). Oikophobia.

écorché (a″kor-sha′) [Fr.]. The figure of a man or animal, in painting or sculpturing, exhibited as deprived of its skin, so that the muscles are exposed for study.

ecosite (e′ko-sīt) [Gr. *oikos* house + *sitos* food]. A stationary parasite to which the host is immune.

ecostate (e-kos′tāt) [L. *e* without + *costa* rib]. Ribless; without ribs.

ecosystem (ek″o-sis′tem). The basic fundamental unit in ecology, comprising the living organisms and the non-living elements interacting in a certain defined area.

écouvillon (a-koo″ve-yaw′) [Fr.]. A stiff brush or swab used for swabbing out cavities and sores.

écouvillonage (a-koo″ve-yŏ-nahzh′) [Fr.]. The scrubbing of a cavity or a sore.

ecphoria (ek-fo′re-ah) [Gr. *ekphoros* to be made known + *-ia*]. The revival of an engram or memory trace.

ecphorize (ek′fo-riz). To revive an engram or memory trace and bring it into the consciousness.

ecphory (ek′fo-re). Ecphoria.

ecphyadectomy (ek″fi-ah-dek′to-me) [Gr. *ekphyas* appendix + *ektomē* excision]. Appendectomy.

ecphyaditis (ek″fi-ah-di′tis) [Gr. *ekphyas* appendix + *-itis*]. Inflammation of the vermiform appendix.

ecphylactic (ek″fi-lak′tik). Pertaining to or marked by ecphylaxis.

ecphylaxis (ek″fi-lak′sis) [Gr. *ek* out of + *phylaxis* a guarding]. A condition of impotency of the antibodies or phylactic agents in the blood.

ecphyma (ek-fi′mah), pl. *ecphy′mata* [Gr. *ek* out + *phyma* growth]. An outgrowth or protuberance. **e. glob′ulus,** a contagious disease of Ireland, characterized by the formation on the skin of tubercles which soften, forming red swellings.

écrasement (a-krahz-maw′) [Fr.]. Removal by means of the écraseur.

écraseur (a-krah-zer′) [Fr. "crusher"]. An instrument containing a chain or cord to be looped about a part and then tightened so as to divide the inclosed part.

ecsomatics (ek″so-mat′iks) [Gr. *ek* out + *sōma* body]. The study by laboratory methods of the materials removed from the body.

ecstasy (ek′stah-se) [Gr. *ekstasis*]. A kind of trance or state of fixed contemplation with mental exaltation, partial abeyance of most of the functions, and rapt expression of countenance.

ecstatic (ek-stat′ik). Pertaining to or characterized by ecstasy.

ecstrophy (ek′stro-fe) [Gr. *ekstrephein* to turn inside out]. Exstrophy.

E.C.T. Abbreviation for *electric convulsive therapy.* See *shock therapy* under *therapy.*

ectacolia (ek″tah-ko′le-ah). Ectasia of a portion of the colon.

ectad (ek′tad) [Gr. *ektos* without]. Outward; the reverse of inward.

ectal (ek′tal) [Gr. *ektos* without]. Superficial or external.

ectasia (ek-ta′ze-ah) [Gr. *ektasis* + *-ia*]. Dilatation, expansion, or distention. **alveolar e.,** vesicular emphysema. **diffuse arterial e.,** cirsoid aneurysm. **hypostatic e.,** dilatation of a blood vessel from the effect of gravity on the blood. **e. i′ridis,** a condition in which the iris is displaced, causing smallness of the pupil. **mammary duct e.,** a condition characterized chiefly by dilatation of the collecting ducts of the mammary gland, inspissation of breast secretion, intraductal inflammation, and marked periductal and interstitial chronic inflammatory reaction in which plasma cells are prominent. **papillary e.,** a circumscribed dilatation of the capillaries, forming a red spot on the skin. **skyrocket capillary e′s,** spider bursts.

ectasin (ek′tah-sin) [Gr. *ektasis* extension]. A substance derivable from tuberculin and having the properties of a vasomotor dilator.

ectasis (ek′tah-sis). Ectasia.

ectasy (ek′tah-se). Ectasia.

ectatic (ek-tat′ik). Distended or stretched; distensible.

ectental (ek-ten′tal) [Gr. *ektos* without + *entos* within]. Pertaining to the ectoderm and entoderm, and to their line of junction.

ecterograph (ek′ter-o-graf) [Gr. *ektos* outside + *graphein* to write]. An apparatus for recording graphically the movements of the intestines.

ectethmoid (ek-teth′moid) [Gr. *ektos* without + *ethmoid*]. One of the paired lateral masses of the ethmoid bone.

ecthyma (ek-thi′mah) [Gr. *ekthyma*]. A pustular eruption, usually seated on a hardened base, and encircled by an inflammatory area. The pustules discharge, leaving spots of pigmented cicatrization. **e. contagio′sum,** sheep pox which sometimes infests human beings. **e. gangreno′sum,** dermatitis gangrenosa infantum. **e. syphilit′icum,** an ecthymiform eruption in tertiary syphilis. **tropical e.,** dermatitis cupoliformis.

ecthymiform (ek-thi′mĭ-form). Resembling ecthyma.

ecthyreosis (ek-thi″re-o′sis) [Gr. *ek* out + *thyroid*]. Absence of the thyroid gland or loss of the function of the gland.

ectiris (ek-ti′ris) [Gr. *ektos* without + *iris*]. The external layer of the iris.

ecto- [Gr. *ektos* outside]. A prefix denoting situated on, without, or on the outside.

ecto-antigen (ek″to-an′te-jen). An antigen which seems to be loosely attached to the outside of bacteria so that it can be readily removed by shaking them in physiologic sodium chloride solution; also an antigen formed in the ectoplasm of a bacterium. Cf. *immunogen.*

ectoblast (ek′to-blast) [*ecto-* + Gr. *blastos* germ]. 1. The ectoderm. 2. An external membrane; a cell wall.

ectocardia (ek-to-kar′de-ah) [*ecto-* + Gr. *kardia* heart]. Congenital displacement of the heart, either inside or outside the thorax.

ectochoroidea (ek″to-ko-roid′e-ah) [*ecto-* + Gr. *chorioeidēs* choroid]. The outer layer of the choroid coat of the eye.

ectocinerea (ek″to-sĭ-ne′re-ah) [*ecto-* + *cinerea*]. The cortical gray matter of the brain.

ectocinereal (ek″to-sĭ-ne′re-al). Relating to the ectocinerea.

ectocolon (ek″to-ko′lon) [Gr. *ektasis* dilatation + *kolon* colon]. Dilatation of the colon.

ectocolostomy (ek″to-ko-los′to-me) [*ecto-* + *colostomy*]. The surgical formation of an opening into the colon through the abdominal wall.

ectocondyle (ek″to-kon′dil). The external condyle of a bone.

ectocornea (ek″to-kor′ne-ah) [*ecto-* + *cornea*]. The outer layer of the cornea.

ectocyst (ek′to-sist). The exterior coat of a dermoid cyst.

ectocytic (ek″to-si′tik) [*ecto-* + Gr. *kytos* hollow vessel]. Outside the cell.

ectoderm (ek′to-derm) [*ecto-* + Gr. *derma* skin]. The outermost of the three primary germ layers of the embryo. From it are developed the epidermis and the epidermal tissues, such as the nails, hair, and glands of the skin, the nervous system, the external sense organs, as the ear, eye, etc., and the mucous membrane of the mouth and anus. Cf. *entoderm* and *mesoderm.* **amniotic e.,** the inner layer of the amnion (and covering of the umbilical cord) that is continuous with body ectoderm. **basal e.,** trophoblast covering the eroded uterine tissue that faces the placental sinuses. **blastodermic e.,** the external layer of a blastula or blastodisk. **chorionic e.,** the trophoblast. **neural e.,** the region of the ectoderm destined to become the neural tube. **primitive e.,** blastodermic e.

ectodermal (ek″to-der′mal) [*ecto-* + Gr. *derma* skin]. Pertaining to or derived from the ectoderm.

ectodermatosis (ek″to-der″mah-to′sis). Ectodermosis.

ectodermic (ek″to-der′mik). Ectodermal.

ectodermoidal (ek″to-der-moid′al). Of the nature of or resembling the ectoderm.

ectodermosis (ek″to-der-mo′sis). A disorder based on congenital maldevelopment of the organs of ectodermal derivation, i.e., nervous system, retina, eyeball, and skin. **e. ero′siva pluriorificia′lis,** a form of erythema multiforme with fever and erosive lesions of the mucosa of the mouth, anus, penis, etc. Called also *dermatostomatitis.*

ecto-entad (ek″to-en′tad). From without inward.

ecto-enzyme (ek″to-en′zīm). An enzyme which is secreted from a cell into the surrounding medium; an extracellular enzyme. Cf. *endoenzyme.*

ectogenic (ek″to-jen′ik). Ectogenous.

ectogenous (ek-toj′e-nus) [*ecto-* + Gr. *gennan* to produce]. Introduced from without; arising from causes outside the organism.

ectoglia (ek-tog′le-ah) [*ecto-* + Gr. *glia* glue]. The thin, external marginal layer of the early medullary tube of the embryo.

ectoglobular (ek″to-glob′u-lar) [*ecto-* + *globule*]. Formed outside the blood cells.

ectogony (ek-tog′o-ne). The influence exerted on the mother by the developing embryo.

ectokelostomy (ek″to-ke-los′to-me) [*ecto-* + Gr. *kēlē* hernia + *stoma* mouth]. Operation of displacing a hernial sac through the abdominal wall and keeping it open with drainage, followed by operation for radical cure.

ectolecithal (ek″to-les′ĭ-thal) [*ecto-* + Gr. *lekithos* yolk]. Having the yolk situated peripherally.

ectoloph (ek′to-lof). The external ridge on an upper molar tooth of the horse.

ectolysis (ek-tol′ĭ-sis) [*ecto*plasm + *lysis*]. Lysis of the ectoplasm.

ectomere (ek′to-mēr) [*ecto-* + Gr. *meros* part]. Any one of the blastomeres which share in the formation of the ectoderm.

ectomesoblast (ek″to-mes′o-blast). The layer of cells which has not yet become differentiated into ectoblast and mesoblast.

-ectomize (ek′to-mīz) [Gr. *ektomē* excision + *-izein* to render]. Word termination denoting deprivation by excision, as in *thyroidectomize,* *adrenalectomize,* etc. By extension used in terms to designate destruction or deprivation by other methods as well.

ectomorph (ek′to-morf). An individual exhibiting ectomorphy.

ectomorphic (ek″to-mor′fik). Pertaining to or characterized by ectomorphy.

ectomorphy (ek′to-mor″fe) [*ecto*blast + Gr. *morphē* form]. A type of body build in which tissues derived from the ectoderm predominate. There is relative preponderance of linearity and fragility, with large surface area and thin muscles and subcutaneous tissue.

ectomy (ek′to-me) [Gr. *ektomē*]. Excision of an organ or part. Used as a word termination to indicate excision of the structure or organ designated by the root to which it is affixed, as *appendectomy, tonsillectomy,* etc. By extension used in terms to designate destruction or deprivation by other methods as well.

ectonuclear (ek″to-nu′kle-ar). Outside the nucleus of a cell.

ectopagus (ek-top′ah-gus) [*ecto-* + Gr. *pagos* something fixed]. A double monster connected along the side of the body, so that the components are definitely right and left, the inner arms and/or legs being represented by a bilateral median limb.

ectoparasite (ek″to-par′ah-sīt) [*ecto-* + *parasite*]. A parasite which lives on the outside of the body of the host.

ectopectoralis (ek″to-pek″to-ra′lis). Musculus pectoralis major.

ectoperitoneal (ek″to-per″ĭ-to-ne′al). Relating to the external or abdominal surface of the peritoneum.

ectoperitonitis (ek″to-per″ĭ-to-ni′tis) [*ecto-* + *peritonitis*]. Inflammation of the external or abdominal side of the peritoneum.

ectophylaxination (ek″to-fi-lak″sĭ-na′shun). The process of rendering immune by the transference to the animal of a prophylactic substance which has been developed in some other animal.

ectophyte (ek′to-fīt) [*ecto-* + Gr. *phyton* plant]. A vegetable parasite or species living on the outside of the body of its host.

ectopia (ek-to′pe-ah) [Gr. *ektopos* displaced + *-ia*]. Displacement or malposition, especially if congenital. **e. cor′dis,** displacement of the heart outside the thoracic cavity. **e. cor′dis, pectoral,** location of the heart outside the chest wall, through a fissure in the lower sternum. **e. cor′dis abdomina′lis,** location of the heart in the abdominal cavity. **e. len′tis,** displacement of the crystalline lens of the eye. **e. pupil′lae congen′ita,** congenital displacement of the pupil. **e. tes′tis,** dislocation of the testicle. **e. vesi′cae,** exstrophy of the bladder.

ectopic (ek-top′ik). 1. Pertaining to or characterized by ectopia. 2. Located away from normal position.

ectopism (ek′to-pizm). Anatopism.

ectoplacenta (ek-to-plah-sen′tah) [*ecto-* + Gr. *placenta* cake]. The actively growing trophoblast that becomes the placenta in rodents.

ectoplasm (ek′to-plazm) [*ecto-* + Gr. *plasma* a thing formed]. The outer, stiffer portion or region of the cytoplasm of a cell which may be differentiated in texture from the inner portion or endoplasm. Called also *exoplasm, ectoplast,* and *plasma membrane.*

ectoplasmatic (ek″to-plaz-mat′ik). Pertaining to ectoplasm; outside of the cell plasma.

ectoplast (ek′to-plast). Ectoplasm.

ectoplastic (ek″to-plas′tik) [*ecto-* + Gr. *plassein* to shape]. Having a formative power on the surface, as, *ectoplastic* cells.

ectopotomy (ek″to-pot′o-me) [Gr. *ektopos* displaced + Gr. *tomē* cut]. Excision of the fetus in extra-uterine pregnancy.

ectopterygoid (ek″to-ter′ĭ-goid). Musculus pterygoideus lateralis.

ectopy (ek′to-pe). Ectopia.

ectoretina (ek″to-ret′ĭ-nah) [*ecto-* + *retina*]. The outermost layer of the retina.

ectosarc (ek′to-sark) [*ecto-* + Gr. *sarx* flesh]. The outer layer of *Amoebae* and *Gregarinidia.*

ectoscopy (ek-tos′ko-pe) [*ecto-* + Gr. *skopein* to examine]. Visual determination of the outlines of the lungs and of localized internal conditions.

ectosite (ek′to-sīt). Ectoparasite.

ectoskeleton (ek″to-skel′ĕ-ton). Exoskeleton.

ectosphere (ek′to-sfēr). The outer zone of the centrosome.

ectosteal (ek-tos′te-al). Pertaining to or situated on the outside of a bone.

ectostosis (ek-tos-to′sis) [*ecto-* + Gr. *osteon* bone]. Ossification beneath the perichondrium.

ectosuggestion (ek″to-sug-jes′chun). A suggestion originating from outside. Cf. *autosuggestion.*

ectothrix (ek′to-thriks) [*ecto-* + Gr. *thrix* hair]. A fungus which grows inside the hair shaft but also produces a sheath of arthrospores on the outside of the hair. Such fungi include *Trichophyton verrucosum* (*large-spored e.*) and *T. mentagrophytes, Microsporum audouinii, M. canis,* and *M. gypseum* (*small-spored e's*).

ectotoxemia (ek″to-tok-se′me-ah) [*ecto-* + *toxemia*]. Toxemia produced by a substance introduced from outside the body.

ectotoxic (ek″to-tok′sik). Pertaining to exotoxin.

ectotoxin (ek″to-tok′sin). Exotoxin.

Ectotrichophyton (ek″to-tri-kof′ĭ-ton) [*ecto-* + Gr. *thrix* hair + *phyton* plant]. A genus of fungi which attack the surface of the hair shaft. Many species have been isolated from various lesions in man.

ectozoa (ek″to-zo′ah). Plural of *ectozoon.*

ectozoal (ek″to-zo′al). Pertaining to or caused by ectozoa.

ectozoon (ek″to-zo′on), pl. *ectozo′a* [*ecto-* + Gr. *zōon* animal]. An animal parasite or species living on the outside of the body of its host.

ectrimma (ek-trim′ah) [Gr. *ektrimma*]. An ulcer caused by friction.

ectrodactylia (ek″tro-dak-til′e-ah). Ectrodactyly.

ectrodactylism (ek″tro-dak′tĭ-lism). Ectrodactyly.

ectrodactyly (ek″tro-dak′tĭ-le) [Gr. *ektrōma* abortion + *daktylos* finger]. Congenital absence of all or of only part of a digit (*partial e.*).

ectrogenic (ek″tro-jen′ik). Pertaining to or characterized by ectrogeny.

ectrogeny (ek-troj′e-ne) [Gr. *ektrōma* abortion + *gennan* to produce]. Congenital absence or defect of a part.

ectromelia (ek″tro-me′le-ah). Gross hypoplasia or aplasia of one or more long bones of one or more limbs. The term includes amelia, hemimelia, and phocomelia. **infectious e.,** a virus disease in mice characterized by gangrene and often loss of one or more of the feet and sometimes of other external parts, and by necrotic areas in the liver, spleen, and other organs; also called mouse pox.

ectromelic (ek″tro-mel′ik). Pertaining to or characterized by ectromelia.

ectromelus (ek-trom′ĕ-lus) [Gr. *ektrōma* abortion + *melos* limb]. An individual exhibiting ectromelia.

ectrometacarpia (ek″tro-met″ah-kar′pe-ah) [Gr. *ektrōma* abortion + *metacarpus* + *-ia*]. Congenital absence of a metacarpal bone.

ectrometatarsia (ek″tro-met″ah-tar′se-ah) [Gr. *ektrōma* abortion + *metatarsus* + *-ia*]. Congenital absence of a metatarsal bone.

ectrophalangia (ek″tro-fah-lan′je-ah). Congenital absence of one or more phalanges of a digit.

ectropion (ek-tro′pe-on) [Gr. "an everted eyelid"; *ektropē* a turning aside]. The turning outward (eversion) of an edge or margin, as of the eyelid, resulting in exposure of the palpebral conjunctiva. **e. cicatri′ceum, cicatricial e.,** eversion of the margin of an eyelid caused by contraction of scar tissue in the lid or by contraction of the skin. **flaccid e.,** ectropion of the lower lid resulting from reduced tone of the orbicularis oculi muscle. **e. luxu'rians,** e. sarcomatosum. **paralytic e., e. paralyt'icum,** eversion of the margin of the lower eyelid as a result of paralysis of the facial nerve, and loss of contractile power of the orbicularis oculi muscle. **e. sarcomato'sum,** eversion of an eyelid resulting from chronic thickening of the palpebral conjunctiva. **senile e., e. seni'lis,** eversion of the lower eyelid associated with relaxation of the fibers of the palpebral portion of the orbicularis oculi muscle as a concomitant of age, or occurring as a result of atrophic changes in the skin. **spastic e., e. spas'ticum,** ectropion caused by tonic spasm of the orbicularis oculi muscle. **e. u'veae,** eversion of the margin of the pupil, often congenital (*e. u'veae congen'itum*), and frequently due to the presence of a newly formed membrane on the anterior layer of the iris, or to the formation of connective tissue in the stroma.

ectropionize (ek-tro'pe-on-īz). To put into a state of eversion.

ectropium (ek-tro'pe-um). Ectropion.

ectrosis (ek-tro'sis) [Gr. *ektrōsis*]. 1. Abortion. 2. Abortive treatment of disease.

ectrosyndactylia (ek″tro-sin″dak-til'e-ah). Ectrosyndactyly.

ectrosyndactyly (ek″tro-sin-dak'tĭ-le) [Gr. *ektrōma* abortion + *syn* together + *daktylos* finger]. A condition in which some of the digits are missing and those that remain are cohesive.

ectrotic (ek-trot'ik). 1. Pertaining to or producing abortion. 2. Arresting the development of a disease.

ectylotic (ek″tĭ-lot'ik) [Gr. *ek* out + *tylos* callus]. 1. Removing warts or calluses. 2. An agent that removes warts or calluses.

ectylurea (ek″til-u-re'ah). Chemical name: 2-ethyl-cis-crotonylurea: used to produce mild depression of the central nervous system.

ectype (ek'tīp). An unusual type of physical or mental constitution.

ectypia (ek-ti'pe-ah). Deviation from type; the possession of an unusual type of constitution.

ecuresis (ek″u-re'sis) [Gr. *ek* out + *ourein* to make water]. Production of absolute dehydration of the body by excessive urinary excretion in relation to the intake of water.

eczema (ek'zĕ-mah) [Gr. *ekzein* to boil out]. An inflammatory skin disease characterized by lesions varying greatly in character, with vesiculation, infiltration, watery discharge, and the development of scales and crusts. The disease is frequently attended with restlessness and fever and other symptoms of constitutional disturbance, as well as by local itching and burning. **allergic e.,** allergic dermatitis. **e. articulo'rum,** flexural e. **atopic e.,** allergic dermatitis. **e. bar'bae,** eczema affecting the beard area of the face and neck. **e. cap'itis,** eczema of the scalp. **crackled e., e. craquelé,** a variety in which the outer epidermis shows superficial cracks. **e. crusto'sum,** a variety with thinnish yellow crusts. **e. diabetico'rum,** a form which accompanies glycosuria. **dry e.,** eczema in which the affected skin is dry and scaly. **e. ep'ilans,** eczema with loss of hair. **e. epizoot'ica,** foot-and-mouth disease. **e. erythemato'sum,** a relatively mild form of eczema with erythematous patches. **flexural e.,** eczema affecting a flexor surface, as of the elbow or knee. **e. herpet'icum,** a vesiculopustular eruption caused by herpes simplex virus superimposed upon areas of pre-existing eczema. **e. hypertroph'icum,** a disease characterized by enlargement of the skin papillae, resulting in a crop of warty outgrowths. **infantile e.,** intrinsic allergic dermatitis, common in infants and occurring especially during dentition. **e. intertri'go,** intertrigo. **lichenoid e.,** a variety characterized by thickening of the epidermis. **linear e.,** eczema with the lesions occurring in lines. **e. mad'idans,** a form, of various subvarieties, marked by hot, moist, and swollen skin. **e. margina'tum,** tinea cruris. **moist e.,** eczema with fluid exudation on the surface of the area affected. **e. neurit'icum,** any eczema appearing in patches limited to defined areas supplied by particular cutaneous nerves. **nummular e., e. nummula're,** eczema in which the patches are coin shaped. **e. papulo'sum,** a form accompanied by the formation of minute papules of firm consistence and deep red color and by severe itching. **e. parasit'icum,** eczema due to presence of a parasitic microorganism. **e. pustulo'sum,** a form marked by the formation of pustules. **e. ru'brum,** a form of eczema marked by infiltration, thickening, often with swelling and sometimes with intermittent edema and variable degrees of redness, and usually with an oozing surface. **e. scrofuloder'ma,** mycosis fungoides. **e. seborrhoe'icum,** seborrhea. **e. sic'cum,** dry e. **solar e., e. sola're,** an eczematous eruption occurring on the exposed areas of the body, due to the sunburn-producing wavelengths of sunlight, and usually occurring in the spring or summer. **e. squamo'sum,** a variety characterized by adherent scales of shed epithelium. **stasis e.,** eczema of the legs due to impeded circulation, with edema, pigmentation, and ulceration. **e. tylot'icum,** eczema of the palms and soles, with keratotic changes producing a resemblance to tylosis or callosity. **e. vaccina'tum,** a vesiculopapular eruption caused by vaccinia virus, superimposed upon areas of pre-existing eczema. **e. verruco'sum,** eczema occurring with wartlike excrescences, affecting chiefly elderly or aged persons. **e. vesiculo'sum,** eczema marked by a vesicular eruption. **weeping e.,** moist e.

eczematid (ek-zem'ah-tid). Any eczema-like lesion caused by allergy to a microorganism or its products.

eczematization (ek-zem″ah-ti-za'shun). Persistent eczema-like lesions of the skin due to continued traumatism and scratching.

eczematogenic (ek-zem″ah-to-jen'ik). Causing eczema.

eczematoid (ek-zem'ah-toid). Resembling eczema.

eczematosis (ek-zem″ah-to'sis). Any eczematous disease.

eczematous (ek-zem'ah-tus). Affected with or of the nature of eczema.

E.D. Abbreviation for *erythema dose,* or for *effective dose.*

$E.D._{50}$. Abbreviation for *median effective dose.*

Eddowes' disease, syndrome (ed'ōz) [Alfred *Eddowes,* British physician, 1850–1946]. See under *syndrome.*

Edebohls' operation, position (ed'e-bōlz) [George M. *Edebohls,* New York surgeon, 1853–1908]. See under *operation* and *position.*

Edelmann's anemia, cell (a'del-manz) [Adolf *Edelmann,* physician in Vienna, 1885–1939]. See under *anemia* and *cell.*

edema (e-de'mah) [Gr. *oidēma* swelling]. The presence of abnormally large amounts of fluid in the intercellular tissue spaces of the body; usually applied to demonstrable accumulation of excessive fluid in the subcutaneous tissues. **acute circumscribed e., acute essential e.,** angioneurotic e. **alimentary e.,** nutritional edema. **ambulant e.** See *Calabar swelling,* under *swelling.* **angioneurotic e.,** a condition characterized by the sudden appearance of temporary edematous areas of the skin or mucous membranes and occasionally of the viscera, often associated with dermographia, urticaria, erythema, and purpura, which may be of allergic, neurotic, or of unknown origin. Called also *acute circumscribed edema, Quincke's edema, wandering edema, giant urticaria, Milton's urticaria,* and *urticaria oedematosa.* **e. artefac'tum,** edema that is artificially produced. **Berlin's e.,** edema around the macular region of the retina, due to a severe blow to the eyeball. **blue e.,** a puffed, bluish appearance of a limb in hysterical paralysis. **brown e.,** hardening and infiltration of the lung with a brownish fluid. **e. bullo'sum vesi'cae,** a condition of the mucous lining of the bladder marked by the formation of clear vesicles with small white particles floating between them. **Calabar e.,** edema produced by filaria. **e. cal'idum,** inflammatory e. **cardiac e.,** edema due to heart disease with the resulting slowing of the peripheral blood flow and the rise in capillary pressure. **circumscribed e.,** angioneurotic e. **collateral e.,** edema of one part of a paired organ, as the lungs, produced by overaction on account of disease of the other part. **e. ex vac'uo,** edema of a part resulting from the vacuum caused by atrophy of some structure in the part. **famine e.,** nutritional e. **fingerprint e.,** edema in which the whorls of the fingerprint are clearly visible after circumferential manipulation of a pressure point on the forehead or sternum, considered indicative of intracellular fluid excess. **e. frig'idum,** noninflammatory e. **e. fu'gax,** edema resulting from transient accumulation of fluid in a specific region. **gaseous e.,** edema accompanied with gas formation, as in gas bacillus infection and subcutaneous emphysema. **giant e.,** angioneurotic e. **hepatic e.,** edema due to faulty functioning of the liver. **Huguenin's e.,** acute congestive edema of the brain. **hunger e.,** nutritional e. **hydremic e.,** edema in conditions marked by hydremia. **hysterical e.,** blue e. **inflammatory e.,** a form due to inflammation, and attended with redness and pain. **insulin e.,** edema which sometimes follows the injection of insulin. **invisible e.,** the accumulation of a considerable amount of fluid in the subcutaneous tissues before it becomes demonstrable. **e. of lungs,** pulmonary e. **lymphatic e.,** edema in which the effused liquid comes from the lymph vessels. **malignant e.,** edema marked by rapid extension, with destruction of tissue and formation of a gas. **migratory e.,** angioneurotic e. **Milroy's e.,** acute attacks of local edema occurring as a result of an inherited tendency. **Milton's e.,** angioneurotic e. **mucous e.,** myxedema. **mycotic e.,** the South African horse sickness; a deadly epizootic of microbic origin. **e. neonato'rum,** a disease of newborn children marked by spreading edema with cold, livid skin. **nephrotic e.,** edema occurring in nephrosis and in the intermediate stage of diffuse nephritis. **neuropathic e.,** pseudolipoma. **noninflammatory e.,** edema without redness and pain, occurring from passive congestion or a watery condition of the blood. **nonpitting e.,** edema in which the tissues cannot be pitted by pressure. **nutritional e.,** a disorder of nutrition due to long-continued diet deficiency and marked by anasarca and edema. Called also *famine e., war e., hunger e., prison e.,* and *nutritional dropsy*. **passive e.,** edema occurring because of obstruction to drainage from the area. **periretinal e.,** retinitis centralis serosa. **Pirogoff's e.,** malignant e. **pitting e.,** edema in which the tissues show prolonged existence of the pits produced by pressure. **prehepatic e.,** edema occurring in prehepatic hypoproteinemia. **pulmonary e.,** an effusion of serous fluid into the air vesicles and interstitial tissue of the lungs. **purulent e.,** a swelling due to the effusion of a purulent fluid. **Quincke's e.,** angioneurotic e. **renal e.,** edema due to nephritis and the consequent hypoproteinemia. **rheumatismal e.,** painful red edematous swellings on the limbs in rheumatism, due to subcutaneous exudation. **salt e.,** edema produced by an increase of sodium chloride in the diet. **solid e.,** myxedema. **terminal e.,** pulmonary edema which tends to hasten death. **toxic e.,** edema from the inhalation of certain gases. **venous e.,** edema in which the effused liquid comes from the blood. **vernal e. of lung,** edema of the lung occurring in spring and considered to be allergic. **wandering e.,** angioneurotic e. **war e.,** nutritional e.

edematigenous (e-dem″ah-tij′e-nus). Edematogenic.

edematin (e-dem′ah-tin). The substance composing the microsomes of a cell.

edematization (e-dem″ah-ti-za′shun). The process of becoming or of making edematous.

edematogenic (e-dem″ah-to-jen′ik). Producing or causing edema.

edematous (e-dem′ah-tus). Pertaining to or affected by edema.

Edentata (e″den-ta′tah). An order of mammals including the armadillo, sloth and anteater.

edentate (e-den′tāt). Edentulous.

edentia (e-den′she-ah) [L. *e* without + *dens* tooth]. Absence of the teeth.

edentulate (e-den′tu-lāt). Edentulous.

edentulous (e-den′tu-lus) [L. *e* without + *dens* tooth]. Without teeth; having lost the natural teeth.

edestan (e-des′tan). An insoluble form of edestin produced by an increase of the hydrogen ion concentration.

edge (ej). A thin side or border. **cutting e.,** the angle formed by the merging of two flat surfaces, by which something may be cut, such as the blade of a knife, or the incisal surface of an anterior tooth. **incisal e.,** the junction of the labial surface of an anterior tooth with a flattened linguoincisal surface created by occlusal wear.

edge-strength (ej′ strength). The resistance offered by an edge to a fracturing force, applied especially in dentistry to such resistance offered by the edge of an amalgam restoration.

Edinger's law, nucleus, etc. (ed′ing-gerz) [Ludwig *Edinger*, German neurologist, 1855–1918]. See under the nouns.

edipism (ed′ĭ-pizm) [from *Oedipus*, King of Thebes. See *Oedipus complex*]. Intentional injury of one's own eyes.

Edlefsen's reagent (ed′lef-senz) [Gustav J. J. F. *Edlefsen*, German physician, 1842–1910]. See under *reagent*.

edrophonium (ed″ro-fo′ne-um). Chemical name: dimethylethyl(3-hydroxyphenyl)ammonium: used as a curare antagonist, and as a diagnostic agent in myasthenia gravis.

Edsall's disease (ed′salz) [David Linn *Edsall*, American physician, 1869–1945]. Heat cramp.

educt (e′dukt). A substance extracted from organic matter without any alteration in its composition.

eduction (e-duk′shun) [L. *e* (*ex*) from + *ducere* to lead]. The process of leading out from or the dissipation of a former state, as the restoration to normal physiological state of an anesthetized patient.

edulcorant (e-dul′ko-rant). Sweetening.

edulcorate (e-dul′ko-rāt). To sweeten.

EEE. Abbreviation for *eastern equine encephalomyelitis.*

EEG. Abbreviation for *electroencephalogram.*

eelworm (ēl′wurm). Any roundworm, such as ascaris.

effacement (ĕ-fās′ment). The obliteration of form or features, applied to that condition of the cervix in labor when it is so changed that only the external os remains.

effect (ĕ-fekt′). The result produced by an action. **additive e.,** the summation of the effects of two or more drugs which produce the same kind of effect when such drugs are administered in combination. **anachoretic e.** See *anachoresis.* **clasp-knife e.,** a sudden complete flexion of the limb in the lengthening reaction. **Compton e.,** a change in the wavelength of scattered rays and emission of recoil electrons in deep radiation. **contrary e.,** Hata's phenomenon. **cumulative e.,** cumulative action. **Danysz e.** See under *phenomenon.* **Deelman e.,** scarification of the skin in artificial carcinogenesis tends to localize the subsequent carcinomata at the scarified area. **Hallberg e.,** the crests and troughs of ultrashort standing-wave field have opposite electrical signs. **Hallwachs e.,** photo-electrical effect. **interpolar e.,** the effect of the electric current which acts throughout the whole region of the body between the two poles, as contrasted with the polar effect. **Mierzejewski e.,** the disharmonious development of gray and white matter of the brain, the gray being in excess. **Nagler e.,** gas-filled tubes, placed in high frequency fields, will act as rectifiers, causing a unidirectional current. **Orbeli e.** See under *phenomenon.* **Pasteur e.,** diminution of fermentation by aeration. **photechic e.,** Russell e. **photoelectrical e.,** the ejection of electrons from matter when light of short wavelengths falls upon it. **polar e.,** the effect of the electric current which is manifested at one of the poles. **position e.,** in genetics, the changed effect produced by alteration of the relative positions of various genes on the chromosomes. **pressure e.,** the sum of the changes that are produced in a tissue by pressure. **Raman e.,** when a substance is irradiated with monochromatic light, the spectrum which the substance scatters contains, in addition to a line of the same wavelength as the incident radiation, lines which are satellites of the primary line moving with it when the wavelength of the primary radiation is altered. **Russell e.,** the rendering of a photographic plate developable by substances other than light. Called also *photechic effect.* **Soret e.,** when a solution is maintained for some time in a temperature gradient, the upper part being warmer than the lower, a difference in concentration between the two parts is set up. **Staub-Traugott e.,** a second dose of dextrose by mouth to a normal person one hour after a first dose does not elevate the blood sugar level. **Tyndall e.** See under *phenomenon.* **Zeeman e.,** separation of a single line in the spectrum by suitable magnetic fields.

effectiveness (ef-fek′tiv-nes). The ability to produce a specific result or to exert a specific measurable influence. **relative biological e.,** an expression of the effectiveness of other types of radiation in comparison with that of 1 r of gamma or roentgen rays.

effector (ef-fek′tor). A nerve end organ which serves to distribute impulses which activate muscle contraction and gland secretion. **somatic e.,** one of the nerve end organs in the striated skeletal muscles. **visceral e.,** one of the end organs in involuntary muscle.

effemination (ĕ-fem″ĭ-na′shun). The presence or production of feminine characteristics in the male.

efferent (ef′er-ent) [L. *ex* out + *ferre* to bear]. Centrifugal; conveying away from a center.

efferential (ef″er-en′shal). Efferent.

effervescent (ef-er-ves′ent) [L. *effervescens*]. Bubbling; sparkling; giving off gas bubbles.

efficiency (e-fish′en-se). Ability to accomplish a desired effect or to perform a certain action. **visual e.,** the ratio of the resolving power of the eye that is being tested to that of a normal eye.

effleurage (ef-loo-rahzh′) [Fr.]. Stroking movement in massage.

efflorescence (ef″lo-res′ens) [L. *efflorescentia*]. 1. The fact or state of being efflorescent. 2. A rash or eruption; any skin lesion.

efflorescent (ef″lo-res′ent) [L. *efflorescere* to bloom]. Becoming powdery in consequence of losing the water of crystallization.

effluve (ef-lo͞ov′). A conductive discharge of a high voltage current through a dielectric.

effluvium (ef-floo′ve-um), pl. *efflu′via* [L. "a flowing out"]. 1. An outflowing, or shedding, as of the hair. 2. An exhalation or emanation, applied especially to one of noxious character. **anagen e.,** abnormal loss of hair in the anagen phase, sometimes resulting from administration of cytotoxic drugs, as in chemotherapy of cancer, or from intravenous administration of colchicine. **e. capillo′rum,** falling out of the hair. **telluric e.,** an emanation arising from the earth. See *miasma* and *tellurium.* **telogen e.,** falling out of the hair resulting from the mass precipitation of telogen, caused by insult or injury of a systemic nature.

effortil (ef′for-til). Chemical name: dl-m-hydroxy-α-(ethylaminomethyl) benzyl alcohol: used as a sympathomimetic and as a pressor agent.

effraction (ef-frak′shun). A breaking open; a weakening.

effumability (ef″u-mah-bil′ĭ-te) [L. *ex* out + *fumus* smoke]. The property of being easily volatilized.

effuse [L. *effusus,* from *ex* out + *fundere* to pour]. 1. (ĕ-fūs′) Spread out, profuse: said of bacterial growth that is thin, veily, and unusually widely spread. 2. (ĕ-fūz′) To pour out and spread widely.

effusion (ĕ-fu′zhun) [L. *effusio* a pouring out]. 1. The escape of fluid into a part or tissue. 2. An effused material. **hemorrhagic e.,** an effusion of bloody fluid. **pleural e.,** the presence of fluid in the pleural space. **purulent e.,** an effusion of purulent material. **serous e.,** an effusion of serous material.

egagropilus (e″gah-grop′ĭ-lus) [Gr. *aigagros* wild goat + *pilos* felt]. Trichobezoar.

egersimeter (e″ger-sim′e-ter). An instrument for testing the electric excitability of nerves and muscles and for measuring chronaxia.

egersis (e-ger′sis) [Gr.]. Abnormal wakefulness.

egesta (e-jes′tah) [L. *e* out + *gerere* to bear]. Excreted matter; waste material thrown out from the body.

egestion (e-jes′chun). The casting out, or excretion from the body, of material which is indigestible.

egg (eg) [L. *ovum*]. An animal ovum, applied especially to an ovum that is extruded from the maternal body before development of the embryo, and sometimes before fertilization.

Eggleston's method (eg′el-stunz) [Cary *Eggleston,* American physician, born 1884]. See under *method.*

egilops (e′jĭ-lops) [Gr. *aix* goat + *ōps* eye]. Perforating abscess at the inner canthus of the eye.

eglandulous (e-gland′u-lus) [L. *e* without + *glandula* glandule]. Having no glands.

ego (e′go) [L. *ego* I]. That portion of the psyche which possesses consciousness, maintains its identity, and recognizes and tests reality.

egobronchophony (e″go-bron-kof′o-ne) [Gr. *aix* goat + *bronchophony*]. The bleating and bronchial voice characteristic of pleuropneumonia.

egocentric (e″go-sen′trik) [L. *ego* I + *centric*]. Having all one's ideas centered about one's self. Cf. *allocentric.*

egomania (e″go-ma′ne-ah) [Gr. *egō* I + *mania* madness]. Morbid self-esteem.

egophony (e-gof′o-ne) [Gr. *aix* goat + *phōnē* voice]. A bleating quality of voice observed in auscultation in certain cases of lung consolidation (Laennec).

egosyntonic (e″go-sin-ton′ik). In harmony with the ego and its standards.

egotropic (e″go-trop′ik) [Gr. *egō* I + *tropos* a turning]. Egocentric.

eH. Symbol for *oxidation-reduction potential.*

Ehlers-Danlos syndrome (a′lerz-dan′los) [Edvard *Ehlers,* Danish dermatologist, 1863–1937; Henri-Alexander *Danlos*]. Danlos syndrome.

Ehrenritter's ganglion (er′en-rit″erz) [Johann *Ehrenritter,* Austrian anatomist, died 1790]. See under *ganglion.*

Ehrlich's reaction (ār′liks) [Paul *Ehrlich,* German bacteriologist, 1854–1915; co-winner, with Elie Metchnikoff, of the Nobel prize for medicine and physiology in 1908]. See under *reaction.* **E.'s**

side-chain theory. See under *theory.* **E.'s "606,"** arsphenamine.

Ehrlich-Hata preparation [Paul *Ehrlich;* Sahachiro *Hata,* Japanese physician, 1872–1938]. Arsphenamine.

Ehrlichia (ār-lik′e-ah) [Paul *Ehrlich*]. A genus of the tribe Ehrlichieae, family Rickettsiaceae, order Rickettsiales. Three species, **E. ca′nis, E. bo′vis,** and **E. ovi′na,** produce disease in dogs, cattle, and sheep, respectively, but are nonpathogenic for man.

Ehrlichieae (ār″lĭ-ki′e-e). A tribe of the family Rickettsiaceae, order Rickettsiales, class Microtatobiotes, made up of rickettsia-like organisms adapted to existence in invertebrates, chiefly arthropods, and pathogenic for certain vertebrates, but not for man. It includes three genera, *Cowdria, Ehrlichia,* and *Neorickettsia.*

Ehrmann's alcohol test meal (ār′mahnz) [Rudolf R. *Ehrmann,* New York internist, 1879–1963]. See under *test meal.*

Eichhorst's corpuscles, neuritis (ik′horsts) [Hermann *Eichhorst,* Swiss physician, 1849–1921]. See under *corpuscle* and *neuritis.*

Eichstedt's disease (ik′stets) [Karl Ferdinand *Eichstedt,* physician in Greifswald, 1816–1892]. Pityriasis versicolor.

Eicken's method (i′kenz) [Carl von *Eicken,* German laryngologist and otologist, 1873–1960]. In examination of the hypopharynx, the cricoid cartilage is drawn forward.

eiconometer (i″ko-nom′e-ter). Eikonometer.

eidetic (i-det′ik) [Gr. *eidos* that which is seen; form or shape]. Pertaining to or characterized by exact visualization of events or of objects previously seen. By extension, sometimes used to designate an individual possessing such an ability.

eidogen (i′do-jen) [Gr. *eidos* form + *genesthai* produced]. A substance elaborated by a second grade inductor, which is capable of modifying the form of an organ already induced.

eidoptometry (i″dop-tom′e-tre) [Gr. *eidos* form + *optos* seen + *metron* measure]. Measurement of the acuteness of vision for the perception of form.

Eijkman's test (ik′manz) [Christiaan *Eijkman,* Dutch physiologist, 1858–1930; discoverer of the causative agent in beriberi, proponent of the vitamin theory, and co-winner, with F. G. Hopkins, of the Nobel prize for medicine in 1929]. See under *test.*

eikonometer (i″ko-nom′e-ter) [Gr. *eikōn* image + *metron* measure]. An instrument used in making an examination for aniseikonia.

eiloid (i′loid) [Gr. *eilein* to roll up + *eidos* form]. Having a coiled appearance.

Eimeria (i-me′re-ah) [Gustav Heinrich Theodor *Eimer,* German zoologist, 1843–1898]. A genus of the order Sporozoa in which an oocyst contains four spores and each spore two sporozoites. Various species are parasitic in the epithelial cells of man and animals, the oocysts being found in the feces. **E. a′vium,** a species found in birds. **E. ca′vae** is found in guinea pigs. **E. clupea′rum** is found almost constantly in the livers of herrings (*Clupea harengus*) and to a lesser extent in the livers of sprat (young herring) and mackerel (*Scomber scomber*). **E. falcifor′mis,** a species found in mice. **E. hom′inis,** a parasite found in the exudate in a case of purulent pleurisy. **E. meliad′igris** is found in the intestines of turkeys. **E. migai′rii** is found in feces of laboratory rats. **E. oxys′pora,** a rare species found in man. **E. per′forans,** a species causing intestinal coccidiosis in rabbits. **E. sardi′nae** is found in large numbers in the testes of sprats (young herrings), to some extent in the "soft roes" of adult herrings (*Clupea harengus*), and in tinned sardines. **E. snij′dersi,** reported from man in Sumatra. **E. sti′edae** is found in the liver of rabbits and mice and rarely in man. **E. tenel′la,** a species causing coccidiosis in fowls. **E. wenyo′ni,** a parasite occasionally found in man. **E. zur′nii,** a species causing intestinal coccidiosis in cattle and severe diarrhea in calves.

Einhorn's saccharimeter, test (īn′hornz) [Max *Einhorn,* physician in New York, 1862–1953]. See under *saccharimeter* and *tests.*

einsteinium (īn-sti′ne-um) [Albert *Einstein,* Austrian-Swiss-American mathematical physicist, 1879–1955; winner of the Nobel prize for physics in 1921]. The chemical element of atomic number 99, atomic weight 254, symbol Es, originally discovered in debris from a thermonuclear explosion in 1952.

Einthoven's string galvanometer (īn′to-venz) [Willem *Einthoven,* Dutch physiologist, 1860–1927; winner of the Nobel prize for medicine in 1924]. See under *galvanometer.*

eisanthema (īs-an′the-mah) [Gr. *eis* into + *anthein* to bloom]. An eruption on a mucous membrane.

Eisenia (i-se′ne-ah). A genus of chaelopod worms. *E. foe′tida,* a species found in the urine.

Eisenmenger's complex (i′sen-meng″erz) [Victor *Eisenmenger,* German physician, 1864–1932]. See under *complex.*

eisodic (i-sod′ik) [Gr. *eis* into + *hodos* way]. Afferent or centripetal.

eisoptrophobia (i-sop″tro-fo′be-ah) [Gr. *eisoptron* mirror + *phobia*]. Fear of mirrors.

Eitelberg's test (i′tel-bergz) [Abraham *Eitelberg,* Austrian physician, born 1847]. See under *tests.*

eiweissmilch (i′vīs-milkh) [Ger.]. Albumin milk.

E.j. Abbreviation for *elbow jerk.*

ejaculate (e-jak′u-lāt). 1. To expel suddenly. 2. Ejaculum.

ejaculatio (e-jak″u-la′she-o) [L.]. Ejaculation. **e. defi′ciens,** defective ejaculation. **e. prae′cox,** ejaculation of the semen immediately after the beginning of the sexual act. **e. retarda′ta,** unduly delayed ejaculation.

ejaculation (e-jak″u-la′shun) [L. *ejaculatio*]. A sudden act of expulsion, as of the semen.

ejaculator (e-jak′u-la″tor) [L.]. That which or one who ejaculates. **e. sem′inis,** musculus bulbospongiosus.

ejaculatory (e-jak′u-lah-to″re) [L. *ejaculatorius*]. Pertaining to ejaculation.

ejaculum (e-jak′u-lum). The fluid discharged at ejaculation in the male, consisting of the secretions of Cowper's gland, epididymis, ductus deferens, seminal vesicles, and prostate, and containing the spermatozoa.

ejecta (e-jek′tah) [L. pl.; from *e* out + *jacere* to cast]. Excrementitious material; refuse.

ejector (e-jek′tor). An apparatus for effecting the forcible expulsion or removal of a material or body. **saliva e.,** an apparatus for removal of saliva from the mouth of the patient during operations on the teeth.

Ejusd. Abbreviation for L. *ejus′dem,* of the same.

eka- (e′kah) [Sanscrit, "one" or "first"]. A prefix added to the name of a known chemical element as a provisional designation of the unknown element which should occur next in the same group in the periodic system.

eka-iodine (e′kah i′o-dīn). The name formerly used to designate element 85, now officially known as astatine.

Ekehorn's operation (a′ka-hornz) [Jol. Gustav *Ekehorn,* Swedish surgeon, 1857–1938]. See under *operation.*

EKG. Abbreviation for *electrocardiogram.*

ekiri (e-ki′ri). An acute and fatal form of endemic infantile diarrhea occurring in Japan.

ekphorize (ek′fo-rīz). Ecphorize.

EKY. Abbreviation for *electrokymogram.*

elaborate (e-lab′o-rāt) [L. *elabora′re* to work out]. To produce complex substances formed out of simpler materials.

elacin (el′ah-sin). Degenerated elastic tissue.

elaeo-. For words beginning thus, see those beginning *eleo-*.

elaioma (e-le-o′mah). Eleoma.

elaiometer (e″la-om′e-ter). Eleometer.

elaiopathia (e″la-o-path′e-ah). Elaiopathy.

elaiopathy (e″la-op′ah-the) [Gr. *elaion* oil + *pathos* disease]. A diffuse fatty edema, usually attacking the joints of the lower extremities, the effect of contusions or distortions incurred in war, and attributed to the formation of an irritating oily substance and its action upon the subcutaneous cellular tissue (C. Blondi, 1917). **pathomimic e.,** the simulation of disease produced by the injection of liquid petrolatum subcutaneously.

elaioplast (e-la′o-plast) [Gr. *elaion* oil + *plassein* to form]. A fat-producing plastid.

Elaps (e′laps). A genus of poisonous snakes, including the harlequin snakes of North America and the coral snakes of tropical America.

elassosis (el″ah-so′sis) [Gr. *elassōn* smaller, less]. A diminutive type of mitosis characteristic of the small cells of the thymus.

elastase (e-las′tās). A factor or enzyme capable of catalyzing the digestion of elastic tissue.

elastic (e-las′tik) [L. *elasticus*]. Susceptible of being stretched, compressed, or distorted, and then tending to assume its original shape.

elastica (e-las′tĭ-kah) [L.]. 1. Gum elastic or caoutchouc. 2. A general term for elastic tissue of the body, such as that found in the tunica elastica of blood vessels. 3. Tunica elastica.

elasticin (e-las′tĭ-sin). Elastin.

elasticity (e″las-tis′ĭ-te). The quality or condition of being elastic.

elastin (e-las′tin). A yellow scleroprotein, the essential constituent of yellow elastic tissue: it is brittle when dry, but when moist is flexible and elastic.

elastinase (e-las′tin-ās). An enzyme that dissolves elastic tissue.

elastofibroma (e-las″to-fi-bro′mah). A tumor consisting of both elastin and fibrous elements. **e. dor′si,** a tumor of subscapular soft tissue, occurring in old age; consisting of an elastin-filled central core and a surrounding elastase-resistant matrix impregnated with elastin.

elastogel (e-las′to-jel). A gel which possesses great elasticity.

elastoid (e-las′toid). A substance formed by the hyaline degeneration of the internal elastic lamina of blood vessels: seen in the vessels of the uterus after delivery.

elastolysis (e″las-tol′ĭ-sis). The digestion of elastic substance or tissue.

elastolytic (e-las″to-lit′ik). Capable of catalyzing the digestion of elastic tissue.

elastoma (e″las-to′mah). A tumor of elastic tissue of the skin. See *pseudoxanthoma elasticum.* **juvenile e.,** a congenital abnormality characterized by hyperplasia of the elastic tissue of the skin.

elastometer (e″las-tom′e-ter). An instrument for determining the elasticity of tissues, and thus measuring the degree of edema.

elastometry (e″las-tom′e-tre). The measurement of elasticity.

elastomucin (e-las″to-mu′sin). A polysaccharide component of elastic tissue.

elastopathy (e″las-top′ah-the). Deficiency of elastic tissue.

elastoplast (e-las′to-plast). Trade mark for an elastic bandage.

elastorrhexis (e-las″to-rek′sis). Rupture of fibers composing elastic tissue.

elastose (e-las′tōs). An albumose formed by treating elastin with ferments, acids, or alkalis.

elastosis (e″las-to′sis). Degeneration of elastic tissue. **e. dystroph′ica,** degeneration of Bruch's membrane producing angioid streaks in the fundus oculi. **senile e., e. seni′lis,** a dermatosis marked by degeneration in the elastic tissue of the skin of old people.

elastotic (e″las-tot′ik). Pertaining to or characterized by elastosis.

elation (e-la′shun). Emotional excitement marked by speeding up of mental and bodily activity.

elbow (el′bo) [L. *cubitus*]. 1. The bend of the arm; the joint which connects the arm and forearm. 2. Any angular bend. **baseball pitchers' e.,** a disorder of the elbow in baseball pitchers due to a piece of cartilage or bone torn from the head of the radius. **capped e.,** hydroma of the elbow; a swelling of the bursa or a hard, fibrous mass on the point of the elbow in horses or cattle. Called also *shoe boil.* **miners' e.,** enlargement of the bursa over the point of the elbow (olecranon bursitis) caused by resting the weight of the body on the elbow in mining. **nursemaids' e.,** pulled e. **pulled e.,** subluxation of the head of the radius distally under the annular ligament. **tennis e.,** epicondylalgia of the humerus caused by strain in playing tennis or other sports; called also *radiohumeral bursitis.*

elcosis (el-ko′sis). Helcosis.

El debab. The native name of an infection of horses and camels in Algeria, caused by *Trypanosoma berberum.*

elder (el′der). The plants, *Sambucus nigra,* of Europe, *S. canadensis,* of America, and other congeneric species: the flowers, which contain a volatile oil, have been used in dressing wounds, burns, ulcers, etc.

eldrin (el′drin). Rutin.

Elec. Abbreviation for *electricity* and *electuary.*

elective (e-lek′tiv). 1. Tending to combine with or act on one substance rather than another. 2. Subject to the choice or decision of the patient or physician, applied to procedures that are only advantageous to the patient but not necessary to save his life.

electric (e-lek′trik). Of the nature of electricity.

electrical (e-lek′trĭ-kal). Pertaining to electricity.

electricity (e-lek-tris′ĭ-te) [Gr. *ēlektron* amber]. One of the fundamental forms of energy. It exists as negative and as positive electricity, both of which are ultimately granular or atomic. The atom of negative electricity is the electron and the atom of positive electricity seems to be the proton. See *atom.* **animal e.,** electricity generated within the animal body as the shock from an electric eel and the electric currents now picked up and recorded as electrocardiography, electroencephalography, etc. **dynamic e.,** electricity generated by a dynamo. **faradic e.** See under *current.* **franklinic e.,** frictional e. **frictional e.,** electricity produced by rubbing various substances together. It has high voltage but little amperage. **galvanic e.** See under *current.* **induced e.** See under *current.* **magnetic e.,** electricity produced by passing a conductor through a magnetic field. **negative e.,** electricity that is the manifestation of an accumulation of electrons. **positive e.,** electricity that is the manifestation of a deficiency of electrons. **resinous e.,** frictional electricity generated by rubbing resin with flannel. **static e.,** a form of frictional electricity generated by a static machine. **vitreous e.,** frictional electricity generated by rubbing glass with flannel. **voltaic e.** See *galvanic current,* under *current.*

electrify (e-lek′trĭ-fi). To charge with electricity.

electrization (e-lek″tri-za′shun). The act of charging with or treatment by electricity. **direct e.,** electrization by applying one electrode to a muscle or to its motor point, and the other to an indifferent point.

electro- [Gr. *ēlektron* amber]. Combining form denoting relationship to electricity.

electro-affinity (e-lek″tro-ah-fin′ĭ-te). The degree of tenacity with which the ions of an element hold their charges.

electro-analysis (e-lek″tro-ah-nal′ĭ-sis). Chemical analysis performed by the aid of the electric current.

electro-anastomosis (e-lek″tro-ah-nas″to-mo′-sis). Electrosurgical intestinal anastomosis.

electro-anesthesia (e-lek″tro-an″es-the′ze-ah). Anesthesia induced by electricity.

electro-appendectomy (e-lek″tro-ap″en-dek′-to-me). Appendectomy with the electrocautery knife.

electrobasograph (e-lek″tro-ba′so-graf) [*electro-* + Gr. *basis* step + *graphein* to record]. An apparatus for recording the duration of weight bearing on the respective part while walking, i.e., a record of the gait.

electrobiology (e-lek″tro-bi-ol′o-je) [*electro-* + *biology*]. The study of electric phenomena in the living body, whether developed by vital or other processes.

electrobioscopy (e-lek″tro-bi-os′ko-pe) [*electro-* + Gr. *bios* life + *skopein* to examine]. The determination of the presence or absence of life by means of an electric current.

electrocardiogram (e-lek″tro-kar′de-o-gram) [*electro-* + Gr. *kardia* heart + *gramma* mark]. A graphic tracing of the electric current produced by the contraction of the heart muscle. The normal electrocardiogram shows upward and downward deflections, the result of auricular and ventricular activity. The first upward deflection, P, is due to contraction of the auricles and is known as the *auricular complex*. The other deflections, Q, R, S, T, are all due to the action of the ventricles, and are known as the *ventricular complexes*.

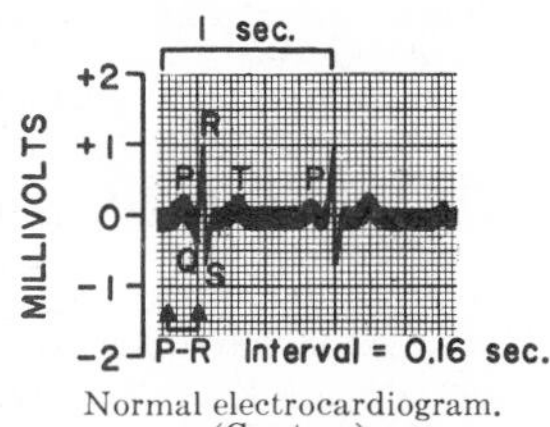

Normal electrocardiogram. (Guyton.)

electrocardiograph (e-lek″tro-kar′de-o-graf). An instrument for performing electrocardiography, i.e., for making electrocardiograms.

electrocardiography (e-lek″tro-kar″de-og′rah-fe). The making of graphic records of the electric currents emanating from heart muscle, as a method for studying the action of the heart muscle. **precordial e.,** electrocardiography which studies the changes in potential over the chest wall near the surface of the heart. See *precordial leads,* under *lead.*

electrocardiophonogram (e-lek″tro-kar″de-o-fo′no-gram). A record of the heart sounds made by an electrocardiophonograph.

electrocardiophonograph (e-lek″tro-kar″de-o-fo′no-graf). An apparatus for recording electrically the heart sounds.

electrocardioscopy (e-lek″tro-kar-de-os′ko-pe) [*electro-* + Gr. *kardia* heart + *skopein* to examine]. Electrocardiography by means of a cathode-ray oscillograph which throws a record on a luminous screen.

electrocatalysis (e-lek″tro-kah-tal′ĭ-sis). The catalytic effect produced by electricity on the bodily processes.

electrocautery (e-lek″tro-kaw′ter-e). An apparatus for cauterizing tissue, consisting of a platinum wire in a holder which may be heated to a red or white heat by a current of electricity when connected in the circuit.

electrochemistry (e-lek″tro-kem′is-tre). Study of chemical changes produced by electric action.

electrochemy (e-lek″tro-kem′e). That branch of physical therapy which embraces those modalities which produce chemical effects in the tissues, such as electrolysis, cataphoresis, and iontophoresis.

electrocholecystectomy (e-lek″tro-ko-le-sis-tek′to-me). Electrosurgical excision of the gallbladder.

electrocholecystocausis (e-lek″tro-ko″le-sis″-to-kaw′sis). Electrosurgical cauterization of the gallbladder.

electrochromatography (e-lek″tro-kro″mah-tog′rah-fe). Chromatography performed under the influence of an electric field.

electrocision (e-lek″tro-sizh′un). Excision of malignant growths after the application to them of oscillatory electricity.

electrocoagulation (e-lek″tro-ko-ag″u-la′shun). Coagulation by means of a biterminal high frequency electric current; a form of surgical diathermy.

electrocontractility (e-lek″tro-kon-trak-til′ĭ-te). Contractility in response to electric stimulation.

electrocorticogram (e-lek″tro-kor′tĭ-ko-gram). The record obtained by electrocorticography.

electrocorticography (e-lek″tro-kor′tĭ-kog′rah-fe). Electroencephalography with the electrodes applied directly to the cortex of the brain.

electrocortin (e-lek″tro-kor′tin). Aldosterone.

electrocryptectomy (e-lek″tro-krip-tek′to-me). Diathermic destruction of tonsillar crypts.

electroculture (e-lek′tro-kul-tūr). The stimulation of growth, flowering and seeding by electrical means.

electrocution (e-lek″tro-ku′shun). The taking of life by passage of electric current through the body.

electrocystography (e-lek″tro-sis-tog′rah-fe). The recording of changes of electric potential in the human urinary bladder.

electrocystoscope (e-lek″tro-sis′to-skōp). A cystoscope which utilizes the electric light.

electrode (e-lek′trōd) [Gr. *ēlektron* amber + *hodos* way]. A medium used between an electric conductor and the object to which the current is to be applied. In electrotherapy, an electrode is an instrument with a point or surface from which to discharge current to the body of a patient. **active e.,** therapeutic e. **brush e.,** a wire brush connected with one of the poles of an electric battery: used for applying electricity to the body. **calomel e.,** an electrode used as a standard in the determination of hydrogen ion concentration because it develops a constant potential. It consists of metallic mercury in contact with calomel and hydrochloric acid. **deglutible e.,** an electrode which may be swallowed: for faradization of the stomach. **depolarizing e.,** one which has a resistance greater than that of the portion of the body inclosed in the circuit. **dispersing e.,** silent e. **exciting e.,** therapeutic e. **hydrogen e.,** an electrode made by depositing platinum black on platinum and then allowing it to absorb hydrogen gas to saturation. It is used in the determination of hydrogen ion concentration. **impregnated e.,** therapeutic e. **indifferent e.,** silent e. **localizing e.,** therapeutic e. **multiple point e.,** an electrode possessing multiple terminals. **negative e.,** the cathode. **point e.,** an electrode with an insulating handle at one end and a metallic point at the other for use in applying sparks. **positive e.,** the anode. **prescription e.,** an electrode impregnated with medicaments according to a physician's prescription. **silent e.,** the electrode which is not therapeutically active. **spark ball e.,** an insulating handle having on one end a metallic ball: used in applying static sparks. **therapeutic e.,** an electrode of carbon cored or filled with materials for medication.

electrodeposition (e-lek″tro-de″po-zish′un). The deposition of metal by electric action (electroplating), sometimes employed in dentistry for the copper coating of inlay impressions, etc.

electrodermogram (e-lek″tro-der′mo-gram). The tracing obtained by electrodermography.

electrodermography (e-lek″tro-der-mog′rah-fe). The recording of the electrical resistance of the skin, which varies with the amount of sweating, and constitutes a sensitive index to the activity of the autonomic nervous system.

electrodesiccation (e-lek″tro-des″ĭ-ka′shun). Dehydration of tissue by the use of a uniterminal high frequency current through a pointed needle electrode. See *fulguration.*

electrodiagnosis (e-lek″tro-di″ag-no′sis). The use of electricity in the diagnosis of pathologic conditions.

electrodiagnostics (e-lek″tro-di″ag-nos′tiks). The science and practice of electrodiagnosis.

electrodialysis (e-lek″tro-di-al′ĭ-sis). Dialysis under the influence of an electric field.

electrodiaphake (e-lek″tro-di-af′ah-ke). An instrument for removing the lens by diathermy.

electrodiaphane (e-lek″tro-di′ah-fān). Diaphanoscope.

electrodiaphany (e-lek″tro-di-af′ah-ne) [*electro-* + Gr. *diaphainein* to show through]. Diaphanoscopy.

electrodynamometer (e-lek″tro-di-nah-mom′e-ter). An instrument used in measuring the strength of electric currents.

electroencephalogram (e-lek″tro-en-sef′ah-lo-gram). The graphic record obtained by electroencephalography.

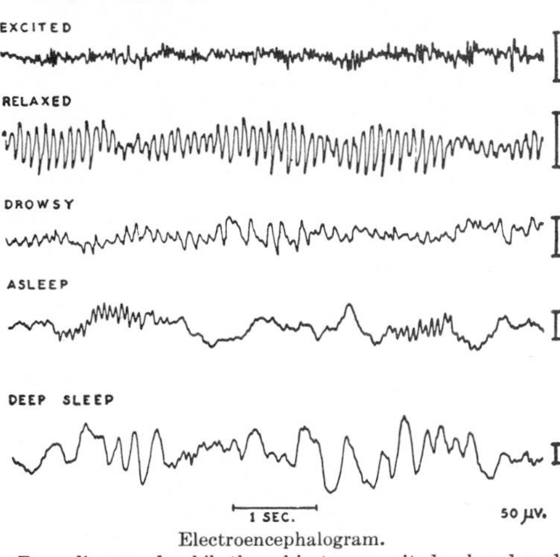

Electroencephalogram.

Recordings made while the subject was excited, relaxed, and in various stages of sleep. During excitement the brain waves are rapid and of small amplitude, whereas in sleep they are much slower and of greater amplitude. The regular waves characteristic of the relaxed state are called alpha waves. (From Jasper, in Epilepsy and Cerebral Localization, by Penfield and Erickson.)

electroencephalograph (e-lek″tro-en-sef′ah-lo-graf). An instrument for performing electroencephalography.

electroencephalography (e-lek″tro-en-sef″ah-log′rah-fe). The recording of the electric currents developed in the brain, by means of electrodes applied to the scalp, to the surface of the brain (*intracranial e.*), or placed within the substance of the brain (*depth e.*).

electro-endosmosis (e-lek″tro-en″dos-mo′sis). Endosmosis under the influence of an electric field.

electro-enterostomy (e-lek″tro-en″ter-os′to-me). Electrosurgical enterostomy.

electrofluoroscopy (e-lek″tro-floo″o-ros′ko-pe). Fluoroscopic electrocardiography.

electrogastroenterostomy (e-lek″tro-gas″tro-en-ter-os′to-me). Gastroenterostomy performed with an electric knife.

electrogastrogram (e-lek″tro-gas′tro-gram). The graphic record obtained by electrogastrography.

electrogastrography (e-lek″tro-gas-trog′rah-fe). The synchronous recording of the electrical and mechanical activity of the stomach.

electrogenesis (e-lek″tro-jen′e-sis) [*electro-* + Gr. *genesis* production]. The production of electricity.

electrogram (e-lek′tro-gram). Electrograph.

electrograph (e-lek′tro-graf). 1. A roentgenogram. 2. A record produced by changes in electric potential.

electrography (e″lek-trog′rah-fe) [*electro-* + Gr. *graphein* to record]. 1. Roentgenography. 2. The graphic recording of changes in electric potential, as in electrocardiography, electroencephalography, etc.

electrohemostasis (e-lek″tro-he-mos′tah-sis) [*electro-* + *hemostasis*]. The arrest of hemorrhage by means of a high frequency current.

electrohysterogram (e-lek″tro-his′ter-o-gram). The graphic record obtained by electrohysterography.

electrohysterography (e-lek″tro-his″ter-og′rah-fe). The recording of the changes in electric potential associated with contractions of the uterine muscle.

electro-ionic (e-lek″tro-i-on′ik). A term applied to medication by driving ions into the skin with electric current.

electrokinetic (e-lek″tro-ki-net′ik). Pertaining to motion produced by an electric current.

electrokymogram (e-lek″tro-ki′mo-gram). The record produced by electrokymography.

electrokymograph (e-lek″tro-ki′mo-graf). An instrument for recording motion of or changes in density of organs by recording variations in intensity of a small beam of roentgen rays; it consists of three essential parts—a fluoroscope, a pick-up unit, and a recording instrument: used especially for showing motion of the cardiac silhouette.

electrokymography (e-lek″tro-ki-mog′rah-fe). The photography on x-ray film of the motion of the heart or of other moving structures which can be visualized radiologically.

electrolepsy (e-lek′tro-lep″se). Electric chorea.

electrolithotrity (e-lek″tro-lĭ-thot′rĭ-te). The disintegration of calculi by an electric current.

electrology (e″lek-trol′o-je) [*electro-* + *-logy*]. That branch of science which deals with the phenomena and properties of electricity.

electrolysis (e″lek-trol′ĭ-sis) [*electro-* + Gr. *lysis* dissolution]. Destruction by passage of an electric current, as disintegration of a chemical compound or removal of excessive hair or of other growths from the body.

electrolyte (e-lek′tro-līt) [*electro-* + Gr. *lytos* that may be dissolved]. 1. A solution that conducts electricity by means of its ions. 2. An electrical conductor in which passage of a current causes production of gas or deposit of a solid at the electrodes. **amphoteric e.,** a substance which dissociates into both hydrogen (H^+) and hydroxyl (OH^-) ions. Called also *ampholyte.* **colloidal e.,** an electrolyte in which one of the ions has been replaced by colloidal units.

electrolytic (e-lek″tro-lit′ik). Pertaining to or characterized by electrolysis.

electrolyzable (e-lek′tro-līz″ah-bl). Susceptible of being decomposed by the electric current.

electromagnet (e-lek″tro-mag′net). A temporary magnet made by passing an electric current through a coil of wire, surrounding a core of soft iron.

electromagnetism (e-lek″tro-mag′net-izm). Magnetism produced by an electric current.

electromassage (e-lek″tro-mah-sahzh′). Massage combined with the application of electricity.

electrometer (e″lek-trom′e-ter) [*electro-* + Gr. *metron* measure]. An instrument for measuring static or other electricity or differences in electric potential. **gold leaf e.,** an instrument for detecting the presence of electricity by the divergence of two slips of gold leaf. **Lippmann's capillary e.,** an instrument for measuring small differences of electric potential (up to 0.95 volt) by means of a thread of mercury.

electrometrogram (e-lek″tro-met′ro-gram) [*electro-* + Gr. *mētra* uterus + *gramma* mark]. An apparatus for recording changes in electric potential associated with contraction of the uterine muscle.

electromigratory (e-lek″tro-mi′grah-to″re). Moving under the influence of electric current.

electromotive (e-lek″tro-mo′tiv). Causing electric activity to be propagated along a conductor.

electromyogram (e-lek″tro-mi′o-gram). The record obtained by electromyography.

electromyography (e-lek″tro-mi-og′rah-fe) [*electro-* + *myography*]. The recording of the changes in electric potential of muscle (1) by means of surface or needle electrodes to determine merely whether the muscle is contracting or not (useful in kinesiology) or (2) by insertion of a needle electrode into the muscle and observing by cathode-ray oscilloscope and loud-speaker the action potentials spontaneously present in a muscle (abnormal) or induced by voluntary contractions, as a means of detecting the nature and location of motor unit lesions; or (3) recording the electrical activity evoked in a muscle by stimulation of its nerve (useful for study of several aspects of neuromuscular function, neuromuscular conduction, extent of nerve lesion, reflex responses, etc.). **ureteral e.,** recording of the action potentials produced by peristalsis of the ureter.

electron (e-lek′tron). The unit or "atom" of negative electricity. It is equivalent to 4.77×10^{-10} absolute electrostatic units or 1.59×10^{-20} absolute electromagnetic units, and its mass when moving at moderate speed is $\frac{1}{1845}$ that of a hydrogen atom or 9×10^{-28} grams. Electrons flowing in a conductor constitute an electric current; when ejected from a radioactive substance, the beta rays; and when revolving about the nucleus of an atom they determine all of its physical and chemical properties except mass and radioactivity. Cf. *atom*. **emission e.,** one of the electrons which give radioactivity to the atom. **free e.,** an electron which is not bound to the nucleus of an atom but may move from one atom nucleus to another. **valency e.,** one of the electrons concerned in the chemical reaction of the atom.

electronarcosis (e-lek″tro-nar-ko′sis). Narcosis or unconsciousness produced by passing an electric current through the brain of a patient by electrodes placed on the temples: used in treating schizophrenia.

electronation (e-lek″tro-na′shun). The addition of an electron or electrons to an element; a term equivalent to "reduction."

electronegative (e-lek″tro-neg′ah-tiv). Negatively electric; bearing a negative electric charge.

electroneurolysis (e-lek″tro-nu-rol′ĭ-sis). Neurolysis by means of the electric needle.

electronic (e″lek-tron′ik). Pertaining to or carrying electrons.

electronics (e″lek-tron′iks). The science which treats of the conduction of electricity through gases or through a vacuum.

electronization (e-lek″tron-i-za′shun). The procedure of restoring electrical equilibrium (healthy cell structure) to diseased cells by irradiation.

electronograph (e″lek-tron′o-graf). An electron micrograph.

electro-osmosis (e-lek″tro-oz-mo′sis). Iontophoresis.

electroparacentesis (e-lek″tro-par″ah-sen-te′sis). Puncture of the eyeball with a needle, using galvanic current and holding the needle in position until bubbles of hydrogen appear in the aqueous humor.

electropathology (e-lek″tro-pah-thol′o-je) [*electro-* + Gr. *pathos* disease + *-logy*]. The study of pathologic conditions of the body as revealed by electricity.

electrophonoide (e-lek″tro-fo′noid). An apparatus which reproduces the tones of the human voice by means of mechanical larynges. It is used in treating chronic deafness.

electrophoresis (e-lek″tro-fo-re′sis). The movement of charged particles suspended in a liquid on various media (e.g., paper, starch, agar), under the influence of an applied electric field.

electrophoretic (e-lek″tro-fo-ret′ik). Pertaining to electrophoresis.

electrophorus (e-lek-trof′o-rus) [*electro-* + Gr. *phoros* bearing]. An instrument for obtaining static electricity by means of induction.

electrophototherapy (e-lek″tro-fo″to-ther′ah-pe). Treatment of disease with the electric light.

electrophysiology (e-lek″tro-fiz″e-ol′o-je). The science of physiology in its relations to electricity; the study of the electric reactions of the body in health.

electropism (e-lek′tro-pizm). Electrotropism.

electroplexy (e-lek′tro-plek″se) [*electro-* + Gr. *plēgē* stroke]. Electric shock.

electropneumatotherapy (e-lek″tro-nu″mah-to-ther′ah-pe). The treatment of weak voice by passing a faradic current into the larynx.

electropneumograph (e-lek″tro-nu′mo-graf). An electric apparatus for recording breathing movements.

electropositive (e-lek″tro-poz′ĭ-tiv) [*electro-* + *positive*]. Positively electric; bearing a positive electric charge.

electroprognosis (e-lek″tro-prog-no′sis). The employment of electricity for the purpose of prognosis.

electropuncture (e-lek′tro-punk-tūr). Electrization by means of needles thrust into the tissues.

electropyrexia (e-lek″tro-pi-rek′se-ah) [*electro-* + *pyrexia*]. The production of high temperature in the body by electrical means through a special apparatus, used in fever therapy.

electroradiology (e-lek″tro-ra″de-ol′o-je). The branch of medicine which has to do with use of electricity and x-ray in therapeutics.

electroradiometer (e-lek″tro-ra-de-om′e-ter). An electroscope for measuring radiant energy.

electroresection (e-lek″tro-re-sek′shun). Excision by electrical means.

electroretinogram (e-lek″tro-ret′ĭ-no-gram). The record obtained by electroretinography.

electroretinography (e-lek″tro-ret″ĭ-nog′rah-fe). The recording of the changes in electric potential in the retina after stimulation by light.

electrosalivogram (e-lek″tro-sah-li′vo-gram). A graphic record or curve showing the action potential of the salivary glands.

electroscission (e-lek″tro-sizh′un). Cutting of tissue by the electric cautery.

electroscope (e-lek′tro-skōp) [*electro-* + Gr. *skopein* to examine]. A device for determining the presence and nature of static electricity.

electroselenium (e-lek″tro-sĕ-le′ne-um). A form of colloidal selenium.

electroshock (e-lek′tro-shok). Shock produced by application of electric current to the brain. See *shock therapy*, under *therapy*.

electrosol (e-lek′tro-sol). A colloidal solution of a metal obtained by passing electric sparks through distilled water between poles formed of the metal.

electrosome (e-lek′tro-sōm). A chondriosome considered as a center of chemical activity.

electrospectrogram (e-lek″tro-spek′tro-gram). A record produced in electrospectrography.

electrospectrography (e-lek″tro-spek-trog′rah-fe). The isolation and recording of the constituent wave systems that are merged in an electroencephalogram.

electrospinogram (e-lek″tro-spi′no-gram). A tracing of the action potential of the spinal cord.

electrostatic (e-lek″tro-stat′ik). Pertaining to static electricity.

electrostatics (e-lek″tro-stat′iks) [*electro-* + Gr.

statikos causing to stand]. The sum of knowledge regarding static electricity.

electrostenolysis (e-lek″tro-stĕ-nol′ĭ-sis). The oxidation and reduction which occur on opposite surfaces of a high resistance membrane in a solution when there is a steep electric potential gradient across the membrane, reduction occurring on the surface facing the anode.

electrostethograph (e-lek″tro-steth′o-graf). An apparatus for recording the amplified heart sounds over the chest.

electrostriatogram (e-lek″tro-stri-āt′o-gram). A record of waves derived by the bipolar technique from the several structures of the corpus striatum.

electrosurgery (e-lek″tro-sur′jer-e). The surgical employment of electricity; surgery performed by the electric knife; surgical diathermy.

electrosynthesis (e-lek″tro-sin′thĕ-sis). Chemical union effected by means of electricity.

electrotaxis (e-lek″tro-tak′sis) [*electro-* + Gr. *taxis* arrangement]. The movement of organisms or cells under the influence of electric currents.

electrothanasia (e-lek″tro-thah-na′ze-ah) [*electro-* + Gr. *thanotos* death]. Death by electricity; electrocution.

electrotherapeutics (e-lek″tro-ther-ah-pu′tiks). Treatment of disease by means of electricity.

electrotherapeutist (e-lek″tro-ther-ah-pu′tist). A physician who specializes in the therapeutic use of electricity.

electrotherapist (e-lek″tro-ther′ah-pist). Electrotherapeutist.

electrotherapy (e-lek″tro-ther′ah-pe). Electrotherapeutics.

electrotherm (e-lek′tro-therm) [*electro-* + Gr. *thermē* heat]. An electric appliance for heating the skin and thus relieving pain.

electrothermotherapy (e-lek″tro-ther″mo-ther′ah-pe). The production of heat within the living tissues for therapeutic purposes by means of bodily resistance to the passing of an electric current.

electrotome (e-lek′tro-tōm) [*electro-* + Gr. *tomē* a cut]. An electric surgical knife.

electrotomy (e-lek-trot′o-me). Diathermy excision with low current, high voltage, and high frequency: in it the tissues are not coagulated.

electrotonic (e-lek″tro-ton′ik). Pertaining to electrotonus.

electrotonus (e″lek-trot′o-nus) [*electro-* + Gr. *tonos* tone]. The condition of a nerve or muscle beyond and between the two electrodes when a galvanic current is applied to a portion of its length.

electrotrephine (e-lek″tro-tre′fīn). A form of trephine operated by electricity.

electrotropism (e″lek-trot′ro-pizm) [*electro-* + Gr. *tropos* a turning, change]. The tendency of a cell or organism to react in a definite manner in response to an electric stimulus. **negative e.,** the tendency of a cell to be repelled by an electric stimulus. **positive e.,** the tendency of a cell to be attracted by an electric stimulus.

electro-ultrafiltration (e-lek″tro-ul″trah-fil-tra′shun). Ultrafiltration in an electric field.

electroureterogram (e-lek″tro-u-re′ter-o-gram). The record obtained by ureteral electromyography.

electrovagogram (e-lek″tro-va′go-gram). Vagogram.

electrozone (e-lek′tro-zōn) [*electro-* + *ozone*]. A nascent oxygen or ozone produced by the electrolysis of salt water, and used as a disinfectant.

electuary (e-lek′tu-a-re) [L. *electuarium,* from *e* out + *legere* to select]. A medicinal preparation consisting of a powdered drug made into a paste with honey or syrup. **e. of senna,** a mixture of senna, syrup and tamarind pulp.

eleidin (el-e′ĭ-din). A substance of peculiar nature, allied to keratin and protoplasm, found in the cells of the stratum lucidum of the skin.

element (el′ĕ-ment) [L. *elementum*]. 1. Any one of the primary parts or constituents of a thing. 2. In chemistry, a simple substance which cannot be decomposed by chemical means and which is made up of atoms which are alike in their peripheral electronic configurations and so in their chemical properties, but which may differ in their nuclei and so in their atomic weight and in their radioactive properties. [See *Table of Elements* on page 476.] **anatomic e.,** morphological e. **appendicular e's,** a set of cartilaginous rods attached to the chondral skull of the embryo; from them are developed the ear bones, the hyoid, and the styloid process. **electronegative e.,** any chemical element that seeks the positive pole or cathode in electrolysis. **electropositive e.,** a chemical element that seeks the negative pole or cathode in electrolysis. **galvanic e.,** the essential parts of an electric battery; the substances which form the generating and collecting plates of a battery. **labile e.,** tissue cells which continue to multiply during the life of the individual. **morphological e.,** any cell, fiber, or other of the ultimate structures which go to make up tissues and organs. **radioactive e.,** a chemical element which spontaneously transmutes into another element with emission of corpuscular or electromagnetic radiations. The natural radioactive elements are all those with atomic number above 83, and some other elements, such as potassium (at. no. 19) and rubidium (at. no. 37), which are very weakly radioactive. **sarcous e.,** any one of the elementary granules into which the primitive fibril of an elementary muscle fiber is divisible. **stable e.** 1. A chemical element which does not spontaneously transmute into another element with emission of corpuscular or electromagnetic radiations. The stable elements are those with atomic number below 84, except for a few, such as potassium and rubidium, which are weakly radioactive. 2. A tissue cell of mature tissues which does not alter by mitosis. **tissue e.,** morphological e. **trace e's,** chemical elements that are distributed throughout the tissues in very small amounts and are either essential in nutrition such as cobalt, copper, magnesium, manganese and zinc, or may be harmful, such as selenium. **tracer e's.** See *radioactive tracer,* under *tracer.* **transcalifornium e's,** the elements with atomic numbers higher than that of californium, and discovered subsequent to its discovery in 1950. They are einsteinium 99, fermium 100, mendelevium 101, nobelium 102, and lawrencium 103. **transuranic e's, transuranium e's,** the elements with atomic numbers higher than that of uranium. Applied originally to neptunium 93, plutonium 94, americium 95, curium 96, berkelium 97, and californium 98, the term now, by definition, includes the transcalifornium elements as well.

elementary (el″ĕ-men′tah-re). Not resolvable or divisible into simpler parts or components.

elemi (el′ĕ-me) [Turkish *eleme* hand picked]. A resinous substance, of extremely various origin, the best coming from *Canarium commune,* of the Philippine Islands. It furnishes a volatile oil, and is used externally, generally in an ointment, for ulcers and sores.

elemicin (e-lem′ĭ-sin). The chief constituent of elemi oil. It is trimethoxy allyl benzene, $(CH_3O)_3$-$C_6H_2.CH_2.CH{:}CH_2$.

eleo- (el′e-o) [Gr. *elaion* oil]. Combining form denoting relationship to oil.

eleoma (el″e-o′mah) [*eleo-* + *-oma*]. A tumor or swelling caused by the injection of oil into the tissues.

eleometer (el″e-om′e-ter) [*eleo-* + Gr. *metron* measure]. An instrument for determining percentage of oil in a mixture, also specific gravity of oils.

eleomyenchysis (el″e-o-mi-en′kĭ-sis) [*eleo-* + Gr. *mys* muscle + *enchysis* infusion]. The injection of oils into muscles for therapeutic purposes, especially for treatment of clonic local spasm.

eleopathy (el″e-op′ah-the). Elaiopathy.

TABLE OF ELEMENTS

NAME	SYMBOL	AT. NO.	AT. WT.*
Actinum	Ac	89	(227)
Aluminum	Al	13	26.982
Americium	Am	95	(243)
Antimony	Sb	51	121.75
Argon	Ar	18	39.948
Arsenic	As	33	74.922
Astatine	At	85	(210)
Barium	Ba	56	137.34
Berkelium	Bk	97	(247)
Beryllium	Be	4	9.012
Bismuth	Bi	83	208.980
Boron	B	5	10.811
Bromine	Br	35	79.909
Cadmium	Cd	48	112.40
Calcium	Ca	20	40.08
Californium	Cf	98	(249)
Carbon	C	6	12.011
Cerium	Ce	58	140.12
Cesium	Cs	55	132.905
Chlorine	Cl	17	35.453
Chromium	Cr	24	51.996
Cobalt	Co	27	58.933
Copper	Cu	29	63.54
Curium	Cm	96	(247)
Dysprosium	Dy	66	162.50
Einsteinium	Es	99	(254)
Erbium	Er	68	167.26
Europium	Eu	63	151.96
Fermium	Fm	100	(253)
Fluorine	F	9	18.998
Francium	Fr	87	(223)
Gadolinium	Gd	64	157.25
Gallium	Ga	31	69.72
Germanium	Ge	32	72.59
Gold	Au	79	196.967
Hafnium	Hf	72	178.49
Helium	He	2	4.003
Holmium	Ho	67	164.930
Hydrogen	H	1	1.008
Indium	In	49	114.82
Iodine	I	53	126.904
Iridium	Ir	77	192.2
Iron	Fe	26	55.847
Krypton	Kr	36	83.80
Lanthanum	La	57	138.91
Lawrencium	Lw	103	(257)
Lead	Pb	82	207.19
Lithium	Li	3	6.939
Lutetium	Lu	71	174.97
Magnesium	Mg	12	24.312
Manganese	Mn	25	54.938
Mendelevium	Md	101	(256)
Mercury	Hg	80	200.59
Molybdenum	Mo	42	95.94
Neodymium	Nd	60	144.24
Neon	Ne	10	20.183
Neptunium	Np	93	(237)
Nickel	Ni	28	58.71
Niobium	Nb	41	92.906
Nitrogen	N	7	14.007
Nobelium	No	102	(253)
Osmium	Os	76	190.2
Oxygen	O	8	15.999
Palladium	Pd	46	106.4
Phosphorus	P	15	30.974
Platinum	Pt	78	195.09
Plutonium	Pu	94	(242)
Polonium	Po	84	(210)
Potassium	K	19	39.102
Praseodymium	Pr	59	140.907
Promethium	Pm	61	(147)
Protactinium	Pa	91	(231)
Radium	Ra	88	(226)
Radon	Rn	86	(222)
Rhenium	Re	75	186.2
Rhodium	Rh	45	102.905
Rubidium	Rb	37	85.47
Ruthenium	Ru	44	101.07
Samarium	Sm	62	150.35
Scandium	Sc	21	44.956
Selenium	Se	34	78.96
Silicon	Si	14	28.086
Silver	Ag	47	107.870
Sodium	Na	11	22.990
Strontium	Sr	38	87.62
Sulfur	S	16	32.064
Tantalum	Ta	73	180.948
Technetium	Tc	43	(99)
Tellurium	Te	52	127.60
Terbium	Tb	65	158.924
Thallium	Tl	81	204.37
Thorium	Th	90	232.038
Thulium	Tm	69	168.934
Tin	Sn	50	118.69
Titanium	Ti	22	47.90
Tungsten	W	74	183.85
Uranium	U	92	238.03
Vanadium	V	23	50.942
Xenon	Xe	54	131.30
Ytterbium	Yb	70	173.04
Yttrium	Y	39	88.905
Zinc	Zn	30	65.37
Zirconium	Zr	40	91.22

* Atomic weights are corrected to conform with the 1961 values of the Commission on Atomic Weights, expressed to the fourth decimal point, rounded off to the nearest thousandth. The numbers in parentheses are the mass numbers of the most stable or most common isotope.

eleoplast (el-e′o-plast) [*eleo-* + Gr. *plastos* formed]. A globular body made up of granular protoplasm and containing drops of oil.

eleopten (el″e-op′ten) [*eleo-* + Gr. *ptēnos* volatile]. The more volatile constituent of a volatile oil, as distinguished from its stearopten.

eleosaccharum (el″e-o-sak′ah-rum), pl. *eleosacch′ara* [Gr. *elaion* oil + *sakcharon* sugar]. A mixture of sugar with a volatile oil; an oil sugar.

eleotherapy (el″e-o-ther′ah-pe) [*eleo-* + *therapy*]. Oleotherapy.

eleothorax (el″e-o-tho′raks) [*eleo-* + *thorax*]. Oleothorax.

elephantiasic (el″ĕ-fan″te-as′ik). Pertaining to elephantiasis.

elephantiasis (el″ĕ-fan-ti′ah-sis) ["elephant disease"]. A chronic disease due to filariasis of the lymphatic channels and characterized by inflammation and obstruction of the lymphatics and hypertrophy of the skin and subcutaneous tissues. The legs and external genitals are principally affected, the disease beginning in attacks of dermatitis, with enlargement of the part, attended by chills and fever (elephantoid fever) and followed by the formation of ulcers and tubercles, with thickening, discoloration, and fissuring of the skin. The disease is most common in tropical regions near the coast (Galen). The term elephantiasis is often applied to hypertrophy and thickening of the tissues from any cause. **e. arab′icum,** true elephantiasis. **e. asturien′sis,** pellagra. **e. chirur′gica,** Halsted's name for massive edema of the arm after mastectomy. **congenital e.,** elephantiasis of the skin occurring at birth. **e. gingi′vae,** fibromatosis gingivae. **e. graeco′rum,** true leprosy. **e. filarien′sis,** true elephantiasis due to filariasis. **e. leishmania′na,** the edema and hypertrophy of tissues caused by leishmaniasis. **lymphangiectatic e.,** elephantiasis of a part due to lymphangiectasis. **e. neuromato′sa,** neurofibroma. **nevoid e.,** a variety marked by great dilatation of the lymph vessels. **e. nos′tras,** chronic streptococcic lymphedema. **e. oc′uli,** thickening and protrusion of the eyelids. **e. scro′ti,** that in which the scrotum is the principal seat of the disease.

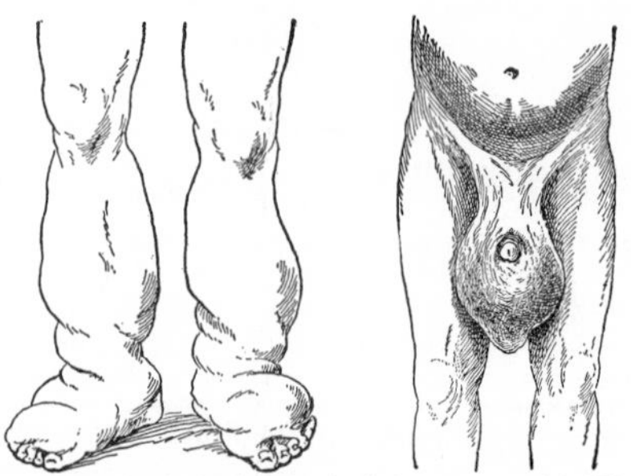

Elephantiasis of the legs and of the scrotum (de Rivas).

e. telangiecto′des, a variety marked by circumscribed hypertrophy of skin and subcutaneous tissue, causing the skin to hang in folds, as in dermatolysis.

elephantoid (el″ĕ-fan′toid). Relating to or resembling elephantiasis.

eleutheromania (e-lu″ther-o-ma′ne-ah) [Gr. *eletheria* freedom]. Abnormal enthusiasm for freedom.

elevation (el″ĕ-va′shun). A raised area, or point of greater height. **dicrotic e.,** the secondary rise of a dicrotic pulse wave in the sphygmogram. **tactile e.,** torulus tactilis.

elevator (el′ĕ-va″tor) [L. *elevare* to lift]. An instrument for lifting a depressed part, or for removing osseous tissue or roots of teeth. **Cryer's e.,** a dental instrument for removing the roots of molar teeth; furnished in pairs, one for mesial and one for distal roots, which are reversed for use on opposite sides of the jaw. **periosteum e.,** a flat steel bar for separating the attachments of the periosteum to bone. **screw e.,** a dental instrument designed to be screwed into a root canal for subsequent removal of the root, usually of the apical third.

elgustometer (el″gus-tom′e-ter). An electrical apparatus for the clinical determination of taste thresholds.

eliminant (e-lim′ĭ-nant). 1. Causing an evacuation. 2. An agent that promotes evacuation.

elimination (e-lim″ĭ-na′shun) [L. *eliminatio*, from *e* out + *limen* threshold]. The act of expulsion or of extrusion, especially of expulsion from the body.

elinguation (e″lin-gwa′shun) [L. *e* out + *lingua* tongue]. The removal of the tongue.

elinin (el′ĭ-nin). A lipoprotein fraction of red cells containing the Rh and A and B factors.

elipten (e-lip′ten). Trade mark for a preparation of amino-glutethimide.

elixir (e-lik′ser) [L., from Arabic]. A clear, sweetened, usually hydroalcoholic liquid containing flavoring substances and sometimes active medicinal agents, used orally as a vehicle or for the effect of the medicinal agent contained. **aromatic e.,** a preparation containing compound orange spirit, sugar, talc, and alcohol: used as a vehicle for dispensing drugs. **gentian e., glycerinated,** a preparation of gentian and taraxacum fluidextracts, compound cardamon tincture, raspberry syrup, sweet orange peel tincture, phosphoric acid, ethyl acetate, glycerin, sucrose, and alcohol, in purified water: used as a flavored vehicle for drugs. **e. I. Q. & S., iron, quinine, and strychnine e.,** a preparation of iron, quinine, and strychnine, with compound orange spirit, alcohol, glycerin, and purified water: used as a bitter tonic. **pepsin e.,** a water preparation containing a proteolytic enzyme from the glandular layer of the fresh stomach of the hog, with lactic acid, glycerin, alcohol, orange oil, and amaranth solution. **terpin hydrate e.,** a preparation of terpin hydrate, sweet orange peel tincture, benzaldehyde, glycerin, alcohol, and syrup, in purified water: used as an expectorant.

elkoplasty (el′ko-plas″te). Helcoplasty.

elkosin (el′ko-sin). Trade mark for preparations of sulfisomidine.

elkosis (el′ko-sis). Helcosis.

Ellermann-Erlandsen method (el′er-mahn-ăr′land-sen) [Wilhelm *Ellermann*, Copenhagen pathologist, born 1871; Alfred *Erlandsen*, Copenhagen hygienist, 1878–1918]. Tuberculin titer test. See under *test*.

Elliot's operation (el′ĭ-ots) [Col. R. H. *Elliot*, of the Indian Medical Service, 1864–1936]. See under *operation*.

Elliot's position [John W. *Elliot*, American surgeon, 1852–1925]. See under *position*.

Elliot's sign [George T. *Elliot*, American dermatologist, 1851–1935]. See under *sign*.

Elliott treatment [Charles Robert *Elliott*, American gynecologist]. See under *treatment*.

ellipsin (e-lip′sin). The insoluble constituents of cells which remain after the removal of the soluble proteins.

ellipsis (e-lip′sis) [Gr. "a leaving out"]. In psychiatry, the omission of words or of ideas by a patient in the course of psychoanalysis.

ellipsoid (e-lip′soid). Any one of the spindle-shaped masses of cells surrounding the second portion of the arterioles of the spleen. See *sheathed artery*, under *artery*. **rod e.,** the outer refractile portion of the inner rod section. **e. of spleen.** See *sheathed artery*, under *artery*.

elliptocytary (e-lip″to-si′tah-re). Pertaining to elliptocytes.

elliptocyte (e-lip′to-sīt). An elliptical erythrocyte.

elliptocytosis (e-lip″to-si-to′sis). A hereditary disorder in which the greater proportion of erythrocytes are elliptical in shape, and which is characterized by varying degrees of increased red cell destruction and anemia.

elliptocytotic (e-lip″to-si-tot′ik). Pertaining to or characterized by elliptocytosis.

Ellis's curve, ligament, line, sign (el′ĭ-sez) [Calvin *Ellis*, Boston physician, 1826–1883]. See under the nouns.

elongation (e″long-ga′shun). The process or condition of increasing in length.

elorine (el′o-rēn). Trade mark for a preparation of tricyclamol.

Elsberg's solution, test (els′bergz) [Charles Albert *Elsberg*, New York surgeon, 1871–1948]. See under *solution* and *test*.

Elschnig bodies (elsh′nig) [Anton *Elschnig*, German ophthalmologist, 1863–1939]. See under *body*.

Elsner's asthma (els′nerz) [Christoph Friedrich *Elsner*, German physician, 1749–1820]. Angina pectoris.

Elsner's medium (els′nerz) [Moritz *Elsner*, German bacteriologist, 1861–1935]. See under *medium*.

eluate (el′u-āt). The substance separated out by, or the product of, elution or elutriation.

eluent (e-lu′ent). A solution used in elution.

elurophobia (e-lu″ro-fo′be-ah). Ailurophobia.

elution (e-lu′shun) [L. *e* out + *luere* to wash]. In chemistry, the separation of material by washing, as in the freeing of an enzyme from its absorbent.

elutriation (e-lu″tre-a′shun) [L. *elutriare* to wash out]. The operation of pulverizing substances and mixing them with water, so as to separate the lighter from the heavier constituents, which settle out in solution.

Ely's sign, test (e′lēz) [Leonard W. *Ely*, American orthopedic surgeon, 1868–1944]. See under *test*.

elytritis (el″ĭ-tri′tis) [*elytro-* + *-itis*]. Colpitis.

elytro- (el′ĭ-tro) [Gr. *elytron* a covering, sheath]. Combining form denoting relationship to the vagina or to a sheath. For words beginning thus, see those beginning *colpo-*.

Elzholz's bodies, mixture (elts′holts-ez) Adolf *Elzholz*, alienist in Vienna, 1863–1925]. See under *body* and *mixture*.

Em. Abbreviation for *emmetropia*.

emaciation (e-ma″se-a′shun) [L. *emaciare* to make lean]. Excessive leanness; a wasted condition of the body.

emaculation (e-mak″u-la′shun) [L. *e* out + *macula* spot]. The removal of freckles and spots from the face.

emailloblast (e-măl′o-blast) [Fr. *émail* enamel + Gr. *blastos* germ]. Ameloblast.

emailloid (e-ma′loid) [Fr. *émail* enamel]. A tumor which develops from the enamel of a tooth.

eman (em′an). A unit for expressing the concentration of radium emanation in solution. It is the concentration present when one tenth of a millimicrocurie of radium emanation is dissolved in 1 liter of air or water, or 10^{-10} curie.

emanation (em-ah-na′shun) [L. *e* out + *manare* to flow]. That which is given off, such as a gaseous disintegration product given off from radioactive substances or an effluvium. **actinium e.,** one member of the radioactive series derived from actinium. It is produced from actinium X, has an atomic weight of 218, its atomic number is

86, and by the loss of alpha particles it becomes actinium A. Called also *actinon.* **radium e.,** radon. **thorium e.,** one member of the radioactive series derived from thorium. It is produced from thorium X, has an atomic weight of 220, its atomic number is 86, and by the loss of alpha particles it changes into thorium A. Called also *thoron.*

emanator (em′ah-na″tor). An instrument for giving off and applying to the body radioactive emanations.

emanatorium (em″ah-na-to′re-um). An institute for treating diseases by radioactive emanations.

emancipation (e-man″si-pa′shun) [L. *emancipare* to release, give up]. The establishment of local autonomy within restricted fields of a developing embryo.

emanotherapy (em″ah-no-ther′ah-pe). Treatment with radium or other emanations.

emansio mensium (e-man′se-o men′se-um) [L. "tardiness of the menses"]. The condition in which menstruation has never taken place.

emasculation (e-mas″ku-la′shun) [L. *emasculare* to castrate]. 1. Excision of the penis. 2. Castration.

Emb. Abbreviation for *embryology.*

Embadomonas (em″bah-dom′o-nas). Retortamonas.

embalming (em-bahm′ing). The treatment of the dead body with antiseptics and preservatives, to prevent putrefaction.

embalmment (em-bahm′ment). See *Merciére's method,* under *method.*

embarras (aw″bar-rah′) [Fr.]. Difficulty; distress. **e. gastrique** (gas-trēk′), an attack of acute gastric pain.

embedding (em-bed′ing). 1. The fixation of a tissue specimen in a firm medium, in order to keep it intact during the cutting of thin sections. 2. Implantation.

embelate (em′bĕ-lāt). Any salt of embelic acid.

Embelia (em-be′le-ah). A genus of myrtaceous East Indian climbing plants. **E. ri′bes, E. robus′ta,** species whose fruit has been used for its anthelminthic and cathartic principles.

embelin (em′bĕ-lin). An active principle, $CH_3(CH_2)_{10}.C_6HO_2(OH)_2$, from *Embelia ribes,* which has been used as a teniacide.

emboitement (aw-bwat′maw) [Fr. "encasement"]. The supposed encasement of miniature individuals within the germ cells of predecessors, advanced as one theory of preformation.

embolalia (em″bo-la′le-ah). Embololalia.

embole (em′bo-le) [Gr. *embolē* a throwing in]. 1. The reducing of a dislocated limb. 2. Emboly.

embolectomy (em″bo-lek′to-me) [*embolus* + Gr. *ektomē* excision]. Surgical removal of an embolus from a blood vessel.

embolemia (em″bo-le′me-ah) [*embolus* + Gr. *haima* blood + *-ia*]. The presence of emboli in the blood.

emboli (em′bo-li) [L.]. Plural of *embolus.*

embolia (em-bo′le-ah). Embole.

embolic (em-bol′ik). Pertaining to an embolus or to embolism.

emboliform (em-bol′ĭ-form). 1. Shaped like a wedge. 2. Resembling an embolus.

embolism (em′bo-lizm) [L. *embolismus,* from Gr. *en* in + *ballein* to throw]. The sudden blocking of an artery or vein by a clot or obstruction which has been brought to its place by the blood current (Virchow). **air e.,** aeroembolism. **bacillary e.,** obstruction of a vessel by an aggregation of bacilli. **bland e.,** that in which the plug is composed of nonseptic material. **capillary e.,** blocking of the capillaries with bacteria. **cerebral e.,** embolism of a cerebral artery. **coronary e.,** embolism in one of the coronary arteries causing obstruction and leading to infarction of the myocardium. **crossed e.,** paradoxical e. **direct e.,** embolism occurring in the direction of the blood stream. **fat e.,** embolism of fat that has entered the circulation. **hematogenous e.,** embolism in a blood vessel. **infective e.,** embolism in which the embolus is infective. **lymph e., lymphogenous e.,** embolism of a lymph vessel. **miliary e.,** that which affects at the same time many small blood vessels. **multiple e.,** embolism by a number of small emboli. **oil e.,** fat e. **paradoxical e.,** blockage of an artery by a thrombus from a systemic vein, which has passed through a defect that permits direct communication between the right and the left side of the heart, notably an open foramen ovale. **pulmonary e.,** the closure of the pulmonary artery or one of its branches by an embolus, resulting in pulmonary edema or hemorrhagic infarction. **pyemic e.,** infective e. **retinal e.,** embolism of the central artery of the retina. **retrograde e.,** one which moves in a direction opposite to that of the blood current. **spinal e.,** embolism of an artery in the spinal cord. **trichinous e.,** embolism due to trichinae. **venous e.,** embolism of a vein.

embololalia (em″bŏ-lo-la′le-ah) [Gr. *emballein* to insert + *lalia* babble]. The interpolation of meaningless words into the speech.

embolomycotic (em″bŏ-lo-mi-kot′ik). Pertaining to or marked by an infectious embolus.

embolophrasia (em″bŏ-lo-fra′ze-ah) [Gr. *emballein* to insert + *phrasis* utterance]. Embololalia.

Embolus impacted at bifurcation of a branch of an artery (Green).

embolus (em′bo-lus) pl. *em′boli* [Gr. *embolos* plug]. 1. A clot or other plug brought by the blood from another vessel and forced into a smaller one so as to obstruct the circulation. 2. The nucleus emboliformis. **air e.,** a bubble of air obstructing a blood vessel. **cancer e.,** a small mass of cells detached from a cancer and carried by the blood stream to lodgment in a distant location. **cellular e.,** an embolus consisting of tissue cells of various kinds, occurring in various acute infectious diseases. **fat e.,** an embolus made up of oil or fat. **foam e.,** an embolus formed by a mixture of gas and blood. **obturating e.,** an embolus completely blocking a vessel. **riding e., saddle e., straddling e.,** an embolus at the bifurcation of an artery, blocking both branches.

emboly (em′bo-le) [Gr. *embolē* a throwing in]. The invagination of the blastula by which the gastrula is formed.

embouchment (aw-boosh-maw′) [Fr.]. The opening of one vessel into another.

embrasure (em-bra′zhur). The interproximal space occlusal to the area of contact of adjacent teeth in the same dental arch. **buccal e.,** the embrasure opening out toward the cheek between molar and premolar teeth. **labial e.,** the embrasure opening toward the lips between canine and incisor teeth. **lingual e.,** one of the openings on the lingual sides of the teeth. **occlusal e.,** the space between the marginal ridges of approximating teeth, mesially and distally, and the point of contact and the occlusal plane.

embrocation (em-bro-ka′shun) [L. *embrocatio*]. 1. The application of a liquid medicament to the surface of the body. 2. A liquid medicine for external use.

embryectomy (em″bre-ek′to-me) [*embryo* + Gr. *ektomē* excision]. Excision of the embryo in extra-uterine pregnancy.

embryo (em-bre-o) [Gr. *embryon*]. 1. The early or developing stage of any organism, especially the developing product of fertilization of an egg. In the human, the embryo is generally considered to be the developing organism from one week after

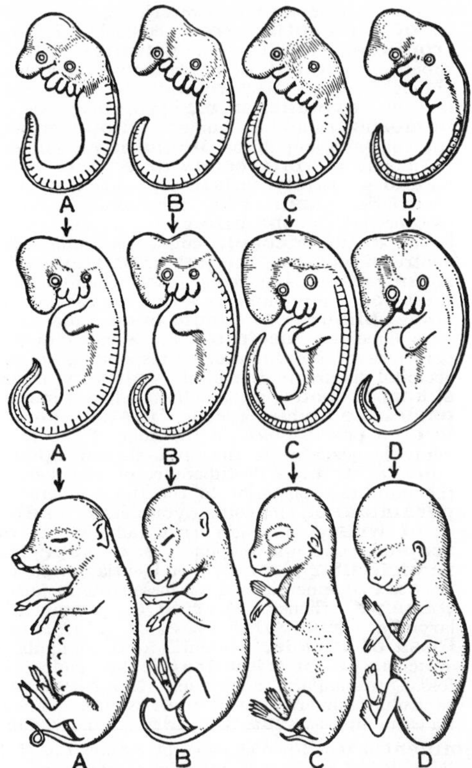

Four mammalian embryos at various stages of development: A, hog; B, calf; C, rabbit; D, human. (Villee: from Romanes' "Darwin and After Darwin," after Haeckel, with the permission of the Open Court Publishing Company.)

conception to the end of the second month. 2. The element in the seed of plants which develops into a new individual. **hexacanth e.,** the embryo of *Taenia saginata* as found in the intestinal tract of cattle. **presomite e.,** the embryo at any stage prior to the appearance of the first somite. **previllous e.,** the embryo at any stage prior to the appearance of the chorionic villi. **somite e.,** the embryo at any stage between the appearances of the first and the last somites. **Spee's e.,** an embryo described by Spee as being between one and two weeks old. **Wilms's e.** See under *tumor*.

embryocardia (em″bre-o-kar′de-ah) [*embryo* + Gr. *kardia* heart]. A symptom in which the sounds of the heart resemble those of fetal life, there being very little difference in the quality of the first and second sounds. **jugular e.,** auricular flutter.

embryoctony (em″bre-ok′tŏ-ne) [*embryo* + Gr. *kteinein* to kill]. The artificial destruction of the living embryo, or of the unborn fetus.

embryogenesis (em″bre-o-jen′e-sis) [*embryo* + *genesis*]. The development of a new individual by means of sexual reproduction, that is, from a fertilized ovum.

embryogenic (em″bre-o-jen′ik). 1. Pertaining to the development of the embryo. 2. Producing an embryo.

embryogenetic (em″bre-o-jĕ-net′ik). Embryogenic.

embryogeny (em″bre-oj′e-ne) [*embryo* + Gr. *gennan* to produce]. The production or origin of the embryo.

embryograph (em′bre-o-graf) [*embryo* + Gr. *graphein* to write]. A combination of a microscope and a camera lucida: used in drawing figures of the embryo.

embryography (em″bre-og′rah-fe) [*embryo* + Gr. *graphein* to write]. A treatise or description of the embryo.

embryoid (em′bre-oid) [*embryo* + Gr. *eidos* form]. Resembling the embryo.

embryoism (em′bre-o-izm). The condition of being an embryo.

embryologist (em″bre-ol′o-jist). An expert in embryology.

embryology (em″bre-ol′o-je) [*embryo* + *-logy*]. The science which treats of the development of the embryo. **causal e.,** experimental e. **descriptive e.,** analysis of the sequential development of embryos and their tissues and organs as established through the study of graded stages. **experimental e.,** the analysis of the factors and relations in development, obtained by subjecting embryos to experimental procedures. Called also *causal embryology*.

embryoma (em″bre-o′mah). A tumor made up of two or more kinds of tissues which may be well differentiated histologically and sometimes functionally but are entirely devoid of organization. Teeth and hair are particularly common. See *embryonal carcinosarcoma*, under *carcinosarcoma*.

embryomorphous (em″bre-o-mor′fus) [*embryo* + Gr. *morphē* form]. Noting certain abnormal tissue elements supposed to be relics of a conception.

embryonal (em′bre-o-nal). Pertaining to the embryo.

embryonate (em′bre-o-nāt). 1. Pertaining to or resembling an embryo. 2. Containing an embryo. 3. Impregnated; fecundated.

embryonic (em″bre-on′ik). Pertaining to the embryo, or to the first trimester of prenatal life in the human; occurring during the first trimester of prenatal life.

embryoniform (em″bre-on′ĭ-form). Resembling an embryo.

embryonism (em′bre-o-nizm). Embryoism.

embryonization (em″bre-o-ni-za′shun). Reversion to the embryonic form on the part of a tissue or cell.

embryonoid (em′bre-o-noid). Resembling an embryo.

embryopathia (em″bre-o-path′e-ah). Embryopathy. **e. rubeola′ris,** developmental anomalies observed in infants of mothers who had rubeola during pregnancy.

embryopathology (em″bre-o-pah-thol′o-je). The study of abnormal embryos or of defective development.

embryopathy (em″bre-op′ah-the) [*embryo-* + Gr. *pathos* disease]. A morbid condition resulting from interference with normal embryonic development.

embryophore (em′bre-o-fōr). A second egg shell formed by the embryo after loss of the first, as seen in the eggs of *Taenia* as they are found in the feces.

embryoplastic (em″bre-o-plas′tik) [*embryo* + Gr. *plassein* to shape]. Pertaining to or concerned in the formation of an embryo.

embryoscope (em″bre-o-skōp) [*embryo* + Gr. *skopein* to examine]. An instrument for observing the development of the embryo, as of birds.

embryotocia (em″bre-o-to′se-ah) [*embryo* + Gr. *tokos* birth]. The delivery of the embryo; abortion.

embryotome (em′bre-o-tōm). A cutting instrument used in embryotomy.

embryotomy (em″bre-ot′o-me) [*embryo* + Gr. *tomē* a cutting]. 1. The dismemberment of a fetus to facilitate delivery. 2. The dissection of embryos and fetuses.

embryotoxon (em″bre-o-tok′son) [*embryo* + Gr. *toxon* a bow, or anything arched]. A congenital opacity of the margin of the cornea; called also *arcus juvenilis*.

embryotroph (em″bre-o-trōf′) [*embryo* + Gr. *trophē* nourishment]. The total nutriment (histotroph and hemotroph) made available to the embryo.

embryotrophy (em″bre-ot′ro-fe) [*embryo* + Gr. *trophē* nourishment]. The nutrition of the embryo.

embryulcia (em″bre-ul′se-ah) [Gr. *embryoulkia*]. The instrumental removal of the fetus from the uterus.

embryulcus (em″bre-ul′kus) [Gr. *embryoulkos*]. A blunt hook for use in embryulcia.

EMC. Abbreviation for *encephalomyocarditis* (virus).

emedullate (e-med′u-lāt) [L. *e* out + *medulla* marrow]. To remove the marrow from.

emergency (e-mer′jen-se) [L. *emergere* to raise up]. An unlooked for or sudden occasion; an accident; an urgent or pressing need.

emergent (e-mer′jent). 1. Pertaining to an emergency. 2. Coming into being through consecutive stages of development.

emery (em′er-e). An abrasive substance, consisting of corundum and various impurities, such as iron oxide.

emesia (ĕ-me′ze-ah). Emesis.

emesis (em′e-sis) [Gr. *emein* to vomit]. Vomiting; an act of vomiting. **e. gravida′rum,** the vomiting of pregnancy.

emetatrophia (em″ĕ-tah-tro′fe-ah) [Gr. *emetos* vomiting + *atrophia* atrophy]. Atrophy or wasting due to persistent vomiting.

emetic (e-met′ik) [Gr. *emetikos;* L. *emeticus*]. 1. Bringing on or causing the act of vomiting. 2. An agent that causes vomiting. **direct e.,** one that acts directly on the nerves of the stomach. **indirect e.,** one that acts on the vomiting center through the blood. **mechanical e.,** direct e. **systemic e.,** indirect e. **tartar e.,** antimony potassium tartrate.

emeticology (e-met″ĭ-kol′o-je). The sum of knowledge regarding emetics.

emetine (em′ĕ-tin). An alkaloid obtained from ipecac or prepared by methylation of cephaeline: used as an antiamebic. **e. bismuth iodide,** $C_{29}H_{40}O_4N_2.2HI.BiI_3.H_2O$, an orange-red powder containing from 17 to 23 per cent of anhydrous emetine and from 15 to 20 per cent of bismuth: used in the treatment of amebic dysentery. **e. hydrochloride,** a salt of emetine, $C_{33}H_{44}O_4N_2.2HCl$, used in amebic dysentery.

emetism (em′ĕ-tizm). Ipecac poisoning.

emetocathartic (em″ĕ-to-kah-thar′tik). 1. Both emetic and cathartic. 2. An agent that is both emetic and cathartic.

emetology (em″ĕ-tol′o-je). Emeticology.

emetophobia (em″e-to-fo′be-ah) [Gr. *emetos* vomiting + *phobia*]. Abnormal fear of vomiting.

E.M.F. Abbreviation of *electromotive force,* and for *erythrocyte maturation factor.*

EMG. Abbreviation for *electromyogram.*

emictory (e-mik′to-re) [L. *e* out + *mingere* to urinate]. Diuretic.

emigration (em″ĭ-gra′shun) [L. *e* out + *migrare* to wander]. The escape of leukocytes through the walls of small blood vessels; diapedesis.

eminence (em′ĭ-nens). A prominence or projection, especially one upon the surface of a bone. Called also *eminentia* [N A]. **antithenar e.,** hypothenar. **arcuate e.,** eminentia arcuata. **articular e. of temporal bone,** tuberculum articulare ossis temporalis. **auditory e.,** eminentia acustica. **bicipital e.,** tuberositas radii. **canine e.,** a prominent bony ridge overlying the root of either canine tooth on the labial surface of both the maxilla and the mandible. **capitate e.,** capitulum humeri. **e. of cartilage of Santorini,** tuberculum corniculatum. **caudate e. of liver,** processus caudatus hepatis. **coccygeal e.,** cornu sacrale. **cochlear e. of sacral bone,** promontorium ossis sacri. **collateral e. of lateral ventricle,** eminentia collateralis ventriculi lateralis. **e. of concha,** eminentia conchae. **cruciform e. of occipital bone,** eminentia cruciformis. **cuneiform e. of head of rib,** crista capitis costae. **deltoid e.,** tuberositas deltoidea humeri. **Doyère's e.,** the papilla marking the entrance of a nerve filament into a muscle fiber. **facial e. of eminentia teres,** colliculus facialis. **frontal e.,** tuber frontale. **genital e.,** genital tubercle. **gluteal e. of femur,** tuberositas glutea femoris. **hypobranchial e.,** copula linguae. **hypothenar e.,** hypothenar. **e. of humerus,** capitulum humeri. **iliopectineal e.,** eminentia iliopubica. **iliopubic e.,** eminentia iliopubica. **intercondylar e., intercondyloid e., intermediate e.,** eminentia intercondylaris. **jugular e.,** tuberculum jugulare ossis occipitalis. **mamillary e.,** corpus mamillare. **e. of Meckel,** eminentia collateralis ventriculi lateralis. **medial e. of rhomboid fossa,** eminentia medialis fossae rhomboideae. **nasal e.,** the prominence above the root of the nose. **oblique e. of cuboid bone,** tuberositas ossis cuboidei. **occipital e.,** a ridge in the paracoele of the embryo, corresponding to the occipital fissure in the adult. **olivary e. of sphenoid bone,** tuberculum sellae turcicae. **parietal e.,** tuber parietale. **postchiasmatic e.,** a protuberance on the floor of the third ventricle posterior to the optic chiasm. **postfundibular e.,** a protuberance on the floor of the interbrain posterior to the tuber cinereum. **pyramidal e.,** eminentia pyramidalis. **radial e. of wrist,** eminentia carpi radialis. **e. of scapha,** eminentia scaphae. **e. of superior semicircular canal,** eminentia arcuata. **terete e.,** eminentia medialis fossae rhomboideae. **thenar e.,** thenar. **thyroid e.,** prominentia laryngea. **triangular e., e. of triangular fossa of auricle,** eminentia fossa triangularis auriculae. **e. of triquetral fossa,** eminentia fossae triangularis auriculae. **trochlear e.,** capitulum humeri. **ulnar e. of wrist,** eminentia carpi ulnaris. **vagal e.,** trigonum nervi vagi.

eminentia (em″ĭ-nen′she-ah), pl. *eminen′tiae* [L.]. [N A, B N A]. A general term for a prominence or projection, especially one on the surface of a bone. Called also *eminence.* **e. abducen′tis, Streeter,** colliculus facialis. **e. annula′ris,** pons. **e. arcua′ta** [N A, B N A], an arched prominence on the internal surface of the petrous part of the temporal bone in the floor of the middle cranial fossa, marking the position of the superior semicircular canal. It is particularly prominent in young skulls. Called also *arcuate eminence.* **e. articula′ris os′sis tempora′lis,** tuberculum articulare ossis temporalis. **e. capita′ta,** capitulum humeri. **e. car′pi radia′lis** [B N A], an eminence on the palmar surface of the radial side of the wrist, formed by the tubercles on the scaphoid and trapezium bones. Omitted in N A. **e. car′pi ulna′ris** [B N A], an eminence on the palmar surface of the ulnar side of the wrist, formed by the pisiform bone and the hook of the hamate bone. Omitted in N A. **e. ciner′ea cuneifor′mis,** trigonum nervi vagi. **e. collatera′lis ventric′uli latera′lis** [N A, B N A], an elevation in the floor of the inferior horn of the lateral ventricle, produced by the collateral sulcus. Called also *collateral eminence of lateral ventricle.* **e. con′chae** [N A, B N A], the projection on the medial surface of the auricle that corresponds to the concha on the lateral surface. Called also *eminence of concha.* **e. crucia′ta** [B N A], **e. crucifor′mis** [N A], the cross-shaped bony prominence on the internal surface of the squama of the occipital bone, at the intersection of the ridges associated with the sulci of the superior sagittal sinus and the transverse sinuses. Called also *cruciate eminence of occipital bone.* **e. facia′lis,** colliculus facialis. **e. fallo′pii,** a ridge on the inner wall of the tympanum, showing the position of the facial nerve. **e. fos′sae triangula′ris auric′ulae** [N A, B N A], the protuberance on the medial surface of the auricle that corresponds to the triangular fossa on the lateral surface. Called also *eminence of triangular fossa of auricle.* **e. grac′ilis,** fasciculus gracilis medullae oblongatae. **e. hypoglos′si,** trigonum nervi hypoglossi. **e. iliopectin′ea** [B N A], **e. iliopu′bica** [N A], a diffuse enlargement just anterior to the acetabulum, marking the junction of the ilium with the superior ramus of the pubis. Called also *iliopubic eminence.* **e. intercondyla'ris** [N A], **e. intercondyloi'dea** [B N A], **e. interme'dia,** an eminence on the proximal extremity of the tibia, surmounted on either side by a prominent tubercle, on to the sides of which the articular facets are prolonged. Called also *intercondylar eminence.* **e. jugula'ris,** tuberculum jugulare ossis occipitalis. **e. latera'lis cartilag'inis cricoi'deae,** facies articularis thyroidea. **e. latera'lis mecke'lii, e. Mecke'li,** e. collateralis ventriculi lateralis. **e. media'lis fos'sae rhomboi'deae** [N A, B N A], an eminence in the medial part of the floor of the fourth ventricle, bounded laterally by the sulcus limitans and produced by the facial colliculus and the trigone of the hypoglossal nerve. Called also *medial eminence of rhomboid fossa.* **e. papilla'ris, e. pyramida'lis** [N A, B N A], the hollow elevation in the inner wall of the middle ear, which contains the stapedius muscle. Called also *pyramidal eminence.* **e. sca'phae** [N A, B N A], the prominence on the medial side of the auricle of the external ear that corresponds to the scapha on the lateral side. **e. styloi'dea,** prominentia styloidea. **e. sym'physis,** the prominent lower border of the middle of the chin. **e. te'res,** e. medialis fossae rhomboideae. **e. triangula'ris,** e. fossae triangularis. **e. trigem'ina, e. trigem'ini,** lamina tecti mesencephali. **e. va'gi,** ala cinerea.

emissaria (em"ĭ-sa're-ah) [L.]. Plural of *emissarium.*

emissarium (em"ĭ-sa're-um), pl. *emissa'ria* [L.]. B N A name for an emissary vein. See *venae emissariae.* **e. condyloi'deum** [B N A], vena emissaria condyloidea. **e. mastoi'deum** [B N A], vena emissaria mastoidea. **e. occipita'le** [B N A], vena emissaria occipitalis. **e. parieta'le** [B N A], vena emissaria parietalis.

emissary (em'ĭ-sa"re) [L. *emissarium* drain]. Affording an outlet, referring especially to the venous outlets from the dural sinuses through the skull.

emission (e-mish'un) [L. *emissio,* a sending out]. A discharge: specifically, an involuntary discharge of semen. **nocturnal e.,** reflex emission of the semen during sleep. **thermionic e.,** the emission of electrons and ions by incandescent bodies.

emissivity (e"mis-siv'ĭ-te). The ratio of emissive power (of radiant energy) of a surface to that of a black surface having the same temperature.

emivan (em'ĭ-van). Trade mark for preparations of ethamivan.

emmenagogic (e-men"ah-goj'ik). Inducing menstruation.

emmenagogue (e-men'ah-gog) [Gr. *emmēna* menses + *agōgos* leading]. An agent or measure that induces menstruation. **direct e.,** an agent that induces menstruation by acting directly upon the reproductive organs. **indirect e.,** an agent or measure that acts to induce menstruation by relieving another condition of which amenorrhea is a secondary result.

emmenia (e-me'ne-ah) [Gr. *emmēna*]. The menses.

emmenic (e-men'ik). Pertaining to the menses.

emmeniopathy (e-me"ne-op'ah-the) [Gr. *emmēnios* menses + *pathos* disease]. Any disorder of menstruation.

emmenology (em"ĕ-nol'o-je) [Gr. *emmēna* menses + *-logy*]. The sum of knowledge regarding menstruation and its disorders.

Emmerich's bacillus (em'er-iks) [Rudolf *Emmerich,* bacteriologist in Munich, 1852–1914]. *Escherichia coli,* var. *neapolitanus.*

Emmet's needle, operation (em'ets) [Thomas Addis *Emmet,* gynecologist in New York, 1828–1919]. See under *needle* and *operation.*

emmetrope (em'e-trōp). An individual who has perfect vision (emmetropid).

emmetropia (em-e-tro'pe-ah) [Gr. *emmetros* in proper measure + *ōpē* sight + *-ia*]. A state of proper correlation between the refractive system of the eye and the axial length of the eyeball, rays of light entering the eye parallel to the optic axis being brought to a focus exactly on the retina.

emmetropic (em"e-trop'ik). Pertaining to or characterized by emmetropia.

emol (e'mol). An emollient, soapy mineral from Perthshire in Scotland: used in various chronic skin diseases and for removing thickened epidermis.

emollient (e-mol'e-ent) [L. *emolliens* softening, from *e* out + *mollis* soft]. 1. Softening or soothing. 2. An agent which softens or soothes the skin, or soothes an irritated internal surface.

emotiometabolic (e-mo"she-o-met"ah-bol'ik). Inducing some metabolism as a result of emotion.

emotiomotor (e-mo"she-o-mo'tor). Inducing some activity as a result of emotion.

emotiomuscular (e-mo"she-o-mus'ku-lar). Pertaining to muscular activity due to emotion.

emotion (e-mo'tion) [L. *emovere* to disturb]. A state of mental excitement characterized by alteration of feeling tone.

emotional (e-mo'shun-al). Pertaining to the emotions.

emotiovascular (e-mo"she-o-vas'ku-lar). Producing a vascular change as a result of emotion.

emotive (e-mo'tiv). Marked by emotion; exciting emotion.

emotivity (e"mo-tiv'ĭ-te). The capacity for emotion; the capacity for reacting to a stimulus.

Emp. Abbreviation for L. *emplas'trum,* a plaster.

empacho (em-pah'cho). A Mexican term for chronic indigestion in children with diarrhea.

empasma (em-paz'mah) [Gr. *en* in + *passein* to sprinkle]. A powder for external use.

empathic (em-path'ik). Pertaining to or characterized by empathy.

empathize (em'pah-thīz). To experience or feel empathy; to enter into another person's feelings.

empathy (em'pah-the) [Gr. *en* into + *pathos* feeling]. The recognition of and entering into the feelings of another person.

emphlysis (em'flĭ-sis) [Gr. *en* in + *phlysis* eruption]. An exanthematous disease in which the lesions become scabby.

emphractic (em-frak'tik) [Gr. *emphraktikos* likely to obstruct]. 1. Tending to obstruct the pores. 2. An agent which closes the pores of the skin.

emphraxis (em-frak'sis) [Gr.]. A stoppage, obstruction, or infraction.

emphysatherapy (em"fiz-ah-ther'ah-pe) [Gr. *emphysan* to inflate + *therapeia* treatment]. The injection of gas into an organ for therapeutical purposes.

emphysema (em"fi-se'mah) [Gr. "an inflation"]. A swelling or inflation due to the presence of air, applied especially to a morbid condition of the lungs (*pulmonary e.*). **alveolar e.,** vesicular e. **atrophic e.,** emphysema with wasting of the lung substance. **compensating e., compensatory e.,** dilatation of one part of the lung to compensate for the consolidation of another part. **ectatic e.,** vesicular e. **false e.,** gas in the tissues due to septic poison or gangrene. **gangrenous e.,** a malignant emphysema of microbic origin. **glass blower's e.,** emphysema of the lungs due to overstrain in glass blowers. **hypertrophic e.,** vesicular emphysema in which from overstretching the contractile energy of the lungs is destroyed, so that they become permanently enlarged, and the thorax assumes a characteristic barrel shape. **interlobular e.,** interstitial e. **interstitial e.,** presence of air in the interstitial tissues of the lungs, as a result of destruction of the walls of the alveoli. **interstitial e., spontaneous,** presence of air in the interstitial tissues of the lungs, following spontaneous rupture of the alveoli. **Jenner's e.,** senile e. **mediastinal e.,** the presence of air in the mediastinal tissue.

pulmonary e., a condition of the lung characterized by increase beyond normal in the size of air spaces distal to the terminal bronchioles, either from dilatation of the alveoli (*vesicular e.*), or from destruction (*interstitial e.*) of their walls. **senile e.,** emphysema due to dilatation of the alveoli occurring with age. **small-lunged e.,** atrophic e. **subcutaneous e.,** the presence of air or gas in the subcutaneous tissues of the body. **surgical e.,** subcutaneous emphysema following surgical operation. **traumatic e.,** distention of the subcutaneous tissues by air escaping from the pleural cavity after intrathoracic injury. **vesicular e.,** increase beyond normal in the size of the air spaces in the lung distal to the terminal bronchioles, as a result of dilatation of the alveoli.

emphysematous (em″fi-sem′ah-tus). Of the nature of or affected with emphysema.

Empiric (em-pir′ik) [Gr. *empeirikos* experimental]. 1. The second of the post-hippocratic schools of medicine, which arose in the second century, B.C., under the leadership of Philinos of Cos and Serapion of Alexandria. As opposed to the Dogmatists, the Empirics declared that the search for the ultimate causes of phenomena was vain, but they were active in endeavoring to discover the immediate causes. They paid particular attention to the totality of symptoms. In their search for a line of treatment to benefit a particular set of symptoms they employed the "tripod of the Empirics": (1) their own chance observations—their own experience; (2) learning obtained from contemporaries and predecessors—the experience of others; and (3), in cases of new diseases, the formation of conclusions from other diseases which they resembled—analogy. The Empirics paid great attention to clinical observation, and were guided in their methods of treatment almost entirely by experience. 2. A believer in or practitioner of the Empiric school of medicine.

empiric (em-pir′ik). 1. Empirical. 2. A practitioner whose skill is based on experience.

empirical (em-pir′e-kal). Based on experience.

empiricism (em-pir′ĭ-sizm) [Gr. *empeiria* experience]. 1. The method of the Empiric school of medicine. 2. Reliance on mere experience; empirical practice. 3. Quackery.

empirin (em′pĭ-rin). Trade mark for tablets containing acetylsalicylic acid, acetophenetidin, and caffeine.

emplastic (em-plas′tik) [Gr. *emplastikos* stopping up]. 1. Adhesive or glutinous. 2. A constipating medicine.

emplastrum (em-plas′trum) [L.; Gr. *emplastron*]. A plaster. **e. adhae′sivum,** adhesive plaster. **e. adhae′sivum steri′le,** sterile adhesive plaster. **e. belladon′nae,** belladonna plaster. **e. cap′sici,** capsicum plaster. **e. hydrargy′ri,** mercurial plaster. **e. o′pii,** opium plaster. **e. plum′bi olea′tis,** lead plaster. **e. resi′nae,** rosin plaster; adhesive plaster. **e. sapo′nis,** soap plaster. **e. sin′apis,** mustard plaster.

emporiatrics (em-po″re-at′riks) [Gr. *emporos* one who goes on shipboard as a passenger + *iatrikē* medicine]. That branch of medicine which treats of the health problems of travelers about the world.

emprosthotonos (em″pros-thot′o-nos) [Gr. *emprosthen* forward + *tonos* tension]. A form of tetanic spasm in which the head and feet are brought forward and the body is rendered tense.

emprosthotonus (em″pros-thot′o-nus). Emprosthotonos.

emptysis (emp′tĭ-sis) [Gr.]. Expectoration, especially of blood.

Empusa (em-pu′sah). A genus of parasitic fungi. **E. mus′cae,** a species developing in the bodies of flies, thus destroying them.

empyema (em″pi-e′mah) [Gr. *empyema*]. Accumulation of pus in a cavity of the body, especially in the chest (pyothorax). **e. artic′uli,** acute suppurative synovitis. **e. benig′num,** a variety in which fever is absent and there is a fair condition of general health, but which is usually incurable. **e. of the chest,** suppuration in the pleural cavity, due to pleurisy or traumatism; pyothorax. The disease is attended by dyspnea, fever, loss of strength, and emaciation. **interlobar e.,** empyema situated between two lobes of the lung. **latent e.,** empyema unaccompanied by any symptoms. **loculated e.,** pus in a group of loculi. **mastoid e.,** suppurative inflammation of the mucous lining of the cavities of the mastoid process. **metapneumonic e.,** empyema developing some time after the subsidence of the pneumonia. **e. necessita′tis,** empyema in which the pus can make a spontaneous escape. **e. of pericardium,** purulent pericarditis. **pneumococcal e.,** that which is due to the pneumococcus. **pulsating e.,** pyothorax in which the movements of the heart produce a visible vibration of the chest wall. **putrid e.,** empyema in which the pus has become more or less decomposed. **streptococcal e.,** a form due to the streptococcus of erysipelas. **synpneumonic e.,** empyema which arises during the course of pulmonary inflammation. Cf. *metapneumonic e.* **thoracic e.,** pyothorax. **tuberculous e.,** a form of empyema due to the tubercle bacillus.

empyemic (em″pi-e′mik). Pertaining to or of the nature of empyema.

empyesis (em″pi-e′sis) [Gr. *empyēsis* suppuration]. 1. An accumulation of pus, as one behind the iris (Marchart), or in the anterior chamber of the eye (Himly). 2. Any disease characterized by phlegmonous vesicles becoming filled with purulent fluid.

empyocele (em′pi-o-sēl) [Gr. *empyein* to suppurate + *kēlē* tumor]. A collection of pus at the umbilicus.

empyreuma (em″pi-roo′mah) [Gr. *empyreuma* a live coal]. The peculiar odor of animal or vegetable matter when charred in a closed vessel.

empyreumatic (em″pi-roo-mat′ik). Pertaining to empyreuma; pertaining to or produced by destructive distillation of organic matter.

E.M.S. Abbreviation for *Emergency Medical Service* (British).

emul. Abbreviation for L. *emul′sum* emulsion.

emulgent (e-mul′jent) [L. *emulgere* to milk or drain out]. 1. Effecting a straining or purifying process. 2. A renal artery or vein. 3. A medicine which stimulates the flow of bile or urine.

emulsifier (e-mul″si-fi′er). An agent that is used to produce an emulsion.

emulsify (e-mul′sĭ-fi). To convert or to be converted into an emulsion.

emulsin (e-mul′sin). A hydrolyzing enzyme which splits amygdalin and other beta glycosides.

emulsion (e-mul′shun) [L. *emulsio, emulsum*]. A preparation of one liquid distributed in small globules throughout the body of a second liquid. The emulsions for which official standards have been promulgated include cod liver oil emulsion, cod liver oil emulsion with malt, liquid petrolatum emulsion, and phenolphthalein in liquid petrolatum emulsion. **bacillary e.** See *new tuberculin, Koch,* under *tuberculin.* **Butschli's e.,** a preparation of potassium carbonate and rancid olive oil: used in microscopical work. **chylomicron e.,** the finely dispersed emulsion of fat which is found in the blood. **kerosene e.,** an emulsion of kerosene in soap solution: used as an insecticide. **photographic e.,** a gelatinous coating incorporating silver halide which is applied to film. **Pusey's e.,** a preparation of powdered tragacanth, glycerin, phenol, oil of bergamot, and olive oil in water: used in infantile eczema.

emulsive (e-mul′siv). 1. Capable of emulsifying a substance. 2. Susceptible of being emulsified. 3. Affording an oil on pressure.

emulsoid (e-mul′soid). An emulsion colloid.

emulsum (e-mul′sum), pl. *emul′sa* [L.]. An emulsion.

emunctory (e-munk'to-re) [L. *emungere* to cleanse]. 1. Excretory or depurant. 2. Any excretory organ or duct.

emundation (e"mun-da'shun) [L. *emundatio* a cleansing]. The rectification of drugs.

emydin (em'ĭ-din). A protein found in the eggs of the tortoise.

emylcamate (e-mil'kah-māt). Chemical name: 3-methyl-3-pentanol carbamate: used as a tranquilizer.

enamel (en-am'el). The white, compact, and very hard substance that covers and protects the dentin of the crown of a tooth. Called also *enamelum* [N A] and *substantia adamantina dentis* [B N A]. **brown e., hereditary,** amelogenesis imperfecta. **curled e.,** enamel in which the columns are bent. **dwarfed e.,** enamel which is less thick than normal: called also *nanoid e.* **gnarled e.,** enamel in which the rods run in bundles, each bundle having a different direction and intertwining with its neighbors. Cf. *straight e.* **mottled e.,** an enamel defect, largely of the permanent teeth, resulting from ingestion of excessive amounts of fluoride in water used for drinking and for food preparation during the period of enamel calcification. The affected teeth have a dull, chalky white appearance on eruption and later, in areas with higher fluoride concentration, may show a brown stain. **nanoid e.,** dwarfed e. **straight e.,** enamel in which the rods pursue an almost straight course Cf. *gnarled e.*

enameloblast (en-am'el-o-blast). Ameloblast.

enameloblastoma (en-am"el-o-blas-to'mah). Ameloblastoma.

enameloma (en-am"el-o'mah) [*enamel* + *-oma*]. A tiny globule of enamel, firmly adherent to a tooth, most frequently found near or in the bifurcation or trifurcation of the roots, or on the root surface near the cemento-enamel junction.

enamelum (e-nam'el-um). [N A] The white, compact, and very hard substance that covers and protects the dentin of the crown of a tooth. Called also *enamel*, and *substantia adamantina dentis* [B N A].

enanthem (en-an'them). Enanthema.

enanthema (en"an-the'ma), pl. *enanthe'mas, enanthem'ata* [Gr. *en* in + *anthema* a blossoming]. An eruption upon a mucous surface.

enanthematous (en"an-them'ah-tus). Pertaining to or of the nature of an enanthema.

enanthesis (en"an-the'sis) [Gr. *en* in + *anthein* to bloom]. Any skin eruption due to an internal disease.

enanthrope (en-an'thrōp) [Gr. *en* in + *anthrōpos* man]. Any source of disease situated within the human body.

enantiobiosis (en-an"te-o-bi-o'sis) [Gr. *enantios* opposite + *bios* life]. The condition in which organisms living together antagonize one another's development. Cf. *symbiosis.*

enantiomorph (en-an'te-o-morf") [Gr. *enantios* opposite + *morphē* form]. A compound exhibiting, or capable of exhibiting, enantiomorphism; an enantiomorphic isomer.

enantiomorphic (en-an"te-o-mor'fik). Pertaining to or exhibiting enantiomorphism.

enantiomorphism (en-an"te-o-mor'fizm) [Gr. *enantios* opposite + *morphē* form]. A special type of optical isomerism in which a nonsuperimposable, mirror-image relationship exists at all times between the respective molecules of the compounds. Enantiomorphic isomers always rotate the plane of polarized light to the same degree but in opposite directions; otherwise most of their chemical and physical properties are identical. The molecules are always asymmetric, very often as the result of possession of one or more asymmetric carbon atoms. Thus lactic acid, CH_3-CHOHCOOH, possessing one such carbon atom, exists in a *dextro* and a *laevo* form. The molecules of some enantiomorphic compounds (e.g., certain biphenyl or spirane compounds) are asymmetric as a whole, but do not possess any asymmetric carbon atoms.

enantiopathia (en-an"te-o-path'e-ah) [Gr. *enantios* opposite + *pathos* suffering]. 1. Any disease or morbid process antagonistic to or curative of another. 2. The curing of one disease by inducing another of an opposite kind.

enantiopathic (en-an"te-o-path'ik). Inducing opposite feelings.

enantiopathy (en-an"te-op'ah-the). Enantiopathia.

enantiothamnosis (en-an"te-o-tham-no'sis). Infection by the fungus Enantiothamnus.

Enantiothamnus (en-an"te-o-tham'nus). A genus of fungi. *E. braul'ti* causes a condition marked by the development of nodules which have a central opening from which pus exudes.

enarkyochrome (en-ar'ke-o-krōm") [Gr. *en* in + *arkys* network + *chrōma* color]. An arkyochrome nerve cell containing a single network of chromatin substance.

enarthritis (en"ar-thri'tis). Inflammation of an enarthrosis.

enarthrodial (en"ar-thro'de-al). Of or pertaining to an enarthrosis.

enarthrosis (en"ar-thro'sis) [Gr. *en* in + *arthrosis* joint]. A joint in which the globular head of one bone is received into a socket in another, as in the hip joint.

en bissac (aw bis-sahk') [Fr.]. A method of reducing strangulated hernia by forcing a congenital hernia into a pouch or diverticulum.

en bloc (aw blok') [Fr.]. In a lump; as a whole.

encanthis (en-kan'this) [Gr. *en* in + *kanthos* the angle of the eye]. A small red excrescence on the semilunar fold of the conjunctiva and inner lacrimal caruncle.

encapsulated (en-kap'su-lāt-ed) [Gr. *en* in + L. *capsula* a little box]. Enclosed within a capsule.

encapsulation (en-kap"su-la'shun). 1. Any act of inclosing in a capsule. 2. A physiologic process of inclosure in a sheath made up of a substance not normal to the part.

encapsuled (en-kap'sūld). Encapsulated.

encarditis (en"kar-di'tis). Endocarditis.

encatarrhaphy (en"kat-ar'ah-fe). Enkatarrhaphy.

enceinte (aw-sawt') [Fr.]. Pregnant; with child.

encelialgia (en"se-le-al'je-ah) [Gr. *en* in + *koilia* belly + *-algia* pain]. Pain in an abdominal viscus.

enceliitis (en-se"le-i'tis) [Gr. *en* in + *koilia* belly + *-itis*]. Inflammation of an intra-abdominal organ.

encelitis (en"se-li'tis). Enceliitis.

encephalalgia (en-sef"ah-lal'je-ah) [*encephalo-* + *-algia*]. Pain within the head.

encephalasthenia (en-sef"al-as-the'ne-ah) [*encephalo-* + Gr. *astheneia* weakness]. Lack of brain power.

encephalatrophy (en-sef"ah-lat'ro-fe) [*encephalo-* + *atrophy*]. Atrophy of the brain.

encephalauxe (en"sef-ah-lawk'se) [*encephalo-* + Gr. *auxē* increase]. Hypertrophy of the brain.

encephalemia (en-sef"ah-le'me-ah) [*encephalo-* + Gr. *haima* blood + *-ia*]. Congestion of the brain.

encephalic (en"se-fal'ik). 1. Pertaining to the encephalon. 2. Within the skull.

encephalin (en-sef'ah-lin). A nitrogenous principle said to be obtainable from brain tissue.

encephalitic (en"sef-ah-lit'ik). Pertaining to or affected with encephalitis.

encephalitides (en"sef-ah-lit'ĭ-dēz). Plural of *encephalitis.*

encephalitis (en"sef-ah-li'tis), pl. *encephalit'ides* [*encephalo-* + *-itis*]. Inflammation of the brain. **e. A,** lethargic e. **acute disseminated e.,** postinfection e. **Australian X e.** See under *disease.* **e. B,** Japanese B e. **Binswanger's e.,** e. subcorticalis chronica. **buffalo e.,** a virus encephalitis of the Asiatic water buffalo. **e. C,**

St. Louis e. **chronic subcortical e.,** e. subcorticalis chronica. **cortical e., e. cortica'lis,** encephalitis affecting the cortex of the brain only. **Economo's e.,** epidemic e. **enzootic e. of horses,** Borna disease. **epidemic e., e. epidem'ica,** a viral disease of obscure pathology, occurring epidemically, and in one of several types. See *Japanese B e., lethargic e., Russian spring-summer e.,* and *St. Louis e.* **equine e.** See *equine encephalomyelitis,* under *encephalomyelitis,* and *Borna disease,* under *disease.* **forest-spring e.,** Russian spring-summer e. **fox e.,** a viral disease of foxes, raccoons, and coyotes. **hemorrhagic e.,** inflammation of the brain with hemorrhagic foci and perivascular exudate. Called also *Strümpell-Leichtenstern type of encephalitis.* **hemorrhagic arsphenamine e.,** a rapidly progressive form which sometimes follows the administration of arsphenamine. **e. hemorrha'gica supe'rior,** polioencephalitis hemorrhagica superior. **herpes e.,** a viral disease resembling equine encephalomyelitis. **e. hyperplas'tica,** an acute nonsuppurating form of encephalitis. Called also *Hayem's type of encephalitis.* **Ilhe'us e.,** a form transmitted by mosquitoes in Brazil. **infantile e.,** inflammation of the brain in children from infectious disease, injury, etc. **influenzal e.,** epidemic e. **Japanese B e.,** a form of epidemic encephalitis occurring in Japan and other Pacific islands, China, Manchuria, U.S.S.R., and probably much of the Far East; it may occur as a symptomless, subclinical infection, or an acute meningoencephalomyelitis with cortical damage and cord lesions resembling those of poliomyelitis. **lead e.,** encephalitis with marked cerebral edema, caused by lead poisoning. **lethargic e., e. lethar'gica,** a form of epidemic encephalitis, the original type described by von Economo, characterized by increasing languor, apathy, and drowsiness, passing into lethargy; observed in various parts of the world between 1915 and 1926. **Murray Valley e.,** Australian X disease. **e. neonato'rum,** encephalitis in the newborn. **e. periaxia'lis diffu'sa,** progressive subcortical encephalopathy. **e. periaxia'lis sclerot'icans,** multiple sclerosis. **porcine virus e.,** Teschen disease. **postinfection e.,** an acute disease of the central nervous system seen in persons who are convalescing from infectious diseases. Called also *acute disseminated e., acute disseminated encephalomyelitis, acute demyelinating disease,* and *acute perivascular myelinoclasis.* **postvaccinal e.,** acute encephalitis sometimes occurring after vaccination. **purulent e., pyogenic e.,** suppurative e. **Russian autumnal e.,** Japanese B e. **Russian endemic e., Russian forest-spring e.,** Russian spring-summer e. **Russian spring-summer e.,** a form of epidemic encephalitis which is acquired in forests from infected ticks, but is also transmitted in other ways, as by ingestion of the flesh of infected mammals and birds, or milk of infected goats. It ranges in severity from mild to fatal cases, with degenerative changes in organs other than those of the nervous system. **Russian tick-borne e., Russian vernal e.,** Russian spring-summer e. **St. Louis e.,** a viral disease first observed in Illinois in 1932, closely similar to western equine encephalomyelitis clinically, occurring in late summer and early fall and transmitted usually by mosquitoes of the Culex genus. It ranges from an abortive type of infection to a severe disease. **Schilder's e.,** progressive subcortical encephalopathy. **Semliki forest e.,** a form due to a virus obtained from mosquitoes in Semliki forest. **e. sid'erans,** a form of epidemic encephalitis terminating fatally in a few hours. **e. subcortica'lis chron'ica,** degeneration of the subcortical white matter of the brain accompanying sclerotic changes in the blood vessels supplying it. **suppurative e.,** encephalitis accompanied by suppuration and abscess formation. **toxoplasmic e.,** encephalitis due to infection with *Toxoplasma.* **vaccinal e.,** postvaccinal e. **vernal e.,** Russian spring-summer e. **Vienna e.,** lethargic e. **West Nile e.,** an encephalitis first recognized in Uganda, but now widespread in Africa and observed also in Israel; it occurs chiefly in summer and is sporadic rather than epidemic in form. **woodcutter's e.,** Russian spring-summer e.

encephalitogenic (en-sef″ah-lit-o-jen′ik) [*encephalitis* + Gr. *gennan* to produce]. Causing encephalitis.

Encephalitozoon (en″sĕ-fal″ĭ-to-zo′on) [*encephalitis* + Gr. *zōon* animal]. A microsporidian parasite. **E. cunic'uli,** the causative agent in spontaneous encephalomyelitis of the rabbit. They are found in intracellular cysts as well as free in the brain, kidney, and other organs. **E. hom'inis,** an organism isolated from granulomatous encephalomyelitis. **E. ra'biei,** Negri bodies.

encephalization (en-sef″ah-li-za′shun). The developmental process by which the cerebral cortex has taken over the functions of the lower (spinal) centers.

encephalo- (en-sef′ah-lo) [Gr. *enkephalos* brain]. A combining form denoting relationship to the brain.

encephalo-arteriography (en-sef″ah-lo-ar-te″re-og′rah-fe). A combination of encephalography and arteriography for examining the blood supply of the brain.

encephalocele (en-sef′ah-lo-sēl) [*encephalo-* + Gr. *kēlē* hernia]. Hernia of the brain, manifested by protrusion of brain substance through a congenital or traumatic opening of the skull.

Encephalocele.

encephaloclastic (en-sef″ah-lo-klas′tik) [*encephalo-* + Gr. *klastōs* broken]. Exhibiting the residues of a destructive lesion in the brain. See under *porencephaly.*

encephalocoele (en-sef″-ah-lo-se′le) [*encephalo-* + Gr. *koilos* hollow]. 1. The entire cavity of the cranium. 2. The ventricles and other spaces of the brain.

encephalocystocele (en-sef″ah-lo-sis′to-sēl) [*encephalo-* + Gr. *kystis* sac, bladder + *kēlē* hernia]. Hernia of the brain, the protrusion being distended by a collection of fluid communicating with the ventricle. Called also *hydrencephalocele.*

Encephalocytozoon (en-sef″ah-lo-si″to-zo′on) [*encephalo-* + Gr. *kytos* hollow vessel + *zōon* animal]. An organism, probably protozoan, found in the brain of rabbits. See *Encephalitozoon.*

encephalodialysis (en-sef″ah-lo-di-al′ĭ-sis) [*encephalo-* + Gr. *dialysis* loosening]. Softening of the brain.

encephalodysplasia (en-sef″ah-lo-dis-pla′se-ah). Any congenital anomaly of the brain.

encephalogram (en-sef′ah-lo-gram″). A roentgenogram of the head.

encephalography (en-sef″ah-log′rah-fe) [*encephalo-* + Gr. *graphein* to write]. The making of x-ray films of the brain.

encephaloid (en-sef′ah-loid) [*encephalo-* + Gr. *eidos* form]. 1. Resembling the brain or brain substance. 2. Encephaloma.

encephalolith (en-sef′ah-lo-lith) [*encephalo-* + Gr. *lithos* stone]. A brain calculus.

encephalology (en″sef-ah-lol′o-je) [*encephalo-* + *-logy*]. The sum of knowledge regarding the brain, its functions, and its diseases.

encephaloma (en″sef-ah-lo′mah). 1. Hernia of the brain. 2. Encephaloid cancer; a malignant growth of brainlike texture. 3. A tumor of the brain.

encephalomalacia (en-sef″ah-lo-mah-la′she-ah) [*encephalo-* + Gr. *malakia* softness]. Morbid softness, or softening, of the brain.

encephalomeningitis (en-sef″ah-lo-men″in-ji′tis) [*encephalo-* + *meningitis*]. Inflammation of the brain and its membranes.

encephalomeningocele (en-sef″ah-lo-me-ning′go-sēl) [*encephalo-* + Gr. *mēninx* membrane + *kēlē* hernia]. Protrusion of the cerebral membranes and brain substance through a defect in the skull.

encephalomeningopathy (en-sef″ah-lo-men″in-gop′ah-the). Disease involving the brain and the meninges.

encephalomere (en-sef′ah-lo-mēr) [*encephalo-* + Gr. *meros* part]. Any one of the succession of segments which make up the embryonic brain.

encephalometer (en-sef″ah-lom′e-ter) [*encephalo-* + Gr. *metron* measure]. An instrument used in locating certain of the regions of the brain.

encephalomyelitis (en-sef″ah-lo-mi″ĕ-li′tis). Inflammation involving both the brain and the spinal cord. **acute disseminated e.,** postinfection encephalitis. **benign myalgic e.,** a disease, usually occurring in epidemics, which is characterized by initial headache, fever, myalgia, muscular weakness, and emotional lability. **equine e.,** a viral disease of horses and mules, occurring as summer epizootics in the Western Hemisphere. Three forms are recognized: *eastern equine e., western equine e.,* and *Venezuelan equine e.* **equine e., eastern,** a viral disease similar to western equine encephalomyelitis, but occurring principally in the Atlantic and Gulf coast states. **equine e., Venezuelan,** a viral disease of horses and mules observed first in South America in 1935, the causative agent being isolated in Venezuela in 1938; the infection in man resembles influenza, with little or no indication of central nervous system involvement. **equine e., western,** a viral disease of horses and mules, communicable to man, occurring chiefly as a meningoencephalitis, with little involvement of the medulla or spinal cord; observed west of the Mississippi River in the United States, but present also along the Gulf and Atlantic coasts. **granulomatous e.,** a disease marked by granulomas and necrosis of the walls of the cerebral and spinal ventricles. **Mengo e.,** a form of encephalomyelitis the virus of which was first isolated from animals in the Mengo region of Uganda. **postvaccinal e.,** inflammation of the brain and spinal cord following vaccination or infection with vaccinia virus. **toxoplasmic e.,** encephalomyelitis due to infection with *Toxoplasma.* **viral e., virus e.,** encephalomyelitis caused by a virus. See *equine e.*

encephalomyelocele (en-sef″ah-lo-mi-el′o-sēl) [*encephalo-* + Gr. *myelon* spinal cord + *kēlē* hernia]. Abnormality of the foramen magnum and absence of the laminae and spinal processes of the cervical vertebrae, with herniation of meninges, brain substance, and spinal cord.

encephalomyeloneuropathy (en-sef″ah-lo-mi″ĕ-lo-nu-rop′ah-the). Disease involving the brain, spinal cord, and nerves.

encephalomyelopathy (en-sef″ah-lo-mi″ĕ-lop′ah-the) [*encephalo-* + Gr. *myelos* marrow + *pathos* disease]. Any disease or diseased condition of the brain and spinal cord.

encephalomyeloradiculitis (en-sef″ah-lo-mi″ĕ-lo-rah-dik″u-li′tis). Inflammation of the brain, spinal cord, and spinal nerve roots.

encephalomyeloradiculoneuritis (en-sef″ah-lo-mi″ĕ-lo-rah-dik″u-lo-nu-ri′tis). Guillain-Barré syndrome.

encephalomyeloradiculopathy (en-sef″ah-lo-mi″ĕ-lo-rah-dik″u-lop′ah-the). Disease involving the brain, spinal cord, and spinal nerve roots.

encephalomyocarditis (en-sef″ah-lo-mi″o-kar-di′tis). A viral disease characterized by degenerative and inflammatory changes in skeletal and cardiac muscle, and lesions of the central nervous system resembling those of poliomyelitis.

encephalon (en-sef′ah-lon) [Gr. *enkephalos*]. [N A, B N A] The mass of nerve tissue contained within the cranium, including the cerebrum, cerebellum, pons, and medulla oblongata.

encephalonarcosis (en-sef″ah-lo-nar-ko′sis) [*encephalo-* + Gr. *narkē* stupor]. Stupor due to brain disease.

encephalopathia (en-sef″ah-lo-path′e-ah). Encephalopathy. **e. alcohol′ica,** polioencephalitis haemorrhagica superior.

encephalopathic (en-sef″ah-lo-path′ik). Pertaining to encephalopathy.

encephalopathy (en-sef″ah-lop′ah-the) [*encephalo-* + Gr. *pathos* illness]. Any degenerative disease of the brain. **demyelinating e.,** a degenerative disease of the brain characterized by demyelination. See *progressive subcortical e.* **hypertensive e.,** a complex of cerebral phenomena (headache, convulsions, coma, etc.) occurring in the course of glomerulonephritis. **lead e.,** brain disorder caused by lead poisoning. **progressive subcortical e.,** a familial disease of unknown etiology, characterized by headache, dysphasia, weakness of the arms and legs, and visual failure progressing to blindness; intracranial pressure is increased, and there are also mental deterioration, stupor, convulsions, and spastic quadriplegia. The white substance of the brain is replaced by brownish gray translucent material, and demyelination occurs. **saturnine e.,** lead e. **Wernicke's e.,** polioencephalitis haemorrhagica superior.

encephalophyma (en-sef″ah-lo-fi′mah) [*encephalo-* + Gr. *phyma* growth]. Any tumor of the brain.

encephalopsy (en-sef′ah-lop″se) [*encephalo-* + Gr. *opsis* vision]. A condition in which the patient associates certain colors with certain words, numbers, flavors, etc.

encephalopsychosis (en-sef″ah-lo-si-ko′sis) [*encephalo-* + *psychosis*]. Any mental disease due to focal brain lesion (Southard).

encephalopuncture (en-sef″ah-lo-punk′tūr). Puncture of the brain.

encephalopyosis (en-sef″ah-lo-pi-o′sis) [*encephalo-* + Gr. *pyōsis* suppuration]. Suppuration or abscess of the brain.

encephalorachidian (en-sef″ah-lo-rah-kid′e-an) [*encephalo-* + Gr. *rhachis* spine]. Cerebrospinal.

encephalorrhagia (en-sef″ah-lo-ra′je-ah) [*encephalo-* + Gr. *rhēgnynai* to burst out]. Hemorrhage within the brain or from the brain, especially cerebral pericapillary hemorrhage.

encephalosclerosis (en-sef″ah-lo-skle-ro′sis) [*encephalo-* + Gr. *sklērōsis* hardness]. Hardening of the brain.

encephaloscope (en-sef′ah-lo-skōp). A speculum for examining cavities (such as abscess cavities) in the brain.

encephaloscopy (en-sef″ah-los′ko-pe) [*encephalo-* + Gr. *skopein* to examine]. Inspection or examination of the brain.

encephalosepsis (en-sef″ah-lo-sep′sis) [*encephalo-* + Gr. *sēpsis* decay]. Gangrene of brain tissue.

encephalosis (en-sef″ah-lo′sis) [*encephalo-* + *-osis*]. Any organic brain disease; as used by Winkelman, the term indicates a degenerative process as distinguished from true encephalitis.

encephalospinal (en-sef″ah-lo-spi′nal). Pertaining to the brain and spinal column.

encephalothlipsis (en-sef″ah-lo-thlip′sis) [*encephalo-* + Gr. *thlipsis* pressure]. Compression of the brain.

encephalotome (en-sef′ah-lo-tōm). An instrument for performing encephalotomy.

encephalotomy (en-sef″ah-lot′o-me) [*encephalo-* + Gr. *tomē* a cutting]. 1. The destruction of the head of a fetus in order to facilitate delivery. 2. The dissection or anatomy of the brain.

encheiresis (en″ki-re′sis) [Gr. *en* in + *cheir* hand]. Any manipulation, especially the introduction of a bougie, sound, or catheter.

enchondral (en-kon′dral). Endochondral.

enchondroma (en″kon-dro′mah) [Gr. *en* in + *chondros* cartilage + *-oma*]. A hyperplastic growth of cartilage tissue remaining in the interior or substance of a cartilage or bone. Called also *true chondroma.* **multiple congenital e.,** dyschondroplasia. **e. petrif′icum,** a cartilaginous tumor with osseous infiltration; osteoenchondroma.

enchondromatosis (en-kon″dro-mah-to′sis). A condition characterized by hamartomatous proliferation of cartilage cells within the metaphysis of several bones, causing thinning of the overlying cortex and distortion of the growth in length.

enchondromatous (en″kon-dro′mah-tus). Of the nature of, or pertaining to, enchondroma.

enchondrosarcoma (en-kon″dro-sar-ko′mah). A sarcoma containing cartilaginous tissue.

enchondrosis (en″kon-dro′sis). 1. An outgrowth from cartilage. 2. An enchondroma.

enchylema (en″ki-le′mah) [Gr. *en* in + *chylos* juice]. See *hyaloplasm.*

enchyma (en′kĭ-mah) [Gr. *en* in + *chymos* juice]. The substance elaborated from absorbed nutritive materials; the formative juice of the tissues.

enclave (en′klāv, aw-klahv′) [Fr.]. A substance detached from its normal connection and enclosed within another organ or tissue.

enclitic (en-klit′ik) [Gr. *enklinein* to incline]. Having the planes of the fetal head inclined to those of the maternal pelvis; not synclitic.

encolpism (en-kol′pizm) [Gr. *en* in + *kolpos* vagina]. Medication by vaginal suppositories and injections.

encolpitis (en″kol-pi′tis) [Gr. *en* in + *kolpos* vagina]. Endocolpitis.

encopresis (en-kop-re′sis). Incontinence of feces not due to organic defect or illness.

encranial (en-kra′ne-al). Situated within the cranium.

encranius (en-kra′ne-us) [Gr. *en* in + *kranion* skull]. A teratoid parasite located within the cranium of the autosite.

encyesis (en″si-e′sis) [Gr. *en* in + *kyēsis* pregnancy]. Normal uterine pregnancy.

encyopyelitis (en-si″o-pi″ĕ-li′tis) [*encyesis* + *pyelitis*]. Inflammation of the renal pelvis occurring in normal pregnancy.

encysted (en-sist′ed) [Gr. *en* in + *kystis* sac, bladder]. Inclosed in a sac, bladder, or cyst.

encystment (en-sist′ment). The process or condition of being or becoming encysted.

end-. See *endo-.*

endadelphos (end″ah-del′fos) [*end-* + Gr. *adelphos* brother]. A monster in which a parasitic twin is inclosed within the body of the autosite, or within a tumor upon the larger twin.

Endamoeba (end″ah-me′bah). A genus of amebas parasitic in the intestines of invertebrates, having a large central area of the nucleus devoid of chromatic material, surrounded by a wide zone of chromatin granules and a thick nuclear membrane. Cf. *Entamoeba.* **E. blat′tae,** a species found in the intestine of the cockroach.

endangiitis (end″an-je-i′tis). Inflammation of the endangium; intimitis.

endangium (end-an′je-um) [*end-* + Gr. *angeion* vessel]. The innermost coat of a blood vessel (tunica intima vasorum [N A].).

endaortic (end″a-or′tik). Pertaining to the interior of the aorta.

endaortitis (end″a-or-ti′tis). Inflammation of the lining membrane of the aorta.

endarterectomize (end″ar-ter-ek′to-miz). To subject to endarterectomy.

endarterectomy (end″ar-ter-ek′to-me). Excision of the thickened, atheromatous tunica intima of an artery.

endarterial (end″ar-te′re-al). Within an artery.

endarteritis (end″ar-ter-i′tis) [*end-* + Gr. *artēria* artery + *-itis*]. Inflammation of the tunica intima of an artery. **e. defor′mans,** chronic endarteritis characterized by fatty degeneration of the arterial tissues, with the formation of deposits of lime salts. **Heubner's specific e.,** syphilitic lesions of the blood vessels in late cerebral syphilis. **e. oblit′erans,** endarteritis followed by collapse and closure of the smaller branches. **e. prolif′erans,** overgrowth of fibrous tissue in the internal layers of the aorta.

endarterium (end″ar-te′re-um) [*end-* + Gr. *artēria* artery]. The tunica intima of an artery.

endarteropathy (end″ar-ter-op′ah-the). Disorder of the innermost coat (tunica intima) of an artery. **digital e.,** disorder of the tunica intima of the arteries of the digits, associated with Raynaud's phenomenon and nutritional lesions of the pulp of the fingers.

end-artery (end′ar-ter-e). An artery which does not anastomose with other arteries.

endaxoneuron (end″ak-so-nu′ron) [*end-* + *axoneuron*]. A neuron the process of which remains within the spinal cord.

end-body (end′bod-e). See *complement.*

end-brain (end′brān). Telencephalon.

end-brush (end′brush). The brushlike or tufted arrangement sometimes forming the termination of the process of a nerve cell.

end-bud (end′bud). 1. An ovoid or spheroid body located at the termination of a nerve fiber, and dispersed in the skin, mucous membranes, muscles, joints, and connective tissue of the internal organs. End-buds show a wide diversity, from simple end knobs to complex sensory end organs with connective tissue sheaths. For names of specific types see under *corpuscle.* 2. Tail bud.

end-bulb (end′bulb). End-bud, def. 1.

endchondral (end-kon′dral). Endochondral.

endeictic (en-dīk′tik) [Gr. *endeixis* a pointing out]. Symptomatic.

endemia (en-de′me-ah). Any endemic disease.

endemial (en-de′me-al). Endemic.

endemic (en-dem′ik) [Gr. *endēmos* dwelling in a place]. 1. Present in a community at all times, but occurring in only small numbers of cases. 2. A disease of low morbidity that is constantly present in a human community.

endemiology (en-de″me-ol′o-je) [*endemic* + *-logy*]. The field of science dealing with all the factors relating to the occurrence of endemic disease.

endemo-epidemic (en″de-mo-ep″ĭ-dem′ik). Endemic, but occasionally becoming epidemic.

endemy (en′dĕ-me). Any endemic disease.

endepidermis (end″ep-ĭ-der′mis). The epithelium or internal epidermis.

endergic (end-er′jik) [*end-* + Gr. *ergon* work]. Taking in work: a term applied to chemical reactions with an increase of free energy. Cf. *exergic.*

endergonic (end″er-gon′ik). Characterized by or accompanied by the absorption of energy.

endermic (en-der′mik) [Gr. *en* in + *derma* skin]. Acting by absorption through the skin; intracutaneous.

endermically (en-der′mĭ-kal-e). By direct application to the skin.

endermism (en′der-mizm). The endermic administration of medicines.

endermosis (en″der-mo′sis) [Gr. *en* in + *derma* skin]. 1. The endermic administration of medicines. 2. Any herpetic affection of the mucous membranes.

enderon (en′der-on) [Gr. *en* in + *deros* skin]. The deeper part of the skin or mucous membrane, as distinguished from the epithelium or epidermis.

enderonic (en″der-on′ik). Pertaining to the enderon or derived from it.

Enders (en′derz), John F. United States microbiologist, born 1897; co-winner, with Thomas H. Weller and Frederick C. Robbins, of the Nobel prize in medicine and physiology for 1954, for the discovery that poliomyelitis viruses multiply in human tissue.

end-feet. Button-like or knoblike terminal enlargements of naked nerve fibers which end in relation to the dendrite of another cell. Called also *terminal buttons, boutons terminaux* and *synaptic knobs.*

end-flake (end′flāk). End-plate.

ending (end′ing). A termination or finish; especially the peripheral termination of a nerve or nerve fiber. **annulospiral e's,** wide, ribbonlike sensory nerve endings which are wrapped around the fibers of a muscle spindle. **encapsulated nerve e's,** corpuscula nervosa terminalia. **epilemmal e's,** sensory nerve endings in striated muscle in which the nerve endings are in close contact with the muscle fibers but do not penetrate the sarcolemma. **flower-spray e's,** branched, slender sensory nerve endings on the sarcolemma of muscle spindles. **free nerve e's,** terminationes nervorum liberae. **grape e's,** sensory nerve endings in muscle which have the form of terminal swellings. **nerve e.,** any terminus of a nerve, especially the peripheral termination.

end-lobe (end′lōb). The occipital lobe.

end-nucleus (end-nu′kle-us). Terminal nucleus.

endo-, end- [Gr. *endon* within]. Prefix denoting an inward situation, within.

Endo's medium (en′dōz) [S. *Endo*, physician in Tokyo, 1869–1937]. See under *medium.*

endo-abdominal (en″do-ab-dom′ĭ-nal). Pertaining to the interior of the abdomen.

endo-aneurysmorrhaphy (en″do-an″u-riz-mor′ah-fe) [*endo-* + Gr. *aneurysma* aneurysm + *rhaphē* suture]. Matas' operation for aneurysm by opening the aneurysmal sac and closing the internal orifice by suture.

endo-angiitis (en″do-an-je-i′tis). Endangiitis.

endo-antitoxin (en″do-an-te-tok′sin). An antitoxin contained within the elaborating cell.

endo-aortitis (en″do-a″or-ti′tis). Endaortitis.

endo-appendicitis (en″do-ah-pen″dĭ-si′tis). Inflammation of the mucous membrane lining the vermiform appendix.

endo-arteritis (en″do-ar″ter-i′tis). Endarteritis.

endo-auscultation (en″do-aws″kul-ta′shun). Auscultation of the stomach and thoracic organs by means of a tube passed into the stomach.

endobacillary (en″do-bas′ĭ-lăr-e). Contained within a bacillus.

endobiotic (en″do-bi-ot′ik) [*endo-* + Gr. *biōsis* living]. Living parasitically within the tissues of the host.

endoblast (en′do-blast) [*endo-* + Gr. *blastos* germ]. Entoderm.

endoblastic (en″do-blas′tik). Pertaining to the endoblast; hypoblastic.

endobronchitis (en″do-brong-ki′tis). Inflammation of the epithelial lining of the bronchi or of the bronchia.

endocardial (en″do-kar′de-al) [*endo-* + Gr. *kardia* heart]. 1. Situated or occurring within the heart. 2. Pertaining to the endocardium.

endocarditic (en″do-kar-dit′ik). Pertaining to endocarditis.

endocarditis (en″do-kar-di′tis). Inflammation of the endocardium (Bouillaud); a disease generally associated with acute rheumatism, sometimes with other acute febrile diseases, and marked by dyspnea, rapid heart action, and peculiar systolic murmurs. Endocarditis is classified as *nonbacterial* (including acute nonrheumatic endocarditis and acute rheumatic endocarditis) and *bacterial* (*mycotic* or *infective*) including acute and subacute forms. **acute bacterial e.,** a rapidly progressive endocarditis which usually is part of an acute septicemia due to a variety of bacteria. **e. benig′na,** vegetative e. **e. chorda′lis,** endocarditis affecting particularly the chordae tendineae. **chronic e.,** a form associated with disease of the heart valves. **fetal e.,** right-side e. **infectious e.,** malignant e. **e. len′ta,** subacute bacterial e. **malignant e.,** a usually, and often rapidly fatal form of acute bacterial endocarditis marked by ulcerated valvular lesions (*ulcerative e.*). **mural e.,** a form affecting the lining of the walls of the heart chambers, as distinguished from *valvular e.* **mycotic e.,** endocarditis caused by a fungus infection. **nonbacterial thrombotic e.,** a form marked by erosion of the valves with deposition of a clot. **plastic e.,** endocarditis with the formation of a fibrous exudate which causes adhesion of the valves to surrounding parts. **polypous e.,** ulcerative endocarditis with the formation of polypoid masses of fibrin. **pulmonic e.,** endocarditis involving the pulmonic valve. **pustulous e.,** ulcerative endocarditis in which minute abscesses occur in the substance of the valves. **rheumatic e.,** endocarditis associated with rheumatic fever. **right-side e.,** primary acute endocarditis of the right side of the heart. Called also *fetal e.* **septic e.,** malignant endocarditis. **subacute bacterial e.,** a protracted form of endocarditis caused by various bacteria, usually in association with the nonhemolytic *Streptococcus viridans.* Called also *e. lenta.* **ulcerative e.,** malignant endocarditis. **valvular e.,** endocarditis affecting the membrane over the valves of the heart only. **vegetative e., verrucous e.,** nonbacterial endocarditis with the formation of shreds of fibrin on the ulcerated valves; frequently found in cases of lupus erythematosus disseminatus. **viridans e.,** subacute bacterial e.

endocardium (en″do-kar′de-um) [*endo-* + Gr. *kardia* heart]. [N A, B N A] The endothelial lining membrane of the heart and the connective tissue bed on which it lies.

endoceliac (en″do-se′le-ak) [*endo-* + Gr. *koilia* cavity]. Inside one of the body cavities.

endocellular (en″do-sel′u-lar). Within a cell.

endocervical (en″do-ser′vĭ-kal). Pertaining to the interior of the cervix uteri.

endocervicitis (en″do-ser″vĭ-si′tis) [*endo-* + L. *cervix* neck]. Inflammation of the mucous membrane of the cervix uteri.

endochondral (en″do-kon′dral). Situated, formed, or occurring within cartilage.

endochorion (en″do-ko′re-on) [*endo-* + Gr. *chorion* chorion]. The inner chorionic layer.

endochrome (en′do-krōm) [*endo-* + Gr. *chrōma* color]. The coloring matter within a cell.

endocolitis (en″do-ko-li′tis). Inflammation of the mucous membrane of the colon.

endocolpitis (en″do-kol-pi′tis) [*endo-* + Gr. *kolpos* vagina]. Inflammation of the mucous membrane of the vagina.

endocomplement (en″do-kom′ple-ment). An endocellular complement; a complement contained in the erythrocytes as distinguished from that contained in the serum.

endocorpuscular (en″do-kor-pus′ku-lar). Situated within a corpuscle.

endocranial (en″do-kra′ne-al). Situated within the cranium.

endocraniosis (en″do-kra″ne-o′sis). Intracranial hyperostosis described by Morgagni.

endocranitis (en″do-kra-ni′tis). Inflammation of the endocranium.

endocranium (en″do-kra′ne-um) [*endo-* + Gr. *kranion* skull]. The dura mater of the brain.

endocrinasthenia (en″do-krin″as-the′ne-ah). Endocrine exhaustion resulting in a psychosis or psychoneurosis.

endocrinasthenic (en″do-krin″as-then′ik). Pertaining to or marked by endocrine exhaustion.

endocrine (en′do-krīn) [*endo-* + Gr. *krinein* to separate]. 1. Secreting internally; applied to organs whose function is to secrete into the blood or lymph a substance that has a specific effect on another organ or part. See *internal secretion,* under *secretion*, and *hormone*. 2. Pertaining to internal secretions.

endocrinic (en″do-krin′ik). Endocrinous.

endocrinid (en′do-krin″id). Any skin affection of endocrine origin.

endocrinism (en-dok′rĭ-nism). Endocrinopathy.

endocrinium (en″do-krin′e-um). The endocrine system.

endocrinogram (en″do-krin′o-gram). A chart recording the observations made by the cycloscope on endocrine disorders.

endocrinologist (en″do-krĭ-nol′o-jist). An individual skilled in endocrinology, and in the diagnosis and treatment of disorders of the glands of internal secretion.

endocrinology (en″do-krĭ-nol′o-je) [*endocrine* + *-logy*]. The study of the glands of internal secretion and their role in the physiology of the body.

endocrinopath (en″do-krin′o-path). A person with disorder of the glands of internal secretion.

endocrinopathic (en″do-krin″o-path′ik). Pertaining to or characterized by endocrinopathy.

endocrinopathy (en″do-krĭ-nop′ah-the) [*endocrine* + Gr. *pathos* disease]. Any disease due to disorder of any of the glands of internal secretion.

endocrinosis (en″do-krĭ-no′sis). A disordered condition due to dysfunction of the glands of internal secretion.

endocrinosity (en″do-krĭ-nos′ĭ-te). The quality or state of secreting internally, or of being endocrine.

endocrinotherapy (en″do-kri″no-ther′ah-pe). Treatment of disease by the administration of endocrine preparations.

endocrinotropic (en″do-kri″no-trop′ik). Having an endocrine tendency.

endocrinous (en-dok′rĭ-nus). Of or pertaining to an internal secretion or to a gland producing such a secretion.

endocritic (en″do-krit′ik). Endocrine.

endocyclic (en″do-sik′lik). A term applied to cyclic compounds in which the bond occurs in the nucleus.

endocystitis (en″do-sis-ti′tis). Inflammation of the lining membrane of the bladder.

endocyte (en′do-sit) [*endo-* + Gr. *kytos* hollow vessel]. Any cell inclusion.

endoderm (en′do-derm) [*endo-* + Gr. *derma* skin]. Entoderm.

endodermal (en″do-der′mal). Pertaining to the entoderm.

Endodermophyton (en″do-der-mof′ĭ-ton) [*endo-* + Gr. *derma* skin + *phyton* a growth]. The former name of a genus of fungi, now called Trichophyton.

endodermoreaction (en″do-der″mo-re-ak′shun). Trambusti's reaction.

endodiascope (en″do-di′ah-skōp). A roentgen-ray tube which may be placed inside a body cavity for roentgenography and radiotherapy.

endodiascopy (en″do-di-as′ko-pe) [*endo-* + Gr. *dia* through + *skopein* to examine]. Roentgenoscopic examination of a body cavity by means of an endodiascope.

endodontia (en″do-don′she-ah). Endodontics.

endodontics (en″do-don′tiks) [*end-* + Gr. *odous* tooth + *-ics*]. That branch of dentistry which is concerned with the etiology, prevention, diagnosis, and treatment of diseases and injuries that affect the tooth pulp and apical periodontal tissues.

endodontist (en″do-don′tist). A dentist who practices endodontics.

endodontitis (en″do-don-ti′tis) [*endo-* + Gr. *odous* tooth]. Pulpitis.

endodontium (en″do-don′she-um). The dental pulp.

endodontologist (en″do-don-tol′o-jist). Endodontist.

endodontology (en″do-don-tol′o-je). Endodontics.

endo-ectothrix (en″do-ek′to-thriks). A ringworm fungus which produces spores both on the interior and exterior of the hairs.

endo-enteritis (en″do-en″ter-i′tis). Inflammation of the mucous membrane of the intestine.

endo-enzyme (en″do-en′zīm). An intracellular enzyme; an enzyme which is retained in a cell and does not normally diffuse out of the cell into the surrounding medium. Cf. *ecto-enzyme.*

endo-erepsin (en″do-e-rep′sin). Endocellular erepsin.

endo-esophagitis (en″do-e-sof″ah-ji′tis). Inflammation of the lining membrane of the esophagus.

endo-exoteric (en″do-ek″so-ter′ik) [*endo-* + Gr. *exōterikos* pertaining to the outside]. Resulting from certain causes internal to the body, and from others of external origin.

endofaradism (en″do-far′ah-dizm). Internal faradism, as of the stomach.

endogain (en′do-gān). The primary gain of emotional illness, which operates on a deeply unconscious level in its initiation.

endogalvanism (en″do-gal′vah-nizm). Internal galvanism, as of the stomach.

endogamy (en-dog′ah-me [*endo-* + Gr. *gamos* marriage]. 1. Fertilization by the union of separate cells having the same chromatin ancestry. Called also *pedogamy*. Cf. *autogamy* and *exogamy*. 2. Restricting marriage to persons within the community.

endogastrectomy (en″do-gas-trek′to-me) [*endo-* + Gr. *gastēr* stomach + *ektomē* excision]. Extirpation of the mucosa of the stomach.

endogastric (en″do-gas′trik). Pertaining to the interior of the stomach.

endogastritis (en″do-gas-tri′tis). Inflammation of the mucous membrane of the stomach.

endogen (en′do-jen). An obsolete term for a monocotyledonous plant.

endogenetic (en″do-je-net′ik). Endogenous.

endogenic (en″do-jen′ik). Endogenous.

endogenous (en-doj′e-nus) [*endo-* + Gr. *gennan* to produce]. 1. Growing from within; in botany, belonging to the class of endogens. 2. Developing or originating within the organism, or arising from causes within the organism.

endoglobar (en″do-glo′bar). Endoglobular.

endoglobular (en″do-glob′u-lar). Situated or occurring within the blood corpuscles.

endognathion (en″do-na′the-on) [*endo-* + Gr. *gnathos* jaw]. The inner segment of the incisive bone.

endogonidium (en″do-go-nid′e-um). A gonidium developed within a cell.

endoherniotomy (en″do-her″ne-ot′o-me). An operation for hernia similar in its technic to endoaneurysmorrhaphy.

endo-intoxication (en″do-in-tok″sĭ-ka′shun). Poisoning caused by an endogenous toxin.

endolabyrinthitis (en″do-lab″ĭ-rin-thi′tis). Inflammation of the membranous labyrinth.

endolaryngeal (en″do-lah-rin′je-al) [*endo-* + Gr. *larynx*]. Situated on or occurring within the larynx.

endolarynx (en′do-lar″inks). The interior or cavity of the larynx.

Endolimax (en″do-li′maks) [*endo-* + Gr. *leimax* a snail]. A genus of amebas sometimes found in the intestine of man. **E. na′na,** a harmless commensal parasite common in the intestine of man and in lower animals. It is distinguished from other amebas by its nucleus which possesses a large irregular karyosome. Cf. *Entamoeba.*

endolumbar (en′do-lum′bar). Within the lumbar portion of the spinal cord.

endolymph (en′do-limf) [*endo-* + *lymph*]. The fluid contained in the membranous labyrinth of the ear. Called also *endolympha* [N A].

endolympha (en″do-lim′fah). [N A, B N A] The fluid contained within the membranous labyrinth of the ear, it is entirely separate from the perilymph. Called also *endolymph.*

endolymphatic (en″do-lim-fat′ik). Pertaining to the endolymph.

endolysin (en-dol′ĭ-sin) [*endo-* + *lysin*]. A bactericidal substance existing in cells, acting directly on bacteria. **leukocytic e.,** leukin, def. 1.

endolysis (en-dol′ĭ-sis) [*endo-* + Gr. *lysis* dissolution]. Dissolution or breaking up of the cytoplasm of a cell.

endomastoiditis (en″do-mas″toid-i′tis). Inflammation within the mastoid cavity and cells.

endomesoderm (en″do-mes′o-derm) [*endo-* + Gr. *mesos* middle + *derma* skin]. Mesoderm originating from the entoderm of the two-layered blastodisk.

endometrectomy (en″do-me-trek′to-me) [*endo-* + Gr. *mētra* womb + *ektomē* excision]. Extirpation of the uterine mucosa.

endometria (en″do-me′tre-ah). Plural of *endometrium.*

endometrial (en″do-me′tre-al). Pertaining to the endometrium.

endometrioid (en″do-me′tre-oid). Resembling endometrium.

endometrioma (en″do-me″tre-o′mah). A solitary, non-neoplastic mass containing endometrial tissue.

endometriosis (en″do-me″tre-o′sis) [*endometrium* + *-osis*]. A condition in which tissue more or less perfectly resembling the uterine mucous membrane occurs aberrantly in various locations in the pelvic cavity. **e. exter′na,** extrauterine occurrence of tissue resembling the uterine mucous membrane. **e. inter′na,** adenomyosis. **ovarian e., e. ova′rii,** occurrence in the ovary of tissue resembling the uterine mucous membrane, either in the form of small superficial islands or in the form of endometrial ("chocolate") cysts of various sizes. **e. uteri′na,** adenomyosis. **e. ves′icae,** endometriosis involving the bladder.

endometriotic (en″do-me″tre-ot′ik). Pertaining to or characterized by endometriosis.

endometritis (en″do-me-tri′tis) [*endometrium* + *-itis*]. Inflammation of the endometrium. **bacteriotoxic e.,** endometritis caused by the toxins of bacteria, as distinguished from that caused by the presence of the organisms themselves. **decidual e.,** inflammation of the decidual membranes of pregnancy. **e. dis′secans,** endometritis with a tendency to the formation of large, deep ulcers. **exfoliative e.,** endometritis with the casting off of portions of the membrane. **glandular e.,** endometritis of the uterine glands. **membranous e.,** endometritis with an exudate which forms a false membrane. **puerperal e.,** endometritis following childbirth.

endometrium (en-do-me′tre-um), pl. *endome′tria* [*endo-* + Gr. *metra* uterus]. The mucous coat of the uterus, the thickness and structure of which vary with the phase of the menstrual cycle. Accepted by N A as an alternative term for *tunica mucosa uteri.* **Swiss-cheese e.,** hyperplasia of the endometrium, under the influence of progesterone, in which the glands vary in size and shape, producing an appearance like that of Swiss cheese, with its large and small holes.

endometry (en-dom′e-tre) [*endo-* + Gr. *metron* measure]. The measurement of the capacity of a cavity.

endomitosis (en″do-mi-to′sis). Reproduction of nuclear elements not followed by chromosome movements and cytoplasmic division.

endomitotic (en″do-mi-tot′ik). Pertaining to or characterized by endomitosis.

endomixis (en″do-miks′is) [*endo-* + Gr. *mixis* mixture]. The disintegration and subsequent reorganization of the macronucleus occasionally observed in a protozoan organism. It may to some extent take the place of conjugation.

endomorph (en′do-morf). An individual exhibiting endomorphy.

endomorphic (en″do-mor′fik). Pertaining to or characterized by endomorphy.

endomorphy (en′do-mor″fe) [*endo*derm + Gr. *morphē* form]. A type of body build in which tissues derived from the endoderm predominate. There is relative preponderance of soft roundness throughout the body, with large digestive viscera and accumulations of fat, the body usually presenting large trunk and thighs and tapering extremities.

Endomyces (en″do-mi′sēz) [*endo-* + Gr. *mykēs* fungus]. A name formerly given a genus of fungi. **E. al′bicans,** *Candida albicans.* **E. capsula′tus, E. epidermat′idis, E. epider′midis,** *Blastomyces dermatitidis.*

endomycosis (en″do-mi-ko′sis). Infection with Endomyces.

endomyocarditis (en″do-mi″o-kar-di′tis) [*endo-* + Gr. *mys* muscle + *kardia* heart]. Inflammation of the endocardium and myocardium.

endomysium (en″do-mis′e-um) [*endo-* + Gr. *mys* muscle]. The sheath of delicate reticular fibrils which surrounds each muscle fiber.

endonasal (en″do-na′zal). Within the nose.

endonephritis (en″do-ne-fri′tis) [*endo-* + *nephritis*]. Pyelitis.

endoneural (en″do-nu′ral). Pertaining to or situated within a nerve.

endoneurial (en″do-nu′re-al). Pertaining to the endoneurium.

endoneuritis (en″do-nu-ri′tis). Inflammation of the endoneurium.

endoneurium (en″do-nu′re-um) [*endo-* + Gr. *neuron* nerve]. The interstitial connective tissue in a peripheral nerve, separating the individual nerve fibers.

endoneurolysis (en″do-nu-rol′ĭ-sis) [*endo-* + Gr. *neuron* nerve + *lysis* dissolution]. Hersage.

endonuclear (en″do-nu′kle-ar). Within a cell nucleus.

endonucleolus (en″do-nu-kle′o-lus). A nonstaining spot near the center of the nucleolus.

endo-oxidase (en″do-ok′sĭ-dās). Oxidase occurring within a cell, such as a bacterium.

endoparasite (en″do-par′ah-sīt) [*endo-* + *parasite*]. A parasite which lives within the body of its host.

endopelvic (en″do-pel′vik). Within the pelvis.

endopeptidase (en″do-pep′tĭ-dās). A proteolytic enzyme that is capable of hydrolyzing peptide linkages in the interior of the peptide chain, as well as terminal linkages.

endoperiarteritis (en″do-per″ĭ-ar″ter-i′tis). Inflammation involving both the internal and the external coat of an artery.

endopericardial (en″do-per″ĭ-kar′de-al). Pertaining to the endocardium and pericardium.

endopericarditis (en″do-per″ĭ-kar-di′tis). Inflammation involving both the endocardium and pericardium.

endoperimyocarditis (en″do-per″ĭ-mi″o-kar-di′tis). Inflammation of the endocardium, pericardium, and myocardium.

endoperineuritis (en″do-per″ĭ-nu-ri′tis). Inflammation of the endoneurium and perineurium.

endoperitoneal (en″do-per″ĭ-to-ne′al). Within the peritoneum.

endoperitonitis (en″do-per″ĭ-to-ni′tis). Inflammation of the serous lining of the peritoneal cavity.

endophasia (en″do-fa′ze-ah). The silent reproduction of a word or words.

endophlebitis (en″do-fle-bi′tis) [*endo-* + Gr. *phleps* vein + *-itis*]. Inflammation of the intima of a vein. **e. hepat′ica oblit′erans,** thrombophlebitis producing obstruction of the hepatic veins. **proliferative e.,** phlebosclerosis.

endophthalmitis (en″dof-thal-mi′tis) [*endo-* + *ophthalmitis*]. Inflammation of the internal structures of the eye. **e. phaco-aller′gica, e. phaco-anaphylac′tica, e. phacogenet′ica,** endophthalmitis occurring as a reaction to the injection of lens substance.

endophylaxination (en″do-fi-lak″si-na′shun). Resistance to intoxication developed entirely within the body of the animal possessing it.

endophyte (en′do-fīt) [*endo-* + Gr. *phyton* plant]. Entophyte.

endophytic (en″do-fit′ik) [*endo-* + Gr. *phyein* to grow]. Growing inward; proliferating on the interior or inside of an organ or other structure.

endoplasm (en′do-plazm) [*endo-* + Gr. *plasma* something formed]. The central portion of the cytoplasm of a cell. Cf. *ectoplasm.*

endoplast (en′do-plast) [*endo-* + Gr. *plassein* to form]. The nucleus of a cell.

endoplastic (en″do-plas′tik). Entoplastic.

endopolyploid (en″do-pol′e-ploid). Having reduplicated chromatin within an intact nucleus, with or without an increase in the number of chromosomes (applied only to cells and tissues).

endopolyploidy (en″do-pol′e-ploi″de) [*endo-* + *polyploidy*]. 1. Endomitosis. 2. Polysomaty. 3. Autopolyploidy resulting from a previous endomitotic cycle.

endorachis (en″do-ra′kis). Endorhachis.

endoradiography (en″do-ra″de-og′rah-fe). The radiographic demonstration of the condition of internal organs and cavities by means of radiopaque materials.

end-organ (end′or-gan). One of the larger, encapsulated endings of the sensory nerves. For names of specific types, see under *corpuscle.*

endorhachis (en″do-ra′kis) [*endo-* + Gr. *rhachis* spine]. Dura mater spinalis.

endorhinitis (en″do-ri-ni′tis) [*endo-* + Gr. *rhis* nose]. Inflammation of the lining membrane of the nasal passages.

endosalpingitis (en″do-sal″pin-ji′tis) [*endosalpinx* + *-itis*]. Inflammation of the endosalpinx.

endosalpingoma (en″do-sal″pin-go′mah). Adenomyoma of the uterine tube.

endosalpingosis (en″do-sal″pin-go′sis). Adenomyosis of the uterine tube.

endosalpinx (en″do-sal′pinks) [*endo-* + Gr. *salpinx* tube]. The mucous membrane lining the uterine tube, arranged in longitudinal rugae, or folds, and continuous with the mucous lining of the uterus (tunica mucosa tubae uterinae [N A]).

endosarc (en′do-sark). Endoplasm.

endoscope (en′do-skōp) [*endo-* + Gr. *skopein* to examine]. An instrument for the examination of the interior of a hollow viscus, such as the bladder.

endoscopic (en″do-skop′ik). Performed by means of an endoscope; pertaining to endoscopy.

endoscopy (en-dos′ko-pe). Inspection of any cavity of the body by means of an endoscope. **peroral e.,** endoscopic examination of organs accessible to observation through an endoscope passed through the mouth.

endosecretory (en-do-se′kre-to-re) [*endo-* + *secretory*]. Pertaining to the internal secretions; secreting internally.

endosepsis (en″do-sep′sis). Septicemia originating within the organism.

endosite (en′do-sīt). An endoparasite.

endoskeleton (en″do-skel′ĕ-ton) [*endo-* + Gr. *skeleton*]. The bony and cartilaginous structures of the body, exclusive of that part of the skeleton only which is of dermal origin.

endosmometer (en″dos-mom′e-ter) [*endosmosis* + Gr. *metron* measure]. An instrument for determining the rate and extent of endosmosis.

endosmosis (en″dos-mo′sis) [*endo-* + Gr. *ōsmos* impulsion]. A movement in liquids separated by a membranous or porous septum, by which one fluid passes through the septum into the cavity which contains another fluid of a different density. Cf. *exosmosis.*

endosmotic (en″dos-mot′ik). Of the nature of endosmosis.

endosoma (en″do-so′mah) [*endo-* + Gr. *sōma* body]. The substance which fills a red blood corpuscle.

endosperm (en′do-sperm). A substance containing reserve food materials, formed within the embryo sac of plants.

endospore (en′do-spōr) [*endo-* + Gr. *sporos* seed]. See *spore.*

endosporium (en″do-spōr′e-um). The inner layer of the envelope of a spore.

endosteitis (en-dos″te-i′tis). Inflammation of the endosteum.

endosteoma (en-dos″te-o′mah) [*endo-* + Gr. *osteon* bone + *-oma*]. A tumor in the medullary cavity of a bone.

endostethoscope (en″do-steth′o-skōp). A stethoscope passed into the esophagus for auscultating the heart.

endosteum (en-dos′te-um) [*endo-* + Gr. *osteon* bone]. The tissue lining the medullary cavity of a bone.

endostitis (en″dos-ti′tis). Endosteitis.

endostoma (en″dos-to′mah). Endosteoma.

endosymbiont (en″do-sim′be-ont) [*endo-* + *symbiont*]. A symbiont which lives within the cells of its partner.

endotendineum (en″do-ten-din′e-um) [*endo-* + L. *tendo, tendines,* after Gr. *tenon*]. The delicate connective tissue separating the secondary bundles (fascicles) of a tendon.

endotenon (en″do-ten′on) [*endo-* + Gr. *tenōn* tendon]. Endotendineum.

endothelia (en″do-the′le-ah). Plural of *endothelium.*

endothelial (en″do-the′le-al). Pertaining to or made up of endothelium.

endotheliitis (en″do-the-le-i′tis). Inflammation of the endothelium.

endothelio-angiitis (en″do-the″le-o-an″je-i′tis). A condition related to lupus erythematosus and attended with fever, arthritis, pleuritis, pericarditis, endocarditis and angiitis (George Baehr).

endothelioblastoma (en″do-the″le-o-blas-to′mah) [*endothelium* + Gr. *blastos* germ + *-oma*]. A tumor of mesenchymal origin, the cells of which tend to differentiate into flat endothelial cells and to line vessels, cavities, and surfaces (Mallory). The term includes angioma, hemangioma, endothelioma, and lymphangioma.

endotheliochorial (en″do-the″le-o-ko′re-al) [*endothelium* + *chorion*]. Denoting a type of placenta in which syncytial trophoblast embeds maternal vessels bared to their endothelial lining.

endotheliocyte (en″do-the′le-o-sīt) [*endothelia* + Gr. *kytos* hollow vessel]. A term for the large mononuclear phagocytic wandering cells of the circulating blood and tissues which are supposed by some to be derived from proliferating vascular endothelium. Called also *endothelial phagocyte.*

endotheliocytosis (en-do-the″le-o-si-to′sis). An abnormal increase in the number of endotheliocytes.

endothelioid (en″do-the′le-oid). Resembling endothelium.

endothelioinoma (en″do-the″le-o-ĭ-no′mah). A fibrous tumor on the endothelium.

endotheliolysin (en″do-the″le-ol′ĭ-sin). An antibody capable of causing disintegration of endothelial tissue.

endotheliolytic (en″do-the″le-o-lit′ik). Capable of destroying endothelial tissue.

endothelioma (en″do-the″le-o′mah) [*endothelium* + *-oma*]. A tumor which originates from the endothelial linings of blood vessels (*hemangio-endo-*

thelioma), lymphatics (*lymphangio-endothelioma*), or serous cavities. **e. cap'itis,** a large multiple endothelioma on the scalp. **e. cu'tis,** endothelioma of the skin, manifested as violaceous papules. **dural e.,** meningioma.

endotheliomatosis (en"do-the"le-o-mah-to'sis). The formation of multiple and diffuse endotheliomas in a tissue.

endotheliomyoma (en"do-the"le-o-mi-o'mah). A myomatous tumor arising from endothelium.

endotheliomyxoma (en"do-the"le-o-mik-so'-mah). A myxomatous tumor arising from endothelium.

endotheliosis (en"do-the"le-o'sis). Proliferation of endothelium.

endotheliotoxin (en"do-the"le-o-tok'sin). A specific toxin which acts on the endothelium of capillaries and small veins, producing hemorrhage. Cf. *hemorrhagin.*

endothelium (en"do-the'le-um), pl. *endothe'lia* [*endo-* + Gr. *thēlē* nipple]. [N A, B N A] The layer of epithelial cells that lines the cavities of the heart and of the blood and lymph vessels, and the serous cavities of the body, originating from the mesoderm. **e. cam'erae anterio'ris bul'bi** [N A], **e. cam'erae anterio'ris oc'uli** [B N A], the mesothelial layer covering the posterior surface of the posterior limiting lamina of the cornea and the anterior surface of the stroma of the iris. **corneal e.,** the portion of the endothelium of the anterior chamber of the eye that covers the posterior surface of the cornea. **extraembryonic e.,** endothelium which arises outside of the body of the embryo, such as that lining the vitelline vessels.

endothermal (en"do-ther'mal). Endothermic.

endothermic (en"do-ther'mik). Characterized by or accompanied by the absorption of heat; heat absorbing; storing up heat or energy in a potential form.

endothermy (en'do-ther"me) [*endo-* + Gr. *thermē* heat]. The production of heat in the tissues from within by the resistance offered by the tissues to the passage of the high-frequency current.

endothoracic (en"do-tho-ras'ik). Within the thorax; situated internal to the ribs.

endothrix (en'do-thriks) [*endo-* + Gr. *thrix* hair]. A fungus whose growth is confined chiefly within the shaft of the hair, without formation of conspicuous external spores. Such fungi include *Trichophyton tonsurans* and *T. violaceum.*

endothyroidopexy (en"do-thi-roi'do-pek"se). Endothyropexy.

endothyropexy (en-do-thi'ro-pek-se). The operation of freeing the thyroid from the trachea, dislocating it forward, and fixing it to one side in a pocket between the sternocleidomastoid muscle and the skin.

endotin (en-do'tin). A purified form of old tuberculin. Called also *tuberculinum purum.*

endotoscope (en-do'to-skōp) [*endo-* + Gr. *ous* ear + *skopein* to examine]. An endoscope for examination of the ear.

endotoxic (en"do-tok'sik). Pertaining to or possessing endotoxin.

endotoxicosis (en"do-tok"sĭ-ko'sis). Poisoning caused by an endotoxin.

endotoxin (en"do-tok'sin). A heat-stable toxin present in the bacterial cell but not in cell-free filtrates of cultures of intact bacteria. They are found primarily in enteric bacilli, in which they are identical with the somatic antigen, but are found also in certain of the gram-negative cocci and in Pasteurella and Brucella species. They occur in the cell wall of enteric bacilli, probably as a lipid-polysaccharide-polypeptide complex extractable in trichloracetic acid and glycols. The endotoxins are pyrogenic and increase capillary permeability, the activity being substantially the same regardless of the species of bacteria from which they are derived. Called also *bacterial pyrogens.*

endotoxoid (en"do-tok'soid). A toxoid prepared from endotoxin.

endotracheal (en"do-tra'ke-al) [*endo-* + *trachea*]. 1. Within or through the trachea. 2. Performed by passage through the lumen of the trachea.

endotracheitis (en"do-tra-ke-i'tis). Inflammation of the mucosa of the trachea.

endotrachelitis (en"do-tra-kel-i'tis) [*endo-* + Gr. *trachēlos* neck]. Endocervicitis.

endotrypsin (en"do-trip'sin) [*endo-* + *trypsin*]. A digestive ferment derived from yeast and resembling trypsin in its action.

endotryptase (en"do-trip'tās). An intracellular ferment from yeast, capable of digesting zymase.

endo-urethral (en"do-u-re'thral). Within the urethra.

endo-uterine (en"do-u'ter-in). Within the uterus.

endovaccination (en"do-vak"sĭ-na'shun) [*endo-* + *vaccination*]. The administration of vaccines by the mouth.

endovasculitis (en"do-vas"ku-li'tis) [*endo-* + L. *vasculum* vessel]. Inflammation of the intima of a blood vessel.

endovenitis (en"do-ve-ni'tis). Endophlebitis.

endovenous (en"do-ve'nus). Intravenous.

endoxan (en-dok'san). Cyclophosphamide.

end-piece (end'pēs). 1. Complement. 2. The albumin or soluble portion in complement splitting.

end-plate (end'plāt). A flattened terminal discoid expansion at the ending of a motor nerve fiber upon a muscle fiber.

end-pleasure (end'plezh-er). The pleasure produced by the sexual orgasm, as contrasted with the fore-pleasure which precedes it.

endyma (en'dĭ-mah). Ependyma.

-ene. A suffix used in chemistry to indicate an unsaturated hydrocarbon containing one double bond.

enelectrolysis (en"e-lek-trol'ĭ-sis). Removal of superfluous hair by pulling out the hair and passing a current through the electric needle into the hole left.

Enem. Abbreviation for *enema.*

enema (en'e-mah), *pl. enemas* or *enem'ata* [Gr.]. A clyster or injection; a liquid injected or to be injected into the rectum. **analeptic e.,** an enema consisting of a pint of tepid water containing ½ teaspoonful of salt. Called also *thirst e.* **barium e.,** a suspension of barium administered as a clyster and retained in the intestines during roentgenologic examination, the presence of deformities of the intestine, produced by neoplasm or other abnormality, being demonstrated by filling defects revealed by the column of radiopaque barium. **blind e.,** the insertion of a soft-rubber tube into the rectum to aid in the expulsion of flatus. **contrast e.,** barium e. **Dobell's e.,** a nutrient enema containing scraped boiled meat, pancreas emulsion, boiled arrowroot, pepsin, and pancreatin. **double contrast e.,** injection and evacuation of a suspension of barium, followed by inflation of the intestines with air under light pressure: used in mucosal relief roentgenography. **Ewald's e.,** a nutrient enema containing eggs, wheat flour boiled in a 20 per cent grape sugar solution, and red wine. **flatus e.,** an enema made of ½ oz. of magnesium sulfate, 1 oz. of glycerin, and 4 oz. of warm water. **Leube's e.,** an enema containing boiled meat, fat, and pancreatin. **nutrient e., nutritive e.,** an enema of predigested nutrient matter. **pancreatic e.,** an enema containing pancreatin. **Rosenheim's e.,** a nutrient enema consisting of peptone, cod liver oil, and sugar in a 0.3 per cent soda solution. **shock e.,** an enema of 1 pint of 5 per cent solution of sodium bicarbonate containing 1 oz. of whisky: given to prevent shock after an operation. **soapsuds e.,** an enema made by dissolving 2 oz. of soap in a pint of warm water. **thirst e.,** analeptic enema. **turpentine e.,** an enema of 1 pint of soapsuds containing 2 oz. olive oil and 1 oz. turpentine.

enemator (en′e-ma″tor). An apparatus for giving enemas.

enepidermic (en″ep-ĭ-der′mik). Used upon or applied to the skin.

energetics (en″er-jet′iks). The study of energy; the science of energy.

energid (en′er-jid). Living, active protoplasm, as distinguished from deutoplasm.

energometer (en″er-gom′e-ter). An apparatus for studying the pulse, measuring—(1) The pressure sufficient to overcome the pulse wave; (2) the energy expended in the cuff to counteract this pressure; (3) the pressure at which the maximal volume of blood meets the cuff; (4) the value of this maximal blood volume; (5) the pressure at which the energy expended in the cuff becomes maximal; and (6) the volume of this maximal energy.

energy (en′er-je) [Gr. *energeia*]. Ability to operate or work; power to produce motion, to overcome resistance, and to effect physical changes. **binding e.,** energy equal to the difference between the weight of the nucleus of an atom and the sum of the weights of its constituent particles. **biotic e.,** the form of energy peculiar to living matter. **chemical e.,** energy which shows itself in chemical transformations. **kinetic e.,** energy in action or engaged in producing work or motion. **nuclear e.,** energy released by the splitting of the atom. **e. of position, potential e.,** energy at rest or not manifested in actual work.

enervation (en″er-va′shun) [L. *enervatio*]. 1. Lack of nervous energy; languor. 2. Removal of a nerve or a section of a nerve.

enflagellation (en″flaj-el-la′shun). The formation of flagella.

engagement (en-gāj′ment). In obstetrics, the entrance of the fetal head, or presenting part, into the superior pelvic strait and beginning descent through the pelvic canal.

engastrius (en-gas′tre-us) [Gr. *en* in + *gastēr* belly]. A fetal monster in which a parasitic twin is contained within the abdomen of the autosite.

Engel's alkalimetry (eng′elz) [Rodolphe Charles *Engel*, Alsatian chemist, 1850–1916]. See under *alkalimetry*.

Engelmann's disks (eng′el-mahnz) [Theodor Wilhelm *Engelmann*, a German physiologist 1843–1909]. See under *disk*.

engine (en′jin). A mechanical apparatus by which energy is converted from one form to another. **dental e.,** a machine operated by foot power or by electricity, for activating drills, burs, burnishers, or other instrument held in the handpiece and used by dentists in procedures on the teeth. **high speed e.,** a dental engine capable of turning the bur in the handpiece at a rate of more than 10,000 revolutions per minute. **ultraspeed e.,** a dental engine which turns burs at a rate of more than 100,000 revolutions per minute.

englobe (en-glōb′). To absorb within the substance of a globe, such as an ameba, leukocyte, or other cell.

Engman's disease (eng′manz) [Martin F. *Engman*, dermatologist in St. Louis, 1869–1953]. Dermatitis infectiosa eczematoides.

engorged (en-gorjd′). Distended or swollen with fluids.

engorgement (en-gorj′ment). Hyperemia; local congestion; excessive fulness of any organ or passage.

engram (en′gram) [Gr. *en* in + *gramma* mark]. A lasting mark or trace. The term is applied to the definite and permanent trace left by a stimulus in the protoplasm of a tissue. In psychology it is the lasting trace left in the psyche by anything that has been experienced psychically; a latent memory picture.

engraphia (en-graf′e-ah). The process hypothesized in the theory that stimuli leave definite traces (engrams) on the protoplasm which, when regularly repeated, induce a habit that persists after the stimuli cease.

enhematospore (en-hem′ah-to-spōr″) [Gr. *en* in + *haima* blood + *sporos* spore]. A spore of the malarial parasite formed in the blood by the breaking up of the amebula and the red corpuscle containing it.

enhemospore (en-hem′o-spōr). Enhematospore.

enhexymal (en-hek′sĭ-mal). Hexobarbital.

enissophobia (en-is″o-fo′be-ah) [Gr. *enissein* to reproach + *phobia*]. Fear of reproach for sin; fear of unpardonable sin.

enkatarrhaphy (en″kah-tar′ah-fe) [Gr. *enkatarrhaptein* to sew in]. The operation of burying a structure by suturing together the sides of the tissues alongside of it.

enol (e′nol). One of two tautomeric forms of a substance, the other being the keto form. The enol is formed from the keto by migration of hydrogen from the adjacent carbon atom to the carbonyl group:

R.CH	R.CH_2
‖	|
R.C.OH	R.C:O
enol form	keto form

enolase (e′no-lās). An enzyme in muscle extract that changes phosphoglyceric acid into phosphopyruvic acid.

enology (e-nol′o-je) [Gr. *oinos* wine + *-logy*]. The scientific study of the production and composition of wine.

enomania (e-no-ma′ne-ah) [Gr. *oinos* wine + *mania* madness]. 1. A periodical or maniacal craving for strong drink. 2. Delirium tremens.

enophthalmos (en-of-thal′mos) [Gr. *en* in + *ophthalmos* eye]. Abnormal retraction of the eye into the orbit.

enophthalmus (en″of-thal′mus). Enophthalmos.

enorchia (en-or′ke-ah) [Gr. *en* in + *orchis* testis]. Cryptorchidism.

enorganic (en-or-gan′ik). Existing as a permanent quality of the organism.

enosimania (en″os-ĭ-ma′ne-ah) [Gr. *enosis* a quaking + *mania* madness]. Insanity characterized by extreme terror.

enostosis (en″os-to′sis) [Gr. *en* in + *osteon* bone]. A morbid bony growth developed within the cavity of a bone or on the internal surface of the bone cortex.

enoxidase (e-nok′sĭ-das) [Gr. *oinos* wine + *oxidase*]. An oxidizing ferment found in spoiled wines.

ens (enz) [L.]. A thing. **e. mor′bi,** the nature or essential principle of a disease considered apart from its causation; the pathology of a disease as distinguished from its etiology.

ensiform (en′sĭ-form) [L. *ensis* sword + *forma* form]. Shaped like a sword. Cf. *xiphoid*.

ensisternum (en″sis-ter′num) [L. *ensis* sword + *sternum*]. Processus xiphoideus.

ensomphalus (en-som′fah-lus) [Gr. *en* in + *sōma* a body + *omphalos* navel]. A double fetal monster with blended bodies, two separate navels, and two umbilical cords.

enstrophe (en′stro-fe) [Gr. *enstrephein* to turn in]. Inversion, especially of the margin of the eyelids.

E.N.T. Abbreviation for *ear, nose,* and *throat*.

entacoustic (en″tah-koos′tik) [Gr. *entos* within + *akoustikos* of hearing]. Pertaining to the organ of hearing.

entad (en′tad). Toward the center; inwardly.

ental (en′tal) [Gr. *entos* within]. Inner; central.

entalação (en″tah-lah-sah′yo). A disease of Brazil characterized by recurrent attacks of severe difficulty in swallowing. Called also *tropical cardiospasm, tropical dysphagia,* and *mal d'engasgo*.

entamebiasis (en″tah-me-bi′ah-sis). Infection with Entamoeba.

Entamoeba (ent″ah-me′bah). A genus of amebas which are parasitic in the intestines of vertebrates. They are distinguished by a more or less spherical nucleus with a relatively small chromosome near its center, and numerous chromatic granules lining the nuclear membrane. Several species, including *E. co′li*, *E. gingiva′lis*, and *E. histolyt′ica*, are commonly parasitic in man. Cf. *Endamoeba*. **E. bucca′lis,** *E. gingivalis*. **E. buetsch′lii,** *Iodamoeba buetschlii*. **E. co′li,** a nonpathogenic form found in the intestinal tract of man. **E. gingiva′lis,** a species found in the mouth, about the gums and in the tartar of the teeth. **E. histolyt′ica,** a species which is the cause of amebic or tropical dysentery and tropical abscess of the liver. Called also *Amoeba dysenteriae*. **E. kartul′isi,** found in the pus of necrotic bone abscesses. **E. na′na,** *Endolimax nana*. **E. nippon′ica,** a species from cases of tropical dysentery in Japan. **E. tetrage′na,** *E. histolytica*. **E. tropica′lis,** *E. histolytica*. **E. un′dulans,** an oval body with an undulating membrane, found in the human intestine.

1, *Entamoeba coli*. 2, *E. histolytica*. (de Rivas.)

entasia (en-ta′ze-ah) [Gr. *entasis*]. A constrictive spasm; spasmodic muscular action.

entasis (en′tah-sis). Entasia.

entelechy (en-tel′ĕ-ke) [Gr. *entelecheia* actuality]. 1. Completion; full development or realization; the complete expression of some function. 2. A supposed vital principle operating in living creatures as a directive spirit.

entepicondyle (en-tep″ĭ-kon′dīl). The internal epicondyle of the humerus.

enteque (en-ta′ka). A disease of animals in South America, characterized by the formation of horny structures in the lungs.

enter-. See *entero-*.

enteraden (en-ter′ad-en) [*enter-* + Gr. *adēn* gland]. Any intestinal gland.

enteradenitis (en″ter-ad″e-ni′tis) [*enteraden* + *-itis*]. Inflammation of the intestinal glands.

enteral (en′ter-al) [Gr. *enteron* intestine]. Within, or by way of, the intestine.

enteralgia (en″ter-al′je-ah) [*enter-* + *-algia*]. Pain or neuralgia of the intestine.

enteramine (en″ter-am′in). Serotonin.

enterangiemphraxis (en″ter-an″je-em-frak′sis) [*enter-* + Gr. *angeion* vessel + *emphraxis* stoppage]. Obstruction of the intestinal blood vessels.

enterauxe (en″ter-awk′se) [*enter-* + Gr. *auxē* increase]. Hypertrophy of the intestinal wall.

enterectasis (en″ter-ek′tah-sis) [*enter-* + Gr. *ektasis* extension]. Distention of the intestines.

enterectomy (en″ter-ek′to-me) [*enter-* + Gr. *ektomē* excision]. The excision of a part of the intestine; resection of the intestine.

enterelcosis (en″ter-el-ko′sis) [*enter-* + Gr. *helkōsis* ulceration]. Ulceration of the intestine.

enterepiplocele (en″ter-e-pip′lo-sēl). Entero-epiplocele.

enteric (en-ter′ik) [Gr. *enterikos* intestinal]. Pertaining to the intestines.

enteric-coated (en-ter″ik-kōt′ed). A trade term designating a special coating applied to tablets or capsules which prevents release and absorption of their contents until they reach the intestines.

entericoid (en-ter′ĭ-koid). Resembling enteric or typhoid fever.

enteritis (en″ter-i′tis) [*enter-* + *-itis*]. Inflammation of the intestine, applied chiefly to inflammation of the small intestine. See also *enterocolitis*. **e. anaphylac′tica,** hemorrhagic inflammation of both the large and the small intestine following a second dose of anaphylactogen in sensitized dogs. **cat e.,** panleukopenia. **choleriform e.,** an acute, cholera-like diarrheal disease with a high case fatality rate, prevalent in epidemic and endemic form in the Western Pacific area since 1938, caused by the El Tor or Celebes vibrio immunologically identical with the cholera vibrio. **cicatrizing e., cicatrizing e., chronic,** regional ileitis. **e. cys′tica chron′ica,** a form marked by cystic dilatation of the intestinal glands, due to closure of the openings of their ducts. **diphtheritic e.,** enteritis characterized by the presence of a false membrane and severe ulceration of the mucosa beneath the membrane. **feline e.,** panleukopenia. **e. gra′vis,** an often fatal disease characterized by acute onset of severe abdominal pain, nausea, vomiting, and bloody diarrhea, with mucosal necrosis and hemorrhage and edema of the submucosa, most prominent in the jejunum and proximal ileum. **e. membrana′cea, membranous e., mucomembranous e., mucous e., myxomembranous e.,** mucous colitis. **e. necrot′icans,** an inflammation of the intestines in man, caused by *Clostridium perfringens* type F, and characterized by necrosis. **e. nodula′ris,** enteritis with enlargement of the lymph nodes. **pellicular e.,** mucous colitis. **phlegmonous e.,** a condition with symptoms resembling those of peritonitis; it may be secondary to other intestinal diseases, as chronic obstruction, strangulated hernia, carcinoma, etc. **e. polypo′sa,** enteritis marked by polypoid growths in the intestine, due to proliferation of the connective tissue. **protozoan e.,** enteritis in which the intestine is infested with protozoan organisms of various species. **pseudomembranous e.,** enteritis without fever and with profuse exudate of mucin. **regional e., segmental e.,** regional ileitis. **streptococcus e.,** primary phlegmonous enteritis, due to *Streptococcus pyogenes*.

entero- (en′ter-o-) [Gr. *enteron* intestine]. A combining form denoting relationship to the intestines.

entero-anastomosis (en″ter-o-ah-nas″to-mo′sis). The surgical formation of an anastomosis between two portions of the intestine.

entero-antigen (en″ter-o-an′tĭ-jen). An antigen derived from the intestine.

entero-apokleisis (en″ter-o-ap″o-kli′sis) [*entero-* + Gr. *apokleisis* a shutting out]. The surgical exclusion of a part of the intestine.

Enterobacteriaceae (en″ter-o-bak-te″re-a′se-e). A family of Schizomycetes (order Eubacteriales), made up of gram-negative rod-shaped organisms, occurring as plant or animal parasites, or as saprophytes. It includes five tribes, *Erwinieae*, *Escherichieae*, *Proteeae*, *Salmonelleae*, and *Serratieae*.

enterobacteriotherapy (en″ter-o-bak-te″re-o-ther′ah-pe). Treatment by vaccine made from intestinal bacteria.

enterobiasis (en″ter-o-bi′ah-sis). Infection with worms of the genus Enterobius.

enterobiliary (en″ter-o-bil′e-er-e). Pertaining to the intestine and the bile passages.

Enterobius (en″ter-o′be-us) [*entero-* + Gr. *bios* life]. A genus of nematode intestinal worms of the family Oxyuridae. **E. vermicula′ris,** the seatworm or pinworm, a small white worm parasitic in the upper part of the large intestine, and occasionally in the female genitals and bladder. It is frequent in the rectum of children, causing itching and reflex disturbance. Formerly called *Oxyuris vermicularis*.

enterobrosis (en″ter-o-bro′sis) [*entero-* + Gr. *brōsis* eating]. Intestinal perforation.

enterocele (en′ter-o-sēl) [*entero-* + Gr. *kēlē* hernia]. 1. Any hernia of the intestine. 2. Posterior vaginal hernia.

enterocentesis (en″ter-o-sen-te′sis) [*entero-* + Gr. *kentēsis* puncture]. Surgical puncture of the intestine.

enterochirurgia (en″ter-o-ki-rur′je-ah) [*entero-* + Gr. *cheirourgia* surgery]. Surgery of the intestine.

enterocholecystostomy (en″ter-o-ko″le-sis-tos′to-me) [*entero-* + Gr. *cholē* bile + *kystis* bladder + *stoma* mouth]. The surgical creation of an opening from the gallbladder to the small intestine.

enterocholecystotomy (en″ter-o-ko″le-sis-tot′-o-me) [*entero-* + *cholecystotomy*]. Incision of the gallbladder and the intestine.

enterocinesia (en″ter-o-si-ne′ze-ah) [*entero-* + Gr. *kinēsis* motion]. Peristalsis.

enterocinetic (en″ter-o-si-net′ik). Pertaining to or stimulating peristalsis.

enterocleisis (en″ter-o-kli′sis) [*entero-* + Gr. *kleisis* closure]. 1. Closure of a wound in the intestine. 2. Occlusion of the lumen of the intestine. **omental e.**, closure of an intestinal perforation by covering it with omentum.

enteroclysis (en″ter-ok′lĭ-sis) [*entero-* + Gr. *klysis* a drenching]. The injection of a nutrient or medicinal liquid into the bowel.

enteroclysm (en′ter-o-klizm) [*entero-* + Gr. *klysmos* a clyster]. Enteroclysis.

enterococcemia (en″ter-o-kok-se′me-ah) [*enterococcus* + Gr. *haima* blood + *-ia*]. The presence of enterococci in the blood.

enterococci (en″ter-o-kok′si). Plural of *enterococcus*.

enterococcus (en″ter-o-kok′us), pl. *enterococ′ci* [*entero-* + *coccus*]. Any streptococcus of the human intestine. The enterococcus group includes *Streptococcus faecalis, Strep. durans, Strep. liquefaciens*, and *Strep. zymogenes*.

enterocoele (en″ter-o-se′le) [*entero-* + Gr. *koilia* belly]. The body cavity formed by the outpouchings from the archenteron.

enterocolectomy (en″ter-o-ko-lek′to-me). Resection of the intestines including the ileum, cecum, and ascending colon.

enterocolitis (en″ter-o-ko-li′tis) [*entero-* + *colitis*]. Inflammation involving both the small intestine and the colon. **hemorrhagic e.**, an inflammation of the small intestine and colon, characterized by hemorrhagic breakdown of the intestinal mucosa with inflammatory-cell infiltration. **necrotizing e.**, pseudomembranous e. **pseudomembranous e.**, an acute superficial necrosis of the mucosa of the small intestine and colon, characterized by profound shock and dehydration, and the passage per rectum of seromucus, often mixed with blood, and shreds or casts of the bowel wall.

enterocolostomy (en″ter-o-ko-los′to-me) [*entero-* + Gr. *kolon* colon + *stoma* mouth]. The operative formation of a communication between the small intestine and the colon.

enterocrinin (en″ter-ok′rĭ-nin). A hormone prepared from the intestines of animals which stimulates the glands of the small intestine to activity.

enterocutaneous (en″ter-o-ku-ta′ne-us). Pertaining to or communicating with the intestine and the cutaneous surface of the body, as an enterocutaneous fistula.

enterocyst (en′ter-o-sist) [*entero-* + Gr. *kystis* sac, bladder]. A benignant cyst proceeding from the subperitoneal tissue.

enterocystocele (en″ter-o-sis′to-sēl) [*entero-* + Gr. *kystis* bladder + *kēlē* hernia]. Hernia of the bladder and intestine.

enterocystoma (en″ter-o-sis-to′mah) [*entero-* + Gr. *kystis* cyst + *-oma*]. A congenital cyst lined with ciliated epithelium occurring along the gastro-intestinal canal; the remains of the omphalomesenteric duct.

enterodynia (en″ter-o-din′e-ah) [*entero-* + Gr. *odynē* pain]. Pain in the intestine.

entero-enterostomy (en″ter-o-en″ter-os′to-me). Surgical anastomosis between two parts of the intestine not normally in relation with each other.

entero-epiplocele (en″ter-o-e-pip′lo-sēl) [*entero-* + Gr. *epiploon* omentum + *kēlē* hernia]. Hernia of the small intestine and omentum.

enterogastritis (en″ter-o-gas-tri′tis) [*entero-* + Gr. *gastēr* stomach + *-itis*]. Inflammation of the small intestine and stomach.

enterogastrone (en″ter-o-gas′trōn). A hormone of the duodenum which mediates the humoral inhibition of gastric secretion and motility produced by the ingestion of fat.

enterogenous (en″ter-oj′e-nus) [*entero-* + Gr. *gennan* to produce]. 1. Arising from the primitive foregut. 2. Originating within the intestine.

enterogram (en′ter-o-gram). A tracing made by an instrument of the movements of the intestine.

enterograph (en′ter-o-graf) [*entero-* + Gr. *graphein* to write]. An instrument for recording the intestinal movements.

enterography (en″ter-og′rah-fe). 1. Recording of the intestinal movements by means of an enterograph. 2. A description of the intestines.

enterohepatitis (en″ter-o-hep-ah-ti′tis) [*entero-* + Gr. *hēpar* liver + *-itis*]. 1. Inflammation of the bowel and liver. 2. An infectious disease of turkeys, caused by *Histomonas meleagridis*, with lesions of the intestine and liver, and a dark discoloration of the comb. Called also *blackhead of turkeys* and *typhlohepatitis*.

enterohepatocele (en″ter-o-hep′ah-to-sēl″). An infantile umbilical hernia which contains intestines and liver.

enterohepatopexy (en″ter-o-hep″ah-to-pek′se). Fixation to the liver of a seromuscular flap of a defunctionalized loop of the proximal small intestine, a step in autotransplantation of the liver.

enterohydrocele (en″ter-o-hi′dro-sēl) [*entero-* + *hydrocele*]. Hernia with hydrocele.

enteroidea (en″ter-oi′de-ah). The intestinal fevers; the fevers caused by intestinal bacteria, including typhoid fever, paratyphoid fever, etc.

entero-intestinal (en″ter-o-in-tes′tĭ-nal) [*entero-* + *intestine*]. Pertaining to two different portions of the intestine.

enterokinase (en″ter-o-ki′nās). An enzyme of the intestinal juice which activates the proteolytic enzyme of the pancreatic juice by converting trypsinogen into trypsin.

enterokinesia (en″ter-o-ki″ne′se-ah). Peristalsis.

enterokinetic (en″ter-o-ki-net′ik). Pertaining to or stimulating peristalsis.

enterolith (en′ter-o-lith″) [*entero-* + Gr. *lithos* stone]. An intestinal calculus; any concretion found in the intestine.

enterolithiasis (en″ter-o-lĭ-thi′ah-sis) [*entero-* + *lithiasis*]. A condition characterized by the presence of intestinal calculi.

enterology (en″ter-ol′o-je) [*entero-* + *-logy*]. The sum of what is known regarding the intestines.

enterolysis (en″ter-ol′ĭ-sis) [*entero-* + Gr. *lysis* dissolution]. The operative freeing of the intestine from adhesions.

enteromegalia (en″ter-o-mĕ-ga′le-ah). Enteromegaly.

enteromegaly (en″ter-o-meg′ah-le) [*entero-* + Gr. *megaleia* bigness]. Enlargement of the intestine.

enteromere (en′ter-o-mēr″) [*entero-* + Gr. *meros* part]. Any segment of the embryonic alimentary tract.

enteromerocele (en″ter-o-me′ro-sēl) [*entero-* + Gr. *mēros* thigh + *kēlē* hernia]. Femoral hernia.

enterometer (en″ter-om′e-ter) [*entero-* + Gr. *metron* measure]. An instrument for measuring the lumen of the small intestine in operations.

Enteromonas (en″ter-o-mo′nas). A genus of flagellate protozoa. **E. hom′inis,** a minute flagellate protozoan, a rare parasite in the intestine of man.

enteromycodermitis (en″ter-o-mi″ko-der-mi′-tis) [*entero-* + Gr. *myxa* mucus + *derma* skin]. Endoenteritis.

enteromycosis (en″ter-o-mi-ko′sis) [*entero-* + Gr. *mykēs* fungus + *-osis*]. Disease of the intestine due to bacteria or fungi. **e. bacteria′cea,** a general name for certain infections of the intestine due to nonspecific bacteria.

enteromyiasis (en″ter-o-mi-i′ah-sis) [*entero-* + Gr. *myia* fly]. Presence of larvae of flies in the intestine.

enteron (en′ter-on) [Gr.]. The intestine or alimentary canal; usually used with specific reference to the small intestine.

enteroneuritis (en″ter-o-nu-ri′tis). Inflammation of the nerves of the intestine.

enteronitis (en″ter-o-ni′tis). Enteritis. **polytropous e.,** a condition characterized by nausea, vomiting, diarrhea, and headache: called also *acute infectious gastro-enteritis* and *Spencer's disease*.

enteroparesis (en″ter-o-par′e-sis) [*entero-* + Gr. *paresis* relaxation]. Relaxation of the intestine resulting in dilatation.

enteropathogen (en″ter-o-path′o-jen). A microorganism which causes a disease of the intestines.

enteropathogenesis (en″ter-o-path″o-jen′e-sis). The production of disease or disorder of the intestines.

enteropathogenic (en″ter-o-path″o-jen′ik). Pertaining to or effective in production of disease of the intestines.

enteropathy (en″ter-op′ah-the) [*entero-* + Gr. *pathos* illness]. Any disease of the intestine.

enteropexy (en′ter-o-pek″se) [*entero-* + Gr. *pēxis* fixation]. Surgical fixation of the intestine to the abdominal wall.

enteroplasty (en′ter-o-plas″te) [*entero-* + Gr. *plassein* to mold]. Plastic surgery of the intestine, especially an operation for enlarging the caliber of the constricted bowel.

enteroplegia (en″ter-o-ple′je-ah) [*entero-* + Gr. *plēgē* stroke]. Paralysis of the intestine.

enteroplex (en′ter-o-pleks″) [*entero-* + Gr. *plexis* weaving]. A device for joining the edges of a divided intestine.

enteroplexy (en′ter-o-plek″se) [*entero-* + Gr. *plexis* weaving]. The union of two portions of the intestine by means of aluminum rings and elastic pegs.

enteroproctia (en″ter-o-prok′she-ah) [*entero-* + Gr. *prōktos* anus]. The condition of having an artificial anus.

enteroptosia (en″ter-op-to′se-ah). Enteroptosis.

enteroptosis (en″ter-op-to′sis) [*entero-* + Gr. *ptōsis* fall]. Descent or downward displacement of the intestine in the abdominal cavity.

enteroptotic (en″ter-op-tot′ik). Pertaining to or characterized by enteroptosis.

enterorenal (en″ter-o-re′nal). Pertaining to the intestine and the kidney.

enterorrhagia (en″ter-o-ra′je-ah) [*entero-* + Gr. *rhēgnynai* to burst forth]. Hemorrhage from the intestine.

enterorrhaphy (en″ter-or′ah-fe) [*entero-* + Gr. *rhaphē* suture]. The act of suturing a gap or wound of the intestine. **circular e.,** the sewing together of two completely divided portions of intestine by the invagination of one portion over the other and stitching or otherwise joining them end to end.

enterorrhea (en″ter-o-re′ah). Diarrhea.

enterorrhexis (en″ter-o-rek′sis) [*entero-* + Gr. *rhēxis* rupture]. Rupture of the intestine.

enteroscope (en′ter-o-skōp″) [*entero-* + Gr. *skopein* to examine]. An endoscope for examining the intestine.

enterosepsis (en″ter-o-sep′sis) [*entero-* + Gr. *sēpsis* putrefaction]. Intestinal sepsis due to putrefaction of the contents of the intestines.

enterosite (en′ter-o-sit″). An intestinal parasite.

enterosorption (en″ter-o-sorp′shun). Accumulation of a substance in the bowel by virtue of its passage from the circulating blood; occurring when its exsorption exceeds its insorption.

enterospasm (en′ter-o-spazm″) [*entero-* + Gr. *spasmos* spasm]. A spasm of the intestine.

enterostasis (en″ter-o-sta′sis) [*entero-* + Gr. *stasis* stoppage]. Intestinal stasis.

enterostaxis (en″ter-o-stak′sis) [*entero-* + Gr. *staxis* dripping]. Slow hemorrhage through the intestinal mucous membrane.

enterostenosis (en″ter-o-ste-no′sis) [*entero-* + Gr. *stenōsis* contraction]. Narrowing or stricture of the intestine.

enterostomy (en″ter-os′to-me) [*entero-* + Gr. *stoma* mouth]. The artificial formation of a permanent opening into the intestine through the abdominal wall. **gun-barrel e.,** enterostomy in which both segments of the divided intestine open outside of the abdominal wall.

enterotome (en′ter-o-tōm″) [*entero-* + Gr. *tomē* a cut]. A knife or scissors for slitting the intestine. **Dupuytren's e.,** a cutting forceps used in making an artificial anus.

enterotomy (en″ter-ot′o-me) [*entero-* + Gr. *temnein* to cut]. 1. Any cutting operation upon the living intestine. 2. The anatomy or dissection of the intestine.

enterotoxemia (en″ter-o-tok-se′me-ah). A condition characterized by presence in the blood of toxins produced in the intestines. **infectious e. of sheep,** an infectious bacterial disease of sheep in West Australia: caused by *Clostridium perfringens* type D.

enterotoxication (en″ter-o-tok″sĭ-ka′shun). Enterotoxism.

enterotoxigenic (en″ter-o-tok″sĭ-jen′ik). Producing or containing a toxin specific for the cells of the intestinal mucosa.

enterotoxin (en″ter-o-tok′sin). 1. A toxin specific for the cells of the intestinal mucosa. 2. A toxin arising in the intestine. 3. An exotoxin that is protein in nature and relatively heat stable, produced by staphylococci, primarily by coagulase-positive *Staphylococcus pyogenes* var. *aureus*. Enterotoxin, which on ingestion produces violent vomiting and diarrhea, is the primary factor in staphylococcal food poisoning.

enterotoxism (en″ter-o-tok′sizm). Auto-intoxication of enteric origin.

enterotropic (en″ter-o-trop′ik) [*entero-* + Gr. *tropos* a turning]. Having a special affinity for or exerting its principal effect upon the intestines.

enterotyphus (en″ter-o-ti′fus). Typhoid fever.

enterovaginal (en″ter-o-vaj′ĭ-nal). Pertaining to or communicating with the intestine and the vagina, as an enterovaginal fistula.

enterovesical (en″ter-o-ves′ĭ-kal). Pertaining to or communicating with the intestine and urinary bladder, as an enterovesical fistula.

entero-vioform (en″ter-o-vi′o-form). Trade mark for a preparation of iodochlorhydroxyquin.

enterovirus (en″ter-o-vi′rus). One of a group of morphologically similar viruses infecting the gastrointestinal tract and discharged in the excreta, including poliovirus, the Coxsackie viruses, and the ECHO viruses.

enterozoic (en″ter-o-zo′ik). Relating to or caused by an enterozoon.

enterozoon (en″ter-o-zo′on), pl. *enterozo′a* [*entero-* + Gr. *zōon* animal]. An animal parasite or species inhabiting or infesting the intestinal canal.

enteruria (en″ter-u′re-ah) [*entero-* + Gr. *ouron* urine + *-ia*]. The presence of fecal constituents in the urine.

enthalpy (en′thal-pe) [Gr. *en* within + *thalpein* to warm]. The heat content of a physical system.

entheomania (en″the-o-ma′ne-ah) [Gr. *entheos* inspired + *mania* madness]. Religious insanity.

enthesis (en′the-sis) [Gr. "a putting in; insertion"]. The use of non-living material in the repair of a defect or deformity of the body.

enthetic (en-thet′ik) [Gr. *enthetikos* fit for implanting]. 1. Pertaining to enthesis. 2. Introduced from without.

enthlasis (en′thlah-sis) [Gr. "a dint caused by pressure"]. Comminuted fracture of the skull, with depression of the bony fragments.

entiris (en-ti′ris) [Gr. *entos* within + *iris* iris]. The posterior pigment layer of the iris.

entity (en′tĭ-te) [L. *ens* being]. An independently existing thing; a reality.

ento- [Gr. *entos* inside]. A prefix signifying within, or inner.

entoblast (en′to-blast) [*ento-* + Gr. *blastos* germ]. 1. Entoderm. 2. A cell nucleolus.

entocele (en′to-sēl) [*ento-* + Gr. *kēlē* hernia]. An internal hernia.

entochondrostosis (en″to-kon″dros-to′sis) [*ento-* + Gr. *chondros* cartilage + *osteon* bone]. The development of bone taking place within cartilage.

entochoroidea (en″to-ko-roid′e-ah) [*ento-* + Gr. *chorioeidēs* choroid]. The inner layer of the choroid coat of the eye.

entocineria (en″to-sĭ-ne′re-ah). The internal or noncortical gray substance of the brain and cord.

entocnemial (en″tok-ne′me-al). On the inner side of the tibia.

entocone (en′to-kōn) [*ento-* + Gr. *kōnos* cone]. The inner posterior cusp of an upper molar tooth.

entoconid (en″to-ko′nid) [*ento-* + Gr. *kōnos* cone]. The inner posterior cusp of a lower molar tooth.

entocornea (en″to-kor′ne-ah) [*ento-* + *cornea*]. Descemet's membrane.

entocranial (en″to-kra′ne-al). Endocranial.

entocuneiform (en″to-ku′ne-ĭ-form). The inner cuneiform bone of the foot.

entocyte (en′to-sīt) [*ento-* + Gr. *kytos* hollow vessel]. The cell contents.

entoderm (en′to-derm) [*ento-* + Gr. *derma* skin]. The innermost of the three primary germ layers of the embryo. From it are derived the epithelium of the pharynx, respiratory tract (except the nose), the digestive tract, bladder and urethra. Cf. *ectoderm* and *mesoderm*. **primitive e.,** the primary internal layer of the gastrula stage that becomes both gut and yolk sac. **yolk-sac e.,** the epithelial lining of the yolk sac.

entodermal (en″to-der′mal). Pertaining to or derived from the entoderm.

entodermic (en″to-der′mik). Entodermal.

ento-ectad (en″to-ek′tad) [*ento-* + Gr. *ektos* without]. Directed or proceeding from within outward.

entome (en′tōm) [Gr. *entemnein* to cut in]. An instrument for cutting urethral strictures.

entomere (en′to-mēr) [*ento-* + Gr. *meros* part]. A blastomere normally destined to become entoderm.

entomesoderm (en″to-mes′o-derm). Endomesoderm.

entomion (en-to′me-on) [Gr. *entomē* notch]. The point at the tip of the mastoid angle of the parietal bone in the parietal notch of the temporal bone.

entomo- (en′to-mo) [Gr. *entomon* insect]. Combining form denoting relationship to an insect, or to insects.

Entomobrya (en″to-mo-bri′ah). A genus of insects, the spring tails, Australian species of which cause irritation by their bite.

entomogenous (en″to-moj′e-nus) [*entomo-* + Gr. *gennan* to produce]. 1. Derived from insects, their bites, emanations, etc. 2. Growing in the body of an insect.

entomologist (en″to-mol′o-jist). An expert in entomology.

entomology (en″to-mol′o-je) [*entomo-* + *-logy*]. That branch of zoology which deals with the study of insects.

entomophilous (en″to-mof′ĭ-lus) [*entomo-* + Gr. *philein* to love]. Fertilized by insect-borne pollen: said of certain flowers.

entomophobia (en″to-mo-fo′be-ah) [*entomo-* + *phobia*]. Morbid dread of insects (mites, ticks, etc.).

Entomospira (en″to-mo-spi′rah) [*entomo-* + Gr. *speira* coil]. A genus name formerly given certain spirochetal microorganisms, now included in the genus Borrelia. **E. glossi′nae,** *Borrelia glossinae.*

entophthalmia (en″tof-thal′me-ah). Inflammation of the inner parts of the eyeball.

entophyte (en′to-fīt) [*ento-* + Gr. *phyton* plant]. A parasitic plant organism living within the body of its host.

entopic (en-top′ik) [Gr. *en* in + *topos* place]. Occurring in the proper place.

entoplasm (en′to-plazm) [*ento-* + Gr. *plasma* something formed]. 1. Endoplasm. 2. The blue-staining, or nonchromatinic, portion of certain bacteria.

entoplastic (en″to-plas′tik) [*ento-* + Gr. *plastikos* formative]. Having a formative power lodged within.

entoptic (en-top′tik) [*ento-* + Gr. *optikos* seeing]. Noting visual phenomena which have their seat within the eye.

entoptoscope (en-top′to-skōp). An instrument for examining the mediums of the eyes, to ascertain their transparency.

entoptoscopy (en″top-tos′ko-pe) [*ento-* + Gr. *ōps* eye + *skopein* to examine]. The observation of the interior of the eye and its light and shadows.

entoretina (en″to-ret′ĭ-nah) [*ento-* + *retina*]. The internal or nervous portion of the retina, disposed in five layers, which are named respectively outer molecular, inner nuclear, inner molecular, ganglion, and nerve fiber layers. Called also *lamina vasculosa retinae* and *nervous layer of Henle.*

entorganism (ent-or′gan-izm) [*ento-* + *organism*]. An internal parasite.

Entorula (en-tor′u-lah). A genus of yeastlike fungi, many species of which have been isolated from blastomycotic lesions in man.

entosarc (en′to-sark) [*ento-* + Gr. *sarx* flesh]. Endoplasm.

entosthoblast (en-tos′tho-blast) [Gr. *entosthen* from within + *blastos* germ]. The hypothetical nucleus of the nucleolus.

entostosis (ent″os-to′sis) [*ento-* + Gr. *osteon* bone]. Enostosis.

entotic (en-tot′ik) [*ento-* + Gr. *ōtikos* of the ear]. Situated in or arising within the ear.

entotympanic (en″to-tim-pan′ik). Within the tympanum of the ear.

entozoa (en″to-zo′ah). Plural of *entozoon.*

entozoal (en″to-zo′al). Pertaining to or caused by entozoa.

entozoon (en″to-zo′on), pl. *entozo′a* [*ento-* + Gr. *zōon* animal]. A parasitic animal organism living within the body of its host.

entripsis (en-trip′sis) [Gr. *en* in + *tripsis* rubbing]. Inunction.

entropion (en-tro′pe-on) [Gr. *en* in + *tropein* to turn]. The turning inward (inversion) of an edge or margin, as of the margin of the eyelid, with the tarsal cartilage turned inward toward the eyeball. **e. cicatric′eum, cicatricial e.,** inversion of the margin of an eyelid caused by contraction of scar tissue in the palpebral conjunctiva or underlying tarsus. **spastic e., e. spas′ticum,** inversion of the eyelid caused by tonic spasm of the orbicularis oculi muscle. **e. u′veae,** inversion of the margin of the pupil, usually the result of an iritis attended with exudate, and occurring rarely as a congenital condition.

entropionize (en-tro′pe-on-īz). To put into a state of entropion or inversion; to turn inward.

entropium (en-tro′pe-um). Entropion.

entropy (en′tro-pe). Diminished capacity for spontaneous change; the measure of that part of the heat or energy of a system which is not available to perform work. Entropy increases in all irreversible mechanical processes.

entwicklungsmechanik (ent″wik-lungs″mĕ-kan′ik) [Ger. "developmental mechanics"]. Experimental embryology.

entypy (en′ti-pe) [Gr. *entypē* pattern]. A method of gastrulation in which the entoderm lies external to the amniotic ectoderm.

enucleate (e-nu′kle-āt) [L. *enucleare*]. To remove whole and clean, as a tumor from its envelope.

enucleation (e-nu″kle-a′shun) [L. *e* out + *nucleus* kernel]. The removal of an organ, of a tumor, or of another body in such a way that it comes out clean and whole, like a nut from its shell. Used in connection with the eye, it denotes removal of the eyeball after the eye muscles and optic nerve have been severed.

enula (en′u-lah). The inner aspect of the gum.

enuresis (en″u-re′sis) [Gr. *enourein* to void urine]. Involuntary discharge of the urine; often used alone with specific reference to involuntary discharge of urine occurring during sleep at night (*nocturnal enuresis*).

enuretic (en″u-ret′ik). 1. Pertaining to enuresis. 2. An agent which causes enuresis.

envelope (en′vĕ-lōp). An encompassing structure or membrane. **egg e.,** egg membrane.

envenomization (en-ven″om-i-za′shun). The poisonous effects caused by the bites, stings, or effluvia of insects and other arthropods, or the bites of snakes.

environment (en-vi′ron-ment) [Fr. *environner* to surround, to encircle]. The sum total of all the conditions and elements which make up the surroundings of an individual.

enzactin (en-zak′tin). Trade mark for preparations of triacetin.

enzootic (en″zo-ot′ik) [Gr. *en* in + *zōon* animal]. 1. Present in an animal community at all times, but occurring in only small numbers of cases. 2. A disease of low morbidity which is constantly present in an animal community.

enzygotic (en″zi-got′ik). Developed from the same fertilized ovum.

enzymatic (en″zi-mat′ik). Relating to an enzyme.

enzyme (en′zīm) [Gr. *en* in + *zymē* leaven]. An organic compound, frequently a protein, capable of accelerating or producing by catalytic action some change in a substrate for which it is often specific. **activating e.,** an enzyme that activates a given amino acid by attaching it to the corresponding transfer ribonucleic acid. **adaptive e.,** induced e. **amylolytic e.,** one that catalyzes the conversion of starch into sugar. **autolytic e.,** one that produces autolysis or digestion of the cell in which it exists. **bacterial e.,** an enzyme existing in or secreted by a bacterium. **branch-point e.,** the enzyme of a reaction that branches off a common pathway to initiate a specific biosynthetic pathway. It is usually subject to feedback inhibition by the endproduct of the specific pathway initiated. **catheptic e.,** any one of a group of proteolytic enzymes characterized by the property of being activated by hydrocyanic acid, hydrogen sulfide and many other substances. They include cathepsin, papain and bromelin. Called also *papainase*. **clotting e., coagulating e.,** an enzyme, such as rennin and fibrin ferment, that catalyzes the conversion of soluble into insoluble proteins. **constitutive e.,** one that is produced by a microorganism regardless of the presence or absence of the specific substrate acted upon. Cf. *induced e.* **curdling e.,** coagulating e. **deamidizing e.,** one that catalyzes the decomposition of amino acids into ammonia compounds. **decarbolizing e.,** one that splits CO_2 from organic acids. **digestive e.,** a substance that catalyzes the process of digestion. **Dubos e.,** tyrothricin. **extracellular e.,** one that exists outside of the cell secreting it. **fat-splitting e.,** lipolytic e. **glycolytic e.,** one which catalyzes the oxidation of sugar. **Haas e.,** one that catalyzes the oxidation of coenzyme II. **hydrolytic e.,** one that catalyzes hydrolysis; a hydrolase. **induced e.,** one whose production requires or is markedly stimulated by a specific small molecule, the *inducer*, which is the substrate of the enzyme or a compound structurally related to it. The inducers studied first were substrates whose utilization thus became possible; hence these enzymes were known earlier as *adaptive enzymes*. **inhibitory e.,** antienzyme. **intracellular e.,** one that is contained within the protoplasm of the cell secreting it. **inverting e.,** one which catalyzes the decomposition of sugar, as invertin. **lipolytic e.,** one that catalyzes the decomposition of fat. **milk-curdling e.,** rennin. **mucolytic e.,** one that catalyzes the depolymerization of mucopolysaccharides. **oxidation e.,** oxidase. **peptolytic e.,** one that catalyzes the decomposition of peptone. **protective e.** See under *ferment*. **proteolytic e.,** one that catalyzes the hydrolysis of proteins and various protein split products, the final product being peptone. **redox e.,** one that catalyzes oxidation-reduction reactions. **reducing e.,** reductase. **respiratory e.,** the enzymic system that catalyzes the oxidation of hexose monophosphoric acid ester by the oxygen of the air. The complete system consists of the hexose monophosphoric acid ester, a between-ferment, a coenzyme, the yellow enzyme and oxygen. **Schardinger's e.** See under *reductase*. **steatolytic e.,** one that catalyzes the decomposition of fat. **Straub e.,** soluble diaphorase. **sucroclastic e.,** one that catalyzes the decomposition of sugar. **urea e.,** urease. **uricolytic e.,** one that catalyzes the conversion of uric acid into urea. **Warburg's respiratory e.,** an organic iron compound present in all tissues, the primary factor in cell respiration. It is similar in character to the cytochromes. Called also *respiratory catalyst* and *atmungsferment*. **yellow e's,** a number of substances which have been isolated from various organs and tissues and which take part in oxidations and reductions in the body. All contain riboflavin in their prosthetic groups.

enzymic (en-zim′ik). Of the nature of an enzyme.

enzymology (en″zi-mol′o-je). The study of enzymes and enzymatic action.

enzymolysis (en″zi-mol′ĭ-sis) [*enzyme* + Gr. *lysis* dissolution]. The disintegrative action or reaction produced by an enzyme.

enzymosis (en″zi-mo′sis) [*enzyme* + *-osis*]. Fermentation induced by an enzyme.

enzymuria (en″zi-mu′re-ah) [*enzyme* + *urine*]. The presence of enzymes in the urine.

eolipyle (e-ol′e-pīl). A form of spirit lamp used to heat cautery irons.

eonism (e′o-nizm) [Chevalier *d'Eon*, French political adventurer, 1728–1810; having adopted woman's dress when sent on a secret mission to Russia in 1755, he was later forced by decree of Louis XVI to wear such apparel to the end of his life]. Transvestism.

eopsia (e-op′se-ah) [Gr. *ēōs* dawn + *opsis* vision]. Orthropsia.

eosin (e′o-sin) [Gr. *ēōs* dawn]. A rose-colored stain or dye, the potassium and sodium salts of tetrabromfluorescein, $C_{20}H_8Br_4O_5$: commercially, several other red coal tar dyes are called eosin, the eosins being bromine derivatives of fluorescein. **water-soluble e., e. W** or **W S, yellowish e., e. Y,** a very important plasma stain, used especially with hematoxylin, methylene blue, and methyl green. It is the sodium salt of tetrabromfluorescein, $NaO.(C_6HBr_2.O)_2C.C_6H_4.COONa$.

eosinocyte (e″o-sin′o-sīt). Eosinophil.

eosinopenia (e″o-sin-o-pe′ne-ah) [*eosinophil* + Gr. *penia* poverty]. Abnormal deficiency of eosinophilic leukocytes in the blood.

eosinophil (e″o-sin′o-fil) [*eosin* + Gr. *philein* to love]. A structure, cell, or histologic element readily stained by eosin; most commonly used to designate an eosinophilic leukocyte.

eosinophile (e″o-sin′o-fīl). 1. Eosinophil. 2. Eosinophilic.

eosinophilic (e″o-sin″o-fil′ik). Readily stainable with eosin.

eosinophilia (e″o-sin″o-fil′e-ah) [*eosin* + Gr. *philein* to love]. 1. The formation and accumulation of an abnormally large number of eosinophils in the blood. 2. The condition of being readily stained with eosin. **tropical e.,** a disease occurring in certain parts of India, characterized clinically by anorexia, malaise, cough, leukocytosis, and an absolute increase in eosinophils.

eosinophilotactic (e″o-sin″o-fil″o-tak′tik). Eosinotactic.

eosinophilous (e″o-sin-of′ĭ-lus). Eosinophilic.

eosinotactic (e″o-sin″o-tak′tik) [*eosinophil* + Gr. taktikos regulating]. Exhibiting an influence on eosinophilic cells. **negatively e.,** repelling eosinophilic cells. **positively e.,** attracting eosinophilic cells.

eosolate (e-o′so-lāt). A salt of a creosote ester.

eosophobia (e-o″so-fo′be-ah) [Gr. *ēōs* dawn + *phobia*]. Morbid fear or dread of day-break.

epacmastic (ep″ak-mas′tik). Pertaining to the epacme.

epacme (ep-ak′me) [Gr. *epakmazein* to come to its height]. The stage or period of increase.

epactal (e-pak′tal) [Gr. *epaktos* brought in]. 1. Supernumerary. 2. A wormian bone.

eparsalgia (ep″ar-sal′je-ah) [Gr. *epairein* to lift + *-algia*]. Any disorder or trouble due to overstrain of a part including dilatation of the heart, hernia, enteroptosis, hemoptysis, etc. (Sterling).

eparterial (ep″ar-te-re-al) [Gr. *epi* upon + *artēria* artery]. Over an artery; applied especially to the first branch of the right primary bronchus which is so situated.

epauxesiectomy (ep″awk-se″ze-ek′to-me) [Gr. *epauxēsis* increase + *ektomē* excision]. The surgical removal of a growth.

epaxial (ep-ak′se-al) [Gr. *epi* upon + *axis*]. Situated upon or above the axis.

epencephal (ep″en-sef′al). Epencephalon.

epencephalic (ep″en-se-fal′ik). Pertaining to the epencephalon.

epencephalon (ep″en-sef′ah-lon) [Gr. *epi* upon + *enkephalos* brain]. 1. Cerebellum. 2. Metencephalon. 3. Myelencephalon.

ependopathy (ep″en-dop′ah-the). Ependymopathy.

ependyma (ep-en′dĭ-mah) [Gr. *ependyma* upper garment]. [N A, B N A] The lining membrane of the ventricles of the brain and of the central canal of the spinal cord.

ependymal (ep-en′dĭ-mal). Pertaining to or composed of ependyma.

ependymitis (ep″en-dĭ-mi′tis). Inflammation of the ependyma.

ependymoblast (ep″en-di′mo-blast). An embryonic ependymal cell; an ependymal spongioblast.

ependymoblastoma (ep-en″dĭ-mo-blas-to′mah). A tumor made up of ependymoblasts.

ependymocyte (ep-en′dĭ-mo-sīt″) [*ependyma* + Gr. *kytos* hollow vessel]. An ependymal cell.

ependymocytoma (ep-en″dĭ-mo-si-to′mah). Ependymoma.

ependymoma (ep-en″dĭ-mo′mah). A tumor containing adult ependymal cells.

ependymopathy (ep-en″dĭ-mop′ah-the). Disease of the ependyma.

Eperythrozoon (ep″e-rith″ro-zo′on) [Gr. *epi* upon + *erythros* red + *zōon* animal]. A genus of microorganisms of the family Bartonellaceae, order Rickettsiales, occurring as seven species, of limited pathogenicity, which infect rodents, cattle, sheep, and swine.

eperythrozoonosis (ep″e-rith″ro-zo″o-no′sis). Infection with organisms of the genus *Eperythrozoon.*

epharmony (ep-har′mo-ne). Development in complete harmony with environment; harmonic relation between structure and environment.

ephebiatrics (e-fe″be-at′riks) [Gr. *ephēbos* one arrived at puberty + *iatrikē* surgery, medicine]. That department of medicine which deals especially with the diagnosis and treatment of the diseases of youth (18–25 years).

ephebic (ĕ-feb′ik) [Gr. *ephēbikos* pertaining to puberty]. Pertaining to youth or the period of puberty.

ephebogenesis (ef″e-bo-jen′e-sis) [Gr. *ephēbos* puberty + *genesis*]. The bodily changes occurring at puberty.

ephebogenic (ef″e-bo-jen′ik). Pertaining to or caused by ephebogenesis.

ephebology (ef″e-bol′o-je) [Gr. *ephēbos* one arrived at puberty + *-logy*]. The study of puberty.

Ephedra (e-fed′rah) [Gr. *epi* upon + *hedra* seat]. A genus of gnetaceous plants. *E. antisyphilit′ica, E. vulga′ris,* and others furnish the Chinese drug ma huang.

ephedrine (e-fed′rin). Chemical name: l-α(1-methylaminoethyl)benzyl alcohol; an alkaloid obtained from *Ephedra equisetina,* or produced synthetically: used as a sympathomimetic, as a pressor substance, to relieve bronchial spasm, or as a central nervous system stimulant.

ephelides (e-fel′ĭ-dēz) [Gr.]. Plural of *ephelis.*

ephelis (e-fe′lis), pl. *ephel′ides* [Gr. *ephēlis*]. A freckle.

ephemera (ĕ-fem′er-ah) [Gr. *ephēmeros* short-lived]. A transitory condition. **e. Brittan′ica,** miliary fever.

ephemeral (ĕ-fem′er-al). Short-lived; transient.

ephidrosis (ef″ĭ-dro′sis) [Gr. *ephidrōsis*]. Excessive sweating; hyperhidrosis. **e. cruen′ta,** the excretion of bloody sweat.

ephippium (ep-hip′e-um) [Gr. *epi* upon + *hippos* horse]. Sella turcica.

ephynal (ef′ĭ-nal). Trade mark for a preparation of vitamin E. See *alpha tocopherol.*

epi- (ep′ĭ) [Gr. *epi* on]. A prefix denoting on or upon.

epiallopregnanolone (ep″ĭ-al″o-preg-nan′o-lōn). A male sex hormone extracted from pregnancy urine, which aids in the development of male sex characteristics.

epiblast (ep′ĭ-blast) [*epi-* + Gr. *blastos* germ]. 1. Ectoderm. 2. Ectoderm, except for the neural plate.

epiblastic (ep″ĭ-blas′tik)). Pertaining to or arising from the epiblast; ectodermal.

epiblepharon (ep″ĭ-blef′ah-ron) [*epi-* + Gr. *blepharon* eyelid]. A condition in which a fold of skin stretches along the border of the lower lid and presses the lashes against the eyeball.

epibole (e-pib′o-le). Epiboly.

epiboly (e-pib′o-le) [Gr. *epibolē* cover]. A method of gastrulation by which the smaller blastomeres at the animal pole of the fertilized ovum grow over and enclose the cells of the vegetal hemisphere.

epibulbar (ep″ĭ-bul′bar). Upon the eyeball.

epicanthal (ep″ĭ-kan′thal). 1. Pertaining to the epicanthus. 2. Overlying the canthus.

epicanthus (ep″ĭ-kan′thus) [*epi-* + Gr. *kanthos* canthus]. A vertical fold of skin on either side of the nose, sometimes covering the inner canthus. It is present as a normal characteristic in persons of certain races and sometimes occurs as a congenital anomaly in others. Called also *epicanthal fold* and *plica palpebronasalis* [N A].

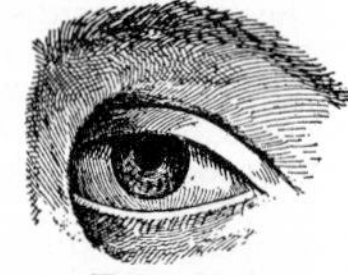

Epicanthus.

epicarcinogen (ep″ĭ-kar-sin′o-jen). An agent which increases the effect of a carcinogen.

epicardia (ep″ĭ-kar′de-ah). The lower portion of the esophagus, extending from the hiatus esophagi to the cardia.

epicardiectomy (ep″ĭ-kar″de-ek′to-me). An operation by which the heart is supplied with a collateral circulation from the pericardium when the normal circulation through the coronary arteries is pathologically or artificially restricted or shut off.

epicardiolysis (ep″ĭ-kar-de-ol′ĭ-sis) [*epicardium* + Gr. *lysis* dissolution]. Harrington's operation of separating the visceral layer of the pericardium (epicardium) from the myocardium.

epicardium (ep″ĭ-kar′de-um) [*epi-* + Gr. *kardia* heart]. B N A term and N A alternative for *lamina visceralis pericardii*, the layer of the pericardium which is in contact with the heart.

epicauma (ep″ĭ-kaw′mah) [Gr. *epikauma*]. 1. A blister caused by a burn. 2. A spot on the cornea of the eye.

epicele (ep′ĭ-sēl). Epicoele.

epicentral (ep″ĭ-sen′tral). Attached to the centrum of a vertebra.

epichitosamine (ep″ĭ-ke-to′sah-min). A hexosamine homologous with glucosamine, but containing mannose instead of *d*-glucose.

epichordal (ep″ĭ-kor′dal). Situated dorsad of the notochord.

epichorion (ep″ĭ-ko′re-on) [*epi-* + *chorion*]. That part of the uterine mucosa which incloses the fertilized ovum.

epicoele (ep′ĭ-sēl) [*epi-* + Gr. *koilia* hollow]. The cavity of the myelencephalon.

epicoeloma (ep″ĭ-se-lo′mah). The portion of the coeloma nearest the notochord.

epicomus (e-pik′o-mus) [*epi-* + Gr. *komē* hair]. A monster with a parasitic twin joined at the summit of the head.

epicondylalgia (ep″ĭ-kon-dĭ-lal′je-ah) [*epicondyle* + *-algia*]. Pain in the muscles attached to the epicondyle of the humerus. It is a functional neurosis due to strains on the forearm.

epicondyle (ep″ĭ-kon′dīl) [*epi-* + Gr. *kondylos* condyle]. An eminence upon a bone, above its condyle. Called also *epicondylus*. **external e. of humerus,** epicondylus lateralis humeri. **internal e. of femur,** epicondylus medialis femoris. **internal e. of humerus,** epicondylus medialis humeri. **lateral e. of femur,** epicondylus lateralis femoris. **lateral e. of humerus,** epicondylus lateralis humeri. **medial e. of femur,** epicondylus medialis femoris. **medial e. of humerus,** epicondylus medialis humeri.

epicondyli (ep″ĭ-kon′dĭ-le) [L.]. Plural of *epicondylus*.

epicondylian, epicondylic (ep″ĭ-kon-di′le-an, ep″ĭ-kon-dil′ik). Pertaining to an epicondyle.

epicondylitis (ep″ĭ-kon″dil-i′tis). Inflammation of the epicondyle or of the tissues adjoining the epicondyle of the humerus. **external humeral e., radiohumeral e.,** tennis elbow.

epicondylus (ep″ĭ-kon′dĭ-lus), pl. *epicon′dyli* [L.]. An eminence upon a bone, above its condyle. Called also *epicondyle*. **e. latera′lis fem′oris** [N A, B N A], a projection from the distal end of the femur, above the lateral condyle, for the attachment of collateral ligaments of the knee. Called also *lateral epicondyle of femur*. **e. latera′lis hu′meri** [N A, B N A], a projection from the distal end of the humerus, giving attachment to a common tendon of origin of the extensor carpi radialis brevis, extensor digitorum communis, extensor digiti quinti proprius, extensor carpi ulnaris, and supinator muscles. Called also *lateral epicondyle of humerus*. **e. media′lis fem′oris** [N A, B N A], a projection from the distal end of the femur, above the medial condyle, for the attachment of collateral ligaments of the knee. Called also *medial epicondyle of femur*. **e. media′lis hu′meri** [N A, B N A], a projection from the distal end of the humerus, giving attachment to the pronator teres above, a common tendon of origin of the flexor c[illegible] maris longus, flexor digitoru[illegible] flexor carpi ulnaris muscles in th[illegible] ulnar collateral ligament bel[illegible] *medial epicondyle of humerus*.

epicoracoid (ep″ĭ-kor′ah-koid). [illegible] the coracoid process.

epicorneascleritis (ep″ĭ-kor″ne-ah-skle-ri′tis). A chronic inflammatory condition affecting the cornea and sclera.

epicostal (ep″ĭ-kos′tal) [*epi-* + L. *costa* rib]. Situated upon a rib.

epicranium (ep″ĭ-kra′ne-um) [*epi-* + Gr. *kranion* skull]. The integument, aponeurosis, and muscular expansions of the scalp.

epicrisis (ep″ĭ-kri′sis) [*epi-* + *crisis*]. 1. A second or supplementary crisis. 2. A critical analysis or discussion of a case of disease after its termination.

epicritic (ep″ĭ-krit′ik) [Gr. *epikrisis* determination]. Relating to or serving the purpose of accurate determination: applied to cutaneous nerve fibers that serve the purpose of perceiving fine variations of touch or temperature. See *epicritic sensibility*.

epicystitis (ep″ĭ-sis-ti′tis) [*epi-* + Gr. *kystis* bladder]. Inflammation of the structures above the bladder.

epicystotomy (ep″ĭ-sis-tot′o-me) [*epi-* + Gr. *kystis* bladder + *tomē* a cut]. Suprapubic operation for stone in the bladder.

epicyte (ep′ĭ-sīt) [*epi-* + Gr. *kytos* hollow vessel]. 1. The membrane which invests a cell. 2. A pneumonocyte. 3. The external protective layer of the ectoplasm of a protozoon.

epicytoma (ep″ĭ-si-to′mah). Epithelioma.

epidemic (ep″ĭ-dem′ik) [Gr. *epidēmios* prevalent]. 1. Attacking many people in any region at the same time; widely diffused and rapidly spreading. 2. A disease of high morbidity which is only occasionally present in a human community. 3. A season of the extensive prevalence of any particular disease.

epidemicity (ep″ĭ-dĕ-mis′ĭ-te). The quality of being widely diffused and rapidly spreading throughout a community.

epidemiogenesis (ep″ĭ-de″me-o-jen′e-sis). The spread of a communicable disease to epidemic proportions.

epidemiography (ep″ĭ-de″me-og′rah-fe) [*epidemic* + Gr. *graphein* to write]. A treatise upon or an account of epidemics.

epidemiology (ep″ĭ-de″me-ol′o-je) [*epidemic* + *-logy*]. The field of science dealing with the relationships of the various factors which determine the frequencies and distributions of an infectious process, a disease, or a physiological state in a human community (Kenneth F. Maxcy).

epiderm (ep′ĭ-derm). Epidermis.

epidermal (ep″ĭ-der′mal). 1. Pertaining to the epidermis. 2. Any material of epidermal origin, such as dandruff, various hairs, etc., which may be productive of allergic response in hypersensitive persons.

epidermatic (ep″ĭ-der-mat′ik). Epidermic.

epidermatomycosis (ep″ĭ-der″mah-to″mi-ko′sis). Dermatomycosis.

epidermatoplasty (ep″ĭ-der-mat′o-plas″te) [*epidermis* + Gr. *plassein* to form]. Skin grafting done with pieces of epidermis with the underlying outer layer of the corium.

epidermatous (ep″ĭ-der′mah-tus). Epidermic.

epidermic (ep″ĭ-der′mik). Pertaining to the epidermis.

epidermicula (ep″ĭ-der-mik′u-lah). A very thin membrane or cuticula, such as that covering a hair.

epidermidalization (ep″ĭ-der″mid-ah-li-za′shun). Development of epidermic cells (stratified epithelium) from mucous cells (columnar epithelium).

epidermides (ep″ĭ-der′mĭ-dēz) [Gr.]. Plural of *epidermis.*

epidermidolysis (ep″ĭ-der″mi-dol′ĭ-sis). Epidermolysis.

epidermidosis (ep″ĭ-der″mi-do′sis). Any skin disease affecting primarily the epidermis.

epidermis (ep″ĭ-der′mis), pl. *epider′mides* [*epi-* + Gr. *derma* skin]. [N A, B N A] The outermost and nonvascular layer of the skin, made up from

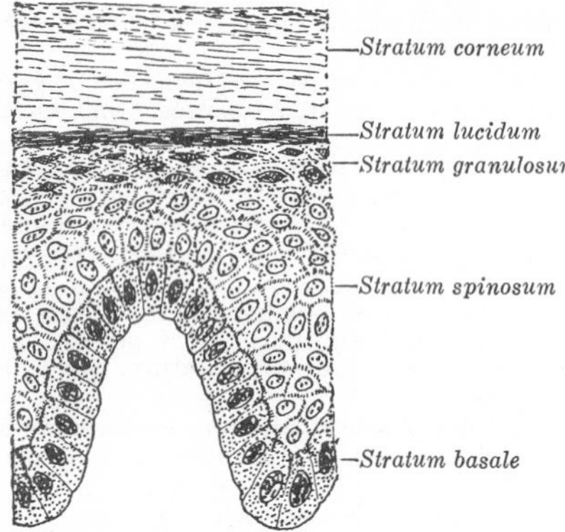

Section of epidermis (after Hill).

without inward of five layers: (1) The *stratum corneum*, or *horny layer*, which consists of flattened horny cells; (2) the *stratum lucidum*, or *layer of Oehl*, consisting of several layers of transparent nucleated cells; (3) the *stratum granulosum*, or *layer of Langerhans*, composed of flattened granular cells; (4) the *stratum spinosum*, or *layer of Malpighi* (rete mucosum), composed of rounded or polygonal pigmented cells; and (5) the *stratum basale* (basal cell layer), composed of columnar cells arranged perpendicularly.

epidermitis (ep″ĭ-der-mi′tis). Inflammation of the epidermis.

epidermization (ep″ĭ-der″mi-za′shun). 1. The process of covering or of becoming covered with epidermis. 2. Skin grafting.

epidermodysplasia (ep″ĭ-der″mo-dis-pla′se-ah). Faulty development of the epidermis. **e. verrucifor′mis,** a familial condition characterized by faulty development of the upper layers of the epidermis, with red or red-violet, smooth round or irregularly shaped papules with perpendicular margins occurring on the hands and feet.

epidermoid (ep″ĭ-der′moid). 1. Resembling the epidermis. 2. A cerebral or meningeal tumor formed by inclusion of epidermal cells from the skin or mucous membrane.

epidermoidoma (ep″ĭ-der″moi-do′mah). A usually benign, slowly growing tumor developing from an ectodermal rest or inclusion located in the scalp, in the diploic space, or between the dura and the inner table of the skull. Histologically it resembles cholesteatoma of the middle ear, but it has no connection with the outer ear or with pneumatic cavities of the middle ear.

epidermolysis (ep″ĭ-der-mol′ĭ-sis) [*epidermis* + Gr. *lysis* dissolution]. A loosened state of the epidermis. Cf. *acantholysis.* **e. acquis′ita,** epidermolysis bullosa occurring during adult life. **e. bullo′sa,** a disease of the skin, usually appearing at birth or soon after and marked by the development of bullae, vesicles and epidermal cysts which appear after irritation. Called also *epidermolysis bullosa hereditaria, acantholysis bullosa, Köbner's disease,* and *Goldscheider's disease.*

epidermoma (ep″ĭ-der-mo′mah). A cutaneous outgrowth, such as a wart.

epidermomycosis (ep″ĭ-der″mo-mi-ko′sis). A general name for any dermatitis caused by microscopical fungi and yeasts.

epidermophytid (ep″ĭ-der-mof′ĭ-tid). A skin eruption caused by Epidermophyton.

epidermophytin (ep″ĭ-der-mof′ĭ-tin). A vaccine for epidermophytosis, being a filtrate from a culture of Epidermophyton.

Epidermophyton (ep″ĭ-der-mof′ĭ-ton) [*epidermis* + Gr. *phyton* plant]. A genus of fungi (dermatophytes). **E. flocco′sum** attacks both skin and nails and is one of the causative organisms of tinea cruris, tinea pedis (athlete's foot) and tinea unguium.

epidermophytosis (ep″ĭ-der″mo-fi-to′sis). Infection by fungi of the genus Epidermophyton; dermatophytosis. **e. cru′ris,** tinea cruris. **e. interdigita′le,** dermatophytosis.

epidermosis (ep″ĭ-der-mo′sis). A skin disease affecting chiefly the epidermis.

epidermotropic (ep″ĭ-der-mo-trop′ik). Having a special affinity for or exerting a particular effect upon epidermal tissues.

epidiascope (ep″ĭ-di′ah-skōp) [*epi-* + Gr. *dia* through + *skopein* to examine]. A lantern for projecting the images of opaque bodies upon a screen by reflected or transmitted light.

epididymal (ep″ĭ-did′ĭ-mal). Pertaining to the epididymis.

epididymectomy (ep″ĭ-did″ĭ-mek′to-me) [*epididymis* + Gr. *ektomē* excision]. Surgical removal of the epididymis.

epididymis (ep″ĭ-did′ĭ-mis), pl. *epididym′ides* [*epi-* + Gr. *didymos* testis]. [N A, B N A] The elongated cordlike structure along the posterior border of the testis, in the ducts of which the spermatozoa are stored. It consists of a head, a body, and a tail.

epididymitis (ep″ĭ-did″ĭ-mi′tis). Inflammation of the epididymis.

epididymodeferentectomy (ep″ĭ-did″ĭ-mo-def″er-en-tek′to-me). Excision of the epididymis and ductus deferens.

epididymodeferential (ep″ĭ-did″ĭ-mo-def″er-en′shal). Pertaining to the epididymis and ductus deferens.

epididymo-orchitis (ep″ĭ-did″ĭ-mo-or-ki′tis). Inflammation of the epididymis and testis.

epididymotomy (ep″ĭ-did″ĭ-mot′o-me) [*epididymis* + Gr. *tomē* a cut]. Incision of the epididymis.

epididymovasectomy (ep″ĭ-did″ĭ-mo-vaz-ek′-to-me). Excision of the epididymis and a large portion of the ductus deferens.

epididymovasostomy (ep-e-did″e-mo-vaz-os′-to-me) [*epididymo-* + *vas* deferens + Gr. *stomoun* to provide with an opening, or mouth]. Surgical creation of a new communication between the epididymis and a formerly distal portion of the vas (ductus) deferens.

epidural (ep″ĭ-du′ral). Situated upon or outside the dura.

epifascial (ep″ĭ-fash′e-al). Upon the fascia.

epifolliculitis (ep″ĭ-fo-lik″u-li′tis). Inflammation of the hair follicles.

epigain (ep′ĭ-gān). The unconscious portion of the secondary external advantage to be derived from an emotional illness.

epigamous (ĕ-pig′ah-mus) [*epi-* + Gr. *gamos* marriage]. Occurring after conception: a term descriptive of the theory that the sex of an embryo is determined by external factors acting on the embryo during its development.

epigaster (ep″ĭ-gas′ter) [*epi-* + Gr. *gastēr* belly]. The hind gut: the embryonic structure from which the large intestine is formed.

epigastralgia (ep″ĭ-gas-tral′je-ah) [*epigastrium* + *-algia*]. Pain in the epigastrium.

epigastric (ep″ĭ-gas′trik) [*epi-* + Gr. *gastēr* belly]. Pertaining to the epigastrium.

epigastrium (ep″ĭ-gas′tre-um) [Gr. *epigastrion*]. The upper middle region of the abdomen, located within the sternal angle. Called also *regio epigastrica* [N A].

epigastrius (ep″ĭ-gas′tre-us) [*epi-* + Gr. *gastēr* belly]. A double monster in which the parasite is small and forms a tumor upon the epigastrium of the autosite.

epigastrocele (ep″ĭ-gas′tro-sēl) [*epigastrium* + Gr. *kēlē* hernia]. Hernia in the epigastric region.

epigastrorrhaphy (ep″ĭ-gas-tror′ah-fe) [*epigastrium* + Gr. *rhaphē* suture]. The closure of an epigastric wound by stitches.

epigenesis (ep″ĭ-jen′e-sis) [*epi-* + *genesis*]. The theory that development starts from a structureless cell, and consists in the successive formation and addition of new parts which do not preexist in the fertilized egg: opposed to the theory of preformation.

epigenetic (ep″ĭ-je-net′ik). Pertaining to epigenesis.

epigenetics (ep″ĭ-je-net′iks). The science concerned with the causal analysis of development.

epiglottectomy (ep″ĭ-glot-tek′to-me). Epiglottidectomy.

epiglottic (ep″ĭ-glot′ik). Pertaining to the epiglottis.

epiglottidean (ep″ĭ-glo-tid′e-an). Pertaining to the epiglottis.

epiglottidectomy (ep″ĭ-glot″ĭ-dek′to-me) [*epiglottis* + Gr. *ektomē* excision]. Excision of the epiglottis.

epiglottiditis (ep″ĭ-glot″ĭ-di′tis). Inflammation of the epiglottis.

epiglottis (ep″ĭ-glot′is) [*epi-* + Gr. *glōttis* glottis]. [N A, B N A] The lidlike structure which covers the entrance to the larynx.

epiglottitis (ep″ĭ-glot-ti′tis). Epiglottiditis.

epignathous (e-pig′nah-thus). Of the nature of an epignathus.

epignathus (e-pig′nah-thus) [*epi-* + Gr. *gnathos* jaw]. A tumor arising from the soft or hard palate in the region of Rathke's pouch, filling the buccal cavity and protruding from the mouth. Because the tumor sometimes shows a certain degree of organization, it has been considered a parasitic fetus.

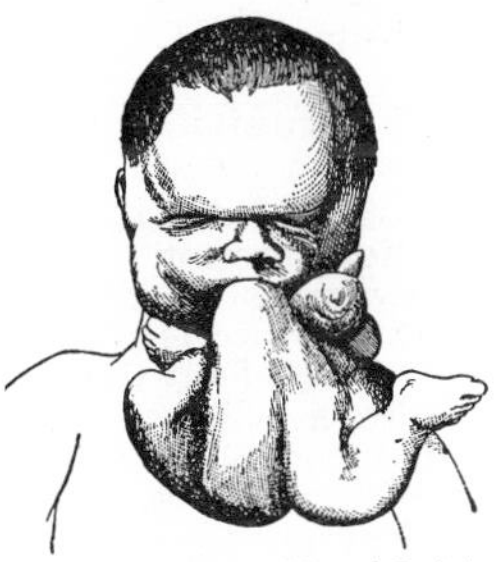

Epignathus (Gould and Pyle).

epigonal (e-pig′o-nal) [*epi-* + Gr. *gonē* seed]. Situated on an embryonic gonad.

epiguanine (ep″ĭ-gwan′in). One of the purine bodies found in the urine after the ingestion of theobromine (cocoa). It is 7-methyl-2-amino-6-oxypurine, $C_6H_7N_5O$.

epihydrinaldehyde (ep″ĭ-hi″drin-al′de-hīd). A chemical compound, one of the substances which give rancid fats their disagreeable odor.

epihyoid (ep″ĭ-hi′oid). Situated upon the hyoid bone.

epilamellar (ep″ĭ-lah-mel′ar). Situated upon the basement membrane.

epilation (ep″ĭ-la′shun) [L. *e* out + *pilus* hair]. The removal of hair by the roots.

epilatory (e-pil′ah-to-re). 1. Pertaining to the removal of hairs. 2. An agent which effects the destruction or removal of hairs.

epilemma (ep″ĭ-lem′ah) [*epi-* + Gr. *lemma* scale]. The endoneurium.

epilemmal (ep″ĭ-lem′al). Pertaining to the epilemma.

epilepidoma (ep″ĭ-lep′ĭ-do′mah) [*epi-* + Gr. *lepis* rind + *-oma*]. A tumor composed of hyperplastic tissue derived from the epiblast.

epilepsia (ep″ĭ-lep′se-ah) [L.; Gr. *epilēpsia*]. Epilepsy. **e. gra′vior,** the convulsive type of epilepsy. Called also *grand mal* and *haut mal.* **e. ma′jor,** e. gravior. **e. mi′nor,** a brief or mild epileptic seizure. Called also *minor epilepsy* and *petit mal.* **e. mit′ior,** e. minor. **e. nu′tans,** head nodding attacks in children, a minor form of astatic seizure. **e. partia′lis contin′ua,** continuous clonic movements, not necessarily epileptic in nature. **e. procur′siva,** a running fit. **e. rotato′ria,** an epileptic seizure in which the body rotates; torsion spasm. **e. tar′da,** epilepsy beginning in middle age or later.

epilepsy (ep′ĭ-lep″se) [Gr. *epilēpsia* seizure]. A disease characterized by one or more of the following symptoms: paroxysmally recurring impairment or loss of consciousness, involuntary excess or cessation of muscle movements, psychic or sensory disturbances, and perturbation of the autonomic nervous system. Symptoms are based on a substrate of paroxysmal disturbance of the electrical activity of the brain. On the basis of origin, epilepsy is genetic (essential, idiopathic, cryptogenic) or acquired (symptomatic). On the basis of mechanism, it is physiologic (biologic) or organic. On the basis of clinical and electroencephalographic phenomena, four subdivisions are recognized. (1) *Grand mal* (convulsions, major e., haut mal)—subgroups: generalized, focal (localized), and jacksonian (rolandic). (2) *Petit mal*—subgroups: petite absence (pyknoepilepsy), myoclonic jerks, and astatic (akinetic, drop, inhibition). (3) *Psychomotor* (psychic, psychic equivalent, or variant)—subgroups: psychomotor proper (tonic with adversive or torsion movements or masticatory phenomena), automatic (with amnesia), and sensory (hallucinations, or dream states or déjà vu). (4) *Autonomic* (diencephalic) with flushing, pallor, tachycardia, hypertension, perspiration, or other visceral symptoms. **abdominal e.,** paroxysmal abdominal pain, the expression of neuronal discharge from the brain. **acquired e.,** epilepsy originating after conception. **activated e.,** epileptic seizures induced by electrical or drug stimulation for the purpose of observing the pattern of response, both brain wave and physical. **automatic e.,** automatisms, often ambulatory with purposive acts, but with amnesia for the events. **Bravais-jacksonian e.,** jacksonian e. **cardiac e.,** epileptic seizures associated with or caused by cardiac disease. **cortical e.,** seizure phenomena localized to cortical areas. **cryptogenic e.,** epilepsy of unknown origin (genetic or biologic). **diurnal e.,** epileptic attacks occurring in the daytime or when the patient is awake. **essential e.,** cryptogenic e. **focal e.,** epileptic seizures that are predominantly one-sided or local, or present localized features. **hysterical e.,** a seizure presenting features of both hysteria and epilepsy. **idiopathic e.,** cryptogenic e. **jacksonian e.,** a progression of involuntary clonic movement (anterior rolandic e.) or of sensation (posterior rolandic e.), with retention of consciousness. **larval e.,** unerupted epileptic seizures, represented only by characteristic waves in the electroencephalogram. **laryngeal e.,** tussive syncope. **latent e.,** larval e. **major e.** See *epilepsy.* **matutinal e.,** epileptic seizures occurring in the morning on awakening. **menstrual e.,** epileptic seizures associated with menstruation. **minor e.,** brief or mild seizures, especially of the petit mal, or psychomotor, variety. **musicogenic e.,** reflex epilepsy occurring in response to a musical stimulus. **myoclonus e.,** a condition characterized by intermittent or continuous clonus of muscle groups with mental deterioration based on progressive neuropathology, often interspersed with convulsive seizures. Called also *Unverricht's disease.* **nocturnal e.,** epileptic attacks occurring at night or while the patient is asleep. **physiologic e.,** biologic or electrobiologic seizures based on physiologic and not on organic or structural abnormalities of the brain. **procursive e.,** running fits. **psychic e.,** a seizure manifested by a predominance of psychic or psychotic features. Called also *psychic equivalent.* **psychomotor e.,** a condition characterized by purposeful motor and/or psychic activity which is irrelevant for the time and place, the patient being amnesic afterward for events occurring during the seizure. **reflex e.,** an epileptic seizure occurring in response to a sensory (tactile, visual, auditory or musical) stimulus. **rolandic e.** See *jacksonian e.* **sensory e.,** seizures manifested by hallucinations of sight, smell, or taste. **serial e.,** seizures occurring in series, with return of consciousness between the individual attacks. **symptomatic e.,** epileptic seizures complicated by presence of organic (structural) changes of the brain (usually acquired) or of a disease process or a toxin (alcohol, lead, metrazol). **tardy e.,** epilepsia tarda. **tonic e.,** a seizure characterized by involuntary movements marked by rigidity. **traumatic e.,** epileptic seizures occurring as the result of trauma (gunshot wound or other injury) to the brain. **uncinate e.,** epileptic seizures originating in the uncinate region of the temporal lobe, especially sensory hallucinations.

epileptic (ep″ĭ-lep′tik) [Gr. *epilēptikos*]. 1. Pertaining to, or affected with, epilepsy. 2. A person affected with epilepsy.

epileptiform (ep″ĭ-lep′tĭ-form). Epileptoid.

epileptogenic (ep″ĭ-lep-to-jen′ik) [*epilepsy* + Gr. *gennan* to produce]. Producing epileptic attacks.

epileptogenous (ep″ĭ-lep-toj′e-nus). Epileptogenic.

epileptoid (ep″ĭ-lep′toid) [Gr. *epilēpsia* seizure + *eidos* form]. 1. Resembling epilepsy or its manifestations. 2. Occurring in severe or sudden paroxysms.

epileptologist (ep″ĭ-lep-tol′o-jist). A practitioner who makes a special study of epilepsy.

epileptology (ep″ĭ-lep-tol′o-je). The study of epilepsy.

epileptosis (ep″ĭ-lep-to′sis). Any mental disease belonging to the epileptic group (Southard).

epiloia (ep″ĭ-loi′ah). Tuberous sclerosis.

epimandibular (ep″ĭ-man-dib′u-lar) [*epi-* + L. *mandibulum* jaw]. Situated upon the lower jaw.

epimenorrhagia (ep″ĭ-men″o-ra′je-ah). Too frequent and too excessive menstruation.

epimenorrhea (ep″ĭ-men″o-re′ah). Abnormally frequent menstruation; menstrual irregularity in which the patient has a menstrual cycle less than the normal twenty-eight days.

epimere (ep′ĭ-mēr) [*epi-* + Gr. *meros* a part]. The dorsal portion of a somite that forms muscles innervated by the dorsal ramus of a spinal nerve.

epimerite (ep″ĭ-mer′ĭt) [*epi-* + Gr. *meros* part]. An organ of certain gregarine protozoa by which they are attached to epithelial cells.

epimicroscope (ep″ĭ-mi′kro-skōp). A microscope in which the specimen is illuminated by light passing through a condenser built around the objective.

epimorphic (ep″ĭ-mor′fik). Pertaining to or characterized by epimorphosis.

epimorphosis (ep″ĭ-mor-fo′sis) [*epi-* + Gr. *morphē* form]. The regeneration of a piece of an organism by proliferation at the cut surface.

Epimys (ep′ĭ-mis) [*epi-* + Gr. *mys* mouse]. A genus of rats. *E. norve′gicus* is the ship rat; *E. rat′tus* is the plague rat of India.

epimysium (ep″ĭ-mis′e-um) [*epi-* + Gr. *mys* muscle]. The fibrous sheath about an entire muscle. Called also *perimysium externum.*

epinasty (ep′ĭ-nas″te) [*epi-* + Gr. *nastos* pressed close]. Downward curvature produced by excessive growth on the upper side of an extended organ.

epinephrectomy (ep″ĭ-ne-frek′to-me). Adrenalectomy.

epinephrine (ep″ĭ-nef′rin). A hormone secreted by the adrenal medulla in response to splanchnic stimulation, and stored in the chromaffin granules, being released predominantly in response to hypoglycemia. It is also produced synthetically. It is the most powerful vasopressor substance known, increasing blood pressure, stimulating the heart muscle, accelerating the heart rate, and increasing cardiac output. It is used pharmaceutically as a sympathomimetic, a cardiac stimulant, a pressor substance, and to relax bronchial smooth muscles.

epinephrinemia (ep″ĭ-nef″rĭ-ne′me-ah). The presence of epinephrine in the blood.

epinephritis (ep″ĭ-ne-fri′tis) [*epi-* + Gr. *nephros* kidney]. Inflammation of an adrenal gland.

epinephroma (ep″ĭ-ne-fro′mah). Hypernephroma.

epinephros (ep″ĭ-nef′ros) [*epi-* + Gr. *nephros* kidney]. An adrenal gland (glandula suprarenalis [N A]).

epineural (ep″ĭ-nu′ral). Situated upon a neural arch.

epineurial (ep″ĭ-nu′re-al). Pertaining to the epineurium.

epineurium (ep″ĭ-nu′re-um) [*epi-* + Gr. *neuron* nerve]. The connective tissue covering of a peripheral nerve.

epinosic (ep″ĭ-no′sik) [*epi-* + Gr. *nosos* disease]. Pertaining to some secondary advantage because of illness.

epinosis (ep″ĭ-no′sis). A psychic or imaginary state of illness secondary to an original illness. Cf. *paranosis.*

epionychium (ep″e-o-nik′e-um). Eponychium.

epiorchium (ep″e-or′ke-um). Lamina visceralis.

epiornitic (ep″e-or-nit′ik). Epornitic.

epiotic (ep″e-ot′ik) [*epi-* + Gr. *ous* ear]. Situated on or above the ear.

epiparonychia (ep″ĭ-par-o-nik′e-ah). A combination of eponychia and paronychia.

epipastic (ep″ĭ-pas′tik) [*epi-* + Gr. *passein* to sprinkle]. 1. Suitable for use as a dusting powder. 2. A powder to be sprinkled upon the surface of the body.

epipharyngeal (ep″ĭ-fah-rin′je-al). Nasopharyngeal.

epipharyngitis (ep″ĭ-far″in-ji′tis). Nasopharyngitis.

epipharynx (ep″ĭ-far′inks). Nasopharynx.

epiphenomenon (ep″ĭ-fe-nom′e-non) [*epi-* + Gr. *phainomenon* phenomenon]. An accessory, exceptional, or accidental occurrence in the course of an attack of any disease.

epiphora (e-pif′o-rah) [Gr. *epiphora* sudden burst]. An abnormal overflow of tears down the cheek: mainly due to stricture of the lacrimal passages.

epiphrenal (ep″ĭ-frē′nal). Above the diaphragm.

epiphylactic (ep″ĭ-fi-lak′tik). Pertaining to or marked by epiphylaxis.

epiphylaxis (ep″ĭ-fi-lak′sis) [*epi-* + Gr. *phylaxis* a guarding]. Increase or reinforcement of normal phylaxis, as seen in the positive phase by opsonic or vaccine therapy.

epiphyseal (ep″ĭ-fiz′e-al). Pertaining to or of the nature of an epiphysis.

epiphyses (e-pif′ĭ-sēz). Plural of *epiphysis.*

epiphysial (ep″ĭ-fiz′e-al). Epiphyseal.

epiphysiodesis (ep″ĭ-fiz″e-od′ĕ-sis) [*epiphysis* + Gr. *desis* a binding]. The operation of fixing a separated epiphysis to its diaphysis.

epiphysioid (ep″ĭ-fiz′e-oid). Resembling epiphyses; a term applied to carpal and tarsal bones which develop like epiphyses from centers of ossification.

epiphysiolysis (ep″ĭ-fiz″e-ol′ĭ-sis) [*epiphysis* + Gr. *lysis* loosening]. Separation of an epiphysis from its bone; especially slipping of the upper femoral epiphysis.

epiphysiopathy (ep″ĭ-fiz″e-op′ah-the) [*epiphysis* + Gr. *pathos* disease]. 1. Any disease of the pineal gland. 2. Any disease of an epiphysis of a bone.

epiphysis (e-pif′ĭ-sis), pl. *epiph′yses* [Gr. "an ongrowth; excrescence"]. [N A, B N A] 1. The end of a long bone, usually wider than the shaft, and either entirely cartilaginous or separated from the shaft by a cartilaginous disc. 2. Part of a bone formed from a secondary center of ossification, commonly found at the ends of long bones, on the margins of flat bones, and at tubercles and processes; during the period of growth epiphyses are separated from the main portion of the bone by cartilage. **e. cer′ebri,** corpus pineale. **slipped e.,** dislocation of the epiphysis of a bone, as of the epiphysis of the head of the femur, which is the cause of coxa vara. **stippled epiphyses,** chondrodystrophia fetalis calcificans.

epiphysitis (e-pif″ĭ-si′tis). Inflammation of an epiphysis or of the cartilage which separates it from the main bone. **vertebral e.,** necrotic inflammation of the vertebral epiphyses; Scheuermann's disease.

epiphyte (ep′ĭ-fit) [*epi-* + Gr. *phyton* plant]. 1. A plant organism growing upon another plant. 2. A plant organism parasitic upon the exterior of the human or an animal body.

epiphytic (ep″ĭ-fit′ik). 1. Pertaining to or caused by epiphytes. 2. A widely diffused outbreak of an infectious disease in plants.

epipial (ep″ĭ-pi′al). Situated on the pia.

epipleural (ep″ĭ-ploo′ral). Situated on a pleural element, or pleurapophysis.

epiplo- (e-pip′lo) [Gr. *epiploon*]. Combining form denoting relationship to the epiploon.

epiplocele (e-pip′lo-sēl) [*epiplo-* + Gr. *kēlē* hernia]. A hernia which contains omentum.

epiplo-ectomy (ep″ĭ-plo-ek′to-me) [*epiplo-* + Gr. *ektomē* excision]. Omentectomy; excision of the omentum.

epiplo-enterocele (e-pip″lo-en′ter-o-sēl) [*epiplo-* + Gr. *enteron* intestine + *kēlē* hernia]. Hernia containing intestine and omentum.

epiploic (ep″ĭ-plo′ik). Pertaining to the epiploon.

epiploitis (e-pip″lo-i′tis). Inflammation of the epiploon.

epiplomerocele (e-pip″lo-me′ro-sēl) [*epiplo-* + Gr. *mēros* thigh + *kēlē* hernia]. Femoral hernia containing omentum.

epiplomphalocele (ep″ĭ-plom-fal′o-sēl) [*epiplo-* + Gr. *omphalos* navel + *kēlē* hernia]. Umbilical hernia containing omentum.

epiploon (e-pip′lo-on) [Gr.]. The omentum. **great e.,** omentum majus. **lesser e.,** omentum minus.

epiplopexy (e-pip′lo-pek″se) [*epiplo-* + Gr. *pēxis* fixation]. Omentopexy.

epiploplasty (e-pip′lo-plas″te) [*epiplo-* + Gr. *plassein* to form]. The use of the epiploon for covering raw surfaces in abdominal surgery.

epiplorrhaphy (e″pip-lor′ah-fe) [*epiplo-* + Gr. *rhaphē* suture]. Omentorrhaphy; suture of the omentum.

epiplosarcomphalocele (e-pip″lo-sar″kom-fal′o-sēl) [*epiplo-* + Gr. *sarx* flesh + *omphalos* navel + *kēlē* hernia]. An umbilical hernia complicated with a local fleshy excrescence.

epiploscheocele (e″pip-los′ke-o-sēl) [*epiplo-* + Gr. *oscheon* scrotum + *kēlē* hernia]. Scrotal hernia containing omentum.

epipygus (ep″ĭ-pi′gus). Pygomelus.

epipyramis (ep″ĭ-pir′ah-mis). A small supernumerary carpal bone, between the triquetrum, lunate, hamate and capitate bones: called also *epitriquetrum*.

epirotulian (ep″ĭ-ro-tu′le-an) [*epi-* + L. *rotula* patella]. Upon the patella.

episarkin (ep″ĭ-sar′kin). One of the alloxur bases, $C_4H_6N_3O$, occurring in the normal urine and the urine of leukemia.

episclera (ep″ĭ-skle′rah). The loose connective tissue forming the external surface of the sclera.

episcleral (ep″ĭ-skle′ral). Overlying the sclera.

episcleritis (ep″ĭ-skle-ri′tis). Inflammation of tissues overlying the sclera; also inflammation of the outermost layers of the sclera. **e. partia′lis fu′gax,** sudden hyperemia of the sclera and overlying conjunctiva, lasting a short time.

episclerotitis (ep″ĭ-skle″ro-ti′tis). Episcleritis.

episcope (ep′ĭ-skōp). 1. A projecting lantern for throwing images of solid objects on a white screen in natural colors. 2. An instrument for examination of the surface of objects.

episio- (e-piz′e-o) [Gr. *epision* the region of the pubes]. Combining form denoting relationship to the vulva.

episioclisia (e-piz″e-o-kli′se-ah) [*episio-* + Gr. *kleisis* closure]. Surgical closure of the vulva.

episio-elytrorrhaphy (e-piz″e-o-el″e-tror′ah-fe) [*episio-* + *elytrorrhaphy*]. The operation of narrowing the vulva and vagina to support a prolapsed uterus.

episioperineoplasty (e-piz″e-o-per″ĭ-ne′o-plas″te) [*episio-* + *perineum* + Gr. *plassein* to form]. Plastic repair of the vulva and perineum.

episioperineorrhaphy (e-piz″e-o-per″ĭ-ne-or′ah-fe). The suturing of the vulva and perineum for the support of a prolapsed uterus.

episioplasty (e-piz′e-o-plas″te) [*episio-* + Gr. *plassein* to shape]. Plastic repair of the vulva.

episiorrhaphy (e-piz″e-or′ah-fe) [*episio-* + Gr. *rhaphē* suture]. 1. The suturing of the labia majora. 2. The sewing up of a lacerated perineum.

episiostenosis (e-piz″e-o-ste-no′sis) [*episio-* + Gr. *stenōsis* contraction]. The narrowing of the vulvar slit.

episiotomy (e-piz″e-ot′o-me) [*episio-* + Gr. *tomē* a cutting]. Surgical incision of the vulvar orifice for obstetrical purposes (Ould, 1742).

episode (ep′ĭ-sōd). A noteworthy happening, for which the time can usually be fixed, occurring in the course of ordinary events. **psycholeptic e.,** a sudden and vivid psychic experience to which a patient attributes the beginning of his illness, and which so possesses his mind that he is unable to shake it off.

epispadia (ep″ĭ-spa′de-ah). Epispadias.

epispadiac (ep″ĭ-spa′de-ak). Pertaining to or exhibiting epispadias. By extension, sometimes used to designate an individual exhibiting epispadias.

epispadial (ep″ĭ-spa′de-al). Pertaining to epispadias.

epispadias (ep″ĭ-spa′de-as) [*epi-* + Gr. *spadōn* a rent]. A congenital defect in which the urethra opens on the dorsum of the penis. **female e.,** a fissure of the upper wall of the urethra in the female.

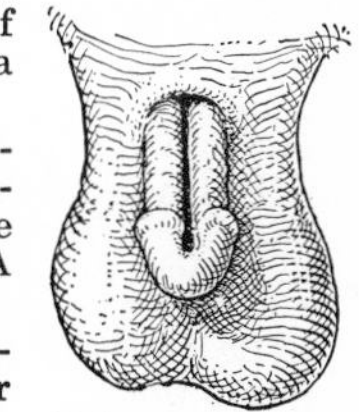

Epispadias (Arey).

epispastic (ep″ĭ-spas′tik) [*epi-* + Gr. *span* to draw]. 1. Causing a blister or serous discharge from a superficial lesion. 2. A blistering agent.

epispinal (ep″ĭ-spi′nal). Situated upon the spinal cord or the spinal column.

episplenitis (ep′ĭ-sple-ni′tis) [*epi-* + Gr. *splēn* spleen + *-itis*]. Inflammation of the capsule of the spleen.

epistasis (e-pis′tah-sis) [*epi-* + Gr. *stasis* a standing]. 1. The checking of any discharge, as of blood, menses, or lochia. 2. A scum or pellicle, as on the surface of urine. 3. Epistasy.

epistasy (e-pis′tah-se) [*epi-* + Gr. *stasis* a standing]. The concealing of one hereditary character by another superimposed upon it.

epistatic (ep″ĭ-stat′ik). 1. Pertaining to or characterized by epistasis. 2. Superimposed.

epistaxis (ep″ĭ-stak′sis) [Gr.]. Nosebleed; hemorrhage from the nose. **Gull's renal e.,** a disease of middle adult life marked by renal hemorrhage, but with no known lesion. Called also *essential renal hematuria, angioneurotic hematuria,* and *renal hemophilia.*

epistemology (ep″ĭ-ste-mol′o-je) [Gr. *epistēmē* knowledge + *-logy*]. The science of the methods and validity of knowledge.

epistemophilia (ep″ĭ-ste-mo-fil′e-ah) [Gr. *epistēmē* knowledge + *philein* to love]. Marked or abnormal interest in learning.

episternal (ep″ĭ-ster′nal). 1. Situated on or over the sternum. 2. Pertaining to the episternum.

episternum (ep″ĭ-ster′num) [*epi-* + Gr. *sternon* sternum]. A bone present in reptiles and monotremes that may be represented as part of the manubrium, or first piece of the sternum.

episthotonos (e″pis-thot′o-nos). Emprosthotonos.

epistropheus (ep″ĭ-stro′fe-us) [Gr. "the pivot"] [B N A]. The second cervical vertebra (axis [N A]).

epitarsus (ep″ĭ-tar′sus) [*epi-* + *tarsus*]. An anomaly of the eye consisting of a fold of conjunctiva passing from the fornix to near the lid border. Called also *congenital pterygium.*

epitela (ep″ĭ-te′lah) [*epi-* + L. *tela* web]. The delicate tissue of Vieussen's valve.

epitendineum (ep″ĭ-ten-din′e-um). The fibrous sheath covering a tendon.

epitenon (ep″ĭ-te′non) [*epi-* + Gr. *tenōn* tendon]. The connective tissue covering a tendon within its sheath.

epithalamic (ep″ĭ-thah-lam′ik). 1. Overlying the thalamus. 2. Pertaining to the epithalamus.

epithalamus (ep″ĭ-thal′ah-mus). [N A, B N A] The part of the thalamencephalon just superior and posterior to the thalamus, comprising the pineal body and the habenular trigone; the stria medullaris is sometimes considered to belong to it.

epithalaxia (ep″ĭ-thah-lak′se-ah) [*epithelium* + Gr. *allaxis* exchange]. Desquamation of the epithelium, especially of the intestinal mucosa.

epithelia (ep″ĭ-the′le-ah). Plural of *epithelium.*

epithelial (ep″ĭ-the′le-al). Pertaining to or composed of epithelium.

epithelialization (ep″ĭ-the″le-al-i-za′shun). The covering of a denuded surface with epithelium; conversion into epithelium.

epithelialize (ep″ĭ-the′le-al-īz). To cover with or change into epithelium.

epithelio- (ep″ĭ-the′le-o). Combining form denoting relationship to the epithelium.

epithelioblastoma (ep″ĭ-the″le-o-blas-to′mah) [*epithelio-* + Gr. *blastos* cell + *-oma*]. An epithelial tumor; a tumor made up of epithelial cells. The term includes papilloma, adenoma, and carcinoma.

epithelioceptor (ep″ĭ-the″le-o-sep′tor). The region in a gland cell which receives a nerve stimulus from the end-organ of the nerve fibril.

epitheliochorial (ep″ĭ-the″le-o-ko′re-al) [*epithelium* + *chorion*]. Denoting a type of placenta in which the uterine lining is not eroded but merely lies in apposition.

epitheliofibril (ep″ĭ-the′le-o-fi″bril). One of the fibrils which run through the protoplasm of epithelial cells.

epitheliogenetic (ep″ĭ-the″le-o-je-net′ik) [*epithelio-* + Gr. *gennan* to produce]. Due to epithelial proliferation.

epitheliogenic (ep″ĭ-the″le-o-jen′ik). Tending to produce epithelium.

epithelioglandular (ep″ĭ-the″le-o-glan′du-lar). Pertaining to the epithelial cells of a gland.

epithelioid (ep″ĭ-the′le-oid). Resembling epithelium.

epitheliolysin (ep″ĭ-the-le-ol′ĭ-sin). A cytolysin formed in the serum of an animal when epithelial cells from an animal of a different species are injected. The epitheliolysin has the power of destroying epithelial cells of an animal of the same species as that from which the epithelial cells were originally taken.

epitheliolysis (ep″ĭ-the″le-ol′ĭ-sis) [*epithelio-* + Gr. *lysis* dissolution]. Destruction of epithelial cells.

epitheliolytic (ep″ĭ-the″le-o-lit′ik). Pertaining to, characterized by, or causing epitheliolysis.

epithelioma (ep″ĭ-the″le-o′mah). An epithelial cancer; a malignant tumor consisting mainly of epithelial cells and primarily derived from the skin or mucous surface. See *carcinoma.* **e. adamanti′num,** adamantinoma. **e. adenoi′des cys′ticum,** multiple benign cystic adenoma; a rare form of basal-cell carcinoma, consisting of epithelial masses showing glandular arrangement and cyst formation, and appearing as heaped-up lesions on the surface, especially on the face. Called also *Brooke's tumor, acanthoma adenoides cysticum, tricho-epithelioma papulosum multiplex.* **e. cap′itis,** multiple benign epithelioma of the scalp. **chorionic e.,** chorioepithelioma. **columnar e., cylindrical e.,** one composed of columnar cells arranged in glandlike tubules. **e. contagio′sum,** a contagious disease of birds characterized by the formation of epithelial nodules upon the skin, especially of the comb and wattles, and sometimes by a pseudomembrane in the respiratory passages. Called also *fowlpox* and *sorehead.* **diffuse e.,** a variety in which the adjacent tissue is infiltrated with the malignant cells. **glandular e.,** a variety consisting of gland cells and affecting mucous surfaces. **e. mollus′cum,** molluscum epitheliale. **multiple benign cystic e.,** epithelioma adenoides cysticum. **e. myxomato′des psammo′sum,** a form occurring in the third ventricle of the brain, composed of myxomalike tissue containing hard, granular matter. **suprarenal e.,** a hypernephroma.

epitheliomatosis (ep″ĭ-the″le-o-mah-to′sis). The state of being subject to or afflicted with epitheliomas.

epitheliomatous (ep″ĭ-the″le-o′mah-tus). Pertaining to or of the nature of epithelioma.

epitheliomuscular (ep″ĭ-the″le-o-mus′ku-lar). Composed of epithelium and muscle.

epitheliosis (ep″ĭ-the″le-o′sis). 1. Proliferation of the epithelium of the conjunctiva. 2. Borrel's name for a disease in which the causative agent is a filtrable virus which exhibits a special affinity for the epithelial structures of the body, including variola, vaccinia, sheeppox, molluscum contagiosum, and contagious epithelioma of birds. **e. desquamati′va conjuncti′vae,** a condition resembling trachoma occurring in the Samoan Islands.

epitheliotoxin (ep″ĭ-the″le-o-tok′sin). A cytotoxin which destroys epithelial cells.

epithelite (ep″ĭ-the′līt). A lesion produced as a reaction to irradiation, in which the epithelium is replaced by a fibrous exudate.

epithelium (ep″ĭ-the′le-um), pl. *epithe′lia* [epi- + Gr. *thēlē* nipple]. [N A, B N A] The covering of internal and external surfaces of the body, including the lining of vessels and other small cavities. It consists of cells joined by small amounts of cementing substances. Epithelium is classified into types on the basis of the number of layers deep and the shape of the superficial cells. **e. ante′rius cor′neae** [N A], the outer epithelial layer of the cornea, consisting of stratified squamous epithelium continuous with that of the conjunctiva. Called also *e. corneae* [B N A] and *anterior e. of cornea.* **ciliated e.,** any type bearing vibratile cilia on the free surface. **columnar e.,** a type composed of tall prismatic cells. **e. cor′neae** [B N A], **corneal e.,** e. anterius corneae. **cubical e., cuboidal e.,** a type composed of cells which have a cubical shape. **e. duc′tus semicircula′ris** [N A], the inner, simple, low epithelium lining the semicircular ducts. **false e.,** the lining of joint cavities. **germinal e.,** a layer of epithelial cells between the primitive mesentery and each mesonephros. It becomes epithelial covering of the gonad and perhaps gives rise to the germ cells. **glandular e.,** epithelium made up of glandular or secreting cells. **laminated e.,** stratified e. **e. of lens, e. len′tis** [N A, B N A], the cuboidal epithelium on the front of the lens. **mesenchymal e.,** the epithelium which lines the subdural and subarachnoid spaces, the perilymphatic spaces in the inner ear and the chamber of the eye. **pavement e.,** epithelium composed of a single layer of flat cells. **pigmentary e., pigmented e.,** epithelium containing granules of pigment. **protective e.,** epithelium that forms a protective covering, as the epidermis. **pyramidal e.,** columnar epithelium whose cells have been modified by pressure into truncated pyramids. **respiratory e.,** the pseudostratified epithelium that lines all but the finer divisions of the respiratory tract. **rod e.,** epithelium the cells of which are rod-shaped. **sense e., sensory e.,** epithelium having relation with a special sense organ; neuro-epithelium. **simple e.,** a type composed of a single layer of cells. **squamous e.,** epithelium composed of thin, platelike cells. **stratified e.,** epithelium in which the cells are arranged in several layers. **subcapsular e.** 1. The epithelioid lining of the capsule of ganglia. 2. Epithelium lentis. **tessellated e.,** simple squamous epithelium. **transitional e.,** epithelium that was originally thought to represent a transition form between stratified squamous and columnar epithelium, found characteristically in the mucous membrane of the excretory passages of the urinary system; in the contracted condition it consists of many cell layers, whereas in the stretched condition usually only two layers can be distinguished.

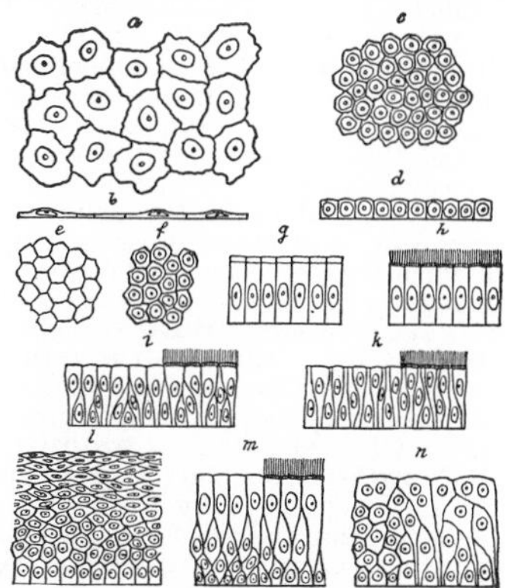

Epithelium of different types: *a, b,* simple squamous; *c, d,* simple cuboidal; *e, f, g,* simple columnar; *h,* simple columnar ciliated; *i, k,* pseudostratified columnar; *l,* stratified squamous; *m,* stratified columnar; *n,* transitional. (Maximow-Bloom.)

epithelization (ep″ĭ-the″li-za′shun). Epithelialization.

epithelize (ep″ĭ-the′līz). Epithelialize.

epithesis (e-pith′ĕ-sis) [Gr. "a laying on"]. 1. The surgical correction of deformity or of crooked limbs. 2. A splint or other appliance to be worn.

epitonic (ep″ĭ-ton′ik) [Gr. *epitonos* strained]. Abnormally tense or tonic; exhibiting an abnormal degree of tension or of tone.

epitoxoid (ep″ĭ-tok′soid). Any toxoid which has less affinity for an antitoxin than the toxin has.

epitoxonoid (ep″ĭ-tok′so-noid). A toxonoid which has the least affinity for its corresponding antitoxin.

epitrichium (ep″ĭ-trik′e-um) [*epi-* + Gr. *trichion* hair]. Periderm, def. 1.

epitriquetrum (ep″ĭ-tri-kwe′trum). Epipyramis.

epitrochlea (ep″ĭ-trok′le-ah) [*epi-* + Gr. *trochilia,* L. *trochlea* pulley]. The inner condyle of the humerus.

epituberculosis (ep″ĭ-tu-ber″ku-lo′sis). 1. A congestive process developing at the beginning of pulmonary tuberculous infection. See *epituberculous infiltration,* under *infiltration.* 2. A benign chronic illness of children characterized by a homogeneous opacity extending from the hilus out into a lobe of a lung.

epiturbinate (ep″ĭ-ter′bĭ-nāt). The soft tissue covering a nasal concha (turbinate bone).

epitympanic (ep″ĭ-tim-pan′ik). 1. Situated upon or over the tympanum. 2. Pertaining to the epitympanum (recessus epitympanicus [N A]).

epitympanum (ep″ĭ-tim′pah-num). Recessus epitympanicus.

epityphlitis (ep″ĭ-tif-li′tis) [*epi-* + Gr. *typhlon* cecum + *-itis*]. 1. Appendicitis. 2. Paratyphlitis.

epityphlon (ep″ĭ-ti′flon) [*epi-* + Gr. *typhlon* cecum]. The vermiform appendix.

epizoa (ep″ĭ-zo′ah). Plural of *epizoon.*

epizoic (ep″ĭ-zo′ik). Pertaining to or caused by epizoa.

epizoicide (ep″ĭ-zo′ĭ-sīd) [*epizoon* + L. *caedere* to kill]. An agent which destroys epizoa.

epizoology (ep″ĭ-zo-ol′o-je). Epizootiology.

epizoon (ep″ĭ-zo′on), pl. *epizo′a* [*epi-* + Gr. *zōon* animal]. An animal parasite living upon the exterior of the body of the host.

epizoonosis (ep″ĭ-zo″o-no′sis). A skin disease caused by an animal parasite.

epizootic (ep″ĭ-zo-ot′ik). 1. Attacking many animals in any region at the same time; widely diffused and rapidly spreading. 2. A disease of high morbidity which is only occasionally present in an animal community.

epizootiology (ep″ĭ-zo-ot″e-ol′o-je). The study of epizootics; the field of science dealing with the relationships of the various factors which determine the frequencies and distributions of infectious diseases among animals.

épluchage (a″ploo-shahzh′) [Fr. "cleaning," "picking"]. Removal of the contused and contaminated tissues of a wound. Cf. *débridement.*

eponychia (ep″o-nik′e-ah) [*eponychium* + *-ia*]. A purulent blister, involving the epidermis at the groove of the nail.

eponychium (ep″o-nik′e-um) [*epi-* + Gr. *onyx* nail]. 1. [N A, B N A] The narrow band of epidermis that extends from the nail wall onto the nail surface. Commonly called *cuticle.* 2. The horny fetal epidermis at the site of the future nail.

eponym (ep′o-nim) [Gr. *epōnymos* named after]. A name or phrase formed from or including the name of a person, as Bright's disease.

eponymic (ep″o-nim′ik). Named from some person; pertaining to an eponym.

epoophorectomy (ep″o-o″fo-rek′to-me) [*epi-* + Gr. *ōophoron* ovary + *ektomē* excision]. Surgical removal of the epoophoron.

epoophoron (ep″o-of′o-ron) [*epi-* + Gr. *ōophoron* ovary]. [N A, B N A] A vestigial structure associated with the ovary, consisting of a more cranial group of mesonephric tubules and a corresponding portion of the mesonephric duct. Called also *parovarium* and *Rosenmüller's body.*

epornithology (ep-or″nĭ-thol′o-je). The scientific study of diseases of high morbidity which are only occasionally present in a bird community.

epornitic (ep″or-nit′ik) [*epi-* + Gr. *ornis* bird]. 1. Attacking many birds in any region at the same time. 2. A disease of high morbidity which is only occasionally present in a bird population.

epoxytropine tropate (e-pok″se-tro′pēn tro′pāt). Methscopolamine.

EPR. Abbreviation for *electrophrenic respiration.*

eprolin (ep′ro-lin). Trade mark for a preparation of vitamin E, consisting of a concentrate of distilled natural tocopherols.

EPS. Abbreviation for *exophthalmos-producing substance.*

Epstein's disease, pearls (ep′stīnz) [Alois *Epstein,* a pediatrician in Prague, 1849–1918]. See under *disease* and *pearl.*

Epstein's nephrosis [Albert Arthur *Epstein,* American physician, born 1880]. See under *nephrosis.*

Epstein's sign, symptom. See under *symptom.*

epulides (ep-u′lĭ-dēz). Plural of *epulis.*

epulis (ep-u′lis), pl. *epu′lides* [Gr. *epoulis* a gum-boil]. A nonspecific term sometimes applied to any growth on the gingiva. **congenital e. of newborn,** a pedunculated lesion of the gingiva, present at birth, apparently arising on the crest of the alveolar ridge or process, and usually occurring in the incisor region. **e. fibromato′sa,** a fibroma arising from the alveolar periosteum and the periodontal membrane. **e. fissura′ta,** granuloma fissuratum. **giant cell e., e. giganto-cellula′ris,** peripheral giant cell reparative granuloma. **e. granulomato′sa,** a small growth on the gingiva resulting from mechanical irritation or infection.

epulo-erectile (ep″u-lo″e-rek′til). Both epuloid and erectile.

epulofibroma (ep″u-lo″fi-bro′mah). A fibroma of the gingiva.

epuloid (ep′u-loid). Resembling an epulis.

epulosis (ep″u-lo′sis) [Gr. *epoulōsis*]. A scarring over; cicatrization.

epulotic (ep″u-lot′ik) [Gr. *epoulōtikos*]. Pertaining to, characterized by, or promoting cicatrization.

equanil (ek′wah-nil). Trade mark for preparations of meprobamate.

equate (e′kwāt). To make equal or equivalent. In color vision, the physiologic faculty of combining two colors to match a third, as to combine red and green to make a homogeneous yellow.

equation (e-kwa′zhun) [L. *aequatio*, from *aequare* to make equal]. An expression made up of two members connected by the sign of equality, =. **Ambard's e.** See under *formula.* **chemical e.,** an equation which expresses a chemical reaction, the symbols on the left of the equation denoting the substances before, and those on the right those after, the reaction. **Harden and Young e.,** an equation showing the chemical reaction in the fermentation of glucose to carbon dioxide, alcohol and hexose diphosphate. **Henderson-Hasselbalch e.,** a formula for calculating the pH of a buffer solution such as blood plasma, $\mathrm{pH} = \mathrm{p}\kappa' + \log \frac{(\mathrm{BA})}{(\mathrm{HA})}$. (HA) is the concentration of a weak acid; (BA) the concentration of a weak salt of this acid; pκ′ the buffer system. **personal e.,** the more or less constant difference between the results of observation depending upon the personal qualities of observers.

equator (e-kwa′tor) [L. *aequator* equalizer]. An imaginary line encircling a globe, equidistant from the poles. Used in anatomical nomenclature to designate such a line on a spherical organ, dividing the surface into two approximately equal parts. Called also *aequator* [B N A]. **e. bul′bi oc′uli** [N A], an imaginary line encircling the eyeball equidistant from the anterior and the posterior poles, dividing the eye into anterior and posterior halves. Called also *e. of eyeball.* **e. of cell,** the boundary of the plane of separation of a dividing cell. **e. of crystalline lens,** e. lentis. **e. of eyeball,** e. bulbi oculi. **e. of lens, e. len′tis** [N A], the rounded peripheral margin of the lens at which the anterior and posterior surfaces meet.

equatorial (e″kwah-to′re-al). Pertaining to an equator; occurring at the same distance from each extremity of an axis.

equiaxial (e″kwe-ak′se-al). Having axes of the same length.

Equidae (ek′wĭ-de) [L. *equus* horse]. A family of mammals containing a single genus, *Equus,* which includes the horse, the ass and the zebra.

equilibration (e″kwĭ-li-bra′shun). The achievement of a balance between opposing elements or forces. **occlusal e.,** modification of the occlusal forms of teeth to equalize occlusal stress or achieve harmonious occlusion.

equilibrator (e″kwĭ-li-bra′tor). An apparatus used to produce or maintain a state of balance between opposing forces.

equilibrium (e″kwĭ-lib′re-um) [L. *aequus* equal + *libra* balance]. A state of balance or equipoise; a condition in which opposing forces exactly counteract each other. **acid-base e.,** a normal ratio between the acid and basic elements of the blood and body fluids; normal hydrogen ion concentration. **body e.,** the condition in which the materials taken into the body are balanced by corresponding excretions. **carbon e.,** the condition in which the total carbon of the excreta is balanced by the carbon of the food. **colloid e.,** a stable condition of the colloids of the body fluids: disturbance of such equilibrium produces colloidoclastic shock or anaphylactoid crisis. **Donnan e.,** the conditions which exist at equilibrium when two solutions are separated by a membrane which is permeable to some of the ions of the solutions, but not to all of them. There is an irregular distribution of the ions between the two solutions, an electrical potential develops between the two sides of the membrane, the two solutions vary in osmotic and in hydrostatic pressure. **dynamic e.,** the condition of balance between varying, shifting, and opposing forces which is characteristic of living processes. **fluid e.** See *water balance,* under *balance.* **homeostatic e.,** the constancy of most vital conditions, such as pH, electrolytic composition, water distribution and various ratios. Cf. *homeostasis.* **membrane e.,** Donnan e. **nitrogen e., nitrogenous e.,** the condition in which the body is metabolizing and excreting as much nitrogen as it is receiving in the food; called also *protein e.* **nutritive e.,** physiologic e. **physiologic e.,** the condition in which the amount of material taken into the body exactly equals the amount discharged. **protein e.,** nitrogen equilibrium. **radioactive e.,** the fixed ratio that results after the lapse of a suitable time between a radioactive element and one of its disintegration products as a result of their half value periods. That of uranium and radium is as 2,380,000 to 1. **water e.** See under *balance.*

equimolar (e″kwĭ-mo′lar). Containing the same number of moles, or having the same molarity.

equimolecular (e″kwĭ-mo-lek′u-lar). Containing the same number of molecules: said of solutions.

equination (e″kwĭ-na′shun) [L. *equinus* equine]. Inoculation with the virus of horsepox.

equine (e′kwin) [L. *equinus* relating to horses]. Pertaining to, characteristic of, or derived from the horse.

equinia (e-kwin′e-ah) [L. *equus* horse]. Glanders. **e. mi′tis,** a mild form of glanders sometimes seen in man and contracted from horses.

equinophobia (e-kwi″no-fo′be-ah) [L. *equinus* relating to horses + Gr. *phobos* fear + *-ia*]. Morbid fear of horses.

equinovarus (e-kwi″no-va′rus). Talipes equinovarus.

equinus (e-kwi′nus). Talipes equinus.

equipotential (e″kwĭ-po-ten′shal) [L. *aequus* equal + *potentia* ability, power]. Possessed of similar and equal power; capable of developing in the same way and to the same extent.

equipotentiality (e″kwe-po-ten″she-al′ĭ-te). The quality or state of having similar and equal power; the capacity for developing in the same way and to the same extent.

equisetosis (ek″wĭ-se-to′sis). Poisoning of horses from eating equisetum.

equisetum (ek″wĭ-se′tum). A common weed, *E. arvense,* horsetail or jointed rush. It causes a form of poisoning in horses that eat it with hay. It is used as a diuretic drug in eclectic practice.

equivalence (e-kwiv′ah-lens). 1. The condition of being equivalent. 2. Quantivalence; the amount of hydrogen which a chemical element can replace in a compound.

equivalent (e-kwiv′ah-lent) [L. *aequivalens,* from *aequus* equal + *valere* to be worth]. 1. Having the same value; neutralizing or counterbalancing each other. 2. Chemical equivalent. 3. In medicine, a symptom that replaces one that is usual in a given disease. **balanotherapeutic e.,** the amount of the chemical constituents of a mineral water which must be taken by an adult in twenty-four hours in order to get the desired therapeutic effect (Kisch). **chemical e.,** the weight of a substance which will combine with or displace 8 parts by weight of oxygen. **combustion e.,** the heat value of a gram of fat or carbohydrate burnt outside the body. It measures the amount of potential energy of the substance available, in the form of food, for the production of heat or the supply of energy. **endosmotic e.,** the number which represents the quantity of water that will pass through a diaphragm by endosmosis in the same time that a unit of any other given substance will pass in the other direction by exosmosis. **epileptic e.,** a disturbance, mental or bodily, that may take the place of an epileptic attack. **glucose e.,** the amount of glucose that can be oxidized with the aid of 1 unit of insulin. **gold e.,** the amount of protective colloid, expressed in milligrams, which is just enough to prevent the precipitation of 10 cc. of a 0.0055 per cent gold solution by 1 cc. of a 10 per cent sodium chloride solution. **gram e.,** the atomic weight of an element divided by its valency. **isodynamic e.,** the ratio, from a food-energy standpoint, between carbohydrate and fat. It is 9.3 to 4.1 or 2.3 to 1; that is, one part of fat is equivalent to 2.3 parts of sugar or starch. **Joule's e.,** the mechanical equivalent of heat or the amount of work expended in raising a pound of water through 1°F.; 772 foot-pounds. **psychic e.,** psychic epilepsy. **starch e.,** a number (nearly 2.4) expressing the amount of oxygen which a given weight of fat will require for its complete combustion as compared with the amount required by the same weight of starch. **toxic e.,** the amount of poison able to kill one kilogram of animal. **water e.,** the product of the weight of an animal by its specific heat, it being also the number which represents the specific heat of an equal weight of water.

E.R. Abbreviation for *external resistance.*

Er. Chemical symbol for *erbium.*

erasion (e-ra′zhun) [L. *erasio*]. Removal by scraping away. **e. of a joint,** arthrectomy.

Erasistratus (er″ah-sis′trah-tus) (c. 300 B.C.). A celebrated Greek anatomist and physician who practiced chiefly in Alexandria. He dissected the human body, and observed the association between ascites and hepatic cirrhosis. He also made many physiological observations, and has been called "The Father of Physiology."

Eratyrus (er″ah-ti′rus). A genus of reduviid bugs which transmit Chagas' disease.

Erb's atrophy, dystrophy, palsy, paralysis, point, sclerosis, etc. (erbz) [Wilhelm Heinrich *Erb*, German internist, 1840–1921]. See under the nouns.

Erben's phenomenon (er′benz) [Siegmund *Erben*, neurologist in Vienna, born 1863]. See under *phenomenon.*

erbium (er′be-um). A rare metallic element: symbol, Er; atomic number, 68; atomic weight, 167.26.

Erdmann's reagent (erd′manz) [H. *Erdmann*, German chemist, 1862–1910]. See under *reagent.*

erectile (e-rek′til). Capable of erection.

erection (e-rek′shun) [L. *erectio*]. The condition of being made rigid and elevated.

erector (e-rek′tor) [L.]. That which or one who erects, such as a muscle which raises or holds up a part.

eredosome (e-red′o-sōm). The amorphous hemoglobin which fills the meshes of the stroma or discoplasm of erythrocytes.

eremacausis (er″ĕ-mah-kaw′sis) [Gr. *ērema* gently + *kausis* burning]. The slow oxidation, combustion, or decay of organic matter.

eremophobia (er″ĕ-mo-fo′be-ah) [Gr. *erēmos* solitary + *phobia*]. Morbid fear of being alone.

erepsin (e-rep′sin) [Gr. *ereptesthai* to feed on]. A group of enzymes in the small intestines which catalyze the hydrolysis of partially digested proteins to produce amino acids. See *peptidase.*

ereptase (e-rep′tās). Erepsin.

ereptic (e-rep′tik). Pertaining to or containing erepsin.

erethin (er′e-thin) [Gr. *erethizein* to irritate]. The poisonous principle of tuberculin.

erethism (er′e-thizm) [Gr. *erethisma* stimulation]. Excessive irritability or sensibility to stimulation.

erethismic (er″ĕ-thiz′mik). Erethistic.

erethisophrenia (er″ĕ-thiz″o-fre′ne-ah) [Gr. *erethizein* to irritate + *phrēn* mind]. Exaggerated mental excitability.

erethistic (er″ĕ-this′tik) [Gr. *erethistikos*]. Pertaining to, characterized by, or producing erethism.

erethitic (er″ĕ-thit′ik). Hunt's term for the excitatory temperament, marked by great activity of mind and body, i.e., responsive, impulsive, emotional, quick tempered, and restless.

ereuth-. For words beginning thus, see those beginning *eryth-.*

ERG. Abbreviation for *electroretinogram.*

erg (erg) [Gr. *ergon* work]. A unit of work or energy, being the work performed when a force of 1 dyne moves its point of operation through a distance of 1 centimeter; equivalent to 2.4×10^{-8} gram calories, or to 0.624×10^{12} electron volts.

ergasia (er-ga′se-ah) [Gr. "work"]. 1. A hypothetical substance which stimulates the activity of body cells. 2. Meyer's term for any mentally integrated function, activity, reaction or attitude of the individual; psychobiological functioning.

ergasiatrics, ergasiatry (er-ga″ze-at′riks, er″-gah-si′ah-tre). Meyer's term for psychiatry.

ergasidermatosis (er-ga″se-der″mah-to′sis) [*ergasia* + *dermatosis*]. Ergodermatosis.

ergasiology (er-ga″se-ol′o-je) [*ergasia* + *-logy*]. Objective psychobiology.

ergasiomania (er-ga″se-o-ma′ne-ah) [*ergasia* + Gr. *mania* madness]. 1. An insane desire to be continually at work. 2. Undue eagerness to perform surgical operations.

ergasiophobia (er-ga″se-o-fo′be-ah) [*ergasia* + *phobia*]. 1. Morbid aversion to work. 2. Undue fear of performing surgical operations.

ergasthenia (er″gas-the′ne-ah) [Gr. *ergon* work + *astheneia* weakness]. A condition of debility from overwork.

ergastic (er-gas′tik) [Gr. *ergastikos*]. 1. Having potential energy; a term applied to passive material formed or stored by a cell, such as starch, fat, and cellulose. 2. Pertaining to ergasia.

ergastoplasm (er-gas′to-plazm) [*ergasia* + *plasm*]. Kinoplasm.

ergo- (er′go) [Gr. *ergon* work]. A combining form denoting relationship to work.

ergobasine (er″go-ba′sin). Ergonovine.

ergocalciferol (er-go-kal-sif′er-ol). Calciferol.

ergodermatosis (er″go-der″mah-to′sis) [*ergo-* + *dermatosis*]. An industrial or occupational dermatosis.

ergodynamograph (er″go-di-nam′o-graf) [*ergo-* + Gr. *dynamis* force + *graphein* to record]. An apparatus for recording the force exhibited and the work done in muscular contraction.

ergo-esthesiograph (er″go-es-the′se-o-graf) [*ergo-* + Gr. *aisthēsis* sensation + *graphein* to record]. An apparatus for recording graphically the muscular aptitude of candidates for aviation.

ergogenic (er″go-jen′ik) [*ergo-* + Gr. *gennan* to produce]. Tending to increase work output.

ergogram (er′go-gram) [*ergo-* + Gr. *gramma* a mark]. A tracing made by an ergograph.

ergograph (er′go-graf) [*ergo-* + Gr. *graphein* to record]. An instrument for recording work done in muscular exertion. **Mosso's e.** (1890), an apparatus for recording the force and frequency of flexion of the fingers.

ergographic (er″go-graf′ik). Pertaining to the ergograph.

ergomania (er″go-ma′ne-ah). Ergasiomania.

ergomaniac (er″go-ma′ne-ak) [*ergo-* + Gr. *mania* madness]. A person morbidly desirous of being continually at work.

ergometer (er-gom′e-ter) [*ergo-* + Gr. *metron* measure]. A dynamometer.

ergometrine (er″go-met′rin). Ergonovine.

ergonomics (er″go-nom′iks) [*ergo-* + Gr. *nomos* law]. The science relating to man and his work, embodying the anatomic, physiologic, psychologic, and mechanical principles affecting the efficient use of human energy.

ergonovine (er″go-no′vin). An ergot alkaloid, N-[α-(hydroxymethyl)ethyl]-D-lysergamide: used as an oxytocic, and to relieve migraine headache.

ergophobia (er-go-fo′be-ah). Ergasiophobia.

ergophore (er″go-fōr) [*ergo-* + Gr. *phoros* bearing]. The group of atoms in a molecule that brings about the specific activity of the substance, as of a toxin, agglutinin, or the like, after the molecule has been properly anchored by the haptophore.

ergoplasm (er′go-plazm). Kinoplasm.

ergostat (er′go-stat). A machine to be worked for muscular exercise, for the cure of obesity, etc.

ergosterol (er-gos′te-rol). A sterol, $C_{28}H_{43}.OH$, occurring in animal and plant tissues which, on irradiation with ultraviolet rays, becomes a potent antirachitic substance, vitamin D_2. The substance was originally isolated by Tanret from ergot and named accordingly. **activated e., irradiated e.,** viosterol.

ergostetrine (er″go-stet′rin). Ergonovine.

ergot (er′got) [Fr.; L. *ergota*]. 1. The dried sclerotium of *Claviceps purpurea:* used in fluidextract as an oxytocic. 2. Calcar avis. 3. A small mass of horn in the tuft of hair at the flexion surface of the fetlock in horses.

ergotamine (er-got′ah-min). An alkaloid derived from ergot, consisting of lysergic acid, ammonia, proline, phenylalanine, and pyruvic acid combined in amide linkages: used as an oxytocic, and in treatment of migraine.

ergotherapy (er″go-ther′ah-pe) [*ergo-* + Gr. *therapeia* treatment]. Treatment of disease by physical effort.

ergothioneine (er″go-thi″o-ne′in). The trimethylbetaine of thiohistidine, $C_3HN_2(SH).CH_2.CH.$-$CO.ON(CH_3)_3$, found in ergot and in the blood and in abnormal amounts in the urine of cancer patients.

ergotism (er′got-izm). Chronic poisoning from excessive or misdirected use of ergot as a medicine, or from eating ergotized grain. It is marked by cerebrospinal symptoms, spasms, and cramps, or by a kind of dry gangrene.

ergotized (er′got-īzd). Diseased or otherwise affected by ergot.

ergotocin (er″go-to′sin). Ergonovine.

ergotrate (er′go-trāt). Trade mark for preparations of ergonovine.

ergotropic (er″go-trop′ik). Pertaining to ergotropy.

ergotropy (er-got′ro-pe) [Gr. *ergon* work + *tropos* a turning]. The reaction of the body cells to the application of nonspecific agents, such as the injection of proteins, counterirritation, baths, etc. As applied in clinical therapeutics the object is to stimulate the general defenses of the body rather than to develop specific antibodies.

ergusia (er-ju′se-ah). A hypothetical lipoid substance which liberated from a cell reduces surface tension and enables the cell to migrate.

Erichsen's disease, ligature, sign (or **test**) (er′ik-senz) [John *Erichsen*, English surgeon, 1818–1896]. See under the nouns.

Eriodictyon (er″e-o-dik′te-on) [Gr. *erion* wool + *diktyon* net]. A genus of hydrophyllaceous plants. *E. califor′nicum* (*E. glutino′sum*), yerba santa, or mountain balm, was once used in bronchitis.

eriodictyon (er″e-o-dik′te-on). The dried leaf of *Eriodictyon californicum.* Its fluidextract and aromatic syrup are used as vehicles for dispensing drugs.

eriometer (er″e-om′e-ter) [Gr. *erion* wool + *metron* measure]. An instrument for measuring the diameter of minute particles of fibers from the size of the colored rings produced by the diffraction of light: used for measuring the diameter of erythrocytes.

eriometry (er″e-om′e-tre). The use of the eriometer.

erisiphake (er-is′ĭ-fāk). Erysiphake.

Eristalis (er-is′tah-lis). A genus of flies. **E. tenax,** the "drone fly," the "rat-tailed" larvae of which may cause severe intestinal myiasis.

Erlangen method, treatment (ār′lang-en). See under *treatment.*

Erlanger, E. Joseph. American physiologist, born 1874, noted for his work on the nervous system; co-winner, with Herbert Spencer Gasser, of the Nobel prize for medicine in 1944.

Erlenmeyer flask (ār′len-mi″er) [Emil *Erlenmeyer*, German chemist, 1825–1909]. See under *flask.*

Erlenmeyer's mixture (ār′len-mi″erz) [F. A. *Erlenmeyer*, German physician, 1849–1926]. See under *mixture.*

erntefieber (ern′te-fe″ber) [Ger. "harvest-fever"]. Schlammfieber.

erode (e-rōd′). To wear away.

erogenous (e-roj′e-nus). Erotogenic.

erose (e-rōs′) [L. *erodere* to gnaw off]. Having an irregularly toothed edge.

erosio (e-ro′se-o) [L.]. Erosion. **e. interdigita′lis blastomycet′ica** or **saccharomycet′ica,** an eroded lesion occurring in the interdigital webs of the fingers and toes, and caused probably by *Candida* (*Monilia*) *albicans.*

erosion (e-ro′zhun) [L. *erosio*, from *erodere* to eat out]. An eating or gnawing away; a kind of ulceration. In dentistry, the wasting away or loss of substance of a tooth by a chemical process that does not involve known bacterial action. **cervical e.,** a condition caused by chemical irritation and characterized by ulceration of the everted columnar epithelium of the endocervix and the squamous epithelium of the vaginal portion of the cervix. **Dieulafoy's e.,** ulcerative gastritis complicating pneumonia.

erosive (e-ro′siv). 1. Causing, characterized by, or producing erosion. 2. An agent that produces erosion.

erotic (e-rot′ik) [Gr. *erōtikos*]. Pertaining to love or to lust.

eroticism, erotism (e-rot′ĭ-sizm, er′o-tizm). A morbid sexual instinct or desire. **anal e.,** sensual or libidinous satisfaction associated with defecation. **muscle e.,** erotism stimulated by muscular exercise. **oral e.,** sensual or libidinous satisfaction associated with eating, or related oral activity.

eroticomania (e-rot″ĭ-ko-ma′ne-ah). Erotomania.

erotize (er′o-tīz). To endow with erotic or libidinous instinct or energy.

eroto- (e-ro′to) [Gr. *erōs* love]. A combining form denoting relationship to love or sexual desire.

erotogenesis (e-ro″to-jen′e-sis). The formation or production of erotic feeling.

erotogenic (e-ro″to-jen′ik) [*eroto-* + Gr. *gennan* to produce]. Producing erotic feelings.

erotographomania (e-ro″to-graf″o-ma′ne-ah) [*eroto-* + Gr. *graphein* to write + *mania* madness]. Morbid interest in writing love letters.

erotology (er″o-tol′o-je) [*eroto-* + *-logy*]. The study of love.

erotomania (e-rot″to-ma′ne-ah) [*eroto-* + Gr. *mania* madness]. Morbid exaggeration of sexual behavior or reaction.

erotomaniac (e-ro″to-ma′ne-ak). A person affected with erotomania.

erotopath (e-ro′to-path). A person with disordered sexual impulse.

erotopathy (er″o-top′ah-the) [*eroto-* + Gr. *pathos* disease]. Disorder of the sexual impulse.

erotophobia (e-ro″to-fo′be-ah) [*eroto-* + *phobia*]. Morbid dislike for sexual love.

erotopsychic (e-ro″to-si′kik) [*eroto-* + Gr. *psyche* soul]. Marked by perversion of the sexual impulse.

erotosexual (e-ro″to-seks′u-al). Pertaining to the sexual love life.

ERPF. Abbreviation for *effective renal plasma flow*.

erratic (ĕ-rat′ik) [L. *errare* to wander]. 1. Roving or wandering. 2. Eccentric; deviating from an accepted course of thought or conduct.

errhine (er′īn) [Gr. *en* in + *rhis* nose]. 1. Promoting a nasal discharge. 2. A medicine which promotes nasal discharge or secretion.

ertron (er′tron). Trade mark for preparations of vitamin D_2. See *calciferol*.

erubescence (er″u-bes′ens) [L. *erubescere* to grow red]. A flushing of the skin.

eructatio (e″ruk-ta′she-o) [L., from *eructare* to belch]. Eructation. **e. nervo′sa,** nervous eructation.

eructation (e-ruk-ta′shun) [L. *eructatio*]. The act of belching, or of casting up wind from the stomach. **nervous e.,** a gastric neurosis marked by air swallowing followed by belching.

eruption (e-rup′shun) [L. *eruptio* a breaking out]. 1. The act of breaking out, appearing, or becoming visible. 2. A visible lesion of the skin due to disease, and marked by redness, prominence, or both. **bullous e.,** an eruption of large blebs or blisters. **creeping e.,** a dermatitis caused by the burrowing of nematodes or larvae in the deeper layers of the skin. See *larva migrans*. **crustaceous e.,** an eruption consisting of crusts. **drug e.,** dermatitis medicamentosa. **erythematous e.,** an eruption consisting of patches of redness. **iodine e.,** an eruption on the skin resulting from the internal use of iodine. **Kaposi's varicelliform e.,** a vesiculopustular eruption, of viral origin, superimposed upon a pre-existing eczema; it may be caused by the virus of herpes simplex (eczema herpeticum), vaccinia (eczema vaccinatum), or by another virus. **macular e.,** an eruption in the form of spots, and due to hemorrhage, congestion, or pigmentation. **medicinal e.,** an eruption due to the ingestion of medicines; a drug eruption. **papular e.,** an eruption of small solid elevations. **petechial e.,** an eruption in spots, due to hemorrhage. **pustular e.,** an eruption of pustules. **sandworm e.,** a form of creeping eruption in South America apparently caused by a small mite. **scaly e., squamous e.,** an eruption consisting of scales. **serum e.,** an eruption or exanthem following the injection of a serum. **tubercular e.,** an eruption of large elevations.

eruptive (e-rup′tiv). Pertaining to, or characterized by, eruption.

ERV. Abbreviation for *expiratory reserve volume*.

Erwinia (er-win′e-ah) [*Erwin* F. Smith, American bacteriologist, 1854–1927]. A genus of microorganisms of the tribe Erwinieae, family Enterobacteriaceae, order Eubacteriales. The 16 described species are pathogenic for plants, causing dry necroses, galls, or wilts, or soft rots.

Erwinieae (er″wĭ-ni′e-e). A taxonomic tribe of the family Enterobacteriaceae, order Eubacteriales, made up of motile rods normally not requiring organic nitrogen compounds for growth and producing acid, with or without visible gas, from a variety of sugars. It includes a single genus, *Erwinia*.

Ery. Abbreviation for *Erysipelothrix*.

erysipelas (er″ĭ-sip′ĕ-las) [Gr. *erythros* red + *pella* skin]. A contagious, infectious disease of skin and subcutaneous tissue, marked by redness and swelling of affected areas, and with constitutional symptoms. Sometimes accompanied by vesicular and bullous lesions. **ambulant e.** is marked by the eruption recurring at various points. **coast e.** (erisipela de la costa), a disease of Guatemala caused by the filarial worm *Onchocerca caecutiens*, marked by the formation of subcutaneous nodules on the head. **facial e.,** erysipelas that affects the face, which is marked by an area of swelling, redness, and itching. **gangrenous e.,** a variety which is characterized by sloughing. It is always fatal. **e. gra′ve inter′num,** erysipelas in the vagina, uterus, and peritoneum: a form of puerperal fever. **idiopathic e.,** that which does not follow a trauma. It occurs usually on the face or scalp, and follows the usual mild course, invariably ending in recovery unless complicated with some other affection. **malignant e.,** one of the forms of puerperal fever. **migrant e.,** a form in which the morbid process disappears successively from various parts of the body, to reappear elsewhere. Called also *wandering e.* **e. per′stans,** an erysipelas-like eruption sometimes seen in conjunction with lupus erythematosus. **phlegmonous e.,** that which is marked by subcutaneous suppuration. **e. pustulo′sum,** vesicular erysipelas in which the vesicles become filled with pus. **recurrent e.,** a mild form, chiefly facial, and prone to recur: considered by some a pseudo-erysipelas. **relapsing e.,** a chronic type of erysipelatous disease, often associated with deep-seated suppuration. **surgical e.,** erysipelas that occurs following a surgical operation. **swine e.,** a contagious disease of young swine, caused by *Erysipelothrix insidiosa* and attended with fever and the formation of red blotches on the neck and body. Called also *rouget du porc* and *red fever of swine*. **traumatic e.,** erysipelas that starts in a wound. **e. verruco′sum,** erysipelas having a warty appearance. **e. vesiculo′sum, vesicular e.,** a variety marked by vesicles or bullae. **wandering e.** migrant e. **white e.,** edema of an erysipelatous nature, but without apparent dilatation of the blood vessels. **zoonotic e.,** erysipeloid.

erysipelatous (er″ĭ-sĭ-pel′ah-tus). Pertaining to or of the nature of erysipelas.

erysipeloid (er″ĭ-sip′ĕ-loid) [*erysipelas* + Gr. *eidos* form]. An infective dermatitis due to infection with *Erysipelothrix insidiosa*. It usually begins in a wound and remains localized, although it may become generalized and septicemic.

Erysipelothrix (er″ĭ-sip′ĕ-lo-thriks) [*erysipelas* + Gr. *thrix* hair]. A genus of microorganisms of the family Corynebacteriaceae, order Eubacteriales, containing a single species. **E. insidio′sa,** a species of microorganisms occurring as gram-positive rods and filaments, the causative agent of swine erysipelas, and also infecting sheep, turkeys, and rats. An erythematous-edematous lesion, commonly on the hand, resulting from contact with infected meat, hides, or bones, represents the usual type of infection in man. **E. rhusiopath′iae,** *E. insidiosa*.

erysipelotoxin (er″ĭ-sip″ĕ-lo-tok′sin). The toxin of erysipelas.

erysiphake (er-is′ĭ-fāk) [Gr. *erysis* a drawing + *phakos* lentil]. Barraquer's instrument for removing the lens in cataract by suction. Cf. *phacoerysis*.

erythema (er″ĭ-the′mah) [Gr. *erythēma* flush upon the skin]. A name applied to redness of the skin produced by congestion of the capillaries, which may result from a variety of causes, the etiology or a special type of lesion often being indicated by a modifying term. **e. ab ig′ne,** redness of the skin caused by exposure to radiant heat. **acrodynic e.,** a condition characterized by reddened painful areas on the palms and soles. **a. annula′re,** a type of erythema multiforme in which the areas of redness are ring-shaped. **e. annula′re centrif′ugum,** a chronic variant of erythema multiforme, with single or multiple edematous and erythematous papules, occurring usually on the thighs and lower legs, the lesions enlarging peripherally and clearing in the center, to produce annular lesions, which may coalesce;

the condition may persist for years, with incomplete remissions and exacerbations. **e. annula're rheumat'icum,** an exanthem associated with rheumatic endocarditis, characterized by red or bluish-red semicircles or rings over the abdomen, the sides of the thorax, and the back. **e. arthrit'icum epidem'icum,** Haverhill fever. **e. brucel'lum,** redness of the skin occurring in brucellosis. **e. bullo'sum,** a type of erythema multiforme characterized by eruption of vesicles or bullae. **e. calor'icum,** a form of erythema resulting from exposure to heat or cold, or both; also to exposure to the chemical rays of light. **e. circina'tum,** a type of erythema multiforme marked by circular grouping of the lesions. **diaper e.,** a nonspecific erythema occurring over the gluteal region in infants. **e. eleva'tum diu'tinum,** erythema characterized by presence of firm, persistent, nodular elevations. **endemic e.,** pellagra. **epidemic e.,** erythredema polyneuropathy. **epidemic arthritic e.,** Haverhill fever. **e. exudati'vum,** a type of erythema multiforme marked by exudative lesions. **e. figura'tum,** a type of erythema multiforme in which the lesions create a bizarre pattern. **e. fu'gax,** redness of the skin that comes and goes quickly. **gluteal e.,** diaper e. **e. gyra'tum,** a type of erythema multiforme in which the lesions have a gyrate appearance. **e. indura'tum,** tuberculosis cutis indurativa. **e. infectio'sum,** a mildly contagious disease, sometimes occurring in epidemics, and marked by a rose-colored maculopapular rash. It occurs chiefly in children between the ages of four and twelve. Called also *fifth disease.* **inflammatory e.,** any form of erythema in which dermatitis is a pronounced feature. **e. intertri'go,** intertrigo. **e. i'ris,** a type of erythema multiforme in which the lesions form concentric rings, producing a target-like appearance. **Jacquet's e.,** diaper e. **e. margina'tum,** a type of erythema multiforme in which the reddened areas are disk-shaped, with elevated edges. **e. mi'grans,** geographic tongue. **Milian's e.,** a scarlatiniform eruption with malaise and fever, occurring seven to nine days after injection of arsphenamine, or as a toxic reaction to other drugs. **e. multifor'me,** a symptom complex characterized by vivid erythematous, urticarial, bullous, and/or purpuric lesions which appear suddenly in a symmetrical distribution; individual attacks are usually self-limited, but recurrences are the rule. **napkin e.,** diaper e. **e. neonato'rum,** a usually temporary diffuse redness of the skin of a newborn infant. **e. neonato'rum tox'icum,** erythema of a toxic origin in a newborn infant. **ninth-day e.,** Milian's e. **e. nodo'sum,** an acute inflammatory skin disease marked by tender red nodules, due to exudation of blood and serum, and accompanied by intense itching and burning. The lesions appear in successive patches during a period of several weeks. **e. nodo'sum syphilit'icum,** a condition resembling erythema nodosum, being a malignant form of syphilis; called also *Mauriac's disease.* **palmar e.,** redness of the skin of the palms, occurring in certain disease states, during pregnancy, or as a hereditary condition. **e. paratrim'ma,** a skin inflammation, the first stage of an incipient decubitus ulcer. **e. per'nio,** chilblain. **e. per'stans,** a persistent reddening of the skin. **e. pudicit'iae,** morbid flushing. **e. puncta'tum,** e. scarlatiniforme. **e. scarlatinifor'me, e. scarlatinoi'des,** a febrile affection attended with a rash resembling that of scarlatina; it may recur frequently, and sometimes leads to exfoliation. **e. sim'plex,** a condition marked only by reddening of the skin, with little or no pruritus. **e. sola're,** erythema due to exposure to rays of the sun. **e. streptog'enes,** a mild condition characterized by nondescript patches of scaling and depigmentation on the face, occurring principally in children. **symptomatic e.,** erythema occurring secondarily to some systemic condition. **toxic e., e. tox'icum,** a generalized, diffuse erythematous eruption or a widespread erythematomacular eruption occurring as a result of administration of a drug, or caused by bacterial toxins or other toxic substances. **e. traumat'icum,** redness of the skin caused by friction or pressure on the area. **e. venena'tum,** toxic e.

erythematous (er″ĭ-them'ah-tus). Of the nature of erythema.

erythemogenic (er″ĭ-the″mo-jen'ik). Causing erythema.

erythermalgia (er″ĭ-ther-mal'je-ah). Erythromelalgia.

erythra (er'ith-rah). An eruption of the skin.

Erythraea (er″ĭ-thre'ah) [Gr. *erythraios* red]. A genus of red-flowered gentianaceous plants. *E. centau'rium* is the lesser (European) centaury. This and various other species are tonic and stomachic. See *centaury.*

erythralgia (er″ĭ-thral'je-ah) [*erythro-* + *-algia*]. A condition marked by pain and redness of the skin.

erythrasma (er″ĭ-thraz'mah). A chronic infection of the skin, marked by the development of red or brownish patches on the inner side of the thigh, on the scrotum, and in the axilla. **Baerensprung's e.,** eczema marginatum affecting the thighs.

erythredema polyneuropathy (er-ith″re-de'mah pol″e-nu-rop'ah-the) [*erythro-* + Gr. *oidēma* swelling]. A condition occurring in infants marked by swollen, bluish-red hands and feet and disordered digestion, followed by multiple arthritis and muscular weakness (W. Swift). Called also *pink disease, Swift's disease, Feer's disease, epidemic erythema, acrodynia, pedionalgia epidemica, trophodermatoneurosis,* and *dermatopolyneuritis.*

erythremia (er″ĭ-thre'me-ah) [*erythro-* + Gr. *haima* blood]. Polycythemia vera.

erythremoid (er″ĭ-thre'moid). Resembling erythremia.

erythremomelalgia (er-ith″re-mo-mel-al'je-ah) [Gr. *erythrēma* redness + *melos* limb + *-algia*]. Erythromelalgia.

erythrin (er'ith-rin). 1. A chromogen from *Roccella tinctoria* and other lichens. 2. An antibacterial peptide derived from erythrocytes.

Erythrina (er″ĭ-thri'nah). A genus of tropical shrubs and trees of the legume family, some species of which contain active alkaloids.

erythrism (e-rith'rizm). Redness of the hair and beard with a ruddy complexion.

erythristic (er″ĭ-thris'tik). Characterized by erythrism.

erythrityl (e-rith'rĭ-til). The univalent radical C_4H_9 from erythritol. **e. tetranitrate,** a synthetic compound, $C_4H_6(NO_3)_4$, with a vasodilator action resembling that of nitroglycerin.

erythro- (e-rith'ro) [Gr. *erythros* red]. A combining form meaning red, or denoting a relationship to red.

Erythrobacillus (e-rith″ro-bah-sil'us). A genus of small aerobic nonpathogenic bacterial organisms which produce red or pink pigments. It is now replaced by the genus *Serratia.*

erythroblast (e-rith'ro-blast) [*erythro-* + Gr. *blastos* germ]. A term used by Ehrlich to indicate any type of nucleated erythrocyte, but now more generally, and somewhat inaccurately, used to designate an immature cell from which a red corpuscle develops. The precise position assigned to it in the red cell lineage varies with the specific theory of blood maturation being propounded. **basophilic e.,** a cell with a slightly clumped nuclear chromatin and basophilic cytoplasm without hemoglobin, which, in the developmental lineage, follows the pronormoblast. Called also *early erythroblast, basophilic* or *early normoblast,* and *prorubricyte.* **early e.,** basophilic e. **late e.,** polychromatophilic e. **polychromatophilic e.,** a cell of the stage following the basophilic erythroblast, in which there is increased chromatin clumping and the earliest appearance of pink cytoplasmic hemoglobin. Called also *late erythroblast, polychromatophilic* or *intermediate normoblast,* and *rubricyte.*

erythroblastemia (e-rith″ro-blas-te′me-ah). The presence in the peripheral blood of abnormally large numbers of nucleated red cells.

erythroblastic (e-rith″ro-blas′tik). Of, or relating to, erythroblasts.

erythroblastoma (e-rith″ro-blas-to′mah). A tumor-like mass composed of nucleated red blood corpuscles.

erythroblastomatosis (e-rith″ro-blas″to-mah-to′sis). A condition marked by the formation of erythroblastomas.

erythroblastopenia (e-rith″ro-blas″to-pe′ne-ah). Abnormal deficiency of the erythroblasts. See *aplastic crisis,* under *crisis.*

erythroblastosis (e-rith″ro-blas-to′sis). 1. The presence of erythroblasts in the circulating blood; erythroblastemia. 2. A disease of fowl marked by an increase in the number of immature red blood cells in the circulating blood. Called also *erythroleukosis.* **e. feta′lis, e. neonato′rum,** a hemolytic anemia of the fetus or newborn infant, caused by the transplacental transmission of maternally formed antibody, usually secondary to an incompatibility between the blood group of the mother and that of her offspring, characterized by increased numbers of nucleated red cells in the peripheral blood, hyperbilirubinemia, and extramedullary hematopoiesis.

erythroblastotic (e-rith″ro-blas-tot′ik). Pertaining to or characterized by erythroblastosis.

erythrocatalysis (e-rith″ro-kah-tal′ĭ-sis). Erythrokatalysis.

erythrochloropia (e-rith″ro-klo-ro′pe-ah) [*erythro-* + Gr. *chlōros* green + *ōps* eye]. Ability to distinguish red and green, but not blue or yellow.

erythrochloropsia (e-rith″ro-klo-rop′se-ah). Erythrochloropia.

erythrochromia (e-rith″ro-kro′me-ah) [*erythro-* + Gr. *chrōma* color]. Hemorrhagic pigmentation of the spinal fluid, giving it a red color.

erythroclasis (er″e-throk′lah-sis) [*erythro-* + Gr. *klasis* a breaking]. Fragmentation or splitting up of red blood cells.

erythroclastic (e-rith″ro-klas′tik). Pertaining to, characterized by, or producing erythroclasis.

erythroconte (e-rith′ro-kōnt) [*erythro-* + Gr. *kontos* a pole]. A small rodlike body found in erythrocytes in pernicious anemia.

erythrocruorin (e-rith″ro-kroo′o-rin). A respiratory protein from the blood of the marine worm, *Spirographis spallanzanii* and certain other worms.

erythrocuprein (e-rith″ro-koo′prin). A copper-protein compound, contained in the erythrocytes, the function of which is unknown.

erythrocyanogenia (e-rith″ro-si″ah-no-je′ne-ah). Erythrocyanosis.

erythrocyanosis (e-rith″ro-si″ah-no′sis) [*erythro-* + Gr. *kyanōsis* dark blue color]. A condition marked by areas of bluish-red discoloration on the skin with irregular swellings, burning, and itching. **e. cru′rum puella′ris, e. frig′ida cru′rum puella′rum, e. supramalleola′ris,** a bluish-red discoloration of the legs of young women due to exposure to cold.

erythrocyte (e-rith′ro-sīt [*erythro-* + Gr. *kytos* hollow vessel]. One of the elements found in peripheral blood. Normally, in the human, the mature form is a non-nucleated, yellowish, circular, biconcave disk, adapted, by virtue of its configuration and its hemoglobin content, to transport oxygen. **achromic e.,** a colorless erythrocyte. See *achromocyte.* **basophilic e.,** one that takes the basic stain. See *basophilia* (def. 1). **burr e.,** a peculiar, often triangular or crescentic poikilocyte with peripheral spiny projections, sometimes observed in patients with azotemia, gastric carcinoma, and bleeding peptic ulcer. **crenated e.,** an erythrocyte which shows a scalloped border. **immature e.,** any erythrocyte prior to achievement of its complete development. **"Mexican hat" e.,** leptocyte. **orthochromatic e.,** one that takes only the acid stain. **polychromatic e., polychromatophilic e.,** an erythrocyte that, on staining, shows various shades of blue, combined with tinges of pink. **target e.,** leptocyte.

erythrocythemia (e-rith″ro-si-the′me-ah). An increase in the number of erythrocytes in the blood. See *erythrocytosis* and *polycythemia vera.*

erythrocytic (e-rith″ro-sit′ik). Pertaining to erythrocytes.

erythrocytin (e-rith″ro-si′tin). A substance, most probably phospholipid in nature, present in red cell hemolysates, which may function in the first stage of coagulation to generate intrinsic thromboplastin.

erythrocytoblast (e-rith″ro-si′to-blast). Erythroblast.

erythrocytolysin (e-rith″ro-si-tol′ĭ-sin). A substance which causes dissolution of erythrocytes and escape of hemoglobin.

erythrocytolysis (e-rith″ro-si-tol′ĭ-sis) [*erythrocyte* + Gr. *lysis* dissolution]. Dissolution of erythrocytes and escape of the hemoglobin.

erythrocytometer (e-rith″ro-si-tom′e-ter) [*erythrocyte* + Gr. *metron* measure]. A device for measuring or counting erythrocytes.

erythrocytometry (e-rith″ro-si-tom′e-tre). The measurement or counting of erythrocytes.

erythrocyto-opsonin (e-rith″ro-si″to-op-so′nin) [*erythrocyte* + *opsonin*]. An opsonin that has opsonic action on red blood corpuscles. Called also *hemopsonin.*

erythrocytopenia (e-rith″ro-si″to-pe′ne-ah). Erythropenia.

erythrocytophagous (e-rith″ro-si-tof′ah-gus). Pertaining to or characterized by erythrocytophagy.

erythrocytophagy (e-rith″ro-si-tof′ah-je) [*erythrocyte* + Gr. *phagein* to devour]. The engulfment or consumption of erythrocytes by other cells, such as the histiocytes of the reticuloendothelial system.

erythrocytopoiesis (e-rith″ro-si″to-poi-e′sis). Erythropoiesis.

erythrocytorrhexis (e-rith″ro-si″to-rek′sis) [*erythrocyte* + Gr. *rhēxis* rending]. A morphological change in erythrocytes, consisting in the escape from the cells of round, shining granules and splitting off of particles.

erythrocytoschisis (e-rith″ro-si-tos′kĭ-sis) [*erythrocyte* + Gr. *schisis* division]. A morphological change in erythrocytes, consisting in the degeneration of the cells into disklike bodies similar to the blood platelets.

erythrocytosis (e-rith″ro-si-to′sis). Increase in the total red cell mass as the result of a known stimulus (secondary polycythemia), in contrast to erythremia (primary polycythemia). **leukemic e., e. megalosplen′ica,** polycythemia vera. **stress e.,** a form of relative polycythemia observed in active, anxiety-prone individuals, in which the increase in the red cell mass, as demonstrated by the elevated peripheral blood hematocrit, is more apparent than real, being the result of a diminished plasma volume.

erythrocytotropic (e-rith″ro-si″to-trop′ik). Having a selective affinity for or exerting a special action on erythrocytes.

erythrocyturia (e-rith″ro-si-tu′re-ah). Hematuria.

erythrodegenerative (e-rith″ro-de-jen′er-a″-tiv). Characterized by degeneration of erythrocytes.

erythroderma (e-rith″ro-der′mah) [*erythro-* + Gr. *derma* skin]. Abnormal redness of the skin, usually applied to a condition of abnormal redness over widespread areas of the body. **atopic e.,**

a chronic diffuse dermatitis occurring in allergic infants. **congenital ichthyosiform e.,** a generalized hereditable dermatitis with marked scaling. **e. desquamati'vum,** a condition in breast-fed infants with symptoms resembling a generalized seborrhea. **e. ichthyosifor'me congen'itum,** congenital ichthyosiform e. **lymphomatous e.,** widespread redness of the skin occurring as a manifestation of lymphoma. **e. psoriat'icum,** a generalized psoriasis vulgaris, showing the clinical characteristics of exfoliative dermatitis. **Sézary e.** See under *syndrome*. **e. squamo'sum,** widespread reddening of the skin, with the appearance of groups of scaly papules.

erythrodermatitis (e-rith″ro-der″mah-ti'tis) [*erythro-* + *dermatitis*]. Inflammation of the skin, with redness.

erythrodermia (e-rith″ro-der'me-ah). Erythroderma.

erythrodextrin (e-rith″ro-deks'trin). A dextrin, *e*-dextrin, which is turned red by iodine and changed by various digestive ferments into maltose.

erythrodiol (er″e-thro'di-ol). A triterpenic monostearate from the fruit of the coca bush.

erythrodontia (e-rith″ro-don'she-ah) [*erythro-* + Gr. *odous* tooth]. Reddish brown pigmentation of the teeth.

erythrogen (e-rith'ro-jen). A fatty, crystalline compound from diseased bile.

erythrogenesis (e-rith″ro-jen'e-sis). The production of erythrocytes. **e. imperfec'ta,** congenital hypoplastic anemia.

erythrogenic (e-rith″ro-jen'ik) [*erythro-* + Gr. *gennan* to produce]. 1. Producing erythrocytes. 2. Producing a sensation of red. 3. Producing or causing a rash.

erythrogone (e-rith'ro-gōn). Erythrogonium.

erythrogonium (e-rith″ro-go'ne-um) [*erythrocyte* + Gr. *gonē* seed]. A very immature erythroblast, regarded by some as the common progenitor of both the pathologic megaloblast and the physiologic normoblast. Called also *erythrogone.*

erythrogranulose (e-rith″ro-gran'u-lōs). An amylodextrin which is colored red by iodine.

erythroid (er″ĭ-throid). Of a red color; reddish.

erythroidine (e-rith'roi-din). An alkaloid, $C_{16}H_{19}NO_3$ from *Erythrina americana:* it has a curare-like action.

erythrokatalysis (e-rith″ro-kah-tal'ĭ-sis) [*erythro-* + Gr. *katalysis* dissolution]. The dissolution of erythrocytes; erythrocytolysis.

erythrokinetics (e-rith″ro-ki-net'iks) [*erythrocyte* + Gr. *kinētikos* of or for putting in motion]. The quantitative, dynamic study of *in vivo* production and destruction of erythrocytes.

erythrol (er'ith-rol). A polyhydric alcohol, $CH_2OH(CHOH)_2CH_2OH$, occurring in algae and mosses. See *erythrityl.* **e. tetranitrate,** erythrityl tetranitrate.

erythrolein (er″ĭ-thro'le-in). A red coloring matter obtained from litmus.

erythroleukemia (e-rith″ro-lu-ke'me-ah). A malignant blood dyscrasia characterized by neoplastic proliferation of both erythroblastic and myeloblastic elements, with atypical erythroblasts and myeloblasts in the peripheral blood; resembling both acute and chronic erythremic myelosis and forming, with the latter entities, a part of the di Guglielmo syndrome.

erythroleukoblastosis (e-rith″ro-lu″ko-blas-to'sis). Icterus gravis neonatorum.

erythroleukosis (e-rith″ro-lu-ko'sis). 1. A condition seen in malaria in which the erythrocytes are changed into brassy bodies. 2. Erythroblastosis, def. 2.

erythro-leuko-thrombocythemia (e-rith″ro-lu″ko-throm″bo-si-the'me-ah). Di Guglielmo's term for hyperplasia of the erythroblastic, leukoblastic, and megakaryocytic tissue with the appearance of immature cells in the blood.

erythrolitmin (e-rith″ro-lit'min). A red crystalline compound, one of the chief ingredients of litmus.

erythrolysin (er″ĭ-throl'ĭ-sin). Erythrocytolysin.

erythrolysis (er″e-throl'ĭ-sis). Erythrocytolysis.

erythromania (e-rith″ro-ma'ne-ah) [*erythro-* + Gr. *mania* madness]. Excessive and uncontrollable blushing.

erythromelalgia (e-rith″ro-mel-al'je-ah) [*erythro-* + Gr. *melos* limb + *-algia*]. A disease affecting chiefly the extremities of the body, the feet more often than the hands, and marked by paroxysmal, bilateral vasodilatation, particularly of the extremities, with burning pain, and increased skin temperature and redness. Also called *erythermalgia* and *acromelalgia.* **e. of the head,** a severe recurring headache caused by vascular dilatation and both induced by and cured by doses of histamine.

erythromelia (e-rith″ro-me'le-ah) [*erythro-* + Gr. *melos* limb]. A disease distinct from erythromelalgia, marked by painless progressive redness of the skin, radiating from the central part to the periphery, and situated on the extensor surfaces of the legs and arms.

erythrometer (er″ĭ-throm'e-ter) [*erythro-* + Gr. *metron* measure]. 1. An instrument or color scale for measuring degrees of redness. 2. Erythrocytometer.

erythrometry (er″ĭ-throm'e-tre). 1. The measurement of the degree of redness. 2. Erythrocytometry.

erythromycin (e-rith″ro-mi'sin). A broad-spectrum antibiotic substance produced by a strain of *Streptomyces erythreus.*

erythron (er'ĭ-thron) [Gr. *erythros* red]. The circulating erythrocytes in the blood, their precursors, and all the elements of the body concerned in their production.

erythroneocytosis (e-rith″ro-ne″o-si-to'sis) [*erythro-* + Gr. *neos* new + *kytos* hollow vessel]. The presence of immature erythrocytes in the blood.

erythronoclastic (e-rith″ro-no-klas'tik). Causing lysis or destruction of erythron.

erythroparasite (e-rith″ro-par'ah-sīt). A parasite of the erythrocytes.

erythropathy (er″ĭ-throp'ah-the) [*erythro-* + Gr. *pathos* disease]. Any disorder of the erythrocytes.

erythropenia (e-rith″ro-pe'ne-ah) [*erythro-* + Gr. *penia* poverty]. Deficiency in the number of erythrocytes.

erythrophage (e-rith'ro-fāj) [*erythro-* + Gr. *phagein* to eat]. A phagocyte that takes up erythrocytes and blood pigments.

erythrophagia (e-rith″ro-fa'je-ah). Erythrocytophagy.

erythrophagocytosis (e-rith″ro-fag″o-si-to'sis). Erythrocytophagy.

erythrophagous (er″ĭ-throf'ah-gus). Erythrocytophagous.

erythrophil (e-rith'ro-fil) [*erythro-* + Gr. *philein* to love]. 1. A cell or other element that is easily stained red. 2. Erythrophilous.

erythrophilous (er″ĭ-throf'ĭ-lus). Easily stained with red.

Erythrophloeum (e-rith″ro-fle'um) [*erythro-* + Gr. *phloios* bark]. A genus of leguminous trees. *E. guineen'se* affords casca, mancona, or sassybark, an African ordeal poison.

erythrophobia (e-rith″ro-fo'be-ah) [*erythro-* + *phobia*]. 1. A neurotic manifestation marked by blushing on the slightest provocation. 2. Morbid fear of blushing. 3. Morbid aversion to red.

erythrophore (e-rith'ro-fōr) [*erythro-* + Gr. *phoros* bearing]. A chromatophore containing granules of a red or brown alcohol-resistant pigment. Called also *allophore.*

erythrophose (e-rith′ro-fōz) [*erythro-* + Gr. *phōs* light]. Any red phose.

erythrophthisis (e-rith″ro-thi′sis) [*erythro-* + Gr. *phthisis* wasting]. A condition characterized by severe impairment of the restorative power of the erythrocyte-forming tissues.

erythrophthoric (e-rith″ro-thor′ik) [*erythro-* + Gr. *phthora* destruction]. Pertaining to rapid total destruction of the erythrocytes by a process other than hemolysis.

erythrophyll (e-rith′ro-fil) [*erythro-* + Gr. *phyllon* leaf]. A red coloring matter occurring in plants.

erythropia (er″e-thro′pe-ah). Erythropsia.

erythroplasia (e-rith″ro-pla′ze-ah). A condition of mucous membrane characterized by erythematous papular lesions. **e. of Queyrat,** a condition characterized by a circumscribed, velvety, erythematous papular lesion on the glans penis, coronal sulcus, or prepuce, leading to scaling and superficial ulceration, and degenerating to squamous cell epithelioma.

erythroplastid (e-rith″ro-plas′tid). A red blood corpuscle of mammalian animals, characterized by having no nucleus.

erythropoiesis (e-rith″ro-poi-e′sis) [*erythro-* + Gr. *poiēsis* making]. The production of erythrocytes.

erythropoietic (e-rith″ro-poi-et′ik). Pertaining to, characterized by, or promoting erythropoiesis.

erythropoietin (e-rith″ro-poi′ĕ-tin). A nondialyzable, relatively heat-stable glycoprotein, migrating electrophoretically as an α_2-globulin, considered to be the humoral plasma factor which stimulates red cell production.

erythroprecipitin (e-rith″ro-pre-sip′ĭ-tin). A precipitin specific for hemoglobin.

erythroprosopalgia (e-rith″ro-pros″o-pal′je-ah) [*erythro-* + Gr. *prosōpon* face + *-algia*]. A nervous disorder, analogous to erythromelalgia, marked by redness and pain in the face.

erythropsia (er″ĭ-throp′se-ah) [*erythro-* + Gr. *opsis* vision + *-ia*]. A visual defect in which all objects appear to have a red tinge.

erythropsin (er″e-throp′sin) [*erythro-* + Gr. *opsis* vision]. Rhodopsin.

erythropyknosis (e-rith″ro-pik-no′sis) [*erythro-* + *pyknosis*]. Pyknosis.

erythrorrhexis (e-rith″ro-rek′sis) [*erythro-* + Gr. *rhēxis* rupture]. Erythrocytorrhexis.

erythrose (er′ĭ-thrōs). 1. Tetrose. 2. [Fr.]. Erythrosis. **e. péribucca′le pigmentaire′,** Brocq's name for a condition marked by erythema and brownish pigmentation around the mouth, and on the chin and cheeks, developing in apparently normal girls at puberty, and waxing and waning with each menstrual period.

erythrosedimentation (e-rith″ro-sed″ĭ-men-ta′shun). The sedimentation of erythrocytes.

erythrosis (er″ĭ-thro′sis). 1. A reddish or purplish discoloration of the skin and mucous membranes seen in polycythemia vera. 2. Hyperplasia of the hematopoietic tissue.

erythrothioneine (e-rith″ro-thi″o-ne′in). Ergothioneine.

erythrotoxin (e-rith″ro-tok′sin). A substance which exerts a deleterious effect on erythrocytes.

erythrulose (e-rith′roo-lōs). A ketose sugar, $C_4H_8O_4$, formed by the oxidation of erythrol.

erythruria (er″ĭ-throo′re-ah) [*erythro-* + Gr. *ouron* urine + *-ia*]. The passing of red urine.

es (es) [L. *esse* to be]. Nietsche's term for the metaphysical incomprehensible something at the very bottom of human nature, being lower than the conscious ego and even lower than the freudian subconscious.

Esbach's reagent (es′bahks) [Georges Hubert *Esbach*, a physician in Paris, 1843–1890]. See under *reagent.*

escape (es-kāp′). The act of becoming free. **ventricular e.,** a condition of vagal arrhythmia in which the atrioventricular impulse becomes effective before the sino-auricular impulse.

escarro-nodulaire (es″kar-ro′nod″u-lār′) [Fr.]. Boutonneuse fever.

Esch. Abbreviation for *Escherichia.*

Esch's medium (esh′ez) [Peter *Esch*, German gynecologist, 1874–1952]. A culture medium for *Vibrio comma.*

eschar (es′kar) [Gr. *eschara* scab]. A slough produced by burning or by a corrosive application. **neuropathic e.,** a decubitus ulcer in disease of the spinal cord.

escharotic (es-kah-rot′ik) [Gr. *escharōtikos*]. 1. Corrosive; capable of producing an eschar. 2. A corrosive or caustic agent.

Escherich's bacillus (esh′er-iks) [Theodor *Escherich*, German physician, 1857–1911]. *Escherichia coli.*

Escherichia (esh″er-i′ke-a). A genus of microorganisms of the tribe Escherichieae, family Enterobacteriaceae, order Eubacteriales, made up of gram-negative, motile or nonmotile short rods, widely distributed in nature, and occasionally pathogenic for man. **E. aures′cens,** a species of organisms isolated from human feces, from an infected eye, and from contaminated water supplies, characterized by the ability to produce yellow-orange carotenoid pigments. **E. co′li,** a species of organisms constituting the greater part of the intestinal flora of man and other animals. Characteristically positive to indol and methyl red tests, and negative to the Voges-Proskauer and citrate tests. Divided into physiological types on the basis of sucrose and salicin fermentation by some workers. Separable into serotypes on the basis of distribution of heat-stable O antigens, envelope antigens of varying heat stability, and flagellar antigens that are heat labile. Usually nonpathogenic, but pathogenic strains, often hemolytic, and predominantly certain serotypes are common. Pathogenic strains are the cause of scours in calves, the hemorrhagic septicemia Winckel's disease in newborn children, one of the most frequently encountered causes of urinary tract infection and of epidemic diarrheal disease, especially in children, and is found infrequently in localized suppurative processes. They often become the predominant bacteria in the flora of the mouth and throat during antibiotic therapy. **E. freun′dii,** a species normally found in soil and water, as well as in the intestinal tract of man and other animals; certain strains have been confused with salmonellas. **E. interme′dia,** a species widely distributed in nature, being found, like others of the genus, in soil, water, and the intestinal tract of man and other animals.

Escherichieae (esh″er-i-ki′e-e). A tribe of the family Enterobacteriaceae, order Eubacteriales, made up of motile or non-motile rods that ferment glucose and lactose with the production of acid and visible gas. It comprises the coliform bacteria and includes five genera, *Aerobacter, Alginobacter, Escherichia, Klebsiella,* and *Paracolobactrum.*

eschrolalia (es-kro-la′le-ah) [Gr. *aischros* shameful + *lalia* babble]. Coprolalia.

Eschscholtzia (esh-skōlt′ze-ah). A genus of papaveraceous plants. *E. califor′nica* (California poppy) is a hypnotic and anodyne.

escin (es′kin). A strongly hemolytic saponin derived from horse-chestnut.

escorcin (es-kor′sin). A product, $C_9H_8O_4$, of the action of sodium amalgam on esculetin. It is used in detecting the corneal and conjunctival lesions.

Escudero's test (es-koo-da′rōz) [Pedro *Escudero*, Buenos Aires physician, born 1877]. See under *test.*

esculapian (es″ku-la′pe-an). Aesculapian.

esculent (es′ku-lent). Edible; fit for eating.

esculoside (es-ku′lo-sīd). A sugar which is derived from esculin.

escutcheon (es-kuch′an) [L. *scutum* a shield]. The pattern of distribution of the pubic hair.

E.S.E. Abbreviation for Ger. *elektrostatische einheit,* electrostatic unit.

eseptate (e-sep′tāt). Having no septa.

E.S.F. Abbreviation for *erythropoietic stimulating factor.*

eserine (es′er-in) [*esere,* an African name of the Calabar bean]. Physostigmine.

esidrix (es′ĭ-driks). Trade mark for a preparation of hydrochlorothiazide.

-esis. Word termination denoting state or condition. See *-sis.*

eskabarb (es′kah-barb). Trade mark for a preparation of phenobarbital.

eskadiazine (es″kah-di′ah-zēn). Trade mark for a preparation of sulfadiazine.

esmarch (es′mark). 1. An Esmarch bandage. 2. To treat with an Esmarch bandage.

Esmarch's bandage, etc. (es′marks) [Johann Friedrich August von *Esmarch,* German surgeon, 1823–1908]. See under *bandage,* etc.

eso- (es′o) [Gr. *esō* inward]. A combining form meaning within.

esocataphoria (es″o-kat-ah-fo′re-ah) [*eso-* + *cataphoria*]. The condition in which the visual axis turns downward and inward.

esocine (es′o-sin). A protamine from the sperm of the pike, *Esox lucius.*

esodeviation (e″so-de″ve-a′shun). A turning inward. In ophthalmology, esophoria.

esodic (e-sod′ik) [Gr. *es* toward + *hodos* way]. Afferent or centripetal.

eso-ethmoiditis (es″o-eth″moid-i′tis) [*eso-* + *ethmoiditis*]. Inflammation within the sinuses of the ethmoid bone.

esogastritis (es″o-gas-tri′tis) [*eso-* + *gastritis*]. Inflammation of the mucous membrane of the stomach.

esophagalgia (e-sof″ah-gal′je-ah) [*esophagus* + *-algia*]. Pain in the esophagus.

esophageal (e-sof″ah-je′al, e-so-fa′je-al). Pertaining to or belonging to the esophagus.

esophagectasia (e-sof″ah-jek-ta′se-ah) [*esophagus* + Gr. *ektasis* distention + *-ia*]. Dilatation of the esophagus.

esophagectasis (e-sof″ah-jek′tah-sis). Esophagectasia.

esophagectomy (e-sof″ah-jek′to-me) [*esophagus* + Gr. *ektomē* excision]. Excision of a portion of the esophagus.

esophagism (e-sof′ah-jism). Spasm of the circular muscular fibers of the esophagus. **hiatal e.,** cardiospasm.

esophagismus (e-sof″ah-jiz′mus). Esophagism.

esophagitis (e-sof″ah-ji′tis) [*esophagus* + *-itis*]. Inflammation of the esophagus. **e. dis′secans superficia′lis,** infection of the esophagus with sloughing of the squamous epithelial lining in the form of a tubular cast. **peptic e.,** inflammation of the esophagus caused by a reflux of acid and pepsin from the stomach; usually associated with hiatus hernia, duodenal ulcer, indwelling tubes, or prolonged vomiting.

esophagocele (e-sof′ah-go-sēl) [*esophagus* + Gr. *kēlē* hernia]. Abnormal distention of the esophagus; hernia of the esophagus: protrusion of the mucous and submucous coats of the esophagus through a rupture in the muscular coat, producing a pouch or diverticulum.

esophagocologastrostomy (e-sof″ah-go-ko″lo-gas-tros′to-me). Surgical creation of a new communication between the esophagus and stomach, with interposition of a segment of colon.

esophagoduodenostomy (e-sof″ah-go-du″o-de-nos′to-me). Surgical anastomosis between the esophagus and the duodenum.

esophagodynia (e-sof″ah-go-din′e-ah) [*esophagus* + Gr. *odynē* pain]. Pain in the esophagus.

esophago-enterostomy (e-sof″ah-go-en″ter-os′to-me) [*esophagus* + Gr. *enteron* intestine + *stomoun* to provide with an opening, or mouth]. The operation of suturing the esophagus to the duodenum and excising the stomach. This is Schlatter's operation for total extirpation of the stomach.

esophagofundopexy (e-sof″ah-go-fun″do-pek′-se). Surgical fixation of the esophagus to the fundus of the stomach.

esophagogastrectomy (e-sof″ah-go-gas-trek′-to-me). Excision of the esophagus and stomach.

esophagogastro-anastomosis (e-sof″ah-go-gas″tro-ah-nas″to-mo′sis). Surgical formation of an anastomosis between the esophagus and the stomach.

esophagogastroplasty (e-sof″ah-go-gas′tro-plas″te). Plastic repair of the esophagus and stomach; cardioplasty.

esophagogastroscopy (e-sof″ah-go-gas-tros′-ko-pe) [*esophagus* + Gr. *gastēr* stomach + *skopein* to examine]. Endoscopic examination of the esophagus and the stomach.

esophagogastrostomy (e-sof″ah-go-gas-tros′to-me) [*esophagus* + Gr. *gastēr* stomach + *stomoun* to provide with an opening, or mouth]. Surgical creation of an artificial communication between the stomach and esophagus.

esophagogram (e-sof′ah-go-gram). A roentgenogram of the esophagus.

esophagography (e-sof″ah-gog′rah-fe). Roentgenography of the esophagus.

esophagojejunogastrostomosis (e-sof″ah-go-je″ju-no-gas″tros-to-mo′sus). The operation of mobilizing a loop of jejunum and implanting its proximal end in the esophagus and its distal end in the stomach: done in cases of esophageal stricture.

esophagojejunogastrostomy (e-sof″ah-go-je-ju″no-gas-tros′to-me). Esophagojejunogastrostomosis.

esophagojejunostomy (e-sof″ah-go-je-ju-nos′-to-me). Surgical anastomosis between the esophagus and the jejunum.

esophagolaryngectomy (e-sof″ah-go-lar″in-jek′to-me). En bloc excision of the upper cervical esophagus and larynx.

esophagology (e-sof″ah-gol′o-je). The study and treatment of diseases of the esophagus.

esophagomalacia (e-sof″ah-go-mah-la′she-ah) [*esophagus* + Gr. *malakia* softness]. Softening of the walls of the esophagus.

esophagometer (e-sof″ah-gom′e-ter) [*esophagus* + Gr. *metron* measure]. An instrument for measuring the length of the esophagus.

esophagomycosis (e-sof″ah-go-mi-ko′sis) [*esophagus* + Gr. *mykēs* fungus]. Any disease of the esophagus caused by fungi.

esophagomyotomy (e-sof″ah-go-mi-ot′o-me). Incision through the muscular coat of the esophagus, the term usually referring clinically to incision through the muscular coat of the distal part of the esophagus.

esophagopharynx (e-sof″ah-go-făr′inks). The distal portion of the pharynx where the fibers of the inferior constrictor are arranged in circular form.

esophagoplasty (e-sof′ah-go-plas″te) [*esophagus* + Gr. *plassein* to form]. A plastic operation on the esophagus.

esophagoplication (e-sof″ah-go-pli-ka′shun). The operation of treating an esophageal pouch by folding in its wall.

esophagoptosis (e-sof″ah-gop-to′sis) [*esophagus* + Gr. *ptōsis* falling]. Prolapse of the esophagus.

esophagosalivation (e-sof″ah-go-sal′ĭ-va′shun). A salivation which accompanies cancer of the esophagus.

esophagoscope (e-sof′ah-go-skōp) [*esophagus* + Gr. *skopein* to examine]. An endoscope for examination of the esophagus.

esophagoscopy (e-sof″ah-gos′ko-pe). Endoscopic examination of the esophagus.

esophagospasm (e″so-fag′o-spazm) [*esophagus* + *spasm*]. Spasm of the esophagus.

esophagostenosis (e-sof″ah-go-ste-no′sis) [*esophagus* + Gr. *stenōsis* constriction]. Stricture or constriction of the esophagus.

esophagostoma (e″sof-ah-gos′to-mah) [*esophagus* + Gr. *stoma* mouth]. The external opening of an artificial passage leading into the esophagus.

esophagostomy (e-sof″ah-gos′to-me) [*esophagus* + Gr. *stoma* mouth]. The creation of an artificial opening into the esophagus.

esophagotome (e″so-fag′o-tōm). A cutting instrument for use in esophagotomy.

esophagotomy (e-sof″ah-got′o-me) [*esophagus* + Gr. *tomē* a cut]. Incision of the esophagus.

esophagram (e-sof′ah-gram). Esophagogram.

esophagus (e-sof′ah-gus) [Gr. *oisophagos*, from *oisein* to carry + *phagēma* food]. [N A] The musculomembranous passage extending from the pharynx to the stomach.

esophoria (es″o-fo′re-ah) [*eso-* + Gr. *phorein* to bear]. Deviation of a visual axis toward that of the other eye when fusion is prevented.

esophoric (es″o-for′ik). Pertaining to or characterized by esophoria.

esophylactic (es″o-fi-lak′tik) [*eso-* + *phylaxis*]. Pertaining to or of the nature of esophylaxis.

esophylaxis (es″o-fi-lak′sis). Prophylaxis against disease performed by the cells and fluids of the body. Cf. *exophylaxis.*

esosphenoiditis (es″o-sfe″noid-i′tis) [*eso-* + *sphenoid* + *-itis*]. Osteomyelitis of the sphenoid bone.

esoteric (es″o-ter′ik) [Gr. *esōterikos* inner]. 1. Designed for the initiated alone; hidden; secret. 2. In physiology, arising within the organism.

esotoxin (es″o-tok′sin). A toxin produced within the organism; an endotoxin.

esotropia (es″o-tro′pe-ah) [*eso-* + Gr. *trepein* to turn]. Deviation of a visual axis toward that of the other eye when fusion is a possibility.

esotropic (es″o-trop′ik). Pertaining to or characterized by esotropia.

ESP. Abbreviation for *extrasensory perception.*

espnoic (esp-no′ik) [Gr. *es* into + *pnoē* vapor, blast]. Pertaining to the injection of vapors or gases.

esponja (es-pong′ah). A granular inflammation of the skin in Brazilian horses, probably due to larval infection by *Habronema muscae.*

espundia (es-poon′de-ah). Naso-oral leishmaniasis.

esquillectomy (es″kwil-lek′to-me) [Fr. *esquille* fragment + Gr. *ektomē* excision]. Excision of fragments of bone following fractures caused by projectiles.

E.S.R. Abbreviation for *erythrocyte sedimentation rate.*

essence (es′ens) [L. *essentia* quality or being]. 1. That which is or necessarily exists as the cause of the properties of a body. 2. A solution of a volatile oil in alcohol. **e. of peppermint,** peppermint spirit (U.S.P.). **pepsin e.,** pepsin and rennin elixir (N.F.).

essentia (ĕ-sen′she-ah). Essence.

essential (ĕ-sen′shal) [L. *essentialis*]. 1. Constituting the necessary or inherent part of a thing; giving a substance its peculiar and necessary qualities. 2. Idiopathic; self-existing; having no obvious external exciting cause.

E.S.T. Abbreviation for *electroshock therapy.*

ester (es′ter). Any compound formed from an alcohol and an acid by the removal of water. The esters are named as if they were salts of the alcohol radicals. Called also *compound ether* and *ethereal salt.* **aceto-acetic e.,** the ethyl ester of aceto-acetic acid, $CH_3.CO.CH_2.CO.O.C_2H_5$, a colorless liquid: used for the synthesis of a great variety of compounds. **Cori e.,** glucose 1-phosphate; a glucopyranose 1-monophosphate, $CH_2.OH.CH(CHOH)_3.CHO.PO(OH)_2$.
└——O——┘
See *hexosephosphoric esters.* **Embden e.,** glucopyranose 6-phosphoric acid. **Harden-Young e.,** a fructofuranose diphosphate, $(OH)_2PO.CH_2O.CHO(CHOH)_2CH.CH_2O.PO(OH)_2$. See
└——O——┘
hexosephosphoric esters. **hexosephosphoric e's,** esters concerned in the chemical processes of muscle contraction and the fermentation of glucose by yeast. They are the Cori ester, the Harden-Young ester, the Neuberg ester and the Robison ester. **Neuberg e.,** fructose 6-phosphate; a fructofuranose monophosphate, $CH_2OH.CHO.(CHOH)_2.CH.CH_2O.PO(OH)_2$. See
└——O——┘
hexosephosphoric e's. **Robison e.,** glucose 6-phosphate; a glucopyranose 6-monophosphate, $CHOH(CHOH)_3.CH.CH_2O.PO(OH)_2$. See *hex-*
└——O——┘
osephosphoric e's.

esterapenia (es″ter-ah-pe′ne-ah) [*esterase* + Gr. *penia* poverty]. Deficiency in the cholinesterase content of the blood.

esterase (es′ter-ās). An enzyme which catalyzes the hydrolysis of an ester into its alcohol and acid. **acetylcholine e.,** cholinesterase.

esterification (es-ter″ĭ-fi-ka′shun). The process of converting an acid into an ester.

esterize (es′ter-iz). To convert, or be converted, into an ester.

esterolysis (es″ter-ol′ĭ-sis) [*ester* + Gr. *lysis* dissolution]. The hydrolysis of an ester into its alcohol and acid.

esterolytic (es″ter-o-lit′ik). Effecting or pertaining to esterolysis.

Estes' operation (es′tēz) [William Lawrence *Estes*, Jr., American surgeon, 1885–1940]. See under *operation.*

esthematology (es″them-ah-tol′o-je) [Gr. *aisthēma* sensation + *-logy*]. The science of the senses and sense organs.

esthesia (es-the′ze-ah) [Gr. *aisthēsis* perception]. 1. Perception, feeling, or sensation. 2. A neurosis of perception or sensation.

esthesic (es-the′sik) [Gr. *aisthēsis* perception]. Pertaining to the mental perception of sensations.

esthesio- (es-the′ze-o) [Gr. *aisthēsis* perception, sensation]. A combining form denoting relationship to feeling or to the perceptive faculties.

esthesioblast (es-the′ze-o-blast) [*esthesio-* + Gr. *blastos* germ]. A ganglioblast; an embryonic cell of the spinal ganglia.

esthesiodic (es-the″ze-od′ik). Esthesodic.

esthesiogen (es-the′ze-o-jen) [*esthesio-* + Gr. *gennan* to produce]. A substance which in certain conditions of the body is supposed to produce symptoms of excitation when brought near or into contact with the person.

esthesiogenic (es-the″ze-o-jen′ik). Producing sensation.

esthesiology (es-the″ze-ol′o-je) [*esthesio-* + *-logy*]. The science of sensation and the senses.

esthesiomania (es-the″ze-o-ma′ne-ah) [*esthesio-* + Gr. *mania* madness]. Insanity with perversion of the senses.

esthesiomene (es-the″ze-om′e-ne). Esthiomene.

esthesiometer (es-the″ze-om′e-ter) [*esthesio-* + Gr. *metron* measure]. An instrument for measuring tactile sensibility.

esthesioneure (es-the′ze-o-nūr) [*esthesio-* + Gr. *neuron* nerve]. A sensory neuron.

esthesioneuroblastoma (es-the″ze-o-nu″ro-blas-to′mah). A radiosensitive glioma occurring in the nasal cavity.

esthesioneurosis (es-the″ze-o-nu-ro′sis) [*esthesio-* + *neurosis*]. Any disorder of the sensory nerves.

esthesionosus (es-the″ze-on′o-sus) [*esthesio-* + Gr. *nosos* disease]. Esthesioneurosis.

esthesiophysiology (es-the″ze-o-fiz″e-ol′o-je). The physiology of the perceptive faculties.

esthesioscopy (es-the″ze-os′ko-pe) [*esthesio-* + Gr. *skopein* to examine]. Delimitation on the skin of areas in which pain is felt or the tissues are tender.

esthesodic (es″the-zod′ik) [*esthesio-* + Gr. *hodos* path]. Conducting or pertaining to the conduction of sensory impulses.

esthetic (es-thet′ik) [Gr. *aisthēsis* sensation]. 1. Pertaining to sensation. 2. Pertaining to beauty, or the improvement of appearance.

estheticokinetic (es-thet″ĭ-ko-ki-net′ik). Both sensory and motor.

esthetics (es-thet′iks). The branch of philosophy dealing with beauty. In dentistry, a philosophy concerned especially with the appearance of a dental restoration, as achieved through its color or form.

esthiomene (es″the-om′ĕ-ne) [Gr. *esthiomenos* eroded]. A chronic ulceration and elephantiasis of the labia and clitoris due to lymphogranuloma venereum.

esthophysiology (es″tho-fiz″e-ol′o-je). The physiology of sensation and sense organs.

estinyl (es′tĭ-nil). Trade mark for a preparation of ethinyl estradiol.

estival (es′tĭ-val) [L. *aestivus*, from *aestas* summer]. Pertaining to or occurring in summer.

estivation (es″tĭ-va′shun) [L. *aestivus* pertaining to summer]. The adaptation or modifications in an animal that enable it to survive a hot, dry summer. Cf. *hibernation.*

estivo-autumnal (es″tĭ-vo-aw-tum′nal). Pertaining to the summer and autumn: a term applied to a form of malaria. See under *malaria* and *Plasmodium.*

Estlander's operation (est′land-erz) [Jakob August *Estlander*, Finnish surgeon, 1831–1881]. See under *operation.*

eston (es′ton). Monobasic aluminum acetate.

estradiol (es″trah-di′ol, es-tra′de-ol). An estrogenic steroid, 1,3,5(10)-estratriene-3,17β-diol, isolated from the liquor folliculi of hog's ovaries and from the urine of pregnant mares and prepared semisynthetically by hydrogenation of estrone. It exists in two forms, α-estradiol and β-estradiol. **e. benzoate,** an estrogenic steroid used for parenteral injection. **e. dipropionate,** the dipropionyl ester of estradiol, which is claimed to be absorbed slowly. **ethynyl e.,** a derivative of estradiol used for oral administration.

estrapentaene (es″trah-pen′tah-ēn). A steroid nucleus with five double bonds and one methyl group, $C_{18}H_{20}$.

estratetraene (es″trah-tet′rah-ēn). A steroid nucleus with four double bonds and one methyl group, $C_{18}H_{22}$.

estratriene (es″trah-tri′ēn). A steroid nucleus with three double bonds and one methyl group, $C_{18}H_{24}$.

estrenol (es′trĕ-nol). A crystalline estrogenic steroid, $C_{18}H_{24}O$, 3-hydroxy Δ1,3,5-estratriene.

estriasis (es-tri′ah-sis). Oestriasis.

Estridae (es′trĭ-de). Oestridae.

estrinization (es″trin-ĭ-za′shun). Production of the cellular changes in the vaginal epithelium characteristic of estrus.

estrogen (es′tro-jen). A generic term for estrus-producing compounds.

estrogenic (es-tro-jen′ik). Producing estrus.

estrogenicity (es″tro-je-nis′ĭ-te). The quality of exerting or the ability to exert an estrus-producing effect.

estrogenous (es-troj′e-nus). Estrogenic.

estrone (es′trōn). An estrogenic steroid, 1,3,5(10)-estratriene-3-ol-17-one, isolated from the urine of pregnant animals.

estrostilben (es″tro-stil′ben). Stilbestrol.

estrous (es′trus). Pertaining to estrus.

estrual (es′troo-al). Pertaining to estrus.

estruation (es″troo-a′shun). Estrus.

estrugenone (es″troo-jen′on). Trade mark for a preparation of estrone.

estrum (es′trum). Any form of recurrent excitement. See *estrus.*

estrus (es′trus) [L. *oestrus* gadfly; Gr. *oistros* anything that drives mad, any vehement desire]. 1. The recurrent, restricted period of sexual receptivity in female mammals, marked by intense sexual urge. 2. The cycle of changes in the genital tract which are produced as a result of ovarian hormonal activity.

estuarium (es″tu-a′re-um) [L.]. A vapor bath.

e.s.u. Abbreviation for *electrostatic unit.*

Et. Chemical symbol for *ethyl.*

etamon (et′ah-mon). Trade mark for a solution of tetraethylammonium (chloride).

état (a-tah′) [Fr.]. State, condition. **é. criblé** (a-tah′ krēb-la′). 1. A condition in which the necrotic Peyer's patches in typhoid fever are riddled with small, irregular perforations. 2. Status cribralis. **é. lacunaire** (a-tah′ lah-ku-nār′), status lacunaris. **é. mammelonné** (a-tah′ mah-mel-un-a′), hyperplasia of the mucous membrane of the stomach in chronic gastritis, resulting in the formation of small elevations. **é. marbré** (a-tah′ mar-bra′), marble state. **é. vermoulu** (a-tah′ vār-moo-lu′) ["worm-eaten state"], an irregularly ulcerated condition of the surface of the brain which is sometimes seen in advanced arteriosclerosis.

Eternod's sinus (a-ter-nōz′) [Auguste François Charles *d'Eternod*, Swiss histologist, 1854–1932]. See under *sinus.*

ethal (eth′al). Cetyl alcohol.

ethamivan (ĕ-thim′ĭ-van). Chemical name: vanillic diethylamide: used as a respiratory stimulant, and to hasten recovery from general anesthesia.

ethane (eth′ān). A gaseous hydrocarbon, C_2H_6, forming a constituent of illuminating gas.

ethanol (eth′ah-nol). Alcohol.

ethaverine (eth″ah-ver′ēn). Chemical name: 6,7-diethoxy-1-(3,4-diethoxybenzyl) isoquinoline: used as a relaxant for vascular smooth muscle.

ethchlorvynol (eth-klōr′vĭ-nol). Chemical name: 1-chloro-3-ethyl-1-penten-4-yn-3-ol: used as a hypnotic and sedative.

ethene (eth-ēn′). Ethylene.

ethenoid (eth′ĕ-noid). Containing an ethene or ethylene linkage.

etheogenesis (e″the-o-jen′e-sis) [Gr. *ētheos* bachelor + *genesis* production]. Nonsexual reproduction in male gametes of protozoa.

ether (e′ther) [L. *aether*, Gr. *aithēr* "the upper and purer air"]. 1. A fluid of the utmost tenuity, which is conceived to fill all space, and to serve as a medium for the transmission of waves of heat and light. 2. A colorless, transparent, mobile, very volatile liquid, $C_4H_{10}O$, with a characteristic odor, and highly inflammable: used by inhalation as a general anesthetic. 3. A term applied to various volatile liquids, mostly containing diethyl ether or resembling it. 4. Any member of a group of compounds derived from two alcohol molecules by the elimination of water. If the alcohol radicals are identical, the compound is a *simple ether;* if they are different it is a *complex*, or *mixed, ether.* **acetic e.,** ethyl acetate. **anesthetic e.,** purified ether used for the purpose of producing anesthesia. **chloric e.,** a mixture of chloroform and alcohol. **complex e.,** a chemical compound derived from two different alcohol radicals by the elimination of water. **compound e.,** ester. **dibromomethyl e.,** a war gas, $BrCH_2O\text{-}CH_2Br$, that irritates the lungs and affects the functioning of the semicircular canals. **dichloromethyl e.,** a form of mustard gas, $(CH_2Cl)_2O$. **diethyl e.,** ether (def. 2). **dimethyl e.,** a liquid, $CH_3.O.CH_3$, with general anesthetic properties. **enanthic e.,** pelargonic e. **ethyl e.,** ether (def. 2). **ethyl-vinyl e.,** an anesthetic compound, $CH_3.CH_2.O.CH{:}CH_2$. **formic e.,** ethyl formate. **hydriodic e.,** ethyl iodide. **hydrobromic e.,** ethyl bromide. **hydrochloric e.,** ethyl chloride. **luminiferous e.,** ether (def. 1). **mitigated e.,** E.-C. mixture. **mixed e.,** complex e. **nitrofurfuryl methyl e.,** 2-(methoxymethyl)-5-nitrofuran: used as a topical fungicide and sporicide in skin infections. **nitrous e.,** ethyl nitrite. **oenanthic e.,** pelargonic e. **pelargonic e.,** an ether of pelargonic acid. It is an oily liquid with the odor of quinces. **petroleum e.,** petroleum benzin. **pyroacetic e.,** acetone. **simple e.,** a chemical compound derived from two identical alcohol radicals by the elimination of water. **thio e.,** an ether in which sulfur replaces oxygen. **thioallylic e.,** allyl sulfide. **vinyl e.,** an anesthetic compound, $CH_2{:}CH.O.CH{:}CH_2$; a clear liquid with a characteristic odor; administered by inhalation to produce general anesthesia.

ethereal (e-the′re-al). 1. Pertaining to, prepared with, containing, or resembling ether. 2. Evanescent; delicate.

etherification (e″ther-ĭ-fi-ka′shun). The formation of an ether from alcohol.

etherin (e′ther-in). A poison extractable by ether from the bodies of tubercle bacilli. Called also *etherobacillin*. See *benzenin, chloroformin,* and *xylenin*.

etherion (e-the′re-on). 1. A gas said to have been discovered in 1898 in the atmosphere: said to be about $\frac{1}{1,000}$ part as dense as hydrogen, and to exist in less than $\frac{1}{1,000,000}$ part of its proportion in the air. 2. Mathews' name for one of the minute spheres which make up the ether.

etherism (e′ther-izm). Etheromania.

etherization (e″ther-i-za′shun). The administration by ether of inhalation, and the consequent production of anesthesia.

etherize (e′ther-īz). To put under the anesthetic influence of ether.

etherobacillin (e″ther-o-bah-sil′in). Etherin.

etheromania (e″ther-o-ma′ne-ah). Uncontrollable addiction to the use of ether as a stimulant.

etherometer (e″ther-om′e-ter) [*ether* + Gr. *metron* measure]. A device for administering ether by which the number of drops per minute can be accurately controlled.

etherrausch (a′ter-rowsh) [Ger.]. See *rausch*.

ethical (eth′ĭ-kal). In accordance with the principles which govern right conduct.

ethics (eth′iks) [Gr. *ēthos* the manner and habits of man or of animals]. The rules or principles which govern right conduct. **medical e.,** the rules or principles governing the professional conduct of physicians.

ethidene (eth′ĭ-dēn). The bivalent radical, CH_3.-CH. **e. chloride,** a colorless, volatile, anesthetic fluid, CH_3CHCl_2, with the taste and smell of chloroform. It is used like chloroform, but is more dangerous. **e. diamine,** a harmful and to hasten recovery from general anesthesia.

ethinamate (ĕ-thin′ah-māt). Chemical name: 1-ethynylcyclohexyl carbamate: used as a central nervous system depressant.

ethinyl trichloride (eth′ĭ-nil tri-klo′rīd). Trichloroethylene.

ethionine (ĕ-thi′o-nin). The ethyl homologue of methionine.

ethiopification (e″the-op″ĭ-fi-ka′shun) [Gr. *Aithiops* an Ethiop + L. *facere* to make]. The blackening of the skin by the use of silver or other metallic agents.

ethisterone (ĕ-this′ter-ōn). Chemical name: 17α-ethynyl-4-androsten-17β-ol-3-one: used as a progestational steroid.

ethmocarditis (eth″mo-kar-di′tis) [Gr. *ēthmos* sieve + *kardia* heart + *-itis*]. Inflammation of the connective tissue of the heart.

ethmocephalus (eth″mo-sef′ah-lus) [Gr. *ēthmos* sieve + *kephalē* head]. A monster with an imperfect head, more or less union of the eyes, and a rudimentary nose, which may often be displaced upward.

ethmofrontal (eth″mo-fron′tal). Pertaining to the ethmoid and frontal bones.

ethmoid (eth′moid) [Gr. *ēthmos* sieve + *eidos* form]. Cribriform; sievelike.

ethmoidal (eth-moi′dal). Of or pertaining to the ethmoid bone.

ethmoidectomy (eth″moi-dek′to-me) [*ethmoid* + Gr. *ektomē* excision]. Excision of the ethmoid cells or of a portion of the ethmoid bone.

ethmoiditis (eth″moid-i′tis). Inflammation of the ethmoid bone.

ethmoidotomy (eth″moid-ot′o-me). Surgical incision into the ethmoid sinus.

ethmolacrimal (eth″mo-lak′rĭ-mal). Pertaining to the ethmoid and the lacrimal bones.

ethmomaxillary (eth″mo-mak′sĭ-lār-e). Pertaining to the ethmoid and the maxillary bones.

ethmonasal (eth″mo-na′zal). Pertaining to the ethmoid and the nasal bones.

ethmopalatal (eth″mo-pal′ah-tal). Pertaining to the ethmoid and palatal bones.

ethmosphenoid (eth″mo-sfe′noid). Pertaining to the ethmoid and the sphenoid bones.

ethmoturbinal (eth″mo-tur′bĭ-nal). The superior and middle nasal conchae.

ethmovomerine (eth″mo-vo′mer-in). Pertaining to the ethmoid bone and the vomer.

ethmyphitis (eth″me-fi′tis) [Gr. *ēthmos* sieve + *hyphē* tissue]. Inflammation of the cellular tissue; cellulitis.

ethnic (eth′nik). Pertaining to race or races of men.

ethnics (eth′niks) [Gr. *ethnikos* of or for a nation]. Ethnology.

ethnography (eth-nog′rah-fe) [Gr. *ethnos* race + *graphein* to write]. A description of the races of men.

ethnology (eth-nol′o-je) [Gr. *ethnos* race + *-logy*]. The science which deals with the races of men, their descent, relationship, etc.

ethobrom (eth′o-brōm). Tribromoethanol.

ethocaine (eth′o-kān). Procaine.

ethoheptazine (eth″o-hep′tah-zēn). Chemical name: 1-methyl-4-carbethoxy-4-phenylhexamethylenimine: used as an analgesic.

ethohexadiol (eth″o-heks-a′de-ol). Chemical name: 2-ethyl-1,3-hexamediol: used as an insect repellant.

ethologist (e-thol′o-jist). An individual skilled in ethology.

ethology (e-thol′o-je) [Gr. *ēthos* the manners and habits of man, or of animals + *-logy*]. The scientific study of animal behavior.

ethopropazine (eth″o-pro′pah-zēn). Chemical name: 10-(2-diethylaminopropyl) phenothiazine: used to produce parasympathetic blockade, and to reduce tremors in parkinsonism.

ethosuximide (eth″o-suk′sĭ-mīd). Chemical name: α-ethyl, α-methyl succinimide: used as an anticonvulsant in treatment of petit mal epilepsy.

ethotoin (ĕ-tho′to-in). Chemical name: 3-ethyl-5-phenylhydantoin: used as an anticonvulsant in grand mal epilepsy.

ethoxazene (eth-ok′sah-zēn). Chemical name: 2,4-diamino-4′-ethoxyazobenzene: used to relieve pain associated with chronic infections of the urinary tract.

ethoxzolamide (eth″oks-ol′ah-mīd). Chemical name: 6-ethoxy-2-benzothiazolesulfonamide: a diuretic of the carbonic anhydrase inhibitor type.

ethyl (eth′il) [*ether* + Gr. *hylē* matter]. The univalent alcohol radical, $CH_3.CH_2$. **e. acetate,** a transparent, colorless liquid, $CH_3COOC_2H_5$, used as a flavoring agent. **e. aminobenzoate,** a white crystalline substance, ethyl para-aminobenzoate, used as a local anesthetic. **e. biscoumacetate,** a white, odorless, bitter, crystalline solid, 3,3′-carboxymethylene bis(4-hydroxycoumarin) ethyl ester, used as an anticoagulant. **e. bromide,** a colorless volatile liquid, C_2H_5Br, of sweetish taste and ethereal odor, and possessing anesthetic properties. **e. butyrate,** the butyric acid ester of ethyl alcohol, $C_3H_7.CO.O.C_2H_5$, with the odor of pineapple. **e. carbamate,** urethan. **e. carbinol,** propyl alcohol. **e. chaulmoograte,** the ethyl esters of the fatty acids of chaulmoogra oil, used in the treatment of leprosy. **e. chloride,** a colorless, mobile, extremely volatile liquid, C_2H_5Cl: used as a general and topical anesthetic. **e. cyanide,** a colorless liquid, C_2H_5CN. **e. diacetate,** a material which has been used in urinary tests. **e. diiodosalicylate,** white crystals of $OH.C_6H_2I_2.CO.O.C_2H_5$: used in place of iodoform. **e. ether.** See *ether* (def. 2). **e. formate,** a volatile antispasmodic and anesthetic liquid, $HCOOC_2H_5$. **e. hydrate,** ordinary, or ethylic, alcohol. **e. iodide,** a colorless liquid, CH_3CH_2I: used as an antispasmodic, alterative, and resorbent. Called also *hydriodic ether*. **e. mercaptan,** a thio-alcohol, C_2H_5SH, which has a revolting odor and which helps to give the odor to feces. **e. nitrate,** a compound, $CH_3.CH_2.NO_3$, sometimes employed as a vasodilator. **e. nitrite,** $C_2H_5NO_2$; a liquid which is mixed with alcohol to form sweet spirit of niter. **e. orange,** a dye, the sodium salt of diethylaniline-azo-benzene-sulfonic acid, $C_6H_4.N(C_2H_5)_2.N_2.C_6H_4.SO_2.ONa$: used as an indicator, being turned red by acids and yellow by alkalis. **e. oxide,** a colorless, transparent, highly volatile liquid, closely similar to ether: used only as a pharmaceutical solvent. **e. pelargonate,** the pelargonic acid ester of ethyl alcohol, $C_8H_{17}.CO.O.C_2H_5$. **e. phenacetin,** a yellow oil, $C_8H_4(OC_2H_5)N(C_2H_5)CH_3CO$: hypnotic. **e. phenylcinchoninate,** a yellowish powder: used to promote elimination of uric acid. **e. phenylephrine,** effortil. **e. pyoktanin,** an auramine derivative: actively antiseptic. **e. salicylate,** the salicylic acid ester of ethyl alcohol, $CH_3.CH_2.O.CO.C_6H_4OH$: used like the salicylates.

ethylamine (eth″il-am′in). A liquid ptomaine, $CH_3CH_2NH_2$, from decaying plant tissue, possessing many of the properties of ammonia. **e. sulfonic acid,** taurine. **e. urate,** a remedy employed in the treatment of gout and gravel.

ethylate (eth′il-āt). Any compound of ethyl alcohol in which the hydrogen of the hydroxyl is replaced by a base.

ethylation (eth″il-a′shun). The act of combining or causing to combine with the ethyl radical.

ethylcellulose (eth″il-sel′u-lōs). An ethyl ether of cellulose, used as an ingredient in preparing pharmaceuticals.

ethylene (eth′ĭ-lēn). A colorless gas, $CH_2{=}CH_2$, somewhat lighter than air, and having a slightly sweet taste and odor: used for inducing general anesthesia.

ethylic (e-thil′ik). Pertaining to or derived from ethyl.

ethylism (eth′il-izm). Poisoning or intoxication by ethyl alcohol.

ethylmorphine hydrochloride (eth″il-mor′fēn hi″dro-klo′rīd). A white or faintly yellow, odorless, microcrystalline powder, $C_{19}H_{23}NO_3.HCl.2H_2O$: used as a narcotic and antitussive.

ethylnoradrenaline (eth″il-nor-ad-ren′ah-lin). Ethylnorepinephrine.

ethylnorepinephrine (eth″ĭl-nor-ep″ĭ-nef′rin). Chemical name: α-(1-aminopropyl) protocatechuyl alcohol: used as a sympathomimetic, and in treatment of bronchial asthma.

ethylnorsuprarenin (eth″il-nor-su″prah-ren′in). Ethylnorepinephrine.

etincelage (a″tĕn-sĕ-lahzh′) [Fr.]. Fulguration.

etiocholanolone (e″te-o-ko-lan′o-lōn). A reduced form of testosterone excreted in the urine.

etiogenic (e″te-o-jen′ik) [Gr. *aitia* cause + *gennan* to produce]. Causative.

etiolation (e″te-o-la′shun) [Fr. *étioler* to blanch]. A blanching or paleness of color in a plant due to lack of chlorophyll when grown in the dark.

etiolin (e-ti′o-lin). A hypothetical pigment or chlorophyll precursor assumed to give the yellow color to etiolated seedlings.

etiologic (e″te-o-loj′ik). Etiological.

etiological (e″te-o-loj′e-kal). Pertaining to etiology, or to the causes of disease.

etiology (e″te-ol′o-je) [Gr. *aitia* cause + *-logy*]. The study or theory of the causation of any disease; the sum of knowledge regarding causes.

etiopathology (e″te-o-pah-thol′o-je). Pathogenesis.

etioporphyrin (e″te-o-por′fir-in). A porphyrin, $C_{32}H_{38}N_4$, obtained from hematoporphyrin.

etiotropic (e″te-o-trop′ik) [Gr. *aitia* cause + *tropos* turning]. Directed against the cause of a disease.

etrohysterectomy (e″tro-his-ter-ek′to-me) [Gr. *ētron* hypogastrium + *hysterectomy*]. Hypogastric excision of uterus.

etrotomy (e-trot′o-me) [Gr. *ētron* hypogastrium + *temnein* to cut]. Pelvic section.

etryptamine (e-trip′tah-min). Chemical name: 3-(2-aminobutyl) indole acetate: used as a psychomotor stimulant.

Eu. Chemical symbol for *europium*.

eu- (u) [Gr. *eu* well]. A combining form meaning well, easily, or good; the opposite of *dys-*.

euangiotic (u″an-je-ot′ik) [*eu-* + Gr. *angeion* vessel]. Well supplied with blood vessels.

Eubacteriales (u″bak-te″re-a′lēz). An order of Schizomycetes, comprising the true bacteria, which are simple undifferentiated, rigid, spherical or rod-shaped cells. It includes 13 families, *Achromobacteraceae, Azotobacteraceae, Bacillaceae, Bacteroidaceae, Brevibacteriaceae, Brucellaceae, Corynebacteriaceae, Enterobacteriaceae, Lactobacillaceae, Micrococcaceae, Neisseriaceae, Propionibacteriaceae*, and *Rhizobiaceae*.

Eubacterium (u″bak-te′re-um). A genus of microorganisms of the tribe Lactobacilleae, family Lactobacillaceae, order Eubacteriales, nonsporulating, gram-positive anaerobic bacilli found in the intestinal tract as parasites and as saprophytes in soil and water. Occasionally found in purulent lesions but of questionable primary pathogenicity.

eubiotics (u″bi-ot′iks) [*eu-* + Gr. *bios* life]. The science of healthy living.

eubolism (u′bo-lizm) [*eu-* + *metabolism*]. A condition of normal body metabolism.

eucalyptol (u″kah-lip′tol). A colorless liquid with a characteristic aromatic, camphoraceous odor, and a cooling, pungent, spicy taste, obtained from eucalyptus oil and other sources: used as an expectorant.

Eucalyptus (u″kah-lip′tus) [*eu-* + Gr. *kalyptos* covered]. A genus of myrtaceous trees and shrubs, chiefly Australian, of many species.

eucapnia (u-kap′ne-ah) [*eu-* + Gr. *kapnos* smoke]. The condition in which the carbon dioxide of the blood is normal.

eucatropine (u-kat′ro-pēn). Chemical name: 1,2,2,6-tetramethyl-4-piperidinol mandelate: used in parasympathetic blockade, as a mydriatic.

euchlorhydria (u″klōr-hi′dre-ah) [*eu-* + *chlorhydric acid*]. The presence of the normal proportion of free hydrochloric acid in the gastric juice.

eucholia (u-ko′le-ah) [*eu-* + Gr. *cholē* bile]. Normal condition of the bile.

euchromatin (u-kro′mah-tin). The gene-bearing fraction of chromatin, composed of desoxyribose nucleic acid with higher proteins of the globulin type.

euchromatopsy (u-kro′mah-top″se) [*eu-* + Gr. *chrōma* color + *opsis* vision]. Normal color vision.

euchromosome (u-kro′mo-sōm) [*eu-* + *chromosome*]. Autosome.

euchylia (u-kil′e-ah) [*eu-* + Gr. *chylos* chyle]. A normal condition of the chyle.

eucolloid (u-kol′oid). A colloid in which each dispersed particle consists of a single large molecule.

eucrasia (u-kra′se-ah) [*eu-* + Gr. *krasis* mixture]. A state of health; proper balance of different factors constituting a healthy state.

eudiaphoresis (u-di″ah-fo-re′sis) [*eu-* + *diaphoresis*]. An easy, natural, or comforting escape of perspiration.

eudiemorrhysis (u″di-ĕ-mor′ĭ-sis) [*eu-* + Gr. *dia* through + *haima* blood + *rhysis* flow]. The normal flow of blood through the capillaries.

eudiometer (u″de-om′e-ter) [Gr. *eudia* fine weather + *metron* measure]. An instrument used in testing the purity of the air.

eudipsia (u-dip′se-ah) [*eu-* + Gr. *dipsa* thirst + *-ia*]. Ordinary, mild thirst.

euergasia (u″er-ga′se-ah) [*eu-* + *ergasia*]. Normal psychobiological functioning.

euesthesia (u″es-the′ze-ah) [*eu-* + Gr. *aisthēsis* perception]. A normal state of the senses.

Euflagellata (u-flaj″ĕ-la′tah). Flagellata.

euflavine (u-fla′vin). Acriflavine.

eugamy (u′gah-me) [Gr. *eu* well + *gamos* marriage]. The union of gametes, each of which contains the proper (haploid) complement of chromosomes.

eugenetics (u″jĕ-net′iks). Eugenics.

Eugenia (u-je′ne-ah). An extensive genus of myrtaceous trees and shrubs. *E. caryophyllata* furnishes clove; *E. chequen* furnishes cheken; and *E. pimenta* (*Pimenta officinalis*) furnishes pimenta.

eugenics (u-jen′iks) [*eu-* + Gr. *gennan* to generate]. The study and control of various possible influences as a means of improving the hereditary characteristics of a race. **negative e.,** that concerned with prevention of the mating of individuals possessing inferior or undesirable traits. **positive e.,** that concerned with promotion of optimal mating of individuals possessing superior or desirable traits.

eugenism (u′jen-izm). That condition of heredity and environment which tends to produce healthy and happy existence.

eugenist (u-jen′ist). A person who is versed in eugenics.

eugenol (u′jen-ol). An oily, liquid principle, $OH.C_6H_3(OCH_3).C_3H_5$, obtainable from oil of cloves, cinnamon, etc.: an antiseptic and anodyne used in dentistry for the treatment of pulp inflammation.

eugenothenics (u-je″no-then′iks). The study of race improvement by the regulation of both heredity and environment.

Euglena (u-gle′nah) [*eu-* + Gr. *glēnē* pupil of the eye]. A genus of infusorian animals. *E. vir′idis* is found in stagnant pools.

euglobulin (u-glob′u-lin). One of a class of globulins characterized by being insoluble in water but soluble in saline solutions. See also under *globulin*.

euglycemia (u″gli-se′me-ah). A normal level of glucose in the blood.

euglycemic (u″gli-se′mik). Pertaining to, characterized by, or conducive to euglycemia.

eugnathic (u-nath′ik) [*eu-* + Gr. *gnathos* jaw]. Pertaining to or characterized by a normal state of the maxilla and mandible.

eugnosia (u-no′se-ah) [*eu-* + Gr. *gnōsis* perception]. Ability to recognize and synthesize sensory stimuli into a normal perception.

eugnostic (u-nos′tik). Pertaining to eugnosia.

eugonic (u-gon′ik) [*eu-* + Gr. *gonē* seed]. Growing luxuriantly: said of bacterial cultures.

eukaryosis (u″kar-e-o′sis) [*eu-* + Gr. *karyon* nucleus + *-osis*]. The state of having a true nucleus, the nuclear material being surrounded by a membrane and containing organelles.

eukaryotic (u″kar-e-ot′ik). Pertaining to or characterized by eukaryosis.

eukeratin (u-ker′ah-tin). A true keratin found in hair, nails, feathers, and horns.

eukinesia (u″ki-ne′se-ah) [Gr. *eu* well + *kinēsis* movement + *-ia*]. The state of possessing normal or proper motor function or activity; normal or proper mobility.

eukinesis (u″ki-ne′sis). Eukinesia.

eukinetic (u″ki-net′ik). Pertaining to or characterized by eukinesia.

eulachon (u′lah-kon). The candle-fish, *Thaleichthys pacificus:* its oil is used like cod liver oil.

Eulenburg's disease (oil′en-burgz) [Albert *Eulenburg*, German neurologist, 1840–1917]. Myotonia congenita.

eumenorrhea (u″men-o-re′ah) [*eu-* + Gr. *mēn* menses + *rhoia* flow]. A normal menstruation.

eumetria (u-me′tre-ah) [Gr. "good measure," "good proportion"]. A normal condition of nerve impulse, so that a voluntary movement just reaches the intended goal; the proper range of movement.

eumorphics (u-mor′fiks). A branch of orthopedics which deals with the re-establishment of normal or proper form.

eumorphism (u-mor′fizm) [*eu-* + Gr. *morphē* form]. Retention of the normal form of a cell.

Eumycetes (u″mi-se′tēz). A class of Thallophyta including all the true fungi.

eunoia (u-noi′ah) [*eu-* + Gr. *nous* mind]. Alertness of mind and will.

eunuch (u′nuk) [Gr. *eunouchos* a castrated person, employed in Asia, and later in Greece, to take charge of the women and act as a chamberlain]. A man or boy deprived of the testes or the external genital organs.

eunuchism (u′nuk-izm) [Gr. *eunouchismos* castration]. The condition of a castrated male. **pituitary e.,** loss of sexual power due to derangement of the pituitary secretion.

eunuchoid (u′nuk-oid) [Gr. *eunouchoeidēs*]. 1. Resembling a eunuch; having the characteristics of a eunuch. 2. A cryptorchid person with defective masculinity of appearance, causing him to resemble a eunuch.

eunuchoidism (u′nuk-oid″izm). A deficiency of the testes or of the testicular secretion, with impaired sexual power and eunuch-like symptoms.

euosmia (u-os′me-ah) [*eu-* + Gr. *osmē* smell]. 1. Normal state of the sense of smell. 2. A pleasant odor.

eupancreatism (u-pan′kre-ah-tizm). A normal condition of the pancreatic function.

Eupatorium (u″pah-to′re-um). A genus of composite-flowered plants. The leaves and tops of *E. perfoliatum*, boneset or thoroughwort, are tonic, diuretic, diaphoretic, and stomachic.

eupepsia (u-pep′se-ah) [*eu-* + Gr. *pepsis* digestion + *-ia*]. Good digestion; particularly the presence of a normal amount of pepsin in the gastric juice.

eupepsy (u′pep-se). Eupepsia.

eupeptic (u-pep′tik). Pertaining to, characterized by, or promoting eupepsia.

euperistalsis (u-per″ĭ-stal′sis). Normal or painless peristalsis.

euphagia (u-fa′je-ah) [*eu-* + Gr. *phagein* to eat]. A normal and proper manner of eating.

euphoretic (u″fo-ret′ik). 1. Pertaining to, characterized by, or producing a condition of euphoria. 2. An agent that produces euphoria.

euphoria (u-fo′re-ah) [Gr. "the power of bearing easily"]. Bodily comfort; well-being; absence of pain or distress. In psychiatry, an abnormal or exaggerated sense of well-being.

euphoriant (u-fo′re-ant). Euphoretic.

euphoric (u-fo′rik). Characterized by euphoria.

euphorigenic (u-fōr″ĭ-jen′ik). Tending to produce euphoria.

euphoristic (u″fo-ris′tik). Causing euphoria.

euphoropsia (u″fōr-op′se-ah) [*euphoria* + Gr. *opsis* vision]. Comfortable vision.

eupiesia (u″pi-e′se-ah). Eupiesis.

eupiesis (u″pi-e′sis) [*eu-* + Gr. *piesis* pressure]. Normal pressure, as normal blood pressure, or normal pressure within a specific organ.

eupietic (u″pi-et′ik). Pertaining to or characterized by eupiesis.

euplastic (u-plas′tik) [*eu-* + Gr. *plastikos* plastic]. Readily becoming organized; adapted to the formation of tissue.

euploid (u′ploid) [*eu-* + *-ploid*]. 1. Having a balanced set or sets of chromosomes, in any number. 2. An individual or cell having a balanced set or sets of chromosomes, in any number.

euploidy (u-ploi′de). The state of having a balanced set or sets of chromosomes, in any number.

eupnea (ūp-ne′ah) [*eu-* + Gr. *pnein* to breathe]. Easy or normal respiration.

eupneic (ūp-ne′ik). Pertaining to or characterized by eupnea.

eupractic (u-prak′tic) [*eu-* + Gr. *praktikos* active, able, effective]. Pertaining to, characterized by, or promoting eupraxia.

eupraxia (u-prak′se-ah) [Gr. "good conduct"]. Intactness of reproduction of coordinated movements.

eupraxic (u-prak′sik). 1. Concerned in the proper performance of a function. 2. Eupractic.

Euproctis (u-prok′tis). A genus of moths. **E. chrysorrhoe′a (phaeorrhoe′a),** the brown-tail moth, which may be the cause of a dermatitis.

eupyrene (u-pi′rēn). Having a normal nucleus or chromatic material: said of certain spermatozoa.

eupyrexia (u″pi-rek′se-ah). A slight fever in the early stage of an infection, regarded as an attempt on the part of the organism to combat the infection.

eupyrous (u′pi-rus). Eupyrene.

eurax (u′raks). Trade mark for preparations of crotamiton.

eurhythmia (u-rith′me-ah) [Gr. "harmony"]. 1. Harmonious relationships in body or organ development. 2. Regularity of the pulse.

europium (u-ro′pe-um). A rare element, atomic number 63, atomic weight 151.96, symbol Eu.

Eurotium (u-ro′she-um) [Gr. *eurōs* mold]. A genus of fungi or molds. **E. re′pens,** a species sometimes seen on bread and on preserved fruits. **E. malig′num,** a species occasionally found in the ear.

eury- (u′re) [Gr. *eurys* wide]. Combining form meaning wide or broad.

eurycephalic (u″re-sĕ-fal′ik) [*eury-* + Gr. *kephalē* head]. Having a wide head.

eurycephalous (u″re-sef′ah-lus). Eurycephalic.

eurycranial (u″re-kra′ne-al). Eurycephalic.

eurygnathic (u″rig-nath′ik). Pertaining to or characterized by eurygnathism.

eurygnathism (u-rig′nah-thizm) [*eury-* + Gr. *gnathos* jaw]. The state of having a wide jaw.

euryon (u′re-on) [Gr. *eurys* wide]. The point at either end of the greatest transverse diameter of the skull.

euryopia (u″re-o′pe-ah) [*eury-* + Gr. *ōps* eye]. Abnormally wide opening of the eyes.

Eurypelma (u″re-pel′mah). A genus of tarantulas. **E. hent′zii,** the American tarantula.

euryphotic (u″re-fo′tik) [*eury-* + Gr. *phōs* light]. Able to see in a wide range of light intensity.

eurysomatic (u″re-so-mat′ik) [*eury-* + Gr. *sōma* body]. Having a squat, thick-set body.

eurythermic (u″re-ther′mik) [*eury-* + Gr. *thermē* heat]. Able to grow through a wide range of temperature: said of bacteria.

euscope (u′skōp) [Gr. *eu* well + *skopein* to examine]. A device for projecting the image from a compound microscope upon a barium screen in a dark chamber so that it may be easily viewed.

Euscorpius (u-skor′pe-us). A genus of scorpions. **E. ital′icus,** the black scorpion of Europe and North Africa.

Eusimulium (u″sĭ-mu′le-um). A genus of flies of the family Simuliidae, various species of which are common hosts of *Onchocerca volvulus*, a filarial worm that is parasitic in man.

eusitia (u-sit′e-ah) [*eu-* + Gr. *sitos* food]. Normal appetite.

eusplanchnia (u-splank′ne-ah) [Gr. *eu* well + *splanchna* viscera + *-ia*]. A normal condition of the internal organs.

eusplenia (u-sple′ne-ah). Normal splenic function.

eustachian (u-sta′ke-an) [named after Bartolommeo *Eustachio* (L. *Eustachius*), an Italian anatomist, 1520–1574]. See under *canal*, *tube*, *valve*, etc.

eustachitis (u″sta-ki′tis). Inflammation of the eustachian tube.

eustachium (u-sta′ke-um). The eustachian tube.

eusthenia (u-sthen′e-ah) [*eu-* + Gr. *sthenos* strength]. A condition of normal sthenia.

eusthenuria (u″sthen-u′re-ah) [*eu* + G. *sthenos* strength + *ouron* urine + *-ia*]. A normal state of the urine as regards osmolality.

Eustis' test (u′stis) [Allan Chotard *Eustis*, American physician, born 1876]. See under *test*.

Eustrongylus (u-stron′jĭ-lus). Former name of a genus of nematode parasites. **E. gi′gas,** *Dioctophyma renale*.

eusystole (u-sis′to-le) [*eu-* + *systole*]. A normal state of the systole of the heart.

eusystolic (u″sis-tol′ik). Pertaining to or characterized by eusystole.

Eutamias (u-tam′e-as). The western chipmunk which harbors the plague-infected fleas, *Monopsyllus eumolpi*, and has been found infected with plague.

eutectic (u-tek′tik) [Gr. *eutēktos* easily melted or dissolved]. Melting readily: said of a mixture that melts more easily than any of its ingredients.

eutelegenesis (u-tel″e-jen′e-sis) [*eu-* + Gr. *tēle* far off + *genesis* reproduction]. Artificial insemination by semen of a donor selected because of special characteristics for the production of superior offspring.

eutelolecithal (u-tel″o-les′ĭ-thal) [*eu-* + *telolecithal*]. Having deutoplasm greatly in excess of the cell protoplasm: said of the ova of birds and many reptiles. Cf. *oligolecithal* and *telolecithal*.

eutexia (u-tek′se-ah) [*eu-* + Gr. *tēxis* a melting]. 1. The state of being stable and well combined. 2. The union of two solids to form a liquid.

euthanasia (u″thah-na′ze-ah) [*eu-* + Gr. *thanatos* death]. 1. An easy or painless death. 2. Mercy death; the putting to death of a person suffering from an incurable disease.

euthenic (u-then′ik). Conducive to race improvement through environment.

euthenics (u-then′iks) [Gr. *euthēnia* well-being]. The science of race improvement through the regulation of environment.

eutherapeutic (u-ther″ah-pu′tik) [*eu-* + *therapeutic*]. Having good therapeutic properties.

euthermic (u-ther′mik) [Gr. *euthermos* very warm]. Characterized by the proper temperature.

euthymism (u-thi′mizm). A normal condition of thymus activity.

euthyphoria (u″the-fo′re-ah) [Gr. *euthys* straight + *pherein* to bear]. Normal relationship of the visual axis, without deviation when fusion is prevented.

euthyroid (u-thi′roid). Having a normally functioning thyroid gland.

euthyroidism (u-thi′roid-ism). A condition of normal thyroid function.

eutocia (u-to′se-ah) [Gr. *eutokia*]. Normal labor, or childbirth.

eutopic (u-top′ik) [*eu-* + Gr. *topos* place]. Situated normally. Cf. *ectopic*.

eutrepisty (u′trĕ-pis″te) [Gr. *eutrepēs* well prepared]. The practice of administering a remedy before an operation to lessen the danger of infection.

Eutriatoma (u″trĭ-at′o-mah). A genus of reduviid bugs, species of which transmit Chagas' disease.

eutrichosis (u″tri-ko′sis) [*eu-* + Gr. *thrix, trichos* hair]. A normal development of the hair.

Eutrombicula (u″trom-bik′u-lah). A genus of mites of the family Trombiculidae. See *chigger.* **E. alfreddugèsi,** the common chigger of the United States.

eutrophia (u-tro′fe-ah) [*eu-* + Gr. *trophē* nourishment + *-ia*]. A state of normal (good) nutrition.

eutrophic (u-trof′ik). Pertaining to, characterized by, or conducive to good nutrition.

euxanthon (u-zan′thon). A ketone, dioxydiphenylene ketone oxide, $CO(C_6H_3OH)_2O$, obtained from Indian yellow.

evacuant (e-vak′u-ant) [L. *evacuans* making empty]. 1. Emptying; serving to clear the bowels. 2. A remedy which empties any organ; a cathartic, emetic, or diuretic.

evacuation (e-vak″u-a′shun) [L. *evacuatio,* from *e* out + *vacuus* empty]. 1. An emptying, as of the bowels. 2. A dejection or stool; material discharged from the bowels.

evacuator (e-vak′u-a-tor). An instrument for compelling an evacuation, as of the bowels or bladder, or for removing fluid or small particles from a cavity.

evagination (e-vaj″ĭ-na′shun). An outpouching of a layer or part. **optic e.,** optic vesicle.

evanescent (ev″ah-nes′ent) [L. *evanescere* to vanish away]. Vanishing; passing away quickly; unstable; unfixed.

evaporation (e-vap″o-ra′shun) [L. *e* out + *vaporare* to steam]. Conversion of a liquid or solid into vapor.

Eve's method (ēvz) [F. C. *Eve,* English physician, 1871–1952]. A method of artificial respiration. See under *respiration, artificial.*

evectics (e-vek′tiks) [L. *evehere* to lift up]. The study of methods of acquiring a good habit of body.

eventration (e″ven-tra′shun) [L. *eventratio* disembowelment, from *e* out + *venter* belly]. 1. Protrusion of the bowels from the abdomen. 2. Removal of the abdominal viscera. **diaphragmatic e.,** elevation of the dome of the diaphragm as the result of congenital atrophy and thinning of the diaphragm on the left side.

Eversbusch's operation (a′vārz-boosh″ez) [Oskar *Eversbusch,* German ophthalmologist, 1853–1912]. See under *operation.*

eversion (e-ver′zhun) [L. *eversio*]. A turning outward or inside out.

evert (e-vert′) [L. *e* out + *vertere* to turn]. To turn inside out; to turn out.

évidement (a-vēd-maw′) [Fr.]. The operation of scooping out a cavity or a diseased portion of an organ.

évideur (a-ve-dur′) [Fr.]. An instrument for performing évidement.

evil (e′vil). An illness or disease. **king's e.,** scrofula. **poll e.,** an abscess behind the ears of a horse, caused by a dual infection of the supra-atlantal bursa by Brucella and Actinomyces. **quarter e.,** symptomatic anthrax. **St. John's e.,** epilepsy. **St. Main's e.,** itch. **St. Martin's e.,** drunkenness.

evipal (e-vi′pal). Trade mark for a preparation of hexobarbital.

eviration (e″vi-ra′shun) [L. *e* out + *vir* man]. 1. Castration. 2. A form of paranoia in which the patient believes he is a woman, and assumes feminine qualities.

evisceration (e-vis″er-a′shun) [L. *evisceratio; e* out + *viscus* the inside of the body]. Removal of the viscera, or internal organs; disembowelment. Used in connection with the eye, it denotes removal of the contents of the eyeball, the sclera being left intact.

E-viton (e-vi′ton). The unit of quantity of biologically effective ultraviolet radiation.

evocation (ev″o-ka′shun) [L. *e* out + *vocare* to call]. The calling forth of morphogenetic potentialities through contact with organizer material, living or dead.

evocator (ev′o-ka″ter). A chemical substance emitted by an organizer region of an embryo that evokes a specific morphogenetic response from embryonic tissue in contact with it.

evolution (ev″o-lu′shun) [L. *evolutio,* from *e* out + *volvere* to roll]. 1. An unrolling. 2. A process of development in which an organ or organism becomes more and more complex by the differentiation of its parts; a continuous and progressive change according to certain laws and by means of resident forces. 3. Preformation. **bathmic e.,** evolution due to something in the organism itself independent of environment. Called also *orthogenic e.* **convergent e.,** the appearance of similar forms and/or functions in two or more lines not sufficiently related phylogenetically to account for the similarity. **Denman's spontaneous e.,** a mechanism of spontaneous version in transverse presentations in which the head rotates behind, and as the breech descends the shoulder ascends in the pelvis, the breech finally coming down and emerging. **determinate e.,** orthogenesis. **emergent e.,** the assumption that each step in evolution produces something new and something that could not be predicted from its antecedents. **organic e.,** the origin and development of species; the theory that existing organisms are the result of descent with modification from those of past times. **orthogenic e.,** bathmic e. **saltatory e.,** evolution showing sudden changes; mutation or saltation. **spontaneous e.,** the unaided expulsion of a transversely placed fetus without the process of version or turning.

evolutive (ev″o-lu′tiv). Relating to evolution; specifically applied to a type of mental defect characterized by retardation of the evolutionary process.

evulsio (e-vul′se-o) [L., from *e* out + *vellere* to pluck]. Evulsion. **e. ner′vi op′tici,** the tearing out of the optic nerve from the eyeball.

evulsion (e-vul′shun) [L. *evulsio*]. The plucking or tearing out, as of a polypus. See *avulsion.*

Ewald's enema, test meal (a′vahlts) [Carl Anton *Ewald,* physician in Berlin, 1845–1915]. See under *enema* and *test meal.*

Ewart's sign (u′arts) [William *Ewart,* English physician, 1848–1929]. See under *sign.*

Ewing's tumor (u′ingz) [James *Ewing,* New York pathologist, 1866–1943]. See under *tumor.*

ex- (eks) [L. *ex;* Gr. *ex* out, away from]. A prefix meaning away from, without, or outside, and sometimes used to denote completely, as in *exacerbation.*

exacerbation (eks-as″er-ba′shun) [*ex-* + L. *acerbus* harsh]. Increase in the severity of any symptoms or disease.

exacrinous (eks-ak′rĭ-nus) [*ex-* + Gr. *krinein* to secrete]. Pertaining to the external secretion of a gland.

exairesis (eks-er′ĕ-sis) [Gr. "a taking out"]. Exeresis.

exaltation (eg″zawl-ta′shun). An abnormal mental state, marked by a feeling of great importance and ecstatic spiritual elevation.

examination (eks-am″ĭ-na′tion) [L. *examinare*]. Inspection or investigation, especially as a means of diagnosing disease, qualified according to the methods employed, as physical examination, roentgen examination, cystoscopic examination, etc. **recto-abdominal e.,** bimanual examination with the fingers of one hand in the rectum and the other hand on the abdomen.

exangia (eks-an′je-ah) [*ex-* + Gr. *angeion* vessel]. Dilatation of a blood vessel.

exania (ek-sa′ne-ah) [*ex-* + L. *anus*]. Prolapse of the rectum.

exanimation (eg-zan″ĭ-ma′shun). Unconsciousness; coma.

exanthem (ek-san′them) [Gr. *exanthēma*]. 1. Any eruptive disease or eruptive fever. 2. The eruption which characterizes an eruptive fever. See *eruption*. **vesicular e.,** a vesicular eruption in horses marked by the formation of nodules, vesicles, and pustules in the mucous membrane of the vagina and the skin of the vulva and penis.

exanthema (eks″an-the′mah), pl. *exanthe′mas, exanthem′ata* [Gr. *exanthēma*]. Exanthem. **e. subitum,** a condition frequently seen in children, marked by remittent fever lasting three days, falling by crisis, and followed a few hours later by a rash on the trunk. Called also *Duke's disease, fourth disease, parascarlatina,* and *roseola infantum.*

exanthematous (ek″san-them′ah-tus). Pertaining to, characterized by, or of the nature of, an exanthem.

exanthrope (ek′zan-thrōp) [*ex-* + Gr. *anthrōpos* man]. Any source of disease not situated within the human body.

exanthropic (ek″zan-throp′ik). Of the nature of an exanthrope; not situated within the human body.

exarteritis (eks″ar-tĕ-ri′tis) [*ex-* + *arteritis*]. Inflammation of the outer arterial coat.

exarticulation (eks″ar-tik-u-la′shun) [*ex-* + L. *articulus* joint]. Amputation at a joint; removal of a portion of a joint.

excalation (eks″kah-la′shun). Absence or exclusion of one member of a normal series, such as a vertebra.

excarnation (eks″kar-na′shun) [*ex-* + L. *caro, carnis* flesh]. Removal of superfluous carneous tissue from a preparation.

excavatio (eks″kah-va′she-o), pl. *excavatio′nes* [L., from *ex* out + *cavus* hollow]. A general term used in anatomical nomenclature to designate a hollowed-out space, or pouchlike cavity. **e. papil′lae ner′vi op′tici** [N A, B N A], a depression in the center of the optic disk. Called also *optic* or *physiological cup.* **e. rectouteri′na** [N A, B N A], a sac or recess formed by a fold of the peritoneum dipping down between the rectum and the uterus. Called also *cul-de-sac of Douglas,* and *rectouterine pouch.* **e. rectovesica′lis** [N A, B N A], the space between the rectum and the bladder in the peritoneal cavity of the male. Called also *rectovesical pouch.* **e. vesicouteri′na** [N A, B N A], the space between the bladder and the uterus in the peritoneal cavity. Called also *uterovesical pouch.*

excavation (eks″kah-va′shun) [L. *excavatio*]. 1. The act of hollowing out. 2. A hollowed-out space, or pouchlike cavity. **atrophic e.,** the cupping of the optic disk, caused by atrophy of the optic nerve fibers. **dental e.,** removal of carious material from a tooth in preparation for filling. **glaucomatous e.,** cupping of the optic disk, which is total and due to abnormally high intraocular pressure. **ischiorectal e.,** fossa ischiorectalis. **e. of optic disk, physiologic e.,** excavatio papillae nervi optici. **rectoischiadic e.,** fossa ischiorectalis. **rectouterine e.,** excavatio rectouterina. **rectovesical e.,** excavatio rectovesicalis. **vesicouterine e.,** excavatio vesicouterina.

excavationes (eks″kah-va″she-o′nēz) [L.]. Plural of *excavatio.*

excavator (eks′kah-va″tor). A form of scoop or gouge for surgeons' use. **dental e.,** an instrument for removing carious material from a tooth and shaping the internal walls of a cavity.

excelsin (ek-sel′sin). A crystalline globulin from the Brazil nut.

excementosis (ek-se″men-to′sis). Hyperplasia of the cementum of the root of a tooth.

excentric (ek-sen′trik). Eccentric.

excerebration (ek″ser-ĕ-bra′shun) [*ex-* + L. *cerebrum* brain]. The removal of the brain, chiefly that of the fetus in embryotomy.

excernant (ek-ser′nant) [L. *excernere* to excrete, to purge]. Causing an evacuation or discharge.

exchanger (eks-chānj′er). An apparatus by which something may be exchanged. **heat e.,** a device which is placed in the circuit of extracorporeal circulation, to induce rapid cooling and rewarming of blood.

excipient (ek-sip′e-ent) [L. *excipiens,* from *ex* out + *capere* to take]. Any more or less inert substance added to a prescription in order to confer a suitable consistency or form to the drug; a vehicle.

excise (ek-sīz′). To cut out or off.

excision (ek-sizh′un) [L. *excisio,* from *ex* out + *caedere* to cut]. An act of cutting away or taking out. **wound e.,** débridement.

excitability (ek-sīt″ah-bil′ĭ-te). Readiness to respond to a stimulus; irritability.

excitable (ek-sīt′ah-b'l) [L. *excitabilis*]. Susceptible of stimulation; responding to a stimulus.

excitant (ek-sīt′ant). Any agent which produces excitation of the vital functions, or of those of the brain.

excitation (ek″si-ta′shun) [L. *excitatio,* from *ex* out + *citare* to call]. An act of irritation or stimulation; a condition of being excited. **anomalous atrioventricular e.,** Wolff-Parkinson-White syndrome. **direct e.,** the stimulation of a muscle by placing an electrode on the muscle itself. **indirect e.,** the stimulation of a muscle through its nerve.

excitatory (ek-si′tah-to″re). 1. Tending to excitation or stimulation. 2. Tending to disassimilation.

excito-anabolic (ek-si″to-an″ah-bol′ik). Stimulating anabolism or constructive metabolism.

excitocatabolic (ek-si″to-kat″ah-bol′ik). Stimulating catabolism or destructive metabolism.

excitoglandular (ek-si″to-glan′du-lar). Causing activity of the glandular functions.

excitometabolic (ek-si″to-met″ah-bol′ik). Producing metabolic changes.

excitomotor (ek-si″to-mo′tor). 1. Tending to produce motion or motor function. 2. An agent which induces motion or functional activity.

excitomotory (ek-si″to-mo′to-re). Excitomotor.

excitomuscular (ek-si″to-mus′ku-lar). Stimulating muscular activity.

excitonutrient (ek-si″to-nu′tre-ent). Exciting or stimulating nutrition.

excitor (ek-si′tor). A nerve, the stimulation of which excites greater action in the part which it supplies.

excitosecretory (ek-si″to-se′kre-to-re). Producing increased secretion.

excitovascular (ek-si″to-vas′ku-lar). Causing vascular changes, with consequent flushings and erections, and probably certain skin diseases.

exclave (eks′klāv) [*ex-* + L. *clavis* key, by analogy with *enclave*]. A detached part of an organ, as of the pancreas or of some other gland.

exclusion (eks-kloo′zhun) [L. *exclusio,* from *ex* out + *claudere* to shut]. The act or process of ejecting, rejecting, or extruding. Specifically, an operation in which a portion of an organ is separated from the rest of the organ, but is not removed from the body.

excochleation (eks-kok″le-a′shun) [*ex-* + L. *cochlea* spoon]. The operation of curetting or scooping out a cavity.

exconjugant (eks-kon′ju-gahnt) [L. *ex* + *conjugare* to unite]. A protozoan that has just undergone conjugation.

excoriation (eks-ko″re-a′shun) [L. *excoriare* to flay, from *ex* out + *corium* skin]. Any superficial loss of substance, such as that produced on the skin by scratching.

excrement (eks′krĕ-ment) [L. *excrementum*, from *ex* out + *cernere* to separate]. Fecal matter; matter cast out as waste from the body.

excrementitious (eks″krĕ-men-tish′us). Pertaining to or of the nature of excrement; fecal.

excrescence (eks-kres′ens) [*ex-* + L. *crescere* to grow]. Any abnormal outgrowth; a projection of morbid origin. **cauliflower e.,** verruca acuminata. **fungating e., fungous e.,** a fungous growth in the umbilicus after separation of the umbilical cord; granuloma of the umbilicus. **Lambl's e's,** small papillary projections on the cardiac valves seen post mortem on many adult hearts, possibly the result of endocarditis.

excrescent (eks-kres′ent). Resembling or of the nature of an excrescence.

excreta (eks-kre′tah) [L., pl.]. Excretion products; waste materials excreted by the body.

excrete (eks-krēt′) [L. *excernere*]. To throw off, as waste matter, by a normal discharge.

excretin (eks′kre-tin). A crystalline compound, $C_{20}H_{36}O$, derivable from human feces.

excretion (eks-kre′shun) [L. *excretio*]. 1. The act, process, or function of excreting. 2. Material which is excreted.

excretory (eks′kre-to-re). Of or pertaining to or subserving excretion.

excurrent (eks-kur′ent). Excretory; efferent.

excursion (eks-kur′zhun) [L. *excursio*, from *ex* out + *currere* to run]. Movements occurring from a normal, or rest, position of a movable part in performance of a function, as those of the mandible to attain functional contact between the cusps of the mandibular and maxillary teeth in mastication, or of the chest wall in respiration. **lateral e.,** sideward movement of the mandible between the position of closure and that in which the tips of the cusps of opposing teeth are in vertical proximity. **protrusive e.,** movement of the mandible between the position of closure and that in which the incisal edges of the anterior teeth are in vertical approximation. **retrusive e.,** the slight backward and return movement of the mandible between the position of closure and one slightly posterior.

excursive (eks-kur′sive). Pertaining to or characterized by excursion.

excyclophoria (ek″si-klo-fo′re-ah). Cyclophoria in which the upper pole of the vertical axis of the eye deviates away from the midline of the face and toward the temple. Called also *positive* (or *plus*) *cyclophoria.*

excyclotropia (ek″si-klo-tro′pe-ah). Cyclotropia in which the upper pole of the vertical axis of the eye deviates away from the midline of the face, and toward the temple. Called also *positive* (or *plus*) *cyclotropia.*

excystation (ek″sis-ta′shun). Escape from a cyst or envelope; especially a stage in the life cycle of parasites occurring after the cystic form has been swallowed by the host.

exelcin (ek-sel′sin). A substance extracted from Brazil nut.

exelcymosis (ek″sel-si-mo′sis) [*ex-* + Gr. *helkyein* to draw]. Extraction, as of a tooth.

exemia (ek-se′me-ah) [*ex-* + Gr. *haima* blood + *-ia*]. Loss of fluid from the blood vessels, the red cells being left behind. Cf. *hemoconcentration.*

exencephalia (eks″en-sĕ-fa′le-ah) [*ex-* + Gr. *enkephalos* brain + *-ia*]. A developmental anomaly characterized by an imperfect cranium, the brain lying outside of the skull.

exencephalon (eks″en-sef′ah-lon). Exencephalus.

exencephalous (eks″en-sef′ah-lus). Characterized by exencephalia.

exencephalus (eks″en-sef′ah-lus) [*ex-* + Gr. *enkephalos* brain]. A fetal monster exhibiting exencephalia.

exencephaly (eks″en-sef′ah-le). Exencephalia.

exenteration (eks-en″ter-a′shun) [*ex-* + Gr. *enteron* bowel]. Surgical removal of the inner organs; commonly used to indicate radical excision of the contents of a body cavity, as of the pelvis. Used in connection with the eye, it denotes removal of the entire contents of the orbit. **pelvic e.,** excision of the organs and adjacent structures of the pelvis. **pelvic e., anterior,** excision en masse of the bladder, lower ureters, vagina, adnexa, pelvic lymph nodes, and pelvic peritoneum, with implantation of the ureters into the intact pelvic colon. **pelvic e., posterior,** excision en masse of the pelvic colon, uterus, vagina, and adnexa, with or without pelvic lymph node excision, the lower urinary tract being undisturbed. **pelvic e., total,** excision en masse of the bladder, lower ureters, vagina, uterus, adnexa, and the pelvic and lower sigmoid colon, with excision of the pelvic lymph nodes and removal of all the pelvic peritoneum.

exenteritis (eks-en″ter-i′tis). Inflammation of the peritoneal covering of the intestine.

exercise (ek′ser-sīz). The performance of physical exertion for improvement of health or the correction of physical deformity. **active e.,** motion imparted to a part by voluntary contraction and relaxation of the muscles controlling the part. **active resistive e.,** that performed voluntarily by the patient against resistance supplied by another or by his own physiologically antagonistic muscles. **corrective e.,** the scientific use of bodily movement to maintain or restore normal function in diseased or injured tissues. **free e.,** active exercise in which no aid is derived from external forces. **muscle-setting e.,** static e. **passive e.,** motion imparted to a segment of the body by another individual, machine, or other outside force, or produced by voluntary effort of another segment of the patient's own body. **static e.,** active contraction and relaxation of a muscle or of a group of muscles without producing motion of the joint which it ordinarily mobilizes. **therapeutic e.,** corrective e. **underwater e.,** exercise performed in a pool or a large tub. Cf. *Hubbard tank.*

exeresis (eks-er′ĕ-sis) [Gr. *exairesis* a taking out]. Removal or excision of a nerve, vessel, or other part or organ.

exergic (ek-ser′jik) [*ex-* + Gr. *ergon* work]. Giving out work: a term applied to chemical reactions which occur with a decrease in free energy. Cf. *endergic.*

exergonic (ek″ser-gon′ik). Characterized or accompanied by the release of energy.

exesion (eg-ze′zhun) [L. *exedere* to eat out]. The gradual destruction of superficial parts of a tissue.

exfetation (eks″fe-ta′shun) [*ex-* + L. *fetus*]. Extrauterine pregnancy.

exflagellation (eks″flaj-ĕ-la′shun) [*ex-* + L. *flagellum*]. The protrusion or formation of flagella by a protozoon, such as the formation of microgametes (male gametes) from a microgametocyte in malaria.

exfoliatio (eks″fo-le-a′she-o) [L., from *ex-* + *folium* leaf]. Exfoliation. **e. area′ta lin′guae,** geographical tongue.

exfoliation (eks″fo-le-a′shun) [L. *exfoliatio*]. A falling off in scales or layers.

exfoliative (eks-fo′le-a″tiv). Characterized by exfoliation.

exhalation (eks″hah-la′shun) [L. *exhalatio*, from *ex* out + *halare* to breathe]. 1. The giving off of watery or other vapor, or of an effluvium. 2. A vapor or other substance exhaled or given off.

exhale (eks-hāl′) [*ex-* + L. *halare* to breathe]. 1. To expel from the lungs by breathing. 2. To give off a watery or other vapor.

exhaustion (eg-zawst′yun) [*ex-* + L. *haurire* to drain]. 1. Privation of energy with consequent inability to respond to stimuli. 2. Withdrawal. 3. Condition of emptiness caused by withdrawal. 4. Emptying by a process of withdrawal. **heat e.,** a form of heat stroke or shock occurring commonly among workers in furnace rooms, foundries, etc., although it may occur from exposure to the sun's heat. It is marked by subnormal temperature, with dizziness, nausea and sometimes collapse. Called also *heat prostration.* **heat e., anhidrotic, heat e., type II,** tropical anhidrotic asthenia. **nervous e.,** depression of vital functions due to excessive demands upon the nervous energy; neurasthenia.

Exhib. Abbreviation for L. *exhibea'tur,* let it be given.

exhibit (eg-zib'it) [L. *exhibere* to administer]. To administer as a remedy. **scientific e.,** a display depicting results of original investigation or scientific correlation of facts: generally held in connection with state or national medical gatherings.

exhibition (ek"sĭ-bish'un). Administration of a drug.

exhibitionism (ek"sĭ-bish'un-izm). The display of one's body or parts (even the genitals) for the purpose, conscious or unconscious, of attracting sexual interest.

exhibitionist (ek"sĭ-bish'un-ist). An individual who is addicted to exhibitionism.

exhilarant (eg-zil'ar-ant) [L. *exhilarare* to gladden]. 1. Causing elevation or gladness. 2. An enlivening or elating agent.

exhumation (eks"hu-ma'shun) [*ex-* + L. *humus* earth]. Disinterment; removal of the dead body from the earth after burial.

exitus (ek'sĭ-tus), pl. *exitus* [L. "a going out"]. 1. Death. 2. An exit or outlet. **e. pel'vis,** apertura pelvis inferior.

Exner's nerve, plexus (eks'nerz) [Siegmund *Exner,* Austrian physiologist, 1846–1926]. See under *nerve* and *plexus.*

exo- (ek'so) [Gr. *exō* outside]. A prefix meaning outside, or outward.

exo-antigen (ek"so-an'te-jen). Ecto-antigen.

exobiology (ek"so-bi-ol'o-je). The science concerned with the study of life on other planets than the earth.

exocardia (ek"so-kar'de-ah). Ectocardia.

exocardial (ek"so-kar'de-al). Situated, occurring, or developed outside the heart.

exocataphoria (ek"so-kat"ah-fo're-ah) [*exo-* + *cataphoria*]. The condition in which the visual axis turns downward and outward.

exochorion (ek"so-ko're-on). That part of the chorion which is derived from the ectoderm.

exocoelom (ek"so-se'lom) [*exo-* + *coelom*]. The portion of the coelom which is situated external to the embryo.

exocoeloma (ek"so-se-lo'mah). Exocoelom.

exocolitis (ek"so-ko-li'tis) [*exo-* + *colitis*]. Inflammation of the outer coat of the colon.

exocrine (ek-so'krin) [*exo-* + Gr. *krinein* to separate]. 1. Secreting outwardly: the opposite of endocrine. 2. The external secretion of a gland.

exocrinology (ek"so-krĭ-nol'o-je). The study of substances secreted externally by individuals which effect integration of a group of organisms.

exocrinosity (ek"so-krĭ-nos'ĭ-te). The quality or state of secreting externally.

exocyclic (ek-so-si'klik). A term applied to cyclic chemical compounds having their double bond in the side chain.

exodeviation (ek"so-de"ve-a'shun). A turning outward. In ophthalmology, exophoria.

exodic (eks-od'ik) [*ex-* + Gr. *hodos* way]. Centrifugal or efferent.

exodontia (ek"so-don'she-ah). Exodontics.

exodontics (ek"so-don'tiks). That branch of dentistry dealing with extraction of the teeth.

exodontist (ek"so-don'tist). A dentist who practices exodontics.

exodontology (ek"so-don-tol'o-je). That department of dentistry which deals with extraction of the teeth.

exo-enzyme (ek"so-en'zīm). An extracellular enzyme; an enzyme which acts outside of the cells in which it originates.

exo-erythrocytic (ek"so-e-rith"ro-si'tik). Outside of the erythrocyte, a term applied to a stage in the development of certain malarial parasites which takes place in tissue cells instead of in erythrocytes.

exogamy (eks-og'ah-me) [*exo-* + Gr. *gamos* marriage]. 1. Protozoon fertilization by the union of elements that are not derived from the same cell. Cf. *autogamy* and *endogamy.* 2. Heterosexuality.

exogastric (ek"so-gas'trik). Pertaining to the external coats of the stomach.

exogastritis (ek"so-gas-tri'tis). Inflammation of the external coat of the stomach.

exogastrula (ek"so-gas'troo-lah) [*exo-* + *gastrula*]. A gastrula in which invagination is hindered and the mesentoderm bulges outward.

exogen (eks'o-jen). An obsolete term for a dicotyledonous plant.

exogenetic (ek"so-je-net'ik) [*exo-* + Gr. *gennan* to produce]. Exogenous.

exogenic (ek"so-jen'ik). Exogenous.

exogenous (eks-oj'ĕ-nus) [*exo-* + Gr. *gennan* to produce]. 1. Growing by additions to the outside; in botany, belonging to the class of the exogens. 2. Developed or originating outside the organism.

exognathia (ek"sog-na'the-ah). Prognathism.

exognathion (ek"sog-na'the-on) [*exo-* + Gr. *gnathos* jaw]. The alveolar process of the upper jaw.

exohemophylaxis (ek"so-he"mo-fi-lak'sis) [*exo-* + Gr. *haima* blood + *phylaxis* a guarding]. A procedure consisting of mixing arsphenamine with some of the patient's blood and then injecting the mixture, the object being to reduce the sensitiveness of the blood.

exohysteropexy (ek"so-his'ter-o-pek"se) [*exo-* + Gr. *hystera* uterus + *pēxis* fixation]. Uterine fixation by implanting the fundus in the abdominal wall.

exolever (ek"so-le'ver). A lever-like instrument for extracting tooth roots.

exometer (eks-om'e-ter). An apparatus for measuring the fluorescent quality of the roentgen ray in comparison with units of candle power.

exometritis (eks"o-me-tri'tis) [*exo-* + Gr. *mētra* womb + *-itis*]. Inflammation of the peritoneal or outer surface of the uterus.

exomphalos (eks-om'fah-los) [*ex-* + Gr. *omphalos* navel]. 1. Hernia of the abdominal viscera into the umbilical cord. 2. Umbilical hernia.

exomysium (eks"o-mis'e-um). Perimysium.

exopathic (ek"so-path'ik). Of the nature of an exopathy; originating outside the body.

exopathy (eks-op'ah-the) [*exo-* + Gr. *pathos* disease]. A disease originating in some cause lying outside the organism.

exopeptidase (ek"so-pep'tĭ-dās). A proteolytic enzyme the action of which is limited to terminal peptide linkages.

exophoria (ek-so-fo're-ah) [*exo-* + Gr. *phorein* to bear]. Deviation of a visual axis away from that of the other eye when fusion is prevented.

exophoric (ek"so-for'ik). Pertaining to or characterized by exophoria.

exophthalmic (ek"sof-thal'mik). Of or pertaining to or characterized by exophthalmos.

exophthalmogenic (ek"sof-thal"mo-jen'ik). Causing or producing exophthalmia.

exophthalmometer (ek"sof-thal-mom'e-ter). An instrument for measuring the amount of exophthalmos.

exophthalmometric (ek"sof-thal"mo-met'rik). Pertaining to exophthalmometry.

exophthalmometry (ek"sof-thal-mom'e-tre). Measurement of the extent of protrusion of the eyeball in exophthalmos.

exophthalmos (ek″sof-thal′mos) [*ex-* + Gr. *ophthalmos* eye]. Abnormal protrusion of the eyeball. **endocrine e.,** exophthalmos associated with disorder of an endocrine gland, commonly thyrotoxicosis. **pulsating e.,** exophthalmos with pulsation and bruit, due to aneurysm pushing the eye forward.

exophthalmus (ek″sof-thal′mus). Exophthalmos.

exophylactic (ek″so-fi-lak′tik). Pertaining to or of the nature of exophylaxis.

exophylaxis (ek″so-fi-lak′sis) [*exo-* + Gr. *phylaxis* a guarding]. Prophylaxis against disease from the outside, such as the protective influence of the skin. Cf. *esophylaxis.*

exophytic (ek″so-fit′ik) [*exo-* + Gr. *phyein* to grow]. Growing outward; proliferating on the exterior or surface of an organ or other structure, in which the growth originated.

exoplasm (ek′so-plazm) [*exo-* + Gr. *plasma* something formed]. Ectoplasm.

exopneumopexy (ek″so-nu′mo-pek″se) [*exo-* + Gr. *pneumōn* lung + *pēxis* fixation]. The operation of exteriorization and fixation of the lung.

exorbitism (ek-sor′bĭ-tizm). Exophthalmos.

exormia (ek-sor′me-ah) [*ex-* + Gr. *hormē* rush]. Any papular disease of the skin.

exosepsis (ek″so-sep′sis) [*ex-* + Gr. *sēpsis* decay]. Septic poisoning which does not originate within the organism.

exoserosis (ek″so-se-ro′sis). An oozing of serum or exudate, as in moist skin diseases and edema.

exoskeleton (ek″so-skel′ĕ-ton) [*exo-* + *skeleton*]. A hard structure developed on the outside of the body, as the shell of a crustacean. In vertebrates the term is applied to structures produced by the epidermis, as hair, nails, hoofs, teeth, etc.

exosmose (ek′sos-mōs). To diffuse from within outward.

exosmosis (ek″sos-mo′sis) [*ex-* + Gr. *ōsmos* impulsion]. Diffusion or osmosis from within outward; movement outward through a diaphragm or through vessel walls.

exosplenopexy (ek″so-sple′no-pek″se) [*exo-* + Gr. *splēn* spleen + *pēxis* fixation]. The operation of suturing the spleen upon the outside of the body or in the wound.

exospore (ek′so-spōr). See *spore.*

exosporium (ek″so-spo′re-um). The external layer of the envelope of a spore.

exostosectomy (ek-sos″to-sek′to-me). Excision of an exostosis.

exostosis (ek″sos-to′sis) [*ex-* + Gr. *osteon* bone]. A bony growth projecting outward from the surface of a bone. **e. bursa′ta,** an exostosis from the epiphyseal portion of a bone, consisting of bone and cartilaginous tissue covered by a connective-tissue capsule. **e. cartilagin′ea,** a variety of osteoma consisting of a layer of cartilage developing beneath the periosteum of a bone. **dental e.,** cementosis. **ivory e.,** a bony growth of great density. **e. mul′tiplex cartilagin′ea,** dyschondroplasia.

exostotic (ek″sos-tot′ik). Pertaining to or of the nature of exostosis.

exoteric (ek″so-ter′ik) [Gr. *exōterikos* outer]. Generated or developed outside the organism.

exothelioma (ek″so-the″le-o′mah). Meningioma.

exothermal (ek″so-ther′mal). Exothermic.

exothermic (ek″so-ther′mik) [*exo-* + Gr. *thermē* heat]. Marked by the evolution of heat; liberating heat or energy from its potential forms. Cf. *endothermic.*

exothymopexy (ek″so-thi′mo-pek″se) [*exo-* + *thymus* + Gr. *pēxis* fixation]. The operation of enucleating the thymus gland from its fossa and suturing it to the top of the sternum.

exothyroidopexy (ek″so-thi-roi′do-pek″se). Exothyropexy.

exothyropexia (ek″so-thi″ro-pek′se-ah). Exothyropexy.

exothyropexy (ek″so-thi′ro-pek-se) [*exo-* + *thyroid* + Gr. *pēxis* fixation]. The operation of drawing out the enlarged thyroid gland through an incision and letting it shrivel on the outside.

exotic (eg-zot′ik). Of foreign origin; not native.

exotospore (ek-so′to-spōr). The needle-like spore (sporozoite) of the malarial parasite by which it enters the blood corpuscle. Called also *oxyspore* and *raphidiospore.*

exotoxic (ek″so-tok′sik) [*exo-* + *toxic*]. Pertaining to or produced by an exotoxin.

exotoxin (ek″so-tok′sin) [*exo-* + *toxin*]. A toxic substance formed by bacteria that is found outside the bacterial cell, or free in the culture medium. Exotoxins are heat-labile, and protein in nature. They are detoxified with retention of antigenicity by treatment with formaldehyde (formol toxoid), and are the most poisonous substances known to man; the $L.D._{50}$ of crystalline botulinum type A toxin for the mouse is 4.5×10^{-9} mg.

exotropia (ek″so-tro′pe-ah) [*exo-* + Gr. *tropos* a turning + *-ia*]. Deviation of a visual axis away from that of the other eye when fusion is a possibility.

exotropic (ek″so-tro′pik). 1. Turning outward. 2. Pertaining to or characterized by exotropia.

expander (eks-pan′der) [L. *expandere* to spread out]. Extender. **plasma volume e.,** plasma extender.

expansion (eks-pan′shun) [L. *expandere* to spread out]. 1. The process or state of being increased in extent, surface, or bulk. 2. A region or area of increased bulk or surface. **e. of the arch,** widening of the palatal arch in orthodontics. **cubical e.,** increase in volume by an increase in all dimensions. **hygroscopic e.,** an increase in dimensions of a body or substance as a result of absorption of moisture. **setting e.,** the increase in dimensions of a material, such as plaster of paris, which occurs concurrently with its hardening. **thermal e.,** an increase in dimensions of a body or substance as a result of exposure to high temperature. **wax e.,** increase in the dimensions of a wax pattern for a dental restoration to compensate for shrinkage of the gold during the casting process.

expansiveness (eks-pan′siv-nes). Behavior marked by euphoria, loquacity, and grandiosity.

expectation (eks″pek-ta′shun) [L. *expectare,* from *ex* out + *spectare* to look at]. That which may be anticipated, or looked forward to. **e. of life,** a figure representing the number of years, based on known statistics, which any person of a given age or class may reasonably expect to live.

expectorant (eks-pek′to-rant) [*ex-* + L. *pectus* breast]. 1. Promoting the ejection by spitting of mucus or other fluids from the lungs and trachea. 2. An agent that promotes the ejection of mucus or exudate from the lungs, bronchi, and trachea; sometimes extended to all remedies that quiet cough (antitussives). **liquefying e.,** an expectorant that promotes the ejection of mucus from the respiratory tract by decreasing the viscosity of that already present. **stimulant e.,** an expectorant that promotes ejection of mucus from the respiratory tract by stimulating its secretion by the respiratory tract mucosa. **Stokes's e.,** a preparation of ammonium carbonate, fluidextracts of senna and of squill, and camphorated tincture of opium in syrup of tolu.

expectoration (eks-pek″to-ra′shun). 1. The act of coughing up and spitting out materials from the lungs, bronchi, and trachea. 2. Sputum.

experiment (eks-per′ĭ-ment) [L. *experimentum* "proof from experience"]. A procedure gone through in order to discover or to demonstrate some fact or general truth. **bulbocapnine e.,** the experimental injection of bulbocapnine into animals which produces in them the motor phenomena typical of catatonia. **check e.,** crucial e. **control e.,** an experiment that is made under standard conditions, to test the correctness of other observations. **crucial e.,** an experiment so designed and so prepared for by previous work that it will definitely settle some point. **Cyon's e.,** a stimulus to an intact anterior spinal nerve root induces a stronger contraction of muscle than the same stimulus to the peripheral end of a divided nerve root. **defect e.,** observation of an embryo, after destruction of a region or part, to ascertain the effect on development. **Goltz's e.,** striking a frog on the abdomen will produce stoppage of the heart's action. **heat puncture e.,** stimulation, mechanical or electrical, of the corpus striatum, which produces a rise of temperature. **Küss's e.,** injection of a solution of opium or belladonna into the bladder produces no symptoms of poisoning, thus proving the impermeability of the bladder epithelium. **Mariotte's e.** (to demonstrate the blind spot of the eye), the eye is fixed on the center of a cross marked on a card on which is also marked a large spot. The card is moved to or from the face, and at a certain distance the image of the spot will disappear. **Müller's e.,** the converse of Valsalva's experiment, that is, making a forced inspiratory effort with the glottis closed. **Nussbaum's e.,** ligation of the renal arteries of an animal in order to isolate the glomeruli of the kidneys from the circulation. **O'Beirne's e.,** the experiment of injecting air or water into a loop of intestine passed through a hole in a sheet of paper: done to demonstrate the causation of strangulated hernia. **Römer's e.,** the placing of abrine in the conjunctiva to show the formation of antitoxins. **Scheiner's e.,** the experiment of looking at an object through two pin holes close together in a card. If the object is in focus, only one image is observed; if it is not, two or more images are seen. **Stensen's e.,** the experiment of cutting off the blood supply from the lumbar region of the spinal cord of an animal by compressing the abdominal aorta: it produces paralysis of the posterior parts of the body. **Toynbee's e.,** the experiment of partially exhausting the air in the tympanic cavity by swallowing while the nose and mouth are closed. **Valsalva's e.** See under *maneuver.*

expiration (eks″pĭ-ra′shun) [*ex-* + L. *spirare* to breathe]. 1. The act of breathing out or expelling air from the lungs. 2. Termination, or death.

expiratory (eks-pi′rah-to″re). Subserving or pertaining to expiration.

expire (ek-spīr′). 1. To breathe out. 2. To die.

expirium (eks-pi′re-um). An expiration.

expiscation (eks″pis-ka′shun). The long-continued study of symptoms for diagnostic purposes.

explant (eks-plant′). 1. To take from the body and place in an artificial medium for growth. 2. Tissue taken from its original site and transferred to an artificial medium for growth.

explode (eks-plōd′) [L. *explodere,* from *ex* out + *plaudere* to clap the hands]. 1. To cause to undergo sudden and violent decomposition. 2. To undergo sudden and violent decomposition.

exploration (eks″plo-ra′shun) [L. *exploratio,* from *ex* out + *plorare* to cry out]. An act of search, investigation, or careful examination, as in diagnosis.

exploratory (eks-plo′rah-to″re) [L. *exploratorius* pertaining to research]. Subserving an exploration.

explorer (eks-plor′er). An instrument for use in exploration.

explosion (eks-plo′zhun) [L. *explosio*]. 1. A sudden and violent outbreak, as of emotion. 2. The discharge of a neural cell.

explosive (eks-plo′siv). Characterized by explosions, or by sudden and violent outbreaks.

exponent (eks′po-nent). A symbol placed above and at the right of another symbol to indicate the power to which the latter is to be raised, as, x^2. **hydrogen e.,** a figure used to express the hydrogen ion concentration of a liquid. It is the logarithm of the figure expressing the concentration. It is represented by the symbol pH.

expression (eks-presh′un) [L. *expressio*]. 1. The facial aspect, or appearance of the face, as determined by the physical or emotional state. 2. The act of squeezing or pressing out: a term used in pharmacy, surgery, and obstetrics. **Kristeller e.** See under *method.*

expressivity (eks″pres-siv′ĭ-te) [L. *expressus*]. The extent to which a heritable trait is manifested by an individual carrying the principal gene conditioning it.

expulsive (eks-pul′siv) [*ex-* + L. *pellere* to drive]. Driving or forcing out; tending to expel.

exsanguinate (eks-sang′gwĭ-nāt) [*ex-* + L. *sanguis* blood]. 1. To deprive of blood. 2. Bloodless; anemic.

exsanguination (eks-sang″wĭ-na′shun). The forcible expulsion of the blood from a part.

exsanguinotransfusion (eks-sang″gwĭ-no-trans-fu′zhun). Exchange transfusion.

exsect (ek-sekt′). To excise; to cut out.

exsection (ek-sek′shun). Excision.

exsector (ek-sek′tor). A cutting instrument for use in performing exsections.

exsiccant (ek-sik′ant). 1. Drying or absorbing moisture. 2. An agent which absorbs moisture.

exsiccate (ek′sĭ-kāt) [L. *exsiccare,* from *ex* out + *siccus* dry]. To dry thoroughly; in chemistry, to deprive of the water of crystallization.

exsiccation (ek″sĭ-ka′shun). The act of drying; in chemistry, the deprival of a crystalline substance of its water of crystallization.

exsiccator (ek′sĭ-ka″tor). A container in which drying is done in chemistry.

exsiccosis (ek″sĭ-ko′sis). The bodily state produced by low water intake.

exsomatize (ek-so′mah-tīz) [*ex-* + Gr. *sōma* body]. To remove from the body.

exsorption (ek-sorp′shun). The movement of a substance out of the blood vessels into adjacent tissues or spaces; used to denote such movement from the circulating blood into the lumen of the gastrointestinal tract.

exstrophy (ek′stro-fe) [*ex-* + Gr. *strephein* to turn oneself]. The congenital eversion or turning inside out of an organ, as the bladder. **e. of the bladder,** a congenital malformation in which, from deficiency of the abdominal wall and bladder, the latter organ appears to be turned inside out, having the internal surface of the posterior wall showing through the opening in the anterior wall.

exsufflation (eks″suf-fla′shun) [*ex-* + L. *sufflatio* a blowing up]. The act of exhausting the air content of a cavity by artificial or mechanical means, especially such action upon the lungs by means of an exsufflator.

exsufflator (eks″suf-fla′tor). An apparatus which, by the sudden production of negative pressure, can reproduce in the bronchial tree the effects of a natural, vigorous cough.

ext. Abbreviation for *extract.*

extender (eks-ten′der) [*ex-* + L. *tendere* to stretch]. Something which enlarges or prolongs. **artificial plasma e.,** a substance which can be transfused, to maintain fluid volume of the blood in event of great necessity, supplemental to the use of whole blood and plasma.

extension (eks-ten′shun) [L. *extensio*]. 1. The movement by which the two ends of any part are pulled asunder. 2. A movement which brings the members of a limb into or toward a straight condition. **Bardenheuer's e.,** extension for fractured limbs with longitudinal, transverse, and rotary pulls, designed to produce extension in all the directions in which the muscles which cause the displacement act. **Buck's e.,** the extension of a fractured leg by weights, the foot of the bed being raised so that the body makes counterextension. **Codivilla's e.,** extension of a fractured limb in which the attachment to the bone is by means of calipers or a nail passed through the lower end of the bone. **nail e.,** extension exerted on the distal fragment of a fractured bone by means of a nail or pin (Steinmann pin) driven into the fragment. **e. per contiguita′tem,** the spreading of a morbid process through one tissue or part into one adjacent to it. **e. per continuita′tem,** the spreading of a morbid process throughout a single tissue or part. **e. per sal′tam,** the spreading of a morbid condition from one part to a part or tissue distant from it, with normal tissues intervening; metastasis.

extensometer (eks″ten-som′e-ter) [L. *extensus* extension + Gr. *metron* measure]. An instrument for measuring distortion of specimens under test.

extensor (eks-ten′sor) [L.]. Any muscle that extends a joint.

exterior (eks-te′re-or) [L.]. Situated on or near the outside; outer.

exteriorize (eks-te′re-or-īz). 1. To form a correct mental reference of the image of an object seen. 2. In psychiatry, to turn one's interest outward. 3. To temporarily expose an organ or part and bring it outside the body.

extern (eks′tern). A medical student or graduate in medicine who assists in the care of patients in a hospital but does not reside in the hospital.

external (eks-ter′nal) [L. *externus* outside]. Situated or occurring on the outside.

externalia (eks″ter-na′le-ah). The external genitals.

externe (eks′tern). Extern.

externus (eks-ter′nus). External; in official anatomical nomenclature, used to designate a structure farther from the center of an organ or cavity.

exteroceptive (eks″ter-o-sep′tiv). Sherrington's term for the external surface field of distribution of receptor organs. See *interoceptive, proprioceptive,* and *receptor.*

exteroceptor (eks″ter-o-sep′tor). A sensory nerve terminal which is stimulated by the immediate external environment, such as those in the skin and mucous membranes. See *interoceptor.*

exterofection (eks″ter-o-fek′shun). The response of the body made to changes in external environment, effected by the cerebrospinal system.

exterofective (eks″ter-o-fek′tiv). Responding to external stimuli: a term applied by Cannon to the cerebrospinal nervous system.

exterogestate (eks″ter-o-jes′tāt). 1. Developing outside the uterus, but still requiring complete care to meet all physical needs. 2. An infant during the period of exterior gestation.

extima (eks′tĭ-mah) [L.]. Outermost. See *tunica intima.*

extinguish (eks-ting′gwish) [L. *extinguere*]. To render extinct.

extirpation (ek″ster-pa′shun) [L. *extirpare* to root out, from *ex* out + *stirps* root]. Complete removal or eradication of a part. **e. of pulp, pulp e.,** complete removal of the dental pulp from the pulp chamber and root canal of a tooth.

extorsion (eks-tor′shun) [L. *ex* from + *torsio* twisting]. Tilting of the upper part of the vertical meridian of the eye away from the midline of the face.

extra- (eks′trah) [L. *exter* outward]. A prefix meaning outside of, beyond, or in addition.

extra-adrenal (eks″trah-ad-re′nal). Situated or occurring outside of the adrenal gland.

extra-anthropic (eks″trah-an-throp′ik). Exanthropic.

extra-articular (eks″trah-ar-tik′u-lar) [*extra-* + L. *articulus* joint]. Situated or occurring outside a joint.

extrabronchial (eks″trah-brong′ke-al). Outside of or independent of the bronchial tubes.

extrabuccal (eks″trah-buk′al). Outside of the mouth.

extrabulbar (eks″trah-bul′bar). Outside of or away from a bulb, as the medulla oblongata or the urethral bulb.

extracapsular (eks″trah-kap′su-lar). Situated or occurring outside a capsule.

extracardial (eks″trah-kar′de-al). Outside the heart.

extracarpal (eks″trah-kar′pal). Just outside the region of the wrist.

extracellular (eks″trah-sel′u-lar). Outside of a cell or cells.

extracerebral (eks″trah-ser′ĕ-bral). Situated or having its origin outside the cerebrum.

extracorporal (eks″trah-kor′po-ral). Extracorporeal.

extracorporeal (eks″trah-kor-po′re-al) [*extra-* + L. *corpus* body]. Situated or occurring outside the body.

extracorpuscular (eks″trah-kor-pus′ku-lar). Outside of the corpuscles.

extracranial (eks″trah-kra′ne-al). Outside of the cranium.

extract (eks′trakt) [L. *extractum*]. A concentrated preparation of a vegetable or animal drug obtained by removing the active constituents therefrom with a suitable menstruum, evaporating all or nearly all the solvent, and adjusting the residual mass or powder to a prescribed standard. Extracts are prepared in three forms: semiliquid or of syrupy consistency, pilular or solid, and as dry powder. **allergenic e.,** an extract of the protein of any substance to which a person may be sensitive: used for diagnosis or desensitization therapy in conditions due to hypersensitivity. They are prepared from a great variety of substances, from food to fungi, and from house dust to horse serum. **animal e.,** one prepared from material of animal origin. **beef e.,** a concentrate from beef broth, used in compounding certain prescriptions. **belladonna e.,** an alcoholic preparation of belladonna leaf, containing in each 100 Gm. 1.15–1.35 Gm. of the alkaloids of belladonna leaf: used as a parasympatholytic. **cascara sagrada e.,** a powdered preparation of cascara sagrada, each gram of which represents 3 Gm. of cascara sagrada: cathartic. **chondodendron tomentosum e.,** an alcoholic extract of a desiccated substance (curare) obtained from the bark and stem of *Chondodendron tomentosum:* used in producing relaxation of skeletal muscle. **chondrus e.,** a tan powder prepared from chondrus: used as a protective. **colocynth e.,** a powdered preparation each gram of which represents 4 Gm. of colocynth: used as a cathartic. **colocynth e., compound,** a preparation of colocynth extract with finely powdered ipomea resin, aloe, and cardamon seed: cathartic. **compound e.,** one prepared from more than one drug. **dry e.,** an extract prepared in a dry form, starch, sucrose, lactose, powdered glycyrrhiza, magnesium carbonate, magnesium oxide, or calcium phosphate being used as a diluent. **glycyrrhiza e.,** a brown powder prepared from the rhizome and roots of species of *Glycyrrhiza:* used as a flavoring agent. **glycyrrhiza e., pure,** a preparation of the dried rhizome and roots of varieties of *glycyrrhiza glabra,* used in the compounding of aromatic cascara sagrada fluidextract. **Goulard's e.,** lead subacetate solution. **henbane e.,** hyoscyamus e. **hyoscyamus e.,** a preparation of hyoscyamus, in pilular or powdered form, each 100 Gm. of which contains 155 mg. of the alkaloids of hyoscyamus. **Irish moss e.,** chondrus e. **licorice root e.,** glycyrrhiza e. **licorice root e., pure,** glycyrrhiza e., pure. **liver e.,** a brownish, somewhat hygroscopic powder prepared from mammalian livers: used as a hematopoietic. **liver e., liquid,** liver solution. **liver e., parenteral,** liver injection. **e. of male fern,** aspidium oleoresin. **malt e.,** a product containing dextrin, maltose, a small amount of glucose, and amylolytic enzymes, obtained by extracting the partially and artificially germinated grain of one or more varieties of *Hordeum vulgare;* used as a nutritive and emulsifying agent. **nux vomica e.,** a powder prepared from nux vomica, each 100 Gm. of which contains 7–7.75 Gm. of strychnine. **ox bile e.,** a brown or brownish or greenish yellow powder, with a characteristic odor and bitter taste: used as a choleretic. **oxgall e., powdered,** ox bile e. **parathyroid e.,** parathyroid injection. **pilular e.,** an extract prepared as a plastic mass, liquid glucose, malt extract, or glycerin being used as a diluent. **poison ivy e.,** a preparation of the fresh leaves of poison ivy, *Rhus toxicodendron,* used in prevention of poison ivy dermatitis. **poison oak e.,** a preparation of the fresh leaves of poison oak, *Rhus diversiloba,* used in prevention of poison oak dermatitis. **pollen e.,** a preparation of the pollen of certain plants, such as ragweed, used in the diagnosis and treatment of inhalant allergy. **powdered e.,** dried e. **Rhamnus purshiana e.,** cascara sagrada e. **rice polishings e.,** a preparation of rice polishings, used as a source of vitamin B_1, or thiamine. **solid e.,** pilular e. **tikitiki e.,** rice polishings e. **yeast e.,** a powder prepared from a water-soluble, peptone-like derivative of yeast cells (*Saccharomyces*).

extraction (eks-trak′shun) [L. *ex* out + *trahere* to draw]. 1. The process or act of pulling or drawing out. 2. The preparation of an extract. **breech e.,** extraction of the infant from the uterus in breech presentation. **breech e., partial,** extraction of the remainder of the infant's body after it has been extruded from the uterus by natural forces as far as the umbilicus. **breech e., total,** extraction of the entire body of the infant from the uterus in cases of breech presentation. **e. of a cataract,** the surgical removal of a cataractous lens. **flap e.,** extraction of cataract by an incision which makes a flap of cornea. **tooth e.,** the removal of a tooth.

extractive (eks-trak′tiv). Any substance present in an organized tissue, or in a mixture in a small quantity, and requiring to be extracted by a special method.

extractor (eks-trak′tor). An instrument used in drawing out, pulling, or extracting.

extractum (eks-trak′tum), gen. *extrac′ti*, pl. *extrac′ta* [L., from *ex* out + *trahere* to draw]. An extract. **e. car′nis,** beef extract. **e. fel′lis bo′vis,** ox bile extract. **e. hep′atis,** liver extract. **e. nu′cis vom′icae,** nux vomica extract. **e. perpolitio′num ory′zae,** rice polishings extract.

extracystic (eks″trah-sis′tik). Outside a cyst or the bladder.

extradural (eks″trah-du′ral). Situated or occurring outside the dura mater.

extra-embryonic (eks″trah-em″bre-on′ik). Not occurring as a part of the embryo proper; applied specifically to the fetal membranes.

extra-epiphysial (eks″trah-ep″ĭ-fiz′e-al). Away from, or unconnected with, an epiphysis.

extra-expiratory (eks″trah-eks-pi′rah-to″re). Relating to forced expiration.

extragenital (eks″trah-jen′ĭ-tal). Unrelated to, not originating in, or remote from the genital organs.

extrahepatic (eks″trah-he-pat′ik). Situated, or occurring, outside of the liver.

extraligamentous (eks″trah-lig″ah-men′tus). Occurring outside a ligament.

extramalleolus (eks″trah-mal-le′o-lus). The outer malleolus of the ankle joint.

extramarginal (eks″trah-mar′jĭ-nal). Below the limit of consciousness.

extramastoiditis (eks″trah-mas″toid-i′tis). Inflammation of the outer surface of the mastoid process and of the superincumbent tissues.

extramedullary (eks″trah-med′u-la″re). Situated or occurring outside any medulla, especially the medulla oblongata.

extrameningeal (eks″trah-mĕ-nin′je-al). Occurring outside the meninges.

extramural (eks″trah-mu′ral) [L. *extra* + *murus* wall]. Situated or occurring outside a wall.

extraneous (eks-tra′ne-us) [L. *extraneus* external]. Existing or belonging outside the organism.

extranuclear (eks″trah-nu′kle-ar). Situated or occurring outside a nucleus.

extraocular (eks″trah-ok′u-lar). Situated outside the eye.

extraoculogram (eks″trah-ok′u-lo-gram). A graphic representation of the changes in the corneofundal electric potential of the eye, recorded by means of electrodes applied to the skin on either side of the orbit; useful in determining disturbances in the metabolic activity of the eye.

extraparenchymal (eks″trah-par-en′kĭ-mal). Occurring or formed outside of the parenchyma.

extrapelvic (eks″trah-pel′vik). Unconnected with the pelvis.

extrapericardial (eks″trah-per″ĭ-kar′de-al). Outside the pericardium.

extraperineal (eks″trah-per″ĭ-ne′al). Away from the perineum.

extraperiosteal (eks″trah-per″e-os′te-al). Outside of or independent of the periosteum.

extraperitoneal (eks″trah-per″ĭ-to-ne′al). Situated or occurring outside the peritoneal cavity.

extraplacental (eks″trah-plah-sen′tal). Independent of the placenta.

extraplantar (eks″trah-plan′tar). On the outside of the sole of the foot.

extrapleural (eks″trah-ploo′ral). Outside the pleural cavity.

extrapolar (eks″trah-po′lar). Situated or occurring outside or not between the poles, as of a battery.

extraprostatic (eks″trah-pros-tat′ik). Not connected with the prostate gland.

extraprostatitis (eks″trah-pros″tah-ti′tis). Paraprostatitis.

extrapulmonary (eks″trah-pul′mo-na″re). Not connected with the lungs.

extrapyramidal (eks″trah-pi-ram′ĭ-dal). Outside of the pyramidal tracts.

extrarectus (eks″trah-rek′tus). Musculus rectus lateralis bulbi.

extraserous (eks″trah-se′rus). Outside of a serous cavity.

extrasomatic (eks″trah-so-mat′ik). Unconnected with the body.

extrasuprarenal (eks″trah-su″prah-re′nal). Extra-adrenal.

extrasyphilitic (eks″trah-sif″ĭ-lit′ik). Superadded to a syphilitic infection or lesion.

extrasystole (eks″trah-sis′to-le). A premature contraction of the heart which is independent of the normal rhythm and arises in response to an impulse in some part of the heart other than the sinoauricular node. **auricular e.,** an extrasystole in which the stimulus is thought to arise in the remains of the cardiac tube incorporated in the auricle elsewhere than at the sinus. **auriculoventricular e.,** one in which the stimulus is supposed to arise in the auriculoventricular node; called also *nodal e.* **infranodal e.,** ventricular extrasystole. **interpolated e.,** a contraction taking place between two normal heart beats. **nodal e.,** auriculoventricular e. **retrograde e.,** a premature ventricular contraction followed by a premature

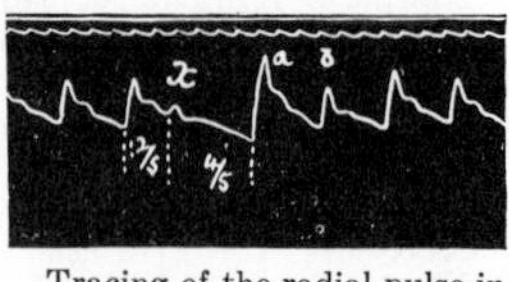

Tracing of the radial pulse in a patient suffering from occasional extrasystoles. The extrasystole occurs at *x*. Note the compensatory pause of four fifths of a second and the large pulse wave terminating this pause (Hay).

auricular contraction, due to transmission of the stimulus backward over the bundle of His. **ventricular e.,** one in which the stimulus arises in the ventricular portion of the auriculoventricular bundle.

extratracheal (eks″trah-tra′ke-al). Situated or occurring outside the trachea.

extratubal (eks″trah-tu′bal). Outside of a tube.

extratympanic (eks″trah-tim-pan′ik). Outside the tympanum of the ear.

extra-uterine (eks″trah-u′ter-in). Situated or occurring outside the uterus.

extravaginal (eks″trah-vaj′ĭ-nal). Outside of the vagina or of a sheath.

extravasation (eks-trav″ah-sa′shun) [*extra-* + L. *vas* vessel]. 1. A discharge or escape, as of blood, from a vessel into the tissues. 2. The process of being extravasated. 3. Blood or other substance which has been extravasated. **punctiform e.,** one which causes a tissue to be covered with minute bloody points.

extravascular (eks″trah-vas′ku-lar). Situated or occurring outside a vessel or the vessels.

extraventricular (eks″trah-ven-trik′u-lar). Situated or occurring outside a ventricle.

extraversion (eks″trah-ver′zhun). 1. The turning outward or objectifying of personal interests, emotions, or psychic trends. 2. In orthodontia, an unusually wide dental arch.

extravert (eks′trah-vert). Extrovert.

extremital (eks-trem′ĭ-tal). Pertaining to or situated at an extremity.

extremitas (eks-trem′ĭ-tas), pl. *extremita′tes* [L.]. 1. A general term used in anatomical nomenclature to indicate a distal or terminal portion of an organ or part. 2. [B N A] The arm or leg. Called *membrum* [N A]. **e. acromia′lis clavic′ulae** [N A, B N A], the lateral end of the clavicle, which articulates with the acromion of the scapula. Called also *acromial extremity of clavicle.* **e. ante′rior lie′nis** [N A], the lower pole of the spleen, which is situated anterior to the upper pole. Called also *e. inferior lienis* [B N A], and *anterior extremity of spleen.* **e. infe′rior** [B N A], membrum inferius. **e. infe′rior lie′nis** [B N A], e. anterior lienis. **e. infe′rior re′nis** [N A, B N A], the lower, smaller pole of the kidney. Called also *inferior extremity of kidney.* **e. infe′rior tes′tis** [N A, B N A], the lower end of the testis, which is attached to the tail of the epididymis. Called also *inferior extremity of testis.* **e. poste′rior lie′nis** [N A], the uppermost pole of the spleen, situated somewhat posterior to the lower pole. Called also *e. superior lienis* [B N A], and *posterior extremity of spleen.* **e. sterna′lis clavic′ulae** [N A, B N A], the medial end of the clavicle, which articulates with the sternum. Called also *sternal extremity of clavicle.* **e. supe′rior** [B N A], membrum superius. **e. supe′rior lie′nis** [B N A], e. posterior lienis. **e. supe′rior re′nis** [N A, B N A], the upper, larger pole of the kidney. Called also *superior extremity of kidney.* **e. supe′rior tes′tis** [N A, B N A], the upper end of the testis, which is attached to the head of the epididymis. Called also *superior extremity of testis.* **e. tuba′ria ova′rii** [N A, B N A], the upper end of the ovary, related to the free end of the uterine tube. Called also *tubal extremity of ovary.* **e. uteri′na ova′rii** [N A, B N A], the lower end of the ovary, directed toward the uterus. Called also *uterine extremity of ovary.*

extremitates (eks-trem″ĭ-tah′tēz) [L.]. Plural of *extremitas.*

extremity (eks-trem′ĭ-te). 1. A distal or terminal portion. See *extremitas.* 2. An arm or leg (membrum [N A]); sometimes applied specifically to a hand or foot. **cartilaginous e. of rib,** cartilago costalis. **external e. of clavicle,** extremitas acromialis claviculae. **fimbriated e. of fallopian tube,** fimbria ovarica. **internal e. of clavicle,** extremitas sternalis claviculae. **lower e.,** membrum inferius. **pelvic e. of ovary,** extremitas uterina ovarii. **proximal e. of phalanx of finger,** basis phalangis digitorum manus. **proximal e. of phalanx of toe,** basis phalangis digitorum pedis. **scapular e. of clavicle,** extremitas acromialis claviculae. **upper e.,** membrum superius. **uterine e. of ovary,** extremitas uterina ovarii.

extrinsic (eks-trin′sik) [L. *extrinsecus* situated on the outside]. Coming from or originating outside; having relation to parts outside the organ or limb where found.

extrogastrulation (eks″tro-gas″troo-la′shun). The formation of an embryonic monster by gastrular evagination instead of invagination.

extrophia (eks-tro′fe-ah). Exstrophy.

extrospection (eks″tro-spek′shun) [*extra-* + L. *spectare* to look]. The continued habit of inspecting one's own skin, associated with mysophobia, or insane dread of dirt.

extroversion (eks″tro-ver′zhun) [L. *extroversio,* from *extra* outside + *vertere* to turn]. 1. A turning inside out; exstrophy. 2. Extraversion.

extrovert (eks′tro-vert). A person whose interest is turned outward toward external values.

extrude (eks-trood′). 1. To force out, or to occupy a position distal to that normally occupied. 2. In dentistry, to occupy a position occlusal to that normally occupied (said of an over-erupted tooth).

extrudoclusion (eks-troo″do-kloo′zhun). Extrusion (def. 2).

extrusion (eks-troo′zhun). 1. A pushing out; a forcing out or expulsion. 2. In dentistry, the condition of a tooth when it extends too far in an occlusal direction.

extubate (eks-tu′bāt) [*ex-* + L. *tuba* tube]. To remove a tube from.

extubation (eks″tu-ba′shun). The removal of a previously inserted tube.

exuberant (eg-zu′ber-ant) [L. *exuberare* to be very fruitful]. Copious or excessive in production; showing excessive proliferation.

exudate (eks′u-dāt) [L. *exsudare* to sweat out]. Material, such as fluid, cells, or cellular debris, which has escaped from blood vessels and been deposited in tissues or on tissue surfaces, usually as a result of inflammation. An exudate, in contrast to a transudate, is characterized by a high content of protein, cells, or solid materials derived from cells.

exudation (eks″u-da′shun). 1. The escape of fluid, cells, and cellular debris from blood vessels and their deposition in or on the tissues, usually as the result of inflammation. 2. An exudate.

exudative (eks-oo′dah-tiv). Of or pertaining to a process of exudation.

exulcerans (eks-ul′ser-anz) [L.]. Ulcerating.

exulceratio (eks-ul″ser-a′she-o) [L.]. Ulceration. **e. sim′plex,** superficial ulceration.

exumbilication (eks″um-bil″ĭ-ka′shun) [*ex-* + *umbilicus*]. 1. Marked protrusion of the navel. 2. Umbilical hernia.

exutory (eks-u′tor-e) [L. *exutum,* from *exuere* to lay aside; remove]. 1. Drawing off. 2. An agent that draws off.

exuviae (eks-u′ve-e) [L., pl.]. 1. Cast-off epidermis. 2. A slough.

exuviation (eks-u″ve-a′shun) [L. *exuere* to divest oneself of]. The shedding of any epithelial structure, as of the deciduous teeth.

eye (i) [L. *oculus;* Gr. *ophthalmos*]. The organ of vision. Called also *oculus* [N A]. In shape the eye (bulbus oculi [N A]) consists of a large sphere, with the segment of a smaller sphere, the *cornea,* in front. It is composed of three coats—the *sclera* and *cornea,* the *choroid,* and the *retina*—each coat being divided into several layers. Within the three coats are the refracting media—namely, the *aqueous humor,* the *crystalline lens,* and the *vitreous humor.* The sclerotic, or external coat, is white

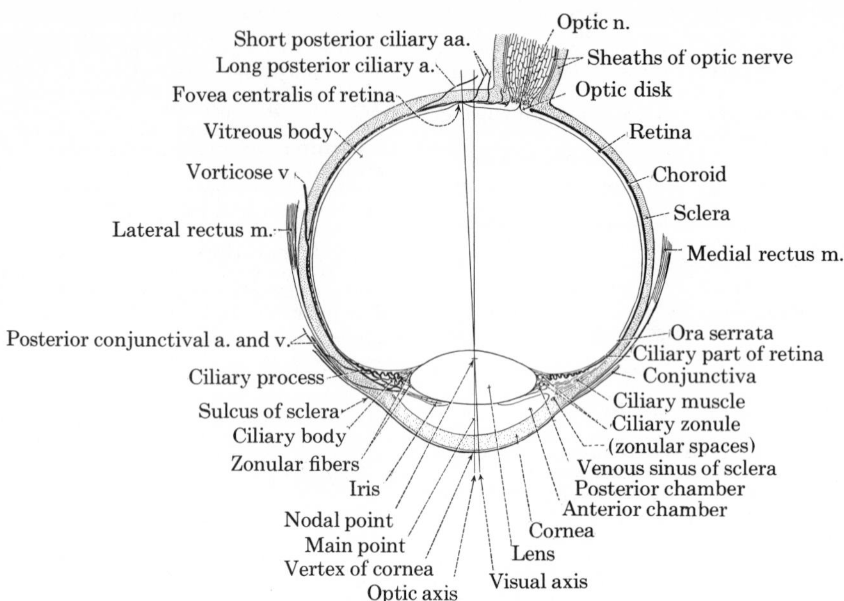

HORIZONTAL SECTION THROUGH RIGHT EYE

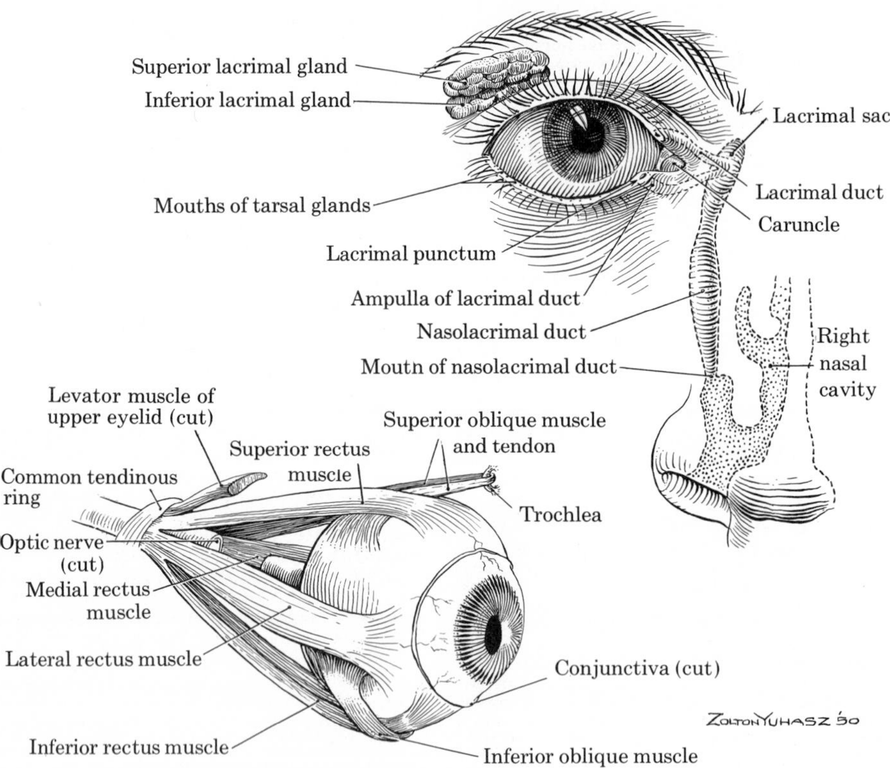

THE EYE AND RELATED STRUCTURES

and fibrous. Posteriorly the fibers of the optic nerve enter through small perforations in the *lamina cribrosa*. The inner surface is attached to the choroid by delicate connective tissue, the *lamina fusca*. The *cornea* is composed of five layers, the internal layer being a serous membrane, and sometimes called *Descemet's membrane*. The *choroid*, or middle coat, is chiefly composed of blood vessels and pigment. Anteriorly, it terminates near the periphery of the lens in folds called the *ciliary processes*. The *retina*, or internal coat, is chiefly composed of nerve tissue, and is made up of three principal layers. The external layer, or Jacob's membrane, is composed of terminal nerve cells, which, from their shape, are called the *rods* and *cones*. The *iris* is a curtain with a central perforation, the *pupil*, and is composed of smooth muscular fibers arranged both in a circular and in a radiating manner. It varies in color, and is suspended in the aqueous humor in front of the lens. The *ciliary ligament* is a ring of connective tissue fibers surrounding the iris. The *ciliary muscle* surrounds the periphery of the iris and controls the convexity of the lens during accommodation. The *aqueous humor* fills the cavity between the cornea in front and the lens behind. The *vitreous humor* fills the space back of the lens, and is a clear, jelly-like substance containing mucin. It is surrounded by the *hyaloid membrane*. The *lens*, or *crystalline humor*, is a double convex transparent body between the vitreous and aqueous humors, and is held in place by an elastic *capsule* and *suspensory* ligament. The arteries of the eye are the short ciliary, the long ciliary, the anterior ciliary, and the central artery of the retina. The nerves are the optic and the long and short ciliary nerves. **blear e.,** marginal blepharitis. **Bright's e.,** the eye as affected in chronic disease of the kidney. **cinema e.,** Klieg e. **crab's e's,** concretions from the digestive tract of a crawfish. **cystic e.,** distention of the eyelid by a large thin-walled sac. **dark-adapted e.,** an eye that has undergone the changes produced by adequate exposure to darkness. It is more sensitive to very weak light. **epiphyseal e.,** parietal e. **exciting e.,** the eye that is primarily injured and from which the influences start which involve the other eye in sympathetic ophthalmia. **fixating e.,** in strabismus, the eye which is directed toward the object of vision. **hare's e.,** lagophthalmos. **hop e.,** conjunctivitis in hop pickers caused by irritation from the spinelike hairs of the hop plant. **Klieg e.,** a condition marked by conjunctivitis, edema of the eyelids, lacrimation, and photophobia due to exposure to the intense lights (Klieg lights) which are used in making moving pictures. Called also *cinema e.* **light-adapted e.,** an eye that has undergone the changes produced by adequate exposure to rather strong light. It is less sensitive to weak light. **monochromatic e.,** an eye which can perceive only one color. **Nairobi e.,** a form of conjunctivitis in East Africa produced by the juice of crushed blister beetles. **parietal e.,** a modification of the pineal body in some lower vertebrates, to form a dorsal median eye; called also *epiphysial e.*, *pineal e.*, and *parietal organ*. **pineal e.,** parietal e. **pink e.,** acute contagious conjunctivitis. **primary e.,** exciting e. **reduced e., schematic e.** 1. An apparatus with two refracting elements, one representing the cornea and the other the lens. 2. A diagrammatic illustration of the structure of the eye. **secondary e.,** sympathizing e. **shipyard e.,** epidemic keratoconjunctivitis. **Snellen's reform e.,** an artificial eye composed of two concavo-convex plates with an empty space between. **squinting e.,** in strabismus, the eye the visual axis of which deviates from the object of vision while the sound eye fixates. **sympathizing e.,** the uninjured eye which becomes secondarily involved in sympathetic ophthalmia.

eyeball (i′bawl). The globe or ball of the eye. Called also *bulbus oculi* [N A]. See description under *eye*.

eyebrow (i′brow). 1. The transverse elevation at the junction of the forehead and the upper eyelid, consisting of five layers: skin, subcutaneous tissue, a layer of interwoven fibers of the orbicularis oculi and occipitofrontalis muscles, a submuscular areolar layer, and pericranium. Called also *supercilium* [N A]. 2. The hairs growing on the transverse elevation at the junction of the forehead and the upper eyelid. Called also *supercilia* [N A].

eyecup (i′kup). 1. A small vessel for application of cleansing or medicated solution to the exposed area of the eyeball. 2. Optic cup.

eyeground (i′ground). The fundus of the eye, which can be seen on ophthalmoscopical examination.

eyelash (i′lash). One of the hairs growing at the edge of an eyelid; collectively called *cilia* [N A].

eyelid (i′lid). Either of the two movable folds (upper and lower) that protect the anterior surface of the eyeball. Called *palpebrae* [N A]. **third e.,** the nictitating membrane. See under *membrane*.

eye-minded (i-mīnd′ed). Remembering chiefly the impressions made on the eye.

eyepiece (i′pēs). The lens or system of lenses in a microscope (or telescope) that is nearest to the eye of the user and that serves to further magnify the image produced by the objective. **comparison e.,** an eyepiece which presents as being in juxtaposition the images of separate objects being transmitted through two different objectives. **compensating e.,** an eyepiece especially designed to correct chromatic and spherical aberrations of the light rays produced by the objective. **demonstration e.,** a device consisting of two eyepieces which may be affixed to the eyepiece tube of a microscope, permitting two observers to see the same field simultaneously. **huygenian e.,** a negative eyepiece consisting of two planoconvex lenses, the convexities being directed toward the objective. **negative e.,** a combination of two lenses, one of which is below the plane in which the real image from the objective is formed. **positive e.,** a single lens combination, consisting of two planoconvex lenses or of an achromatic doublet or triplet, the combination being above the plane in which the real image from the objective is formed. **Ramsden's e.,** a positive eyepiece consisting of two planoconvex lenses with the convexities turned toward each other. **wide-field e.,** a positive eyepiece consisting of a doublet and a single element, giving a wider field of view than that afforded by other eyepieces.

eyepoint (i′point). A point above the eyepiece in which all the beams of light emerging from the microscope intersect.

eyestrain (i′strān). Fatigue of the eye from overuse or from uncorrected defect in focus of the eye.

F

F. 1. Abbreviation for *Fahrenheit, fiat, field of vision, French* (catheter size), *Fusiformis,* and *formula.* 2. The chemical symbol of *fluorine;* the symbol for *gilbert.*

F_1. 1. The "first filial generation" produced by crossing two individuals. 2. A fluorescent substance found in small amounts in normal urine, and in larger quantities in the urine of pellagrins. Said to be present in larger amounts after the ingestion of thiamine.

F_2. 1. The "second filial generation" produced by mating two members of the F_1 generation. 2. A substance in urine which develops fluorescence after alkali is added. It may appear in small amounts in normal urine or in large amounts in the urine of normal persons after the ingestion of nicotinic acid.

F 710, 710F. See under *Fourneau.*

FA. Abbreviation for *fatty acid.*

F. A. Abbreviation for *field ambulance.*

F. and R. Abbreviation for *force and rhythm* (of pulse).

fabella (fah-bel′lah), pl. *fabel′lae* [L. "little bean"]. A sesamoid fibrocartilage on the gastrocnemius muscle, which is visible roentgenographically as a small, bony shadow behind the knee joint.

fabellae (fah-bel′le) [L.]. Plural of *fabella.*

Faber's anemia (fah′berz) [Knud Helge *Faber,* Danish physician, 1862–1956]. Achylanemia.

fabism (fa′bizm) [L. *faba* bean]. Favism.

fabrication (fab″rĭ-ka′shun). The telling of imaginary events or tales as if they were true; confabulation.

Fabricius (fah-bris′e-us), Hieronymus [It. Girolamo *Fabrizio*] (1537–1619). An Italian anatomist and surgeon who was the pupil and successor (at Padua) of Gabriele Falloppio. He was the teacher of William Harvey, and the discoverer of the valves of the veins.

F.A.C.D. Abbreviation for *Fellow of the American College of Dentists.*

face (fās) [L. *facies*]. 1. The anterior aspect of the head from the forehead to the chin inclusive. 2. Any presenting aspect, or surface. See also *facies.* **adenoid f.,** adenoid facies. **bovine f., cow f.,** facies bovina. **dish f., dished f.,** a facial deformity characterized by a prominence of the forehead, a recession of the midface and lower half of the nose, a lengthening of the upper lip, and a prognathic chin; called also *facies scaphoidea.* **frog f.,** flatness of the face due to intranasal disease. **hippocratic f.,** facies hippocratica. **hippopotamus f.,** a condition resulting from excessive hypertrophy of the gums. **moon f., moon-shaped f.,** the peculiar rounded face observed in various conditions, such as Cushing's syndrome, or following administration of adrenal corticoids.

face-bow (fās′bo). A device used in dentistry to record the positional relationship of the maxillary ridge to the temporomandibular joints and to transfer this relationship to the articulator, for the purpose of orienting the casts and dentures so that they will function on the articulator in the same manner as in the patient's mouth. **adjustable axis f.-b.,** one that can be adjusted to permit location of the axis of rotation of the mandible. **kinematic f.-b.,** adjustable axis f.-b.

faceometer (fās-om′e-ter). An instrument for measuring the dimensions of the face.

facet (fas′et) [Fr. *facette*]. A small plane surface on a hard body, as on a bone. See also *fovea.* **articular f.,** a small plane surface on a bone at the site where it articulates with another structure. See terms beginning *facies articularis,* under *facies.* **articular f. of atlas, circular,** fovea dentis atlantis. **articular f. of atlas, inferior,** fovea articularis inferior atlantis. **articular f. of atlas, superior,** fovea articularis superior atlantis. **articular f's for rib cartilages,** incisurae costales sterni. **f. of calcaneus, posterior, medial,** facies articularis talaris media calcanei. **clavicular f.,** incisura clavicularis sterni. **costal f., anterior, costal f., inferior,** facies articularis tuberculi costae. **costal f., posterior, costal f., superior,** facies articularis capitis costae. **costal f's of sternum,** incisurae costales sterni. **costal f. of vertebra, superior,** fovea costalis superior. **lateral f's of sternum,** incisurae costales sterni. **malleolar f. of tibia, internal,** facies articularis malleolaris tibiae. **squatting f.,** a smooth area observed on the anterior surface of the lower end of the tibia in races whose members habitually sit in the squatting position. **f. for tubercle of rib,** fovea costalis transversalis.

facetectomy (fas″e-tek′to-me) [*facet* + Gr. *ektomē* excision]. Excision of the articular facet of a vertebra.

facette (fah-set′) [Fr.]. Facet.

facial (fa′shal) [L. *facialis*]. Pertaining to the face.

facies (fa′she-ēz), pl. *fa′cies* [L.]. 1. A term used in anatomical nomenclature to designate (*a*) the anterior aspect of the head, from forehead to chin, inclusive, and also (*b*) a specific surface of a body structure, part, or organ. 2. The expression or appearance of the face. **f. abdomina′lis,** the expression of the face characteristic of abdominal disease. It is a pinched, anxious, furrowed face, with nose and upper lip drawn up. **adenoid f.,** the stupid expression, with open mouth, seen in children with adenoid growths. **f. ante′rior antebra′chii** [N A], the ventral, or front, surface of the forearm. Called also *f. volaris antibrachii* [B N A]. **f. ante′rior bra′chii** [N A, B N A], the ventral, or front, surface of the upper arm. **f. ante′rior cor′neae** [N A, B N A], the anterior surface of the cornea. **f. ante′rior cru′ris** [N A, B N A], the ventral, or front, surface of the leg. **f. ante′rior den′tium premola′rium et mola′rium** [N A], the contact surface of the premolar and molar teeth that is directed toward the midline of the dental arch. **f. ante′rior fem′oris** [N A, B N A], the ventral, or front, surface of the thigh. **f. ante′rior glan′dulae suprarena′lis** [N A, B N A], the anterior, or front, surface of the adrenal gland. **f. ante′rior i′ridis** [N A, B N A], the anterior surface of the iris, directed toward the anterior chamber of the eye. **f. ante′rior latera′lis hu′meri** [N A, B N A], the anterolateral surface of the humerus, which provides attachment to the deltoid muscle and lateral part of the brachialis muscle. **f. ante′rior len′tis** [N A, B N A], the surface of the lens directed toward the anterior surface of the eye. **f. ante′rior maxil′lae** [N A, B N A], the surface of the body of the maxilla that is directed forward and somewhat laterally. It is bounded roughly by the infraorbital margin, root of the frontal process, nasal notch, alveolar process, and zygomatic process. **f. ante′rior media′lis hu′meri** [N A, B N A], the surface of the humerus that begins above at the intertubercular groove and spreads out inferiorly to form the wide smooth area for origin of the brachialis muscle. Called also *anteromedial surface of humerus.* **f. ante′rior palpebra′rum** [N A, B N A], the anterior, or external, surface of the eyelids. **f. ante′rior pancre′atis** [N A, B N A], the front, or anterior, surface of the pancreas, directed toward the ventral surface of the body. **f. ante′rior par′tis**

petro'sae os'sis tempora'lis [N A], the surface of the petrous part of the temporal bone that forms the posterior portion of the floor of the middle cranial fossa. Called also *f. anterior pyramidis ossis temporalis* [B N A]. **f. ante'rior patel'lae** [N A], the slightly convex, longitudinally striated anterior, or front, surface of the patella, which is perforated by small openings for the nutrient vessels. **f. ante'rior prosta'tae** [N A, B N A], the anterior, or ventral, surface of the prostate, separated from the pubic symphysis by the pudendal venous plexus. **f. ante'rior pyram'idis os'sis tempora'lis** [B N A], f. anterior partis petrosae ossis temporalis. **f. ante'rior ra'dii** [N A], the anterior, or volar, surface of the radius, which gives attachment to the flexor pollicis longus and pronator quadratus muscles. Called also *f. volaris radii* [B N A]. **f. ante'rior re'nis** [N A, B N A], the anterior, peritoneum-covered surface of the kidney which is directed toward the viscera. **f. ante'rior ul'nae** [N A], the front, or anterior, surface of the ulna. Called also *f. volaris ulnae* [B N A]. **f. anterolatera'lis cartilag'inis arytenoi'deae** [N A], the external surface of the arytenoid cartilage, which bears the triangular pit, the oblong pit, and the arcuate crest. **f. antoni'na,** a facial appearance common in advanced leprosy, with ectropion, paralysis of the extraocular muscles, lagophthalmic keratitis, and loss of tear secretion creating a facial expression of empty stare (rotunditas oculorum). **aortic f.,** the facial appearance of persons with aortic insufficiency: the cheeks are somewhat shrunken, the complexion pale and sallow, and the sclera pale and bluish. **f. articula'ris acromia'lis clavic'ulae** [N A, B N A], the smooth area on the lateral end of the clavicle for articulation with the acromion of the scapula. **f. articula'ris acro'mii** [N A, B N A], a small variable area on the acromion of the scapula, for articulation with the acromial end of the clavicle. **f. articula'ris ante'rior ax'is** [N A], an oval facet on the ventral surface of the odontoid process of the axis, articulating with the fovea dentis of the atlas. Called also *f. articularis anterior epistrophei* [B N A] and *anterior articular facet of axis.* **f. articula'ris ante'rior calca'nei** [B N A], f. articularis talaris anterior calcanei. **f. articula'ris ante'rior epistroph'ei** [B N A], f. articularis anterior axis. **f. articula'ris arytenoi'dea cartilag'inis cricoi'deae** [N A], the surface of the cricoid cartilage that articulates with the arytenoid cartilage. **f. articula'ris calca'nea ante'rior ta'li** [N A, B N A], the small surface on the head of the talus that rests upon the anterior articular surface of the calcaneus. **f. articula'ris calca'nea me'dia ta'li** [N A, B N A], the convex part of the head of the talus that articulates with the sustentaculum tali of the calcaneus. **f. articula'ris calca'nea poste'rior ta'li** [N A, B N A], a transverse concavity on the inferior surface of the talus, articulating with the calcaneus. **f. articula'ris cap'itis cos'tae** [N A], the surface on the head of a rib where it articulates with the body of a vertebra. Typically it is divided into two facets by a transverse crest, the lower facet articulating with the corresponding vertebra, and the upper facet with the suprajacent vertebra. The articular surfaces of the heads of the first, tenth, eleventh, and twelfth ribs generally consist of only one facet. Called also *f. articularis capituli costae* [B N A]. **f. articula'ris cap'itis fib'ulae** [N A], the medial surface of the head of the fibula, which articulates with the lateral condyle of the tibia. Called also *f. articularis capituli fibulae* [B N A]. **f. articula'ris capit'uli cos'tae** [B N A], f. articularis capitis costae. **f. articula'ris capit'uli fib'ulae** [B N A], f. articularis capitis fibulae. **f. articula'ris car'pea ra'dii** [N A, B N A], the concave part of the distal end of the radius, which articulates with the lunate and scaphoid carpal bones. Called also *carpal articular surface of radius.* **f. articula'ris cartilag'inis arytenoi'dea** [N A], the surface of the arytenoid cartilage that articulates with the cricoid cartilage. **f. articula'ris cuboi'dea calca'nei** [N A, B N A], the saddle-shaped area on the anterior surface of the calcaneus where it articulates with the cuboid bone. Called also *cuboid articular surface of calcaneus.* **f. articula'ris fibula'ris tib'iae** [N A], the articular surface on the posteroinferior aspect of the lateral condyle of the tibia, which articulates with the head of the fibula. **f. articula'ris fos'sae mandibula'ris** [B N A], f. articularis ossis temporalis. **f. articula'res inferio'res atlan'tis** [B N A]. See *fovea articularis inferior atlantis.* **f. articula'ris infe'rior tib'iae** [N A, B N A], the surface on the distal end of the tibia where it articulates with the talus. **f. articula'res inferio'res vertebra'rum** [B N A], the surfaces on the inferior articular processes of the vertebrae. Omitted in N A. **f. articula'ris malleola'ris tib'iae** [N A, B N A], the lateral aspect of the medial malleolus, which articulates with the talus. **f. articula'ris malle'oli fib'ulae** [N A, B N A], the anterosuperior surface of the lateral malleolus, which articulates with the lateral side of the talus. **f. articula'ris me'dia calca'nei** [B N A], f. articularis talaris media calcanei. **f. articula'ris navicula'ris ta'li** [N A, B N A], the surface of the head of the talus that articulates with the navicular bone. **f. articula'ris os'sis tempora'lis** [N A], the articular surface found in the deep part of the mandibular fossa of the temporal bone. Called also *f. articularis fossae mandibularis* [B N A]. **f. articula'ris os'sium** [N A, B N A], the surface by which a bone articulates with another. Called also *articular surface.* **f. articula'ris patel'lae** [N A, B N A], the posterior, or back, surface of the patella, which is largely covered by a thick cartilaginous layer. **f. articula'ris poste'rior ax'is** [N A], a smooth groove on the dorsal surface of the odontoid process of the axis, which lodges the transverse ligament of the atlas. Called also *f. articularis posterior epistrophei* [B N A]. **f. articula'ris poste'rior calca'nei** [B N A], f. articularis talaris posterior calcanei. **f. articula'ris poste'rior epistroph'ei** [B N A], f. articularis posterior axis. **f. articula'ris sterna'lis clavic'ulae** [N A, B N A], a triangular surface on the medial end of the clavicle for articulation with the sternum. **f. articula'ris supe'rior tib'iae** [N A, B N A], the surface on the proximal end of the tibia that articulates with the condyles of the femur. **f. articula'res superio'res vertebra'rum** [B N A], the articular facets on the superior articular processes of the vertebrae. Omitted in N A. **f. articula'ris tala'ris ante'rior calca'nei** [N A], the small area on the superior surface of the calcaneus just anterior to the middle articular surface, which articulates with the talus. Called also *f. articularis anterior calcanei* [B N A]. **f. articula'ris tala'ris me'dia calca'nei** [N A], the area on the superior surface of the calcaneus just in front of the calcaneal sulcus, which articulates with the talus. Called also *f. articularis media calcanei* [B N A]. **f. articula'ris tala'ris poste'rior calca'nei** [N A], the area on the superior surface of the calcaneus just posterolateral to the calcaneal sulcus, which articulates with the talus. Called also *f. articularis posterior calcanei* [B N A]. **f. articula'ris thyroi'dea cartilag'inis cricoi'deae** [N A], the surface of the cricoid cartilage that articulates with the thyroid cartilage. **f. articula'ris tuber'culi cos'tae** [N A, B N A], the convex facet on the costal tubercle that articulates with the transverse process of a vertebra. **f. auricula'ris os'sis il'ii** [N A], **f. auricula'ris os'sis il'ium** [B N A], a somewhat ear-shaped area on the sacropelvic surface of the ilium, which articulates with the auricular surface of the sacrum to form the sacroiliac joint. **f. auricula'ris os'sis**

sac′ri [N A, B N A], the broad irregular surface on the superior half of the lateral aspect of the sacrum, which articulates with the ilium. Called also *auricular surface of sacrum.* **f. bovi′na** [L. "cow face"], a term sometimes applied to the appearance of the face in craniofacial dysostosis. **f. bucca′lis den′tis** [N A, B N A], the surface of a posterior tooth that is directed outward toward the cheek. **cardiac f.,** the anxious expression of patients with heart disease, marked by bright, watery, staring eyes, wide palpebral slits, tensely held mouth, and face slightly shrunken. **f. cerebra′lis a′lae mag′nae** [B N A], **f. cerebra′lis a′lae majo′ris** [N A], the smooth, concave part of the great wing of the sphenoid bone that forms the anterior part of the floor of the middle cranial fossa, lying in front of the petrous and squamous parts of the temporal bone. **f. cerebra′lis os′sis fronta′lis** [B N A], f. interna ossis frontalis. **f. cerebra′lis os′sis parieta′lis** [B N A], f. interna ossis parietalis. **f. cerebra′lis par′tis squamo′sae os′sis tempora′lis** [N A], **f. cerebra′lis squa′mae tempora′lis** [B N A], the inner surface of the squamous part of the temporal bone, forming the lateral wall of the middle cranial fossa. **f. co′lica lie′nis** [N A], the surface of the spleen that is in contact with the colon. **f. contac′tus den′tis** [N A, B N A], the surface of a tooth that is in contact with an adjacent tooth in the same dental arch. **f. convex′a cer′ebri** [B N A], f. superolateralis cerebri. **Corvisart's f.,** the facial expression characteristic of cardiac insufficiency. **f. costa′lis pulmo′nis** [N A, B N A], the surface area of each lung adjacent to the rib cage. **f. costa′lis scap′ulae** [N A, B N A], the anteromedially facing, concave surface of the scapula. Called also *costal surface of scapula.* **f. diaphragmat′ica cor′dis** [N A, B N A], the surface of the heart that rests on the diaphragm and is directed inferiorly and posteriorly. It is formed by the two ventricles, the left ventricle contributing a little more than the right. **f. diaphragmat′ica hep′atis** [N A], the surface of the liver that lies in contact with the diaphragm, being composed of the superior, anterior, right, and posterior aspects. **f. diaphragmat′ica lie′nis** [N A, B N A], the convex posterolateral surface of the spleen which is directed toward the diaphragm. **f. diaphragmat′ica pulmo′nis** [N A, B N A], the surface area of each lung that is adjacent to the diaphragm. **f. doloro′sa,** the facial expression of a patient experiencing pain or severe sickness. **f. dorsa′lis antibra′chii** [B N A], f. posterior antebrachii. **f. dorsa′les digito′rum ma′nus** [N A, B N A], the posterior, or back (dorsal), surfaces of the fingers. **f. dorsa′les digito′rum pe′dis** [N A, B N A], the superior, or upper (dorsal), surfaces of the toes. **f. dorsa′lis os′sis sac′ri** [N A, B N A], the markedly convex and rough posterior, or dorsal, surface of the sacrum, which gives origin to the sacrospinalis muscle. **f. dorsa′lis ra′dii** [B N A], f. posterior radii. **f. dorsa′lis scap′ulae** [N A, B N A], the convex posterior surface of the scapula, which is divided into two unequal parts (superior and inferior) by the spine of the scapula. **f. dorsa′lis ul′nae** [B N A], f. posterior ulnae. **f. exter′na os′sis fronta′lis** [N A], the external surface of the squama of the frontal bone. Called also *f. frontalis ossis frontalis* [B N A]. **f. ex′terna os′sis parieta′lis** [N A], the externally directed surface of the parietal bone. Called also *f. parietalis ossis parietalis* [B N A]. **f. fibula′ris cru′ris,** N A alternative for *f. lateralis cruris.* **f. fronta′lis os′sis fronta′lis** [B N A], f. externa ossis frontalis. **f. gas′trica lie′nis** [N A, B N A], the surface of the spleen that is in contact with the stomach. **f. glu′tea os′sis il′ii** [N A], the large external, or dorsal, surface of the ala of the ilium, on which are located the three gluteal lines. Called also *gluteal surface of ilium.* **f. hepat′ica,** a thin face with sunken eyeballs, sallow complexion, and yellow conjunctivae, characteristic of certain chronic disorders of the liver. **f. hippocrat′ica,** a drawn, pinched, and livid appearance of the face, indicative of approaching death. **Hutchinson's f.,** a peculiar appearance in ophthalmoplegia externa, the eyeballs being fixed, the eyebrows raised, and the lids drooping. **f. infe′rior cer′ebri** [N A], the lower, or inferior, surface of the cerebrum. Called also *basis cerebri* [B N A]. **f. infe′rior hemisphe′rii cerebel′li** [N A], the inferior surface of the cerebellar hemisphere, formed by the inferior semilunar lobule, the biventral lobule, the tonsilla, and the flocculus. **f. infe′rior hemisphe′rii cer′ebri** [N A], the part of the cerebral hemisphere that rests on the tentorium and in the anterior and middle cranial fossae. **f. infe′rior hep′atis** [B N A], f. visceralis hepatis. **f. infe′rior lin′guae** [N A, B N A], the under surface of the body of the tongue. **f. infe′rior mesenceph′ali** [B N A], the inferior surface of the mesencephalon. Omitted in N A. **f. infe′rior pancre′atis** [N A, B N A], the inferior surface of the pancreas. **f. infe′rior par′tis petro′sae os′sis tempora′lis** [N A], **f. infe′rior pyram′idis os′sis tempora′lis** [B N A], that surface of the petrous part of the temporal bone which appears on the external surface of the base of the cranium. **f. infero-latera′lis prosta′tae** [N A], the convex inferolateral surface of the prostate, separated from the superior fascia of the pelvic diaphragm by a venous plexus. **f. infratempora′lis maxil′lae** [N A, B N A], the posterior convex surface of the body of the maxilla, bounded roughly by the inferior orbital fissure, the zygomatic process and associated ridge, maxillary tuberosity, and posterior margin of the nasal surface. **f. interlo-ba′res pulmo′nis** [N A], the surface area of each lung lying within the oblique and horizontal fissures. **f. inter′na os′sis fronta′lis** [N A], the vertically situated, concave cerebral surface of the frontal bone. In its midline the sagittal sulcus is seen superiorly and the frontal crest inferiorly. Called also *f. cerebralis ossis frontalis* [B N A]. **f. inter′na os′sis parieta′lis** [N A], the internal, or cerebral, surface of the parietal bone. Called also *f. cerebralis ossis parietalis* [B N A]. **f. intestina′lis u′teri** [N A, B N A], the convex posterior surface of the uterus, adjacent to the intestine. **f. labia′lis den′tis** [N A, B N A], the surface of an anterior tooth that is directed outward toward the lip. **f. latera′lis bra′chii** [N A, B N A], the outer, or lateral, surface of the upper arm. **f. latera′lis cru′ris** [N A], the outer, or lateral, surface of the leg. **f. latera′lis den′tium incisivo′rum et canino′rum** [N A, B N A], the contact surface of the incisor and canine teeth that is directed away from the midline of the dental arch. **f. latera′les digito′rum ma′nus** [N A], the lateral surfaces of the fingers. Called also *margines radiales digitorum manus* [B N A], and *facies radiales digitorum manus.* **f. latera′les digito′rum pe′dis** [N A], the lateral surfaces of the toes. Called also *margines laterales digitorum pedis* [B N A]. **f. latera′lis fem′oris** [N A, B N A], the outer, or lateral, surface of the thigh. **f. latera′lis fib′ulae** [N A, B N A], the area between the anterior and posterior borders of the body of the fibula. **f. latera′lis os′sis zygomat′ici** [N A], the anterior convex surface of the zygomatic bone. Called also *f. malaris ossis zygomatici* [B N A]. **f. latera′lis ova′rii** [N A, B N A], the surface of the ovary in contact with the lateral pelvic wall. **f. latera′lis ra′dii** [N A, B N A], the surface of the radius that gives attachment to the supinator and pronator teres muscles proximally, and underlies the tendons of the extensor carpi radialis longus and brevis muscles distally. **f. latera′lis tes′tis** [N A, B N A], the surface of the testis that is directed away from its fellow of the opposite side. **f. latera′lis tib′iae** [N A, B N A], the surface of the body of the tibia between the interosseous and anterior borders. **f. leonti'na** [L. "lion's face"], a peculiar, lion-like appearance of the face, seen in certain cases of leprosy. See *leontiasis*. **f. lingua'lis den'tis** [N A, B N A], the surface of a tooth that faces inward toward the tongue. **f. luna'ta acetab'uli** [N A, B N A], the articular portion of the acetabulum. **f. mala'ris os'sis zygomat'ici** [B N A], f. lateralis ossis zygomatici. **f. malleola'ris latera'lis ta'li** [N A, B N A], the large triangular facet on the talus that articulates with the lateral malleolus. **f. malleola'ris media'lis ta'li** [N A, B N A], the narrow facet on the talus continuous with the superior surface. It articulates with the medial malleolus. **Marshall Hall's f.,** the facies of hydrocephalus. **f. masticato'ria den'tis** [N A, B N A], the surface of a tooth which is directed toward the teeth of the opposing dental arch; the occlusal surface. **f. maxilla'ris a'lae majo'ris** [N A], a small surface on the inferior part of the great wing of the sphenoid bone above the pterygoid processes. It is perforated by the foramen rotundum. Called also *f. sphenomaxillaris alae magnae* [B N A]. **f. maxilla'ris lam'inae perpendicula'ris os'sis palati'ni** [N A], **f. maxilla'ris par'tis perpendicula'ris os'sis palati'ni** [B N A], the lateral surface of the perpendicular plate of the palatine bone, which is in relation to the maxilla. Posteriorly the greater palatine sulcus is seen. **f. media'lis bra'chii** [N A, B N A], the inner, or medial, surface of the upper arm. **f. media'lis cartilag'inis arytenoi'deae** [N A], the surface of the arytenoid cartilage that faces medially, toward the opposite arytenoid cartilage. **f. media'lis cer'ebri** [N A, B N A], the surface of the cerebrum directed toward the midline of the body. **f. media'lis cru'ris** [N A], the inner, or medial, surface of the leg. **f. media'lis den'tium incisivo'rum et canino'rum** [N A, B N A], the contact surface of the incisor and canine teeth that is directed toward the midline of the dental arch. **f. media'les digito'rum ma'nus** [N A], the medial surfaces of the fingers. Called also *margines ulnares digitorum manus* [B N A], and *facies ulnares digitorum manus*. **f. media'les digito'rum pe'dis** [N A], the medial surfaces of the toes. Called also *margines mediales digitorum pedis* [B N A]. **f. media'lis fem'oris** [N A, B N A], the inner, or medial, surface of the thigh. **f. media'lis fib'ulae** [N A, B N A], the narrow area on the body of the fibula between the interosseous and anterior borders. **f. media'lis hemisphe'rii cer'ebri** [N A], the surface of the cerebral hemisphere that is directed toward the opposite hemisphere. **f. media'lis ova'rii** [N A, B N A], the side of the ovary in contact with the fimbriated end of the uterine tube and the intestine. **f. media'lis pulmo'nis** [N A], the surface area of each lung lying medially next to the vertebral column and mediastinum. Called also *f. mediastinalis pulmonis* [B N A]. **f. media'lis tes'tis** [N A, B N A], the surface of the testis that is directed toward its fellow of the opposite side. **f. media'lis tib'iae** [N A, B N A], the slightly convex surface of the body of the tibia between the anterior and medial borders. **f. media'lis ul'nae** [N A, B N A], the smooth, rounded, internal surface of the ulna. **f. mediastina'lis pulmo'nis** [B N A], f. medialis pulmonis. **mitral f., mitrotricuspid f.,** the appearance of the face of patients with mitral disease, marked by rosy, flushed cheeks and dilated capillaries. **myasthenic f.,** the characteristic facial expression in myasthenia gravis, caused by ptosis and weakness of the facial muscles. **myopathic f.,** the peculiar facial expression produced by relaxation of the facial muscles. **f. nasa'lis lam'inae horizonta'lis os'sis palati'ni** [N A], the superior surface of the horizontal part of the palatine bone; it forms the posterior part of the floor of the nasal cavity. Called also *f. nasalis partis horizontalis ossis palatini* [B N A]. **f. nasa'lis lam'inae perpendicula'ris os'sis palati'ni** [N A], the medial surface of the perpendicular plate of the palatine bone. It articulates with the middle and inferior nasal conchae. Called also *f. nasalis partis perpendicularis ossis palatini* [B N A]. **f. nasa'lis maxil'lae** [N A, B N A], the surface of the body of the maxilla that helps form the lateral wall of the nasal cavity. It is bounded roughly by the following medial margin of the orbital surface, medial margin of the infratemporal surface, the palatine process, and the nasal notch. **f. nasa'lis par'tis horizonta'lis os'sis palati'ni** [B N A], f. nasalis laminae horizontalis ossis palatini. **f. nasa'lis par'tis perpendicula'ris os'sis palati'ni** [B N A], f. nasalis laminae perpendicularis ossis palatini. **f. orbita'lis a'lae mag'nae** [B N A], **f. orbita'lis a'lae majo'ris** [N A], the quadrilateral surface on the great wing of the sphenoid bone that forms the major part of the lateral wall of the orbit. **f. orbita'lis maxil'lae** [N A, B N A], a triangular surface on the body of the maxilla that forms the greater part of the floor of the orbit. **f. orbita'lis os'sis fronta'lis** [N A, B N A], the triangularly shaped plates of the frontal bone that form most of the roof of each orbit and the floor of the anterior cranial fossa. They are separated by the ethmoidal notch. **f. orbita'lis os'sis zygomat'ici** [N A, B N A], the part of the zygomatic bone that helps form the lateral wall of the orbit. **f. [os'sea] cra'nii** [B N A], the bony skeleton of the face. Omitted in N A. **f. ova'rica, f. ovari'na,** an anxious expression of the face characteristic of ovarian disease. **f. palati'na lam'inae horizonta'lis os'sis palati'ni** [N A], **f. palati'na par'tis horizonta'lis os'sis palati'ni** [B N A], the inferior surface of the horizontal part of the palatine bone; it forms the posterior part of the hard palate. **f. palma'res digito'rum ma'nus** [N A], the ventral, or front (palmar), surfaces of the fingers. Called also *f. volares digitorum manus*. **f. parieta'lis os'sis parieta'lis** [B N A], f. externa ossis parietalis. **Parkinson's f.,** a stolid expression of the face pathognomonic of paralysis agitans. **f. patella'ris fem'oris** [N A, B N A], the smooth anterior continuation of the condyles that forms the surface of the femur articulating with the patella. **f. pelvi'na os'sis sac'ri** [N A, B N A], the smooth, concave, ventrocaudally directed surface of the sacrum that helps form the posterior wall of the pelvis. **f. planta'res digito'rum pe'dis** [N A, B N A], the inferior, or lower (plantar), surfaces of the toes. **f. poplit'ea fem'oris** [N A], the triangular area forming the superior part of the floor of the popliteal fossa. Called also *planum popliteum femoris* [B N A]. **f. poste'rior antebra'chii** [N A], the dorsal, or back, surface of the forearm. Called also *f. dorsalis antibrachii* [B N A]. **f. poste'rior bra'chii** [N A, B N A], the dorsal, or back, surface of the upper arm. **f. poste'rior cartilag'inis arytenoi'deae** [N A], the concave dorsal surface of the arytenoid cartilage, to which various laryngeal muscles are attached. **f. poste'rior cor'neae** [N A, B N A], the posterior surface of the cornea, which forms the anterior boundary of the anterior chamber. **f. poste'rior cru'ris** [N A, B N A], the dorsal, or back, surface of the leg. **f. poste'rior den'tium premola'rium et mola'rium** [N A], the contact surface of the premolar and the molar teeth that is directed away from the midline of the dental arch. **f. poste'rior fem'oris** [N A, B N A], the dorsal, or back, surface of the thigh. **f. poste'rior fib'ulae** [N A, B N A], the large area between the posterior and interosseous borders of the body of the fibula, presenting the medial crest. **f. poste'rior glan'dulae suprarena'lis** [N A, B N A], the portion of the adrenal gland that is directed toward the posterior body wall. **f. poste'rior hep'atis** [B N A], pars posterior facies diaphragmaticae hepatis. **f. poste'rior hu'meri** [N A, B N A], the surface of the humerus that is subdivided obliquely by the radial groove to give attachment to the lateral and medial heads of the triceps muscle. **f. poste′rior i′ridis** [N A, B N A], the posterior surface of the iris, directed toward the posterior chamber of the eye. **f. poste′rior len′tis** [N A, B N A], the posterior surface of the lens, directed toward the vitreous body of the eye. **f. poste′rior palpebra′rum** [N A, B N A], the internal surface of the eyelids, in contact with the eyeball and covered by the conjunctiva. **f. poste′rior pancre′atis** [N A, B N A], the posterior surface of the pancreas. **f. poste′rior par′tis petro′sae os′sis tempora′lis** [N A], the surface of the petrous part of the temporal bone that forms part of the anterior portion of the floor of the posterior cranial fossa. Called also *f. posterior pyramidis ossis temporalis* [B N A]. **f. poste′rior prosta′tae** [N A, B N A], the dorsal surface of the prostate, separated by fascia from the anterior wall of the rectum. **f. poste′rior pyram′idis os′sis tempora′lis** [B N A], f. posterior partis petrosae ossis temporalis. **f. poste′rior ra′dii** [N A], the dorsal surface of the radius, which gives attachment to the supinator, abductor pollicis longus, and extensor pollicis brevis muscles. Called also *f. dorsalis radii* [B N A]. **f. poste′rior re′nis** [N A, B N A], the dorsal surface of the kidney, directed toward the posterior body wall, and not covered by peritoneum. **f. poste′rior tib′iae** [N A, B N A], the surface of the body of the tibia between the medial and interosseous borders; in the proximal third presenting the soleal line. **f. poste′rior ul′nae** [N A], the posterolaterally directed surface of the ulna. Called also *f. dorsalis ulnae* [B N A]. **f. pulmona′lis cor′dis** [N A], the surface of the heart that comes in contact with the left lung; contributed mainly by the left ventricle and to a much lesser degree by the left atrium. **f. radia′les digito′rum ma′nus,** N A alternative for *f. laterales digitorum manus.* **f. rena′lis glan′dulae suprarena′lis** [N A], the surface of the adrenal gland that is directed toward the kidney, being separated from it by a layer of fat. Called also *basis glandulae suprarenalis* [B N A]. **f. rena′lis lie′nis** [N A, B N A], the surface of the spleen that is in contact with the left kidney. **f. sacropelvi′na os′sis il′ii** [N A], an irregular area on the inner surface of the ala of the ilium, posterior to the iliac fossa; it contains the iliac tuberosity and the auricular surface. **f. scaphoi′dea,** dish face. **f. sphenomaxilla′ris a′lae mag′nae** [B N A], f. maxillaris alae majoris. **f. sternocosta′lis cor′dis** [N A, B N A], the convex surface of the heart, which in general is directed ventrally and somewhat superiorly, being formed mainly by the right ventricle, and to a lesser degree by the left ventricle and the atria. **f. supe′rior hemisphe′rii cerebel′li** [N A], the superior surface of the cerebellar hemisphere, consisting of the ala of the lobulus centralis, the lobulus quadrangularis, the lobulus simplex, and the superior semilunar lobule. **f. supe′rior hep′atis** [B N A], pars superior faciei diaphragmaticae hepatis. **f. supe′rior troch′leae ta′li** [N A, B N A], the broad, smooth surface of the talus that articulates with the tibia. **f. superolatera′lis cer′ebri** [N A], the convex outer surface of the cerebrum, which faces the flat bones of the skull. Called also *f. convexa cerebri* [B N A]. **f. symphys′eos os′sis pu′bis** [B N A], **f. symphysia′lis** [N A], the rough, ovoid, medial surface of the body of the pubic bone, by which it articulates at the pubic symphysis with its fellow of the opposite side. **f. tempora′lis a′lae mag′nae** [B N A], **f. tempora′lis a′lae majo′ris** [N A], the lateral and inferior surface of the great wing of the sphenoid bone, divided by the infratemporal crest into a superior part that forms a portion of the floor of the temporal fossa, and an inferior part that is directed inferiorly toward the infratemporal fossa. **f. tempora′lis os′sis fronta′lis** [N A, B N A], the slightly concave surface of the frontal bone that forms the upper part of the floor of the temporal fossa and gives attachment to the anterosuperior part of the temporalis muscle. **f. tempora′lis os′sis zygomat′ici** [N A, B N A], the internal, concave surface of the zygomatic bone, facing the temporal and infratemporal fossae. **f. tempora′lis par′tis squamo′sae** [N A], **f. tempora′lis squa′mae tempora′lis** [B N A], the external surface of the squamous part of the temporal bone, the anterior part of which forms a portion of the temporal fossa. **f. tibia′lis cru′ris,** N A alternative for *f. medialis cruris.* **typhoid f., f. typho′sa,** the vacant and bewildered, often wild and defiant, expression, with face flushed and a dusky, leaden hue, seen in early stages of typhoid fever. **f. ulna′res digito′rum ma′nus,** N A alternative for *f. mediales digitorum manus.* **f. urethra′lis pe′nis** [N A, B N A], the surface of the penis overlying the urethra, and opposite the dorsum penis. **f. uteri′na,** the facial expression characteristic of uterine disease. **f. vesica′lis u′teri** [N A, B N A], the flat anterior surface of the uterus, adjacent to the urinary bladder. **f. viscera′lis hep′atis** [N A], the posteroinferior surface of the liver, which is in contact with various abdominal viscera. Called also *f. inferior hepatis* [B N A]. **f. viscera′lis lie′nis** [N A], the surface of the spleen which comes in contact with various other viscera, including the colon (facies colica), kidney (facies renalis), and stomach (facies gastrica). **f. vola′ris antibra′chii** [B N A], f. anterior antebrachii. **f. vola′res digito′rum ma′nus** [B N A], f. palmares digitorum manus. **f. vola′ris ra′dii** [B N A], f. anterior radii. **f. vola′ris ul′nae** [B N A], f. anterior ulnae. **Wells′ f.,** f. ovarica.

facilitation (fah-sil″ĭ-ta′shun) [L. *facilis* easy]. 1. The promotion or hastening of any natural process; the reverse of inhibition. 2. Specifically, the effect produced in nerve tissue by the passage of an impulse. The resistance of the nerve is diminished so that a second application of the stimulus evokes the reaction more easily. Called also *bahnung.* Cf. *law of facilitation.* **Wedensky f.,** facilitation across a block; when there is a complete block to nerve conduction the threshold of the nerve below the block to electric stimulation is lowered.

facilitory (fah-sil′ĭ-tōr-e). Making easier; promoting or hastening a natural process.

facing (fās′ing). A piece of porcelain or resin fashioned to represent the outer surface of a tooth and to be reinforced by gold so as to restore the full form of the natural tooth.

facio- (fa′she-o) [L. *facies* face]. A combining form denoting relationship to the face.

faciobrachial (fa″she-o-bra′ke-al) [*facio-* + Gr. *brachiōn* arm]. Pertaining to the face and arm.

faciocephalalgia (fa″she-o-sef″ah-lal′je-ah) [*facio-* + Gr. *kephalē* head + *-algia*]. Neuralgic pain in the face and neck attributed to disorders of the autonomic (vegetative) nervous system.

faciocervical (fa″she-o-ser′ve-kal) [*facio-* + L. *cervix* neck]. Affecting the face and neck.

faciolingual (fa″she-o-ling′gwal) [*facio-* + L. *lingua* tongue]. Pertaining to the face and tongue.

facioplasty (fa″she-o-plas′te) [*facio-* + Gr. *plassein* to form]. Plastic surgery of the face.

facioplegia (fa″she-o-ple′je-ah) [*facio-* + Gr. *plēgē* stroke]. Facial paralysis.

facioscapulohumeral (fa″she-o-skap″u-lo-hu′mer-al). Pertaining to the face, scapula, and arm.

F.A.C.P. Abbreviation for *Fellow of the American College of Physicians.*

F.A.C.S. Abbreviation for *Fellow of the American College of Surgeons.*

factitial (fak-tish′al). Produced by artificial means; unintentionally produced.

factitious (fak-tish′us) [L. *factitiosus*]. Artificial; not natural.

factor (fak′tor) [L. "maker"]. An agent or element that contributes to the production of a result, such as a chemical compound that is essential to a reaction (e.g., a coagulation factor), a quantity or symbol which is employed in a specific formula, or, in the study of heredity, a particular gene. **accelerator f.** See *factor V*, under *coagulation f's*. **accessory f., accessory food f.,** a vitamin. **activation f.** See *factor XII*, under *coagulation f's*. **alpha f.,** a name formerly given the hormone that governs the estrous phase of the ovarian cycle. **anabolism-promoting f.,** a principle which enhances protein utilization, permitting growth or tissue restitution with a lower level of protein intake than possible without it, an activity noted in various antibiotics and ataraxics. **animal protein f.,** an element in animal proteins found to be essential to maximal growth of animals. **antiachromotrichia f.,** pantothenic acid. **antiacrodynia f.,** pyridoxine. **antialopecia f.,** inositol. **antianemia f.,** an element which is essential for the maturation of erythrocytes and the prevention of anemia. See under *Castle's f's*. **antianemia f. for chicks,** a vitamin in spinach and other green leaves, which prevents anemia in chicks: possibly folic acid. **anti-black tongue f.,** nicotinic acid. **anticanities f., antidermatitis f. of chicks,** pantothenic acid. **antidermatitis f. of rats,** pyridoxine. **anti-egg white f.,** biotin. **anti-gray hair f.,** pantothenic acid. **antihemophilic f.** See *factor VIII*, under *coagulation f's*. See also *hemophilic f.* **antihemorrhagic f.,** vitamin K. **anti-insulin f.,** a substance of unknown constitution in extracts of the anterior pituitary which when injected into rabbits neutralizes the effect of insulin subsequently injected. **antineuritic f.,** thiamine. **antipellagra f.,** nicotinic acid. **anti-pernicious anemia f.,** cyanocobalamin. **antirachitic f.,** vitamin D. **antiscorbutic f.,** ascorbic acid. **antisterility f.,** vitamin E. **antistiffness f.,** a factor present in raw cream, crude molasses, and unheated cane juice, lack of which in animals causes stiffness of the wrist, and later emaciation, weakness, and death. **antixerophthalmia f., antixerotic f.,** vitamin A. **beta f.,** a name formerly given the hormone that governs the progestational phase of the ovarian cycle. **Bittner milk f.,** mouse mammary tumor agent. **bone f.,** a fundamental factor in periodontoclasia, being the systemic regulatory influence upon the response of alveolar bone to local irritants. **Bx f.,** para-aminobenzoic acid. **Castle's f's,** the factors, absence of any of which is responsible for the development of pernicious anemia. The normal gastric juice contains a mucoprotein (*intrinsic factor*) which is necessary for the assimilation and absorption of cyanocobalamin (*extrinsic factor*) contained in food, an essential for the production of the *antianemia* or *erythrocyte maturation factor* (EMF). **chemotactic f.,** the substance that brings about chemotaxis. **chick antidermatitis f.,** pantothenic acid. **chick antipellagra f.,** pantothenic acid. **chick growth f. S,** strepogenin. **Christmas f.** See *factor IX*, under *coagulation f's*. **chromotrichial f.,** para-aminobenzoic acid. **citrovorum f.,** a dietary element found necessary for the growth of *Leuconostoc citrovorum*. See *folinic acid*. **coagulation f's,** substances in the blood that are essential to the maintenance of normal hemostasis; the absence, diminution, or excess of any one of them may lead to abnormality of the clotting mechanism. Twelve factors have been recognized and identified by Roman numerals: *factor I*, a high molecular weight plasma protein which is converted to fibrin through the action of thrombin and which participates in stages 3 and 4 of blood coagulation. Called also *fibrinogen*. *factor II*, a glycoprotein present in the plasma that is converted to thrombin by extrinsic thromboplastin during the second stage of blood coagulation. Called also *prothrombin*. *factor III*, a material that has a number of sources in the body and is important in the formation of extrinsic thromboplastin. Called also *tissue thromboplastin*. *factor IV*, an appellation that is, in the scheme of hemostasis, assigned to calcium, because of its requirement in the first, second, and probably the third stage of blood coagulation. *factor V*, a heat- and storage-labile material, present in plasma and not in serum, not adsorbed by aluminum hydroxide or barium sulfate, and functioning in the formation of intrinsic and extrinsic thromboplastins. Called also *Ac-globulin*, *labile factor*, *proaccelerin*, *accelerator factor*, and *plasma converting factor*. *factor VI*, a factor previously called accelerin and thought to be an intermediary product of prothrombin conversion; it no longer is considered in the scheme of hemostasis, and hence it is assigned neither a name nor a function at this time. *factor VII*, a heat- and storage-stable material, present in serum but not in plasma, adsorbed by aluminum hydroxide and barium sulfate, and participating only in the formation of extrinsic thromboplastin. Called also *proconvertin*, *stable factor*, *serum prothrombin conversion accelerator* (*SPCA*), *prothrombinogen*, *autoprothrombin I*, and *prothrombinokinase*. *factor VIII*, a relatively storage-labile material, present in plasma and not in serum, not adsorbed by aluminum hydroxide or barium sulfate, and participating only in the formation of intrinsic thromboplastin; a primary deficiency of this factor causes classical, sex-linked hemophilia A. Called also *antihemophilic factor* (*AHF*), *antihemophilic globulin* (*AHG*), *hemophilic factor A*, *platelet cofactor I*, *thromboplastinogen*, and *thrombocytolysin*. *factor IX*, a relatively storage-stable substance present in normal serum but not in plasma, adsorbed by aluminum hydroxide and barium sulfate, and involved in the generation of intrinsic thromboplastin; a deficiency of this factor results in a hemorrhagic syndrome called hemophilia B which is similar to classical hemophilia A. Called also *plasma thromboplastin component* (*PTC*), *Christmas factor*, *hemophilic factor B*, and *autoprothrombin II*. *factor X*, a heat-labile material with limited storage stability at room temperature, present in serum but not in plasma, which functions in the formation of both intrinsic and extrinsic thromboplastin. Called also *Stuart factor*, and *Stuart-Prower factor*. *factor XI*, a stable factor, present in both plasma and serum, adsorbed partially or not at all by aluminum hydroxide or barium sulfate; together with factor XII it forms a complex which then activates factor IX in the formation of intrinsic thromboplastin. Called also *plasma thromboplastin antecedent* (*PTA*), and *hemophilic factor C*. *factor XII*, a stable factor, present in plasma and serum and poorly adsorbed by alkaline earths, which is activated by contact with glass or other foreign surfaces and initiates the process of blood coagulation *in vitro*. Its precise role during *in vivo* hemostasis remains unclear. Called also *Hageman factor* (*HF*), *glass factor*, *contact factor*, and *activation factor*. *platelet factor 1*, a substance with factor V activity on the surface of the platelets, probably identical to factor V adsorbed from the plasma. *platelet factor 2*, an accelerator of the thrombin-fibrinogen reaction, attached to platelets. *platelet factor 3*, a substance, probably phospholipid in nature, extracted from platelets, important in the generation of intrinsic thromboplastin. *platelet factor 4*, a component of blood platelets, found also in other cells, which is capable of neutralizing the antithrombin activity of heparin in the fibrinogen-fibrin reaction and the inhibitory effect of heparin on thromboplastin generation. **co-enzyme f.,** diaphorase. **complementary f.,** pyridoxine. **contact f.** See *factor XII*, under *coagulation f's*. **Curling f.,** griseofulvin. **Day's f.,** folic acid. **diabetogenic f.,** a substance of unknown constitution in extracts of the anterior pituitary which, when injected into normal dogs, causes them to become diabetic. **diffusion f.,** hyaluronidase. **Duran-Reynals permeability f.,** hyaluronidase. **eluate f.,** pyridoxine. **eryth-**

rocyte maturation f., an element that promotes the maturation of red blood cells. See under *Castle's f's.* **erythropoietic stimulating f.**, a name given a factor in the body which stimulates the production of erythrocytes; probably identical with erythropoietin. **etiologic f's**, the elements or influences that can be assigned as the cause of a disease or lesion. **excess f.**, a characteristic of the electroencephalogram of schizophrenic patients, indicative of the degree of psychosis in the patient. **extrinsic f.** See under *Castle's f's.* **fermentation L. casei f.**, folic acid. **fibrin f's**, fibrinogen and paraglobulin. **filtrate f.**, **filtrate f. II**, pantothenic acid. **galactopoietic f.**, prolactin. **glass f.** See *factor XII*, under *coagulation f's.* **glycotropic f.**, anti-insulin f. **growth f.**, an organic compound which is required by an organism for growth and which cannot be synthesized by it. **f. H.**, biotin. **Hageman f.** See *factor XII*, under *coagulation f's.* **hemophilic f. A.** See *factor VIII*, under *coagulation f's.* **hemophilic f. B.** See *factor IX*, under *coagulation f's.* **hemophilic f. C.** See *factor XI*, under *coagulation f's.* **hyperglycemic-glycogenolytic f.** See *glucagon.* **f. I.** 1. See under *coagulation f's.* 2. Pyridoxine. **f. II.** 1. See under *coagulation f's.* 2. Pantothenic acid. **f. III.** See under *coagulation f's.* **intrinsic f.** See under *Castle's f's.* **f. IV.** See under *coagulation f's.* **f. IX.** See under *coagulation f's.* **ketogenic f.**, orophysin. **labile f.** See *factor V*, under *coagulation f's.* **Lactobacillus bulgaricus f.**, an element contained in many natural products which is necessary for the growth of several strains of *Lactobacillus bulgaricus* and possibly for animal growth. **Lactobacillus casei f.**, folic acid. **Lactobacillus lactis Dorner f.**, cyanocobalamin. **lactogenic f.**, prolactin. **LE f.**, the material in the gamma globulin fraction of serum that has the potential to induce the formation of the LE cell. **leukocytosis-promoting f.**, Menkin's name for a substance or factor liberated by injured cells, which is responsible for the leukocytosis accompanying inflammatory processes. Called also *LPF.* **leukopenic f.**, Menkin's name for a factor in inflammatory exudates which may be the cause of the initial leukopenia accompanying inflammatory processes. **liver filtrate f.**, pantothenic acid. **liver Lactobacillus casei f.**, folic acid. **LLD f.**, cyanocobalamin. **lysogenic f.**, bacteriophage. **maturation f.**, a substance which causes cells to mature. **milk f.**, mouse mammary tumor agent. **mouse antialopecia f.**, inositol. **mouse mammary tumor f.**, mouse mammary tumor agent. **multiple f's**, in heredity, two or more genes which cooperate or blend or cumulate to produce a certain character. **N f.**, a factor occurring in yeast, meat, liver and wheat germ, the absence of which from an otherwise complete diet causes rats to voluntarily consume more alcohol than they do when factor N is present in the diet. **Nebenthau f.**, a chemical group, $N:C(OH).CH_2$, derived from urea; an essential constituent of the barbituric acid hypnotics. **necrotizing f.**, necrotoxin. **norite eluate f.**, folic acid. **pellagra-preventive f.**, nicotinic acid. **Peter's f.**, vitamin B_5. **plasma converting f.** See *factor V*, under *coagulation f's.* **platelet f's**, factors important in hemostasis which are contained in or attached to the platelets. See *platelet factor 1, platelet factor 2, platelet factor 3*, and *platelet factor 4*, under *coagulation f's.* See also *platelet cofactors*, under *cofactor.* **P.-P. f.**, nicotinic acid. **f. R.**, folic acid. **rat acrodynia f.**, pyridoxine. **Readors' f.**, vitamin B_4. **reducing f.**, ascorbic acid. **restropic f.**, a substance in the blood which stimulates the activity of the reticuloendothelial system. **Rh f.**, **Rhesus f.**, a factor present in the blood. See *blood type.* **rheumatoid f.**, a protein of high molecular weight appearing in the serum in most patients with rheumatoid arthritis and detectable by serological tests. **f. S**, biotin. **Simon's septic f.**, decrease of eosinophils and increase of neutrophils in the blood in pyogenic infections. **skin f.**, biotin. **SLR f.**, folic acid. **spreading f.**, hyaluronidase. **stable f.** See *factor VII*, under *coagulation f's.* **Streptococcus lactis R f.**, folic acid. **Stuart f.**, **Stuart-Prower f.** See *factor X*, under *coagulation f's.* **Trapp's f.**, the last two figures expressive of the specific gravity of urine; when multiplied by 2 they give the number of parts of solids per 1000. **f. U**, folic acid. **f. V.** 1. See under *coagulation f's.* 2. One of the factors necessary for the growth of influenza and other organisms; it is Warburg's co-enzyme, pyridine nucleotide phosphate. **f. VI.** See under *coagulation f's.* **f. VII.** See under *coagulation f's.* **f. VIII.** See under *coagulation f's.* **f. W**, biotin. **Wills f.**, a substance present in crude yeast and liver that is therapeutically effective in certain cases of nutritional macrocytic anemia; thought not to be identical with vitamin B_{12} or folic acid. **f. X.** 1. See under *coagulation f's.* 2. Biotin. **f. XI.** See under *coagulation f's.* **f. XII.** See under *coagulation f's.* **f. Y**, pyridoxine. **yeast eluate f.**, pyridoxine. **yeast filtrate f.**, pantothenic acid. **yeast L. casei f.**, folic acid.

facultative (fak′ul-ta″tiv). Not obligatory; voluntary; potential; pertaining to or characterized by the ability to adjust to particular circumstances or to assume a particular role.

faculty (fak′ul-te) [L. *facultas*]. 1. Any normal power or function, especially a mental one. 2. The corps of professors and instructors of a college or university. **fusion f.**, the power of blending into one the two images seen by the two eyes.

fadenreaction (fah″den-re-ak′shun) [Ger.]. Mandelbaum's reaction.

faenum graecum (fe′num gre′kum) [L. "Greek hay"]. Fenugreek.

Faget's sign (fazh-āz′) [Jean Charles *Faget*, a French physician, 1818–1884]. See under *sign.*

fagopyrism (fag-op′ĭ-rizm) [L. *fagopyrum* buckwheat]. Poisoning by buckwheat.

Fahr. Abbreviation for *Fahrenheit.*

Fahraeus reaction, test (fah-re′us) [Robin *Fahraeus*, Swedish pathologist, born 1888]. See under *tests.*

Fahrenheit scale, thermometer (far′en-hīt) [Gabriel Daniel *Fahrenheit*, a German physicist, 1686–1736]. See under *thermometer.*

failure (fāl′yer). Inability to perform. **heart f.** See *heart-failure.*

faint (fānt). Syncope.

falcadina (fal″kah-de′nah). A disease of Istria characterized by the formation of papillomas.

falcate (fal′kāt). Falciform.

falces (fal′sēz) [L.]. Plural of *falx.*

falcial (fal′shal). Pertaining to a falx.

falciform (fal′sĭ-form) [L. *falx* sickle + *forma* form]. Shaped like a sickle.

falcula (fal′ku-lah) [L.]. The falx cerebelli.

falcular (fal′ku-lar) [L. *falx* sickle]. Sickle-shaped.

fallectomy (fah-lek′to-me). Salpingectomy.

fallopian aqueduct, ligament, tube (fal-lo′pe-an) [Gabriele *Falloppio* (L. *Fallopius*), 1523–1562; an important Italian anatomist, pupil of Vesalius, and later professor at Padua]. See under the nouns.

fallostomy (fah-los′to-me). Salpingostomy.

Fallot's tetrad, tetralogy (fal-ōz′) [Étienne-Louis Arthur *Fallot*, French physician, 1850–1911]. See *tetralogy of Fallot.*

fallotomy (fah-lot′o-me). Division of the fallopian tube.

Falls's test (fawlz) [Frederick Howard *Falls*, Chicago obstetrician and gynecologist, born 1885]. See under *tests.*

false (fawls) [L. *falsus*]. Not true; not genuine; apparent, but not real.

Falta's triad (fahl′taz) [Wilhelm *Falta*, Vienna physician, born 1875]. See under *triad.*

falx (falks), pl. *fal'ces* [L. "sickle"]. A sickle-shaped organ or structure; used as a general term in anatomical nomenclature to designate such a structure. **aponeurotic f., f. aponeurot'ica,** f. inguinalis. **f. cerebel'li** [N A, B N A], **f. of cerebellum,** the small fold of dura mater in the midline of the posterior cranial fossa, projecting forward toward the vermis of the cerebellum. **f. cer'ebri** [N A, B N A], **f. of cerebrum,** the sickle-shaped fold of dura mater that extends downward in the longitudinal cerebral fissure and separates the two cerebral hemispheres. **inguinal f., f. inguina'lis** [N A, B N A], the united tendons of the transversalis and internal oblique muscles going to the linea alba and pectineal line of the pubic bone. Called also *tendo conjunctivus.* **ligamentous f., f. ligamen-to'sa,** processus falciformis ligamenti sacrotuberosi. **f. sep'ti,** N A alternative for *valvula foraminis ovalis.*

F.A.M.A. Abbreviation for *Fellow of the American Medical Association.*

fames (fa'mēz) [L.]. Hunger.

familial (fah-mil'e-al) [L. *familia* family]. Occurring in or affecting different members of the same family.

family (fam'ĭ-le). 1. A group of individuals descended from a common ancestor. 2. A taxonomic subdivision subordinate to an order (or suborder) and superior to a tribe (or subfamily). **degenerate f.,** a family that produces many socially unfit members and only few desirable members. **Jukes f.,** a family located mostly in New York State; the history covers five generations. **Kallikak f.,** an American family with two branches; one unfit, the other highly respectable; history from the American Revolution. **systematic f.** See *family* (def. 2). **Zero f.,** a Swiss family of three branches, two of which are respected and one very unfit. A very complete history from the 17th century.

fang (fang). 1. The root of a tooth. 2. A carnassial tooth of a beast or the envenomed tooth of a serpent.

Fannia (fan'e-ah). A genus of flies, the larvae of which have caused both intestinal and urinary myiasis in man. **F. canicula'ris,** a species of small grayish flies, visibly different from the housefly; they lay their eggs on decaying vegetable matter or animal manure, from which the eggs or larvae may gain access to human hosts. **F. scala'ris,** a species of flies similar to but larger than *F. canicularis,* and commonly depositing its eggs in excrement, rather than in vegetable matter.

fantascope (fan'tah-skōp) [*fantasy* + Gr. *skopein* to examine]. An apparatus for enabling a person to converge the eyes, and so observe certain phenomena of binocular vision.

fantast (fan'tast). A psychopathic person in whom fantasy and day-dreaming usurp the place of real experience and activity.

fantasy (fan'tah-se). Phantasy.

Fantus' antidote (fan'tus) [Bernard *Fantus,* Chicago pharmacologist, 1874–1904]. See under *antidote.*

F.A.P.H.A. Abbreviation for *Fellow of the American Public Health Association.*

Far. Abbreviation for *faradic.*

Farabeuf's triangle (far"ah-bufs') [Louis Hubert *Farabeuf,* French surgeon, 1841–1910]. See under *triangle.*

farad (far'ad) [Michael *Faraday*]. The unit of electrical capacity. The capacity of a condenser which, charged with 1 coulomb, gives a difference of potential of 1 volt. This unit is so large that one-millionth part of it has been adopted as a practical unit called a microfarad.

Faraday's constant, law, space (far'ah-dāz) [Michael *Faraday,* English physicist, 1791–1867]. See under the nouns.

faradic (fah-rad'ik). Pertaining to faradism.

faradimeter (far"ah-dim'e-ter) [*farad* + Gr. *metron* measure]. An instrument for measuring faradic electricity.

faradipuncture (far"ad-ĭ-punk'tūr). The application of the faradic current by means of needle electrodes thrust into the tissues.

faradism (far'ah-dizm). 1. Induced electricity. 2. Induced electricity in a rapidly alternating current. 3. Faradization. **surging f.,** a faradic current of gradually increasing and decreasing amplitude.

faradization (far"ah-di-za'shun). The therapeutic use of an interrupted current for the stimulation of muscles and nerves. Such a current is derived from an induction coil, usually from the secondary though occasionally from the primary. **galvanic f.,** the use of a galvanic or continuous electric current conjoining with that of an alternating current.

faradize (far'ah-dīz). To treat with faradism.

faradocontractility (far"ah-do-kon"trak-til'ĭ-te). Contractility in response to faradic stimulus.

faradomuscular (far"ah-do-mus'ku-lar). Resulting from application of the faradic current to a muscle.

faradonervous (far"ah-do-ner'vus). Resulting from the application of the faradic current to a nerve.

faradopalpation (far"ah-do-pal-pa'shun). Galvanopalpation.

faradotherapy (far"ah-do-ther'ah-pe). Treatment by the use of faradism.

farcin (far-să') [Fr.]. Farcy. **f. du boeuf** (far-să' doo buf), cattle farcy.

farcinoma (far"sĭ-no'mah). A glanderous tumor.

farcy (far'se). The more chronic and constitutional form of glanders, marked by thickening of the superficial lymph vessels. See *glanders.* **button f.,** farcy characterized by the formation of small tubercular nodules in the skin of the limbs, thorax, and abdomen. **cattle f.,** a disease of cattle which is caused by infection with *Nocardia farcinica,* and characterized by the formation of cheesy nodules in the subcutaneous tissue and the organs. **cryptococcus f.,** lymphangitis epizootica. **Japanese f., Neapolitan f.,** lymphangitis epizootica. **f. pipes,** acute farcy along the lymphatic vessels. **water f.,** inflammation of the lymphatics of a horse's leg.

fardel-bound (far'del-bownd). Having an inflamed abomasum and distended omasum, so that chewing of the cud is impossible; a condition seen in cattle and sheep.

farina (fah-re'nah) [L.]. 1. Meal or flour. 2. A starchy food prepared from maize. **f. ave'na,** oatmeal. **f. trit'ici,** wheaten flour.

farinaceous (far"ĭ-na'shus) [L. *farinaceus*]. 1. Of the nature of flour or meal. 2. Starchy; containing starch.

farinometer (far"ĭ-nom'e-ter). An instrument for determining the percentage of gluten in flour.

Farr's law (farz) [William *Farr,* English medical statist, 1807–1883]. See under *law.*

Farre's line (farz) [Arthur *Farre,* British obstetrician, 1811–1887]. See under *line.*

Farre's tubercles (farz) [John Richard *Farre,* an English physician, 1775–1862]. See under *tubercle.*

farsighted (far-sīt'ed). Hyperopic.

farsightedness (far-sit'ed-nes). Hyperopia.

Fasc. Abbreviation for L. *fascic'ulus,* bundle.

fascia (fash'e-ah), pl. *fas'ciae* [L. "band"]. 1. [N A, B N A] A sheet or band of fibrous tissue such as lies deep to the skin or forms an investment for muscles and various organs of the body. 2. A bandage. **abdominal f., internal,** f. transversalis. **Abernethy's f.,** f. iliaca. **anal f.,** f. diaphragmatis pelvis inferior. **anoscrotal f.,** f. superficialis perinei. **antebrachial f., f. antebra'chii** [N A], the investing fascia of the forearm. **aponeurotic f.,** deep f. **f. of arm,** f. brachii. **f. axilla'ris** [N A, B N A],

axillary f., the investing fascia of the armpit which passes between the lateral borders of the pectoralis major and latissimus dorsi muscles. **bicipital f.,** aponeurosis musculi bicipitis brachii. **brachial f., f. bra'chii** [N A, B N A], the investing fascia of the arm. **buccinator f., f. buccopharyn'gea** [N A, B N A], **buccopharyngeal f.,** a fibrous membrane forming the external covering of the constrictor muscles of the pharynx, and passing forward superiorly to the surface of the buccinator muscle. **Buck's f.,** the deep fascia of the penis, being continuous with Colles' fascia of the perineum and with Scarpa's fascia of the abdominal wall. **bulbar f., f. bul'bi [Tenoni]** [B N A]. See *vaginae bulbi.* **f. of Camper,** the superficial layer of the superficial fascia of the abdomen. **cervical f.,** f. cervicalis. **cervical f., deep,** f. nuchae. **f. cervica'lis** [N A], the fascia of the neck, comprising a superficial layer deep to the skin, a pretracheal layer anterior to the trachea, and a prevertebral layer anterior to the vertebrae; it also forms a sheath enclosing the carotid vessels and vagus nerve. Called also *f. colli* [B N A], and *cervical f.* **f. cine'rea,** a band extending from the lateral striae of the corpus callosum to the fascia dentata. **clavipectoral f., f. clavipectora'lis** [N A], a fascial sheet investing the subclavius muscle, attaching to the clavicle above and continuing to the pectoralis minor muscle below. Called also *f. coracoclavicularis* [B N A]. **f. clitor'idis** [N A, B N A], **f. of clitoris,** the dense fibrous tissue that encloses the two corpora cavernosa of the clitoris. **Cloquet's f.,** the condensation of extraperitoneal tissue closing the femoral ring (septum femorale). **Colles' f.,** f. diaphragmatis urogenitalis inferior. **f. col'li** [B N A], f. cervicalis. **fasciae of colon,** teniae coli. **Cooper's f.** 1. Fascia cremasterica. 2. See *fibrae intercrurales.* **coracoclavicular f., f. coracoclavicula'ris** [B N A], **coracocostal f.,** f. clavipectoralis. **cremasteric f., f. cremaster'ica** [N A, B N A], the thin covering of the spermatic cord formed by the investing fascia of the cremasteric muscle. It is adjacent to the external surface of the internal spermatic fascia. **cribriform f.** 1. Fascia cribrosa. 2. Septum femorale. **f. cribro'sa** [N A, B N A], the part of the superficial fascia of the thigh that covers the saphenous opening. **crural f., f. cru'ris** [N A, B N A], the investing fascia of the leg. **Cruveilhier's f.,** f. superficialis perinei. **dartos f. of scrotum,** tunica dartos. **deep f.,** a dense, firm, fibrous membrane investing the trunk and limbs, and giving off sheaths to the various muscles. **deep f. of arm,** f. brachii. **deep f. of back,** f. thoracolumbalis. **deep f. of forearm,** f. antebrachii. **deep f. of perineum,** diaphragma urogenitale. **deep f. of thigh,** f. lata femoris. **Denonvilliers' f.,** septum rectovesicale. **f. denta'ta hippocam'pi** [B N A], **dentate f.,** gyrus dentatus. **f. diaphrag'matis pel'vis infe'rior** [N A, B N A], the fascia that covers the lower surface of the coccygeus and levator ani muscles, forming the medial wall of the ischiorectal fossa. **f. diaphrag'matis pel'vis supe'rior** [N A, B N A], the fascia forming the inner sheath of the levator ani and coccygeus muscles. **f. diaphrag'matis urogenita'lis infe'rior** [N A, B N A], the investing fascia on the superficial surface of the urogenital diaphragm, which is continuous with the fascia covering the external oblique muscle and the sheath of the rectus abdominis. Called also *membrana perinei.* **f. diaphrag'matis urogenita'lis supe'rior** [N A, B N A], the investing fascia on the deep surface of the urogenital diaphragm, continuous with the membranous layer of the subcutaneous tissue covering the front and sides of the lower part of the abdomen. **dorsal f., deep,** f. thoracolumbalis. **dorsal f. of foot,** f. dorsalis pedis. **dorsal f. of hand, f. dorsa'lis ma'nus** [N A, B N A], the investing fascia of the back of the hand. **f. dorsa'lis pe'dis** [N A, B N A], the investing fascia on the dorsum of the foot. **endoabdominal f.,** f. transversalis. **endopelvic f., f. endopelvi'na,** a name given in Basle Nomina Anatomica to fascia forming part of the general layer lining the pelvic walls and serving as a packing for the pelvic organs, as well as ensheathing the blood vessels, various specific parts of which have been unofficially known by various names. Omitted in N A. **endothoracic f., f. endothora'cica** [N A, B N A], the fascial sheet beneath the serous lining of the thoracic cavity. **extrapleural f.,** a prolongation of the endothoracic fascia sometimes found at the root of the neck, which is important as possibly modifying the auscultatory sounds at the apex of the lung. **femoral f.,** f. lata femoris. **fibroareolar f.,** superficial f. **f. of forearm,** f. antebrachii. **f. of head,** galea aponeurotica. **hypogastric f.,** f. pelvis. **iliac f.** 1. Fascia iliaca. 2. Arcus iliopectineus. **f. ili'aca** [N A, B N A], a strong fascia covering the inner surface of the iliac and psoas muscles. **f. iliopectin'ea** [B N A], **iliopectineal f.,** arcus iliopectineus. **f. infraspina'ta** [B N A], omitted in N A. **infundibuliform f.,** f. spermatica interna. **intercolumnar f.** 1. Fascia cremasterica. 2. See *fibrae intercrurales.* **ischioprostatic f.,** f. diaphragmatis urogenitalis inferior. **ischiorectal f.,** f. diaphragmatis pelvis inferior. **f. la'ta fem'oris** [N A, B N A], the external investing fascia of the thigh. **f. of leg,** f. cruris. **longitudinal f., anterior,** ligamentum longitudinale anterius. **longitudinal f., posterior,** ligamentum longitudinale posterius. **lumbodorsal f., f. lumbodorsa'lis** [B N A], f. thoracolumbalis. **masseteric f., f. masseter'ica** [N A], a layer of deep cervical fascia covering the masseter muscle. **muscular fasciae of eye, fas'ciae muscula'res bul'bi** [N A], **fas'ciae muscula'res oc'uli** [B N A], the sheets of fascia investing the extraorbital muscles, continuous with the vaginae bulbi. **f. of nape,** f. nuchae. **f. of neck,** f. cervicalis. **f. nu'chae** [N A, B N A], **nuchal f.,** the fascia on the muscles in the dorsal region of the neck. **obturator f., f. obturato'ria** [N A, B N A], the part of the parietal fascia of the pelvis covering the internal obturator muscle. **orbital fasciae, fas'ciae orbita'les** [N A, B N A], fibrous tissue surrounding the posterior part of the eyeball, supporting and binding together the structures within the orbit. **palmar f.,** aponeurosis palmaris. **palpebral f., f. palpebra'lis,** septum orbitale. **parietal f. of pelvis,** f. pelvis parietalis. **parotid f., f. parotide'a** [N A], a layer of cervical fascia enclosing the parotid gland. **f. parotideomasseter'ica** [B N A], the fascia enclosing the parotid gland and masseter muscle; separately called *f. parotidea* and *f. masseterica* in the new Nomina Anatomica. **f. pectin'ea** [B N A], **pectineal f.,** the pubic portion of the fascia lata. Omitted in N A. **pectoral f., f. pectora'lis** [N A, B N A], the sheet of fascia investing the pectoralis major muscle. **pelvic f.,** f. pelvis. **pelvic f., parietal,** f. pelvis parietalis. **pelvic f., visceral,** f. pelvis visceralis. **pelviprostatic f.,** f. prostatae. **f. pel'vis** [N A, B N A], fascia that forms part of the general layer lining the walls of the pelvis and invests the pelvic organs. **f. pel'vis parieta'lis** [N A], the fascia on the wall of the pelvis. **f. pel'vis viscera'lis** [N A], the fascia that covers the organs and vessels of the pelvis. **f. pe'nis profun'da** [N A], the firm inner fascial layer that surrounds the corpora cavernosa and the corpus spongiosum collectively. **f. pe'nis superficia'lis** [N A], the loose external layer of fascial tissue of the penis, continuous with the tunica dartos and with the superficial perineal fascia. **perineal f., deep,** diaphragma urogenitale. **perineal f., middle,** f. diaphragmatis urogenitale superior. **perineal f., superficial,** f. superficialis perinei. **pharyngobasilar f., f. pharyngobasila'ris** [N A, B N A], a strong fibrous membrane in the wall of the pharynx, lined internally with mucous membrane and incompletely covered on its outer surface by the overlapping constrictor muscles of the pharynx. It blends with the periosteum at the base of the skull. **phrenicopleural f., f. phrenicopleura'lis** [N A], the fascial layer on the upper surface of the diaphragm, beneath the pleura. **plantar f.,** aponeurosis plantaris. **prevertebral f.,** lamina prevertebralis. **proper f. of neck, f. pro'pria col'li,** f. cervicalis. **f. pro'pria coo'peri,** fascia spermatica interna. **f. prosta'tae** [N A, B N A], **f. of prostate,** the reflection of the superior fascia of the pelvic diaphragm onto the prostate. **rectal f.,** f. diaphragmatis pelvis superior. **rectoabdominal f.,** vagina musculi recti abdominis. **rectovesical f.,** f. diaphragmatis pelvis superior. **Richet's f.,** a fold of extraperitoneal fascia enveloping the obliterated umbilical vein. **scalene f.,** membrana suprapleuralis. **Scarpa's f.** See *fibrae intercrurales.* **semilunar f.,** aponeurosis musculi bicipitis brachii. **Sibson's f.,** membrana suprapleuralis. **spermatic f., external,** f. spermatica externa. **spermatic f., internal,** f. spermatica interna. **f. spermat'ica exter'na** [N A], the thin outer covering of the spermatic cord, which is continuous with the investing fascia of the external oblique muscle. **f. spermat'ica inter'na** [N A], the thin innermost covering of the spermatic cord, derived from the transversalis fascia of the abdominal wall. Called also *tunica vaginalis communis* [*testis et funiculi spermatici*] [B N A]. **subperitoneal f.** 1. Fascia subperitonealis. 2. Tela subserosa peritonei. **f. subperitonea'lis** [N A], the thin layer of connective tissue separating the peritoneum from the transversalis fascia. **f. subscapula'ris** [B N A], omitted in N A. **superficial f.** 1. Fascia superficialis. 2. Tela subcutanea. **superficial f. of perineum,** f. superficialis perinei. **f. superficia'lis** [B N A], a fascial sheet lying directly beneath the skin. Omitted in N A. **f. superficia'lis perine'i** [N A, B N A], the subcutaneous tissue of the urogenital region, comprising a superficial fatty and a deep membranous layer. **f. supraspina'ta** [B N A], omitted in N A. **f. of Tarin, f. tari'ni,** gyrus dentatus. **temporal f., f. tempora'lis [lam'ina profun'da et lam'ina superficia'lis]** [N A], a strong fibrous sheet covering the temporalis muscle. It has a deep and a superficial part which attach inferiorly to the zygomatic arch. **f. of Tenon.** See *vaginae bulbi.* **f. of thigh,** f. lata femoris. **f. thoracolumba'lis** [N A], **thoracolumbar f.,** the fascia of the back that attaches medially to the vertebral column for its entire length and blends laterally with the aponeurosis of the transversus abdominis muscle. Inferiorly it attaches to the iliac crest and the sacrum. Called also *f. lumbodorsalis* [B N A]. **thyrolaryngeal f.,** fascia investing the thyroid body and attaching to the cricoid cartilage. **f. transversa'lis** [N A, B N A], **transverse f.,** part of the inner investing layer of the abdominal wall, continuous with the fascia of the other side behind the rectus abdominis and the rectus sheath, and continuous also with the diaphragmatic fascia, iliac fascia, and the parietal pelvic fascia. **triangular f. of abdomen,** ligamentum inguinale reflexum. **triangular f. of Macalister,** musculus pyramidalis. **triangular f., of Quain,** ligamentum inguinale reflexum. **Tyrrell's f.,** septum rectovesicale. **f. of urogenital trigone,** diaphragma urogenitale. **visceral f. of pelvis,** f. pelvis visceralis. **volar f.,** aponeurosis palmaris.

fasciae (fash'e-e) [L.]. Plural of *fascia.*

fasciagram (fash'e-ah-gram). A roentgenogram obtained by fasciagraphy.

fasciagraphy (fash"e-ag'rah-fe). Roentgenography of fasciae after the injection of air into them.

fascial (fash'e-al). Pertaining to or of the nature of a fascia.

fasciaplasty (fash'e-ah-plas"te) [*fascia* + Gr. *plassein* to form]. A plastic operation on a fascia.

fascicle (fas'ĭ-k'l). A small bundle or cluster, especially of nerve or muscle fibers. See also *fasciculus.* **longitudinal f. of cerebrum, medial,** fasciculus longitudinalis medialis cerebri. **longitudinal f's of cruciform ligament,** fasciculi longitudinales ligamenti cruciformis atlantis.

fascicular (fah-sik'u-lar). 1. Pertaining to a fascicle. 2. Fasciculated.

fasciculated (fah-sik'u-lāt-ed). Clustered together or occurring in bundles.

fasciculation (fah-sik"u-la'shun). 1. The formation of fasciculi. 2. A small local contraction of muscles, visible through the skin, representing a spontaneous discharge of a number of fibers innervated by a single motor nerve filament.

fasciculi (fah-sik'u-li) [L.]. Plural of *fasciculus.*

fasciculus (fah-sik'u-lus), pl. *fascic'uli* [L. dim. of *fascis* bundle]. A small bundle or cluster; used as a general term in anatomical nomenclature to designate a small bundle of nerve or muscle fibers. Called also *fascicle.* **f. aberrans of Monokow,** rubrospinal tract. **f. acus'ticus,** one of a series of white striae extending transversely across the floor of the fourth ventricle of the brain. **f. ante'rior pro'prius [Flech'sigi]** [B N A], a name given the white fibers (part of the fasciculi proprii) anterior to the gray matter of the spinal cord. **f. anterolatera'lis superficia'lis [Gower'si]** [B N A], tractus spinocerebellaris anterior. **f. arcua'tus,** f. longitudinalis superior cereberi. **f. atrioventricula'ris** [N A], a small band of atypical cardiac muscle fibers originating in the atrioventricular node. See *bundle of His.* **f. of Burdach,** pars temporalis radiationis corporis callosi. **cerebellospinal f., f. cerebellospina'lis** [B N A], tractus spinocerebellaris posterior. **f. cerebrospina'lis ante'rior** [B N A], tractus corticospinalis anterior. **cerebrospinal f., lateral, f. cerebrospina'lis latera'lis** [B N A], tractus corticospinalis lateralis. **fascic'uli cor'poris restifor'mis** [B N A], omitted in N A. **cuneate f. of Burdach,** f. cuneatus medullae spinalis. **cuneate f. of medulla oblongata,** f. cuneatus medullae oblongatae. **cuneate f. of spinal cord,** f. cuneatus medullae spinalis. **f. cunea'tus [Burda'chi]** [B N A], f. cuneatus medullae spinalis. **f. cunea'tus medul'lae oblonga'tae** [N A], the continuation into the medulla oblongata of the fasciculus cuneatus of the spinal cord. Called also *funiculus cuneatus medullae oblongatae* [B N A]. **f. cunea'tus medul'lae spina'lis** [N A], the lateral portion of the posterior funiculus of the spinal cord, composed of ascending fibers that terminate in the nucleus cuneatus of the medulla oblongata. Called also *f. cuneatus* [*Burdachi*] [B N A]. **dorsolateral f., f. dorsolatera'lis,** tractus dorsolateralis. **f. ex'ilis,** a cluster of muscle fibers connecting the flexor pollicis longus with the inner condyle of the humerus, or with the coronoid process of the ulna. **extrapyramidal motor f.,** rubrospinal tract. **fibrous f. of biceps muscle,** aponeurosis musculi bicipitis brachii. **Flechsig's f.** 1. Fasciculus anterior proprius. 2. Fasciculus lateralis proprius. **f. of Foville,** tractus spinocerebellaris posterior. **f. of Goll,** f. gracilis medullae spinalis. **f. of Gowers,** tractus spinocerebellaris anterior. **f. gra'cilis medul'lae oblonga'tae** [N A], the continuation into the medulla oblongata of the fasciculus gracilis of the spinal cord. Called also *funiculus gracilis medullae oblongatae* [B N A]. **f. gra'cilis medul'lae spina'lis** [N A], the median portion of the posterior funiculus of the spinal cord, composed of ascending fibers that terminate in the nucleus gracilis of the medulla oblongata. Called also *f. gracilis* [*Golli*] [B N A]. **interfascicular f., f. interfascicula'ris,** a collection of fibers situated between the fasciculus gracilis and the fasciculus cuneatus, containing some of the descending branches of the fibers of the medial division of the dorsal roots of the spinal nerves. **f. latera′lis plex′us brachia′lis** [N A, B N A], a collection of fibers arising from the anterior divisions of the superior and middle trunks of the brachial plexus, C5 through C7, and passing to the lateral pectoral and musculocutaneous nerves and the lateral root of the median and the ulnar nerves. **f. latera′lis pro′prius [Flech′sigi]** [B N A], a name given the white fibers (part of the fasciculi proprii) lateral to the gray matter of the spinal cord. **longitudinal f., dorsal,** f. longitudinalis dorsalis. **longitudinal f., medial,** f. longitudinalis medialis. **longitudinal f. of cerebrum, inferior,** f. longitudinalis inferior cerebri. **longitudinal f. of cerebrum, posterior,** f. longitudinalis medialis cerebri. **longitudinal f. of cerebrum, superior,** f. longitudinalis superior cerebri. **longitudinal f. of colon.** See *teniae coli.* **longitudinal fasciculi of cruciform ligament,** fasciculi longitudinales ligamenti cruciformis atlantis. **longitudinal f. of medulla oblongata, posterior,** f. longitudinalis medialis medullae oblongatae. **f. longitudina′lis dorsa′lis** [N A], a lightly myelinated fiber bundle that runs in the periventricular gray substance throughout the extent of the mesencephalon, near the medial longitudinal fasciculus. **f. longitudina′lis infe′rior cer′ebri** [N A, B N A], a bundle of association fibers extending through the occipital and temporal lobes of the cerebrum, consisting chiefly of geniculocalcarine projection fibers. Called also *inferior longitudinal f. of cerebrum.* **fascic′uli longitudina′les ligamen′ti crucifor′mis atlan′tis** [N A], vertical midline longitudinal fibers that, together with the transverse ligament of the atlas, form the cruciform ligament of the atlas. The fibers arise in two groups from the root of the dens—one group extending cranially to the anterior margin of the foramen magnum, the other caudally to the body of the axis. Called also *longitudinal fasciculi of cruciform ligament.* **f. longitudina′lis media′lis** [N A, B N A], a well-defined fiber tract extending through the mesencephalon, into the spinal cord, and carrying vestibular internuclear and extrapyramidal fibers. Throughout most of its course it lies just lateral to the midline in the dorsal part of the tegmentum. **f. longitudina′lis media′lis cer′ebri,** B N A term for the portion of the fasciculus longitudinalis medialis within the cerebrum. **f. longitudina′lis media′lis medul′lae oblonga′tae,** B N A term for the portion of the fasciculus longitudinalis medialis within the medulla oblongata. **f. longitudina′lis media′lis pon′tis,** B N A term for the portion of the fasciculus longitudinalis medialis within the pons. **fascic′uli longitudina′les pon′tis** [N A], **fascic′uli longitudina′les [pyramida′les] pon′tis** [B N A], the corticopontine, corticonuclear, and corticospinal fibers that are found in the pars basilaris of the pons. **f. longitudina′lis supe′rior cer′ebri** [N A, B N A], a bundle of association fibers in the cerebrum, extending from the frontal lobe to the posterior end of the lateral sulcus, and interrelating the cortex of the frontal, temporal, parietal, and occipital lobes. **maculary f.,** a system of nerve fibers originating in the macula lutea; some are uncrossed (on the temporal side) and others are crossed fibers (on the nasal side of the retina). **mamillothalamic f., f. mamillothalam′icus** [N A], a stout bundle of fibers from the mamillary body to the anterior nucleus of the thalamus. Called also *f. thalamomamillaris* [*Vicq d' Azyri*] [B N A]. **f. margina′lis ventra′lis,** a fasciculus made up of the tectospinal tract and the vestibulospinal tract. **f. media′lis plex′us brachia′lis** [N A, B N A], a collection of fibers arising from the anterior division of the inferior trunk, C8–T1, and passing to the medial pectoral, medial brachial cutaneous, and medial antebrachial cutaneous nerves, and the medial root of the ulnar and the median nerve: general sensory and motor. **Meynert's f.,** f. retroflexus. **muscular fasciculi of colon,** teniae coli. **f. obli′quus [pon′tis]** [B N A], omitted in N A. **f. occipitofronta′lis,** tapetum. **olivary f.,** a fillet beneath and enclosing the olivary body. **optic f.,** the optic nerve. **oval f.,** an area of descending fibers in the posterior funiculus of the spinal cord near the posterior septum; called also *median root zone.* **fascic′uli pedunculomamilla′res** [B N A], omitted in N A. **f. poste′rior plex′us brachia′lis** [N A, B N A], a collection of fibers arising from the posterior divisions of the superior, middle, and inferior trunks of the brachial plexus, C5 through C8 and sometimes T1, and passing to the subscapular, thoracodorsal, radial, and axillary nerves: general sensory and motor. **fascic′uli pro′prii** [N A], that part of the white matter of the spinal cord bordering the gray matter, and containing fibers that travel for a distance of only a few segments of the cord. **pyramidal f., anterior,** tractus corticospinalis anterior. **pyramidal f., direct,** tractus corticospinalis anterior. **pyramidal f., lateral,** tractus corticospinalis lateralis. **f. pyramida′lis ante′rior,** tractus corticospinalis anterior. **f. pyramida′lis latera′lis,** tractus corticospinalis lateralis. **f. retroflex′us** [B N A], a small bundle of nerve fibers running from the habenula to the interpeduncular nucleus; called also *Meynert's bundle* or *fasciculus*, and *habenulopeduncular tract.* **f. of Rolando,** the enlarged head of the posterior cornu of gray matter in the medulla oblongata. **f. rotun′dus,** tractus solitarius medullae oblongatae. **septomarginal f.,** a collection of fibers situated near the posterior median septum of the spinal cord, containing some of the descending branches of the fibers of the medial division of the dorsal roots of the spinal nerves. **solitary f.,** tractus solitarius medullae oblongatae. **f. subcallo′sus,** a tract of long association fibers beneath the callosum, running to the frontal, occipital, and parietal lobes. **sulcomarginal f., f. sulcomargina′lis,** a layer of descending branches of dorsal root fibers situated in the anterior funiculus of the spinal cord, along the border of the anterior fissure. **f. te′res,** f. longitudinalis medialis pontis. **f. thalamomamilla′ris [Vicq d'Azyri]** [B N A], f. mamillothalamicus. **fascic′uli transver′si aponeuro′sis palma′ris** [N A, B N A], the transverse fascial bands that support the webs between the fingers. Called also *transverse f. of palmar aponeurosis.* **fascic′uli transver′si aponeuro′sis planta′ris** [N A, B N A], transverse bundles in the plantar asponeurosis near the toes. Called also *transverse fasciculi of plantar aponeurosis.* **f. of Türck,** tractus corticospinalis anterior. **unciform f., uncinate f., f. uncina′tus** [N A, B N A], a collection of fibers connecting the frontal and temporal lobes of the cerebrum. **f. of Vicq d'Azyr,** f. mamillothalamicus.

fasciectomy (fas″e-ek′to-me) [*fascia* + Gr. *ektomē* excision]. Excision of fascia.

fasciitis (fas″e-i′tis). Inflammation of fascia. **exudative calcifying f.,** calcinosis. **nodular f.,** proliferative f. **proliferative f.,** a benign reactive proliferation of fibroblasts with a distinct microscopic pattern superficially resembling that of sarcoma; the lesions are located in the subcutaneous tissues and commonly associated with the deep fascia. **pseudosarcomatous f.,** a benign soft-tissue tumor occurring subcutaneously and sometimes arising from deep muscle and fascia, and histologically resembling a malignant sarcoma.

fasciodesis (fas″e-od′ĕ-sis) [L. *fascia* + Gr. *desis* binding]. The operation of suturing a fascia to skeletal attachment.

Fasciola (fah-si′o-lah) [L. *fasciola* a band]. A genus of flukes. **F. gigan′tica,** the giant liver fluke of Africa and Asia which occasionally infects man. **F. hepat′ica,** the common liver fluke of sheep, oxen, goats, horses, and other herbivorous animals. It is occasionally found in the human liver, where it may cause dangerous symptoms by obstructing the biliary passages, causing enlargement of the liver, with degeneration and cyst formation. Several snails of the genus Lymnaea act as invertebrate hosts. Called also *Fasciola humana, F. venarum,* and *Distoma hepaticum.* **F. heteroph′yes,** *Heterophyes heterophyes.* **F. mag′na,** *Fascioloides magna.*

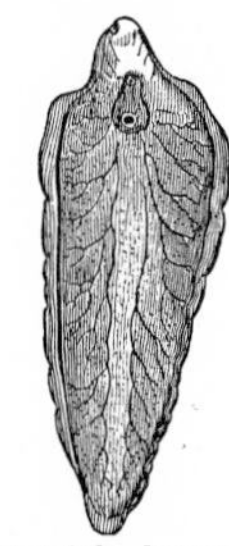
Fasciola hepatica (Mitchell).

fasciola (fah-se′o-lah), pl. *fasci′olae* [L., dim. of *fascia*]. 1. A small band or striplike structure. 2. A small bandage. **f. cine′rea** [B N A], **f. cine′rea cin′guli,** gyrus fasciolaris. **f. dentata,** gyrus dentatus.

fasciolae (fah-se′o-le) [L.]. Plural of *fasciola.*

fasciolar (fah-se′o-lar). Pertaining to a fasciola.

Fascioletta (fas″e-o-let′tah). A name formerly given a genus of parasitic flukes. **F. ilioca′na,** *Echinostoma iliocanum.*

fascioliasis (fas″e-o-li′ah-sis). Infection with *Fasciola hepatica, Fascioloides,* or *Fasciolopsis.*

Fascioloides (fas″e-o-loi′dēz). A genus of flukes. **F. mag′na,** the large American liver fluke; a trematode found in the liver and lungs of herbivorous animals in North America.

fasciolopsiasis (fas″e-o-lop-si′ah-sis). The state of being infected with flukes of the genus Fasciolopsis.

Fasciolopsis (fas″e-o-lop′sis) [*fasciola* + Gr. *opsis* appearance]. A genus of trematode worms. **F. bus′ki,** a trematode worm found in the gallbladder and duodenum of residents in Asia. It is the largest of the intestinal flukes, and is said to cause indigestion, nausea, headache, and diarrhea. The intermediate hosts are the mussels, *Planorbis coenosus* and *Segmentina largillierti.* Other names that have been given this species are *F. fuelleborni* from Calcutta and Egypt, *F. goddardi* from China, *F. rathouisi* from Asia, *F. spinifera* from China.

fascioplasty (fash′e-o-plas″te). Any plastic operation on fascia.

fasciorrhaphy (fash″e-or′ah-fe) [*fascia* + Gr. *rhaphē* suture]. The suturing together of torn fascia.

fasciotomy (fash″e-ot′o-me) [*fascia* + Gr. *temnein* to cut]. Surgical incision of a fascia.

fascitis (fah-si′tis). Inflammation of a fascia.

fast (fast). Immovable, or unchangeable; resistant to the action of a specific drug or to staining.

fastidium (fas-tid′e-um) [L. "loathing, disgust"]. Repugnance to food.

fastigatum (fas″tĭ-ga′tum) [L.]. Pointed; sharpened to a point.

fastigium (fas-tij′e-um) [L. "gable end"]. 1. [B N A] The highest point in the roof of the fourth ventricle, at the junction between the superior medullary velum and the nodulus. 2. The acme, or highest point, as of a fever.

fastness (fast′nes). The quality of being immovable or unchangeable, as the property of bacteria to resist the action of stains or of destructive agents.

fat (fat). 1. Adipose tissue; a white or yellowish tissue which forms soft pads between various organs of the body, serves to smooth and round out bodily contours, and furnishes a reserve supply of energy. 2. An ester of glycerol with fatty acids, usually oleic acid, palmitic acid, or stearic acid. **bound f.,** masked f. **brown f.,** interscapular gland. **chyle f.,** fat in the form of an extremely fine emulsion taken into the chyle by the lymphatics of the intestine. **corpse f., grave f.,** adipocere. **masked f.,** fat that can be detected in a cell or tissue by chemical methods but is not revealed by staining methods. **milk f.,** the suspension in milk which tends to separate out as cream. **molecular f.,** fat occurring in fine specks within the cells. **moruloid f., mulberry f.,** interscapular gland. **neutral f.,** a compound of a fatty acid and glycerin. **protein f.,** soap albumin. **wool f.,** the purified, anhydrous, fatlike substance from the wool of sheep, *Ovis aries,* used as a water-absorbable ointment base. Called also *anhydrous lanolin* and *refined wool fat.* **wool f., hydrous,** the purified fatlike substance from the wool of sheep, *Ovis aries,* containing 25 to 30 per cent of water, used as a water-absorbable ointment base. **wool f., refined.** See *wool f.*

fatal (fa′tal). Causing death; deadly; mortal.

fate (fāt) [L. *fatum* what is ordained by the gods]. The ultimate disposition or decreed outcome. In pharmacology, the intermediate and ultimate disposition of a drug in the body. **prospective f.,** the development normally achieved by any region of the egg or early embryo when there is no interference.

fatigability (fat″ĭ-gah-bil′ĭ-te). Easy susceptibility to fatigue.

fatigue (fah-tēg′) [Fr.; L. *fatigatio*]. A state of increased discomfort and decreased efficiency resulting from prolonged or excessive exertion. **convoy f.,** the condition of seamen in the merchant marine, whose ships have been torpedoed, bombed or sunk and who are unable to sleep or rest because of the constant threat of another similar experience. **pilot f.,** progressive decrease of efficiency together with a feeling of loss of control, occurring in aviators. **stance f.,** the fatigue produced by quiet standing. **stimulation f.,** decreased excitability of a nerve from repeated stimulation.

fatty (fat′e). Pertaining to fat.

fauces (faw′sēz) [L., pl. of *faux* "a gorge, narrow pass"]. The passage from the mouth to the pharynx, including both the lumen and its boundaries.

Fauchard's disease (fo-sharz′) [Pierre *Fauchard,* French dentist, 1678–1761]. Periodontitis.

faucial (faw′shal). Pertaining to the fauces.

faucitis (faw-si′tis). Inflammation of the fauces.

fauna (faw′nah) [L. *Faunus* mythical deity of herdsmen]. The animal life present in or characteristic of a given region or locality. It may be discernible with the unaided eye (macrofauna), or only with the aid of a microscope (microfauna).

Fauvel's granules (fo-velz′) [Sulpice Antoine *Fauvel,* French physician, 1813–1884]. Peribronchitic abscesses.

faveolar (fa-ve′o-lar). Pertaining to the faveolus.

faveolate (fa-ve′o-lāt) [L. *faveolus,* from *fa′vus* honeycomb]. Honeycombed; alveolate.

faveoli (fa-ve′o-li) [L.]. Plural of *faveolus.*

faveolus (fa-ve′o-lus), pl. *fave′oli* [L.]. Foveola.

favid (fa′vid). A secondary skin eruption due to allergy in favus.

favism (fa′vism) [Italian *fava* bean]. An acute hemolytic anemia caused by ingestion of fava beans or inhalation of the pollen of the plant, occurring in certain individuals as a result of a hereditary biochemical lesion of the erythrocytes and a consequent enzyme deficiency. See *glucose-6-phosphate dehydrogenase anemia.*

favus (fa′vus) [L. "honeycomb"]. A distinctive type of tinea capitis, caused by *Trichophyton schoenleini,* and characterized by the formation of yellow, cup-shaped crusts composed of dense mats of mycelia and epithelial debris, which enlarge to form prominent honeycomb-like masses. **f. circina′tus,** favus occurring in a circinate patch. **f. herpet′icus,** favus in which the lesion is papulovesicular and studded with small yellow points. **f. herpetifor′mis,** mouse favus.

mouse f., a disease of mice, caused by the fungus *Achorion quinkeanum;* it may be transmitted to man. **f. mu′rium,** mouse f. **f. pila′ris,** favus of the scalp.

F-cortef (ef-kor′tef). Trade mark for a preparation of fludrocortisone.

F.D. Abbreviation for *focal distance,* and for *fatal dose.*

F.D.$_{50}$. Abbreviation for *median fatal dose,* or that quantity of an agent which is fatal to 50 per cent of the test subjects.

F.D.A. Abbreviation for *fronto-dextra anterior* (right fronto-anterior) position of the fetus.

F.D.I. Abbreviation for *Fédération Dentaire Internationale* [Fr. International Dental Association].

F.D.P. Abbreviation for *fronto-dextra posterior* (right frontoposterior) position of the fetus.

F.D.T. Abbreviation for *fronto-dextra transversa* (right frontotransverse) position of the fetus.

Fe. Chemical symbol for *iron* (L. *ferrum*).

Feb. dur. Abbreviation for L. *feb′re duran′te,* while the fever lasts.

febricant (feb′rĭ-kant). Causing fever.

febricide (feb′rĭ-sīd) [*febris* + L. *caedere* to kill]. 1. Lowering bodily temperature in fever. 2. An agent that reduces fever.

febricity (fe-bris′ĭ-te). Feverishness; the quality of being febrile.

febricula (fe-brik′u-lah) [L.]. A slight or temporary attack of fever.

febrifacient (feb″rĭ-fa′shent) [*febris* + L. *facere* to make]. Producing fever.

febrific (feb-rif′ik). Producing fever.

febrifugal (feb-rif′u-gal) [*febris* + L. *fugare* to put to flight]. Dispelling or relieving fever.

febrifuge (feb′rĭ-fūj). An agent that reduces body temperature in fever.

febrile (feb′ril) [L. *febrilis*]. Pertaining to or characterized by fever.

febriphobia (feb-re-fo′be-ah) [L. *febris* fever + *phobia*]. Anxiety produced by a rise in body temperature.

febris (fe′bris) [L.]. Fever. **f. colomben′sis,** a fever occurring in Ceylon. **f. endem′ica rose′ola,** dengue. **f. entericoi′des,** entericoid fever. **f. meliten′sis,** brucellosis. **f. pal′lida,** an acute infectious malignant endocarditis occurring in Switzerland. **f. quinta′na,** trench fever. **f. recur′rens,** relapsing fever. **f. ru′bra,** scarlatina. **f. sudora′lis,** brucellosis. **f. tritae′a,** tertian intermittent fever. **f. un′dulans.** 1. Brucellosis. 2. Typhomalarial fever. **f. uveoparotide′a,** uveoparotid fever. **f. wolhynica,** trench fever.

fecal (fe′kal). Pertaining to or of the nature of feces.

fecalith (fe′kah-lith) [*feces* + Gr. *lithos* stone]. An intestinal concretion formed around a center of fecal matter.

fecaloid (fe′kal-oid). Resembling fecal matter.

fecaloma (fe″kah-lo′mah) [*feces* + *-oma*]. Stercoroma.

fecaluria (fe″kah-lu′re-ah) [*feces* + Gr. *ouron* urine + *-ia*]. The presence of fecal matter in the urine.

feceometer (fe″se-om′e-ter). An instrument for measuring the rate of defecation and the amount of the feces.

feces (fe′sēz) [L. *faeces,* pl. of *faex* refuse]. The excrement discharged from the intestines, consisting of bacteria, cells exfoliated from the intestines, secretions, chiefly of the liver, and a small amount of food residue.

Fechner's law (fek′nerz) [Gustav Theodor *Fechner,* Prussian natural philosopher, 1801–1887]. See under *law.*

$FeCO_3$. Ferrous carbonate.

fecula (fek′u-lah) [L. *faecula* lees, dregs]. 1. Lees or sediment. 2. Starch; also the starchy part of a seed.

feculent (fek′u-lent) [L. *faeculentus*]. 1. Having dregs or a sediment. 2. Excrementitious.

fecundate (fe′kun-dāt) [L. *fecundere* to make fruitful]. To impregnate or fertilize.

fecundatio (fe″kun-da′she-o) [L.]. Fecundation. **f. ab ex′tra,** impregnation occurring without entrance of the penis into the vagina.

fecundation (fe″kun-da′shun) [L. *fecundatio*]. Impregnation or fertilization. **artificial f.,** artificial insemination.

fecundity (fe-kun′dĭ-te) [L. *fecunditas*]. Ability to produce offspring rapidly and in large numbers.

Fede's disease (fa′daz) [Francesco *Fede,* an Italian physician, 1832–1913]. See under *disease.*

Federici's sign (fe-de-re′chēz) [Cesare *Federici,* an Italian physician, 1832–1892]. See under *sign.*

fee (fe). A charge fixed by custom or by law. **capitation f.,** the annual fee per person on a practitioner's panel under the National Insurance Act of Great Britain.

feeblemindedness (fe″b'l-mīnd′ed-nes). Mental deficiency from arrested mental development. The feebleminded are divided into three grades: idiots, with a mental age below two years; imbeciles, with a mental age between two and seven years; and morons, with a mental age between seven and twelve years.

feedback (fēd′bak). The return of some of the output of a system as input. See also *feedback inhibition.*

feeding (fēd′ing). The taking or giving of food. **artificial f.,** feeding of a baby with food other than mother's milk. **breast f.,** the feeding of an infant at the breast. **extrabuccal f.,** the administration of nutriment other than by mouth. **Finkelstein's f.,** feeding of infants based upon decrease in the milk sugar of the food. **forced f., forcible f.,** the administration of food by force to those who cannot or will not receive it. **sham f.,** feeding in which the food is chewed and swallowed but does not enter the stomach, being diverted to the exterior by an esophageal fistula or other device.

Feer's disease (fairz) [Emil *Feer,* Swiss pediatrician, 1864–1955]. See under *disease.*

fee-splitting (fe-split′ing). The division of moneys received by a specialist, such as a surgeon, between himself and the physician who referred the patient to him.

fefe (fe-fe) [Samoan]. Elephantiasis.

Fehleisen's streptococcus (fa′līs-enz) [Friedrich *Fehleisen,* German (later American) physician, 1854–1924]. The streptococcus of erysipelas.

Fehling's solution (fa′lingz) [Hermann von *Fehling,* German chemist, 1812–1885]. See under *solution.*

fel (fel), gen. *fel′lis* [L. "bile," "gall"]. The bile. **f. bo′vis,** oxgall. **f. bo′vis inspis′satum,** dried oxgall. **f. bo′vis purifica′tum, f. tau′ri purifica′tum,** purified oxgall: laxative, tonic, and digestant.

Feleki's instrument (fa-la′kēz) [Hugo von *Feleki,* Budapest urologist, 1861–1932]. An instrument for massaging the prostate.

fellatio (fĕ-la′she-o) [L. *fellare* to suck]. Oral stimulation or manipulation of the penis.

felo-de-se (fa″lo-da-sa′) [Sp. "felon of one's self"]. A person who commits suicide.

felon (fel′on). A purulent infection or abscess involving the pulp of the distal phalanx of the finger. Cf. *paronychia* and *eponychia.* **bone f.,** a subperiosteal felon causing necrosis of the bone. **deep f.,** a term which includes subcutaneous, thecal and subperiosteal felons. **frog f.,** an abscess in the web space of the hand. **subcutaneous f.,** a deep felon situated beneath the skin. **subcuticular f., subepithelial f.,** a pustule located between the cuticle and the true skin. **subperiosteal f.,** a felon involving the periosteum of the terminal phalanx. **superficial f.,** subcuticular felon. **thecal f.,** a felon that involves the synovial sheath, producing a suppurative tenosynovitis.

Felsen's treatment (fel′senz) [Joseph *Felsen*, New York gastroenterologist, 1892–1955]. See under *treatment*.

Felton's serum, unit (fel′tunz) [Lloyd D. *Felton*, Boston physician, 1885–1953]. See under *serum* and *unit*.

feltwork (felt′werk). A complex of closely interwoven fibers, as of nerve fibrils.

Felty's syndrome (fel′tēz) [A. R. *Felty*, American physician, born 1895]. See under *syndrome*.

Fem. intern. Abbreviation for L. *femor′ibus inter′nus*, at the inner side of the thighs.

female (fe′māl) [L. *femella* young woman]. 1. An individual organism of the sex that bears young or that produces ova or eggs. 2. Feminine.

feminilism (fem-in′il-izm). Feminism.

feminine (fem′ĭ-nin). Pertaining to the female sex, or possessing qualities normally characteristic of the female.

femininity (fem″ĭ-nin′ĭ-te). Womanhood; the possession of normal female qualities by a woman.

feminism (fem′ĭ-nizm). The appearance or existence of female secondary sex characters in the male. **mammary f.,** gynecomastia.

feminization (fem″ĭ-ni-za′shun). The induction or development of female secondary sex characters in the male. **testicular f.,** a condition in which the subject is phenotypically female but lacks nuclear sex chromatin and is of XY chromosomal sex; the uterus and tubes are absent or rudimentary, and the gonads are typically testes and may be abdominal or inguinal in position.

feminonucleus (fem″ĭ-no-nu-kle′us). The female pronucleus.

femme (fahm) [Fr.]. Woman. **sage f.** (sahzh-fahm′) [Fr. "wise woman"], a midwife.

femora (fem′o-rah) [L.]. Plural of *femur*.

femoral (fem′or-al) [L. *femoralis*]. Pertaining to the femur, or to the thigh.

femorocele (fem′o-ro-sēl) [L. *femur* thigh + Gr. *kēlē* hernia]. Femoral hernia.

femoro-iliac (fem″o-ro-il′e-ak). Pertaining to the femur and the ilium.

femorotibial (fem″o-ro-tib′e-al). Pertaining to the femur and the tibia.

femur (fe′mur), pl. *fem′ora* [L.] [N A, B N A]. 1. The proximal portion of the lower member of the body, situated between the pelvis and the knee. 2. The bone that extends from the pelvis to the knee, being the longest and largest bone in the body. Called also *thigh bone*.

fenestra (fĕ-nes′trah), pl. *fenes′trae* [L. "window"]. A window-like opening; an opening or open area, as in an anatomical structure, or in a bandage or cast, or in the blade of a forceps. **f. choled′ocha,** a gridlike opening created in the wall of the duodenum by removal of the biliary and pancreatic ducts. **f. of cochlea, f. coch′leae** [N A, B N A], a round opening in the inner wall of the middle ear below and a little behind the fenestra vestibuli. It is covered by the secondary tympanic membrane. Called also *round window*. **f. nov-ova′lis,** a surgically created oval window in the vestibular dome in Lempert's fenestration operation. **f. ova′lis,** f. vestibuli. **f. rotun′da,** f. cochleae. **f. vestib′uli** [N A, B N A], an oval opening in the inner wall of the middle ear, which is closed by the base of the stapes. Called also *oval window*.

fenestrae (fĕ-nes′tre) [L.]. Plural of *fenestra*.

fenestrated (fen′es-trāt″ed) [L. *fenestratus*]. Pierced with one or more openings.

fenestration (fen″es-tra′shun) [L. *fenestratus* furnished with windows]. 1. The act of perforating, or the condition of being perforated. 2. The surgical creation of a new opening in the labyrinth of the ear for the restoration of hearing in cases of otosclerosis. **aortopulmonary f.,** a congenital anomaly consisting of a communication between the aorta and the pulmonary artery just above the semilunar valves.

Fenwick's disease (fen′wiks) [Samuel *Fenwick*, English physician, 1821–1902]. Primary atrophy of the stomach.

Fe_2O_3. Ferric oxide.

$FeOH_3$. Ferric hydroxide.

feosol (fe′o-sol). Trade mark for preparations of ferrous sulfate.

feral (fe′ral) [L. *feralis*]. Savage; wild; deadly.

fer-de-lance (fār-dĕ-lahs′) [Fr. "lance head"]. A large venomous snake, *Bothrops atrox*, of South and Central America, Mexico and the West Indies.

Féréol's nodes (fa″ra-ōlz′) [Louis Henri Felix *Féréol*, French physician, 1825–1891]. See under *node*.

fergon (fer′gon). Trade mark for preparations of ferrous gluconate.

Fergusson's incision, speculum (fer′gus-unz) [Sir William *Fergusson*, British surgeon, 1808–1877]. See under *incision* and *speculum*.

ferment [L. *fermentum* leaven]. 1. (fer-ment′). To undergo fermentation; the term is applied to decomposition of carbohydrates. 2. (fer′ment). Any substance that causes fermentation in other substances with which it comes in contact. See *enzyme*. **chemical f.,** one which is not a living organism; an enzyme. **curdling f.,** rennin. **defensive f's.** See *Abderhalden's reaction*, under *reaction*. **diastatic f.,** a ferment that changes starch into sugar. **digestive f.,** a ferment which participates in the digestion of food. **fibrin f.,** thrombin. **heteroform f.,** a bacteriolytic ferment which destroys those bacteria which produce it and others as well. **lab f.,** rennin. **lactic f.,** a ferment which decomposes lactose into lactic acid and carbon dioxide. **leukocytic f.,** the ferment or cytase of leukocytes. **living f.,** an organized ferment. **metallic f.,** a colloidal metal. **milk-curdling f.,** rennin. **myosin f.,** one occurring in muscle plasma which converts myosinogen into myosin. **organized f.,** a living plant or animal organism, such as a microbe, which acts as a ferment. **protective f.,** a ferment formed in the body as a result of the presence in the blood of foreign substances, and capable of splitting up the foreign substance and thus protecting the organism. Called *abwehrfermente*. Cf. *Abderhalden's reaction*, under *reaction*. **soluble f., unorganized f.,** an enzyme. **urea f.** See *urease* and *nephrozymase*. **Warburg's f.** See under *enzyme*.

fermental (fer-men′tal). Pertaining to or arising from a ferment.

fermentation (fer″men-ta′shun) [L. *fermentatio*]. Enzymic decomposition, especially of carbohydrates as used in the production of alcohol, bread, vinegar, and other food or industrial materials. **acetic f.,** the conversion of a weak alcoholic solution into acetic acid or vinegar. **alcoholic f.,** the production of ethylic alcohol from carbohydrates. **ammoniacal f.,** the formation of ammonia and carbon dioxide from urea. **amylic f.,** the fermentation which produces amyl alcohol from sugar. **butyric f.,** the change of carbohydrates, milk, etc., into butyric acid. **caseous f.,** the coagulation of soluble casein under the influence of rennet ferment. **dextran f.,** the fermentation by which dextrose is converted into dextran. **diastatic f.,** the change of starch into glucose, under the influence of ptyalin, the glycolytic ferment, etc. **frog spawn f.,** dextran f. **intestinal f.,** a form of intestinal dyspepsia marked by abdominal distention, discomfort and pain, with watery stools and impaired starch digestion. **lactic f., lactic acid f.,** the souring of milk, caused by various bacilli. **propionic f.,** the production of propionic acid from saccharine solutions by the *Bacillus cavicidus*. **saccharobutyric f.,** intestinal fermentation of carbohydrates, with the formation of butyric acid, produced by the *Bacillus aerogenes-capsulatus*. **stormy f.,** the rapid fermentation of milk produced by *Clostridium welchii*, marked by rupture of the clotted milk by the pressure of the gas which develops. **viscous f.**, the production of gummy substances, as in the urine, in milk, and in wine, under the influence of various bacilli.

fermentemia (fer″men-te′me-ah) [*ferment* + Gr. *haima* blood + *-ia*]. The presence of a ferment in the blood.

fermentogen (fer-men′to-jen) [*ferment* + Gr. *gennan* to produce]. A substance which may be converted into a ferment.

fermentoid (fer-men′toid) [*ferment* + Gr. *eidos* form]. A ferment which has been altered so as to lose its active properties.

fermentum (fer-men′tum) [L. "ferment"]. Yeast.

fermium (fer′me-um) [Enrico *Fermi*, Italian physicist, 1901–1954; winner of the Nobel prize for physics in 1938]. The chemical element number 100, atomic weight 253, symbol Fm, originally discovered in debris from thermonuclear explosion in 1952.

Ferrata's cell (fer-at′az) [Adolfo *Ferrata*, Italian physician, 1880–1946]. Hemohistioblast.

ferrated (fer-āt′ed). Charged with iron.

Ferrein's cords, foramen, ligament, pyramid, tubes, etc. (fer′in) [Antoine *Ferrein*, French physician, 1693–1769]. See under the nouns.

ferri (fer′e) [L. gen. of *ferrum*]. See *iron*.

ferri-albuminic (fer″e-al-bu-min′ik). Containing iron and albumin.

Ferribacterium (fer″re-bak-te′re-um). A genus of microorganisms of the family Siderocapsaceae, suborder Pseudomona dineae, order Pseudomonadales, occurring as rods with rounded or square ends, singly, or in pairs or short chains. It includes two species, *F. du′plex* and *F. rectangula′re*.

ferric (fer′ik) [L. *ferrum*]. Containing iron in its trivalent form (Fe ≡), and yielding trivalent ions (Fe^{+++}) in aqueous solution.

ferricyanide (fer″e-si′ah-nīd). A salt of hydroferricyanic acid.

ferricyanogen (fer″e-si-an′o-jen). A hexad radical, $(FeC_6N_6)_2$.

Ferrier's method, treatment (fer′e-erz) [P. *Ferrier*, French physician]. See under *treatment*.

ferrin (fer′in). An iron-containing substance found in some bile pigments.

ferritin (fer′ĭ-tin). The iron-apoferritin complex, which is one of the forms in which iron is stored in the body.

Ferrobacillus (fer″ro-bah-sil′lus). A genus of microorganisms of the family Siderocapsaceae, suborder Pseudomonadineae, order Pseudomonadales, occurring as short rod-shaped cells, singly or in pairs, which oxidize ferrous iron to the ferric state. The type species is *F. ferroox′idans*.

ferrocholinate (fer″ro-ko′lin-āt). A compound prepared by reacting equimolar quantities of freshly precipitated ferric chloride with choline dihydrogen citrate, the metallic ion being sequestered and firmly bound into a ring within the molecule: used as a hematinic.

ferrocyanide (fer″o-si′ah-nīd). A salt of hydroferrocyanic acid.

ferrocyanogen (fer″o-si-an′o-jen). A tetravalent radical, $Fe(CN)_6$.

ferrokinetics (fer″ro-ki-net′iks). The turnover, or rate of change, of iron in the body.

ferrolip (fer′ro-lip). Trade mark for preparations of ferrocholinate.

ferrometer (fer-om′e-ter) [*ferrum* + Gr. *metron* measure]. An instrument for estimating the amount of iron in the blood.

ferropectic (fer″o-pek′tik). Fixing iron.

ferropexy (fer′o-pek″se) [*ferrum* + Gr. *pēxis* fixation]. The fixation of iron.

ferroprotein (fer″o-pro′te-in). A protein combined with an iron-containing radical. The ferroproteins are respiratory carriers. Cf. *Warburg's enzyme*, under *enzyme*, and *cytochrome*.

ferrosilicon (fer″o-sil′ĭ-kon). Steel in which silicon has been incorporated, giving a substance of great tensile strength.

ferrosoferric (fer-o″so-fer′ik). Combining a ferrous with a ferric compound.

ferrotherapy (fer″o-ther′ah-pe) [*ferrum* + *therapy*]. Therapeutic use of iron and iron compounds.

ferrous (fer′us). Containing iron in its divalent form (Fe =) and yielding divalent ions (Fe^{++}) in aqueous solution. **f. lactate,** iron lactate. **f. sulfate,** iron sulfate.

ferruginous (fer-u′jĭ-nus) [L. *ferruginosus*; *ferrugo* iron rust]. 1. Containing iron or iron rust; chalybeate. 2. Of the color of iron rust.

ferrule (fer′ool). A ring or band of metal applied to the root or crown of a tooth in order to strengthen it, or to protect the margin of the prepared area during placement of a restoration.

fertile (fer′til) [L. *fertilis*]. Fruitful; susceptible of being developed into a new individual (of ova); not sterile or barren.

fertility (fer-til′ĭ-te). The capacity to conceive or induce conception.

fertilization (fer′tĭ-lĭ-za′shun). The act of rendering fertile; fecundation. It consists of the fusion of a spermatozoon with an ovum, this being the natural stimulus which starts the development of the zygote thus formed. It results in the restoration of the diploid number of chromosomes, the paternal participation in inheritance, the determination of sex, and the initiation of cleavage. **cross f.,** the fertilization of one flower by the pollen of another.

fertilizin (fer″tĭ-li′zin). A substance of the plasma membrane and gelatinous coat of the ovum. It is considered to possess the specific receptor groups that bind the spermatozoon to the ovum, and may also be concerned in engulfment of the spermatozoon by the ovum. In sea-urchins it has been characterized chemically as a glycoprotein of about 300,000 molecular weight.

Ferula (fer′u-lah) [L.]. A genus of umbelliferous plants. *F. asafoetida*, *F. foetida*, *F. narthex*, and *F. scorodosma* yield asafetida. *F. galbaniflua* and *F. rubricaulis* yield galbanum.

Ferv. Abbreviation for L. *fer′vens*, boiling.

fervescence (fer-ves′ens) [L. *fervescere* to become hot]. Development of an increased body temperature, or fever.

fester (fes′ter). To suppurate superficially.

festinant (fes′tĭ-nant). Accelerating.

festination (fes″tĭ-na′shun) [L. *festinatio*]. An involuntary tendency to increase the speed in walking, as seen in paralysis agitans and other nervous diseases.

festoon (fes-toon′). The curvature of the gingival margin around the teeth, a feature that is reproduced in an artificial denture by carvings in the base material.

festschrift (fest′shrift) [Ger.]. A memorial volume; a book made up of articles contributed by pupils or associates and friends of a scientist or leader, published usually to honor some special occasion, such as a birthday or other anniversary.

fetal (fe′tal). Pertaining to a fetus; in the human, usually pertaining to the young developing in utero after the second month of gestation.

fetalism (fe′tal-izm). Fetalization.

fetalization (fe″tal-i-za′shun). The retention, into adult life, of bodily characters which at some earlier stage of evolutionary history were actually only infantile and were rapidly lost as the organism attained maturity.

fetation (fe-ta′shun). The development of a fetus within the uterus.

feticide (fe′tĭ-sid) [*fetus* + L. *caedere* to kill]. The destruction of the fetus in the uterus.

feticulture (fe′tĭ-kul″tūr). The hygiene of pregnancy.

fetid (fe′tid) [L. *foetidus*]. Having a rank or disagreeable smell.

fetish (fe′tish). An object believed to be endowed with supernatural powers or regarded with unreasoning devotion.

fetishism (fe′tish-izm). The worship or adoration of an inanimate object as a symbol of a loved person.

fetishist (fe′tish-ist). A person who secures erotic gratification from a fetish.

fetlock (fet′lok). The metacarpophalangeal and metatarsophalangeal regions in the horse.

fetography (fe-tog′rah-fe) [*fetus* + Gr. *graphein* to write]. Roentgenography of the fetus in utero.

fetometry (fe-tom′e-tre) [*fetus* + Gr. *metron* measure]. The measurement of the fetus, especially of the diameters of the fetal head. **roentgen f.,** measurement of the fetal head in the uterus by means of the roentgen ray.

fetoplacental (fe″to-plah-sen′tal). Pertaining to the fetus and placenta.

fetor (fe′tor) [L.]. Stench, or offensive odor. **f. ex o′re,** halitosis. **f. hepat′icus,** the peculiar odor of the breath characteristic of hepatic disease. **f. o′ris,** halitosis.

fetuin (fe′tu-in). A low molecular globulin which constitutes nearly the total globulin in the blood of the fetus and newborn of ungulates.

fetus (fe′tus) [L.]. The unborn offspring of any viviparous animal; the developing young in the human uterus after the end of the second month. Before 8 weeks it is called an embryo; it becomes an infant when it is completely outside the body of the mother, even before the cord is cut. **f. acardi′acus,** acardius. **f. amor′phus,** holoacardius amorphus. **calcified f.,** lithopedion. **f. compres′sus,** f. papyraceus. **harlequin f.,** a fetus with congenital ichthyosis. **f. in fe′tu,** a small, imperfect fetus, incapable of independent life, contained within the body of another fetus, the autosite. **mummified f.,** a shriveled and dried-up fetus. **paper-doll f., papyraceous f.,** f. papyraceus. **f. papyra′ceus,** a dead fetus pressed flat by the growth of a living twin. **parasitic f.,** an incomplete minor fetus attached to a larger, more completely developed fetus, or autosite. **f. sanguinolen′tis,** a dead fetus which has undergone maceration. **sireniform f.,** a sirenomelus, or sympus.

Feulgen reaction, test (foil′gen) [Robert *Feulgen*, German physiologic chemist, 1884–1955]. See under *test.*

fever (fe′ver) [L. *febris*]. 1. Abnormally high bodily temperature; pyrexia. 2. Any disease characterized by marked increase of temperature, acceleration of the pulse, increased tissue destruction, restlessness, delirium, etc. **abortus f.,** brucellosis. **absorption f.,** a fever often seen during the first twelve hours after parturition. **acclimation f.** 1. A disease caused by a change of climate. 2. A disease of horses and cattle due to a change of surroundings, as from pasture in the country to stables in the city. **Aden f.,** dengue. **adenotyphus f.,** typhus fever with swelling of mesenteric glands. **adynamic f.,** asthenic f. **African coast f.,** Rhodesian f. **African tick f.,** a relapsing fever caused by *Borrelia duttonii.* **algid pernicious f.,** pernicious malaria with symptoms of collapse. **alimentary f.,** the fever which accompanies gastrointestinal disturbance. **American mountain f.,** Colorado tick f. **Andaman A f.,** a leptospiral fever occurring in the Netherlands East Indies. **aphthous f.,** foot and mouth disease. **Archibald's f.,** a fever occurring in the Soudan, characterized by high fever and drowsiness. **artificial f.,** elevation of bodily temperature produced by artificial means, such as the high-frequency heater or malariotherapy. **aseptic f.,** surgical fever from aseptic wounds, supposed to be due to the disintegration of leukocytes. **Assam f.,** kala-azar. **asthenic f.,** a fever with nervous depression, feeble pulse, and a cool, moist skin. **Australian Q f.** See *Q fever.* **autumn f.,** nanukayami. **Bangkok hemorrhagic f.,** dengue. **barbiero f.,** a disease produced by the bite of *Panstrongylus megistus.* **biduotertian f.,** tertian malaria with two broods of parasites segmenting on alternate days, so the febrile paroxysms are nearly continuous. **biliary f. of dogs,** a condition in dogs, caused by the *Piroplasma canis.* Called also *malignant jaundice of dogs.* **biliary f. of horses,** a disease of horses due to infection with the *Piroplasma equi,* and marked by pigmentation of the mucous membranes with bile. **bilious f.,** one with apparent liver complications and attended with the vomiting of bile. **bilious f. of cattle,** galziekte. **black f.,** Rocky Mountain spotted f. **black-water f.,** a dangerous and little understood complication or malaria, especially of the falciparum type, characterized by the passage of dark red to black urine, severe toxicity, and high mortality, especially for Europeans. **blister f.,** pemphigus acutus. **blue f.,** Rocky Mountain spotted f. **boohoo f.,** a disease of Hawaii and other Pacific islands marked by depression of spirits and gastrointestinal disorder. **bouquet f.,** dengue. **boutonneuse f.,** a form of rickettsiosis endemic in southern Europe and northern Africa, transmitted by the dog tick, *Rhipicephalus sanguineus.* **brain f.,** cerebral meningitis or cerebritis, or both together. **Brazilian f., Brazilian spotted f.,** exanthematic typhus of São Paulo. See under *typhus.* **breakbone f.,** dengue. **Bullis f.,** a febrile disease observed in soldiers who had been at Camp Bullis, Texas, marked by very low white blood count with neutropenia, postorbital and occipital headache, and constant lymphadenitis. It is probably caused by a species of *Rickettsia,* and transmitted by the bites of the Lone Star tick, *Amblyomma americanum.* **bullous f.,** the fever that accompanies pemphigus. **Bushy creek f.,** pretibial f. **Bwamba f.,** a mild febrile disease occurring in African natives in Uganda caused by a virus. **cachectic f., cachexial f.,** kala-azar. **Cameroon f.,** malarial f. **camp f.,** typhus f. **canicola f.,** a disease of dogs caused by *Leptospira canicola.* **canine yellow f.,** nambi-uvua. **Canton f.,** Chinese typhus fever of a malarial type. **carbohydrate f.,** food f. **carbuncular f.,** a variety of anthrax affecting cattle and horses, marked by the formation of circumscribed swellings in the skin, which at first are hard, hot, and painful, but later become gangrenous. **Carter's f.,** Asiatic relapsing f. **catarrhal f.,** herpetic f. **cat bite f.,** rat bite f. **cat-scratch f.,** a benign, subacute, regional lymphadenitis which may proceed to sterile suppuration or subside spontaneously. It occurs in people who have contact with cats. and usually follows a scratch or bite. **Cavité f.,** an endemic fever, resembling dengue, of Cavité in the Philippine Islands and the neighborhood. It is marked by abrupt onset, high fever, muscular pain, and tenderness of the eyeballs. **cerebrospinal f.,** epidemic cerebrospinal meningitis. **cesspool f.,** typhoid f. **Chagres f.,** a malignant type of malarial fever occurring along the Chagres River in South America. **channel f.,** land f. **Charcot's f.,** intermittent hepatic f. **childbed f.,** puerperal f. **Chitral f.,** an acute infectious fever (pappataci fever) occurring in the Chitral Valley in India. **Choix f.,** a disease observed in northern Mexico, identical with Rocky Mountain spotted fever. **Cobb's pigmentary f.,** a disease occurring in India marked by a sudden and rapidly rising fever, headache, nausea, vomiting, and pigmentation of the cheeks and nose. **Colombian tick f.,** a variety of spotted fever occurring in Colombia, identical with Rocky Mountain spotted fever. **Colorado tick f.,** a non-exanthematous febrile disease occurring in the Rocky Mountain regions of the United States where the tick vector of the causative virus is prevalent. **Congolian red f.,** murine typhus. **continued f.,** one which does not vary more than 1–1½°F. in twenty-four hours. **Corsican f.,** a sort of malarial fever occurring in Corsica. **cot-**

ton-mill f., byssinosis. **Cyprus f.**, brucellosis. **dandy f.**, dengue. **Danube f.**, a remittent fever endemic along the river Danube. **deer fly f.**, tularemia. **dehydration f.**, inanition f. **dengue f.**, dengue. **desert f.**, coccidioidomycosis. **digestive f.**, a slight rise of temperature during the process of digestion. **double continued f.**, a fever resembling typhoid fever occurring in China. **double quartan f.**, a form of malaria in which the paroxysms occur on two successive days with a one day interval. **Dumdum f.**, kala-azar. **Dutton's relapsing f.**, the central African form of relapsing fever caused by *Borrelia duttonii.* **dust f.**, brucellosis. **East Coast f.**, Rhodesian f. **elephantoid f.**, a recurrent acute febrile condition occurring with filariasis; it may be associated with elephantiasis or lymphangitis, or may occur without inflammatory phenomena. **enteric f.**, typhoid f. **entericoid f.**, any fever which resembles typhoid fever in its clinical manifestations. **ephemeral f.**, a slight fever persisting or lasting only a day or two. **ephemeral f. of horses,** stiff sickness; three-day sickness: an acute infectious disease which affects horses in South Africa. **epidemic catarrhal f.**, influenza. **epidemic hemorrhagic f.**, an acute infectious disease characterized by fever, purpura, peripheral vascular collapse, and acute renal failure, caused by a filtrable agent thought to be transmitted to man by mites or chiggers. **equine biliary f.**, a disease of horses caused by *Babesia equi.* It is marked by jaundice and high fever, with enlargement of the spleen and lymph nodes. **eruptive f., exanthematous f.**, any fever accompanied by an eruption on the skin. **eruptive Mediterranean f.**, Mediterranean exanthematous fever. **essential f.**, fever for which no cause has been found. **estivo-autumnal f.**, malarial fever. **exanthematic f. of Marseille,** boutonneuse f. **famine f.** 1. Relapsing fever. 2. Typhus. **Far East hemorrhagic f.**, epidemic hemorrhagic f. **fatigue f.**, a febrile attack due to overexercise and the absorption of waste products. **ferment f.**, a fever produced by the subcutaneous injection of an unorganized ferment. **fermentation f.**, fever due to the absorption of the products of septic fermentation. **field f.**, harvest f. **five-day f.**, trench f. **flood f.**, scrub typhus. **food f.**, sudden fever with digestive disturbance lasting from a few days to some weeks, and attributed to intestinal auto-intoxication. **Fort Bragg f.**, pretibial f. **foundryman's f.**, metal fume f. **gastric f.**, any acute abdominal attack associated with gastric disturbances. **Gibraltar f.**, brucellosis. **glandular f.**, infectious mononucleosis. **goat f., goat's milk f.**, brucellosis. **Hankow f.**, schistosomiasis japonica. **harvest f.**, a form of spirochetosis affecting harvest workers: it is marked by fever, conjunctivitis, stupor, diarrhea, vomiting, and abdominal pains. **Hasami f.**, a mild fever of Japan caused by *Leptospira autumnalis.* **Haverhill f.**, an acute febrile disease caused by *Streptobacillus moniliformis,* transmitted by the bite of an infected rat, and characterized by an erythematous eruption and more or less severe generalized arthritis, with adenitis, headache, and vomiting; first described in Haverhill, Mass., in 1926. **Hawaiian f.**, a disease coming on with malaise and chill, followed by remittent fever, with splenic enlargement, jaundice, and headache. It occurs in the Hawaiian Islands. **hay f.**, an acute conjunctivitis with nasal catarrh, and often with asthmatic symptoms, regarded as an anaphylactic or allergic condition excited by a specific antigen to which the individual is sensitized. Called also *hay asthma* and *pollenosis.* **hay f., nonseasonal, hay f., perennial,** hay fever which is not restricted to a particular season of the year but is caused by an allergen to which the patient is more or less exposed all the year round, such as dusts and foods. **hay f., seasonal,** hay fever which recurs at about the same time each year and is caused by some specific allergen present at that season, such as various pollens. **hectic f.**, a daily recurring fever with profound sweating, chills, and flushed countenance, associated with tuberculosis and septic poisoning. **hematuric f.**, any malarial fever that is associated with hematuria. **hemoglobinuric f.**, any malarial fever attended with hemoglobinuria. See *black-water f.* **hepatic f.**, catarrhal angiocholitis. **herpetic f.**, a condition characterized by chills, fever, sore throat, and a herpetic eruption on the face. The condition is apparently infectious. **Herxheimer f.**, a fever that sometimes accompanies a Herxheimer reaction. **hospital f.**, epidemic typhus. **hugli f.**, a severe malarial fever endemic in Bengal. Called also *endemic glandular f.* **hyperpyrexial f.**, a peculiar fever with very high temperature (104 to 107°F.) occurring in the West Coast of Africa and in Ceylon. **hysterical f.**, an irregular elevation of temperature without general symptoms, sometimes seen in hysteria. **icterohemorrhagic f.**, Weil's disease. **Ikwa f.**, trench f. **inanition f.**, a transitory fever which frequently occurs in infants during the first few days of life. It is believed to be due to dehydration and is also called *dehydration f.* **intermenstrual f.**, fever sometimes seen in tuberculous women between the menstrual periods. **intermittent f.**, an attack of malaria or other fever that is broken up into recurring paroxysms of elevated temperature separated by intervals during which the temperature is normal. **intermittent hepatic f.**, a fever occurring intermittently as the result of intermittent impaction of stone in the common duct and inflammation of the bile ducts. Called also *Charcot fever* and *Charcot syndrome.* **inundation f.**, scrub typhus. **irritation f.**, a febrile condition due to the presence of irritant materials in the body. **island f.**, scrub typhus. **Jaccoud's dissociated f.**, fever with slow and irregular pulse in tuberculous meningitis of adults. **jail f.**, epidemic typhus. **Japanese flood f., Japanese river f.**, scrub typhus. **jessor f.**, a long-standing intermittent fever common in parts of India. **jungle f.**, a form of pernicious malarial fever occurring in the East Indies. **jungle yellow f.**, a form of yellow fever endemic in parts of Africa and South America. It occurs in or near uncut forest or jungle in areas where *Aedes aegypti* is not found. **Kagami f.**, infectious mononucleosis. **Kedani f.**, scrub typhus. **Kenya f.**, Kenya typhus. **Kew Gardens spotted f.**, rickettsialpox. **Kinkiang f.**, Katayama disease. **Korin f.**, epidemic hemorrhagic f. **kriim f.**, an endemic fever of Iceland, Faroe, and Greenland. **Kumaon f.**, a form of typhus fever in India. **Kyoto f.**, a seven-day fever occurring in Kyoto, Japan. **land f.**, a set of symptoms resembling seasickness sometimes experienced when, after an ocean voyage, the ship enters a relatively landlocked body of water; called also *channel f.* **lechuguilla f.**, a plant toxemia of sheep and goats in western Texas, commonly called swellhead: caused by eating *Agave lechuguilla.* **lent f.**, typhoid f. **leprotic f.**, the irregular febrile disturbances seen in the early stages of leprosy. **Levant f.**, a fever endemic in the Levant; by some believed to be of malarial origin. **Lone Star f.**, Bullis f. **low f.** 1. Asthenic fever. 2. Typhoid fever. **lung f.**, croupous or other pneumonia. **macular f.** 1. A fever characterized by the presence of macules. 2. Typhus fever. **malarial f.**, malaria. **malarial catarrhal f. of sheep,** heartwater disease. **malignant f.**, fever in which the blood undergoes rapid degenerative changes. **Malta f., Maltese f.**, brucellosis. **Manchurian f.**, a disease similar to typhoid or typhus, occurring in Manchuria. **Marseilles f.**, boutonneuse f. **marsh f.** 1. Leptospiral jaundice. 2. Malaria. **Mediterranean f.**, brucellosis. **Mediterranean exanthematous f.**, boutonneuse f. **Mediterranean yellow f.**, Weil's disease. **metal fume f.**, an occupational disorder occurring in those engaged in welding and other metallic operations and due to the volatilized metals. It includes *brass chills, zinc chills, zinc fume f., braziers' chills*, and *brassfounders' ague*. **Meuse f.**, trench f. **mianeh f.**, a form of relapsing fever in Iran. **miliary f.**, an acute infectious disease characterized by fever, profuse sweating, and the formation of a great many papules, succeeded by a crop of pustules. Called also *sweating sickness*. **milk f.** 1. A mild form of puerperal septicemia. 2. A fever said to attend the establishment of lactation after delivery. 3. An endemic fever said to be caused by the use of unwholesome cow's milk. 4. A disease of cows. See *cerebral anemia*, under *anemia*, and *parturient paralysis*, under *paralysis*. **mite f.**, typhus f. **mosquito f.**, a febrile disease affecting unacclimated persons in Herzegovina at the beginning of the mosquito season. **Mossman f.**, a febrile disease endemic in Queensland, Australia, caused by *Leptospira australis*. **mountain f.** 1. Colorado tick fever. 2. Rocky Mountain spotted fever. 3. Brucellosis. **mountain tick f.**, Colorado tick f. **mouse f.**, mouse septicemia. **mud f.**, leptospiral jaundice. **muma f.**, myositis purulenta tropica. **Murchison-Pel-Ebstein f.**, a type of fever observed on occasion in patients with Hodgkin's disease, characterized by irregular episodes of pyrexia of several days' duration, with intervening periods in which the temperature is normal. **Naegele's f.**, fever associated with urticarial eruption described by Naegele in southwest Africa. **nakra f.**, nasa f. **nanukayami f.**, nanukayami. **nasa f., nasha f.** [Hind. *násá* nose], a remittent fever of India attended with brain congestion and a pathognomonic turgescence of the vessels of the schneiderian membrane. **Neapolitan f.**, brucellosis. **nicobar f.**, a violent type of jungle fever. **night-soil f.**, typhoid f. **nine-mile f.**, a name formerly given to Q fever in mice and laboratory workers. See *Q fever*. **nodal f., nodular f.**, erythema nodosum. **nonexanthematous tick f.**, Colorado tick f. **Oroya f.**, the acute febrile anemic stage of Carrion's disease. **Pahvant Valley f.**, tularemia. **paludal f.**, malaria. **Panama f.**, Chagres f. **pappataci f.**, phlebotomus f. **papular f.**, a disorder marked by fever, papular eruption, and rheumatic pains. **paramalta f.**, paramelitensis f. **paramelitensis f.**, a disease resembling clinically Malta fever, but caused by an organism which differs from the *Brucella melitensis*. **paratyphoid f.**, a continued fever with symptoms resembling those of typhoid fever, but with the Widal reaction negative. It is caused by *Salmonella paratyphi*, the paratyphoid, or paracolon bacillus of which there are three types, A, B, and C. See *Salmonella paratyphi, S. schottmülleri*, and *S. hirschfeldii*. **para-undulant f.**, a fever resembling a mild undulant fever, but not caused by the organism of undulant fever. **parenteric f.**, a fever resembling clinically typhoid fever and paratyphoid fever, but due to bacteria other than the bacteria of these diseases. **parrot f.**, psittacosis. **peach f.**, irritation of the skin, with nasal and bronchial catarrh and conjunctivitis, occurring in those who deal in or handle peaches. **periodic f.**, a hereditary condition characterized by repetitive febrile episodes and autonomic disturbances, occurring in precise or irregular cycles of days, weeks, or months; it may begin at any time of life and may last for decades with temporary remissions, or may cease. **petechial f.**, cerebrospinal meningitis. **Pfeiffer's glandular f.**, a mild type of glandular fever occurring in children, marked by swelling of the lymph glands, prostration, and anemia. **pharyngoconjunctival f.**, a febrile disease of viral etiology, occurring in epidemic form, largely in school children, and characterized by fever, pharyngitis, rhinitis, conjunctivitis, and enlarged cervical lymph nodes. **Philippine hemorrhagic f.**, dengue. **phlebotomus f.**, a febrile disease of short duration, resembling dengue in many of its symptoms, occurring in Mediterranean countries, caused by a virus which is transmitted by a species of sandfly, *Phlebotomus papatasii*, and its geographical distribution being limited by occurrence of the vector. **pinta f.**, a disease observed in northern Mexico, identical with Rocky Mountain spotted fever. **pneumonic f.**, croupous pneumonia. **polyleptic f.**, recurrent f. **Pomona f.**, a leptospiral infection occurring in Australia. **pretibial f.**, a virus infection marked by a rash on the pretibial region accompanied by lumbar and postorbital pain, malaise, coryza and fever. **Pretoria f.**, a fever with symptoms resembling abortive typhoid, observed in South Africa. **prison f.**, typhus f. **protein f.**, heightened temperature produced by the injection of protein material into the body. **puerperal f.**, septic poisoning occurring in childbed. **pulmonary f.**, croupous pneumonia. **putrid f.**, epizootic cerebrospinal meningitis. **pythogenic f.**, typhoid f. **Q f.** [Q for *query*], a febrile rickettsial infection, usually respiratory, described in Australia but world wide in distribution and including Balkan grippe in the Mediterranean area; caused by *Coxiella burnettii* (*Rickettsia diaporica*). **quartan f.**, a form of malarial fever caused by the *Plasmodium malariae*, which completes its life cycle in seventy-two hours, so that the paroxysm recurs every three days. **quinine f.**, a fever attended with skin eruption, seen among those who work in quinine. **quintan f., quintana f.**, trench f. **quotidian f.**, a fever that recurs every day. **rabbit f.**, tularemia. **railway f.**, a condition marked by fever and malaise seen in cattle that have been on a long railway journey without proper care and feeding. **rat-bite f.**, an infectious disease following the bite of a rat or other rodent. There are two forms of this disease: *Haverhill fever* and *sodoku*. **recurrent f.**, relapsing f. **red f.**, dengue. **red f. of Congo,** murine typhus. **red f. of swine,** swine erysipelas. **red-water f.**, Texas f. **relapsing f.**, any one of a group of acute infectious diseases caused by various species of *Borrelia*, and marked by alternating periods of fever and apyrexia, each lasting from five to seven days. The disease begins abruptly with chill, headache, neuromuscular pains, fever, and sometimes vomiting. During the febrile periods there is enlargement of the liver and spleen. The organism causing the disease varies in different countries. **remittent f.**, a fever in which the diurnal variation is 2°F. or more, but in which the temperature never falls to a normal level. See *malarial f.* **rheumatic f.**, a disease, probably infectious, associated with the presence of hemolytic streptococci in the body. Beginning with an attack of sore throat, pharyngitis and cervical adenitis, there develop chilliness, rapid rise of temperature, prostration and painful inflammation of the joints (polyarthritis). There is usually cardiac involvement and the development of subcutaneous nodules is characteristic. Called also *acute rheumatic fever, acute articular rheumatism*, and *polyarthritis rheumatica*. **Rhodesian f.**, a form of piroplasmosis of cattle in Africa, caused by the *Piroplasma* (*Theileria*) *parva*, and marked by high fever and swelling of the lymph nodes. The organism is transmitted by the bite of several ticks of the genus *Rhipicephalus*. Called also *East African coast f., Rhodesian red-water f.*, and *Rhodesian tick f.* **rice-field f.**, a fever affecting workers in the rice harvest in Italy and in Sumatra. It is caused by a species of *Leptospira*. **Rift Valley f.**, a febrile disease of viral etiology first observed in domestic animals and man in the Rift Valley of South Africa; its symptoms resemble those of dengue, and it is rarely fatal. **Rio Grande f.**, brucellosis. **river f. of Japan,** pappataci f. **Robb's heat f.**, a noninfective cerebrospinal fever occurring in East Africa. **Robles' f.**, a condition characterized by irregular fever and mild general symptoms, and continuing from two weeks to three months. It occurs in British Honduras. **rock f.**, brucellosis. **Rocky Mountain spotted f.**, an infectious disease formerly believed to be peculiar to the region of the Rocky Mountains but now known to occur in other parts of the western hemisphere. It is characterized by high fever, pains in the bones and muscles, headache, a red, spotted eruption which may become dark and confluent, and by mental symptoms. It is caused by *Rickettsia rickettsii*, which is transmitted by the ticks, *Dermacentor andersoni* (*venus'tus*), the American dog tick, *Dermacentor variabilis*, *Amblyomma americanum* and the rabbit tick, *Haemaphysalis leporispalustris*. **Roman f.,** a virulent type of malarial fever prevailing in the Campagna of Rome. **Russian headache f.,** a dengue-like disease. **sakushu f.,** seven-day fever occurring in autumn epidemics in the Okayama Prefecture of Japan. **Salmonella f.,** a condition resembling mild typhoid fever caused by some member of the genus *Salmonella*. **Salonica f.,** trench f. **salt f.,** fever associated with excess of salt in the body, due to the retention by the salt of the water normally eliminated in the perspiration. **sandfly f.,** phlebotomus f. **San Joaquin f.,** coccidioidomycosis. **São Paulo f.,** exanthematic typhus of São Paulo. See under *typhus*. **scarlet f.,** scarlatina; an acute contagious and exanthematous disease with a scarlet eruption, or rash (Sydenham, 1675). It is caused by a specific strain of hemolytic streptococcus, *S. scarlatinae*. It begins with chills, vomiting, and sore throat, followed by pyrexia and rapid pulse. After about twenty-four hours the eruption appears as a rash of thickly set red spots, which begin to fade in two or three days, and is often gone by the end of the first week. The fever departs in favorable cases with the disappearance of the eruption, which is attended by a desquamation of the skin in fine, branny scales and in large flakes. Recovery may often be looked for in two or three weeks, but is seldom complete in less than six weeks, and it is during this stage that kidney complications are liable to occur, chiefly as a result of exposure to cold or wet. The nephritis is liable to lead to dropsy and uremia. Throat, ear, and eye complications are not infrequent, and often prove chronic. **septic f.,** one due to the entrance of septic poisons in the blood. **seven-day f.** 1. A fever affecting Europeans in India, and marked by symptoms similar to those of dengue. 2. Nanukayami. **sheep f.,** heartwater. **shin bone f.,** trench f. **ship f.,** epidemic typhus. **shipping f.,** pasteurellosis in cattle. **shoddy f.,** a febrile disease, with cough, dyspnea, and headache caused by the dust in shoddy factories. **shouten f.,** a disease which is probably a form of dengue. **simple continued f.,** a noncontagious fever with neither remissions nor intermissions. **slime f.,** leptospiral jaundice. **slow f.,** brucellosis. **solar f.,** dengue. **Songo f.,** epidemic hemorrhagic f. **South African tick-bite f.,** a rickettsial infection observed in South Africa, similar to boutonneuse fever; transmitted by the dog tick, *Haemaphysalis leachi* and by larvae of *Rhipicephalus evertsi* and *Amblyomma hebraeum*. **spirillum f.,** relapsing f. **splenic f.,** true anthrax. **spotted f.,** a febrile disease that is typically characterized by a skin eruption, such as Rocky Mountain spotted fever, boutonneuse fever, and other infections caused by tick-borne rickettsiae, and typhus and epidemic cerebrospinal meningitis. **sthenic f.,** fever characterized by a full, strong pulse, hot and dry skin, high temperature, thirst, and active delirium. **stiff-neck f.,** epidemic cerebrospinal meningitis. **stockyards f.,** pasteurellosis in cattle. **Sumatran mite f.,** a form of scrub typhus transmitted by larvae of *Trombicula deliensis*. **sun f.,** dengue. **swamp f.** 1. Leptospiral jaundice. 2. Equine infectious anemia. 3. Malaria. **sweat f.,** miliaria. **swine f.,** hog cholera. **swine f., African,** a viral disease similar to but more severe than hog cholera, and caused by an immunologically distinct agent; recognized first in Africa and found also in western Europe. **Tachamocho f.,** a fever described as occurring at Tachamocho, Colombia; marked by high fever, vomiting, headache, and diarrhea. **tertian f.,** a form of malarial fever caused by the *Plasmodium vivax*, which completes its life cycle in forty-eight hours, thus causing the paroxysm to recur every two days. **tetanoid f.,** cerebrospinal meningitis. **Texas f.,** an infectious cattle disease caused by the presence in the blood of *Babesia bigemina*, which is introduced by the bite of the tick, *Boophilus annulatus*. **Texas tick f.,** Bullis f. **therapeutic f.,** pyretotherapy. **thermic f.,** sunstroke. **three-day f.,** phlebotomus f. **threshing f.,** a form of pneumoconiosis with irritation of the respiratory tract, headache, and fever, occurring in workers at threshing grain. **tibialgic f.,** trench f. **tick f.,** any infectious disease transmitted by the bite of a tick. The causative parasite may be a rickettsia, as in Rocky Mountain spotted fever; a piroplasma, as in Texas fever; a Borrelia, as in relapsing fever; or a virus, as in Colorado tick fever. **Tobia f.,** a disease observed in Colombia, identical with Rocky Mountain spotted fever. **Tokushima f.,** infectious mononucleosis. **traumatic f.,** one which follows a wound or injury. **trench f.,** a relapsing fever, marked by headache, dizziness, and pain in the back and legs. It is a germ disease (probably rickettsial), the infection being transmitted by the body louse. Called also *quintan f.*, *five-day f.*, *Meuse f.*, *shin bone f.*, *Volhynia f.*, *His-Werner disease*. **trypanosome f.,** trypanosomiasis. **tsutsugamushi f.,** scrub typhus. **twelve-day f. of Nigeria,** a dengue-like or typhus-like fever, characterized by abundant rash for several weeks, slight albuminuria, and fever terminating by lysis. **typhoid f.,** a specific eruptive communicable fever, due to *Salmonella typhosa*, and marked by inflammation and ulceration of Peyer's patches, enlargement of the spleen and mesenteric glands, and catarrhal inflammation of the intestinal mucous membrane. **typhoid f., abenteric,** typhoid fever in which the intestinal tract is not involved. **typhoid f., abortive,** a variety in which the symptoms are developed in a few days. **typhoid f., ambulatory,** a form in which the symptoms are not severe enough to confine the patient to bed. **typhoid f., apyretic,** a form in which the fever does not rise above 100°F., often remaining normal. **typhoid f., foudroyant,** a severe form with convulsions and other nervous disturbances. **typhoid f., hemorrhagic,** a highly fatal variety with hemorrhage from the mouth, intestine, and kidneys. **typhomalarial f.,** a fever showing typhoid symptoms, but believed to be malarial in origin. **typhus f.** See *typhus*. **undulant f.,** brucellosis. **urethral f., urinary f.,** fever following the use of the urethral bougie, catheter, or sound. **urticarial f.,** a febrile disease marked by urticarial rash. **uveoparotid f.,** a manifestation of sarcoidosis, marked by chronic inflammation of the parotid gland and the uvea. It is attended also by chronic iridocyclitis, unilateral facial paralysis, lassitude, and a subfebrile temperature. Called also *Heerfordt's disease*. **vaccinal f.,** the slight fever that sometimes follows vaccination. **valley f.,** coccidioidomycosis. **van der Scheer's f.,** trench f. **vesicular f.** 1. A disorder marked by fever, localized pain, and a generalized vesicular eruption, occurring in Ceylon. 2. Pemphigus. **Volhynia f.,** trench f. **war f.,** epidemic typhus. **water f.** 1. Fever following the intravenous injection of aqueous solutions, as of salvarsan, due probably to the hemolytic effect of the water. 2. Leptospiral jaundice. **West African f.,** black-water f. **Whitmore's f.,** melioidosis. **Woolley's f.,** a fever accompanied by jaundice, described by Woolley as occurring in the Andaman Islands. **wound f.,** traumatic f. **Yangtze Valley f.,** Katayama disease. **yellow f.,** an acute infectious disease due to a virus, transmitted by mosquitoes and marked by fever, jaundice and albuminuria, the jaundice resulting from necrosis of the liver. The disease is endemic in Central West Africa and many parts of South America. Classic yellow fever is an urban disease (*urban yellow fever*) and is transmitted by

Aedes aegypti. Jungle yellow fever occurs in jungle regions of South America and Africa and is transmitted in South America by *Aedes leucocelaenus* and *Haemagogus capricorni* and in Africa by *Aedes simpsoni.* **Zambesi f.,** an indeterminate nonmalarial fever of Kaffirs in the Zambesi Valley (Bruce, 1910). **zinc fume f.,** metal fume f.

feveret (fe-ver-et′). 1. Influenza or grippe. 2. Ephemeral fever.

fexism (fek′sizm). Cretinism.

F.F.A. Abbreviation for *free fatty acids.*

F.F.T. Abbreviation for *flicker fusion threshold.*

F.h. Abbreviation for L. *fi′at haus′tus,* let a draught be made.

fiat (fi′at), pl. *fi′ant* [L.]. Let there be made.

fiber (fi′ber). An elongated, threadlike structure. See also *fibra.* **A f's,** fibers of the somatic nervous system having conduction velocities of 20–100 meters per second. Cf. *alpha, beta,* and *gamma f's.* **accelerating f's,** nerve fibers that transmit the impulses that accelerate the heart beat. **accessory f's,** those fibers of the zonule of Zinn running perpendicularly to the chief fibers and not reaching the lens; supporting fibers running from the ciliary body to the chief fibers and bracing them, including the interciliary fibers and the orbiculociliary fibers. Called also *association* or *auxiliary fibers.* **adrenergic f's,** nerve fibers that liberate adrenalin-like substances at the time of passage of nerve impulses across a synapse. **alpha f's,** motor fibers and proprioceptor fibers of the somatic nervous system having conduction velocities of 100 meters per second. **alveolar f's,** fibers of the periodontal membrane extending from the cementum of the tooth root to the walls of the alveolus, distinguished as alveolar crest, horizontal, oblique, and apical fibers. **alveolar crest f's,** fibers of the periodontal membrane extending from the cementum of the tooth root to the alveolar crest. **anastomosing f's, anastomotic f's,** fibers extending from one muscle bundle or nerve trunk to another. **apical f's,** fibers of the periodontal membrane extending from the cementum of the tooth root to the deepest portion of the alveolus. **archiform f's,** fibrae intercrurales. **arcuate f's, external,** fibrae arcuatae externae. **arcuate f's, internal,** fibrae arcuatae internae. **arcuate f's of cerebrum,** fibrae arcuatae cerebri. **argentaffine f's, argentophil f's,** reticular f's. **asbestos f's,** fibers formed in degenerating hyaline cartilage by ossification of the collagen fibers. **association f's.** 1. Fibrae arcuatae cerebri. 2. Accessory fibers. **association f's of cerebrum, short,** fibrae arcuatae cerebri. **augmentor f's,** accelerating f's. **auxiliary f's,** accessory f's. **axial f.,** the axis-cylinder of a nerve fiber. **B f's,** unmyelinated fibers of the autonomic nervous system that have a conduction velocity of 4.5 meters per second. **basilar f's,** fibers that form the middle layer of the zona arcuata and the zona pectinata of the organ of Corti: called also *auditory strings.* **Beale's f.,** a spiral nerve fiber. **Bergmann's f's,** processes which radiate from certain superficial glia cells of the cerebellum and enter the pia. **Berneheimer's f's,** a tract of nerve fibers of the brain running from the optic tract to Luys' body. **beta f's,** touch and temperature fibers of the somatic nervous system having conduction velocities of 40 meters per second. **Bogrow's f's,** nerve fibers of the cerebrum running from the optic tract to the thalamus. **bone f's,** Sharpey's f's. **Brücke's f's,** fibrae meridionales musculi ciliaris. **bulbospiral f's,** spiral muscular fibers forming a portion of the musculature of the auricles and ventricles of the heart. **Burdach's f's,** nerve fibers connected with Burdach's nucleus. **C f's,** unmyelinated fibers of the autonomic nervous system that have a conduction velocity of 0.6 meters per second. **capsular f's,** the nerve fibers within the internal capsule of the brain. **cerebrospinal f's,** the fibers in the internal capsule of the brain which run from the motor region of the cortex to the pyramids of the medulla oblongata. **chief f's,** those fibers of the zonule of Zinn which run from the ciliary body to the lens, including the orbiculoposterocapsular, the orbiculo-anterocapsular, the cilioposterocapsular, and cilio-equatorial fibers. Called also *principal* or *main fibers.* **cholinergic f's,** nerve fibers that liberate acetylcholine at the time of passage of a nerve impulse across a synapse. **chromatic f.,** the long fiber of chromatin into which the nucleus is resolved during the early stages of karyokinesis and which afterward separates into the chromosomes. **chromosomal f.,** traction f. **cilio-equatorial f's,** those chief fibers which pass from the summits of the ciliary processes to the equator of the lens. **cilioposterocapsular f's,** the most numerous of the chief zonular fibers, arising from the tips and sides of the ciliary processes, passing posteriorly and crossing the anteriorly directed fibers, to insert into the posterior capsule anterior to the insertion of the orbiculoposterocapsular fibers. **circular f's of ciliary muscle,** fibrae circulares musculi ciliaris. **circular f's of ear drum.** See *stratum circulare membranae tympani.* **collagenous f's,** the soft, flexible, white fibers which are the most characteristic constituents of all types of connective tissue. **collateral f's of Winslow,** fibrae intercrurales. **commissural f's,** the nerve fibers which pass between the cortex of opposite hemispheres of the brain. **cone f's,** the fiber-like extensions of the cone cells on either side of their nuclei which connect the retinal cones with the outer molecular layers of the retina. **continuous f's,** the spindle fibers in mitosis which extend from pole to pole. **Corti's f's,** rods of Corti. **corticonuclear f's,** fibrae corticonucleares. **corticopontine f's,** fibrae corticopontinae. **corticospinal f's,** fibrae corticospinales. **dark f's,** muscle fibers rich in sarcoplasm and having a dark appearance. **Darkschewitsch's f's,** nervous fibers of the cerebrum running from the optic tract to the habenular ganglion. **decussating f's,** those which cross in the center of the optic commissure, connecting the retina of each eye with the opposite cerebral hemisphere. **dendritic f's,** fibers which pass in a treelike form from the cortex to the white substance of Schwann. **dentinal f's,** Tomes' f's. **dentinogenic f's,** Korff's f's. **depressor f's,** afferent nerve fibers which, when stimulated, cause diminished tone of the vasoconstrictor center and, therefore, decreased arterial pressure. **Edinger's f's,** fibers in the cerebrum of amphibia, forming part of the visual paths. **elastic f's,** yellowish fibers of elastic quality traversing the intercellular substance of connective tissue. **endogenous f's,** nerve fibers of the spinal cord which arise from cells the bodies of which are situated inside the cord. **exogenous f's,** fibers of the spinal cord which arise from cells the bodies of which are situated outside the cord. **extraciliary f's.** See *fleece.* **forklike f's,** branching fibers in the tunica media of arteries. **gamma f's,** fibers of the somatic nervous system that conduct pain impulses at 20 meters per second. **geminal f's,** the pair of fibers formed by division of the pyramidal fibers of the cord, one fiber of each pair continuing on the same side of the cord, and the other passing to the opposite side. **Gerdy's f's,** the fibers of the superficial ligament connecting the clefts of the palmar surfaces of the fingers. **Goll's f's,** fibers extending from Goll's nucleus to the vermis of the cerebellum. **Gottstein's f's,** the external hair cells, and nerve fibers associated with them, forming a part of the expansion of the auditory nerve in the cochlea. **Gratiolet's radiating f's,** fibers that radiate from the optic center in the occipital lobe to the external geniculatum and pulvinar. **gray f's,** nonmedullated nerve fibers, found largely, but not exclusively, in the sympathetic nerves. **hair f.,** any one of the horny fibers, each containing relics of a nucleus, which make up the main substance of a hair. **half-spindle f's,** spindle fibers in mitosis which extend from one pole to the chromosomes. **Henle's f's,** the fibers of the fenestrated membrane which exists in certain arteries between the external and middle coats: a part are elastic, others nucleated. **Herxheimer's f's,** minute spiral fibers in the stratum mucosum of the skin. **heterodesmotic f's,** white fibers connecting dissimilar gray structures of the nervous system. **homodesmotic f's,** white fibers connecting similar gray structures of the central nervous system. **horizontal f's.** 1. See raphe medullae oblongatae. 2. Fibers of the periodontal membrane extending horizontally from the cementum of the tooth root to the walls of the alveolus. **impulse-conducting f's,** Purkinje's f's. **interciliary f's,** those accessory fibers running between the ciliary processes. **intercolumnar f's,** fibrae intercrurales. **intercrural f's,** fibrae intercrurales. **interzonal f's,** the delicate fibers of achromatin forming the central spindle during karyokinesis. **intraciliary f's,** a set of fibers passing from the anterior peduncles of the cerebellum to the dentatum. **intrafusal f's,** modified muscle fibers which, surrounded by fluid and enclosed in a connective tissue envelope, compose the muscle spindle. **itinerant f's,** projection f's. **Korff's f's,** thickened radial argentophilic collagen fibers at the periphery of the pulp of a tooth, entering the dentin and condensing to form the matrix. **lattice f's,** reticular f's. **f's of lens,** fibrae lentis. **light f's,** muscle fibers poor in sarcoplasm and therefore more transparent than dark fibers. **longitudinal f's of pons,** fasciculi longitudinales pontis. **main f's,** chief f's. **mantle f.,** any one of the cytoplasmic filaments which assist in drawing the daughter chromosomes toward the poles of the central spindles. **Mauthner's f.,** an axon that extends from the metencephalon to the caudal end of the spinal cord of fishes and amphibians, and provides the final common path for impulses to the tail. **medullated f's,** grayish-white nerve fibers whose axis-cylinders are surrounded by a medulla (or white substance of Schwann). **meridional f's of ciliary muscle,** fibrae meridionales musculi ciliaris. **Meynert's f's,** nerve fibers conveying light sensations from the anterior corpora quadrigemina to the oculomotor nuclei. **moss f.,** a peculiar form of nerve fiber. **motor f.,** a fiber in a mixed nerve which transmits motor impulses only. **Müller's f's,** elongated neuroglial elements in the retina extending between the limiting membranes. **muscle f.,** any one of the cells comprising the linear elements of muscular tissue. **myelinated f's,** medullated f's. **Nélaton's f's,** Nélaton's sphincter. **nerve f.,** a slender process of a neuron, especially the prolonged axon which conducts nerve impulses. **neuroglial f.,** one of the fibrillar structures embedded in the cytoplasm and expansions of the neuroglial cells. **nonmedullated f's,** nerve fibers which lack the myelin sheath. **oblique f's,** fibers of the periodontal membrane which extend obliquely from the cementum of the tooth root to the alveolar bone. **oblique f's of stomach,** fibrae obliquae ventriculi. **odontogenic f's,** the fibers forming the layer of connective tissue of the matrix of a tooth surrounding the pulp. **olivocerebellar f's.** See *tractus olivocerebellaris.* **orbiculo-anterocapsular f's,** those chief fibers which have the most posterior and internal position, lying in close relation to the anterior boundary of the vitreous. **orbiculociliary f's,** those accessory fibers which pass from the pars orbicularis to the ciliary processes. **orbiculoposterocapsular f's,** those chief fibers which spring from the prolongation of the hyaloid membrane investing the ciliary ring. **osteocollagenous f's,** fibers gathered together into bundles and united by a special binding substance in the interstitial substance of bone. **osteogenetic f's,** osteogenic f's. **osteogenic f's,** precollagenous fibers formed by osteoclasts and becoming the fibrous component of bone matrix. **oxytalan f.,** a connective tissue fiber, resistant to acid hydrolysis, found in structures subjected to mechanical stress, such as tendons, ligaments, adventitia, and connective tissue sheaths that surround the skin appendages. **pectinate f's,** musculi pectinati. **perforating f's,** Sharpey's f's. **periventricular f's,** fibrae periventriculares. **Perlia f's,** nerve fibers of optical function in the cerebrum running to the medulla oblongata. **pilomotor f's,** unmyelinated nerve fibers going to the small muscles of the hair follicles. **postcommissural f's,** the fibers of the postcommissure lying just behind the peduncle of the epiphysis. **postganglionic f's,** fibers constituting a postganglionic neuron. **precollagenous f's,** a name given reticular fibers on the supposition that they are immature collagenous fibers. **precommissural f's,** fibers of the precommissure in the lamina terminalis. **preganglionic f's,** fibers constituting a preganglionic neuron. **pressor f's,** afferent nerve fibers which, when stimulated, cause excitation of the vasoconstrictor center and consequently a rise of arterial pressure. **principal f's,** chief f's. **projection f's,** a term applied to all the bundles of axon fibers which connect the cerebral cortex with the brain stem; called also *projection tract.* **Prussak's f's,** two short fibers from the end of the short process of the malleus to the notch of Rivinus. **Purkinje's f's,** beaded muscular fibers forming a network in the subendocardial tissue of the ventricles of the heart. They are thought to be concerned in the conduction of stimuli from the atria to the ventricles. **pyramidal f's of medulla oblongata,** fibrae pyramidales medullae oblongatae. **radiating f's of anterior chondrosternal ligaments,** ligamenta sternocostalia radiata. **radiating f's of ear drum.** See *stratum radiatum membranae tympani.* **Reissner's f.,** a free fiber in the central canal of the spinal cord. **f's of Remak,** gray f's. **reticular f's,** immature connective tissue fibers, staining with silver, forming the reticular framework of lymphoid and myeloid tissue and occurring also in the interstitial tissue of glandular organs, the papillary layer of the skin, and elsewhere: called also *argentophilic f's, lattice f's,* and *Gitterfasern.* **Retzius' f's,** the stiff filaments of Deiters' cells in the organ of Corti. **Ritter's f.,** a fiber in the axis of a retinal rod: probably a nerve fiber. **rod f's,** the fiber portion of the rod cells of the retina. **Rolando's f's,** the external arcuate fibers of the medulla oblongata. **Sappey's f's,** smooth muscle fibers in the check ligaments of the eye near their orbital attachments. **scattered fillet f's,** fibers lying internal to the lemniscus of the brain. **Sharpey's f's,** fibers that pass from the periosteum and embed in the periosteal lamellae. **short association f's,** fibers in the cerebrum connecting adjacent convolutions. **sinospiral f's,** spiral muscular fibers forming a portion of the musculature of the atria and ventricles of the heart. **spindle f's,** achromatic filaments extending between the poles of a dividing cell and, as a whole, making a spindle-shaped configuration. **Stilling's f's,** association fibers of the cerebellum. **sustentacular f's,** Müller's f's. **sweat f.,** a nerve fiber which activates a sweat gland. **T f.,** a nerve fiber that branches at right angles from the axon of a nerve cell. **Tomes' f's,** branching processes of the odontoblasts in the dentinal canals. **traction f's,** the fibers of the spindle in mitosis along which the daughter chromosomes move apart. **transilient f's,** nerve fibers that pass from one convolution to another not next to it. **transseptal f's,** fibers of the periodontal membrane extending interproximally over the interdental septum, their ends being embedded in the cementum of adjacent teeth. **ultraterminal f.,** a thin unmyelinated twig given off from the ramifications of the axon in the motor plate. **varicose f's,** certain medullated fibers which have no neurilemma; after death a fluid accumulates between the myelin and the axon, giving the fibers a varicose appearance. **von Monakow's f's,** nerve fibers of the cerebrum running from the optic tract to the lenticular ganglion. **Weissmann's f's,** fibers within the muscle spindle. **Wernicke's f's,** Gratiolet's radiating f's. **white f's,** collagenous f's. **yellow f's,** elastic f's. **zonular f's,** fibrae zonulares.

Fibiger (fi′bĭ-ger), Johannes Andreas Grib. Danish pathologist, 1867–1928; winner of the Nobel prize in physiology and medicine for 1926.

fibra (fi′brah), pl. *fi′brae* [L.]. [N A, B N A] A general term designating an elongated, threadlike structure. Called also *fiber*. **fi′brae annula′res.** See *pars anularis vaginae fibrosae digitorum manus* and *pars anularis vaginae fibrosae digitorum pedis*. **fi′brae arcua′tae cer′ebri** [N A, B N A], short association fibers within the cerebral cortex, connecting adjacent gyri. Called also *arcuate fibers of cerebrum*. **fi′brae arcua′tae exter′nae** [N A, B N A], fibers that arise from various nuclei and run over the surface of the medulla to reach the inferior cerebellar peduncle. Called also *external arcuate fibers*. **fi′brae arcua′tae inter′nae** [N A, B N A], fibers that arise from the nucleus cuneatus and nucleus gracilis and pass ventromedially around the central gray substance of the medulla oblongata to form the decussation of the lemniscus. Called also *internal arcuate fibers*. **fi′brae cerebel′lo-oliva′res** [B N A]. See *tractus olivocerebellaris*. **fi′brae circula′res mus′culi cilia′ris** [N A], fibers running parallel with the margin of the cornea, in the anterior and inner portion of the ciliary body. **fi′brae corticonuclea′res** [N A], longitudinal fibers in the pars basilaris of the pons that originate in the cerebral cortex and synapse in the various nuclei of the medulla oblongata. Called also *corticonuclear fibers*. **fi′brae corticopon′tinae** [N A], longitudinal fibers in the pars basilaris of the pons that originate in the cerebral cortex and synapse in the pontine nuclei of the same side. Called also *corticopontine fibers*. **fi′brae corticospina′lis** [N A], longitudinal fibers in the pars basilaris of the pons that originate in the cerebral cortex, course through the pons, enter the medulla oblongata in the pyramids, and form the corticospinal tracts in the spinal cord. Called also *corticobulbar* or *corticospinal fibers*. **fi′brae intercrura′les** [N A, B N A], fibers joining the medial and lateral crura of the superficial inguinal ring. Called also *intercrural fibers*. **fi′brae len′tis** [N A, B N A], long bands, derived from the epithelium, that make up the substance of the lens. Called also *fibers of lens*. **fi′brae meridiona′les mus′culi cilia′ris** [N A], fibers of the ciliary muscle that run from the pectinate ligament toward the ciliary processes. Called also *fibrae meridionales* [*Brueckei*] [B N A], and *meridional fibers of ciliary muscle*. **fi′brae obli′quae ventric′uli** [N A, B N A], the inner, obliquely coursing fibers of the muscular tunic of the stomach. Called also *oblique fibers of stomach*. **fi′brae periventricula′res** [N A], fibers that arise from the hypothalamus, then descend along the third ventricle and through the tegmentum of the mesencephalon and the reticular formation of the pons and medulla oblongata. Called also *periventricular fibers*. **fi′brae pon′tis profun′dae** [B N A], fibrae pontis transversae. **fi′brae pon′tis superficia′les** [B N A], omitted in N A. **fi′brae pon′tis transver′sae** [N A], fibers within the pars basilaris of the pons which arise from the pontine nuclei and run laterally to form the middle cerebellar peduncles. Most of these fibers cross the midline. Called also *fibrae pontis profundae* [B N A], and *transverse fibers of pons*. **fi′brae pro′priae,** fibrae arcuatae cerebri. **fi′brae pyramida′les medul′lae oblonga′tae** [N A], nerve fibers in the ventromedial part of the medulla oblongata, which originate at the cerebral cortex and go to the spinal cord and medulla oblongata. On the surface they are seen as the pyramid. Called also *fasciculi pyramidales medullae oblongatae* [B N A], and *pyramidal fibers of medulla oblongata*. **fi′brae zonula′res** [N A, B N A], the fibers that anchor the lens capsule to the ciliary body and the retina. Called also *zonular fibers*.

fibrae (fi′bre) [L.]. Plural of *fibra*.

fibralbumin (fi″bral-bu′min). Globulin.

fibre (fi′ber). Fiber.

fibremia (fi-bre′me-ah) [L. *fibra* fiber + Gr. *haima* blood + *-ia*]. The presence of fibrin in the blood.

fibril (fi′bril) [L. *fibrilla*]. A minute fiber or filament; often a component of a compound fiber. **collagen f's,** delicate fibrils of collagen in connective tissue, usually cemented together in wavy bundles. Cf. *fibroblast*. **dentinal f's,** component fibrils of the dentinal matrix. **Dirck's f's,** fibrils of elastic tissue binding together the layers of elastic fibers of the tunica media of an artery. **Ebner's f's,** threadlike fibrils in the dentin and in the cementum of a tooth. **fibroglia f's.** See *fibroglia*. **muscle f., muscular f.,** myofibril. **nerve f.,** an axon. **side f. of Golgi,** a delicate twig given off at right angles from a neuraxon near its junction with the ganglion cells. **Tomes' f's,** dentinal f's.

fibrilla (fi-bril′ah), pl. *fibril′lae* [L.]. A fibril.

fibrillae (fi-bril′e) [L.]. Plural of *fibrilla*.

fibrillar, fibrillary (fi′brĭ-lar, fi′brĭ-lăr-e). Pertaining to a fibril or to fibrils.

fibrillated (fi′brĭ-lāt-ed). Made up of fibrils.

fibrillation (fi-brĭ-la′shun). 1. The quality of being fibrillar. 2. A small local contraction of muscles, invisible under the skin, resulting from spontaneous activation of single muscle cells or muscle fibers. **atrial f., auricular f.,** a condition characterized by irregular convulsive movements of the atria of the heart, the number of impulses being very great, and individual fibers acting independently. **ventricular f.,** a condition characterized by fibrillary twitching of the ventricular muscle, the impulses traversing the ventricles so rapidly that coordinated contractions cannot occur.

fibrilloblast (fi-bril′o-blast) [*fibril* + Gr. *blastos* germ]. Odontoblast.

fibrilloceptor (fi-bril′o-sep″tor). Any one of the specific receptors at the terminals of the neurofibrils of the peripheral sensory neuron which receive the stimuli.

fibrillogenesis (fi-bril″o-jen′e-sis). The formation of fibrillae.

fibrillolysis (fi″brĭ-lol′ĭ-sis). The destruction or dissolution of fibrils or fibrillae.

fibrillolytic (fi″bril-o-lit′ik). Destroying or dissolving fibrillae.

fibrin (fi′brin). A whitish, insoluble protein formed from fibrinogen by the action of thrombin (fibrin ferment), as in the clotting of blood. Fibrin forms the essential portion of the blood clot. Cf. *fibrinogen*. A spongelike material of human fibrin, prepared from a foam of a solution of human fibrinogen clotted with thrombin, in the form of foam or film, may be used in various surgical procedures to induce hemostasis. **gluten f.,** a form of fibrin from the seeds of various plants. **Henle's f.,** fibrin formed by precipitating semen with water. **myosin f.,** an insoluble variety of myosin. **stroma f.,** fibrin obtained from the stroma of blood corpuscles. **vegetable f.,** gluten f.

fibrination (fi″brĭ-na′shun). The acquisition of an abnormally large amount of fibrin; applied to coagulation within, and of, the circulating blood.

fibrinemia (fi″brĭ-ne′me-ah). Fibremia.

fibrin-globulin (fi″brin-glob′u-lin). Fibrinoglobulin.

fibrinocellular (fi″brĭ-no-sel′u-lar). Made up of fibrin and cells.

fibrinogen (fi-brin′o-jen) [*fibrin* + Gr. *gennan* to produce]. A plasma protein of high molecular weight that is converted to fibrin through the action of thrombin. Called also *coagulation factor I.* A sterile compound, derived from normal human plasma and dried from the frozen state, is used to increase coagulability of the blood.

fibrinogenase (fi″brin-oj′e-nās) [*fibrinogen* + *-ase*]. An enzyme which influences coagulation of protein.

fibrinogenemia (fi-brin″o-jĕ-ne′me-ah). The presence of an excessive amount of fibrinogen in the blood.

fibrinogenesis (fi″brĭ-no-jen′e-sis). The production or formation of fibrin.

fibrinogenic (fi″brĭ-no-jen′ik). Producing or causing the formation of fibrin.

fibrinogenolysis (fi″brĭ-no-jĕ-nol′ĭ-sis) [*fibrinogen* + Gr. *lysis* dissolution]. The dissolution or inactivation of fibrinogen in the blood.

fibrinogenolytic (fi″brĭ-no-jen″o-lit′ik). Pertaining to or inducing fibrinogenolysis.

fibrinogenopenia (fi-brin″o-jen″o-pe′ne-ah). Deficiency of fibrinogen in the blood.

fibrinogenopenic (fi″brin-o-jen″o-pe′nik). Pertaining to or caused by fibrinogenopenia.

fibrinogenous (fi″brĭ-noj′e-nus). Caused by fibrin, or resulting from the formation of fibrin.

fibrinoglobulin (fi″brĭ-no-glob′u-lin). A globulin entering into the composition of fibrinogen.

fibrinoid (fi′brĭ-noid) [*fibrin* + Gr. *eidos* form]. 1. Resembling fibrin. 2. A homogeneous, eosinophilic, refractile, relatively acellular material with some of the tinctorial properties of fibrin.

fibrinokinase (fi″brĭ-no-ki′nās). A non-water-soluble plasminogen activator derived from animal tissues.

fibrinolysin (fi″brĭ-no-li′sin). Any enzyme that catalyzes the digestion of fibrin. See also *plasmin.* **seminal f.,** an enzyme in human semen which liquefies the clotted semen.

fibrinolysis (fi″brĭ-no-li′sis) [*fibrin* + Gr. *lysis* dissolution]. The splitting up of fibrin by enzyme action.

fibrinolytic (fi″brĭ-no-lit′ik). Pertaining to, characterized by, or causing fibrinolysis.

fibrinopenia (fi″brĭ-no-pe′ne-ah) [*fibrin* + Gr. *penia* poverty]. Deficiency of fibrin and fibrinogen in the blood.

fibrinopeptide (fi″brĭ-no-pep′tīd). A substance split off from fibrinogen, during coagulation, by the action of thrombin.

fibrinoplastic (fi″brĭ-no-plas′tik). Of the nature of fibrinoplastin.

fibrinoplastin (fi″brĭ-no-plas′tin). Paraglobulin. **Schmidt's f.,** serum globulin.

fibrinopurulent (fi″brĭ-no-pu′roo-lent). Characterized by the presence of both fibrin and pus.

fibrinorrhoea (fi″brĭ-no-re′ah). A profuse discharge containing fibrin. **f. plas′tica,** membranous dysmenorrhea.

fibrinoscopy (fi-brĭ-nos′ko-pe) [*fibrin* + Gr. *skopein* to examine]. Inoscopy.

fibrinose (fi′brĭ-nōs). An albumose derived from fibrin.

fibrinosis (fi″brĭ-no′sis). A condition characterized by excess of fibrin in the blood.

fibrinous (fi′brĭ-nus). Pertaining to or of the nature of fibrin.

fibrinuria (fi″brin-u′re-ah). The presence of fibrin in the urine.

fibro- (fi′bro) [L. *fibra* fiber]. A combining form denoting relationship to fibers.

fibroadamantoblastoma (fi″bro-ad″ah-man″-to-blas-to′mah). Ameloblastic fibroma.

fibroadenia (fi″bro-ah-de′ne-ah) [*fibro-* + Gr. *adēn* gland]. Fibroid degeneration of gland tissue, especially the reduction in lymphocytes and increase in stroma in the malpighian bodies in Banti's disease.

fibroadenoma (fi″bro-ad″e-no′mah). Adenoma containing fibrous tissue. **giant f. of the breast,** a fibroadenoma of large size that involves much of the mammary glands.

fibroadenosis (fi″bro-ad″e-no′sis). A nodular condition of the breast not due to neoplasm.

fibroadipose (fi″bro-ad′ĭ-pōs). Both fibrous and fatty.

fibroangioma (fi″bro-an″je-o′mah). An angioma containing much fibrous tissue.

fibroareolar (fi″bro-ah-re′o-lar) [*fibro-* + L. *areola*]. Both fibrous and areolar.

fibroblast (fi′bro-blast) [*fibro-* + Gr. *blastos* germ]. A connective tissue cell; a flat elongated cell with cytoplasmic processes at each end, having a flat, oval, vesicular nucleus. Fibroblasts, which differentiate into chondroblasts, collagenoblasts, and osteoblasts, form the fibrous tissues in the body, tendons, aponeuroses, supporting and binding tissues of all sorts. Called also *fibrocyte* and *desmocyte.*

fibroblastic (fi″bro-blas′tik). 1. Pertaining to fibroblasts. 2. Fibroplastic.

fibroblastoma (fi″bro-blas-to′mah). A tumor arising from the ordinary connective tissue cell or fibroblast. It includes fibroma and fibrosarcoma. **arachnoid f., meningeal f.,** meningioma. **perineural f.,** a fibroma growing from the connective tissue sheath of a nerve.

fibrobronchitis (fi″bro-brong-ki′tis). Plastic bronchitis.

fibrocalcific (fi″bro-kal-sif′ik). Pertaining to or characterized by partially calcified fibrous tissue.

fibrocarcinoma (fi″bro-kar″sĭ-no′mah). Carcinoma containing fibrous tissue.

fibrocartilage (fi″bro-kar′tĭ-lij). A type of cartilage made up of typical cartilage cells (chondrocytes), with parallel thick, compact collagenous bundles forming the interstitial substances, separated by narrow clefts enclosing the encapsulated cells. For names of specific structures composed of such tissue, see under *fibrocartilago.* **acetabular f.,** ligamentum acetabuli. **basal f.,** fibrocartilago basalis. **basilar f.,** synchondrosis sphenooccipitalis. **circumferential f.,** fibrocartilage which forms a rim about a joint cavity. **connecting f.,** a disk of fibrocartilage which attaches opposing bones to each other by synchondrosis. **cotyloid f.,** labrum glenoidale. **elastic f.,** fibrocartilage containing elastic fibers. **interarticular f.,** an articular disk. See terms beginning *discus articularis,* under *discus.* **intervertebral f.,** discus intervertebralis. **semilunar f's,** crescent-shaped structures resting on the articulating surfaces of the upper end of the tibia, increasing the concavity of the tibial condyles and acting as cushions or shock absorbers; the lateral and medial menisci. **spongy f.,** connecting f. **stratiform f.,** cartilage such as that lining the bony grooves lodging certain tendons. **white f.,** fibrocartilage in which strong bundles of white fibrous tissue predominate. **yellow f.,** fibrocartilage containing bundles of yellow elastic fibers but with little or no white fibrous tissue.

fibrocartilagines (fi″bro-kar″tĭ-laj′ĭ-nēz) [L.]. Plural of *fibrocartilago.*

fibrocartilaginous (fi″bro-kar″tĭ-laj′ĭ-nus). Pertaining to or composed of fibrocartilage.

fibrocartilago (fi″bro-kar″tĭ-lah′go), pl. *fibrocartilag′ines* [L.]. [N A, B N A] A general term for an anatomical structure composed of cartilage the matrix of which contains a considerable amount of fibrous tissue. Called also *fibrocartilage.* **f. basa′lis** [B N A], the cartilage that fills the foramen lacerum of the skull. Omitted in N A. **f. basila′ris,** synchrondrosis sphenooccipitalis. **fibrocartilag′ines intervertebra′les** [B N A], disci intervertebrales. **f. navicula′ris** [B N A], omitted in N A.

fibrocaseous (fi″bro-ka′se-us). Both fibrous and caseous.

fibrocellular (fi″bro-sel′u-lar). Partly fibrous and partly cellular.

fibrochondritis (fi″bro-kon-dri′tis) [*fibro-* + *chondritis*]. Inflammation of a fibrocartilage.

fibrochondroma (fi″bro-kon-dro′mah) [*fibro-* + *chondroma*]. A mixed fibroma and chondroma.

fibrocyst (fi′bro-sist) [*fibro-* + Gr. *kystis* sac, bladder]. A fibroma that has suffered cystic degeneration.

fibrocystic (fi″bro-sis′tik). Characterized by the development of cystic spaces, especially in relation to some duct or gland, accompanied by an overgrowth of fibrous tissue.

fibrocystoma (fi″bro-sis-to′mah). Fibroma blended with cystoma; a tumor containing fibromatous and cystomatous elements.

fibrocyte (fi′bro-sit) [*fibro-* + Gr. *kytos* hollow vessel]. Fibroblast.

fibrocytogenesis (fi″bro-si″to-jen′e-sis) [*fibrocyte* + Gr. *genesis* production]. The development of connective tissue fibrils.

fibroelastic (fi″bro-e-las′tik). Composed of fibrous and elastic tissue.

fibroelastosis (fi″bro-e″las-to′sis). Overgrowth of fibroelastic elements. **endocardial f.,** a condition characterized by hypertrophy of the wall of the left ventricle and conversion of the endocardium into a thick fibroelastic coat, with reduction in the capacity of the ventricle. The leaflets of the aortic valve are often irregular in size or number, and thickened and covered with hyalinized verrucous overgrowths.

fibro-enchondroma (fi″bro-en″kon-dro′mah). Enchondroma containing fibrous elements.

fibrofascitis (fi″bro-fah-si′tis). Fibrositis.

fibrofatty (fi″bro-fat′e). Both fibrous and fatty.

fibrofibrous (fi″bro-fi′brus). Joining or connecting fibers.

fibrogenesis (fi″bro-jen′e-sis) [*fibro-* + *genesis*]. The development of fibers.

fibrogenic (fi″bro-jen′ik). Conducive to the development of fibers.

fibroglia (fi-brog′le-ah) [*fibro-* + Gr. *glia* glue]. Border fibrils in close relation to the surface of fibroblasts, and thought by some to be transformations of the ectoplasm.

fibroglioma (fi″bro-gli-o′mah). Fibroma blended with glioma.

fibrohemorrhagic (fi″bro-hem″o-raj′ik). Attended with hemorrhage and fibrin formation.

fibroid (fi′broid) [*fibro-* + Gr. *eidos* form]. 1. Having a fibrous structure; resembling a fibroma. 2. A fibroma. 3. A myoma of the uterus. **Paget's recurrent f.,** spindle-shaped sarcoma of the subcutaneous tissue.

fibroidectomy (fi″broid-ek′to-me) [fibroid + Gr. *ektomē* excision]. Excision of a fibroid tumor (myoma) of the uterus.

fibroin (fi-bro′in). A white albuminoid, $C_{15}H_{23}N_3O_6$, from spiders' webs and the cocoons of insects.

fibrolipoma (fi″bro-lĭ-po′mah) [*fibro-* + Gr. *lipos* fat + *-oma*]. A fibrous tumor that is in part fatty.

fibrolipomatous (fi″bro-lĭ-po′mah-tus). Pertaining to fibrolipoma.

fibrolymphoangioblastoma (fi″bro-lim″fo-an″je-o-blas′to-mah). A hard, freely movable tumor of the breast, partially adherent to the skin, composed of fibrous tissue with precollagenous and collagenous fibers, and numerous small communicating vessels forming cavities lined with endothelium-like cells. Called also *Bajardi-Taddei disease.*

fibroma (fi-bro′mah). A tumor composed mainly of fibrous or fully developed connective tissue. **ameloblastic f.,** an odontogenic tumor characterized by the simultaneous proliferation of both epithelial and mesenchymal tissue, without the formation of enamel or dentin. **f. caverno′sum,** a fibroma containing greatly dilated blood vessels. **chondromyxoid f. of bone,** a benign neoplasm with distinct histologic characteristics, apparently derived from cartilage-forming connective tissue, and sometimes mistaken for chondrosarcoma. **concentric f.,** a uterine fibroma surrounding the uterine cavity. **f. cu′tis,** fibroma of the skin. **cystic f.,** a fibroma which has undergone cystic degeneration. **f. du′rum,** hard f. **f. emato′des cys′ticum,** a fibroma of the nares formed by cysts which arise from distended alveoli lined with overgrowing cells. **f. fungoi′des,** mycosis fungoides. **hard f.,** one composed of fibrous tissue with few cells. **intracanalicular f.,** adenocele. **f. lipoi′dicum, f. lipomato′des,** xanthoma. **f. mol′le,** soft fibroma. **f. mollus′cum,** molluscum fibrosum. **f. mucino′sum,** a fibroma affected with mucoid degeneration. **multiple f.,** a condition marked by numerous fibrous tumors of the skin. See *molluscum fibrosum.* **f. myxomato′des,** a myxofibroma. **non-osteogenic f.,** a common degenerative and proliferative lesion of the medullary and cortical tissues of bone, occurring most commonly near the ends of the diaphyses of the large long bones, particularly of the lower extremities, often causing no symptoms and discovered only incidentally in roentgenograms of the skeleton made for other reasons. **odontogenic f.,** a benign tumor of the jaw, arising from the embryonic portion of the tooth germ, the dental papilla, or dental follicle, or originating later from the periodontal membrane. **parasitic f.,** a pedunculated, subperitoneal fibroid of the uterus which obtains part or all of its blood supply from the omentum. **f. pen′dulum,** a pendulous fibroma of the skin. **f. sarcomato′sum,** fibrosarcoma. **soft f.,** one containing copious cells. **telangiectatic f.,** angiofibroma. **f. thecocellula′re xanthomato′des,** theca-cell tumor. **f. xantho′ma,** fibroxanthoma.

fibromatogenic (fi-bro″mah-to-jen′ik). Producing or causing the formation of fibroma.

fibromatoid (fi-bro′mah-toid) [*fibroma* + Gr. *eidos* form]. Resembling fibroma; fibroma-like.

fibromatosis (fi″bro-mah-to′sis). A tendency to the development of fibromas; the formation of multiple fibromas. **f. gingi′vae,** a diffuse fibroma involving the gingivae and palate, manifested as a dense, diffuse, smooth or nodular overgrowth of the tissues. **f. ventric′uli,** linitis plastica.

fibromatous (fi-bro′mah-tus). Pertaining to or of the nature of fibroma.

fibromectomy (fi″bro-mek′to-me) [*fibroma* + Gr. *ektomē* excision]. Excision of a fibroma.

fibromembranous (fi″bro-mem′brah-nus). Composed of membrane containing much fibrous tissue.

fibromuscular (fi″bro-mus′ku-lar). Composed of fibrous and muscular tissue.

fibromyectomy (fi″bro-mi-ek′to-me). Fibromyomectomy.

fibromyitis (fi″bro-mi-i′tis) [*fibro-* + Gr. *mys* muscle + *-itis*]. Inflammation and fibrous degeneration of a muscle.

fibromyoma (fi″bro-mi-o′mah) [*fibro* + Gr. *mys* muscle + *-oma*]. A tumor containing both fibrous and muscular tissue; a myoma containing fibrous elements.

fibromyomectomy (fi″bro-mi″o-mek′to-me). Excision of a fibromyoma.

fibromyositis (fi″bro-mi″o-si′tis) [*fibro-* + Gr. *mys* muscle + *-itis*]. Inflammation of fibromuscular tissue. **nodular f.,** a disease marked by inflammation and the formation of nodules in the muscles.

fibromyotomy (fi″bro-mi-ot′o-me). Excision of a fibromyoma.

fibromyxoma (fi″bro-mik-so′mah). Fibroma blended with myxoma.

fibromyxosarcoma (fi″bro-mik″so-sar-ko′mah). A sarcoma containing fibrous and myxoid tissue.

fibroneuroma (fi″bro-nu-ro′mah). A neuroma containing fibrous elements.

fibronuclear (fi″bro-nu′kle-ar). Made up of nucleated fibers.

fibro-osteoma (fi″bro-os″te-o′mah). Osteofibroma.

fibropapilloma (fi″bro-pap″ĭ-lo′mah). A papilloma containing much fibrous tissue.

fibropericarditis (fi″bro-per″ĭ-kar-di′tis). Fibrinous pericarditis.

fibroplasia (fi″bro-pla′se-ah). The formation of fibrous tissue, as in the healing of wounds. **retrolental f.,** a condition characterized by the presence of opaque tissue behind the lens, leading to detachment of the retina and arrest of growth of the eye, generally attributed to use of high concentrations of oxygen in the care of premature infants. Called also *Terry's syndrome,* and *RLF.*

fibroplastic (fi″bro-plas′tik) [*fibro-* + Gr. *plassein* to form]. Giving origin to fibrous tissue.

fibroplastin (fi″bro-plas′tin). Paraglobulin.

fibroplate (fi′bro-plāt). An interarticular fibrocartilage.

fibropolypus (fi″bro-pol′ĭ-pus). A polyp containing fibrous elements.

fibropsammoma (fi″bro-sah-mo′mah). A tumor containing fibrous and psammomatous elements.

fibropurulent (fi-bro-pu′roo-lent). Characterized by the presence of both fibers and pus.

fibroreticulate (fi″bro-re-tik′u-lāt). Composed of a network of fibers.

fibrosarcoma (fi″bro-sar-ko′mah). A sarcoma containing fibrous elements. **odontogenic f.,** a malignant tumor of the jaws, originating from one of the mesenchymal components of the tooth or tooth germ, and histologically identical with other fibrosarcomas; the malignant counterpart of odontogenic fibroma. **f. ova′rii mucocellula′re carcinomato′des,** Krukenberg's tumor.

fibrose (fi′brōs). To form fibrous tissue.

fibroserous (fi″bro-se′rus). Composed of both fibrous and serous elements.

fibrosis (fi-bro′sis). The formation of fibrous tissue; fibroid degeneration. **arteriocapillary f.,** the narrowing or closure of minute arteries and capillaries by inflammatory internal fibrosis. **cystic f.,** a pathological change in an organ, involving overgrowth of fibrous tissue, accompanied by the development of cystic spaces. **cystic f. of the pancreas,** a generalized, hereditary disorder of infants, children, and young adults, in which there is widespread dysfunction of the exocrine glands; characterized by signs of chronic pulmonary disease, pancreatic deficiency, abnormally high levels of electrolytes in the sweat, and occasionally by biliary cirrhosis. The degree of involvement of organs and glandular systems may vary greatly, with consequent variations in the clinical picture. **diffuse interstitial pulmonary f.** See *pulmonary f.* **mediastinal f.,** development of whitish, hard fibrous tissue in the upper mediastinum, causing compression, distortion, or obliteration of the superior vena cava, and sometimes constriction of the bronchi and large pulmonary vessels. **neoplastic f.,** proliferative f. **nodular subepidermal f.,** the formation, beneath the epidermis, of multiple fibrous nodules as the result of productive inflammation. **panmural f. of the bladder,** chronic interstitial cystitis. **periureteric f.,** progressive development of fibrous tissue, spreading laterally from the great midline vessels, gradually engulfing, distorting, and finally causing strangulation of one or both ureters. **postfibrinous f.,** fibrosis occurring in tissues in which fibrin has been deposited. **proliferative f.,** fibrosis in which the fibrous elements continue to proliferate after the original causative factor has ceased to operate. **pulmonary f., interstitial, diffuse,** a peculiar, progressive fibrosis of the pulmonary alveolar walls, of undetermined etiology, leading to deficient aeration of the blood, with resulting dyspnea and cyanosis, and to cor pulmonale. **replacement f.,** the development of fibrous tissues to replace tissue that has been damaged. **retroperitoneal f.,** deposition of fibrous tissue in the retroperitoneal space, producing vague abdominal discomfort, and often causing blockage of the ureters, with resultant hydronephrosis, azotemia, and weakness. **f. u′teri,** a morbid condition characterized by overgrowth of the smooth muscle and increase in the collagenous fibrous tissue, producing a thickened, coarse, tough myometrium.

fibrositis (fi″bro-si′tis) [*fibrous* tissue + *-itis*]. Inflammatory hyperplasia of the white fibrous tissue of the body, especially of the muscle sheaths and facial layers of the locomotor system. It is marked by pain and stiffness. Called also *muscular rheumatism.*

fibrothorax (fi″bro-tho′raks). A condition characterized by adhesion of the two layers of pleura, the lung being covered by a thick layer of non-expansible fibrous tissue; often a consequence of traumatic hemothorax or of tuberculous effusion or emphysema, and sometimes produced artificially.

fibrotic (fi-brot′ik). Pertaining to or characterized by fibrosis.

fibrotuberculosis (fi″bro-tu-ber″ku-lo′sis). Fibroid phthisis (def. 1).

fibrous (fi′brus). Composed of or containing fibers.

fibroxanthoma (fi″bro-zan-tho′mah). A type of xanthoma containing fibromatous elements.

fibula (fib′u-lah) [L. "buckle"]. [N A, B N A] The outer and smaller of the two bones of the leg.

fibular (fib′u-lar). Pertaining to the fibula.

fibularis (fib″u-la′ris). Fibular; in official anatomical nomenclature, designating relationship to the fibula.

fibulocalcaneal (fib″u-lo-kal-ka′ne-al). Pertaining to the fibula and calcaneus.

F.I.C.D. Abbreviation for *Fellow of the International College of Dentists.*

fici (fi′si) [L. *ficus* fig]. Grease in horses.

Fick's bacillus (fiks) [Rudolph Armin *Fick,* German physician, 1866–1939]. *Proteus vulgaris.*

Ficker's diagnosticum (fik′erz) [Philip Martin *Ficker,* German bacteriologist, born 1868]. See *diagnosticum.*

ficosis (fi-ko′sis). Sycosis.

F.I.C.S. Abbreviation for *Fellow of the International College of Surgeons.*

fidicinales (fi-dis″ĭ-na′lez) [pl., from L. *fidicen, fidicinis,* a player on the harp]. Musculi lumbricales manus.

fieber (fe′ber) [Ger.]. Fever. **gelb f.,** yellow fever. **rück′fall f.,** relapsing fever.

Fiedler's disease, myocarditis (fēd′lerz) [Carl Ludwig Alfred *Fiedler,* German physician, 1835–1921]. See *leptospiral jaundice* and under *myocarditis.*

field (fēld). 1. An area or open space. 2. In embryology, the condition or group of factors to which any living system owes its typical organization. **absolute f.,** that area of the cerebral cortex injury of which always causes paralysis or spasm. **auditory f.,** the space or range within which stimuli may be perceived as sound. **Cohnheim's f's,** small polygonal areas of myofibrillae seen in a transverse section of a muscle fiber. **f. of consciousness,** the total sum of experiences at a given instant. **dark f.** See *ultramicroscope.* **deaf f.,** deaf point. **f. of fixation,** the region bounded by the utmost limits of central or clear vision, the eye being allowed to move, but the head being fixed. **Flechsig's f.,** the myelinogenetic field. **Forel's f.,** the most dorsal of the strata of the subthalamus, which is in direct relation with the thalamus and consists of fine longitudinal fibers. **individuation f.,** a region in which an organizer influences adjacent tissue to become a part of a total embryo. **Krönig's**

f., the area of resonance on the chest due to the apices of the lungs. **magnetic f.,** that portion of space about a magnet in which its action is perceptible. **f. of a microscope,** the area that can be seen through a microscope at one time. The *high-power field* is that area which is visible under the high-power objective; the *low-power field* is that which is visible under low power. **morphogenetic f.,** an embryonic region, larger than its main derivatives, out of which definite structures normally develop. **myelinogenetic f.,** a collection of fibers in the neuraxis which at a definite stage of development receive myelin sheaths; called also *field of Flechsig*. **primary nail f.,** a flat area on the terminal phalanx in the embryo where the nail is to develop. **relative f.,** an area of the cerebral cortex in which a lesion may or may not cause paralysis. **surplus f.,** the portion of the field of vision in partial hemianopia which passes beyond the point of fixation. **tactile f.,** sensory circle. **f. of vision,** that portion of space which the fixed eye can see. **f. of vision, cribriform,** a field of vision over which a number of isolated scotomas lie dispersed. **f. of vision, overshot,** a condition in which the line of separation between the halves of the field of vision does not pass through the point of fixation. **Wernicke's f.,** Wernicke's area.

Fielding's membrane (fēld'ingz) [George Hunsley *Fielding*, English anatomist, 1801–1871]. The tapetum.

fièvre (fe-evr') [Fr.]. Fever. **f. boutonneuse** (fe-evr' boo-ton-uz'), boutonneuse fever. **f. caprine** (fe-evr' kah-prēn), brucellosis. **f. exanthematique de Marseille** (fe-evr' eks-an"thĕ-mah-tēk') boutonneuse fever. **f. jaune** (fe-evr' zhōn), yellow fever. **f. récurrente** (fe-evr' ra"kuh-rant'), relapsing fever.

FIGLU. Abbreviation for *formiminoglutamic acid*.

Figueira's syndrome (fe-ga-e'rahz) [Fernandes *Figueira*, pediatrician in Rio de Janeiro, died 1928]. See under *syndrome*.

figuratus (fig"u-ra'tus) [L.]. Figured.

figure (fig'ūr) [L. *figura*, from *fingere* to shape or form]. 1. An object of a particular form. 2. A number, or numeral. **fortification f's,** a form of migraine aura characterized by scintillating, colored lights or zigzag luminous bands suggestive of the walls of a turret. **Minkowski's f.,** a numerical expression of the relation between dextrose and nitrogen in the urine on a pure meat diet, and when fasting. It is 2.8 : 1. **mitotic f's,** stages exhibiting a pattern characteristic of mitosis. **Purkinje's f's.** See under *image*. **Stifel's f.,** a black disk having a white spot in the center, used for locating and measuring the blind spot in the eye. **Zöllner's f's.** See under *line*.

fila (fi'lah) [L.]. Plural of *filum*.

filaceous (fi-la'shus). Made up of filaments.

filament (fil'ah-ment) [L. *filamentum*]. A delicate fiber or thread. **f's of Ammon,** fine hairs, or cilia, on the inner surface of the ciliary body of the eye. **axial f.,** the central thread of the flagellum of a spermatozoon. **bacterial f.,** a threadlike form unsegmented or without constrictions between the segments. **linin f.,** a network of linin spread throughout the cell nucleus. **spermatic f.,** the naked caudal filament of a spermatozoon. **terminal f.,** filum terminale. **terminal f. of spinal dura mater,** filum durae matris spinalis.

filamenta (fil"ah-men'tah) [L.]. Plural of *filamentum*.

filamentous (fil-ah-men'tus). Composed of long, threadlike structures: said of bacterial colonies.

filamentum (fil"ah-men'tum), pl. *filamen'ta* [L.]. A filament.

filar (fi'lar) [L. *filum* thread]. Threadlike; filamentous.

Filaria (fĭ-la're-ah) [L. *filum* thread]. A former loosely applied generic name for members of the superfamily Filarioidea. **F. bancrof'ti,** *Wuchereria bancrofti*. **F. conjuncti'vae,** a species found in the eye of horses and asses, and sometimes in man. **F. demarquay'i,** *F. juncea*. **F. diur'na,** the larval form of *Loa loa*. **F. equi'na,** a common parasite of the abdominal cavity of horses and asses; sometimes found in man. **F. hom'inis o'ris,** a species found in the mouth. **F. immit'is,** *Dirofilaria immitis*. **F. jun'cea,** a very small species found in the West Indies. **F. labia'lis,** a species found in the lip. **F. len'tis,** a species found in the lens of the eye. **F. lo'a,** *Loa loa*. **F. lymphat'ica,** a species found in the bronchial lymph glands. **F. magalhae'si,** *Dirofilaria magalhaesi*. **F. medinen'sis,** *Dracunculus medinensis*. **F. noctur'na,** *Wuchereria bancrofti*. **F. oc'uli,** *Loa loa*. **F. ozzar'di,** *Mansonella ozzardi*. **F. palpebra'lis,** a species found in the upper eyelid. **F. per'stans,** *Acanthocheilonema perstans*. **F. philippinen'sis,** *Wuchereria bancrofti*. **F. recon'dita,** a species found in the blood of dogs, and passing its intermediary cycle in the thoracic muscles of *Culex fatigans*. **F. san'guinis-hom'inis,** *Wuchereria bancrofti*. **F. vol'vulus,** *Onchocerca volvulus*.

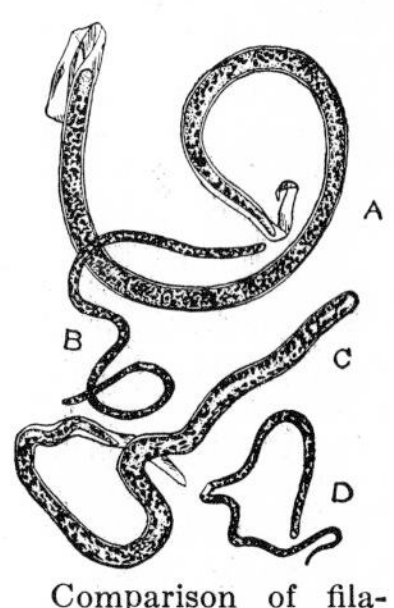

Comparison of filariae. *A*, *bancrofti* (large with sheath); *B*, *perstans* (small, blunt tail, no sheath); *C*, *loa* (large with sheath); *D*, *juncea* (*demarquayi*) (small, sharp tail, with sheath) (× 75). (Manson.)

filaria (fĭ-la're-ah), pl. *fila'riae* [L. *filum* thread]. A nematode worm of the superfamily Filarioidea. **blood f.,** *Wuchereria bancrofti*. **Brug's f.,** *Wuchereria malayi*.

filariae (fĭ-la're-e) [L.]. Plural of *filaria*.

filarial (fĭ-la're-al). Pertaining to or caused by filariae.

filariasis (fil"ah-ri'ah-sis). A diseased state due to the presence of filariae within the body. **Bancroft's f.,** infestation of the lymphatics and connective tissue with the adult form of *Wuchereria bancrofti*. **Brug's f., f. malayi,** infestation with *Wuchereria malayi*. **Ozzard's f.,** infestation with *Mansonella ozzardi*.

filaricidal (fĭ-lăr"ĭ-sīd'al) [*filaria* + L. *caedere* to kill]. Destructive to filariae.

filaricide (fĭ-lăr'ĭ-sīd). An agent that is destructive to filariae.

filariform (fĭ-lăr'ĭ-form). Threadlike; resembling filariae.

Filarioidea (fĭ-lăr"e-oi'de-ah). A superfamily or order of nematode parasites, the adults being threadlike worms which invade the tissues and body cavities where the female deposits embryonated eggs (prelarvae) known as microfilaria. These microfilariae are ingested by blood-sucking insects in whom they pass their developmental stage and are returned to man by the bites of such insects. The filaria of man belong to the genera *Wuchereria*, *Onchocerca*, *Loa*, *Acanthocheilonema*, *Mansonella*, and *Dirofilaria*.

Filatov's (Filatow's) disease, spots (fĭ-lat'ofs) [Nil Féodorowich *Filatov*, pediatrician in Moscow, 1847–1902]. See under the nouns.

file (fīl). A surgical or a dental instrument with a finely serrated surface, for reducing surplus hard substance such as bone or materials used in dental restorations, or for smoothing roughened surfaces.

filiform (fil'ĭ-form) [L. *filum* thread + *forma* form]. 1. Thread shaped. 2. An extremely slender bougie.

filioma (fil-e-o'mah). Fibroma of sclera.

filioparental (fil"e-o-pah-ren'tal). Pertaining to the relationships between children and their parents.

Filipovitch's (Filipowicz's) sign (fĭ-le'po-vich"ez) [Casimir *Filipovitch*, Polish physician]. See under *sign*.

filipuncture (fil′ĭ-punk-tūr) [L. *filum* thread + *punctura* puncture]. The insertion of a wire or thread into an aneurysm.

filix (fi′liks), pl. *fil′ices* [L.]. A fern. **f. mas,** male fern. See *aspidium.*

fillet (fil′et). 1. A loop, as of cord or tape, for making traction. 2. A loop-shaped structure, such as a band of nerve fibers in the brain. **acoustic f.,** lemniscus lateralis. **bulbar f.,** lemniscus medialis. **lateral f., lower f.,** lemniscus lateralis. **medial f., mesial f.,** lemniscus medialis. **olivary f.,** the nerve fasciculus surrounding the olivary nucleus. **pontile f.,** lemniscus lateralis.

filling (fil′ing). 1. The material which is inserted into a prepared tooth cavity; usually gold, amalgam, cement, or a synthetic resin. 2. The restoration of the crown with appropriate material after removal of the carious tissue from a tooth. **combination f.,** one made up of two or more materials, usually placed one over the other. **complex f.,** a filling for a complex cavity. **composite f.,** combination f. **compound f.,** a filling for a cavity that involves two surfaces of a tooth. **contour f.,** a filling that is shaped to restore the anatomical form of a tooth. **direct f.,** one that is formed and completed directly in the tooth cavity. **direct resin f.,** a direct filling made from a synthetic resin. **indirect f.,** one that is constructed on a die that has been made from an accurate impression of the tooth and is then inserted into the tooth cavity. **Mosetig-Moorhof f.** See *Mosetig-Moorhof bone wax,* under *wax.* **nonleaking f.,** a filling so well adapted to the wall of the tooth cavity as to prevent the penetration of moisture between the filling and the tooth. **permanent f.,** a filling intended to provide complete function while the tooth remains in the oral cavity. **provisional f.,** temporary f. **temporary f.,** a filling, as of gutta percha, zinc oxide–eugenol pastes, self-curing acrylic resin, or zinc phosphate or silicate cement, which is placed in a tooth cavity with the intention of removing it within a short period of time.

film (film). 1. A thin layer or coating. 2. A thin sheet specially processed for use in photography or roentgenography; used also to designate such a sheet after exposure to light rays or other radiant energy to which it is sensitive. **fixed blood f.,** a thin film of blood spread on a slide, dried quickly, and fixed. **gelatin f., absorbable,** a sterile, non-antigenic, absorbable, water-insoluble gelatin film: used as an aid in the surgical closure and repair of defects in dura and pleura. **lateral jaw f.,** an x-ray film showing either the ramus or the body of the mandible. **occlusal f.,** an x-ray film showing topographic and cross-sectional views of the maxillary or mandibular dental structure and adjacent tissue. **periapical f.,** an x-ray film showing a particular tooth and the tissues adjacent to the apex of its root. **sulfa f.,** a film made from an emulsion of sulfadiazine, sulfanilamide, and methyl cellulose: used as a dressing for burns, cuts, and skin grafts. **x-ray f.,** a sheet specially prepared for use in roentgenography after exposure to roentgen rays and appropriate processing; a roentgenogram.

filoma (fĭ-lo′mah). Fibroma of the sclera.

filopod (fil′o-pod). Filopodium.

filopodium (fi″lo-po′de-um), pl. *filopo′dia* [L. *filum* thread + Gr. *pous* foot]. A pseudopodium which is slender and pointed at the tip.

filopressure (fi′lo-presh″ūr) [L. *filum* thread + *pressura* pressure]. The compression of a blood vessel by a thread.

filovaricosis (fi′lo-var″ĭ-ko′sis). The development of varicosities on the axis-cylinder of a nerve fiber.

filter (fil′ter) [L. *filtrum*]. 1. A device for the straining of water or other liquid. 2. In radiation therapy, a screen made of some substance which permits passage of some wavelengths while absorbing others. **Berkefeld f.,** one made of infusorial earth, available in three porosities: V (*viel,* or coarse), N (normal), and W (*wenig,* or fine). Most bacteria are removed by the V filter; all are usually removed by the N; and the W is used for exceedingly small organisms. **Chamberland f.,** one made of unglazed porcelain, available in several graded porosities, L1, L2, L3, etc., the L3 being roughly equivalent to the Berkefeld N. **Coors f.,** a filter cylinder of unglazed porcelain. **Darnall f.,** the filter used in the United States Army. The water is mechanically filtered through Canton flannel after being treated with a precipitant. **Gooch f.,** a platinum or porcelain crucible the bottom of which is perforated with holes and covered with a layer of asbestos fibers. **Haen f.,** a form of bacterial filter which employs a membrane. **intermittent sand f.,** a sand filter to which sewage is applied for only a short time and then is allowed to drain away so that aeration and oxidation may take place. **Jenkins' f.,** a bacterial filter for small quantities of material, the medium being a porous porcelain block which is held tightly by compression between a metallic cylinder and a metal funnel. **Kitasato's f.,** a bacteriological filter in which the liquids are drawn by suction through an unglazed porcelain bougie. **Mandler f.,** a filter for household and for laboratory use which is made from diatomaceous earth. **mechanical f.,** a filter of sand or other porous material through which water is forced rapidly to remove gross particles. These particles may be the precipitate caused by the addition to the water of some coagulant. **Pasteur-Chamberland f.,** a hollow column of unglazed porcelain through which liquids are forced by pressure or by vacuum exhaustion. **percolating f.,** trickling filter. **Reichel's f.,** a bacteriological filter in which the liquid is placed in a receiver of unglazed porcelain and drawn through the walls of the receiver by suction. **roughing f., scrubbing f.,** a coarse-grained filter through which turbid water is passed to remove the larger particles and thus protect the sand filter from clogging. **Seitz f., Seitz-Werke f.,** one in which the filtering element is an asbestos pad, which is the equivalent of the Berkefeld N filter. **sintered glass f.,** a filter of sintered glass, available in various porosities, sometimes designed C (coarse), M (medium), F (fine), and UF (ultrafine); only the ultrafine is bacteria-proof. **slow sand f.,** a filter made of sand and gravel through which water passes slowly and is purified largely by the action of the microorganisms growing on the surface of the grains of sand near the top of the filter. **sprinkling f.,** a trickling filter in which the sewage is applied by spray. **trickling f.,** beds of porous material on which sewage is distributed and allowed to percolate through to drains laid on a tight floor. The purpose is to so oxidize the organic material as to make it nonputrescible. **Wood's f.,** a filter of glass containing nickel oxide, which eliminates visible light waves and passes ultraviolet wavelengths of about 3650 A, used in both diagnosis and treatment of various dermatologic conditions. The fluorescence of infected hairs under such light is an important aid in the diagnosis of tinea capitis.

filterable (fil′ter-ah-b′l). Capable of passing through the pores of a filter: applied to elements that can pass through a filter which will not permit the passage of the usual microorganisms.

filtrable (fil′trah-b′l). Filterable.

filtrate (fil′trāt). A liquid which has passed through a filter. **glomerular f.,** the fluid that passes from the blood through the glomeruli of a kidney and is excreted as urine.

filtration (fil-tra′shun). 1. The passage of a liquid through a filter, accomplished by a pressure differential which may be produced by positive pressure on the liquid to be filtered or negative pressure on the filtrate. 2. In radiotherapy, the passing of the roentgen ray through a sheet of aluminum or other metal by which the non-penetrating or soft rays are removed, only the penetrating or hard rays passing through.

filtratometer (fil″trah-tom′e-ter). An instrument for measuring gastric filtrates.

filtros (fil′tros). An artificial porous stone made by compacting silicious sand and used as a filtering element in purifying sewage.

fil′trum ventric′uli [L.]. A depression between the two projections formed in the lateral wall of the vestibule of the larynx by the arytenoid and cuneiform cartilages. Called also *Merkel's filtrum.*

filum (fi′lum), pl. *fi′la* [L.]. [N A, B N A] A threadlike structure or part. **fi′la anastomot′ica ner′vi acus′tici** [B N A], omitted in N A. **f. du′rae ma′tris spina′lis** [N A, B N A], the part of the filum terminale between the point of its dural investment and its attachment to the dorsal surface of the coccyx. Called also *f. of spinal dura mater.* **f. latera′lia pon′tis** [B N A], omitted in N A. **fi′la olfacto′ria,** nervi olfactorii. **fi′la radicula′ria nervo′rum spina′lium** [N A, B N A], the threadlike filaments by which the dorsal and ventral roots of each spinal nerve are attached to the spinal cord. Called also *root filaments of spinal nerves.* **f. of spinal dura mater,** f. durae matris spinalis. **f. termina′le** [N A, B N A], a slender, threadlike prolongation from the end of the conus medullaris, anchoring the spinal cord to the coccyx. It consists of a prolongation of the pia mater that pierces the dural sac caudally, where both are attached to the coccygeal ligament.

fimbria (fim′bre-ah) [L. *fimbriae* (pl.) a fringe]. One of the individual components making up a fringe, or a structure resembling such a component. **f. hippocam′pi,** the band of white matter along the median edge of the ventricular surface of the hippocampus. **ovarian f., f. ova′rica,** the longest of the processes that make up the fimbriae tubae uterinae, extending along the free border of the mesosalpinx. **fim′briae of tongue,** papillae foliatae. **fim′briae tu′bae uteri′nae** [N A, B N A], **fimbriae of uterine tube,** the numerous divergent fringelike processes on the distal part of the infundibulum of the uterine tube.

Fimbriaria (fim″bre-a′re-ah). A genus of tapeworms. **F. fasciola′ris,** a tapeworm infecting wild and domestic fowl.

fimbriated (fim′bre-āt-ed) [L. *fimbriatus*]. Fringed.

fimbriation (fim″bre-a′shun). The formation of or the possession of fimbriae.

fimbriatum (fim″bre-a′tum) [L.]. Fringed.

fimbriocele (fim′bre-o-sēl″) [*fimbria* + Gr. *kēlē* hernia]. Hernia containing fimbriae of the uterine tube.

Finckh test (fink) [Johann *Finckh*, German psychiatrist, born 1873]. See under *tests.*

finder (fīnd′er). A device on a microscope to facilitate the finding of some object in the field.

finding (fīnd′ing). An observation; a condition discovered.

finger (fing′ger). Any one of the five digits of the hand. **baseball f.,** partial flexion of the terminal phalanx of a finger caused by the ball striking the end or back of the finger in playing baseball. **bolster f's,** the swollen fingers that result from a monilia infection in workers who handle sugar. **Brodie's f.,** herpes zoster infection of the finger. **clubbed f.,** a deformity produced by proliferation of the soft tissues about the terminal phalanx, with no constant osseous changes: seen in various cases of chronic disease of the thoracic organs. **dead f.,** a numb, mottled finger, such as one seen in acrocyanosis. **drop f.,** mallet f. **drumstick f.,** clubbed f. **first f.,** the thumb. **giant f.,** macrodactyly. **hammer f.,** mallet f. **hippocratic f's,** enlargement of the terminal phalanges, with coarse nails curving over the ends of the fingers. See *hypertrophic pulmonary osteoarthropathy,* under *osteo-arthropathy.* **index f.,** the second digit of the hand, the thumb being considered the first. **insane f.,** chronic whitlow in certain cases of confirmed insanity. **lock f.,** one that is fixed in a flexed position, owing to the presence of a small fibrous growth in the sheath of the tendon of the extensor. **Madonna f's,** the thin, delicate fingers seen in pituitary acromicria. **mallet f.,** permanent flexion of the distal phalanx. **Morse f.,** a deformity of the finger due to constant use of the Morse telegraph key. **ring f.,** the fourth digit of the hand. **snapping f.,** trigger f. **spider f.,** arachnodactylia. **spring f.,** a condition in which flexion and extension of the finger beyond certain points are difficult. **stuck f.,** a vasospastic condition of the fingers sometimes seen in users of vibratory tools. **trigger f.,** a finger liable to be affected with a momentary spasmodic arrest of flexion or extension, followed by a snapping into place: it is due to stenosing tendovaginitis. **tulip f's,** fingers affected by dermatitis after handling tulip bulbs. **washerwoman's f's,** the dry shrunken fingers of patients with fatal cases of cholera. **waxy f.,** dead f. **webbed f's,** fingers united to a greater or less extent by a fold of skin; syndactylia. **white f.,** dead f.

fingeragnosia (fing″ger-ag-no′se-ah) [*finger* + *agnosia*]. Inability to recognize, indicate on command, name or choose the individual fingers of one's own hand or of the hands of others.

fingerprint (fing′ger-print). An impression of the cutaneous ridges of the fleshy distal portion of a finger, made by applying ink and pressing the finger on paper. Such records (as well as prints of hand or foot) are used as means of establishing identification.

Finikoff's method or **treatment** (fin′ĭ-kofs) [*Finikoff*, Leningrad surgeon]. See under *treatment.*

Finkelstein's albumin milk [Heinrich *Finkelstein*, German pediatrician. 1865–1942]. See *albumin milk,* under *milk.*

Finney's operation (fin′ēz) [John M. T. *Finney*, Baltimore surgeon, 1863–1942]. See under *operation.*

Finochietto's stirrup (fe-no″ke-at′ōz) [Enrique *Finochietto*, surgeon in Buenos Aires, 1881–1948]. See under *stirrup.*

Finsen bath, light (fin′sen) [Neils Ryberg *Finsen*, Danish physician, 1860–1904; the first to discover the curative effects of ultraviolet rays, and winner of the Nobel prize for medicine and physiology in 1903]. See under *bath* and *light.*

fire (fīr). Fever. **grass f.,** stalk disease of cattle. **St. Anthony's f.** 1. Ergot poisoning. 2. Erysipelas. **St. Francis' f.,** erysipelas.

firpene (fir′pēn). Pinene.

Fischer's murmur, sign (fish′erz) [Louis *Fischer*, pediatrician in New York, 1864–1944]. See under *murmur* and *sign.*

Fischer's solution, treatment [Martin Henry *Fischer*, American physician, born 1879]. See under *solution* and *treatment.*

Fischer's test [Emil *Fischer*, German chemist, 1852–1919]. See under *tests.*

Fisher bed [Frederick Richard *Fisher*, British orthopedist, 1844–1932]. See under *bed.*

fissile (fis′il). Capable of being split; fissionable.

fission (fish′un) [L. *fissio*]. 1. The act of splitting. 2. A form of asexual reproduction in which the cell simply divides into two approximately equal parts. It is seen in bacteria and other low forms of life. 3. The splitting of the nucleus of an atom, releasing a great quantity of kinetic energy. **binary f.,** the halving of the nucleus and then of the cytoplasm of the cell, as in protozoa. **bud f.,** reproduction by the protrusion of a portion of the protoplasm; seen in some rhizopods. **cellular f.** See *fission,* 2nd def. **nuclear f.** See *fission,* 3rd def.

fissionable (fish′un-ah-b′l). Capable of undergoing fission.

fissiparous (fi-sip′ah-rus) [L. *fissus* cleft + *parere* to produce]. Propagated by fission.

fissula (fish′u-lah) [L., dim. of *fissum*]. A little cleft. **f. an′te fenes′tram,** an irregular ribbon of connective tissue that extends through the bony otic capsule from the vestibule just anterior to the oval window, to the tympanic cavity near the processus cochleariformis.

fissura (fis-su'rah), pl. *fissu'rae* [L.]. [N A, B N A] A general term for a cleft or groove, especially a deep fold in the cerebral cortex that involves its entire thickness. Called also *fissure*. **f. in a'no,** anal fissure. **f. antitragohelici'na** [N A, B N A], a fissure in the auricular cartilage between the cauda helicis and the antitragus. Called also *antitragohelicine fissure*. **f. au'ris congen'ita,** a congenital fissure of the auricle. **f. calcari'na** [B N A], sulcus calcarinus. **fissu'rae cerebel'li** [N A], the numerous shallow grooves in the cortex of the cerebellum, on the surface and within the deep fissures, which divide the cortex into folia. Called also *sulci cerebelli* [B N A], and *sulci of cerebellum*. **f. cer'ebri latera'lis [Syl'vii]** [B N A], sulcus lateralis cerebri. **f. choroi'dea** [N A], the line in the lateral ventricle along which the choroid plexus invaginates. Called also *choroid fissure*. **f. collatera'lis** [B N A], sulcus collateralis. **f. hippocam'pi** [B N A], sulcus hippocampi. **f. horizonta'lis cerebel'li** [N A], the fissure that separates the superior from the inferior semilunar lobule of the cerebellum. Called also *horizontal fissure of cerebellum* and *sulcus horizontalis cerebelli* [B N A]. **f. horizonta'lis pulmo'nis dex'tri** [N A], the cleft that extends forward from the oblique fissure in the right lung, separating the upper and middle lobes. Called also *horizontal fissure of right lung*. **f. ligamen'ti tere'tis** [N A], the fossa on the visceral surface of the liver lodging the ligamentum teres in the adult, and helping separate the right and left lobes of the liver. Called also *fissure for ligamentum teres* and *fossa venae umbilicalis* [B N A]. **f. ligamen'ti veno'si** [N A], a fossa on the posterior part of the diaphragmatic surface of the liver lodging the ligamentum venosum in the adult. Called also *fissure for ligamentum venosum*. **f. longitudina'lis cer'ebri** [N A, B N A], the deep fissure between the cerebral hemispheres extending inferiorly to the corpus callosum. Called also *longitudinal fissure of cerebrum*. **f. media'na ante'rior medul'lae oblonga'tae** [N A, B N A], the continuation of the anterior median fissure of the spinal cord on the ventral aspect of the medulla oblongata. Called also *anterior median fissure of medulla oblongata*. **f. media'na ante'rior medul'lae spina'lis** [N A, B N A], the fissure in the midline of the anterior, or ventral, surface of the spinal cord. Called also *anterior median fissure of spinal cord*. **f. obli'qua pulmo'nis** [N A]. 1. The cleft that separates the lower from the middle lobe in the right lung. 2. The cleft that separates the upper from the lower lobe in the left lung. Called also *oblique fissure of lung*. **f. orbita'lis infe'rior** [N A, B N A], a cleft in the inferolateral wall of the orbit bounded by the great wing of the sphenoid and the orbital process of the maxilla. It transmits the infraorbital and zygomatic nerves and the infraorbital vessels. Called also *inferior orbital fissure*. **f. orbita'lis supe'rior** [N A, B N A], an elongated cleft between the small and great wings of the sphenoid bone, which transmits various nerves and vessels. Called also *superior orbital fissure*. **f. parietooccipita'lis** [B N A], sulcus parietooccipitalis. **f. petrooccipita'lis** [N A, B N A], a fissure extending backward from the foramen lacerum between the basioccipital and the posterior and inner border of the petrous portion of the occipital bone. Called also *petrooccipital fissure*. **f. petrosquamo'sa** [N A, B N A], a slight fissure of varying distinctness in the floor of the middle cranial fossa, marking the line of fusion between the squamous and petrous portions of the temporal bone. Called also *petrosquamous fissure*. **f. petrotympan'ica** [N A, B N A], a narrow transversely running slit just posterior to the articular surface of the mandibular fossa of the temporal bone; an arteriole and the chorda tympani nerve pass through it, and it lodges a portion of the malleus. Called also *petrotympanic fissure*. **f. posterolatera'lis cerebel'li** [N A], the fissure which separates the nodulus from the uvula and the flocculus from the tonsilla of the cerebellum. Called also *posterolateral fissure*. **f. pri'ma cerebel'li** [N A], the fissure that separates the anterior from the posterior lobe in the cerebellum. It lies between the culmen and declive of the vermis, and between the part of the hemisphere that is continuous with the culmen and the lobulus simplex in the hemisphere. Called also *primary fissure*. **f. pterygoi'dea** [B N A], a fissure on the inferior portion of each pterygoid process where the pyramidal process of the palate is inserted between the diverging medial and lateral pterygoid plates. Omitted in N A. Called also *pterygoid notch*. **f. pterygomaxilla'ris** [N A], a cleft just behind the inferior orbital fissure between the lateral pterygoid plate and the maxilla. Called also *pterygomaxillary fissure*. **f. sphenooccipita'lis** [B N A], the fissure between the basilar part of the occipital bone and the body of the sphenoid bone. Omitted in N A. **f. sphenopetro'sa** [N A, B N A], a fissure in the floor of the middle cranial fossa between the posterior edge of the great wing of the sphenoid bone and the petrous part of the temporal bone. Called also *sphenopetrosal fissure*. **f. transver'sa cerebel'li** [B N A], omitted in N A. **f. transver'sa cer'ebri** [N A, B N A], the fissure between the dorsal surface of the diencephalon and the ventral surface of the cerebral hemispheres, produced by the folding back of the hemispheres during their development. Called also *transverse fissure of cerebrum*. **f. tympanomastoi'dea** [N A, B N A], an external fissure on the inferior and lateral aspect of the skull between the tympanic portion and the mastoid process of the temporal bone. The auricular branch of the vagus nerve often passes through it. Called also *tympanomastoid fissure*. **f. tympanosquamo'sa** [N A], a line seen on the posterior wall of the external acoustic meatus at the junction between the tympanic and squamous parts of the temporal bone. Called also *tympanosquamous fissure*.

fissurae (fis-su're) [L.]. Plural of *fissura*.

fissural (fish'u-ral). Pertaining to a fissure.

fissure (fish'ūr) [L. *fissura*]. 1. Any cleft or groove, normal or otherwise; especially a deep fold in the cerebral cortex which involves the entire thickness of the brain wall. Cf. *sulcus*. 2. In dentistry, a fault in the surface of a tooth caused by the imperfect joining of the enamel of the different lobes. To be distinguished from a groove or sulcus (A.D.A.). See *fissura*. **abdominal f.,** a congenital cleft in the abdominal wall. **adoccipital f.,** a fissure which sometimes crosses the caudal part of the precuneus and joins the occipital fissure. Called also *entolambdoid f.* **Ammon's f.,** a pear-shaped aperture in the sclera at an early fetal period. **amygdaline f.,** a cerebral fissure near the extremity of the temporal lobe. **anal f.,** a painful linear ulcer at the margin of the anus. **angular f.,** fissura sphenopetrosa. **ansate f.,** a small fissure on the superior aspect of the anterior part of the brain. **antitragohelicine f.,** fissura antitragohelicina. **ape f.,** a term applied to any fissure in the human brain that is found also in apes, especially to the sulcus lunatus. **f. of aqueduct of vestibule,** apertura externa aqueductus vestibuli. **f. of auricle, posterior,** fissura antitragohelicina. **auricular f. of temporal bone,** fissura tympanomastoidea. **basilar f.,** fissura sphenooccipitalis. **basisylvian f.,** the part of the fissure of Sylvius between the temporal lobe and the orbital surface of the frontal bone. **f. of Bichat,** fissura transversa cerebri. **branchial f.,** branchial cleft. **Broca's f.,** the fissure that surrounds the left inferior frontal gyrus. **Burdach's f.,** a fissure between the lateral surface of the insula and the inner surface of the operculum. **calcarine f.,** sulcus calcarinus. **callosal f.,** sulcus corporis callosi. **callosomarginal f.,** sulcus cinguli. **central f.,** sulcus centralis. **cerebral f's, f's of cere-**

brum, sulci cerebri. **cerebral f., lateral,** sulcus lateralis cerebri. **choroid f.** 1. A ventral fissure formed by invagination of the optic vesicle and its stalk in the embryo, permitting the ingrowth of the mesoblast for the formation of the vitreous humor, etc. 2. Fissura choroidea. **collateral f.,** sulcus collateralis. **corneal f.,** rima cornealis. **craniofacial f.,** a vertical fissure separating the mesethmoid into two parts. **dentate f.,** sulcus hippocampi. **f. of ductus venosus,** fossa ductus venosi. **Ecker's f.,** a transverse fissure on the dorsal surface of the occipital lobe of the brain, forming part of the paroccipital fissure. Called also *transverse occipital f.* **ectorhinal f.,** a fissure separating the rhinencephalon from the rest of the hemisphere. **enamel f.,** a fault in the enamel surface of a tooth. See *fissure* (def. 2). **entolambdoid f.,** adoccipital f. **entorbital f.,** a fissure occasionally seen between the orbital and olfactory fissures. **ethmoid f.,** meatus nasi superior. **exoccipital f.,** Wernicke's f. **fimbriodentate f.,** fimbriodentate sulcus. **glaserian f.,** fissura petrotympanica. **f. of glottis,** rima glottidis. **great f. of cerebrum,** fissura transversa cerebri. **great horizontal f.,** fissura horizontalis cerebelli. **Henle's f's,** spaces filled with connective tissue between the muscular fibers of the heart. **hippocampal f., f. of hippocampus.** 1. Sulcus hippocampi. 2. Sulcus calcarinus. **horizontal f. of cerebellum,** fissura horizontalis cerebelli. **horizontal f. of right lung,** fissura horizontalis pulmonis dextri. **incisive f.,** sutura incisiva. **inferofrontal f.,** one between the middle and inferior frontal convolutions of the brain. **intercerebral f.,** one separating the two hemispheres of the brain. **interparietal f.,** sulcus intraparietalis. **intraprecuneal f.,** a fissure in the precuneal region of the brain, anterior to the cuneus. **intratonsillar f.,** fossa supratonsillaris. **lacrimal f.,** sulcus lacrimalis ossis lacrimalis. **lateral f. of cerebrum,** sulcus lateralis cerebri. **f. for ligamentum teres,** fissura ligamenti teretis. **f. for ligamentum venosum,** fissura ligamenti venosi. **linguogingival f.,** an occasional fissure in the lingual surface of an upper incisor tooth. **longitudinal f.** 1. Fissura longitudinalis cerebri. 2. Tenia omentalis. **longitudinal f. of cerebellum,** vallecula cerebelli. **longitudinal f. of cerebrum,** fissura longitudinalis cerebri. **mandibular f's,** the two lowest facial fissures of the embryo. **median f. of medulla oblongata, anterior,** fissura mediana anterior medullae oblongatae. **median f. of medulla oblongata, posterior,** sulcus medianus posterior medullae oblongatae. **median f. of spinal cord, anterior,** fissura mediana anterior medullae spinalis. **median f. of spinal cord, posterior,** sulcus medianus posterior medullae spinalis. **f. of Monro,** sulcus hypothalamicus. **oblique f. of lung,** fissura obliqua pulmonis. **occipital f.,** sulcus parietooccipitalis. **occipital f., anterior,** the depression between the occipitotemporal and inferior sphenoid lobes. **occipital f., perpendicular,** sulcus calcarinus. **occipital f., perpendicular, external,** stria medialis trigoni olfactorii. **occipitosphenoidal f.,** fissura sphenooccipitalis. **oral f.,** rima oris. **orbital f., inferior,** fissura orbitalis inferior. **orbital f., superior,** fissura orbitalis superior. **f. of palpebrae, palpebral f.,** rima palpebrarum. **Pansch's f.,** a fissure in the brain extending from the lower end of the central fissure to near the end of the occipital lobe. **paracentral f., anterior,** sulcus precentralis. **parallel f.,** sulcus temporalis superior. **parietal f.,** the parietal portion of the sulcus intraparietalis. **parietooccipital f.,** sulcus parietooccipitalis. **parietosphenoid f.,** incisura parietalis ossis temporalis. **paroccipital f.,** the posterior portion of the sulcus intraparietalis. **petrobasilar f.,** fissura petrooccipitalis. **petromastoid f.,** fissura tympanomastoidea. **petrooccipital f.,** fissura petrooccipitalis. **petrosal f., superficial,** hiatus canalis nervi petrosi majoris. **petrosphenoidal f.,** fissura sphenopetrosa. **petrosquamosal f., petrosquamous f.,** fissura petrosquamosa. **petrotympanic f.,** fissura petrotympanica. **portal f.,** porta hepatis. **postcentral f.,** one of the sulci of the cerebellum. **posterolateral f.,** fissura posterolateralis cerebelli. **posthippocampal f.,** sulcus calcarinus. **postrhinal f.,** a fissure between the hippocampal and subcollateral convolutions. **postseptal f.,** a cerebral fissure in the posterior part of the occipital lobe. **precentral f.,** a fissure that is parallel to the central sulcus and anterior to it. **prelimbic f.,** the anterior part of the sulcus cinguli. **prepyramidal f.,** a fissure in front of the pyramid, between the tonsil and the cuneate lobule. **primary f.,** fissura prima cerebelli. **pterygoid f.,** fissura pterygoidea. **pterygomaxillary f.,** fissura pterygomaxillaris. **pterygopalatine f.,** fissura pterygomaxillaris. **pterygopalatine f. of palatine bone,** sulcus palatinus major ossis palatini. **pterygotympanic f.,** fissura petrotympanica. **f. of Rolando,** sulcus centralis. **f. of round ligament,** fissura ligamenti teretis. **sagittal f. of liver,** fossa sagittalis sinistra hepatis. **Santorini's f's,** incisurae cartilaginis meatus acustici. **Schwalbe's f's,** the supercentral and anterior occipital fissures. **sphenoidal f.,** fissura orbitalis superior. **sphenoidal f., inferior,** fissura orbitalis inferior. **sphenoidal f., superior,** fissura orbitalis superior. **sphenomaxillary f.** 1. Fissura orbitalis inferior. 2. Fossa pterygopalatina. **sphenooccipital f.,** fissura sphenooccipitalis. **sphenopetrosal f.,** fissura sphenopetrosa. **squamotympanic f.,** fissura petrotympanica. **subfrontal f.,** inferofrontal f. **subsylvian f.** 1. An occasional fissure on the ventral surface of the frontal lobe of the brain. 2. Ramus posterior sulci lateralis cerebri. **subtemporal f.,** an occasional fissure in the inferior and middle temporal convolutions. **supercallosal f.,** sulcus cinguli. **supercentral f.,** a cleft of the cerebrum situated above and parallel to the dorsal part of the central fissure. **superfrontal f.,** a fissure on the lateral aspect of the frontal lobe, which demarcates the middle frontal gyrus. **superoccipital f.,** a fissure in the upper part of the occipital portion of the posterior lobe of the cerebrum. **superseptal f.,** a fissure in the cuneus nearly parallel with the occipital fissure. **supertemporal f.,** sulcus temporalis superior. **sylvian f., f. of Sylvius,** sulcus lateralis cerebri. **tentorial f.,** sulcus collateralis. **transtemporal f.,** an occasional short fissure on the lateral surface of the temporal lobe. **transverse f.,** porta hepatis. **transverse f. of cerebrum,** fissura transversa cerebri. **transverse f. of cerebrum, anterior,** sulcus centralis. **transverse f. of cerebrum, great,** fissura transversa cerebri. **tympanic f.,** fissura petrotympanica. **tympanomastoid f.,** fissura tympanomastoidea. **tympanosquamous f.** 1. Fissura tympanosquamosa. 2. Fissura petrotympanica. **umbilical f.,** fossa venae umbilicalis. **f. of the venous ligament,** fossa ductus venosi. **f. of the vestibule,** rima vestibuli. **Wernicke's f.,** a fissure that sometimes demarcates the parietal and temporal lobes from the occipital lobes. **zygal f.,** a fissure that consists of two portions united by a third portion. **zygomaticosphenoid f.,** a fissure between the orbital surface of the great wing of the sphenoid bone and the zygomatic bone.

fistula (fis'tu-lah), pl. *fistulas* or *fis'tulae* [L. "pipe"]. An abnormal passage or communication, usually between two internal organs, or leading from an internal organ to the surface of the body; frequently designated according to the organs or parts with which it communicates, as anovaginal, bronchocutaneous, hepatopleural, pulmonoperitoneal, rectovaginal, urethrovaginal, and the like (see illustrations). Such passages are frequently

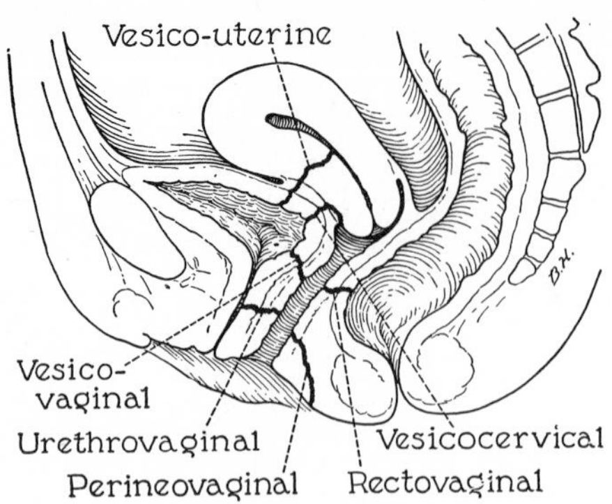

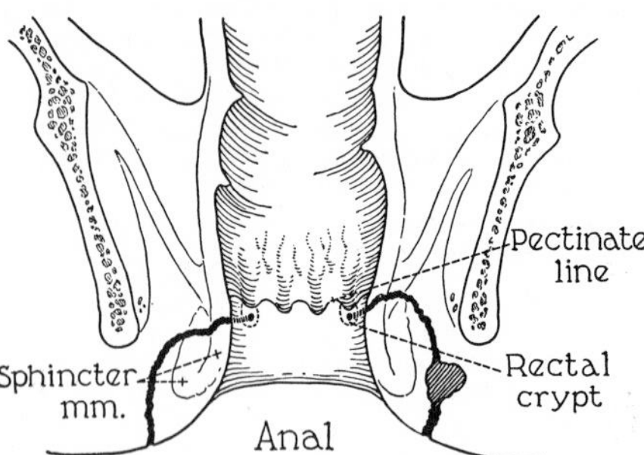

Various types of fistula, designated according to the site, or the organs with which they communicate.

created experimentally for the purpose of obtaining body secretions for physiologic study. **abdominal f.,** an abnormal passage leading from one of the hollow abdominal viscera to the surface of the abdomen. **alveolar f.,** dental f. **amphibolic f.,** an opening made into the gallbladder of an animal in order to obtain bile for study, with the common bile duct left intact so that the bile may flow through it when the fistula is closed. **anal f., f. in a'no,** one opening on the cutaneous surface near the anus, which may or may not communicate with the rectum. **arteriovenous f.,** an abnormal communication between an artery and a vein; it may result from injury (*traumatic arteriovenous f.*), or occur as a congenital abnormality (*congenital arteriovenous fistula*). **f. au'ris congen'ita,** preauricular f., congenital. **biliary f.,** an abnormal passage communicating with the biliary tract. **f. bimuco'sa,** a complete fistula of the anus, both ends of which open on the mucous surface of the anal canal. **blind f.,** a fistula that is open at one end only; it may open only upon the cutaneous surface of the body (*external blind f.*), or on an internal mucous surface (*internal blind f.*). **branchial f.,** an abnormal passage resulting from failure of closure of a branchial cleft. **cervical f.** 1. Branchial fistula. 2. An abnormal passage communicating with the canal of the cervix uteri. **f. cervicovagina'lis laqueat'ica,** a fistula in the vaginal portion of the cervix uteri, communicating with the cervical canal and the vagina. **f. ciba'lis,** the esophagus. **f. col'li congen'ita,** a congenital fistula in the neck, opening into the pharynx. **colonic f.,** an abnormal passage communicating with the colon and the cutaneous surface of the body (*external colonic f.*), or with the colon and another hollow organ (*internal colonic f.*). **complete f.,** an abnormal passage in the body, each end of which opens on a mucous surface or on the cutaneous surface of the body. **f. cor'neae,** an orifice remaining after failure of a corneal ulcer to heal. **craniosinus f.,** a fistula between the intracranial space and one of the paranasal sinuses, permitting the escape of cerebrospinal fluid into the nose. **dental f.,** an abnormal passage communicating with the apical periodontal area of a tooth, which permits egress on the mucous membrane or the skin of an inflammatory or suppurative discharge. **Eck's f.,** an artificial communication made between the portal vein and the vena cava (Eck, 1877). **Eck's f. in reverse,** an artificial communication created to route all the blood from the posterior (lower) part of the body through the portal vein and liver. **external f.,** an abnormal communication between a hollow organ and the external surface of the body. **fecal f.,** a colonic fistula opening on the external surface of the body and discharging feces. **gastric f.,** an abnormal passage communicating with the stomach; often applied to an artificially created opening, through the abdominal wall, into the stomach. **gingival f.,** a dental fistula opening on the ging va. **hepatic f.,** an abnormal communication between the liver and another body part or organ. **horseshoe f.,** a semicircular fistulous tract near the anus, both openings being on the cutaneous surface. **incomplete f.,** blind f. **internal f.,** an abnormal communication between two internal organs. **intestinal f.,** an abnormal passage communicating with the intestine, often designating an artificially created opening, through the abdominal wall, into the intestine. **lacrimal f.,** an abnormal passage communicating with the lacrimal sac or duct. **lacteal f.,** an abnormal passage communicating with a lacteal duct. **lymphatic f., f. lymphat'ica,** an abnormal passage communicating with a lymphatic vessel. **Mann-Bollman f.,** an artificial opening into an isolated segment of intestine, the proximal end of which is sutured to the abdominal wall and the other end is attached by side-by-side anastomosis to the duodenum or other part of the small intestine. **parietal f.,** an abnormal passage in the body wall, ending blindly or communicating with an internal organ or body cavity. **pharyngeal f.,** an abnormal passage communicating with the pharynx. **pilonidal f.,** pilonidal sinus. **preauricular f., congenital,** an epidermal-lined tract communicating with a pitlike depression just in front of the helix and above the tragus (ear pit), resulting from imperfect fusion of the first and second branchial arches in formation of the auricle. **pulmonary f.,** an abnormal passage communicating with the lung. **pulmonary arteriovenous f., congenital,** a congenital anomaly characterized by existence of a direct communication between the pulmonary arterial and venous systems, allowing unoxygenated blood to enter the systemic circulation. **salivary f.,** an abnormal passage communicating with a salivary duct. **spermatic f.,** an abnormal passage communicating with the seminal ducts. **stercoral f.,** fecal f. **submental f.,** a salivary fistula opening below the chin. **Thiry's f.,** an artificial opening into an isolated segment of intestine, the proximal end of which is sutured to the abdominal wall and the other end is closed. **Thiry-Vella f.,** an artificial opening into an internal closed loop of intestine, communication to the abdominal wall being through an intestinal segment. **thoracic f.,** an abnormal passage communicating with the thoracic cavity. **tracheal f.,** an abnormal passage communicating with the trachea. **umbilical f.,** an abnormal passage communicating with the gut or with the urachus at the umbilicus. **urachal f.,** an abnormal passage communicating with the urachus. **urinary f.,** an abnormal passage communicating with the urinary tract. **Vella's f.,** an artificial opening into an isolated segment of intestine, each end of which is sutured to the abdominal wall. **vesical f.,** an abnormal passage communicating with the urinary bladder.

fistulation (fis″tu-la'shun). Fistulization.

fistulatome (fis'tu-lah-tōm) [*fistula* + Gr. *temnein* to cut]. Syringotome.

fistulatomy (fis″tu-lat′o-me) [*fistula* + Gr. *tomē* a cut]. Fistulotomy.

fistulectomy (fis″tu-lek′to-me) [*fistula* + Gr. *ektomē* excision]. The excision of a fistulous tract.

fistulization (fis″tu-li-za′shun). 1. The process of becoming fistulous. 2. The surgical creation of an opening into a hollow organ, or of an opening between two structures which were not previously connected.

fistulo-enterostomy (fis″tu-lo-en″ter-os′to-me). The operation of making a biliary fistula empty permanently into the intestine.

fistulotomy (fis″tu-lot′o-me). Incision of a fistula.

fistulous (fis′tu-lus) [L. *fistulosus*]. Pertaining to or of the nature of a fistula.

fit (fit). 1. An episode characterized by inappropriate and involuntary motor or psychic activity. 2. The adaptation of one structure into another, as the adaptation of any dental restoration to its site in the mouth. **running f.,** an episode observed in an animal, characterized by uncontrolled running.

Fitz's law, syndrome (fitz′ez) [Reginald Heber *Fitz*, physician in Boston, 1843–1913]. See under *law* and *syndrome.*

Fitz Gerald method, treatment [William H. *Fitz Gerald*, American physician, 1872–1939]. Zone therapy.

fix (fiks). To fasten or hold firm. See *fixation.*

fixateur (fēks-ah-ter′) [Fr.]. Amboceptor.

fixation (fiks-a′shun) [L. *fixatio*]. 1. The act or operation of holding, suturing, or fastening in a fixed position. 2. The condition of being held in a fixed position. 3. In psychiatry, the cessation of the development of personality at a stage short of complete maturity. 4. In microscopy, the treatment of material so that its structure may be examined in the greatest detail with minimal alteration of the normal state, and also to provide information concerning the chemical properties (as of cell constituents) by interpretation of fixation reactions. 5. In chemistry, the rendering of a compound non-volatile or solid. 6. In ophthalmology, direction of the gaze so that the image of the object looked at falls on the fovea centralis. **alexin f.,** f. of the complement. **binocular f.,** training both eyes on the same object as in ordinary vision. **f. of the complement,** when antigen unites with its specific antibody, complement, if present, is taken into the combine and becomes inactive or fixed. Its presence or absence as free, active complement can be shown by adding sensitized blood cells or blood cells and hemolytic amboceptor to the mixture. If free complement is present, hemolysis occurs; if not, no hemolysis is observed. This reaction is the basis of many tests for infection, including the Wassermann test for syphilis, and reactions for gonococcus infection, glanders, typhoid fever, tuberculosis, amebiasis, etc. Called also *complement fixation* and *Bordet-Gengou phenomenon.* **father f.,** inordinate attachment of a person to the male parent. **freudian f.,** arrest of an emotional progression at some intermediate level of psychosexual development. **internal f.,** the fastening together of the ends of a fractured bone by means of wires, plates, screws, or nails applied directly to the fractured bone. **mother f.,** inordinate attachment of a person to the female parent. **nitrogen f.,** the union of the free atmospheric nitrogen with other elements to form chemical compounds, such as ammonia and nitrates or amino groups. It is done mostly by certain organisms in the soil, by electric power in special machines, and by catalysis. **parent f.,** inordinate attachment of an individual for a parent, persisting into adult life and preventing normal development of interest in a person of the opposite sex.

fixative (fik′sah-tiv). 1. An agent employed in the preparation of a histologic or pathologic specimen, for the purpose of maintaining the existing form and structure of all its constituent elements. Great numbers of such agents are used, the most important being composed of formalin, potassium bichromate, bichloride of mercury, osmic acid, or picric acid (trinitrophenol), alone or in various combinations. See also under *fluid* and *solution.* 2. See *amboceptor.* **Kaiserling's f.** See under *solution.* **Maximow's f.,** a solution composed of Zenker's stock solution, formol, and osmic acid, used in preserving vertebrate cells for study with the visible light microscope. **Zenker's f.,** a fixative solution containing corrosive mercuric chloride, potassium bichromate, sodium sulfate, glacial acetic acid, and water; the sodium sulfate is frequently omitted. The most widely used variations of this fixative are the modifications by Maximow and by Custer, in which formalin replaces the acetic acid. **Zenker-formol f.,** a solution composed of Zenker's stock solution with added formaldehyde.

fixator (fiks-a′tor). Amboceptor.

Fl. Abbreviation for *fluid.*

F.L.A. Abbreviation for *fronto-laeva anterior* (left fronto anterior) position of the fetus.

F.l.a. Abbreviation for L. *fi'at le'ge ar'tis,* let it be done according to rule.

flabellum (flah-bel′um) [L. "fan"]. A set of radiating fibers in the corpus striatum.

flaccid (flak′sid) [L. *flaccidus*]. Weak, lax, and soft.

flacherie (flash-er-e′) [Fr.]. A disease of silkworms caused by a microparasite.

Flack's node (flaks) [Martin Flack, physiologist in London, 1882–1931]. See *Keith-Flack's node,* under *node.*

flagella (flah-jel′ah) [L.]. Plural of *flagellum.*

Flagellata (flaj″ĕ-la′tah). A subdivision of the class *Mastigophora* of the order *Protozoa,* containing forms with a definite anterior end on which there are one or more flagella.

flagellate (flaj′ĕ-lāt). 1. Furnished with slender, whiplike processes. 2. A form of microorganism observed in the blood of typhoid patients.

flagellation (flaj″ĕ-la′shun). 1. A form of massage by tapping a part with the fingers. 2. Erotic pleasure derived from whipping or being whipped. 3. The protrusion of flagella; exflagellation.

Flagellidia (flaj″ĕ-lid′e-ah). Flagellata.

flagelliform (flah-jel′ĭ-form) [L. *flagellum* whip + *forma* shape]. Shaped like a flagellum, or lash.

flagellosis (flaj″ĕ-lo′sis). Infestation with a flagellate protozoan.

flagellospore (flah-jel′o-spōr). A spore provided with one or more flagella. Called also *flagellula.*

flagellula (flah-jel′u-lah). Flagellospore.

flagellum (flah-jel′um), pl. *flagel'la* [L. "whip"]. A mobile, whiplike process or stout cilium, especially a coiled, filamentous appendage, originating in the cell wall or outer layers of cytoplasm of some rod-shaped bacteria, and serving as an organ of locomotion. The movement is a rhythmic contraction moving helicoidally over the flagellum, the substance of which is similar to myosin.

Flajani's disease (flah-jan′ēz) [Giuseppe *Flajani,* Italian surgeon, 1741–1808]. Exophthalmic goiter.

flame (flām). 1. The luminous, irregular appearance usually accompanying combustion, or an appearance resembling it. 2. To render sterile by exposure to a flame. **capillary f's,** telangiectatic spots sometimes seen on the face of a newborn infant; called also *stork bites.* **manometric f.,** a gas flame in an enclosed box arranged so that it pulsates with the vibration of air. Such pulsations may be seen on a mirror or recorded photographically (flame picture).

flammentachygraph (flam″men-tak′ĭ-graf). An instrument for recording morbid conditions of the circulation.

flange (flanj). A projecting border or edge. In dentistry, applied to that part of the denture base which extends from around the embedded teeth to the border of the denture. **buccal f.,** the portion of the flange of a denture which extends toward the cheek. **labial f.,** the portion of the flange of a denture which adjoins the lips. **lingual f.,** the portion of the flange of a mandibular denture which occupies the space in the concavity of the dental arch, extending toward the tongue.

flank (flank). The part of the body below the ribs and above the ilium.

flap (flap). 1. A partly detached mass of tissue, especially one partially detached by the knife, to be used in repair of defects in a remote part of the body. Also see *graft.* 2. An uncontrolled movement. **cellulocutaneous f.,** a surgical flap cut from skin and subcutaneous tissue. **circular f.,** a surgical flap of somewhat circular outline. **island f.,** a skin graft consisting of the skin and subcutaneous tissue with a pedicle made up of only the nutrient vessels. **jump f.,** a graft cut from abdomen and attached to a flap of the same size on the forearm. The forearm flap is transferred later to some other part of the body. **liver f.,** asterixis. **musculocutaneous f.,** a surgical flap cut from skin and muscle. **skin f.,** a thin surgical flap containing little or no subcutaneous tissue. **sliding f.,** a flap carried to its new position by sliding. **surgical f.,** a mass of tissue partially detached from one part of the body and attached, directly or as a jump flap, to a remote part, for repair of a defect.

flaps (flaps). Severe swelling of the lips in horses.

flare (flār). 1. A spreading flush or area of redness on the skin, spreading out around an infective lesion or extending beyond the main point of reaction to an irritant. 2. A sudden appearance of a new lesion, such as a pulmonary tuberculosis lesion, in a previously apparently healthy area.

flarimeter (flār-im′e-ter). An instrument for detecting heart disease in its early stages by measuring shortness of breath.

flash (flash). Excess material extruded from a die when material is being molded, as in the molding of denture bases.

flask (flask). 1. A container, such as a narrow-necked vessel of glass for containing liquid. 2. A metal case in which the materials used in the creation of artificial dentures are placed for processing. 3. To place a denture in a flask for processing. **casting f.,** refractory f. **crown f.,** denture f. **culture f.,** a flask for growing cultures of bacteria or of other cells. **denture f.,** a boxlike case of metal which can be tightly closed, and in which dentures or other resinous restorations can be compressed and cured. **Erlenmeyer f.,** a glass flask with a conical body, broad base, and narrow neck. **molding f.,** a metal case in which plastic denture base material is molded around the artificial teeth. **refractory f.,** a metal tube in which a refractory mold is made for casting metal dental restorations or appliances. **volumetric f.,** a narrow-necked vessel of glass calibrated to contain or deliver an exact volume at a given temperature.

flasking (flask′ing). The enclosure of a denture in a flask for the purpose of vulcanizing it.

flat (flat). 1. Lying in one plane; having an even surface. 2. Having little or no resonance. 3. Slightly below the normal pitch of sound. **optical f.,** a glass plate so perfectly flat that only an interferometer can measure its unevenness.

Flatau's law (flat-owz′) [Edward *Flatau,* Polish neurologist, 1869–1932]. See under *law.*

flatfoot (flat′foot). A condition in which one or more of the arches of the foot have flattened out. **spastic f.,** a painful form of flatfoot due to spasm of the pronator muscles.

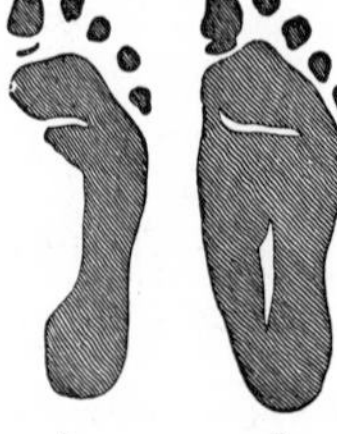

Print of the sole of a normal foot (A) and of one with flatfoot (B) (Albert).

flatness (flat′nes). A peculiar quality of sound obtained by percussing a part that is abnormally solid.

flatulence (flat′u-lens) [L. *flatulentia*]. Distention of the stomach or the intestines with air or gases.

flatulent (flat′u-lent) [L. *flatulentus*]. Pertaining to or characterized by flatulence; distended with gas.

flatus (fla′tus) [L. "a blowing"]. 1. Gas or air in the gastrointestinal tract. 2. The air expired in breathing; an act of expelling air from the lungs. **f. vagina′lis,** noisy expulsion of gas from the vagina.

flatworm (flat′werm). Any worm belonging to the group Platyhelminthes.

flavanone (fla′vah-nōn). A compound formed by reduction of the 2:3 double bond of a flavone.

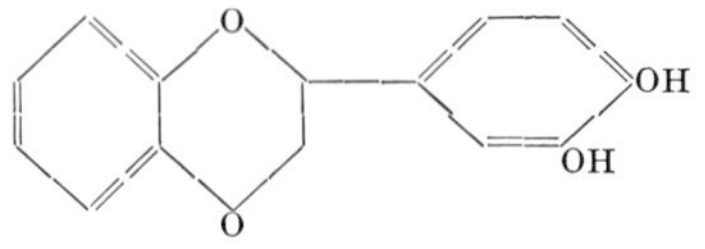

flavedo (flah-ve′do) [L.]. Yellowness, as of the skin.

flavescens (flah-ves′enz) [L. *flavescere* to become gold colored]. Yellowish.

flavine (fla′vīn). See *acriflavine.*

flavism (fla′vism) [L. *flavus* yellow]. Yellowness of hair.

Flavobacterium (fla″vo-bak-te′re-um). A genus of microorganisms of the family Achromobacteraceae, order Eubacteriales, made up of gram-negative rod-shaped bacteria characteristically producing yellow, orange, red, or yellow-brown pigmentation, and found in soil and water. It includes 26 species, some of which are said to be pathogenic.

flavone (fla′vōn). A colorless crystalline substance, with a benzenoid ring (A) fused to a γ-pyrone ring (B), and a benzenoid ring (C) attached to the carbon atom adjacent to the pyrone ring oxygen; related to vitamin P and able to reverse increased capillary fragility. Numerous yellow dyestuffs having similar properties are derived from it.

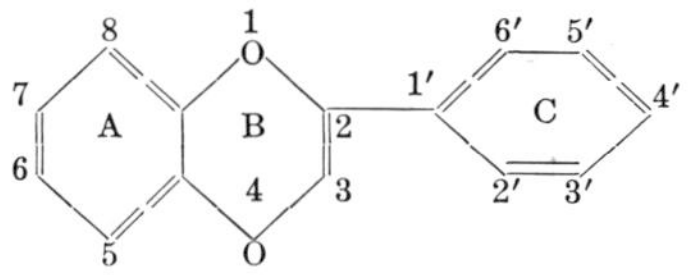

flavonoid (fla′vo-noid). A generic term for a group of compounds with properties resembling those of vitamin P. See also *bioflavonoid.*

flavonol (fla′vo-nol). A yellow-crystalline substance, formed by introduction of an OH group at C-3 of a flavone.

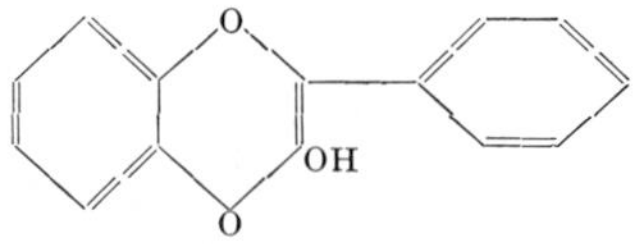

flavoprotein (fla″vo-pro′te-in). A conjugated protein in which the prosthetic group contains a flavin.

flavor (fla′vor). 1. That quality of any substance which affects the taste. 2. A pharmaceutical or other preparation for improving the taste of a food or medicine.

flavoxanthin (fla″vo-zan′thin). A yellow pigment, $C_{40}H_{56}O_3$, from the petals of ranunculaceous plants.

flaxseed (flaks′sēd). Linseed.

fld. Abbreviation for *fluid.*

fl.dr. Abbreviation for *fluid dram.*

flea (fle). Any insect of the order *Siphonaptera;*

many are parasitic and may act as carriers of disease. The genera of medical importance are: *Cediopsylla, Ceratophyllus, Ctenocephalides, Ctenophthalmus, Ctenopsyllus, Diamanus, Echidnophaga, Hoplopsyllus, Monopsyllus, Nosopyllus, Oropsylla, Pulex, Rhopalopsyllus, Tunga, Xenopsylla.* **Asiatic rat f.,** *Xenopsylla cheopis.* **burrowing f.,** *Tunga penetrans.* **cat f.,** *Ctenocephalides felis.* **chigoe f.,** *Tunga penetrans.* **common f.,** *Pulex.* **common rat f.,** *Nosopsyllus.* **dog f.,** *Ctenocephalides canis.* **European rat f.,** *Ceratophyllus fasciatus.* **human f.,** *Pulex.* **Indian rat f.,** *Xenopsylla.* **jigger f.,** *Tunga penetrans.* **mouse f.,** *Ctenopsyllus segnis.* **sand f.,** *Tunga penetrans.* **squirrel f.,** *Hoplopsyllus.* **sticktight f.,** *Echidnophaga.* **suslik f.,** a Russian flea which infests squirrels. **tropical rat f.,** *Xenopsylla.*

Flechsig's area, cuticula, fasciculus, field, tract, etc. (flek′sigz) [Paul Emil *Flechsig,* alienist in Leipzig, 1847–1929]. See under the nouns.

fleckfieber (flek-fe′ber) [Ger.]. Epidemic typhus. See under *typhus.*

fleckmilz (flek′milts) [Ger.]. A condition of the spleen in malignant nephrosclerosis in which necrotic follicles appear as translucent areas.

flection (flek′shun). Flexion.

fleece (flēs). A network of interlacing fibers. **f. of Stilling,** the lacework of white fibers surrounding the dentate nucleus.

Fleischl's hemometer, test (fli′shelz) [Ernest von *Fleischl* von Marxow, Austrian pathologist, 1846–1891]. See under *hemometer* and *test.*

Fleischmann's bursa (flīsh′manz) [Godfried *Fleischmann,* German anatomist, 1777–1853]. See under *bursa.*

Fleitmann's test (flit′manz) [Theodore *Fleitmann,* German chemist]. See under *tests.*

Fleming (flem′ing), Sir Alexander. A Scottish bacteriologist, 1881–1955; co-winner, with Ernest Boris Chain and Sir Howard Walter Florey, of the Nobel prize in medicine and physiology for 1945 for the discovery of penicillin and its curative effect in infectious disease.

flemingen (flĕ-min′jin). An orange-red powder, in small prismatic needles, from waras, a product of *Flemin′gia grahamia′na;* a strong stain.

flesh (flesh). The soft, muscular tissue of the animal body. **goose f.,** cutis anserina.

fletcherism (flech′er-izm) [Horace *Fletcher,* American dietitian, 1849–1919]. The thorough mastication of solid food and the taking of liquids by sips.

flex (fleks) [L. *flexus* bent]. To bend or put in a state of flexion.

flexibilitas (flek-sĭ-bil′ĭ-tas) [L.]. Flexibility. **f. ce′rea,** a cataleptic state in which the limbs retain any position in which they may be placed.

flexibility (flek″sĭ-bil′ĭ-te) [L. *flexibilitas*]. The quality of being flexible.

flexible (flek′sĭ-bl) [L. *flexibilis, flexilis*]. Readily bent without tendency to break.

flexile (fleks′il). Flexible.

fleximeter (fleks-im′e-ter). An instrument for measuring the amount of flexion of a joint.

flexion (flek′shun) [L. *flexio*]. The act of bending or condition of being bent.

Flexner's bacillus, serum (fleks′nerz) [Simon *Flexner,* American pathologist, 1863–1946]. See under *bacillus* and *serum.*

flexor (flek′sor) [L.]. Any muscle that flexes a joint. See *Table of Musculi.* **f. retinac′ulum.** See *retinaculum flexorum manus* and *retinaculum musculorum flexorum pedis.*

flexuose (fleks′u-ōs). Winding or wavy.

flexura (flek-shoo′rah), pl. *flexu′rae* [L.]. A bending; used as a general term in anatomical nomenclature to designate a bent portion of a structure or organ. Called also *flexure.* **f. co′li dex′tra** [N A, B N A], the bend in the large intestine between the ascending and transverse parts. Called also *hepatic,* or *right, flexure of colon.* **f. co′li sinis′tra** [N A, B N A], the bend in the large intestine at the junction between the transverse and descending parts of the colon. Called also *left,* or *splenic, flexure of colon.* **f. duode′ni infe′rior** [N A, B N A], the bend in the duodenum at the junction of the descending and horizontal parts. Called also *inferior flexure of duodenum.* **f. duode′ni supe′rior** [N A, B N A], the bend in the first or superior part of the duodenum. Called also *superior flexure of duodenum.* **f. duodenojejuna′lis** [N A, B N A], the bend in the small intestine at the junction between the duodenum and jejunum. The suspensory muscle of the duodenum attaches to this point. Called also *duodenal flexure.* **f. hepat′ica co′li,** f. coli dextra. **f. liena′lis co′li,** f. coli sinistra. **f. perinea′lis rec′ti** [N A, B N A], the dorsal and caudal bend at the caudal end of the rectum. Called also *perineal flexure of rectum.* **f. sacra′lis rec′ti** [N A, B N A], the ventrally concave first bend in the rectum. Called also *sacral flexure of rectum.*

flexurae (flek-shoo′re) [L.]. Plural of *flexura.*

flexural (flek′shur-al). Pertaining to or affecting a flexure.

flexure (flek′sher). A bending; a bent portion of a structure or organ. **basicranial f.,** pontine f. **caudal f.,** the bend at the aboral end of the embryo. **cephalic f.,** the curve in the midbrain of the embryo. **cerebral f.,** one of the bends in the embryonic brain. **cervical f.,** a bend in the neural tube of the embryo at the junction of the brain and spinal cord. **cranial f.,** cephalic f. **dorsal f.,** one of the flexures of the embryo in the mid-dorsal region. **duodenojejunal f.,** flexura duodenojejunalis. **hemal f.,** a curvature of the cerebral vesicles toward the hemal or ventral aspect. **hepatic f. of colon,** flexura coli dextra. **iliac f. of colon,** colon sigmoideum. **inferior f. of duodenum,** flexura duodeni inferior. **left f. of colon,** flexura coli sinistra. **longitudinal f. of duodenum,** plica longitudinalis duodeni. **lumbar f.,** the ventral curvature of the back in the lumbar region. **mesencephalic f.,** a flexure in the neural tube of the vertebrate embryo at the level of the mesencephalon. **nuchal f.,** cervical f. **perineal f. of rectum,** flexura perinealis recti. **pontine f.,** a flexure in the hindbrain of the embryo. **right f. of colon,** flexura coli dextra. **sacral f.,** caudal f. **sacral f. of rectum,** flexura sacralis recti. **sigmoid f. of colon,** colon sigmoideum. **splenic f. of colon,** flexura coli sinistra. **superior f. of duodenum,** flexura duodeni superior.

flicker (flik′er). The visual sensation produced by intermittent flashes of light. At a certain rate of such flashes a sensation of continuous brightness is experienced and this rate is called *critical fusion frequency* or *c.f.f.*

Fliess therapy, treatment (flēs) [Wilhelm *Fliess,* Berlin physician, 1858–1928]. See under *treatment.*

flight (flit). Swift and unhampered movement. **f. of ideas,** mental activity characterized by repeated changes in the line or type of thought.

Flindt's spots (flints) [N. *Flindt,* Danish physician, 1843–1913]. Koplik's spots.

Flint's arcade, law (flints) [Austin *Flint,* American physiologist, 1836–1915]. See under *arcade* and *law.*

Flint's murmur (flints) [Austin *Flint,* American physician, 1812–1886]. See under *murmur.*

floccilegium (flok″sĭ-le′je-um). Floccillation.

floccillation (flok″sĭ-la′shun) [L. *floccilatio*]. The picking at the bedclothes by a delirious patient.

floccose (flok′ōs) [L. *floccosus* full of flocks of wool]. Woolly: said of a bacterial growth which is composed of short, curved chains variously oriented.

floccular (flok′u-lar). Pertaining to the flocculus.

flocculation (flok″u-la′shun). A colloid phenomenon in which the disperse phase separates in discrete, usually visible, particles rather than in a continuous mass, as in coagulation. **Ramon f.,** a method of standardizing antitoxic serums by the *in vitro* precipitation of toxin and antitoxin when mixed.

floccule (flok'ūl). Flocculus. **toxoid-antitoxin f.,** a suspension of the precipitate which is formed when toxoid and antitoxin are mixed.

flocculent (flok'u-lent). Containing downy or flaky masses.

flocculoreaction (flok"u-lo-re-ak'shun). A serum reaction characterized by flocculation.

flocculus (flok'u-lus), pl. *floc'culi* [L. "tuft"]. 1. A small tuft, as of wool or similar material, or a small mass of other fibrous material such as one of the flakes of a flocculent solution. 2. [N A, B N A] A small lobe on the lower side of either cerebellar hemisphere, continuous with the nodule of the vermis. **accessory f., f. seconda'rii** [B N A], **secondary f.,** a small lobe sometimes seen near the flocculus in the inferior process of the cerebellum. Omitted in N A.

Flood's ligament (fludz) [Valentine *Flood*, Irish surgeon, 1800–1847]. See under *ligament.*

Flor. Abbreviation for L. *flo'res*, flowers.

flora (flo'rah) [L. *Flora*, the goddess of flowers]. The plant life present in or characteristic of a special location. It may be discernible with the unaided eye (macroflora), or only with the aid of a microscope (microflora). **intestinal f.,** the bacteria normally residing within the lumen of the intestine.

florantyrone (flo-ran'ti-rōn). Chemical name: γ-oxo-γ-(8-fluoranthene)butyric acid: used as a hydrocholeretic.

floraquin (flor'ah-kwin). Trade mark for a preparation of diiodohydroxyquin.

Florence's reaction, test (flor-ahns') [Albert *Florence*, French physician, 1851–1927]. See under *tests.*

florentium (flo-ren'she-um). Promethium.

flores (flo'rēz) [L., pl. of *flos* flower]. 1. The blossoms or flowers of a plant. 2. A drug after sublimation. **f. benzoi'ni,** benzoic acid. **f. ci'nae,** Russian wormwood. **f. sul'furis,** sublimed sulfur.

Florey unit (flor'ē) [Sir Howard W. *Florey*, English pathologist, born 1898; co-winner, with Ernest Boris Chain and Sir Alexander Fleming, of the Nobel prize for medicine in 1945]. See *Oxford unit*, under *unit.*

florid (flor'id) [L. *floridus* blossoming]. 1. In full bloom; occurring in fully developed form. 2. Having a bright red color.

floridin (flor'ĭ-din). A purplish or violet coloring matter occurring in the blood of invertebrates.

florinef (flor'ĭ-nef). Trade mark for preparations of fludrocortisone.

floropryl (flor'o-pril). Trade mark for preparations of isoflurophate.

Florschütz formula (flor'shitz) [Georg *Florschütz*, German physician, born 1859]. See under *formula.*

Flourens' doctrine, theory (floo-ranz') [Marie Jean Pierre *Flourens*, French physiologist, 1794–1867]. See under *theory.*

Flower's index (flow'erz) [Sir William Henry *Flower*, British physician, 1831–1899]. See under *index.*

flowers (flow'erz). 1. The blossoms of a plant. 2. A sublimed drug, as sulfur or benzoin. 3. The menses. **f. of arsenic,** arsenic trioxide. **f. of benzoin,** benzoic acid. **f. of camphor,** powdered camphor prepared by sublimation. **f. of sulfur,** sublimed sulfur.

flowmeter (flo'me-ter). An apparatus for measuring the rate of flow of liquids or gases.

fl.oz. Abbreviation for *fluid ounce.*

F.L.P. Abbreviation for *fronto-laeva posterior* (left fronto posterior) position of the fetus.

F.L.T. Abbreviation for *fronto-laeva transversa* (left fronto transverse) position of the fetus.

flucticuli (fluk-tik'u-li) [L.]. Plural of *flucticulus.*

flucticulus (fluk-tik'u-lus), pl. *fluctic'uli* [L., dim. of *fluctus* wave]. One of the many markings, like small waves, on the lateral wall of the third ventricle behind the anterior commissure.

fluctuant (fluk'tu-ant). 1. Showing varying levels. 2. Conveying the sensation of or exhibiting, on palpation, wavelike motion, owing to a liquid content.

fluctuation (fluk"tu-a'shun) [L. *fluctuatio*]. 1. A variation, as about a fixed value or mass. 2. A wavelike motion, as of a fluid in a cavity of the body after succussion.

fludrocortisone (floo"dro-kor'tĭ-sōn). A synthetic adrenal corticoid, 9α-fluoro-17-hydroxycorticosterone, with effects similar to those of hydrocortisone and desoxycorticosterone.

flügelplatte (fle"gel-plah'teh). [Ger.]. Lamina alaris.

Fluhmann's test (floo'manz) [C. Frederic *Fluhmann*, American gynecologist, born 1898]. See under *tests.*

Fluhrer's probe (floo'rerz) [William Francis *Fluhrer*, New York physician, 1870–1932]. See under *probe.*

fluid (floo'id) [L. *fluidus*]. 1. A liquid or a gas. 2. Composed of elements or particles which freely change their relative positions without their separating. **allantoic f.,** the fluid contained in the allantois. **Altmann's f.,** a histologic fixing fluid composed of equal parts of 2 per cent osmic acid solution and a 5 per cent potassium dichromate solution. **amniotic f.,** fluid produced by the amnion at the very earliest period of fetation; at first crystal clear, it later becomes cloudy. The amount at term normally varies from 500 to 2,000 ml. **ascitic f.,** the serous fluid which accumulates in the peritoneal cavity in ascites. **Bamberger's f.,** an albuminous mercuric solution for use in the treatment of syphilis. **Berthollet's f.,** a mixture of sodium chloride and sodium hypochlorite solutions. **bleaching f.,** a fluid prepared by passing chlorine gas into an emulsion of calcium hydrate. **Bouin's f.,** a fixing fluid for histologic work, consisting of formaldehyde solution, glacial acetic acid, and saturated solution of trinitrophenol. **Burnett's disinfecting f.,** a strong aqueous solution of zinc chloride. **Callison's f.,** a solution of distilled water, Löffler's aniline methylene blue, solution of formaldehyde, glycerin, ammonium oxalate, and sodium chloride: used as a diluent in counting red blood corpuscles. **cephalorachidian f.,** cerebrospinal f. **cerebrospinal f.,** the fluid contained within the four ventricles of the brain, the subarachnoid space, and the central canal of the spinal cord. Called also *liquor cerebrospinalis.* **chlorpalladium f.,** a decalcifying fluid for anatomical and other specimens, containing palladium chloride and hydrochloric acid. **Coley's f.,** a mixture of erysipelas and prodigiosus toxins: used in the treatment of malignant tumors. **Condy's f.,** a disinfecting solution of sodium and potassium permanganates. **Dakin's f.,** a buffered aqueous solution of sodium hypochlorite: used as a bactericide. See *sodium hypochlorite solution*, under *solution*, and *Carrel-Dakin treatment*, under *treatment.* **decalcifying f.,** a solution of formic acid and formalin. **Delafield's f.,** a fixing fluid for delicate histologic tissues, containing osmic acid, chromic acid, acetic acid, and alcohol. **Flemming's fixing f.,** Flemming's solution. **follicular f.,** liquor folliculi. **formol-Müller f.,** Müller's fluid to which formaldehyde has been added. **Fralick's f.,** a germicidal fluid containing nascent chlorine and ozone: used by venous injection in tuberculosis. **Gauvain's f.,** a mixture of guaiacol, iodoform, ether, and sterile olive oil: for lavage in empyema. **Helly's f.,** a histological fixative consisting of Zenker's fluid in which the glacial acetic acid is replaced by formalin. The most widely used formula consists of 9 parts Zenker stock solution and 1 part neutral formalin (Zenker-Helly-Maximow) and is usually called Zenker formol. **interstitial f.**, that portion of the body water outside of the cells and outside of the plasma volume; the extracellular water minus the plasma volume. **Kaiserling's f.** See under *solution.* **labyrinthine f.**, perilymph. **Lang's f.**, a hardening fluid containing corrosive mercuric chloride, sodium chloride, and acetic acid, in water. **Locke's f.** See under *solution.* **Mitchell's f.**, a mixture of sodium chloride, bromine, hydrochloric acid, and water acted on by an electric current: used in pulmonary tuberculosis. **Morton's f.**, a mixture of iodine, potassium iodide, and glycerin: formerly used by injection in spinal meningocele. **Müller's f.**, a hardening solution consisting of potassium dichromate, sodium sulfate, and water. **Parker's f.**, a hardening fluid composed of formaldehyde and alcohol. **Pasteur's f.** See under *solution.* **pericardial f.**, liquor pericardii. **Piazza's f.**, a blood-coagulating fluid composed of sodium chloride and ferric chloride in water. **Pitfield's f.**, a diluting fluid for counting leukocytes; made by dissolving acacia gum in distilled water and adding glacial acetic acid and gentian violet. **Purdy's f.** See under *solution.* **Rees and Ecker diluting f.**, a solution of sodium citrate, formaldehyde solution, brilliant cresyl blue, and distilled water, used as a diluting fluid for blood platelets. **Scarpa's f.**, endolymph of the ear. **Schaudinn's f.**, a hardening fluid consisting of mercury bichloride, alcohol, and distilled water. **seminal f.**, semen. **subarachnoid f.**, cerebrospinal f. **synovial f.**, synovia. **Tellyesniczky's f.**, a fixing solution consisting of potassium dichromate, water, and glacial acetic acid. **Thoma's f.**, a decalcifying fluid for histologic work, consisting of alcohol and pure nitric acid. **tissue f.**, the extracellular fluid which constitutes the environment of the body cells. It is low in protein, it is formed by filtration through the capillaries, and it drains away as lymph. **Toison's f.** See under *solution.* **ventricular f.**, that portion of the cerebrospinal fluid contained in the cerebral ventricles. **Waldeyer's f.**, chlorpalladium fluid. **Wickersheimer's f.**, a fluid composed of arsenic trioxide, sodium chloride, and the sulfate, carbonate, and nitrate of potassium in a mixture of water, alcohol, and glycerin: used for preserving anatomical specimens. **Zenker's f.** See under *fixative.*

fluidextract (floo″id-eks′trakt). A liquid preparation of a vegetable drug containing alcohol as a solvent or as a preservative, or both, of such strength that each milliliter contains 1 Gm. of the standard drug which it represents.

fluidextractum (floo″id-eks-trak′tum), gen. *fluidextrac′ti*, pl. *fluidextrac′ta* [L.]. Fluidextract.

fluidism (floo′id-izm). Humoralism.

fluidounce (floo-id-ouns′). Fluid ounce. See under *ounce.*

fluidrachm (floo″id-ram′). Fluid dram.

fluidram (floo-id-ram′). Fluid dram. See under *dram.*

fluke (flo͝ok). Any parasitic trematode worm. See *Trematoda.* **blood f.**, *Schistosoma.* **intestinal f's.** See *Amphistoma, Dicrocoelium, Echinostoma, Fasciolopsis, Gastrodiscus, Heterophyes, Metagonimus*, and *Watsonius.* **liver f's.** See *Clonorchis, Fasciola*, and *Opisthorchis.* **lung f.** See *Paragonimus.*

flumen (floo′men), pl. *flu′mina* [L.]. A stream. **flu′mina pilo′rum** [N A, B N A], continuous lines formed by the pattern of hair growth on various parts of the body, the hairs lying in the same direction. Called also *hair streams.*

flumethiazide (floo″mĕ-thi′ah-zīd). Chemical name: 6-trifluoromethyl-1,2,4-benzothiadiazine-7-sulfonamide-1,1-dioxide: used as a diuretic and antihypertensive.

flumina (floo′mĭ-nah) [L.]. Plural of *flumen.*

fluocinolone acetonide (floo″o-sin′o-lōn ah-set′o-nīd). Chemical name: $6\alpha,9\alpha$-difluoro-16α-hydroxyprednisolone-16,17-acetonide: used as a steroid compound with anti-inflammatory action, and for topical application to skin lesions.

fluohydrisone (floo″o-hi′drĭ-sōn). Fludrocortisone.

fluohydrocortisone (floo″o-hi″dro-kor′ti-sōn). Fludrocortisone.

fluor (floo′or) [L. *fluore* to flow]. A discharge. **f. al′bus**, leukorrhea.

fluorane (floo′or-ān). The mother substance from which fluorescein and its derivatives are obtained. It is $C_6H_4.O(C_6H_4.CO)_2$.

fluorescein (floo″o-res′e-in). The simplest of the fluorane dyes and the mother substance of eosin, $C_{20}H_{12}O_5$: used intravenously in tests to indicate by its fluorescence the adequacy of the circulation, and combined with radioactive iodine in localization of brain tumors, etc. **f. sodium, soluble f.**, an odorless, orange-red powder, $C_{20}H_{10}Na_2O_5$, used in dilute solution to reveal lesions of the cornea and suggested as a test of circulation in the extremities.

fluoresceinuria (floo″o-res″e-in-u′re-ah). The presence of fluorescein in the urine.

fluorescence (floo″o-res′ens) [first observed in *fluor spar*]. The property of emitting light after exposure to light, the wavelength of the emitted light being longer than that of the light absorbed.

fluorescent (floo″o-res′ent). Exhibiting fluoresence.

fluorescin (floo″o-res′in). A light yellow powder, $C_{20}H_{14}O_5$, freely soluble in water, slightly soluble in alcohol and ether: used as a dye.

fluoridation (floo-or″ĭ-da′shun). Treatment with fluorides; specifically, the addition of fluoride to the public water supply as part of the public health program to prevent or reduce the incidence of dental caries.

fluoride (floo′o-rīd). A binary compound of fluorine.

fluoridization (floo-or″ĭ-di-za′shun). 1. Application of fluoride solution to the teeth. 2. Fluoridation.

fluoridize (floo-or′ĭ-dīz). 1. To apply a solution of fluoride to the teeth as a means of controlling or preventing caries. 2. To add fluorides to a substance.

fluorine (floo′o-rēn) [from *fluor spar*, from which it is derived]. A nonmetallic, gaseous element, belonging to the halogen group; symbol, F; atomic number, 9; atomic weight, 18.998.

fluorocyte (floo-or′o-sīt). A reticulocyte showing red fluorescence.

fluorography (floo″or-og′rah-fe). Fluororoentgenography.

fluorometer (floo″or-om′e-ter). 1. An apparatus for measuring the quantity of rays given out by a roentgen-ray tube. 2. An attachment to the fluoroscope, enabling the operator to secure a correct and undistorted shadow of the object and to locate exactly the position of the object.

fluorometholone (floor″o-meth′o-lōn). Chemical name: 9α-fluoro-$11\beta,17\alpha$-dihydroxy-6α-methyl-1,4-pregnadiene-3,20-dione: used as a glucocorticoid with anti-inflammatory effects on the skin.

fluorophosphate (floo-or″o-fos′fāt). An organic compound containing fluorine and phosphorus. **diisopropyl f.**, isoflurophate.

fluororoentgenography (floo″o-ro-rent″gen-og′rah-fe). The photographic recording of fluoroscopic images on small films, using a fast lens: used in mass roentgenography of the chest. Called also *photofluorography.*

fluoroscope (floo-o′ro-skōp) [*fluorescence* + Gr. *skopein* to examine]. A device used for examining deep structures by means of the roentgen rays: it consists of a screen (*fluorescent screen*) covered with crystals of calcium tungstate. **biplane f.**, a fluoroscope by which examinations can be made in two planes, horizontal and vertical.

fluoroscopical (floo′o-ro-skop″ĭ-kal). Pertaining to fluoroscopy.

fluoroscopy (floo″or-os′ko-pe). Examination by means of the fluoroscope.

fluorosis (floo″o-ro′sis). A condition resulting from ingestion of excessive amounts of fluorine. **dental f.,** a mottled discoloration of the tooth enamel occurring in chronic endemic fluorosis. **endemic f., chronic,** a condition caused by long-continued ingestion of excessive amounts of fluorine as a result of high levels of the element in the natural water supply, usually manifest by a mottled discoloration of the enamel of the teeth.

fluothane (floo′o-thān). Trade mark for a preparation of halothane.

fluoxymesterone (floo-ok″se-mes′ter-ōn). Chemical name: 9α-fluoro-11β-hydroxy-17α-methyltestosterone: used as an anabolic androgen in palliative treatment of certain cancers.

fluphenazine (floo-fen′ah-zēn). Chemical name: 4-{3-[2-(trifluoromethyl)phenothiazin-10-yl]-propyl}-1-piperazineethanol, or 10-{3-[4-(2-hydroxyethyl)piperazinyl]propyl}-2-trifluoromethyl phenothiazine: used as a tranquilizer and antiemetic.

fluprednisolone (floo″pred-nis′o-lōn). Chemical name: 6α-fluoroprednisolone: used as an anti-inflammatory corticosteroid in treatment of joint diseases and allergic disturbances.

flurandrenolone (floor″an-dren′o-lōn). Chemical name: 6α-fluoro-16α-hydroxyhydrocortisone-16,-17-acetonide: a corticosteroid applied locally to skin lesions.

flush (flush). A redness of the face and neck. **atropine f.,** flushing and dryness of the skin of the face and neck from overdosage with atropine. **breast f.,** a condition sometimes occurring in the early puerperium marked by a tense and flushed state of the breasts with pronounced veining. **hectic f.,** the peculiar flush of the febrile state of hectic fever. **mahogany f.,** a deep red or mahogany-colored, circumscribed spot seen on one cheek in some cases of lobal pneumonia. **malar f.,** hectic flush at the malar eminence in pulmonary tuberculosis.

flutter (flut′er). A quick vibration or pulsation. **atrial f., auricular f.,** a condition of cardiac arrhythmia in which the auricular contractions are extremely rapid (180 to 400 per minute), but are rhythmic and of uniform amplitude. The ventricles are unable to respond to each auricular impulse, so that a partial or complete block is set up, the impulses no longer arise from the sino-auricular node, but from some other portion of the auricle. **impure f.,** a form of auricular flutter in which the auricular rhythm is irregular. **mediastinal f.,** a condition of motility of the mediastinum in which each inspiration of the healthy lung draws the mediastinum toward itself. **pure f.,** a form of auricular flutter in which the auricular rhythm is regular.

flux (fluks) [L. *fluxus*]. 1. An excessive flow or discharge. 2. A borax-containing substance that maintains the cleanliness of metals to be united and facilitates the easy flow and attachment of solder. **alvine f.,** diarrhea. **bilious f.,** tropical dysentery with a copious discharge of bile. **black f.,** a mixture of potassium carbonate and powdered charcoal. **bloody f.** See *dysentery.* **celiac f.,** diarrhea accompanied by the discharge of undigested food. **hepatic f.,** bilious f. **luminous f.,** the rate of passage of radiant energy evaluated by reference to the luminous sensation produced by it. **menstrual f.,** the menses. **neutral f.,** a fusible material, usually an inorganic salt, which does not unite with the combined oxygen in the metal (barium chloride, sodium chloride). **oxidizing f.,** a material which, when heated, gives up oxygen that may unite with base metals and form oxides (as potassium nitrate, potassium chlorate). **reducing f.,** a flux which unites with the oxygen of metallic oxides and frees the metal from such combinations.

fluxion (fluk′shun). A flowing; especially an abnormal or excessive flow of fluid to a part.

fly (flī). A dipterous, or two-winged, insect. **black f.,** a name given various individuals of the family Simuliidae. **bloodsucking f's.** See *Chrysops* and *Tabanus.* **blow f., bluebottle f.** See *Calliphora.* **bot f.** See *Dermatobia, Gasterophilus,* and *Hypoderma.* **caddis f.,** a fly of the order Trichoptera; hairs and scales from these flies are an exciting cause of allergic coryza and asthma. **cheese f.** See *Piophila.* **Columbacz f.,** *Simulium columbaczense.* **crane f.** See *Tipulidae.* **deer f.,** *Chrysops discalis.* **drone f.,** *Eristalis tenax.* **dung f.,** *Sepsis violacea.* **eye f.,** any fly which attacks the eye. See *Hippelates* and *Siphunculina funicola.* **filth f.,** *Musca domestica.* **flesh f.** See *Sarcophaga* and *Wohlfahrtia.* **frit f.** Same as *eye f.* **fruit f.** See *Drosophilia.* **gad f.** See *Tabanus.* **gold f.,** *Lucilia caesar.* **greenbottle f.** See *Lucilia.* **heel f.** See *Hypoderma.* **horn f.** See *Hematobium.* **horse f.** See *Tabanus.* **house f.,** *Musca domestica.* **hover f.** See *Helophilus* and *Tubifera.* **lake f.** See *Hexagenia.* **latrine f.,** *Fannia scalaris.* **mango f., mangrove f.** See *Chrysops.* **moth f.,** a fly of the family Psychodidae. **Motuca f.** See *Lepidoselaga.* **owl f.,** a name given individuals of the family Psychodidae. **phlebotomus f.** See *Phlebotomus.* **pomace f.** See *Drosophila.* **Russian f.,** *Cantharis.* **sand f.** See *sandfly.* **screw-worm f.** See *Cochliomyia.* **Seroot f.,** *Tabanus gratus.* **soldier f.,** *Hermetia illucens,* the larvae of which sometimes cause intestinal myiasis in man. **Spanish f.,** *Cantharis.* **stable f.** See *Stomoxys.* **tick f.** See *Hippobosca.* **tsetse f.** See *Glossina.* **tumbu f.,** *Cordylobia anthropophaga.* **typhoid f.,** *Musca domestica.* **vinegar f.** See *Drosophila.* **warble f.** See *Dermatobia.*

F.M. Abbreviation for L. *fi′at mistu′ra,* make a mixture.

focal (fo′kal). Pertaining to or occupying a focus.

Fochier's abscess (fosh″e-āz′) [Alphonse *Fochier,* French gynecologist, 1845–1903]. See under *abscess.*

foci (fo′si) [L.]. Plural of *focus.*

focil, focile (fo′sil, fo′sĭ-le) [L. *fusillus,* a little spindle]. One of the bones of the forearm or leg.

focimeter (fo-sim′e-ter). An apparatus for finding the focus of a lens.

focus (fo′kus), pl. *fo′ci* [L. "fire-place"]. 1. The point of convergence of light rays or of the waves of sound. 2. The chief center of a morbid process. **aplanatic f.,** that focus or point from which rays diverging pass the lens without spherical aberration. **Assmann f.,** the early exudative lesion of pulmonary tuberculosis occurring most frequently in the subapical region. **conjugate f.,** the point at which rays that come from some definite point are brought together. **epileptogenic f.,** the area of the cortex responsible for causing epileptic seizures, as revealed in the encephalogram. **principal foci,** points of convergence of rays parallel with the principal axis of a lens, or system: in the *eye* (approx.), 18 mm. from the anterior nodal point, and 24 mm. from the posterior nodal point, and holding the ratio of the indices of air and vitreum (Fording). **real f.,** the point at which convergent rays intersect. **Simon's foci,** hematogenous areas in the apices of the lungs of children regarded as precursors of apical tuberculosis in later life. **virtual f.,** the point at which divergent rays would intersect if prolonged backward.

Fodéré's sign (fod″a-rāz′) [François-Emmanuel *Fodéré,* French physician, 1764–1835]. See under *sign.*

Foerster. See *Förster.*

fog (fog). A colloid system in which the dispersion medium is a gas and the disperse particles are liquid.

fogging (fog′ing). A method employed in testing

vision, the patient being first made artificially myopic by means of plus spheres, in order to relax all accommodation before using cylinders.

fogo (fo'go) [Port. "fire"]. A name given to a skin condition in Brazil. **f. selva'gem** [Port. "wild fire"], Brazilian pemphigus.

foil (foil). Metal in the form of an extremely thin, pliable sheet. **gold f.,** pure gold rolled into an extremely thin sheet, used in the restoration of carious or fractured teeth. **platinum f.,** pure platinum rolled into an extremely thin sheet, used as a matrix for various soldering procedures, and also in the construction of porcelain restorations, to provide internal form during their fabrication. **tin f.,** tin rolled into an extremely thin sheet, used to separate other materials, as separating the cast and denture-base material while it is being flasked and cured.

Fol. Abbreviation for L. *fo'lia*, leaves.

fold (fōld). A thin, recurved margin, or doubling. **alar f's,** plicae alares. **amniotic f.,** the folded edge of the amniotic membrane where it rises over and finally encloses the embryo. **Arnold's f.,** Béraud's valve. **aryepiglottic f.,** plica aryepiglottica. **aryepiglottic f. of Collier,** plica triangularis. **axillary f's,** the folds of skin bounding the armpit, the plica axillaris anterior and plica axillaris posterior. **Brachet's mesolateral f.,** mesolateral f. **bulboventricular f.,** a fold between the bulbus cordis and the ventricle that disappears as the bulbus cordis is absorbed into the right ventricle. **caval f.,** a ridge that contains the superior segment of the embryonic inferior vena cava. **cecal f's,** plicae cecales. **cholecystoduodenocolic f.,** an unusual fold of peritoneum sometimes uniting the colon, duodenum, and gallbladder. **ciliary f's,** plicae ciliares. **circular f's of Kerckring,** plicae circulares. **conjunctival f.,** the cul-de-sac formed where the conjunctiva is reflected from the eyeball to the upper or lower eyelid. **costocolic f.,** a fold of peritoneum from the diaphragm to the splenic flexure of the colon, forming a shelflike structure above the spleen. **Douglas' f.** 1. Plica rectouterina. 2. Linea arcuata vaginae musculi recti abdominis. **Duncan's f's,** the loose folds of peritoneum which cover the uterus immediately following delivery. **duodenojejunal f.,** plica duodenalis superior. **duodenomesocolic f.,** plica duodenalis inferior. **epicanthal f., epicanthine f.,** epicanthus. **epigastric f.,** plica umbilicalis lateralis. **falciform f. of fascia lata,** margo falciformis. **fimbriated f.,** plica fimbriata. **gastric f's,** plicae gastricae. **gastropancreatic f.,** plica gastropancreatica. **genital f.** See *urogenital ridge*. **glosso-epiglottic f's,** folds of mucous membrane extending from the base of the tongue to the epiglottis. **gluteal f.,** the crease separating the buttock from the thigh. **Guérin's f.,** a fold of mucous membrane occasionally seen in the fossa navicularis of the urethra. **Hasner's f.,** plica lacrimalis. **head f.,** a crescentic, ventral fold of the blastoderm at the future head end of the embryo. **Heister's f.,** Heister's valves. **Hensing's f.,** the superior ligament of the cecum. **horizontal f's of rectum,** plicae transversalis recti. **ileocecal f.,** plica ileocecalis. **ileocolic f.,** a crescentic fold of peritoneum forming a part of the mesentery, mesocecum, and mesocolon. **incudal f.,** plica incudis. **inferior duodenal f.,** plica duodenalis inferior. **interarticular f. of hip,** ligamentum capitis femoris. **interureteric f.,** plica interureterica. **iridial f's,** plicae iridis. **Jonnesco's f., Juvara's f.,** parietoperitoneal f. **Kerckring's f's,** plicae circulares. **Kohlrausch's f.,** a name sometimes given one of the transverse folds of the rectum, projecting into its lumen from the right side. **lacrimal f.,** plica lacrimalis. **f's of large intestine,** plicae semilunares coli. **longitudinal f. of duodenum,** plica longitudinalis duodeni. **Luschka's f.,** ileocolic f. **mallear f. of mucous membrane of tympanum, anterior,** plica mallearis anterior tunicae mucosae cavi tympani. **mallear f. of tympanic membrane, anterior,** plica mallearis anterior membranae tympani. **mallear f. of tympanic membrane, posterior,** plica mallearis posterior membranae tympani. **mammary f.,** the primordium of the mammary gland in the early embryo. It extends from the root of the upper extremity to the inguinal fold. **Marshall's f.,** plica venae cavae sinistrae. **medullary f.,** neural f. **mesenteriomesocolic f.,** a fold of peritoneum extending from the mesentery into the mesocolon of the sigmoid flexure. **mesolateral f.,** the right lamella of the primitive mesentery running to the right lobe of the liver. **mesonephric f.,** mesonephric ridge. **mesouterine f.,** a fold of peritoneum supporting the uterus. **mucobuccal f., mucosobuccal f.,** the cul-de-sac formed where the mucous membrane is reflected from the upper or lower jaw to the cheek. **mucous f.,** plica mucosa. **mucous f's of rectum,** columnae anales. **nail f.,** the fold of tissue around the base and sides of the nail. **nasopharyngeal f.,** plica salpingopalatina. **Nélaton's f.,** a transverse fold of mucous membrane in the rectum, marking the junction of its lower and middle thirds. **neural f.,** one of the paired folds, lying one on either side of the neural plate, that form the neural tube. **opercular f.,** a fold of tissue constituting an adhesion between the tonsil and the anterior pillar of the fauces. **palatine f's, transverse,** plicae palatinae transversae. **palmate f's,** plicae palmatae. **palpebral f's,** conjunctival f's. **palpebronasal f.,** plica palpebronasalis. **pancreaticogastric f.,** plica gastropancreatica. **paraduodenal f.,** plica paraduodenalis. **parietocolic f.,** Hensing's f. **parietoperitoneal f.,** a fold of peritoneum in the fetus, arising at the left side of the ascending colon and attached to the parietal peritoneum at the right of the ascending colon. **Pawlik's f's,** two columns in the vagina forming the lateral boundaries of Pawlik's triangle: they serve to mark the openings of the ureters. **pharyngoepiglottic f.,** a fold of mucous membrane running backward from the epiglottis. **pituitary f's,** the folds of the dura mater enclosing the hypophysis cerebri. **primitive f.,** one of the two ridges flanking the primitive groove, one on either side. **Rathke's f's,** two fetal folds of mesoderm which unite at the median line to form Douglas' septum and to render the rectum a complete canal. **rectal f's,** plicae transversales rectae. **rectouterine f.,** plica rectouterina. **rectovaginal f.,** a fold of peritoneum interposed between the rectum and vagina. **rectovesical f.,** a fold of peritoneum interposed between the rectum and urinary bladder. **retrotarsal f.,** conjunctival f. **Rindfleisch's f's,** folds in the serous surface of the pericardium around the beginning of the aorta. **sacrogenital f.,** plica rectouterina. **salpingopalatine f.,** plica salpingopalatina. **salpingopharyngeal f.,** plica salpingopharyngea. **Schultze's f.,** a sickle-shaped fold of the amnion extending from the point of insertion of the cord into the placenta to the remains of the umbilical vesicle. **semilunar f.,** plica semilunaris. **semilunar f's of colon,** plicae semilunares coli. **semilunar f. of conjunctiva,** plica semilunaris conjunctivae. **semilunar f. of transversalis fascia,** ligamentum interfoveolare. **serous f.,** plica serosa. **sigmoid f's of colon,** plicae semilunares coli. **spiral f. of cystic duct,** plica spiralis. **sublingual f.,** plica sublingualis. **superior duodenal f.,** plica duodenalis superior. **synovial f.,** plica synovialis. **synovial f. of hip,** ligamentum capitis femoris. **synovial f., infrapatellar, synovial f., patellar,** plica synovialis infrapatellaris. **tail f.,** a crescentic, ventral fold of the blastoderm, at the future caudal end of the embryo. **transverse f's of rectum,** plicae transversales recti. **Treves' f.,** plica ileocecalis. **triangular f.,** plica triangularis. **tubal f's of uterine tube,** plicae tubariae tubae uterinae. **umbilical f., lateral,** plica umbilicalis lateralis. **umbilical f., medial,** plica umbilicalis medialis. **umbilical f., median, umbilical f., middle,** plica umbilicalis mediana. **urogenital f.,** urogenital ridge. **vaginal f's,** rugae vaginales. **vascular cecal f.,** plica cecalis vascularis. **ventricular f.,** plica vestibularis. **Veraguth's f.,** an angularly distorted fold of skin on the lateral third of the upper eyelid; described by Veraguth as occurring in melancholia. **vesical f., transverse,** plica vesicalis transversa. **vestibular f.,** plica vestibularis. **vestigial f. of Marshall,** plica venae cavae sinistrae. **villous f's of stomach,** plicae villosae ventriculi. **vocal f.,** plica vocalis. **vocal f., false,** plica vestibularis.

folia (fo′le-ah). Plural of *folium.*

folian (fo′le-an). Denoting a structure named for Caecilius *Folius.* See *Folius' process.*

foliaceous (fo″le-a′shus) [L. *folia* leaves]. Pertaining to or resembling leaves.

folie (fo-le′) [Fr.]. Psychosis. **f. à deux** (ah-duh′), occurrence of psychosis simultaneously in two closely associated persons. **f. circulaire** (seer-ku-lair′), the circular form of manic-depressive psychosis. **f. du doute** (du-doot′), pathologic inability to make even the most trifling decisions. **f. du pourquoi** (du-poor-kwah′), psychopathological constant questioning. **f. gemellaire** (zha″mĕ-lār′), psychosis occurring simultaneously in twins. **f. musculaire** (mus″ku-lār′), severe chorea. **f. raisonnante** (rez-un-ahnt′), the delusional form of any psychosis.

Folin's test (fol′inz) [Otto *Folin,* American physiologic chemist, 1867–1934]. See under *tests.*

foliosan (fo′le-o-san). Phyllosan.

folium (fo′le-um), pl. *fo′lia* [L. "leaf"]. A general term used in anatomical nomenclature to designate a leaflike structure, especially one of the leaflike subdivisions of the cerebellar cortex. **f. cacu′minis,** f. vermis. **fo′lia cerebel′li** [N A], **folia of cerebellum,** the numerous long, narrow folds of the cerebellar cortex, separated by sulci and supported by white laminae. They are aggregated into the various subdivisions of the cerebellum. Called also *gyri cerebelli* [B N A]. **lingual f.,** a foliate papilla of the tongue. **f. ver′mis** [N A, B N A], the part of the vermis of the cerebellum between the declive and the tuber vermis.

Folius' process (fo′le-us) [Caecilius *Folius,* anatomist of Venice, 1615–1650]. See under *process.*

follicle (fol′lĭ-k'l). A very small excretory or secretory sac or gland. Called also *folliculus.* **aggregated f's,** folliculi lymphatici aggregati. **aggregated f's of vermiform appendix,** folliculi lymphatici aggregati appendicis vermiformis. **atretic f.,** a graafian follicle which has involuted. **dental f.,** the structure within the substance of the jaws enclosing the tooth before its eruption; the dental sac and its contents. **Fleischmann's f.,** an occasional follicle in the mucosa of the floor of the mouth, near the anterior border of the genioglossus muscle. **gastric f's.** 1. Glandulae gastricae [propriae]. 2. The lymphoid masses in the gastric mucosa. **graafian f's,** folliculi ovarici vesiculosi. **hair f.,** folliculus pili. **intestinal f's,** the intestinal glands. See *glandulae intestinales intestini crassi, glandulae intestinales intestini recti,* and *glandulae intestinales intestini tenuis.* **lenticular f's,** lymphatic follicles of the mucous membrane of the stomach. **Lieberkühn's f's,** intestinal glands. See *glandulae intestinales intestini crassi, glandulae intestinales intestini recti,* and *glandulae intestinales intestini tenuis.* **lingual f's,** folliculi linguales. **lymph f.,** folliculus lymphaticus. **lymph f's of stomach,** folliculi lymphatici gastrici. **lymphatic f's, aggregated, of Peyer,** folliculi lymphatici aggregati. **lymphatic f's, laryngeal,** folliculi lymphatici laryngei. **lymphatic f's of large intestine, solitary,** folliculi lymphatici solitarii intestini crassi. **lymphatic f's of tongue,** folliculi linguales. **Montgomery's f's,** Naboth's f's. **mucous f's, nasal,** glandulae nasales. **Naboth's f's, nabothian f's,** cystlike formations caused by occlusion of the lumina of glands in the mucosa of the uterine cervix, causing them to be distended with retained secretion. **ovarian f.,** the egg and its encasing cells, at any stage of its development. **ovarian f's, primary,** folliculi ovarici primarii. **ovarian f's, vesicular,** folliculi ovarici vesiculosi. **primordial f.,** an ovarian follicle consisting of an egg enclosed by a single layer of cells. **sebaceous f.,** a sebaceous gland of the skin. **solitary f's.** See *folliculi lymphatici solitarii intestini crassi* and *folliculi lymphatici solitarii intestini tenuis.* **f. of Stannius,** a lymphoid unit resembling the thymus, developing from nodules formed by proliferation of points of the epithelium of the bursa of Fabricius in chicks. **thyroid f's, f's of thyroid gland,** folliculi glandulae thyroideae. **f's of tongue,** folliculi linguales.

folliclis (fol′ĭ-klis). Tuberculosis papulonecrotica.

follicular (fo-lik′u-lar) [L. *follicularis*]. Of or pertaining to a follicle or follicles.

folliculi (fo-lik′u-li) [L.]. Plural of *folliculus.*

folliculin (fo-lik′u-lin). Estrone.

folliculitis (fo-lik″u-li′tis). Inflammation of a follicle or follicles; used ordinarily in reference to hair follicles, but sometimes in relation to follicles of other kinds. **f. absce′dens et suffo′diens,** perifolliculitis abscedens et suffodiens. **agminate f.,** inflammation of a number of follicles in one area. **f. bar′bae,** inflammation of the hair follicles in the bearded area of the face and neck. **f. cheloida′lis,** keloidal f. **f. decal′vans,** a rare condition tending to occur in individuals with bristly hair, a cluster of follicular pustules or papules forming in a localized area; the process spreads peripherally, involving other follicles, with central scar formation and permanent hair loss. **f. decal′vans et li′chen spinulo′sus,** lichen planus et acuminatus atrophicus. **f. gonorrhoe′ica,** littritis caused by gonococci. **keloidal f., f. keloida′lis,** a chronic condition characterized by development of persistent hard follicular papules which eventually fuse, with reparative activity leading to development of typical keloidal plaques, which give the disease its name; occurring usually on the back of the neck. Called also *dermatitis papillaris capillitii, acne chéloidique, acne keloid,* and *sycosis nuchae necrotisans.* **f. na′res per′forans,** inflammation of a hair follicle in the nose, with pustulation and destruction of the follicle, leading to extension of the process through the tissues to the external surface. **f. ulerythemato′sa reticula′ta,** a condition occurring primarily in youth, and characterized by appearance on the face of numerous closely crowded, small areas of atrophy, separated by narrow ridges, the affected area being erythematous and the skin stretched and hard. **f. variolifor′mis,** acne varioliformis.

folliculoma (fo-lik″u-lo′mah). A tumor of the ovary formed from the epithelium of the graafian follicles, and containing structures that resemble follicles; an oophoroma or granulosa cell tumor.

folliculosis (fo-lik″u-lo′sis). A disease characterized by excessive development of lymph follicles.

folliculus (fo-lik′u-lus), pl. *follic′uli* [L., dim. of *follis* a leather bag]. [N A, B N A] A general term used in anatomical nomenclature to designate a very small excretory or secretory sac or gland. Called also *follicle.* **follic′uli glan′dulae thyroi′deae** [N A], discrete, cystlike units of the thyroid gland that are lined with cuboidal epithelium and are filled with a colloid substance. There are about 30 to each lobule. Called also *follicles of thyroid gland.* **follic′uli lingua′les** [N A, B N A], projections on the mucosa of the root of the tongue, caused by underlying nodular masses of lymphoid tissue, making up the lingual tonsil. Called also *lingual follicles*. **f. lymphat′icus** [N A]. 1. A small collection of lymphoid tissue found in such places as the mucosa of the gut. Called also *nodulus lymphaticus* [B N A], and *lymph follicle*. 2. A small transient collection of actively proliferating lymphocytes in the cortex of a lymph node, expressing the cytogenetic and defense functions of the lymphatic tissue. Called also *lymphatic nodule*. **follic′uli lymphat′ici aggrega′ti** [N A], oval elevated areas of lymphoid tissue on the mucosa of the small intestine, composed of many lymphoid follicles closely packed together. Called also *noduli lymphatici aggregati* [*Peyeri*] [B N A], and *Peyer's patches*. **follic′uli lymphat′ici aggrega′ti appen′dicis vermifor′mis** [N A], oval elevated areas of lymphoid tissue occupying the greater part of the submucosa of the vermiform appendix. Called also *noduli aggregati processus vermiformis* [B N A]. **follic′uli lymphat′ici gas′trici** [N A], small lymphocytic aggregates in the interstitial tissue of the lamina propria of the stomach, especially in the pyloric region. Called also *noduli lymphatici gastrici* [B N A]. **follic′uli lymphat′ici laryn′gei** [N A], lymphatic aggregations in the mucosa of the ventricle of the larynx and on the posterior surface of the epiglottis. Called also *noduli lymphatici laryngei* [B N A]. **follic′uli lymphat′ici liena′les** [N A], aggregations of lymphatic tissue that ensheath the arteries in the spleen; often called the *white pulp*. Called also *noduli lymphatici lienales* [*Malpighii*] [B N A]. **follic′uli lymphat′ici rec′ti** [N A], concentrations of lymphoid tissue in the tunica mucosa of the rectum. Called also *noduli lymphatici recti* [B N A]. **follic′uli lymphat′ici solita′rii intesti′ni cras′si** [N A], the areas of concentrated lymphatic tissue in the tunica mucosa of the colon. Called also *noduli lymphatici solitarii intestini crassi* [B N A], and *solitary lymph follicles of large intestine*. **follic′uli lymphat′ici solita′rii intesti′ni ten′uis** [N A], small lymph follicles scattered throughout the mucosa and submucosa of the small intestine. Called also *noduli lymphatici solitarii intestini tenuis* [B N A]. **follic′uli ooph′ori prima′rii** [B N A], folliculi ovarici primarii. **follic′uli ooph′ori vesiculo′si [Graaf′i]** [B N A], folliculi ovarici vesiculosi. **follic′uli ovar′ici prima′rii** [N A], immature ovarian follicles, each comprising an immature ovum and the few specialized epithelial cells (follicle cells) that surround it. Called also *folliculi oophori primarii* [B N A]. **follic′uli ovar′ici vesiculo′si** [N A], maturing ovarian follicles, each comprising a theca filled with follicular fluid, the inner part of one side of which bears the cumulus, containing the germ cell, or ovum. Called also *folliculi oophori vesiculosi* [*Graafi*] [B N A], and *graafian follicles*. **f. pi′li** [N A, B N A], the epithelial tube within which each hair grows. Called also *hair follicle*.

follutein (fol-lu′te-in). Trade mark for a preparation of chorionic gonadotropin.

Foltz's valve (fōlts′ez) [J. C. E. *Foltz*, French ophthalmologist, 1822–1876]. See under *valve*.

folvite (fōl′vīt). Trade mark for preparations of folic acid.

fomentation (fo″men-ta′shun) [L. *fomentatio; fomentum*, a poultice]. Treatment by warm and moist applications; also the substance thus applied.

fomes (fo′mēz), pl. *fo′mites* [L. "tinder"]. An object, such as a book, wooden object, or an article of clothing, that is not in itself corrupted but is able to harbor pathogenic microorganisms which may by that means be transmitted to others.

fomite (fo′mīt). Fomes.

fomites (fo′mĭ-tēz). Plural of *fomes*.

Fonsecae′a pedro′soi. *Hormodendrum pedrosoi.*

fontactoscope (fon-tak′to-skōp). An instrument for measuring the radioactivity of water and gas.

Fontana's canals, markings, spaces (fon-tah′nahz) [Abada Felix *Fontana*, Italian naturalist, 1730–1805]. See under *marking* and *space*.

fontanel (fon″tah-nel). Fontanelle.

fontanelle (fon″tah-nel′) [Fr., dim. of *fontaine* spring, filter]. A soft spot, such as one of the membrane-covered spaces remaining in the incompletely ossified skull (*fonticuli cranii* [N A]). **anterior f.**, fonticulus anterior. **anterolateral f.**, fonticulus sphenoidalis. **bregmatic f.**, fonticulus anterior. **Casser's f., Casserian f.**, fonticulus mastoideus. **cranial f's**, fonticuli cranii. **frontal f.**, fonticulus anterior. **Gerdy's f.**, a fontanelle occasionally occurring in the sagittal suture. **mastoid f.**, fonticulus mastoideus. **occipital f., posterior f.**, fonticulus posterior. **posterolateral f., posterotemporal f.**, fonticulus mastoideus. **quadrangular f.**, fonticulus anterior. **sagittal f.**, Gerdy's f. **sphenoidal f.**, fonticulus sphenoidalis. **triangular f.**, fonticulus posterior.

fonticuli (fon-tik′u-li) [L.]. Plural of *fonticulus*.

fonticulus (fon-tik′u-lus), pl. *fontic′uli* [L., dim. of *fons* fountain]. [N A, B N A] A soft spot; used in anatomical nomenclature to designate one of the membrane-covered spaces remaining in the incompletely ossified skull. Called also *fontanelle*. **f. ante′rior** [N A], the unossified area of the skull situated at the junction of the frontal, coronal, and sagittal sutures. Called also *f. frontalis* [*major*] [B N A], and *anterior fontanelle*. **fontic′uli cra′nii** [N A], the membrane-covered spaces, or soft spots, remaining at the incomplete angles of the parietal and adjacent bones, until ossification of the skull is completed. Called also *fontanelles*. **f. fronta′lis** [B N A], f. anterior. **f. guttu′ris**, fossa jugularis. **f. ma′jor**, f. anterior. **f. mastoi′deus** [N A, B N A], the unossified area of the skull at the junction of the lambdoidal, parietomastoid, and occipitomastoid sutures. Called also *mastoid fontanelle*. **f. mi′nor**, f. posterior. **f. occipita′lis** [B N A], **f. poste′rior** [N A], the unossified area of the skull at the junction of the sagittal and lambdoidal sutures. Called also *f. minor* and *posterior fontanelle*. **f. sphenoida′lis** [N A, B N A], the unossified area at the junction of the parietal and frontal bones, the greater wing of the sphenoidal, and the squamous part of the temporal bones. Called also *sphenoidal fontanelle*.

food (fo͞od). Anything which, when taken into the body, serves to nourish or build up the tissues or to supply heat; aliment. **isodynamic f's**, foods which generate equal amounts of energy in heat units.

foot (foot) [L. *pes*]. The terminal organ of the leg. **athlete's f.**, tinea pedis. **broad f.**, metatarsus latus. **burning feet**, a deficiency disease, probably riboflavin deficiency, occurring among the poor in South India and West Africa. It is marked by burning sensations in the soles and palms and by inflammation of the angles of the mouth. Called also *barasheh* and *chacaleh*. **buttress f.**, a condition of periostitis or ostitis in the region of the pyramidal process of the os pedis of a horse with fracture of the process, deformity of the hoof, and alteration of the normal angle of the joint. Called also *pyramidal disease* and *low ringbone*. **Charcot's f.**, the deformed foot seen in tabetic arthropathy. **cleft f.**, a deformed foot in which the division between the third and fourth toes extends into the metatarsal region. **contracted f.** See *hoof-bound*. **crooked f.**, a condition of a horse's hoof in which one wall is concave and the opposite wall convex, giving the hoof a bent appearance. It is due to improper trimming and shoeing. **dangle f., drop f.**, a condition in which the foot hangs in a plantar-flexed position, due to lesion of the peroneal nerve. **end f.** See *end-foot*. **forced f.**, a painful swelling of the feet of soldiers after forced marches, due to fracture of the fourth metatarsal bone. **Friedreich's f.**, pes cavus, with hyperextension of the toes: seen in hereditary ataxia. **fungus f.**, maduromycosis. **Hong Kong f.**, an infectious mycotic disease (dermatophytosis) of the foot occurring in China. **immersion f.**, a condition resembling trench foot occurring in shipwrecked persons who have spent protracted periods in water-logged boats. **Madura f.**, maduromycosis. **march f.**, painful swelling of the forefoot, often associated with fracture of one of the metatarsal bones, following excessive foot strain. **Morand's f.**, a foot having eight toes. **Morton's f.**, metatarsalgia. **mossy f.**, an infective verrucotic condition of the skin of the feet, endemic in the Amazon region of South America. **pricked f.**, a condition in a horse in which the sole or the frog has been punctured either in the forge or by the animal treading on a nail or some other object. **pumiced f.**, a condition in which the sole of a horse's hoof projects beyond the level of the wall, the horn being porous and brittle in quality. Called also *dropped sole* and *convex sole*. **reel f.**, clubfoot. **sag f.**, sagging of the arch of the foot. **shelter f.**, a swollen condition of the feet occurring among persons who spend the night in air-raid shelters. **shuffle f.**, a condition marked by the steppage gait of spastic paralysis. **spread f.**, metatarsus latus. **sucker f.**, a pyramidal expansion of a process of an astrocyte by which the latter is attached to a small blood vessel: called also *sucker apparatus*, *podium*, and *vascular foot plate*. **tabetic f.**, the flat, distorted foot seen in tabes, and due to disease of the tarsus. **taut f.**, a shortening and contraction of the calf muscles and plantar flexors of the foot, due to high-heeled shoes. **trench f.**, a condition of the feet of soldiers in the trenches resembling frostbite. It is due to the prolonged action of water on the skin combined with circulatory disturbance due to cold and inaction. Called also *water-bite*, *foot stasis*, and *local frigorism*. **weak f.**, an early stage of flatfoot.

foot-candle (foot kan′d'l). A unit of illumination, being 1 lumen per foot or equivalent to 1.0764 milliphots.

foot lambert (foot lam′bert). See *lambert*.

foot-pound (foot-pownd′). The work done in raising a mass of one pound the distance of one foot against gravity. Abbreviated f.p.

forage (fo-rahzh′) [Fr. "boring, drilling"]. Surgical creation of a V-shaped longitudinal trench in the prostate by means of the electric current, thereby removing obstruction caused by its hypertrophy. The term is applied to similar cutting operations on other parts.

foramen (fo-ra′men), pl. *foram′ina* [L.]. A natural opening or passage; used as a general term in anatomical nomenclature to designate such a passage, especially one into or through a bone. **accessory f.**, the orifice on the surface of a root opening into an accessory root canal of a tooth. **alveolar foramina of maxilla, foram′ina alveola′ria maxil′lae** [N A, B N A], the openings of the alveolar canals on the infratemporal surface of the maxilla. **aortic f.**, hiatus aorticus. **apical f. of tooth, f. a′picis den′tis** [N A, B N A], an aperture at or near the apex of the root of a tooth, giving passage to the blood vessels and nerves supplying the pulp. **arachnoid f.**, apertura mediana ventriculi quarti. **auditory f., external,** meatus acusticus externus. **auditory f., internal,** porus acusticus internus. **Bartholin's f.**, f. obturatum. **Bichat's f.**, a canal extending from the subarachnoid space to the third ventricle. **f. of Bochdalek,** hiatus pleuroperitonealis. **Botallo's f.**, f. ovale cordis. **Bozzi's f.**, the macula lutea of the retina. **f. cae′cum lin′guae** [B N A], f. cecum linguae. **f. cae′cum medul′lae oblonga′tae** [B N A], a depression under the edge of the pons, formed by the termination of the anterior fissure of the medulla oblongata. Omitted in N A. **f. cae′cum poste′rius, f. caecum of Vicq d'Azyr,** f. caecum medullae oblongatae. **caroticotympanic foramina,** canaliculi caroticotympanici. **carotid f.**, the inferior aperture of the carotid canal, giving passage to the carotid vessels. **cavernous f.**, a passage for the median vertebral vein in the sphenoid bone. **cecal f., f. ce′cum,** f. cecum ossis frontalis. **f. cecum of frontal bone,** f. cecum ossis frontalis. **f. ce′cum lin′guae** [N A], a depression on the dorsum of the tongue at the end of the median sulcus, representing the remains of the upper end of the thyroglossal duct of the embryo. **f. ce′cum os′sis fronta′lis** [N A], a blind opening formed between the frontal crest and the crista galli. It sometimes transmits a vein from the nasal cavity to the superior sagittal sinus. **f. cecum of tongue,** f. cecum linguae. **f. centra′le,** fovea centralis. **cervical f.**, f. transversarium. **condyloid f., anterior,** canalis hypoglossi. **condyloid f., posterior,** canalis condylaris. **conjugate f.**, a foramen formed by a notch in each of two opposed bones. **f. costotransversa′rium** [N A, B N A], the narrow space which is present between the dorsal surface of the neck of a rib and the ventral surface of the transverse process of the corresponding vertebra. Called also *costotransverse f.* **cotyloid f.**, a passage between the margin of the acetabulum and the transverse ligament. **cribroethmoid f.**, f. ethmoidale anterius. **dental foramina.** See *foramina alveolaria maxillae* and *foramina mandibulae*. **f. diaphrag′matis [sel′lae]** [B N A], the opening in the center of the diaphragm of the sella through which the infundibulum passes. Omitted in N A. **Duverney's f.**, f. epiploicum. **emissary f.**, any foramen in a cranial bone that gives passage to an emissary vein. **epiploic f., f. epiplo′icum** [N A], an opening connecting the two sacs of the peritoneum, situated below and behind the porta hepatis. **esophageal f.**, hiatus esophageus. **ethmoidal foramina,** foramina ethmoidalia. **ethmoidal f., anterior,** f. ethmoidale anterius. **ethmoidal f., posterior,** f. ethmoidale posterius. **foram′ina ethmoida′lia** [N A, B N A], small openings in the ethmoid bone at the junction of the medial wall with the roof of the orbit, the anterior transmitting the nasal branch of the ophthalmic nerve and the anterior ethmoid vessels, the posterior transmitting the posterior ethmoid vessels. Called also *ethmoidal foramina*. **f. ethmoida′le ante′rius** [N A, B N A], a small opening on the medial wall of the orbit, on the line of the frontoethmoidal suture, that transmits the anterior ethmoidal nerve and vessels. **f. ethmoida′le poste′rius** [N A, B N A], a small opening on the medial wall of the orbit, on the line of the frontoethmoidal suture, that transmits the posterior ethmoidal nerve and vessels. Called also *posterior ethmoidal f.* **f. of Fallopio,** hiatus canalis nervi petrosi majoris. **Ferrein's f.**, hiatus canalis nervi petrosi majoris. **frontal f.**, incisura frontale. **frontoethmoidal f.**, a foramen on the line of the frontoethmoidal suture. **Galen's f.**, the opening of the anterior cardiac vein into the right atrium. **glandular foramina of Littre,** lacunae urethrales. **glandular f. of Morgagni, glandular f. of tongue,** f. cecum linguae. **great f.**, f. magnum. **Hartigan's f.**, a foramen said to exist in the base of the transverse process of a lumbar vertebra seldom persisting to adult life. **Huschke's f.**, a perforation found near the inner extremity of the tympanal plate: caused by arrest of development. **incisive f., f. incisi′vum** [N A, B N A], one of the openings in the incisive fossa of the hard palate that transmit the nasopalatine nerves. **incisor f., median,** Scarpa's f. **infraorbital f., f. infraorbita′le** [N A, B N A], the opening of the infraorbital canal on the anterior surface of the maxilla giving passage to the infraorbital nerve and vessels. **innominate f.**, an occasional opening in the temporal bone for passage of the small superficial petrosal nerve. **intersacral foramina,** foramina intervertebralia ossis sacri. **interventricular f., f. interventricula′re**

[N A], **f. interventricula're [Monro'i]** [B N A], a communication between the lateral and the third ventricle. Called also *f. of Monro.* **intervertebral f.,** f. intervertebrale. **f. intervertebra'le** [N A, B N A], the passage formed by the inferior and superior notches on the pedicles of adjacent vertebrae. It transmits a spinal nerve and vessels. **foramina intervertebra'lia os'sis sa'cri** [N A, B N A], the four short, forked tunnels in each lateral wall of the sacral canal, connecting it with the pelvic and dorsal sacral foramina. Called also *intervertebral foramina of sacrum.* **ischiadic f., greater,** f. ischiadicum majus. **ischiadic f., lesser,** f. ischiadicum minus. **f. ischia'dicum ma'jus** [N A, B N A], a hole converted from the major sciatic notch by the sacrotuberal and sacrospinal ligaments. Called also *greater sciatic f.* **f. ischia'dicum mi'nus** [N A, B N A], a hole converted from the minor sciatic notch by the sacrotuberal and sacrospinal ligaments. Called also *lesser sciatic f.* **ischiopubic f.,** f. obturatum. **jugular f., f. jugula're** [N A, B N A], the opening formed by the jugular notches on the temporal and occipital bones, for the transmission of various veins, arteries, and nerves. **f. of Key and Retzius,** apertura lateralis ventriculi quarti. **lacerate f., anterior,** fissura orbitalis superior. **lacerate f., middle,** f. lacerum. **lacerate f., posterior,** f. jugulare. **f. lac'erum** [N A, B N A], an irregular gap formed at the junction of the great wing of the sphenoid bone, the tip of the petrous part of the temporal bone, and the basilar part of the occipital bone. In life its inferior aspect is filled with fibrocartilage, superior to which the internal carotid artery lies. **f. lac'erum ante'rius,** fissura orbitalis superior. **f. lac'erum me'dium,** f. lacerum. **f. lac'erum poste'rius,** f. jugulare. **lateral f.,** accessory f. **left f., inferior,** hiatus aorticus. **left f., superior,** hiatus esophageus. **f. of Luschka,** apertura lateralis ventriculi quarti. **f. of Magendie,** apertura mediana ventriculi quarti. **f. mag'num** [N A], the large opening in the anterior and inferior part of the occipital bone, interconnecting the vertebral canal and the cranial cavity. Called also *f. occipitale magnum* [B N A]. **malar f.,** f. zygomaticofaciale. **f. mandib'ulae** [N A], **f. mandibula're** [B N A], the opening on the medial surface of the ramus of the mandible, leading into the mandibular canal. **mastoid f., f. mastoi'deum** [N A, B N A], a prominent opening in the temporal bone posterior to the mastoid process and near its occipital articulation. An artery and vein usually pass through it. **maxillary f.,** hiatus maxillaris. **maxillary f., anterior,** f. mentale. **maxillary f., inferior,** f. ovale basis cranii. **maxillary f., internal, maxillary f., posterior,** f. mandibulae. **maxillary f., superior,** f. rotundum ossis sphenoidalis. **medullary f.,** f. vertebrale. **meibomian f.,** f. cecum linguae. **mental f., f. menta'le** [N A, B N A], an opening on the lateral part of the body of the mandible, opposite the second bicuspid tooth, for passage of the mental nerve and vessels. **f. of Monro,** f. interventriculare. **Morand's f.,** f. cecum linguae. **Morgagni's f., morgagnian f.** 1. A small gap on either side, between the sternal and costal portions of the diaphragm, for the passage of the superior epigastric blood vessels and a few lymphatic vessels. 2. Foramen cecum linguae. 3. Foramen singulare. **nasal foramina, foram'ina nasa'lia** [B N A], openings on the outer surface of each nasal bone for the transmission of blood vessels. Omitted in N A. **foram'ina nervo'sa lim'bus lam'inae spira'lis** [N A], numerous small openings in the labium limbi tympanicum for the passage of the cochlear nerves. Called also *foramina nervosa laminae spiralis* [B N A]. **f. nutric'ium** [N A, B N A], **nutrient f.,** any one of the passages that admit the nutrient vessels to the medullary cavity of a bone. **obturator f., f. obtura'tum** [N A, B N A], the large opening between the os pubis and the ischium. **occipital f., great, occipital f., inferior,** f. magnum. **f. occipita'le mag'num** [B N A], f. magnum. **olfactory f.,** any one of the many openings of the cribriform plate of the ethmoidal bone. **optic f. of sclera,** lamina cribrosa sclerae. **optic f. of sphenoid bone, f. op'ticum os'sis sphenoida'lis** [B N A], canalis opticus. **orbitomalar f.,** f. zygomaticoorbitale. **oval f. of fetus,** fossa ovalis cordis. **oval f. of hip bone,** f. obturatum. **oval f. of sphenoid bone,** f. ovale basis cranii. **f. ova'le ba'sis cra'nii** [N A], an opening in the posterior part of the medial portion of the great wing of the sphenoid bone. It transmits the mandibular branch of the trigeminal nerve and some vessels. Called also *f. ovale ossis sphenoidalis* [B N A]. **f. ova'le cor'dis** [N A], the aperture in the septum secundum of the fetal heart that provides a communication between the atria. **f. ova'le os'sis sphenoida'lis** [B N A], f. ovale basis cranii. **f. of Pacchioni, pacchionian f.,** f. diaphragmatis [sellae]. **palatine foramina, accessory,** foramina palatina minora. **palatine f., anterior,** f. incisivum. **palatine f., greater,** f. palatinum majus. **palatine formina, lesser,** foramina palatina minora. **palatine f., posterior,** f. palatinum majus. **foramina of palatine tonsil,** fossulae tonsillares. **f. palati'num ma'jus** [N A, B N A], the inferior opening of the great palatine canal, found laterally on the horizontal plate of each palatine bone opposite the root of each third molar tooth. It transmits a palatine nerve and artery. Called also *greater palatine f.* **foram'ina palati'na mino'ra** [N A, B N A], the openings of the palatine canals behind the palatine crest and the greater palatine foramina. Called also *lesser palatine foramina.* **foram'ina papilla'ria re'nis** [N A, B N A], **papillary foramina of kidney,** minute openings in the summit of each renal papilla, the orifices of the collecting tubules. **parietal f., f. parieta'le** [N A, B N A], an opening on the posterior part of the superior portion of the parietal bone for the passage of a vein and arteriole. **pleuroperitoneal f.** 1. Hiatus pleuroperitonealis. 2. Morgagni's f. (def. 1). **pterygopalatine f.,** f. palatinum majus. **pulpal f.,** f. apicis dentis. **quadrate f.,** f. venae cavae. **f. rad'icis den'tis,** f. apicis dentis. **Retzius' f.,** apertura lateralis ventriculi quarti. **right f.,** f. venae cavae. **rivinian f.,** incisura tympanica. **root f.,** f. apicis dentis. **f. rotun'dum os'sis sphenoida'lis** [N A, B N A], a round opening in the medial part of the great wing of the sphenoid bone that transmits the maxillary branch of the trigeminal nerve. **sacral foramina, anterior,** foramina sacralia pelvina. **f. of sacral canal,** hiatus sacralis. **sacral foramina, internal,** foramina sacralia pelvina. **sacral foramina, posterior,** foramina sacralia dorsalia. **foram'ina sacra'lia anterio'ra** [B N A], foramina sacralia pelvina. **foram'ina sacra'lia dorsa'lia** [N A], the eight openings (four on each side) on the dorsal surface of the sacrum for the dorsal rami of the sacral nerves. Called also *dorsal sacral foramina* and *foramina sacralia posteriora* [B N A]. **foram'ina sacra'lia pelvi'na** [N A], the eight openings (four on each side) on the pelvic surface of the sacrum for the ventral rami of the sacral nerves. Called also *anterior sacral foramina* and *foramina sacralia anteriora* [B N A]. **foram'ina sacra'lia posterio'ra** [B N A], foramina sacralia dorsalia. **sacrosciatic f., great,** f. ischiadicum majus. **sacrosciatic f., small,** f. ischiadicum minus. **f. of saphenous vein,** hiatus saphenus. **Scarpa's f.,** one of the two foramina, one behind either upper medial incisor, for transmission of the nasopalatine nerves. **Schwalbe's f.,** f. caecum medullae oblongatae. **sciatic f., greater,** f. ischiadicum majus. **sciatic f., lesser,** f. ischiadicum minus. **f. singula're** [N A, B N A], the opening in the inferior vestibular area of the fundus of the internal acoustic meatus that gives passage to the nerves of the ampulla of the posterior semicircular duct. **foramina of smallest veins of heart,** foramina venarium minimarum cordis. **Soemmering's f.,** fovea centralis retinae. **sphenopalatine f.** 1. Foramen sphenopalatinum. 2. Foramen palatinum majus. **f. sphenopalati'num** [N A, B N A], an opening on the medial wall of the pterygopalatine fossa, interconnecting this fossa with the nasal cavity, and transmitting the sphenopalatine artery and nasal nerves. **sphenotic f.,** f. lacerum. **spinal f., f. of spinal cord,** f. vertebrale. **f. spino'sum** [N A, B N A], **spinous f.,** an opening in the great wing of the sphenoid bone, near its posterior angle, for the middle meningeal artery. **Spöndel's f.,** a small foramen in the cartilaginous base of the skull between the ethmoid bone and the lower wings of the sphenoid and the anterior ethmoid. **f. of Stenson.** 1. Foramen incisivum. 2. Canalis incisivus. **stylomastoid f., f. stylomastoi'deum** [N A, B N A], a foramen on the inferior part of the temporal bone between the styloid and mastoid processes, for the facial nerve and the stylomastoid artery. **suborbital f.,** the orifice at the anterior end of the infra-orbital canal for the infra-orbital artery and nerve. **supraorbital f., f. supraorbita'le** [B N A], **f. supraorbita'lis** [N A], an opening in the frontal bone in the supraorbital margin, giving passage to the supraorbital artery and nerve. It is often present as a notch (incisura frontale) bridged only by fibrous tissue. **suprapyriform f.,** an opening above the pyramidalis muscle through which the gluteal vessels and superior gluteal nerve pass out of the pelvis. **f. of Tarin,** hiatus canalis nervi petrosi majoris. **temporal f., superior,** linea temporalis superior ossis parietalis. **temporomalar f.,** f. zygomaticotemporale. **terminal f. of pelvis,** linea terminalis pelvis. **thebesian foramina, foram'ina thebes'ii,** foramina venarum minimarum cordis. **thyroid f., f. thyroi'deum** [N A], an inconstantly present opening in the upper part of the lamina of the thyroid cartilage, resulting from incomplete union of the fourth and fifth branchial cartilages. **tonsillar foramina,** fossulae tonsillares. **f. transversa'rium** [N A, B N A], **transverse f.,** the passage in either process of a cervical vertebra that, in the upper six vertebrae, transmits the vertebral vessels. It is small or may be absent in the seventh. **vena caval f., f. ve'nae ca'vae** [N A, B N A], the opening in the respiratory diaphragm that transmits the inferior vena cava and some branches of the right vagus nerve. **foram'ina vena'rum minima'rum cor'dis** [N A], minute openings in the walls of the right atrium of the heart, through which small veins, the venae cordis minimae, empty their blood directly into the heart. **venous f.,** f. venae cavae. **vertebral f.** 1. Foramen vertebrale. 2. Foramen transversarium. **f. vertebra'le** [N A, B N A], the large opening in a vertebra formed by its body and arch. **vertebroarterial f.,** f. transversarium. **f. of Vesalius,** an opening at the inner side of the foramen ovale of the sphenoid. **f. of Vicq d'Azyr,** f. caecum medullae oblongatae. **Vieussen's foramina,** foramina venarum minimarum cordis. **Weitbrecht's f.,** an opening in the capsule of the shoulder joint through which passes the synovial membrane to the bursa that lines the under surface of the subscapularis muscle. **f. of Winslow,** f. epiploicum. **zygomatic f., anterior, zygomatic f., external, zygomatic f., facial,** f. zygomaticofaciale. **zygomatic f., inferior, zygomatic f., internal, of Arnold,** f. zygomaticoorbitale. **zygomatic f., internal, of Meckel,** f. zygomaticotemporale. **zygomatic f., orbital,** f. zygomaticoorbitale. **zygomatic f., posterior,** f. zygomaticotemporale. **zygomatic f., superior,** f. zygomaticoorbitale. **zygomatic f., temporal,** f. zygomaticotemporale. **zygomaticofacial f., f. zygomaticofacia'le** [N A, B N A], the opening on the anterior surface of the zygomatic bone for the zygomaticofacial nerves and vessels. **zygomaticoorbital f., f. zygomaticoorbita'le** [N A, B N A], either of the two openings on the orbital surface of each zygomatic bone, which transmit branches of the zygomatic branch of the trigeminal nerve and branches of the lacrimal artery. **zygomaticotemporal f., f. zygomaticotempora'le** [N A, B N A], the opening on the temporal surface of the zygomatic bone for passage of the zygomaticotemporal nerve.

foramina (fo-ram'ĭ-nah) [L.]. Plural of *foramen.*

foraminiferous (for″am-ĭ-nif'er-us) [*foramen* + L. *ferre* to bear]. Having foramina.

foraminotomy (for″am-ĭ-not'o-me) [*foramina* + Gr. *tomē* a cut]. The operation of removing the roof of intervertebral foramina, done for the relief of nerve root oppression.

foraminulum (for″ah-min'u-lum), pl. *foramin'ula* [L.]. A minute foramen.

foration (fo-ra'shun) [L. *forare* to bore]. The act or process of trephination or boring.

force (fōrs) [L. *fortis* strong]. Energy, or power; that which originates or arrests motion. **catabolic f.,** energy derived from the metabolism of food. **chewing f.,** masticatory f. **electromotive f.,** the force which, by reason of differences in potential, causes a flow of electricity from one place to another, giving rise to an electric current. It is measured in volts and is abbreviated E.M.F. **field f's,** hypothetical forces which have part in the individuation processes of the early embryo. **masticatory f.,** the force applied by the muscles of mastication during the chewing of food. **nerve f., nervous f.** 1. The ability of nerve tissue to conduct stimuli. 2. In psychiatry, the amount of nervous capital or stamina a person possesses. **occlusal f.,** the force exerted on opposing teeth when the jaws are brought into approximation. **reserve f.,** energy above that required for normal functioning. In the heart it is the power which will take care of the additional circulatory burden imposed by bodily exertion. **rest f.,** the power of the heart necessary to maintain the circulation when the patient is at rest. **vital f.,** the energy which characterizes a living organism.

forceps (fōr'seps) [L.]. 1. An instrument with two blades and handles for pulling, grasping, or compressing. 2. Any forcipate organ or part, particularly the terminal fibers of the corpus callosum. **alligator f.,** strong toothed forceps having a double clamp. **f. ante'rior,** f. minor. **artery f.,** forceps for grasping and compressing an artery. **aural f.,** forceps for operations of the ear. **axis-traction f.,** obstetrical forceps so constructed that the traction may be made in the line of the pelvic axis. **Barton f.,** an obstetrical forceps with a hinge in the right blade. **bayonet f.,** a forceps whose blades are offset from the axis of the handles. **bone f.,** forceps used for cutting bone. **bulldog f.,** spring forceps for seizing an artery or other part to arrest hemorrhage. **bullet f.,** a forceps for extracting bullets. **capsule f.,** forceps for removing the lens capsule in membranous cataract. **Chamberlen f.,** the original form of obstetrical forceps, invented by Peter Chamberlen (1560–1631), and disclosed by Hugh Chamberlen (1664–1728). **clamp f.** 1. A forceps with an automatic lock, used for compressing arteries, the pedicle of a tumor, etc. 2. In dentistry, forceps used to hold and open the rubber-dam clamp while it is being placed on a tooth. **clip f.,** small forceps with broad ends to the blades fastened by a spring catch, used to close the end of a severed artery during operations. **Cornet's f.,** a forceps for holding a cover-glass. **DeLee f.,** a modified Simpson forceps. **dental f.,** forceps for the extraction of teeth. **disk f.,** a forceps for grasping the scleral disk in trephining the eyeball. **dressing f.,** forceps with scissor-like handles for grasping lint, drainage tubes, etc., in dressing wounds. **ear f.,** delicate forceps for extracting foreign bodies from the auditory canal. **epilating f.,** forceps for use in plucking out hairs. **extracting f.,** dental f. **fixation f.,** forceps for holding a part during an operation. **galea f.,** Willett f. **hammer f.,** a combined hammer and forceps for surgeons' use. **hemostatic f.,** forceps for controlling hemorrhage. **high f.** See *forceps delivery, high,* under *delivery.* **Hodge's f.,** a variety of obstetrical forceps. **Kielland's f., Kjelland's f.,** obstetrical forceps having short handles, no axis tractor, a marked cephalic curve, and an articulation permitting a gliding movement of one blade over the other. **Knapp's f.,** forceps with roller blades: used to express trachomatous granules from the conjunctiva. **Kocher's f.,** strong forceps for holding tissues during operation or for compressing bleeding tissue. **Laborde's f.,** forceps for grasping the tongue in Laborde's method of stimulating respiration. **Laplace's f.,** forceps used in enterostomy for holding the portions of the intestines together while they are being sutured. **Levret's f.,** modified Chamberlen forceps, curved to correspond with the curve of the parturient canal. **Liston's f.,** a type of bone-cutting forceps. **lithotomy f.,** forceps for removing stone from the bladder in lithotomy. **low f.** See *forceps delivery, low,* under *delivery.* **Löwenberg's f.,** forceps for removing adenoid growths. **Luikart f.,** an obstetrical forceps with unfenestrated blades. **f. ma'jor,** the terminal fibers of the callosum that pass into the occipital lobe. **mid f.** See *midforceps delivery,* under *delivery.* **f. mi'nor,** the terminal fibers of the callosum that pass from the splenium into the frontal lobe. **mosquito f.,** a small hemostatic forceps. **mouse-tooth f.,** forceps with two or more fine teeth at the tip of each blade. **obstetrical f.,** an instrument designed to extract the child by the head from the maternal passages without injury to it or to the mother. **Péan's f.,** a clamp for hemostasis. **Piper f.,** a special obstetrical forceps for an aftercoming head. **f. poste'rior,** f. major. **roller f.,** forceps with a roller at the end of each blade: used for compressing the granulations in trachoma. **rongeur f.,** a forceps designed for use in cutting bone. **sequestrum f.,** forceps with small but strong serrated jaws for removing the portions of bone forming a sequestrum. **Simpson's f.,** a form of obstetrical forceps. **speculum f.,** long slender forceps for use through a speculum. **suture f.,** forceps used to hold the needle in passing a suture. **Tarnier's f.,** a form of axis-traction forceps. **tenaculum f.,** forceps having a sharp hook at the end of each jaw. **torsion f.,** forceps for making torsion on an artery to arrest hemorrhage. **tracheal f.,** long slender forceps for removing foreign bodies from the trachea. **trachoma f.,** roller f. **tubular f.,** slender forceps for use through a tubular instrument. **Tucker-McLean f.,** a long obstetrical forceps with a solid blade. **vulsella f., vulsellum.,** vulsella, vulsellum. **Willett f.,** a vulsellum forceps for applying scalp traction in the control of hemorrhage from placenta praevia.

Forchheimer's sign (forch'hi-merz) [Frederick *Forchheimer,* physician in Cincinnati, 1853–1913]. See under *sign.*

forcipate (for'sĭ-pāt). Shaped like forceps.

Forcipomyia (for″sĭ-po-mi'yah). A genus of Chironomidae. *F. townsendi* and *F. utae* are thought to transmit uta by their bites.

forcipressure (for'sĭ-presh-ur). Pressure with forceps, chiefly for the arrest of hemorrhage.

Fordyce's disease, spot (for'dīs-es) [John Addison *Fordyce,* New York dermatologist, 1858–1925]. See under *disease* and *spot.*

forearm (fōr'arm). The part of the upper member of the body between the elbow and the wrist. Called also *antebrachium* [N A].

forebrain (fōr'brān). The prosencephalon.

foreconscious (fōr-kon'shus). 1. Incapable of becoming conscious until certain conditions are fulfilled. 2. That part of the mind which contains memory impressions which may be brought into consciousness under certain conditions.

forefinger (fōr-fing'ger). The index finger.

forefoot (fōr'foot). One of the front feet of a quadruped.

foregilding (fōr'gild-ing). The treatment of fresh nerve tissue with salts in histologic technic.

foregut (fōr'gut). The embryonic organ from which are derived the pharynx, esophagus, stomach, and duodenum.

forehead (fōr'hed). The part of the face above the eyes. **bony f.,** the skeleton of the forehead, formed by the anterior part of the skull (frontal bone).

forekidney (fōr-kid'ne). Pronephros.

Forel's commissure, decussation, field, fornix (fo-relz') [Auguste *Forel,* Swiss psychiatrist, 1848–1931]. See under the nouns.

fore-pleasure (fōr'plezh-er). Sexual pleasure which precedes orgasm. Cf. *end-pleasure.*

foreskin (fōr'skin). The prepuce (preputium penis).

foretop (fōr'top). The anterior portion of the mane of a horse, covering the forehead.

forewaters (fōr'wat-erz). The amniotic fluid that presents at the cervix uteri.

Forlanini's treatment (fōr″lah-ne'nēz) [Carlo *Forlanini,* Italian physician, 1847–1918]. See under *treatment.*

form (form) [L. *forma*]. The characteristic of a structure or entity generally determined by its shape and size, or other external or visible feature. **accolé f.** (ak″o-la'), appliqué f. **appliqué f.** (ap″lĭ-ka'), the early form of *Plasmodium falciparum* which appears as a fine blue line with a chromatin dot apparently applied to the margin of an erythrocyte; called also *accolé form.* **band f's,** leukocytes with bandlike or horseshoe-shaped nuclei, constituting about 4 per cent of the total leukocytes. **involution f's,** abnormal forms of bacteria arising through death of the cells and dissolution of their structure. **racemic f.** See *racemate.* **retention f.,** adaptation of the form of a tooth cavity in such a way as to help maintain the filling material in the cavity. **spherical f. of occlusion,** an arrangement of teeth which places their occlusal surfaces on the surface of an imaginary sphere (usually 8 inches in diameter) with its center above the level of the teeth. **tooth f.,** the characteristic curves, lines, angles, and contours of a tooth which permits it to be differentiated from other teeth and its identity to be established.

Formad's kidney (fōr'madz) [Henry F. *Formad,* American physician, 1847–1892]. See under *kidney.*

formaldehyde (fōr-mal'de-hīd). A powerfully disinfectant gas, HCHO, sometimes used as a disinfectant for rooms, clothing, etc. A 40 per cent solution of formaldehyde gas in water is widely used as a fixing fluid or preservative, and has also been used as a surgical and general antiseptic.

formaldehydogenic (for-mal″de-hīd″o-jen'ik) [*formaldehyde* + *-genic*]. Producing formaldehyde; pertaining to the production of formaldehyde by certain compounds when subjected to chemical reactions (i.e., steroids with α-ketol grouping in the C-17 position which on treatment with periodic acid liberate formaldehyde).

formalin (fōr'mah-lin). A 40 per cent solution of gaseous formaldehyde: used as an antiseptic and disinfectant in 1:2000 to 1:200 solutions, and as a fixing agent for histological specimens.

formalith (fōr'mah-lith). A porous block charged with solution of formaldehyde; disinfectant.

formalize (fōr'mal-īz). To treat with formaldehyde.

formant (fōr'mant). In phonology, the special partial tone of constant pitch for each vowel.

formate (fōr′māt). Any salt of formic acid.

formatio (for-ma′she-o), pl. *formatio′nes* [L.]. [N A, B N A] A general term designating a structure of definite shape. Called also *formation*. **f. al′ba,** the light-colored middle part of the formatio reticularis medullae spinalis. **f. bulla′ris,** the tissue composing the primary olfactory center in the olfactory bulb; that is, the glomeruli, granule cells, and mitral cells. **f. claustra′lis,** the fifth layer of the gray matter of the cerebral cortex. **f. gris′ea,** the darker-colored lateral part of the formatio reticularis medullae spinalis. **f. reticula′ris medul′lae oblonga′tae** [N A], the part of the medulla oblongata that fills the interspaces among the major nuclei and fiber tracts. It consists of intermingled fibers and gray substance, the latter often subdivided into specifically named nuclei. Called also *reticular formation of medulla oblongata*. **f. reticula′ris medul′lae spina′lis** [N A, B N A], a mixture of white and gray substance in the angle between the posterior horn and the lateral horn where the latter is present, and between the posterior and anterior horns elsewhere. Called also *reticular formation of spinal cord*. **f. reticula′ris mesenceph′ali** [N A], **f. reticula′ris pedun′culi cer′ebri** [B N A], the part of the cerebral peduncle that fills the interspaces among the major nuclei and fiber tracts. It is composed of intermingled fibers and gray substance. Called also *f. reticularis pedunculi cerebri* [B N A], and *reticular formation of mesencephalon*. **f. reticula′ris pon′tis** [N A, B N A], the part of the pars dorsalis of the pons that fills the interspaces among the major nuclei and fiber tracts. It consists of intermingled fibers and gray substance. Called also *reticular formation of pons*. **f. vermicula′ris,** the tonsilla and flocculus of the cerebellum considered as one structure (Bolk).

formation (fōr-ma′shun). 1. The process of giving shape or form; the creation of an entity, or of a structure of definite shape. 2. A structure of definite shape. See *formatio*. **coffin f.,** the surrounding of dead nerve cells by satellite cells in neuronophagia. **compromise f.,** the creation of an adjustment between a conscious intention and an unconscious opposing wish, producing the symptoms of a neurosis. **gray reticular f.,** substantia reticularis grisea. **palisade f.,** an arrangement in cells of glioma, the fusiform cells being arranged in compact manner pointing radially from a central area comparatively free of vessels. **reaction f.,** the development of attributes which hold in check and repress the unconscious components of infantile sexuality. **reticular f. of medulla oblongata,** formatio reticularis medullae oblongatae. **reticular f. of mesencephalon,** formatio reticularis mesencephali. **reticular f. of pons,** formatio reticularis pontis. **reticular f. of spinal cord,** formatio reticularis medullae spinalis. **rouleaux f.,** the aggregation of erythrocytes in structures resembling piles of coins, caused by adhesion of their flat surfaces. **spore f.,** sporulation. **white reticular f.,** substantia reticularis alba.

formative (fōr′mah-tiv). Concerned in the origination of an organism, part, or tissue.

formboard (fōrm′bōrd). A board containing variously shaped cut-outs into which blocks corresponding to the cut-outs are to be fitted: used as a test in mental deficiency.

forme (fōrm), pl. *formes* [Fr.]. Form. **f. fruste** (fōrm froost), pl. *formes frustes* [Fr. "defaced"], an atypical form, as of a disease. **f. tardive** (fōrm tahr-dēv′) [Fr. "late"], a late-occurring form of a disease that usually makes its appearance at an earlier age.

formication (fōr″mĭ-ka′shun) [L. *formica* ant]. A sensation as of small insects crawling over the skin.

formiciasis (for″mĭ-si′ah-sis) [L. *formica* ant]. A condition produced by poisoning resulting from ant bites.

formilase (fōr′mĭ-lās). A ferment which converts acetic acid into unstable formic acid.

formin (fōr′min). A brand of methenamine.

formol (fōr′mol). Formalin.

formolage (fōr″mo-lahzh′). Flushing hydatid cysts with a 2 per cent solution of formalin.

formose (fōr′mōs). A mixture of sugars having the formula $C_6H_{12}O_6$, formed by polymerizing sugar.

formula (fōr′mu-lah), pl. *formulas* or *formulae* [L., dim. of *forma* form]. A specific statement, using numerals and other symbols, of the composition of, or of the directions for preparing, a compound, such as a medicine, or of a procedure to follow for obtaining a desired value or result; a simplified statement, using numerals and symbols, of a single concept. See also *chemical formula*. **acoustic f.,** Brenner's f. **Ambard's f.,** a formula for finding the urea index (K) in kidney disease: $\frac{Ur}{\sqrt{D \times \frac{70}{P} \times \sqrt{\frac{C}{25}}}} = K$, in which Ur represents the proportion of urea in the blood; D, the total urea for twenty-four hours in grams; P, the body weight of the patient in kilograms; C, the proportion of urea in the urine. **antigenic f.,** an expression of the different components making up the antigenic structure of a bacterial cell. **Arneth's f.,** an expression of the normal ratio of different types of polymorphonuclear leukocytes, depending on the number of lobes (1 to 5) that the nucleus shows, which is as follows: 1 lobe, 5 per cent; 2 lobes, 35 per cent; 3 lobes, 41 per cent; 4 lobes, 17 per cent; 5 lobes, 2 per cent. **Arrhenius' f.,** $\log x = \theta_c$, in which x is the viscosity of the solution relative to that of the medium of suspension, c the percentage of volume occupied by the suspended particles, and θ a constant. **Beckmann's f.,** a formula used in cryoscopy, $M = KP/\triangle$, in which M is the molecular weight of dissolved substances, K the constant for each solvent, P the percentage strength of the solution, and $\triangle$ the lowering of the freezing point in degrees. **Bernhardt's f.,** the ideal weight of an adult in kilograms equals height in centimeters multiplied by chest circumference in centimeters divided by 240. **Bird's f.,** the last two figures expressive of the specific gravity of urine closely represent the number of grains of solids in each ounce. **Black's f.,** $F = (W + C) - H$. W represents the weight in pounds; C, the chest measurement in inches at full inspiration; and H, the height in inches. When F is over 120 a man is classed as very strong; between 110 and 120, strong; between 100 and 110, good; between 90 and 100, fair; between 80 and 90, weak; under 80, very weak. Cf. *Pignet's f.* **Brenner's f.,** with the cathode in the external meatus, a loud sound is heard on closing the circuit, intensity is diminished during closure, and the sound ceases when the circuit is broken. With the anode in the meatus, no sound is heard on closing or during closure; a weak sound is heard at the break. **Broca's f.,** the ideal weight of a full-grown man in kilograms equals the number of centimeters by which his height exceeds 1 meter. **chemical f.,** a combination of symbols used to express the chemical constitution of a substance. In practice, different types of formulas, of varying complexity, are employed. See *empirical f.*, *molecular f.*, *spatial f.*, *structural f.* **Christison's f.,** Trapp's f. **configurational f.,** spatial f. **constitutional f.,** structural f. **Demoivre's f.,** the expectation of life is equal to two thirds of the difference between the age of the person and eighty. **dental f.,** an expression in symbols of the arrangement of teeth in the jaws. The human dental formula is, for the 20 deciduous teeth, $i.\ \frac{2-2}{2-2}\ c.\ \frac{1-1}{1-1}\ m.\ \frac{2-2}{2-2}$, and, for the 32 permanent teeth, $i.\ \frac{2-2}{2-2}\ c.\ \frac{1-1}{1-1}\ pm.\ \frac{2-2}{2-2}\ m.\ \frac{3-3}{3-3}$, in which *c.* represents the canine, *i.* the incisor, *m.* the molar, and *pm.* the premolar teeth, and the upper and lower figures represent their number in the maxilla and mandible, respectively. **digital f.,** a formula expressing the relative lengths of the digits, usually $3 > 4 > 2 > 5 > 1$, or $3 > 2 > 4 > 5 > 1$, for the fingers, and $1 > 2 > 3 > 4 > 5$, or $2 > 1 > 3 > 4 > 5$, for the toes. **Dreser's f.,** a formula comparing the molecular concentration of the urine with that of the blood, to show the work done by the kidney. **Dreyer's f.,** a formula for expressing vital capacity of the lungs as a function of the body surface: $W^{0.72}/V.C. = K$, in which W is body weight; V. C., the vital capacity in cubic centimeters; and K a constant which at 0.69 represents 100 per cent fitness. **Du Bois' f.,** the surface area, O, is equal to $P^{0.425} \times L^{0.725} \times 71.84$, in which P represents weight, and L, height of the body. **Einthoven's f.,** $e^1 + e^3 \times e^2$. See *Einthoven's triangle,* under *triangle.* **electric f.,** a series of symbols expressing an electric reaction. **empirical f.,** a chemical formula which expresses the proportions of the elements present in a substance. For substances composed of discrete molecules, it expresses the relative numbers of atoms present in a molecule of the substance in the smallest whole numbers. For example, the *empirical formula* for ethane is written CH_3, whereas its actual *molecular formula* is C_2H_6. **Florschütz's f.,** L:(2B − L), in which L represents body length, and B, circumference of abdomen. An index of 5 is normal; an index below 5 indicates the degree of overweight. **Gale's f.,** pulse rate − pulse pressure − 111 closely represents the basal metabolic rate. **graphic f.,** a term occasionally used to describe a "complete" structural formula, i.e., one in which every individual atom and bond is represented in the formula. The distinction is made because structural formulas are frequently written in a simplified or shortened form. See *structural f.* **Guthrie's f.,** the ideal weight of an adult in pounds equals 110 + (5.5 × number of inches body height exceeds five feet). **Haines' f.,** the product obtained by multiplying the last two digits of the number expressing its specific gravity by 1.1 (Haines' coefficient) closely represents the number of grains of solids in one fluid ounce of urine. **Häser's f.,** the product obtained by multiplying the last two digits of the number expressing its specific gravity by 2.33 (Häser's coefficient) closely represents the number of grains of solids in 1,000 ml. of urine. **Katz f.,** the average erythrocyte sedimentation rate equals $\left(S_1 + \frac{S_2}{2}\right) / 2$, in which S_1 is the height in mm. of the column of clear fluid at the end of one hour, and S_2 its height at the end of two hours. **Loebisch's f.,** the product obtained by multiplying the last two digits of the number expressing its specific gravity by 2.2 (Loebisch's coefficient) closely represents the number of grains of solids in 1,000 ml. of urine. **Long's f.,** the product obtained by multiplying the last two digits of the number expressing its specific gravity by 2.6 (Long's coefficient) closely represents the number of grains of solids in 1,000 ml. of urine. **Mall's f.,** the age (in days) of an embryo is equal to the square root of its length (in millimeters) from vertex to breech multiplied by 100. **McLean's f.,** a modification of Ambard's formula for finding the urea index in kidney disease:

$$\frac{\text{gm. urea per 24 hrs.} \sqrt{\text{gm. urea per L. of urine}} \times 8.96}{\text{weight in kilos} \times (\text{gm. urea per L. of blood})^2}.$$

Meeh's f., the surface area, *O*, is equal to $K\sqrt[3]{P^2}$, in which *K* is a constant (12.3), and *P* is the weight of the body. **molecular f.,** a chemical formula giving the number of atoms of each element present in a molecule of a substance, without indicating how they are linked up. **paretic f.,** the findings in the cerebrospinal fluid characteristic of dementia paralytica. They are normal or slightly increased pressure; moderate pleocytosis; moderate increase in protein; change in the colloidal gold test; and positive cerebrospinal fluid Wassermann test. **Pignet's f.,** F = H − (C + W). *H* represents the height in centimeters; *C,* the chest measurement in centimeters at greatest expiration; and *W,* the weight in kilograms. When *F* is less than 10 a person is classed as very strong; between 10 and 15, strong; between 15 and 20, good; between 20 and 25, medium; between 25 and 30, weak; above 30, very weak. Cf. *Black's f.* **Poisson-Pearson f.,** a formula for calculating the percentage of error in determining the endemic index of malaria: $\frac{200}{n}\sqrt{\frac{2 \times (n - x)}{n}}\sqrt{1 - \frac{n-1}{N-1}}$, in which *N* is number of children under fifteen years in the locality; *n,* the number examined for the spleen rate; *x,* the number having enlarged spleens; and *x/n* is the spleen rate. **projection f.,** a planar, and therefore simplified, representation of a spatial formula. **psychobiologic f.,** Meyer's term for the steps in studying and dealing with psychic disorders: What are the facts? Under what conditions do they occur? What are the factors in their working, and how do they group themselves? What are the results? How far are they modifiable? How can they be reconstructed and brought to a test? **Ranke's f.,** the number expressive of the specific gravity − 1000 × 0.52 − 5.406 closely represents the amount in grams of the albumin per liter of a serous fluid. **rational f.,** structural f. **Read's f.,** 0.75 × pulse rate + 0.75 × pulse pressure − 72 closely represents the basal metabolic rate. **Reuss' f.,** $\frac{3}{8}(S - 1000) - 2.8$, in which *S* is the specific gravity, closely represents the percentage of albumin present in a pathologic fluid exudate or transudate. **Rollier's f.,** a formula for gradually increasing exposure of the body to ultraviolet rays of the sun. **Runeberg's f.,** a modification of Reuss' formula in which 2.8 is replaced by 2.73 in case of a transudate and by 2.88 in case of an inflammatory exudate. **spatial f.,** a chemical formula giving the numbers of atoms of each element present in a molecule of a substance, which atom is linked to which, the types of linkages involved, and the relative positions of the atoms in space. **stereochemical f.,** spatial f. **structural f.,** a chemical formula

```
    H  H
    |  |
H—C—C—O—H          C2H5OH
    |  |
    H  H
"Complete"         "Abbreviated"
```

Structural formulas for ethyl alcohol.

telling how many atoms of each element are present in a molecule of a substance, which atom is linked to which, and the type of linkages involved. For convenience, abbreviated structural formulas are sometimes used. Called also *constitutional f.* and *graphic f.* **Trapp's f.,** the product obtained by multiplying the last two digits of the number expressing its specific gravity by 2 (Trapp's coefficient) closely represents the number of grains of solids in 1,000 ml. of urine. **Van Slyke's f.,** the urinary coefficient of various substances is equal to $D/(Bl \times \sqrt{Wt \times V})$, in which *D* is the daily output in grams of the substance in the urine; *Bl,* the grams of the same substance per liter of blood; *Wt,* the weight of the patient in kilograms; and *V,* the total volume of urine in twenty-four hours. **vertebral f.,** an expression in symbols of the number of vertebrae in each region of the spinal column. For man it is $C_7T_{12}L_5S_5Cd_4 = 33$. **Vierordt-Mesh f.,** the body surface, *O,* is equal to $mP^{\frac{2}{3}}$, in which *m* represents the height, and *P* the weight.

formulary (fŏr′mu-lār″e). A collection of recipes, formulas, and prescriptions. **National F.,** a book of standards for certain pharmaceutics and preparations which are not included in the U. S. Pharmacopeia. It is compiled by a Committee of the American Pharmaceutical Association, and is recognized as a book of official standards by the Pure Food and Drugs Act of 1906.

formyl (fŏr′mil) [L. *formic* + Gr. *hylē* matter]. The radical, CHO or H.C:O—, of formic acid. **f.**

phenetidin, colorless crystals, para-ethoxyformanilid, $C_2H_5O.C_6H_4.NH.COH$: antiseptic and analgesic. **f. piperidine,** an oily liquid with an aromatic, agreeable odor, produced from formamide and piperidine.

Fornet's reaction (fōr-nāz′) [Walter *Fornet*, German physician, born 1877]. See under *reaction*.

fornicate (fōr′nĭ-kāt). 1. [L. *fornicatus* arched]. Shaped like an arch. 2. [L. *fornix*, a brothel]. To engage in illicit sexual intercourse.

fornicolumn (fōr′nĭ-kol″um). The anterior pillar of the fornix cerebri.

fornicommissure (fōr″nĭ-kom′ĭ-sūr). The commissure of the fornix vaginae.

fornix (for′niks), pl. *for′nices* [L. "arch"]. [N A, B N A] A general term designating an archlike structure or the vaultlike space created by such a structure. **anterior f.** See *f. vaginae.* **f. cer′ebri** [N A, B N A], **f. of cerebrum,** an arched fiber tract having two lateral halves that are united under the corpus callosum and separate at either end. It comprises two columns, a body, and two crura. **f. conjuncti′vae infe′rior** [N A, B N A], the inferior line of reflection of the conjunctiva from the eyelid to the eyeball. Called also *inferior conjunctival f.* **f. conjuncti′vae supe′rior** [N A, B N A], the superior line of reflection of the conjunctiva from the eyelid to the eyeball. It receives the openings of the lacrimal duct. Called also *superior conjunctival f.* **f. pharyn′gis** [N A, B N A], **f. of pharynx,** the vault of the pharynx. **posterior f.** See *f. vaginae.* **f. sac′ci lacrima′lis** [N A, B N A], the upper, blind extremity of the lacrimal sac. Called also *f. of lacrimal sac.* **f. vagi′nae** [N A, B N A], the recess formed between the vaginal wall and the vaginal part of the cervix; sometimes spoken of as *anterior f.* or *posterior f.*, depending on its relation to the anterior or posterior wall of the vagina.

foroblique (fōr″ob-lek′). A registered trade-mark designating an obliquely forward visual telescopic system used in certain cystoscopes.

Forssell's sinus (fōr′selz) [Gösta *Forssell*, Swedish radiologist, 1876–1950]. See under *sinus*.

Forssman's antigen (fōrs′manz) [John *Forssman*, Swedish pathologist, 1868–1947]. See under *antigen*.

Forssmann (fors′man), Werner Theodor Otto. German surgeon, born 1904; co-winner, with André F. Cournand and Dickinson W. Richards, of the Nobel prize in medicine and physiology for 1956, for developing new techniques in the diagnosis and treatment of heart disease.

Förster's choroiditis, disease, photometer (fers′terz) [Richard *Förster*, German ophthalmologist, 1825–1902]. See under *choroiditis* and *photometer*.

Förster's operation (fers′terz) [Otfried *Förster*, German neurologist, 1873–1941]. See under *operation*.

Förster-Penfield operation (fers′ter-pen′fēld) [Otfried *Förster;* Wilder *Penfield*, American neurosurgeon, born 1891]. See under *operation*.

forthane (for′thān). Trade mark for a preparation of methylhexaneamine.

fortuitous (fōr-tu′ĭ-tus). Pertaining to chance.

Foshay's serum [Lee *Foshay*, American bacteriologist, born 1896]. See under *serum*.

fossa (fos′sah), pl. *fos′sae* [L.]. A trench or channel; used in anatomical nomenclature as a general term to denote a hollow or depressed area. **acetabular f., f. acetab′uli** [N A, B N A], a rough non-articular area in the floor of the acetabulum above the acetabular notch. **adipose fossae,** spaces in the female breast, just beneath the skin, which contain fat. **Allen's f.,** a fossa on the neck of the femur. **amygdaloid f.,** the depression between the pillars of the fauces, on either side, which lodges the tonsil. **anconal f., anconeal f.,** f. olecrani. **antecubital f.,** f. cubitalis. **f. anthel′icis** [N A, B N A], **f. of anthelix,** the depression on the medial surface of the auricle that corresponds to the anthelix on the lateral surface. **articular f. of atlas, inferior,** fovea articularis inferior atlantis. **articular f. of atlas, superior,** fovea articularis superior atlantis. **articular f. of mandible,** f. mandibularis. **articular f. for odontoid process of axis,** fovea dentis atlantis. **articular f. of temporal bone,** f. mandibularis. **f. axilla′ris** [N A, B N A], **axillary f.,** the small hollow, underneath the arm, where it joins the body at the shoulder. Called also *axilla.* **Biesiadecki's f.,** f. iliacosubfascialis. **Broesike's f.,** parajejunal f. **f. caeca′lis** [B N A], a peritoneal recess at the beginning of the colon. Omitted in N A. **f. cani′na** [N A, B N A], **canine f.,** a wide depression on the external surface of the maxilla superolateral to the canine tooth socket. The levator anguli oris muscle arises from it. **f. capitel′li,** the depression for the head of the malleus. **f. cap′itis fem′oris,** fovea capitis femoris. **f. carot′ica** [B N A], trigonum caroticum. **cerebellar f.,** f. cranii posterior. **cerebral f.,** any one of the depressions on the floor of the cranial cavity. See *f. cranii anterior, f. cranii media,* and *f. cranii posterior.* **f. cer′ebri latera′lis [Syl′vii]** [B N A], f. lateralis cerebri. **f. chor′dae duc′tus veno′si,** f. ductus venosi. **Claudius' f.,** ovarian f. **cochleariform f.,** semicanalis musculi tensoris tympani. **condylar f., f. condyla′ris** [N A], **condyloid f.,** either of two pits situated on the lateral portions of the occipital bone, one on either side of the foramen magnum, posterior to the occipital condyle. Called also *f. condyloidea* [B N A]. **condyloid f., posterior,** f. condylaris. **condyloid f. of atlas,** fovea articularis superior atlantis. **condyloid f. of mandible,** f. mandibularis. **condyloid f. of temporal bone,** f. mandibularis. **f. condyloi′dea** [B N A], f. condylaris. **coronoid f. of humerus, f. coronoi′dea hu′meri** [N A, B N A], the cavity in the humerus that receives the coronoid process of the ulna. **f. of coronoid process,** f. coronoidea humeri. **costal f., inferior,** fovea costalis inferior. **costal f., superior,** fovea costalis superior. **costal f., transverse,** fovea costalis transversalis. **cranial f., anterior,** f. cranii anterior. **cranial f., middle,** f. cranii media. **cranial f., posterior,** f. cranii posterior. **f. cra′nii ante′rior** [N A, B N A], the anterior subdivision of the floor of the cranial cavity, supporting the frontal lobes of the brain. **f. cra′nii me′dia** [N A, B N A], the middle subdivision of the floor of the cranial cavity, supporting the temporal lobes of the brain and the hypophysis. **f. cra′nii poste′rior** [N A, B N A], the posterior subdivision of the floor of the cranial cavity, supporting the cerebellum, pons, and medulla oblongata. **cribriform f.,** tuberositas sacralis. **crural f.,** anulus femoralis. **cubital f.** 1. Fossa cubitalis. 2. Fossa coronoidea humeri. **f. cubita′lis** [N A, B N A], the depression in the anterior region of the elbow. **f. cys′tidis fel′leae,** f. vesicae felleae. **digastric f., f. digas′trica** [N A, B N A], a depression on the posterior surface of the base of the mandible on each side of the symphysis to which is attached the anterior belly of the digastric muscle. **digital f. of femur,** f. trochanterica. **digital f., inferior,** anulus femoralis. **digital f., superior,** f. inguinalis medialis. **f. duc′tus veno′si** [N A, B N A], **f. of ductus venosus,** an impression on the posterior part of the diaphragmatic surface of the liver in the fetus, lodging the ductus venosus. **duodenal f., inferior,** recessus duodenalis inferior. **duodenal f., superior,** recessus duodenalis superior. **duodenojejunal f.,** recessus duodenalis superior. **epigastric f.** 1. Fossa epigastrica. 2. The urachal fossa. **f. epigas′trica** [N A], a fossa in the epigastric region. Called also *scrobiculus cordis* [B N A]. **ethmoid f.,** a groove situated in the cribriform plate of the ethmoid bone in which lodges the olfactory lobe of the brain. **f. of eustachian tube,** f. scaphoidea ossis sphenoidalis. **femoral f.,** anulus femoralis. **floccular f.,** f. subarcuata ossis temporalis. **f. of gallbladder,** f. vesicae felleae. **f. of gasserian ganglion,** impressio trigemini ossis temporalis. **Gerdy's hyoid f.,** superior carotid triangle. **f. glan'dulae lacrima'lis** [N A, B N A], a shallow depression in the lateral part of the roof of the orbit, lodging the lacrimal gland. Called also *lacrimal f.* **glandular f. of frontal bone,** f. glandulae lacrimalis. **glenoid f.,** f. mandibularis. **glenoid f. of scapula,** cavitas glenoidalis. **glenoid f. of temporal bone,** f. mandibularis. **greater f. of Scarpa,** trigonum femorale. **Gruber's f.,** a diverticulum in the suprasternal space alongside of the inner end of the clavicle. **Gruber-Landzert f.,** a recess in the peritoneum in the same situation as the duodenojejunal fossa, but extending downward behind the duodenojejunal angle. **harderian f.,** the depression in which the harderian glands are lodged. **Hartmann's f.,** f. ileocecalis infima. **f. of head of femur,** fovea capitis femoris. **f. hel'icis,** scapha. **f. hemiellip'tica,** recessus ellipticus vestibuli. **f. hemisphe'rica,** recessus sphericus vestibuli. **hyaloid f., f. hyaloi'dea** [N A, B N A], a depression on the anterior surface of the vitreous body, in which the lens is lodged. Called also *lenticular f. of vitreous body.* **hypogastric f.,** a depression on the interior surface of the anterior abdominal wall, between the hypogastric folds. **hypophyseal f., f. hypophys'eos** [B N A], **f. hypophysia'lis** [N A], a deep depression in the middle of the sella turcica of the sphenoid bone, lodging the hypophysis cerebri. **ileocecal f., inferior,** recessus ileocecalis inferior. **ileocecal f., superior,** recessus ileocecalis superior. **f. ileoceca'lis infi'ma,** a peritoneal recess between the meso-appendix and Tuffier's inferior ligament. **ileocolic f.,** recessus ileocecalis superior. **iliac f., f. ili'aca** [N A, B N A], a large, smooth concave area occupying much of the inner surface of the ala of the ilium, especially anteriorly. From it arises the iliacus muscle. **iliacosubfascial f., f. iliacosubfascia'lis** [B N A], a depression on the inner surface of the abdomen between the psoas muscle and the crest of the ilium. Omitted in N A. **f. iliopecti'nea** [B N A], **iliopectineal f.,** a depression between the iliopsoas and pectineus muscles in the center of Scarpa's triangle. Omitted in N A. **incisive f. of maxilla,** a depression in the maxilla above the incisor teeth. **incudal f., f. incu'dis** [N A, B N A], **f. of incus,** a groove in the posterior wall of the tympanic cavity, lodging the short limb of the incus. **infraclavicular f.,** trigonum deltoideopectorale. **infraduodenal f.,** a recess in the peritoneum below the third portion of the duodenum. **f. infraspina'ta** [N A, B N A], **infraspinous f.,** the lower of two recesses on the dorsal surface of the scapula. **infratemporal f., f. infratempora'lis** [N A, B N A], the area on the side of the cranium limited superiorly by the infratemporal crest, posteriorly by the mandibular fossa, anteriorly by the infratemporal surface of the maxilla, and laterally by the zygomatic arch and part of the ramus of the mandible. **inguinal f., external,** f. inguinalis lateralis. **inguinal f., internal,** f. inguinalis medialis. **inguinal f., lateral,** f. inguinalis lateralis. **inguinal f., medial, inguinal f., middle,** f. inguinalis medialis. **f. inguina'lis latera'lis** [N A], the depression on the inside of the anterior abdominal wall lateral to the lateral umbilical fold. Called also *lateral inguinal f.* and *fovea inguinalis lateralis* [B N A]. **f. inguina'lis media'lis** [N A], the depression on the inside of the anterior abdominal wall between the medial and lateral umbilical folds. Called also *medial inguinal f.* and *fovea inguinalis medialis* [B N A]. **innominate f. of auricle,** cavum conchae. **intercondylar f. of femur,** f. intercondylaris femoris. **intercondylar f. of femur, anterior,** facies patellaris femoris. **intercondylar f. of tibia, anterior,** area intercondylaris anterior tibiae. **intercondylar f. of tibia, posterior,** area intercondylaris posterior tibiae. **f. intercondyla'ris fem'oris** [N A], the posterior depression between the condyles of the femur. Called also *intercondylar f. of femur* and *f. intercondyloidea femoris* [B N A]. **f. intercondyl'ica,** f. intercondylaris femoris. **intercondyloid f.** See *f. intercondylaris femoris, area intercondylaris anterior tibiae,* and *area intercondylaris posterior tibiae.* **f. intercondyloi'dea ante'rior tib'iae** [B N A], area intercondylaris anterior tibiae. **f. intercondyloi'dea fem'oris** [B N A], f. intercondylaris femoris. **f. intercondyloi'dea poste'rior tib'iae** [B N A], area intercondylaris posterior tibiae. **intercrura'lis f.,** f. interpeduncularis. **f. intermesocol'ica transver'sa,** a recess of the peritoneum in the same situation as the duodenojejunal fossa, but extending transversely. **interpeduncular f., f. interpeduncula'ris** [N A], **f. interpeduncula'ris [Tarini]** [B N A], a depression on the inferior surface of the mesencephalon, between the two cerebral peduncles, the floor of which is the posterior perforated substance. **intersigmoid f.,** recessus intersigmoideus. **ischiorectal f., f. ischiorecta'lis** [N A, B N A], the potential space between the pelvic diaphragm and the skin below it. An anterior recess extends a variable distance between the pelvic and urogenital diaphragms, sometimes reaching the retropubic space. **Jobert's f.,** the fossa in the popliteal region bounded above by the adductor magnus and below by the gracilis and sartorius, best seen when the knee is bent and the thigh strongly rotated outward. **f. of Jonnesco,** recessus duodenalis superior. **jugular f., f. jugula'ris** [B N A], the depression at the base of the neck just above the sternum. Omitted in N A. **jugular f. of temporal bone, f. jugula'ris os'sis tempora'lis** [N A, B N A], a prominent depression on the inferior surface of the petrous part of the temporal bone, forming the major part of the jugular notch. It forms the anterior and lateral wall of the jugular foramen and lodges the superior bulb of the internal jugular vein. **lacerate f.,** an irregularly shaped opening in the orbit just above the disphenoid. **lacrimal f.** 1. Fossa glandulae lacrimalis. 2. Sulcus lacrimalis ossis lacrimalis. **f. of lacrimal gland,** f. glandulae lacrimalis. **f. of lacrimal sac,** f. sacci lacrimalis. **Landzert's f.,** a fossa formed by two folds of peritoneum enclosing the left colic artery and the inferior mesenteric vein at the side of the duodenum. **lateral f. of cerebrum,** f. lateralis cerebri. **f. of lateral malleolus,** f. malleoli lateralis. **f. latera'lis cer'ebri** [N A], a depression, in fetal life, on the lateral surface of each cerebral hemisphere at the bottom of which lies the insula; later it is closed over by the operculum, the edges of which form the lateral sulcus. Called also *f. cerebri lateralis* [*Sylvii*] [B N A]. **lenticular f.,** f. hyaloidea. **lesser f. of Scarpa,** f. iliopectinea. **f. for ligamentum teres,** fissura ligamenti teretis. **f. of little head of radius.** 1. Fossa coronoidea humeri. 2. Fovea capituli radii. **longitudinal fossae of liver, right,** fossae sagittales dextrae hepatis. **f. longitudina'lis hep'atis,** f. sagittalis sinistra hepatis. **Luschka's f.,** recessus ileocecalis superior. **Malgaigne's f.,** the superior carotid triangle. **f. malle'oli latera'lis** [N A], a depression on the medial aspect of the lateral malleolus behind its articular surface. Called also *f. of lateral malleolus.* **mandibular f., f. mandibula'ris** [N A, B N A], a prominent depression in the inferior surface of the squamous part of the temporal bone at the base of the zygomatic process, in which the condyloid process of the mandible rests. **mastoid f. of temporal bone,** f. subarcuata ossis temporalis. **maxillary f.,** f. canina. **mesentericoparietal f.,** parajejunal f. **mesocranial f.,** f. cranii media. **mesogastric f.,** recessus duodenalis superior. **middle cranial f.,** f. cranii media. **Mohrenheim's f.,** trigonum deltoideopectorale. **f. of Morgagni,** f. navicularis urethrae. **f. mus'culi biven'teris,** f. digastrica. **mylohyoid f. of mandible,** fovea sublingualis. **myrtiform f.,** f. praenasalis. **nasal f.,** the portion of the nasal cavity anterior to the middle meatus. **navicular f. of Cruveilhier,** f. scaphoidea ossis sphenoidalis. **navicular f. of male urethra,** f. navicularis urethrae. **navicular f. of sphenoid bone,** f. scaphoidea ossis sphenoidalis. **f. navicula'ris ure'thrae** [N A], **f. navicula'ris ure'thrae [Morgag'nii]** [B N A], the lateral expansion of the urethra in the glans penis. **f. navicula'ris [vestib'uli vagi'nae]** [B N A], f. vestibuli vaginae. **occipital f., inferior,** f. cranii media. **occipital f., superior,** f. cranii posterior. **f. occipita'lis cerebra'lis,** f. lateralis cerebri. **f. olec'rani** [N A, B N A], **olecranon f.,** a depression on the posterior surface of the humerus, above the trochlea, for lodging the olecranon of the ulna. **olfactory f.,** a depression on the inner surface of the cranium for the olfactory lobes. **f. of omental sac, inferior,** recessus inferior omentalis. **f. of omental sac, superior,** recessus superior omentalis. **oral f.,** stomodeum. **oval f. of heart,** fossa ovalis cordis. **oval f. of thigh,** hiatus saphenus. **f. ova'lis,** recessus ellipticus vestibuli. **f. ova'lis cor'dis** [N A, B N A], a depression on the right side of the interatrial septum of the heart, representing the remains of the fetal foramen ovale. **f. ova'lis fem'oris** [B N A], hiatus saphenus. **ovarian f., f. ova'rica,** a shallow pouch on the posterior surface of the broad ligament, in which the ovary is located. **paraduodenal f.,** recessus duodenalis superior. **parajejunal f.,** a pouch of peritoneum below the lower end of the first part of the jejunum. **parietal f.,** the deepest portion of the inner surface of the parietal bone. **patellar f.,** f. hyaloidea. **patellar f. of femur,** facies patellaris femoris. **patellar f. of tibia,** area intercondylaris anterior tibiae. **perineal f.,** f. ischiorectalis. **petrosal f., f. for petrosal ganglion,** fossula petrosa. **piriform f.,** recessus piriformis. **pituitary f.,** f. hypophysialis. **f. poplit'ea** [N A, B N A], **popliteal f.,** the depression in the posterior region of the knee. **popliteal f. of femur,** f. intercondylaris femoris. **popliteal f. of tibia,** area intercondylaris posterior tibiae. **postcondyloid f.,** f. condylaris. **posterior f. of humerus,** f. olecrani. **f. praenasalis** [B N A], **prenasal f.,** the incisive fossa of the maxilla. Omitted in N A. **prescapular f., prespinous f.,** a depression in the anterior surface of the spine of the scapula. **f. provesica'lis,** f. ileocecalis infima. **pterygoid f. of inferior maxillary bone,** fovea pterygoidea mandibulae. **pterygoid f. of sphenoid bone, f. pterygoi'dea os'sis sphenoida'lis** [N A, B N A], the posteriorly facing fossa which is formed by the divergence of the medial and lateral pterygoid plates of the sphenoid bone, and lodges the internal pterygoid and tensor veli palatini muscles. **pterygomaxillary f.,** f. pterygopalatina. **f. pterygopalati'na** [N A, B N A], **pterygopalatine f.,** a small depression between the front of the root of the pterygoid process of the sphenoid bone and the back of the maxilla. **radial f. of humerus, f. radia'lis hu'meri** [N A, B N A], a depression on the anterior surface of the humerus just above the capitulum. **retrocecal f.,** recessus retrocecalis. **retroduodenal f.,** a pouch of peritoneum below and behind the third portion of the duodenum. **retromandibular f., f. retromandibula'ris** [B N A], the depression behind the angle of the jaw, on either side, beneath the auricle. Omitted in N A. **rhomboid f., f. rhomboi'dea** [N A, B N A], the floor of the fourth ventricle of the brain, made up of the dorsal surfaces of the medulla and pons. **Rosenmüller's f.,** recessus pharyngeus. **f. sac'ci lacrima'lis** [N A, B N A], the fossa that lodges the lacrimal sac, formed by the lacrimal sulcus of the lacrimal bone and the frontal process of the maxilla. **fossae sagitta'les dex'trae hep'atis** [B N A], a longitudinal fissure in the right lobe of the liver. Omitted in N A. **fossae sagitta'les hep'atis,** f. sagittalis sinistra hepatis. **f. sagitta'lis sinis'tra hep'atis** [B N A], a longitudinal fissure in the left lobe of the liver. Omitted in N A. **scaphoid f., f. scaphoi'dea.** 1. Scapha. 2. Fossa triangularis auriculae. **scaphoid f. of sphenoid bone, f. scaphoi'dea os'sis sphenoida'lis** [N A, B N A], a depression on the superior part of the posterior portion of the medial plate of the pterygoid process of the sphenoid bone, giving attachment to the tensor veli palatini muscle. **f. scar'pae ma'jor** [B N A], trigonum femorale. **sellar f.,** f. hypophysialis. **semilunar f. of ulna,** incisura trochlearis ulnae. **sigmoid f.,** sulcus sinus transversi. **sigmoid f. of temporal bone,** sulcus sinus sigmoidei ossis temporalis. **sigmoid f. of ulna,** incisura trochlearis ulnae. **sigmoid f. of ulna, lesser,** incisura radialis ulnae. **sphenoidal f.,** apertura sinus sphenoidalis. **sphenomaxillary f.,** f. pterygopalatina. **splenic f. of omental sac,** recessus lienalis. **f. subarcua'ta os'sis tempora'lis** [N A, B N A], **subarcuate f. of temporal bone,** a small fossa on the internal surface of the petrous part of the temporal bone just below the arcuate eminence, most prominent in the fetus. In the adult it lodges a piece of dura and transmits a small vein. **subcecal f.,** recessus ileocecalis inferior. **f. subinguina'lis** [B N A], a depression in the anterior surface of the thigh beneath the groin. Omitted in N A. **sublingual f.,** fovea sublingualis. **submandibular f.,** fovea submandibularis. **submaxillary f.,** fovea submandibularis. **subpyramidal f.,** a fossa on the internal wall of the middle ear, behind the round window and below the pyramid. **subscapular f., f. subscapula'ris** [N A, B N A], the concave ventral surface of the body of the scapula. **subsigmoid f.,** a fossa between the mesentery of the sigmoid flexure and that of the descending colon. **supraclavicular f., greater,** f. supraclavicularis major. **supraclavicular f., lesser,** f. supraclavicularis minor. **f. supraclavicula'ris ma'jor** [N A, B N A], a depression on the surface of the body, located above and behind the clavicle, lateral to the tendon of the sternocleidomastoid muscle. **f. supraclavicula'ris mi'nor** [N A, B N A], the region of the neck in the depression behind the clavicle, about the interval between the two tendons of the sternocleidomastoid muscle. Called also *lesser supraclavicular fossa* and *Zang's space*. **supracondyloid f.,** a depression on the femur between the internal tuberosity and the internal supracondyloid tubercle. **supramastoid f.,** a small depression at the junction of the posterior and superior borders of the external auditory canal. **suprasphenoidal f.,** f. hypophysialis. **f. supraspina'ta** [N A, B N A], **supraspinous f.,** the upper of two recesses on the dorsal surface of the scapula. **supratonsillar f., f. supratonsilla'ris** [N A, B N A], the space between the palatoglossal and palatopharyngeal arches above the tonsil. **supratrochlear f., posterior,** f. olecrani. **supravesical f., f. supravesica'lis** [N A], the depression on the inside of the anterior abdominal wall between the median and the medial umbilical fold. Called also *fovea supravesicalis peritonaei* [B N A]. **sylvian f., f. of Sylvius.** 1. Fossa lateralis cerebri. 2. Sulcus lateralis cerebri. **Tarin's f.,** f. interpeduncularis. **temporal f.** 1. Fossa temporalis. 2. Fossa cranii media. **f. tempora'lis** [N A, B N A], the area on the side of the cranium outlined posteriorly and superiorly by the temporal lines, anteriorly by the frontal and zygomatic bones, laterally by the zygomatic arch, and inferiorly by the infratemporal crest. **terminal f.,** f. navicularis urethrae. **tibiofemoral f.,** a palpable space between the articular surfaces of the tibia and femur mesial (internal tibiofemoral f.) or lateral (external tibiofemoral f.) to the inferior pole of the patella. **tonsillar f., f. tonsilla′ris** [N A], the depression between the palatoglossal and palatopharyngeal arches in which the palatine tonsil is located. Called also *sinus tonsillaris* [B N A]. **f. transversa′lis hep′atis,** porta hepatis. **f. of Treitz,** recessus duodenalis superior. **triangular f. of auricle, f. triangular′is auric′ulae** [N A, B N A], the cavity just above the concha of the ear between the crura of the anthelix. **trochanteric f., f. trochanter′ica** [N A, B N A], a deep depression on the medial surface of the greater trochanter that receives the insertion of the tendon of the obturator externus muscle. **trochlear f., f. trochlea′ris,** fovea trochlearis. **ulnar f.,** f. coronoidea humeri. **umbilical f., medial,** f. inguinalis medialis. **f. umbilica′lis hep′atis,** fissura ligamenti teretis. **urachal f.,** a depression on the inner surface of the anterior abdominal wall, between the urachus and the hypogastric artery. **f. ve′nae ca′vae** [B N A], sulcus venae cavae. **f. ve′nae umbilica′lis** [B N A], fissura ligamenti teretis. **f. veno′sa,** a fold of peritoneum situated at the duodenojejunal angle. **f. vesi′cae fel′leae** [N A, B N A], the fossa on the posteroinferior surface of the liver that lodges the gallbladder. It helps separate the left and right lobes. Called also *f. of gallbladder.* **vestibular f., f. of vestibule of vagina, f. vestib′uli vagi′nae** [N A], the part of the vestibule between the orifice of the vagina and the frenulum of the pudendal labia. Called also *f. navicularis vestibuli vaginae* [B N A]. **Waldeyer's f.,** the recessus duodenalis inferior and recessus duodenalis superior considered as one space. **zygomatic f.,** f. infratemporalis.

fossae (fos′e) [L.]. Plural of *fossa.*

fossette (fos-set′) [Fr.]. 1. A small depression. 2. A small and deep corneal ulcer.

fossula (fos′su-lah), pl. *fos′sulae* [L., dim. of *fossa*]. A small fossa; used in anatomical nomenclature as a general term to designate a slight depression in the surface of a structure or organ. **f. of cochlear window,** f. fenestrae cochleae. **costal f., inferior,** fovea costalis inferior. **costal f., superior,** fovea costalis superior. **f. fenes′trae coch′leae** [N A, B N A], a depression on the medial wall of the tympanic cavity, at the bottom of which is the fenestra cochleae. Called also *f. of cochlear* or *round window.* **f. fenes′trae vestib′uli** [N A, B N A], a depression on the medial wall of the tympanic cavity, at the bottom of which is the fenestra vestibuli. Called also *f. of vestibular* or *oval window.* **f. petro′sa** [N A, B N A], **petrosal f., f. of petrous ganglion,** a small depression on the under surface of the petrous portion of the temporal bone, on a small ridge separating the jugular fossa from the external carotid foramen. **f. post fenes′tram,** a connective tissue tract just behind the oval window, resembling the fissula ante fenestram, but smaller and less constant. **tonsillar fossulae of palatine tonsil,** fossulae tonsillares tonsillae palatinae. **tonsillar fossulae of pharyngeal tonsil,** fossulae tonsillares tonsillae pharyngeae. **fos′sulae tonsilla′res ton′sillae palati′nae** [N A, B N A], the mouths of the tonsillar crypts of the palatine tonsils. **fos′sulae tonsilla′res ton′sillae pharyn′geae** [N A, B N A], the mouths of the tonsillar crypts of the pharyngeal tonsil

fossulae (fos′u-le) [L.]. Plural of *fossula.*

fossulate (fos′u-lāt). Marked by a small fossa; hollowed or grooved.

Fothergill's disease, neuralgia, pill (foth′er-gilz) [John *Fothergill,* English physician, 1712–1780]. See *scarlatina anginosa, trigeminal neuralgia,* and under *pill.*

Fouchet's test (foo-shāz′) [A. *Fouchet,* French physician]. See under *tests.*

foudroyant (foo″drah-yaw′) [Fr.]. Fulminant.

foulage (foo-lahzh′) [Fr. "treading, pressing of grapes"]. Massage in which the muscles are kneaded and pressed.

foul brood (fowl-brood). A contagious disease of honey bees caused by *Bacillus alvei.*

foundation (foun-da′shun). The structure or basis on which something is built. **denture f.,** the portion of the structures and tissues of the mouth that is available to support a denture.

founder (fown′der). The crippled condition of a horse afflicted with laminitis. **chest f.,** founder accompanied by atrophy of the chest muscles. **grain f.,** a condition of indigestion or overloaded stomach in the horse due to overeating.

fourchette (foor-shet′) [Fr. "a fork-shaped object"]. Frenulum labiorum pudendi.

Fourneau 190 [foor-no′) [Earnest François Auguste *Fourneau,* French physician, 1872–1949]. Stovarsol. **F. 270,** tryparsamide. **F. 309,** suramin sodium. **F. 664,** a synthetic organic compound closely resembling plasmochin and used in the treatment of malaria. It is 8-(3-diethylamino-2,2-dimethylpropyl-amino)-6-methoxy-quinoline, $CH_3O.C_8H_5N.NH.CH_2.C(CH_3)_2CH_2.N(C_2H_5)_2$. **F. 693,** pamaquine. **F. 710,** neostibosan. **F. 883,** 2-diethylamino-ethyl-1,4-benzodioxan: it is adrenolytic. **F. 993,** an adrenolytic drug, 2-piperidinomethyl-1,4-benzodioxan. **F. 1262,** a drug that slows heart action and lowers blood pressure, 2-diethylamino-ethoxydiphenyl.

Fournier's disease, sign, test (foor-ne-āz′) [Jean Alfred *Fournier,* dermatologist in Paris, 1832–1914]. See under the nouns.

fovea (fo′ve-ah), pl. *fo′veae* [L.]. A pit or depression; used in anatomical nomenclature as a general term to denote a small pit in the surface of a structure or organ. **anterior f. of humerus, greater,** fossa coronoidea humeri. **anterior f. of humerus, lesser,** fossa radialis humeri. **articular foveae for rib cartilages,** incisurae costales sterni. **articular f., of temporal bone,** fossa mandibularis. **f. articula′ris infe′rior atlan′tis** [N A], either of the two inferior articular surfaces (facies articulares inferiores atlantis [B N A]) found on the lateral masses of the atlas. Called also *inferior articular f. of atlas.* **f. articula′ris supe′rior atlan′tis** [N A], either of the two superior articular surfaces (facies articulares superiores atlantis [B N A]) found on the lateral masses of the atlas. Called also *superior articular surface of atlas.* **calcaneal f.,** sulcus calcanei. **f. cap′itis fem′oris** [N A, B N A], a depression in the head of the femur where the ligamentum teres is attached. **f. capit′uli ra′dii** [B N A], a shallow cup on the upper surface of the head of the radius for articulation with the capitulum of the humerus. Omitted in N A. **f. cardi′aca.** 1. Fossa epigastrica. 2. Anterior intestinal portal. **central f. of retina, f. centra′lis ret′inae** [N A, B N A], a tiny pit, about 1 degree wide, in the center of the macula lutea, composed of slim, elongated cones; it is the area of clearest vision, because here the layers of the retina are spread aside, permitting light to fall directly on the cones. **f. of condyloid process,** f. pterygoidea mandibulae. **f. of coronoid process,** fossa coronoidea humeri. **costal f., inferior,** f. costalis inferior. **costal f., superior,** f. costalis superior. **costal f., transverse,** f. costalis transversalis. **costal foveae of sternum,** incisurae costales sterni. **f. costa′lis infe′rior** [N A, B N A], a small facet on the lower edge of the body of a vertebra articulating with the head of a rib. **f. costa′lis supe′rior** [N A, B N A], a small facet on the upper edge of the body of a vertebra articulating with the head of a rib. Called also *superior costal facet.* **f. costa′lis transversa′lis** [N A, B N A], a facet on the transverse process of a vertebra for articulation with the tubercle of a rib. Called also *transverse costal f.* **crural f.,** anulus femoralis. **dental f. of atlas, f. den′tis atlan′tis** [N A, B N A], the facet on the inner surface of the anterior arch of the atlas for the articulation of the dens of the axis. **digastric f.,** fossa digastrica. **femoral f.,** anulus femoralis. **f. of fourth ventricle,** f. inferior fossae rhomboideae. **glandular foveae of Luschka,** foveolae granulares. **f. of head of femur,** f. capitis femoris. **f. for head of radius,** fossa radialis humeri. **f. hemiellip′tica,** recessus ellipticus vestibuli. **f. hemisphe′rica,** recessus sphericus vestibuli. **inferior f. of floor of fourth ventricle,** f. inferior fossae rhomboideae. **f. infe′rior fos′sae rhomboi′deae** [N A, B N A], a slight depression in the sulcus limitans of the fourth ventricle just caudal to the striae medullares. Called also *inferior f. of sulcus limitans.* **inferior f. of sulcus limitans,** f. inferior fossae rhomboideae. **inguinal f., external,** fossa inguinalis lateralis. **inguinal f., internal,** fossa inguinalis medialis. **inguinal f., lateral,** fossa inguinalis lateralis. **inguinal f., medial,** fossa inguinalis medialis. **inguinal f., middle,** fossa inguinalis medialis. **f. inguina′lis latera′lis** [B N A], fossa inguinalis lateralis. **f. inguina′lis media′lis** [B N A], fossa inguinalis medialis. **interligamentous f. of peritoneum,** fossa supravesicalis. **f. of lateral malleolus,** facies articularis malleolaris tibiae. **f. lim′bica,** a sulcus marking the lateral border of the lateral area olfactoria and gyrus hippocampi in the lower mammals. **f. of little head of radius,** f. capituli radii. **malleolar f., lateral, of fibula,** facies articularis malleoli fibulae. **f. of Morgagni,** f. navicularis urethrae. **f. nu′chae** [B N A], a depression at the nape of the neck, below the external occipital protuberance. Omitted in N A. **oblong f. of arytenoid cartilage,** f. oblonga cartilaginis arytenoideae. **f. oblon′ga cartilag′inis arytenoi′deae** [N A], a depression on the anterolateral surface of the arytenoid cartilage, separated from the triangular pit above by the arcuate crest. Called also *oblong pit of arytenoid cartilage.* **oval f. of femur,** hiatus saphenus. **pterygoid f., f. pterygoi′dea mandib′ulae** [N A], **f. pterygoi′dea proces′sus condyloi′dei** [B N A], a depression on the inner side of the neck of the condyloid process of the mandible, for attachment of the external pterygoid muscle. **sublingual f., f. sublingua′lis** [N A, B N A], a depression on the inner surface of the body of the mandible, lodging the sublingual gland. **submandibular f., f. submandibula′ris** [N A], **f. submaxilla′ris** [B N A], a depression on the medial aspect of the body of the mandible, lodging the submandibular gland. **f. supe′rior fos′sae rhomboi′deae** [N A, B N A], a slight depression in the sulcus limitans just rostral to the striae medullares. Called also *superior f. of sulcus limitans.* **superior f. of sulcus limitans,** f. superior fossae rhomboideae. **supratrochlear f., anterior,** fossa coronoidea humeri. **supratrochlear f. of humerus,** fossa coronoidea humeri. **f. supravesica′lis peritonae′i** [B N A], fossa supravesicalis. **f. of talus,** sulcus tali. **f. of tooth of atlas,** f. dentis atlantis. **f. triangula′ris cartilag′inis arytenoi′deae** [N A], a depression on the anterolateral surface of the arytenoid cartilage, separated from the oblong pit below by the arcuate crest. Called also *triangular pit of arytenoid cartilage.* **trochlear f., f. trochlea′ris** [N A, B N A], a depression on the anteromedial part of the orbital surface of the frontal bone for the attachment of the trochlea of the superior oblique muscle. It is often replaced by the trochlear spine.

foveate (fo′ve-āt) [L. *foveatus*]. Pitted.

foveation (fo″ve-a′shun). A pitted condition.

foveola (fo-ve′o-lah), pl. *fove′olae* [L., dim. of *fovea*]. A small pit; used in anatomical nomenclature as a general term to denote an extremely small depression. **f. coccyg′ea** [N A, B N A], **coccygeal f.,** a dermal pit near the tip of the coccyx, indicatory of the site of attachment of the embryonic neural tube to the skin. **fove′olae gas′tricae** [N A, B N A], the numerous pits in the gastric mucosa marking the openings of the gastric glands. Called also *gastric pits.* **granular foveolae, fove′olae granula′res** [N A], **fove′olae granula′res [Pacchioni]** [B N A], small pits on the internal surface of the cranial bones on either side of the groove for the superior sagittal sinus. They are occupied by the arachnoidal granulations. **fove′olae papil′lae,** foramina papillaria.

foveolate (fo-ve′o-lāt). Pitted.

Foville's syndrome (fo-vēlz′) [Achille Louis François *Foville,* French psychiatrist, 1831–1887]. See under *syndrome.*

Foville's tract (fo-vēlz′) [Achille Louis *Foville,* French neurologist, 1799–1878]. See under *tract.*

Fowler's operation, position (fow′lerz) [George Ryerson *Fowler,* American surgeon, 1848–1906]. See under *operation* and *position.*

Fowler's solution (fow′lerz) [Thomas *Fowler,* English physician, 1736–1801]. Potassium arsenite solution.

Fowler-Murphy treatment [G. R. *Fowler;* John Benjamin *Murphy,* Chicago surgeon, 1857–1916]. See under *treatment.*

fowlpox (fowl′poks). Epithelioma contagiosum.

Fox's impetigo [William Tilbury *Fox,* English dermatologist, 1836–1879]. Impetigo contagiosa.

Fox-Fordyce disease (foks-for′dis) [George Henry *Fox,* New York dermatologist, 1846–1937; John Addison *Fordyce,* New York dermatologist, 1858–1925]. See under *disease.*

foxglove (foks′glov). See *digitalis.* **purple f.,** digitalis.

F.p. 1. Abbreviation for L. *fi′at po′tio,* let a potion be made. 2. Abbreviation for *freezing point.*

F.pil. Abbreviation for L. *fi′ant pil′ulae,* let pills be made.

F.R. Abbreviation for *flocculation reaction.* See *Sachs-Georgi test,* under *tests.*

Fr. Chemical symbol for *francium.*

Fracastorius (frak″as-to′re-us) [It. Girolamo *Fracastoro*] (1478–1553). A Veronese physician, poet, and geologist, who published in 1530 a medical poem, *Syphilis sive morbus gallicus,* in which the name syphilis was first given to the disease.

Fract.dos. Abbreviation for L. *frac′ta do′si,* in divided doses.

fraction (frak′shun). In chemistry, one of the separable constituents of a substance. **Dakin and West's liver f.,** an extract from the liver efficient in the treatment of pernicious anemia. **mol f.,** the ratio of mols of a solute to total mols in the solution. **plasma f's,** the various proteins separated from blood plasma.

fractional (frak′shun-al) [L. *fractio* a breaking]. Accomplished by repeated divisions.

fractography (frak-tog′rah-fe) [L. *fractus* broken + Gr. *graphein* to record]. A technique of photography which permits observation of jagged surfaces at high magnification.

fracture (frak′tūr) [L. *fractura,* from *frangere* to break]. 1. The breaking of a part, especially a bone. 2. A break or rupture in a bone. **agenetic f.,** spontaneous fracture due to imperfect osteogenesis. **apophysial f.,** one in which a small smear fragment or a bony prominence is torn from the bone. **articular f.,** a fracture of the joint surface of a bone. **atrophic f.,** a spontaneous fracture resulting from atrophy of the bone. **avulsion f.,** an indirect fracture caused by avulsion. **Barton's f.,** fracture of the distal end of the radius. **bending f.,** an indirect fracture caused by bending of the limb. **Bennett's f.,** a longitudinal fracture of the first metacarpal bone running into the carpometacarpal joint and complicated by subluxation. Called also *stave of the thumb.* **boxers' f.,** fracture of one of the extremities of the first metacarpal bone. **bucket-handle f.,** a tear in the semilunar cartilage, along the middle

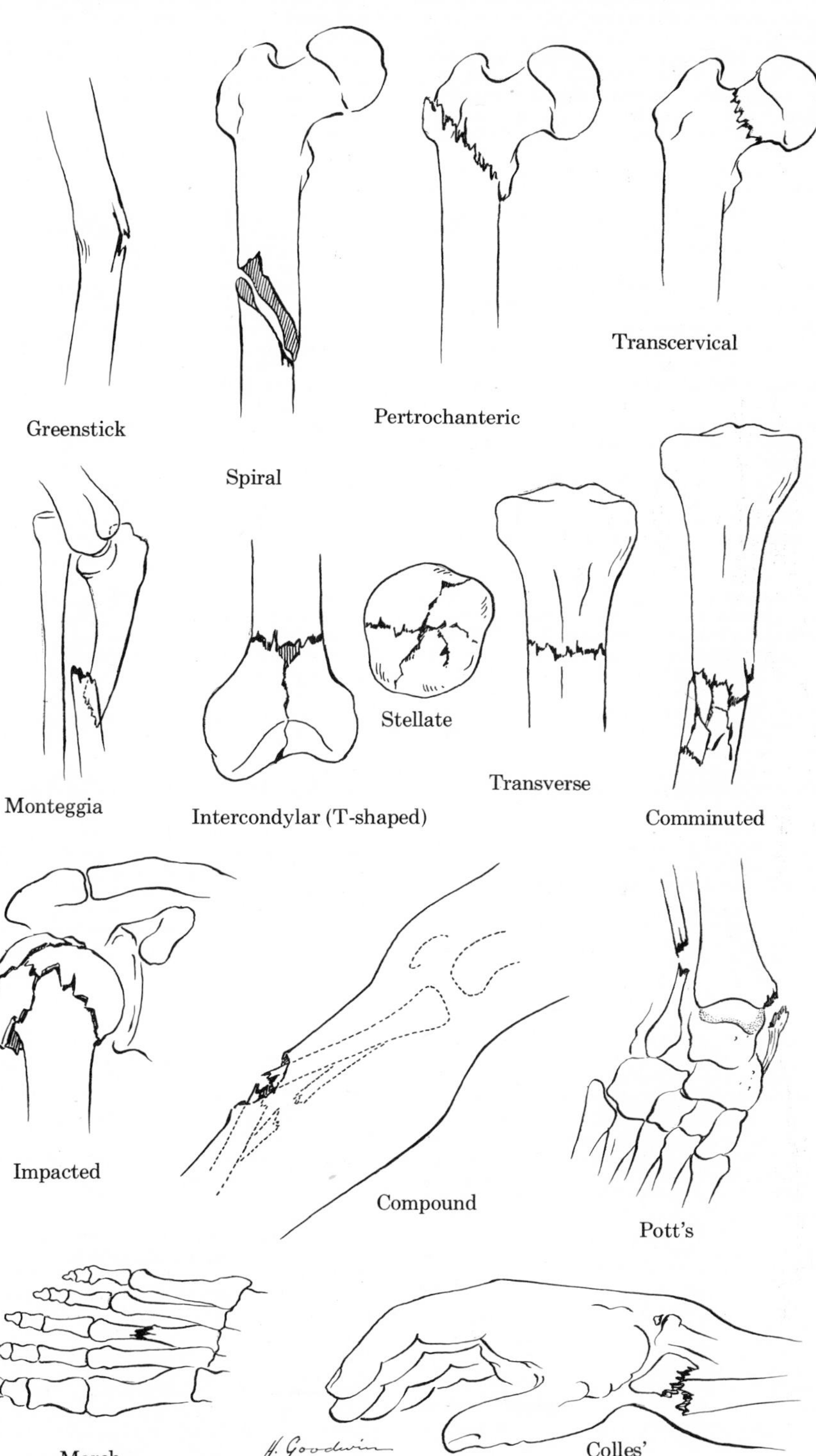

VARIOUS TYPES OF FRACTURES

portion, leaving a loop of cartilage lying in the intercondylar notch. **bumper f.**, fracture of one or both legs immediately below the knee caused by an automobile bumper. **bursting f.**, a comminuted fracture of the distal phalanx. **butterfly f.**, a comminuted fracture in which there are two fragments on each side of a main fragment, somewhat resembling the wings of a butterfly. **buttonhole f.**, fracture in which the bone is perforated by a missile. **capillary f.**, a fracture that appears in the roentgenogram as a fine hairlike line, the segments of bone not being separated; sometimes seen in fractures of the skull. **chisel f.**, oblique detachment of a piece from the head of the radius. **cleavage f.** (*abschälungsfractur*), shelling off of cartilage with a small fragment of bone from the upper surface of the capitellum humeri (Kocher). **closed f.**, a fracture which does not produce an open wound in the skin. Called also *simple f.* **Colles' f.**, fracture of the lower end of the radius in which the lower fragment is displaced posteriorly. (See illustration.) If the lower fragment is displaced anteriorly, it is a *reverse Colles' fracture* (Smith's fracture). **comminuted f.**, one in which the bone is splintered or crushed. **complete f.**, one in which the bone is entirely broken across. **complicated f.**, fracture with injury of the adjacent parts. **compound f.**, open f. **compression f.**, one produced by compression. **condylar f.**, fracture of the humerus in which a small fragment including the condyle is separated from the inner or outer aspect of the bone. **congenital f.**, intra-uterine f. **f. by contrecoup,** a fracture of the skull at a distance from the point struck. **depressed f.**, a fracture of the skull in which a fragment is depressed below the surface. **diacondylar f.**, transcondylar f. **direct f.**, a fracture at the point of injury. **double f.**, fracture of a bone in two places. **Dupuytren's f.** 1. Pott's fracture. 2. (of forearm). Galeazzi's fracture. **Duverney's f.**, fracture of the ilium just below the anterior superior spine. **dyscrasic f.**, fracture due to weakening of the bone from debilitating disease. **f. en coin** (ah kwahn), a V-shaped fracture. **f. en rave** (ah rahv), a fracture in which the break is transverse at the surface, but not within. **endocrine f.**, fracture of a bone weakened by endocrine disorder, such as hyperparathyroidism. **epiphysial f.**, fracture at the point of union of an epiphysis with the shaft of a bone. **extracapsular f.**, a fracture of the humerus or femur outside of the capsular ligament. **fatigue f.**, a fracture of the upper end of the tibia attributed to the strain of prolonged walking. **fissure f., fissured f.**, a crack extending from a surface into, but not through, a long bone. **Galeazzi's f.**, fracture of the radius above the wrist combined with dislocation of the distal end of the ulna. **Gosselin's f.**, a V-shaped fracture of the distal end of the tibia, extending into the ankle joint. **greenstick f.,** fracture in which one side of a bone is broken, the other being bent; an infraction. **grenade-thrower's f.**, fracture of the humerus caused by muscular contraction in throwing a grenade. **Guérin's f.**, bilateral horizontal fracture of the maxilla. **gunshot f.**, a fracture produced by a bullet or other missile. **gutter f.**, a fracture of the skull in which the depression is elliptic in form. **hickory-stick f.**, greenstick f. **impacted f.,** fracture in which one fragment is firmly driven into the other. **incomplete f.**, one which does not entirely destroy the continuity of the bone. **indirect f.**, a fracture at a point distant from the site of injury. **inflammatory f.**, fracture of a bone weakened by inflammatory disease. **interperiosteal f.**, incomplete or greenstick fracture. **intra-articular f.**, a fracture of the articular surface of a bone. **intracapsular f.**, one within the capsule of a joint. **intraperiosteal f.**, a fracture without rupture of the periosteum. **intra-uterine f.**, fracture of a fetal bone occurring in utero. **joint f.**, articular fracture. **lead pipe f.**, fracture in which the cortex of the bone is slightly compressed and bulged on one side with a slight crack on the opposite side of the bone. **Le Fort's f.**, bilateral horizontal fracture of the maxilla. **linear f.**, a fracture extending lengthwise of the bone. **longitudinal f.**, a break in a bone extending in a longitudinal direction. **loop f.**, bucket-handle f. **loose f.**, a fracture in which the bone is completely broken so that the broken ends have free play. **march f.**, fracture of a bone of the lower extremity, developing after repeated stresses, such as is seen in soldiers. Cf. *march foot*, under *foot*. **Monteggia's f.**, fracture in the proximal half of the shaft of the ulna, with dislocation of the head of the radius. Sometimes called parry fracture because it is often caused by attempts to fend off blows with the forearm. **Moore's f.**, fracture of the lower end of the radius with dislocation of the head of the ulna and imprisonment of the styloid process beneath the annular ligaments. **multiple f.**, a variety in which there are two or more lines of fracture of the same bone not communicating with each other. **neoplastic f.**, fracture due to weakening of the bone as a result of a malignant process. **neurogenic f.**, fracture due to weakening of the bone as a result of tabes, paresis, etc. **oblique f.**, fracture in which the break extends in an oblique direction. **open f.**, one in which there is an external wound leading to the break of the bone. Called also *compound f.* **paratrooper f.**, fracture of the posterior articular margin of the tibia and/or of the internal or external malleolus. **parry f.**, Monteggia f. **pathologic f.**, spontaneous f. **perforating f.**, buttonhole f. **periarticular f.**, a fracture extending close to, but not into, a joint. **pertrochanteric f.**, fracture of the femur passing through the great trochanter. **pillion f.**, a fracture of the lower end of the femur occurring when the knee of a person riding pillion on a motorcycle is struck in a collision. It is a T-shaped fracture with displacement of the condyles behind the femoral shaft. **ping-pong f.**, an indented fracture of the skull, resembling the indentation that can be produced with the finger in a ping-pong ball; when elevated it resumes and retains its normal position. **pond f.**, fracture of the skull in which a fissure circumscribes the radiating lines, giving the depressed area a circular form. **Pott's f.**, fracture of the lower part of the fibula, with serious injury of the lower tibial articulation, usually a chipping off of a portion of the inner malleolus, or rupture of the internal lateral ligament. **pressure f.**, one caused by pressure on the bone from an adjoining tumor. **Quervain's f.**, fracture of the navicular bone together with a volar luxation of the os lunatum. **resecting f.**, a fracture in which a piece of the bone is taken out, as by a rifle-ball. **secondary f.**, a fracture occurring spontaneously as a result of weakening of the bone by disease. **Shepherd's f.**, fracture of the astragalus, with detachment of the outer protecting edge. **silver-fork f.**, fracture of the lower ends of the radius: so called from the shape of the deformity that it causes. **simple f.**, closed f. **simple f., complex,** a closed fracture in which there is considerable injury to adjacent soft tissues. **Skillern's f.**, complete fracture of the lower third of the radius with greenstick fracture of the lower third of the ulna. **Smith's f.**, a fracture of the lower end of the radius near its articular surface with forward displacement of the lower fragment; sometimes called *reverse Colles' fracture*. **spiral f.**, one in which the bone has been twisted apart. **splintered f.**, a comminuted fracture in which the bone is splintered into thin, sharp fragments. **spontaneous f.**, one occurring as a result of disease of a bone or from some undiscoverable cause, and not due to trauma. **sprain f.**, the separation of a tendon or ligament from its insertion, taking with it a piece of bone. **sprinter's f.**, fracture of the anterior superior or of the anterior inferior spine of the ilium, a fragment of the bone being pulled off by muscular violence, as at the start of a sprint. **stellate f.**, a fracture with a central point of injury, from which radiate numerous fissures.

Stieda's f., fracture of the internal condyle of the femur. **subcapital f.**, fracture of a bone just below its head; especially an intracapsular fracture of the neck of the femur at the junction of the head and neck. **subcutaneous f.**, simple f. **subperiosteal f.**, a crack through a bone without alteration in its alignment or contour, the supposition being that the periosteum is not broken. **supracondylar f.**, fracture of the humerus in which the line of fracture is through the lower end of the shaft of the humerus. **torsion f.**, spiral f. **torus f.**, a fracture in which there is a localized expansion or torus of the cortex, with little or no displacement of the lower end of the bone. **transcervical f.**, fracture through the neck of the femur. **transcondylar f.**, fracture of the humerus in which the line of fracture is at the level of the condyles, traverses the fossae, and is in part within the capsule of the joint. **transverse f.**, a fracture at right angles to the axis of the bone. **trimalleolar f.**, fracture of the medial and lateral malleoli and the posterior tip of the tibia. **trophic f.**, one due to a trophic disturbance. **tuft f.**, bursting f. **Wagstaffe's f.**, separation of the internal malleolus. **willow f.**, greenstick f.

fracture-dislocation (frak′tūr dis″lo-ka′shun). A fracture of a bone near a joint, also involving dislocation.

Fraenkel (freng′kel). See *Fränkel.*

fragiform (fraj′ĭ-form) [L. *fraga* strawberry + *forma* shaped]. Shaped like a strawberry.

fragilitas (frah-jil′ĭ-tas) [L.]. Fragility. **f. crin′ium,** a brittle condition of the hair. **f. os′sium,** abnormal brittleness of the bones. See *osteogenesis imperfecta.* **f. san′guinis** [L. "fragility of the blood"]. See *erythrocyte fragility.* **f. un′guium** [L. "fragility of the nails"], abnormal brittleness of the nails.

fragility (frah-jil′ĭ-te). Susceptibility, or lack of resistance, to factors capable of causing disruption of continuity or integrity. **f. of blood,** erythrocyte f. **capillary f.,** susceptibility, or lack of resistance, of capillaries to disruption under conditions of increased stress. **erythrocyte f.,** the susceptibility, or lack of resistance, of erythrocytes to hemolysis when exposed to increasingly hypotonic saline solutions (*osmotic f.*) or when subjected to mechanical trauma (*mechanical f.*). **hereditary f. of bone,** idiopathic osteopsathyrosis. **mechanical f.** See *erythrocyte f.* **osmotic f.** See *erythrocyte f.*

fragilocyte (frah-jil′o-sīt). An erythrocyte which is less than normally resistant to hypotonic salt solution.

fragilocytosis (frah-jil″o-si-to′sis). The presence of fragilocytes in the blood.

fragmentation (frag″men-ta′shun). A division into fragments. **f. of myocardium,** transverse rupture of the muscle fibers of the heart.

fragment (frag′ment). One of the small pieces into which a larger entity has been broken. **Spengler's f's,** small round bodies seen in tuberculous sputum.

fraise (frāz) [Fr. "strawberry"]. A conical or hemispherical burr for cutting osteoplastic flaps or enlarging trephine openings.

frambesia (fram-be′ze-ah) [Fr. *framboise* raspberry]. Yaws. **f. trop′ica,** yaws.

frambesin (fram-be′sin). Cultures of *Spirochaeta pertenue* heated to 60°C.: used as a skin test for frambesia.

frambesioma (fram-be″ze-o′mah). The primary lesion of frambesia consisting of a large single projecting nodule.

framboesia (fram-be′ze-ah). Yaws.

framboesioma (fram-be″ze-o′mah). Frambesioma.

frame (frām). A structure, usually rigid, designed for giving support to or for immobilizing a part. **Balkan f.** See under *splint.* **Bradford f.,** a rectangular frame of gas pipe to which is attached a sheet of heavy canvas: used as a bed frame in tuberculosis of the spine and fracture of the thigh. **Deiters' terminal f.,** plates in the lamina reticularis uniting Deiters' phalanges with the cells of Hensen. **Hibbs' f.,** a frame used in the application of traction plaster jackets in the treatment of scoliosis. **occluding f.,** a dental articulator. **quadriplegic standing f.,** a device for supporting in the upright position a patient whose four limbs are paralyzed. **spectacle f.,** a frame of metal or plastic for holding lenses before the eyes. **trial f.,** a spectacle frame specially devised to permit easy insertion of different lenses used in testing vision. **Whitman's f.,** a frame similar to Bradford's frame except that it is curved.

framework (frām′werk). The basic structure about which something is formulated or built; as the supporting elements of a prosthesis (such as a partial denture) to which the remaining portions are attached. **scleral f.,** the larger and coarser part of the angle of the iris which is adjacent to the sclera. **uveal f.,** ligamentum pectinatum anguli iridocornealis.

Francis' disease (fran′siz) [Edward *Francis,* American physician, born 1872]. Tularemia.

Francis' triplex pill [John Wakefield *Francis,* American physician, 1789–1861]. Compound pill of aloes, mercury, and scammony.

francium (fran′se-um). The chemical element of atomic number 87, atomic weight 223, symbol Fr.

Francke's needle, sign, symptom (frang′kez) [Karl Ernst *Francke,* German physician, 1859–1920]. See under the nouns.

franghi (fran′ge). Venereal syphilis in Syria.

Frank's operation. 1. [Fritz *Frank,* German gynecologist, 1856–1923]. Subcutaneous symphysiotomy. 2. [Rudolf *Frank,* Vienna surgeon, 1862–1913]. See under *operation.*

Franke's operation (frang′kez) [Felix *Franke,* German surgeon, born 1860]. See under *operation.*

Fränkel's sign (freng′kelz) [Albert *Fränkel,* German physician, 1848–1916]. See under *sign.*

Fränkel's speculum, test (freng′kelz) [Bernhard *Fränkel,* German laryngologist, 1837–1911]. See under *speculum* and *tests.*

Fränkel's treatment (freng′kelz) [Albert *Fränkel,* Heidelberg physician, 1864–1938]. See under *treatment.*

Fränkel-Weichselbaum pneumococcus (freng′kel-vīk′sel-bawm). *Diplococcus pneumoniae.*

Frankenhäuser's ganglion (frang′ken-hoy″-zerz) [Ferdinand *Frankenhäuser,* German gynecologist, died 1894]. See under *ganglion.*

Frankl-Hochwart's disease (frank′l-hoch′-warts) [Lothar von *Frankl-Hochwart,* Vienna neurologist, 1862–1914]. Polyneuritis cerebralis menieriformis.

Franklin glasses (frangk′lin) [Benjamin *Franklin,* American patriot, 1706–1790]. Bifocal glasses.

franklinism (frangk′lin-izm) [B. *Franklin*]. 1. Static or frictional electricity. 2. Franklinization.

franklinization (frangk″lin-i-za′shun). The therapeutic use of static electricity.

Frasera (fra′zer-ah) [after John *Fraser,* 1750–1817]. 1. A genus of gentianaceous plants. 2. The root of *F. walteri,* or American calumba: a bitter tonic.

Fraunhofer's lines (frown′hof-erz) [Joseph von *Fraunhofer,* German optician, 1787–1826]. See under *line.*

Frazier's needle (fra′zherz) [Charles H. *Frazier,* American surgeon, 1870–1936]. See under *needle.*

Frazier-Spiller operation (fra′zher-spil′er) [Charles H. *Frazier;* William Gibson *Spiller,* American neurologist, 1864–1940]. See under *operation.*

FRC. Abbreviation for *functional residual capacity.*

F.R.C.P. Abbreviation for *Fellow of the Royal College of Physicians.*

F.R.C.P.(C.) Abbreviation for *Fellow of the Royal College of Physicians of Canada.*

F.R.C.P.E. Abbreviation for *Fellow of the Royal College of Physicians of Edinburgh.*

F.R.C.P.(Glasg.). Abbreviation for *Fellow of the Royal College of Physicians and Surgeons of Glasgow* qua *Physician.*

F.R.C.P.I. Abbreviation for *Fellow of the Royal College of Physicians in Ireland.*

F.R.C.S. Abbreviation for *Fellow of the Royal College of Surgeons.*

F.R.C.S.(C.) Abbreviation for *Fellow of the Royal College of Surgeons of Canada.*

F.R.C.S.E. Abbreviation for *Fellow of the Royal College of Surgeons of Edinburgh.*

F.R.C.S.(Glasg.). Abbreviation for *Fellow of the Royal College of Physicians and Surgeons of Glasgow* qua *Surgeon.*

F.R.C.S.I. Abbreviation for *Fellow of the Royal College of Surgeons in Ireland.*

F.R.C.V.S. Abbreviation for *Fellow of the Royal College of Veterinary Surgeons.*

freckle (frek′l). A brownish pigmented spot on the skin due to discrete accumulation of melanin as a result of the stimulant effect of sunlight, without increase in the number of melanocytes at the epidermodermal junction. **cold f.,** lentigo.

Frédéricq's sign (fra-da-rēks′) [Louis Auguste *Frédéricq*, Belgian physician, 1815–1853]. See under *sign.*

Fredet-Ramstedt operation (frĕ-da′ rahm′-stet] [Pierre *Fredet*, French surgeon, 1870–1946; Conrad *Ramstedt*, German surgeon, born 1867]. See under *operation.*

freemartin (fre′mar-tin). A female calf born as a twin to a male calf. It is commonly sterile and intersexual as the result of male hormone reaching it through anastomosed placental vessels.

Frei's bubo, disease, test (frīz) [Wilhelm Siegmund *Frei*, German dermatologist, 1885–1943]. See *lymphogranuloma venereum*, and under *test.*

Freiberg's infraction (fri′bergz) [Albert Henry *Freiberg*, American surgeon, 1868–1940]. See *Köhler's bone disease* (def. 2), under *disease.*

fremitus (frem′ĭ-tus) [L.]. A thrill or vibration, especially one that is perceptible on palpation. **bronchial f.,** rhonchal f. **dental f.,** stridor dentium. **friction f.,** the thrill caused by the rubbing together of two dry surfaces. **hydatid f.,** a tremulous impulse felt on palpation over a hydatid cyst. **pectoral f.,** vocal f. **pericardial f.,** a thrill of the chest wall due to the friction of the surfaces of the pericardium over each other. **pleural f.,** a vibration of the wall of the thorax due to friction of the opposing surfaces of the pleura over each other. **rhonchal f.,** vibrations produced by the passage of air through a large bronchial tube filled with mucus. **subjective f.,** a thrill felt by the patient on humming with his mouth closed. **tactile f.,** a thrill, as in the chest wall, which may be felt by a hand applied to the thorax while the patient is speaking. **tussive f.,** a thrill felt on the chest when the patient coughs. **vocal f.,** a thrill caused by speaking, and perceived by the ear of the auscultator applied to the chest.

frenal (fre′nal). Pertaining to a frenum.

French (french′). See *French scale*, under *scale.*

frenectomy (fre-nek′to-me). Excision of a frenum.

frenetic (frĕ-net′ik). Pertaining to mental disease.

Frenkel's movements, treatment (freng-kelz′) [Heinrich S. *Frenkel*, Berlin neurologist, 1860–1931]. See under *movement.*

frenosecretory (fre″no-se′kre-to″re) [L. *fraenum* bridle + *secretory*]. Exercising an inhibitory or restraining power over the secretions.

frenotomy (fre-not′o-me) [L. *fraenum* frenum + Gr. *tomē* a cutting]. Incision of a frenum or frenulum, as of the frenulum linguae in treatment of tonguetie.

frenulum (fren′u-lum), pl. *fren′ula* [L., dim. of *fraenum*]. A small bridle; used in anatomical nomenclature as a general term to designate a small fold of integument or mucous membrane that checks, curbs, or limits the movements of an organ or part. **f. of anterior medullary velum,** f. veli medullaris superior. **f. clitor′idis** [N A, B N A], **f. of clitoris,** a fold formed by the union of the labia posterior with the clitoris. **f. of ileocecal valve,** f. valvae ileocecalis. **f. of inferior lip, f. la′bii inferio′ris** [N A, B N A], the fold of mucous membrane on the inside of the middle of the lower lip, connecting the lip with the gums. **f. la′bii superio′ris** [N A, B N A], the fold of mucous membrane on the inside of the middle of the upper lip, connecting the lip with the gums. **f. labio′rum puden′di** [N A, B N A], the posterior union of the labia minora, anterior to the posterior commissure. Called also *f. of pudendal labia.* **f. lin′guae** [N A, B N A], the vertical fold of mucous membrane under the tongue, attaching it to the floor of the mouth. Called also *f. of tongue.* **f. lin′geae cerebel′li,** vincula lingulae cerebelli. **frenula of Morgagni.** See *f. valvae ileocecalis.* **f. of prepuce of penis, f. prepu′tii pe′nis** [N A], the fold on the lower surface of the glans penis that connects it with the prepuce. **f. of pudendal labia, f. puden′di,** f. labiorum pudendi. **f. of superior lip,** f. labii superioris. **f. of superior medullary velum,** f. veli medullaris superior. **f. of tongue,** f. linguae. **f. val′vae ileoceca′lis** [N A], **fren′ula val′vulae co′li** [B N A], a fold formed by the joined extremities of the ileocecal valve, extending partly around the lumen of the colon. Called also *f. of ileocecal valve.* **f. ve′li medulla′ris anterioris** [B N A], **f. ve′li medulla′ris supe′rior** [N A], a band that lies in the superior medullary velum at its attachment to the inferior colliculi. Called also *f. of superior medullary velum.*

frenum (fre′num), pl. *fre′na* [L. *fraenum* bridle]. A restraining structure or part. See *frenulum.* **f. of labia,** frenulum labiorum pudendi. **Macdowel's f.,** a group of fibers attached to the tendon of the pectoralis muscle and strengthening the intermuscular septum. **f. of Morgagni,** frenulum valvulae ileocecalis. **f. of tongue,** frenulum linguae. **f. of valve of colon,** frenulum valvulae ileocecalis.

frenzy (fren′ze) [Gr. *phrenitizein* to be delirious or frantic]. Violent maniacal excitement.

frequency (fre′kwen-se). 1. In statistics, the number of occurrences of a determinable entity per unit of time or of population. 2. The number of vibrations made by a particle or ray in one second; in electricity, the rate of oscillation or alternation in an alternating current; the number of complete cycles produced by an alternating current generator per second. **audio f.,** any frequency corresponding to a normally audible sound wave. **fusion f.** See *flicker phenomenon* under *phenomenon.* **high f.,** the rate of oscillation in an alternating current exceeding the rate at which muscular contraction ceases—approximately 10,-000 per second. See *high-frequency current*, under *current.* **infrasonic f.,** any frequency below the audio frequency range. **low f.,** an alternating current where frequency in cycles per second is low in reference to a certain standard, such as the pitch frequency of middle C. **subsonic f.,** infrasonic f. **supersonic f.,** ultrasonic f. **ultrasonic f.,** any frequency above the audio frequency range.

Frerichs' theory (fra′riks) [Friedrich Theodor *Frerichs*, Berlin physician, 1819–1885]. See under *theory.*

fressreflex (fres′re-fleks) [Ger. "eating reflex"]. Rhythmic sucking, chewing and swallowing movements elicited by stroking of the lips and cheeks.

freta (fre′tah) [L.]. Plural of *fretum.*

fretum (fre′tum), pl. *fre′ta* [L.]. A constriction, or

strait. **f. hal'leri,** a constriction between the atria and ventricles of the fetal heart.

Freud's cathartic method, theory (froids) [Sigmund *Freud*, neurologist in Vienna, 1856–1939]. See *catharsis*, and under *theory*.

freudian (froid'e-an). 1. Pertaining to Sigmund Freud and his doctrines regarding the causes of certain nervous disorders, that they are based on the existence of unconscious sexual impressions, and that the cure of such disorders can be secured by bringing these impressions into the consciousness by psychoanalysis; the term also is applied to the theory that dreams are the expression under symbolic forms of suppressed wishes, many of which are of a sexual nature. See *unconscious* and *psychoanalysis*. 2. One who follows the teaching and theories of Sigmund Freud.

Freund adjuvant (froind) [Jules *Freund*, Hungarian-born bacteriologist in the United States, 1890–1960]. See under *adjuvant*.

Freund's anomaly, reaction (froinds) [Hermann Wolfgang *Freund*, German gynecologist, 1859–1925]. See under *anomaly* and *reaction*.

Freund's law, operation (froinds) [Wilhelm Alexander *Freund*, German gynecologist, 1833–1917]. See under *law* and *operation*.

Freund-Kaminer reaction (froind'kah'min-er) [Ernst *Freund*, Vienna (later London) physician, 1863–1946; Gisa *Kaminer*, Vienna physician, born 1887]. See under *reaction*.

Frey's hairs (frīz) [Max von *Frey*, German physiologist, 1852–1932]. See under *hair*.

Frey's syndrome (frīz) [Lucie *Frey*, Polish physician]. Auriculotemporal syndrome. See under *syndrome*.

Freyer's operation (fri'erz) [Sir Peter Johnston *Freyer*, British surgeon, 1851–1921]. See under *operation*.

F.R.F.P.S.G. Abbreviation for *Fellow of the Royal Faculty of Physicians and Surgeons of Glasgow*.

friable (fri'ah-b'l) [L. *friabilis*]. Easily pulverized or crumbled.

Fricke's bandage (frik'ez) [Johann Karl Georg *Fricke*, German surgeon, 1790–1841]. See under *bandage*.

friction (frik'shun) [L. *frictio*]. The act of rubbing; attrition.

Fridenberg's card, test (frid'en-bergz) [Percy H. *Fridenberg*, American ophthalmologist, born 1868–1960]. See *stigmometric test card*.

Friedländer's bacillus (frēd'len-derz) [Carl *Friedländer*, German pathologist, 1847–1887]. See under *bacillus*.

Friedländer's disease (frēd'len-derz) [Max *Friedländer*, German physician, born 1841]. Endarteritis obliterans.

Friedman's test (frēd'manz) [Maurice H. *Friedman*, American physician, born 1903]. See under *test*.

Friedman-Lapham test (frēd'man-lap'ham) [Maurice H. *Friedman;* Maxwell E. *Lapham*, New Orleans obstetrician, born 1899]. See *Friedman's test*, under *test*.

Friedreich's ataxia, disease, sign, etc. (frēd'riks) [Nikolas *Friedreich*, Heidelberg physician, 1825–1882]. See under the nouns.

friente (fre-en'te). An erythematous dermatitis common among wood choppers and field workers, and probably caused by *Ustilago hypodytes* or by *Aclerda berlesei*.

frigidity (frĭ-jid'ĭ-te). Coldness; especially sexual indifference, usually applied to sexual indifference in the female.

frigolabile (frig"o-la'bil) [L. *frigor* cold + *labilis* unstable]. Easily affected or destroyed by cold.

frigorific (frig"o-rif'ik) [L. *frigorificus*]. Producing coldness.

frigorism (frig'o-rizm) [L. *frigor* cold]. A condition due to circulatory disturbance from long exposure to cold. **local f.,** trench foot.

frigostabile (frig"o-sta'bil). Frigostable.

frigostable (frig"o-sta'bl) [L. *frigor* cold + *stabilis* firm]. Resistant to cold or low temperature.

frigotherapy (frig'o-ther'ah-pe). Cryotherapy.

frina (fre'nah). Furunculus orientalis.

frit (frit). Imperfectly fused material used as a basis for making glass, and used in the formation of porcelain teeth.

Fritsch's catheter (frich'es) [Heinrich *Fritsch*, German gynecologist, 1844–1915]. See under *catheter*.

frog (frog). 1. A tailless, leaping amphibian with a smooth skin and fully webbed feet, commonly used as a laboratory animal. 2. The band of horny substance in the middle of the sole of a horse's foot, dividing into two branches and running toward the heel in the form of a fork. **Cohnheim's f., salt f.,** a frog from which the blood has been removed and replaced by normal salt solution. **rheoscopical f.,** the condition obtained when the nerve of a muscle nerve preparation is laid across a contracting muscle, causing the muscle in the former to contract and thus ascertaining the passage of an electric current, as in the rheoscope.

frog stay (frog sta). See *spine* (def. 3).

Fröhlich's syndrome (fra'liks) [Alfred *Fröhlich*, Vienna neurologist, 1871–1953]. See under *syndrome*.

Frohn's reagent (frohnz) [Damianus *Frohn*, German physician, born 1843]. See under *reagent*.

Froin's syndrome (frow-ăn') [Georges *Froin*, French physician, born 1874]. See under *syndrome*.

frolement (frōl-maw') [Fr.]. 1. A rustling sound often heard in auscultation in disease of the pericardium. 2. A massage movement consisting of light brushing with the palm of the hand.

Froment's paper sign (fro-mahz') [Jules *Froment*, French physician]. See under *sign*.

Frommann's lines (from'anz) [Carl *Frommann*, anatomist in Heidelberg, 1831–1892]. See under *line*.

Frommel's disease, operation (from'elz) [Richard *Frommel*, German gynecologist, 1854–1912]. See under the nouns.

frondose (fron'dōs) [L. *frondosus* leafy]. Bearing fronds, or villi, as the chorion frondosum.

frons (fronz) [L. "the front, forepart"]. [N A, B N A] The region of the face above the eyes. Called also *forehead*. **f. cra'nii** [N A, B N A], **f. of cranium,** the anterior extremity of the brain case; the bony forehead.

frontad (fron'tad). Toward a frontal aspect.

frontal (fron'tal) [L. *frontalis*]. Pertaining to the forehead.

frontalis (fron-ta'lis) [L.]. Frontal; in official anatomical nomenclature it designates a relationship to the frontal or coronal plane.

frontipetal (fron-tip'ĕ-tal) [L. *frontalis* in front + *petere* to seek]. Directed to the front; moving in a frontal direction.

frontomalar (fron"to-ma'lar). Pertaining to the frontal and malar bones.

frontomaxillary (fron"to-mak'sĭ-lār"e). Pertaining to the frontal bone and the upper jaw.

frontonasal (fron"to-na'zal). Pertaining to the frontal sinus and the nose.

fronto-occipital (fron"to-ok-sip'ĭ-tal). Pertaining to the forehead and the occiput.

frontoparietal (fron"to-pah-ri'e-tal). Pertaining to the frontal and parietal bones.

frontotemporal (fron"to-tem'po-ral). Pertaining to the frontal and temporal bones.

Froriep's ganglion (fro'rēps) [August von *Froriep*, German anatomist, 1849–1917]. See under *ganglion*.

Fröschel's symptom (fresh'elz) [Emil *Fröschel*, Vienna otologist, born 1883]. See under *symptom*.

frost (frost). A deposit resembling that of frozen dew or vapor. **urea f.,** the appearance on the skin of salt crystals left by evaporation of the sweat in urhidrosis.

frostbite (frost′bīt). Damage to tissues as the result of exposure to low environmental temperatures. **deep f.,** damage resulting from exposure to extremely low temperatures, involving not only the skin and subcutaneous tissue but also deeper tissues and even underlying bone, sometimes leading to loss of affected parts. **superficial f.,** damage resulting from exposure to low temperatures, involving only the skin or extending to the tissue immediately beneath it.

frost-itch (frost′ich). Pruritus hiemalis.

frottage (fro-tahzh′) [Fr. "rubbing"]. Rubbing movement in massage.

F.R.S. Abbreviation for *Fellow of the Royal Society.*

fructivorous (fruk-tiv′o-rus). Subsisting on or eating fruits.

fructofuranose (fruk″to-fu′rah-nōs). The combining and more reactive form of fructose, $CH_2OH.CH.(CHOH)_2.CHO.CH_2OH$ (ring through O).

fructokinase (fruk″to-ki′nās). An enzyme that catalyzes the transfer of a high-energy phosphate group from a donor to D-fructose, producing D-fructose-1-phosphate.

fructolysis (fruk-tol′ĭ-sis). The splitting up of fructose.

fructopyranose (fruk″to-pi′rah-nōs). Fructose.

fructosamine (fruk″to-sa′min). An amino sugar formed by the reduction of the osazone of glucosamine.

fructosan (fruk′to-san). A hexosan, $C_6H_{10}O_5$, an anhydride of fructose.

fructosazone (fruk″to-sa′zōn). Levulosazone.

fructose (fruk′tōs) [L. *fructus* fruit]. Levulose, or fruit sugar, a ketohexose, $CH_2OH.(CHOH)_3.CO.CH_2OH$, found in all sweet fruits. **f. diphosphate, f. 1,6-diphosphate,** the Harden-Young ester. **f. 6-phosphate,** the Neuberg ester.

fructosidase (fruk-to′si-dās). Invertin.

fructoside (fruk-to′sīd). A compound which bears the same relation to fructose as a glucoside does to glucose.

fructosuria (fruk″to-su′re-ah) [*fructose* + Gr. *ouron* urine + *-ia*]. The presence of fructose in the urine.

fructovegetative (fruk″to-vej′ĕ-ta″tiv). Composed of or pertaining to fruits and vegetables.

frugivorous (froo-jiv′o-rus) [L. *frux* fruit + *vorare* to eat]. Eating or subsisting on fruit.

fruit (froot) [L. *fructus*]. The developed ovary of a plant, including the seed and its envelopes.

fruitarian (froo-ta′re-an). A person whose diet consists chiefly of fruits.

fruitarianism (froo-ta′re-an-izm). The use of an exclusively fruit diet.

Frust. Abbreviation for L. *frustilla′tim,* in small pieces.

frustration (frus-tra′shun). A condition of increased emotional tension resulting from failure to achieve sought gratifications or satisfactions, ordinarily as a result of forces outside of one's self.

F. s. a. Abbreviation for L. *fi′at secun′dum ar′tem,* let it be made skilfully.

FSH. Abbreviation for *follicle-stimulating hormone.*

ft. Abbreviation for L. *fi′at* or *fi′ant,* let there be made, and for *foot.*

Ft. mas. div. in pil. Abbreviation for L. *fi′at mas′sa dividen′da in pil′ulae,* let a mass be made and divided into pills.

Ft. pulv. Abbreviation for L. *fi′at pul′vis,* let a powder be made.

fuadin (fu′ah-din). Trade mark for a preparation of stibophen.

Fuchs's coloboma (fooks) [Ernest *Fuchs,* German oculist, 1851–1930]. See under *coloboma.* **F.'s dystrophy.** See under *dystrophy.* **F.'s optic atrophy,** peripheral atrophy of the optic nerve.

Fuchs's protein test (H. J. *Fuchs,* German physician]. See under *tests.*

fuchsin (fook′sin) [Leonard *Fuchs,* German botanist, 1501–1566]. 1. A powerful red dye. 2. A dark brown pigment resembling melanin in the pigment layer of the retina. **acid f.,** a mixture of sulfonated fuchsins used in Andrade's indicator and in various complex stains. **basic f.,** a mixture of rosaniline and pararosaniline hydrochlorides, used as a topical germicide. **new f.,** a basic dye with staining properties much like basic fuchsin. It is triaminotritolylmethane chloride, or trimethyl fuchsin, $[CH_3(NH_2).C_6H_3]_2C.C_6H_3(CH_3).NH_2Cl$.

fuchsinophil (fook-sin′o-fil) [*fuchsin* + Gr. *philein* to love]. 1. Any cell or other element readily stained with fuchsin. 2. Fuchsinophilic.

fuchsinophilia (fook″sin-o-fil′e-ah). The property of staining readily with fuchsin dyes; especially the affinity of infarcted areas of the heart for acid fuchsin, which is an aid in determining diagnosis in cases of unexplained death.

fuchsinophilic (fook″sin-o-fil′ik). Readily stained by fuchsin; pertaining to or characterized by fuchsinophilia.

fuchsinophilous (fook″sin-of′ĭ-lus). Fuchsinophilic.

fucosan (fu′ko-san). A pentosan which is a constituent of the cell wall of many seaweeds.

fucose (fu′kōs). A crystalline methyl pentose, deoxygalactose, $CH_3.CH(CHOH)_3.CO$ (ring through O); the dextro form is from convolvulin, the levo form from seaweed.

Fuerbringer (fer′bring-er). See *Fürbringer.*

fugacity (fu-gas′ĭ-te) [L. *fugacitas,* from *fugere* to flee]. The tendency to escape; specifically, in physiology, the tendency for fluid to leave a local region or given point of the body.

-fugal (fu′gal). 1. [L., *fugare* to put to flight]. Word termination implying banishing, or driving away, affixed to a stem designating the object of banishment, as *culicifugal,* driving away mosquitoes and gnats (Culex), or *febrifugal,* relieving or dispelling fever. 2. [L., *fugere* to flee from]. Word termination implying traveling away from, affixed to a stem designating the object from which flight is made, as *centrifugal* traveling away from a center, or *corticipital,* directed away from the cortex.

fugitive (fu′jĭ-tiv) [L. *fugitivus*]. 1. Wandering. 2. Transient.

fugue (fūg) [L. *fuga* a flight]. A disturbance of consciousness in which the patient performs purposeful acts. After the state has passed, however, he has no conscious remembrance of his actions during this period. **epileptic f.,** a condition of clouded consciousness which may take the place of or follow an epileptic seizure.

fuguism (foo′goo-izm) [Jap. *fugu* the tetraodon fish + *-ism*]. Tetraodontoxism.

fuguismus (foo″goo-iz′mus) [see *fuguism*]. Tetraodontoxism.

fugutoxin (foo-goo-tok′sin). Tetraodontoxin.

Fukala's operation (foo-kah′lahz) [Vincenz *Fukala,* Vienna ophthalmologist, 1847–1911]. See under *operation.*

Fuld's test [Ernst *Fuld,* German internist, born 1873]. See under *test.*

fulgurant (ful′gu-rant) [L. *fulgurans,* from *fulgur* lightning]. Coming and going like a flash of lightning.

fulgurate (ful′gu-rāt). 1. To come and go like a flash of lightning. 2. To subject to destruction by electric sparks. See *fulguration.*

fulguration (ful″gu-ra′shun) [L. *fulgur* lightning]. Destruction of animal tissue by electric sparks whose action is controlled by a movable electrode.

This may be direct or indirect. *Direct:* An insulated fulguration electrode with a metal point is connected to the uniterminal of the high frequency apparatus and a spark of electricity is allowed to impinge on the area to be treated. *Indirect:* In this procedure the patient is connected directly by means of a metal handle to the uniterminal and the operator draws, by means of a lead pencil, an arc from the patient. **Keating-Hart's f.,** fulguration of external cancer.

fulgurize (ful′gu-rīz). To treat by fulguration.

fuliginous (fu-lij′ĭ-nus) [L. *fuligo* soot]. Sooty in color or appearance.

Fülleborn's method (fēl′ĕ-bornz) [Friedrich *Fülleborn*, German parasitologist, 1866–1933]. See under *method.*

Fuller's operation [Eugene *Fuller*, New York urologist, 1858–1930]. Incision of the seminal vesicles.

füllkörper (fēl′ker-per) [Ger., pl., "fill-bodies"]. Glia cells which have become degenerated.

fulminant (ful′mĭ-nant) [L. *fulminare* to flare up]. Sudden, severe; occurring suddenly and with great intensity.

fulminate (ful′mĭ-nāt). To occur suddenly with great intensity.

fulvicin (ful′vĭ-sin). Trade mark for a preparation of griseofulvin.

fumagillin (fu″mah-jil′in). An antibiotic elaborated by strains of *Aspergillus fumigatus:* used as an amebicide.

fumarase (fu′mah-rās). An enzyme which catalyzes the equilibrium between fumaric and malic acid.

fumarate (fu′mar-āt). A salt of fumaric acid. **ferrous f.,** the anhydrous salt of a combination of ferrous iron and fumaric acid: used as a hematinic.

fumigant (fu′mĭ-gant). A substance used in fumigation.

fumigation (fu″mĭ-ga′shun) [L. *fumus* smoke, steam, vapor]. Exposure of an area or object to disinfecting fumes.

fuming (fūm′ing) [L. *fumus* smoke]. Smoking; emitting a visible vapor.

fumiron (fūm′i-ron). Trade mark for a preparation of ferrous fumarate.

functio (funk′she-o) [L.]. Function. **f. lae′sa,** loss of function.

function (funk′shun) [L. *functio* a performance]. The special, normal, or proper action of any part or organ. **allomeric f.,** the function of the spinal cord which depends on the integrative action of their several parts. **antixenic f.,** the reactivity of living tissue to any foreign substance. **Carnot's f., carnotic f.,** the relation between the quantity of heat lost by a body and the work which can be done by it. **isomeric f.,** the individual function of the several sections of the spinal cord and brain stem.

functional (funk′shun-al). Of, or pertaining to, a function; affecting the functions, but not the structure.

functionating (funk′shun-āt-ing). In a condition of performing the proper function.

fundal (fun′dal). Pertaining to a fundus.

fundament (fun′dah-ment) [L. *fundamentum*]. 1. A base or foundation, such as the breech or rump. 2. The anus and parts adjacent to it.

fundamental (fun″dah-men′tal). Pertaining to a base or foundation.

fundectomy (fun-dek′to-me). Excision of the fundus of an organ, as the fundus of the uterus.

fundi (fun′di) [L.]. Plural of *fundus.*

fundic (fun′dik). Pertaining to a fundus.

fundiform (fun′dĭ-form) [L. *funda* sling + *forma* form]. Shaped like a sling.

fundoplication (fun″do-pli-ka′shun). Mobilization of the lower end of the esophagus and plication of the fundus of the stomach up around it, in treatment of reflux esophagitis.

Fundulus (fun′du-lus). A genus of killifish of the order Cyprinodontidae. The common or green killifish, *F. heteroclitus*, is much used in biological research.

fundus (fun′dus), pl. *fun′di* [L.]. The bottom or base of anything; used in anatomical nomenclature as a general term to designate the bottom or base of an organ, or the part of a hollow organ farthest from its mouth. **albinotic f.,** an eye fundus which is colorless due to lack of pigment in the pigment epithelium. **f. of bladder.** 1. Fundus vesicae urinariae. 2. Apex vesicae urinariae. **f. follic′uli pi′li** [B N A], the deepest part of a hair follicle. Omitted in N A. **f. of gallbladder,** f. vesicae felleae. **f. of internal acoustic meatus, f. mea′tus acus′tici inter′ni** [N A, B N A], the laterally placed end or bottom of the internal acoustic meatus. **f. oc′uli,** the posterior part, or back of the eye. **f. of stomach,** f. ventriculi. **tessellated f.,** an eye fundus in which the choroid and its blood vessels are visible, giving the appearance of islands of pigment situated between the vessels. **f. tigré** (te-gra′), leopard retina. **f. tym′pani,** paries jugularis cavi tympani. **f. of urinary bladder.** 1. Fundus vesicae urinariae. 2. Apex vesicae urinariae. **f. u′teri** [N A, B N A], **f. of uterus,** the part of the uterus above the orifices of the uterine tubes. **f. of vagina, f. vagi′nae,** fornix vaginae. **f. ventric′uli** [N A, B N A], that part of the stomach to the left and above the level of the entrance of the esophagus. Called also *f. of stomach.* **f. ves′icae fel′leae** [N A, B N A], the inferior, dilated portion of the gallbladder. Called also *f. of gallbladder.* **f. ves′icae urina′riae** [N A, B N A], the base or posterior surface of the bladder. Called also *f. of urinary bladder.*

funduscope (fun′dus-skōp) [*fundus* + Gr. *skopein* to examine]. An instrument for examining the fundus of the eye.

funduscopy (fun-dus′ko-pe). Examination or inspection of the fundus of the eye.

fundusectomy (fun″dus-ek′to-me) [*fundus* + Gr. *ektomē* excision]. Excision of the fundus of the stomach.

fungal (fung′gal). Pertaining to or caused by a fungus.

fungate (fung′gāt). To produce fungus-like growths; to grow rapidly, like a fungus.

fungemia (fun-je′me-ah). The presence of fungi in the blood stream.

fungi (fun′ji) [L.]. Plural of *fungus.*

Fungi Imperfecti (fun′ji im″per-fek′ti) [L., pl. "imperfect fungi"]. A large group of fungi having septate mycelium in which the sexual stage is unknown. This group includes many of the fungi which are pathogenic for animals and plants, among them Candida, Cryptococcus, Blastomyces, Histoplasma, Trichophyton, Actinomyces, etc.

fungicidal (fun″jĭ-si′dal) [*fungus* + L. *caedere* to kill]. Destroying fungi.

fungicide (fun′jĭ-sīd). An agent that destroys fungi.

fungicidin (fun″jĭ-si′din). Nystatin.

fungiform (fun′jĭ-form). Shaped like a fungus or mushroom.

fungistasis (fun-jĭ-sta′sis) [*fungus* + Gr. *stasis* a stopping]. Inhibition of growth of fungi.

fungistat (fun′jĭ-stat). A substance that checks the growth of fungi.

fungistatic (fun″jĭ-stat′ik). Inhibiting the growth of fungi.

fungisterol (fun-jis′ter-ol). A sterol, $C_{25}H_{40}O$, found in ergot and other fungi.

fungitoxic (fun″jĭ-tok′sik). Exerting a toxic effect upon fungi.

fungitoxicity (fun″jĭ-tok-sis′ĭ-te). The quality of exerting a toxic effect upon fungi.

fungizone (fun′jĭ-zōn). Trade mark for a preparation of amphotericin B.

fungoid (fung′goid) [*fungus* + Gr. *eidos* form]. Resembling a fungus, or mushroom. **chignon f.,** a nodular growth often occurring on human hair.

fungosity (fun-gos′ĭ-te). A fungoid growth or excrescence.

fungous (fung′gus) [L. *fungosus*]. Of the nature of or resembling a fungus.

fungus (fung′gus), pl. *fun′gi* [L.]. 1. Any one of a class of vegetable organisms of a low order of development, including mushrooms, toadstools, molds, etc. 2. A growth on the body resembling a fungus; a spongy mass of morbid granulation tissue. **alpha f.,** the fungus, *Achorion arloingi*, of favus herpetiformis. **beta f.,** the fungus, *Achorion schoenleinii*. **f. of the brain,** hernia cerebri. **chignon f.** See under *fungoid*. **cutaneous f.,** dermatomyces. **disease f.,** a fungus capable of producing disease. **fission f.,** schizomycete. **foot f.,** the fungus that produces mycetoma. **gamma f.,** a strain of the fungus *Achorion schoenleinii*. **f. haemato′des,** a soft, bleeding, malignant tumor. **kefir fungi,** a mixture of bacteria and yeasts capable of causing lactic acid fermentation of milk of the kefir type. **mold f.,** a fungus of the order Mucorales. **mosaic f.,** a fungus-like intercellular deposit of cholesterol sometimes seen in scrapings from the skin of the foot. **ray f.,** actinomyces. **slime f.,** mycetozoa. **f. tes′tis,** protrusion from a scrotal sinus of a mass of granulation tissue in tuberculous epididymitis. **thread f.,** a general term for the fungi of pityriasis, favus, etc. **umbilical f.,** granulation tissue on the stem of the umbilical cord in newborn infants. **yeast f.,** saccharomyces.

funic (fu′nik). Pertaining to the funis.

funicle (fu′nĭ-kl). Funiculus.

funicular (fu-nik′u-lar). Pertaining to a funiculus.

funiculitis (fu-nik″u-li′tis). 1. Inflammation of the spermatic cord. 2. Inflammation of that portion of a spinal nerve root which lies within the intervertebral canal. **endemic f.,** a disease occurring in Ceylon and southern India, marked by painful swelling of the spermatic cord, chills, nausea, and vomiting. It results in death unless operation is performed.

funiculopexy (fu-nik′u-lo-pek″se) [L. *funiculus* cord + Gr. *pēxis* fixation]. Surgical fixation of the spermatic cord to the tissues in the correction of undescended testes.

funiculus (fu-nik′u-lus), pl. *funic′uli* [L.]. A cord; used in anatomical nomenclature as a general term to indicate a cordlike structure or part. **f. am′nii,** a cord of tissue by which the amnion and chorion are temporarily united in certain ruminant animals. **f. ante′rior medul′lae spina′lis** [N A, B N A], **anterior f. of spinal cord,** the white substance of the spinal cord that lies on either side between the anterior median fissure and the ventral root; formerly called *anterior columns*. **cuneate f., f. cunea′tus** [B N A], fasciculus cuneatus medullae spinalis. **f. cunea′tus externa′lis,** sulcus centralis. **f. cunea′tus latera′lis,** a longitudinal ridge on the oblongata between the line of roots of the spinal accessory nerve and the funiculus cuneatus. **dorsal f., f. dorsa′lis.** 1. A name sometimes applied to the spinal cord. 2. Funiculus posterior medullae spinalis. **f. gra′cilis,** fasciculus gracilis medullae spinalis. **f. grac′ilis medul′lae oblonga′tae** [B N A], fasciculus gracilis medullae oblongatae. **hepatic f.,** ductus choledochus. **hepatic f. of Rauber,** arteria hepatica propria. **lateral f. of medullae oblongata, f. latera′lis medul′lae oblonga′tae** [N A, B N A], the continuation into the medulla oblongata of all the fiber tracts of the lateral funiculus of the spinal cord, with the exception of the lateral corticospinal tract. **f. latera′lis medul′lae spina′lis** [N A, B N A], the white substance of the spinal cord that lies on either side between the dorsal and ventral roots; formerly called *lateral columns*. Called also *lateral f. of spinal cord*. **ligamentous f.,** ligamentum collaterale carpi ulnare. **funic′uli medul′lae spina′lis** [N A, B N A], the large bundles of fiber tracts that make up the white substance of the spinal cord. Called also *funiculi of spinal cord*. **f. poste′rior medul′lae spina′lis** [N A, B N A], **posterior f. of spinal cord,** the white substance of the spinal cord that lies on either side between the posterior median sulcus and the dorsal root. **f. of Rolando,** fasciculus cuneatus medullae spinalis. **f. scler′ae** [B N A], omitted in N A. **f. sil′iquae,** f. lateralis medullae oblongatae. **f. solita′rius,** tractus solitarius medullae oblongatae. **f. spermat′icus** [N A], the structure that extends from the abdominal inguinal ring to the testis. See *spermatic cord*. **funiculi of spinal cord,** funiculi medullae spinalis. **f. of spinal cord, anterior,** f. anterior medullae spinalis. **f. of spinal cord, lateral,** f. lateralis medullae spinalis. **f. of spinal cord, posterior,** f. posterior medullae spinalis. **f. of sternum,** incisura jugularis sterni. **f. te′res,** eminentia medialis. **f. umbilica′lis** [N A, B N A], the flexible structure connecting the umbilicus with the placenta and giving passage to the umbilical arteries and vein. See *umbilical cord*. **ventral f., f. ventra′lis,** f. anterior medullae spinalis.

funiform (fu′nĭ-form) [L. *funis* rope + *forma* shape]. Resembling a rope or cord.

funis (fu′nis) [L. "cord"]. Any cordlike structure; particularly the umbilical cord. **f. argen′teus,** the spinal cord. **f. bra′chii,** the median cephalic vein of the arm. **f. hippoc′ratis,** the Achilles tendon.

funnel (fun′el). A conic, hollow structure with an opening at the apex, such as the vessels used in chemistry and pharmacy in filtering and for other purposes. **accessory müllerian f.,** a rudiment similar to the primordial uterine tube. **drainage f.,** one employed in the drainage of wounds. **Golgi's f's,** spiral fibrillary coils said to surround the axon of myelinated nerve fibers: they are probably artefacts. **mitral f.,** a state of the mitral valve in mitral stenosis in which the valve and the left auricle take the form of a hollow cone; called also *mitral buttonhole*. **muscular f.,** the funnel-shaped space bounded by the four straight muscles of the eye. **pial f.,** a sheath of adventitia, extended from the pia mater, loosely surrounding the blood vessels of the substance of the brain or cord. **Renver's f.,** an appliance used in treating urethral stricture. **vascular f.,** the light colored depression at the center of the disk of the retina.

F.U.O. Abbreviation for *fever of undetermined origin*.

furacin (fu′rah-sin). Trade mark for preparations of nitrofurazone.

furadantin (fur″ah-dan′tin). Trade mark for preparations of nitrofurantoin.

furaltadone (fūr-al′tah-dōn). Chemical name: 5-(4-morpholinylmethyl)-3-(5-nitro-2-furfurylideneamino)-2-oxazolidinone: used as an antibacterial.

furan, furane (fu′ran). A colorless liquid, CH:CH.CH:CH (ring closed by O), from wood tar.

furanose (fu′rah-nōs). A sugar in which the oxygen ring bridges carbon atoms 1 and 4 in the aldoses or carbon atoms 2 and 5 in the ketoses.

furaspor (fur′ah-spōr). Trade mark for a preparation of nitrofurfuryl methyl ether.

furazolidone (fu″rah-zol′ĭ-dōn). Chemical name: 3-(4-nitro-2-furfurylideneamino)-2-oxazolidinone: used as a local antibacterial and antiprotozoal.

Fürbringer's sign, test (fer′bring-erz) [Paul *Fürbringer*, Berlin physician, 1849–1930]. See under *sign* and *tests*.

furca (fur′kah), pl. *fur′cae* [L. "fork"]. The area lying between and at the base of normally divided tooth roots. See *bifurca* and *interfurca.*

furcae (fur′ke) [L.]. Plural of *furca.*

furcal (fur′kal) [L. *furca* fork]. Shaped like a fork; forked.

furcocercous (fur″ko-ser′kus) [L. *furca* fork + Gr. *kerkos* tail]. Having a forked tail.

furcula (fur′ku-la) [L. "little fork"]. A horseshoe-shaped ridge in the embryonic larynx, bounding the pharyngeal aperture in front and laterally.

furfur (fur′fur), pl. *fur′fures* [L. "bran"]. An epidermic scale, such as dandruff.

furfuraceous (fur″fu-ra′shus) [L. *furfur* bran]. Resembling bran or dandruff.

furfuran (fur′fu-ran). Furan.

furibund (fu′rĭ-bund). Full of fury; raging; maniacal.

furmethonol (fur-meth′o-nol). Furaltadone.

furor (fu′ror) [L.]. Fury; rage. **f. epilep′ticus,** an attack of intense anger occurring in epilepsy. **f. secan′di,** tomomania. **f. uteri′nus,** nymphomania.

furoxone (fur-ok′sōn). Trade mark for preparations of furazolidone.

furrow (fur′o). A groove or trench. **atrioventricular f.,** the transverse groove marking off the atria of the heart from the ventricles. **digital f.,** any one of the transverse lines on the palmar surface of a finger. **genital f.,** a groove that appears on the genital tubercle of the fetus at the end of the second month. **gluteal f.,** the furrow which separates the nates. **interventricular f.,** interventricular groove. **Jadelot's f's.** See under *line.* **Liebermeister's f's,** depressions sometimes seen on the upper surface of the liver from pressure of the ribs, generally from tight lacing. **mentolabial f.,** the hollow just above the chin. **nympholabial f.,** a groove separating the labium majus and labium minus on either side. **primitive f.,** primitive groove. **Schmorl's f.,** a depression over the apex of the lung, said to be indicative of a tendency to tuberculosis. **scleral f.,** scleral sulcus. **Sibson's f.,** the under border of the pectoralis major muscle. **skin f's,** sulci cutis.

Fürstner's disease (ferst′nerz) [Carl *Fürstner,* German psychiatrist, 1848–1906]. See under disease.

furuncle (fu′rung-k'l) [L. *furunculus*]. A painful nodule formed in the skin by circumscribed inflammation of the corium and subcutaneous tissue, inclosing a central slough or "core." It is caused by bacteria, which enter through the hair follicles or sudoriparous glands, and its formation is favored by constitutional or digestive derangement and local irritation.

furuncular (fu-rung′ku-lar). Pertaining to or of the nature of a furuncle or boil.

furunculoid (fu-rung′ku-loid). Resembling a furuncle or boil.

furunculosis (fu-rung″ku-lo′sis). The occurrence of a number of furuncles. **f. blastomycet′ica, f. cryptococ′cica,** a form of blastomycosis in which the lesions resemble furuncles.

furunculous (fu-rung′ku-lus). Furuncular.

furunculus (fu-rung′ku-lus), pl. *furun′culi* [L.]. Furuncle. **f. orienta′lis,** cutaneous leishmaniasis. **f. vulga′ris,** carbuncle.

Fusarium (fu-sa′re-um). A genus of molds belonging to the class of Ascomycetes. **F. equi′num** is believed to be the cause of itch disease, a dermatomycosis in horses in Oregon.

fuscin (fus′in) [L. *fuscus* brown]. A brown pigment of the retinal epithelium.

fuse (fūz). A bar, strip or wire of easily fusible metal inserted for safety in an electric circuit. When the current increases beyond a safe strength the metal melts, thus breaking the circuit and thereby saving an apparatus from overload.

fuseau (fĕ-zō′), pl. *fuseaux* [Fr.]. A spindle-shaped spore characteristic of fungi of the genus *Trichophyton.*

fusi (fu′si) [L.]. Plural of *fusus.*

fusible (fu′sĭ-b'l). Susceptible of being melted.

fusicellular (fu″sĭ-sel′u-lar). Fusocellular.

fusiform (fu′sĭ-form) [L. *fusus* spindle + *forma* form]. Spindle shaped.

Fusiformis (fu″sĭ-for′mis). A name formerly given to the genus *Fusobacterium.*

fusion (fu′zhun) [L. *fusio*]. 1. The act or process of melting. 2. The abnormal coherence of adjacent parts or bodies. 3. The coordination of the separate images of the same object in the two eyes into one. 4. The operative formation of an ankylosis (*f. of joint*). **binocular f.** See *fusion,* def. 3. **diaphyseal-epiphyseal f.,** operative establishment of bony union between the diaphysis and epiphysis, to arrest growth in length of a bone. **nerve f.,** a method of nerve anastomosis done for the purpose of inducing a regeneration which will resupply empty tracts of a nerve by new growths of fibers. **spinal f.,** spondylosyndesis.

fusional (fu′zhun-al). Marked by fusion.

Fusobacterium (fu″so-bak-te′re-um). A genus of nonsporulating obligate anaerobic filamentous bacteria occurring as normal flora in the mouth and large bowel; often found in necrotic tissue, probably as secondary invaders. **F. plauti-vincen′ti,** an organism found in necrotizing ulcerative gingivitis and stomatitis (trench mouth).

fusocellular (fu″so-sel′u-lar) [L. *fu′sus* spindle + *cellular*]. Having spindle-shaped cells.

fusospirillary (fu″so-spi′rĭ-lār″e). Pertaining to or caused by fusiform bacilli and spirillae, as in necrotizing ulcerative gingivitis.

fusospirillosis (fu″so-spi″rĭ-lo′sis). Necrotizing ulcerative gingivitis.

fusospirochetal (fu″so-spi″ro-ke′tal). Pertaining to or caused by fusiform bacilli and spirochetes.

fusospirochetosis (fu″so-spi″ro-ke-to′sis). Infection with fusiform bacilli and spirochetes.

fusostreptococcicosis (fu″so-strep″to-kok-sĭ-ko′sis). Infection with fusiform bacilli and streptococci.

fustic (fus′tik). A yellow dye wood from a South American tree, *Morus tinctoria.*

fustigation (fus″tĭ-ga′shun) [L. *fustigatio*]. Therapeutic treatment by flagellation. **electric f.,** therapeutic treatment by beating with rods or by the strokes of electrodes.

fusus (fu′sus), pl. *fu′si* [L.]. A spindle-like object; applied especially to minute air vesicles in a hair shaft. **cortical fusi,** the delicate air spaces appearing among the cells of the cortex as a hair grows out, produced by drying out of the fluid which fills the spaces in the living portion of the hair root. **fracture fusi,** minute rifts or ruptures observed between the keratinized cells of the cortex of a mature hair shaft which has been subjected to pressure sufficient to dissociate the cells of the particular region.

fututrix (fu-tu′triks). A female who practices tribadism.

F. vs. Abbreviation for L. *fi′at venaesec′tio,* let the patient be bled.

G

G. 1. Abbreviation for *gram, gingival,* and *gonidial* colony. 2. A symbol for the Newtonian constant of gravitation.

g. 1. Abbreviation for *gram* or *grams.* 2. A symbol used in aviation medicine for the unit of force which is exerted upon the aviator's body during acceleration in flying.

γ. The third letter of the Greek alphabet. See *gamma.* Used as a symbol for *microgram.*

G.A. Abbreviation for *gingivo-axial.*

Ga. Chemical symbol for *gallium.*

gadfly (gad′fli). See *Tabanus.*

gadinin (gad′ĭ-nin). A ptomaine, $C_7H_{16}NO_2$, from decaying fish and from bacterial cultures of human feces.

gadolinium (gad″o-lin′e-um). A rare element of atomic number 64, atomic weight 157.25, and symbol Gd.

gaduhiston (gad″u-his′ton) [L. *gadus* cod + *histon*]. A histon occurring in the spermatozoa of the codfish.

Gadus (ga′dus) [L.; Gr. *gados*]. A genus of fishes. **G. mor′rhua,** the codfish: from its liver, cod liver oil is prepared.

Gaenslen's sign, test (genz′lenz) [Frederick Julius *Gaenslen,* Milwaukee surgeon, 1877–1937]. See under *sign.*

Gaertner. See *Gärtner.*

gafeira (gaf″a-ir′ah) [Port.]. Leprosy.

Gaffky scale, table (gaf′ke) [Georg Theodor August *Gaffky,* German bacteriologist, 1850–1918]. See under *scale.*

Gaffkya (gaf′ke-ah) [G. T. A. *Gaffky*]. A genus of microorganisms of the family Micrococcaceae, order Eubacteriales, occurring as spherical cells in tetrads, often appearing to be enclosed in a common capsule. **G. homa′ri,** a species which is pathogenic for lobsters but is not known to occur in man. **G. tetrag′ena,** a part of the normal flora of the upper respiratory tract, but often pathogenic for mice, and other species.

gag (gag). 1. A surgical device for holding the mouth open. 2. To retch, or strive to vomit.

gage (gāj). Gauge.

gaile (gal) [Fr.]. Scabies.

Gaillard's suture (ga-yahrz′) [François Lucien *Gaillard,* French physician, 1805–1869]. See under *suture.*

Gairdner's test (gārd′nerz) [Sir William Tennant *Gairdner,* Scotch physician, 1824–1907]. Coin test. See under *tests.*

Gaisböck's disease, syndrome (gīs′bekz) [Felix *Gaisböck,* German physician, born 1868]. Polycythemia hypertonica.

gait (gāt). The manner or style of walking. **antalgic g.,** the limp characteristic of cured cases of coxalgia, marked by the avoidance of weight-bearing on the affected side. **ataxic g.,** a walk in which the foot is raised high and the entire sole strikes the ground at once and very suddenly. **cerebellar g.,** a staggering gait indicative of cerebellar disease. **Charcot's g.,** the peculiar gait of hereditary ataxia. **equine g.,** a walk accomplished mainly by flexing the hip joint: seen in peroneal paralysis. **festinating g.,** a gait in which the patient moves with short, hurrying steps, often on tiptoe. **gluteal g.,** the gait characteristic of paralysis of the gluteus medius muscle, marked by a listing of the trunk toward the affected side at each step. **helicopod g.,** a gait in which the feet describe half-circles, as in some cases of hysterical disorder and in certain cases of hemiplegia. **hemiplegic g.,** the helicopod gait of hemiplegia. **multiple sclerotic g.,** spastic gait with rigidity of the lower limbs. **Oppenheim's g.,** a gait marked by irregular oscillation of the head, limbs, and body: seen in some cases of disseminated sclerosis. **paralytic g.,** a gait in which the feet are dragged loosely along the ground. **scissor g.,** a gait in which one foot is passed in front of the other, producing a cross-legged progression. **spastic g.,** a walk in which the legs are held together and move in a stiff manner, the toes seeming to drag and catch. **steppage g.,** a gait in which the advancing foot hangs with the toes pointing toward the ground, the leg being lifted high in order that the toes may clear the ground. It is due to paralysis of the peroneal nerve and is seen in lesions of the lower motor neuron, such as multiple neuritis, lesions of the anterior motor horn cells, and lesions of the cauda equina. **swaying g.,** cerebellar g. **tabetic g.,** ataxic g.

gakhuri (gak-hoo′re). The plant, *Tribulus lanuginosus,* of India: used locally as a medicine.

galact-. See *galacto-.*

galacta-. See *galacto-.*

galactacrasia (gal″ak-tah-kra′se-ah) [*galact-* + *a* neg. + Gr. *krasis* mixture + *-ia*]. Abnormal condition of the breast milk.

galactagogin (gah-lak″tah-gog′in). The hypothetical galactagogue hormone of the placenta.

galactagogue (gah-lak′tah-gog) [*galact-* + Gr. *agōgos* leading]. 1. Increasing the flow of milk. 2. An agent that promotes the flow of milk.

galactan (gah-lak′tan). A hemicellulose carbohydrate that yields galactose upon hydrolysis. Agar is a well-known example.

galactase (gah-lak′tās). A proteolytic enzyme which hydrolyzes caseinogen in the stomach.

galactemia (gal″ak-te′me-ah) [*galact-* + Gr. *haima* blood + *-ia*]. A morbid condition of the blood in which it contains milk.

galactic (gah-lak′tik). 1. Pertaining to milk. 2. Galactagogue.

galactidrosis (gah-lak″tid-ro′sis) [*galact-* + Gr. *hidrōs* sweat]. The sweating of a fluid resembling milk.

galactin (gah-lak′tin). Prolactin.

galactischia (gal″ak-tisk′e-ah) [*galact-* + Gr. *ischein* to suppress]. Suppression of the secretion of milk.

galactite (gah-lak′tīt). Ethyl galactose.

galacto-, galact-, galacta- (gah-lak′to, gah-lakt′, gah-lak′tah) [Gr. *gala, galaktos* milk]. Combining form denoting relationship to milk.

galactoblast (gah-lak′to-blast) [*galacto-* + Gr. *blastos* germ]. A colostrum corpuscle found in the acini of the mammary gland.

galactocele (gah-lak′to-sēl) [*galacto-* + Gr. *kēlē* tumor]. 1. A cystic enlargement of the mammary gland containing milk. 2. A hydrocele filled with a milky fluid.

galactochloral (gah-lak-to-klo′ral). A derivative, $C_8H_4Cl_3O_6$, of chloral and galactose in glossy scales: it is used as a hypnotic.

galactococcus (gah-lak″to-kok′us) [*galacto-* + *coccus*]. A staphylococcus found in cases of inflammation of the udder in cows.

galactocrasia (gah-lak-to-kra′se-ah). Galactacrasia.

galactogen (gah-lak′to-jen). A polysaccharide in the eggs of snails which yields galactose on hydrolysis.

galactogenous (gal″ak-toj′e-nus) [*galacto-* + Gr. *gennan* to produce]. Favoring the production of milk.

galactogogue (gah-lak″to-gog). Galactagogue.

galactokinase (gah-lak″to-ki′nās). An enzyme

that catalyzes the transfer of a high-energy phosphate group from a donor to D-galactose, producing D-galactose-1-phosphate.

galactolipid (gah-lak″to-lip′id). Galactolipin.

galactolipin, galactolipine (gah-lak″to-li′pin). 1. Any compound of a fatty acid containing nitrogen but no phosphorus, and combined with galactose. 2. Cerebroside.

galactoma (gal″ak-to′mah) [*galact-* + *-oma*]. Galactocele.

galactometastasis (gah-lak″to-mĕ-tas′tah-sis). Galactoplania.

galactometer (gal″ak-tom′e-ter) [*galacto-* + Gr. *metron* measure]. An instrument for measuring the specific gravity of milk.

galactopathy (gal″ak-top′ah-the) [*galacto-* + Gr. *pathos* disease]. Milk cure.

galactopexic (gah-lak″to-pek′sik). Fixing or holding galactose.

galactopexy (gah-lak′to-pek″se). The fixation of galactose by the liver.

galactophagous (gal″ak-tof′ah-gus) [*galacto-* + Gr. *phagein* to eat]. Feeding upon milk.

galactophlebitis (gah-lak″to-fle-bi′tis) [*galacto-* + *phlebitis*]. Phlegmasia alba dolens.

galactophlysis (gal″ak-tof′lĭ-sis) [*galacto-* + Gr. *phlysis* eruption]. A vesicular eruption containing a milky fluid.

galactophore (gah-lak′to-for). 1. Galactophorous. 2. A milk duct.

galactophoritis (gah-lak″to-fo-ri′tis) [*galacto-* + Gr. *pherein* to carry + *-itis*]. Inflammation of the milk ducts.

galactophorous (gal″ak-tof′o-rus) [*galacto-* + Gr. *pherein* to bear]. Conveying milk.

galactophthisis (gal″ak-tof′thĭ-sis) [*galacto-* + *phthisis*]. Phthisis or emaciation due to or brought on by overlactation.

galactophygous (gal-ak-tof′ĭ-gus) [*galacto-* + Gr. *phygē* flight]. Arresting the milk secretion.

galactoplania (gah-lak″to-pla′ne-ah) [*galacto-* + Gr. *planē* wandering]. The secretion of milk in some abnormal part; the metastasis of milk.

galactopoietic (gah-lak″to-poi-et′ik) [*galacto-* + Gr. *poiein* to make]. 1. Pertaining to, characterized by, or promoting the production of milk. 2. An agent that promotes the secretion of milk.

galactopyra (gah-lak″to-pi′rah) [*galacto-* + Gr. *pyr* fire]. Milk fever.

galactopyranose (gah-lak″to-pi′rah-nōs). The pyranose form of galactose, $CH_2OH.$-CH.CH.$(CHOH)_3$.CHOH (ring through O from first CH to CHOH).

galactorrhea (gah-lak″to-re′ah) [*galacto-* + Gr. *rhoia* flow]. Excessive or spontaneous flow of milk.

galactosamine (gah-lak″to-sam′in). An amino sugar, $NH_2.CH_2.C(CHOH)_4CHOH$ (ring through O from C to CHOH).

galactosan (gah-lak′to-san). A polysaccharide occurring in plants, yielding galactose on hydrolysis.

galactosazone (gah-lak″to-sa′zōn). The phenylosazone of galactose, $CHOH(CHOH)_3C(:N.NH.C_6H_5).CH.N.NH.C_6H_5$. It is a yellow, crystalline substance which is formed by treating galactose with phenylhydrazine and acetic acid. The crystals melt at 193°C. and may be used in identifying galactose.

galactoschesis (gal″ak-tos′kĕ-sis) [*galacto-* + Gr. *schesis* suppression]. Suppression of the milk secretion.

galactoscope (gah-lak′to-skōp) [*galacto-* + Gr. *skopein* to examine]. A device for showing the proportion of cream in the milk.

galactose (gah-lak′tōs). An aldohexose, $CH_2OH(CHOH)_4CHO$, obtained from lactose or milk sugar by the action of an enzyme or by boiling with a mineral acid. It is a white crystalline substance, resembles glucose in most of its properties, but is less soluble, less sweet, and forms mucic acid when oxidized with nitric acid. *d*-Galactose is found in milk sugar, in the cerebrosides of the brain, in the raffinose of the sugar beet, and in many gums and seaweeds; *l*-galactose in flaxseed mucilage.

galactosemia (gah-lak″to-se′me-ah). 1. A hereditary disorder of carbohydrate metabolism, characterized by vomiting, diarrhea, jaundice, poor weight gain, and malnutrition in early infancy. 2. The presence of galactose in the blood.

galactosidase (gah-lak″to-si′dās). An enzyme which catalyzes the splitting of galactosides.

galactoside (gah-lak′to-sīd). A glycoside containing galactose. **beta g.,** lactose.

galactosis (gal″ak-to′sis). The formation of milk by the lacteal glands.

galactostasia (gah-lak″to-sta′se-ah). Galactostasis.

galactostasis (gal″ak-tos′tah-sis) [*galacto-* + Gr. *stasis* halt]. 1. Cessation of the milk secretion. 2. An abnormal collection of milk.

galactosuria (gah-lak″to-su′re-ah) [*galactose* + Gr. *ouron* urine + *-ia*]. Presence of galactose in the urine.

galactotherapy (gah-lak″to-ther′ah-pe) [*galacto-* + Gr. *therapeia* treatment]. 1. The treatment of suckling children by giving remedies to the mother or wet nurse. 2. Milk cure. 3. The hypodermic injection of the milk of a syphilitic patient for the cure of syphilis.

galactotoxicon (gah-lak″to-tok′sĭ-kon). A poisonous compound formed in decomposed milk.

galactotoxin (gah-lak″to-tok′sin) [*galacto-* + Gr. *toxikon* poison]. A basic substance formed in milk.

galactotoxism (gah-lak″to-tok′sizm). Poisoning by milk.

galactotrophy (gal″ak-tot′ro-fe) [*galacto-* + Gr. *trophē* nutrition]. Feeding with milk.

galactoxism (gal″ak-tok′sizm). Galactotoxism.

galactoxismus (gah-lak″tok-siz′mus). Galactotoxism.

galactozymase (gah-lak″to-zi′mās) [*galacto-* + Gr. *zymē* leaven]. A starch-liquefying ferment.

galacturia (gal″ak-tu′re-ah) [*galact-* + Gr. *ouron* urine + *-ia*]. The discharge of milklike urine; chyluria.

galalith (gal′ah-lith) [Gr. *gala* milk + *lithos* stone]. A material for the manufacture of absorbable anastomosis buttons, consisting of paracasein hardened by solution of formaldehyde.

galea (ga′le-ah) [L.]. A helmet, or helmetlike structure. **g. aponeurot′ica** [N A, B N A], the aponeurotic structure of the scalp, connecting the frontal and occipital bellies of the occipitofrontalis muscle. **tendinous g.,** g. aponeurotica.

galeanthropy (ga″le-an′thro-pe) [Gr. *galē* cat + *anthrōpos* man]. A mental delusion that one has become a cat.

Galeati's glands (gal″e-ah′tēz) [Domenico Maria *Galeati*, Italian physician, 1686–1775]. Intestinal glands.

galeatus (gal″e-a′tus) [L. *galea* helmet]. Born with a caul.

Galeazzi's fracture, sign (gal″e-at′zēz) [Riccardo *Galeazzi*, Italian orthopedic surgeon, 1866–1952]. See under the nouns.

Galen (ga′len) [Claudius Galenus] (130–200 A.D.). The celebrated Greek physician and medical writer, born at Pergamum (Asia Minor); latterly he practiced in Rome, where he became physician to the Emperor, Marcus Aurelius. Although he did not dissect the human cadaver, he made many valuable anatomical and physiological observations on animals, and his writings on these and other subjects are extensive. His influence on medicine was profound for many centuries—his teleology ("nature does nothing in vain") being particularly attractive to the medieval mind, although it was stultifying as regards advances in medical thought and practice.

galenic (gah-len′ik). Pertaining to the ancient system of medicine taught and practiced by Galenus, or Galen.

galenica (gah-len′ĭ-kah). Galenicals.

galenicals (gah-len′ĭ-kalz). Medicines prepared according to the formulas of Galen. The term is now used to denote standard preparations containing one or several organic ingredients, as contrasted with pure chemical substances.

galenics (gah-len′iks). Galenicals.

galenism (ga′len-izm). Galen's system of medicine, being a blend of the humoral theory and Pythagorean number lore.

Galeodes araneoides (gal″e-o′dēz ah-ra″ne-oi′dēz). A spiderlike animal of the Old World, with a venomous bite.

galeophilia (gal″e-o-fil′e-ah). Ailurophilia.

galeophobia (gal″e-o-fo′be-ah). Ailurophobia.

galeropia, galeropsia (gal″er-o′pe-ah, gal″er-op′se-ah) [Gr. *galeros* cheerful + *opsis* vision]. Abnormal clearness of vision.

gall (gawl) [L. *galla*]. 1. The bile. 2. Nutgall. **Aleppo g.,** nutgall. **ox g.,** fel bovis. **Smyrna g.,** nutgall. **wind g.,** vessicnon.

Gall's craniology (gawlz) [Franz Joseph *Gall*, anatomist in Vienna and Paris, 1758–1828]. Phrenology.

gallacetophenone (gal-as″e-to-fe′non). A yellowish powder, $CH_3.CO.C_6H_2(OH)_3$, or trioxyacetophenone.

gallamine triethiodide (gal′lah-mĭn tri″ĕ-thi′o-dīd). Chemical name: [v-phenenyltris(oxyethylene)] tris [triethylammonium iodide]. Used to relax skeletal muscles.

gallate (gal′āt). Any salt of gallic acid.

gallbladder (gawl′blad-der). The pear-shaped reservoir for the bile on the posteroinferior surface of the liver, between the right and the quadrate lobe. Called also *vesica fellea* [N A]. **Courvoisier's g.,** a chronically obstructed gallbladder. **fish-scale g.,** a gallbladder presenting a fish-scale-like appearance from multiple small cysts of the mucosa. **folded fundus g.,** a gallbladder showing a complete bend or a constriction in the x-ray picture; called also *phrygian cap*. **sandpaper g.,** a rough state of the mucous membrane of the gallbladder caused by the presence of the cholesterin crystals. **stasis g.,** a gallbladder in which there is increased inflow of bile and retardation of the outflow. **strawberry g.,** a gallbladder presenting a strawberry-like appearance, due to fine grains of cholesterin-fat material embedded in the mucosa as a result of chronic catarrhal inflammation. **wandering g.,** abnormal mobility of the fundus and body of the gallbladder.

gallein (gal′e-in). Dioxyfluorescein, an aniline dye indicator which is changed in color by an alkali to red and by an acid to yellow.

Gallie transplant (gal′e) [William Edward *Gallie*, Toronto surgeon, 1882–1959]. Strips of fascia lata of the thigh employed as sutures in hernia operations.

Galli Mainini test (gal′e mi-ne′ne) [Carlos *Galli Mainini*, physician in Buenos Aires]. See under *test*.

Gallionella (gal″le-o-nel′lah) [Benjamin *Gaillon*, French zoologist, 1782–1839]. A genus of microorganisms of the family Caulobacteraceae, suborder Pseudomonadineae, order Pseudomonadales, occurring as stalked, kidney-shaped or rounded cells, growing only in iron-containing fresh or salt water. It includes five species, *G. ferrugin'ea*, *G. infurca'ta*, *G. ma'jor*, *G. mi'nor*, and *G. umbella'ta*.

gallipot (gal′ĭ-pot). A small pot for ointments or confections.

gallisin (gal′ĭ-sin). A substance analogous to dextrin.

gallium (gal′e-um) [L., from *Gallia* Gaul]. A rare metal; atomic number, 31, atomic weight, 69.72; symbol, Ga: some of its compounds are poisonous.

gallon (gal′on) [L. *congius*]. A measure of volume, four quarts (3785 cc.); in the United States, 231 cubic inches.

gallsickness (gawl-sik′nes). A disease of cattle marked by high temperature, anemia, and icterus. Caused by *Anaplasma marginale*.

gallstone (gawl′stōn). A concretion, usually of cholesterol, formed in the gallbladder or bile duct.

Galton's delta, law, whistle (gawl′tonz) [Francis *Galton*, English scientist, 1822–1911]. See under the nouns.

Galv. Abbreviation for *galvanic*.

galvanic (gal-van′ik). 1. Named for or discovered by Luigi *Galvani*, Italian physician and physiologist, 1737–1798. 2. Pertaining to galvanism.

galvanism (gal′vah-nizm) [Luigi *Galvani*]. 1. Galvanic electricity: uninterrupted current electricity derived from a chemical battery. 2. The therapeutical use of direct current.

galvanization (gal″vah-ni-za′shun). Treatment by galvanic electricity. **spinogastric g.,** galvanization in which the negative pole is placed over the stomach, and the positive is moved up and down the spine.

galvanocautery (gal″vah-no-kaw′ter-e). Cautery by a wire heated with a galvanic current.

galvanochemical (gal″vah-no-kem′e-kal). Pertaining to the chemical action of the galvanic current.

galvanocontractility (gal″vah-no-kon″trak-til′ĭ-te). Contractility in response to a galvanic stimulus.

galvanofaradization (gal″vah-no-far″ah-di-za′shun). The simultaneous use of continuous and interrupted electric currents.

galvanogustometer (gal″vah-no-gus-tom′e-ter). An apparatus for the clinical determination of taste thresholds by the use of a galvanic current.

galvanoionization (gal″vah-no-i″on-i-za′shun). Iontophoresis.

galvanolysis (gal″vah-nol′ĭ-sis) [*galvanism* + Gr. *lysis* dissolution]. Electrolysis.

galvanometer (gal″vah-nom′e-ter) [*galvanism* + Gr. *metron* measure]. An instrument for measuring current by electromagnetic action. **Einthoven's g., string g., thread g.,** an apparatus for detecting very minute electric currents, consisting of a delicate thread of silvered quartz or platinum stretched between the poles of a strong magnet. The thread may be illuminated by an arc light and the shadow of the thread thrown upon a screen after being magnified by a microscope.

galvanomuscular (gal″vah-no-mus′ku-lar). Produced by the application of the galvanic current directly to a muscle.

galvanonarcosis (gal″vah-no-nar-ko′sis). Electronarcosis.

galvanonervous (gal″vah-no-ner′vus). Produced by application of the galvanic current to a nerve trunk.

galvanopalpation (gal″vah-no-pal-pa′shun). A method of testing the sensory and vasomotor nerves of the skin by applying a sharp-pointed anode electrode to the part of the skin to be tested, the cathode being applied to some other part of the body.

galvanopuncture (gal″vah-no-pungk′tūr). The introduction of needles to complete a galvanic circuit.

galvanoscope (gal-van′o-skōp) [*galvanism* + Gr. *skopein* to examine]. An instrument that shows the presence of a galvanic current.

galvanoscopy (gal″vah-nos′ko-pe). Diagnostic examination by means of galvanism.

galvanosurgery (gal″vah-no-sur′jer-e). The employment of galvanism in surgery.

galvanotaxis (gal″vah-no-tak′sis). The tendency of a living organism to arrange itself in a medium so that its axis bears a certain relation to the direction of the current in the medium.

galvanotherapeutics, galvanotherapy (gal-vah-no-ther″ah-pu′tiks, gal″vah-no-ther′ah-pe). The therapeutical employment of galvanic current.

galvanothermy (gal″vah-no-ther′me) [*galvanism* + Gr. *thermē* heat]. Heating or burning by means of a galvanic current.

galvanotonic (gal″vah-no-ton′ik). Of the nature of galvanotonus; both galvanic and tonic.

galvanotonus (gal″vah-not′o-nus) [*galvanism* + Gr. *tonos* tension]. Tonic response to galvanism.

galvanotropism (gal″vah-not′ro-pizm) [*galvanism* + Gr. *tropos* a turn]. The tendency of an organism to turn or move under the action of an electric current.

galziekte (gahl-zēk′te) [Dutch *gal* gall + *ziekte* sickness]. South African name for gallsickness.

gam-. See *gamo-*.

Gamaleia's spirillum (gam″ah-la′yahz) [M. *Gamaleia*, Russian bacteriologist, [1859–1949]. *Vibrio metchnikovii*.

gamasid (gam′ah-sid). A mite of the family Gamasidae.

Gamasidae (gah-mas′ĭ-de). A family of mites of the order Acarina; the spider mites or beetle mites. They are parasitic on birds and animals.

gamasoidosis (gam″ah-soi-do′sis). Infestation by a mite of the family Gamasidae, such as the dermatitis caused by the fowl mite, *Dermanyssus*.

Gambian horse sickness (gam′be-an) [*Gambia*, a British colony of the west coast of Africa]. See under *sickness*.

gamboge (gam-bōj′, gam-booj′). See *cambogia*.

Gambusia (gam-bu′se-ah). A genus of fish effective in destroying mosquito larvae. **G. affin′is,** a top minnow which has been introduced into every major malarious region in the world. It feeds upon the larvae of Anopheles mosquitoes along the surface of the water.

gamefar (gah′mĕ-fahr). Pamaquine.

gamete (gam′ēt) [Gr. *gametē* wife, *gametēs* husband]. 1. A reproductive element; one of two cells, male and female, whose union is necessary, in sexual reproduction, to initiate the development of a new individual. 2. The malarial parasite in its sexual form in the stomach of a mosquito, either male (microgamete) or female (macrogamete). The latter is fertilized by the former to develop into an ookinete.

gametic (gah-met′ik). Pertaining to gametes or the primitive sexual elements.

gameto- (gam′ĕ-to). Combining form denoting relationship to a gamete.

gametoblast (gam′ĕ-to-blast) [*gameto-* + Gr. *blastos* germ]. A sporozoite.

gametocidal (gam″ĕ-to-si′dal). Capable of destroying gametes or gametocytes.

gametocide (gam′ĕ-to-sīd) [*gameto-* + L. *caedere* to kill]. An agent that destroys gametes or gametocyte.

gametocinetic (gam″ĕ-to-si-net′ik). Gametokinetic.

gametocyte (gah-met′o-sīt) [*gameto-* + Gr. *kytos* hollow vessel]. The sexual plasmodial cell in malarial blood which may produce gametes when taken into the mosquito host. It may be male (microgametocyte) or female (macrogametocyte).

gametocytemia (gah-me″to-si-te′me-ah). The presence of malarial gametocytes in the blood corpuscles.

gametogenesis (gam″ĕ-to-jen′e-sis) [*gameto-* + Gr. *genesis* production]. The development of the male and female sex cells or gametes.

gametogenic (gam″ĕ-to-jen′ik). Favoring the production of germ cells.

gametogonia (gam″ĕ-to-go′ne-ah). 1. The phase of the development cycle of the malarial parasite in man in which male and female gametocytes are formed which infect the mosquito. 2. Reproduction by means of gametes.

gametogony (gam″ĕ-tog′o-ne). Gametogonia.

gametoid (gam′ĕ-toid). Resembling gametes or reproductive cells.

gametokinetic (gam″ĕ-to-ki-net′ik) [*gameto-* + Gr. *kinein* to move]. Stimulating gamete action.

gametologist (gam″ĕ-tol′o-jist). A scientist whose special study is gametology.

gametology (gam″ĕ-tol′o-je) [*gamete* + Gr. *logos* discourse]. The study of gametes.

gametophagia (gam″ĕ-to-fa′je-ah). Gamophagia.

gametophyte (gam′ĕ-to-fīt) [*gameto-* + Gr. *phyton* plant]. The haploid or sexual stage in the antithetic alternation of generations.

gametotropic (gam″ĕ-to-trop′ik). Having affinity for gametes.

Gamgee tissue (gam′je) [Sampson *Gamgee*, British surgeon, 1828–1886]. See under *tissue*.

gamic (gam′ik). Sexual: applied to eggs which develop only after fertilization.

gamma (gam′mah). 1. The third letter in the Greek alphabet, γ; used as part of a chemical name to distinguish the third in a series of compounds or to designate the position of the third carbon atom of an aliphatic chain or the position opposite the alpha position on the naphthalene ring. 2. Microgram. 3. A unit of intensity of magnetic field, $\gamma = 0.00001$ gauss. 4. A numerical expression of the degree of development of a photographic negative.

gamma benzene hexachloride (gam′mah ben′zēn hek″sah-klōr′īd). Lindane.

gammacism (gam′ah-sizm) [Gr. *gamma* the letter G]. The imperfect utterance of G sounds.

gammagraphic (gam″ah-graf′ik). Pertaining to the recording of gamma rays in the study of organs after the administration of radioactive isotopes.

gammagram (gam′ah-gram). A graphic record of the gamma rays emitted by an object or substance.

gamma-lactone (gam″mah-lak′tōn). A compound having a five-membered ring structure formed by internal reaction of a carboxylic acid group with a hydroxyl group on the gamma carbon of a carbon chain.

gammaloidosis (gam″mah-loi-do′sis). Amyloidosis.

gamma-pipradol (gam″ah-pip′rah-dol). Azacyclonol.

gammot (gam′ot). An old form of surgical knife.

gamo-, gam- (gam′o, gam′) [Gr. *gamos* marriage]. Combining form denoting relationship to marriage or sexual union.

gamobium (gah-mo′be-um) [*gamo-* + Gr. *bios* life]. In biology, the sexually reproducing generation in cases of alternation of generation. Cf. *agamobium*.

gamogenesis (gam″o-jen′e-sis) [*gamo-* + Gr. *genesis* production]. Sexual reproduction.

gamogenetic (gam″o-jĕ-net′ik). Pertaining to or exhibiting sexual reproduction.

gamogonia (gam″o-go′ne-ah). Gametogonia.

gamomania (gam″o-ma′ne-ah). A morbid desire to marry.

gamont (gam′ont) [*gam-* + Gr. *ōn* being]. Either of the conjugating individuals in gregarine reproduction.

gamophagia (gam″o-fa′je-ah) [*gamo-* + Gr. *phagein* to eat]. The disappearance of the male or female element in the conjugation of unicellular organisms.

gamophobia (gam″o-fo′be-ah) [*gamo-* + *phobia*]. Morbid fear of marriage.

gampsodactylia (gamp″so-dak-til′e-ah) [Gr. *gampsos* crooked + *daktylos* digit + *-ia*]. Deformity of the toes marked by hyperextension of the first phalanx on the metatarsal and flexion of the other two phalanges. Called also *clawfoot*.

Gandy-Gamna nodule. See *Gamna nodules*, under *nodule*.

ganga (gang′gah). A preparation of the pistillate flowers of *Cannabis sativa:* used for smoking.

gangli-. See *ganglio-*.
ganglia (gang′gle-ah). Plural of *ganglion*.
ganglial (gang′gle-al). Pertaining to a ganglion.
gangliasthenia (gang″gle-as-the′ne-ah). Asthenia due to ganglionic disease.
gangliated (gang′gle-āt″ed). Ganglionated.
gangliectomy (gang″gle-ek′to-me). Ganglionectomy.
gangliform (gang′glĭ-form). Having the form of a ganglion.
gangliitis (gang″gle-i′tis). Ganglionitis.
ganglio-, gangli- (gang′gle-o, gang′gle) [Gr. *ganglion* knot]. Combining form denoting relationship to a ganglion.
ganglioblast (gang′gle-o-blast) [*ganglio-* + Gr. *blastos* germ]. An embryonic cell of the cerebrospinal ganglia.
gangliocyte (gang′gle-o-sīt) [*ganglio-* + Gr. *kytos* hollow vessel]. A ganglion cell.
gangliocytoma (gang″gle-o-si-to′mah). A tumor containing ganglion cells.
glioform (gang′gle-o-form). Gangliform.
ganglioglioma (gang″gle-o-gli-o′mah). A glioma rich in mature neurons or ganglion cells.
ganglioglioneuroma (gang″gle-o-gli″o-nu-ro′-mah). A nerve tumor containing ganglion cells, glia cells, and nerve fibers.
gangliolytic (gang″gle-o-lyt′ik). Ganglioplegic.
ganglioma (gang″gle-o′mah) [*ganglio-* + *-oma*]. A tumor of a lymphatic ganglion.
ganglion (gang′gle-on), pl. *ganglia* or *ganglions* [Gr. "knot"]. 1. A knot, or knotlike mass; used in anatomical nomenclature as a general term to designate a group of nerve cell bodies located outside of the central nervous system. In older terminology the term was occasionally applied to certain nuclear groups within the brain or spinal cord. 2. A form of cystic tumor occurring on an

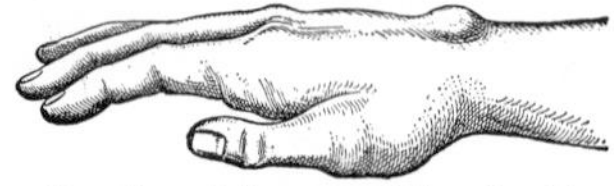

Ganglion of the wrist (Moorhead).

aponeurosis or tendon, as in the wrist. **abdominal ganglia,** ganglia celiacum. **acousticofacial g.,** a ganglion of early embryonic life, a portion of which persists as the geniculate ganglion. **Acrel's g.,** a cystic tumor on an extensor tendon of the wrist. **Andersch's g.,** g. inferius nervi glossopharyngei. **anterior g. of thalamus,** the anterior tubercle of the thalamus. **aorticorenal g., g. aorticorena′le** [N A], a more or less detached inferior portion of the celiac ganglion. **Arnold's g.** 1. Ganglion oticum. 2. Glomus caroticum. **auditory g.** See *nuclei nervi cochlearis, ventralis et dorsalis*. **Auerbach's g.,** any one of the small ganglia of Auerbach's plexus. **auricular g.,** g. oticum. **basal ganglia,** masses of gray matter centrally embedded with the thalamus in the cerebral hemisphere, comprising the corpus striatum (caudate and lentiform nuclei), amygdaloid body, and claustrum. Sometimes the thalamus is considered as part of the basal ganglia; the tuber cinereum, geniculate bodies, and even the corpora quadrigemina have also been included. Called also *basal nuclei*. **Bezold's g.,** a series of ganglion cells in the interatrial septum. **Bidder's ganglia,** two ganglia of the auricular septum of a frog's heart. **Blandin's g.,** g. submandibulare. **Bochdalek's g., g. Bochdalek′ii,** plexus dentalis superior. **Bock's g.,** carotid g. **cardiac ganglia, gan′glia cardi′aca** [N A], ganglia usually found connected with the cardiac plexus on the right side of the arterial ligament. **carotid g.,** a ganglion in the lower part of the cavernous sinus. **carotid g., inferior,** a ganglion of the lower part of the carotid canal. **carotid g., superior,** one in the upper part of the carotid canal. **casserian g.,** g. trigeminale. **celiac g., g. celi′acum** [N A], a group of postganglionic sympathetic nerve cell bodies associated with the celiac plexus, lying on the crus of the diaphragm and innervating abdominal viscera. It receives preganglionic fibers from the greater and lesser splanchnic nerves. **central g. of brain,** the thalamus and corpus striatum. **cephalic g.,** the ciliary, otic, sphenopalatine, and submaxillary ganglia, all mainly of the sympathetic, or trisplanchnic, system. **cerebral g., g. cer′ebri,** thalamus. **cerebrospinal ganglia,** the ganglia associated with the cranial and spinal nerves. **cervical g., inferior,** g. cervicothoracicum. **cervical g., middle,** g. cervicale medium. **cervical g., superior,** g. cervicale superius. **cervical g. of uterus,** a ganglion situated near the cervix uteri. **g. cervica′le infe′rius** [B N A], g. cervicothoracicum. **g. cervica′le me′dium** [N A, B N A], a ganglion on the sympathetic trunk at about the level of the cricoid cartilage. Its postganglionic fibers are distributed mainly to the heart, cervical region, and upper member. **g. cervica′le supe′rius** [N A, B N A], a ganglion on the thoracic trunk in front of the second and third cervical vertebrae; the highest ganglion on the sympathetic trunk, it gives rise to postganglionic fibers to the head. **cervicothoracic g., g. cervicothora′cicum** [N A], a ganglion on the sympathetic trunk anterior to the lowest cervical or first thoracic vertebra. It is formed by a union of the seventh and eighth cervical and the first thoracic ganglia. Called also *g. cervicale inferius* [B N A], and *stellate g.* **cervico-uterine g.,** Frankenhäuser's g. **g. cilia′re** [N A, B N A], **ciliary g.,** a parasympathetic ganglion in the posterior part of the orbit, from which the smooth muscles of the eye are innervated. It receives preganglionic fibers from the oculomotor nerve. **Cloquet's g.,** an enlargement of the nasopalatine nerve in the anterior palatine canal. **coccygeal g.,** glomus coccygeum. **compound g.,** a cystic tumor of a tendon sheath that has been compressed into two parts by a ligament. **Corti's g.,** g. spirale partis cochlearis nervi octavi. **Darkschewitsch's g.,** Darkschewitsch's nucleus. **diaphragmatic ganglia,** ganglia phrenica. **diffuse g.,** a swelling of several adjoining tendon sheaths due to inflammatory effusion. **dorsal root g.,** spinal g. **g. ectomamilla′re,** corpus mamillare. **Ehrenritter's g.,** g. superius nervi glossopharyngei. **g. extracrania′le,** g. inferius nervi glossopharyngei. **g. of facial nerve.** See *g. impar* and *ganglia intermedia trunci sympathici*. **false g.,** an enlargement on a nerve that does not have a true ganglionic structure. **Frankenhäuser's g.,** a ganglion near the cervix uteri. Called also *cervico-uterine g.* **Froriep's g.,** the ganglion of the lowest occipital segment in the human embryo. **Ganser's g.,** nucleus interpeduncularis. **gasserian g.,** g. trigeminale. **geniculate g., g. genic′uli ner′vi facia′lis** [N A, B N A], the sensory ganglion of the facial nerve, situated on the geniculum of that nerve. **g. of Gudden,** nucleus interpeduncularis. **g. of habenulae,** nucleus habenulae. **hepatic g.,** a ganglion situated near the hepatic artery. **hypogastric g.,** either of two ganglia on each side of the cervix uteri, connected with the sacral and hypogastric plexuses. **hypoglossal g.,** a ganglion of the dorsal root of the hypoglossal nerve; rarely found in the human subject. **g. im′par** [N A], the ganglion commonly found in front of the coccyx, where the sympathetic trunks of the two sides unite. **inferior g. of glossopharyngeal nerve,** g. inferius nervi glossopharyngei. **inferior g. of vagus,** g. inferius nervi vagi. **g. infe′rius ner′vi glossopharyn′gei** [N A], a ganglion on the glossopharyngeal nerve at the lower border of the petrous bone. It and the superior ganglion contain cell bodies for sensory fibers of the nerve. Called also *g. petrosum* [B N A]. **g. infe′rius ner′vi va′gi** [N A], a general sensory ganglion of the vagus nerve located below the superior ganglion, opposite the transverse processes of the first and second cervical vertebrae. Called also *g. nodosum* [B N A]. **inframaxillary g., anterior,** a ganglion situated near the incisor teeth, and giving off filaments to the teeth. **inframaxillary g., posterior,** a ganglion situated near the last molar teeth. **inhibitory g.,** any ganglion performing an inhibitory function. **intercarotid g.,** glomus caroticum. **g. intercrania'le,** g. superius nervi glossopharyngei. **intercrural g., intercrural g. of Arnold,** nucleus interpeduncularis. **gan'glia interme'dia** [N A], **intermediate ganglia,** small groups of sympathetic nerve cell bodies commonly found on communicating branches of the spinal nerves in the cervical and lumbar regions. **interpeduncular g.,** nucleus interpeduncularis. **intervertebral g. of head, posterior,** g. superius nervi glossopharyngei. **g. intervertebra'le,** g. spinale. **g. isth'mi,** nucleus interpeduncularis. **jugular g., inferior,** g. inferius nervi glossopharyngei. **jugular g. of glossopharyngeal nerve,** g. superius nervi glossopharyngei. **jugular g. of vagus nerve, g. jugula're ner'vi va'gi** [B N A], g. superius nervi vagi. **Küttner's g.,** a large lymphatic gland on the internal jugular vein immediately beneath the posterior belly of the digastric muscle, forming the principal lymphatic terminus of the tongue. Called also *hauptganglion*. **Langley's g.,** a collection of nerve cells in the hilus of the submaxillary gland. **Laumonier's g.,** carotid g. **Lee's g.,** cervical g. of the uterus. **lenticular g.,** g. ciliare. **lesser g. of Meckel,** g. submandibulare. **lingual g.,** g. submandibulare. **lobar g.,** the ganglion of the cerebral lobes. **Lobstein's g.,** a small enlargement on the great splanchnic nerve above the diaphragm. **Loetwig's g.,** bulbus cordis. **lower g. of glossopharyngeal nerve,** g. inferius nervi glossopharyngei. **lower g. of vagus nerve,** g. inferius nervi vagi. **Ludwig's g.,** a ganglion connected with the cardiac plexus and situated near the right atrium of the heart. **gan'glia lumba'lia** [N A, B N A], **lumbar ganglia,** the ganglia on the lumbar part of the sympathetic trunk, usually numbering four on either side. **Luschka's g.,** glomus coccygeum. **gan'glia lymphat'ica,** lymph nodes. See *nodus lymphaticus*. **maxillary g.,** g. submandibulare. **Meckel's g.,** g. pterygopalatinum. **Meissner's g.,** one of the small ganglionic nodes in Meissner's plexus. **mesenteric g., inferior,** g. mesentericum inferius. **mesenteric g., superior,** g. mesentericum superius. **g. mesenter'icum infe'rius** [N A], a sympathetic ganglion in the inferior mesenteric plexus near the beginning of the inferior mesenteric artery. **g. mesenter'icum supe'rius** [N A, B N A], a subdivision of the celiac ganglion found near the superior mesenteric artery. **Meynert's g.,** a mass of cells within the tuber cinereum near the optic tract. Called also *basal optic g.* **g. of Müller,** g. superius nervi glossopharyngei. **nasal g.,** g. pterygopalatinum. **nephrolumbar g.,** a ganglion at the junction of branches of the spermatic and lumbar nerves, giving off branches to the kidney and lumbar region. **g. ner'vi splanch'nici,** g. splanchnicum (def. 1). **Neubauer's g.,** the ganglion formed by the lower cervical and first thoracic ganglia. **nodose g., g. nodo'sum** [B N A], g. inferius nervi vagi. **olfactory g.,** a mass of tissue in the embryo which develops into the olfactory nerves. **ophthalmic g.,** g. ciliare. **optic g., orbital g.,** g. ciliare. **otic g., g. o'ticum** [N A, B N A], a parasympathetic ganglion next to the medial surface of the mandibular division of the trigeminal nerve, just inferior to the foramen ovale, formed by postganglionic cell bodies that synapse with preganglionic fibers from the lesser petrosal nerve. **pelvic ganglia, gan'glia pelvi'na** [N A], small sympathetic and parasympathetic ganglia located within the pelvic plexus. **periosteal g.,** periostitis albuminosa. **petrosal g., petrosal g., inferior, g. petro'sum, petrous g.,** g. inferius nervi glossopharyngei. **pharyngeal g.,** a ganglion on an anterior branch of the carotid plexus. **phrenic ganglia, gan'glia phren'ica** [N A, B N A], small sympathetic ganglia sometimes found within the phrenic plexus. **gan'glia plex'uum autonomico'rum** [N A], **gan'glia plex'uum sympathico'rum** [B N A], groups of nerve cell bodies found in the autonomic plexuses, composed primarily of sympathetic postganglionic neurons. Called also *ganglia of autonomic plexuses*. **prevertebral g.,** sympathetic ganglia of the thorax and abdomen other than those of the sympathetic trunk. **primary g.,** a ganglion on a tendon or aponeurosis that does not follow a local inflammation. **prostatic g.,** a ganglion situated on the prostate gland, and connected with the prostatic plexus. **pterygopalatine g., g. pterygopalati'num** [N A], a parasympathetic ganglion in the pterygopalatine fossa, formed by postganglionic cell bodies that synapse with preganglionic fibers from the facial nerve via the nerve of the pterygopalatine canal. Called also *g. sphenopalatinum* [B N A]. **Remak's g.,** a sympathetic ganglion in the heart tissue near the superior vena cava. **renal ganglia, gan'glia rena'lia** [N A], small sympathetic ganglia within the renal plexus. **g. ret'inae,** the outer of the two subdivisions of the internal nuclear layer of the retina. **Ribes' g.,** the alleged upper termination of the sympathetic nerve surrounding the anterior communicating artery of the brain. **sacral ganglia, gan'glia sacra'lia** [N A, B N A], the ganglia of the sacral part of the sympathetic trunk, usually four on either side. **Scarpa's g.,** g. vestibulare. **Schacher's g.,** g. ciliare. **Schmiedel's g.,** inferior carotid g. **semilunar g.** 1. Ganglion trigeminale. 2. Ganglion celiacum. **semilunar g., abdominal, g. semiluna're [Gas'seri],** g. trigeminale. **sensory g.,** a name sometimes applied to the collective masses of nerve cell bodies in the brain subserving the function of sensation. **simple g.,** a cystic tumor in a tendon sheath. **sinoatrial g.,** Remak's g. **sinus g.,** a group of nerve cells around the junction of the coronary sinus and the right atrium of the heart. **Soemmering's g.,** substantia nigra. **solar ganglia,** ganglia celiacum. **sphenomaxillary g., sphenopalatine g., g. sphenopalati'num,** g. pterygopalatinum. **spinal g., g. spina'le** [N A, B N A], the ganglion found on the dorsal root of each spinal nerve, composed of the unipolar nerve cell bodies of the sensory neurons of the nerve. **spiral g., spiral g. of cochlea,** g. spirale cochleae. **spiral g. of cochlear nerve,** g. spirale partis cochlearis nervi octavi. **g. spira'le coch'leae** [N A, B N A], the ganglion of the cochlear nerve, located within the modiolus and sending fibers through the foramina nervosa to the spiral organ. **g. spira'le ner'vi coch'leae** [B N A], **g. spira'le par'tis cochlea'ris ner'vi octa'vi** [N A], the sensory ganglion of the pars cochlearis of the eighth cranial nerve, found near the medial border of the osseous spiral lamina. **splanchnic g.** 1. Ganglion splanchnicum. 2. Plexus celiacus. **g. splanch'nicum** [N A, B N A], a small ganglion formed on the greater splanchnic nerve near the twelfth thoracic vertebra. **stellate g.,** g. cervicothoracicum. **g. stella'tum,** N A alternative for *g. cervicothoracicum*. **submandibular g., g. submandibula're** [N A], **g. submax'illare** [B N A], **submaxillary g.,** a ganglion located superior to the deep part of the submandibular gland, on the lateral surface of the hyoglossus muscle; it receives a parasympathetic root from the lingual nerve, and a sympathetic root derived from the plexus on the facial artery. **superior g. of glossopharyngeal nerve,** g. superius nervi glossopharyngei. **superior g. of vagus nerve,** g. superius nervi vagi. **g. supe'rius, g. supe'rius ner'vi glossopharyn'gei** [N A, B N A], a small ganglion of the glossopharyngeal nerve at the jugular foramen. It and the inferior ganglion contain cell bodies for sensory fibers of the nerve. Called also *superior g. of glossopharyngeal nerve.* **g. supe′rius ner′vi va′gi** [N A], a small general sensory ganglion on the vagus in the jugular foramen, giving off a meningeal and an auricular branch. Called also *g. jugulare nervi vagi* [B N A], and *superior g. of vagus nerve.* **suprarenal g.,** a ganglion at the junction of the great splanchnic nerves. **ganglia of sympathetic plexuses,** ganglia plexuum autonomicorum. **ganglia of sympathetic trunk,** ganglia trunci sympathici. **synovial g.,** a synovial cyst. **terminal g., g. termina′le** [N A], a group of nerve cells found along the terminal nerves, medial to the olfactory bulb. **gan′glia thoraca′lia** [B N A], **thoracic ganglia, gan′glia thora′cica** [N A], the ganglia on the thoracic portion of the sympathetic trunk, usually about ten on either side. **g. thora′cicum pri′mum,** g. cervicothoracicum. **thyroid g., inferior, thyroid g., superior,** names formerly applied to g. cervicale medium. **trigeminal g., g. of trigeminal nerve, g. trigemina′le** [N A], a ganglion on the sensory root of the fifth cranial nerve, situated in a cleft within the dura mater (trigeminal cave) on the anterior part of the petrous portion of the temporal bone, and giving off the ophthalmic and maxillary and part of the mandibular nerve. Called also *g. semilunare* [*Gasseri*] [B N A]. **Troisier's g.,** an enlarged lymphatic gland sometimes seen above the clavicle in cases of retrosternal tumor. **gan′glia trun′ci sympath′ici** [N A, B N A], groups of nerve cell bodies found along each sympathetic trunk, about twenty on either side. Called also *ganglia of sympathetic trunk.* **tympanic g.,** g. tympanicum. **tympanic g. of Valentin,** intumescentia tympanica. **g. tympan′icum** [N A], a ganglion on the tympanic branch of the glossopharyngeal nerve. **upper g.,** g. superius nervi glossopharyngei. **vagal g., inferior,** g. inferius nervi vagi. **vagal g., superior,** g. superius nervi vagi. **Valentin's g.,** intumescentia tympanica. **ventricular g.,** Bidder's g. **vertebral g., g. vertebra′le.** 1. [N A] A small ganglion on one of the branches interconnecting the middle and inferior cervical ganglia of the sympathetic trunk. 2. Ganglion cervicothoracicum. **vestibular g., g. vestibula′re** [N A, B N A], the sensory ganglion of the pars vestibularis of the eighth cranial nerve. It consists of bipolar cells and is located in the superior part of the lateral end of the internal acoustic meatus. **Walther's g.,** glomus coccygeum. **Wrisberg's g., g. Wrisbergi.** See *ganglia cardiaca.* **wrist g.,** cystic enlargement of a tendon sheath on the back of the wrist.

ganglionated (gang′gle-o-nāt-ed). Provided with ganglia.

ganglionectomy (gang″gle-o-nek′to-me) [*ganglio-* + Gr. *ektomē* excision]. Excision of a ganglion.

ganglionervous (gang″gle-o-ner′vus). Pertaining to the sympathetic nerve.

ganglioneure (gang′gle-o-nūr) [*ganglio-* + Gr. *neuron* nerve]. Any cell of a nervous ganglion.

ganglioneuroblastoma (gang″gle-o-nu″ro-blas-to′mah). Ganglioneuroma of immature cells.

ganglioneuroma (gang″gle-o-nu-ro′mah). A tumor made up of ganglion cells.

ganglionic (gang″gle-on′ik). Pertaining to a ganglion.

ganglionitis (gang″gle-on-i′tis). Inflammation of a ganglion. **acute posterior g.,** herpes zoster.

ganglionoplegic (gang″gle-on″o-ple′jik). Ganglioplegic.

ganglionostomy (gang″gle-o-nos′to-me) [*ganglio-* + Gr. *stomoun* to provide with an opening, or mouth]. Surgical creation of an opening into a cystic tumor on a tendon sheath or aponeurosis.

ganglioplegic (gang″gle-o-ple′jik) [*ganglio-* + Gr. *plēgē* stroke]. 1. Blocking transmission of impulses through the sympathetic and parasympathetic ganglia. 2. An agent that blocks the transmission of impulses through the sympathetic and parasympathetic ganglia.

ganglioplexus (gang″gle-o-plek′sus). A plexus of nerve fibers in a ganglion.

ganglioside (gang′gle-o-sīd). A general designation for a member of a class of galactose cerebrosides found in the tissues of the central nervous system.

gangliosympathectomy (gang″gle-o-sim″pah-thek′to-me). Excision of a sympathetic ganglion.

Gangolphe's sign (gahn-golfs′) [Louis *Gangolphe,* French surgeon]. See under *sign.*

gangosa (gang-go′sah) [Sp. "muffled voice"]. A form of treponematosis manifested as a destructive ulceration of the nose, nasopharynx and hard palate, being one of the late lesions of yaws. Called also *ogo* and *rhinopharyngitis mutilans.*

gangrene (gang′grēn) [L. *gangraena;* Gr. *gangraina* an eating sore, which ends in mortification]. Death of tissue, usually in considerable mass and generally associated with loss of vascular (nutritive) supply and followed by bacterial invasion and putrefaction. Cf. *necrosis* and *necrobiosis.* **anaphylactic g.,** gangrene occurring as a result of anaphylactic reaction to the injection of serum. **angioneurotic g.,** a disease observed in early life, due to thrombosis and sclerosis of the arteries and veins, and occurring chiefly in cold regions. Called also *spontaneous g.* **angiosclerotic g.,** dry gangrene caused by vascular sclerosis. **circumscribed g.,** gangrene which is clearly separated from the normal tissue by a zone of inflammatory reaction. **cold g.,** gangrene that is not preceded by inflammation. **cutaneous g.,** a form of pyodermatitis of young children due to a staphylococcus. **diabetic g.,** moist gangrene occurring in a person with diabetes. **disseminated cutaneous g.,** widespread gangrene of the skin of nervous origin. **dry g.,** necrosis occurring without subsequent bacterial decomposition, the tissues becoming dry and shriveled. **embolic g.,** that which follows the cutting off of the blood supply by an embolism. **emphysematous g.,** gas g. **epidemic g.,** ergotism. **fulminating g.,** malignant edema. **gas g., gaseous g.,** a condition often resulting from dirty, lacerated wounds in which the muscles and subcutaneous tissues become filled with gas and a serosanguineous exudate. The condition is due to bacteria among which are *Clostridium oedematis maligni* (*vibrion septique*), *Cl. perfringens, Cl. oedematiens,* and other species of *Clostridium.* **glycemic g., glykemic g.,** diabetic g. **hot g.,** gangrene which follows an inflammation. **humid g.,** moist g. **inflammatory g.,** gangrene due to acute inflammation. **mephitic g.,** gas g. **moist g.,** necrosis of tissues, with proteolytic decomposition resulting from bacterial action. **oral g.,** cancrum oris. **presenile g.,** thromboangiitis obliterans. **pressure g.,** gangrene due to pressure, as in decubitus ulcer. **primary g.,** gangrene occurring without preceding inflammation of the part. **progressive g.,** gangrene in which an effective limiting zone of inflammatory reaction does not form. **progressive bacterial synergistic g.,** a superficial spreading infection caused by the association of two organisms, neither one of which is capable of producing significant infection alone. **Raynaud's g.,** Raynaud's disease, def. 1. **secondary g.,** a form which follows a local inflammation. **spontaneous g.,** angioneurotic g. **static g.,** gangrene that results from stasis of blood in a part. **symmetric g.,** gangrene of corresponding parts on either side, due to vasomotor disturbances. **sympathetic g.,** gangrene which results from some primary condition. **thrombotic g.,** gangrene from thrombosis of an artery. **traumatic g.,** gangrene which occurs as a consequence of accidental injury. **trophic g.,** gangrene due to lesion of the trophic nerve supply of a part. **venous g.,** static g.

gangrenosis (gang″grĕ-no′sis). The development of gangrene.

gangrenous (gang′grĕ-nus). Pertaining to, characterized by, or of the nature of gangrene.

ganoblast (gan′o-blast). Ameloblast.

Ganser's ganglion, symptom, syndrome (gan′serz) [Sigbert Joseph Maria *Ganser*, psychiatrist in Dresden, 1853–1931]. See under the nouns.

Gant's clamp (gants) [Samuel Goodwin *Gant*, New York proctologist, 1870–1944]. See under *clamp*.

Gant's line, operation (gants) [Frederick James *Gant*, English surgeon, 1825–1905]. See under *line* and *operation*.

gantrisin (gan′trĭ-sin). Trade mark for preparations of sulfisoxazole.

gap (gap). An unoccupied interval in time or an opening in space. **air-bone g.**, the lag between the audiographic curves for air- and bone-conducted stimuli, as an indication of loss of bone conduction of the ear. **auscultatory g.**, time in which sound is not heard in the auscultatory method of sphygmomanometry, occurring in hypertension and in aortic stenosis. Also called *trou auscultatoire*. **Bochdalek's g.**, hiatus pleuroperitonealis. **chromatid g.**, a non-staining region in a chromatid, the portions of the chromatid immediately proximal and distal to the site remaining in alignment. **interocclusal g.**, interocclusal distance. See under *distance*. **isochromatid g.**, a non-staining region of the same level in two sister chromatids, the distal segments remaining in alignment with the proximal portions. **quenched spark g.**, a multiple spark gap with numerous electrodes about 0.3 mm. apart and equipped with a copper air-cooling device. **silent g.**, auscultatory g. **spark g.**, the space between the terminals of a high-tension circuit across which the spark is to jump.

gapes (gāps). A disease of young fowls and turkeys caused by the gapeworm, *Syngamus trachea*.

Gardiner-Brown's test [Alfred *Gardiner-Brown*, English otologist]. See under *tests*.

Garel's sign (gar-elz′) [Jean *Garel*, French physician, 1852–1931]. See under *sign*.

Garg. Abbreviation for L. *gargaris′mus*, gargle.

gargalanesthesia (gar″g′l-an″es-the′ze-ah). Absence of the tickle sense.

gargalesthesia (gar″g′l-es-the′ze-ah). The sense which perceives tickling sensations.

gargalesthetic (gar″g′l-es-thet′ik). Pertaining to the tickle sense.

gargarism (gar′gar-izm) [L., Gr., *gargarisma*]. A gargle or throat wash.

garget (gar′get). 1. Mastitis in the cow. 2. A disease of swine characterized by loss of appetite and staggering gait.

gargle (gar′g′l) [L. *gargarisma*]. A solution used for rinsing the mouth and throat.

gargoylism (gar′goil-izm). A rare hereditary condition characterized by peculiar facies and skeletal changes of varying degrees of severity, thought to result from inability of the body cells to metabolize certain substances of high molecular weight, which consequently accumulate in the body.

Gariel's pessary (gar″e-elz′) [Maurice *Gariel*, French physician, 1812–1878]. See under *pessary*.

Garland's curve, triangle (gar′landz) [George Minot *Garland*, American physician, 1848–1926]. See under *curve* and *triangle*.

garnet (gar′net). A silicate of any combination of aluminum, cobalt, magnesium, iron, and manganese, usually coated on paper or cloth, commonly used in dentistry for polishing dentures.

garotilha (gar″o-til′hah). Anthrax of cattle in Brazil.

Garré's osteomyelitis (gar-āz′) [Carl *Garré*, Swiss surgeon, 1857–1928]. See under *osteomyelitis*.

Garrod's test (gar′ods). 1. (For hematoporphyrin in urine) [Sir Archibald Edward *Garrod*, British physician, 1858–1936]. 2. (For uric acid in blood) [Alfred Baring *Garrod*, London physician, 1819–1907]. See under *tests*.

garrot (gar′ot). An instrument for compressing an artery by twisting a circular bandage about a part; a form of tourniquet.

Gärtner's bacillus (gairt′nerz) [August *Gärtner*, German bacteriologist, 1848–1934]. *Salmonella enteritidis*.

Gartner's canal, cyst, duct (gart′nerz) [Hermann Treschow *Gartner*, Danish surgeon and anatomist, 1785–1827]. See under the nouns.

Gärtner's phenomenon, tonometer (gairt′nerz) [Gustav *Gärtner*, Austrian physician, 1855–1937]. See under *phenomenon* and *tonometer*.

gas (gas). Any elastic aeriform fluid in which the molecules are separated from one another and so have free paths. **coal g.**, a gas produced by the destructive distillation of coal and much used for domestic cooking. It is poisonous because it contains carbon monoxide. **ethyl g.**, tetra-ethyl lead. **hemolytic g.**, arsin. **inert g.**, gases without chemical activity found in the atmosphere in small amounts. They are helium, neon, argon, krypton, xenon, and niton. **lacrimator g.**, tear g. **laughing g.**, nitrous oxide. **marsh g.**, methane. **mustard g.**, dichlorodiethyl sulfide. **noble g.**, any one of the inert gases. **olefiant g.**, ethylene. **sewer g.**, the mixture of gases and vapors from a sewer; often dangerous from the contained materials resulting from the decay of organic matter. **sneezing g.**, diphenylchlorarsine. **sweet g.**, carbon monoxide. **tear g.**, a gas which produces severe lacrimation by irritating the conjunctivae. **vesicating g.**, dichlorodiethyl sulfide. **vomiting g.**, chloropicrin. **war g.**, any noxious gas manufactured for possible use in warfare.

gaseous (gas′e-us). Of the nature of a gas.

gasiform (gas′ĭ-form). Gaseous.

Gaskell's bridge (gas′kelz) [Walter Holbrook *Gaskell*, English physiologist, 1847–1914]. See under *bridge*.

gaskin (gas′kin). The thigh of a horse.

gasogenic (gas-o-jen′ik). Producing gas.

gasometer (gas-om′e-ter). A calibrated container for measuring volume of gases.

gasometric (gas″o-met′rik). Pertaining to gasometry.

gasometry (gas-om′e-tre) [*gas* + Gr. *metron* measure]. The chemical determination of the amount of gas present in a mixture.

Gasser, Herbert Spencer (gas′er). American physiologist, born 1888, noted for his work on the nervous system; co-winner, with E. Joseph Erlanger, of the Nobel prize for medicine and physiology in 1944.

gasserectomy (gas″er-ek′to-me). Surgical removal of the gasserian ganglion.

gasserian (gas-se′re-an) [Johann Laurentius *Gasser*, professor of anatomy in Vienna from 1757 to 1765]. See under *ganglion*.

gaster (gas′ter) [Gr. *gastēr*]. Stomach.

gasteralgia (gas-ter-al′je-ah). Gastralgia.

gasterangiemphraxis (gas″ter-an″je-em-frak′sis) [*gaster* + Gr. *angeion* vessel + *emphraxis* obstruction]. Obstruction of the blood vessels of the stomach.

gasterasthenia (gas″ter-as-the′ne-ah). Gastrasthenia.

gasteremphraxis (gas″ter-em-frak′sis). 1. Gasterangiemphraxis. 2. Distention of the stomach.

gasterhysterotomy (gas″ter-his″ter-ot′o-me). Abdominal hysterotomy.

Gasterophilus (gas″ter-of′ĭ-lus) [*gaster* + Gr. *philein* to love]. A genus of dipterous insects. *G.*

equi is the bot fly whose larva infests horses. The larvae of *G. intestinalis* are supposed to cause creeping eruption (larva migrans). *G. hemorrhoidalis,* the horse bot fly, found in Russia, sometimes infests man. *G. mericionalis* produces tumors of the duodenum of horses in Spain.

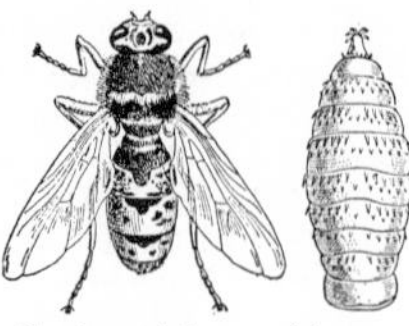
Gasterophilus and larva.

gastr-. See *gastro-*.

gastradenitis (gas″trad-ĕ-ni′tis) [*gastr-* + Gr. *adēn* gland + *-itis*]. Inflammation of the stomach glands.

gastralgia (gas-tral′je-ah) [*gastr-* + *-algia*]. Pain in the stomach. **appendicular g.,** pain in the stomach due to lesion of the vermiform appendix.

gastralgokenosis (gas-tral″go-ke-no′sis) [*gastr-* + Gr. *algos* pain + *kenōsis* emptiness]. Paroxysmal gastric pain when the stomach is empty, and which is easily relieved by taking food.

gastramine (gas′trah-min). Betazole.

gastraneuria (gas″trah-nu′re-ah) [*gastr-* + *a* neg. + Gr. *neuron* nerve]. Impaired nervous tone of the stomach.

gastrasthenia (gas″tras-the′ne-ah) [*gastr-* + *asthenia*]. A feeble or weak state of the functions of the stomach.

gastratrophia (gas″trah-tro′fe-ah) [*gastr-* + Gr. *atrophia* atrophy]. Atrophy of the stomach.

gastrectasia (gas-trek-ta′ze-ah) [*gastr-* + Gr. *ektasis* stretching + *-ia*]. Dilatation of the stomach.

gastrectasis (gas-trek′tah-sis). Gastrectasia.

gastrectomy (gas-trek′to-me) [*gastr-* + Gr. *ektomē* excision]. The cutting out or removal of the whole or part of the stomach. **partial g., subtotal g.,** excision of a large portion, but not all, of the stomach; gastric resection.

gastrectosis (gas″trek-to′sis). Gastrectasia.

gastric (gas′trik) [L. *gastricus;* Gr. *gastēr* stomach]. Pertaining to the stomach.

gastricism (gas′trĭ-sizm). Any gastric disorder, such as dyspepsia or indigestion.

gastricsin (gas-trik′sin). A proteolytic enzyme isolated from the gastric juice. Originating from the same precursor (pepsinogen) as pepsin, it is of heavier molecular weight than pepsin, and possesses different amino acids at the N terminal.

gastrin (gas′trin). A hormone obtained from the pyloric mucosa which on injection increases the flow of gastric juice.

gastritic (gas-trit′ik). Pertaining to or affected with gastritis.

gastritis (gas-tri′tis) [*gastr-* + *-itis*]. Inflammation of the stomach. **antral g., antrum g.,** inflammation affecting the antrum of the stomach. **atrophic g.,** chronic gastritis with atrophy of the mucous membrane and glands. **catarrhal g.,** inflammation of the mucous membrane of the stomach, with hypertrophy of the membrane, secretion of an excessive quantity of mucus, and alteration of the gastric juice. The condition is marked by loss of appetite, nausea, pain, vomiting, and tympanitic distention of the stomach. **exfoliative g.,** chronic gastritis in which bits of the surface of the mucous membrane are shed. **follicular g.,** inflammation of the glands of the stomach. **giant hypertrophic g.,** gastritis characterized by marked and wide-spread enlargement of the gastric folds. **g. granulomato′sa fibroplas′tica,** benign hypertrophy of the pylorus; linitis plastica. **hyperpeptic g.,** hyperpepsia. **hypertrophic g.,** gastritis with infiltration and enlargement of the glands. **interstitial g.,** linitis plastica. **mycotic g.,** gastritis caused by fungi. **phlegmonous g.,** a variety with abscesses in the stomach walls. **polypous g.,** hypertrophic gastritis with polypus-like projections into the stomach. **pseudomembranous g.,** a variety in which a false membrane occurs in patches within the stomach. **purulent g., suppurating g.,** gastritis in which pus is produced. **toxic g.,** gastritis caused by the action of a poison or a corrosive agent.

gastro-, gastr- (gas′tro, gas′tr-) [Gr. *gastēr* stomach]. Combining form denoting relationship to the stomach or to the abdomen.

gastroacephalus (gas″tro-a-sef′ah-lus) [*gastro-* + *a* priv. + Gr. *kephalē* head]. A twin monster, the autosite bearing a headless parasite on its abdomen.

gastroadenitis (gas″tro-ad″e-ni′tis). Gastradenitis.

gastroadynamic (gas″tro-a″di-nam′ik). Marked by an adynamic condition of the stomach.

gastroalbumorrhea (gas″tro-al-bu″mo-re′ah) [*gastro-* + *albumin* + Gr. *rhoia* flow]. The secretion of protein matter by the stomach.

gastroamorphus (gas″tro-a-mor′fus) [*gastro-* + Gr. *a* priv. + *morphē* form]. A presumptive twin monster in which the parasite consists of fetal parts concealed within the abdomen of the autosite.

gastroanastomosis (gas″tro-ah-nas″to-mo′sis). Gastrogastrostomy.

gastroatonia (gas″tro-ah-to′ne-ah). Atony of the stomach.

gastroblennorrhea (gas″tro-blen″o-re′ah) [*gastro-* + *blennorrhea*]. Excessive secretion of mucus by the stomach.

gastrobrosis (gas″tro-bro′sis) [*gastro-* + Gr. *brōsis* eating]. Perforation of the stomach wall by a corrosive or ulcerative process.

gastrocamera (gas″tro-kam′er-ah). A small camera which can be swallowed and thereby make photographs of the inside of the stomach.

gastrocardiac (gas″tro-kar′de-ak). Pertaining to the stomach and the heart.

gastrocele (gas′tro-sēl) [*gastro-* + Gr. *kēlē* hernia]. Hernial protrusion of the stomach or of a gastric pouch.

gastrochronorrhea (gas″tro-kron″o-re′ah) [*gastro-* + Gr. *chronos* time + *rhoia* flowing]. Chronic gastric hypersecretion.

gastrocnemius (gas″trok-ne′me-us) [*gastro-* + Gr. *knēmē* leg]. See *Table of Musculi.*

gastrocoele (gas′tro-sēl) [*gastro-* + Gr. *koilos* hollow]. The archenteron.

gastrocolic (gas″tro-kol′ik). Pertaining to or communicating with the stomach and colon, as a gastrocolic fistula.

gastrocolitis (gas″tro-ko-li′tis) [*gastro-* + Gr. *kolon* colon + *-itis*]. Inflammation of the stomach and colon.

gastrocoloptosis (gas″tro-ko″lop-to′sis) [*gastro-* + *colon* + Gr. *ptōsis* falling]. Downward displacement of the stomach and colon.

gastrocolostomy (gas″tro-ko-los′to-me) [*gastro-* + Gr. *kolon* colon + *stomoun* to provide with an opening, or mouth]. The creation of an artificial passage from the stomach to the colon.

gastrocolotomy (gas″tro-ko-lot′o-me) [*gastro-* + Gr. *kolon* colon + *tomē* a cut]. Incision of the stomach and colon.

gastrocolpotomy (gas″tro-kol-pot′o-me) [*gastro-* + Gr. *kolpos* vagina + *temnein* to cut]. Cesarean section with incision into the vagina.

gastrocutaneous (gas″tro-ku-ta′ne-us). Pertaining to the stomach and skin, or communicating with the stomach and the cutaneous surface of the body, as a gastrocutaneous fistula.

gastrodialysis (gas″tro-di-al′ĭ-sis) [*gastro-* + Gr. *dialysis* separation]. Sloughing of the gastric mucous membrane.

gastrodiaphane (gas″tro-di′ah-fān) [*gastro-* + Gr. *dia* through + *phainein* to show]. A small electric lamp to be introduced into the stomach in gastrodiaphany.

gastrodiaphanoscopy (gas″tro-di-af″ah-nos′ko-pe) [*gastro-* + Gr. *dia* through + *phainein* to show + *skopein* to examine]. Gastrodiaphany.

gastrodiaphany (gas″tro-di-af′ah-ne) [*gastro-* + Gr. *dia* through + *phainein* to show]. The exploration of the stomach by means of an electric lamp passed down the esophagus.

gastrodidymus (gas″tro-did′ĭ-mus) [*gastro-* + Gr. *didymos* twin]. Symmetrical conjoined twins joined in the abdominal region.

gastrodisciasis (gas″tro-dis-ki′ah-sis). Infection caused by *Gastrodiscoides hominis.*

Gastrodiscoides (gas″tro-dis-koi′dēz) [*gastro-* + Gr. *diskos* disk + *eidos* form]. A genus of trematodes parasitic in the intestinal tract. **G. hom′-inis,** a species of trematode common in the cecum and large intestine of pigs and occasionally in man, in Cochin China, India, and the Malay States.

Gastrodiscus (gas″tro-dis′kus). Gastrodiscoides.

gastrodisk (gas′tro-disk). The germinal disk.

gastroduodenal (gas″tro-du″o-de′nal). Pertaining to or communicating with the stomach and duodenum, as a gastroduodenal fistula.

gastroduodenitis (gas″tro-du-od″e-ni′tis) [*gastro-* + *duodenitis*]. An inflammation of the stomach and duodenum.

gastroduodenoenterostomy (gas″tro-du″o-de″no-en″ter-os′to-me). Gastroduodenostomy.

gastroduodenoscopy (gas″tro-du″o-dĕ-nos′ko-pe) [*gastro-* + *duodenum* + Gr. *skopein* to examine]. Examination of the stomach and duodenum through the gastroscope by an incision through the stomach wall.

gastroduodenostomy (gas″tro-du″o-dĕ-nos′to-me) [*gastro-* + *duodenum* + Gr. *stomoun* to provide with an opening, or mouth]. Surgical creation of an anastomosis between the stomach and the duodenum.

gastrodynia (gas″tro-din′e-ah) [*gastro-* + Gr. *odynē* pain]. Pain in the stomach.

gastroenteralgia (gas″tro-en″ter-al′je-ah) [*gastro-* + Gr. *enteron* intestine + *-algia*]. Pain in the stomach and intestines.

gastroenteric (gas″tro-en-ter′ik) [*gastro-* + Gr. *enteron* intestine]. Pertaining to the stomach and intestines.

gastroenteritis (gas″tro-en-ter-i′tis) [*gastro-* + *enteritis*]. Inflammation of the stomach and intestines. **acute infectious g.,** polytropous enteronitis. **g. hemorrha′gica,** black tongue in dogs. **g. paratypho′sa B,** a condition caused by the *Bacillus paratyphosus B.* **g. typho′sa,** a form of gastroenteritis caused by the typhoid bacillus.

gastroenteroanastomosis (gas″tro-en″ter-o-ah-nas″to-mo′sis). Anastomosis between the intestine and the stomach in gastroenterostomy.

gastroenterocolitis (gas″tro-en″ter-o-ko-li′tis). Inflammation of the stomach, small intestine, and colon.

gastroenterocolostomy (gas″tro-en″ter-o-ko-los′to-me) [*gastro-* + Gr. *enteron* intestine + *kolon* colon + *stomoun* to provide with an opening, or mouth]. Surgical creation of a passage between the stomach, intestine, and colon.

gastroenterologist (gas″tro-en″ter-ol′o-jist). A practitioner who specializes in diseases of the stomach and intestine.

gastroenterology (gas″tro-en″ter-ol′o-je) [*gastro-* + Gr. *enteron* intestine + *-logy*]. The study of the stomach and intestines and their diseases.

gastroenteropathy (gas″tro-en″ter-op′ah-the). Any disease of the stomach and intestines.

gastroenteroplasty (gas″tro-en′ter-o-plas″te). Gastroplasty combined with enteroplasty.

gastroenteroptosis (gas″tro-en″ter-op-to′sis) [*gastro-* + Gr. *enteron* intestine + *ptōsis* falling]. Falling down, or prolapse, of the stomach and intestines.

gastroenterostomy (gas″tro-en-ter-os′to-me)

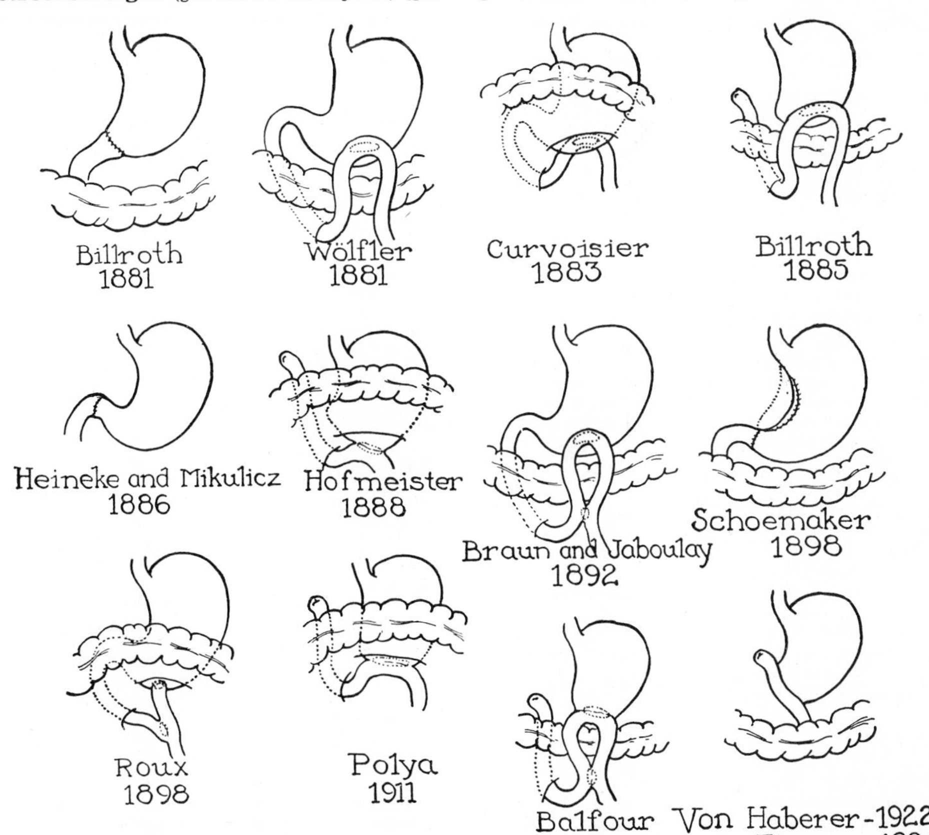

Types of gastroenterostomy.

[*gastro-* + Gr. *enteron* intestine + *stomoun* to provide with an opening, or mouth]. Surgical creation of an artificial passage (anastomosis) between the stomach and intestines.

gastroenterotomy (gas″tro-en″ter-ot′o-me) [*gastro-* + Gr. *enteron* intestine + *temnein* to cut]. Surgical incision of the stomach and intestine.

gastroepiploic (gas″tro-ep″ĭ-plo′ik) [*gastro-* + Gr. *epiploon* caul]. Pertaining to the stomach and epiploon.

gastroesophageal (gas″tro-e-sof″ah-je′al) [*gastro-* + Gr. *oisophagos* gullet]. Pertaining to the stomach and esophagus.

gastroesophagitis (gas″tro-e-sof″ah-ji′tis). Inflammation of the stomach and esophagus.

gastroesophagostomy (gas″tro-e-sof″ah-gos′to-me). Surgical creation of an anastomosis between the stomach and the esophagus: done for stricture of the lower end of the esophagus.

gastrofaradization (gas″tro-far″ah-di-za′shun). The therapeutical application of faradism to the stomach.

gastrogalvanization (gas″tro-gal″vah-ni-za′shun). The therapeutical application of galvanism to the stomach.

gastrogastrostomy (gas″tro-gas-tros′to-me) [*gastro-* + *gastro-* + Gr. *stomoun* to provide with an opening, or mouth]. Surgical creation of an anastomosis between the pyloric and cardiac ends of the stomach, performed for hourglass contraction of the stomach.

gastrogavage (gas″tro-gah-vazh′) [*gastro-* + Fr. *gavage* cramming]. The introduction of nutriment into the stomach by means of a tube passed through the esophagus.

gastrogenic (gas″tro-jen′ik). Formed or originating in the stomach.

gastrograph (gas′tro-graf) [*gastro-* + Gr. *graphein* to record]. An apparatus for recording the motions of the stomach.

gastrohelcoma (gas″tro-hel-ko′mah). A stomach ulcer.

gastrohelcosis (gas″tro-hel-ko′sis) [*gastro-* + Gr. *helkos* ulcer]. Ulceration of the stomach.

gastrohepatic (gas″tro-he-pat′ik) [*gastro-* + Gr. *hēpar* liver]. Pertaining to the stomach and liver.

gastrohepatitis (gas″tro-hep-ah-ti′tis). Inflammation of the stomach and liver.

gastrohydrorrhea (gas″tro-hi″dro-re′ah) [*gastro-* + Gr. *hydōr* water + *rhoia* flow]. The secretion by the stomach of a quantity of watery fluid deficient in hydrochloric acid and gastric enzymes.

gastrohypernervia (gas″tro-hi″per-ner′ve-ah). Gastrohyperneuria.

gastrohyperneuria (gas″tro-hi″per-nu′re-ah) [*gastro-* + Gr. *hyper* over + *neuron* nerve + *-ia*]. Excessive activity of the nerves of the stomach.

gastrohypertonic (gas″tro-hi″per-ton′ik). Marked by excessive tonicity of the stomach.

gastrohyponervia (gas″tro-hi″po-ner′ve-ah). Gastrohyponeuria.

gastrohyponeuria (gas″tro-hi″po-nu′re-ah) [*gastro-* + Gr. *hypo* under + *neuron* nerve + *-ia*]. Defective activity of the nerves of the stomach.

gastrohysterectomy (gas″tro-his″ter-ek′to-me) [*gastro-* + Gr. *hystera* womb + *ektomē* excision]. Removal of the uterus through an incision in the abdominal wall.

gastrohysteropexy (gas″tro-his′ter-o-pek″se) [*gastro-* + Gr. *hystera* womb + *pēxis* fixation]. Fixation of the displaced uterus to the ventral wall.

gastrohysterorrhaphy (gas″tro-his″ter-or′ah-fe) [*gastro-* + Gr. *hystera* womb + *rhaphē* suture]. Gastrohysteropexy.

gastrohysterotomy (gas″tro-his″ter-ot′o-me) [*gastro-* + Gr. *hystera* womb + *temnein* to cut]. Cesarean section; delivery of a fetus through an incision of the abdominal and uterine walls.

gastroileitis (gas″tro-il-e-i′tis). Inflammation of the stomach and ileum.

gastroileostomy (gas″tro-il-e-os′to-me). Surgical creation of an anastomosis between the stomach and ileum.

gastrointestinal (gas″tro-in-tes′tĭ-nal) [*gastro-* + *intestinal*]. Pertaining to or communicating with the stomach and intestine, as a gastrointestinal fistula.

gastrojejunocolic (gas″tro-jĕ-ju″no-kol′ik). Pertaining to or communicating with the stomach, jejunum, and colon, as a gastrojejunocolic fistula.

gastrojejuno-esophagostomy (gas″tro-jĕ-ju″-no-e-sof″ah-gos′to-me). Esophagojejunogastrostomosis.

gastrojejunostomy (gas″tro-jĕ-ju-nos′to-me) [*gastro-* + *jejunostomy*]. Surgical creation of an anastomosis between the stomach and jejunum.

gastrokateixia (gas″tro-kah-tik′se-ah) [*gastro-* + Gr. *kata* down + *eixis* a giving way]. Gastroptosis.

gastrokinesograph (gas″tro-ki-nes′o-graf) [*gastro-* + Gr. *kinēsis* motion + *graphein* to record]. A device for recording the mechanical motions of the stomach.

gastrolienal (gas″tro-li′en-al) [*gastro-* + L. *lien* spleen]. Pertaining to the stomach and spleen.

gastrolith (gas′tro-lith) [*gastro-* + Gr. *lithos* stone]. A calcareous or other concretion formed in the stomach.

gastrolithiasis (gas″tro-lĭ-thi′ah-sis) [*gastro-* + Gr. *lithos* stone + *-iasis*]. The presence or formation of gastroliths.

gastrologist (gas-trol′o-jist). A specialist in diseases of the stomach.

gastrology (gas-trol′o-je) [*gastro-* + *-logy*]. The sum of knowledge regarding the stomach.

gastrolysis (gas-trol′ĭ-sis) [*gastro-* + Gr. *lysis* loosening]. The operation of loosening the stomach from adhesions.

gastromalacia (gas″tro-mah-la′she-ah) [*gastro-* + Gr. *malakia* softening]. An abnormal softening or softness of the wall of the stomach.

gastromegaly (gas″tro-meg′ah-le) [*gastro-* + Gr. *megas* large]. Enlargement of the stomach.

gastromelus (gas-trom′ĕ-lus) [*gastro-* + Gr. *melos* limb]. A fetal monster with a supernumerary leg attached to the abdomen.

gastromenia (gas″tro-me′ne-ah) [*gastro-* + Gr. *mēniaia* menses]. Vicarious menstruation through the stomach.

gastromeningitis (gas″tro-men″in-ji′tis). Inflammation of the stomach and the cerebral meninges.

gastromycosis (gas″tro-mi-ko′sis) [*gastro-* + Gr. *mykēs* fungus]. A disease of the stomach caused by fungi.

gastromyotomy (gas″tro-mi-ot′o-me) [*gastro-* + Gr. *mys* muscle + *temnein* to cut]. Pylorotomy.

gastromyxorrhea (gas″tro-mik″so-re′ah) [*gastro-* + Gr. *myxa* mucus + *rhoia* flow]. Excessive secretion of mucus by the stomach.

gastronephritis (gas″tro-ne-fri′tis). Inflammation of the stomach and kidney.

gastronesteostomy (gas″tro-nes″te-os′to-me) [*gastro-* + Gr. *nēstis* jejunum + *stomoun* to provide with a mouth or opening]. Gastrojejunostomy.

gastropancreatitis (gas″tro-pan″kre-ah-ti′tis). Inflammation of the stomach and pancreas.

gastroparalysis (gas″tro-pah-ral′ĭ-sis). Paralysis of the stomach.

gastroparesis (gas″tro-par′e-sis) [*gastro-* + Gr. *paresis* paralysis]. Paralysis of the stomach.

gastroparietal (gas″tro-pah-ri′ĕ-tal). Pertaining to the stomach and the body wall.

gastropathic (gas″tro-path′ik). Pertaining to disease of the stomach.

gastropathy (gas-trop′ah-the) [*gastro-* + Gr. *pathos* disease]. Any disease of the stomach.

gastroperiodynia (gas″tro-per″e-o-din′e-ah) [*gastro-* + Gr. *periodos* period + *odynē* pain]. Periodical attacks of pain in the stomach.

gastroperitonitis (gas″tro-per″ĭ-to-ni′tis). Inflammation of the stomach and peritoneum.

gastropexy (gas′tro-pek″se) [*gastro-* + Gr. *pēxis* fixation]. Surgical fixation of the stomach to the abdominal wall for the cure of displacement.

Gastrophilus (gas-trof′ĭ-lus). Gasterophilus.

gastrophore (gas′tro-fōr) [*gastro-* + Gr. *phoros* bearing]. An instrument for fixing the stomach and coaptating its walls during operations upon that organ.

gastrophotography (gas″tro-fo-tog′rah-fe). Photography of the stomach by means of a camera introduced into it.

gastrophotor (gas″tro-fo′tor). An instrument for gastrophotography.

gastrophrenic (gas″tro-fren′ik) [*gastro-* + Gr. *phrēn* diaphragm]. Pertaining to the stomach and diaphragm.

gastrophthisis (gas″tro-this′is) [*gastro-* + Gr. *phthisis* wasting]. 1. Hyperplasia of the gastric mucosa and submucosa, leading to thickening of the stomach walls and diminution of its cavity. 2. Emaciation due to abdominal disease.

gastroplasty (gas′tro-plas″te) [*gastro-* + Gr. *plassein* to form]. Plastic operation on the stomach.

gastroplegia (gas″tro-ple′je-ah) [*gastro-* + Gr. *plēgē* stroke]. Paralysis of the stomach.

gastropleuritis (gas″tro-plu-ri′tis). Inflammation of the stomach and the pleura.

gastroplication (gas″tro-pli-ka′shun) [*gastro-* + L. *plicare* to fold]. The surgical treatment of a dilated stomach by means of stitching a fold in the stomach or by the removal of a fold of its walls.

gastropneumonic (gas″tro-nu-mon′ik). Pertaining to the stomach and lungs.

gastropod (gas′tro-pod). A mollusk of the class Gastropoda which contains the snails and slugs. See *snail.*

gastroptosia (gas″tro-to′se-ah). Gastroptosis.

gastroptosis (gas″tro-to′sis) [*gastro-* + Gr. *ptosis* falling]. Downward displacement of the stomach. Cf. *enteroptosis.*

gastroptyxis (gas″tro-tik′sis) [*gastro-* + Gr. *ptyxis* a folding]. An operation for reducing a dilated stomach.

gastroptyxy (gas″tro-tik″se). Gastroptyxis.

gastropulmonary (gas″tro-pul′mo-nar-e) [*gastro-* + L. *pulmo* lung]. Pertaining to the stomach and lungs.

gastropylorectomy (gas″tro-pi″lo-rek′to-me) [*gastro-* + Gr. *pylōros* pylorus + *ektomē* excision]. Excision of the pyloric portion of the stomach.

gastropyloric (gas″tro-pi-lor′ik). Pertaining to the stomach and pylorus.

gastroradiculitis (gas″tro-rah-dik″u-li′tis) [*gastro-* + L. *radix* root + *-itis*]. Inflammation of the posterior roots of spinal nerves involving irritation of the sensory fibers in them which are connected with the stomach.

gastrorrhagia (gas″tro-ra′je-ah) [*gastro-* + Gr. *rhēgnynai* to break forth]. Hemorrhage from the stomach.

gastrorrhaphy (gas-tror′ah-fe) [*gastro-* + Gr. *rhaphē* suture]. 1. The suture of a wound of the stomach. 2. Gastroplication.

gastrorrhea (gas″tro-re′ah) [*gastro-* + Gr. *rhoia* flow]. Excessive secretion of mucus or gastric juice in the stomach. **g. contin′ua chron′ica,** gastrosuccorrhea.

gastrorrhexis (gas″tro-rek′sis) [*gastro-* + Gr. *rhēxis* rupture]. Rupture of the stomach.

gastrosalpingotomy (gas″tro-sal″pin-got′o-me) [*gastro-* + *salpingotomy*]. Incision of the uterine tube through the abdominal wall.

gastroschisis (gas-tros′kĭ-sis) [*gastro-* + Gr. *schisis* cleft]. A congenital fissure of the abdominal wall.

gastroscope (gas′tro-skōp) [*gastro-* + Gr. *skopein* to examine]. An endoscope for inspecting the interior of the stomach.

gastroscopic (gas″tro-skop′ik). Pertaining to gastroscopy or the gastroscope.

gastroscopy (gas-tros′ko-pe) [*gastro-* + Gr. *skopein* to examine]. The inspection of the interior of the stomach by means of the gastroscope. **lower g.,** laparogastroscopy.

gastrosia (gas-tro′se-ah). A disease of the stomach. **g. fungo′sa,** a disease of the stomach caused by fungi or molds.

gastrosis (gas-tro′sis). Any disease of the stomach.

gastrospasm (gas′tro-spazm) [*gastro-* + *spasm*]. Spasm of the stomach.

gastrospiry (gas′tro-spi″re) [*gastro-* + L. *spirare* to breathe]. Aerophagy.

gastrosplenic (gas″tro-splen′ik). Pertaining to the stomach and spleen.

gastrostaxis (gas″tro-stak′sis) [*gastro-* + Gr. *staxis* a dripping]. The oozing of blood from the mucous membrane of the stomach.

gastrostenosis (gas″tro-ste-no′sis) [*gastro-* + Gr. *stenōsis* narrowing]. Contraction or shrinkage of the stomach.

gastrostogavage (gas-tros″to-gah-vahzh′). Introduction of nutriment into the stomach by means of a tube passed through a gastric fistula.

gastrostolavage (gas-tros″to-lah-vahzh′). Washing of the stomach through a gastric fistula.

gastrostoma (gas-tros′to-mah) [*gastro-* + Gr. *stoma* mouth]. A gastric fistula.

gastrostomize (gas-tros′to-mīz). To perform gastrostomy upon.

gastrostomosis (gas-tros″to-mo′sis). Gastrostomy.

gastrostomy (gas-tros′to-me) [*gastro-* + Gr. *stomoun* to provide with an opening, or mouth]. Surgical creation of an artificial gastric fistula. **Beck's g.,** the operation of forming an opening into the stomach through a tube formed from the greater curvature of the stomach.

gastrosuccorrhea (gas″tro-suk″o-re′ah) [*gastro-* + L. *succus* juice + Gr. *rhoia* flow]. Excessive and continuous secretion of gastric juice. Called also *Reichmann's disease.* **digestive g.,** a condition in which there is excessive secretion of gastric juice during digestion only. **g. muco′sa,** excessive secretion of mucus by the stomach.

gastrotherapy (gas″tro-ther′ah-pe) [*gastro-* + Gr. *therapeia* treatment]. 1. The use of an extract of the gastric mucosa of hogs in the treatment of pernicious anemia. 2. The treatment of stomach disease.

gastrothoracopagus (gas″tro-tho″rah-kop′ah-gus) [*gastro-* + Gr. *thōrax* chest + *pagos* thing fixed]. A double monster joined at the abdomen and thorax. **g. dipy′gus,** a double monster in which there is attached to the abdomen of the autosite a parasite consisting of the pelvis and lower extremities only.

gastrotome (gas′tro-tōm). A cutting instrument used in gastrotomy.

gastrotomy (gas-trot′o-me) [*gastro-* + Gr. *temnein* to cut]. Operative incision into the stomach.

gastrotonometer (gas″tro-to-nom′e-ter) [*gastro-* + Gr. *tonos* tension + *metron* measure]. An instrument for measuring intragastric pressure.

gastrotonometry (gas″tro-to-nom′e-tre). The measurement of intragastric pressure.

gastrotoxin (gas″tro-tok′sin). A substance that exerts a toxic effect on the stomach.

gastrotrachelotomy (gas″tro-tra″kel-ot′o-me) [*gastro-* + Gr. *trachēlos* neck + *temnein* to cut]. Cesarean section in which the uterus is opened by an incision in the cervix.

gastrotropic (gas″tro-trop′ik) [*gastro-* + Gr. *tropos* a turning]. Having an affinity for or exerting a special effect upon the stomach.

gastrotubotomy (gas″tro-tu-bot′o-me). Gastrosalpingotomy.

gastrotympanites (gas″tro-tim″pah-ni′tēz) [*gastro-* + *tympanites*]. Tympanitic distention of the stomach.

gastroxia (gas-trok′se-ah) [*gastr-* + Gr. *oxys* sour]. Gastroxynsis.

gastroxynsis (gas″troks-in′sis) [*gastr-* + Gr. *oxynein* to sharpen, exacerbate]. Excessive secretion of hydrochloric acid by the stomach; hyperchlorhydria. **g. fungo′sa,** a form due to the presence of molds in the stomach.

gastrula (gas′troo-lah). That early embryonic stage which follows the blastula. The simplest type consists of two layers, the ectoderm and the mesentoderm, and of two cavities, one lying between the ectoderm and the entoderm; the other (the archenteron) formed by invagination so as to lie within the entoderm and having an opening (the blastopore).

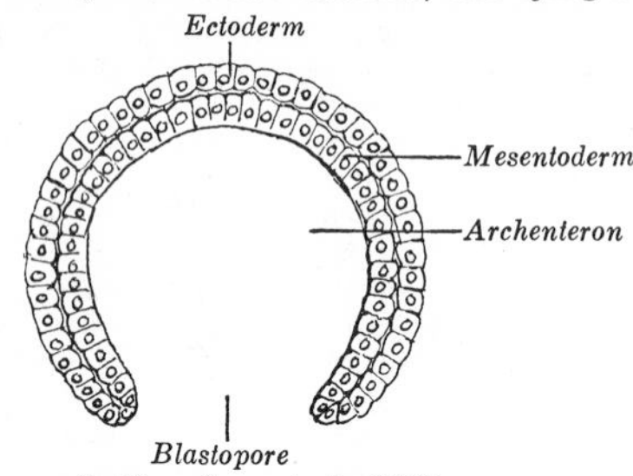

Section of a gastrula (Hill).

gastrulation (gas″troo-la′shun). The process by which the young embryo acquires its three germ layers.

Gatch bed (gach) [Willis Dew *Gatch,* American surgeon, born 1878]. See under *bed.*

gatism (ga′tizm) [Fr. *gâter* to spoil]. Rectal, vesical, or rectovesical incontinence.

gatophilia (gat″o-fil′e-ah). Ailurophilia.

gatophobia (gat″o-fo′be-ah). Ailurophobia.

gattine (gat′ēn). A disease of silkworms caused by a mixed infection with a filtrable virus and *Streptococcus bombycis.*

Gaucher's cells, disease (go-shāz) [Phillipe Charles Ernest *Gaucher,* French physician, 1854–1918]. See under *cell* and *disease.*

gauge (gāj). An instrument for determining the dimensions or caliber of anything. **Boley g.,** a watchmaker's gauge used in dentistry to measure tooth dimensions and to make other measurements important in prosthetic dentistry. **catheter g.,** a plate with graduated perforations for measuring the outside diameter of catheters.

Gaultheria (gawl-the′re-ah) [Jean François *Gaultier,* Quebec physician and botanist, 1708–1756]. A genus of ericaceous plants. The leaves of *G. procumbens,* of North America, afford a fragrant volatile oil rich in methyl salicylate.

gauntlet (gawnt′let) [Fr. *gant* glove]. A bandage which covers the hand and fingers like a glove.

gauss (gows) [Johann Karl F. *Gauss,* German physicist, 1777–1855]. The unit of magnetic flux density; symbol *B.*

Gauss's sign (gows′ez) [Carl J. *Gauss,* Würzburg gynecologist, 1875–1957]. See under *sign.*

gaussian curve (gow′shun) [J. K. F. *Gauss*]. See under *curve.*

Gauvain's fluid (go-vānz′) [E. Almore *Gauvain,* American dermatologist, born 1893]. See under *fluid.*

gauze (gawz). A light, open-meshed fabric of muslin or similar material. Before use in surgery it is usually rendered sterile and is frequently impregnated with various antiseptics, as iodoform gauze, borated gauze, sublimated gauze, etc. **absorbable g.,** gauze made from oxidized cellulose. **absorbent g.,** a well-bleached cotton cloth of plain weave, of various thread counts (20–44 per inch warp, 12–36 filling) and various weights (17.2–44.5 Gm. per yard). **absorbent g., sterile,** absorbent gauze which has been sterilized and subsequently protected from contamination. **petrolatum g.,** absorbent gauze saturated with white petrolatum: used as a protective covering for wounds.

gavage (gah-vahzh′) [Fr. "cramming"]. 1. Feeding through a tube passed into the stomach. 2. The therapeutic use of a very full diet.

Gavard's muscle (gah-vahrz′) [Hyacinthe *Gavard,* French anatomist, 1753–1802]. See under *muscle.*

Gay-Lussac's law (ga″lū-sahks′) [Joseph Louis *Gay-Lussac,* French naturalist, 1778–1850]. See under *law.*

Gayet's disease (ga-yāz′) [Prudent *Gayet,* French surgeon]. See under *disease.*

gayle (ga′le). A sort of puerperal fever in ewes during the lambing season. It is caused by *Staphylococcus haemorrhagicus* and is communicable to man in the form of a local skin eruption on the hands of those who skin the ewes.

Gaza's operation (gah′zahz) [Wilhelm von *Gaza,* German surgeon, 1883–1936]. Ramisection.

G.B.A. Abbreviation for *gingivobuccoaxial.*

GC. Abbreviation for *gonococcus,* or *gonococcal.*

g.-cal. Abbreviation for *gram calorie,* or small calorie.

g-cm. Abbreviation for *gram-centimeter.*

Gd. Chemical symbol for *gadolinium.*

Ge. Chemical symbol for *germanium.*

Gee's disease (gēz) [Samuel Jones *Gee,* London physician, 1839–1911]. A celiac (intestinal) disorder of children probably identical with sprue.

geeldikkop (gēl-dik′kop) [Dutch "yellow, thick head"]. A disorder of sheep caused by eating the poisonous plant, *Tribulus terrestris.*

Gegenbaur's cell (ga′gen-bow″erz) [Carl *Gegenbaur,* German anatomist, 1826–1903]. Osteoblast.

Geigel's reflex (gi′gelz) [Richard *Geigel,* German physician, 1859–1930]. See under *reflex.*

Geiger counter, Geiger-Müller counter (gi′ger, gi′ger-mil′er) [Hans *Geiger,* German physicist in England, 1882–1945]. See under *counter.*

Geissler's test (gīs′lerz) [Ernst *Geissler,* German physician in 19th century]. See under *tests.*

Geissler's tube (gīs′lerz) [Heinrich *Geissler,* German physicist, 1814–1879]. See under *tube.*

gel (jel). A colloid which is firm in consistency, although containing much liquid; a colloid in a gelatinous form. See *sol.* **aluminum hydroxide g.,** a preparation consisting of a suspension of 3.6 to 4.4 per cent of aluminum oxide, in the form of the hydrated oxide: used to reduce gastric acidity, as a demulcent and protective for gastric mucosa, as a vehicle to increase absorption of orally administered penicillin, and in conjunction with a low phosphorus diet in the treatment of renal disease. Called also *dried aluminum hydroxide gel.* **aluminum phosphate g.,** a water suspension of aluminum phosphate and some flavoring agents: used as a gastric antacid, astringent and demulcent. **corticotropin g.,** repository corticotropin injection (U.S.P.).

Gel. quav. Abbreviation for L. *gelati′na qua′vis,* in any kind of jelly.

gelase (jel′ās). An enzyme which is able to split agar-agar.

gelasmus (jĕ-las′mus) [Gr. *gelasma* a laugh]. Hysterical laughter.

gelate (jel′āt). To form a gel.

gelatification (jĕ-lat″ĭ-fi-ka′shun). Conversion into gelatin.

gelatigenous (jel″ah-tij′e-nus). Producing or forming gelatin.

gelatin (jel′ah-tin) [L. *gelatina,* from *gelare* to congeal]. A product obtained by partial hydrolysis of collagen derived from the skin, white connective tissue, and bones of animals. Used as a food, and pharmaceutically in the manufacture of capsules and in emulsions and suppositories. **agar g.,** nutrient bouillon solidified with gelatin and agar. **carbolized g.,** nutrient gelatin containing phenol. **g. compound phenolized,** a mixture of gelatin, zinc oxide, glycerin and water in phenol: used in preparing bandages (jelly bandages) for chronic ulcers and burns, and for producing pressure on varicose veins. **dextrose g.,** nutrient gelatin containing dextrose. **Elsner's potato g.,** potato g. **fish g.,** fish bouillon solidified with 10 per cent of gelatin. **glucose-formate g.,** nutrient gelatin containing glucose and sodium formate. **glycerinated g.,** a preparation of gelatin and glycerin. **Goadsby's potato g.,** potato g. **Guarniari's agar g.,** agar g. **Heller's urine g.,** urine g. **Japanese g.,** agar. **Kitasato's glucose-formate g.,** glucose-formate g. **lactose litmus g.,** nutrient gelatin containing lactose and sufficient litmus solution to color the medium a deep lavender. **litmus g.,** nutrient gelatin containing sufficient litmus to give it a deep lavender color. **litmus whey g.,** litmus whey when solidified with gelatin. **meat extract g.,** meat extract bouillon solidified with gelatin. **meat infusion g.,** nutrient g. **medicated g.,** gelatin mixed with medicated substances: for local application. **nutrient g.,** a bacteriological culture medium consisting of nutrient bouillon solidified with gelatin. **Piorkowski's g.,** a medium for cultivating typhoid bacilli, consisting of peptone, gelatin, and urine. **potato g.** 1. A cold water extract of grated potatoes containing potassium iodide and solidified with gelatin. 2. Glycerin potato broth solidified with gelatin. **silk g.,** sericin. **sulfindigotate g.,** nutritive gelatin containing glucose and sodium sulfindigotate. **urine g.** 1. (Heller). Plain urine gelatin containing peptone and salt, and made neutral to litmus. 2. (plain). Freshly passed urine solidified with gelatin. **vegetable g.,** a gelatin-like matter obtained from vegetable tissues. See *agar.* **Weyl's sulfindigotate g.,** sulfindigotate g. **g. of Wharton,** Wharton's jelly. **whey g.,** whey, obtained from fresh milk which has been curdled with rennet, solidified with 10 per cent of gelatin. **wort g.,** beerwort culture medium solidified with 10 per cent of gelatin. **Würtz's lactose litmus g.,** lactose litmus g. **zinc g.,** a preparation of zinc oxide, gelatin, glycerin, and purified water, applied topically as a protective.

gelatinase (jĕ-lat′ĭ-nās). An enzyme which liquefies gelatin, but does not affect fibrin of egg albumin. It occurs among bacteria, molds, yeasts, etc.

gelatiniferous (jel″ah-tĭ-nif′er-us) [L. *gelatina* gelatin + *ferre* to bear]. Producing gelatin.

gelatinize (jĕ-lat′ĭ-nīz). 1. To convert into gelatin. 2. To become converted into gelatin.

gelatinoid (jĕ-lat′ĭ-noid). Resembling gelatin.

gelatinolytic (jel″ah-tĭ-no-lit′ik) [*gelatin* + Gr. *lysis* dissolution]. Dissolving or splitting up gelatin.

gelatinosa (jel″ah-tĭ-no′sah) [L.]. Gelatinous. See *substantia gelatinosa.*

gelatinous (jĕ-lat′ĭ-nus) [L. *gelatinosus*]. Like jelly or softened gelatin.

gelatinum (jel-ah-ti′num) [L.]. Gelatin. **g. glycerina′tum,** glycerinated gelatin.

gelation (je-la′shun). The conversion of a sol into a gel.

gelatose (jel′ah-tōs). An albumose formed by hydrolyzing gelatin by acid, alkalis, or an enzyme.

gelatum (jĕ-la′tum) [L.]. Jelly, or gel.

gelfilm (jel′film). Trade mark for absorbable gelatin film.

gelfoam (jel′fōm). Trade mark for preparations of absorbable gelatin sponge.

gelidusi (ga″le-doo′se). Pelidisi.

geliqua (ga-le′kwah). Pirquet's word formula representing ten times two thirds of the body weight.

Gellé's test (zhel-āz′) [Marie Ernest *Gellé,* French aurist, 1834–1923]. See under *tests.*

Gellhorn pessary (gel′horn) [George *Gellhorn,* St. Louis gynecologist, 1870–1936]. See under *pessary.*

gelodiagnosis (je″lo-di″ag-no′sis). A method of distinguishing between colon and typhoid bacilli, based on fermentation by the former of lactose in the culture medium.

gelose (jel′ōs). Agar.

gelosis (je-lo′sis), pl. *gelo′ses* [L. *gelare* to freeze]. A hard lump in a tissue, especially such a lump in a muscle.

gelotherapy, gelototherapy (jel″o-ther′ah-pe, jel″o-to-ther′ah-pe) [Gr. *gelōs* laughter + *therapeia* cure]. Treatment of disease by provoking laughter.

gelotripsy (jel′o-trip″se) [*gelosis* + Gr. *tripsis* a rubbing]. The breaking up of geloses in muscle by massage.

Gély's suture (zha-lēz′) [Jules Aristide *Gély,* French surgeon, 1806–1861]. See under *suture.*

gemästete (gĕ-mes′tĕ-tĕ) [Ger.]. Swollen, or bloated: a term applied to enlarged astrocytes in the region of a degenerated area.

gemellary (jem′ĕ-lār″e). Pertaining to twins.

gemellipara (jem″el-lip′ah-rah) [L. *gemelli* twins + *parere* to produce]. A woman who has given birth to twins.

gemellology (gem″el-ol′o-je) [L. *gemellus* twin + *-logy*]. The scientific study of twins and twinning.

geminate (jem′ĭ-nāt). [L. *geminatus*]. Paired; occurring in pairs.

gemini (jem′ĭ-ni) [L.]. Plural of *geminus.*

geminous (jem′ĭ-nus). Geminate.

geminus (jem′ĭ-nus), pl. *gem′ini* [L.]. A twin. **gem′ini aequa′les,** monozygotic twins.

gemistocytic (jem-is″to-si′tik). Composed of large round cells: a term applied to astrocytomas composed of such cells.

gemma (jem′ah) [L. "bud"]. 1. A budlike body or structure. 2. Micelle.

gemmangioma (jem″an-je-o′mah). A vascular tumor composed of embryonal cells or angioblasts.

gemmation (jem-a′shun) [L. *gemmare* to bud]. Reproduction by budding; a kind of reproduction in cells in which a portion of the cell body is thrust out and then becomes separated, forming a new individual.

gemmule (jem′ūl) [L. *gemmula,* dim. of *gemma* bud]. 1. A reproductive bud; the immediate product of gemmation. 2. Any one of the many little excrescences upon the protoplasmic process of a nerve cell. 3. Hypothetical units assumed to be thrown off by the somatic cells, to be stored in the germ cells, and to determine the development of certain characters.

gemonil (jem′o-nil). Trade mark for a preparation of metharbital.

gen (jēn). Gene.

-gen (jen′) [Gr. *gennan* to produce]. Word termination denoting an agent productive of the object or state indicated by the word stem to which it is affixed, as allergen (allergy), cryogen (cold), and pathogen (disease).

genal (je′nal) [L. *gena* cheek]. Pertaining to the cheek.

gene (jēn) [Gr. *gennan* to produce]. The biologic unit of heredity, self-reproducing and located in a definite position (locus) on a particular chromosome. **allelic g's,** genes situated at corresponding loci in a pair of chromosomes. **dominant g.,** one which produces an effect in the organism, regardless of the state of the corresponding allele. **holandric g's,** genes in the non-homologous region of the Y chromosome. **lethal g.,** a gene the presence of which brings about the death of the organism. **operator g.,** one that is believed to control, through interaction with a repressor, the activity of an adjacent sequence of structural genes. **recessive g.,** a gene that will produce an effect in the organism only when it is transmitted by both parents. **repressor g.,** a gene that controls the formation of a repressor which in turn controls the function of a structural gene. **sex-linked g.,** a gene that is carried on the X or Y chromosome. **structural g.,** a gene that governs the formation of an enzyme.

geneogenous (je″ne-oj′e-nus) [Gr. *genea* birth + *gennan* to produce]. Congenital.

genera (jen′er-ah) [L.]. Plural of *genus*.

general (jen′er-al) [L. *generalis*]. Affecting many parts or all parts of the organism; not local.

generalize (jen′er-al-īz). To convert from a local to a general disease; to render general.

generation (jen″er-a′shun) [L. *generatio*]. 1. The act or process of reproduction. 2. A class composed of all individuals removed by the same number of successive ancestors from a common predecessor, or occupying positions on the same level in a genealogical chart. **alternate g.,** the alternate reproduction by asexual and sexual means in an animal or plant species. **asexual g.,** production of a new individual (organism) not originating from the union of sexual elements (gametes). **direct g.,** asexual g. **filial g., first,** all of the offspring produced by the mating of two individuals, as in a hybrid cross. Symbol F_1. **filial g., second,** all of the offspring produced by the mating of two individuals of the first filial generation. Symbol F_2. **nonsexual g.,** asexual g. **parental g.,** the generation with which a particular genetic study is begun. Symbol P_1. **sexual g.,** production of a new individual (organism) by the union of male and female elements (gametes). **spontaneous g.,** the generation of living organisms from nonliving matter; abiogenesis.

generative (jen′er-a″tiv). Pertaining to the reproduction of the species.

generic (jĕ-ner′ik) [L. *genus, generis* kind]. 1. Pertaining to a genus. 2. Distinctive.

genesial, genesic (jĕ-ne′ze-al, jĕ-nes′ik). Pertaining to generation or to origin.

genesiology (jĕ-ne″ze-ol′o-je) [*genesis* + *-logy*]. The sum of what is known concerning reproduction.

genesis (jen′e-sis) [Gr. *genesis* production, generation]. The coming into being of anything; the process of originating. Often used as a word termination to denote the production, formation, or development of the object or state indicated by the word stem to which it is affixed, as biogenesis, gametogenesis, and pathogenesis.

genesistasis (jen″e-sis′tah-sis) [*genesis* + Gr. *stasis* a stopping]. Interruption of the reproduction of organisms by chemotherapy so as to permit the body cells or fluids to dispose of them.

genestatic (gen″e-stat′ik). Tending to prevent sporulation.

genetic (je-net′ik). 1. Pertaining to reproduction, or to birth or origin. 2. Inherited.

geneticist (je-net′ĭ-sist). A specialist in genetics.

genetics (je-net′iks) [Gr. *gennan* to produce]. The study of heredity.

genetopathy (jen-ĕ-top′ah-the) [Gr. *genesis* reproduction + *pathos* disease]. Disease affecting the reproductive functions.

genetotrophic (je-net″o-trōf′ik). Pertaining to genetics and nutrition; relating to problems of nutrition which are hereditary in nature, or transmitted through the genes.

genetous (je-net′us). Dating from fetal life.

Geneva Convention. An international agreement of 1864, whereby the signatory nations pledged themselves to treat the wounded and the army medical and nursing staffs as neutrals on the field of battle.

Gengou phenomenon (zhaw-goo′) [Octave *Gengou*, French bacteriologist, 1875–1957]. Fixation of the complement.

Gengou-Moreschi phenomenon (zhaw-goo′ mo-res′ke) [Octave *Gengou;* Carlo *Moreschi*, Italian pathologist]. Fixation of the complement.

genial, genian (je-ni′al, je-ni′an) [Gr. *geneion* chin]. Pertaining to the chin.

genic (jen′ik). Pertaining to or caused by genes.

-genic (jen′ik) [Gr. *gennan* to produce]. Word termination meaning producing, or productive of.

genicula (je-nik′u-lah) [L.]. Plural of *geniculum*.

genicular (je-nik′u-lar). Pertaining to the knee.

geniculate (je-nik′u-lāt) [L. *geniculatus*]. Bent, like a knee.

geniculum (je-nik′u-lum), pl. *genic′ula* [L., dim. of *genu*]. A little knee; used in anatomical nomenclature as a general term to designate a sharp, kneelike bend in a small structure or organ, such as a nerve. **g. cana′lis facia′lis** [N A, B N A], **g. of facial canal,** the bend in the facial canal which lodges the geniculum nervi facialis. Called also *genu of facial canal.* **g. of facial nerve, g. ner′vi facia′lis** [N A, B N A], the part of the facial nerve at the lateral end of the internal acoustic meatus, where the fibers turn sharply posteroinferiorly, and where the geniculate ganglion is found. Called also *genu of facial nerve.*

genin (jen′in). Aglycone.

genioglossus (je″ne-o-glos′us). See *Table of Musculi.*

geniohyoglossus (je″ne-o-hi″o-glos′us). Musculus genioglossus.

geniohyoid (je″ne-o-hi′oid). Pertaining to the chin and hyoid bone.

geniohyoideus (je″ne-o-hi-oi′de-us). See *Table of Musculi.*

genion (je-ni′on) [Gr. *geneion* chin]. A craniometric point situated at the apex of the mental protuberance.

genioplasty (je-ni′o-plas″te) [Gr. *geneion* chin + Gr. *plassein* to shape]. Plastic surgery of the chin.

genital (jen′ĭ-tal) [L. *genitalis* belonging to birth]. 1. Pertaining to reproduction, or to the organs of generation. 2. [Pl.]. The reproductive organs (organa genitalia [N A]).

genitalia (jen″ĭ-ta′le-ah) [L., pl.]. The reproductive organs (organa genitalia [N A]). **external g.** See *partes genitales femininae externae* and *partes genitales masculinae externae.* **indifferent g.,** the reproductive organs of the embryo prior to the establishment of definitive sex.

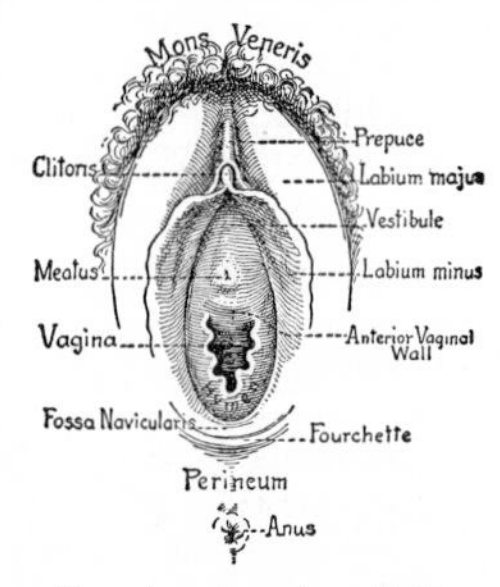

Female external genitalia (J. C. Hirst).

genitaloid (jen′ĭ-tal-oid) [*genitalia* + Gr. *eidos* form]. Pertaining to the primordial sex cells, before future sexuality is distinguishable.

genito- (jen′ĭ-to) [L. *genitalis* belonging to birth]. Combining form denoting relationship to the organs of reproduction.

genitocrural (jen″ĭ-to-kroo′ral) [*genital* + *crural*]. Pertaining to the genitalia and the leg.

genitofemoral (jen″ĭ-to-fem′or-al). Genitocrural.

genitoinfectious (jen″ĭ-to-in-fek′shus). Venereal.

genitoplasty (jen′ĭ-to-plas″te) [*genital* + Gr. *plassein* to mold]. Plastic surgery on the genital organs.

genitourinary (jen″ĭ-to-u′rĭ-nar-e). Pertaining to the genital and urinary organs.

genius (jēn′yus). 1. Distinctive character or peculiar nature. 2. Superlative aptitude or ability. **g. epidem′icus,** Sydenham's theory of "epidemic constitutions," that contagious diseases are influenced by cosmic or atmospheric conditions which may change the character of and produce variations in these diseases. **g. lo′ci,** the particular susceptibility of a tissue to develop secondary tumors. **g. mor′bi,** the predominant character of a disease.

Gennari's band, line (jen-nah′rēz) [Francisco *Gennari*, Italian anatomist of the 18th century]. See *line of Gennari*, under *line*.

Gennerich's treatment (gen′ĕ-riks) [Wilhelm *Gennerich*, German dermatologist, 1877–1951]. See under *treatment*.

geno- (jen′o) [Gr. *gennan* to produce]. Combining form denoting relationship to reproduction or to sex.

genoblast (jen′o-blast) [*geno-* + Gr. *blastos* germ]. 1. The nucleus of the fertilized ovum. 2. A mature germ cell.

genodermatology (jen″o-der″mah-tol′o-je). That branch of dermatology which treats of hereditary skin diseases.

genodermatosis (jen″o-der-mah-to′sis) [*geno-* + *dermatosis*]. A genetically determined disorder of the skin.

genome (je′nōm) [Gr. *gennan* to produce + *-ōma* mass, abstract entity]. The complete set of hereditary factors, as contained in the haploid assortment of chromosomes.

genomic (je-nom′ik). Pertaining to the genome.

genoneme (jen′o-nēm) [*geno-* + Gr. *nēma* a thread]. Axoneme.

genophobia (jen″o-fo′be-ah) [*geno-* + *phobia*]. Morbid dread of sex and sexuality.

genotype (jen′o-tīp) [*geno-* + Gr. *typos* type]. 1. The fundamental hereditary constitution (or assortment of genes) of an individual. Cf. *phenotype*. 2. The type species of a genus.

genotypic (jen″o-ti′pik). Pertaining to or expressive of the genotype.

Gensoul's disease (zhan-soolz′) [Joseph *Gensoul*, French surgeon, 1797–1858]. Ludwig's angina.

gentian (jen′shun). The dried rhizome and roots of *Gentiana lutea*: used as a bitter tonic.

gentianase (jen′shen-ās). An enzyme which catalyzes the hydrolysis of gentianose.

gentianin (jen′shah-nin) [L. *gentianinum*]. Various substances extracted from gentian root; gentianic acid, or a mixture of the latter and gentiopicrin.

gentianophil (jen′shan-o-fil). 1. An element staining readily with gentian violet. 2. Gentianophilic.

gentianophilic (jen″shan-o-fil′ik) [*gentian* + Gr. *philein* to love]. Staining readily with gentian violet.

gentianophilous (jen″shan-of′ĭ-lus). Gentianophilic.

gentianophobic (jen″shan-o-fo′bik). Not staining readily with gentian violet.

gentianophobous (jen″shan-of′o-bus). Gentianophobic.

gentiavern (jen′shah-vern). Methylrosaniline.

gentisate (jen′tĭ-sāt). A salt of gentisic acid.

gentran (jen′tran). Trade mark for a preparation of dextran.

genu (je′nu), gen. *ge′nus*, pl. *gen′ua* [L.] [N A, B N A]. 1. The site of articulation between the thigh (femur) and leg. Called also *knee*. 2. A general term used to designate any anatomical structure bent like the knee. **g. cap′sulae inter′nae** [N A, B N A], the blunt angle formed by the union of the two limbs of the internal capsule, situated posterior to the caudate nucleus, anterior to the thalamus, and medial to the lentiform nucleus. **g. cor′poris callo′si** [N A, B N A], **g. of corpus callosum,** the sharp ventral curve at the anterior end of the trunk of the corpus callosum. **g. extror′sum,** g. varum. **g. of facial canal,** geniculum canalis facialis. **g. of facial nerve.** 1. Genu nervi facialis. 2. Geniculum nervi facialis. **g. impres′sum,** a flattening and bending of the knee joint to one side, with consequent displacement of the patella up and to the same side. **g. of internal capsule,** g. capsulae internae. **g. [inter′num] ra′dicis ner′vi facia′lis** [B N A], g. nervi facialis. **g. intror′sum,** g. valgum. **g. ner′vi facia′lis** [N A], the bend in the fibers arising from the nucleus of the facial nerve, which produces the facial eminence in the floor of the fourth ventricle. It is at this point that the fibers loop around the abducent nucleus. Called also *g. of facial nerve* and *g. [internum] radicis nervi facialis* [B N A]. **g. recurva′tum,** abnormal hyperextensibility of the knee joint. **g. val′gum,** a deformity in which the knees are abnormally close together and the space between the ankles is increased. Known also as *knock knee*. **g. va′rum,** a deformity in which the knees are abnormally separated and the lower extremities are bowed inwardly. The deformity may be in the thigh or leg, or both. Known also as *bowleg*.

genua (jen′u-ah) [L.]. Plural of *genu*.

genual (jen′u-al). Relating to or resembling a genu.

genuclast (jen′u-klast) [L. *genu* knee + Gr. *klan* to break]. An instrument for breaking up knee joint adhesions.

genucubital (jen″u-ku′bĭ-tal) [L. *genu* knee + *cubitus* elbow]. Pertaining to or resting on the knees and elbows.

genufacial (jen″u-fa′shal) [L. *genu* knee + *facies* face]. Pertaining to or resting upon the knees and face.

genupectoral (jen″u-pek′tor-al) [L. *genu* knee + *pectus* breast]. Pertaining to or resting on the knees and chest.

genus (je′nus), pl. *gen′era* [L.]. A taxonomic category subordinate to a tribe (or subtribe) and superior to a species (or subgenus).

geny- (jen′e) [Gr. *genys* jaw]. A combining form denoting relationship to the jaw.

genyantralgia (jen″e-an-tral′je-ah) [*geny-* + *antrum* + *-algia*]. Pain in the maxillary sinus.

genyantritis (jen″e-an-tri′tis) [*geny-* + *antrum* + *-itis*]. Inflammation of the maxillary sinus.

genyantrum (jen″e-an′trum) [*geny-* + Gr. *antron* cave]. The antrum of Highmore, or maxillary sinus.

genycheiloplasty (jen″e-ki′lo-plas″te) [*geny-* + Gr. *cheilos* lip + *plassein* to form]. Plastic surgery of the jaw and lip.

genyplasty (jen′e-plas″te) [*geny-* + Gr. *plassein* to mold]. Surgical reconstruction of the jaw.

geo- (je′o) [Gr. *gē* earth]. A combining form denoting relationship to the earth, or to soil.

geobiology (je″o-bi-ol′o-je) [*geo-* + *biology*]. The biology of terrestrial life.

geochemistry (je″o-kem′is-tre) [*geo-* + *chemistry*]. The science concerned with study of the elements in the earth's crust.

Geocyclus (je″o-si′klus). A genus of schizomycetes with flagella-like filaments.

geode (je′ōd) [Gr. *geōdes* earthlike: so called from a fancied resemblance to a mineral geode]. A dilated lymph space.

geomedicine (je″o-med′ĭ-sin) [*geo-* + *medicine*]. That branch of medicine that has to do with the influence of climatic and environmental conditions on health.

geopathology (je″o-pah-thol′o-je) [*geo-* + *pathology*]. The study of the peculiarities of disease in relation to topography, climate, food habits, etc. of various regions of the earth.

geophagia (je-o-fa′je-ah) [*geo-* + Gr. *phagein* to eat]. The habit of eating clay or earth.

geophagism (je-of′ah-jizm). Geophagia.

geophagist (je-of′ah-jist). One who eats earth habitually.

geophagy (je-of′ah-je). Geophagia.

Georgi's test (ga-or′gēz) [Walter *Georgi*, German bacteriologist, 1889–1920]. Sachs-Georgi test.

geotaxis (je″o-tak′sis) [*geo-* + Gr. *taxis* arrangement]. Geotropism.

geotragia (je″o-tra′je-ah) [*geo-* + Gr. *trōgein* to chew]. Geophagia.

geotrichosis (je″o-tri-ko′sis). Infection by a species of *Geotrichum* which may attack the bronchi, lungs, mouth, or intestinal tract.

Geotrichum (je-ot′rĭ-kum). A genus of yeastlike fungi of the family Eremascaceae, various species of which have been isolated from pulmonary lesions.

geotropic (je″o-trop′ik). Influenced in growth by gravity.

geotropism (je-ot′ro-pizm) [*geo-* + Gr. *tropos* a turning]. A tendency of growth or movement toward or away from the earth; the influence of gravity on growth. A tendency to grow toward the earth is *positive g.;* to grow away from the earth, *negative g.*

gephyrophobia (je-fi″ro-fo′be-ah) [Gr. *gephyra* bridge + *phobia*]. Fear of walking on a bridge, river bank, or other structure near the water.

Geraghty's test (ger′ah-tēz) [John T. *Geraghty*, American physician, 1876–1924]. The phenolsulfonphthalein test.

Gerardinus (jĕ-rar′dĭ-nus). A genus of minnows. **G. poeciloi′des,** a species of minnows used in Barbados and Central America to eat the larvae of Anopheles mosquitoes.

geratic (je-rat′ik) [Gr. *gēras* old age]. Pertaining to old age.

geratology (jer″ah-tol′o-je). Gereology.

gerbil (jer′bil). A small burrowing rodent, *Gerbillus iateronia*, native on the veldt of South Africa, which is one of the chief agents for transmitting plague.

Gerdy's fibers, etc. (zher-dēz′) [Pierre Nicolas *Gerdy*, French physician, 1797–1856]. See under *fiber*, etc.

gereology (jer″e-ol′o-je) [Gr. *gēras* old age + *-logy*]. The science which deals with old age and its phenomena.

Gerhardt's disease, reaction, sign, test (ger′harts) [Carl J. *Gerhardt*, German physician, 1833–1902]. See under *disease, sign,* and *tests.*

Gerhardt's test (zher-harts′) [Charles Frédéric *Gerhardt*, French chemist, 1816–1856]. See under *tests.*

Gerhardt-Semon law (Carl J. *Gerhardt;* Sir Felix *Semon*, German laryngologist in London, 1849–1921]. See under *law.*

geriatric (jer″e-at′rik). Pertaining to the treatment of the aged.

geriatrics (jer″e-at′riks) [Gr. *gēras* old age + *iatrikē* surgery, medicine]. That branch of medicine which treats all problems peculiar to old age and the aging, including the clinical problems of senescence and senility. **dental g.,** gerodontics.

geriodontics (jer″e-o-don′tiks). Gerodontics.

geriodontist (jer″e-o-don′tist). Gerodontist.

geriopsychosis (jer″e-o-si-ko′sis) [Gr. *gēras* old age + *psychosis*]. Any one of the presenile and senile groups of mental diseases (Southard).

Gerlach's network, valve (ger′laks) [Joseph von *Gerlach*, German anatomist, 1820–1896]. See under *network* and *valve.*

Gerlier's disease (zher-le-āz′) [Felix *Gerlier*, French physician, 1840–1914]. See under *disease.*

germ (jerm) [L. *germen*]. 1. A pathogenic microorganism. 2. Living substance capable of developing into an organ, part, or organism as a whole; a primordium. **dental g.,** the collective tissues from which an entire tooth is formed, including the dental sac, dental organ, and dental papilla. **enamel g.,** the epithelial rudiment of the enamel organ. **hair g.** See *hair matrix*, under *matrix.* **wheat g.,** the embryo of wheat, which contains tocopherol, thiamine, riboflavin, and other vitamins.

germanin (jer′mah-nin). Suramin sodium.

germanium (jer-ma′ne-um). A very rare white metal; atomic number 32, atomic weight 72.59; symbol, Ge. **g. dioxide,** GeO_2, has erythropoietic properties and has been used in treating anemia in 0.2 per cent aqueous solution.

germicidal (jer″mĭ-si′dal) [L. *germen* germ + *caedere* to kill]. Destructive to pathogenic microorganisms.

germicide (jer′mĭ-sīd). An agent that destroys pathogenic microorganisms.

germiculture (jer′mĭ-kul″tūr) [L. *germen* germ + *cultura* culture]. The artificial cultivation of pathogenic microorganisms.

germinal (jer′mĭ-nal) [L. *germinalis*]. Pertaining to or of the nature of a germ.

germination (jer″mĭ-na′shun) [L. *germinatio*]. The sprouting of a seed or spore or of a plant embryo.

germinative (jer′mĭ-na″tiv) [L. *germinativus*]. Pertaining to germination or to a germ.

germogen (jer′mo-jen) [*germ* + Gr. *gennan* to produce]. A mass of protoplasm from which reproductive cells arise.

gero-, geronto- (jer′o, jer-on′to) [Gr. *gerōn, gerontos* old man]. Combining form denoting relationship to old age or to the aged.

gerocomia (jer″o-ko′me-ah) [*gero-* + Gr. *komein* to care for]. The care of old men; the hygiene of old age.

gerocomy (jer′o-ko″me). Gerocomia.

geroderma, gerodermia (jer-o-der′mah, jer-o-der′me-ah) [*gero-* + Gr. *derma* skin]. Dystrophy of the skin and genitals, producing the appearance of old age (Rummo and Ferrannini, 1897).

gerodontia (jer-o-don′she-ah). Gerodontics.

gerodontic (jer″o-don′tik) [*gero-* + Gr. *odous* tooth]. 1. Pertaining to changes in the dental tissues with age. 2. Pertaining to the practice of gerodontics.

gerodontics (jer″o-don′tiks). The treatment of dental problems of aging persons, or peculiar to advanced age.

gerodontist (jer″o-don′tist). A dentist who practices gerodontics.

gerodontology (jer″o-don-tol′o-je). The study of the dentition and dental problems in the aged or aging.

gerokomy (jer-o′ko-me). Gerocomia.

geromarasmus (jer″o-mah-raz′mus) [*gero-* + Gr. *marasmos* a wasting]. The emaciation sometimes characteristic of old age.

geromorphism (jer″o-mor′fizm) [*gero-* + Gr. *morphē* form]. Premature decrepitude and senility. **cutaneous g.,** a condition in which the skin shows at a very early age the characteristics of old age.

gerontal (jer-on′tal). Pertaining to an old man or old age; senile.

gerontin (jer-on′tin). A base from the nuclei of the cells of a dog's liver, identical with spermin.

geronto-. See *gero-.*

gerontologist (jer″on-tol′o-jist). A specialist in gerontology.

gerontology (jer″on-tol′o-je) [*geronto-* + *-logy*]. The scientific study of the problems of aging in all their aspects—clinical, biological, historical, and sociological.

gerontophile (jer-on′to-fīl). A person who manifests gerontophilia.

gerontophilia (jer″on-to-fil′e-ah) [*geronto-* + Gr. *philein* to love]. Special fondness for old people.

gerontopia (jer″on-to′pe-ah) [*geronto-* + Gr. *opsis* vision]. Senopia.

gerontotherapeutics (jer-on″to-ther″ah-pu′tiks) [*geronto-* + *therapeutics*]. Therapeutic management of aging persons designed to retard and prevent the development of many of the aspects of senescence.

gerontotherapy (jer-on″to-ther′ah-pe). Gerontotherapeutics.

gerontotoxon, gerontoxon (jer-on″to-tok′son, jer-on-tok′son) [*geronto-* + Gr. *toxon* bow]. The arcus senilis. **g. len′tis,** equatorial couching of the lens in the aged.

Gerota's capsule, method (ga-ro′tahz) [Dumitru *Gerota*, anatomist in Bucharest, 1867–1939]. See under *capsule* and *method.*

Gerson diet, Gerson-Herrmannsdorfer diet (gār′son, har′mans-dor-fer) [Max *Gerson*, German physician in New York, born 1881; Adolph *Herrmannsdorfer*, German surgeon, born 1889]. See under *diet.*

Gerstmann's syndrome (garst′manz) [Josef *Gerstmann*, Vienna neurologist, born 1887]. See under *syndrome.*

Gersuny's phenomenon, symptom (gar-su′nēz) [Robert *Gersuny*, surgeon in Vienna, 1844–1924]. See under *symptom.*

gerüstmark (gĕ-rist′mark) [Ger. *gerüst* scaffolding + *mark* marrow]. A unique, collagen-poor zone of connective tissue lying across the bone marrow adjoining the growing ends of bones; observed in scurvy.

gesarol (ges′ah-rol). Swiss name for DDT.

gestagen (jes′tah-jen). A hormone with progestational activity.

gestaltism (ges-tawlt′izm) [Ger. *Gestalt* form]. That theory in psychology which claims that the objects of mind, as immediately presented to direct experience, come as complete unanalyzable wholes or forms (Gestalten) which cannot be split up into parts. Called also *gestalt theory.*

gestation (jes-ta′shun) [L. *gestatio*, from *gestare* to bear]. The period of development of the young in viviparous animals, from time of fertilization of the ovum. **exterior g.,** the development of an infant after emergence from the uterus, until the time of quadrupedal locomotion, or about the age of nine months, during the period when it is in need of fetal care and might still be regarded as a fetus. **interior g.,** the development of an infant before emergence from the uterus.

gestosis (jes-to′sis), pl. *gesto′ses* [L. *gestare* to bear] Any toxemic manifestation of pregnancy.

geumaphobia (gu″mah-fo′be-ah) [Gr. *geuma* taste + *phobos* fear + *-ia*]. A morbid fear of tastes.

G.F.R. Abbreviation for *glomerular filtration rate.*

G.G.G. Abbreviation for L. *gum′mi gut′tae gam′biae*, gamboge.

Ghilarducci's reaction (ge″lar-doot′shēz) [Francesco *Ghilarducci*, Italian physician, 1857–1924]. See under *reaction.*

Ghon lesion, tubercle [Anton *Ghon*, Prague pathologist, 1866–1936]. See under *tubercle.*

Ghon-Sachs bacillus [Anton *Ghon;* Anton *Sachs*]. *Clostridium septicum.*

ghost (gōst). A faint or shadowy figure, lacking the customary substance of reality. **blood g.,** phantom corpuscle.

G.I. Abbreviation for *gastrointestinal* and for *globin insulin.*

Giacomini's band (jah-ko-me′nēz) [Carlo *Giacomini*, Italian anatomist, 1841–1898]. See under *band.*

Giannuzzi's cells, crescents, demilunes (jah-noot′zēz) [Guiseppe *Giannuzzi*, Italian anatomist, 1839–1876]. See under *crescent.*

giant (ji′ant) [Gr. *gigas*]. A person or organism of very great size.

giantism (ji′ant-izm). 1. Gigantism. 2. Excessive size, as of cells or nuclei.

Giardia (je-ar′de-ah) [Alfred *Giard*, biologist in Paris, 1846–1908]. A genus of flagellate protozoan organisms found in the intestinal tract of man and of animals, but not known to be pathogenic, although infection by it is frequently accompanied by a severe diarrhea. **G. lamb′lia,** the species found in man, is a symmetrical, pear-shaped organism with a sucking disk and four pairs of flagella. Called also *G. intestinalis, Cercomonas intestinalis, Dicercomonas muris, Lamblia intestinalis,* and *Megastoma entericum.*

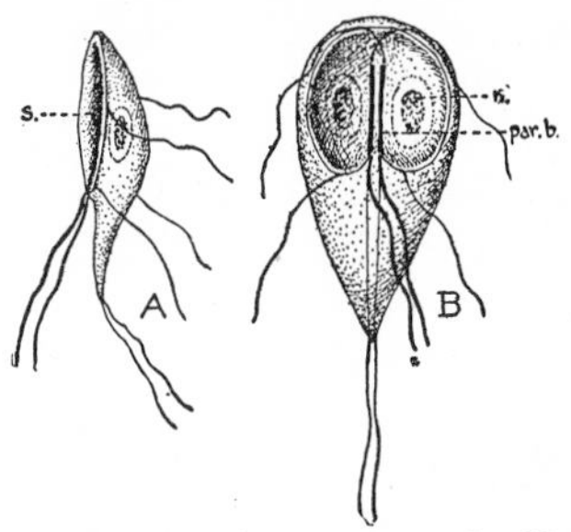

Giardia lamblia: A, side view (s., sucker-like depression); B, ventral view (par. b., parabasal bodies; n., nucleus) (Wenyon).

giardiasis (ji″ar-di′ah-sis). Infection with *Giardia.*

Gibbon's hernia (gib′onz) [Q. V. *Gibbon*, American surgeon, 1813–1894]. See under *hernia.*

gibbosity (gib-bos′ĭ-te) [L. *gibbosus* crooked]. The condition of being humped.

gibbous (gib′us) [L. *gibbosus*]. Convex; humped; protuberant; humpbacked.

Gibbs's theorem (gibz) [Josiah Willard *Gibbs*, American physicist, 1839–1903]. See under *theorem.*

gibbus (gib′us) [L.]. A hump.

Gibert's disease (zhe-bārz′) [Camille Melchior *Gibert*, French dermatologist, 1797–1866]. Pityriasis rosea.

Gibney's bandage, perispondylitis, strapping [Virgil P. *Gibney*, New York surgeon, 1847–1927]. See under *bandage* and *perispondylitis.*

Gibson's bandage (gib′sunz) [William *Gibson*, American surgeon, 1788–1868]. See under *bandage.*

Gibson's murmur, rule (gib′sunz) [George Alexander *Gibson*, Edinburgh physician, 1854–1913]. See under *murmur* and *rule.*

gid (gid). Staggers.

giddiness (gid′e-nes). Dizziness.

Giemsa's stain (gēm′sahz) [Gustav *Giemsa*, chemist and bacteriologist in Hamburg, 1867–1948]. See *table of stains and staining methods.*

Gierke's corpuscles (gēr′kez) [Hans Paul Bernard *Gierke*, German anatomist, 1847–1886]. See under *corpuscle.*

Gierke's disease (gēr′kez) [Edgar von *Gierke*, German pathologist, born 1877]. Glycogenosis.

Gieson (ge′son). See *van Gieson.*

Gifford's operation, reflex, sign (gif′ordz) [Harold *Gifford*, American oculist, 1858–1929]. See under the nouns.

giga- (ji′gah) [Gr. *gigas* mighty]. Combining form designating gigantic size; used in naming units of measurement to indicate a quantity one billion (10^9) times the unit designated by the root with which it is combined.

gigantism (ji′gan-tizm) [Gr. *gigas* giant]. Abnormal overgrowth; excessive or monstrous size and stature. **acromegalic g.,** gigantism in which the body has the changes in the short and flat bones characteristic of acromegaly. **eunuchoid g.,** gigantism in which the body shows the proportion of a eunuch and sexual deficiency. **normal g.,** gigantism in which the body proportions and sexual development are normal.

giganto- (ji-gan′to) [Gr. *gigas, gigantos* huge]. A combining form meaning huge.

gigantoblast (ji-gan′to-blast) [*giganto-* + Gr. *blastos* germ]. A very large nucleated erythroblast.

gigantochromoblast (ji-gan″to-kro′mo-blast) [*giganto-* + *chromoblast*]. Gigantoblast.

gigantocyte (ji-gan′to-sīt) [*giganto-* + Gr. *kytos* hollow vessel]. An erythrocyte of enormous size, measuring over 16 micra in diameter. Cf. *megalocyte.*

gigantosoma (ji-gan″to-so′mah) [*giganto-* + Gr. *sōma* body]. Gigantism, or great size and stature.

Gigli's operation, saw (jēl′yēz) [Leonardo *Gigli*, gynecologist in Florence, 1863–1908]. See under *operation* and *saw*.

gikiyami (ge″ke-yam′e). Nanukayami.

gilbert (gil′bert) [W. *Gilbert*, English physicist, 1544–1603]. The unit of magnetomotive force; symbol, *F*.

Gilbert's disease, sign (zhēl-bārz′) [Nicolas Augustin *Gilbert*, French physician, 1858–1927]. See under *disease* and *sign*.

Gilchrist's disease, mycosis (gil′krists) [Thomas Casper *Gilchrist*, American dermatologist, 1862–1927]. Blastomycosis.

gildable (gil′dah-b'l). Susceptible of being colored with gold stains.

Gill's operation [A. Bruce *Gill*, American orthopedic surgeon]. See under *operation*.

Gillenia (jil-le′ne-ah) [L.; after Arnold *Gill*]. A genus of rosaceous plants. The root of *G. trifoliata* and *G. stipulacea*, of North America, is mildly emetic and aperient.

Gilles de la Tourette's disease [Georges *Gilles de la Tourette*, French physician, 1857–1904]. See under *disease*.

Gilliam's operation [David Tod *Gilliam*, Columbus gynecologist, 1844–1923]. See under *operation*.

Gillies' graft, operation (gil′ēz) [Sir Harold Delf *Gillies*, British plastic surgeon, 1882–1960]. See under *graft* and *operation*.

Gilmer's splint (gil′merz) [Thomas Lewis *Gilmer* American oral surgeon, 1849–1931]. See under *splint*.

Gimbernat's ligament (him-ber-nats′) [Antonio de *Gimbernat*, Spanish surgeon, 1734–1790]. See under *ligament*.

ginger (jin′jer) [L. *zingiber;* Gr. *zingiberis*]. The dried rhizome of *Zingiber officinale:* used as a flavoring agent.

gingiva (jin′jĭ-vah). [L. "gum of the mouth"]. See *gingivae*. **alveolar g.,** that portion of the gingivae which covers the alveolar process. **areolar g.,** that portion of the gingivae which overlies the alveolar process, being bound to it by loose areolar connective tissue. **buccal g.,** that portion of the gingivae which is applied to the buccal surfaces of the posterior teeth. **cemented g.,** that portion of the gingivae which is firmly attached to the neck of a tooth. **free g.,** the portion of the gingivae covering part of the crowns of the teeth, but not attached to them. **labial g.,** that portion of the gingivae which is applied to the labial surfaces of the anterior teeth. **lingual g.,** that portion of the gingivae which is applied to the lingual surfaces of the teeth. **marginal g.,** free g. **septal g.,** that portion of the gingivae which occupies the interproximal spaces.

gingivae (jin-jĭ′ve) [L., plural of *gingiva*]. [N A] The mucous membrane, with the supporting fibrous tissue, which overlies the crowns of unerupted teeth and encircles the necks of those that have erupted. See also under *gingiva*.

gingival (jin′jĭ-val). Pertaining to the gingivae.

gingivalgia (jin″jĭ-val′je-ah) [*gingiva* + *-algia*]. Pain in the gingivae.

gingivally (jin″jĭ-val″le). Toward the gingivae.

gingivectomy (jin″jĭ-vek′to-me) [*gingiva* + Gr. *ektomē* excision]. Surgical excision of all loose infected and diseased gingival tissue to eradicate periodontal infection and reduce the depth of the gingival sulcus.

gingivitis (jin-jĭ-vi′tis) [*gingiva* + *-itis*]. Inflammation involving the gingival tissue only. **atrophic g., senile,** a condition characterized by hyperkeratinization and areas of desquamation in the gingiva. **bismuth g.,** inflammation of the gingivae caused by local deposit of bismuth from the blood stream, after its administration for systemic disease. **"cotton-roll" g.,** secondary infection of denuded areas of gingivae caused by adherence of epithelium to cotton rolls placed in the mouth during dental procedures. **desquamative g.,** a chronic inflammatory condition characterized by tendency of the surface epithelium of the gingivae to desquamate. **fusospirochetal g.,** necrotizing ulcerative g. **herpetic g.,** infection of gingivae by the herpetic virus. **marginal g., simple,** hyperemia of the gingivae with edema of the margins and gingival papillae, resulting from slight trauma or neglected dental hygiene. **marginal g., suppurative, g. margina′lis suppurati′va,** inflammation of the gingival margins, with formation of a purulent discharge. **necrotizing ulcerative g.,** an acute or chronic gingival infection characterized by redness and swelling, necrosis extending from the interdental papillae along the gingival margins, pain, hemorrhage, a necrotic odor, and often a pseudomembrane. **phagedenic g.,** rapidly progressive ulcerative inflammation of the gums. **streptococcal g.,** inflammation of the gingival margins caused by streptococcal infection. **ulceromembranous g.,** necrotizing ulcerative g. **Vincent's g.,** necrotizing ulcerative g.

gingivo- (jin′jĭ-vo) [L. *gingiva* gum]. Combining form denoting relationship to the gingivae.

gingivoaxial (jin″jĭ-vo-ak′se-al). Pertaining to or formed by the gingival and axial walls of a tooth cavity.

gingivobuccoaxial (jin″jĭ-vo-buk″ko-ak′se-al). Pertaining to or formed by the gingival, buccal, and axial walls of a tooth cavity.

gingivoectomy (jin″jĭ-vo-ek′to-me). Gingivectomy.

gingivoglossitis (jin″jĭ-vo-glos-si′tis) [*gingiva* + Gr. *glōssa* tongue + *-itis*]. Inflammation of gingivae and tongue.

gingivolabial (jin″jĭ-vo-la′be-al). Pertaining to the gingivae and lips.

gingivolinguoaxial (jin″jĭ-vo-ling″gwo-ak′se-al). Pertaining to or formed by the gingival, lingual, and axial walls of a tooth cavity.

gingivoplasty (jin′jĭ-vo-plas″te) [*gingivo-* + Gr. *plassein* to form]. Surgical modeling of the gingival margin and papillae to obtain a normal gingival contour.

gingivosis (jin″jĭ-vo′sis) [*gingivo-* + *-osis*]. A chronic diffuse inflammation of the gingivae, with desquamation of papillary epithelium and mucous membrane.

gingivostomatitis (jin″jĭ-vo-sto″mah-ti′tis). Inflammation involving both the gingivae and the oral mucosa. **herpetic g.,** an infection of the gingivae and oral mucosa by the herpetic virus, characterized by fever and by redness and swelling, without necrosis, of the gingival papillae or gingival margins; localized ulcerative lesions may be present.

ginglyform (jin′glĭ-form). Ginglymoid.

ginglymo-arthrodial (jin″glĭ-mo-ar-thro′de-al). Partly ginglymoid and partly arthrodial.

ginglymoid (jin′glĭ-moid) [*ginglymus* + Gr. *eidos* form]. Resembling a ginglymus.

ginglymus (jin′glĭ-mus) [L.; Gr. *ginglymos* hinge]. [N A, B N A] A type of synovial joint that allows movement in but one plane, forward and backward, as the hinge of a door. Called also *hinge joint*.

Giordano's sphincter (jor-dan′ōz) [Davide *Giordano*, Italian surgeon, 1864–1954]. See under *sphincter*.

Giovannini's disease (jo″vah-ne′nēz) [Sabastiano *Giovannini*, Italian dermatologist, 1851–1920]. See under *disease*.

Giraldés' organ (he-ral′dās) [Jachim Albin Cardozo Cazado *Giraldés*, Portuguese surgeon in Paris, 1808–1875]. See under *organ*.

Girard's method, treatment (jir-ardz′) [Brig. Gen. Alfred C. *Girard*, Swiss surgeon, 1850–1916]. See under *treatment*.

girdle (ger′d'l) [L. *cingulum;* Gr. *zōstēr*]. An encircling structure, or part; anything that encircles a body. Called also *cingulum*. **Hitzig's g.,** an encircling zone of analgesia at the level of the breasts, in the area supplied by the third and sixth dorsal nerves, seen in the early stages of tabes dorsalis. **g. of inferior extremity,** pelvic g. (cingulum membri inferioris [N A]). **limbus g.,** a corneal degeneration in the form of an opaque line concentric with the limbus. **Neptune g.,** an abdominal band used in applying a wet-pack. **pelvic g.,** the encircling bony structure supporting the lower limbs. See *cingulum membri inferioris* [N A]. **shoulder g.,** the encircling bony structure supporting the upper limbs. See *cingulum membri superioris* [N A]. **g. of superior extremity, thoracic g.,** shoulder g. (cingulum membri superioris [N A]). **Venus' g.,** mercurial plaster spread on leather or linen: used in the treatment of syphilis. Called also *balteum venereum*.

Girdner's probe (gerd′nerz) [John Harvey *Girdner*, physician in New York, 1856–1933]. See under *probe*.

gitaligin (jĭ-tal′ĭ-jin). Trade mark for a preparation of amorphous gitalin.

gitalin (jit′ah-lin). A cardiac glycoside, $C_{35}H_{56}O_{12}$, from the leaves of *Digitalis purpurea*. **amorphous g.,** a glycosidal constituent of the leaves of *Digitalis purpurea:* used as a cardiotonic.

githagism (gith′ah-jizm). Poisoning by the seeds of *Agrostemma githago*, or corn cockle.

gitogenin (jit-oj′ĕ-nin). A sapogenin, $C_{27}H_{44}O_4$, from gitonin.

gitonin (jit′o-nin). A neutral saponin, $C_{50}H_{82}O_{23}$, from digitalis seed.

gitoxigenin (ji-tok′sĭ-jen-in). An aglycone, $C_{23}H_{34}O_5$, from digitalis.

gitterfasern (git′er-fas″ern) [Ger.]. The reticular lattice fibers of the corium.

Giuffrida-Ruggieri stigma (joof-re″dah-roo″je-er′e) [Vincenzo *Giuffrida-Ruggieri*, Italian anthropologist, 1872–1922]. See under *stigma*.

GIX. An insecticidal compound, similar to DDT, but with fluorine replacing chlorine in the paraphenyl position.

gizzard (giz′ard). The strong muscular stomach of a bird.

GL. Abbreviation for *greatest length*, a measurement used for small flexed embryos.

Gl. Chemical symbol for *glucinium*.

gl. Abbreviation for L. *glan′dula* and *glan′dulae* (gland, glands).

G.L.A. Abbreviation for *gingivolinguoaxial*.

glabella (glah-bel′ah) [L. *glaber* smooth]. 1. The smooth area on the frontal bone between the superciliary arches. 2. The most prominent point in the midsagittal plane between the eyebrows: used as an anthropometric landmark.

glabellad (glah-bel′ad). Toward the glabella.

glabellum (glah-bel′um). Glabella.

glabrificin (glah-brif′ĭ-sin) [L. *glaber* smooth + *facere* to make]. An antibody: so called from the property of rendering bacteria smooth or glabrous.

glabrous (gla′brus) [L. *glaber* smooth]. Smooth and bare.

glacial (gla′shal) [L. *glacialis*]. Resembling ice; vitreous; solid.

gladiate (gla′de-āt) [L. *gladius* sword]. Sword-shaped.

gladioline (glah-di′o-lin). An alkaloid or leukomaine from the brain tissue.

gladiolus (glah-di′o-lus) [L., dim. of *gladius* sword]. Corpus sterni.

gladiomanubrial (glad″e-o-mah-nu′bre-al). Pertaining to gladiolus and manubrium.

glairin (glār′in) [L. *clarus* clear]. A gelatinous substance of bacterial origin found in the water of certain sulfur springs.

glairy (glār′e). Resembling the white of an egg.

gland (gland) [L. *glans* acorn]. An aggregation of cells, specialized to secrete or excrete materials not related to their ordinary metabolic needs. Called also *glandula*. **absorbent g.,** nodus lymphaticus. **accessory g.,** a detached mass of glandular tissue situated near or at some distance from a gland of similar structure. **acid g's,** glandulae gastricae [propriae]. **acinotubular g.,** one that is both acinous and tubular. **acinous g.,** a gland made up of a number of acini. **admaxillary g.,** an accessory salivary gland emptying into the parotid duct. **adrenal g.,**

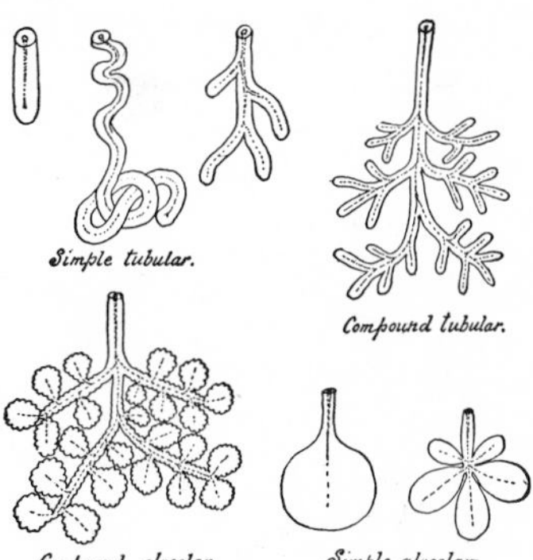

Diagrams of different forms of glands (Hill).

a flattened body situated in the retroperitoneal tissues at the superior pole of either kidney. Called also *glandula suprarenalis* [N A]. **adrenal g's, accessory,** glandulae suprarenales accessoriae. **aggregate g's, agminated g's,** folliculi lymphatici aggregati. **Albarran's g.,** that part of the median lobe of the prostate underneath the uvula vesicae. **albuminous g's,** certain glands of the digestive tract that secrete a watery fluid. **alveolar g.,** acinous g. **anacrine g.,** exocrine g. **anal g's,** glandulae circumanales. **angular g.,** glandula submandibularis. **anomalous g.,** ductless g. **anteprostatic g.** 1. Glandula bulbourethralis. 2. Glandula vestibularis major. **aortic g.,** aortic body. **apical g's of tongue,** glandulae linguales anteriores. **apocrine g.,** one the discharged secretion of which contains part of the secreting cells. **aporic g.,** ductless g. **areolar g's,** glandulae areolares. **arterial g.,** any knot of small arteries, or mass of vascular tissue, such as the glomus coccygeum. **arteriococcygeal g.,** glomus coccygeum. **arytenoid g's,** glandulae laryngeae posteriores. **atrabiliary g.,** glandula suprarenalis. **Avicenna's g.,** an encapsulated tumor. **axillary g's,** nodi lymphatici axillares. **Bartholin's g.,** one of the two small bodies on either side of the vaginal orifice, homologues of the bulbourethral glands in the male. Called also *glandula vestibularis major* [N A]. **Bauhin's g's,** glandulae linguales anteriores. **Baumgarten's g's,** tubular glands of the conjunctiva situated on the nasal side of the eyelids. **Berman's g's,** glands with greatly enlarged ducts and thin epithelial lining. **g's of biliary mucosa,** glandulae mucosae biliosae. **Blandin and Nuhn's g's,** glandulae linguales anteriores. **blood g., blood vessel g.,** endocrine g. **Bochdalek's g's,** cysts in the tongue derived from the primitive thyroglossal duct. **Boerhaave's g's,** glandulae sudoriferae. **Bonnot's g.,** interscapular g. **Bowman's g's,** glandulae olfactoriae. **brachial g's,** nodi lymphatici cubitales. **bronchial g's,** glandulae bronchiales. **Bruch's g's,** the lymph follicles of the conjunctiva of the lower lid. **Brunner's g's,** glandulae duodenales. **buccal g's,** glandulae buccales. **bulbocavernous g., bulbourethral g.,** one of two glands embedded in the substance of the sphincter of the urethra, just posterior to the membranous part of the urethra. Called also *glandula bulbourethralis* [N A]. **cardiac g's.** 1. The glands of the cardiac extremity of the stomach. 2. Glandulae

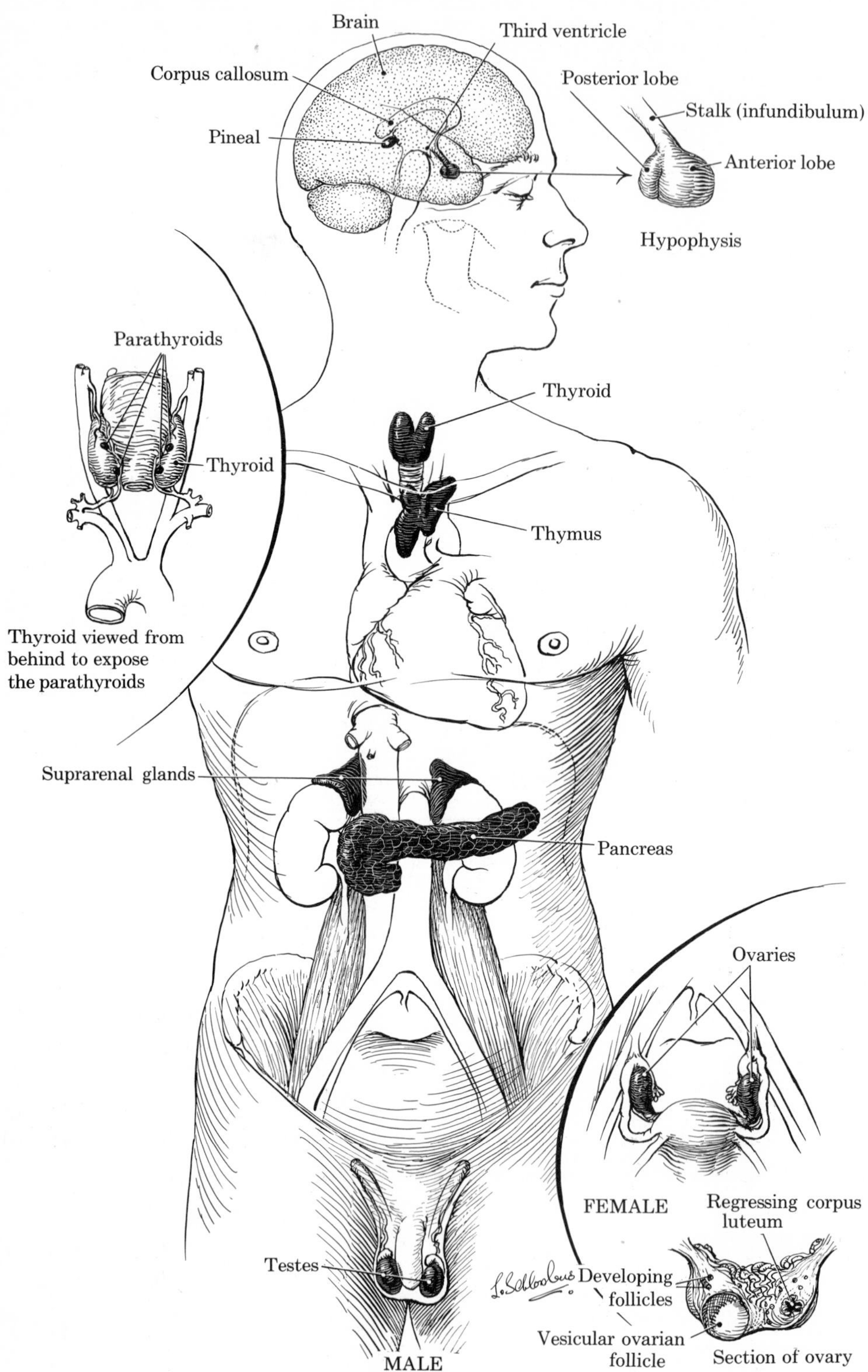

THE ENDOCRINE GLANDS

esophageae. **carotid g.,** glomus caroticum. **celiac g's,** lymph glands anterior to the abdominal aorta. **ceruminous g's,** the glands in the skin of the external auditory canal that secrete the cerumen. Called also *glandulae ceruminosae* [N A]. **cervical g's of uterus,** glandulae cervicales uteri. **cheek g's,** glandulae buccales. **choroid g.,** the choroid plexus, regarded as the secretor of the cerebrospinal fluid. **Ciaccio's g's,** glandulae lacrimales accessoriae. **ciliary g's, ciliary g's of conjunctiva,** glandulae ciliares conjunctivales. **circumanal g's,** specialized sweat and sebaceous glands situated around the anus. Called also *glandulae circumanales* [N A]. **closed g.,** ductless g. **Cobelli's g's,** mucous glands in the mucosa of the esophagus just above the cardia. **coccygeal g.,** glomus coccygeum. **compound g.,** one made up of a number of smaller units whose excretory ducts combine to form ducts of progressively higher order. **conglomerate g.,** compound g. **conjunctival g's,** glandulae conjunctivales. **convoluted g's,** glandulae sudoriferae. **Cowper's g.** 1. Glandula bulbourethralis. 2. Glandula vestibularis major. **cutaneous g's,** glands in the skin. See *glandulae cutis.* **cytogenic g.,** a term applied to the testis and the ovary because they form and secrete living cells. **dental g.,** one of the white areas on the mucous membrane of the jaw over the point of emergence of the tooth. **ductless g.,** one without a duct. See *endocrine g's.* **duodenal g's,** glandulae duodenales. **Duverney's g.,** glandula bulbourethralis. **Ebner's g's,** albuminous or serous secreting glands in the posterior part of the tongue near the vallate papillae. **eccrine g.,** a gland which produces a simple fluid secretion without admixture of cell plasm or cell contents. **Eglis' g's,** glandulae mucosae ureteris. **endocrine g's,** organs that secrete specific substances (hormones) which are released directly into the circulatory system and which influence metabolism and other body processes. See Plate XVII. Called also *glandulae sine ductibus* [N A]. **endo-epithelial g.,** a gland situated in an epithelial layer. **enterochromaffin g.,** a type of gland found in the mucosa of the intestinal canal, characterized by the presence in the cell protoplasm of granules which stain with chromium salts and are impregnable with silver. **esophageal g's,** glandulae esophageae. **excretory g.,** any gland that excretes waste products from the system. **exepithelial g.,** a gland situated below the epithelial layer. **exocrine g.,** a gland which discharges its secretion through a duct. **follicular g's of tongue,** folliculi linguales. **Fränkel's g's,** minute glands that open below the edge of the vocal cords. **fundic g's, fundus g's,** glandulae gastricae [propriae]. **Galeati's g's,** glandulae duodenales. **gastric g's,** the secreting glands of the stomach, including the fundus glands, cardiac glands, and pyloric glands. **gastric g's, proper,** glandulae gastricae [propriae]. **gastro-epiploic g's,** nodi lymphatici gastrici [dextri et sinistri]. **g's of Gay,** numerous highly developed sweat glands in the circumanal region. **genal g's,** glandulae buccales. **genital g.** 1. Ovary (ovarium [N A]). 2. Testis. **gingival g's,** glandlike infoldings of epithelium at the junction of gingiva and tooth. **Gley's g's,** glandulae thyroideae accessoriae. **globate g.,** nodus lymphaticus. **glomerate g's, glomiform g's,** glandulae glomiformes. **glossopalatine g's,** mucous glands at the posterior end of the smaller sublingual glands. **Guérin's g's,** ductus paraurethrales. **gustatory g's,** Ebner's g's. **guttural g.,** one of the mucous glands of the pharynx. **hair g.,** the sebaceous gland of a hair follicle. **g's of Haller,** glandulae preputiales. **Harder's g's, harderian g's,** accessory lacrimal glands at the inner corner of the eye in animals that possess nictitating membranes. They excrete an unctuous fluid that facilitates the movement of the third eyelid. They are rudimentary in man. **haversian g's,** villi synoviales. **hedonic g's,** glands in some of the lower animals which function during the season of sexual activity. **hemal g's,** hemolymph glands that have blood-vascular connections only. **hemal lymph g's,** hemolymph glands that contain lymph sinuses. **hematopoietic g's,** certain glandlike bodies which take a part in the making of the blood, such as the spleen, thyroid, and lymphatic glands. **hemolymph g's,** minute nodes resembling small lymphatic glands but red or brown in color and containing blood sinuses instead of or alongside of lymph spaces. They occur especially in the retroperitoneal tissue near the origin of the superior mesenteric and renal arteries, but are found elsewhere. They are believed to take part in blood destruction and formation. Two varieties are distinguished—*splenolymph* glands and *marrow-lymph* glands. **Henle's g's,** tubular glands in the conjunctiva of the eyelids. **hepatic g's,** glandulae mucosae biliosae. **heterocrine g's,** glands having a mixed (mucous and albuminous) secretion. **hibernating g.,** a collection of brown fatty tissue found in various regions of the body in hibernating animals. See *interscapular g.* **holocrine g.,** one the discharged secretion of which contains the entire secreting cells. **Huguier's g's,** two minor vaginal glands. **incretory g's,** endocrine g's. **intercarotid g.,** glomus caroticum. **interscapular g.,** a narrow lobulated mass of tissue in the neck and scapular region of embryos, of the newborn, and sometimes of adult mammals. Its probable function is the storage of fat and the formation of blood. This tissue has been called *brown fat* from its color, and *moruloid* or *mulberry fat* from its microscopical appearance. Called also *Bonnot's g.* **interstitial g.,** Leydig's cell. **intestinal g's,** straight tubular glands in the mucous membrane of the intestines, opening, in the small intestine, between the bases of the villi, and containing argentaffin cells. **intraepithelial g.,** endo-epithelial g. **intramuscular g's of tongue,** glandulae linguales anteriores. **jugular g.,** a lymph gland behind the clavicular insertion of the sternomastoid muscle. **Krause's g's,** glandulae conjunctivales. **labial g's of mouth,** glandulae labiales oris. **lacrimal g.,** glandula lacrimalis. **lacrimal g's, accessory,** glandulae lacrimales accessoriae. **lactiferous g.,** corpus mammae. **g's of large intestine,** glandulae intestinales intestini crassi. **large sweat g.,** an apocrine gland which usually produces an odoriferous secretion. **laryngeal g's,** glandulae laryngeae. **lenticular g's of stomach,** folliculi lymphatici gastrici. **lenticular g's of tongue,** folliculi linguales. **g's of Lieberkühn,** intestinal glands. **lingual g's,** glandulae linguales. **lingual g's, anterior, of Blandin and Nuhn,** glandulae linguales anteriores. **Littre's g's.** 1. Glandulae preputiales. 2. Glandu-

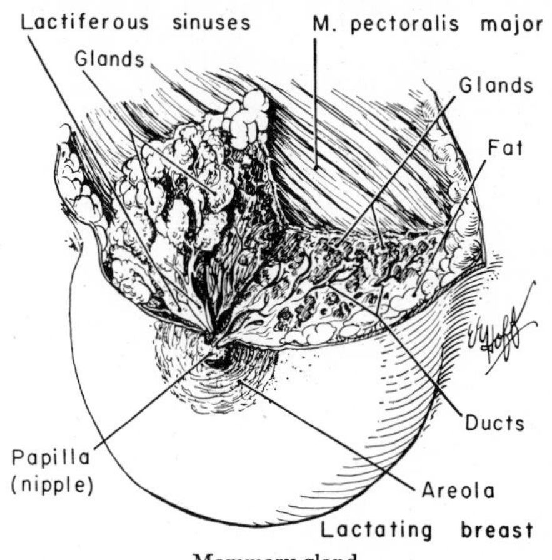

Mammary gland.

lae urethrales urethrae masculinae. **Luschka's g.,** glomus coccygeum. **lymph g., lymphatic g.,** nodus lymphaticus. **lymphatic g's, extraparotid,** lymph nodes overlying the parotid gland, between the superficial and deep fasciae. **malar g's,** glandulae buccales. **mammary g.,** corpus mammae. **mandibular g.,** glandula submandibularis. **Manz' g's,** glandular depressions on the borders of the eyelids. **marrow-lymph g's,** hemolymph glands that have a marrow-like tissue. **maxillary g.,** glandula submandibularis. **meibomian g's,** glandulae tarsales. **merocrine g.,** one the discharged secretion of which contains no part of the secreting cells. **Méry's g.** 1. Glandula bulbourethralis. 2. Glandula vestibularis major. **mesenteric g's,** nodi lymphatici mesenterici. **mesocolic g's,** glands in the mesentery of the colon. See *nodi lymphatici colici dextri, medii,* and *sinistri, nodi lymphatici ileocolici,* and *nodi lymphatici mesenterici inferiores.* **miliary g's,** glandulae sudoriferae. **mixed g's,** glands that are both mucous and serous. **molar g's,** glandulae molares. **Moll's g's,** glandulae ciliares conjunctivales. **monoptychic g.,** a gland in which the tubules or alveoli are lined with a single layer of secreting cells. **Montgomery's g's,** glandulae areolares. **Morgagni's g's,** glandulae urethrales urethrae masculinae. **g's of mouth,** glandulae oris. **mucilaginous g's,** villi synoviales. **muciparous g., mucous g.,** a gland that secretes a slimy, chemically inert material. Called also *glandula mucosa* [N A]. **mucous g's, lingual,** glandulae linguales. **mucous g's of auditory tube,** glandulae tubariae. **mucous g's of duodenum,** glandulae duodenales. **mucous g's of eustachian tube,** glandulae tubariae. **myometrial g.,** a tissue supposed to develop in the wall of the uterus at the site of implantation of the placenta and to last until the end of pregnancy. **Naboth's g's,** Naboth's follicles. **nasal g's,** glandulae nasales. **g. of neck,** tonsilla pharyngea. **Nuhn's g's,** glandulae linguales anteriores. **odoriferous g's of prepuce,** glandulae preputiales. **oil g's,** glandulae sebaceae. **open g.,** exocrine g. **oxyntic g's,** glandulae gastricae [propriae]. **pacchionian g's,** granulationes arachnoideales. **palatine g's,** glandulae palatinae. **palpebral g's,** glandulae tarsales. **pancreaticosplenic g.,** nodi lymphatici pancreaticolienales. **parafrenal g's,** glands opening near the frenum of the prepuce. **parathyroid g's,** small bodies in the region of the thyroid gland, developed from the entoderm of the branchial clefts, numbering one to four, commonly two (glandula parathyroidea inferior and glandula parathyroidea superior [N A]); they are concerned chiefly with the metabolism of calcium and phosphorus. **paraurethral g's,** ductus paraurethrales. **parotid g.,** the largest of the three chief, paired salivary glands. See *glandula parotis* [N A]. **parotid g., accessory,** glandula parotis accessoria. **pectoral g's.** See *nodi lymphatici axillares.* **peptic g's,** a set of mucous glands on the mucous membrane of the stomach, believed to secrete the gastric juice. **perspiratory g's,** glandulae sudoriferae. **Peyer's g's,** folliculi lymphatici aggregati. **pharyngeal g's,** glandulae pharyngeae. **Philip's g's,** enlarged glands above the clavicle, seen in children with tuberculosis. **pilous g.,** the sebaceous gland of a hair follicle. **pineal g.,** corpus pineale. **pituitary g.,** the epithelial body of dual origin located at the base of the brain in the sella turcica. It is attached by a stalk to the hypothalamus, from which it receives an important neural outflow. The hypophysis is composed of two main lobes, the *anterior lobe* (lobus anterior hypophyseos [N A], pars anterior, pars distalis), which arises from the buccal epithelium in the embryo, and the *posterior lobe* (lobus posterior hypophyseos [N A], pars posterior, neurohypophysis, infundibular body), which originates in the embryo as an evagination from the floor of the diencephalon. Other portions of this body are the *pars tuberalis,* which is an extension of the pars anterior up around the infundibular stalk, and the *pars intermedia,* a part of uncertain function wedged in between the two main lobes. The entire gland is often called the governing endocrine gland of the body. Its anterior lobe secretes several important hormones which regulate the proper functioning of the thyroid, gonads, adrenal cortex, and other organs of internal secretion. As a consequence, it is of vital importance to the growth, maturation, and reproduction of the individual. The posterior lobe, formerly thought to be the source of hormones having antidiuretic and oxytocic action, is now known to serve only as a reservoir for them. Called also *hypophysis cerebri* [N A]. **Poirier's g's,** lymph nodes on the conoid ligament at the upper border of the isthmus of the thyroid. **polyptychic g.,** a gland in which the tubules or alveoli are lined with more than one layer of secreting cells. **preen g.,** a large, compound alveolar structure present on the back of birds, above the base of the tail, which secretes an oily "water-proofing" material that the bird applies to its feathers and skin by preening. **pregnancy g's,** the glands containing female genital hormone, that is, the ovarian follicle, corpus luteum, and placenta. **prehyoid g's,** glandulae thyroidea accessoriae. **preputial g's,** glandulae preputiales. **prostate g.,** prostata. **puberty g's,** Steinach's name for the interstitial cells of Leydig in the male and the lutein cells of the ovary in the female. **pyloric g's,** glandulae pyloricae. **racemose g's,** glands composed of acini arranged like grapes on a stem. **retrolingual g.,** a rather large gland in some animals situated near the mandibular gland. **retromolar g's,** glandulae molares. **Rivini's g's,** glandulae sublinguales. **Rosenmüller's g.** 1. Glandula lacrimalis inferior. 2. See *lymphoglandulae subinguinales profundae.* **saccular g.,** a gland consisting of a sac or sacs, lined with glandular epithelium. **salivary g's,** the glands of the oral cavity whose combined secretion constitutes the saliva. They include the parotid, sublingual, and submandibular glands, as well as numerous small glands in the tongue, lips, cheeks, and palate. **salivary g., abdominal,** pancreas. **salivary g., external,** glandula parotis. **salivary g., internal.** See *glandula sublingualis* and *glandula submandibularis.* **Sandstroem's g's,** glandulae thyroideae accessoriae. **Schüller's g's,** diverticula of the ducts of Gartner. **sebaceous g's,** glandulae sebaceae. **sebaceous g's of conjunctiva,** glandulae sebaceae conjunctivales. **sebiferous g's,** glandulae sebaceae. **sentinel g.,** an enlarged lymph node, considered to be pathognomonic of some pathological condition elsewhere. **seromucous g.,** one that contains both serous and mucous secreting cells. Called also *glandula seromucosa* [N A]. **serous g.,** a gland that secretes a watery albuminous material commonly but not always containing enzymes. Called also *glandula serosa* [N A]. **Serres' g's,** pearly masses of epithelial cells near the surface of the gum of the infant. **sexual g.** See *testis* and *ovarium.* **Sigmund's g's,** the epitrochlear lymph glands. **Skene's g.,** ductus paraurethrales. **g's of small intestine,** glandulae intestinales intestini tenuis. **solitary g's of small intestine,** folliculi lymphatici solitarii. **splenoid g.,** an apparently compensatory new growth that sometimes follows extirpation of the spleen. **splenolymph g's,** hemolymph glands which have more of the splenic type of tissue. **Stahr's g.,** a lymph gland situated on the facial artery. **staphyline g's,** glandulae palatinae. **subauricular g.,** nodi lymphatici retroauriculares. **sublingual g.,** the smallest of the three chief, paired salivary glands. See *glandula sublingualis* [N A]. **submandibular g., submaxillary g.,** one of the three chief, paired salivary glands. See *glandula submandibularis* [N A]. **sudoriparous g's,** glandulae sudoriferae. **suprarenal g.,** glandula suprarenalis. **suprarenal g's, accessory,** glandulae suprarenales accessoriae. **Suzanne's g.,** a mucous gland of the mouth, beneath the alveololingual groove. **sweat g's,** the glands that secrete sweat. See *glandulae sudoriferae* [N A]. **synovial g's,** villi synoviales. **target g.,** a gland specifically affected by a pituitary hormone. Such glands include the thyroid, adrenals, and gonads. **tarsal g's, tarsoconjunctival g's,** glandulae tarsales. **Theile's g's,** glandlike formations in the walls of the cystic duct and in the pelvis of the gallbladder. **thymus g.,** thymus. **thyroid g.,** glandula thyroidea. **thyroid g's, accessory,** glandulae thyroideae accessoriae. **Tiedemann's g.,** glandula vestibularis major. **g's of tongue,** glandulae linguales. **tracheal g's,** glandulae tracheales. **trachoma g's,** lymphoid follicles of the conjunctiva, found chiefly near the inner canthus of the eye. **tubular g.,** any gland made up of or containing a tubule or a number of tubules. **tympanic g's,** glandulae tympanicae. **tympanic g. of Krause,** intumescentia tympanica. **g's of Tyson,** glandulae preputiales. **unicellular g.,** a cell which performs a secretory function, as a goblet cell. **urethral g's,** glandulae urethrales. **urethral g's of female urethra,** glandulae urethrales urethrae femininae. **uropygial g.,** preen g. **uterine g's,** tubular glands of the endometrium. **utricular g's,** glandulae uterinae. **vaginal g.,** any gland occurring exceptionally in the vaginal mucous membrane. **vascular g.** 1. Glomus. 2. A hemolymph gland. **vestibular g., greater,** glandula vestibularis major [N A]. **vestibular g's, lesser,** glandulae vestibulares minores. **Virchow's g.,** signal node. **vitelline g.** See *vitellarium*. **vulvovaginal g.,** glandula vestibularis major. **Waldeyer's g's,** acinotubular glands in the inner skin of the attached edge of the eyelid. **Wasmann's g's,** peptic g's. **Weber's g's,** the tubular mucous glands of the tongue. **Willis' g's,** corpora albicantia. **g's of Wolfring,** small tubulo-alveolar glands in the subconjunctival tissue above the upper border of the tarsal plate, their ducts opening on the conjunctival surface. **g's of Zeis,** sebaceous glands on the free edges of the eyelids. **Zuckerkandl's g.,** a small yellow mass occasionally seen between the two geniohyoid muscles, thought to be an accessory thyroid gland.

glandebalae (glan-deb′ah-le) [L., pl.]. The hairs of the axilla; called also *hirci* [N A].

glanderous (glan′der-us). Of the nature of or affected with glanders.

glanders (glan′derz) [L. *malleus*]. A disease of horses communicable to man, and caused by the glanders bacillus, *Malleomyces mallei*. It is marked by a purulent inflammation of mucous membranes and an eruption of nodules on the skin which coalesce and break down, forming deep ulcers, which may end in necrosis of cartilages and bones. Called also *equinia*. **African g., Japanese g.,** lymphangitis epizootica.

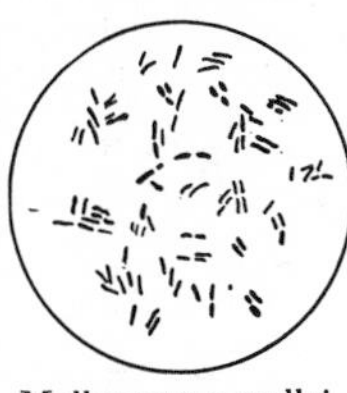

Malleomyces mallei.

glandes (glan′dēz) [L.]. Plural of *glans*.

glandilemma (glan″dĭ-lem′ah) [*gland* + Gr. *lemma* sheath]. The capsule or outer envelope of a gland.

glandula (glan′du-lah), pl. *glan′dulae* [L.]. [N A, B N A] An aggregation of cells, specialized to secrete or excrete materials not related to their ordinary metabolic needs. Called also *gland*. **glan′dulae areola′res** [N A], **glan′dulae areola′res [Montgomer′ii]** [B N A], sebaceous glands of the mammary areola. Called also *areolar glands*. **glan′dulae bronchia′les** [N A, B N A], mixed seromucous glands in the mucosa and submucosa of the bronchial walls. Called also *bronchial glands*. **glan′dulae bucca′les** [N A, B N A], the serous and mucous glands on the inner surface of the cheeks. Called also *buccal glands*. **g. bulbourethra′lis** [N A], **g. bulbourethra′lis [Cow′peri]** [B N A], either of two glands embedded in the substance of the sphincter of the male urethra, just posterior to the membranous part of the urethra. They are homologues of the greater vestibular glands in the female. Called also *bulbourethral gland*. **glan′dulae cerumino′sae** [N A, B N A], the glands in the skin of the external auditory canal that secrete the cerumen. Called also *ceruminous glands*. **glan′dulae cervica′les u′teri** [N A, B N A], highly branched mucous glands in the wall of the uterine cervix. Called also *cervical glands of uterus*. **glan′dulae cilia′res conjunctiva′les** [N A], **glan′dulae cilia′res [Molli]** [B N A], modified sudoriferous glands on the free margin of the eyelids near the eyelashes. Called also *ciliary glands of conjunctiva*. **glan′dulae circumana′les** [N A, B N A], specialized sweat and sebaceous glands situated in an annular zone around the anus. Called also *circumanal glands*. **g. clau′sa,** a ductless gland. **glan′dulae conjunctiva′les** [N A], mucous glands of the middle portion of the conjunctiva. Called also *glandulae mucosae conjunctivae [Krausei]* [B N A] and *conjunctival glands*. **glan′dulae cu′tis** [N A, B N A], the glands of the skin, including the glomiform, sudoriferous, circumanal, ceruminous, and sebaceous glands. **glan′dulae duodena′les** [N A], **glan′dulae duodena′les [Brunneri]** [B N A], tubuloalveolar glands in the submucous layer of the duodenum. Called also *duodenal glands*. **glan′dulae esophage′ae** [N A], the mucous glands in the submucosa of the esophagus. Called also *esophageal glands*. **glan′dulae gas′tricae [pro′priae]** [N A, B N A], very numerous, nearly straight tubular glands located in the mucosa of the fundus and body of the stomach. They secrete the gastric juice. Called also *gastric glands proper*. **glan′dulae glomifor′mes** [N A, B N A], glomiform arteriovenous shunts found in the skin, which are called glands although they appear to be non-glandular. Called also *glomiform glands*. **glan′dulae hepat′icae,** glandulae mucosae biliosae. **g. inci′siva,** a small intraoral gland in the median line of the upper jaw near the incisors. **g. intercarot′ica,** glomus caroticum. **glan′dulae intestina′les intesti′ni cras′si** [N A], simple mucous glands in the tunica mucosa of the large intestine. **glan′dulae intestina′les intesti′ni ten′uis** [N A], simple tubular glands in the small intestine, opening between the bases of the villi. **glan′dulae intestina′les rec′ti** [N A], the scattered mucous glands in the tunica mucosa of the rectum. **glan′dulae labia′les o′ris** [N A, B N A], the serous and mucous glands on the inner part of the lips. **g. lacrima′lis** [N A], one of the glands that lie at the upper outer angle of the orbit and secrete the tears. They are divided into two portions, the orbital and palpebral, by the orbital fascia. Called also *lacrimal gland*. **glan′dulae lacrima′les accesso′riae** [N A, B N A], portions of the lacrimal gland sometimes found near the superior fornix of the conjunctiva. Called also *accessory lacrimal glands*. **g. lacrima′lis infe′rior** [B N A], pars palpebralis glandulae lacrimalis. **g. lacrima′lis supe′rior** [B N A], pars orbitalis glandulae lacrimalis. **glan′dulae laryn′geae** [N A, B N A], the mucous glands in the mucosa of the larynx. **glan′dulae laryn′geae anterio′res** [B N A], mucous glands in the anterior of the larynx. Omitted in N A. **glan′dulae laryn′geae me′diae** [B N A], mucous glands located in the aryteno-epiglottic fold. Omitted in N A. **glan′dulae laryn′geae posterio′res** [B N A], mucous glands in the posterior wall of the larynx. Omitted in N A. **glan′dulae lingua′les** [N A, B N A], the mucous and serous glands on the surface of the tongue. **glan′dulae lingua′les ante-**

rio′res [N A, B N A], deeply placed mucoserous glands near the apex of the tongue. Called also *anterior lingual glands.* **g. mamma′ria** [N A], the collective glandular elements of the mamma, or breast, which secrete milk for nourishment of the young. Called also *mammary gland.* **glan′dulae mola′res** [N A, B N A], the glands on the external aspect of the buccinator muscle, their ducts piercing it to open on the internal aspect of the cheek. Called also *molar glands.* **g. muco′sa** [N A, B N A], a gland that secretes a slimy, chemically inert material. Called also *mucous gland.* **glan′dulae muco′sae bilio′sae** [N A, B N A], tubuloalveolar glands in the mucosa of the bile ducts and the neck of the gallbladder. Called also *glands of biliary mucosa.* **glan′dulae muco′sae conjuncti′vae [Kraus′ei]** [B N A], glandulae conjunctivales. **glan′dulae muco′sae ure′teris** [B N A], mucous glands of the ureter. Omitted in N A. **glan′dulae nasa′les** [N A, B N A], numerous large mucous and serous glands in the respiratory part of the nasal cavity. Called also *nasal glands.* **glan′dulae olfacto′riae** [N A, B N A], small mucous glands in the olfactory mucosa. Called also *olfactory glands.* **glan′dulae o′ris** [N A, B N A], the glands of the mouth. **glan′dulae palati′nae** [N A, B N A], the mucous glands on the soft palate and the posteromedial part of the hard palate. Called also *palatine glands.* **glan′dulae parathyroi′deae** [N A, B N A], small bodies in the region of the thyroid gland occurring in a variable number of pairs, commonly two, named *glandula parathyroidea superior* and *glandula parathyroidea inferior*, according to their position. See *parathyroid glands.* **g. paro′tis** [N A, B N A], the largest of the three chief, paired glands which, together with numerous small glands in the mouth, constitute the salivary glands; it is located below the zygomatic arch, below and in front of the external acoustic meatus. Called also *parotid gland.* **g. paro′tis acces-so′ria** [N A, B N A], a more or less detached portion of the parotid gland that is frequently present. **glan′dulae pel′vis rena′lis** [B N A], mucous glands in the wall of the kidney pelvis. Omitted in N A. **glan′dulae pharyn′geae** [N A, B N A], mucous glands beneath the tunica mucosa of the pharynx. Called also *pharyngeal glands.* **g. pituita′ria,** N A alternative for *hypophysis cerebri.* See also *pituitary gland.* **glan′dulae preputia′les** [N A], small sebaceous glands of the corona of the penis and the inner surface of the prepuce, which secrete smegma. Called also *preputial glands.* **g. prosta′ta, g. prostat′ica,** prostata. **glan′dulae pylo′ricae** [N A, B N A], the secreting glands of the pyloric part of the stomach. Called also *pyloric glands.* **glan′dulae seba′ceae** [N A, B N A], glands secreting an oily substance, sebum, and situated chiefly in the corium. Called also *sebaceous glands.* **glan′dulae seba′ceae conjunctiva′les** [N A], sebaceous glands on the free margin of the eyelids. **glan′dulae seba′ceae la′bii majo′ris pudenda′lis** [B N A], sebaceous glands in the skin of the labia majora. Omitted in N A. **glan′dulae seba′ceae mam′mae** [B N A], the sebaceous glands located in the skin of the breasts. Omitted in N A. **g. seromuco′sa** [N A], a gland composed of both mucous and serous secreting cells, such as the labial glands. Called also *seromucous gland.* **g. sero′sa** [N A], a gland that secretes a watery albuminous material, commonly but not always containing enzymes. Called also *serous gland.* **glan′dulae si′ne duc′tibus** [L. "glands without ducts"] [N A], the endocrine glands, including the thyroid and parathyroid glands, the hypophysis, corpus pineale, thymus, and glandula suprarenalis. **g. sublingua′lis** [N A, B N A], the smallest of the three chief, paired salivary glands, predominantly mucous in type, and draining into the oral cavity through 10 to 30 sublingual ducts. Called also *sublingual gland.* **g. submandibu-la′ris** [N A], **g. submaxilla′ris** [B N A], one of the three chief, paired salivary glands, predominantly serous, lying partly above and partly below the posterior half of the base of the mandible. Called also *submandibular gland.* **glan′dulae sudorif′erae** [N A, B N A], the glands that secrete sweat, consisting of coiled tubes situated in the subcutaneous tissue and opening by a duct on the surface of the skin. Called also *sweat glands.* **g. suprarena′lis** [N A, B N A], a flattened body situated in the retroperitoneal tissues at the superior pole of either kidney. See *adrenal gland.* **glan′dulae suprarena′les accesso′riae** [N A, B N A], accessory adrenal glandular tissue found in the abdomen or pelvis. Called also *accessory suprarenal glands.* **glan′dulae suprarena′les sic′cae,** desiccated adrenal glands. **glan′dulae tarsa′les** [N A], **glan′dulae tarsa′les [Meibo′mi]** [B N A], sebaceous follicles between the tarsi and the conjunctiva of the eyelids. Called also *tarsal glands.* **g. thyroi′dea** [N A], a large, ductless organ, normally situated in front of and on either side of the trachea. See *thyroid gland,* under *gland.* **glan′dulae thyroi′deae accesso′riae** [N A], small exclaves of the thyroid gland that may be found any place along the course of the thyroglossal duct, as well as in the thorax. Called also *accessory thyroid glands.* **glan′dula thyroi′dea accesso′ria suprahyoi′dea** [B N A], accessory thyroid tissue found above the hyoid bone. Omitted in N A. **glan′dulae thyroi′deae sic′cae,** desiccated thyroid glands. **glan′dulae trachea′les** [N A, B N A], mucous glands in the elastic submucous coat between the cartilaginous rings and on the posterior wall of the trachea. Called also *tracheal glands.* **glan′dulae tuba′riae** [N A], mucous glands within the mucosa of the auditory tube, especially near its nasopharyngeal end. Called also *glandulae mucosae tubae auditivae* [B N A], and *mucous glands of auditory tube.* **g. tympan′icae** [B N A], a small mass situated on Jacobson's nerve in the tympanic canal. Omitted in N A. **glan′dulae urethra′les [Lit′trei]** [B N A], glandulae urethrales urethrae masculinae. **glan′dulae urethra′les ure′thrae femini′nae** [N A], numerous small mucous glands in the mucosa of the female urethra, some of which on either side are drained by the inconstant paraurethral duct opening into the vestibule. Called also *urethral glands of female urethra.* **glan′dulae urethra′les ure′thrae masculi′nae** [N A], mucous glands in the wall of the male urethra. Called also *Littre's glands.* **glan′dulae ure-thra′les ure′thrae mulie′bris** [B N A], glandulae urethrales urethrae femininae. **g. uropy-gia′lis,** preen gland. **glan′dulae uteri′nae** [N A, B N A], simple tubular glands throughout the entire thickness and extent of the endometrium, which become enlarged during the premenstrual period. **glan′dulae vesica′les ves′icae urina′riae** [B N A], mucous glands in the wall of the urinary bladder. Omitted in N A. **g. vestibula′ris ma′jor** [N A], either of two small reddish yellow bodies in the vestibular bulbs, one on each side of the vaginal orifice. They are homologues of the bulbourethral glands in the male. Called also *Bartholin's gland* and *greater vestibular gland.* **glan′dulae vestibu-la′res mino′res** [N A, B N A], small mucous glands opening upon the vestibular mucous membrane between the urethral and the vaginal orifice. Called also *lesser vestibular glands.*

glandulae (glan′du-le) [L.]. Plural of *glandula.*

glandular (glan′du-lar). 1. Pertaining to or of the nature of a gland. 2. Pertaining to the glans penis.

glandule (glan′dūl) [L. *glandula*]. A small gland.

glandulous (glan′du-lus) [L. *glandulosus*]. Abounding in kernels or small glands.

glans (glanz), pl. *glan′des* [L. "acorn"]. A small rounded mass, or glandlike body. **g. clitor′idis** [N A, B N A], **g. of clitoris,** erectile tissue at the end of the clitoris, which is continuous with the intermediate part of the vestibular bulbs.

g. pe′nis [N A, B N A], the cap-shaped expansion of the corpus spongiosum at the end of the penis.

glare (glār). A condition of discomfort in the eye and of depression of central vision produced when a bright light enters the field of vision, especially when the eye is adapted to dark. The amount of glare is directly proportional to the candle power of the light and inversely proportional to the square of the distance of the light from the eye and to its angular distance from the visual axis. *Direct g.*, when the image of the light falls on the fovea; *peripheral g.*, when it falls outside of the fovea.

glarometer (glār-om′e-ter). An instrument for measuring a person's resistance to glare from the lights of an approaching automobile.

glaserian artery, fissure, etc. (gla-se′re-an) [named for or described by Johann Heinrich *Glaser* (Glaserius), Swiss anatomist, 1629–1675]. See under the nouns.

Glasgow's sign (glas′gōz) [William Carr *Glasgow*, American physician, 1845–1907]. See under *sign*.

glass (glas) [L. *vit′rum*]. 1. A hard, brittle, and often transparent substance, usually consisting of the fused amorphous silicates of potassium or sodium, and of calcium, with silica in excess. 2. (Pl.) Lenses worn to aid or improve vision. See also *spectacles* and *lens*. **bifocal g's,** lenses which have two different refracting powers, one for distant and one for near vision. **contact g's.** See *contact lens*. **cover g.,** a thin glass plate used to cover an object for microscopical examination. **crown g.,** a hard glass, being a silicate of sodium (or potassium) with lime and alumina. **crutch g's,** spectacles which will elevate and support the upper lid of patients with ptosis. **cupping g.,** a vessel of glass from which the air has been or can be exhausted, applied to the body for the purpose of drawing blood to the surface. **flint g.,** a soft glass, mainly composed of lead and potassium silicates. **Franklin g's,** bifocal g's. **Hallauer's g's,** grayish-green spectacle glasses which prevent the passage of blue and ultraviolet rays. **holvi g.,** a glass more transparent than ordinary glass to ultraviolet rays. **hyperbolic g's,** lenses ground with a section of a hyperbolic curve. **lithium g.,** glass containing lithium, used in grenz ray x-ray tubes. **object g.** See *objective*. **optical g.,** glass of high quality and controlled composition, used for lenses. **quartz g.,** pure crystalline quartz, SiO_2; used for prisms, lenses, and other purposes (1) because its index of thermal expansion is so small that it does not crack when heated or cooled, and (2) because it transmits more of the ultraviolet radiation than does ordinary glass. **snow g's,** glasses with special lenses to prevent snow blindness. **soluble g.,** a potassium or sodium silicate which is sometimes used in preparing immovable bandages. **sun g's,** glasses with special lenses which filter the rays of the sun. **test g.,** a small glass vessel, resembling a beaker, used in a chemical laboratory. **trifocal g's,** lenses which have three different refracting powers, one for distant, one for intermediate, and one for near vision. **water g.,** soluble g. **Wood's g.** See under *filter*.

glassy (glas′e). Like glass; hyaline or vitreous.

Glauber's salt (glow′berz) [Johann Rudolf *Glauber*, German physician and chemist, 1604–1668]. Sodium sulfate.

glaucarubin (glaw″kah-ru′bin). A crystalline glycoside obtained from the fruit of *Simaruba glauca:* used as an amebicide.

glaucoma (glaw-ko′mah) [Gr. *glaukōma* opacity of the crystalline lens (from the dull gray gleam of the affected eye)]. A condition of the eye characterized by increased intraocular pressure. **g. absolu′tum,** the final stage of glaucoma characterized by pain in the eye and blindess. **apoplectic g.,** hemorrhagic g. **auricular g.,** that associated with increased intralabyrinthine pressure. **g. consumma′tum,** g. absolutum. **Donders' g.,** g. simplex. **fulminant g.,** a sudden and intensely acute form of inflammatory glaucoma with immediate loss of sight and light perception (von Graefe). **hemorrhagic g.,** that which is caused by pressure from retinal hemorrhage (von Graefe). **g. im′minens,** an impending glaucoma. **infantile g.,** hydrophthalmos. **inflammatory g.,** a form attended with ciliary congestion, corneal opacity, and blindness, recurring in paroxysmal attacks. **malignant g.,** glaucoma that grows rapidly worse in spite of iridectomy. **narrow-angle g.,** a form of primary glaucoma in an eye characterized by a shallow anterior chamber and a narrow angle, in which filtration is compromised as a result of the iris blocking the angle. **open-angle g.,** a form of primary glaucoma in an eye in which the angle remains open, but filtration is gradually diminished because of the tissues of the angle. **primary g.,** increased intraocular pressure occurring in an eye without previous disease. See *narrow-angle g.* and *open-angle g.* **secondary g.,** increased intraocular pressure resulting from a disease or injury. **g. sim′plex,** a form with no pronounced inflammatory symptoms, but attended with progressive loss of vision.

glaucomatous (glaw-ko′mah-tus). Pertaining to or of the nature of glaucoma.

glaucosis (glaw-ko′sis). Blindness caused by glaucoma.

glaucosuria (glaw″ko-su′re-ah) [Gr. *glaukos* silvery + *ouron* urine + *-ia*]. Indicanuria.

glaze (glāz). In dentistry, a ceramic veneer added to a porcelain restoration after it has been fired, to give a completely nonporous, glossy or semiglossy surface.

gleet (glēt). A chronic form of gonorrheal urethritis. **nasal g.,** a chronic catarrhal discharge from the nose of horses, having a bluish, creamy appearance and a bad odor.

gleety (glēt′e). Pertaining to or of the nature of gleet.

Glegg's mixture [Wilfrid *Glegg*, English laryngologist, died 1940]. See under *mixture*.

Glénard's disease, test (gla-narz′) [Frantz *Glénard*, French physician, 1848–1920]. See *splanchnoptosis*, and *girdle test*, under *tests*.

glenohumeral (gle″no-hu′mer-al). Pertaining to the glenoid cavity and to the humerus.

glenoid (gle′noid) [Gr. *glēnē* socket + *eidos* form]. Resembling a pit or socket; see under *cavity*.

Glenospora (gle-nos′po-rah). A genus of fungi. *G. graphii* has been found in otomycosis.

Glenosporella (gle″no-spo-rel′ah). A genus of parasitic hyphomycetes.

glenosporosis (gle″no-spo-ro′sis). Infection with Glenospora.

Gley's cells, glands (glāz) [Marcel Eugène Émile *Gley*, French physiologist, 1857–1930]. See under *cell* and *gland*.

glia (gli′ah) [Gr. "glue"]. The neuroglia. Used as a word termination to denote a gluelike structure or tissue. **ameboid g.,** degenerated neuroglia cells which are rich in pale protoplasm, possess few processes, and have densely staining nuclei. **cytoplasmic g.,** enlarged neuroglia cells, rich in cytoplasm, containing vacuoles and supplied with fibrils: seen in degeneration of the spinal cord. **g. of Fañana,** a form of neuroglia cells occurring in the molecular layer of the cerebellar cortex. **fibrillary g.,** degenerated neuroglia cells containing an abundance of fibrils.

gliacyte (gli′ah-sīt) [*glia* + Gr. *kytos* hollow vessel]. A cell of the neuroglia.

gliadin (gli′ah-din) [Gr. *glia* glue]. An alcohol-soluble protein obtainable from wheat.

glial (gli′al). Pertaining to glia or neuroglia.

gliarase (gli′ah-rās). An aggregation of astrocytes whose cytoplasm has undergone incomplete fission.

glio- (gli′o) [Gr. *glia* glue]. A combining form denoting relationship to a gluey substance or specifically to the neuroglia.

gliobacteria (gli″o-bak-te′re-ah) [*glio-* + *bacteria*]. Rod-shaped schizomycetes which are surrounded by a zooglea.

glioblast (gli′o-blast). Spongioblast.

glioblastoma (gli″o-blas-to′mah) [*glio-* + Gr. *blastos* germ + *-oma*]. Spongioblastoma. **g. multifor′me,** a cerebral glioma characterized by the presence of a great variety of cellular types.

gliococcus (gli″o-kok′us) [*glio-* + Gr. *kokkos* berry]. A micrococcus forming gelatinous matter.

gliocyte (gli′o-sīt). Gliacyte.

gliocytoma (gli″o-si-to′mah). A tumor composed of glia cells; a neurogliocytoma.

gliogenous (gli-oj′e-nus) [*glio-* + Gr. *gennan* to produce]. Produced or formed by glia (neuroglia) cells.

glioma (gli-o′mah) [*glio-* + *-oma*]. A tumor composed of tissue which represents neuroglia in any one of its stages of development. **ameboid g.,** a glioma which has undergone hyaline and fatty degeneration. **g. endoph′ytum,** glioma of the retina beginning in the inner layers. **ependymal g.,** a bulky, solid, rather firm but vascular tumor of the fourth ventricle. **g. exoph′ytum,** glioma of the retina beginning in the outer layers. **ganglionic g.,** a glioma which contains also ganglion cells of nearly adult type. See *neuroblastoma.* **g. multifor′me,** spongioblastoma multiforme. **nasal g.,** a tumor of the superior nasal sinus which may arise from the olfactory bulb. **peripheral g.,** schwannoma. **g. ret′inae,** a tumor of the retina resembling glioma of the cerebrum. Called also *fungus medullaris oculi.* **g. sarcomato′sum,** a gliosarcoma. **telangiectatic g.,** glioma containing blood vessels.

gliomatosis (gli″o-mah-to′sis). Excessive development of the neuroglia, especially of the spinal cord, in certain cases of syringomyelia.

gliomatous (gli-o′mah-tus). Affected with or of the nature of glioma.

gliomyoma (gli″o-mi-o′mah). A tumor containing gliomatous and myomatous elements.

gliomyxoma (gli″o-mik-so′mah). A tumor containing gliomatous and myxomatous elements.

glioneuroma (gli″o-nu-ro′mah). A tumor containing both gliomatous and neuromatous elements.

gliophagia (gli″o-fa′je-ah) [*glio-* + Gr. *phagein* to eat]. Phagocytosis of neuroglia cells.

gliopil (gli′o-pil) [*glio-* + Gr. *pilos* felt]. A dense feltwork of glial processes, as in the subependymal matrix of the ventricular system.

gliosa (gli-o′sah). The gray matter of the spinal cord which covers the head of the dorsal horn and surrounds the central canal.

gliosarcoma (gli″o-sar-ko′mah) [*glio-* + *sarcoma*]. A spindle-cell glioma. See also *spongioblastoma.* **g. ret′inae,** glioma retinae.

gliosis (gli-o′sis). The disease condition associated with the presence of gliomas or with the development of neuroglia tissue. **basilar g.,** gliosis affecting the brain stem, thalamus, and corpus striatum. **cerebellar g.,** gliosis affecting the cerebellum. **diffuse g.,** gliosis affecting the whole of the cerebral tissue, or widely scattered through it. **hemispheric g.,** gliosis affecting one of the cerebral hemispheres. **hypertrophic nodular g.,** a form of gliosis in which the brain is symmetrically enlarged because of hyperplasia of the neuroglial tissue. **lobar g.,** gliosis affecting a single lobe of the brain. **perivascular g.,** a form of arteriosclerosis of the cerebral vessels, marked by increase of the neuroglia about the vessels. **spinal g.,** syringomyelia. **unilateral g.,** hemispheric gliosis.

gliosome (gli′o-sōm) [*glio-* + Gr. *sōma* body]. One of the small cytoplasmic granules seen in neuroglia cells.

gliotoxin (gli″o-tok′sin). An antibiotic substance obtained from several unrelated species of fungi.

Gliricola (gli-rik′o-lah). A genus of lice. **G. porcel′li,** a biting louse found on guinea pigs.

glischrin (glis′krin) [Gr. *glischros* gluey]. A mucin produced in urine by bacterial activity.

glischruria (glis-kroo′re-ah) [Gr. *glischros* gluey + *ouron* urine + *-ia*]. The presence of glischrin in the urine.

Glisson's capsule, sling (glis′unz) [Francis *Glisson,* English physician and anatomist, 1597–1677, one of the founders of the Royal Society]. See under *capsule* and *sling.*

glissonitis (glis″o-ni′tis). Inflammation of Glisson's capsule.

globi (glo′bi) [L.]. Plural of *globus.*

globin (glo′bin). The protein constituent of hemoglobin; also any member of a group of proteins similar to the typical globin.

globinometer (glo″bĭ-nom′e-ter). An instrument used in determining the proportion of oxyhemoglobin in the blood.

globomyeloma (glo″bo-mi″ĕ-lo′mah). A roundcelled sarcoma.

globose (glo′bōs) [L. *globus* a ball]. Globe-shaped, spherical.

globular (glob′u-lar). 1. Like a globe or globule. 2. Pertaining to red blood corpuscles.

Globularia (glob″u-la′re-ah). A European shrub.

globulariacitrin (glob″u-la″re-ah-sit′rin). Rutin.

globule (glob′ūl) [L. *globulus* a globule]. 1. A small spherical mass; a little globe or pellet, as of medicine. 2. A blood disk or corpuscle; a lymph corpuscle; a fat corpuscle in milk. **dentin g's,** small spherical bodies in the peripheral dentin, created by beginning calcification of the matrix about discrete foci. **Dobie's g.,** a minute stainable mass in the middle of the transparent disk of a muscle fibril. **Marchi's g's,** fragments and particles of broken-up myelin which stain by Marchi's method, seen in degenerations of the spinal cord. **milk g's,** the small round masses of fat in milk which tend to separate out as cream. **Morgagni's g's,** minute hyaline spheres sometimes found between the eye lens and its capsule, chiefly in cases of cataract. **myelin g's,** colorless globules resembling fat droplets and sometimes spirally marked, seen in some sputa. **polar g's,** polar bodies.

globuli (glob′u-li) [L.]. Plural of *globulus.*

globulicidal (glob″u-lĭ-si′dal) [L. *globulus* globule + *caedere* to kill]. Destructive to blood corpuscles.

globulicide (glob′u-lĭ-sīd″). An agent that destroys blood corpuscles.

globuliferous (glob″u-lif′er-us). Taking up or destroying the blood corpuscles.

globulimeter (glob″u-lim′e-ter) [*globule* + Gr. *metron* measure]. An instrument for counting and measuring blood corpuscles.

globulin (glob′u-lin) [L. *globulus* globule]. A class of proteins characterized by being insoluble in water, but soluble in saline solutions (euglobulins), or water soluble proteins (pseudoglobulins) whose other physical properties closely resemble true globulins. **AC g., accelerator g.,** factor V. See under *coagulation factors.* **alpha g's,** globulins of plasma which in neutral or alkaline solutions have the greatest electrophoretic mobility, in this respect most nearly resembling the albumins. **antidiphtheritic g.,** the globulin which is the active constituent of antidiphtheritic serum. **antihemophilic g.,** factor VIII. See under *coagulation factors.* **antitoxic g.,** the globulin which is the active constituent of an antitoxic serum. **beta g's,** globulins of plasma which have an electrophoretic mobility in neutral or alkaline solutions intermediate between that of the alpha and the gamma globulins. **gamma g's,** globulins of plasma which in neutral or alkaline solutions have the slowest electrophoretic mobility: used in the prophylaxis of measles and epidemic hepatitis. Most antibodies are gamma globulins. **immune serum g.,** a sterile solution of globulins which contains those antibodies normally present in adult human blood: used as an immunizing agent. **g. X,** a globulin occurring in the intracellular spaces of muscle.

globulinemia (glob″u-lin-e′me-ah) [*globulin* + Gr. *haima* blood + *-ia*]. The presence of globulin in the blood.

globulinuria (glob″u-lin-u′re-ah) [*globulin* + Gr. *ouron* urine + *-ia*]. The presence of globulin in the urine.

globulism (glob′u-lizm). Polyglobulism.

globulolysis (glob″u-lol′ĭ-sis) [*globule* + Gr. *lysis* dissolution]. Destruction of red blood corpuscles.

globulolytic (glob″u-lo-lit′ik). Pertaining to, characterized by, or causing globulolysis.

globulose (glob′u-lōs). A proteose produced by action of pepsin on the globulins; several varieties have been described.

globulus (glob′u-lus), pl. *glob′uli* [L.]. 1. The nucleus globosus. 2. A pill, bolus, or spherical suppository. **glob′uli os′sei,** globules of bone tissue contained within lacunae of the calcified cartilage matrix in intrachondrial bone.

globulysis (glo-bu′lĭ-sis). Globulolysis.

globus (glo′bus), pl. *glo′bi* [L.]. 1. A sphere or ball; a large spherical mass. 2. A subjective sensation as of a lump or mass. **g. abdomina′lis,** the sensation of a lump in the lower abdomen. **g. of the heel,** that portion of the wall of a horse's hoof where it curves around the heel to form the bar. **g. hyster′icus,** the subjective sensation of a lump in the throat; a condition frequently seen in hysteria. **g. ma′jor epididym′idis,** caput epididymidis. **g. mi′nor epididym′idis,** cauda epididymidis. **g. pal′lidus** [N A, B N A], the smaller and more medial part of the lentiform nucleus, separated from the putamen by the external medullary lamina and subdivided by the medial medullary lamina into internal and external parts.

glomangioma (glo-man″je-o′mah) [*glomus* + Gr. *angeion* vessel + *-oma*]. An extremely painful, small, firm, slightly elevated, rounded red-blue tumor, usually occurring on the distal portions of the fingers and toes, in the skin or in deeper structures.

glome (glōm). Either of the two prominences on the posterior edge of the frog of a horse's foot.

glomectomy (glo-mek′to-me). Excision of a glomus.

glomera (glom′er-ah) [L.]. Plural of *glomus*.

glomerate (glom′er-āt) [L. *glomeratus* wound into a ball]. Crowded together into a ball.

glomerular (glo-mer′u-lar). Pertaining to or of the nature of a glomerulus.

glomerule (glom′er-ūl). Glomerulus.

glomeruli (glo-mer′u-li) [L.]. Plural of *glomerulus*.

glomerulitis (glo-mer″u-li′tis). Inflammation of the glomeruli of the kidney with proliferation of glomerular endothelium and the presence of mononuclear cells in the capillaries.

glomerulonephritis (glo-mer″u-lo-ne-fri′tis) [*glomerulus* + *nephritis*]. A variety of nephritis characterized by inflammation of the capillary loops in the glomeruli of the kidney. It occurs in acute, subacute and chronic forms and is usually secondary to an infection, especially with the hemolytic streptococcus.

glomerulopathy (glo-mer″u-lop′ah-the). Noninflammatory disease of the kidney glomeruli. **diabetic g.,** intercapillary glomerulosclerosis.

glomerulosclerosis (glo-mer″u-lo-skle-ro′sis). Arteriolar nephrosclerosis. **intercapillary g.,** a degenerative complication of diabetes, manifested as albuminuria, nephrotic edema, hypertension, renal insufficiency, and retinopathy.

glomerulose (glo-mer′u-lōs). Glomerular.

glomerulus (glo-mer′u-lus), pl. *glomer′uli* [L., dim. of *glomus* ball]. A tuft or cluster; used in anatomical nomenclature as a general term to designate such a structure, as one composed of blood vessels or nerve fibers. Often used alone to designate one of the glomeruli of the kidney (glomeruli renis [N A]). **arterial glomeruli, coccygeal.** See *glomus coccygeum*. **glomer′uli arterio′si coch′leae** [N A, B N A], an arterial network surrounding the cochlea. **caudal glomeruli.** See *glomus coccygeum*. **glomeruli of kidney, malpighian glomeruli,** glomeruli renis. **nonencapsulated nerve g.,** a nerve ending in the connective tissue of various organs in which the terminal branches of the nerve form spherical or elongated structures resembling glomeruli. **olfactory g.,** one of the small globular masses of dense neuropil in the olfactory bulb containing the first synapse in the olfactory pathway. **glomer′uli re′nis** [N A, B N A], coils of blood vessels, one projecting into the expanded end or capsule of each of the uriniferous tubules. Called also *glomeruli of kidney*. **Ruysch's glomeruli,** glomeruli renis.

glomic (glo′mik). Pertaining to or affecting a glomus.

glomoid (glo′moid). Resembling a glomus.

glomus (glo′mus), pl. *glom′era* [L. "a ball"]. [N A, B N A] A small, histologically recognizable body, composed primarily of fine arterioles connecting directly with veins, and possessing a rich nerve supply. **glom′era aor′tica,** corpora para-aortica. **g. carot′icum** [N A, B N A], **carotid g., g. carotid′eum,** a small, neurovascular structure at the bifurcation of the common carotid, which contains chemoreceptors that respond to changes in the blood. Called also *carotid body*. **choroid g., g. choroi′deum** [N A], an enlargement of the choroid plexus of the lateral ventricle where the inferior horn joins the central part. **coccygeal g., g. coccyge′um** [N A, B N A], a collection of arteriovenous anastomoses formed, close to the tip of the coccyx, by the middle sacral artery. **cutaneous g., digital g., neuromyo-arterial g.,** the total unit making up a Sucquet-Hoyer anastomosis. It is an organ located in the derma and cutaneous tissue, chiefly beneath the nails, and acting to control the circulation in the peripheral tissues.

glonoin (glon′o-in). Glyceryl trinitrate.

glonoinism (glon′o-in-izm″). The toxic effect produced by glyceryl trinitrate.

gloss-. See *glosso-*.

glossa (glos′ah) [Gr. *glōssa*]. The tongue (lingua [N A]).

glossagra (glos-sa′grah, glos′ag-rah) [*gloss-* + Gr. *agra* seizure]. Gouty pain of the tongue.

glossal (glos′al). Pertaining to the tongue.

glossalgia (glos-sal′je-ah) [*gloss-* + *-algia*]. Pain in the tongue.

glossanthrax (glos-san′thraks) [*gloss-* + *anthrax*]. Carbuncle of the tongue.

glossectomy (glos-sek′to-me) [*gloss-* + Gr. *ektomē* excision]. Surgical removal of the tongue (*total g.*) or of a portion of it (*partial g.*).

Glossina (glos-si′nah). A genus of biting flies; the tsetse flies. **G. mor′sitans,** a fly of South Africa which transmits by its bite the *Trypanosoma brucei*, the cause of nagana in horses, and is also the transmitter of *T. rhodesiense*, the cause of the sleeping sickness of Rhodesia. **G. pallid′ipes,** a fly which transmits *Trypanosoma brucei*. **G.**

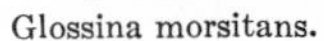

Glossina morsitans.

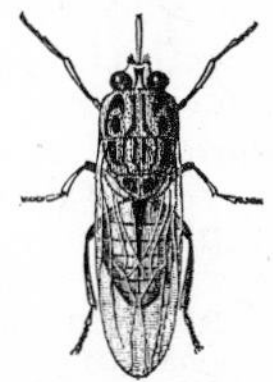

Glossina palpalis.

palpa'lis, a species of Central Africa which transmits by its bite *Trypanosoma gambiense*, the organism of Africa sleeping sickness. Other species which probably transmit trypanosomes to animals and to man are: *G. brevipalpis, G. brevipennis, G. fusca, G. longipalpis, G. longipennis, G. pallicera, G. swynnertoni, G. tachinoides*.

glossitis (glos-si'tis) [*gloss-* + *-itis*]. Inflammation of the tongue. **g. area'ta exfoliati'va,** geographic tongue. **g. dis'secans, dissecting g.,** a chronic form in which the tongue is deeply furrowed. **Hunter's g.,** a condition of the tongue seen in pernicious anemia, marked by smooth atrophy of the surface and edges. **idiopathic g.,** inflammation of the substance of the tongue and its mucous membrane. **Moeller's g.,** chronic superficial glossitis, or glossodynia exfoliativa; an affection of the tongue sometimes extending to the cheeks and palate, affecting middle-aged people, especially women, and marked by burning pain and by red irregular patches, thinning of the papillae, and desquamation of the stratum corneum. Called also *chronic lingual papillitis, slick tongue, glossy tongue*, and *glazed tongue*. **parasitic g., g. parasit'ica,** black tongue. **parenchymatous g.,** idiopathic g. **rhomboid g., median, g. rhomboi'dea media'na,** a congenital anomaly of the tongue, with a flat or slightly raised ovoid-, diamond-, or rhomboid-shaped reddish patch or plaque on the dorsal surface, immediately anterior to the circumvallate papillae.

glosso-, gloss- (glos'o, glos) [Gr. *glōssa* tongue]. Combining form denoting relationship to the tongue.

glossocele (glos'o-sēl) [*glosso-* + Gr. *kēlē* tumor]. Swelling and protrusion of the tongue.

glossocinesthetic (glos″o-sin-es-thet'ik). Glossokinesthetic.

glossocoma (glŏ-sok'o-mah). Retraction of the tongue.

glossodynamometer (glos″o-di″nah-mom'e-ter) [*glosso-* + *dynamometer*]. An instrument for recording the power of the tongue to resist pressure.

glossodynia (glos″o-din'e-ah) [*glosso-* + Gr. *odynē* pain]. Pain in the tongue. **g. exfoliati'va,** Moeller's glossitis.

glosso-epiglottic (glos″o-ep-ĭ-glot'ik). Glossoepiglottidean.

glosso-epiglottidean (glos″o-ep-ĭ-glo-tid'e-an). Pertaining to the tongue and epiglottis.

glossograph (glos'o-graf) [*glosso-* + Gr. *graphein* to record]. An apparatus for recording the tongue movements in speech.

glossohyal (glos″o-hi'al) [*glosso-* + *hyoid*]. Pertaining to the tongue and hyoid bone.

glossokinesthetic (glos″o-kin″es-thet'ik) [*glosso-* + *kinesthetic*]. Pertaining to the subjective perception of the movements of the tongue in speech.

glossolalia (glos″o-la'le-ah) [*glosso-* + Gr. *lalein* to babble]. Speech in unknown or imaginary language.

glossology (glŏ-sol'o-je) [*glosso-* + *-logy*]. 1. The sum of knowledge regarding the tongue. 2. A treatise on nomenclature.

glossolysis (glŏ-sol'ĭ-sis) [*glosso-* + Gr. *lysis* loosening]. Paralysis of the tongue.

glossomantia (glos″o-man-ti'ah) [*glosso-* + Gr. *manteia* divination]. Prognosis based on the appearance of the tongue.

glossoncus (glŏ-song'kus) [*glosso-* + Gr. *onkos* mass]. A swelling of the tongue.

glossopalatinus (glos″o-pal″ah-ti'nus). Musculus palatoglossus.

glossopathy (glŏ-sop'ah-the) [*glosso-* + Gr. *pathos* disease]. Any disease of the tongue.

glossopharyngeal (glos″o-fah-rin'je-al) [*glosso-* + *pharynx*]. Pertaining to the tongue and pharynx.

glossopharyngeum (glos″o-fah-rin'je-um) [*glosso-* + *pharynx*]. The tongue and pharynx together.

glossopharyngeus (glos″o-fah-rin'je-us). See *Table of Musculi*.

glossophobia (glos″o-fo'be-ah). Lalophobia.

glossophytia (glos″o-fit'e-ah) [*glosso-* + Gr. *phyton* plant]. Black tongue.

glossoplasty (glos'o-plas″te) [*glosso-* + Gr. *plassein* to mold]. Plastic operation on the tongue.

glossoplegia (glos″o-ple'je-ah) [*glosso-* + Gr. *plēgē* stroke]. Paralysis of the tongue.

glossoptosis (glos″op-to'sis) [*glosso-* + Gr. *ptōsis* fall]. Downward displacement or retraction of the tongue.

glossopyrosis (glos″o-pi-ro'sis) [*glosso-* + Gr. *pyrōsis* burning]. A burning sensation in the tongue.

glossorrhaphy (glŏ-sor'ah-fe) [*glosso-* + Gr. *rhaphē* suture]. Suture of the tongue.

glossoscopy (glŏ-sos'ko-pe) [*glosso-* + Gr. *skopein* to examine]. Examination of the tongue.

glossospasm (glos'o-spazm) [*glosso-* + Gr. *spasmos* spasm]. Spasm of the tongue muscles.

glossosteresis (glos″o-ster-e'sis). Glossectomy.

glossotilt (glos'o-tilt) [*glosso-* + Gr. *tillein* to pull]. A lever which holds the tongue in one of the processes for artificial respiration.

glossotomy (glŏ-sot'o-me) [*glosso-* + Gr. *temnein* to cut]. Incision of the tongue.

glossotrichia (glos″o-trik'e-ah) [*glosso-* + Gr. *thrix* hair]. Hairy tongue.

glottic (glot'ik). 1. Pertaining to the glottis. 2. Pertaining to the tongue.

glottides (glot'ĭ-dēz). Plural of *glottis*.

glottis (glot'is), pl. *glot'tides* [Gr. *glōttis*]. [N A, B N A] The vocal apparatus of the larynx, consisting of the true vocal cords (vocal folds) and the opening between them (rima glottidis). **false g.,** rima vestibuli. **intercartilaginous g., respiratory g.,** pars intercartilaginea rimae glottidis. **true g.,** rima glottidis.

glottitis (glŏ-ti'tis). Glossitis.

glottology (glŏ-tol'o-je). Glossology.

glou-glou (gloo'gloo) [Fr.]. 1. A gurgling sound produced in the stomach by various causes, such as the pressure of a corset. 2. A rattling sound sometimes heard in auscultation of the heart.

Glover's organism (glov'erz) [T. J. *Glover*, Canadian bacteriologist, born 1887]. A gram-positive microorganism isolated by Glover from various types of malignant tumor.

glow (glo). Incandescence; also brightness or warmth of color. **negative g.,** the luminous glow that envelops the cathode in a discharge tube at moderately low gas pressure. **salt g.,** a rubbing of the entire body with moist salt, producing a vivid pink glow of the skin and having a gently stimulative effect.

glucagon (gloo'kah-gon). A hyperglycemic-glycogenolytic factor thought to be secreted by the pancreas in response to hypoglycemia or to stimulation by the growth hormone of the anterior pituitary. **g. hydrochloride,** a pharmaceutical preparation used in treatment of hypoglycemia, acting to produce a prompt elevation of the glucose concentration of the blood by mobilizing glycogen stored in the liver.

glucal (gloo'kal). An aldehyde derivative, $C_6H_{10}O_4$, of glucose.

glucase (gloo'kās). An enzyme from plants and microorganisms, changing starch into dextroglucose.

glucatonia (gloo-kah-to'ne-ah). Reduction of blood sugar to a point where pathologic symptoms are produced.

glucemia (gloo-se'me-ah). Glycemia.

glucide (gloo'sīd). An organic substance consisting in whole or in part of carbohydrates; a general term, embracing the carbohydrates and glycosides.

glucidtemns (gloo'sid-tems). A collective name

for the products produced by the digestion of starch, namely, dextrin, maltose, and glucose.

glucinium (gloo-sin′e-um). Beryllium.

gluciphore (gloo′sĭ-fōr). Glucophore.

gluck (gluk). A clucking noise sometimes made by a horse, due to spasm of the velum palati.

gluco- (gloo′ko) [Gr. *gleukos* sweetness]. Combining form denoting relationship to sweetness, or to glucose. Cf. *glyco-*.

glucocinin (gloo″ko-sin′in). Glucokinin.

glucocorticoid (gloo″ko-kor′tĭ-koid). A corticoid which increases gluconeogenesis, raising the concentration of liver glycogen and blood sugar (S hormone).

gluco-ferrum (gloo″ko-fer′rum). Trade mark for preparations of ferrous gluconate.

glucofuranose (gloo″ko-fu′rah-nōs). A form of glucose in which carbon atoms 1 and 4 are bridged by an oxygen atom.

glucogenesis (gloo″ko-jen′e-sis). The formation of glucose by the breakdown of glycogen.

glucogenic (gloo″ko-jen′ik). Giving rise to or producing glucose.

glucohemia (gloo″ko-he′me-ah). Glycohemia.

glucokinetic (gloo″ko-ki-net′ik). Activating sugar so as to maintain the sugar level of the blood.

glucokinin (gloo″ko-kin′in) [*gluco-* + Gr. *kinein* to move]. A hormone-like substance obtained from vegetable tissues and yeast, subcutaneous injection of which produces hypoglycemia in animals and acts on depancreatized dogs in a manner similar to insulin; called also *plant insulin*.

glucolactone (gloo″ko-lak′tōn). A lactone from gluconic acid.

glucolysis (gloo-kol′ĭ-sis). Glycolysis.

glucolytic (gloo″ko-lit′ik). Glycolytic.

gluconate (gloo′ko-nāt). A salt of gluconic acid, containing the $HOCH_2(CHOH)_5COO$— radical. **ferrous g.,** a compound used in the treatment of iron deficiency anemia.

gluconeogenesis (gloo″ko-ne″o-jen′e-sis). Glyconeogenesis.

glucopenia (gloo-ko-pe′ne-ah). Glycopenia.

glucophenetidin (gloo″ko-fĕ-net′ĭ-din). A derivative from paraphenetidin and dextrose, in silky white needles.

glucophore (gloo′ko-fōr) [*gluco-* + Gr. *phoros* bearing]. The group of atoms in a molecule of a compound which is responsible for its sweet taste.

glucoprotein (gloo″ko-pro′te-in). Glycoprotein.

glucoproteinase (gloo″ko-pro′te-in-ās). An enzyme which catalyzes the hydrolysis of glucoproteins.

glucopyranose (gloo″ko-pi′rah-nōs). A form of glucose in which carbon atoms 1 and 5 are bridged by an oxygen atom.

glucosamine (gloo″ko-sam′in). An alpha-amino derivative of dextrose (δ-glucose), obtained from mucin and chitin by hydrolysis. Called also *glycosamine* and *dextrosamine*. **acetyl g.,** the structural unit of chitin.

glucosan (gloo′ko-san). An anhydro-polymer which on hydrolysis yields a hexose.

glucosazone (gloo″ko-sa′zōn). A yellow, crystalline substance, $CH_2OH(CHOH)_3C(:N.NH.C_6H_5).CH:N.NH.C_6H_5$, produced by treating dextrose with phenylhydrazine and acetic acid. The crystals melt at 205°C. and may be used in the identification of glucose.

glucose (gloo′kōs) [Gr. *gleukos* sweetness; *glykys* sweet]. 1. A thick syrupy, sweet liquid generally made by incomplete hydrolysis of starch. See *liquid g.* 2. A term frequently used by chemists and biologists for *d-glucose,* which is dextrose. In pharmacy glucose should refer to the syrup, the term dextrose should be employed when referring to the pure hexose as described in the U. S. Pharmacopeia. **Brun's g.,** a histologic clearing solution composed of glucose, distilled water, camphor, and glycerin. **gamma g.,** a very reactive form of glucose that can be isolated only as a derivative. **liquid g.,** an odorless, colorless or yellowish, thick syrupy liquid, with a sweet taste, consisting chiefly of dextrose, with dextrins, maltose, and water, and obtained by the incomplete hydrolysis of starch. **g. 1-phosphate,** an intermediate in carbohydrate metabolism, $CH_2OH.CH(CHOH)_3CH.O.PO.(OH)_2$ (ring closed through O). **g. 6-phosphate,** an intermediate in carbohydrate metabolism, $CHOH(CHOH)_3.CH.CH_2O.PO(OH)_2$ (ring closed through O).

glucosidase (gloo′ko-si-dās). An enzyme which splits a glucoside. **alpha g.,** maltase. **beta g.,** emulsin.

glucoside (gloo′ko-sīd). A glycoside in which the sugar constituent is glucose. Originally the term glucoside was given to any one of a variety of natural plant products containing a sugar, but it is now generally restricted to those in which the sugar is glucose. See *glycoside.*

glucosidolytic (gloo″ko-si″do-lit′ik). Causing the splitting up of glucosides.

glucosin (gloo′ko-sin). Any one of a group of bases derived from dextrose by the action of ammonia: some are highly toxic.

glucosone (gloo′ko-sōn). An aldehyde ketone, $CH_2OH.(CHOH)_3.CO.CHO$, suggested as a possible substitute for insulin.

glucosum (gloo-ko′sum). Glucose.

glucosuria (gloo″ko-su′re-ah) [*glucose* + Gr. *ouron* urine + *-ia*]. The presence of glucose in the urine.

glucoxylose (gloo″ko-zi′lōs). A disaccharide, $C_{11}H_{20}O_{10}$, occurring in the leaves and branches of *Daviesia latifolia.*

glucurolactone (gloo″ku-ro-lak′tōn). Chemical name: γ-lactone of D-glucofuranuronic acid: used in treatment of arthritis, neuritis, and fibrositis.

glucuronate (gloo-ku′ro-nāt). A salt of glucuronic acid.

glucuronidase (gloo″ku-ron′ĭ-dās). An enzyme which catalyzes the splitting of glucuronides. **beta g.,** an enzyme found in the liver and the spleen where it catalyzes the hydrolysis of conjugated glucuronides.

glucuronide (gloo-ku′ron-īd). Any compound with glucuronic acid.

glucuronolactone (gloo″ku-ro″no-lak′tōn). Glucurolactone.

glue (gloo). An adhesive preparation in the form of impure gelatin derived from boiling certain animal substances, such as hoofs, in water. **fish g.,** glue made from the swimming bladder of fishes. **Sinclair's g.,** a mixture of ordinary glue, water, glycerin, calcium chloride, and thymol.

Gluge's corpuscles (gloo′gez) [Gottlieb *Gluge,* German pathologist, 1812–1898]. See under *corpuscle.*

glutamate (gloo′tah-māt). A salt of glutamic acid.

glutaminase (gloo-tam′ĭ-nās). An enzyme which catalyzes the splitting of glutamine into glutamic acid and ammonia.

glutamine (gloo-tam′in). The mono-amide of amino-glutaric acid, $COOHCHNH_2(CH_2)_2CONH_2$, found in the juices of many plants. It is an essential element in the nutrition of *Streptococcus haemolyticus.*

glutan H-C-L (gloo′tan ăch se el). Trade mark for capsules containing glutamic acid hydrochloride.

glutathione (gloo″tah-thi′ōn) [*glutamic* acid + Gr. *theion* sulfur]. A tripeptide, gamma-glutamylcysteyl-glycine, $HOOC.CH(NH_2).CH_2.CH_2.CO.NH.CH(CH_2.SH).CO.NH.CH_2.COOH$, composed of glutamic acid, cysteine, and aminoacetic acid, and isolated from animal and plant tissues. It is the co-enzyme of glyoxalase and acts as a respiratory carrier of oxygen. **oxidized g.,** the precursor of reduced glutathione. **reduced g.,** a tripeptide present in red cells, a deficiency of which most probably predisposes erythrocytes to the oxidant and hemolytic effects of certain drugs, such as the antimalarial agents. It is functionally associated with glucose-6-phosphate dehydrogenase and reduced triphosphopyridine nucleotide in the maintenance of red cell integrity.

glutathionemia (gloo″tah-thi″o-ne′me-ah). The presence of glutathione in the blood.

gluteal (gloo′te-al) [Gr. *gloutos* buttock]. Pertaining to the buttocks.

glutelin (gloo′tĕ-lin). A simple protein, insoluble in all neutral solvents, but readily soluble in very dilute acids and alkalis and coagulable by heat. It occurs in seeds of cereals.

gluten (gloo′ten) [L. "glue"]. The protein of wheat and other grains which gives to the dough its tough elastic character. **g.-casein,** a protein preparation employed in intestinal surgery to excite adhesive inflammation.

glutenin (gloo′tĕ-nin). The glutelin of wheat.

gluteofemoral (gloo″te-o-fem′or-al) [*gluteal* + *femoral*]. Pertaining to the buttock and thigh.

gluteoinguinal (gloo″te-o-in′gwĭ-nal). Pertaining to the buttock and groin.

glutethimide (gloo-teth′ĭ-mīd). Chemical name: 2-ethyl-2-phenylglutarimide: used as a central nervous system depressant.

glutin (gloo′tin). 1. A viscid substance from the glutelin of wheat: gluten-casein. 2. Gelatin in its soft, dissolved, or gelatinous state.

glutinous (gloo′tĭ-nus) [L. *glutinosus*]. Sticky; adhesive; gluey.

glutitis (gloo-ti′tis) [Gr. *gloutos* buttock + *-itis*]. Inflammation of the buttock.

glutolin (gloo′to-lin). An albuminoid substance found in paraglobulin and thought to be a constant constituent of blood plasm.

glutoscope (gloo′to-skōp). An apparatus for observing agglutination.

glutose (gloo′tōs). An artificial glucoside that resembles glucose in many of its chemical reactions, but which seems to be inert in the body.

Gluzinski's test (gloo-zin′skēz) [Wladyslaw Antoni *Gluzinski*, a physician in Lemberg, 1856–1935]. See under *tests*.

glycal (gli′kal). An unsaturated sugar, —CH=CH—.

glycase (gli′kās). An enzyme which converts maltose and maltodextrin into dextrose.

glycemia (gli-se′me-ah) [Gr. *glykys* sweet + Gr. *haima* blood + *-ia*]. The presence of sugar in the blood.

glycemin (gli′sĕ-min). A substance, secreted by the liver, in the blood of diabetics which has an antagonistic action toward insulin by inhibition to fixation of dextrose by erythrocytes.

glyceraldehyde (glis″er-al′de-hīd). A compound, glyceric aldehyde, $CH_2OHCHOHCHO$, formed by the oxidation of glycerol. **g. phosphate,** a triosephosphate which results from the decomposition of hexosephosphate in the chemistry of muscle contraction.

glycerate (glis′er-āt). A salt or ester of glyceric acid.

glyceridase (glis′er-ĭ-dās). Lipase.

glyceride (glis′er-īd). An organic acid ester of glycerol. The natural fats are glycerides of the higher fatty acids. **medullary g.,** a marrow extract used in anemia.

glycerin (glis′er-in) [L. *glycerinum*]. A clear, colorless, syrupy liquid, 1,2,3-propanetriol: used as an emollient and as a solvent for drugs.

glycerinated (glis′er-in-āt-ed). Treated with or preserved in glycerin.

glycerinum (glis″er-i′num) [L.]. Glycerin.

glycerite (glis′er-īt) [L. *glyceritum*]. A solution or mixture of a medicinal substance in glycerin. The glycerites for which official standards have been promulgated are boroglycerin, starch, and tannic acid glycerites.

glyceritum (glis″er-i′tum), gen. *glyceri′ti*, pl. *glyceri′ta* [L.]. Glycerite. **g. ac′idi tan′nici,** tannic acid glycerite (N.F.). **g. am′yli,** starch glycerite (U.S.P.). **g. boroglyceri′ni,** boroglycerin glycerite (N.F.).

glycerogel (glis′er-o-jel). A gel in which glycerin is the dispersed medium.

glycerogelatin (glis″er-o-jel′ah-tin). Glycerin jelly.

glycerol (glis′er-ol). Glycerin. **acetanilid g.,** a mixture of glycerin and acetanilid powder. **g. boroglycerite,** boroglycerin glycerite. **g. phosphate,** an intermediate in alcoholic fermentation, $CH_2OH.CHOH.CH_2.O.PO(OH)_2$.

glycerophilic (glis″er-o-fil′ik). Having a special affinity for glycerin.

glycerophosphatase (glis″er-o-fos′fah-tās). An enzyme which catalyzes the decomposition of glycerophosphates.

glycerophosphate (glis″er-o-fos′fāt). Any salt of glycerophosphoric acid: several of them are used as so-called nerve tonics.

glycerose (glis′er-ōs). A sugar formed by oxidizing glycerin. There are two glyceroses, glyceric aldehyde and dioxyacetone.

glyceryl (glis′er-il). The trivalent radical, C_3H_5, of glycerin. **g. margarate,** intarvin. **g. triacetate,** triacetin. **g. trinitrate,** a colorless or yellowish, oily liquid, $C_3H_5(O.NO_2)_3$, formed by the action of nitric and sulfuric acids on glycerin. It is poisonous and highly explosive. Physiologically, it has the actions of nitrites and is a vasodilator: used principally in angina pectoris and asthma. Called also *nitroglycerin* and *glonoin*.

glycide (gli′sid). The oxide of hydroxypropene, isomeric with lactic aldehyde and acetol.

glycidol (glis′id-ol). Glycide.

glycinate (gli′sin-āt). Any salt of glycine (aminoacetic acid).

glycine (gli′sin). Aminoacetic acid.

glycinin (glis′ĭ-nin). A globulin which constitutes 90 to 95 per cent of the protein content of soy bean.

Glyciphagus (gli-sif′ah-gus) [Gr. *glykys* sweet + *phagein* to eat]. A genus of mites. See also *Tyroglyphus*. **G. bus′ki,** a species which has caused large sores on the foot of a Negro in England. **G. domes′ticus (G. pruno′rum),** a species which infests sugar and causes grocers' itch.

glyco- [Gr. *glykys* sweet]. Combining form denoting relationship to sugar. Cf. *gluco-*.

glycobiarsol (gli″ko-bi-ar′sol). Chemical name: bismuth p-glycolylarsanilate: used in treatment of intestinal amebiasis.

glycocholaneresis (gli″ko-ko″lan-er′ĕ-sis) [*glycocholic acid* + Gr. *hairesis* a taking]. Increase in the output or elimination of glycocholic acid in the bile. Cf. *cholaneresis*.

glycocholate (gli″ko-kol′āt). A salt of glycocholic acid.

glycocine (gli′ko-sin). Aminoacetic acid.

glycoclastic (gli″ko-klas′tik) [*glyco-* + Gr. *klan* to break]. Glycolytic.

glycocoll (gli′ko-kol) [*glyco-* + Gr. *kolla* glue]. Aminoacetic acid.

glycocyaminase (gli″ko-si′am″ĭ-nās). An enzyme in the liver which hydrolyzes glycocyamine into urea and aminoacetic acid.

glycocyamine (gli″ko-si′ah-min). A nitrogenous compound, guanidine-acetic acid, $NH_2.C(NH).NH.CH_2.COOH$, formed by heating guanidine with glycine. When methylated it becomes creatine.

glycogelatin (gli″ko-jel′ah-tin). An ointment base containing glycerin and gelatin.

glycogen (gli′ko-jen) [*glyco-* + Gr. *gennan* to produce]. A polysaccharide, $(C_6H_{10}O_5)_x$, which is the chief carbohydrate storage material in animals.

It is formed by and largely stored in the liver, being depolymerized to glucose and liberated as needed. Called also *animal starch.* **hepatic g.,** glycogen stored in the liver. **tissue g.,** glycogen stored in the tissues other than the liver, especially that in the muscles.

glycogenal (gli″ko-jen′al). A compound which occurs in the organism along with glycogen.

glycogenase (gli-ko′jĕ-nās). An enzyme which hydrolyzes glycogen to lower saccharides. See *Cori ester,* under *ester.*

glycogenesis (gli″ko-jen′e-sis) [*glyco-* + *genesis*]. 1. The formation or synthesis of glycogen. 2. The production of sugar.

glycogenetic (gli″ko-je-net′ik). Pertaining to, characterized by, or promoting glycogenesis.

glycogenic (gli″ko-jen′ik). Pertaining to glycogenesis or to glycogen.

glycogenolysis (gli″ko-jĕ-nol′ĭ-sis) [*glycogen* + Gr. *lysis* dissolution]. The splitting up of glycogen in the body tissues.

glycogenolytic (gli″ko-jen″o-lit′ik). Pertaining to, characterized by, or promoting glycogenolysis.

glycogenosis (gli″ko-je-no′sis). A chronic metabolic abnormality of childhood characterized by enormous enlargement of the liver (due to storage of glycogen), hypoglycemia, and failure of epinephrin to mobilize glycogen (due to enzyme shortage in the liver). Called also *glycogen disease, von Gierke's disease, glycogenic hepatomegaly, glycogen accumulation,* and *glycogenic thesaurismosis.*

glycogenous (gli-koj′ĕ-nus). Glycogenetic.

glycogeny (gli-koj′ĕ-ne). Glycogenesis.

glycogeusia (gli″ko-ju′se-ah) [*glyco-* + Gr. *geusis* taste]. A condition in which there is a sweet taste in the mouth.

glycohemia (gli″ko-he′me-ah) [*glyco-* + Gr. *haima* blood + *-ia*]. Glycemia.

glycohistechia (gli″ko-his-tek′e-ah) [*glyco-* + Gr. *histos* tissue + *echein* to hold]. The presence of an abnormally large amount of sugar in a tissue (Urbach).

glycol (gli′kol). Any one of a group of aliphatic dihydric alcohols, having marked hygroscopic properties and useful as solvents and plasticizers. *Diethylene g.* should not be used for oral administration.

glycolate (gli′ko-lāt). A salt or ester of glycolic acid.

glycoleucine (gli″ko-lu′sin). Norleucine.

glycolipid (gli″ko-lip′id). A lipid containing carbohydrate radicals. They are esters of aliphatic acids and carbohydrates and include galactoside and cerebrosides.

glycolipide (gli″ko-lip′īd). Glycolipid.

glycolipin (gli″ko-li′pin). Glycolipid.

glycolyl (gli′ko-lil). 1. The radical $HOCH_2CO$—. 2. The radical $=C_2H_2O$.

glycolysis (gli-kol′ĭ-sis) [*glyco-* + Gr. *lysis* solution]. The breaking down of sugars into simpler compounds.

glycolytic (gli″ko-lit′ik). Pertaining to, characterized by, or promoting glycolysis.

glycometabolic (gli″ko-met-ah-bol′ik). Pertaining to the metabolism of sugar.

glycometabolism (gli″ko-mĕ-tab′o-lizm). The metabolism of sugar.

glycone (gli′kōn). A glycerin suppository.

glyconeogenesis (gli″ko-ne″o-jen′e-sis) [*glyco-* + Gr. *neos* new + *gennan* to produce]. The formation of carbohydrates from molecules which are not themselves carbohydrates, as protein or fat.

glyconucleoprotein (gli″ko-nu″kle-o-pro′te-in). A nucleoprotein having the carbohydrate group largely developed.

glycopenia (gli″ko-pe′ne-ah) [*glyco-* + Gr. *penia* poverty]. A deficiency of sugar in the tissues.

glycopexic (gli″ko-pek′sik). Pertaining to, characterized by, or promoting glycopexis.

glycopexis (gli″ko-pek′sis) [*glyco-* + Gr. *pēxis* fixation]. The fixation or storing of sugar or glycogen.

Glycophagus (gli-kof′ah-gus). A genus of sugar mites which may cause itch.

glycophenol (gli″ko-fe′nol). Glucide.

glycophilia (gli″ko-fil′e-ah) [*glyco-* + Gr. *philein* to love]. A condition in which a very small amount of dextrose produces hyperglycemia.

glycophospholipin (gli″ko-fos″fo-li′pin). A phospholipin containing carbohydrate radicals; found in the liver.

glycopolyuria (gli″ko-pol″e-u′re-ah) [*glyco-* + Gr. *polys* much + *ouron* urine + *-ia*]. Diabetes with a moderate increase of the sugar of the urine and with a marked increase of uric acid in the blood.

glycoprival (gli″ko-pri′val) [*glyco-* + L. *privus* deprived of]. Pertaining to or characterized by deprivation of carbohydrates.

glycoprotein (gli″ko-pro′te-in). Any one of a class of conjugated proteins consisting of a compound of protein with a carbohydrate group. They are distinguished by yielding in decomposition a product capable of reducing cupric oxide. The glycoproteins include the mucins, the mucoids, and the chondroproteins.

glycoptyalism (gli″ko-ti′al-izm) [*glyco-* + Gr. *ptyalon* saliva]. Glycosialia.

glycopyrrolate (gli″ko-pir′ro-lāt). Chemical name: 1-methyl-3-pyrrolidyl-α-phenylcyclopentaneglycolate: used to produce parasympathetic blockade, and to reduce gastric acid secretion and hypermotility.

glycoregulation (gli″ko-reg″u-la′shun). The control of sugar metabolism.

glycoregulatory (gli″ko-reg′u-lah-to″re). Pertaining to the control of sugar metabolism.

glycorrhachia (gli″ko-ra′ke-ah) [*glyco-* + Gr. *rhachis* spine + *-ia*]. Presence of sugar in the cerebrospinal fluid.

glycorrhea (gli″ko-re′ah) [*glyco-* + Gr. *rhoia* flow]. Any sugary discharge, as of urine.

glycosamine (gli″ko-sam′in). Glucosamine.

glycosecretory (gli″ko-se′kre-to-re). Causing or concerned in the secretion of glycogen.

glycoseen (gli′ko-sēn). An anhydrosugar in which there is a double bond between two adjacent carbon atoms having hydroxyl groups in the *trans*-position.

glycosemia (gli-ko-se′me-ah). Glycemia.

glycosialia (gli″ko-si-a′le-ah) [*glyco-* + Gr. *sialon* saliva + *-ia*]. Presence of sugar in the saliva.

glycosialorrhea (gli″ko-si″ah-lo-re′ah) [*glyco-* + Gr. *sialon* saliva + *rhoia* flow]. Excessive flow of saliva containing sugar.

glycosidase (gli′co-sĭ-dās). An enzyme which catalyzes the decomposition of a glycoside.

glycoside (gli′ko-sīd). A compound which contains a carbohydrate molecule (sugar), particularly any such natural product in plants. Cf. *glucoside.* **cardiac g.,** any one of a group of glycosides occurring in certain plants (Digitalis, Strophanthus, Scilla, and others), which have a characteristic action on the heart. **cyanophoric g.,** a glycoside which on hydrolysis yields hydrocyanic acid. **sterol g.,** phytosterolin.

glycosine (gli-ko′sin). 1. A ring compound formed by the action of concentrated ammonia on glyoxal which sometimes unites with urea in the kidneys, forming uric acid. 2. An extract from the pancreas.

glycosometer (gli″ko-som′e-ter) [*glyco-* + Gr. *metron* measure]. An instrument used in determining the proportion of sugar in the urine.

glycostatic (gli″ko-stat′ik). Tending to maintain a constant sugar level.

glycosuria (gli″ko-su′re-ah) [*glyco-* + Gr. *ouron* urine + *-ia*]. The presence of an abnormal amount of glucose in the urine; especially the excretion of an abnormally large amount of sugar (glucose) in the urine; i.e. of more than 1 Gm. in twenty-four hours. **alimentary g.,** digestive g. **benign g.,** renal g. **digestive g.,** normal glycosuria following the ingestion of sugar. **emotional g.,** glycosuria induced by violent emotion. **epinephrine g.,** glycosuria following the injection of epinephrine. **hyperglycemic g.,** glycosuria associated with hyperglycemia. **magnesium g.,** glycosuria due to high concentration of magnesium in the blood. **nervous g.,** glycosuria produced by puncture of the fourth ventricle of the brain or by stimulation of the great splanchnic nerve. **non-diabetic g., non-hyperglycemic g., normoglycemic g., orthoglycemic g.,** renal g. **pathologic g.,** a condition in which large amounts of sugar appear in the urine for a considerable period of time. **phloridzin g., phlorhizin g.,** glycosuria following the administration of phlorhizin. **pituitary g.,** glycosuria and hyperglycemia due to hypersecretion of the posterior lobe of the hypophysis. **renal g.,** glycosuria occurring when there is only the normal amount of sugar in the blood. **toxic g.,** glycosuria produced by poisons.

glycotaxis (gli″ko-tak′sis) [*glyco-* + Gr. *taxis* arrangement]. The metabolic distribution of glucose to the body tissues.

glycotropic (gli″ko-trop′ik) [*glyco-* + Gr. *tropos* a turning]. Having an affinity for or attracting sugar; mediated by sugar; causing hyperglycemia.

glycuresis (gli″ku-re′sis). The normal increase in the glucose content of the urine which follows an ordinary carbohydrate meal.

glycuronate (gli-ku′ro-nāt). A compound formed by the union of glycuronic acid and some other substance, frequently an aromatic body.

glycuronuria (gli-ku″ro-nu′re-ah). The presence of glucuronic acid in the urine.

glycyl (glis′il). The univalent acid radical, H_2NCHC_2O, derived from aminoacetic acid.

glycylglycine (glis″il-glis′in). The simplest polypeptide, $CH_2(NH_2).CO.NH.CH_2.CO_2.H$.

glycyltryptophan (glis″il-trip′to-fan). A dipeptide consisting of glycine and tryptophan radicals: used as a test for cancer of stomach. See under *tests*.

Glycyrrhiza (glis″ĭ-ri′zah) [Gr. *glykys* sweet + *rhiza* root]. A genus of leguminous plants.

glycyrrhiza (glis″ir-ri′zah). The dried rhizome and roots of *Glycyrrhiza glabra:* used in a fluidextract or syrup as a flavored vehicle for drugs.

glycyrrhizin (glis″ĭ-ri′zin) [L. *glycyrrhizinum*]. A sweet substance from licorice root.

glykemia (gli-ke′me-ah). Glycemia.

glyoxal (gli-ok′sal). A yellow crystalline compound, O:HC.CH:O, prepared by the oxidation of acetaldehyde.

glyoxalase (gli-ok′sah-lās). A hydrase which catalyzes the change of methylglyoxal to lactic acid by the addition of water.

glyoxalin (gli-ok′sah-lin). Iminazole.

glyphylline (gli-fil′lin). Dyphylline.

Glyptocranium (glip″to-kra′ne-um). A genus of spiders. **G. gasteracanthoi′des,** a venomous spider of Peru.

glysal (gli′sal). Spirosal.

glytheonate (gli-the′o-nāt). Trade mark for a preparation of theophylline sodium glycinate.

Gm. Abbreviation for *gram.*

G.M.C. Abbreviation for *General Medical Council* (British).

Gmelin's test (ma′linz) [Leopold *Gmelin*, German physiologist, 1788–1853]. See under *tests.*

gnat (nat). A small dipterous insect. In England the term is applied to mosquitoes; in America to insects smaller than mosquitoes. See *Chironomidae.* **buffalo g.,** a name given various individuals of the family Simuliidae. **eye g.,** *Hippelates pusio.* **turkey g.,** a name given various individuals of the family Simuliidae.

gnath-. See *gnatho-.*

gnathalgia (nath-al′je-ah) [*gnath-* + *-algia*]. Pain in the jaw.

gnathic (nath′ik). Pertaining to the jaw or cheek.

gnathion (nath′e-on). The lowest point on the median line of the lower jaw.

gnathitis (nath-i′tis) [*gnath-* + *-itis*]. Inflammation of the jaw.

gnatho-, gnath- (nath′o, nath) [Gr. *gnathos* jaw]. Combining form denoting relationship to the jaw.

Gnathobdellidae (nath″o-del′ĭ-de). A family of the Hirudinea which includes the genus *Hirudo*, the leech.

gnathocephalus (nath″o-sef′ah-lus) [*gnatho-* + Gr. *kephalē* head]. A fetal monster with no part of the head except the jaws.

gnathodynamics (nath″o-di-nam′iks) [*gnatho-* + Gr. *dynamis* power]. The study of the physical forces used in mastication.

gnathodynamometer (nath″o-di″nah-mom′e-ter) [*gnatho-* + *dynamometer*]. An instrument for measuring the force exerted in closing the jaws. **bimeter g.,** a gnathodynamometer equipped with a central-bearing point of adjustable height.

gnathodynia (nath″o-din′e-ah) [*gnatho-* + Gr. *odynē* pain]. Pain in the jaw.

gnathography (nath-og′rah-fe) [*gnatho-* + Gr. *graphein* to record]. The recording of the strength of a patient's bite by a tracing of the changes in the flow of an electric current through a bite gauge.

gnathology (nath-ol′o-je). A science which deals with the masticatory apparatus as a whole, including morphology, anatomy, histology, physiology, pathology, and therapeutics.

gnathoplasty (nath′o-plas″te) [*gnatho-* + Gr. *plassein* to mold]. Plastic surgery of the jaw or cheek.

gnathoschisis (nath-os′kĭ-sis) [*gnatho-* + Gr. *schisis* splitting]. Congenital cleft of the upper jaw, as in cleft palate.

gnathostatics (nath″o-stat′iks) [*gnatho-* + Gr. *statikē* the art of weighing]. A method of orthodontic diagnosis based on determination of the craniometric relationships between the teeth and their supporting structures.

Gnathostoma (nath-os′to-mah) [*gnatho-* + Gr. *stoma* mouth]. A genus of nematode worms parasitic in cats, swine, cattle, and sometimes in man. **G. his′pidum,** a species found in the stomach of pigs in China, which occasionally produces a form of "creeping disease" in man. **G. siamen′se, G. spinig′erum,** a nematode parasitic in the stomach of cats, dogs, cattle, and swine.

gnathostomatics (nath″o-sto-mat′iks). The physiology of the mouth and jaws.

gnathostomiasis (nath″o-sto-mi′ah-sis). Infection with Gnathostoma.

Gnathostomum (nath-os′to-mum). Gnathostoma.

G.N.C. Abbreviation for *General Nursing Council.*

gnosia (no′se-ah). The faculty of perceiving and recognizing.

gnosis (no′sis) [Gr. *gnōsis* knowledge]. Edinger's term for the arousal of associative mnemonic complexes by sensory pallial impulses; one of the functions of the cerebral cortex. Cf. *praxis.*

gnotobiota (no″to-bi-o′tah). The specifically and entirely known microfauna and microflora of a specially reared laboratory animal.

gnotobiote (no″to-bi′ōt). A specially reared laboratory animal the microfauna and microflora of which are specifically known in their entirety.

gnotobiotic (no″to-bi-ot′ik). Pertaining to a gnotobiote or to gnotobiotics.

gnotobiotics (no″to-bi-ot′iks) [Gr. *gnotos* known + *biota* the fauna and flora of a region]. The science of rearing laboratory animals the microfauna and microflora of which are specifically known in their entirety.

Goa powder (go′ah) [*Goa* a city of India]. See under *powder.*

goatpox (gōt′poks). An acute infectious disease of goats marked by a vesicular eruption with catarrh of the respiratory mucous membranes. Called also *variola caprina.*

Godélier's law (go-da-lyāz′) [Charles Pierre *Godélier*, French physician, 1813–1877]. See under *law.*

Goetsch's skin reaction (gech′ez) [Emil *Goetsch*, American physician, born 1883]. See under *reaction.*

Goffe's operation (gofs) [J. Riddle *Goffe*, American gynecologist, 1851–1932]. See under *operation.*

goiter (goi′ter). An enlargement of the thyroid gland, causing a swelling in the front part of the neck. **aberrant g.,** enlargement of an ectopic or supernumerary thyroid gland. **adenomatous g.,** enlargement of the thyroid gland caused by an adenoma of the gland. **basedow g.,** a colloid goiter which has become hyperfunctioning after administration of iodine. **colloid g.,** a large and soft form of goiter in which the follicles of the gland are greatly distended with colloid. **congenital g.,** enlargement of the thyroid gland which is present at birth, or which results from a congenital absence of enzymes leading to inadequate production of thyroxine. **cystic g.,** an enlarged thyroid gland containing cysts formed by mucoid or colloid degeneration. **diffuse g.,** a thyroid gland which is diffusely enlarged. **diving g.,** a goiter which is movable and is located sometimes above and sometimes below the sternal notch. **endemic g.,** enlargement of the thyroid gland occurring in certain districts, particularly in the mountain regions of the Alps, Pyrenees, Carpathians, Andes, and Himalayas, and other areas where the iodine content of the normal diet is low. **exophthalmic g.,** a disorder marked by an enlarged pulsating thyroid gland, marked acceleration of the pulse rate, exophthalmos, a tendency to profuse sweats, nervous symptoms, including fine muscular tremors, psychic disturbance, emaciation, and increased basal metabolism. Called also *Flajani's, Graves', Parry's,* and *Basedow's disease, hyperthyroidism, thyrotoxicosis, toxic goiter.* **fibrous g.,** enlargement of the thyroid gland caused by hyperplasia of the capsule and stroma. **follicular g.,** parenchymatous g. **intrathoracic g.,** goiter in which a portion of the enlarged thyroid is situated in the thoracic cavity. **lingual g.,** an enlargement of the upper end of the original thyroglossal duct, forming a tumor at the posterior part of the dorsum of the tongue. **nodular g.,** an enlarged thyroid gland containing circumscribed nodules within its substance. **papillomatous g.,** adenomatous g. **parenchymatous g.,** goiter marked by increase in the follicles and proliferation of the epithelium. **perivascular g.,** one which surrounds a large blood vessel. **plunging g.,** diving g. **simple g.,** simple hyperplasia of the thyroid gland. **substernal g.,** goiter in which a portion of the enlarged gland is situated beneath the sternum. **toxic g.,** exophthalmic g. **vascular g.,** enlargement of the thyroid gland due chiefly to dilatation of the blood vessels. **wandering g.,** diving g.

Exophthalmic goiter.

goitre (goi′ter) [Fr.]. Goiter.

goitrin (goi′trin). A goitrogenic substance isolated from rutabagas and turnips.

goitrogen (goi′tro-jen). A goiter-producing compound.

goitrogenic (goi-tro-jen′ik). Producing goiter.

goitrogenicity (goi″tro-jĕ-nis′ĭ-te). The tendency to produce goiter.

goitrogenous (goi-troj′e-nus). Producing goiter.

gold (gōld). A yellow metallic element occurring in masses or veins in rocks or in grains in the sand of rivers. Its symbol is Au (L. *au′rum*); atomic number, 79; atomic weight, 196.967; specific gravity, 19.32. Gold and many of its compounds are used in medicine, chiefly as alteratives, and all the compounds are poisonous. **adhesive g.,** annealed gold with cohesive properties which make it suitable for use in dental restorations. **annealed g.,** gold which has been heated in a flame to drive off any contaminating gases and increase its cohesive properties. **g. aurothiosulfate,** g. sodium thiosulfate. **cohesive g.,** a chemically pure gold which can be made to form a solid block when properly packed or condensed into a tooth cavity. **crystal g., crystalline g.,** mat g. **Dutch g.,** an alloy of copper and zinc. **fibrous g.,** mat g. **mat g.,** a type of pure gold composed of flakelike crystals formed by electrodeposition. **g. monobromide,** a yellowish-gray compound, AuBr: antiseptic antisyphilitic, and anodyne. **non-cohesive g.,** gold which does not weld because of a gaseous contaminant on its surface. **Nürnberg g.,** a preparation containing 2.5 per cent gold, 7.5 per cent aluminum, and 90 per cent copper. **g. sodium thiomalate,** an odorless, fine, white to yellowish white powder with a metallic taste, $C_4H_3AuNa_2O_4S.H_2O$: used in treatment of rheumatoid arthritis and nondisseminated lupus erythematosus. **g. sodium thiosulfate,** white needle-like or prismatic small glistening crystals, $Na_3Au(S_2B_3)_2.2H_2O$: used in treatment of rheumatoid arthritis. **g. thioglucose,** aurothioglucose. **g. tribromide,** an antisyphilitic, anti-epileptic, and anodyne substance, $AuBr_3$.

Goldberger's diet (gōld′ber-gerz) [Joseph *Goldberger*, American physician, 1874–1929]. See under *diet.*

Goldblatt's clamp, hypertension [Harry *Goldblatt*, Cleveland physician, born 1891]. See under *clamp* and *hypertension.*

Golden's sign (gōl′denz) [W. W. *Golden*, American physician]. See under *sign.*

Goldflam's disease (gōlt′flahmz) [Samuel V. *Goldflam*, Polish neurologist, 1852–1932]. Myasthenia gravis pseudoparalytica.

Goldscheider's disease, percussion, test (gōld′shi-derz) [Alfred *Goldscheider*, Berlin physician, 1858–1935]. See under the nouns.

Goldstein's disease, hematemesis, hemoptysis, sign (gōld′stīnz) [Hyman I. *Goldstein*, American physician, 1887–1954]. See under the nouns.

Goldstein rays (gōld′stīn) [Eugene *Goldstein*, German physicist, 1850–1930]. See under *ray.*

Goldthwait's sign, symptom (gōld′thwāts) [Joel E. *Goldthwait*, American orthopedic surgeon, born 1866]. See under *sign.*

Golgi's cell, complex, etc. (gol′jēz) [Camillo *Golgi*, Italian histologist, 1843–1926; co-winner, with Santiago Ramon y Cajal, of the Nobel prize for medicine and physiology in 1906]. See under *cell, complex,* etc.

Goll's columns, fibers, nucleus (golz) [Friedrich *Goll*, Swiss anatomist, 1829–1904]. See under the nouns.

Goltz's experiment (gōlts′ez) [Friedrich Leopold *Goltz*, German physician, 1834–1902]. See under *experiment.*

Gombault's degeneration, neuritis (gom-bōz′) [François Alexis Albert *Gombault*, French neurologist, 1844–1904]. See under *neuritis.*

Gombault-Philippe triangle (gom-bo′ fe-lēp′) [F. A. A. *Gombault;* Claudius *Philippe*, French pathologist, 1866–1903]. See under *triangle.*

Gomori method, stain [George *Gomori*, Hungarian histochemist in Chicago, 1904–1957]. See *Table of Stains and Staining Methods*, under *stain.*

gomphiasis (gom-fi′ah-sis) [Gr. "tooth ache," "gnashing of the teeth"]. 1. Looseness of the teeth. 2. Odontalgia.

gomphosis (gom-fo′sis) [Gr. *gomphōsis* a bolting

together]. [N A, B N A] A type of fibrous joint in which a conical process is inserted into a socket-like portion, such as the styloid process in the temporal bone, or the teeth in the dental alveoli.

gon- (gon). 1. [Gr. *gonē* seed]. Combining form denoting relation to seed or to the semen. 2. [Gr. *gony* knee]. Combining form denoting relationship to the knee.

gonacratia (gon″ah-kra′she-ah) [*gon-*(1) + Gr. *akrateia* incontinence]. Spermatorrhea.

gonad (gon′ad) [L. *gonas*, from Gr. *gonē* seed]. A gamete-producing gland; an ovary or testis. **indifferent g.,** the sexually undifferentiated gonad of the early embryo, the male and female potentialities being represented, respectively, by two specific histological elements, medulla and cortex, which have alternative roles in gonadogenesis. Development of the cortex, with suppression of the medulla, produces the ovary; development of the medulla, with suppression of the cortex, produces the testis. **third g.,** the adrenal gland, so called because of the interrelationship between it and the sex glands.

gonadal (gon′ad-al). Pertaining to a gonad.

gonadectomize (go″nad-ek′to-mīz). To deprive of the gonads by surgical excision.

gonadectomy (go″nad-ek′to-me) [*gonad* + Gr. *ektomē* excision]. Removal of an ovary or testis.

gonadial (go-nad′e-al). Pertaining to a gonad.

gonadogenesis (gon″ah-do-jen′e-sis) [*gonado-* + Gr. *genesis* production]. The development of the gonads in the embryo, especially the development of gonads typical of one or the other sex.

gonado-inhibitory (gon″ah-do-in-hib′ĭ-to-re). Inhibiting or preventing gonadal activity.

gonadokinetic (gon″ah-do-ki-net′ik) [*gonad* + Gr. *kinēsis* motion]. Stimulating gonadal activity.

gonadopathy (gon″ah-dop′ah-the) [*gonad* + Gr. *pathos* disease]. Any disease of the gonads.

gonadopause (go-nad′o-paws). The loss of gonadal activity which accompanies the aging process.

gonadotherapy (gon″ah-do-ther′ah-pe). Treatment by the use of hormones from the ovary or testis.

gonadotrope (go-nad′o-trop). 1. A person who exhibits gonadotropism. 2. A gonadotropic substance.

gonadotrophic (gon″ah-do-tro′fik). Gonadotropic.

gonadotrophin (gon″ah-do-tro′fin). Gonadotropin.

gonadotropic (gon″ah-do-trōp′ik) [*gonad* + Gr. *tropos* a turning]. Stimulating the gonads: applied to hormones of the anterior pituitary which influence the gonads.

gonadotropin (gon″ah-do-tro′pin). A substance having affinity for or a stimulating effect on the gonads. There are three varieties: 1, anterior pituitary; 2, chorionic from human pregnancy urine; and 3, chorionic from the serum of pregnant mares (*equine g.*). **chorionic g.,** the gonadotropic substance from human or equine placentas: used in treatment of underdevelopment of sex glands.

gonadotropism (gon″ad-ot′ro-pizm) [*gonad* + Gr. *tropos* a turning]. An endocrine constitution in which the gonads or sex glands exercise a dominating influence.

gonaduct (gon′ah-dukt). The duct of a gonad; an oviduct, or sperm duct.

gonagra (gon-ag′rah) [*gon-*(2) + Gr. *agra* seizure]. Gout in the knee.

gonalgia (go-nal′je-ah) [*gon-*(2) + *-algia*]. Pain in the knee.

gonangiectomy (gon″an-je-ek′to-me). Vasectomy.

gonarthritis (gon″ar-thri′tis) [*gon-*(2) + Gr. *arthron* joint + *-itis*]. Inflammation of a knee or knee joint.

gonarthrocace (gon″ar-throk′a-se) [*gon-*(2) + Gr. *arthron* joint + *kakē* evil]. An inflamed condition of the knee joint; white swelling.

gonarthromeningitis (gon-ar″thro-men″in-ji′tis) [*gon-*(2) + Gr. *arthron* joint + *mēninx* membrane]. Inflammation of the synovial membrane of the knee joint.

gonarthrotomy (gon″ar-throt′o-me) [*gon-*(2) + Gr. *arthron* joint + *temnein* to cut]. Surgical incision of the knee joint.

gonatagra (gon″ah-tag′rah). Gonagra.

gonatocele (go-nat′o-sēl) [*gon-*(2) + Gr. *kēlē* tumor]. Tumor of the knee.

gonecyst, gonecystis (gon′e-sist, gon″e-sis′tis) [Gr. *gonē* seed + *kystis* bladder]. Vesicula seminalis.

gonecystitis (gon″e-sis-ti′tis). Inflammation of a seminal vesicle.

gonecystolith (gon″e-sis′to-lith) [*gonecyst* + Gr. *lithos* stone]. A concretion in a seminal vesicle.

gonecystopyosis (gon″e-sis″to-pi-o′sis) [*gonecyst* + Gr. *pyōsis* suppuration]. Suppuration in a seminal vesicle.

goneitis (gon″e-i′tis) [*gon-*(2) + *-itis*]. Inflammation of the knee.

gonepoiesis (gon″e-poi-e′sis) [Gr. *gonē* seed + *poiein* to make]. The secretion or formation of the semen.

gonepoietic (gon″e-poi-et′ik). Pertaining to, characterized by, or promoting gonepoiesis.

Gongylonema (gon″jĭ-lo-ne′mah) [Gr. *gongylos* round + *nēma* thread]. A genus of filarial nematodes. **G. ingluvic′ola** has been found in chickens. **G. neoplas′ticum** occurs in the anterior portion of the digestive tract of rats. **G. pul′chrum** is a common parasite in the esophageal mucosa of sheep, goats, cattle and pigs in the United States. It has been found on the lips and mouth of man. **G. scuta′tum** occurs in cattle and sheep.

gongylonemiasis (gon″jĭ-lo-ne-mi′ah-sis). Infestation with *Gongylonema*.

gonia (go′ne-ah). Plural of *gonion*.

gonidangium (gon″id-an′je-um). A cell within which gonidia are formed.

gonidia (go-nid′e-ah). Plural of *gonidium*.

gonidiospore (go-nid′e-o-spōr). An endospore formed within a spore capsule, as in *Mucor*.

gonidium (go-nid′e-um), pl. *gonid′ia* [Gr. *gonē* seed]. 1. A spore which is not born free, but is formed in a case or receptacle; an endospore. 2. One of the chlorophyll-bearing elements of lichens.

Gonin's operation (go-nāz′) [Jules *Gonin*, Swiss ophthalmic surgeon, 1870–1935]. See under *operation*.

gonio- (go′ne-o) [Gr. *gōnia* angle]. Combining form denoting relationship to an angle.

goniocraniometry (go″ne-o-kra″ne-om′e-tre) [*gonio-* + *craniometry*]. The measurement of the cranial angles.

gonioma (gon″e-o′ma) [*gon-*(1) + *-oma*]. A tumor developed from sexual cells.

goniometer (go″ne-om′e-ter) [*gonio-* + Gr. *metron* measure]. 1. An instrument for measuring angles. 2. A plank, one end of which may be tilted to any height: used for testing for labyrinthine disease. **finger g.,** an apparatus for measuring the limits of flexion and extension of the interphalangeal joints of the fingers.

gonion (go′ne-on), pl. *go′nia* [Gr. *gōnia* angle]. A cephalometric landmark, being the most inferior, posterior, and lateral point on the external angle of the mandible.

goniophotography (go″ne-o-fo-tog′rah-fe). Photography of the angle of the anterior chamber of the eye.

goniopuncture (go″ne-o-punk′tūr). A filtering operation for glaucoma, done by inserting a knife blade through clear cornea just within the limbus, across the anterior chamber, and through the opposite corneoscleral wall.

gonioscope (go′ne-o-skōp″) [*gonio-* + Gr. *skopein*

to examine]. A kind of ophthalmoscope for examining the angle of the anterior chamber and for demonstrating ocular motility and rotation.

gonioscopy (go″ne-os′ko-pe). Examination of the angle of the anterior chamber of the eye with the gonioscope.

goniotomy (go″ne-ot′o-me) [*gonio-* + Gr. *tomē* a cutting]. Barkan's operation for that type of glaucoma which is characterized by an open angle and normal depth of the anterior chamber: it consists of the opening of Schlemm's canal under direct vision secured by a contact glass.

gonite (gon′īt). Any one of the reproductive elements of bacteria.

gonitis (go-ni′tis) [*gon-*(2) + *-itis*]. Inflammation of the knee. **fungous g.,** inflammation of the knee joint in which the capsule is diffusely thickened. **g. tuberculo′sa,** tuberculosis of the knee joint.

gono- (gon′o) [Gr. *gonē* seed]. Combining form denoting relationship to semen or seed.

gonoblennorrhea (gon″o-blen″o-re′ah). Gonorrheal conjunctivitis.

gonocampsis (gon″o-kamp′sis). Permanent flexion of the knee.

gonocele (gon′o-sēl). Spermatocele.

gonochorism (gon-ok′o-rizm) [*gono-* + Gr. *chōrizein* to separate]. Differentiation of the gonads with normal development of the reproductive organs appropriate to the sex; the opposite of hermaphroditism.

gonococcal (gon″o-kok′al). Pertaining to gonococci.

gonococcemia (gon″o-kok-se′me-ah) [L. *gonococci* + Gr. *haima* blood + *-ia*]. The presence of gonococci in the blood.

gonococci (gon″o-kok′si). Plural of *gonococcus.*

gonococcic (gon″o-kok′sik). Gonococcal.

gonococcide (gon″o-kok′sīd) [*gonococcus* + L. *caedere* to kill]. An agent that destroys gonococci.

gonococcocide (gon″o-kok′o-sīd) [*gonococcus* + L. *caedere* to kill]. Gonococcide.

gonococcus (gon″o-kok′us), pl. *gonococ′ci* [*gono-* + *coccus*]. An individual microorganism of the species *Neisseria gonorrhoeae,* the organism causing gonorrhea.

gonocyte (gon′o-sīt) [*gono-* + Gr. *kytos* hollow vessel]. 1. The primitive reproductive cell of the embryo. 2. A secondary gamete-producing cell.

gonocytoma (gon″o-si-to′mah). A tumor derived from gonocytes.

gonodeviation (gon″o-de″ve-a′shun). The complement-deviation reaction for gonorrheal infections.

gonohemia (gon″o-he′me-ah) [*gonorrhea* + Gr. *haima* blood + *-ia*]. General gonorrheal infection.

gonomery (gon-om′er-e) [*gono-* + Gr. *meros* part]. The condition in which the paternal and the maternal chromosomes remain in separate groups and do not completely fuse, as occurs in certain hybrids.

gononephrotome (gon″o-nef′ro-tōm) [*gono-* + Gr. *nephros* kidney + *tomē* section]. That part of the mesoderm which develops into the reproductive and excretory organs of the embryo.

gonophage (gon′o-fāj). The bacteriophage elaborated by the gonococcus in culture.

gonophore (gon′o-fōr) [*gono-* + Gr. *phoros* bearing]. An accessory generative organ, such as the uterine tube and uterus, in the female, or spermiduct and seminal vesicle, in the male.

gonorrhea (gon″o-re′ah) [*gono-* + Gr. *rhein* to flow]. A contagious catarrhal inflammation of the genital mucous membrane, transmitted chiefly by coitus, and due to *Neisseria gonorrhoeae.* The disease is marked by pain, ardor urinae, and a mucopurulent discharge; there may be complications, such as prostatitis, epididymitis, orchitis, cystitis, etc. It may also produce arthritis and endocarditis.

gonorrheal (gon″o-re′al). Of or pertaining to gonorrhea.

gonotokont (gon″o-to′kont). Auxocyte.

gonotome (gon′o-tōm) [*gono-* + Gr. *tomē* section]. That part of the mesoderm which develops into the reproductive organs of the embryo.

gonotoxemia (gon″o-tok-se′me-ah). Toxemia caused by gonococcus infection.

gonotoxic (gon″o-tok′sik). Due to gonorrheal infection or to the toxin of gonococcus.

gonotoxin (gon″o-tok′sin). The toxin of the gonococcus.

gony- (gon′e) [Gr. *gony* knee]. Combining form denoting relationship to the knee.

Gonyaulax (gon″e-aw′laks). A genus of protozoa. **G. catanel′la,** a poisonous flagellate protozoon which may cause mussel poisoning and which helps to form the destructive red tide in the ocean.

gonycampsis (gon″e-kamp′sis) [*gony-* + Gr. *kampsis* bending]. Abnormal curvature of the knee.

gonycrotesis (gon″e-kro-te′sis) [*gony-* + Gr. *krotēsis* striking]. Genu valgum.

gonyectyposis (gon″e-ek″tĭ-po′sis) [*gony-* + Gr. *ektypōsis* a modelling in relief]. Genu varum.

gonyocele (gon′e-o-sēl″) [*gony-* + Gr. *kēlē* tumor]. Synovitis or tuberculous arthritis of the knee.

gonyoncus (gon″e-ong′kus) [*gony-* + Gr. *onkos* bulk]. Tumor of the knee.

Goodell's sign (good′elz) [William *Goodell,* American gynecologist, 1829–1894]. See under *sign.*

Goodpasture's stain (good-pas′churs) [Ernest William *Goodpasture,* American pathologist, 1886–1960]. See *Table of Stains and Staining Methods,* under *stain.*

Goormaghtigh apparatus, cells [Norbert *Goormaghtigh,* Belgian physician, 1890–1960]. See under *apparatus.*

Gordiacea (gor″de-a′se-ah). An order of the Nemathelminthes commonly called "horse hair" or "hair eels."

Gordius (gor′de-us) [Gordian knot]. A genus of the Gordiacea, the hair snakes or horsehair worms. **G. aquat′icus, G. medinen′sis,** *Dracunculus medinensis.* **G. robus′tus,** a species found as a parasite in man, which apparently causes intestinal and nervous symptoms.

Gordon (gor′don), Alexander (1752–1799). Scottish obstetrician who, in his *Treatise on the Epidemic Puerperal Fever of Aberdeen* (1795), first demonstrated the contagiousness of this disease.

Gordon's bodies, test (gor′donz) [Mervyn Henry *Gordon,* English physician, 1872–1953]. See under *body* and *tests.*

Gordon's reflex, sign (gor′donz) [Alfred *Gordon,* American neurologist, 1874–1953]. See *flexor reflex, paradoxical,* under *reflex,* and *finger phenomenon,* def. 1, under *phenomenon.*

Gordon's sign (gor′donz) [William *Gordon,* English physician, 1863–1929]. Cardiac sign.

gorget (gor′jet). A wide-grooved lithotome director.

gorondou (go-ron′doo). Goundou.

Goslee tooth (goz′le) [Hart J. *Goslee,* American dentist, 1871–1930]. See under *tooth.*

Gosselin's fracture (gos-laz′) [Léon Athanase *Gosselin,* French surgeon, 1815–1887]. See under *fracture.*

gossypii (gŏ-sip′e-i) [L.]. Genitive of *gossypium.* **g. radi′cis cor′tex,** cotton root bark.

Gossypium (gŏ-sip′e-um) [L.]. A genus of malvaceous plants; cotton plants. The bark of the root of various species (*cotton root bark*) is diuretic, emmenagogic, and oxytocic. See *cotton, cotton oil.*

gossypium (gŏ-sip′e-um), gen. *gossyp′ii* [L.]. Cotton. **g. asep′ticum, g. depura′tum, g. purifica′tum,** purified cotton.

gossypol (gos′ĭ-pol). A yellow pigment found in cottonseed.

GOT. Abbreviation for *glutamic-oxalacetic transaminase.*

Göthlin's index, test (get′linz) [Gustaf *Göthlin,* Swedish physiologist]. See under *tests.*

Gottlieb's epithelial attachment (got′lēbz) [Bernhard *Gottlieb,* Vienna dentist, 1885–1950]. The epithelial tissue which attaches the gingiva to the surface of a tooth.

Gottschalk's operation (got′shalks) [Sigmund *Gottschalk,* German surgeon, 1860–1914]. See under *operation.*

Gottstein's fibers, process (got′stīnz) [Jacob *Gottstein,* otologist in Breslau, 1832–1895]. See under *fiber* and *process.*

gouge (gowj). A hollow chisel used in cutting and removing bone.

Gougerot's syndrome (goo″zher-ōz′) [Henri *Gougerot,* French dermatologist, 1881–1955]. See under *syndrome.*

Goulard's extract, lotion, water (goo-larz′) [Thomas *Goulard,* French surgeon, 1724–1784]. See *lead subacetate solution* and *diluted lead subacetate solution.*

Gould's sign (go͞oldz) [George Milbry *Gould,* American ophthalmologist, 1848–1922]. See under *sign.*

Gould's suture (go͞oldz) [Sir Alfred Pearce *Gould,* English surgeon, 1852–1922]. See under *suture.*

Gouley's catheter (goo′lēz) [John Williams Severin *Gouley,* American surgeon, 1832–1920]. See under *catheter.*

goundou (go͞on′doo). Osteoplastic periostitis of the nose: a disease seen in the natives of Central Africa and South America, and marked by headache, purulent nasal discharge, and the formation of symmetrical painless swellings (bony exostoses) at the sides of the nose. It is thought to be a sequel of yaws. Called also *henpue, gundo, henpuys,* and *anakhré.*

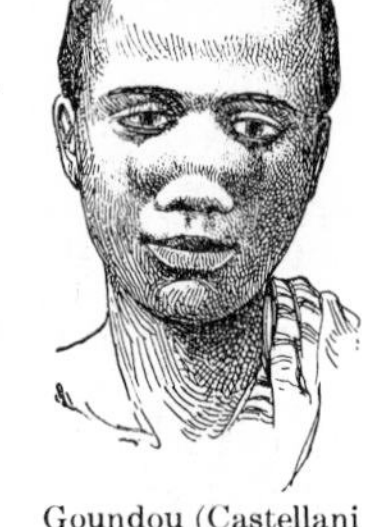
Goundou (Castellani and Chalmers).

gousiekte (goo-sek′te) [Dutch "rapid disease"]. A condition in sheep marked by myocarditis, dilatation and heart failure, caused by eating the poisonous plant *Vangueria pygmora.*

gout (gowt) [L. *gutta* a drop, because of the ancient belief that the disease was due to a "noxa" falling drop by drop into the joint]. A condition characterized by perversion of the purine metabolism, by an excess of uric acid in the blood, by attacks of acute arthritis and by the formation of chalky deposits in the cartilages of the joints, which deposits, however, consist mostly of urates. Called also *podagra.* **abarticular g.,** that which does not affect the joints. **articular g.,** gout affecting the joints. **calcium g.,** calcinosis. **chalky g.,** tophaceous g. **irregular g.,** abarticular g. **latent g., masked g.,** lithemia without the typical features of gout. **lead g.,** gout ascribed to lead poisoning. **lipoid g.,** xanthoma tuberosum. **misplaced g.,** gout in which the arthritic symptoms have disappeared and are followed by severe constitutional disturbances. **oxalic g.,** oxalism. **polyarticular g.,** an atypical form of gout which attacks many joints and which resembles rheumatic fever in that an attack may last for weeks. **poor man's g.,** gout ascribed to hard work, exposure, ill feeding, and excess in the use of malt liquors. **regular g.,** articular g. **retrocedent g.,** misplaced g. **rheumatic g.,** atrophic arthritis. **saturnine g.,** lead g. **tophaceous g.,** gout in which there are tophi or chalky deposits of sodium urate. **visceral g.,** a disease of hens due to vitamin A deficiency and curable by the administration of carotene or cod liver oil.

gouty (gow′te). Affected with, or of the nature of, gout.

Gowers' column, contraction, process, tract, etc. (gow′erz) [Sir William R. *Gowers,* English neurologist, 1845–1915]. See under the nouns.

Goyrand's hernia (gwar-ahndz′) [Jean Gaspar Blaise *Goyrand,* French surgeon, 1803–1866]. See under *hernia.*

G.P. Abbreviation for *general paresis* and *general practitioner.*

G.P.I. Abbreviation for *general paralysis of the insane.*

GPT. Abbreviation for *glutamic-pyruvic transaminase.*

gr. Abbreviation for *grain.*

graafian follicle, vesicle (graf′e-an) [Reijnier (Regner) de *Graaf,* a celebrated Dutch physician and anatomist, 1641–1673]. See *folliculi ovarici vesiculosi.*

gracile (gras′il) [L. *gracilis*]. Slender or delicate.

Grad. Abbreviation for L. *grada'tim,* by degrees.

gradatim (gra-da′tim) [L.]. Gradually; by degrees.

Gradenigo's syndrome (grah-dĕ-ne′gōz) [Giuseppe *Gradenigo,* Italian physician, 1859–1926]. See under *syndrome.*

gradient (gra′de-ent). The rate of increase or decrease of a variable magnitude; also the curve which represents it. **axial g.** 1. The topographical variation in the rate of metabolism. 2. Development in the direction of the axis of the body or of any of its parts in relation to the rate of metabolism in the various parts. **physiologic g.,** a line of decreasing intensity of vital reactions to stimulation.

graduate (grad′u-āt) [L. *graduatus*]. 1. A person who has received a degree from a university or college. 2. A measuring vessel marked by a series of lines.

graduated (grad′u-āt-ed) [L. *gradus* step]. Marked by a succession of lines, steps, or degrees.

Graefe's disease, sign, etc. (gra′fēz) [Albrecht von *Graefe,* German ophthalmologist, 1828–1870]. See under *disease* and *sign.*

Grafenberg ring (graf′en-burg) [Ernst *Grafenberg,* German gynecologist in United States, born 1881]. See under *ring.*

graft (graft). A slip of skin or of other tissue for implantation. **accordion g.,** a full-thickness graft in which multiple slits have been made so that the graft may be stretched to cover a large area. **activated g.,** hyperplastic g. **animal g.,** a graft of tissue transferred from one of the lower animals to man. Called also *zooplastic g.* **autodermic g., auto-epidermic g.,** a skin graft taken from the patient's own body. **autologous g.,** autograft. **avascular g.,** a graft of tissue in which not even transient vascularization is achieved. **Blair-Brown g.,** a split skin graft of intermediate thickness. **bone g.,** a piece of bone taken from an animal or from some bone of the patient and used to take the place of a removed bone or bony defect. **Braun g.,** a thick skin graft. **Braun-Wangensteen g.,** implanted grafts of skin cut from a large graft. **brephoplastic g.,** the transplantation of tissue from an embryo or newborn to an adult animal. **cable g.,** a nerve graft made up of several sections of nerve in the manner of a cable. **chorio-allantoic g.,** the placing of cells, tissues or parts on the chorio-allantoic membrane of the embryonic chick. **cutis g.,** skin from which epidermis and subcutaneous fat have been removed, used instead of fascia in various plastic procedures. **Davis g.,** pinch g. **delayed g.,** a graft or flap of skin which is sutured back into its bed and subsequently shifted. **dermic g.,** a graft composed of a bit of the derma, or true skin. **double-end g.,** a pedicle graft or rope graft. **Douglas's g.,** sieve g. **Dragstedt g.,** accordion g. **epidermic g.,** a piece of epidermis implanted upon a raw surface. **Esser g.,** a full-thickness graft applied by spreading the graft over a mold of Stent preparation and suturing the graft and mold into a prepared pocket. **fascia g.,** a graft taken from the fascia lata or from the lumbar fascia. **fascicular g.,** a nerve graft in which the bundles of nerve fibers are approximated and sutured separately. **fat g.,** a graft of fat freed from its bed: used in filling depressions. **free g.,** a graft of tissue completely freed from its bed. **full-thickness g.,** a skin graft consisting of the full thickness of the skin, with none of the subcutaneous tissue. **gauntlet g.,** pedicle g. **Gillies' g.,** rope g. **heterodermic g.,** a skin graft taken from the body of a person other than the patient. **heterologous g.,** heterograft. **homologous g.,** homograft. **hyperplastic g.,** a skin graft which is in a state of active repair, as in recovery from inflammation. **implantation g.,** a graft in which small pieces of skin are embedded in granulation tissue. **island g.,** a flap of skin and subcutaneous tissue with a pedicle containing the nutrient vessels. **isologous g.,** isograft. **jump g.,** a pedicle graft transferred from one location to another in successive stages. **Krause-Wolfe g.,** a graft of full thickness of the skin. **lamellar g.,** replacement of the superficial layers of an opaque cornea by a thin layer of clear cornea from a donor eye. **Ollier-Thiersch g.,** a very thin graft including the epidermis and nearly always some of the derma. **omental g's,** strips of omentum to cover the line of enterorrhaphy. **osseous g.,** bone g. **pedicle g.,** a graft consisting of the full thickness of the skin and the subcutaneous tissue attached by a pedicle. **penetrating g.,** a full-thickness corneal transplant. **periosteal g.,** a piece of periosteum applied to a denuded area of a bone. **pinch g.,** a piece of skin about ¼ in. in diameter, obtained by elevating the skin with a needle and slicing it off with a knife. The thickness of the graft may vary, but it is always free of fat. **Reverdin g.,** epidermic g. **rope g.,** a graft made by elevating a long strip of tissue from its bed except at the two extremities, the cut edges then being sutured together to form a tube. **seed g.,** implantation g. **sieve g.,** a graft in which the portion of skin to be removed has had circular islands cut out of it, these islands being left on the donor area. **skin g.,** a bit of skin implanted to replace a lost part of the integument. **sleeve g.,** a graft for repairing traumatic gaps in nerves by a sleevelike extension from the distal stump which is sutured to the central stump. **split-skin g.,** a skin graft consisting of only half the skin thickness. **Stent g.,** Esser g. **thick-split g.,** a skin graft cut in large pieces, often including about two thirds of the full thickness of the skin. **Thiersch's g.,** Ollier-Thiersch g. **thyroid g.,** a piece of the thyroid body implanted in the tissues as a remedy for myxedema. **tube g., tunnel g.,** rope g. **white g.,** avascular g. **Wolfe's g., Wolfe-Krause g.,** Krause-Wolfe g. **zooplastic g.,** animal g.

grafting (graft'ing). The implantation of skin or other tissue, from a different site or source, to replace damaged structures.

Graham's law (gra'amz) [Thomas *Graham*, English chemist, 1805–1869]. See under *law*.

Graham's test (gra'amz) [Evarts Ambrose *Graham*, American surgeon, 1883–1957]. See under *test*.

Graham Steell murmur (gra'am stēl) [Graham *Steell*, English physician, 1851–1942]. See under *murmur*.

Grahamella (gra″am-el'lah). A genus of the family Bartonellaceae, order Rickettsiales, made up of Bartonella-like microorganisms, and occurring as two species, *G. peromys'ci* and *G. tal'pae*, infecting deer mice and moles, respectively.

grahamellosis (gra″am-el-o'sis). Infection with organisms of the genus *Grahamella*.

grain (grān) [L. *gra'num*]. 1. A seed, especially of a cereal plant. 2. The twentieth part of a scruple: 0.065 gram. **cayenne pepper g's,** brown crystals of uric acid in the urine. **V-shaped g's,** a system of separate grains of colorable material (each grain united with an achromatic thread) in the ovum.

grainage (grān'ij). Weight in grains or parts of a grain.

gram (gram) [Fr. *gramme*]. The basic unit of mass (weight) of the metric system, being the equivalent of 15.432 grains. Abbreviated G. or Gm.

-gram (gram') [Gr. *gramma* that which is written; a mark]. Word termination meaning that which is written or recorded.

Gram's method, stain, solution (gramz) [Hans Christian Joachim *Gram*, Danish physician, 1853–1938]. See *Table of Stains and Staining Methods*, under *stain*, and also under *solution*.

gramicidin (gram″ĭ-si'din). An antibacterial substance produced by the growth of *Bacillus brevis*, one of the two principal components of tyrothricin. Called also *gramicidin D*.

gramine (gram'in). A crystalline indole alkaloid, $C_{11}H_{14}N_2$, from barley.

graminin (gram'ĭ-nin). A fructosan from rye flour.

gram-ion (gram-i'on). A quantity of an ion whose weight in grams in numerically equal to the atomic weight of the ion.

gramme (gram) [Fr.]. Gram.

grammeter (gram'me-ter). A unit of work, representing the energy expended in raising 1 Gm. of weight 1 meter vertically against gravitational force. It is one thousandth of a kilogrammeter, or about 98,000 ergs.

grammole (gram'mol). Gram-molecule.

gram-molecule (gram-mol'ĕ-kūl). As many grams of a substance as are numerically equal to its molecular weight.

gram-negative (gram-neg'ah-tiv). Losing the stain or decolorized by alcohol in Gram's method of staining, a primary characteristic of certain microorganisms (see Table).

gram-positive (gram-poz'ĭ-tiv). Retaining the stain or resisting decolorization by alcohol in Gram's method of staining, a primary characteristic of certain microorganisms (see Table).

TABLE OF GRAM-NEGATIVE AND GRAM-POSITIVE BACTERIA
(After Waksman and Schatz)

Gram-Negative

Aerobacter aerogenes	Neisseria intracellularis
Brucella abortus	Pasteurella lepiseptica
Brucella melitensis	Pasteurella pestis
Brucella suis	Pasteurella tularensis
Eberthella typhi	Proteus vulgaris
Escherichia coli	Pseudomonas aeruginosa
Escherichia communior	Salmonella aertrycke
Hemophilus influenzae	Salmonella enteritidis
Hemophilus pertussis	Salmonella schottmülleri
Klebsiella ozogenes	Salmonella suipestifer
Klebsiella pneumoniae	Shigella paradysenteriae
Malleomyces mallei	Vibrio comma
Neisseria gonorrhoeae	

Gram-Positive

Actinomyces bovis	Erysipelothrix muriseptica
Bacillus anthracis	Mycobacterium tuberculosis
Clostridium butyricum	Staphylococcus aureus
Clostridium septicum	Streptococcus faecalis
Clostridium sordelli	Strept. hemolyticus
Clostridium tetani	Strept. lactis
Clostridium welchii	Strept. salivarius
Corynebacterium diphtheriae	Strept. viridans
Diplococcus pneumoniae	

granatonin (gran-ah-to'nin). Pseudopelletierin.

granatum (grah-na'tum), gen. *grana'ti* [L.]. Pomegranate.

Grancher's disease, system (grahn-shāz) [Jacques Joseph *Grancher*, French physician, 1843–1907]. See under *disease* and *system*.

grandiosity (gran″de-os'ĭ-te). A condition characterized by delusions of grandeur.

grand mal (grahn mahl). See *epilepsy*.

Grandry's corpuscles (grahn'drēz) [French anatomist of the 19th century]. See under *corpuscle*.

Granger line, sign (grān′jer) [Amedee *Granger,* New Orleans radiologist, 1879–1939]. See under *line* and *sign.*

granoplasm (gran′o-plazm). Granular protoplasm.

Granström's sign (gran′stremz) [K. O. *Granström,* British ophthalmologist]. See under *sign.*

granula (gran′u-lah), pl. *gran′ulae* [L.]. Granule, def. 2.

granular (gran′u-lar) [L. *granularis*]. Made up of or marked by presence of granules or grains.

granulase (gran′u-lās). A ferment thought to be present in grain and to have the power of splitting starch into achroodextrin and maltose.

granulatio (gran″u-la′she-o), pl. *granulatio′nes* [L.]. A granule, or granular mass. **granulatio′nes arachnoidea′les** [N A], **granulatio′nes arachnoidea′les [Pacchio′ni]** [B N A], enlarged arachnoid villi, visible to the naked eye, projecting into the venous sinuses and creating slight depressions on the inner surface of the cranium. Called also *arachnoidal granulations.* **granulatio′nes cerebra′les, granulatio′nes pacchio′ni,** granulationes arachnoideales.

granulation (gran″u-la′shun) [L. *granulatio*]. 1. The division of hard or metallic substances into small particles. 2. The formation in wounds of small, rounded, fleshy masses; also a mass so formed. 3. A small, round, abnormal mass of lymphoid tissue, as on the conjunctiva of the lids or within the pharynx. **arachnoidal g's,** granulationes arachnoideales. **Bayle's g's,** gray tubercular nodules of the lung that have undergone fibroid degeneration. **Bright's g's,** the granulations of large white kidney. **cell g's,** small masses seen in the cytoplasm of certain cells that give the latter a characteristic appearance when stained. See the various granules, under *granule.* **exuberant g's,** excessive proliferation of granulation tissue in the healing of a wound. **pacchionian g's,** granulationes arachnoideales. **pyroninophilic g's,** structures seen in liver and other cells, which stain red with methyl green–pyronine by Pappenheim's stain. They are one of the early effects of carbon tetrachloride poisoning. **Virchow's g's,** granulations containing ependymal and glia fibers, found in the walls of the cerebral ventricles in general paralysis.

granulationes (gran″u-la″she-o′nēz) [L.]. Plural of *granulatio.*

granule (gran′ūl) [L. *granulum*]. 1. A small particle or grain. 2. A small pill made from sucrose. **acidophil g's,** granules staining with acid dyes. **agminated g's,** small protoplasmic particles occurring in the blood, supposed to be disintegrated blood corpuscles. **albuminous g's,** granules seen in the cytoplasm of many normal cells, which optically disappear on the addition of acetic acid, but are not affected by ether or chloroform. **aleuronoid g's,** colorless myeloid colloidal bodies found in the base of pigment cells. **alpha g's.** 1. The coarse, highly refractive, eosinophil granules of leukocytes. They are composed of albuminous matter. Called also *eosinophil g's* and *oxyphil g's.* 2. The acidophil granules in the cells of the hypophysis. **Altmann's g's,** mitochondria. **amphophil g's,** beta g's. **argentaffine g's,** granules which stain with silver. **azur g., azurophil g.,** a granule which stains easily with azure dyes; they are coarse reddish granules and are seen in many lymphocytes. **Babes-Ernst g's,** metachromatic g's. **Balfour's infective g.,** a small refractive granule seen in the red blood corpuscles in spirochetosis of fowls. **basal g.,** blepharoplast. **basophil g's,** granules staining with basic dyes. **beta g's,** presecretion granules found in the hypophysis and pancreatic islands. **Bettelheim's g's,** small mobile granules seen in the blood. **Bollinger's g's.** 1. Bollinger's bodies. 2. Small yellowish-white granules in mulberry-like masses, containing micrococci, seen in the granulation tissue of botryomycosis. **Bütschli's g's,** swellings on the bipolar rays of the amphiaster in the ovum. **carbohydrate g's,** particles of carbohydrate matter in the body fluids in the course of being assimilated. **chromatic g's, chromophilic g's,** Nissl's bodies. **cone g's,** the nuclei of the visual cells of the retina in its outer nuclear layer which are connected with the cones. **cortical g's,** special structures in the cortex of the ovum of many animals, which break up during fertilization and supply the material for the development of the fertilization membrane. **cytoplasmic g's,** albuminous g's. **delta g's,** fine basophilic granules occurring in the lymphocytes. **Dioscorides' g.,** a granule of lactose and gum arabic with arsenious acid. **Ehrlich's g's, Ehrlich-Heinz g's,** cell granules which stain with Ehrlich's triacid stain. **elementary g's,** hemokoniae. **eosinophil g's,** granules staining with eosin. **epsilon g's,** neutrophil granules from the protoplasm of polynuclear leukocytes. **Fauvel's g's,** peribronchitic abscesses. **fuchsinophil g's,** granules staining with fuchsin. **gamma g's,** a name applied to basophilic granules found in the blood, marrow, and in the tissues. **Grawitz's g's,** minute granules seen in the red blood corpuscles in the basophilia of lead poisoning. **hyperchromatin g.,** azur g. **infective g.,** a small granular body which carries the infection in trypanosomiasis. **iodophil g's,** granules staining brown with iodine, seen in polymorphonuclear leukocytes in various acute infectious diseases. **Isaac's g's,** small highly refractive granules seen in some of the erythrocytes of normal blood: they represent the final stage in the maturation of the erythrocyte. **juxtaglomerular g's,** stainable osmophilic secretory granules present in the juxtaglomerular cells, closely resembling zymogen granules. **kappa g.,** azur g. **Kölliker's interstitial g's,** various sized granules seen in the sarcoplasm of muscle fibers. **Kretz's g's,** granules found in the liver in cirrhosis. **Langley's g's,** granules seen in secreting serous glands. **meningeal g's,** granulationes arachnoideales. **metachromatic g's,** nucleoprotein granules, present in many bacterial cells, which have an avidity for basic dyes and cause irregular staining of the cell. **Mezei g's,** spherical brownish granules seen in smears from the lesions of cutaneous actinomycosis. **Much's g's,** granules and rods found in tuberculous sputum which do not stain by the usual processes for acid-fast bacilli, but do stain with Gram stain; regarded as modified tubercle bacilli. **Neusser's g's,** basophil granules seen about the nuclei of leukocytes. **neutrophil g's,** epsilon g's. **Nissl's g's,** Nissl's bodies. **oxyphil g's,** acidophil g's. **pigment g's,** small masses of coloring matter occurring in pigment cells. **Plehn's g's,** basophil granules in the conjugating form of malarial parasite. **polar g's,** metachromatic g's. **protein g's,** minute particles of various proteins, some anabolic and others catabolic. **rod g's,** the nuclei of rod visual cells in the outer nuclear layer of the retina which are connected with the rods. **Schridde's g's,** granules similar to Altmann's granules, but smaller, found in plasma cells and lymphocytes. **Schrön's g.,** a small body, of doubtful origin, seen in the germinal spot of the ovum. **Schrön-Much g's,** Much's g's. **Schüffner's g's,** Schüffner's dots. **Schüle's g's,** Plehn's g's. **secretory g's,** granules in secretory cells which apparently represent material that helps to form the secretion. **seminal g's,** the small granular bodies seen in the spermatic fluid. **sphere g.,** a large granular cell or corpuscle seen in serous exudation. **sulfur g's,** peculiar granular bodies of a yellow color found in actinomycotic lesions and discharges. **thread g's,** mitochondria. **toxic g's,** basophilic cytoplasmic granules appearing in the leukocytes in cases of infection. **volutin g's,** metachromatic g's. **zymogen g's,** secretory granules in certain cells, containing the antecedents of enzymes that become active after they have left the cell.

granuliform (gran′u-lĭ-form). In the form of, or resembling, small grains.

granulitis (gran″u-li′tis). Miliary tuberculosis.

granulo-adipose (gran″u-lo-ad′ĭ-pōs). Showing fatty degeneration which contains granules of fat.

granuloblast (gran′u-lo-blast). An embryonic blood cell containing granules and developing into a granulocyte.

granuloblastosis (gran″u-lo-blas-to′sis). A disease of fowl marked by an increase in the circulating blood of immature blood cells of the granular series. There may be infiltration of the liver or spleen.

granulocorpuscle (gran″u-lo-kor′pus-l). A small corpuscle observed in the infected tissue of venereal lymphogranuloma.

granulocyte (gran′u-lo-sit) [*granular* + Gr. *kytos* hollow vessel]. Any cell containing granules, especially a leukocyte containing neutrophil, basophil or eosinophil granules in its cytoplasm. **band-form g.,** a stage in the development of the granulocytic leukocyte, in which the nuclear indentation is more than half the width of the hypothetical round nucleus, and its opposite ends become approximately parallel for an appreciable distance.

granulocytemia (gran″u-lo-si-te′me-ah). The presence of an excess of granulocytes in the blood. **dysplastic g.,** qualitative dysfunction of the neutrophil leukocytes.

granulocytopenia (gran″u-lo-si″to-pe′ne-ah) [*granulocyte* + Gr. *penia* poverty]. Deficiency of granulocytes in the blood.

granulocytopoiesis (gran″u-lo-si″to-poi-e′sis). The production of granulocytes.

granulocytopoietic (gran″u-lo-si″to-poi-et′ik). Pertaining to, characterized by, or stimulating granulocytopoiesis.

granulocytosis (gran″u-lo-si-to′sis). An abnormally large number of granulocytes in the blood.

granulofatty (gran″u-lo-fat′e). Granulo-adipose.

granulofilocyte (gran″u-lo-fil′o-sīt) [*granule* + *filum* thread + Gr. *kytos* hollow vessel]. A reticulocyte.

granuloma (gran″u-lo′mah). A tumor or neoplasm made up of granulation tissue (Virchow). **amebic g.,** granulomatous lesions of the colon sometimes seen in amebiasis. **g. annula′re,** a granuloma consisting of hard, reddish nodules arranged in a circle which enlarge until they form a ring. **benign g. of thyroid,** a chronic inflammation of the thyroid gland which changes it into a bulky tumor which later becomes extremely hard. **coccidioidal g.,** the secondary, progressive, chronic (granulomatous) stage of coccidioidomycosis. **dental g.,** a mass of granulation tissue usually surrounded by a fibrous sac continuous with the periodontal membrane and attached to the apex of a root; thought to be the result of a chronic periapical abscess. **Durck's g.,** malarial g. **g. endem′icum,** cutaneous leishmaniasis. **eosinophilic g.,** a type of xanthomatosis characterized by the presence of rarefactions or cysts in one or more bones and sometimes associated with eosinophilia. **g. fissura′tum,** a peculiar circumscribed, firm, whitish, fissured, fibrotic granuloma of the gum and buccal mucosa, occurring in the fold between the jaw and cheek. **g. fungoi′des,** mycosis fungoides. **g. gangraenes′cens,** a condition beginning with the formation of proliferating granulations in the nasal mucous membrane which invade the adjacent tissues and soon become gangrenous. **Hodgkins' g.,** Hodgkin's disease. **infectious g.,** granuloma caused by a specific microorganism, as tubercle. **g. inguina′le,** a granulomatous venereal disease characterized by deep purulent ulcerations of the skin of the external genitals, caused by *Donovania granulomatis;* prevalent in the tropics of North and South America and India, affecting especially dark-skinned people. Called also *granuloma venereum, pudendal ulcer,* and *ulcerating granuloma of the pudenda.* **g. i′ridis,** a nonmalignant and highly vascular growth of the iris, of various forms. **lipoid g.,** a granuloma containing lipoid cells; xanthoma. **lipophagic g.,** a granuloma attended by the loss of subcutaneous fat. **lycopodium g.,** a granulomatous lesion developing after an operation as a result of the introduction of lycopodium spores into the operative field. **Majocchi's g.,** a condition characterized by the development of nodules at the borders of rather indistinct scaling patches on the lower half of the lower leg, caused by *Trichophyton rubrum* infection; after persisting for three or four months the lesions are slowly absorbed, or undergo necrosis, leaving a depressed scar. **malarial g.,** a granulomatous lesion sometimes seen in the brain in fatal cases of cerebral malaria. **malignant g., g. malig′num,** Hodgkin's disease. **Mignon's eosinophilic g.,** a solitary destructive lesion affecting the skull and other bones of children and young adults. **paracoccidioidal g.,** South American blastomycosis. **peripheral giant cell reparative g.,** a pedunculated or sessile lesion apparently arising from periodontal membrane or mucoperiosteum, and usually resulting from trauma, such as tooth extraction, or denture irritation. **g. puden′di,** granuloma inguinale. **g. pyogen′icum,** a fungating pedunculated growth in which the granulations consist of masses of pyogenic organisms: called also *septic g.* and *botryomycosis hominis.* **rheumatic g's,** nodules occurring in various parts of the body in rheumatism. **g. sarcomato′des,** mycosis fungoides. **septic g.,** granuloma pyogenicum. **g. telangiectat′icum,** a form characterized by numerous dilated blood vessels. **trichophytic g., g. trichophyt′icum,** a variety consisting of round or flat nodules, from a rose red to a cyanotic hue, disseminated or arranged in chains, and caused by a trichophyton. **g. trop′icum,** yaws. **ulcerating g. of the pudenda,** granuloma inguinale. **venereal g., g. vene′reum,** granuloma inguinale. **Wegener's g.,** a progressive disease, characterized by granulomatous lesions of the respiratory tract, focal necrotizing arteriolitis, and, finally, widespread inflammation of all the organs of the body.

granulomatosis (gran″u-lo″mah-to′sis). The formation of multiple granuloma. **lipoid g.,** xanthomatosis. **malignant g.,** Hodgkin's disease. **g. siderot′ica,** a condition in which brownish nodules (Gamna nodules) are seen in the enlarged spleen.

granulomatous (gran″u-lom′ah-tus). Composed of granulomas.

granulomere (gran′u-lo-mēr). The center portion of a platelet in a dry, stained blood smear, apparently filled with fine purplish red granules, thought possibly to be an artefact. Cf. *hyalomere.*

granulopectic (gran″u-lo-pek′tik). Pertaining to or characterized by granulopexis.

granulopenia (gran″u-lo-pe′ne-ah). Granulocytopenia.

granulopexis (gran″u-lo-pek′sis) [*granulo-* + Gr. *pēxis* fixation]. The fixation of granules.

granulopexy (gran′u-lo-pek″se). Granulopexis.

granulophilocyte (gran″u-lo-fil′o-sīt). A circulating reticulocyte.

granulophthisis (gran″u-lo-thi′sis) [*granulo-* + Gr. *phthisis* wasting]. Degeneration or destruction of the granulopoietic tissue.

granuloplasm (gran′u-lo-plazm). Entosarc.

granuloplastic (gran″u-lo-plas′tik) [*granule* + Gr. *plassein* to form]. Forming granules.

granulopoiesis (gran″u-lo-poi-e′sis) [*granulocyte* + Gr. *poiein* to make]. The formation of granulocytes.

granulopoietic (gran″u-lo-poi-et′ik). Pertaining to or concerned in the formation of granulocytes.

granulopotent (gran″u-lo-po′tent). Capable of forming granules.

granulosa (gran″u-lo′sah). Membrana granulosa.

granulosarcoid (gran″u-lo-sar′koid). Mycosis fungoides.

granulosarcoma (gran″u-lo-sar-ko′mah). Mycosis fungoides.

granulose (gran′u-lōs). 1. The more soluble portion of starch. See *amylose.* 2. A bacterial polysaccharide occurring as cytoplasmic granules and staining red to blue with iodine.

granulosis (gran″u-lo′sis). The formation of a mass of granules. **g. ru′bra na′si,** a disease of the skin of the nose, which sometimes extends to the cheeks, marked by a bright red color of the part, over which are scattered reddish specks and papules. It is associated with hyperhidrosis of the area and is due to chronic inflammation of the vessels around the sweat glands.

granulosity (gran″u-los′ĭ-te). A mass of granulations.

granulotherapy (gran″u-lo-ther′ah-pe). The production of hyperleukocytosis by the intravenous injection of carbon or other material: for the treatment of infectious processes.

granum (gra′num), pl. *gra′na* [L.]. Grain.

grapes (grāps). 1. Granulations forming in severe cases of grease-heel in horses. 2. Bovine tuberculosis. **Carswell's g's,** tuberculous infiltration distributed in masses around the smaller bronchi like bunches of grapes: seen in pulmonary tuberculosis.

graph (graf) [Gr. *graphein* to write, or record]. A diagram or curve representing clinical or experimental data. Often used as a word termination denoting an instrument for writing or recording.

graphesthesia (graf″es-the′ze-ah) [Gr. *graphein* to write + *aisthēsis* perception]. The sense by which are recognized figures or numbers written on the skin.

graphic (graf′ik) [Gr. *graphein* to write]. Written or drawn; pertaining to representation by diagrams.

graphite (graf′it) [L. *graphites,* from Gr. *graphis* a style, or writing instrument]. Plumbago: a form of native mineralized carbon.

grapho- (graf′o) [Gr. *graphein* to record]. Combining form denoting relationship to writing or to a record.

grapho-analysis (graf″o-ah-nal′ĭ-sis). Psychoanalysis in which the patients write out their thoughts.

graphocatharsis (graf″o-kah-thar′sis). Graphoanalysis.

graphokinesthetic (graf″o-kin″es-thet′ik) [*grapho-* + Gr. *kinein* to move + *aisthēsis* perception]. Pertaining to the sensation aroused by the act of writing.

graphology (graf-ol′o-je) [*grapho-* + *-logy*]. The study of the handwriting.

graphomania (graf″o-ma′ne-ah). An obsessive urge or desire to write.

graphomotor (graf″o-mo′tor) [*grapho-* + *motor*]. Pertaining to, or affecting, the movements required in writing.

graphopathology (graf″o-pah-thol′o-je). The study of handwriting as an indication of mental or physical disorder.

graphophobia (graf″o-fo′be-ah) [*grapho-* + *phobia*]. Abnormal dread of writing.

graphorrhea (graf″o-re′ah) [*grapho-* + Gr. *rhoia* flow]. A morbid mental condition marked by the writing of a long succession of meaningless and unconnected words.

graphoscope (graf′o-skōp) [*grapho-* + Gr. *skopein* to examine]. An instrument for treating myopia and asthenopia.

graphospasm (graf′o-spazm) [*grapho-* + Gr. *spasmos* spasm]. Writers' cramp.

-graphy (graf′e) [Gr. *graphein* to write, record]. Word termination meaning the act of writing or recording.

Graser's diverticulum (grah′serz) [Ernst *Graser,* German surgeon, 1860–1929]. See under *diverticulum.*

Grashey's aphasia (grash′ēz) [Hubert von *Grashey,* Munich psychologist, 1839–1911]. See under *aphasia.*

grass (gras). Any plant of the order Gramineae. Some of the grasses which by their pollen are important causes of hay fever are: Bermuda **g.,** *Cynodon dactylon;* June g., *Poa pratensis;* Johnson g., *Sorghum halepense;* Orchard g., *Dactylis glomerata;* Redtop g., *Agrostis alba;* Sweet vernal g., *Anthoxanthum odoratum;* and Timothy g., *Phleum pratense.* **scurvy g.,** a cruciferous plant, *Cochlearia officinalis,* once used as a remedy for scurvy.

Grasset's law, phenomenon, sign (grah-sāz′) [Joseph *Grasset,* French physician, 1849–1918]. See under *law* and *phenomenon.*

Grasset-Gaussel phenomenon (grah-sa′go-sel′) [Joseph *Grasset;* Amans *Gaussel,* French physician, 1871–1937]. Grasset's phenomenon.

gratification (grat″ĭ-fi-ka′shun). The lowering of an emotional tension which follows the fulfillment of an instinctual aim.

Gratiola (grah-ti′o-lah). A genus of plants. **G. officina′lis,** the hedge hyssop, a scrophulariaceous plant of Europe: purgative, emetic, and diuretic.

Gratiolet's optic radiation (grah-te″o-lāz′) [Louis Pierre *Gratiolet,* French anatomist, 1815–1865]. Radiatio optica.

grattage (grah-tahzh′) [Fr.]. The removal of granulations (as in trachoma) by scraping or by friction with a stiff brush.

Gräupner's test (groip′nerz) [Sigurd (Solo) *Gräupner,* German physician, 1861–1916]. See under *tests.*

grave (grāv) [L. *gravis*]. Severe or serious.

gravedo (gra-ve′do) [L.]. Cold in the head, or nasal catarrh.

gravel (grav′el). A term applied to fairly coarse concretions of mineral salts, as from the kidneys or bladder, of smaller size than the so-called stones.

Graves' disease (grāvz) [Robert James *Graves,* Irish physician, 1797–1853]. Exophthalmic goiter.

grave-wax (grāv′waks). Adipocere.

gravid (grav′id) [L. *gravida* heavy, loaded]. Pregnant; containing developing young.

gravida (grav′ĭ-dah). A pregnant woman. Called *gravida I* or *primigravida* during the first pregnancy, *gravida II* during the second pregnancy, *gravida III* during the third pregnancy, etc.

gravidic (grah-vid′ik). Occurring in pregnancy.

gravidin (grav′ĭ-din). Kyestein.

gravidism (grav′id-izm). Pregnancy, or the sum of symptoms, signs, and conditions associated with it.

graviditas (grah-vid′ĭ-tas). Pregnancy. **g. examnia′lis,** pregnancy in which the amnion has burst and is retracted around the insertion of the umbilical cord, but the chorion is intact. **g. exochoria′lis,** pregnancy in which the membranes have burst and shrunk, leaving the fetus in the uterus but outside of the chorion.

gravidity (grah-vid′ĭ-te) [L. *graviditas*]. The condition of being with child; pregnancy.

gravidocardiac (grav″ĭ-do-kar′de-ak) [L. *gravida* + Gr. *kardia* heart]. Pertaining to heart disease of pregnancy.

gravidopuerperal (grav″ĭ-do-pu-er′per-al). Pertaining to pregnancy and the puerperium.

gravimeter (grah-vim′e-ter) [L. *gravis* heavy + *metrum* measure]. An instrument for determining specific gravities.

gravimetric (grav″ĭ-met′rik). Pertaining to measurement by weight; performed by weight, as gravimetric method.

gravistatic (grav″ĭ-stat′ik). Due to gravitation, as, *gravistatic* pulmonary congestion.

gravitation (grav″ĭ-ta′shun). The force that tends to draw all bodies together.

gravitometer (grav″ĭ-tom′e-ter). A balance for measuring specific gravity.

gravity (grav′ĭ-te) [L. *gravitas*]. Weight; tendency toward the center of the earth. **specific g.,** the weight of a substance compared with that of an equal volume of another substance taken as a standard.

Grawitz's cachexia, tumor (grah′vits-ez) [Paul *Grawitz*, pathologist in Greifswald, 1850–1932]. See under *cachexia* and *tumor*.

gray (gra). 1. Of a hue between white and black. 2. The gray matter of the nervous system. **central g.,** relatively undifferentiated gray matter which retains its primitive position near the ventricles. **nervous g.,** Nissl's term for the unknown specific constituent of the gray matter of the nervous system. **silver g., steel g.,** nigrosin.

grease (grēs). An inflammatory swelling in a horse's leg in the region of the fetlocks and pasterns, with the formation of cracks in the skin and the excretion of oily matter.

grease-heel (grēs-hēl′). Grease.

green (grēn). 1. Having the color of fresh leaves or of grass. 2. A green coloring matter or dye. **acid g.,** light g. S F. **benzaldehyde g.,** malachite g. **brilliant g.,** a basic dye having powerful bacteriostatic properties for gram-positive organisms. **bromcresol g.,** an indicator used in the determination of hydrogen ion concentration, being yellow at pH 4.0 and blue at pH 5.6. **Brunswick g.,** copper subcarbonate. **chrome g.** 1. Chromium sesquioxide, Cr_2O_3. 2. A mixture of chrome yellow and prussian blue. **diazin g.,** Janus g. **ethyl g.,** brilliant g. **fast acid g. N,** light g. S F. **Hoffman g.,** iodine g. **indocyanine g.,** a dye used in tests of cardiovascular function. **iodine g.,** a dye used as a chromatin stain. **Janus g.,** a dye used as a histologic and bacteriologic stain. **Janus g. B,** an azo dye used supravitally for the demonstration of mitochondria. **light g., 2 G, 3 G, 4 G,** or **2 G N,** light g. S F. **light g. N,** malachite g. **light g. S F, yellowish,** an acid dye used as a plasma stain. **malachite g.,** a triphenylmethane dye used as a stain for bacteria and as an antiseptic for wounds. **malachite g. G,** brilliant g. **methyl g.,** a mixture of hepta and hexa methyl-pararosaniline. **methylene g.,** one of the constituents of polychrome methylene blue. It is a mononitromethylene blue, $(CH_3)_2.N.-C_6H_3(SN)C_6H_2(NO_2).N(CH_3)_2Cl$. **new solid g.,** a bacteriostatic dye, tetramethyldiaminotriphenylmethane chloride. **Paris g.,** a double salt of copper acetate and copper meta-arsenite, $Cu(C_2H_3O_2)_2.3Cu(AsO_2)_2$. **Schweinfurt g.,** Paris g. **solid g.,** malachite g. **Victoria g.,** a dye having powerful bacteriostatic properties.

Greene's sign (grēnz) [Charles Lyman *Greene*, American physician, 1863–1929]. See under *sign*.

Greenhow's disease (grēn′howz) [Edward Headlam *Greenhow*, English physician, 1814–1888]. See under *disease*.

greffotome (gref′o-tōm) [Fr. *greffe* graft + Gr. *temnein* to cut]. An instrument for cutting grafts of tissue.

gregaloid (greg′ah-loid) [L. *grex* flock + Gr. *eidos* form]. Formed by casual union of independent cells: said of a colony of protozoa.

Gregarina (greg″ah-ri′nah) [L. *gregarius*, crowding together]. A genus of Sporozoa, species of which are common parasites in the digestive tract and body cavities of insects. No species is positively known to inhabit the human body, but it is said that they are found in some cancers of the human subject.

gregarina (greg″ah-ri′nah), pl. *gregari′nae*. An organism of the genus Gregarina.

gregarine (greg′ah-rīn). Pertaining to the Gregarina.

gregarinosis (greg″ah-rĭ-no′sis). A disease condition due to infestation with gregarinae.

Gregory's powder (greg′o-rēz) [James *Gregory*, Scotch physician, 1753–1821]. See under *powder*.

grenz rays [Ger. *Grenze*, boundary]. See under *ray*.

Greve's tumor reaction or **test.** See under *tests*.

grid (grid). 1. A grating; in electricity, (*a*) a perforated lead plate for conducting current and containing the active material of the plates of a storage battery; (*b*) the control electrode of an electron tube. 2. A chart with horizontal and perpendicular lines for plotting curves. **baby g.,** a direct reading control chart on infant growth. **Wetzel g.,** a direct reading chart for evaluating physical fitness in terms of body build, developmental level, and basal metabolism.

Griesinger's disease, sign, symptom (gre′zing-erz) [Wilhelm *Griesinger*, German neurologist, 1817–1868]. See under *disease* and *sign*.

griffado (grĭ-fah′do). A person one of whose parents is white and the other a quadroon, and who thus has one-eighth Negro blood.

griffe (grēf) [Fr.]. Talon. **g. des orteils** (grēf da zor-ta′), clawfoot.

Grignard's compound, reaction, reagent (grēn-yahrz′) [François August Victor *Grignard*, French chemist, 1871–1935]. See under *reagent*.

Grindelia (grin-de′le-ah) [H. *Grindel*, 1776–1836]. A genus of American composite-flowered plants. The leaves and flowering tops of *G. camporum*, *G. cuneifolia*, and *G. squarrosa*, of the western United States, have been used in medicine.

grip (grip). 1. [Fr. *grippe*]. Influenza. 2. A grasping or seizing. **Dabney's g.,** epidemic pleurodynia. **devil's g.,** epidemic pleurodynia. **Pawlik's g.,** a grasping of the fetus through the abdominal wall in order to feel what part is situated above the pelvic brim, thus determining the progress of labor.

grippal (grip′al). Pertaining to grip, or influenza.

grippe (grip). Influenza. **g. aurique′,** a polyneuritis sometimes resulting from the therapeutic use of gold salts. **Balkan g.,** a febrile rickettsial infection occurring in the Mediterranean area. See *Q fever*.

griseofulvin (griz″e-o-ful′vin). An antibiotic substance first isolated from *Penicillium griseofulvum:* effective in the treatment of superficial fungus infections of the skin.

Grisolle's sign (gre-zolz′) [Augustin *Grisolle*, French physician, 1811–1869]. See under *sign*.

Gritti's amputation (gre′tēz) [Rocco *Gritti*, surgeon in Milan, 1857–1920]. See under *amputation*.

Gritti-Stokes amputation (gre′te stōks) [Rocco *Gritti;* Sir William Stokes]. See under *amputation*.

Grocco's sign, triangle (grok′ōz) [Pietro *Grocco*, physician in Florence, 1857–1916]. See under *sign*.

grog (grog). Navicular disease.

groin (groin) [L. *inguen*]. The lowest part of the abdominal wall, near its junction with the thigh.

Grönblad-Strandberg syndrome (gren′blad-strand′berg) [Ester *Grönblad*, Swedish ophthalmologist; James *Strandberg*, Swedish dermatologist]. See under *syndrome*.

groove (gro͞ov). 1. A shallow linear depression, especially one appearing during embryonic development or persisting in definitive bone. See also *fissure* and *sulcus*. 2. In dentistry, a linear channel or sulcus, especially on the surface of a tooth (A.D.A.). **alveolingual g.,** the groove between the lower jaw and the tongue. **anterolateral g. of medulla,** sulcus lateralis anterior medullae oblongatae. **anterolateral g. of spinal cord,** sulcus lateralis anterior medullae spinalis. **anteromedian g. of spinal cord,** fissura mediana anterior medullae spinalis. **arterial g's,** sulci arteriosi. **atrioventricular g., auriculoventricular g.,** sulcus coronarius cordis. **basilar g.,** sulcus basilaris pontis. **basilar g. of occipital bone,** clivus ossis occipitalis. **basilar g. of sphenoid bone,** clivus cranii. **bicipital g. of humerus,** sulcus intertubercularis humeri. **Blessig's g.,** a trace in the eye of the developing embryo corresponding in position with the future ora serrata. **branchial g.,** an external furrow, lined with ectoderm, occurring in the embryo between two branchial arches. **carotid g. of sphenoid bone, cavernous g. of sphenoid bone,** sulcus caroticus. **costal g.,** sulcus costae. **dental g., primitive,** a groove in the border of the jaws of the embryo. **developmental g's,** fine grooves in the enamel which mark the junction of the primitive lobes of a tooth. **digastric g.,** incisura mastoidea ossis temporalis. **enamel g's,** the grooves bounding the enamel knot. **g. for eustachian tube,** sulcus tubae auditivae. **genital g.,** urethral g. **gingival g., free,** a shallow groove on the facial surface of the gingiva, running parallel to the margin of the gingiva at a distance of 0.5 to 1.5 mm., and usually at the level of, or somewhat apical to, the bottom of the gingival sulcus. **g. of great superficial petrosal nerve,** sulcus nervi petrosi majoris. **hamular g.,** sulcus hamuli pterygoidei. **Harrison's g.,** a horizontal depression along the lower border of the chest, corresponding to the costal insertion of the diaphragm: seen in children with rickets and with chronic respiratory affections. **infraorbital g. of maxilla,** sulcus infraorbitalis maxillae. **interosseous g. of calcaneus,** sulcus calcanei. **intertubercular g. of humerus,** sulcus intertubercularis humeri. **interventricular g., anterior,** sulcus interventricularis anterior. **interventricular g., posterior,** sulcus interventricularis posterior. **labial g.,** a groove produced by degeneration of the central cells of the labial lamina, which later becomes the vestibule of the oral cavity. **lacrimal g.,** fossa sacci lacrimalis. **g. of lacrimal bone,** sulcus lacrimalis ossis lacrimalis. **laryngotracheal g.,** a furrow at the caudal end of the embryonic pharynx that develops into the respiratory tract. **lateral g. for lateral sinus of occipital bone,** sulcus sinus transversi. **lateral g. for lateral sinus of parietal bone,** sulcus sinus sigmoidei ossis parietalis. **lateral g. for sigmoidal part of lateral sinus,** sulcus sinus sigmoidei ossis temporalis. **Liebermeister's g's,** anteroposterior grooves on the surface of the liver due to irregular development. **medullary g.,** neural g. **mesal g.,** a groove on the floor of the fourth ventricle. **mesiolingual g.,** a groove over the junction of the fifth cusp on an upper molar tooth. **g. for middle temporal artery,** sulcus arteriae temporalis mediae. **musculospiral g.,** sulcus nervi radialis. **mylohyoid g. of inferior maxillary bone,** sulcus mylohyoideus mandibulae. **nail g.,** sulcus matricis unguis. **nasal g., g. for nasal nerve,** sulcus ethmoidalis ossis nasalis. **nasolacrimal g.,** an epithelial ingrowth parallel with but medial to the nasomaxillary groove of the embryo, which marks the site of later development of the nasolacrimal duct. **nasomaxillary g.,** a furrow located between the maxillary and the lateral nasal process of the same side in the embryo. **nasopalatine g.,** a furrow on the lateral surface of the vomer for the nasopalatine nerve. **nasopharyngeal g.,** a faint line between the nasal cavity and the nasopharynx. **neural g.,** the groove produced by the invagination of the neural plate during the process of formation of the neural tube. Called also *medullary g.* **obturator g.,** sulcus obturatorius ossis pubis. **occipital g.,** sulcus arteriae occipitalis. **occlusal g's,** the developmental grooves on the occlusal surface of a posterior tooth. **olfactory g.,** a groove on the cribriform plate of the ethmoid bone on each side of the crista galli for the olfactory lobe of the cerebrum. **optic g.,** sulcus chiasmatis. **palatine g., anterior,** canalis incisivus. **palatine g's of maxilla,** sulci palatini maxillae. **palatine g. of palatine bone,** sulcus palatinus major ossis palatini. **palatomaxillary g. of palatine bone,** sulcus palatinus major ossis palatini. **paraglenoid g's of hip bone,** sulci paraglenoidales ossis coxae. **paramedian g. of spinal cord, anterior,** sulcus intermedius anterior medullae spinalis. **paramedian g. of spinal cord, posterior,** sulcus intermedius posterior medullae spinalis. **posterolateral g. of spinal cord,** sulcus lateralis posterior medullae spinalis. **preauricular g's of ilium,** sulci paraglenoidales ossis coxae. **primitive g.,** a lengthwise furrow on the outer surface of the primitive streak. **pterygopalatine g. of pterygoid plate,** sulcus pterygopalatinus processus pterygoidei. **radial g., g. for radial nerve,** sulcus nervi radialis. **sagittal g.,** a groove on the inner surface of the skull for the superior longitudinal sinus. **Sibson's g.,** a furrow sometimes seen at the lower border of the pectoralis major muscle. **sigmoid g. of temporal bone,** sulcus sinus sigmoidei ossis temporalis. **g's of skin,** sulci cutis. **g. of small superficial petrosal nerve,** sulcus nervi petrosi minoris. **subclavian g.,** a furrow along the middle of the clavicle for the subclavius muscle. **subcostal g.,** sulcus costae. **g. for superior longitudinal sinus,** sulcus sagittalis ossis parietalis. **supplemental g's,** grooves on the surface of a tooth which do not mark (as do the developmental grooves) the junction of the primitive lobes of the tooth. **g. for tibialis posticus muscle,** sulcus malleolaris tibiae. **trigeminal g.,** the embryonic structure which develops into the gasserian ganglion. **ulnar g., g. of ulnar nerve,** sulcus nervi ulnaris. **urethral g.,** the urogenital groove on the primitive phallus which, in the male, becomes the urethra. **venous g's,** sulci venosi. **Verga's lacrimal g.,** a groove running downward from the lower orifice of the nasal duct. **vertebral g.,** the depression on each side of the spine.

gross (grōs) [L. *grossus* rough]. Coarse or large; macroscopic; taking no account of minutiae.

Gross's disease, pill (grōs'ez) [Samuel D. *Gross*, American surgeon, 1805–1884]. See under *disease* and *pill*.

Grossich's method (grōs'iks) [Antonio *Grossich*, surgeon in Fiume, 1849–1926]. See under *method*.

Grossman's sign (grōs'manz) [Morris *Grossman*, American neurologist, born 1881]. See under *sign*.

group (gro͞op). 1. An assemblage of objects having certain things in common. 2. A number of atoms forming a recognizable and usually a transferable portion of a molecule. **alcohol g.,** a combination of carbon, hydrogen, and oxygen atoms in a molecule which is characteristic of a chemical compound known as an alcohol. There are three: —CH_2OH, the primary, =CHOH, the secondary, and ≡COH, the tertiary alcohol group. **azo g.,** a bivalent chemical group composed of two nitrogen atoms, —N:N—. **blood g.** See *blood type*, under *B*. **coli-aerogenes g.,** a group of microorganisms which includes *Escherichia coli, Aerobacter aerogenes,* and a variety of forms intermediate between these two organisms. Called also *coliform bacilli* or *coliform bacteria*. **colon-typhoid-dysentery g.,** a group of gram-negative bacteria more or less resembling *Escherichia coli*. **complementophil g.,** the group of the amboceptor by means of which it is attached to the complement. **cytophil g.,** the group of the amboceptor by means of which it is anchored to the sensitive cell. **ergophore g.** See *ergophore*. **glucophore g.** See *glucophore*. **haptophore g.** See *haptophore*. **heboid-paranoid g.,** a group of mental disorders, including the juvenile insanities, dementia precox, and paranoia. **hemorrhagic-septicemia g.,** a group of bacteria of which *Pasteurella pestis* is the type organism. **hog cholera g.,** paratyphoid enteritidis g. **methyl g.,** a monovalent chemical group, —CH_3. **osmophore g.** See *osmophore.* **paratyphoid-enteritidis g.,** a group of organisms which cause food poisoning in man and various diseases in animals. **peptide g.,** the bivalent radical, —CO.NH—, formed by reaction between the NH_2 and COOH groups of adjacent amino acids, and by such linkage building up compounds known as di-, tri-, tetra-[etc.]peptides, depending on the number of amino acids making up the molecule. **prosthetic g.,** the non-amino acid portion of a protein molecule. **proteus g.,** a group of bacteria of which *Proteus vulgaris* is the type organism. **saccharide g.,** a combination of carbon, hydrogen, and oxygen atoms in a hypothetical molecule, $C_6H_{10}O_5$, the number of which in the compound determines the specific name of the polysaccharide, as di-, tri-, or tetrasaccharide. **salmonella g.,** paratyphoid-enteritidis group. **sapophore g.** See *sapophore.* **sulfonic g.,** a monovalent radical, —SO_2OH. **toxophore g.** See *toxophore.* **zymophore g.** See *zymophore.*

grouping (gro͝op′ing). The classification of individual entities according to certain common characteristics. **antigenic structural g.,** haptene. **blood g.,** the classification of blood according to the type to which it belongs; employed in determination of the suitability of blood for transfusion in a particular recipient, in cases of disputed paternity, and in certain criminal cases. **haptenic g.,** haptene.

group-specific (gro͝op″spě-sif′ik). Specific for a given blood group: said of agglutinins.

Grove's cell (grōv) [Sir William Robert *Grove,* English physicist, 1811–1896]. See under *cell.*

growth (grōth). 1. A normal process of increase in size, produced by accretion of tissue of a constitution similar to that originally present. 2. An abnormal formation, such as a tumor. **absolute g.,** an expression of the actual increase in size of an organism, or of a particular organ or part. **accretionary g.,** increase in size resulting from increase in number of special cells by mitotic division, other more differentiated cells which perform various physiological functions having lost the ability to proliferate. **allometric g.,** the growth of different organs or parts of an organism at different rates. **appositional g.,** growth by addition at the periphery of a particular structure or part. Cf. *interstitial g.* **auxetic g.,** increase in the size of an organism, organ, or part, resulting from increase in the size of the cells, their number remaining the same. **differential g.,** an expression of the comparison of the increases in size of dissimilar organisms, organs, or parts. **heterogonous g.,** growth of such a nature that, when it is plotted logarithmetically, it gives a straight line. **histiotypic g.,** uncontrolled growth of cells as occurs in tissue cultures. **interstitial g.,** growth occurring in the interior of parts or structures already formed. Cf. *appositional g.* **intussusceptive g.,** auxetic g. **isometric g.,** the growth of different organs or parts of an organism at the same rate. **multiplicative g.,** increase in the size of an organism, organ, or part, resulting from increase in the number of cells brought about by their mitotic division, the average size of the cells remaining about the same. **new g.,** a neoplasm, or tumor. **organotypic g.,** controlled growth of cells as occurs normally in the production of organs and parts. **postnatal g.,** growth occurring subsequent to birth. **prenatal g.,** growth occurring before birth. **relative g.,** an expression of the comparison of the increases in size of similar organisms, organs, or parts.

grübelsucht (gre′bel-so͝okt) [Ger.]. The drawing of fine distinctions (hair-splitting) in argument or in reasoning.

Gruber's bougies, speculum (groo′berz) [Josef *Gruber,* Austrian aurist, 1827–1900]. See under *bougie* and *speculum.*

Gruber's fossa (groo′berz) [Wenaslaus Leopold *Gruber,* Russian anatomist, 1814–1890]. See under *fossa.*

Gruber's reaction (groo′berz) [Max von *Gruber,* bacteriologist in Munich, 1853–1927]. See under *reaction.*

Gruby's disease (groo′bēz) [David *Gruby,* Hungarian physician in Paris, 1810–1898]. See under *disease.*

Grubyella (groo″be-el′ah). A genus of fungi. **G. ferrugin′ea,** *Microsporon ferrugineum.*

gruel (groo′el). A thin paste or porridge made of cereal grain.

gruffs (grufs). The coarse part of a drug.

grumose, grumous (groo′mōs, groo′mus) [L. *grumus* heap]. Clotted or lumpy.

Grünbaum's test (grēn′bowmz) [Albert S. *Grünbaum,* English physician, born 1869]. See under *tests.*

grundplatte (groont-plaht′tě) [Ger.]. Lamina basalis.

grutum (groo′tum) [L.]. Milium.

Grynfelt's hernia, triangle (grin′felts) [Joseph Casimir *Grynfelt,* French surgeon, 1840–1913]. See under *hernia* and *triangle.*

gryochrome (gri′o-krōm) [Gr. *gry* morsel + *chrōma* color]. A nerve cell in which the stainable matter of the cell body appears as fine granules: used also adjectively.

gryposis (grĭ-po′sis) [Gr. *grypōsis* a crooking, hooking]. Abnormal curvature. **g. pe′nis,** chordee. **g. un′guium,** onychogryposis.

GSH. Abbreviation for *reduced glutathione.*

G6PD. Abbreviation for *glucose-6-phosphate dehydrogenase.*

GSSG. Abbreviation for *oxidized glutathione.*

G.S.W. Abbreviation for *gunshot wound.*

gt. Abbreviation for L. *gut′ta,* drop.

gtt. Abbreviation for L. *gut′tae,* drops.

g.u. Abbreviation for *genitourinary.*

guaco (gwah′ko) [Spanish American]. A name given to many South American plants, and especially to *Mikania guaco:* used in asthma, dyspepsia, gout, rheumatism, and in skin diseases.

guanase (gwan′ās). A deaminizing enzyme which catalyzes the change of guanine into xanthine and ammonia.

guanazola (gwan″ah-zo′lah). A chemical compound said to check the growth of certain types of cancer in mice and to be effective against *Miyagawanella psittaci.*

guanethidine (gwan-eth′ĭ-dēn). Chemical name: [2-(octahydro-1-azocinyl) ethyl]guanidine sulfate: used as an antihypertensive.

guanidase (gwan′ĭ-dās). An enzyme formed by *Aspergillus niger,* which hydrolyzes guanidine into urea and ammonia.

guanidine (gwan′ĭ-din). A poisonous base, the amidine of amino carbamic acid, $NH:C.(NH_2)_2$. **g. hydrochloride,** a compound used in the treatment of myasthenia gravis.

guanidinemia (gwan″ĭ-din-e′me-ah). The presence of guanidine in the blood.

guanine (gwan′in). A white, crystalline base, 2-amino-6-oxypurine, $C_5H_5N_5O$, found in guano, fish scales, leguminous seedlings, and various animal tissues. It is one of the decomposition products of nuclein and occurs as a white deposit in the tissues of swine affected with a kind of gout. **g. nucleotide,** guanylic acid.

guanophore (gwan′o-for) [*guanine* + Gr. *phoros* bearing]. A cell filled with guanine crystals which produce interference in the light and thus give the cell a silvery appearance.

guanosine (gwan′o-sin). A nucleoside, guanine riboside, $C_{10}H_{13}O_5N_5$, from the leaves and unripe berries of the coffee plant.

guarana (gwah-rah′nah) [Tupi-Guarani]. A dried paste prepared from the seeds of *Paullinia cupana,* a tree of Brazil: used as an astringent in diarrhea.

guaranine (gwah-rah′nin). Caffeine.

Guarnieri's bodies, corpuscles (gwar″ne-er′ēz) [Guiseppi *Guarnieri*, Italian physician, 1856–1918]. See under *body.*

guayule (gwi-oo′la). The Mexican rubber plant, *Parthenium argentatum*, which may produce a severe dermatitis.

gubernacular (gu″ber-nak′u-lar). Pertaining to a gubernaculum.

gubernaculum (gu″ber-nak′u-lum) [L. "helm"]. Something which guides. **chorda g.,** a portion of the gubernaculum testis and round ligament that develops in the body wall of the embryo. **g. den′tis,** a band of connective tissue connecting the dental sac of the unerupted permanent tooth with the gingiva. **Hunter's g.,** g. testis. **g. tes′tis** [N A], the fetal ligament attached to the lower end of the epididymis and to the bottom of the scrotum that is present during the descent of the testis.

Gubler's hemiplegia, icterus, line, etc. (gōōb′lerz) [Adolphe *Gubler*, French physician, 1821–1879]. See under the nouns.

Gubler-Robin typhus [*A. Gubler;* Albert Edouard Charles *Robin*, French physician, 1847–1928]. The renal form of typhus.

Gudden's commissure, ganglion, etc. [Bernard Alloys von *Gudden*, German neurologist, 1824–1886]. See under the nouns.

Guelpa diet, treatment (gwel′pah) [Guglielmo *Guelpa*, Italian physician in Paris, 1850–1930]. See under *diet* and *treatment.*

Guéneau de Mussy's point (ga-no′dŭ-mis-sēz′) [Noel François Odon *Guéneau de Mussy*, French physician, 1813–1885]. See *de Mussy's point,* under *point.*

Guenz (gints). See *Günz.*

Guenzburg (gints′boorg). See *Günzburg.*

Guérin's fold, fracture, glands, sinus, etc. (ga-ranz′) [Alphonse François Marie *Guérin*, French surgeon, 1816–1895]. See under the nouns.

guha (gu′hah). A sort of bronchial asthma, endemic in the island of Guam.

guide (gīd). A device by which another object is led in its proper course, such as a grooved sound, or a filiform bougie over which a tunneled sound is passed, as in stricture of the urethra.

Guidi's canal (gwe′dēz) [Guido *Guidi* (L., *Vidius*), Italian physician, 1500–1569]. Vidian canal.

Guillain-Barré syndrome (ge-yan′ bar-ra′) [Georges *Guillain*, French neurologist, 1876–1961; Jean Alexander *Barré*, French neurologist, born 1880]. See under *syndrome.*

guillotine (gil′o-tēn) [Fr.]. An instrument for excising a tonsil or the uvula.

Guinard's method, treatment (ge-narz′) [Aimé *Guinard*, French surgeon, 1856–1911]. See under *treatment.*

guinea pig (gin′e pig). A small rodent, *Cavia cobaya*, used extensively for experimental work.

Guinon's disease (ge-nawz′) [George *Guinon*, French physician, 1859–1929]. See under *disease.*

Guiteras' disease (ge-ta′ras) [Juan *Guiteras*, Cuban physician, 1852–1925]. See under *disease.*

Gull's disease (gulz) [Sir William Withey *Gull*, English physician, 1816–1890]. See under *disease.*

Gull-Sutton disease [W. W. *Gull;* Henry Gawen *Sutton*, London physician, 1837–1891]. Arteriocapillary fibrosis.

gullet (gul′et). The passage leading to the stomach, including both the pharynx and esophagus.

Gullstrand's slit lamp (gul′strandz) [Allvar *Gullstrand*, Swedish ophthalmologist, 1862–1930; winner of the Nobel prize for physiology and medicine in 1911]. See under *lamp.*

gulose (gu′lōs). A hexose, $CH_2OH(CHOH)_4CHO$, isomeric with glucose but nonfermentable.

gum (gum) [L. *gummi*]. 1. A mucilaginous excretion from various plants. On hydrolysis gums yield hexoses, pentoses, and uronic acids. 2. See *gingivae.* **acaroid g.,** a resin derived from *Xanthorrhoea hastilis* and *X. arborea*, tall liliaceous plants growing in Australia. **animal g.,** a polysaccharide isolated from various proteins and tissues; possibly an impure chondroitin. **g. arabic,** acacia. **Australian g.,** wattle g. **Bassora g.,** a gum resembling gum arabic, from Persia. **g. benjamin, g. benzoin,** benzoin. **blackboy g.,** acaroid g. **blue g.** 1. Eucalyptus. 2. The bluish discoloration of the gums seen in lead poisoning. **Botany Bay g.,** acaroid gum. **British g.,** dextrin. **g. camphor,** camphor. **cape g.,** a gum from *Acacia horrida.* **chagual g.,** a gum like gum arabic, derived from *Puya lanuginosa*, a tree of Chile. **Cowdie g.,** a gum or resin from the New Zealand tree, *Dammara australis.* **doctor g.,** hog g. **eucalyptus g.,** red g. **ghatli g.,** a gum from the dhava tree of India: used like gum arabic. **g. guaiacum,** the resin of guajacum. **hog g.,** a gum from *Rhus metopium* of South America. **Indian g.,** karaya g. **karaya g.,** sterculia g. **Kordofan g.,** the best variety of acacia from Kordofan and adjacent region. **mesquite g.,** a gum from *Prosopis juliflora*, of Texas. **g. opium,** opium. **Orenburg g.,** an edible, sweetish, gummy, and somewhat resinous substance collected in Russia from larch trees after forest fires: it is soluble in water. **red g.,** an exudation from the bark of *Eucalyptus rostrata:* used as an astringent and in throat affections. **g. senegal,** acacia. **sterculia g.,** the dried gummy exudation from *Sterculia urens*, or other species of Sterculia, used as a bulk cathartic. **succory g.,** a narcotic, resinous exudation from *Chondrilla juncea*, a composite-flowered plant. **g. thus,** turpentine. **g. tragacanth,** tragacanth. **wattle g.,** the gum of several Australian species of *Acacia*, an excellent substitute for true gum arabic.

gumanin (gu′mah-nin). White dammar.

gumma (gum′ah), pl. *gummas* or *gum′mata* [L. *gummi* gum]. A soft, gummy tumor, such as that occurring in tertiary syphilis, made up of tissue resembling granulation tissue. **tuberculous g.,** a soft gummy tumor of tuberculous origin, occurring in scrofuloderma gummosa.

gummate (gum′āt). An arabate.

gummatous (gum′ah-tus). Of the nature of gumma.

gummi (gum′i) [L.]. Gum (of plants).

gummose (gum′ōs). A sugar, $C_6H_{12}O_6$, formed by the action of dilute acids upon animal gum.

gummy (gum′e). Resembling a gum or a gumma.

Gumprecht's shadows (goom′prekts) [Ferdinand *Gumprecht*, German physician, born 1864]. See under *shadow.*

gum-resin (gum-rez′in). A concrete juice exuding from various trees. The gum-resins consist of a principle soluble in water and insoluble in alcohol, combined with a volatile oil or resin soluble in alcohol, but not in water, and include ammoniac, asafetida, euphorbium, galbanum, gamboge, myrrh, olibanum, and scammony.

guncotton (gun-kot′n). Pyroxylin.

gundo (goon′do). Goundou.

Gunn's dots, phenomenon, syndrome (gunz) [Robert Marcus *Gunn*, English ophthalmologist, 1850–1909]. See under *dot* and *syndrome.*

Gunning's reaction, test (gun′ingz) [Jan Willem *Gunning*, Dutch chemist, 1827–1901]. See under *test.*

Gunning's splint (gun′ingz) [Thomas Brian *Gunning*, American dentist, 1813–1889]. See under *splint.*

Günz's ligament (gints′ez) [Justus Gottfried *Günz*, German anatomist, 1714–1789]. See under *ligament.*

Günzburg's test (gints′boorgz) [Alfred *Günzburg*, German physician, born 1861]. See under *tests.*

gurgulio (gur-gu′le-o) [L. "gullet"]. The uvula.

guru (goo′roo). Kola.

Gussenbauer's clamp, operation, suture (goos′en-bow″erz) [Carl *Gussenbauer*, German surgeon, 1842–1903]. See under the nouns.

gustation (gus-ta′shun) [L. *gustatio*, from *gustare* to taste]. The act of tasting or the sense of taste. **colored g.,** the association of colors with tastes.

gustatism (gus′tah-tizm). A sensation of taste produced indirectly by other than gustatory stimuli.

gustatory (gus′tah-to″re) [L. *gustatorius*]. Pertaining to the sense of taste.

gustometer (gus-tom′e-ter) [L. *gustare* to taste + Gr. *metron* measure]. An apparatus used in the quantitative determination of taste thresholds. **electronic g.,** an electronic apparatus used in the determination of taste thresholds.

gustometry (gus-tom′e-tre). The clinical determination of thresholds of the sense of taste.

gut (gut). 1. The intestine or bowel. 2. The primitive digestive tube, consisting of the fore-, mid-, and hindgut. 3. Catgut. **blind g.,** the cecum. **postanal g.,** a temporary extension of the embryonic gut caudal to the cloaca. **preoral g.,** Seesel's pouch. **primitive g.,** archenteron. **ribbon g.,** an absorbable ribbon of the intestinal tissue of animals used for suturing where broad support is to be secured. **silkworm g.** See *silkworm -gut,* under *S.* **tail g.,** postanal g.

Guterman's test (go͝ot′er-manz) [Henry Samuel *Guterman*, American physician]. See under *test.*

Guthrie's formula (guth′rēz) [Clyde G. *Guthrie*, American physician, 1880–1931]. See under *formula.*

Guthrie's muscle (guth′rēz) [George James *Guthrie*, English surgeon, 1785–1856]. Sphincter urethrae membranaceae.

gutta (gut′ah), pl. *gut′tae* [L.]. A drop. **g. rosa′cea,** acne rosacea. **g. sere′na,** amaurosis.

guttadiaphot (gut″ah-di′ah-fōt) [L. *gutta* drop + Gr. *dia* through + *phōs* light]. A process for demonstrating changes in the blood by the appearance of the blood stains on three strips of absorbent paper: red, green, and blue.

gutta-percha (gut″ah-per′chah). The coagulated milky juice of various tropical trees of the family Sapotaceae.

Guttat. Abbreviation for L. *guttatim*, drop by drop.

guttate (gut′āt). Characterized by lesions that are drop-shaped.

guttatim (gut-ta′tim) [L.]. Drop by drop.

guttering (gut′er-ing). The operation of cutting a gutter-like excision in a bone.

gutti (gut′i). Gamboge.

gut-tie (gut′ti). 1. A twisting of the intestine of animals, causing colicky pains. 2. A condition in cattle in which a loop of intestine passes through a tear in the peritoneum and is held there, producing obstruction of the bowels.

Guttmann's sign (goot′mahnz) [Paul *Guttmann*, Berlin physician, 1834–1893]. See under *sign.*

Gutt. quibusd. Abbreviation for L. *gut′tis quibus′dam*, with a few drops.

guttur (gut′ur) [L.]. Throat.

guttural (gut′ur-al). Pertaining to the throat.

gutturophony (gut″ur-of′o-ne) [*guttur* + Gr. *phōnē* voice]. Throaty quality of the voice.

gutturotetany (gut″ur-o-tet′ah-ne) [*guttur* + *tetany*]. A guttural spasm, resulting in a kind of stutter.

Gutzeit's test (goot′zītz) [Max Adolf *Gutzeit*, Leipzig chemist, 1847–1915]. See under *test.*

Guy de Chauliac. See *Chauliac.*

Guyon's amputation, sign (ge-yonz′) [Felix Jean Casimir *Guyon*, surgeon in Paris, 1831–1920]. See under *amputation* and *sign.*

Gwathmey's oil-ether anesthesia (gwath′mēz) [James Taylor *Gwathmey*, New York surgeon, 1863–1944]. See under *anesthesia.*

gymnastics (jim-nas′tiks) [Gr. *gymnastikos* pertaining to athletics]. Systematic muscular exercise. **ocular g.,** systematic exercise of the eye muscles in order to secure proper movement, accommodation, or fixation. **Swedish g.,** a system of exercise following a rigid pattern of carefully chosen free, active, deliberate movement, utilizing little equipment and stressing correct bodily posture, based on the effect of exercise on the various vital organs. **vocal g.,** methodical exercise of the voice for the purpose of increasing the lung expansion.

Gymnema (jim-ne′mah). A genus of trees. The leaves of *G. sylvestre*, of Africa, are used to disguise the taste of unpleasant medicines.

gymno- (jim′no) [Gr. *gymnos* naked]. Combining form meaning naked or denoting relationship to nakedness.

Gymnoascaceae (jim″no-as-ka′se-e). A family of the ascomycetous fungi in which the reproductive organs are in the form of naked asci.

Gymnoascus (jim″no-as′kus). A genus of fungi, some species of which have been isolated from skin lesions of domestic animals and man.

gymnobacteria (jim″no-bak-te′re-ah) [*gymno-* + *bacteria*]. Plural of *gymnobacterium.*

gymnobacterium (jim″no-bak-te′re-um), pl. *gymnobacteria.* A microorganism which has no flagella.

gymnocarpous (jim″no-kar′pus) [*gymno-* + Gr. *karpos* fruit]. Having the hymenium exposed during spore formation: said of certain fungi.

gymnocolon (jim′no-ko″lon). Irrigation of the colon.

gymnocyte (jim′no-sīt) [*gymno-* + Gr. *kytos* hollow vessel]. A cell with no cell wall.

gymnophobia (jim″no-fo′be-ah) [*gymno-* + *phobia*]. Morbid aversion to the sight of the naked body.

gymnoplast (jim′no-plast) [*gymno-* + Gr. *plastos* formed]. A mass of protoplasm without an enclosing wall.

gymnoscopic (jim″no-skop′ik) [*gymno-* + Gr. *skopein* to examine]. Inclined to or concerned with viewing the naked body.

gymnosophy (jim-nos′o-fe) [*gymno-* + Gr. *sophia* wisdom]. The cult of nakedness; nudism.

gymnosperm (jim′no-sperm) [*gymno-* + Gr. *sperma* seed]. A plant in which the seeds are not enclosed in an ovary.

gymnospore (jim′no-spōr). A spore without any protective envelope.

gymnosporidia (jim″no-spo-rid′e-ah) [*gymno-* + *sporidium*]. A group of animal microorganisms, examples of which have been found in human blood.

Gymnothorax (jim″no-tho′raks) [*gymno-* + Gr. *thōrax* chest]. A genus of moray eels whose flesh is sometimes used as food.

gyn-. See *gyneco-.*

gynaeco-. For words beginning thus, see those beginning *gyneco-.*

gynaecophorus (jin″e-kof′o-rus). Bilharzia.

gynander (jĭ-nan′der) [*gyn-* + Gr. *anēr, andros* man]. 1. A hermaphrodite. 2. A masculine woman.

gynandria (jĭ-nan′dre-ah). Gynandrism.

gynandrism (jĭ-nan′drizm) [*gyn-* + *andr-* + *-ism*]. 1. Hermaphroditism. 2. Pseudohermaphroditism in the female, characterized by hypertrophy of the clitoris and union of the labia majora, simulating in general appearance the penis and scrotum.

gynandroblastoma (jĭ-nan″dro-blas-to′mah) [*gyn-* + *andro-* + *blastoma*]. A rare ovarian tumor containing histological features of both arrhenoblastoma and granulosa cell tumor.

gynandroid (jĭ-nan′droid) [*gyn-* + *andr-* + Gr. *eidos* form]. An individual exhibiting gynandrism.

gynandromorphism (jĭ-nan″dro-mor′fizm) [*gyn-* + *andro-* + Gr. *morphē* form]. 1. The quality of having both male and female characteristics in certain parts of the body other than the gonads. 2. Hermaphroditism. **bilateral g.,** bilateral hermaphroditism.

gynandromorphous (jĭ-nan″dro-mor′fus). Having both male and female qualities.

gynandry (jĭ′nan-dre). Gynandrism.

gynanthropia (ji″nan-thro′pe-ah). Gynandrism.

gynanthropism (jĭ-nan′thro-pizm). Gynandrism.

gynase (jin′ās) [*gyn-* + *-ase*]. A hypothetical enzyme-like substance regarded as the material basis of femaleness in heredity. Cf. *andrase.*

gynatresia (jin″ah-tre′ze-ah) [*gyn-* + *a* neg. + Gr. *trēsis* perforation]. Occlusion of some part of the female genital tract, especially of the vagina.

gynecic (jĭ-nes′ik). Pertaining to women.

gynecium (jĭ-ne′se-um) [*gyn-* + Gr. *oikos* house]. The female part of a flower.

gyneco-, gyn-, gyne-, gyno- [Gr. *gynē, gynaikos* woman]. Combining form denoting relationship to woman or to the female sex.

gynecogen (jin′ĕ-ko-jen). Any substance (female sex hormones) which produces or stimulates female characteristics.

gynecogenic (jin″ĕ-ko-jen′ik) [*gyneco-* + Gr. *gennan* to produce]. Causing or producing female characteristics.

gynecography (jin″e-kog′rah-fe). Roentgenography of the female reproductive tract.

gynecoiatry (jin″ĕ-ko-i′ah-tre). Gyniatrics.

gynecoid (jin′ĕ-koid) [*gyneco-* + Gr. *eidos* form]. Woman-like; resembling a woman.

gynecologic (jin″ĕ-ko-loj′ik). Pertaining to or affecting the female reproductive tract.

gynecological (jin″ĕ-ko-loj′e-k'l). Pertaining to gynecology.

gynecologist (jin″ĕ-kol′o-jist). A person skilled in gynecology.

gynecology (jin″ĕ-kol′o-je) [*gyneco-* + *-logy*]. That branch of medicine which treats of diseases of the genital tract in women.

gynecomania (jin″ĕ-ko-ma′ne-ah) [*gyneco-* + Gr. *mania* madness]. Satyriasis.

gynecomastia (jin″ĕ-ko-mas′te-ah) [*gyneco-* + Gr. *mastos* breast]. Excessive development of the male mammary glands, even to the functional state. **nutritional g.,** refeeding g. **refeeding g.,** transitory enlargement of the male breast developing during rehabilitation and recovery from a state of malnutrition. **rehabilitation g.,** refeeding g.

gynecomastism (jin″ĕ-ko-mas′tizm). Gynecomastia.

gynecomasty (jin′ĕ-ko-mas″te). Gynecomastia.

gynecomazia (jin″ĕ-ko-ma′ze-ah). Gynecomastia.

gynecopathy (jin″ĕ-kop′ah-the) [*gyneco-* + Gr. *pathos* disease]. A disease peculiar to women.

gynecotokology (jin″ĕ-ko-to-kol′o-je) [*gyneco-* + Gr. *tokos* birth + *-logy*]. A name suggested for the combined specialities of gynecology and obstetrics.

gyneduct (jin′ĕ-dukt) [*gyne-* + *duct*]. The primitive female duct; müllerian duct.

gynephobia (jin″ĕ-fo′be-ah) [*gyne-* + *phobia*]. Dread of or morbid aversion to the society of women.

gyneplasty (jin′ĕ-plas″te). Gynoplastics.

gynergen (jin′ĕr-jen). Trade mark for preparations of ergotamine tartrate.

gynesin (jin′ĕ-sin). Trigonelline.

gyniatrics (jin″e-at′riks) [*gyn-* + Gr. *iatrikē* surgery, medicine]. Gynecology.

gyniatry (jin″e-at′re). Gyniatrics.

gyno-. See *gyneco-.*

gynogamon (ji-no′gam-on). A gamete hormone that is given off from female gametes.

gynogenesis (jin″o-jen′e-sis) [*gyno-* + Gr. *genesis* production]. Development of an egg that is stimulated by a sperm in the absence of any participation of the sperm nucleus.

gynomerogon (jin″o-mer′o-gon). An organism developed from a fertilized ovum containing the female pronucleus only, the cells, as a result, containing only the maternal set of chromosomes.

gynomerogone (jin″o-mer′o-gon). Gynomerogon.

gynomerogony (jin″o-mĕ-rog′o-ne) [*gyno-* + Gr. *meros* part + *gonos* procreation]. Development of a portion of a fertilized ovum containing the female pronucleus only.

gynopathic (jin″o-path′ik) [*gyno-* + Gr. *pathos* disease]. Caused by or pertaining to disease of women.

gynopathy (jin-op′ah-the). Any disease of women.

gynophobia (ji″no-fo′be-ah). Gynephobia.

gynoplastics (ji″no-plas′tiks) [*gyno-* + Gr. *plastos* formed]. The plastic surgery of the female reproductive organs.

gynoplasty (ji′no-plas″te). Gynoplastics.

gynotermon (ji-no′ter-mon). The gamete hormone that is given off from female gametes and that tends to cause the zygote to be female.

gypsum (jip′sum) [L.; Gr. *gypsos* chalk]. Calcium sulfate; when calcined, it becomes plaster of paris, much used in making permanent dressings for fractures.

gyrate (ji′rāt) [L. *gyratus* turned round]. Twisted in a ring or spiral shape.

gyration (ji-ra′shun). Revolution in a circle or in circles.

gyre (jīr). Gyrus.

gyrectomy (ji-rek′to-me). Excision or resection of a cerebral gyrus, or of a portion of the cerebral cortex. **frontal g.,** topectomy.

gyrencephala (ji″ren-sef′ah-lah) [*gyrus* + Gr. *enkephalos* brain]. A group of higher mammals in which the brain is characteristically marked by convolutions.

gyrencephalic (ji″ren-sĕ-fal′ik). 1. Pertaining to the gyrencephala. 2. Having a brain marked by convolutions. Cf. *lissencephalic.*

gyri (ji′ri) [L.]. Plural of *gyrus.*

gyro- (ji′ro) [Gr. *gyros* ring or circle]. Combining form meaning round or denoting relationship to a gyrus.

gyrochrome (ji′ro-krōm) [*gyro-* + Gr. *chrōma* color]. A nerve cell in which the Nissl bodies have a ringlike arrangement in the cytoplasm. Cf. *arkyochrome, perichrome,* and *stichochrome.*

gyroma (ji-ro′mah) [*gyro-* + *-oma*]. A form of tumor of the ovary, consisting of a convoluted, highly refracting mass.

gyromele (ji′ro-mēl). A flexible catheter tipped with sponge: also a stomach tube with a rotating center, used in treating the stomach.

gyrometer (ji-rom′e-ter) [*gyro-* + Gr. *metron* measure]. An instrument for measuring the cerebral gyri.

Gyropus (ji′ro-pus). A genus of lice. **G. ova′lis,** a biting louse found on guinea pigs.

gyrosa (ji-ro′sah) [L.]. Gastric vertigo in which everything seems to turn round.

gyrose (ji′rōs). Marked by curved lines or circles.

gyrospasm (ji′ro-spazm) [*gyro-* + Gr. *spasmos* spasm]. Rotatory spasm of the head.

gyrotrope (ji′ro-trōp). Rheotrope.

gyrous (ji′rus). Gyrose.

gyrus (ji′rus), pl. *gy′ri* [L.; Gr. *gyros* ring or circle]. [N A, B N A] One of the tortuous elevations (convolutions) of the surface of the brain caused by infolding of the cortex. See *gyri cerebri.* **angular g., g. angula′ris** [N A, B N A], a convolution of the inferior parietal lobule, arching over the posterior end of the superior temporal sulcus and continuous with the middle temporal gyrus. **annectant gyri, gy′ri annecten′tes,** gyri transitivi cerebri. **gy′ri bre′ves in′sulae** [N A, B N A], the short, rostrally placed gyri on the surface of the insula. Called also *short gyri of insula.* **Broca's g.,** the inferior frontal gyrus of the left hemisphere of the cerebrum. **callosal g., g. callo'sus,** g. cinguli. **central g., anterior,** g. precentralis. **central g., posterior,** g. postcentralis. **g. centra'lis ante'rior** [B N A], g. precentralis. **g. centra'lis poste'rior** [B N A], g. postcentralis. **g. cerebel'li** [B N A], folia cerebelli. **gy'ri cere'bri** [N A, B N A], **gyri of cerebrum,** the tortuous elevations (convolutions) of the surface of the cerebral hemisphere, caused by infolding of the cortex and separated by the fissures or sulci. Many of them are constant enough that they have been given special names. **cingulate g., g. cin'guli** [N A, B N A], arch-shaped convolution closely related to the surface of the corpus callosum, from which it is separated by the callosal sulcus. **dentate g.** 1. Gyrus dentatus (def. 1). 2. Gyrus fasciolaris. **g. denta'tus.** 1. [N A] A serrated strip of gray matter under the medial border of the hippocampus. Called also *fascia dentata hippocampi* [B N A]. 2. Gyrus fasciolaris. **g. fasciola'ris** [N A], the upward extension of the dentate gyrus. Called also *fasciola cinerea* [B N A]. **g. fornica'tus** [B N A], a name given the marginal portion of the cerebral cortex on the medial aspect of the hemisphere, including the gyrus cinguli, gyrus hippocampi, isthmus, and uncus. Omitted in N A. **frontal g., ascending,** g. precentralis. **frontal g., inferior,** g. frontalis inferior. **frontal g., middle,** g. frontalis medius. **frontal g., superior,** g. frontalis superior. **g. fronta'lis infe'rior** [N A, B N A], a convolution of the frontal lobe below the inferior frontal sulcus. It consists of a pars opercularis, pars triangularis, and pars orbitalis. **g. fronta'lis me'dius** [N A, B N A], a convolution of the frontal lobe between the superior and inferior frontal sulci. **g. fronta'lis supe'rior** [N A, B N A], a convolution of the frontal lobe above the superior frontal sulcus. **fusiform g., g. fusifor'mis** [B N A], a gyrus of the temporal lobe on the inferior surface of the hemisphere between the inferior temporal gyrus and the parahippocampal gyrus. It consists of a lateral and a medial part, called [N A] *g. occipitotemporalis lateralis* and *g. occipitotemporalis medialis.* **hippocampal g., g. hippocam'pi** [B N A], g. parahippocampalis. **infracalcarine g., g. infracalcari'nus,** g. lingualis. **gy'ri in'sulae** [N A, B N A], the gyri that are found on the surface of the insula, including the *gyrus longus insulae* and the *gyri breves insulae.* **g. lim'bicus,** gyrus fornicatus. **lingual g., g. lingua'lis** [N A, B N A], a gyrus of the occipital lobe on the inferior surface of the hemisphere, which is continuous rostrally with the parahippocampal gyrus. **long g. of insula, g. lon'gus in'sulae** [N A, B N A], the long, occipitally placed gyrus on the surface of the insula. **marginal g.,** g. parahippocampalis. **marginal g. of Turner,** g. frontalis superior. **g. margina'lis,** g. parahippocampalis. **occipital gyri, lateral,** gyri occipitales laterales. **occipital gyri, superior,** gyri occipitales superiores. **gy'ri occipita'les latera'les** [B N A], the convolutions on the inferior and lateral portions of the convex surface of the occipital lobe. Omitted in N A. **gy'ri occipita'les superio'res** [B N A], the convolutions on the convex surface of the occipital lobe, superior to the lateral occipital sulcus. Omitted in N A. **occipitotemporal g., lateral,** g. occipitotemporalis lateralis. **occipitotemporal g., medial,** g. occipitotemporalis medialis. **g. occipitotempora'lis latera'lis** [N A], the lateral portion of a gyrus (g. fusiformis [B N A]) on the inferior surface of the cerebral hemisphere, between the inferior temporal gyrus and the parahippocampal gyrus. **g. occipitotempora'lis media'lis** [N A], the medial portion of a gyrus (g. fusiformis [B N A]) on the inferior surface of the cerebral hemisphere, between the inferior temporal gyrus and the parahippocampal gyrus. **g. olfacto'rius latera'lis of Retzius,** limen insulae. **g. olfacto'rius media'lis,** area subcallosa. **g. olfacto'rius media'lis of Retzius,** area subcallosa. **gy'ri oper'ti,** gyri breves insulae. **orbital gyri, gy'ri orbita'les** [N A, B N A], the various irregular convolutions lateral to the olfactory sulcus on the orbital surface of the frontal lobe. **paracentral g., g. paracentra'lis,** lobulus paracentralis. **parahippocampal g., g. parahippocampa'lis** [N A], a convolution on the inferior surface of each cerebral hemisphere, lying between the hippocampal and collateral sulci. Called also *g. hippocampi* [B N A]. **paraterminal g., g. paratermina'lis** [N A], a thin sheet of gray substance covering the under surface of the rostrum of the corpus callosum. Called also *g. subcallosus* [B N A]. **parietal g.,** any one of the convolutions into which the surface of the parietal lobe is divided. **parietal g., ascending, postcentral g., g. postcentra'lis** [N A], the convolution of the parietal lobe lying between the central and postcentral sulci. Called also *g. centralis posterior* [B N A]. **precentral g., g. precentra'lis** [N A], the convolution of the frontal lobe lying between the precentral and central sulci. Called also *g. centralis anterior* [B N A]. **preinsular gyri,** gyri breves insulae. **gy'ri profun'di cer'ebri** [B N A], the deep cerebral convolutions. Omitted in N A. **quadrate g.,** precuneus. **g. rec'tus** [N A, B N A], a convolution on the orbital surface of the frontal lobe, medial to the olfactory sulcus and continuous with the superior frontal gyrus on the medial surface. **short gyri of insula,** gyri breves insulae. **subcallosal g., g. subcallo'sus,** g. paraterminalis. **subcollateral g.,** a convolution on the temporal lobe of the brain, between the collateral and the inferior temporal (occipitotemporal [N A]) sulci, and connecting the occipital and temporal lobes. **supracallosal g., g. supracallo'sus,** indusium griseum. **supramarginal g., g. supramargina'lis** [N A, B N A], the convolution of the inferior parietal lobe that curves around the upper end of the posterior branch of the lateral fissure and is continuous behind it with the superior temporal gyrus. **temporal g., inferior,** g. temporalis inferior. **temporal g., middle,** g. temporalis medius. **temporal g., superior,** g. temporalis superior. **temporal gyri, transverse,** gyri temporales transversi. **g. tempora'lis infe'rior** [N A, B N A], the convolution of the temporal lobe lying between the sulci called the inferior temporal and the occipitotemporal according to the N A nomenclature. **g. tempora'lis me'dius** [N A, B N A], the convolution of the temporal lobe lying between the superior and the inferior [N A] temporal sulci. **g. tempora'lis supe'rior** [N A, B N A], the convolution of the temporal lobe lying between the superior temporal sulcus and the lateral fissure. **gy'ri tempora'les transver'si** [N A, B N A], the transverse convolutions marking the posterior extremity of the superior temporal gyrus and extending down into the lateral fissure. **gy'ri transiti'vi cer'ebri** [B N A], various small folds on the cerebral surface that are too inconstant to bear special names. Called also *annectant gyri.* **uncinate g., g. uncina'tus,** g. parahippocampalis.

H

H. 1. Chemical symbol for *hydrogen*. 2. Abbreviation for *haustus* (a draft), *henry, horizontal, ho'ra* (hour), *hypermetropia*, and *Holzknecht unit*.

H. 1. The symbol for *oersted*. 2. A symbol for *Hauch*, denoting the motile or flagellate type of a microorganism, as contrasted with the O (*ohne Hauch*) or nonmotile type.

H^+. Symbol for hydrogen ion.

[H^+]. Symbol for hydrogen ion concentration.

h. Abbreviation for *Planck's constant*.

H^2. Chemical symbol for heavy hydrogen. See under *hydrogen*.

H & E. Abbreviation for *hematoxylin and eosin stain*.

Haab's magnet, reflex (hahbz) [O. *Haab*, professor of ophthalmology in Zurich, 1850–1931]. See under *magnet* and *reflex*.

habena (hah-be'nah), pl. *habe'nae* [L. "rein"]. See *habenula* (def. 2).

habenal, habenar (hah-be'nal, hah-be'nar). Pertaining to the habena.

habenula (hah-ben'u-lah), pl. *haben'ulae* [L., dim. of *habena*]. 1. A frenulum, or reinlike structure, such as one of a set of such structures in the cochlea. 2. [N A, B N A] The small eminence on the dorsomedial eminence of the thalamus, just in front of the posterior commissure. **h. arcua'ta,** the inner portion of the basilar membrane of the cochlea. **h. cona'rii,** the peduncle of the pineal body. **Haller's h.,** vestigium processus vaginalis. **h. pectina'ta,** the outer portion of the basilar membrane of the cochlea. **h. perfora'ta,** foramen nervosum. **h. urethra'lis,** either of two whitish lines extending from the urinary meatus to the clitoris in girls and young women.

habenular (hah-ben'u-lar). Pertaining to the habenula.

habit (hab'it) [L. *habitus*, from *habere* to hold]. 1. A fixed or constant practice established by frequent repetition. 2. Predisposition or bodily temperament. See under *type*. **apoplectic h.,** habitus apoplecticus. **asthenic h.** See under *type*. **drug h.,** the habitual use of a drug; drug addiction. **endothelioid h.,** a condition in which the nucleus of a cell is relatively small as compared with the cytoplasm. **full h.,** habitus apoplecticus. **glaucomatous h.,** shallowness of the anterior chamber of the eye with dilated pupil: seen in persons who have a predisposition to glaucoma. **leptosomatic h.,** a light, thin build of body. **leukocytoid h.,** endothelioid habit. **opium h.,** opiumism. **physiologic h.,** an acquired modification of behavior or response to stimulation brought about and permanently fixed by constant repetition. **pycnic h.,** a short, stocky build of body.

habitat (hab'ĭ-tat). The natural abode or home of an animal or plant species.

habituation (hah-bit"u-a'shun). 1. The gradual adaptation to a stimulus or to the environment. 2. The extinction of a conditioned reflex by repetition of the conditioned stimulus: called also *negative adaptation*. 3. A condition resulting from the repeated consumption of a drug, with a desire to continue its use, but with little or no tendency to increase the dose; there may be psychic, but no physical dependence on the drug, and detrimental effects, if any, are primarily on the individual.

habitus (hab'ĭ-tus) [L. "habit"]. Physique. See also under *habit* and *type*. **h. apoplec'ticus,** a full, heavy, thick-set body build indicating a possible tendency to apoplexy. **h. enteroptot'icus,** the bodily conformation seen in enteroptosis, marked by a long narrow abdomen. **h. phthis'icus,** a bodily habit predisposing to pulmonary tuberculosis, marked by pallor, emaciation, poor muscular development, and small bones.

habromania (hab"ro-ma'ne-ah) [Gr. *habros* graceful + *mania* madness]. Amenomania; mental disorder with marked gaiety or cheerfulness.

Habronema (hab"ro-ne'mah) [Gr. *habros* graceful + *nema* thread]. A genus of nematode worms parasitic in the stomach of horses. The larval forms are taken up from the feces of horses by flies and the flies, swallowed by horses with their feed, transmit the larvae to the horses' stomachs. The larvae may also be transmitted to the skin of horses where they produce a dermatitis and a form of granuloma; in the conjunctiva they produce bungeye. The species are *H. megastoma, H. muscae*, and *H. microstoma*.

habronemiasis (hab"ro-ne-mi'ah-sis). Infection with Habronema, causing summer dermatitis (esponja) and granuloma in Brazilian horses.

habronemic (hab"ro-ne'mik). Pertaining to or caused by Habronema.

hachement (ash-maw') [Fr.]. A chopping or hacking stroke in massage.

Hackenbruch's experience (hah'ken-brŏŏks) [Peter Theodor *Hackenbruch*, German surgeon, 1865–1924]. The area of anesthesia produced by the injection of a local anesthetic is rhombic-shaped.

hadephobia (ha"de-fo'be-ah) [Gr. *Hades* + *phobos* fear + *-ia*]. Morbid fear of hell.

hadernkrankheit (hahd'ern-krahnk-hīt) [Ger.]. A disease affecting rag-pickers, variously regarded as anthrax or malignant edema.

hae-. For words beginning thus, see also those beginning *he-*.

Haeckel's law (hek'elz) [Ernst Heinrich *Haeckel*, German naturalist, 1834–1919]. See under *law*.

haem (hēm). Heme.

haem-, haema-. See *hemo-*. For words beginning thus, see also those beginning *hem-*.

Haemadipsa (he"mah-dip'sah) [*haema-* + Gr. *dipsa* thirst]. A genus of leeches. **H. ceylon'ica,** a species common in Ceylon, which is annoying to man and animals because of its painful bite. **H. japon'ica,** a species found in Japan.

Haemagogus (hem"ah-go'gus) [*haem-* + Gr. *agōgos* leading]. A genus of mosquitoes some of which transmit jungle yellow fever in tropical South America.

Haemamoeba (hem"ah-me'bah). Haemosporidia.

Haemaphysalis (hem"ah-fis'ah-lis) [Gr. *haima* blood + *physallis* bubble]. A genus of ticks. **H. humero'sa,** the bandicoot tick, one of the vectors of *Coxiella burnetii*. **H. leach'i,** the common dog tick of South Africa. It transmits tick-bite fever. **H. lep'oris-palus'tris,** a rabbit tick which is one of the agents for the spread of spotted fever and tularemia among rabbits. **H. puncta'ta,** a species of tick which acts as a vector of tick paralysis of sheep in Crete.

Haemapium (hĕ-ma'pe-um). A genus of plasmocytes. *H. riedyi* occurs in the erythrocytes of certain salamanders.

haemato-. See *hemo-*. For words beginning thus, see also those beginning *hemato-*.

Haematobium (hem"ah-to'be-um). A genus of flies. **H. ir'ritans,** a genus of small flies, "horn flies," which are very troublesome to cattle.

Haematopinus (hem"ah-to-pi'nus) [*haemato-* + Gr. *pinein* to drink]. A genus of sucking lice, species of which infest horses, swine, and cattle.

Haematoxylon (he"mah-tok'sĭ-lon) [*haemato-* + Gr. *xylon* wood]. A genus of leguminous trees. The heart wood of *H. campechianum*, or logwood, contains tannin and is astringent.

Haementeria (hem″en-te′re-ah). A genus of leeches. **H. ghilian′ii,** a species found in Brazil. **H. officina′lis,** a species used for medicinal purposes in Mexico and South America.

haemo-. See *hemo-*. For words beginning thus, see also those beginning *hemo-*.

Haemobartonella (he″mo-bar″to-nel′lah). A genus of the family Bartonellaceae, order Rickettsiales, occurring in eight species which are parasitic for various lower animals. **H. ca′nis,** a species which infects dogs. **H. mu′ris,** a common parasite of the laboratory rat, in which the infection is activated by splenectomy.

Haemocytozoa (hem″o-si″to-zo′ah). Haemosporidia.

Haemodipsus (hem″o-dip′sus). A genus of lice. **H. ventrico′sus,** the common sucking louse of the rabbit which transmits the infective agent of tularemia from rabbit to rabbit.

Haemogregarina (hem″o-greg″ah-ri′nah). A genus of sporozoan parasites found in the blood corpuscles of reptiles, amphibians, and some warm-blooded animals. Part of their life cycle is passed in another host, usually an insect.

Haemonchus (he-mon′kus). A genus of parasitic worms. **H. contor′tus,** a nematode intestinal parasite of sheep, reported as having been found in man. **H. pla′cei,** a species found in cattle.

Haemophilus (he-mof′ĭ-lus). A genus of microorganisms of the family Brucellaceae, order Eubacteriales characterized by the nutritional requirement of di- or triphosphopyridine nucleotide. **H. aegyp′tius,** an organism that is related to *H. influenzae* and is the cause of acute contagious conjunctivitis. **H. ducrey′i,** the causative agent of chancroid. **H. du′plex,** the causative agent of a chronic or acute blepharoconjunctivitis in man. **H. influen′zae,** a species once thought to be the cause of epidemic influenza in man; it produces a serious form of meningitis, especially in infants. **H. vagina′lis,** a hemophilic bacterium associated, possibly causally, with human vaginitis.

Haemophoructus (hem″o-fo-ruk′tus). A genus of blood-sucking flies of the family Heleidae.

Haemopis (he-mo′pis). A genus of leeches. *H. paludum* is parasitic in the nose and throat in Ceylon. *H. sanguisuga* of Europe and North Africa infests the nasal passages.

Haemoproteus (hem″o-pro′te-us). A genus of sporozoa parasitic in the blood corpuscles of birds. **H. colum′bae,** a sluggish ameboid organism found in the red blood cells of pigeons. Its invertebrate host is a biting fly (*Pseudolychnia maura* or *P. lividocolor*). Other species are: *H. danielews′kyi*, found in the crow (*Corvus cornix*), *H. noc′tuae*, found in the little owl (*Glaucidium noctuae*); *H. pas′seris*, found in the blood of the sparrow.

haemorrhagia (hem″o-ra′je-ah) [L.]. Hemorrhage. **h. per rex′in,** hemorrhage from rupture of a blood vessel.

Haemosporidia (hem″o-spo-rid′e-ah) [*haemo-* + Gr. *sporos* seed, spore]. An order of sporozoa which live parasitically in the red blood corpuscles of vertebrate animals. It includes the genera *Plasmodium, Haemoproteus, Leukocytozoon, Babesia, Theileria* and possibly *Toxoplasma, Cytamoeba,* and *Anaplasma.*

haemosporidium (hem″o-spo-rid′e-um), pl. *haemosporidia*. An individual organism of the order Haemosporidia.

Haen's pills (hah′enz) [Anton de *Haen*, Dutch physician in Vienna, 1811–1884]. See under *pill.*

Haenel's symptom (ha′nelz) [Hans *Haenel*, German neurologist, born 1874]. See under *symptom.*

Haeser (ha′ser). See *Häser.*

Haff disease (haf) [named from the Frisches *Haff*, where epidemics occurred in 1924–5, 1932–3, and 1940]. See under *disease.*

hafnium (haf′ne-um) [L. *Hafniae*, Copenhagen]. A chemical element of atomic number 72 and atomic weight 17849; symbol Hf. Discovered in a zircon, in 1923, by Coster and Hevesy of Copenhagen.

Hagedorn needle (hahg′ĕ-dorn) [Werner *Hagedorn*, German surgeon, 1831–1894]. See under *needle.*

hagiotherapy (ha″je-o-ther′ah-pe) [Gr. *hagios* sacred + Gr. *therapeia* treatment]. Miraculous healing by a holy man.

Haglund's disease (hahg′loondz) [Sims Emil Patrik *Haglund*, Swedish orthopedist, born 1870]. See under *disease.*

Hagner's bag, operation (hag′nerz) [Francis R. *Hagner*, American surgeon, 1873–1940]. See under *bag* and *operation.*

Hahn's cannula (hahnz) [Eugene *Hahn*, Berlin surgeon, 1841–1902]. See under *cannula.*

hahnemannian (hah″nĕ-man′e-an). Pertaining to Christian Friedrich Samuel *Hahnemann* (1755–1843), founder of homeopathy.

hahnemannism (hah′nĕ-man″izm). Homeopathy.

Haidinger's brushes (hi′ding-erz) [Wilhelm von *Haidinger*, Austrian mineralogist, 1795–1871]. Two conical, brushlike images, with apexes touching, seen on looking through a Nicol prism.

Haines' coefficient, formula, reagent, test (hānz′) [Walter Stanley *Haines*, Chicago chemist, 1850–1923]. See under *formula* and *tests.*

hair (hār) [L. *pilus;* Gr. *thrix*]. A long slender filament. Applied especially to such filamentous appendages of the skin (pili [N A]), consisting of modified epidermal tissue; also the aggregate of such filaments, especially that of the scalp. Each hair consists of a cylindrical *shaft* and a root, which is contained in a flasklike depression (*hair follicle*) in the corium and subcutaneous tissue. The base of the root is expanded into the *hair bulb*, which rests upon the *hair papilla.* **auditory h's,** hairlike attachments of the specialized epithelial cells of the cristae acusticae and the maculae acusticae. **h's of axilla,** hirci. **beaded h.,** hair marked with alternate swellings and constrictions; as seen in monilethrix. **burrowing h.,** one which grows horizontally in the skin, instead of penetrating its surface. **club h.,** a hair the root of which is surrounded by a bulbous enlargement composed of completely keratinized cells, preliminary to normal loss of the hair from the follicle. **h's of ear,** tragi. **embedded h.,** burrowing h. **exclamation point h.,** a hair which, when pulled out, shows atrophy and attenuation of the bulb. **h's of eyebrow,** supercilia. **Frey's h's,** stiff hairs mounted in a handle: used for testing the sensitiveness of the pressure points of the skin. **ingrown h.,** one which has curved and reentered the skin, exciting a foreign body papule, which may become infected. **knotted h.,** trichonodosis. **lanugo h.,** the fine hair growing on the body of the fetus, constituting the lanugo. **moniliform h.,** beaded h. **h's of nose,** vibrissae. **h's of pubis,** pubes. **resting h.,** one that has ceased growing, but has not yet been shed from the follicle. **ringed h.,** a condition in which a hair appears to be marked by alternating bands of white, as a result of some barrier in the hair which prevents passage of light and causes the rays to be reflected back, giving the effect of the white bands. **h's of scalp,** capilli. **Schridde's cancer h's,** occasional deep black, coarse, dull hairs on the beard and temples, seen in patients with cancer and other cachectic conditions. **sensory h's,** hairlike projections on the surface of sensory epithelial cells. **stellate h.,** a hair split at the end in a starlike form. **tactile h's,** hairs which are sensitive to touch, as the vibrissae of certain animals. **taste h's,** short hairlike processes projecting freely into the lumen of the pit of a taste bud from the peripheral ends of the taste cells. **terminal h.,** the coarse hair growing on various areas of the body during adult years. **twisted h.,** a hair which at spaced intervals is twisted through an axis of 180 degrees, being abnormally flattened at the site of twisting. **vellus h.,** the downy hair growing on the body during the prepuberal years, constituting the vellus. **wooly h.,** lanugo.

hairball (hăr′bawl). Trichobezoar.

haircap (hăr′kap). Polytrichum.

haircast (hăr′kast). A trichobezoar filling and assuming the shape of the stomach.

halation (hal-a′shun). Indistinctness or blurring of the visual image by strong illumination coming from the same direction as the viewed object.

halazone (hal-ah-zōn). Chemical name: p-dichlorosulfamylbenzoic acid: used as a disinfectant for water supplies.

Halban's sign (hal′banz) [Joseph *Halban*, Vienna gynecologist, 1870–1937]. See under *sign*.

Haldane apparatus, chamber (hawl′dān) [John Scott *Haldane*, English physiologist, 1860–1936]. See under *chamber*.

haldrone (hal′drōn). Trade mark for a preparation of paramethasone acetate.

Hales's piezometer (hālz) [Stephen *Hales*, English physiologist, 1677–1761]. See under *piezometer*.

half-life (haf′lif). The time in which the radioactivity originally associated with an isotope will be reduced by one half through radioactive decay.

half-retinal (haf-ret′ĭ-nal). Pertaining to or affecting one half of the retina.

halide (hal′īd). 1. Haloid. 2. A salt of an alkali metal, as lithium, sodium, potassium, with one of the halogens (fluorine, chlorine, bromine, or iodine).

hali-ichthyotoxin (hal″ĭ-ik″the-o-tok′sin). A poisonous base of bacterial origin from stale fish.

halisteresis (hah-lis″ter-e′sis) [Gr. *hals* salt + *sterēsis* privation]. Osteomalacia; a loss or lack of the lime salts (calcium) of bone. **h. ce′rea,** waxy softening of the bones.

halisteretic (hah-lis″ter-et′ik). Affected with, or of the nature of, halisteresis.

halitosis (hal-ĭ-to′sis) [L. *halitus* exhalation]. Offensive breath; bad breath.

halituous (hah-lit′u-us) [L. *halitus* exhalation]. Covered with moisture or vapor.

halitus (hal′i-tus) [L.]. An exhalation or vapor; an expired breath. **h. saturni′nus,** lead breath.

Hall's disease (hawlz) [Marshall *Hall*, English physician, 1790–1857]. See under *disease*.

hallachrome (hal′ah-krōm). A compound formed from dihydroxy phenylalanine by tyrosinase.

Hallauer's glasses (hal′ow-erz) [Otto *Hallauer*, Basel ophthalmologist, born 1866]. See under *glasses*.

Hallberg effect (hawl′berg) [J. Henry *Hallberg*, American radiologist]. See under *effect*.

Hallé's point (al-āz′) [Adrien Joseph Marie Noël *Hallé*, French physician, born 1859]. See under *point*.

Haller's ansa, arch, circle, fretum, layer, line, etc. (hal′erz) [Albrecht von *Haller*, Swiss physiologist, 1708–1777, the master physiologist of his time]. See under the nouns.

hallex (hal′eks), pl. *hal′lices*. Hallux.

Hallion's law, test (al-yawz′) [Louis *Hallion*, French physiologist, 1862–1940]. See under *law* and *tests*.

Hallopeau's disease (al-o-pōz′) [François Henri *Hallopeau*, French dermatologist, 1842–1919]. Lichen sclerosus et atrophicus.

hallucal (hal′u-kal). Pertaining to the hallux, or great toe.

hallucination (hah-lu″sĭ-na′shun) [L. *hallucinatio;* Gr. *alyein* to wander in the mind]. A sense perception not founded upon objective reality. **auditory h.,** the hearing of unreal sounds. **depressive h.,** a condition of acute depression with hallucinations. **gustatory h.,** a hallucination of taste. **haptic h.,** a tactile hallucination. **hypnagogic h.,** a hallucination occurring between sleeping and awakening. **lilliputian h.,** a hallucination in which things seem smaller than they actually are. **olfactory h.,** hallucination of smell. **reflex h.,** arousal of a secondary sensation by a sensation of a different modality. **stump h.,** the sensation of the existence of a limb or part of a limb after its amputation. **tactile h.,** hallucination of touch. **visual h.,** a sensation of seeing not stimulated by actual presence of the object seen.

hallucinative, hallucinatory (hah-lu′sĭ-na-tiv, hah-lu′sĭ-nah-to″re). Characterized by hallucinations.

hallucinogen (hah-lu′sĭ-no-jen) [*hallucin*ation + Gr. *gennan* to produce]. An agent which produces hallucinations.

hallucinogenesis (hah-lu″sĭ-no-jen′e-sis). The production of hallucinations.

hallucinogenetic (hah-lu″sĭ-no-je-net′ik). Pertaining to or characterized by hallucinogenesis.

hallucinogenic (hah-lu″sĭ-no-jen′ik). Producing hallucinations.

hallucinosis (hah-lu″sĭ-no′sis). A psychosis marked by hallucinations. **acute h., alcoholic h.,** a form of alcoholic psychosis, marked by auditory hallucinations and loose delusions of persecution.

hallucinotic (hah-lu″sĭ-not′ik). Pertaining to or characterized by hallucinosis.

hallux (hal′uks), pl. *hal′luces* [L.]. The great toe, or first digit of the foot. **h. doloro′sa,** a painful disease of the great toe usually associated with flatfoot. **h. flex′us,** h. rigidus. **h. mal′leus,** hammer toe of the great toe. **h. rig′idus,** painful flexion deformity of the great toe in which there is limitation of motion at the metatarsophalangeal joint. **h. val′gus,** angulation of the great toe away from the midline of the body, or toward the other toes. **h. va′rus,** angulation of the great toe toward the midline of the body, or away from the other toes.

Hallux valgus.

Hallwachs effect (hal′vaks) [Franz *Hallwachs*, physiologist in Dresden, 1859–1922]. See under *effect*.

halmatogenesis (hal″mah-to-jen′e-sis) [Gr. *halma* a jump + *genesis* production]. A sudden alteration of type from one generation to another. Called also *saltatory variation*.

halo (ha′lo) [L.; Gr. *halōs*]. 1. A luminous or colored circle, such as the colored circle seen around a light in glaucoma. 2. A ring seen around the macula lutea in ophthalmoscopical examination. 3. The imprint of the ciliary processes upon the vitreous body. **Fick's h.,** a colored circle appearing around a light, caused by the wearing of contact lenses. See *Fick's phenomenon*. **h. glaucomato′sus, glaucomatous h.,** a narrow pinkish yellow or yellowish white zone completely surrounding the optic papilla in glaucoma, caused by atrophy and contraction of the underlying choroid. **h. saturni′nus,** lead line. **senile h.,** a zone of variable width surrounding the optic papilla, caused by exposure of various elements of the choroid as a result of senile atrophy of the pigmented epithelium.

halo- (hal′o) [Gr. *hals* salt]. Combining form denoting relationship to a salt.

Halobacterium (hal″o-bak-te′re-um). A genus of halophilic microorganisms of the family Pseudomonadaceae, suborder Pseudomonadineae, order Pseudomonadales, occurring as highly pleomorphic rod-shaped cells. It includes five species, *H. cutiru′brum*, *H. halo′bium*, *H. marismor′tui*, *H. salina′rium*, and *H. trapan′icum*.

haloduric (hal″o-du′rik) [Gr. *hals* salt + L.

durare to endure]. Capable of existing in a medium containing a high concentration of salt.

halogen (hal′o-jen) [*halo-* + Gr. *gennan* to produce]. An element of a closely related chemical family, all of which form similar (saltlike) compounds in combination with sodium. The halogens are bromine, chlorine, fluorine, and iodine.

haloid (hal′oid) [*halo-* + Gr. *eidos* form]. Saltlike; derived from a halogen.

halometer (hah-lom′e-ter) [*halo-* + Gr. *metron* measure]. 1. An instrument for measuring ocular halos. 2. An instrument for estimating the size of red corpuscles by measuring the diffraction halos which they produce.

halometry (hah-lom′e-tre). 1. The measurement of halos. 2. The measurement of the size of red blood corpuscles by utilizing the blood smear as a diffraction grating.

halophil (hal′o-fil). A microorganism that requires a high concentration of salt for optimal growth.

halophile (hal′o-fil). 1. Halophil. 2. Halophilic.

halophilic (hal″o-fil′ik) [Gr. *hals* salt + *philein* to love]. Pertaining to or characterized by an affinity for salt; applied to microorganisms which require a high concentration of salt for optimal growth.

halosteresis (hah-los″ter-e′sis). Halisteresis.

halotestin (hal″o-tes′tin). Trade mark for a preparation of fluoxymesterone.

halothane (hal′o-thān). Chemical name: 2-bromo-2-chloro-1,1,1-trifluoroethane. Use: inhalation anesthetic.

Halsted's operation, suture (hal′stedz) [William Stewart *Halsted*, Baltimore surgeon, 1852–1922]. See under *operation* and *suture*.

Haly Abbas. See *Ali Abbas*.

halzoun (hal′zun). A disease of Syria caused by *Fasciola hepatica*, which attaches itself to the pharyngeal mucous membrane.

hamamelose (ham-am′e-lōs). A natural sugar, $CH_2OH(CHOH)_2.COH(CH_2OH).COH$, from the bark of *Hamamelis virginiana*.

hamarthritis (ham″ar-thri′tis) [Gr. *hama* together + *arthritis*]. Arthritis of all the joints at the same time.

hamartia (ham-ar′she-ah) [Gr. "defect"]. A defect in tissue combination during development.

hamarto- (ham′ar-to) [Gr. *hamartia* defect, sin]. Combining form denoting relationship to a defect.

hamartoblastoma (ham-ar″to-blas-to′mah) [*hamarto-* + Gr. *blastos* germ + *-oma*]. A tumor developing from a hamartoma.

hamartoma (ham″ar-to′mah) [*hamarto-* + *-oma*]. Albrecht's term for a tumor-like nodule of superfluous tissue.

hamartomatosis (ham″ar-to-mah-to′sis). The development of multiple hamartomas.

hamartomatous (ham″ar-to′mah-tus). Pertaining to a disturbance in growth of a tissue in which the cells of a circumscribed area outstrip those of the surrounding areas.

hamartophobia (ham″ar-to-fo′be-ah) [*hamarto-* + *phobia* fear]. Morbid fear of error or sin.

hamartoplasia (ham″ar-to-pla′se-ah) [*hamarto-* + Gr. *plassein* to form]. Overdevelopment of a tissue as a reaction to the attempts of that tissue to repair.

hamatum (hah-ma′tum) [L. "hooked"]. The os hamatum, or unciform bone.

Hamberger's schema (ham′ber-gerz) [Georg Ehrhard *Hamberger*, German physician, 1697–1755]. See under *schema*.

Hamburger interchange (ham′boor-ger) [Hartog Jacob *Hamburger*, Dutch physiologist, 1859–1924]. The ionic interchange between the corpuscles and plasma of the blood which regulates the reaction of the blood. Called also *secondary buffering*.

Hamilton's bandage, pseudophlegmon, test (ham′il-tonz) [Frank Hastings *Hamilton*, American surgeon, 1813–1875]. See under the nouns.

Hamman's disease, sign (ham′anz) [Louis *Hamman*, American physician, 1877–1946]. See under *disease* and *sign*.

Hamman-Rich syndrome (ham′an rich) [Louis *Hamman;* Arnold R. Rich, American pathologist, born 1893]. Diffuse interstitial pulmonary fibrosis.

Hammarsten's test (ham′er-stenz) [Olof *Hammarsten*, physiologist in Upsala, 1841–1932]. See under *tests*.

hammer (ham′er). 1. An instrument with a head designed for striking blows. 2. The hammer-shaped bone of the middle ear; the malleus. **Major's h.,** a metal hammer intended to be heated in boiling water and applied to the skin as a counterirritant. **Neef's h., Wagner's h.,** an instrument for the rapid opening and closing of a galvanic circuit.

Hammerschlag's test (ham′er-shlahgz) [Albert *Hammerschlag*, physician in Vienna, 1863–1935]. See under *tests*.

Hammond's disease (ham′undz) [William Alexander *Hammond*, American neurologist, 1828–1900]. Athetosis.

hamster (ham′ster). A ratlike rodent, *Cricetus cricetus* of Europe and Western Asia, bred and used extensively as a laboratory experimental animal.

hamstring (ham′string). Either of the tendons which laterally bound the popliteal space. **inner h.,** the tendons of the gracilis, sartorius, and two other muscles. **outer h.,** the tendon of the biceps flexor femoris.

hamular (ham′u-lar). Shaped like a hook.

hamulus (ham′u-lus), pl. *ham′uli* [L. "little hook"]. A hook-shaped process. **h. coch′leae,** h. laminae spiralis. **h. of ethmoid bone,** processus uncinatus ossis ethmoidalis. **frontal h., h. fronta′lis,** ala cristae galli. **h. of hamate bone,** h. ossis hamati. **lacrimal h., h. lacrima′lis** [N A, B N A], the hooklike process on the anterior part of the inferolateral border of the lacrimal bone, articulating with the maxilla. **h. lam′inae spira′lis** [N A, B N A], the hooklike upper end of the osseous spiral lamina. **h. os′sis hama′ti** [N A, B N A], a hooklike process on the volar surface of the hamate bone, to which numerous structures are attached. Called also *hook of hamate bone*. **palatine h.,** processus uncinatus ossis ethmoidalis. **pterygoid h., h. pterygoi′deus** [N A, B N A], a hooklike process on the inferior extremity of the medial pterygoid plate of the sphenoid bone, around which the tendon of the tensor veli palatini muscle passes. **trochlear h.,** spina trochlearis.

hand (hand) [L. *manus*]. The carpus, metacarpus, and fingers together. **accoucheur's h.,** obstetrician's h. **ape h.,** a hand with the thumb permanently extended. **benediction h.,** a hand in which the ring and little fingers are flexed, the thumb and other two fingers remaining normal: seen in ulnar paralysis and syringomyelia. **claw h.** See *clawhand*. **cleft h.,** malformation of the hand in which the division between the fingers extends into the metacarpus; also a hand in which the middle digits are absent, and the remaining fingers are abnormally large; called also *lobster-claw hand* and *main fourche*. **dead h.,** an occupational disorder seen sometimes in those who use vibratory tools, and apparently caused by the multitude of concussions. The hands are painful and dark blue in color, but blanch on exposure to cold. **drop h.** See *wristdrop*. **flat h.,** manus plana. **ghoul h.,** a condition in which the skin of the palm is depigmented and of a dead-white, tallow-yellow color, with blotchy areas of brownish hyperpigmentation, observed in Nigeria and thought to be associated with tertiary yaws. **Krukenberg's h.,** a forklike stump created by separating the distal ends of the ulna and radius and covering them with skin, after amputation proximal to the carpus. **lobster-claw h.,**

cleft h. **Marinesco's succulent h.**, a hand marked by edema with lividity and coldness of the skin; seen in syringomyelia. **mirror h's**, a deformity in which there are two crude hands growing from a common wrist. **monkey h.**, a hand showing atrophy of the thenar muscles; called also *main en singe*. **obstetrician's h.**, the contraction of the hand in tetany; the hand is flexed at the wrist, the fingers at the metacarpophalangeal joints but extended at the interphalangeal joints, the thumb being strongly flexed into the palm. **opera-glass h.**, a pawlike hand marked by telescoping of the fingers caused by absorption of the phalanges: occurs in chronic arthritis. **phantom h.**, a paresthetic feeling as if the hand were still present after amputation. **preacher's h.**, benediction h. **skeleton h.**, a hand markedly atrophied and held in a position of extension: seen in progressive muscular atrophy; called also *main en squelette*. **spade h.**, the thick square hand of myxedema and acromegaly. **split h.**, cleft hand. **trench h.**, contracture or other incapacity of the hand from frost-bite in the trenches; called also *main de tranchées*. **trident h.**, the characteristic hand of achondroplasia: the fingers are relatively of the same length, and there is a peculiar separation of the second and third fingers at the second phalangeal joint, causing the fingers to spread out. **washerwoman's h.**, the blanched, corrugated hand of washerwomen; found also in the hands of the drowned. **writing h.**, a peculiar position of the hand seen in paralysis agitans.

Hand's disease, syndrome (handz) [Alfred *Hand*, Philadelphia pediatrician, 1868–1949]. Hand-Schüller-Christian disease.

Hand-Schüller-Christian disease (hand-shil′er-kris′chan) [Alfred *Hand;* Artur *Schüller;* Henry A. *Christian*]. See under *disease*.

handedness (hand′ed-nes). The preferential use, in all voluntary motor acts, of the hand of one side. **left h.**, the preferential use, in all voluntary motor acts, of the left hand. **right h.**, the preferential use, in all voluntary motor acts, of the right hand.

Handley's method (hand′lēz) [W. Sampson *Handley*, English surgeon, born 1872]. Treatment of elephantiasis by draining by means of long cotton and silk threads inserted into the tissues.

handpiece (hand′pēs). That part of a dental engine which is held in the hand of the operator and which engages the bur or working point while it is being revolved.

Hanger's test (hang′erz) [Franklin M. *Hanger*, Jr., American physician, born 1894]. See under *tests*.

Hannover's canal (han′o-verz) [Adolph *Hannover*, Danish anatomist, 1814–1894]. See under *canal*.

Hanot's cirrhosis (an-ōz′) [Victor Charles *Hanot*, French physician, 1844–1896]. Biliary cirrhosis.

Hansen's bacillus, disease (han′sunz) [Gerhard Armauer *Hansen*, Norwegian physician, 1841–1912]. See *Mycobacterium leprae*, and *leprosy*.

hansenaria (han″sĕ-na′re-ah). Plural of *hansenarium*.

hansenarium (han″sĕ-na′re-um), pl. *hansena′ria* [G. A. *Hansen*]. A term suggested to replace leprosarium as the name of an institution devoted to the care of patients with leprosy (Hansen's disease).

Hanson's extract, unit (han′sunz) [Adolph M. *Hanson*, American surgeon, born 1888]. See under *extract* and *unit*.

hapalonychia (hap″ah-lo-nik′e-ah) [Gr. *hapalos* soft + Gr. *onyx* nail]. A soft, uncornified condition of the nails.

haphalgesia (haf″al-je′ze-ah) [Gr. *haphē* touch + *algēsis* sense of pain + *-ia*]. The sensation of pain on touching nonirritating objects or when the skin is lightly touched.

haphephobia (haf″e-fo′be-ah) [Gr. *haphē* touch + *phobia*]. Morbid dread of being touched.

Hapke's phenomenon (hap′kez) [Franz *Hapke*, German physician]. See under *phenomenon*.

haplo- (hap′lo) [Gr. *haploos* simple, single]. Combining form meaning simple or single.

haplobacteria (hap″lo-bak-te′re-ah) [*haplo-* + *bacteria*]. Bacteria which are not filamentous.

Haplochilus (hap″lo-ki′lus). A genus of fish. **H. pan′chax**, a small fish, called *ikan kapala timah* in Malay, which is placed in fishponds in the Netherlands East Indies to eat the larvae of Anopheles mosquitoes.

haplodermatitis (hap″lo-der″mah-ti′tis) [*haplo-* + Gr. *derma* skin + *-itis*]. An uncomplicated inflammation of the skin.

haplodermitis (hap″lo-der-mi′tis). Haplodermatitis.

haplodont (hap′lo-dont) [*haplo-* + Gr. *odous* tooth]. Having molar teeth without cusps or ridges.

Haplographiaceae (hap″lo-graf″e-a′se-e). A family of fungi.

haploid (hap′loid). 1. Having a single set of chromosomes, as normally carried by a gamete, or having one complete set of nonhomologous chromosomes. Cf. *diploid*. 2. An individual or cell having only one member of each pair of homologous chromosomes.

haploidy (hap′loi-de). The state of having only one member of each pair of homologous chromosomes.

haplomycosis (hap″lo-mi-ko′sis). Infection with Haplosporangium.

haplont (hap′lont). A haploid individual.

haplopathy (hap-lop′ah-the) [*haplo-* + Gr. *pathos* disease]. An uncomplicated disease.

haplophase (hap′lo-fāz). That phase in the life history of germ cells when the nuclei are haploid.

haplopia (hap-lo′pe-ah) [*haplo-* + Gr. *ōps* vision]. Single vision; the condition in which an object looked at is seen single and not double.

haploscope (hap′lo-skōp) [*haplo-* + Gr. *skopein* to examine]. A form of stereoscope used for testing the visual axes. **mirror h.**, an instrument for making experiments, with different degrees of convergence of the visual axes.

haploscopic (hap-lo-skop′ik). Pertaining to a haploscope; stereoscopic.

haplosporangin (hap″lo-spo-ran′jin). An antigen derived from the fungus *Haplosporangium parvum*.

Haplosporangium parvum (hap″lo-spo-ran′je-um par′vum). A fungus which is associated with granulomatous lesions of the lungs in certain rodents.

Haplosporidia (hap″lo-spo-rid′e-ah) [*haplo-* + Gr. *sporos* seed, spore]. An order of Sporidia found as parasites in the intestines of marine annelides and in tumors of fishes. Only one species infests man. See *Rhinosporidium seeberi*.

hapt-, hapte-. See *hapto-*.

hapten (hap′ten). Haptene.

haptene (hap′tēn). That portion of an antigenic molecule or antigenic complex that determines its immunological specificity. Commonly polysaccharide in naturally occurring antigens, and a low molecular weight substance (e.g., arsenilic acid derivatives) in artificial antigens. It reacts specifically in vivo and in vitro with homologous antibody. Called also *antigenic determinant, antigenic structural grouping*, and *haptenic grouping*. **bacterial h.**, a complex carbohydrate (polysaccharide) which can be extracted from various bacteria, which is highly type specific and which gives specific precipitation in homologous antiserums but which is not antigenic when injected into animals. **group A h.**, a viscous substance made up of polysaccharides, hexose, acetyl glucosamine and amino acids.

haptenic (hap-ten′ik). Pertaining to or caused by haptenes.

haptephobia (hap″te-fo′be-ah). Haphephobia.

haptic (hap′tik) [Gr. *haptikos* able to lay hold of]. Tactile.

haptics (hap′tiks). The science of touch, or the sense of contact.

haptin (hap′tin). Haptene.

hapto-, hapt-, hapte- [Gr. *haptein* to touch, seize upon, or hold fast]. Combining form denoting relationship to touch or to seizure.

haptoglobin (hap″to-glo′bin). A serum α_2-globulin glycoprotein that binds free hemoglobin. Three types, distinguished on the basis of electrophoretic patterns, are determined by the interaction of two codominant somatic genes, Hp^1 and Hp^2. Other variants have also been described.

haptometer (hap-tom′e-ter) [*hapto-* + Gr. *metron* measure]. An instrument for measuring sensitivity to touch.

haptophil, haptophile (hap′to-fil) [*hapto-* + Gr. *philein* to love]. Having a peculiar affinity for a haptophore.

haptophore (hap′to-fōr) [*hapto-* + Gr. *phoros* bearing]. The specific group of the molecule of toxins, agglutinins, precipitins, opsonins, and lysins by which they become attached to their antibodies, antigens, or the receptors of cells, thus making possible their specific activity. See *Ehrlich's side-chain theory*, under *theory*.

haptophoric (hap″to-fōr′ik). Haptophorous.

haptophorous (hap-tof′o-rus). Causing the combination of an antitoxin with cells. See *haptophore*.

haptotaxis (hap″to-tak′sis). Thigmotaxis.

haramaitism (har″ah-ma′ĭ-tizm). Child marriage among the Hindus.

harara (hah-rar′ah). A skin disease on the backs of the hands of visitors in Palestine caused by the bites of sand flies of the genus *Phlebotomus*.

hardening (hard′en-ing). The procedure of rendering tissue firm, so that it may be more readily cut for purposes of microscopical examination.

Harder's glands (hard′erz) [Johann Jacob *Harder*, Swiss anatomist, 1656–1711]. See under *gland*.

hardness (hard′nes). 1. A quality of water produced by soluble salts of calcium and magnesium or other substances which form an insoluble curd with the soap and thus interfere with its cleansing power. 2. The quality of firmness produced by cohesion of the particles composing a substance, as evidenced by its inflexibility or resistance to indentation or distortion. 3. The penetrating power of roentgen rays depending on their wavelength: the shorter the wavelength the harder the rays and the greater their penetrating power. 4. The degree of refraction of the residual gas in a glass tube: the higher the vacuum the shorter the wavelength of the resulting roentgen rays. **permanent h.,** hardness of water not removed by boiling; it is usually due to sulfates and chlorides. **temporary h.,** hardness of water removed by boiling; it is due to soluble bicarbonates, which lose CO_2 on boiling and precipitate as normal carbonates.

Hardy's lotion (ar-dēz′) [Louis Phillipe Alfred *Hardy*, French physician, 1811–1893]. See under *lotion*.

Hare's syndrome (hārz) [Edward Selleck *Hare*, British surgeon, 1812–1838]. See under *syndrome*.

harelip (hār′lip). A congenital cleft or defect in the upper lip, usually due to failure of the median nasal and maxillary processes to unite. The maxilla and palate may also be involved. **acquired h.,** a cleft of the upper lip caused by trauma. **double h.,** a cleft on either side of the upper lip as a result of bilateral failure of closure of the cleft between the median nasal and the maxillary process. **median h.,** a midline defect of the lip caused by failure of the median nasal processes to unite. **single h.,** a lateral cleft of the upper lip caused by failure of the median nasal and the maxillary process to unite.

harlequin (hahr′lĕ-kwin). A venomous snake belonging to the genus *Elaps*.

Harley's disease (har′lēz) [George *Harley*, English physician, 1829–1896]. Paroxysmal hemoglobinuria.

harmonia (har-mo′ne-ah) [L.]. [B N A] The immovable articulation of bones by surfaces that are nearly smooth. Called also *sutura plana* [N A].

harmony (har′mo-ne). The state of working together smoothly. **occlusal h.,** proper occlusion of the teeth occurring in various positions of the mandible. **occlusal h., functional,** such occlusion of the teeth in all positions of the mandible during mastication as will provide the greatest masticatory efficiency without imposing undue strain or trauma on the supporting tissues.

harmonyl (har′mo-nil). Trade mark for preparations of deserpidine.

harpoon (har-po͞on′) [Gr. *harpazein* to seize]. An instrument for removing small pieces of living tissue for diagnostic examination.

Harpyrynchus (har″pe-ring′kus) [Gr. *harpē* bird of prey + Gr. *rhynchos* snout]. A genus of mites parasitic on birds.

Harrington's solution (har′ing-tonz) [Charles *Harrington*, American physician, 1856–1908]. See under *solution*.

Harris' bands, membranes, segregator, separator (har′is) [Malcolm La Selle *Harris*, Chicago surgeon, 1862–1936]. See under *band* and *segregator*.

Harrison antinarcotic act. A Federal law, enacted March 1, 1915, which regulates the possession, sale, purchase, and prescription of habit-forming drugs, such as cocaine, morphine, opium, etc.

Harrison's groove, sulcus (har′ĭ-sunz) [Edwin *Harrison*, London physician, 1779–1847]. See under *groove*.

Harrower's hypothesis, test (har′o-erz) [Henry R. *Harrower*, American physician, born 1883]. See under *hypothesis* and *tests*.

harrowing (har′o-ing). Hersage.

Hartel method, technic, treatment (har′tel) [F. *Hartel*, German surgeon]. See under *treatment*.

Hartley-Krause operation (hart′le-krows) [Frank *Hartley*, New York surgeon, 1857–1913; Fedor *Krause*, German surgeon, 1857–1937]. See under *operation*.

Hartmanella (hart″man-el′ah). A genus of amebae. **H. hyali′na,** a coprozoic ameba found in human feces.

Hartmann's curet, speculum (hart′manz) [Arthur *Hartmann*, laryngologist in Berlin, 1849–1931]. See under *curet* and *speculum*.

Hartmann's fossa, point (hart′manz) [Henri *Hartmann*, French surgeon, 1860–1952]. See under the nouns.

Hartmann's pouch (hart′manz) [Robert *Hartmann*, German anatomist, 1831–1893]. See under *pouch*.

Hartmann's solution (hart′manz) [Alexis F. *Hartmann*, American physician, born 1898]. See under *solution*.

hartshorn (harts′horn). 1. The horn of the stag or hart; cornu cervi. 2. A popular name for ammonia water.

harveian (har′ve-an). Named in honor of William *Harvey*.

Harvey (har′ve), William (1578–1657). A celebrated English physician whose brilliant inductive reasoning and inductive experiments, described in his *De motu cordis* (1628), establish him as the true discoverer of the circulation of the blood. He was also one of the first to disbelieve the doctrine of preformation of the fetus.

Häser's coefficient, formula (ha′zerz) [Heinrich *Häser*, German physician, 1811–1885]. See under *formula*.

Hashimoto's disease, struma, thyroiditis

(hash″ĭ-mo′tōz) [Hakaru *Hashimoto*, Japanese surgeon, 1881–1934]. Struma lymphomatosa.

hashish (hash-ēsh′) [Arabic "herb"]. The stalks and leaves of *Cannabis indica*. See *cannabis*.

hashishin (hash-e′shin). A hashish addict.

hashishism (hash′ēsh-izm). Hashish addiction.

Hasner's fold, valve (hahs′nerz) [Joseph Ritter von Artha *Hasner*, an ophthalmologist in Prague, 1819–1892]. See *plica lacrimalis*.

Hassall's corpuscles (has′alz) [Arthur Hill *Hassall*, English chemist and physician, 1817–1894]. See under *corpuscle*.

Hassin's sign, treatment (has′inz) [George Boris *Hassin*, Russian neurologist in the United States, 1873–1951]. See under *sign* and *treatment*.

Hata's phenomenon, preparation (hah′tahs) [Sahachiro *Hata*, Japanese physician, 1873–1938]. See under *phenomenon* and *preparation*.

Hauch (howkh) [Ger. "breath"]. See *H*.

Haudek's niche, sign (haw′deks) [Martin *Haudek*, roentgenologist in Vienna, 1880–1931]. See under *niche*.

haunch (hawnch). The hip and buttock.

hauptganglion of Küttner (howpt′gang″gle-on). Küttner's ganglion.

Haust. Abbreviation for L. *haus′tus*, a draft.

haustorium (haws-to′re-um), pl. *hausto′ria* [L. *haustor* a drawer]. An organ of certain parasitic protozoa by which they attach themselves to the host for the purpose of obtaining nourishment.

haustra (haws′trah). Plural of *haustrum*.

haustral (haws′tral). Pertaining to the haustra of the colon.

haustration (haws-tra′shun). 1. The formation of a haustrum. 2. A haustrum.

haustrum (haws′trum), pl. *haus′tra* [L. *haustor* drawer]. A recess. **haus′tra co′li** [N A, B N A], **haustra of colon,** sacculations in the wall of the large intestine produced by adaptation of its length to that of the tenia coli, or by the arrangement of the circular muscle fibers.

haustus (haws′tus) [L.]. Draft. **h. ni′ger,** black draft.

haut-mal (o-mahl′) [Fr.]. An epileptic attack in its full development; epilepsia gravior.

Haverhill fever (ha′ver-il) [*Haverhill*, Mass., where an epidemic occurred in 1925]. See under *fever*.

Haverhillia multiformis (ha″ver-il′e-ah mul″-tĭ-for′mis). The name given to a slender gram-negative streptobacillus which was found in cases of Haverhill fever: now called *Streptobacillus muris-ratti*.

haversian canal, system (ha-ver′shan) [Clopton *Havers*, English physician and anatomist, 1650–1702; known for his researches on the minute structure of bone, which were recorded in his *Osteologia nova* (1691)]. See under *canal* and *system*.

Hawkins's keloid (haw′kinz) [Caesar Henry *Hawkins*, London surgeon, 1798–1884]. False keloid.

Hay's test (hāz) [Matthew *Hay*, Scotch physician, 1855–1932]. See under *tests*.

Hayem's solution, type (a-yawz′) [Georges *Hayem*, physician in Paris, 1841–1933]. See under *solution* and *type*.

Hayem-Widal syndrome (a-yaw-ve′dal) [Georges *Hayem;* Georges Fernand Isidore *Widal*, French physician, 1862–1929]. Hemolytic jaundice.

hay fever (ha fe′ver). See under *fever*.

Haygarth's nodes, nodosities (ha′garths) [John Haygarth, English physician, 1740–1827]. See under *node*.

Haynes' operation (hānz) [Irving S. *Haynes*, New York surgeon, 1861–1946]. See under *operation*.

Hazen's theorem (ha′zenz) [Allen *Hazen*, American civil engineer, born 1869]. See under *theorem*.

Hb. Symbol for *hemoglobin*.

H_3BO_3. Boric acid.

HBr. Hydrobromic acid.

H.C. Abbreviation for *hospital corps*.

HCHO. Formaldehyde.

HCl. Hydrochloric acid.

HCN. Hydrocyanic acid.

HCO_3. The bicarbonate radical.

H_2CO_3. Carbonic acid.

HCT. Abbreviation for *hematocrit*.

H.D. Abbreviation for *hearing distance*.

H. d. Abbreviation for L. *ho′ra decu′bitus*, at bedtime.

H.D.L.W. Distance at which a watch is heard by the left ear.

HDN. Abbreviation for *hemolytic disease of the newborn*.

H.D.R.W. Distance at which a watch is heard by the right ear.

He. Chemical symbol for *helium*.

he-. For words beginning thus, see also those beginning *hae-*.

head (hed) [L. *caput;* Gr. *kephalē*]. The upper, anterior, or proximal extremity of a structure or body, especially that part of an organism which contains the brain and the organs of special sense. See also *caput*. **angular h. of quadratus labii superioris muscle,** musculus levator labii superioris alaeque nasi. **articular h.,** an eminence on a bone by which it articulates with another bone. **h. of astragalus,** caput tali. **big h.,** swelled h. **h. of blind colon,** cecum. **h. of caudate nucleus,** caput nuclei caudati. **h. of condyloid process of mandible,** caput mandibulae. **coronoid h. of pronator radii teres muscle,** caput ulnare musculi pronatoris teretis. **deep h. of triceps extensor cubiti muscle,** caput mediale musculi tricipitis brachii. **drum h.,** membrana tympani. **h. of epididymis,** caput epididymidis. **external h. of triceps extensor cubiti muscle,** caput laterale musculi tricipitis brachii. **h. of femur,** caput femoris. **h. of fibula,** caput fibulae. **first h. of triceps extensor cubiti muscle,** caput longum musculi tricipitis brachii. **great h. of adductor hallucis muscle,** caput obliquum musculi adductoris hallucis. **great h. of triceps extensor cubiti muscle,** caput laterale musculi tricipitis brachii. **great h. of triceps femoris muscle,** musculus adductor magnus. **hot cross bun h.,** caput natiforme. **hourglass h.,** a head in which the coronal suture is depressed. **humeral h. of flexor carpi ulnaris muscle,** caput humerale musculi flexoris carpi ulnaris. **humeral h. of flexor digitorum sublimis muscle,** caput humeroulnare musculi flexoris digitorum superficialis. **humeral h. of pronator teres muscle,** caput humerale musculi pronatoris teretis. **h. of humerus,** caput humeri. **infraorbital h. of quadratus labii superioris muscle,** musculus levator labii superioris. **inner h. of gastrocnemius muscle,** caput mediale musculi gastrocnemii. **internal h. of biceps flexor cubiti muscle,** caput breve musculi bicipitis brachii. **internal h. of triceps extensor cubiti muscle,** caput mediale musculi tricipitis brachii. **lateral h. of gastrocnemius muscle,** caput laterale musculi gastrocnemii. **lateral h. of triceps brachii muscle,** caput laterale musculi tricipitis brachii. **little h. of humerus,** capitulum humeri. **little h. of mandible,** processus condyloideus mandibulae. **little h. of metatarsal bone,** caput ossis metatarsalis. **long h. of adductor hullucis muscle,** caput obliquum musculus adductoris hallucis. **long h. of adductor triceps muscle,** musculus adductor longus. **long h. of biceps brachii muscle,** caput longum musculi bicipitis brachii. **long h. of**

biceps femoris muscle, caput longum musculi bicipitis femoris. **long h. of biceps flexor cruris muscle,** caput longum musculi bicipitis femoris. **long h. of biceps flexor cubiti muscle,** caput longum musculi bicipitis brachii. **long h. of triceps brachii muscle,** caput longum musculi tricipitis brachii. **long h. of triceps extensor cubiti muscle,** caput longum musculi tricipitis brachii. **long h. of triceps femoris muscle,** musculus adductor longus. **h. of malleus,** caput mallei. **h. of mandible.** 1. Caput mandibulae. 2. Processus condyloideus mandibulae. **medial h. of gastrocnemius muscle,** caput mediale musculi gastrocnemii. **medial h. of triceps brachii muscle,** caput mediale musculi tricipitis brachii. **medusa h.,** caput medusae. **h. of metacarpal bone,** caput ossis metacarpalis. **h. of metatarsal bone,** caput ossis metatarsalis. **middle h. of triceps extensor cubiti muscle,** caput longum musculi tricipitis brachii. **h. of muscle,** caput musculi. **nasal h. of levator labii superioris alaeque nasi muscle,** musculus levator labii superioris alaeque nasi. **nerve h.,** discus nervi optici. **oblique h. of adductor hallucis muscle,** caput obliquum musculus adductoris hallucis. **outer h. of gastrocnemius muscle,** caput laterale musculi gastrocnemii. **h. of pancreas,** caput pancreatis. **h. of penis,** glans penis. **h. of phalanx of fingers,** caput phalangis digitorum manus. **h. of phalanx of toes,** caput phalangis digitorum pedis. **plantar h. of flexor digitorum pedis longus muscle,** musculus quadratus plantae. **quadrate h. of flexor digitorum pedis longus muscle,** musculus quadratus plantae. **radial h. of flexor digitorum sublimis muscle,** caput radiale musculi flexoris digitorum superficialis. **radial h. of humerus,** capitulum humeri. **h. of radius,** caput radii. **h. of rib,** caput costae. **saddle h.,** a head with a sunken crown. **scapular h. of triceps extensor cubiti muscle,** caput longum musculi tricipitis brachii. **second h. of triceps extensor cubiti muscle,** caput laterale musculi tricipitis brachii. **short h. of biceps brachii muscle,** caput breve musculi bicipitis brachii. **short h. of biceps femoris muscle,** caput breve musculi bicipitis femoris. **short h. of biceps flexor cruris muscle,** caput breve musculi bicipitis femoris. **short h. of biceps flexor cubiti muscle,** caput breve musculi bicipitis brachii. **short h. of coracoradialis muscle,** caput breve musculi bicipitis brachii. **short h. of triceps extensor cubiti muscle,** caput mediale musculi tricipitis brachii. **short h. of triceps femoris muscle,** musculus adductor brevis. **h. of spleen,** extremitas posterior lienis. **h. of stapes,** caput stapedis. **steeple h.,** oxycephaly. **swelled h.,** a condition in young rams, caused by infection by *clostridium novyi,* and characterized by intense edematous swelling of the head, face, and neck. **h. of talus,** caput tali. **tower h.,** oxycephaly. **transverse h. of adductor hallucis muscle,** caput transversum musculi adductoris hallucis. **h. of ulna,** caput ulnae. **ulnar h. of flexor carpi ulnaris muscle,** caput ulnare musculi flexoris carpi ulnaris. **ulnar h. of pronator radii teres muscle,** caput ulnare musculi pronatoris teretis. **ulnar h. of pronator teres muscle,** caput ulnare musculi pronatoris teretis. **white h.,** witkop. **zygomatic h. of quadratus labii superior muscle,** musculus zygomaticus minor.

Head's zones [Henry *Head,* London neurologist, 1861–1940]. See under *zone.*

headache (hed′āk). Pain in the head; cephalagia. **anemic h.,** headache due to anemia, local or general. **bilious h., blind h.,** migraine. **congestive h.,** headache due to congestion or hyperemia. **dynamite h.,** a severe headache occurring in persons handling high explosives. **helmet h.,** pain involving the upper half of the head. **histamine h., Horton's h.,** histamine cephalalgia. **hyperemic h.,** congestive h. **miners' h.,** headache due to the gases produced by exploded nitroglycerin. **organic h.,** headache due to structural disease of the cerebral membranes. **puncture h.,** the headache and associated symptoms following puncture of the spinal canal and removal of cerebrospinal fluid. **pyrexial h.,** that due to fever. **reflex h.,** that due to disease of some organ, as the stomach, eyes, etc. **rhinogenous h.,** headache due to nasal disease. **sick h.,** migraine. **symptomatic h.,** reflex h. **toxic h.,** headache due to systemic poisoning. **vacuum h.,** headache due to obstruction of the outlet of the frontal sinus. **vasomotor h.,** histamine cephalalgia.

headgrit (hed′grit). Cholera of sheep.

headgut (hed′gut). The foregut.

healing (hēl′ing). A process of cure; the restoration of wounded parts. **h. by first intention,** healing in which the parts unite directly without the intervention of granulations. **h. by granulation,** healing by third intention. **h. by second intention,** union by the adhesion of granulating surfaces. **h. by third intention,** union by the filling of a wound with granulations. **mental h.,** psychotherapy. **metaphysical h.,** psychotherapy.

health (helth). A state of complete physical, mental, and social wellbeing, and not merely the absence of disease and infirmity.

healthy (hel′the). Pertaining to, characterized by, or promoting health.

hearing (hēr′ing) [L. *auditus*]. The sense by which sounds are appreciated. **color h.,** chromesthesia. **double disharmonic h.,** diplacusis. **monaural h.,** hearing with one ear. **visual h.,** lip reading.

heart (hart) [L. *cor;* Gr. *kardia*]. The viscus of cardiac muscle that maintains the circulation of the blood. Called also *cor* [N A, B N A]. It is divided into four cavities—two atria and two ventricles. The left atrium receives oxygenated blood from the lungs. From there the blood passes to the left ventricle, which forces it via the aorta through the arteries to supply the tissues of the body. The right atrium receives the blood after it has passed through the capillaries and given up much of its oxygen. The blood then passes to the right ventricle, and then to the lungs, to be oxygenated. The major valves are four in number: the *left atrioventricular valve* (*biscuspid,* or *mitral*), between the left atrium and ventricle; the *right atrioventricular valve* (*tricuspid*), between the right atrium and ventricle; the aortic, at the orifice of the aorta in the left ventricle; and the *pulmonary,* at the orifice of the pulmonary trunk in the right ventricle. **abdominal h.,** a heart displaced into the abdominal cavity. **armored h., armour h.,** a condition marked by calcareous deposits in the pericardium. **athletic h.,** hypertrophy of the heart with no disease of the valves, sometimes seen in athletes. **beer h.,** Tübingen h. **beriberi h.,** heart failure from avitaminosis. **boat-shaped h.,** the heart of aortic regurgitation due to dilatation and hypertrophy of the left ventricle. **bony h.,** a heart containing calcareous patches. **cervical h.,** one situated high up in the neck. **chaotic h.,** a heart which exhibits frequent premature systoles arising from multiple foci. **encased h.,** a heart affected with chronic constrictive pericarditis. **fat h., fatty h.** 1. A heart affected with fatty degeneration. 2. A condition in which there is an excessive layer of fat deposited about and in the heart muscle. **fibroid h.,** a heart affected with a chronic myocarditis in which fibrous tissue is developed within the muscular tissue of the organ. **flask-shaped h.,** the x-ray appearance of the heart in pericarditis with effusion. **frosted h.,** a condition in which the pericardium is thickened, giving the heart the appearance of being frosted like a cake. **hairy h.,** cor villosum. **hanging h.,** a condition as seen in the roentgenogram in cardioptosis, in which the heart appears as if hanging straight down from

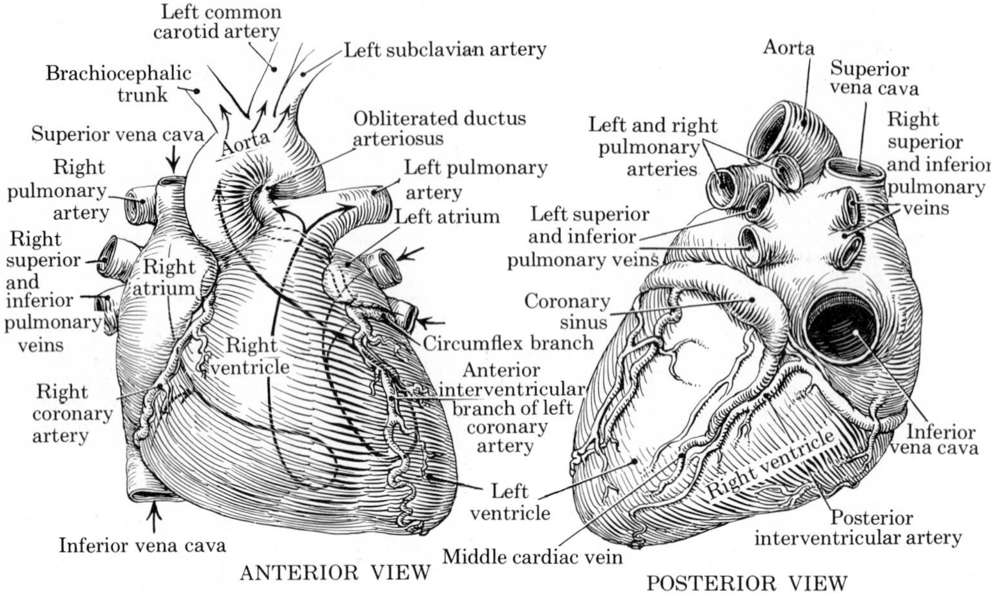

ANTERIOR VIEW

POSTERIOR VIEW

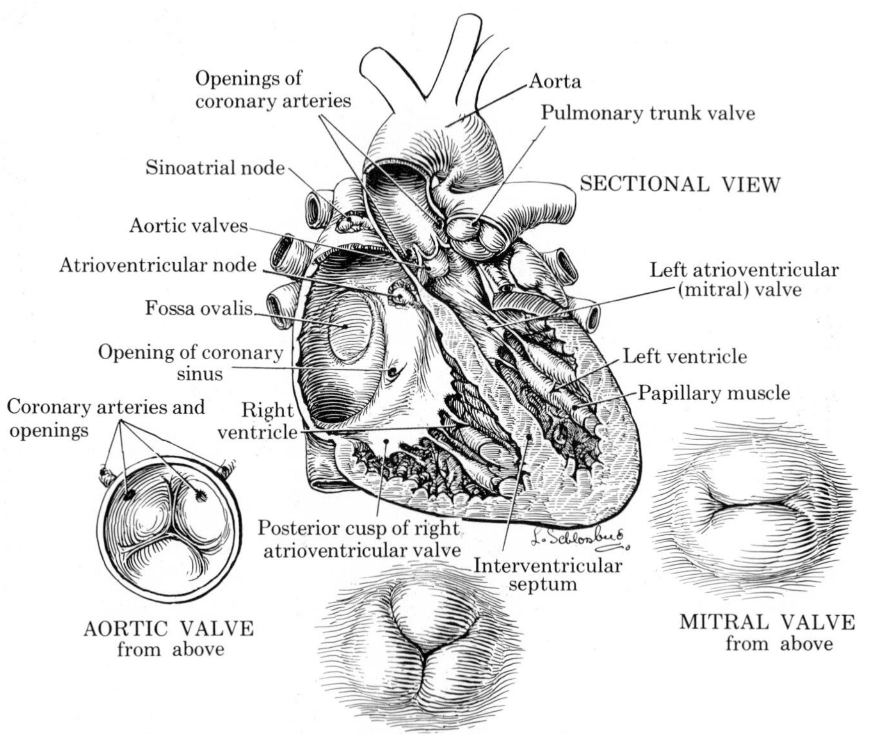

SECTIONAL VIEW

AORTIC VALVE from above

MITRAL VALVE from above

RIGHT ATRIOVENTRICULAR (TRICUSPID) VALVE from above

DETAILS OF STRUCTURE OF THE HEART

the aorta. **hypoplastic h.,** a heart of small size. **icing h.,** frosted h. **irritable h.,** neurocirculatory asthenia. **left h.,** the left atrium and ventricle; that portion of the heart which propels the blood in the systemic circulation. **luxus h.,** dilatation of the left ventricle of the heart, conjoined with hypertrophy. **lymph h.,** an organ in frogs and fishes concerned in the distribution of lymph. **myxedema h.,** an enlarged heart associated with hypothyroidism. **ox h.,** cor bovinum. **pear-shaped h.,** the x-ray appearance of the heart in combined aortic and mitral disease. **pectoral h.,** a heart situated in the front of the chest where it produces a bulging area. **pendulous h.,** drop heart. **pulmonary h.,** right heart. **Quain's fatty h.,** a fatty degeneration of the heart muscle. **right h.,** the right atrium and ventricle; that portion of the heart which propels the blood in the pulmonary circulation. **round h.,** the x-ray appearance of the heart in mitral stenosis and regurgitation. **sabot h.,** coeur en sabot. **soldier's h.** neurocirculatory asthenia. **stony h.,** a heart rigidly contracted in ventricular systole: it occurs in heat stroke. **systemic h.,** left heart. **tabby cat h.,** a condition of the heart in which the inner surface of the ventricular wall and the papillary muscles are streaked and spotted: seen in marked cases of fatty degeneration. Called also *thrush breast h., tiger h.,* and *tiger lily h.* **thrush breast h., tiger h., tiger lily h.,** tabby cat h. **tobacco h.,** a heart showing irregularity of action as a result of excessive use of tobacco. **Traube's h.,** heart disease resulting from kidney disorder. **triatrial h.,** cor triatriatum. **Tübingen h.,** dilatation and hypertrophy of the heart from excessive beer drinking. **turtle h.,** sino-auricular heart block. **wandering h.,** an abnormally movable heart. **wooden-shoe h.,** coeur en sabot.

heart-block (hart′blok). The condition in which the muscular interconnection between the auricle and ventricle (auriculoventricular band or band of His) is interrupted, so that the auricle and ventricle beat independently of each other (Gaskell). The condition is marked by permanent or paroxysmal bradycardia, epileptiform, vertiginous, or syncopal attacks, and pulsations of the cervical veins exceeding in rate those of the arteries. The condition is known as *Adams-Stokes disease.* **arborization h.,** a form in which there is interference with the fine terminal subendocardial fibers of the Purkinje system. The electrocardiogram shows a diphasic curve absent and a negative T wave and a splintered R wave present. **atrioventricular h., auriculoventricular h.,** a form in which the blocking is at the auriculoventricular junction. **bundle-branch h.,** interventricular h. **complete h.,** a condition in which the functional relation between the parts of the bundle of His is destroyed by a lesion, so that the auricles and ventricles act independently of each other. **interventricular h.,** a form in which one ventricle contracts without the other on account of obstruction in one of the branches of the bundle of His; called also *bundle-branch block.* **sino-auricular h.,** a form in which the blocking is located between the auricles and the mouths of the great veins and coronary sinus.

heartburn (hart′burn). A burning sensation in the esophagus; pyrosis.

heart-failure (hart′fāl-yer). 1. Sudden fatal cessation of the heart's action. 2. The clinical condition resulting from inability of the myocardium of the ventricles to maintain an adequate flow of blood to all the tissues of the body. **backward h.,** that produced by passive engorgement of the venous system caused by a backward rise in pressure proximal to the heart. **congestive h.,** prolonged impairment of the ability of the heart to maintain an adequate flow of blood to the tissues. **forward h.,** diminution in the amount of blood propelled in a forward direction by the heart, resulting in inadequate supply of blood to the tissues. **left ventricular h.,** failure of proper output by the left ventricle, with dyspnea, orthopnea, etc. **right ventricular h.,** failure of proper functioning of the right ventricle, with venous engorgement, hepatic enlargement, and subcutaneous edema.

heartometer (hart-om′e-ter). An instrument serving as a combined sphygmotonograph and plethysmograph.

heartwater (hart-wot′er). A fatal disease of cattle, sheep, and goats, marked by fluid accumulation in the pleura, pericardium and pleural cavity. It is caused by *Cowdria ruminantium,* which is transmitted by the ticks *Amblyomma hebraeum* and *A. variagata.*

heartworm (hart′werm). *Dirofilaria immitis.*

HEAT. Abbreviation for *human erythrocyte agglutination test.*

heat (hēt) [L. *calor;* Gr. *thermē*]. 1. The sensation of an increase in temperature. 2. The energy which produces the sensation of heat. It exists in the form of molecular or atomic vibration (thermal agitation) and may be transferred by conduction through a substance, by convection by a substance, and by radiation as electromagnetic waves. 3. Sexual ardor of animals. **atomic h.,** the amount of heat required to raise an atom from 0 to 1°C. **conductive h.,** heat applied to the body by continuity from a heated object, such as a hot water bag. **convective h.,** heat thrown on to the surface of the body from some outside source. In physical therapy, heating of the body surface by rays from the visible and infra-red regions of the spectrum. **conversive h.,** heat which is developed in the tissues by the resistance of the tissues to the passage of high-frequency waves through them. **delayed h.,** recovery heat. **dry h.,** heat that is not moist. Heated dry air is used in an apparatus such as a covered "baker," designed for the production of hyperemia. The dry air rapidly absorbs from the skin the moisture of perspiration induced in the apparatus during treatment. **initial h.,** the heat produced in muscle at the very beginning of muscular contraction. Cf. *recovery h.* **latent h.,** that which apparently disappears when it is absorbed by bodies which thereby are not rendered warmer; the heat which a body may absorb without changing its temperature. **molecular h.,** the product of the molecular weight of a substance multiplied by its specific heat. **prickly h.,** miliaria. **radiant h.,** electromagnetic waves longer than the waves of red light and shorter than the Hertzian waves. **recovery h.,** that part of the heat developed by muscular contraction which is evolved after shortening has begun. Cf. *initial h.* **sensible h.,** the heat which, when absorbed by a body, produces a rise in temperature. **specific h.,** the amount of energy required to raise the temperature of unit mass of a substance one degree.

Heath's operation (hēths) [Christopher *Heath,* English surgeon, 1835–1905]. See under *operation.*

Heaton's operation (he′tonz) [George *Heaton,* Boston surgeon, 1808–1879]. See under *operation.*

heaves (hēvz). A respiratory disturbance, most common in the Equidae, resulting from reduced elasticity in and rupture of the elastic network of the respiratory bronchioles and pulmonary alveoli and characterized by partly forced expiration.

Hebdom. Abbreviation for L. *hebdom′ada,* a week.

hebeosteotomy (heb″e-os″te-ot′o-me). Pubiotomy.

hebephrenia (heb″ĕ-fre′ne-ah) [Gr. *hēbē* youth + *phrēn* mind]. A clinical form of dementia praecox (schizophrenia) coming on soon after the onset of puberty and marked by rapid deterioration, hallucinations, absurd delusion, senseless laughter, and silly mannerisms. See *dementia praecox.* **grafted h.,** hebephrenia grafted, as it were, on feeblemindedness.

hebephreniac (heb″ĕ-fre′ne-ak). An individual exhibiting hebephrenia.

Heberden's asthma, disease, nodes (he′ber-denz) [William *Heberden*, English physician, 1710–1801]. See under the nouns.

hebetic (he-bet′ik) [Gr. *hēbētikos* youthful]. Pertaining to or occurring at the time of puberty.

hebetomy (he-bet′o-me). Pubiotomy.

hebetude (heb′ĕ-tūd) [L. *hebetudo*]. Mental dullness with impairment of the special senses, such as is seen in asthenic fevers.

hebiatrics (he″be-at′riks). Ephebiatrics.

heboid (heb′oid) [Gr. *hēbē* youth + *eidos* form]. The simple form of dementia praecox.

heboidophrenia (heb″oi-do-fre′ne-ah). Dementia praecox marked by simple dementia.

hebosteotomy (he-bos″te-ot′o-me). Pubiotomy.

hebotomy (he-bot′o-me). Pubiotomy.

Hebra's disease, ointment, etc. (he′brahs) [Ferdinand von *Hebra*, Austrian dermatologist, 1816–1880, founder of the histologic school of dermatology]. See under the nouns.

hecatomeral (hek″ah-tom′er-al). Hecatomeric.

hecatomeric (hek″ah-to-mer′ik) [Gr. *hekateron* each of two + *meros* part]. Having processes which divide into two, one going to each side of the spinal cord: used of certain neurons.

Hecht's phenomenon (hekts) [Adolf *Hecht*, Vienna pediatrist, born 1876]. Rumpel-Leede phenomenon.

Hecht's test (hekts) [Hugo *Hecht*, Prague physician, in Cleveland, born 1883]. See under *tests*.

Hecker's law (hek′erz) [Karl v. *Hecker*, German obstetrician, 1827–1882]. See under *law*.

hectic (hek′tik) [L. *hecticus;* Gr. *hektikos* consumptive]. Associated with tuberculosis or with septic poisoning.

hecto- (hek′to) [Fr., from Gr. *hekaton* one hundred]. Combining form designating one hundred; used in naming units of measurement to indicate a quantity 100 (10^2) times the unit designated by the root with which it is combined.

hectogram (hek′to-gram). A unit of mass of the metric system, being 10^2 grams; the equivalent of 3.527 ounces avoirdupois, or 3.215 ounces apothecaries' weight.

hectoliter (hek′to-le-ter). A unit of capacity of the metric system, being 10^2 liters; the equivalent of 26.4 United States or 22 Imperial gallons.

hectometer (hek-tom′e-ter). A unit of linear measure of the metric system, being 10^2 meters, or the equivalent, roughly, of 328 feet and one inch.

H.E.D. Abbreviation for German *Haut-Einheits-Dosis* (unit skin dose), a unit of roentgen-ray dosage established by Seitz and Wintz.

hederiform (hed′er-ĭ-form) [L. *hedera* ivy + *forma* shape]. Ivy-shaped: a term applied to certain nerve endings in the malpighian layer of the skin.

hedonia (he-do′ne-ah). Abnormal cheerfulness.

hedonic (he-don′ik). Pertaining to pleasure.

hedonics (he-don′iks) [Gr. *hēdonē* pleasure]. The study of pleasurable and unpleasurable feelings.

hedonism (he′don-izm) [Gr. *hēdonē* pleasure]. Devotion to pleasure; the doctrine that regards pleasure and happiness as the highest good.

hedonophobia (he-don″o-fo′be-ah) [Gr. *hēdonē* pleasure + *phobia*]. Fear of pleasure.

hedratresia (hed″rah-tre′se-ah) [Gr. *hedra* anus + *atresia*]. Imperforation of the anus.

hedrocele (hed′ro-sēl) [Gr. *hedra* anus + *kēlē* hernia]. Hernia, or prolapse, of the intestine through the anus.

hedulin (hed′u-lin). Trade mark for a preparation of phenindione.

heel (hēl) [L. *calx*]. The hindmost part of the foot. **anterior h.,** a triangular-shaped piece of leather fastened obliquely across the ball of the shoe just behind the heads of the metatarsal bones, the object being to support the heads, equalize the pressure, and support the anterior arch. **big h.,** epidemic enlargement of the os calcis occurring in parts of Africa. **contracted h.,** hoof-bound. **cracked h's,** keratodermia plantare sulcatum. **gonorrheal h.,** the development of exostoses on the heel, attributed to gonorrheal infection. **painful h.,** a condition in which pain is caused by pressure on the heel. **policeman's h.,** calcanodynia in a policeman. **prominent h.,** a swelling on the back of the heel due to thickening of the periosteum of the os calcis. **Thomas h.,** a shoe correction consisting a heel $\frac{1}{2}$ in. longer and $\frac{1}{6}$–$\frac{1}{8}$ in. higher on the inside, used to bring the heel of the foot into varus and to prevent depression in the region of the head of the talus. **weak h.,** a condition of the wall of a horse's hoof in which, owing to the softness of the horn and the oblique direction of the horn fibers, the heels are unable to bear the body weight.

Heerfordt's disease (hār′forts) [C. F. *Heerfordt*, Danish ophthalmologist]. Uveoparotid fever.

hefeflavin (hef′ĕ-fla″vin). A lyochrome pigment from yeast.

Hegar's dilator, operation, sign (ha′garz) [Alfred *Hegar*, gynecologist in Freiburg, 1830–1914]. See under the nouns.

hegemony (hĕ-jem′o-ne) [Gr. *hēgemōn* leader]. Leadership; the state of being chief.

Heiberg-Esmarch maneuver (hi′berg es′-mark) [Jacob *Heiberg*, Norwegian surgeon, 1843–1888; Johann Friedrich August von *Esmarch*, German surgeon, 1823–1908]. See under *maneuver*.

Heichelheim's test (hi′kel-hīmz) [Rudolf *Heichelheim*, German physician]. See under *tests*.

Heidenhain's cells, law, rods, stain, etc. (hi′den-hīnz) [Rudolph P. *Heidenhain*, German physiologist, 1834–1897]. See under the nouns.

height (hīt). The vertical measurement of an object or body. **apex h.,** the magnitude of the ordinates of the summated twitches of a muscle following application of electric or other stimulation. **h. of contour,** a line surrounding the crown of a tooth and marking the junction of the surfaces sloping occlusally and those sloping cervically. **sitting h.,** sitting vertex h. **sitting suprasternal h.,** the distance from the middle of the anterior-superior border of the manubrium sterni to the surface on which the subject is seated. **sitting vertex h.,** the distance from the highest point of the head in the sagittal plane to the surface on which the subject is seated; commonly called *sitting height.* **standing h.,** the distance from the highest point of the head in the sagittal plane to the surface on which the individual is standing, measured when the subject is not wearing shoes.

Heilbronner's sign, thigh (hīl′bron-erz) [Karl *Heilbronner*, Dutch physician, 1870–1914]. See under *thigh*.

Heim's pill (hīmz) [Ernst Ludwig *Heim*, German physician, 1747–1834]. See under *pill*.

Heim-Kreysig sign (hīm-kri′sig) [E. L. *Heim;* Friedrich Ludwig *Kreysig*, German physician, 1770–1839]. See under *sign*.

Heine's operation (hi′nez) [Leopold *Heine*, German oculist, 1870–1940]. See under *operation*.

Heine-Medin disease (hi′nĕ ma′din) [Jacob *Heine*, German physician, 1800–1879; Karl Oskar *Medin*, Swedish physician, 1847–1928]. See under *disease*.

Heineke-Mikulicz operation (hi′nĕ-kĕ mik′-u-lich) [Walter Hermann *Heineke*, German surgeon, 1834–1901; Johann von *Mikulicz*-Radecki, Polish surgeon, 1850–1905]. See under *operation*.

Heinz bodies, granules (hints) [Robert *Heinz*, German pathologist, 1865–1924]. See under *body*.

Heiser's treatment (hi′serz) [Victor G. *Heiser*, American physician, born 1873]. See under *treatment*.

Heisrath's operation (hīs′raths) [Friedrich *Heisrath*, German ophthalmologist, 1850–1904]. See under *operation*.

Heister's diverticulum, valve (hīs′terz) [Lorenz *Heister*, German anatomist, 1683–1758]. See under *diverticulum* and *valve*.

Hektoen phenomenon (hek′tōn) [Ludvig *Hektoen*, Chicago pathologist, 1863–1951]. See under *phenomenon*.

HeLa cells (he′lah) [from the name of the patient from whose carcinoma of the cervix uteri the parent carcinoma cells were isolated in 1951 at Johns Hopkins Hospital by Dr. George O. Gey]. See under *cell*.

helcoid (hel′koid) [Gr. *helkos* ulcer + *eidos* form]. Resembling an ulcer.

helcology (hel-kol′o-je) [Gr. *helkos* ulcer + *-logy*]. The scientific study of ulcers.

helcoma (hel-ko′mah) [Gr.]. Corneal ulcer (Hippocrates).

helcoplasty (hel′ko-plas″te) [Gr. *helkos* ulcer + *plassein* to form]. Plastic surgery of ulcer sites.

helcosis (hel-ko′sis) [Gr. *helkōsis*]. Ulceration; the formation of an ulcer.

Helcosoma tropicum (hel″ko-so′mah trop′ĭ-kum). *Leishmania tropica.*

Heleidae (hĕ-le′ĭ-de). A family of flies of the order Diptera, containing, among others, the four genera *Culicoides, Haemophoructus, Lasiohelea,* and *Leptoconops,* various species of which suck the blood of man, and may serve as vectors of disease. Formerly called *Ceratopogonidae.*

helianthin (he-le-an′thin). An orange-yellow aniline dye, the sodium salt of para-dimethyl-amino-azo-benzene-sulfonic acid: an indicator with a pH range of 3.1–4.4, being red at 3.1 and yellow at 4.4. Called also *tropeolin D, methyl orange,* and *Poirrier's orange.*

heliation (he″le-a′shun). Treatment by exposure to the sun's rays.

helicin (hel′ĭ-sin). A glycoside formed by oxidizing salicin, which on hydrolysis yields glucose and salicylic aldehyde.

helicine (hel′ĭ-sīn). 1. Of a spiral form. 2. Of or pertaining to the helix.

helico- (hel′ĭ-ko) [Gr. *helix* coil]. Combining form denoting relationship to a coil, or to a snail (Helix).

helicoid (hel′ĭ-koid) [*helico-* + Gr. *eidos* form]. Resembling a coil or helix.

helicopepsin (hel″ĭ-ko-pep′sin) [*helico-* + *pepsin*]. An enzyme resembling pepsin, from snails.

helicopodia (hel″ĭ-ko-po′de-ah). Helicopod gait.

helicoprotein (hel″ĭ-ko-pro′te-in) [*helico-* + *protein*]. A glucoprotein substance obtained from the snail, *Helix pomata.*

helicorubrin (hel″ĭ-ko-roo′brin). A respiratory pigment (hemochromogen), occurring in the liver and gut of the snail, *Helix pomata,* and other articulates and mollusks.

helicotrema (hel″ĭ-ko-tre′mah) [*helico-* + Gr. *trēma* hole]. [N A, B N A] The passage that connects the scala tympani and scala vestibuli at the apex of the cochlea.

helide (he′lid). A compound of an element with helium.

helio- (he′le-o) [Gr. *hēlios* sun]. Combining form denoting relationship to the sun.

helioaerotherapy (he″le-o-a″er-o-ther′ah-pe) [*helio-* + Gr. *aēr* air + *therapeia* treatment]. Treatment by exposure to the sun's rays and to fresh air.

helion (he′le-on). Helium.

heliopathia (he″le-o-path′e-ah) [*helio-* + Gr. *pathos* disease]. Any pathological disturbance caused by sunlight.

heliophobe (he′le-o-fōb). A person morbidly sensitive to the sun's rays.

heliophobia (he″le-o-fo′be-ah) [*helio-* + *phobia*]. Morbid avoidance or dread of sunlight.

heliosensitivity (he″le-o-sen″sĭ-tiv′ĭ-te). Sensitivity to sunlight.

heliosin (he″le-o′sin). A compound containing keratin and various inorganic salts.

heliosis (he″le-o′sis) [*helio-* + *-osis*]. Sunstroke.

heliotaxis (he″le-o-tak′sis) [*helio-* + Gr. *taxis* arrangement]. The motile response of an organism to the stimulus of light. **negative h.,** the motile response of an organism in the opposite direction from the source of the light stimulus. **positive h.,** the motile response of an organism toward the source of the light stimulus.

heliotherapy (he″le-o-ther′ah-pe) [*helio-* + *therapy*]. The treatment of disease by exposing the body to the sun's rays; the therapeutic use of the sun bath.

heliotrope B (he′le-o-trōp″be). Amethyst violet. See under *violet.*

heliotropism (he″le-ot′ro-pizm) [*helio-* + Gr. *tropē* a turn, turning]. The tendency of an organism to orient itself in relation to the stimulus of light. **negative h.,** the tendency of an organism to orient itself away from the source of the light stimulus. **positive h.,** the tendency of an organism to orient itself toward the source of the light stimulus.

helisterine (hĕ-lis′ter-in) [Gr. *helix* snail]. A sterol from snails.

helium (he′le-um) [Gr. *hēlios* sun]. A colorless, odorless, tasteless gas, one of the inert, gaseous elements which was first detected in the sun and is now obtained from natural gas. Symbol, He; atomic number, 2; atomic weight, 4.003. Used in medicine as a diluent for other gases.

helix (he′liks) [Gr. "snail," "coil"]. 1. A coiled structure, such as the coil of wire in an electromagnet. 2. [N A, B N A] The superior and posterior free margin of the pinna of the ear.

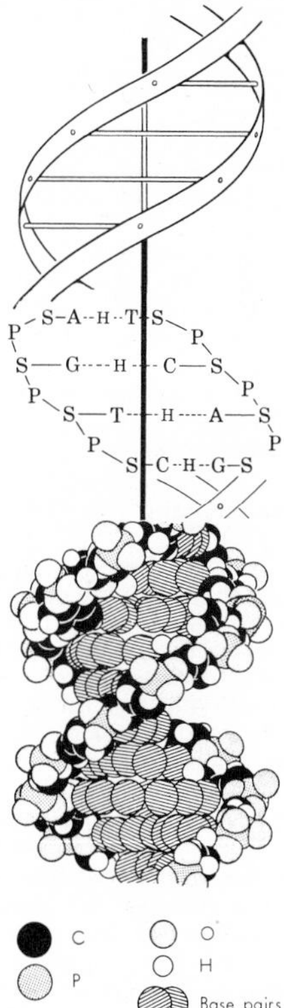

The DNA helix, representing the structure of deoxyribonucleic acid. *Upper:* as a spiral staircase. *Middle:* as an arrangement of organic molecules (A = adenine, C = cystine, G = guanine, P = phosphate, S = sugar, T = thymine) and hydrogen bonds. *Lower:* as an arrangement of atoms of carbon, hydrogen, oxygen, and phosphorus, and base pairs as shown. (From Swanson: The Cell, Prentice-Hall, Inc., 1960.)

Watson-Crick h., a double helix, each chain of which contains information completely specifying the other chain, representing a structural formulation of the mechanism by which the genetic information in DNA reproduces itself.

Helkesimastix (hel″kĕ-sĭ-mas′tiks). A genus of coprozoic flagellates. **H. fecic′ola**, an oval coprozoic flagellate which has been grown from human feces.

Hellat's sign (hel′ats) [Piotr *Hellat*, Russian otologist, 1857–1912]. See under *sign*.

Hellendall's sign (hel′en-dahlz) [Hugo *Hellendall*, gynecologist in Düsseldorf, born 1872]. Cullen's sign.

Heller's test (hel′erz) [Johann Florenz *Heller*, Vienna pathologist, 1813–1871]. See under *tests*.

Hellin's law (hel′inz) [Dyonizy *Hellin*, Polish pathologist, 1867–1935]. See under *law*.

Helmholtz's ligament, theory (helm′holtz-ez) [Hermann Ludwig Ferdinand von *Helmholtz*, German physiologist, 1821–1894]. See under *ligament* and *theory*.

helminth (hel′minth) [Gr. *helmins* worm]. A worm or wormlike parasite.

helminthagogue (hel-min′thah-gog) [*helminth* + Gr. *agōgos* leading]. Vermifuge.

helminthemesis (hel″min-them′ĕ-sis) [*helminth* + Gr. *emesis* vomiting]. The vomiting of worms.

helminthiasis (hel″min-thi′ah-sis). A morbid state due to infection with worms. **cutaneous h.**, larva migrans. **h. elas′tica**, the occurrence of elastic tumors in the groin and axilla, probably due to filariae. **h. wuchere′ri**, a term proposed by V. Pereira for all forms of filariasis.

helminthic (hel-min′thik). Pertaining to or caused by worms.

helminthicide (hel-min′thĭ-sīd) [*helminth* + L. *caedere* to kill]. Vermicide.

helminthism (hel′min-thizm). The presence of worms in the body.

helminthochorton (hel-min″tho-kor′ton) [*helminth* + Gr. *chortos* grass]. A mixture of pigments of seaweeds obtained in Corsica: vermifuge and antipyretic.

helminthoid (hel-min′thoid) [*helminth* + Gr. *eidos* form]. Wormlike.

helminthology (hel″min-thol′o-je) [*helminth* + *-logy*]. The scientific study of worms.

helminthoma (hel″min-tho′mah) [*helminth* + *-oma*]. A tumor caused by a parasitic worm.

helminthophobia (hel-min″tho-fo′be-ah) [*helminth* + *phobia*]. Morbid fear of being infected with worms.

helminthous (hel-min′thus). Pertaining to or infected with worms.

helo- (he′lo) [Gr. *hēlos* nail]. Combining form denoting relationship to a nail, or to a wart or callus.

Heloderma (he″lo-der′mah) [*helo-* + Gr. *derma* skin]. A genus of venomous lizards of Arizona and New Mexico. *H. hor′ridum*, the Mexican caltelepon. *H. suspec′tum*, the Gila monster.

heloma (he-lo′mah) [*helo-* + *-oma*]. A corn or callosity on the hand or foot.

Helophilus (hĕ-lof′ĭ-lus). A genus of flies, hover flies, whose larvae may cause nasal and intestinal myiasis.

helosis (he-lo′sis). The condition of having corns.

helotomeia (he″lo-to-mi′ah). Helotomy.

helotomy (he-lot′o-me) [*helo-* + Gr. *temnein* to cut]. The excision of corns or of calluses.

Helweg's bundle, tract (hel′vegz) [Hans Kristian Saxtorph *Helweg*, Danish physician, 1847–1901]. Olivospinal tract.

hem (hēm). Heme.

hem-, hema-. See *hemo-*.

hemabarometer (hem″ah-bah-rom′e-ter) [*hema-* + *barometer*]. An instrument for ascertaining the specific gravity of the blood.

hemachromatosis (hem″ah-kro″mah-to′sis). Hemochromatosis.

hemachrome (hem′ah-krōm). Hemochrome.

hemachrosis (hem″ah-kro′sis) [*hema-* + Gr. *chrōsis* coloring]. Abnormal or excessive redness of the blood.

hemacyanine (hem″ah-si′ah-nin). Hematocyanine.

hemacyte (hem′ah-sīt). Hemocyte.

hemacytometer (hem″ah-si-tom′e-ter) [*hema-* + Gr. *kytos* hollow vessel + Gr. *metron* measure]. An instrument used in counting the blood corpuscles.

hemacytometry (hem″ah-si-tom′e-tre). The counting of blood corpuscles by means of a hemacytometer.

hemacytopoiesis (hem″ah-si″to-poi-e′sis). Hematopoiesis.

hemacytozoon (hem″ah-si″to-zo′on), pl. *hemacytozo′a*. Hemocytozoon.

hemad (he′mad). 1. Toward the hemal or ventral aspect. 2. A blood corpuscle.

hemaden (hem′ah-den) [*hem-* + Gr. *adēn* gland]. A ductless gland.

hemadenology (hem″ad-e-nol′o-je) [*hem-* + Gr. *adēn* gland + *-logy*]. The study of the relations of the internal secretions to general diseases.

hemadostenosis (hem″ad-o-ste-no′sis) [Gr. *haimas* blood stream + *stenōsis* narrowing]. The narrowing or obliteration of a blood vessel.

hemadromograph (hem″ah-drom′o-graf). Hemodromograph.

hemadromometer (hem″ah-dro-mom′e-ter). Hemodromometer.

hemadynamometer (hem″ah-di″nah-mom′e-ter). Hemodynamometer.

hemadynamometry (hem″ah-di″nah-mom′e-tre). Measurement of blood pressure.

hemafacient (hem″ah-fa′shent). Hematopoietic.

hemafecia (hem″ah-fe′se-ah) [*hema-* + *feces*]. Blood in the feces.

hemagglutination (hem″ah-gloo″tĭ-na′shun). Agglutination of erythrocytes, which may be caused by antibodies (see *hemagglutinin*) or by certain virus particles (e.g., the viruses of influenza and mumps). **passive h.**, the agglutination of erythrocytes on which antigen has been adsorbed in the presence of antiserum to that antigen. **viral h.**, the agglutination of erythrocytes (usually chicken) in the presence of hemagglutinating viruses, e.g., influenza, mumps, etc.

hemagglutinative (hem″ah-gloo′tĭ-na″tiv). Pertaining to, characterized by, or causing agglutination of erythrocytes.

hemagglutinin (hem″ah-gloo′tĭ-nin) [*hem-* + *agglutinin*]. An antibody that agglutinates erythrocytes, classified according to the cells which it agglutinates as *autologous* (cells of the same organism), *heterologous* (cells of individuals of other species), and *homologous* (cells of other individuals of the same species). Some hemagglutinins are effective with erythrocytes suspended in 0.85 per cent sodium chloride solution; others are ineffective unless hydrophilic colloids (e.g., albumin, fibrinogen) are added, or the erythrocytes have been treated with a proteolytic enzyme. **cold h.**, one which acts only at temperatures near 4°C. **warm h.**, one which acts only at temperatures near 37°C.

hemagogic (hem″ah-goj′ik). Of the nature of a hemagogue; promoting the discharge of blood.

hemagogue (hem′ah-gog) [*hem-* + Gr. *agōgos* leading]. An agent that promotes a sanguineous discharge.

hemagonium (hem″ah-go′ne-um) [*hema-* + Gr. *gonē* seed]. Hemoblast, def. 1.

hemal (he′mal). Pertaining to the blood.

hemalexin (hem″ah-lek′sin). An alexin of the blood.

hemalexis (hem″ah-lek′sis) [*hem-* + Gr. *alexein*

to protect]. The production of alexins or protective elements of the blood.

hemalum (hem-al′um). A compound containing hematoxylin and alum, widely used as a nuclear stain, especially in combination with eosin.

hemanalysis (hem″ah-nal′ĭ-sis) [*hem-* + *analysis*]. Analysis or examination of the blood.

hemangiectasia (hem″an-je-ek-ta′se-ah). Hemangiectasis.

hemangiectasis (hem″an-je-ek′tah-sis) [*hem-* + Gr. *angeion* vessel + *ektasis* dilatation]. Dilatation of blood vessels.

hemangioameloblastoma (hĕ-man″je-o-ah-mel″o-blas-to′mah). Ameloblastic hemangioma.

hemangioblast (hĕ-man′je-o-blast). A mesodermal cell which gives rise to both vascular endothelium and hemocytoblasts.

hemangioblastoma (hĕ-man″je-o-blas-to′mah). A capillary hemangioma of the brain consisting of proliferated blood vessel cells or angioblasts.

hemangioendothelioblastoma (hĕ-man″je-o-en″do-the″le-o-blas-to′mah) [*hem-* + Gr. *angeion* vessel + *endothelium* + Gr. *blastos* germ + *-oma*]. A tumor of mesenchymal origin of which the cells tend to form endothelial cells and line blood vessels.

hemangioendothelioma (hĕ-man″je-o-en″do-the″le-o′mah) [*hemangioma* + *endothelioma*]. A tumor formed by malignant proliferation of the endothelium of the capillary vessels. **h. tubero′sum mul′tiplex,** a hyperplasia of the endothelium of the cutaneous blood vessels producing an eruption of nodules and papules.

hemangiofibroma (hĕ-man″je-o-fi-bro′mah). A hemangioma containing fibrous tissue.

hemangioma (hĕ-man″je-o′mah) [*hem-* + *angioma*]. A benign tumor made up of new-formed blood vessels. Cf. *angioma* and *lymphangioma*. **ameloblastic h.,** a tumor composed of an ameloblastoma and hemangioma occurring concomitantly. **capillary h.,** nevus flammeus. **cavernous h.,** angioma cavernosum. **h. congenita′le,** h. simplex. **h. hypertroph′icum cu′tis,** a cellular form of capillary hemangioma occurring chiefly on the skin. **h. sim′plex,** a vascular nevus made up of red elevations composed of aggregations of small blood vessels, present at or appearing soon after birth.

hemangiomatosis (hĕ-man″je-o-mah-to′sis). A condition in which multiple hemangiomas are developed.

hemangiopericyte (hĕ-man″je-o-per′ĭ-sit). Pericyte.

hemangiopericytoma (hĕ-man″je-o-per″ĕ-si-to′mah). A tumor composed of spindled cells with a rich vascular network, which apparently arises from pericytes. It is related to a glomus tumor but, unlike the latter, has no nerve elements.

hemangiosarcoma (hĕ-man″je-o-sar-ko′mah). A malignant tumor formed by proliferation of endothelial and fibroblastic tissue.

hemapheic (hem″ah-fe′ik). Pertaining to or characterized by hemaphein.

hemaphein (hem″ah-fe′in) [*hema-* + Gr. *phaios* dusky, gray]. A brown coloring matter of the blood and urine.

hemapheism (hem″ah-fe′izm). The presence of hemaphein in the urine.

hemaphobia (hem″ah-fo′be-ah). Hemophobia.

hemaphotograph (hem″ah-fo′to-graf). Hemophotograph.

hemapoiesis (hem″ah-poi-e′sis) [*hema-* + Gr. *poiēsis* formation]. Hematopoiesis.

hemapoietic (hem″ah-poi-et′ik). Hematopoietic.

hemapophysis (hem″ah-pof′ĭ-sis) [*hem-* + *apophysis*]. A costal cartilage regarded as an apophysis of the hemal spine.

hemarthros (hem-ar′thros). Hemarthrosis.

hemarthrosis (hem″ar-thro′sis) [*hem-* + Gr. *arthron* joint]. Extravasation of blood into a joint or its synovial cavity.

hemartoma (hem″ar-to′mah). A tumor of new-formed blood vessels.

hemase (hem′ās) [*hem-* + *-ase*]. A catalase found in the blood.

hemasthenosis (hem″as-the-no′sis) [*hem-* + Gr. *astheneia* weakness]. 1. Defective circulation of the blood. 2. A defective state of the blood.

hemastrontium (hem″as-tron′she-um). A tissue stain prepared by adding strontium chloride to a solution of hematein and aluminum chloride in alcohol and citric acid.

hemat-, hemata-. See *hemo-*.

hematachometer (hem″ah-tah-kom′e-ter). Hemotachometer.

hemataerometer (hem″at-a″er-om′e-ter) [*hemat-* + Gr. *aēr* air + *metron* measure]. An instrument for measuring the pressure of gases in the blood.

hematal (hem′ah-tal). Pertaining to blood or blood vessels.

hematalloscopy (hem″at-ah-los′ko-pe) [*hemat-* + Gr. *allos* other + *skopein* to examine]. The examination of blood to distinguish one kind from another.

hematapostasis (hem″at-ah-pos′tah-sis) [*hemat-* + Gr. *apostasis* standing away]. The metastasis of blood.

hematapostema (hem″at-ah-pos-te′mah) [*hemat-* + Gr. *apostēma* abscess]. An abscess containing effused blood.

hemate (hem′āt). A compound of hematein.

hemateikon (hem″ah-ti′kon) [*hemat-* + Gr. *eikōn* image]. The blood picture, or appearance of the blood under the microscope.

hematein (hem″ah-te′in). A brownish-red, crystalline substance, $C_{16}H_{12}O_6$, derived from hematoxylin by oxidation.

hematemesis (hem″at-em′e-sis) [*hemat-* + Gr. *emesis* vomiting]. The vomiting of blood. **Goldstein's h.,** hematemesis due to bleeding telangiectases in the stomach. **h. puella′ris,** blood vomiting in girls or young women with no stomach lesion.

hematencephalon (hem″at-en-sef′ah-lon). The effusion of blood into the brain.

hematherapy (hem″ah-ther′ah-pe). Hemotherapy.

hemathermal (hem″ah-ther′mal). Hematothermal.

hemathermous (hem″ah-ther′mus). Hematothermal.

hemathorax (hem″ah-tho′raks). Hemothorax.

hematic (he-mat′ik). 1. Pertaining to or contained in blood. 2. Hematinic.

hematicum (he-mat′ĭ-kum). An aqueous alcoholic solution of iron compounds.

hematid (hem′ah-tid). 1. A red blood corpuscle. 2. A skin eruption of hematic origin.

hematidrosis (hem″at-i-dro′sis) [*hemat-* + Gr. *hidrōsis* sweating]. The excretion of bloody sweat.

hematimeter (hem″ah-tim′e-ter). Hemacytometer.

hematimetry (hem″ah-tim′e-tre). Hemacytometry.

hematin (hem′ah-tin). Heme.

hematinemia (hem″ah-tin-e′me-ah) [*hematin* + Gr. *haima* blood + *-ia*]. The presence of hematin (heme) in the blood.

hematinic (hem″ah-tin′ik). 1. Pertaining to hematin. 2. An agent which improves the quality of the blood, increasing the hemoglobin level and the number of erythrocytes.

hematinogen (hem″ah-tin′o-jen). A substance that produces blood.

hematinometer (hem″ah-tin-om′e-ter). Hemoglobinometer.

hematinuria (hem″ah-tin-u′re-ah) [*hematin* + Gr. *ouron* urine + *-ia*]. The presence of hematin in the urine.

hematischesis (hem″ah-tis′ke-sis) [*hemat-* + Gr. *schesis* checking]. Arrest of bleeding.

hematischetic (hem″ah-tis-ket′ik). Pertaining to, characterized by, or promoting hematischesis.

hemato-. See *hemo-*.

hemato-aerometer (hem″ah-to-a″er-om′e-ter). Hemataerometer.

hematobilia (hem″ah-to-bil′e-ah). Bleeding into the biliary passages.

hematobium (hem″ah-to′be-um), pl *hemato′bia* [*hemato-* + Gr. *bios* life]. Any organism that lives in the blood, especially an animal microorganism.

hematoblast (hem′ah-to-blast) [*hemato-* + Gr. *blastos* germ]. 1. A cell or mass from which a red blood corpuscle is developed, whether found in the blood or in a hematopoietic tissue; called also *erythrogonium* and *proerythroblast*. 2. Hayem's name for a blood platelet.

hematocatharsis (hem″ah-to-kah-thar′sis) [*hemato-* + Gr. *katharsis* purging]. The ridding of the blood of toxic substances; blood lavage.

hematocele (hem′ah-to-sēl) [*hemato-* + Gr. *kēlē* tumor]. An effusion of blood into a cavity, especially into the tunica vaginalis testis. **parametric h., pelvic h.,** a tumor formed by effusion of blood into Douglas' pouch. **pudendal h.,** a sanguineous tumor in a labium of the pudenda. **retro-uterine h.,** parametric h. **scrotal h.,** effusion of blood into the tissues of the scrotum. **vaginal h.,** effusion of blood into the tunica vaginalis testis.

hematocelia (hem″ah-to-se′le-ah). Hematocoelia.

hematocephalus (hem″ah-to-sef′ah-lus) [*hemato-* + Gr. *kephalē* head]. A fetus born with a head distended with blood.

hematochezia (hem″ah-to-ke′ze-ah) [*hemato-* + Gr. *chezein* to go to stool]. The passage of bloody stools.

hematochlorine (hem″ah-to-klo′rin) [*hemato-* + Gr. *chlōros* green]. A green coloring matter occurring in the placenta and derived from hemoglobin.

hematochromatosis (hem″ah-to-kro″mah-to′sis) [*hemato-* + Gr. *chrōma* color]. Staining of the tissues with blood pigment; hemochromatosis.

hematochyluria (hem″ah-to-ki-lu′re-ah) [*hemato-* + Gr. *chylos* chyle + *ouron* urine + *-ia*]. The discharge of blood and chyle with the urine, due to *Filaria sanguinis-hominis*.

hematoclasis (hem″ah-tok′lah-sis). Hemoclasis.

hematoclastic (hem″ah-to-klas′tik). Hemoclastic.

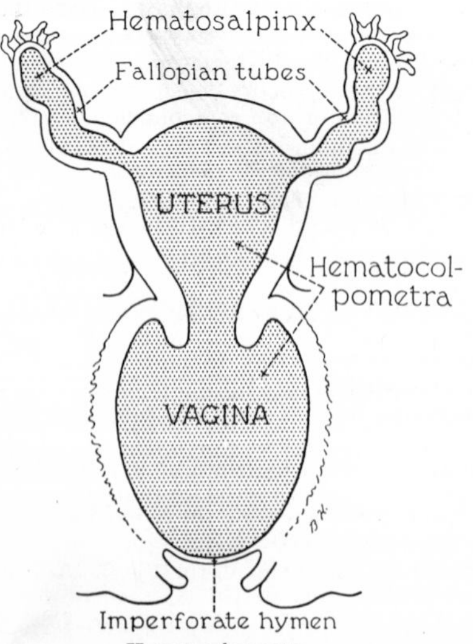

Hematocolpometra.

hematocoelia (hem″ah-to-se′le-ah) [*hemato-* + Gr. *koilia* cavity]. Effusion of blood into the peritoneal cavity.

hematocolpometra (hem″ah-to-kol″po-me′trah) [*hemato-* + Gr. *kolpos* vagina + *mētra* uterus]. Accumulation of menstrual blood in the vagina and uterus.

hematocolpos (hem″ah-to-kol′pos) [*hemato-* + Gr. *kolpos* vagina]. An accumulation of menstrual blood in the vagina.

hematocrit (he-mat′o-krit) [*hemato-* + Gr. *krinein* to separate]. The volume percentage of erythrocytes in whole blood. Originally applied to the apparatus or procedure used in its determination, but later used to designate the result of the determination. **large vessel h.,** the fraction of blood, sampled from a large vessel, that is occupied by the erythrocytes as measured upon centrifugation. **whole body h.,** the fraction of the total blood volume, as measured by suitable dilution of a plasma component and an erythrocyte component, that is occupied by the erythrocytes, expressed as a percentage, showing the ratio of erythrocyte volume to total blood volume.

hematocryal (hem″ah-tok′re-al) [*hemato-* + Gr. *kryos* cold]. Cold blooded.

hematocrystallin (hem″ah-to-kris′tal-in). Hemoglobin.

hematocyanin (hem″ah-to-si′ah-nin) [*hemato-* + Gr. *kyanos* blue]. A chromoprotein occurring in the blood of mollusks and arthropods. It is a blue respiratory pigment and contains 0.17 to 0.38 per cent of copper.

hematocyst (hem′ah-to-sist) [*hemato-* + Gr. *kystis* sac, bladder]. An effusion of blood into the bladder or into a cyst.

hematocystis (hem″ah-to-sis′tis). Hematocyst.

hematocyte (hem′ah-to-sīt). Hemocyte.

hematocytoblast (hem″ah-to-si′to-blast). Myeloblast.

hematocytolysis (hem″ah-to-si-tol′ĭ-sis). Hemocytolysis.

hematocytometer (hem″ah-to-si-tom′e-ter). Hemacytometer.

hematocytopenia (hem″ah-to-si″to-pe′ne-ah) [*hematocyte* + Gr. *penia* poverty]. Deficiency in all the cellular elements of the blood.

hematocytosis (hem″ah-to-si-to′sis) [*hematocyte* + *-osis*]. An increase in the cellular elements of the blood.

hematocyturia (hem″ah-to-si-tu′re-ah) [*hematocyte* + Gr. *ouron* urine + *-ia*]. The occurrence of blood corpuscles in the urine.

hematodialysis (hem″ah-to-di-al′ĭ-sis). Hemodialysis.

hematodynamometer (hem″ah-to-di-nah-mom′e-ter). Hemodynamometer.

hematodystrophy (hem″ah-to-dis′tro-fe). Hemodystrophy.

hematoencephalic (hem″ah-to-en″se-fal′ik) [*hemato-* + Gr. *enkephalos* brain]. Pertaining to the blood and the brain.

hematogen (hem′ah-to-jen) [*hemato-* + Gr. *gennan* to produce]. A substance that produces blood.

hematogenesis (hem″ah-to-jen′e-sis) [*hemato-* + *genesis*]. The production of blood.

hematogenic (hem″ah-to-jen′ik). 1. Hematopoietic. 2. Hematogenous.

hematogenous (hem″ah-toj′e-nus). Produced by or derived from the blood; disseminated by the circulation or through the blood stream.

hematoglobin (hem″ah-to-glo′bin). Hemoglobin.

hematoglobinuria (hem″ah-to-glo-bin-u′re-ah). Hemoglobinuria.

hematoglobulin (hem″ah-to-glob′u-lin). Hemoglobin.

hematogone (hem′ah-to-gōn). Hemocytoblast.

hematohidrosis (hem″ah-to-hid-ro′sis). Hematidrosis.

hematohistioblast (hem″ah-to-his′te-o-blast). Hemohistioblast.

hematohiston (hem″ah-to-his′ton). The globin of the blood.

hematohyaloid (hem″ah-to-hi′ah-loid) [*hemato-* + *hyaloid*]. The hyaline matter formed by degeneration of thrombi through conglutination of the red corpuscles or blood platelets.

hematoid (hem′ah-toid) [*hemato-* + Gr. *eidos* form]. Resembling blood.

hematoidin (hem-ah-toid′in). A yellow-brown, crystalline substance, $C_{16}H_{18}N_2O_3$, from blood clots.

hematokolpos (hem″ah-to-kol′pos). Hematocolpos.

hematokrit (he-mat′o-krit). Hematocrit.

hematolin (hem″ah-to′lin). A compound, $C_{68}H_{78}O_7N_8$, from hematin.

hematolith (hem′ah-to-lith). Hemolith.

hematologist (hem″ah-tol′o-jist). A specialist in the study of the blood.

hematology (hem″ah-tol′o-je) [*hemato-* + *-logy*]. That branch of biology which treats of the morphology of the blood and blood-forming tissues.

hematolymphangioma (hem″ah-to-lim″fan-je-o′mah) [*hemato-* + L. *lympha* lymph + Gr. *angeion* vessel + *-oma*]. A tumor composed of blood vessels and lymph vessels.

hematolysis (hem″ah-tol′ĭ-sis). Hemolysis.

hematolytic (hem″ah-to-lit′ik). Hemolytic.

hematoma (hem″ah-to′mah), pl. *hemato′mas* [*hemato-* + *-oma*]. A tumor containing effused blood. **aneurysmal h.,** false aneurysm. **h. au′ris,** a blood tumor of the perichondrium of the ear. **dural h.,** a circumscribed subdural effusion of the blood occurring in layers. **pelvic h.,** an effusion of blood into the pelvic cellular tissue. **perianal h.,** a hematoma under the perianal skin, caused by rupture of a subcutaneous vessel, the blood being kept localized by the fibroelastic septa and causing much pain. **pulsatile h.,** false aneurysm. **retrouterine h.,** an effusion of blood into the retrouterine connective tissue.

hematomancy (hem′ah-to-man-se) [*hemato-* + Gr. *manteia* divination]. Diagnosis by examination of the blood.

hematomanometer (hem″ah-to-mah-nom′e-ter). Sphygmomanometer.

hematomediastinum (hem″ah-to-me″de-as-ti′-num) [*hemato-* + *mediastinum*]. An effusion of blood in the mediastinum.

hematometachysis (hem″ah-to-mĕ-tak′ĭ-sis) [*hemato-* + Gr. *meta* across + *chysis* shedding]. Blood transfusion.

hematometakinesis (hem″ah-to-met″ah-ki-ne′-sis) [*hemato-* + Gr. *meta* across + *kinesis* movement]. The phenomenon of the shifting of blood from one part of the body to another: called also *borrowing-lending hemodynamic phenomenon.*

hematometer (hem″ah-tom′e-ter) [*hemato-* + Gr. *metron* measure]. 1. A hemoglobinometer. 2. A hemadynamometer.

hematometra (hem″ah-to-me′trah) [*hemato-* + Gr. *mētra* uterus]. An accumulation of blood in the uterus.

hematometry (hem″ah-tom′e-tre) [*hemato-* + Gr. *metron* measure]. Measurement of the hemoglobin and estimation of the percentage of the various cells in the blood.

hematomole (he-mat′o-mōl). Breus' mole.

Hematomonas (hem″ah-tom′o-nas) [*hemato-* + Gr. *monas* monad]. A genus of protozoan parasites living in the blood.

hematomphalocele (hem″at-om-fal′o-sēl) [*hemat-* + *omphalocele*]. An umbilical hernia containing blood.

hematomphalus (hem″at-om′fah-lus). 1. Hematomphalocele. 2. Blue navel. See *Cullen's sign,* under *sign.*

hematomycosis (hem″ah-to-mi-ko′sis). The presence of fungi in the blood.

hematomyelia (hem″ah-to-mi-e′le-ah) [*hemato-* + Gr. *myelos* marrow + *-ia*]. An effusion of blood within or upon the spinal cord.

hematomyelitis (hem″ah-to-mi″e-li′tis) [*hemato-* + *myelitis*]. Acute myelitis with bloody effusion.

hematomyelopore (hem″ah-to-mi′el-o-pōr) [*hemato-* + Gr. *myelos* marrow + *poros* opening]. A disease marked by the formation of canals in the spinal cord, due to hemorrhage.

hematoncometry (hem″at-on-kom′e-tre) [*hemat-* + Gr. *onkos* mass + *metron* measure]. Measurement of blood volume.

hematonephrosis (hem″ah-to-ne-fro′sis). Presence of blood in the pelvis of the kidney.

hematonic (hem″ah-ton′ik). A blood tonic.

hematonosis (hem″ah-ton′o-sis). Any disease of the blood.

hematopathology (hem″ah-to-pah-thol′o-je). Hemopathology.

hematopenia (hem″ah-to-pe′ne-ah) [*hemato-* + Gr. *penia* poverty]. Deficiency of blood.

hematopericardium (hem″ah-to-per″ĭ-kar′de-um). Hemopericardium.

hematoperitoneum (hem″ah-to-per″ĭ-to-ne′-um). Hemoperitoneum.

hematopexin (hem″ah-to-pek′sin). Hemopexin.

hematopexis (hem″ah-to-pek′sis). Hemopexis.

hematophage (hem′ah-to-fāj). Hemophagocyte.

hematophagia (hem″ah-to-fa′je-ah). 1. Blood drinking. 2. The act of subsisting on the blood of another animal. 3. Hemophagocytosis.

hematophagocyte (hem″ah-to-fag′o-sīt). Hemophagocyte.

hematophagous (hem″ah-tof′ah-gus) [*hemato-* + Gr. *phagein* to eat]. Pertaining to or characterized by hematophagia.

hematophagy (hem″ah-tof′ah-je). Hematophagia.

hematophilia (hem″ah-to-fil′e-ah). Hemophilia.

hematophobia (hem″ah-to-fo′be-ah). Hemophobia.

hematophyte (hem′ah-to-fīt) [*hemato-* + Gr. *phyton* plant]. Any vegetable microorganism or species living in the blood.

hematophytic (hem″ah-to-fit′ik). Pertaining to or caused by hematophytes.

hematopiesis (hem″ah-to-pi′e-sis) [*hemato-* + Gr. *piesis* pressure]. Blood pressure.

hematoplania (hem″ah-to-pla′ne-ah) [*hemato-* + Gr. *planē* wandering]. Vicarious menstruation.

hematoplasmopathy (hem″ah-to-plaz-mop′ah-the) [*hemato-* + *plasma* + Gr. *pathos* disease]. Any disorder due to alteration of the protein constitution of the blood.

hematoplast (hem′ah-to-plast). Hematoblast.

hematoplastic (hem″ah-to-plas′tik) [*hemato-* + Gr. *plassein* to mold]. Concerned in the elaboration of the blood.

hematopneic (hem″ah-to-ne′ik) [*hemato-* + Gr. *pnein* to breathe]. Pertaining to the oxygenation of the blood.

hematopoiesis (hem″ah-to-poi-e′sis) [*hemato-* + Gr. *poiein* to make]. The formation and development of blood cells. **extramedullary h.,** the formation and development of blood cells outside the bone marrow, as in the spleen, liver, and lymph nodes.

hematopoietic (hem″ah-to-poi-et′ik) [*hemato-* + Gr. *poiein* to make]. 1. Pertaining to or affecting the formation of blood cells. 2. An agent that promotes the formation of blood cells.

hematopoietin (hem″ah-to-poi′e-tin). Hemopoietin.

hematoporphyria (hem″ah-to-por-fi′re-ah). A constitutional state marked by abnormal quantity of porphyrin (uroporphyrin and coproporphyrin) in the tissues and secreted in the urine, pigmentation of the face (and later of the bones), sensitiveness of the skin to light, vomiting, and intestinal disturbance. Called also *porphyria*.

hematoporphyrin (hem″ah-to-por′fĭ-rin) [*hemato-* + Gr. *porphyra* purple]. An iron-free derivative, $C_{34}H_{38}O_6N_4$, of heme. It is a dark violet powder, a product of the decomposition of hemoglobin.

hematoporphyrinemia (hem″ah-to-por-fĭ-rin-e′me-ah). The presence of hematoporphyrin in the blood.

hematoporphyrinism (hem″ah-to-por′fĭ-rin-izm). A state characterized by hematoporphyrinemia and a sensitiveness to sunlight.

hematoporphyrinuria (hem″ah-to-por″fĭ-rin-u′re-ah). The occurrence of hematoporphyrin in the urine.

hematoporphyroidin (hem″ah-to-por″fĭ-roi′-din). A product of the decomposition of hematoporphyrin.

Hematopota (hem″ah-top′o-tah). A former name of the genus now known as *Chrysozona*.

hematorrhachis (hem-ah-tor′ah-kis) [*hemato-* + Gr. *rhachis* spine]. Hemorrhage into the vertebral canal.

hematorrhea (hem″ah-to-re′ah) [*hemato-* + Gr. *rhoia* flow]. A free or copious hemorrhage.

hematosalpinx (hem″ah-to-sal′pinks). An accumulation of blood in the uterine tube.

hematoscheocele (hem″ah-tos′ke-o-sēl) [*hemato-* + Gr. *oscheon* scrotum + *kēlē* tumor]. A collection of blood within the scrotum.

hematoscope (hem′ah-to-skōp) [*hemato-* + Gr. *skopein* to examine]. An instrument for the optical or spectroscopic examination of the blood.

hematoscopy (hem″ah-tos′ko-pe). Examination of the blood, as with a spectroscope.

hematosepsis (hem″ah-to-sep′sis). Septicemia.

hematosin (hem″ah-to′sin). Heme.

hematosis (hem″ah-to′sis). 1. The formation of the blood. 2. The aeration of the blood in the lungs.

hematospectrophotometer (hem″ah-to-spek″-tro-fo-tom′e-ter). A spectrophotometer for determining the amount of hemoglobin in the blood.

hematospectroscope (hem″ah-to-spek′tro-skōp) [*hemato-* + *spectroscope*]. A spectroscope for examining thin layers of blood.

hematospectroscopy (hem″ah-to-spek-tros′ko-pe) [*hemato-* + *spectroscopy*]. The spectroscopic examination of the blood.

hematospermatocele (hem″ah-to-sper-mat′o-sēl) [*hemato-* + Gr. *sperma* seed + *kēlē* tumor]. A spermatocele containing blood.

hematospermia (hem″ah-to-sper′me-ah). Hemospermia.

hematospherinemia (hem″ah-to-sfēr″ĭ-ne′me-ah) [*hemato-* + Gr. *sphaira* sphere + *haima* blood + *-ia*]. Hemoglobinemia.

hematosporidia (hem″ah-to-spo-rid′e-ah). A suborder of *Sporozoa* which contains the parasite of malaria.

hematostatic (hem″ah-to-stat′ik) [*hemato-* + Gr. *stasis* standing]. Due to, or characterized by, stagnation of the blood.

hematosteon (hem″ah-tos′te-on) [*hemat-* + Gr. *osteon* bone]. Hemorrhage into the medullary cavity of a bone.

hematotherapy (hem″ah-to-ther′ah-pe). Hemotherapy.

hematothermal (hem″ah-to-ther′mal) [*hemato-* + Gr. *thermē* heat]. Having warm blood.

hematothorax (hem″ah-to-tho′raks). Hemothorax.

hematotic (hem″ah-tot′ik). Pertaining to hematosis.

hematotoxic (hem″ah-to-tok′sik) [*hemato-* + *toxic*]. 1. Pertaining to hematotoxicosis. 2. Poisonous to the blood and hematopoietic system.

hematotoxicosis (hem″ah-to-tok″sĭ-ko′sis). Toxic damage to the hematopoietic system.

hematotoxin (hem″ah-to-tok′sin). Hemotoxin.

hematotrachelos (hem″ah-to-trah-ke′los) [*hemato-* + Gr. *trachēlos* neck]. Distention of the cervix of the uterus with blood, owing to atresia of the external os or of the vagina.

hematotropic (hem″ah-to-trop′ik) [*hemato-* + Gr. *tropos* a turning]. Having a special affinity for or exerting a specific effect on the blood or blood corpuscles.

hematotympanum (hem″ah-to-tim′pah-num) [*hemato-* + *tympanum*]. A hemorrhagic exudation into the drum cavity of the ear.

hematoxic (hem″ah-tok′sik). Hematotoxic.

hematoxin (hem″ah-tok′sin). Hemotoxin.

hematoxylin (hem″ah-tok′sĭ-lin). A crystalline stain, $C_{16}H_{14}O_6 + 3H_2O$, obtained by extracting logwood with ether. It may be used as an indicator with a pH range of 5–6. **alum h.,** hemalum. **Delafield's h.,** a staining fluid containing hematoxylin, alcohol, ammonia alum, water, glycerin, and methyl alcohol. **iron h.** See *Heidenhain* and *Weigert's stain*, under *stains* and *staining*.

hematoxylon (he″mah-tok′sĭ-lon). Haematoxylon.

hematozemia (hem″ah-to-ze′me-ah) [*hemato-* + Gr. *zēmia* loss]. A gradual loss of blood.

hematozoa (hem″ah-to-zo′ah). Plural of *hematozoon*.

hematozoon (hem″ah-to-zo′on), pl. *hematozo′a* [*hemato-* + Gr. *zōon* animal]. Any animal microorganism or species living in the blood.

hematozoic (hem″ah-to-zo′ik). Pertaining to or caused by hematozoa.

hematozymosis (hem″ah-to-zi-mo′sis) [*hemato-* + Gr. *zymōsis* fermentation]. Fermentation of the blood.

hematuresis (hem″ah-tu-re′sis). Hematuria.

hematuria (hem″ah-tu′re-ah) [*hemat-* + Gr. *ouron* urine + *-ia*]. The discharge of blood in the urine. **angioneurotic h.,** Gull's renal epistaxis. **endemic h.,** urinary schistosomiasis. **enzootic bovine h.,** a disease of cattle marked by passing of blood in the urine, anemia, and debilitation. **essential h.,** hematuria for which a cause cannot be determined. **false h.,** redness of the urine due to food or drugs containing pigment. **microscopic h.,** blood in the urine, the presence of which can be discovered only by the microscope. **renal h.,** hematuria in which the blood comes from the kidney. **urethral h.,** hematuria in which the blood comes from the urethra. **vesical h.,** hematuria in which the blood comes from the bladder.

hema-urochrome (hem″ah-u′ro-krōm) [*hema-* + *urochrome*]. A substance found in the urine in such diseases as carcinoma and sarcoma, and thought to be a derivative of heme from blood destruction.

hemautograph (hem-aw′to-graf) [*hem-* + Gr. *autos* self + *graphein* to record]. A tracing made by an arterial blood jet.

hemautography (hem″aw-tog′rah-fe). The recording of a hemautograph.

hembra (hem′brah). The ulcerative type of dermal leishmaniasis.

heme (hēm). The nonprotein, insoluble, iron protoporphyrin constituent of hemoglobin, various other respiratory pigments and of many cells, both animal and vegetable. It is $C_{34}H_{33}O_4N_4FeOH$, an iron compound of protoporphyrin and so constitutes the pigment portion or protein-free part of the hemoglobin molecule. Heme was formerly known as hematin.

hemelytrometra lateralis (hem-el″e-tro-me′-trah lat″er-a′lis) [*hem-* + Gr. *elytron* sheath + *mētra* womb]. Accumulation of menstrual blood in a pouch formed by the rudimentary half of a double vagina.

hemendothelioma (hem″en-do-the″le-o′mah). A form of endothelioma containing blood vessels.

Hementaria (he″men-ta′re-ah). A genus of leeches. **H. officiana′lis,** a leech commonly used in Mexico and Central America for therapeutic purposes.

hemeralope (hem′er-al-ōp). A person affected with hemeralopia.

hemeralopia (hem″er-al-o′pe-ah) [Gr. *hēmera* day + *alaos* blind + *ōps* eye]. Day blindness; defective vision in a bright light. The term has been used incorrectly for nyctalopia.

Hemerocampa (hem″er-o-kam′pah). A genus of moths. **H. leukostig′ma,** the white-marked tussock moth. In the larval stage the smaller white hairs are poisonous and may produce severe urticaria.

hemerythrin (hēm″e-rith′rin) [*hem-* + Gr. *erythros* red]. The coloring matter of the blood of earthworms which is contained in the plasma.

hemetaboly (he″mĕ-tab′o-le) [*hem-* + *metaboly*]. The metabolism of blood elements.

hemi- (hem′e) [Gr. *hēmi-* half]. A prefix signifying one half.

hemiablepsia (hem″e-ah-blep′se-ah). Hemianopia.

hemiacardius (hem″e-ah-kar′de-us) [*hemi-* + *a* neg. + Gr. *kardia* heart]. One of twin fetuses in which only a part of the circulation is accomplished by its own heart.

hemiacephalus (hem″e-ah-sef′ah-lus) [*hemi-* + *a* neg. + Gr. *kephalē* head]. A fetal monster whose head lacks a brain and calvarium.

hemiachromatopsia (hem″e-ak″ro-mah-top′-se-ah) [*hemi-* + *achromatopsia*]. Color blindness in one half, or in corresponding halves, of the visual field.

hemiageusia (hem″e-ah-gu′ze-ah) [*hemi-* + *a* neg. + Gr. *geusis* taste + *-ia*]. Loss or absence of the sense of taste on one side of the tongue.

hemiageustia (hem″e-ah-gūs′te-ah). Hemiageusia.

hemialbumin (hem″e-al-bu′min) [*hemi-* + *albumin*]. Hemialbumose.

hemialbumose (hem″e-al′bu-mōs). A crystallizable product of the digestion of certain proteins; normally found in bone marrow, and occurring in the urine of osteomalacia and diphtheria.

hemialbumosuria (hem″e-al-bu″mo-su′re-ah) [*hemialbumose* + Gr. *ouron* urine + *-ia*]. The presence of hemialbumose in the urine.

hemialgia (hem″e-al′je-ah) [*hemi-* + *-algia*]. Pain affecting one side of the body only.

hemiamaurosis (hem″e-am″aw-ro′sis). Hemianopsia.

hemiamblyopia (hem″e-am″ble-o′pe-ah) [*hemi-* + *amblyopia*]. Impairment of the visual power of one half of the retina.

hemiamyosthenia (hem″e-ah-mi″os-the′ne-ah) [*hemi-* + *a* neg. + Gr. *mys* muscle + *sthenos* strength + *-ia*]. Lack of muscular power on one side of the body.

hemianacusia (hem″e-an″ah-ku′ze-ah) [*hemi-* + *an* neg. + Gr. *akousia* hearing]. Loss of hearing in one ear only.

hemianalgesia (hem″e-an″al-je′ze-ah) [*hemi-* + *analgesia*]. Analgesia of one side of the body.

hemianencephaly (hem″e-an″en-sef′ah-le) [*hemi-* + Gr. *an* neg. + *enkephalos* brain]. Congenital absence of one side of the brain.

hemianesthesia (hem″e-an″es-the′ze-ah). Anesthesia affecting only one side of the body. **alternate h.,** h. cruciata. **cerebral h.,** that which is due to lesion of the internal capsule of the lenticular nucleus. **crossed h.,** h. cruciata. **h. crucia′ta,** loss of sensation on one side of the face with contralateral loss of pain and temperature sense on the body, resulting from a lateral lesion in the pons or medulla, affecting both the sensory root of the trigeminal nerve and the spinothalamic tract. **mesocephalic h., pontile h.,** that which is due to disease of the pons. **spinal h.,** that which is due to a lesion of the spinal cord.

hemianopia (hem″e-ah-no′pe-ah) [*hemi-* + *an-* neg. + Gr. *ōpē* vision + *-ia*]. Defective vision or blindness in half of the visual field. **absolute h.,** blindness to light, color, and form, in half of the visual field. **altitudinal h.,** defective vision or blindness in a horizontal half of the visual field. **bilateral h.,** true h. **binasal h.,** heteronymous hemianopia in which the defects are in the nasal half of the field of vision in each eye. **binocular h.,** true h. **bitemporal h.,** heteronymous hemianopia in which the defects are in the temporal half of the field of vision in each eye. **h. bitempora′lis fu′gax,** transient bitemporal hemianopia, sometimes seen in syphilitic patients. **complete h.,** hemianopia affecting an entire half of the visual field of each eye. **congruous h.,** homonymous hemianopia in which the defects in the field of vision in each eye are symmetrical in position and identical in all other respects. **crossed h.,** heteronymous h. **equilateral h.,** homonymous h. **heteronymous h.,** hemianopia affecting the nasal or the temporal half of the field of vision of each eye. **homonymous h.,** hemianopia affecting the right halves or the left halves of the visual fields of the two eyes. **horizontal h.,** altitudinal h. **incomplete h.,** hemianopia affecting less than an entire half of the visual field. **incongruous h.,** homonymous hemianopia in which the defects in the field of vision in the two eyes differ in one or more respects, as in extent or intensity. **nasal h.,** defective vision or blindness in the medial vertical half of the visual field, that is the half nearest the nose. **quadrant h., quadrantic h.,** defective vision or blindness in one fourth of the visual field in each eye. **relative h.,** defective vision or blindness to form or color in half of the visual field, the perception of light being retained. **temporal h.,** defective vision or blindness in the lateral vertical half of the visual field, that is, the half nearest the temple. **true h.,** defective vision or blindness in one vertical half of each eye, due to a single lesion of the optic tract, at or above the level of the chiasm. **unilateral h.,** defective vision or blindness in half of the visual field of one eye only. **uniocular h.,** unilateral h. **vertical h.,** defective vision or blindness in a lateral half of the visual field.

hemianopic (hem″e-ah-no′pik). Pertaining to or characterized by hemianopia.

hemianopsia (hem″e-an-op′se-ah). Hemianopia.

hemianoptic (hem″e-an-op′tik). Hemianopic.

hemianosmia (hem″e-an-oz′me-ah) [*hemi-* + *anosmia*]. Loss of the sense of smell in one of the nostrils.

hemiapraxia (hem″e-ah-prak′se-ah) [*hemi-* + *apraxia*]. Loss of ability to perform coordinated movements on one side of the body only.

hemiarthrosis (hem″e-ar-thro′sis) [*hemi-* + *arthrosis*]. A spurious synchondrosis.

hemiasynergia (hem″e-ah″sin-er′je-ah) [*hemi-* + *asynergia*]. Asynergia affecting one side of the body only.

hemiataxia (hem″e-ah-tak′se-ah) [*hemi-* + *ataxia*]. Ataxia affecting one side of the body only.

hemiataxy (hem″e-ah-tak′se). Hemiataxia.

hemiathetosis (hem″e-ath″e-to′sis) [*hemi-* + *athetosis*]. Athetosis affecting one side of the body only.

hemiatrophy (hem″e-at′ro-fe) [*hemi-* + *atrophy*]. Atrophy of one side of the body or of one half of an organ or part. **facial h.,** atrophy of one lateral half of the face: sometimes progressive, and due to a nervous disorder. **progressive lingual h.,** progressive atrophy of one lateral half of the tongue.

hemiautotroph (hem″e-aw′to-trōf). An organism which can build up protein from inorganic nitrogen but requires organic carbon.

hemiautotrophic (hem″e-aw″to-trof′ik) [*hemi-* + *autotrophic*]. Partly self-nourishing: a term applied to microorganisms which can build up protein from inorganic nitrogen but require organic carbon.

hemiballism (hem″e-bal′izm). Hemiballismus.

hemiballismus (hem″e-bal-iz′mus) [*hemi-* + Gr. *ballismos* jumping]. A violent form of motor restlessness involving only one side of the body and being most marked in the upper extremity, resulting from a destructive lesion of the subthalamus.

hemibilirubin (hem″e-bil″ĭ-roo′bin). A modified bile pigment found in the urine, possibly a urobilinogen.

hemic (hem′ik) [Gr. *haima* blood]. Pertaining to the blood.

hemicanities (hem″e-kah-nish′e-ēz). Grayness of the hair on one side of the body.

hemicardia (hem″e-kar′de-ah) [*hemi-* + Gr. *kardia* heart]. A congenital anomaly characterized by the presence of only half of a four-chambered heart. **h. dex′tra,** hemicardia in which the right side of the heart is present. **h. sinis′tra,** hemicardia in which the left side of the heart is present.

hemicardius (hem″e-kar′de-us). A free twin fetus whose development is greatly reduced but whose body form and various parts are still recognizable.

hemicellulase (hem″e-sel′u-lās). An enzyme which catalyzes the hydrolysis of hemicellulose.

hemicellulose (hem″e-sel′u-lōs). A general name for a group of high molecular carbohydrates that resemble cellulose but are more soluble and more easily decomposed. They can be extracted by dilute alkali and precipitated with dilute acid. They usually contain a hexose, a pentose and a uronic acid.

hemicentrum (hem″e-sen′trum) [*hemi-* + *centrum*]. Either lateral half of a vertebral centrum.

hemicephalia (hem″e-se-fa′le-ah) [*hemi-* + Gr. *kephalē* head]. Congenital absence of the cerebrum.

hemicephalus (hem″e-sef′ah-lus). A fetal monster exhibiting hemicephalia.

hemicerebrum (hem″e-ser′e-brum) [*hemi-* + *cerebrum*]. A cerebral hemisphere.

hemichorea (hem″e-ko-re′ah) [*hemi-* + *chorea*]. Chorea which affects only one side.

hemichromatopsia (hem″e-kro″mah-top′se-ah) [*hemi-* + *chromatopsia*]. Color blindness in one half of the visual field.

hemichromosome (hem″e-kro′mo-sōm) [*hemi-* + *chromosome*]. A body formed by the longitudinal division of a chromosome.

hemicolectomy (hem″e-ko-lek′to-me) [*hemi-* + *colectomy*]. Excision of approximately half of the colon. **left h.,** resection of the entire left half of the colon, from the middle of the transverse colon to the rectum. **right h.,** resection of the entire right colon, from the ileum to the middle of the transverse colon.

hemicollin (hem″e-kol′in) [*hemi-* + Gr. *kolla* glue]. A substance formed by the digestion of gelatin.

hemicorporectomy (hem″e-kor″po-rek′to-me) [*hemi-* + L. *corpus* body + Gr. *ektomē* excision]. Surgical removal of the lower part of the body, including the bony pelvis, external genitals, and the lower part of the rectum and anus.

hemicrania (hem″e-kra′ne-ah) [*hemi-* + Gr. *kranion* skull]. 1. Pain or aching in one side of the head. 2. Incomplete anencephaly.

hemicraniectomy (hem″e-kra″ne-ek′to-me) [*hemi-* + Gr. *kranion* skull + *ektomē* excision]. Doyen's operation of sectioning the vault of the skull from before backward, near the median line, and forcing the entire side outward, thus exposing half of the brain.

hemicraniosis (hem″e-kra″ne-o′sis). A condition marked by hyperostosis on one half of the cranium or face, with cerebral involvement. The condition is believed to be due to endothelioma of the dura.

hemicraniotomy (hem″e-kra″ne-ot′o-me) [*hemi-* + Gr. *kranion* skull + *temnein* to cut]. Hemicraniectomy.

hemidecortication (hem″e-de-kor″tĭ-ka′shun). Removal of one half of the cerebral cortex.

Hemidesmus (hem″e-des′mus). A genus of asclepiadaceous plants. The root of *H. in′dicus* has been used like sarsaparilla.

hemidiaphoresis (hem″e-di″ah-fo-re′sis) [*hemi-* + *diaphoresis*]. Excessive sweating of one side of the body only.

hemidiaphragm (hem″e-di′ah-fram). One half of the diaphragm.

hemidrosis (hem″ĭ-dro′sis). Hemihidrosis.

hemidysergia (hem″e-dis-er′je-ah). Dysergia affecting one side of the body.

hemidysesthesia (hem″e-dis″es-the′ze-ah) [*hemi-* + *dys-* + *aisthēsis* feeling]. A disorder of sensation affecting one side of the body only.

hemidystrophy (hem″e-dis′tro-fe). Unequal development of the two sides of the body.

hemiectromelia (hem″e-ek-tro-me′le-ah). A developmental anomaly characterized by imperfect development of the limbs of one side of the body.

hemielastin (hem″e-e-las′tin). A substance formed by the digestion or hydrolysis of elastin.

hemiencephalus (hem″e-en-sef′ah-lus) [*hemi-* + Gr. *enkephalos* brain]. A fetus that lacks one cerebral hemisphere.

hemiepilepsy (hem″e-ep′ĭ-lep-se) [*hemi-* + *epilepsy*]. Epilepsy affecting one side of the body only.

hemifacial (hem″e-fa′shal). Pertaining to or affecting one half of the face.

hemigastrectomy (hem″e-gas-trek′to-me). Excision of one half of the stomach.

hemigeusia (hem″e-gu′se-ah) [*hemi-* + Gr. *geusis* taste + *-ia*]. Presence of taste perception on one side of the tongue only.

hemiglossal (hem″e-glos′sal) [*hemi-* + Gr. *glōssa* tongue]. Affecting one side of the tongue.

hemiglossectomy (hem″e-glos-sek′to-me) [*hemi-* + Gr. *glōssa* tongue + *ektomē* excision]. Resection of one side of the tongue.

hemiglossitis (hem″e-glos-si′tis) [*hemi-* + Gr. *glōssa* tongue + *-itis*]. Inflammation involving only one side of the tongue.

hemignathia (hem″e-nath′e-ah) [*hemi-* + Gr. *gnathos* jaw + *-ia*]. A developmental anomaly characterized by partial to complete lack of the lower jaw on one side.

hemihepatectomy (hem″e-hep″ah-tek′to-me). Excision of part of the liver.

hemihidrosis (hem″e-hĭ-dro′sis) [*hemi-* + Gr. *hidrōs* sweat]. Sweating on one side of the body only.

hemihypalgesia (hem″e-hi″pal-je′ze-ah). Hypalgesia affecting one side of the body.

hemihyperesthesia (hem″e-hi″per-es-the′ze-ah) [*hemi-* + *hyperesthesia*]. Abnormally increased acuteness of sensation on one side of the body.

hemihyperidrosis (hem″e-hi″per-ĭ-dro′sis) [*hemi-* + Gr. *hyper* over + *hidrōs* sweat]. Excessive sweating on one side of the body only.

hemihypermetria (hem″e-hi″per-me′tre-ah). Exaggerated extension of one half of a part. Cf. *hypermetria.*

hemihyperplasia (hem″e-hi″per-pla′ze-ah). Overdevelopment of one side of the body, or of one half of an organ or part, as of the cranium.

hemihypertonia (hem″e-hi″per-to′ne-ah) [*hemi-* + Gr. *hyper* over + *tonos* tension + *-ia*]. Increased tonicity of the muscles of one side, resulting in tonic contractions: sometimes seen after apoplectic attacks. Called also *hemitonia.*

hemihypertrophy (hem″e-hi-per′tro-fe) [*hemi-* + *hypertrophy*]. Overgrowth of one half of the body or unilateral hypertrophy of a part. **facial h.,** hypertrophy of half of the face.

hemihypesthesia (hem″e-hi″pes-the′ze-ah). Abnormally decreased acuteness of sensation on one side of the body.

hemihypo-esthesia (hem″e-hi″po-es-the′ze-ah). Hemihypesthesia.

hemihypoplasia (hem″e-hi″po-pla′ze-ah). Underdevelopment of one side of the body, or of one half of a part or organ, as of the brain.

hemihypotonia (hem″e-hi″po-to′ne-ah) [*hemi-* + Gr. *hypo* under + *tonos* tension + *-ia*]. Defective tonicity of one side of the body.

hemikaryon (hem″e-kar′e-on) [*hemi-* + Gr. *karyon* nucleus]. A nucleus which contains the haploid number of chromosomes.

hemilaminectomy (hem″e-lam″ĭ-nek′to-me). Removal of the vertebral laminae on one side only.

hemilaryngectomy (hem″e-lar″in-jek′to-me). Excision of one half of the larynx.

hemilateral (hem″e-lat′er-al). Affecting one half of one side.

hemilesion (hem″e-le′zhun). A lesion of one side of the spinal cord only.

hemilingual (hem″e-ling′gwal) [*hemi-* + L. *lingua* tongue]. Affecting one side of the tongue.

hemimacroglossia (hem″e-mak″ro-glos′e-ah). Enlargement of one side of the tongue.

hemimandibulectomy (hem″e-man-dib-u-lek′-to-me). Surgical excision of half of the mandible.

hemimelia (hem″e-me′le-ah) [*hemi-* + Gr. *melos* limb + *-ia*]. A developmental anomaly characterized by absence of all or part of the distal half of a limb. **fibular h.**, hemimelia of the lower limb in which the fibular side is absent. **radial h.**, hemimelia of the upper limb in which the radial side is absent. **tibial h.**, hemimelia of the lower limb in which the tibial side is absent. **ulnar h.**, hemimelia of the upper limb in which the ulnar side is absent.

hemimelus (hem-im′ĕ-lus). An individual exhibiting hemimelia.

hemin (he′min) [Gr. *haima* blood]. The crystalline chloride of heme, $C_{34}H_{33}N_4O_4FeCl$, of which Teichmann's crystals are composed.

heminephrectomy (hem″e-ne-frek′to-me). Excision of a portion of a kidney.

heminephro-ureterectomy (hem″e-nef″ro-u-re″ter-ek′to-me). Excision of a portion of a kidney and ureter.

hemineurasthenia (hem″e-nu″ras-the′ne-ah). Neurasthenia affecting one side of the body only.

hemiobesity (hem″e-o-bēs′ĭ-te) [*hemi-* + *obesity*]. Obesity of one side of the body only.

hemiopalgia (hem″e-op-al′je-ah) [*hemi-* + Gr. *ōps* eye + *-algia*]. Pain in one side of the head and in one eye.

hemiopia (hem″e-o′pe-ah). 1. Hemianopia (Plenk). 2. Absence of visual power in one half of the retina.

hemiopic (hem″e-op′ik) [*hemi-* + Gr. *ōps* eye]. 1. Affecting one eye. 2. Pertaining to hemiopia.

hemipagus (hem-ip′ah-gus) [*hemi-* + Gr. *pagos* thing fixed]. Twin fetuses united laterally at the thorax.

hemiparalysis (hem″e-pah-ral′ĭ-sis). Hemiplegia.

hemiparanesthesia (hem″e-par″an-es-the′ze-ah) [*hemi-* + Gr. *para* below + *anesthesia*]. Anesthesia of the lower half of one side of the body.

hemiparaplegia (hem″e-par″ah-ple′je-ah) [*hemi-* + *paraplegia*]. Paralysis of the lower half of one side of the body.

hemiparesis (hem″e-par′e-sis) [*hemi-* + *paresis*]. Muscular weakness affecting one side of the body.

hemiparesthesia (hem″e-par″es-the′ze-ah) [*hemi-* + *paresthesia*]. Perverted sensation on one side of the body.

hemiparkinsonism (hem″e-par′kin-son-izm). Parkinsonism (paralysis agitans) affecting only one side of the body.

hemipelvectomy (hem″e-pel″vek′to-me). Amputation of a lower limb through the sacroiliac joint.

hemipeptone (hem″e-pep′tōn) [*hemi-* + *peptone*]. One of the intermediate products of pepsin digestion of protein. It is formed along with antipeptone, and differs from the latter in being convertible into amino-acids by trypsin.

hemiphalangectomy (hem″e-fal″an-jek′to-me). The excision of part of a digital phalanx.

hemipinta (hem″ĭ-pin′tah). A rare form of pinta in which the pigmentary disturbances affect only one half of the body.

hemiplacenta (hem″e-plah-sen′tah) [*hemi-* + *placenta*]. An organ, composed of the chorion, yolk sac, and, usually, allantois, which puts marsupial embryos into temporary relation with the maternal uterus.

hemiplegia (hem″e-ple′je-ah) [*hemi-* + Gr. *plēgē* stroke]. Paralysis of one side of the body. **h. al′ternans hypoglos′sica,** hemiplegia due to lesion of the hypoglossal nerve on the side opposite the paralyzed part. **alternate h.,** that which affects a part on one side of the body and another part on the opposite side. Called also *crossed h.* **ascending h.,** ascending paralysis of one lateral half of the body. **capsular h.,** hemiplegia due to lesion of the internal capsule. **cerebral h.,** that which is due to a lesion of the brain. **contralateral h.,** hemiplegia on the side of the body opposite to the site of the brain lesion causing it. **crossed h.,** alternate hemiplegia. **h. crucia′ta,** alternate hemiplegia. **facial h.,** paralysis of one side of the face, the body being unaffected. **faciobrachial h.,** paralysis of one half of the face and of the arm on the same side. **faciolingual h.,** paralysis of one side of the face and tongue. **flaccid h.,** hypotonia. **Gubler's h.** 1. Alternate hemiplegia. 2. Apparent hemiplegia occurring as a symptom in hysteria. **infantile h.,** hemiplegia due to cerebral hemorrhage at delivery or occurring before birth. **spastic h.,** hemiplegia with spasms and atrophy: usually infantile. **spinal h.,** a form due to a lesion of the spinal cord.

hemiplegic (hem″e-ple′jik). Pertaining to or of the nature of hemiplegia.

hemiprostatectomy (hem″e-pros″tah-tek′to-me). Removal of one lateral half of the prostate.

hemiprotein (hem″e-pro′te-in) [*hemi-* + *protein*]. Antialbumin.

Hemiptera (he-mip′ter-ah) [*hemi-* + Gr. *pteron* wing]. An order of insects which may be winged or wingless, including ordinary bugs and lice, characterized by having the mouth parts adapted to piercing or sucking.

hemipylorectomy (hem″e-pi″lor-ek′to-me). Excision of a portion of the pylorus.

hemipyocyanin (hem″e-pi″o-si′ah-nin). An antibiotic produced by the growth of *Pseudomonas pyocyanea* which is active against *Achorion schoenleini* and *Candida albicans.*

hemipyonephrosis (hem″e-pi″o-ne-fro′sis). A hydronephrotic sac in a portion of the kidney; or pyonephrosis of half of a double kidney.

hemirachischisis (hem″e-rah-kis′kĭ-sis). Rachischisis without prolapse of the spinal cord.

hemisacralization (hem″e-sa″kral-i-za′shun). Fusion of the fifth lumbar vertebra to the first segment of the sacrum on only one side.

hemiscotosis (hem″e-sko-to′sis). Hemianopia.

hemisection (hem″e-sek′shun). 1. Bisection. 2. A section or cutting of one half.

hemiseptum (hem″e-sep′tum). Either half of a septum; especially the lamina of the septum lucidum. **h. auricula′re,** the lateral half of the septum between the auricles of the heart. **h. cer′ebri,** the lateral half of the septum lucidum of the brain. **h. ventricula′re,** the lateral half of the septum between the ventricles of the heart.

hemisomnambulism (hem″e-som-nam′bu-lizm). Somnambulism in which the subject retains consciousness and his normal personality.

hemisomus (hem″e-so′mus) [*hemi-* + Gr. *sōma* body]. A fetal monster with body imperfectly developed.

hemisotonic (hem″i-so-ton′ik) [Gr. *haima* blood + *isotonic*]. Having the same osmotic pressure as the blood.

hemispasm (hem′e-spazm). Spasm affecting one side only.

hemisphaeria (hem″ĭ-sfe′re-ah) [L.]. Plural of *hemisphaerium*.

hemisphaerium (hem″ĭ-sfe′re-um), pl. *hemisphae′ria* [L.]. Hemisphere. **hemisphae′ria bul′bi ure′thrae** [B N A], the lateral halves of the bulb of the urethra. Omitted in N A.

hemisphere (hem′ĭ-sfēr) [*hemi-* + Gr. *sphaira* a ball or globe]. Half of any spherical or roughly spherical structure or organ, as demarcated by passing a plane through the poles or along the equator, or otherwise dividing it into approximately equal portions. **animal h.,** the half of the mass of cells formed by cleavage of a fertilized telolecithal ovum that is nearest the animal pole. **cerebellar h.,** hemispherium cerebelli. **cerebral h.,** one of the pair of structures constituting the largest part of the brain in the human, formed by the evagination of the lateral wall of the embryonic telencephalon. Called also *hemispherium* [N A]. It consists of the extensive cerebral cortex, corpus striatum, and rhinencephalon, and contains the lateral ventricle. **dominant h.,** that cerebral hemisphere which is more concerned than the other in the integration of sensations and the control of many functions, such as the preferential use of one or the other of paired organs in voluntary movements, e.g. the left cerebral hemisphere in right-handed persons, and vice versa. However, the left hemisphere is usually dominant for speech, regardless of the handedness. **vegetal h.,** the half of the mass of cells formed by cleavage of a fertilized telolecithal ovum that is nearest the vegetal pole.

hemispherectomy (hem″ĭ-sfēr-ek′to-me) [*hemisphere* + Gr. *ektomē* excision]. Resection of a cerebral hemisphere.

hemispherium (hem″ĭ-sfe′re-um), pl. *hemisphe′ria* [L.]. [N A] The largest part of the brain in the human. See *cerebral hemisphere*, under *hemisphere*. **h. cerebel′li** [N A], the part of the cerebellum lateral to the vermis; each hemisphere being composed of an ala of the lobulus centralis, the lobulus quadrangularis, lobulus simplex, the superior and inferior semilunar lobules, the biventral lobule, tonsilla, and flocculus.

hemisphygmia (hem″ĭ-sfig′me-ah) [*hemi-* + Gr. *sphygmos* pulse]. A condition in which there are twice as many pulse beats as there are heart beats.

Hemispora stellata (hem-is′po-rah stel-la′tah). A fungus found in cases of mycosis resembling sporotrichosis.

hemispore (hem′e-spōr). A spore formed by the differentiation and division of the terminal portion of a hypha.

hemisporosis (hem″e-spo-ro′sis). A mycosis due to infection with the *Hemispora stellata*, characterized by gummatous swellings in the bones and other tissues.

hemistrumectomy (hem″e-stroo-mek′to-me). Hemithyroidectomy.

hemisyndrome (hem″e-sin′drōm). A syndrome indicative of a unilateral lesion of the spinal cord.

hemisystole (hem″e-sis′to-le) [*hemi-* + *systole*]. Failure of the left ventricle to contract every other time, resulting in only one pulse beat for every two beats of the heart.

hemiterata (hem″e-ter′ah-tah) [*hemi-* + Gr. *teras* monster]. Pl. A group of congenitally deformed individuals who cannot be classed as teratisms or monstrosities.

hemiteratic (hem″e-ter-at′ik). Congenitally deformed, but not monstrous.

hemiterpene (hem″e-ter′pēn). A terpene having the formula C_5H_8.

hemitetany (hem″e-tet′ah-ne). Tetany limited to one side of the body.

hemithermo-anesthesia (hem″e-ther″mo-an″-es-the′ze-ah). Absence of sensibility to temperature on one side of the body.

hemithorax (hem″e-tho′raks) [*hemi-* + *thorax*]. One side of the chest.

hemithyroidectomy (hem″e-thi″roid-ek′to-me). Excision of one lobe of the thyroid gland.

hemitomias (hem″ĭ-to′me-as) [Gr. *hēmitomias* half a eunuch]. A person deprived of one testis.

hemitonia (hem″ĭ-to′ne-ah) [*hemi-* + Gr. *tonos* tension + *-ia*]. Hemihypertonia.

hemitoxin (hem″ĭ-tok′sin). A toxin the toxicity of which has been reduced by one half.

hemitremor (hem″e-tre′mor). Tremor of one side of the body.

hemivagotony (hem″e-va-got′o-ne). Hyperexcitability of the vagus nerve on one side.

hemivertebra (hem″e-ver′te-brah). 1. A developmental anomaly characterized by incomplete development of one side of a vertebra. 2. (Pl., *hemiver′tebrae*.) A vertebra which is incompletely developed on one side.

hemizygosity (hem″e-zi-gos′ĭ-te). The state of possessing only one of a pair of genes that influence the determination of a particular trait, as the existence in a male of a mutant X gene which is not opposed by a normal allele.

hemizygote (hem″e-zi′gōt). An individual or cell possessing only one of a pair of genes that influence the determination of a particular trait.

hemizygous (hem″e-zi′gus). Possessing only one of a pair of genes that influence the determination of a particular trait.

hemlock (hem′lok). 1. Conium. 2. Any fir tree of the genus *Tsuga*, especially *T. canadensis*, the source of Canada pitch, of the volatile oil of hemlock, and of an astringent extract.

hemo-, haemo-, hem-, haem-, hema-, hemato- (he′mo, hem, he′mah, hem′ah-to) [Gr. *haima*, *haimatos* blood]. Combining form denoting relationship to the blood.

hemoagglutination (he″mo-ah-gloo″tĭ-na′shun). Hemagglutination.

hemoagglutinin (he″mo-ah-gloo′tĭ-nin). Hemagglutinin.

hemoalkalimeter (he″mo-al″kah-lim′e-ter). An instrument for ascertaining the alkalinity of the blood.

hemobilia (he″mo-bil′e-ah). Hematobilia.

hemobilinuria (he″mo-bi-lin-u′re-ah) [*hemo-* + *bilin* + Gr. *ouron* urine + *-ia*]. The presence of urobilin in the blood and urine.

hemoblast (he′mo-blast). Hemocytoblast. **lymphoid h. of Pappenheim,** proerythroblast.

hemoblastosis (he″mo-blas-to′sis). Proliferation of the blood-forming tissues: the term includes leukosis, erythrosis, and reticulo-endotheliosis. Called also *hemolymphadenosis* and *hemomyelosis*.

hemocatatonistic (he″mo-kat″ah-to-nis′tik). Lessening the cohesion between the hemoglobin and the erythrocytes of the blood.

hemocatharsis (he″mo-kah-thar′sis). Hematocatharsis.

hemocatheresis (he″mo-kah-ther′ĕ-sis) [*hemo-* + Gr. *kathairesis* destruction]. The destruction of blood, especially of erythrocytes.

hemocatheretic (he″mo-kath″er-et′ik). Pertaining to, characterized by, or promoting hemocatheresis.

hemocelom (he″mo-se′lom). Hemocoelom.

hemocholecyst (he″mo-ko′le-sist). Non-traumatic hemorrhage of the gallbladder.

hemocholecystitis (he″mo-ko-le-sis-ti′tis). Cholecystitis with hemorrhage into the gallbladder.

hemochorial (he″mo-ko′re-al) [*hemo-* + *chorion*]. Denoting a type of placenta in which maternal blood comes in direct contact with the chorion.

hemochromatosis (he″mo-kro″mah-to′sis). 1. A disorder of iron metabolism, considered to be genetically determined, and characterized by excess deposition of iron in the tissues, especially in the liver, and by pigmentation of the skin, hepatic cirrhosis, and decreased carbohydrate tolerance. Called also *idiopathic hemochromatosis, iron storage disease, bronze diabetes,* and *pigmentary cirrhosis.* 2. A similar condition occurring in patients with refractory hemolytic anemia as the result of excessive blood transfusions or of iron salt administration, excess iron absorption, or defective iron utilization.

hemochromatotic (he″mo-kro″mah-tot′ik). Pertaining to or characterized by hemochromatosis.

hemochrome (he′mo-krōm) [*hemo-* + Gr. *chrōma* color]. An oxygen-carrying pigment found in the blood of various animals; the hemochromes include hemoglobin, erythrocruorin, chlorocruorin, hematocyanin and hemoerythrin.

hemochromogen (he″mo-kro′mo-jen) [*hemo-* + Gr. *chrōma* color + *gennan* to produce]. A general term for a compound of heme with various proteins and other substances. **hemoglobin h.,** a hemoglobin in which the globin has been denatured.

hemochromometer (he″mo-kro-mom′e-ter) [*hemo-* + Gr. *chrōma* color + *metron* measure]. An instrument for making color tests of the blood to determine the proportion of hemoglobin.

hemochromometry (he″mo-kro-mom′e-tre). The measurement of the quantity of hemoglobin in the blood.

hemochromoprotein (he″mo-kro″mo-pro′te-in). A colored, conjugated protein, with respiratory functions, found in the blood of animals.

hemocidal (he″mo-si′dal) [*hemo-* + L. *caedere* to kill]. Destroying blood cells; marked by destruction of blood.

hemoclasia (he″mo-kla′se-ah). The occurrence of postalimentary leukopenia. See *hemoclastic crisis,* under *crisis.*

hemoclasis (he-mok′lah-sis) [*hemo-* + Gr. *klasis* a breaking]. Hemolysis.

hemoclastic (he-mo-klas′tik). Pertaining to, characterized by, or causing destruction or dissolution of erythrocytes.

hemocoagulin (he″mo-ko-ag′u-lin). A constituent of the venom of certain snakes which causes coagulation of the blood.

hemococcidium (he″mo-kok-sid′e-um). Plasmodium.

hemocoelom (he-mo-se′lom) [*hemo-* + *coelom*]. The part of the coelom in which the heart is developed.

hemocoeloma (he″mo-se-lo′mah) [*hemo-* + *coeloma*]. Hemocoelom.

hemoconcentration (he″mo-kon″sen-tra′shun). Decrease of the fluid content of the blood, with resulting increase in its concentration.

hemoconia (he″mo-ko′ne-ah). Hemokonia.

hemoconiosis (he″mo-ko″ne-o′sis). The presence of an abnormal amount of hemoconiae in the blood.

hemocrine (he′mo-krin). Having an endocrine influence in the blood.

hemocrinia (he″mo-krin′e-ah) [*hemo-* + *endocrine*]. The presence of endocrine substances (hormones) in the blood.

hemocrinotherapy (he″mo-krin″o-ther′ah-pe). Treatment by injection of the patient's own blood mixed with an endocrine extract.

hemocryoscopy (he″mo-kri-os′ko-pe) [*hemo-* + *cryoscopy*]. Cryoscopy of the blood; the ascertaining of the freezing point of the blood.

hemocrystallin (he″mo-kris′tal-in). Hemoglobin.

hemoculture (he′mo-kul′tūr) [*hemo-* + *culture*]. A bacteriological culture of the blood.

hemocuprein (he″mo-ku′pre-in). An organic copper and protein compound isolated from erythrocytes.

hemocyanin (he″mo-si′ah-nin). Hematocyanin.

hemocyte (he′mo-sīt) [*hemo-* + Gr. *kytos* hollow vessel]. Any blood corpuscle, or formed element of the blood.

hemocytoblast (he″mo-si′to-blast) [*hemocyte* + Gr. *blastos* germ]. The free stem cell from which, according to the monophyletists, by development along different lines, all the other cells of the blood are derived.

hemocytoblastoma (he″mo-si″to-blas-to′mah). A tumor containing all the cells typical of bone marrow.

hemocytocatheresis (he″mo-si″to-kah-ther′e-sis) [*hemocyte* + Gr. *kathairesis* destruction]. The destruction of erythrocytes.

hemocytogenesis (he″mo-si″to-jen′e-sis) [*hemocyte* + *genesis*]. The formation or production of blood cells.

hemocytology (he″mo-si-tol′o-je) [*hemocyte* + *-logy*]. The study of the cellular elements of the blood.

hemocytolysis (he″mo-si-tol′ĭ-sis). Hemolysis.

hemocytolytic (he″mo-si″to-lit′ik). Hemolytic.

hemocytometer (he″mo-si-tom′e-ter). Hemacytometer.

hemocytophagic (he″mo-si″to-faj′ik). Pertaining to or characterized by hemocytophagy.

hemocytophagy (he″mo-si-tof′ah-je) [*hemocyte* + Gr. *phagein* to devour]. The ingestion and destruction of blood corpuscles by the histiocytes of the reticuloendothelial system.

hemocytopoiesis (he″mo-si″to-poi-e′sis). Hematopoiesis.

hemocytotripsis (he″mo-si″to-trip′sis) [*hemocyte* + Gr. *tribein* to rub]. The disintegration of the blood corpuscles by reason of pressure.

hemocytozoa (he″mo-si″to-zo′ah). Plural of *hemocytozoon.*

hemocytozoon (he″mo-si″to-zo′on), pl. *hemocytozo′a* [*hemo-* + Gr. *kytos* hollow vessel + *zōon* animal]. Any animal microorganism parasitic in the blood cells.

hemodia (he-mo′de-ah) [Gr. *haimōdia* condition of having the teeth on edge]. Unusual sensitiveness of the teeth.

hemodiagnosis (he″mo-di″ag-no′sis) [*hemo-* + *diagnosis*]. Diagnosis by examination of the blood.

hemodialysis (he″mo-di-al′ĭ-sis). The removal of certain elements from the blood by virtue of the difference in the rates of their diffusion through a semipermeable membrane.

hemodialyzer (he″mo-di′ah-līz″er). An apparatus by which hemodialysis may be performed, blood being separated by a semipermeable membrane from another solution of composition designed to secure diffusion of certain elements out of the blood. **ultrafiltration d.,** one in which differences in fluid pressure bring about diffusion (usually) of protein-free fluid from the blood.

hemodiapedesis (he″mo-di″ah-pe-de′sis) [*hemo-* + *diapedesis*]. The extravasation of blood through the skin.

hemodiastase (he″mo-di′as-tās) [*hemo-* + *diastase*]. An amylolytic enzyme in the blood.

hemodilution (he″mo-di-lu′shun). Increase of the fluid content of the blood with resulting decrease in its concentration.

hemodipsia (he″mo-dip′se-ah) [*hemo-* + Gr. *dipsa* thirst + *-ia*]. The desire to drink blood to assuage thirst.

hemodromograph (he″mo-drom′o-graf). A recording hemodromometer.

hemodromometer (he″mo-dro-mom′e-ter) [*hemo-* + Gr. *dromos* course + *metron* measure]. An instrument for measuring the speed of the blood current.

hemodynamic (he″mo-di-nam′ik). Pertaining to the movements involved in the circulation of the blood.

hemodynamics (he″mo-di-nam′iks) [*hemo-* + Gr. *dynamis* power]. The study of the movements of the blood and of the forces concerned therein.

hemodynamometer (he″mo-di″nah-mom′e-ter) [*hemo-* + Gr. *dynamis* strength + *metron* measure]. An apparatus for measuring the pressure of the blood.

hemodynamometry (he″mo-di″nah-mom′e-tre). Measurement of blood pressure.

hemodystrophy (he″mo-dis′tro-fe) [*hemo-* + *dys-* + Gr. *trophē* nutrition]. Any blood disease due to faulty blood nutrition.

hemo-endocrinopathic (he″mo-en″do-krin-o-path′ik). Pertaining to disease of blood formation and of endocrine function.

hemoendothelial (he″mo-en-do-the′le-al) [*hemo-* + *endothelium*]. Denoting a type of placenta in which maternal blood comes in contact with the endothelium of chorionic vessels.

hemoerythrin (he″mo-e-rith′rin) [*hemo-* + Gr. *erythros* red]. A red respiratory pigment found in the blood of certain worms.

hemoferrum (he″mo-fer′um). Oxyhemoglobin.

hemoflagellate (he″mo-flaj′ĕ-lāt). Any flagellate protozoan parasite of the blood. The term includes the trypanosomes and leishmanias.

hemofuscin (he″mo-fūs′in) [*hemo-* + L. *fuscus* brown]. A brownish-yellow pigment that results from the decomposition of hemoglobin. It gives the urine a deep ruddy color.

hemogenesis (he″mo-jen′e-sis). Hematogenesis.

hemogenia (he″mo-je′ne-ah) [*hemo-* + Gr. *gennan* to produce]. An archaic term for a condition thought to be identical with angiohemophilia.

hemogenic (he″mo-jen′ik). Hematogenic.

hemoglobic (he″mo-glo′bik). Producing or containing hemoglobin.

hemoglobin (he″mo-glo′bin). The oxygen-carrying pigment of the erythrocytes, formed by the developing erythrocyte in bone marrow. A molecule of hemoglobin contains four different globin polypeptide chains, designated α, β, γ, δ, each composed of several hundred amino acids. Different types of hemoglobin are determined by the specific combination of these chains, the number of chains of the different types in the molecule being indicated by subscript numerals. For example, *hemoglobin F* (*fetal h.*), which is the predominant type in the newborn, may be written as $\alpha_2^A\gamma_2^F$. *Hemoglobin A* (*adult h.*), which is normally predominant in the adult, is designated $\alpha_2^A\beta_2^A$. Another hemoglobin, *hemoglobin* A_2 (designated $\alpha_2^A\delta_2^{A_2}$), is usually present in limited minor concentrations. Many hemoglobins with differing electrophoretic mobilities and characteristics have been reported, for example, S, C, D, E, G, H, I, J, K, L, M, N, Q, Norfolk, and Barts. (See also *hemoglobinopathy*.) Because refined biochemical techniques may lead to the discovery of still other hemoglobins, certain standards for nomenclature have been devised. The hemoglobin electrophoretic mobility is designated by a capital letter; if two or more hemoglobins have the same mobility, the geographic area of discovery is indicated as a subscript, for example, hemoglobin M_S, or $M_{Saskatoon}$, and hemoglobin M_M, or $M_{Milwaukee}$. To restrict the increasing use of capital letters new hemoglobins are named simply for the laboratory, hospital, or town where they were discovered, for example, hemoglobin$_{Norfolk}$. When known, the number of each kind of polypeptide chain in the molecule should be indicated by the appropriate subscript numeral. **h. carbamate,** a compound of hemoglobin and CO_2. It is the principal form in which CO_2 is transported from the tissues to the lungs. **inactive h.,** hemoglobin which does not combine with oxygen. **muscle h.,** myohemoglobin. **nitric oxide h.,** a stable compound of nitric oxide and hemoglobin. **oxidized h., oxygenated h.,** the hemoglobin of arterial blood, combined with oxygen. **reduced h.,** the hemoglobin of venous blood, which has given up its oxygen in the tissues.

hemoglobinated (he″mo-glo′bin-āt-ed). Containing hemoglobin.

hemoglobinemia (he″mo-glo″bĭ-ne′me-ah) [*hemoglobin* + Gr. *haima* blood]. The presence of hemoglobin in the plasma of the blood.

hemoglobiniferous (he″mo-glo″bĭ-nif′er-us). Carrying or yielding hemoglobin.

hemoglobinocholia (he″mo-glo″bĭ-no-ko′le-ah) [*hemoglobin* + Gr. *cholē* bile + *-ia*]. The occurrence of hemoglobin in the bile.

hemoglobinogenous (he″mo-glo″bĭ-noj′e-nus). Producing hemoglobin.

hemoglobinolysis (he″mo-glo″bĭ-nol′ĭ-sis) [*hemoglobin* + Gr. *lysis* dissolution]. Splitting up of hemoglobin.

hemoglobinometer (he″mo-glo″bĭ-nom′e-ter) [*hemoglobin* + Gr. *metron* measure]. An instrument for measuring the hemoglobin of the blood.

hemoglobinometry (he″mo-glo″bĭ-nom′e-tre). The measurement of the hemoglobin of the blood.

hemoglobinopathy (he″mo-glo″bĭ-nop′ah-the) [*hemoglobin* + Gr. *pathos* disease]. A hematologic disorder caused by alteration in the genetically determined molecular structure of hemoglobin, which results in a characteristic complex of clinical and laboratory abnormalities and often, but not always, overt anemia. The specific features of these hemoglobin abnormalities are related to variation of the composite globin polypeptide chains, designated α, β, γ, δ, and to changes in the sequential arrangement of the amino acids constituting these chains. When analysis has revealed the site of biochemical aberration the abnormality of the peptide chain and the number of the altered amino acid and nature of its replacement also should be indicated. For example, hemoglobin S is expressed as $\alpha_2^A\beta_2^S$, or $\alpha_2^A\beta_2^{6\ valine}$, and, more completely, hemoglobin $G_{Philadelphia}$ is expressed as $\alpha_2^G\beta_2^A$, or $\alpha_2^{6\ lysine}\beta_2^A$. If more than one hemoglobin is present, the phenotype should be designated by listing them in order of decreasing concentrations; for example, the phenotype for sickle cell trait is expressed as AS, for sickle cell anemia as SS, and for sickle cell–hemoglobin C disease as SC.

hemoglobinopepsia (he″mo-glo″bĭ-no-pep′se-ah) [*hemoglobin* + Gr. *pepsis* digestion]. Hemoglobinolysis.

hemoglobinophilia (he″mo-glo″bĭ-no-fil′e-ah) [*hemoglobin* + Gr. *philein* to love]. Fondness for hemoglobin.

hemoglobinophilic (he″mo-glo″bĭ-no-fil′ik). Living on hemoglobin. In bacteriology, growing especially well in culture media containing hemoglobin.

hemoglobinorrhea (he″mo-glo″bĭ-no-re′ah) [*hemoglobin* + Gr. *rhoia* flow]. Escape of hemoglobin from the blood vessels.

hemoglobinous (he″mo-glo′bĭ-nus). Containing hemoglobin.

hemoglobinuria (he″mo-glo″bĭ-nu′re-ah) [*hemoglobin* + Gr. *ouron* urine + *-ia*]. The presence of free hemoglobin in the urine. **bovine h.** 1. Texas cattle fever. 2. British redwater. **epidemic h.,** hemoglobinuria of young infants: attended with cyanosis, jaundice, etc. Called also *Winckel's disease* and *maladie bronzée*. **epidemic h. of cattle,** a disease said to be due to a microbe, *Neisseria babesi*. **intermittent h.,** hemoglobinuria occurring in isolated episodes. See *paroxysmal cold h.* and *paroxysmal nocturnal h.* **malarial h.,** blackwater fever of hot climates. **march h.,** hemoglobinuria following prolonged and rapid marching. **paroxysmal cold h.,** a condition characterized by the sudden passage of hemoglobin in the urine following local or general exposure to cold. **paroxysmal nocturnal h.,** a rare, chronic, paroxysmal form of hemolysis of unknown cause characterized by episodic hemoglobinuria occurring chiefly, but not always, at night, and by hemosiderinuria, increased amounts of plasma hemoglobin, and a positive acid-serum (Ham) test. **h. of sheep,** heart-water disease.

toxic h., that which is consequent upon the ingestion of various poisons.

hemoglobinuric (he″mo-glo″bĭ-nu′rik). Pertaining to or characterized by hemoglobinuria.

hemogram (he′mo-gram) [*hemo-* + Gr. *gramma* a writing]. The blood picture; a written record or a graphic representation of the differential blood count.

hemohistioblast (he″mo-his′te-o-blast) [*hemo-* + Gr. *histos* tissue + *blastos* germ]. Ferrata's name for the hypothetical stem cell of all blood cells. Cf. *hemocytoblast.*

hemohydraulics (he″mo-hi-draw′liks). The branch of science which deals with blood in motion; the hydraulics of the blood.

hemoid (he′moid) [*hem-* + Gr. *eidos* form]. Resembling blood.

hemokinesis (he″mo-ki-ne′sis) [*hemo-* + Gr. *kinēsis* movement]. The flow of blood in the body.

hemokinetic (he″mo-ki-net′ik). Pertaining to or promoting the flow of blood in the body.

hemokonia (he″mo-ko′ne-ah). Small, round or dumbbell-shaped particles, demonstrating Brownian movement, observed in blood platelets under dark-field microscopy. Called also *blood dust of Müller.*

hemokoniosis (he″mo-ko″ne-o′sis). Hemoconiosis.

hemoleukocyte (he″mo-lu′ko-sīt). A leukocyte.

hemoleukocytic (he″mo-lu″ko-si′tik). Pertaining to the leukocytes.

hemolipase (he″mo-lip′ās). A ferment of the blood capable of saponifying fats.

hemolith (he′mo-lith) [*hemo-* + Gr. *lithos* stone]. A concretion in the wall of a blood vessel.

hemology (he-mol′o-je). Hematology.

hemolutein (he″mo-lu′te-in). A yellow pigment from the blood serum of certain animals.

hemolymph (he′mo-limf) [*hemo-* + *lymph*]. 1. The blood and lymph. 2. The nutrient fluid, or blood, of certain invertebrates.

hemolymphadenosis (he″mo-limf-ad″e-no′sis). Hemoblastosis.

hemolymphangioma (he″mo-lim-fan″je-o′mah). Hematolymphangioma.

hemolymphocytotoxin (he″mo-lim″fo-si″to-tok′sin). A toxin which destroys blood and lymph corpuscles.

hemolysate (he-mol′ĭ-sāt). The product resulting from hemolysis.

hemolysin (he-mol′ĭ-sin) [*hemo-* + Gr. *lysis* dissolution]. A substance which liberates hemoglobin from red blood corpuscles. Hemolysins may be present naturally in the body or they may be formed therein as a result of injections of foreign red corpuscles. The hemolysin formed by the injection of blood from the same species of animal is called *isolysin* or *isohemolysin*, that by the injection from another species, a *heterolysin;* one which destroys cells of the animal's own body is an *autolysin.* **acid h.,** one which reacts optimally at a pH below 7. **alpha h.,** a staphylococcic lysin that rapidly lyses both sheep and rabbit cells at 37°C. **bacterial h.,** a toxic substance produced by bacteria which lyses erythrocytes. **beta h.,** a staphylococcic hemolysin that hemolyzes sheep cells but only after a hot-cold lysis. **heterophile h.,** a hemolysin which has affinity for the red cells of some animal besides the one for which it is specific. **hot-cold h.,** a hemolytic toxic substance of bacterial origin that lyses erythrocytes in the cold following preliminary warm incubation. **immune h.,** a hemolysin made by injecting an animal with blood or with blood corpuscles.

hemolysis (he-mol′ĭ-sis) [*hemo-* + Gr. *lysis* dissolution]. The liberation of hemoglobin. Hemolysis consists of the separation of the hemoglobin from the corpuscles and its appearance in the fluid in which the corpuscles are suspended. It may be caused by hemolysins, by chemicals, by freezing or heating, or by distilled water. **alpha h.,** the production of a zone of greenish discoloration surrounding a bacterial colony on blood-agar medium, caused by partial decomposition of hemoglobin and characteristic of pneumococci and certain streptococci. **beta h.,** the production of a clear zone immediately surrounding a bacterial colony on blood-agar medium, which is characteristic of certain pathogenic bacteria. **biologic h.,** hemolysis by lysins produced in animals and plants. **contact h.,** the hastened hemolysis of corpuscles in contact with a surface. **immune h.,** the lysis of erythrocytes by complement in the presence of antibody to the erythrocyte. **passive h.,** the lysis of erythrocytes on which antigen has been adsorbed in the presence of complement and antiserum to that antigen. **siderogenous h.,** portal cirrhosis of liver associated with hemochromatosis; bronze diabetes. **venom h.,** hemolysis produced by snake poison.

hemolysoid (he-mol′ĭ-soid). A hemolysin the toxophore group of which has been destroyed. It is able to unite with the blood cell, but not to destroy it.

hemolysophilic (he″mo-li″so-fil′ik). Uniting readily with hemolysin.

hemolytic (he″mo-lit′ik). Pertaining to, characterized by, or producing hemolysis.

hemolytopoietic (he″mo-lit″o-poi-et′ik) [*hemo-* + Gr. *lysis* dissolution + *poiein* to make]. Regulating or pertaining to the formation and destruction of blood cells: a term applied to the system or mechanism in the body which controls the cellular elements of the blood by maintaining a proper balance between blood cell formation and destruction.

hemolyzable (he″mo-līz′ah-b′l). Capable of undergoing hemolysis.

hemolyzation (he″mo-li-za′shun). The production of hemolysis.

hemolyze (he′mo-līz). To subject to or to undergo hemolysis.

hemomanometer (he″mo-mah-nom′e-ter). A manometer for determining blood pressure.

hemomediastinum (he″mo-me″de-as-ti′num). Hematomediastinum.

hemometer (he-mom′e-ter). Hemoglobinometer.

hemometra (he″mo-me′trah). Hematometra.

hemometry (he-mom′ĕ-tre). Hematometry.

hemomyelosis (he″mo-mi″ĕ-lo′sis). Hemoblastosis.

hemonephrosis (he″mo-ne-fro′sis). Hematonephrosis.

hemo-opsonin (he″mo-op-so′nin). Hemopsonin.

hemopathic (he″mo-path′ik). Pertaining to disease of the blood; due to blood disorder.

hemopathology (he″mo-pah-thol′o-je) [*hemo-* + *pathology*]. Study of diseases of the blood.

hemopathy (he-mop′ah-the) [*hemo-* + Gr. *pathos* disease]. Any disease of the blood.

hemopericardium (he″mo-per″ĭ-kar′de-um) [*hemo-* + *pericardium*]. An effusion of blood within the pericardium.

hemoperitoneum (he″mo-per″ĭ-to-ne′um) [*hemo-* + *peritoneum*]. An effusion of blood in the peritoneal cavity.

hemopexin (he″mo-pek′sin). A ferment which coagulates blood.

hemopexis (he″mo-pek′sis) [*hemo-* + Gr. *pēxis* fixation]. Coagulation of blood.

hemophage (he′mo-fāj). Hematophage.

hemophagocyte (he″mo-fag′o-sīt) [*hemo-* + *phagocyte*]. A phagocyte which destroys blood corpuscles.

hemophagocytosis (he″mo-fag″o-si-to′sis). Hemocytophagy.

hemophil (he′mo-fil) [*hemo-* + Gr. *philein* to love]. 1. Thriving on blood. 2. A microorganism which grows best in media containing hemoglobin.

hemophilia (he″mo-fil′e-ah) [*hemo-* + Gr. *philein* to love + *-ia*]. A hereditary hemorrhagic diathesis characterized by hemarthroses and deep tissue bleeding, due to deficient generation of intrinsic thromboplastin. **h. A.,** hemophilia due to a lack in the blood of coagulation factor VIII; transmitted by the female to the male as a sex-linked recessive abnormality. **h. B,** a hereditary hemorrhagic diathesis due to lack in the blood of coagulation factor IX; like hemophilia A, transmitted by the female to the male as a sex-linked recessive abnormality. Called also *Christmas disease*. **h. C,** a term applied to a hemorrhagic diathesis due to a lack in the blood of coagulation factor XI; the condition resembles hemophilias A and B clinically, but is transmitted as an autosomal dominant. **h. calcipri'va,** a term applied to a bleeding tendency due to deficiency of calcium in the blood. **classical h.,** hemophilia A. **hereditary h.,** a bleeding tendency resulting from a genetically determined deficiency of some factor in the blood. **h. neonato'rum,** purpura in newborn children. **renal h.,** Gull's renal epistaxis. **sporadic h.,** hemorrhage occurring spontaneously and not as a result of a genetically determined deficiency in the blood. **vascular h.,** angiohemophilia.

hemophiliac (he″mo-fil′e-ak). An individual exhibiting hemophilia.

hemophilic (he-mo-fil′ik). 1. Fond of blood; living in blood. In bacteriology, growing especially well in culture media containing hemoglobin. 2. Pertaining to or characterized by hemophilia.

hemophilioid (he″mo-fil′e-oid) [*hemophilia* + Gr. *eidos* form]. Resembling classical hemophilia clinically. Applied to a number of congenital or acquired hemorrhagic disorders that are not due solely to a deficiency of blood coagulation factor VIII.

Hemophilus (he-mof′ĭ-lus). A genus name formerly given a taxon of microorganisms growing best (or only) in the presence of hemoglobin. **H. bo′vis,** *Moraxella bovis*. **H. bronchisep′ticus,** *Bordetella bronchiseptica*. **H. parapertus′sis,** *Bordetella parapertussis*. **H. pertus′sis,** *Bordetella pertussis*.

hemophilus (he-mof′ĭ-lus). A hemophilic microorganism. **h. of Koch-Weeks,** *Haemophilus aegyptius*. **h. of Morax-Axenfeld,** *Haemophilus duplex*.

hemophobia (he″mo-fo′be-ah) [*hemo-* + Gr. *phobos* fear + *-ia*]. Morbid dread of blood.

hemophoric (he″mo-for′ik) [*hemo-* + Gr. *phoros* bearing]. Carrying or conveying blood.

hemophotograph (he″mo-fo′to-graf). A photograph of blood corpuscles.

hemophthalmia, hemophthalmos, hemophthalmus (he″mof-thal′me-ah, he″mof-thal′mos, he″mof-thal′mus) [*hemo-* + Gr. *ophthalmos* eye]. An extravasation of blood within the eye.

hemophthisis (he-mof′thĭ-sis) [*hemo-* + Gr. *phthisis* wasting]. A term once used to indicate anemia due to insufficient nutrition of blood cells.

hemopiezometer (he″mo-pi″e-zom′e-ter) [*hemo-* + Gr. *piesis* pressure + *metron* measure]. Any apparatus for measuring blood pressure.

hemoplasmodium (he″mo-plaz-mo′de-um). The plasmodium of a blood parasite.

hemoplasmopathy (he″mo-plaz-mop′ah-the). Hematoplasmopathy.

hemoplastic (he″mo-plas′tik). Hematoplastic.

hemopleura (he″mo-ploo′rah). Hemothorax.

hemopneumopericardium (he″mo-nu″mo-per″ĭ-kar′de-um). Pneumopericardium with hemorrhagic effusion.

hemopneumothorax (he″mo-nu″mo-tho′raks). Pneumothorax with hemorrhagic effusion.

hemopoiesic (he″mo-poi-e′sik). Hematopoietic.

hemopoiesis (he″mo-poi-e′sis). Hematopoiesis. **heteroplastic h.,** the production of blood cells directly from their stem cells. **homoplastic h.,** the production of new mature blood cells by young elements of the same type.

hemopoietic (he″mo-poi-et′ik). Hematopoietic.

hemopoietin (he″mo-poi-e′tin) [*hemo-* + Gr. *poein* to make]. 1. A supposed substance in hog's stomach which acts upon a substance in protein food to produce a hematopoietic substance similar to the active principle of liver. See *Castle's factors*, under *factor*. 2. Hemopoietine.

hemopoietine (he″mo-poi-e′tin). A name originally given to a substance which stimulated erythropoiesis; probably the same as erythropoietin.

hemoporphyrin (he″mo-por′fĭ-rin). A compound $C_{34}H_{38}O_4N_4$, derived from hematoporphyrin.

hemoposia (he″mo-po′ze-ah) [*hemo-* + Gr. *posis* drinking + *-ia*]. The drinking of blood.

hemoprecipitin (he″mo-pre-sip′ĭ-tin). A blood precipitin.

hemoproctia (he″mo-prok′she-ah) [*hemo-* + Gr. *prōktos* anus]. Hemorrhage from the rectum.

Hemoproteus (he″mo-pro′te-us). Haemoproteus.

hemopsonin (he″mop-so′nin) [*hemo-* + *opsonin*]. An opsonin which acts on red blood corpuscles to render them susceptible of phagocytosis.

hemoptic, hemoptoic (he-mop′tik, he-mop-to′ik). Hemoptysic.

hemoptysic (he″mop-ti′sik). Pertaining to or marked by hemoptysis.

hemoptysis (he-mop′tĭ-sis) [*hemo-* + Gr. *ptyein* to spit]. The expectoration of blood or of blood-stained sputum. **cardiac h.,** that due to disturbed arterial tension in persons with heart disease. **endemic h.,** paragonimiasis. **Goldstein's h.,** hemoptysis due to bleeding telangiectases in the tracheo-bronchial tree. **Manson's h.,** hemoptysis due to parasitic infection of the lungs. **parasitic h.,** a disease caused by infection of the lungs with *Paragonimus westermanii*. It is marked by cough and spitting of blood and by gradual deterioration of health. Called also *pulmonary distomatosis* and *lung fluke disease*. **vicarious h.,** that which occurs instead of a menstruation.

hemopyelectasis (he″mo-pi-ĕ-lek′tah-sis) [*hemo-* + Gr. *pyelos* pelvis + *ektasis* dilatation]. Dilatation of the renal pelvis with an accumulation of bloody fluid.

hemopyrrol (he″mo-pir′ol). A pyrrole produced by the reduction of hematoporphyrin.

hemorrhachis (he-mor′ah-kis). Hematorrhachis.

hemorrhage (hem′or-ij) [*hemo-* + Gr. *rhēgnynai* to burst forth]. A copious escape of blood from the vessels; bleeding. **alveolar h.,** hemorrhage from a dental alveolus. **arterial h.,** the escape of blood from an artery or a ruptured aneurysm. **capillary h.,** the oozing of blood from the minute vessels. **capsuloganglionic h.,** hemorrhage into the basal ganglia and internal and external capsule of the brain. **cerebral h.,** a hemorrhage into the cerebrum or occurring within the cranium. It may be dural, meningeal, supradural, epidural, subdural, etc. **concealed h.,** internal h. **essential h.,** one not due to an injury. **external h.,** one in which blood escapes from the body. **extradural h.,** hemorrhage into the epidural space. **fibrinolytic h.,** hemorrhage resulting from abnormalities in the fibrinolytic system, and not dependent on hypofibrinogenemia. **gravitating h.,** hemorrhage into the spinal canal, in which the blood settles to the lower part of the canal from the force of gravity. **intermediary h., intermediate h.,** recurring h. **internal h.,** hemorrhage in which the extravasated blood remains within the body. **intradural h.,** hemorrhage into the intradural space. **intrapartum h.,** hemorrhage occurring during parturition. **massive h.,** loss of blood so rapid and profuse as to bring on surgical shock. **nasal h.,** epistaxis. **parenchymatous h.,** capillary hemorrhage into the substance of an organ. **h. per rhexin,** hemorrhage from rupture of a blood vessel. **petechial h.,** hemorrhage that occurs in minute points beneath the skin. **plasma h.,** the loss of the fluid portion (plasma) of the blood. **postpartum h.,** that which occurs soon after labor or childbirth. **primary h.,** that which occurs as an immediate result of an injury. **pulmonary h.,** hemorrhage from the lungs; pneumorrhagia. **punctate h.,** spots of blood effused into the tissues from capillary hemorrhage. **recurring h.,** that which has been once stopped by clots, but returns after the period of reaction, the clots being displaced by the blood current. **renal h.,** hemorrhage from the kidney; nephrorrhagia. **secondary h.,** that which follows an accident or injury after a considerable lapse of time. **splinter h's,** Blumer's name for linear hemorrhages beneath the nail seen in certain cases of subacute bacterial endocarditis. **spontaneous h.,** the bleeding of hemophilia. **subarachnoid h.,** hemorrhage into the subarachnoid space. **unavoidable h.,** that which results from the detachment of a placenta praevia. **uterine h., essential,** a condition marked by hemorrhage from the uterus, and usually showing hypertrophy of the uterine mucosa and cystic disease of the ovary. Called also *metropathia haemorrhagica.* **venous h.,** the escape of blood from a wounded vein; phleborrhagia. **vicarious h.,** a discharge of blood from any part in consequence of the suppression of a discharge from another part.

hemorrhagenic (hem″o-rah-jen′ik) [*hemorrhage* + Gr. *gennan* to produce]. Causing hemorrhage.

hemorrhagic (hem″o-raj′ik). Pertaining to or characterized by hemorrhage.

hemorrhagin (hem″o-ra′jin). A cytolysin existing in certain venoms and poisons, such as snake venom and ricin, which is destructive to endothelial cells and blood vessels.

hemorrhagiparous (hem″o-rij-ip′ah-rus) [*hemorrhage* + L. *parere* to produce]. Causing hemorrhage.

hemorrhaphilia (hem″o-rah-fil′e-ah). Hemophilia.

hemorrhea (hem-o-re′ah). Hematorrhea.

hemorrheology (he″mo-re-ol′o-je) [*hemo-* + Gr. *rhoia* flow + *logos* treatise]. The scientific study of the deformation and flow properties of cellular and plasmatic components of blood in macroscopic, microscopic, and sub-microscopic dimensions, and the rheological properties of vessel structure with which the blood comes in direct contact.

hemorrhoid (hem′o-roid) [Gr. *haimorrhois*]. A varicose dilatation of a vein of the superior or inferior hemorrhoidal plexus. **combined h.,** mixed h. **external h.,** a varicose dilatation of a vein of the inferior hemorrhoidal plexus, situated

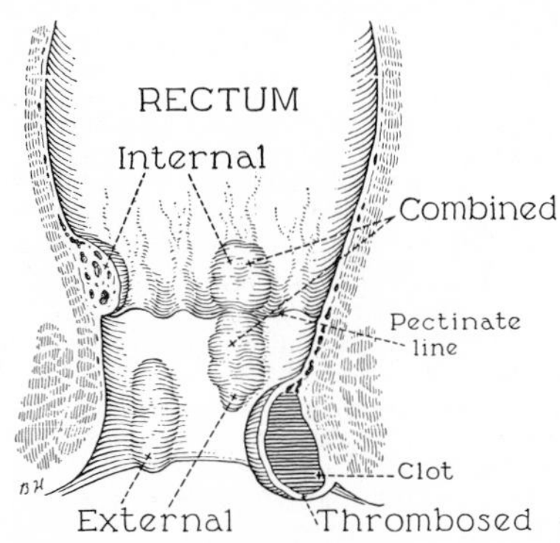

Hemorrhoids.

distal to the pectinate line and covered with modified anal skin. **internal h.,** a varicose dilatation of a vein of the superior hemorrhoidal plexus, originating above the pectinate line, and covered by mucous membrane. **lingual h.,** a varicose dilatation of a vein at the root of the tongue. **mixed h.,** a varicose dilatation of a vein connecting the superior and inferior hemorrhoidal plexuses, forming an external and an internal hemorrhoid in continuity. **mucocutaneous h.,** mixed h. **prolapsed h.,** an internal hemorrhoid which has descended below the pectinate line and protruded outside the anal sphincter. **strangulated h.,** an internal hemorrhoid which has been prolapsed sufficiently and for long enough time for its blood supply to become occluded by the constricting action of the anal sphincter. **thrombosed h.,** one containing clotted blood.

hemorrhoidal (hem″o-roi′dal). Pertaining to, or of the nature of, hemorrhoids.

hemorrhoidectomy (hem″o-roid-ek′to-me). Excision of hemorrhoids.

hemorrhoidolysis (hem″o-roid-ol′ĭ-sis) [*hemorrhoid* + Gr. *lysis* dissolution]. The dissolution of hemorrhoids by chemical or electrical means.

hemosalpinx (he″mo-sal′pinks) [*hemo-* + Gr. *salpinx* tube]. Hematosalpinx.

hemoscope (he′mo-skōp). Hematoscope.

hemosialemesis (he″mo-si″al-em′e-sis) [*hemo-* + Gr. *sialon* saliva + *emesis* vomiting]. The discharge of bloody saliva.

hemosiderin (he″mo-sid′er-in) [*hemo-* + Gr. *sidēros* iron]. An insoluble form of storage iron in which the micelles of ferric hydroxide are so arranged as to be visible microscopically both with and without the use of specific staining methods.

hemosiderinuria (he″mo-sid″er-in-u′re-ah). The presence of hemosiderin in the urine.

hemosiderosis (he″mo-sid″er-o′sis). A focal or general increase in tissue iron stores without associated tissue damage.

hemosite (he′mo-sīt). A blood parasite.

hemosozic (he″mo-so′zik) [*hemo-* + Gr. *sōzein* to save]. Preventing hemolysis; antihemolytic.

hemosozin (he″mo-so′zin). A sozin in the blood.

hemospasia (he″mo-spa′ze-ah) [*hemo-* + Gr. *span* to draw]. The drawing of blood, especially by cupping.

hemospast (he′mo-spast). A cup or other device for drawing blood.

hemospastic (he″mo-spas′tik). Serving to draw or extract blood.

hemospermia (he″mo-sper′me-ah) [*hemo-* + Gr. *sperma* seed + *-ia*]. The presence of blood in the semen.

Hemosporidia (he″mo-spo-rĭd′e-ah). Haemosporidia.

hemostasia (he″mo-sta′ze-ah). Hemostasis.

hemostasis (he-mos′tah-sis) [*hemo-* + Gr. *stasis* halt]. 1. The arrest of an escape of blood. 2. The checking of the flow of blood through any part or vessel.

hemostat (he′mo-stat). 1. An instrument for constricting a blood vessel to check the flow or escape of blood. 2. An agent which checks hemorrhage.

hemostatic (he″mo-stat′ik) [*hemo-* + Gr. *statikos* standing]. 1. Checking the flow of blood. 2. An agent that arrests the flow of blood. **capillary h.,** an agent which reduces capillary bleeding time by increasing the contractility and resistance and decreasing the permeability of the capillary wall. **Martin's h.,** surgeon's agaric impregnated with ferric chloride. **Wright's h.,** a mixture of formaldehyde solution and gelatin: used as a dental hemostatic.

hemostyptic (he″mo-stip′tik). Hemostatic.

hemotachometer (he″mo-tah-kom′e-ter) [*hemo-* + Gr. *tachos* swiftness + *metron* measure]. An instrument for measuring the swiftness of the blood current.

hemotherapeutics (he″mo-ther″ah-pu′tiks). Hemotherapy.

hemotherapy (he″mo-ther′ah-pe) [*hemo-* + Gr. *therapeia* treatment]. Treatment of disease by the administration of blood or blood products, such as blood plasma.

hemothigmic (he″mo-thig′mik) [*hemo-* + Gr. *thigma* touch]. Touching blood without inducing coagulation of the latter. Cf. *anhemothigmic.*

hemothorax (he″mo-tho′raks) [*hemo-* + Gr. *thōrax* chest]. A collection of blood in the pleural cavity.

hemothymia (he″mo-thi′me-ah) [*hemo-* + Gr. *thymos* spirit + *-ia*]. An uncontrollable tendency to murder.

hemotonia (he″mo-to′ne-ah) [*hemo-* + Gr. *tonos* tension + *-ia*]. The tonus of the solid elements of the blood.

hemotoxic (he″mo-tok′sik). Hematotoxic.

hemotoxin (he″mo-tok′sin). An exotoxin characterized by hemolytic activity. **cobra h.,** the constituent of cobra venom which is able to lyse red blood cells of man and of various other animals without the presence of blood serum.

hemotroph (he′mo-trof) [*hemo-* + Gr. *trophē* nourishment]. The sum total of the nutritive substances supplied to the embryo from the maternal blood during gestation.

hemotrophe (he′mo-trof). Hemotroph.

hemotrophic (he″mo-trōf-ik). Pertaining to or derived through hemotroph.

hemotropic (he″mo-trop′ik). Hematotropic.

hemotropin (he-mot′ro-pin). Hemopsonin.

hemotrypsia (he″mo-trip′se-ah). A condition in which a hemorrhage, especially an internal one, provokes hemorrhage in another part.

hemotympanum (he″mo-tim′pah-num). Hematotympanum.

hemovolumetry (he″mo-vol-u′me-tre). The measurement of the volume of the blood.

hemoxometer (he″mok-som′e-ter) [*hemo-* + *oxygen* + Gr. *metron* measure]. An instrument for measuring the oxygen content of the blood.

hemozoin (he″mo-zo′in). The pigment found in malarial parasites.

hemozoon (he″mo-zo′on). Hematozoon.

hemuresis (hem″u-re′sis) [*hem-* + *uresis*]. The voiding of bloody urine.

henbane (hen′bān). Hyoscyamus. Called also *black henbane.*

Hench-Aldrich index, test (hench al′drich) [Philip S. *Hench*, American physician, born 1896, co-winner, with E. C. Kendall and Tadeus Reichstein, of the Nobel prize for medicine and physiology in 1950; Martha *Aldrich*, American biochemist, born 1897]. See under *test.*

Henderson's test (hen′der-sonz) [Yandell *Henderson*, American physiologist, 1873–1944]. See under *test.*

Henderson-Jones disease (hen′der-son-jōnz′) [Melvin S. *Henderson*, American orthopedic surgeon, 1883–1954; Hugh T. *Jones*, American orthopedic surgeon, born 1892]. See under *disease.*

Henke's space, triangle (hen′kēz) [Wilhelm *Henke*, German anatomist, 1834–1896]. See under *space* and *triangle.*

Henle's layer, loop, membrane, sheath, etc. (hen′lēz) [Friedrich Gustav Jakob *Henle*, German anatomist, 1809–1885, a celebrated anatomist and histologist]. See under the nouns.

Henle-Coenen sign, test (hen′le-ke′nan) [Adolf R. *Henle*, German surgeon, born 1864; Hermann *Coenen*, German surgeon, born 1875]. See under *tests.*

henna (hen′ah). The dried and powdered leaves of *Lawsonia inermis:* a cosmetic and hair dye, and an astringent.

Hennebert's sign (en-bārz′) [Belgian otologist]. See under *sign.*

Henoch's purpura (hen′ōks) [Edouard Heinrich *Henoch*, German pediatrist, 1820–1910]. See under *purpura.*

henogenesis (hen″o-jen′e-sis) [Gr. *hen* one + *genesis* origin]. The developmental course of an individual; ontogenesis.

henosis (he-no′sis) [Gr. *henōsis* combination into one, union]. Healing or union.

henotic (he-not′ik) [Gr. *henōtikos* serving to unite]. Promoting healing, tending to heal.

henpox (hen′poks). A disease of fowls, pigeons, and turkeys, marked by an eruption of yellow, warty nodules, chiefly on the head.

henpue, henpuye (hen-poo′ye) [West African]. Goundou.

henry (hen′re) [Joseph *Henry*, American physicist, 1797–1878]. The unit of electric induction.

Henry's law (hen′rēz) [William *Henry*, English chemist, 1775–1837]. See under *law.*

Hensen's canal, cells, disk, knot, stripe, etc. [Victor *Hensen*, German anatomist and physiologist, 1835–1924]. See under the nouns.

Henshaw test (hen′shaw) [Russell *Henshaw*, New York physician]. See under *tests.*

Hensing's ligament (hen′singz) [Frederich Wilhelm *Hensing*, German anatomist, 1719–1745]. See under *ligament.*

hepaptosis (hep″ap-to′sis). Hepatoptosis.

hepar (he′par) [Gr. *hēpar* liver]. 1. [N A, B N A] A large gland of a dark-red color situated in the upper part of the abdomen on the right side. See *liver.* 2. The liver of certain animals, used in pharmaceutical preparations. 3. A liver-like or liver-colored substance. **h. adipo′sum,** fatty liver. **h. loba′tum,** a liver divided into numerous lobes by deep fissures produced by syphilis. **h. sicca′tum,** the dried and powdered liver of pigs: used as a food and medicine in organic diseases of the liver. **h. sul′furis,** sulfurated potash.

heparin (hep′ah-rin). A mucopolysaccharide acid occurring in various tissues, but most abundantly in the liver. In pharmacy, a mixture of active principles obtained from the livers or lungs of domestic animals; injected intravenously, it renders the blood incoagulable, most probably by interfering with the formation of intrinsic thromboplastin and the action of thrombin. Used in the prevention and treatment of thrombosis and in bacterial endocarditis, postoperative pulmonary embolism, frostbite, and also in repair of vascular injury.

heparinate (hep′ah-rin-āt). Any salt of heparin.

heparinemia (hep″ah-rin-e′me-ah). The presence of heparin in the blood.

heparinize (hep′ah-rin-īz). To treat with heparin in order to increase the clotting time of the blood.

hepat-. See *hepato-.*

hepatalgia (hep″ah-tal′je-ah) [*hepat-* + Gr. *algos* pain + *-ia*]. Pain in the liver.

hepatargia (hep″ah-tar′je-ah) [*hepat-* + Gr. *argia* inactivity]. Auto-intoxication from defective liver action.

hepatargy (hep″ah-tar′je). Hepatargia.

hepatase (hep′ah-tās). A hypothetical detoxicating ferment of the liver.

hepatatrophia (hep″at-ah-tro′fe-ah) [*hepat-* + Gr. *atrophia* atrophy]. Atrophy of the liver.

hepatatrophy (hep″at-at′ro-fe). Hepatatrophia.

hepatauxe (hep″at-awk′se) [*hepat-* + Gr. *auxē* increase]. Hepatomegaly.

hepatectomize (hep″ah-tek′to-mīz). To deprive of the liver by surgical removal.

hepatectomy (hep″ah-tek′to-me) [*hepat-* + Gr. *ektomē* excision]. Excision of a portion of the liver, or of a lesion of the liver.

hepatic (he-pat′ik) [L. *hepaticus;* Gr. *hēpatikos*]. Pertaining to the liver.

hepatico- (he-pat′ĭ-ko) [Gr. *hēpatikos* of the liver]. Combining form denoting relationship to a hepatic duct.

hepaticocholangiocholecystenterostomy (he-pat″ĭ-ko-ko-lan″je-o-ko″le-sis″ten-ter-os′to-me). Surgical creation of a new communication between the gallbladder and a hepatic duct and between the intestine and gallbladder.

hepaticocholangiojejunostomy (he-pat″ĭ-ko-ko-lan″je-o-je″ju-nos′to-me). Surgical creation of a new communication between the gallbladder, a hepatic duct, and the jejunum.

hepaticodochotomy (he-pat″ĭ-ko-do-kot′o-me). Surgical incision of a hepatic duct and the common bile duct.

hepaticoduodenostomy (he-pat″ĭ-ko-du″o-de-nos′to-me). Surgical creation of a new communication between a hepatic duct and the duodenum.

hepatico-enterostomy (he-pat″ĭ-ko-en″ter-os′-to-me) [*hepatico-* + Gr. *enteron* intestine + *stomoun* to provide with an opening, or mouth]. Surgical creation of a new communication between a hepatic duct and the intestine.

hepaticogastrostomy (he-pat″ĭ-ko-gas-tros′to-me) [*hepatico-* + Gr. *gastēr* stomach + *stomoun* to provide with an opening, or mouth]. Surgical creation of a new communication between a hepatic duct and the stomach.

hepaticojejunostomy (he-pat″ĭ-ko-je″ju-nos′-to-me) [*hepatico-* + *jejunum* + Gr. *stomoun* to provide with an opening, or mouth]. Surgical creation of a new communication between a hepatic duct and the jejunum.

Hepaticola (hep″ah-tik′o-lah) [*hepat-* + *colere* to inhabit]. A genus of nematodes parasitic in the liver of rats. *H. hepatica* has been found in the liver of man in India.

hepaticoliasis (he-pat″ĭ-ko-li′ah-sis). Infestation with *Hepaticola.*

hepaticolithotomy (he-pat″ĭ-ko-lĭ-thot′o-me). Incision of a hepatic duct with removal of calculus.

hepaticolithotripsy (he-pat″ĭ-ko-lith′o-trip-se). The operation of crushing a stone in a hepatic duct.

hepaticopulmonary (he-pat″ĭ-ko-pul′mo-nar″-e). Pertaining to the liver and the lungs.

hepaticostomy (he-pat″ĭ-kos′to-me) [*hepatico-* + Gr. *stomoun* to provide with an opening, or mouth]. Surgical creation of an artificial opening into a hepatic duct.

hepaticotomy (he-pat″ĭ-kot′o-me) [*hepatico-* + Gr. *tomē* cutting]. Incision of a hepatic duct.

hepatin (hep′ah-tin). Glycogen.

hepatism (hep′ah-tizm). Ill health due to liver disease.

hepatitides (hep″ah-tit′ĭ-dēz). Plural of *hepatitis.*

hepatitis (hep″ah-ti′tis), pl. *hepatit′ides* [*hepat-* + *-itis*]. Inflammation of the liver. **acute parenchymatous h.,** acute yellow atrophy of the liver. **chronic interstitial h.,** cirrhosis of the liver. **h. contagio′sa ca′nis,** a highly fatal virus disease of dogs characterized by sore throat, fever, cough, weakness, and collapse. **enzootic h.,** Rift Valley fever. **epidemic h.,** infectious h. **familial h.,** progressive lenticular degeneration. **homologous serum h.,** serum h. **infectious h.,** a subacute disease of worldwide distribution, caused by a virus, and tending to occur in children and young adults; the liver is diffusely enlarged, and the symptoms include fever, gastrointestinal distress, headache, anorexia, and jaundice. The incubation period varies from 1 to 6 weeks. **infectious necrotic h. of sheep,** black disease. **h. seques′trans,** hepatitis with necrosis and distintegration of the liver tissue. **serum h.,** a condition indistinguishable clinically from infectious hepatitis, but caused by an immunologically distinct virus which is transmitted by inadequately sterilized syringes and needles, by procedures such as tattooing, and by administration of infectious blood, plasma, or blood products. The incubation period is 8 to 22 weeks. **suppurative h.,** inflammation of the liver attended by abscess formation. **toxipathic h.,** hepatitis caused by direct action of a poison on the liver cells. **transfusion h.,** serum h. **trophopathic h.,** hepatitis caused by deficiency of a nutritive factor.

hepatization (hep″ah-ti-za′shun). 1. The change of tissue into a liver-like substance. 2. Impregnation with hydrogen sulfide. **gray h.,** hepatization of the lung in which the affected tissue has a gray color. **red h.,** a form in which the affected tissue is red from excess of blood. **yellow h.,** a stage in hepatization in which the exudate is purulent.

hepatized (hep′ah-tīzd). Changed into a liver-like substance.

hepato-, hepat- [Gr. *hēpar, hēpatos* liver]. Combining form denoting relationship to the liver.

hepatobiliary (hep″ah-to-bil′e-ār″e). Pertaining to the liver and the bile or the biliary ducts.

hepatobronchial (hep″ah-to-brong′ke-al). Pertaining to or communicating with the liver and a bronchus, as a hepatobronchial fistula.

hepatocarcinogenesis (hep″ah-to-kar″si-no-jen′e-sis). The production of carcinoma of the liver.

hepatocarcinogenic (hep″ah-to-kar″sĭ-no-jen′-ik). Causing carcinoma of the liver.

hepatocele (he-pat′o-sēl) [*hepato-* + Gr. *kēlē* hernia]. Hernial protrusion of a part of the liver.

hepatocellular (hep″ah-to-sel′u-lar). Pertaining to or affecting liver cells.

hepatocholangeitis (hep″ah-to-ko-lan″je-i′tis). Inflammation of the liver and bile ducts.

hepatocholangiocystoduodenostomy (hep″-ah-to-ko-lan″je-o-sis″to-du″o-de-nos′to-me). The operation of establishing drainage of the bile ducts into the duodenum by way of the gallbladder.

hepatocholangioduodenostomy (hep″ah-to-ko-lan″je-o-du″o-de-nos′to-me). The operation of establishing drainage of the bile ducts into the duodenum.

hepatocholangioenterostomy (hep″ah-to-ko-lan″je-o-en″ter-os′to-me) [*hepato-* + Gr. *cholē* bile + *angeion* vessel + *enteron* intestine + *stomoun* to provide with an opening, or mouth]. Surgical creation of a new communication between the bile ducts and the intestine.

hepatocholangiogastrostomy (hep″ah-to-ko-lan″je-o-gas-tros′to-me). The operation of establishing drainage of the bile ducts into the stomach.

hepatocholangiostomy (hep″ah-to-ko-lan″je-os′to-me). The operation of establishing drainage of the bile ducts either through the abdominal wall (*external h.*) or into some part of the gastro-intestinal tract (*internal h.*).

hepatocirrhosis (hep″ah-to-si-ro′sis) [*hepato-* + *cirrhosis*]. Cirrhosis of the liver.

hepatocolic (hep″ah-to-kol′ik). Pertaining to the liver and the colon.

hepatocuprein (hep″ah-to-koo′prin). A copper-containing compound present in liver tissue.

hepatocystic (hep″ah-to-sis′tik). Pertaining to the liver and gallbladder.

hepatoduodenostomy (hep″ah-to-du″o-de-nos′-to-me) [*hepato-* + *duodenum* + Gr. *stomoun* to provide with an opening, or mouth]. The surgical creation of a new communication between the liver and the duodenum.

hepatodynia (hep″ah-to-din′e-ah) [*hepato-* + Gr. *odynē* pain]. Pain in the liver.

hepatodysentery (hep″ah-to-dis′en-ter-e). Dysentery due to inflammation of the liver.

hepatodystrophy (hep″ah-to-dis′tro-fe). Acute yellow atrophy of the liver.

hepato-enteric (hep″ah-to-en-ter′ik). Pertaining to the liver and intestine.

hepato-enterostomy (hep″ah-to-en″ter-os′to-me). Surgical creation of a communication between the cut surface of a liver graft and the intestine, permitting drainage of bile from the grafted tissue directly into the lumen of the intestine.

hepatoflavin (hep″ah-to-fla′vin). Riboflavin obtained from liver tissue.

hepatofugal (hep″ah-tof′u-gal) [*hepato-* + L. *fugere* to flee from]. Directed or flowing away from the liver.

hepatogastric (hep″ah-to-gas′trik). Pertaining to the liver and stomach.

hepatogenic (hep″ah-to-jen′ik). 1. Giving rise to or forming liver tissue. 2. Hepatogenous.

hepatogenous (hep″ah-toj′e-nus). 1. Produced in or originating in the liver. 2. Hepatogenic.

hepatoglobin (hep″ah-to-glo′bin). A protein which is one of the fractions of blood plasma. It is said to be increased in infections, malignancy and certain endocrine disorders.

hepatoglobinemia (hep″ah-to-glo-bĭ-ne′me-ah). Abnormal increase in hepatoglobin in the blood plasma.

hepatoglycemia glycogenetica (hep″ah-to-gli-se′me-ah gli″ko-je-net′ĭ-kah). Glycogenosis.

hepatogram (hep′ah-to-gram). 1. A tracing of the liver pulse in the sphygmogram. 2. A roentgenogram of the liver.

hepatography (hep″ah-tog′rah-fe) [*hepato-* + Gr. *graphein* to record]. 1. A treatise on the liver. 2. The recording of a tracing of the liver pulse. 3. The making of a roentgenogram of the liver.

hepatohemia (hep″ah-to-he′me-ah) [*hepato-* + Gr. *haima* blood]. Congestion of the liver.

hepatoid (hep′ah-toid) [*hepato-* + Gr. *eidos* form]. Resembling the liver in structure.

hepatolenticular (hep″ah-to-len-tik′u-lar). Pertaining to the liver and the lenticular nucleus.

hepatolienal (hep″ah-to-li′e-nal). Pertaining to the liver and spleen.

hepatolienography (hep″ah-to-li″ĕ-nog′rah-fe) [*hepato-* + L. *lien* spleen + Gr. *graphein* to record]. Roentgenography of the liver and spleen after intravenous injection of an opaque medium.

hepatolienomegaly (hep″ah-to-li″ĕ-no-meg′-ah-le). Hepatosplenomegaly.

hepatolith (hep′ah-to-lith) [*hepato-* + Gr. *lithos* stone]. A gallstone, especially one within the liver.

hepatolithectomy (hep″ah-to-lĭ-thek′to-me) [*hepato-* + Gr. *lithos* stone + *ektomē* excision]. The excision of a calculus from the liver or the hepatic duct.

hepatolithiasis (hep″ah-to-lĭ-thi′ah-sis) [*hepato-* + *lithiasis*]. The formation or presence of calculi in the intrahepatic biliary ducts.

hepatologist (hep″ah-tol′o-jist). A specialist in hepatology.

hepatology (hep″ah-tol′o-je) [*hepato-* + *-logy*]. The study of the liver.

hepatolysin (hep″ah-tol′ĭ-sin). A cytolysin destructive to liver cells.

hepatolysis (hep″ah-tol′ĭ-sis) [*hepato-* + Gr. *lysis* dissolution]. Destruction of the liver cells.

hepatolytic (hep″ah-to-lit′ik). Pertaining to, characterized by, or causing hepatolysis.

hepatoma (hep″ah-to′mah). A tumor of the liver: Sabourin's term for a transition stage between adenoma and carcinoma of the liver.

hepatomalacia (hep″ah-to-mah-la′she-ah) [*hepato-* + Gr. *malakia* softening]. Softening of the liver.

hepatomegalia (hep″ah-to-mĕ-ga′le-ah) [*hepato-* + Gr. *megas* big]. Hepatomegaly. **h. glycogen′ica,** glycogenosis.

hepatomegaly (hep″ah-to-meg′ah-le). Enlargement of the liver. **glycogenic h.,** glycogenosis.

hepatomelanosis (hep″ah-to-mel″ah-no′sis). Melanosis of the liver.

hepatometry (hep″ah-tom′e-tre). Determination of the size of the liver.

hepatomphalos (hep″ah-tom′fah-los) [*hepat-* + Gr. *omphalos* navel]. Projection of the liver through the abdominal wall near the umbilicus.

hepatomphalocele (hep″ah-tom′fah-lo-sēl). Omphalocele with liver also in the membranous sac outside the abdomen.

hepatonephric (hep″ah-to-nef′rik). Pertaining to the liver and kidney.

hepatonephritic (hep″ah-to-ne-frit′ik). Pertaining to or characterized by hepatonephritis.

hepatonephritis (hep″ah-to-ne-fri′tis) [*hepato-* + Gr. *nephros* kidney]. A form of severe icterus due to simultaneous inflammation of the liver and kidneys from the same cause.

hepatonephromegaly (hep″ah-to-nef″ro-meg′-ah-le) [*hepato-* + Gr. *nephros* kidney + *megas* large]. Enlargement of the liver and kidney.

hepatopath (hep′ah-to-path). A person with liver disease.

hepatopathy (hep″ah-top′ah-the) [*hepato-* + Gr. *pathos* disease]. Any disease of the liver.

hepatoperitonitis (hep″ah-to-per″ĭ-to-ni′tis) [*hepato-* + *peritonitis*]. Inflammation of the peritoneum covering the liver.

hepatopetal (hep″ah-top′ĕ-tal) [*hepato-* + L. *petere* to seek]. Directed or flowing toward the liver.

hepatopexy (hep′ah-to-pek″se) [*hepato-* + Gr. *pēxis* fixation]. Surgical fixation of the displaced liver to the abdominal wall.

hepatophage (hep′ah-to-fāj) [*hepato-* + Gr. *phagein* to eat]. A giant cell supposed to destroy the liver cells.

hepatophlebitis (hep″ah-to-fle-bi′tis). Inflammation of the veins of the liver.

hepatophlebotomy (hep″ah-to-fle-bot′o-me) [*hepato-* + *phlebotomy*]. The aspiration of blood from the liver.

hepatophyma (hep″ah-to-fi′mah) [*hepato-* + Gr. *phyma* growth]. Abscess of the liver.

hepatopleural (hep″ah-to-ploo′ral). Pertaining to the liver and the pleura, or communicating with the liver and pleural cavity, as a hepatopleural fistula.

hepatopneumonic (hep″ah-to-nu-mon′ik) [*hepato-* + Gr. *pneumonikos* of the lungs]. Pertaining to, affecting, or communicating with the liver and lungs.

hepatoportal (hep″ah-to-por′tal). Pertaining to the portal system of the liver.

hepatoptosia (hep″ah-to-to′se-ah). Hepatoptosis.

hepatoptosis (hep″ah-to-to′sis) [*hepato-* + Gr. *ptōsis* falling]. Dislocation of the liver; movable liver.

hepatopulmonary (hep″ah-to-pul′mo-nar″e). Hepatopneumonic.

hepatorecurrence (hep″ah-to-re-kur′ens). Recurrence of syphilis attacking the liver.

hepatorenal (hep″ah-to-re′nal). Pertaining to the liver and kidneys.

hepatorrhagia (hep″ah-to-ra′je-ah) [*hepato-* + Gr. *rhēgnynai* to burst forth]. Hemorrhage from the liver.

hepatorrhaphy (hep″ah-tor′ah-fe) [*hepato-* + Gr. *rhaphē* suture]. The suturing of the liver.

hepatorrhea (hep″ah-to-re′ah) [*hepato-* + Gr. *rhoia* flow]. A morbidly excessive secretion of bile; any morbid flow from the liver.

hepatorrhexis (hep″ah-to-rek′sis) [*hepato-* + Gr. *rhēxis* rupture]. Rupture of the liver.

hepatoscopy (hep″ah-tos′ko-pe) [*hepato-* + Gr. *skopein* to examine]. Examination of the liver.

hepatosis (hep″ah-to′sis). Any functional disorder of the liver. **serous h.,** veno-occlusive disease of the liver.

hepatosolenotropic (hep″ah-to-so-le″no-trop′-ik) [*hepato-* + Gr. *sōlēn* a channel, gutter, pipe + *tropē* a turn, turning]. Having an affinity for or exerting a specific effect on the cholangioles and interlobular ducts of the liver.

hepatosplenitis (hep″ah-to-sple-ni′tis). Inflammation of the liver and spleen.

hepatosplenography (hep″ah-to-sple-nog′rah-fe). Roentgenography of the liver and spleen.

hepatosplenomegaly (hep″ah-to-sple″no-meg′-ah-le) [*hepato-* + Gr. *splēn* spleen + *megas* big]. Enlargement of the liver and spleen.

hepatosplenometry (hep″ah-to-sple-nom′e-tre). Determination of the size of the liver and spleen.

hepatosplenopathy (hep″ah-to-sple-nop′ah-the). Any combined disorder of the liver and spleen.

hepatostomy (hep″ah-tos′to-me) [*hepato-* + Gr. *stoma* mouth]. The making of an opening into the liver, as for the removal of gallstones.

hepatotherapy (hep″ah-to-ther′ah-pe) [*hepato-* + Gr. *therapeia* treatment]. Treatment of disease by the administration of liver or liver extract.

hepatothrombin (hep″ah-to-throm′bin) [*hepato-* + *thrombin*]. Wolf's name for a fibrin factor formed by the liver and existing in the blood, which unites with leukothrombin to form thrombin.

hepatotomy (hep″ah-tot′o-me) [*hepato-* + Gr. *tomē* cut]. Surgical incision of the liver. **transthoracic h.,** the operation of incising the liver for abscess by resecting a rib, opening the pleural sac, and incising the diaphragm.

hepatotoxemia (hep″ah-to-tok-se′me-ah) [*hepato-* + *toxemia*]. Blood poisoning originating in the liver.

hepatotoxic (hep″ah-to-tok′sik). Toxic to liver cells.

hepatotoxicity (hep″ah-to-toks-is′ĭ-te). The quality or property of exerting a destructive or poisonous effect upon liver cells.

hepatotoxin (hep″ah-to-tok′sin) [*hepato-* + *toxin*]. A toxin destructive to liver cells; especially an antibody produced by injecting an animal with liver cells.

hepatotropic (hep″ah-to-trop′ik) [*hepato-* + Gr. *tropos* a turning]. Having a special affinity for or exerting a specific effect on the liver.

hepatoxic (hep″ah-tok′sik). Hepatotoxic.

Hepatozoon (hep″ah-to-zo′on) [*hepato-* + Gr. *zōon* animal]. A genus of parasites found in blood corpuscles. *H. canis* is transmitted to dogs by the tick *Rhipicephalus appendiculatus*. *H. muris* occurs in the liver cells of rats.

hephestic (he-fes′tik) [Gr. *Hēphaistos* Greek god of fire]. Characteristic of blacksmiths.

hephestiorrhaphy (he-fes″te-or′ah-fe) [Gr. *Hēphaistos* Greek god of fire + *rhaphē* suture]. Cauterization of the edges of a wound to produce adhesions.

hephormone (hep′hor-mōn). Glycogen.

hepta-, hept- [Gr. *hepta* seven]. Combining form meaning seven.

heptabarbital (hep″tah-bar′bĭ-tal). Chemical name: 5-(1-cyclohepten-1-yl)-5-ethylbarbituric acid: used as a sedative and hypnotic.

heptachromic (hep″tah-kro′mik) [*hepta-* + Gr. *chrōma* color]. 1. Pertaining to or exhibiting seven colors. 2. Able to distinguish all seven colors of the spectrum; possessing full color vision.

heptad (hep′tad). Any element having a valency of seven.

heptadactylia (hep″tah-dak-til′e-ah) [*hepta-* + Gr. *daktylos* finger + *-ia*]. The occurrence of seven digits (fingers or toes) on one limb.

heptadactylism (hep″tah-dak′tĭ-lizm). Heptadactylia.

heptadactyly (hep″tah-dak′tĭ-le). Heptadactylia.

heptaldehyde (hep-tal′de-hīd). A compound which can produce liquefaction of carcinomas in mice.

heptane (hep′tān). A hydrocarbon, C_7H_{16}, from pine resin and petroleum: identical with abietene.

heptapeptide (hep″tah-pep′tīd). A polypeptide containing seven amino acids.

heptaploid (hep′ta-ploid). 1. Pertaining to or characterized by heptaploidy. 2. An individual or cell having seven sets of chromosomes.

heptaploidy (hep′tah-ploi″de). The state of having seven sets of chromosomes (7n).

heptargia (hep-tar′je-ah). Hepatargia.

heptatomic (hep″tah-tom′ik). Septivalent.

heptavalent (hep-tav′ah-lent) [*hepta-* + L. *valere* to be able]. Septivalent.

heptose (hep′tōs) [*hept-* + *-ose*]. A monosaccharide containing seven carbon atoms in a molecule.

heptosuria (hep″to-su′re-ah). Presence of a heptose in the urine.

herb (erb, herb) [L. *herba*]. Any leafy plant without a woody stem, especially one used as a household remedy or as a flavoring. **death's h.,** belladonna leaf. **vulnerary h.,** an herb anciently regarded as healing wounds.

herbaceous (her-ba′shus). Having the characters of an herb.

herbal (her′bal). A book on herbs.

herbalist (her′bal-ist). A herb doctor.

Herbert's operation (her′berts) [Major Herbert *Herbert*, Indian Medical Service]. See under *operation*.

herbicide (her′bĭ-sīd) [L. *herba* herb + *caedere* to kill]. An agent that is destructive to weeds.

herbivorous (her-biv′o-rus) [L. *herba* herb + *vorare* to eat]. Subsisting upon grasses and herbs.

Herb. recent. Abbreviation for L. *herba′rium recen′tium*, of fresh herbs.

Herbst's corpuscles (herbsts) [Ernst Friedrich Gustav *Herbst*, German physician, 1803–1893]. See under *corpuscle*.

hereditary (he-red′ĭ-ter-e) [L. *hereditarius*]. Derived from ancestry or obtained by inheritance; in relation to disease, denoting a condition that may be genetically transmitted from parent to offspring.

heredity (he-red′ĭ-te) [L. *hereditas*]. 1. Organic resemblance based on descent (Castle). 2. The genetic transmission of a particular quality or trait from parent to offspring. **autosomal h.,** the transmission of a quality or trait by a gene located on an autosome. **sex-linked h.,** the transmission of a quality or trait by a gene located on a sex-chromosome; often implying transmission of a trait from mother to son by a gene carried on the X chromosome.

heredo-ataxia (her″e-do-ah-tak′se-ah). Hereditary ataxia, as in Friedreich's ataxia or Marie's disease.

heredobiologic (her″e-do-bi″o-loj′ik). Pertaining to or due to hereditary endogenic factors.

heredodegeneration (her″e-do-de-jen″er-a′shun). A hereditary degeneration due to disease or defect of the hyaloplasm; heredocerebellar ataxia (Marie).

heredodiathesis (her″e-do-di-ath′e-sis). Hereditary diathesis or predisposition.

heredofamilial (her″e-do-fah-mil′e-al). Hereditary in certain families.

heredo-immunity (her″e-do-ĭ-mu′nĭ-te). Hereditary or inherited immunity.

heredo-infection (her″e-do-in-fek′shun). Germinal infection.

heredolues (her″e-do-lu′ēz). Congenital syphilis.

heredoluetic (her″e-do-lu-et′ik). Pertaining to congenital syphilis.

heredopathia (her″e-do-path′e-ah). An inherited pathological condition. **h. atac′tica polyneuritifor′mis,** Refsum's disease.

heredosyphilis (her″e-do-sif′ĭ-lis). Congenital syphilis.

heredosyphilitic (her″e-do-sif″ĭ-lit′ik). A person affected with congenital syphilis.

heredosyphilology (her″e-do-sif″ĭ-lol′o-je). The study of congenital syphilis.

heredotrophedema (her″e-do-trof″e-de′mah). Hereditary edema.

heredotuberculosis (her″e-do-tu-ber″ku-lo′sis). Inherited tuberculosis.

hereism (he′re-izm) [Gr. *Hēra* or *Hērē* the queen of the Greek gods; the sister and wife of Zeus]. Faithfulness to the marriage vows.

Hérelle. See *d'Hérelle*.

Herff's clamp (herfs) [Otto von *Herff*, Swiss gynecologist, 1856–1916]. A variety of wound clamp.

Hering's law, test, theory (her′ingz) [Ewald *Hering*, physiologist in Leipzig, 1834–1918]. See under the nouns.

Hering's phenomenon (her′ingz) [Ewald *Hering*, physiologist in Cologne, born 1866]. See under *phenomenon*.

heritable (her′ĭ-tah-b'l). Capable of being inherited.

hermaphrodism (her-maf′ro-dizm). Hermaphroditism.

hermaphrodite (her-maf′ro-dit) [Gr. *hermaphroditos*]. An individual organism possessing gonadal tissue typical of both sexes. See also *intersex*.

hermaphroditism (her-maf′ro-dit-izm) [Gr. *hermaphroditos* a person partaking of the attributes of both sexes]. A state characterized by the presence of both male and female sex organs. In man it is caused by failure of differentiation of the gonads, with presence of both ovarian and testicular tissue and presence of contradictory morphologic criteria of sex. See also *intersexuality*. **bilateral h.**, that in which gonadal tissue typical of both sexes occurs on each side of the body. **dimidiate h.**, lateral h. **h. with excess**, a condition characterized by the presence of the normal organs typical of one sex with some that pertain to the opposite sex. **false h.**, pseudohermaphroditism. **lateral h.**, presence of gonadal tissue typical of one sex on one side of the body and tissue typical of the other sex on the opposite side. **neuter h., neutral h.**, a condition of anomalous sexual development, without gonadal tissue typical of either sex (gonadal aplasia). **protandrous h.**, the state of an organism having generative organs typical of both sexes, in which the male organs develop first, and those typical of the female sex develop later. **protogynous h.**, the state of an organism having generative organs typical of both sexes, in which the female organs develop first, and those typical of the male sex develop later. **spurious h.**, pseudohermaphroditism. **transverse h.**, a condition in which the external genital organs are characteristic of one sex and the gonads are typical of the other. **true h.**, coexistence, in the same individual, of both ovarian and testicular tissue, with somatic characters typical of both sexes. **unilateral h.**, presence of gonadal tissue typical of both sexes on one side and of an ovary or testis on the other.

hermaphroditismus (her-maf″ro-di-tiz′mus). Hermaphroditism. **h. ve′rus**, true hermaphroditism. **h. ve′rus bilatera′lis**, bilateral hermaphroditism. **h. ve′rus latera′lis**, lateral hermaphroditism. **h. ve′rus unilatera′lis**, unilateral hermaphroditism.

Hermetia illucens (her-me′she-ah il-lu′senz). The soldier fly, the larvae of which cause intestinal myiasis in man.

hermetic (her-met′ik) [L. *hermeticus*]. Impervious to air; airtight.

hermetically (her-met′ĭ-kal-le). In an air-tight manner.

hermodactyl (her″mo-dak′til) [Gr. *hermodaktylos*]. The root of *Colchicum variegatum*: cathartic.

hernia (her′ne-ah) [L.]. The protrusion of a loop or knuckle of an organ or tissue through an abnormal opening (Celsus). **abdominal h.**, the protrusion of some internal body structure through the abdominal wall. **acquired h.**, one brought on by lifting or by a strain or other injury. **h. adipo′sa**, fat h. **Barth's h.**, hernia of loops of intestine between the serosa of the abdominal wall and that of a persistent vitelline duct. **Béclard's h.**, femoral hernia through the saphenous opening. **Birkett's h.**, synovial h. **h. of the bladder**, protrusion of a part of the bladder through any normal or other opening. **cecal h.**, one that contains the cecum or a part of it. **h. cere′bri**, the protrusion of the brain substance through the skull. **Cloquet's h.**, crural h., pectineal. **complete h.**, one in which the sac and its contents have passed through the orifice. **concealed h.**, hernia not perceptible on palpation. **congenital h.**, that which exists at birth, most commonly scrotal. **Cooper's h.**, retroperitoneal hernia. **crural h.**, femoral h. **crural h., pectineal**, hernia within and behind the femoral vessels, the tumor resting upon the pectineus muscle. **cystic h.**, cystocele. **diaphragmatic h.**, hernia through the diaphragm. **direct h.** See under *inguinal h.* **diverticular h.**, the protrusion of a congenital diverticulum of the gut. **dry h.**, a hernia in which the sac and its contents have become intimately adherent to each other. **duodenojejunal h.**, Treitz's h. **encysted h.**, scrotal or oblique inguinal hernia in which the bowel, enveloped in its own proper sac, passes into the tunica vaginalis in such a way that the bowel has three coverings of peritoneum. **epigastric h.**, a hernia through the linea alba above the navel. **external h.** See under *inguinal h.* **extrasaccular h.**, sliding h. **fat h.**, hernial protrusion of properitoneal fat through the abdominal wall; called also *h. adiposa.* **femoral h.**, hernia into the femoral canal. **foraminal h.**, hernia through the foramen of Winslow. **funicular h.**, hernia of the umbilical or spermatic cord. **gastro-esophageal h.**, a form of hiatal hernia in which the lower end of the esophagus and the adjacent part of the stomach herniate into the thorax. **Gibbon's h.**, hydrocele with large hernia. **gluteal h.**, femoral h. **Goyrand's h.**, inguinal hernia that does not descend into the scrotum. **Gruber's h.**, internal mesogastric hernia. **Grynfelt h.**, congenital hernia through the superior lumbar space. **Hesselbach's h.**, hernia with a diverticulum through the cribriform fascia. **Hey's h.**, encysted h. **hiatal h., hiatus h.**, protrusion of any structure through the esophageal hiatus of the diaphragm. **Holthouse's h.**, an inguinal hernia which has turned outward into the groin. Called also *inguinocrural h.* **incarcerated h.**, hernia so occluded as to be not reducible. **incisional h.**, hernia occurring through an old abdominal incision. **incomplete h.**, one which has not passed quite through the orifice. **indirect h.** See under *inguinal h.* **infantile h.**, oblique inguinal hernia behind the funicular process of the peritoneum. **inguinal h.**, hernia into the inguinal canal. An *indirect* inguinal hernia (*external* or *oblique* hernia) leaves the abdomen through the internal ring, and passes down obliquely through the inguinal canal, external to the deep epigastric artery. A *direct* inguinal hernia (*internal* hernia) emerges between the deep epigastric artery and the edge of the rectus muscle. **inguinocrural h.**, Holthouse's h. **inguinofemoral h.**, a combined inguinal and femoral hernia. **inguinoproperitoneal h.**, hernia that is partly inguinal and partly properitoneal. Called also *Krönlein's h.* **inguinosuperficial h.**, interstitial hernia which passes through the internal inguinal ring, the inguinal canal, and the external inguinal ring, but at this point is deflected upward and outward so as to lie upon the aponeurosis of the external oblique. Called also *Kürster's h.* **h. in rec′to**, a hernia into the wall of the rectum. **intermuscular h., interparietal h.**, an interstitial hernia which lies between one or another of the fascial or muscular planes of the abdomen. **internal h.** 1. A hernia which lies within the abdomen without involving the abdominal wall. 2. See under *inguinal h.* **intersigmoid h.**, hernia of the intestine through the intersigmoid fossa. **interstitial h.**, a hernia in which a knuckle of intestine lies between two layers of the abdominal wall. **h. of the iris**, protrusion of a part of the iris. **irreducible h.**, hernia that cannot be restored by taxis. **ischiatic h.**, hernia through the sacrosciatic foramen. **ischiorectal h.**, a protrusion of the abdominal viscera between fibers of

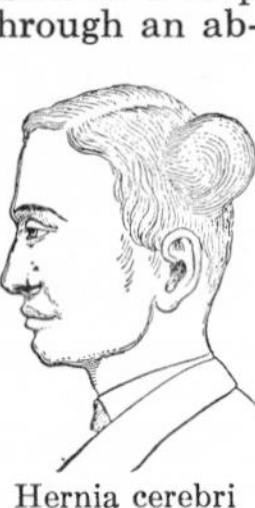
Hernia cerebri (Moorhead).

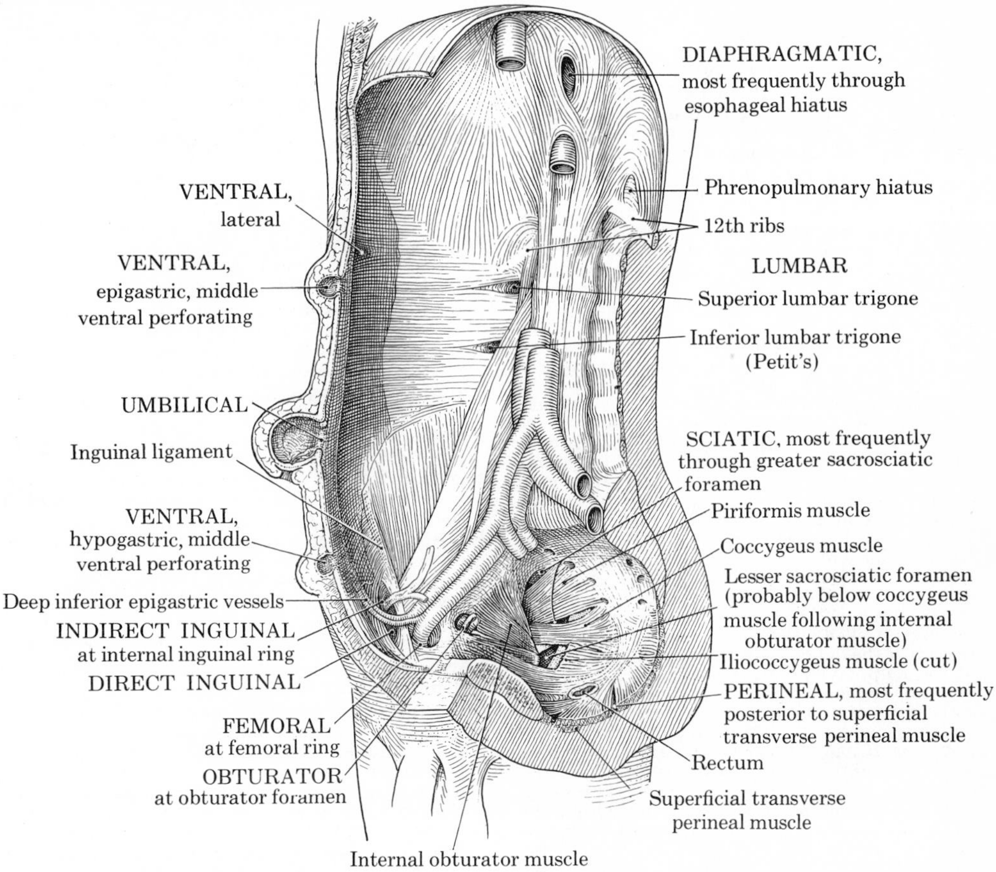

DIAPHRAGMATIC,
most frequently through
esophageal hiatus
VENTRAL,
lateral
Phrenopulmonary hiatus
12th ribs
VENTRAL,
epigastric, middle
ventral perforating
LUMBAR
Superior lumbar trigone
Inferior lumbar trigone
(Petit's)
UMBILICAL
Inguinal ligament
SCIATIC, most frequently
through greater sacrosciatic
foramen
VENTRAL,
hypogastric, middle
ventral perforating
Piriformis muscle
Coccygeus muscle
Lesser sacrosciatic foramen
(probably below coccygeus
muscle following internal
obturator muscle)
Deep inferior epigastric vessels
INDIRECT INGUINAL
at internal inguinal ring
DIRECT INGUINAL
Iliococcygeus muscle (cut)
PERINEAL, most frequently
posterior to superficial
transverse perineal muscle
FEMORAL
at femoral ring
OBTURATOR
at obturator foramen
Rectum
Superficial transverse
perineal muscle
Internal obturator muscle

TYPES OF INTESTINAL HERNIA: ABDOMINAL AND PELVIC OPENINGS

Abdominal peritoneum
Loop of intestine
Internal
inguinal ring
External
inguinal ring
Closed
vaginal process
Patent
process
Testis
INFANTILE
FUNICULAR
CONGENITAL, SCROTAL

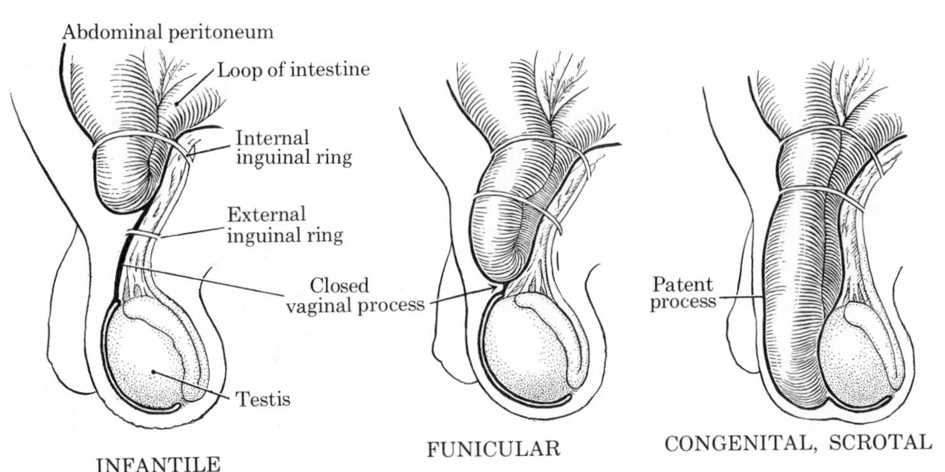

TYPES OF INDIRECT INGUINAL HERNIA

the levator ani muscle. **Krönlein's h.,** inguinoproperitoneal h. **Küster's h.,** inguinosuperficial h. **labial h.,** the protrusion of a knuckle of the gut into a labium majus. **labial h., posterior,** vaginolabial h. **Laugier's h.,** a femoral hernia perforating Gimbernat's ligament. **levator h.,** pudendal h. **Littre's h.,** diverticular h. **lumbar h.,** hernia in the loin. **mesenteric h.,** the passage of a portion of the gut through an opening in the mesentery. **mesocolic h.,** hernia into a pouch of the mesocolon. **mucosal h.,** hernia of the mucous membrane of the intestine through an opening in the muscular coat. **oblique h.** See under *inguinal h.* **obturator h.,** protrusion through the obturator foramen. **omental h.,** a protrusion of a knuckle of omentum. **ovarian h.,** hernial protrusion of an ovary. **paraesophageal h.,** a form of hiatal hernia in which part of the stomach, but not of the esophagus, herniates into the thorax. **paraperitoneal h.,** hernia of the bladder in which only a part of the protruded bladder is covered by the peritoneum of the sac. **parasaccular h.,** sliding h. **h. par glissement** (glĕs-maw'), sliding h. **parietal h.,** Richter's h. **parumbilical h.,** hernia in the region of the navel. **pectineal h.,** hernia situated beneath the pectineal fascia. **perineal h.,** ischiorectal h. **Petit's h.,** lumbar hernia in Petit's triangle. **properitoneal h.,** an interstitial hernia which is located between the parietal peritoneum and the transversalis fascia. **pudendal h.,** a hernia located in the pudendum, having passed through a rent in the levator muscle and its fascia. Called also *levator h.* **h. of pulp,** protrusion of the dental pulp through the dentin wall of the pulp cavity. **pulsion h.,** a hernia produced by sudden increase of intra-abdominal pressure. **rectal h.,** hernia in recto. **reducible h.,** one that may be returned by manipulation. **retrocecal h.,** protrusion of the intestine into a pouch behind the cecum. **retrograde h.,** herniation of two loops of intestine, the portion of intestine between the two loops lying within the abdominal cavity. **retroperitoneal h.,** hernia of the intestine into the duodenojejunal fossa. **Richter's h.,** one in which only a part of the lumen of the gut is protruded. **Riex's h.,** retrocecal h. **Rokitansky's h.,** protrusion of a sac of mucous membrane or of the peritoneum through separated muscular fibers of the intestine. **sciatic h.,** hernia through the great sacrosciatic foramen. **scrotal h.,** an inguinal hernia which has descended into the scrotum. **sliding h., slip h., slipped h.,** hernia of the colon in which a portion of the part is drawn into or slips into a hernial sac by the inclusion in the sac of the parietal peritoneum to which it is attached. **spigelian h.,** abdominal hernia through the linea semilunaris. **strangulated h.,** one which is tightly constricted and has become or is likely to become sphacelated. **subpubic h.,** obturator h. **synovial h.,** protrusion of the inner lining membrane through the stratum fibrosum of a joint capsule. **thyroidal h.,** obturator h. **tonsillar h.,** the extrusion of the tonsilla cerebelli through the foramen magnum. **Treitz's h.,** a retroperitoneal hernia through the duodenojejunal recess. **tunicary h.,** mucosal h. **umbilical h.,** protrusion of part of the intestine at the umbilicus, the defect in the abdominal wall and protruding bowel being covered with skin and subcutaneous tissue. **uterine h.,** hernial protrusion of the uterus. **vaginal h.,** hernia into the vagina. **vaginal h., posterior,** downward protrusion of the pouch of Douglas, with its intestinal contents, between the posterior vaginal wall and the rectum; called also *enterocele.* **vaginolabial h.,** hernia of a viscus into the posterior end of the labium majus. **Velpeau's h.,** femoral hernia in front of the femoral vessels. **ventral h.,** hernia through the abdominal wall. **vesical h.,** protrusion of the bladder. **Von Bergmann's h.,** a small, generally intermittent form of hiatus hernia. **w h.,** retrograde hernia.

hernial (her'ne-al). Pertaining to a hernia.

herniary (her'ne-a-re). Pertaining to or associated with hernia.

herniated (her'ne-āt"ed). Protruding like a hernia; enclosed in a hernia.

herniation (her"ne-a'shun). The abnormal protrusion of an organ or other body structure through a defect or natural opening in a covering membrane, muscle, or bone. **h. of nucleus pulposus,** rupture or prolapse of the nucleus pulposus into the spinal canal.

hernio-appendectomy (her"ne-o-ap"en-dek'to-me). Herniotomy combined with appendectomy.

hernio-enterotomy (her"ne-o-en"ter-ot'o-me). Herniotomy conjoined with enterotomy.

hernioid (her'ne-oid). Resembling hernia.

herniolaparotomy (her"ne-o-lap"ah-rot'o-me). Laparatomy for the cure of hernia.

herniology (her"ne-ol'o-je) [*hernia* + *-logy*]. The study and science of hernias.

hernioplasty (her'ne-o-plas"te). Operation for the radical cure of hernia.

herniopuncture (her"ne-o-pungk'tūr) [*hernia* + *puncture*]. Surgical puncture of a hernia.

herniorrhaphy (her"ne-or'ah-fe) [*hernia* + Gr. *rhaphē* suture]. Suture of a hernia; the radical operation for hernia.

herniotome (her"ne-o-tōm). A knife for operating on hernia.

herniotomy (her"ne-ot'o-me) [*hernia* + Gr. *temnein* to cut]. A cutting operation for the repair of hernia; kelotomy.

heroin (her'o-in). Diacetylmorphine.

heroinism (her'o-in-izm). Addiction to the use of heroin, with its morbid effects.

heroinomania (her"o-in"o-ma'ne-ah). Heroinism.

Herophilus (hĕ-rof'ĭ-lus) (c. 300 B.C.). A renowned Greek physician and anatomist of Alexandria who performed dissection of the human body, and whose important anatomical observations (e.g., on the brain, duodenum, and genitalia, and on the differentiation between nerves and blood vessels) have led many to regard him as "the Father of Anatomy."

herpangina (herp"an-ji'nah) [*herpes* + *angina*]. A specific infectious disease characterized by sudden onset of fever of short duration and appearance of typical vesicular or ulcerated lesions in the faucial area or on the soft palate; caused by a virus of the Coxsackie A group.

herpes (her'pēz) [L.; Gr. *herpēs*]. An inflammatory skin disease characterized by the formation of small vesicles in clusters (Galen). As commonly used, the term alone refers to *herpes simplex.* **h. catarrha'lis,** h. simplex. **h. circina'tus,** tinea circinata. **h. cor'neae,** herpetic inflammation involving the cornea. **h. des'quamans,** tinea imbricata. **h. digita'lis,** herpes simplex of the fingers. **h. facia'lis,** herpes occurring on the face. **h. farino'sus,** a variety of ringworm. **h. febri'lis,** eruption of skin lesions characteristic of herpes, as a concomitant of fever, commonly occurring about the lips or nose. Called also *fever blisters* and *cold sores.* **h. generalisa'tus,** herpes scattered over the body. **h. genita'lis,** herpes simplex involving the genital mucosa. **h. gestatio'nis,** a herpes peculiar to pregnant women. **h. i'ris,** a form occurring in rings on the hands and feet. **h. labia'lis,** herpes of the lips. **h. menstrua'lis,** a form that recurs at the menstrual period. **h. menta'lis,** herpes simplex of the submental region. **h. o'ticus,** herpes infection of the ear. **h. phlyctaeno'des,** dermatitis herpetiformis. **h. praeputia'lis,** a form that occurs on the male genitals. **h. progenita'lis,** herpes of the genitals. **h. recur'rens,** herpes occurring in repeated attacks. **h. sim'plex,** an acute virus disease marked by groups of watery blisters on the skin and mucous membranes, such as the borders of the lips or the nares (*h. labialis,* cold sores), the mucous surface of the genitals (*h. genitalis*). It often accompanies fever (*h. febrilis,* fever blisters). **h. ton'surans,**

tinea tonsurans. **h. ton′surans maculo′sus,** pityriasis rosea. **h. veg′etans,** pemphigus vegetans. **h. zos′ter,** an acute inflammatory disease of the cerebral ganglia and ganglia of the posterior nerve roots, caused by the virus of chickenpox. It is characterized by groups of small vesicles on inflammatory bases occurring in the cutaneous areas supplied by certain nerve trunks, and associated with neuralgic pain. Called also *acute posterior ganglionitis, shingles, zoster,* and *zona.* **h. zos′ter o′ticus,** herpetic inflammation involving the ear drum. **h. zos′ter varicello′-sus,** herpes zoster with secondary varicelliform eruption.

herpesencephalitis (her″pēz-en-sef″ah-li′tis). See under *encephalitis.*

herpesvirus (her″pēz-vi′rus). The causative viral agent of herpes simplex (herpes labialis). Two types are distinguished on the basis of the effects produced on cells in tissue culture, the *GC strain* causing the formation of giant cells, the *P strain* causing proliferative changes, with the rounding and piling up of cells.

herpetic (her-pet′ik) [L. *herpeticus*]. Pertaining to or of the nature of herpes.

herpetiform (her-pet′ĭ-form) [L. *herpes* herpes + *forma* form]. Resembling herpes.

herpetism (her′pĕ-tizm). A predisposition to herpes.

Herpetomonas (her″pĕ-tom′o-nas) [Gr. *herpeton* creeper + *monas* monad]. A genus of flagellate animal microparasites found in invertebrate hosts. They closely resemble one of the developmental forms of trypanosomes.

herpetomoniasis (her-pet″o-mo-ni′ah-sis). Infection with a species of Herpetomonas.

Herrick's anemia (her′iks) [James B. *Herrick,* Chicago physician, 1861–1954]. Sickle cell anemia. See under *anemia.*

Herring bodies (her′ing) [Percy Theodore *Herring,* English physiologist, born 1889]. See under *body.*

Herrmannsdorfer diet (her″mans-dor′fer) [Adolf *Herrmannsdorfer,* Berlin surgeon, born 1889]. See *Gerson-Herrmannsdorfer diet,* under *diet.*

hersage (ār-sahzh′) [Fr. "combing"]. Surgical dissociation of the fibers of a peripheral nerve by splitting the sheath and separating the nerve, throughout the diseased area, into a ribbon of fine free fibers.

Herter's disease, infantilism (her′terz) [Christian Archibald *Herter,* American physician, 1865–1910]. Intestinal infantilism.

Hertig-Rock ovum (her′tig rok) [Arthur T. *Hertig,* American pathologist, born 1904; John *Rock,* American gynecologist, born 1890]. See under *ovum.*

Hertwig's sheath (hert′vigz) [Richard *Hertwig,* German zoologist, 1850–1937]. See under *sheath.*

Hertwig-Magendie phenomenon (hert′vig mah-jen′de) [Richard *Hertwig;* François *Magendie*]. Skew deviation.

hertzian waves (hertz′e-an) [Heinrich Rudolf *Hertz,* German physicist, 1857–1894]. See under *wave.*

Herxheimer's fibers, reaction, spirals (herks′hīm-erz) [Karl *Herxheimer,* German dermatologist, born 1861]. See under *fiber* and *reaction.*

Heryng's sign (her′ingz) [Théodor *Heryng,* Polish laryngologist, 1847–1925]. See under *sign.*

herzstoss (hārz′stos) [Ger.]. A phenomenon in which, during systole, there is no definite point of maximum impulse but the whole precordium rises en masse.

Heschl's gyrus (hesh′l'z) [Richard L. *Heschl,* Austrian pathologist, 1824–1881]. Transverse temporal convolution.

hesperanopia (hes″per-ah-no′pe-ah) [Gr. *hespera* evening + *an* neg. + *ops* eye]. Nyctalopia.

hesperidin (hes-per′ĭ-din). A flavone glycoside, $C_6H_{11}O_6.C_6H_2(OH)_2.C:O.CH:C_6H_3OH.O.CH_3$, in vitamin P, which with its chalcone and a protein forms an oxidation-reduction couple.

Hess (hes), Walter Rudolf. Swiss physiologist, born 1881, noted for research on the nervous system; co-winner, with Antonio Egas Moniz, of the Nobel prize in medicine and physiology for 1949.

Hesselbach's hernia, triangle (hes′el-bahks) [Franz Kaspar *Hesselbach,* German surgeon, 1759–1816]. See under *hernia* and *triangle.*

heter-. See *hetero-.*

heteradelphia (het″er-ah-del′fe-ah) [*heter-* + Gr. *adelphos* brother]. A joined twin monstrosity in which one fetus is much more fully developed than the other.

heteradelphus (het″er-ah-del′fus). A monster exhibiting heteradelphia.

heteradenia (het″er-ah-de′ne-ah) [*heter-* + Gr. *adēn* gland]. Any abnormality of the gland tissue.

heteradenic (het″er-ah-den′ik). Pertaining to, affected with, or of the nature of, heteradenia.

heteradenoma (het″er-ad″e-no′mah) [*heter-* + *adenoma*]. Any hyaline cylindroma.

Heterakis gallinae (het″er-a′kis gah-li′ne). A nematode parasite in the ceca of wild and domestic fowl.

heteralius (het″er-a′le-us) [*heter-* + Gr. *halios* fruitless]. An extreme example of heteradelphia.

heterauxesis (het″er-awk-ze′sis) [*heter-* + Gr. *auxēsis* growth]. Disproportionate growth of a part in relation to another part.

heteraxial (het″er-ak′se-al) [*heter-* + *axis*]. Having axes of unequal length.

heterecious (het″er-e′shus) [*heter-* + Gr. *oikos* house]. Living upon one host in one stage or generation and upon another in the next.

heterecism (het″er-e′sizm). The state of being heterecious.

heteresthesia (het″er-es-the′ze-ah) [*heter-* + Gr. *aisthēsis* perception]. Variation in the degree of cutaneous sensibility on adjoining areas of the body surface.

hetero-, heter- [Gr. *heteros* other]. Combining form meaning other, or denoting relationship to another.

heteroagglutination (het″er-o-ah-gloo″tĭ-na′-shun). Heterohemagglutination.

heteroagglutinin (het″er-o-ah-gloo′tĭ-nin). Heterohemagglutinin.

heteroalbumose (het″er-o-al′bu-mōs) [*hetero-* + *albumose*]. A form of hemialbumose that is not soluble in water, but is soluble in hydrochloric acid and sodium chloride solutions.

heteroalbumosuria (het″er-o-al″bu-mo-su′re-ah) [*heteroalbumose* + Gr. *ouron* urine + *-ia*]. The presence of heteroalbumose in the urine.

heteroantibody (het″er-o-an″tĭ-bod′e). An antibody combining with antigens originating from a species foreign to the antibody producer.

heteroantigen (het″er-o-an′tĭ-jen). An antigen originating from a species foreign to the antibody producer.

heteroatom (het″er-o-at′om). Any atom of a ring-shaped chemical nucleus other than the carbon atoms.

heteroautoplasty (het″er-o-aw′to-plas″te) [*hetero-* + *autoplasty*]. The surgical transfer of tissue from one part of the body to another.

heteroauxin (het″er-o-auk′sin). A compound occurring in urine which acts as a plant growth hormone.

heteroblastic (het″er-o-blas′tik) [*hetero-* + Gr. *blastos* germ]. Having origin in different kinds of tissue.

heterocellular (het″er-o-sel′u-lar). Composed of cells of different kinds.

heterocentric (het″er-o-sen′trik) [*hetero-* + L. *centrum* center]. Made up of rays that are neither parallel nor meet in one point: said of a ray of light.

heterocephalus (het″er-o-sef′ah-lus) [*hetero-* + Gr. *kephalē* head]. A fetal monster with two unequal heads.

heterochiral (het″er-o-ki′ral) [*hetero-* + Gr. *cheir* hand]. Reversed as regards right and left, but otherwise the same in form and size.

heterochromatin (het″er-o-kro′mah-tin). A genetically inert chromatin fraction which consists of histone, deoxyribonucleic acid, and ribonucleic acid.

heterochromatosis (het″er-o-kro″mah-to′sis). Heterochromia.

heterochromia (het″er-o-kro′me-ah) [*hetero-* + Gr. *chrōma* color + *-ia*]. Diversity of color in a part or parts that should normally be of one color. **h. i′ridis,** difference of color in the two irides, or in different areas of the same iris.

heterochromosome (het″er-o-kro′mo-sōm) [*hetero-* + *chromosome*]. Allosome, def. 1.

heterochromous (het″er-o-kro′mus). Marked by diversity of color; exhibiting heterochromia.

heterochron (het″er-o-krōn′). Having different or varying chronaxie.

heterochronia (het″er-o-kro′ne-ah) [*hetero-* + Gr. *chronos* time + *-ia*]. 1. The formation of parts or tissues, or the occurrence of a phenomenon, at an unusual time. 2. A difference in the rate or time of occurrence between two processes. 3. Difference of more than 100 per cent between the chronaxie of a muscle and that of its nerve.

heterochronic (het″er-o-kron′ik) [*hetero-* + Gr. *chronos* time]. Pertaining to or characterized by heterochronia.

heterochronous (het″er-ok′ro-nus). Heterochronic.

heterochthonous (het″er-ok′tho-nus) [*hetero-* + Gr. *chthōn* a particular land or country]. Originating in a region other than that in which it is found. Cf. *autochthonous.*

heterochylia (het″er-o-ki′le-ah). The sudden varying of the gastric secretion from normal acidity to hyperacidity or anacidity.

heterocinesia (het″er-o-sĭ-ne′se-ah) [*hetero-* + Gr. *kinēsis* movement]. A condition in which the patient performs movements other than those he is instructed to perform.

heterocladic (het″er-o-klad′ik) [*hetero-* + Gr. *klados* branch]. Indicating an anastomosis between terminal branches from different arteries.

heterocomplement (het″er-o-kom′ple-ment) [*hetero-* + *complement*]. A complement derived from an animal of a species different from the one which furnishes the amboceptor.

heterocomplementophilic (het″er-o-kom″plemen″to-fil′ik). Having an affinity for heterocomplements.

heterocrine (het′er-o-krin) [*hetero-* + Gr. *krinein* to separate]. Secreting more than one kind of matter.

heterocrisis (het″er-ok′rĭ-sis) [*hetero-* + Gr. *krisis* division]. An abnormal crisis.

heterocyclic (het″er-o-sik′lik) [*hetero-* + Gr. *kyklos* circle]. Having or pertaining to a closed chain or ring formation which includes atoms of different elements.

heterocytolysin (het″er-o-si-tol′ĭ-sin). Heterolysin.

heterocytotoxin (het″er-o-si″to-tok′sin). A toxin which destroys cells from an animal of another species.

Heterodera radicicola (het″er-od′er-ah rad″ĭ-sik′o-lah). A nematode parasitic on the common root vegetables, such as radishes, carrots, turnips, potatoes, etc., as well as on celery. When infested vegetables are eaten ova of the parasite may appear in the stools and may lead to incorrect diagnosis.

heterodermic (het″er-o-der′mik) [*hetero-* + Gr. *derma* skin]. Performed with another person's skin. See *dermatoheteroplasty.*

heterodesmotic (het″er-o-des-mot′ik) [*hetero-* + Gr. *desmos* a bond]. Joining dissimilar parts of the central nervous system. See under *fiber.*

heterodidymus (het″er-o-did′ĭ-mus). Heterodymus.

heterodont (het′er-o-dont) [*heter-* + Gr. *odous* tooth]. Having teeth of different types, such as incisors and molars.

Heterodoxus longitarsus (het″er-o-dok′sus lon″jĭ-tar′sus). A kangaroo louse found sometimes on dogs.

heterodrome (het′er-o-drōm) [*hetero-* + Gr. *dromos* running]. A negative induction current.

heterodromous (het″er-od′ro-mus) [*hetero-* + Gr. *dromos* running]. Moving or acting in the opposite direction.

heterodymus (het″er-od′ĭ-mus) [*hetero-* + Gr. *didymos* twin]. A fetal monster with a second head, neck, and thorax attached to the thorax.

hetero-erotism (het″er-o-er′o-tizm) [*hetero-* + Gr. *erōs* love]. Sexual feeling directed toward another individual. Cf. *auto-erotism.*

heterogametic (het″er-o-gah-met′ik). Characterized by the production of gametes of different kinds in respect to the sex chromosomes.

heterogamous (het″er-og′ah-mus). Having the conjugating elements (gametes) unlike in size and structure.

heterogamy (het″er-og′ah-me) [*hetero-* + Gr. *gamōs* marriage]. Reproduction resulting from the union of two cells (gametes) which differ in size and structure.

heteroganglionic (het″er-o-gang″gle-on′ik) [*hetero-* + Gr. *ganglion* ganglion]. Connecting various ganglia: used of the sympathetic nervous system.

heterogeneity (het″e-o-je-ne′ĭ-te). The state or quality of being heterogeneous.

heterogeneous (het″er-o-je′ne-us) [*hetero-* + Gr. *genos* kind]. Consisting of or composed of dissimilar elements or ingredients; not having a uniform quality throughout.

heterogenesis (het″er-o-jen′e-sis) [*hetero-* + Gr. *genesis* generation]. 1. Alternation of generation; reproduction that differs in character in successive generations. 2. Asexual generation. 3. The development of a living thing from some other kind of living thing, as a virus from a cell.

heterogenetic (het″er-o-je-net′ik). 1. Pertaining to heterogenesis. 2. Not arising within the organism.

heterogenic (het″er-o-jen′ik). 1. Occurring in the wrong sex, as a beard upon a woman. 2. Derived from a different source or species.

heterogenicity (het″er-o-je-nis′ĭ-te). Heterogeneity.

heterogenote (het′er-o-je″nōt) [*hetero-* + *gene* (analogy with zygote)]. A cell which has an additional genetic fragment, different from its intact genotype. It usually results from transduction.

heterogenous (het″er-oj′e-nus). Derived from a different source or species.

heteroglobulose (het″er-o-glob′u-lōs). A heteroalbumose obtained from a globulin.

heterogony (het″er-og′o-ne) [*hetero-* + Gr. *gonos* procreation]. Heterogenesis.

heterograft (het′er-o-graft). A graft of tissue obtained from the body of an animal of a species other than that of the recipient.

heterography (het″er-og′rah-fe) [*hetero-* + Gr. *graphein* to record]. The writing of words other than those intended by the writer.

heterohemagglutination (het″er-o-hem″ah-gloo″tĭ-na′shun). Agglutination of erythrocytes by a hemagglutinin derived from an individual of a different species.

heterohemagglutinin (het″er-o-hem″ah-gloo′tĭ-nin). A hemagglutinin that agglutinates erythrocytes of organisms of other species.

heterohemolysin (het″er-o-he-mol′ĭ-sin). A hemolysin occurring spontaneously in the blood of an untreated animal that will hemolyze the blood cells of an animal of another species.

heterohexosan (het″er-o-hek′so-san). Any one of a class of heterosaccharides which contain hexose units. They are lignocellulose, pectocellulose, and lipocellulose.

heteroimmune (het″er-o-ĭ-mūn′). Immune to the cells of an animal of a different species from the one which furnishes the immune serum.

heteroinfection (het″er-o-in-fek′shun). Infection from outside the organism; exogenous infection.

heteroinoculable (het″er-o-in-ok′u-lah-b′l). Susceptible of being inoculated from one individual to another.

heteroinoculation (het″er-o-in-ok″u-la′shun). Inoculation from one individual to another.

heterointoxication (het″er-o-in-tok″sĭ-ka′shun). Poisoning by material introduced from outside the body.

heterokaryon (het″er-o-kar′e-on) [*hetero-* + Gr. *karyon* nucleus]. A cell or hypha containing two or more nuclei of different genetic constitutions.

heterokeratoplasty (het″er-o-ker′ah-to-plas″-te) [*hetero-* + *keratoplasty*]. Grafting of corneal tissue from an individual of a species other than that of the recipient.

heterokinesis (het″er-o-ki-ne′sis) [*hetero-* + Gr. *kinēsis* motion]. The differential distribution of the sex chromosomes in the developing gametes of a heterogametic organism.

heterolalia (het″er-o-la′le-ah) [*hetero-* + Gr. *lalia* utterance]. Heterophasia.

heterolateral (het″er-o-lat′er-al) [*hetero-* + L. *latus* side]. Relating to the opposite side.

heteroliteral (het″er-o-lit′er-al). Marked by the substitution of one letter for another in pronouncing words.

heterolith (het′er-o-lith) [*hetero-* + Gr. *lithos* stone]. An intestinal concretion not formed of mineral matter.

heterologous (het″er-ol′o-gus) [*hetero-* + Gr. *logos* due relation, proportion]. 1. Made up of tissue not normal to the part. 2. Derived from an individual of a different species or one having a different genetic constitution. See *heterograft*.

heterology (het″er-ol′o-je). Abnormality in structure, arrangement, or manner of formation. In chemistry, the relationship between substances of partial identity of structure but of different properties.

heterolysin (het″er-ol′ĭ-sin). A lysin which dissolves cells of other species than the one in which it is formed; one that is formed on the introduction of antigen from a different species.

heterolysis (het″er-ol′ĭ-sis) [*hetero-* + Gr. *lysis* dissolution]. Lysis of the cells of one species by lysin from a different species.

heterolytic (het″er-o-lit′ik). Pertaining to or caused by heterolysis or a heterolysin.

heteromastigote (het″er-o-mas′tĭ-gōt) [*hetero-* + Gr. *mastix* lash]. Having several forward flagella together with one directed backward.

heteromeral (het″er-om′er-al). Heteromeric.

heteromeric (het″er-o-mer′ik) [*hetero-* + Gr. *meros* part]. Sending processes through one of the commissures to the white matter of the other side of the spinal cord: said of nerve cells.

heteromerous (het″er-om′er-us). Heteromeric.

heterometaplasia (het″er-o-met″ah-pla′se-ah) [*hetero-* + *metaplasia*]. Development of tissue into a variety foreign to the part where it is produced.

heterometropia (het″er-o-mĕ-tro′pe-ah). The state in which there is a different kind of refraction in the two eyes; antimetropia.

heteromorphic (het″er-o-mor′fik). Heteromorphous.

heteromorphosis (het″er-o-mor-fo′sis) [*hetero-* + Gr. *morphōsis* a forming]. The development, in regeneration, of an organ or structure different from the one that was lost.

heteromorphous (het″er-o-mor′fus) [*hetero-* + Gr. *morphē* form]. 1. Of abnormal shape or structure; differing from the type. 2. Having synaptic chromosome mates which differ in size, form, or structure.

heteronephrolysine (het″er-o-ne-frol′ĭ-sin) [*hetero-* + *nephrolysine*]. A nephrolysine which acts on the cells of animals from a different species.

heteronomous (het″er-on′o-mus) [*hetero-* + Gr. *nomos* law]. 1. In biology, subject to different laws of growth; specialized along different lines. 2. In psychology, subject to another will, as in hypnotism.

heteronymous (het″er-on′ĭ-mus) [*hetero-* + Gr. *onyma* name]. 1. Having names indicative of correlation. 2. Standing in opposite relations. See under *hemianopia*.

hetero-osteoplasty (het″er-o-os′te-o-plas″te) [*hetero-* + Gr. *osteon* bone + *plassein* to shape]. The surgical grafting of a bone with a piece taken from one individual to another.

heteropagus (het″er-op′ah-gus) [*hetero-* + Gr. *pagos* thing fixed]. A twin fetal monster in which one component (the parasite) is much smaller than and dependent on the other (the autosite).

heteropancreatism (het″er-o-pan′kre-ah-tizm). An irregular condition of functioning on the part of the pancreas.

heteropathy (het″er-op′ah-the) [*hetero-* + Gr. *pathos* disease]. 1. Abnormal or morbid sensitiveness to stimuli. 2. Allopathy.

heteropentosan (het″er-o-pen′to-san). A heterosaccharide which contains pentose units, such as gums, mucilages, and pectic substances.

heterophany (het″er-of′ah-ne) [*hetero-* + Gr. *phainein* to appear]. A difference in the manifestations of the same condition.

heterophasia (het″er-o-fa′ze-ah) [*hetero-* + Gr. *phasis* speech + *-ia*]. The uttering of words other than those intended by the speaker.

heterophasis (het″er-o-fa′sis). Heterophasia.

heterophemia (het″er-o-fe′me-ah) [*hetero-* + Gr. *phēmē* word]. Heterophasia.

heterophil (het′er-o-fil). 1. A finely granular polymorphonuclear leukocyte represented by neutrophils in man but characterized in other mammals by granules which have variable sizes and staining characteristics. 2. Heterophilic.

heterophilic (het″er-o-fil′ik) [*hetero-* + Gr. *philein* to love]. 1. Having affinity for other antigens or antibodies besides the one for which it is specific. 2. Staining with a type of stain other than the usual one.

heterophonia (het″er-o-fo′ne-ah) [*hetero-* + Gr. *phōnē* voice]. Any abnormality of the voice or of phonation.

heterophony (het″er-of′o-ne). Heterophonia.

heterophoralgia (het″er-o-fo-ral′je-ah) [*hetero-* + Gr. *phoros* bearing + *-algia*]. Heterophoria associated with pain.

heterophoria (het″er-o-fo′re-ah) [*hetero-* + Gr. *pherein* to bear + *-ia*]. Failure of the visual axes to remain parallel after the visual fusional stimuli have been eliminated. See *esophoria*, *exophoria*, *hyperphoria*, and *hypophoria*.

heterophoric (het″er-o-fo′rik). Pertaining to or characterized by heterophoria.

heterophosphatase (het″er-o-fos′fah-tās). Hexokinase.

heterophthalmia (het″er-of-thal′me-ah) [*hetero-* + Gr. *ophthalmos* eye + *-ia*]. Difference in the direction of the axes, or in the color, of the two eyes.

heterophthalmos (het″er-of-thal′mos). Heterophthalmia.

heterophthongia (het″er-of-thon′je-ah) [*hetero-* + Gr. *phthongos* utterance + *-ia*]. Any abnormality of speech.

heterophydiasis (het″er-o-fi-di′ah-sis). Heterophyiasis.

Heterophyes (het″er-of′ĭ-ēz) [*hetero-* + Gr. *phyē* stature]. A genus of minute trematode worms found in the middle third of the small intestine of man, dogs, and cats in Egypt (*H. heterophyes*) and Japan (*H. katsuradai*).

heterophyiasis (het″er-o-fi-i′ah-sis). Infection with trematodes of the genus *Heterophyes*, characterized by abdominal pain with mucous diarrhea.

heteroplasia (het″er-o-pla′ze-ah) [*hetero-* + Gr. *plassein* to mold]. The replacement of normal by abnormal tissue; malposition of normal cells.

heteroplasm (het′er-o-plazm). Any heterologous tissue.

heteroplastic (het″er-o-plas′tik). Pertaining to heteroplasia or to heteroplasty.

heteroplastid (het″er-o-plas′tid). A surgical graft derived from another person or from a lower animal.

heteroplasty (het′er-o-plas″te) [*hetero-* + Gr. *plassein* to mold]. Operative replacement of lost parts or tissues by material derived from an individual of a different species, or by synthetic or nonorganic material.

heteroploid (het′er-o-ploid). 1. Pertaining to or characterized by heteroploidy. 2. An individual or cell with an abnormal number of chromosomes.

heteroploidy (het′er-o-ploi″de). The state of having an abnormal number of chromosomes.

Heteropoda (het″er-op′o-dah). A genus of large spiders sometimes confused with tarantulas. **H. venato′ria,** a large spider found in shipments of tropical fruit, particularly bananas. Its bite is painful, but not serious.

heteropodal (het″er-op′o-dal) [*hetero-* + Gr. *pous* foot]. Having branches or processes of different kinds: said of nerve cells.

heteroprosopus (het″er-o-pro′so-pus) [*hetero-* + Gr. *prosōpon* face]. Janiceps.

heteroproteose (het″er-o-pro′te-ōs). A primary proteose which is insoluble in water, but soluble in dilute salt solution.

heteropsia (het″er-op′se-ah) [*hetero-* + Gr. *opsis* vision]. Unequal vision in the two eyes.

heteropsychologic (het″er-o-si″ko-loj′ik). Pertaining to ideas formed outside the individual mind.

Heteroptera (het″er-op′ter-ah) [*hetero-* + Gr. *pteron* wing]. A suborder of the Hemiptera characterized by the possession of two pairs of wings, one horny, the other membranous. There are two genera: *Cimex* and *Lamus*.

heteroptics (het″er-op′tiks) [*hetero-* + Gr. *optikos* optic]. False or perverted vision.

heteropyknosis (het″er-o-pik-no′sis) [*hetero-* + Gr. *pyknōsis* condensation]. 1. The quality of showing variations in density throughout. 2. A state of differential condensation observed in comparison of different chromosomes, or of different regions of the same chromosome. **negative h.,** attenuation of condensation observed in comparison of different chromosomes, or of different regions of the same chromosome. **positive h.,** accentuation of condensation observed in comparison of different chromosomes, or of different regions of the same chromosome.

heteropyknotic (het″er-o-pik-not′ik). Pertaining to or characterized by heteropyknosis. **negatively h.,** showing areas of lesser condensation than normal. **positively h.,** showing areas of greater condensation than normal.

heterosaccharide (het″er-o-sak′ah-rid). A polysaccharide containing a carbohydrate and a noncarbohydrate unit.

heteroscope (het′er-o-skōp) [*heterophoria* + Gr. *skopein* to examine]. A pair of fusion tubes so mounted as to subserve the observation of the progress of cases of heterophoria.

heteroscopy (het″er-os′ko-pe). Inequality of vision in the two eyes.

heteroserotherapy (het″er-o-se″ro-ther′ah-pe). Treatment of a patient by serum derived from some other individual.

heterosexual (het″er-o-seks′u-al). Pertaining to the opposite sex; directed toward a person of the opposite sex.

heterosexuality (het″er-o-seks″u-al′ĭ-te). Love or sexual desire directed toward persons of the opposite sex.

heterosis (het″er-o′sis) [Gr. *heterōsis* alteration]. The condition in which the first generation hybrid shows more vigor than either of the parent strains.

heterosmia (het″er-os′me-ah) [*hetero-* + Gr. *osmē* smell]. A condition in which odors are incorrectly interpreted.

heterosome (het″er-o-sōm) [*hetero-* + Gr. *sōma* body]. A sex chromosome.

heterosporous (het″er-os′po-rus) [*hetero-* + Gr. *sporos* seed]. Having two kinds of spores.

heterostimulation (het″er-o-stim″u-la′shun). Stimulation of an animal with antigenic material originating from foreign species.

heterosuggestion (het″er-o-sug-jes′chun) [*hetero-* + *suggestion*]. Suggestion received from another person.

heterotaxia (het″er-o-tak′se-ah) [*hetero-* + Gr. *taxis* arrangement]. Anomalous placement or transposition of viscera or parts.

heterotaxic (het″er-o-tak′sik). Affected with heterotaxia.

heterotaxis (het″er-o-tak′sis). Heterotaxia.

heterotaxy (het′er-o-tak″se). Heterotaxia.

heterotherapy (het″er-o-ther′ah-pe) [*hetero-* + Gr. *therapeia* treatment]. Treatment of disease by remedies which are antagonistic to the principal symptoms of the disease; nonspecific therapy.

heterotherm (het′er-o-therm). An animal which exhibits heterothermy.

heterothermic (het″er-o-ther′mik). Pertaining to or characterized by heterothermy.

heterothermy (het′er-o-ther″me) [*hetero-* + Gr. *thermē* heat]. The exhibition of widely different body temperatures at different times or under different conditions, as certain species of birds, marsupials, or hibernating species.

heterotonia (het″er-o-to′ne-ah) [*hetero-* + Gr. *tonos* tension + *-ia*]. A state characterized by variations in tension or tone.

heterotonic (het″er-o-ton′ik). Pertaining to or characterized by heterotonia.

heterotopia (het″er-o-to′pe-ah) [*hetero-* + Gr. *topos* place + *-ia*]. 1. Displacement or misplacement of parts or organs; the presence of a tissue in an abnormal location. 2. A jumbling of sounds in words.

heterotopic (het″er-o-top′ik). Occurring at an abnormal place or upon the wrong part of the body.

heterotopy (het″er-ot′o-pe). Heterotopia.

heterotoxic (het″er-o-tok′sik). Pertaining to heterotoxin.

heterotoxin (het″er-o-tok′sin) [*hetero-* + *toxin*]. A toxin formed outside of the body.

heterotoxis (het″er-o-tok′sis). Poisoning by toxic matter introduced into the system from without.

heterotransplant (het″er-o-trans′plant). Heterograft.

heterotransplantation (het″er-o-trans″plan-ta′shun). Heteroplasty.

heterotrichosis (het″er-o-tri-ko′sis) [*hetero-* + Gr. *trichōsis* growth of hair]. Growth of hair of different colors on the body. **h. supercilio′rum,** difference in color of the hairs of the two eyebrows (von Walther).

heterotrichous (het″er-ot′rĭ-kus). Having irregular cilia, in size, shape, function, or distribution.

heterotroph (het′er-o-trōf). A heterotrophic organism, such as an animal or a chlorophyll-free plant.

heterotrophia (het″er-o-tro′fe-ah) [*hetero-* + Gr.

trophē nourishment]. Any disorder or fault of nutrition.

heterotrophic (het″er-o-trof′ik) [*hetero-* + Gr. *trophē* nutrition]. Not self-sustaining: said of organisms which require a reduced form of carbon for energy and synthesis. Cf. *autotrophic.*

heterotrophy (het″er-ot′ro-fe). 1. The state of being heterotrophic; heterotrophic nutrition. 2. Heterotrophia.

heterotropia (het″er-o-tro′pe-ah) [*hetero-* + Gr. *tropē* a turn, turning + *-ia*]. Failure of the visual axes to remain parallel when fusion is a possibility. See *esotropia, exotropia, hypertropia,* and *hypotropia.*

heterotropy (het″er-ot′ro-pe). Heterotropia.

heterotrypsin (het″er-o-trip′sin). An enzyme of the pancreatic juice.

heterotypic (het″er-o-tip′ik). Pertaining to, characteristic of, or belonging to a different type.

heterotypical (het″er-o-tip′e-k'l). Of a type differing from that usually or normally encountered; having characteristics peculiar to a different type; sometimes applied to the first meiotic division of the germ cells.

heterovaccine (het″er-o-vak′sēn). A vaccine made from some bacterium other than the one causing the disease for which the vaccine is used. It is one form of nonspecific therapy.

heteroxenous (het″er-ok′se-nus) [*hetero-* + Gr. *xenos* guest-friend, stranger]. Requiring more than one host in order to complete the life cycle: said of parasitic organisms. Cf. *monoxenous.*

heteroxeny (het″er-ok′se-ne). The quality or condition of being heteroxenous.

heterozoic (het″er-o-zo′ik) [*hetero-* + Gr. *zōon* animal]. Pertaining to another animal or species of animal.

heterozygosis (het″er-o-zi-go′sis). The formation of a zygote by the union of gametes of unlike genetic constitution.

heterozygosity (het″er-o-zi-gos′ĭ-te) [*hetero-* + *-zygosity*]. The state of possessing different alleles in regard to a given character.

heterozygote (het″er-o-zi′gōt) [*hetero-* + *zygote*]. An individual possessing different alleles in regard to a given character.

heterozygous (het″er-o-zi′gus). Possessing different alleles in regard to a given character.

HETP. Hexaethyltetraphosphate.

hetrazan (het′rah-zan). Trade mark for preparations of diethylcarbamazine.

hettocyrtosis (het″o-sir-to′sis) [Gr. *hētton* less + *kyrtōsis* curvature]. A slight curvature.

Heublein method (hoib′līn) [Arthur C. *Heublein*, New York radiologist, 1879–1932]. See under *method.*

Heubner's disease (hoib′nerz) [Johann Otto L. *Heubner*, pediatrician in Berlin, 1843–1926]. See under *disease.*

heuristic (hu-ris′tik) [Gr. *heuriskein* to find out, discover]. Encouraging or promoting investigation; conducive to discovery.

heurteloup (her′tel-o͞op, Fr., urt-loo′) [Baron Charles Louis Stan *Heurteloup*, French surgeon, 1793–1864]. An artificial leech, or cupping apparatus.

Heuser's membrane (hoi′zerz) [Chester *Heuser*, American embryologist, born 1885]. See under *membrane.*

hex-, hexa- [Gr. *hex* six]. Combining form meaning six.

hexabasic (hek″sah-ba′sik) [*hexa-* + *basic*]. Having six atoms replaceable by a base.

hexa-betalin (hek″sah-be′tah-lin). Trade mark for preparations of pyridoxine hydrochloride.

hexabiose (hek″sah-bi′ōs). Disaccharide.

hexachlorophene (hek″sah-klo′ro-fēn). Chemical name: 2,2′-methylenebis-(3,4,6-trichlorophenol): used as a local antiseptic and detergent for application to the skin.

hexachromic (hek″sah-kro′mik) [*hexa-* + Gr. *chrōma* color]. 1. Pertaining to or exhibiting six colors. 2. Able to distinguish only six of the seven colors of the spectrum.

hexacosane (heks-ak′o-sān) [*hexa-* + Gr. *eikosi* twenty]. An aliphatic hydrocarbon, $C_{26}H_{58}$, extracted from plant waxes.

hexad (hek′sad). 1. A group or combination of six similar or related entities. 2. Any element having a valency of six.

hexadactylia (hek″sah-dak-til′e-ah) [*hexa-* + Gr. *daktylos* finger + *-ia*]. The occurrence of six digits (fingers or toes) on one limb.

hexadactylism (hek″sah-dak′tĭ-lizm). Hexadactylia.

hexadactyly (hek″sah-dak′tĭ-le). Hexadactylia.

hexadimethrine (hek″sah-di-meth′rēn). Chemical name: poly(1,5-dimethyl-1,5-diazaundecamethylene): used to neutralize the anticoagulant action of heparin.

hexaethyltetraphosphate (hek″sah-eth″il-tet″rah-fos′fāt). A powerful anticholinesterase which has been tried in the treatment of myasthenia gravis.

Hexagenia bilineata (hek″sah-je′ne-ah bi-lin″-e-a′tah). A mayfly of the shores of Lake Erie whose cast skins may cause asthma.

hexahydric (hek″sah-hi′drik). Containing six atoms of hydrogen.

hexahydrohematoporphyrin (hek″sah-hi″-dro-hem″ah-to-por′fĭ-rin). One of the resulting products of the treatment of hematin with alcohol and a reducing agent.

hexamethonium (hek″sah-mĕ-tho′ne-um). Chemical name: hexamethylenebis(trimethylammonium): used in blockade of autonomic ganglia, and to produce hypotension.

hexamethylated (hek″sah-meth′ĭ-lāt-ed). Containing six methyl groups.

hexamethylenamine (hek″sah-meth″il-ēn-am′-in). Methenamine.

hexamethylendiamine (hek″sah-meth″il-ēn-di′am-in). A ptomaine, $NH_2(CH_2)_6NH_2$, from decomposing pancreas and muscle.

hexamine (hek′sam-in). Methenamine.

Hexamita (heks-am′ĭ-tah). A genus of flagellate parasites found in various animals. **H. meleag′ridis,** a species found in turkeys. **H. mu′ris,** a species found in the intestines of rats and mice.

hexamitiasis (heks-am″ĭ-ti′ah-sis). A morbid condition resulting from infestation with parasites of the genus Hexamita.

hexamylose (heks-am′ĭ-lōs). A crystalline amylose, $(C_6H_{10}O_5)_6$.

hexane (hek′sān). A liquid hydrocarbon, C_6H_{14}.

hexaploid (hek′sah-ploid). 1. Pertaining to or characterized by hexaploidy. 2. An individual or cell having six sets of chromosomes.

hexaploidy (hek′sah-ploi″de). The state of having six sets of chromosomes (6 n).

Hexapoda (heks-ap′o-dah) [*hexa-* + Gr. *pous* foot]. The true or six-footed insects.

hexatomic (hek″sah-tom′ik) [*hex-* + *atom*]. 1. Containing six atoms of an element, or six replaceable univalent atoms. 2. In immunology, having the power of binding six complements of different strains.

hexavaccine (hek″sah-vak′sēn). A vaccine containing six different organisms.

hexavalent (hek″sah-va′lent). Having a valency of six.

hexavibex (hek″sah-vi′beks). Trade mark for a preparation of pyridoxine hydrochloride.

hexavitamin (hek″sah-vi′tah-min). A preparation, in capsule or tablet form, containing vitamin A, vitamin D, ascorbic acid, thiamine hydrochloride, riboflavin, and nicotinamide.

hexenmilch (hek′sen-milkh) [Ger. "witches' milk"]. A milklike secretion from the breast of a newborn infant.

hexestrol (heks-es′trol). Chemical name: 4′4′-(1,2-diethylethylene)diphenol: used as an estrogenic substance.

hexetidine (heks-et′ĭ-dēn). Chemical name: 5-amino-1,3-bis(β-ethylhexyl)-5-methylhexahydropyrimidine: used as an antibacterial, antifungal, and antitrichomonal agent.

hexhydric (heks-hi′drik). Containing six atoms of replaceable hydrogen.

hexiology (hek-se-ol′o-je) [Gr. *hexis* habit + *-logy*]. The science of study of the relations of an organism to its environment.

hexobarbital (hek″so-bar′bĭ-tal). Chemical name: 5-(1-cyclohexen-1-yl)-1,5-dimethylbarbituric acid: used as a sedative and hypnotic of short duration.

hexobarbitone (hek″so-bar′bĭ-tōn). Hexobarbital.

hexocyclium (hek″so-si′kle-um). Chemical name: N-(β-cyclohexyl-β-hydroxy-β-phenylethyl)-N′-methylpiperazine: used in parasympathetic blockade, and as an antispasmodic.

hexokinase (hek″so-ki′nās). An enzyme that catalyzes the transfer of a high-energy phosphate group of a donor to D-glucose, producing D-glucose-6-phosphate.

hexonic (heks-on′ik). Pertaining to the hexone bases.

hexosamine (hek′sōs-am″in). A nitrogenous sugar in which an amino group replaces a hydroxyl group.

hexosan (hek′so-san). An anhydride or a polymerized form of a hexose.

hexosazone (hek″so-sa′zōn). An osazone formed from a hexose.

hexose (hek′sōs). A monosaccharide containing six carbon atoms in a molecule. **h. diphosphate.** See *Harden-Young ester* under *ester*. **h. monophosphate.** See *hexosephosphate*.

hexosephosphatase (hek″sōs-fos′fah-tās). An enzyme which catalyzes the oxidation of hexosephosphate.

hexosephosphate (hek″sōs-fos′fāt). An ester of glucose with phosphoric acid, which aids in the absorption of sugars and which, as the Cori, Embden, Harden-Young, Neuberg and Robison esters, is important in carbohydrate metabolism. See under *ester*.

hexoxidase (heks-ok′sĭ-dās). An enzyme which catalyzes the oxidation of hexuronic (ascorbic) acid.

hexyl (hek′sil) [*hex-* + Gr. *hylē* matter]. A hydrocarbon, C_6H_{13}, in many isomeric forms.

hexylcaine (hek′sil-kān). Chemical name: 1-cyclohexylamino-2-propanol benzoate: used as a local anesthetic.

hexylresorcinol (hek″sil-re-zor′sĭ-nol). Chemical name: 4-hexyl-1,3-dihydroxybenzene: used as an anthelmintic.

Hey's amputation, hernia, ligament, operation, saw (hāz) [William *Hey*, English surgeon, 1736–1819]. See under the nouns.

Heyd's syndrome (hādz) [Charles Gordon *Heyd*, New York surgeon]. Hepatorenal syndrome.

Heymans, Corneille (hay′manz). French-Belgian physiologist, born 1892; winner of the Nobel prize for medicine and physiology in 1938.

Heynsius' test (hīn′se-oos) [Adrian *Heynsius*, Dutch physician, 1831–1885]. See under *tests*.

HF. Abbreviation for *Hageman factor*.

Hf. Chemical symbol for *hafnium*.

Hg. 1. Chemical symbol for mercury (L. *hydrargyrum*). 2. Abbreviation for *hemoglobin*.

Hgb. Abbreviation for *hemoglobin*.

$HgCl_2$. Corrosive mercuric chloride.

Hg_2Cl_2. Mild mercurous chloride.

HGF. Abbreviation for *hyperglycemic-glycogenolytic factor* (glucagon).

HgI_2. Mercuric iodide.

Hg_2I_2. Mercurous iodide.

$Hg(NO_3)_2$. Mercuric nitrate.

HgO. Mercuric oxide.

Hg_2O. Mercurous oxide.

HgS. Mercuric sulfide.

$HgSO_4$. Mercuric sulfate.

HHb. Chemical symbol for un-ionized hemoglobin.

H. + Hm. Compound hypermetropic astigmatism.

HI. Hydriodic acid.

hiant (hi′ant) [L. *hiare* to yawn]. Yawning or gaping; opening wide.

hiatal (hi-a′tal). Pertaining to or affecting a hiatus.

hiation (hi-a′shun). The act of yawning.

hiatopexia, hiatopexy (hi″at-o-pek′se-ah, hi-at′o-pek″se) [*hiatus* + Gr. *pēxis* fixation]. Surgical fixation or repair of a genital hiatus.

hiatus (hi-a′tus) [L.]. A gap, cleft, or opening. **adductor h.,** h. tendineus. **h. adducto′rius,** N A alternative for *h. tendineus*. **aortic h., h. aor′ticus** [N A, B N A], the opening in the diaphragm through which the aorta and thoracic duct pass. **Breschet's h.,** helicotrema. **h. of canal for greater petrosal nerve,** h. canalis nervi petrosi majoris. **h. of canal for lesser petrosal nerve,** h. canalis nervi petrosi minoris. **h. cana′lis facia′lis** [B N A], **h. cana′lis ner′vi petro′si majo′ris** [N A], an opening in the petrous part of the temporal bone in the floor of the middle cranial fossa that transmits the greater petrosal nerve and a branch of the middle meningeal artery. Called also *h. of canal for greater petrosal nerve*. **h. cana′lis ner′vi petro′si mino′ris** [N A], the small, laterally placed opening on the anterior surface of the pyramid of the temporal bone that transmits the lesser petrosal nerve. Called also *h. of canal for lesser petrosal nerve*. **esophageal h., h. esophage′us** [N A], the opening in the diaphragm for the passage of the esophagus and the vagus nerves. **h. of facial canal, h. of fallopian canal, h. fallo′pii, false h. of fallopian canal,** h. canalis nervi petrosi majoris. **h. femora′lis,** anulus femoralis. **h. fina′lis sacra′lis,** a cleft in the lowermost sacral vertebra. **h. for greater superficial petrosal nerve,** h. canalis nervi petrosi majoris. **h. interme′dius lumbosacra′lis,** a cleft in the region of the first sacral vertebra, considered to represent a normally delayed ossification in young subjects. **h. interosse′us,** the opening above the interosseous membrane of the forearm for the passage of the posterior interosseous vessels. **h. leukae′micus,** a condition observed in acute myeloblastic leukemia in which there are numerous myeloblasts and a number of mature neutrophils in the peripheral blood, with few or no intermediate forms. Called also *hiatus leukaemicus of Naegeli*. **h. lumbosacra′lis,** the gap between the arches of the fifth lumbar and first sacral vertebrae, which is greater than the space between any vertebrae at a higher level. **h. maxilla′ris** [N A, B N A], **maxillary h., h. of maxillary sinus,** a very irregular opening on the medial surface of the maxillary sinus, in the articulated skull being largely filled by parts of several adjoining bones. **neural h.,** an opening in the neural tube during the process of closure. **h. oesophage′us** [B N A], h. esophageus. **h. pleuroperitonea′lis,** an opening in the fetal diaphragm. Its failure to close leaves a congenital defect which may become a site for congenital diaphragmatic hernia. Called also *foramen of Bochdalek*. **sacral h., h. sacra′lis** [N A, B N A], the opening at the inferior end of the sacral canal formed by failure of the laminae of the fifth and sometimes the fourth sacral vertebrae to meet in the midline. **saphenous h., h. saphe′nus** [N A], the depression in the fascia lata that is bridged by the cribriform fascia and perforated by the great saphenous vein. Called also *fossa ovalis femoris* [B N A]. **Scarpa's h.,** helicotrema. **semilunar h., h. semiluna′ris** [N A, B N A], the deep semilunar groove anterior and inferior to the bulla of the ethmoid bone; the anterior ethmoidal air cells, the maxillary sinus, and sometimes the frontonasal duct drain into it. **subarcuate h.,** fossa subarcuata ossis temporalis. **h. tendin'eus** [N A, B N A], the opening between the long tendon of the adductor magnus and the femur, marking the distal end of the adductor canal. Called also *h. adductorius.* **h. tota'lis sacra'lis,** a cleft in all of the sacral vertebrae, sometimes also involving one or several of the contiguous lumbar vertebrae. **vena caval h.,** foramen venae cavae. **h. of Winslow,** foramen epiploicum.

Hibbs' frame, operation (hibz) [Russell H. *Hibbs,* New York surgeon, 1869–1932]. See under *frame* and *operation.*

hibernation (hi″ber-na′shun) [L. *hiberna* winter]. The dormant state in which certain animals pass the winter. Cf. *estivation.* **artificial h.,** a state of reduced metabolism, muscle relaxation, and a twilight sleep resembling narcosis, produced pharmacodynamically by controlled inhibition of the sympathetic nervous system and causing attenuation of the homeostatic reactions of the organism.

hibernoma (hi″ber-no′mah). A rare tumor made up of large polyhedral cells with a coarsely granular cytoplasm, occurring on the back or around the hips. So called because it is considered by some to be a manifestation of a vestigial fat storage organ and comparable to the dorsal fat pads of hibernating animals.

hiccup (hik′up). An involuntary spasmodic contraction of the diaphragm, causing a beginning inspiration which is suddenly checked by closure of the glottis, causing the characteristic sound. **epidemic h.,** a condition frequently seen in epidemic encephalitis.

Hicks' sign, version (hiks) [John Braxton *Hicks,* English gynecologist, 1823–1897]. See under *sign* and *version.*

hidebound (hīd′bownd). Affected with scleroderma.

hidradenitis (hi″drad-e-ni′tis) [Gr. *hidrōs* sweat + *adēn* gland + *-itis*]. Inflammation of a sweat gland. **h. suppurati'va,** a disease of the sweat glands marked by the development of one or more cutaneous, shotlike nodules, which gradually enlarge to the size of a pea, and undergo softening and suppuration, with subsequent discharge.

hidradenoma (hi″drad-e-no′mah). Syringocystadenoma.

hidro- (hid′ro) [Gr. *hidrōs* sweat]. Combining form denoting relation to sweat or to a sweat gland.

hidroa (hid-ro′ah) [Gr. *hidrōa* sudamina; *hidrōs* sweat]. 1. Sudamina or other skin affection accompanied by sweating. 2. Hydroa.

hidroadenoma (hid″ro-ad″e-no′mah). Syringocystadenoma.

hidrocystoma (hid″ro-sis-to′mah) [*hidro-* + *cystoma*]. A retention cyst of a sweat gland.

hidromancy (hid′ro-man″se) [*hidro-* + Gr. *manteia* divination]. Prognosis based upon the character of the sweat.

hidropoiesis (hid″ro-poi-e′sis) [*hidro-* + Gr. *poiēsis* formation]. The formation of sweat.

hidropoietic (hid″ro-poi-et′ik). Pertaining to, characterized by, or promoting hidropoiesis.

hidrorrhea (hid-ro-re′ah) [*hidro-* + Gr. *rhoia* flow]. Profuse perspiration.

hidrosadenitis (hi″dros-ad″e-ni′tis) [*hidro-* + Gr. *adēn* gland + *-itis*]. Inflammation of the sweat glands. **h. axilla'ris,** inflammation of the sweat glands of the axilla. **h. des'truens suppurati'va,** Pollitzer's name for a form of necrotic acneiform tuberculide, acne agminata: called also *Pollitzer's disease.*

hidroschesis (hid-ros′kĕ-sis) [*hidro-* + Gr. *schesis* holding]. Suppression of the perspiration.

hidrosis (hid-ro′sis). 1. The secretion and excretion of the sweat. 2. Any skin disease affecting primarily the sweat glands. 3. Too profuse sweating.

hidrotic (hid-rot′ik). Pertaining to, characterized by, or causing hidrosis.

hiemalis (hi″ĕ-ma′lis). Pertaining to or occurring in winter.

hier-. See *hiero-.*

hiera picra (hi′er-ah pi′krah) ["holy bitters"]. Powder of aloes and canella, used as a condiment and antiscorbutic in the West Indies.

hieralgia (hi″er-al′je-ah) [*hier-* + *-algia*]. Pain in the sacrum.

hiero-, hier- (hi′er-o, hi′er) [Gr. *hieron* sacred, or sacrum]. Combining form denoting relationship to the sacrum, or to religion.

hierolisthesis (hi″er-o-lis-the′sis) [*hier-* + Gr. *olisthanein* to slip]. Displacement of the sacrum.

hieromania (hi″er-o-ma′ne-ah) [*hiero-* + Gr. *mania* madness]. Religious insanity or frenzy.

hierophobia (hi″er-o-fo′be-ah) [*hiero-* + Gr. *phobos* fear + *-ia*]. Fear of sacred or religious things.

hierotherapy (hi″er-o-ther′ah-pe) [*hiero-* + Gr. *therapeia* therapy]. The treatment of disease by religious exercises.

Higginson's syringe (hig′in-sonz) [Alfred *Higginson,* Liverpool surgeon of 19th century]. See under *syringe.*

Highmore's antrum, body, etc. (hi′mōrz) [Nathaniel *Highmore,* English surgeon, 1613–1685]. See under the nouns.

highmoritis (hi″mōr-i′tis). Inflammation of the maxillary sinus (antrum of Highmore).

higueron (hig-wer′on). The plant *Ficus laurifolia;* the milk of the plant has been used in ancylostomiasis.

hila (hi′lah) [L.]. Plural of *hilum.*

hilar (hi′lar). Pertaining to a hilus.

hilastic (hi-las′tik) [Gr. *hilasmos* atonement]. In Greek medicine, prophylactic, in the sense of diverting disease by rites of propitiation.

Hildebrandt's test (hil′de-brants) [Fritz *Hildebrandt,* German pharmacologist, born 1887]. See under *tests.*

Hildenbrand's disease (hil′den-brands) [Johann Valentin von *Hildenbrand,* Austrian physician, 1763–1818]. Typhus.

hili (hi′li) [L.]. Plural of *hilus.*

hilitis (hi-li′tis). Inflammation of a hilus, especially of the hilus of the lung.

Hill (hil′), Archibald Vivian. English biochemist, born 1886, noted for work on heat loss in muscle contraction; co-winner, with Otto Fritz Meyerhof, of the Nobel prize for medicine and physiology in 1922.

hillock (hil′ok). A small prominence or elevation. **auricular h's,** tubercles adjoining the first branchial groove that give rise to the auricle of the ear. **axon h.,** the conical expansion of an axon at its point of attachment to the body of the nerve cell. **Doyère's h.,** the elevation where a nerve fiber enters a muscle. **germ h., germ-bearing h.,** cumulus oophorus. **seminal h.,** colliculus seminalis.

Hilton's law, muscle, sac, etc. (hil′tunz) [John *Hilton,* English surgeon, 1804–1878]. See under the nouns.

hilum (hi′lum), pl. *hi'la* [L.]. Hilus.

hilus (hi′lus), pl. *hi'li* [L. "a small thing"]. A depression or pit at that part of an organ where the vessels and nerves enter. **h. glan'dulae suprarena'lis** [N A, B N A], the depression on the anterior surface of the suprarenal gland where the suprarenal vein enters the gland. **h. hep'atis,** porta hepatis. **h. of kidney,** h. renalis. **h. lie'nis** [N A, B N A], the fissure on the gastric surface of the spleen where the vessels and nerves enter. **h. of lung,** h. pulmonis. **h. of lymph node,** h. nodi lymphatici. **h. no'di lymphat'ici** [N A], the indentation on a lymph node where the arteries enter and the veins and efferent lymphatic vessels leave. Called also *h. lymphoglandulae* [B N A]. **h. nu'clei denta'ti** [N A, B N A], the fibrous core of the dentate nucleus of the cerebellum. **h. nu'clei oliva'ris** [N A, B N A], the white core of the inferior olivary nucleus, most prominent medially. **h. of olivary nucleus,** h. nuclei olivaris. **h. ova'rii** [N A, B N A], **h. of ovary,** the point on the mesovarial border of the ovary where the vessels and nerves enter. **h. pulmo'nis** [N A, B N A], the depression on the mediastinal surface of the lung where the bronchus, and the blood vessels and nerves enter. **h. rena'lis** [N A, B N A], the point on the medial margin of the kidney where the vessels, nerves, and ureter enter. **h. of spleen,** h. lienis. **h. of suprarenal gland,** h. glandulae suprarenalis.

himantosis (hi″man-to'sis) [Gr. *himantōsis*, from *himas* strap]. Elongation of the uvula.

hinchazon (hinch″ah-zon') [Cuban]. Beriberi.

hindbrain (hīnd'brān). 1. Metencephalon. 2. Rhombencephalon.

Hindenlang's test (hin'den-lahngz) [Karl *Hindenlang*, German physician, 1854–1884]. See under *tests*.

hindgut (hīnd'gut). The embryonic structure from which chiefly the colon is formed.

hind-kidney (hīnd-kid'ne). The metanephros.

Hinton test (hin'ton) [William A. *Hinton*, American bacteriologist, born 1883]. See under *tests*.

HIO_3. Iodic acid.

hip (hip). The region of the articulation of the femur and innominate bone, on either side of the pelvis. **snapping h.,** a condition marked by a slipping around of the hip joint, sometimes with an audible snap, due to the slipping of a tendinous band over the great trochanter.

hippanthropia (hip″an-thro'pe-ah) [Gr. *hippos* horse + *anthrōpos* man]. A condition in which the patient believes himself to be, and makes movements in imitation of, a horse.

hipped (hipt). Having a fracture at the point of the hip: said of horses.

Hippel's disease (hip'elz) [Eugen von *Hippel*, German ophthalmologist, 1867–1939]. Angiomatosis of the retina.

Hippelates (hip″ĕ-la'tēz). A genus of insects of the order Diptera. **H. pu'sio,** the "eye gnat" of Coachella Valley, California, which is the mechanical vector of epidemic conjunctivitis, usually of a severe, follicular type.

hippiater (hip'e-a″ter). A veterinarian.

hippiatric (hip″e-at'rik). Veterinary.

hippiatrics (hip″e-at'riks) [Gr. *hippos* horse + *iatrikē* surgery, medicine]. Veterinary medicine and surgery.

hippiatry (hip'e-ah-tre). Hippiatrics.

hippo (hip'po). Ipecac.

hippo- (hip'o) [Gr. *hippos* horse]. Combining form denoting relationship to a horse.

Hippobosca (hip-o-bos'kah) [*hippo-* + Gr. *boskein* to feed]. The typical genus of the family Hippoboscidae. They are pupiparous, dipterous, parasitic insects, called the winged tick fly of the horse. **H. ru'fipes,** the species which is thought to transmit galziekte.

hippocamp (hip'o-kamp). Hippocampus.

hippocampal (hip″o-kam'pal). Pertaining to the hippocampus.

hippocampus (hip″o-kam'pus) [Gr. *hippokampos* sea horse]. [N A, B N A] A curved structure in the medial part of the floor of the inferior horn of the lateral ventricle. It is a submerged gyrus forming the larger part of the olfactory cerebral cortex. Called also *hippocampus major*, *Ammon's horn*, and *cornu Ammonis*. **h. leo'nis,** hippocampus. **h. ma'jor,** hippocampus. **h. mi'nor,** calcar avis. **h. nu'dus,** a small part of the hippocampus on the median surface of the brain, in the cavity formed by the splenial bending of the fascia dentata.

hippocoprosterol (hip″o-ko-pros'ter-ol) [*hippo-* + Gr. *kopros* dung + *sterol*]. A sterol found in the feces of herbivorous animals and derived from the phytosterol of grass and other food plants, $C_{27}H_{54}O$.

Hippocrates (hip-pok'rah-tēz) **of Cos** (late 5th century B.C.). The famous Greek physician who is generally regarded as the "Father of Medicine." Many of the writings of Hippocrates and his school have survived—the so-called *Corpus Hippocraticum*, but it is not certain which were written by Hippocrates himself; these writings are usually characterized by the stress laid on treatment and prognosis. An oath which appears in the body of work attributed to Hippocrates and his school, and known as the Hippocratic oath, has been the ethical guide of the medical profession since those days. It is as follows:

"I swear by Apollo the physician, by Æsculapius, Hygeia, and Panacea, and I take to witness all the gods, all the goddesses, to keep according to my ability and my judgment the following Oath:

"To consider dear to me as my parents him who taught me this art; to live in common with him and if necessary to share my goods with him; to look upon his children as my own brothers, to teach them this art if they so desire without fee or written promise; to impart to my sons and the sons of the master who taught me and the disciples who have enrolled themselves and have agreed to the rules of the profession, but to these alone, the precepts and the instruction. I will prescribe regimen for the good of my patients according to my ability and my judgment and never do harm to anyone. To please no one will I prescribe a deadly drug, nor give advice which may cause his death. Nor will I give a woman a pessary to procure abortion. But I will preserve the purity of my life and my art. I will not cut for stone, even for patients in whom the disease is manifest; I will leave this operation to be performed by practitioners (specialists in this art). In every house where I come I will enter only for the good of my patients, keeping myself far from all intentional ill-doing and all seduction, and especially from the pleasures of love with women or with men, be they free or slaves. All that may come to my knowledge in the exercise of my profession or outside of my profession or in daily commerce with men, which ought not to be spread abroad, I will keep secret and will never reveal. If I keep this oath faithfully, may I enjoy my life and practice my art, respected by all men and in all times; but if I swerve from it or violate it, may the reverse be my lot."

hippocratic (hip″po-krat'ik). Pertaining to or described by Hippocrates of Cos, or pertaining to the school of medicine founded by him.

hippocratism (hip-pok'rah-tizm). The system of medicine attributed to Hippocrates and his school, based on imitating the processes of nature, and emphasizing treatment and prognosis.

hippocratist (hip-pok'rah-tist). A believer in or practitioner of the system of medicine attributed to Hippocrates and his school.

hippolite (hip'o-līt). Hippolith.

hippolith (hip'o-lith) [*hippo-* + Gr. *lithos* stone]. A bezoar, or concretion, from the alimentary tract of the horse.

hippomane (hĭ-pom'ah-ne). 1. Small, rounded bodies found in the allantoic fluid of various animals, especially the ungulates. 2. The discharge from the vagina of a mare in heat.

hippomelanin (hip″o-mel'ah-nin) [*hippo-* + Gr. *melas* black]. A black pigment from tumors and marrow of horses affected with melanosis.

hippostercorin (hip″o-ster'ko-rin). Hippocoprosterol.

hippulin (hip'u-lin). A crystalline estrogenic steroid, $C_{18}H_{20}O_2$, with four double bonds; an isomer of equilin. Obtained from the urine of pregnant mares.

hippurase (hip'u-rās). Hippuricase.

hippurate (hip'u-rāt). Any salt of hippuric acid.

hippuria (hĭ-pu're-ah) [*hippo-* + Gr. *ouron* urine + *-ia*]. Excess of hippuric acid in the urine.

hippuric (hĭ-pu'rik) [*hippo-* + Gr. *ouron* urine]. Derivable from the urine of horses. See under *acid*.

hippuricase (hĭ-pu'ri-kās). An enzyme which catalyzes the hydrolysis of hippuric acid to benzoic acid and glycine.

hippus (hip'us) [Gr. *hippos* a complaint of the eyes, such that they are always winking]. A condition characterized by abnormal exaggeration of the rhythmic contraction and dilation of the pupil, independent of changes in illumination or in fixation of the eyes.

hip-shot (hip′shot). Deformed by fracture of the haunch: said of a horse.

hirci (hir′se) [L.]. Plural of *hircus*. Used in anatomical nomenclature [N A, B N A] to designate the hair growing in the axilla.

hircin (hir′sin) [L. *hircus* goat]. An ill-smelling principle from the suet of goats.

hircismus (hir-siz′mus) [L. *hircus* goat]. The strong odor of the axillae.

hircus (hir′kus), pl. *hir′ci* [L. "a goat"]. 1. See *hirci*. 2. Tragus.

Hirschberg's magnet, method (hirsh′bergz) [Julius *Hirschberg*, German ophthalmologist, 1843–1925]. See under *magnet* and *method*.

Hirschberg's reaction (hirsh′bergz) [Leonard Keene *Hirschberg*, American physician, born 1877]. See under *reaction*.

Hirschfeld's canals (hirsh′feldz) [I. *Hirschfeld*, American dentist]. Interdental canals.

Hirschfeld's disease [Felix *Hirschfeld*, German physician, born 1863]. Acute diabetes mellitus.

Hirschfelder's tuberculin (hirsh′fel-derz) [Joseph Oakland *Hirschfelder*, American physician, 1854–1920]. See under *tuberculin*.

Hirschsprung's disease (hirsh′sproongz) [Harold *Hirschsprung*, a Danish physician, 1830–1916]. See under *disease*.

hirsute (her′sūt) [L. *hirsutus*]. Shaggy; having long hair.

hirsuties (her-su′she-ēz) [L.]. Excessive hairiness.

hirsutism (her′sūt-izm). Abnormal hairiness, especially in women.

hirudicidal (hĭ-roo″dĭ-si′dal). Destructive to leeches.

hirudicide (hĭ-roo′dĭ-sīd). An agent that is destructive to leeches.

hirudin (hĭ-roo′din) [L. *hirudo* leech]. The active principle of the secretion of the buccal glands of leeches. It has the power of preventing coagulation of the blood by acting as an antithrombin.

Hirudinea (hir″u-din′e-ah). A class of the Annelida; the leeches.

hirudiniasis (hir″u-dĭ-ni′ah-sis). Invasion of the nose, mouth, pharynx, or larynx by leeches.

hirudinization (hĭ-roo″dĭ-ni-za′shun) [L. *hirudo* leech]. 1. The process of rendering the blood noncoagulable by the injection of hirudin. 2. The application of leeches.

hirudinize (hĭ-roo′dĭ-nīz). To render the blood noncoagulable by the injection of hirudin.

Hirudo (hĭ-roo′do), pl. *hiru′dines* [L. "leech"]. A genus of the Hirudinea. **H. aegypti′aca** is pathogenic when drunk with water. **H. japon′ica,** the medicinal leech of Japan. **H. javan′ica,** a leech of Java, Batavia, and Burma. It may also be parasitic in the body cavities. **H. medicina′lis,** the well-known olive-gray leech that was formerly used extensively for therapeutic purposes. **H. quinquestria′ta,** a leech occurring in Australia. **H. sanguisor′ba,** *Haemopis sanguisuga*. **H. trocti′na,** the common European leech, which is marked with green, orange, and black somewhat like a trout.

His's band, bundle, disease, spindle (his′ez) [Wilhelm *His*, Jr., German physician, 1863–1934]. See under *bundle*, *disease*, and *spindle*.

His's bursa, canal, rule, spaces, zone, etc. [Wilhelm *His*, eminent German anatomist and embryologist, 1831–1904]. See under the nouns.

hist-. See *histo-*.

histadyl (his′tah-dil). Trade mark for preparations of methapyrilene.

histaffine (his-taf′in) [Gr. *histos* tissue + L. *affinis* having affinity for]. 1. Having affinity for tissues. 2. A substance present in the blood serum of animals affected with certain diseases that combines with certain constituents of the tissues to produce the phenomenon of fixation of the complement.

histalog (his′tah-log). Trade mark for a preparation of betazole.

histaminase (his-tam′ĭ-nās). An enzyme which has the power of inactivating histamine. It has been used in the treatment of allergic dermatoses and intestinal intoxications.

histamine (his′tah-min). An amine, beta-imidazolylethyl-amine, $CH.NH.CH{:}N.C.CH_2.CH_2.NH_2$, occurring in all animal and vegetable tissues. It is a powerful dilator of the capillaries and a stimulator of gastric secretion. A pharmaceutical preparation is used to reduce sensitivity to allergens and as a diagnostic aid in testing gastric acid formation. **h. dihydrochloride,** a compound, $C_5H_5N_2.2HCl$. **h. phosphate,** a colorless, odorless compound, $C_5H_9N_3.2H_3PO_4$, used as a diagnostic acid in the study of gastric secretion.

histaminemia (his-tam″ĭ-ne′me-ah). The presence of histamine in the blood.

histaminia (his″tah-min′e-ah). A condition of shock caused by excess of histamine development in the body.

histanoxia (his″tan-ok′se-ah) [*hist-* + *anoxia*]. Oxygen deprivation of the tissues due to a lessening of the blood supply.

histase (his′tās). An enzyme that digests tissue.

histenzyme (his-ten′zīm). An enzyme from the kidney which catalyzes the splitting of hippuric acid into benzoic acid and glycocoll.

histic (his′tik). Pertaining to or of the nature of tissue.

histidase (his′tĭ-dās). An enzyme in the liver which opens the imidazole ring of histidine, liberating ammonia.

histidinase (his′tĭ-dĭ-nās). An enzyme of the liver which acts specifically on histidine, splitting it into ammonia, glutamic acid, and formic acid.

histidine (his′tĭ-din). An alpha-amino acid, beta-4-imidazolyl alanine, $N{:}CH.NH.CH{:}C.CH_2\text{-}CH(NH_2)COOH$, essential for optimal growth in infants; first found as a decomposition product of the protamine of sturgeon testes (Kossel, 1896), obtainable from any protein by the action of sulfuric acid and water. **h. monohydrochloride,** a preparation used in the treatment of peptic ulcer.

histidinemia (his″tĭ-dĭ-ne′me-ah). The presence of excessive amounts of histidine in the blood.

histidinuria (his″tĭ-dĭ-nu′re-ah). The presence of histidine in the urine.

histio- (his′te-o) [Gr. *histion*, diminutive of *histos* web, tissue]. Combining form denoting relationship to tissue.

histioblast (his′te-o-blast). A local histiocyte.

histioblastoma (his″te-o-blas-to′mah). Reticuloendothelioma.

histiocyte (his′te-o-sīt) [*histio-* + Gr. *kytos* hollow vessel]. A large phagocytic interstitial cell forming part of the reticuloendothelial system and corresponding to the macrophage or clasmatocyte. **cardiac h.,** Anitschkow's myocyte. **wandering h's,** the storage cells of the connective tissue.

histiocytoma (his″te-o-si-to′mah) [*histiocyte* + *-oma*]. A tumor containing histiocytes. **lipoid h.,** fibroxanthoma.

histiocytomatosis (his″te-o-si-to″mah-to′sis). Any generalized disorder of the reticuloendothelial system, such as xanthomatosis, Gaucher's disease, Niemann-Pick disease, lymphogranulomatosis, etc.

histiocytosis (his″te-o-si-to′sis). A condition marked by the abnormal appearance of histiocytes in the blood. **lipid h.,** Niemann-Pick disease. **h. X,** a generic term embracing eosinophilic granuloma, Letterer-Siwe disease, and Hand-Schüller-Christian disease, and indicating a shared common origin for the three entities.

Histiogaster entomophagus (his′te-o-gas″ter en″to-mof′ah-gus). An acarid mite which may cause a cutaneous vanillism.

histiogenic (his″te-o-jen′ik). Histogenous.

histioid (his′te-oid). Histoid.

histio-irritative (his″te-o-ir′ĭ-ta″tiv) [*histio-* + *irritative*]. Having an irritative effect on connective tissue.

histioma (his″te-o′mah). Histoma.

histionic (his″te-on′ik). Pertaining to or derived from a tissue.

histo-, hist- (his′to, hist-) [Gr. *histos* web, tissue]. Combining form denoting relationship to tissue.

histoblast (his′to-blast) [*histo-* + Gr. *blastos* germ]. A tissue-forming cell.

histochemistry (his″to-kem′is-tre). That branch of histology which deals with the disposition of chemical components in cells and in the intracellular materials of tissues.

histochemotherapy (his″to-ke″mo-ther′ah-pe). See *chemotherapy.*

histochromatosis (his″to-kro″mah-to′sis) [*histo-* + Gr. *chrōma* color]. A general term for affections of the reticuloendothelial system, including xanthochromatosis, Gaucher's disease and lymphogranulomatosis.

histoclastic (his″to-klas′tik) [*histo-* + Gr. *klastos* broken]. Breaking down tissue: said of certain cells.

histocompatibility (his″to-kom-pat″ĭ-bil′ĭ-te). The quality or state of being histocompatible.

histocompatible (his″to-kom-pat′ĭ-b'l). Capable of being accepted and remaining functional, applied to cells or tissues showing these characteristics when grafted in another organism.

histocyte (his′to-sīt). Histiocyte.

histodiagnosis (his″to-di″ag-no′sis) [*histo-* + *diagnosis*]. Diagnosis by microscopical examination of the tissues.

histodialysis (his″to-di-al′ĭ-sis) [*histo-* + *dialysis*]. The disintegration or breaking down of tissues.

histodifferentiation (his″to-dif″er-en″she-a′-shun). The acquisition of tissue characteristics by cell groups.

histofluorescence (his″to-floo″o-res′ens). Fluorescence produced in the body by the administration of some substance previous to exposure to the roentgen rays.

histogenesis (his″to-jen′e-sis) [*histo-* + Gr. *genesis* production]. The formation or development of tissues from the undifferentiated cells of the germ layers of the embryo.

histogenetic (his″to-je-net′ik). Pertaining to histogenesis.

histogenous (his-toj′e-nus) [*histo-* + Gr. *gennan* to produce]. Formed by the tissues.

histogeny (his-toj′e-ne). Histogenesis.

histogram (his′to-gram). A diagram or graphic representation of frequency distributions.

histography (his-tog′rah-fe) [*histo-* + Gr. *graphein* to write]. Description of the tissues.

histohematin (his″to-hem′ah-tin) [*histo-* + *hematin*]. Cytochrome.

histohematogenous (his″to-hem″ah-toj′e-nus) [*histo-* + Gr. *haima* blood + *gennan* to produce]. Formed from both the tissues and the blood.

histohydria (his″to-hi′dre-ah) [*histo-* + Gr. *hydōr* water]. The presence of an excessive amount of water in body tissue.

histohypoxia (his″to-hi-pok′se-ah). An abnormally diminished concentration of oxygen in the tissues.

histoid (his′toid) [*histo-* + Gr. *eidos* form]. 1. Weblike. 2. Developed from but one kind of tissue. 3. Like one of the tissues of the body.

histoincompatibility (his″to-in″kom-pat″ĭ-bil′-ĭ-te). The quality or state of being histoincompatible.

histoincompatible (his″to-in″kom-pat′ĭ-b'l). Not being accepted or remaining functional, applied to cells or tissues which are rejected or die when grafted in another organism.

histokinesis (his″to-ki-ne′sis) [*histo-* + Gr. *kinēsis* motion]. Movement in the tissues of the body.

histologist (his-tol′o-jist). A person who is learned in histology.

histology (his-tol′o-je) [*histo-* + *-logy*]. That department of anatomy which deals with the minute structure, composition and function of the tissues. Called also *microscopical anatomy.* **normal h.,** the histology of normal tissues. **pathologic h.,** the histology of diseased tissues.

histolysate (his-tol′ĭ-zāt). A substance formed by histolysis.

histolysis (his-tol′ĭ-sis) [*histo-* + Gr. *lyein* to loosen]. The dissolution or the breaking down of tissues.

histolytic (his″to-lit′ik). Pertaining to, characterized by, or causing histolysis.

histoma (his-to′mah) [*histo-* + *-oma*]. Any tissue tumor, as a fibroma.

histometaplastic (his″to-met″ah-plas′tik). Pertaining to, characterized by, or stimulating metaplasia of tissue.

Histomonas meleagridis (his-to′mo-nas mel″-e-ag′rĭ-dis). A flagellate protozoan causing enterohepatitis (blackhead) of turkeys.

histomorphology (his″to-mor-fol′o-je). The morphology of tissues; histology.

histone (his′tōn). A simple protein, soluble in water and insoluble in dilute ammonia. The globin of hemoglobin is a histone. Some are decidedly poisonous and contain a considerable amount of phosphorus. Combined with leukonuclein they form nucleohistone. Blood treated with histone is altered so that it coagulates with difficulty. Histone has been found in the urine in leukemia and febrile conditions. Cf. *protamine.* **h. nucleinate,** a compound of nucleic acid and histone, the characteristic constituent of lymph glands, spleen, and thymus.

histonectomy (his″to-nek′to-me) [*histo-* + Gr. *ektomē* excision]. Periarterial sympathectomy.

histoneurology (his″to-nu-rol′o-je) [*histo-* + *neurology*]. The histology of the nervous system; neurohistology.

histonomy (his-ton′o-me) [*histo-* + Gr. *nomos* law]. The scientific study of tissues based on the translation, into biological terms, of quantitative laws derived from histological measurement.

histonuria (his-tōn-u′re-ah) [*histone* + Gr. *ouron* urine + *-ia*]. The presence of histone in the urine.

histopathology (his″to-pah-thol′o-je) [*histo-* + *pathology*]. Pathologic histology.

histophysiology (his″to-fiz″e-ol′o-je) [*histo-* + *physiology*]. The physiology of the minute elements of the tissues.

Histoplasma (his″to-plaz′mah). A genus of fungi imperfecti. **H. capsula′tum,** a species of pathogenic fungi which may cause infection in man.

histoplasmin (his″to-plaz′min). A sterile broth filtrate of a culture of *Histoplasma capsulatum:* injected intracutaneously as a test for histoplasmosis.

histoplasmosis (his″to-plaz-mo′sis). Infection with *Histoplasma capsulatum*, which may produce different clinical pictures: a systemic febrile disease with splenomegaly, septic fever, anemia, and leukopenia, simulating kala-azar; lymphatic involvement resembling Hodgkin's disease, lymphosarcoma, leukemia, or aplastic anemia; pulmonary symptoms with cavitation and fibrous adhesions of the pleura, sometimes complicating tuberculosis; or ulcerative lesions of the skin and mucosa. Because of the characteristic intracellular location of the causative organisms, sometimes called *cytomycosis*, or *reticuloendothelial cytomycosis*.

histoplast (his′to-plast). Wassermann's preparation containing extract of live staphylococcus: used locally in treatment of furuncle.

historadiography (his″to-ra″de-og′rah-fe) [*histo-* + *radiography*]. Roentgenography of microscopic sections of tissue.

historetention (his″to-re-ten′shun). Retention of matter by the tissues.

historrhexis (his″to-rek′sis) [*histo-* + Gr. *rhēxis* rupture]. Breaking up of tissue; Southard's term for focal destruction of nerve tissue of noninfectious nature.

histosiphon (his″to-si′fon) [*histo-* + Gr. *siphōn* tube]. A burrow in the tissue of a host, such as that caused by *Sarcoptes scabiei*.

histosite (his′to-sīt). A tissue parasite.

histoteliosis (his″to-tel″e-o′sis) [*histo-* + Gr. *tēle* + *-osis*]. The final differentiation of cells whose fate has already been determined irreversibly.

histotherapy (his″to-ther′ah-pe) [*histo-* + *therapy*]. The treatment of disease by the administration of animal tissues.

histothrombin (his″to-throm′bin). Thrombin from connective tissue.

histotome (his′to-tōm) [*histo-* + Gr. *tomē* a cut]. A cutting instrument used in microtomy.

histotomy (his-tot′o-me) [*histo-* + Gr. *temnein* to cut]. The dissection of the tissues; microtomy.

histotoxic (his″to-tok′sik) [*histo-* + Gr. *toxikon* poison]. Poisonous to tissue or tissues.

histotribe (his′to-trīb) [*histo-* + Gr. *tribein* to crush]. A strong forceps for clamping on a mass of tissue containing blood vessels to secure hemostasis.

histotripsy (his′to-trip″se) [*histo-* + Gr. *tripsis* crushing]. The crushing of tissue with a histotribe.

histotroph (his′to-trōf) [*histo-* + Gr. *trophē* nourishment]. The sum total of nutritive substances supplied to the embryo in viviparous animals from sources other than the mother's blood. Cf. *hemotroph*.

histotrophic (his″to-trof′ik). 1. Encouraging the formation of tissue. 2. Pertaining to histotroph; with reference to nutrition through histotroph.

histotropic (his″to-trop′ik) [*histo-* + Gr. *tropos* a turning]. Having special affinity for tissue cells.

histozoic (his″to-zo′ik) [*histo-* + Gr. *zōē* life]. Living on or within the tissues: said of parasites.

histozyme (his′to-zīm) [*histo-* + Gr. *zymē* leaven]. Hippuricase.

histrionic (his″tre-on′ik). Pertaining to or characterized by histrionism.

histrionism (his′tre-o-nizm) [L. *histrio* actor]. The morbid or hysterical adoption of an exaggerated manner and gestures.

Hittorf number, tube (hit′orf) [Johann Wilhelm *Hittorf*, German physicist, 1824–1914]. See under *number* and *tube*.

Hitzig's girdle, test (hits′igz) [Eduard *Hitzig*, German psychiatrist, 1838–1907]. See under *girdle* and *tests*.

Hl. Symbol for *latent hypermetropia*.

Hm. Symbol for *manifest hypermetropia*.

HN2. Mechlorethamine.

HNO_2. Nitrous acid.

HNO_3. Nitric acid.

Ho. Chemical symbol for *holmium*.

H_2O. Water.

H_2O_2. Hydrogen dioxide or peroxide.

hoarseness (hōrs′nes). A rough quality of voice.

Hoboken's nodules, valves (ho′bo-kenz) [Nicolas von *Hoboken*, Dutch anatomist and physician, 1632–1678]. See under the nouns.

Hoche's bandelette (hōk′ez) [Alfred Erich *Hoche*, German psychiatrist, 1865–1943]. A small bundle of nerve fibers forming part of the fasciculus posterior proprius.

Hochenegg's operation, symptom (hōk′en-egz) [Julius von *Hochenegg*, Vienna surgeon, 1859–1940]. See under *operation* and *symptom*.

Hochsinger's phenomenon, sign (hōk′sing-erz) [Karl *Hochsinger*, Austrian pediatrician]. See under *phenomenon* and *sign*.

hock (hok). The tarsal joint or region of the tarsus in the hind leg of the horse or ox. **capped h.**, a cyst or a thickening of the skin over the point of the calcaneum in the horse. **curby h.**, a hock affected with curb. **spring h.**, a swelling above and below the hock of a horse, due to inflammation of the ligaments.

Hodara's disease (ho-dar′ahz) [Menahem *Hodara*, Turkish physician]. See under *disease*.

hodegetics (hod″e-jet′iks) [Gr. *hodēgētikos* fitted for guiding]. Medical etiquette.

Hodge's forceps, pessary, plane, etc. (hoj′-ez) [Hugh Lenox *Hodge*, American gynecologist, 1796–1873]. See under the nouns.

Hodgen apparatus, splint (hoj′en) [John Thompson *Hodgen*, American surgeon, 1826–1882]. See under *splint*.

Hodgkin (hoj′kin), Alan Lloyd. English physiologist, born 1914; co-winner, with John Carew Eccles and Andrew Fielding Huxley, of the Nobel prize in medicine and physiology for 1963, for discoveries concerning the ionic mechanisms involved in excitation and inhibition in the peripheral and central portions of the nerve cell membrane.

Hodgkin's disease, granuloma (hoj′kinz) [Thomas *Hodgkin*, English physician, 1798–1866]. See under *disease*.

Hodgson's disease (hoj′sonz) [Joseph *Hodgson*, English physician, 1788–1869]. See under *disease*.

hodi-potsy (ho″de-pot′se). A skin disease of Madagascar resembling pityriasis versicolor.

hodology (ho-dol′o-je) [Gr. *hodos* path + *-logy*]. That department of neurology which deals with the pathways of the nervous system.

hodoneuromere (ho″do-nu′ro-mēr) [Gr. *hodos* path + *neuron* nerve + *meros* part]. A segment of the embryonic trunk with its pair of nerves and their branches.

Hoehne's sign (ha′nez) [Ottomar *Hoehne*, German gynecologist, 1871–1932]. See under *sign*.

hof [Ger. "court"]. The area of the cytoplasm of a cell encircled by the concavity of the nucleus.

Hofacker-Sadler law (hof-ak′er sad′ler) [Johann D. *Hofacker*, German obstetrician, 1788–1828; Michael Thomas *Sadler*, English obstetrician, 1834–1923]. See under *law*.

Hofbauer cells (hof′bow-er) [J. Isfred Isidore *Hofbauer*, American gynecologist, born 1878]. See under *cell*.

Hoff. See *van't Hoff*.

Hoffa's disease, operation (hof′az) [Albert *Hoffa*, German surgeon, 1859–1907]. See under *disease* and *operation*.

Hoffmann's anodyne (hof′manz) [Friedrich *Hoffmann*, German physician, 1660–1742]. See under *anodyne*.

Hoffmann's atrophy, sign [Johann *Hoffmann*, Heidelberg neurologist, 1857–1919]. See under *atrophy* and *sign*.

Hoffmann's duct [Moritz *Hoffmann*, German anatomist, 1622–1698]. The pancreatic duct.

Hoffmann's violet [August Wilhelm *Hoffmann*, German chemist, 1818–1892]. Dahlia.

Hofmann's bacillus [Georg von *Hofmann*-Wellenhof, Austrian bacteriologist]. *Corynebacterium pseudodiphtheriticum*.

Hofmann's reaction, test [H. *Hofmann*, German obstetrician]. See under *tests*.

Hofmeister's test (hōf′mīs-terz) [Franz *Hofmeister*, German physiologic chemist, 1850–1922]. See under *tests*.

Högyes's treatment (hed′yes-ez) [Endre *Högyes*, Hungarian physician, 1847–1906]. See under *treatment*.

hol-. See *holo-*.

holagogue (hol′ah-gog) [*hol-* + Gr. *agōgos* leading]. A medicine capable of expelling all disease humors; a drastic or radical remedy.

holandric (hol-an′drik) [Gr. *holos* entire + *aner* man]. Inherited exclusively through the male descent; transmitted through genes located on the Y chromosome.

holarthritis (hol″ar-thri′tis). Hamarthritis.

Holden's line (hōl′denz) [Luther *Holden*, English surgeon, 1815–1905]. See under *line*.

holergasia (hol″er-ga′ze-ah). Meyer's term for the major psychoses. Cf. *holergastic*.

holergastic (hol′er-gas″tik) [*hol-* + Gr. *ergon* work]. Meyer's term for sweeping disorders of psychic function, i.e., major psychoses, in which the socially organized personality is deranged. Cf. *merergastic*.

holism (hōl′izm) [Gr. *holos* whole]. The conception of man as a functioning whole.

holistic (ho-lis′tik). Considering man as a functioning whole, or relating to the conception of man as a functioning whole.

hollow (hol′o). A depressed area or concavity. **Sebileau's h.,** a depressed area beneath the tongue, formed by the oral mucosa and the sublingual glands.

hollow-back (hol′o-bak). Lordosis.

Holmes (hōmz), Oliver Wendell (1809–1894). Noted American physician, anatomist, and writer, whose paper *On the Contagiousness of Puerperal Fever* (1843) antedated the work of Semmelweis in its appeal for surgical cleanliness to combat this disease.

Holmes's operation (hōmz) [Timothy *Holmes*, English surgeon, 1825–1907]. See under *operation*.

Holmes's phenomenon (hōmz) [Gordon *Holmes*, British neurologist]. See *rebound phenomenon*, under *phenomenon*.

Holmgren's test (holm′grenz) [Alarik Fritniof *Holmgren*, Swedish physiologist, 1831–1897]. See under *tests*.

holmium (hol′me-um). One of the rare earths; symbol, Ho; atomic number, 67; atomic weight, 164.930.

holo- (hol′o) [Gr. *holos* entire]. Combining form meaning entire, or denoting relationship to the whole.

holoacardius (hol″o-ah-kar′de-us) [*holo-* + *a* neg. + Gr. *kardia* heart]. A separate, monozygotic twin

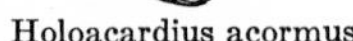
Holoacardius acormus.

Holoacardius acephalus.

represented by a more or less shapeless and unidentifiable mass; the vascular systems of the two fetuses are connected, and the circulation in utero is accomplished solely by the heart of the more perfect twin. **h. aceph′alus,** an imperfectly formed free twin fetus lacking the cranial part of the body. **h. acor′mus,** an imperfectly formed free twin fetus lacking the caudal part of the body. **h. amor′phus,** an imperfectly formed free twin fetus entirely without form and recognizable parts.

holo-antigen (hol″o-an′tĭ-jen). Whole antigen.

holoblastic (hol″o-blas′tik) [*holo-* + Gr. *blastos* germ]. Undergoing cleavage in which the entire ovum participates; completely dividing.

holocaine (ho′lo-kān). Trade mark for a preparation of phenacaine.

holocephalic (hol″o-sĕ-fal′ik) [*holo-* + Gr. *kephalē* head]. Having the head entire: said of a monster fetus.

holocrine (hol′o-krĭn) [*holo-* + Gr. *krinein* to separate]. Wholly secretory: noting that type of glandular secretion in which the entire secreting cell, along with its accumulated secretion, forms the secreted matter of the gland, as in the sebaceous glands. See *merocrine* and *apocrine*.

holodiastolic (hol″o-di″as-tol′ik) [*holo-* + *diastole*]. Pertaining to the entire diastole.

holoendemic (hol″o-en-dem′ik) [*holo-* + Gr. *endēmos* dwelling in a place]. Affecting practically all of the residents of a particular area.

holoenzyme (hol″o-en′zīm). The functional compound formed by the combination of an apoenzyme and its appropriate coenzyme.

hologamy (ho-log″ah-me) [*holo-* + Gr. *gamos* marriage]. The condition in which the gametes are of the same size and structural type as the somatic cells.

hologastroschisis (hol″o-gas-tros′kĭ-sis) [*holo-* + Gr. *gaster* belly + *schisis* cleft]. A developmental anomaly characterized by a fissure extending the entire length of the abdomen.

hologenesis (hol″o-jen′e-sis) [*holo-* + Gr. *genesis* formation]. The theory that man originated everywhere on earth, instead of in certain special region or regions.

hologynic (hol″o-jin′ik) [*holo-* + Gr. *gynē* woman]. Inherited exclusively through the female descent; transmitted through genes located on attached X chromosomes.

holomastigote (hol″o-mas′tĭ-gōt) [*holo-* + Gr. *mastix* lash]. Having numerous flagella scattered over the body.

holomorphosis (hol″o-mor-fo′sis) [*holo-* + Gr. *morphōsis* formation]. The complete regeneration of a lost part.

holomyarial (hol″o-mi-a′re-al). A type of arrangement of the muscular system in the Nematoda. The muscle cells are small, numerous, close together, and form a band below the cuticle.

holophytic (hol″o-fit′ik) [*holo-* + Gr. *phyton* plant]. Obtaining food like a plant: said of certain protozoa.

holorachischisis (hol″o-rah-kis′kĭ-sis) [*holo-* + Gr. *rhachis* spinal column + *schisis* cleft]. Fissure of the entire spinal cord.

holosaccharide (hol″o-sak′ah-rīd). A polysaccharide composed of sugar units only. Cf. *heterosaccharide*.

holoschisis (hol″o-ski′sis) [*holo-* + Gr. *schisis* cleft]. Amitosis.

Holospora (hol″o-spo′rah) [*holo-* + Gr. *sporos* seed]. A genus of microorganisms of uncertain affinities which are parasitic on protozoa.

holosystolic (hol″o-sis-tol′ik) [*holo-* + *systole*]. Pertaining to the entire systole.

holotetanus (hol″o-tet′ah-nus) [*holo-* + *tetanus*]. General tetanus.

holothurin (ho″lo-thu′rin). A hemotoxic substance derived from sea cucumbers (holothurians).

Holothyrus (hol″o-thi′rus). A genus of ticks. *H. coccinella*, of Mauritius, is found on geese, and is poisonous to human subjects, causing a painful swelling of the tongue and throat.

holotonia (hol″o-to′ne-ah) [*holo-* + Gr. *tonos* tension + *-ia*]. Muscular spasm of the whole body.

holotonic (hol″o-ton′ik). Pertaining to, characterized by, or causing holotonia.

holotopy (ho-lot′o-pe) [*holo-* + Gr. *topos* place]. The position of an organ in relation to the whole body.

holotrichous (ho-lot′rĭ-kus) [*holo-* + Gr. *thrix* hair]. Covered uniformly with cilia.

holotyphlon (hol″o-tif′lon). Superior colic ventriculus.

holozoic (hol″o-zo′ik) [*holo-* + Gr. *zōon* animal]. Having nutritional characters of an animal, i.e. digesting protein. Cf. *holophytic*.

holozymase (hol″o-zi′mās). The complete enzyme, including both the co-enzyme and the apozymase.

Holten's test (hol′tenz) [Cai *Holten*, Danish physician]. See under *test*.

Holthouse's hernia (holt′howz-es) [Carsten *Holthouse*, English surgeon, 1810–1901]. See under *hernia*.

Holzknecht space, stomach, unit (holts-knekt) [Guido *Holzknecht*, radiologist in Vienna, 1872–1931]. See under the nouns.

homalocephalus (hom″ah-lo-sef′ah-lus) [Gr. *homalos* level + *kephalē* head]. A person with a flat head.

homalography (hom″ah-log′rah-fe) [Gr. *homalos* level + *graphein* to write]. The study of anatomy by means of plane sections of the parts.

Homalomyia (ho″mah-lo-mi′yah). A genus of flies whose maggots sometimes infest the human intestine.

homaluria (hom″ah-lu′re-ah) [Gr. *homalos* level, even + *ourein* to make water + *-ia*]. Production and excretion of urine at a normal, even rate.

homarine (hom′ah-rin). An organic nitrogen compound which is found in lobster muscle. It is the methyl betaine of picolinic acid, $C_5H_4N(CO).CH_3$.

homatropine (ho-mat′ro-pin). An alkaloid, obtained by the condensation of tropine and mandelic acid: used to produce parasympathetic blockade, and as a mydriatic. **h. hydrobromide,** an extremely poisonous compound, $C_{16}H_{21}NO_3.HBr$: used topically in the eye as a cycloplegic and mydriatic. **h. methylbromide,** a compound, $C_{17}H_{24}BrNO_3$, parasympatholytic: used in the treatment of gastrointestinal spasm and hyperchlorhydria.

homaxial (ho-mak′se-al). Having axes of the same length.

homeo-, homoeo-, homoio- (ho′me-o-) [Gr. *homois* like, resembling; always the same, unchanging]. Combining form denoting sameness, similarity, or a constant, unchanging state.

homeochrome (ho′me-o-krōm″) [*homeo-* + Gr. *chrōma* color]. Staining with mucin stains after formol-bichromate fixation: applied to certain serous cells of the salivary glands. Cf. *tropochrome*.

homeocyte (ho-me′o-sīt). Lymphocyte.

homeograft (ho′me-o-graft). Homeotransplant.

homeokinesis (ho″me-o-ki-ne′sis) [*homeo-* + Gr. *kinēsis* motion]. The stage of miosis in which the daughter cells receive equal amounts and kinds of chromatin.

homeomorphous (ho″me-o-mor′fus) [*homeo-* + Gr. *morphē* form]. Of like form and structure.

homeo-osmosis (ho″me-o-os-mo′sis). The maintenance, by a cell, tissue, organ, or organism, of its fluid milieu at relatively constant and stable osmotic pressure (or tonicity), independent of the tonicity of the surrounding medium.

homeo-osteoplasty (ho″me-o-os″te-o-plas′te) [*homeo-* + Gr. *osteon* bone + *plassein* to mold]. The surgical implantation of a piece of a bone similar to the bone receiving the graft.

homeopath (ho′me-o-path). Homeopathist.

homeopathic (ho″me-o-path′ik). Pertaining to homeopathy.

homeopathist (ho″me-op′ah-thist). One who practices homeopathy.

homeopathy (ho″me-op′ah-the) [*homeo-* + Gr. *pathos* disease]. A system of therapeutics founded by Samuel Hahnemann (1755–1843), in which diseases are treated by drugs which are capable of producing in healthy persons symptoms like those of the disease to be treated, the drug being administered in minute doses.

homeoplasia (ho″me-o-pla′ze-ah) [*homeo-* + Gr. *plassein* to form]. The formation of new tissue like that adjacent to it and normal to the part.

homeoplastic (ho″me-o-plas′tik). 1. Resembling in structure the adjacent parts. 2. Pertaining to, characterized by, or stimulating homeoplasia.

homeostasis (ho″me-o-sta′sis) [*homeo-* + Gr. *stasis* standing]. A tendency to uniformity or stability in the normal body states (internal environment or fluid matrix) of the organism (Cannon).

homeostatic (ho″me-o-stat′ik). Pertaining to homeostasis.

homeotherapy (ho″me-o-ther′ah-pe) [*homeo-* + Gr. *therapeia* treatment]. Treatment of disease with a substance similar to but not the same as the causative agent of the disease.

homeotherm (ho′me-o-therm). Homoiotherm.

homeothermal (ho″me-o-ther′mal) [*homeo-* + Gr. *thermē* heat]. Homoiothermic.

homeotransplant (ho″me-o-trans′plant). A piece of tissue taken from one individual and transplanted into another individual of the same species.

homeotransplantation (ho″me-o-trans″plan-ta′shun) [*homeo-* + *transplantation*]. Transplantation of tissue from one individual to another of the same species.

homeotypic, homeotypical (ho″me-o-tip′ik, ho″me-o-tip′e-k'l) [*homeo-* + Gr. *typos* type]. Resembling the normal or usual type; applied to the second miotic division of the germ cells.

homergy (hom′er-je) [Gr. *homos* same + *ergon* work]. Normal metabolism.

homicide (hom′ĭ-sīd) [L. *homo* man + *caedere* to kill]. The taking of the life of another individual.

homicidomania (hom″ĭ-sīd-o-ma′ne-ah). Impulsive desire to commit murder.

homiculture (hom′ĭ-kul″tūr) [L. *homo* man + *cultura* culture]. Positive eugenics.

homilophobia (hom″ĭ-lo-fo′be-ah). Dread of sermons.

hominal (hom′ĭ-nal) [L. *homo* man]. Pertaining to man; pertaining to human beings.

homininoxious (hom″in-e-nok′shus). Injurious to man.

homme (um) [Fr.]. Man. **h. rouge** (um-roozh′) [Fr. "red man"], a stage in mycosis fungoides in which the red plaques become infiltrated and coalesce over a wide area of the body.

homo-. 1. [Gr. *homos* same]. Combining form meaning the same. 2. A prefix in chemical names indicating the addition of one CH_2 group to the main compound.

homoarterenol (ho″mo-ar″tĕ-re′nol). Nordefrin.

homocentric (ho″mo-sen′trik) [*homo-* + Gr. *kentron* center]. Having the same center or focus.

homocerebrin (ho″mo-ser′e-brin) [*homo-* + *cerebrin*]. A principle like cerebrin from the brain substance.

homochrome (ho″mo-krōm) [*homo-* + Gr. *chrōma* color]. Taking the same color as the stain.

homochronous (ho-mok′ro-nus) [*homo-* + Gr. *chronos* time]. Occurring at the same age in successive generations.

homocinchonine (ho″mo-sin′ko-nin). An alkaloid, $C_{19}H_{22}ON_2$, from cinchona, isomeric with cinchonine.

homocladic (ho″mo-klad′ik) [*homo-* + Gr. *klados* branch]. Formed between small branches of the same artery: said of such an anastomosis.

homocyclic (ho″mo-sik′lik). Having or pertaining to a closed chain or ring formation which includes only atoms of the same element.

homocystine (ho″mo-sis′tin). A synthetic alpha-alpha′-dithiobis alpha-aminobutyric acid, $[S.CH_2.CH_2.CH(NH_2).COOH]_2$, which results from the demethylation of methionine. It is homologous with cystine and able to function as a source of sulfur in the body.

homodesmotic (ho″mo-des-mot′ik) [*homo-* + Gr. *desmos* bond]. Joining similar parts of the central nervous system. See under *fiber*.

homodont (ho′mo-dont) [*hom-* + Gr. *odous* tooth]. Having teeth of only one type.

homodromous (ho-mod′ro-mus) [*homo-* + Gr. *dromos* running]. Moving or acting in the same direction.

homoerotic (ho″mo-e-rot′ik). Pertaining to homoeroticism; homosexual.

homoeroticism (ho″mo-e-rot′ĭ-sizm). Eroticism directed toward a person of the same sex, especially when the role assumed by the affected person is passive.

homogametic (ho″mo-gah-met′ik). Having but one class of gametes with respect to the sex chromosomes, as the human female.

homogenate (ho-moj′ĕ-nāt). Material obtained by homogenation.

homogeneity (ho″mo-jĕ-ne′ĭ-te). The state or quality of being homogeneous.

homogeneization (ho″mo-je″ne-i-za′shun). Homogenization.

homogeneous (ho″mo-je′ne-us) [*homo-* + Gr. *genos* kind]. Consisting of or composed of similar elements or ingredients; of a uniform quality throughout.

homogenesis (ho″mo-jen′e-sis) [*homo-* + Gr. *genesis* production]. The reproduction by the same process in each generation, as contrasted with heterogenesis.

homogenetic (ho″mo-je-net′ik). Pertaining to or characterized by homogenesis.

homogenic (ho″mo-jen′ik). Homozygous.

homogenicity (ho″mo-je-nis′ĭ-te). Homogeneity.

homogenization (ho-moj″e-ni-za′shun). The act or process of rendering homogeneous.

homogenize (ho-moj′e-nīz). To render homogeneous, or of uniform quality or consistency throughout.

homogenous (ho-moj′e-nus). Having a similarity of structure because of descent from a common ancestor.

homogentisuria (ho″mo-jen″tĭ-su′re-ah). The excretion of homogentisic acid in the urine. See *alkaptonuria*.

homogeny (ho-moj′e-ne). Homogenesis.

homoglandular (ho″mo-glan′du-lar). Pertaining to the same gland.

homograft (ho′mo-graft). A graft of tissue obtained from the body of another animal of the same species but with a genotype differing from that of the recipient.

homohemotherapy (ho″mo-he-mo-ther′ah-pe). Treatment by the injection of blood from another individual of the same species.

homoio-. See *homeo-*.

homoioplasia (ho″moi-o-pla′se-ah). Homeoplasia.

homoiopodal (ho″moi-op′o-dal) [*homoio-* + Gr. *pous* foot]. Having processes of one kind only: said of nerve cells.

homoiostasis (ho″moi-os′tah-sis). Homeostasis.

homoiotherm (ho-moi′o-therm). An animal which exhibits homoiothermy; a so-called warm-blooded animal.

homoiothermal (ho″moi-o-ther′mal). Homoiothermic.

homoiothermic (ho-moi″other′mik). Pertaining to or characterized by homoiothermy.

homoiothermism (ho″moi-o-ther′mizm). Homoiothermy.

homoiothermy (ho-moi′o-ther″me) [*homoio-* + Gr. *thermē* heat]. The maintenance of a constant body temperature despite changes in the environmental temperature.

homoiotoxin (ho-moi′o-tok-sin). A toxin from one individual which is toxic for other individuals of the same species.

homokeratoplasty (ho″mo-ker′ah-to-plas″te). Corneal grafting with tissue derived from another individual of the same species.

homolateral (ho″mo-lat′er-al). Ipsilateral.

homologen (ho-mol′o-jen). Homologue, def. 2.

homologous (ho-mol′o-gus) [Gr. *homologos* agreeing, correspondent]. 1. Corresponding in structure, position and origin. Cf. *analogous*. 2. Derived from an animal of the same species but of different genotype. See *homograft*.

homologue (hom′o-log). 1. Any homologous organ or part; an organ similar in structure, position, and origin to another organ. See *analogue*. 2. In chemistry, one of a series of compounds, each of which is formed from the one before it by the addition of a constant element. Called also *homologen*.

homology (ho-mol′o-je) [Gr. *homologia* agreement]. The quality of being homologous; the morphological identity of corresponding parts; structural similarity due to descent from a common form.

homolysin (ho-mol′ĭ-sin). See *hemolysin*.

homolysis (ho-mol′ĭ-sis) [*homo-* + Gr. *lysis* dissolution]. Lysis of a cell by extracts of the same type of tissue.

homomorphic (ho-mo-mor′fik) [*homo-* + Gr. *morphē* form]. Having synaptic chromosome mates of similar size and form.

homomorphosis (ho″mo-mor-fo′sis) [*homo-* + Gr. *morphōsis* formation]. Regenerative replacement of a lost part by a similar part.

homonomous (ho-mon′o-mus) [*homo-* + Gr. *nomos* law]. 1. Subject to the same law. 2. Designating homologous serial parts, such as somites.

homonymous (ho-mon′ĭ-mus) [*homo-* + Gr. *onoma* name]. 1. Having the same or corresponding sound or name. 2. Standing in the same relation. See under *hemianopia*.

homophilic (ho″mo-fil′ik) [*homo-* + Gr. *philein* to love]. Having affinity for, or reacting with, a specific antigen: said of an antibody.

homoplastic (ho″mo-plas′tik) [*homo-* + Gr. *plassein* to form]. Denoting a transplantation or grafting of tissue taken from another individual of the same species.

homoplasty (ho′mo-plas″te). 1. Operative replacement of lost parts or tissues by similar parts from another individual of the same species. 2. Similarity between organs or their parts not due to common ancestry.

homorganic (hom″or-gan′ik) [*homo-* + Gr. *organon* organ]. Produced by the same or by homologous organs.

homosexual (ho″mo-seks′u-al). 1. Pertaining to the same sex. 2. An individual who is sexually attracted toward a person of the same sex.

homosexuality (ho″mo-seks″u-al′ĭ-te) [*homo-* + *sexuality*]. Sexual attraction toward those of the same sex. **female h.**, lesbianism.

homosporous (ho-mos′po-rus) [*homo-* + Gr. *sporos* seed]. Having only one kind of spores.

homostimulant (ho″mo-stim′u-lant). 1. Stimulating the same organ from which it is derived. 2. An extract from an organ which, on injection into the body, stimulates the same organ from which it is derived.

homostimulation (ho″mo-stim″u-la′shun). Treatment by a homostimulant.

homothermal (ho″mo-ther′mal). Homoiothermic.

homothermic (ho″mo-ther′mik). Homoiothermic.

homotonia (ho″mo-to′ne-ah). Isotonia.

homotonic (ho″mo-ton′ik). Isotonic.

homotopic (ho″mo-top′ik) [*homo-* + Gr. *topos* place]. Occurring at the same place upon the body.

homotransplant (ho″mo-trans′plant). A homoplastic graft.

homotropism (ho-mot′ro-pizm) [*homo-* + Gr. *tropos* a turning]. The property of cells to attract cells of a like order.

homotype (hom′o-tīp) [*homo-* + Gr. *typos* type]. A part that has a reversed symmetry with its fellow of the opposite side of the body.

homotypic (ho″mo-tip′ik). Pertaining to, characteristic of, or belonging to the same type.

homozoic (ho″mo-zo′ik) [*homo-* + Gr. *zōon* animal]. Pertaining to the same animal or same species.

homozygosis (ho″mo-zi-go′sis). The formation of a zygote by the union of gametes of similar genetic constitution.

homozygosity (ho″mo-zi-gos′ĭ-te) [*homo-* + *zygosity*]. The state of possessing an identical pair of alleles in regard to a given character or to all characters.

homozygote (ho″mo-zi′gōt) [*homo-* + *zygote*]. An individual possessing an identical pair of alleles in regard to a given character or to all characters.

homozygous (ho″mo-zi′gus). Possessing an identical pair of alleles in regard to a given character or to all characters.

homunculus (ho-munk′u-lus) [L. "a little man"]. 1. In psychiatry, a little man created by the imagination. 2. A dwarf without deformity or disproportion of parts.

honorarium (on″o-ra′re-um), pl. *honora′ria* [L.]. A gratuity that substitutes for a professional fee.

hood (hood). A flexible covering. **tooth h.,** dental operculum.

hoof (ho͞of) [L. *ungula*]. The hard, horny casing of the foot or ends of the digits of many animals which are, because of this feature, designated ungulates. **curved h.,** a condition in which the hoof has the wall of one side concave and the other convex. **dished h.,** a hoof which is concave from the coronet to the plantar surface. **false h.,** the hoof of an unused digit. **ribbed h., ringed h.,** a condition in which the wall of a horse's hoof is marked by ridges running parallel with the coronary margin.

hoof-bound (ho͞of′bound). Dryness and contraction of a horse's hoof, causing lameness. Called also *contracted foot* and *contracted heel*.

hook (hook). A curved instrument used for holding or catching, or for exerting traction on a part. **blunt h.,** an instrument for exercising traction upon the fetus in certain cases of breech presentation. **Bose's h's,** small hooks used in tracheostomy. **Braun's h.,** a hook for decapitating the fetus. **fixation h.,** a hook for fixing a part. **Loughnane's h.,** a double-pronged hook for removing fragments of the prostate in transurethral prostatectomy. **Malgaigne's h's,** two pairs of hooks connected by a screw for approximating the pieces of a broken patella. **Pajot's h.,** a hook for decapitating the fetus. **palate h.,** a hook for raising the palate in rhinoscopy. **Rambotham's h.,** a hook for decapitating the fetus. **squint h.,** a hook for stretching an eye tendon in tenotomy. **tracheostomy h.,** a hook for use in tracheostomy. **Tyrrell's h.,** a slender hook used in eye surgery.

hook-up (hook′up). The method of arranging circuits, appliances, and electrodes, in the giving of any particular treatment.

hookworm (hook′werm). A worm of the family Strongylidae, parasitic in the intestine of man and animals. **American h.,** *Necator americanus*. **h. of the dog,** *Ancylostoma canina*. **European h.,** *Ancylostoma duodenale*. **h. of the rat,** *Nippostrongylus miris*. **h. of ruminants,** Monodontus.

hoolamite (hoo′lah-mīt). A chemical detector for carbon monoxide. It contains fuming sulfuric acid, iodine pentoside, and powdered pumice. It changes from light gray to green under the influence of carbon monoxide.

Hooper's pills (hoo′perz) [John *Hooper*, English apothecary of the 18th century]. See under *pill*.

hoose (ho͞oz). A disease of sheep, cattle, goats and swine, caused by the presence of *Strongylus filaria* in the bronchial tubes or in the lungs. It is marked by cough, dyspnea, anorexia, and constipation. Called also *sheep cough*.

hoove, hooven (ho͞ov, hoo′ven). Hoven.

Hoover's sign (hoo′verz) [Charles Franklin *Hoover*, American physician, 1865–1927]. See under *sign*.

HOP. Abbreviation for *high oxygen pressure*.

Hope's mixture (hōps) [John *Hope*, English physician, 1725–1786]. See under *mixture*.

Hopkins (hop′kinz), Sir Frederick Gowland. English biologist, 1861–1947, noted for his pioneering work in vitamin research and nutritional chemistry; co-winner, with Christiaan Eijkman, of the Nobel prize for medicine and physiology in 1929.

Hoplopsyllus anomalus (hop″lo-sil′us ah-nom′ah-lus). A species of flea found in the ground squirrels of western United States and transmitting plague.

Hopmann's polyp (hop′manz) [Carl Melchior *Hopmann*, German rhinologist, 1849–1925]. See under *polyp*.

Hoppe-Seyler's test (hop″ĕ-si′lerz) [Ernst Felix Immanuel *Hoppe-Seyler*, German physiologic chemist, 1825–1895]. See under *tests*.

Hor. decub. Abbreviation for L. *ho′ra decu′bitus*, at bedtime.

hordein (hor′de-in) [L. *hordeum*, barley]. A simple native protein from barley, a prolamine insoluble in water, but soluble in 80 per cent alcohol.

hordeolum (hor-de′o-lum) [L. "barleycorn"]. See *sty*.

hordeum (hor′de-um), gen. *hor′dei* [L.]. Barley.

horehound (hōr′hound). The labiate plant, *Marrubium vulgare*, also its leaves and tops (L. *marrubium*): used in coughs and dyspnea and as a vermifuge.

Hor. interm. Abbreviation for L. *ho′ris interme′diis*, at the intermediate hours.

horismascope (ho-ris′mah-skōp). A variety of albumoscope consisting of a U-shaped tube, one arm of which is of small caliber and has a funnel-like top, the other arm being of larger caliber and having a black area against which traces of albumin may be seen.

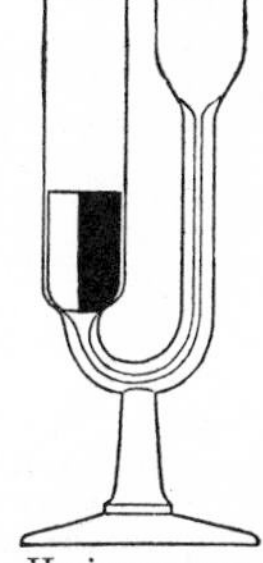
Horismascope.

horismology (hor″iz-mol′o-je) [Gr. *horismos* the definition of a word + *-logy*]. The art of defining words; the science concerned with establishing the definitions of terms.

horizocardia (ho-ri″zo-kar′de-ah) [Gr. *horizōn* horizon + *kardia* heart]. A horizontal position of the heart.

horizontalis (hor″ĭ-zon-ta′lis). Horizontal, or parallel to the plane of the horizon; in official anatomical nomenclature the term relates to this orientation when the body is in the anatomical, that is, the upright position.

horme (hor′ma). Monakow's term for the central source of instincts.

hormesis (hor-me′sis) [Gr. *hormēsis* rapid motion]. The stimulating effect of subinhibitory concentrations of any toxic substance on any organism.

hormic (hor′mik) [Gr. *hormē* an urge]. A term applied to the theory that organic phenomena are determined by inborn instincts, tendencies and dispositions.

hormion (hor′me-on) [Gr. *hormos* a wreath]. The median anterior point of the spheno-occipital bones.

hormocardiol (hor″mo-kar′de-ol) [*hormone* + Gr. *kardia* heart]. An extract from the sinus of the frog's heart that stimulates the contraction of the frog's ventricle.

Hormodendrum (hor″mo-den′drum). A genus of fungi. The species *H. pedrosoi* and *H. compactum* are causes of chromoblastomycosis.

hormonagogue (hor-mōn′ah-gog) [*hormone* + Gr. *agōgos* leading]. An agent that stimulates the production of hormones.

hormonal (hor′mo-nal). Pertaining to or of the nature of a hormone.

hormone (hor′mōn) [Gr. *hormaein* to set in motion, spur on]. A chemical substance, produced in the body, which has a specific effect on the activity of a certain organ; originally applied to substances secreted by various endocrine glands and transported in the blood stream to the target organ on which their effect was produced, the term was later applied to various substances not produced by special glands but having similar action. **adaptive h.,** one, such as ACTH or the corticoids, which is secreted during adaptation to unusual circumstances. **adrenocortical h.,** one of the steroids produced by the adrenal cortex, belonging, on the basis of biological activity and structure, to four main types: (1) estrogen; (2) androgens; (3) progesterone; (4) corticoids. **adrenocorticotropic h.,** a secretion of the anterior pituitary which is the most important regulator of the production and secretion of all of the hormones of the adrenal cortex except aldosterone. **adrenomedullary h's,** substances secreted by the adrenal medulla, including epinephrine and norepinephrine. **androgenic h's,** the masculinizing hormones, androsterone and testosterone. **anterior pituitary h.,** one of the several protein or polypeptide hormones secreted by the anterior lobe of the pituitary gland, including the adrenocorticotropic, somatotropic, thyrotropic, and the gonadotropic hormones. **antidiuretic h.,** vasopressin; so called because of its specific effect on the epithelial cells of the distal portion of the uriniferous tubule, stimulating reabsorption of water independently of solids, and resulting in concentration of urine. **A.P.L. h.** (*a*nterior *p*ituitary–*l*ike *h*ormone), chorionic gonadotropin. **Aschheim-Zondek h.,** luteinizing h. **chondrotropic h.,** growth h. **chromaffin h.,** epinephrine. **chromatophorotropic h.,** intermedin. **corpus luteum h.,** progesterone. **cortical h.** See *adrenocortical h.* **estrogenic h's,** substances capable of producing certain biological effects, the most characteristic of which are the changes which occur in mammals at estrus; the naturally occurring estrogenic hormones are β-estradiol, estrone, and estriol. **follicle h.,** an estrogenic hormone produced by the graafian follicle. **follicle-stimulating h.,** one of the gonadotropic hormones of the anterior pituitary, which stimulates the growth and maturation of graafian follicles in the ovary, and stimulates spermatogenesis in the male. **follicular h.,** one produced by the graafian follicle. **galactopoietic h.,** lactogenic h. **gonadotropic h.,** any hormone which has an influence on the gonads. **gonadotropic h's, pituitary,** three hormones secreted by the anterior pituitary which have an influence on the gonads, including follicle-stimulating hormone, luteinizing hormone, and lactogenic hormone. **growth h.,** any substance that stimulates growth, especially one secreted by the anterior pituitary, which exerts a direct effect on protein, carbohydrate, and lipid metabolism, and controls the rate of skeletal and visceral growth. **inhibitory h.,** a substance which exerts a depressing influence on certain of its target organs. **interstitial cell-stimulating h.,** luteinizing h.; so called because it also stimulates the Leydig (interstitial) cells of the testis. **lactation h.,** lactogenic h. **lactogenic h.,** one of the gonadotropic hormones of the anterior pituitary, which is responsible for lactation in the postpartum woman, the breast having been prepared by estrogen and progesterone; it is also necessary for stimulation of functional activity of the corpus luteum. **langerhansian h.,** one of the hormones secreted by the islets of Langerhans of the pancreas, including both insulin and glucagon. **local h.,** a substance with hormone-like properties, produced from blood or other body fluid precisely when and where it is needed, and usually rapidly destroyed. **luteal h.,** one secreted by the corpus luteum. See *progesterone.* **luteinizing h.,** a gonadotropic hormone of the anterior pituitary which acts with the follicle-stimulating hormone to cause ovulation of mature follicles and secretion of estrogen by thecal and granulosa cells. It is also concerned with corpus luteum formation and, in the male, stimulates the development and functional activity of Leydig (interstitial) cells. **luteotropic h.,** lactogenic h.; so called because it is also necessary for stimulation of functional activity of the corpus luteum in certain species. **mammotropic h.,** lactogenic h. **melanin-stimulating h.,** a substance derived from the posterior pituitary which influences the formation or deposition of melanin in the body. **orchidic h.,** one secreted by the testis. **ovarian h.,** one secreted by the ovary. **parathyroid h.,** a substance secreted by the parathyroid glands, which exerts an influence on calcium and phosphorus metabolism and on the formation of bone. **placental h.,** a hormone produced by the placenta during pregnancy, including chorionic gonadotrophin, relaxin, and other substances having estrogenic, progesteronic, or adrenocorticoid activity. **posterior pituitary h's,** hormones derived from the posterior lobe of the pituitary, including vasopressin and oxytocin; now believed to be formed in the neuronal cells of the hypothalamic nuclei and to be stored in nerve cell endings in the posterior pituitary (neurohypophysis). **progestational h.,** progesterone; so called because, in the latter half of the menstrual cycle, it is concerned mainly with preparing the endometrium for nidation of the fertilized ovum if conception has occurred. **P. U. h.** (pregnancy urine h.), the chorionic gonadotropin found in the urine in pregnancy. **sex h's,** hormones having estrogenic (*female sex h's*) or androgenic (*male sex h's*) activity. **somatotrophic h., somatotropic h.,** growth h. **testicular h., testis h.,** one secreted by the testis. **thyrotropic h.,** a hormone of the anterior lobe of the pituitary which exerts a stimulating influence on the thyroid gland.

hormonic (hor-mon′ik). Pertaining to or acting as a hormone; having the exciting influence of a hormone.

hormonogenesis (hor″mo-no-jen′e-sis). Hormonopoiesis.

hormonogenic (hor″mo-no-jen′ik). Hormonopoietic.

hormonology (hor″mo-nol′o-je). The science of hormones; clinical endocrinology.

hormonopexic (hor″mo-no-pek′sik) [*hormone* + Gr. *pēxis* fixation]. Fixing hormones.

hormonopoiesis (hor″mo-no-poi-e′sis) [*hormone* + Gr. *poiesis* a making, creation]. The production of hormones.

hormonopoietic (hor″mo-no-poi-et′ik). Pertaining to, characterized by, or stimulating hormonopoiesis.

hormonoprivia (hor-mōn″o-priv′e-ah) [*hormone* + L. *privus* without, deprived of]. Lack of hormone, or the condition produced by a deficiency of hormone in the body.

hormonotherapy (hor″mo-no-ther′ah-pe). Treatment by the use of hormones.

hormopoiesis (hor″mo-poi-e′sis). Hormonopoiesis.

hormopoietic (hor″mo-poi-et′ik). Hormonopoietic.

horn (horn) [L. *cornu*]. A pointed projection such as the paired processes on the head of various animals, or other structure resembling them in shape. **h. of Ammon,** hippocampus. **anterior h. of lateral ventricle,** cornu anterius ventriculi lateralis. **anterior h. of spinal cord,** cornu anterius medullae spinalis. **cicatricial h.,** a hard, dry outgrowth from a cicatrix, commonly scaly and very rarely osseous. **h. of clitoris,** an occasional formation of a horny mass, resembling a talon, under the prepuce of the clitoris. **coccygeal h.,** cornu coccygeum. **cutaneous h.,** cornu cutaneum. **gray h. of spinal cord,**

anterior, columna anterior medullae spinalis. **gray h. of spinal cord, lateral,** columna lateralis medullae spinalis. **gray h. of spinal cord, posterior,** columna posterior medullae spinalis. **greater h. of hyoid bone,** cornu majus ossis hyoidei. **inferior h. of falciform margin,** cornu inferius marginis falciformis. **inferior h. of lateral ventricle,** cornu inferius ventriculi lateralis. **inferior h. of thyroid cartilage,** cornu inferius cartilaginis thyroideae. **lateral h. of hyoid bone,** cornu majus ossis hyoidei. **lateral h. of spinal cord,** cornu laterale medullae spinalis. **lesser h. of hyoid bone,** cornu minus ossis hyoidei. **posterior h. of lateral ventricle,** cornu posterius ventriculi lateralis. **posterior h. of spinal cord,** cornu posterius medullae spinalis. **h. of pulp.,** an extension of the pulp into an accentuation of the roof of the pulp chamber directly under a cusp or a developmental lobe of the tooth. **sacral h.,** cornu sacrale. **sebaceous h.,** a hard outgrowth of the contents of a sebaceous cyst. **superior h. of falciform margin,** cornu superius marginis falciformis. **superior h. of hyoid bone,** cornu minus ossis hyoidei. **superior h. of thyroid cartilage,** cornu superius cartilaginis thyroideae. **h. of uterus,** tuba uterina. **warty h.,** a hard pointed outgrowth of a wart.

Horn's sign (hornz) [C. ten *Horn,* Dutch surgeon]. See under *sign.*

Horner's law, syndrome (hor′nerz) [Johann Friedrich *Horner,* Swiss ophthalmologist, 1831–1886]. See under *law* and *syndrome.*

Horner's muscle (hor′nerz) [William Edmonds *Horner,* American anatomist, 1793–1853]. Pars lacrimalis musculi orbicularis oculi.

hornification (hor″nĭ-fi-ka′shun). Cornification; change into horny tissue, a process which occurs in the secondary enamel cuticle.

hornskin (horn′skin). Animal skin or hide, dried and varnished: used in orthopedic surgery.

horny (hor′ne). Having the nature and appearance of horn.

horopter (ho-rop′ter) [Gr. *horos* limit + *optēr* observer]. The sum of all the points in space, the images of which fall on corresponding points of the retina. **Vieth-Müller h.,** a circle which joins the fixation point with the nodal points of the two eyes.

horopteric (hor″op-ter′ik). Pertaining to a horopter.

horrida cutis (hor′ĭ-dah ku′tis). Cutis anserina.

horripilation (hor″ĭ-pi-la′shun) [L. *horrere* to bristle, to stand on end + *pilus* hair]. Erection of the fine hairs of the skin, as in cutis anserina.

Horrocks' maieutic (hor′oks) [Peter *Horrocks,* London obstetrician, 1852–1901]. See under *maieutic.*

horror (hor′or) [L.]. Dread; terror. **h. autotox′icus** [L. "fear of self poisoning"], a term coined by Ehrlich and Morgenroth in 1900 to express the refusal of a normal animal to form autoantibodies; it was believed that formation of such antibodies might result in self-destruction of the antibody producer as a result of the reaction between autoantibody and the corresponding antigen present in tissues. **h. fusio′nis** [L. "horror of fusion"], antipathy to single binocular fusion, manifested in the tendency of one eye to move away from the fixation state in which the retinal image falls on the macula in each eye.

horsepower (hors′pow″er). A unit of power, being the equivalent of that expended in raising 33,000 pounds one foot in one minute.

horsepox (hors′poks). Modified smallpox occurring in the horse.

horse-sickness (hors-sik′nes). An infectious disease of horses and mules in South Africa, marked by serous exudations. Called also *pferdepest.*

Horsley's putty, test, trephine, wax (hors′lēz) [Sir Victor Alexander Haden *Horsley,* English surgeon, 1857–1916]. See under *tests, trephine,* and *wax.*

Hortega cell (hor-ta′gah) [Pio del Rio *Hortega,* Spanish histologist in Buenos Aires, 1882–1945]. A microglia cell. **H. method,** ammoniacal silver carbonate staining for microglia.

hortobezoar (hor″to-be-zōr′). Phytobezoar.

Horton's headache, syndrome (hōr′tunz) [Bayard T. *Horton,* American physician, born 1895]. Histamine cephalalgia.

hortungskörper (hor″tungs-ker′per) [Ger., pl., "storage substances"]. Material deposited in body organs as one of the manifestations of aging.

Hor. un. spatio. Abbreviation for L. *ho′rae uni′us spa′tio,* at the end of one hour.

H_2OsO_4. Osmic acid.

hospital (hos′pit-′l) [L. *hospitalium; hospes* host, guest]. An institution for the treatment of the sick. "An institution suitably located, constructed, organized, managed and personneled, to supply, scientifically, economically, efficiently and unhindered, all or any recognized part of the complex requirements for the prevention, diagnosis, and treatment of physical, mental, and the medical aspect of social ills; with functioning facilities for training new workers in the many special professional, technical and economic fields essential to the discharge of its proper functions; and with adequate contacts with physicians, other hospitals, medical schools and all accredited health agencies engaged in the better health program."—Council on Medical Education. **banian h.,** a hospital for animals. **base h.,** a hospital unit within the line of communication of the army, usually in a permanent building, designed for the reception of wounded and other patients received via the field hospitals from the front, and for cases originating within the line of communication itself. **camp h.,** an immobile military unit organized and equipped for the care of the sick and wounded in camp in order to prevent immobilization of field hospitals or other mobile sanitary organizations. **closed h.,** a hospital in which only members of the staff are permitted to treat patients. **cottage h.,** a hospital consisting of a number of detached cottages. **evacuation h.,** a mobile advance hospital unit within the line of communication, designed to take over the functions of field hospitals when they move away with their divisions and to supplement base hospitals in their functions. **field h.,** a portable military hospital, manned by noncommissioned officers and men, located beyond the zone of conflict, 3–4 miles beyond the dressing stations, designed to shelter and care for wounded brought in by ambulance companies until they can be transported to the line of communications.

hospitalism (hos′pit-′l-izm″). 1. The morbid conditions due to the assembling of diseased persons in a hospital. 2. A psychoneurotic habit of attending hospital dispensaries as a patient.

hospitalization (hos″pit-′l-i-za′shun). The confinement of a patient in a hospital, or the period of such confinement.

hospitalize (hos′pit-′l-īz). To place a patient in a hospital.

host (hōst) [L. *hospes*]. 1. An animal or plant which harbors or nourishes another organism (parasite). 2. The recipient of an organ or other tissue transplanted from another organism. **alternate h.,** intermediary h. **definitive h., final h.,** the animal in which a parasite passes its adult and sexual existence. **intermediary h., intermediate h.,** the animal in which a parasite passes its larval or nonsexual existence. **h. of predilection,** the host which is preferred by a parasite. **primary h.,** definitive h. **reservoir h.,** an animal which serves as a host for organisms that are also parasitic for man, and from which man may become infected. **secondary h.,** intermediary h.

hot (hot). 1. Characterized by high temperature.

2. Containing dangerous radioactive material; dangerously radioactive.

Hotchkiss' operation (hoch′kis) [Lucien W. *Hotchkiss*, American surgeon, 1859–1926]. See under *operation.*

hottentotism (hot′en-tot-izm). An exaggerated form of stuttering.

hough (hok). Hock.

Houghton's test (how′tonz) [E. M. *Houghton*, American physician, 1867–1937]. See under *tests.*

Houssay's phenomenon (how-sāz′) [Bernardo Alberto *Houssay*, physiologist in Buenos Aires, born 1887; co-winner, with C. F. and G. T. Cori, of the Nobel prize in medicine and physiology for 1947]. See under *phenomenon.*

Houston's muscle, valve (hu′stonz) [John *Houston*, Irish surgeon, 1802–1845]. See under *muscle* and *valve.*

hoven (ho′ven). A kind of indigestion in cattle and sheep, marked by an abnormal collection of gas in the first stomach. Called also *hoove, hooven, bloat, blown* and *tympany of the stomach.*

Hovius' canal (ho′ve-us) [Jacob *Hovius*, Dutch ophthalmologist, b. circa 1675]. See under *canal.*

Howard's method (how′ardz) [Benjamin Douglas *Howard*, American physician, 1840–1900]. See under *respiration, artificial.*

Howell's bodies (how′elz) [William Henry *Howell*, American physiologist, 1860–1945]. See under *body.*

Howell-Jolly bodies [W. H. *Howell; Justin Jolly*, French histologist, 1870–1953]. Howell's bodies.

Howship's lacunae, sign, symptom (how′ships) [John *Howship*, English surgeon, 1781–1841]. See under *lacuna*, and *Romberg-Howship sign*, under *sign.*

Hp. Abbreviation for *haptoglobin.*

hpf. Abbreviation for *high-power field.*

HPO_3. Metaphosphoric acid.

H_3PO_2. Hypophosphorous acid.

H_3PO_3. Phosphorous acid.

H_3PO_4. Orthophosphoric acid; phosphoric acid.

$H_4P_2O_6$. Hypophosphoric acid.

$H_4P_2O_7$. Pyrophosphoric acid.

H.S. Abbreviation for *house surgeon.*

h.s. Abbreviation for L. *ho′ra som′ni*, at bedtime.

H_2S. Hydrogen sulfide.

H_2SiO_3. Metasilicic acid.

H_4SiO_4. Orthosilicic acid.

H_2SO_3. Sulfurous acid.

H_2SO_4. Sulfuric acid.

5-HT (fīv āch te). Serotonin.

Ht. Symbol for *total hypermetropia.*

htone na (hut-to′ne-nah). A peripheral neuritis of malarial origin occurring in Burma.

HU. Abbreviation for *hyperemia unit.*

Huchard's disease, sign (e-sharz′) [Henri *Huchard*, physician in Paris, 1844–1910]. See under *disease* and *sign.*

Hueck's ligament (heks) [Alexander Friedrich *Hueck*, German anatomist, 1802–1842]. See under *ligament.*

Huenefeld's mixture (he′nĕ-felts) [Friedrich Ludwig *Huenefeld*, German chemist, 1798–1882]. See under *mixture.*

Hueppe's disease (he′pez) [Ferdinand *Hueppe*, German bacteriologist, 1852–1938]. Hemorrhagic septicemia.

Hueter's bandage, line, maneuver, sign (he′terz) [Karl *Hueter*, German surgeon, 1838–1882]. See under the nouns.

Hufnagel operation (huf′na-gel) [Charles A. *Hufnagel*, American surgeon, born 1916]. See under *operation.*

Huggins operation, test (hug′inz) [Charles Brenton *Huggins*, Chicago urologist, born 1901]. See under *operation* and *tests.*

Huguenin's edema (e-gen-az′) [Gustave *Huguenin*, Swiss psychiatrist, 1841–1920]. See under *edema.*

Huguier's canal, circle, disease, glands, etc. (e-ge-āz′) [Pierre Charles *Huguier*, French surgeon, 1804–1873]. See under the nouns.

Huhner test (hoon′er) [Max *Huhner*, New York urologist, 1873–1947]. See under *tests.*

hum (hum). An indistinct, low, prolonged sound. **venous h.,** a continuous blowing, singing, or humming murmur heard on auscultation over the right jugular vein in anemia, chlorosis, and occasionally in health. Called also *bruit de diable* and *humming-top murmur.*

humatin (hu′mah-tin). Trade mark for preparations of paromomycin sulfate.

humectant (hu-mek′tant) [L. *humectus*, from *humectare* to be moist]. 1. Moistening. 2. A moistening or diluent substance.

humectation (hu″mek-ta′shun). The act of moistening.

humeral (hu′mer-al) [L. *humeralis*]. Of or pertaining to the humerus.

humeri (hu′mer-i) [L.]. Plural of *humerus.*

humeroradial (hu″mer-o-ra′de-al). Pertaining to the humerus and the radius.

humeroscapular (hu″mer-o-skap′u-lar). Pertaining to the humerus and the scapula.

humero-ulnar (hu″mer-o-ul′nar). Pertaining to the humerus and the ulna.

humerus (hu′mer-us), pl. *hu′meri* [L.]. [N A, B N A] The bone that extends from the shoulder to the elbow. **h. va′rus,** a bent humerus.

humidifier (hu-mid′ĭ-fi″er). An apparatus for controlling humidity by adding to the content of moisture in the air of a room.

humidity (hu-mid′ĭ-te) [L. *humiditas*]. The degree of moisture, especially of that in the air. **absolute h.,** the actual amount of vapor in the atmosphere expressed in grains per cubit foot. **relative h.,** the percentage of moisture in the air as compared to the amount necessary to cause saturation, which is taken as 100.

humin (hu′min). 1. Humic acid. 2. The dark amorphous material which is formed during the acid hydrolysis of a protein, chiefly from trypsin.

humor (hu′mor), pl. *humors, humo′res* [L. "a liquid"]. 1. A fluid or semifluid substance; used in anatomical nomenclature to designate certain fluid materials in the body. See also *humoralism.* 2. Any chronic cutaneous disease. **aqueous h., h. aquo′sus** [N A], the fluid produced in the eye, occupying the anterior and posterior chambers, and diffusing out of the eye into the blood; regarded as the lymph of the eye, its composition varies from that of lymph in the body generally. **h. cristalli′nus, crystalline h.** 1. The crystalline lens. 2. The vitreous body. **ocular h.,** one of the humors of the eye—the aqueous or vitreous. **vitreous h.** 1. Corpus vitreum. 2. Humor vitreus. **h. vit′reus** [N A, B N A], the watery substance, resembling aqueous humor, contained within the interstices of the stroma in the vitreous body.

humoral (hu′mor-al). Pertaining to the humors of the body.

humoralism (hu′mor-al-izm). The obsolete doctrine that all diseases arise from some change of the humors. See *humoral theory*, under *theory.*

humorism (hu′mor-izm). Humoralism.

humorsol (hu′mor-sol). Trade mark for a solution of demecarium bromide.

humpback (hump′bak). Kyphosis.

humulin (hu′mu-lin). 1. Lupulin. 2. A dry, concentrated preparation of hops.

humulon (hu′mu-lon). An antibacterial substance derived from hops.

humulus (hu′mu-lus), gen. *hu′muli* [L.]. See *hops.*

humus (hu′mus) [L.]. A dark mold of decayed vegetable tissue: used therapeutically in certain forms of the bath.

hunchback (hunch′bak). 1. Kyphosis. 2. An individual characterized by a rounded deformity of the back, or kyphosis.

hundstaupe (hoont′stow-pĕ) [Ger.]. Dog distemper.

hunger (hung′ger). A craving, as for food. **air h.,** a distressing dyspnea occurring in paroxysms, and often forerunning an attack of diabetic coma (Kussmaul, 1874). **calcium h.,** a condition due to calcium defect, marked by severe headache during and after menstruation. **chlorine h.,** a desire for salt due to deficiency of chlorine in the blood. **hormone h.,** deficiency in the supply to any organ of the special hormone on which its proper functioning depends.

Hunner's ulcer (hun′erz) [Guy LeRoy *Hunner*, American surgeon, born 1868]. See under *ulcer*.

Hunt's atrophy, disease, neuralgia, phenomenon, syndrome [James Ramsay *Hunt*, American neurologist, 1874–1937]. See under the nouns.

Hunt's reaction, test [Reid *Hunt*, American pharmacologist, 1870–1948]. See under *reaction*.

Hunter's canal, operation (hunt′erz) [John *Hunter*, English anatomist and surgeon, 1728–1793]. See under *canal* and *operation*.

Hunter's glossitis [William *Hunter*, English physician, 1861–1937]. See under *glossitis*.

Hunter's ligament, line [William *Hunter*, English anatomist, 1718–1783, brother of John Hunter]. See under *ligament* and *line*.

hunterian (hun-te′re-an). Named for or described by, John Hunter. See under *chancre*.

Huntington's chorea (hunt′ing-tunz) [George *Huntington*, American physician, 1850–1916]. See under *chorea*.

Huppert's disease, test (hoop′erts) [Hugo *Huppert*, Bohemian physician, 1832–1904]. See *multiple myeloma*, and under *tests*.

Hurler's disease, syndrome (hoor′lerz) [Gertrud *Hurler*, Austrian pediatrician]. Gargoylism.

Hürthle cell (her′tel) [Karl *Hürthle*, German histologist, born 1860]. See under *cell*.

Huschke's canal, foramen, valve, etc. (hoosh′kez) [Emil *Huschke*, German anatomist, 1797–1858]. See under the nouns.

husk (husk). Hoose.

Hutchinson's disease, facies, mask, pupil, syndrome, teeth, triad (huch′in-sunz) [Sir Jonathan *Hutchinson*, English surgeon, 1828–1913]. See under the nouns.

hutchinsonian (huch″in-so′ne-an). Named for or described by Sir Jonathan Hutchinson.

Hutchison type (huch′ĭ-son) [Sir Robert *Hutchison*, English pediatrician, 1871–1960]. See under *type*.

Hutinel's disease (e-tin-elz′) [Victor Henri *Hutinel*, pediatrician in Paris, 1849–1933]. See under *disease*.

Huxley (huks′le), Andrew Fielding. English physiologist, born 1917; co-winner, with John Carew Eccles and Alan Lloyd Hodgkin, of the Nobel prize in medicine and physiology for 1963, for discoveries concerning the ionic mechanism involved in excitation and inhibition in peripheral and central parts of the nerve cell membrane.

Huxley's layer (huks′lēz) [Thomas Henry *Huxley*, English physiologist and naturalist, 1825–1895]. See under *layer*.

huygenian (hi-jen′e-an). Named for Christian *Huygens*, a Dutch physicist, 1629–1695. See under *eyepiece*.

HVL. Abbreviation for *half-value layer*.

Hy. Abbreviation for *hypermetropia*.

hyal (hi′al). Hyoid.

hyal-. See *hyalo-*.

hyalin (hi′ah-lin) [Gr. *hyalos* glass]. 1. A translucent albuminoid substance, one of the products of amyloid degeneration. 2. A substance composing the walls of hydatid cysts. **hematogenous h.,** hematohyaloid.

hyaline (hi′ah-līn) [Gr. *hyalos* glass]. Glassy and transparent or nearly so.

hyalinization (hi″ah-lin″i-za′shun). Conversion into a substance resembling glass.

hyalinosis (hi″ah-lin-o′sis). Hyaline degeneration.

hyalinuria (hi″ah-lin-u′re-ah). The discharge of hyalin in the urine.

hyalitis (hi″ah-li′tis). 1. Inflammation of a hyaloid membrane. 2. Inflammation of the vitreous body. **asteroid h.,** inflammation of the vitreous body marked by the presence of spherical or star-shaped inclusions. **h. puncta′ta,** inflammation of the vitreous body marked by the formation of small opacities. **h. suppurati′va,** a purulent inflammation of the vitreous body.

hyalo-, hyal- (hi′ah-lo, hi′al) [Gr. *hyalos* glass]. Combining form denoting resemblance to glass.

hyaloenchondroma (hi″ah-lo-en″kon-dro′mah). A chondroma of hyaline cartilage.

hyalogen (hi-al′o-jen) [*hyalo-* + Gr. *gennan* to produce]. An albuminous substance occurring in cartilage, the vitreous body, etc., and convertible into hyalin.

hyaloid (hi′ah-loid) [*hyal-* + Gr. *eidos* form]. Resembling glass.

hyaloidin (hi″ah-loid′in). A carbohydrate radical from mucoproteins. It resembles chondroitin, but contains no sulfuric acid.

hyaloiditis (hi″ah-loid-i′tis). Hyalitis.

hyaloma (hi″ah-lo′mah) [*hyal-* + *-oma*]. Colloid milium.

hyalomere (hi′ah-lo-mēr) [*hyalo-* + Gr. *meros* part]. A zone of homogeneous or finely fibrillar pale blue cytoplasm surrounding the central granular portion (granulomere) of a platelet in a dry, stained blood smear; thought possibly to be an artefact.

hyalomitome (hi″ah-lo-mit′ōm). Hyaloplasm.

Hyalomma (hi″ah-lom′ah) [*hyal-* + Gr. *omma* eye]. A genus of ticks. *H. aegyp′tium* is a cattle tick of Africa, India, and southern Europe. *H. mauritan′icum* transmits *Theileria dispar* in northern Africa.

hyalomucoid (hi″ah-lo-mu′koid). The mucoid of the vitreous body.

hyalonyxis (hi″ah-lo-nik′sis) [*hyalo-* + Gr. *nyxis* pricking]. The act of puncturing the vitreous body.

hyalophagia (hi″ah-lo-fa′je-ah) [*hyalo-* + Gr. *phagein* to eat]. The eating of glass.

hyalophagy (hi″ah-lof′ah-je). Hyalophagia.

hyalophobia (hi″ah-lo-fo′be-ah) [*hyalo-* + Gr. *phobos* + *-ia*]. Morbid fear of glass.

hyaloplasm (hi′ah-lo-plazm) [*hyalo-* + Gr. *plasma* anything formed]. 1. The more fluid, finely granular substance of the cytoplasm of cells. Called *paraplasm, interfilar mass, interfilar substance, interfibrillar substance of Flemming, paramitome, enchylema*, and *cytolymph*. 2. The conducting medium of the axon. **nuclear h.,** karyolymph.

hyaloserositis (hi″ah-lo-se″ro-si′tis) [*hyalo-* + *serum* + *-itis*]. A form of inflammation of serous membranes marked by hyalinization of the serous exudate into a pearly investment of the organ concerned. Cf. *frosted heart* and *perihepatitis chronica hyperplastica*. **progressive multiple h.,** polyorrhymenitis.

hyalosome (hi-al′o-sōm) [*hyalo-* + Gr. *sōma* body]. A structure resembling the nucleolus of a cell, but staining only slightly.

hyalotome (hi-al′o-tōm). Paramitome.

hyalurate (hi″ah-lu′rāt). A salt or ester of hyaluronic acid.

hyaluronidase (hi″ah-lu-ron′ĭ-dās). An enzyme that catalyzes the hydrolysis of hyaluronic acid, the cement substance of the tissues. It is found in leeches, in snake and spider venom, and in testes and malignant tissues, and is produced by a variety of pathogenic bacteria. Called also *Duran-Reynals factor*, or *spreading factor*. **h. for injection,** a soluble enzyme product prepared from mammalian testes, capable of catalyzing the hydrolysis of mucopolysaccharides of the type of hyaluronic acid: used to promote absorption and diffusion of solutions injected subcutaneously.

hyazyme (hi′ah-zīm). Trade mark for a preparation of hyaluronidase for injection.

hybrid (hi′brid) [L. *hybrida* mongrel]. An animal or plant produced from parents different in kind, such as parents belonging to two different species. **false h.,** an individual produced by a form of gynogenesis in which the foreign spermatozoon enters the ovum, activates it to cell division, but does not fuse with the egg nucleus.

hybridism (hi′brid-izm). 1. The state of being a hybrid. 2. The production of hybrids.

hybridity (hi-brid′ĭ-te). The state of being a hybrid.

hybridization (hi″brid-i-za′shun). The act or process of producing hybrids.

hydantoin (hi-dan′to-in). A crystalline base, CO.NH.CH_2.CO.NH, derivable from allantoin.

hydantoinate (hi″dan-to′in-āt). Any salt of hydantoin.

hydatid (hi′dah-tid) [L. *hydatis*, a drop of water]. 1. A hydatid cyst. 2. Any cyst-like structure. **alveolar h's.** See *hydatid disease, alveolar*, under *disease*. **h. of Morgagni,** a cystlike remnant of the müllerian duct attached to a testis or to the oviduct. See *appendix testis* and *appendices vesiculosi epoophori*. **sessile h.,** appendix testis. **stalked h's,** appendices vesiculosi epoophori.

hydatidiform (hi″dah-tid′ĭ-form). Resembling a hydatid cyst.

hydatidocele (hi″dah-tid′o-sēl) [*hydatid* + Gr. *kēlē* tumor]. A tumor of the scrotum containing hydatids.

hydatidoma (hi″dah-tid-o′mah). A tumor containing hydatids or one caused by hydatids.

hydatidosis (hi″dah-tid-o′sis). Hydatid disease; infestation with echinococcus.

hydatidostomy (hi″dah-tid-os′to-me) [*hydatid* + Gr. *stoma* mouth]. The opening and draining of a hydatid cyst.

hydatiduria (hi″dah-tid-u′re-ah). The excretion of hydatid cysts in the urine.

Hydatigera (hi″dah-tij′er-ah). A genus of tapeworms resembling *Taenia*, but with a massive rostellum without a neck and found mostly in the intestines of carnivorous animals. *H. infantis* has been reported from man in Argentina.

hydatism (hi′dah-tizm) [Gr. *hydatis* water]. The sound caused by the presence of fluid in a cavity.

hydatoid (hi′dah-toid). 1. The aqueous humor. 2. The hyaloid membrane. 3. Pertaining to the aqueous humor.

Hyde's disease (hīdz) [James Nevin *Hyde*, American dermatologist, 1840–1910]. Prurigo nodularis.

hydeltra (hi-del′trah). Trade mark for preparations of prednisolone.

hydnocarpate (hid-no-kar′pāt). A salt of hydnocarpic acid.

hydr-. See *hydro-*.

hydracetin (hi-dras′ĕ-tin). Acetylphenylhydrazine.

hydracid (hi-dras′id). Haloid acid.

hydradenitis (hi″drad-e-ni′tis). Hidradenitis.

hydradenoma (hi″drad-e-no′mah). Syringocystadenoma.

hydraeroperitoneum (hi-dra″e-ro-per″ĭ-to-ne′-um) [*hydr-* + Gr. *aēr* air + *peritoneum*]. A collection of watery fluid and gas in the peritoneal cavity.

hydragogue (hi′drah-gog) [*hydr-* + Gr. *agōgos* leading]. 1. Producing watery discharge, especially from the bowels. 2. A cathartic which causes watery purgation.

hydralazine (hi-dral′ah-zēn). Chemical name: 1-hydrazinophthalazine: used as a hypotensive agent.

hydramine (hi′drah-min). An amine derived from a glycol in which one hydroxyl is replaced by an amino group.

hydramnion (hi-dram′ne-on). Hydramnios.

hydramnios (hi-dram′ne-os) [*hydr-* + *amnion*]. Excess of amniotic fluid.

hydranencephaly (hi″dran-en-sef′ah-le). Complete or almost complete absence of the cerebral hemispheres, the space they normally occupy being filled with cerebrospinal fluid.

Hydrangea (hi-dran′je-ah). A genus of saxifragaceous trees and shrubs. The root of *H. arborescens* is diuretic.

hydrangiography (hi-dran″je-og′rah-fe) [*hydr-* + Gr. *angeion* vessel + *graphein* to write]. 1. A description of the lymphatic vessels. 2. Lymphangiography.

hydrangiology (hi-dran″je-ol′o-je) [*hydr-* + Gr. *angeion* vessel + *-logy*]. Lymphangiology.

hydrangiotomy (hi-dran″je-ot′o-me) [*hydr-* + Gr. *angeion* vessel + *tomē* a cutting]. Lymphangiotomy.

hydrargyri (hi-drar′jĭ-ri). Genitive of L. *hydrargyrum*, mercury. **h. bichlo′ridum,** mercury bichloride. **h. chlo′ridum corro′sivum,** mercury bichloride. **h. iodi′dum fla′vum,** mercurous iodide, yellow. **h. iodi′dum ru′brum,** mercuric iodide, red. **h. ox′idum fla′vum,** mercuric oxide, yellow. **h. sali′cylas,** mercuric salicylate.

hydrargyria (hi″drar-jir′e-ah). Mercurialism.

hydrargyrism (hi-drar′jĭ-rizm). Mercurialism.

hydrargyromania (hi-drar″jĭ-ro-ma′ne-ah). Mental disorder due to mercury poisoning.

hydrargyrorelapsing (hi-drar″jĭ-ro-re-laps′-ing). Relapsing after apparently successful mercurial treatment.

hydrargyrosis (hi-drar″jĭ-ro′sis). Mercurialism.

hydrargyrum (hi-drar′jĭ-rum), gen. *hydrar′gyri* [L. "liquid silver"]. Mercury. **h. ammonia′tum,** ammoniated mercury. **h. chlo′ridum mi′te,** mercurous chloride, mild. **h. olea′tum,** mercury oleate.

hydrarthrodial (hi″drar-thro′de-al). Pertaining to hydrarthrosis.

hydrarthrosis (hi″drar-thro′sis) [*hydr-* + Gr. *arthron* joint + *-osis*]. An accumulation of watery fluid in the cavity of a joint. **intermittent h.,** serous effusion into a joint occurring periodically.

hydrase (hi′drās). An enzyme which catalyzes the addition of water to a compound without producing hydrolysis.

hydrate (hi′drāt) [L. *hydras*]. 1. Any compound of a radical with H_2O. 2. Any salt or other compound that contains water of crystallization.

hydrated (hi′drāt-ed) [L. *hydratus*]. Combined with water; forming a hydrate or a hydroxide.

hydration (hi-dra′shun). 1. The act of combining or causing to combine with water. 2. The condition of being combined with water.

hydraulics (hi-draw′liks) [*hydr-* + Gr. *aulos* pipe]. The branch of physics which treats of the action of liquids under physical laws.

hydrazine (hi′drah-zin). A colorless, gaseous diamine, $H_2N.NH_2$; also any member of a group of its substitution derivatives.

hydrazone (hi-drah-zōn). A compound formed from a sugar by the action of phenylhydrazine. It may be converted into an osazone by further treatment with phenylhydrazine.

hydremia (hi-dre′me-ah) [*hydr-* + Gr. *haima* blood]. Excess of water in the blood; a condition in which the proportion of the serum in the blood to the corpuscles is excessive.

hydrencephalocele (hi″dren-sef′ah-lo-sēl) [*hydr-*

+ *encephalocele*]. Hernial protrusion through a cranial defect of brain substance containing cerebrospinal fluid.

hydrencephalomeningocele (hi″dren-sef″ah-lo-mĕ-nin′go-sēl). Hernial protrusion through a cranial defect of the meninges containing cerebrospinal fluid and brain substance.

hydrencephalus (hi″dren-sef′ah-lus). Hydrocephalus.

hydrepigastrium (hi″drep-ĭ-gas′tre-um) [*hydr-* + *epigastrium*]. A collection of watery fluid between the peritoneum and the abdominal wall.

hydriatric (hi″dre-at′rik) [*hydr-* + Gr. *iatikos, iatrikos* healing]. Pertaining to hydrotherapy.

hydriatrics (hi″dre-at′riks). Hydrotherapy.

hydriatrist (hi″dre-at′rist). A specialist in hydrotherapy.

hydric (hi′drik). Pertaining to or combined with hydrogen; containing replaceable hydrogen.

hydride (hi′drīd) [Gr. *hydōr* water]. Any compound of hydrogen with an element or radical.

hydriodate (hi-dri′o-dāt). A salt of hydriodic acid.

hydrion (hi-dri′on). Hydrogen ion.

hydro-, hydr- [Gr. *hydōr* water]. Combining form denoting relationship to water or to hydrogen.

hydroa (hid-ro′ah). A skin disease marked by red, irregular patches on which form groups of vesicles. The disease is attended with intense itching, debility, and nervous symptoms. Called also *dermatitis herpetiformis* and *pemphigus pruriginosus*. **h. aestiva′le,** h. puerorum. **h. febri′le,** herpes simplex. **h. gestatio′nis, h. gravida′rum,** dermatitis herpetiformis occurring during pregnancy or the puerperium. **h. puero′rum, h. vaccinifor′me,** a disease of children marked by the development of vesicles upon patches of erythema and often associated with porphyrinuria. The disease may recur every summer. **h. vesiculo′sum,** herpes iris.

hydroadipsia (hi″dro-ah-dip′se-ah) [*hydro-* + *a* neg. + Gr. *dipsa* thirst]. Absence of thirst for water.

hydroaestivale (hi″dro-es-tĭ-va′le). Hydroa puerorum.

hydroappendix (hi″dro-ah-pen′diks). Distention of the vermiform appendix with a watery fluid.

hydrobilirubin (hi″dro-bil″ĭ-ru′bin) [*hydro-* + *bilirubin*]. A brownish-red pigment, $C_{32}H_{40}N_4O_7$, derivable from bilirubin by reduction. It is believed to be identical with stercobilin and urobilin.

hydroblepharon (hi″dro-blef′ah-ron) [*hydro-* + Gr. *blepharon* eyelid]. Edema of the eyelids.

hydrobromate (hi″dro-bro′māt). Any salt of hydrobromic acid.

hydrobromide (hi″dro-bro′mid). An addition salt of hydrobromic acid. Cf. *hydrochloride*.

hydrocal (hi′dro-kal). Trade mark for an artificial stone used in dentistry.

hydrocalycosis (hi″dro-kal″ĭ-ko′sis) [*hydro-* + *calyx* + *-osis*]. Distention of a single calyx of the kidney with accumulated urine.

hydrocarbarism (hi″dro-kar′bar-izm). Hydrocarbonism.

hydrocarbon (hi″dro-kar′bon). An organic compound that contains carbon and hydrogen only. The hydrocarbons are divided into *alicyclic, aliphatic,* and *aromatic* hydrocarbons, according to the arrangement of the atoms and the chemical properties of the compounds. **alicyclic h.,** a hydrocarbon that has cyclic structure and aliphatic properties. **aliphatic h.,** a hydrocarbon in which no carbon atoms are joined to form a ring. **aromatic h.,** a hydrocarbon that has cyclic structure and a closed conjugated system of double bonds that gives it the characteristic chemical properties of the parent aromatic hydrocarbon, benzene (C_6H_6); other typical aromatic hydrocarbons are toluene (C_7H_8), naphthalene ($C_{10}H_8$), anthracene ($C_{14}H_{10}$), and phenanthrene ($C_{14}H_{10}$). **carcinogenic h.,** a condensed nuclear aromatic hydrocarbon that tends to cause cancer when applied to the skin or when it is otherwise administered. **Diels' h.,** methyl cyclopentenophenanthrene. **saturated h.,** a hydrocarbon that has the maximum number of hydrogen atoms for a given carbon structure, such as methane, ethane, propane, cyclopropane, and the butanes. **unsaturated h.,** an aliphatic or alicyclic hydrocarbon that has less than the maximum number of hydrogen atoms for a given carbon structure, such as ethylene, acetylene, propylene, cyclohexene, and the butenes.

hydrocarbonism (hi″dro-kar′bon-izm). Poisoning by hydrocarbons.

hydrocardia (hi″dro-kar′de-ah). Hydropericardium.

hydrocele (hi′dro-sēl) [*hydro-* + Gr. *kēlē* tumor]. A circumscribed collection of fluid, especially a collection of fluid in the tunica vaginalis of the testicle or along the spermatic cord. **cervical h.,** a serous dilatation of a persistent cervical cleft or duct, or sometimes of a deep cervical lymph space. **chylous h.,** a form in which the fluid is milky in appearance. **h. col′li,** cervical h. **congenital h.,** hydrocele in the unobliterated canal between the peritoneal cavity and that of the tunica vaginalis. **diffused h.,** a collection of fluid diffused in the loose connective tissue of the spermatic cord. **Dupuytren's h.,** bilocular hydrocele of the tunica vaginalis testis. **encysted h.,** one which occurs in cysts outside the cavity of the tunica vaginalis testis. **h. fem′inae,** an affection of the round ligament of the female resembling ordinary hydrocele. **funicular h.,** hydrocele of the tunica vaginalis of the spermatic cord in a space closed toward the testis and open toward the peritoneal cavity. **Gibbon's h.,** hydrocele with voluminous hernia. **hernial h.,** distention of the hernial sac with a fluid. **Maunoir's h.,** cervical hydrocele. **h. mulie′bris,** a watery dilatation of the canal of Nuck. **h. of neck,** cervical h. **Nuck's h.,** h. muliebris. **scrotal h.,** a circumscribed collection of fluid in the scrotum. **h. spina′lis,** spina bifida.

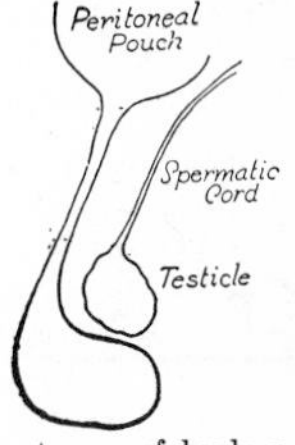

Anatomy of hydrocele (Morse).

hydrocelectomy (hi″dro-se-lek′to-me) [*hydrocele* + Gr. *ektomē* excision]. Excision of a hydrocele.

hydrocenosis (hi″dro-se-no′sis) [*hydro-* + Gr. *kenōsis* emptying]. Removal of a dropsical fluid.

hydrocephalic (hi″dro-se-fal′ik). Pertaining to or affected with hydrocephalus.

hydrocephalocele (hi″dro-sef′ah-lo-sēl). Hydrencephalocele.

hydrocephaloid (hi″dro-sef′ah-loid). 1. Resembling hydrocephalus. 2. A state resembling infantile hydrocephalus, but attended with depression of the fontanels: it follows diarrhea.

hydrocephalus (hi-dro-sef′ah-lus) [*hydro-* + Gr. *kephalē* head]. A condition characterized by abnormal accumulation of fluid in the cranial vault, accompanied by enlargement of the head, prominence of the forehead, atrophy of the brain, mental weakness, and convulsions. **acute h.,** tubercular meningitis. **chronic h.,** a slowly progressing form occurring in infancy. **communicating h.,** hydrocephalus in which there is no obstruction in the ventricular system and cerebrospinal fluid passes readily out of the brain into the spinal canal. **congenital h.,** chronic h. **external h.,** abnormal accumulation of fluid between the brain and dura mater. **infantile h.,** chronic h. **internal h.,** abnormal accumulation of fluid in the ventricular system of the brain. **noncommunicating h., obstructive h.,** hydrocephalus with obstruction in the ventricular system, preventing free passage of the cerebrospinal fluid from the brain into the spinal canal. **otitic h.,** acute hydrocephalus caused by spread of the inflammation of otitis media to the cranial cavity. **primary h.,** chronic h. **secondary h.,** hydrocephalus resulting from meningitis or obstruction of the venous outflow.

hydrochinonuria (hi″dro-kin″o-nu′re-ah). The presence of hydroquinone in the urine as a result of administration of salol, resorcinol, phenol, or uva-ursi.

hydrochlorate (hi″dro-klo′rāt). Hydrochloride.

hydrochloride (hi″dro-klo′rīd). An addition salt of hydrochloric acid, for instance with quinine, the hydrochloric acid adds on in such a way that the valence of the basic nitrogen is changed from three to five. In a sense the alkaloid hydrochlorides may be looked on as derivatives of ammonium chloride:

$$\begin{matrix} H \\ H \\ H \end{matrix} \gt N \lt \begin{matrix} H \\ Cl \end{matrix}$$

hydrochlorothiazide (hi″dro-klo″ro-thi′ah-zīd). Chemical name: 6-chloro-7-sulfamyl-2H-3,4-dihydro-1,2,4-benzothiadiazine-1,1-dioxide: used as a diuretic and antihypertensive.

hydrocholecystis (hi″dro-ko″le-sis′tis) [*hydro-* + Gr. *cholē* bile + *kystis* bladder]. Distention of the gallbladder with watery fluid.

hydrocholeresis (hi″dro-ko″ler-e′sis) [*hydro-* + Gr. *cholē* bile + *hairesis* a taking]. Choleresis characterized by increase in water output, or induction of the excretion of bile relatively low in specific gravity, viscosity, and total solid content.

hydrocholeretic (hi″dro-ko″ler-et′ik). Pertaining to, characterized by, or producing hydrocholeresis.

hydrocholesterol (hi″dro-ko-les′ter-ol). A reduced form of cholesterol.

hydrocinchonidine (hi″dro-sin-kon′ĭ-din). An alkaloid, $C_{19}H_{24}ON_2$, isomeric with cinchonine.

hydrocirsocele (hi″dro-sir′so-sēl) [*hydro-* + *cirsocele*]. Hydrocele combined with varicocele.

hydrocodone (hi″dro-ko′dōn). Dihydrocodeinone.

hydrocollidine (hi″dro-kol′ĭ-din) [*hydro-* + *collidine*]. A poisonous oily ptomaine, $C_8H_{13}N$, from nicotine, decayed flesh, and from stale fish.

hydrocolloid (hi″dro-kol′loid) [*hydro-* + *colloid*]. A colloid system in which water is the dispersion medium. **irreversible h.,** a hydrocolloid which can be converted from the sol to the gel condition but cannot be reverted to a sol by any simple means. **reversible h.,** a hydrocolloid which can be reverted from the gel to the sol condition by increase in temperature.

hydrocolpos (hi″dro-kol′pos) [*hydro-* + Gr. *kolpos* vagina]. A collection of watery fluid in the vagina.

hydroconion (hi″dro-ko′ne-on) [*hydro-* + Gr. *konis* dust]. An atomizer or vaporizer for throwing liquids in a fine spray.

hydrocortamate (hi″dro-kor′tah-māt). Chemical name: 17-hydroxycorticosterone-21-diethylaminoacetate: used in treatment of dermatoses.

hydrocortisone (hi″dro-kor′tĭ-sōn). A compound, 4-pregnene-3,20-dione-11β,17α,21-triol, an adrenocortical steroid with glucogenic action, isolated from adrenal glands or produced synthetically. In physiological studies it is commonly referred to as cortisol. **h. acetate,** the acetate ester of hydrocortisone, $C_{23}H_{32}O_6$, a poorly absorbed compound, used topically or by intra-articular injection. **h. tertiary-butylacetate,** an ester of hydrocortisone especially suited for intrasynovial use.

hydrocortone (hi″dro-kor′tōn). Trade mark for preparations of hydrocortisone.

hydrocyanism (hi″dro-si′an-izm). Poisoning with hydrocyanic acid.

hydrocyst (hi′dro-sist) [*hydro-* + Gr. *kystis* sac, bladder]. A cyst with watery contents.

hydrocystadenoma (hi″dro-sis″tad-e-no′mah). Syringocystadenoma.

hydrocystoma (hi″dro-sis-to′mah) [*hydro-* + Gr. *kystis* cyst + *-ōma* tumor]. A cystic condition of the sweat glands of the face, resulting from excessive exposure to high temperatures and humidity.

hydrodiascope (hi″dro-di′ah-skōp) [*hydro-* + Gr. *dia* through + *skopein* to see]. An instrument used in the treatment of astigmatism.

hydrodictiotomy (hi″dro-dik″te-ot′o-me). An operation for displacement of the retina (R. Secondi).

hydrodiffusion (hi″dro-dĭ-fu′zhun). Diffusion in an aqueous medium.

hydrodipsia (hi″dro-dip′se-ah). Thirst for water.

hydrodipsomania (hi″dro-dip″so-ma′ne-ah). An epileptic condition characterized by attacks of insatiable thirst.

hydrodiuresis (hi″dro-di″u-re′sis) [*hydro-* + *diuresis*]. Copious secretion of urine of low specific gravity.

hydrodiuril (hi″dro-di′u-ril). Trade mark for a preparation of hydrochlorothiazide.

hydrodynamics (hi″dro-di-nam′iks) [*hydro-* + *dynamics*]. That branch of the science of mechanics which treats of liquids.

hydroelectric (hi″dro-e-lek′trik). Pertaining to water and electricity.

hydroelectrization (hi″dro-e-lek″tri-za′shun). Treatment by the hydroelectric bath.

hydroencephalocele (hi″dro-en-sef′ah-lo-sēl). Hydrencephalocele.

hydroergotinine (hi″dro-er-got′ĭ-nin). Ergotoxine.

hydrogel (hi′dro-jel). A gel that has water as its dispersion medium.

hydrogen (hi′dro-jen) [*hydro-* + Gr. *gennan* to produce]. The lightest element. It is an odorless, tasteless, colorless gas which is inflammable and explosive when mixed with air. It is found in water and in all organic compounds. Its ion is the active constituent of all acids. Its symbol is H; atomic number, 1; atomic weight, 1.00797; and specific gravity, 0.069. Hydrogen exists in three isotopes: ordinary hydrogen is the mass 1 isotope; also called *protium;* heavy hydrogen is the mass 2 isotope, also called *deuterium* or *deutium;* mass 3 isotope is *tritium.* **arseniuretted h.** See under *arsine.* **h. dioxide,** h. peroxide. **h. disulfide,** an ill-smelling liquid, H_2S_2. **double weight h., heavy h.** See *hydrogen.* **h. monoxide,** water, H_2O. **h. peroxide,** a strongly disinfectant cleansing and bleaching liquid, H_2O_2; used mainly as a wash or spray. **h. selenide,** a poisonous gas, H_2Se: its inhalation causes an obstinate coryza and destroys the sense of smell. **h. sulfide, sulfuretted h.,** hydrosulfuric acid.

hydrogenase (hi′dro-jen-ās). An enzyme which catalyzes the reduction of various substances by means of molecular hydrogen. **fumaric h.,** a yellow enzyme which catalyzes the reduction of fumaric acid to succinic acid.

hydrogenate (hi′dro-jen-āt). To cause to combine with hydrogen; to reduce.

hydrogenide (hi′dro-jen-id). A hydride.

hydrogenize (hi′dro-jen-īz). Hydrogenate.

hydrogenlyase (hi″dro-jen-li′ās). An adaptive enzyme formed by many strains of *Escherichia coli* that catalyzes the breakdown of formic acid to carbon dioxide and hydrogen.

hydrogenoid (hi-droj′ĕ-noid). A homeopathic term denoting a constitution or temperament that will not tolerate much moisture.

Hydrogenomonas (hi-dro″jĕ-no-mo′nas). A genus of microorganisms of the family Methanomonadaceae, suborder Pseudomonadineae, order Pseudomonadales, occurring as facultative chemoautotrophic short rod-shaped cells obtaining energy from the oxidation of hydrogen. It includes four species, *H. fa′cilis, H. fla′va, H. panto′tropha,* and *H. vit′rea.*

hydroglossa (hi″dro-glos′ah) [*hydro-* + Gr. *glōssa* tongue]. Ranula.

hydrogymnasium (hi″dro-jim-na′ze-um). A pool for exercise under water.

hydrogymnastic (hi″dro-jim-nas′tik). Pertaining to exercises performed in the water.

hydrohematonephrosis (hi″dro-hem″ah-to-ne-fro′sis) [*hydro-* + Gr. *haima* blood + *nephros* kidney]. Distention of the pelvis of the kidney with an accumulation of bloody urine.

hydrohepatosis (hi″dro-hep″ah-to′sis) [*hydro-* + Gr. *hēpar* liver]. A condition in which there is a collection of watery fluid in the liver.

hydrohymenitis (hi″dro-hi″men-i′tis) [*hydro-* + Gr. *hymēn* membrane + *-itis*]. The inflammation of a serous membrane.

hydrokinesitherapy (hi″dro-ki-ne″se-ther′ah-pe) [*hydro-* + Gr. *kinēsis* movement + *therapeia* treatment]. Treatment by under-water exercise.

hydrokinetic (hi″dro-ki-net′ik). Relating to the movement of water or other fluid, as in a whirlpool bath.

hydrokinetics (hi″dro-ki-net′iks) [*hydro-* + Gr. *kinēsis* motion]. That branch of mechanics which treats of fluids in motion.

hydrokollag (hi″dro-kol′ag). A suspension of finely particulate graphite, used in experimental study of ciliary action and lymphatic drainage.

hydrol (hi′drol). 1. Hydrone. 2. A final mother liquor obtained in the manufacture of glucose from cornstarch.

hydrolabile (hi″dro-la′bil). Having a tendency to lose weight under carbohydrate or salt restriction or following infections or gastrointestinal disease.

hydrolability (hi″dro-lah-bil′ĭ-te) [*hydro-* + L. *labilis* liable to change]. A condition in which tissue fluids tend to vary in quantity.

hydrolabyrinth (hi″dro-lab′ĭ-rinth). Abnormal accumulation of endolymph in the inner ear.

hydrolase (hi′dro-lās). An enzyme that catalyzes the hydrolytic cleavage of a compound, such as esters, peptides, glycosides, and amides. **guanosine h.,** an enzyme which catalyzes the conversion of guanosine into guanine and sugar.

hydrology (hi-drol′o-je) [*hydro-* + *-logy*]. The sum of knowledge regarding water and its uses.

hydrolose (hi′dro-lōs). Trade mark for a preparation of methylcellulose.

hydrolymph (hi′dro-limf) [*hydro-* + *lymph*]. The thin, watery nutritive fluid of certain of the lower animals.

hydrolysate (hi-drol′ĭ-zāt). A compound produced by hydrolysis. **protein h.,** a mixture of amino acids prepared by splitting a protein with acid, alkali, or enzyme. Such preparations provide the nutritive equivalent of the original material (casein, lactalbumin, fibrin, etc.) in the form of its constituent amino acids: used in special diets or for patients unable to take the ordinary food proteins.

hydrolysis (hi-drol′ĭ-sis), pl. *hydrol′yses* [*hydro-* + Gr. *lysis* dissolution]. The splitting of a compound into fragments by the addition of water, the hydroxyl group being incorporated in one fragment, and the hydrogen atom in the other.

hydrolyst (hi′dro-list). An agent that promotes hydrolysis.

hydrolyte (hi′dro-līt). A substance undergoing hydrolysis.

hydrolytic (hi-dro-lit′ik). Pertaining to, characterized by, or promoting hydrolysis.

hydrolyze (hi′dro-līz). To subject to hydrolysis.

hydroma (hi-dro′mah). Hygroma.

hydromania (hi″dro-ma′ne-ah) [*hydro-* + Gr. *mania* madness]. Mental disorder marked by a tendency to commit suicide by drowning.

hydromassage (hi″dro-mah-sahzh′). Massage by means of moving water.

hydromeningitis (hi″dro-men″in-ji′tis) [*hydro-* + *meningitis*]. 1. Meningitis with serous effusion. 2. Descemetitis or cyclitis.

hydromeningocele (hi″dro-mĕ-nin′go-sēl) [*hydro-* + Gr. *mēninx* membrane + *kēlē* hernia]. Protrusion of the meninges through a defect in the skull or spine, forming a sac containing cerebrospinal fluid.

hydrometer (hi-drom′e-ter) [*hydro-* + Gr. *metron* measure]. An instrument for determining the specific gravities of a fluid.

hydrometra (hi″dro-me′trah) [*hydro-* + Gr. *mētra* uterus]. A collection of watery fluid in the uterus.

hydrometric (hi″dro-met′rik). Pertaining to hydrometry.

hydrometrocolpos (hi″dro-me″tro-kol′pos) [*hydro-* + Gr. *mētra* uterus + *kolpos* vagina]. A collection of watery fluid in the uterus and vagina.

hydrometry (hi-drom′e-tre). The measurement of the specific gravity of a fluid by means of the hydrometer.

hydromicrocephaly (hi″dro-mi″kro-sef′ah-le). Microcephaly with an abnormal amount of cerebrospinal fluid.

hydromphalus (hi-drom′fah-lus) [*hydro-* + Gr. *omphalos* navel]. A cystic accumulation of watery fluid at the umbilicus.

hydromyelia (hi″dro-mi-e′le-ah). A pathologic condition characterized by accumulation of fluid in the enlarged central canal of the spinal cord.

hydromyelocele (hi″dro-mi-el′o-sēl) [*hydro-* + *myelocele*]. Hydromyelomeningocele.

hydromyelomeningocele (hi″dro-mi″ĕ-lo-mĕ-nin′go-sēl) [*hydro-* + Gr. *myelos* marrow + *mēninx* membrane + *kēlē* hernia]. A defect of the spine marked by protrusion of the membranes and tissue of the spinal cord, forming a fluid-filled sac.

hydromyoma (hi″dro-mi-o′mah) [*hydro-* + *myoma*]. A cystic (usually uterine) myoma containing fluid.

hydronaphthylamine (hi″dro-naf″thil-am′in). A powerfully mydriatic substance, $C_{10}H_{11}NH_2$.

hydrone (hi′drōn). The unassociated water molecule, H_2O.

hydronephrosis (hi″dro-ne-fro′sis) [*hydro-* + Gr. *nephros* kidney]. Distention of the pelvis and calyces of the kidney with urine, as a result of obstruction of the ureter, with accompanying atrophy of the parenchyma of the organ. **closed h.,** a permanent condition, resulting from complete obstruction of the ureter. **open h.,** an intermittent condition, resulting from sporadic or incomplete obstruction of the ureter.

hydronephrotic (hi″dro-ne-frot′ik). Pertaining to or characterized by hydronephrosis.

hydro-oligocythemia (hi″dro-ol″ĭ-go-si-the′me-ah) [*hydro-* + Gr. *oligos* few + *kytos* hollow vessel + *haima* blood]. A condition characterized by both an absolute increase in the fluid portion of the blood and an absolute decrease in the number of erythrocytes.

hydropancreatosis (hi″dro-pan″kre-ah-to′sis). The accumulation of watery fluid in the pancreas.

hydroparasalpinx (hi″dro-par″ah-sal′pinks) [*hydro-* + Gr. *para* beside + *salpinx* tube]. A collection of watery fluid in the wall of the uterine tube.

hydroparotitis (hi″dro-par″o-ti′tis). Distention of the parotid gland with watery fluid.

hydropathic (hi″dro-path′ik). Pertaining to hydropathy.

hydropathy (hi-drop′ah-the) [*hydro-* + Gr. *pathos* disease]. Treatment of disease by the application of water; particularly a system of treatment which professes to cure all diseases by the use of water; water cure.

hydropenia (hi″dro-pe′ne-ah) [*hydro-* + Gr. *penia* poverty]. Deficiency of water in the body.

hydropenic (hi′dro-pe″nik). Relating to hydropenia.

hydropericarditis (hi″dro-per″ĭ-kar-di′tis). Pericarditis attended with a watery effusion in the pericardial sac.

hydropericardium (hi″dro-per″ĭ-kar′de-um) [*hydro-* + *pericardium*]. Abnormal accumulation of serous fluid in the pericardial cavity.

hydroperinephrosis (hi″dro-per″ĭ-ne-fro′sis)

[*hydro-* + Gr. *peri* around + *nephros* kidney + *-osis*]. A collection of fluid in the retroperitoneal connective tissue and opening into the pelvis of the kidney.

hydroperion (hi″dro-per′e-on) [*hydro-* + Gr. *peri* around + *ōon* egg]. The fluid between the decidua reflexa and the decidua vera.

hydroperitoneum (hi″dro-per″ĭ-to-ne′um) [*hydro-* + *peritoneum*]. Ascites, or abnormal accumulation of fluid in the peritoneal cavity.

hydroperitonia (hi″dro-per″ĭ-to′ne-ah). Ascites.

hydropexia (hi″dro-pek′se-ah). Hydropexis.

hydropexic (hi″dro-pek′sik) [*hydro-* + Gr. *pēxis* fixation]. Fixing or holding water; pertaining to the holding of water.

hydropexis (hi″dro-pek′sis). The fixation or holding of water.

hydrophagocytosis (hi″dro-fag″o-si-to′sis) [*hydro-* + *phagocytosis*]. The absorption by macrophages of plasma surrounding them.

Hydrophidae (hi-drof′ĭ-de). A family of poisonous sea snakes of the Indian and tropical Pacific oceans.

hydrophil (hi′dro-fil). Hydrophilic.

hydrophilia (hi-dro-fil′e-ah) [*hydro-* + Gr. *philein* to love + *-ia*]. The property of absorbing water.

hydrophilic (hi″dro-fil′ik). Readily absorbing moisture; hygroscopic.

hydrophilism (hi-drof′ĭ-lizm). Hydrophilia.

hydrophilous (hi-drof′ĭ-lus). Hydrophilic.

hydrophobia (hi″dro-fo′be-ah) [*hydro-* + Gr. *phobos* fear + *-ia*]. Rabies. **paralytic h.,** rabies with symptoms not unlike those of acute ascending paralysis.

hydrophobic (hi″dro-fo′bik). 1. Pertaining to or affected with hydrophobia. 2. Not readily absorbing water, or being adversely affected by water, as a hydrophobic colloid.

hydrophobin (hi″dro-fo′bin). Lyssin.

hydrophobophobia (hi″dro-fo″bo-fo′be-ah) [*hydrophobia* + Gr. *phobos* fear + *-ia*]. Lyssophobia.

hydrophorograph (hi″dro-fo′ro-graf) [*hydro-* + Gr. *phora* a being borne, or carried along + *graphein* to record]. An instrument for measuring and recording the pressure and/or flow of a fluid, especially the flow of urine or the pressure of the spinal fluid.

hydrophthalmia (hi″drof-thal′me-ah). Hydrophthalmos.

hydrophthalmos (hi″drof-thal′mos) [*hydro-* + Gr. *ophthalmos* eye]. Dropsy of the eye; distention of the eyeball by a watery effusion, producing buphthalmos, keratoglobus, staphyloma, etc. **h. ante′rior,** that which affects the anterior portion of the eyeball only. **h. poste′rior,** that affecting the posterior part of the eyeball only. **h. tota′lis,** that which affects the entire eyeball.

hydrophthalmus (hi″drof-thal′mus). Hydrophthalmos.

hydrophysometra (hi″dro-fi″so-me′trah) [*hydro-* + *physometra*]. Physohydrometra.

hydropic (hi-drop′ik) [L. *hydropicus;* Gr. *hydrōpikos*]. Pertaining to or affected with dropsy.

hydropigenous (hi″dro-pij′e-nus). Causing dropsy.

hydroplasma (hi″dro-plaz′mah) [*hydro-* + Gr. *plasma* something formed]. The watery or liquid part of the protoplasm.

hydroplasmia (hi″dro-plaz′me-ah). A thinning or dilution (increased water content) of the blood plasma.

hydropneumatosis (hi″dro-nu″mah-to′sis) [*hydro-* + Gr. *pneumatōsis* inflation]. A collection of fluid and gas within the tissues.

hydropneumogony (hi″dro-nu-mo′go-ne) [*hydro-* + Gr. *pneuma* air + *gony* knee]. The injection of air into a joint with a view to obtaining information with regard to the presence of effusion in the joint.

hydropneumopericardium (hi″dro-nu″mo-per″ĭ-kar′de-um) [*hydro-* + Gr. *pneuma* air + *pericardium*]. A collection of watery fluid and gas within the pericardium.

hydropneumoperitoneum (hi″dro-nu″mo-per″ĭ-to-ne′um) [*hydro-* + Gr. *pneuma* air + *peritoneum*]. A collection of watery fluid and gas in the peritoneal cavity.

hydropneumothorax (hi″dro-nu″mo-tho′raks) [*hydro-* + Gr. *pneuma* air + *thōrax* chest]. A collection of fluid and gas within the pleural cavity.

hydroporphin (hi″dro-por′fin). A partially or fully reduced porphyrin or porphin; a porphyrinogen.

hydroposia (hi″dro-po′ze-ah) [*hydro-* + Gr. *posis* drinking + *-ia*]. The drinking of water.

hydropotherapy (hi″dro-po-ther′ah-pe) [Gr. *hydrōps* dropsy + *therapeia* treatment]. The therapeutic injection of ascitic fluid.

hydrops (hi′drops) [L.; Gr. *hydrōps*]. The abnormal accumulation of serous fluid in the tissues or in a body cavity. Called also *dropsy.* **h. abdom′inis,** ascites. **h. ad mat′ulam,** polyuria. **h. am′nii,** polyhydramnios. **h. an′tri,** effusion of serous fluid into the maxillary sinus. **h. artic′uli,** hydrarthrosis. **h. asthmat′icus,** beriberi. **endolymphatic h.,** Meniere's syndrome. **fetal h., h. feta′lis,** accumulation of fluid in the entire body of the newborn infant, in hemolytic disease caused by antibodies present in the blood of the Rh-negative mother. **h. follic′uli,** accumulation of fluid in the graafian follicle. **h. hypos′trophos,** angioneurotic edema. **h. labyrin′thi, labyrinthine h.,** Meniere's syndrome. **h. pericar′dii,** hydropericardium. **h. spu′rius,** pseudomyxoma peritonaei. **h. tu′bae,** hydrosalpinx. **h. tu′bae prof′luens,** a condition in which the abdominal opening of the uterine tube becomes closed, and the tube may reach enormous proportions as it fills with serum; peristaltic action of the tube causes colicky pain, until the fluid escapes through the uterine opening. Called also *intermittent hydrosalpinx.*

hydropyonephrosis (hi″dro-pi″o-ne-fro′sis [*hydro-* + Gr. *pyon* pus + *nephros* kidney + *-osis*]. The accumulation of urine and pus in the pelvis of the kidney.

hydrorachis (hi-dror′ah-kis) [*hydro-* + Gr. *rhachis* spine]. A collection of water in the vertebral canal.

hydrorachitis (hi″dro-rah-ki′tis) [*hydro-* + Gr. *rhachis* spine + *-itis*]. Inflammation within the vertebral canal, attended with a watery effusion.

hydrorheostat (hi″dro-re′o-stat) [*hydro-* + *rheostat*]. A rheostat in which resistance is furnished by water.

hydrorrhea (hi″dro-re′ah) [*hydro-* + Gr. *rhoia* flow]. A copious watery discharge. **h. gravida′rum,** a periodic or intermittent discharge of clear, yellowish, or bloody fluid from the uterus, caused by escape of amniotic fluid or resulting from decidual metritis. **nasal h.,** watery discharge from the nose.

hydrosalpinx (hi″dro-sal′pinks) [*hydro-* + Gr. *salpinx* trumpet]. A collection of watery fluid in a uterine tube, occurring as the end-stage of pyosalpinx. **h. follicula′ris,** hydrosalpinx in which there is no central cystic cavity, the lumen being broken up into compartments as the result of fusion of the tubal plicae. **intermittent h.,** hydrops tubae profluens. **h. sim′plex,** hydrosalpinx characterized by excessive distention and thinning of the wall of the tube, the plicae being few and widely separated.

hydrosarcocele (hi″dro-sar′ko-sēl) [*hydro-* + *sarcocele*]. Combined hydrocele and sarcocele.

hydroscheocele (hi-dros′ke-o-sēl) [*hydro-* + Gr. *oscheon* scrotum + *kēlē* hernia]. A scrotal hernia containing a collection of serous fluid.

hydroscope (hi″dro-skōp) [*hydro-* + Gr. *skopein* to examine]. An instrument for detecting the presence of water.

hydrosis (hi-dro′sis). Hidrosis.

hydrosol (hi′dro-sol). A sol in which the continuous phase (dispersion medium) is water.

hydrosoluble (hi″dro-sol′u-b'l). Soluble in water.

hydrosphygmograph (hi-dro-sfig′mo-graf) [*hydro-* + Gr. *sphygmos* pulse + *graphein* to record]. A sphygmograph with water for an index.

hydrospirometer (hi″dro-spi-rom′e-ter) [*hydro-* + L. *spirare* to breathe + Gr. *metron* measure]. A spirometer in which a column of water serves as an index.

hydrostabile (hi″dro-sta′bil). Preserving a stable weight under diet restrictions or gastrointestinal disease. Cf. *hydrolabile.*

hydrostat (hi′dro-stat) [*hydro-* + Gr. *histanai* to halt]. A device by which the height of fluid in a container (column or reservoir) is regulated.

hydrostatic (hi″dro-stat′ik) [*hydro-* + Gr. *statikos* standing]. Pertaining to a liquid in a state of equilibrium.

hydrostatics (hi″dro-stat′iks). The science of liquids in a state of rest or equilibrium.

hydrosudopathy (hi″dro-su-dop′ah-the) [*hydro-* + L. *sudor* sweat + Gr. *pathos* disease]. Hydrosudotherapy.

hydrosudotherapy (hi″dro-su″do-ther′ah-pe). Hydrotherapy with the induction of perspiration.

hydrosynthesis (hi″dro-sin′the-sis). A chemical reaction in which water is formed.

hydrosyringomyelia (hi″dro-sĭ-ring″go-mi-e′le-ah) [*hydro-* + Gr. *syrinx* tube + *myelos* marrow]. Coexistence of hydromyelia and syringomyelia.

hydrotaxis (hi″dro-tak′sis) [*hydro-* + Gr. *taxis* arrangement]. An orientation movement of motile organisms or cells in response to stimulation by water or moisture.

Hydrothaea (hi″dro-the′ah). A genus of flies. **H. meteor′ica,** a species which attacks the eyes and nostrils of man and animals.

hydrotherapeutics (hi″dro-ther″ah-pu′tiks). Hydrotherapy.

hydrotherapy (hi-dro-ther′ah-pe) [*hydro-* + Gr. *therapeia* service done to the sick]. The application of water in any form, either internally or externally, in the treatment of disease.

hydrothermic (hi″dro-ther′mik). Relating to the temperature effects of water, as in hot baths.

hydrothionammonemia (hi″dro-thi″o-nam″o-ne′me-ah) [*hydro-* + Gr. *theion* sulfur + *ammonium* + *haima* blood]. The occurrence of ammonium hydrosulfide in the blood.

hydrothionemia (hi″dro-thi″o-ne′me-ah) [*hydro-* + Gr. *theion* sulfur + *haima* blood]. The presence of hydrogen sulfide in the blood.

hydrothionuria (hi″dro-thi″o-nu′re-ah) [*hydro-* + Gr. *theion* sulfur + *ouron* urine + *-ia*]. The presence of hydrogen sulfide in the urine.

hydrothorax (hi″dro-tho′raks) [*hydro-* + Gr. *thorax* chest]. A collection of watery fluid in the pleural cavity. **chylous h.,** the presence of chyle in the thoracic cavity, due to a wound or rupture of the thoracic duct.

hydrotis (hi-dro′tis) [*hydro-* + Gr. *ous* ear]. A watery effusion within the ear.

hydrotomy (hi-drot′o-me) [*hydro-* + Gr. *tomē* a cutting]. The dissection or separation of parts by the forcible injection of water.

hydrotropism (hi″dro-tro′pizm) [*hydro-* + Gr. *tropē* a turn, turning]. A growth response of a nonmotile organism elicited by the presence of water or moisture.

hydrotympanum (hi″dro-tim′pah-num) [*hydro-* + *tympanum*]. A collection of watery fluid in the middle ear.

hydro-ureter (hi″dro-u-re′ter). Abnormal distention of the ureter with urine or with a watery fluid.

hydro-ureterosis (hi″dro-u-re″ter-o′sis). Hydroureter.

hydro-uria (hi″dro-u′re-ah) [*hydro-* + Gr. *ouron* urine + *-ia*]. Increase in the amount of urinary secretion with normal or reduced amount of solids.

hydrous (hi′drus). Containing water.

hydrovarium (hi″dro-va′re-um) [*hydro-* + L. *ovarium* ovary]. A collection of serous fluid in an ovary.

hydroxide (hi-drok′sīd). Any compound of hydroxyl (OH) with another radical.

hydroxidion (hi-drok″sĭ-di′on). Hydroxyl ion.

hydroxy- (hi-drok′se). A prefix in chemical terms indicating presence of the univalent radical, OH.

hydroxyacetanilide (hi-drok″se-as″ĕ-tan′ĭ-lid). Acetaminophen.

hydroxyamphetamine (hi-drok″se-am-fet′ah-min). Chemical name: p-(2-aminopropyl)phenol: used as a sympathomimetic, nasal decongestant, pressor, and mydriatic.

hydroxyapatite (hi-drok″se-ap′ah-tīt). A compound, $Ca_{10}(PO_4)_6(OH)_2$, probably the main inorganic constituent of bone and teeth.

hydroxybenzene (hi-drok″se-ben′zēn). Phenol.

hydroxychloroquine (hi-drok′se-klo′ro-kwin). Chemical name: 7-chloro-4-{4-[ethyl(2-hydroxyethyl)amino]-1-methylbutylamino}-quinoline: used as a suppressant for lupus erythematosus.

17-hydroxycorticosterone (hi-drok″se-kor″tĭ-ko′ster-ōn). Cortisol.

hydroxydione (hi-drok″se-di′ōn). Chemical name: 21-hydroxypregnane-3,20-dione: used as a basal anesthetic.

hydroxyestrin benzoate (hi-drok″se-es′trin ben′zo-āt). Progynon B.

hydroxyethylamine (hi-drok″se-eth″il-am′in). A base found in kephalin.

hydroxyethylapocupreine (hi-drok″se-eth″il-ap″o-ku′pre-in). A quinine derivative used in the treatment of pneumonia.

hydroxyethylapoquinine (hi-drok″se-eth″il-ap″o-kwi′nīn). A derivative of quinine which has been used in pneumonia.

hydroxyl (hi-drok′sil). The univalent radical OH, which, in combination with other radicals, forms hydroxides.

hydroxylamine (hi-drok″sil-am′in). An amine, NH_3O, whose hydrochloride, $NH_2OH.HCl$, is antiseptic and is used in skin diseases.

hydroxylysine (hi″drok-sil′ĭ-sin). One of the alpha amino acids, $NH_2.CH_2.CHOH(CH_2)_2.CH(NH_2).COOH$.

hydroxynervone (hi-drok″se-ner′vōn). A cerebroside occurring in brain tissue.

hydroxyphenylethylamine (hi-drok″se-phen″-il-eth″il-am′in). Tyramine.

hydroxyprogesterone (hi-drok″se-pro-jes′ter-ōn). A long-acting progesterone used in treatment of corpus luteum deficiency.

hydroxyproline (hi-drok″se-pro′lin). An amino acid, gamma-hydroxy-alpha-pyrrolidin-carboxylic acid, produced in the digestion or hydrolytic decomposition of proteins.

hydroxystilbamidine (hi-drok″se-stil-bam′ĭ-dēn). Chemical name: 2-hydroxy-4,4′-stilbenedicarboxamidine: used in treatment of leishmaniasis and blastomycosis.

hydroxytetracycline (hi-drok″se-tet″rah-si′-klēn). Oxytetracycline.

hydroxyvaline (hi-drok″se-val′in). An amino acid produced by protein hydrolysis.

hydroxyzine (hi-drok′sĭ-zēn). Chemical name: 1-(p-chlorobenzhydryl)-4[2-(2-hydroxyethoxy)-ethyl]piperazine: used as a psychotherapeutic agent.

hydruria (hi-droo′re-ah) [*hydr-* + Gr. *ouron* urine + *-ia*]. Polyuria; diabetes insipidus.

hydruric (hi-droo′rik). Characterized by hydruria.

hyenanchin (hi″ĕ-nan′kin). A poisonous substance from the outer envelopes of the fruit of *Toxicodendron capense,* of South Africa. It somewhat resembles strychnine in its action.

hyetometry (hi″ĕ-tom′e-tre) [Gr. *hyetos* rain + *metron* measure]. Measurement of the rainfall.

Hygeia (hi-je′ah) [Gr. *Hygieia*]. The goddess of health, one of the daughters of Æsculapius, the mythical god of healing, who assisted in the rites at the early temples of healing.

hygeiolatry (hi″je-ol′ah-tre) [Gr. *Hygieia* + *latreia* servitude]. Excessive attention to one's own health.

hygieist (hi-je′ist). Hygienist.

hygiene (hi′je-ēn) [Gr. *hygieia* health]. The science of health and of its preservation. **industrial h.,** that branch of preventive medicine which is concerned with the protection of health of the industrial population. **mental h.,** the science which deals with the development of healthy mental and emotional reactions and habits. **oral h.,** the proper care of the mouth and teeth for the maintenance of health and the prevention of disease. **sex h.,** that department of hygiene which deals with sex, sexual conduct and personal sex hygiene as these are related to individual and community health. **social h.,** that department of hygiene which deals with the promotion of sexual health, embracing personal sex hygiene, healthy marriage and family relations, and sex education. The term is sometimes used as a euphemism for venereal disease control.

hygienic (hi″je-en′ik). Pertaining to hygiene, or conducive to health.

hygienics (hi″je-en′iks). A system of principles for promoting health; hygiene.

hygienism (hi-je′en-izm). Devotion to the observance of hygienic rules.

hygienist (hi′je-en-ist). A specialist in hygiene. **dental h.,** an auxiliary member of the dental profession who has been trained in the art of removing calcareous deposits and stains from the surfaces of the teeth and in providing additional services and information on the prevention of oral disease; such persons are employed in private dental offices or are active in school or public health programs.

hygienization (hi″je-en-i-za′shun). The establishment of hygienic conditions.

hygieology (hi″je-ol′o-je) [Gr. *hygieia* health + *-logy*]. The complete science upon which the arts of hygiene and sanitation are based.

hygiogenesis (hi″je-o-jen′e-sis) [Gr. *hygiēs* healthy + *gennan* to produce]. The mechanism of the processes which lead to maintenance of health.

hygiology (hi″je-ol′o-je). Hygieology.

hygrechema (hi″gre-ke′mah). An auscultation sound caused by the presence of water.

hygremometry (hi-gre-mom′e-tre) [Gr. *hygros* moist + *haima* blood + *metron* measure]. Estimation of the dried substance of the blood for the purpose of determining the proportion of hemoglobin.

hygric (hi′grik) [Gr. *hygros* moist]. Pertaining or relating to moisture.

hygro- (hi′gro) [Gr. *hygros* moist]. Combining form meaning moist or denoting relationship to moisture.

hygroblepharic (hi″gro-blĕ-far′ik) [*hygro-* + Gr. *blepharon* eyelid]. Noting the excretory ducts of the lacrimal canals.

hygroma (hi-gro′mah), pl. *hygro′mas* or *hygro′mata* [*hygro-* + *-oma*]. A sac, cyst, or bursa distended with a fluid. **cystic h., h. cys′ticum,** an endothelium-lined, fluid-containing lesion of lymphatic origin, encountered most often in infancy and childhood, and occurring in various regions of the body, including the axilla, chest wall, and groin, but most frequently in the posterior triangle of the neck, behind the sternocleidomastoideus muscle (*h. col′li cys′ticum*). **Fleischmann's h.,** enlargement of a bursa in the floor of the mouth, to the outer side of the genioglossus muscle. **h. praepatella′re,** housemaid's knee. **subdural h.,** a hygroma situated beneath the dura mater.

hygromatous (hi-gro′mah-tus). Pertaining to or of the nature of hygroma.

hygromedry (hi-grom′ĕ-dre). Measurement of the vapor given off from a definite area of the skin.

hygrometer (hi-grom′e-ter) [*hygro-* + Gr. *metron* measure]. An instrument for measuring the moisture of the atmosphere. **hair h., Saussure's h.,** a hygrometer whose action is determined by the elongation and contraction of a hair under the influence of moisture.

hygrometric (hi″gro-met′rik). Pertaining to hygrometry.

hygrometry (hi-grom′e-tre) [*hygro-* + Gr. *metron* measure]. The measurement of the proportion of moisture in the air.

hygrophobia (hi″gro-fo′be-ah) [*hygro-* + *phobia* fear]. Morbid dread of dampness.

hygrostomia (hi″gros-to′me-ah) [*hygro-* + Gr. *stoma* mouth]. Ptyalism or salivation.

hygroton (hi′gro-ton). Trade mark for a preparation of chlorthalidone.

hyla (hi′lah). A lateral extension of the mesocele, or aqueduct of Sylvius. Called also *paraqueduct*.

hyle (hi′le) [Gr. *hylē* matter]. The primitive substance from which all matter is composed. See *protyl*.

Hylemyia (hi″lĕ-mi′ah). A genus of flies, the larvae of which infest vegetables and may be swallowed if the latter are eaten raw. *H. anti′qua*, onion root maggot. *H. bras′sicae*, the cabbage root maggot.

hylephobia (hi″lĕ-fo′be-ah) [Gr. *hylē* matter + *phobos* fear + *-ia*]. Morbid fear of materialism.

hylergography (hi″ler-gog′rah-fe) [Gr. *hylē* matter + *ergon* work + *graphein* to write]. A recording of the effect of the environmental materials on a cell.

hylic (hi′lik) [Gr. *hylē* matter]. Composed of matter: a term applied by Adami to the pulp tissues of the embryo.

hylo, hyl-, hyle- (hi′lo, hīl, hi′le) [Gr. *hylē* matter]. Combining form denoting relationship to matter (material or substance). Cf. *-yl*.

hylogenesis (hi″lo-jen′e-sis) [*hylo-* + Gr. *genesis* formation]. The formation of matter.

hylogeny (hi-loj′e-ne). Hylogenesis.

hylology (hi-lol′o-je) [*hylo-* + *-logy*]. The study of elementary or crude materials.

hyloma (hi-lo′mah) [*hyl-* + *-oma*]. A tumor formed in one of the original hylic tissues. **atypical h.,** gliosarcoma. **mesenchymal h.,** a tumor composed of tissue derived from the mesenchyma. **mesothelial h.,** a tumor formed from tissue of mesothelial origin. **typical h.,** a neuroma or glioma.

hylopathism (hi-lop′ah-thizm) [*hylo-* + Gr. *pathos* disease]. The doctrine that disease is due to changes in the constitution of matter.

hylopathist (hi-lop′ah-thist). A believer in the theory of hylopathism.

hylotropic (hi″lo-trop′ik). Pertaining to or characterized by hylotropy.

hylotropy (hi-lot′ro-pe) [Gr. *hylē* matter + *tropē* a turn, turning]. The ability of a substance to change from one physical form to another (e.g., solid to liquid, liquid to gas) without change in chemical composition.

hylozoism (hi-lo′zo-izm) [*hylo-* + Gr. *zōon* animal]. The doctrine that all matter in the universe is alive.

hymen (hi′men) [Gr. *hymēn* membrane]. [N A] The membranous fold which partially or wholly occludes the external orifice of the vagina. **annular h.,** circular g. **h. bifenestra′tus, h. bifo′ris,** a hymen with two openings side by side and a broad septum between them. **circular h.,** a hymen with a circular opening. **cribriform h.,** a hymen pierced by many small perforations. **denticular h.,** a hymen with an opening which has serrate edges. **falciform h.,** a sickle-shaped hymen. **fenestrated h.,** cribriform h. **imperforate h.,** one which completely closes the vaginal orifice. **infundibuliform h.,** a hymen that has a central opening with sloping sides. **lunar h.,** a moon-shaped hymen. **septate h., h. sep'tus,** a form of hymen in which the opening is divided by a narrow septum. **h. subsep'tus,** a form of hymen in which the opening is partially filled by a septum growing out of one wall, but not reaching the other.

hymenal (hi'men-al). Pertaining to the hymen.

hymenectomy (hi"men-ek'to-me) [Gr. *hymēn* membrane, hymen + *ektomē* excision]. Excision of the hymen.

hymenitis (hi"men-i'tis) [Gr. *hymēn* membrane + *-itis*]. Inflammation of the hymen.

hymenium (hi-me'ne-um) [*dim.* of Gr. *hymēn* membrane]. The spore-forming surface of the hyphae of fungi.

hymenolepiasis (hi"mĕ-no-lep-i'ah-sis). Infection with Hymenolepis.

Hymenolepis (hi"mĕ-nol'e-pis) [Gr. *hymēn* membrane + *lepis* rind]. A genus of cestode worms. **H. diminu'ta,** a tapeworm of rats and mice, occasionally found in man. **H. frater'na,** the rodent form of **H.** *nana.* **H. lanceola'ta,** a tapeworm of ducks and geese once reported from man. **H. muri'na,** H. *nana.* **H. na'na,** the dwarf tapeworm, a species about 1 inch long, found in the adult form in the human intestine, and frequently causing local disturbance.

hymenology (hi"men-ol'o-je) [Gr. *hymēn* membrane + *-logy*]. The sum of what is known regarding the membranes.

Hymenoptera (hi"men-op'ter-ah) [Gr. *hymēn* membrane + *pteron* wing]. An order of insects having usually two pairs of well developed wings, as the bees, wasps, ants, etc.

hymenopterism (hi"men-op'ter-izm). Poisoning by the stings or bites of insects of the order Hymenoptera, as of a bee or wasp.

hymenorrhaphy (hi"men-or'ah-fe) [Gr. *hymēn* hymen + *rhaphē* seam]. The closure of the vagina by sutures at the hymen.

hymenotome (hi-men'o-tōm) [Gr. *hymēn* membrane + *tomē* a cut]. An instrument for cutting membranes.

hymenotomy (hi"men-ot'o-me) [Gr. *hymēn* membrane + *temnein* to cut]. Surgical incision of the hymen.

hyobasioglossus (hi"o-ba"se-o-glos'us). The basal part of the hyoglossus muscle.

hyodesoxycholaneresis (hi"o-des-ok"se-ko"-lah-ner'e-sis) [*hyodesoxycholic* acid + Gr. *hairesis* a taking]. Increase in the output or elimination of hyodesoxycholic acid in the bile. Cf. *cholaneresis.*

hyo-epiglottic (hi"o-ep"ĭ-glot'ik). Pertaining to the hyoid bone and the epiglottis.

hyo-epiglottidean (hi"o-ep"ĭ-glo-tid'e-an). Hyo-epiglottic.

hyoglossal (hi"o-glos'al) [*hyo*id bone + Gr. *glōssa* tongue]. Pertaining to the hyoid bone and the tongue.

hyoid (hi'oid) [Gr. *hyoeides* U-shaped]. 1. Shaped like the Greek letter upsilon (*υ*). 2. Pertaining to the hyoid bone.

hyoscine (hi'o-sin) [L. *hyoscina*]. Scopolamine.

hyoscyamine (hi"o-si'ah-min). An alkaloid usually obtained from species of *Hyoscyamus* Linné or other genera of the family *Solanaceae:* used to produce parasympathetic blockade and in treatment of parkinsonism.

Hyoscyamus (hi"o-si'ah-mus) [L.; Gr. *hys* swine + *kyamos* bean]. A genus of solanaceous plants. The leaves, seeds, flowers, and tops of *H. ni'ger* are narcotic, mydriatic, and analgesic.

hyoscyamus (hi"o-si'ah-mus). The dried leaf of *Hyoscyamus niger:* used in tincture or extract to produce parasympathetic blockade.

hyospondylotomy (hi"o-spon"dĭ-lot'o-me) [*hyoid* + Gr. *spondylos* vertebra + *temnein* to cut]. Hypospondylotomy.

Hyostrongylus rubidus (hi"o-stron'jĭ-lus roo'-bĭ-dus). A small red worm found in the stomach of pigs.

hyothyroid (hi"o-thi'roid). Pertaining to the hyoid bone and the thyroid cartilage.

hyovertebrotomy (hi"o-ver"te-brot'o-me). Hypospondylotomy.

hypacidemia (hi-pas"ĭ-de'me-ah) [Gr. *hypo* under + *acid* + *haima* blood]. Deficiency of an acid in the blood.

hypacidity (hi"pah-sid'ĭ-te) [Gr. *hypo* under + *acidity*]. Deficiency of acid: lack of normal acidity.

hypacusia (hi"pah-ku'ze-ah). Hypacusis.

hypacusis (hi"pah-ku'sis) [Gr. *hypo* under + *akousis* hearing]. A slightly diminished acuity of the sense of hearing.

hypadrenia (hi"pad-re'ne-ah). Adrenal insufficiency.

hypalbuminemia (hi"pal-bu"mĭ-ne'me-ah). Hypoalbuminemia.

hypalbuminosis (hi"pal-bu-mĭ-no'sis). Hypoalbuminosis.

hypalgesia (hi"pal-je'ze-ah) [Gr. *hypo* under + *algēsis* pain]. Diminished sensitiveness to pain.

hypalgesic (hi"pal-je'sik). Pertaining to, characterized by, or producing hypalgesia.

hypalgetic (hi"pal-jet'ik). Hypalgesic.

hypalgia (hi-pal'je-ah). Hypalgesia.

hypamnion (hi-pam'ne-on). Hypamnios.

hypamnios (hi-pam'ne-os) [Gr. *hypo* under + *amnion*]. Deficiency of the amniotic fluid.

hypanakinesia (hi-pan"ah-ki-ne'ze-ah) [Gr. *hypo* under + *anakinēsis* exercise + *-ia*]. Deficiency of motor activity; hypokinesia. **h. ventric'uli,** deficiency of motor activity of the stomach.

hypanakinesis (hi-pan"ah-ki-ne'sis). Hypanakinesia.

hypaphorine (hi-paf'o-rin). A crystalline alkaloid originally obtained from *Erythrina hypaphorus.*

hypaphrodisia (hi-paf"ro-diz'e-ah). Decreased or deficient sexual desire.

hyparterial (hi"par-te're-al) [Gr. *hypo* under + *artēria* artery]. Beneath an artery, applied especially to the bronchi which are so situated.

hypasthenia (hi"pas-the'ne-ah) [Gr. *hypo* under + *asthenia* weakness]. Slight asthenia.

hypaxial (hi-pak'se-al). Situated ventrad to the body axis.

hypazoturia (hi-paz"o-tu're-ah) [Gr. *hypo* under + *azoturia*]. Deficient elimination of nitrogen in the urine.

hypemia (hi-pe'me-ah). Anemia.

hypencephalon (hi"pen-sef'ah-lon) [Gr. *hypo* under + *enkephalos* brain]. The mesencephalon, pons, and medulla.

hypenchyme (hi'pen-kīm). The primitive embryonic tissue formed in the cavity of the archenteron.

hypengyophobia (hi-pen"je-o-fo'be-ah) [Gr. *hypengyos* responsible + *phobos* fear + *-ia*]. Morbid fear of responsibility.

hypeosinophil (hi-pe"o-sin'o-fil) [*hypo-* + *eosinophil*]. 1. A cell or other structural element imperfectly stainable with eosin; specifically, one of the leukocyte granules which stain with eosin, but may be decolorized by alkalis or acids. 2. Imperfectly stainable with eosin.

hyper- (hi'per) [Gr. *hyper* above]. A prefix signifying above, beyond, or excessive.

hyperacanthosis (hi"per-ak"an-tho'sis) [*hyper-* + Gr. *akantha* prickle + *-osis*]. Hypertrophy of the prickle layer of the skin.

hyperacid (hi"per-as'id) [*hyper-* + L. *acidus* sour]. Abnormally or excessively acid.

hyperacidaminuria (hi"per-as"id-am"ĭ-nu're-ah). Excess of amino acids in the urine.

hyperacidity (hi"per-ah-sid'ĭ-te). An excessive degree of acidity. **gastric h.,** hyperchlorhydria. **larval h.,** gastric hyperacidity which is not revealed.

hyperacousia (hi″per-ah-koo′ze-ah). Hyperacusis.

hyperaction (hi″per-ak′shun). Hyperactivity.

hyperactivity (hi″per-ak-tiv′ĭ-te). Abnormally increased activity.

hyperacusia (hi″per-ah-ku′ze-ah). Hyperacusis.

hyperacusis (hi″per-ah-ku′sis) [*hyper-* + Gr. *akousis* hearing]. Abnormal acuteness of the sense of hearing, or a painful sensitiveness to sounds.

hyperacute (hi″per-ah-kūt′). Extremely acute.

hyperadenosis (hi″per-ad″e-no′sis) [*hyper-* + Gr. *adēn* gland + *-osis*]. A condition characterized by enlargement of the glands.

hyperadiposis (hi″per-ad″ĭ-po′sis) [*hyper-* + *adiposis*]. Extreme adiposity or fatness.

hyperadiposity (hi″per-ad″ĭ-pos′ĭ-te). Hyperadiposis.

hyperadrenalemia (hi″per-ad-re″nal-e′me-ah). The presence of an abnormally increased amount of adrenal secretion in the blood.

hyperadrenalism (hi″per-ad-re′nal-izm). Abnormally increased secretory activity of the adrenal gland.

hyperadrenia (hi″per-ad-re′ne-ah). Hyperadrenalism.

hyperadrenocorticism (hi″per-ad-re″no-kor′tĭ-sizm). A condition characterized by abnormally increased functional activity of the cortex of the adrenal gland.

hyperaffective (hi″per-af-fek′tiv). Pertaining to or characterized by hyperaffectivity.

hyperaffectivity (hi″per-af″fek-tiv′ĭ-te). Abnormally increased sensibility to mild superficial stimuli; the quality of abnormally heightened emotional reactivity.

hyperakusis (hi″per-ah-koo′sis). Hyperacusis.

hyperalbuminemia (hi″per-al-bu″mĭ-ne′me-ah). An abnormally high albumin content of the blood.

hyperalbuminosis (hi″per-al-bu″mĭ-no′sis). A condition characterized by presence of an excess of albuminoids.

hyperaldosteronemia (hi″per-al″do-stēr″ōn-e′me-ah). Abnormal increase in the level of aldosterone in the blood.

hyperaldosteronuria (hi″per-al″do-stēr″ōn-u′re-ah). The presence of excessive amounts of aldosterone in the urine.

hyperalgesia (hi″per-al-je′ze-ah) [*hyper-* + Gr. *algēsis* pain]. Excessive sensitiveness or sensibility to pain. **auditory h.,** the condition in which slight noises cause pain. **muscular h.,** the condition in which slight exertion causes great weariness or pain.

hyperalgesic (hi″per-al-je′sik). Pertaining to or characterized by hyperalgesia.

hyperalgetic (hi″per-al-jet′ik). Hyperalgesic.

hyperalgia (hi-per-al′je-ah) [*hyper-* + *-algia*]. Hyperalgesia.

hyperalimentation (hi″per-al″ĭ-men-ta′shun). The ingestion or administration of a greater than optimal amount of nutrients.

hyperalimentosis (hi″per-al″ĭ-men-to′sis). Disease due to excess in eating.

hyperalkalescence (hi″per-al″kah-les′ens). An excess of alkalinity.

hyperalkalinity (hi″per-al″kah-lin′ĭ-te). Excessive alkalinity.

hyperallantoinuria (hi″per-ah-lan″to-in-u′re-ah). An excess of allantoin in the urine.

hyperalonemia (hi″per-al″o-ne′me-ah) [*hyper-* + Gr. *hals* salt + *haima* blood]. Excess of salts in the blood.

hyperaminoacidemia (hi″per-am″ĭ-no-as″ĭ-de′me-ah). Presence of amino acids in the blood in excess of the normal amount.

hyperammonemia (hi″per-am″mo-ne′me-ah). An abnormally high level of ammonia in the blood.

hyperammoniemia (hi″per-ah-mo″ne-e′me-ah). Hyperammonemia.

hyperammonuria (hi″per-am″mo-nu′re-ah). Increased excretion of ammonia in the urine.

hyperamylasemia (hi″per-am″il-ās-e′me-ah). Abnormally high elevation of amylase in the blood serum.

hyperanacinesia (hi″per-an″ah-si-ne′ze-ah). Hyperanakinesia.

hyperanakinesia (hi″per-an-ah-ki-ne′ze-ah) [*hyper-* + Gr. *anakinēsis* exercise + *-ia*]. Excessive motor activity; hyperkinesia. **h. ventric′uli,** excessive motor activity of the stomach.

hyperanakinesis (hi″per-an″ah-ki-ne′sis). Hyperanakinesia.

hyperandrogenism (hi″per-an′dro-jen-izm). A state characterized or caused by an excessive secretion of androgens.

hyperaphia (hi″per-a′fe-ah) [*hyper-* + Gr. *haphē* touch]. Excessive tactile sensibility; hyperpselaphesia.

hyperaphic (hi″per-af′ik). Pertaining to or characterized by hyperaphia.

hyperazotemia (hi″per-az″o-te′me-ah) [*hyper-* + *azotemia*]. An excess of nitrogenous matter in the blood.

hyperazoturia (hi″per-az″o-tu′re-ah). Presence of an excessive amount of nitrogenous matter in the urine.

hyperbaric (hi″per-bār′ik) [*hyper-* + Gr. *baros* weight]. Characterized by greater than normal pressure or weight; applied to gases under greater than atmospheric pressure, or to a solution of greater specific gravity than another taken as a standard of reference.

hyperbilirubinemia (hi″per-bil″ĭ-roo″bĭ-ne′me-ah). An excess of bilirubin in the blood.

hyperblastosis (hi″per-blas-to′sis) [*hyper-* + Gr. *blastos* germ]. An overgrowth of some specific tissue.

hyperbrachycephalic (hi″per-brak″e-sĕ-fal′ik). Having a cephalic index of 85.5 or more.

hyperbrachycephaly (hi″per-brak″e-sef′ah-le). The condition of being hyperbrachycephalic.

hyperbulia (hi″per-bu′le-ah) [*hyper-* + Gr. *boulē* will]. Morbid development of the will; excessive wilfulness.

hypercalcemia (hi″per-kal-se′me-ah) [*hyper-* + *calcium* + Gr. *haima* blood]. An excess of calcium in the blood. **idiopathic h.,** a condition of infants, associated with vitamin D intoxication, and characterized by elevated serum calcium levels and increased density of the skeleton, with mental deterioration progressing to idiocy, and nephrocalcinosis causing chronic uremia.

hypercalcinemia (hi″per-kal″sĭ-ne′me-ah). Hypercalcemia.

hypercalcinuria (hi″per-kal″sĭ-nu′re-ah). Hypercalciuria.

hypercalcipexy (hi″per-kal′sĭ-pek″se). Excessive fixation of calcium.

hypercalciuria (hi″per-kal″sĭ-u′re-ah). Excess of calcium in the urine.

hypercapnia (hi″per-kap′ne-ah) [*hyper-* + Gr. *kapnos* smoke]. Excess of carbon dioxide in the blood.

hypercapnic (hi″per-kap′nik). Pertaining to or characterized by hypercapnia.

hypercarbia (hi″per-kar′be-ah). Hypercapnia.

hypercarotenemia (hi″per-kar″o-tēn-e′me-ah). An excess of carotene in the blood.

hypercarotinemia (hi″per-kar″o-tĭ-ne′me-ah). Hypercarotenemia.

hypercatabolic (hi″per-kat″ah-bol′ik). Pertaining to, characterized by, or causing hypercatabolism.

hypercatabolism (hi″per-kah-tab′o-lizm). Abnormally increased catabolism.

hypercatharsis (hi″per-kah-thar′sis) [*hyper-* + Gr. *katharsis* purge]. Excessive purgation.

hypercathartic (hi″per-kah-thar′tik) [*hyper-* + Gr. *kathartikos* purgative]. Excessively cathartic.

hypercellular (hi″per-sel′u-lar). Pertaining to or characterized by hypercellularity.

hypercellularity (hi″per-sel″u-lār′ĭ-te). A state characterized by an abnormal increase in the number of cells present, as in bone marrow.

hypercementosis (hi″per-se″men-to′sis). Excessive development of secondary cementum on the surfaces of tooth roots.

hypercenesthesia (hi″per-se″nes-the′ze-ah) [*hyper-* + *cenesthesia*]. A feeling of exaggerated well being such as is seen in general paralysis and sometimes in mania.

hyperchloremia (hi″per-klo-re′me-ah). An excess of chloride in the blood.

hyperchloremic (hi″per-klo-re′mik). Pertaining to or characterized by hyperchloremia.

hyperchlorhydria (hi″per-klōr-hid′re-ah). Excessive secretion of hydrochloric acid by the stomach cells. **larval h.,** hyperchlorhydria without any symptoms.

hyperchloridation (hi″per-klo″ri-da′shun). The administration of an excess of sodium chloride to the patient.

hyperchloride (hi″per-klo′rīd). A perchloride.

hyperchloruration (hi″per-klōr″u-ra′shun). An excess of chlorides in the body.

hyperchloruria (hi″per-klōr-u′re-ah). Excess of chlorides in the urine.

hypercholesteremia (hi″per-ko-les″ter-e′me-ah). Hypercholesterolemia.

hypercholesteremic (hi″per-ko-les′ter-e″mik). Hypercholesterolemic.

hypercholesterinemia (hi″per-ko-les″ter-in-e′-me-ah). Hypercholesterolemia.

hypercholesterolemia (hi″per-ko-les″ter-ol-e′-me-ah) [*hyper-* + *cholesterol* + Gr. *haima* blood]. Excess of cholesterol in the blood.

hypercholesterolemic (hi″per-ko-les″ter-ol-e′-mik). Pertaining to, characterized by, or tending to produce hypercholesterolemia.

hypercholesterolia (hi″per-ko-les″ter-ol′e-ah). Abnormally high cholesterol content of the bile.

hypercholia (hi″per-ko′le-ah) [*hyper-* + Gr. *cholē* bile + *-ia*]. Excessive secretion of bile.

hyperchondroplasia (hi″per-kon″dro-pla′se-ah). Excessive development of cartilage.

hyperchromaffinism (hi″per-kro-maf′ĭ-nizm). A condition caused by excessive secretion of chromaffin in the body, marked by paroxysms of arterial hypertension.

hyperchromasia (hi″per-kro-ma′se-ah). Hyperchromatism.

hyperchromatic (hi″per-kro-mat′ik). 1. Staining more intensely than is normal. 2. Pertaining to or marked by hyperchromatism.

hyperchromatin (hi″per-kro′mah-tin). The part of the chromatin that stains with blue aniline dyes.

hyperchromatism (hi″per-kro′mah-tizm) [*hyper-* + Gr. *chrōma* color]. Excessive pigmentation; especially a form of degeneration of a cell nucleus in which it becomes filled with particles of pigment, or chromatin. **macrocytic h.,** hyperchromatic macrocythemia.

hyperchromatopsia (hi″per-kro″mah-top′se-ah) [*hyper-* + Gr. *chrōma* color + *opsis* vision]. A condition in which all objects appear colored.

hyperchromatosis (hi″per-kro″mah-to′sis). 1. Increased staining capacity. 2. Hyperchromatism.

hyperchromemia (hi″per-kro-me′me-ah) [*hyper-* + Gr. *chrōma* color + *haima* blood + *-ia*]. A high color index of the blood.

hyperchromia (hi″per-kro′me-ah). 1. Abnormal increase in the hemoglobin content of the erythrocytes. 2. Hyperchromatism.

hyperchromic (hi″per-kro′mik). Highly or excessively stained or colored.

hyperchylia (hi″per-ki′le-ah). Excessive secretion of gastric juice.

hyperchylomicronemia (hi″per-ki″lo-mi″kro-ne′me-ah). The presence in the blood of an excessive number of particles of fat (chylomicrons).

hypercinesia (hi″per-si-ne′ze-ah). Hyperkinesia.

hypercoagulability (hi″per-ko-ag″u-lah-bil′ĭ-te). The state of being more readily coagulated than normal.

hypercoagulable (hi″per-ko-ag′u-lah-bl). Characterized by abnormally increased coagulability.

hypercoria (hi″per-ko′re-ah). Hyperkoria.

hypercorticalism (hi″per-kor′tĭ-kal-izm). Hyperadrenocorticism.

hypercorticism (hi″per-kor′tĭ-sizm). Hyperadrenocorticism.

hypercortisonism (hi″per-kor′tĭ-sōn″izm). A morbid condition resulting from the effects of an excess of cortisone.

hypercrine (hi″per-krin′). Due to endocrine hyperfunction.

hypercrinemia (hi″per-krin-e′me-ah). Hypercrinism.

hypercrinia (hi″per-krin′e-ah). Hypercrinism.

hypercrinism (hi″per-kri′nizm) [*hyper-* + Gr. *krinein* to separate]. The bodily state caused by excessive secretion of any endocrine gland.

hypercrisia (hi″per-kris′e-ah). Hypercrinism.

hypercryalgesia (hi″per-kri″al-je′ze-ah) [*hyper-* + Gr. *kryos* cold + *algēsis* pain]. Excessive sensitiveness to cold.

hypercryesthesia (hi″per-kri″es-the′ze-ah) [*hyper-* + Gr. *kryos* cold + *aisthēsis* perception]. Hypercryalgesia.

hypercupremia (hi″per-ku-pre′me-ah). An excess of copper in the blood.

hypercupriuria (hi″per-ku″pre-u′re-ah). An excess of copper in the urine.

hypercyanotic (hi″per-si″ah-not′ik). Extremely cyanotic.

hypercyesis (hi″per-si-e′sis) [*hyper-* + Gr. *kyēsis* gestation]. Superfetation.

hypercythemia (hi″per-si-the′me-ah) [*hyper-* + Gr. *kytos* hollow vessel + *haima* blood + *-ia*]. Abnormal increase in the number of erythrocytes in the blood.

hypercytochromia (hi″per-si″to-kro′me-ah) [*hyper-* + Gr. *kytos* hollow vessel + *chrōma* color]. Increased staining capacity of a blood cell.

hypercytosis (hi″per-si-to′sis) [*hyper-* + Gr. *kytos* hollow vessel + *-osis*]. A condition characterized by an abnormally increased number of cells, especially of leukocytes.

hyperdactylia (hi-per-dak-til′e-ah) [*hyper-* + Gr. *daktylos* finger + *-ia*]. The presence of more than the normal number of fingers or toes.

hyperdactylism (hi″per-dak′tĭ-lizm). Hyperdactylia.

hyperdactyly (hi″per-dak′tĭ-le). Hyperdactylia.

hyperdiastole (hi″per-di-as′to-le) [*hyper-* + *diastole*]. Active dilatation of the heart.

hyperdicrotic (hi″per-di-krot′ik) [*hyper-* + *dicrotic*]. Exhibiting marked dicrotism.

hyperdicrotism (hi″per-dik′ro-tizm) [*hyper-* + *dicrotism*]. The quality of being hyperdicrotic; extreme dicrotism.

hyperdiemorrhysis (hi″per-di″e-mor′ĭ-sis) [*hyper-* + Gr. *dia* through + *haima* blood + *rhysis* flowing]. Capillary hyperemia.

hyperdiploid (hi′per-dip″loid). 1. Pertaining to or characterized by hyperdiploidy. 2. An individual or cell with more than the diploid number of chromosomes.

hyperdiploidy (hi′per-dip″loi-de). The state of having more than the diploid number of chromosomes ($> 2n$).

hyperdipsia (hi″per-dip′se-ah) [*hyper-* + Gr. *dipsa* thirst + *-ia*]. Intense thirst of relatively brief duration.

hyperdistention (hi″per-dis-ten′shun). Excessive distention.

hyperdiuresis (hi″per-di″u-re′sis) [*hyper-* + *diuresis*]. Excessive secretion of urine.

hyperdontia (hi″per-don′she-ah). A condition characterized by the presence of supernumerary teeth.

hyperdontogeny (hi″per-don-toj′e-ne). The development of supernumerary teeth.

hyperdynamia (hi″per-di-na′me-ah) [*hyper-* + Gr. *dynamis* force]. Excessive muscular activity. **h. u′teri,** excessive uterine contractions in labor.

hyperdynamic (hi″per-di-nam′ik). Pertaining to or characterized by hyperdynamia.

hypereccrisia (hi″per-ek-kris′e-ah) [*hyper-* + Gr. *ekkrisis* excretion + *-ia*]. A state characterized by abnormally increased excretion.

hypereccrisis (hi″per-ek′krĭ-sis). Hypereccrisia.

hypereccritic (hi-per-ek-krit′ik). Pertaining to or exhibiting hypereccrisia.

hyperechema (hi″per-e-ke′mah) [*hyper-* + Gr. *ēchēma* sound]. Exaggeration of auditory sensations.

hyperelectrolytemia (hi-per-e-lek″tro-līt-e′me-ah). An abnormally high concentration of electrolytes in the blood.

hyperemesis (hi″per-em′e-sis) [*hyper-* + Gr. *emesis* vomiting]. Excessive vomiting. **h. gravida′rum,** the pernicious vomiting of pregnancy. **h. hi′emis,** an illness, usually of short duration, characterized by brief nausea followed by repeated vomiting, with epigastric pain and some collapse, and later a few loose, pale stools. **h. lacten′tium,** the vomiting of nursing babies.

hyperemia (hi″per-e′me-ah) [*hyper-* + Gr. *haima* blood + *-ia*]. An excess of blood in a part. **active h.,** excess of blood in a part due to local or general relaxation of the arterioles. **arterial h.,** active h. **Bier's passive h.,** the induction of venous congestion by applying a thin rubber band, for the treatment of joint affections and inflammatory conditions. **collateral h.,** increased flow of blood through collateral vessels when the flow through the main artery is arrested. **constriction h.,** Bier's passive h. **fluxionary h.,** active h. **leptomeningeal h.,** congestion of the pia-arachnoid. **passive h.,** an excess of blood in a part resulting from obstruction to its outflow from the area. **reactive h.,** an excess of blood in a part following restoration of its flow after having been temporarily arrested. **staungs h.,** Bier's passive h. **venous h.,** passive h.

hyperemization (hi″per-e″mi-za′shun). The production of hyperemia, especially when employed for therapeutic purposes.

hyperemotivity (hi″per-e″mo-tiv′ĭ-te). Hyperaffectivity.

hyperencephalus (hi″per-en-sef′ah-lus) [*hyper-* + Gr. *enkephalos* brain]. A monster fetus with the cranial vault absent and the brain exposed.

hyperendocrinia (hi″per-en″do-krin′e-ah). Hyperendocrinism.

hyperendocrinism (hi″per-en-dok′rĭ-nizm) [*hyper-* + Gr. *endon* within + *krinein* to separate]. Abnormally increased activity of an organ of internal secretion.

hyperendocrisia (hi″per-en″do-kris′e-ah). Hyperendocrinism.

hyperenergia (hi″per-en-er′je-ah). Excessive energy or activity.

hypereosinophilia (hi″per-e″o-sin-o-fil′e-ah). Excessive eosinophilia.

hyperephidrosis (hi″per-ef″ĭ-dro′sis) [*hyper-* + Gr. *epi* upon + *hidrōs* sweat]. Excessive sweating.

hyperepinephrinemia (hi″per-ep″ĭ-nef″rin-e′me-ah) [*hyper-* + *epinephrine* + Gr. *haima* blood]. An excess of epinephrine in the blood.

hyperepinephry (hi″per-ep″ĭ-nef′re). Excessive secretion of epinephrine by the adrenal gland.

hyperequilibrium (hi″per-e″kwĭ-lib′re-um). An excessive tendency to vertigo.

hypererethism (hi″per-er′e-thizm). Extreme irritability.

hyperergasia (hi″per-er-ga′se-ah) [*hyper-* + Gr. *ergon* work]. Abnormally increased functional activity.

hyperergia (hi″per-er′je-ah). 1. Hyperergasia. 2. Hypersensitivity to allergens.

hyperergic (hi″per-er′jik). 1. More energetic than normal. 2. Pertaining to or characterized by hyperergy.

hyperergy (hi′per-er″je) [*hyper-* + *allergy*]. Excessive reactivity.

hypererythrocythemia (hi″per-e-rith″ro-si-the′me-ah). Hypercythemia.

hyperesophoria (hi″per-es″o-fo′re-ah) [*hyper-* + Gr. *esō* inward + *phorein* to bear]. A tendency of the visual axis to deviate upward and inward.

hyperesthesia (hi″per-es-the′ze-ah) [*hyper-* + Gr. *aisthēsis* sensation + *-ia*]. Abnormally increased sensitiveness of the skin or of an organ of special sense. **acoustic h., auditory h.,** hyperacusis. **cerebral h.,** that which is due to a cerebral lesion. **gustatory h.,** hypergeusia. **muscular h.,** muscular oversensitiveness to pain or fatigue. **olfactory h.,** hyperosmia. **oneiric h.,** increase of sensitiveness or of pain during sleep and dreams. **optic h.,** abnormal sensitiveness of the eye to light. **sexual h.,** abnormal increase of the sexual impulse. **tactile h.,** hyperaphia.

hyperesthetic (hi″per-es-thet′ik). Pertaining to or characterized by hyperesthesia.

hyperestrinemia (hi″per-es-trin-e′me-ah). Hyperestrogenemia.

hyperestrinism (hi″per-es′trin-izm). A condition due to excessive secretion of estrin and characterized by functional uterine bleeding (menometrorrhagia).

hyperestrogenemia (hi″per-es″tro-jen-e′me-ah). An excessive amount of estrogens in the blood.

hyperestrogenism (hi″per-es′tro-jen-izm). A state characterized or caused by excessive secretion of estrogen.

hyperestrogenosis (hi″per-es″tro-jen-o′sis). An abnormally elevated level of estrogens in the body.

hypereuryopia (hi″per-u″re-o′pe-ah) [*hyper-* + Gr. *eurys* wide + *ōps* eye + *-ia*]. Abnormally wide opening of the eyes.

hyperevolutism (hi″per-e-vol′u-tizm). A condition characterized by development in excess of the normal.

hyperexcretory (hi″per-eks′kre-to-re). Marked by excessive secretion.

hyperexophoria (hi″per-ek″so-fo′re-ah) [*hyper-* + Gr. *exō* outward + *phorein* to bear + *-ia*]. A tendency of the visual axis to deviate upward and outward.

hyperextension (hi″per-eks-ten′shun). Extreme or excessive extension of a limb or part.

hyperferremia (hi″per-fer-re′me-ah). An excess of iron in the blood.

hyperferremic (hi″per-fer-re′mik). Pertaining to or characterized by hyperferremia.

hyperferricemia (hi″per-fer″ĭ-se′me-ah). Hyperferremia.

hyperflexion (hi″per-flek′shun). Forcible overflexion of a limb or part.

hyperfolliculinemia (hi″per-fo-lik″u-lin-e′me-ah). The presence of an excessive amount of estrogen in the blood.

hyperfolliculinism (hi″per-fo-lik′u-lin-izm). Any condition caused by the presence in the body of excessive quantities of estrogen.

hyperfolliculinuria (hi″per-fo-lik″u-lin-u′re-ah). The presence of an excessive amount of estrogen in the urine.

hyperfunctioning (hi″per-funk′shun-ing). Excessive functioning of an organ.

hypergalactia (hi″per-gah-lak′she-ah) [*hyper-* + Gr. *gala* milk]. Excessive secretion of milk.

hypergalactosis (hi″per-gal″ak-to′sis). Hypergalactia.

hypergalactous (hi″per-gah-lak′tus). Pertaining to, characterized by, or causing hypergalactia.

hypergammaglobulinemia (hi″per-gam″ah-glob″u-lin-e′me-ah). An excess of gamma globulin in the blood.

hypergasia (hip″er-ga′se-ah). Hypoergasia.

hypergenesis (hi″per-jen′e-sis) [*hyper-* + Gr. *genesis* development]. Excessive development, hypertrophy, or redundancy.

hypergenetic (hi″per-je-net′ik). Pertaining to or characterized by hypergenesis.

hypergenitalism (hi″per-jen′ĭ-tal-izm). Hypergonadism.

hypergeusesthesia (hi″per-gūs″es-the′ze-ah). [*hyper-* + Gr. *geusis* taste + *aisthēsis* perception + *-ia*]. Excessive or abnormal acuteness of the sense of taste.

hypergeusia (hi″per-gu′se-ah). Hypergeusesthesia.

hypergia (hi-per′je-ah). 1. Hypergasia. 2. Diminished sensitivity in allergy.

hypergigantosoma (hi″per-ji-gan″to-so′mah) [*hyper-* + Gr. *gigas* giant + *sōma* body]. Excessive tallness, or gigantism.

hyperglandular (hi″per-glan′du-lar). Marked by abnormally increased glandular activity.

hyperglobulia (hi″per-glo-bu′le-ah) [*hyper-* + L. *globulus* globule]. Excess in the number of red cells in the blood; erythrocytosis.

hyperglobulinemia (hi″per-glob″u-lin-e′me-ah). Abnormally high globulin content of the blood.

hyperglobulism (hi″per-glob′u-lizm). Hyperglobulia.

hyperglycemia (hi″per-gli-se′me-ah) [*hyper-* + Gr. *glykys* sweet + *haima* blood + *-ia*]. Abnormally increased content of sugar in the blood.

hyperglycemic (hi″per-gli-se′mic). Pertaining to, characterized by, or causing hyperglycemia.

hyperglyceridemia (hi″per-glis″er-id-e′me-ah). An excess of glycerides in the blood.

hyperglyceridemic (hi″per-glis′er-id-e″mik). Pertaining to, characterized by, or producing hyperglyceridemia.

hyperglycinemia (hi″per-gli″sĭ-ne′me-ah). The presence of excessive glycine in the blood, accompanied by episodic vomiting, lethargy, dehydration, and ketosis, with hypogammaglobulinemia, neutropenia, increased susceptibility to infection, thrombocytopenia, and periodic purpura, and leading to developmental retardation.

hyperglycistia (hi″per-gli-sis′te-ah) [*hyper-* + Gr. *glykys* sweet + *histos* tissue]. Excess of sugar in the bodily tissues.

hyperglycodermia (hi″per-gli″ko-der′me-ah) [*hyper-* + Gr. *glykys* sweet + *derma* skin + *-ia*]. The presence of an excessive amount of sugar in the skin.

hyperglycogenolysis (hi″per-gli″ko-jen-ol′ĭ-sis). Excessive splitting up of glycogen, resulting in an excess of dextrose in the body.

hyperglycoplasmia (hi″per-gli″ko-plaz′me-ah). The presence of a greater amount than normal of sugar in the blood plasma.

hyperglycorrhachia (hi″per-gli″ko-ra′ke-ah) [*hyper-* + Gr. *glykys* sweet + *rhachis* spine]. The presence of a greater than normal concentration of glucose in the cerebrospinal fluid.

hyperglycosemia (hi″per-gli″ko-se′me-ah). Hyperglycemia.

hyperglycosuria (hi″per-gli″ko-su′re-ah) [*hyper-* + *glycosuria*]. Extreme glycosuria.

hyperglycystia (hi″per-gli-sis′te-ah). Hyperglycistia.

hyperglykemia (hi″per-gli-ke′me-ah). Hyperglycemia.

hypergnosia (hi″per-no′se-ah) [*hyper-* + Gr. *gnōsis* knowledge]. A paranoic condition marked by distortion of perception with a tendency to project psychic conflicts to the environment.

hypergography (hi″per-gog′rah-fe). The branch of physical chemistry which deals with the effects of substances on cells.

hypergonadism (hi″per-go′nad-izm). A condition resulting from or characterized by abnormally increased functional activity of the gonads, with excessive growth and precocious sexual development.

hyperguanidinemia (hi″per-gwan″ĭ-din-e′me-ah). The presence of an excess of guanidine in the blood.

hyperhedonia (hi″per-he-do′ne-ah) [*hyper-* + Gr. *hēdonē* pleasure]. Morbid increase of the feeling of pleasure in agreeable acts.

hyperhedonism (hi″per-he′do-nizm). Hyperhedonia.

hyperhemoglobinemia (hi″per-he″mo-glo″bin-e′me-ah). The presence of an excessive amount of hemoglobin in the blood.

hyperheparinemia (hi″per-hep″ah-rin-e′me-ah). The presence of an excessive amount of heparin in the blood.

hyperhepatia (hi″per-he-pat′e-ah) [*hyper-* + Gr. *hēpar* liver]. Hyperfunction of the liver.

hyperhidrosis (hi″per-hi-dro′sis) [*hyper-* + Gr. *hidrōsis* sweating]. Excessive perspiration. **h. latera′lis,** excessive sweating on one side of the body only.

hyperhidrotic (hi″per-hi-drot′ik). Pertaining to, characterized by, or causing hyperhidrosis.

hyperhormonal (hi-per-hōr′mo-nal). Excessive in hormone; due to hormone excess.

hyperhormonic (hi″per-hōr-mon′ik). Hyperhormonal.

hyperhormonism (hi″per-hōr′mōn-izm). Endocrine hyperfunction.

hyperhydration (hi″per-hi-dra′shun). A state of increased water content of the body.

hyperhydrochloria (hi″per-hi-dro-klo′re-ah). Hyperchlorhydria.

hyperhydrochloridia (hi″per-hi-dro-klo-rid′e-ah). Hyperchlorhydria.

hyperhydropexia (hi″per-hi″dro-pek′se-ah). Hyperhydropexis.

hyperhydropexis (hi″per-hi′dro-pek″sis). The fixation of an abnormal amount of water.

hyperhydropexy (hi″per-hi′dro-pek″se). Hyperhydropexis.

hyperhypercytosis (hi″per-hi″per-si-to′sis). Leukocytosis in which the proportion of neutrophils is abnormally increased.

hyperhypocytosis (hi″per-hi″po-si-to′sis). Leukopenia in which the proportion of neutrophils is abnormally increased.

hyperhypophysism (hi″per-hi-pof′ĭ-sizm). Hyperpituitarism.

hyperidrosis (hi″per-i-dro′sis). Hyperhidrosis.

hyperimmunity (hi″per-ĭ-mu′nĭ-te). A degree of immunity greater than is usually found under similar circumstances.

hyperimmunization (hi″per-im″u-ni-za′shun). Immunization to an unusually high degree; immunization of a convalescent individual with active virus of the disease.

hyperingestion (hi″per-in-jes′chun). Ingestion of a greater than optimal amount of nutrients.

hyperinosemia (hi″per-in″o-se′me-ah) [*hyper-* + Gr. *is*, *inos* fiber + *haima* blood + *-ia*]. An abnormally increased content of fibrin in the blood.

hyperinosis (hi″per-in-o′sis). Hyperinosemia.

hyperinsulinar (hi″per-in′su-lin-ar). Pertaining to or characterized by excessive secretion of insulin.

hyperinsulinemia (hi″per-in″su-lin-e′me-ah). The presence of an excessive amount of insulin in the blood.

hyperinsulinism (hi″per-in′su-lin-izm). 1. Excessive secretion of insulin by the pancreas, resulting in hypoglycemia. 2. Insulin shock from overdosage of insulin.

hyperinterrenal (hi″per-in″ter-re′nal). Pertaining to or resulting from overactivity of the adrenal glands.

hyperinterrenopathy (hi″per-in″ter-re-nop′ah-the) [*hyper-* + *interrenal* + Gr. *pathos* disease]. Any disease due to overactivity of the adrenal glands; hyperadrenocorticism.

hyperinvolution (hi″per-in″vo-lu′shun). Too complete involution; superinvolution.

hyperiodemia (hi″per-i″o-de′me-ah). The presence of an excessive amount of iodine in the blood.

hyperisotonia (hi″per-i″so-to′ne-ah) [*hyper-* + Gr. *isos* equal + *tonos* tension]. Marked equality of tone or of tonicity.

hyperisotonic (hi″per-i″so-ton′ik) [*hyper-* + Gr. *isos* equal + *tonos* tension, or tone]. Noting a serum containing more salt than is necessary to preserve the red corpuscles.

hyperkalemia (hi″per-kah-le′me-ah). Abnormally high potassium content of the blood.

hyperkaliemia (hi″per-kal″e-e′me-ah). Hyperkalemia.

hyperkeratinization (hi″per-ker″ah-tin″i-za′-shun) [*hyper-* + *keratinization*]. The excessive development of keratin in the epidermis.

hyperkeratomycosis (hi″per-ker″ah-to-mi-ko′-sis) [*hyperkeratosis* + Gr. *mykēs* fungus]. Hypertrophy of a corneous tissue, due to a microphyte.

hyperkeratosis (hi″per-ker″ah-to′sis) [*hyper-* + Gr. *keras* horn]. 1. Hypertrophy of the corneous layer of the skin, or any disease characterized by it. 2. Hypertrophy of the cornea. 3. See *x-disease*, 2nd def., under *disease*. **h. congenita′lis palma′ris et planta′ris,** keratosis palmaris et plantaris. **h. excen′trica,** porokeratosis. **h. figura′ta centrif′uga atroph′ica,** porokeratosis. **h. lacuna′ris,** a condition in which the tonsillar crypts contain hard, firmly attached masses. **h. lin′guae,** black tongue. **h. pen′-etrans,** a keratotic skin lesion in which conical pegs extend down toward or into the corium. **h. subungua′lis,** hyperkeratosis affecting the nail beds. **h. universa′lis congen′ita,** ichthyosis.

hyperketonemia (hi″per-ke″to-ne′me-ah). An abnormally increased concentration of ketone bodies in the blood.

hyperketonuria (hi″per-ke″to-nu′re-ah). The presence of an excessive quantity of ketone in the urine.

hyperketosis (hi″per-ke-to′sis). The formation of an excess of ketone.

hyperkinemia (hi″per-ki-ne′me-ah) [*hyper-* + Gr. *kinein* move + *haima* blood + *-ia*]. Abnormally high cardiac output (blood circulation) when at rest and supine.

hyperkinemic (hi″per-ki-ne′mik). 1. Increasing blood flow through a tissue. 2. An agent which increases the flow of blood through a tissue area.

hyperkinesia (hi″per-ki-ne′ze-ah) [*hyper-* + Gr. *kinēsis* motion + *-ia*]. Abnormally increased mobility; abnormally increased motor function or activity. **professional h.,** occupation neurosis.

hyperkinesis (hi″per-ki-ne′sis). Hyperkinesia.

hyperkinetic (hi″per-ki-net′ik). Pertaining to or characterized by hyperkinesia.

hyperkoria (hi″per-ko′re-ah) [*hyper-* + Gr. *koros* satiety + *-ia*]. An early sense of satiety.

hyperlactacidemia (hi″per-lakt″as-ĭ-de′me-ah). An excessive amount of lactic acid in the blood.

hyperlactation (hi″per-lak-ta′shun). Lactation in greater than normal amount or for a longer than usual period.

hyperlecithinemia (hi″per-les″ĭ-thin-e′me-ah). Excess of lecithin in the blood.

hyperlethal (hi″per-le′thal). More than sufficient to cause death.

hyperleukocytosis (hi″per-lu″ko-si-to′sis) (*hyper-* + *leukocyte* + *-osis*]. An abnormally excessive increase in the number of leukocytes in the blood.

hyperleydigism (hi″per-li′dig-izm). Overactivity of Leydig's interstitial cells.

hyperlipemia (hi″per-li-pe′me-ah) [*hyper-* + Gr. *lipos* fat + *haima* blood + *-ia*]. An excess of fat in the blood.

hyperlipidemia (hi″per-lip″ĭ-de′me-ah) [*hyper-* + *lipid* + Gr. *haima* blood + -ia]. An abnormally high concentration of lipids in the blood.

hyperlipoidemia (hi″per-li″poi-de′me-ah). Hyperlipidemia.

hyperlipoproteinemia (hi″per-lip″o-pro″te-in-e′me-ah). An excess of lipoproteins in the blood.

hyperliposis (hi″per-lĭ-po′sis). An excess of fat in the blood serum or tissues.

hyperlithemia (hi″per-li-the′me-ah). Presence in the blood of a high concentration of lithium.

hyperlithic (hi″per-lith′ik). Pertaining to or characterized by an excess of lithic (uric) acid.

hyperlithuria (hi″per-lith-u′re-ah). Excess of lithic (uric) acid in the urine.

hyperlordosis (hi″per-lor-do′sis). An extremely marked lordosis.

hyperluteinization (hi″per-lu″te-in-i-za′shun). Excessive luteinization of the cystic follicles of the ovary.

hyperlutemia (hi″per-lu-te′me-ah). An increased amount of luteal hormone (progesterone) in the blood.

hypermagnesemia (hi″per-mag″nes-e′me-ah). An abnormally large magnesium content of the blood plasma.

hypermania (hi″per-ma′ne-ah). Intense mania with overwhelming tensions and marked disorientation.

hypermastia (hi″per-mas′te-ah) [*hyper-* + Gr. *mastos* breast]. 1. The presence of one or more supernumerary mammary glands. 2. Hypertrophy of the mammary gland.

hypermature (hi″per-mah-tūr′). Past the stage of maturity.

hypermegasoma (hi″per-meg″ah-so′mah) [*hyper-* + Gr. *megas* great + *sōma* body]. Excessive tallness and size.

hypermelanotic (hi″per-mel″ah-not′ik). Characterized by an excessive deposit of melanin.

hypermenorrhea (hi″per-men″o-re′ah) [*hyper-* + Gr. *mēn* month + *rhein* to flow]. Excessive uterine bleeding occurring at regular intervals, the period of flow being of usual duration.

hypermesosoma (hi″per-mes″o-so′mah) [*hyper-* + Gr. *mesos* middle + *sōma* body]. A stature somewhat exceeding the ordinary.

hypermetabolism (hi″per-mĕ-tab′o-lizm). Abnormally increased utilization of material by the body; increased metabolism. **extrathyroidal h.,** abnormally elevated basal metabolism unassociated with thyroid disease.

hypermetamorphosis (hi″per-met″ah-mor-fo′-sis). Too rapid drift of thought activity, leading to mental distraction and confusion, and forming a chief element in mania.

hypermetaplasia (hi″per-met″ah-pla′se-ah). Abnormally increased metaplasia.

hypermetria (hi″per-me′tre-ah) [Gr. "a passing all measure, overflow"]. A condition in which voluntary muscular movement overreaches the intended goal; excessive range of movement.

hypermetrope (hi″per-met′rōp). Hyperope.

hypermetropia (hi″per-me-tro′pe-ah) [*hyper-* + Gr. *metron* measure + *ōps* eye + *-ia*]. Hyperopia.

hypermicrosoma (hi″per-mi″kro-so′mah) [*hyper-* + Gr. *mikros* small + *sōma* body]. Extreme smallness of body; marked dwarfishness.

hypermimia (hi″per-mim′e-ah) [*hyper-* + Gr. *mimia* representation by means of art]. Excessive use of gestures when speaking.

hypermineralization (hi″per-min″er-al-i-za′-

shun). The presence of an excess of mineral elements in the body.

hypermnesia (hi″perm-ne′ze-ah) [*hyper-* + Gr. *mnēmē* memory]. Excessive crowding or unusual clarity of memory images.

hypermnesic (hi″perm-ne′sik). 1. Pertaining to or characterized by hypermnesia. 2. Marked by excessive mental activity.

hypermodal (hi″per-mo′dal). In statistics, relating to the values or items located to the right of the mode in a variations curve.

hypermorph (hi′per-morf) [*hyper-* + Gr. *morphē* form]. A person who is tall but of low sitting height, with bony and narrow arms and legs, slender body, narrow nose, shoulders, thorax, and lips. Cf. *mesomorph.*

hypermotility (hi″per-mo-til′ĭ-te). Excessive or abnormally increased motility.

hypermyotonia (hi″per-mi″o-to′ne-ah) [*hyper-* + Gr. *mys* muscle + *tonos* tension + *-ia*]. Excess of muscular tonicity.

hypermyotrophy (hi″per-mi-ot′ro-fe) [*hyper-* + Gr. *mys* muscle + *trophē* nourishment]. Excessive development of the muscular tissue.

hypernanosoma (hi″per-na″no-so′mah) [*hyper-* + Gr. *manos* dwarf + *sōma* body]. A very low but not absolutely dwarfish stature.

hypernatremia (hi″per-nah-tre′me-ah) [*hyper-* + L. *natron* sodium + Gr. *haima* blood + *-ia*]. Excessive amount of sodium in the blood.

hypernatremic (hi″per-na-tre′mik). Pertaining to, characterized by, or causing hypernatremia.

hypernatronemia (hi″per-nat″ro-ne′me-ah). Hypernatremia.

hypernea (hi″per-ne′ah). Hypernoia.

hyperneocytosis (hi″per-ne″o-si-to′sis) [*hyper-* + Gr. *neos* new + *kytos* hollow vessel + *-osis*]. Leukocytosis in which an excessive number of immature forms of leukocytes are present.

hypernephritis (hi″per-ne-fri′tis). Inflammation of the adrenal body.

hypernephroid (hi″per-nef′roid). Resembling the adrenal body.

hypernephroma (hi″per-ne-fro′mah) [*hyper-* + Gr. *nephros* kidney + *-oma*]. A tumor of the kidney whose structure resembles that of the cortical tissue of the adrenal gland.

hyperneurotization (hi″per-nu-rot″i-za′shun) [*hyper-* + Gr. *neuron* nerve]. The implantation of a foreign motor nerve into a muscle possessing its normal innervation in order to increase the energy force of the muscle.

hypernitremia (hi″per-ni-tre′me-ah) [*hyper-* + *nitrogen* + Gr. *haima* blood]. Excessive quantity of nitrogen in the blood.

hypernoia (hi″per-noi′ah) [*hyper-* + Gr. *nous* mind]. Excessive mental activity.

hypernomic (hi″per-nom′ik) [*hyper-* + Gr. *nomos* law]. Above the law; unrestrained, excessive.

hypernormal (hi″per-nor′mal). In excess of what is normal.

hypernormocytosis (hi″per-nor″mo-si-to′sis) [*hyper-* + *normocytosis*]. Excessive increase in the proportion of neutrophils in the blood.

hypernutrition (hi″per-nu-trish′un). Overfeeding and its ill effects.

hyperontomorph (hi″per-on′to-morf) [*hyper-* + Gr. *ōn* being + *morphē* form]. A person with a tendency to hyperthyroidism.

hyperonychia (hi″per-o-nik′e-ah) [*hyper-* + Gr. *onyx* nail + *-ia*]. Hypertrophy of the nails.

hyperonychosis (hi″per-on″e-ko′sis). Hyperonychia.

hyperope (hi″per-ōp). An individual exhibiting hyperopia.

hyperopia (hi″per-o′pe-ah) [*hyper-* + Gr. *ōps* eye + *-ia*]. That error of refraction in which rays of light entering the eye parallel to the optic axis are brought to a focus behind the retina, as a result of the eyeball being too short from front to back. Called also farsightedness because the near point is more distant than it is in emmetropia with an equal amplitude of accommodation. **absolute h.,** that which can be partially corrected by accommodation. **axial h.,** that which is due to shortness of the anteroposterior axis of the eye. **curvature h.,** hyperopia due to insufficient convexity of the refracting surfaces. **facultative h.,** that which can be entirely corrected by the unaided accommodative power of the eye. **index h.,** hyperopia caused by deficient refractive power in the mediums of the eye. **latent h.,** that part of the total hyperopia that is constantly concealed by accommodative effort. **manifest h.,** that which may be corrected by accommodation aided by convex lenses. **relative h.,** that in which vision is distinct only when excessive convergence is made. **total h.,** manifest and latent hyperopia combined.

hyperopic (hi″per-o′pik). Pertaining to or exhibiting hyperopia.

hyperorchidism (hi″per-or′kĭ-dizm) [*hyper-* + Gr. *orchis* testicle]. Abnormally increased functional activity of the testes.

hyperorexia (hi″per-o-rek′se-ah) [*hyper-* + Gr. *orexis* appetite + *-ia*]. An abnormally increased appetite.

hyperorthocytosis (hi″per-or″tho-si-to′sis) [*hyper-* + Gr. *orthos* straight + *kytos* hollow vessel + *-osis*]. Leukocytosis in which the proportion of the various forms of leukocytes is normal.

hyperosmia (hi″per-oz′me-ah) [*hyper-* + Gr. *osmē* smell]. Abnormally increased sensitiveness to odors.

hyperosmotic (hi″per-os-mot′ik). 1. Producing or caused by abnormally rapid osmosis. 2. Containing a higher concentration of osmotically active components.

hyperosphresia (hi″per-os-fre′ze-ah) [*hyper-* + Gr. *osphrēsis* smell + *-ia*]. Hyperosmia.

hyperosteogeny (hi″per-os″te-oj′e-ne) [*hyper-* + Gr. *osteon* bone + *gennan* to produce]. Excessive development of bone.

hyperostosis (hi″per-os-to′sis) [*hyper-* + Gr. *osteon* bone + *-osis*]. Hypertrophy of bone; exostosis. **h. cra′nii,** hyperostosis involving the cranial bones. **h. fronta′lis inter′na,** a new formation of bone tissue protruding in patches on the internal surface of the cranial bones in the frontal region. **infantile cortical h.,** a disease of young infants characterized by soft tissue swellings over the affected bones, fever, and irritability, and marked by periods of remission and exacerbation. **Morgagni's h.,** h. frontalis interna.

hyperostotic (hi″per-os-tot′ik). Pertaining to or exhibiting hyperostosis.

hyperovaria (hi″per-o-va′re-ah) [*hyper-* + L. *ovarium* ovary]. Sexual precocity in girls from excessive ovarian secretion.

hyperovarianism (hi″per-o-va′re-an-izm). Hyperovaria.

hyperovarism (hi″per-o′vah-rizm). Hyperovaria.

hyperoxaluria (hi″per-ok″sah-lu′re-ah). The excretion of an excessive amount of oxalate in the urine. **primary h.,** a genetic disorder characterized by urinary excretion of oxalate, with nephrolithiasis, nephrocalcinosis and often a generalized deposit of calcium oxalate, resulting from a defect in glyoxalate metabolism.

hyperoxemia (hi″per-ok-se′me-ah) [*hyper-* + Gr. *oxys* sharp + *haima* blood]. Excessive acidity of the blood.

hyperoxia (hi″per-ok′se-ah). An excess of oxygen in the system.

hyperoxic (hi″per-ok′sik). Pertaining to or characterized by hyperoxia.

hyperoxidation (hi″per-ok″sĭ-da′shun). Excess in the amount of oxygen present.

hyperpallesthesia (hi″per-pal″es-the′ze-ah) [*hyper-* + *pallesthesia*]. Abnormally increased sensibility to vibrations.

hyperpancreorrhea (hi″per-pan″kre-o-re′ah). Excessive secretion from the pancreas.

hyperparasite (hi″per-par′ah-sit) [*hyper-* + *parasite*]. A parasite that preys on a parasite. **second degree h.,** a parasite that preys on a hyperparasite.

hyperparathyroidism (hi″per-par″ah-thi′roid-izm). Abnormally increased activity of the parathyroids, causing loss of calcium from the bones and resulting in a condition marked by pain and tenderness in the bones, spontaneous fractures, muscular weakness, abdominal cramps, and osteitis fibrosa.

hyperparotidism (hi″per-pah-rot′ĭ-dizm). Excessive activity of the parotid gland.

hyperpathia (hi″per-path′e-ah). Abnormally exaggerated subjective response to painful stimuli.

hyperpepsia (hi″per-pep′se-ah) [*hyper-* + Gr. *pepsis* digestion]. Impairment of digestion, due to hyperchlorhydria.

hyperpepsinemia (hi″per-pep″sin-e′me-ah). An abnormally high level of pepsin in the blood.

hyperpepsinia (hi″per-pep-sin′e-ah). Abnormally profuse secretion of pepsin in the stomach.

hyperpepsinuria (hi″per-pep″sin-u′re-ah). An abnormally high level of pepsin in the urine.

hyperperistalsis (hi″per-per″ĭ-stal′sis). Excessively active peristalsis.

hyperpermeability (hi″per-per″me-ah-bil′ĭ-te). Undue or abnormal permeability.

hyperpexia (hi″per-pek′se-ah) [*hyper-* + Gr. *pēxis* fixation + *-ia*]. Fixation of an excessive amount of a substance by a tissue.

hyperpexy (hi″per-pek′se). Hyperpexia.

hyperphagia (hi″per-fa′je-ah) [*hyper-* + Gr. *phagein* to eat]. Ingestion of a greater than optimal quantity of food.

hyperphalangia (hi″per-fah-lan′je-ah). Presence of more than the normal number of phalanges in the longitudinal axis of a digit.

hyperphalangism (hi″per-fah-lan′jizm). Hyperphalangia.

hyperphasia (hi″per-fa′ze-ah) [*hyper-* + Gr. *phasis* speech]. Excessive talkativeness.

hyperphonesis (hi″per-fo-ne′sis) [*hyper-* + Gr. *phōnēsis* sounding]. An increase in intensity of the vocal sound in auscultation, or of the percussion note.

hyperphonia (hi″per-fo′ne-ah) [*hyper-* + Gr. *phōnē* voice]. Excessively energetic phonation, as seen in stammerers.

hyperphoria (hi″per-fo′re-ah) [*hyper-* + Gr. *phorein* to bear]. Upward deviation of the visual axis of an eye when fusion is prevented.

hyperphosphatasia (hi″per-fos″fah-ta′ze-ah). Abnormal elevation of the level of phosphatase in the body.

hyperphosphatemia (hi″per-fos″fah-te′me-ah). An excessive amount of phosphates in the blood.

hyperphosphaturia (hi″per-fos″fah-tu′re-ah). An excessive amount of phosphates in the urine.

hyperphosphoremia (hi″per-fos″for-e′me-ah). An excessive amount of phosphorus compounds in the blood.

hyperphrenia (hi″per-fre′ne-ah) [*hyper-* + Gr. *phrēn* mind]. 1. Great mental excitement. 2. Excessive mental activity.

hyperpiesia (hi″per-pi-e′se-ah). Abnormally high blood pressure occurring independently of any discoverable organic disease.

hyperpiesis (hi″per-pi′e-sis) [*hyper-* + Gr. *piesis* pressure]. Abnormally high pressure, as elevated blood pressure.

hyperpietic (hi″per-pi-et′ik). Pertaining to, characterized by, or causing hyperpiesis.

hyperpigmentation (hi″per-pig″men-ta′shun). Abnormally increased pigmentation.

hyperpinealism (hi″per-pi′ne-al-izm). Abnormally increased activity of the pineal body.

hyperpituitarism (hi″per-pĭ-tu′ĭ-tah-rizm). A condition due to pathologically increased activity of the pituitary gland, either of (1) the basophilic cells **(basophilic h.)** which results in basophil adenoma causing compression of the pituitary or hypopituitarism; or (2) of the eosinophilic cells **(eosinophilic h.)** which produces overgrowth, acromegaly and gigantism or true hyperpituitarism.

hyperplasia (hi″per-pla′ze-ah) [*hyper-* + Gr. *plasis* formation]. The abnormal multiplication or increase in the number of normal cells in normal arrangement in a tissue. Cf. *hypertrophy*. **cementum h.,** hypercementosis. **chronic perforating h. of pulp,** internal resorption of a tooth. **endometrial h., h. endome′trii,** abnormal overgrowth of the endometrium. **inflammatory h.,** hyperplasia brought about by inflammation. **lipoid h.,** increased formation of lipoid-containing cells. **neoplastic h.,** hyperplasia brought about by a new growth. **polar h.,** excessive development at either extremity of the embryo, producing a monster either with two heads or with three or more lower limbs. **Swiss-cheese h.,** hyperplasia of a tissue which on section shows openings as in Swiss cheese.

hyperplasmia (hi″per-plaz′me-ah) [*hyper-* + *plasma*]. 1. Excess in the proportion of blood plasm to corpuscles. 2. Abnormally large size of erythrocytes through the absorption of plasma.

hyperplasminemia (hi″per-plaz″min-e′me-ah). An excess of plasmin in the circulating blood.

hyperplastic (hi″per-plas′tik). Pertaining to or characterized by hyperplasia.

hyperploid (hi′per-ploid) [*hyper-* + *-ploid*]. 1. Having more than the typical number of chromosomes in unbalanced sets. 2. An individual or cell having more than the typical number of chromosomes in unbalanced sets.

hyperploidy (hi″per-ploi′de). The state of having more than the typical number of chromosomes in unbalanced sets.

hyperpnea (hi″perp-ne′ah) [*hyper-* + Gr. *pnoia* breath]. Abnormal increase in the depth and rate of the respiratory movements.

hyperpneic (hi″perp-ne′ik). Pertaining to or characterized by hyperpnea.

hyperpolypeptidemia (hi″per-pol″e-pep″tĭ-de′-me-ah). Excess of polypeptids in the blood.

hyperponesis (hi″per-po-ne′sis) [*hyper-* + Gr. *ponēsis* oppressed by toils]. A condition of being abnormally weighed down by one's duties and responsibilities.

hyperponetic (hi″per-po-net′ik). Pertaining to or characterized by hyperponesis.

hyperporosis (hi″per-po-ro′sis). Excessive callus formation.

hyperposia (hi″per-po′ze-ah) [*hyper-* + Gr. *posis* drinking + *-ia*]. Abnormally increased ingestion of fluids for relatively brief periods.

hyperpostpituitary (hi″per-pōst″pĭ-tu′ĭ-ter″e). Pertaining to excess of posterior pituitary hormone.

hyperpotassemia (hi″per-pot″ah-se′me-ah). Excess of potassium in the blood.

hyperpragic (hi″per-praj′ik). Characterized by excessive activity.

hyperpraxia (hi″per-prak′se-ah) [*hyper-* + Gr. *praxis* exercise]. Abnormal or maniacal activity.

hyperpresbyopia (hi″per-pres″be-o′pe-ah). Excessive presbyopia.

hyperprochoresis (hi″per-pro″ko-re′sis) [*hyper-* + Gr. *prochōrēsis* a going forth]. Abnormal increase of a motor propulsive function; specifically, hyperperistalsis.

hyperprolanemia (hi″per-pro″lan-e′me-ah). An excessive amount of prolan A in the blood.

hyperprolinemia (hi″per-pro″lin-e′me-ah). An excessive amount of proline in the blood.

hyperprosexia (hi″per-pro-sek′se-ah) [*hyper-* + Gr. *prosechein* to heed]. A condition in which the mind is occupied by one idea to the exclusion of others.

hyperproteinemia (hi″per-pro″te-in-e′me-ah)

[*hyper-* + *protein* + Gr. *haima* blood + *-ia*]. The presence of an abnormally high amount of protein in the blood.

hyperproteosis (hi″per-pro″te-o′sis). A condition caused by an excess of protein in the diet.

hyperpselaphesia (hi″perp-sel″ah-fe′ze-ah) [*hyper-* + Gr. *psēlaphēsis* touch + *-ia*]. Hypersensitivity to touch.

hyperpsychosis (hi″per-si-ko′sis) [*hyper-* + Gr. *psychē* soul]. Exaggeration of mental activity with abnormal rapidity of the flow of thought.

hyperptyalism (hi″per-ti′al-izm) [*hyper-* + Gr. *ptyalon* spittle]. Abnormally increased secretion of saliva.

hyperpyremia (hi″per-pi-re′me-ah) [*hyper-* + Gr. *pyreia* fuel + *haima* blood + *-ia*]. Excess of unoxidized carbonaceous matter in the blood.

hyperpyretic (hi″per-pi-ret′ik). Pertaining to, exhibiting, or causing hyperpyrexia.

hyperpyrexia (hi″per-pi-rek′se-ah) [*hyper-* + Gr. *pyressein* to be feverish]. A highly elevated body temperature.

hyperpyrexial (hi″per-pi-rek′se-al). Pertaining to hyperpyrexia.

hyperreactive (hi″per-re-ak′tiv). Pertaining to or characterized by a greater than normal response to stimuli.

hyperreflexia (hi″per-re-flek′se-ah) [*hyper-* + *reflex* + *-ia*]. Exaggeration of reflexes.

hyperresonance (hi″per-rez′o-nans). An exaggerated resonance.

hyperrhinoplaty (hi″per-ri′no-plat″e) [*hyper-* + Gr. *rhis* nose + *platys* wide]. Abnormally great breadth of the bridge of the nose, sometimes accompanied by hypertrophy of the bone. **interocular h.,** ocular hypertelorism.

hypersalemia (hi″per-sal-e′me-ah). Abnormally increased content of salt in the blood.

hypersaline (hi″per-sa′līn). Excessively saline: a term applied to treatment by the administration of large doses of sodium chloride.

hypersalivation (hi″per-sal″ĭ-va′shun). Hyperptyalism.

hypersarcosis (hi″per-sar-ko′sis) [*hyper-* + Gr. *sarx* flesh]. Excessive formation of granulation tissue.

hypersecretion (hi″per-se-kre′shun). Excessive secretion. **gastric h.,** hyperchlorhydria.

hypersegmentation (hi″per-seg″men-ta′shun). The appearance of being divided into multiple segments or lobes. **hereditary h. of neutrophils,** a hereditary condition in which the neutrophils are multilobed.

hypersensibility (hi″per-sen″sĭ-bil′ĭ-te). Excessive sensibility or sensitivity to a substance or stimulus.

hypersensitive (hi″per-sen′sĭ-tiv). 1. Exhibiting abnormally increased sensitivity. 2. Having the specific or general ability to react with characteristic symptoms to the application or contact with certain substances (allergens) in amounts innocuous to normal individuals.

hypersensitiveness (hi″per-sen′sĭ-tiv″nes). A state of altered reactivity in which the body reacts to a foreign agent more strongly than normal. Cf. *anaphylaxis* and *allergy*.

hypersensitization (hi″per-sen″sĭ-ti-za′shun). The process of rendering or the condition of being abnormally sensitive. See *anaphylaxis*.

hypersialosis (hi″per-si″ah-lo′sis). Hyperptyalism.

hyperskeocytosis (hi″per-ske″o-si-to′sis) [*hyper-* + Gr. *skaios* left + *kytos* hollow vessel + *-osis*]. Hyperneocytosis.

hypersomia (hi″per-so′me-ah) [*hyper-* + Gr. *sōma* body]. Gigantism.

hypersomnia (hi″per-som′ne-ah) [*hyper-* + L. *somnus* sleep]. Uncontrollable drowsiness; pathologically excessive sleep.

hypersphyxia (hi″per-sfik′se-ah) [*hyper-* + Gr. *sphyxis* pulse + *-ia*]. Increased activity of the circulation with increased blood pressure.

hypersplenia (hi″per-sple′ne-ah). Hypersplenism.

hypersplenism (hi″per-splen′izm). A condition characterized by exaggeration of the suggested inhibitory or destructive functions of the spleen, resulting in deficiency of the peripheral blood elements, singly or in combination, hypercellularity of the bone marrow, and usually, but not always, splenomegaly.

hypersplenotrophy (hi″per-sple-not′ro-fe). Splenomegaly.

hyperspongiosis (hi-per-spon″je-o′sis). Proliferation of the substantia spongiosa.

hypersteatosis (hi″per-ste-ah-to′sis). Increased sebaceous secretion.

hyperstereoroentgenography (hi″per-ste″re-o-rent″gen-og′rah-fe). Stereoroentgenography with great distance between the homologous points.

hyperstereoskiagraphy (hi″per-ste″re-o-ski-ag′rah-fe). Hyperstereoroentgenography.

hypersthenia (hi″per-sthe′ne-ah) [*hyper-* + Gr. *sthenos* strength]. Exalted strength or tonicity.

hypersthenic (hi″per-sthen′ik). Pertaining to or characterized by hypersthenia.

hypersthenuria (hi″per-sthĕ-nu′re-ah) [*hyper-* + Gr. *sthenos* strength + *ouron* urine + *-ia*]. Increased osmolality of the urine.

hypersuprarenalemia (hi″per-su″prah-re″nal-e′me-ah). Hyperadrenalemia.

hypersuprarenalism (hi″per-su″prah-re′nal-izm). Hyperadrenalism.

hypersusceptibility (hi″per-sŭ-sep″tĭ-bil′ĭ-te). A condition of abnormally increased susceptibility to poisons, infective agents, or agents which in the normal individual are entirely innocuous.

hypersympathicotonus (hi″per-sim-path″e-ko-to′nus). An increased tone of the sympathetic nervous system.

hypersystole (hi″per-sis′to-le). Abnormal exaggeration of the systole.

hypersystolic (hi″per-sis-tol′ik). Characterized by hypersystole; having heart beats of excessive force.

hypertarachia (hi″per-tar-ak′e-ah) [*hyper-* + Gr. *tarachē* confusion]. Extreme irritability of the nervous system.

hypertelorism (hi-per-te′lor-izm) [*hyper-* + Gr. *tēlouros* distant]. Abnormally increased distance between two organs or parts. **ocular h., orbital h.,** a condition characterized by abnormal increase in the interorbital distance, often associated with cleidocranial or craniofacial dysostosis, and occasionally accompanied by mental deficiency.

hypertensin (hi″per-ten′sin). Angiotensin.

hypertensinogen (hi″per-ten-sin′o-jen). A name given a globulin of the blood plasma which, when acted on by renin, gives rise to hypertensin (angiotensin).

hypertension (hi″per-ten′shun) [*hyper-* + *tension*]. Abnormally high tension; especially high blood pressure. **adrenal h.,** arterial hypertension caused by adrenal ischemia. **benign h.,** essential hypertension which exists for years without producing symptoms. **essential h.,** high blood pressure occurring without discoverable organic cause. **Goldblatt h.,** renal hypertension due to occlusion of the renal arteries. **malignant h.,** essential hypertension with an acute stormy onset, the development of neuroretinitis, a progressive course, and a poor prognosis. **neuromuscular h.,** a condition of hyperexcitability and hyperirritability of reflex response. **pale h.,** malignant hypertension. **portal h.,** abnormally increased blood pressure in the portal venous system, a frequent complication of cirrhosis of the liver. **pulmonary h.,** increased pressure within the pulmonary circulation. **red h.,** benign hypertension. **renal h.,**

hypertension due to or associated with renal damage or defective renal function. **vascular h.,** high blood pressure.

hypertensive (hi″per-ten′siv). 1. Characterized by or causing increased tension or pressure, as abnormally high blood pressure. 2. A person with abnormally high blood pressure.

hypertensor (hi″per-ten′sor). A substance that raises the blood pressure.

hyperthecosis (hi″per-the-ko′sis). Hyperplasia with excessive luteinization of the cells of the inner stromal layer, the theca interna, of the ovary.

hyperthelia (hi″per-the′le-ah) [*hyper-* + Gr. *thēlē* nipple]. The presence of supernumerary nipples.

hyperthermal (hi″per-ther′mal). Marked by abnormally high temperature.

hyperthermalgesia (hi″per-ther″mal-je′ze-ah) [*hyper-* + Gr. *thermē* heat + *algēsis* pain]. Abnormally increased sensitiveness to heat.

hyperthermesthesia (hi″per-ther″mes-the′ze-ah) [*hyper-* + Gr. *thermē* heat + *aisthēsis* perception + *-ia*]. Increased sensibility for heat.

hyperthermia (hi″per-ther′me-ah) [*hyper-* + Gr. *thermē* heat]. An abnormally high body temperature; fever.

hyperthermo-esthesia (hi″per-ther″mo-es-the′ze-ah). Hyperthermesthesia.

hyperthermy (hi″per-ther′me). Hyperthermia.

hyperthrombinemia (hi″per-throm″bin-e′me-ah). Abnormally high thrombin content of the blood.

hyperthrombocytemia (hi″per-throm″bo-si-te′me-ah). An abnormally high blood platelet count.

hyperthymergasia (hi″per-thi″mer-ga′ze-ah) [*hyper-* + Gr. *thymos* spirit + *ergon* work]. Meyer's term for overactivity of mood, marked by excitement, agitation, elation, and exaggerated self-feeling.

hyperthymergastic (hi″per-thi″mer-gas′tik). Pertaining to or characterized by hyperthymergasia.

hyperthymia (hi″per-thi′me-ah) [*hyper-* + Gr. *thymos* spirit + *-ia*]. Excessive emotionalism.

hyperthymic (hi″per-thi′mik). Marked by hyperthymia.

hyperthymism (hi″per-thi′mizm). A condition attributed to excessive activity of the thymus gland.

hyperthyrea (hi″per-thi′re-ah). Hyperthyroidism.

hyperthyreosis (hi″per-thi″re-o′sis). Hyperthyroidism.

hyperthyroid (hi″per-thi′roid). Marked by, or due to, hyperthyroidism.

hyperthyroidism (hi″per-thi′roid-izm). Excessive functional activity of the thyroid gland, characterized by increased basal metabolism, by exophthalmos, and by disturbances in the vegetative nervous system and in creatine metabolism. **masked h.,** hyperactivity of the thyroid gland without the classic symptoms but manifested by symptoms restricted to a single system, as by cardiovascular symptoms.

hyperthyroidosis (hi″per-thi″roi-do′sis). Hyperthyroidism.

hyperthyroxinemia (hi″per-thi-rok″sin-e′me-ah). Excess of thyroxin in the blood.

hypertonia (hi″per-to′ne-ah) [*hyper-* + Gr. *tonos* tension]. A condition of excessive tone, tension, or activity. See also *hypertension.* **h. oc′uli,** high intraocular pressure. **h. polycythae′mica,** increased blood pressure associated with polycythemia.

hypertonic (hi″per-ton′ik). 1. Pertaining to or characterized by an abnormally increased tonicity or tension. 2. Having an osmotic pressure greater than that of the solution with which it is compared.

hypertonicity (hi″per-to-nis′ĭ-te). The state or quality of being hypertonic.

hypertonus (hi″per-to′nus). Hypertonia.

hypertoxic (hi″per-tok′sik). Excessively toxic.

hypertoxicity (hi″per-tok-sis′ĭ-te). The state or quality of being excessively toxic.

hypertrichiasis (hi″per-trik-i′ah-sis) [*hyper-* + Gr. *thrix* hair + *-iasis*]. Hypertrichosis. **h. lanugino′sa,** an unusually heavy growth of the lanugo over the body. **h. partia′lis,** the occurrence of excessive hair in patches where it does not normally grow. **h. universa′lis,** the presence of excessive hair over all the body and limbs.

hypertrichophrydia (hi″per-trik″ŏ-frid′e-ah) [*hyper-* + Gr. *thrix* hair + *ophrys* eyebrow]. Excessive growth of the eyebrows.

hypertrichosis (hi″per-trik-o′sis) [*hyper-* + Gr. *thrix* hair + *-osis*]. An abnormally excessive growth of hair. **h. pin′nae au′ris,** an abnormally excessive growth of hair on the pinna of the ear, a trait which is thought to be transmitted by a gene on the Y chromosome.

hypertriglyceridemia (hi″per-tri-glis″er-i-de′-me-ah). An excess of triglycerides in the blood.

hypertrophia (hi″per-tro′fe-ah). Hypertrophy.

hypertrophic (hi″per-trof′ik). Pertaining to or marked by hypertrophy.

hypertrophy (hi-per′tro-fe) [*hyper-* + Gr. *trophē* nutrition]. The morbid enlargement or overgrowth of an organ or part due to an increase in size of its constituent cells. **adaptive h.,** increase in size in response to changed conditions, as, for example, increased thickness of the walls of a hollow organ when the outflow is obstructed. **Billroth h.,** idiopathic benign hypertrophy of the pylorus. **compensatory h.,** that which results from increased functional activity due to some physical defect. **complementary h.,** increase in size of the remaining part of an organ to take the place of a portion which has been lost. **concentric h.,** increased thickness of the walls of an organ, with no enlargement and with diminished capacity. **eccentric h.,** hypertrophy of a hollow organ, with dilatation of its cavity. **false h.,** enlargement that is due to an increase in only one constituent element of an organ or part, more commonly the stroma. **functional h.,** hypertrophy of an organ or part caused by its increased activity. **Marie's h.,** enlargement of the soft parts of the joints resulting from periostitis. **numeric h.,** that which is due to an increased number of structural elements. **physiologic h.,** temporary increase in the size of an organ produced by physiologic activity, as in the female breast during pregnancy and lactation. **pseudomuscular h.,** pseudohypertrophic muscular dystrophy. **quantitative h.,** hyperplasia. **simple h.,** that which is due to a simple increase of the number of structural elements. **simulated h.,** apparent increase in the size of a part, due to absence of normal attrition, as in the teeth. **true h.,** enlargement that is due to an increase of all the component elements of an organ or part. **ventricular h.,** hypertrophy of the myocardium of a ventricle, causing undue deviation of the axis of the electrocardiogram in the direction of the side affected. **vicarious h.,** hypertrophy of an organ in consequence of the failure of action of another organ of allied function.

hypertropia (hi″per-tro′pe-ah) [*hyper-* + Gr. *trepein* to turn]. Upward deviation of the visual axis of an eye when fusion is a possibility.

hyperuresis (hi″per-u-re′sis). Polyuria.

hyperuricacidemia (hi″per-u″rik-as″ĭ-de′me-ah). Hyperuricemia.

hyperuricaciduria (hi″per-u″rik-as″ĭ-du′re-ah). Hyperuricuria.

hyperuricemia (hi″per-u″rĭ-se′me-ah). Excess of uric acid in the blood.

hyperuricemic (hi″per-u″rĭ-se′mik). Pertaining to or characterized by hyperuricemia.

hyperuricuria (hi″per-u″rik-u′re-ah). Excess of uric acid in the urine.

hypervaccination (hi″per-vak″sĭ-na′shun). A

second inoculation of an immunized animal with enough vaccine to enable it to afford a serum protective to other animals.

hypervascular (hi″per-vas′ku-lar). Extremely vascular.

hypervegetative (hi″per-vej″e-ta′tiv) [*hyper-* + L. *vegetativus* plant-fashion]. Denoting a constitutional body type in which the visceral, nutritional functions predominate.

hypervenosity (hi″per-ve-nos′ĭ-te). Excessive development of the venous system.

hyperventilation (hi″per-ven″tĭ-la′shun). 1. A state in which there is an increased amount of air entering the pulmonary alveoli, resulting in reduction of the carbon dioxide tension. 2. Abnormally prolonged, rapid, and deep breathing, frequently used as a test procedure in epilepsy and tetany.

hyperviscosity (hi″per-vis-kos′ĭ-te). Excessive viscosity.

hypervitaminosis (hi″per-vi″tah-min-o′sis). A condition due to an excess of one or more vitamins. **h. A,** a symptom complex resulting from ingestion of excessive amounts of vitamin A, with skin pigmentation, generalized pruritus, and changes in the horny structures of the skin and loss of hair. **h. D,** a symptom complex resulting from ingestion of excessive amounts of vitamin D, with weakness, fatigue, loss of weight, and other symptoms.

hypervitaminotic (hi″per-vi″tah-min-ot′ik). Pertaining to or characterized by hypervitaminosis.

hypervolemia (hi″per-vo-le′me-ah) [*hyper-* + *volume* + Gr. *haima* blood + *-ia*]. Abnormal increase in the volume of circulating fluid (plasma) in the body.

hypervolemic (hi″per-vo-le′mik). Pertaining to or characterized by hypervolemia.

hypesthesia (hip″es-the′ze-ah). Hypoesthesia.

hypha (hi′fah), pl. *hy′phae* [L.]. One of the filaments composing the mycelium of a fungus.

hyphae (hi′fe) [L.]. Plural of *hypha*.

hyphedonia (hīp″he-do′ne-ah) [*hypo-* + Gr. *hēdonē* pleasure + *-ia*]. Morbid diminution of the feeling of pleasure in acts that normally give pleasure.

hyphema (hi-fe′mah) [Gr. *hyphaimos* suffused with blood, blood-shot; especially of the eyes]. Hemorrhage into the anterior chamber of the eye.

hyphemia (hi-fe′me-ah) [*hypo-* + Gr. *haima* blood + *-ia*]. Oligemia, or deficiency of blood.

hyphephilia (hif″e-fil′e-ah) [Gr. *hyphē* web + *philein* to love]. Sexual gratification by contact with fabrics, such as velvet, silk, etc. See also *frottage.*

hyphidrosis (hīp″hid-ro′sis) [*hypo-* + Gr. *hidrōs* sweat + *-osis*]. Too scanty perspiration.

Hyphomicrobiaceae (hi″fo-mi-kro″be-a′se-e). A family of Schizomycetes (order Hyphomicrobiales), made up of cells attached to one another by a slender filament, daughter cells arising from such filaments or from one growing out of the pole of a mature cell. It includes two genera, *Hyphomicrobium* and *Rhodomicrobium.*

Hyphomicrobiales (hi″fo-mi-kro″be-a′lēz). An order of Schizomycetes, made up of ovoid, ellipsoidal, spherical, or pyriform cells which commonly occur in aggregates but may occur singly or in pairs, and which multiply by budding or by budding and longitudinal fission. It includes two families, *Hyphomicrobiaceae* and *Pasteuriaceae.*

Hyphomicrobium (hi″fo-mi-kro′be-um). A genus of microorganisms of the family Hyphomicrobiaceae, order Hyphomicrobiales, made up of ovoid cells growing in a dense clump from which filaments radiate outward. The type species is *H. vulga′re.*

hyphomycete (hi″fo-mi-sēt′). An organism belonging to the Hyphomycetes.

Hyphomycetes (hi″fo-mi-se′tēz) [pl., Gr. *hyphē* web + Gr. *mykēs* fungus]. A group of fungi not otherwise classified, because their life history is not well known. Called also *Fungi Imperfecti.*

hyphomycetic (hi″fo-mi-set′ik). Due to the presence of mold fungi.

hyphomycetoma (hi″fo-mi″se-to′mah). A tumor caused by hyphomycetes.

hyphomycosis (hi″fo-mi-ko′sis). Infection with hyphomycetes. **h. des′truens e′qui,** leeches.

hypinosis (hip″e-no′sis). Hypoinosemia.

hypinotic (hip″e-not′ik). Pertaining to, or characterized by, hypinosis.

hypisotonic (hīp″i-so-ton′ik). Less than isotonic.

hypnagogic (hip″nah-goj′ik). 1. Producing sleep. 2. Occurring just before sleep: said of dreams.

hypnagogue (hip′nah-gog) [*hypno-* + Gr. *agōgos* leading]. 1. Hypnotic; pertaining to drowsiness. 2. An agent which induces sleep or drowsiness.

hypnalgia (hip-nal′je-ah) [*hypno-* + Gr. *algos* pain + *-ia*]. Pain that occurs during sleep.

hypnapagogic (hip″nap-ah-goj′ik) [*hypno-* + Gr. *apo* away + *agōgos* leading]. Preventing sleep.

hypnesthesia (hip″nes-the′ze-ah) [*hypno-* + Gr. *aisthēsis* perception + *-ia*]. Sleepiness.

hypnic (hip′nik) [Gr. *hypnikos*]. Inducing or pertaining to sleep.

hypno- (hip′no) [Gr. *hypnos* sleep]. Combining form denoting a relationship to sleep.

hypnoanalysis (hip″no-ah-nal′ĭ-sis) [*hypno-* + *analysis*]. A method of psychotherapy in which psychoanalysis is employed in a setting controlled by the therapist.

hypnoanesthesia (hip″no-an″es-the′ze-ah). Induction of the anesthetic state by hypnosis.

hypnobatia (hip″no-ba′she-ah) [*hypno-* + Gr. *bainein* to walk]. Somnambulism.

hypnocinematograph (hip″no-sin″e-mat′o-graf) [*hypno-* + Gr. *kinēma* movement + *graphein* to record]. An apparatus for recording the movements made by a sleeping person.

hypnocyst (hip′no-sist) [*hypno-* + *cyst*]. A quiescent cyst.

hypnodontia (hip″no-don′she-ah). Hypnodontics.

hypnodontics (hip″no-don′tiks) [*hypnosis* + Gr. *odous* tooth]. The application of controlled suggestion and hypnosis in the practice of dentistry.

hypnogenetic (hip″no-je-net′ik). Hypnogenic.

hypnogenic (hip-no-jen′ik) [*hypno-* + Gr. *gennan* to produce]. Inducing sleep or hypnotism.

hypnogenous (hip-noj′e-nus). Hypnogenic.

hypnoid (hip′noid). Resembling hypnosis or the hypnotic state.

hypnoidal (hip-noi′dal). Pertaining to a state resembling hypnosis.

hypnoidization (hip″noi-di-za′shun). The production of light hypnosis or of the hypnoid state.

hypnolepsy (hip′no-lep″se) [*hypno-* + Gr. *lēpsis* seizure]. Abnormal sleepiness.

hypnology (hip-nol′o-je) [*hypno-* + *-logy*]. The sum of what is known regarding sleep and hypnotism.

hypnonarcoanalysis (hip″no-nar″ko-ah-nal′ĭ-sis). Psychoanalysis with the patient hypnotized and narcotized with a sedative drug.

hypnonarcosis (hip″no-nar-ko′sis). Light hypnosis combined with narcosis.

hypnopompic (hip″no-pom′pik) [*hypno-* + Gr. *pompē* a sending away, a sending home]. Persisting after sleep; applied to visions or dreams that persist prior to complete awakening.

hypnosia (hip-no′ze-ah). Uncontrollable drowsiness.

hypnosis (hip-no′sis). An artificially induced passive state in which there is increased amenability and responsiveness to suggestions and commands, provided that these do not conflict seriously with the subject's own conscious or unconscious wishes.

hypnosophy (hip-nos′o-fe) [*hypno-* + Gr. *sophia* wisdom]. The study of sleep and its phenomena.

hypnotherapy (hip″no-ther′ah-pe) [*hypno-* + Gr. *therapeia* treatment]. The use of hypnosis in the treatment of disease.

hypnotic (hip-not′ik) [Gr. *hypnōtikos*]. 1. Inducing sleep. 2. Pertaining to or of the nature of hypnotism. 3. A drug that acts to induce sleep. **indirect h's,** agents that induce sleep by relieving conditions that may interfere with it, as iron in anemia, digitalis in vascular relaxation, etc.

hypnotism (hip′no-tizm). 1. The method or practice of inducing hypnosis. 2. Hypnosis.

hypnotist (hip′no-tist). One who induces hypnosis.

hypnotization (hip″no-ti-za′shun). The induction of hypnosis.

hypnotize (hip′no-tīz). To put into a state of hypnosis.

hypnotoxin (hip″no-tok′sin). 1. A toxin which is supposed to accumulate during the waking hours, until finally it is sufficient to inhibit the activity of the cortical cells and thus induce sleep. 2. A toxic substance derived from the tentacles of the hydrozoan, *Physalia*, characteristically causing a central nervous system depression, affecting both motor and sensory elements.

hypo (hi′po). 1. A popular designation of hypochondriasis. 2. A contraction for sodium thiosulfate, used as a photographic fixing agent.

hypo- (hi′po) [Gr. *hypo* under]. A prefix signifying beneath, under, or deficient. In chemistry, it denotes that the principal element in the compound is combined in its lowest state of valence.

hypoacidity (hi″po-ah-sid′ĭ-te). Deficiency of acid; lack of normal acidity.

hypoactivity (hi″po-ak-tiv′ĭ-te). Abnormally diminished activity.

hypoadenia (hi″po-ah-de′ne-ah) [*hypo-* + Gr. *adēn* gland + *-ia*]. Abnormally diminished glandular activity.

hypoadrenalemia (hi″po-ad-re″nal-e′me-ah). The presence of an abnormally decreased amount of adrenal secretion in the blood.

hypoadrenalism (hi″po-ad-re′nal-izm). Abnormally diminished activity of the adrenal gland.

hypoadrenia (hi″po-ad-re′ne-ah). Hypoadrenalism.

hypoadrenocorticism (hi″po-ad-re″no-kor′tĭ-sizm). Abnormally diminished secretion of the adrenal cortex.

hypoaffective (hi″po-af-fek′tiv). Pertaining to or characterized by hypoaffectivity.

hypoaffectivity (hi″po-af″fek-tiv′ĭ-te). Abnormally diminished sensibility to superficial stimuli; the quality of abnormally decreased emotional reactivity.

hypoalbuminemia (hi″po-al-bu″min-e′me-ah). An abnormally low albumin content of the blood.

hypoalbuminosis (hi″po-al-bu″mĭ-no′sis). A condition characterized by an abnormally low level of albumin.

hypoaldosteronemia (hi″po-al″do-stĕr″ōn-e′-me-ah). An abnormally low level of aldosterone in the blood.

hypoaldosteronism (hi″po-al″do-stĕr′ōn-izm). Aldosteronopenia.

hypoaldosteronuria (hi″po-al″do-stĕr″ōn-u′re-ah). Presence of an abnormally low level of aldosterone in the urine.

hypoalgesia (hi″po-al-je′se-ah). Hypalgesia.

hypoalimentation (hi″po-al″ĭ-men-ta′shun). Insufficient nourishment.

hypoalkaline (hi″po-al′kah-līn). Less alkaline than normal.

hypoalkalinity (hi″po-al″kah-lin′ĭ-te). The state of being less alkaline than normal.

hypoalonemia (hi″po-al″o-ne′me-ah) [*hypo-* + Gr. *hals* salt + *haima* blood + *-ia*]. A deficiency of salts in the blood.

hypoaminoacidemia (hi″po-am″ĭ-no-as″ĭ-de′-me-ah). The presence of less than the normal amount of amino acids in the blood.

hypoandrogenism (hi″po-an-dro′jen-izm). Deficiency of androgen.

hypoazoturia (hi″po-az″o-tu′re-ah) [*hypo-* + L. *azotum* nitrogen + Gr. *ouron* urine + *-ia*]. Diminished excretion of nitrogenous material in the urine.

hypobaric (hi″po-bār′ik) [*hypo-* + Gr. *baros* weight]. Characterized by less than normal pressure or weight; applied to gases under less than atmospheric pressure or to a solution of lower specific gravity than another taken as a standard of reference. See under *solution*.

hypobaropathy (hi″po-bār-op′ah-the) [*hypo-* + Gr. *baros* pressure + *pathos* disease]. The disturbances experienced in high altitudes due to reduced air pressure. See *altitude anoxia*, under *anoxia*, and *mountain sickness*, under *sickness*.

hypobasophilism (hi″po-ba-sof′ĭ-lizm). Hypopituitarism.

hypobilirubinemia (hi″po-bil″ĭ-ru″bĭ-ne′me-ah). Abnormal diminution of bilirubin in the blood.

hypoblast (hi′po-blast) [*hypo-* + Gr. *blastos* germ]. Entoderm.

hypoblastic (hi″po-blas′tik). Pertaining to the hypoblast.

Hypobosca rufipes (hi″po-bos′kah roo′fĭ-pēz). A fly of South Africa whose bite transmits the *Trypanosoma theileri*.

hypobranchial (hi″po-brang′ke-al) [*hypo-* + Gr. *branchia* gills]. Located beneath the branchial arches.

hypobromite (hi″po-bro′mīt). Any salt of hypobromous acid.

hypobulia (hi″po-bu′le-ah) [*hypo-* + Gr. *boulē* will + *-ia*]. Abnormal feebleness of the will.

hypocalcemia (hi″po-kal-se′me-ah) [*hypo-* + *calcium* + Gr. *haima* blood + *-ia*]. Reduction of the blood calcium below normal.

hypocalcia (hi″po-kal′se-ah). Deficiency of calcium.

hypocalcipectic (hi″po-kal″sĭ-pek′tik). Pertaining to or characterized by hypocalcipexy.

hypocalcipexy (hi″po-kal′sĭ-pek″se). Deficient calcium fixation.

hypocalciuria (hi″po-kal″se-u′re-ah). An abnormally diminished amount of calcium in the urine.

hypocapnia (hi″po-kap′ne-ah) [*hypo-* + Gr. *kapnos* smoke + *-ia*]. Deficiency of carbon dioxide in the blood. See *acapnia*.

hypocapnic (hi″po-kap′nik). Pertaining to or characterized by hypocapnia.

hypocarbia (hi″po-kar′be-ah). Hypocapnia.

hypocatalasemia (hi″po-kat″ah-la-se′me-ah). A diminished content of catalase in the blood.

hypocatalasia (hi″po-kat″ah-la′ze-ah). A condition characterized by reduced levels of catalase in all or most of the tissues of the body, caused by heterozygosity for the gene for acatalasia.

hypocellular (hi″po-sel′u-lar). Pertaining to or characterized by hypocellularity.

hypocellularity (hi″po-sel″u-lăr′i-te). A state of abnormal decrease in the number of cells present, as in bone marrow.

hypocelom (hi″po-se′lom). Hypocoelom.

hypocenesthesia (hi″po-sen″es-the′ze-ah) [*hypo-* + *cenesthesia*]. Lack of the normal sense of well being, such as is seen in hypochondria.

hypocenter (hi″po-sen′ter). The spot immediately beneath the exact site of explosion of an atomic bomb.

hypochloremia (hi″po-klo-re′me-ah). An abnormally diminished level of chloride in the blood.

hypochloremic (hi″po-klo-re′mik). Pertaining to or characterized by hypochloremia.

hypochlorhydria (hi″po-klor-hid′re-ah) [*hypo-* + Gr. *chlōros* green + *hydōr* water + *-ia*]. Deficiency of hydrochloric acid in the gastric juice. Cf. *achlorhydria*.

hypochloridation (hi″po-klo″ri-da′shun). Chloride deficiency in the system.

hypochloridemia (hi″po-klo″rid-e′me-ah). Hypochloremia.

hypochlorite (hi″po-klo′rit) [*hypo-* + Gr. *chlōros* green]. Any salt of hypochlorous acid.

hypochlorization (hi″po-klo″ri-za′shun). Reduction of the amount of sodium chloride in the diet.

hypochloruria (hi″po-klo-ru′re-ah) [*hypo-* + *chloride* + Gr. *ouron* urine + *-ia*]. Deficiency of chlorides in the urine.

hypocholesteremia (hi″po-ko-les″ter-e′me-ah). Hypocholesterolemia.

hypocholesteremic (hi″po-ko-les″ter-e′mik). Hypocholesterolemic.

hypocholesterinemia (hi″po-ko-les″ter-in-e′me-ah). Hypocholesterolemia.

hypocholesterolemia (hi″po-ko-les″ter-ol-e′me-ah). An abnormally diminished amount of cholesterol in the blood.

hypocholesterolemic (hi″po-ko-les″ter-ol-e′mik). Pertaining to, characterized by, or producing hypocholesterolemia.

hypocholia (hi-po-ko′le-ah). Oligocholia.

hypocholuria (hi″po-ko-lu′re-ah). Abnormal reduction in the amount of bile in the urine.

hypochondria (hi″po-kon′dre-ah). 1. Plural of *hypochondrium*. 2. Hypochondriasis.

hypochondriac (hi″po-kon′dre-ak). 1. Pertaining to the hypochondrium or to hypochondriasis. 2. A person affected with hypochondriasis.

hypochondriacal (hi″po-kon-dri′ah-kal). Affected with hypochondriasis.

hypochondriasis (hi″po-kon-dri′ah-sis) [so called because the hypochondrium, and especially the spleen, was supposed to be the seat of this disorder]. Morbid anxiety about the health, often associated with a simulated disease and more or less pronounced melancholia.

hypochondrium (hi″po-kon′dre-um), pl. *hypochon′dria* [*hypo-* + Gr. *chondros* cartilage]. Regio hypochondriaca [dextra et sinistra].

hypochordal (hi″po-kor′dal). Situated ventral to the notochord.

hypochromasia (hi″po-kro-ma′ze-ah) [*hypo-* + Gr. *chrōma* color]. 1. The condition of staining less intensely than normal. 2. Decrease of hemoglobin in the erythrocytes so that they are abnormally pale in color.

hypochromatic (hi″po-kro-mat′ik). Containing an abnormally small number of chromosomes; marked by hypochromatism.

hypochromatism (hi″po-kro′mah-tizm) [*hypo-* + *chromatin*]. Abnormally deficient pigmentation; especially deficiency of the chromatin in a cell nucleus.

hypochromatosis (hi″po-kro″mah-to′sis). The gradual fading and disappearance of the nucleus (the chromatin) of a cell. Called also *nuclear solution.*

hypochromemia (hi″po-kro-me′me-ah) [*hypo-* + Gr. *chrōma* color + *haima* blood + *-ia*]. A condition in which the blood has an abnormally low color index. **idiopathic h.,** idiopathic hypochromic anemia.

hypochromia (hi″po-kro′me-ah) [*hypo-* + Gr. *chrōma* color + *-ia*]. 1. Abnormal decrease in the hemoglobin content of the erythrocytes. 2. Hypochromatism.

hypochromic (hi″po-kro′mik). Pertaining to or marked by hypochromia.

hypochromotrichia (hi″po-kro″mo-trik′e-ah). Abnormally reduced pigmentation of the hair.

hypochrosis (hi″po-kro′sis) [*hypo-* + Gr. *chrōma* color + *-osis*]. Anemia in which there is an abnormally small amount of hemoglobin in the blood.

hypochylia (hi″po-ki′le-ah) [*hypo-* + Gr. *chylos* chyle + *-ia*]. Deficient secretion of gastric juice.

hypocinesia (hi″po-si-ne′ze-ah). Hypokinesia.

hypocinesis (hi″po-si-ne′sis). Hypokinesia.

hypocist (hi′po-sist). Hypocistis.

hypocistis (hi″po-sis′tis). The juice and extract of various species of *Cytinus*, as of *C. hypocistis* of southern Europe: astringent.

hypocitremia (hi″po-sit-re′me-ah) [*hypo-* + *citric* acid + Gr. *haima* blood + *-ia*]. Abnormally low content of citric acid in the blood.

hypocitruria (hi″po-sit-roo′re-ah) [*hypo-* + *citric* acid + Gr. *ouron* urine + *-ia*]. Excretion of urine containing an abnormally small amount of citric acid.

hypocoagulability (hi″po-ko-ag″u-lah-bil′ĭ-te). The state of being less readily coagulated than normal.

hypocoagulable (hi″po-ko-ag′u-lah-bl). Characterized by abnormally decreased coagulability.

hypocoelom (hi″po-se′lom) [*hypo-* + Gr. *koilōma* hollow]. The ventral portion of the coelom of any embryonic vertebrate.

hypocolasia (hi″po-ko-la′ze-ah). Hypokolasia.

hypocondylar (hi″po-kon′dĭ-lar). Below a condyle.

hypocone (hi′po-kōn) [*hypo-* + Gr. *kōnos* cone]. The distolingual cusp of an upper molar tooth.

hypoconid (hi″po-ko′nid). The distobuccal cusp of a lower molar tooth.

hypoconule (hi″po-kon′ūl). The distal, or fifth, cusp of an upper molar tooth.

hypoconulid (hi″po-kon′u-lid). The distal, or fifth, cusp of a lower molar tooth.

hypocorticalism (hi″po-kor′tĭ-kal-izm). Hypoadrenocorticism.

hypocorticism (hi″po-kor′tĭ-sizm). Hypoadrenocorticism.

hypocrine (hi′po-krin). Due to endocrine hypofunction.

hypocrinia (hi″po-krin′e-ah). Hypocrinism.

hypocrinism (hi″po-kri′nism) [*hypo-* + Gr. *krinein* to secrete]. A bodily state due to deficient secretion of any endocrine gland.

hypocupremia (hi″po-ku-pre′me-ah). An abnormally diminished concentration of copper in the blood.

hypocyclosis (hi″po-si-klo′sis) [*hypo-* + Gr. *kyklos* circle + *-osis*]. Insufficiency of accommodation due either to undue rigidity of the crystalline lens (*lenticular h.*) or to weakness of the ciliary muscle (*ciliary h.*).

hypocystotomy (hi″po-sis-tot′o-me) [*hypo-* + *cystotomy*]. The surgical opening of the bladder through the perineum.

hypocythemia (hi″po-si-the′me-ah) [*hypo-* + Gr. *kytos* cell + *haima* blood + *-ia*]. A deficiency in the number of erythrocytes in the blood, especially that in aplastic anemia.

hypocytosis (hi″po-si-to′sis) [*hypo-* + *-cyte* + *-osis*]. Defect or scantiness of corpuscles in the blood.

hypodactylia (hi″po-dak-til′e-ah). The presence of less than the normal number of fingers or toes.

hypoderm (hi′po-derm) [*hypo-* + Gr. *derma* skin]. 1. Hypodermis. 2. A hypodermic injection.

Hypoderma (hi″po-der′mah) [*hypo-* + Gr. *derma* skin]. A genus of warble flies of the family Oestridae which cause myiasis of the skin. **H. bo′vis,** a species which infests cattle, seriously damaging the hide and interfering with the nutrition of the animal. It sometimes causes a creeping eruption in man. **H. linea′ris, H. linea′tus,** a warble fly of cattle in the United States.

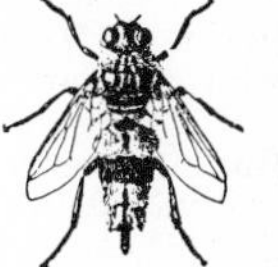

Hypoderma bovis and its larva.

hypodermatic (hi″po-der-mat′ik). Hypodermic.

hypodermatoclysis (hi″po-der-mah-tok′lĭ-sis). Hypodermoclysis.

hypodermatomy (hi″po-der-mat′o-me) [*hypo-* + Gr. *derma* skin + *temnein* to cut]. Incision of subcutaneous tissues.

hypodermiasis (hi″po-der-mi′ah-sis). Infection by *Hypoderma*; larva migrans.

hypodermic (hi″po-der′mik) [*hypo-* + Gr. *derma* skin]. Applied or administered beneath the skin.

hypodermis (hi″po-der′mis) [*hypo-* + Gr. *derma* skin]. 1. The layer of superficial fascia (tela subcutanea). 2. The outer layer of the body of invertebrates which secretes the cuticular exoskeleton.

hypodermoclysis (hi″po-der-mok′lĭ-sis) [*hypo-* + Gr. *derma* skin + *klyzein* to wash out]. The introduction, into the subcutaneous tissues, of fluids, especially physiologic sodium chloride solution, in large quantity.

hypodermolithiasis (hi″po-der″mo-lĭ-thi′ah-sis) [*hypo-* + Gr. *derma* skin + *lithos* stone + *-iasis*]. The formation or presence of subcutaneous calcareous nodes.

hypodiaphragmatic (hi″po-di″ah-frag-mat′ik). Below the diaphragm.

hypodiploid (hi′po-dip″loid). 1. Pertaining to or characterized by hypodiploidy. 2. An individual or cell with less than the diploid number of chromosomes.

hypodiploidy (hi′po-dip″loi-de). The state of having less than the diploid number of chromosomes ($<2n$).

hypodipsia (hi″po-dip′se-ah) [*hypo-* + Gr. *dipsa* thirst + *-ia*]. Abnormally diminished thirst.

hypodontia (hi″po-don′she-ah). Partial anodontia.

hypodynamia (hi″po-di-na′me-ah) [*hypo-* + Gr. *dynamis* force]. Diminished power. **h. cor′dis,** diminished cardiac power.

hypodynamic (hi″po-di-nam′ik). Pertaining to or characterized by hypodynamia.

hypoeccrisia (hi″po-ek-kris′e-ah) [*hypo-* + Gr. *ekkrisis* excretion + *-ia*]. A state characterized by abnormally diminished excretion.

hypoeccrisis (hi″po-ek′krĭ-sis). Hypoeccrisia.

hypoeccritic (hi″po-ek-krit′ik). Pertaining to or characterized by hypoeccrisia.

hypoelectrolytemia (hi″po-e-lek″tro-lit-e′me-ah). Abnormally decreased electrolyte content of the blood.

hypoemotivity (hi″po-e″mo-tiv′ĭ-te). Hypoaffectivity.

hypoendocrinia (hi″po-en″do-krin′e-ah). Hypoendocrinism.

hypoendocrinism (hi″po-en-dok′rĭ-nizm) [*hypo-* + Gr. *endon* within + *krinein* to secrete]. Abnormally decreased activity of an organ of internal secretion.

hypoendocrisia (hi″po-en″do-kris′e-ah). Hypoendocrinism.

hypoeosinophilia (hi″po-e″o-sin″o-fil′e-ah). Eosinopenia.

hypoepinephrinemia (hi″po-ep″ĭ-nef″rin-e′me-ah). An abnormally low level of epinephrine in the blood.

hypoepinephry (hi″po-ep″ĭ-nef′re). Abnormally diminished secretion by the adrenal gland.

hypoequilibrium (hi″po-e″kwĭ-lib′re-um). Unusual freedom from tendency to vertigo.

hypoergasia (hi″po-er-ga′se-ah) [*hypo-* + Gr. *ergon* work]. Abnormally decreased functional activity.

hypoergia (hi″po-er′je-ah). 1. Hypoergasia. 2. Hyposensitivity to allergens.

hypoergic (hi″po-er′jik). 1. Less energetic than normal. 2. Pertaining to or characterized by hypoergy.

hypoergy (hi″po-er′je). Abnormally diminished reactivity.

hypoesophoria (hi″po-es″o-fo′re-ah). A tendency of the visual axis to deviate downward and medially when fusion is prevented.

hypoesthesia (hi″po-es-the′ze-ah) [*hypo-* + Gr. *aisthēsis* sensation + *-ia*]. Abnormally decreased sensitiveness of the skin or of a special sense. **acoustic h., auditory h.,** hypacusis. **gustatory h.,** hypogeusesthesia. **olfactory h.,** hyposmia. **tactile h.,** hypopselaphesia.

hypoesthetic (hi″po-es-thet′ik). Pertaining to or characterized by hypoesthesia.

hypoestrinemia (hi″po-es″trĭ-ne′me-ah). Hypoestrogenemia.

hypoestrogenemia (hi″po-es″tro-jen-e′me-ah). An abnormally diminished amount of estrogen in the blood.

hypoevolutism (hi″po-e-vol′u-tizm). A condition characterized by abnormally retarded development.

hypoexophoria (hi″po-ek″so-fo′re-ah). A tendency of the visual axis to deviate downward and laterally when fusion is prevented.

hypoferremia (hi″po-fer-re′me-ah). Deficiency of iron in the blood.

hypoferrism (hi″po-fer′izm) [*hypo-* + L. *ferrum* iron]. Deficiency of iron in the system.

hypofibrinogenemia (hi″po-fi-brin″o-jen-e′me-ah). Abnormally low fibrinogen content of the blood.

hypofunction (hi″po-funk′shun). Diminished function.

hypogalactia (hi″po-gah-lak′she-ah). Deficiency of milk secretion.

hypogalactous (hi″po-gah-lak′tus) [*hypo-* + Gr. *gala* milk]. Producing a deficient secretion of milk.

hypogammaglobulinemia (hi″po-gam″ah-glob″u-lin-e′me-ah). An abnormally low level of gamma globulin in the blood. **acquired h.,** hypogammaglobulinemia which becomes manifest after early childhood; the condition may be *primary* (i.e., without discoverable underlying cause) or *secondary* (i.e., associated with such conditions as multiple myeloma, lymphoma, and chronic lymphatic leukemia, in which there is failure of gamma globulin synthesis). **congenital h.,** hypogammaglobulinemia in which the manifestations of immunological inadequacy appear shortly after birth. **primary h., secondary h.** See *acquired h.*

hypogastric (hi″po-gas′trik) [L. *hypogastricus*]. 1. Situated below the stomach. 2. Pertaining to the hypogastrium (regio hypogastrica).

hypogastrium (hi″po-gas′tre-um) [*hypo-* + Gr. *gastēr* stomach]. Regio hypogastrica.

hypogastropagus (hi″po-gas-trop′ah-gus) [*hypo-* + Gr. *gastēr* belly + *pagos* thing fixed]. Conjoined twins united at the hypogastric region.

hypogastroschisis (hi″po-gas-tros′kĭ-sis) [*hypo-* + Gr. *gastēr* belly + *schisis* cleft]. A developmental anomaly in which an abdominal fissure is restricted to the hypogastric region.

hypogenesis (hi″po-jen′e-sis) [*hypo-* + Gr. *genesis* production]. Defective growth or development. **polar h.,** defective development at either extremity of the embryo, resulting in deformity.

hypogenetic (hi″po-je-net′ik). Pertaining to or characterized by hypogenesis.

hypogenitalism (hi″po-jen′ĭ-tal-izm). Hypogonadism.

hypogeusesthesia (hi″po-gūs″es-the′ze-ah) [*hypo-* + Gr. *geusis* taste + *aisthēsis* perception + *-ia*]. Abnormally diminished acuteness of the sense of taste.

hypogeusia (hi″po-gu′ze-ah). Hypogeusesthesia.

hypogigantosoma (hi″po-ji-gan″to-so′mah) [*hypo-* + Gr. *gigas* giant + *sōma* body]. Abnormally increased height and size, not amounting to true gigantism.

hypoglandular (hi″po-glan′du-lar). Marked by abnormally decreased glandular activity.

hypoglobulia (hi″po-glo-bu′le-ah) [*hypo-* + *glob-*

ule]. Deficiency in the number of red cells in the blood.

hypoglossal (hi″po-glos′al) [*hypo-* + Gr. *glōssa* tongue]. Situated under the tongue.

hypoglottis (hi″po-glot′is) [*hypo-* + Gr. *glōssa* tongue]. 1. The under side or part of the tongue. 2. Ranula.

hypoglycemia (hi″po-gli-se′me-ah) [*hypo-* + Gr. *glykys* sweet + *haima* blood + *-ia*]. An abnormally diminished content of glucose in the blood.

hypoglycemic (hi″po-gli-se′mik). 1. Pertaining to, characterized by, or producing hypoglycemia. 2. An agent that acts to lower the level of glucose in the blood.

hypoglycemosis (hi″po-gli″se-mo′sis). Abnormally diminished glucose content in blood and tissues.

hypoglycogenolysis (hi″po-gli″ko-jen-ol′ĭ-sis). Defective glycogenolysis.

hypoglycorrhachia (hi″po-gli″ko-ra′ke-ah) [*hypo-* + Gr. *glykys* sweet + *rhachis* spine + *-ia*]. Less than the normal content of glucose in the cerebrospinal fluid.

hypognathous (hi-pog′nah-thus). 1. Having a protruding lower jaw. 2. Of the nature of a hypognathus.

hypognathus (hi-pog′nah-thus) [*hypo-* + Gr. *gnathos* jaw]. A parasitic monster attached to the lower jaw of the autosite.

hypogonadia (hi″po-go-nad′e-ah). Hypogonadism.

hypogonadism (hi″po-go′nad-izm). A condition resulting from or characterized by abnormally decreased functional activity of the gonads, with retardation of growth and sexual development.

hypogranulocytosis (hi″po-gran″u-lo-si-to′sis). Reduction in the number of granular leukocytes in the blood. Cf. *agranulocytosis.*

hypohemia (hi″po-he′me-ah) [*hypo-* + Gr. *haima* blood + *-ia*]. Anemia.

hypohepatia (hi″po-he-pat′e-ah) [*hypo-* + Gr. *hēpar* liver]. Deficient functioning of the liver.

hypohidrosis (hi″po-hid-ro′sis) [*hypo-* + Gr. *hidrōsis* sweating]. Abnormally diminished perspiration.

hypohidrotic (hi″po-hĭ-drot′ik). Pertaining to, characterized by, or causing hypohidrosis.

hypohormonal (hi″po-hōr′mo-nal). Deficient in hormone; due to hormone deficiency.

hypohormonic (hi″po-hōr-mon′ik). Hypohormonal.

hypohormonism (hi-po-hor′mōn-izm). Endocrine hypofunction.

hypohydration (hi″po-hi-dra′shun). A state of decreased water content of the body; dehydration.

hypohydrochloria (hi″po-hi″dro-klo′re-ah). Hypochlorhydria.

hypohyloma (hi″po-hi-lo′mah). A tumor due to hyperplasia of hylic tissues.

hypohypnotic (hi″po-hip-not′ik). Marked by light sleep or hypnosis.

hypohypophysism (hi″po-hi-pof′ĭ-sizm). Hypopituitarism.

hypoidrosis (hi″po-id-ro′sis). Hypohidrosis.

hypoimmunity (hi″po-ĭ-mu′nĭ-te). Lowered immunity.

hypoinosemia (hi″po-in″o-se′me-ah) [*hypo-* + Gr. *is, inos* fiber + *haima* blood + *-ia*]. An abnormally decreased content of fibrin in the blood.

hypoinosis (hi″po-ĭ-no′sis). Hypoinosemia.

hypoinsulinemia (hi″po-in″su-lin-e′me-ah). A deficiency of insulin in the blood.

hypoinsulinism (hi″po-in′su-lin-izm). Deficient secretion of insulin by the pancreas, resulting in hyperglycemia.

hypoiodidism (hi″po-i-o′dĭ-dizm) [*hypo-* + *iodide* + *-ism*]. Deficiency of iodide in the body.

hypoisotonic (hi″po-i″so-ton′ik). Less than isotonic; said of a solution having a lesser osmotic power than another.

hypokalemia (hi″po-ka-le′me-ah). Abnormally low potassium content of the blood.

hypokalemic (hi″po-ka-le′mik). Pertaining to or characterized by hypokalemia.

hypokaliemia (hi″po-kal″e-e′me-ah). Hypokalemia.

hypokinemia (hi″po-ki-ne′me-ah) [*hypo-* + Gr. *kinein* to move + *haima* blood + *-ia*]. Subnormal cardiac output.

hypokinesia (hi″po-ki-ne′ze-ah) [*hypo-* + Gr. *kinēsis* motion + *-ia*]. Abnormally decreased mobility; abnormally decreased motor function or activity.

hypokinesis (hi″po-ki-ne′sis). Hypokinesia.

hypokinetic (hi″po-ki-net′ik). Pertaining to or characterized by hypokinesia.

hypokolasia (hi″po-ko-la′ze-ah) [*hypo-* + Gr. *kolazein* to curtail, to correct + *-ia*]. Functional weakness of the inhibiting mechanism.

hypolarynx (hi″po-lar′inks). The infraglottic compartment of the larynx from the true vocal cords to the first tracheal ring.

hypolemmal (hi″po-lem′al) [*hypo-* + Gr. *lemma* sheath]. Located beneath a sheath, as the end-plates of motor nerves under the sarcolemma of muscle.

hypolepidoma (hi″po-lep″ĭ-do′mah) [*hypo-* + Gr. *lepis* scale + *-oma*]. A tumor formed by hyperplasia of a hypoblastic tissue.

hypolethal (hi″po-le′thal). Not sufficient to cause death.

hypoleukemia (hi″po-lu-ke′me-ah). Hypoleukocytosis.

hypoleukia (hi″po-lu′ke-ah). Hypoleukocytosis.

hypoleukocytosis (hi″po-lu″ko-si-to′sis) [*hypo-* + Gr. *leukos* white + *kytos* cell + *-osis*]. A deficiency of leukocytes in the blood.

hypoleydigism (hi″po-li′dig-izm). Abnormally diminished functional activity of Leydig's interstitial cells.

hypoliposis (hi″po-li-po′sis). A deficiency of fat in the blood or tissues.

hypolutemia (hi″po-lu-te′me-ah). A decreased amount of luteal hormone (progesterone) in the blood.

hypolymphemia (hi″po-lim-fe′me-ah) [*hypo-* + *lymph* + Gr. *haima* blood + *-ia*]. Abnormal deficiency in the proportion of lymphocytes in the blood.

hypomagnesemia (hi″po-mag″nēs-e′me-ah). An abnormally low magnesium content of the blood plasma.

hypomania (hi″po-ma′ne-ah) [*hypo-* + Gr. *mania* madness]. Mania of a moderate type.

hypomaniac (hi″po-ma′ne-ak). A person affected with hypomania.

hypomanic (hi″po-ma′nik). Pertaining to or resembling hypomania.

hypomastia (hi-po-mas′te-ah) [*hypo-* + Gr. *mastos* breast + *-ia*]. Abnormal smallness of the mammary glands.

hypomazia (hi″po-ma′ze-ah). Hypomastia.

hypomegasoma (hi″po-meg″ah-so′mah) [*hypo-* + Gr. *megas* great + *sōma* body]. Tallness; tall stature.

hypomelancholia (hi″po-mel″an-ko′le-ah) [*hypo-* + Gr. *melancholia* melancholia]. Melancholia with but slight mental disorder.

hypomenorrhea (hi″po-men″o-re′ah) [*hypo-* + Gr. *mēn* month + *rhein* to flow]. Uterine bleeding of less than the normal amount occurring at regular intervals, the period of flow being of the same or less than usual duration.

hypomere (hi′po-mēr). 1. The ventrolateral portion of a myotome, innervated by an anterior ramus of a spinal nerve. 2. The lateral plate of mesoderm that develops into the walls of the body cavities.

hypomesosoma (hi″po-mes″o-so′mah) [*hypo-* +

Gr. *mesos* middle + *sōma* body]. A stature somewhat below the medium.

hypometabolism (hi″po-mĕ-tab′o-lizm) [*hypo-* + *metabolism*]. Abnormally decreased utilization of any substance by the body in metabolism; low metabolic rate.

hypometria (hi″po-me′tre-ah) ["a deficiency"; by analogy with Gr. *eumetria, hypermetria*]. A condition in which voluntary muscular movement falls short of reaching the intended goal; diminished range of movement.

hypomicron (hi″po-mi′kron). Submicron.

hypomicrosoma (hi″po-mi-kro-so′mah) [*hypo-* + Gr. *mikros* small + Gr. *sōma* body]. The very smallest normal stature.

hypomineralization (hi″po-min″er-al-i-za′-shun). Deficiency of mineral elements in the body.

hypomnesis (hi″pom-ne′sis) [*hypo-* + Gr. *mnēmē* memory]. Defective memory.

hypomodal (hi″po-mo′dal). In statistics, relating to the values or items located to the left of the mode in a variations curve.

hypomorph (hi′po-morf) [*hypo-* + Gr. *morphē* form]. A person who is short in standing height as compared with his sitting height. Cf. *hypermorph* and *mesomorph*.

hypomotility (hi″po-mo-til′ĭ-te). Deficient power of movement in any part.

hypomyotonia (hi″po-mi″o-to′ne-ah) [*hypo-* + Gr. *mys* muscle + *tonos* tension + *-ia*]. Deficient muscular tonicity.

hypomyxia (hi″po-mik′se-ah) [*hypo-* + Gr. *myxa* mucus + *-ia*]. Decreased secretion of mucus.

hyponanosoma (hi″po-na″no-so′mah) [*hypo-* + Gr. *nanos* dwarf + *sōma* body]. The extreme of dwarfishness, or nanism.

hyponatremia (hi″po-nah-tre′me-ah). Deficiency of sodium in the blood; salt depletion.

hyponatruria (hi″po-nah-troo′re-ah). An abnormally low level of sodium in the urine.

hyponea (hi″po-ne′ah). Hyponoia.

hyponeocytosis (hi″po-ne″o-si-to′sis) [*hypo-* + Gr. *neos* new + *-cyte* + *-osis*]. Leukopenia with immature forms of leukocytes present in the blood.

hyponitremia (hi″po-ni-tre′me-ah). Deficiency of nitrogen in the blood.

hyponoderma (hi″po-no-der′mah). Larva migrans.

hyponoia (hi″po-noi′ah) [*hypo-* + Gr. *nous* mind + *-ia*]. Sluggish mental activity.

hyponoic (hi″po-no′ik). Arising from early formed but unconscious processes.

hyponomoderma (hi″po-nom″o-der′mah). Larva migrans.

hyponychial (hi″po-nik′e-al). Beneath a nail.

hyponychium (hi″po-nik′e-um) [*hypo-* + Gr. *onyx* nail]. [N A] The thickened epidermis underneath the free distal end of the nail.

hyponychon (hi-pon′ĭ-kon) [*hypo-* + Gr. *onyx* nail]. Ecchymosis beneath the nail.

hypo-orchidia (hi″po-or-kid′e-ah). Defective endocrine activity of the testes.

hypo-orthocytosis (hi″po-or″tho-si-to′sis) [*hypo-* + Gr. *orthos* regular + *-cyte* + *-osis*]. Leukopenia in which the proportion of the various forms of leukocytes is normal.

hypo-ovaria (hi″po-o-va′re-ah). Defective endocrine activity of the ovaries.

hypo-ovarianism (hi″po-o-va′re-an-izm). Hypo-ovaria.

hypopallesthesia (hi″po-pal″es-the′ze-ah) [*hypo-* + *pallesthesia*]. Abnormally decreased sensibility to vibrations.

hypopancreatism (hi″po-pan′kre-ah-tizm). Diminished pancreatic activity.

hypopancreorrhea (hi″po-pan″kre-o-re′ah). Abnormally diminished secretion from the pancreas.

hypoparathyreosis (hi″po-par″ah-thi″re-o′sis). Hypoparathyroidism.

hypoparathyroidism (hi″po-par″ah-thi′roid-izm). The condition produced by defective action of the parathyroids or by the removal of those bodies.

hypopepsia (hi″po-pep′se-ah) [*hypo-* + Gr. *pepsis* digestion + *-ia*]. Impairment of digestion, due to hypochlorhydria.

hypopepsinia (hi″po-pep-sin′e-ah). Deficiency in the pepsin secretion of the stomach.

hypoperistalsis (hi″po-per″ĭ-stal′sis). Abnormally sluggish peristalsis.

hypopexia (hi″po-pek′se-ah) [*hypo-* + Gr. *pēxis* fixation + *-ia*]. The fixation by a tissue of a deficient amount of a substance.

hypopexy (hi′po-pek″se). Hypopexia.

hypophalangism (hi″po-fah-lan′jizm). Less than the usual number of phalanges of a finger or toe.

hypophamine (hi-pof′ah-min). The active principle of the posterior lobe of the hypophysis. **alpha h.**, oxytocin. **beta h.**, vasopressin.

hypopharyngoscope (hi″po-fah-ring′go-skōp). An instrument for inspecting the lower part of the pharynx.

hypopharyngoscopy (hi″po-far″in-gos′ko-pe). Examination of the lower part of the pharynx.

hypopharynx (hi″po-far′inks). That division of the pharynx which lies below the upper edge of the epiglottis and opens into the larynx and esophagus.

hypophobia (hi″po-fo′be-ah). Lack of fear.

hypophonesis (hi″po-fo-ne′sis) [*hypo-* + Gr. *phōnēsis* sounding]. Diminished intensity of the sound in auscultation or percussion.

hypophonia (hi″po-fo′ne-ah) [*hypo-* + Gr. *phōnē* voice + *-ia*]. Defective speech due to lack of phonation and resulting in whispering.

hypophoria (hi″po-fo′re-ah) [*hypo-* + Gr. *phorein* to bear + *-ia*]. Downward deviation of the visual axis of an eye when fusion is prevented.

hypophosphatasia (hi″po-fos″fah-ta′ze-ah). An inborn error of metabolism with a genetic basis, characterized by lowered phosphatase activity of the serum, due, apparently, to lack of alkaline phosphatase in the cells, and resulting in defective rebuilding and mineralization of bone.

hypophosphate (hi″po-fos′fāt). A salt of hypophosphoric acid.

hypophosphatemia (hi″po-fos″fah-te′me-ah). An abnormally decreased amount of phosphate in the blood.

hypophosphaturia (hi″po-fos″fah-tu′re-ah). An abnormally decreased amount of phosphate in the urine.

hypophosphite (hi″po-fos′fīt). Any salt of hypophosphorous acid.

hypophosphoremia (hi″po-fos″fo-re′me-ah). An abnormally decreased amount of phosphorus compounds in the blood.

hypophrenia (hi″po-fre′ne-ah) [*hypo-* + Gr. *phrēn* mind + *-ia*]. Feeblemindedness.

hypophrenic (hi″po-fren′ik) [*hypo-* + Gr. *phrēn* diaphragm, mind]. 1. Below the diaphragm. 2. Feebleminded.

hypophrenium (hi″po-fre′ne-um). A peritoneal space between the diaphragm and the transverse colon.

hypophrenosis (hi″po-fre-no′sis). Southard's term for feeblemindedness, including idiocy, imbecility, moronity, and subnormality.

hypophyseal (hi″po-fiz′e-al). Pertaining to a hypophysis, especially to the hypophysis cerebri, or pituitary gland.

hypophysectomize (hi″po-fiz-ek′to-mīz). To deprive of the hypophysis, or pituitary gland, by surgical removal.

hypophysectomy (hi″po-fiz-ek′to-me) [*hypophysis* + Gr. *ektomē* excision]. Surgical removal of the hypophysis or pituitary gland.

hypophysial (hi″po-fiz′e-al). Hypophyseal.

hypophysiectomy (hi″po-fiz″e-ek′to-me). Hypophysectomy.

hypophysin (hi-pof′ĭ-sin). A phosphorous substance secreted by the posterior lobe of the hypophysis and having the power of increasing the action of the heart: used in endocrine therapy.

hypophysioprivic (hi″po-fiz″e-o-priv′ik). Pertaining to deficiency of the internal secretion of the hypophysis.

hypophysis (hi-pof′ĭ-sis) [*hypo-* + Gr. *phyein* to grow]. Any process or outgrowth, especially the hypophysis cerebri. **h. cer′ebri** [N A, B N A], an epithelial body of dual origin located at the base of the brain in the sella turcica. See *pituitary gland.*

hypophysitis (hi-pof″ĭ-si′tis). Inflammation of the hypophysis cerebri.

hypophysoma (hi-pof″ĭ-zo′mah). A tumor of the hypophysis cerebri.

hypophysoprivic (hi-pof″ĭ-zo-pri′vik). Hypophysioprivic.

hypopiesia (hi-po-pi-e′se-ah). Abnormally low blood pressure occurring independently of any discoverable organic disease.

hypopiesis (hi″po-pi-e′sis) [*hypo-* + Gr. *piesis* pressure]. Abnormally low pressure, as abnormally low blood pressure.

hypopietic (hi″po-pi-et′ik). Pertaining to, characterized by, or causing hypopiesis.

hypopigmentation (hi″po-pig″men-ta′shun). Abnormally decreased pigmentation.

hypopigmenter (hi″po-pig-men′ter). An agent that reduces pigmentation of the skin.

hypopinealism (hi″po-pi′ne-al-izm). Defective functional activity of the pineal body.

hypopituitarism (hi″po-pĭ-tu′ĭ-tah-rizm). A condition due to pathologically diminished activity of the hypophysis due to pressure from basophil adenoma and marked by excessive deposit of fat and the persistence or acquirement of adolescent characteristics. See also *hyperpituitarism.*

hypoplasia (hi″po-pla′ze-ah) [*hypo-* + Gr. *plasis* formation + *-ia*]. Defective or incomplete development. **enamel h.,** incomplete or defective development of the enamel of the teeth. **enamel h., hereditary,** amelogenesis imperfecta. **h. of mesenchyme,** osteogenesis imperfecta. **Turner's h.** See *Turner's teeth.*

hypoplastic (hi″po-plas′tik). Marked by hypoplasia.

hypoplasty (hi′po-plas″te). Hypoplasia.

hypopnea (hi″po-ne′ah) [*hypo-* + Gr. *pnoia* breath]. Abnormal decrease in the depth and rate of the respiratory movements.

hypopneic (hi″po-ne′ik). Pertaining to or characterized by hypopnea.

hypoporosis (hi″po-po-ro′sis) [*hypo-* + Gr. *pōros* callus + *-osis*]. Deficient formation of callus.

hypoposia (hi″po-po′ze-ah) [*hypo-* + Gr. *posis* drinking + *-ia*]. Abnormally diminished ingestion of fluids.

hypopotassemia (hi″po-po″tah-se′me-ah). Hypokalemia.

hypopotassemic (hi″po-po″tah-se′mik). Hypokalemic.

hypopotentia (hi″po-po-ten′she-ah) [*hypo-* + L. *potentia* power]. A condition of diminished power, especially of diminished electrical activity of the cerebral cortex.

hypopraxia (hi″po-prak′se-ah) [*hypo-* + Gr. *praxis* action + *-ia*]. Abnormally diminished activity.

hypoprolanemia (hi″po-pro″lan-e′me-ah). A lessened amount of prolan A in the blood.

hypoprosody (hi″po-pros′o-de). Diminution of the normal variation of stress, pitch, and rhythm of speech.

hypoproteinemia (hi″po-pro″te-in-e′me-ah). Abnormal decrease in the amount of protein in the blood. **prehepatic h.,** hypoproteinemia occurring as a result of prolonged ingestion of faulty low-protein diet.

hypoproteinia (hi″po-pro″te-in′e-ah). A subnormal protein status of the body.

hypoproteinic (hi″po-pro″te-in′ik). Pertaining to or characterized by hypoproteinia.

hypoproteinosis (hi″po-pro″te-in-o′sis). Deficiency of proteins or protein foods.

hypoprothrombinemia (hi″po-pro-throm″bin-e′me-ah). Deficiency of prothrombin in the blood.

hypopselaphesia (hi″pop-sel″ah-fe′ze-ah) [*hypo-* + Gr. *psēlaphēsis* touch + *-ia*]. Diminution or dulness of the tactile sense.

hypopsychosis (hi″po-si-ko′sis) [*hypo-* + Gr. *psychē* mind, soul + *-osis*]. Diminution of the function of thought; blunting of the thought processes.

hypopteronosis cystica (hi″po-ter-on′o-sis sis′tĭ-kah) [*hypo-* + Gr. *pteron* feather]. A disease of canaries, known commonly as "lumps." The lesion consists of a cyst, single or multilocular, of a feather follicle which arises during a moult.

hypoptyalism (hi″pop-ti′al-izm) [*hypo-* + Gr. *ptyalon* spittle]. Abnormally decreased secretion of saliva.

hypopus (hi-po′pus). A stage in the development of the grain mites (Tyroglyphidae) between the first and the second nymph stages.

hypopyon (hi-po′pe-on) [*hypo-* + Gr. *pyon* pus]. An accumulation of pus in the anterior chamber of the eye.

hyporeactive (hi″po-re-ak′tiv). Pertaining to or characterized by a less than normal response to stimuli.

hyporeflexia (hi″po-re-flek′se-ah). Weakening of the reflexes.

hyporrhea (hi″po-re′ah) [*hypo-* + Gr. *rhoia* flow]. Slight hemorrhage.

hyposalemia (hi″po-sal-e′me-ah) [*hypo-* + L. *sal* salt + Gr. *haima* blood + *-ia*]. Abnormally decreased concentration of salt in the blood.

hyposalivation (hi″po-sal″ĭ-va′shun). Hypoptyalism.

hyposarca (hi″po-sar′kah). Anasarca.

hyposcheotomy (hi-pos″ke-ot′o-me) [*hypo-* + Gr. *oscheon* scrotum + *tomē* cut]. Puncture of a hydrocele at the lower portion of the tunica vaginalis.

hyposcleral (hi″po-skle′ral). Under the sclerotic coat of the eye.

hyposecretion (hi″po-se-kre′shun). Diminished secretion.

hyposensitive (hi″po-sen′sĭ-tiv). 1. Exhibiting abnormally decreased sensitivity. 2. Having the specific or general ability to react to a specific allergen reduced by repeated and gradually increasing doses of the offending substance.

hyposensitization (hi″po-sen″sĭ-ti-za′shun). The act or process of making hyposensitive; desensitization.

hyposexuality (hi″po-seks″u-al′ĭ-te). Deficiency in sexuality.

hyposiagonarthritis (hi″po-si-ag″on-ar-thri′tis). Inflammation of the temporomandibular joint.

hyposialadenitis (hi″po-si″al-ad″e-ni′tis) [*hypo-* + Gr. *sialon* saliva + *adēn* gland + *-itis*]. Inflammation of the submaxillary salivary gland.

hyposialosis (hi″po-si″ah-lo′sis). Hypoptyalism.

hyposkeocytosis (hi″po-ske″o-si-to′sis) [*hypo-* + Gr. *skaios* left + *-cyte* + *-osis*]. Hyponeocytosis.

hyposmia (hi-poz′me-ah) [*hypo-* + Gr. *osmē* smell + *-ia*]. Abnormally decreased sensitiveness to odors.

hyposmosis (hi″pos-mo′sis). Decreased speed of osmosis.

hyposomia (hi″po-so′me-ah) [*hypo-* + Gr. *sōma* body + *-ia*]. Inadequate bodily development.

hyposomnia (hi″po-som′ne-ah). Insomnia.

hypospadia (hi″po-spa′de-ah). Hypospadias.

hypospadiac (hi″po-spa′de-ak). A person affected with hypospadias.

hypospadias (hi″po-spa′de-as) [*hypo-* + Gr. *spadōn* a rent]. A developmental anomaly in the male in which the urethra opens on the under side of the penis or on the perineum. **female h.,** a developmental anomaly in the female in which the urethra opens into the vagina.

hyposphresia (hi″pos-fre′ze-ah) [*hypo-* + Gr. *osphrēsis* smell + *-ia*]. Hyposmia.

hyposphyxia (hi″po-sfik′se-ah) [*hypo-* + Gr. *sphyxis* pulse + *-ia*]. Decreased activity of the circulation, with lowered blood pressure.

hypospondylotomy (hi″po-spon″dil-ot′o-me) [*hypo-* + Gr. *spondylos* vertebra + *temnein* to cut]. The veterinary operation of incising the guttural pouch.

hypostasis (hi-pos′tah-sis) [*hypo-* + Gr. *stasis* halt]. 1. A deposit or sediment. 2. The formation of a deposit; especially a settling of the blood due to a feeble blood current.

hypostatic (hi″po-stat′ik). 1. Pertaining to, caused by, or associated with, hypostasis. 2. Abnormally static, said of certain inherited characters which are liable to be suppressed by other characters.

hyposteatolysis (hi″po-ste″ah-tol′ĭ-sis). Inadequate hydrolysis of fats during digestion.

hyposteatosis (hi″po-ste″ah-to′sis). Deficient secretion of sebum.

hyposthenia (hi″pos-the′ne-ah) [*hypo-* + Gr. *sthenos* strength + *-ia*]. An enfeebled state; weakness.

hyposthenianț (hi″pos-the′ne-ant). Reducing the strength; debilitant.

hyposthenic (hi″pos-then′ik). Pertaining to or characterized by hyposthenia.

hyposthenuria (hi″pos-thĕ-nu′re-ah) [*hypo-* + Gr. *sthenos* strength + *ouron* urine + *-ia*]. Decreased osmolality of the urine. **tubular h.,** decreased osmolality of the urine as a result of injury to the epithelial cells of the renal tubules.

hypostomia (hi″po-sto′me-ah) [*hypo-* + Gr. *stōma* mouth + *-ia*]. A developmental anomaly characterized by abnormal smallness of the mouth, the slit being vertical instead of horizontal.

hypostosis (hip″os-to′sis) [*hypo-* + Gr. *osteon* bone + *-osis*]. Deficient development of bone.

hypostypsis (hi″po-stip′sis) [*hypo-* + Gr. *stypsis* contraction]. Moderate astringency.

hypostyptic (hi″po-stip′tik). Moderately or mildly styptic.

hyposulfite (hi″po-sul′fit). Sodium thiosulfate.

hyposuprarenalemia (hi″po-su″prah-re″nal-e′me-ah). Hypoepinephrinemia.

hyposuprarenalism (hi″po-su″prah-re′nal-izm). Hypoadrenalism.

hyposympathicotonus (hi″po-sim-path″ĭ-ko-to′nus). A decreased tone of the sympathetic nervous system.

hyposynergia (hi″po-sin-er′je-ah) [*hypo-* + *synergia*]. Defective coordination.

hyposystole (hi″po-sis′to-le) [*hypo-* + *systole*]. Abnormal diminution of the systole.

hypotaxia (hi″po-tak′se-ah) [*hypo-* + Gr. *taxis* arrangement + *-ia*]. A condition of diminished control over the will and actions, such as occurs in the first stage of hypnotism.

hypotelorism (hi″po-tel′o-rizm) [*hypo-* + Gr. *tēlouros* distant]. Abnormally decreased distance between two organs or parts. **ocular h., orbital h.,** a condition characterized by abnormal decrease in the intraorbital distance, consistently present in trigonocephaly.

hypotension (hi″po-ten′shun). Diminished tension; lowered blood pressure. **orthostatic h.,** lowered blood pressure when the person changes from a supine to an erect position.

hypotensive (hi″po-ten′siv). 1. Characterized by or causing diminished tension or pressure, as abnormally low blood pressure. 2. A person with abnormally low blood pressure.

hypotensor (hi″po-ten′sor). A substance that lowers the blood pressure.

hypothalamotomy (hi″po-thal″ah-mot′o-me) [*hypothalamus* + Gr. *temnein* to cut]. Production of lesions in the posterolateral part of the hypothalamus, in the treatment of psychotic disorders.

hypothalamus (hi″po-thal′ah-mus). [N A, B N A] The portion of the diencephalon which forms the floor and part of the lateral wall of the third ventricle. It includes the optic chiasm, mammillary bodies, tuber cinereum, infundibulum, and hypophysis. The nuclei of this region exert control over visceral activities, water balance, temperature, sleep, etc.

hypothenar (hi-poth′e-nar) [*hypo-* + Gr. *thenar* palm]. [N A, B N A] The ridge on the palm along the bases of the fingers and the ulnar margin.

hypothermal (hi″po-ther′mal) [*hypo-* + Gr. *thermē* heat]. Pertaining to or characterized by reduced temperature.

hypothermia (hi″po-ther′me-ah) [*hypo-* + Gr. *thermē* heat + *-ia*]. Low temperature; especially a state of low body temperature induced as a means of decreasing metabolism of tissues and thereby need for oxygen, as used in various surgical procedures, especially on the heart. **endogenous h.,** abnormally reduced body temperature resulting from physiological causes, due to dysfunction of the central nervous system or of the endocrine system.

hypothermy (hi″po-ther′me). Hypothermia.

hypothesis (hi-poth′ĕ-sis). A supposition assumed as a basis of reasoning. **cardionector h.,** the hypothesis that there are two pacemakers or cardionectors in the heart; one, the atrionector, controls the atria, and the other, the ventriculonector, the ventricles. **Gad's h.,** the arterial and portal venous communications in the portal canal meet at an acute angle, leaving a wedge-shaped valve between them at their junction. **Harrower's h.,** hormone hunger. **insular h.,** the supposition that diabetes is due to disordered function of the islands of Langerhans in the pancreas. **lattice h.,** a theory of the nature of the antigen-antibody reaction which postulates reaction between multivalent antigen and divalent antibody to give an antigen-antibody complex of a lattice-like structure. **Makeham's h.,** the assumption that death is due to two co-existing causes: (1) chance, which is constant; (2) inability to withstand destruction, which progresses geometrically. **Planck's quantum h.,** that energy is radiated or absorbed only in integral units equal to *hn*, in which *h* is Planck's constant, and *n* is the frequency of vibration. **Starling's h.,** the direction and rate of transfer between plasma in the capillary and fluid in the tissue spaces depend on the hydrostatic pressure on each side of the capillary wall, on the osmotic pressure of protein in plasma and in tissue fluid, and on the properties of the capillary wall as a filtering membrane. **unitarian h.,** the theory that antibody is a single species of modified serum globulin regardless of the overt consequences of its reaction with homologous antigen, e.g., agglutination, precipitation, complement fixation, etc. **Woods-Fildes h.,** that the sulfonamides tend to replace para-aminobenzoic acid which is an essential metabolite for certain bacteria.

hypothrepsia (hi″po-threp′se-ah). Malnutrition.

hypothrombinemia (hi″po-throm″bin-e′me-ah). A deficiency of thrombin in the blood, resulting in a tendency to bleeding.

hypothymergasia (hi″po-thi″mer-ga′se-ah) [*hypo-* + Gr. *thymos* spirit + *ergon* work + *-ia*]. Meyer's term for underactivity of mood, marked by depression, stupor, sadness, and anxiety.

hypothymergastic (hi″po-thi″mer-gas′tik). Pertaining to or characterized by hypothymergasia.

hypothymia (hi″po-thi′me-ah) [*hypo-* + Gr. *thy-*

mos spirit + *-ia*]. Abnormal diminution of emotional tone: diminution of feeling tone.

hypothymic (hi″po-thi′mik). Marked by hypothymia.

hypothymism (hi″po-thi′mizm). Abnormally deficient thymus activity.

hypothyrea (hi″po-thi′re-ah). Hypothyroidism.

hypothyreosis (hi″po-thi″re-o′sis). Hypothyroidism.

hypothyroid (hi″po-thi′roid). Marked by or due to hypothyroidism.

hypothyroidation (hi″po-thi″roid-a′shun). The induction of hypothyroidism.

hypothyroidea (hi″po-thi-roi′de-ah). Hypothyroidism.

hypothyroidism (hi″po-thi′roid-izm). Deficiency of thyroid activity or the condition resulting therefrom.

hypothyrosis (hi″po-thi-ro′sis). Hypothyroidism.

hypotonia (hi″po-to′ne-ah) [*hypo-* + Gr. *tonos* tone + *-ia*]. A condition of abnormally diminished tone, tension, or activity. See also *hypotension*. **h. oculi,** low intraocular pressure.

hypotonic (hi-po-ton′ik). 1. Having an abnormally reduced tonicity or tension. 2. Having an osmotic pressure lower than that of the solution with which it is compared.

hypotonicity (hi″po-to-nis′ĭ-te). The state or quality of being hypotonic.

hypotonus (hi-pot′o-nus). Hypotonia.

hypotony (hi-pot′o-ne). Hypotonia.

hypotoxicity (hi″po-tok-sis′ĭ-te) [*hypo-* + Gr. *toxikon* poison]. The state or quality of possessing mitigated or diminished toxicity.

hypotrichosis (hi″po-trik-o′sis) [*hypo-* + Gr. *thrix* hair + *-osis*]. Presence of less than the normal amount of hair.

hypotrichous (hi-po′trĭk-us) [*hypo-* + Gr. *thrix* hair]. Having no cilia on the dorsal surface: said of certain infusoria.

hypotrophic (hi″po-trof′ik). Pertaining to or characterized by hypotrophy.

hypotrophy (hi-pot′ro-fe) [*hypo-* + Gr. *trophē* nutrition]. 1. Bacterial nutrition in which the organism is nourished by its host's nutrition. 2. Abiotrophy.

hypotropia (hi″po-tro′pe-ah) [*hypo-* + Gr. *tropos* a turning + *-ia*]. Downward deviation of the visual axis of an eye when fusion is a possibility.

hypotryptophanic (hi″po-trip-to-fan′ik). Caused by deficiency of tryptophan in the diet.

hypotympanotomy (hi″po-tim″pah-not′o-me). Surgical opening of the hypotympanum.

hypotympanum (hi″po-tim′pah-num). A space in the middle ear, below the lower edge of the sulcus tympanicus.

hypouremia (hi″po-u-re′me-ah). An abnormally low level of urea in the blood.

hypouresis (hi″po-u-re′sis). Deficient urination.

hypouricuria (hi″po-u″rik-u′re-ah). Deficiency of uric acid in the urine.

hypourocrinia (hi″po-u″ro-krin′e-ah) [*hypo-* + Gr. *ouron* urine + *krinein* to secrete + *-ia*]. Deficient secretion of urine.

hypovaria (hi″po-va′re-ah). Deficiency of the internal secretion of the ovary.

hypovarianism (hi″po-va′re-an-izm). Hypovaria.

hypovegetative (hi″po-vej″e-ta′tiv) [*hypo-* + L. *vegetativus* plant-fashion]. Denoting a constitutional body type in which somatic systems predominate in contrast to visceral organs.

hypovenosity (hi″po-ve-nos′ĭ-te). Incomplete development of the venous system in any area.

hypoventilation (hi″po-ven″tĭ-la′shun). A state in which there is a reduced amount of air entering the pulmonary alveoli, resulting in elevation of the carbon dioxide tension.

hypovertebrotomy (hi″po-ver″te-brot′o-me). Hypospondylotomy.

hypovitaminosis (hi″po-vi″tah-min-o′sis). A condition due to a deficiency of one or more essential vitamins.

hypovolemia (hi″po-vo-le′me-ah) [*hypo-* + *volume* + Gr. *haima* blood + *-ia*]. Abnormally decreased volume of circulating fluid [plasma] in the body.

hypovolemic (hi″po-vo-le′mik). Pertaining to or characterized by hypovolemia.

hypoxemia (hi″pok-se′me-ah) [*hypo-* + *oxygen* + Gr. *haima* blood + *-ia*]. Deficient oxygenation of the blood.

hypoxia (hi-pok′se-ah). Low oxygen content or tension; deficiency of oxygen in the inspired air.

hypoxic (hi-pok′sik). Pertaining to or characterized by hypoxia.

hypsarhythmia (hip″sah-rith′me-ah). Gibbs' term for an electroencephalographic abnormality sometimes observed in infants, with random, high-voltage slow waves and spikes that arise from multiple foci and spread to all cortical areas. The disorder is usually characterized by spasms or quivering spells, and is commonly associated with mental retardation.

hypsarrhythmia (hip″sah-rith′me-ah) [Gr. *hypsi* high + *arrhythmos* unrhythmical + *-ia*]. See *hypsarhythmia*.

hypsi- (hip′se) [Gr. *hypsi* high]. Combining form meaning high.

hypsibrachycephalic (hip″se-brak″e-se-fal′ik) [*hypsi-* + Gr. *brachys* broad + *kephalē* head]. Having the head broad and high.

hypsicephalic (hip″se-se-fal′ik) [*hypsi-* + Gr. *kephalē* head]. Having a vertical index over 75.

hypsicephaly (hip″se-sef′ah-le). Oxycephaly.

hypsiconchous (hip″se-kong′kus) [*hypsi-* + Gr. *konchē* shell]. Having an orbital index over 85.

hypsiloid (hip′sĭ-loid) [Gr. *hypsiloeidēs* in the shape of an Υ]. Shaped like the Greek letter Υ.

hypsiphobia (hip″sĭ-fo′be-ah). Hypsophobia.

hypsistaphylia (hip″sĭ-stah-fil′e-ah) [*hypsi-* + Gr. *staphylē* uvula + *-ia*]. Highness and narrowness of the palate.

hypsistenocephalic (hip″se-sten″o-se-fal′ik) [*hypsi-* + Gr. *stenos* narrow + *kephalē* head]. Having a high, curved vertex, cheek bones prominent, and jaws prognathic: said of a form of skull common among Copts, Fellahs, and Abyssinians.

hypso- (hip′so) [Gr. *hypsos* height]. Combining form denoting relationship to height.

hypsocephalous (hip″so-sef′ah-lus) [*hypso-* + Gr. *kephalē* head]. Having a high vertex; having a breadth-height index of the head of over 75.

hypsodont (hip′so-dont) [*hypso-* + Gr. *odous* tooth]. Having prism-shaped teeth with high crowns.

hypsokinesis (hip″so-ki-ne′sis) [*hypso-* + Gr. *kinēsis* motion]. A backward swaying, retropulsion or falling when in erect posture, seen in cases of paralysis agitans and other forms of the amyostatic syndrome.

hypsonosus (hip-so′no-sus) [*hypso-* + Gr. *nosos* disease]. Mountain sickness; balloon sickness.

hypsophobia (hip″so-fo′be-ah) [*hypso-* + Gr. *phobos* fear + *-ia*]. Morbid fear of great heights.

hypsotherapy (hip″so-ther′ah-pe) [*hypso-* + *therapy*]. The therapeutic use of high altitude.

hypurgia (hi-pur′je-ah) [L.; Gr. *hypourgiai* medical services]. The sum of the minor or subsidiary factors that make for recovery in any particular case.

hyrtenal (her′tĭ-nal). A terpene aldehyde, $(CH_3)_2C{:}C_6H_7.CHO$, from *Hernandia peltata*.

Hyrtl's loop, recess, sphincter, etc. (hēr′tlz) [Joseph *Hyrtl*, eminent anatomist at Prague and Vienna, 1810–1894]. See under the nouns.

hysteralgia (his″ter-al′je-ah) [*hystero-* + *-algia*]. Pain in the uterus.

hysteratresia (his″ter-ah-tre′ze-ah). Atresia of the uterus.

hysterectomy (his″ter-ek′to-me) [*hystero-* + Gr. *ektomē* excision]. The operation of excising the uterus, performed either through the abdominal wall (*abdominal h.*) or through the vagina (*vaginal h.*). **cesarean h.,** cesarean section followed by removal of the uterus, oviducts, and ovaries. **chemical h.,** destruction of the endometrium by means of caustic chemicals. **paravaginal h.,** excision of the uterus through a perineal incision. **Porro h.,** cesarean h. **radical h.,** Wertheim's operation. **subtotal h.,** hysterectomy in which the cervix is left in place. **supracervical h., supravaginal h.,** subtotal hysterectomy.

hysteresis (his″ter-e′sis) [Gr. *hysterēsis* a lagging behind]. The failure of coincidence of two associated phenomena, such as that exhibited in the differing temperatures of gelation and of liquefaction of a reversible colloid.

hystereurynter (his″ter-u-rin′ter) [*hystero-* + Gr. *eurynein* to widen]. An instrument for dilating the os uteri: a metreurynter.

hystereurysis (his″ter-u-rĭ-sis). Dilatation of the os uteri.

hysteria (his-tēr′e-ah) [Gr. *hystera* uterus + *-ia*]. A psychoneurosis, the symptoms of which are based on conversion and which is characterized by lack of control over acts and emotions, by morbid self-consciousness, by anxiety, by exaggeration of the effect of sensory impressions, and by simulation of various disorders. Symptoms of the disease are hyperesthesia: pain and tenderness in the region of the ovaries, spine, and head; anesthesia and other sensory disturbances; choking sensation; dimness of vision; paralysis; tonic spasms; convulsions; retention of urine; vasomotor disturbances; fever, hallucinations, and catalepsy. **anxiety h.,** hysteria showing conversion phenomena with recurring attacks of anxiety. **canine h.,** fright disease. **conversion h.,** a condition in which psychic energy from a repressed idea or complex is converted into nervous stimuli giving rise to physical symptoms. **fixation h.,** hysteria in which the symptoms are based on those of an organic disease. **h. libidino′sa,** Cullen's term for acute uterine pruritus or nymphomania. **h. ma′jor,** hysteria characterized by the sudden onset of dream states, stupors, and paralyses. **h. mi′nor,** hysteria with mild convulsions in which consciousness is not lost. **monosymptomatic h.,** hysteria which manifests itself by one symptom only.

hysteriac (his-tēr′e-ak). A person affected with hysteria.

hysteric (his-ter′ik). Pertaining to or characterized by hysteria.

hysterical (his-ter′ĭ-kal). Characterized by hysteria.

hystericism (his-ter′ĭ-sizm). A tendency toward hysteria.

hystericoneuralgic (his-ter″ĭ-ko-nu-ral′jik). Resembling neuralgia, but of the nature of hysteria.

hysteriform (his-ter′ĭ-form). Having the appearance of hysteria.

hysterism (his′ter-izm). Hysteria.

hysteritis (his″ter-i′tis). Metritis.

hystero- (his′ter-o) [Gr. *hystera* uterus]. Combining form denoting relationship to the uterus, or to hysteria. See also *metro-*.

hysterobubonocele (his″ter-o-bu-bon′o-sēl). An inguinal hernia containing the uterus.

hysterocarcinoma (his″ter-o-kar″sĭ-no′mah). Uterine carcinoma.

hysterocatalepsy (his″ter-o-kat′ah-lep″se). Hysteria with cataleptic symptoms.

hysterocele (his′ter-o-sēl) [*hystero-* + Gr. *kēlē* hernia]. Hernia of the uterus.

hysterocervicotomy (his″ter-o-ser″vĭ-kot′o-me) [*hystero-* + *cervix* + Gr. *tomē* a cutting]. Incision of the cervix uteri and lower segment of the uterus in difficult labor.

hysterocleisis (his″ter-o-kli′sis) [*hystero-* + Gr. *kleisis* closure]. Surgical closure of the os uteri.

hysterocolpectomy (his″ter-o-kol-pek′to-me) [*hystero-* + Gr. *kolpos* vagina + *ektomē* excision]. Vaginal hysterectomy with total colpectomy.

hysterocolposcope (his″ter-o-kol′po-skōp) [*hystero-* + Gr. *kolpos* vagina + *skopein* to examine]. An electrically lighted device for viewing the interior of the uterus.

hysterocystic (his″ter-o-sis′tik). Pertaining to the uterus and the bladder.

hysterocystocleisis (his″ter-o-sis″to-kli′sis) [*hystero-* + Gr. *kystis* bladder + *kleisis* closure]. The operation of turning the cervix uteri into the bladder and suturing it: done for the relief of vesico-uterovaginal fistula or for uretero-uterine fistula.

hysterocystopexy (his″ter-o-sis′to-pek″se) [*hystero-* + Gr. *kystis* bladder + *pēxis* fixation]. Ventrovesicofixation.

hysterodynia (his″ter-o-din′e-ah) [*hystero-* + Gr. *odynē* pain]. Pain in the uterus.

hysteroepilepsy (his″ter-o-ep′ĭ-lep″se). A severe type of hysteria with convulsions simulating those of epilepsy. At first there occur loss of consciousness and spasms, followed by a stage of violent spasmodic movements and mental disturbance, and finally a condition marked by delirium, erotic symptoms, etc.

hysteroepileptogenic (his″ter-o-ep″ĭ-lep″to-jen′ik) [*hysteroepilepsy* + Gr. *gennan* to produce]. Producing hysteroepilepsy.

hysteroerotic (his″ter-o-e-rot′ik). Both hysteric and erotic.

hysterogastrorrhaphy (his″ter-o-gas-tror′ah-fe) [*hystero-* + Gr. *gastēr* stomach + *rhaphē* suture]. Suture of the uterus to the abdominal wall.

hysterogenic (his″ter-o-jen′ik) [*hystero-* + Gr. *gennan* to produce]. Causing hysterical phenomena or symptoms.

hysterogram (his′ter-o-gram). A roentgenogram of the uterus.

hysterograph (his′ter-o-graf) [*hystero-* + Gr. *graphein* to record]. An apparatus for measuring the strength of uterine contractions in labor.

hysterography (his″ter-og′rah-fe) [*hystero-* + Gr. *graphein* to record]. 1. Graphic recording of the strength of uterine contractions in labor. 2. Roentgenography of the uterus after instillation of a contrast medium.

hysteroid (his′ter-oid) [*hystero-* + Gr. *eidos* form]. Resembling hysteria.

hysterolaparotomy (his″ter-o-lap″ah-rot′o-me) [*hystero-* + Gr. *lapara* flank + *tomē* a cutting]. Incision of the uterus through the abdominal wall.

hysterolith (his′ter-o-lith) [*hystero-* + Gr. *lithos* stone]. A uterine calculus.

hysterology (his″ter-ol′o-je) [*hystero-* + *-logy*]. The sum of what is known regarding the uterus.

hysterolysis (his″ter-ol′ĭ-sis) [*hystero-* + Gr. *lysis* dissolution]. The operation of loosening the uterus from its attachments or adhesions.

hysteromania (his″ter-o-ma′ne-ah) [*hystero-* + Gr. *mania* madness]. 1. Hysterical mania. 2. Nymphomania.

hysterometer (his″ter-om′e-ter) [*hystero-* + Gr. *metron* measure]. An instrument for measuring the uterus.

hysterometry (his″ter-om′e-tre) [*hystero-* + Gr. *metron* measure]. The measurement of the dimensions of the uterus.

hysteromyoma (his″ter-o-mi-o′mah). Myoma of the uterus.

hysteromyomectomy (his″ter-o-mi″o-mek′to-me) [*hystero-* + *myoma* + Gr. *ektomē* excision]. Excision of a uterine myoma.

hysteromyotomy (his″ter-o-mi-ot′o-me) [*hystero-* + Gr. *mys* muscle + *tomē* a cutting]. Incision of the uterus for the purpose of removing a solid tumor.

hysteronarcolepsy (his″ter-o-nar′ko-lep″se). Narcolepsy caused by hysteria.

hysteroneurasthenia (his″ter-o-nu″ras-the′ne-ah). Neurasthenia occurring in association with hysteria.

hysteroneurosis (his″ter-o-nu-ro′sis) [*hystero-* + *neurosis*]. A reflex nervous disorder due to a uterine lesion.

hystero-oophorectomy (his″ter-o-o″of-o-rek′-to-me) [*hystero-* + *oophorectomy*]. Excision of the uterus and ovaries.

hystero-ovariotomy (his″ter-o-o-va″re-ot′o-me). Hystero-oophorectomy.

hysteropathy (his″ter-op′ah-the) [*hystero-* + Gr. *pathos* disease]. Any uterine disease or disorder.

hysterope (his′ter-ōp). A person affected with hysteropia.

hysteropexia (his″ter-o-pek′se-ah). Hysteropexy.

hysteropexy (his′ter-o-pek-se) [*hystero-* + Gr. *pēxis* fixation]. The fixation of a displaced uterus by a surgical operation. It may be done by ventrosuspension, shortening of the round ligaments, shortening of the sacro-uterine ligaments, shortening of the endopelvic fascia (Manchester type operation). It is distinguished as *abdominal* or *vaginal*, according as the uterus is fastened to the abdominal wall or to the vagina.

hysteropia (his″ter-o′pe-ah) [*hystero-* + Gr. *ōps* eye]. Hysteric disorder of the vision.

hysteropsychosis (his″ter-o-si-ko′sis) [*hystero-* + Gr. *psychē* mind]. A mental disorder due to uterine disease.

hysteroptosia (his″ter-op-to′ze-ah). Metroptosis.

hysteroptosis (his″ter-op-to′sis). Metroptosis.

hysterorrhaphy (his-ter-or′ah-fe) [*hystero-* + Gr. *rhaphē* suture]. 1. Hysteropexy. 2. The operation of suturing of the lacerated uterus.

hysterorrhexis (his″ter-o-rek′sis). Metrorrhexis.

hysterosalpingectomy (his″ter-o-sal″pin-jek′-to-me) [*hystero-* + Gr. *salpinx* tube + *ektomē* excision]. Excision of the body of the uterus and uterine tubes.

hysterosalpingography (his″ter-o-sal″ping-gog′rah-fe) [*hystero-* + Gr. *salpinx* tube + *graphein* to record]. Roentgenography of the uterus and uterine tubes after the injection of opaque material. Called also *uterosalpingography*, *uterotubography*, *hysterotubography*, *metrosalpingography*, *metrotubography*.

hysterosalpingo-oophorectomy (his″ter-o-sal-ping″go-o″of-o-rek′to-me). Excision of the uterus, uterine tubes, and ovaries.

hysterosalpingostomy (his″ter-o-sal″ping-gos′-to-me). The operation of forming an anastomosis between the uterus and the distal portion of the uterine tube after excision of a strictured or obstructed portion of the tube.

hysteroscope (his′ter-o-skōp) [*hystero-* + Gr. *skopein* to examine]. An endoscope used in direct visual examination of the canal of the uterine cervix and the cavity of the uterus.

hysteroscopy (his″ter-os′ko-pe). Inspection of the uterus.

hysterospasm (his′ter-o-spazm). Spasm of the uterus.

hysterostat (his′ter-o-stat) [*hystero-* + Gr. *statikos* stopping]. A mechanical device for holding radium tubes in any desired distribution in the uterus in the treatment of cancer.

hysterostomatocleisis (his″ter-o-sto″mah-to-kli′sis) [*hystero-* + Gr. *stoma* mouth + *kleisis* closure]. An operation for vesicovaginal fistula consisting of closure of the cervical canal and conversion of the vesical and uterine cavities into one common cavity by means of an opening between them.

hysterostomatome (his″ter-o-sto′mah-tōm). A knife used in hysterostomatomy.

hysterostomatomy (his″ter-o-sto-mat′o-me) [*hystero-* + Gr. *stoma* mouth + *temnein* to cut]. Incision of the os or cervix uteri.

hysterosyphilis (his″ter-o-sif′ĭ-lis). A hysterical neurosis due to syphilitic disease.

hysterosystole (his″ter-o-sis′to-le) [Gr. *hysteros* too late + *systole*]. A contraction of the heart occurring after its normal time. Cf. *proiosystole*.

hysterotabetism (his″ter-o-ta′bĕ-tizm). Combined hysteria and tabes.

hysterothermometry (his″ter-o-ther-mom′e-tre). Uterothermometry.

hysterotokotomy (his″ter-o-to-kot′o-me) [*hystero-* + Gr. *tokos* birth + *temnein* to cut]. Cesarean section.

hysterotome (his″ter-o-tōm) [*hystero-* + Gr. *tomē* a cutting]. An instrument for incising the uterus.

hysterotomotokia (his″ter-o-to″mo-to′ke-ah) [*hystero-* + Gr. *tomē* a cutting + *tokos* birth]. Cesarean section.

hysterotomy (his″ter-ot′o-me) [*hystero-* + Gr. *temnein* to cut]. Incision of the uterus. **abdominal h.,** incision of the uterus through the wall of the abdomen. **vaginal h.,** incision of the uterus through the wall of the vagina.

hysterotrachelectasia (his″ter-o-tra″kel-ek-ta′se-ah). Surgical dilation of the cervix and uterus.

hysterotrachelectomy (his″ter-o-tra″kel-ek′to-me). Amputation of the cervix uteri; trachelectomy.

hysterotracheloplasty (his″ter-o-tra′kel-o-plas″te). Plastic repair of the cervix uteri; tracheloplasty.

hysterotrachelorrhaphy (his″ter-o-tra″kel-or′-ah-fe) [*hystero-* + Gr. *trachēlos* neck + *rhaphē* suture]. The operation of suturing the cervix uteri.

hysterotrachelotomy (his″ter-o-tra″kel-ot′o-me) [*hystero-* + Gr. *trachelos* neck + *tomē* a cutting]. Incision of the cervix uteri.

hysterotraumatic (his″ter-o-traw-mat′ik) [*hystero-* + Gr. *trauma* wound]. Pertaining to or associated with hysterotraumatism.

hysterotraumatism (his″ter-o-traw′mah-tizm). Hysteric symptoms following traumatism.

hysterotubography (his″ter-o-tu-bog′rah-fe). Hysterosalpingography.

hysterovagino-enterocele (his″ter-o-vaj″ĭ-no-en′ter-o-sēl) [*hystero-* + *vagina* + Gr. *enteron* intestine + *kēlē* hernia]. Hernia containing the uterus, vagina, and intestine.

hystriciasis (his″tri-si′ah-sis) [Gr. *hystrix* hedgehog + *-iasis*]. 1. Morbid erection of the hairs. 2. Ichthyosis hystrix.

hystricism (his′trĭ-sizm). Hystriciasis.

hystrix (his′triks) [Gr. "hedgehog"]. Ichthyosis hystrix.

hytakerol (hi-tak′er-ol). Trade mark for preparations of dihydrotachysterol.

hyther (hi′ther) [Gr. *hydōr* water + *thermē* heat]. The combined effect upon the body of the humidity and temperature of the air.

hyzone (hi′zōn). An unstable triatomic form of hydrogen, H_3.

I

I. 1. Chemical symbol for *iodine.* 2. Abbreviation for *intensity of magnetism.*

I^{131}. A radioactive isotope of iodine with atomic weight of 131 and a half-life of 8.04 days.

I^{132}. A radioactive isotope of iodine with atomic weight of 132 and a half-life of 2.4 hours.

i. Abbreviation for *optically inactive.*

I.A. Symbol for *impedance angle.*

-ia. Word termination used in names of diseases, indicating state or condition.

iamatology (i″am-ah-tol′o-je) [Gr. *iama, iamatos* remedy + *-logy*]. The study or science of remedies.

ianthinopsia (i-an″thĭ-nop′se-ah) [Gr. *ianthinos* violet + *opsis* vision]. Violet vision; a condition in which objects seem to be violet colored.

-iasis (i′ah-sis). Word termination meaning a process or the condition resulting therefrom, particularly a morbid condition. See *-sis.*

iateria (i″ah-te′re-ah) [Gr. *iatērion* a mode of cure]. Therapeutics.

iathergy (i-ath′er-je) [Gr. *iathēnai* to have been cured + *ergon* work]. The state of immunity existing in an immunized organism in which the tuberculin skin sensitivity has been abolished by specific desensitization.

iatraliptic (i″ah-trah-lip′tik) [Gr. *iatreia* cure + *aleiphein* to anoint]. Pertaining to the application of remedies by friction.

iatraliptics (i″ah-trah-lip′tiks). Treatment by inunction and friction.

iatrarchy (i′ah-trar″ke) [Gr. *iatros* physician + *archē* rule]. Government by physicians.

iatreusiology (i″ah-troo″se-ol′o-je) [Gr. *iatreusis* treatment + *-logy*]. The science of treatment; therapeutics.

iatreusis (i″ah-troo′sis) [Gr.]. Treatment.

iatric (i-at′rik) [Gr. *iatrikos*]. Pertaining to medicine or to a physician.

iatro- [Gr. *iatros* physician]. Combining form denoting relationship to a physician or to medicine.

Iatrobdella (i″at-ro-del′ah). Hirudo.

iatrochemical (i-at″ro-kem′e-kal). Pertaining to iatrochemistry.

iatrochemist (i-at″ro-kem′ist). A person belonging to the school of iatrochemistry.

iatrochemistry (i-at″ro-kem′is-tre) [*iatro-* + *chemistry*]. The name of a school of medicine of the 17th century, which espoused the theory that all the phenomena of life and disease were based on chemical action.

iatrogenesis (i″at-ro-jen′e-sis) [*iatro-* + Gr. *genesis* production]. The creation of additional problems resulting from the activity of physicians, as those related to an increasing number of aging persons as a result of the increased life span achieved by medical advances.

iatrogenic (i″at-ro-jen′ik) [*iatro-* + Gr. *gennan* to produce]. Resulting from the activity of physicians. Originally applied to disorders induced in the patient by autosuggestion based on the physician's examination, manner, or discussion, the term is now applied to any condition in a patient occurring as the result of treatment by a physician or surgeon.

iatrology (i″ah-trol′o-je) [*iatro-* + *-logy*]. The science of medicine.

iatromathematical (i-at″ro-math″ĕ-mat′ĭ-kal). Iatrophysical.

iatromechanical (i-at″ro-mĕ-kan′ĭ-kal). Iatrophysical.

iatrophysical (i-at″ro-fiz′ĭ-kal). The name of a school of medicine in the 17th century which thought all the phenomena of life and disease were based on the laws of physics.

iatrophysicist (i-at″ro-fiz′ĭ-sist). A person belonging to the iatrophysical school.

iatrophysics (i-at″ro-fiz′iks) [*iatro-* + Gr. *physikos* natural]. 1. The physics of medicine or of medical and surgical treatment. 2. The treatment of diseases by physical or mechanical means; physiatry.

iatrotechnics (i-at″ro-tek′niks) [*iatro-* + Gr. *technē* art]. The technics of medical and surgical practice.

iatrotechnique (i-at″ro-tek-nēk′). Iatrotechnics.

I.B. Abbreviation for *inclusion body.*

IC. Abbreviation for *inspiratory capacity.*

ice (īs). A solid produced by reduction of the temperature of water: used as a refrigerant. **dry i.,** carbon dioxide snow.

Iceland moss (īs′land maws′). See *Cetraria.* **I. spar,** a crystalline form of calcium carbonate: used in making Nicol prisms.

ichnogram (ik′no-gram) [Gr. *ichnos* a footprint + *gramma* mark]. A footprint.

ichor (i′kor) [Gr. *ichōr*]. A thin, serous, or sanious fluid from a sore or wound.

ichoremia (i″kor-e′me-ah) [*ichor* + Gr. *haima* blood + *-ia*]. Septicemia.

ichoroid (i′ko-roid) [*ichor* + Gr. *eidos* form]. Resembling ichor or pus.

ichorous (i′kor-us). Of the nature of a serum or ichor.

ichorrhea (i-ko-re′ah) [*ichor* + Gr. *rhoia* flow]. A copious discharge of ichorous fluid or sanies.

ichorrhemia (i″ko-re′me-ah) [*ichor* + Gr. *haima* blood + *-ia*]. Septicemia.

ichthammol (ik′tham-mol). A reddish brown to brownish black viscous fluid, with a strong, characteristic odor, obtained by the destructive distillation of certain bituminous schists, sulfonation of the distillate, and neutralization of the product with ammonia: used as a local antibacterial and irritant to the skin.

ichthyism (ik′the-izm). Ichthyismus.

ichthyismus (ik″the-iz′mus) [Gr. *ichthys* fish]. Ichthyotoxism. **i. exanthemat′icus,** a form in which the gastrointestinal irritation is accompanied by a scarlatinous rash.

ichthyo- (ik′the-o) [Gr. *ichthys* fish]. Combining form denoting relationship to fish.

ichthyoacanthotoxin (ik″the-o-ah-kan″tho-tok′sin) [*ichthyo-* + Gr. *akantha* prickle + *toxikon* poison]. The venom secreted by venomous fishes, in connection with stings, spines, or "teeth."

ichthyoacanthotoxism (ik″the-o-ah-kan″tho-tok′sizm). Intoxication resulting from injuries produced by the stings, spines, or "teeth" of venomous fishes.

ichthyocolla (ik″the-o-kol′ah) [*ichthyo-* + Gr. *kolla* glue]. A form of gelatin prepared from the swimming-bladders of the Russian sturgeon, *Acipenser huso:* used as a clarifying agent.

ichthyohemotoxin (ik″the-o-he″mo-tok′sin) [*ichthyo-* + Gr. *haima* blood + *toxikon* poison]. A toxic substance that is found in the blood of certain fish.

ichthyohemotoxism (ik″the-o-he″mo-tok′sizm). Intoxication caused by ichthyohemotoxin.

ichthyoid (ik′the-oid) [*ichthyo-* + Gr. *eidos* form]. Resembling a fish; shaped like a fish.

ichthyolsulfonate (ik″the-ol-sul′fo-nāt). A salt of ichthyolsulfonic acid.

ichthyootoxin (ik″the-o″o-tok′sin) [*ichthyo-* + Gr. *ōon* egg + *toxikon* poison]. A toxic substance derived from the roe of certain fish.

ichthyootoxism (ik″the-o″o-tok′sizm). Intoxication caused by ichthyootoxin.

ichthyophagous (ik″the-of′ah-gus). Eating or subsisting on fish.

ichthyophagy (ik″the-of′ah-je) [*ichthyo-* + Gr. *phagein* to eat]. The practice of subsisting on fish.

ichthyophobia (ik″the-o-fo′be-ah) [*ichthyo-* + *phobia*]. Abnormal aversion to fish.

Ichthyophthirius multifiliis (ik″the-o-thir′e-us mul″ti-fil′e-is). A ciliate protozoan which causes pustules in the skin of fresh-water fish.

ichthyosarcotoxin (ik″the-o-sar″ko-tok′sin) [*ichthyo-* + Gr. *sarx, sarkos* flesh + *toxikon* poison]. The poison found in the flesh of poisonous fishes, excluding toxins which may result from bacterial contamination.

ichthyosarcotoxism (ik″the-o-sar″ko-tok′sizm). Intoxication resulting from the ingestion of the flesh of poisonous fishes, excluding ordinary bacterial food poisoning.

ichthyosis (ik″the-o′sis) [*ichthyo-* + *-osis*]. A disease characterized by dryness, roughness, and scaliness of the skin, due to hypertrophy of the horny layer. Called also *fish skin disease* and *xeroderma*. **i. congen′ita,** a congenital anomaly of the skin characterized by diffuse hyperkeratosis and abnormal cornification and resulting in the formation of thick horny scales. Called also *hyperkeratosis congenita, keratosis diffusa foetalis*. **i. cor′nea,** keratosis pilaris. **follicular i., i. follicula′ris,** keratosis follicularis. **i. hys′trix,** a variety with dry and warty knobs (Machin, 1733). **i. intrauteri′na,** i. congenita. **linear i.,** ichthyosis occurring in bands or streaks. **i. lin′guae,** leukoplakia. **nacreous i.,** a form which is marked by pearly scales. **i. palma′ris, i. palma′ris et planta′ris, i. planta′ris,** keratosis palmaris et plantaris. **i. sauroder′ma,** severe ichthyosis in which the skin is covered with thick plates like the skin of a crocodile. Called also *crocodile skin*. **i. scutula′ta,** a form with lozenge-shaped scales. **i. seba′cea cor′nea,** keratitis follicularis. **i. serpenti′na,** ichthyosis with an eruption resembling a serpent's skin. **i. sim′plex,** xeroderma. **i. spino′sa,** ichthyosis hystrix in which the scales are spiny. **i. thysanotrich′ica,** trichostasis spinulosa. **i. u′teri,** a condition marked by the transformation of the columnar epithelium of the endometrium into stratified epithelium.

Ichthyosis in newborn (Arey).

ichthyosismus (ik″the-o-sis′mus). Ichthyotoxism.

ichthyotic (ik″the-ot′ik). Pertaining to or characterized by ichthyosis.

ichthyotoxic (ik″the-o-tok′sik). Caused by the toxic principle of fish.

ichthyotoxicology (ik″the-o-tok″sĭ-kol′o-je) [*ichthyo-* + Gr. *toxikon* poison + *-logy*]. The science of poisons derived from certain fish, their cause, detection, and effects, and the treatment of conditions produced by them.

ichthyotoxicum (ik″the-o-tok′sĭ-kum) [*ichthyo-* + Gr. *toxikon* poison]. An obsolete term proposed (1889) to designate a toxic substance found in eel serum.

ichthyotoxin (ik″the-o-tok′sin) [*ichthyo-* + *toxin*]. A general term applied to any type of toxic substance derived from fish.

ichthyotoxism (ik″the-o-tok′sizm) [*ichthyo-* + *toxin* + *-ism*]. A general term applied to intoxication caused by any toxic substance derived from fish.

I.C.N. Abbreviation for *International Council of Nurses*.

iconolagny (i-kon′o-lag″ne) [Gr. *eikōn* image + *lagneia* lust]. Sexual stimulation aroused by pictures or statues.

iconomania (i-kon″o-ma′ne-ah) [Gr. *eikon* image + *mania* madness]. Morbid interest in images, real or symbolic.

ICSH. Abbreviation for *interstitial cell–stimulating hormone* (luteinizing hormone).

I.C.T. Abbreviation for *inflammation of connective tissue*, and *insulin-coma therapy*.

ictal (ik′tal) [L. *ictus* stroke]. Pertaining to, characterized by, or caused by a stroke, such as an acute epileptic seizure.

icterepatitis (ik″ter-ep″ah-ti′tis). Icterohepatitis.

icteric (ik-ter′ik). Pertaining to or affected with jaundice.

icteritious (ik″ter-ish′us). 1. Affected with jaundice. 2. Of a yellow or jaundiced hue.

ictero-anemia (ik″ter-o-ah-ne′me-ah). A disease marked by the development of icterus and anemia, with splenic enlargement, urobilinuria, and a hemolysis associated with fragility of the red blood corpuscles. Called also *hemolytic icteroanemia* and *Widal's syndrome*.

icterode (ik′ter-ōd). Icteroid.

icterogenic (ik″ter-o-jen′ik) [*icterus* + Gr. *gennan* to produce]. Causing icterus.

icterogenicity (ik″ter-o-je-nis′ĭ-te). Ability to cause icterus.

icterohematuria (ik″ter-o-hem″ah-tu′re-ah). Heartwater.

icterohematuric (ik″ter-o-hem″ah-tu′rik). Pertaining to icterohematuria; marked by jaundice and hematuria.

icterohemoglobinuria (ik″ter-o-he″mo-glo″-bin-u′re-ah). Combined icterus and hemoglobinuria.

icterohepatitis (ik″ter-o-hep″ah-ti′tis). Inflammation of the liver with marked jaundice.

icteroid (ik′ter-oid) [*icterus* + Gr. *eidos* form]. Resembling jaundice.

icterus (ik′ter-us) [L.; Gr. *ikteros*]. Jaundice. **acholuric hemolytic i. with splenomegaly,** hemolytic jaundice. **bilirubin i.,** retention jaundice. **i. castren′sis gra′vis,** Weil's disease occurring among troops in camp. **i. castren′sis le′vis,** catarrhal jaundice affecting troops in camp. **i. catarrha′lis,** catarrhal jaundice. **congenital family i.,** hemolytic jaundice. **cythemolytic i.,** icterus due to excessive formation of bile from destruction of red blood corpuscles. **epidemic catarrhal i.,** a mild form of Weil's disease. **febrile i., i. febri′lis,** acute infectious jaundice. **i. gra′vis,** acute yellow atrophy of the liver. **i. gra′vis neonato′rum,** severe jaundice in the newborn, usually a form of iso-immunization with the Rh factor. **Gubler's i.,** a kind of hematogenous jaundice believed by Gubler to be due to excessively rapid hemolysis. **Hayem's i.,** hemolytic jaundice. **i. hemolyt′icus,** hemolytic jaundice. **i. infectio′sus,** leptospiral jaundice. **Liouville's i.,** i. neonatorum. **i. me′las** ["black jaundice"], Winckel's disease. **i. neonato′rum,** the jaundice sometimes seen in newborn children. **nuclear i.,** kernicterus. **i. prae′cox,** jaundice in secondary syphilis. **i. sim′plex,** catarrhal jaundice. **spirochetal i.,** leptospiral jaundice. **i. typhoi′des,** acute yellow atrophy of the liver. **urobilin i.,** regurgitation jaundice. **i. vir′idans,** green jaundice.

ictometer (ik-tom′e-ter) [*ictus* + Gr. *metron* measure]. An instrument for measuring the heart's impulse over the chest wall.

ictus (ik′tus), pl. *ic′tus* [L. "stroke"]. A stroke, blow, or sudden attack. **i. cor′dis,** the heart beat. **i. epilep′ticus,** an epileptic attack. **i. immunisato′rius,** the injection of a large quantity of bacteria or toxin for the purpose of inducing the formation of a large quantity of antibody. **i. paralyt′icus,** a paralytic stroke. **i. san′guinis,** an apoplectic attack. **i. so′lis,** a sunstroke.

ID. Abbreviation for *intradermal*, and *inside diameter*.

I.D. Abbreviation for *infective dose.*

I.D.$_{50}$. Abbreviation for *median infective dose*, being that amount of pathogenic microorganisms which will produce infection in 50 per cent of the test subjects.

Id. Abbreviation for L. *i'dem*, the same.

id (id). 1. Chromomere, def. 1. 2. Freud's term for the self-preservative tendencies and the instincts as a totality; the true unconscious. It is the reservoir of instinctive impulses and is dominated by the pleasure principle. 3. A skin rash associated with but remote from the main lesion of the disease: considered to be an allergic reaction following cutaneous sensitization to the causative agent of the disease. Often used as a word termination in combination with a root representing the causative factor, as syphilid, dermatophytid, etc.

-id (id) [Gr. *eidos* form, shape]. Word termination meaning having the shape of, or resembling. See also *id*, def. 3.

idant (i'dant). Weismann's name for the unit of germ plasm made up of simple units of ids. Cf. *biophore.*

-ide. A suffix signifying a binary compound of a nonmetallic element, such as a chloride or a sulfide.

Ide reaction, test [Sobei *Ide;* Tamao *Ide*, physicians in Tokyo]. See under *reaction.*

idea (i-de'ah) [Gr. "form"]. A mental impression or conception. **autochthonous i.,** an idea which comes into the mind in some unaccountable way, independently of trains of thought, and which is strange, but cannot be accounted for by a hallucination. **compulsive i.,** an idea which intrudes, recurs, and persists despite reason and will, and which impels toward some inappropriate act. **dominant i.,** a morbid or other impression that controls or colors every action and thought. **fixed i.,** a morbid impression or belief which stays in the mind and cannot be changed by reason. **hyperquantivalent i.,** an idea which has become of the utmost importance to the patient, absorbing his thought, and excluding anything which might tend to discredit its truth. **imperative i.,** compulsive i. **i. of reference, referential i.,** the assumption by a patient that the words and actions of others refer to himself or the projection of the causes of his own imaginary difficulties upon someone else.

ideal (i-de'al). Having some relation to ideas, impressions, or imaginations. **ego i.,** the standard of perfection unconsciously created by an individual for himself.

ideation (i"de-a'shun). The distinct mental presentation of objects. **incoherent i.,** a mental condition in which the patient is unable to express a definite idea because there are other ideas rushing into consciousness; called also *flow of ideas.*

ideational (i"de-a'shun-al). Relating to ideation or the formation of objects and images in the mind.

idée (id-a') [Fr.]. Idea. **i. fixe** (id-a' fēks'), fixed idea.

identification (i-den"tĭ-fi-ka'shun). A mental mechanism of the unconscious by which (1) the ego attaches or transfers to itself qualities or properties belonging to other persons or objects; or (2) the ego transfers to one person the representation it holds of another person or of itself. **cosmic i.,** identification of one's self with the universe, as in schizophrenic delusions of omnipotence.

ideodynamism (i-de"o-di'nah-mizm) [*idea* + Gr. *dynamis* power]. The stimulation, through the cerebral cells, by an idea, of those nerve fibers which are to realize that idea.

ideogenetic (i"de-o-je-net'ik). Induced by or related to vague sense impressions rather than organized images.

ideogenous (i"de-oj'e-nus). Ideogenetic.

ideoglandular (i"de-o-glan'du-lar). Arousing glandular activity as a result of some recollection or thought.

ideokinetic (i-de"o-ki-net'ik). Ideomotor.

ideology (id"e-ol'o-je) [Gr. *idea* + *-logy*]. 1. The science of the development of ideas. 2. The body of ideas characteristic of an individual or of a social unit.

ideometabolic (i"de-o-met-ah-bol'ik). Producing some metabolism as a result of mental action, normal or other.

ideometabolism (i"de-o-mĕ-tab'o-lizm). Metabolism produced by mental influence.

ideomotion (i"de-o-mo'shun). Motion or muscular action which is neither reflex nor volitional, but is induced by some dominant idea.

ideomotor (i"de-o-mo'tor). Aroused by an idea or thought: said of involuntary motion so aroused.

ideomuscular (i"de-o-mus'ku-lar). Producing involuntary muscular action as a result of some ideation, memory, or hallucination.

ideophrenia (i"de-o-fre'ne-ah). A morbid mental state characterized by marked perversion of ideas.

ideophrenic (i"de-o-fren'ik). Pertaining to or exhibiting ideophrenia.

ideoplastia (i"de-o-plas'te-ah) [*idea* + Gr. *plassein* to form]. The passive inert condition of a patient under complete hypnosis in which he is capable of receiving suggestions of ideas from the hypnotist.

ideovascular (i"de-o-vas'ku-lar). Producing vascular change as a result of some ideation, memory, or hallucination.

idio- (id'e-o) [Gr. *idios* own, peculiar]. Combining form denoting relationship to self or to one's own, or to something separate and distinct.

idio-agglutinin (id"e-o-ah-gloo'tĭ-nin) [*idio-* + *agglutinin*]. An agglutinin which originates in the animal independently of any transfer or artificial means.

idioblapsis (id"e-o-blap'sis) [*idio-* + Gr. *blapsis* a harming, damage]. Coca's name for a nonreaginic food allergy in which (1) the hereditary influence controlling it is independent of atopic inheritance, (2) allergic antibodies are not demonstrable, (3) many symptoms are not represented in the atopic group, and (4) the allergic reaction practically always causes acceleration of the pulse.

idioblaptic (id"e-o-blap'tik) [*idio-* + Gr. *blastikos* hurtful]. Pertaining to, or characterized by, idioblapsis.

idioblast (id'e-o-blast) [*idio-* + Gr. *blastos* germ]. Any one of the hypothetical ultimate units of a cell: a biophore.

idiochromatin (id"e-o-kro'mah-tin) [*idio-* + *chromatin*]. The chromatin which is concerned in reproduction; the chromatin which bears the ids.

idiochromidia (id"e-o-kro-mid'e-ah) [*idio-* + *chromidia*]. That part of the chromidia or extranuclear chromatin which takes part in the reproduction of the cell. Cf. *trophochromidia.*

idiochromosome (id"e-o-kro'mo-sōm). An accessory chromosome.

idiocrasy (id"e-ok'rah-se). Idiosyncrasy.

idiocratic (id"e-o-krat'ik). Idiosyncratic.

idiocy (id'e-o-se). Complete congenital imbecility; extreme mental deficiency. See *idiot.* **absolute i.,** the lowest type of mental deficiency. **amaurotic familial i.** (Tay, 1881; Sachs, 1887), a disease of infants and children, marked by changes in the macula lutea, increasing failure of vision, paralysis, and death. **athetosic i.,** athetosis. **Aztec i.,** microcephalic i. **cretinoid i.,** cretinism. **developmental i.,** idiocy due to arrest of brain development. **diplegic i.,** paralysis in infancy affecting all the extremities. **eclamptic i.,** idiocy associated with convulsions. **epileptic i.,** idiocy combined with epilepsy. **genetous i.,** idiocy dating from fetal life. **hemiplegic i.,** idiocy combined with hemiplegia. **hydrocephalic i.,** idiocy combined with chronic hydrocephalus. **intrasocial i.,** idiocy in which the patient is capable of performing some regular occupation. **Kulmuk i.,** Mongolian i. **microcephalic i.,** idiocy associated with microcephalia. **Mongolian i.,** marked mental deficiency associated with mongolism. **paralytic i.,** idiocy with paralysis. **paraplegic i.,** idiocy associated with paraplegia. **plagiocephalic i.,** idiocy associated with distortion of the cranium. **scaphocephalic i.,** idiocy associated with scaphocephaly. **sensorial i.,** mental defect due to early loss of any of the special senses. **traumatic i.,** that which results from an injury received at birth or in infancy.

idiogamist (id″e-og′ah-mist) [*idio-* + Gr. *gamos* marriage]. A person who is capable of coitus with only one particular woman, or with only a few selected ones, being impotent with all others.

idiogenesis (id″e-o-jen′e-sis) [*idio-* + Gr. *genesis* production]. The spontaneous origin of disease.

idioglossia (id″e-o-glos′e-ah) [*idio-* + Gr. *glōssa* tongue + *-ia*]. Imperfect articulation, with the utterance of meaningless vocal sounds.

idioglottic (id″e-o-glot′ik). Pertaining to idioglossia.

idiogram (id′e-o-gram″) [*idio-* + *-gram*]. A diagrammatic representation of a chromosome complement, based on measurement of the chromosomes of a number of cells.

idiohetero-agglutinin (id″e-o-het″er-o-ah-gloo′tĭ-nin) [*idio-* + Gr. *heteros* other + *agglutinin*]. A hetero-agglutinin normally present in the blood.

idioheterolysin (id″e-o-het-er-ol′ĭ-sin). A heterolysin normally present in the blood.

idiohypnotism (id″e-o-hip′no-tizm) [*idio-* + *hypnotism*]. Spontaneous or self-induced hypnotism.

idio-imbecile (id″e-o-im′bĕ-sil). A grade of mental deficiency between idiot and imbecile.

idio-iso-agglutinin (id″e-o-i″so-ah-gloo′tĭ-nin). An iso-agglutinin normally present in the blood, and not produced by artificial means.

idio-isolysin (id″e-o-i-sol′ĭ-sin). A lysin normally present which destroys the cells of an animal of the same species as that in which it is formed.

idiolalia (id″e-o-la′le-ah). A condition marked by the use of invented language.

idiolysin (id″e-ol′ĭ-sin) [*idio-* + *lysin*]. A lysin which is normally present in the blood and is not produced by artificial means.

idiomere (id′e-o-mēr). Chromomere.

idiometritis (id″e-o-me-tri′tis) [*idio-* + Gr. *mētra* womb + *-itis*]. Inflammation of the parenchyma of the uterus.

idiomuscular (id″e-o-mus′ku-lar) [*idio-* + L. *musculus* muscle]. Pertaining to the muscular tissue apart from any nerve stimulus; a term applied to certain muscular contractions which occur in degenerated muscles only.

idioneural (id″e-o-nu′ral) [*idio-* + Gr. *neuron* nerve]. Pertaining to a single nerve, or to the nervous system exclusively.

idioneurosis (id″e-o-nu-ro′sis) [*idio-* + Gr. *neuron* nerve]. Any neurosis arising from the nerves themselves; an idiopathic neurosis.

idioparasite (id″e-o-par′ah-sīt). A parasite generated within the body of the host.

idiopathetic (id″e-o-pah-thet′ik). Idiopathic.

idiopathic (id″e-o-path′ik). Of the nature of an idiopathy; self-originated; of unknown causation.

idiopathy (id″e-op′ah-the) [*idio-* + Gr. *pathos* disease]. A morbid state of spontaneous origin: one neither sympathetic nor traumatic. **toxic i.,** any one of a group of diseases due to sensitization to particular proteins, and including asthma, hay fever, urticaria, angioneurotic edema, and some forms of eczema and gastrointestinal disorder.

idiophone (id′e-o-fōn) [*idio-* + Gr. *phōnē* voice]. An apparatus by means of which vibrations of the singing voice will produce flower-pictures on a membrane covered with colored dust.

idiophonia (id″e-o-fo′ne-ah). Unpleasant quality of voice.

idiophore (id′e-o-fōr) [*idio-* + Gr. *pherein* to bear]. The (theoretical) primary form of living cell substance.

idiophrenic (id″e-o-fren′ik) [*idio-* + Gr. *phrēn* mind]. Pertaining to the brain itself.

idioplasm (id′e-o-plazm) [*idio-* + Gr. *plasma* anything formed]. The active, vital, or reproductive part of a cell contained in the chromosomes of the nucleus; on it depend the peculiar characters of the cell. Called also *germ plasm*.

idiopsychologic (id″e-o-si″ko-loj′ik). Pertaining to ideas formed within one's own mind.

idioreflex (id″e-o-re′fleks) [*idio-* + *reflex*]. A reflex brought about by a cause within the same organ.

idioretinal (id″e-o-ret′ĭ-nal). Pertaining to the retina alone: a term applied to a visual sensation occurring without any visual stimulus.

idiosome (id′e-o-sōm) [*idio-* + Gr. *sōma* body]. 1. A supposed ultimate element of living matter; micelle. 2. The centrosome of a spermatocyte, together with surrounding Golgi apparatus and mitochondria.

idiospasm (id′e-o-spazm). A spasm of a limited area or region.

idiosyncrasy (id″e-o-sin′krah-se) [*idio-* + Gr. *synkrasis* mixture]. 1. A habit or quality of body or mind peculiar to any individual. 2. An abnormal susceptibility to some drug, protein, or other agent which is peculiar to the individual.

idiosyncratic (id″e-o-sin-krat′ik). Pertaining to or characterized by idiosyncrasy.

idiot (id′e-ot) [Gr. *idiōtēs* one in private station, ignoramus]. A person without intellect and understanding; a feebleminded person whose mental age is below two years. **erethistic i.,** an idiot who is active and restless. **Mongolian i.,** a person affected with Mongolian idiocy. **pithecoid i.,** an idiot with an apelike face. **profound i.,** the lowest type of mental defective with practically no mentality, usually of small size and physically abnormal. **i.-savant,** a person who is idiotic in some respects, yet has some special faculty well developed, such as memory, mathematics, or music. **superficial i.,** an idiot higher in the scale than a profound idiot: he can speak, though imperfectly, and has fair motor coordination. **torpid i.,** an idiot who is dull and inactive.

idiotism (id′e-ot-izm). The state or condition of being an idiot.

idiotopy (id′e-o-top″e) [*idio-* + Gr. *topos* place]. The position and relation of the parts of an organ among themselves.

idiotoxin (id″e-o-tok′sin). Allergen; atopen; an antigen which causes an allergic reaction.

idiotrophic (id″e-o-trof′ik) [*idio-* + Gr. *trophē* nutrition]. Capable of selecting its own nourishment.

idiotropic (id″e-o-trop′ik) [*idio-* + Gr. *tropos* a turning]. A term applied to the type of personality which is satisfied with its own inner intellectual and emotional experiences.

idiotype (id′e-o-tīp). Genotype.

idiovariation (id″e-o-var″e-a′shun). A mutation or change in the germ plasm, the cause of which is unknown.

idioventricular (id″e-o-ven-trik′u-lar). Relating to or affecting the cardiac ventricle alone.

idiozome (id′e-o-zōm). Idiosome.

iditol (i′dĭ-tol). A hexahydric alcohol, CH_2OH-$(CHOH)_4CH_2OH$, isomeric with dextrose.

idorgan (id′or-gan). A potential organ or organism containing at least two plastids, but not possessed of individuality.

idose (i′dōs). A hexose isomeric with dextrose.

idrosis (id-ro′sis). Hidrosis.

I.E. Abbreviation for Ger. *immunitäts Einheit*, immunizing unit.

I-em-hotep. Imhotep.

ignatia (ig-na′she-ah) [L.]. The beanlike seed of *Strychnos ignatii*. It is poisonous, and contains the alkaloids strychnine and brucine.

igniextirpation (ig″ne-eks″ter-pa′shun) [L. *ignis* fire + *extirpatio* extirpation]. The excision of an organ by the hot cautery.

ignioperation (ig″ne-op″er-a′shun) [L. *ignis* fire + *operation*]. An operation performed by hot cautery.

ignipedites (ig″ne-pe-di′tez). Beriberi.

ignipuncture (ig′ne-punk″tūr) [L. *ignis* fire + *punctura* puncture]. Therapeutic puncture with hot needles.

ignis (ig′nis) [L.]. Fire. **i. inferna′lis** ["infernal fire"], ergotism. **i. sa′cer** ["sacred fire"]. 1. Ergotism. 2. Erysipelas. 3. Herpes zoster.

ignisation (ig″ni-za′shun) [L. *ignis* fire]. The hyperthermia produced by exposure to artificial sources of heat.

ignition (ig-nish′un) [L. *ignis* fire]. The act of burning or of taking fire.

ignotin (ig′no-tin). A principle obtained from Liebig's extract of meat. See *carnosin.*

igramide (ig′rah-mid). Sulfanilamide.

I.H. Abbreviation for *infectious hepatitis.*

II-para. Abbreviation for *secundipara.*

III-para. Abbreviation for *tertipara.*

I.K. Abbreviation for Ger. *immune Körper*, immune bodies. See *tuberculin,* and *Spengler's immune bodies*, under *body.*

Il. Chemical symbol of *illinium.*

ileac (il′e-ak). 1. Of the nature of ileus. 2. Pertaining to the ileum.

ileadelphus (il″e-ah-del′fus). Iliadelphus.

ileal (il′e-al). Pertaining to the ileum.

ileectomy (il″e-ek′to-me) [*ileum* + Gr. *ektomē* excision]. Surgical removal of the ileum.

ileitis (il″e-i′tis). Inflammation of the ileum. **distal i., regional i., terminal i.,** a disease in which the terminal 12 to 14 inches of the ileum becomes cicatrized following a chronic inflammation: it frequently leads to intestinal obstruction.

ileo- (il′e-o) [L. *ileum*]. Combining form denoting relationship to the ileum.

ileocecal (il″e-o-se′kal). Pertaining to the ileum and cecum.

ileocecostomy (il″e-o-se-kos′to-me). Surgical creation of an opening between the ileum and the cecum.

ileocecum (il″e-o-se′kum). The ileum and cecum considered as one organ.

ileocolic (il″e-o-kol′ik). Pertaining to the ileum and colon.

ileocolitis (il″e-o-ko-li′tis). Inflammation of the ileum and colon. **i. ulcero′sa chron′ica,** a chronic form characterized by fever, rapid pulse, anemia, diarrhea and right iliac pain.

ileocolonic (il″e-o-ko-lon′ik). Ileocolic.

ileocolostomy (il″e-o-ko-los′to-me) [*ileo-* + *colon* + Gr. *stoma* mouth]. Surgical creation of an opening between the ileum and colon.

ileocolotomy (il″e-o-ko-lot′o-me) [*ileo-* + *colon* + Gr. *temnein* to cut]. Surgical incision of the ileum and colon.

ileocystoplasty (il″e-o-sis′to-plas″te) [*ileo-* + Gr. *kystis* bladder + *plassein* to form]. Suture of an isolated segment of the ileum to the urinary bladder, to increase the bladder size and capacity.

ileoileostomy (il″e-o-il″e-os′to-me) [*ileo-* + *ileo-* + Gr. *stoma* mouth]. Surgical creation of an opening between two parts of the ileum.

ileoproctostomy (il″e-o-prok-tos′to-me) [*ileo-* + Gr. *prōktos* rectum + *stoma* mouth]. Surgical creation of an opening between the ileum and rectum.

ileorectal (il″e-o-rek′tal). Pertaining to or communicating with the ileum and rectum, as an ileorectal fistula.

ileorectostomy (il″e-o-rek-tos′to-me). Ileoproctostomy.

ileorrhaphy (il″e-or′ah-fe) [*ileo-* + Gr. *rhaphē* suture]. The operation of suturing the ileum.

ileosigmoid (il″e-o-sig′moid). Pertaining to the ileum and the sigmoid.

ileosigmoidostomy (il″e-o-sig″moid-os′to-me) [*ileo-* + *sigmoid flexure* + Gr. *stoma* mouth]. Surgical creation of an opening between the ileum and the sigmoid colon.

ileostomy (il″e-os′to-me) [*ileo-* + Gr. *stoma* mouth]. Surgical creation of an opening into the ileum.

ileotomy (il″e-ot′o-me) [*ileo-* + Gr. *temnein* to cut]. Incision of the ileum through the abdominal wall.

ileotransversostomy (il″e-o-trans″vers-os′to-me). Surgical creation of an opening between the ileum and the transverse colon.

ileotyphus (il″e-o-ti′fus). Typhoid fever.

iletin (il′ĕ-tin). Trade mark for preparations of insulin for injection. **lente i.,** trade mark for a preparation of intermediate-acting insulin free of modifying protein (insulin zinc suspension). **NPH i.,** trade mark for a preparation of insulin, protamine, and zinc, with a time activity similar to that of lente insulin. See *insulin isophane suspension.*

ileum (il′e-um) [L.]. [N A] The distal portion of the small intestine, extending from the jejunum to the cecum. Called also *intestinum ileum* [B N A]. **duplex i.,** congenital duplication of the ileum.

ileus (il′e-us) [L.; Gr. *eileos*, from *eilein* to roll up]. Obstruction of the intestines. **adynamic i.,** ileus resulting from inhibition of bowel motility, which may be produced by numerous causes, most frequently by peritonitis. **dynamic i., hyperdynamic i.,** spastic i. **mechanical i.,** obstruction of the intestines resulting from mechanical causes. **meconium i.,** ileus in the newborn due to blocking of the bowel with thick meconium. **occlusive i.,** mechanical i. **paralytic i., i. paralyt′icus,** adynamic i. **spastic i.,** obstruction of the bowel resulting from persisting contraction of the intestinal musculature. See *Ogilvie's syndrome*, under *syndrome.* **i. subpar′ta,** ileus due to pressure of the gravid uterus on the pelvic colon.

ilexanthine (i″lĕ-zan′thin). A yellow, crystalline principle, $C_{17}H_{23}O_{11}$, from holly leaves.

iliac (il′e-ak) [L. *iliacus*]. Pertaining to the ilium.

iliadelphus (il″e-ah-del′fus). Iliopagus.

ilicin (il′ĭ-sin). A bitter antiperiodic compound derived from holly, *Ilex aquifolium.*

ilidar (il′ĭ-dar). Trade mark for a preparation of azapetine.

ilio- (il′e-o) [L. *ilium*]. Combining form denoting relationship to the ilium or flank.

iliococcygeal (il″e-o-kok-sij′e-al). Pertaining to the ilium and coccyx.

iliocolotomy (il″e-o-ko-lot′o-me). Surgical incision of the colon in the iliac region.

iliocostal (il″e-o-kos′tal) [*ilio-* + L. *costa* rib]. Connecting or pertaining to the ilium and ribs.

iliofemoral (il″e-o-fem′or-al). Pertaining to the ilium and femur.

iliofemoroplasty (il″e-o-fem′or-o-plas″te). Operative fusion of a tuberculous hip joint by splitting the great trochanter from the shaft of the femur and inserting into the fissure a flap of bone bent down from the lateral surface of the ilium.

iliohypogastric (il″e-o-hi″po-gas′trik). Pertaining to the ilium and hypogastrium.

ilio-inguinal (il″e-o-in′gwĭ-nal). Pertaining to the iliac and inguinal regions.

iliolumbar (il″e-o-lum′ber). Pertaining to the iliac and lumbar regions, or to the flank and loin.

iliolumbocosto-abdominal (il″e-o-lum″bo-kos″to-ab-dom′ĭ-nal). Pertaining to the iliac, lumbar, costal, and abdominal regions.

iliometer (il″e-om′e-ter) [*iliac* spines + Gr. *metron* measure]. An instrument for determining the relative heights of the iliac spines and their relative distance from the center of the spinal column.

iliopagus (il″e-op′ah-gus) [*ilio-* + Gr. *pagos* thing fixed]. Symmetrical conjoined twins united in the iliac region.

iliopectineal (il″e-o-pek-tin′e-al). Pertaining to the ilium and pubes.

iliopelvic (il″e-o-pel′vik). Pertaining to the iliac region or muscle and to the pelvis.

iliopsoas (il″e-o-so′as). See *Table of Musculi.*

iliopubic (il″e-o-pu′bik). Iliopectineal.

iliosacral (il″e-o-sa′kral). Pertaining to the ilium and the sacrum.

iliosciatic (il″e-o-si-at′ik). Pertaining to the ilium and the ischium.

iliospinal (il″e-o-spi′nal). Pertaining to the ilium and the spinal column.

iliothoracopagus (il″e-o-tho″rah-kop′ah-gus) [*ilium* + Gr. *thōrax* chest + *pagos* thing fixed]. Symmetrical conjoined twins fused from the pelvis to the thorax.

iliotibial (il″e-o-tib′e-al). Pertaining to or extending between the ilium and tibia.

iliotrochanteric (il″e-o-tro-kan-ter′ik). Pertaining to the ilium and a trochanter.

ilioxiphopagus (il″e-o-zi-fop′ah-gus). Symmetrical conjoined twins fused from the pelvis to the xiphoid process.

ilium (il′e-um), pl. *il′ia* [L.]. The expansive superior portion of the hip bone. It is a separate bone in early life. Called also *os ilium* [N A].

ill (il). 1. Not well; sick. 2. A disease or disorder. **colt i.,** an infectious, catarrhal fever of young horses. **föhn i.,** the headache, weariness and depression that are felt when the föhn (a special wind from the south in Central Europe) blows. It is not known just what produces the symptoms but they are relieved by breathing washed air. **joint i.,** pyemia affecting the joints of foals soon after birth, due to infection with *Shigella equirulis.* **leaping i.,** staggers. **leg i.,** inflammation of the interdigital spaces in sheep, producing lameness. **louping i.,** a disease primarily affecting sheep in Great Britain and Ireland, characterized by encephalomyelitis, and caused by a virus which is transmitted by the tick, *Ixodes ricinus.* **navel i.,** omphalophlebitis. **thorter i.,** staggers.

illacrimation (il″ak-rĭ-ma′shun). Epiphora.

illaqueation (il″ak-we-a′shun) [L. *illaqueare* to ensnare]. The cure of an ingrowing eyelash by drawing it out with a loop.

Illicium (il-is′e-um) [L.]. A genus of magnoliaceous trees and shrubs.

illinition (il-ĭ-nish′un) [L. *illinire* to smear]. The application of an ointment or liniment with rubbing.

illinium (il-lin′e-um) [University of *Illinois*]. Former name of the element *promethium.*

illness (il′nes). A condition marked by pronounced deviation from the normal healthy state; sickness. **compressed air i.,** decompression sickness.

illumination (ĭ-lu″mĭ-na′shun) [L. *illuminatio*]. The lighting up of a part, cavity, organ, or object for inspection. The illumination at any point of a surface is the density of the luminous flux at that point. **axial i.,** the transmission or reflection of light along the axis of a microscope. **central i.,** axial i. **contact i.,** illumination of the eye by means of an instrument which is pressed directly to the cornea and conjunctiva. **critical i.,** the focusing of light precisely upon an object inspected. **darkfield i., darkground i.,** the throwing of peripheral rays of light upon a microscopical object from the side, the center rays being blocked out. The object appears bright upon a dark background. See *ultramicroscope.* **direct i.,** the throwing of light upon a microscopical object from above or from the direction of observation. **focal i.,** the throwing of light upon the focus of a lens or mirror. **Köhler i.,** an improved method of illumination, for obtaining the best image detail in microscopical work. **lateral i., oblique i.,** illumination in which the light enters the microscope obliquely. **through i.,** the transmission of light through an object, or from the direction opposite to that of observation. **vertical i.,** direct i.

illuminism (ĭ-lu′min-izm). A state marked by delusions of communication with supernatural beings.

illusion (ĭ-lu′zhun) [L. *illusio*]. A false or misinterpreted sensory impression; a false interpretation of a real sensory image. **Kuhnt's i.,** similar intervals seem smaller in the temporal field than in the nasal field of a single eye. **passive i.,** an illusion determined by the nature of the sense organs and the environment, as double vision of a single object.

illusional (ĭ-lu′zhun-al). Pertaining to, or characterized by, illusions.

illutation (il″u-ta′shun) [L. *in* in + *lutum* mud]. Treatment by mud baths.

ilotycin (i″lo-ti′sin). Trade mark for preparations of erythromycin.

I.M. Abbreviation for *intramuscularly* (by intramuscular injection).

im-. A prefix in chemical names indicating the bivalent group >NH.

ima (i′mah) [L.]. Lowest.

image (im′ij) [L. *imago*]. A picture or conception with more or less likeness to an objective reality. **accidental i.,** after-image. **acoustic i.,** a concept corresponding to something heard. **aerial i.,** an image seen as in the air by use of the ophthalmoscope. **auditory i.,** acoustic i. **body i.,** a three-dimensional concept of one's self, recorded in the cortex by the perception of ever-changing postures of the body, and constantly changing with them. **direct i., erect i.,** a picture from rays not yet focused. **false i.,** the one formed by the deviating eye in strabismus. **heteronymous i.,** the two images seen when the eyes are focused on a point beyond the object. **homonymous i.,** the two images seen when the eyes are focused on a point nearer than the object. **incidental i.,** the impression of an image which remains on the retina after the object has been removed. **inverted i.,** real i. **memory i.,** a sensation or sense perception as it is pictured in the memory. **mental i.,** any concept corresponding to an object appreciated by the senses. **mirror i.** 1. The image of light made visible by the reflecting surface of the cornea and lens when illuminated through the slit lamp. 2. An identical reproduction of an object except for transposition of right and left relations, as appears in the reflection of an object in a mirror. **motor i.,** the organized cerebral model of the possible movements of the body. **negative i.,** after-image. **ocular i.,** visual i. **optical i.,** one formed by the reflection or refraction of rays of light. **Purkinje's i.,** an image upon the retina produced by the shadow of the blood vessels. **Purkinje-Sanson i's,** three pairs of images of one object seen in observing the pupil. **real i.,** one formed where the emanating rays are collected, in which the object is pictured as being inverted. **retinal i.,** the representation formed upon the retina of an object seen. **sensory i.,** a representation formed by means of one or more of the sense organs. **specular i.,** mirror i., def. 1. **tactile i.,** a mental concept corresponding to an object perceived by the sense of touch. **virtual i.,** direct i. **visual i.,** a mental concept corresponding to an object perceived by the sense of sight.

imagines (ĭ-maj′ĭ-nēz). Plural of *imago.*

imago (ĭ-ma′go), pl. *ima′goes,* or *imag′ines* [L.]. 1. The final or adult stage of an insect. Cf. *larva, pupa.* 2. In psychoanalysis, a childhood memory or phantasy of a loved person which remains in adult life.

imagocide (ĭ-ma′go-sīd) [*imago* + L. *caedere* to kill]. An agent which destroys adult insects, especially adult mosquitoes.

imapunga (im-ah-pung′ah). A disease of cattle in South Africa.

imbalance (im-bal′ans). Lack of balance; especially lack of balance between muscles, as in insufficiency of ocular muscles. **autonomic i.,** autonomic ataxia; any disturbance of the involuntary nervous system. **sympathetic i.,** vagotonia. **vasomotor i.,** autonomic imbalance.

imbecile (im′bĕ-sil). 1. Defective mentally. 2. One who is mentally defective; a feebleminded person whose mental age is between two and seven years. **moral i.,** an imbecile who is morally as well as mentally deficient.

imbecility (im″bĕ-sil′ĭ-te) [L. *imbecillitas*]. Feebleness of mind, congenital or acquired. **phenylpyruvic i.,** phenylpyruvic oligophrenia.

imbed (im-bed′). Embed.

imbibition (im″bi-bish′un) [L. *imbibere* to drink]. The absorption of a liquid. **hemoglobin i.,** absorption by the tissue of free hemoglobin.

imbricated (im′brĭ-kāt″ed) [L. *imbricatus; imbrex* tile]. Overlapping like tiles or shingles.

imbrication (im″brĭ-ka′shun). The overlapping of apposing surfaces, like shingles on a roof.

Imhoff tank (im′hof) [Karl *Imhoff*, German sanitarian, born 1876]. See under *tank*.

Imhotep (im′ho-tep) (c. 2600 B.C.). An Egyptian physician of the third dynasty (founded by Zoser) who was later worshipped as a healing god. He is the first physician whose name is known.

imidamine (im″id-am′in). Antazoline.

imidazole (im″id-az′ōl). Iminazole.

imide (im′īd). A secondary amine; any compound containing the bivalent group, >NH.

imido- (ĭ-me′do). A prefix used to denote the presence in a compound of the bivalent group >NH attached to an acid radical.

imidogen (ĭ-me′do-jen). The bivalent radical >NH.

iminazole (im″in-az′ōl). A radical,

```
HC—N
||   H\
      >CH, occurring in histidine.
HC—N//
```

iminazolyl-ethylamine (im″in-az″o-lil-eth″il-am′in). Histamine.

imino- (ĭ-me′no). A prefix used to denote the presence of the bivalent group >NH attached to a nonacid radical.

imino-urea (ĭ-me″no-u-re′ah). Guanidine.

imipramine (ĭ-mip′rah-mēn). Chemical name: 5-(3-dimethylaminopropyl)-10,11-dihydro-5H-dibenz(b,f)azepine: used as a psychic energizer.

Imlach's plug (im′laks) [Francis *Imlach*, Scottish physician, 1819–1891]. See under *plug*.

immature (im″ah-tūr′) [L. *in* not + *maturus* mature]. Unripe or not fully developed.

immediate (ĭ-me′de-āt) [L. *in* not + *mediatus* mediate]. Direct; with nothing intervening.

immedicable (im-med′ĭ-kah-b′l) [L. *immedicabilis*]. Beyond the hope of cure.

immersion (ĭ-mer′shun) [L. *immersio*]. 1. The plunging of a body into a liquid. 2. The use of the microscope with the object and object glass both covered with a liquid. **homogeneous i.,** the employment in microscopy of a liquid of nearly the same refractive power as the cover glass. **oil i.,** the covering of the microscopical objective and the object with oil. **water i.,** the covering of the microscopical objective and the object with water.

immiscible (ĭ-mis′ĭ-b′l). Not susceptible of being mixed.

immobility (im″mo-bil′ĭ-te). 1. The state of being immovable. 2. Chronic hydrocephalus of cattle.

immobilization (im-mo″bil-i-za′shun). The act of rendering immovable.

immobilize (im-mo′bil-īz) [L. *in* not + *mobilis* movable]. To render incapable of being moved.

immune (ĭ-mūn′) [L. *immunis* safe]. 1. Protected against any particular disease, as by inoculation. 2. A person or animal that is protected against any particular disease or poison.

immunifacient (ĭ-mu″nĭ-fa′shent). Producing immunity: said of diseases, such as diphtheria and typhoid, which for a time produce immunity against themselves.

immunifaction (ĭ-mu″nĭ-fak′shun). Immunization.

immunisin (ĭ-mu′nĭ-zin). Amboceptor.

immunity (ĭ-mu′nĭ-te) [L. *immunitas*]. The condition of being immune; security against any particular disease or poison, specifically, the power which an individual sometimes acquires to resist and/or overcome an infection to which most or many of its species are susceptible. See *resistance*. **acquired i.,** specific immunity attributable to the presence of antibody and to a heightened reactivity of antibody-forming cells and of phagocytic cells, following prior exposure to an infectious agent or its antigens, or passive transfer of antibody. **active i.,** acquired immunity attributable to the presence of antibody formed by the animal in response to antigenic stimulus. **actual i.,** active i. **antibacterial i.,** immunity against the action of bacteria. **antiblastic i.,** immunity due to forces antagonistic to the growth of the microorganism in the body of the host organism. **antimicrobic i.,** antibacterial i., **antitoxic i.,** immunity against toxins. **antiviral i.,** immunity against viruses. **artificial i.,** passive i. **athreptic i.,** immunity due to the absence of a specific substance which is necessary for growth of the infecting organism. **bacteriolytic i.,** antibacterial i. **cellular i.,** acquired immunity (usually to an infectious agent) in which the role of phagocytic cells is predominant. **community i.,** herd i. **congenital i.,** the immunity which an individual possesses at birth. **cross i.,** immunity produced by inoculation with an organism different from, but belonging to the same group as, the organism of the disease. **familial i.,** immunity occurring as a characteristic in certain families. **herd i.,** the resistance of a group to attack by a disease to which a large proportion of the members are immune, thus lessening the likelihood of a patient with the disease coming into contact with a susceptible individual. **humoral i.,** acquired immunity in which the role of circulating antibody is predominant. **infection i.,** resistance to infection by reason of an already existing infection by the same or a homologous organism. **inherent i.,** a natural inborn immunity. **inherited i.,** immunity transmitted from the parents through the germ cells. **innate i.,** natural i. **intra-uterine i.,** a passive immunity acquired by the fetus through the placenta from an immune mother. **local i.,** immunity manifested predominantly in a restricted anatomical region or type of tissue. **maturation i.,** increase in resistance to disease that comes with development to maturity. **mixed i.,** acquired i. **natural i.,** the resistance of the normal animal to infection, in contrast to specific acquired immunity. **nonspecific i.,** immunity, or increase of antibodies, resulting from the injection of some nonspecific antigen. **opsonic i.,** immunity due to the presence of opsonins. **passive i.,** acquired immunity produced by administration of preformed antibody. **phagocytic i.,** immunity dependent on the formation in the body of substances which prepare the bacteria for phagocytosis. **placental i.,** intra-uterine i. **postoncolytic i.,** immunity to tumor development following lysis of a previously existing tumor. **preemptive i.,** a form of interference phenomenon. **Profeta's i.,** the alleged immunity against syphilitic infection possessed by some children of syphilitic parents. **racial i.,** the resistance which all or most of the members of a species or other natural group manifest toward a certain infection. **residual i.,** immunity which remains in the body for varying periods after the complete disappearance of the infection. **solid i.,** immunity against the various strains of a pathogenic microorganism. **species i.,** racial i. **specific i.,** immunity against a particular disease, e.g., scarlet fever, or against a particular antigen. **tissue i.,** local i. **toxin-antitoxin i.,** an active antitoxic immunity produced by injecting subcutaneously a nearly neutral mixture of diphtheria toxin and antitoxin.

immunization (im″u-ni-za′shun). The process of rendering a subject immune, or of becoming immune. **active i.,** inoculation with a specific antigen to promote antibody formation in the body. **collateral i.,** inoculation of a patient with an organism other than the one causing an existing infection. **isopathic i.,** active i. **occult i.,** immunization produced in some unknown, spontaneous way. **passive i.,** transient immunization produced by the introduction into the system of the blood serum of animals already rendered immune. **side-to-side i.,** an immunization method in which the antigen is injected into one side of the body and the corresponding antibody into the other side.

immunizator (im″u-ni-za′tor). That which renders immune.

immunocatalysis (im″u-no-kah-tal′ĭ-sis). Catalysis which participates in immunity reactions.

immunochemistry (im″u-no-kem′is-tre). That department of chemistry which deals with the substances and reactions concerned in immunity.

immunodiagnosis (im″u-no-di″ag-no′sis). Diagnosis by the reactions of immunity; serum diagnosis.

immunoelectrophoresis (ĭ-mu″no-e-lek″tro-fo-re′sis). A method combining electrophoresis and double diffusion for distinguishing between proteins and other materials by means of differences in their electrophoretic mobility and antigenic specificities. The supporting medium may be agar gel, cellulose acetate film, or other material. In general the antigen is placed in a central well and subjected to electrophoresis. The antibody is then placed in rectangular wells which are parallel to the direction of the electrophoresis. Double diffusion occurs between the antibody in the rectangular wells and the antigen. **reverse i.,** a procedure identical to immunoelectrophoresis, with the positions of the antigen and antibody being interchanged.

immunogenetic (ĭ-mu″no-je-net′ik). Pertaining to or concerned with the interrelations of immune reactions and genetic constitution, as in the study of blood groups.

immunogenetics (im″u-no-je-net′iks) [*immuno-* + *genetics*]. The branch of genetics concerned with the inheritance of antigenic and other characters related to the immune response.

immunogenic (im″u-no-jen′ik). Producing immunity.

immunohematology (ĭ-mu″no-hem″ah-tol′o-je). That branch of medicine dealing with diseases of the blood of which the cause, the pathogenesis, or the clinical manifestations have been shown to be determined by an antigen-antibody reaction.

immunologist (im″u-nol′o-jist). A person who makes a special study of immunology.

immunology (im″u-nol′o-je). The department of biology which concerns itself with the study of immunity.

immunopolysaccharide (ĭ-mu″no-pol″e-sak′-ah-rid). A polysaccharide obtained from bodies of various bacteria. These compounds have specific immunologic properties, such as the ability to precipitate homologous antisera and to act as antigens.

immunoprotein (im″u-no-pro′te-in). Immunprotein.

immunoreaction (ĭ-mu″no-re-ak′shun). The reaction that takes place between an antigen and its antibody.

immunosurgery (ĭ-mu″no-ser′jer-e). The employment of specific immune therapy in surgical practice.

immunotherapy (ĭ-mu″no-ther′ah-pe). Treatment by the production of immunity.

immunotoxin (im″u-no-tok′sin). Any antitoxin.

immunotransfusion (ĭ-mu″no-trans-fu′zhun). Transfusion of blood from donors previously immunized by the patient's bacteria or from the specific infection or of blood from persons recently recovered from the specific infection.

immunprotein (ĭ-mūn-pro′te-in). Protein concerned in immunity and its antibody action.

impact (im′pakt) [L. *impactus*]. A sudden and forcible collision.

impacted (im-pakt′ed) [L. *impactus*]. Driven firmly in; closely or firmly lodged in position.

impaction (im-pak′shun) [L. *impactio*]. The condition of being firmly lodged or wedged. **ceruminal i.,** an accumulation of cerumen in the external auditory canal. **dental i.,** the condition in which a tooth is embedded in the alveolus so that its eruption is prevented, or is locked in position by bone, restoration, or surfaces of adjacent teeth, preventing either its normal occlusion or its routine removal. **fecal i.,** a collection of putty-like or hardened feces in the rectum or sigmoid.

impalpable (im-pal′pah-b'l) [L. *in* not + *palpare* to feel]. Impossible of being detected by touch; extremely fine, or small.

impaludation (im″pal-u-da′shun). The application of malariotherapy.

impaludism (im-pal′u-dizm) [L. *in* into + *palus* marsh]. Malarial cachexia.

impar (im′par) [L. "unequal"]. Not paired; having no fellow; azygous.

imparidigitate (im-par″ĭ-dij′ĭ-tāt) [L. *impar* unequal + *digitus* finger]. Perissodactylous.

impatency (im-pa′ten-se). The condition of being closed or obstructed.

impatent (im-pa′tent). Not open; closed or obstructed.

impedance (im-pēd′ans). The opposition to the flow of an alternating current which is the vector sum of ohmic resistance plus additional resistance, if any, due to induction, to capacity, or to both. Its symbol is Z. The resistance due to the inductive and condenser characteristics of a circuit is called reactance.

impedin (im′pe-din). An agent which antagonizes the antimicrobic powers of the body.

imperative (im-per′ah-tiv) [L. *imperativus*]. Dominant; not subject to control by the will.

imperception (im″per-sep′shun). Defective power of perception.

imperforate (im-per′fo-rāt) [L. *imperforatus*]. Not open; abnormally closed.

imperforation (im-per″fo-ra′shun). The state of being abnormally closed. **otic i.,** ankylotia.

imperialine (im-pe′re-al-in). A crystalline alkaloid, $C_{35}H_{60}NO_4$, from *Fritillaria imperialis*.

imperious (im-per′e-us). Overruling or compulsive; said of acts or motions that are not under control of the will.

impermeable (im-per′me-ah-b'l) [L. *in* not + *per* through + *meare* to move]. Not permitting a passage, as for fluid.

impervious (im-per′ve-us) [L. *impervius*]. Impenetrable; not affording a passage.

impetiginization (im″pe-tij″ĭ-ni-za′shun). The development of impetigo upon an area previously affected with some other skin disease.

impetiginous (im″pe-tij′ĭ-nus) [L. *impetiginosus*]. Pertaining to or of the nature of impetigo.

impetigo (im″pe-ti′go) [L.]. A bacterial, inflammatory skin disease, characterized by the appearance of pustules. **Bockhart's i.,** superficial pustular perifolliculitis. **i. bullo′sa, bullous i.,** impetigo in which the developing vesicles do not rupture, but progress to form bullae, which collapse and become covered with crusts; sometimes occurring epidemically in hospital nurseries.

i. contagio'sa, a contagious disease, caused by coagulase-positive micrococci and sometimes by beta hemolytic streptococci; the initial lesion, a small reddish macule, soon becomes a vesicle, which ruptures readily, presenting a weeping spot on which the fluid dries, to form a crust. **i. contagio'sa bullo'sa,** a contagious skin condition characterized by appearance of bullae which rupture and become covered with crusts. **i. eczemato'des,** pustular eczema. **follicular i., i. follicula'ris,** superficial pustular perifolliculitis. **furfuraceous i.,** erythema streptogenes. **i. herpetifor'mis,** a severe disease affecting pregnant women, and characterized by the appearance of groups of pustules. **i. neonato'rum,** bullous impetigo in newborn infants due to staphylococcus infection; called also *pemphigus neonatorum, pemphigoid,* and *impetigo of the newborn.* **i. sim'plex, i. staphylog'enes,** impetigo due to pathogenic staphylococci. **i. syphilit'ica,** a pustular eruption in syphilis. **i. variolo'sa,** a pustular eruption occurring between the drying lesions of smallpox.

impf-malaria (impf'mah-la"re-ah) [Ger.]. Malaria produced by injection of infectious material.

impf-tetanus (impf'tet-ah-nus) [Ger.]. Inoculated tetanus: cultures from it afford a special form of pathogenic bacillus.

impilation (im"pi-la'shun). Rouleau formation.

Implacentalia (im"plas-en-ta'le-ah). A division of the class Mammalia, including the mammals that do not have a placenta.

implant[1] (im-plant'). To insert or to graft, especially into the intact tissues of the recipient, or host.

implant[2] (im'plant). Material which is inserted or grafted into the body, such as tissue, or a small container holding radon or radium, for internal application of its radiation. **endometrial i's,** fragments of endometrial mucosa transferred through the oviducts and implanted on the uterus, ovaries, or pelvic peritoneum.

implantation (im"plan-ta'shun) [L. *in* into + *plantare* to set]. 1. The insertion of a part or tissue, such as skin, nerve, or tendon, in a new site in the body. 2. Attachment of the blastocyst to the epithelial lining of the uterus, its penetration through the epithelium, and its embedding in the compact layer of the endometrium, occurring six or seven days after fertilization of the ovum. 3. The introduction of a solid medicine beneath the skin. 4. The inoculation of the bacteria into the blood or other fluid which is being tested for its bactericidal power. After a suitable interval portions of the mixture are transferred to culture mediums (explantation) or the mixture may be incubated directly if it is nutritive (inculturing). **central i.,** superficial i. **circumferential i.,** superficial i. **eccentric i.,** embedding of the blastocyst within a recess of the uterine cavity. **end-to-end i.,** surgical repair, as of the bowel or of a nerve, by bringing together the divided ends. **filigree i.,** the insertion of a silver network in the abdominal wall for the purpose of closing a large abdominal hernia. **hypodermic i.,** the placing of a medicine in the subcutaneous tissue. **interstitial i.,** complete embedding of a blastocyst within the endometrium. **nerve i.,** the operation of inserting and attaching a nerve into the sheath of another nerve. **parenchymatous i.,** the introduction of a medicine into the substance of a tumor. **periosteal i.,** the operation of inserting a normal tendon into the periosteum of a joint at the insertion of a paralyzed tendon to take the place of the latter. **silk i.,** the operation of restoring a paralyzed tendon by implanting strands of sterile silk so that they will stimulate the formation of fascial sheaths along the line of the paralyzed tendon. **superficial i.,** embedding of the blastocyst so that the blastocyst, and later the chorionic sac, comes to occupy the uterine cavity. **teratic i.,** the partial blending of an imperfect with a nearly perfect fetus.

imponderable (im-pon'der-ah-b'l) [L. *in* not + *pondus* weight]. Having no weight.

impotence (im'po-tens) [L. *in* not + *potentia* power]. Lack of power: chiefly of copulative power or virility. It may be *atonic,* due to paralysis of the motor nerves (nervi erigentes) without evidence of lesion of the central nervous system; *paretic,* due to lesion in the central nervous system, particularly in the spinal cord; *psychic,* dependent on mental complex; *symptomatic,* due to some other disorder, such as injury to nerves in the perineal region, by virtue of which the sensory portion of the erection reflex arc is blocked out.

impotency (im'po-ten"se). Impotence.

impotentia (im"po-ten'she-ah) [L.]. Impotence. **i. coeun'di,** inability of the male to perform the sexual act. **i. erigen'di,** inability to have an erection of the penis. **i. generan'di,** inability to reproduce.

impregnate (im-preg'nāt) [L. *impregnare*]. 1. To render pregnant. 2. To saturate or charge with.

impregnation (im"preg-na'shun) [L. *impregnatio*]. 1. The act of fecundation or of rendering pregnant. 2. The process or act of saturation; a saturated condition.

impressio (im-pres'se-o), pl. *impressio'nes* [L.]. An indentation, or concavity; used in anatomical nomenclature as a general term to designate an indentation produced in the surface of one organ by pressure exerted by another. **i. cardi'aca hep'atis** [N A, B N A], a depression on the superior part of the diaphragmatic surface of the liver, corresponding to the position of the heart. Called also *cardiac impression of liver.* **i. cardi'aca pulmo'nis** [N A], the indentation on the medial surface of either lung produced by the heart and pericardium. Called also *cardiac impression of lung.* **i. col'ica hep'atis** [N A, B N A], a variable concavity in the right lobe of the liver, where it is in contact with the right flexure of the colon. Called also *colic impression of liver.* **impressio'nes digita'tae** [N A, B N A], poorly defined depressions on the inner surface of the cranium, corresponding to the gyri of the brain. Called also *digitate impressions.* **i. duodena'lis hep'atis** [N A, B N A], a concavity on the right lobe of the liver where it is in contact with the descending part of the duodenum. Called also *duodenal impression of liver.* **i. esophage'a hep'atis** [N A], a concavity on the left lobe of the liver corresponding to the position of the abdominal part of the esophagus. Called also *esophageal impression of liver.* **i. gas'trica hep'atis** [N A, B N A], a large concavity in the left lobe of the liver where it is in contact with the anterior surface of the stomach. Called also *gastric impression of liver.* **i. gas'trica re'nis** [B N A], a concavity on the anterior surface of the left kidney where it is in contact with the stomach. Omitted in N A. **i. hepat'ica re'nis** [B N A], an impression on the anterior surface of the left kidney where it is in contact with the liver. Omitted in N A. **i. ligamen'ti costoclavicula'ris** [N A], the point on the inferior surface of the clavicle where the costoclavicular ligament is attached. Called also *impression of costoclavicular ligament* and *tuberositas costalis claviculae* [B N A]. **i. meningea'lis.** See *foveolae granulares.* **i. muscula'ris re'nis** [B N A], a depression on the posterior surface of the kidney where it is in contact with the psoas muscle. Omitted in N A. **i. oesophage'a hep'atis** [B N A], i. esophagea hepatis. **i. petro'sa pal'lii** [B N A], a groove on the base of the brain corresponding to the superior angle of the petrous portion of the temporal bone. Omitted in N A. **i. rena'lis hep'atis** [N A, B N A], the concavity on the right lobe of the liver where it is in contact with the right kidney. **i. suprarena'lis hep'atis** [N A, B N A], a small concavity on the right lobe of the liver, superior to the renal impression, caused by contact with the right suprarenal gland. **i. trigem'ini os'sis tempora'lis** [N A, B N A], the shallow impression in the floor of the middle cranial fossa on the petrous part of the temporal bone, lodging the semilunar ganglion of the trigeminal nerve. Called also *trigeminal impression.*

impression (im-presh′un) [L. *impressio*]. 1. A slight indentation or depression. See *impressio.* 2. A negative copy or counterpart of some object made by bringing into contact with the object, with varying degrees of pressure, some plastic material which later becomes solidified. 3. An effect produced upon the mind, body, or senses by some external stimulus, or agent. **angular i. for gasserian ganglion,** impressio trigemini ossis temporalis. **basilar i.,** a developmental deformity of the occipital bone and upper end of the cervical spine, in which the latter appears to have pushed the floor of the occipital bone upward. Called also *platybasia* and *basilar invagination.* **cardiac i.,** an impression made by the heart on another organ. See *impressio cardiaca hepatis* and *impressio cardiaca pulmonis.* **cardiac i. of liver,** impressio cardiaca hepatis. **cardiac i. of lung,** impressio cardiaca pulmonis. **cleft palate i.,** an impression made of a cleft palate, to facilitate construction of a prosthetic appliance. **colic i. of liver,** impressio colica hepatis. **complete denture i.,** one made of the entire maxilla or mandible, for the purpose of construction of a complete denture. **i. of costoclavicular ligament,** impressio ligamenti costoclavicularis. **deltoid i. of humerus,** tuberositas deltoidea humeri. **dental i.,** an impression of the jaw and/or teeth made in some plastic substance, such as plaster of paris, special waxes, modeling compound, zinc oxide paste, reversible colloids, or alginate materials, which is later filled in with plaster of paris to produce a facsimile of the oral structures present. **digastric i.,** fossa digastrica. **digital i's, digitate i's,** impressiones digitatae. **direct bone i.,** one made of the denuded jaw bone, for the purpose of constructing an implant denture. **duodenal i. of liver,** impressio duodenalis hepatis. **esophageal i. of liver,** impressio esophagea hepatis. **final i.,** one which is used for making the master cast for a dental prosthesis. **gastric i.,** an impression made by the stomach on another organ. See *impressio gastrica hepatis* and *impressio gastrica renis.* **gastric i. of liver,** impressio gastrica hepatis. **hydrocolloid i.,** one made of a hydrocolloid material. **lower i., mandibular i.,** an impression of the lower jaw and/or teeth. **maxillary i.,** an impression of the upper jaw and/or teeth. **meningeal i.** See *foveolae granulares.* **mental i.,** an effect produced upon the mind by stimuli received from outside the body. **partial denture i.,** one made of a partially edentulous arch for the purpose of constructing a partial denture. **preliminary i., primary i.,** one which is made for the purpose of study or for the construction of a tray. **renal i. of liver,** impressio renalis hepatis. **rhomboid i. of clavicle,** impressio ligamenti costoclavicularis. **sectional i.,** a dental impression that is made in sections. **sensory i.,** an effect produced upon the mind as a result of stimuli received from outside the body by a special sense organ. **snap i.,** preliminary i. **suprarenal i. of liver,** impressio suprarenalis hepatis. **trigeminal i. of temporal bone,** impressio trigemini ossis temporalis. **upper i.,** maxillary i.

impressiones (im-pres″e-o′nēz) [L.]. Plural of *impressio.*

improcreant (im-pro′kre-ant). Unable to procreate.

impuberal (im-pu′ber-al). Destitute of pubic hairs; not yet having reached puberty.

impuberism (im-pu′ber-izm). The condition of not having reached puberty.

impulse (im′puls). 1. A sudden pushing force. 2. A sudden uncontrollable determination to act. **cardiac i.** 1. The impulse or beat of the heart at the fifth intercostal space at the left side of the sternum. 2. Excitation wave. **episternal i.,** an aortic impulse felt at the episternal notch. **morbid i.,** an uncontrollable wish to do some abnormal act. **nerve i., nervous i., neural i.,** the impulse or activity propagated along nerve fibers.

impulsion (im-pul′shun). An abnormal impulse to perform certain acts, usually of a disagreeable nature. **wandering i.,** fugue.

imputability (im-pu″tah-bil′ĭ-te). Soundness of mind; unimpaired responsibility.

im-pyeng (im′pi-eng). Collapsing typhus.

Imre's treatment (im′rāz) [Josef *Imre,* Budapest ophthalmologist, 1884–1945]. See under *treatment.*

I.M.S. Abbreviation for *Indian Medical Service.*

imu (e′moo). A disorder endemic among the Ainu of Japan, marked by a mental state that renders the patient liable to attacks of psychomotor disorder precipitated by some emotional shock.

IMViC, imvic. A mnemonic indicating the tests used in classifying coliform bacteria, namely indol, methyl red, Voges-Proskauer, and citrate.

In. Chemical symbol for *indium.*

in. Abbreviation for *inch.*

in- [L. *in* in, into]. 1. A prefix signifying in, within, or into. 2. A negative or privative prefix. 3. An intensive prefix.

inacidity (in″ah-sid′ĭ-te). Absence of acidity.

inaction (in-ak′shun) [L. *in* not + *actio* act]. Imperfect response to a normal stimulus.

inactivate (in-ak′tĭ-vāt). To render inactive; to destroy the activity of.

inactivation (in-ak″tĭ-va′shun). The destruction of the activity of a serum by the action of heat or other means. **i. of the complement,** the destruction of activity of the complement, usually produced by heating serum to 56°C. for 30 minutes.

inactose (in-ak′tōs). A variety of optically inactive plant sugar.

inadequacy (in-ad′ĕ-kwah-se) [L. *in* not + *adaequare* to make equal]. Inability to perform an allotted function; insufficiency.

inagglutinable (in-ah-gloo′tĭ-nah-b'l). Not agglutinable.

inalimental (in″al-ĭ-men′tal) [L. *in* not + *alimentum* food]. Not nutritious; not serviceable as food.

inanimate (in-an′ĭ-māt) [L. *in* not + *animatus* alive]. 1. Without life. 2. Lacking in animation.

inanition (in″ah-nish′un) [L. *inanis* empty]. The physical condition which results from complete lack of food.

inappetence (in-ap′ĕ-tens) [L. *in* not + *appetere* to desire]. Lack of desire or appetite.

inarticulate (in″ar-tik′u-lāt) [L. *in* not + *articulatus* joined]. Not joined; disjointed; not uttered like articulate speech.

in articulo mortis (in ar-tik′u-lo mor′tis) [L.]. At the very point of death.

inassimilable (in″ah-sim′ĭ-lah-b'l) [L. *in* not + *assimilable*]. Not susceptible of being utilized as nutriment.

inaxon (in-ak′son) [Gr. *is, inos* fiber + *axōn* axis]. A nerve cell whose axon breaks up into terminal filaments at a considerable distance from the cell. Cf. *dendraxon.*

inborn (in′born). Formed or implanted during intrauterine life.

inbreeding (in′brēd-ing). The mating of closely related individuals, or of individuals having closely similar genetic constitutions.

incallosal (in″kah-lo′sal). Characterized by absence of the corpus callosum, and usually by consequent idiocy.

incandescent (in″kan-des′ent) [L. *incandescens* glowing]. Glowing with heat and light.

incarcerated (in-kar′ser-āt″ed) [L. *incarceratus* imprisoned]. Imprisoned; constricted.

incarceration (in-kar″ser-a′shun) [L. *in* in + *carcer* prison]. Unnatural retention or confinement of a part, as may occur in hernia.

incarial (in-ka′re-al). Pertaining to or characteristic of the Incas in Peru or of the Peruvian race.

incarnant (in-kar′nant) [L. *incarnare* to invest in flesh]. Incarnative.

incarnatio (in″kar-na′she-o) [L. *incarnare* to invest in flesh]. Ingrowth. **i. un′guis,** ingrowth of a toenail; ingrown toenail.

incarnative (in-kar′nah-tiv) [L. *incarnare* to invest in flesh]. 1. Promoting the formation of granulations. 2. An agent that promotes granulations.

incasement (in-kās′ment). The act of surrounding or state of being surrounded, as with a case. See *preformation.*

incendiarism (in-sen′de-ar-izm). A criminal tendency to set fires. Cf. *pyromania.*

incest (in′sest). Sexual intercourse between persons too closely related to contract a legal marriage.

inch (inch). A unit of linear measure, one-twelfth of a foot, or one thirty-sixth of a yard, being the equivalent of 25.4 mm.

inchacao (in-chah-kah′o) [Brazilian]. Beriberi.

incidence (in′sĭ-dens) [L. *incidere* (*in* + *cadere*), to occur, to happen]. An expression of the rate at which a certain event occurs, as the number of new cases of a specific disease occurring during a certain period.

incident (in′sĭ-dent) [L. *incidens* falling upon]. 1. Falling or striking upon. 2. Afferent.

incineration (in-sin″er-a′shun) [L. *in* into + *cineres* ashes]. The act of burning to ashes; cremation.

incipient (in-sip′e-ent). Beginning to exist; coming into existence.

incisal (in-si′zal). Cutting.

incised (in-sīzd′) [L. *incisus*]. Cut; made by cutting.

incision (in-sizh′un) [L. *incidere* (*in* + *caedere*), to cut open, to cut through]. 1. A cut, or wound produced by cutting. 2. The act of cutting. **Auvray i.,** an incision for splenectomy: the usual incision is made along the outer border of the left rectus muscle and up to the costal cartilages; this is extended upward and posteriorly over the lower ribs to the level of the eighth interspace. **Bar's i.,** an incision for cesarean section made in the midline of the abdomen above the umbilicus, the uterus being incised longitudinally. **Battle's i., Battle-Jalaguier-Kammerer i.,** incision for abdominal section, consisting of a vertical incision of the skin and fascia, vertical division of the anterior layer of the sheath of the rectus, with retraction of the rectus inward, vertical division of the posterior layer of the rectal sheath nearer the median line, together with the subserous areolar tissue and peritoneum: used in quiescent stage of appendicitis and in some operations on the stomach, liver, and gallbladder. **Bergmann's i.,** an incision for exposing the kidney, made from the outer border of the erector spinae at the level of the twelfth rib, toward the junction of the outer and middle third of Poupart's ligament. **Bevan's i.,** one for exposing the gallbladder. See illustration. **celiotomy i.,** an incision made through the abdominal wall to give access to the peritoneal cavity. **confirmatory i.,** an incision into an organ made for the purpose of confirming a diagnosis. **crucial i.,** a cross-shaped incision. **Deaver's i.** (*for appendicitis*), incision through the sheath of the right rectus muscle, the muscle being then pushed inward. **Dührssen's i's,** deep incisions made in the cervix uteri to facilitate delivery; hysterostomatotomy. **Fergusson's i.,** an incision for excision of the upper jaw. It runs along the junction of the nose with the cheek, around the ala of the nose to the median line, and descends to bisect the upper lip. **Fowler's angular i.,** an incision for anterolateral abdominal section. **hockey stick i.,** Meyer's hockey stick i. **Kehr's i.,** an abdominal incision for opening up a wide field. It extends from the xiphoid cartilage to the umbilicus in the median line, and obliquely downward to the right or left of the umbilicus, and again vertically downward. **Kocher's i.,** a gallbladder incision 10 cm. long, parallel with and 4 cm. below the right costal margin. **Küstner's i.,** a semilunar abdominal incision with the concavity above, through the fat above the symphysis pubis, following one of the natural folds of the skin. The upper flap is detached from the aponeurosis of the external oblique, and then the usual incision is made parallel to the rectus muscle. **Langenbeck's i.,** an abdominal incision through the linea semilunaris parallel to the fibers of the rectus abdominis muscle: used for operations of the kidney, spleen, colon, tail of pancreas, etc. **lateral rectus i.** See illustration. **Longuet's i.** See under *operation.* **McArthur's i.,** a vertical upper transrectus incision, with transverse division of the posterior sheath and peritoneum. **McBurney's i.,** an abdominal incision parallel to the fibers of the external oblique muscle and about 1 inch from the anterior superior spine of the ilium. The skin and subcutaneous fat are incised down to the external oblique, the fibers of which are split; the internal oblique is exposed, its fibers, along with those of the transversalis, being split and separated. **Mackenrodt's i.,** a transverse semilunar abdominal incision, its lowest point about 2 cm. above the pubes. **median i.,** one in the midline of the body. **Meyer's hockey stick i.,** one for entering the lower anterior abdomen, partly by intramuscular separation, partly by transverse division of muscle, by an incision shaped somewhat like a hockey

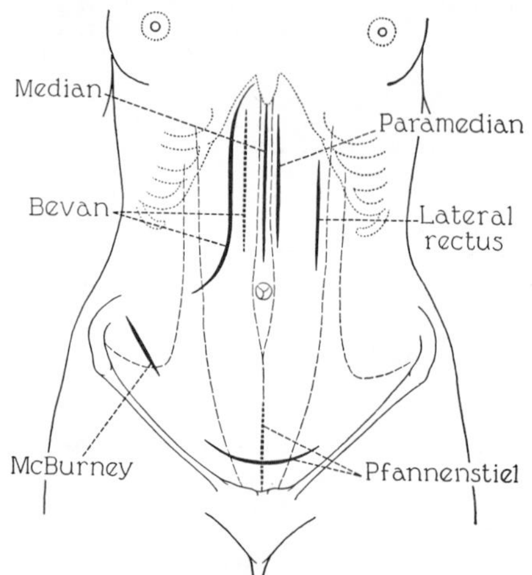

Various abdominal incisions (Partipilo).

stick: used in complicated appendicitis. **paramedian i.** See illustration. **Parker's i.,** one over the area of dullness in appendiceal abscess, nearly parallel with Poupart's ligament. **Perthes' i.,** a gallbladder incision: a vertical right rectus incision from ensiform to umbilicus: from the lower end a horizontal extension crosses the rectus to costal margin. **Pfannenstiel's i.,** an abdominal incision, consisting of a curved incision, the convexity directed downward, just above the symphysis, passing through skin, superficial fascia, and aponeurosis, exposing the pyramidalis and recti muscles, which muscles are separated from each other in the median line, the peritoneum being opened vertically. **relief i.,** one made to relieve tension in a part. **Vischer's lumbo-iliac i.,** separation of the muscular and tendinous fibers of the abdominal muscles of the lumbo-iliac region, just above the center of the iliac crest, in their cleavage lines, without transverse division of the muscle fibers or harm to the abdominal nerves. **Warren's i.,** an incision following the thoracomammary fold, permitting access to any part of the breast. **Wilde's i.,** exposure of the mastoid process by an incision behind the auricle, the bone being opened if necessary: done for mastoid abscess.

incisive (in-si′siv) [L. *incisivus*]. 1. Having the power or quality of cutting. 2. Pertaining to the incisor teeth.

incisolabial (in-si″zo-la′be-al). Noting the incisal and labial surfaces of an anterior tooth.

incisolingual (in-si″zo-ling′gwahl). Noting the incisal and lingual surfaces of an anterior tooth.

incisoproximal (in-si″zo-prok′sĭ-mal). Noting the incisal and proximal surfaces of an anterior tooth.

incisor (in-si′zer) [L. *incidere* to cut into]. Adapted for cutting. See under *tooth*. **central i., first i.,** medial i. **lateral i.,** that one of the incisor teeth on either side of either jaw, located farther from the midline of the body. **medial i.,** that one of the incisor teeth on either side of either jaw, located closer to the midline of the body. **second i.,** lateral i. **shovel-shaped i's,** large upper medial incisor teeth that are concave on the lingual side.

incisura (in-si-su′rah), pl. *incisu′rae* [L.]. A cut, notch, or incision; used in anatomical nomenclature as a general term to indicate an indention or depression, chiefly on the edge of a bone or other structure. Called also *incisure* and *notch*. **i. acetab′uli** [N A, B N A], a deficiency in the inferior portion of the lunate surface of the acetabulum. **i. angula′ris ventric′uli** [N A], the lowest point on the lesser curvature of the stomach, marking the junction of the cranial two-thirds and caudal one-third of the stomach. Called also *gastric notch*. **i. ante′rior au′ris** [N A, B N A], a depression between the crus of the helix and the tragus. Called also *anterior incisure of ear*. **i. ap′icis cor′dis** [N A, B N A], a slight notch found at the site where the anterior and posterior interventricular sulci become continuous and cross the right margin of the heart. Called also *incisure of apex of heart*. **i. cardi′aca pulmo′nis sinis′tri** [N A], a depression in the anterior border of the left lung for the apex of the heart. Called also *cardiac notch*. **i. cardi′aca ventric′uli** [N A], the point on the stomach where it articulates with the clavicle. Called also greater curvature. Called also *cardiac incisure of stomach*. **incisu′rae cartilag′inis mea′tus acus′tici exter′ni** [N A, B N A], two vertical fissures in the anterior part of the cartilage of the external acoustic meatus. **i. cerebel′li ante′rior** [B N A], a notch on the anterior surface of the cerebellum. Omitted in N A. **i. cerebel′li poste′rior** [B N A], a notch between the cerebellar hemispheres posteriorly, containing the falx cerebelli. Omitted in N A. **i. clavicula′ris ster′ni** [N A, B N A], a hollow at each side of the cranial surface of the manubrium of the sternum, where it articulates with the clavicle. Called also *clavicular notch of sternum*. **incisu′rae costa′les ster′ni** [N A, B N A], the facets on the sternum, seven on each lateral edge, for articulation with the costal cartilages. Called also *costal notches of sternum*. **i. ethmoida′lis os′sis fronta′lis** [N A, B N A], a space between the orbital parts of the frontal bone, in which the ethmoid bone is lodged. Called also *ethmoid notch of frontal bone*. **i. fastig′ii,** a transverse furrow on the ventricular surface of the cerebellar lamina of the developing cerebellum. **i. fibula′ris tib′iae** [N A, B N A], a hollow on the outer surface of the lower end of the tibia, in which the lower end of the fibula rests. Called also *fibular notch*. **i. fronta′lis** [N A, B N A], a notch in the frontal bone, located in the supraorbital margin medial to the supraorbital notch or foramen, for transmission of branches of the supraorbital nerve and vessels; frequently converted into a foramen (foramen frontale) by a bridge of osseous tissue. Called also *frontal notch*. **i. interarytenoi′dea laryn′gis** [N A], the posterior portion of the aditus laryngis between the two arytenoid cartilages. Called also *interarytenoid notch*. **i. interloba′ris hep′atis,** i. ligamenti teretis. **i. interloba′ris pulmo′nis** [B N A], an incisure separating adjacent lobes of a lung. See *fissura obliqua pulmonis* and *fissura horizontalis pulmonis dextri*. **i. intertrag′ica** [N A, B N A], the notch at the lower part of the pinna of the ear between the tragus and the antitragus. Called also *intertragic incisure*. **i. ischiad′ica ma′jor** [N A, B N A], the large notch on the posterior border of the hip bone, where the posterior borders of the ilium and the ischium become continuous. Called also *greater sciatic notch*. **i. ischiad′ica mi′nor** [N A, B N A], the notch on the posterior border of the ischium just inferior to the ischiadic spine. Called also *lesser sciatic notch*. **i. jugula′ris os′sis occipita′lis** [N A, B N A], a notch on the anterior surface of a jugular process of the occipital bone, forming the posterior wall of the jugular foramen. Called also *jugular notch of occipital bone*. **i. jugula′ris os′sis tempora′lis** [N A, B N A], a prominent depression on the inferior surface of the petrous part of the temporal bone. It forms the anterior and lateral wall of the jugular foramen and lodges the superior bulb of the internal jugular vein in its lateral part and the glossopharyngeal, vagus, and accessory nerves in its medial part. Called also *jugular notch of temporal bone*. **i. jugula′ris ster′ni** [N A, B N A], the notch on the upper border of the sternum between the clavicular notches. Called also *jugular notch of sternum*. **i. lacrima′lis maxil′lae** [N A, B N A], an indentation on the nasal part of the maxilla, just inferior to the lacrimal border of the frontal process. Called also *lacrimal notch of maxilla*. **i. ligamen′ti tere′tis** [N A], a notch in the inferior border of the liver, occupied by the ligamentum teres in the adult. Called also *i. umbilicalis* [B N A] and *notch of the ligamentum teres*. **i. mandib′ulae** [N A, B N A], a deep notch on the upper edge of the ramus of the mandible between the condyle and the coronoid process. Called also *mandibular notch*. **i. mastoi′dea os′sis tempora′lis** [N A, B N A], a deep groove on the medial surface of the mastoid process of the temporal bone, which gives origin to the posterior belly of the digastric muscle. Called also *mastoid notch*. **i. nasa′lis maxil′lae** [N A, B N A], the large notch in the anterior border of the maxilla that with its fellow forms the anterior opening of the nasal fossae. Called also *nasal notch of maxilla*. **i. pancre′atis** [N A, B N A], a notch at the junction of the left half of the head of the pancreas and the neck of the pancreas. Called also *pancreatic notch*. **i. parieta′lis os′sis tempora′lis** [N A, B N A], the notch found on the upper margin of the temporal bone where the squamous and parietomastoid sutures meet. Called also *parietal notch of temporal bone*. **i. perone′a tib′iae,** i. fibularis tibiae. **i. preoccipita′lis** [N A], a notch near the posterior end of the inferolateral border of the cerebral hemisphere. A line joining it to the parietooccipital sulcus serves to delineate the parietal and temporal lobes from the occipital lobe. Called also *preoccipital incisure*. **i. radia′lis ul′nae** [N A, B N A], the cavity on the outer side of the coronoid process, articulating with the rim of the head of the radius. Called also *radial notch*. **i. Rivi′ni,** i. tympanica [Rivini]. **i. Santori′ni.** 1. Incisura anterior auris. 2. See *incisurae cartilaginis meatus acustici*. **i. scap′ulae** [N A, B N A], a notch, converted into a foramen by a ligament, on the upper border of the scapula at the base of the coracoid process. Called also *scapular notch*. **i. semiluna′ris tib′iae,** i. fibularis tibiae. **i. semiluna′ris ul′nae** [B N A], i. trochlearis ulnae. **i. sphenopalatin′a os′sis palati′ni** [N A, B N A], a notch between the oribital and sphenoid processes of the palatine bone: it is converted into a foramen by the under surface of the sphenoid bone. Called also *sphenopalatine notch of palatine bone.* **i. supraorbita'lis** [N A, B N A], a palpable notch in the frontal bone, at the junction of the medial one-third and lateral two-thirds of the supraorbital margin, for transmission of the supraorbital nerve and vessels to the forehead. In life it is bridged by fibrous tissue, which is sometimes ossified, forming a bony aperture (foramen supraorbitale). Called also *supraorbital notch.* **i. tempora'lis,** a slight fissure between the incus of the hippocampal gyrus and the apex of the temporal lobe. **i. tento'rii cerebel'li** [N A, B N A], an opening in the anteromedial part of the cerebellar tentorium, occupied by the upper part of the pons and by the mesencephalon. Called also *tentorial notch.* **i. termina'lis au'ris** [N A, B N A], a deep notch separating the lamina tragi and cartilage of the external acoustic meatus from the main auricular cartilage. Called also *terminal incisure of ear.* **i. thyroi'dea infe'rior** [N A], a notch at the lower part of the anterior border of the thyroid cartilage. Called also *inferior thyroid notch.* **i. thyroi'dea supe'rior** [N A], a deep notch in the upper portion of the anterior border of the thyroid cartilage. Called also *superior thyroid notch.* **i. trag'ica,** i. intertragica. **i. trochlea'ris ul'nae** [N A], a large concavity on the anterior surface at the proximal end of the ulna, formed by the olecranon and coronoid processes, for articulation with the trochlea of the humerus. Called also *i. semilunaris ulnae* [B N A], and *trochlear notch of ulna.* **i. tympan'ica [Rivi'ni]** [B N A], a defect in the upper portion of the tympanic part of the temporal bone, between the greater and lesser tympanic spines, which is filled in by the pars flaccida of the tympanic membrane. Omitted in N A. **i. ulna'ris ra'dii** [N A, B N A], a concavity on the medial side of the distal extremity of the radius, articulating with the head of the ulna. Called also *ulnar notch.* **i. umbilica'lis** [B N A], i. ligamenti teretis. **i. vertebra'lis infe'rior** [N A, B N A], the indentation found below each pedicle of a vertebra which, with the indentation located above the pedicle of the vertebra below, forms the intervertebral foramen. Called also *inferior vertebral notch.* **i. vertebra'lis supe'rior** [N A, B N A], the indentation found above each pedicle of a vertebra which, with the indentation located below the corresponding pedicle of the vertebra above, forms the intervertebral foramen. Called also *superior vertebral notch.*

incisurae (in″si-su're) [L.]. Plural of *incisura.*

incisure (in-si'zhŭr). A cut, notch, or incision. Called also *incisura* [N A]. **i. of acetabulum,** incisura acetabuli. **i. of apex of heart,** incisura apicis cordis. **i. of calcaneus,** sulcus tendinis musculi flexoris hallucis longi calcanei. **cardiac i. of lung,** incisura cardiaca pulmonis sinistra. **cardiac i. of stomach,** incisura cardiaca ventriculi. **clavicular i. of sternum,** incisura clavicularis sterni. **costal i's of sternum,** incisurae costales sterni. **cotyloid i.,** incisura acetabuli. **digastric i. of temporal bone,** incisura mastoidea ossis temporalis. **ethmoidal i. of frontal bone,** incisura ethmoidalis ossis frontalis. **falciform i. of fascia lata,** margo falciformis fasciae latae. **fibular i. of tibia,** incisura fibularis tibiae. **frontal i.,** incisura frontalis. **humeral i. of ulna,** incisura trochlearis ulnae. **iliac i., lesser,** incisura ischiadica minor. **interarytenoid i. of larynx,** incisura interarytenoidea laryngis. **interclavicular i.,** incisura jugularis sterni. **ischiadic i., greater,** incisura ischiadica major. **ischiadic i., lesser,** incisura ischiadica minor. **jugular i. of occipital bone,** incisura jugularis ossis occipitalis. **jugular i. of sternum,** incisura jugularis sterni. **jugular i. of temporal bone,** incisura jugularis ossis temporalis. **lacrimal i. of maxilla,** incisura lacrimalis maxillae. **i's of Lanterman, i's of Lanterman-Schmidt,** oblique lines or slashes on the sheaths of medullated nerve fibers. **lateral i. of sternum,** incisura clavicularis sterni. **i. of mandible,** incisura mandibulae. **mastoid i. of temporal bone,** incisura mastoidea ossis temporalis. **maxillary i., inferior,** margo lacrimalis maxillae. **nasal i. of frontal bone,** margo nasalis ossis frontalis. **nasal i. of maxilla,** incisura nasalis maxillae. **obturator i. of pubic bone,** sulcus obturatorius ossis pubis. **palatine i.,** fissura pterygoidea. **palatine i. of Henle,** incisura sphenopalatina ossis palatini. **parietal i. of temporal bone, parietosphenoidal i.,** incisura parietalis ossis temporalis. **patellar i. of femur,** facies patellaris femoris. **peroneal i. of tibia,** incisura fibularis tibiae. **popliteal i.,** fossa intercondylaris femoris. **preoccipital i.,** incisura preoccipitalis. **pterygoid i.,** fissura pterygoidea. **radial i. of ulna,** incisura radialis ulnae. **Rivinus' i.,** incisura tympanica [Rivini]. **i. of scapula,** incisura scapulae. **Schmidt-Lanterman i's,** i's of Lanterman. **semilunar i.,** incisura scapulae. **semilunar i., greater, of ulna,** incisura trochlearis ulnae. **semilunar i, lesser, of ulna,** incisura radialis ulnae. **semilunar i. of mandible,** incisura mandibulae. **semilunar i. of radius,** incisura ulnaris radii. **semilunar i. of scapula,** incisura scapulae. **semilunar i. of sternum,** incisura clavicularis sterni. **semilunar i. of sternum, superior,** incisura jugularis sterni. **semilunar i. of tibia,** incisura fibularis tibiae. **semilunar i. of ulna,** incisura trochlearis ulnae. **sigmoid i. of mandible,** incisura mandibulae. **sigmoid i. of ulna,** incisura trochlearis ulnae. **sphenopalatine i. of palatine bone,** incisura sphenopalatina ossis palatini. **sternal i.,** incisura jugularis sterni. **supraorbital i.,** foramen supraorbitalis. **suprascapular i.,** incisura scapulae. **i. of talus,** sulcus tendinis musculi flexoris hallucis longi tali. **i. of tentorium of cerebellum,** incisura tentorii cerebelli. **terminal i. of ear,** incisura terminalis auris. **thoracic i.,** angulus infrasternalis thoracis. **thyroid i., inferior,** incisura thyroidea inferior. **thyroid i., superior,** incisura thyroidea superior. **trochlear i. of ulna,** incisura trochlearis ulnae. **ulnar i. of radius,** incisura ulnaris radii. **umbilical i.,** incisura ligamenti teretis. **vertebral i., greater, vertebral i., inferior,** incisura vertebralis inferior. **vertebral i., lesser, vertebral i., superior,** incisura vertebralis superior.

incitogram (in-si'to-gram). The neural conditions which organize and initiate efferent impulses.

inclinatio (in″klĭ-na'she-o), pl. *inclinatio'nes* [L.]. Inclination. **i. pel'vis** [N A, B N A], the angle between the plane of the superior aperture of the minor pelvis and the horizontal plane, when the body is in the erect position. Called also *pelvic incline.*

inclination (in″klĭ-na'shun) [L. *inclinatio* a leaning]. A sloping or leaning; the angle of slope from a particular line or plane of reference. Applied especially in dentistry to the deviation of a tooth from the vertical. **pelvic i., i. of pelvis,** inclinatio pelvis.

incline (in'klīn). Inclination. **pelvic i., i. of pelvis,** inclinatio pelvis.

inclinometer (in″klĭ-nom'e-ter). An instrument for determining the ocular diameter.

inclusion (in-klu'zhun) [L. *inclusio*]. 1. The act of enclosing or condition of being enclosed. 2. Anything that is enclosed. **cell i.,** a usually lifeless, often temporary, constituent in the cytoplasm of a cell, such as an accumulation of proteins, fats, carbohydrates, pigments, secretory granules, or crystals. **dental i.,** a tooth which is so surrounded with bony material that it is unable to erupt. **fetal i.,** a partially developed embryo enclosed within the body of its twin. **intranuclear i's,** inclusion bodies. **leukocyte i's,** Döhle's inclusion bodies. **Walthard's i's.** See under *islet.*

incoagulability (in″ko-ag″u-lah-bil′ĭ-te). The state of being incapable of coagulation.

incoagulable (in″ko-ag′u-lah-b′l). Not susceptible to coagulation.

incoherent (in″ko-hēr′ent) [L. *in* not + *cohaerere* to cling together]. Without proper sequence; incongruous.

incompatibility (in″kom-pat″ĭ-bil′ĭ-te). The quality of being incompatible. **chemical i.,** the quality of not being miscible with another given substance without a chemical change. **physiologic i.,** the quality of not being administrable with another given remedy on account of their antagonistic effects. **therapeutic i.,** opposition in therapeutic effect between two or more medicines.

incompatible (in″kom-pat′ĭ-b′l) [L. *incompatibilis*]. Not suitable for combination or simultaneous administration; mutually repellent.

incompensation (in″kom-pen-sa′shun). Lack of compensation.

incompetence (in-kom′pe-tens) [L. *in* not + *competens* sufficient]. Inadequacy or insufficiency. **aortic i.** See under *insufficiency*. **i. of the cardiac valves.** See under *insufficiency*. **ileocecal i.,** inability of the ileocecal valve to prevent the flow of material from the colon to the ileum. **muscular i.,** incompetence of a cardiac valve due to defective action of the papillary muscles (musculi papillares). **pyloric i.** See under *insufficiency*. **relative i.,** defective closure of a cardiac valve due to dilatation of the corresponding cavity of the heart. **valvular i.** See *insufficiency of the valves*, under *insufficiency*.

incompetency (in-kom′pe-ten″se). Incompetence.

incompetent (in-kom′pe-tent). 1. Unable to perform the required functions. 2. An individual who is unable to perform the required functions of everyday living.

incompressible (in″kom-pres′ĭ-b′l). Not susceptible of being squeezed together.

incontinence (in-kon′tĭ-nens) [L. *incontinentia*]. Inability to refrain from yielding to normal impulses, as sexual desire, or the urge to defecate or urinate. **active i.,** incontinence in which the bowels or bladder are emptied involuntarily, but at regular intervals and in the normal way. **fecal i., i. of the feces,** failure of voluntary control of the anal sphincters, with involuntary passage of feces and flatus. **intermittent i.,** loss of control of the urine on a sudden movement or on pressure on the bladder, due to interruption of the voluntary path above the lumbar center. **i. of milk,** galactorrhea. **overflow i.,** urinary incontinence due to pressure of retained urine in the bladder. **paradoxical i.,** dribbling overflow of urine from a bladder too greatly distended as a result of obstruction of the bladder neck or urethra. **paralytic i.,** fecal and urinary incontinence caused by relaxation of the sphincters from destruction of the lumbar centers. **passive i.,** incontinence of urine in which the bladder is full and cannot be emptied in the normal way, but the urine dribbles away from mere pressure. **rectal i.,** fecal i. **stress i.,** involuntary discharge of urine due to anatomic displacement which exerts an opening pull on the bladder orifice, as in straining or coughing. **urinary i., i. of urine,** failure of voluntary control of the vesical and urethral sphincters, with constant or frequent involuntary passage of urine.

incontinent (in-kon′tĭ-nent). Unable to refrain from yielding to normal impulses, as sexual desire, or the urge to defecate or urinate.

incontinentia (in-kon″tĭ-nen′she-ah) [L.]. 1. Incontinence. 2. Immoderation, or excess. **i. al′vi,** fecal incontinence. **i. pigmen′ti,** a pigmentary anomaly marked by irregular shaped patches on the skin due to excessive deposit of melanin. The condition occurs in females only and is often associated with defects of the eyes, teeth and hair. **i. uri′nae,** urinary incontinence. **i. vul′vae,** flatus vaginalis.

incoordination (in″ko-or″dĭ-na′shun) [L. *in* not + *coordination*]. Lack of the normal adjustment of muscular motions; failure of organs to work harmoniously. **jerky i.,** that which leads to great and sudden irregularity of movement.

incorporation (in-kor″po-ra′shun) [L. *in* into + *corpus* body]. The union of one substance with another, or with others, in a composite mass.

incostapedial (ing″ko-sta-pe′de-al). Pertaining to the incus and stapes.

increment (in′kre-ment) [L. *incrementum*]. Addition, or increase; the amount by which a given quantity or value is increased. **absolute i.,** the exact amount by which anything is increased. **relative i.,** the amount by which anything is increased, in relation to the original size or volume.

incretion (in-kre′shun). An internal secretion. **negative i.,** an internal secretion which does not act as a hormone, but is supposed to act as a neutralizer of poisonous substances circulating in the blood.

incretodiagnosis (in-kre″to-di″ag-no′sis). Diagnosis of disease of internal secretions.

incretogenous (in″kre-toj′e-nus). Caused by an internal secretion or hormone.

incretology (in″kre-tol′o-je) [*incretion* + *-logy*]. The branch of medicine which deals with the internal secretion; endocrinology.

incretopathy (in″kre-top′ah-the) [*incretion* + Gr. *pathos* disease]. Any disease of internal secretions.

incretory (in′kre-to-re). Pertaining to internal secretion; endocrine.

incretotherapy (in-kre″to-ther′ah-pe). Treatment by the administration of endocrines.

incrustation (in″krus-ta′shun) [L. *in* on + *crusta* crust]. 1. The formation of a crust. 2. A crust, scale, or scab.

incubate (in′ku-bāt) [L. *incubare* to lie in or on; to watch over jealously]. 1. To place in an optimal situation for development, as by provision of the proper temperature and humidity for the growth of living cells, such as ova, microorganisms, or tissue cells. 2. Material which has been incubated.

incubation (in″ku-ba′shun) [L. *incubatio*]. 1. The induction of development, as the development of disease-producing microorganisms in an intermediate or in the ultimate host, or the development of microorganisms or other cells in appropriate media. 2. The development of the embryo in the eggs of oviparous animals. 3. In Greek medicine, the rite of sleeping in the Æsculapian temples, medical advice being rendered in a dream, or by the priests, if patients waked.

incubator (in′ku-ba-ter). 1. An apparatus for maintaining a premature infant in an environment of proper temperature and humidity. 2. An apparatus for maintaining a constant and suitable temperature for the development of eggs, cultures of microorganisms, or other living cells.

incubus (in′ku-bus) [L.]. 1. A nightmare. 2. A heavy mental burden.

incudal (ing′ku-dal) [L. *incus* anvil]. Pertaining to the incus.

incudectomy (ing″ku-dek′to-me) [L. *incus* anvil + Gr. *ektomē* excision]. Surgical removal of the incus.

incudiform (ing-ku′dĭ-form). Anvil-shaped.

incudomalleal (ing″ku-do-mal′e-al). Pertaining to the incus and malleus.

incudostapedial (ing″ku-do-sta-pe′de-al). Pertaining to the incus and stapes.

inculturing (in-kul′chūr-ing). Implantation, def. 4.

incurable (in-ku′rah-b′l). Not susceptible of being cured.

incurvation (in″kur-va′shun) [L. *incurvare* to bend in]. A condition of being bent in.

incus (ing′kus) [L. "anvil"]. [N A, B N A] The

middle of the three ossicles of the ear. Called also *anvil*.

incyclophoria (in-si″klo-fo′re-ah). Cyclophoria in which the upper pole of the vertical axis of the eye deviates toward the midline of the face, or toward the nose.

incyclotropia (in-si″klo-tro′pe-ah). Cyclotropia in which the upper pole of the vertical axis of the eye deviates toward the midline of the face, or toward the nose.

in d. Abbreviation for L. *in di′es*, daily.

indagation (in″dah-ga′shun) [L. *indagatio*]. A careful search, inquiry, or examination.

Indecidua (in″de-sid′u-ah). A division of the class Mammalia, including the mammals without a decidua.

indenization (in-den″i-za′shun). Innidiation.

indentation (in″den-ta′shun) [L. *indentatio; dens* tooth]. 1. A condition of being notched; a notch, pit, or depression. 2. The act of indenting, as with the finger.

index (in′deks), pl. *indexes* or *in′dices* [L.]. 1. [N A, B N A] The second digit of the hand, or forefinger; the finger adjacent to the thumb. 2. An expression of the ratio of one dimension of an object to another dimension, or of one measurable value to another, usually determined by multiplying the smaller value by 100 and dividing by the larger value. 3. A formula based on measurable values to express a value incapable of precise determination. 4. A core or mold used in dentistry to record or maintain the relative position of a tooth or teeth to one another and/or to a cast, to ensure reproduction in the dental prosthesis of their original position. **ACH i.**, an index for nutritional condition of children based on measurements of arm girth, chest depth, and hip width. **acidosis i.**, a number representing the degree of intensity of acidosis. **altitudinal i.**, the relation of the cranial height to the cranial length; called also *height i.* and *length-height i.* **alveolar i.**, gnathic i. **antibacterial i.**, the minimal value of the ratio of inhibitor to metabolite just sufficient to prevent the growth of the organism. **antitryptic i.**, a number representing the increased viscosity of a solution of casein treated with trypsin to which the blood serum of a cancer patient has been added, as compared with the viscosity after the same procedure in which the blood serum is normal. **Arneth i.** See under *formula*. **auricular i.**, the relation of the width to the height of the auricle. **auriculo-parietal i.**, the ratio of the breadth of the skull between the auricular points to its greatest breadth. **auriculovertical i.**, the ratio of the height of the skull above the auricular point to its greatest height. **Ayala i.** See under *quotient*. **Barach's i.**, a formula for determining the operability of a patient based on his cardiac efficiency: it is (SP × PR) + (DP × PR), in which *SP* is systolic pressure, *DP* diastolic pressure, *PR* pulse rate. The limits of operability are 13,000 and 20,000. **baric i.**, 100 times the body weight divided by the cube of the stature. **basilar i.**, the ratio of the distance between the basion and the alveolar point to the total length of the skull. **Becker-Lennhoff i.**, Lennhoff's i. **biochemical racial i.**, the ratio of the percentage of persons having agglutinogen A in their erythrocytes to the percentage having agglutinogen B, or the ratio of persons of blood group II to those of blood group III. **Bodecker i.**, the ratio between the number of tooth surfaces affected by caries (five surfaces to a tooth) and the total number of surfaces that could be so affected. **body build i.**, body weight divided by the square of the stature. **Bouchard's i.** (of adiposity or emaciation), the weight in kilograms divided by the height in decimeters. In a normal adult male each decimeter of height weighs 4200 Gm. **brachial i.**, 100 times the length of the forearm divided by the length of the upper arm. **Broders' i.**, an index of malignancy based on the fact that the more undifferentiated or embryonic the cells of a tumor, the more malignant is the tumor. Grade 1 contains one fourth undifferentiated cells; Grade 2, one half undifferentiated cells; Grade 3, three fourths undifferentiated cells; Grade 4, all cells undifferentiated. **Brown's vasomotor i.**, definite increase of the cutaneous temperature of the extremities over the increase of the mouth temperature after typhoid vaccine has been administered. **Brugsch i.**, chest circumference × 100 divided by body length. **buffer i.**, the ratio of a small increment of alkali to the small increment in pH thus produced. **calcium i.**, the relative amount of calcium in the blood compared with that in a 1:6000 solution of calcium oxide. **cardiac i.**, the minute volume of blood per square meter of body surface. A normal average is 2.2 liters. **cardio-thoracic i.**, the size of the heart in relation to the size of the chest, being the greatest transverse diameter of the heart shadow as compared with the greatest transverse diameter of the chest shadow on radioscopy. **catalase i.**, a number representing the proportion between the amount (in grams) of hydrogen peroxide decomposed by 1 cc. of blood, as compared with the erythrocyte count of the same blood. **cephalic i.**, 100 times the maximal head breadth divided by the maximal head length. **cephalo-orbital i.**, 100 times the capacity of the cranium divided by the capacity of the two orbits. **cephalorhachidian i.**, cerebrospinal i. **cephalospinal i.**, the ratio of the area of the foramen magnum in square meters and the cranial capacity in cubic centimeters. **cerebral i.**, the ratio of the greatest transverse to the greatest anteroposterior diameter of the cranial cavity. **cerebrospinal i.**, the figure obtained by multiplying the final cerebrospinal pressure by the quantity of fluid withdrawn in spinal puncture and then dividing by the initial pressure. **chemotherapeutic i.**, an index indicating the toxicity of a drug for the body as compared with its toxicity for a parasite: it is the maximal tolerated dose per Kg. of body weight divided by the minimal curative dose per Kg. of body weight. **color i.**, an expression of the relative amount of hemoglobin contained in a red blood corpuscle compared with that of a normal individual of the patient's age and sex. Divide the percentage of hemoglobin by the percentage of erythrocytes. **coronofrontal i.**, the ratio of the greatest frontal to the greatest coronal breadth of the head. **cranial i.**, 100 times the maximal breadth of the skull divided by its length. **cytophagic i.**, the relative phagocytic power of leukocytes from a given source, as compared with that of leukocytes from a different source used as a standard. **degenerative i.**, an index indicating the proportion of granulocytes showing toxic granules in the cytoplasm. **dental i.**, the result obtained by multiplying the dental length by 100 and dividing by the length of the basinasal line. **effective temperature i.**, an index indicating the warmth due to air temperature, air movement, and humidity. **empathic i.**, the degree of empathy felt by one person toward another. **endemic i.**, the percentage of persons in any locality affected with an endemic disease. **i. of excursion of uterus**, the distance in centimeters that the uterus, held by forceps, can be displaced upward and downward from its normal location by means of light pulling and pushing motions. **facial i.**, the relation of the length of the face to its width, obtained by multiplying by 100 the bizygomatic width and dividing the product by the distance from the ophryon to the alveolar point. **femorohumeral i.**, 100 times the length of the upper arm divided by the length of the thigh. **Flower's i.**, dental i. **forearm-hand i.**, 100 times the length of the hand divided by the length of the forearm. **Fourmentin's thoracic i.**, the number obtained by multiplying the transverse diameter of the thorax by 100 and dividing by the anteroposterior diameter. **generation i.**, the number that shows the rate of increase from generation to generation. In the binary division of bacteria, if all survive the rate will be 2; if some die the rate will be less. **gnathic i.,** the degree of prominence of the jaws; the distance from the basion to the front of the jaw expressed as a percentage of the distance from the basion to the midpoint of the nasal suture. **habitus i.,** 100 times the sum of the chest girth and the abdominal girth divided by the stature. **hair i.,** the figure obtained by dividing the least diameter of the cross section of a hair by its greatest diameter and multiplying by 100; a high index indicates an approximately round shape; a low index indicates an ovoid cross section. **hand i.,** 100 times the breadth of the hand divided by the length of the hand. **hematopneic i.,** a figure denoting the intensity of blood oxygenation. **hemolytic i.,** a formula devised to help calculate increased erythrocyte destruction: the average of a 4-day quantitation of fecal urobilinogen (in mg.) multiplied by 100 is divided by the hemoglobin (in Gm. per 100 ml.) multiplied by total blood volume divided by 100. **hemophagocytic i.,** the relative phagocytic power of the entire blood, including both leukocytes and serum. Called also *opsonocytophagic i.* **hemorenal i., hemorenal salt i.,** the ratio of the amount of inorganic salts in the urine to that in the blood, obtained by dividing the electric resistance of the blood by that of the urine. **Hench-Aldrich i.** See under *test.* **icteric i., icterus i.,** a figure expressing the amount of bilirubin in the blood, determined by comparing the color of the blood serum with an arbitrary standard potassium dichromate solution: indicative of liver function. **intermembral i.,** 100 times the length of the entire arm divided by the length of the entire leg. **iron i.,** an index of iron in the blood calculated by dividing the figure for the whole blood iron by the red blood cell count in millions of cells per cubic millimeter; the normal figure is between 8 an 9. **juxtaglomerular i.,** a semiquantitative estimation of the degree of granulation of juxtaglomerular cells obtained by a counting method and expressed as a ratio to the number of glomeruli. **Kaup i.,** weight divided by the length of the body squared. **Krebs' leukocyte i.,** the number obtained by dividing the percentage of neutrophils by the percentage of lymphocytes. **length-breadth i.,** the breadth of the skull expressed as a percentage of its length. **length-height i.,** the height of the skull expressed as a percentage of its length. **Lennhoff's i.,** the number obtained by dividing 100 times the distance from the sternal notch to the symphysis pubis by the greatest circumference of the abdomen. **leukopenic i.,** the variation from normal of the leukocyte count. If ingestion of food is followed by a significant fall in the total leukocyte count, allergic hypersensitiveness to that food is indicated. Cf. *hemoclastic crisis,* under *crisis.* **Livi's i.,** $100 \times \sqrt[3]{P{:}6}$, in which P = body weight in grams × body length in centimeters. **lower leg-foot i.,** 100 times the length of the foot divided by the length of the lower leg. **lymphocyte-monocyte i.,** the ratio of lymphocytes to endothelial leukocytes, used to indicate the extent of tuberculous invasion compared with the resistance of the patient. **Macdonald i.,** the proportion of children with enlarged spleen that also show malarial parasites by microscopical examination. **McLean's i.** See under *formula.* **maxillo-alveolar i.,** 100 times the distance between the two most lateral points on the surface of the alveolar margins, usually opposite the middle of the second molar teeth, divided by the maxillo-alveolar length. **metacarpal i.,** the average of the figures obtained by dividing the lengths of the right second, third, fourth, and fifth metacarpal bones by their respective breadths at the exact midpoint; stated to range normally between 5.4 and 7.9. A value above 8.4 is diagnostic of arachnodactylia. **mitotic i.,** an expression of the number of mitoses found in a stated number of cells. **monocyte-leukocyte i.,** the number obtained by dividing the number of lymphocytes by the number of the monocytes. **morphological i.,** the volume of the trunk divided by the length of the limbs. **morphologic face i.,** 100 times the distance from the nasion to the gnathion divided by the bizygomatic breadth. **nasal i.,** 100 times the maximal breadth of the nasal aperture divided by the nasion-nasospinale height. **nucleoplasmic i.,** the relation of the size of the nucleus of a cell to that of the cytoplasm, expressed numerically by the quotient of the nuclear volume divided by the difference between the volume of the cell and the nuclear volume. **obesity i.,** body weight divided by body volume. **opsonic i.,** the opsonic power of the blood of a patient for any particular microorganism compared with the normal as measured by in vitro phagocytosis. **opsonocytophagic i.,** hemophagocytic i. **orbital i. (of Broca),** 100 times the height of the opening of the orbit, divided by its width. **palatal i., palatine i., palatomaxillary i.,** 100 times the maximal palatal breadth divided by the maximal palatal length. **parasite i.,** the percentage of individuals in a population whose blood smears show the presence of malarial parasites. **pelvic i.,** the number obtained by multiplying the anterior-posterior diameter of the pelvis by 100 and dividing by the greatest transverse width across the inlet. **permanganate i.,** a figure expressing the total amount of organic matter in the cerebrospinal fluid as measured by the reduction of a solution of potassium permanganate of known strength. **phagocytic i.** 1. The average number of bacteria ingested per leukocyte of a patient's blood. 2. (*Of Arneth.*) The proportion in the blood of multinuclear neutrophil leukocytes with nuclei having three or more lobes. **physiognomonic upper face i.,** 100 times the distance from the nasion to the stomion divided by the bizygomatic breadth. **Pignet i.** See under *formula.* **Pirquet's i.** (of nutritional status), multiply the weight in grams by 10, divide this product by the sitting height in centimeters and extract the cube root of this quotient. A result lower than 0.945 indicates faulty nutrition. **ponderal i.,** 100 times the cube root of the body weight divided by the stature. **prothrombin i.,** the time of clotting of control plasma, divided by the time of clotting of the patient's blood. **Quarterly Cumulative I. Medicus,** a former publication of the American Medical Association, in which was indexed most of the medical literature in the world. **radiohumeral i.,** 100 times the maximal length of the radius divided by the maximal length of the humerus. **refractive i.,** the refractive power of a medium compared with that of air, which is assumed to be 1. **i. of resistance,** an index obtained by comparing the percentage of neutrophil cells of the blood with the total leukocyte count; the percentage of neutrophils represents the severity of the infection, while the leukocyte count indicates the power of resistance. **Röhrer's i.** (of the state of nutrition), multiply the weight in grams by 100 and divide the product by the cube of the height in centimeters. **sacral i.,** 100 times the breadth of the sacrum, divided by the length. **salivary urea i.** See *Hench-Aldrich test,* under *test.* **saturation i.,** a number indicating the hemoglobin content of a person's red blood cells as compared with the normal, obtained by dividing the percentage of hemoglobin by the percentage by volume of the cells. **sedimentation i.,** the logarithm of the number of millimeters of sedimentation of erythrocytes that would have occurred in 100 minutes at the maximum rate of sedimentation observed at 10 minute intervals over a 2–2½ hour period. **splanchnoptotic i.,** the distance of the jugulum from the upper margin of the pubic symphysis divided by the minimal circumference of the abdomen, the quotient being multiplied by 100. **spleen i.,** the percentage of individuals in the population having enlarged spleens: used in malaria surveys. **splenometric i.,** an index of the amount of malarial infection:

obtained by multiplying the spleen rate by the average enlarged spleen. **staphylo-opsonic i.,** the opsonic index in staphylococcic infection. **stephanozygomatic i.,** the relation of the interstephanic and bizygomatic diameters. **thoracic i.,** the ratio of the anteroposterior diameter of the thorax to the transverse diameter. **tibiofemoral i.,** 100 times the length of the lower leg divided by the length of the thigh. **tibioradial i.,** 100 times the length of the forearm divided by the length of the lower leg. **trunk i.,** 100 times the bi-acromial breadth divided by the sitting suprasternale height. **tuberculo-opsonic i.,** the opsonic index in tuberculous infection. **urea i.** See *Ambard's formula* and *McLean's formula,* under *formula.* **ureosecretory i.** See *Ambard's formula,* under *formula.* **uricolytic i.,** the percentage of uric acid which is oxidized to allantoin before being secreted. **ventilation i.,** the ratio of the residual volume of the lung to total lung capacity. **vertical i.,** 100 times the height of the skull divided by the length. **vital i.,** the ratio of births to deaths within a given time in a population; called also *birth-death ratio.* **volume i.,** the index indicating the size of an erythrocyte as compared with the normal. It is the quotient obtained by dividing the volume of red corpuscles (expressed in percentage of the normal) by the number of red corpuscles (expressed in percentage of the normal). **xanthoproteic i.** See *Mulder's test,* under *test.* **zygomatico-auricular i.,** the ratio between the zygomatic and auricular diameters of the skull.

indican (in′dĭ-kan). 1. A yellow indoxyl glycoside, $C_6H_4.NH.CH:C.O.C_6H_{11}O_5$, from the plants that yield indigo. On hydrolysis it yields dextrose and indoxyl. 2. Potassium indoxyl sulfate, C_6H_4-NH.CH.CO.SO_2.OK, formed by decomposition of trytophan in the intestines and found in the urine.

indicanemia (in″dĭ-kan-e′me-ah) [*indican* + Gr. *haima* blood + *-ia*]. The presence of indican in the blood.

indicanhidrosis (in″dĭ-kan″hid-ro′sis) [*indican* + Gr. *hidrōs* sweat + *-osis*]. Blue sweat.

indicanidrosis (in″dĭ-kan″id-ro′sis). Indicanhidrosis.

indicanmeter (in′dĭ-kan-me″ter). An instrument for estimating the amount of indican in the urine.

indicanorachia (in″dĭ-kan-o-ra′ke-ah). The presence of indican in the spinal fluid.

indicant (in′dĭ-kant). 1. Indicating. 2. A symptom which indicates the true diagnosis or treatment.

indicanuria (in″dĭ-kan-u′re-ah) [*indican* + Gr. *ouron* urine + *-ia*]. The presence in the urine of indican in excessive quantity.

indicarmine (in″dĭ-kar′mīn). Indigo carmine.

indicatio (in″dĭ-ka′she-o) [L.]. Indication. **i. causa′lis,** an indication as to the treatment of a disease afforded by its cause. **i. curati′va, i. mor′bi,** an indication as to treatment afforded by the nature of the morbid processes observed. **i. symptomat′ica,** an indication as to disease afforded by the symptoms that may arise.

indication (in″dĭ-ka′shun) [L. *indicatio*]. A sign or circumstance which points to or shows the cause, pathology, treatment, or issue of an attack of disease; that which points out; that which serves as a guide or warning.

indicator (in′dĭ-ka″ter) [L.]. 1. The forefinger; index finger. 2. The extensor indicis muscle. 3. Any substance which, when added in small quantities, shows the appearance or disappearance of a chemical individual by a conspicuous change of color or the attainment of a certain pH. **anaerobic i.,** a dilute solution of methylene blue is decolorized in the absence of oxygen. **Andrade's i.,** a solution of acid fuchsin in water, decolorized to a yellow color by sodium hydrate solution, and added to sugar bouillon culture medium. An acid-producing organism cultivated on this bouillon turns the medium magenta red. **complex i.,** in psychoanalysis, anything that discloses or indicates the working of a complex. **radioactive i.** See under *tracer.* **redox i.,** a pigment which indicates by a change of color the change in pH. **Schneider's i.,** an index giving a cardiovascular rating based on circulation data as a measure of physical fatigue and efficiency.

indicophose (in′dĭ-ko″fōz). An indigo-colored phose.

Indiella (in″de-el′ah). A genus of fungi several species of which (*I. brumpti, I. mansoni, I. reynieri*) cause white mycetoma.

indifférence (ahn-de″fa-rahns′) [Fr.]. Indifference. **belle i.** (bel″ahn-de″fa-rahns′) [Fr. "beautiful indifference"], a complacent attitude toward their condition and symptoms shown by hysterical patients and patients with other states, such as schizophrenia.

indifferent (in-dif′er-ent) [L. *indifferens*]. Not tending one way or another; neutral; having no preponderating affinity.

indigenous (in-dij′e-nus) [L. *indigenus*]. Native, or not exotic; native to a particular place or country.

indigestible (in″di-jes′tĭ-b'l) [*in-* neg. + *digestible*]. Not susceptible of being digested.

indigestion (in″di-jes′chun). Lack or failure of digestion. **acid i.,** hyperchlorhydria. **fat i.,** inability to digest fat; steatorrhea. **gastric i.,** indigestion taking place in or due to some disorder of the stomach. **intestinal i.,** imperfect performance of the digestive function of the intestine. **nervous i.,** nervous dyspepsia. **psychic i.,** digestive disturbance due to psychic or mental disquietude. **sugar i.,** defective ability to digest sugar, resulting in fermentative diarrhea.

indigitation (in-dij″ĭ-ta′shun) [L. *in* into + *digitus* finger]. Intussusception or invagination.

indiglucin (in″dĭ-gloo′sin). A sugar formed together with indigo on the decomposition of indican.

indigo (in′dĭ-go) [Gr. *Indikon* Indian dye]. A blue dyeing material from various leguminous and other plants, as *Indigofera tinctoria,* etc., being the aglycone of indican; also made synthetically. It is found in the sweat and the urine, being derived from the indican.

indigogen (in′dĭ-go-jen). A crystalline principle from indigo.

indigopurpurine (in″dĭ-go-pur′pu-rin). A purple pigment occasionally found in the urine.

indigotin (in″dĭ-go′tin). A neutral, tasteless, dark blue powder, $C_{16}H_{10}N_2O_2$, the principal ingredient of commercial indigo. Called also *indigo blue.*

indigotindisulfonate (in″dĭ-go″tin-di-sul′fo-nāt). A dye, $C_{16}H_8N_2Na_2O_8S_2$, used in tests for measurement of kidney function.

indigouria (in″dĭ-go-u′re-ah). Indiguria.

indiguria (in″dig-u′re-ah) [*indigo* + Gr. *ouron* urine + *-ia*]. The presence of indigo in the urine.

indirect (in″di-rekt′) [L. *indirectus*]. 1. Not immediate or straight. 2. Acting through an intermediary agent.

indirubin (in″di-roo′bin). A red pigment occasionally found in the urine.

indirubinuria (in″di-roo″bin-u′re-ah). The presence of indirubin in the urine.

indiscriminate (in″dis-krim′ĭ-nāt) [L. *in* not + *discrimen* distinction]. Affecting various parts.

indisposition (in″dis-po-zish′un). The condition of being slightly ill; a slight illness.

indium (in′de-um) [L. *indicum* indigo]. A metallic element; atomic number, 49; atomic weight, 114.82; symbol, In; named from its blue line in the spectrum. Its use in medicine is mainly homeopathic.

individuation (in″dĭ-vid″u-a′shun). 1. The process of developing individual characteristics. 2. Differential regional activity in the embryo occurring in response to organizer influence.

indolaceturia (in″do-las″ĕ-tu′re-ah). The presence of indolacetic acid in the urine. It is usually associated with pathologic conditions of the intestinal tract.

indole (in′dōl). A compound, $C_6H_4CH{:}CH.NH$, from indigo, and from the decomposition of tryptophan in the intestines; it is also found in cultures of the spirillum of cholera and other bacteria. It gives part of their peculiar odor to the feces; it is found in large quantities in the urine and accumulates in the intestine in cases of intestinal obstruction.

indolent (in′do-lent) [L. *in* not + *dolens* painful]. Causing little pain, as, an *indolent* tumor.

indologenous (in″do-loj′e-nus) [*indole* + Gr. *gennan* to produce]. Causing the formation of indole.

indoluria (in″dōl-u′re-ah). The presence of indole in the urine.

indophenol (in″do-fe′nol). Any one of a series of dyes which are nitrogen derivatives of quinone.

indophenolase (in″do-fe′nōl-ās). Cytochrome oxidase.

indophenol-oxidase (in″do-fe″nol-ok′sĭ-dās). An oxidizing enzyme occurring in the pancreas, salivary glands, spleen, bone marrow, and thymus, whose action is to influence the formation of indophenol in the body.

indoxyl (in-dok′sil) [Gr. *indikon* indigo + *oxys* sharp]. An oily substance, $C_6H_4.C(OH){:}CH.NH$, soluble in water, existing normally in the urine of some persons and formed by decomposition of tryptophan.

indoxylemia (in-dok″sil-e′me-ah) [*indoxyl* + Gr. *haima* blood + *-ia*]. The presence of indoxyl in the blood.

indoxyl-sulfate (in-dok′sil-sul′fāt). A compound found in the urine in some cases in which great putrefactive changes are occurring in the intestine.

indoxyluria (in″dok-sil-u′re-ah) [*indoxyl* + Gr. *ouron* urine + *-ia*]. The presence of an excess of indoxyl in the urine.

induced (in-dūst′) [L. *inducere* to lead in]. 1. Produced artificially. 2. Produced by induction.

inducer (in-dūs′er). Something that induces. In biosynthesis, a compound that induces the synthesis of a specific enzyme or sequence of enzymes, by antagonizing the action of the corresponding repressor.

inductance (in-duk′tans). That property of a circuit by virtue of which a magnetic field is associated with the circuit when the circuit is carrying current. The unit of inductance, or "self-induction," is the henry.

induction (in-duk′shun) [L. *inductio*]. 1. The act or process of inducing or causing to occur, especially the production of a specific morphogenetic effect in the developing embryo through the influence of evocators or organizers, or the production of anesthesia or unconsciousness by use of appropriate agents. 2. The appearance of an electric current or of magnetic properties in a body because of the presence of another electric current or magnetic field nearby. **autonomous i.,** induction in which the inductor forms no part of the portion produced. **complementary i.,** induction in which the inductor forms a part of the portion produced. **somatic i.,** the production of new characters through the influence of the soma on the germ cells. **Spemann's i.,** the stimulating and directing effect shown by certain tissues on neighboring tissues or parts in early development of the embryo. **spinal i.,** that process by which one reflex lowers the threshold of another reflex which otherwise cannot be penetrated.

inductogram (in-duk′to-gram). Roentgenogram.

inductopyrexia (in-duk″to-pi-rek′se-ah). Electropyrexia.

inductor (in-duk′ter). A tissue elaborating a chemical substance which acts to determine the growth and differentiation of embryonic parts. Cf. *organizer*.

inductorium (in″duk-to′re-um). An apparatus for generating currents of induced electricity.

indulin (in′du-lĭn). A coal tar dye, used as a histologic stain.

indulinophil (in″du-lin′o-fil). 1. An element easily stainable with indulin. 2. Indulinophilic.

indulinophilic (in″du-lin-o-fil′ik) [*indulin* + Gr. *philein* to love]. Stainable with indulin.

indurated (in′du-rāt″ed) [L. *indurare* to harden]. Hardened; rendered hard.

induration (in″du-ra′shun) [L. *induratio*]. 1. The quality of being hard; the process of hardening. 2. An abnormally hard spot or place. **black i.,** the hardening and pigmentation of lung tissue seen in pneumonia. **brown i.** 1. A deposit of altered blood pigment in the lung in pneumonia. 2. Marked increase of the connective tissue of the lung and excessive pigmentation, due to long-continued congestion from valvular heart disease or to anthracosis. **cyanotic i.,** a congested, dense, and purple state of the kidney in which the blood current is slowed and the transudation of fluid through the glomeruli is impeded. **fibroid i.,** cirrhosis. **Froriep's i.,** myositis fibrosa. **granular i.,** cirrhosis. **gray i.,** an induration of lung tissue in or after pneumonia, without pigmentation. **laminate i.,** a thin layer of round-cell infiltration of the corium in chancre. **parchment i.,** laminate i. **penile i.,** Peyronie's disease. **plastic i.,** sclerosis of the corpora cavernosa of the penis. **red i.,** interstitial pneumonia in which the lung is red and congested.

indurative (in′du-ra″tiv). Pertaining to or marked by induration.

indusium griseum (in-du′ze-um gris′e-um) [L.]. [N A] A thin layer of gray substance on the dorsal aspect of the corpus callosum. Called also *supracallosal gyrus*.

-ine. A suffix indicating an alkaloid, an organic base, or a halogen.

inebriant (in-e′bre-ant) [L. *inebriare* to make drunk]. 1. Causing intoxication. 2. An intoxicating agent.

inebriation (in-e″bre-a′shun) [L. *inebriatio*]. The condition of being drunk.

inebriety (in″e-bri′ĕ-te) [L. *in* intensive + *ebrietas* drunkenness]. Habitual drunkenness.

inemia (in-e′me-ah) [Gr. *is* fiber + *haima* blood + *-ia*]. The presence of fibrin in the blood.

inert (in-ert′). Having no action.

inertia (in-er′she-ah) [L.]. Inactivity; inability to move spontaneously. **colonic i.,** weak muscular activity of the colon, leading to distension of the organ and constipation. **i. u′teri,** sluggishness of the uterine contractions during labor.

in extremis (in eks-tre′mis) [L. "at the end"]. At the point of death.

Inf. Abbreviation for L. *infun′de*, pour in.

infancy (in′fan-se). The early period of life; generally considered to designate the first 12 to 14 months of life.

infant (in′fant) [L. *infans; in* neg. + *fans* speaking]. A young child; generally considered to designate the human young from birth or from the termination of the newborn period (the first four weeks of life) to the time of assumption of erect posture (12 to 14 months). **immature i.,** one expelled from the uterus early in the course of gestation and weighing 500 to 999 grams (17 ounces to 2.2 pounds) at birth, with an extremely poor chance of survival. **mature i.,** one weighing 2500 grams (5.5 pounds) or more at birth, and having an optimum chance of survival. **postmature i., post-term i.,** one weighing more than 4082 grams (9 pounds) at birth and having an accurate history of a prolonged gestation period, and parents who are not unusually tall or heavy. Such an infant has a large head and hard bones, and often presents in an abnormal position. Delivery is often difficult, and fetal mortality and maternal morbidity are increased. **premature i.,** one born early in the course of gestation and weighing 1000 to 2499 grams (2.2 to 5.5 pounds) at birth, having poor to good chance of survival, depending on the weight.

infanticide (in-fan′tĭ-sīd) [L. *infans* infant + *caedere* to kill]. The taking of the life of an infant.

infanticulture (in-fan′tĭ-kul″tūr). Puericulture.

infantile (in′fan-tīl) [L. *infantilis*]. Pertaining to an infant or to infancy.

infantilism (in-fan′tĭ-lizm). A condition in which the characters of childhood persist in adult life. It is marked by mental retardation, underdevelopment of the sexual organs, and often, but not always, by dwarfness of stature. Cf. *ateleiosis* and *progeria*. **angioplastic i.,** infantilism attributed to defective development of the vascular system. **Brissaud's i.,** infantile myxedema. **cachetic i.,** infantilism due to chronic infection or poisoning. **celiac i.,** infantilism resulting from celiac disease. **dysthyroidal i.,** infantilism due to defective thyroid activity. **hepatic i.,** infantilism associated with hepatic cirrhosis. **Herter's i.,** intestinal i. **hypophysial i.,** a type of dwarfism, with retention of infantile characteristics, due to undersecretion of the growth-promoting and the gonadotropic hormones of the anterior hypophysis. Called also *pituitary infantilism*, *pituitary dwarfism*, *Levi-Lorain dwarfism*, *Paltauf's dwarfism*, *ateleiosis* and *pituitaria*. **idiopathic i.,** a form of arrested development of unknown causation. **intestinal i.,** a diarrheal disease of young children tending to be accompanied by failure of growth and marked by large pale stools containing much fat, probably identical with sprue. See *sprue*. **Levi-Lorain i., Lorain's i.,** hypophysial i. **lymphatic i.,** infantilism associated with lymphantism. **myxedematous i.,** cretinism. **pancreatic i.,** a form caused by defective pancreatic action. **partial i.,** arrested development of a single part or tissue. **regressive i.,** reversion to an infantile state after body growth has been completed. **renal i.,** renal osteodystrophy. **reversive i.,** regressive i. **sex i.,** continuance of the prepuberal sex characters and behavior beyond the usual age of puberty. **static i.,** a state occurring in children characterized by hypotonia of the trunk muscle and hypertonia of the muscles of the extremities. **symptomatic i.,** infantilism due to general defective development of tissues. **tardy i.,** regressive i. **toxemic i.,** intestinal i. **universal i.,** general dwarfishness in stature with absence of the secondary sexual characteristics.

infantorium (in″fan-to′re-um). A hospital for the newborn and young infants.

infarct (in′farkt) [L. *infarctus*]. An area of coagulation necrosis in a tissue due to local anemia resulting from obstruction of circulation to the area. **anemic i.,** an area of necrosis in a tissue produced by sudden arrest of circulation in a vessel; called also *pale i.* and *white i.* **bilirubin i's,** masses of crystals of bilirubin in the pyramids of the kidneys, especially in newborn infants. **bland i.,** an uninfected infarct. **bone i.,** an area of bone tissue which has become necrotic as a result of loss of its arterial blood supply. **Brewer's i's,** dark-red, wedge-shaped areas, resembling infarcts, seen on section of a kidney in pyelonephritis. **calcareous i.,** a deposit of calcium salt in the tissues. **cystic i.,** an infarct which is enclosed in a membrane. **embolic i.,** one caused by an embolus. **hemorrhagic i.,** an infarct which is red in color owing to the oozing of red corpuscles into the dead area; called also *red i.* **pale i.,** anemic i. **red i.,** hemorrhagic i. **thrombotic i.,** one caused by a thrombus. **uric acid i.,** a deposit of uric acid crystals in the renal tubules of the newborn. **white i.,** anemic i.

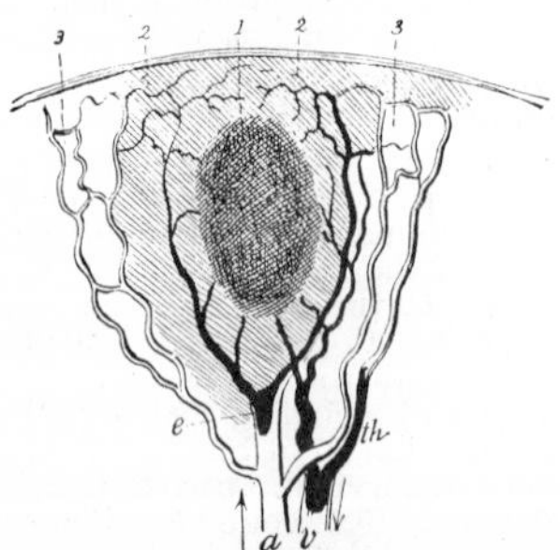

Diagram of a hemorrhagic infarct: *a*, Artery obliterated by an embolus (*e*); *v*, vein filled with a secondary thrombus (*th*); 1, center of infarct, which is becoming disintegrated; 2, area of extravasation; 3, area of collateral hyperemia. (O. Weber.)

infarction (in-fark′shun) [L. *infarcire* to stuff in]. 1. The formation of an infarct. 2. An infarct. **cardiac i.,** myocardial i. **cerebral i.,** an ischemic condition of the brain, producing a persistent focal neurological deficit in the area of distribution of one of the major cerebral arteries. **intestinal i.,** occlusion of an artery or arteriole in the wall of the intestine, resulting in the formation of an area of coagulation necrosis. **myocardial i.,** the formation of an infarct in the myocardium, as a result of interruption of the blood supply to the area, as in coronary thrombosis. **pulmonary i.,** infiltration of an airless area of lung with blood cells, resulting from obstruction of the pulmonary artery by an embolus or thrombus.

infaust (in′fowst) [L. *infaustus* unlucky]. Unfavorable.

infectible (in-fek′tĭ-b'l). Capable of being infected.

infection (in-fek′shun). 1. Invasion of the body by pathogenic microorganisms and the reaction of the tissues to their presence and to the toxins generated by them; often applied to presence of microorganisms within the tissues, whether or not this results in detectable pathologic effects. 2. A general term applied to invasion of the body by bacteria, protozoa, and helminths. Cf. *infestation*. **aerial i.,** air-borne i. **agonal i.,** terminal i. **air-borne i.,** infection by agents transmitted through the air. **apical i.,** infection situated at the apex of the root of a tooth. **autochthonous i.,** an infection acquired locally. **consecutive i.,** septic infection implanted upon a morbid process already established. **contact i.,** direct i. **cross i.,** infection transmitted between patients infected with different pathogenic microorganisms. **cryptogenic i.,** bacterial infection without discoverable entrance of the infective agent. **diaplacental i.,** infection acquired through the placenta. **direct i.,** infection produced by direct contact with another person. **droplet i.,** infection by means of small droplets of moisture expelled into the air during talking or by coughing and sneezing, and which remain suspended for some time. **dust-borne i.,** infection by agents which have become affixed to particles of dust and are transmitted by that means. **ectogenous i.,** infection caused by organisms which have gained entrance to the body from outside, as through surgical or accidental wounds, or natural orifices. **endogenous i.,** infection caused by bacteria normally present within the body but which by some combination of circumstances have become pathogenic. **exogenous i.,** infection caused by bacteria not normally present in the body but which have gained entrance from the environment. **falciparum i.,** infection with *Plasmodium falciparum*. **focal i.,** infection in which bacteria exist in circumscribed areas or foci in certain tissues, and from there are sent out into the blood stream. The common sites of focal infection are the tonsils, periodontal tissue, nasal sinuses, fallopian tubes, and prostate gland. **gas gan-**

grene i., infection of wounds by bacteria producing gas gangrene. **germinal i.,** transmission of infection to the child by means of the ovum or sperm of the parent. **hand-borne i.,** infection carried on a person's hands. **herd i.,** the presence of an infection in a herd or community. **inapparent i.,** subclinical i. **indirect i.,** infection transmitted by water, food, or other means of conveyance. **latent i.,** a condition in which pathogenic microorganisms persist in the tissues for long periods, during most of which there is no obvious manifestation of disease; the term is not intended to apply to the period of incubation of an organism, even when of long duration. **mass i.,** infection produced by a large number of pathogenic organisms in the circulation. **mixed i.,** infection with more than one organism at the same time. **phytogenic i.,** infection caused by plant organisms. **pyogenic i.,** an infection caused by a pus-producing organism. **Salinem i.,** a form of leptospirosis occurring in Salinem. **secondary i.,** infection by a microorganism following an infection by another kind of microorganism. **septic i.,** septicemia. **silent i.,** subclinical i. **simple i.,** infection by a single variety of microorganism. **subclinical i.,** infection which produces no detectable symptoms. **terminal i.,** an acute infection occurring near the end of a disease and frequently causing death. **Vincent's i.,** necrotizing ulcerative gingivitis. **water-borne i.,** infection caused by microorganisms which may be transmitted through water and acquired through ingestion, bathing, or other means. **zoogenic i.,** infection caused by animal organisms.

infectiosity (in-fek″she-os′ĭ-te). The degree of infectiousness of a microbe.

infectious (in-fek′shus). Caused by or capable of being communicated by infection. An infectious disease is one caused by parasites, such as bacteria, protozoa, or fungi.

infectiousness (in-fek′shus-nes). The state or quality of being infectious.

infective (in-fek′tiv) [L. *infectivus*]. Of the nature of an infection; infectious.

infectivity (in″fek-tiv′ĭ-te). Infectiousness.

infecundity (in″fe-kun′dĭ-te) [L. *infecunditas*]. Sterility or barrenness.

inferent (in′fer-ent). Afferent.

inferior (in-fe′re-or) [L. "lower"; neut. *inferius*]. Situated below, or directed downward; in official anatomical nomenclature, used in reference to the lower surface of an organ or other structure.

inferolateral (in″fer-o-lat′er-al) [L. *inferus* low + *latus* side]. Situated below and to one side.

inferomedian (in″fer-o-me′de-an) [L. *inferus* low + *medius* middle]. Situated in the middle of the under side.

inferoposterior (in″fer-o-pos-te′re-or). Situated below and behind.

infertilitas (in″fer-til′ĭ-tas). Infertility. **i. fem′inis,** absence in a woman of the ability to become pregnant.

infertility (in″fer-til′ĭ-te) [L. *in* not + *fertilis* fruitful, prolific]. Absence of the ability to conceive, or to induce conception.

infestation (in-fes-ta′shun). Invasion of the body by arthropods, including insects, mites, and ticks. Cf. *infection.*

infibulation (in-fib-u-la′shun) [L. *infibulare* to buckle together]. The act of buckling, or fastening as if with buckles, especially fastening of the prepuce or labia majora with clasps or stitches to prevent copulation.

infiltrate (in-fil′trāt). 1. To penetrate the interstices of a tissue or substance. 2. Material deposited by infiltration. **Assmann's tuberculous i.** See under *focus.*

infiltration (in″fil-tra′shun) [L. *in* into + *filtration*]. The diffusion or accumulation in a tissue of substances not normal to it. **adipose i.,** fatty i. **albuminous i.,** infiltration of tissue with albuminous material. **amyloid i.,** infiltration with amyloid substance. **calcareous i.,** a deposit of lime and magnesium salts in the tissues. **calcium i.,** a deposit of calcium salts within the tissues of the body. **cellular i.,** an infiltration of round cells within the tissues. **epituberculous i.,** a collateral hyperemia and inflammatory infiltration surrounding a tuberculous focus: called also *epituberculosis.* **fatty i.** 1. A deposit of fat in the tissues, especially between the cells. 2. The presence of fat globules or oil in the cells. **gelatinous i.,** gray i. **glycogenic i.,** the deposition of granules of glycogen in the cells. **gray i.,** a condition of the lungs in acute tuberculosis in which, after death, they assume a gray appearance. **inflammatory i.,** that which is formed by an inflammatory exudation penetrating the interstices of a tissue. **paraneural i.,** paraneural anesthesia. **peripheral annular i.,** ring abscess. **pigmentary i.,** an abnormal deposit of pigment in a tissue. **purulent i.,** the presence of pus in the tissues, as in diffuse abscess. **saline i.,** the deposit of mineral salts in a living tissue. **sanguineous i.,** infiltration with extravasated blood. **serous i.,** the abnormal presence of lymph in a tissue. **tuberculous i.,** the formation of a group or of groups of tuberculous cells and bacilli in a tissue. **urinous i.,** an extravasation of urine into a tissue. **waxy i.,** amyloid i.

infirm (in-firm′) [L. *infirmis; in* not + *firmus* strong]. Weak; feeble, as from disease or old age.

infirmary (in-fir′mah-re) [L. *infirmarium*]. A hospital or institution where sick or infirm persons are maintained or treated. **camp i.,** a mobile military unit, officered by a sergeant of the hospital corps, designed to furnish dispensary facilities during field service or to become the nucleus of an immobile camp hospital when necessary.

infirmity (in-fir′mĭ-te) [L. *infirmitas*]. 1. A feeble or weak state of the body or mind. 2. A disease or condition producing weakness.

inflammation (in″flah-ma′shun) [L. *inflammatio; inflammare* to set on fire]. The condition into which tissues enter as a reaction to injury (Adami). To the classical signs of inflammation—pain (dolor), heat (color), redness (rubor), and swelling (tumor)—is sometimes added loss of function (functio laesa). Histologically inflammation is characterized by hyperemia, stasis, changes in the blood and walls of the small vessels, and by various exudations. **acute i.,** one in which the inflammatory processes are active. **adhesive i.,** that which promotes the adhesion of contiguous surfaces. **atrophic i.,** a form which results in atrophy and deformity. **catarrhal i.,** a form which affects principally a mucous surface, and which is marked by a discharge of mucopus and epithelial debris. **chronic i.,** inflammation of slow progress and marked by the formation of new connective tissue. **cirrhotic i.,** atrophic i. **croupous i.,** a fibrinous inflammation leading to the formation of a false membrane. **diffuse i.,** one that is both interstitial and parenchymatous or is spread over a large area. **disseminated i.,** one that has a number of distinct foci. **exudative i.,** one in which the prominent feature is an exudate. **fibrinous i.,** one that is characterized by an exudate of coagulated fibrin. **fibroid i.,** atrophic i. **focal i.,** one that is confined to a single spot or to a few limited spots. **granulomatous i.,** chronic inflammation in which there is a formation of granulation tissue. **hyperplastic i.,** one which leads to the formation of new connective tissue fibers. **hypertrophic i.,** inflammation which is marked by increase in the size of the elements composing the affected tissue. **interstitial i.,** one that primarily affects the stroma of an organ. **metastatic i.,** one that is reproduced in a distant part by the conveyance of infectious material through the blood vessels and lymph organs. **necrotic i.,** inflammation attended by death of the affected tissue. **obliterative i.,** inflammation of the lining membrane of a cavity or vessel, producing adhesions between the surfaces and consequent obliteration of the lumen. **parenchymatous i.**, one that primarily affects the essential tissue elements of an organ. **plastic i., productive i., proliferous i.**, hyperplastic i. **reactive i.**, inflammation occurring about a foreign body or a focus of degeneration. **sclerosing i.**, atrophic i. **seroplastic i.**, inflammation accompanied by both serous and plastic exudation. **serous i.**, one which produces an exudation of serum. **simple i.**, that in which there is no flow of pus or other product of inflammation. **specific i.**, one that is due to a particular microorganism. **suppurative i.**, one characterized by the formation of pus. **toxic i.**, one that is caused by a poison, such as a bacterial product. **traumatic i.**, one that is caused by an injury.

inflammatory (in-flam′ah-to″re). Pertaining to or characterized by inflammation.

inflation (in-fla′shun) [L. *in* into + *flare* to blow]. 1. Distention with air, gas, or a fluid. 2. The act of distending with air or with a gas.

inflator (in-fla′tor). An instrument for inflating any organ for therapeutic or diagnostic purposes.

inflexion (in-flek′shun) [L. *inflexio; in* in + *flectere* to bend]. The act of bending inward or state of being bent inward.

inflorescence (in″flo-res′ens). The structure or arrangement of the flowers of a plant.

influenza (in″flu-en′zah) [Ital. "influence"]. An acute infectious, epidemic disease marked by depression, distressing fever, acute catarrhal inflammation of the nose, larynx, and bronchi, neuralgic and muscular pains, gastrointestinal disorder and nervous disturbances, such as headache, insomnia, convulsions, and delirium. The disease is primarily due to a filtrable virus, although *Haemophilus influenzae* and other organisms are often present as secondary invaders. There are two varieties of the disease, designated influenza A and influenza B. The duration of the disease is from a few days to one or two weeks; relapses frequently occur, the patient being left weak for a long time and subject to colds, etc. According to the organs chiefly affected the disease is said to be respiratory, nervous, or gastrointestinal in form. Complications are frequent, the chief ones being pneumonia and various affections of the ear and eye. The disease occurs in extensive epidemics or pandemics. **abdominal i.**, influenza marked especially by abdominal symptoms, such as tympanites, diarrhea, or symptoms resembling those of typhoid fever. **clinical i.**, a condition with the clinical features of influenza but in which no specific virus can be isolated. **endemic i.**, a disease resembling epidemic influenza, but less severe in character, occurring during the winter season; called also *influenza nostras, acute catarrhal fever*, and *winter grip*. **epidemic i.**, influenza occurring in localized outbreaks. **horse i.**, a highly contagious disease in horses which is caused by a filtrable virus and which tends to the development of complications. **laryngeal i.**, influenza in horses in which sore throat is the chief symptom. **i. lymphat′ica**, infectious mononucleosis. **i. nos′tras**, endemic influenza. **pandemic i.**, influenza occurring in waves that spread widely over the world at irregular intervals. **Spanish i.**, a name given to the acute influenza-like disease, a pandemic of which passed over Europe and America during the summer and autumn of 1918. **summer i. of Italy**, phlebotomus fever. **swine i.**, a highly contagious disease of hogs caused by two infectious agents, *Haemophilus influenzae* and filtrable virus, in cooperation.

influenzal (in″flu-en′zal). Pertaining to influenza.

infolding (in-fōld′ing). 1. The folding inward of a layer, as in the formation of the neural tube in the embryo. 2. The enclosing of redundant tissue by suturing together the walls of the organ on either side of it.

infra- (in′frah) [L. *infra* beneath]. A prefix meaning situated, formed, or occurring beneath the element indicated by the word stem to which it is affixed.

infra-axillary (in″frah-ak′sĭ-lār″e). Below the axilla.

infrabulge (in′frah-bulj). The surfaces of a tooth gingival to the height of contour, or sloping cervically.

infraclavicular (in″frah-klah-vik′u-lar). Beneath a clavicle.

infraclusion (in″frah-kloo′zhun). The condition in which the occluding surface of a tooth does not reach the normal occlusal plane.

infracommissure (in″frah-kom′ĭ-sūr). The inferior commissure.

infraconstrictor (in″frah-kon-strik′tor). The inferior constrictor of the pharynx.

infracortical (in″frah-kor′tĭ-kal). Beneath the cortex, as of the brain.

infracostal (in″frah-kos′tal) [*infra-* + L. *costa* rib]. Below a rib or below the ribs.

infracotyloid (in″frah-kot′ĭ-loid). Beneath the cotyloid cavity or acetabulum.

infraction (in-frak′shun) [L. *in* into + *frac′tio* break]. Incomplete fracture of a bone without displacement of the fragments. **Freiberg's i.** See *osteochondrosis of head of second metatarsal bone.*

infradentale (in″frah-den-ta′le). A cephalometric landmark, being the highest anterior point on the gingiva between the mandibular medial incisors.

infradiaphragmatic (in″frah-di″ah-frag-mat′ik). Below the diaphragm.

infraduction (in″frah-duk′shun). The turning downward of a part, especially of the eye.

infraglenoid (in″frah-gle′noid). Below the fossa of the glenoid cavity.

infraglottic (in″frah-glot′ik). Below the glottis.

infrahyoid (in″frah-hi′oid). Below the hyoid bone.

inframamillary (in″frah-mam′ĭ-lār″e). Below the nipple.

inframammary (in″frah-mam′ah-re). Below the mammary gland.

inframandibular (in″frah-man-dib′u-lar). Beneath the lower jaw.

inframarginal (in″frah-mar′jĭ-nal). Situated below a margin or border.

inframaxillary (in″frah-mak′sĭ-lār″e). Beneath the jaw.

inframicrobe (in″frah-mi′krōb). A filtrable virus.

infranuclear (in″frah-nu′kle-ar). Below a nucleus.

infraocclusion (in″frah-ŏ-kloo′zhun). Infraclusion.

infraorbital (in″frah-or′bĭ-tal). Lying under or on the floor of the orbit.

infrapatellar (in″frah-pah-tel′ar). Below the patella.

infraplacement (in″frah-plās′ment). Infraclusion.

infrapsychic (in″frah-si′kik). Below the psychic level; automatic.

infrared (in-frah-red′). Noting rays of energy beyond the red end of the spectrum, between the red waves and the radio waves, having wavelengths between 7700 and 120,000 angstroms. **long-wave i.**, infrared radiation of the longest wavelength, that is, furthest from the visible spectrum (wavelength 15,000–120,000 angstroms). **short-wave i.**, infrared radiation of the shortest wavelength, that is, closest to the visible spectrum (wavelength 7700–15,000 angstroms).

infrascapular (in″frah-skap′u-lar). Beneath the scapula.

infrasonic (in″frah-son′ik). Below the frequency range of the waves normally perceived as sound by the human ear.

infraspinous (in″frah-spi′nus). Beneath the spine of the scapula.

infrasternal (in″frah-ster′nal). Below the sternum.

infratemporal (in″frah-tem′po-ral). Below the temporal fossa.

infratonsillar (in″frah-ton′sĭ-lar). Below the faucial tonsil.

infratracheal (in″frah-tra′ke-al). Beneath the trachea.

infratrochlear (in″frah-trok′le-ar). Beneath the trochlea.

infratubal (in″frah-tu′bal). Beneath a tube.

infraturbinal (in″frah-tur′bĭ-nal). The inferior turbinate bone.

infra-umbilical (in″frah-um-bil′ĭ-kal). Beneath the umbilicus.

infraversion (in″frah-ver′shun) [*infra-* + *version*]. 1. Downward deviation of an eye. 2. Infraclusion.

infriction (in-frik′shun) [L. *in* on + *frictio* rubbing]. The rubbing of medicaments upon the skin.

infundibula (in″fun-dib′u-lah) [L.]. Plural of *infundibulum.*

infundibular (in″fun-dib′u-lar). Of the nature of or resembling an infundibulum.

infundibuliform (in″fun-dib′u-lĭ-form) [L. *infundibulum* funnel + *forma* form]. Shaped like a funnel.

infundibuloma (in″fun-dib-u-lo′mah). A tumor of the infundibulum hypothalami.

infundibulopelvic (in″fun-dib″u-lo-pel′vik). Pertaining to an infundibulum and a pelvis, as of the kidney.

infundibulum (in″fun-dib′u-lum), pl. *infundib′ula* [L. "funnel"]. 1. A funnel-shaped passage; used in anatomical nomenclature as a general term to designate such a structure. 2. N A alternative for *conus arteriosus.* **crural i., i. crura′le,** canalis femoralis. **ethmoidal i. of cavity of nose,** i. ethmoidale cavi nasi. **ethmoidal i. of ethmoid bone,** infundibulum ethmoidale ossis ethmoidalis. **i. ethmoida′le ca′vi na′si** [N A, B N A], a passage connecting the cavity of the nose with the anterior ethmoidal cells and the frontal sinus. **i. ethmoida′le os′sis ethmoida′lis** [N A, B N A], a variable sinuous passage extending upward from the middle nasal meatus through the ethmoidal labyrinth, communicating with the anterior ethmoidal cells and often with the frontal sinus. **i. of fallopian tube,** i. tubae uterinae. **i. of heart,** conus arteriosus. **i. hypothal′ami** [N A, B N A], **i. of hypothalamus,** a hollow, funnel-shaped mass in front of the tuber cinereum, which extends to the posterior lobe of the hypophysis. **infundibula of kidney,** calices renales minores. **i. na′si, i. of nose.** 1. Infundibulum ethmoidale cavi nasi. 2. Infundibulum ethmoidale ossis ethmoidalis. **i. pulmo′nis, i. pulmo′num.** See *ductuli alveolares.* **infundib′ula re′num** [B N A], calices renales minores. **i. tu′bae uteri′nae** [N A, B N A], the funnel-like dilation at the distal end of the uterine tube. **i. of urinary bladder,** fundus vesicae urinariae. **i. of uterine tube,** i. tubae uterinae.

infusible (in-fu′zĭ-b′l). Incapable of being melted.

infusion (in-fu′zhun). 1. [L. *infusio;* from *in* into + *fundere* to pour]. The steeping of a substance in water for obtaining its proximate principles. 2. [L. *infusum,* gen. *infusi*]. The product of the process of steeping a drug for the extraction of its medicinal principles. 3. The therapeutic introduction of a fluid, as saline solution, into a vein. NOTE—An *infusion* flows in by gravity, an *injection* is forced in by a syringe, an *instillation* is dropped in, an *insufflation* is blown in and an *infection* slips in unnoticed. **cold i.,** the product of steeping a drug in cold water. **meat i.** (for bacteriological use), fresh lean meat free from fat is ground and extracted with water. The mixture is infused over night in the icebox, gradually raised to the boiling point, and filtered. **saline i.,** introduction, either subcutaneously or intravenously, of saline solution.

infusodecoction (in-fu″so-de-kok′shun). A mixture of the infusion and the decoction of a substance.

Infusoria (in″fu-so′re-ah) [L. pl., so called because found in *infusions,* after exposure to air]. A class of Protozoa characterized by the presence of cilia.

infusoriotoxin (in″fu-so″re-o-tok′sin). A toxin destructive to Infusoria.

infusum (in-fu′sum) [L.]. An infusion, def. 2.

ingesta (in-jes′tah) [L. pl., *in* into + *gerere* to carry]. Food and drink taken into the stomach.

ingestant (in-jes′tant). A substance that is or may be taken into the body by way of the mouth, or through the digestive system.

ingestion (in-jes′chun). The act of taking food, medicines, etc., into the body, by mouth.

ingestive (in-jes′tiv). Pertaining to or effecting an ingestion.

ingluveosis (in-gloo″ve-o′sis) [L. *ingluvies* gizzard]. Cardiospasm.

ingluvies (in-gloo′ve-ēz) [L.]. 1. The craw or crop of birds. 2. The first stomach of ruminant animals.

Ingrassia's process (in-grah′se-ahs) [Giovanni Filippo *Ingrassia,* Italian anatomist, 1510–1580]. Ala minor ossis sphenoidalis.

ingravescent (in″grah-ves′ent) [L. *in* upon + *gravesci* to grow heavy]. Gradually increasing in severity.

inguen (ing′gwen), pl. *in′guina* [L.]. [N A, B N A] The lowest part of the abdominal wall, near the junction of the trunk and thigh. Called also *groin.*

inguinal (ing′gwĭ-nal) [L. *inguinalis*]. Pertaining to the inguen, or groin.

inguino-abdominal (ing″gwĭ-no-ab-dom′ĭ-nal). Pertaining to the groin and the abdomen.

inguinocrural (ing″gwĭ-no-kroo′ral). Pertaining to the groin and the thigh.

inguinodynia (ing″gwĭ-no-din′e-ah). Pain in the groin: a common symptom of hysteria.

inguinolabial (ing″gwĭ-no-la′be-al). Pertaining to the groin and labium.

inguinoscrotal (ing″gwĭ-no-skro′tal). Pertaining to the groin and the scrotum.

INH (i′en-āch). Trade mark for preparations of isoniazid.

inhalant (in-ha′lant). A substance that is or may be taken into the body by way of the nose and trachea, or through the respiratory system. **antifoaming i.,** an agent that is inhaled as a vapor to prevent the formation of foam in the respiratory passages of a patient with pulmonary edema.

inhalation (in″hah-la′shun) [L. *inhalatio*]. 1. The drawing of air or other vapor into the lungs. 2. A substance to be inhaled as a vapor.

inhalatorium (in″ha-lah-to′re-um). An institution for treating disease by inhalation methods.

inhale (in-hāl′) [L. *inhalare*]. To take into the lungs by breathing.

inhaler (in-ha′ler). 1. An apparatus for administering vapor or volatilized remedies by inhalation. 2. An apparatus to prevent dust, smoke, or the like from entering the lungs, or to enable a person with affected lungs to breathe cold or damp air with less danger and discomfort. **Allis' i.,** an apparatus for administering ether by the drop method. **ether i.,** a form of apparatus for administering the vapor of ether as an anesthetic. **H. H. i.,** an oxygen inhaler used in treating gassed patients: named from the inventors, Henderson and Haggard.

inherent (in-hēr′ent) [L. *inhaerens* sticking fast]. Implanted by nature; intrinsic; innate.

inheritance (in-her′ĭ-tans). 1. The acquisition of characters or qualities by transmission from parent to offspring. 2. That which is transmitted from parent to offspring. **alternative i.,** inheritance in which the characters are inherited from one parent. **amphigonous i.,** inheritance of characteristics from both parents. **biparental i.,** amphigonous i. **blending i.,** inheritance in which the characters of mother and father seem to blend in the offspring. **crisscross i.,** inheritance by offspring of characters from the parent of the opposite sex. **cytoplasmic i.,** transmission of characters dependent on self-perpetuating elements not nuclear in origin. **duplex i.,** amphigonous i. **extrachromosomal i.,** transmission of characters dependent on some factor not connected with the chromosomes. **holandric i.,** inheritance carried only by the males and not by the females. **hologynic i.,** inheritance carried only by the females and not by males. **homochronous i.,** the inheritance of characteristics which appear in the offspring at the same age as they appeared in the parent. **homotropic i.,** the alleged inheritance of acquired characteristics. **maternal i.,** the transmission of characters that are dependent on peculiarities of the egg cytoplasm produced, in turn, by nuclear genes. **mendelian i.** See *Mendel's law*, under *law*. **monofactorial i.,** the acquisition of a characteristic or quality, the transmission of which depends on a single gene. **multifactorial i.,** the acquisition of a characteristic or quality, the manifestation of which is subject to modification by a number of genes.

inhibin (in-hib'in). 1. Any bacteria-transforming enzyme. 2. A water-soluble hormone secreted by the testicles that is supposed to restrain the stimulating effect of the pituitary upon the interstitial cells of the testes.

inhibition (in″hĭ-bish'un) [L. *inhibere* to restrain; *in* in + *habere* to have]. Arrest or restraint of a process. **competitive i.,** prevention of the action of an effector substance (or agent) by another substance (or agent) that enters into combination with the element on which the effector substance acts or which is essential to its action. **i. of complement,** complement is inhibited by 15 to 25 per cent salt solution and can be thus kept in the refrigerator for weeks, resuming its activity when diluted to isotonicity with distilled water. **endproduct i.,** inhibition by the endproduct of a biosynthetic pathway of the action of the initial, branchpoint enzyme of that pathway. **false feedback i.,** inhibition of the action of the initial branchpoint enzyme of a biosynthetic pathway by an analogue of the endproduct of that pathway. **feedback i.,** endproduct i. **reflex i.,** a condition in which a negative response is evoked by a stimulus. **selective i.,** the reduction of the physiological function of an essential metabolite which results from its being replaced by a similar but inactive compound. **specific i.,** a condition in which a precipitoid is combined with all the available precipitinogen, so that when fresh precipitin is added no precipitate will occur. **Wedensky i.,** a partial block to conduction in a nerve may transmit impulses at low frequencies but not at higher frequencies.

inhibitive (in-hib'ĭ-tiv). Inhibitory.

inhibitor (in-hib'ĭ-tor). 1. Any substance which interferes with a chemical reaction. 2. A chemical substance which acts to inhibit, or hold in check, the action of a tissue organizer or the growth of microorganisms. 3. A mechanical device for curing mouth breathing. **aldosterone i.,** an agent that blocks the action of aldosterone on the renal tubules. **cholesterol i.,** an agent which suppresses the production of cholesterol or decreases the level of cholesterol in the blood. **cholinesterase i.,** an agent that inhibits the action of cholinesterase. **competitive i.,** a closely similar but inactive compound which tends to replace an essential metabolite. **mitotic i.,** a substance which inhibits mitosis, e.g., colchicine. **serum i.,** antiplasmin.

inhibitory (in-hib'ĭ-tor″e) [L. *inhibere* to restrain]. Restraining or arresting any process: effecting a stay or arrest, partial or complete.

inhibitrope (in-hib'ĭ-trōp). One in whom certain stimuli tend to produce arrest of function.

inhomogeneity (in-ho″mo-je-ne'ĭ-te). Lack of normal homogeneity.

inhomogeneous (in″ho-mo-je'ne-us). Lacking homogeneity.

iniac (in'e-ak). Pertaining to the inion.

iniad (in'e-ad). Toward the inion.

inial (in'e-al). Iniac.

iniencephalus (in″e-en-sef'ah-lus). A fetus exhibiting iniencephaly.

iniencephaly (in″e-en-sef'ah-le) [Gr. *inion* occiput + *enkephalos* brain]. A developmental anomaly characterized by enlargement of the foramen magnum, and absence of the laminal and spinal processes of the cervical, dorsal, and sometimes lumbar vertebrae, with vertebrae reduced in number and irregularly fused, the brain and much of the cord occupying a single cavity.

inio- (in'e-o) [Gr. *inion* occiput]. Combining form denoting relationship to the occiput.

iniodymus (in″e-od'ĭ-mus) [*inio-* + Gr. *didymos* twin). Iniopagus.

inion (in'e-on) [Gr. "the back of the head"]. [N A] The most prominent point of the external occipital protuberance.

iniopagus (in″e-op'ah-gus) [*inio-* + Gr. *pagos* thing fixed]. Conjoined symmetrical twins fused at the occiput.

iniops (in'e-ops) [*inio-* + Gr. *ōps* eye]. A double-faced monster with the posterior face incomplete.

initial (ĭ-nish'al) [L. *initialis*, from *initium* beginning]. Pertaining to the very first stage of any process.

initis (in-i'tis) [Gr. *is*, *inos* fiber]. Inflammation of the substance of a muscle.

Inj. Abbreviation for *injection.*

injectable (in-jek'tah-b'l). 1. Capable of being injected. 2. A substance which may be injected.

injected (in-jekt'ed). 1. Filled by injection. 2. Thrown in by injection. 3. Congested.

injectio (in-jek'she-o), pl. *injectio'nes* [L., from *in* into + *jacere* to throw]. Injection.

injection (in-jek'shun) [L. *injectio*]. 1. The act of forcing a liquid into a part, such as the rectum or a blood vessel. 2. A substance forced into a part or organ; an enema. Officially, in pharmacy, a solution of a medicament suitable for injection. 3. The condition of being injected; congestion. **adrenal cortex i.,** a preparation containing a mixture of the endocrine principles derived from the cortex of adrenal glands: used in treatment of adrenal insufficiency. **anatomical i.,** an injection into the vessels or organs of the cadaver, designed to facilitate dissection or demonstration. **Brown-Séquard i.,** injection of testicular extract. **capillary i.,** a hyperemia which makes the small blood vessels visible. **circumcorneal i.,** dilatation of the conjunctival blood vessels close to the limbus, and diminishing toward the periphery. **coarse i.,** an anatomical injection that fills only the larger vessels. **dextrose i.,** a sterile solution of dextrose in water for injection; used as a fluid and nutrient replenisher. **endermic i.,** intracutaneous i. **epifascial i.,** one made upon the surface of a fascia, particularly the injection of arsphenamine upon the fascia lata. **exciting i.,** sensitizing i. **fine i.,** an anatomical injection that fills even the smallest vessels. **fructose i.,** a sterile solution of fructose in water: used as a fluid and nutrient replenisher. **gaseous i.,** injection of gas or air for therapeutic purposes as in collapse therapy; for diagnostic purposes, as in ventriculography; or to assist in anatomical demonstrations. **gelatin i.,** a preservative injection of which gelatin is the base. **hypodermic i.,** an injection made into the subcutaneous tissues; called also *subcutaneous i.* **insulin i.,** a sterile solution of the active principle of the pancreas which affects the metabolism of glucose: a prompt-acting preparation used in treatment of diabetes mellitus. **intracardiac**

i., one into the cavity of the heart. **intracutaneous i., intradermal i., intradermic i.,** one made into the corium or substance of the skin. **intramuscular i.,** an injection into the substance of the muscles. **intravascular i.,** an injection made into a vessel. **intravenous i.,** an injection made into a vein. **jet i.,** injection through the intact skin of a drug in solution by an extremely fine jet of the solution under high pressure. **liver i.,** a sterile preparation of the soluble thermostable fraction of mammalian livers that stimulates hematopoiesis in patients with pernicious anemia, administered intramuscularly. **opacifying i.,** the injection of a radiopaque substance into the vessels or into some body cavity for diagnostic radiological study. **oxytocin i.,** a sterile solution of an oxytocic principle prepared by synthesis or obtained from the posterior lobe of the pituitary gland of domestic animals: used to stimulate contraction of smooth muscle, particularly the pregnant uterus. **parathyroid i.,** a sterile solution of water-soluble principles of the parathyroid glands, administered intramuscularly to maintain the level of calcium in the blood. **parenchymatous i.,** one made into the substance of an organ. **posterior pituitary i.,** a sterile solution of the principles from the posterior lobe of the pituitary of domestic animals used for food by man. **potassic saline i., lactated,** a sterile solution of potassium chloride, sodium chloride, and sodium lactate in water for injection: used as a fluid and electrolyte replenisher. **preparatory i.,** sensitizing i. **preservative i.,** an injection that serves to protect a cadaver or specimen from decay. **protamine sulfate i.,** a sterile isotonic solution prepared from the sperm or from the mature testes of fish belonging to the genus *Oncorhynchus*, *Salmo*, or *Trutta:* used to counteract the action of heparin. **protein hydrolysate i.,** a sterile solution of amino acids and short-chain peptides, used as a parenteral nutrient. **radiochromate sodium i.,** a sterile solution of radioactive chromium, in the form of $Na_2Cr^{51}O_4$: used in estimation of blood volume. **Ringer's i.,** a sterile solution of sodium chloride, potassium chloride, and calcium chloride in water for injection, used as a fluid and electrolyte replenisher. **Ringer's i., lactated,** a sterile solution of calcium chloride, potassium chloride, and sodium lactate in water for injection, used as a fluid and electrolyte replenisher. **Schlösser i.,** alcohol injection of main branches of the trigeminal nerve at their deep foramina of exit for trigeminal neuralgia. **sclerosing i.,** the injection into a blood vessel of material (e.g., sodium citrate) which will obliterate the vessel; used in varicose veins, angioma, etc. **sensitizing i.,** the first injection of protein or other sensitizing antigen. **sodium chloride i.,** a sterile isotonic solution of sodium chloride in water for injection, used as a fluid and electrolyte replenisher. **subcutaneous i.,** hypodermic i. **vasopressin i.,** a sterile solution in water for injection of the water-soluble, pressor principle of the posterior lobe of the pituitary of healthy domestic animals.

injector (in-jek′tor) [L. *injicere* to inject]. An instrument used in making injections.

Inj. enem. Abbreviation for L. *injiciatur enema*, let an enema be injected.

injury (in′ju-re) [L. *injuria; in* not + *jus* right]. Harm or hurt; a wound or maim. Usually applied to damage inflicted to the body by an external force. **egg-white i.,** biotin deficiency. **Goyrand's i.,** pulled elbow. **steering-wheel i.,** contusion of the heart in motorists caused by being thrown forward with the precordium against the steering wheel. **whiplash i.,** a nonspecific term applied to injury to the spine and spinal cord at the junction of the fourth and fifth cervical vertebrae, occurring as the result of rapid acceleration or deceleration of the body. Because of their greater mobility, the four upper vertebra act as the lash, and the lower three act as the handle of the whip.

inlay (in′la). Material laid into a defect in tissue. In dentistry, a filling that is made outside the tooth to correspond with the form of a cavity and then cemented into the tooth. **cast i.,** gold i. **epithelial i.,** a method of securing epithelialization of a wound cavity. A mold of the cavity is taken, and this is covered with a Thiersch graft of epidermis, the whole being inserted into the wound cavity, the edges being approximated with sutures. The mold is removed after ten days, leaving the cavity completely epithelialized. **gold i.,** one made of gold or of a gold alloy. **porcelain i.,** an inlay made of porcelain. **wax i.,** the inlay pattern created by forcing wax into the cavity of a tooth, this pattern being invested and the gold inlay subsequently cast in the mold.

inlet (in′let). An avenue of ingress. **pelvic i.,** the superior aperture of the minor pelvis, bounded by the crest and pecten of the pubic bones, the arcuate lines of the ilia, and the anterior margin of the base of the sacrum. Called also *apertura pelvis superior* [N A].

Inman's disease (in′manz) [Thomas *Inman*, English physician, 1820–1876]. Myalgia.

innate (in′nāt) [L. *in* in + *nasci* to be born]. Inborn; hereditary; congenital.

innervation (in″er-va′shun) [L. *in* into + *nervus* nerve]. 1. The distribution or supply of nerves to a part. 2. The supply of nervous energy or of nerve stimulus sent to a part. **double i.,** innervation of voluntary muscles by both encephalospinal and sympathetic fibers. **reciprocal i.,** the innervation of muscles around the joints, where the motor centers are so connected in pairs that when one is excited the center of the corresponding antagonist is inhibited.

innidiation (ĭ-nid″e-a′shun) [L. *in* into + *nidus* nest]. The development of cells in a part to which they have been carried by metastasis; called also *colonization* and *indenization.*

innocent (in′o-sent) [L. *innocens; in* not + *nocere* to harm]. Not malignant; benign; not tending of its own nature to a fatal issue.

innocuous (ĭ-nok′u-us). Harmless.

innominatal (ĭ-nom″ĭ-na′tal). Pertaining to the innominate artery or to the innominate bone.

innominate (ĭ-nom′ĭ-nāt) [L. *innominatus* nameless; *in* not + *nomen* name]. Not having a name; nameless.

innoxious (ĭ-nok′shus) [L. *in* not + *noxius* harmful]. Not injurious; not hurtful.

innutrition (in″nu-trish′un). Want of nutrition.

ino- (in′o) [Gr. *is, inos* fiber]. Combining form denoting relationship to a fiber, or fibrous material.

inoblast (in′o-blast) [*ino-* + Gr. *blastos* germ]. Any connective tissue cell in the formative stage.

inoccipitia (in-ok″sĭ-pit′e-ah). Absence or deficiency of the occipital lobe of the brain.

inochondritis (in″o-kon-dri′tis) [*ino-* + Gr. *chondros* cartilage + *-itis*] Inflammation of a fibrocartilage.

inochondroma (in″o-kon-dro′mah) [*ino-* + Gr. *chondros* cartilage + *-oma*]. A fibrochondroma.

inocula (in-ok′u-lah). Plural of *inoculum.*

inoculability (in-ok″u-lah-bil′ĭ-te). The quality or state of being inoculable.

inoculable (in-ok′u-lah-b′l). 1. Susceptible of being inoculated; transmissible by inoculation. 2. Not immune against a disease transmissible by inoculation.

inoculate (in-ok′u-lāt). To communicate a disease by inserting its virus; to implant microbes or infectious materials in or on culture mediums; to introduce immune serum, vaccines of various kinds and other antigenic materials for preventive, curative or experimental purposes.

inoculation (in-ok″u-la′shun) [L. *inoculatio*, from *in* into + *oculus* bud]. Introduction of microorganisms, infective material, serum and other substances into tissues of living plants and animals, or culture mediums; introduction of a disease agent into a healthy individual to produce a mild form of the disease followed by immunity, e.g., vaccine virus. **curative i.,** the injection of an antiserum for curative purposes. **protective i.,** the injection of an antiserum to protect against a disease; vaccination against a disease. **side-to-side i.,** the injection of virus into one side of an animal and the specific antiserum into the other.

inoculum (in-ok′u-lum), pl. *inoc′ula* [L.]. The substance used in inoculation.

inocystoma (in″o-sis-to′mah) [*ino-* + Gr. *kystis* cyst + *-oma*]. A fibrous tumor affected with cystic degeneration.

inocyte (in′o-sīt) [*ino-* + *-cyte*]. A cell of fibrous tissue.

ino-epithelioma (in″o-ep″ĭ-the″le-o′mah). Epithelioma with fibrous elements.

inogen (in′o-jen) [*ino-* + Gr. *gennan* to produce]. A hypothetical substance of the muscular tissue, the sudden breaking up of which was once supposed to cause muscular contraction.

inogenesis (in″o-jen′e-sis). The formation of fibrous tissue.

inogenous (in-oj′e-nus). Produced from or producing fibrous tissue.

inoglia (in-og′le-ah) [*ino-* + Gr. *glia* glue]. Fibroglia.

inohymenitis (in″o-hi″men-i′tis) [*ino-* + Gr. *hymēn* membrane + *-itis*]. Inflammation of any fibrous membrane.

inoleiomyoma (in″o-li″o-mi-o′mah) [*ino-* + Gr. *leios* smooth + *mys* muscle + *-oma*]. A tumor composed of unstriped muscular tissue.

inolith (in′o-lith) [*ino-* + Gr. *lithos* stone]. A fibrous concretion.

inoma (in-o′mah). Fibroma.

inomyoma (in″o-mi-o′mah). Fibromyoma.

inomyositis (in″o-mi″o-si′tis). Fibromyositis.

inomyxoma (in″o-mik-so′mah). Fibromyxoma.

inoneuroma (in″o-nu-ro′mah). Fibroneuroma.

inoperable (in-op′er-ah-b'l). Not suitable to be operated upon.

inopexia (in″o-pek′se-ah) [*ino-* + Gr. *pēxis* fixation + *-ia*]. A tendency toward spontaneous coagulation of the blood.

inophragma (in″o-frag′mah) [*ino-* + Gr. *phragmos* a fencing in]. Ground membrane; a name given to Krause's membrane and Hensen's line because they continue uninterruptedly as transverse membranes through all the adjoining fibrils of a muscle fiber. See *mesophragma* and *telophragma*.

inorganic (in″or-gan′ik) [*in-* not + *organic*]. 1. Having no organs. 2. Not of organic origin. 3. Pertaining to substances not of organic origin.

inorgoxydant (in″or-gok′sĭ-dant). A microorganism which lives in and obtains energy from the oxidation of inorganic materials. The group includes the sulfur, nitrite, nitrate, and perhaps also the iron bacteria.

inosclerosis (in″o-skle-ro′sis) [*ino-* + Gr. *sklēros* hard]. Sclerosis or induration by increase of fibrous tissue.

inoscopy (in-os′ko-pe) [*ino-* + Gr. *skopein* to examine]. The diagnosis of disease by artificial digestion and examination of the fibers or fibrinous matter of the sputum, blood, effusions, etc.

inosculate (in-os′ku-lāt) [L. *in* into + *osculum* little mouth]. To unite or communicate by means of small openings or anastomoses.

inosculation (in-os″ku-la′shun). The establishment of communication, by means of small openings or anastomoses, applied especially to establishment of such communication between already existing blood vessels or other tubular structures that come in contact.

inose (in′ōs). Inositol.

inosemia (in″o-se′me-ah) [*ino-* + Gr. *haima* blood + *-ia*]. 1. An excess of fibrin in the blood. 2. The presence of inose (inositol) in the blood.

inosinate (in-o′sĭ-nāt). A salt of inosinic acid.

inosine (in′o-sin). A nucleoside, $C_{10}H_{12}O_5N_4$, resulting from the decomposition of inosinic acid. It is a compound of hypoxanthine and ribose.

inosite (in′o-sīt). Inositol.

inositis (in″o-si′tis) [*ino-* + *-itis*]. Inflammation of fibrous tissue.

inositol (in-o′sĭ-tol). A crystalline substance, hexahydroxycyclohexane, $CHOH(CHOH.CHOH)_2$-$CHOH$, resembling a sugar, that is found in muscle, urine, the viscera, and various plant substances. It is a vitamin of the B complex concerned in the growth of yeast, and curative of mouse alopecia and said to inhibit tumor growth.

inositoluria (in″o-si″tol-u′re-ah). Inosituria.

inosituria (in″o-si-tu′re-ah) [*inosite* + Gr. *ouron* urine + *-ia*]. The occurrence of inositol in the urine.

inosteatoma (in″o-ste″ah-to′mah) [*ino-* + Gr. *stear* fat + *-oma*]. A fatty tumor containing fibrous elements.

inostosis (in″os-to′sis). The re-formation of bony tissue to replace such tissue which has been destroyed.

inosuria (in″o-su′re-ah). 1. An excess of fibrin in the urine. 2. Inosituria.

inotagma (in″o-tag′mah) [*ino-* + Gr. *tagma* arrangement]. A linear arrangement of the contractile structural elements of a muscle cell.

inotropic (in″o-trop′ik) [*ino-* + Gr. *trepein* to turn or influence]. Affecting the force or energy of muscular contractions. **negatively i.,** weakening the force of muscular contraction. **positively i.,** increasing the strength of muscular contraction.

inotropism (in-ot′ro-pizm). The quality of influencing the contractility of muscle fibers.

in ovo (in o′vo) [L.]. In the egg; referring specifically to various experimental procedures involving the use of chick embryos.

In. pulm. Abbreviation for L. *in pulmen′to*, in gruel.

inquest (in′kwest) [L. *in* into + *quaerere* to seek]. Inquiry before a coroner into the manner of a death.

inquiline (in′kwĭ-līn) [L. *inquilinus* a lodger]. An organism which lives within the body of another, but does not derive its nourishment from the host.

inquisition (in″kwĭ-zish′un) [L. *inquisitio; in* into + *quaerere* to seek]. An investigation.

inructation (in″ruk-ta′shun). Abnormal and noisy swallowing of air.

insalivation (in″sal-ĭ-va′shun) [L. *in* in + *saliva* spittle]. The saturation of the food with saliva in mastication.

insalubrious (in″sah-lu′bre-us). Not salubrious; not conducive to health.

insane (in-sān′) [L. *in* not + *sanus* sound]. Mentally deranged.

insanitary (in-san′ĭ-ter-e). Not in a good sanitary condition.

insanity (in-san′ĭ-te) [L. *insanitas*, from *in* not + *sanus* sound]. Mental derangement or disorder. The term is a social and legal rather than a medical one, and indicates a condition which renders the affected person unfit to enjoy liberty of action because of the unreliability of his behavior with concomitant danger to himself and others. **adolescent i.,** dementia praecox. **affective i.,** affective psychosis. **alcoholic i.,** alcoholic psychosis. **alternating i.,** manic-depressive psychosis. **anticipatory i.,** that which appears in a patient at an earlier age than that at which it attacked the parent. **choreic i.,** Huntington's chorea. **circular i.,** manic-depressive psychosis that is characterized by alternating manic and depressive phases without any quiescent intervals. **climacteric i.,** involution melancholia. **communicated i.,** folie à deux. **compound i.,** the concurrence of two or more forms of insanity. **compulsive i.,** insanity in which the patient is completely dominated by impulse or obsessions. **consecutive i.,** that which follows some neurosis or other disease. **cyclic i.,** circular i. **doubting i.,** insanity characterized by morbid doubt, suspicion, and indecision. **emotional i.,** affective psychosis. **hereditary i.,** that which is inherited from a parent or grandparent. **homicidal i.,** insanity marked by a desire to take human life. **homochronous i.,** that which appears in the patient at the same age at which it appeared in the patient's father or mother. **hysteric i.,** anxiety hysteria. **idiophrenic i.,** insanity due to disease of the brain itself. **impulsive i.,** an insane tendency to acts of violence. **manic-depressive i.,** manic-depressive psychosis. **moral i.,** that which is marked by impairment of the moral sense. **perceptional i.,** a form marked by hallucinations and illusions. **periodic i.,** that which recurs at regular intervals. **polyneuritic i.,** Korsakoff's syndrome. **primary i.,** any insanity not known to be consequent upon some previous attack or disease. **puerperal i.,** mental derangement coming on after childbirth. **recurrent i.,** mental aberration with lucid intervals. **senile i.,** senile psychosis. **simultaneous i.,** folie à deux. **toxic i.,** toxic psychosis.

insanoid (in-sa′noid). Resembling insanity.

inscriptio (in-skrip′she-o), pl. *inscriptio′nes* [L., from *in* upon + *scribere* to write]. Inscription. **i. tendin′ea** [B N A], intersectio tendinea. **inscriptio′nes tendin′eae mus′culi rec′ti abdom′inis** [B N A], intersectiones tendineae musculi recti abdominis.

inscription (in-skrip′shun) [L. *inscriptio*]. 1. A mark, or line. 2. That part of a prescription which contains the names and amounts of the ingredients. **tendinous i.,** intersectio tendinea. **tendinous i's of rectus abdominis muscle,** intersectiones tendineae musculi recti abdominis.

inscriptiones (in-skrip″she-o′nēz) [L.]. Plural of *inscriptio.*

Insecta (in-sek′tah) [L. from *in* + *sectum* cut]. A class of the Arthropoda characterized by division into three parts, head, thorax, and abdomen; there are three orders of medical interest; Hemiptera, Diptera, and Siphonaptera.

insectarium (in″sek-ta′re-um). A place for breeding and raising insects.

insecticide (in-sek′tĭ-sīd) [L. *insectum* insect + *caedere* to kill]. 1. Destructive to insects. 2. Any substance poisonous to insects.

insectifuge (in-sek′tĭ-fūj) [*insect* + L. *fugare* to put to flight]. A preparation which repels insects.

Insectivora (in″sek-tiv′o-rah) [*insect* + L. *vorare* to devour]. An order of small, terrestrial and nocturnal mammals which feed on insects.

insectivore (in-sek′tĭ-vōr). An individual of the order Insectivora.

insectivorous (in″sek-tiv′o-rus). Subsisting on insects.

insectology (in″sek-tol′o-je). The study of insects as they are related to human activities.

insemination (in-sem″ĭ-na′shun) [L. *inseminatus* sown, from *in* into + *semen* seed]. The deposit of seminal fluid within the vagina. **artificial i.,** introduction of semen into the vagina by artificial means. **donor i., heterologous i.,** artificial insemination in which the semen used is that of a man other than the woman's husband. Also called A.I.D. **homologous i.,** artificial insemination in which the husband's semen is used. Also called A.I.H.

insenescence (in″se-nes′ens). The process of growing old.

insensible (in-sen′sĭ-b′l) [L. *in* not + *sensibilis* appreciable]. 1. Not appreciable by or perceptible to the senses. 2. Devoid of consciousness or of sensibility.

insertio (in-ser′she-o) [L.]. Insertion. **i. velamento′sa,** velamentous insertion.

insertion (in-ser′shun) [L. *insertio;* from *in* into + *serere* to join]. 1. The act of implanting, or the condition of being implanted. 2. The place of attachment of a muscle to the bone which it moves. **parasol i.,** insertion of the umbilical cord in the placenta, in which the vessels of the cord separate before they join the placenta and resemble the ribs of a parasol. **velamentous i.,** attachment of the umbilical cord to the membranes, with the vessels coursing for a long or short distance between the amnion and the chorion to the body of the placenta.

insheathed (in-shēthd′). Enclosed within a sheath.

insidious (in-sid′e-us) [L. *insidiosus* deceitful, treacherous]. Coming on in a stealthy manner.

insight (in′sīt). In psychiatry, the patient's knowledge that his symptoms are abnormal.

in situ (in si′tu) [L.]. In the natural or normal place; confined to the site of origin without invasion of neighboring tissues.

insolation (in″so-la′shun) [L. *insolare* to expose to the sun; *in* in + *sol* sun]. 1. Treatment by exposure to the sun's rays; the sun bath. 2. Sunstroke; thermic fever due to exposure to the sun's rays. **asphyxial i.,** sunstroke with low temperature, cold skin, and feeble pulse. **hyperpyrexial i.,** thermic fever with very high temperature, coma, and congested skin.

insoluble (in-sol′u-b′l) [L. *insolubilis,* from *in* not + *solvere* to dissolve]. Not susceptible of being dissolved.

insomnia (in-som′ne-ah) [L. *in* not + *somnus* sleep + *-ia*]. Inability to sleep; abnormal wakefulness.

insomniac (in-som′ne-ak). An individual exhibiting insomnia.

insomnic (in-som′nik). Characterized by insomnia; unable to sleep.

insorption (in-sorp′shun). The movement of a substance into the blood; used to denote such movement from the contents of the gastrointestinal tract into the circulating blood.

inspection (in-spek′shun) [L. *inspectio, inspicere* to behold]. Examination by the eye.

inspectionism (in-spek′shun-izm). Sexual pleasure experienced by looking at the genitals or at sexual objects; scoptophilia.

inspersion (in-sper′zhun) [L. *inspersio; in* upon + *spargere* to sprinkle]. The act of sprinkling, as with a powder.

inspiration (in″spĭ-ra′shun) [L. *inspirare,* from *in* in + *spirare* to breathe]. The act of drawing air into the lungs.

inspirator (in′spĭ-ra″tor) [L.]. A form of inhaler or respirator.

inspiratory (in-spi′rah-to″re). Pertaining to or subserving inspiration.

inspirium (in-spi′re-um). An inspiration.

inspirometer (in″spi-rom′e-ter) [*inspire* + Gr. *metron* measure]. An apparatus for measuring the amount of air inspired.

inspissated (in-spis′āt-ed) [L. *inspissatus,* from *in* intensive + *spissare* to thicken]. Being thickened, dried, or rendered less fluid.

inspissation (in″spis-sa′shun) [L. *inspissatio*]. 1. The act or process of rendering dry or thick by the evaporation of readily vaporizable parts. 2. The condition of being rendered less thin by evaporation.

inspissator (in-spis′a-tor). An apparatus for inspissating fluids, such as blood serum.

instar (in′stahr) [L. "a form"]. Any one of the larval stages of an insect between molts.

instep (in′step). The dorsal part of the arch of the foot.

instillation (in″stil-la′shun) [L. *instillatio*, from *in* into + *stillare* to drop]. The act or process of dropping a liquid into a cavity.

instillator (in′stil-la″tor). An instrument for performing instillations.

instinct (in′stinkt) [L. *instinctus; in* on + *stinguere* to prick]. A propensity that urges an animal or human being, without the exercise of reason, to the performance of actions which are for the most part normally useful or beneficial. **death i.,** in psychiatry the latent instinctive impulse toward death. **ego i.,** any instinct that is not sexual. **herd i.,** the instinct or urge to be one of a group and to conform to the standards of that group in conduct and opinion. **mother i.,** the complex behavior in a mother which accomplishes the care of the young. It is absent in certain endocrine deficiencies.

instinctive (in-stink′tiv). Of the nature of an instinct; performed apparently without the exercise of the reason.

institutes (in′stĭ-tūts) [L. *institutum* established regulation]. Established or fundamental principles. **i. of medicine,** the fundamental principles of medical science; especially physiology, pathology, and the kindred branches of medical education.

instrument (in′stroo-ment) [L. *instrumentum; instruere* to furnish]. Any mechanical tool, appliance, or apparatus.

instrumental (in″stroo-men′tal). Pertaining to or performed by instruments.

instrumentarium (in″stroo-men-ta′re-um). The equipment or instruments required for any particular operation or purpose; the physical adjuncts with which a physician combats disease.

instrumentation (in″stroo-men-ta′shun). The use of instruments; work performed with instruments.

insuccation (in″sŭ-ka′shun) [L. *insuccare* to soak in; *in* into + *succus* juice]. The thorough soaking of a drug before preparing an extract from it.

insufficiency (in″sŭ-fish′en-se) [L. *insufficientia*, from *in* not + *sufficiens* sufficient]. The condition of being insufficient or inadequate to the performance of the allotted duty. **active i.,** the inability of a muscle to act owing to the abnormal (or other) approximation of its insertion to its origin. **adrenal i.,** Addison's disease. **aortic i.,** insufficiency of the aortic valve. See *i. of the valves.* **capsular i.,** hypoadrenalism. **cardiac i.,** inability of the heart to perform its function properly. **i. of the externi,** insufficient power in the externi muscles of the eye, so that they are overbalanced by the interni, producing esophoria. **i. of the eyelids,** a condition in which the eyes are closed only by a conscious effort. **gastric i., gastromotor i.,** inability of the stomach to empty itself, although it is not dilated; myasthenia gastrica. **hepatic i.,** inability of the liver properly to perform its functions. **i. of the interni,** insufficient power in the interni muscles of the eye, so that they are overbalanced by the externi, producing exophoria. **mitral i.,** insufficiency of the mitral valve. See *i. of the valves.* **muscular i.,** the inability of a muscle to do its normal work by a normal contraction. **myocardial i.,** insufficiency or breakdown of the heart muscle. **myovascular i.,** insufficiency of the heart with increased arterial tension. **parathyroid i.,** hypoparathyroidism. **proteopexic i.** See *hemoclastic crisis,* under *crisis.* **pseudoaortic i.,** a condition marked by some of the symptoms of aortic insufficiency, but due to arteriosclerosis. **pulmonary i.,** insufficiency of the pulmonary valve. See *i. of the valves.* **pyloric i.,** defective closure of the pylorus, producing inability of the stomach to prevent the too rapid escape of the food into the bowel. **renal i.,** a state in which the kidneys are unable to remove a sufficient proportion of the effete matter of the blood. **thyroid i.,** hypothyroidism. **tricuspid i.,** insufficiency of the tricuspid valve. See *i. of the valves.* **uterine i.,** weakness of the contractile power of the uterus, due to muscular atony. **i. of the valves, valvular i.,** a condition in which the valves do not close perfectly, so that the blood passes back through the orifices at each diastole: named, according to the valve affected, *aortic, mitral, pulmonary,* or *tricuspid.* **venous i.,** an edematous condition of the lower extremities due to stasis of the venous blood flow. Called also *stasis edema, stasis eczema,* or *stasis ulcer,* according to the type of lesion produced.

insufficientia (in″sŭ-fish″e-en′she-ah) [L.]. Insufficiency. **i. ver′tebrae,** functional disorder based on spinal injury which does not produce organic disease of the spine.

insufflation (in″sŭ-fla′shun) [L. *in* into + *sufflatio* a blowing up]. The act of blowing a powder, vapor, gas, or air into a cavity, as into the lungs. **cranial i.,** the forcing of air into the subdural space and the cerebral ventricles. **endotracheal i.,** introduction of air into the trachea through a tube passed into the larynx: employed to avoid collapse of the lung in intrathoracic operations. **i. of the lungs,** the act of blowing air into the lungs for the purpose of artificial respiration. **perirenal i.,** the injection of air around the kidneys for the purpose of roentgen visualization of the adrenal glands. **tubal i.** See *Rubin's test,* under *test.*

insufflator (in′sŭ-fla″tor). An instrument used in performing insufflation.

insula (in′su-lah), pl. *in′sulae* [L. "island"]. [N A, B N A] A triangular area of the cerebral cortex which forms the floor of the lateral cerebral fossa. It is covered over and hidden from view by the juxtaposition of the opercula, which thus forms the lateral cerebral fissure. Called also *island of Reil* and *central lobe.* **insulae of Peyer,** folliculi lymphatici aggregati. **i. of Reil, i. Rei′lii,** insula.

insulae (in′su-le) [L.]. Plural of *insula.*

insular (in′su-lar). Pertaining to an island, especially to the insula or to the islands of Langerhans.

insularine (in′su-lar-in). A yellow amorphous alkaloid, $C_{37}H_{38}O_6N_2$, from *Cissampelos insularis.*

insular-pancreatotropic (in″su-lar-pan″kre-ah-to-trop′ik). Having affinity for or a stimulating action on the islands of Langerhans in the pancreas.

insulation (in″su-la′shun) [L. *insulare* to make an island of]. The state in which the communication of electricity to other bodies is prevented by the interposition of a nonconductor; also, the material or substance which insulates. The electrical resistance of an insulator is expressed in megohms, a unit representing a million ohms.

insulator (in′su-la″tor). Any substance or appliance of such nonconducting properties that it can be used to secure insulation.

insulin (in′su-lin) [L. *insula* island (of the pancreas) + *-in* ending indicating chemical compound]. A protein hormone formed by the islet cells of Langerhans in the pancreas and secreted into the blood, where it regulates carbohydrate (sugar) metabolism. Also a preparation of the active principle of the pancreas, used therapeutically in diabetes and sometimes in other conditions. **globin i.,** a combination of insulin with the globin of erythrocytes. In rapidity of onset and duration of action it seems to be midway between insulin and protamine zinc insulin. **globin zinc i.,** a preparation of insulin modified by addition of zinc chloride and globin, with an intermediate period of action. **hexamine i.,** a combination of hexamine tetramine with insulin: used in juvenile diabetes. **histone zinc i.,** a mixture of insulin, histone and zinc. **isophane i.,** a proprietary preparation of insulin made from zinc-insulin crystals modified by addition of protamine. **i. lente,** a sterile suspension of insulin modified by the addition of zinc chloride. **NPH i.,** isophane i. **oral i., peroral i.,** insulin prepared for oral use, by administration along with a substance which will protect it from the enzymes of the gastrointestinal tract. **plant i.,** glucokinin. **protamine i., i. protaminate,** insulin precipitated from a solution of insulin hydrochloride with a monoprotamine compound and suitably buffered. It is more slowly absorbed than ordinary insulin and its action is correspondingly prolonged. **protamine zinc i.,** a mixture of protamine, zinc and insulin, said to have a more prolonged hypoglycemic action than insulin or protamine insulin. **i. tannate,** a salt of insulin claimed to have certain advantages over regular insulin. **three-to-one i.,** a combination of regular insulin and protamine zinc insulin, having the activity of three parts of the former and one part of the latter. **vegetable i.,** glucokinin. **zinc-protamine i.,** protamine zinc insulin.

insulinase (in′su-lin-ās). An enzyme in body tissues which destroys or inactivates insulin.

insuline (in′su-lin). Insulin.

insulinemia (in″su-lin-e′me-ah) [*insulin* + Gr. *haima* blood + *-ia*]. The presence of insulin in the blood.

insulinization (in″su-lin″i-za′shun). Treatment with insulin.

insulinlipodystrophy (in″su-lin-li″po-dis′tro-fe). The local disappearance of fat in diabetic patients on insulin treatment.

insulinogenesis (in″su-lin-o-jen′e-sis). The formation and release of insulin by the pancreas.

insulinogenic (in″su-lin″o-jen′ik). Pertaining to, characterized by, or promoting insulinogenesis.

insulinoid (in′su-lin-oid). 1. Resembling insulin. 2. Any substance with hypoglycemic properties like those of insulin.

insulinoma (in″su-lin-o′mah). A tumor consisting of tissue from the islands of Langerhans.

insulism (in′su-lizm). Hyperinsulinism.

insulitis (in″su-li′tis). Cellular infiltration of the islands of Langerhans, possibly in response to invasion by an infectious agent.

insulogenic (in″su-lo-jen′ik). Insulinogenic.

insuloma (in″su-lo′mah) [L. *insula* island (of Langerhans) + *-oma*]. An adenoma of the islands of Langerhans of the pancreas; called also *islet adenoma* and *langerhansian adenoma.*

insulopathic (in″su-lo-path′ik). Pertaining to, or due to, abnormal insulin secretion.

insultus (in-sul′tus) [L.]. An attack. **i. hyster′icus,** hysterical attack.

insusceptibility (in″sŭ-sep″tĭ-bil′ĭ-te). The quality of not being susceptible; immunity.

intake (in-tāk′). The substances or quantities thereof taken in and utilized by the body. **caloric i.,** the food ingested or otherwise taken into the body. **fluid i.,** the fluid taken into the body by drinking or parenterally.

integration (in″te-gra′shun). 1. Assimilation; anabolic action or activity. 2. The combination of different acts so that they cooperate toward a common end. **biological i.,** the acquisition of functional coordination during embryonic development through humoral and nervous influences. **primary i.,** the recognition by a child that his body is a unit apart from the environment. **secondary i.,** the sublimation of the separate elements of the early sexual instinct into the mature psychosexual personality.

integrator (in′te-gra″tor). An instrument for measuring body surfaces.

integument (in-teg′u-ment) [L. *integumentum*]. A covering or investment. **common i.,** the covering of the body, or skin. See *integumentum commune.*

integumentary (in-teg-u-men′tar-e). 1. Pertaining to or composed of skin. 2. Serving as a covering, like the skin.

integumentum (in-teg″u-men′tum) [L., from *in* on + *tegere* to cover]. A covering, or investment. **i. commu′ne** [N A, B N A], the covering of the body, or skin, including its various layers and the accessory structures (hair, nails, and skin glands, including the breast, or mammary gland). Called also *common integument.*

intellect (in′te-lekt) [L. *intellectus*, from *intelligere* to understand]. The mind, thinking faculty, or understanding.

intellection (in″te-lek′shun). The objectively appreciable evaluation of relationships by the mind.

intelligence (in-tel′ĭ-jens) [L. *intelligere* to understand]. The ability to comprehend or understand.

intemperance (in-tem′per-ans) [L. *in* not + *temperare* to moderate]. Excess or lack of self-control in respect of food and drink; immoderate indulgence in the use of alcoholic drinks.

intensification (in-ten″sĭ-fi-ka′shun) [L. *intensus* intense + *facere* to make]. 1. The act of making anything intense. 2. The process of becoming intense.

intensimeter (in″ten-sim′e-ter). Fürstenau's device for measuring the intensity of roentgen rays; it is based on the variation of electric resistance of a selenium cell under influence of irradiation at different intensities.

intensionometer (in-ten″se-o-nom′e-ter). An ionometric instrument for measuring the intensity of roentgen rays. Two series of plates, separated by an air gap that serves as the dielectric, are connected to opposite terminals in a closed chamber. An electric circuit is completed when the air becomes ionized by the roentgen rays, and the difference in electric potential is registered by deflection of a galvanometer needle.

intensity (in-ten′sĭ-te) [L. *intensus* intense; *in* on + *tendere* to stretch]. The condition or quality of being intense; a high degree of tension, activity, or energy. **i. of electric field,** the force exerted on a unit charge in an electric field. **luminous i.,** the light-giving power of a source of light. Cf. *candle power.* **i. of roentgen rays,** the roentgen-ray energy passing per unit time through unit area normal to the direction of propagation.

intensive (in-ten′siv) [L. *in* on + *tendere* to stretch]. Of increasing force or intensity.

intention (in-ten′shun) [L. *intentio*, from *in* upon + *tendere* to stretch]. A natural or other process; a process of healing. See under *healing.*

inter- (in′ter) [L. *inter* between]. A prefix meaning situated, formed, or occurring between elements indicated by the word stem to which it is affixed.

interaccessory (in″ter-ak-ses′o-re). Connecting the accessory processes of the vertebrae.

interacinar (in″ter-as′ĭ-nar). Situated between acini.

interacinous (in″ter-as′ĭ-nus). Interacinar.

interagglutination (in″ter-ah-gloo-tĭ-na′shun). Agglutination of one kind of cells by the agglutinins of a nearly related kind.

interalveolar (in″ter-al-ve′o-lar). Between alveoli.

interangular (in″ter-ang′gu-lar). Situated or occurring between two or more angles.

interannular (in″ter-an′u-lar) [*inter-* + L. *annulus* ring]. Situated between two rings or constrictions, or between two nodes of Ranvier.

interarticular (in″ter-ar-tik′u-lar) [*inter-* + L. *articulus* joint]. Situated between articular surfaces.

interarytenoid (in″ter-ar″e-te′noid). Between the arytenoid cartilages.

interatrial (in″ter-a′tre-al). Situated between the atria.

interauricular (in″ter-aw-rik′u-lar). Interatrial.

interbody (in′ter-bod″e). An amboceptor.

interbrain (in′ter-brān). 1. Thalamencephalon. 2. Diencephalon.

intercadence (in″ter-ka′dens) [*inter-* + L. *cadere* to fall]. The occurrence of an additional or supernumerary beat between two full beats of the pulse.

intercadent (in″ter-ka′dent). Marked by intercadence; having an irregular rhythm.

intercalary (in-ter′kah-ler″e) [L. *intercalarius; inter-* + *calare* to call]. Inserted or placed between; interposed.

intercalate (in-ter′kah-lāt) [L. *intercalatus*]. To insert between.

intercalation (in-ter″kah-la′shun). A speech neurosis in which a word or sound is interposed between words or phrases.

intercalatum (in″ter-kah-la′tum). Substantia nigra.

intercanalicular (in″ter-kan″ah-lik′u-lar). Between canaliculi.

intercapillary (in″ter-kap′ĭ-lār-e). Among or between capillaries.

intercarotic (in″ter-kah-rot′ik). Between the carotid arteries.

intercarotid (in″ter-kah-rot′id). Intercarotic.

intercarpal (in″ter-kar′pal). Between the carpal bones.

intercartilaginous (in″ter-kar″tĭ-laj′ĭ-nus). Connecting or situated between two or more cartilages.

intercavernous (in″ter-kav′er-nus). Between two cavities.

intercellular (in″ter-sel′u-lar). Situated between the cells of any structure.

intercentral (in″ter-sen′tral). Situated between or connecting two or more nerve centers.

intercerebral (in″ter-ser′e-bral). Connecting or situated between the two cerebral hemispheres.

interchondral (in″ter-kon′dral). Intercartilaginous.

intercilium (in″ter-sil′e-um) [*inter-* + L. *cilium* eyelash]. The space between the eyebrows.

interclavicular (in″ter-klah-vik′u-lar) [*inter-* + L. *clavicula* clavicle]. Situated between the clavicles.

interclinoid (in″ter-kli′noid). Pertaining to, or passing between, the clinoid processes.

intercoccygeal (in″ter-kok-sij′e-al). Situated between the segments of the coccyx.

intercolumnar (in″ter-ko-lum′nar) [*inter-* + L. *columna* column]. Situated between columns or pillars.

intercondylar (in″ter-kon′dĭ-lar). Situated between two condyles.

intercondyloid (in″ter-kon′dĭ-loid). Intercondylar.

intercondylous (in″ter-kon′dĭ-lus). Intercondylar.

intercostal (in″ter-kos′tal) [*inter-* + L. *costa* rib]. Situated between the ribs.

intercostohumeral (in″ter-kos-to-hu′mer-al). Pertaining to an intercostal space and the humerus.

intercostohumeralis (in″ter-kos″to-hu″mer-a′lis) [L.]. The lateral cutaneous branch of the second intercostal nerve going to the skin of the arm.

intercourse (in′ter-kōrs) [L. *intercursus* running between]. Mutual exchange. **sexual i.,** coitus.

intercricothyrotomy (in″ter-kri″ko-thi-rot′o-me) [*inter-* + *cricothyroid* + Gr. *temnein* to cut]. Incision of the larynx through the cricothyroid membrane; inferior laryngotomy.

intercristal (in″ter-kris′tal). Between two crests.

intercrural (in″ter-kru′ral). Between two crura.

intercurrent (in″ter-kur′ent) [L. *intercurrens*, from *inter-* + *currere* to run]. Breaking into and modifying the course of an already existing disease.

intercuspation (in″ter-kus-pa′shun). The fitting together of the cusps of opposing teeth in occlusion.

intercutaneomucous (in″ter-ku-ta″ne-o-mu′kus). Between the skin and mucous membrane.

interdeferential (in″ter-def″er-en′shal). Between the two ductus deferentes.

interdental (in″ter-den′tal) [*inter-* + L. *dens* tooth]. Situated between the proximal surfaces of adjacent teeth in the same dental arch. Cf. *interocclusal.*

interdentium (in″ter-den′she-um). The interproximal space.

interdigit (in″ter-dij′it). The space between any two contiguous fingers or toes.

interdigital (in″ter-dij′ĭ-tal) [*inter-* + L. *digitus* finger]. Situated between two adjacent fingers or toes.

interdigitate (in″ter-dij′ĭ-tāt) [*inter-* + L. *digitus* finger]. To interlock and interrelate, as the fingers of clasped hands.

interdigitation (in″ter-dij″ĭ-ta′shun) [*inter-* + L. *digitus* digit]. 1. An interlocking of parts by finger-like processes. 2. Any one of a set of finger-like processes. 3. In dentistry, intercuspation.

interface (in′ter-fās). In chemistry, the surface of separation or boundary between two phases of a heterogeneous system. **dineric i.,** the interface between two immiscible liquids.

interfacial (in″ter-fa′shal). Pertaining to an interface.

interfascicular (in″ter-fah-sik′u-lar) [*inter-* + L. *fasciculus* bundle]. Situated between fasciculi.

interfeminium (in″ter-fĕ-min′e-um) [L.]. The space between the thighs, or the inside of the thighs.

interfemoral (in″ter-fem′o-ral). Between the thighs.

interfemus (in″ter-fe′mus) [L.]. Interfeminium.

interference (in″ter-fēr′ens) [*inter-* + L. *ferire* to strike]. 1. A merging of two waves of light or of sound, producing in the first instance darkness, in the other, silence. 2. A disturbance in the conduction of the heart impulse due to the impulse reaching the conduction region while it is still in its refractory state. When this state lasts for several beats it is called *dissociation by interference.*

interfering (in″ter-fēr′ing). Brushing; the striking or rubbing of the fetlock of a horse by the opposite foot.

interferometer (in″ter-fēr-om′e-ter). An instrument for measuring lengths or movements by means of the phenomena caused by the interference of two rays of light.

interferometry (in″ter-fēr-om′e-tre). The use of the interferometer for measuring distances or movements.

interferon (in″ter-fēr′on). A protein formed during the interaction of animal cells with viruses, which is capable of conferring on fresh animal cells of the same species resistance to infection with a wide range of viruses.

interfibrillar (in″ter-fi′bril-ar) [*inter-* + L. *fibrilla* small fiber]. Between or among fibrils.

interfibrillary (in″ter-fi′brĭ-lār″e). Interfibrillar.

interfibrous (in″ter-fi′brus). Between fibers.

interfilamentous (in″ter-fil″ah-men′tus). Between filaments.

interfilar (in″ter-fi′lar) [*inter-* + L. *filum* thread]. Between or among the fibrils of a reticulum.

interfrontal (in″ter-fron′tal). Between the halves of the frontal bone.

interfurca (in″ter-fur′kah), pl. *interfur′cae* [*inter-* + L. *furca* fork]. The area lying between and at the base of three or more normally divided tooth roots.

interfurcae (in″ter-fur′ke). Plural of *interfurca.*

interganglionic (in″ter-gang″gle-on′ik) [*inter-* + *ganglion*]. Between ganglia.

intergemmal (in″ter-jem′al) [*inter-* + L. *gemma* bud]. Between taste buds or other buds.

interglobular (in″ter-glob′u-lar) [*inter-* + L. *globulus* globule]. Between or among globules, as of the dentin.

intergluteal (in″ter-gloo′te-al). Between the buttocks.

intergonial (in″ter-go′ne-al). Between the tips of the two angles of the mandible.

intergrade (in′ter-grād) [*inter-* + L. *gradus* a step]. A step or stage between two other stages. **sex i.,** an individual showing characteristics between the typical male and female condition. Called also *intersex*.

intergranular (in″ter-gran′u-lar). Between the granule cells of the brain.

intergyral (in″ter-ji′ral). Between cerebral gyri or convolutions.

interhemicerebral (in″ter-hem″ĭ-ser′e-bral). Intercerebral.

interhemispheric (in″ter-hem″ĭ-sfer′ik). Intercerebral.

interictal (in″ter-ik′tal). Occurring between attacks or paroxysms.

interior (in-tēr′e-or) [L. "inner"; neut. *interius*]. 1. Situated inside; inward. 2. An inner part or cavity.

interischiadic (in″ter-is″ke-ad′ik). Between the two ischia.

interkinesis (in″ter-ki-ne′sis) [*inter-* + Gr. *kinēsis* motion]. A period intervening between the first and second divisions in meiosis, similar to the interphase in mitosis.

interlabial (in″ter-la′be-al) [*inter-* + L. *labium* lip]. Between the lips, or between two labia.

interlamellar (in″ter-lah-mel′ar) [*inter-* + L. *lamella* layer]. Situated between lamellae.

interligamentary (in″ter-lig″ah-men′tār-e). Between or among ligaments.

interligamentous (in″ter-lig″ah-men′tus). Interligamentary.

interlobar (in″ter-lo′bar) [*inter-* + L. *lobus* lobe]. Situated or occurring between lobes.

interlobitis (in″ter-lo-bi′tis). Inflammation of the pleura lying between lobes of the lung.

interlobular (in″ter-lob′u-lar) [*inter-* + L. *lobulus* lobule]. Situated or occurring between lobules.

interlocking (in″ter-lok′ing). A complication of twin labor in which the chins are hooked or one twin may sit astride its fellow: called also *locking* or *collision*.

intermalleolar (in″ter-mah-le′o-lar). Between the malleoli.

intermamillary (in″ter-mam′ĭ-lār″e). Between the nipples.

intermammary (in″ter-mam′ah-re). Between the breasts.

intermarriage (in″ter-mar′ij) [*inter-* + L. *maritare* to wed]. 1. The marriage of persons related by blood or consanguinity. 2. The marriage of persons of different races.

intermaxilla (in″ter-mak-sil′ah). The intermaxillary bone.

intermaxillary (in″ter-mak′sĭ-lār″e). Situated between the two maxillae.

intermediary (in″ter-me′de-ār″e) [*inter-* + L. *medius* middle]. Performed or occurring in a median stage; neither early nor late.

intermediate (in″ter-me′de-āt) [*inter-* + L. *medius* middle]. Placed between; intervening.

intermedin (in″ter-me′din). A proteohormone secreted by the pars intermedia of the pituitary, a chromatophore-expanding hormone which produces the color changes in the skin of amphibia, reptiles, and fish when they are placed in the dark.

intermediolateral (in″ter-me″de-o-lat′er-al). Both intermediate and lateral.

intermedius (in″ter-me′de-us). Intermediate; in official anatomical nomenclature it designates the middle of three structures, one of which is situated closer to and the other farther from the midline of the body or part.

intermembranous (in″ter-mem′brah-nus). Situated or occurring between membranes.

intermeningeal (in″ter-mĕ-nin′je-al). Situated or occurring between the meninges.

intermenstrual (in″ter-men′stroo-al) [*inter-* + *menstrual*]. Occurring between the menstrual periods.

intermenstruum (in″ter-men′stroo-um). The interval between two menstrual periods.

intermetacarpal (in″ter-met″ah-kar′pal) [*inter-* + *metacarpal*]. Situated between the metacarpal bones.

intermetameric (in″ter-met″ah-mer′ik). Between two metameres.

intermetatarsal (in″ter-met″ah-tar′sal). Situated or occurring between the metatarsal bones.

intermission (in″ter-mish′un) [L. *intermissio; inter* between + *mittere* to send]. An interval; a period of temporary cessation, as between two occurrences or paroxysms.

intermitotic (in″ter-mi-tot′ik). Pertaining to or occurring during the interval between successive mitoses.

intermittent (in″ter-mit′ent) [L. *intermittens; inter* between + *mittere* to send]. Occurring at separated intervals; having periods of cessation of activity.

intermural (in-ter-mu′ral) [*inter-* + L. *murus* wall]. Situated between the walls of an organ or organs.

intermuscular (in″ter-mus′ku-lar). Situated between muscles.

intern (in′tern) 1. [Fr. *interne*]. A graduate of a medical school serving and residing in a hospital preparatory to being licensed to practice medicine. 2. [Fr. *interner*]. To confine within certain geographical or physical boundaries.

internal (in-ter′nal) [L. *internus*]. Situated or occurring within or on the inside.

internarial (in″ter-na′re-al) [*inter-* + L. *nares* nostrils]. Situated between the nostrils.

internasal (in″ter-na′zal). Situated between the nasal bones.

internatal (in″ter-na′tal) [*inter-* + L. *nates* buttocks]. Between the buttocks, or gluteal prominences.

internation (in″ter-na′shun). The act of confining within certain physical boundaries, as the confinement of a mental patient.

interne (in-tern′) [Fr.]. Intern.

interneuron (in″ter-nu′ron). Any neuron, in a chain of neurons, which is situated between the primary afferent neuron and the final motor neuron.

internist (in-ter′nist). A physician who specializes in the diagnosis and medical treatment of diseases and disorders of the internal structures of the human body.

internodal (in″ter-no′dal). Between two nodes.

internode (in′ter-nōd) [*inter-* + L. *nodus* knot]. A space between two nodes. **i. of Ranvier,** the segment of a nerve fiber between two nodes of Ranvier.

internodular (in″ter-nod′u-lar). Internodal.

internship (in′tern-ship). The position or term of service of an intern in a hospital.

internuclear (in″ter-nu′kle-ar). 1. Situated between or among nuclei. 2. Between the nuclear layers of the retina.

internuncial (in″ter-nun′she-al) [*inter-* + L. *nuncius* messenger]. Serving as a medium of communication between nerve neurons or centers.

internus (in-ter′nus). Internal; in official anatomical nomenclature, used to designate something situated nearer to the center of an organ or a cavity.

interocclusal (in″ter-ŏ-kloo′zal). Situated between the occlusal surfaces of opposing teeth in the two dental arches. Cf. *interdental*.

interoceptive (in″ter-o-sep′tiv). Sherrington's term for the internal surface field of distribution of receptor organs. See *receptor*, *exteroceptive*, and *proprioceptive*.

interoceptor (in″ter-o-sep′tor). Any one of the sensory nerve terminals which are located in and transmit impulses from the viscera.

interofection (in″ter-o-fek′shun). The responses of the body to changes in the internal environment of the body effected by the sympathetic system.

interofective (in″ter-o-fek′tiv). Affecting the interior of the organism: a term applied by Cannon to the autonomic nervous system.

interogestate (in″ter-o-jes′tāt). 1. Developing within the uterus. 2. An infant developing within the uterus, or during the period of internal gestation.

interoinferiorly (in″ter-o-in-fēr′e-or″le). Inwardly and in a downward position or direction.

interolivary (in″ter-ol′ĭ-vār″e). Situated between the olivary bodies.

interorbital (in″ter-or′bĭ-tal) [*inter-* + L. *orbita* orbit]. Situated between the orbits.

interosculate (in″ter-os′ku-lāt) [*inter-* + L. *osculum* little mouth]. To form a communication between two structures.

interosseal (in″ter-os′e-al) [*inter-* + L. *os* bone]. 1. Situated between bones. 2. Pertaining to the interossei muscles.

interosseous (in″ter-os′e-us) [L. *interosseus; inter* between + *os* bone]. Between bones.

interpalpebral (in″ter-pal′pe-bral). Between the eyelids.

interparietal (in″ter-pah-ri′ĕ-tal) [*inter-* + L. *paries* wall]. 1. Intermural. 2. Situated between the parietal bones.

interparoxysmal (in″ter-par″ok-siz′mal). Occurring between paroxysms.

interpediculate (in″ter-pe-dik′u-lāt). Between the pedicles of a vertebra, as interpediculate distance.

interpeduncular (in″ter-pe-dunk′u-lar) [*inter-* + L. *pedunculus* peduncle]. Situated between two peduncles.

interphalangeal (in″ter-fah-lan′je-al) [*inter-* + *phalangeal*]. Situated between two contiguous phalanges.

interphase (in′ter-fāz). The period during which a cell is not dividing; the interval between production of a new cell and its mitosis.

interphyletic (in″ter-fi-let′ik) [*inter-* + *phyletic*]. Intermediate in form between two types of cell.

interpial (in″ter-pi′al). Situated between the two layers of the pia.

interplant (in′ter-plant) [*inter-* + L. *plantare* to set]. An embryonic part isolated by transference to an indifferent environment provided by another embryo.

interpleural (in″ter-ploor′al). Between two layers of the pleura, as between the visceral and the parietal pleura.

interpolar (in″ter-po′lar) [*inter-* + L. *polus* pole]. Situated between two poles.

interpolation (in-ter″po-la′shun). 1. Surgical implantation of tissue. 2. The determination of intermediate values in a series on the basis of observed values.

interpositum (in″ter-poz′i-tum) [L.]. Interposed.

interprotometamere (in″ter-pro″to-met′ah-mēr) [*inter-* + Gr. *prōtos* first + *meta* across + *meros* part]. The structure between the primary segments of the embryo.

interproximal (in″ter-prok′sĭ-mal). Between adjoining surfaces.

interpubic (in″ter-pu′bik) [*inter-* + L. *pubes*]. Between the pubic bones.

interpupillary (in″ter-pu′pĭ-lār″e). Between the pupils.

interradial (in″ter-ra′de-al). Situated between rays.

interrenal (in″ter-re′nal) [*inter-* + *renal*]. Between the kidneys.

interrenalin (in″ter-ren′ah-lin). The name applied to the life-sustaining principle of the adrenal cortex (interrenal gland) by its discoverers, J. M. Rogoff and G. N. Stewart.

interrenalism (in″ter-re′nal-izm). A condition of virilism due to hyperplasia of the tissue of the adrenal cortex.

interrenalopathy (in″ter-re″nal-op′ah-the). Any disorder of the function of the cortex of the adrenal gland.

interrenalotropic (in″ter-re″nal-o-trop′ik). Interrenotropic.

interrenin (in″ter-ren′in). 1. Goldzieher's name for the hormone of the cortex of the adrenal gland. 2. A commercial adrenal extract claimed to contain the life-sustaining principle of the adrenal cortex.

interrenotropic (in″ter-re″no-trop′ik) [*interrenal* system + Gr. *tropikos* turning]. Having affinity for or a stimulating action on the adrenal cortex.

interrenotropin (in″ter-re-not′ro-pin). A substance having affinity for or a stimulating effect on the adrenal cortex.

interrupted (in″ter-rupt′ed) [L. *interruptus; inter* between + *ruptus* broken]. Not continuous; marked by intermissions or breaches of continuity.

interrupter (in″ter-rup′ter). A device for making and breaking the electric circuit at regular intervals.

interscapilium (in″ter-skah-pil′e-um) [L.]. The space between the scapulae.

interscapular (in″ter-skap′u-lar) [*inter-* + L. *scapula* shoulder blade]. Situated between the scapulae.

interscapulum (in″ter-skap′u-lum). The interscapilium.

intersciatic (in″ter-si-at′ik). Between the two ischia.

intersectio (in″ter-sek′she-o), pl. *intersectio′nes* [*inter-* + L. *secare* to cut]. A cutting across, or between; a site at which one structure cuts across another. **i. tendin′ea** [N A], a fibrous band that crosses the belly of a muscle and more or less completely divides it into two parts. Called also *inscriptio tendinea* [B N A], and *tendinous intersection.* **intersectio′nes tendin′eae mus′culi rec′ti abdom′inis** [N A], three or more fibrous bands that cross the front of the rectus abdominis muscle, fusing with the anterior layer of its sheath. Called also *inscriptiones tendineae musculi recti abdominis* [B N A], and *tendinous intersections of rectus abdominis muscle.*

intersection (in″ter-sek′shun). A site at which one structure cuts across another. **tendinous i.,** intersectio tendinea.

intersectiones (in″ter-sek″she-o′nēz) [L.]. Plural of *intersectio.*

intersegment (in″ter-seg′ment). 1. Any one of a series of segments, like the angiotomes, etc. 2. A metamere.

intersegmental (in″ter-seg-men′tal). Between segments.

interseptal (in″ter-sep′tal). Between two septums.

interseptum (in″ter-sep′tum) [L.]. The diaphragm.

intersex (in′ter-seks). 1. Intersexuality. 2. An individual who shows one or more contradictions of the morphological criteria of sex. Such individuals are categorized in three classes: Class I—the gonadal sex agrees with the nuclear sex; Class II—the nuclear sex contradicts the gonadal sex; Class III—nuclear sex may be either male or female, but gonadal sex cannot be determined. **female i.,** an individual who shows one or more contradictions of the morphological criteria of sex but who has only female gonadal tissue and shows sex chromatin in the somatic cells. **male i.,** an individual who shows one or more contradictions of the morphological criteria of sex but who has only male gonadal tissue and shows no sex chromatin in the somatic cells. **true i.,** an individual who shows one or more contradictions of the morphological criteria of sex and possesses both male and female gonadal tissue; the chromatin test may be either positive or negative.

intersexual (in″ter-seks′u-al). Pertaining to or characterized by intersexuality.

intersexuality (in″ter-seks″u-al′ĭ-te). The intermingling, in varying degrees, of the characters of each sex, including physical form, reproductive organs, and sexual behavior, in one individual, as a result of some flaw in embryonic development.

interspace (in′ter-spās). A space between two similar structures. **dineric i.,** the surface between two liquid phases.

interspinal (in-ter-spi′nal). Between two spinous processes.

interspinous (in″ter-spi′nus). Interspinal.

intersternal (in″ter-ster′nal). Between parts of the sternum.

interstice (in-ter′stis) [L. *interstitium*]. A small interval, space, or gap in a tissue or structure.

interstitial (in″ter-stish′al) [L. *interstitialis; inter* between + *sistere* to set]. Pertaining to or situated in the interstices of a tissue.

interstitialoma (in″ter-stish″e-ah-lo′ma). A tumor or mass of interstitial tissue.

intersystole (in″ter-sis′to-le). The interval which exists between the end of the auricular and the beginning of the ventricular systole.

intertarsal (in″ter-tar′sal). Situated between the tarsal bones.

intertinctus (in″ter-tink′tus). Colored differentially.

intertransverse (in″ter-trans-vers′) [*inter-* + L. *transversus* turned across]. Situated between or connecting the transverse processes of the vertebrae.

intertriginous (in″ter-trij′ĭ-nus). Affected with or of the nature of intertrigo.

intertrigo (in″ter-tri′go) [*inter-* + L. *terere* to rub]. A chafe or chafed patch of the skin which occurs especially on opposed surfaces; also the erythema or eczema that may result from a chafe of the skin. **i. labia′lis,** chafing and maceration at the external commissures of the lips. **i. saccharomycet′ica,** intertrigo due to yeast infection.

intertrochanteric (in″ter-tro″kan-ter′ik) [*inter-* + *trochanter*]. Situated in or pertaining to the space between the greater and the lesser trochanter.

intertubercular (in″ter-tu-ber′ku-lar). Between tubercles.

intertubular (in″ter-tu′bu-lar) [*inter-* + L. *tubulus* tubule]. Situated between or among tubules.

interureteral (in″ter-u-re′ter-al). Interureteric.

interureteric (in″ter-u″re-ter′ik) [*inter-* + *ureter*]. Situated between the ureters.

intervaginal (in″ter-vaj′ĭ-nal). Situated between sheaths.

interval (in′ter-val) [*inter-* + L. *vallum* rampart]. The space between two objects or parts; the lapse of time between two recurrences or paroxysms. **a.-c. i., atriocarotid i.,** the time between the start of the atrial and of the carotid wave in a jugular pulse tracing. Called *intersystolic period.* **atrioventricular i.,** the time between atrial and ventricular systole. **auriculocarotid i.,** atriocarotid i. **auriculoventricular i., a.-v. i.,** atrioventricular i. **c.-a. i., cardioarterial i.,** the time between the apex beat and arterial pulsation. **focal i.,** the distance from the anterior to the posterior focal point. **lucid i.,** a brief period of remission of symptoms in a psychosis. **passive i.,** the time when neither the atria nor the ventricles of the heart are expanding or contracting. **postsphygmic i.** See under *period.* **PR i.,** the portion of the electrocardiogram between the P complex and the QRS complex. **presphygmic i.** See under *period.* **QRST i.,** the ventricular complex of the electrocardiogram. **Sturm's i.,** focal i.

intervalvular (in″ter-val′vu-lar). Between valves.

intervascular (in″ter-vas′ku-lar). Between blood vessels.

interventricular (in″ter-ven-trik′u-lar) [*inter-* + L. *ventriculum* ventricle]. Situated between ventricles.

intervertebral (in″ter-ver′te-bral) [*inter-* + *vertebra*]. Situated between two contiguous vertebrae.

intervillous (in″ter-vil′us) [*inter-* + L. *villus* tuft]. Situated between or among villi.

intestinal (in-tes′tĭ-nal) [L. *intestinalis*]. Pertaining to the intestine.

intestine (in-tes′tin) [L. *intesti′nus* inward, internal; Gr. *enteron*]. The portion of the alimentary canal extending from the pyloric opening of the stomach to the anus. See *intestinum.* **blind i.,** cecum. **empty i.,** jejunum. **iced i.,** peritonitis chronica fibrosa incapsulans. **jejunoileal i.,** intestinum tenue mesenteriale. **large i.,** the distal portion of the intestine. See *intestinum crassum* [N A]. **mesenterial i.,** intestinum tenue mesenteriale. **pancreatic i.,** duodenum. **segmented i.,** colon. **small i.,** the proximal portion of the intestine. See *intestinum tenue* [N A]. **straight i.,** rectum. **twisted i.,** ileum.

intestinotoxin (in-tes″tĭ-no-tok′sin). Enterotoxin.

intestinum (in″tes-ti′num), pl. *intesti′na* [L., from *intestinus* inward, internal]. The portion of the alimentary canal extending from the pyloric opening of the stmoach to the anus; a membranous tube, comprising the intestinum tenue and the intestinum crassum. Called also *intestine.* **i. cae′cum** [B N A], cecum. **i. cras′sum** [N A, B N A], the distal portion of the intestine, about five feet long, extending from its junction with the small intestine to the anus; it comprises the cecum, colon, rectum, and anal canal. Called also *large intestine.* **i. il′eum** [B N A], ileum. **i. jeju′num** [B N A], jejunum. **i. rec′tum** [B N A], rectum. **i. ten′ue** [N A, B N A], the proximal portion of the intestine, smaller in caliber and about twenty feet long, extending from the pylorus to the cecum; it comprises the duodenum, jejunum, and ileum. Called also *small intestine.* **i. ten′ue mesenteria′le** [B N A], the portion of the small intestine which has a mesentery, comprising the jejunum and ileum. Omitted in N A.

intima (in′tĭ-mah) [L.]. Innermost. See *tunica intima.*

intimal (in′tĭ-mal). Pertaining to the tunica intima.

intima-pia (in″tĭ-mah-pi′ah). The combined intima of blood vessels and pia mater which surrounds the arteries of the brain.

intimectomy (in″tĭ-mek′to-me) [*intima* + Gr. *ektomē* excision]. Excision of the tunica intima of an artery; endarterectomy.

intimitis (in″tĭ-mi′tis). Inflammation of the tunica intima of an artery. **proliferative i.,** a skin condition due to inflammation of the tunica intima of small arteries and veins of the skin and marked by livedo and dermal ulcers.

intocostrin (in″to-kos′trin). Trade mark for a preparation of chondodendron tomentosum extract.

intoe (in′to). Hallux valgus.

intolerance (in-tol′er-ans) [L. *in* not + *tolerare* to bear]. Inability to endure or withstand. **alcoholic i.,** the inability to take alcohol without going on to excess.

intorsion (in-tor′shun) [L. *in* toward + *torsio* twisting]. Tilting of the upper part of the vertical meridian of the eye toward the midline of the face.

intorter (in′tor-ter). An internal rotator.

intoxation (in″tok-sa′shun). Poisoning.

intoxication (in-tok″sĭ-ka′shun) [L. *in* intensive + Gr. *toxikon* poison]. 1. Poisoning; the state of being poisoned. 2. The condition produced by excessive use of alcoholic stimulants. **acid i.,** acidosis of a severe grade. **alkaline i.,** alkalosis of a severe grade. **anaphylactic i.,** the train of symptoms which follows the second injection of antigen in anaphylaxis. **bongkrek i.,** poisoning from bongkrek, a native Javanese dish, prepared by means of molds from copra press cake. When the fermentation process is faulty, severe poisoning occurs, with vomiting, profuse perspiration, muscle cramps, and coma. **intestinal i.,** auto-intoxication. **menstrual i.,** a condition characterized by headache, vomiting, skin eruptions and other symptoms appearing during the menstrual period. **premenstrual i.** See under *tension.* **roentgen i.,** a condition sometimes produced by intensive irradiation with roentgen rays. It is marked by uneasiness, vertigo, nausea, and vomiting. Called also *roentgenkater.* **septic i.,** sapremia. **serum i.,** a condition of temporary intoxication which sometimes follows the injection of serum. **water i.,** the condition induced by the undue retention of water: it is marked by vomiting, depression of temperature, convulsions, coma and may end in death.

intra- (in′trah) [L. *intra* within]. A prefix meaning situated, formed, or occurring within the element indicated by the word stem to which it is affixed.

intra-abdominal (in″trah-ab-dom′ĭ-nal). Within the abdomen.

intra-acinous (in″trah-as′ĭ-nus). Within an acinus.

intra-appendicular (in″trah-ap′en-dik′u-lar). Within the appendix.

intra-arachnoid (in″trah-ah-rak′noid). Within or underneath the arachnoid.

intra-arterial (in″trah-ar-te′re-al). Within an artery or arteries.

intra-articular (in″trah-ar-tik′u-lar) [*intra-* + L. *articulus* joint]. Within a joint.

intra-atomic (in″trah-ah-tom′ik). Within an atom.

intra-atrial (in″trah-a′tre-al). Within an atrium.

intra-aural (in″trah-aw′ral). Within the ear.

intra-auricular (in″trah-aw-rik′u-lar). Intra-atrial.

intrabronchial (in″trah-brong′ke-al). Situated or occurring within a bronchus.

intrabuccal (in″trah-buk′al). Within the mouth or within the cheek.

intracanalicular (in″trah-kan″ah-lik′u-lar). Within canaliculi.

intracapsular (in″trah-kap′su-lar). Within a capsule.

intracardiac (in″trah-kar′de-ak). Within the heart.

intracarpal (in″trah-kar′pal). Within the wrist.

intracartilaginous (in″trah-kar″tĭ-laj′ĭ-nus). Within a cartilage; endochondral.

intracavitary (in″trah-kav′ĭ-tār″e). Within a cavity, as that of the cervix or of the uterus.

intracelial (in″trah-se′le-al). Within one of the body cavities.

intracellular (in″trah-sel′u-lar) [*intra-* + L. *cellula* cell]. Situated or occurring within a cell or cells.

intracephalic (in″trah-se-fal′ik). Within the brain.

intracerebellar (in″trah-ser″e-bel′ar). Situated within the cerebellum.

intracerebral (in″trah-ser′e-bral). Situated within the cerebrum.

intracervical (in″trah-ser′ve-kal). Situated within the canal of the cervix uteri.

intrachondral (in″trah-kon′dral). Endochondral.

intrachondrial (in″trah-kon′dre-al). Endochondral.

intrachordal (in″trah-kor′dal). Within the notochord.

intracisternal (in″trah-sis-ter′nal). Within a cistern, especially the cisterna magna.

intracolic (in″trah-kol′ik). Within the colon.

intracordal (in″trah-kor′dal) [*intra-* + L. *cor* heart]. Within the heart.

intracorporal (in″trah-kor′po-ral). Intracorporeal.

intracorporeal (in″trah-kor-po′re-al). Situated or occurring within the body.

intracorpuscular (in″trah-kor-pus′ku-lar). Occurring within corpuscles.

intracostal (in″trah-kos′tal). On the inner surface of the rib.

intracranial (in″trah-kra′ne-al). Situated within the cranium.

intracrureus (in″trah-kroo-re′us). The internal part of the crureus.

intracutaneous (in″trah-ku-ta′ne-us). Intradermal.

intracystic (in″trah-sis′tik). Within a cyst.

intracytoplasmic (in″trah-si″to-plaz′mik). Within the cytoplasm of a cell.

intrad (in′trad) [Old Lat.]. Within; inward in situation or direction.

intradermal (in″trah-der′mal). Within the dermis.

intradermic (in″trah-der′mik). Intradermal.

intradermoreaction (in″trah-der″mo-re-ak′-shun). Intradermal reaction.

intraductal (in″trah-duk′tal). Situated or occurring within the duct of a gland.

intraduodenal (in″trah-du″o-de′nal). Within the duodenum.

intradural (in″trah-du′ral). Within or beneath the dura.

intra-epidermal (in″trah-ep″ĭ-der′mal). Within the epidermis.

intra-epidermic (in″trah-ep′ĭ-der′mik). Intra-epidermal.

intra-epiphyseal (in″trah-ep″ĭ-fiz′e-al). Within an epiphysis.

intra-epithelial (in″trah-ep″ĭ-the′le-al). Situated among the cells of the epithelium.

intraerythrocytic (in″trah-e-rith″ro-sit′ik). Located or occurring within the erythrocyte.

intrafaradization (in″trah-far″ad-i-za′shun). The faradization of the inner surface of the stomach or other viscus.

intrafascicular (in″trah-fah-sik′u-lar). Within a fascicle.

intrafebrile (in″trah-feb′rĭl). During the febrile stage.

intrafetation (in″trah-fe-ta′shun). The development of a fetus within another fetus.

intrafilar (in″trah-fi′lar) [*intra-* + L. *filum* thread]. Situated within a reticulum.

intrafissural (in″trah-fish′u-ral). Within a cerebral fissure.

intrafistular (in″trah-fis′tu-lar). Within a fistula.

intrafollicular (in″trah-fo-lik′u-lar). Within a follicle.

intrafusal (in″trah-fu′zal) [*intra-* + L. *fusus* spindle]. Pertaining to the striated fibers within a muscle spindle.

intragalvanization (in″trah-gal″van-i-za′shun). The galvanization of the inner surface of any organ.

intragastric (in″trah-gas′trik). Situated or occurring within the stomach.

intragemmal (in″trah-jem′al) [*intra-* + L. *gemma* bud]. Situated within a bud, as a taste bud.

intraglandular (in″trah-glan′du-lar). Within a gland.

intraglobular (in″trah-glob′u-lar). Within a globe or globule, as within an erythrocyte.

intragyral (in″trah-ji′ral). Within a cerebral gyrus.

intrahepatic (in″trah-he-pat′ik). Within the liver.

intrahyoid (in″trah-hi′oid). Within the hyoid bone.

intra-intestinal (in″trah-in-tes′tĭ-nal). Within the intestine.

intrajugular (in″trah-jug′u-lar). Internal to the jugular foramen, process, or vein.

intralamellar (in″trah-lah-mel′ar). Within lamellae.

intralaryngeal (in″trah-lah-rin′je-al). Within the larynx.

intralesional (in″trah-le′shun-al). Occurring in or introduced directly into a localized lesion.

intraleukocytic (in″trah-lu″ko-si′tik). Within a leukocyte.

intraligamentous (in″trah-lig″ah-men′tus). Within a ligament.

intralingual (in″trah-ling′gwal). Within the tongue.

intralobar (in″trah-lo′bar). Within a lobe.

intralobular (in″trah-lob′u-lar). Within a lobule.

intralocular (in″trah-lok′u-lar). Within the loculi of a structure.

intralumbar (in″trah-lum′bar). Endolumbar.

intraluminal (in″trah-lu′mĭ-nal). Within the lumen of a tube.

intramammary (in″trah-mam′ah-re). Within the breast.

intramarginal (in″trah-mar′jĭ-nal). Within a margin.

intramastoiditis (in″trah-mas″toid-i′tis). Inflammation of the antrum and cells of the mastoid process.

intramatrical (in″trah-mat′re-kal). Within a matrix.

intramedullary (in″trah-med′u-lār″e). 1. Within the spinal cord. 2. Within the medulla oblongata. 3. Within the marrow cavity of a bone.

intramembranous (in″trah-mem′brah-nus). Within a membrane.

intrameningeal (in″trah-mĕ-nin′je-al). Within the meninges.

intramolecular (in″trah-mo-lek′u-lar). Within the molecule.

intramural (in″trah-mu′ral) [*intra-* + L. *murus* wall]. Within the wall of an organ.

intramuscular (in″trah-mus′ku-lar) [*intra-* + L. *musculus* muscle]. Within the substance of a muscle.

intramyocardial (in″trah-mi″o-kar′de-al). Within the myocardium.

intranarial (in″trah-na′re-al). Within the nostrils.

intranasal (in″trah-na′zal) [*intra-* + L. *nasus* nose]. Within the nose.

intranatal (in″trah-na′tal). Occurring during birth.

intraneural (in″trah-nu′ral). Within or into a nerve.

intranuclear (in″trah-nu′kle-ar). Within a nucleus.

intraocular (in″trah-ok′u-lar) [*intra-* + L. *oculus* eye]. Within the eye.

intraoperative (in″trah-op′er-a″tiv). Performed or occurring during the course of a surgical operation.

intra-oral (in″trah-o′ral). Within the mouth.

intra-orbital (in″trah-or′bĭ-tal) [*intra-* + L. *orbita* orbit]. Within the orbit.

intra-osseous (in″trah-os′e-us). Within a bone.

intra-osteal (in″trah-os′te-al). Intra-osseous.

intra-ovarian (in″trah-o-va′re-an). Within the ovary.

intraparenchymatous (in″trah-par″en-kim′ah-tus). Within the parenchyma of an organ.

intraparietal (in″trah-pah-ri′ĕ-tal) [*intra-* + L. *paries* wall]. 1. Intramural. 2. Situated in the parietal region of the brain.

intrapartum (in′trah-par′tum). Occurring during childbirth, or during delivery.

intrapelvic (in″trah-pel′vik). Within the pelvis.

intrapericardial (in″trah-per″ĭ-kar′de-al). Within the pericardium.

intraperineal (in″trah-per″ĭ-ne′al). Within the tissues of the perineum.

intraperitoneal (in″trah-per″ĭ-to-ne′al). Within the peritoneal cavity.

intraphyletic (in″trah-fi-let′ik). Occurring during the development of a cell.

intrapial (in″trah-pe′al). Within or beneath the pia mater.

intraplacental (in″trah-plah-sen′tal). Within the placenta.

intrapleural (in″trah-ploor′al). Within the pleura.

intrapolar (in″trah-po′lar). Within the space between the two poles.

intrapontine (in″trah-pon′tīn) [*intra-* + L. *pons*]. Within the substance of the pons.

intraprostatic (in″trah-pros-tat′ik). Within the prostate gland.

intraprotoplasmic (in″trah-pro″to-plaz′mik). Within the protoplasm.

intrapsychic (in-trah-si′kik). Within the mind; originating or operating within the mental or psychic field.

intrapsychical (in″trah-si′ke-kal). Intrapsychic.

intrapulmonary (in″trah-pul′mo-ner″e). Situated in the substance of the lung.

intrapyretic (in″trah-pi-ret′ik) [*intra-* + Gr. *pyretos* fever]. During the stage of fever.

intrarachidian (in″trah-rah-kid′e-an). Intraspinal.

intrarectal (in″trah-rek′tal). Within the rectum.

intrarenal (in″trah-re′nal). Within the kidney.

intraretinal (in″trah-ret′ĭ-nal). Within the retina.

intrascleral (in″trah-skle′ral). Within the sclera.

intrascrotal (in″trah-skro′tal). Within the scrotum.

intrasellar (in″trah-sel′ar). Within the sella turcica.

intraserous (in″trah-se′rus). Within the blood serum.

intraspinal (in″trah-spi′nal). Situated or occurring within the vertebral column.

intrasplenic (in″trah-sple′nik). Within the spleen.

intrasternal (in″trah-ster′nal). Within the sternum.

intrastitial (in″trah-stish′al). Within the cells or fibers of a tissue.

intrastromal (in″trah-stro′mal). Within the stroma of an organ.

intrasynovial (in″trah-sĭ-no′ve-al). Within the synovial cavity of a joint.

intratarsal (in″trah-tar′sal). Within or on the inner side of the tarsus.

intratesticular (in″trah-tes-tik′u-lar). Within the testicle.

intrathecal (in″trah-the′kal). Within a sheath.

intrathenar (in″trah-the′nar). Situated between the thenar and hypothenar eminences.

intrathoracic (in″trah-tho-ras′ik). Endothoracic.

intratonsillar (in″trah-ton′sĭ-lar). Within the tonsil.

intratrabecular (in″trah-trah-bek′u-lar). Within the trabeculae.

intratracheal (in″trah-tra′ke-al). Endotracheal.

intratubal (in″trah-tu′bal). Situated or occurring within a tube, especially within a uterine tube.

intratubular (in″trah-tu′bu-lar). Within the tubules of an organ.

intratympanic (in″trah-tim-pan′ik). Within the tympanic cavity.

intra-ureteral (in″trah-u-re′ter-al). Within the ureter.

intra-urethral (in″trah-u-re′thral). Within the urethra.

intra-uterine (in″trah-u′ter-in). Within the uterus.

intravaginal (in″trah-vaj′ĭ-nal). Within the vagina.

intravasation (in-trav″ah-za′shun). The entrance of foreign material into a blood vessel.

intravascular (in″trah-vas′ku-lar) [*intra-* + L. *vasculum* vessel]. Within a vessel or vessels.

intravenation (in″trah-ve-na′shun). The entrance or injection of foreign matter into a vein.

intravenous (in″trah-ve′nus). Within a vein or veins.

intraventricular (in″trah-ven-trik′u-lar). Within a ventricle.

intraversion (in″trah-ver′zhun). Unusual narrowness of the dental arch.

intravertebral (in″trah-ver′te-bral). Intraspinal.

intravesical (in″trah-ves′e-kal) [*intra-* + L. *vesica* bladder]. Situated within the bladder.

intravillous (in″trah-vil′us). Situated within a villus.

intravital (in″trah-vi′tal). Occurring during life.

intra vitam (in′trah vi′tam) [L.]. During life.

intravitelline (in″trah-vi-tel′in). Within the vitellus or yolk.

intravitreous (in″trah-vit′re-us). Into or within the vitreous.

intrinsic (in-trin′sik) [L. *intrinsecus* situated on the inside]. Situated entirely within or pertaining exclusively to a part.

intro- (in′tro) [L. *intro* within]. A prefix meaning into or within.

introducer (in″tro-du′ser). An intubator.

introfier (in′tro-fi″er). A liquid which has the property of lowering the interfacial tension of emulsions.

introflexion (in″tro-flek′shun). A bending inward.

introgastric (in″tro-gas′trik) [*intro-* + Gr. *gastēr* stomach]. Conveyed into the stomach.

introitus (in-tro′ĭ-tus), pl. *intro′itus* [L., from *intro* within + *ire* to go]. The entrance to a cavity or space. **i. oesoph′agi,** the entrance into the esophagus. **i. pel′vis,** apertura pelvis superior. **i. vagi′nae,** ostium vaginae.

introjection (in″tro-jek′shun) [*intro-* + L. *jacere* to throw]. A mental operation by which a person appropriates an occurrence or characteristic and makes it a part of himself or turns against himself the hostility felt toward another.

intromission (in″tro-mish′un) [*intro-* + L. *mittere* to send]. The insertion of one part or thing into another.

introrsus (in-tror′sus) [L.]. Turned in.

introspection (in″tro-spek′shun) [*intro-* + L. *spicere* to look]. The contemplation or observation of one's own thoughts and feelings; self-analysis.

introsusception (in″tro-sus-sep′shun) [*intro-* + L. *suscipere* to receive]. Intussusception.

introversion (in″tro-ver′shun) [*intro-* + L. *versio* a turning]. 1. The turning outside in, more or less completely, of an organ. 2. A turning inward of the libido, so that interest does not move toward an object, but turns inward to the self.

introvert (in′tro-vert). 1. A person whose libido is turned inward upon himself. 2. To turn one's interest toward one's self.

intrude (in-tro͞od′). To project inward.

intrusion (in-troo′zhun). Inward projection.

intubate (in′tu-bāt). To treat by intubation.

intubation (in″tu-ba′shun) [L. *in* into + *tuba* tube]. The insertion of a tube; especially the introduction of a tube into the larynx through the glottis, performed in diphtheria and edema of the glottis for the introduction of air. **endotracheal i.,** insertion of a tube through the trachea to assure a clear airway and prevent entrance of foreign material into the tracheobronchial tree. **nasal i.,** insertion of a tube into the respiratory or gastrointestinal tract through the nose. **oral i.,** insertion of a tube into the respiratory or gastrointestinal tract through the mouth.

intubationist (in-tu-ba′shun-ist). One who performs an intubation.

intubator (in′tu-ba-tor). An instrument used in intubation.

intumesce (in-tu-mes′). To swell up.

intumescence (in-tu-mes′ens) [L. *intumescentia*]. 1. A swelling, normal or abnormal. 2. The process of swelling.

intumescent (in-tu-mes′ent) [L. *intumescens*]. Swelling or becoming swollen.

intumescentia (in-tu-mĕ-sen′she-ah), pl. *intumescen′tiae* [L.]. An enlargement or swelling. **i. cervica′lis** [N A, B N A], the enlargement of the spinal cord in the cervical region, at the level of attachment of the nerves to the upper limbs. **i. gangliofor′mis ner′vi va′gi,** ganglion inferius nervi vagi. **i. lumba′lis** [N A, B N A], the enlargement of the spinal cord in the lumbar region, at the level of attachment of the nerves to the lower limbs. **i. tympan′ica** [B N A], an enlargement on the tympanic branch of the glossopharyngeal nerve. Omitted in N A.

intussusception (in″tus-sus-sep′shun) [L. *intus* within + *suscipere* to receive]. A receiving within: specifically, (1) The prolapse of one part of the intestine into the lumen of an immediately adjoining part (Treves, 1899). There are four varieties: *colic,* involving segments of the large intestine; *enteric,* involving only the small intestine; *ileocecal,* in which the ileocecal valve prolapses into the cecum, drawing the ileum along with it; and *ileocolic,* in which the ileum prolapses through the ileocecal valve into the colon. (2) In physiology, the reception into an organism of matter, such as food, and its transformation into new protoplasm. **agonic i., postmortem i.,** intussusception occurring in the death agony. **retrograde i.,** the invagination of a distal part of the bowel into a proximal part.

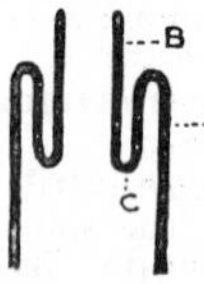

B
A
C

Schema of an intussusception: A, Intussuscipiens; B, entering layer; C, intussusceptum (Stevens).

intussusceptum (in″tus-sus-sep′tum) [L.]. The portion of intestine that has been invaginated within another part in intussusception.

intussuscipiens (in″tus-sus-sip′e-ens) [L.]. The portion of intestine into which another portion has invaginated in intussusception.

Inula (in′u-lah) [L.]. A genus of composite-flowered plants.

inula (in′u-la), gen. *in′ulae* [L.]. The root of *Inula helenium.* See *elecampane.*

inulase (in′u-lās). An enzyme occurring in *Aspergillus niger* and *Penicillium glaucum,* which changes inulin into levulose. **inosine i.,** an enzyme which hydrolyzes inosine into hypoxanthine and sugar.

inulin (in′u-lin). A vegetable starch, $(C_6H_{10}O_5)_4$, a fructose polysaccharide occurring in the rhizome of certain plants (Compositae). It is a polymerized form of fructofuranose, yields levulose on hydrolysis, and is used in a test for determining renal function.

inulinase (in′u-lin-ās). Inulase.

inuloid (in′u-loid). A colorless compound, $C_6H_{10}O_5$, resembling inulin, but more soluble.

inulol (in′u-lol). Alantol.

inunction (in-ungk′shun) [L. *in* into + *unguere* to anoint]. 1. The act of anointing or of applying an ointment with friction. 2. An ointment made with lanolin as a menstruum.

inunctum (in-ungk′tum). Inunction, def. 2. **i. men′tholis compos′itum,** compound menthol ointment.

inustion (in-us′chun) [L. *in* into + *urere* to burn]. The application of actual cautery.

in utero (in u′ter-o) [L.]. Within the uterus.

invaccination (in-vak″sĭ-na′shun). Inoculation with some other disease during vaccination.

invaginate (in-vaj′ĭ-nāt). To infold one portion within another portion of the same thing.

invagination (in-vaj″ĭ-na′shun) [L. *invaginatio*, from *in* within + *vagina* sheath]. 1. The infolding of one part within another, specifically a process of gastrulation in which one region infolds to form a double-layered cup. 2. An obliterative operation for the cure of hernia. 3. Intussusception. **basilar i.,** basilar impression.

invaginator (in-vaj′ĭ-na″tor). An instrument for turning in the tissues in the surgical repair of hernia.

invalid (in′vah-lid) [L. *invalidus; in* not + *validus* strong]. 1. Not well and strong. 2. A person who is disabled by illness or infirmity.

invasin (in-va′zin). Hyaluronidase.

invasion (in-va′zhun) [L. *invasio; in* into + *vadere* to go]. 1. The attack or onset of a disease. 2. The simple harmless entrance of bacteria into the body or their deposition in the tissues, as distinguished from infection.

invasiveness (in-va′siv-nes). The ability of a microorganism to enter the body and to spread more or less widely throughout the tissues. The organism may or may not cause an infection or a disease. See *hyaluronidase.*

invermination (in-ver″mĭ-na′shun). Helminthiasis.

inversine (in-ver′sēn). Trade mark for a preparation of mecamylamine.

inversion (in-ver′zhun) [L. *inversio; in* into + *vertere* to turn]. A turning inward, inside out, upside down, or other reversal of the normal relation of a part. In psychiatry, the condition of being an invert, homosexuality. In genetics, the inverted reunion of the intervening segment after breakage of one chromosome at two points. **carbohydrate i.,** hydrolysis of the complex carbohydrates to simple sugars. **sexual i.,** homosexuality. **thermic i.,** the state in which a patient's temperature is highest in the morning. **i. of uterus,** a turning of the uterus inside out or upside down. **visceral i.,** the more or less complete right and left transposition of the viscera. See *situs inversus viscerum.*

inversus (in-ver′sus) [L.; *in* into + *vertere* to turn]. Opposite to, or inverted from, the normal. See *situs inversus viscerum.*

invert (in′vert). A person whose sexual interests and impulses are directed toward a person of the same sex.

invertase (in-ver′tās). Invertin.

Invertebrata (in-ver″te-bra′tah). A division of the animal kingdom, including all forms that have no spinal column.

invertebrate (in-ver′te-brāt). 1. One of the Invertebrata. 2. Having no spinal column.

invertin (in-ver′tin). An enzyme produced by yeasts and the intestinal mucosa, which catalyzes the hydrolysis of cane sugar to invert sugar. Also called *sucrase.*

invertor (in-ver′tor). A muscle which turns in a part.

invertose (in′ver-tōs). Invert sugar.

investment (in-vest′ment). The material in which a denture, tooth, crown, or pattern for a dental restoration is enclosed before curing, soldering, or casting, or the process of enclosing it in such material.

inveterate (in-vet′er-āt) [L. *inverteratus; in* intensive + *vetus* old]. Chronic and confirmed; long established and of difficult cure.

inviscation (in″vis-ka′shun) [L. *in* among + *viscum* slime]. The mixing of the food with the mucous secretion of the mouth in mastication.

in vitro (in vi′tro) [L.]. Within a glass; observable in a test tube.

in vivo (in vi′vo) [L.]. Within the living body.

involucre (in′vo-lu″ker). An involucrum.

involucrum (in″vo-lu′krum), pl. *involu′cra* [L.; *in* in + *volvere* to wrap]. A covering or sheath, such as contains the sequestrum of a necrosed bone.

involuntary (in-vol′un-ter″e) [L. *involuntarius; in* against + *voluntas* will]. Performed independently of the will.

involuntomotory (in-vol″un-to-mo′tor-e). Pertaining to motion that is not voluntary.

involute (in′vo-lūt) [L. *in* into + *volvere* to roll]. 1. To return to normal size after enlargement. 2. To regress; to change to an earlier or more primitive condition.

involution (in″vo-lu′shun) [L. *involutio; in* into + *volvere* to roll]. 1. A rolling or turning inward over a rim. 2. One of the movements involved in the gastrulation of many animal types. 3. A retrograde change, the reverse of evolution; applied especially to a lessening of the size of a tissue caused by a reduction in the number of its component cells, without degeneration. **senile i.,** the shriveling of an organ in an aged person.

involutional (in″vo-lu′shun-al). Pertaining to, due to, or occurring in involution.

Iodamoeba (i″o-dah-me′bah). A genus of amebas. **I. buetsch′lii,** a species of nonpathogenic amebas found in the intestinal tract. The cysts (formerly called iodine cysts or I-cysts) usually contain a large glycogen mass which stains intensely with iodine. Called also *Endolimax williamsi, Entamoeba buetschlii,* and *E. williamsi.* **I. wil′liamsi,** *I. buetschlii.*

iodate (i′o-dāt). Any salt of iodic acid.

iod-Basedow (i-ōd-bas′e-dow). Jodbasedow.

iodemia (i″o-de′me-ah) [*iodine* + Gr. *haima* blood + *-ia*]. The presence of iodides in the blood.

iodeosin (i″o-de′o-sin). Erythrosin.

iodide (i′o-dīd). Any binary compound of iodine: a compound of iodine with an element or radical.

iodimetry (i″o-dim′e-tre) [*iodine* + Gr. *metron* measure]. The estimation of the quantity of iodine in a mixture or compound.

iodinate (i-o′dĭ-nāt). To combine or compound with iodine.

iodine (i′o-din) [Gr. *ioeides* violet-like, from the color of its vapor]. A halogen element of a peculiar odor and acrid taste; symbol, I; atomic number, 53; atomic weight, 126.904. It is a nonmetallic element, occurring in heavy, grayish black plates or granules. Iodine is essential in nutrition, being especially abundant in the colloid of the thyroid gland. **povidone-i.** See *povidone-iodine.*

iodinin (i-od′ĭ-nin). A purple pigment which is antibiotic in high dilution to *Streptococcus hemolyticus.*

iodinophil (i″o-din′o-fil) [*iodine* + Gr. *philein* to love]. 1. Any cell or other element readily stainable with iodine. 2. Iodinophilous.

iodinophilous (i″o-din-of′ĭ-lus). Readily stainable with iodine.

iodipamide (i″o-dip′ah-mīd). Chemical name: N,-N′-adipyl-bis(3-amino-2,4,6-triiodobenzoic acid): used as a radiopaque medium in cholecystography.

iodism (i′o-dizm). Ill health resulting from injudicious use of iodine or iodine compounds. It is marked by atrophy of the glands and glandular organs, coryza, ptyalism, frontal headache, emaciation, weakness, and eruptions on the skin.

iodize (i′o-dīz). To impregnate with iodine or to put under its influence.

iodobrassid (i-o″do-bras′sid). Chemical name:

ethyl diiodobrassidate: used in iodide therapy, and as a radiopaque medium.

iodochlorhydroxyquin (i-o″do-klōr″hi-drok′se-kwin). Chemical name: 5-chloro-7-iodo-8-quinolinol: used as an anti-amebic.

ioderma (i″o-do-der′mah) [*iodine* + Gr. *derma* skin]. Any skin eruption resulting from iodism.

iodoform (i-o′do-form) [*iodine* + *formyl*]. A yellow, crystalline substance, triiodomethane (CHI_3), having a strong, penetrating odor, containing about 96 per cent of iodine, and soluble in chloroform and ether and somewhat in alcohol and water: used as a local antibacterial.

iodoformism (i′o-do-form″izm). Poisoning by iodoform.

iodoformize (i″o-do-form′īz). To treat or impregnate with iodoform.

iodoformum (i″o-do-for′mum). Iodoform.

iodogenic (i″o-do-jen′ik) [*iodine* + Gr. *gennan* to produce]. Yielding or producing iodine.

iodoglobulin (i″o-do-glob′u-lin). An iodine-containing globulin (protein).

iodohydrargyrate (i″o-do-hi-drar′jĭ-rāt). A compound of iodine and mercury with another substance.

iodolography (i″o-do-log′rah-fe). Roentgenologic visualization of an organ or part after the injection into it of iodized oil.

iodomethamate (i-o″do-meth′ah-māt). Chemical name: 3,5-diiodo-1-methylchelidamic acid: used as a radiopaque medium for urography.

iodometric (i″o-do-met′rik). Pertaining to iodometry.

iodometry (i″o-dom′e-tre) [*iodine* + Gr. *metron* measure]. Estimation of the quantity of a chemical by titration with iodine.

iodophenol (i″o-do-fe′nol). 1. A mono-iodophenol, $OH.C_6H_5I$. 2. A preparation of iodine, phenol, and glycerin: antiseptic.

iodophil (i′o-do-fil). Iodinophil.

iodophilia (i″o-do-fil′e-ah) [*iodine* + Gr. *philein* to love + *-ia*]. The reaction shown by leukocytes in certain conditions when treated with iodine or iodides. Normal leukocytes are colored bright yellow, but in certain pathologic conditions, as toxemia and severe anemia, the polymorphonuclears show diffuse brownish coloration. When the staining affects the leukocytes themselves, it is termed *intracellular;* when only the particles around the leukocytes are affected, it is *extracellular.*

iodophthalein (i-o″do-thal′e-in). Chemical name: tetraiodophenolphthalein: used as a radiopaque medium for cholecystography.

iodopsin (i″o-dop′sin) [Gr. *iōdēs* violet colored + *opsis* vision]. A photosensitive violet retinal pigment found in the retinal cones of some animals and important for vision.

iodopyracet (i-o″do-pi′rah-set). Chemical name: diethanolammonium-3,5-diiodo-4-pyridone-N-acetate: used as a radiopaque medium for urography.

iodosulfate (i″o-do-sul′fāt). A combination of a base with iodine and sulfuric acid.

iodotherapy (i″o-do-ther′ah-pe) [*iodine* + Gr. *therapeia* treatment]. Treatment with iodine or the iodides.

iodothyrine (i″o-do-thi′rin). Thyroiodine.

iodothyroglobulin (i″o-do-thi″ro-glob′u-lin). Thyroglobulin.

iodoventriculography (i″o-do-ven-trik″u-log′-rah-fe). Ventriculography with iodine contrast medium.

iodovolatilization (i″o-do-vol″ah-til-i-za′shun). The liberation of free iodine by living epidermal cells in the iodogenic layer of certain algae.

iodum (i-o′dum), gen. *io′di* [L.]. Iodine.

ioduria (i″o-du′re-ah). The presence of iodides in the urine.

iometer (i-om′e-ter). An instrument for determining the constancy of roentgen-ray output.

ion (i′on) [Gr. *iōn* going]. An atom or a group of atoms having a charge of positive (cation) or negative (anion) electricity. See *ionic theory*, under *theory*. **dipolar i.,** zwitterion. **gram i.,** the weight in grams of an ion numerically equal to the atomic or molecular weight of the ion. **hydrogen i.,** the nucleus of the hydrogen atom or a hydrogen atom that has lost its electron. It bears a positive charge equivalent to the negative charge of the electron and is called a proton. **hydronium i.,** a combination of a hydrogen ion (H^+) with a molecule of water, giving H_3O^+. **hydroxyl i.,** the hydroxyl group, OH, in solution bearing a negative electric charge.

ionic (i-on′ik). Pertaining to an ion or to ions.

ionium (i-o′ne-um) [*ion*]. A radioactive isotope of thorium, of atomic weight 230.5. It emits both alpha and gamma rays.

ionization (i″on-i-za′shun). 1. The dissociation of a substance in solution into its constituent ions. 2. Iontophoresis. **medical i.,** iontophoresis.

ionize (i′on-īz). To separate into ions.

ionocolorimeter (i″o-no-kol″or-im′e-ter). An apparatus for measuring the ionic acidity of a solution.

ionogen (i-on′o-jen) [*ion* + Gr. *gennan* to form]. A substance which may be ionized.

ionogenic (i-on″o-jen′ik). Forming or supplying ions.

ionometer (i″o-nom′e-ter). An instrument for the measurement of the intensity or quantity of roentgen rays.

ionometry (i″o-nom′e-tre). Roentgenometry.

ionone (i′on-ōn) [Gr. *ion* violet]. An odoriferous derivative of orris root, prepared commercially from citral and used as a perfume.

ionophose (i′o-no-fōz″) [Gr. *ion* violet + *phose*]. A violet phose.

ionoscope (i-on′o-skōp). An instrument for detecting alkaline or acid impurity in nitrous oxide.

ionotherapy (i″o-no-ther′ah-pe). 1. [*ion* + *therapy*]. Iontophoresis. 2. [Gr. *ion* violet + *therapy*]. Treatment by means of ultraviolet rays.

ion-protein (i-on-pro′te-in). A protein molecule combined with an inorganic ion, which is the form in which protein takes part in vital processes.

iontherapy (i″on-ther′ah-pe). Iontophoresis.

iontophoresis (i-on″to-fo-re′sis). The introduction, by means of the electric current, of ions of soluble salts into the tissues of the body for therapeutic purposes. Called also *iontherapy, galvanoionization, ionic medication,* and *medical ionization.*

iontoquantimeter (i-on″to-quan-tim′e-ter) [*ion* + *quantimeter*]. Ionometer.

iontoradeometer (i-on″to-ra″de-om′e-ter). Ionometer.

iontotherapy (i-on″to-ther′ah-pe). The use simultaneously of direct current and diathermy from the same electrodes.

IOP. Abbreviation for *intraocular pressure.*

iophendylate (i″o-fen′dĭ-lāt). Chemical name: ethyl iodophenylundecylate: used as a radiopaque medium for roentgenography of the spine and of the biliary tract.

iophobia (i″o-fo′be-ah) [Gr. *ios* poison + *phobia*]. A morbid fear of poisons.

iotacism (i-o′tah-sizm) [Gr. *iōta* letter I]. Excessive use of the sound of the Greek letter iota (English e, as in be) in speaking.

iothiouracil (i″o-thi″o-u′rah-sil). Chemical name: 5-iodo-2-thiouracil: used in preparation for thyroidectomy, and in treatment of hyperthyroidism when thyroidectomy is contraindicated.

I.P. Abbreviation for *incisoproximal, intraperitoneally,* and *isoelectric point.*

I-para. Abbreviation for *primipara.*

ipecac (ip′e-kak). The dried rhizome and roots of *Cephaëlis ipecacuanha*, used in fluid extract and syrup as an emetic and expectorant agent.

ipomea (i″po-me′ah). The dried root of *Ipomoea orizabensis:* used as a cathartic.

Ipomoea (i″po-me′ah). A genus of herbs and shrubs of the family Convolvulaceae, comprising some 300 species.

IPPB. Abbreviation for *intermittent positive pressure breathing:* active inflation of the lungs during inspiration under positive pressure from a cycling valve.

ipral (ip′ral). Trade mark for preparations of probarbital.

iproniazid (i″pro-ni′ah-zid). Chemical name: 1-isonicotinoyl-2-isopropylhydrazine: used as a psychic energizer, antituberculotic, and antihypertensive.

ipsation (ip-sa′shun) [L. *ipse* himself]. Masturbation.

ipsilateral (ip″sĭ-lat′er-al) [L. *ipse* self + *latus* side]. Situated on or pertaining to the same side.

ipsism (ip′sizm). Masturbation.

I.Q. Abbreviation for *intelligence quotient.*

I.R. Abbreviation for *internal resistance.*

Ir. Chemical symbol for *iridium.*

irascibility (ĭ-ras″ĭ-bil′ĭ-te) [L. *irascibilis* ill tempered]. Morbid irritability and quickness of temper.

ircon (ir′kon). Trade mark for a preparation of ferrous fumarate.

irid- (ir′id). See *irido-.*

iridal (i′rĭ-dal). Iridic.

iridauxesis (ir″id-awk-se′sis) [*irid-* + Gr. *auxēsis* increase]. Thickening of the iris.

iridectasis (ir″ĭ-dek′tah-sis) [*irid-* + Gr. *ektasis* dilatation]. Dilatation of the iris, or pupil of the eye.

iridectome (ir″id-ek′tōm) [*irid-* + Gr. *ektemnein* to cut out]. A cutting instrument for use in iridectomy.

iridectomesodialysis (ir″id-ek″to-me″so-di-al′ĭ-sis) [*irid-* + Gr. *ektomē* excision + *mesos* middle + *dialysis* loosening]. Excision and separation of adhesions around the inner edge of the iris.

iridectomize (ir″id-ek′to-mīz). To deprive of part of the iris by excision.

iridectomy (ir″ĭ-dek′to-me) [*irid-* + Gr. *ektomē* excision]. Surgical excision of part of the iris. **optic i.,** excision of part of the iris as a means of enlarging an abnormally small pupil and improving vision. **preliminary i., preparatory i.,** iridectomy that is performed prior to removal of the lens in cataract surgery. **stenopeic i.,** excision of a small part of the iris, with preservation of the sphincter. **therapeutic i.,** iridectomy that is performed for the cure of disease of the eye.

iridectopia (ir″id-ek-to′pe-ah) [*irid-* + Gr. *ektopos* displaced + *-ia*]. Displacement of the iris of the eye.

iridectropium (ir″id-ek-tro′pe-um). Ectropion uveae.

iridemia (ir″ĭ-de′me-ah) [*irid-* + Gr. *haima* blood + *-ia*]. Hemorrhage from the iris.

iridencleisis (ir″ĭ-den-kli′sis) [*irid-* + Gr. *enklein* to lock in]. The formation of an artificial pupil by strangulation of a slip of the iris in a corneal incision.

iridentropium (ir″ĭ-den-tro′pe-um). Entropion uveae.

irideremia (ir″ĭ-der-e′me-ah) [*irid-* + Gr. *erēmia* want of, absence]. Congenital absence of the iris.

irides (ir′ĭ-dēz) [Gr.]. Plural of *iris.*

iridescence (ir″ĭ-des′ens) [L. *iridescere* to gleam like a rainbow]. The condition of gleaming with bright and changing colors.

iridescent (ir″ĭ-des′ent) [L. *iridescens*]. Gleaming with bright colors like those of the rainbow.

iridesis (i-rid′ĕ-sis) [*iris* + Gr. *desis* a binding]. The operation of forming a new pupil or changing the position of the old by tying a slip or slips of the iris in an opening made in the cornea.

iridiagnosis (i″rĭ-di-ag-no′sis). Iridodiagnosis.

iridial (i-rid′e-al). Iridic.

iridian (i-rid′e-an). Iridic.

iridic (i-rid′ik). Pertaining to the iris.

iridium (i-rid′e-um) [L. *iris* rainbow, from the tints of its salts]. A very hard white metal; symbol, Ir; atomic number, 77; atomic weight, 192.2.

iridization (ir″ĭ-di-za′shun). The subjective perception of iridescent halos about lights, occurring in glaucoma.

irido-, irid- [Gr. *iris, iridos* rainbow, colored circle]. Combining form denoting relationship to the iris of the eye, or to a colored circle.

irido-avulsion (ir″ĭ-do-ah-vul′shun). Complete tearing away of the iris from its periphery.

iridocapsulitis (ir″ĭ-do-kap-su-li′tis). Inflammation of the iris and the capsule of the lens.

iridocele (i-rid′o-sēl) [*irido-* + Gr. *kēlē* hernia]. Hernial protrusion of a slip of the iris.

iridochoroiditis (ir″ĭ-do-ko″roid-i′tis). Inflammation of the iris and the choroid.

iridocoloboma (ir″ĭ-do-kol″o-bo′mah) [*irido-* + Gr. *kolobōma* mutilation]. Congenital fissure or coloboma of the iris.

iridoconstrictor (ir″ĭ-do-kon-strik′tor). A muscle element or an agent which acts to constrict the pupil of the eye.

iridocorneosclerectomy (ir″ĭ-do-kor″ne-o-skle-rek′to-me). Surgical excision of a portion of the iris, cornea, and sclera for glaucoma.

iridocyclectomy (ir″ĭ-do-si-klek′to-me) [*irido-* + Gr. *kyklos* circle + *ektomē* excision]. Surgical removal of the iris and of the ciliary body.

iridocyclitis (ir″ĭ-do-si-kli′tis) [*irido-* + Gr. *kyklos* circle + *-itis*]. Inflammation of the iris and of the ciliary body.

iridocyclochoroiditis (ir″ĭ-do-si″klo-ko″roid-i′tis) [*irido-* + Gr. *kyklos* circle + *choroiditis*]. Inflammation of the iris, ciliary body, and choroid coat.

iridocystectomy (ir″ĭ-do-sis-tek′to-me). A plastic operation on the iris devised by Knapp.

iridocyte (i-rid′o-sit) [*irido-* + *-cyte*]. One of the cells in the connective tissue of cold-blooded animals which give the iridescent appearance to the skin of fishes.

iridodesis (ir″ĭ-dod′e-sis). Iridesis.

iridodiagnosis (ir″ĭ-do-di″ag-no′sis). Diagnosis of disease by the appearance of the iris, its color, markings, changes, etc.

iridodialysis (ir″ĭ-do-di-al′ĭ-sis) [*irido-* + Gr. *dialysis* loosening]. 1. Coredialysis. 2. The separation or loosening of the iris from its attachment. 3. Division or splitting of the iris, congenital or other, producing more than one pupil.

iridodiastasis (ir″ĭ-do-di-as′tah-sis). A defect of the peripheral border of the iris, but not affecting the pupillary margin, producing the clinical appearance of more than one pupil.

iridodilator (ir″ĭ-do-di-la′tor). A muscle element or an agent which acts to dilate the pupil of the eye.

iridodonesis (ir″ĭ-do-do-ne′sis) [*irido-* + Gr. *donēsis* tremor]. Abnormal tremulousness of the iris on movements of the eye, occurring in subluxation of the lens, depriving the iris of this support.

iridokeratitis (ir″ĭ-do-ker″ah-ti′tis) [*irido-* + Gr. *keras* horn, cornea + *-itis*]. Inflammation of the iris and cornea.

iridokinesia (ir″ĭ-do-ki-ne′ze-ah). Iridokinesis.

iridokinesis (ir″ĭ-do-ki-ne′sis) [*irido-* + Gr. *kinēsis* movement]. The contraction and expansion of the iris.

iridokinetic (ir″ĭ-do-ki-net′ik). Pertaining to iridokinesis.

iridoleptynsis (ir″ĭ-do-lep-tin′sis) [*iris* + Gr. *leptynsis* attenuation]. Thinning or atrophy of the iris.

iridology (ir″ĭ-dol′o-je) [*irido-* + *-logy*]. The study of the iris, particularly of its color, markings, changes, etc., as associated with disease.

iridolysis (ir″ĭ-dol′ĭ-sis) [*irido-* + Gr. *lysis* a loosening]. The surgical release of adhesions of the iris.

iridomalacia (ir″ĭ-do-mah-la′she-ah) [*irido-* + Gr. *malakia* softness]. Softening of the iris.

iridomesodialysis (ir″ĭ-do-me″so-di-al′ĭ-sis) [*irido-* + Gr. *mesos* middle + *dialysis* loosening]. Loosening of adhesions around the inner edge of the iris.

iridomotor (ir″ĭ-do-mo′tor). Pertaining to movements of the iris; affecting contraction or dilation of the pupil of the eye.

iridoncus (ir″ĭ-dong′kus) [*irid-* + Gr. *onkos* bulk]. Tumor or swelling of the iris.

iridoparalysis (ir″ĭ-do-pah-ral′ĭ-sis). Iridoplegia.

iridopathy (ir″ĭ-dop′ah-the) [*irido-* + Gr. *pathos* disease]. Disease of the iris.

iridoperiphakitis (ir″ĭ-do-per″e-fa-ki′tis) [*irido-* + Gr. *peri* around + *phakos* lens]. Inflammation of the capsule of the crystalline lens.

iridoplegia (ir″ĭ-do-ple′je-ah) [*iris* + Gr. *plēgē* stroke + *-ia*]. Paralysis of the sphincter of the iris, with lack of contraction or dilation of the pupil. **accommodation i.,** failure of the pupil to contract when an accommodative effort is made. **complete i.,** paralysis of the sphincter of the pupil, with failure to react to any stimulus. **reflex i.,** failure of the pupil to contract under the influence of light or when skin is stimulated. **sympathetic i.,** failure of the pupil to dilate when the skin is stimulated.

iridoptosis (ir″ĭ-dop-to′sis) [*irido-* + Gr. *ptōsis* falling]. Prolapse of the iris.

iridopupillary (ir″ĭ-do-pu′pĭ-ler″e). Pertaining to the iris and the pupil.

iridorhexis (ir″ĭ-do-rek′sis) [*irido-* + Gr. *rhēxis* rupture]. 1. Rupture of the iris. 2. The tearing away of the iris.

iridoschisis (ir″ĭ-dos′kĭ-sis). Coloboma of the iris.

iridosclerotomy (ir″ĭ-do-skle-rot′o-me) [*irido-* + *sclera* + Gr. *tomē* a cutting]. Incision of the sclera and of the edge of the iris in treatment of glaucoma.

iridosteresis (ir″ĭ-do-ste-re′sis) [*irido-* + Gr. *sterēsis* loss]. The removal of part or all of the iris.

iridotasis (ir″ĭ-dot′ah-sis) [*irido-* + Gr. *tasis* stretching]. The operation of stretching the iris in treatment of glaucoma.

iridotomy (ir″ĭ-dot′o-me) [*irido-* + Gr. *tomē* a cutting]. Incision of the iris, as in creating an artificial pupil.

Iris (i′ris). A genus of perennial herbs. The roots of several species, *I. florentina*, *I. germanica* and *I. pallida*, are the source of orris. *I. versicolor*, a plant indigenous to America, which is the source of a substance used as a cathartic and emetic.

iris (i′ris), pl. *ir′ides* [Gr. "rainbow," "halo"]. 1. [N A, B N A] The circular pigmented membrane behind the cornea, perforated by the pupil; the most anterior portion of the vascular tunic of the eye, it is made up of a flat bar of circular muscular fibers surrounding the pupil, a thin layer of plain muscle fibers by which the pupil is dilated, and posteriorly of two layers of pigmented epithelial cells. 2. The rhizome of *Iris versicolor*, formerly considered purgative, emetic, and diuretic. **i. bombé,** a condition in which the iris is bowed

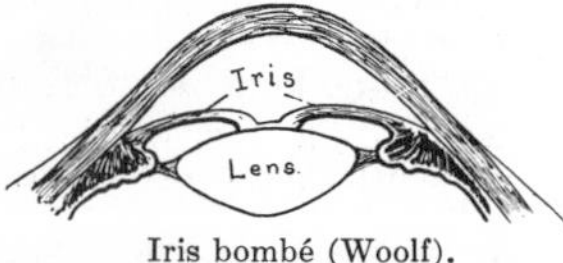

Iris bombé (Woolf).

forward by the collection of aqueous humor between the iris and lens in total posterior synechia. **Florentine i.,** orris root, the fragrant rhizome of *I. florentina* and other European species of iris: astringent, aromatic, and pectoral. **tremulous i.,** one characterized by abnormal tremulousness. See *iridodonesis*. **umbrella i.,** i. bombé.

irisin (i′rĭ-sin). A fructose polysaccharide $(C_6H_{10}O_5)_n$, from *Iris pseudo-acorus:* aperient and cholagogue.

irisopsia (i″ris-op′se-ah) [Gr. *iris* rainbow + *opsis* vision]. A visual defect in which objects appear surrounded by rings of colored light.

iritic (i-rit′ik). Pertaining to or of the nature of iritis.

iritis (i-ri′tis) [*iris* + *-itis*]. Inflammation of the iris, usually marked by pain, congestion in the ciliary region, photophobia, contraction of the pupil, and discoloration of the iris. **i. blennorrhagique à rechutes,** recurrent hypopyon. **i. catamenia′lis,** iritis recurring before each menstrual period. **diabetic i.,** iritis marked by the deposit of glycogen in diabetic patients. **follicular i.,** iritis marked by multiple small nodules the size of a pinhead. **gouty i.,** painful iritis occurring in gouty patients; uratic iritis. **i. papulo′sa,** iritis with papules in the iris; usually syphilitic. **plastic i.,** a variety in which the exudate consists of fibrinous matter which forms new tissue. **purulent i.,** iritis in which the exudate is purulent. **quiet i.,** iritis without pain or ciliary congestion. **i. recid′ivans staphylococco-aller′gica,** recurrent hypopyon. **serous i.,** iritis in which the exudate consists of serum. **spongy i.,** iritis with a fibrinous exudate, forming a spongy mass in the anterior chamber. **sympathetic i.,** a variety affecting a previously sound eye from sympathy with the other eye, which has been injured. **uratic i.,** gouty i.

iritoectomy (i″rĭ-to-ek′to-me) [*iris* + Gr. *ektomē* excision]. Removal of a portion of the iris.

iritomy (i-rit′o-me). Iridotomy.

irium (ir′e-um). Sodium lauryl sulfate.

iron (i′ern) [A. S. *iren;* L. *ferrum*]. A metallic element found in certain minerals, in nearly all soils, and in mineral waters: atomic number, 26; atomic weight, 55.847; specific gravity, 7.85–7.88; symbol, Fe. Iron occurs in the blood, especially in the hemoglobin, and is used to build up the blood in anemia. The compounds of iron are astringent and styptic. **i. acetate,** a compound, $Fe(C_2H_3O_2)_3$, used as an astringent. **alcoholized i.,** pulverized i. **i. alginate,** a tasteless, brown, insoluble powder; a salt especially valuable for its blandness and assimilability; a sedative and laxative tonic. **i. and ammonium citrate,** a substance in transparent garnet scales. **i. and ammonium sulfate,** $FeNH_4(SO_4)_2 + 12H_2O$; a powerful styptic. **i. and ammonium tartrate,** ammonio-tartrate of iron; a mild chalybeate. **i. and magnesium citrate,** a salt in greenish-yellow scales. **i. and potassium tartrate,** a salt, $C_4H_4O_6(FeO)K$, in brown, red, or garnet scales: a pleasant chalybeate. **i. and quinine citrate,** a preparation in dark greenish golden scales. **i. and strychnine citrate,** a bitter tonic substance in red scales. **i. arsenate,** ferrous arsenate, $Fe_3(AsO_4)_2.6H_2O$. **i. arsenite,** ferric arsenite, $4Fe_2O_3.As_2O_3.5H_2O$, a brownish-yellow powder, used in anemia and in pellagra. **i. ascorbate,** a compound which has been used intravenously in the treatment of anemia. **available i.,** that portion of iron in the food which can be separated from the total iron content by digestive processes. **i. benzoate,** an orange-brown powder, $Fe_26C_7H_5O_2 + 6H_2O$. **i. bromide,** a brick-red, deliquescent body, $FeBr_2$: tonic, alterative, and styptic. **i. carbonate,** a white, flocculent or crystalline salt, $FeCO_3$: readily convertible into ferric oxide. **i. caseinate,** i. nucleo-albuminate. **i. chloride,** an orange-colored, crystalline body, $FeCl_3 + 12H_2O$. **i. choline citrate,** ferrocholinate. **i. citrate,** $Fe_2(C_6H_5O_7)_2 + 6H_2O$: an agent in clear, garnet-colored scales. **i. citrate green,** a complex ferric ammonium citrate: used for intramuscular and subcutaneous injection. **dialyzed i.,** an aqueous solution of ferric oxychloride prepared by dialysis. **i. gluconate,** ferrous gluconate. **i. glycerophosphate,** a salt, $(CH_2OH.CHOH.CHO.PO_3)_3Fe_2$, in yellow plates or in a greenish-gray powder; a nerve tonic. **i. hydroxide,** the hydrated oxide of iron, $Fe(OH)_3$, a reddish-brown substance, used as an antidote in poisoning by arsenous acid. **i. hypophosphite,** $Fe(H_2PO_2)_3$: a white or grayish salt. **i. iodate,** $Fe_2O_3.2I_2O_5.8H_2O$: a tasteless compound claimed not to injure the teeth. **i. iodide,** FeI_2, in clear, greenish, deliquescent, tabular crystals: especially useful in scrofulous conditions. **i. iodobehanate,** an amorphous, reddish-brown powder, useful in scrofula, chlorosis, rachitis, etc. **i. lactate,** $Fe(C_3H_5O_3)_2.3H_2O$, a salt in minute, whitish-green crystals. **i. magnesium sulfate,** a greenish-white powder, $FeSO_4.MgSO_4 + 7H_2O$: used in anemia. **"masked" i.,** iron occurring in the form of a complexion. **i. nucleo-albuminate,** a tasteless preparation of casein and iron. **i. oleate,** a waxy solid; astringent and tonic. **i. oxalate,** $FeC_2O_4 + H_2O$; a yellowish, crystalline powder. **i. phosphate,** a compound of ferric and ferrous phosphates, Fe_22PO_4, $FePO_4 + 12H_2O$. **i. phosphate, soluble,** ferric phosphate rendered soluble by sodium citrate. **i. protosulfate,** ferrous sulfate. **pulverized i.,** metallic iron mechanically powdered. **i. pyrophosphate,** $Fe_4(P_2O_7)_3$. **Quevenne's i.,** reduced iron. **reduced i.,** finely powdered metallic iron obtained by precipitation with hydrogen from a solution of the oxide or carbonate. **i. subcarbonate,** an amorphous, brownish powder, consisting mainly of iron hydroxide. **i. subsulfate,** a compound, $Fe_4O(SO_4)_5$: in reddish-brown, transparent scales or in an amorphous mass; a powerful styptic. **i. succinate,** a green-gray substance: said to be useful in cholelithiasis. **i. sulfate,** $FeSO_4 + 7H_2O$: an astringent tonic; used also as a deodorizer and disinfectant. **i. tannate,** a salt in crimson scales or plates. **i. valerianate,** a dark red, amorphous powder, $Fe_2(C_5H_9O_2)_6$: tonic and sedative. **i. vitellinate,** a therapeutical preparation of egg yolk and iron. See *oviferrin*.

ironate (i′ron-āt). Trade mark for a preparation of ferrous sulfate.

irosul (i′ro-sul). Trade mark for various preparations of ferrous sulfate.

irotomy (i-rot′o-me). Iridotomy.

irradiate (ir-ra′de-āt). To treat with roentgen rays or other form of radioactivity.

irradiation (ir-ra″de-a′shun) [L. *in* into + *radiare* to emit rays]. 1. A phenomenon in which, owing to the difference in the illumination of the field of vision, objects appear to be much larger than they really are. 2. Treatment by roentgen rays or other form of radioactivity. 3. The dispersion of a nervous impulse beyond the normal path of conduction. 4. The application of rays, such as ultraviolet rays, to a substance to increase its vitamin efficiency. **interstitial i.,** therapeutical irradiation by the insertion into the tissues of capillary tubes of glass, gold or platinum containing radium or radon. **Medinger-Craver i.,** irradiation of the entire body.

irreducible (ir″re-dūs′ĭ-b′l). Not susceptible of being reduced.

irregular (ir-reg′u-lar) [L. *in* not + *regula* rule]. Not in conformity with the rule of nature; not recurring at regular intervals.

irregularity (ir-reg″u-lar′ĭ-te). The quality of not conforming with the rule of nature, or of not occurring at regular intervals. **i. of pulse,** arrhythmia.

irreinoculability (ir″re-in-ok″u-lah-bil′ĭ-te). Immunity due to the effects of a previous inoculation beyond the possibility of successful reinoculation.

irrespirable (ir″re-spīr′ah-b′l). Not possible of being breathed with safety.

irresuscitable (ir″re-sus′ĭ-tah-b′l). Beyond the possibility of being revived.

irreversibility (ir″re-ver″sĭ-bil′ĭ-te). The quality of being incapable of being reversed. **i. of conduction,** the principle that the pathway for every reflex permits passage of the nerve impulse in one direction only.

irreversible (ir″re-ver′sĭ-b′l). Incapable of being reversed; not capable of recovery.

irrigate (ir′ĭ-gāt). To wash out.

irrigation (ir″ĭ-ga′shun) [L. *irrigatio; in* into + *rigare* to carry water]. Washing by a stream of water or other fluid. **continuous i.,** the steady maintenance of a stream of water over an inflamed surface. **mediate i.,** the passing of a stream of hot or cold water through a flexible tube coiled around a part.

irrigator (ir′ĭ-ga″tor) [L. "waterer"]. An apparatus for performing irrigation.

irrigoradioscopy (ir″ĭ-go-ra″de-os′ko-pe). Roentgenoscopy of the intestines during the introduction of a contrast enema.

irrigoscopy (ir″ĭ-gos′ko-pe). Irrigoradioscopy.

irritability (ir″ĭ-tah-bil′ĭ-te) [L. *irritabilitas*, from *irritare* to tease]. 1. The quality of being irritable or of responding to stimuli. 2. Abnormal responsiveness to slight stimuli. **i. of the bladder,** a condition in which the presence of a small amount of urine in the bladder produces a desire to urinate. **chemical i.,** responsiveness to a stimulus that acts by producing a chemical change in the tissues. **electric i.,** responsiveness of nerve or muscle to the stimulus of an electric current passed through it. **faradic i.,** muscular responsiveness to faradic currents. **galvanic i.,** a condition in which a galvanic current will cause a muscular response. **mechanical i.,** responsiveness to a mechanical stimulus. **muscular i.,** the normal contractile quality of muscular tissue. **myotatic i.,** the power of a muscle to contract in response to stretching. **nervous i.** 1. The ability of a nerve to transmit impulses. 2. Morbid excitability of the nervous system. **specific i.** See *law of specific irritability*. **i. of the stomach,** a condition of the stomach in which vomiting is caused by normal amounts of digestible food. **tactile i.,** a condition of cells that repels foreign particles; negative chemotaxis.

irritable (ir′ĭ-tah-b′l) [L. *irritabilis; irritare* to tease]. 1. Capable of reacting to a stimulus. 2. Abnormally sensitive to a stimulus.

irritant (ir′ĭ-tant) [L. *irritans*]. 1. Giving rise to irritation. 2. An agent that produces irritation.

irritation (ir″ĭ-ta′shun) [L. *irritatio*]. 1. The act of stimulating. 2. A state of overexcitation and undue sensitiveness. **cerebral i.,** the second stage of brain concussion. **direct i.,** irritation due to direct stimulation of a part. **functional i.,** that which is attended with functional derangement without organic lesion; also overexcitability due to excessive functional activity. **spinal i.,** any condition of functional derangement and nervous irritability accompanied by tenderness along the spinal column.

irritative (ir′ĭ-ta″tiv). Dependent on or caused by irritation.

Irukandji sting (ir″u-kan′je) [*Irukandji*, an aboriginal tribe in the vicinity of Cairns, Queensland, Australia]. See under *sting*.

IRV. Abbreviation for *inspiratory reserve volume*.

I.S. Abbreviation for *intercostal space*.

isaconatine (i″sah-kon′ah-tēn). Benzaconine.

Isambert's disease (e-zahm-bārz′) [Emile *Isambert*, French physician, 1828–1876]. See under *disease*.

isatin (i′sah-tin). A crystalline compound, $C_8H_5O_2N$, in the form of yellowish red crystals, soluble in alcohol and ether, slightly soluble in water: used as a reagent.

isauxesis (is″awk-se′sis) [Gr. *isos* equal + *auxēsis* increase]. Growth of a part or parts at the same rate as the growth of the whole.

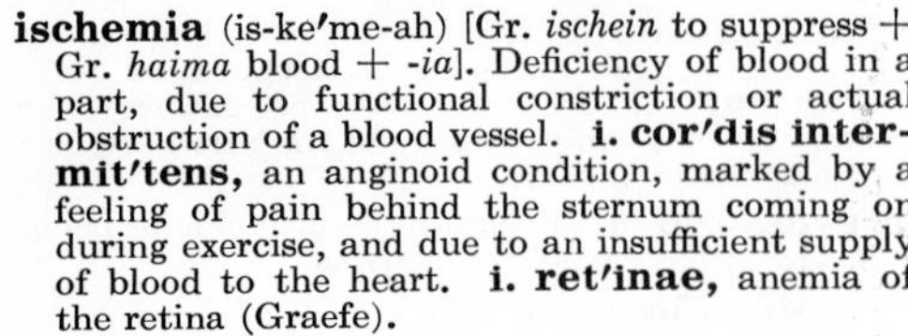

ischemia (is-ke′me-ah) [Gr. *ischein* to suppress + Gr. *haima* blood + *-ia*]. Deficiency of blood in a part, due to functional constriction or actual obstruction of a blood vessel. **i. cor′dis intermit′tens,** an anginoid condition, marked by a feeling of pain behind the sternum coming on during exercise, and due to an insufficient supply of blood to the heart. **i. ret′inae,** anemia of the retina (Graefe).

ischemic (is-kem′ik). Pertaining to, or affected with, ischemia.

ischesis (is-ke′sis) [Gr. *ischein* to suppress]. Retention or suppression of a discharge.

ischia (is′ke-ah). Plural of *ischium.*

ischiac (is′ke-ak). Ischiatic.

ischiadelphus (is″ke-ah-del′fus) [*ischio-* + Gr. *adelphos* brother]. Ischiodidymus.

ischiadic (is″ke-ad′ik). Ischiatic.

ischialgia (is″ke-al′je-ah) [*ischio-* + *-algia*]. Pain in the hip.

ischias (is′ke-as). Ischialgia.

ischiatic (is″ke-at′ik) [L. *ischiaticus*]. Pertaining to the ischium or to the haunch.

ischiatitis (is″ke-ah-ti′tis). Inflammation of the ischiatic nerve.

ischidrosis (is″kid-ro′sis) [Gr. *ischein* to suppress + *hidrōs* sweat + *-osis*]. Suppression of the secretion of sweat.

ischio- (is′ke-o) [Gr. *ischion* hip]. Combining form denoting relationship to the ischium, or to the hip.

ischioanal (is″ke-o-a′nal) [*ischio-* + *anus*]. Pertaining to ischium and anus.

ischiobulbar (is″ke-o-bul′bar) [*ischio-* + L. *bulbus* bulb]. Pertaining to the ischium and the bulb of the urethra.

ischiocapsular (is″ke-o-kap′su-lar) [*ischio-* + L. *capsula* capsule]. Pertaining to the ischium and the capsular ligament of the hip joint.

ischiocele (is′ke-o-sēl) [*ischio-* + Gr. *kēlē* hernia]. Hernia through the sacrosciatic notch.

ischiococcygeal (is″ke-o-kok-sij′e-al). Pertaining to the ischium and coccyx.

ischiococcygeus (is″ke-o-kok-sij′e-us) [*ischio-* + Gr. *kokkyx* coccyx]. 1. The coccygeus muscle. 2. The posterior part of the levator ani.

ischiodidymus (is″ke-o-did′ĭ-mus) [*ischio-* + Gr. *didymos* twin]. Symmetrical conjoined twins united at the pelvis.

ischiodymia (is″ke-o-dim′e-ah) [*ischio-* + Gr. *didymos* twin + *-ia*]. The condition of symmetrical conjoined twins united at the pelvis.

ischiodynia (is″ke-o-din′e-ah) [*ischio-* + Gr. *odynē* pain]. Ischialgia.

ischiofemoral (is″ke-o-fem′o-ral) [*ischio-* + *femur*]. Pertaining to the ischium and femur.

ischiofibular (is″ke-o-fib′u-lar). Pertaining to the ischium and the fibula.

ischiohebotomy (is″ke-o-he-bot′o-me) [*ischio-* + Gr. *hēbē* pubes + *temnein* to cut]. The operation of dividing the ischiopubic ramus and the ascending ramus of the pubes.

ischiomelus (is″ke-om′e-lus) [*ischio-* + Gr. *melos* limb]. A fetal monster with an extra limb attached at the base of the spine.

ischiomenia (is″ke-o-me′ne-ah). Ischomenia.

ischioneuralgia (is″ke-o-nu-ral′je-ah) [*ischio-* + *neuralgia*]. Neuralgia of the hip; sciatica.

ischionitis (is″ke-o-ni′tis). Inflammation of the tuberosity of the ischium.

ischiopagia (is″ke-o-pa′je-ah). The condition exhibited by an ischiopagus.

ischiopagus (is-ke-op′ah-gus) [*ischio-* + Gr. *pagos* thing fixed]. Conjoined twins fused at the ischia, the axes of the two bodies extending in a straight line but in opposite directions.

Ischiopagus.

ischiopagy (is″ke-op′ah-je). Ischiopagia.

ischioperineal (is″ke-o-per″ĭ-ne′al). Pertaining to the ischium and perineum.

ischiopubic (is″ke-o-pu′bik). Pertaining to the ischium and pubis.

ischiopubiotomy (is″ke-o-pu″be-ot′o-me). Obstetrical division of the ischiopubic and horizontal branches of the os pubis.

ischiorectal (is″ke-o-rek′tal). Pertaining to the ischium and rectum.

ischiosacral (is″ke-o-sa′kral). Pertaining to the ischium and sacrum.

ischiothoracopagus (is″ke-o-tho″rah-kop′ah-gus). Iliothoracopagus.

ischiovaginal (is″ke-o-vaj′ĭ-nal). Pertaining to the ischium and vagina.

ischiovertebral (is″ke-o-ver′te-bral). Pertaining to the ischium and the vertebral column.

ischium (is′ke-um), pl. *is′chia* [L.; Gr. *ischion* hip]. The inferior dorsal part of the hip bone. It is a separate bone in early life. Called also *os ischii* [N A].

ischo- (is′ko) [Gr. *ischein* to suppress]. Combining form meaning suppressed, or denoting relationship to suppression.

ischocholia (is″ko-ko′le-ah) [*ischo-* + Gr. *cholē* bile + *-ia*]. Suppression of bile.

ischochymia (is″ko-kim′e-ah) [*ischo-* + Gr. *chymos* chyme + *-ia*]. Suppression of gastric digestion; Einhorn's term for dilatation of the stomach, so called because stagnation of the food is the essential symptom of the disease.

ischogalactic (is″ko-gah-lak′tik) [*ischo-* + Gr. *gala* milk]. 1. Suppressing the secretion of milk. 2. An agent which suppresses the secretion of milk.

ischogyria (is″ko-ji′re-ah) [*ischo-* + *gyrus*]. A condition in which the cerebral convolutions have a jagged appearance: seen in bulbar sclerosis.

ischomenia (is″ko-me′ne-ah) [*ischo-* + Gr. *mēniaia* menses]. Suppression of the menses.

ischuretic (is″ku-ret′ik). Pertaining to ischuria.

ischuria (is-ku′re-ah) [*ischo-* + Gr. *ouron* urine + *-ia*]. Suppression or retention of the urine. **i. paradox′a,** a condition in which the bladder is overdistended with urine, although the patient continues to urinate. **i. spas′tica,** ischuria caused by spasm of the sphincter urinae.

iseiconia (īs″i-ko′ne-ah). Iso-iconia.

iseiconic (īs″i-kon′ik). Iso-iconic.

iseikonia (is″i-ko′ne-ah). Iso-iconia.

Ishihara's test (ish″ĭ-hah′rahz) [Shinobu *Ishihara,* Japanese ophthalmologist, born 1879]. See under *tests.*

Isidora (i″sĭ-do′rah). A genus of snails, species of which are intermediate hosts of *Schistosoma.*

isinglass (i′sin-glas). Ichthyocolla. **Japanese i.,** agar.

island (i′land). A cluster of cells or an isolated piece of tissue. Cf. *islet.* **blood i's,** aggregations of mesenchyme cells in the angioblast of the early embryo, which develop into vascular endothelium and blood corpuscles. **i's of Calleja.** See under *islet.* **cartilage i's.** See *intrachondrial bone,* under *bone.* **i's of Langerhans,** irregular structures in the pancreas composed of cells smaller than the ordinary secreting cells. These masses of cells produce an internal secretion, insulin, which is connected with the metabolism of carbohydrates, and their degeneration is one of the causes of diabetes. **olfactory i's,** masses of distorted pyramidal cells in the gray matter of the olfactory portion of the brain. **Pander's i's,** reddish-yellow cords of corpuscular matter in the splanchnopleure of the embryo which develop into blood and blood vessels. **i. of Reil,** insula.

islet (i′let). A cluster of cells or an isolated piece of tissue. Cf. *island.* **blood i's.** See under *island.* **Calleja's i's,** masses of pyramidal and stellate cells in the cortex of the gyrus hippocampi. **i's of Langerhans.** See under *island.* **Walthard's i's,** rests of squamous epithelium in the ovary to which is attributed the development of Brenner tumor.

-ism (iz'm) [Gr. *-izō* + *-mos*]. Word termination meaning state, condition, or fact of being, or the process or result of an action.

ismelin (is′me-lin). Trade mark for a preparation of guanethidine.

iso- (i′so) [Gr. *isos* equal]. A prefix or combining form meaning equal, alike, or the same. In bacteriology, it indicates *from* individuals of the same species. In chemistry, it signifies *isomeric with* another compound.

isoadrenocorticism (i″so-ad-re″no-kōr′tĭ-sizm). The normal state of secretion of the cells of the adrenal cortex, as distinguished from hypo- or hyperadrenocorticism.

isoagglutination (i″so-ah-gloo″tĭ-na′shun). Isohemagglutination.

isoagglutinin (i″so-ah-gloo′tĭ-nin). Isohemagglutinin.

isoamyl nitrite (i″so-am′il ni-trīt). Amyl nitrite.

isoamylamine (i″so-am″il-am′in). A liquid ptomaine, $(CH_3)_2CH.CH_2CH_2NH_2$, obtainable from stale yeast, cod liver oil, and other sources, especially the distillation of horn with potassium hydroxide. Leucine by the loss of CO_2 becomes isoamylamine.

isoanaphylaxis (i″so-an″ah-fi-lak′sis). Anaphylaxis produced by the administration of serum from the same species, as in man by the administration of human serum.

isoandrosterone (i″so-an-dro′stēr-ōn). An androgenic steroid, 3 (3 beta-hydroxyetho-allocholane-17-one), isolated from some adrenal cortical tumors.

isoantibody (i-so-an′tĭ-bod″e). An antibody combining with an antigen present in tissues of some but not all individuals of the same species as the antibody producer.

isoantigen (i″so-an′tĭ-jen). An antigen present in tissues of some but not all individuals of the same species as the antibody producer. The best known isoantigens are the blood group antigens of man and animals.

isobar (i′so-bar) [*iso-* + Gr. *baros* weight]. 1. One of two or more chemical species with the same atomic weight but different atomic numbers. 2. A line on a map or chart depicting the boundaries of an area in which the atmospheric pressure is the same.

isobaric (i″so-bār′ik) [*iso-* + Gr. *baros* weight]. See under *solution.*

isobody (i′so-bod″e). An antibody which is active for antigens of other animals of the same species as the animal from which it is derived.

isobolism (i-sob′o-lizm) [*iso-* + Gr. *ballein* to throw]. The tendency of motor nerve fibers to undergo maximal excitation on stimulation.

isobornyl thiocyanoacetate (i″so-bor′nil thi″o-si″ah-no-as′e-tāt). Chemical name: terpinyl thiocyanoacetate: used as a pediculicide.

isobutanol (i″so-bu′tah-nol″). Isobutyl alcohol.

isocaloric (i″so-kah-lo′rik). Containing or providing the same number of calories; equicaloric.

isocarboxazid (i″so-kar-bok′sah-zid). Chemical name: 1-benzyl-2-(5-methyl-3-isoxazolylcarbonyl)-hydrazine: used as a psychic energizer, and to reduce pain of angina pectoris.

isocellobiose (i″so-sel″o-bi′ōs). A disaccharide formed in the degradation of cellulose.

isocellular (i″so-sel′u-lar) [*iso-* + L. *cellula* cell]. Composed of cells of the same kind and size.

isocholesterin (i″so-ko-les′ter-in). Isocholesterol.

isocholesterol (i″so-ko-les′ter-ol). 1. An isomeric form of cholesterol found in lanolin. 2. Phrenosterol.

isochromatic (i″so-kro-mat′ik) [*iso-* + Gr. *chrōma* color]. Of the same color throughout.

isochromatophil (i″so-kro-mat′o-fil) [*iso-* + Gr. *chrōma* color + *philein* to love]. Staining equally with the same dye.

isochromosome (i″so-kro′mo-sōm). A chromosome in which the two arms are exact duplicates.

isochron (i′so-kron). Having equal chronaxie.

isochronal (i-sok′ro-nal). Isochronous.

isochronia (i-so-kro′ne-ah). 1. A condition of correspondence between processes with respect to their time, rate, or frequency. 2. The condition of having the same chronaxie as between a muscle and its nerve.

isochronic (i″so-kron′ik). Isochronous.

isochronism (i-sok′ro-nizm). Isochronia.

isochronous (i-sok′ro-nus) [*iso-* + Gr. *chronos* time]. Performed in equal times: said of vibrations of one thing that take place at the same time and continue as long as those in another.

isochroous (i-sok′ro-us) [*iso-* + Gr. *chroa* color]. Isochromatic.

isocolloid (i-so-kol′oid). A colloid having the same composition in both phases—the disperse phase and the dispersion medium.

isocomplement (i″so-kom′plĕ-ment). A complement from the same individual, or one of the same species, which furnishes the amboceptor.

isocomplementophilic (i″so-kom″plĕ-men-to-fil′ik). Having affinity for isocomplements.

isocoria (i″so-ko′re-ah) [*iso-* + Gr. *korē* pupil]. Equality in size of the two pupils.

isocortex (i″so-kor′teks). That portion of the cerebral cortex which is made up of the layers, six in number, which develop between the sixth and eighth fetal months. Cf. *allocortex.*

isocreatinine (i″so-kre-at′ĭ-nin). A base similar to creatinine found in the muscle of fish.

isocyanide (i″so-si′ah-nid). One of a class of organic cyanides characterized by their disagreeable odor and formed by heating silver cyanide with alkyl iodides. Called also *carbylamine.*

isocyclic (i″so-si′klik) [*iso-* + Gr. *kyklos* circle]. Homocyclic.

isocytolysine (i″so-si-tol′ĭ-sin) [*iso-* + *cytolysine*]. A cytolysine which acts on the cells of animals of the same species as that from which it is derived.

isocytosis (i″so-si-to′sis) [*iso-* + *-cyte* + *-osis*]. Equality of the size of cells, especially red blood corpuscles.

isocytotoxin (i″so-si″to-tok′sin). A cytotoxin which is toxic for homologous cells of the same species.

isodactylism (i-so-dak′til-izm) [*iso-* + Gr. *daktylos* finger + *-ism*]. A condition in which the fingers are of relatively even length.

isodiagnosis (i″so-di″ag-no′sis). Diagnosis of a condition by inoculation of a susceptible animal with blood from a patient suspected of having an inapparent infection.

isodiametric (i″so-di″ah-met′rik) [*iso-* + Gr. *dia* through + *metron* measure]. Having the same diameter in all directions.

isodispersoid (i″so-dis-per′soid). Isocolloid.

isodontic (i″so-don′tik) [*iso-* + Gr. *odous* tooth]. Having all the teeth of the same size and shape.

isodulcite (i″so-dul′sīt). Rhamnose.

isodynamic (i″so-di-nam′ik) [*iso-* + Gr. *dynamis* power]. Exhibiting equal force or power.

isodynamogenic (i″so-di-nam″o-jen′ik) [*iso-* + Gr. *dynamis* power + *gennan* to produce]. Producing equal force or power.

iso-electric (i″so-e-lek′trik) [*iso-* + *electric*]. Uniformly electric throughout, or having the same electric potential, and hence giving off no current.

iso-energetic (i″so-en″er-jet′ik). Exhibiting equal energy.

isoenzyme (i″so-en′zīm). One of the multiple forms in which a protein catalyst may exist in a single species, the various forms differing chemically, physically, and/or immunologically. Called also *isozyme.*

isoflurophate (i″so-floo′ro-fāt). Chemical name: diisopropyl fluorophosphate: used as an anticholinesterase inhibitor, and as a miotic in glaucoma.

isogame (i-sog′ah-me). Isogamy.

isogamete (i″so-gam′ēt). A gamete of the same size as the gamete with which it unites.

isogamous (i-sog′ah-mus). Having the conjugating elements similar and equal in all respects.

isogamy (i-sog′ah-me) [*iso-* + Gr. *gamos* marriage]. Reproduction resulting from the union of two cells (gametes) that are identical in size and structure, as occurs in protozoa.

isogeneric (i″so-je-ner′ik). Of the same kind; pertaining to or obtained from individuals of the same genus.

isogenesis (i″so-jen′e-sis) [*iso-* + Gr. *genesis* production]. Similarity in the processes of development.

isogenous (i-soj′e-nus). Developed from the same cell.

isograft (i′so-graft). A graft of tissue obtained from the body of another individual of the same genotype as the recipient.

isohemagglutination (i″so-hem″ah-gloo″tĭ-na′shun). Agglutination of erythrocytes caused by a hemagglutinin from another individual of the same species.

isohemagglutinin (i″so-hem″ah-gloo′tĭ-nin). A hemagglutinin that agglutinates the erythrocytes of other individuals of the same species.

isohemolysin (i″so-he-mol′ĭ-sin) [*iso-* + *hemolysin*]. A hemolysin which acts on the blood of animals of the same species as that from which it is derived.

isohemolysis (i″so-he-mol′ĭ-sis). Hemolysis of the blood corpuscles of an animal by the serum from another animal of the same species.

isohemolytic (i″so-he″mo-lit′ik). Pertaining to or characterized by isohemolysis.

isohydria (i″so-hi′dre-ah) [*iso-* + Gr. *hydōr* water + *-ia*]. Water equilibrium in the body.

isohydric (i″so-hi′drik). A term applied to the series or cycle of chemical reactions in the erythrocyte in which carbon dioxide is take up and oxygen released without the production of an excess of hydrogen.

isohypercytosis (i″so-hi″per-si-to′sis) [*iso-* + Gr. *hyper* over + *-cyte* + *-osis*]. Increase in the number of leukocytes, with normal proportion of neutrophil cells.

isohypocytosis (i″so-hi″po-si-to′sis) [*iso-* + Gr. *hypo* under + *-cyte* + *-osis*]. Decrease in the number of leukocytes, with normal relation between the number of the various forms.

iso-iconia (i″so-i-ko′ne-ah) [*iso-* + Gr. *eikōn* image]. A condition in which the image of an object is the same in both eyes.

iso-iconic (i″so-i-kon′ik). Marked by iso-iconia.

iso-immunization (i″so-im″u-ni-za′shun). Development of antibodies against an antigen derived from an individual of the same species. **Rh i.,** the development of anti-Rh agglutinins in an Rh− person in response to transfusion of Rh+ blood or to being pregnant with an Rh+ fetus.

iso-ionia (i″so-i-o′ne-ah). Constancy of the ionic concentration of a solution.

isokreatinin (i″so-kre-at′ĭ-nin). A ptomaine from decaying fish, crystallizable in a yellow powder, $C_4H_7N_3O$.

isolactose (i″so-lak′tōs). A disaccharide formed from lactose by the action of an enzyme.

isolate (i′so-lāt). 1. To separate from other persons, materials, or objects. 2. A population or other material that has been obtained by isolation, such as living organisms (bacteria or other cells) obtained in pure culture, or (higher organisms) separated by geographical, genetic, ecological, or social barriers which prevent their interbreeding with other individuals beyond those barriers, and so differentiated from others of their kind by the accumulation of new characteristics.

isolateral (i″so-lat′er-al). 1. Equilateral. 2. Ipsilateral.

isolation (i″so-la′shun). The process of isolating, or the state of being isolated, such as (*a*) the physiologic separation of a part, as by tissue culture or by interposition of inert material; (*b*) the separation from contact with others of patients having a communicable disease; or (*c*) the successive propagation of a growth of microorganisms until a pure culture is obtained.

isolecithal (i″so-les′ĭ-thal) [*iso-* + *lekithos* yolk]. Having a small amount of yolk evenly distributed throughout the cyloplasm of the ovum.

isoleucine (i″so-lu′sin). An amino acid, ethylmethyl-alpha-amino-propionic acid, $CH_3(C_2H_5)$.-CHCH(NH_2).COOH, a decomposition product of fibrin and other proteins: essential for optimal growth in infants and for nitrogen equilibrium in human adults.

isoleukocytosis (i″so-lu″ko-si-to′sis). Leukocytosis with normal distribution of leukocytes in the blood picture.

isologous (i-sol′o-gus). Characterized by an identical genotype. See *isograft.*

isolophobia (i″so-lo-fo′be-ah) [*isolation* + *phobia*]. Abnormal dread of being alone.

isolysin (i-sol′ĭ-sin). Isohemolysin.

isolysis (i-sol′ĭ-sis). Isohemolysis.

isolytic (i″so-lit′ik). Pertaining to isolysis.

isomaltose (i″so-mawl′tōs). An isomeric form of maltose formed by treating glucose with strong acids or by the action of maltase on glucose. It occurs in beer, urine, blood, honey, liver and other natural substances.

isomastigote (i″so-mas′tĭ-gōt) [*iso-* + Gr. *mastix* lash]. Having two equal and similar flagella at the anterior pole.

isomer (i′so-mer) [*iso-* + Gr. *meros* part]. Any compound exhibiting, or capable of exhibiting, isomerism.

isomerase (i-som′er-ās). An enzyme that catalyzes the process of isomerization, such as the interconversion of aldoses and ketoses.

isomeric (i″so-mer′ik). Pertaining to or exhibiting isomerism.

isomeride (i-som′er-īd). Isomer.

isomerism (i-som′er-izm) [*iso-* + Gr. *meros* part]. The possession by two or more distinct compounds of the same molecular formula, each molecule possessing an identical number of atoms of each element, but in different arrangement. Isomerism is divided into two broad classifications: *structural isomerism* and *stereochemical isomerism,* or *stereoisomerism.* **chain i.,** a type of structural isomerism in which the compounds differ in regard to the linkages in the basic chain of carbon atoms. See illustration. **dynamic i.,** tautomerism. **functional group i.,** a type of structural isomerism dependent upon the presence of different functional groups, such compounds being of distinct chemical types. For example, ethyl alcohol, C_2H_5OH, and dimethyl ether, CH_3OCH_3. **geometric i.,** a type of stereoisomerism usually described as being dependent upon some form of restricted rotation, enabling the component parts of the molecule to occupy different spatial positions. Thus, *cis-* and *trans-*dichloroethylene are said to be geometric isomers, the isomerism resulting from the lack of freedom of rotation about the

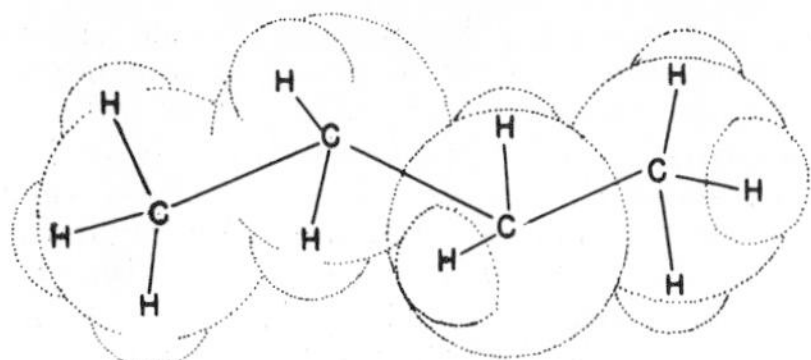

Normal butane

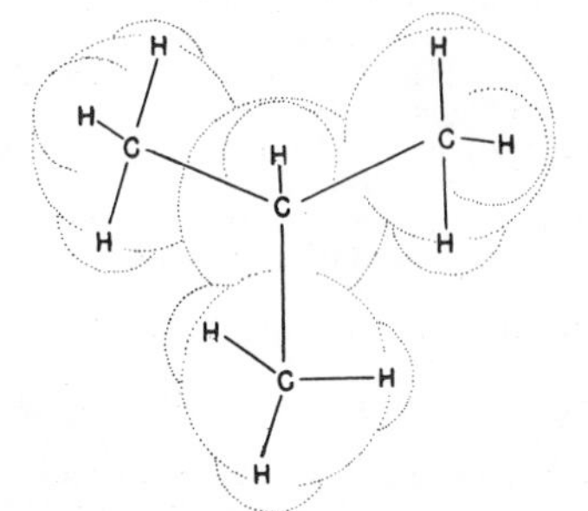

Isobutane

Chain isomerism. (Luder, Vernon, and Zuffanti.)

double bond. In the case of *cis-* and *trans-*decalin, however, the rigidity of the fused ring structure is responsible for the isomerism. **nuclear i.,** chain i. **optical i.,** a type of stereoisomerism in which an appreciable number of molecules exhibit any of the following effects on polarized light: the isomers (*a*) rotate the plane of polarization to the *same* degree in *opposite* directions (enantiomorphism); or the isomers (*b*) rotate the plane of polarization to a *different* degree in either the same direction or in opposite directions, or (*c*) have no effect on the plane because of so-called internal compensation (diastereoisomerism). **position i.,** a type of structural isomerism in which the position occupied by an atom or group differs with reference to the same fundamental carbon chain. For example, *n*-propyl chloride, $CH_3CH_2CH_2Cl$, and isopropyl chloride, $CH_3CHClCH_3$. **spatial i.,** stereoisomerism. **stereochemical i.,** stereoisomerism. **structural i.,** the possession by two or more compounds of the same molecular formula but of different structural formulas, the linkages of the atoms being different, in contrast to stereoisomerism, in which the structural arrangements of the atoms are the same. **substitution i.,** position i.

isomerization (i-som″er-i-za′shun). The process whereby any isomer, whether structural or spatial, is converted into another, usually requiring special conditions of temperature, pressure, or catalysts.

isometheptene (i″so-meth′ep-tēn). Chemical name: 2-methylamino-6-methyl-5-heptene: used as a sympathomimetic and antispasmodic.

isometric (i″so-met′rik) [*iso-* + Gr. *metron* measure]. 1. Of equal dimensions. 2. Not isotonic.

isometropia (i″so-me-tro′pe-ah) [*iso-* + Gr. *metron* measure + *ōps* eye]. Equality in the refraction of the two eyes.

isomicrogamete (i″so-mi″kro-gam′ēt) [*iso-* + *microgamete*]. A protozoan sexual cell or gamete of a small size, but equal in size to the gamete with which it conjugates.

isomorphic (i″so-mor′fik). Isomorphous.

isomorphism (i″so-mor′fizm) [*iso-* + Gr. *morphē* form]. The quality of being isomorphous.

isomorphous (i″so-mor′fus) [*iso-* + Gr. *morphē* form]. Having the same form. In genetics, referring to genotypes of polyploid organisms which produce similar gametes even though containing genes in different combinations on homologous chromosomes.

isomuscarine (i″so-mus′kah-rin). A basic substance formed by oxidizing choline. It is isomeric with muscarine, but has different physiologic properties.

isonaphthol (i″so-naf′thol). Betanaphthol.

isonephrotoxin (i″so-nef″ro-tok′sin) [*iso-* + *nephrotoxin*]. A nephrotoxin which acts on cells of the animals of the same species from which it is derived.

isoniazid (i″so-ni′ah-zid). An odorless compound, isonicotinic acid hydrazide, occurring in colorless or white crystals or as a white crystalline powder: used in treatment of tuberculosis.

isonicotinoylhydrazine (i″so-nik″o-tin″o-il-hi′-drah-zēn). Isoniazid.

isonicotinylhydrazine (i″so-nik″o-tin″il-hi′-drah-zēn). Isoniazid.

isonipecaine (i″so-nip′e-kān). Meperidine.

isonitril (i″so-ni′tril). Isocyanide.

isonormocytosis (i″so-nor″mo-si-to′sis). The condition in which the leukocytes of the blood are normal, both in actual number and in the relative proportion of the various sorts. Called also *dinormocytosis* and *normonormocytosis.*

iso-oncotic (i″so-on-kot′ik). Having the same oncotic pressure.

iso-osmotic (i″so-oz-mot′ik). Isosmotic.

Isoparoichis trisimilitubis (i″so-par-oi′kis tri-sim″ĭ-li-tu′bis). A fluke, commonly parasitic in the air bladder of fish in India and China and sometimes found in man.

isopathy (i-sop′ah-the) [*iso-* + Gr. *pathos* disease]. The treatment of disease by means of products of the disease or with the organ affected, e.g., smallpox by giving minute doses of variolous matter, disease of the liver by giving extract of liver, etc.

isopatin (i-sop′ah-tin). An immunizing agent of animal origin which gives no biuret reaction and yet is active in small amounts.

isopepsin (i″so-pep′sin). Pepsin modified by heat.

isophagy (i-sof′ah-je) [*iso-* + Gr. *phagein* to eat]. Autolysis.

isophan (i′so-fan) [*iso-* + Gr. *phainein* to show]. A hybrid which looks like other hybrids, but yet has a different germinal constitution.

isophenolization (i″so-fe″nol-i-za′shun). The injection of isophenol to produce paralysis or destruction of a sympathetic nerve.

isophoria (i″so-fo′re-ah) [*iso-* + Gr. *phoros* bearing + *-ia*]. Equality in the tension of the vertical muscles of each eye; absence of hyperphoria and of hypophoria.

isophrin (i′so-frin). Trade mark for a preparation of phenylephrine.

isopia (i-so′pe-ah) [*iso-* + Gr. *ōps* vision]. Equality of vision in the two eyes.

isoplassont (i″so-plas′ont) [*iso-* + Gr. *plassein* to form]. Either of two things which have certain features in common.

isoplastic (i″so-plas′tik) [*iso-* + *plastic*]. Taken from another animal of the same species: said of tissue transplants or grafts.

isoprecipitin (i″so-pre-sip′ĭ-tin). A precipitin which is active against the serum of animals of the same species as the animal from which it is derived.

isopregnenone (i″so-preg′ne-nōn). Chemical name: 9-β,10α-pregna-4,6-diene,3,20-dione: used as a progestational agent, and as a test of pregnancy.

isoprenaline (i″so-pren′ah-lēn). Isoproterenol.

isopressor (i′so-pres″or). Having the ability to raise the blood pressure to the same extent.

isopropamide (i″so-pro′pah-mīd). Chemical name: (3-carbamoyl-3,3-diphenylpropyl)diisopropylmethylammonium: used in parasympathetic blockade, and as an antispasmodic.

isopropanol (i″so-pro′pah-nol). Isopropyl alcohol.

isopropyl (i″so-pro′pil). The univalent radical, $(CH_3)_2CH$.

isopropylarterenol (i″so-pro″pil-ar″tě-re′nol). Isoproterenol.

isopropyl-benzanthracene (i″so-pro″pil-benz-an′thrah-sēn). 6-isopropyl 1:2-benzanthracene, a carcinogenic hydrocarbon.

isopropyl meprobamate (i″so-pro′pil mep″ro-bam′āt). Carisoprodol.

isoproterenol (i″so-pro″tě-re′nol). Chemical name: α-(isopropylaminomethyl)-3,4-dihydroxy-benzyl alcohol: used as a sympathomimetic, cardiac stimulant, and antispasmodic, and in relief of bronchospasm.

isopter (i-sop′ter) [*iso-* + Gr. *optēr* observer]. A line depicting the area in the field of vision in which the visual acuity is the same.

isopyknosis (i″so-pik-no′sis) [*iso-* + Gr. *pyknōsis* condensation]. The state of being of uniform density; applied especially to a state of uniform condensation observed in comparison of different chromosomes, or of different regions of the same chromosome.

isopyknotic (i″so-pik-not′ik). Pertaining to or characterized by isopyknosis.

isordil (i′sor-dil). Trade mark for preparations of isosorbide dinitrate.

isorhodeose (i″so-ro′de-ōs). A sugar, *d*-glucomethylose, $CH_2(CHOH)_4CHO$, from cinchona bark.

isoriboflavin (i″so-ri″bo-fla′vin). A compound, dichlororibityl isoalloxazine, which can produce riboflavin deficiency.

isorrhea (i″so-re′ah) [*iso-* + Gr. *rhein* to flow]. A steady equilibrium between the intake and output, by the body, of water and/or solutes.

isorrheic (i″so-re′ik). Pertaining to or characterized by isorrhea.

isorrhopic (i″so-rop′ik) [*iso-* + Gr. *rhopē* momentum]. Of equal value.

isorubin (i″so-ru′bin). New fuchsin.

isoscope (i″so-skōp) [*iso-* + Gr. *skopein* to examine]. An apparatus for observing the changes of position of the horizontal and vertical lines in the movements of the eyeball.

isoserine (i″so-se′rin). A compound, CH_2NH_2.-CHOH.COOH, isomeric with serine.

isoserotherapy (i″so-se″ro-ther′ah-pe). Treatment by use of an isoserum.

isoserum (i″so-se′rum) [*iso-* + *serum*]. A serum obtained from a person who has had the same disease as the patient who is being treated.

isosexual (i″so-seks′u-al) [*iso-* + *sexual*]. Pertaining to or characteristic of the same sex.

isosmotic (i″sos-mot′ik). Having the same osmotic pressure.

isosmoticity (i″sos-mo-tis′ĭ-te). The state or quality of being isosmotic.

isosorbide dinitrate (i″so-sor′bid di-ni′trāt). Chemical name: 1,4,3,6-dianhydro-sorbitol-2,5-dinitrate: used in treatment of coronary insufficiency.

isospermotoxin (i″so-sper″mo-tok′sin). A toxin against sperm developed in the blood after injection of sperm; a spermotoxin that will act on the spermatozoa of the same species as that in which it was formed.

Isospora (i-sos′po-rah) [*iso-* + Gr. *sporos* spore]. A genus of coccidia characterized by the two tetrazoic spores in the oocyst. **I. bel′li,** a species causing a coccidial diarrhea in man. **I. bigem′ina,** a form found in dogs and cats. **I. fe′lis,** a species causing intestinal coccidiosis in cats. **I. hom′inis,** a nonpathogenic coccidian sometimes temporarily present in the small intestine of man. Called also *Coccidium bigeminum, C. hominis, C. perforans, Cytospermium hominis, Eimeria stiedae, Isospora bigemina.* **I. laca′zei,** a species causing intestinal coccidiosis in birds. **I. rivol′ta,** a species causing intestinal coccidiosis in dogs.

isospore (i′so-spōr) [*iso-* + Gr. *sporos* spore]. A nonsexual spore that develops directly into an adult without conjugation. See *anisospore.*

isostere (i′so-stēr). A substance which stands in the same place as or in place of another compound. See *competitive inhibitor* under *inhibitor.*

isosthenuria (i″sos-thě-nu′re-ah) [*iso-* + Gr. *sthenos* strength + *ouron* urine + *-ia*]. Maintenance of a constant osmolality of the urine, regardless of changes in the osmotic pressure of the blood.

isostimulation (i″so-stim″u-la′shun). Stimulation of an animal with antigenic material originating from other animals of the same species.

isotamieutic (i″so-tam″e-u′tik) [*iso-* + Gr. *tamieuein* to save]. Sparing equally.

isothebaine (i″so-the′ba-in). An alkaloid, $C_{19}H_{21}$-O_3N, from *Papaver orientalis.*

isotherapy (i″so-ther′ah-pe) [*iso-* + Gr. *therapeia* treatment]. Isopathy.

isotherm (i′so-therm). A line on a map or chart depicting the boundaries of an area in which the temperature is the same.

isothermal (i″so-ther′mal) [*iso-* + Gr. *thermē* heat]. Isothermic.

isothermic (i″so-ther′mik). Having the same temperature.

isothermognosis (i″so-ther″mo-no′sis) [*iso-* + Gr. *thermē* heat + *gnōsis* recognition]. Disordered sense perception in which pain, cold, and heat stimuli are all perceived as heat.

isothiazine (i″so-thi′ah-zēn). Ethopropazine.

isothiocyanate (i″so-thi″o-si′ah-nāt). A salt of isothiocyanic acid. **acrynyl i.,** a compound, $C_7H_7O.NCS$, found in white mustard. **allyl i.,** a compound, $C_3H_5.NCS$, found in oil of mustard. **butyl i.,** a compound, $CH_3.CH_2(CH_3)NCS$, found in horseradish. **phenyl-ethyl i.,** a compound, $CH_3.CH_2(C_6H_5)NCS$, found in oil of mignonette.

isothipendyl (i″so-thi′pen-dil). Chemical name: [10-(2-dimethylaminopropyl)-9-thia-1,10-diaza-anthracene]: used as an antihistaminic.

isotonia (i″so-to′ne-ah) [*iso-* + Gr. *tonos* tone]. 1. A condition of equal tone, tension, or activity. 2. Equality of osmotic pressure between two elements of a solution or between two different solutions.

isotonic (i″so-ton′ik) [*iso-* + Gr. *tonos* tone]. Pertaining to or characterized by isotonia.

isotonicity (i″so-to-nis′ĭ-te). The quality of being isotonic.

isotope (i′so-tōp) [*iso-* + Gr. *topos* place]. A chemical element having the same atomic number as another (that is, the same number of nuclear protons) but possessing a different atomic mass (that is, a different number of nuclear neutrons). **radioactive i.,** an isotope that transmutes into another element with emission of corpuscular or electromagnetic radiations. Such isotopes occur naturally or may be produced by bombardment of a common chemical element with high velocity particles. **stable i.,** an isotope which does not transmute into another element with emission of corpuscular or electromagnetic radiations.

isotopology (i″so-to-pol′o-je). The scientific study of isotopes, and of their uses and applications.

isotoxic (i″so-tok′sik). Pertaining to an isotoxin.

isotoxin (i″so-tok-sin) [*iso-* + *toxin*]. A toxin active on other animals of the same species.

isotransplant (i″so-trans′plant) [*iso-* + *transplant*]. A piece of tissue taken from one individual and transplanted into another individual of the same species.

isotransplantation (i″so-trans″plan-ta′shun). The making of an isotransplant.

Isotricha intestinalis (i-sot′rĭ-kah in-tes″tĭ-na′lis). A ciliate organism found in the stomachs of cattle.

isotrimorphism (i″so-tri-mor′fizm) [*iso-* + Gr. *treis* three + *morphē* form]. Isomorphism between the three forms of two trimorphous substances.

isotrimorphous (i″so-tri-mor′fus). Pertaining to or characterized by isotrimorphism.

isotron (i′so-tron). An apparatus for separating isotopes electromagnetically.

isotropic (i″so-trop′ik) [*iso-* + Gr. *tropos* a turning]. 1. Having like properties in all directions, as in a cubic crystal or in an egg without predetermined axis. 2. Being singly refractive.

isotropous (i-sot′ro-pus). Isotropic.

isotropy (i-sot′ro-pe). The quality or condition of being isotropic.

isotypical (i″so-tip′e-kal) [*iso-* + *typical*]. Of the same type.

isouretin (i″so-u-re′tin). Formamidoxim, NH_2-CH:NOH, a compound isomeric with urea.

isoxsuprine (i-sok′su-prēn). Chemical name: 1-(p-hydroxyphenyl)-2-[(1′-methyl-2′-phenoxy)-ethylamino]-1-propanol: proposed as a vasodilator and uterine relaxant.

isozyme (i′so-zīm). Isoenzyme.

Israelson's reaction, test (iz′rel-sonz). See under *tests*.

issue (is′u). A suppurating sore made and kept open by inserting an irritant substance.

istarin (is′tah-rin). A substance said to be obtainable from brain tissue.

isthmectomy (is-mek′to-me) [*isthmus* + Gr. *ektomē* excision]. Excision of an isthmus; particularly excision of median goiter by removal of the isthmus of the thyroid gland.

isthmian (is′me-an). Isthmic.

isthmic (is-mik). Pertaining to an isthmus.

isthmitis (is-mi′tis). Inflammation of the isthmus of the fauces.

isthmocholosis (is″mo-ko-lo′sis) [*isthmus* + Gr. *cholē* bile + *-osis*]. Faucial catarrh with bilious disturbance.

isthmoparalysis (is″mo-pah-ral′ĭ-sis). Isthmoplegia.

isthmoplegia (is″mo-ple′je-ah) [*isthmus* + Gr. *plēgē* stroke]. Paralysis of the isthmus faucium.

isthmospasm (is′mo-spazm″). Spasm of an isthmus, as of the isthmus of a uterine tube or of the fauces.

isthmus (is′mus), pl. *isth′mi* [Gr. *isthmos*]. A narrow connection between two larger bodies or parts; used in anatomical nomenclature as a general term to designate such a connecting structure or region. **anterior i. of fauces,** i. faucium. **i. of aorta, i. aor′tae** [N A, B N A], **aortic i.,** a narrowed portion of the aorta, especially noticeable in the fetus, at the point where the ductus arteriosus is attached. **i. of cartilage of auricle, i. cartilag′inis au′ris** [N A, B N A], a bridge of cartilage connecting the cartilage of the external acoustic meatus with the main part of the cartilage of the auricle of the external ear. **i. of cingulate gyrus,** i. gyri cinguli. **i. of eustachian tube,** i. tubae auditivae. **i. of fallopian tube,** i. tubae uterinae. **i. of fauces, i. fau′cium** [N A, B N A], the constricted aperture between the cavity of the mouth and the pharynx. **i. glan′dulae thyroi′deae** [N A], the band of tissue connecting the lobes of the thyroid gland. Called also *i. of thyroid gland.* **i. gy′ri cin′guli** [N A], **i. gy′ri fornica′ti** [B N A], the constricted portion of the cingulate gyrus, connecting with the parahippocampal gyrus in the region of the splenium of the corpus callosum. Called also *i. of cingulate gyrus.* **Haller's i.,** fretum halleri. **i. of His,** i. rhombencephali. **Krönig's i.,** a narrow, ribbon-like area of resonance extending over the shoulder and connecting the larger areas of resonance on the chest and back, overlying the apex of the lung (Krönig's fields). **i. of limbic lobe,** i. gyri cinguli. **oropharyngeal i., pharyngooral i.,** i. faucium. **i. prosta′tae** [N A, B N A], **i. of prostate,** the commissure on the base of the prostate, between the right and the left lateral lobe. **i. rhombenceph′ali** [N A, B N A], **i. of rhombencephalon,** a narrow segment of the brain in the fetus, forming the plane of separation between the rhombencephalon and the cerebrum. **i. of thyroid gland,** i. glandulae thyroideae. **i. tu′bae auditi′vae** [N A, B N A], the narrowest part of the auditory tube, at the junction of the pars ossea and the pars cartilaginea of the tube. Called also *i. of auditory tube.* **i. tu′bae uteri′nae** [N A, B N A], the narrow part of the uterine tube at its junction with the uterus. **i. ure′thrae,** a constricted part of the urethra, at the junction of the cavernous with the membranous urethra. **i. u′teri** [N A], **i. of uterus,** the constricted part of the uterus between the cervix and the body. **i. of Vieussens,** limbus fossae ovalis.

isuprel (i′su-prel). Trade mark for a preparation of isoproterenol.

isuria (i-su′re-ah) [Gr. *isos* equal + *ouron* urine + *-ia*]. Excretion of urine at a uniform rate.

Itard's catheter (e-tarz′) [Jean Marie Gaspard *Itard*, French otologist, 1774–1838]. See under *catheter.*

Itard-Cholewa sign (e-tar′ ko-la′vah) [J. M. G. *Itard;* Erasmus Rudolph *Cholewa*, German physician, born 1845]. See under *sign.*

itate (i′tāt). A substance in milk which oxidizes nitrite to nitrate.

itch (ich). 1. A skin disorder marked by itching. 2. Scabies. **Caripito i.,** a condition accompanied by rash and itching, developing in seamen visiting the harbor of Caripito (on the San Juan river, in Venezuela), caused by dust or hairs from the wings of moths. **copra i.,** a dermatitic eruption affecting those who unload cocoanuts and caused by an acarus (Tyroglyphus). **Cuban i.,** variola minor. **dhobie i.,** a contact dermatitis caused by the marking fluid (bhilawanol oil) used on laundry by the native washermen (dhobie) of India. **grain i.,** a dermatitis accompanied by itching, caused by a mite, *Pediculoides ventricosus*, which preys on the larvae of a certain insect which lives on straw. The disease affects persons who sleep on mattresses containing infected straw. Called also *acarodermatitis urticarioides,* and *dermatitis schambergi.* **ground i.,** the itching eruption caused by the entrance into the skin of the larvae of *Necator americanus* or *Ancylostoma duodenale.* **mad i.,** a disease developing suddenly in cattle and caused by a filtrable virus: it is marked by severe pruritus, convulsions and coma. Called also *bovine pseudorabies.* **Moeller's i., Norway i.,** radesyge. **Philippine i.,** variola minor. **seven-year i.,** scabies. **swimmers' i.,** schistosome dermatitis.

itching (ich′ing). An unpleasant cutaneous sensation which provokes the desire to scratch or rub the skin. Present as a symptom in various skin diseases, it may also occur idiopathically. See also *pruritus.*

iter (i′ter) [L.]. A way or tubular passage. **i. ad infundib′ulum,** the passage from the third ventricle to the infundibulum. **i. den′tium,** the area through which a permanent tooth makes its appearance. **i. e ter′tio ad quar′tum ventric′ulum,** aqueductus cerebri. **i. of Sylvius,** aqueductus cerebri.

iteral (i′ter-al). Pertaining to an iter.

iteroparity (it″er-o-par′ĭ-te) [L. *iterare* to repeat + *parere* to bear]. The state, in an individual organism, of reproducing repeatedly, or more than once in a lifetime.

iteroparous (it″er-op′ah-rus). Reproducing more than once in a lifetime.

-ites [Gr. *-itēs*, a masculine termination agreeing with *hydrōps* dropsy (understood)—e.g., tympanites, the windy dropsy]. A word termination indicating dropsy of the part indicated by the word stem to which it is attached.

ithycyphos (ith″e-si′fōs). Ithyokyphosis.

ithylordosis (ith″e-lor-do′sis) [Gr. *ithys* straight + *lordōsis* bending forward]. Lordosis without any lateral curvature.

ithyokyphosis (ith″e-o-ki-fo′sis) [Gr. *ithys* straight + *kyphos* humped + *-osis*]. Backward projection of the spinal column.

-itis, pl. *-it′ides* [*-itis,* a feminine adjectival termination agreeing with Gr. *nosos* (understood)—e.g., neuritis = Gr. *hē neuritis nosos,* the disease of the nerves, which soon becomes the inflammatory disease]. A word termination denoting inflammation of the part indicated by the word stem to which it is attached.

Ito-Reenstierna test (e′to rēn-stēr′nah) [Hayazo *Ito,* Japanese pathologist born 1865; John *Reenstierna,* Swedish dermatologist, born 1882]. See under *tests.*

ITP. Abbreviation for *idiopathic thrombocytopenic purpura.*

itrosyl (it′ro-sil). Concentrated nitrous ether.

itrumil (it′roo-mil). Trade mark for a preparation of iothiouracil.

ittiolo (it″e-o′lo) [Italian]. Ichthyol.

I.U. Abbreviation for *immunizing unit* and for *international unit.*

I.V. Abbreviation for *intravenously* (by intravenous injection).

ivain (i′va-in). A bitter, yellow substance from *Achillea moschata.*

ivaol (i′va-ol). A thick, fragrant, oily substance obtained by distillation from *Achillea moschata.*

ivory (i′vo-re) [L. *ebur, eburneus*]. 1. The bonelike substance of the tusks or teeth of elephants. 2. Dentin (substantia dentinum [N A]).

I.V.T. Abbreviation for *intravenous transfusion.*

Iwanoff's (Iwanow's) retinal edema (e-wan′ofs) [Wladimir P. *Iwanoff* (Iwanow), Russian ophthalmologist, born 1861]. See *Blessig's cysts,* under *cyst.*

Ixodes (iks-o′dēz) [Gr. *ixōdes* like bird-lime]. A genus of ticks that become parasitic on man and beasts. **I. bicor′nis,** a Mexican tick that infests the cougar. Its bite may cause a high fever in an adult and may kill a child. **I. calvepal′pus,** an African tick that infests monkeys and native children. **I. fre′quens,** a species that infests cattle, horses, and man in Japan. **I. hexag′onus,** a species that infests burrowing animals in Europe and ground squirrels in California. It may transmit plague. **I. holocy′clus,** a tick particularly of marsupials but which causes a tick paralysis in young cattle in New South Wales. **I. persulca′tus,** a species that is a reservoir and vector of Russian spring-summer encephalitis. **I. pilo′sus,** a species which causes tick paralysis in sheep in South Africa, and infests many other animals. **I. pu′tus,** a species that infests the nests of many marine birds. **I. ra′sus,** a species that attacks the badger, other carnivores and man in Africa. **I. rici′nus,** the castor bean tick, which is parasitic on cattle, sheep and wild animals, and transmits *Babesia bovis* and the virus of louping ill. **I. rubicun′dus,** a species that may cause a tick paralysis in sheep in West Africa. **I. spinipal′pus,** a species that infests rabbits and squirrels in British Columbia.

ixodiasis (iks″o-di′ah-sis). Any disease or lesion due to the bite of ticks; infestation with ticks.

ixodic (ik-sod′ik). Caused by ticks.

Ixodidae (iks-od′ĭ-de). A family of the Acarina, made up of the hard ticks which are characterized by the presence of a scutum. It includes the following genera: *Amblyomma, Aponomma, Boophilus, Dermacentor, Haemaphysalis, Hyalomma, Ixodes, Margaropus, Rhipicephalus.*

Ixodiphagus (iks″o-dif′ah-gus). A genus of flies. **I. caucur′tei,** a fly which is parasitic on ticks of the family Ixodidae.

ixodism (iks′o-dizm). Ixodiasis.

Ixodoidea (iks″o-doi′de-ah). A superfamily of the class Arachnida; the ticks. It embraces the families Argasidae, or soft ticks, and Ixodidae, or hard ticks.

ixomyelitis (ik″so-mi″ĕ-li′tis) [Gr. *ixys* waist + Gr. *myelos* marrow + *-itis*]. Inflammation of the lumbar part of the spinal cord.

Izar's reagent (i′zarz) [Guido *Izar,* Italian pathologist, born 1883]. See under *reagent.*

-ize [Gr. *-izō*]. Word termination denoting subjection to the specific action or treatment indicated by the stem to which it is affixed, as *adrenalectomize, thyroidectomize,* etc.

J

J. Symbol for *Joule's equivalent.*

jaagsiekte (yahg-zēk′te). Jagziekte.

Jaboulay's button, operation (zhah″boo-lāz′) [Mathieu *Jaboulay,* French surgeon, 1860–1913]. See under *button* and *operation.*

Jaccoud's fever, sign (zhah-ko͞oz′) [Sigismond *Jaccoud,* French physician, 1830–1913]. See under *fever* and *sign.*

jacket (jak′et). An enveloping structure or garment, especially a covering for the trunk or for the upper part of the body. See also *jacket crown.* **Minerva j.,** a plaster-of-paris jacket reaching from the crest of the ilia to the chin: for fracture of the vertebrae. **plaster-of-paris j.,** a casing of plaster of paris enveloping the body for the purpose of correcting deformities. **porcelain j.,** a jacket crown of porcelain. **Sayre's j.,** a plaster-of-paris jacket used as a support for the spinal column. **strait j.,** a contrivance for restraining the limbs, especially the arms, of a violently disturbed person. **Willock's respiratory j.,** a sort of jacket used to strengthen the movements of respiration in emphysema of the lungs.

jackscrew (jak′skroo). A device operated by means of a screw in a threaded socket, used in orthodontics to expand the dental arch.

Jackson's law, rule, sign, syndrome (jak′sunz) [John Hughlings *Jackson,* London neurologist, 1835–1911]. See under the nouns.

Jackson's membrane [Jabez North *Jackson,* surgeon in Kansas City, 1868–1935]. See under *membrane.*

Jackson's safety triangle, sign [Chevalier *Jackson,* American laryngologist, 1865–1958]. See under *triangle,* and *asthmatoid wheeze,* under *wheeze.*

Jackson's sign [James *Jackson,* Jr., Boston physician, 1810–1834]. See under *sign,* def. 3.

jacksonian epilepsy (jak-so′ne-an) [John Hughlings *Jackson*]. See under *epilepsy.*

Jacob's membrane, ulcer (ja′kubz) [Arthur *Jacob,* Irish ophthalmologist, 1790–1874]. See *bacillary membrane,* and under *ulcer.*

Jacobaeus operation (yah″ko-ba′us) [Hans Christian *Jacobaeus,* Swedish surgeon, 1879–1937]. See under *operation.*

jacobine (ja′ko-bin). A poisonous alkaloid, $C_{18}H_{25}O_6N$, from *Senecio jacobea.* It may cause necrosis of the liver.

Jacobson's anastomosis, canal, cartilage, nerve, organ, plexus, etc. (ja′kub-sunz) [Ludwig Levin *Jacobson,* Danish anatomist, 1783–1843]. See under the nouns.

Jacobson's retinitis [Julius *Jacobson,* German ophthalmologist, 1829–1889]. Syphilitic retinitis.

Jacobson's solution (jah′kob-sunz) [Jacob *Jacobson*, French ophthalmologist]. See under *solution*.

Jacobsthal's test (yak′obz-talz) [Erwin Wolfgang Jakob *Jacobsthal*, Hamburg bacteriologist, born 1879]. See under *tests*.

Jacquemier's sign (zhahk-me-āz′) [Jean Marie *Jacquemier*, French obstetrician, 1806–1879]. See under *sign*.

jactatio (jak-ta′she-o) [L.]. Jactitation. **j. cap′itis noctur′na,** rhythmic rolling of the head of a child just before falling asleep.

jactation (jak-ta′shun). Jactitation.

jactitation (jak″tĭ-ta′shun) [L. *jactitatio; jactitare* to toss]. The tossing to and fro of a patient in acute disease.

jaculiferous (jak″u-lif′er-us) [L. *jaculum* dart + *ferre* to bear]. Bearing prickles.

Jadassohn's disease, test (yah′das-ōnz) [Josef *Jadassohn*, German dermatologist in Bern, 1863–1936]. See *maculopapular erythrodermia*, and under *tests*.

Jadelot's furrows, lines (zhad-lōz′) [Jean François Nicolas *Jadelot*, physician in Paris, 1791–1830]. See under *line*.

Jaeger's test types (ya′gerz) [Edward *Jaeger* von Jastthal, Austrian oculist, 1818–1884]. See under *test types*.

Jaffé's test (zhah-fāz′) [Max *Jaffé*, German physiologic chemist, 1841–1911]. See under *tests*.

jagziekte (yahg-zēk′te) [Dutch *jagen* go quickly + *ziekte* sickness]. A fatal pulmonary adenosis of sheep, apparently caused by a filtrable virus.

Jakob's disease (yak′obz) [Alfons *Jakob*, German psychiatrist, 1884–1931]. Spastic pseudosclerosis.

Jakob-Creutzfeldt disease (yak′ob-kroits′-felt) [Alfons *Jakob;* Hans Gerhard *Creutzfeldt*, German psychiatrist, born 1885]. Spastic pseudosclerosis.

Jaksch's anemia, disease, test (yaksh) [Rudolf von *Jaksch*, physician in Prague, 1855–1947]. See *anemia infantum pseudoleukaemica*, and under *tests*.

jalap (jal′ap) [Sp. *jalapa*, from *Jalapa*, a city of Mexico]. The dried tuberous root of *Exogonium purga:* used as a cathartic.

Janet's disease, test (zhah-nāz′) [Pierre Marie Felix *Janet*, French physician, 1859–1947]. See under *disease* and *tests*.

Janeway's pill (jān′wāz) [Edward Gamaliel *Janeway*, American physician, 1841–1911]. Compound pill of aloes and podophyllin.

Janeway's sphygmomanometer, spots (jān′wāz) [Theodore C. *Janeway*, American physician, 1872–1917]. See under the nouns.

janiceps (jan′ĭ-seps) [L. *Janus* a two-faced god + *caput* head]. A double monster with one head and two opposite faces. **j. asym′metros,** a janiceps with one imperfect and one more complete face. **j. parasit′icus,** a double fetal monster in which there is partial duplication of the head in the frontal plane.

Janin's tetanus (zhah-naz′) [Joseph *Janin*, French physician, born 1864]. Kopf-tetanus.

Janosik's embryo (yan′o-siks) [Jan *Janosik*, Prague anatomist, 1856–1927]. A human embryo having three aortic arches and two gill pouches.

Jansen's operation (yan′senz) [Albert *Jansen*, German otologist]. See under *operation*.

Jansen's test [W. Murk *Jansen*, Dutch orthopedic surgeon, 1863–1935]. See under *tests*.

Jansky's classification (jan′skēz) [Jan *Jansky*, Czech psychiatrist, 1873–1921]. A classification of blood types, designating them by roman numerals I to IV, corresponding with O, A, B, and AB, respectively, in the international, or Landsteiner, classification.

Janthinosoma (jan″thĭ-no-so′mah). A genus of mosquitoes. **J. lut′zi,** a species which transports the eggs of bot flies (Dermatobia) glued to its abdomen. **J. postica′ta,** a species which also transports the eggs of a bot fly.

Jaquet's apparatus (zhah-kāz′) [Alfred *Jaquet*, Swiss pharmacologist, 1865–1937]. A recording apparatus for venous and cardiac impulse.

jararaca (jah″rah-rak′ah). A small venomous snake of Brazil belonging to the genus *Bothrops*.

Jarcho's pressometer (jahr′kōz) [Julius *Jarcho*, New York obstetrician, born 1882]. See under *pressometer*.

jargonaphasia (jar″gon-ah-fa′ze-ah). A speech defect in which several words are run into one.

Jarisch's ointment (yah′rish-ez) [Adolf *Jarisch*, Austrian dermatologist, 1850–1902]. See under *ointment*.

Jarotzky's diet (yar-ot′skēz) [Alexander *Jarotzky*, Moscow physician, born 1866]. See under *diet*.

Jarvis' snare (jahr′vis) [William Chapman *Jarvis*, New York laryngologist, 1855–1895]. See under *snare*.

Jatropha (jat′ro-fah) [Gr. *iatros* physician + *trophē* nourishment]. A genus of tropical euphorbiaceous plants. **J. cur′cas** affords the physic nut or purging nut. See *Curcas*. **J. man′ihot** produces tapioca and casareep. **J. u′rens,** ortiga, bears white hairs which may cause intense itching.

jaundice (jawn′dis) [Fr. *jaunisse*, from *jaune* yellow]. A syndrome characterized by hyperbilirubinemia and deposition of bile pigment in the skin and mucous membranes with resulting yellow appearance of the patient. **absorption j.,** that due to absorption of bile into the blood vessels. **acathetic j.,** jaundice due to pathologic changes in the liver cells, which become unable to retain their secretions. **acholuric j.,** jaundice without bile pigments in urine or with only minute quantities of them. **acholuric familial j.** See *hemolytic j.* **acute febrile j., acute infectious j.,** infectious hepatitis. **anhepatic j., anhepatogenous j.,** yellow appearance of the skin and mucous membranes not caused by liver disease. **black j.,** Winckel's disease. **blue j.,** cyanosis. **Budd's j.,** acute parenchymatous hepatitis. **catarrhal j.,** infectious hepatitis. **cholangietic j.,** obstructive j. **complete j.,** the presence of both bile pigments and bile salts in the blood. **dissociated j., dissociation j.,** jaundice in which either the pigment or the salts of bile formed within the liver are separately shunted from the biliary path into the lymph vessels or blood vessels of the liver. See *hepatic dissociation j.* and *renal dissociation j.* **dynamic j.,** hemolytic j. **emotional j.,** jaundice resulting from deep emotion, such as great anxiety. **epidemic catarrhal j.,** infectious hepatitis. **familial acholuric j.** See *hemolytic j.* **febrile j.,** leptospiral j. **functional j.,** hemolytic j. **Hayem's j.,** hemolytic j. **hemapheic j.,** urobilin j. **hematogenous j.,** hemolytic j. **hematohepatogenous j.,** jaundice that is partly hematogenous and partly hepatogenous. This form includes toxemic jaundice and the jaundice seen in malaria, yellow fever, typhoid, typhus, acute malaria, yellow atrophy of the liver, etc. **hemolytic j.,** a rare, chronic, and generally hereditary disease characterized by periods of excessive hemolysis due to abnormal fragility of the red corpuscles which are small and spheroidal. It is accompanied by enlargement of the spleen and by jaundice. The hereditary or congenital form is known as *congenital family icterus, familial acholuric j.,* and *Minkowski-Chauffard syndrome;* the acquired form is known as *acquired hemolytic j.* and *Hayem-Widal syndrome*. Called also *spherocytic anemia, hemolytic splenomegaly, acholuric hemolytic icterus with splenomegaly, anemia icterohemolytica.* **hemorrhagic j.,** leptospiral j. **hepatic dissociation j.,** the presence of bilirubin or bile salts separately in the blood stream. **hepatocellular j.,** jaundice caused by injury to or disease of the liver cells. **hepatogenic j.,** that which is due to some disease or disorder of the liver. **homologous serum j., human serum j.,** serum hepatitis.

infectious j., infective j. 1. Infectious hepatitis. 2. Leptospiral jaundice. **inogenous j.,** icterus neonatorum due to change of the hemoglobin in the tissues. **latent j.,** hyperbilirubinemia without yellow staining of the tissues. **leptospiral j.,** an acute infectious disease characterized by nephritis, jaundice, fever, muscular pain, and enlargement of the liver and spleen, and caused by a spirochete, *Leptospira icterohaemorrhagiae*. The symptoms last from ten days to two weeks, and recovery is usually uneventful. Called also *Weil's disease, infectious spirochetal jaundice, icterogenic spirochetosis, spirochetosis icterohaemorrhagica, leptospirosis icterohaemorrhagica,* and *Fiedler's disease*. **lutein j.,** carotinemia. **malignant j.,** acute yellow atrophy of the liver. **malignant j. of dogs,** biliary fever of dogs. **mechanical j.,** obstructive j. **j. of the newborn,** icterus neonatorum. **nuclear j.,** kernicterus. **obstructive j.,** that which is due to an impediment to the flow of the bile from the liver to the duodenum. **occult j.,** bile in the blood in such small quantity as to cause no symptoms. **physiologic j.,** mild icterus neonatorum lasting during the first few days after birth. **picric acid j.,** jaundice due to picric acid poisoning in munition workers or to its ingestion by malingering soldiers. **pleiochromic j., polychromic j.,** hemolytic j. **post-arsphenamine j.,** jaundice following the administration of arsphenamine. **regurgitation j.,** jaundice due to escape of bile from the bile canaliculi into the blood stream and marked by urobilinogen in the urine. **renal dissociation j.,** the presence of bile pigments in the blood due to separation of the biliary elements through renal filtration of the bile salts. **retention j.,** a form of jaundice due to inability of the liver to dispose of the bilirubin provided by the circulating blood. **Schmorl's j.,** kernicterus. **spherocytic j.,** a term proposed by Krumbhaar for typical hemolytic jaundice because the erythrocytes become smaller than normal and spherical in form. **spirochetal j.,** leptospiral j. **Sumatra j.,** a form of infectious jaundice endemic in Sumatra and caused by *Leptospira pyrogenes*. **toxemic j., toxic j.,** jaundice produced by poisons, such as phosphorus, arseniuretted hydrogen, picric acid, snake poison, etc. **urobilin j.,** jaundice due to the presence of urobilin in the blood. **xanthochromic j.,** jaundice marked by yellow discoloration of the palms, soles, and mucous membranes, but without bile pigment in the urine.

Javal's ophthalmometer (zhah-valz′) [Louis Emile *Javal*, French oculist, 1839–1907]. See under *ophthalmometer*.

javellization (jav″el-i-za′shun). The purification of water supplies by treatment with Javelle solution of hypochlorites.

jaw (jaw). One of the bony structures in the head of vertebrates, bearing the teeth and enabling lower animals to seize their prey and others to bite and chew food. **big j.,** actinomycosis in cattle. **crackling j.,** chronic subluxation of the jaw in which a crackling sound accompanies closure after wide opening. **drop j.,** the paralytic stage of rabies in a dog, in which the jaw falls. **Hapsburg j.,** a mandibular prognathous jaw such as is seen in many members of the Hapsburg family. **lower j.,** mandibula. **lumpy j.,** actinomycosis in cattle. **parrot j.,** the condition produced by protrusion of the upper jaw. **phossy j.,** phosphonecrosis. **pig j.,** an abnormal protrusion of the upper jaw of the horse, with hypertrophy of the teeth. **pipe j.,** a painful condition of the jaws caused by carrying a tobacco pipe in the mouth. **rubber j.,** a softened condition of the jaw in animals, caused by resorption and replacement of the bone by fibrous tissue, occurring in association with renal osteodystrophy. **upper j.,** maxilla.

Jaworski's bodies, corpuscles, test (yahwor′skēz) [Velary *Jaworski*, Polish physician, 1849–1925]. See under *corpuscle* and *tests*.

Jeanselme's nodules (zhah-selmz′) [Edouard *Jeanselme*, French dermatologist, 1858–1935]. See under *nodule*.

jecorize (jek′o-rīz) [L. *jecur* liver]. To impart to a food the therapeutical qualities of cod liver oil, as by treating milk with ultraviolet ray.

jecur (je′kur) [L.]. Liver.

Jeddah ulcer (jed′ah) [*Jeddah*, a town of Arabia]. Furunculus orientalis.

Jeffersonia (jef″er-so′ne-ah) [named for T. *Jefferson*, 1743–1826]. A genus of berberidaceous herbs. The root of *J. diphylla*, of North America, is tonic, diuretic, and expectorant: emetic in large doses.

jejunal (je-joo′nal). Pertaining to the jejunum.

jejunectomy (je″joo-nek′to-me) [*jejuno-* + Gr. *ektomē* excision]. Excision of the jejunum or a part of it.

jejunitis (je″joo-ni′tis). Inflammation of the jejunum.

jejuno- (je-joo′no) [L. *jejunum* empty]. Combining form denoting relationship to the jejunum.

jejunocecostomy (je-joo″no-se-kos′to-me) [*jejuno-* + *cecum* + Gr. *stoma* opening]. The operation of forming an anastomosis between the jejunum and cecum.

jejunocolostomy (je-joo″no-ko-los′to-me) [*jejuno-* + *colon* + Gr. *stoma* mouth]. The formation of an anastomosis between the jejunum and the colon.

jejuno-ileitis (je-joo″no-il″e-i′tis). Inflammation of the jejunum and ileum together.

jejuno-ileostomy (je-joo″no-il″e-os′to-me) [*jejuno-* + *ileum* + Gr. *stoma* mouth]. The formation of an anastomosis between jejunum and colon.

jejunojejunostomy (je-joo″no-je″joo-nos′tome). The operative formation of an anastomosis between two portions of the jejunum.

jejunorrhaphy (je″joo-nor′ah-fe) [*jejuno-* + Gr. *rhaphē* suture]. The operation of suturing the jejunum.

jejunostomy (je″joo-nos′to-me) [*jejuno-* + Gr. *stoma* mouth]. The surgical creation of a permanent opening through the abdominal wall into the jejunum.

jejunotomy (je″joo-not′o-me) [*jejuno-* + Gr. *temnein* to cut]. Surgical incision of the jejunum.

jejunum (je-joo′num) [L. "empty"]. [N A] That portion of the small intestine which extends from the duodenum to the ileum. Called also *intestinum jejunum* [B N A].

Jellinek's sign, symptom (yel′ĭ-neks) [Stefan *Jellinek*, physician in Vienna, born 1871]. See under *sign*.

jelly (jel′e) [L. *gelatina*]. A soft substance which is coherent, tremulous, and more or less translucent; generally, a colloidal semisolid mass. **cardiac j.,** a jelly, present between the endothelium and myocardium of the embryonic heart, that transforms into the connective tissue of the endocardium. **contraceptive j.,** a nongreasy jelly for introduction into the vagina to prevent conception. **enamel j.,** stellate reticulum. **glycerin j.,** a compound of glycerin, zinc oxide, and gelatin: used in cases of eczema. **mineral j.,** a soft, semisolid substance prepared from petroleum, used as a basis for salves and ointments; petrolatum. **petroleum j.,** mineral j. **Wharton's j.,** the soft, jelly-like, homogeneous intercellular substance of the umbilical cord; it gives the reaction for mucin and contains thin collagenous fibers which increase in number with the age of the fetus.

Jendrassik's maneuver (yen-drah′siks) [Ernst *Jendrassik*, physician in Budapest, 1858–1921]. See under *maneuver*.

Jenner's stain (jen′erz) [Louis *Jenner*, London physician, 1866–1904]. See *table of stains and staining methods*.

jennerian (jen-ne′re-an). Named for Edward *Jenner* (English physician, 1749–1823), the discoverer of vaccination.

jennerization (jen″er-i-za′shun). Production of

immunity to a disease by inoculation of an attenuated form of the virus producing the disease.

Jensen's classification (yen′senz) [Orla *Jensen,* Danish physiologic chemist]. A classification of bacteria based upon the nutritive characteristics of the organisms.

Jensen's sarcoma, tumor (yen′senz) [Carl Oluf *Jensen,* Danish veterinary pathologist, 1864–1934]. See under *sarcoma.*

jerk (jerk). A sudden reflex or involuntary movement. **Achilles j., ankle j.,** triceps surae j. **biceps j.,** biceps reflex. **crossed j.,** movement of the leg when attempt is made to elicit the quadriceps jerk on the opposite side. **jaw j.,** jaw reflex. **knee j.,** quadriceps j. **quadriceps j.,** a twitchlike contraction of the quadriceps muscle, elicited by sharply tapping the patellar ligament when the leg hangs loosely flexed at a right angle. **tendon j.,** tendon reaction. **triceps surae j.,** a twitchlike contraction of the triceps surae muscle, elicited by sharply tapping the muscle or the Achilles tendon.

Jesionek lamp (yes-e′o-nek) [Albert *Jesionek,* Giessen dermatologist, 1870–1935]. See under *lamp.*

jessur (jes′er). Native Bengal name for Russell's viper.

Jesu Haly. See *Ali ben Iza.*

Jewett nail (joo′et) [Eugene Lyon *Jewett,* American surgeon, born 1900]. See under *nail.*

jhin jhinia (jin jin′e-ah). An epidemic condition, perhaps a neuromimesis, which was first noticed in 1935 in Calcutta. It is characterized by a tingling sensation in the sole of one or both feet, especially in the great toe, and often by a feeling of pressure in the head and by trembling of the whole body.

jigger (jig′ger). *Tunga penetrans.*

Jobert's fossa, suture (zho-bārz′) [Antoine Joseph *Jobert* de Lamballe, French surgeon, 1799–1867]. See under *fossa* and *suture.*

Jochmann's test (yōk′manz) [Georg *Jochmann,* Berlin internist, 1874–1915]. Müller-Jochmann test.

jodbasedow (i″od-bas′e-do). Iodine-induced hyperthyroidism.

Joest's bodies (yests) [Ernst *Joest,* Dresden veterinary pathologist, 1873–1926]. See under *body.*

Joffroy's reflex (zhof-rwhahz′) [Alexis *Joffroy,* French physician, 1844–1908]. See under *reflex.*

Johannseniella sordidella (jo-han″sen-e-el′ah sor″dĭ-del′ah). A midge which is a veritable pest in Greenland.

Johne's bacillus, disease (yo′nez) [Heinrich Albert *Johne,* German pathologist, 1839–1910]. See *Mycobacterium paratuberculosis* and under *disease.*

johnin (yo′nin). A filtrate of cultures of Johne's bacillus (*Mycobacterium paratuberculosis*) used in testing cattle for Johne's disease.

Johnson's test (john′sonz) [Sir George *Johnson,* English physician, 1818–1896]. See under *tests.*

joint (joint) [L. *junctio* a joining, connection]. The place of union between two or more bones of the skeleton. Called also *articulatio* and *junctura.* For English names of other specific joints not included here, see under *articulation.* **amphidiarthrodial j.,** amphidiarthrosis. **arthrodial j.,** plane j. **ball-and-socket j.,** spheroidal j. **biaxial j.,** one permitting movement in two of the assumed three mutually perpendicular axes, or having two degrees of freedom. **bilocular j.,** a joint in which the synovial cavity is divided into two compartments by an interarticular cartilage. **bleeders' j.,** hemorrhage into a joint in persons of a hemorrhagic diathesis. **Brodie's j.,** hysteric j. **Budin's j.,** a band of cartilage seen at birth between the squamous and the two condylar portions of the occipital bone. **cartilaginous j.,** junctura cartilaginea. **Charcot's j.,** neurogenic arthropathy. **Chopart's j.,** articulatio tarsi transversa. **Clutton's j.,** painless symmetrical hydrarthrosis, especially of the knee joints: seen in hereditary syphilis. **cochlear j.,** a form of hinge joint which permits of some lateral motion. **coffin j.,** the second interphalangeal joint of the foot of a horse. **composite j., compound j.,** a joint in which several bones articulate. **condyloid j.,** one in which an ovoid head of one bone moves in an elliptical cavity of another, permitting all movements except axial rotation. **Cruveilhier's j.,** articulatio atlantooccipitalis. **diarthrodial j.,** synovial j. **dry j.,** one affected with chronic villous arthritis. **elbow j.,** the joint between the arm and forearm. See *articulatio cubiti* [N A]. **ellipsoidal j.,** a biaxial joint resembling a ball-and-socket joint, but with the articulating surfaces much longer in one direction than in the direction at right angles, the circumference of the joint thus resembling an ellipse. **enarthrodial j.,** spheroidal j. **false j.,** pseudarthrosis. **fibrocartilaginous j.,** one in which the participating elements are united by fibrocartilage, usually separated from the bones by thin plates of hyaline cartilage. Called also *symphysis,* and *secondary cartilaginous joint.* **fibrous j.,** one in which the components are connected by fibrous tissue. See *junctura fibrosa* [N A]. **flail j.,** one showing abnormal mobility. **freely movable j.,** synovial j. **fringe j.,** one affected with chronic villous arthritis. **ginglymoid j.,** ginglymus. **gliding j.,** plane j. **hemophilic j.,** bleeders' j. **hinge j.,** ginglymus. **hip j.,** the articulation of the femur and pelvis. Called also *articulatio coxa.* **hysteric j.,** a condition which resembles arthritis but is of psychic origin. **immovable j.,** junctura fibrosa. **intercarpal j's,** the articulations between the carpal bones. Called also *articulationes intercarpeae.* **irritable j.,** a joint which is subject to attacks of inflammation without discoverable cause. **knee j.,** the compound joint between the femur, patella, and tibia. See *articulatio genus* [N A]. **ligamentous j.,** syndesmosis. **Lisfranc's j.** See *articulationes tarsometatarseae.* **midcarpal j.,** the joint between the scaphoid, semilunar, and cuneiform bones and the second row of the carpal bones. Called also *articulatio mediocarpea.* **mixed j.,** one combining features of different types of joints. **multiaxial j.,** one permitting movement in each of the assumed three mutually perpendicular axes, or having three degrees of freedom. Called also *articulatio spheroidea.* **open j.,** a veterinary term for a joint in which the surface of the bones is exposed, as a result of inflammation and sloughing of the tissues. **pivot j.,** a uniaxial joint in which one bone pivots within a bony or an osseoligamentous ring. **plane j.,** a type of synovial joint in which the opposed surfaces are flat or only slightly curved. Called also *articulatio plana* [N A]. **polyaxial j.,** multiaxial j. **rotary j.,** pivot j. **sacrococcygeal j.,** junctura sacrococcygea. **saddle j.,** a joint having two saddle-shaped surfaces at right angles to each other. **scapuloclavicular j.,** articulatio acromioclavicularis. **sellar j.,** saddle j. **shoulder j.,** articulatio humeri. **simple j.,** a joint

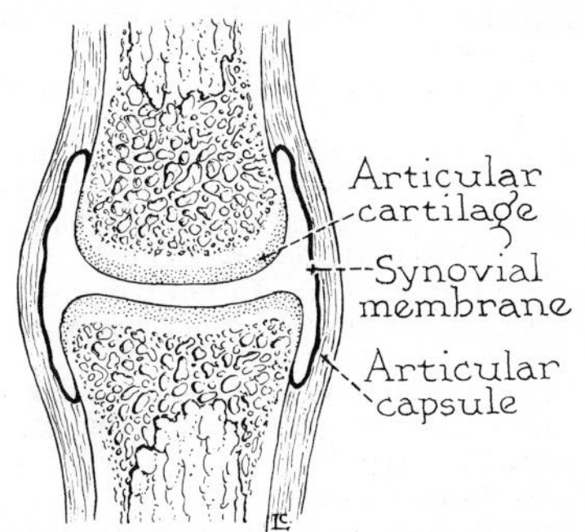

Section of synovial joint.
(King and Showers.)

in which only two bones articulate. **socket j. of tooth,** gomphosis. **spheroidal j.,** a type of synovial joint in which a spheroidal surface on one bone ("ball") moves within a concavity ("socket") on the other bone. Called also *articulatio spheroidea* [N A]. **spiral j.,** cochlear j. **stifle j.,** the articulation in quadrupeds corresponding with the knee joint of man, consisting actually of two joints, that between the femur and tibia, and that between the femur and patella. **synarthrodial j.,** junctura fibrosa. **synovial j.,** a special form of articulation permitting more or less free movement. See *junctura synovialis.* **tarsal j., transverse,** articulatio tarsi transversa. **through j.,** junctura synovialis. **trochoid j.,** pivot j. **uniaxial j.,** one permitting movement in only one of the assumed three mutually perpendicular axes, or having only one degree of freedom. **unilocular j.,** a synovial joint having only one cavity. **von Gies j.,** a chronic syphilitic chondro-osteoarthritis.

Jolles' test (yol′ez) [Adolf *Jolles*, Austrian chemist, born 1864]. See under *tests.*

Jolly's bodies (zho-lēz′) [Justin *Jolly*, French histologist, 1870–1953]. Howell's bodies.

Jolly's reaction (yo′lēz) [Friedrich *Jolly*, German neurologist, 1844–1904]. See under *reaction.*

Jonas' symptom (yo′nas) [Siegfried *Jonas*, Austrian physician, born 1874]. Spasm of the pylorus in babies.

Jones's cylinder, protein, etc. See *Bence Jones albumin*, etc.

Jones's nasal splint [John *Jones*, American surgeon, 1729–1791]. See under *splint.*

Jones's position, splint [Sir Robert *Jones*, English surgeon, 1858–1933]. See under *position* and *splint.*

Jonnesco's fold, fossa, operation (jo-nes′-kōz) [Thoma *Jonnesco*, Rumanian surgeon, 1860–1926]. See under the nouns.

Jonston's arc [Johns *Jonston*, Polish physician, 1603–1675]. Alopecia areata.

Jorissenne's sign (zhor-ĭ-senz′) [Gustav *Jorissenne*, Belgian physician]. See under *sign.*

joule (jo͞ol) [James Prescott *Joule*, English physicist, 1818–1899]. The M.K.S. unit of work or energy. It is the work done in moving a body a distance of one meter against a force of one newton, or the energy expended by a current of one ampere flowing for one second through a resistance of one ohm. Adopted in 1948 as the unit of heat.

Joule's equivalent (jo͞olz) [J. P. *Joule*]. See under *equivalent.*

Jourdain's disease (zhoor-daz′) [Anselme Louis Bernard *Jourdain*, French surgeon, 1734–1816]. See under *disease.*

juccuya (ŭ-koo′yah). The ulcerative type of dermal leishmaniasis.

juga (joo′gah) [L.]. Plural of *jugum.*

jugal (joo′gal) [L. *jugalis; jugum* yoke]. 1. Connecting like a yoke. 2. Pertaining to the cheek.

jugale (joo-ga′le). The jugal point.

jugate (joo′gāt). 1. Locked together. 2. Marked by ridges.

jugged (jugd). Having glanderous swellings: said of horses.

Juglans (joo′glans) [L. "Jove's nut," walnut]. A genus of juglandaceous trees: the walnuts.

juglans (joo′glans). The root bark of *J. cinerea*, the butternut tree: aperient.

juglone (jug′lōn). An antibiotic derived from the leaves and husks of the black walnut tree: active against certain fungi.

jugomaxillary (joo″go-mak′sĭ-lār″e). Pertaining to the zygomatic bone and the maxilla.

jugular (jug′u-lar) [L. *jugularis: jugulum* neck]. Pertaining to the neck.

jugulation (jug″u-la′shun) [L. *jugulare* to cut the throat of]. The sudden and rapid arrest of disease by therapeutical measures.

jugum (joo′gum), pl. *ju′ga* [L. "a yoke"]. A depression or ridge connecting two structures. **ju′ga alveola′ria mandib′ulae** [N A, B N A], depressions on the anterior surface of the alveolar process of the mandible, between the ridges caused by the roots of the incisor teeth. Called also *alveolar ridges of mandible.* **ju′ga alveola′ria maxil′lae** [N A, B N A], the depressions on the anterior surface of the alveolar process of the maxilla, between the ridges caused by the roots of the incisor teeth. Called also *alveolar ridges of maxilla.* **ju′ga cerebra′lia os′sium cra′nii** [B N A], variable ridges on the inner surface of the cranium, corresponding to the sulci of the brain. Called also *cerebral ridges of cranium.* Omitted in N A. **j. pe′nis,** a forceps for compressing the penis. **j. sphenoida′le** [N A], the portion of the body of the sphenoid bone that connects the lesser wings.

juice (jo͞os′) [L. *jus* broth]. Any fluid from an animal or plant tissue. **appetite j.,** gastric juice secreted during eating and varying in character with the appetite for the food which is being eaten. **cancer j.,** a milky juice obtained from cancerous tissue, and containing cancer cells. **cherry j.,** liquid expressed from the fresh ripe fruit of *Prunus cerasus:* used as an ingredient in preparing flavored vehicles for pharmaceuticals. **gastric j.,** succus gastricus. **intestinal j.,** succus entericus. **pancreatic j.,** succus pancreaticus. **press j.,** liquid obtained by submitting finely ground tissue to great pressure. **raspberry j.,** the liquid expressed from the fresh ripe fruit of varieties of *Rubus idaeus* or *Rubus strigosus:* used in a syrup as a flavored vehicle for drugs. **testicle j., testicular j.,** spermine.

julep (joo′lep) [L. *julapium*]. A sweetened alcoholic drink or cordial of various kinds.

Julliard's mask (zho͞ol-yahrz′) [Gustave *Jullaird*, Belgian surgeon, 1836–1911]. See under *mask.*

jumentous (joo-men′tus) [L. *jumentum*, a beast of burden]. Having a strong animal odor.

jumping (jump′ing). Gilles de la Tourette's disease.

junction (junk′shun). The place of meeting or of coming together, as of two different organs or types of tissue. See also *joint* and *junctura.* **amelodentinal j.,** dentinoenamel j. **cementoenamel j.,** the line at which the cementum covering the root of a tooth and the enamel covering its crown meet, designated anatomically as the cervical line. **dentinocemental j.,** the plane of meeting between the dentin and cementum on the root of a tooth. **dentinoenamel j.,** the plane of meeting between the dentin and enamel on the crown of a tooth. **manubriogladiolar j.,** synchondrosis sternalis. **mucogingival j.,** the scalloped line marking the separation of the gingiva from the oral mucosa overlying the dental alveoli. **myoneural j.,** the point of junction of a nerve fiber with the muscle which it innervates. **osseous j's,** the sites of union of different bones. Called also *articulationes* [N A]. **sclerocorneal j.,** the junction between the sclera and the cornea, marked on the outer surface of the eyeball by a slight furrow. **tendinous j's.** See *connexus intertendineus.*

junctional (junk′shun-al). Pertaining to a junction.

junctura (junk-tu′rah), pl. *junctu′rae* [L. "a joining"]. A general term used in anatomical nomenclature to designate the site of union between different structures. See also *articulatio* and *joint.* **j. cartilagin′ea** [N A], a form of articulation in which the union of the bony elements is by intervening cartilage. It includes synchondrosis and symphysis. Called also *amphiarthrosis* [B N A], and *cartilaginous joint.* **junctu′rae cin′guli mem′bri inferio′ris** [N A], the articulations of the girdle of the inferior member. **junctu′rae cin′guli mem′bri superio′ris** [N A], the articulations of the girdle of the superior member. **junctu'rae colum'nae vertebra'lis, thora'cis, et cra'nii** [N A], the articulations of the vertebral column, thorax, and cranium. **j. fibro'sa** [N A], a form of articulation in which the union of the bony elements is by continuous intervening fibrous connective tissue. It includes suture, syndesmosis, and gomphosis. Called also *synarthrosis* [B N A], and *fibrous joint*. **junctu'rae mem'bri inferio'ris li'beri** [N A], the articulations of the free inferior member, that is, of the thigh, leg, and foot. **junctu'rae mem'bri superio'ris li'beri** [N A], the articulations of the free superior member, that is, of the arm, forearm, and hand. **j. os'sium** [B N A], a joint. See also *articulatio*. **junctu'rae os'sium,** N A alternative for *articulationes*. **juncturae os'sium cin'guli extremita'tis pelvi'nae,** juncturae cinguli membri inferioris. **junctu'rae os'sium cin'guli extremita'tis thora'cicae,** juncturae cinguli membri superioris. **j. sacrococcyg'ea** [N A], the articulation between the coccyx and the sacrum. Called also *symphysis sacrococcygea* [B N A], and *sacrococcygeal joint*. **j. synovia'lis** [N A], a specialized form of articulation permitting more or less free movement, the union of the bony elements being surrounded by an articular capsule enclosing a cavity lined by synovial membrane. Called also *diarthrosis* [B N A], and *synovial joint*. **junctu'rae tendi'num** [B N A]. See *connexus intertendineus*.

juncturae (junk-tu're) [L.]. Plural of *junctura*.

Jung's method (yoongz) [Carl Gustav *Jung*, Swiss psychiatrist, 1875–1961]. Psychoanalysis.

Jung's muscle (yoongz) [Karl Gustav *Jung*, Swiss anatomist, 1793–1864]. Musculus pyramidalis auriculae.

Jungbluth's vasa propria (yoong'bloots) [Hermann *Jungbluth*, German physician]. See *vasa propria*.

Jüngling's disease (yeng'lingz) [Otto *Jüngling*, German surgeon, born 1884]. Osteitis tuberculosa multiplex cystica.

juniper (joo'nĭ-per). The dried ripe fruit of *Juniperus communis*, or juniper tree.

junk (junk). 1. A form of cushion used in dressing fractures. 2. Oakum, sometimes used in surgical dressings.

Junker apparatus, bottle, inhaler (junk'er) [F. E. *Junker*, English physician of 19th century]. A bottle-like inhaler for administration of chloroform (1867).

Junod's boot (zhoo-nōz') [Victor Theodor *Junod*, French physician, 1809–1881]. See under *boot*.

jurisprudence (joor"is-proo'dens) [L. *juris prudentia* knowledge of law]. The scientific study or application of the principles of law and justice. **dental j.,** the application of the principles of law and justice as they relate to the practice of dentistry. **medical j.,** the application of the principles of law and justice as they relate to the practice of medicine and the relations of physicians to each other and to society in general.

jury-mast (joor'e-mast). An upright bar used in supporting the head in cases of Pott's disease.

juscul. Abbreviation for L. *jus'culum*, broth.

jusculum (jus'ku-lum) [L.]. Soup or broth.

justo major (jus'to ma'jor). See *pelvis aequabiliter justo major*.

justo minor (jus'to mi'nor). See *pelvis aequabiliter justo minor*.

Justus' test (joos'toos) [J. *Justus*, Hungarian dermatologist]. See under *tests*.

jute (joot). The fibers of *Corchorus olitorius:* formerly used in surgical dressings.

juvantia (joo-van'she-ah) [L. pl.]. Adjuvant and palliative medicines or appliances.

juvenile (joo'vĕ-nīl). Pertaining to youth or childhood; young or immature.

juxta-articular (juks"tah-ar-tik'u-lar) [L. *juxta* near + *articulus* joint]. Situated near a joint or in the region of a joint.

juxta-epiphyseal (juks"tah-ep-ĭ-fiz'e-al). Near to or adjoining an epiphysis.

juxtaglomerular (juks"tah-glo-mer'u-lar). Near to or adjoining a glomerulus of the kidney.

juxtangina (juks-tan'jĭ-nah) [L. "almost quinsy"]. Inflammation involving the muscles of the pharynx.

juxtaposition (juks"tah-po-zish'un) [L. *juxta* near + *positio* place]. Apposition.

juxtapyloric (juks"tah-pi-lor'ik). Situated near the pylorus or near the pyloric vein.

juxtaspinal (juks-tah-spi'nal) [L. *juxta* near + *spine*]. Close to the spinal column.

K

K. 1. Chemical symbol for *potassium* [L. *kalium*]. 2. Abbreviation for *electrostatic capacity, kathode*, and *Kelvin* (scale; absolute zero).

k. Abbreviation for *constant*.

κ. Symbol for *magnetic susceptibility*.

K stoff [Ger.]. A gas, chloromethyl chloroformate.

Ka. Abbreviation for *kathode* (*cathode*).

kabure (kah-boo're). A skin disease found in Japan; probably caused by the burrowing of the cercariae of *Schistosoma japonica* in the skin.

Kader's operation (kah'ders) [Bronislaw *Kader*, Polish surgeon, 1863–1937]. See under *operation*.

Kaes's feltwork (kiz'ez) [Theodor *Kaes*, German neurologist, 1852–1913]. A dense network of nerve fibers in the cerebral cortex.

Kaes-Bechterew layer [Theodor *Kaes;* Vladimir Mikhailovich von *Bechterew*, 1857–1927]. Bechterew's layer.

Kafka's reaction, test (kaf'kaz) [Victor *Kafka*, German physician, 1881–1955]. See under *tests*.

Kahlbaum's disease (kahl'bowmz) [Karl Ludwig *Kahlbaum*, German physician, 1828–1899]. Catatonia.

Kahler's disease, law (kah'lerz) [Otto *Kahler*, Austrian physician, 1849–1893]. See *multiple myeloma*, and under *law*.

Kahn's albumin A reaction, test [Herbert *Kahn*, German physician]. See under *tests*, def. 2.

Kahn's test (kahnz) [Reuben Leon *Kahn*, American bacteriologist, born 1887]. See under *tests*, def. 1.

kahweol (kah'we-ol) [Turkish *galweh* coffee]. A white crystalline lipid which forms the principal part of the unsaponifiable fraction of coffee.

kaif (kif) [Arabic]. Dreamy tranquillity from the use of drugs.

kainophobia (ki-no-fo'be-ah) [Gr. *kainos* new + *phobia*]. Fear of new things.

kaiserling (ki'zer-ling). 1. Kaiserling's solution. 2. A specimen preserved in Kaiserling's solution.

Kaiserling's solution (ki'zer-lings) [Karl *Kaiserling*, German pathologist, 1869–1942]. See under *solution*.

kakergasia (kak-er-ga'se-ah). Cacergasia.

kakergastic (kak-er-gas'tik). Cacergastic.

kakesthesia (kak-es-the'ze-ah). Cacesthesia.

kakidrosis (kak-i-dro'sis) [Gr. *kakos* bad + *hidrōs*

perspiration + *-osis*]. An extremely disagreeable odor of the sweat.

kakke (kahk′ka) [Japanese]. Beriberi.

kakodyl (kak′o-dil). Cacodyl.

kakon (kak′on). J. Monakow's term for an abnormal reaction in anxiety neuroses.

kakosmia (kak-oz′me-ah) [Gr. *kakos* bad + *osmē* smell + *-ia*]. A foul or disagreeable odor.

kakotrophy (kak-ot′ro-fe). Cacotrophy.

kala-azar (kah′lah ah-zar′) [Hindu, black fever]. An infectious disease with a high fatality rate, occurring along the Mediterranean shore, in West Africa, Mesopotamia, southern Russia, India, North China and Brazil. It is marked by fever, progressive anemia, wasting, enlargement of the spleen and liver, and dropsy, and is caused by the parasite *Leishmania donovani*, which infests the endothelial cells, especially of the spleen and liver. It seems to be transmitted to man by the bite of the sandfly, *Phlebotomus argentipes*, and other species of this genus. The disease is also called *febrile tropical splenomegaly, visceral leishmaniasis, Dumdum fever, cachectic fever, black fever, ponos*, and *nonmalarial remittent fever*. **canine k., infantile k., Mediterranean k.,** a form affecting infants, chiefly in countries bordering on the Mediterranean, formerly ascribed to *Leishmania infantum*, which is now regarded as identical with *L. donovani*. Called also *ponos*.

kaladana (kal-ah-da′nah). The dried seeds of *Ipomoea nil:* purgative or anthelmintic.

kalagua (kah-lah′gwah). A South American drug used in tuberculosis.

kalemia (kah-le′me-ah) [L. *kalium* potassium + Gr. *haima* blood + *-ia*]. The presence of potassium in the blood.

kali (ka′li, kah′le) [Ger.]. Potash. **k. arsenico′sum,** Fowler's solution.

kaliemia (ka-le-e′me-ah). Kalemia.

kaligenous (ka-lij′e-nus) [*kalium* + Gr. *gennan* to produce]. Producing potash.

kalimeter (kah-lim′e-ter). Alkalimeter.

kaliopenia (ka″le-o-pe′ne-ah) [L. *kalium* potassium + Gr. *penia* poverty]. A deficiency of potassium in the body.

kaliopenic (ka″le-o-pe′nik). Pertaining to, characterized by, or producing kaliopenia.

kalium (ka′le-um) [L.]. Potassium.

kaliuresis (ka″le-u-re′sis) [L. *kalium* potassium + Gr. *ourēsis* a making water]. The excretion of potassium in the urine.

kaliuretic (ka″le-u-ret′ik). 1. Pertaining to, characterized by, or promoting kaliuresis. 2. An agent that promotes kaliuresis.

kallak (kal′ak) [Eskimo for disease of the skin]. A pustular dermatitis common among the Eskimos.

kallidin (kal′lĭ-dĭn). A type of kinin liberated by the action of kallikrein on a globulin of blood plasma. Two forms of kallidin have been identified: one of them (*kallidin I*) is the same as bradykinin; the other (*kallidin II*) is a decapeptide composed of bradykinin with an N-terminal lysine added.

Kallikak (kal′ĭ-kak) [Gr. *kallos* beauty + *kakos* bad]. A pseudonym applied by H. H. Goddard to a family described by him which had two lines of descendants, one of normal or superior individuals, the other of feebleminded and degenerate ones.

kallikrein (kal″lĭ-kre′in). A type of enzyme present in pancreas, saliva, urine, blood plasma, etc., which liberates kallidin from a globulin of blood plasma and hence has vasodilator and whealing actions.

kallikreinogen (kal″lĭ-kri′no-jin). The inactive precursor of kallikrein which is normally present in blood; its conversion into kallikrein may be triggered by a variety of physical or chemical changes.

Kalmia (kal′me-ah). A genus of shrubs, leaves of which have been used in syphilis, diarrhea, and chronic inflammatory disorders.

Kalmuk idiocy (kal′mook) [*Kalmuk*, a Mongolian people in Asia and Russia]. See under *idiocy*.

kalopsia (kal-op′se-ah) [Gr. *kalos* beautiful + *opsis* sight + *-ia*]. A condition in which all objects appear more beautiful than they really are.

kaluresis (kal″u-re′sis). Kaliuresis.

kaluretic (kal″u-ret′ik). Kaliuretic.

kalymana-bacterium (kal″ĭ-ma′na bak-te′re-um). A Brazilian term for the organism causing venereal granuloma.

kamala (kam′ah-lah). The glands and hairs of the capsules of *Mallotus philippinensis*, an East Indian shrub: purgative, used mainly against taenia and lumbrici.

kamaline (kam′ah-lin). An alkaloid from kamala.

Kaminer reaction (kam′ĭ-ner) [Gisa *Kaminer*, Vienna physician, 1883–1941]. Freund's reaction.

kanagugui (kan″ah-goo′gwe). A Japanese plant, *Lindera erythrocarpa;* its fluidextract is used in secondary syphilis.

kanamycin (kan″ah-mi′sin). A substance produced by *Streptomyces kanamyceticus:* used as a broad-spectrum antibiotic.

Kanavel's sign (kan-a′velz) [Allen Buchner *Kanavel*, Chicago surgeon, 1874–1938]. See under *sign*.

kangaroo (kang″gah-roo′). A marsupial mammal of Australasia, of many species; from its tail a tendon is derived that is valued as a ligature.

kansasiin (kan-sas′e-in). A product prepared from *Mycobacterium kansasii*, comparable to tuberculin, used in a cutaneous test of hypersensitivity.

kantrex (kan′treks). Trade mark for preparations of kanamycin.

kanyemba (kan″e-em′bah). Chiufa.

kaodzera (kah″od-ze′rah). Rhodesian trypanosomiasis; a disease prevalent in Rhodesia, similar to sleeping sickness and due to *Trypanosoma rhodesiense*.

kaoliang (ka″o-le′ang). A sorghum grain of Africa and India whose seed can be milled into a flour.

kaolin (ka′o-lin). A native hydrated aluminum silicate, powdered and freed from gritty particles by elutriation: used as an ingredient in kaolin mixture with pectin.

kaolinosis (ka″o-lin-o′sis). A kind of pneumoconiosis caused by inhaling particles of kaolin.

Kaplan's test (kap′lanz) [David M. *Kaplan*, New York physician, born 1876]. See under *tests*.

Kaposi's disease, sarcoma, varicelliform eruption (kap′o-sēz) [Moritz Kohn *Kaposi*, Austrian dermatologist, 1837–1902]. See under *disease, eruption*, and *sarcoma*.

kappadione (kap″pah-di′ōn). Trade mark for a preparation of menadiol sodium diphosphate.

Kappeler's maneuver (kap′ĕ-lerz) [Otto *Kappeler*, German surgeon, 1841–1909]. See under *maneuver*.

kaps-. For words beginning thus, see also those beginning *caps-*.

kapselcoccus (kap″sel-kok′us). A microbe found in pyosalpinx.

kara-kurt (kah′rah-koort″). The Russian spider *Latrodectus lugubris*.

karaya (kar′a-ah). A gum from the bark of a tree of the genus *Astragalus:* used in setting fluids for the hair, in certain foods, and in laxatives. In sensitive individuals it may cause hay fever, asthma, and skin eruptions.

Karell's cure, treatment (kah′relz) [Philip *Karell*, Russian physician, 1806–1886]. See under *treatment*.

Karroo syndrome (kah-roo′) [*Karroo*, region of South Africa]. See under *syndrome*.

Kartagener's syndrome, triad (kar-tag′e-nerz) [M. *Kartagener*, German physician]. See under *syndrome*.

Karyamoebina (kar″e-am-e-bi′nah). An ameba

with the peripheral chromatin clumped in a few large, elongated masses. **K. falca'ta,** a species found in the intestinal tract of man in California.

karyapsis (kar"e-ap'sis) [*karyo-* + Gr. *hapsis* joining]. Union of nuclei in a conjugating cell.

karyenchyma (kar"e-en'kĭ-mah) [*karyo-* + Gr. *enchymos* juicy]. Karyolymph.

karyo- (kar'e-o) [Gr. *karyon* nucleus, or nut]. Combining form denoting relationship to a nucleus. See also words beginning *caryo-*.

karyoblast (kar'e-o-blast) [*karyo-* + Gr. *blastos* germ]. A cell at the beginning of the erythrocyte series.

karyochromatophil (kar"e-o-kro-mat'o-fil) [*karyo-* + Gr. *chrōma* color + *philein* to love]. Having a stainable nucleus.

karyochrome (kar'e-o-krōm") [*karyo-* + Gr. *chrōma* color]. A nerve cell the nucleus of which is deeply stainable, while the body is not; its nucleus is larger than that of a cytochrome, and there are varieties designated by Greek letters.

karyochylema (kar"e-o-ki-le'mah). Nuclear sap.

karyoclastic (kar"e-o-klas'tik). Karyoklastic.

karyocyte (kar'e-o-sīt) [*karyo-* + *-cyte*]. 1. A nucleated cell. 2. An early normoblast.

karyogamic (kar"e-o-gam'ik) [*karyo-* + Gr. *gamos* marriage]. Pertaining to, or characterized by, union of nuclei.

karyogamy (kar"e-og'ah-me) [*karyo-* + Gr. *gamos* marriage]. Cell conjugation with union of nuclei.

karyogen (kar'e-o-jen") [*karyo-* + Gr. *gennan* to produce]. An organic iron compound found in certain cell nuclei, especially the head of the spermatozoon.

karyogenesis (kar"e-o-jen'e-sis) [*karyo-* + Gr. *genesis* production]. The development of the nucleus of a cell.

karyogenic (kar"e-o-jen'ik). Forming the nucleus of a cell; pertaining to karyogenesis.

karyogonad (kar"e-o-go'nad) [*karyo-* + Gr. *gonē* seed]. Micronucleus.

karyokinesis (kar"e-o-ki-ne'sis) [*karyo-* + Gr *kinesis* motion]. The phenomena involved in division of the nucleus, in the process of indirect cell division, or mitosis. **asymmetrical k.,** mitosis in which the chromosomes divide unequally and into dissimilar masses. **hyperchromatic k.,** mitosis in which the number of chromosomes is abnormally large. **hypochromatic k.,** mitosis in which the number of chromosomes is abnormally small.

karyokinetic (kar"e-o-ki-net'ik). Pertaining to or of the nature of karyokinesis.

karyoklasis (kar"e-ok'lah-sis) [*karyo-* + Gr. *klasis* breaking]. The breaking down of the cell nucleus.

karyoklastic (kar"e-o-klas'tik). 1. Breaking down cell nuclei. 2. Arresting mitosis.

karyolobic (kar"e-o-lo'bik). Having a lobe-shaped nucleus.

karyolobism (kar"e-o-lo'bizm). A lobed condition of a cell nucleus, especially the nucleus of a leukocyte.

karyology (kar"e-ol'o-je) [*karyo-* + *-logy*]. The branch of cytology which deals with the cell nucleus.

karyolymph (kar'e-o-limf) [*karyo-* + *lymph*]. The liquid part of a cell nucleus, as contrasted with the chromatin and linin.

karyolysis (kar"e-ol'ĭ-sis) [*karyo-* + Gr. *lysis* dissolution]. A form of necrobiosis in which the nucleus of a cell swells and gradually loses its chromatin.

Karyolysus lacertarum (kar-e-ol'ĭ-sus las-er-ta'rum) [*karyo-* + Gr. *lyein* to loose]. A hemogregarina from the blood of lizards.

karyolytic (kar"e-o-lit'ik). Producing or pertaining to karyolysis; destroying cell nuclei.

karyomere (kar'e-o-mēr"). 1. Chromomere, def. 1. 2. A vesicle containing only a small portion of the typical nucleus, usually following abnormal mitosis.

karyometry (kar"e-om'e-tre) [*karyo-* + Gr. *metron* measure]. Measurement of a cell nucleus.

karyomicrosome (kar"e-o-mi'kro-sōm) [*karyo-* + *microsome*]. Nucleomicrosome.

karyomit (kar'e-o-mit) [*karyo-* + Gr. *mitos* thread]. A chromatin thread of the nuclear network.

karyomitome (kar"e-om'ĭ-tōm). The nuclear chromatin network.

karyomitosis (kar"e-o-mi-to'sis). Mitosis.

karyomitotic (kar"e-o-mi-tot'ik). Pertaining to karyomitosis.

karyomorphism (kar"e-o-mor'fizm) [*karyo-* + Gr. *morphē* form]. The shape of a cell nucleus, especially that of a leukocyte.

karyon (kar'e-on) [Gr. *karyon* nucleus]. 1. The nucleus of a cell. 2. An extract of the leaves of the walnut tree which has been used in the treatment of tuberculosis.

karyonide (kar'e-o-nīd) [Gr. *karyon* nucleus]. A clone of which all the nuclei are derived from a single nucleus by vegetative reproduction.

karyophage (kar'e-o-fāj) [*karyo-* + Gr. *phagein* to eat]. A cell that exercises phagocytic action on the nucleus of the infested cell.

karyoplasm (kar'e-o-plazm) [*karyo-* + Gr. *plasma* plasm]. The nucleoplasm, or protoplasm of the nucleus of a cell.

karyoplasmic (kar"e-o-plaz'mik). Pertaining to karyoplasm.

karyoplast (kar'e-o-plast). The nucleus of a cell.

karyoplastin (kar"e-o-plas'tin). The substance of a mitotic spindle; the parachromatin.

karyopyknosis (kar"e-o-pik-no'sis). Shrinkage of a cell nucleus, with condensation of the chromatin into a solid, structureless mass or masses.

karyopyknotic (kar"e-o-pik-not'ik). Pertaining to, characterized by, or causing karyopyknosis.

karyoreticulum (kar"e-o-re-tik'u-lum) [*karyo-* + *reticulum*]. The fibrillar part of the karyoplasm as distinguished from the fluid part of karyolymph.

karyorrhectic (kar"e-o-rek'tik). Pertaining to, characterized by, or causing karyorrhexis.

karyorrhexis (kar"e-o-rek'sis) [*karyo-* + Gr. *rhēxis* a breaking]. The rupture of the cell nucleus in which the chromatin disintegrates into formless granules which are extruded from the cell.

karyosome (kar'e-o-sōm) [*karyo-* + Gr. *sōma* body]. One of the masses of chromatin aggregated as knots in the chromatin network. Called also *net knot, false nucleolus, chromatin nucleolus,* and *chromatin reservoir.*

karyospherical (kar"e-o-sfer'e-kal). Possessing a spherical nucleus.

karyostasis (kar"e-os'tah-sis) [*karyo-* + Gr. *stasis* halt]. The so-called resting stage of the nucleus between mitotic divisions.

karyota (kar"e-o'tah). Nucleated cells.

karyotheca (kar"e-o-the'kah) [*karyo-* + Gr. *thēkē* sheath]. The membrane enclosing a cell nucleus.

karyotin (kar'e-o-tin). Chromatin.

karyotype (kar'e-o-tīp) [*karyo-* + *type*]. A systematized arrangement of the chromosomes of a single cell, typical of an individual or a species.

karyotypic (kar"e-o-tip'ik). Pertaining to or representative of the karyotype.

karyozoic (kar"e-o-zo'ik) [*karyo-* + Gr. *zōon* animal]. Existing in or inhabiting the nuclei of cells, as do certain protozoa.

kasai (kah-si'). A syndrome seen in the Belgian Congo, characterized by anemia, depigmentation of the skin, and edema, all of which may be secondary to iron deficiency.

kat-, kata- [Gr. *kata* down]. Prefix meaning down, against. For words beginning thus, see also those beginning *cat-, cata-*.

katachromasis (kat"ah-kro'mah-sis). The process by which the daughter chromosomes reconstruct the daughter nuclei.

katadidymus (kat″ah-did′ĭ-mus) [*kata-* + Gr. *didymos* twin]. A twin fetal monster divided above, but single toward the podalic pole (monstra duplicia katadidyma—Förster).

katakinetomere (kat″ah-kin′e-to-mēr) [*kata-* + Gr. *kinēsis* motion + *meros* part]. A. P. Mathews' name for matter in which the molecules and atoms are poor in energy content and therefore dead. Cf. *anakinetomere.*

katakinetomeric (kat″ah-kin″e-to-mer′ik). Poor in energy content. Cf. *anakinetomeric.*

katalase (kat′ah-lās). Peroxidase.

kataphraxis (kat″ah-frak′sis). The operation of enclosing or surrounding an organ with metal supports to keep it in place.

kataphylaxis (kat″ah-fi-lak′sis). 1. The transport of phylactic agents to the site of infection. 2. The increased activity of certain bacterial spores when injected along with an ionizable salt of calcium. The washed spores injected alone are innocuous but injected with a calcium salt produce a typical and fatal infection.

katathermometer (kat″ah-ther-mom′e-ter). A pair of alcoholic thermometers, one with a dry bulb and one with a wet bulb. They are heated to 110 F., exposed to the air, and the time noted that it takes each bulb to fall from 100 to 90 F. From this the temperature as it affects the body can be deduced.

Katayama (kat″ah-yah′mah). A genus of snails. **K. nosopoh′ra,** a snail which is the intermediate host of *Schistosoma japonicum.*

Katayama disease (kat″ah-yah′mah). Schistosomiasis japonica.

Katayama's test (kat″ah-yah′mahz) [Kunika *Katayama,* Japanese physician, 1856–1931]. See under *tests.*

katechin (kat′e-chin). Blum's term for a blood constituent which has an antithyroid effect. Called also *Blum substance.*

katharometer (kath″ah-rom′e-ter). An instrument for electrometric determination of basal metabolic rates.

kathepsin (kah-thep′sin). An intracellular protease present in mammalian organs.

kathisophobia (kath″i-so-fo′be-ah). Akathisia.

katholysis (kah-thol′ĭ-sis). Electrolysis with the cathode needle.

katine (ka′tin). An alkaloid, $C_{10}H_{18}ON_2$, from *Catha edulis.* It acts on the nervous system like cocaine, but has no local anesthetic properties.

kation (kat′e-on). Cation.

katolysis (kah-tol′ĭ-sis) [Gr. *katō* below + *lysis* dissolution]. The incomplete or intermediate conversion of complex chemical bodies into simpler compounds; applied especially to digestive processes.

katophoria (kat″o-fo′re-ah). Katotropia.

katotropia (kat″o-tro′pe-ah) [Gr. *katō* below + *trepein* to turn]. A tendency of the visual axes to fall below the object looked at. Called also *katophoria.*

Katz formula [Johann Rudolf *Katz,* German colloid chemist, 1880–1938]. See under *formula.*

katzenjammer (kats′en-yam′er) [Ger.]. Symptoms of headache, acute gastric catarrh, possibly cerebral edema, and functional neuritis, following ingestion of alcohol.

Katzenstein's test (kats′en-stīnz) [Moritz *Katzenstein,* German surgeon, 1872–1932]. See under *tests.*

Kauffmann's test (kowf′manz) [Friedrich *Kauffmann,* Berlin internist, born 1893]. See under *tests.*

Kaufmann's method or **treatment** [Fritz *Kaufmann,* German neurologist, born 1875]. See under *treatment.*

Kayser's disease (ki′zers) [Bernhard *Kayser,* German ophthalmologist, 1869–1954]. See under *disease.*

Kayser-Fleischer ring (ki′zer flish′er) [Bernhard *Kayser;* Richard *Fleischer,* Munich physician, 1848–1909]. See under *ring.*

KBr. Potassium bromide.

KC. Abbreviation for *kathodal* (*cathodal*) *closing.*

kc. Abbreviation for *kilocycle.*

KCC. Abbreviation for *kathodal* (*cathodal*) *closing contraction.*

$KC_2H_3O_2$. Potassium acetate.

KCl. Potassium chloride.

KClO. Potassium hypochlorite.

$KClO_3$. Potassium chlorate.

K_2CO_3. Potassium carbonate.

kc.p.s. Abbreviation for *kilocycles per second.*

KCT. Abbreviation for *kathodal* (*cathodal*) *closing tetanus.*

KD. Abbreviation for *kathodal* (*cathodal*) *duration.*

KDT. Abbreviation for *kathodal* (*cathodal*) *duration tetanus.*

Keating-Hart's method, treatment (ke′-ting-harts) [Walter Valentine de *Keating-Hart,* French physician, 1870–1922]. See *fulguration.*

kebocephaly (keb″o-sef′ah-le). Cebocephaly.

ked (ked). The sheep tick, *Melophagus ovinus.*

keel (kēl). A septicemic enteritis of ducklings caused by *Salmonella anatum.*

Keeley cure (ke′le) [Leslie E. *Keeley,* American physician, 1834–1900]. See under *cure.*

Keen's operation, sign (kēnz) [William Williams *Keen,* Philadelphia surgeon, 1837–1932]. See under *operation* and *sign.*

keeper (kēp′er). The armature of a magnet.

kefyr (kef′er). Kefir.

Kehr's incision, operation (kārz) [Hans *Kehr,* German surgeon, 1862–1916]. See under *incision* and *operation.*

Kehrer's reflex, sign (kār′erz) [Ferdinand *Kehrer,* German neurologist, born 1883]. See under *reflex* and *sign.*

keirospasm (ki′ro-spazm) Gr. *keirein* to shear + *spasm*]. An occupational neurosis occurring in barbers, characterized by spasmodic contraction of muscles of the fingers, hand, and forearm.

Keith's bundle, node (kēths) [Sir Arthur *Keith,* London anatomist, 1866–1955]. See under *bundle* and *node.*

Keith's diet [Norman M. *Keith,* American physician, born 1885]. See under *diet.*

Keith-Flack node [Sir Arthur *Keith;* Martin *Flack,* physiologist in London, 1882–1931]. See under *node.*

kelectome (ke′lek-tōm) [Gr. *kēlē* tumor + *ektomē* excision]. A device used in removing specimens of tissue from tumors.

kelis (ke′lis) [Gr. *kēlē* tumor]. 1. Morphea. 2. Keloid.

Keller's test (kel′erz) [Philipp *Keller,* German dermatologist, born 1891]. See under *tests.*

Kelling's test (kel′ings) [Georg *Kelling,* German physician, born 1866]. See under *tests.*

Kelly's operation, sign, speculum (kel′ēz) [Howard Atwood *Kelly,* American surgeon, 1858–1943]. See under the nouns.

keloid (ke′loid) [Gr. *kēlē* tumor + *eidos* form]. A new growth or tumor of the skin, consisting of whitish ridges, nodules, and plates of dense tissue. These growths tend to recur after removal and are sometimes tender or painful. **acne k.,** keloidal folliculitis. **Addison's k.,** morphea. **Alibert's k., cicatricial k., false k.,** a growth resembling a true keloid, but resulting from hypertrophy of a cicatrix.

keloidosis (ke″loi-do′sis). A condition marked by the formation of multiple keloids or keloid-like growths.

keloma (ke-lo′mah). Keloid.

keloplasty (ke′lo-plas″te) [Gr. *kēlē* tumor]. Plastic operation on a scar.

kelos (ke′los). Keloid.

kelosomus (ke-lo-so′mus). Celosomia.

kelotomy (ke-lot′o-me) [Gr. *kēlē* a rupture + *temnein* to cut]. The surgical division of the stricture in strangulated hernia.

Kelvin scale (kel′vin) [Lord *Kelvin* (William Thompson), British physicist, 1824–1907]. See under *scale.*

kemadrin (kem′ah-drin). Trade mark for a preparation of tricyclamol.

Kempner diet (kemp′ner) [Walter *Kempner*, American physician, born 1903]. See under *diet.*

kenacort (ken′ah-kort). Trade mark for preparations of triamcinolone.

kenalog (ken′ah-log). Trade mark for preparations of triamcinolone acetonide.

Kendall (ken′dahl), Edward Calvin. American chemist, born 1886, noted for his work on hormones, especially the adrenal steroids; co-winner, with P. S. Hench and T. Reichstein, of the Nobel prize for physiology and medicine in 1950.

Kennedy's syndrome (ken′ĕ-dēz) [Foster *Kennedy*, New York neurologist, 1884–1952]. See under *syndrome.*

Kenny method, treatment (ken′e) [Sister Elizabeth *Kenny* of Brisbane, Australia, later in U.S.A., 1886–1952]. See under *treatment.*

keno- (ken′o) [Gr. *kenos* empty]. Combining form denoting empty. See also words beginning *ceno-.*

kenophobia (ken″o-fo′be-ah) [*keno-* + *phobia* fear]. Morbid dread of large open spaces.

kenotoxin (ke′no-tok-sin) [*keno-* + *toxin*]. The toxin of fatigue; produced in muscle by muscular contractions.

kenotron (ken′o-tron). An electric valve consisting of a vacuum tube having for one electrode a hot filament: often used in rectifying alternating to direct current, as in roentgen generators.

Kent's bundle (kents) [Albert Frank Stanley *Kent*, English physiologist, born 1863]. See under *bundle.*

Kent-His bundle [A. F. S. *Kent;* Wilhelm *His*, Jr.]. Bundle of His.

kentrokinesis (ken″tro-ki-ne′sis). Centrokinesia.

kentrokinetic (ken″tro-ki-net′ik). Centrokinetic.

kenurenin (ken″u-re′nin). An alpha amino acid closely related to tryptophan.

kephal- (kef′ahl). For words beginning thus, see those beginning *cephal-.*

kephir, kephyr (kef′er). Kefir.

keracele (ker′ah-sēl) [Gr. *keras* horn + *kēlē* tumor]. A horny tumor.

Kerandel's symptom (ker″an-delz′) [Jean François *Kerandel*, French colonial physician, born 1873]. See under *sign.*

keraphyllocele (ker″ah-fil′o-sēl) [Gr. *keras* horn + *phyllon* leaf + *kēlē* tumor]. A horny tumor on the inner surface of the wall of a horse's hoof.

kerasin (ker′ah-sin). A galactoside, probably $C_{48}H_{93}O_8N$, obtained from brain substance. It yields on hydrolysis galactose, sphingosine, and lignoceric acid.

keratalgia (ker″ah-tal′je-ah) [*kerato-* + *-algia*]. Pain in the cornea.

keratectasia (ker″ah-tek-ta′ze-ah) [*kerato-* + Gr. *ektasis* extension]. Protrusion of the cornea.

keratectomy (ker″ah-tek′to-me) [*kerato-* + Gr. *ektomē* excision]. Excision of a portion of the cornea: usually done for anterior staphyloma.

keratiasis (ker″ah-ti′ah-sis). The presence of horny warts on the skin.

keratic (ker-at′ik). 1. Pertaining to horn. 2. Pertaining to the cornea.

keratin (ker′ah-tin). A scleroprotein which is the principal constituent of epidermis, hair, nails, horny tissues, and the organic matrix of the enamel of the teeth. It is a very insoluble protein, contains sulfur, and yields tyrosine and leucine on decomposition. Its solution is sometimes used in coating pills when the latter are desired to pass through the stomach unchanged.

keratinase (ker′ah-tĭ-nās). A proteolytic enzyme which enables the clothes moth to digest wool keratin.

keratinization (ker″ah-tin″i-za′shun). 1. The development of or conversion into keratin. 2. The process of becoming horny.

keratinize (ker′ah-tin-īz). To make or become horny.

keratinocyte (kĕ-rat′ĭ-no-sit). The epidermal cell which synthesizes keratin; constituting 95 per cent of the epidermal cells and, with the melanocyte, forming the binary cell system of the epidermis. In its various successive stages it is known as basal cell, prickle cell, and granular cell.

keratinoid (ker′ah-tin-oid). A form of tablet not soluble in the stomach, but readily soluble in the intestine.

keratinose (ker′ah-tin-ōs). An albumose obtained from keratin by hydrolyzing with an acid, alkali, or ferment.

keratinous (ke-rat′ĭ-nus). Containing or of the nature of keratin; horny.

keratitis (ker″ah-ti′tis) [*kerato-* + *-itis*]. Inflammation of the cornea. **acne rosacea k.,** a severe keratitis associated with acne rosacea of the cornea and eyelids. **actinic k.,** a form due to the action of ultraviolet light. **alphabet k.,** striate k. **artificial silk k.,** keratitis occurring among workers in artificial silk manufacture. It is marked by blurring of vision with the appearance of haloes around lights. **band k., band-shaped k., k. bandelette,** ribbon-like k. **k. bullo′sa,** the formation of large or small bullae or blebs upon the cornea. **deep k.,** interstitial k. **dendriform k., dendritic k.,** that which results in a dendriform ulceration of the cornea. **Dimmer's k.,** k. nummularis. **k. discifor′mis,** keratitis with the formation of a round or oval, disk-like opacity of the cornea. **fascicular k.,** keratitis attended by the formation of a band of blood vessels. **k. filamento′sa,** keratitis with twisted filaments of mucoid material on the surface of the cornea. **furrow k.,** dendritic keratitis. **herpetic k.,** keratitis occurring along with herpes zoster. **hypopyon k.,** suppurative keratitis associated with purulent infiltration and hypopyon. See *ulcus serpens corneae.* **interstitial k.,** a chronic variety of keratitis with deep deposits in the substance of the cornea, which becomes hazy throughout and has a ground-glass appearance (Sichel, 1837). The disease is associated with congenital syphilis, and occurs in children before the fifteenth year. Called also *parenchymatous k.* and *deep k.* **lagophthalmic k.,** that which accompanies lagophthalmos; it is due to exposure of the eyeball to the air. **lattice k.,** familial degeneration of the cornea with lattice-like areas. **marginal k.,** phlyctenular keratitis in which the papules are arranged around the margin of the cornea. **mycotic k.,** keratomycosis. **neuroparalytic k.,** that which follows disease of the trifacial nerve. **k. nummula′ris,** keratitis marked by corneal deposits which are circular areas with sharply defined edges surrounded by a halo of less dense character; called also *Dimmer's k.* **oyster shuckers' k.,** a kind of suppurative keratitis produced by pieces of oyster shell which have entered the cornea. **parenchymatous k.,** interstitial k. **k. petrif′icans,** keratitis with calcareous changes. **phlyctenular k.,** a variety characterized by the formation of pustules or papules on the cornea. **k. profun′da,** interstitial k. **k. puncta′ta, punctate k.,** an old term for the formation of cellular and fibrinous deposits (keratic precipitates) on the posterior surface of the cornea, occurring after injury or iridocyclitis and giving an appearance of fine drops of dew. **k. puncta′ta subepithelia′lis,** a form with gray areas on the cornea under Bowman's membrane, with an intact superficial epithelium. **purulent k.,** keratitis in which there is formed either a suppurating ulcer or an abscess. **k. pustulifor'mis profun'da,** a painful keratitis marked by deep-seated yellow intracorneal spots, hypopyon and purulent iritis. **k. ramifica'ta superficia'lis,** a disease of the tropics marked by superficial loss of the epithelium of the cornea. **reapers' k.,** suppurative keratitis due to the wounding of the cornea by the awn of some grain, as barley. **reticular k.,** familial degeneration of the cornea with reticular areas. **ribbon-like k.,** the formation of a transverse film on the cornea. **rosacea k.,** acne rosacea k. **sclerosing k.,** keratitis associated with scleritis, leading to hyperplasia. **scrofulus k.,** phlyctenular keratitis. **secondary k.,** keratitis due to disease of some other part of the eye. **serpiginous k.,** ulcus serpens corneae. **k. sic'ca,** keratoconjunctivitis sicca. **striate k.,** keratitis marked by parallel and intersecting lines on the corneal epithelium; called also *alphabet k.* **suppurative k.,** keratitis attended with, or associated with, suppuration. **trachomatous k.,** pannus. **traumatic k.,** that which results from a wound. **trophic k.,** neuroparalytic k. **vascular k.,** keratitis accompanied by the formation of blood vessels beneath the conjunctiva and outer layers of the cornea. **vasculonebulous k.,** pannus. **vesicular k.,** keratitis with the development of small vesicles on the surface. **xerotic k.,** softening of the cornea.

kerato- (ker'ah-to) [Gr. *keras* horn, cornea]. A combining form denoting relationship to the cornea, or to horny tissue.

keratoacanthoma (ker"ah-to-ak"an-tho'mah) [*kerato-* + *acanthoma*]. A rapidly growing papular lesion, with a superficial crater filled with a keratin plug, usually situated on the face, which reaches maximum size and then resolves spontaneously within four to six months from onset.

kerato-angioma (ker"ah-to-an"je-o'mah). Angiokeratoma.

keratocele (ker'ah-to-sēl) [*kerato-* + Gr. *kēlē* hernia]. Hernia of the innermost layer of the cornea (Descemet's membrane).

keratocentesis (ker"ah-to-sen-te'sis) [*kerato-* + Gr. *kentēsis* puncture]. Puncture of the cornea.

keratoconjunctivitis (ker"ah-to-kon-junk"tĭ-vi'tis). Inflammation of the cornea and conjunctiva. **epidemic k.,** a highly infectious disease characterized by relatively little ocular exudate, development of round subepithelial opacities in association with the keratitis, and often swelling of regional lymph nodes; systemic symptoms, especially headache, may also be present. Adenovirus type 8 has been repeatedly isolated from patients with the disease. **epizootic k.,** a keratoconjunctivitis of cattle, caused by *Moraxella bovis* and characterized by discharge and clouding or destruction of the cornea. **flash k.,** keratoconjunctivitis caused by exposure to a welding arc or other source of ultraviolet rays. **k. sic'ca,** a condition marked by hyperemia of the conjunctiva, lacrimal deficiency, thickening of the corneal epithelium, itching and burning of the eye and reduced visual acuity. **virus k.,** epidemic k.

keratoconus (ker"ah-to-ko'nus) [*kerato-* + Gr. *kōnos* cone]. A conical protrusion of the cornea.

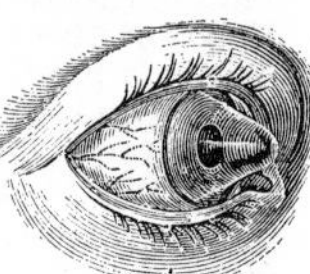
Keratoconus.

keratoderma (ker"ah-to-der'mah) [*kerato-* + Gr. *derma* skin]. 1. A horny skin or covering. 2. The cornea. 3. Hypertrophy of the horny layer of the skin. **k. blennorrha'gica,** a symptom complex characterized by presence of peculiar crusted, hornlike lesions on hands and feet, and sometimes elsewhere on the body; frequently associated with gonococcal urethritis and arthritis but occurring also in nonspecific infections or in response to different etiological stresses. **k. climacter'icum, endocrine k.,** circumscribed hyperkeratosis of the palms and soles, occurring in menopausal women. **k. palma'ris et planta'ris, symmetric k.,** keratosis palmaris et plantaris.

keratodermatitis (ker"ah-to-der"mah-ti'tis) [*kerato-* + Gr. *derma* skin + *-itis*]. Inflammation of the skin associated with hypertrophy of the horny layer.

keratodermia (ker"ah-to-der'me-ah) [*kerato-* + Gr. *derma* skin + *-ia*]. Keratoderma. **k. blennorrha'gica,** keratoderma blennorrhagica. **k. excen'trica,** porokeratosis. **k. palma'ris et planta'ris,** keratosis palmaris et plantaris. **k. planta're sulca'tum,** a disease of India marked by thickening and deep fissuring of the skin of the heel and sole of the foot, and between the toes; called also *chaluni, haja, cracked heels,* and *panki.*

keratoectasia (ker"ah-to-ek-ta'ze-ah). Protrusion of the cornea.

keratogenesis (ker"ah-to-jen'e-sis). The formation or production of horny material.

keratogenetic (ker"ah-to-je-net'ik). Pertaining to keratogenesis.

keratogenous (ker"ah-toj'e-nus) [*kerato-* + Gr. *gennan* to produce]. Giving rise to a growth of horny material.

keratoglobus (ker"ah-to-glo'bus) [*kerato-* + L. *globus* globe]. A globular enlargement and protrusion of the anterior segment of the eye, in the absence of elevated intraocular pressure.

keratohelcosis (ker"ah-to-hel-ko'sis) [*kerato-* + Gr. *helkōsis* ulceration]. Ulceration of the cornea.

keratohemia (ker"ah-to-he'me-ah) [*kerato-* + Gr. *haima* blood + *-ia*]. The presence of deposits of blood in the cornea.

keratohyalin (ker"ah-to-hi'ah-lin). A form of hyalin found in the skin.

keratohyaline (ker"ah-to-hi'ah-līn). Both horny and hyaline, like the material of the stratum granulosum of the epidermis.

keratoid (ker'ah-toid) [*kerato-* + Gr. *eidos* form]. Resembling horn or corneal tissue.

keratoiditis (ker"ah-toid-i'tis). Keratitis.

kerato-iridocyclitis (ker"ah-to-ir"ĭ-do-sik-li'tis). Inflammation of the cornea, iris, and ciliary body.

kerato-iridoscope (ker"ah-to-i-rid'o-skōp) [*kerato-* + Gr. *iris* iris + *skopein* to examine]. A form of compound microscope for examining the eye.

kerato-iritis (ker"ah-to-i-ri'tis) [*kerato-* + Gr. *iris* iris + *-itis*]. Inflammation of the cornea and iris. **hypopyon k.,** hypopyon keratitis.

keratoleptynsis (ker"ah-to-lep-tin'sis) [*kerato-* + Gr. *leptynsis* attenuation]. Removal of the anterior thickness of the cornea and covering of the denuded area with bulbar conjunctiva. An operation for preserving a nonfunctioning eye for esthetic purposes.

keratoleukoma (ker"ah-to-lu-ko'mah) [*kerato-* + *leukoma*]. A white opacity of the cornea.

keratolysis (ker"ah-tol'ĭ-sis) [*kerato-* + Gr. *lysis* dissolution]. Separation or peeling of the horny layer of the epidermis. **k. exfoliati'va,** a disease marked by a peeling or separation of the epidermis, particularly of the palms and soles. **k. neonato'rum,** dermatitis exfoliativa infantum.

keratolytic (ker"ah-to-lit'ik). 1. Pertaining to, characterized by, or producing keratolysis. 2. An agent that promotes keratolysis.

keratoma (ker"ah-to'mah), pl. *keratomas* or *kerato'mata* [*kerato-* + *-oma*]. A growth of horny tissue. See also *keratosis.* **k. diffu'sum,** ichthyosis congenita. **k. heredita'ria mu'tilans,** spontaneous amputation by encircling bands associated with hyperkeratosis. **k. malig'num congenita'le,** ichthyosis. **k. palma're et planta're,** keratosis palmaris et plantaris. **k. planta're sulca'tum,** a thickened fissured condition of the skin of the soles of the feet. It may be the tertiary lesion of framboesia tropica. **k. seni'le,** senile keratosis.

keratomalacia (ker"ah-to-mah-la'she-ah) [*kerato-* + Gr. *malakia* softness]. Softening of the cornea.

keratome (ker'ah-tōm) [*kerato-* + Gr. *temnein* to cut]. A knife for incising the cornea.

keratometer (ker"ah-tom'e-ter) [*kerato-* + Gr. *metron* measure]. An instrument for measuring the curves of the cornea.

keratometric (ker"ah-to-met'rik). Pertaining to keratometry, or to measurements made with a keratometer.

keratometry (ker"ah-tom'e-tre). The measurement of the cornea.

keratomycosis (ker"ah-to-mi-ko'sis) [*kerato-* + Gr. *mykēs* fungus + *-osis*]. Fungus disease of the cornea. **k. lin'guae,** black tongue.

keratonosis (ker"ah-to-no'sis). Any anomaly in the horny structure of the epidermis.

keratonosus (ker"ah-ton'o-sus) [*kerato-* + Gr. *nosos* disease]. Any disease of the cornea.

keratonyxis (ker"ah-to-nik'sis) [*kerato-* + Gr. *nyssein* to puncture]. Puncture of the cornea, as in certain operations on the cornea.

keratopathy (ker"ah-top'ah-the). A noninflammatory disease of the cornea. **band k.,** a condition characterized by an abnormal circumcorneal band, as the paralimbal corneal infiltrate of calcium observed in the milk-alkali syndrome.

keratoplasty (ker'ah-to-plas"te) [*kerato-* + Gr. *plassein* to form]. Plastic surgery of the cornea; corneal grafting. **optic k.,** transplantation of corneal material to replace scar tissue which interferes with vision. **tectonic k.,** transplantation of corneal material to replace tissue which has been lost.

keratoprotein (ker"ah-to-pro'te-in) [*kerato-* + *protein*]. The protein of the horny tissues of the body, such as the hair, nails, and epidermis.

keratorhexis (ker"ah-to-rek'sis) [*kerato-* + Gr. *rhēxis* rupture]. Rupture of the cornea.

keratoscleritis (ker"ah-to-skle-ri'tis). Inflammation of the cornea and sclera.

keratoscope (ker'ah-to-skōp) [*kerato-* + Gr. *skopein* to examine]. An instrument for examining the cornea.

keratoscopy (ker"ah-tos'ko-pe). The examination of the cornea; more especially the study of the reflections of light from its anterior surface.

keratose (ker'ah-tōs). Horny.

keratosic (ker"ah-to'sik). Keratotic.

keratosis (ker"ah-to'sis) pl. *kerato'ses* [*kerato-* + *-osis*]. 1. Any horny growth, such as a wart or callosity. 2. Any condition attended by horny growths. **k. blennorrha'gica,** keratoderma blennorrhagica. **k. diffu'sa feta'lis,** ichthyosis congenita. **k. follicula'ris,** a rare hereditary condition manifested by areas of crusting verrucous papular growths, usually occurring symmetrically on the trunk, axillae, neck, face, scalp, and retroauricular areas. Called also *Darier's disease* and *dyskeratosis follicularis.* **k. follicula'ris conta'giosa,** Brooke's name for a rare form of cornification of the skin, thought to be of a contagious nature. **gonorrheal k.,** keratoderma blennorrhagica. **k. labia'lis,** a condition marked by indurated keratinized patches on the mucosa of the lips. **k. lin'guae,** leukoplakia linguae. **nevoid k.,** a condition characterized by horny nevi disseminated over the body. **k. ni'gricans,** acanthosis nigricans. **k. obtu'rans,** a condition characterized by a mass of epidermic scales and cerumen obstructing the external auditory meatus. **k. palma'ris et planta'ris,** a congenital, often hereditary condition characterized by thickening of the stratum corneum of the skin of the palms and soles, sometimes with painful lesions resulting from the formation of fissures. **k. pharynge'us,** a condition characterized by projection of numerous white horny masses from the tonsils and from the orifices of the lymph follicles in the wall of the pharynx. **k. pila'ris,** a condition in which the disorder of keratinization is limited to the hair follicles, usually on the extensor surfaces of the thighs and arms, but occurring anywhere, with discrete follicular papules which re-form after removal. Called also *ichthyosis follicularis, lichen pilaris, pityriasis pilaris,* and *follicular xeroderma.* **k. puncta'ta,** keratosis, with localization of the lesions in multiple points. **seborrheic k., k. seborrhe'ica,** a benign, noninvasive tumor of epidermal origin, characterized by hyperplasia of the keratinocytes, ordinarily developing as a small yellow or brown, sharply marginated, slightly raised lesion, covered by a thin greasy scale. **senile k., k. seni'lis,** a sharply outlined, gray to grayish black, slightly elevated flat papule, depending more on exposure to actinic radiation than on age, and histologically considered a squamous cell carcinoma, grade ½. **k. suprafollicula'ris,** k. pilaris. **k. veg'etans,** k. follicularis.

keratotic (ker"ah-tot'ik). Pertaining to, characterized by, or promoting keratosis.

keratotome (ker-at'o-tōm). Keratome.

keratotomy (ker"ah-tot'o-me) [Gr. *keras* cornea + *temnein* to cut]. Surgical incision of the cornea. **delimiting k.,** incision of the cornea in ulcus serpens by a cut tangential to the advancing border of the ulcer and made to emerge at a corresponding point in the other side.

keraunoneurosis (kĕ-raw"no-nu-ro'sis) [Gr. *keraunos* lightning + *neurosis*]. A nervous disorder due to lightning stroke.

keraunophobia (kĕ-raw"no-fo'be-ah) [Gr. *keraunos* lightning + *phobia*]. Morbid dread of lightning.

Kerckring's folds, ossicles, valves (kerk'ringz) [Theodorus *Kerckring,* Dutch anatomist, 1640–1693]. See *valvulae conniventes* and under *ossicle.*

kerectasis (ke-rek'tah-sis) [Gr. *keras* cornea + *ektasis* distention]. A uniform bulging or protrusion of the cornea.

kerectomy (ke-rek'to-me) [Gr. *keras* cornea + *ektomē* excision]. Removal of a part of the cornea.

kerion (ke're-on) [Gr. *kērion* honeycomb]. A nodular, boggy, exudative, circumscribed tumefaction which is covered with pustules. **k. cel'si, Celsus' k.,** pustular inflammation of the hair follicles of the scalp in tinea tonsurans.

keritherapy (ker"ĭ-ther'ah-pe) [Gr. *kēros* wax + *therapeia* treatment]. 1. Treatment by baths of liquid paraffin. 2. Treatment of extensive burns with paraffin solutions.

kermes (ker'mēz) [Arabic, Persian]. The *Coccus ilicis,* an insect found on the leaves of various oaks, chiefly on *Quercus coccifera* (kermes-oak). It furnishes a red pigment which is used as a dyestuff.

kernel (ker'nel). That part of an atom left after removal of the ionizable electrons.

kernicterus (kārn-ik'ter-us) [Ger. "nuclear jaundice"]. A condition with severe neural symptoms, associated with high levels of bilirubin in the blood. It is characterized by deep yellow staining of the basal nuclei, globus pallidus, putamen, and caudate nucleus, as well as the cerebellar and bulbar nuclei, and the white and gray substance of the cerebrum, and is accompanied by widespread destructive changes.

Kernig's sign (ker'nigz) [Vladimir *Kernig,* Russian physician, 1840–1917]. See under *sign.*

kernschwund (kārn'shvoont) [Ger.]. Congenital faulty development or absence of nuclei in the cells of the central nervous system; e.g., in congenital ophthalmoplegia (Moebius).

keroid (ker'oid) [Gr. *keroeidēs* hornlike]. 1. Resembling horn. 2. Resembling the cornea.

Kerona pediculus (kĕ-ro'nah pe-dik'u-lus). A ciliate parasitic on the fresh-water *Hydra.*

kerosene (ker'o-sēn). A colorless liquid distilled

from petroleum. It is used to destroy the aquatic larvae of mosquitoes and mixed with vinegar or with olive oil for the treatment of head lice.

kerotherapy (ker″o-ther′ah-pe). Keritherapy.

kerril (ker′il). A venomous sea snake, *Hydrophis jerdoni*, of the Indian Ocean.

keten (ke′ten). Ketene.

ketene (ke′tēn). A colorless gas of penetrating odor, carbomethane, $H_2C{:}CO$, also any one of several derivatives from it. The simplest of the ketones, it combines with water to form acetic acid.

ketimine (ke′tĭ-min). A ketone in which oxygen is replaced by the imino group.

keto- (ke′to). A prefix which denotes possession of the carbonyl group, :C:O.

keto-acid (ke″to-as′id). See under *acid*.

keto-aldehyde (ke″to-al′de-hīd). See under *aldehyde*.

ketogenesis (ke″to-jen′e-sis) [*ketone* + Gr. *genesis* production]. The production of ketone (acetone) bodies.

ketogenetic (ke″to-je-net′ik). Forming ketones.

ketogenic (ke″to-jen′ik). Forming ketone; capable of being converted into ketone. The ketogenic substances in metabolism are the fatty acids and certain of the amino acids of protein.

ketoheptose (ke″to-hep′tōs). A ketone sugar of the heptose group, $C_2H_{14}O_7$.

ketohexose (ke″to-hek′sōs). A hexose which is a ketone derivative. Cf. *aldohexose*.

ketohydroxyestratriene (ke″to-hi-drok″se-es′trah-tri″ēn). Estrone.

ketohydroxyestrin (ke″to-hi-drok″se-es′trin). Estrone.

ketol (ke′tol). See *indole*.

ketolysis (ke-tol′ĭ-sis) [*ketone* + Gr. *lysis* dissolution]. The splitting up of acetone bodies.

ketolytic (ke″to-lit′ik). Pertaining to, characterized by, or promoting ketolysis.

ketone (ke′tōn). Any compound containing the carbonyl group, CO. **dimethyl k.,** acetone. **methyl phenyl k.,** acetophenone.

ketonemia (ke″to-ne′me-ah) [*ketone* + Gr. *haima* blood + *-ia*]. The presence of ketone (acetone) bodies in the blood.

ketonic (ke-to′nik). Pertaining to or developed from a ketone.

ketonization (ke″to-ni-za′shun). Conversion into a ketone.

ketonuria (ke″to-nu′re-ah) [*ketone* + Gr. *ouron* urine + *-ia*]. The presence of ketone (acetone) bodies in the urine.

ketonurine (ke″tōn-u′rin). The urine excreted after administration of a ketogenic diet.

ketoplasia (ke″to-pla′se-ah). The formation of ketone (acetone) bodies.

ketoplastic (ke″to-plas′tik) [*ketone* + Gr. *plassein* to form]. Pertaining to, characterized by, or promoting the formation of ketone (acetone) bodies.

ketoreductase (ke″to-re-duk′tās). An enzyme in liver, muscle, and kidney which transforms aceto-acetic acid into 1-β-oxybutyric acid.

ketose (ke′tōs). A sugar which is the ketone of a hexatomic alcohol; any sugar which contains a carbonyl group.

ketoside (ke′to-sīd). Any glycoside which yields ketose on hydrolysis.

ketosis (ke-to′sis). A condition characterized by an abnormally elevated concentration of ketone (acetone) bodies in the body tissues and fluids.

ketosteroid (ke-to′ste-roid). A steroid which possesses ketone groups on functional carbon atoms. The 17-ketosteroids have a ketone group on the 17th carbon atom. They are found in the urine of normal men and women and in excess in certain adrenal cortex and ovarian tumors. The principal ketosteroids are androsterone, iso-androsterone, etiocholanol-3-alpha-17-one, dehydro-isoandrosterone, estrone, corticosterone, and Kendall's compound E. Called also *urinary androgens*.

ketosuria (ke″to-su′re-ah). The presence of ketose in the urine.

keto-tetrahydrophenanthrene (ke″to-tet″rah-hi″dro-fe-nan′thrēn). 1-keto-1,2,3,4-tetrahydrophenanthrene, a carcinogenic substance.

ketotetrose (ke″to-tet′rōs). A ketose that contains 4 carbon atoms.

ketotic (ke-tot′ik). Pertaining to, characterized by, or causing ketosis.

keto-urine (ke″to-u′rin). Ketonurine.

ketoxime (ke-tok′sīm). A ketonic oxime.

kev. Abbreviation for *kilo* (1,000) *electron volts;* the equivalent of 3.82×10^{-17} gram calories, or 1.6×10^{-9} ergs.

key (ke). 1. An instrument for opening a lock, or a device for making or breaking an electric circuit; by extension, any tool for revealing specific information. **blood k.,** a chart illustrating the principal normal and abnormal conditions of the blood. **DuBois-Reymond's k.,** an appliance by means of which electric currents can be sent through both electrodes or through a short circuit.

keynote (ke′nōt). In homeopathy, the characteristic property of a drug which indicates its use in treating a similar symptom of disease.

Key-Retzius foramen (ke′ ret′ze-us) [Ernst Axel Henrik *Key*, Swedish physician, 1832–1901; Magnus Gustaf *Retzius*, Swedish histologist, 1842–1919]. Apertura lateralis ventriculi quarti.

kg. Abbreviation for *kilogram*.

kg.-cal. Abbreviation for *kilogram-calorie*, or *large calorie*.

kg.-m. Abbreviation for *kilogram-meter*.

$KHCO_3$. Potassium bicarbonate.

khellin (kel′in). An active principle, di-methoxy-methyl-furano-chromone, from the fruit of *Ammi visnaga*, an umbelliferous plant of Eastern Mediterranean regions: used as a coronary and bronchial dilator.

khosam (ko′sam). Kosam.

KH_2PO_4. Potassium dihydrophosphate.

K_2HPO_4. Potassium hydrophosphate (dipotassium phosphate, monoacid phosphate).

$KHSO_4$. Potassium bisulfate; potassium acid sulfate.

KI. Potassium iodide.

kibe (kīb). Chilblain.

kibisitome (ki-bis′ĭ-tōm) [Gr. *kibisis* pouch + *tomē* a cut]. Cystitome.

kidinga pepo (kid-in′gah pe′po) ["cramplike pains"]. A disease of Zanzibar, probably the same as dengue.

kidney (kid′ne) [L. *ren;* Gr. *nephros*]. One of two glandular bodies in the lumbar region that secrete the urine. Called also *ren* [N A]. Each kidney is about four inches long, two inches wide, and one inch thick, and weighs from four to six ounces. The kidney is of characteristic shape, and presents a notch on the inner, concave, border, known as the *hilus*, which communicates with the cavity or sinus of the kidney and through which the vessels, nerves, and ureter pass. The kidney consists of a *cortex* and a *medulla*. The medullary substance forms pyramids, whose bases are in the cortex and whose apices, which are called *papillae*, project into the calices of the kidney. The renal pyramids number from ten to fifteen. The parenchyma of the kidney is composed of *renal tubules* (nephrons), held together by a little connective tissue. Each tubule begins blindly in a renal corpuscle, consisting of a glomerulus and its capsule, situated within the cortex. After a neck or constriction below the capsule, it becomes the proximal convoluted tubule, Henle's loop, distal convoluted tubule, arched collecting tubule, and then the straight collecting tubule, which opens at the apex of a renal papilla. The straight collecting tubules converge as they descend, forming

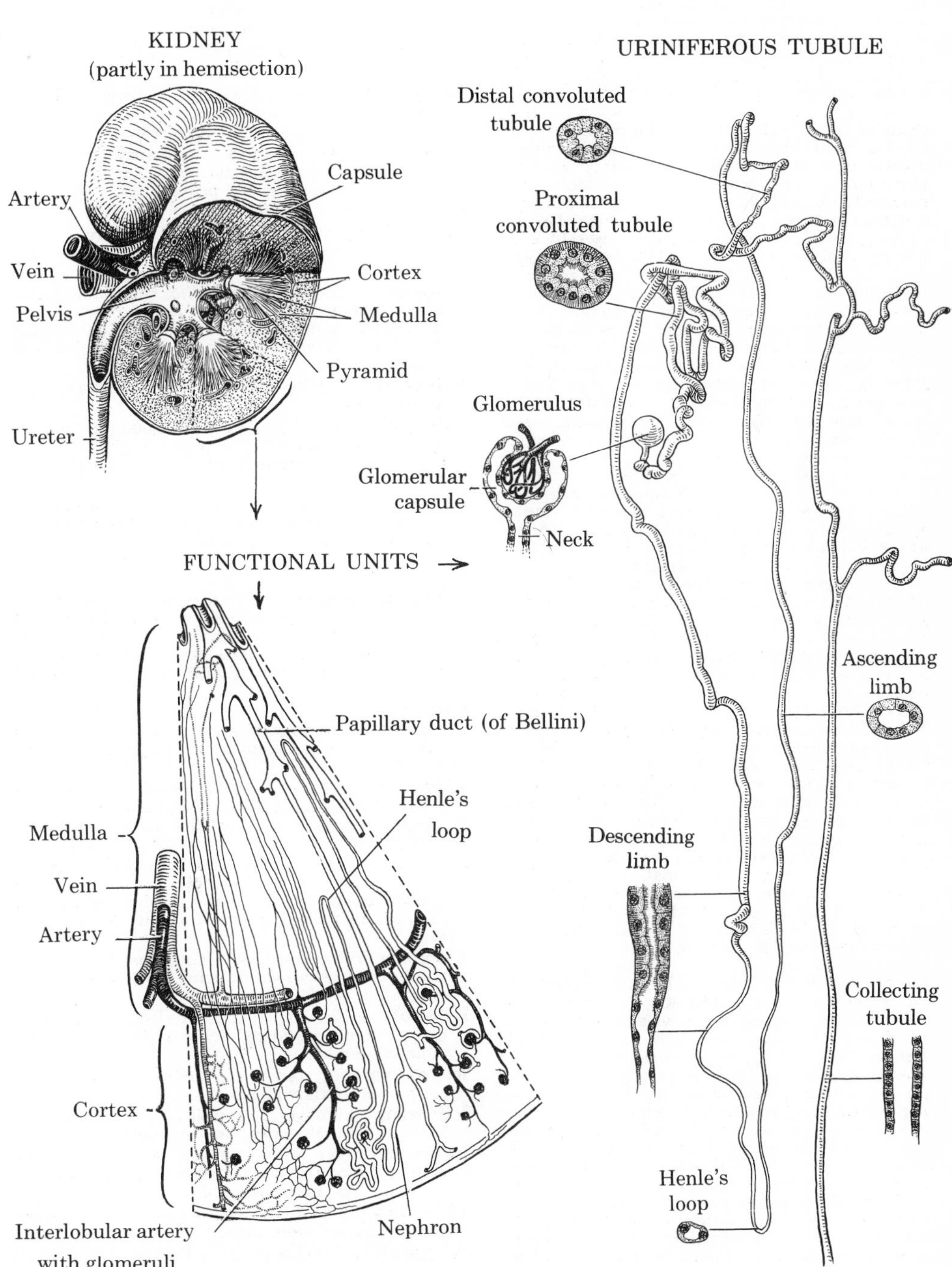

DETAILS OF STRUCTURE OF THE KIDNEY

groups in the center, known as *medullary rays.* **amyloid k.,** one that is the site of amyloid or waxy degeneration. **arteriosclerotic k.,** a kidney contracted as a result of sclerosis of the renal arteries. **artificial k.,** a popular name for a device employed to remove from the blood, while being circulated outside the body, elements which are usually excreted in the urine. See *hemodialyzer.* **atrophic k.,** a kidney affected with diffuse chronic nephritis. **cake k.,** a solid, irregularly lobed organ of bizarre shape, usually situated in the pelvis toward the midline, developed as result of fusion of the two renal anlagen. **cicatricial k.,** a shriveled, irregular, and scarred kidney, resulting from suppurative pyelonephritis. **cirrhotic k.,** granular k. **clump k.,** cake k. **contracted k.,** granular k. **cyanotic k.,** passive congestion of the kidney. **cystic k.,** a kidney containing cysts. **definite k.,** metanephros. **disk k.,** a disk-shaped organ produced by fusion of both poles of the contralateral kidney anlagen. **doughnut k.,** an anomalous organ resulting from bipolar fusion of the renal anlagen before rotation begins, both kidneys being on the same level. **fatty k.,** a kidney affected with fatty degeneration. **floating k.,** one that is misplaced and freely movable. **Formad's k.,** an enlarged and deformed kidney, sometimes seen in chronic alcoholism. **fused k.,** a single anomalous organ developed as a result of fusion of the renal anlagen. **granular k.,** one affected with chronic interstitial inflammation. See *interstitial nephritis, chronic,* under *nephritis.* **head k.,** pronephros. **hind k.,** metanephros. **horseshoe k.,** an anomalous organ developed as a result of fusion of the corresponding poles of the renal anlagen. **lardaceous k.,** amyloid k. **large red k.,** one affected with acute diffuse glomerulonephritis. **large white k.,** one affected with chronic interstitial nephritis. **lump k.,** cake k. **middle k.,** mesonephros. **mortar k.,** one which, as a result of renal tuberculosis, has become a calcified mass of caseous material. **movable k.,** one that is freely movable. **mural k.,** a kidney located in a pocket of peritoneum in the abdominal wall. **myelin k.,** a kidney infiltrated with myelin, producing minute whitish specks or streaks on its surface. **pelvic k.,** a kidney misplaced into the pelvis. **polycystic k.,** a congenital condition characterized by nodular enlargement of the organ, usually occurring bilaterally. **primordial k.,** pronephros. **putty k.,** one containing caseous material trapped by stricture of the ureter by tuberculous granulations in renal tuberculosis. **red contracted k.,** granular k. **Rokitansky's k.,** amyloid k. **Rose-Bradford k.,** a form of fibrotic kidney of inflammatory origin found in young subjects. **sacciform k.,** a distended kidney. **sclerotic k.,** granular k. **sigmoid k.,** a deformed and fused kidney, the upper pole of one kidney being fused with the lower pole of the other. **small red k.,** the kidney in nephrosclerosis. **small white k.,** an atrophied and degenerated state of the kidney resulting from chronic interstitial nephritis. **soapy k.,** a large white kidney which contains myelins instead of simple fats. **sponge k.,** a rare congenital condition, anatomically characterized by multiple small cystic dilatations of the collecting tubules of the medullary portion of the renal pyramids, giving the organ a spongy, porous feeling and appearance. **supernumerary k.,** a kidney in addition to the two usually present, developed as the result of splitting of the nephrogenic blastema, or from separate metanephric blastemas into which partially or completely reduplicated ureteral stalks enter to form separate capsulated kidneys. In some cases the separation of the reduplicated organ is incomplete (*fused supernumerary k.*). **wandering k.,** amyloid k. **waxy k.,** amyloid k.

Kielland (kyel′and). See *Kjelland.*

Kienböck atrophy, disease, phenomenon, unit (kēn′bek) [Robert *Kienböck,* Austrian roentgenologist, 1871–1953]. See under the nouns.

Kiernan's spaces (kēr′nanz) [Francis *Kiernan,* English physician, 1800–1874]. See under *space.*

Kiesselbach's area, space (ke′sel-bahks) [Wilhelm *Kiesselbach,* German laryngologist, 1839–1902]. See under *area.*

kiestein (ki-es′te-in). Kyestein.

kikekunemalo (ki″ke-ku″ne-mah′lo). A resin much resembling copal: used for varnishes.

kil (kil). A white, sticky, soapy clay from the Black Sea region; when sterilized, is employed as an ointment base for use in skin diseases.

Kilian's line, pelvis (kil′e-anz) [Hermann Friedrich *Kilian,* German gynecologist, 1800–1863]. See under *line* and *pelvis.*

killeen (kil′lēn). Chondrus.

Killian's operation (kil′e-anz) [Gustav *Killian,* German laryngologist, 1860–1921]. See under *operation.*

kilo- (kil′o) [Fr., from Gr. *chilioi* thousand]. Combining form used in naming units of measurement to indicate a quantity one thousand (10^3) times the unit designated by the root with which it is combined.

kilocalorie (kil′o-kal″o-re). Large calorie. See under *calorie.*

kilocycle (kil′o-si″kl). A unit of 1,000 (10^3) cycles, e.g., 1,000 cycles per second, applied to the frequency of electromagnetic waves. Abbreviated kc.

kilogram (kil′o-gram). A unit of mass (weight) of the metric system, being 1,000 (10^3) grams, or the equivalent of 2.204623 pounds avoirdupois and of 2.679229 pounds apothecaries' weight. Abbreviated kg.

kilogram-meter (kil′o-gram-me″ter). A unit of work, representing the energy required to raise 1 kg. of weight 1 meter vertically against gravitational force, equivalent to about 7.2 foot-pounds and equal to 1,000 gram-meters. Abbreviated kg.-m.

kiloliter (kil′o-le″ter) [Fr. *kilolitre*]. A unit of capacity of the metric system, being 1,000 (10^3) liters, or the equivalent of 264.18 gallons. Abbreviated kl.

kilomegacycle (kil″o-meg″ah-si′kl). A unit of 1,000 (10^3) megacycles (10^9 cycles), e.g., 1,000 megacycles per second, applied to the frequency of electromagnetic waves. Abbreviated kMc.

kilometer (kil′o-me″ter) [Fr. *kilomètre*]. A unit of linear measurement of the metric system, being 1,000 (10^3) meters, or the equivalent of 3280.83 feet, or about five-eighths of a mile. Abbreviated km.

kilonem (kil′o-nem) [*kilo* + Gr. *nemesthai* to feed]. A unit of nutritive value, being 1,000 nems, or the equivalent of 667 calories.

kilovolt (kil′o-vōlt). A unit of electrical pressure or electromotive force, being 1,000 (10^3) volts. Abbreviated kv.

kilovoltmeter (kil-o-volt′me-ter). A voltmeter calibrated in kilovolts.

kilowatt (kil′o-wat). A unit of electric power, being 1,000 (10^3) watts. Abbreviated kw.

kilowatt-hour (kil′o-wat owr). A unit of energy equivalent to the work done by one kilowatt in one hour. Abbreviated kw.-hr.

kilurane (kil′u-rān). A unit of radioactivity, being 1,000 (10^3) uranium units.

Kimmelstiel-Wilson syndrome (kim′el-stēl wil′son) [Paul *Kimmelstiel,* German pathologist in the United States, born 1900; Clifford *Wilson,* English physician, born 1906]. See under *syndrome.*

Kimpton-Brown tube (kimp′ton brown′) [Arthur Ronald *Kimpton,* Boston surgeon]. See under *tube.*

kimputu (kēm-poo′too) [African]. Relapsing fever.

kinanesthesia (kin″an-es-the′ze-ah) [Gr. *kinēsis* motion + *anesthesia*]. Loss of power of perceiving the sensation of movement, due to derangement of deep sensibility.

kinase (ki′nās). 1. An enzyme that catalyzes the transfer of a high-energy group of a donor, usually adenosine triphosphate, to some acceptor, and variously named, according to the acceptor, as *creatine kinase, fructokinase, galactokinase, hexokinase,* and *phosphoglycerate kinase.* Called also *phosphotransferase* and *transphosphorylase.* 2. An enzyme that activates a zymogen, variously named, according to its source, as *enterokinase, staphylokinase,* and *streptokinase.* **bacterial k.,** an enzyme of bacterial origin that activates a precursor (plasminogen) of a plasma protease (plasmin). **creatine k.,** an enzyme that catalyzes the transfer of a high-energy phosphate group from a donor to creatine, producing phosphocreatine. **insulin k.,** an enzyme assumed to exist in the liver which activates insulin. **phosphoglycerate k.,** an enzyme that catalyzes the transfer of a high-energy phosphate group from a donor to D-3-phosphoglycerate, producing D-1,3-diphosphoglycerate. **tissue k.,** fibrinokinase.

kine-. See *kinesio-.* For words beginning thus see also words beginning *cine-.*

kinematics (kin″e-mat′iks) [Gr. *kinēma* motion]. That phase of mechanics which deals with the possible motions of a material body.

kinematograph (kin″e-mat′o-graf) [Gr. *kinēma* motion + *graphein* to record]. An instrument for exhibiting pictures of objects in motion: it is of considerable service in diagnosis.

kinemia (ki-ne′me-ah). Cardiac output.

kinemic (ki-ne′mik) [*kine-* + Gr. *haima* blood]. Pertaining to cardiac output.

kineplastics (kin″e-plas′tiks). Kineplasty.

kineplasty (kin′e-plas″te) [Gr. *kinein* to move + *plassein* to form]. Plastic amputation; amputation in which the stump is so formed as to be utilized for motor purposes.

kinergety (kin′er-jet-e). The capacity for kinetic energy.

kinesalgia (kin″e-sal′je-ah) [*kinesio-* + *-algia*]. Pain on muscular exertion.

kinescope (kin′e-skōp) [*kine-* + Gr. *skopein* to examine]. An instrument for measuring ocular refraction, in which the patient observes a fixed object through a slit in a moving disk.

kinesia (ki-ne′se-ah). Kinetosis.

kinesialgia (ki-ne″se-al′je-ah). Kinesalgia.

kinesiatrics (ki-ne″se-at′riks) [*kinesio-* + Gr. *iatrikē* surgery, medicine]. Kinesitherapy.

kinesi-esthesiometer (ki-ne″se-es-the″ze-om′e-ter) [*kinesio-* + Gr. *aisthēsis* perception + *metron* measure]. An instrument for estimating or measuring the muscular sense.

kinesimeter (kin″e-sim′e-ter) [*kinesio-* + Gr. *metron* measure]. 1. An instrument for the quantitative measurement of movements. 2. An instrument for exploring the surface of the body to test cutaneous sensibility.

kinesio, kine- (ki-ne′se-o, kin′e) [Gr. *kinēsis* movement]. Combining form denoting relationship to movement.

kinesiodic (ki-ne″se-od′ik). Kinesodic.

kinesiology (ki-ne″se-ol′o-je) [*kinesio-* + *-logy*]. The sum of what is known regarding human motion.

kinesiometer (ki-ne″se-om′e-ter). Kinesimeter.

kinesioneurosis (ki-ne″se-o-nu-ro′sis) [*kinesio-* + *neurosis*]. A functional nervous disorder characterized by derangement of the nervous system. **external k.,** one that affects the muscles of external relation. **internal k.,** one that affects the muscles of the viscera. **vascular k.,** angioneurosis. **visceral k.,** internal k.

kinesiotherapy (ki-ne″se-o-ther′ah-pe). Kinesitherapy.

kinesiphony (kin″e-sif′o-ne) [*kinesio-* + Gr. *phōnē* sound]. The employment of a buzzer in restraining the hearing.

kinesitherapy (ki-ne″se-ther′ah-pe) [*kinesio-* + Gr. *therapeia* cure]. The treatment of disease by movements or exercise.

kinesodic (kin″e-sod′ik) [*kinesio-* + Gr. *hodos* way]. Conducting or pertaining to the conduction of motor impulses.

kinesophobia (ki-ne″so-fo′be-ah) [*kinesio-* + *phobia*]. Dread of movement.

kinesthesia (kin″es-the′ze-ah) [*kine-* + Gr. *aisthēsis* perception + *-ia*]. The sense by which muscular motion, weight, position, etc., are perceived.

kinesthesiometer (kin″es-the″ze-om′e-ter) [*kinesthesia* + Gr. *metron* measure]. A device by which to test the muscular sensibility.

kinesthesis (kin″es-the′sis). Kinesthesia.

kinesthetic (kin″es-thet′ik). Pertaining to kinesthesia or the muscular sense.

kinetia (ki-ne′te-ah). Kinetosis.

kinetic (ki-net′ik) [Gr. *kinētikos*]. Pertaining to or producing motion.

kinetics (ki-net′iks) [Gr. *kinētikos* of or for putting in motion]. The branch of dynamics that pertains to the turnover, or rate of change, of a specific factor (e.g. erythrocytes—erythrokinetics, leukocytes—leukokinetics, or iron—ferrokinetics), commonly expressed as units of amount per unit time. **chemical k.,** the study of the rates at which chemical reactions proceed.

kinetism (kin′e-tizm). The ability to perform or initiate muscular action.

kineto- (ki-ne′to) [Gr. *kinētos* movable]. Combining form meaning movable.

kinetocardiogram (ki-ne″to-kar′de-o-gram). The graphic record obtained by kinetocardiography.

kinetocardiography (ki-ne″to-kar″de-og′rah-fe). The technique of recording the vibrations or pulsations at various sites over the anterior chest wall, as a means of study in heart disease.

kinetochore (ki-ne′to-kōr) [*kineto-* + Gr. *chora* space]. A clear region where the arms of a chromosome meet.

kinetocyte (ki-ne′to-sīt) [*kineto-* + *-cyte*]. A term once applied to one of the round or oval bodies about the size of a blood platelet, as forming a fourth element in the blood, where they move actively among the corpuscles (Edelmann).

kinetocythemia (ki-ne″to-si-the′me-ah) [*kinetocyte* + Gr. *haima* blood + *-ia*]. Kinetocytosis.

kinetocytopenia (ki-ne″to-si″to-pe′ne-ah) [*kinetocyte* + Gr. *penia* poverty]. Deficiency of kinetocytes in the blood.

kinetocytosis (ki-ne″to-si-to′sis) [*kinetocyte* + *-osis*]. The presence of an abnormally large proportion of kinetocytes in the blood.

kinetogenic (ki-ne″to-jen′ik) [*kineto-* + Gr. *gennan* to produce]. Causing or producing movement.

kinetographic (ki-ne″to-graf′ik) [*kineto-* + Gr. *graphein* to record]. Recording graphically the movements of parts and features.

kinetonucleus (ki-ne″to-nu′kle-us) [*kineto-* + *nucleus*]. Kinetoplast.

kinetoplasm (ki-ne′to-plazm) [*kineto-* + Gr. *plasma* something formed]. The most highly contractile portion of the cytoplasm of a cell; the energy plasm: the term is applied to the chromatophilic elements in the nervous tissue.

kinetoplast (ki-ne′to-plast) [*kineto-* + Gr. *plassein* to form]. An accessory body, often referred to as the micronucleus, found in many protozoa, and consisting of two portions, the blepharoplast and the parabasal body, that are united by a delicate fibril.

kinetoscope (ki-ne′to-skōp) [*kineto-* + Gr. *skopein* to examine]. A form of chromophotograph: useful in diagnosis and in physiologic study.

kinetoscopy (ki″ne-tos′ko-pe). Serial photography which exhibits the motions of the limbs or features: used in diagnosis.

kinetoses (ki″ne-to′sēz). Plural of *kinetosis.*

kinetosis (ki″ne-to′sis), pl. *kineto′ses* [*kineto-* +

-*osis*]. Any disorder caused by unaccustomed motion. See *motion sickness.*

kinetotherapy (ki-ne″to-ther′ah-pe). Kinesitherapy.

kingdom (king′dum) [Anglosaxon *cyningdom*]. One of the three categories into which natural objects are usually classified: the *animal kingdom*, including all animals; the *plant kingdom*, including all plants; and the *mineral kingdom*, including all objects and substance without life.

kinin (ki′nin). One of a group of endogenous peptides acting on blood vessels, smooth muscles, and nociceptive nerve endings, such as bradykinin or kallidin. **venom k.,** a peptide found in the venom of insects. **wasp k.,** a potent, pain-provoking peptide present in wasp venom.

kink (kink′). A bend or twist. **ileal k., Lane's k.,** obstruction of the small intestine caused by kinking of Lane's band.

kino- (ki′no) [Gr. *kinein* to move]. Combining form denoting relationship to movement.

kino (ki′no). The dried juice of *Pterocarpus marsupium*, of southern Asia, and of various other trees: astringent.

kinocentrum (ki″no-sen′trum). Centrosome.

kinocilia (ki″no-sil′e-ah). Plural of *kinocilium.*

kinocilium (ki″no-sil′e-um), pl. *kinocil′ia.* A motile, protoplasmic filament on the free surface of a cell. Cf. *stereocilium.*

kinohapt (ki′no-hapt) [*kino-* + Gr. *haptein* to touch]. An esthesiometer for making several tactile stimulations at definite intervals of time or space.

kinoin (ki′no-in). A principle, $C_{14}H_{12}O_6$, from kino.

kinology (ki-nol′o-je). Kinesiology.

kinometer (ki-nom′e-ter) [*kino-* + Gr. *metron* measure]. An instrument for measuring uterine displacements.

kinomometer (ki″no-mom′e-ter) [*kino-* + Gr. *metron* measure]. An instrument for estimating the degree of motion in fingers and wrist.

kinoplasm (ki′no-plazm) [*kino-* + Gr. *plasma* plasm]. The specific kinetic or motor substance of a cell; functional protoplasm. Called also *archoplasm* and *ergastoplasm.*

kinoplastic (ki″no-plas′tik). Pertaining to kinoplasm.

kinosphere (ki′no-sfēr) [*kino-* + *sphere*]. Aster.

kinotoxin (ki″no-tok′sin) [*kino-* + *toxin*]. A fatigue toxin.

kinovin (kin-o′vin). Quinovin.

kiono- (ki′on-o). For words beginning thus, see those beginning *ciono-.*

kiotome (ki′o-tōm) [Gr. *kiōn* column + *temnein* to cut]. A knife for amputating the uvula.

kiotomy (ki-ot′o-me). The use of the kiotome; amputation of the uvula.

Kirchner's diverticulum (kērk′nerz) [Wilhelm *Kirchner*, Würzburg otologist, 1849–1935]. A diverticulum of the eustachian tube.

Kirk's amputation (kirks) [Major General Norman Thomas *Kirk*, former Surgeon General of U. S. Army, 1888–1960]. See under *amputation.*

Kirmisson's operation (kēr″me-sawz′) [Edouard *Kirmisson*, French surgeon, 1848–1927]. See under *operation.*

kirrhonosis (kir″o-no′sis). Kirronosis.

kirronosis (kir″o-no′sis) [Gr. *kirrhos* tawny, orange-tawny + *nosos* disease]. Lobstein's term for fetal jaundice, affecting the serous membranes exclusively.

Kirschner wire (kērsh′ner) [Martin *Kirschner*, German surgeon, 1879–1942]. See under *wire.*

Kirstein's method (ker′stinz) [Alfred *Kirstein*, German physician, 1863–1922]. See under *method.*

Kisch's reflex (kish′ez) [Bruno *Kisch*, German physiologist, born 1890]. See under *reflex.*

Kitasato's filter (ke-tah-sah′tōz) [Shibasaburo *Kitasato*, Japanese bacteriologist, 1852–1931]. See under *filter.*

Kite apparatus (kīt) [Joseph Hiram *Kite*, American orthopedic surgeon, born 1891]. A device for exercising and retraining the muscle of the forearm and hand.

kitol (ki′tol) [Gr. *kētos* sea monster, big fish]. A substance from whale oil which yields vitamin A on heating.

Kittel's treatment (kit′elz) [M. J. *Kittel*, German physician]. See under *treatment.*

k.j. Abbreviation for *knee jerk.*

Kjeldahl's method (kel′dahlz) [Johan Gustav Christoffer *Kjeldahl*, Danish chemist, 1849–1900]. See under *method.*

Kjelland's forceps (kel′landz) [Christian *Kjelland*, Norwegian obstetrician and gynecologist, born 1871]. See under *forceps.*

k.k. Abbreviation for *knee kicks* (knee jerks).

kl. Abbreviation for *klang* and *kiloliter.*

klang (klahng) [Ger.]. A compound musical tone; a fundamental tone combined with its over-tones.

Klapp's creeping treatment (klaps) [Rudolf *Klapp*, surgeon in Berlin, 1873–1949]. See under *treatment.*

Klausner's reaction or **test** (klows′nerz) [Erwin *Klausner*, dermatologist in Prague, born 1883]. See under *tests.*

Klebs-Löffler bacillus (klebz′ lef′ler) [Edwin *Klebs*, German bacteriologist, 1834–1913; Friederich A. J. *Löffler*, German bacteriologist, 1852–1915]. *Corynebacterium diphtheriae.*

Klebsiella (kleb″se-el′lah) [Edwin *Klebs*]. A genus of microorganisms of the tribe Escherichieae, family Enterobacteriaceae, order Eubacteriales, made up of plump short rods with rounded ends, usually occurring singly, and frequently found in the respiratory or intestinal tract in man. **K. friedlän′deri,** *K. pneumoniae.* **K. ozae′nae,** an organism isolated from patients with ozena and also from patients with atrophic rhinitis. **K. pneumo′niae,** an organism closely similar to *Aerobacter aerogenes*, but occurring in patients with lobar pneumonia and other infections of the respiratory tract. **K. rhinoscleroma′tis,** an organism isolated from the nasal secretions of patients with rhinoscleroma.

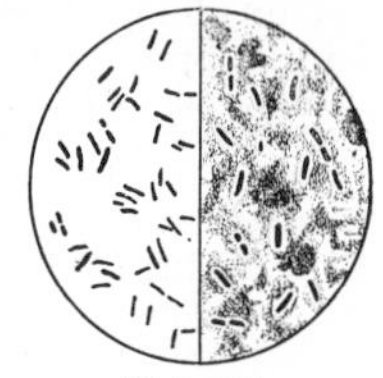
Klebsiella pneumoniae.

Klein's bacillus (klīnz) [Edward Emanuel *Klein*, Hungarian bacteriologist in London, 1844–1925]. *Bacillus enteritidis sporogenes.*

Klemm's tetanus (klemz) [Paul *Klemm*, surgeon in Riga, 1861–1921]. Kopf-tetanus.

Klemperer's tuberculin (klem′per-erz) [Felix (1866–1931) and Georg (1865–1946) *Klemperer*, Berlin physicians]. See under *tuberculin.*

klepto- (klep′to) [Gr. *kleptein* to steal]. Combining form denoting relationship to theft or stealing.

kleptohemodeipnonism (klep″to-he″mo-dēp′-no-nizm) [*klepto-* + Gr. *haima* blood + *deipnon* meal + *-ism*]. A term suggested for the feeding of unfed nymphs of certain species of blood-sucking insects on colony mates which are engorged with blood.

kleptolagnia (klep″to-lag′ne-ah) [*klepto-* + *lagneia* lust]. Sexual gratification produced by theft.

kleptomania (klep″to-ma′ne-ah) [*klepto-* + Gr. *mania* madness]. An uncontrollable impulse to steal, the objects taken usually having a symbolic value of which the subject is unconscious, rather than an intrinsic value.

kleptomaniac (klep″to-ma′ne-ak). An individual exhibiting kleptomania.

kleptophobia (klep″to-fo′be-ah) [*klepto-* + Gr. *phobos* fear + *-ia*]. Insane dread of becoming a thief or of being stolen.

Klieg eye (klēg) [named from *Kliegal*, the manufacturer of electric lamps used in moving picture making]. See under *eye*.

Klimow's test (klim′ofs) [Iwan Alex. *Klimow*, Russian physician, born 1865]. See under *tests*.

Kline test (klīn) [Benjamin S. *Kline*, American pathologist, born 1886]. See under *tests*.

Klinefelter's syndrome (klīn′fel-terz) [Harry F. *Klinefelter*, Jr., American physician, born 1912]. See under *syndrome*.

Klinophilus (kli-nof′ĭ-lus). Cimex.

Klippel-Feil disease, sign, syndrome (klĭ-pel′fīl) [Maurice *Klippel*, French neurologist, 1858–1942; André *Feil*, French physician, born 1884]. See under *disease*, *sign*, and *syndrome*.

kliseometer (klis″e-om′e-ter). Cliseometer.

Kluge's method (kloo′gez) [Karl Alexander Ferdinand *Kluge*, German obstetrician, 1782–1844]. See under *method*.

Klumpke's paralysis (kloomp′kez) [Madame A. *Klumpke* Dejerine, Parisian neurologist, 1859–1927, wife of Joseph Jules Dejerine]. See under *paralysis*.

Klumpke-Dejerine paralysis, syndrome (kloomp′kĕ-dezh″er-ēn′) [Madame A. *Klumpke* Dejerine; Joseph Jules *Dejerine*, French neurologist, 1849–1917]. Klumpke's paralysis.

km. Abbreviation for *kilometer*.

kMc. Abbreviation for *kilomegacycle*.

kMc.p.s. Abbreviation for *kilomegacycles per second*.

$KMnO_4$. Potassium permanganate.

Knapp's forceps, operation, streaks (naps) [Herman Jakob *Knapp*, New York ophthalmologist, 1832–1911]. See under the nouns.

Knapp's test (knaps) [Karl *Knapp*, German chemist]. See under *tests*.

kneading (nēd′ing). A movement in massage consisting of grasping and pressing of muscles.

knee (ne). 1. The site of articulation between the thigh (femur) and leg. Called also *genu* [N A]. 2. Any structure bent like the knee. **k. of aquaeduc′tus fallo′pii,** geniculum canalis facialis. **back k.,** genu recurvatum. **beat k.,** a subcutaneous cellulitis over the kneecap. **big k.** 1. Bursitis over the knee in cattle. 2. A tumor of the bony parts of the knee joint in horses. **Brodie's k.,** a chronic synovitis of the knee joint in which the affected parts acquire a soft and pulpy consistency. **broken k.,** an injury of the knee of a horse due to violence. **capped k.,** distention of the synovial bursa over the knee joint of horses or cattle. **football k.,** a swollen, relaxed, somewhat tender condition of the knee seen in football players. **hooped k.,** the presence of exostoses in the knee of a horse. **housemaid's k.,** inflammation of the bursa in front of the patella, with fluid accumulating within it. **in k.,** genu valgum. **k. of internal capsule,** genu capsulae internae. **knock k.,** genu valgum. **locked k.,** inability to extend the leg fully as a result of tear of the medial semilunar cartilage. **out k.,** genu varum, or bowleg. **Rugby k.,** Schlatter's disease. **septic k.,** a suppurating knee joint. **sprung k.,** forward bending of the knee of a horse, due to shortening of the flexor tendons.

kneippism (nīp′izm) [Rev. Father Sebastian *Kneipp*, 1821–1897, who introduced the practice]. Cure by walking barefoot in the morning dew, cold bathing, etc.

knife (nīf). A cutting instrument, of various shapes and sizes, for surgeons' and dissectors' use. **Beer's k.,** a knife with a triangle-shaped blade, used in operations for cataract and for excising staphyloma of the cornea. **cataract k.,** a knife for cutting the cornea in operations for cataract. **cautery k.,** a knife having the blade connected with an electric battery, so that the tissues may be seared while cutting, thus preventing bleeding. **electric k., endotherm k.,** high-frequency current electrode in the form of a steel needle which cuts through tissues with a searing effect on them. **Graefe's k.,** a slender knife used in linear extraction of cataract. **Groff k.,** an electrosurgery knife. **hernia k.,** herniotome. **Liston's knives,** long-bladed amputation knives.

knismogenic (nis″mo-jen′ik) [Gr. *knismos* tickling + *gennan* to produce]. Producing a tickling sensation.

knitting (nit′ing). The physiological process of repair of a fractured bone.

KNO_3. Potassium nitrate.

knob (nob). A bulbous mass or protuberance. **synaptic k's,** end-feet.

knock (nok). A sound as of a blow against a firm surface. **pericardial k.,** a clear, metallic clicking sound heard over the precordium in certain cases of penetrating chest wounds in the neighborhood of the pericardium; ascribed to emphysema of the mediastinal connective tissue or to free air in the interstitial connective tissue of the lung. Cf. *clicking pneumothorax*, under *pneumothorax*.

Knoepfelmacher's butter meal (knep′fel-mahk′erz) [Wilhelm *Knoepfelmacher*, pediatrist in Vienna, born 1866]. A preparation of milk, flour, butter, and sugar, used in child feeding.

knokkelkoorts (nok′el-koorts) [Dutch "knuckle fever"]. Dengue fever in the Netherlands East Indies.

Knopf's method, treatment (nopfs) [Sigard Adolphus *Knopf*, New York physician, 1857–1940]. See under *treatment*.

knot (not). An intertwining of the ends or parts of one or more cords so they cannot easily be separated. **clove-hitch k.,** a knot consisting of two contiguous loops that are applied around an object, the ends of the cord being toward each other: used for making traction on a part for the reduction of dislocations. **double k.,** friction k. **enamel k.,** a small dense group of epithelial cells in the stellate reticulum of a developing tooth, which disappears before enamel formation begins. **false k.** 1. A local bulge on the umbilical cord caused by protuberant vessels. Cf. *true k.* 2. Granny k. **friction k.,** a knot in which the ends of the cord are twisted twice around each other before being tied. **granny k.,** a double knot in the second loop of which the end of one cord is over, and the other under, its fellow, so that the loops do not lie in the same line. **Hensen's k.,** primitive k. **net k.,** karyosome. **primitive k.,** a mass of cells, at the cranial end of the primitive streak, related to the organization of an embryo. **protochordal k.,** primitive k. **reef k.,** a double knot in which the free ends of the second knot lie in the same plane as the ends of the first knot. **sailors' k., square k.,** reef k. **Staffordshire k.,** a knot for tying pedicles, as of the ovary. It is made by passing a ligature through the pedicle by a needle, which is withdrawn so as to leave a loop which is passed over the pedicle. One of the ends of the ligature is drawn through the loop, and the two ends are tied by a reef knot. **stay k.,** a knot made with two or more ligatures, each being tied with the first half of a reef knot; then all the ends of one side are taken in one hand, and all the ends on the other side in the other hand, and tied as if they formed one single thread. **surgeons' k., surgical k.,** a knot in which the thread is passed twice through the same loop. **syncytial k's,** protuberances of syncytium along the chorionic villi. **Tait's k.,** Staffordshire k. **true k.,** a simple knot produced in the looped umbilical cord during pregnancy. Cf. *false k.*

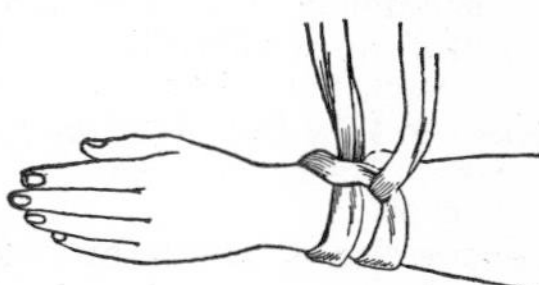

Clove-hitch knot (Erichsen).

knuckle (nuk″l). The dorsal aspect of any phalangeal joint, especially of the metacarpophalangeal joints of the flexed fingers. By extension sometimes applied to any anatomical structure of similar appearance, such as an extruded loop of intestine in hernia.

knuckling (nuk′ling). A condition in which the fetlock joint of a horse is pushed upward and forward, due to shortening of the tendons behind.

Kobelt's tubes (ko′belts) [George L. *Kobelt*, German physician, 1804–1857]. See under *tube*.

Kobert's test (ko′bārts) [Eduard Rudolf *Kobert*, German chemist, 1854–1919]. See under *tests*.

Köbner's disease (keb′nerz) [Heinrich *Köbner*, dermatologist in Breslau and Berlin, 1838–1904]. Epidermitis bullosa.

KOC. Abbreviation for *kathodal* (*cathodal*) *opening contraction*.

Koch's bacillus, lymph, phenomenon, postulates, etc. (kōks) [Robert *Koch*, German bacteriologist, 1843–1910, the discoverer of the tubercle bacillus; winner of the Nobel prize for medicine in 1905]. See under the nouns.

Koch's node (kōks) [Walter *Koch*, German surgeon, born 1880]. Atrioventricular node.

Koch-Weeks bacillus (kōk-wēks) [Robert *Koch;* John Elmer *Weeks*, New York oculist, 1853–1949]. *Haemophilus aegyptius*.

Kocher's forceps, operation (kōk′erz) [Emil Theodor *Kocher*, Swiss surgeon, 1841–1917], the first surgeon to excise the thyroid gland; winner of the Nobel prize for medicine in 1909]. See under *forceps* and *operation*.

kocherization (kōk″er-i-za′shun). Operative reflexion of a flap of the duodenum for exposure of the ampulla of the common bile duct.

Kocks' operation (kōks) [Joseph *Kocks*, German surgeon, 1846–1916]. See under *operation*.

Koeberle's forceps (ke″ber-lāz′) [Eugene *Koeberle*, French surgeon, 1828–1915]. Hemostatic forceps.

Koenecke's reaction, test (ke-nek′ez). See under *tests*.

KOH. Potassium hydroxide.

koha (ko′hah). A Japanese drug derived from cyanine: given intravenously it is said to stimulate the formation of leukocytes and of new tissue and thus hasten wound healing. Called also *rainbow wave drug*.

Köhler's disease (ka′lerz) [Alban *Köhler*, German physician, 1874–1947]. See under *disease*.

Kohlrausch's fold or **valve** (kōl′rowsh-ez) [Otto Ludwig Bernhard *Kohlrausch*, German physician, 1811–1854]. See under *fold*.

Kohn's pores (kōnz) [Hans *Kohn*, German pathologist, born 1866]. See under *pore*.

Kohnstamm's phenomenon (kōn′stahmz) [Oskar *Kohnstamm*, German physician, 1871–1917]. After-movement.

koilo- (koi′lo) [Gr. *koilos* hollow]. Combining form meaning hollow or concave.

koilonychia (koi″lo-nik′e-ah) [*koilo-* + *onyx* nail + *-ia*]. A condition in which the nail is concave; spoon nail.

koilorrhachic (koi″lo-rak′ik) [*koilo* + Gr. *rhachis* spine]. Having a curved lumbar spine with the concavity forward.

koilosternia (koi″lo-ster′ne-ah) [*koilo-* + *sternum* + *-ia*]. Funnel chest.

koinonia (koi-no′ne-ah) [Gr. *koinōnia* community]. 1. Associated or common action as of like cells in the same tissue. 2. Coitus.

koinoniphobia (koi-no″nĭ-fo′be-ah) [Gr. *koinōnia* community + *phobia*]. Morbid fear of a room filled with people.

koinotropic (koi′no-trop″ik) [Gr. *koinos* common + *tropos* a turning]. Syntropic, def. 3.

koinotropy (koi-not′ro-pe). Interest in social or public relationships.

koktigen (kok′tĭ-jen) [L. *coctus* cooked + Gr. *gennan* to produce]. A vaccine made by boiling a salt solution emulsion of an organism.

Kölliker's cells, gland, layer, nucleus, etc. (kel′ĭ-kerz) [Rudolf Albrecht von *Kölliker*, eminent Swiss anatomist, histologist and zoologist, professor at Zurich and Würzburg, 1817–1905]. See under the nouns.

Kollmann's dilator (kol′manz) [Arthur *Kollmann*, Leipzig urologist, born 1858]. A flexible urethral dilator.

kolloxylin (kol-ok′sĭ-lin). A substance resembling celloidin, used in histologic work.

Kolmer's test (kōl′merz) [John A. *Kolmer*, Philadelphia pathologist. born 1886]. See under *tests*.

kolp-. For words beginning thus, see those beginning *colp-*.

kolyone (ko′le-ōn). Colyone.

kolypeptic (ko″le-pep′tik) [Gr. *kōlyein* to hinder + *peptikos* peptic]. Hindering or checking digestion.

kolyphrenia (ko″le-fre′ne-ah) [Gr. *kōlyein* to hinder + *phrēn* mind + *-ia*]. A state of abnormal mental inhibition.

kolyseptic (ko″le-sep′tik) [Gr. *kōlyein* to hinder + *sēptikos* septic]. Checking or hindering septic processes.

kolytic (ko-lit′ik). Hunt's term for the inhibitory temperament, marked by calmness, self-control, with a tendency to passivity of mind and body. Cf. *erethitic*.

konakion (kon″ah-ki′on). Trade mark for a preparation of vitamin K_1. See *phytonadione*.

Kondoleon's operation (kon-do′le-onz) [Emmerich (Emmanuel) *Kondoleon*, surgeon in Athens, 1879–1939]. See under *operation*.

König's operation (ken′igz) [Franz *König*, German surgeon, 1832–1910]. See under *operation*.

König's rods (ken′igz) [Charles Joseph *König*, German otologist, born 1868]. See under *rod*.

konimeter (ko-nim′e-ter). Konometer.

koniocortex (ko″ne-o-kor′teks) [Gr. *konis* dust + *cortex*]. The granular cortex of sensory areas.

koniology (ko″ne-ol′o-je). Coniology.

konometer (ko-nom′e-ter) [Gr. *konis* dust + *metron* measure]. An apparatus for counting the number of dust particles in the air.

Konsuloff's test (kon′soo-lofz) [S. *Konsuloff*, physician in Sofia]. See under *tests*.

konsyl (kon′sil). Trade mark for a preparation of plantago ovata coating.

kontrastin (kon-tras′tin). Zirconium oxide.

koomis (koo′mis). Koumiss.

kopflichtbad (kopf-likt′bad) [Ger.]. A box fitted with electric light bulbs, to go over the head to apply heat to the eyes.

kopf-tetanus (kopf-tet′ah-nus) [Ger. *Kopf* head + *tetanus*]. Tetanus following a wound of the head, especially one near the eyebrow; it is marked by trismus, facial paralysis on one side, and marked dysphagia, the symptoms resembling those of rabies. It is often fatal. Called also *head tetanus* and *hydrophobic tetanus*.

kophemia (ko-fe′me-ah) [Gr. *kōphos* deaf]. Word deafness.

kopiopia (ko″pe-o′pe-ah). Copiopia.

Koplik's spots (kop′liks) [Henry *Koplik*, New York pediatrician, 1858–1927]. See under *spot*.

kopophobia (kop″o-fo′be-ah) [Gr. *kopos* weariness + *phobos* fear + *-ia*]. Morbid fear of fatigue.

Kopp's asthma (kops) [Johann Heinrich *Kopp*, German physician, 1777–1858]. See under *asthma*.

kopr-, kopro-. For words beginning thus, see also those beginning *copr-*, *copro-*.

kopratin (kop′rah-tin) [Gr. *kopros* dung]. The chemical substance which produces the so-called pyridine-hemochromogen spectrum in the pyridine test for blood. It is produced from alphahematin by putrefaction.

koprosterin (kop″ro-ste′rin). Stercorin.

Korányi's auscultation, percussion, treatment (ko-ran′yēz) [Baron F. von *Korányi*, Hungarian physician, 1829–1913]. See under *auscultation* and *treatment*.

Kornberg (korn′berg), Arthur. United States physician and biochemist, born 1918; co-winner, with Severo Ochoa, of the Nobel prize in medicine and physiology for 1959, for work in the discovery of enzymes for producing nucleic acids artificially.

korocyte (ko′ro-sīt) [Gr. *koros* a youth + *-cyte*]. A stab neutrophil leukocyte.

koronion (ko-ro′ne-on), pl. *koro′nia* [Gr. *korōnē* crow, crown]. A point at the apex of the coronoid processes of the mandible.

koroscopy (ko-ros′ko-pe). Coroscopy.

Korotkoff's method, sounds, test (ko-rot′kofs) [Nicolai *Korotkoff*, Russian physician, born 1874]. See under the nouns.

Korsakoff's psychosis, syndrome (kor-sak′ofs) [Sergei Sergeyevich *Korsakoff*, Russian neurologist, 1854–1900]. See under *psychosis*.

Körte-Ballance operation (kĕr′te-bal′ans) [Werner *Körte*, Berlin surgeon, 1853–1937; Charles A. *Ballance*, London surgeon]. See under *operation*.

kosam (ko′sam). The seeds of *Brucea sumatrana*, of southeastern Asia: a Chinese remedy for dysentery and uterine hemorrhage.

Koshevnikoff's (Koschewnikow's) disease (ko-shev′ne-kofs) [Alexei Jakovlevich *Koshevnikoff*, Russian neurologist, 1836–1902]. A mild continuous epilepsy.

Kossel's test (kos′elz) [Albrecht *Kossel*, German physiologist, 1853–1927; winner of the Nobel prize for physiology and medicine in 1910, for his contributions to the chemistry of the cell through works on proteins, including the nucleic substances]. See under *tests*.

Köster's nodule (kes′terz) [Karl *Köster*, German pathologist, 1843–1904]. See under *nodule*.

Kottmann's reaction, test (kot′manz) [K. *Kottmann*, German physician, 1877–1952]. See under *tests*.

koumiss (koo′mis) [Tartarian]. A fermented alcoholic drink prepared from cow's milk; originally from mare's milk by the Tartars. **kefir k.,** milk fermented with kefir fungi.

Kovalevsky's canal (ko″val-ev′skēz) [Alexander Onoufrievich *Kovalevsky*, Russian embryologist, 1840–1901]. See under *canal*.

Kowarsky's test (ko-var′skēz) [A. *Kowarsky*, physician in Berlin]. See under *tests*.

Koyter's muscle (koi′terz) [Volcherus *Koyter*, Dutch anatomist, 1534–1600]. Musculus corrugator supercilii.

K.P. Abbreviation for keratitic precipitates. See *keratitis punctata*, under *keratitis*.

K_3PO_4. Normal ortho- or tribasic potassium phosphate.

Kr. Chemical symbol for *krypton*.

Krabbe's disease (krab′ēz) [Knud H. *Krabbe*, Danish neurologist, 1885–1961]. A form of diffuse infantile familial sclerosis.

Kraepelin's classification (kra′pa-linz) [Emil *Kraepelin*, Munich psychiatrist, 1856–1926]. A classification of the manic-depressive and schizophrenic groups of mental disease.

krait (krāt). An extremely venomous snake of India of the genus *Bungarus*.

Krameria (krah-me′re-ah) [J. G. H. and W. H. *Kramer*, German botanists]. A genus of polygalaceous shrubs and herbs. The roots of *K. triandra*, or Peruvian rhatany, and of *K. argentea*, or Brazilian rhatany, have astringent properties.

Kraske's operation (kras′kēz) [Paul *Kraske*, German surgeon, 1851–1930]. See under *operation*.

kratom (krah′tom). A masticatory containing the leaves of *Mitragyna speciosa*, which is chewed in Siam.

kratometer (kra-tom′e-ter). A prism-refracting instrument for use in orthoptic training.

krauomania (kraw″o-ma′ne-ah). A tic marked by rhythmic movements, such as balancing, head rotation, etc.

kraurosis (kraw-ro′sis) [Gr. *krauros* brittle]. A dry, shriveled condition of a part, especially of the vulva. **k. pe′nis,** balanitis xerotica obliterans. **k. vul′vae,** dryness and shriveling of the vulva. Called also *leukokraurosis, leukoplakia vulvae, leukoplakic vulvitis* and *pruritus vulvae*.

Krause's corpuscles, membrane (krow′zez) [Wilhelm Johann Friedrich *Krause*, German anatomist, 1833–1910]. See *corpuscula bulboidea*, and under *membrane*.

Krause's gland, ligament, valve (krow′zez) [Karl Friedrich Theodor *Krause*, German anatomist, 1797–1868]. See under the nouns.

Krause's operation (krow′zez) [Fedor *Krause*, German surgeon, 1857–1937]. See under *operation*.

kreatin (kre′ah-tin). Creatine.

krebiozen (krĕ-bi′o-zen). An unidentified substance isolated from the blood of horses injected with *Actinomyces bovis*, claimed to be effective in the treatment of cancer.

Krebs cycle (krebz) [Hans Adolf *Krebs*, German biochemist in England, born 1900; co-winner, with F. A. Lipmann, of the Nobel prize for medicine and physiology in 1953]. Tricarboxylic acid cycle.

Krebs' leukocyte index (krebz) [Carl *Krebs*, Copenhagen pathologist, born 1892]. See under *index*.

kreo-. For words beginning thus, see also those beginning *creo-*.

kreotoxicon (kre″o-tok′sĭ-kon). The substance in poisonous meat that produces the toxic symptoms.

kreotoxin (kre″o-tok′sin). Any basic poison generated in a flesh food by a plant microorganism.

kreotoxism (kre″o-tok′sizm) [Gr. *kreas* meat + *toxikon* poison]. Poisoning by meat.

kresofuchsin (kres″o-fo͞ok′sin). A blue-gray powder used as a stain in histology. Its aqueous solution is red, the alcoholic solution blue.

kresol (kres′ol). Cresol.

Kretschmann's space (krech′mahnz) [Friedrich *Kretschmann*, German otologist, 1858–1934]. See under *space*.

Kretschmer types (krech′mer) [Ernst *Kretschmer*, German psychiatrist, born 1888]. See under *type*.

Kretz's granules, paradox (krets′ez) [Richard *Kretz*, German pathologist, 1865–1920]. See under *granule* and *paradox*.

Kreysig's sign (kri′zigs) [Friedrich Ludwig *Kreysig*, physician in Dresden, 1770–1839]. See under *sign*.

krimpsiekte (krimp-zēk′te). A disease of cattle in South Africa caused by poisoning with the plant *Cotyledon wallachii*.

krinin (krin′in). Crinin.

krinosin (kri′no-sin). An amino-lipin, $C_{38}H_{79}NO_5$, obtained from brain substance.

Krishaber's disease (krēs″hab-ārz′) [Maurice *Krishaber*, Hungarian physician in France, 1836–1883]. See under *disease*.

Kristeller method, technic (kris′tel-er) [Samuel *Kristeller*, Berlin gynecologist, 1820–1900]. See under *method*.

Krogh (krōg), August. Danish physiologist, 1874–1949, noted for his research on the capillaries; winner of the Nobel prize for medicine and physiology in 1920.

Kromayer's lamp (kro′mi-erz) [Ernst Ludwig Franz *Kromayer*, German dermatologist, 1862–1933]. See under *lamp*.

Krompecher's carcinoma, tumor (krōm′pekerz) [Edmund *Krompecher*, pathologist in Budapest, 1870–1926]. Rodent ulcer.

kromskop (krōm′skōp) [German, from Gr. *chrōma* color + *skopein* to examine]. An apparatus used for color photography of pathological specimens.

Kronecker's center (kro′nek-erz) [Karl Hugo *Kronecker*, Swiss pathologist, 1839–1914]. See under *center.*

Krönig's area, field, isthmus, steps (kra′-nigz) [Georg *Kronig*, physician in Berlin, 1856–1911]. See under *field, isthmus,* and *steps.*

Krönig's method (kra′nigz) [Bernhard *Krönig*, German gynecologist, 1863–1918]. See under *method.*

Krönlein's hernia, operation (krān′līnz) [Rudolf Ulrich *Krönlein*, surgeon in Zurich, 1847–1910]. See under *hernia* and *operation.*

Krukenberg's arm, hand (kroo′ken-bergz) [Hermann *Krukenberg*, German surgeon, born 1863]. See under *hand.*

Krukenberg's spindle, tumor (kroo′ken-bergz) [Friedrich *Krukenberg*, German pathologist, born 1871]. See under *spindle* and *tumor.*

Krukenberg's vein (kroo′ken-bergz) [Adolph *Krukenberg*, German anatomist, 1816–1877]. See under *vein.*

Kruse's brush (kroo′zez) [Walther *Kruse*, German bacteriologist, 1864–1943]. See under *brush.*

krymotherapy (kri″mo-ther′ah-pe). Crymotherapy.

kryoscopy (kri-os′ko-pe). Cryoscopy.

krypto- (krip′to). For words beginning thus, see also those beginning *crypto-.*

krypton (krip′ton) [Gr. *kryptos* hidden]. An inert gaseous chemical element found in the atmosphere; atomic number, 36; atomic weight, 83.80; symbol, Kr.

KSC. Abbreviation for *kathodal (cathodal) closing contraction.*

K_2SO_4. Potassium sulfate.

KST. Abbreviation for *kathodal (cathodal) closing tetanus.*

kuatsu (koo-at′soo). The Japanese method of reviving unconscious persons.

K.U.B. Abbreviation for *kidney, ureter,* and *bladder.*

kubisagari, kubisgari (koo-bis″ah-gah′re, koo′-bis-gah′re). A form of paralytic vertigo endemic in Japan (Gerlier-Nakano, 1884).

Kugel's artery (koo′gelz). A large anastomotic artery in the heart.

Kuhn's mask (ko͝onz) [Ernst *Kuhn*, Prussian physician, 1873–1920]. See under *mask.*

Kuhn's tube (ko͝onz) [Franz *Kuhn*, Berlin surgeon, 1866–1929]. See under *tube.*

Kühne's fiber, phenomenon, plates, spindle, etc. (ke′nez) [Wilhelm Friedrich (Willy) *Kühne*, German physiologist, 1837–1900]. See under the nouns.

Kühne's methylene blue (ke′nez) [Heinrich *Kühne*, German histologist]. See *methylene blue.*

Kuhnt's illusion, operation (ko͝onts) [Hermann *Kuhnt*, German ophthalmologist, 1850–1925]. See under *illusion* and *operation.*

kukuruku (koo″koo-roo′koo). A disease of Nigeria marked by fever and jaundice.

Kulchitsky's cells (kool-chits′kēz) [Nicholas *Kulchitsky*, Russian histologist, 1856–1925]. See under *cell.*

Kulenkampff's anesthesia (koo′len-kahmpfs) [Dietrich *Kulenkampff*, German surgeon, born 1880]. See under *anesthesia.*

Külz's cylinder, test (kiltsez) [Rudolph Eduard *Külz*, German physician, 1845–1895]. See under *cylinder* and *tests.*

kumiss (koo′mis). Koumiss.

Kümmell's disease, point, spondylitis (kim′elz) [Hermann *Kümmell*, surgeon in Hamburg, 1852–1937]. See under *disease* and *point.*

Kümmell-Verneuil disease (kim′el-ver″-na′e). Kümmell's disease.

kumyss (koo′mis). Koumiss.

Kundrat's lymphosarcoma (kund′rats) [Hans *Kundrat*, German pathologist, 1845–1893]. See under *lymphosarcoma.*

Küntscher nail (kint′sher) [Gerhard *Küntscher*, German surgeon]. See under *nail.*

Kupffer's cells (koop′ferz) [Karl Wilhelm *Kupffer*, German anatomist, 1829–1902]. See under *cell.*

kupramite (ku′prah-mīt). A gas mask adsorbent for ammonia fumes.

Kupressoff's center (koo-pres′ofs) [J. *Kupressoff*, Russian physician of the 19th century]. See under *center.*

Kurella's powder (koo-rel′ahz) [Ernst G. *Kurella*, Berlin physician, 1725–1799]. Compound powder of glycyrrhiza.

kurhaus (koor′hows) [Ger. *Kur* cure + *Haus* house]. A house designed for the convenience of patients at mineral springs.

Kurloff's (Kurlow's) bodies (koor′lofs) [Mikhail Georgiyevitch *Kurloff*, Russian physician, born 1859]. See under *body.*

Kurthia (kur′the-ah) [Heinrich *Kurth*, German bacteriologist, 1860–1901]. A genus of microorganisms of the family Brevibacteriaceae, order Eubacteriales, made up of long rods with rounded ends, found in decomposing material. It includes three species, *K. besson′ii, K. varia′bilis,* and *K. zop′fii.*

kuru (koo′roo). A chronic, progressive, apparently heredofamilial degenerative disorder of the central nervous system, characterized by tremor, ataxia, dysarthria, strabismus, terminal dysphagia, and fasciculations, with death in less than one year in most patients. The condition is restricted to Melanesian natives of one region of the Eastern Highlands of the Australian Trust Territory of New Guinea, where it causes the death of over 1 per cent of the Fore people (some 12,000 natives) annually and affects nearby linguistic groups who intermarry with the Fore. Three-fourths of the patients are adult women and most of the remaining are children of both sexes.

Kurunegala ulcer (koo″roo-na-gah′lah) [the name of a district in Ceylon]. Pyosis tropica.

Küss' experiment (kes) [Emil *Küss*, German physiologist, 1815–1871]. See under *experiment.*

Kussmaul's coma, disease, pulse, symptom, etc. (koos′mowlz) [Adolf *Kussmaul*, German physician, 1822–1902]. See under the nouns.

Kussmaul-Kien respiration (koos′mowl-kēn) [Adolf *Kussmaul;* Alphonse M. J. *Kien*, German physician]. See under *respiration.*

Kussmaul-Landry paralysis (koos′mowl-lan′dre) [Adolf *Kussmaul;* Jean Baptiste Octave *Landry*, French physician, 1826–1865]. Landry's paralysis.

Kussmaul-Maier disease (koos′mowl-mi′er) [Adolf *Kussmaul;* Rudolf *Maier*, German physician, 1824–1888]. Periarteritis nodosa.

Küster's operation (kis′terz) [Ernst Georg Ferdinand *Küster*, German surgeon, 1839–1930]. See under *operation.*

Küstner's law, sign (kist′nerz) [Otto Ernst *Küstner*, gynecologist in Breslau, 1850–1931]. See under *law* and *sign.*

kutrol (ku′trol). Trade mark for a preparation of urogastrone.

kuttarosome (kut-tar′o-sōm) [Gr. *kyttaros* cell of a honeycomb + *soma* body]. A structure at the neck of a retinal cone composed of a series of parallel bars.

kv. Abbreviation for *kilovolt.*

kvp. Abbreviation for *kilovolt peak* (the maximum amount of voltage that an x-ray machine is using).

kw. Abbreviation for *kilowatt.*

kwashiorkor (kwash-e-or′kor) [local name in Gold Coast, Africa, "golden boy" or "red boy"]. A syndrome produced by severe protein deficiency, with characteristic changes in pigmentation of the skin and hair; first reported from Africa, it is now known to occur throughout the world, but mainly in the tropics and subtropics. In the wet, or classic, form, the skin may exhibit darkened, thickened patches on limbs and back which may desquamate, leaving pink, almost raw surfaces of a pellagroid appearance, or there may be generalized desquamation. **marasmic k.,** a condition in which there is deficiency of both calories and protein, with severe tissue wasting, loss of subcutaneous fat, and usually dehydration.

kwell (kwel). Trade mark for preparations of lindane.

kw.-hr. Abbreviation for *kilowatt-hour*.

kyano- (ki′ah-no). For words beginning thus see also those beginning *cyano-*.

kyanophane (ki′ah-no-fān) [Gr. *kyanos* blue + *phainein* to appear]. A supposed bluish pigment from the oil globules of the retinal cones.

kyestein (ki-es′te-in). A film sometimes seen on stale urine, formerly thought a sign of pregnancy.

kyllosis (kil-lo′sis) [Gr. *kyllōsis* a crippling]. Clubfoot, or other deformity of the foot.

kymatism (ki′mah-tizm). Myokymia.

kymocyclograph (ki″mo-si′klo-graf). An apparatus for recording movement.

kymogram (ki′mo-gram). A tracing or other graphic record made by a kymograph.

kymograph (ki′mo-graf) [Gr. *kyma* wave + *graphein* to record]. An instrument for recording variations or undulations, arterial or other (Carl Ludwig, 1847).

kymographion (ki″mo-gra′fe-on). One form of kymograph.

kymography (ki-mog′rah-fe). The use of the kymograph. **roentgen k.,** the graphic recording of the movements of an organ or structure on a single x-ray film.

kymoscope (ki′mo-skōp) [Gr. *kyma* wave + *skopein* to examine]. A device for observing the blood current.

kymotrichous (ki″mo-trik′us) [Gr. *kyma* wave + *thrix* hair]. Having wavy hair.

kynex (ki′neks). Trade mark for preparations of sulfamethoxypyridazine.

kynocephalus (ki″no-sef′ah-lus) [Gr. *kyōn* dog + *kephalē* head]. A fetal monster with a head like that of a dog.

kynophobia (ki″no-fo′be-ah) [Gr. *kyōn* dog + *phobos* fear + *-ia*]. Morbid fear of dogs or of hydrophobia.

kynurenin (kin″u-re′nin). Kynurenine.

kynurenine (ki-nu′ren-in) [Gr. *kyon* dog + L. *ren* kidney]. A crystalline nitrogenous base, frst isolated from dog urine; $NH_2C_6H_4CO.CH_2CH(NH_2)COOH$ (3-anthraniloylalanine), a metabolite of tryptophan found in microorganisms and in the urine of normal animals, and a precursor of kynurenic acid. It is also an intermediate in the conversion of tryptophan to nicotinic acid, one of the B-vitamin compounds.

kyogenic (ki″o-jen′ik) [Gr. *kyēsis* pregnancy + *gennan* to produce]. Pregnancy producing: a term used by Wiesner to describe the anterior hypophysis hormone which stimulates the corpora lutea to secrete progestin.

kyphos (ki′fos) [Gr. "a hump"]. The convex prominence of the spine in kyphosis.

kyphoscoliosis (ki″fo-sko″le-o′sis) [*kyphosis* + *scoliosis*]. Backward and lateral curvature of the spinal column, such as that seen in vertebral osteochondrosis (Scheuermann's disease).

kyphosis (ki-fo′sis) [Gr. *kyphōsis* humpback]. A condition characterized by an abnormally increased convexity in the curvature of the thoracic spine as viewed from the side. **k. dorsa′lis juveni′lis, juvenile k., Scheuermann's k.,** osteochondrosis of the vertebrae.

kyphotic (ki-fot′ik). Affected with or pertaining to kyphosis.

kyphotone (ki′fo-tōn) [Gr. *kyphos* a hump + *tonos* brace]. An apparatus for reducing deformity in Pott's disease.

kyrin (ki′rin). A basic tripeptid obtained by Siegfried by the partial hydrolysis of proteins.

kyrtorrhachic (ker″to-rak′ik) [Gr. *kyrtos* curved + *rhachis* spine]. Having a curved lumbar spine with the concavity backward.

kysth-, kystho- [Gr. *kysthos* vagina]. Combining form formerly used to designate reference to the vagina. For words beginning thus see those beginning *colpo-*.

kyto- [Gr. *kytos* hollow vessel]. For words beginning thus, see those beginning *cyto-*.

L

L. 1. An abbreviation for *Latin*, *Lactobacillus*, *left*, *light sense*, *libra* (pound, balance), *liter*, *length*, *lumbar* (in vertebral formulas), and *coefficient of induction*. 2. Ehrlich's symbol for *lethal* (fatal).

L_0. Ehrlich's symbol for *limes nul*, i.e., a toxin-antitoxin mixture which is completely neutralized and therefore will not kill an animal.

L+. Ehrlich's symbol for *limes tod*, i.e., a toxin-antitoxin mixture which contains one fatal dose in excess and which will kill the experimental animal.

L- (el-). Chemical prefix (small capital) which specifies that the substance corresponds in configuration to the standard substance L-glyceraldehyde, that is, belongs to the same configurational family. In carbohydrate nomenclature, the symbol refers to the configurational family of the *highest numbered* asymmetric carbon atom, as in L-rhamnose. In amino acid nomenclature, under rules adopted in 1947, the symbol refers to the configurational family to which the *lowest numbered* asymmetric carbon atom, i.e., the 2-carbon atom or α-carbon atom, belongs, as in L-threonine. Opposed to D-.

L_g- (el-sub-je). See L-; this chemical prefix (with the subscript *g*) is occasionally used to emphasize that the rules of carbohydrate nomenclature are being employed. The subscript refers to the standard substance glyceraldehyde. Opposed to D_g-.

L_s- (el-sub-es). See L-; this chemical prefix (with the subscript *s*) is used where needed in amino acid nomenclature to avoid possible confusion with carbohydrate nomenclature, as in L_s-threonine. The subscript refers to the standard substance serine. Opposed to D_s-.

l- (el). 1. Chemical abbreviation for *levo-* (i.e., left or counterclockwise) with reference to the direction in which the plane of polarized light is rotated when passed through a solution of the substance or through the substance itself if a liquid: opposed to *d-* (*dextro-*). 2. A prefix used with one of the additional symbols (+) or (−), especially in amino acid nomenclature in the literature from 1923 until 1947 or a little later, with reference to the configurational family to which the 2-carbon atom or α-carbon atom of the amino acid belongs, the actual direction of the rotation in a specified solvent being indicated by the plus or minus sign, as in $l(+)$-alanine; opposed to $d(+)$- or $d(-)$-, as in $d(-)$-alanine or $d(+)$-cystine.

L.A. Abbreviation for *linguoaxial*.

La. Chemical symbol for *lanthanum*.

L. & A. Abbreviation for *light and accommodation* (reaction of pupils).

lab [Ger.]. Rennet.

Labarraque's solution (lab″ah-raks′) [Antoine Germain *Labarraque*, French chemist, 1777–1850]. See under *solution*.

Labbé's triangle, vein (lab-āz′) [Léon *Labbé*, French surgeon, 1832–1916]. See under the nouns.

labia (la′be-ah) [L.]. Plural of *labium*.

labial (la′be-al) [L. *labialis*]. Pertaining to a lip, or labium.

labialism (la′be-al-izm). Defective speech, with use of labial sounds.

labially (la′be-al-e). Toward the lips.

labichorea (la″be-ko-re′ah). Labiochorea.

labile (la′bil) [L. *labilis* unstable, from *labi* to glide]. 1. Gliding; moving from point to point over the surface; unstable. 2. Chemically unstable. **heat l.,** thermolabile.

lability (lah-bil′ĭ-te). The quality of being labile. In psychiatry, emotional instability; a tendency to show alternating states of gaiety and somberness.

labio- (la′be-o) [L. *labium* lip]. Combining form denoting relationship to a lip, especially to the lips of the mouth.

labio-alveolar (la″be-o-al-ve′o-lar). 1. Pertaining to the lip and the dental alveoli. 2. Pertaining to the labial side of a dental alveolus.

labiocervical (la″be-o-ser′vĭ-kal). 1. Pertaining to the labial surface of the neck of an anterior tooth. 2. Labiogingival.

labiochorea (la″be-o-ko-re′ah) [L. *labium* lip + *chorea*]. A choreic stiffening of the lips in speech, with stammering.

labioclination (la″be-o-kli-na′shun). Deviation of an anterior tooth from the vertical, in the direction of the lips.

labiodental (la″be-o-den′tal). Pertaining to the lips and the teeth.

labiogingival (la″be-o-jin′jĭ-val). Pertaining to or formed by the labial and gingival walls of a tooth cavity.

labioglossolaryngeal (la″be-o-glos″o-lah-rin′je-al) [L. *labium* lip + Gr. *glōssa* tongue + *larynx*]. Pertaining to the lips, tongue, and larynx.

labioglossopharyngeal (la″be-o-glos″o-fah-rin′je-al). Pertaining to the lips, tongue, and pharynx.

labiograph (la′be-o-graf) [L. *labium* lip + Gr. *graphein* to record]. An instrument for recording the motions of the lips in speaking.

labioincisal (la″be-o-in-si′zal). Pertaining to or formed by the labial and incisal surfaces of a tooth.

labiolingual (la″be-o-ling′gwal). 1. Pertaining to the lips and the tongue. 2. Pertaining to the labial and lingual surfaces of an anterior tooth.

labiologic (la″be-o-loj′ik). Pertaining to labiology.

labiology (la″be-ol′o-je). The study of the movements of the lips in speaking and singing.

labiomancy (la′be-o-man″se) [L. *labium* lip + Gr. *manteia* foretelling]. Lip reading.

labiomental (la″be-o-men′tal). Pertaining to the lip and chin.

labiomycosis (la″be-o-mi-ko′sis) [L. *labium* lip + Gr. *mykēs* fungus]. Any disease of the lips due to a fungus, such as perlèche and thrush.

labionasal (la″be-o-na′zal). Pertaining to the lip and nose.

labiopalatine (la″be-o-pal′ah-tin). Pertaining to the lip and palate.

labioplacement (la″be-o-plās′ment). Displacement of a tooth toward the lip.

labioplasty (la′be-o-plas″te) [L. *labium* lip + Gr. *plassein* to mold]. Cheiloplasty.

labiotenaculum (la″be-o-te-nak′u-lum) [L. *labium* lip + *tenaculum*]. An instrument for holding the lip.

labioversion (la″be-o-ver′zhun). The state of being displaced labially from the line of occlusion: said of a tooth.

labitome (lab′ĭ-tōm) [Gr. *labis* forceps + *temnein* to cut]. A cutting forceps.

labium (la′be-um), pl. *la′bia* [L.]. A fleshy border or edge; used in anatomical nomenclature as a general term to designate such a structure. Called also *lip*. **l. ante′rius orific′ii exter′ni u′teri** [B N A], l. anterius ostii uteri. **l. ante′rius os′tii pharyn′gei tu′bae auditi′vae** [B N A], the anterior lip of the pharyngeal opening of the auditory tube. Omitted in N A. **l. ante′rius os′tii u′teri** [N A], the anterior projection of the cervix into the vagina. It is shorter and thicker than the posterior lip. Called also *l. anterius orificii externi uteri* [B N A], and *anterior lip of ostium of uterus*. **l. cer′ebri,** an edge of the cerebral hemisphere overlying the corpus callosum. **l. exter′num cris′tae ili′acae** [N A, B N A], the outer margin or lip of the iliac crest. **l. infe′rius o′ris** [N A, B N A], the fleshy margin of the inferior border of the mouth. **l. infe′rius val′vulae co′li** [B N A], the inferior lip of the valve between the ileum and cecum. Omitted in N A. **l. inter′num cris′tae ili′acae** [N A, B N A], the inner margin or lip of the iliac crest. **l. latera′le lin′eae as′perae fem′oris** [N A, B N A], the outer part of the linea aspera, which becomes continuous with the gluteal tuberosity and ends at the greater trochanter. Called also *lateral lips of linea aspera of femur*. **l. lim′bi tympan′icum lam′inae spira′lis** [N A], the lower border of the internal spiral sulcus, formed by the lower extremity of the limbus laminae spiralis. Called also *l. tympanicum laminae spiralis* [B N A]. **l. lim′bi vestibula′re lam′inae spira′lis** [N A], the upper border of the internal spiral sulcus, formed by the upper extremity of the limbus laminae spiralis. Called also *l. vestibulare laminae spiralis* [B N A]. **l. ma′jus puden′di** [N A, B N A], pl. *la′bia majo′ra puden′di*, an elongated fold running downward and backward from the mons pubis in the female, one on either side of the median pudendal cleft. **l. mandibula′re,** l. inferius oris. **l. maxilla′re,** l. superius oris. **l. media′le lin′eae as′perae fem′oris** [N A, B N A], the inner part of the linea aspera, which becomes continuous with the intertrochanteric line. Called also *medial lip of linea aspera of femur*. **l. mi′nus puden′di** [N A, B N A], pl. *la′bia mino′ra puden′di*, a small fold of skin located on either side, between the labium majus and the opening of the vagina. **la′bia o′ris** [N A, B N A], the fleshy upper and lower margins of the mouth. Called also *lips*. **l. poste′rius orific′ii exter′ni u′teri** [B N A], l. posterius ostii uteri. **l. poste′rius os′tii pharyn′gei tu′bae auditi′vae** [B N A], the posterior lip of the pharyngeal opening of the auditory tube. Omitted in N A. **l. poste′rius os′tii u′teri** [N A], the posterior projection of the cervix into the vagina. Called also *l. posterius orificii externi uteri* [B N A], and *posterior lip of ostium of uterus*. **l. supe′rius o′ris** [N A, B N A], the fleshy margin of the superior border of the mouth. **l. supe′rius val′vulae co′li** [B N A], the superior lip of the valve between the ileum and cecum. Omitted in N A. **l. tympan′icum lam′inae spira′lis** [B N A], l. limbi tympanicum laminae spiralis. **l. ure′thrae,** either lateral margin of the external urinary meatus. **l. vestibula′re lam′inae spira′lis** [B N A], l. limbi vestibulare laminae spiralis. **l. voca′le** [B N A], a projection at each side of the rima glottidis. Omitted in N A.

labor (la′bor) [L. "work"]. The function of the female organism by which the product of conception is expelled from the uterus through the vagina to the outside world. Called also *accouchement, childbirth, confinement, parturition*, and *travail*. **artificial l.,** induced l. **atonic l.,** labor protracted because of atony of the uterus. **complicated l.,** labor in which convulsions, hemorrhage, or some other untoward event occurs.

dry l., labor in which the amniotic fluid escapes before the onset of uterine contractions. **false l.** See *false pains.* **immature l.,** labor taking place between the sixteenth and the twenty-eighth week of pregnancy. **induced l.,** labor which is brought on by mechanical or other extraneous means. **instrumental l.,** labor in which expulsion of the product of conception is facilitated by the use of instruments. **mimetic l.** See *false pains.* **missed l.,** retention of a dead fetus in the uterus beyond the period of normal gestation. **multiple l.,** labor in which two or more infants are born. **obstructed l.,** labor hindered by some mechanical obstruction, such as a tumor or contraction in some region of the parturient canal. **postponed l.,** labor occurring later than the expected date. **precipitate l.,** labor which occurs with undue celerity. **premature l.,** expulsion of a viable infant before the normal end of gestation, usually applied to interruption of pregnancy between the twenty-eighth and the thirty-seventh week. **premature l., habitual,** delivery occurring in at least three successive pregnancies at about the same stage of development and prior to completion of the full gestation period. **prolonged l., protracted l.,** labor which is prolonged beyond the ordinary limit. **spontaneous l.,** labor in which no artificial aid is required.

laboratorian (lab″o-rah-to′re-an). A person who devotes himself to laboratory work, as distinguished from a clinician.

laboratory (lab′o-rah-to″re) [L. *laboratorium*]. A place equipped for performing experimental work or certain investigative procedures.

Laborde's forceps, method, sign (lah-bordz′) [Jean Baptiste Vincent *Laborde*, French physician, 1830–1903]. See under the nouns.

labra (la′brah) [L.]. Plural of *labrum.*

labrale (lah-bra′le). An anthropometric landmark on the border of the lip. **l. infe′rius,** the lowest point, in the midsagittal plane, on the vermilion border of the lower lip. **l. supe′rius,** the highest point, in the midsagittal plane, on the vermilion border of the upper lip.

labrocyte (lab′ro-sit) [Gr. *labros* greedy + *-cyte*]. A mast cell.

labrum (la′brum), pl. *la′bra* [L.]. An edge, brim, or lip. **l. acetabula′re** [N A], a ring of fibrocartilage attached to the rim of the acetabulum of the hip bone, increasing the depth of the cavity. Called also *l. glenoidale articulationis coxae* [B N A], and *acetabular lip.* **l. glenoida′le** [N A], a ring of fibrocartilage attached to the rim of the glenoid cavity of the scapula, increasing the depth of the cavity. Called also *l. glenoidale articulationis humeri* [B N A], and *glenoid lip.* **l. glenoida′le articulatio′nis cox′ae** [B N A], l. acetabulare. **l. glenoida′le articulatio′nis hu′meri** [B N A], l. glenoidale.

labyrinth (lab′ĭ-rinth) [Gr. *labyrinthos*]. A system of intercommunicating cavities or canals, such as that constituting the internal ear. **acoustic l.,** cochlea. **bony l.,** the bony part of the internal ear. Called also *labyrinthus osseus* [N A]. **cortical l.,** a network of tubules and blood vessels in the cortex of the kidney. **l. of ethmoid, ethmoidal l.,** labyrinthus ethmoidalis. **Ludwig's l's,** spaces between Bertin's columns and the cortical arches. **membranous l.,** a system of communicating epithelial sacs and ducts within the osseous labyrinth. See *labyrinthus membranaceus* [N A]. **nonacoustic l.,** statokinetic l. **olfactory l.,** labyrinthus ethmoidalis. **osseous l.,** bony l. **statokinetic l.,** the vestibule and semicircular canals.

labyrinthectomy (lab′ĭ-rin-thek′to-me) [*labyrinth* + Gr. *ektomē* excision]. Excision of the labyrinth of the ear.

labyrinthi (lab″ĭ-rin′thi) [L.]. Plural of *labyrinthus.*

labyrinthine (lab″ĭ-rin′thin). Pertaining to a labyrinth.

labyrinthitis (lab″ĭ-rin-thi′tis). Inflammation of the labyrinth; otitis interna.

labyrinthotomy (lab″ĭ-rin-thot′o-me) [*labyrinth* + Gr. *temnein* to cut]. Surgical incision into the labyrinth.

labyrinthus (lab″ĭ-rin′thus), pl. *labyrin′thi* [L.; Gr. *labyrinthos*]. A system of intercommunicating cavities or canals. Called also *labyrinth.* **l. ethmoida′lis** [N A, B N A], either of the paired lateral masses of the ethmoid bone, consisting of numerous thin-walled cellular cavities, the ethmoidal cells. Called also *ethmoidal labyrinth.* **l. membrana′ceus** [N A, B N A], a system of communicating epithelial sacs and ducts, including the endolymphatic duct, utricle, and semicircular ducts, lodged within the bony labyrinth and containing endolymph. Called also *membranous labyrinth.* **l. os′seus** [N A, B N A], the bony part of the internal ear. Called also *bony labyrinth.*

lac (lak), pl. *lac′ta*, gen. *lac′tis* [L.]. 1. Milk. 2. Any milklike medicinal preparation. 3. A wax collected from various tropical trees, caused by an insect, *Coccus lactis.* **l. femini′num** [B N A], the secretion of the human mammary gland. Omitted in N A. **l. fermen′tum,** koumiss. **l. humaniza′tum,** humanized milk. **l. sulfu′ris,** precipitated sulfur. **l. vacci′num,** cow's milk. **l. virgina′le** ["virgin's milk"], a strained liquor of litharge; an ancient remedial wash, variously prepared, but now entirely obsolete. **zapon l.,** a varnish of pyroxylin dissolved in amyl alcohol and amyl acetate.

laccase (lak′ās). An oxidizing enzyme found in the latex of the lac trees and in many vegetables. It oxidizes the latex to Japanese lacquer and many phenols to ortho and para quinones.

lacerable (las′er-ah-b′l). Capable of becoming lacerated.

lacerated (las′er-āt″ed) [L. *lacerare* to tear]. Torn; of the nature of a rent.

laceration (las″er-a′shun) [L. *laceratio*]. 1. The act of tearing. 2. A wound made by tearing.

lacertofulvin (lah-ser″to-ful′vin) [L. *lacertus* lizard + *fulvus* yellow]. A yellow coloring matter from the skin of certain reptiles.

lacertus (lah-ser′tus) [L., "lizard," because of a fancied resemblance]. A name applied to certain fibrous attachments of muscles. **l. cor′dis.** See *trabeculae carneae cordis.* **l. fibro′sus mus′culi bicip′itis bra′chii** [B N A], aponeurosis musculi bicipitalis brachii. **l. me′dius Weitbrech′tii, l. me′dius Wrisber′gii,** ligamentum longitudinale anterius. **l. mus′culi rec′ti latera′lis bul′bi** [N A], the check ligament of the lateral rectus muscle, which is attached to the lateral palpebral ligament.

Lachesis (lak′e-sis) [L.; Gr. *Lachesis* one of the three Fates]. A genus of venomous snakes. *L. lanceola′tus* is the fer-de-lance; *L. mu′tus* is the bushmaster.

lachry- (lak′re). For words beginning thus, see those beginning *lacri-.*

lacinia (lah-sin′e-ah) [L. "fringe"]. Fimbria.

lacmus (lak′mus) [Ger. *Lackmus*]. Litmus.

lacrima (lak′rĭ-mah), pl. *lacrimae* [L.]. See *tears.*

lacrimae (lak′rĭ-me) [L.]. Plural of *lacrima;* B N A name for the watery secretion of the lacrimal glands. Omitted in N A. See *tears.*

lacrimal (lak′rĭ-mal) [L. *lacrimalis; lacrima* tear]. Pertaining to the tears.

lacrimalin (lak-rim′ah-lin). A substance obtained from the secretion of the lacrimal gland: said to have induced a flow of tears.

lacrimase (lak′rĭ-mās). A ferment obtained from the secretion of the lacrimal gland.

lacrimation (lak″rĭ-ma′shun) [L. *lacrimatio*]. The secretion and discharge of tears.

lacrimator (lak′rĭ-ma″tor). A substance which increases the flow of tears, such as certain gases.

lacrimatory (lak′rĭ-mah-to″re). Causing a flow of tears.

lacrimonasal (lak″rĭ-mo-na′zal). Pertaining to the lacrimal sac and the nose.

lacrimotome (lak′rĭ-mo-tōm). A knife for incising the lacrimal sac or duct.

lacrimotomy (lak″rĭ-mot′o-me) [L. *lacrima* tear + Gr. *tomē* a cutting]. Incision of the lacrimal sac or duct.

lactacidase (lak-tas′ĭ-dās). An enzyme of lactic acid bacteria which produces lactic acid fermentation.

lactacidemia (lak-tas″ĭ-de′me-ah) [*lactic acid* + Gr. *haima* blood + *-ia*]. The presence of lactic acid in the blood.

lactacidin (lak-tas′ĭ-din). A food preservative composed of lactic and salicylic acids.

lactacidogen (lak″tah-sid′o-jen) [*lactic acid* + Gr. *gennan* to produce]. See *hexosephosphate.*

lactaciduria (lak-tas″ĭ-du′re-ah) [*lactic acid* + Gr. *ouron* urine + *-ia*]. The presence of lactic acid in the urine.

lactagogue (lak′tah-gog) [L. *lac* milk + Gr. *agōgos* leading]. Galactagogue.

lactalase (lak′tah-lās). A ferment which converts dextrose into lactic acid.

lactalbumin (lak″tal-bu′min). An albumin found in milk and resembling serum albumin.

lactam (lak′tam). A cyclic amide formed from aminocarboxylic acids by the elimination of water. They are isomeric with lactims, which are enol forms of lactams.

```
—C=O          —C—OH
 |              ||
—NH            —N
lactam        lactim
```

lactamide (lak-tam′id). The amide of lactic acid, $CH_3CHOH.CONH_2$.

lactamine (lak-tam′in). Alanine.

lactaroviolin (lak″tah-ro-vi′o-lin). An antibiotic pigment isolated from the fungus *Lactarius deliciosus.*

lactase (lak′tās). An intestinal enzyme that splits lactose into glucose and galactose.

lactate (lak′tāt). Any salt of lactic acid.

lactation (lak-ta′shun) [L. *lactatio*, from *lactare* to suckle]. 1. The secretion of milk. 2. The period of the secretion of milk. 3. Suckling.

lactational (lak-ta′shun-al). Pertaining to lactation.

lacteal (lak′te-al) [L. *lacteus* milky]. 1. Pertaining to milk. 2. Any one of the intestinal lymphatics that take up chyle.

lactein (lak′te-in). Lactolin.

lactenin (lak′tĕ-nin). A bacteriostatic substance in milk.

lactescence (lak-tes′ens) [L. *lactescere* to become milky]. Resemblance to milk; milkiness.

lactic (lak′tik). Pertaining to milk.

lacticemia (lak″tĭ-se′me-ah). The presence of lactic acid in the blood.

lactiferous (lak-tif′er-us) [L. *lac* milk + *ferre* to bear]. Producing or conveying milk.

lactification (lak″tĭ-fi-ka′shun). The production of lactic acid by the lactic acid bacteria.

lactifuge (lak′tĭ-fūj) [L. *lac* milk + *fugare* to expel]. 1. Checking or stopping the secretion of milk. 2. An agent that checks the secretion of milk.

lactigenous (lak-tij′e-nus) [L. *lac* milk + Gr. *gennan* to produce]. Producing or secreting milk.

lactigerous (lak-tij′er-us) [L. *lac* milk + *gerere* to carry]. Lactiferous.

lactim (lak′tim). See under *lactam.*

lactimorbus (lak″tĭ-mor′bus) [L. *lac* milk + *morbus* disease]. Milk sickness.

lactin (lak′tin). 1. Lactose, or sugar of milk. 2. A proprietary sterile milk in ampules for injection in nonspecific protein therapy.

lactinated (lak′tĭ-nāt″ed). Prepared with sugar of milk.

lactivorous (lak-tiv′o-rus) [L. *lac* milk + *vorare* to devour]. Feeding or subsisting upon milk.

lacto- (lak′to) [L. *lac, lactis* milk]. Combining form denoting relationship to milk.

Lactobacillaceae (lak″to-bas″il-la′se-e). A family of Schizomycetes (order Eubacteriales), made up of long or short rods or cocci which divide in one plane only, producing chains or tetrads. It includes two tribes, *Lactobacilleae* and *Streptococceae.*

Lactobacilleae (lak″to-bah-sil′e-e). A tribe of microorganisms of the family Lactobacillaceae, order Eubacteriales, made up of straight or curved rods occurring usually singly or in chains, but sometimes in filaments. It includes five genera, *Catenabacte′rium, Cillobacte′rium, Eubacte′rium, Lactobacil′lus,* and *Ramibacte′rium.*

lactobacillin (lak″to-bah-sil′in). A preparation of lactic acid bacteria to be added to milk to cause lactic acid fermentation.

Lactobacillus (lak″to-bah-sil′lus). A genus of microorganisms of the tribe Lactobacilleae, family Lactobacillaceae, order Eubacteriales, occurring as large gram-positive, anaerobic or microaerophilic bacilli, some of which are considered to be etiologically related to dental caries but are otherwise non-pathogenic. They are separable into 15 species falling into two groups, the homofermentative group producing only lactic acid, and the heterofermentative group producing other end-products of fermentation. **L. acidoph′ilus,** a homofermentative lactobacillus producing the fermented product, acidophilus milk. **L. bif′idus,** a homofermentative lactobacillus predominating in the intestinal flora of breast-fed infants. **L. bulgar′icus,** a homofermentative lactobacillus producing the fermented product known as Bulgarian or bulgaricus milk.

lactobacillus (lak″to-bah-sil′us), pl. *lactobacilli.* An organism of the genus Lactobacillus. **l. of Boas-Oppler,** an organism first isolated from the gastric juice of patients with gastric carcinoma, similar to if not identical with *Lactobacillus bulgaricus.*

Lactobacteriaceae (lak″to-bak-te″re-a′se-e). A former name of a family of Schizomycetes now called Lactobacillaceae.

lactobiose (lak″to-bi′ōs). Lactose.

lactobutyrometer (lak″to-bu″tĭ-rom′e-ter) [*lacto-* + *butyrometer*]. An instrument for measuring the proportion of cream in milk.

lactocele (lak′to-sēl). Galactocele.

lactochrome (lak′to-krōm) [*lacto-* + Gr. *chrōma* color]. Riboflavin.

lactoconium (lak-to-ko′ne-um) [*lacto-* + Gr. *konis* dust]. One of the small particles, of unknown nature, seen with the ultramicroscope in the milk of animals.

lactocrit (lak′to-krit) [*lacto-* + Gr. *kritēs* judge]. An instrument for estimating the amount of fat in milk.

lactodensimeter (lak″to-den-sim′e-ter). Lactometer.

lactofarinaceous (lak″to-far″ĭ-na′shus). Composed of milk and farinaceous foods: said of a diet.

lactoflavin (lak′to-fla″vin) [*lacto-* + L. *flavus* yellow]. Riboflavin.

lactogenic (lak″to-jen′ik). Stimulating the production of milk.

lactoglobulin (lak″to-glob′u-lin). A globulin occurring in milk. **immune l′s,** antibodies occurring in the colostrum of animals.

lactolase (lak′to-lās). A vegetable enzyme which causes the formation of lactic acid.

lactolin (lak′to-lin). Condensed milk.

lactometer (lak-tom′e-ter) [*lacto-* + Gr. *metron* measure]. An instrument for ascertaining the specific gravity of milk.

lactone (lak′tōn). 1. An aromatic liquid, $C_{10}H_8O_4$, prepared by distillation from lactic acid. 2. Tablets containing lactic acid bacteria: used in preparing buttermilk.

lactophenin (lak″to-fe′nin). A bitter, crystalline powder, $C_6H_4(OC_2H_5).NH.CO.CH(OH)CH_3$, derived from phenetidin and lactic acid, soluble in 500 parts of cold and in 55 parts of boiling water: sedative and antipyretic.

lactophosphate (lak″to-fos′fāt) [*lacto-* + L. *phosphas* phosphate]. Any salt of lactic and phosphoric acids.

lactoprecipitin (lak″to-pre-sip′ĭ-tin). A precipitin which will precipitate the casein of milk.

lactoprotein (lak″to-pro′te-in). A protein derived from milk.

lactorrhea (lak″to-re′ah). Galactorrhea.

lactosazone (lak″to-sa′zōn). The phenylosazone of lactose. It is a yellow crystalline substance made by treating lactose with phenylhydrazine and acetic acid. The crystals melt at 200°C. and may be used in identifying lactose.

lactoscope (lak′to-skōp) [*lacto-* + Gr. *skopein* to examine]. A device showing the proportion of cream in milk.

lactose (lak′tōs) [L. *saccharum lactis*]. Beta-glucopyranose 4-beta-galactopyranoside, $C_{12}H_{22}O_{11} + H_2O$, a white crystalline disaccharide which on hydrolysis with acids or certain enzymes yields glucose and galactose. Called also *milk sugar*. **beta l.,** a disaccharide obtained by allowing a solution of lactose to crystallize above 93°C. It is sweeter and more soluble than lactose.

lactoserum (lak″to-se′rum). The serum of an animal into which has been injected milk from another animal. This serum precipitates milk from an animal of the same species as that from which the milk was taken.

lactosum (lak-to′sum). Lactose.

lactosuria (lak″to-su′re-ah) [*lactose* + Gr. *ouron* urine + *-ia*]. The presence of lactose in the urine, observed frequently during lactation.

lactotherapy (lak″to-ther′ah-pe) [*lacto-* + *therapy*]. Treatment by milk diet.

lactotoxin (lak″to-tok′sin). A toxic substance found in milk.

lactovegetarian (lak″to-vej″ĕ-ta′re-an). 1. Pertaining to, consisting of, or subsisting on milk (or other dairy products) and vegetables. 2. A vegetarian who uses dairy products in addition to vegetables in his diet.

Lactuca (lak-tu′kah) [L.]. A genus of composite-flowered plants, including *L. sati′va*, common lettuce, and *L. viro′sa*, the principal source of lactucarium.

lacuna (lah-ku′nah), pl. *lacunae* [L.]. 1. A small pit or hollow cavity; used in anatomical nomenclature as a general term to designate such a compartment within or between other body structures. Called also *lake*. 2. A defect or gap, as in the field of vision (scotoma). **absorption l.,** a pit or groove in developing bone that is undergoing resorption, frequently found to contain osteoclasts. **air l.,** a cavity filled with air, such as those occurring in the hairs. **Blessig's l.** See *Blessig's cysts*. **blood l.,** any one of the blood-filled spaces in the trophoblast of the embryo that serve hemotrophic nutrition. **great l. of urethra,** fossa navicularis urethrae masculinae. **Howship's l.,** absorption l. **intervillous l.,** one of the blood spaces of the placenta in which the fetal villi are found. **lateral lacunae, lacu′nae latera′les** [N A], venous meshworks on the inner aspect of the calvarium, on either side of the superior sagittal sinus. Arachnoidal granulations project into them. **l. mag′na,** fossa navicularis urethrae masculinae. **lacunae of Morgagni,** lacunae urethrales in the male urethra. **lacu′nae Morga′gnii ure′thrae mulie′bris,** glandulae urethrales urethrae femininae. **l. of muscles, l. musculo′rum** [N A, B N A], a compartment beneath the inguinal ligament for the passage of the iliopsoas muscle and femoral nerve, separated from the lacuna vasorum by the iliopectineal arch. **parasinoidal l's,** lacunae laterales. **l. pharyn′gis,** a depression at the pharyngeal end of the auditory tube. **trophoblastic l.,** intervillous l. **lacunae of urethra, urethral lacunae,** lacunae urethrales. **urethral lacunae of Morgagni,** lacunae urethrales in the male urethra. **lacu′nae urethra′les** [N A], numerous small depressions or pits in the mucous membrane of the urethra, with their openings usually directed distally. Some contain openings of ducts of the urethral glands. Applied in B N A to such depressions in the male urethra. **l. vaso′rum** [N A, B N A], a compartment for the passage of the femoral vessels, separated from the lacuna musculorum by the iliopectineal arch. **l. of vessels,** l. vasorum.

lacunae (lah-ku′ne) [L.]. Plural of *lacuna*.

lacunar (lah-ku′nar). Pertaining to or containing lacunae; of the nature of a lacuna.

lacunule (lah-ku′nūl) [L. *lacunula*]. A small lacuna.

lacus (la′kus), pl. *la′cus* [L.]. Lake. **l. lacrima′lis** [N A, B N A], the triangular space at the medial angle of the eye, where the tears collect. Called also *lacrimal lake*.

Ladendorff's test (lah′den-dorfs) [August *Ladendorff*, German physician of the 19th century]. See under *tests*.

Ladin's sign (la′dinz) [Louis Julius *Ladin*, American gynecologist, born 1862]. See under *sign*.

lae-. For words beginning thus, see also those beginning *le-*.

Laelaps (le′laps). A genus of tick mites found on rats and in stable litter. Its bite causes intense itching.

Laennec's cirrhosis, pearls, etc. (la″en-neks′) [René Théophile Hyacinthe *Laennec*, distinguished French physician and inventor of the stethoscope, 1781–1826]. See under the nouns.

laeve (le′vĕ) [L. *levis* smooth]. Nonvillous, as the *chorion laeve*.

laevo- (le′vo). For words beginning thus, see those beginning *levo-*.

Lafora's sign (lah-fo′rahz) [Gonzalo Rodríguez *Lafora*, Spanish physician, born 1887]. See under *sign*.

LaG. Abbreviation for *labiogingival*.

Lag. Abbreviation for L. *lage′na*, a flask.

lag (lag). 1. The period of time elapsing between the application of a stimulus and the resulting reaction. 2. The early period following a bacterial inoculation into a culture medium, in which the growth is slow: called also *lag phase*. **nitrogen l.,** the time that elapses after the administration of a protein before there appears in the urine an amount of nitrogen equivalent to that administered.

lagena (lah-je′nah) [L. "flask"]. The curved, flask-shaped organ of hearing in vertebrates lower than mammals.

lageniform (lah-jen′ĭ-form) [L. *lagena* flask + *form*]. Flask-shaped.

lagnesis (lag-ne′sis) [Gr. *lagneia* salaciousness]. Erotomania.

lagnosis (lag-no′sis) [Gr. *lagnos* salacious, lustful]. Excessive sexual desire, especially in the male; satyriasis.

Lagochilascaris minor (lag″o-ki-las′kah-ris mi′nor). A nematode worm found in the intestine of man in Trinidad.

lagophthalmos (lag″of-thal′mos) [Gr. *lagōs* hare + *ophthalmos* eye]. A condition in which the eye cannot be completely closed; called also *hare's eye*.

lagophthalmus (lag″of-thal′mus). Lagophthalmos.

Lagrange's operation (lah-grah′zez) [Pierre

Felix *Lagrange*, French ophthalmologist, 1857–1928]. Sclerecto-iridectomy.

la grippe (lah grip′) [Fr.]. Influenza.

La.I. Abbreviation for *labioincisal.*

Lain's disease (lānz′) [Everett Samuel *Lain*, American dermatologist, born 1876]. See under *disease.*

laiose (li′ōs). A pale-yellow substance, $C_6H_{12}O_6$, found in the urine in diabetes mellitus. It is nonfermentable and levorotatory.

lake (lāk) [L. *lacus*]. 1. To undergo separation of hemoglobin from the erythrocytes; a phenomenon sometimes occurring in blood. 2. A circumscribed collection of fluid in a hollow or depressed area. **lacrimal l.,** lacus lacrimalis.

Lake's pigment (lāks′) [Richard *Lake*, English otorhinolaryngologist, 1861–1949]. See under *pigment.*

laliatry (lal-i′ah-tre) [Gr. *lalia* talking + *iatria* therapy]. The study and treatment of disorders of speech.

laliophobia (lal″e-o-fo′be-ah) [Gr. *lalia* talking + *phobia*]. Morbid fear of talking and stuttering.

lallation (lal-a′shun) [L. *lallatio*]. A babbling, infantile form of speech.

Lallemand's bodies (lal-mahz′) [Claude François *Lallemand*, French surgeon, 1790–1853]. See under *body.*

lalo- (lal′o) [Gr. *lalein* to babble, speak]. Combining form denoting relationship to speech, or babbling.

lalognosis (lal″og-no′sis) [*lalo-* + Gr. *gnōsis* knowledge]. The understanding of speech.

laloneurosis (lal″o-nu-ro′sis) [*lalo-* + *neurosis*]. Any nervous speech disorder.

lalopathology (lal″o-pah-thol′o-je) [*lalo-* + *pathology*]. The branch of medicine which deals with disorders of speech.

lalopathy (lal-op′ah-the) [*lalo-* + Gr. *pathos* illness]. Any disorder of speech.

lalophobia (lal″o-fo′be-ah) [*lalo-* + *phobia*]. Morbid or extreme dislike of speaking, often associated with stuttering.

laloplegia (lal″o-ple′je-ah) [*lalo-* + Gr. *plēgē* stroke]. Paralysis of the organs of speech.

lalorrhea (lal″o-re′ah) [*lalo-* + Gr. *rhoia* flow]. An abnormal or excessive flow of words.

Lalouette's pyramid (lal″oo-ets′) [Pierre *Lalouette*, French physician, 1711–1742]. See under *pyramid.*

Lamarck's theory (lah-marks′) [Jean Baptiste Pierre Antoine de *Lamarck*, French naturalist, 1744–1829]. See under *theory.*

lambda (lam′dah) [the fourteenth letter of the Greek alphabet, Λ or λ]. The point at the site of the posterior fontanel where the lambdoid and sagittal sutures meet.

lambdacism, lambdacismus (lam′dah-sizm, lam-dah-siz′mus) [Gr. *lambdakismos*]. 1. The substitution of *l* for *r* in speaking. 2. Inability to utter correctly the sound of *l.*

lambdoid (lam′doid) [Gr. *lambda* + *eidos* form]. Shaped like the Greek letter Λ or λ.

lambert (lam′bert) [Johann Heinrich *Lambert*, German mathematician and physicist, 1728–1777]. A unit of brightness, being the brightness of a perfect diffuser emitting one lumen per square centimeter. The unit generally used is one one-thousandth of this and is called a *millilambert.* When the area chosen is one square foot the unit is called a *foot lambert.*

Lambert's cosine law (lam′berts) [J. H. *Lambert*]. See under *law.*

Lambert's treatment (lam′berts) [Alexander *Lambert*, American physician, 1861–1939]. See under *treatment.*

Lamblia (lam′ble-ah) [Vilem Dusan *Lambl*, Bohemian physician, 1824–1895]. See *Giardia.* **L. intestina′lis,** *Giardia lamblia.*

lambliasis, lambliosis (lam-bli′ah-sis, lam-ble-o′sis). Infection with *Giardia lamblia.*

Lambotte's treatment (lam-bots′) [Albin *Lambotte*, Belgian surgeon, 1856–1912]. See under *treatment.*

lamel (lam′el). Lamella, def. 2.

lamella (lah-mel′ah), pl. *lamel′lae* [L., dim. of *lamina*]. 1. A thin leaf or plate, as of bone. 2. A medicated disk or wafer prepared from gelatin, glycerin, and distilled water, and containing a small quantity of an alkaloid, to be inserted under the eyelid. Those for which official standards have been established by the British Pharmacopoeia include lamellae of atropine, cocaine, homatropine, and physostigmine. **articular l.,** the layer of bone to which an articular cartilage is attached. **circumferential l.,** one of the bony plates that underlie the periosteum and endosteum. **concentric l.,** haversian l. **enamel lamellae,** thin dark bands visible in ground sections of teeth viewed with transmitted light; they extend through the entire thickness of the enamel and are thought to be organic matter or light-absorbing cracks. **endosteal l.,** one of the bony plates lying beneath the endosteum. **ground l.,** interstitial l. **haversian l.,** one of the concentric bony plates surrounding a haversian canal. **intermediate l.,** interstitial l. **interstitial l.,** one of the bony plates that fill in between the haversian systems; called also *ground l.* or *intermediate l.* **osseous l.,** any one of the thin plates into which bone can be divided. **periosteal l., peripheral l.,** the layer of bone lying next to the periosteum. **triangular l.,** the layer that joins the choroid plexuses of the third ventricle. **vitreous l.,** lamina basalis.

lamellae (lah-mel′e) [L.]. Plural of *lamella.*

lamellar (lah-mel′ar). Pertaining to or resembling lamellae.

lamina (lam′ĭ-nah), pl. *lam′inae* [L.]. A thin flat plate, or layer; used in anatomical nomenclature as a general term to indicate such a structure, or a layer of a composite structure. Called also *layer.* **l. affix′a** [N A, B N A], a plate in the floor of the pars centralis of the lateral ventricle, covering the thalamostriate vein and stria terminalis. **alar l., l. ala′ris** [N A], either of the pair of longitudinal zones of the embryonic neural tube dorsal to the sulcus limitans, from which are developed the dorsal gray columns of the spinal cord and the sensory centers of the brain. Called also *alar plate.* **lam′inae al′bae cerebel′li** [N A], the core of white substance that supports a folium of the cerebellar cortex. Called also *laminae medullares cerebelli* [B N A], and *white laminae of cerebellum.* **anterior limiting l.,** l. limitans anterior corneae. **l. ante′rior vagi′nae mus′culi rec′ti abdo′minis** [N A], the portion of its sheath lying anterior to the rectus abdominis muscle, formed by aponeuroses of the internal and external oblique above the arcuate line and by the aponeuroses of the internal oblique and transversus, below the arcuate line. **l. ar′cus ver′tebrae** [N A], one of the paired dorsal parts of the vertebral arch connected to the pedicles of the vertebra. Called also *l. of vertebral arch.* **basal l.,** l. basalis. **basal l. of choroid,** l. basalis choroideae. **basal l. of ciliary body,** l. basalis corporis ciliaris. **l. basa′lis** [N A], either of the pair of longitudinal zones of the embryonic neural tube ventral to the sulcus limitans, from which are developed the ventral gray columns of the spinal cord and the motor centers of the brain. Called also *basal plate.* **l. basa′lis cerebel′li** [B N A]. Omitted in N A. **l. basa′lis chorioi′deae** [B N A], **l. basa′lis choroi′deae** [N A], the transparent inner layer of the choroid, in contact with the pigmented layer of the retina and connecting the choroid and the retina. Called also *basal l. of choroid.* **l. basa′lis cor′poris cilia′ris** [N A], the innermost layer of the ciliary body, continuous with the basal lamina of the choroid. Called also *basal l. of ciliary body.* **l. basila′ris duc′tus**

cochlea'ris [N A, B N A], the posterior wall of the cochlear duct, which separates it from the scala tympani; the spiral organ lies against it. Called also *basilar membrane of cochlear duct.* **Bowman's l.,** l. limitans anterior corneae. **l. cartilag'inis cricoi'deae** [N A, B N A], the broad posterior part of the cricoid cartilage. Called also *l. of cricoid cartilage.* **l. cartilag'inis latera'lis tu'bae auditi'vae** [N A], the smaller of the two laminae that compose the tubal cartilage; it lies in the lateral wall of the auditory tube. Called also *lateral lamina of cartilage of auditory tube.* **l. cartilag'inis media'lis tu'bae auditi'vae** [N A], the larger of the two laminae that compose the tubal cartilage; it lies in the medial wall of the auditory tube. Called also *medial lamina of cartilage of auditory tube.* **l. cartilag'inis thyroi'deae [dex'tra et sinis'tra]** [N A, B N A], either of the broad plates that form the sides (right and left) of the thyroid cartilage, converging anteriorly to meet at the midline. Called also *l. of thyroid cartilage.* **l. choriocapilla'ris** [N A, B N A], **choriocapillary l.,** the choroid layer just deep to the basal lamina, consisting of a single-layered network of small capillaries. **l. chorioi'dea epithelia'lis thal'ami** [B N A], an epithelial layer lining the roof of the thalamus. Omitted in N A. **l. chorioi'dea epithelia'lis ventric'uli latera'lis** [B N A], the thin epithelial layer lining the roof of the lateral ventricle. Omitted in N A. **l. chorioi'dea epithelia'lis ventric'uli quar'ti** [B N A], the thin epithelial layer lining the roof of the fourth ventricle. Omitted in N A. **l. cine'rea termina'lis,** l. terminalis hypothalami. **cribriform l.,** fascia cribrosa. **cribriform l. of ethmoid bone,** lamina cribrosa ossis ethmoidalis. **cribriform l. of transverse fascia,** septum femorale. **l. cribro'sa os'sis ethmoida'lis** [N A, B N A], the horizontal plate of the ethmoid bone that forms the roof of the nasal cavity; it is perforated by many foramina for the passage of the olfactory nerves. Called also *cribriform plate of ethmoid bone.* **l. cribro'sa scle'rae** [B N A], the perforated portion of the sclera through which pass the axons of the ganglion cells of the retina. Omitted in N A. **l. of cricoid cartilage,** l. cartilaginis cricoideae. **dental l.,** a thickened epithelial band along the margin of the gum, in the embryo, from which the enamel organs are developed. **dental l., lateral,** a perpendicular layer of cells connecting the developing tooth germ to the dental lamina. **l. denta'lis,** dental l. **l. denta'ta,** labium limbi vestibulare. **dentogingival l.,** dental l. **descending l. of sphenoid bone,** processus pterygoideus ossis sphenoidalis. **l. elas'tica ante'rior [Bow'mani]** [B N A], l. limitans anterior corneae. **l. elas'tica poste'rior [Demour'si, Descem'eti]** [B N A], l. limitans posterior corneae. **episcleral l., l. episclera'lis** [N A], loose connective and elastic tissue covering the sclera and anteriorly connecting it with the conjunctiva. **epithelial l., l. epithelia'lis** [N A], the layer of ependymal cells covering the choroid plexus. **l. exter'na os'sium cra'nii** [N A, B N A], the outer compact layer of bone of the flat bones of the head. Called also *outer table of bones of skull.* **external l. of peritoneum,** peritoneum parietale. **external l. of pterygoid process,** lateralis processus pterygoidei. **l. fibrocartilagin'ea interpu'bica** [B N A], discus interpubicus. **l. fus'ca scle'rae** [N A, B N A], a thin layer of loose, pigmented connective tissue on the inner surface of the sclera, connecting it with the choroid. **l. horizonta'lis os'sis palati'ni** [N A], the horizontal part of the palatine bone, forming the posterior part of the hard palate. Called also *horizontal plate of palatine bone.* **inferior l. of sphenoid bone,** processus pterygoideus ossis sphenoidalis. **l. inter'na os'sium cra'nii** [N A, B N A], the inner compact layer of bone of the flat bones of the head. Called also *inner table of bones of skull.* **internal l. of pterygoid process,** l. medialis processus pterygoidei. **interpubic l., fibrocartilaginous,** discus interpubicus. **labial l.,** the ectodermal plate that on splitting separates lip from gum. **lateral l. of cartilage of auditory tube,** l. cartilaginis lateralis tubae auditivae. **lateral l. of pterygoid process,** l. lateralis processus pterygoidei. **l. latera'lis cartilag'inis tu'bae auditi'vae** [B N A], l. cartilaginis lateralis tubae auditivae. **l. latera'lis proces'sus pterygoi'dei** [N A, B N A], either of a pair of bony plates projecting downward from the roots of the greater wings of the sphenoid bone and forming the medial wall of the ipsilateral infratemporal fossa. Called also *lateral plate of pterygoid process.* **l. lim'itans ante'rior cor'neae** [N A], a thin layer of the cornea beneath the outer layer of stratified epithelium, between it and the substantia propria. Called also *anterior limiting l.* and *l. elastica anterior* [*Bowmani*] [B N A]. **l. lim'itans poste'rior cor'neae** [N A], a thin membrane between the substantia propria and the endothelial layer of the cornea. Called also *l. elastica posterior* [*Demoursi, Descemeti*] [B N A], and *posterior limiting l.* **limiting l., anterior,** l. limitans anterior corneae. **limiting l., posterior,** l. limitans posterior corneae. **medial l. of cartilage of auditory tube,** l. cartilaginis medialis tubae auditivae. **medial l. of pterygoid process,** l. medialis processus pterygoidei. **l. media'lis cartilag'inis tu'bae auditi'vae** [B N A], l. cartilaginis medialis tubae auditivae. **l. media'lis proces'sus pterygoi'dei** [N A, B N A], either of a pair of bony plates projecting downward from the roots of the greater wings of the sphenoid bone and forming the lateral boundary of the ipsilateral posterior aperture of the nasal cavity and the most posterior part of the lateral wall of the nasal cavity. Called also *medial plate of pterygoid process.* **lam'inae mediastina'les** [B N A], the mediastinal layers of the pleura. Omitted in N A. **lam'inae medulla'res cerebel'li** [B N A], laminae albae cerebelli. **l. medulla'ris latera'lis cor'poris stria'ti** [N A], a layer of fibers running through the globus pallidus and dividing it into a lateral and a medial part. Called also *lateral medullary l.* **l. medulla'ris media'lis cor'poris stria'ti** [N A], a layer of fibers separating the putamen from the globus pallidus. Called also *medial medullary l.* **lam'inae medulla'res thal'ami** [N A, B N A], sheets of white fibers covering the surface and separating the nuclei of the thalamus. Called also *medullary l. of thalamus.* **l. medulla'ris transver'sa cor'poris quadrigem'ini,** stratum album profundum corporis quadrigemini. **medullary l., lateral,** l. medullaris lateralis. **medullary l., medial,** l. medullaris medialis. **medullary laminae of thalamus,** laminae medullares thalami. **l. membrana'cea tu'bae auditi'vae** [N A, B N A], **membranous l. of auditory tube,** the connective tissue lamina that supports the inferior and lateral parts of the auditory tube. **l. mesenter'ii pro'pria** [B N A], the proper layer of the mesentery. Omitted in N A. **l. modi'oli** [N A, B N A], a bony plate extending upward toward the cupula as a continuation of the modiolus and of the bony spiral lamina of the cochlea. **l. muscula'ris muco'sae** [N A, B N A], the thin layer of smooth muscle fibers usually found as a part of the tunica mucosa deep to the lamina propria mucosae. **l. muscula'ris muco'sae co'li** [N A, B N A], the muscular layer of the tunica mucosa of the colon. **l. muscula'ris muco'sae esoph'agi** [N A], the muscular layer of the tunica mucosa of the esophagus. **l. muscula'ris muco'sae intesti'ni cras'si** [N A, B N A], the muscular layer of the tunica mucosa of the large intestine. **l. muscula'ris muco'sae intesti'ni rec'ti** [B N A], l. muscularis mucosae recti. **l. muscula'ris muco'sae intesti'ni ten'uis** [N A, B N A], the muscular layer of the tunica mucosa of the small intestine. **l. muscula'ris muco'sae rec'ti** [N A], the muscular layer of the tunica mucosa of the rectum. **l. muscula'ris muco'sae ventric'uli** [N A, B N A], the muscular layer of the tunica mucosa of the stomach. **orbital l., l. orbita'lis os'sis ethmoida'lis** [N A], a thin plate of bone laterally bounding the ethmoid labyrinth on either side and forming part of the medial wall of the orbit. Called also *l. papyracea* [B N A]. **palatine l. of maxilla,** processus palatinus maxillae. **l. papyra'cea** [B N A], l. orbitalis ossis ethmoidalis. **l. parieta'lis pericar'dii** [N A], the parietal layer of the serous pericardium, which is in contact with the fibrous pericardium. **l. parieta'lis tu'nicae vagina'lis pro'priae tes'tis** [B N A], **l. parieta'lis tu'nicae vagina'lis tes'tis** [N A], the outer layer of the tunica vaginalis of the testis, separated from the visceral layer by a cavity. Called also *parietal layer of tunica vaginalis of testis.* **periclaustral l.,** capsula externa. **perpendicular l. of ethmoid bone,** l. perpendicularis ossis ethmoidalis. **l. perpendicula'ris os'sis ethmoida'lis** [N A, B N A], a thin bony plate that descends from the inferior surface of the cribriform plate of the ethmoid bone and participates in forming the nasal septum. Called also *perpendicular plate of ethmoid bone.* **l. perpendicula'ris os'sis palati'ni** [N A], the flat, vertical, bony plate that extends superiorly from either side of the palatine bone. It is surmounted by the orbital and sphenoidal processes. Called also *pars perpendicularis ossis palatini* [B N A], and *perpendicular plate of palatine bone.* **posterior limiting l.,** l. limitans posterior corneae. **l. poste'rior vagi'nae mus'culi rec'ti abdo'minis** [N A], the portion of its sheath lying posterior to the rectus abdominis muscle, formed by the transversus abdominis and its aponeurosis at the level of the xiphoid process; below the xiphoid process, to the arcuate line, it is formed by the aponeuroses of the internal oblique and the transversus. **l. pretrachea'lis fas'ciae cervica'lis** [N A], the layer of the cervical fascia that is anterior to the trachea. **l. prevertebra'lis fas'ciae cervica'lis** [N A], the layer of the cervical fascia that is anterior to the vertebrae. Called also *fascia praevertebralis* [B N A]. **l. profun'da fas'ciae tempora'lis** [N A], the deep portion of the fascia investing the temporal muscle. **l. profun'da mus'culi levato'ris palpe'brae superio'ris** [N A], the deeper of the two layers of the levator palpebrae superioris muscle. **proper l. of mesentery,** lamina mesenterii propria. **l. pro'pria membra'nae tym'pani,** the middle fibrous basis of the tympanic membrane, attached, except anterosuperiorly, to the tympanic plate of the temporal bone. **l. pro'pria muco'sae** [N A, B N A], the connective tissue coat of a mucous membrane just deep to the epithelium and basement membrane. **l. quadrigem'ina** [B N A], l. tecti mesencephali. **rostral l., l. rostra'lis** [B N A], the thin terminal part of the rostrum of the corpus callosum passing down in front of the anterior commissure to the anterior perforated substance and the paraterminal gyrus. Omitted in N A. **l. sep'ti pellu'cidi** [N A, B N A], **l. of septum pellucidum,** either of the thin, vertical sheets, separated by a cleftlike space, which constitute the septum pellucidum. **spiral l., bony,** l. spiralis ossea. **spiral l., secondary,** l. spiralis secundaria. **l. spira'lis os'sea** [N A, B N A], a double plate of bone winding spirally around the modiolus and dividing the spiral canal of the cochlea incompletely into two parts, the scala tympani and the scala vestibuli. Called also *bony spiral l.* **l. spira'lis secunda'ria** [N A, B N A], a bony projection on the outer wall of the osseous spiral lamina in the lower part of the first turn of the cochlea. Called also *secondary spiral l.* **submucous l. of stomach,** tela submucosa ventriculi. **l. superficia'lis fas'ciae cervica'lis** [N A], the layer of the cervical fascia that lies deep to the skin. **l. superficia'lis fas'ciae tempora'lis** [N A], the superficial portion of the fascia investing the temporal muscle. **l. superficia'lis mus'culi levato'ris palpe'brae superio'ris** [N A], the superficial of the two layers of the levator palpebrae superioris muscle. **l. suprachorioi'dea** [B N A], **suprachoroid l., l. suprachoroi'dea** [N A], the outermost layer of the choroid, which connects it with the sclera. **l. supraneuropor'ica,** the part of the membranous roof of the diencephalon covering the foramen of Monro. **tectal l. of mesencephalon, l. tec'ti mesenceph'ali** [N A], the layer of mingled gray and white substance from which arise the superior and inferior colliculi. Called also *l. quadrigemina* [B N A]. **terminal l. of hypothalamus, l. termina'lis hypothal'ami** [N A, B N A], a thin plate derived from the telencephalon, passing upward in front of the optic chiasm and forming the anterior wall of the third ventricle. **l. tra'gi** [N A, B N A], **l. tra'gica,** the longitudinal curved lamina of cartilage in the tragus of the auricle, at the beginning of the cartilaginous portion of the external acoustic meatus. **ungual laminae,** cristae matricis unguis. **vascular l. of choroid,** l. vasculosa choroideae. **vascular l. of stomach,** tela submucosa ventriculi. **l. vasculo'sa chorioi'deae** [B N A], **l. vasculo'sa choroi'deae** [N A], the layer of the choroid between the suprachoroid and choriocapillary layers, containing the largest blood vessels. **l. of vertebra,** pediculus arcus vertebrae. **l. of vertebral arch,** l. arcus vertebrae. **l. viscera'lis pericar'dii** [N A], the inner layer of the serous pericardium, which is in contact with the heart. Called also *epicardium.* **l. viscera'lis tu'nicae vagina'lis pro'priae tes'tis** [B N A], **l. viscera'lis tu'nicae vagina'lis tes'tis** [N A], the inner part of the tunica vaginalis of the testis, firmly attached to the testis and epididymis. Called also *visceral layer of tunica vaginalis of testis.* **l. vit'rea,** l. basalis choroideae. **white laminae of cerebellum,** laminae albae cerebelli.

laminae (lam'ĭ-ne) [L.]. Plural of *lamina.*

laminagram (lam'ĭ-nah-gram). A roentgenogram of a selected layer of the body made by laminagraphy.

laminagraphy (lam"ĭ-nag'rah-fe) [L. *lamina* layer + Gr. *graphein* to record]. See *body section roentgenography,* under *roentgenography.*

laminar (lam'ĭ-nar) [L. *laminaris*]. Made up of, or arranged in, laminae.

laminated (lam'ĭ-nāt"ed). Made up of thin layers or laminae; disposed in laminae or layers.

lamination (lam"ĭ-na'shun). 1. A laminated structure or arrangement. 2. The slicing of the fetal head in embryotomy.

laminectomy (lam"ĭ-nek'to-me) [L. *lamina* layer + Gr. *ektomē* excision]. Excision of the posterior arch of a vertebra.

laminitis (lam"ĭ-ni'tis). Inflammation of a lamina, and especially of the laminae of a horse's foot; a form of founder.

laminogram (lam'ĭ-no-gram). Laminagram.

laminograph (lam'ĭ-no-graf). Laminagraph.

laminography (lam"ĭ-nog'rah-fe). Laminagraphy.

laminotomy (lam"ĭ-not'o-me) [*lamina* + Gr. *tomē* a cutting]. The operation of dividing the lamina of a vertebra.

lamp (lamp). An apparatus for furnishing heat or light. **annealing l.,** an alcohol lamp for heating and purifying gold leaf to be used for filling tooth cavities. **arc l.,** a source of light consisting of gaseous particles from the electrodes of an electric arc which are raised to a temperature of incandescence by an electric current. **Birch-Hirschfeld l.,** a lamp for light treatment in eye diseases. **carbon arc l.,** an open flame lamp with carbon arcs: used in artificial light therapy. **cold quartz mercury vapor l.**, an ultraviolet radiation lamp having a low vapor pressure, low amperage and a high potential glow discharge. **cold red-light l.**, a lamp with a neon glow tube. **Duke-Elder l.**, a lamp for ultraviolet treatment in ophthalmology. **Eldridge-Green l.**, an arrangement of lights for testing color vision. **Finsen l.**, a carbon arc lamp operating at 50 volts and 50 amperes so constructed that radiation is concentrated on an area 1 inch square: a water-cooled quartz system to remove caloric radiation and a compression quartz piece to dehematize the skin. **Finsen-Reya l.**, a modification of the Finsen lamp in which the electrodes are placed at right angles to each other. **Gullstrand's slit l.**, one embodying a diaphragm containing a slitlike opening, by means of which a narrow flat beam of intense light may be projected into the eye. It gives intense illumination so that microscopic study may be made of the conjunctiva, cornea, iris, lens, and vitreous, the special feature being that it illuminates a section through the substance of these structures. **Jesionek l.**, a light for giving artificial sunlight baths. **Kromayer's l.**, a small metal, mercury vapor, water-cooled lamp with a quartz window for the generation of ultraviolet rays. **Lortet l.**, an electric lamp used in Finsen light treatment. **mercury vapor l.**, a lamp in which the arc is struck in mercury and is enclosed in a quartz burner: used in light therapy. There are two types, the air cooled and water cooled (*Kromayer's l.*). **mignon l.** (min′yun), a minute electric light used in cystoscopy, etc. **Nernst l.**, an incandescent electric lamp the filament of which is made of metallic oxides. **quartz l.**, a mercury vacuum lamp made of melted quartz glass embedded in a running water-bath: used for applying light treatment. **Simpson l.** See under *light.* **slit l.**, Gullstrand's slit l. **tungsten arc l.**, a lamp having highly compressed tungsten electrodes. **ultra-violet l.**, an electric light bulb made of glass that transmits ultraviolet rays. **uviol l.**, an electric lamp with a globe of uviol glass, which is unusually transparent to ultraviolet rays. **zoalite l.**, a device for producing radiant heat for therapeutic purposes.

lampas (lam′pas). A swelling and hardening of the mucosa of the hard palate, immediately behind the upper incisors in horses.

lampblack (lamp′blak). Finely powdered carbon derived from the burning of oils, rosin, etc.

Lamprocystis (lam″pro-sis′tis). A genus of microorganisms of the family Thiorhodaceae, suborder Rhodobacteriineae, order Pseudomonadales, made up of spherical to ovoid cells embedded in a common gelatinous capsule. The type species is *L. roseopersi′cina.*

lamprophonia (lam″pro-fo′ne-ah) [Gr. *lampros* clear + *phōnē* voice + *-ia*]. Clearness of voice.

lamprophonic (lam″pro-fon′ik). Pertaining to or characterized by lamprophonia.

Lamus (la′mus). A former genus name of predatory insects of the family Reduviidae now placed under the genera *Panstrongylus* and *Triatoma.*

lamziekte (lam′zēk-te) [Dutch "lame-sickness"]. A disease of cattle in South Africa secondary to bovine osteophagia. The cattle chew putrefying bones and thus absorb the toxin of *Clostridium botulinum.*

lana (lan′ah), pl. and gen. *lan′ae* [L.]. Wool.

lanatoside (lan-at′o-sīd). A glycoside obtained from the leaves of *Digitalis lanata.* Lanatoside C, $C_{49}H_{76}O_{20}$, is used as a cardiotonic.

lanaurin (lan′aw-rin). A pyrrole pigment found in the sweat and urine of sheep which may color the wool yellow.

lance (lans) [L. *lancea*]. 1. Lancet. 2. To cut or open with a lancet. **Mauriceau's l.**, a pointed knife used in embryotomy.

Lancefield classification (lans′fēld) [Rebecca C. *Lancefield,* New York bacteriologist, born 1895]. A classification of the hemolytic streptococci based on the precipitin test. The natural habitat of these groups is as follows: *group A*, pathogenic for man; *group B*, for the most part from cases of mastitis; *group C*, from pathologic conditions of lower animals; *group D*, isolated from cheese; *group E*, isolated from milk; *group F*, isolated from human throats; *group G*, isolated from man, dogs, and monkeys; *groups H* and *K*, non-pathogenic from throat and nose.

lanceolate (lan′se-o-lāt). Shaped like a lance.

Lancereaux's diabetes, treatment, etc. (lahn″ser-ōz′) [Étienne *Lancereaux,* physician in Paris, 1829–1910]. See under the nouns.

lancet (lan′set) [L. *lancea* lance]. A small pointed and two-edged surgical knife. **abscess l.**, a wide-bladed lancet with one convex and one concave edge. **acne l.**, a form with a narrow blade for puncturing the papules of acne. **gum l.**, a knife for incising the gums. **laryngeal l.**, a delicate knife for operations within the larynx: it is operated through a cannula. **spring l.**, one the blade of which is held by a spring. **thumb l.**, one with a wide, two-edged blade.

Lancet coefficient (lan′set) [*The Lancet,* a British medical periodical]. See under *coefficient.*

lancinating (lan′sĭ-nāt″ing) [L. *lancinas*]. Tearing, darting, or sharply cutting. See under *pain.*

Lancisi's nerve, stria (lan-che′sēz) [Giovanni Maria *Lancisi,* Italian physician, 1654–1720]. Stria longitudinalis medialis corporis callosi.

Landau's test (lahn′dowz) [Leopold *Landau,* German surgeon, 1848–1920]. See under *tests.*

Landerer's treatment (lahn′der-erz) [Albert Sigmund *Landerer,* German surgeon, 1854–1904]. See under *treatment.*

landmark (land′mark). A readily recognizable anatomical structure used as a point of reference in establishing the location of another structure or in determining certain measurements.

Landolfi's paste (lan-dol′fēz) [Nicolà *Landolfi,* Neapolitan physician of the 19th century]. See under *paste.*

Landolt's bodies (lahn-dolts′) [Edmund *Landolt,* oculist in Paris, 1846–1926]. See under *body.*

Landouzy's disease (lan-doo′zēz) [Louis Théophile Joseph *Landouzy,* French physician, 1845–1917]. Leptospiral jaundice.

Landouzy-Dejerine dystrophy, type (lan-doo′ze-deh″zher-ēn′) [L. T. J. *Landouzy;* Joseph Jules *Dejerine,* French neurologist, 1849–1917]. See under *dystrophy.*

Landouzy-Grasset law (lan-doo′ze-gras-sa′) [L. T. J. *Landouzy;* Joseph *Grasset,* French physician, 1849–1918]. See under *law.*

Landry's paralysis (lan-drēz′) [Jean Baptiste Octave *Landry,* French physician, 1826–1865]. See under *paralysis.*

Landsteiner's classification (land′sti-nerz) [Karl *Landsteiner,* Austrian biologist in the United States, 1868–1943, winner of the Nobel prize for physiology and medicine in 1930]. A classification of blood types (q.v.) in which they are designated O, A, B, and AB, depending on the presence or absence of agglutinogens A and B in the erythrocytes. Called also *International classification.*

Landström's muscle (lahnd′stremz) [John *Landström,* Swedish surgeon, 1869–1910]. See under *muscle.*

Lane's band, disease, kink, operation, plates (lānz) [Sir W. Arbuthnot *Lane,* English surgeon, 1856–1943]. See under the nouns.

Langdon-Down's disease [John Langdon Haydon *Langdon-Down,* British physician, 1828–1896]. Mongolism.

Lange's operation (lahng′ez) [Fritz *Lange,* German orthopedist, born 1864]. See under *operation.*

Lange's solution, test (lahng′ez) [Carl *Lange,* German physician, born 1883]. See under *solution* and *tests.*

Langenbeck's incision, triangle (lahng′en-beks) [Bernard Rudolf Konrad von *Langenbeck*, German surgeon, 1810–1887]. See under *incision* and *triangle*.

Langer's arch, lines, muscle (lang′erz) [Carl Ritter von Edenberg von *Langer*, Austrian anatomist, 1819–1887]. See under the nouns.

Langerhans' cells, islands (lahng′er-hanz) [Paul *Langerhans*, German pathologist, 1847–1888]. See under *cell* and *island*.

Langhans' cells, layer (lahng′hahnz) [Theodor *Langhans*, German pathologist, 1839–1915]. See under *cell* and *layer*.

Langley's ganglion, granulations, nerves (lang′lēz) [John Newport *Langley*, English physiologist, 1852–1925]. See under the nouns.

laniary (lan′e-a″re) [L. *laniare* to tear to pieces]. Suitable for lacerating, or tearing to pieces, applied to canine teeth.

Lankesterella ranarum (lan-kes″ter-el′ah rah-na′rum) [Sir Edwin Ray *Lankester*, British zoologist, 1847–1930]. A sporozoan parasite of the red blood cells of the frog.

Lankesteria culicis (lan″kes-te′re-ah ku′lĭ-sis). A gregarine sporozoon parasitic in the gut of the mosquito *Aedes aegypti*.

Lannelongue's operation (lan″e-longs′) [Odilon Marc *Lannelongue*, French surgeon, 1840–1911]. See under *operation*.

lanolin (lan′o-lin) [L. *lanolinum; lana* wool + *oleum* oil]. Hydrous wool fat: used as an excipient for remedies for external use. **anhydrous l.,** wool fat.

lanoxin (lan-ok′sin). Trade mark for preparations of digoxin.

lanthanin (lan′thah-nin). Oxychromatin.

lanthanum (lan′thah-num) [Gr. *lanthanein* to be concealed]. A rare metallic element: symbol, La; atomic number, 57; atomic weight, 138.91.

lanuginous (lan-u′jĭ-nus) [L. *lanuginosus*]. Covered with lanugo.

lanugo (lan-u′go) [L.]. [N A, B N A] The fine hair on the body of the fetus. Called also *down* and *wooly hair*.

lanum (la′num) [L. *lana* wool]. Hydrous wool fat.

Lanz's operation, point (lahnts) [Otto *Lanz*, surgeon in Amsterdam, 1865–1935]. See under *operation* and *point*.

L.A.O. Abbreviation for *Licentiate in Obstetric Science*.

LAP. Abbreviation for *lyophilized anterior pituitary* (tissue).

lapactic (lah-pak′tik) [Gr. *lapaktikos, lapassein* to discharge]. Pertaining to or effecting a removal; purgative.

laparectomy (lap″ah-rek′to-me) [*laparo-* + Gr. *ektomē* excision]. Excision of a portion or of portions of the abdominal wall: performed for the purpose of overcoming laxity of the walls and to gain support.

laparo- (lap′ah-ro) [Gr. *lapara* flank]. Combining form denoting relationship to the loin or flank. Sometimes used loosely in reference to the abdomen.

laparocele (lap′ah-ro-sēl). Ventral hernia.

laparocholecystotomy (lap″ah-ro-ko″le-sis-tot′o-me) [*laparo-* + Gr. *cholē* bile + *kystis* bladder + *tomē* a cutting]. Incision of the gallbladder through an abdominal section.

laparocolectomy (lap″ah-ro-ko-lek′to-me) [*laparo-* + Gr. *kolon* colon + *ektomē* excision]. Colectomy.

laparocolostomy (lap″ah-ro-ko-los′to-me) [*laparo-* + Gr. *kolon* colon + *stomoun* to provide with an opening, or mouth]. Surgical creation of a permanent opening into the colon by an incision in the anterolateral wall of the abdomen.

laparocolotomy (lap″ah-ro-ko-lot′o-me) [*laparo-* + Gr. *kolon* colon + *tomē* a cutting]. Colotomy through the abdominal wall.

laparocolpohysterotomy (lap″ah-ro-kol″po-his″ter-ot′o-me) [*laparo-* + Gr. *kolpos* vagina + *hystera* uterus + *tomē* a cutting]. Cesarean section by a combined vaginal and abdominal method.

laparocystectomy (lap″ah-ro-sis-tek′to-me) [*laparo-* + Gr. *kystis* cyst + *ektomē* excision]. Removal of a cyst by an abdominal incision.

laparocystidotomy (lap″ah-ro-sis″tĭ-dot′o-me) [*laparo-* + Gr. *kystis* bladder + *tomē* a cutting]. Incision into the bladder through the abdominal wall just above the pubes.

laparocystotomy (lap″ah-ro-sis-tot′o-me) [*laparo-* + Gr. *kystis* bladder + *tomē* a cutting]. 1. The removal of an extrauterine fetus, the sac being allowed to remain. 2. Laparotomy with removal of the contents of a cyst.

laparo-enterostomy (lap″ah-ro-en″ter-os′to-me) [*laparo-* + Gr. *enteron* intestine + *stomoun* to provide with an opening, or mouth]. The creation of an artificial opening into the intestine through the abdominal wall.

laparo-enterotomy (lap″ah-ro-en″ter-ot′o-me) [*laparo-* + Gr. *enteron* intestine + *tomē* a cutting]. Laparotomy with incision into the intestine.

laparogastroscopy (lap″ah-ro-gas-tros′ko-pe) [*laparo-* + *gastroscopy*]. Examination of the interior of the stomach through a gastrotomy incision.

laparogastrostomy (lap″ah-ro-gas-tros′to-me) [*laparo-* + Gr. *gastēr* stomach + *stomoun* to provide with an opening, or mouth]. The creation of a permanent gastric fistula through the abdominal wall.

laparogastrotomy (lap″ah-ro-gas-trot′o-me) [*laparo-* + Gr. *gastēr* stomach + *tomē* a cutting]. Incision into the stomach through the abdominal wall.

laparohepatotomy (lap″ah-ro-hep″ah-tot′o-me) [*laparo-* + *hepatotomy*]. Incision of the liver through the abdominal wall.

laparohysterectomy (lap″ah-ro-his″ter-ek′to-me) [*laparo-* + Gr. *hystera* uterus + *ektomē* excision]. Removal of the uterus through an opening in the abdominal wall.

laparohystero-oophorectomy (lap″ah-ro-his″ter-o-o″of-o-rek′to-me) [*laparo-* + Gr. *hystera* uterus + *oophorectomy*]. Laparotomy with removal of the uterus and ovaries.

laparohysteropexy (lap″ah-ro-his′ter-o-pek″-se) [*laparo-* + Gr. *hystera* uterus + *pēxis* fixation]. Ventrofixation.

laparohysterosalpingo-oophorectomy (lap″ah-ro-his″ter-o-sal-ping″go-o″of-o-rek′to-me). Removal of the uterus, uterine tubes, and ovaries through an abdominal incision.

laparohysterotomy (lap″ah-ro-his″ter-ot′o-me) [*laparo-* + Gr. *hystera* uterus + *tomē* a cutting]. Laparotomy with incision of the uterus.

laparo-ileotomy (lap″ah-ro-il″e-ot′o-me) [*laparo-* + *ileum* + Gr. *tomē* a cutting]. Laparotomy with incision of the ileum.

laparokelyphotomy (lap″ah-ro-kel″ĭ-fot′o-me) [*laparo-* + Gr. *kelyphos* egg-shell + *tomē* a cutting]. Laparotomy with incision of the sac of an extrauterine gestation.

laparomonodidymus (lap″ah-ro-mon″o-did′ĭ-mus) [*laparo-* + Gr. *monos* single + *didymos* twin]. A monster fetus, double above but single below the pelvis.

laparomyitis (lap″ah-ro-mi-i′tis) [*laparo-* + Gr. *mys* muscle + *-itis*]. Inflammation of the abdominal or lumbar muscles.

laparomyomectomy (lap″ah-ro-mi″o-mek′to-me) [*laparo-* + Gr. *mys* muscle + *ektomē* excision]. The removal of a myoma by an abdominal incision.

laparonephrectomy (lap″ah-ro-ne-frek′to-me) [*laparo-* + Gr. *nephros* kidney + *ektomē* excision]. Removal of a kidney by an incision in the loin.

laparorrhaphy (lap-ah-ror′ah-fe) [*laparo-* + Gr. *rhaphē* suture]. Suturation of the abdominal wall.

laparosalpingectomy (lap″ah-ro-sal″pin-jek′to-me) [*laparo-* + Gr. *salpinx* tube + *ektomē* excision]. Removal of a uterine tube through an abdominal incision.

laparosalpingo-oophorectomy (lap″ah-ro-sal-ping″go-o″of-o-rek′to-me). Removal of a uterine tube and ovary through an abdominal incision.

laparosalpingotomy (lap″ah-ro-sal″pin-got′o-me) [*laparo-* + Gr. *salpinx* tube + *tomē* a cutting]. Incision of a uterine tube through an abdominal incision.

laparoscope (lap′ah-ro-skōp″). An endoscope by means of which the peritoneal cavity, especially the surface of the liver and the peritoneum, can be inspected.

laparoscopy (lap″ah-ros′ko-pe) [*laparo-* + Gr. *skopein* to examine]. Endoscopic examination of the interior of the abdomen by means of a laparoscope.

laparosplenectomy (lap″ah-ro-sple-nek′to-me) [*laparo-* + Gr. *splēn* spleen + *ektomē* excision]. Laparotomy with excision of the spleen.

laparosplenotomy (lap″ah-ro-sple-not′o-me) [*laparo-* + Gr. *splēn* + *tomē* a cutting]. The operation of making an incision into the side to gain access to the spleen, usually for the purpose of draining a cyst or abscess of the spleen.

laparothoracoscopy (lap″ah-ro-tho″rah-kos′-ko-pe) [*laparo-* + Gr. *thōrax* chest + *skopein* to examine]. The inspection of the peritoneal and pleural cavities through an instrument resembling a cystoscope pushed into them through the body wall.

laparotomaphilia (lap″ah-rot″o-mah-fil′e-ah) [*laparotomy* + Gr. *philein* to love + *-ia*]. A morbid desire to undergo abdominal surgery for the relief of simulated distress. Cf. *Munchausen's syndrome.*

laparotome (lap′ah-ro-tōm). A knife used in laparotomy.

laparotomize (lap″ah-rot′o-mīz). To subject to laparotomy.

laparotomy (lap-ah-rot′o-me) [*laparo-* + Gr. *tomē* a cutting]. Surgical incision through the flank: less correctly, but more generally, abdominal section at any point.

laparotrachelotomy (lap″ah-ro-tra″kĕ-lot′o-me) [*laparo-* + Gr. *trachēlos* neck + *tomē* a cutting]. Cesarean section done by incising the cervix and lower uterine segment; low or cervical cesarean section.

laparotyphlotomy (lap″ah-ro-tif-lot′o-me) [*laparo-* + Gr. *typhlon* cecum + *tomē* a cutting]. Incision into the cecum through the flank.

laparo-uterotomy (lap″ah-ro-u″ter-ot′o-me). Laparohysterotomy.

Lapicque's constant, law (lah-pēks′) [Louis *Lapicque*, French physiologist, 1866–1952]. See under *constant* and *law.*

lapinization (lap″in-i-za′shun) [Fr. *lapin* rabbit]. Passage of a virus through rabbits as a means of modifying its characteristics.

lapis (la′pis) [L.]. Stone. **l. al′bus,** the native silicofluoride of calcium: also its homeopathic preparation. **l. calamina′ris,** calamine. **l. caus′ticus,** fused potash. **l. divi′nus,** ammoniated copper. **l. imperia′lis, l. inferna′lis, l. luna′ris,** silver nitrate. **l. ophthal′micus,** l. divinus.

lapnus (lap′nus). A nonfebrile disease of the Philippines beginning with anorexia, abdominal pain, and vomiting—later, burning sensation in hands and feet with blackish-red patches on feet, toes, and fingers; desquamation always follows, sometimes deafness and blindness.

lapsus (lap′sus) [L., from *labi* to slip or fall]. 1. An error, or slip, thought to be revealing of an unconscious wish or association. 2. Falling or dropping of a part; ptosis. **l. cal′ami,** a slip of the pen. **l. lin′guae,** a slip of the tongue. **l. memo′riae,** a lapse of memory.

laqueus (lak′we-us) [L. "a noose"]. Lemniscus.

Larat's treatment (lah-raz′) [Jules Louis François Adrien *Larat*, French physician, born 1857]. See under *treatment.*

larbish (lar′bish). A creeping eruption occurring in Senegal; called also *oerbiss.*

lard (lard) [L. *lardum*]. The purified internal fat of the abdomen of the hog. **benzoinated l.,** a preparation of lard and benzoin.

lardacein (lar-da′se-in). A protein found in tissues affected with amyloid degeneration. It is characterized by being insoluble in nearly all reagents, not acted upon by the gastric juice, and not readily subject to putrefaction. It gives a brown color with iodine and sulfuric acid.

lardaceous (lar-da′shus). 1. Resembling lard. 2. Containing lardacein.

Lardennois' button (lar″den-wahz′) [Henri *Lardennois*, French surgeon, born 1872]. See under *button.*

largon (lar′gon). Trade mark for a preparation of propiomazine hydrochloride.

larithmics (lah-rith′miks) [Gr. *laos* people + *arithmos* number]. The study which deals with population in its quantitative aspects.

Larix (la′riks) [L.]. A genus of coniferous trees, the larches. The astringent bark of *L. europaea* is useful in skin diseases and in pectoral complaints.

larixin (la-rik′sin). Laricic acid.

Laroyenne's operation (lar″oi-enz′) [Lucien *Laroyenne*, French surgeon, born 1876]. See under *operation.*

Larrey's bandage, operation, etc. (lar-rāz′) [Dominique Jean (Baron de) *Larrey*, French surgeon, 1766–1842; the greatest military surgeon of his time, serving in the Napoleonic wars]. See under the nouns.

Larsen-Johansson disease (lar′sen-yo-han′-son) [Sinding *Larsen*, Sven *Johansson*, Swedish surgeons]. See under *disease.*

larva (lar′vah), pl. *lar′vae* [L.]. An immature stage in the life history of an animal in which it is unlike the parent; especially the first stage of insect development after leaving the egg. **l. mi′grans,** a disease marked by the presence of a thin, red, papular, or vesicular line of eruption which gradually extends from one end while fading at the other. It is due to the presence of larvae of the dog and cat hookworm, which burrow beneath the skin. The term is also applied to similar lesions caused by larvae of *Gasterophilus* and *Gnathostoma.* Called also *creeping eruption, sandworm disease, hyponomoderma, hypodermyiasis, ox warble disease, larbish, myiasis linearis,* and *dermamyiasis linearis migrans oestrosa.* **l. migrans, visceral,** a condition caused by prolonged migration of larvae of animal nematodes in human tissues other than skin, characterized by persistent hypereosinophilia, hepatomegaly, and frequently by pneumonitis; commonly caused by *Toxocara canis* or *Toxocara cati.* **rat-tailed l.** See *Eristalis tenax.*

larvaceous (lar-va′shus). Larvate.

larvae (lar′ve) [L.]. Plural of *larva.*

larval (lar′val). 1. Pertaining to larvae. 2. Larvate.

larvascope (lar′vah-skōp). An apparatus for viewing insect larvae.

larvate (lar′vāt) [L. *larva* mask]. Masked; concealed: said of a disease or a symptom of a disease.

larvicide (lar′vĭ-sīd) [*larva* + L. *caedere* to kill]. An agent destructive to insect larvae. **Panama l.,** a mixture of crude carbolic acid, rosin, and caustic soda, heated to a uniform dark colored soap: used to kill Anopheles larvae.

larviphagic (lar″vĭ-fa′jik). Larvivorous.

larviposition (lar″vĭ-po-zish′un). The act of depositing larvae (living maggots) in the tissues of a host.

larvivorous (lar-viv′o-rus) [*larva* + L. *vorare* to eat]. Feeding on or consuming larvae; used especially of fish which ingest mosquito larvae.

laryngalgia (lar″in-gal′je-ah) [*laryngo-* + *-algia*]. Pain in the larynx.

laryngeal (lah-rin′je-al). Of or pertaining to the larynx.

laryngect (lar′in-jekt″). Laryngectomee.

laryngectomee (lar″in-jek′to-me). A person whose larynx has been removed.

laryngectomy (lar″in-jek′to-me) [*laryngo-* + Gr. *ektomē* excision]. Extirpation of the larynx.

laryngemphraxis (lar″in-jem-frak′sis) [*laryngo-* + Gr. *emphraxis* stoppage]. Obstruction or closure of the larynx.

laryngendoscope (lar″in-jen′do-skōp) [*laryngo-* + Gr. *endon* within + *skopein* to examine]. An instrument for viewing the larynx.

laryngismal (lar″in-jiz′mal). Pertaining to laryngismus.

laryngismus (lar″in-jiz′mus) [L.; Gr. *laryngismos* a whooping]. Spasm of the larynx. **l. paralyt′icus,** roaring. **l. strid′ulus,** a condition marked by sudden laryngeal spasm, with a crowing inspiration and the development of cyanosis. It occurs in laryngeal inflammations and as an independent disease, especially in connection with rickets.

laryngitic (lar″in-jit′ik). Pertaining to laryngitis.

laryngitis (lar″in-ji′tis). Inflammation of the larynx, a condition attended with dryness and soreness of the throat, hoarseness, cough, and dysphagia. **acute catarrhal l.,** a form characterized by aphonia or hoarseness, pain and dryness of the throat, dyspnea, a wheezy cough, and more or less fever. **atrophic l.,** chronic catarrhal l. **chronic catarrhal l.,** a form of laryngitis due to recurring inflammation or more frequently a sequel of acute catarrhal laryngitis, characterized by atrophy of the glands of the mucous membrane. **croupous l.,** laryngeal diphtheria. **diphtheritic l.,** laryngitis caused by diphtheria: true or membranous croup. **membranous l.,** laryngitis attended with the formation of a false membrane. **phlegmonous l.,** a usually fatal complication of erysipelas, smallpox, etc., attended with submucous suppuration and edema. **l. sic′ca,** chronic laryngitis. **l. stridulo′sa,** laryngismus stridulus. **subglottic l.,** inflammation of the under surface of the vocal cords. **syphilitic l.,** a chronic form due to syphilitic involvement of the larynx. **tuberculous l.,** a chronic form due to tuberculous ulceration of the larynx.

laryngo- (lah-ring′go) [Gr. *larynx* larynx]. Combining form denoting relationship to the larynx.

laryngocele (lah-ring′go-sēl) [*laryngo-* + Gr. *kēlē* hernia]. An anomalous air sac communicating with the cavity of the larynx and producing a tumor-like lesion visible on the outside of the neck.

laryngocentesis (lah-ring″go-sen-te′sis) [*laryngo-* + Gr. *kentēsis* puncture]. Surgical puncture of the larynx.

laryngofission (lah-ring″go-fish′un). Laryngofissure.

laryngofissure (lah-ring″go-fish′ūr). The operation of opening the larynx by a median incision through the thyroid cartilage with the formation of a wide window: for the removal of cancer of the larynx; median laryngotomy.

laryngogram (lah-ring′go-gram). A roentgenogram of the larynx.

laryngograph (lah-ring′go-graf). A device for registering the laryngeal movements.

laryngography (lar″ing-gog′rah-fe) [*laryngo-* + Gr. *graphein* to record]. 1. The description of the larynx. 2. Roentgenography of the larynx after instillation of a radiopaque substance into it.

laryngology (lar″ing-gol′o-je) [*laryngo-* + *-logy*]. That branch of medicine which has to do with the throat, pharynx, larynx, nasopharynx, and tracheobronchial tree.

laryngometry (lar″ing-gom′e-tre) [*laryngo-* + Gr. *metron* measure]. Measurement of the larynx.

laryngoparalysis (lah-ring″go-pah-ral′ĭ-sis) [*laryngo-* + *paralysis*]. Paralysis of the larynx.

laryngopathy (lar″ing-gop′ah-the) [*laryngo-* + Gr. *pathos* disease]. Any disorder of the larynx.

laryngophantom (lar″ing-go-fan′tom) [*laryngo-* + Gr. *phantasma* phantom]. An artificial model of the larynx.

laryngopharyngeal (lah-ring″go-fah-rin′je-al). Pertaining to the larynx and pharynx.

laryngopharyngectomy (lah-ring″go-far″in-jek′to-me). Excision of the larynx and pharynx.

laryngopharyngeus (lah-ring″go-fah-rin′je-us). The inferior constrictor of the pharynx.

laryngopharyngitis (lah-ring″go-far″in-ji′tis). Inflammation of the larynx and pharynx.

laryngopharynx (lah-ring″go-far′inks) [*laryngo-* + *pharynx*]. The portion of the pharynx which lies below the upper edge of the epiglottis and opens into the larynx and esophagus (pars laryngea pharyngis [N A]).

laryngophony (lar″ing-gof′o-ne) [*laryngo-* + Gr. *phōnē* voice]. The vocal sound as heard in auscultation of the larynx.

laryngophthisis (lar″ing-gof′thĭ-sis) [*laryngo-* + Gr. *phthisis* phthisis]. Tuberculosis of the larynx.

laryngoplasty (lah-ring′go-plas″te) [*laryngo-* + Gr. *plassein* to mold]. Plastic surgery of the larynx.

laryngoplegia (lar″ing-go-ple′je-ah) [*laryngo-* + Gr. *plēgē* stroke + *-ia*]. Paralysis of the larynx.

laryngoptosis (lah-ring″go-to′sis) [*laryngo-* + Gr. *ptōsis* fall]. A lowering and mobilization of the larynx as sometimes seen in the aged.

laryngopyocele (lah-ring″go-pi′o-sēl). A laryngocele containing pus.

laryngorhinology (lah-ring″go-ri-nol′o-je) [*laryngo-* + Gr. *rhis* nose + *-logy*]. The sum of what is known regarding the larynx and nose and their diseases.

laryngorrhagia (lar″ing-go-ra′je-ah) [*laryngo-* + Gr. *rhēgnynai* to break]. Hemorrhage from the larynx.

laryngorrhaphy (lar″ing-gor′ah-fe) [*laryngo-* + Gr. *rhaphē* suture]. The operation of suturing the larynx.

laryngorrhea (lar″ing-go-re′ah) [*laryngo-* + Gr. *rhoia* flow]. Excessive secretion of mucus whenever the voice is used.

laryngoscleroma (lah-ring″go-skle-ro′mah) [*laryngo-* + *scleroma*]. Scleroma of the larynx.

laryngoscope (lah-ring′go-skōp) [*laryngo-* + Gr. *skopein* to examine]. An endoscope for use in direct ocular examination of the larynx.

laryngoscopic (lar″ing-go-skop′ik). Pertaining to laryngoscopy.

laryngoscopist (lar″ing-gos′ko-pist). An expert in laryngoscopy.

laryngoscopy (lar″ing-gos′ko-pe) [*laryngo-* + Gr. *skopein* to view]. Examination of the interior of the larynx, especially that performed with the laryngoscope (*direct laryngoscopy*). **direct l.,** direct ocular examination of the larynx performed with a speculum or with a laryngoscope. **indirect l.,** examination of the larynx by observation of the reflection of it in a laryngeal mirror. **mirror l.,** indirect l. **suspension l.,** examination of the larynx performed with the head of the patient hanging over the edge of the examination table.

laryngospasm (lah-ring′go-spazm) [*laryngo-* + Gr. *spasmos* spasm]. Spasmodic closure of the larynx.

laryngostasis (lar″ing-gos′tah-sis) [*laryngo-* + Gr. *stasis* stoppage]. Croup.

laryngostat (lah-ring′go-stat). An appliance for holding a capsule of radium within the larynx.

laryngostenosis (lah-ring″go-ste-no′sis) [*laryngo-* + Gr. *stenōsis* contracture]. Narrowing or stricture of the larynx.

laryngostomy (lar″ing-gos′to-me) [*laryngo-* +

Gr. *stomoun* to provide with an opening, or mouth]. The creation of an artificial opening into the larynx.

laryngostroboscope (lar″ing-go-strob′o-skōp) [*laryngo-* + Gr. *strophos* whirl + *skopein* to examine]. An apparatus for observing the intralaryngeal phenomena of phonation.

laryngotome (lah-ring′go-tōm). An instrument used in incising the larynx.

laryngotomy (lar″ing-got′o-me) [*laryngo-* + Gr. *tomē* a cutting]. Surgical incision of the larynx. **complete l.,** the longitudinal slitting of the entire larynx. **inferior l.,** incision of the larynx through the cricothyroid membrane. **median l.,** incision of the larynx through the thyroid cartilage. **subhyoid l.,** incision of the larynx through the thyrohyoid membrane. **superior l., thyrohyoid l.,** subhyoid l.

laryngotracheal (lah-ring″go-tra′ke-al). Pertaining to the larynx and trachea.

laryngotracheitis (lah-ring″go-tra″ke-i′tis). 1. Inflammation of the larynx and trachea. 2. A disease of fowls due, probably, to a filtrable virus.

laryngotracheobronchitis (lah-ring″go-tra″ke-o-brong-ki′tis). Inflammation of the larynx, trachea, and bronchi.

laryngotracheobronchoscopy (lah-ring″go-tra″ke-o-bron-kos′ko-pe). Endoscopic examination of the trachea and bronchi.

laryngotracheoscopy (lah-ring″go-tra″ke-os′ko-pe). Peroral tracheoscopy.

laryngotracheotomy (lah-ring″go-tra″ke-ot′o-me) [*laryngo-* + *tracheotomy*]. Incision of the larynx and trachea.

laryngotyphoid (lar″ing-go-ti′foid). Typhoid fever with laryngeal complications.

laryngovestibulitis (lah-ring″go-ves-tib″u-li′tis). Inflammation of the vestibule of the larynx.

laryngoxerosis (lah-ring″go-ze-ro′sis) [*laryngo-* + Gr. *xērōsis* a drying up]. Dryness of the throat.

larynx (lar′inks) [Gr. "the upper part of the windpipe"]. [N A, B N A] The musculocartilaginous structure, lined with mucous membrane, situated at the top of the trachea and below the root of the tongue and the hyoid bone; the essential sphincter guarding the entrance into the trachea and functioning secondarily as the organ of voice. It is formed by nine cartilages—the thyroid, cricoid, epiglottis, two arytenoid, two corniculate, and two cuneiform cartilages, connected by ligaments.

lasanum (las′ah-num) [L. "a night commode"]. An obstetric chair.

lascivia (lah-siv′e-ah) [L. "wantonness"]. Satyriasis.

Lasègue's disease, sign (lah-sāgz′) [Ernest Charles *Lasègue*, French physician, 1816–1883]. See under *disease* and *sign*.

laser (la′zer) [*l*ight *a*mplification by *s*timulated *e*mission of *r*adiation]. A device which produces an extremely intense, small, and nearly nondivergent beam of monochromatic radiation in the visible region with all the waves in phase. Capable of mobilizing immense heat and power when focused at close range, it may be used as a tool in surgical procedures.

Lasiohelea (las″e-o-he′le-ah). A genus of blood-sucking flies of the family Heleidae.

Lassar's paste (las′arz) [Oskar *Lassar*, German dermatologist, 1849–1907]. See under *paste*.

lassitude (las′ĭ-tūd) [L. *lassitudo* weariness]. Weakness; exhaustion.

latah (lah′tah). Gilles de la Tourette's disease.

Lat. dol. Abbreviation for L. *lat′eri dolen′ti*, to the painful side.

latebra (lat′e-brah) [L. "hiding place"]. A flask-shaped mass of white yolk extending from the blastodisk to the center of eggs such as those of birds.

latency (la′ten-se). A state of seeming inactivity, such as that occurring between the instant of stimulation and the beginning of response.

latent (la′tent) [L. *latens* hidden]. Concealed; not manifest; potential.

laterad (lat′er-ad). Toward a side or a lateral aspect.

lateral (lat′er-al) [L. *lateralis*]. 1. Denoting a position farther from the median plane or midline of the body or of a structure. 2. Pertaining to a side.

lateralis (lat″er-a′lis). Lateral; in official anatomical nomenclature it designates a structure situated farther from the midline of the body.

laterality (lat″er-al′ĭ-te). A relationship to one side, such as a tendency, in voluntary motor acts, to use preferentially the organs (hand, foot, ear, eye) of the same side. **crossed l.,** the preferential use, in voluntary motor acts, of heterolateral members of the different pairs of organs, as the right eye and the left hand. **dominant l.,** the preferential use, in voluntary motor acts, of ipsilateral members of the different pairs of organs, as the right ear, eye, hand, and leg (dextrality) or of the left ear, eye, hand, and leg (sinistrality).

latericeous (lat″er-ish′us). Lateritious.

lateritious (lat″er-ish′us) [L. *lateritius; later* brick]. Resembling brick dust.

latero- (lat′er-o) [L. *latus* side]. Combining form denoting relationship to the side.

latero-abdominal (lat″er-o-ab-dom′ĭ-nal). Pertaining to the side and the abdomen.

laterodeviation (lat″er-o-de″ve-a′shun). Deviation or slight displacement to one side.

lateroduction (lat″er-o-duk′shun) [*latero-* + L. *ducere* to draw]. Movement of an eye to either side.

lateroflexion (lat″er-o-flek′shun). Flexion to either side.

lateroposition (lat″er-o-po-zish′un). Displacement to one side.

lateropulsion (lat″er-o-pul′shun) [*latero-* + L. *pellere* to drive]. An involuntary tendency to go to one side while walking.

laterotorsion (lat″er-o-tor′shun) [*latero-* + L. *torquere* to turn]. Twisting of the vertical meridian of the eye to the right or to the left.

lateroversion (lat″er-o-ver′shun) [*latero-* + *version*]. A turning to one side.

latex (la′teks) [L. "fluid"]. A viscid, milky juice secreted by some seed plants.

latexed (lat-eksd′). Bent to one side.

latexion (la-tek′shun). Lateral flexion.

Latham's circle (la′thamz) [Peter Mere *Latham*, English physician, 1789–1875]. See under *circle*.

lathyrism (lath′ĭ-rizm). A morbid condition resulting from ingestion of the seeds of plants of the genus Lathyrus, characterized by spastic paraplegia, pain, hyperesthesia, and paresthesia.

lathyritic (lath″ĭ-rit′ik). Pertaining to or characterized by lathyrism.

lathyrogenic (lath″ĭ-ro-jen′ik). Capable of producing the symptoms characteristic of lathyrism.

latissimus (lah-tis′ĭ-mus) [L.]. Widest.

latrine (lah-trēn′) [Fr.]. A privy or water closet, especially a public one.

latrodectism (lat″ro-dek′tizm) [*Latrodectus* + *-ism*]. Intoxication caused by venom of spiders of the genus Latrodectus.

Latrodectus (lat″ro-dek′tus) [L. *latro* robber + Gr. *daknein* to bite]. A genus of poisonous spiders. *L. mac′tans*, a species found in the United States; it is commonly known as the "black widow." Its bite may cause severe symptoms or even death. *L. curarien′sis* is found in Brazil and Argentina; *L. lugu′bris* in Russia; *L. geomet′ricus* in California; *L. hassel′tii* in New Zealand; *L. macula′tus* in South Africa; *L. malmigniat′tus* in Europe; and *L. tredecimgutta′tus* in Southern Europe and Asiatic Russia.

lattice (lat′is). A framework of regularly placed, intersecting narrow strips, such as the geometrical arrangement of the atoms in a crystal as shown by x-ray analysis.

latus (la′tus) [L.]. 1. Broad, wide. 2. [N A, B N A] The side; flank.

laudable (law′dah-bl) [L. *laudabilis*]. Commendable; healthy.

laugh (laf). An act or paroxysm of laughter. **canine l., sardonic l.,** risus sardonicus.

Laughlen's test (lawk′lins) [George Franklin *Laughlen*, Canadian pathologist, born 1888]. See under *tests*.

laughter (laf′ter). A series of spasmodic and partly involuntary expirations with inarticulate vocalization, normally indicative of merriment, often a hysteric manifestation or a reflex result of tickling. **compulsive l., forced l., obsessive l.,** hearty laughter for which there is no occasion; a symptom in schizophrenia.

Laugier's hernia, sign (lo″zhe-āz′) [Stanislaus *Laugier*, French surgeon, 1799–1872]. See under *hernia* and *sign*.

Laumonier's ganglion (lo-mon″e-āz′) [Jean Baptiste *Laumonier*, French surgeon, 1749–1818]. Carotid ganglion.

Launois-Clérat syndrome (lo-nwah′kla-rah′) [Pierre-Emile *Launois*, French physician, 1856–1914]. Fröhlich's syndrome.

lauranga (law-rang′ah). Bush disease.

Laurence-Biedl syndrome (law′rens-be′del) J. Z. *Laurence*, British ophthalmologist, 1830–1874; Arthur *Biedl*, Prague endocrinologist, 1869–1933]. See under *syndrome*.

Laurence-Moon-Biedl syndrome [J. Z. *Laurence;* R. C. *Moon;* A. *Biedl*]. See under *syndrome*.

laurocerasus (law″ro-ser′ah-sus) [L. *laurus* laurel + *cerasus* cherry]. The European cherry laurel, an evergreen cherry tree, *Prunus laurocerasus*.

lauron (law′ron). Trade mark for a preparation of aurothioglycanide.

Lauth's canal, sinus (lowts) [Ernst Alexander *Lauth*, Strasbourg physiologist, 1803–1837]. Sinus venosus sclerae.

Lauth's ligament (lowts) [Thomas *Lauth*, Strasbourg anatomist and surgeon, 1758–1826]. See under *ligament*.

Lauth's violet (lawths) [Charles *Lauth*, English chemist, 1836–1913]. See under *violet*.

lava (lah′vah) [Ital.]. The scoria ejected from volcanoes; a homeopathic remedy. **hecla l.,** lava from the volcano, Mount Hecla: a homeopathic remedy for promoting the healing of wounds.

lavage (lah-vahzh′) [Fr.]. 1. The irrigation or washing out of an organ, such as the stomach or bowel. 2. To wash out, or irrigate. **l. of the blood, blood l.,** the washing out of toxic matters from the blood by injecting serum into the veins. **electric l.,** injection of a saline enema that has been electrized by a continuous current. **ether l.** See *Souligoux-Morestin method*, under *method*. **gastric l.,** lavage of the stomach. **intestinal l.,** vividialysis by instillation and withdrawal of a rinsing fluid in the intestine for the removal, through the intestinal mucosa, of elements which are not being excreted by the kidneys. **peritoneal l.,** vividialysis by instillation and withdrawal of a rinsing fluid in the peritoneal cavity. **pleural l.,** removal of a pleural exudate by means of a trocar, followed by irrigation. **systemic l.,** lavage of the blood.

Lavandula (lah-van′du-lah) [L.]. A genus of labiate plants; lavenders. The true lavender, *L. ve′ra*, is carminative and stimulant.

lavation (la-va′shun) [L. *lavatio*]. Lavage.

Lavdovski's nucleoid (lav-dov′skēz) [Michail Dorimentow *Lavdovski*, Russian histologist, 1846–1902]. Centrosome.

lavema (lah-ve′mah). Trade mark for preparations of oxyphenisatin.

lavement (lāv′ment). Lavage.

Laveran's bodies, corpuscles (lav-ranz′) [Charles Louis Alphonse *Laveran*, French physician, 1845–1922, noted for discovery of the parasite causing malaria; winner of the Nobel prize for medicine in 1907]. Plasmodia.

Laverania (lav″er-a′ne-ah) [C. L. A. *Laveran*]. A name formerly applied to the malarial parasite, Plasmodium.

laveur (lah-vur′) [Fr.]. An instrument for performing lavage or irrigation.

law (law). A uniform or constant fact or principle. **all or none l.** See *all or none*. **Allen's paradoxic l.,** whereas in normal individuals the more sugar is given the more is utilized, the reverse is true in diabetes. **Ambard's l's.** 1. With the urinary urea concentration constant, the output of urea varies directly as the square of the concentration of the blood urea. 2. With the blood urea concentration constant, the output of urea varies inversely as the square root of the urinary concentration. **Ampère's l.,** the force of an electric current on a movable magnet deviates the austral pole of the latter to the left. **Angström's l.,** the wavelengths of the light absorbed by a substance are the same as those given off by it when luminous. **l. of anticipation,** Mott's l. **Aran's l.,** fractures of the base of the skull (except those by contrecoup) result from injuries to the vault, the fractures extending by radiation along the line of shortest circle. **Arndt-Schulz l.,** weak stimuli increase physiologic activity and very strong stimuli inhibit or abolish activity. **Arrhenius' l.,** only solutions of high osmotic pressure are electrically conductive. **l's of articulation,** a set of rules formulated by R. L. Hanau, to be followed in arranging teeth to produce a balanced articulation. **l. of avalanche,** hypothetical law assumed by Ramón y Cajal, that multiple sensations may be aroused in the brain by a simple sensation at the periphery. **l. of average localization,** visceral pain is most accurately localized in the least mobile viscus. **Avogadro's l.,** equal volumes of all perfect gases at the same temperature and pressure contain the same number of molecules or, in the case of monatomic gases, of atoms. **Babinski's l.,** the law of voltaic vertigo that a normal subject inclines to the side of the positive pole; one with disease of the labyrinth falls to the side to which he tends to incline spontaneously. If the labyrinth is destroyed there is no reaction. **Baer's l.,** the more general features that are common to all the members of a group of animals are, in the embryo, developed earlier than the more special features which distinguish the various members of the group. **Barfurth's l.,** the axis of the tissue in a regenerating structure is at first perpendicular to the cut. **Baruch's l.,** when the temperature of the water used in a bath is above or below that of the skin the effect is stimulating; when both temperatures are the same the effect is sedative. **Bastian's l., Bastian-Bruns l.,** if there is a complete transverse lesion in the spinal cord cephalad to the lumbar enlargement, the tendon reflexes of the lower extremities are abolished. **Baumès's l.,** Colles' l. **Behring's l.,** the blood and serum of an immunized person, when transferred to another subject, will render the latter immune. **Bell's l., Bell-Magendie l.,** the anterior roots of the spinal nerves are motor roots and the posterior are sensory. **Bergonie-Tribondeau l.,** the sensitivity of cells to radiation varies directly with the reproductive capacity of the cells and inversely with their degree of differentiation. **Berthollet's l.,** if two salts in solution by double decomposition can produce a salt less soluble than either, such a salt will be produced. **biogenetic l.,** ontogeny is a recapitulation of phylogeny. **Bordet's l.,** when blood corpuscles are added to a hemolytic medium in bulk, they are more rapidly dissolved than when added in fractions. **Boudin's l.,** there is antagonism between malaria and tuberculosis. **Bowditch's l.** 1. Any stimulus that will produce a contraction of the heart muscle will cause as powerful a pulsation as the most powerful stimulus. 2. Nerves cannot be tired out by stimulation. **Boyle's l.,** at a constant temperature the volume of a perfect gas varies inversely as the pressure, and the pressure varies inversely as the volume. **Breton's l.,** there is a parabolic relation between stimulus and just noticeable difference, expressed by the formula $S = (R/C)\frac{1}{2}$. **Buhl-Bittrich l.,** the supposed principle that in every case of acute miliary tuberculosis there exists within the body at least one old focus of caseation. **Bunge's l.,** the secreting cells of the mammary gland in the dog, cat, and rabbit take from the blood plasma mineral salts in the exact proportion in which they are needed for developing and building up the offspring. **Bunsen-Roscoe l.,** the photochemical effect produced is equal to the product of the intensity of the illumination and the duration of exposure. **Camerer's l.,** children of the same weight have the same food requirements regardless of their ages. **Charles' l.,** at a constant pressure the volume of a given mass of perfect gas varies directly with the absolute temperature. **Clapeyron's l.,** a law of thermodynamics according to which any action sets up forces which tend to counteract it. **Cohn's l.,** the specific forms of bacteria have a fixed and unchanging basis. **Colles' l.,** a child that is affected with congenital syphilis, its mother showing no signs of the disease, will not infect its mother (1837). **Colles-Baumès l.,** Colles' l. **l. of contrary innervation,** Meltzer's l. **Cope's l.,** genera with little specialization originate many types of organisms; highly specialized genera produce but few biological variations. **Coulomb's l.,** the force of attraction or repulsion between two electrified bodies is proportional directly to the quantities of electric charge, and inversely as the square of their distance apart. **Courvoisier's l.,** when the common bile duct is obstructed by a stone, dilatation of the gallbladder is rare; when the duct is obstructed in some other way, dilatation is common. **Curie's l.,** all substances may be rendered radioactive by the influence of the emanations of radium, and substances thus influenced hold their radioactivity longer when inclosed in some material through which the emanations cannot pass. **Cushing's l.,** increase of intracranial tension causes increase of blood pressure to a point slightly above the pressure exerted against the medulla. **Dalton's l.,** the pressure exerted by a mixture of nonreacting gases is equal to the sum of the partial pressures of the separate components. **Dalton-Henry l.,** when a fluid absorbs a mixture of gases, it will absorb as much of each gas as it would have absorbed of either gas separately. **Dastre-Morat l.,** dilatation of the splanchnic vessels is usually accompanied by constriction of the surface vessels of the body, and vice versa. **l. of definite proportions,** any compound always contains the same kind of elements in the same proportions; called also *Proust's l.* **l. of denervation,** denervation of a structure increases its sensitivity to chemical stimulation. **Descartes' l.,** the sine of the angle of incidence bears a constant relation to the sine of the angle of refraction for two given media. **Desmarres' l.,** when the visual axes are crossed the images are uncrossed; when the axes are uncrossed (diverging) the images are crossed. **Diday's l.,** a woman whose first pregnancy results in a stillbirth may have a living child with active syphilis and later a living child with latent syphilis or one entirely unaffected. **l. of diffusion,** any process set up in the nerve centers affects the organism throughout by a process of diffused motion. **Dollo's l.,** phyletic development is irreversible, i.e., reversion to an ancestral peculiarity (atavism) is impossible. **Donders' l.,** the rotation of the eye around the line of sight is not voluntary; when attention is fixed upon a remote object, the amount of rotation is determined entirely by the angular distance of the object from the median plane and from the horizon. **Draper's l.,** only the rays that are absorbed by a photochemical substance will produce a chemical change in it. **DuBois-Reymond l.,** it is the variation of current density, and not the absolute value of current density at any given moment, that acts as a stimulus to a muscle or motor nerve. **Dulong and Petit's l.,** that the atoms of all elements have exactly the same capacity for heat. **Edinger's l.,** a gradual increase in the function of the neuron causes at first increased growth, but if irregular and excessive, then it leads to atrophy and degeneration. **Elliott's l.,** the activity of epinephrine is due to a stimulation of the endings of the sympathetic nerve. **Ewald's l.,** nystagmus resulting from endolymph currents in a semicircular canal is in a direction parallel with the plane of that canal and opposite to the current, and in the horizontal canals the amount of ocular motor impulse derived from the canals whose hair cells are bent toward the utricle is twice as great as from the other (short end); but in the vertical canals the reverse is true. **l. of excitation,** a motor nerve responds by the contraction of its muscle to the alterations of the strength of an electric current and not to its absolute strength. **l. of facilitation,** when an impulse has passed once through a certain set of neurons to the exclusion of others, it will tend to take the same course on a future occasion, and each time it traverses this path the resistance in the path will be smaller. **Faget's l.,** in yellow fever the pulse is at first accelerated, but, as the temperature rises, it shows a marked tendency to fall. **Fajans' l.,** the product left after the emission of alpha rays has a valance less by two than that of the parent radioactive substance; the product left after the emission of beta rays has a valence greater by one than that of the parent radioactive substance. **Faraday's l.,** in electrolysis the amount of an ion liberated in any given time is proportional to the strength of the current. **Farr's l.,** "subsidence is a property of all zymotic diseases"; the gradually decreasing increase of incidence in an epidemic disease, in virtue of which the epidemic curve first ascends rapidly, then more slowly to a maximum, with a descent more rapid than the ascent. **l. of fatigue (Houghton's),** when the same muscle or group of muscles is kept in constant action until fatigue sets in, the total work done, multiplied by the rate of work, is constant. **Fechner's l.,** the intensity of a sensation produced by a varying stimulus varies directly as the logarithm of that stimulus. **Ferry-Porter l.,** critical fusion frequency is directly proportional to the logarithm of the light intensity. **Fildes' l.,** the presence of syphilitic reagin in the blood of the newborn is diagnostic, not of syphilis in the infant but of syphilis in the mother. **Fitz's l.,** acute pancreatitis is to be suspected when a previously healthy person is suddenly affected with violent epigastric pain, vomiting, and collapse, followed inside of twenty-four hours by epigastric swelling, tympanites, or resistance, with slight elevation of temperature. **Flatau's l.,** the greater the length of the fibers of the spinal cord, the closer are they situated to the periphery. **Flechsig's myelogenetic l.,** myelogenetic l. **Flint's l.,** the ontogeny of an organ is the phylogeny of its blood supply. **Flourens' l.,** stimulation of the semicircular canal causes nystagmus in the plane of that canal. **Freund's l.,** during growth ovarian tumors change their position; when pelvic, they tend to grow downward behind the uterus; when they have arisen out of the pelvis, they tend to fall forward toward the abdominal wall. **Froriep's l.,** the skull is developed by the annexation of true vertebrae, the head growing at the expense of the neck. **Galton's l.,** each parent contributes, on an average, one fourth, or $(0.5)^2$, of an individual's heritage, each grandparent one sixteenth, or $(0.5)^4$, each greatgrandparent one sixty-fourth, or $(0.5)^6$, etc., the occupier of each ancestral place in the *n*th degree, whatever the value of *n*, contributing $(0.5)^{2n}$ of the heritage. **Galton's l. of regression,** average parents tend to produce average children; minus parents tend to produce minus children; plus parents tend to produce plus children; but the offspring of extreme parents, whether plus or minus, inherit the parental peculiarities in a less marked degree than the latter were manifested in the parents themselves. **Gay-Lussac's l.,** Charles' l. **Gerhardt-Semon l.,** various peripheral and central lesions affecting the recurrent laryngeal nerve cause the vocal cord to assume a position between abduction and adduction, the paralysis of the parts being incomplete. **Giraud-Teulon l.,** binocular retinal images are formed at the intersection of the primary and secondary axes of projection. **Godélier's l.,** tuberculosis of the peritoneum is invariably associated with tuberculosis of the pleura. **Golgi's l.,** the severity of a malarial attack depends upon the number of parasites in the blood. **Gompertz's l.,** there is a quantitative relation between the probability of death from a given disease and age. **Goodell's l.,** when the cervix is hard as the tip of one's nose, pregnancy does not exist; when it is as soft as one's lips, pregnancy is probable. **Graham's l.,** the rate of diffusion of a gas through porous membranes is in inverse ratio to the square root of their density. **Grasset's l.,** Landouzy-Grasset l. **l. of gravitation,** all bodies attract each other with a force that is directly proportional to their masses and inversely proportional to the square of their distance apart. Called also *Newton's l.* **Grotthus' l.,** only those rays of ultraviolet light that are absorbed produce a chemical effect. **Gudden's l.,** the degeneration of the proximal end of a divided nerve is cellulipetal. **Guldberg and Waage's l.,** the velocity of a chemical reaction is proportional to the active masses of the reacting substances; called also *l. of mass action*, *mass l.*, and *l. of chemical kinetics*. **Gull-Toynbee l.,** in otitis media the lateral sinus and cerebellum are liable to involvement in mastoid disease, and the cerebrum may be attacked when the roof of the tympanum becomes carious. **Gullstrand's l.,** if when the patient is made to turn the head while fixing a distant object the corneal reflex from either eye moves in the direction in which the head is turning, it moves toward the weaker muscle. **Gunn's l.,** in treating a dislocation the limb must be placed in the same position as at the time of injury and force exerted on the displaced bone in the reverse direction to that which caused the dislocation. **Haeckel's l.,** an organism, in developing from the ovum, goes through the same changes as did the species in developing from the lower to the higher forms of animal life. **Hallion's l.,** extracts of an organ when injected into the body exert a stimulating influence on that same organ. **Hamberger's l.,** when the blood is rendered acid, albumins and phosphates pass from the red corpuscles to the serum, and chlorides pass from the serum to the cells; the reverse occurs when the blood is rendered alkaline. **Hanau's l's of articulation,** a set of purely physical laws that must be observed in the formation of the masticatory surfaces of natural or artificial dentures, to assure establishment or production of balanced articulation. **l. of the heart,** the energy set free at each contraction of the heart is a simple function of the length of the fibers composing its muscular walls (Starling). **Hecker's l.,** in every successive childbirth the weight of the infant exceeds that of the predecessor by 150 to 200 Gm. **Heidenhain's l.,** glandular secretion always involves change in the structure of the gland. **Hellin's l.,** one in about 89 pregnancies ends in the birth of twins; one in 89 × 89, or 7921, of triplets; one in 89 × 89 × 89, or 704,969, of quadruplets. **Henry's l.,** the solubility of a gas in a liquid solution is proportional to the partial pressure of the gas. **Hering's l.** 1. The principle of bilateral ocular innervation; equal innervation is sent to the muscles of the two eyes so that one eye is never moved independently of the other. 2. The clearness or purity of any conception or sensation depends on the proportion existing between its intensity and the sum total of the intensities of all the simultaneous conceptions and sensations. **Heyman's l.,** the threshold value of a visual stimulus is increased in proportion to the strength of the inhibitory stimulus. **Hilton's l.,** a nerve trunk which supplies the muscles of any given joint also supplies the muscles which move the joint and the skin over the insertions of such muscles. **Hofacker-Sadler l.,** when the father is older than the mother the ratio of male births is 113 to 100; when the parents are of equal age the ratio is 93.5 males to 100 females; when the mother is older than the father the ratio is 88.2 males to 100 females. **Hoff's l.,** van't Hoff's l. **Hoorweg's l.,** there is a duration of electric discharge above which time does not count, and a duration of discharge below which the time does count, in the provocation of neuromuscular response. **Horner's l.,** ordinary color-blindness is transmitted from males to males through normal females. **l. of independent assortment,** the members of gene pairs segregate independently during miosis. **l. of the intestines,** the presence of a bolus in the intestine induces contraction above and inhibition below the stimulus, thereby producing a progression of the intestinal contents. **l. of inverse square,** the intensity of radiation is inversely proportional to the square of the distance between the point of source and the irradiated surface. **l. of isochronism,** a nerve and its innervated muscle have identical chronaxie values. **isodynamic l.,** in the production of heat in the body the different foodstuffs are interchangeable in accordance with their heat-producing values. **l. of isolated conduction,** the wave of change or nervous impulse which passes through a neuron is never communicated to other neurons except at the terminals. **Jackson's l.,** the nerve functions that are latest developed are the earliest to be destroyed. **Kahler's l.,** the ascending branches of the posterior roots of the spinal nerves pass within the cord in succession from the root zone toward the mesial plane. **Kassowitz's l.,** Diday's l. **Keith's l.,** ligaments are never used for the continuous support of any joint or part. **Koch's l.** See *Koch's postulates*, under *postulate*. **Küstner's l.,** if an ovarian tumor is left-sided, torsion of its pedicle takes place toward the right; if right-sided, toward the left. **Lambert's cosine l.,** the intensity of radiation on an absorbing surface varies as the cosine of the angle of incidence for parallel rays. **Lancereaux's l.,** marantic thrombosis always takes place at points where the tendency to stasis is greatest, and especially at points where the influence of thoracic aspiration and cardiac propulsion is smallest. **Landouzy-Grasset l.,** in lesion of one cerebral hemisphere the head is turned to the side of the brain lesion if there is paralysis, and to that of the affected muscles if there is spasticity. **Lapicque's l.,** the chronaxia is inversely proportional to the diameter of the nerve fiber. **Leopold's l.,** when the placenta is inserted upon the posterior wall of the uterus, the oviducts assume directions converging upon the anterior wall; but if the insertion be on the anterior wall during recumbency, the tubes turn backward and become parallel to the axis of the body. **Levret's l.,** the insertion of the cord is marginal in placenta praevia. **Listing's l.,** when the eyeball is moved from a resting position, the rotational angle in the second position is the same as if the eye were turned about a fixed axis perpendicular to the first and second position of the visual line. **Lössen's l.,** hemophiliac males do not transmit the condition to their offspring. **Louis' l.** 1. Pulmonary tuberculosis generally begins in the left lung. 2. Tuberculosis of any part is attended by localization in the lungs. **Magendie's l.,** Bell's l. **Malthu-**

sian l., the hypothesis that population tends to outrun the means available to sustain it. **Marey's l.,** a pulse of high tension is slow. **Mariotte's l.,** Boyle's l. **l. of mass action, mass l.,** Guldberg and Waage's l. **Meltzer's l.** (*of contrary innervation*), all living functions are continually controlled by two opposing forces: augmentation or action on the one hand, and inhibition on the other. **Mendel's l., mendelian l.,** in the inheritance of certain traits or characters, the offspring are not intermediate in character between the parents but inherit from one or the other parent in this respect. For example, if a pea plant with the factor tallness (TT) is mated with one with the factor shortness (SS) then some of the offspring will inherit TT, some TS, and some SS in the ratio: TT, 2TS, SS. The TT are homozygous (pure) tall, the SS are homozygous short and the TS are heterozygous. Which parent the TS ones resemble will depend on whether T or S is dominant. The TT's mated with TT's breed pure as do the SS's with SS's. The TS's mated with TS's again produce TT's, TS's and SS's in the same ratio as above. TS's mated with TT's or SS's give the same combinations but in a different ratio. **Mendeléeff's l.,** periodic l. **Metchnikoff's l.,** whenever the body is attacked by bacteria, the polymorphonuclear leukocytes and the large mononuclear leukocytes quickly become protective phagocytes. **Meyer's l.,** the internal structure of fully developed normal bone represents the lines of greatest pressure or traction and affords the greatest possible resistance with the least possible amount of material. **Minot's l.,** organisms age fastest when young. **Mott's l. of anticipation,** when the children of the insane become insane they do so at a much earlier age than did their parents. **Müller's l.,** l. of specific irritability. **Müller-Haeckel l.,** biogenetic l. **l. of multiple variants,** any variation from the normal in the bones of the hand or foot is always multiple. **Murri's l.,** a law of the physicopathologic compensation in the heart. **myelogenetic l.** (of Flechsig), the myelination of the nerve fibers of the developing brain takes place in a definite sequence so that fibers belonging to particular functional systems mature at the same time. **Nägeli's l.,** a disease in which eosinophils are present in one-half normal, normal, or increased numbers cannot be typhoid; and the appearance of even a few of such cells must incite caution in the diagnosis. **Nernst's l.,** the current required to stimulate muscle action varies as the square root of its frequency. **Neumann's l.,** the molecular heat in compounds of analogous constitution is always the same. **Newland's l.,** periodic l. **Newton's l.,** l. of gravitation. **Nysten's l.,** rigor mortis affects first the muscles of mastication, next those of the face and neck, then those of the upper trunk and arms, and last of all those of the legs and feet. **Ohm's l.,** the strength of an electric current varies directly as the electromotive force, and inversely as the resistance. **Ollier's l.,** in the case of two parallel bones which are joined at their extremities by ligaments, arrest of growth in one of them involves growth disturbance in the other. **orbital-canine l.,** in the normal denture the orbital line intersects the cusps of the canine teeth. **orbital-gnathion l.,** in the normal denture the gnathion lies in the orbital line. **Pajot's l.,** a solid body contained within another body having smooth walls will tend to conform to the shape of those walls: this law governs the rotating movements of the child during labor. **Pascal's l.,** pressure applied to a liquid at any point is transmitted equally in all directions. **periodic l.,** if the elements are arranged in the sequence of the weight of their atoms, and divided into groups of seven or eight, the corresponding members of each group show relationship in chemical properties: thus, elements having characters alike recur at regular intervals throughout the series. Called also *Mendeléeff's l.* **Peter's l.,** atheroma most commonly affects blood vessels at their angles or turns. **Pfeiffer's l.,** the blood serum of an animal immunized against a disease will, when introduced into the body of another animal, destroy the bacteria of that disease. **Pflüger's l.,** a nerve tract is stimulated when catelectrotonus develops or anelectrotonus disappears, but not under the reverse conditions. **Poiseuille's l.,** the velocity of flow in a tube is proportional to the cross-sectional area of the tube. **Prévost's l.,** in a lateral cerebral lesion the head is turned toward the side involved. **Profeta's l.,** a nonsyphilitic child born of syphilitic parents is immune. **Proust's l.,** l. of definite proportions. **psychophysical l.,** Weber-Fechner l. **Raoult's l.** 1. (*for freezing points*). The depression of the freezing point for the same type of electrolyte dissolved in a given solvent is proportional to the molecular concentration of the solute. 2. (*for vapor pressures*). (*a*) The vapor pressure of a volatile substance from a liquid solution is equal to the mole fraction of that substance times its vapor pressure in the pure state. (*b*) When a non-volatile non-electrolyte is dissolved in a solvent the decrease in vapor pressure of that solvent is equal to the mole fraction of the solute times the vapor pressure of the pure solvent. **l. of reciprocal proportions,** two chemical elements that unite with a third element do so in proportions that are multiples of those in which they unite with each other. **l. of referred pain,** referred pain only arises from irritation of nerves which are sensitive to those stimuli that produce pain when applied to the surface of the body. **l. of refraction,** rays of light passing from a rarer to a denser medium are deflected toward a perpendicular to the surface of incidence: while rays passing from a denser to a rarer medium are deflected away from the perpendicular. **l. of refreshment,** the refreshment of a laboring muscle depends on the rate of supply of arterial blood. **l. of regression,** Galton's l. of regression. **l. of relativity,** simultaneous and successive sensations modify each other. **Ricco's l.,** the relation between intensity and area of illumination; intensity times area equals constant. **Ritter's l.,** both the opening and the closing of an electric current produce stimulation in a nerve. **Ritter-Valli l.,** the primary increase and secondary loss of irritability in a nerve, produced by a section which separates from the nerve center, travel in a peripheral direction. **Rommelaere's l.,** in cases of carcinoma there is a constant diminution of the nitrogen in the urine. **Rosa's l.,** the possibilities of phyletic variation in an organism decrease in proportion to the extent of its development. **Rosenbach's l.,** in lesions of the nerve centers and nerve trunks paralysis appears in the extensor muscles before it does in flexor muscles. **Roussel's l.,** a French law initiated by Theophile Roussel (1874) for the protection of friendless children. **Rubner's l.** 1. (*Law of constant energy consumption.*) The rapidity of growth is proportional to the intensity of the metabolic process. 2. (*Law of constant growth quotient.*) The same fractional part of the entire energy is utilized for growth. This fractional part is called the "growth quotient." **Schroeder van der Kolk's l.,** the sensory fibers of a mixed nerve are distributed to the parts moved by muscles which are stimulated by the motor fibers of the same nerve. **Schütz's l., Schütz-Borissov l.,** the intensity of enzyme action is directly proportional to the square root of its concentration. **l. of segregation,** in each generation the ratio of pure dominants, dominants giving descendants in the proportion of three dominants to one recessive, and pure recessives is 1 : 2 : 1. **Semon's l.,** in progressive organic diseases of the motor laryngeal nerves the abductors of the vocal cords (posterior crico-arytenoids) are the first, and occasionally the only, muscles affected. **Semon-Rosenbach l.,** Semon's l. **Sherrington's l.** 1. Every posterior spinal nerve root supplies a special region of the skin, although fibers from adjacent spinal segments may invade such a region. 2. When a muscle receives a nerve impulse to contract, its antagonist receives simultaneously an impulse to relax. **l. of similars.** See *homeopathy.* **l. of sines,** the sine of the angle of incidence is equal to the sine of the angle of reflection multiplied by a constant quantity. **Snell's l.,** Descartes' l. **Spallanzani's l.,** the law that regeneration is more complete in younger individuals than in older ones. **l. of specific irritability,** every sensory nerve reacts to one form of stimulus and gives rise to one form of sensation only, though if under abnormal conditions it be excited by other forms of stimuli, the sensation evoked will be the same. Called also *Müller's l.* **Starling's l.,** the heart output per beat is directly proportional to the diastolic filling. **Stokes' l.,** a muscle situated above an inflamed membrane is often affected with paralysis. **surface l.,** temperature remaining constant, the heat production, heat loss, and oxygen consumption in an animal are inversely proportional to the free surface or to the square of a linear dimension. **Tait's l.,** in every case of pelvic or abdominal disease in which life is endangered or the health ruined, exploration by celiotomy should be made, except when the disease is known to be malignant. **Talbot's l.,** when complete fusion occurs and the sensation is uniform, the intensity is the same as would occur were the same amount of light spread uniformly over the disk. **Teevan's l.,** fractures of bones occur in the line of extension, and not in the line of compression. **Toynbee's l.,** in cases of brain disease due to otitis the cerebellum and lateral sinuses are affected from the mastoid, and the cerebrum from the tympanic roof. **van der Kolk's l.,** Schroeder van der Kolk's l. **van't Hoff's l.** 1. Many substances in solution exert an osmotic pressure equal to the gas pressure that they would exert if their molecules were in a gaseous state and occupied a volume equal to that of the solution under the same conditions of temperature and pressure. 2. van't Hoff's rule. See under *rule.* **Virchow's l.,** the cell elements of tumors are derived from normal and preexisting tissue cells. **Vulpian's l.,** when a portion of the brain is destroyed the functions of that part are carried on by the remaining parts. **Waller's l., wallerian l.,** if the sensory fibers of the root of a spinal nerve be divided on the central side of the ganglion, the fibers on the peripheral side of the cut do not degenerate; while those that remain connected with the cord degenerate. **Walton's l.,** l. of reciprocal proportions. **Weber's l.,** the variation of stimulus which causes the smallest appreciable change in sensation maintains an approximately fixed ratio to the whole stimulus. **Weber-Fechner l.,** for a sensation to increase by equal amounts (arithmetical progression), the stimulus must increase by geometrical progression. Called also *psychophysical l.* **Weigert's l.,** loss or destruction of elements in the organic world is apt to be followed by overproduction of such elements in the reparative process. **Wien's displacement l.,** in radiation therapy, the wavelengths become shorter as the temperature of the body increases. **Wilder's l. of initial value,** the more intense the function of a vegetative organ, the weaker its capacity for being excited by stimuli and the stronger its reaction to depressing factors; with extremely high or low initial value there is marked tendency to paradoxic reactions (reversal of direction of reaction). **Wolff's l.,** all changes which may occur in the function of a bone are attended by definite alterations in its internal structure. **Wundt-Lamansky l.,** the line of vision in moving through a vertical plane parallel to the frontal plane moves in straight lines in the vertical and horizontal directions, but in curved paths in all other movements. **Wyssakovitsch's l.,** the cells covering any part of the body, so long as they preserve their integrity, protect the underlying tissues. **Zeune's l.,** the proportion of cases of blindness is less in the temperate than in the frigid zone, and increases in the torrid zone as the equator is approached.

lawrencium (law-ren′se-um) [Ernest Orlando *Lawrence,* American physicist, 1901–1958; builder of the first cyclotron for the production of high-energy particles, and winner of the Nobel prize for physics in 1939]. The chemical element of atomic number 103, atomic weight 257, symbol Lw; produced in 1961 by bombardment of californium isotopes of mass 250, 251, and 252.

Lawson Tait. See *Tait.*

laxation (laks-a′shun). Defecation.

laxative (laks′ah-tiv) [L. *laxativus*]. 1. Aperient; mildly cathartic. 2. An agent that acts to promote evacuation of the bowel. **bulk l.,** an agent that acts to promote evacuation of the bowel by increasing the volume of the feces.

laxator (laks-a′tor) [L. *laxare* to unloose or relax]. That which slackens or relaxes. **l. tym′pani ma′jor,** ligamentum mallei anterius. **l. tym′pani mi′nor,** ligamentum mallei laterale.

laxoin (laks′o-in). Phenolphthalein.

layer (la′er). A sheetlike mass of substance of nearly uniform thickness, several of which may be superimposed, one above another, as in the epidermis. Called also *lamina* and *stratum.* **adamantine l.,** enamelum. **ambiguous l.,** the second layer of the cerebral cortex, counting from without: named from the indefinite shapes of many of its cells. **ameloblastic l.,** the inner layer of cells of the enamel organ, created by its invagination, which forms the enamel prisms. **bacillary l.,** l. of rods and cones. **Baillarger's l.,** Baillarger's line. **basal l.** 1. Lamina basalis choroideae. 2. Stratum basale. **basement l.,** basement membrane. **Bechterew's l.,** a layer of fibers in the cerebral cortex between Baillarger's line and the tangential fibers. **Bernard's glandular l.,** a layer of cells which line the acini of the pancreas. **blastodermic l.,** germ l. **Bowman's l.,** lamina limitans anterior corneae. **Bruch's l.,** lamina basalis choroideae. **cerebral l.,** a term applied to the fifth to ninth layers of the retina. **Chievitz l.,** a transient fiber layer separating the inner and outer neuroblastic layers of the optic cup. **choriocapillary l.,** lamina choriocapillaris. **circular l. of ear drum,** stratum circulare membranae tympani. **circular l. of muscular tunic of small intestine,** stratum circulare tunicae muscularis intestini tenuis. **circular l. of muscular tunic of stomach,** stratum circulare tunicae muscularis ventriculi. **circular l. of tympanic membrane,** stratum circulare membranae tympani. **claustral l.,** the layer of gray matter between the external capsule and the insula. **clear l.,** stratum lucidum epidermidis. **columnar l.** 1. Layer of rods and cones. 2. Mantle layer. **compact l.,** stratum compactum. **cortical l.,** the cortex of an organ, as of the brain or ovary. **cutaneous l. of tympanic membrane,** stratum cutaneum membranae tympani. **cuticular l.,** a striate border of modified cytoplasm at the free end of some columnar cells. **deep l. of triangular ligament,** fascia diaphragmatis urogenitalis superior. **Dierk's l.,** a zone of cornification in the vaginal epithelium during its period of greatest thickness in the midinterval period of the menstrual cycle. **Dobie's l.,** Krause's membrane. **enamel l.,** the outermost layer of cells of the enamel organ. **ependymal l.,** the innermost layer of the wall of the primitive neural tube, bounding the central canal, which differentiates regionally into the roof plate and the floor plate. **epitrichial l.,** the most superficial layer of the epidermis of the embryo. **fibrous l. of articular capsule,** membrana fibrosa capsulae articularis. **fillet l.,** stratum interolivare lemnisci. **Floegel's l.,** a granular layer in each transparent lateral disk of a muscle fibril. **ganglion cell l.,** a layer of the retina, situated between the inner molecular layer and the stratum opticum, or nerve fiber layer, consisting essentially of the ganglion cells of the retina, and containing also the fibers of Müller, neuroglia, and branches of the retinal vessels. **ganglionic l. of cerebellum,** stratum gangliosum cerebelli. **Gennari's l.** See *Baillarger's line.* **germ l.,** one of the three primary layers of cells of the embryo (ectoderm, entoderm, or mesoderm), from which the tissues and organs develop. **germinative l. of epidermis,** stratum germinativum epidermidis [Malpighii]. **granular l. of cerebellum,** stratum granulosum cerebelli. **granular l. of follicle of ovary,** stratum granulosum folliculi ovarici vesiculosi. **granular l. of Tomes,** a zone of imperfectly calcified dentrin in apposition with the cementum of teeth. **granule l.,** stratum granulosum cerebelli. **gray l. of superior colliculus,** stratum griseum colliculi superioris. **half-value l.,** the thickness of a given substance which, when introduced in the path of a given beam of rays, will reduce its intensity to one half of the initial value. Called also *half-value thickness.* **Haller's l.,** that portion of the vascular layer of the choroid which is made up of large vessels. **Henle's l.,** the outer layer of cells of the inner root sheath of a hair follicle, lying between the outer root sheath and Huxley's layer of a hair follicle. **horny l. of epidermis,** stratum corneum epidermidis. **Huxley's l.,** a layer of the inner root sheath of a hair follicle, lying between Henle's layer and the inner sheath cuticle. **inferior l. of pelvic diaphragm,** fascia diaphragmatis pelvis inferior. **Kaes-Bechterew's l.,** Bechterew's l. **keratohyaline l.,** stratum granulosum epidermidis. **Kölliker's fibrous l.,** the mesiris. **Langerhans' l.,** stratum granulosum epidermidis. **Langhans' l.,** cytotrophoblast. **latticed l.,** a cortical cell layer of the hippocampus. **longitudinal l. of muscular tunic of small intestine,** stratum longitudinale tunicae muscularis intestini tenuis. **longitudinal l. of muscular tunic of stomach,** stratum longitudinale tunicae muscularis ventriculi. **malpighian l.,** stratum germinativum epidermidis [Malpighii]. **mantle l.,** the middle layer of the wall of the primitive neural tube, containing primitive nerve cells and later forming the gray substance of the central nervous system. **marginal l.,** the outermost layer of the wall of the primitive neural tube, a fibrous mesh into which the nerve fibers later grow, forming the white substance of the central nervous system. **medullary l's of optic thalamus, internal,** laminae medullares thalami. **Meynert's l.,** a layer of pyramidal cells in the cortex of the cerebrum. **molecular l., inner,** the inner plexiform layer of the retina, between the inner nuclear layer and the ganglion cell layer, consisting essentially of the arborization of the axons of the bipolar cells with the dendrites of the ganglion cells. **molecular l., outer,** the outer plexiform layer of the retina, between the outer nuclear layer and the inner nuclear layer, consisting essentially of the arborization of the axons of the rod and cone granules with the dendrites of the bipolar cells. **molecular l. of cerebellum,** stratum moleculare cerebelli. **mosaic l.,** the mesoretina. **mucous l.,** stratum germinativum epidermidis [Malpighii]. **mucous l. of tympanic membrane,** stratum mucosum membranae tympani. **muscular l. of fallopian tube,** tunica muscularis tubae uterinae. **muscular l. of stomach, inner,** stratum circulare tunicae muscularis ventriculi. **nerve fiber l.,** a layer of the retina, situated between the ganglion cell layer and the internal limiting membrane, consisting essentially of the axons of the ganglion cells which pass through the lamina cribrosa to form the optic nerve. **nervous l.,** all of the retina except the pigment layer; the inner layer of the optic cup. **Nitabuch's l.,** Nitabuch's stria. **nuclear l., inner,** a layer of the retina, situated between the outer and inner molecular layers, consisting essentially of the sensory bipolar cells. **nuclear l., outer,** a layer of the retina, situated between the external limiting membrane and the outer molecular layer, consisting essentially of the rod and cone granules (nuclei). **odontoblastic l.,** the epithelioid layer of odontoblasts in contact with the dentin of teeth. **Oehl's l.,** stratum lucidum epidermidis. **Ollier's l., osteogenetic l.,** the innermost layer of the periosteum. **palisade l.,** the basal layer of the stratum mucosum. **Pander's l.,** the splanchnopleural layer of the mesoblast. **papillary l.,** stratum papillare corii. **parietal l. of pelvic fascia,** fascia diaphragmatis pelvis superior. **peripheral l.,** the outer portion of the molecular layer of the cerebral cortex. **perpendicular l. of ethmoid bone,** lamina perpendicularis ossis ethmoidalis. **pigmented l. of ciliary body,** stratum pigmenti corporis ciliaris. **pigmented l. of eyeball,** stratum pigmenti bulbi oculi. **pigmented l. of iris,** stratum pigmenti iridis. **pigmented l. of retina,** stratum pigmenti retinae. **plexiform l's,** the two molecular layers of the retina. **prickle cell l.,** stratum germinativum epidermidis [Malphigii]. **Purkinje l.,** the layer of Purkinje cells in the cerebellar cortex, between the superficial molecular layer and the subjacent granular layer. **radiate l. of tympanic membrane,** stratum radiatum membranae tympani. **Rauber's l.,** the most external of the three layers of cells which form the blastodisk in the young embryo. Called also *blastodermic ectoderm* and *primitive ectoderm.* **Renaut's l.,** a thin hyaline membrane between the corium and the epidermis. **reticular l. of corium,** tunica propria corii. **l. of rods and cones,** a layer of the retina, situated immediately beneath the pigment epithelium, between it and the external limiting membrane, containing the sensitive elements of the retina, the cones, containing a visual pigment, iodopsin, and the rods, containing visual purple, or rhodopsin. **Rohr's l.,** Rohr's stria. **Sattler's l.,** that portion of the vascular layer of the choroid which is made up of medium-sized vessels. **sclerotogenous l., skeletogenous l.,** the layer of mesoderm cells surrounding the notochord of the embryo and developing into the axial skeleton. **somatic l.,** the external layer of the lateral mesoderm after the coelomic split occurs; the inner component of somatopleure. **splanchnic l.,** the internal layer of the lateral mesoderm after the coelomic split occurs; the component of splanchnopleure outside the entoderm. **spongy l.** See *stratum spongiosum.* **subcallosal l.,** the layer of nerve fibers on the lower side of the callosum. **subendocardial l.,** the layer of loose fibrous tissue uniting the endocardium and myocardium. **subendothelial l.,** a middle, fibrous layer of the tunica intima of typical blood vessels, located between the endothelium and internal elastic membrane. **subepicardial l.,** the layer of loose connective tissue uniting the epicardium and myocardium. **submantle l.,** a layer of interglobular dentin situated just below the cover (mantle) dentin. **submucous l.,** tela submucosa. **submucous l. of bladder,** tela submucosa vesicae urinariae. **submucous l. of colon,** tela submucosa coli. **submucous l. of esophagus,** tela submucosa esophagi. **submucous l. of pharynx,** tela submucosa pharyngis. **submucous l. of small intestine,** tela submucosa intestini tenuis. **submucous l. of stomach,** tela submucosa ventriculi. **subodontoblastic l.,** Weil's l. **subpapillary l.,** the vascular layer of the corium. **subserous l.,** tela subserosa. **subserous l. of peritoneum,** tela subserosa peritonei. **superficial l. of fascia of perineum,** fascia superficialis perinei. **superficial l. of triangular ligament,** fascia diaphragmatis urogenitalis inferior. **superior l. of pelvic diaphragm,** fascia diaphragmatis pelvis superior. **superpapillary l.,** stratum germinativum epidermidis [Malpighii]. **suprachorioid l.,** lamina suprachoroidea. **synovial l. of articular capsule,** membrana synovialis capsulae articularis. **Tomes' granular l.,** granular l. of Tomes. **trophic l.,** the entoderm. **Unna's l.,** stratum granulosum epidermidis. **vegetative l.,** the entoderm. **vertical l. of ethmoid bone,** lamina perpendicularis ossis ethmoidalis. **visceral l. of pelvic fascia,** fascia endopelvina. **visceral l. of pericardium,** lamina visceralis pericardii. **Waldeyer's l.,** the vascular layer of the ovary. **Weil's basal l.,** a clear layer relatively free of cells, just inside of the layer of odontoblasts of the tooth pulp, made up of delicate fibrils of connective tissue communicating with the processes of odontoblasts. **white l's of cerebellum,** laminae albae cerebelli. **yellow l.,** crusta phlogistica. **Zeissel's l.,** a layer in the stomach wall between the tunica muscularis mucosae and the tela submucosa. **zonal l. of quadrigeminal body,** stratum zonale corporis quadrigemini. **zonal l. of thalamus,** stratum zonale thalami.

layette (la-et'). The outfit of garments prepared for a new-born child.

lazar (laz'ar) [*Lazarus*, the leper of the Bible]. Leper.

lazaretto (laz"ah-ret'o). 1. A pesthouse or hospital for contagious diseases. 2. A quarantine station.

lb. Abbreviation for L. *li'bra*, pound.

LBF. Abbreviation for *Lactobacillus bulgaricus factor.*

L.Ch. Abbreviation for *Licentiate in Surgery.*

L.D. Abbreviation for *lethal dose, linguodistal,* and for *perception of light difference.*

L.D.50. Abbreviation for *median lethal dose;* a dose which is lethal for 50 per cent of the test subjects.

L.D.A. Abbreviation for *left dorso-anterior* position of the fetus.

L.D.P. Abbreviation for *left dorsoposterior* position of the fetus.

L.D.S. Abbreviation for *Licentiate in Dental Surgery.*

L.E. Abbreviation for *left eye,* and *lupus erythematosus.*

leaching (lēch'ing). Lixiviation.

lead[1] (led) [L. *plumbum*]. A soft, grayish-blue metal with poisonous salts; symbol, Pb; atomic number, 82; atomic weight, 207.19. **l. acetate,** a sweetish, white, basic salt: astringent, anodyne, and discutient. **arsenate of l.,** a mixture of arsenate of soda and acetate of lead in water: used as an insecticide. **l. bitannate,** l. tannate. **black l.,** graphite. **l. carbonate,** a basic salt, $(PbCO_3)_2.Pb(OH)_2$: used as an application to burns and inflamed surfaces. **l. chloride,** a compound, $PbCl_2$: anodyne and astringent. **l. chromate,** a lemon-yellow powder, $PbCrO_4$. Called also *chrome yellow.* **l. iodide,** a yellow, crystalline powder, PbI_2; resolvent and astringent. **l. monoxide,** a binary compound, PbO, called *litharge* when crystalline and *massicot* when amorphous: much used in plasters, etc., and in the treatment of burns. **l. nitrate,** a sweetish, crystalline agent, $Pb(NO_3)_2$: astringent, detergent, and deodorant. **l. oleate,** a white powder, $3Pb(C_{18}H_{33}O_2)_2$: used in diachylon ointment, etc. **l. oxide.** See *l. monoxide* and *l. tetroxide.* **l. phenolsulfonate,** white needles, astringent and antiseptic, $Pb(OH.C_6H_4.SO_2.O)_2.5H_2O$: used in skin diseases. **red l.,** lead tetroxide. **l. selinide,** a compound suggested for use in cancer therapy. **l. subacetate,** a basic acetate of lead. **sugar of l.,** l. acetate. **l. tannate,** a yellowish-gray powder; anodyne and astringent. **tetra-ethyl l.,** a highly poisonous organic lead compound, $Pb(C_2H_5)_4$, used as an antiknock agent in internal combustion motors. It can be absorbed through the skin and may cause mental symptoms and death. Called also *ethyl gas.* **l. tetroxide,** a compound, Pb_3O_4, which may be used like the monoxide. **white l.,** a basic lead carbonate.

lead[2] (lēd). Any one of the records made by the electrocardiograph, varying with the part of the body from which the current is led off. It is customary to use the following three leads: lead I, right arm and left arm, in which the current is derived largely from the base of the heart; lead II, right arm and left leg, corresponding essentially to the long axis of the heart; lead III, left arm and left leg, representing chiefly the left side

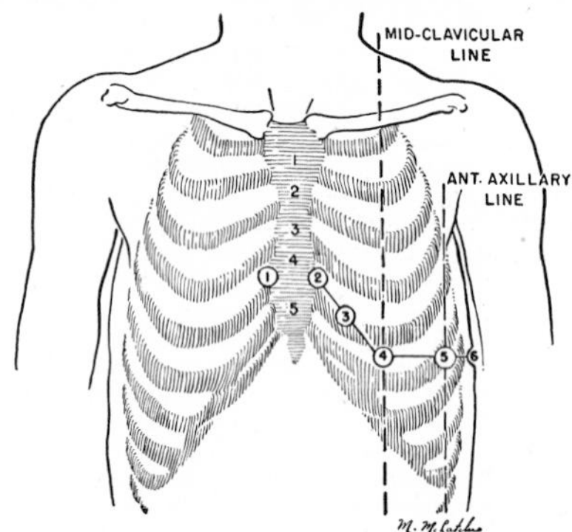

Precordial leads (Graybiel and White).

of the heart; lead IV is taken from the precordial region. Called also *derivation.* **precordial l's,** leads in which one electrode is placed on the chest and the other on an extremity. Such leads are indicated as follows: CR = chest + right arm; CL = chest + left arm; CF = chest and left leg. Subscript numbers 1 to 6 indicate at which points on the chest the lead is taken.

leakage (lēk'ij). The escape of fluid from a vessel or other container. In psychiatry, the discussion by a patient of his own analysis with a person other than the analyst.

leash (lēsh). A bundle of cordlike structures, as nerves, blood vessels, fibers, etc.

leben (leb'en) [Arabic]. A ferment drink of Egypt made from the milk of cows, buffaloes, and goats.

Leber's corpuscles, disease, plexus (la-berz') [Theodor *Leber*, German ophthalmologist, 1840–1917]. See under the nouns.

Lebistes (lĕ-bis'tēz). A genus of small fish, the guppy. **L. reticula'tus,** a species of top-feeding minnows, commonly known as "millions," cultivated in the Barbados to eliminate mosquito larvae.

lecanopagus (lek"an-op'ah-gus) [Gr. *lekanē* basin + *pagos* thing fixed]. Symmetrical conjoined twins fused at the pelvis.

Lecat's gulf (lĕ-kahz') [Claude Nicolas *Lecat*, French surgeon, 1700–1768]. The hollow of the bulbous portion of the urethra.

leche de higuerón (la'cha da ēg"a-ron') [Sp. milk of fig]. The sap or latex of wild fig trees of Central and South America: vermifuge.

lechopyra (lek"o-pi'rah) [Gr. *lechō* parturient woman + *pyr* fever]. Puerperal fever.

lecithal (les'ĭ-thal) [Gr. *lekithos* yolk]. Having a yolk. Used as a word termination, affixed to a word stem descriptive of the state of the yolk substance, as *centrolecithal, isolecithal,* etc.

lecithalbumin (les"ĭ-thal'bu-min). A compound of albumin and lecithin, found in the stomach, liver, kidney, lungs, and spleen.

lecithid (les'ĭ-thid). A compound of lecithin with venom hemolysin. **cobra l.,** a hemolytic compound formed by cobra toxin and the lecithin of the blood.

lecithin (les'ĭ-thin) [Gr. *lekithos* yolk of egg]. A monoaminomonophosphatide, $CH_2(R).CH(R').CH_2.O.PO(OH).O.CH_2.N(OH)(CH_3)_3$ (R and R' being fatty acids), found in animal tissues especially nerve tissue, semen, yolk of egg, and in smaller amount in bile and blood. It is a colorless, crystalline compound, soluble in alcohol, and is chemically the stearyloleylglycerophosphate of choline. Other substances of similar constitution are grouped as lecithins. Lecithins are said to have the therapeutic properties of phosphorus, and have been given in rickets, dyspepsia, neurasthenia, diabetes, anemia, and tuberculosis.

lecithinase (les′ĭ-thin-ās). An enzyme which catalyzes the splitting of lecithin. **cobra l.,** one of the constituents of the hemolysin of cobra venom.

lecithinemia (les″ĭ-thin-ē′me-ah). The presence of lecithin in the blood.

lecitho- (les′ĭ-tho) [Gr. *lekithos* yolk]. Combining form denoting relationship to the yolk of an egg or ovum.

lecithoblast (les′ĭ-tho-blast) [*lecitho-* + Gr. *blastos* germ]. The primitive entoderm of a two-layered blastodisk.

lecithoprotein (les″ĭ-tho-pro′te-in). A compound of the protein molecule with a lecithin. Lecithoproteins occur in all cells.

lecithovitellin (les″ĭ-tho-vi-tel′in). A suspension of egg yolk in a solution of sodium chloride. It reacts with the toxin of *Clostridium welchii* to produce a precipitate or an opacity.

Leclanché's cell (lĕ″klan-shāz′) [Georges *Leclanché*, French physicist, 1839–1882]. See under *cell.*

lectin (lek′tin). A general term applied to hemagglutinating substances extracted from certain plant seeds.

lectual (lek′tu-al) [L. *lectualis; lectus* bed]. Pertaining to a bed or couch.

lectulum (lek′tu-lum) [L., dim. of *lectus* bed]. A little bed. **l. un′guis,** matrix unguis.

LED. Abbreviation for *lupus erythematosus disseminata.*

ledbänder (led′ben-der) [Ger.]. Büngner's bands.

Le Dentu's suture (lĕ-den-tūz′) [Jean-François-Auguste *Le Dentu*, Paris surgeon, 1841–1926]. See under *suture.*

Lederberg (led′er-berg), Joshua. United States biochemist, born 1925; co-winner, with George Wells Beadle and Edward Lawrie Tatum, of the Nobel prize in medicine and physiology for 1958, for work in genetics and heredity.

ledercillin (led″er-sil′lin). Trade mark for preparations of penicillin G procaine.

Lederer's anemia, disease (led′er-erz) [Max *Lederer*, Brooklyn pathologist, 1885–1952]. See under *anemia.*

Ledran's suture (lĕ-draz′) [Henri François *Ledran*, French surgeon, 1685–1770]. See under *suture.*

Leduc's current (lĕ-dooks′) [Stéphane Armand Nicolas *Leduc*, French physicist, 1853–1939]. See under *current.*

Lee's ganglion (lēz) [Robert *Lee*, English physician, 1793–1877]. See under *ganglion.*

leech (lēch) [L. *hirudo*]. 1. An aquatic annelid, *Hirudo medicinalis;* used for drawing blood. An aqueous therapeutic extract of the heads of leeches is employed to prevent the formation of blood clots, etc. Some species, chiefly tropical, may become semiparasitic upon man and animals. See also *Placobdella.* 2. To apply leeches. 3. An old name for physician. **American l.,** the *Sanguisuga decora*, a small species sometimes used in drawing blood. **artificial l.,** an apparatus for drawing blood by artificial suction. **Heurteloup's l.,** an artificial leech. **horse l.** See *Limnatis* and *Haemopis.* **Hungarian l.,** the *Sanguisuga officinalis*, a species locally used in drawing blood. **land l.,** Haemadipsa. **Swedish l.,** the *Sanguisuga medicinalis*, or official leech.

leeches (lēch′ez). An infectious disease of horses in Florida and India, with local lesions on the skin, which begin with slight lumps and grow in size until there is a large raw surface. Called also *hyphomycosis destruens equi*, and in India *bursautee.*

leeching (lēch′ing). 1. The application of a leech for the withdrawal of blood. 2. Leeches.

Leeuwenhoekia australiensis (lu″en-ho′ke-ah aus-tra″le-en′sis) [Antonj van *Leeuwenhoek*, Dutch microscopist, 1632–1723]. A mite found at Sydney, New South Wales, which may cause great irritation by burrowing in the skin.

left-handed (left-hand′ed). Using the left hand preferentially in voluntary motor acts, or more skillfully than the right.

leg (leg). The lower extremity, especially the part from knee to foot. Called also *crus* [N A]. **Anglesey l.,** a form of jointed artificial leg; named from a marquis of Anglesey. **badger l.,** inequality in the length of the legs. **baker l.,** genu valgum. **bandy l.,** genu varum. **Barbados l.,** elephantiasis of the leg. **bayonet l.,** uncorrected backward displacement of the bones of the leg at the knee, followed by ankylosis at the joint. **black l.,** symptomatic anthrax. **bow l.,** genu varum. **deck l's,** edema of the lower legs, occurring in ship passengers in tropical zones. **elephant l.,** elephantiasis. **milk l.,** phlegmasia alba dolens. **red l.,** a fatal septicemia in frogs apparently caused by *Proteus hydrophilus.* **restless l's,** a condition characterized by a disagreeable, creeping, irritating sensation deep inside both legs, usually between the knee and the ankle. The subject can obtain relief only by walking about or keeping his legs moving (Ekbom). **rider's l.,** strain of the adductor muscles of the thigh in horse-back riders. **scaly l.,** an enlarged and encrusted condition of the legs in fowls caused by *Cnemidocoptes mutans.* **tropical l's,** deck l's. **white l.,** phlegmasia alba dolens.

Legal's disease, test (la-galz′) [Emmo *Legal*, German physician, 1859–1922]. See under *disease* and *tests.*

Legg's disease (legz) [Arthur T. *Legg*, Boston surgeon, 1874–1939]. Osteochondritis deformans juvenilis.

Legg-Calvé-Perthes disease (leg′kal-va′-per′tez) [Arthur T. *Legg;* Jacques *Calvé*, French orthopedist, 1875–1954; Georg Clemens *Perthes*, German surgeon, 1869–1927]. Osteochondritis deformans juvenilis.

leghemoglobin (leg″he-mo-glo′bin). A pigment found in leguminous root nodules.

leg-ill (leg′il). Inflammation of the interdigital space of sheep, producing lameness.

legume (leg′ūm). The pod or fruit of a leguminous plant, such as peas and beans.

legumelin (leg″u-me′lin). A simple albumin from lentils, beans, and other leguminous seeds.

legumin (leg′u-min) [L. *legumen* pulse]. A globulin from the seeds of various plants, chiefly of the order *Leguminosae.*

leguminivorous (lĕ-gu″mĭ-niv′o-rus). Feeding on legumes (beans and peas).

leiasthenia (li″as-the′ne-ah) [*leio-* + *asthenia*]. Asthenia of smooth muscle.

Leichtenstern's phenomenon, sign (lĭk′ten-sternz) [Otto Michael *Leichtenstern*, German physician, 1845–1900]. See under *sign.*

Leiner's disease, test (li′nerz) [Karl *Leiner*, Austrian pediatrician, 1871–1930]. Desquamative erythroderma in infants, and see under *tests.*

leio- (li′o) [Gr. *leios* smooth]. Combining form meaning smooth.

leiodermia (li″o-der′me-ah) [*leio-* + Gr. *derma* skin]. Abnormal glossiness and smoothness of the skin.

leiodystonia (li″o-dis-to′ne-ah) [*leio-* + *dystonia*]. Dystonia of smooth muscle.

Leiognathus bacoti (li-og′nah-thus bah-ko′te). *Liponyssus bacoti.*

leiomyoblastoma (li″o-mi″o-blas-to′mah). Leiomyoma.

leiomyofibroma (li″o-mi″o-fi-bro′mah). A tumor with leiomatous, myomatous, and fibromatous elements.

leiomyoma (li″o-mi-o′mah) [*leio-* + Gr. *mys* muscle + *-oma*]. A benign tumor derived from smooth muscle. **l. cu'tis,** a disease characterized by numerous translucent nodules, the size of peas, on the extensor surfaces of the extremities, the nodules containing masses of smooth muscle fibers.

leiomyosarcoma (li″o-mi″o-sar-ko′mah). A sarcoma containing large spindle cells of unstriped muscle.

leiothric (li-o′thrik) [*leio-* + Gr. *thrix* hair]. Having smooth hair.

leiphemia (li-fe′me-ah) [Gr. *leipein* to fail + *haima* blood + *-ia*]. Thinness and poverty of the blood.

leipo- (lip′o). For words beginning thus, see those beginning *lipo-*.

Leishman's cells, stain (lēsh′manz) [Sir William Boog *Leishman*, English army surgeon, 1865–1926]. See under *cell* and *table of stains.*

Leishman-Donovan body (lēsh′man-don′o-van) [Sir William B. *Leishman;* Charles *Donovan*, Irish physician, formerly in Sanitary Service in India, born 1863]. See under *body*.

Leishmania (lēsh-man′e-ah) [Sir William B. *Leishman*]. A genus of flagellate protozoans parasitic in the human and animal bodies, where they are found as small oval or round intracellular organisms, chiefly in the reticuloendothelial cells of the skin or the viscera. In the insect host they develop into slender elongated, nucleated organisms (leptomonad stage). **L. brazilien'sis,** a form

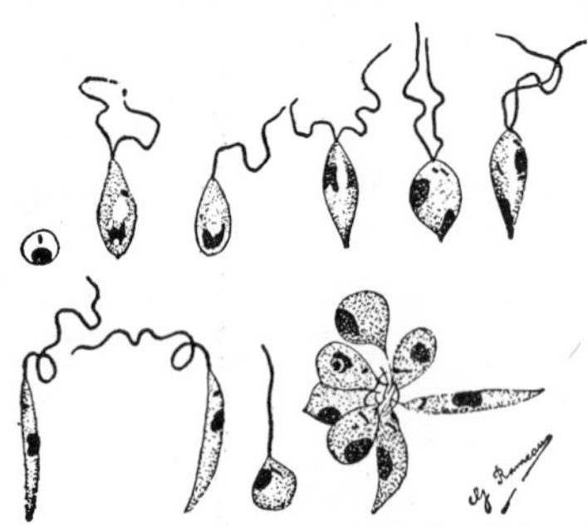

Leishmania tropica (Ch. Nicolle).

morphologically identical with *L. donovani* and which causes American leishmaniasis. **L. donova'ni,** the organism causing visceral leishmaniasis, or kala-azar. **L. enriet'tii,** a species causing an infection in guinea pigs. **L. farcimino'sa,** *Blastomyces farciminosus.* **L. furunculo'sa,** *L. tropica.* **L. infan'tum,** the organism causing Mediterranean kala-azar or infantile splenomegaly, morphologically identical with *L. donovani.* **L. mediterra'nea,** *L. infantum.* **L. nilot'ica,** Brumpt's name for the *L. tropica* found in the keloid form of oriental sore. **L. trop'ica,** the parasite which causes cutaneous leishmaniasis. It is morphologically identical with *L. donovani* and has a similar life history. See *cutaneous leishmaniasis*, under *leishmaniasis*.

leishmaniasis (lēsh″mah-ni′ah-sis). Infection caused by Leishmania. **American l., l. americа'na, Brazilian l.,** mucocutaneous l. **canine l.,** disease of dogs and children in the Mediterranean region caused by *L. infantum.* **cutaneous l., dermal l.,** a chronic ulcerative granuloma endemic chiefly in Asia, Africa, Mediterranean countries, and parts of South America, and marked by the development on the exposed parts of the body of a papule which passes successively through the stage of tubercle, scab, and circumscribed ulcer. It is caused by a protozoan parasite, *Leishmania tropica*, which is transmitted by the sandfly (Phlebotomus). The disease has received various names, according to the locality of its occurrence, as Aleppo boil, Delhi sore, Penjdeh sore, Natal boil, Bagdad sore, Biskra button, Lahore sore, Kandahar sore, furunculus orientalis, oriental button, oriental sore, tropical ulcer, etc., but the conditions occurring under the various names are practically one and the same disease. **infantile l.,** infantile kala-azar. **mucocutaneous l., naso-oral l., nasopharyngeal l.,** a disease widely distributed in Central and South America, caused by *Leishmania braziliensis*, and probably transmitted by a sandfly of the genus *Phlebotomus.* It is characterized by ulceration of the mucous membranes of the nose and throat and may cause wide destruction of tissue in the nasal and oral regions. It is called *forest yaws, bouba braziliana, espundia,* and *uta.* **visceral l.,** kala-azar.

leishmanicidal (lēsh″man-ĭ-si′dal). Destructive to Leishmania.

leishmanid (lēsh′man-id). The early cutaneous nodule of cutaneous leishmaniasis.

leishmaniosis (lēsh″man-e-o′sis). Leishmaniasis.

leishmanoid (lēsh′mah-noid). An eruption of whitish patches along with nodules and papules following partially cured kala-azar: called also *dermal leishmanoid.*

leistungskern (līs′toongs-kern) [Ger.]. The functional part or active center of a cell.

Leiter's coil (li′terz) [Joseph *Leiter*, Austrian instrument maker, died 1892]. See under *coil.*

Lelaps (le′laps). A genus of mites. **L. echidni'nus,** a mite which is parasitic in rats and which acts as the intermediate host of *Hepatozoon perniciosum.*

Leloir's disease (lĕl-warz′) [Henri Camille *Leloir*, French dermatologist, 1855–1896]. Lupus erythematosus.

lema (le′mah) [Gr. *lēmē* a humor that gathers in the corner of the eye]. Sebum palpebrale.

Lembert's suture (lah-bārz′) [Antoine *Lembert*, French surgeon, 1802–1851]. See under *suture.*

lememia (le-me′me-ah) [Gr. *loimos* plague + *haima* blood + *-ia*]. The presence of plague germs in the blood.

lemic (le′mik) [Gr. *loimos* plague]. Pertaining to an epidemic disease, as the plague.

lemmoblast (lem′o-blast). A primitive or immature lemmocyte.

lemmoblastic (lem″o-blas′tik). Forming or developing into neurilemma tissue.

lemmoblastoma (lem″o-blas-to′mah). Spongioblastoma.

lemmocyte (lem′o-sīt) [Gr. *lemma* husk + *-cyte*]. A cell derived from the neural crest and developing into a neurilemma cell.

lemniscus (lem-nis′kus), pl. *lemnis'ci* [L.; Gr. *lēmniskos* fillet]. A ribbon or band; currently used in anatomical nomenclature as a general term to designate a band or bundle of fibers in the central nervous system. **acoustic l., l. acus'ticus,** l. lateralis. **lateral l., l. latera'lis** [N A], a tract of longitudinal fibers extending upward through the lateral part of the tegmental substance of the pons, formed in part by fibers arising from the trapezoid body, and ascending to terminate in the inferior colliculus. Called also *acoustic l.* or *l. acusticus.* **medial l., l. media'lis** [N A], a tract arising from the internal arcuate fibers of the nuclei gracilis and cuneatus, and crossing to the opposite side in the lower part of the medulla oblongata to ascend between the two olives. In the pons, it lies just dorsal to the pontine nuclei. It terminates in the posterior part of the thalamus. Called also *sensory l.* or *l. sensitivus.* **optic l.,** tractus opticus. **l. sensiti'vus, sensory l.,** l. medialis. **spinal l., l. spina'lis** [N A], the part of the spinothalamic tract within the mesencephalon, forming a diffuse bundle just lateral to the medial lemniscus. **l. tempora'lis et occipita'lis,** a bundle of fibers connecting the cortex of the temporal and occipital lobes of the brain. **trigeminal l., l. trigemina'lis** [N A], ascending secondary trigeminal fibers passing to the ventral region of the thalamus; the connections and course of these fibers are not clear, but they are probably related to the fibers of the medial lemniscus.

lemography (le-mog′rah-fe) [Gr. *loimos* plague + *graphein* to write]. A treatise on the plague or other epidemic disease.

lemology (le-mol′o-je) [Gr. *loimos* plague + *-logy*]. The science of contagious and epidemic diseases, especially the plague.

lemon (lem′un). The fruit of *Citrus limon* (Linné) Burmann filius (Fam. *Rutaceae*).

lemoparalysis (le″mo-pah-ral′ĭ-sis) [Gr. *laimos* gullet + *paralysis*]. Paralysis of the gullet.

lemostenosis (lem″o-ste-no′sis) [Gr. *laimos* gullet + *stenōsis* narrowing]. Stenosis of the pharynx or esophagus.

Lemuroidea (lem″u-roi′de-ah). A suborder of Primates, consisting of the lemurs, animals resembling monkeys but having, usually, a sharp, foxlike muzzle and a tail which is usually long and furry, but never prehensile.

Lenard ray (len-ard′) [Philipp *Lenard*, Hungarian physicist, born 1862]. See under *ray*.

length (length). An expression of the longest dimension of an object, or of the measurement between the two ends. **crown-heel l.**, an expression of measurement from the crown of the head to the heel in embryos, fetuses, and infants; the equivalent of *standing height* in older individuals. **crown-rump l.**, an expression of measurement from the crown of the head to the breech in embryos, fetuses, and infants; the equivalent of *sitting height* in older individuals. **dental l.**, an expression of the distance between the mesial surface of the first premolar and the distal surface of the third molar of the upper jaw, or maxilla. **greatest l.**, an expression of measurement in young embryos which are nearly straight. **sitting l.**, the distance from the crown of the head to the coccyx, called by Pirquet Si. **stem l.**, the distance from the vertex to a line joining the ischial tuberosities.

Lenhartz treatment (len′harts) [Hermann Albert Dietrich *Lenhartz*, physician in Hamburg, 1854–1910]. See under *treatment*.

Lenhossék's bundle (len′ho-sheks) [Mihály (Michael) von *Lenhossék*, Hungarian anatomist, 1863–1937]. See under *bundle*.

leniceps (len′ĭ-seps) [L. *lenis* mild + *capere* to seize]. A short-handled obstetric forceps.

lenitive (len′ĭ-tiv) [L. *lenire* to soothe]. 1. Demulcent or soothing. 2. A demulcent remedy.

Lennander's operation (len-an′derz) [Karl Gustav *Lennander*, Swedish surgeon, 1857–1908]. See under *operation*.

Lennhoff's index, sign (len′hofs) [Rudolf *Lennhoff*, German physician, 1866–1933]. See under *index* and *sign*.

lens (lenz) [L. "lentil"]. 1. A piece of glass or other transparent substance so shaped as to converge or scatter the rays of light, especially the glass used in appropriate frames or other instruments to increase the visual acuity of the human eye. See also *glasses* and *spectacles*. 2. [N A] The transparent biconvex body of the eye situated between the posterior chamber and the vitreous body, constituting part of the refracting mechanism of the eye. Called also *l. crystallina* [B N A]. **achromatic l.**, one corrected for chromatic aberration. **acrylic l.**, a plastic replacement for the lens of the eye after cataract surgery. **adherent l.**, contact l. **aplanatic l.**, one that serves to correct spherical aberration. **apochromatic l.**, one corrected for chromatic and spherical aberration. **artificial l.**, a lenticular body of glass or methacrylate inserted in the eyeball after extraction of the crystalline lens in cataract. **biconcave l.**, a lens that has both surfaces concave. **biconvex l.**, a lens that has both surfaces convex. **bicylindrical l.**, one that has both surfaces cylindrical. **bifocal l.**, a spectacle lens made up of two segments with different refractive powers, ordinarily with the upper for far and the lower segment for near vision. **bispherical l.**, one that is spherical on both sides. **Brücke l.**, a combination of a double convex and double concave lens arranged so as to give considerable working distance. **cataract l.**, a powerful lens for spectacles to be used after cataract operation. **compound l.**, a lens that is made up of two or more segments. **concave l.**, dispersing l. **concavoconcave l.**, biconcave l. **contact l.**, a thin curved shell of glass or plastic that is applied directly over the eyeball to correct refractive errors. **converging l.**, **convex l.**, one which brings light to a focus. **convexoconcave l.**, one which has one convex and one concave surface. **Coquille plano l.**, one that is +8D on one side and −8D on the other. **Crookes' l.**, one made from glass rendered opaque to the ultraviolet and infrared rays and still transparent to light. **crossed l.**, one with front and back surfaces of different curvatures. **crystalline l.**, the lens of the eye. See *lens*, def. 2. **cylindrical l.**, one which is a section of a cylinder cut parallel to its axis, with one surface plane and the other concave or convex. **decentered l.**, one in which the visual line does not pass through the center. **dispersing l.**, one that disperses the rays of light. **immersion l.**, immersion objective. See under *objective*. **iseikonic l.**, one which is used to correct aniseikonia. Such lenses affect the focus of the rays entering the eye and also the magnification of the images formed on the retina. **meniscus l.**, a lens which has one convex and one concave surface. **meter l.**, one which focuses parallel rays at a distance of one meter. **minus l.**, a concave lens. **omnifocal l.**, a spectacle lens the power of which increases continuously and regularly in a downward direction, thereby avoiding the discontinuity in field and power which is apparent in bifocal and trifocal lenses. **orthoscopic l.**, one which gives a very flat and undisturbed field of vision. **periscopic l.**, a concavoconvex or concavoconcave lens. **planoconcave l.**, a lens with one plane and one concave side. **planoconvex l.**, a lens with one plane and one convex side. **plus l.**, a convex lens. **prosthetic l.**, artificial l. **punktal l.**, a toric lens which is corrected for astigmatism over the entire field of vision. **retroscopic l.**, one that is tilted inward at the top. **spherical l.**, one that is the segment of a sphere. **Stokes' l.**, a combination of a concave cylindrical and a convex cylindrical lens, used in the diagnosis of astigmatism. **toric l.**, a lens which is cut from a torus by a cut parallel to its axis of formation. Such a lens has power in all meridians, but different amounts on the same side. **trial l.**, any one of a set of lenses used in testing the vision. **trifocal l.**, a spectacle lens made up of three segments with different refractive powers, ordinarily with the upper for distant, the middle for intermediate, and the lower for near vision.

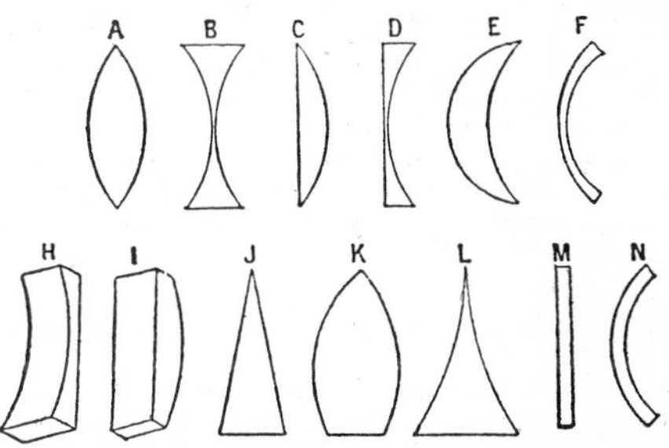

Lenses: A–F, Spherical lenses: A, biconvex; B, biconcave; C, planoconvex; D, planoconcave; E, periscopic convex; F, periscopic concave; H, I, cylindrical lenses, concave and convex; J, K, L, prismatic lenses; M, ordinary flat lens; N, planocoquille (Larousse).

lentectomize (len-tek′to-mīz). To deprive of the crystalline lens by surgical excision.

lentectomy (len-tek′to-me) [*lens* + Gr. *ektomē* excision]. Surgical excision of the crystalline lens.

lenticel (len′tĭ-sel). A lens-shaped gland, especially one of those at the base of the tongue.

lenticonus (len″tĭ-ko′nus) [*lens* + L. *conus* cone]. A conical protrusion of the substance of the crystalline lens, covered by capsule or connective tissue, occurring more frequently on the posterior surface, and usually affecting only one eye.

lenticula (len-tik′u-lah) [L.]. 1. The lenticular nucleus. 2. A freckle.

lenticular (len-tik′u-lar) [L. *lenticularis*]. 1. Pertaining to or shaped like a lens. 2. Pertaining to the crystalline lens. 3. Pertaining to the lenticular nucleus.

lenticulo-optic (len-tik″u-lo-op′tik). Pertaining to the lenticular nucleus and the optic thalamus.

lenticulostriate (len-tik″u-lo-stri′āt). Pertaining to the lenticular nucleus and the corpus striatum.

lenticulothalamic (len-tik″u-lo-thah-lam′ik). Relating to the lenticular nucleus and the optic thalamus.

lentiform (len′tĭ-form). Shaped like a lens.

lentigines (len-tij′ĭ-nēz) [L.]. Plural of *lentigo*.

lentiginosis (len-tij″ĭ-no′sis). The presence of multiple lentigines.

lentiglobus (len″tĭ-glo′bus) [*lens* + L. *globus* sphere]. An exaggerated curvation of the crystalline lens, producing a spherical bulging on its anterior surface.

lentigo (len-ti′go), pl. *lentigines* [L. "freckle"]. A brownish pigmented spot on the skin due to increased deposition of melanin and associated with an increased number of melanocytes at the epidermodermal junction.

lentigomelanosis (len-ti″go-mel″ah-no′sis) [*lentigo* + *melanosis*]. A disease of the skin characterized by presence of lentigines that increase in size and darken in color.

lentitis (len-ti′tis). Phakitis.

lentoptosis (len″to-to′sis) [*lens* + Gr. *ptōsis* falling]. Phacocele.

Lenzmann's point (lents′mahnz) [Richard *Lenzmann*, German physician, 1856–1927]. See under *point*.

Leo's test (la′ōz) [Hans *Leo*, German physician, 1854–1928]. See under *tests*.

Leonicenus (le-on″ĭ-se′nus) [It. Niccolò Leoniceno] (1428–1524). Professor of medicine at Padua, Bologna, and Ferrara; renowned for translating Hippocrates and Galen from Greek into Latin, for an early (1497) work on syphilis, and for a controversial book (1492) in which he courageously corrected many of the errors (particularly botanical) in Pliny's famous *Historia naturalis*.

Leonides (le-on′ĭ-dēz) (2nd–3rd century A.D.). A Greek surgeon who flourished in Rome, and whose writings are cited by Aëtius.

leontiasis (le″on-ti′ah-sis) [Gr. *leōn* lion]. 1. A bilateral and symmetrical hypertrophy of the bones of the face and cranium, leading to a lion-like facial expression. Called also *l. ossea* or *l. ossium*. 2. The facies leonina of leprosy.

Leontodon (le-on′to-don) [Gr. *leōn* lion + *odous* tooth]. Taraxacum.

Leopold's law (la′o-poldz) [Christian Gerhard *Leopold*, German physician, 1846–1911]. See under *law*.

leotropic (le″o-trop′ik) [Gr. *laios* left + *tropos* a turning]. Running spirally from right to left. Cf. *dexiotropic*.

Leotta's sign (la-ot′ahz) [Nicolò *Leotta*, Italian surgeon, born 1878]. See under *sign*.

leper (lep′er). A person afflicted with leprosy.

lepidic (lĕ-pid′ik) [Gr. *lepis* scale]. 1. Pertaining to scales. 2. Pertaining to embryonic layers.

lepido- (lep′ĭ-do) [Gr. *lepis* flake or scale]. Combining form meaning flake or scale.

lepidoma (lep″ĭ-do′mah) [*lepido-* + *-oma*]. A tumor derived from lepidic tissue: called also *rind tumor*. **endothelial l.,** a tumor originating from the endothelium of the blood vessels or lymphatics.

Lepidophyton (lep″ĭ-do-fi′ton) [*lepido-* + Gr. *phyton* plant]. A fungus said to be the cause of Tokelau ringworm.

Lepidoptera (lep″ĭ-dop′ter-ah) [*lepido-* + Gr. *pteron* wing]. An order of insects including the butterflies and moths.

Lepidoselaga (lep″ĭ-do-sĕ-lag′ah). A genus of the tabanid flies. *L. lepido′ta*, the common "motuca fly" of Brazil.

lepidosis (lep″ĭ-do′sis) [*lepido-* + *-osis*]. Any scaly eruption.

lepocyte (lep′o-sīt) [Gr. *lepos* rind + *-cyte*]. Any nucleated cell having a cell wall.

lepothrix (lep′o-thriks) [Gr. *lepos* scale + *thrix* hair]. Trichomycosis axillaris.

lepra (lep′rah) [Gr. *lepra* the leprosy, which makes the skin scaly]. Leprosy. **l. al′ba,** leprosy with absence of pigment from the skin. **l. alphoi′des, l. al′phos,** psoriasis. **l. anaesthet′ica,** leprosy with anesthetic spots. **l. ar′abum,** true leprosy. **l. conjuncti′vae,** leprosy with lesions of the conjunctiva. **l. graeco′rum,** a term vaguely applied to various diseases bearing more or less resemblance to true leprosy. **l. maculo′sa,** leprosy characterized by maculae (spots) of the skin. **l. mu′tilans,** leprosy with mutilation. **l. nervo′rum,** leprosy with nervous complications. **l. nervo′sa,** anesthetic leprosy. **l. tuberculoi′des** (Jadassohn), leprosy with flat intracutaneous granulomas resembling tuberculosis. **Willan's l.,** psoriasis.

lepraphobia (lep″rah-fo′be-ah) [Gr. *lepra* leprosy + *phobia*]. Morbid dread of leprosy.

leprid (lep′rid). An erythematous macule which is the earliest evidence of neural leprosy.

lepride (lep′rid). Leprid.

leprologist (lep-rol′o-jist). An expert in the study and treatment of leprosy.

leprology (lep-rol′o-je). The study of leprosy.

leproma (lep-ro′mah). A superficial granulomatous nodule, the characteristic lesion of leprosy.

lepromatous (lep-ro′mah-tus). Pertaining to leproma.

leprosarium (lep″ro-sa′re-um) [L.]. Leprosary.

leprosary (lep′ro-sār″e) [L. *leprosa′rium*]. A hospital or colony for lepers.

leprosy (lep′ro-se) [Gr. *lepros* scaly, scabby, rough]. A chronic communicable disease, caused by a specific microorganism, the *Mycobacterium leprae*, which produces various granulomatous lesions in the skin, the mucous membranes, and the peripheral nervous system. Two clinical types are recognized: (1) cutaneous, lepromatous, or nodular, and (2) neural or maculo-anesthetic. A combination of these types is called *mixed leprosy*. Called also *lepra* and *elephantiasis graecorum*. **anesthetic l.,** a variety of leprosy marked by hyperesthesia, followed by anesthesia, paralysis, ulceration, and gangrene. **Asturian l.,** pellagra. **cutaneous l.,** nodular l. **Italian l.,** pellagra. **Kabyle l.,** a hereditary disease of Kabyle, probably tertiary syphilis. **lazarine l.,** a clinical form of leprosy characterized by bullous formations followed by eschars and mutilating ulcers. **lepromatous l.,** nodular l. **Lombardy l.,** pellagra. **macular l., maculo-anesthetic l.,** neural l. **murine l.,** rat l. **neural l.,** a form in which nerves are affected, with loss of nerve function and of sensation in the area of distribution of the nerve, with atrophy of tissue and sometimes spontaneous amputation. **nodular l.,** a form of leprosy marked by the development of masses of granulation tissue, called leproma, which may appear superficially, causing great distortion. **rat l.,** a disease found occasionally in rats. It much resembles human leprosy and the lesions contain a *Mycobacterium leprae murium* that is very similar to *M. tuberculosis hominis* but not identical. **trophoneurotic l.,** anesthetic leprosy. **tuberculoid l.,** neural leprosy in which the tissue reaction resembles that of tuberculosis. **water-buffalo l.,** a slowly developing and chronic condition in water buffalo characterized by the presence of acid-fast bacilli in cells of the reticuloendothelial system. **white l.,** lepra alba.

leprotic (lep-rot′ik). Pertaining to or affected with leprosy.

leprotine (lep′ro-tin). A carotenoid provitamin from acid-fast bacteria from a case of leprosy. It gives thin copper-red needles melting at 198–200°F.

leprous (lep′rus) [L. *leprosus*]. Affected with leprosy.

leptandra (lep-tan′drah) [Gr. *leptos* thin + *anēr* anther]. The rhizome and rootlets of *Veronica virginica:* aperient, cholagogue, and tonic.

leptandrin (lep-tan′drin). A bitter glycoside from leptandra, whose active properties it possesses.

leptazol (lep′tah-zol). Pentylenetetrazol.

lepto- (lep′to) [Gr. *leptos* slender]. Combining form meaning slender, thin, or delicate.

leptocephalia (lep″to-se-fa′le-ah). Abnormal tallness and narrowness of the head.

leptocephalic (lep″to-se-fal′ik). Characterized by leptocephalia.

leptocephalous (lep″to-sef′ah-lus). Leptocephalic.

leptocephalus (lep″to-sef′ah-lus) [*lepto-* + Gr. *kephalē* head]. A person with an abnormally tall, narrow head.

leptochroa (lep-to-kro′ah) [*lepto-* + Gr. *chroa* skin]. Abnormal delicacy of skin.

leptochromatic (lep″to-kro-mat′ik) [*lepto-* + *chromatin*]. Having a fine chromatin network.

leptochymia (lep-to-ki′me-ah) [*lepto-* + Gr. *chymos* juice + *-ia*]. Meagerness of the body fluids.

Leptoconops (lep″to-ko′nops). A genus of blood-sucking flies of the family Heleidae.

leptocyte (lep′to-sīt) [*lepto-* + Gr. *kytos* cell]. An erythrocyte characterized by a hemoglobinated peripheral border, surrounding a clear area containing a "bull's-eye" center of pigment; observed in certain hemoglobinopathies, particularly that involving hemoglobin C and the thalassemia syndromes. Called also *target,* or "*Mexican hat,*" *erythrocyte.*

leptocytosis (lep″to-si-to′sis). The presence of leptocytes in the blood.

leptodactylous (lep″to-dak′tĭ-lus) [*lepto-* + Gr. *daktylos* finger]. Possessing slender digits.

leptodactyly (lep″to-dak′tĭ-le). Abnormal slenderness of the digits.

Leptodera pellio (lep-to′der-ah pel′e-o). *Rhabditis genitalis.*

leptodermic (lep″to-der′mik) [*lepto-* + Gr. *derma* skin]. Thin skinned.

leptodontous (lep″to-don′tus) [*lepto-* + Gr. *odous* tooth]. Having slender teeth.

leptomeninges (lep″to-me-nin′jēz). Plural of *leptomeninx.*

leptomeningioma (lep″to-me-nin″je-o′mah). A tumor of the leptomeninges.

leptomeningitis (lep″to-men″in-ji′tis) [*leptomeninx* + *-itis*]. Inflammation of the pia and arachnoid of the brain or spinal cord. Leptomeningitis is variously qualified as acute, basilar, cerebrospinal, chronic, epidemic, external, infantile, intracranial, purulent, nonpurulent, serous, tuberculous, etc. **l. exter′na,** arachnitis. **l. inter′na,** inflammation of the pia mater. **sarcomatous l.,** diffuse sarcomatous infiltration of the pia mater.

leptomeningopathy (lep″to-men″in-gop′ah-the) [*leptomeninges* + Gr. *pathos* disease]. Any disease of the leptomeninges.

leptomeninx (lep″to-men′inks), pl. *leptomenin′ges* [*lepto-* + Gr. *mēninx* membrane]. The pia-arachnoid.

Leptomitus (lep-tom′ĭ-tus). A genus of mycetic fungi. *L. epider′midis* has been found in pustules on the hand. *L. uroph′ilus* has been found in the urine. *L. vagi′nae* has been found in chronic vaginitis.

leptomonad (lep″to-mo′nad). The simple flagellate stage of a trypanosome or of an organism of the genus Leishmania.

leptomonas (lep″to-mo′nas). Leptomonad.

leptonema (lep″to-ne′mah) [*lepto-* + Gr. *nēma* thread]. A presynaptic stage of miosis in which the chromatin is in the form of fine spireme threads.

leptonomorphology (lep″to-no-mor-fol′o-je). The morphology of membranes.

leptopellic (lep″to-pel′ik) [*lepto-* + Gr. *pella* bowl]. Having a narrow pelvis.

leptophonia (lep″to-fo′ne-ah) [*lepto-* + Gr. *phōnē* voice]. Weakness or feebleness of the voice.

leptophonic (lep″to-fon′ik). Pertaining to or characterized by leptophonia.

leptoprosope (lep-top′ro-sōp). An individual exhibiting leptoprosopia.

leptoprosopia (lep″to-pro-so′pe-ah) [*lepto-* + Gr. *prosōpon* face + *-ia*]. Narrowness of the face, with slender features, round, open orbits, long nose, narrow nostrils, and small mouth.

leptoprosopic (lep″to-pro-so′pik). Pertaining to or characterized by leptoprosopia.

Leptopsylla musculi (lep″to-sil′ah mus′ku-li). *Ctenopsylla segnis.*

leptorrhine (lep′to-rīn) [*lepto-* + Gr. *rhis* nose]. Having a nasal index below 48.

leptoscope (lep′to-skōp) [*lepto-* + Gr. *skopein* to examine]. An optical apparatus for examining and measuring the thickness of a monomolecular film of tissue placed on a glass slide.

leptosomatic (lep″to-so-mat′ik) [*lepto-* + Gr. *sōma* body]. Having a light, thin body.

leptosome (lep′to-sōm). A person with a slender light physique.

Leptospira (lep″to-spi′rah) [*lepto-* + Gr. *speira* coil]. A genus of microorganisms of the family Treponemataceae, order Spirochaetales, made up of finely coiled organisms 6 to 20 μ long, the spirals measuring 0.3 μ in depth and 0.5 μ in amplitude. Separated into antigenic varieties or serotypes given species status. The organisms are pathogenic for man and other mammals, and usually occur in rodent reservoirs of infection. **L. austra′lis,** the etiologic agent of canefield fever in Australia and Indonesia. **L. autumna′lis,** the etiologic agent of akiyama and Hasami-Netsu seven-day fever in Japan, and of Fort Bragg fever in the United States. **L. canico′la,** the etiologic agent of canine leptospirosis or Stuttgart disease in dogs and canicola fever in man. **L. grippotypho′sa,** the etiologic agent of mud fever, field fever, and Schlammfieber in western Europe. **L. hy′os,** an etiologic agent of swineherd's disease. **L. icterohaemorrha′giae,** the etiologic agent of infectious jaundice, or Weil's disease, in man and yellows disease in dogs. **L. pomo′na,** an etiologic agent of swineherd's disease and Pomona fever.

leptospire (lep′to-spīr). An individual organism belonging to the genus Leptospira.

leptospirosis (lep″to-spi-ro′sis). The disease produced by Leptospira in the blood. **l. ictero-hemorrha′gica,** leptospiral jaundice.

leptostaphyline (lep″to-staf′ĭ-līn) [*lepto-* + Gr. *staphylē* bunch of grapes, uvula]. Having a palatal index of 79.9 or less.

leptotene (lep′to-tēn) [*lepto-* + Gr. *tainia* ribbon]. In miosis, the stage in which the chromosomes are slender, like threads.

leptothricosis (lep″to-thri-ko′sis). Leptotrichosis.

Leptothrix (lep′to-thriks) [*lepto-* + Gr. *thrix* hair]. A genus of microorganisms of the family Chlamydobacteriaceae, order Chlamydobacteriales, made up of attached or unattached, straight or spirally twisted trichomes, with a sheath originally thin and colorless but later becoming thicker and yellow or brown, with the deposition of ferric hydroxide. Widely distributed, and usually found in fresh water, it includes 12 species: *L. discoph′ora, L. echi′nata, L. epiphyt′ica, L. lopho′lea, L.*

ma'jor, L. ochra'cea, L. pseudovacuola'ta, L. side'ropous, L. sku'jae, L. therma'lis, L. volu'bilis, and *L. winograd'skii.*

Leptotrichia (lep″to-trik′e-ah) [*lepto-* + Gr. *triches* hairs]. A former name of a genus of bacterial organisms, no longer recognized as a valid genus. **L. bucca′lis,** a nonpathogenic species found in the healthy mouth. Called also *Vignal's bacillus.* **L. placoi′des,** a species found in a tooth canal.

leptotrichosis (lep″to-trĭ-ko′sis). Infection with any leptothrix. **l. conjuncti′vae,** Parinaud's conjunctivitis.

Leptotrombidium akamushi (lep″to-trom-bid′e-um ak″ah-moo′she). *Trombicula akamushi.*

leptuntic (lep-tun′tik) [Gr. *leptynein* to thin]. A medicine that thins the blood.

Leptus (lep′tus) [L.]. A name for the larval form of mites of the genus *Trombicula* and *Eutrombicula.* **L. akamu′shi,** *Trombicula akamushi.*

Lerch's percussion [Otto *Lerch,* physician in New Orleans]. See under *percussion.*

leresis (ler-e′sis) [Gr. *lērēsis*]. Agitated or senile loquacity or garrulousness.

Leri's sign (la′rēz) [André *Leri,* French physician, 1875–1930]. See under *sign.*

Leriche's disease, operation (lĕ-rēsh′ez) [René *Leriche,* French surgeon, 1879–1955]. See under *disease,* and *periarterial sympathectomy,* under *sympathectomy.*

leritine (ler′ĭ-tīn). Trade mark for preparations of anileridine.

Lermoyez's syndrome (ler″moi-yāz′) [Marcel *Lermoyez,* French otolaryngologist, 1858–1929]. See under *syndrome.*

Leroux's method (ler-ooz′) [Laurent Charles Pierre *Leroux,* French accoucheur, 1730–1792]. See under *method.*

l.e.s. Abbreviation for *local excitatory state.*

lesbian (les′be-an). 1. Pertaining to homosexuality between females. 2. A female homosexual.

lesbianism (les′be-an-izm). Homosexuality between women.

Leschke's syndrome (lesh′kez) [Erich *Leschke,* Berlin physician, 1877–1933]. See under *syndrome.*

Lesieur-Privey sign (leh′se-er-pre-va′e) [Charles *Lesieur,* French physician, 1876–1919; Paul *Privey,* French physician]. Albuminoreaction.

lesion (le′zhun) [L. *laesio; laedere* to hurt]. Any pathological or traumatic discontinuity of tissue or loss of function of a part. **coarse l.,** macroscopical l. **coin l.,** a rounded coinlike tumor. **Councilman l.,** a noninflammatory hyaline necrosis seen in liver cells in yellow fever, which forms a dense acidophilic mass in the cytoplasm. **degenerative l.,** one caused by or characterized by degeneration. **depressive l.,** one that causes diminution of functional activity. **destructive l.,** one which leads to the obliteration of an organ or the abolishment of its functions. **diffuse l.,** one that spreads widely and irregularly. **discharging l.,** one attended with great and sudden liberation of energy. **disseminated l.,** one that involves a number of separate spots. **Duret's l.,** effusion of blood in the region of the fourth ventricle as a result of slight injury. **Ebstein's l.,** hyaline degeneration and insular necrosis of epithelial cells of the renal tubules in diabetes mellitus. **focal l.,** one that has a small area and definite limits. **functional l.,** one which leads to no obvious or discoverable change of structure, but which causes disturbances of function. **Ghon's primary l.,** Ghon tubercle. **gross l.,** a lesion that is visible to the naked eye. **histologic l.,** microscopical l. **impaction l.,** an osteopathic term for a lesion of any spinal joint in which there is present abnormal thickening of the intervertebral disk with approximation of all the bony parts. **indiscriminate l.,** a lesion affecting different distinct parts or systems of the body. **initial syphilitic l.,** true or hard chancre. **irritative l.,** one which stimulates the functions of the part where it is situated. **local l.,** one in the nervous system giving origin to distinctive local symptoms. **macroscopical l.,** one that is attended by changes obvious to the unaided eye. **microscopical l., minute l.,** one that is discoverable only by the microscope. **mixed l.,** indiscriminate l. **molar l.,** macroscopical lesion. **molecular l.,** a lesion not visible even with the aid of a microscope. **nervous l.,** one which affects nervous tissue. **organic l.,** structural l. **partial l.,** one which involves a part only of an organ or of the diameter of a conducting tract. **peripheral l.,** a lesion of the nerve endings. **precancerous l.,** a lesion in a tissue in which the cells are likely to become malignant. **primary l.,** chancre, the earliest lesion of syphilis. **ring-wall l.,** multiple small ring hemorrhages which simulate proliferation of a glial ring; seen in pernicious anemia. **structural l.,** one that produces an obvious change in a tissue. **systemic l.,** one limited to a system or set of organs with a common function. **total l.,** one involving the whole of an organ or of the diameter of a conducting tract. **toxic l.,** one due to a poison. **traumatic l.,** one produced by injury. **trophic l.,** a lesion manifested by a disturbance in the nutrition of a part. **vascular l.,** one which affects a vessel or vessels. **wire-loop l.,** thickened capillary walls of some parts of a glomerular tuft in disseminated lupus erythematosus.

lesocupethy (les″o-ku′peh-the) [*le*arning, *so*ciety, *cu*lture, and *pe*rsonality *th*eor*y*]. A term suggested by Murdock to embrace the unified psychological and social sciences.

Lesser's test (les′erz) [Fritz *Lesser,* Berlin dermatologist, born 1873]. See under *tests.*

Lesshaft's space, triangle (les′hafts) [Pyotr Frantsovich *Lesshaft,* Russian physician, 1836–1909]. See under *space.*

lethal (le′thal) [L. *lethalis,* from *lethum* death]. Deadly; fatal.

lethality (le-thal′ĭ-te). The ratio of deaths from a given disease to existing cases of that disease.

lethargus (le-thar′gus) [Gr. *lēthargos* lethargic, forgetful]. African sleeping sickness.

lethargy (leth′ar-je) [Gr. *lēthargia* drowsiness]. A condition of drowsiness of mental origin. **African l.,** Congo trypanosomiasis. **hysteric l.,** the sleep stage of hypnosis. **induced l.,** hypnotic trance. **lucid l.,** loss of will power with consequent inability to act, although intellectually conscious.

lethe (le′the) [Gr. *lēthē* forgetfulness]. Amnesia; complete loss of memory.

letheomania (le″the-o-ma′ne-ah) [Gr. *lēthaios* oblivious + *mania* madness]. Narcotic addiction.

letheral (le′ther-al). Pertaining to lethe.

lethologica (leth-o-loj′ĭ-kah) [Gr. *lēthē* forgetfulness + *logos* word]. Inability to remember the proper word.

Letterer-Siwe disease (let′ter-er si′we) [Erich *Letterer,* German physician, born 1895; Sture August *Siwe,* German physician, born 1897]. See under *disease.*

leuceine (lu-se′in). One of a series of compounds related to leucine, but having two atoms less of hydrogen in the molecule.

leucemia (lu-se′me-ah). Leukemia.

leucine (lu′sin) [Gr. *leukos* white]. A crystallizable amino acid, $C_6H_{13}NO_2$, or amino-isocaproic acid; essential for optimal growth in infants and for nitrogen equilibrium in human adults. It is formed by the digestion or hydrolytic cleavage of protein and found normally in the spleen and pancreas, in various tissues, and in the urine in disease, especially in cases of acute yellow atrophy of the liver (Proust, 1818; Braconnot, 1820). In the liver it is converted into urea.

leucinethylester (lu″sin-eth″il-es′ter). An oily liquid, $(CH_3)_2.CH.CH_2CH(NH_2).CO_2.C_2H_5$.

leucinimide (lu″sin-im′id). The anhydride of leucine, $C_{12}H_{22}N_2O_2$, a decomposition product of certain proteins.

leucinosis (lu″sĭ-no′sis). Any condition in which leucine appears in the urine.

leucinuria (lu″sin-u′re-ah) [*leucine* + Gr. *ouron* urine + *-ia*]. The presence of leucine in the urine.

leucismus (lu-siz′mus) [Gr. *leukos* white + *-izō* + *-mos*]. A state of whiteness. **l. pilo′rum,** an abnormal streak or spot of white in the hair of the scalp.

leucitis (lu-si′tis). Scleritis.

leuco- (lu′ko) [Gr. *leukos* white]. Combining form meaning white. See also words beginning *leuko-*.

leucocyte (lu′ko-sīt). Leukocyte.

Leucocytozoon (lu″ko-si″to-zo′on). A genus of sporozoan parasites found in the blood cells of birds. **L. danilews′kyi,** a species found in the little owl (*Glaucidium noctuae*) and in the wood owl (*Syrnium aluco*). Its invertebrate host is the mosquito, *Culex pipiens*. **L. maclean′i,** a species found in the common pheasant (*Phasianus colchicus*). **L. pal′lidum.** See *Ross' bodies*, under *body*. **L. sakharof′fi,** a species found in the crow (*Corvus cornix*). **L. smith′i,** a species found in the domestic turkey (*Meleagris gallopavo*). **L. syphil′idis,** a sporogenic coccidioidal protozoon believed by McDonough to be the cause of syphilis, the *Treponema pallidum* being one stage of its life cycle.

Leucoium (lu-ko′ĭ-um) [L.; Gr. *leukos* white + *ion* violet]. A genus of old world amaryllidaceous plants. *L. aesti′vum* and *L. ver′num* (called snowflake) are common in garden culture: emetic and poisonous.

leucon (lu′kon). Leukon.

Leuconostoc (lu″ko-nos′tok). A genus of microorganisms of the tribe Streptococceae, family Lactobacillaceae, order Eubacteriales, made up of three species of slime-forming saprophytic bacteria found in milk and fruit juices, including *L. citrovo′rum*, *L. dextran′icum*, and *L. mesenteroi′des*.

leucopterin (lu-kop′ter-in). A yellow pigment, $C_{19}H_{19}O_{11}N_5$, isolated from butterfly wings.

leucosin (lu′ko-sin). An albumin found in the cereal grains.

leucotine (lu-ko′tin). An alkaloid, $C_{21}H_{20}O_6$, from paracoto.

leucotomy (lu-kot′o-me). Leukotomy.

Leucotrichaceae (lu″ko-trĭ-ka′se-e). A systematic family of schizomycetes (order Beggiatoales), made up of short cylindrical cells occurring in long trichomes, found in fresh and salt water containing decomposing algae. It includes a single genus, *Leucothrix*. These microorganisms resemble the blue-green algae but do not contain photosynthetic pigments.

leucovorin (lu″ko-vo′rin). A derivative of folic acid, which is effective against folic acid antagonists: used in treatment of megaloblastic anemias.

Leudet's bruit, tinnitus (led-āz′) [Théodor Emile *Leudet*, physician at Rouen, 1825–1887]. See under *tinnitus*.

leukapheresis (lu″kah-fĕ-re′sis) [*leuk*ocyte + Gr. *aphairesis* removal]. The selective removal of leukocytes from withdrawn blood, which is then retransfused in the patient.

leukasmus (lu-kaz′mus). 1. Albinism. 2. Leukoderma.

leukemia (lu-ke′me-ah) [Gr. *leukos* white + *haima* blood + *-ia*]. A fatal disease of the blood-forming organs, characterized by a marked increase in the number of leukocytes and their precursors in the blood, together with enlargement and proliferation of the lymphoid tissue of the spleen, lymphatic glands, and bone marrow. The disease is attended with progressive anemia, internal hemorrhage (as into the retina, etc.), and increasing exhaustion. Leukemia is classified clinically on the basis of (1) the duration and character of the disease—*acute* or *chronic;* (2) the type of cell involved—*myeloid* (*myelogenous*), *lymphoid* (*lymphogenous*) or *monocytic;* (3) increase or nonincrease in the number of abnormal cells in the blood—*leukemic* or *aleukemic* (*subleukemic*). **aleukemic l., aleukocythemic l.,** leukemia in which the white blood cell count is either normal or below normal. **aplastic l.,** leukemia with diminution of both red and white cells with an increase of the proportion of large atypical leukocytes. **basophilic l., basophilocytic l.,** leukemia in which many basophilic granulocytes (mast cells) are present in the blood. **l. cu′tis,** involvement of the skin in leukemia, with tumor-like lesions composed of small round cells resembling leukocytes. **Ebstein's l.,** leukemia which follows an extremely rapid course. **embryonal l.,** stem cell l. **eosinophilic l.,** a form of leukemia in which the eosinophil is the predominating cell. Although resembling chronic myelocytic leukemia in many ways this form of leukemia may follow an acute course despite the absence of predominantly blast forms in the peripheral blood. **l. of fowls,** an infectious disease of the hematopoietic organs of fowls with atrophy of the bone marrow and changes in the viscera. **Fränkel's l.,** acute leukemia with long mononuclear lymphocytes. **granulocytic l.,** myelocytic l. **hemoblastic l., hemocytoblastic l.,** stem cell l. **histiocytic l.,** acute monocytic l. **leukopenic l.,** leukemia in which the white blood cell count is normal or below normal. It may be lymphogenous, monocytic, or myelogenous. **lienomyelogenous l.,** myelocytic l. **lymphatic l., lymphoblastic l., lymphocytic l., lymphogenous l., lymphoid l.,** leukemia associated with hyperplasia and overactivity of the lymphoid tissue, in which the leukocytes are lymphocytes or lymphoblasts. **lymphoidocytic l.,** stem cell l. **lymphosarcoma cell l.,** a form of lymphocytic or lymphoblastic lymphoma characterized by the presence of neoplastic lymphocytes in the peripheral blood. **Mallory l.,** leukemia caused by tar, indole, and benzol. **mast cell l.,** a condition similar to other types of leukemia but characterized by the presence of overwhelming numbers of tissue mast cells in the peripheral blood. **megakaryocytic l.,** hemorrhagic thrombocythemia. **micromyeloblastic l.,** a form of granulocytic leukemia in which the immature, nucleoli-containing cells are small and are distinguishable from lymphocytes only by supravital staining. **mixed l.,** myelocytic l. **monocytic l.,** leukemia in which the predominating leukocytes are identified as monocytes. The disease is generally divided into two main categories: the Naegeli type, in which many of the cells resemble myeloblasts, or cells of the myeloid series; and the Schilling type, in which the cells more truly resemble monocytes or histiocytes. **Moore's infectious l.,** fowl typhoid. **myeloblastic l.,** leukemia in which myeloblasts predominate. **myelocytic l., myelogenous l., myeloid granulocytic l.,** leukemia arising from myeloid tissue in which the granular, polymorphonuclear leukocytes predominate. **Naegeli l.** See *monocytic l.* **plasma cell l.,** leukemia in which the predominating cell in the peripheral blood is the plasma cell; whether this is a distinct form of leukemia or a phase of multiple myeloma remains moot. **Rieder cell l.,** a form of myeloblastic leukemia in which the blood contains asynchronously developed cells with immature cytoplasm and a lobulated, indented, comparatively more mature nucleus. **Schilling's l.** See *monocytic l.* **splenomedullary l., splenomyelogenous l.,** myelocytic l. **stem cell l.,** a form of leukemia in which the predominating cell is so immature and primitive that its classification becomes exceedingly difficult. Called also *embryonal l.*, *hemoblastic l.*, *hemocytoblastic l.*, *lymphoidocytic l.*, and *undifferentiated cell l.* **subleukemic l.,** aleukemic l. **undifferentiated cell l.,** stem cell l.

leukemic (lu-ke′mik). Pertaining to or affected with leukemia.

leukemid (lu-kem′id). A heteromorphic, nonspecific skin lesion of leukemia which does not represent cutaneous infiltrations with leukemic cells.

leukemogen (lu-ke′mo-jen). Any substance which causes or produces leukemia.

leukemogenesis (lu-ke″mo-jen′e-sis). The induction of or development of leukemia.

leukemogenic (lu-ke″mo-jen′ik). Causing leukemia.

leukemoid (lu-ke′moid) [*leukemia* + Gr. *eidos* form]. Characterized by blood and sometimes clinical findings resembling true leukemia to such a degree that initial differentiation between the process causing the observed alterations and leukemia becomes extremely difficult.

leukencephalitis (lūk″en-sef″ah-li′tis) [*leuko-* + *encephalitis*]. Inflammation of the white matter of the brain.

leukergic (lu-ker′jik). Pertaining to or characterized by leukergy.

leukergy (lu′ker-je) [*leuk*ocytes + Gr. *ergon* work]. Appearance in the blood of peculiar (leukergic) leukocytes, which are recognizable by their adhesiveness and tendency to agglomerate in cytologically homogeneous groups; by their large glycogen and alkaline phosphate content; by their greater motility and stronger phagocytic power; and by their ability to shift to the foci of infection as well as to the blood depots (lung, spleen, liver). Leukergy is a defense mechanism, working in various inflammatory states, in some infections, in normal pregnancy, and after profuse bleeding, as well as in some other cases of stress.

leukexosis (lu″kek-so′sis). An aggregation of dead leukocytes in one of the channels of the body.

leukin (lu′kin). 1. A relatively thermostabile lytic substance that can be extracted from polymorphonuclear leukocytes and that attacks particularly *Bacillus anthracis* and other spore-bearing aerobes. Called also *leukocytic alexin* and *leukocytic endolysin.* 2. Leucine.

leuko- (lu′ko) [Gr. *leukos* white]. Combining form meaning white, or denoting relationship to a white corpuscle or leukocyte.

leuko-agglutinin (lu″ko-ah-gloo′tĭ-nin). An agglutinin which acts upon a leukocyte.

leukoblast (lu′ko-blast) [*leuko-* + Gr. *blastos* germ]. An immature leukocyte. **granular l.,** premyelocyte.

leukoblastosis (lu″ko-blas-to′sis). A general term for proliferation of leukocytes, including myelosis and lymphadenosis.

leukochloroma (lu″ko-klo-ro′mah). A disease of fowls resembling chloroma of man.

leukocidin (lu″ko-si′din) [*leuko*cyte + L. *caedere* to kill]. A substance produced by some pathogenic bacteria that is toxic to polymorphonuclear leukocytes, killing the cells with or without lysis.

leukocytal (lu″ko-si′tal). Pertaining to leukocytes.

leukocyte (lu′ko-sit) [*leuko-* + Gr. *kytos* cell]. Any colorless, amoeboid cell mass. Applied especially to one of the formed elements of the blood, consisting of a colorless granular mass of protoplasm, having ameboid movements, and varying in size between 0.005 and 0.015 mm. in diameter. The following varieties of leukocytes are found in normal blood: I. **Agranular, nongranular,** or **lymphoid l's** (*agranulocytes* or *lymphocytes*): (1) *Lymphocytes,* possessing a round, chromatic nucleus; (2) *monocytes,* possessing a pole-indented nucleus. II. **Granular l's** (*granulocytes*): (3) The *polymorphonuclear* or *polynuclear neutrophil l's* (*heterophil l's*), finely granular neutrophil cells with an irregularly lobed nucleus; (4) *eosinophil l's,* coarsely granular eosinophil cells with a bilobed nucleus; (5) *basophil l's,* coarsely granular basophil cells with a bent lobed nucleus. Other forms of leukocytes are found in disease, among which are myelocytes, myeloblasts, lymphoblasts, plasma cells, and various degenerated forms of cells. **endothelial l.,** Mallory's name for the large wandering cells of the circulating blood and the tissues which have notable phagocytic properties. See *endotheliocyte.* **globular l's,** small wandering lymphocytes found in the epithelium of the crypts of the intestines. They have a small dark nucleus and a swollen body and contain large droplets that stain bright red with eosin. **heterophil l's,** the most numerous group of granular leukocytes in the blood of all vertebrates. The granules vary in size and staining property in the different species, being acidophilic in some, amphophilic in others, neutrophilic in some, including man, and basophilic in other groups. In still other species the granules are invisible. **hyaline l.,** monocyte. **leukergic l's,** peculiar leukocytes appearing in the blood in leukergy (q. v.). **mast l.,** a name sometimes used to designate the circulating blood basophil, which is morphologically and histogenetically different from the tissue mast cell. **motile l.,** a leukocyte which has the power of ameboid movement. **nonmotile l.,** a leukocyte which has not the power of ameboid movement. **transitional l.,** monocyte. **Türk's irritation l.,** Türk cell.

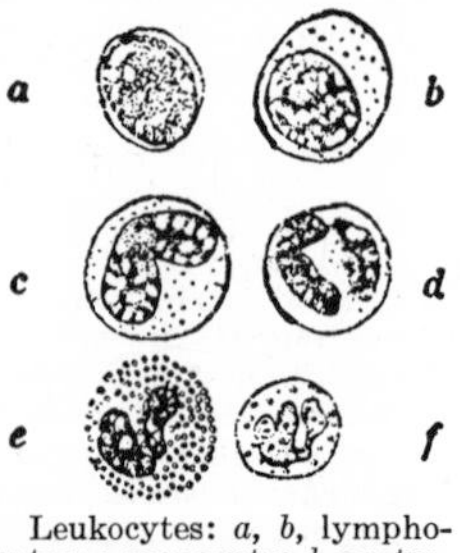

a b c d e f

Leukocytes: *a, b,* lymphocytes; *c,* monocyte; *d,* neutrophil; *e,* eosinophil; *f,* basophil.

leukocythemia (lu″ko-si-the′me-ah) [*leuko-* + *-cyte* + Gr. *haima* blood + *-ia*]. Leukemia.

leukocytic (lu″ko-sit′ik). Pertaining to leukocytes.

leukocytoblast (lu″ko-si′to-blast) [*leukocyte* + Gr. *blastos* germ]. A cell from which a leukocyte develops.

leukocytogenesis (lu″ko-si″to-jen′e-sis) [*leukocyte* + Gr. *genesis* production]. The formation of leukocytes.

leukocytoid (lu′ko-si″toid) [*leukocyte* + Gr. *eidos* form]. Resembling a leukocyte.

leukocytology (lu″ko-si-tol′o-je). The study of leukocytes.

leukocytolysin (lu″ko-si-tol′ĭ-sin). A lysin which causes dissolution of leukocytes.

leukocytolysis (lu″ko-si-tol′ĭ-sis) [*leukocyte* + Gr. *lysis* dissolution]. The breaking down or destruction of leukocytes. **venom l.,** destruction of leukocytes with snake venom.

leukocytolytic (lu″ko-si″to-lit′ik). 1. Pertaining to, characterized by, or causing leukocytolysis. 2. An agent that causes leukocytolysis.

leukocytoma (lu″ko-si-to′mah) [*leukocyte* + *-oma*]. A tumor-like mass of leukocytes.

leukocytometer (lu″ko-si-tom′e-ter) [*leukocyte* + Gr. *metron* measure]. An instrument used in counting the leukocytes.

leukocytopenia (lu″ko-si″to-pe′ne-ah) [*leukocyte* + Gr. *penia* poverty]. Leukopenia.

leukocytophagy (lu″ko-si-tof′ah-je) [*leukocyte* + Gr. *phagein* to devour]. The ingestion and destruction of leukocytes by histiocytes of the reticulo-endothelial system.

leukocytoplania (lu″ko-si″to-pla′ne-ah) [*leukocyte* + Gr. *planē* wandering]. The wandering of leukocytes or their passage through a membrane.

leukocytopoiesis (lu″ko-si″to-poi-e′sis) [*leukocyte* + Gr. *poiein* to make]. The production of leukocytes.

leukocytoreaction (lu″ko-si″to-re-ak′shun). Leukocytic reaction.

leukocytosis (lu″ko-si-to′sis). An increase in the number of leukocytes in the blood. It occurs normally during digestion and in pregnancy, and is seen as a pathologic condition in inflammation, traumatic anemia, various fevers, etc. **absolute l.,** increase in the total number of leukocytes in the blood. **active l.,** one in which the increased leukocytes are capable of spontaneous movement and of active emigration into the blood. **agonal l.**, leukocytosis occurring just before death. **basophilic l.**, increase of the basophilic leukocytes in the blood. **emotional l.**, a high white cell count associated with emotional disturbance. **mononuclear l.**, mononucleosis. **neutrophilic l.**, an increase in the number of polymorphonuclear neutrophil leukocytes in the blood. **passive l.**, leukocytosis in which the increased leukocytes are not capable of motion and have been washed into the blood by mechanical forces. **pathologic l.**, that occurring as the result of some morbid condition, such as infection or trauma. **physiologic l.**, that caused by factors other than disease or trauma. **pure l.**, increase of the polymorphonuclear leukocytes of the blood. **relative l.**, increase in the proportion of any variety of leukocytes in the blood, without increase of the total number of leukocytes. **terminal l.**, agonal l. **toxic l.**, leukocytosis occurring in intoxication with blood poisons.

leukocytotactic (lu″ko-si″to-tak′tik). Pertaining to or marked by leukotaxis.

leukocytotaxis (lu″ko-si″to-tak′sis). Leukotaxis.

leukocytotherapy (lu″ko-si″to-ther′ah-pe). Treatment by the administration of leukocytes.

leukocytotoxin (lu″ko-si″to-tok′sin). A toxin which destroys leukocytes.

leukocytotropic (lu″ko-si″to-trop′ik). Having a selective affinity for leukocytes.

Leukocytozoon (lu″ko-si″to-zo′on) [*leuko-* + *cyto-* + Gr. *zoon* animal]. A genus of Haemosporidia containing numerous species parasitic in the blood corpuscles of birds.

leukocyturia (lu″ko-si-tu′re-ah) [*leukocyte* + Gr. *ouron* urine + *-ia*]. The discharge of leukocytes in the urine.

leukoderivative (lu″ko-de-riv′ah-tiv). Any white derivative from a pigment or coloring matter.

leukoderma (lu″ko-der′mah) [*leuko-* + Gr. *derma* skin]. An acquired type of localized loss of melanin pigmentation of the skin, differing from vitiligo only in that the cause may be more or less apparent. **l. acquisi′tum centrif′ugum,** depigmentation of the skin appearing about a pigmented nevus. Called also *Sutton's disease*.

leukodermatous (lu″ko-der′mah-tus). Pertaining to or characterized by leukoderma.

leukodermia (lu″ko-der′me-ah). Leukoderma.

leukodermic (lu″ko-der′mik). Leukodermatous.

leukodextrin (lu″ko-deks′trin). A compound formed in the transformation of starch into sugar.

leukodiagnosis (lu″ko-di″ag-no′sis). Diagnosis based on the number, proportion of varieties, or specific sensitiveness of leukocytes.

leukodystrophy (lu″ko-dis′tro-fe). Disturbance of the white substance of the brain. **hereditary cerebral l.**, familial centrolobar sclerosis.

leukoedema (lu″ko-e-de′mah). An abnormality of buccal mucosa, resembling early leukoplakia, consisting of an increase in thickness of the epithelium, with intracellular edema of the spinous or malpighian layer.

leukoencephalitis (lu″ko-en-sef″ah-li′tis) [*leuko-* + Gr. *enkephalos* brain + *-itis*]. 1. Inflammation of the white substance of the brain. 2. Forage poisoning; a contagious disease of horses, the lesion of which is softening of the white matter of the brain. It is marked by drowsiness, dimmed vision, unsteady gait, and paralysis of the throat.

leukoencephalopathy (lu″ko-en-sef″ah-lop′ah-the). Disease of the white substance of the brain.

leukoerythroblastosis (lu″ko-e-rith″ro-blas-to′sis). Presence in the circulating blood of numerous immature red and white cells.

leukoferment (lu″ko-fer′ment). A ferment that digests or disintegrates leukocytes.

leukogram (lu′ko-gram). A diagram or tabulation representing the leukocytes of a specimen of blood.

leukokeratosis (lu″ko-ker″ah-to′sis) [*leuko-* + *keratosis*]. Leukoplakia.

leukokinesis (lu″ko-ki-ne′sis). The movement of the leukocytes within the circulatory system.

leukokinetic (lu″ko-ki-net′ik). Pertaining to leukokinesis.

leukokinetics (lu″ko-ki-net′iks) [*leuko*cyte + Gr. *kinētikos* of or for putting in motion]. The quantitative, dynamic study of *in vivo* production, circulation, and destruction of leukocytes.

leukokoria (lu″ko-ko′re-ah) [*leuko-* + Gr. *korē* pupil + *-ia*]. A condition characterized by appearance of a whitish reflex or mass in the pupillary area back of the lens.

leukokraurosis (lu″ko-kraw-ro′sis). Kraurosis vulvae.

leukolymphosarcoma (lu″ko-lim″fo-sar-ko′-mah). Lymphosarcoma cell leukemia.

leukolysin (lu-kol′ĭ-sin). Leukocytolysin.

leukolysis (lu-kol′ĭ-sis). Leukocytolysis.

leukolytic (lu-ko-lit′ik). Leukocytolytic.

leukoma (lu-ko′mah) [Gr. *leukōma* whiteness]. 1. A dense white opacity of the cornea. 2. Leukoplakia buccalis. **l. adhae′rens,** a white tumor of the cornea enclosing a prolapsed adherent iris.

leukomaine (lu′ko-mān) [Gr. *leukōma* whiteness]. Any one of a large group of basic substances or alkaloids normally present in the tissues which are products of metabolism and are probably excrementitious. Some of them, at least, may become toxic, and many are physiologically active.

leukomainemia (lu″ko-mān-e′me-ah) [*leukomaine* + Gr. *haima* blood + *-ia*]. Excess of leukomaines in the blood.

leukomainic (lu″ko-mān′ik). Pertaining to, caused by, or characterized by a leukomaine.

leukomatous (lu-ko′mah-tus). Affected with or of the nature of leukoma.

leukomonocyte (lu″ko-mon′o-sīt) [*leuko-* + Gr. *monos* single + *-cyte*]. A lymphocyte.

leukomyelitis (lu″ko-mi″ĕ-li′tis) [*leuko-* + Gr. *myelos* marrow + *-itis*]. Inflammation of the white substance of the spinal cord.

leukomyelopathy (lu″ko-mi″ĕ-lop′ah-the) [*leuko-* + Gr. *myelos* marrow + *pathos* disease]. Any disease of the white substance of the spinal cord.

leukomyoma (lu″ko-mi-o′mah). Lipomyoma.

leukon (lu′kon). A general term for the circulating leukocytes and the cells from which they arise.

leukonecrosis (lu″ko-ne-kro′sis) [*leuko-* + Gr. *nekrōsis* necrosis]. Gangrene resulting in the formation of a white slough.

leukonuclein (lu″ko-nu′kle-in). An acid nucleoprotein derivable from nucleohiston: when conjugated with histon it again forms nucleohiston.

leukonychia (lu″ko-nik′e-ah) [*leuko-* + Gr. *onyx* nail + *-ia*]. A whitish discoloration of the nails.

leukopathia (lu″ko-path′e-ah) [*leuko-* + Gr. *pathos* illness]. 1. Leukodermia. 2. A disease of the leukocytes or a condition produced by aggregation of dead leukocytes. **l. un′guium,** leukonychia.

leukopathy (lu-kop′ah-the). Leukopathia.

leukopedesis (lu″ko-pe-de′sis) [*leuko*cyte + Gr. *pēdan* to leap]. Diapedesis of leukocytes through the walls of the blood vessels.

leukopenia (lu″ko-pe′ne-ah) [*leuko*cyte + Gr. *penia* poverty]. Reduction in the number of leukocytes in the blood, the count being 5,000 or less. **basophil l., basophilic l.,** abnormal reduction in the number of basophil leukocytes in the blood. **malignant l., pernicious l.,** agranulocytosis.

leukopenic (lu″ko-pe′nik). Pertaining to, characterized by, or causing leukopenia.

leukophagocytosis (lu″ko-fag″o-si-to′sis). Leukocytophagy.

leukophlegmasia (lu″ko-fleg-ma′ze-ah) [*leuko-* + *phlegmasia*]. A variety of white, nondropsical edema, such as phlegmasia alba dolens.

leukophyl (lu′ko-fil). Leukophyll.

leukophyll (lu′ko-fil) [*leuko-* + Gr. *phyllon* leaf]. A colorless substance in plant tissues which becomes converted into protochlorophyll.

leukoplakia (lu″ko-pla′ke-ah) [*leuko-* + Gr. *plax* plate + *-ia*]. A disease marked by the development upon the mucous membrane of the cheeks (*l. buccalis*), gums, or tongue (*l. lingualis*) of white, thickened patches which sometimes show a tendency to fissure. It is common in smokers and sometimes becomes malignant. Called also *leukokeratosis, leukoma, smokers' tongue, smokers' patches, psoriasis buccalis*, and *psoriasis of the tongue.* **l. pe′nis,** kraurosis of the penis. **l. vul′vae,** kraurosis vulvae.

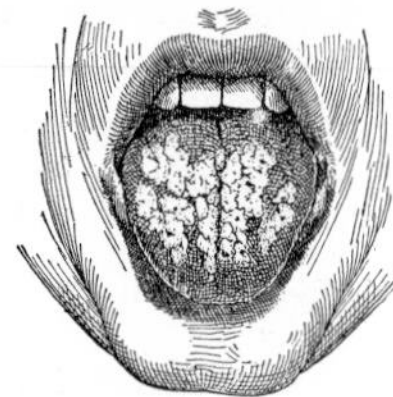
Leukoplakia of the tongue (Homans).

leukoplasia (lu″ko-pla′ze-ah). Leukoplakia.

leukoplast (lu′ko-plast). Leukoplastid.

leukoplastid (lu″ko-plas′tid) [*leuko-* + Gr. *plassein* to form]. A colorless granule of the plant cells whence the starch-producing elements are formed.

leukopoiesis (lu″ko-poi-e′sis). Production of leukocytes.

leukopoietic (lu″ko-poi-et′ik) [*leuko*cyte + Gr. *poiein* to make]. Forming or producing leukocytes.

leukoprecipitin (lu″ko-pre-sip′ĭ-tin). A precipitin specific for leukocytes.

leukoprophylaxis (lu″ko-pro″fĭ-lak′sis). The increase by artificial means of the number of leukocytes in the blood in order to secure immunity to surgical infection.

leukoprotease (lu″ko-pro′te-ās). A protein-splitting enzyme found in polymorphonuclear leukocytes.

leukopsin (lu-kop′sin) [*leuko-* + Gr. *ōps* eye]. Visual white; the colorless matter into which rhodopsin is changed by exposure to white light. It is reconvertible into rhodopsin under proper conditions.

leukorrhagia (lu″ko-ra′je-ah) [*leuko-* + Gr. *rhēgnynai* to break forth]. Profuse leukorrhea.

leukorrhea (lu″ko-re′ah) [*leuko-* + Gr. *rhoia* flow]. A whitish, viscid discharge from the vagina and uterine cavity. **menstrual l., periodic l.,** leukorrhea in place of or along with the menses.

leukorrheal (lu″ko-re′al). Pertaining to or marked by leukorrhea.

leukosarcoma (lu″ko-sar-ko′mah) [*leuko-* + *sarcoma*]. 1. Lymphosarcoma cell leukemia. 2. Any colorless or unpigmented sarcoma.

leukosarcomatosis (lu″ko-sar-ko″mah-to′sis). A condition marked by the development of multiple sarcomas composed of leukocytes.

leukoscope (lu′ko-skōp) [*leuko-* + Gr. *skopein* to examine]. An instrument of Helmholtz's, modified by A. König, for testing color blindness.

leukosis (lu-ko′sis), pl. *leuko′ses.* Proliferation of leukocyte-forming tissue, including myelosis and lymphadenosis. Such proliferation forms the basis of leukemia. **avian l., avian l. complex,** a group of diseases in chickens characterized by proliferation of immature myeloid or lymphoid cells. It includes *erythroblastosis, granuloblastosis, lymphomatosis,* and *myelocytomatosis.* Some conditions included in the group are transmissible. Called also *fowl leukosis.* **fowl l.,** avian l. **lymphoid l.,** a form of leukosis involving chiefly the lymphocytes. **myeloblastic l.,** a form involving chiefly the myeloblasts. **myelocytic l.,** a form involving chiefly the myelocytes.

leukotactic (lu″ko-tak′tik). Pertaining to leukotaxis; having the power of attracting leukocytes.

leukotaxin (lu″ko-tak′sin). Leukotaxine.

leukotaxine (lu″ko-tak′sin). A crystalline nitrogenous substance that appears when tissue is injured, that can be recovered from inflammatory exudates and that increases capillary permeability and the diapedesis of leukocytes.

leukotaxis (lu″ko-tak′sis) [*leuko-* + Gr. *taxis* arrangement]. The cytotaxis of leukocytes; the tendency of leukocytes to collect in regions of injury and inflammation.

leukotherapy (lu″ko-ther′ah-pe) [*leuko-* + Gr. *therapeia* treatment]. Treatment by the administration of leukocytes. **preventive l.,** leukoprophylaxis.

leukothrombopenia (lu″ko-throm″bo-pe′ne-ah). Abnormal lowness of the leukocyte and the thrombocyte counts of the blood.

leukotome (lu′ko-tōm) [*leuko-* + Gr. *tomē* a cut]. A cannula through which a loop of wire is passed to perform the operation of leukotomy.

leukotomy (lu-kot′o-me). The operation of cutting the white matter in the oval center of the frontal lobe of the brain; prefrontal lobotomy. **transorbital l.,** leukotomy performed by way of the orbital plate.

leukotoxic (lu″ko-tok′sik). Destructive to leukocytes.

leukotoxicity (lu″ko-tok-sis′ĭ-te). The quality of having a toxic or deleterious effect on leukocytes.

leukotoxin (lu″ko-tok′sin) [*leuko*cyte + *toxin*]. A cytotoxin destructive to the leukocytes.

leukotrichia (lu″ko-trik′e-ah) [*leuko-* + Gr. *thrix* hair + *-ia*]. Whiteness of the hair. **l. annula′ris,** ringed hair.

leuko-urobilin (lu″ko-u-ro-bi′lin) [*leuko-* + *urobilin*]. A product of the decomposition of urobilin said to occur in light-colored stools.

Leunbach's paste (loi″en-bakhs′) [Jonathan Hugh *Leunbach*, Danish physician, born 1884]. See under *paste.*

Levaditi's stain (lev″ah-de′tēz) [Constantin *Leavditi*, Roumanian bacteriologist in Paris, 1874–1928]. See *stains, table of.*

levallorphan (lev″al-lor′fan). Chemical name: 1-N-allyl-3-hydroxymorphinan: used as an antagonist to narcotics.

levan (lev′an). A hexosan from various grasses which on hydrolysis yields levulose.

levansucrase (lev″an-su′krās). An enzyme which synthesizes levan from sucrose.

levarterenol (lev″ar-tĕ-re′nol). Norepinephrine. **l. bitartrate,** l-α-(aminomethyl)-3,4-dihydroxybenzyl alcohol bitartrate: used as a sympathomimetic and as a pressor agent.

levator (le-va′tor), pl. *levato′res* [L. *levare* to raise]. That which raises or lifts up, such as a muscle or instrument (elevator) for raising an organ or part.

levatores (lev″ah-to′rēz) [L.]. Plural of *levator.*

level (lev′el). 1. A cerebrospinal center for combining or integrating impulses. The first level is spinal, the second is brainstem, the third is cortical. 2. In psychology, the sphere in which a tendency shows itself toward consciousness and adult activity. 3. Functional levels in the bone marrow that in the production of erythrocytes are more or less similar to the layers in the cutaneous epithelium: stratum mucosum, s. granulosum, s. lucidum. **iso-electric l.,** the baseline of the electrocardiogram.

Lévi's syndrome (la′vez) [Léopold *Lévi*, Paris endocrinologist, 1868–1933]. Paroxysmal hyperthyroidism.

levicellular (lev″ĭ-sel′u-lar) [L. *levis* smooth + *cellula* cell]. Smooth celled.

levidulinose (le-vid′u-lin-ōs). A naturally occurring trisaccharide found in manna. On hydrolysis it yields one molecule of glucose and two molecules of mannose.

levigation (lev″ĭ-ga′shun) [L. *levigare* to render smooth]. The grinding to a powder of a hard or moistened substance.

Levin's tube (lĕ-vinz′) [Abraham Louis *Levin*, New Orleans physician, 1880–1940]. See under *tube.*

levitation (lev″ĭ-ta′shun) [L. *levis* light]. A hallucinatory sensation of floating or rising in the air.

levo- (le′vo) [L. *laevus* left]. 1. Combining form meaning left, to the left. 2. Chemical prefix, for which the symbol (−) is frequently substituted, used to emphasize that the substance is the levorotatory enantiomorph, whether the configurational family is known or not. This practice avoids possible confusion with the occasional erroneous use of *l*- standing alone to designate the configurational family to which the substance belongs. Opposed to *dextro-*.

levocardia (le″vo-kar′de-ah) [*levo-* + Gr. *kardia* heart]. Location of the heart in the left hemithorax, with the apex pointing to the left, associated with transposition (situs inversus) of the abdominal viscera, congenital structural anomaly of the heart, and usually with absence of the spleen.

levocardiogram (le″vo-kar′de-o-gram) [*levo-* + *cardiogram*]. That part of the normal cardiogram representing action of the left ventricle.

levoclination (le″vo-kli-na′shun) [*levo-* + L. *clinatus* leaning]. Rotation of the upper poles of the vertical meridians of the two eyes to the left. Cf. *dextroclination.*

levocycloduction (le″vo-si″klo-duk′shun). Levoduction.

levo-dromoran (le″vo-dro′mo-ran). Trade mark for preparations of levorphanol tartrate.

levoduction (le″vo-duk′shun). Movement of either eye to the left.

levoglucose (le″vo-gloo′kōs). Levulose.

levogram (lev′o-gram) [*levo-* + Gr. *graphein* to record]. An electrocardiographic tracing showing left axis deviation, indicative of left ventricular hypertrophy.

levogyral (le″vo-ji′ral) [*levo-* + L. *gyrare* to turn]. Levorotatory.

levogyration (le″vo-ji-ra′shun). Levorotation.

levonordefrin (le″vo-nor′dĕ-frin). Chemical name: l-1-(3′,4′-dihydroxyphenyl)-2-amino-1-propanol: used as a vasoconstrictor.

levophed (lev′o-fed). Trade mark for a preparation of levarterenol.

levophobia (le″vo-fo′be-ah) [*levo-* + *phobia*]. Dread of objects on the left side of the body.

levopropoxyphene (le″vo-pro-pok′se-fēn). Chemical name: α-l-4-dimethylamino-1,2-diphenyl-3-methyl-2-propionoxybutane 2-naphthalene sulfonate: used as an antitussive.

levorotation (le″vo-ro-ta′shun). A turning to the left.

levorotatory (le″vo-ro′tah-to-re) [*levo-* + L. *rotare* to turn]. Turning the plane of polarization, or rays of light, to the left.

levorphanol (lēv-or′fah-nol). Chemical name: l-3-hydroxy-N-methylmorphinan: used as a narcotic analgesic.

levosin (le′vo-sin). A starch occurring in wheat flour, rye, bran, and stubble.

levothyroxine (le″vo-thi-rok′sēn). Chemical name: l-3-[4-(hydroxy-3,5-diiodophenoxy)-3,5-diiodophenyl] alanine: used as replacement therapy in hypothyroidism.

levotorsion (le″vo-tor′shun). Levoclination.

levoversion (le″vo-ver′zhun). An act of turning to the left; in ophthalmology, movement of the eyes to the left.

Levret's forceps, law, etc. (lev-rāz′) [André *Levret*, French accoucheur, 1703–1780]. See under the nouns.

levulan (lev′u-lan). Fructosan.

levulin (lev′u-lin). A starchlike compound, $C_6H_{10}O_5$, occurring in certain plant tubers.

levulosan (lev″u-lo′san). A carbohydrate, $C_6H_{10}O_5$, obtained by heating levulose.

levulosazone (lev″u-lo′sa-zōn). A phenyl-osazone of levulose identical with glucosazone. See also *methyl-phenyl-levulosazone*, under *methyl.*

levulose (lev′u-lōs) [L. *laevus* left + *-ose*]. Fruit sugar; a levorotatory ketohexose, $CH_2OH.(CHOH)_3CO.CH_2OH$, in the form of a colorless, syrupy liquid, from fruits and honey. It occurs also in the intestines, and is sometimes found in the urine. Ordinary cane sugar is changed into dextrose and levulose by digestion. Called also *fructose.*

levulosemia (lev″u-lo-se′me-ah) [*levulose* + Gr. *haima* blood + *-ia*]. The presence of levulose in blood.

levulosuria (lev″u-lo-su′re-ah) [*levulose* + Gr. *ouron* urine + *-ia*]. The occurrence of levulose in urine.

levurid (lev′u-rid). A chronic scaly dermatitis caused by infection with Monilia, Oidium, or Cryptococcus.

levuride (lev′u-rid). Levurid.

Lewandowsky's disease (lev-an-dov′skēz) [Felix *Lewandowsky*, Hamburg dermatologist, 1879–1921]. Rosacea-like tuberculid.

lewisite (lu′ĭ-sīt) [named for W. Lee *Lewis*, American chemist, 1879–1943]. A lethal war gas, being a mixture of dibetachlorovinyl chloroarsine, $AsCl.(OH:CHCl)_2$, and betachlorovinyl dichloroarsine, $AsCl_2.CH:CHCl$. It is a vesicant, lacrimator, and lung irritant.

Lewisohn's method (lu′ĭ-sonz) [Richard *Lewisohn*, New York surgeon, born 1875]. See under *method.*

Lewisonella (lu″ĭ-so-nel′ah). A genus of trypanosomes.

Lexer's operation (leks′erz) [Erich *Lexer*, German surgeon, 1867–1937]. See under *operation.*

Leyden's ataxia, crystals, disease, etc. (li′denz) [Ernst Victor von *Leyden*, German physician, 1832–1910]. See under the nouns.

Leyden jar (li′den). A glass jar partially covered inside and out with tinfoil or other metal: used as a condenser or collector of electricity.

Leydig's cells, cylinders, duct (li′digz) [Franz von *Leydig*, German anatomist, 1821–1908]. See under the nouns.

leydigarche (li″dig-ar′ke) [*Leydig* cells + Gr. *archē* beginning]. The establishment or beginning of gonadal function in the male.

Lf. Abbreviation for *limit flocculation.* See *Lf unit*, under *unit.*

L.F.A. Abbreviation for *left fronto-anterior* (left mento-anterior) position of the fetus.

L.F.D. Abbreviation for *least fatal dose* of a toxin.

L.F.P. Abbreviation for *left frontoposterior* (left mentoposterior) position of the fetus.

L.F.P.S. Abbreviation for *Licentiate of the Faculty of Physicians and Surgeons.*

L.F.T. Abbreviation for *left frontotransverse* (left mentotransverse) position of the fetus.

L.G. Abbreviation for *linguogingival.*

L.H. Abbreviation for *luteinizing hormone.*

Lhermitte's sign (lār′mits) [Jean *Lhermitte*, Paris neurologist, 1877–1959]. See under *sign.*

L.I. Abbreviation for *linguoincisal.*

Li. Chemical symbol for *lithium.*

Lib. Abbreviation for L. *li′bra*, a pound.

liberomotor (lib″er-o-mo′tor) [L. *liber* free + *motor* mover]. Pertaining to voluntary and conscious movements or actions.

libidinal (lĭ-bid′ĭ-nal). Pertaining to or of the nature of libido; erotic.

libidinous (lĭ-bid′ĭ-nus) [L. *libidinosus*]. Lustful or salacious.

libido (lĭ-bi′do), pl. *libid′ines* [L.]. 1. Sexual desire. 2. The energy derived from the primitive impulses. In psycho-analysis the term is applied to the motive power of the sex life; in freudian psychology to psychic energy in general. **bisexual l.,** the fixation of the sexual impulse on both masculine and feminine. **ego l.,** self-love; narcissism.

libidogen (lĭ-bid′o-jen). A supposed erogenous substance secreted by the testicles.

Libman-Sacks disease, syndrome (lib′man-saks′) [Emmanuel *Libman*, New York physician, 1872–1946; Benjamin *Sacks*, New York physician]. See under *disease*.

LiBr. Lithium bromide.

libra (li′brah) [L.]. 1. Pound. 2. Balance.

librium (lib′re-um). Trade mark for preparations of chlordiazepoxide.

license (li′sens) [L. *licere* to be permitted]. A permit to perform acts which without it would be illegal.

licentiate (li-sen′she-āt) [L. *licentia* license]. One holding a license entitling him to practice a particular profession.

lichen (li′ken) [Gr. *leichēn* a tree-moss]. 1. Any species or plant of a group believed to be composed of symbiotic algae and fungi. 2. A name applied to many different kinds of papular skin diseases, the specific type usually being indicated by a modifying term. Frequently used alone to designate *lichen planus*. **l. al′bus,** l. sclerosus et atrophicus. **l. amyloido′sus,** a condition characterized by localized cutaneous amyloidosis. **l. annula′ris,** granuloma annulare. **l. chron′icus sim′plex,** localized neurodermatitis. **l. fibromucinoido′sus,** l. myxedematosus. **l. frambesia′nus,** a name sometimes applied to the lesions in the secondary stage of yaws. **l. lepro′sus,** a manifestation of lepromatous leprosy, with lichenoid papules appearing in groups, usually upon the abdomen. **l. myxedemato′sus,** a condition characterized by abnormal amounts of mucin in the interstices of the cutis, and a widespread eruption of asymptomatic soft, pale-red or yellowish papules 2 to 3 mm. in diameter, which do not coalesce. Although the condition resembles myxedema, it is not associated with thyroid dysfunction. **l. nit′idus,** a rare skin disease in which the lesions are small, usually flat, sharply marginated papules scarcely raised above the level of the skin, pale-red or yellowish brown in color. **l. pila′ris,** l. spinulosus. **l. planopila′ris,** a variant of lichen planus characterized by formation, around the hair follicles, of acuminate horny papules, in addition to the typical lesions of ordinary lichen planus; in its full-blown form there is also loss of hair from the scalp and other regions of the body. **l. pla′nus,** an inflammatory skin disease with wide, flat papules occurring in circumscribed patches, and often very persistent. **l. pla′nus et acumina′tus atroph′icans,** cicatricial alopecia with an eruption of follicular spinous papules. **l. ru′ber, l. ru′ber acumina′tus,** pityriasis rubra pilaris. **l. ru′ber monilifor′mis,** a variant of lichen simplex chronicus, the supposed beaded arrangement of papules being the prominent alveolar pattern of the skin between the deepened furrows. **l. ru′ber pla′nus,** l. planus. **l. sclero′sus et atroph′icus,** a skin disease characterized by the presence of irregular, flat-topped papules, often polygonal in shape with keratotic plugging and sometimes delling. **l. scrofuloso′rum, l. scrofulo′sus,** a form, consisting of reddish papules, peculiar to persons of a tuberculous diathesis. **l. sim′plex chron′icus,** localized neurodermatitis. **l. spinulo′sus,** a condition in which there is a horn or spine in the center of each hair follicle. **l. stria′tus,** a condition characterized by a linear lichenoid eruption, usually occurring in children. **l. trop′icus,** miliaria. **l. urtica′tus,** papular urticaria.

lichenase (li′ken-ās). An enzyme which catalyzes the conversion of lichenin to glucose.

licheniasis (li″ken-i′ah-sis). The formation or development of lichen.

lichenification (li″ken-ĭ-fi-ka′shun). Thickening of the skin, with exaggeration of its normal markings so that the striae form a criss-cross pattern, enclosing flat-topped, shiny, smooth quadrilateral facets between them.

lichenin (li′kĕ-nin). A starchy demulcent polysaccharide, $(C_6H_{10}O_5)_n$, which yields glucose on hydrolysis. It occurs abundantly in Iceland moss, *Citraria islandica,* and in Irish moss, *Chondrus crispus.* Called also *lichen starch* and *moss starch.*

lichenization (li″ken-i-za′shun). The development of patches of lichen.

lichenoid (li′ken-oid) [*lichen* + Gr. *eidos* form]. 1. Resembling the disease called lichen. 2. A disease of the tongue in young children, consisting of whitish patches surrounded by yellow rings.

Lichtheim's disease, plaque, sign, syndrome (likt′hīmz) [Ludwig *Lichtheim*, German physician, 1845–1928]. See under the nouns.

Lichtheimia corymbifera (lik-thi′me-ah kor″-im-bif′er-ah). A genus of the Mucoraceae. It is pathogenic for rabbits and has been found in man in mycosis of the lungs, ear, and pharynx.

Lic.Med. Abbreviation for *Licentiate in Medicine.*

Li_2CO_3. Lithium carbonate.

licorice (lik′o-ris). Glycyrrhiza. **Russian l.,** *Glycyrrhiza glabra glandulifera.* **Spanish l.,** *Glycyrrhiza glabra typica.*

lid (lid). An eyelid. **granular l's,** trachoma. **tucked l. of Collier,** a retraction of the upper eyelid in cases of ophthalmoplegia due to a supranuclear lesion in the brain stem.

lidocaine (li′do-kān). Chemical name: 2-diethylamino-2′,6′-aceto-xylidide: used as a local anesthetic.

Lieben's test (le′benz) [Adolf *Lieben*, Austrian chemist, 1836–1914]. See under *tests.*

lieberkühn (le′ber-kēn). An apparatus attached to the microscope for the purpose of concentrating a ray of light upon a field.

Lieberkühn's crypts, follicles, glands (le′-ber-kēnz) [Johann Nathaniel *Lieberkühn*, German anatomist, 1711–1756]. Intestinal glands.

Liebermann's test (le′ber-mahnz) [Leo von Szentlörincz *Liebermann*, Hungarian physician, 1852–1926]. See under *tests.*

Liebermeister's rule (le′ber-mis″terz) [Carl von *Liebermeister*, German physician, 1833–1901]. See under *rule.*

Liebig's test, theory (le′bigz) [Baron Justus von *Liebig*, German chemist, 1803–1873]. See under *tests* and *theory.*

lien (li′en) [L.]. [N A, B N A] A large glandlike but ductless organ situated in the upper part of the abdomen. See *spleen.* **l. accesso′rius** [N A, B N A], a connected or detached outlying portion, or exclave, of the spleen. Called also *accessory spleen.* **l. mo′bilis,** an abnormally movable spleen.

lienal (li-e′nal). Pertaining to the spleen.

lienculus (li-en′ku-lus). An accessory spleen.

lienectomy (li″ĕ-nek′to-me). Splenectomy.

lienitis (li″ĕ-ni′tis). Splenitis.

lieno- (li-e′no) [L. *lien* spleen]. Combining form denoting relationship to the spleen.

lienocele (li-e′no-sēl). Splenocele.

lienography (li″e-nog′rah-fe). Splenography.

lienomalacia (li-e″no-mah-la′she-ah). Splenomalacia.

lienomedullary (li-e″no-med′u-la″re). Splenomedullary.

lienomyelogenous (li-e″no-mi″ĕ-loj′e-nus). Splenomyelogenous.

lienomyelomalacia (li-e″no-mi″ĕ-lo-mah-la′-she-ah). Splenomyelomalacia.

lienopancreatic (li-e″no-pan″kre-at′ik). Splenopancreatic.

lienopathy (li″e-nop′ah-the). Splenopathy.

lienorenal (li-e″no-re′nal). Pertaining to the spleen and the kidney.

lienotoxin (li-e″no-tok′sin) [*lieno-* + *toxin*]. Splenotoxin.

lienteric (li″en-ter′ik). Affected by or of the nature of a lientery.

lientery (li′en-ter″e) [Gr. *leienteria; leios* smooth + *enteron* intestine]. Diarrhea in which the stools contain undigested food.

lienunculus (li″en-ung′ku-lus). A detached mass or exclave of splenic tissue.

Liepmann's apraxia (lēp′manz) [Hugo Carl *Liepmann*, Berlin neurologist, 1863–1925]. See under *apraxia.*

Liesegang phenomenon, striae, waves (le′-zĕ-gahng) [Ralph Eduard *Liesegang*, German chemist, 1869–1947]. See under *phenomenon.*

Lieutaud's body, sinus, uvula, etc. (lu-toz′) [Joseph *Lieutaud*, French physician, 1703–1780]. See under the nouns.

L.I.F. Abbreviation for *left iliac fossa.*

life (lif) [L. *vita;* Gr. *bios* or *zōe*]. The aggregate of vital phenomena; a certain peculiar stimulated condition of organized matter; that obscure principle whereby organized beings are peculiarly endowed with certain powers and functions not associated with inorganic matter. **animal l.,** vegetative life conjoined with the employment of the senses and with spontaneous movements. **intellectual l., mental l., psychic l.,** that which is attended by conscious exercise of feelings, impulses, and will, and by reason. **intra-uterine l., uterine l.,** the period of life spent in the uterus. **vegetative l.,** that which is manifested in automatic acts requisite for the maintenance of the individual and the propagation of the species.

lig. Abbreviation for *ligament,* or *ligamentum.*

ligament (lig′ah-ment). A band of tissue that connects bones or supports viscera. See *ligamentum.* **accessory l.,** any ligament that strengthens or supports another. See *ligamenta accessoria.* **accessory l's, volar,** ligamenta palmaria. **accessory l's of digits of hand,** ligamenta palmaria. **accessory l. of Henle, lateral,** ligamentum laterale articulationis temporomandibularis. **accessory l. of Henle, medial,** ligamentum sphenomandibulare. **accessory l. of humerus,** ligamentum coracohumerale. **accessory l's of metacarpophalangeal joints,** ligamenta collateralia articulationum metacarpophalangearum. **acromioclavicular l.,** ligamentum acromioclaviculare. **acromiocoracoid l.,** ligamentum coracoacromiale. **adipose l. of knee, of Cruveilhier,** plica synovialis infrapatellaris. **alar l's,** ligamenta alaria. **alar l's of knee,** plicae alares. **alveolodental l.,** periodontium. **annular l., dorsal common,** retinaculum extensorum manus. **annular l., inferior,** ligamentum arcuatum pubis. **annular l., internal,** retinaculum musculorum extensorum pedis inferius. **annular l's, tracheal,** ligamenta anularia trachealia. **annular l. of ankle, external,** retinaculum musculorum peroneorum superius. **annular l. of ankle, internal,** retinaculum musculorum flexorum pedis. **annular l. of base of stapes,** ligamentum anulare stapedis. **annular l. of carpus, posterior,** retinaculum extensorum manus. **annular l's of digits of foot.** See *pars anularis vaginae fibrosae digitorum pedis.* **annular l's of digits of hand.** See *pars anularis vaginae fibrosae digitorum manus.* **annular l. of femur,** zona orbicularis articulationis coxae. **annular l. of finger,** pars anularis vaginae fibrosae digitorum manus. **annular l. of malleolus, external,** retinaculum musculorum extensorum pedis inferius. **annular l. of malleolus, internal,** retinaculum musculorum flexorum pedis. **annular l. of radius,** ligamentum anulare radii. **annular l. of stapes,** ligamentum anulare stapedis. **annular l. of tarsus, anterior,** retinaculum musculorum extensorum pedis inferius. **annular l's of tendon sheaths of fingers.** See *pars anularis vaginae fibrosae digitorum manus.* **annular l. of wrist, dorsal posterior,** retinaculum extensorum manus. **anococcygeal l.,** ligamentum anococcygeum. **anterior l. of colon,** tenia omentalis. **anterior l. of head of fibula,** ligamentum capitis fibulae anterius. **anterior l. of head of rib,** ligamentum capitis costae radiatum. **anterior l. of malleus,** ligamentum mallei anterius. **anterior l. of neck of rib.** See *ligamentum costotransversarium superius.* **anterior l. of radiocarpal joint,** ligamentum radiocarpeum palmare. **l. of antibrachium, of Weitbrecht,** chorda obliqua membranae interosseae antebrachii. **apical dental l., apical odontoid l.,** ligamentum apicis dentis. **appendiculo-ovarian l.,** a fold of mesentery extending between the appendix and the broad ligament. **Arantius' l.,** ligamentum venosum. **arcuate l.,** ligamentum flavum. **arcuate l., lateral,** ligamentum arcuatum laterale. **arcuate l., medial,** ligamentum arcuatum mediale. **arcuate l., median,** l. arcuatum medianum. **arcuate l., pubic,** ligamentum arcuatum pubis. **arcuate l. of diaphragm, external,** ligamentum arcuatum laterale. **arcuate l. of diaphragm, internal,** ligamentum arcuatum mediale. **arcuate l. of diaphragm, lateral,** ligamentum arcuatum laterale. **arcuate l. of knee,** ligamentum popliteum arcuatum. **arcuate l. of pubis, inferior,** ligamentum arcuatum pubis. **Arnold's l.,** ligamentum incudis superius. **articular l. of vertebrae,** capsula articularis articulationum vertebrarum. **arytenoepiglottic l.,** plica aryepiglottica. **atlantooccipital l., anterior, atlantooccipital l., deep,** membrana atlantooccipitalis anterior. **atlantooccipital l., posterior,** membrana atlantooccipitalis posterior. **l's of auditory ossicles,** ligamenta ossiculorum auditus. **l's of auricle of external ear,** ligamenta auricularia. **auricular l., anterior,** ligamentum auriculare anterius. **auricular l., posterior,** ligamentum auriculare posterius. **auricular l., superior,** ligamentum auriculare superius. **Bardinet's l.,** the posterior portion of the annular ligament of the elbow. **Barkow's l.,** the anterior and posterior parts of the elbow joint capsule. **Bellini's l.,** a band passing as part of the capsule of the hip joint to the greater trochanter. **Bérard's l.,** the suspensory ligament of the pericardium, extending to the third and fourth thoracic vertebrae. **Berry's l.,** ligamentum thyrohyoideum. **Bertin's l.,** ligamentum iliofemorale. **Bichat's l.,** the lower bundle of the dorsal sacroiliac ligament. **bifurcate l.,** ligamentum bifurcatum. **bifurcate l's, deep,** ligamenta metatarsea plantaria. **bifurcate l's of Arnold, deep,** ligamenta tarsometatarsea plantaria. **Bigelow's l.,** ligamentum iliofemorale. **bigeminate l's of Arnold,** ligamenta tarsometatarsea dorsalia. **Borgery's l.,** ligamentum popliteum obliquum. **l. of Botallo,** ligamentum arteriosum. **brachiocubital l.,** ligamentum collaterale ulnare. **brachioradial l.,** ligamentum collaterale radiale. **broad l. of liver,** ligamentum falciforme hepatis. **broad l. of lung,** ligamentum pulmonale. **broad l. of uterus,** the peritoneal fold that supports the uterus on either side. Called also *ligamentum latum uteri.* **Brodie's l.,** the transverse humeral ligament. **Burn's l.,** margo falciformis hiatus saphenus. **calcaneocuboid l.,** ligamentum calcaneocuboideum. **calcaneocuboid l., plantar,** ligamentum calcaneocuboideum plantare. **calcaneofibular l.,** ligamentum calcaneofibulare. **calcaneonavicular l.,** ligamentum calcaneonaviculare. **calcaneonavicular l., dorsal,** ligamentum calcaneonaviculare dorsale. **calcaneonavicular l., plantar,** ligamentum calcaneonaviculare plantare. **calcaneotibial l.,** pars tibiocalcanea ligamenti medialis. **Caldani's l.,** a band passing from the inner border of the coracoid process to the lower border of the clavicle, the first rib, and the tendon of the subclavius. **Campbell's l.,** suspensory l. of axilla. **Camper's l.,** diaphragma urogenitale. **canthal l's.** See *ligamentum* *palpebrale mediale* and *raphe palpebralis lateralis*. **capitular l., volar,** ligamentum metacarpeum transversum profundum. **capsular l.,** capsula articularis. **capsular l., internal,** ligamentum capitis femoris. **capsular l., pelviprostatic,** fascia prostatae. **Carcassonne's l.,** ligamentum puboprostaticum. **cardinal l.,** part of a thickening of the visceral pelvic fascia beside the cervix and vagina, passing laterally to merge with the upper fascia of the pelvic diaphragm. **carpal l., dorsal.** See *ligamenta intercarpea dorsalia*. **carpal l., oblique accessory,** ligamentum radiocarpeum palmare. **carpal l., ulnar,** ligamentum collaterale carpi ulnare. **carpometacarpal l's, anterior,** ligamenta carpometacarpea palmaria. **carpometacarpal l's, dorsal,** ligamenta carpometacarpea dorsalia. **carpometacarpal l's, oblique palmar,** ligamenta carpometacarpea palmaria. **carpometacarpal l's, palmar,** ligamenta metacarpea palmaria. **carpometacarpal l's, posterior,** ligamenta carpometacarpea dorsalia. **carpometacarpal l's, volar,** ligamenta carpometacarpea palmaria. **Casserian l.,** ligamentum mallei laterale. **caudal l. of common integument,** retinaculum caudale. **central l.,** filum terminale. **central l. of spinal dura mater,** filum durae matris spinalis. **cervical l., anterior,** membrana tectoria. **cervical l., lateral,** cardinal l. **cervical l., posterior,** ligamentum nuchae. **cervical l. of sinus tarsi,** a strong band behind the bifurcate ligament, extending upward to the neck of the talus. **cervicobasilar l.,** membrana tectoria. **check l's of axis,** ligamenta alaria. **chondrosternal l., interarticular,** ligamentum sternocostale intraarticulare. **chondroxiphoid l's,** ligamenta costoxiphoidea. **l. of Civinini,** ligamentum pterygospinale. **Clado's l.,** appendiculo-ovarian l. **clavicular l., external capsular,** ligamentum acromioclaviculare. **Cloquet's l.,** vestigium processus vaginalis. **coccygeal l., superior,** ligamentum iliofemorale. **collateral l., fibular,** ligamentum collaterale fibulare. **collateral l., radial,** ligamentum collaterale radiale. **collateral l., tibial,** ligamentum collaterale tibiale. **collateral l., ulnar,** ligamentum collaterale ulnare. **collateral l. of carpus, radial,** ligamentum collaterale carpi radiale. **collateral l. of carpus, ulnar,** ligamentum collaterale carpi ulnare. **collateral l's of interphalangeal articulations of foot,** ligamenta collateralia articulationum interphalangearum pedis. **collateral l's of interphalangeal articulations of hand,** ligamenta collateralia articulationum interphalangearum manus. **collateral l's of joints of fingers,** ligamenta collateralia articulationum interphalangearum manus. **collateral l's of joints of toes,** ligamenta collateralia articulationum interphalangearum pedis. **collateral l's of metacarpophalangeal articulations,** ligamenta collateralia articulationum metacarpophalangearum. **collateral l's of metatarsophalangeal articulations,** ligamenta collateralia articulationum metatarsophalangearum. **Colles' l.,** ligamentum inguinale reflexum. **l's of colon,** teniae coli. **common l. of knee, of Weber,** ligamentum transversum genus. **common l. of wrist joint, deep,** ligamentum collaterale carpi radiale. **conoid l.,** ligamentum conoideum. **Cooper's l.,** ligamentum pubicum superius. **Cooper's suspensory l's,** ligamenta suspensoria mammae. **coracoacromial l.,** ligamentum coracoacromiale. **coracocapsular l's,** ligamenta cinguli extremitatis superioris. **coracoclavicular l.,** ligamentum coracoclaviculare. **coracoclavicular l., external,** ligamentum trapezoideum. **coracoclavicular l., internal,** ligamentum conoideum. **coracohumeral l.,** ligamentum coracohumerale. **coracoid l. of scapula,** ligamentum transversum scapulae superius. **cordiform l. of diaphragm,** centrum tendineum. **coronary l. of liver,** ligamentum coronarium hepatis. **coronary l. of radius,** ligamentum anulare radii. **costocentral l., anterior,** ligamentum capitis costae radiatum. **costocentral l., interarticular,** ligamentum capitis costae intraarticulare. **costoclavicular l.,** ligamentum costoclaviculare. **costocolic l.,** ligamentum phrenicolicum. **costocoracoid l.,** ligamentum transversum scapulae superius. **costopericardiac l.,** a ligament joining the upper costosternal articulation with the pericardium. **costosternal l's, radiate,** ligamenta sternocostalia radiata. **costotransverse l.,** ligamentum costotransversarium. **costotransverse l., anterior.** See *ligamentum costotransversarium superius*. **costotransverse l., lateral,** ligamentum costotransversarium laterale. **costotransverse l., posterior.** See *ligamentum costotransversarium superius*. **costotransverse l., superior,** ligamentum costotransversarium superius. **costotransverse l. of Krause, posterior,** ligamentum costotransversarium laterale. **costovertebral l.,** ligamentum capitis costae radiatum. **costoxiphoid l's,** ligamenta costoxiphoidea. **cotyloid l.,** labrum acetabulare. **Cowper's l.,** fascia pectinea. **cricoarytenoid l., posterior,** ligamentum cricoarytenoideum posterius. **cricopharyngeal l., cricosantorinian l.,** ligamentum cricopharyngeum. **cricothyroarytenoid l.,** conus elasticus laryngis. **cricothyroid l.,** ligamentum cricothyroideum. **cricotracheal l.,** ligamentum cricotracheale. **crucial l's of fingers.** See *pars cruciformis vaginae fibrosae digitorum manus*. **crucial l. of foot,** retinaculum musculorum extensorum pedis inferius. **cruciate l. of atlas,** ligamentum cruciforme atlantis. **cruciate l's of fingers.** See *pars cruciformis vaginae fibrosae digitorum manus*. **cruciate l's of knee,** ligamenta cruciata genus. **cruciate l. of knee, anterior,** ligamentum cruciatum anterius genus. **cruciate l. of knee, posterior,** ligamentum cruciatum posterius genus. **cruciate l. of leg,** retinaculum musculorum extensorum pedis inferius. **cruciate l's of toes.** See *pars cruciformis vaginae fibrosae digitorum pedis*. **cruciform l. of atlas,** ligamentum cruciforme atlantis. **crural l.,** ligamentum inguinale. **Cruveilhier's l's,** ligamenta palmaria. **cubitoradial l.,** chorda obliqua membranae interosseae antibrachii. **cubitoulnar l.,** ligamentum collaterale ulnare. **cuboideometatarsal l's, short,** ligamenta tarsometatarsea plantaria. **cuboideonavicular l., dorsal,** ligamentum cuboideonaviculare dorsale. **cuboideonavicular l., oblique,** ligamentum cuboideonaviculare plantare. **cuboideonavicular l., plantar,** ligamentum cuboideonaviculare plantare. **cubonavicular l.,** ligamentum cuboideonaviculare plantare. **cuboscaphoid l., plantar,** ligamentum cuboideonaviculare plantare. **cuneocuboid l., dorsal,** ligamentum cuneocuboideum dorsale. **cuneocuboid l., interosseous,** ligamentum cuneocuboideum interosseum. **cuneocuboid l., plantar,** ligamentum cuneocuboidum plantare. **cuneometatarsal l's, interosseous,** ligamenta cuneometatarsea interossea. **cuneonavicular l's, dorsal,** ligamenta cuneonavicularia dorsalia. **cuneonavicular l's, plantar,** ligamenta cuneonavicularia plantaria. **cutaneophalangeal l's,** ligamentous fibers from the sides of the phalanges near the joints to the skin. **cysticoduodenal l.,** an anomalous fold of peritoneum extending between the gallbladder and the duodenum. **deep l's of tarsus,** ligamenta tarsi profunda. **deltoid l. of ankle,** ligamentum mediale. **deltoid l. of elbow,** ligamentum collaterale ulnare. **dentate l. of spinal cord, denticulate l.,** ligamentum denticulatum. **Denuce's l.,** a short, wide band connecting the radius and the ulna at the wrist. **diaphragmatic l.,** the involuting urogenital ridge that becomes the suspensory ligament of the ovary.

dorsal l's, carpal, ligamenta intercarpea dorsalia. **dorsal l., talonavicular,** ligamentum talonaviculare. **dorsal l's of bases of metacarpal bones,** ligamenta metacarpea dorsalia. **dorsal l's of bases of metatarsal bones,** ligamenta metatarsea dorsalia. **dorsal l. of radiocarpal joint,** ligamentum radiocarpeum dorsale. **dorsal l's of tarsus,** ligamenta tarsi dorsalia. **dorsal l. of wrist,** retinaculum extensorum manus. **Douglas' l.,** plica rectouterina. **duodenohepatic l.,** ligamentum hepatoduodenale. **duodenorenal l.,** ligamentum duodenorenale. **Ellis' l.,** that portion of the rectovesical fascia which extends to the sides of the rectum. **epihyal l.,** ligamentum stylohyoideum. **external l's of Barkow, plantar,** ligamenta intercuneiformia plantaria. **external l. of mandibular articulation,** ligamentum laterale articulationis temporomandibularis. **external l. of neck of rib,** ligamentum costotransversarium posterius. **falciform l.,** processus ligamenti sacrotuberosi. **falciform l. of liver,** ligamentum falciforme hepatis. **fallopian l., l. of Fallopius,** ligamentum inguinale. **false l.,** any suspensory ligament that is a peritoneal fold and not of true ligamentous structure. **Ferrein's l.,** the thick external part of the capsule of the temporomandibular joint. **fibrous l., anterior,** ligamentum sternoclaviculare anterius. **fibrous l. posterior,** ligamentum sternoclaviculare posterius. **flaval l.,** ligamentum flavum. **Flood's l.,** the superior glenohumeral ligament. **fundiform l. of penis,** ligamentum fundiforme penis. **gastrocolic l.,** ligamentum gastrocolicum. **gastrohepatic l.,** ligamentum hepatogastricum. **gastrolienal l.,** ligamentum gastrolienale. **gastropancreatic l. of Huschke,** plica gastropancreatica. **gastrophrenic l.,** ligamentum gastrophrenicum. **gastrosplenic l.,** ligamentum gastrolienale. **genitoinguinal l.,** ligamentum genitoinguinale. **Gerdy's l.,** suspensory l. of axilla. **Gimbernat's l.,** ligamentum lacunare. **l's of girdle of inferior extremity,** ligamenta cinguli extremitatis inferioris. **l's of girdle of superior extremity,** ligamenta cinguli extremitatis superioris. **glenohumeral l's,** ligamenta glenohumeralia. **glenoid l's of Cruveilhier,** ligamenta plantaria articulationum metatarsophalangearum. **glenoid l. of humerus, glenoid l. of Macalister,** labrum glenoidale. **glenoid l. of mandibular fossa,** a ring of fibrocartilage connected with the rim of the mandibular fossa. **Güntz's l.,** part of the obturator membrane. **hamatometacarpal l.,** fibers connecting the hamulus of the unciform bone with the base of the fifth metacarpal bone. **l. of head of femur,** ligamentum capitis femoris. **Helmholtz's l.,** that part of the anterior ligament of the malleus which is attached to the greater tympanic spine. **l's of Helvetius,** ligamenta pylori. **Henle's l.,** falx inguinalis. **Hensing's l.,** a small serous fold from the upper end of the descending colon to the abdominal wall. **hepatic l's,** folds of peritoneum extending from the liver to adjacent structures. **hepatocolic l.,** ligamentum hepatocolicum. **hepatoduodenal l.,** ligamentum hepatoduodenale. **hepatogastric l.,** ligamentum hepatogastricum. **hepatogastroduodenal l.,** omentum minus. **hepatorenal l.,** ligamentum hepatorenale. **hepatoumbilical l.,** ligamentum teres hepatis. **Hesselbach's l.,** ligamentum interfoveolare. **Hey's l.,** margo falciformis hiatus saphenus. **Hueck's l.,** ligamentum pectinatum anguli iridocornealis. **Hunter's l.,** ligamentum teres uteri. **Huschke's l's,** plicae gastropancreaticae. **hyaloideocapsular l.,** the tissue connecting the vitreous body to the peripheral zone of the lens capsule. **hyoepiglottic l.,** ligamentum hyoepiglotticum. **iliocostal l.,** ligamentum lumbocostale. **iliofemoral l.,** ligamentum iliofemorale. **iliolumbar l.,** ligamentum iliolumbale. **iliopectineal l.,** arcus iliopectineus. **iliopubic l.,** ligamentum inguinale. **iliosacral l's, anterior,** ligamenta sacroiliaca ventralia. **iliosacral l's, interosseous,** ligamenta sacroiliaca interossea. **iliosacral l., long,** ligamentum sacroiliacum posterius longum. **iliotibial l. of Maissiat,** tractus iliotibialis. **iliotrochanteric l.,** a portion of the articular capsule of the hip joint. **inferior l. of epididymis,** ligamentum epididymidis inferius. **inferior l. of neck of rib,** ligamentum costotransversarium posterius. **inferior l. of neck of rib of Henle,** ligamentum costotransversarium. **inferior l. of tubercle of rib,** ligamentum costotransversarium laterale. **infundibulopelvic l.,** ligamentum suspensorium ovarii. **inguinal l.,** ligamentum inguinale. **inguinal l., anterior,** crus mediale anuli inguinalis superficialis. **inguinal l., external,** ligamentum inguinale. **inguinal l., internal.** 1. Ligamentum inguinale reflexum. 2. Crus mediale anuli inguinalis superficialis. **inguinal l., posterior,** ligamentum interfoveolare. **inguinal l., reflex,** ligamentum inguinale reflexum. **inguinal l. of Blumberg,** ligamentum interfoveolare. **inguinal l. of Cooper,** ligamentum lacunare. **interarticular l.,** any ligament situated within the capsule of a joint. **interarticular l. of articulation of humerus,** caput longum musculi bicipitis brachii. **interarticular l. of head of rib,** ligamentum capitis costae intraarticulare. **interarticular l. of hip joint,** ligamentum capitis femoris. **intercarpal l's, dorsal,** ligamenta intercarpea dorsalia. **intercarpal l's, interosseous,** ligamenta intercarpea interossea. **intercarpal l's, palmar,** ligamenta intercarpea palmaria. **intercarpal l's, volar,** ligamenta intercarpea palmaria **interclavicular l.,** ligamentum interclaviculare. **intercostal l's, external.** See *membrana intercostalis externa.* **intercostal l's, internal.** See *membrana intercostalis interna.* **intercuneiform l's, dorsal,** ligamenta intercuneiformia dorsalia. **intercuneiform l's, interosseous,** ligamenta intercuneiformia interossea. **intercuneiform l's, plantar,** ligamenta intercuneiformia plantaria. **interfoveolar l.,** ligamentum interfoveolare. **intermaxillary l.,** raphe pterygomandibularis. **intermetacarpal l's, anterior, intermetacarpal l's, distal.** See *ligamentum metacarpeum transversum profundum.* **intermetacarpal l's, dorsal,** ligamenta metacarpea dorsalia. **intermetacarpal l's, interosseous,** ligamenta metacarpea interossea. **intermetacarpal l's, palmar.** 1. Ligamenta metacarpea palmaria. 2. See *ligamentum metacarpeum transversum profundum.* **intermetacarpal l's, proximal, anterior,** ligamenta metacarpea palmaria. **intermetacarpal l's, proximal, posterior,** ligamenta metacarpea dorsalia. **intermetacarpal l's, transverse, dorsal,** ligamenta metacarpea dorsalia. **intermetacarpal l's, transverse, volar,** ligamenta metacarpea palmaria. **intermetatarsal l's, interosseous,** ligamenta metatarsea interossea. **intermetatarsal l's, plantar, distal.** See *ligamentum metatarseum transversum profundum.* **intermetatarsal l's, proximal, dorsal,** ligamenta metatarsea dorsalia. **intermetatarsal l's, proximal, plantar,** ligamenta metatarsea plantaria. **intermetatarsal l's, transverse, dorsal,** ligamenta metatarsea dorsalia. **intermetatarsal l's, transverse, plantar,** ligamenta metatarsea plantaria. **intermuscular l., fibular,** septum intermusculare anterius cruris. **intermuscular l. of arm, external,** septum intermusculare brachii laterale. **intermuscular l. of arm, internal,** septum intermusculare brachii mediale. **intermuscular l. of arm, lateral,** septum intermusculare brachii laterale. **intermuscular l. of arm, medial,** septum intermusculare brachii mediale. **intermuscular l. of thigh, external,** septum intermusculare femoris laterale. **intermus-**

cular l. of thigh, lateral, septum intermusculare femoris laterale. **intermuscular l. of thigh, medial,** septum intermusculare femoris mediale. **internal l. of neck of rib,** ligamentum costotransversarium superius. **interosseous l., radioulnar,** membrana interossea antebrachii. **interosseous l's, transverse metacarpal,** ligamenta metacarpea interossea. **interosseous l's of Barkow, internal,** ligamenta intercuneiformia plantaria. **interosseous l's of bases of metacarpal bones,** ligamenta metacarpea interossea. **interosseous l's of bases of metatarsal bones,** ligamenta metatarsea interossea. **interosseous l. of Cruveilhier, costovertebral,** ligamentum capitis costae intraarticulare. **interosseous l. of Cruveilhier, transversocostal,** ligamentum costotransversarium. **interosseous l's of knee,** ligamenta cruciata genus. **interosseous l. of leg,** membrana interossea cruris. **interosseous l. of pubis,** discus interpubicus. **interosseous l. of pubis, of Winslow,** ligamentum transversum perinei. **interosseous l's of tarsus,** ligamenta tarsi interossea. **interprocess l.,** a ligament that connects two processes on the same bone. **interpubic l.,** discus interpubicus. **interspinal l., interspinous l.,** ligamentum interspinale. **intertarsal l's, dorsal,** ligamenta metatarsea dorsalia. **intertarsal l's, interosseous,** ligamenta metatarsea interossea. **intertarsal l's, plantar,** ligamenta metatarsea plantaria. **intertransverse l.,** ligamentum intertransversarium. **interureteral l.,** plica interureterica. **intervertebral l's,** disci intervertebrales. **intraarticular l. of head of rib,** ligamentum capitis costae intraarticulare. **ischiocapsular l., ischiofemoral l.,** ligamentum ischiofemorale. **ischioprostatic l.,** diaphragma urogenitale. **ischiosacral l's.** See *ligamentum sacrospinale* and *ligamentum sacrotuberale.* **Krause's l.,** ligamentum transversum perinei. **laciniate l.,** retinaculum musculorum flexorum pedis. **laciniate l., external,** retinaculum musculorum seroneorum superius. **lacunar l., lacunar l. of Gimbernat,** ligamentum lacunare. **lambdoid l.,** retinaculum musculorum extensorum pedis inferius. **lateral l. of carpus, radial,** ligamentum collaterale carpi radiale. **lateral l. of carpus, ulnar,** ligamentum collaterale carpi ulnare. **lateral l. of colon,** tenia omentalis. **lateral l's of joints of fingers,** ligamenta collateralia articulationum interphalangearum manus. **lateral l's of joints of toes,** ligamenta collateralia articulationum interphalangearum pedis. **lateral l. of knee,** ligamentum collaterale fibulare. **lateral l's of liver.** See *ligamentum triangulare dextrum hepatis* and *ligamentum triangulare sinistrum hepatis.* **lateral l. of malleus,** ligamentum mallei laterale. **lateral l's of metacarpophalangeal joints,** ligamenta collateralia articulationum metacarpophalangearum. **lateral l's of metatarsophalangeal joints,** ligamenta collateralia articulationum metatarsophalangearum. **lateral l. of temporomandibular articulation,** ligamentum laterale articulationis temporomandibularis. **lateral l. of temporomandibular joint, external,** ligamentum laterale articulationis temporomandibularis. **lateral l. of temporomandibular joint, internal,** ligamentum sphenomandibulare. **lateral l. of wrist joint, external,** ligamentum collaterale carpi radiale. **lateral l. of wrist joint, internal,** ligamentum collaterale carpi ulnare. **Lauth's l.,** ligamentum transversum atlantis. **l. of left superior vena cava,** plica venae cavae sinistrae. **lienophrenic l.,** ligamentum phrenicolienale. **lienorenal l.,** a fold of peritoneum connecting the spleen and the left kidney. **Lisfranc's l.,** a fibrous band running from the lower external surface of the medial cuneiform bone to the internal surface of the base of the second metatarsal bone. **Lockwood's l.,** the thickened area of contact between Tenon's capsule and the sheaths of the inferior rectus and inferior oblique muscles. **longitudinal l., anterior,** ligamentum longitudinale anterius. **longitudinal l., posterior,** ligamentum longitudinale posterius. **longitudinal l. of abdomen,** linea alba. **lumbocostal l.,** ligamentum lumbocostale. **l's of Luschka,** ligamenta sternopericardiaca. **Mackenrodt's l.,** plica rectouterina. **l. of Maissiat,** tractus iliotibialis. **Mauchart's l's,** ligamenta alaria. **maxillary l., lateral,** ligamentum laterale articulationis temporomandibularis. **maxillary l., middle,** ligamentum sphenomandibulare. **l. of Mayer,** ligamentum carpi radiatum. **Meckel's l.,** Meckel's band. **medial l.,** ligamentum mediale. **medial l. of elbow joint,** ligamentum collaterale ulnare. **medial l. of wrist,** ligamentum collaterale carpi ulnare. **meniscofemoral l., anterior,** ligamentum meniscofemorale anterius. **meniscofemoral l., posterior,** ligamentum meniscofemorale posterius. **mesenteriomesocolic l.,** mesenteriomesocolic fold. **mesocolic l. of colon,** tenia mesocolica. **metacarpal l's, dorsal,** ligamenta metacarpea dorsalia. **metacarpal l's, interosseous,** ligamenta metacarpea interossea. **metacarpal l's, palmar,** ligamenta metacarpea palmaria. **metacarpal l's, transverse, deep,** ligamenta metacarpeum transversum profundum. **metacarpal l., transverse, superficial,** ligamentum metacarpeum transversum superficiale. **metacarpophalangeal l's, anterior, metacarpophalangeal l's, palmar,** ligamenta palmaria. **metatarsal l., anterior,** ligamentum metatarseum transversum profundum. **metatarsal l's, dorsal,** ligamenta metatarsea dorsalia. **metatarsal, l's, interosseus,** ligamenta metatarsea interossea. **metatarsal l's, lateral,** ligamenta metacarpea interossea. **metatarsal l's, lateral proper, of Weber, metatarsal l's, lateral, of Weitbrecht,** ligamenta metatarsea interossea. **metatarsal l's, plantar,** ligamenta metatarsea plantaria. **metatarsal l., plantar, anterior,** ligamentum metatarseum transversum profundum. **metatarsal l., transverse, deep,** ligamentum metatarseum transversum profundum. **metatarsal l., transverse, interosseous,** ligamenta metatarsea interossea. **metatarsal l., transverse, superficial,** ligamentum metatarseum transversum superficiale. **metatarsophalangeal l's, inferior,** ligamenta plantaria articulationum metatarsophalangearum. **metatarsophalangeal l's, plantar,** ligamenta plantaria articulationum metatarsophalangearum. **middle l. of neck of rib,** ligamentum costotransversarium. **mucous l.,** plica synovialis. **l. of nape,** ligamentum nuchae. **navicularicuneiform l's, plantar,** ligamenta cuneonavicularia plantaria. **nephrocolic l.,** fasciculi from the fatty capsule of the kidney passing down on the right side to the posterior wall of the ascending colon and on the left side to the posterior wall of the descending colon. **nuchal l.,** ligamentum nuchae. **oblique l. of Cooper, oblique l. of forearm,** chorda obliqua membranae interosseae antebrachii. **oblique l's of knee,** ligamenta cruciata genus. **oblique l. of knee, posterior,** ligamentum popliteum obliquum. **oblique l. of scapula,** ligamentum transversum scapulae superius. **oblique l. of superior radioulnar joint,** chorda obliqua membranae interosseae antebrachii. **obturator l., atlantooccipital,** membrana atlantooccipitalis anterior. **obturator l. of atlas,** membrana atlantooccipitalis anterior et posterior. **obturator l. of pelvis,** membrana obturatoria. **occipitoaxial l.,** membrana tectoria. **occipitoodontoid l's,** ligamenta alaria. **odontoid l., middle,** ligamentum apicis dentis. **odontoid l's of axis,** ligamenta alaria. **orbicular l. of radius,** ligamentum anulare radii. **ovarian l.,** ligamentum ovarii proprium. **palmar l's.**

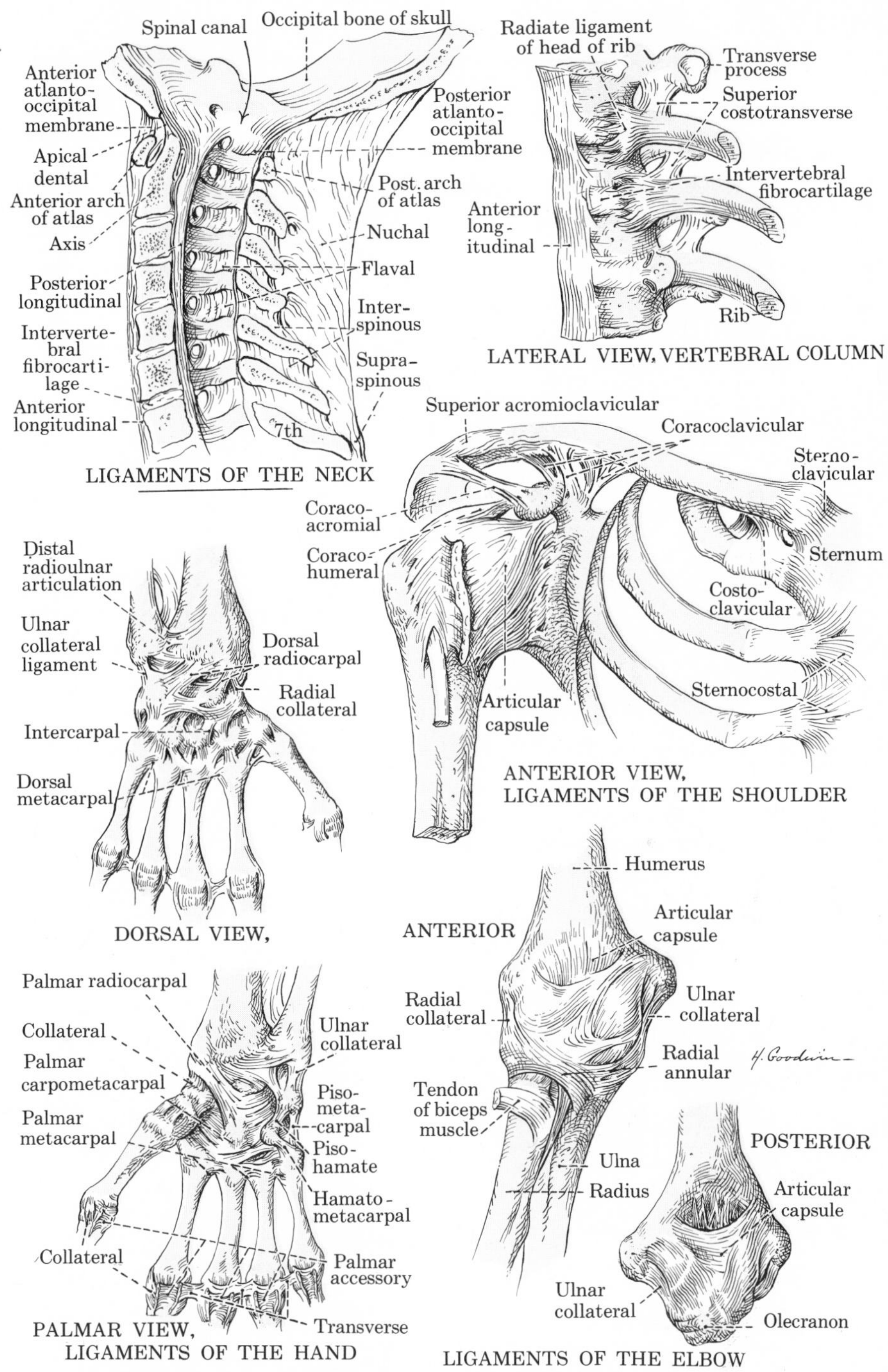

ARTICULAR LIGAMENTS

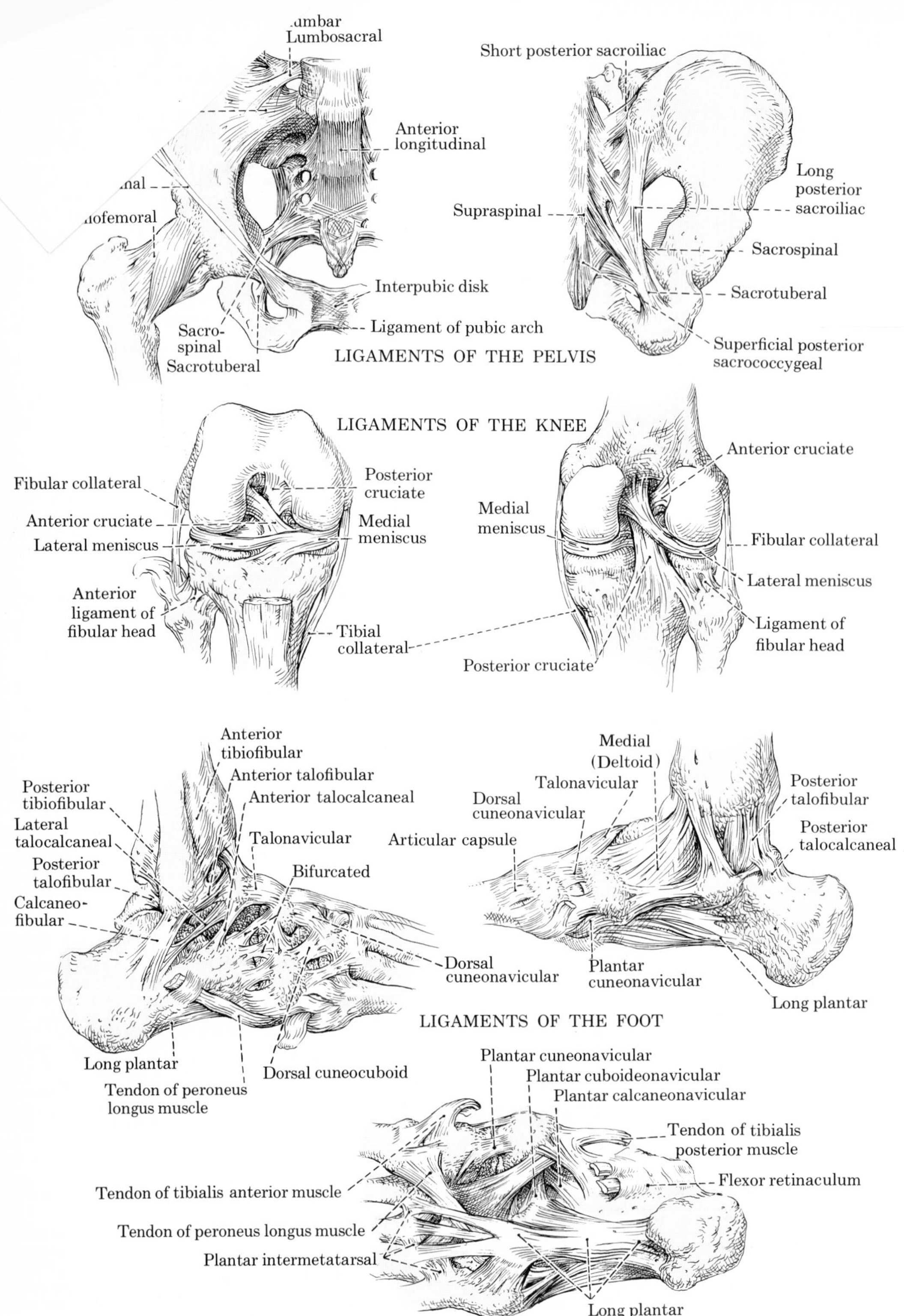

ARTICULAR LIGAMENTS

1. Ligamenta palmaria. 2. See *aponeurosis palmaris.* **palmar l., transverse, deep,** ligamentum metacarpeum transversum profundum. **palmar l. of carpus,** ligamentum carpi radiatum. **palmar l. of radiocarpal joint,** ligamentum radiocarpeum palmare. **palpebral l., medial,** ligamentum palpebrale mediale. **pancreaticosplenic l.,** a fold of peritoneum extending from the pancreas to the spleen. **patellar l.,** ligamentum patellae. **patellar l., internal,** retinaculum patellae mediale. **patellar l., lateral,** retinaculum patellae laterale. **pectinate l. of iridocorneal angle,** ligamentum pectinatum anguli iridocornealis. **pectineal l.,** ligamentum pectineale. **pelvic l., posterior, great,** ligamentum sacrotuberale. **pelvic l., posterior, short,** ligamentum sacrospinale. **pelvic l., transverse,** ligamentum transversum perinei. **l's of pelvic girdle,** ligamenta cinguli extremitatis inferioris. **pelviprostatic l., basal,** fascia prostatae. **perineal l., transverse,** ligamentum transversum perinei. **perineal l. of Carcassone,** ligamentum transversum perinei. **Petit's l.,** uterosacral l. **petrosphenoid l.,** synchondrosis sphenooccipitalis. **petrosphenoid l., anterior.** 1. Synchondrosis sphenopetrosa. 2. Synchondrosis sphenooccipitalis. **pharyngeal l., pharyngeal l., middle,** raphe pharyngis. **phrenicocolic l.,** ligamentum phrenicocolicum. **phrenicolienal l., phrenicosplenic l.,** ligamentum phrenicolienale. **phrenocolic l.,** ligamentum phrenicocolicum. **pisimetacarpal l.,** ligamentum pisometacarpeum. **pisohamate l.,** ligamentum pisohamatum. **pisometacarpal l.,** ligamentum pisometacarpeum. **pisounciform l., piso-uncinate l.,** ligamentum pisohamatum. **plantar l's,** ligamenta plantaria articulationum metatarsophalangearum. **plantar l., long,** ligamentum plantare longum. **plantar l's of bases of metatarsal bones,** ligamenta metatarsea plantaria. **plantar l's of little heads of metacarpal bones.** See *ligamentum metacarpeum transverum profundum.* **plantar l. of second metatarsal bone.** See *ligamenta tarsometatarsea plantaria.* **plantar l. of tarsus,** ligamentum tarsi plantaria. **popliteal l., arcuate,** ligamentum popliteum arcuatum. **popliteal l., external,** retinaculum ligamenti arcuati. **popliteal l., oblique,** ligamentum popliteum obliquum. **posterior l. of head of fibula,** ligamentum capitis fibulae posterius. **posterior l. of incus,** ligamentum incudis posterius. **posterior l. of pinna,** ligamentum auriculare posterius. **posterior l. of radiocarpal joint,** ligamentum radiocarpeum dorsale. **Poupart's l.,** ligamentum inguinale. **preurethral l. of Waldeyer,** ligamentum transversum perinei. **prismatic l. of Weitbrecht,** ligamentum capitis femoris. **proper l's of costal cartilages.** See *membrana intercostalis externa.* **pterygomandibular l.,** raphe pterygomandibularis. **pterygomaxillary l.,** raphe pterygomandibularis. **pterygospinal l.,** ligamentum pterygospinale. **pubic l., inferior.** 1. Ligamentum arcuatum pubis. 2. Ligamentum suspensorium ovarii. **pubic l., superior,** ligamentum pubicum superius. **pubic l. of Cowper,** ligamentum inguinale. **pubic l. of Cruveilhier, anterior,** discus interpubicus. **pubocapsular l.,** ligamentum pubofemorale. **pubofemoral l.,** ligamentum pubofemorale. **puboischiadic l. of prostate gland,** fascia diaphragmatis urogenitalis superior. **puboprostatic l.,** ligamentum puboprostaticum. **puborectal l.** 1. Ligamentum puboprostaticum. 2. Ligamentum pubovesicale. **pubovesical l.,** ligamentum pubovesicale. **pulmonary l.,** ligamentum pulmonale. **quadrate l.,** ligamentum quadratum. **radial l., lateral,** ligamentum collaterale carpi radiale. **radial l. of cubitocarpal articulation,** ligamentum collaterale carpi radiale. **radiate l.,** ligamentum capitis costae radiatum. **radiate l., lateral,** ligamentum collaterale carpi ulnare. **radiate l. of carpus,** ligamentum carpi radiatum. **radiate l. of head of rib,** ligamentum capitis costae radiatum. **radiate l. of Mayer,** ligamentum carpi radiatum. **radiocarpal l., anterior,** ligamentum radiocarpeum palmare. **radiocarpal l., dorsal,** ligamentum radiocarpeum dorsale. **radiocarpal l., palmar,** ligamentum radiocarpeum palmare. **radiocarpal l., volar,** ligamentum radiocarpeum palmare. **rectouterine l.** musculus rectouterinus. **reflex l. of Gimbernat,** ligamentum inguinale reflexum. **reinforcing l's,** ligaments that serve to reinforce joint capsules. **rhomboid l. of clavicle,** ligamentum costoclaviculare. **rhomboid l. of wrist,** ligamentum radiocarpeum dorsale. **ring l. of hip joint,** zona orbicularis articulationis coxae. **round l. of acetabulum,** ligamentum capitis femoris. **round l. of Cloquet,** ligamentum capitis costae intraarticulare. **round l. of femur,** ligamentum capitis femoris. **round l. of forearm,** chorda obliqua membranae interosseae antebrachii. **round l. of uterus,** ligamentum teres uteri. **sacciform l.,** capsula articularis radioulnaris distalis. **sacrococcygeal l., dorsal, deep,** ligamentum sacrococcygeum dorsale profundum. **sacrococcygeal l., dorsal, superficial,** ligamentum sacrococcygeum dorsale superficiale. **sacrococcygeal l., lateral,** ligamentum sacrococcygeum laterale. **sacrococcygeal l., ventral,** ligamentum sacrococcygeum ventrale. **sacroiliac l's, anterior,** ligamenta sacroiliaca ventralia. **sacroiliac l's, dorsal,** ligamenta sacroiliaca dorsalia. **sacroiliac l's, interosseous,** ligamenta sacroiliaca interossea. **sacroiliac l., posterior, long, sacroiliac l., posterior, short.** See *ligamenta sacroiliaca dorsalia.* **sacroiliac l's, ventral,** ligamenta sacroiliaca ventralia. **sacrosciatic l., anterior,** ligamentum sacrospinale. **sacrosciatic l., great,** ligamentum sacrotuberale. **sacrosciatic l., internal,** ligamentum sacrospinale. **sacrosciatic l., least,** ligamentum sacrospinale. **sacrospinal l.,** ligamentum sacrospinale. **sacrotuberal l., sacrotuberous l.,** ligamentum sacrotuberale. **salpingopharyngeal l.,** plica salpingopharyngea. **Santorini's l.,** ligamentum cricopharyngeum. **Sappey's l.,** the thicker posterior part of the capsule of the temporomandibular joint. **scaphocuneiform l's, plantar,** ligamenta cuneonavicularia plantaria. **l. of Scarpa,** cornu superius marginis falciformis. **Schlemm's l's,** two ligamentous bands strengthening the capsule of the shoulder joint. **scrotal l. of testis,** gubernaculum testis. **serous l.,** ligamentum serosum. **l's of shoulder girdle,** ligamenta cinguli extremitatis superioris. **sphenoidal l., external,** ligamentum intercuneiformia plantaria. **sphenoideotarsal l's,** ligamenta tarsometatarsea plantaria. **sphenomandibular l.,** ligamentum sphenomandibulare. **spinoglenoid l.,** ligamentum transversum scapulae inferius. **spinosacral l.,** ligamentum sacrospinale. **spiral l. of cochlea,** ligamentum spirale cochleae. **splenogastric l.,** ligamentum gastrolienale. **splenophrenic l.,** ligamentum phrenicolienale. **spring l.,** ligamentum calcaneonaviculare plantare. **stapedial l.,** l. anulare stapedis. **stellate l., anterior,** ligamentum capitis costae radiatum. **sternoclavicular l., anterior,** ligamentum sternoclaviculare anterius. **sternoclavicular l., posterior,** ligamentum sternoclaviculare posterius. **sternocostal l's,** ligamenta sternocostalia radiata. **sternocostal l., interarticular, sternocostal l., intraarticular,** ligamentum sternocostale intraarticulare. **sternocostal l's, radiate,** ligamenta sternocostalia radiata. **sternopericardiac l's,** ligamenta sternopericardiaca. **stylohyoid l.,** ligamentum stylohyoideum. **stylomandibular l., stylomaxillary l., stylomylohyoid l.,** ligamentum stylomandibulare. **subflaval l.,** ligamentum flavum. **subpubic l.,** ligamentum

arcuatum pubis. **superficial l. of carpus.** 1. Ligamentum radiocarpeum dorsale. 2. Ligamentum radiocarpeum palmare. **superior l. of epididymis,** ligamentum epididymidis superius. **superior l. of hip,** ligamentum iliofemorale. **superior l. of incus,** ligamentum incudis superius. **superior l. of malleus,** ligamentum mallei superius. **superior l. of neck of rib, anterior,** the anterior part of the superior costotransverse ligament. **superior l. of neck of rib, external,** the posterior part of the superior costotransverse ligament. **superior l. of pinna,** ligamentum auriculare superius. **suprascapular l.,** ligamentum transversum scapulae superius. **supraspinal l., supraspinous l.,** ligamentum supraspinale. **suspensory l., marsupial,** plica synovialis infrapatellaris. **suspensory l. of axilla,** a layer ascending from the axillary fascia and ensheathing the pectoralis minor muscle; so called because traction by it, when the arm is abducted, produces the hollow of the armpit. **suspensory l. of axis,** ligamentum apicis dentis. **suspensory l. of bladder,** plica umbilicalis mediana. **suspensory l's of breast,** ligamenta suspensoria mammae. **suspensory l. of clitoris,** ligamentum suspensorium clitoridis. **suspensory l. of humerus,** ligamentum coracohumerale. **suspensory l. of lens,** zonula ciliaris. **suspensory l. of liver,** ligamentum falciforme hepatis. **suspensory l's of mammary gland,** ligamenta suspensoria mammae. **suspensory l. of ovary,** ligamentum suspensorium ovarii. **suspensory l. of penis,** ligamentum suspensorium penis. **suspensory l. of spleen,** ligamentum phrenicolienale. **sutural l.,** a band of fibrous tissue between the opposed bones of a suture or immovable joint. **synovial l.,** a large synovial fold. **synovial l. of hip,** ligamentum capitis femoris. **talocalcaneal l., anterior,** ligamentum talocalcaneum anterius. **talocalcaneal l., interosseous,** ligamentum talocalcaneum interosseum. **talocalcaneal l., lateral,** ligamentum talocalcaneum laterale. **talocalcaneal l., medial,** ligamentum talocalcaneum mediale. **talocalcaneal l., posterior,** ligamentum talocalcaneum posterius. **talofibular l., anterior,** ligamentum talofibulare anterius. **talofibular l., posterior,** ligamentum talofibulare posterius. **talotibial l., anterior,** pars tibiotalaris anterius. **talotibial l., posterior,** pars tibiotalaris posterius. **tarsal l., anterior,** retinaculum musculorum extensorum pedis inferius. **tarsometatarsal l's, dorsal,** ligamenta tarsometatarsea dorsalia. **tarsometatarsal l's, plantar,** ligamenta tarsometatarsea plantaria. **temporomandibular l.,** ligamentum laterale articulationis temporomandibularis. **tendinotrochanteric l.,** a portion of the capsule of the hip joint. **tensor l.,** musculus tensor tympani. **Teutleben's l's,** lateral folds joining the pericardium and diaphragm. **thyroepiglottic l.,** ligamentum thyroepiglotticum. **thyrohyoid l.,** ligamentum thyrohyoideum. **thyrohyoid l., median,** ligamentum thyrohyoideum medianum. **tibiofibular l.,** syndesmosis tibiofibularis. **tibiofibular l., anterior,** ligamentum tibiofibulare anterius. **tibiofibular l., posterior,** ligamentum tibiofibulare posterius. **tibionavicular l.,** pars tibionavicularis ligamenti medialis. **Toynbee's l.,** musculus tensor tympani. **transverse l. of acetabulum,** ligamentum acetabuli. **transverse l. of atlas,** ligamentum transversum atlantis. **transverse l. of carpus,** ligamentum carpi transversum. **transverse l. of knee,** ligamentum transversum genus. **transverse l. of leg,** retinaculum musculorum extensorum pedis superius. **transverse l's of little heads of metacarpal bones.** See *ligamentum metacarpeum transversum profundum.* **transverse l's of little heads of metatarsal bones.** See *ligamentum metatarseum transversum profundum.* **transverse l. of little head of rib,** ligamentum capitis costae intraarticulare. **transverse l. of pelvis,** ligamentum transversum perinei. **transverse l. of scapula, inferior,** ligamentum transversum scapulae inferius. **transverse l. of scapula, superior,** ligamentum transversum scapulae superius. **transverse l. of tibia,** retinaculum musculorum extensorum pedis superius. **transverse l. of wrist,** ligamentum carpi transversum. **transverse l's of wrist, dorsal,** ligamenta intercarpea dorsalia. **transverse humeral l.,** a band of fibers bridging the intertubercular groove of the humerus and holding the tendon of the biceps muscle in the groove. **transversocostal l., superior,** ligamentum costotransversarium superius. **trapezoid l.,** ligamentum trapezoideum. **l. of Treitz,** musculus suspensorius duodeni. **triangular l. of abdomen,** ligamentum inguinale reflexum. **triangular l. of Colles,** fascia diaphragmatis urogenitalis superior. **triangular l. of linea alba,** adminiculum lineae albae. **triangular l. of liver, left,** ligamentum triangulare sinistrum hepatis. **triangular l. of liver, right,** ligamentum triangulare dextrum hepatis. **triangular l. of pubis, anterior,** ligamentum arcuatum pubis. **triangular l. of scapula,** ligamentum transversum scapulae inferius. **triangular l. of thigh,** ligamentum inguinale reflexum. **triangular l. of urethra,** ligamentum puboprostaticum. **trigeminate l's of Arnold,** ligamenta tarsometatarsea dorsalia. **triquetral l.** 1. Ligamentum cricoarytenoideum posterius. 2. Ligamentum coracoacromiale. **triquetral l. of foot,** ligamentum calcaneofibulare. **triquetral l. of scapula,** ligamentum transversum scapulae inferius. **trochlear l.,** ligamentum metacarpeum transversum profundum. **trochlear l's of foot,** ligamenta plantaria articulationum metatarsophalangearum. **trochlear l's of hand,** ligamenta palmaria. **trochlear l's of little heads of metacarpal bones,** ligamenta metacarpeum transversum profundum. **true l. of bladder, anterior.** 1. Ligamentum puboprostaticum. 2. Ligamentum pubovesicale. **tuberososacral l.,** ligamentum sacrotuberale. **tubopharyngeal l. of Rauber,** plica salpingopharyngea. **Tuffier's inferior l.,** that part of the mesentery which is connected with the wall of the iliac fossa. **ulnar l., lateral, ulnar l. of carpus,** ligamentum collaterale carpi ulnare. **ulnocarpal l., palmar,** ligamentum ulnocarpeum palmare. **umbilical l., lateral,** ligamentum umbilicale laterale. **umbilical l., median, umbilical l., middle,** ligamentum umbilicale medianum. **utero-ovarian l.,** ligamentum ovarii proprium. **uteropelvic l's,** expansions of muscular tissue in the broad ligament of the uterus, radiating from the fascia over the obturator internus to the side of the uterus and the vagina. **uterosacral l.,** a part of the thickening of the visceral pelvic fascia beside the cervix and vagina, passing posteriorly in the rectouterine fold to attach to the front of the sacrum. **vaginal l.,** ligamentum vaginale. **vaginal l's of fingers,** vaginae fibrosae digitorum manus. **vaginal l's of toes,** vaginae fibrosae digitorum pedis. **l. of vaginal sheaths,** ligamentum vaginale. **l's of vaginal sheaths of fingers,** vaginae fibrosae digitorum manus. **l's of vaginal sheaths of toes,** vaginae fibrosae digitorum pedis. **l's of Valsalva,** ligamenta auricularia. **venous l. of liver,** ligamentum venosum. **ventricular l. of larynx,** ligamentum vestibulare. **vertebropleural l.,** membrana suprapleuralis. **l. of Vesalius,** ligamentum inguinale. **vesical l., lateral,** ligamentum umbilicale laterale. **vesicopubic l.,** ligamentum pubovesicale. **vesico-umbilical l.,** ligamentum umbilicale laterale. **vesico-uterine l.,** a ligament that extends from the anterior aspect of the uterus to the bladder. **vestibular l.,** ligamentum vestibulare. **vocal l.,** ligamentum vocale.

volar l's of bases of metacarpal bones, ligamenta metacarpea palmaria. **volar l. of carpus, proper,** ligamentum carpi transversum. **volar l's of carpus, transverse, deep,** ligamenta metacarpea palmaria. **volar l's of little heads of metacarpal bones.** See *ligamentum metacarpeum transversum profundum.* **volar l. of wrist, anterior,** ligamentum carpi transversum. **Walther's oblique l.,** ligamentum talofibulare posterius. **Weitbrecht's l.,** chorda obliqua membranae interosseae antebrachii. **Winslow's l.,** ligamentum popliteum obliquum. **Wrisberg's l.,** ligamentum meniscofemorale posterius. **xiphicostal l's of Macalister, xiphoid l's,** ligamenta costoxiphoidea. **Y l.,** ligamentum iliofemorale. **yellow l.,** ligamentum flavum. **Zinn's l.,** anulus tendineus communis. **zonal l. of thigh,** zona orbicularis articulationis coxae.

ligamenta (lig″ah-men′tah) [L.]. Plural of *ligamentum.*

ligamentopexis (lig″ah-men″to-pek′sis) [*ligament* + Gr. *pēxis* fixation]. Ligamentopexy.

ligamentopexy (lig″ah-men″to-pek′se). Ventrosuspension by shortening or suturing the round ligaments of the uterus.

ligamentous (lig″ah-men′tus). Pertaining to or of the nature of a ligament.

ligamentum (lig″ah-men′tum), pl. *ligamen′ta* [L. "a bandage," from *ligare* to bind]. [N A, B N A] A band of tissue that connects bones or supports viscera. Called also *ligament.* Some ligaments are distinct fibrous structures; some are folds of fascia or of indurated peritoneum; still others are relics of fetal organs. For names of specific structures, see *Table of Ligamenta.*

TABLE OF LIGAMENTA

Descriptions of ligaments are given on N A terms. B N A terms, when different, are cross referred to names used in Nomina Anatomica.

ligamen′ta accesso′ria planta′ria [B N A], ligamenta plantaria articulationum metatarsophalangearum.

ligamen′ta accesso′ria vola′ria [B N A], ligamenta palmaria.

l. acromioclavicula′re [N A, B N A], a dense band that joins the superior surface of the acromion and the acromial extremity of the clavicle together, and strengthens the superior part of the articular capsule.

ligamen′ta ala′ria [N A, B N A], two strong bands that pass from the posterolateral part of the tip of the dens of the axis upward and laterally to the condyles of the occipital bone. They limit rotation of the head.

l. annula′re ba′seos stape′dis [B N A], l. anulare stapedis.

ligamen′ta annula′ria digito′rum ma′nus [B N A]. See *pars anularis vaginae fibrosae digitorum manus.*

ligamen′ta annula′ria digito′rum pe′dis [B N A]. See *pars anularis vaginae fibrosae digitorum pedis.*

l. annula′re ra′dii [B N A], l. anulare radii.

ligamen′ta annula′ria [trachea′lia] [B N A], ligamenta anularia trachealia.

l. anococcyg′eum [N A, B N A], a fibrous band connecting the posterior fibers of the sphincter of the anus to the coccyx. Called also *anococcygeal ligament.*

l. anula′re ra′dii [N A], a strong fibrous band that encircles the head of the radius and holds it in position. It is attached to the anterior and posterior margins of the ulnar notch of the radius, forming, with the notch, a complete ring. Called also *l. annulare radii* [B N A].

l. anula′re stape′dis [N A], a ring of fibrous tissue that attaches the base of the stapes to the fenestra vestibuli of the inner ear. Called also *l. annulare baseos stapedis* [B N A], and *annular ligament of stapes.*

ligamen′ta anula′ria trachea′lia [N A], circular horizontal ligaments that join the tracheal cartilages together. Called also *ligamenta annularia [trachealia]* [B N A], and *tracheal annular ligaments.*

l. a′picis den′tis ax′is [N A], a cord of tissue extending from the tip of the dens of the axis to the occipital bone, near the anterior margin of the foramen magnum. It is usually delicate, but is sometimes well developed. Called also *l. apicis dentis epistrophei* [B N A].

l. a′picis den′tis epistro′phei [B N A], l. apicis dentis axis.

l. arcua′tum latera′le [N A], the ligamentous arch, formed by the fascia of the quadratus lumborum muscle, constituting part of the lumbar portion of the diaphragm. Called also *arcus lumbocostalis lateralis [Halleri]* [B N A], and *lateral arcuate ligament of diaphragm.*

l. arcua′tum media′le [N A], the ligamentous arch, formed by the fascia of the psoas muscle, constituting part of the lumbar portion of the diaphragm. Called also *arcus lumbocostalis medialis [Halleri]* [B N A], and *medial arcuate ligament.*

l. arcua′tum media′num [N A], the ligamentous arch across the front of the aorta, interconnecting the crura of the diaphragm. Called also *median arcuate ligament.*

l. arcua′tum pu′bis [N A, B N A], a thick archlike band of fibers situated along the inferior margin of the symphysis pubis. Its fibers are attached to the medial borders of the inferior rami of the pubic bones and thus it rounds out and forms the summit of the pubic arch. Called also *arcuate ligament of pubis.*

l. arterio′sum [N A], a short, thick, strong fibromuscular cord extending from the pulmonary artery to the arch of the aorta. It is the remains of the ductus arteriosus. Called also *l. arteriosum arteriae pulmonalis* [B N A].

l. arterio′sum arte′riae pulmona′lis [B N A], l. arteriosum.

ligamen′ta auricula′ria [N A], the three ligaments, anterior, superior, and posterior, that help attach the auricle to the side of the head. Called also *ligaments of auricle of external ear.*

ligamen′ta auricula′ria [Valsal′vae] [B N A], ligamenta auricularia.

l. auricula′re ante′rius [N A], the auricular ligament that passes from the helix and tragus to the zygoma. Called also, *anterior auricular ligament.*

l. auricula′re ante′rius [Valsal′vae] [B N A], l. auriculare anterius.

l. auricula′re poste′rius [N A], the auricular ligament that passes from the eminence of the concha to the mastoid part of the temporal bone. Called also *posterior auricular ligament.*

l. auricula′re poste′rius [Valsal′vae] [B N A], l. auriculare posterius.

l. auricula′re supe′rius [N A], the auricular ligament that passes from the spine of the helix to the superior margin of the bony external acoustic meatus. Called also *superior auricular ligament.*

l. auricula′re supe′rius [Valsal′vae] [B N A], l. auriculare superius.

ligamen′ta ba′sium [os′sium metacarpa′lium] dorsa′lia [B N A], ligamenta metacarpea dorsalia.

ligamenta ba′sium [os′sium metacarpa′lium] interos′sea [B N A], ligamenta metacarpea interossea.

ligamen′ta ba′sium [os′sium metacarpa′lium] vola′ria [B N A], ligamenta metacarpea palmaria.

ligamen'ta ba'sium [os'sium metatarsa'lium] dorsa'lia [B N A], ligamenta metatarsea dorsalia.

ligamen'ta ba'sium [os'sium metatarsa'lium] interos'sea [B N A], ligamenta metatarsea interossea.

ligamen'ta ba'sium [os'sium metatarsa'lium] planta'ria [B N A], ligamenta metatarsea plantaria.

l. bifurca'tum [N A, B N A], a Y-shaped ligament on the dorsum of the foot, comprising the calcaneonavicular and calcaneocuboid ligaments.

l. calcaneocuboi'deum [N A], the band of fibers connecting the superior surface of the calcaneus and the dorsal surface of the cuboid bone. Called also *pars calcaneocuboidea ligamenti bifurcati* [B N A], and *calcaneocuboid ligament.*

l. calcaneocuboi'deum planta're [N A, B N A], a short, wide, strong band connecting the plantar surfaces of the calcaneus and the cuboid bone. Called also *plantar calcaneocuboid ligament.*

l. calcaneofibula're [N A, B N A], a band of fibers arising from the lateral surface of the lateral malleolus of the fibula just anterior to the apex and passing inferiorly and posteriorly to be attached to the lateral surface of the calcaneus.

l. calcaneonavicula're [N A], the band of fibers connecting the superior surface of the calcaneus and the lateral surface of the navicular bone. Called also *pars calcaneonavicularis ligamenti bifurcati* [B N A], and *calcaneonavicular ligament.*

l. calcaneonavicula're dorsa'le [B N A], the dorsal portion of the calcaneonavicular part of the bifurcate ligament, connecting the dorsal surfaces of the calcaneus and the navicular bone. Omitted in N A.

l. calcaneonavicula're planta're [N A, B N A], a broad, thick band passing from the anterior margin of the sustentaculum tali to the plantar surface of the navicular bone. It bears on its deep surface a fibrocartilage that helps to support the head of the talus.

l. calcaneotibia'le [B N A], pars tibiocalcanea ligamenti medialis.

l. cap'itis cos'tae intraarticula're [N A], a horizontal band of fibers that is attached to the crest separating the two articular facets on the head of the rib, and to the intervertebral disk, thus dividing the joint of the head of the rib into two cavities. It is lacking in the joints of the first, tenth, eleventh, and twelfth ribs. Called also *l. capituli costae interarticulare* [B N A].

l. cap'itis cos'tae radia'tum [N A], fibers that from their attachment on the ventral surface of the head of a rib radiate medially, in a fanlike manner, to attach to the two adjacent vertebrae and to the intervertebral disk between them. Called also *l. capituli costae radiatum* [B N A], and *radiate ligament of head of rib.*

l. cap'itis fem'oris [N A], a curved triangular or V-shaped fibrous band, attached by its apex to the anterosuperior part of the fovea of the head of the femur and by its base to the sides of the acetabular notch and the intervening transverse ligament of the acetabulum. Called also *l. teres femoris* [B N A], *round ligament of femur*, and *ligament of head of femur.*

l. cap'itis fib'ulae ante'rius [N A], a band of fibers that passes obliquely superiorly from the anterior part of the head of the fibula to the lateral condyle of the tibia. Called also *anterior ligament of head of fibula.*

l. cap'itis fib'ulae poste'rius [N A], a band of fibers that passes obliquely superiorly from the posterior part of the head of the fibula to the lateral condyle of the tibia. Called also *posterior ligament of head of fibula.*

l. capit'uli cos'tae interarticula're [B N A], l. capitis costae intraarticulare.

l. capit'uli cos'tae radia'tum [B N A], l. capitis costae radiatum.

ligamen'ta capit'uli fib'ulae [B N A]. See *l. capitis fibulae anterius* and *l. capitis fibulae posterius.*

ligamen'ta capitulo'rum [os'sium metacarpa'lium] transver'sa [B N A]. See *l. metacarpeum transversum profundum.*

ligamen'ta capitulo'rum [os'sium metatarsa'lium] transver'sa [B N A]. See *l. metatarseum transversum profundum.*

l. car'pi dorsa'le [B N A], retinaculum extensorum manus.

l. car'pi radia'tum [N A, B N A], a group of about seven fibrous bands which diverge in all directions on the palmar surface of the mediocarpal joint; the majority radiate from the capitate to the scaphoid, lunate, and triquetral bones. Called also *radiate carpal ligament.*

l. car'pi transver'sum [B N A], retinaculum flexorum manus.

l. car'pi vola're [B N A], transverse reinforcing fibers in the antebrachial fascia over the palmar surface of the wrist. Omitted in N A.

ligamen'ta carpometacar'pea dorsa'lia [N A, B N A], a series of bands on the dorsal surface of the carpometacarpal articulations, joining the carpal bones to the bases of the second to fifth metacarpals. The second metacarpal bone is thus joined to the trapezium, trapezoid, and capitate, the third to the capitate, the fourth to the capitate and hamate, and the fifth to the hamate. Called also *dorsal carpometacarpal ligaments.*

ligamen'ta carpometacar'pea palma'ria [N A], a series of bands on the palmar surface of the carpometacarpal articulations, joining the carpal bones to the second to fifth metacarpals. The second is thus joined to the trapezium, the third to the trapezium, capitate, and hamate, the fourth to the hamate, and the fifth to the hamate. Called also *ligamenta carpometacarpea volaria* [B N A], and *palmar carpometacarpal ligaments.*

ligamen'ta carpometacar'pea vola'ria [B N A], ligamenta carpometacarpea palmaria.

l. cauda'le integumen'ti commu'nis [B N A], retinaculum caudale.

l. ceratocricoi'deum ante'rius [B N A], a fibrous band that extends from the anterior surface of the tip of the inferior cornu of the thyroid cartilage forward and downward and is attached to the side of the arch of the cricoid cartilage. Omitted in N A.

ligamen'ta ceratocricoi'dea latera'lia [B N A], fibrous bands that extend downward and back from the tip of the inferior cornu of the thyroid cartilage and are attached to the lower, lateral, outer surface of the lamina of the cricoid cartilage. Omitted in N A.

ligamen'ta ceratocricoi'dea posterio'ra [B N A], fibrous bands that extend from the posterior surface of the inferior cornu of the thyroid cartilage near its tip upward, backward, and medially, and are attached to the superior lateral margin of the lamina of the cricoid cartilage. Omitted in N A.

ligamen'ta cin'guli extremita'tis inferio'ris [B N A], the ligaments of the pelvic girdle, including (intrinsic) the iliolumbar, sacrotuberous, and sacrospinous ligaments and the superior and arcuate ligaments of the symphysis pubis, and (extrinsic) those of the sacroiliac and hip joints.

ligamen'ta cin'guli extremita'tis superio'ris [B N A], the ligaments of the shoulder girdle, including (intrinsic) the coracoacromial and the inferior and superior transverse scapular ligaments and (extrinsic) those of the sternoclavicular articulation.

ligamen'ta collatera'lia articulatio'num digito'rum ma'nus [B N A], ligamenta collateralia articulationum interphalangearum manus.

ligamen'ta collatera'lia articulatio'num digito'rum pe'dis [B N A], ligamenta collateralia articulationum interphalangearum pedis.

ligamen'ta collatera'lia articulatio'num interphalangea'rum ma'nus [N A], massive fibrous bands on each side of the interphalangeal joints of the fingers. They are placed diagonally, the proximal ends being near the dorsal, and the distal ends near the palmar margins of the digits. Called also *ligamenta collateralia articulationum digitorum manus* [B N A], and *collateral ligaments of interphalangeal articulations of hand.*

ligamen'ta collatera'lia articulatio'num interphalangea'rum pe'dis [N A], fibrous bands, one on either side of each of the interphalangeal joints of the toes. Called also *ligamenta collateralia articulationum digitorum pedis* [B N A], and *collateral ligaments of interphalangeal articulations of foot.*

ligamen'ta collatera'lia articulatio'num metacarpophalangea'rum [N A, B N A], massive, strong fibrous bands on either side of each metacarpophalangeal joint, holding the two bones involved in each joint firmly together. Called also *collateral ligaments of metacarpophalangeal articulations.*

ligamen'ta collatera'lia articulatio'num metatarsophalangea'rum [N A, B N A], strong fibrous bands on either side of each metatarsophalangeal joint, holding the two bones involved in each joint firmly together. Called also *collateral ligaments of metatarsophalangeal articulations.*

l. collatera'le car'pi radia'le [N A, B N A], a short, thick band that passes from the tip of the styloid process of the radius to attach to the scaphoid bone. Called also *radial carpal collateral ligament.*

l. collatera'le car'pi ulna're [N A, B N A], a strong fibrous band that passes from the tip of the styloid process of the ulna and is attached to the triquetral and pisiform bones. Called also *ulnar carpal collateral ligament.*

l. collatera'le fibula're [N A, B N A], a strong, round fibrous cord on the lateral side of the knee joint, entirely independent of the capsule of the knee joint; it is attached superiorly to the posterior part of the lateral epicondyle of the femur and inferiorly to the lateral side of the head of the fibula just in front of the styloid process. Called also *collateral fibular ligament.*

l. collatera'le radia'le [N A, B N A], a large bundle of fibers arising from the lateral epicondyle of the humerus and fanning out to be attached to the lateral side of the annular ligament of the radius. Called also *collateral radial ligament.*

l. collatera'le tibia'le [N A, B N A], a broad, flat, longitudinal band on the medial side of the knee joint. It is attached superiorly to the medial epicondyle of the femur, inferiorly to the medial surface of the body of the tibia, and in between to the medial meniscus. Called also *collateral tibial ligament.*

l. collatera'le ulna're [N A, B N A], a triangular bundle of fibers attached proximally to the medial epicondyle of the humerus, distally to the coronoid process of the ulna and the medial surface of the olecranon, and to a ridge running between the two. Called also *collateral ulnar ligament.*

l. col'li cos'tae [B N A], l. costotransversarium.

ligamen'ta colum'nae vertebra'lis et cra'nii [B N A], ligaments of the vertebral column and cranium.

l. conoi'deum [N A, B N A], the conical, posteromedial portion of the coracoclavicular ligament, attached inferiorly by its tip to the base of the coracoid process of the scapula and superiorly by its base to the inferior surface of the clavicle. Called also *conoid ligament.*

l. coracoacromia'le [N A, B N A], one of three intrinsic ligaments of the scapula, a strong broad triangular band that is attached by its base to the lateral border of the coracoid process and by its tip to the summit of the acromion just in front of the articular facet for the clavicle.

l. coracoclavicula're [N A, B N A], a strong band that joins the coracoid process of the scapula and the acromial extremity of the clavicle. It is divided into two parts, the trapezoid and conoid ligaments.

l. coracohumera'le [N A, B N A], a broad band that arises from the lateral border of the coracoid process of the scapula and passes downward and laterally to be attached to the major tubercle of the humerus.

l. corniculopharyn'geum [B N A], the upper part of the ligamentum jugale between the Y and the corniculate cartilage. Omitted in N A.

l. corona'rium hep'atis [N A, B N A], the line of reflection of the peritoneum from the diaphragmatic surface of the liver to the under surface of the diaphragm. Called also *coronary ligament of liver.*

l. costoclavicula're [N A, B N A], a short, powerful ligament that extends from the superior margin of the first costal cartilage to the inferior surface at the sternal end of the clavicle.

l. costotransversa'rium [N A], short fibers that connect the dorsal surface of the neck of a rib with the anterior surface of the transverse process of the corresponding vertebra. Called also *l. colli costae* [B N A], and *costotransverse ligament.*

l. costotransversa'rium ante'rius [B N A]. See *l. costotransversarium superius.*

l. costotransversa'rium latera'le [N A], a fibrous band that passes transversely from the posterior surface of the tip of a transverse process of a vertebra to the nonarticular part of the tubercle of the corresponding rib. Called also *l. tuberculi costae* [B N A], and *lateral costotransverse ligament.*

l. costotransversa'rium poste'rius [B N A]. See *l. costotransversarium superius.*

l. costotransversa'rium supe'rius [N A], a strong band of fibers ascending from the crest of the neck of a rib to the transverse process of the vertebra above. It may be divided into a stronger anterior portion and a weaker posterior portion. It is lacking for the first rib. Called also *superior costotransverse ligament.*

ligamen'ta costoxiphoi'dea [N A, B N A], inconstant strandlike bands that pass obliquely from the anterior surface of the seventh and sometimes from the sixth costal cartilage to the anterior surface of the xiphoid process of the sternum. Some bands may also be present on the posterior surface.

l. cricoarytenoi'deum poste'rius [N A], the ligament extending from the lamina of the cricoid cartilage to the medial surface of the base and muscular process of the arytenoid cartilage. Called also *posterior cricoarytenoid cartilage.*

l. cricopharyn'geum [N A, B N A], a ligament extending from the cricoid lamina to the midline of the pharynx. Called also *cricopharyngeal ligament.*

l. cricothyreoi'deum [me'dium] [B N A], l. cricothyroideum.

l. cricothyroi'deum [N A], a flat band of white fibrous tissue extending from the inferior thyroid notch down to the arcus of the cricoid cartilage, thus forming the conus elasticus. Called also *l. cricothyreoideum [medium]* [B N A], and *cricothyroid ligament.*

l. cricotrachea'le [N A, B N A], a narrow fibrous ring that connects the lower margin of the cricoid cartilage with the upper tracheal cartilage. It is continuous behind with the membranous wall of the trachea. Called also *cricotracheal ligament.*

l. crucia'tum ante'rius ge'nu [B N A], l. cruciatum anterius genus.

l. crucia'tum ante'rius ge'nus [N A], a strong band that arises from the posteromedial portion of the lateral condyle of the femur, passes anteriorly and inferiorly between the condyles, and is attached to the depression in front of the intercondylar eminence of the tibia. Called also *l. cruciatum anterius genu* [B N A], and *anterior cruciate ligament of knee.*

l. crucia'tum atlan'tis [B N A], l. cruciforme atlantis.

l. crucia'tum cru'ris [B N A], retinaculum musculorum extensorum pedis inferius.

ligamen'ta crucia'ta digito'rum ma'nus

[B N A]. See *pars cruciformis vaginae fibrosae digitorum manus.*

ligamen'ta crucia'ta digito'rum pe'dis [B N A]. See *pars cruciformis vaginae fibrosae digitorum pedis.*

ligamen'ta crucia'ta ge'nu [B N A], ligamenta cruciata genus.

ligamen'ta crucia'ta ge'nus [N A], strong, thick bundles situated in the knee joint between the condyles of the femur, which together form a somewhat cross-shaped structure. Called also *ligamenta cruciata genu* [B N A], and *cruciate ligaments of knee.* See *l. cruciatum anterius genus* and *l. cruciatum posterius genus.*

l. crucia'tum poste'rius ge'nu [B N A], l. cruciatum posterius genus.

l. crucia'tum poste'rius ge'nus [N A], a strong band that arises from the anterolateral surface of the medial condyle of the femur, passes posteriorly and inferiorly between the condyles, and is inserted into the posterior intercondylar area of the tibia. Called also *l. cruciatum posterius genu* [B N A], and *posterior cruciate ligament of knee.*

l. crucifor'me atlan'tis [N A], a ligament in the form of a cross, of which the transverse ligament of the atlas forms the horizontal bar, and the longitudinal fascicles the vertical bar of the cross. Called also *l. cruciatum atlantis* [B N A], and *cruciform ligament of atlas.*

l. cuboideonavicula're dorsa'le [N A, B N A], a fibrous bundle connecting the dorsal surfaces of the cuboid and navicular bones. Called also *dorsal cuboideonavicular ligament.*

l. cuboideonavicula're planta're [N A, B N A], a fibrous band connecting the plantar surfaces of the cuboid and navicular bones. Called also *plantar cuboideonavicular ligament.*

l. cuneocuboi'deum dorsa'le [N A, B N A], fibers connecting the dorsal surfaces of the cuboid and lateral cuneiform bones. Called also *dorsal cuneocuboid ligament.*

l. cuneocuboi'deum interos'seum [N A, B N A], fibers connecting the central portions of the adjacent surfaces of the cuboid and lateral cuneiform bones, between the articular surfaces. Called also *interosseous cuneocuboid ligament.*

l. cuneocuboi'deum planta're [N A, B N A], a band of fibers connecting the plantar surfaces of the cuboid and lateral cuneiform bones. Called also *plantar cuneocuboid ligament.*

ligamen'ta cuneometatar'sea interos'sea [N A, B N A], fibrous bands that join the adjacent surfaces of the cuneiform and the metatarsal bones.

ligamen'ta cuneonavicula'ria dorsa'lia [N A], bands that join the dorsal surface of the navicular bone to the dorsal surfaces of the three cuneiform bones. Called also *ligamenta navicularicuneiformia dorsalia* [B N A], and *dorsal cuneonavicular ligaments.*

ligamen'ta cuneonavicula'ria planta'ria [N A], bands that join the plantar surface of the navicular bone to the adjacent plantar surfaces of the three cuneiform bones. Called also *ligamenta navicularicuneiformia plantaria* [B N A], and *plantar cuneonavicular ligaments.*

l. deltoi'deum [B N A], N A alternative for *l. mediale.*

l. denticula'tum [N A, B N A], a fold of pia mater of the spinal cord, beginning in a longitudinal line along the spinal cord between the lines of attachment of the anterior and posterior roots. The lateral edge is scalloped and has about 21 pointed processes that extend through the arachnoid to become continuous with the inner surface of the dura mater. Called also *denticulate ligament.*

l. duodenorena'le [B N A], a fold of peritoneum that passes from the duodenum to the right kidney. Called also *duodenorenal ligament.* Omitted in N A.

l. epididym'idis infe'rius [N A, B N A], a strand of fibrous tissue, covered with a reflection of the tunica vaginalis, which connects the lower end of the body of the epididymis with the testis. Called also *inferior ligament of epididymis.*

l. epididym'idis supe'rius [N A, B N A], a strand of fibrous tissue, covered with a reflection of the tunica vaginalis, which connects the upper end of the body of the epididymis with the testis. Called also *superior ligament of epididymis.*

l. falcifor'me hep'atis [N A, B N A], a sickle-shaped sagittal fold of peritoneum that helps to attach the liver to the diaphragm, separates the right and left lobes of the liver, and extends from the coronary ligament of the liver behind to the umbilicus in front. Called also *falciform ligament of liver.*

ligamen'ta fla'va [B N A]. See *l. flavum.*

l. fla'vum [N A], one of a series of bands of yellow elastic tissue attached to and extending between the ventral portions of the laminae of two adjacent vertebrae, from the junction of the axis and the third cervical vertebra to the junction of the fifth lumbar vertebra and the sacrum. They assist in maintaining or regaining the erect position and serve to close in the spaces between the arches. Called also *arcuate, flaval,* or *yellow ligament.*

l. fundifor'me pe'nis [N A, B N A], a broad elastic band of fascial fibers that arises from the linea alba and from the fibrae intercrurales just above the symphysis pubis and then passes down to the penis, where it divides and passes around the penis and on into the scrotum. Called also *fundiform ligament of penis.*

l. gastrocol'icum [N A, B N A], the omental folds of the peritoneum that extend from the greater curvature of the stomach to the transverse colon. Called also *gastrocolic ligament.*

l. gastroliena'le [N A, B N A], a peritoneal fold extending from the greater curvature of the stomach to the hilus of the spleen and containing blood vessels, nerves, and lymph nodes. Called also *gastrosplenic ligament.*

l. gastrophren'icum [N A], a fold of peritoneum continuous with the gastrosplenic ligament, extending from the diaphragm to the stomach. Called also *gastrophrenic ligament.*

l. genitoinguina'le [N A], the embryonic precursor of the gubernaculum testis. Called also *genitoinguinal ligament.*

ligamen'ta glenohumera'lia [N A], bands, usually three in number, on the inner surface of the articular capsule of the humerus, attached to the margin of the glenoid cavity and to the anatomical neck of the humerus. Called also *glenohumeral ligaments.*

l. hepatocol'icum [N A, B N A], a fold of peritoneum sometimes passing from the lower surface of the liver near the gallbladder to the right colic flexure. Called also *hepatocolic ligament.*

l. hepatoduodena'le [N A, B N A], a peritoneal fold that passes from the porta hepatis to the superior portion of the duodenum. It is continuous on the left with the gastrohepatic ligament, and on the right it forms one of the borders of the epiploic foramen. It contains the hepatic artery, portal vein, bile duct, nerves, and lymphatics. Called also *hepatoduodenal ligament.*

l. hepatogas'tricum [N A, B N A], a peritoneal fold, part of the lesser omentum, that passes from the under surface of the liver to the lesser curvature of the stomach. Called also *gastrohepatic ligament.*

l. hepatorena'le [N A, B N A], a fold of peritoneum that passes from the back part of the lower surface of the liver to the front of the right kidney and forms the right margin of the epiploic foramen. Called also *hepatorenal ligament.*

l. hyoepiglot'ticum [N A, B N A], a triangular elastic band with its base attached to the upper border of the body of the hyoid bone and its tip to the anterosuperior surface of the epiglottis. Called also *hyoepiglottic ligament.*

l. hyothyreoi'deum latera'le [B N A], l. thyrohyoideum.

l. hyothyreoi'deum me'dium [B N A], l. thyrohyoideum medianum.

l. iliofemora'le [N A, B N A], a very strong triangular or inverted Y-shaped band that covers the anterior and superior portions of the hip joint. It arises by its apex from the lower part of the anterior inferior iliac spine and is inserted by its base into the intertrochanteric line of the femur. Called also *iliofemoral ligament.*

l. iliolumba'le [N A, B N A], a strong band that passes from the transverse processes of the fourth and fifth lumbar vertebrae to the internal lip of the adjacent portion of the iliac crest. Called also *iliolumbar ligament.*

l. in'cudis poste'rius [N A, B N A], a fibrous band by which the cartilaginous tip of the short crus of the incus is fixed to the fossa incudis. Called also *posterior ligament of incus.*

l. in'cudis supe'rius [N A, B N A], a fibrous band that passes from the body of the incus to the roof of the tympanic cavity just back of the superior ligament of the malleus. Called also *superior ligament of incus.*

l. inguina'le [N A], a fibrous band running from the anterior superior spine of the ilium to the spine of the pubis. Called also *inguinal ligament.*

l. inguina'le [Poupar'ti] [B N A], l. inguinale.

l. inguina'le reflex'um [N A], a triangular band of fibers arising from the lacunar ligament and the pubic bone and passing diagonally upward and medially behind the superficial abdominal ring and in front of the inguinal aponeurotic falx to the linea alba.

l. inguina'le reflex'um [Colle'si] [B N A], l. inguinale reflexum.

ligamen'ta intercar'pea dorsa'lia [N A, B N A], several bands that extend transversely across the dorsal surfaces of the carpal bones, connecting various ones together. Called also *dorsal intercarpal ligaments.*

ligamen'ta intercar'pea interos'sea [N A, B N A], short fibrous bands that join the adjacent surfaces of the various carpal bones. Called also *interosseous intercarpal ligaments.*

ligamen'ta intercar'pea palma'ria [N A], several bands that extend transversely across the palmar surfaces of the carpal bones, connecting various ones together. Called also *ligamenta intercarpea volaria* [B N A], and *palmar intercarpal ligaments.*

ligamen'ta intercar'pea vola'ria [B N A], ligamenta intercarpea palmaria.

l. interclavicula're [N A, B N A], a flattened band that passes from the superior surface of the sternal end of one clavicle across the superior margin of the sternum to the same position on the other clavicle.

ligamen'ta intercosta'lia [B N A]. See *membrana intercostalis externa* and *membrana intercostalis interna.*

ligamen'ta intercosta'lia exter'na [B N A]. See *membrana intercostalis externa.*

ligamen'ta intercosta'lia inter'na [B N A]. See *membrana intercostalis interna.*

ligamen'ta intercuneifor'mia dorsa'lia [N A], fibrous bands connecting the dorsal surfaces of the three cuneiform bones. Called also *dorsal intercuneiform ligaments.*

ligamen'ta intercuneifor'mia interos'sea [N A, B N A], short fibrous bands that join the adjacent surfaces of the medial and intermediate, and the intermediate and lateral, cuneiform bones. Called also *interosseous intercuneiform ligaments.*

ligamen'ta intercuneifor'mia planta'ria [N A, B N A], fibrous bands that join the plantar surfaces of the cuneiform bones. Called also *plantar intercuneiform ligaments.*

l. interfoveola're [N A], a thickening in the transversalis fascia on the medial side of the deep inguinal ring. It is connected above to the transversus muscle and below to the inguinal ligament. Called also *interfoveolar ligament.*

l. interfoveola're [Hesselba'chi] [B N A], l. interfoveolare.

l. interspina'le [N A], any of several fine fibrous membranes that extend from one vertebral spinous process to the next. They extend obliquely from the yellow ligaments ventrally to the supraspinous ligament dorsally, and contain white fibrous and yellow elastic tissue. They are lacking in the cervical region. Called also *interspinal ligament.*

ligamen'ta interspina'lia [B N A]. See *l. interspinale.*

l. intertransversa'rium [N A], any of several poorly developed fibrous bands that extend from one vertebral transverse process to the next. They consist of fine membranes in the lumbar region and of small cords in the thoracic region, and are lacking in the cervical region. Called also *intertransverse ligament.*

ligamen'ta intertransversa'ria [B N A]. See *l. intertransversarium.*

l. ischiocapsula're [B N A], l. ischiofemorale.

l. ischiofemora'le [N A], a broad triangular band on the posterior surface of the hip joint. Its base is attached to the ischium posterior and inferior to the acetabulum; its fibers pass superiorly, laterally, and anteriorly across the capsule, bend over the neck, and in part are inserted into the inner side of the trochanteric fossa of the femur and in part blend into the zona orbicularis. Called also *l. ischiocapsulare* [B N A], and *ischiofemoral ligament.*

l. lacinia'tum [B N A], retinaculum musculorum flexorum pedis.

l. lacuna're [N A], a small triangular membrane with its base just medial to the femoral ring. One side is attached to the inguinal ligament and the other to the pectineal line of the pubis. Called also *lacunar ligament.*

l. lacuna're [Gimberna'ti] [B N A], l. lacunare.

l. latera'le articulatio'nis temporomandibula'ris [N A], a strong triangular fibrous band that is attached superiorly by its base to the zygomatic process of the temporal bone, passes down on the lateral side of the joint in contact with the capsule, and is inserted by its apex into the lateral and posterior surfaces of the neck of the condyloid process of the mandible. Called also *l. temporomandibulare* [B N A], and *lateral ligament of temporomandibular articulation.*

l. la'tum u'teri [N A, B N A], a broad fold of peritoneum extending from the side of the uterus to the wall of the pelvis. It is divided into the mesometrium, mesosalpinx, and mesovarium. Called also *broad ligament of uterus.*

l. lienorena'le, N A alternative for *l. phrenicolienale.*

l. longitudina'le ante'rius [N A, B N A], a single long, fibrous band in the midline, attached to the ventral surfaces of the bodies of the vertebrae. It extends from the occipital bone and the anterior tubercle of the atlas down to the sacrum. Called also *anterior longitudinal ligament.*

l. longitudina'le poste'rius [N A, B N A], a single mid-line fibrous band attached to the dorsal surfaces of the bodies of the vertebrae, extending from the occipital bone to the coccyx. Called also *posterior longitudinal ligament.*

l. lumbocosta'le [N A, B N A], a strong fascial band that passes from the twelfth rib to the tips of the transverse processes of the first and second lumbar vertebrae. Called also *lumbocostal ligament.*

l. mal'lei ante'rius [N A, B N A], a fibrous band that extends from the neck of the malleus just above the anterior process to the anterior wall of the tympanic cavity close to the petrotympanic fissure. Some of the fibers pass through the fissure to the spina angulares of the sphenoid bone. Called also *anterior ligament of malleus.*

l. mal'lei latera'le [N A, B N A], a triangular fibrous band that passes from the posterior portion of the incisura tympanica to the head or neck of the malleus. Called also *lateral ligament of malleus.*

l. mal'lei supe'rius [N A, B N A], a delicate fibrous strand passing from the roof of the tympanic cavity to the head of the malleus. Called also *superior ligament of malleus.*

l. malle'oli latera'lis ante'rius [B N A], l. tibiofibulare anterius.

l. malle'oli latera'lis poste'rius [B N A], l. tibiofibulare posterius.

l. media'le [N A], a large fan-shaped ligament on the medial side of the ankle, passing from the medial malleolus of the tibia down onto the tarsal bones. It comprises four parts: pars tibionavicularis, pars tibiocalcanea, pars tibiotalaris anterior, and pars tibiotalaris posterior. Called also *l. deltoideum* [B N A], and *medial ligament.*

l. meniscofemora'le ante'rius [N A], a small fibrous band of the knee joint, attached to the posterior area of the lateral meniscus and passing superiorly and medially, anterior to the posterior cruciate ligament, to attach to the anterior cruciate ligament. Called also *anterior meniscofemoral ligament.*

l. meniscofemora'le poste'rius [N A], a small fibrous band of the knee joint, attached to the posterior area of the lateral meniscus and passing superiorly and medially, posterior to the posterior cruciate ligament, to the medial condyle of the femur. Called also *posterior meniscofemoral ligament.*

ligamen'ta metacar'pea dorsa'lia [N A], bands that interconnect the bases of the second to fifth metacarpal bones by passing transversely from bone to bone on their dorsal surfaces. Called also *ligamenta basium [ossium metacarpalium] dorsalia* [B N A], and *dorsal metacarpal ligaments.*

ligamen'ta metacar'pea interos'sea [N A], short, strong fibrous bands situated between the adjacent surfaces of the bases of the second to fifth metacarpal bones, just distal to the articular surfaces. Called also *ligamenta basium [ossium metacarpalium] interossea* [B N A], and *interosseous metacarpal ligaments.*

ligamen'ta metacar'pea palma'ria [N A], bands that interconnect the bases of the second to fifth metacarpal bones by passing transversely from bone to bone on their palmar surfaces. Called also *ligamenta basium [ossium metacarpalium] volaria* [B N A], and *palmar metacarpal ligaments.*

l. metacar'peum transver'sum profun'dum [N A], a narrow fibrous band that extends across and is attached to the palmar surfaces of the heads of the second to fifth metacarpal bones, joining them together. Called also *ligamenta capitulorum [ossium metacarpalium] transversa* [B N A], and *deep transverse metacarpal ligament.*

l. metacar'peum transver'sum superficia'le [N A], transverse fibers occupying the intervals between the diverging longitudinal bands of the palmar aponeurosis. Called also *superficial transverse metacarpal ligament.*

ligamen'ta metatar'sea dorsa'lia [N A], light transverse bands on the dorsal surfaces of the bases of the second to fifth metatarsal bones, similar to the corresponding ligaments on the metacarpal bones. Called also *ligamenta basium [ossium metatarsalium] dorsalia* [B N A], and *dorsal metatarsal ligaments.*

ligamen'ta metatar'sea interos'sea [N A], bands between the bases of the second to fifth metatarsal bones, similar to the corresponding ligaments of the hand. Called also *ligamenta basium [ossium metatarsalium] interossea* [B N A], and *interosseous metatarsal ligaments.*

ligamen'ta metatar'sea planta'ria [N A], strong transverse bands on the plantar surfaces of the bases of the second to fifth metatarsal bones. Called also *ligamenta basium [ossium metatarsalium] plantaria* [B N A], and *plantar metatarsal ligaments.*

l. metatar'seum transver'sum profun'dum [N A], a narrow fibrous band that extends across, is attached to the plantar surfaces of, and thus joins together the heads of all the metatarsal bones. Called also *ligamenta capitulorum [ossium metatarsalium] transversa* [B N A], and *deep transverse metatarsal ligament.*

l. metatar'seum transver'sum superficia'le [N A], fibers that lie in the superficial fascia of the sole of the foot beneath the heads of the metatarsal bones. Called also *superficial transverse metatarsal ligament.*

ligamen'ta navicularicuneifor'mia dorsa'lia [B N A], ligamenta cuneonavicularia dorsalia.

ligamen'ta navicularicuneifor'mia planta'ria [B N A], ligamenta cuneonavicularia plantaria.

l. nu'chae [N A, B N A], a broad, fibrous, roughly triangular sagittal septum in the back of the neck, separating the right and left sides. It extends from the tips of the spinous processes of all the cervical vertebrae to attach to the entire length of the external occipital crest. Caudally it is continuous with the supraspinous ligament.

ligamen'ta ossiculo'rum audi'tus [N A, B N A], the ligaments of the auditory ossicles, comprising the anterior, lateral, and superior ligaments of the malleus, the posterior and superior ligaments of the incus, and the annular ligament of the stapes. Called also *ligaments of auditory ossicles.*

l. ova'rii pro'prium [N A, B N A], a musculofibrous cord in the broad ligament, joining the ovary to the upper part of the lateral margin of the uterus just below the attachment of the uterine tube. Called also *ovarian ligament.*

ligamen'ta palma'ria [N A], thick, dense fibrocartilaginous plates on the palmar surfaces of the metacarpophalangeal articulations, between the collateral ligaments. They are firmly connected to the bases of the proximal phalanges but only loosely connected to the metacarpal bones. Called also *ligamenta accessoria volaria* [B N A], and *palmar ligaments.*

l. palpebra'le latera'le [N A], a ligament that anchors the lateral end of the superior and inferior tarsal plates to the margin of the orbit.

l. palpebra'le media'le [N A, B N A], fibrous bands that connect the medial ends of the tarsi to the bones of the orbit, an anterior bundle passing in front of the lacrimal sac and being attached to the frontal process of the maxilla, and a posterior bundle passing behind the lacrimal sac and being attached to the posterior crest of the lacrimal bone. Called also *medial palpebral ligament.*

l. patel'lae [N A, B N A], the continuation of the central portion of the tendon of the quadriceps femoris muscle distal to the patella. It extends from the patella to the tuberosity of the tibia. Called also *patellar ligament.*

l. pectina'tum an'guli iridocornea'lis [N A], a few poorly developed fibers found in the iridocorneal angle, interconnecting the cornea, iris, and ciliary muscle. Called also *l. pectinatum iridis* [B N A], and *pectinate ligament of iridocorneal angle.*

l. pectina'tum i'ridis [B N A], l. pectinatum anguli iridocornealis.

l. pectinea'le [N A], a strong aponeurotic lateral continuation of the lacunar ligament along the pectineal line of the pubis. Called also *pectineal ligament.*

l. phrenicocol'icum [N A, B N A], a peritoneal fold that passes from the left colic flexure to the adjacent costal portion of the diaphragm. Called also *phrenicocolic ligament.*

l. phrenicoliena'le [N A, B N A], a peritoneal fold that passes from the diaphragm to the concave surface of the spleen. Called also *l. lienorenale* and *phrenicosplenic ligament.*

l. pisohama'tum [N A, B N A], a fibrous band extending from the pisiform bone to the hook of the hamate bone. Called also *pisohamate ligament.*

l. pisometacar′peum [N A, B N A], a fibrous band extending from the pisiform bone to the bases of the fifth, usually the fourth, and sometimes the third metacarpal bone. Called also *pisometacarpal ligament.*

ligamen′ta planta′ria articulatio′num metatarsophalangea′rum [N A], thick, dense bands situated on the plantar surfaces of the metatarsophalangeal articulations between the collateral ligaments. Called also *ligamenta accessoria plantaria* [B N A].

l. planta′re lon′gum [N A, B N A], the longest ligament of the foot, arising from the lower surface of the calcaneus as far back as the lateral and the medial processes, passing forward over the tendon of the peroneus longus, and inserting into the bases of the second through fifth metatarsal bones. Called also *long plantar ligament.*

l. poplite′um arcua′tum [N A, B N A], a band of variable and ill-defined fibers at the posterolateral part of the knee joint. It is attached inferiorly to the apex of the head of the fibula, arches superiorly and medially over the popliteal tendon, and merges with the articular capsule. Called also *popliteal arch* and *arcuate popliteal ligament.*

l. poplite′um obli′quum [N A, B N A], a broad band of fibers that arises from the medial condyle of the tibia, merges more or less with the tendon of the semimembranosus, and passes obliquely across the back of the knee joint to the lateral epicondyle of the femur. It contains large openings for the passage of vessels and nerves. Called also *oblique popliteal ligament.*

l. pterygospina′le [N A], a band of fibers extending from the upper part of the superior border of the lateral pterygoid plate to the spine of the sphenoid bone. Called also *l. pterygospinosum* [B N A], and *pterygospinal ligament.*

l. pterygospino′sum [B N A], l. pterygospinale.

l. pu′bicum supe′rius [N A, B N A], fibers that pass transversely across the superior margin of the symphysis pubis; attached to the bone and to the interpubic disk, they extend laterally as far as the pubic tubercle. Called also *superior pubic ligament.*

l. pubocapsula′re [B N A], l. pubofemorale.

l. pubofemora′le [N A], a band that arises from the entire length of the obturator crest of the pubic bone and passes laterally and inferiorly to merge into the capsule of the hip joint, some fibers reaching to the lower part of the neck of the femur. Called also *l. pubocapsulare* [B N A], and *pubofemoral ligament.*

l. puboprostat′icum [N A], a thickening of the superior fascia of the pelvic diaphragm in the male that, laterally, extends from the prostate to the tendinous arch of the pelvic fascia and, medially, is a forward continuation of the tendinous arch to the pubis. Called also *puboprostatic ligament.*

l. puboprostat′icum latera′le [B N A]. See *l. puboprostaticum.*

l. puboprostat′icum me′dium [B N A]. See *l. puboprostaticum.*

l. pubovesica′le [N A], a thickening of the superior fascia of the pelvic diaphragm in the female that, laterally, extends from the neck of the bladder to the tendinous arch of the pelvic fascia and, medially, is a forward continuation of the tendinous arch to the pubis. Called also *pubovesical ligament.*

l. pubovesica′le latera′le [B N A]. See *l. pubovesicale.*

l. pubovesica′le me′dium [B N A]. See *l. pubovesicale.*

l. pulmona′le [N A, B N A], a vertical pleural fold that extends from the hilus down to the base on the medial surface of the lung, forming the posterior boundary of the impressio cardiaca. Called also *pulmonary ligament.*

ligamen′ta pylo′ri [B N A], thickened bands of the longitudinal muscular layer of the stomach situated on the anterior and the posterior surfaces of the antrum pyloricum. Omitted in N A.

l. quadra′tum [N A], a fibrous bundle connecting the distal margin of the radial notch of the ulna to the neck of the radius. Called also *quadrate ligament.*

l. radiocar′peum dorsa′le [N A, B N A], a fibrous band that passes obliquely from the posterior border of the distal extremity of the radius to the dorsal surfaces of the proximal row of carpal bones, especially the triquetral and lunate, and to the dorsal intercarpal ligaments. Called also *dorsal radiocarpal ligament.*

l. radiocar′peum palma′re [N A], several bundles of fibers that pass obliquely from the styloid process and the distal anterior margin of the radius to the lunate, triquetral, capitate, and hamate bones. Called also *l. radiocarpeum volare* [B N A], and *palmar radiocarpal ligament.*

l. radiocar′peum vola′re [B N A], l. radiocarpeum palmare.

l. sacrococcyg′eum ante′rius [B N A], l. sacrococcygeum ventrale.

l. sacrococcyg′eum dorsa′le profun′dum [N A], the terminal portion of the posterior longitudinal ligament of the vertebral column. It helps to unite the dorsal surfaces of the fifth sacral and the coccygeal vertebrae. Called also *l. sacrococcygeum posterius profundum* [B N A], and *deep dorsal sacrococcygeal ligament.*

l. sacrococcyg′eum dorsa′le superficia′le [N A], a fibrous band continuous with the supraspinous ligament of the vertebral column; attached cranially to the margin of the sacral hiatus, and diverging as it passes caudally to attach to the dorsal surface of the coccyx. Called also *l. sacrococcygeum posterius superficiale* [B N A], and *superficial dorsal sacrococcygeal ligament.*

l. sacrococcyg′eum latera′le [N A, B N A], a fibrous band, homologous with the intertransverse ligaments, that passes from the transverse process of the first coccygeal vertebra to the lower lateral angle of the sacrum, thus helping to complete the foramen of the fifth sacral nerve. Called also *lateral sacrococcygeal ligament.*

l. sacrococcyg′eum poste′rius profun′dum [B N A], l. sacrococcygeum dorsale profundum.

l. sacrococcyg′eum poste′rius superficia′le [B N A], l. sacrococcygeum dorsale superficiale.

l. sacrococcyg′eum ventra′le [N A], a flat band, homologous with the anterior longitudinal ligament of the vertebral column, that passes from the lower part of the sacrum over onto the anterior part of the coccyx. Called also *l. sacrococcygeum anterius* [B N A], and *ventral sacrococcygeal ligament.*

ligamen′ta sacroili′aca anterio′ra [B N A], ligamenta sacroiliaca ventralia.

ligamen′ta sacroili′aca dorsa′lia [N A], numerous strong bands that pass from the tuberosity of the ilium and the posterior inferior and posterior superior iliac spines to the intermediate sacral crest and adjacent areas of the sacrum. Called also *dorsal sacroiliac ligaments.*

ligamen′ta sacroili′aca interos′sea [N A, B N A], numerous short, strong bundles connecting the tuberosities and adjacent surfaces of the sacrum and the ilium. Called also *interosseous sacroiliac ligaments.*

l. sacroili′acum poste′rius bre′ve [B N A]. See *ligamenta sacroiliaca dorsalia.*

l. sacroili′acum poste′rius lon′gum [B N A]. See *ligamenta sacroiliaca dorsalia.*

ligamen′ta sacroili′aca ventra′lia [N A], numerous thin fibrous bands passing from the ventral margin of the auricular surface of the sacrum to the adjacent portions of the ilium. Called also *ligamenta sacroiliaca anteriora* [B N A], and *ventral sacroiliac ligaments.*

l. sacrospina′le [N A], a deep, thin triangular band, attached by its apex to the spine of the ischium and by its base to the lateral margins of the sacrum and the coccyx. Called also *l. sacrospinosum* [B N A], and *sacrospinal ligament.*

l. sacrospino'sum [B N A], l. sacrospinale.

l. sacrotubera'le [N A], a large, flat band that is attached below to the ischial tuberosity, spreads out as it ascends, and is attached to the lateral margins of the sacrum and the coccyx and to the posterior inferior iliac spine. Called also *l. sacrotuberosum* [B N A], and *sacrotuberal ligament.*

l. sacrotubero'sum [B N A], l. sacrotuberale.

l. sero'sum [B N A], a fold of peritoneum or other serous membrane that helps to hold an organ or part in position and transmits blood vessels and nerves. Omitted in N A.

l. sphenomandibula're [N A, B N A], a thin aponeurotic band that extends from the angular spine of the sphenoid bone downward medial to the temporomandibular articulation and attaches to the lingula of the mandible. Called also *sphenomandibular ligament.*

l. spira'le coch'leae [N A, B N A], the thickened outer or centrifugal portion of the periosteum of the cochlear duct, forming a spiral band to which the basal membrane is attached. Called also *spiral ligament of cochlea.*

l. sternoclavicula're [B N A]. See *l. sternoclaviculare anterius* and *l. sternoclaviculare posterius.*

l. sternoclavicula're ante'rius [N A], a thick reinforcing band on the anterior portion of the articular capsule of the sternoclavicular articulation. It is attached superiorly to the anterior and superior parts of the sternal extremity of the clavical and inferiorly to the anterior surface of the manubrium of the sternum. Called also *anterior sternoclavicular ligament.*

l. sternoclavicula're poste'rius [N A], a thick reinforcing band on the posterior portion of the articular capsule of the sternoclavicular articulation. It is attached superiorly to the posterior and superior parts of the sternal extremity of the clavicle and inferiorly to the posterior surface of the manubrium of the sternum. Called also *posterior sternoclavicular ligament.*

l. sternocosta'le interarticula're [B N A], l. sternocostale intraarticulare.

l. sternocosta'le intraarticula're [N A], a horizontal fibrocartilaginous plate in the center of the second sternocostal joint, which joins the tip of the costal cartilage to the fibrous junction between the manubrium and the body of the sternum, and thus divides the joint into two parts. Called also *l. sternocostale interarticulare* [B N A], and *intraarticular sternocostal ligament.*

ligamen'ta sternocosta'lia radia'ta [N A, B N A], fibrous bands attached to the sternal end of a costal cartilage, radiating from there out onto the ventral part of the sternum.

ligamen'ta sternopericardi'aca [N A, B N A], two (superior and inferior) or more fibrous bands that attach the pericardium to the dorsal surface of the sternum. Called also *sternopericardiac ligaments.*

l. stylohyoi'deum [N A, B N A], a vertical fibroelastic aponeurotic cord attached above to the tip of the styloid process of the temporal bone and below to the lesser horn of the hyoid bone. Called also *stylohyoid ligament.*

l. stylomandibula're [N A, B N A], an aponeurotic band attached superiorly to the tip of the styloid process of the temporal bone and inferiorly to the angle and posterior margin of the ramus of the mandible. Called also *stylomandibular ligament.*

l. supraspina'le [N A, B N A], a single long, vertical fibrous band passing over and attached to the tips of the spinous processes of the vertebrae from the seventh cervical to the sacrum. It is continuous above with the ligamentum nuchae. Called also *supraspinal ligament.*

l. suspenso'rium clitor'idis [N A, B N A], a strong fibrous band that comes from the external deep investing fascia and attaches the root of the clitoris to the linea alba, symphysis pubis, and arcuate pubic ligament. Called also *suspensory ligament of clitoris.*

ligamen'ta suspenso'ria mam'mae [N A], fibrous processes, extending from the corpus mammae to the corium, homologous with the retinacula cutis of other regions of the body. Called also *suspensory ligaments of mammary gland.*

l. suspenso'rium ova'rii [N A, B N A], the portion of the broad ligament lateral to and above the ovary. It contains the ovarian vessels and nerves and passes upward over the iliac vessels. Called also *suspensory ligament of ovary.*

l. suspenso'rium pe'nis [N A, B N A], a strong fibrous band that comes from the external deep investing fascia and attaches the root of the penis to the linea alba, symphysis pubis, and arcuate pubic ligament. Called also *suspensory ligament of penis.*

l. talocalca'neum ante'rius [B N A], a fibrous band passing from the front and lateral surface of the neck of the talus to the superior surface of the calcaneus. It forms the posterior border of the sinus tarsi. Called also *anterior calcaneal ligament.* Omitted in N A.

l. talocalca'neum interos'seum [N A, B N A], fibrous bands in the sinus tarsi, passing between the opposed surfaces of the calcaneus and the talus. Called also *interosseous talocalcaneal ligament.*

l. talocalca'neum latera'le [N A, B N A], a fibrous band passing from the lateral surface of the talus to that of the calcaneus. Called also *lateral talocalcaneal ligament.*

l. talocalca'neum media'le [N A, B N A], a fibrous band connecting the medial tubercle of the talus with the sustentaculum tali of the calcaneus.

l. talocalca'neum poste'rius [B N A], a fibrous band connecting the processus posterior tali with the upper and medial part of the calcaneus. Called also *posterior talocalcaneal ligament.* Omitted in N A.

l. talofibula're ante'rius [N A, B N A], one or more fibrous bands that pass from the anterior surface of the lateral malleolus of the fibula to the anterior margin of the lateral articular surface of the talus. Called also *anterior talofibular ligament.*

l. talofibula're poste'rius [N A, B N A], a strong fibrous horizontal band passing from the posteromedial face of the lateral malleolus of the fibula to the area of the posterior process of the talus. Called also *posterior talofibular ligament.*

l. talonavicula're [N A], a broad, thin fibrous band passing from the dorsal and lateral surfaces of the neck of the talus to the dorsal surface of the navicular bone. Called also *l. talonaviculare* [*dorsale*] [B N A], and *talonavicular ligament.*

l. talonavicula're [dorsa'le] [B N A], l. talonaviculare.

l. talotibia'le ante'rius [B N A], pars tibiotalaris anterior ligamenti medialis.

l. talotibia'le poste'rius [B N A], pars tibiotalaris posterior ligamenti medialis.

ligamen'ta tar'si dorsa'lia [N A, B N A], the dorsal ligaments of the foot, including the bifurcate, the dorsal cuboideonavicular, cuneocuboid, cuneonavicular, and intercuneiform, and the talonavicular ligaments. Called also *dorsal ligaments of tarsus.*

ligamen'ta tar'si interos'sea [N A, B N A], the interosseous ligaments of the tarsus, including the interosseous cuneocuboid, intercuneiform, talocalcaneal ligaments. Called also *interosseous ligaments of tarsus.*

ligamen'ta tar'si planta'ria [N A, B N A], the inferior ligaments of the foot, comprising the long plantar and the plantar calcaneocuboid, calcaneonavicular, cuneonavicular, cuboideonavicular, intercuneiform, and cuneocuboid ligaments. Called also *plantar ligaments of tarsus.*

ligamen'ta tar'si profun'da [B N A], the deep ligaments of the tarsus. Omitted in N A.

ligamen'ta tarsometatar'sea dorsa'lia [N A, B N A], fibrous bands passing from the dorsal surfaces of the bases of the metatarsal bones to the dorsal surfaces of the cuboid and the three cuneiform bones.

ligamen'ta tarsometatar'sea planta'ria [N A, B N A], fibrous bands passing from the plantar surfaces of the bases of the metatarsal bones to the plantar surfaces of the cuboid and the three cuneiform bones.

l. temporomandibula're [B N A], l. laterale articulationis temporomandibularis.

l. te'res fem'oris [B N A], l. capitis femoris.

l. te'res hep'atis [N A, B N A], a fibrous cord, the remains of the left umbilical vein, extending from the porta hepatis, where it is attached to the left branch of the portal vein, out through the fissure of the ligamentum teres and the falciform ligament to the umbilicus.

l. te'res u'teri [N A, B N A], a fibromuscular band in the female that is attached to the uterus near the attachment of the uterine tube, passing then along the broad ligament, out through the inguinal ring, and into the labium majus. Called also *round ligament of uterus.*

l. thyreoepiglot'ticum [B N A], l. thyroepiglotticum.

l. thyroepiglot'ticum [N A], a fibrous band that attaches the petiolus of the epiglottis to the thyroid cartilage just below the superior notch. Called also *l. thyreoepiglotticum* [B N A], and *thyroepiglottic ligament.*

l. thyrohyoi'deum [N A], a round elastic cord that forms the posterior margin of the thyrohyoid membrane. It extends from the tip of the superior horn of the thyroid cartilage upward to the tip of the greater horn of the hyoid bone. Called also *l. hyothyreoideum laterale* [B N A], and *thyrohyoid ligament.*

l. thyrohyoi'deum media'num [N A], the central, thicker portion of the thyrohyoid membrane. Its broader upper part is attached to the body of the hyoid bone and its narrow lower end to the superior incisure of the thyroid cartilage. Called also *l. hyothyreoideum medium* [B N A], and *median thyrohyoid ligament.*

l. tibiofibula're ante'rius [N A], a flat triangular band that passes diagonally, inferiorly, and laterally from the anterior portion of the lateral surface of the distal end of the tibia to the anterior surface of the distal end of the fibula. Called also *l. malleoli lateralis anterius* [B N A], and *anterior tibiofibular ligament.*

l. tibiofibula're poste'rius [N A], a fibrous band that passes diagonally, inferiorly, and laterally from the posterior surface of the distal end of the tibia to the adjacent posterior surface of the distal end of the fibula. Called also *l. malleoli lateralis posterius* [B N A], and *posterior tibiofibular ligament.*

l. tibionavicula're [B N A], pars tibionavicularis ligamenti medialis.

l. transver'sum acetab'uli [N A, B N A], a fibrous band continuous with the acetabular lip of the hip joint, which bridges the acetabular notch and converts it into a foramen. Called also *transverse ligament of acetabulum.*

l. transver'sum atlan'tis [N A, B N A], the strong horizontal portion of the cruciform ligament of the atlas. It is attached at each end to the lateral masses of the atlas and curves posteriorly around the dens of the axis. It thus divides the atlantal ring into a smaller anterior division for the dens and a larger posterior division for the spinal cord and related structures. Called also *transverse ligament of atlas.*

l. transver'sum cru'ris [B N A], retinaculum musculorum extensorum pedis superius.

l. transver'sum ge'nu [B N A], l. transversum genus.

l. transver'sum ge'nus [N A], a more or less distinct bundle of fibers in the knee joint, joining together the anterior convex margin of the lateral meniscus and the anterior concave margin or anterior end of the medial meniscus. Called also *l. transversum genu* [B N A], and *transverse ligament of knee.*

l. transver'sum pel'vis [B N A], l. transversum perinei.

l. transver'sum perine'i [N A], the strengthened fused portion of the superior and inferior fasciae of the urogenital diaphragm at the anterior border of the diaphragm. Called also *l. transversum pelvis* [B N A], and *transverse perineal ligament.*

l. transver'sum scap'ulae infe'rius [N A, B N A], one of three intrinsic ligaments of the scapula, composed of more or less distinct fascial fibers that pass from the lateral border of the spine of the scapula to the adjacent margin of the glenoid cavity, thus converting the notch at the base of the spine into a foramen for the passage of the suprascapular vessels and nerves to the infraspinous fossa. Called also *inferior transverse ligament of scapula.*

l. transver'sum scap'ulae supe'rius [N A, B N A], one of three intrinsic ligaments of the scapula, a band of fibers that bridges the scapular notch, thus forming a foramen for the passage of the suprascapular nerve. One end is attached to the base of the coracoid process, the other end to the medial border of the scapular notch. Called also *superior transverse ligament of scapula.*

l. trapezoi'deum [N A, B N A], a broad, flat band forming the anterolateral portion of the coracoclavicular ligament. It is attached inferiorly to the superior surface of the coracoid process of the scapula and superiorly to the oblique ridge on the inferior surface of the clavicle. Called also *trapezoid ligament.*

l. triangula're dex'trum hep'atis [N A, B N A], the pointed right extremity of the coronary ligament of the liver where the superior and the inferior layer join in their attachment to the diaphragm. Called also *right triangular ligament of liver.*

l. triangula're sinis'trum hep'atis [N A, B N A], a triangular extension of the left extremity of the coronary ligament, which helps to fasten the left lobe of the liver to the diaphragm. Called also *left triangular ligament of liver.*

l. tuber'culi cos'tae [B N A], l. costotransversarium laterale.

l. ulnocar'peum palma're [N A], bundles of fibers that pass from the styloid process of the ulna to the carpal bones. Called also *palmar ulnocarpal ligament.*

l. umbilica'le latera'le [N A, B N A], a fibrous cord, the remains of the obliterated umbilical artery, that is situated in and produces the lateral umbilical fold. Called also *lateral umbilical ligament.*

l. umbilica'le media'num [N A], a fibrous cord, the remains of the partially obliterated urachus, that extends from the bladder to the umbilicus. It is situated in and produces the median umbilical fold. Called also *l. umbilicale medium* [B N A], and *median umbilical ligament.*

l. umbilica'le me'dium [B N A], l. umbilicale medianum.

l. vagina'le [N A, B N A], a fibrous band sometimes found in the inguinal canal, being the remains of the obliterated processus vaginalis. Called also *vaginal ligament.*

ligamen'ta vagina'lia digito'rum ma'nus [B N A], vaginae fibrosae digitorum manus.

ligamen'ta vagina'lia digito'rum pe'dis [B N A], vaginae fibrosae digitorum pedis.

l. ve'nae ca'vae sinis'trae [B N A], plica venae cavae sinistrae.

l. veno'sum [N A], a fibrous cord, the remains of the fetal ductus venosus, lying in the fissure of the ligamentum venosum of the liver.

l. veno'sum [Aran'tii] [B N A], l. venosum.

l. ventricula're [B N A], l. vestibulare.

l. vestibula're [N A], the membrane that extends from the thyroid cartilage in front to the anterolateral surface of the arytenoid cartilage behind. It lies within the vestibular fold, above the vocal ligament. Called also *l. ventriculare* [B N A], and *vestibular ligament.*

l. voca'le [N A, B N A], the elastic tissue membrane that extends from the thyroid cartilage in front to the vocal process of the arytenoid cartilage behind. It lies within the vocal fold, below the vestibular ligament. Called also *vocal ligament.*

---

ligate (li'gāt). To tie or bind with a ligature.

ligation (li-ga'shun) [L. *ligatio*]. The application of a ligature. **Desault's l.,** ligation of the femoral artery as it passes through the adductor muscle: done for popliteal aneurysm. **distal l.,** ligation of an artery on the side of an aneurysm farthest from the heart. **double l.,** the ligation of an artery at two places and division between them. **immediate l.,** ligation of an artery directly around the artery without including any of the surrounding tissues. **mediate l.,** ligation of an artery, including also some of the surrounding tissue. **pole l.,** ligation of both poles of the thyroid gland for the purpose of limiting the amount of blood to and from the gland: employed in Basedow's disease. **proximal l.,** ligation of an artery on the side of an aneurysm nearest the heart.

ligator (li'ga-tor). An instrument used in ligating in parts that are not easily accessible.

ligature (lig'ah-tūr) [L. *ligatura*]. 1. A thread or wire for tying a vessel or strangulating a part. 2. The act of ligation. 3. In orthodontics, a string or wire used to fasten a tooth to an orthodontic appliance or to another tooth. **chain l.,** a kind of ligature used in tying an ovarian pedicle in several places, a long thread being carried through the pedicle in several places, then cut and tied. **elastic l.,** a band of caoutchouc used to strangulant hemorrhoids and pedunculated growths. **Erichsen's l.,** a double thread of white and black for ligating nevi. **interlacing l., interlocking l.,** a ligature applied to a pedicle formed by interlocking loops. **kangaroo l.,** the prepared tendon of a kangaroo's tail: used as a ligature. **lateral l.,** a ligature so applied as to check, but not to interrupt, the blood current. **McGraw's elastic l.,** a ligature used in performing intestinal anastomosis. **occluding l.,** a ligature which includes every blood channel leading to the distal tissue. **provisional l.,** one applied at the beginning of an operation, but removed before its close. **soluble l.,** a ligature of fresh animal membrane applied with a view to its ultimate absorption or incorporation with the tissues. **l. of Stannius** (1852), a ligature tied around a frog's heart, between the sinus venosus and the auricle. It causes the auricle and ventricle to cease beating. **starvation l.,** a ligature applied to a blood vessel to reduce the supply of blood to the part. **suboccluding l.,** a ligature which obstructs the main blood supply, but leaves unobstructed a portion of tissue capable of establishing capillary anastomosis. **terminal l.,** a ligature applied to the cut end of a vessel. **Woodbridge's l.,** a ligature of silk drawn about the auricles of the heart at the junction with the ventricles: done to isolate the ventricles.

ligg. Abbreviation for *ligaments*, or *ligamenta.*

light (līt). The electromagnetic radiation having a velocity of about 3×10^{10} cm., or 186,284 miles, per second, and the vibrations in space being at right angles to the direction of transmission. Frequently construed as limited to the range of wavelength between 3900 and 7700 angstroms, which provides the stimulus for the subjective sensation of sight, but sometimes considered as including part of the ultraviolet and infrared as well. **actinic l.,** light rays capable of producing chemical effects. **axial l., central l.,** light whose rays are parallel to each other and to the optic axis. **cold l.,** light from a 750 watt electric bulb which is covered by a wall of circulating water: this lamp may be applied directly to the skin and is used for transillumination of the tissues for cancer diagnosis. **l. difference,** the difference between the two eyes in their sensitiveness to light: often abbreviated L.D. **diffused l.,** that which has been scattered by reflection and refraction. **Finsen l.,** light consisting principally of the violet and ultraviolet rays given off by a Finsen lamp: used in the treatment of lupus and similar diseases. **idioretinal l.,** sensation of light that occurs in the complete absence of the electromagnetic waves which ordinarily stimulate the sensation. **infrared l.** See under *ray.* **intrinsic l.** (of the retina), the dim light always present in the visual field. **Landeker-Steinberg l.,** a light which emits a spectrum similar to that of the sun except that the ultraviolet waves are eliminated: used therapeutically. **l. minimum,** the smallest degree of light perceived by the eye; often abbreviated to L.M. **Minin l.,** a therapeutic lamp for the administration of violet and ultraviolet light. **monochromatic l.,** one of the colors of the spectrum into which light is divided by a prism. **neon l.,** a light which contains no ultraviolet and no infrared rays. **oblique l.,** the light that falls obliquely on a surface. **polarized l.,** light the vibrations of which are made over one plane or in circles or ellipses. **reflected l.,** light whose rays have been turned back from an illuminated surface. **refracted l.,** light whose rays have been bent out of their original course by passing through a transparent membrane. **Simpson l.,** an electric arc light in which the electrodes are made of tungstate of iron and manganese. The light emitted consists of rays of two kinds: visible rays and invisible rays. The latter consist of heat rays and ultraviolet rays. Used in the treatment of rodent ulcer, lupus, eczema, wounds, rhinitis, and sinusitis. **transmitted l.,** light the rays of which have passed through an object. **Tyndall l.,** the light that is reflected or dispersed by particles suspended in a gas or liquid. See *Tyndall phenomenon*, under *phenomenon.* **ultraviolet l.** See under *ray.* **white l.,** that produced by a mixture of all wavelengths of electromagnetic energy perceptible as light. **Wood l.** See under *filter.*

lightening (līt'en-ing). The sensation of decreased abdominal distention produced by the descent of the uterus into the pelvic cavity occurring from two to three weeks before labor begins.

ligneous (lig'ne-us). Woody; having a wooden feeling.

Lignières' test (lēn-yārz') [José *Lignières*, physician in Buenos Aires, died 1934]. See under *tests.*

lignin (lig'nin). A cyclic unsaturated compound which in connection with cellulose forms the cell wall of plants and thus of wood.

lignocaine (lig'no-kān). Lidocaine.

Lignognathoides (lig"no-nah-thoi'dēz). A genus of lice. **L. monta'nus,** the common sucking louse of the California ground squirrel, *Citellus beecheyi.*

lignum (lig'num), gen. *lig'ni* [L.]. Wood. **l. sanc'tum, l. vi'tae,** the heartwood of *Guajacum officinale* Linne or of *G. sanctum* Linne.

ligula (lig'u-lah) [L. "strap"]. Tenia ventriculi quarti.

ligule (lig'ūl). Ligula.

ligustrin (lĭ-gus'trin). Syringin.

lilacin (li'lah-sin). Syringin.

Lilienthal's probe (lil'e-en-thalz") [Howard *Lilienthal*, surgeon in New York, 1861–1946]. See under *probe.*

limatura (li"mah-tu'rah) [L. *limare* to file]. Filings. **l. fer'ri,** iron filings.

limb (lim). 1. An arm or a leg with all its component parts. Called also *membrum* [N A], and *extremitas* [B N A]. 2. A structure or part resembling an arm or leg. Called also *crus.* **anacrotic l.,** the ascending portion of a tracing of the pulse wave obtained by sphygmography. **l's of anthelix,** crura anthelicis. **catacrotic l.,** the descending portion of a tracing of the pulse wave obtained by sphygmography. **l. of incus, long,** crus longum incudis. **l. of incus, short,** crus breve incudis. **l. of internal capsule, anterior,** crus anterius capsulae internae. **l. of internal capsule, posterior,** crus posterius capsulae internae. **pectoral l.,** the arm (membrum superius), or a homologous part. **pelvic l.,** the leg (membrum inferius), or a homologous part. **phantom l.,** a model of an absent part of an arm or leg, subjectively perceived as real and active. **l. of stapes, anterior,** crus anterius stapedis. **l. of stapes, posterior,** crus posterius stapedis. **thoracic l.,** pectoral l.

limbal (lim′bal). Pertaining to a limbus; limbic; occurring at the junction of the cornea and conjunctiva.

limberneck (lim′ber-nek). A disease of fowl resulting from ingestion of food contaminated with *Clostridium botulinum*, and characterized by a flaccid paralysis which gives the condition its name.

limbi (lim′bi) [L.]. Plural of *limbus*.

limbic (lim′bik). Pertaining to a limbus, or margin; forming a border around. See under *system*.

limbus (lim′bus), pl. *lim′bi* [L.]. A border, hem, fringe; used in anatomical nomenclature as a general term to designate the border of certain structures. See also *labium* and *margo*. **alveolar l. of mandible,** arcus alveolaris mandibulae. **alveolar l. of maxilla,** arcus alveolaris maxillae. **l. alveola′ris mandib′ulae** [B N A], arcus alveolaris mandibulae. **l. alveola′ris maxil′lae** [B N A], arcus alveolaris maxillae. **l. angulo′sus,** linea obliqua cartilaginis thyroideae. **l. chorioi′deus,** the innermost arch of the gyrus fornicatus. **l. conjuncti′vae.** 1. Limbus corneae. 2. Anulus conjunctivae. **l. of cornea, l. cor′neae** [N A, B N A], the edge of the cornea where it joins the sclera. **l. cortica′lis,** the outermost arch of the gyrus fornicatus. **l. fos′sae ova′lis** [N A], **l. fos′sae ova′lis [Vieussen′ii]** [B N A], the prominent rounded margin of the fossa ovalis cordis. **l. lam′inae spira′lis os′seae** [N A], the thickened periosteum of the osseous spiral lamina at the attachment of the vestibular membrane. **l. lu′teus ret′inae,** macula retinae. **l. medulla′ris,** the middle arch of the gyrus fornicatus. **l. membra′nae tym′pani.** 1. [B N A] The thickened margin of the tympanic membrane attached to the tympanic sulcus. Omitted in N A. 2. Anulus fibrocartilagineus membranae tympani. **lim′bi palpebra′les anterio′res** [N A, B N A], the rounded anterior edges of the free margin of the eyelids, from which the eyelashes arise. **lim′bi palpebra′les posterio′res** [N A, B N A], the sharp posterior edges of the free margin of the eyelids, closely applied to the eyeball. **l. of Vieussens,** l. fossae ovalis.

lime (līm) [L. *calx*]. 1. Calcium oxide. 2. The acid fruit of *Citrus acida:* its juice is antiscorbutic and refrigerant. **l. arsenate,** a solution of white arsenic and sal soda in water, used as an insecticide. **bird l.,** a viscid or gummy substance of variable composition and origin that is used to capture small birds. **chlorinated l.** See *calx chlorata*. **slaked l.,** calcium hydroxide. **soda l.,** a mixture of quicklime and sodium hydroxide. **sulfurated l.** See *calx sulfurata*.

limen (li′men), pl. *lim′ina* [L.]. Threshold; used in anatomical nomenclature as a general term to designate the beginning point, boundary, or threshold of a structure. **l. of insula, l. in′sulae** [N A, B N A], the point at which the cortex of the insula is continuous, on the inferior surface of the cerebral hemisphere, with the cortex of the frontal lobe. **l. na′si** [N A, B N A], the boundary line between the bony and cartilaginous portions of the walls of the nasal cavity. **l. of twoness,** the distance between two points of contact on the skin necessary for their recognition as giving rise to separate stimuli.

limina (lim′ĭ-nah) [L.]. Plural of *limen*.

liminal (lim′ĭ-nal) [L. *limen* threshold]. Barely appreciable to the senses: pertaining to a threshold.

liminometer (lim″ĭ-nom′e-ter) [*limen* + Gr. *metron* measure]. An instrument for measuring the strength of stimulus applied over a tendon and determining the reflex threshold.

limit (lim′it) [L. *limes* boundary]. A boundary, as one that confines. **Anstie's l.** See under *rule*. **assimilation l.,** the amount of carbohydrate that the organism can metabolize without causing glycosuria. Called also *saturation limit*. **audibility l.,** the extremes of vibration beyond which the human ear perceives no sound: lower 16–20 cycles per second; upper 18,000–20,000. **elastic l.,** the extent to which elastic material may be deformed without impairing its ability to return to original dimensions. **l. of flocculation,** a term used in expressing the strength of toxin, toxoid, and antitoxin. See *Lf dose*, under *dose*. **l. of perception,** the minimum visual angle below which perception is impossible: an object to be perceived must subtend a visual angle of four or five minutes, thus making its image on the retina about the size of a retinal cone of 3.3–3.6 microns in diameter. **quantum l.,** minimum wavelength. **saturation l.,** assimilation l.

limitans (lim′ĭ-tanz) [L.]. Limiting. See *membrana limitans*.

limitation (lim-ĭ-ta′shun). Circumscription; the act of limiting, or state of being limited. **eccentric l.,** a circumscribed condition of the visual field, more pronounced at some parts of the periphery than at others. **genetic l.,** the necessity that all cells react in accordance with the standards of the particular species to which they belong.

limitrophes (lim′ĭ-trōfs) [Fr. *limitrophe*, "bordering"]. The sympathetic ganglia and their connections.

limitrophic (lim″ĭ-trof′ik). Controlling nutrition.

Limnatis (lim-na′tis). A genus of the Hirudinea. **L. granulo′sa, L. myso′melas,** species occasionally found parasitic in the nasal passages. **L. nilot′ica,** an African species that sometimes becomes lodged in the pharynx. It may be found in the normal cavities of animals.

limnemia (lim-ne′me-ah) [Gr. *limnē* marsh + *haima* blood + *-ia*]. Malarial cachexia.

limnemic (lim-ne′mik). Pertaining to or characterized by limnemia.

limo (li′mo), gen. *limo′nis* [L.]. Lemon.

limonene (lim′o-nēn). An essential oil found in the peel of oranges and lemons. It is a terpene, $C_3H_5.C_6H_8.CH_3$.

limonis (li-mo′nis) [L.]. Genitive of *limo*, lemon. **l. cor′tex,** lemon peel. **l. suc′cus,** lemon juice.

limonite (lim′o-nīt). Hydrous ferric oxide, $2Fe_2O.$-$3H_2O$, an ore of iron.

limophthisis (li-mof′thĭ-sis) [Gr. *limos* hunger + *phthisis* wasting]. Wasting from lack of food or starvation.

limosis (li-mo′sis) [Gr. *limos* hunger]. Abnormal or morbid hunger.

limotherapy (li″mo-ther′ah-pe) [Gr. *limos* hunger + *therapeia* cure]. Hunger cure; the treatment of disease by fasting or by a meager diet: used in dyspepsia, aneurysm, syphilis, and cancer.

Linacre (lin′ah-ker), Thomas (1460–1524). A noted English physician and classicist, who was physician to Henry VIII and the first president of the Royal College of Physicians of London. He was also renowned for his translations of Greek classics (e.g., Galen) into Latin.

linalool (lin-al′o-ol). The olefinic terpene alcohol, dimethyl octadianol, $(CH_3)_2C:CH:CH_2.CH_2.C$-$(CH_3)(OH)CH:CH_2$, of oil of lign aloe; found also in oil of coriander and various other volatile oils.

lincture (lingk′tūr). An electuary.

linctus (lingk′tus) [L. "a licking"]. An electuary.

lindane (lin′dān). Chemical name: 1,2,3,4,5,6-hexachlorocyclohexane: used in treatment of scabies and pediculosis; also to rid animals of ectoparasites.

Lindau's disease (lin′dowz) [Arvid *Lindau*, Swedish pathologist, born 1892]. See under *disease*.

Lindbergh pump [Charles A. *Lindbergh*, American aviator, born 1902]. See under *pump*.

Lindemann's cannula, method (lin′dĕ-manz) [August *Lindemann*, German surgeon, born 1880]. See under *cannula* and *method*.

line (lin) [L. *lin′ea*]. 1. A stripe, streak, mark, or narrow ridge. Often an imaginary line connecting different anatomical landmarks. Called also *linea*. 2. A measure equal to one twelfth of an inch. **abdominal l.,** any line upon the surface of the abdomen, such as one indicating the boundary of a muscle. **absorption l's,** dark lines in the spectrum due to absorption of light by the substance (usually an incandescent gas or vapor) through which the light has passed. Cf. *absorption bands*, under *band*. **accretion l's,** microscopic lines seen in sections of dental enamel, marking successive layers of calcification. **adrenal l.,** Sergent's white adrenal l. **alveolar l.,** a line from the nasion to the alveolar point. **alveolobasilar l.,** a line from the basion to the alveolar point. **alveolonasal l.,** a line from the alveolar point to the nasal point. **Amberg's l.,** a line dividing into two halves the angle formed by the anterior border of the mastoid process and the temporal line. It indicates the most easily accessible part of the lateral sinus for a mastoid operation. Called also *lateral sinus line*. **l. of Amici,** Krause's membrane. **angular l.,** an irregular jagged line dividing the anterior surface of the iris into two regions. **anococcygeal l., white,** ligamentum anococcygeum. **anocutaneous l.,** pectinate l. **arcuate l., external superior,** linea nuchae superior. **arcuate l. of ilium,** linea arcuata ossis ilii. See also *linea glutea anterior, linea glutea inferior,* and *linea glutea posterior*. **arcuate l. of occipital bone, highest,** linea nuchae suprema. **arcuate l. of occipital bone, inferior,** linea nuchae inferior. **arcuate l. of occipital bone, superior,** linea nuchae superior. **arcuate l. of occipital bone, supreme,** linea nuchae suprema. **arcuate l. of pelvis,** linea terminalis pelvis. **arcuate l. of sheath of rectus abdominis muscle,** linea arcuata vaginae musculi recti abdominis. **atropic l.,** one normal to the plane of the axes of rotation of the eye. **auriculobregmatic l.,** a line from the auricular point to the bregma. **axillary l.,** linea axillaris. **Baillarger's l's,** two bands of white fibers seen on section of the cerebral cortex, running parallel to the surface of the cortex. These lines are distinguished as *inner* and *outer*. In the area striata of the cortex only one of these lines (the outer) is visible and here it is known as the *l. of Gennari*. **base l.,** one from the infraorbital ridge to the external auditory meatus and the middle line of the occiput. **base-apex l.,** a line perpendicular to the edge of a prism and bisecting the refracting angle of the prism. **basinasal l.,** one from the basion to the nasion. **basiobregmatic l.,** one from the basion to the bregma. **Baudelocque's l.,** the external conjugate diameter of the pelvis. **Beau's l's,** transverse furrows occurring on the finger nails after wasting diseases. **biauricular l.,** a line passing over the vertex from one auditory meatus to the other. **bi-iliac l.,** one joining the most prominent points of the two iliac crests. **blood l.,** a line of direct descent through several generations. **blue l.,** the characteristic line on the gingiva showing chronic lead poisoning. **Borsieri's l.,** a white mark made upon the skin by the finger nail in the early stages of scarlet fever. **Bridgett's l.,** one drawn on the premastoid lamina after a simple mastoid operation to show the course of the facial canal in order to prevent injury to the facial nerve in doing the radical mastoid operation. **Brödel's white l.,** a longitudinal white line on the anterior surface of the kidney near the convex border. **Bruecke's l's,** broad bands alternating with Krause's membranes in the fibrils of the striated muscles. **Bryant's l.** 1. The vertical side of the iliofemoral triangle. 2. A test line for detecting shortening of the femur. **Burton's l.,** blue l. **calcification l's,** accretion l's. **Camper's l.,** an imaginary line from the inferior border of the ala nasi to the superior border of the tragus of the ear. **cement l.,** a name applied to a line, visible in microscopical examination of bone in cross section, marking the boundary of an osteon (haversian system). **cervical l.,** an anatomical landmark determined by the junction of the enamel- and the cementum-covered portions of a tooth (the cementoenamel junction). **Chaussier's l.,** the median raphe of the callosum. **Chiene's l's,** a set of lines established to aid in localizing the cerebral centers. **Clapton's l.,** a green line on the gums in copper poisoning. **clavicular l.,** one following the course of the clavicles. **cleavage l's,** linear clefts in the skin indicative of direction of the fibers. **Conrad's l.,** a line from the base of the xiphoid process to the point on the chest at which the apex beat is felt, indicating the upper limit of percussion dullness of the left lobe of the liver. **contour l's,** l's of Owen. **copper l.,** a greenish or red line at the border of the gums in copper poisoning. **Correra's l.,** a line in the roentgenogram of the chest, around the outline of the thorax, and bounding the lung fields. **Corrigan's l.,** a purplish line observed on the gums in copper poisoning. **costo-articular l.,** a line from the sternoclavicular joint to a point on the eleventh rib. **costoclavicular l.,** linea parasternalis. **Crampton's l.,** a line on the abdomen indicating the position of the common iliac artery; it extends from the apex of the cartilage of the last rib nearly to the crest of the ilium, then forward to a point just below the anterior superior spine. **cricoclavicular l.,** a line from the cricoid cartilage of the larynx to the point at which the upward projection of the anterior axillary line intersects the clavicle. **cruciate l.,** eminentia cruciformis. **curved l. of ilium,** linea arcuata ossis ilii. **curved l. of ilium, inferior,** linea glutea inferior. **curved l. of ilium, middle,** linea glutea anterior. **curved l. of ilium, superior,** linea glutea posterior. **curved l. of occipital bone, highest,** linea nuchae suprema. **curved l. of occipital bone, inferior,** linea nuchae inferior. **curved l. of occipital bone, superior,** linea nuchae superior. **curved l. of occipital bone, supreme,** linea nuchae suprema. **Czermak's l's,** spatia interglobularia. **Daubenton's l.,** a line from the opisthion to the basion. **dentate l.,** pectinate l. **De Salle's l.,** nasal l. **Dobie's l.,** Krause's membrane. **l. of Douglas,** linea arcuata vaginae musculi recti abdominis. **Duhot's l.,** a line from the superior iliac spine to the apex of the sacrum. **Eberth's l's,** microscopic broken or scalariform lines at the junction of the cardiac muscle cells. **ectental l.,** the line of junction between the ectoderm and entoderm. **Ellis' l., Ellis-Garland l.,** an S-shaped line on the chest, showing the upper border of pleuritic effusions. **embryonic l.,** the primitive tract in the center of the germinal area. **epiphyseal l.,** 1. Linea epiphysialis. 2. A strip of lesser density apparent in the roentgenogram of a long bone, representing the non-calcified portion of the cartilaginous growth plate between the epiphysis and the diaphysis. **facial l.,** a straight line connecting the nasion and pogonion. **Farre's white l.,** the boundary of the insertion of the mesovarium at the hilus of the ovary. **Feiss' l.,** a line from the internal malleolus to the plantar surface of the first metarsophalangeal joint. **l. of fixation,** a straight line extending through the center of rotation of the eye to the object of vision. **focal l., anterior,** a line whose direction is perpendicular to the meridian of greatest curvature of a refracting surface. **focal l., posterior,** a line whose direction is perpendicular to the meridian of least curvature of a refracting surface. **Fraunhofer's l's,** dark lines of the solar spectrum. **Frommann's l's,** transverse marks on the axon of a medullated nerve fiber, rendered visible by silver nitrate. **fulcrum l.,** the imaginary axis around which a removable partial denture tends to rotate. **fulcrum l., retentive,** an imaginary line connecting the retentive points of clasp arms on retaining teeth adjacent to mucosa-borne denture bases, around which a denture tends to rotate when subjected to forces such as the pull of sticky foods. **fulcrum l., stabilizing,** an imaginary line connecting occlusal rests, around which a denture tends to rotate during mastication. **Gant's l.,** one described on the femur below the greater trochanter, for service as a guide in surgical operations. **genal l.,** one of Jadelot's lines, extending from the nasal line near the mouth toward the malar bone. **l. of Gennari.** See *Baillarger's l's.* **gingival l.** 1. A line determined by the level to which the gingiva extends on a tooth; although it follows the curvature of the cervical line, the two rarely coincide. 2. Any linear mark visible on the surface of the gingiva, such as the discoloration resulting from the ingestion of lead (lead l.). **gluteal l., anterior,** linea glutea anterior. **gluteal l., inferior,** linea glutea inferior. **gluteal l., posterior,** linea glutea posterior. **Gottinger's l.,** a line along the upper border of the zygomatic arch. **Granger l.,** a curved line seen in roentgenograms of skulls, indicating the position of the optic groove. **Gubler's l.,** a line connecting the apparent origins of the roots of the fifth nerve. **gum l.,** gingival l. (def. 1.). **Haller's l.,** fissura anterior medullae spinalis. **heave l.,** a groove appearing along the costal arch coincidental with forced contraction of the abdominal muscles following the normal passive expiratory movement in an animal with heaves. **Helmholtz's l.,** a line perpendicular to the plane of the axis of rotation of the eyes. **Hensen's l.,** a light line in the middle of the dark band of a sarcomere: called also *mesophragma* and *M band* or *disk.* **Hilton's white l.,** pectinate l. **Holden's l.,** a sulcus below the inguinal fold, crossing the capsule of the hip joint. **Hudson's l.,** linea corneae senilis. **Hueter's l.,** a straight line connecting the epicondyle of the humerus with the top of the olecranon when the arm is extended. **Hunter's l.,** linea alba. **iliopectineal l.,** linea arcuata ossis illii. **incremental l's,** lines supposedly showing the successive layers deposited in a tissue, as in the enamel, dentin, or cementum of a tooth. **infracostal l.,** one connecting the lower borders of the tenth costal cartilages. **infrascapular l.,** a horizontal line at the level of the inferior angles of the scapulae. **intercondylar l., intercondyloid l.,** linea intercondylaris femoris. **intermediate l. of iliac crest,** linea intermedia cristae iliacae. **interspinal l.,** a line on the abdomen connecting the two anterior superior iliac spines. **intertrochanteric l., intertrochanteric l., anterior,** linea intertrochanterica. **intertrochanteric l., posterior,** crista intertrochanterica. **intertuberal l.,** a line drawn between the prominences of the frontal bone. **intertubercular l.,** an imaginary line drawn transversely across the abdomen at the level of the iliac crests. **isothermal l's,** lines on a map or chart indicating areas of uniform temperature. **Jadelot's l's,** lines of the face in young children, described as being indicative of specific types of disease: the genal, labial, nasal, and oculozygomatic lines. Called also *Jadelot's furrows* or *traits.* **K l's, L l's, M l's, N l's, O l's, P l's,** groups of lines in a roentgen-ray spectrum, determined by the stability level to which the replacement electron "drops"; the K lines come from the level nearest the nucleus of the atom and have the shortest wavelength. **l. of Kaes,** a thin zone or strip of fibers in the supraradiary zone of white matter of the cerebral cortex. **Kilian's l.,** a prominent line on the promontory of the sacrum. **Krause's l.,** Krause's membrane. **L l's.** See under *K lines.* **labial l.,** one of Jadelot's lines, extending laterally from the angle of the mouth: said to indicate disease of the lungs. **Langer's l's,** cleavage l's. **lateral sinus l.,** Amberg's l. **lead l.,** a bluish line at the edge of the gums in lead poisoning. **lip l.,** a line at the level to which the margin of either lip extends on the teeth. **lip l., high,** the highest level on the teeth reached by the upper lip in normal function or during a broad smile. **lip l., low,** the lowest level on the teeth reached by the lower lip in normal function or during a broad smile. **Lizars' l.** 1. A line from the posterior superior spine of the ilium to the midpoint between the tuberosity of the ischium and the greater trochanter; the gluteal artery emerges at the point of junction of its upper and middle thirds. 2. A line from the posterior superior spine of the ilium to the tuberosity of the ischium; the sciatic and pubic arteries emerge at the point of junction of its middle and lower thirds. **lower lung l.,** a horizontal line in roentgenograms of the upper part of the abdomen, running from the lateral chest wall toward the first lumbar vertebra on each side, and representing the lower posterior boundary of the pleural cavity. **M l's.** See discussion under *K l's.* **McKee's l.,** a line drawn from the tip of the cartilage of the eleventh rib to a point an inch and a half to the inner side of the anterior superior spine, then curving downward and forward and inward to a point just above the abdominal ring: used as a guide to the common iliac artery. **magnetic l's of force,** lines indicating direction of force in a magnetic field. **mamillary l.,** linea mamillaris. **mammary l.** 1. A line from one nipple to the other. 2. Milk line. **median l.,** a vertical line dividing the body equally into right and left parts. **median l., anterior,** linea mediana anterior. **median l., posterior,** linea mediana posterior. **mesenteric l.** See *mesenteric triangle,* under *triangle.* **Meyer's l.,** the axial line of the big toe which if extended passes through the center of the heel if shoes have never been worn. **midaxillary l.,** linea axillaris. **midclavicular l.,** linea mamillaris. **middle l. of scrotum,** raphe scroti. **midspinal l.,** a perpendicular line down the middle of the vertebral column. **midsternal l.,** a line passing through the middle of the sternum from the cricoid cartilage to the xiphoid. **milk l.,** the line of thickened epithelium in the embryo along which the mammary glands are developed. **Monro's l.,** one from the umbilicus to the anterior superior spine of the ilium. **Monro-Richter l.,** one from the umbilicus to the left anterior superior iliac spine. **Moyer's l.,** a line from the middle of the body of the third sacral vertebra to a point midway between the anterior superior iliac spines. **muscular l's of scapula,** lineae musculares scapulae. **mylohyoid l. of mandible, mylohyoidean l.,** linea mylohyoidea mandibulae. **N l's.** See under *K l's.* **nasal l.,** one of Jadelot's lines, extending from the ala nasi in a semicircle around the mouth. **nasobasilar l.,** a line through the basion and nasal point. **nasolabial l.,** a line extending from the ala nasi to the angle of the mouth. **Nélaton's l.,** a line from the anterior superior process of the ilium to the most prominent part of the tuberosity of the ischium. **neonatal l.,** a line in the enamel and dentin of a tooth at a position corresponding to the surface of enamel and dentin present at the time of birth. **nigra l.,** linea nigra. **nipple l.,** linea mamillaris. **nuchal l., highest,** linea nuchae suprema. **nuchal l., inferior,** linea nuchae inferior. **nuchal l., middle,** crista occipitalis externa. **nuchal l., superior,** linea nuchae superior. **nuchal l., supreme,** linea nuchae suprema. **O l's.** See under *K l's.* **oblique l.,** one which follows an oblique course. See terms beginning *linea obliqua.* **oblique l. of femur,** linea intertrochanterica. **oblique l. of fibula.** 1. Crista anterior fibulae. 2. Margo anterior fibulae. **oblique l. of mandible,** linea obliqua mandibulae. **oblique l. of mandible, internal,** linea mylohyoidea mandibulae. **oblique l. of thyroid cartilage,** linea obliqua cartilaginis thyroideae. **oblique l. of tibia,** linea musculi solei. **l. of occlusion,** Angle's term for "the line with which, in form and position according to type, the teeth must be in harmony if in normal occlusion"; the line of contact between the maxillary and mandibular teeth when the jaws are closed. **oculozygomatic l.,** one of Jadelot's lines, extending outward from the medial canthus toward the zygoma: said to be a sign of some disorder of the nervous system. **Ogston's l.,** a line from the tubercle of the femur to the intercondylar notch. **omphalospinous l.,** a line on the abdomen connecting the umbilicus and the superior spine of the ilium; a guide to the location of McBurney's point. **l's of Owen,** lines seen on longitudinal section, demarcating layers of interglobular spaces in the deeper parts of the dentin of the crown of a tooth. **P l's.** See under *K l's.* **papillary l.,** linea mamillaris. **parasternal l.,** linea parasternalis. **Pastia's l's.** See under *sign.* **pectinate l.,** a sinuous line following the level of the anal valves and crossing the bases of the columns between them, marking the junction of the zone of the anal canal lined with stratified squamous epithelium and the zone lined with columnar epithelium. Called also *anocutaneous l.* and *dentate l.* **pectineal l.** 1. Linea pectinea femoris. 2. Pecten ossis pubis. **Pickerill's imbrication l's,** horizontal lines on the surface of tooth enamel. **Poirier's l.,** a line running from the nasofrontal angle to a point just above the lambda. **popliteal l. of femur,** linea intercondylaris femoris. **popliteal l. of tibia,** linea musculi solei. **Poupart's l.,** an imaginary line on the surface of the abdomen, passing perpendicularly through the midpoint on Poupart's ligament. **precentral l.,** a line on the head, extending from a point midway between the inion and glabella downward and forward. **primitive l.,** primitive streak. **profile l.,** Camper's l. **pupillary l.,** pupillary axis. **quadrate l.,** a line on the posterior surface of the femur. **recessional l's,** lines or markings on the teeth due to the recession, in the formative period of the teeth, of the soft tissue which gives place to the dentin. **respiratory l.,** a line that connects the bases of the upstrokes in a sphygmogram. **Retzius' l's,** accretion l's. **Robson's l.,** an imaginary line drawn from the nipple to the umbilicus. **Rolando's l.,** a line on the head marking the position of the fissure of Rolando beneath. **Roser's l.,** Nélaton's l. **rough l. of femur,** linea aspera femoris. **Salter's l's,** incremental lines in dentin. **scapular l.,** linea scapularis. **Schoemaker's l.,** one connecting the point of the trochanter with the anterior superior iliac spine; the extension of this line normally runs above the umbilicus, but runs below the umbilicus when the trochanter is higher than normal. **Schreger's l's.** 1. Lines of Owen. 2. Bands of Schreger. **semicircular l., supreme,** linea nuchae suprema. **semicircular l. of Douglas,** linea arcuata vaginae musculi recti abdominis. **semicircular l. of frontal bone,** linea temporalis ossis frontalis. **semicircular l. of occipital bone, highest,** linea nuchae suprema. **semicircular l. of occipital bone, middle,** linea nuchae superior. **semicircular l. of occipital bone, superior,** linea nuchae superior. **semicircular l. of parietal bone, inferior,** linea temporalis inferior ossis parietalis. **semicircular l. of parietal bone, superior,** linea temporalis superior ossis parietalis. **semilunar l.,** linea semilunaris. **Sergent's white adrenal l.,** a white line on the abdomen caused by drawing the finger nail across it: seen in cases of deficient adrenal activity. **Shenton's l.,** a curved line seen in the roentgenogram of the normal hip joint, formed by the top of the obturator foramen. **l. of sight,** a straight line from the center of the pupil to the object viewed. **Skinner's l.,** Shenton's l. **soleal l.,** linea musculi solei. **Spieghel's l., Spigelius' l.,** linea semilunaris. **Stähli's pigment l.,** linea corneae senilis. **sternal l., sternal l., lateral,** linea sternalis. **sternomastoid l.,** one from the heads of the sternomastoid to the mastoid process. **subcostal l.,** a transverse line on the surface of the abdomen at the level of the lower edge of the tenth costal cartilage. **subscapular l's,** lineae musculares scapulae. **supra-orbital l.,** a line across the forehead, just above the root of the external angular process of the frontal bone. **sylvian l.,** a line on the head extending from the external angular process of the frontal bone to a point three fourths of an inch below the most prominent point of the parietal bone. It coincides with the direction of the fissure of Sylvius. **temporal l. of frontal bone,** linea temporalis ossis frontalis. **temporal l. of parietal bone, inferior,** linea temporalis inferior ossis parietalis. **temporal l. of parietal bone, superior,** linea temporalis superior ossis parietalis. **terminal l. of pelvis,** linea terminalis pelvis. **Thompson's l.,** a red line observed on the gingivae in pulmonary tuberculosis. **thyroid red l.,** an erythematous line produced by irritation of the skin on the front of the neck and upper part of the chest in patients with hyperthyroidism. **Topinard's l.,** a line between the glabella and the mental point. **transverse l's of sacral bone,** lineae transversae ossis sacri. **trapezoid l.,** linea trapezoidea. **Trümmerfeld l.,** a zone of metaphyseal degeneration sometimes seen in the bones in infantile scurvy. **Ullmann's l.,** in cases of spondylolisthesis a line extended upward at a right angle from the anterior edge of the first sacral vertebra to the superior surface of the sacrum will pass through the last lumbar vertebra. **umbilico-iliac l.,** a line from the umbilicus to the anterior superior spine of the ilium. **l. of Venus,** the principal transverse line on the palmar surface of the wrist. **vibrating l.,** an imaginary line marking the division between the movable and immovable tissues of the palate. **Virchow's l.,** a line from the root of the nose to the lambda. **visual l.,** axis opticus. **Voigt's boundary l's,** lines which delimit the areas of distribution of peripheral nerves. **Wagner's l.,** a thin, whitish line at the junction of the epiphysis and diaphysis of a bone, formed by preliminary calcification. **Waldeyer's l.,** Farre's white l. **white l.,** linea alba. **white adrenal l.,** Sergent's white adrenal l. **white l. of ischiococcygeal muscle,** ligamentum anococcygeum. **white l. of pelvic fascia,** arcus tendineus fasciae pelvis. **white l. of pelvis,** arcus tendineus musculi levatoris ani. **white l. of pharynx,** raphe pharyngis. **Wrisberg's l's.** See *nervus intermedius.* **l's of Zahn,** laminations visible in antemortem blood clots, caused by alternating layers of gray-white fibrin interspersed with narrow zones of apparent red-blue clot. **Zöllner's l's,** a set of lines of peculiar arrangement designed to be used as an ocular test.

linea (lin′e-ah), pl. *lin′eae* [L.]. A stripe, streak, mark, or narrow ridge; used in anatomical nomenclature as a general term to designate a streak or narrow ridge on the surface of some structure. Called also *line.* **l. al′ba** [N A, B N A], **l. al′ba abdom′inis,** the tendinous mesial line on the anterior abdominal wall between the two rectus muscles, formed by the decussating fibers of the aponeuroses of the three flat abdominal muscles. **l. al′ba cervica′lis,** the mesial line of the neck where the fascial sheaths of the sternohyoid and sternohyoid muscles blend. **lin′eae albican′tes,** striae atrophicae. **l. arcua′ta os′sis il′ii** [N A], the iliac portion of the terminal line, limiting the ala of the ilium inferiorly on its medial surface. Called also *arcuate line of ilium.* **l. arcua'ta vagi'nae mus'culi rec'ti abdom'inis** [N A], a crescentic line marking the termination of the posterior layer of the sheath of the rectus abdominis muscle, just below the level of the iliac crest. Called also *l. semicircularis [Douglasi]* [B N A], and *arcuate line of sheath of rectus abdominis muscle.* **l. as'pera fem'oris** [N A, B N A], a roughened longitudinal line with two lips, on the posterior surface of the shaft of the femur; it gives attachment to various muscles. **lin'eae atroph'icae,** fine reddish lines on the abdomen in Cushing's syndrome. See also *striae atrophicae.* **l. axilla'ris** [N A, B N A], an imaginary vertical line passing through the middle of the axilla, dividing the body into an anterior and a posterior portion. Called also *axillary line.* **l. cor'neae seni'lis,** a horizontal brown line in the lower part of the cornea in senile degeneration. **l. epiphysia'lis** [N A], a line on the surface of an adult long bone marking the site of junction of the epiphysis and diaphysis. Called also *epiphyseal line.* **l. glu'tea ante'rior** [N A], the middle of three rough curved lines on the gluteal surface of the ala of the ilium; it begins from the iliac crest about an inch posterior to the anterior superior iliac spine and arches more or less posteriorly to the greater sciatic notch. Called also *anterior gluteal line.* **l. glu'tea infe'rior** [N A], a rough curved line, often indistinct, on the gluteal surface of the ala of the ilium. It runs from the notch between the anterior superior and anterior inferior iliac spines posteriorly to the anterior part of the greater sciatic notch. Called also *inferior gluteal line.* **l. glu'tea poste'rior** [N A], a rough curved line on the gluteal surface of the ala of the ilium; it begins from the iliac crest about two inches anterior to the posterior superior iliac spine and runs downward to the greater sciatic notch. Called also *posterior gluteal line.* **l. iliopectin'ea,** l. arcuata ossis ilii. **l. innom'inata,** l. terminalis pelvis. **l. intercondyla'ris fem'oris** [N A], **l. intercondyloi'dea fem'oris** [B N A], a transverse ridge separating the floor of the intercondylar fossa from the popliteal surface of the femur, and giving attachment to the posterior portion of the capsular ligament of the knee. Called also *intercondylar line.* **l. interme'dia cris'tae ili'acae** [N A, B N A], the area between the inner and outer lips of the iliac crest. Called also *intermediate line of iliac crest.* **l. intertrochanter'ica** [N A, B N A], a line running obliquely downward and medially from the tubercle of the femur, winding around the medial side of the body of the bone. Called also *intertrochanteric line.* **l. intertrochanter'ica poste'rior,** crista intertrochanterica. **l. mamilla'ris** [N A, B N A], an imaginary vertical line on the anterior surface of the body, passing through the center of the nipple. Called also *mamillary line,* and *l. medioclavicularis.* **l. media'na ante'rior** [N A, B N A], an imaginary line on the anterior surface of the body, dividing it into symmetrical right and left halves. Called also *anterior median line.* **l. media'na poste'rior** [N A, B N A], an imaginary line on the posterior surface of the body, dividing it into symmetrical right and left halves. Called also *posterior median line.* **l. medioclavicula'ris,** N A alternative for *l. mamillaris.* **l. mensa'lis,** any one of the lines on the palm of the hand caused by flexion of the middle, ring, and little fingers. **lin'eae muscula'res scap'ulae** [B N A], low ridges on the costal surface of the scapula, marking the site of attachment of muscle fibers. Omitted in N A. **l. mus'culi sol'ei** [N A], a line extending from the fibular facet downward and inward across the posterior surface of the tibia, giving attachment to fibers of the soleus muscle. Called also *l. poplitea tibiae* [B N A], and *soleal line of tibia.* **l. mylohyoi'dea mandib'ulae** [N A, B N A], a ridge on the inner surface of the mandible from the base of the symphysis to the ascending ramus behind the last molar tooth; it affords attachment to the mylohyoid muscle and superior constrictor of the pharynx. Called also *mylohyoid line of mandible.* **l. ni'gra,** a name given the tendinous mesial line of the abdomen (l. alba) when it has become pigmented in pregnancy. **l. nu'chae infe'rior** [N A, B N A], the lowest of the three nuchal lines found on the outer surface of the occipital bone, extending laterally from the middle of the external occipital crest to the jugular process. Called also *inferior nuchal line.* **l. nu'chae supe'rior** [N A, B N A], a curved line on the outer surface of the occipital bone, extending from the external occipital protuberance toward the lateral angle, and giving attachment medially to the trapezius muscle and laterally to the sternocleidomastoid muscle. Called also *superior nuchal line.* **l. nu'chae supre'ma** [N A, B N A], a sometimes indistinct line arching upward from the external occipital protuberance and running toward the lateral angle of the occipital bone. The epicranial aponeurosis attaches to it. Called also *highest nuchal line.* **l. obli'qua cartilag'inis thyroi'deae** [N A], a line on the external surface of the lamina of the thyroid cartilage, extending between the two thyroid tubercles. Called also *oblique line of thyroid cartilage.* **l. obli'qua fib'ulae,** margo anterior fibulae. **l. obli'qua mandib'ulae** [N A, B N A], a ridge on the external surface of the body of the mandible extending from the mental tubercle to the anterior border of the ascending ramus on either side. Called also *oblique line of mandible.* **l. obli'qua tib'iae,** l. musculi solei. **l. parasterna'lis** [B N A], an imaginary line on the anterior surface of the body midway between the mamillary line and the border of the sternum. Omitted in N A. **l. pectin'ea fem'oris** [N A, B N A], a line running down the posterior surface of the shaft of the femur, giving attachment to the pectineus muscle. Called also *pectineal line.* **l. poplite'a tib'iae** [B N A], l. musculi solii. **l. scapula'ris** [N A, B N A], an imaginary vertical line on the posterior surface of the body, passing through the lower angle of the scapula. Called also *scapular line.* **l. semicircula'ris [Doug'lasi]** [B N A], l. arcuata vaginae musculi recti abdominis. **l. semiluna'ris** [N A], **l. semiluna'ris [Spige'li]** [B N A], a curved line along the lateral border of each rectus abdominis muscle, corresponding to the meeting of the aponeuroses of the internal oblique and transverse abdominal muscles. Called also *semilunar line* and *Spieghel's line.* **l. spira'lis,** l. intertrochanterica. **l. splen'dens, Macal'ister,** fissura anterior medullae spinalis. **l. sterna'lis** [B N A], an imaginary vertical line on the ventral surface of the body, corresponding to the lateral border of the sternum. Omitted in N A. **l. tempora'lis infe'rior os'sis parieta'lis** [N A, B N A], a curved line on the external surface of the parietal bone, marking the limit of attachment of the temporal muscle. Called also *inferior temporal line.* **l. tempora'lis os'sis fronta'lis** [N A, B N A], a ridge extending upward and backward from the zygomatic process of the frontal bone, dividing into superior and inferior parts that are continuous with corresponding lines on the parietal bone, and giving attachment to the temporal fascia. Called also *temporal line of frontal bone.* **l. tempora'lis supe'rior os'sis parieta'lis** [N A, B N A], a curved line on the external surface of the parietal bone, above and parallel to the inferior temporal line, giving attachment to the temporal fascia. Called also *superior temporal line.* **l. termina'lis pel'vis** [N A, B N A], a line on the inner surface of either pelvic bone, extending from the sacroiliac joint to the iliopubic eminence anteriorly, and marking the plane separating the false from the true pelvis. **lin'eae transver'sae os'sis sa'cri** [N A, B N A], four transverse ridges on the pelvic surface of the sacrum, running between the pairs of pelvic sacral foramina, marking the positions of the former intervertebral disks. Called also *transverse lines of sacrum.* **l. trapezoi'dea** [N A], a ridge extending anterolaterally from the conoid tubercle on the inferior surface of the clavicle, giving attachment to the trapezoid portion of the coracoclavicular ligament. Called also *trapezoid line.* **l. vi'sus** [B N A], an imaginary line from the fovea centralis of the retina to the point of fixation of the eye. Omitted in N A. **l. vita'lis** [L. "line of life"], a line on the palm of the hand curving around the thenar eminence.

lineae (lin'e-e) [L.]. Plural of *linea.*

lineage (lin'e-ij) [L. *linea* line]. Descent traced down from or back to a common ancestor. **cell l.,** cytogeny, def. 2.

linear (lin'e-ar) [L. *linearis*]. Pertaining to or resembling a line.

liner (līn'er). Material applied to the inside of the walls of a cavity or container, for protection or insulation of the surface. **cavity l.,** a substance applied to the tooth surface exposed by caries, to protect the dentin and insulate the pulp.

lingism (ling'izm) [Peter H. *Ling,* Swedish poet and gymnast, 1776–1839]. The movement cure; kinesitherapy.

lingua (ling'gwah), pl. *lin'guae* [L. "tongue"]. 1. [N A, B N A] The movable, muscular organ on the floor of the mouth, subserving the special sense of taste and aiding in mastication, deglutition, and the articulation of sound. Called also *tongue.* 2. A structure or part having a shape similar to that of the oral organ of the same name. **l. dissec'ta,** geographic tongue. **l. fraena'ta,** tonguetie. **l. geograph'ica,** geographic tongue. **l. ni'gra,** black tongue. **l. plica'ta,** fissured tongue. **l. villo'sa ni'gra,** black tongue.

linguae (ling'gwe) [L.]. Plural of *lingua.*

lingual (ling'gwal) [L. *lingualis*]. Pertaining to the tongue.

linguale (ling-gwa'le). The point at the upper end of the symphysis of the lower jaw on its lingual surface.

lingualis (ling-gwa'lis), pl. *lingua'les* [L.]. Relating to the tongue.

lingually (ling'gwal-le). Toward the tongue.

Linguatula (ling-gwat'u-lah). A genus of arthropods which, in the adult form, inhabit the frontal, nasal, and maxillary sinuses of animals and sometimes of man. Their larval form (known as *Pentastoma* and *Porocephalus*) infests the digestive organs and lungs. Called also *tongue worms.* **L. rhina'ria (serra'ta),** the species found in man; both the larval and the adult forms have been found.

Linguatula, larval form (Mitchell).

linguatuliasis (ling-gwat"u-li'ah-sis). Invasion of the body by *Linguatula.*

linguatulosis (ling-gwat"u-lo'sis). Linguatuliasis.

linguiform (ling'gwĭ-form). Tongue-shaped.

lingula (ling'gu-lah), pl. *lin'gulae* [L., dim. of *lingua*]. A small tongue-like structure. **l. cerebel'li** [N A, B N A], **l. of cerebellum,** the part of the vermis of the cerebellum, on the ventral surface, where the superior medullary velum attaches. **l. of left lung,** l. pulmonis sinistri. **l. of lower jaw,** l. mandibulae. **l. of mandible, l. mandib'ulae** [N A, B N A], the sharp medial boundary of the mandibular foramen, to which is attached the sphenomandibular ligament. **l. pulmo'nis sinis'tri** [N A], a projection from the lower portion of the upper lobe of the left lung, just beneath the cardiac notch, between the cardiac impression and the inferior margin. Called also *l. of left lung.* **l. of sphenoid, sphenoidal l., l. sphenoida'lis** [N A, B N A], a slender ridge of bone on the lateral margin of the carotid sulcus, projecting backward between the body and great wing of the sphenoid bone.

lingulae (ling'gu-le) [L.]. Plural of lingula.

lingular (ling'gu-lar). Pertaining to a lingula.

lingulectomy (ling"gu-lek'to-me). Excision of the lingula pulmonis sinistri.

linguoaxial (ling"gwo-ak'se-al). Pertaining to or formed by the lingual and axial walls of a tooth cavity.

linguocervical (ling"gwo-ser'vĭ-kal). 1. Pertaining to the lingual surface of the neck of a tooth. 2. Linguogingival.

linguoclination (ling"gwo-kli-na'shun). Deviation of a tooth from the vertical, in the direction of the tongue.

linguoclusion (ling"gwo-kloo'zhun). Malocclusion in which the tooth is lingual to the line of the normal dental arch.

linguodental (ling"gwo-den'tal). Pertaining to the tongue and the teeth.

linguodistal (ling"gwo-dis'tal). Pertaining to or formed by the lingual and distal surfaces of a tooth, or the lingual and distal walls of a tooth cavity.

linguogingival (ling"gwo-jin'jĭ-val). Pertaining to the tongue and gingiva; pertaining to or formed by the lingual and gingival walls of a tooth cavity.

linguoincisal (ling"gwo-in-si'zal). Pertaining to or formed by the lingual and incisal surfaces of a tooth.

linguomesial (ling"gwo-me'ze-al). Pertaining to or formed by the lingual and mesial surfaces of a tooth, or the lingual and mesial walls of a tooth cavity.

linguo-occlusal (ling"gwo-ŏ-kloo'zal). Pertaining to or formed by the lingual and occlusal surfaces of a tooth.

linguopapillitis (ling"gwo-pap"ĭ-li'tis) [L. *lingua* tongue + *papillitis*]. Small painful ulcers around the papillae of the edges of the tongue.

linguoplacement (ling'gwo-plās"ment) [L. *lingua* tongue + *displacement*]. Displacement of a tooth toward the tongue.

linguopulpal (ling"gwo-pul'pal). Pertaining to or formed by the lingual and pulpal walls of a tooth cavity.

linguotrite (ling'gwo-trīt). An instrument for seizing the tongue and drawing it forward.

linguoversion (ling"gwo-ver'zhun). The state of being displaced lingually from the line of occlusion: said of a tooth.

Linim. Abbreviation for *liniment.*

liniment (lin'ĭ-ment) [L. *linimentum; linere* to smear]. An oily liquid preparation to be used on the skin. **camphor l.,** a preparation of camphor and cottonseed oil: used as a local irritant to the skin. **camphor and soap l.,** a preparation of hard soap, camphor, rosemary oil, and alcohol: used as a local irritant to the skin. **chloroform l.,** a preparation of chloroform with camphor and soap linament: used as a local irritant to the skin. **medicinal soft soap l.,** a preparation of medicinal soft soap, lavender oil, and alcohol: used externally as a detergent.

linimentum (lin"ĭ-men'tum) [L.]. Liniment. **l. cam'phorae,** camphor liniment. **l. cam'phorae et sapo'nis,** camphor and soap liniment. **l. chlorofor'mi,** chloroform liniment. **l. sapo'nis mol'lis,** medicinal soft soap liniment.

linin (li'nin) [L. *linum* thread]. The faintly staining substance composing the fine, netlike threads found in the nucleus of a cell, where it bears the chromatin in the form of granules. Cf. *achromatin.*

linitis (lin-i'tis) [Gr. *linon* thread + *-itis*]. Inflammation of the gastric cellular tissue. **l. plas'tica,** diffuse hypertrophy of the submucous connective tissue of the stomach, rendering the walls of the stomach rigid, thick, and hard, like a leather bag. Called also *Brinton's disease, hypertrophic* *gastritis, gastric sclerosis, cirrhosis of the stomach, fibromatosis ventriculi, cirrhotic gastritis,* and *leather bottle stomach.*

linkage (lingk′ij). 1. The connection between different atoms in a chemical compound, or the symbol representing it in structural formulas. See also *bond.* 2. In genetics, the tendency for a group of genes in a chromosome to remain in continuous association from generation to generation. 3. In psychology, the connection between a stimulus and its response.

linked (linkt). United. In genetics, referring to characters which are united so as invariably to be inherited together.

Linognathus (lin-og′nah-thus). A genus of sucking lice: *L. peda′lis* infests sheep. *L. pilif′erus* the dog, *L. sten′opis* the goat, and *L. vilu′li* is the long-nosed louse of the ox.

linolein (lin-o′le-in) [L. *linum* flax + *oleum* oil]. A neutral fat from linseed oil; the glyceride of linoleic acid.

linoxanthine (li″no-zan′thin) [L. *linum* flax + Gr. *xanthos* yellow]. An orange-yellow pigment produced by *Sarcina aurantiaca;* it is the coloring matter of orange pus.

linseed (lin′sēd). The dried ripe seed of *Linum usitatissimum:* used as a protective.

Linser's method (lin′serz) [Paul *Linser,* German dermatologist, born 1871]. Treatment of varicose veins by the injection of corrosive mercuric chloride.

lint (lint) [L. *linteum,* from *linum,* flax]. An absorbent dressing material made by scraping or picking apart old woven linen; also a specially finished woven fabric for surgical dressing. **cotton l.,** a lint of inferior quality prepared from cotton fabrics. **patent l.,** sheet l. **picked l.,** lint prepared by hand. **scraped l.,** lint prepared by scraping. **sheet l.,** a form of lint in sheets, prepared by machinery.

Lint. Abbreviation for L. *lin′teum,* lint.

lintin (lin′tin). A loose fabric of prepared absorbent cotton: used in dressing wounds.

lintine (lin′tēn). Cotton lint from which the oil has been removed.

linum (li′num) [L. "flax"]. Linseed.

lio- (li′o). For words beginning thus, see also those beginning *leio-.*

Li_2O. Lithium oxide.

LiOH. Lithium hydroxide.

liothyronine (li″o-thi′ro-nēn). Chemical name: 1-3[4-(4-hydroxy-3-iodophenoxy)-3,5-diiodophenyl] alanine. Use: treatment of hypothyroidism.

Liouville's icterus (le-oo′vēlz) [Henri *Liouville,* French physician, 1837–1887]. Icterus neonatorum.

lip (lip). 1. Either the upper or lower fleshy margin of the mouth, together called *labia oris* [N A]. 2. A marginal part. Called also *labium.* **acetabular l.,** labrum acetabulare. **anterior l. of cervix of uterus,** labium anterius ostii uteri. **anterior l. of pharyngeal opening of auditory tube,** labium anterius ostii pharyngei tubae auditivae. **cleft l.,** harelip. **double l.,** redundancy of the submucous tissue and mucous membrane of the lip on either side of the median line. **external l. of iliac crest,** labium externum cristae iliacae. **external l. of linea aspera of femur,** labium laterale lineae asperae femoris. **fibrocartilaginous l. of acetabulum,** labrum acetabulare. **glenoid l.,** labrum glenoidale. **glenoid l. of articulation of hip,** labrum acetabulare. **glenoid l. of articulation of humerus,** labrum glenoidale. **greater l. of pudendum,** labium majus pudendi. **Hapsburg l.,** a thick overdeveloped lower lip that often accompanies a Hapsburg jaw. **inferior l.,** labium inferius oris. **inferior l. of ileocecal valve,** labium inferius valvulae coli. **internal l. of iliac crest,** labium internum cristae iliacae. **lateral l. of linea aspera of femur,** labium laterale lineae asperae femoris. **lesser l. of pudendum,** labium minus pudendi. **lower l.,** labium inferius oris. **medial l. of linea aspera of femur,** labium mediale lineae asperae femoris. **l's of mouth,** labia oris. **posterior l. of cervix of uterus,** labium posterius ostii uteri. **posterior l. of pharyngeal opening of auditory tube,** labium posterius ostii pharyngei tubae auditivae. **rhombic l.,** the lateral boundary of the rhombencephalon during embryonic life. **superior l.,** labium superius oris. **superior l. of ileocecal valve,** labium superius valvulae coli. **tympanic l. of limb of spiral lamina,** labium tympanicum limbi laminae spiralis. **upper l.,** labium superius oris. **vestibular l. of limb of spiral lamina,** labium vestibulare limbi laminae spiralis.

lipacidemia (lip″as-ĭ-de′me-ah) [*lipo-* + L. *acidus* acid + Gr. *haima* blood + *-ia*]. The presence of any fatty acid in the blood.

lipaciduria (lip″as-ĭ-du′re-ah) [*lipo-* + L. *acidus* acid + Gr. *ouron* urine + *-ia*]. The presence of any fatty acid in the urine.

liparocele (lip-ar′o-sēl) [Gr. *liparos* oily + *kēlē* tumor]. A fatty scrotal tumor; also a hernia containing fatty material.

liparodyspnea (lip″ah-ro-disp′ne-ah). The dyspnea of the obese.

liparoid (lip′ah-roid). Fatty; resembling fat.

liparomphalus (lip″ah-rom′fah-lus) [Gr. *liparos* oily + *omphalos* navel]. A fatty tumor of the navel.

liparthritis (li″par-thri′tis) [Gr. *leipein* to fail + *arthritis*]. A form of arthritis caused by cessation of the ovarian function.

lipase (lip′ās) [Gr. *lipos* fat + *-ase*]. An enzyme that catalyzes the hydrolysis of ester linkages between the fatty acids and glycerol of the triglycerides and phospholipids.

lipasic (li-pa′sik). 1. Pertaining to lipase. 2. Lipolytic.

lipasuria (lip″ās-u′re-ah). The presence of lipase in the urine.

lipectomy (lip-ek′to-me) [*lipo-* + Gr. *ektomē* excision]. Excision of fatty tissue or of a lesion of the subcutaneous fatty tissue.

lipedema (lip″e-de′mah) [*lipo-* + *edema*]. An accumulation of excess fat and fluid in subcutaneous tissues.

lipemia (lip-e′me-ah) [*lipo-* + Gr. *haima* blood + *-ia*]. The presence of an abnormally high concentration of fat or lipid in the blood; hypercholesteremia. **alimentary l.,** that occurring after the ingestion of food. **l. retina′lis,** a high level of lipids in the blood, manifested by a milky appearance of the veins and arteries of the retina.

lipese (lip′ēs). An enzyme which brings about the synthesis of fats.

lipfanogen (lip-fan′o-jen) [Gr. *lipos* fat + *phaneros* visible + *gennan* to produce]. A substance that produces visible fat; applied to a special group of lipoid substances which, when in a free state, are taken up by living cells and converted into visible fat.

lipid (lip′id). Any one of a group of organic substances which are insoluble in water, but soluble in alcohol, ether, chloroform and other fat solvents and which have a greasy feel. As used in the United States, the term embraces fatty acids and soaps, neutral fats, waxes, steroids, and phosphatides. In Great Britain the term is restricted to those compounds which yield by hydrolysis an alcohol or a sugar, a base, and a fatty acid and does not include the neutral fats, fatty acids, or sterols.

lipidase (lip′ĭ-dās). An enzyme that catalyzes the splitting up of lipids.

lipide (lip′id). Lipid.

lipidemia (lip″ĭ-de′me-ah). The presence of an excess of lipids in the blood.

lipidic (lip-id′ik). Pertaining to or containing lipids.

lipidol (lip′ĭ-dol). A lipid alcohol; an aliphatic fatty alcohol.

lipidolysis (lip″ĭ-dol′ĭ-sis). The splitting up of lipids.

lipidolytic (lip″ĭ-do-lit′ik). Pertaining to, characterized by, or causing lipidolysis.

lipidosis (lip″ĭ-do′sis). A general term for disorders of cellular lipid metabolism.

lipidtemns (lip′id-temz). A collective name for the products formed by the digestion of fats, namely, glycerin and fatty acids.

lipiduria (lip″ĭ-du′re-ah) [*lipid* + Gr. *ouron* urine + *-ia*]. The presence of lipids in the urine.

lipin (lip′in) [Gr. *lipos* fat]. Lipid.

Lipmann (lip′man), Fritz Albert. German biochemist in America, born 1899, noted for discovery of importance of vitamin A in biological processes; co-winner, with Hans Adolph Krebs, of the Nobel prize in medicine and physiology for 1953.

lipo- (lip′o) [Gr. *lipos* fat]. Combining form denoting relationship to fat.

lipo-arthritis (lip″o-ar-thri′tis) [*lipo-* + *arthritis*]. Inflammation of the fatty tissue of a joint.

lipo-atrophia (lip″o-ah-tro′fe-ah). Atrophy of fatty tissues of the body. **l. circumscrip′ta,** localized atrophy of the subcutaneous fat, producing a condition of cutis laxa or dermatolysis.

lipoblast (lip′o-blast) [*lipo-* + Gr. *blastos* germ]. A specialized connective tissue cell which develops into a fat cell.

lipoblastoma (lip″o-blas-to′mah) [*lipo-* + Gr. *blastos* germ + *-oma*]. A tumor made up of lipoblasts or embryonic fat cells.

lipocaic (lip″o-ka′ik) [*lipo-* + Gr. *kaiein* to burn]. A substance extracted from the pancreas which prevents the deposition of fat in the livers of animals after pancreatectomy and after other experimental procedures.

lipocardiac (lip″o-kar′de-ak) [*lipo-* + Gr. *kardia* heart]. Relating to a fatty heart.

lipocatabolic (lip″o-kat″ah-bol′ik). Pertaining to or effecting the destructive metabolism of fat.

lipocele (lip′o-sēl) [*lipo-* + Gr. *kēlē* tumor]. Adipocele.

lipoceratous (lip″o-ser′ah-tus). Adipoceratous.

lipocere (lip′o-sēr) [*lipo-* + L. *cera* wax]. Adipocere.

lipochondrodystrophy (lip″o-kon″dro-dis′tro-fe) [*lipo-* + Gr. *chondros* cartilage + *dystrophy*]. A lipoid disturbance, probably congenital, involving the cartilage, bones, skin, subcutaneous tissues, brain, cornea, liver and spleen. It is characterized by dwarf stature, shortness of the neck and trunk, kyphosis of the spine, depression of the bridge of the nose, stiffness of the joints, shortness of the fingers, mental deficiency and clouding of the cornea.

lipochondroma (lip″o-kon-dro′mah) [*lipo-* + Gr. *chondros* cartilage + *-oma*]. A chondroma containing fatty elements.

lipochrin (lip′o-krin) [*lipo-* + Gr. *ōchros* sallow]. A pigment from the retinal fat globules.

lipochrome (lip′o-krōm) [*lipo-* + Gr. *chrōma* color]. Any one of a group of fat-soluble hydrocarbon pigments, such as carotin, xanthophyll, lutein, chromophane and the natural coloring material of butter, egg yolk, and yellow corn. They are also known as carotenoids.

lipochromemia (lip″o-kro-me′me-ah) [*lipochrome* + Gr. *haima* blood + *-ia*]. The presence of an excess of lipochrome in the blood.

lipochromogen (lip″o-kro′mo-jen). A substance which becomes converted into lipochrome.

lipoclasis (lip-ok′lah-sis) [*lipo-* + Gr. *klasis* breaking]. Lipolysis.

lipoclastic (lip″o-klas′tik) [*lipo-* + Gr. *klastikos* breaking up]. Lipolytic.

lipocorticoid (lip″o-kor′tĭ-koid). A corticoid effective in causing deposition of fat, especially in the liver.

lipocyanine (lip″o-si′ah-nin) [*lipo-* + Gr. *kyanos* blue]. A blue pigment resulting from the action of strong sulfuric acid on lipochrome.

lipocyte (lip′o-sīt) [*lipo-* + *-cyte*]. A fat cell.

lipodieresis (lip″o-di-er′ĕ-sis) [*lipo-* + Gr. *diairesis* a taking]. The splitting up or the decomposition of fat.

lipodieretic (lip″o-di-er-et′ik). Pertaining to, characterized by, or causing lipodieresis.

lipodystrophia (lip″o-dis-tro′fe-ah). Lipodystrophy. **l. intestina′lis,** intestinal lipodystrophy. **l. progressi′va,** a disease characterized by the progressive and symmetrical disappearance of subcutaneous fat from the parts above the pelvis, facial emaciation, and abnormal accumulation of fat about the thighs and buttocks (A. Simons, 1911).

lipodystrophy (lip″o-dis′tro-fe) [*lipo-* + Gr. *dystrophia* dystrophy]. Any disturbance of fat metabolism. **inferior l.,** lipodystrophy of the lower limbs. **insulin l.,** a local reduction of the subcutaneous fat in a region repeatedly injected with insulin. **intestinal l.,** a disease marked by diarrhea with fatty stools, arthritis, emaciation, and loss of strength. It is attended with deposit of fat in the intestinal lymphatic tissue. Called also *Whipple's disease* and *lipophagia granulomatosis.* **progressive l.,** lipodystrophia progressiva.

lipoferous (lip-of′er-us) [*lipo-* + L. *ferre* to carry]. 1. Carrying fat. 2. Sudanophil.

lipofibroma (lip″o-fi-bro′mah). A fibroma containing fatty elements.

lipofuscin (lip″o-fus′sin). Any one of a class of fatty pigments formed by the solution of a pigment in fat. Cf. *lipochrome.*

lipogenesis (lip″o-jen′e-sis) [*lipo-* + *genesis*]. The formation of fat; the transformation of nonfat food materials into body fat.

lipogenetic (lip″o-je-net′ik). Forming, producing, or caused by fat.

lipogenic (lip″o-jen′ik). 1. Lipogenous. 2. Lipogenetic.

lipogenous (lip-oj′e-nus) [*lipo-* + Gr. *gennan* to produce]. Producing fatness.

lipogranuloma (lip″o-gran-u-lo′mah) [*lipo-* + *granuloma*]. A nodule of lipoid material; a foreign body inflammation of adipose tissue containing granulation tissue and oil cysts.

lipogranulomatosis (lip″o-gran″u-lo-mah-to′-sis). A condition of faulty lipid metabolism in which yellow nodules of lipoid matter are deposited in the skin and mucosae, giving rise to granulomatous reactions.

lipohemarthrosis (lip″o-hem″ar-thro′sis) [*lipo-* + Gr. *haima* blood + *arthron* joint + *-osis*]. The presence of fat-containing blood in a joint.

lipohemia (lip″o-he′me-ah). Lipemia.

lipohistiodieresis (lip″o-his″te-o-di-er′ĕ-sis). The disappearance of stored fat from body tissue.

lipoid (lip′oid) [*lipo-* + Gr. *eidos* form]. 1. Fatlike; resembling fat. 2. Lipid. **acetone-insoluble l's,** lipids, consisting largely of lecithins, precipitated from an ethereal extract of dried ox heart by adding an excess of acetone: used as an antigen in the Wassermann test after being brought into solution in a mixture of 1 part of ether and 9 parts of methanol. **anisotropic l.,** a lipid having doubly refractive properties. **brain l.,** an impure cephalin extracted from brain substance and used in checking hemorrhage by accelerating the coagulation of the blood. **Forssman's l.,** Forssman's antigen.

lipoidal (lip-oi′dal). Fatlike; resembling fat.

lipoidase (lip′oi-dās). Lipidase.

lipoidemia (lip″oi-de′me-ah). Lipidemia.

lipoidic (lip-oi′dik). Fatlike; resembling fat.

lipoidolytic (lip-oi″do-lit′ik). Lipidolytic.

lipoidosis (lip″oi-do′sis). Any disturbance of lipid metabolism; the presence of lipids in the cells.

arterial l., atherosclerosis. **cerebroside l.,** Gaucher's disease. **cholesterol l.,** Hand-Schüller-Christian disease. **l. cu'tis et muco'sae,** lipid proteinosis. **phosphatide l.,** Niemann-Pick disease. **renal l.,** lipoid nephrosis. **symmetrical l.,** Madelung's neck.

lipoidproteinosis (lip″oid-pro″te-in-o′sis). A familial disease occurring in the course of latent diabetes, marked by yellowish nodules on the skin and mucosae, keratotic lesions on the extremities, and hoarseness due to faulty lipid metabolism.

lipoidsiderosis (lip″oid-sid-er-o′sis). The absorption of iron by lipids.

lipoiduria (lip″oi-du′re-ah). Lipiduria.

lipoitrin (lip″o-it′rin). A hormone of the posterior pituitary concerned in fat metabolism.

lipolipoidosis (lip″o-lip″oi-do′sis). The presence of lipoids and neutral fats in the cells.

lipo-lutin (li″po-lu′tin). Trade mark for preparations of progesterone.

lipolysis (lip-ol′ĭ-sis) [*lipo-* + Gr. *lysis* dissolution]. The decomposition or splitting up of fat.

lipolytic (lip″o-lit′ik). Pertaining to, characterized by, or causing lipolysis.

lipoma (lip-o′mah) [*lipo-* + *-oma*]. A fatty tumor; a tumor made up of fat cells. Lipomas are painless and benign, but may become the seat of gangrene or fat necrosis. **l. annula're col'li,** diffuse lipomatosis in the neck producing a collar-like enlargement in the region. **l. arbore'cens,** a lipoma within a joint having a treelike form. **l. capsula're,** a fatty tumor due to increase of the fat adjacent to the mamma. **l. caverno'sum,** a lipoma containing blood spaces. **diffuse l.,** a tumor in the form of an irregular mass of fatty tissue without a capsule. **l. diffu'sum re'nis,** lipomatous nephritis. **l. du'rum,** steatoma. **l. fibro'sum,** a fatty tumor with framework of fibrous tissue. **l. lipomato'des,** essential xanthoma. **l. myxomato'des,** a myxolipoma. **nevoid l.,** a lipoma containing many blood vessels. **l. ossif'icans,** a lipoma containing bony tissue. **l. petrif'icans,** a calcified lipoma. **l. petrif'icum ossif'icans,** an ossified lipoma. **l. sacomato'des,** liposarcoma. **telangiectatic l., l. telangiecto'des,** a lipoma containing dilated blood vessels.

lipomatoid (lip-o′mah-toid). Resembling a lipoma.

lipomatosis (lip″o-mah-to′sis). A condition characterized by abnormal localized, or tumor-like, accumulations of fat in the tissues. **l. atroph'icans,** localized accumulations of fat in certain tissues, associated with emaciation of the rest of the body. **diffuse l.,** abnormal increase of subcutaneous fat in the parts above the pelvis, usually in males. **l. doloro'sa,** lipomatosis in which the adipose deposits are tender or painful. **l. gigan'tea,** a form in which the adipose deposits form large masses. **nodular circumscribed l.,** the formation of multiple circumscribed or encapsulated lipomas. They are often accompanied by local tenderness and constitutional symptoms. **l. re'nis,** lipomatous nephritis.

Diffuse lipomatosis (Babcock).

lipomatous (lip-o′mah-tus). Affected with, or of the nature of, lipoma.

lipomeria (li″po-me′re-ah) [Gr. *leipein* to leave + *meros* a part]. Monstrosity consisting of the congenital absence of a limb.

lipometabolic (lip″o-met″ah-bol′ik). Pertaining to metabolism of fat.

lipometabolism (lip″o-mĕ-tab′o-lizm) [*lipo-* + *metabolism*]. The metabolism of fat; utilization of fat.

lipomicron (lip″o-mi′kron). A microscopic fat particle in the blood.

lipomyoma (lip″o-mi-o′mah). A myoma containing fatty tissue.

lipomyxoma (lip″o-miks-o′mah). A myxoma containing fatty elements.

liponephrosis (lip″o-ne-fro′sis). Lipoid nephrosis.

liponeurocyte (lip″o-nu′ro-sit). The name given by Cramer to cells found in the pituitary body of rats.

Liponyssus (lip″o-nis′us) [*lipo-* + Gr. *nyssein* to pierce]. A genus of mites. **L. baco'ti,** a species which transmits epidemic typhus. **L. bur'sa,** the tropical fowl mite. **L. sylvia'rum,** the northern fowl mite.

lipopectic (lip″o-pek′tik). Pertaining to, characterized by, or causing lipopexia.

lipopenia (lip″o-pe′ne-ah). [*lipo-* + Gr. *penia* poverty]. Deficiency of the lipids of the body.

lipopenic (lip″o-pe′nik). Pertaining to, characterized by, or causing lipopenia.

lipopeptid (lip″o-pep′tid). A compound of amino acids and fatty acids.

lipopexia (lip″o-pek′se-ah) [*lipo-* + Gr. *pēxis* fixation]. The accumulation of fat in the tissues.

lipopexic (lip″o-pek′sik). Lipopectic.

lipophage (lip′o-fāj). A cell which ingests or absorbs fat.

lipophagia (lip″o-fa′je-ah). Liphophagy. **l. granulomato'sis,** intestinal lipodystrophy.

lipophagic (lip″o-fa′jik) [*lipo-* + Gr. *phagein* to eat]. Pertaining to, characterized by, or causing lipophagy.

lipophagy (lip-of′ah-je). The destruction of fat; lipolysis.

lipophil (lip′o-fil). An element which has an affinity for fat.

lipophilia (lip″o-fil′e-ah) [*lipo-* + Gr. *philein* to love + *-ia*]. 1. Affinity for fat. 2. A tendency of the obese for fat fixation (Bergman).

lipophilic (lip″o-fil′ik). Having an affinity for fat; pertaining to or characterized by lipophilia.

lipophore (lip′o-fōr) [*lipo-* + Gr. *phoros* bearing]. Xanthophore.

lipophrenia (li″po-fre′ne-ah) [Gr. *leipein* to fail + *phrēn* mind]. Failure of the mental powers.

lipoprotein (lip″o-pro′te-in). A combination of a lipid and protein, possessing the general properties (e.g., solubility) of proteins. Practically all of the lipids of the plasma are present as lipoprotein complexes, α- and β-lipoproteins being distinguished by electrophoresis. The β-lipoproteins transport more of the total plasma cholesterol, contain a higher concentration of both free and esterified cholesterol, and have a higher cholesterol/phospholipid ratio than α-lipoproteins.

liporhodin (lip″o-ro′din) [*lipo-* + Gr. *rhodon* rose]. A red lipochrome.

liposarcoma (lip″o-sar-ko′mah) [*lipo-* + *sarcoma*]. Sarcoma containing fatty elements.

lipose, liposin (lip′ōs, lip-o′sin). A lipase occurring in the blood.

liposis (lip-o′sis) [Gr. *lipos* fat + *-osis*]. Lipomatosis.

liposoluble (lip″o-sol′u-b'l) [*lipo-* + *soluble*]. Soluble in fats.

liposome (lip′o-sōm) [*lipo-* + Gr. *sōma* body]. One of the particles of lipoidal material held emulsified in tissues in the form of "invisible fat."

liposteatosis (lip″o-ste″ah-to′sis). A form of xanthoma in which the lipoid in the foam cells is a phosphatid or cerebroside.

lipostomy (li-pos′to-me) [Gr. *leipein* to fail + *stoma* mouth]. Atrophy of the mouth.

lipotamponade (lip″o-tam′po-nād) [*lipo-* + *tamponade*]. Surgical creation of an extrapleural cavity and filling it with a mass of fat: done to compress the lung in pulmonary tuberculosis.

lipothymia (li″po-thi′me-ah) [Gr. *leipein* to fail + *thymos* mind]. Faintness or swooning; a swoon or faint.

lipotrophic (lip″o-trof′ik). Pertaining to, characterized by, or causing lipotrophy.

lipotrophy (lip-ot′ro-fe) [*lipo-* + Gr. *trophē* nutrition]. Increase of bodily fat.

lipotropic (lip″o-trop′ik). Having an affinity for fats or oils, and thus acting on fat metabolism by hastening the removal of or decreasing the deposit of fat in the liver.

lipotropism (lip-ot′ro-pizm). Affinity for fat, especially that of certain agents which are capable of decreasing the deposits of fat in the liver.

lipotropy (lip-ot′ro-pe) [*lipo-* + Gr. *tropē* a turning]. Affinity for oils and fats or for fatty tissue.

lipotuberculin (lip″o-tu-ber′ku-lin). A lipovaccine for tuberculosis.

lipovaccine (lip″o-vak′sēn) [*lipo-* + *vaccine*]. A vaccine prepared with a vegetable oil as the menstruum.

lipoxanthine (lip″o-zan′thin) [*lipo-* + Gr. *xanthos* yellow]. A yellow lipochrome.

lipoxenous (li-poks′ĕ-nus). Pertaining to or characterized by lipoxeny.

lipoxeny (li-pok′sĕ-ne) [Gr. *leipein* to leave + *xenos* host]. The desertion of the host by a parasite.

lipoxidase (lip-ok′sĭ-dās). An enzyme which catalyzes the addition of oxygen to the double bonds of unsaturated fatty acids.

lipoxidemia (lip″ok-sĭ-de′me-ah). Lipacidemia.

lipoxysm (lip-oks′izm) [Gr. *lipos* fat + *oxys* sharp, acid]. Poisoning by oleic acid.

lippa (lip′ah). Marginal blepharitis.

lipping (lip′ing). 1. A wedge-shaped shadow in the roentgenogram of chondrosarcoma between the cortex and the elevated periosteum. 2. The development of a bony lip in osteoarthrosis.

lippitude (lip′ĭ-tūd) [L. *lippitudo; lippus* bleareyed]. Marginal blepharitis.

Lippmann's electrometer (lip′manz) [Gabriel *Lippmann*, French physicist, 1845–1921]. See under *electrometer*.

Lipschütz bodies, cell, disease, ulcer (lip′shitz) [Benjamin *Lipschütz*, Austrian dermatologist, 1878–1931]. See under the nouns.

lipsis (lip′sis) [Gr. *leipein* to leave]. Ending; cessation. **l. an′imi,** fainting.

lipsitol (lip′sĭ-tol). A compound containing inositol, galactose, fatty acids, phosphoric acid, and ethanolamine.

lipsotrichia (lip″so-trik′e-ah) [Gr. *leipein* to leave + *thrix* hair]. Falling of the hair.

lipuria (lip-u′re-ah) [Gr. *lipos* fat + *ouron* urine + *-ia*]. The presence of oil or fat in the urine.

lipuric (lip-u′rik). Pertaining to or characterized by lipuria.

Liq. Abbreviation for *liquor*.

liquaemin (lik′wah-min). Trade mark for preparations of heparin.

liquamar (lik′wah-mar). Trade mark for a preparation of phenprocoumon.

liquefacient (lik″wĕ-fa′shent) [L. *liquefaciens*]. Having the quality to convert a solid material into a liquid, producing liquefaction.

liquefaction (lik″wĕ-fak′shun) [L. *liquefactio; liquere* to flow + *facere* to make]. The conversion of a material into a liquid form.

liquefactive (lik″wĕ-fak′tiv). Pertaining to, characterized by, or causing liquefaction.

liquescent (lik-wes′ent) [L. *liquescere* to become liquid]. Tending to become liquid; becoming liquid.

liquid (lik′wid) [L. *liquidus; liquere* to flow]. 1. A substance that flows readily in its natural state. 2. Flowing readily; neither solid nor gaseous. **blistering l.,** liquor epispasticus. **Bonain's l.,** an anesthetic for operations on the ear, consisting of phenol, menthol, and cocaine hydrochloride. **Cohn's l.,** a culture liquid for bacteria, consisting of a mixture of ashes of yeast and ammonium tartrate in distilled water. **Declat's l.,** a solution of carbolate of ammonia for external and internal use in cholera. **Dutch l.,** ethylene dichloride. **Ebner's l.,** a decalcifying liquid for microscopical objects consisting of hydrochloric acid, distilled water, and cold saturated solution of sodium chloride. **Pasteur's l.** See under *solution*.

liquiform (lik′wĕ-form). Resembling a liquid.

liquogel (lik′wo-jel). A gel which after melting gives a sol of low viscosity. Cf. *viscagel*.

liquor (lik′er, li′kwor), pl. *liquors, liquo′res* [L.]. 1. A liquid, especially an aqueous solution, or a solution not obtained by distillation. 2. A general term used in anatomical nomenclature for certain fluids of the body. **l. am′nii,** amniotic fluid. **l. cerebrospina′lis** [N A], the fluid contained within the four ventricles of the brain, the subarachnoid space, and the central canal of the spinal cord. Called also *cerebrospinal fluid*. **l. cho′rii,** a fluid which separates the amnion from the chorion in the early stages of gestation. **l. cor′neae,** a fluid occupying the lymph spaces of the cornea. **l. cotun′nii,** perilymph (perilympha [N A]). **l. enter′icus,** succus entericus. **l. follic′uli** [B N A], an albuminous fluid in the vesicular ovarian follicle. Omitted in N A. **l. gas′tricus,** succus gastricus. **Morgagni's l.,** a fluid between the eye lens and its capsule. **mother l.,** the liquid from which any substance has been separated by crystallization. **l. pancreat′icus,** succus pancreaticus. **l. pericar′dii** [B N A], a fluid found in small amount in the potential space between the parietal and visceral laminae of the serous pericardium. Omitted in N A. **l. prostat′icus,** succus prostaticus. **l. pu′ris,** the fluid portion of pus. **l. san′guinis,** the fluid portion of the blood; the blood plasma. **l. of Scarpa, l. scar′pae,** endolymph (endolympha [N A]). **l. sem′inis,** the fluid portion of the semen.

liquores (li-kwo′rēz) [L.]. Plural of *liquor*.

liquorice (lik′er-is). See *Glycyrrhiza*.

liquorrhea (li″kwo-re′ah) [L. *liquor* liquid + Gr. *rhoia* flow]. An excessive discharge of any body fluid, e.g., liquorrhea nasalis.

lirellate (lir′el-lāt) [L. *lira* a ridge]. Ridgelike; marked with ridges or furrows.

lirelliform, lirelline, lirellous (lir-el′ĭ-form, lir′ĕ-lin, lir′ĕ-lus). Lirellate.

Lisfranc's amputation, joint, ligament, tubercle (lis-frahnks′) [Jacques *Lisfranc*, French surgeon, 1790–1847]. See under the nouns.

Lissauer's angle, paralysis, tract (lis′owerz) [Heinrich *Lissauer*, German neurologist, 1861–1891]. See under the nouns.

Lissencephala (lis″en-sef′ah-lah) [Gr. *lissos* smooth + *enkephalos* brain]. A group of placental mammals in which the brain is characteristically smooth or is marked by few convolutions.

lissencephalia (lis″en-se-fa′le-ah). Agyria.

lissencephalic (lis″en-se-fal′ik). 1. Pertaining to the Lissencephala. 2. Having cerebral hemispheres without or with only shallow convolutions, the normal appearance of the brain of many animals (e.g., bats, rodents). 3. Agyric.

lissencephaly (lis″sen-sef″ah-le). Agyria.

lissive (lis′siv) [Gr. *lissos* smooth]. Relieving muscle spasm without interfering with function.

Lissoflagellata (lis″o-flaj″ĕ-la′tah) [Gr. *lissos* smooth + *flagellum*]. A class of flagellate organisms having no protoplasmic collar at the base of the flagellum.

lissothricic (lis″o-thris′ik) [Gr. *lissos* smooth + *thrix* hair]. Having smooth, straight hair.

Lister (lis′ter), Baron Joseph (1827–1912). The last and greatest of an interesting line of English Quaker physicians, who was the father of modern antiseptic surgery.

Listerella (lis″ter-el′ah). Listeria.

listerellal (lis″ter-el′al). Listerial.

listerellosis (lis″ter-el-lo′sis). Listeriosis.

Listeria (lis-ter′e-ah) [Baron Joseph *Lister*]. A genus of microorganisms of the family Corynebacteriaceae, order Eubacteriales, made up of coccoid to bacillary gram-positive microorganisms apparently occurring primarily in lower animals, in which it produces septicemic or encephalomyelitic disease in sporadic or epizootic form. It infects man to produce an upper respiratory disease with angina, lymphadenitis, and conjunctivitis, or a septicemic disease which may be transmitted transplacentally in pregnant women, or it may assume an encephalitic form. Human disease is often, but not invariably, associated with a monocytosis. There is a single species, *L. monocytog′enes.*

listerial (lis-ter′e-al). Pertaining to or caused by organisms of the genus Listeria.

listeriosis (lis-ter″e-o′sis). Infection caused by organisms of the genus Listeria.

listerism (lis′ter-izm). The principles and practice of antiseptic and aseptic surgery.

Listing's law (lis′tingz) [Johann Benedict *Listing*, German physiologist, 1808–1882]. See under *law.*

Liston's forceps, knives, operation, etc. (lis′tonz) [Robert *Liston*, Scottish surgeon in London, 1794–1847]. See under the nouns.

liter (le′ter, li′ter) [Fr. *litre*]. The basic unit of capacity in the metric system, being the volume occupied by 1 kilogram of pure water at its temperature of maximum density and under standard atmospheric pressure. It is the equivalent of 1.0567 quarts liquid measure. Abbreviated l.

lithagogectasia (lith″ah-go″jek-ta′se-ah) [*litho-* + Gr. *agōgos* leading + *ektasis* stretching]. Lithectasy.

lithagogue (lith′ah-gog) [*litho-* + Gr. *agōgos* leading]. 1. Expelling calculi. 2. A remedy that expels calculi.

lithangiuria (lith″an-je-u′re-ah) [*litho-* + Gr. *angeion* vessel + *ouron* urine + *-ia*]. Calculous disease of the urinary tract.

litharge (lith′arj) [Gr. *lithargyros; lithos* stone + *argyros* silver]. Fused lead protoxide, PbO.

lithate (lith′āt). A urate.

lithecbole (lith-ek′bo-le) [*litho-* + Gr. *ekbolē* expulsion]. Expulsion of a calculus.

lithectasy (lith-ek′tah-se) [*litho-* + Gr. *ektasis* stretching]. The extraction of calculi through the mechanically dilated urethra.

lithectomy (lith-ek′to-me). Lithotomy.

lithemia (lith-e′me-ah) [*lithic acid* + Gr. *haima* blood + *-ia*]. Excess of lithic or uric acid and the urates in the blood. It is due to imperfect metabolism of the nitrogenous elements.

lithemic (lith-e′mik). Pertaining to, affected with, or of the nature of, lithemia.

lithia (lith′e-ah). Lithium oxide, Li_2O: an alkali.

lithiasic (lith″e-as′ik). Pertaining to lithiasis.

lithiasis (lith-i′ah-sis) [*litho-* + *-iasis*]. 1. A condition characterized by the formation of calculi and concretions. 2. The gouty diathesis. **appendicular l.,** a condition in which the lumen of the vermiform appendix becomes obstructed with calculi. The condition is said to run in families, and to be akin to gout and rheumatism. **l. conjuncti′vae,** a condition marked by the formation of white, calcareous concretions in the acini of the meibomian glands. **pancreatic l.,** the presence of concretions in the pancreas. It is attended with colic, fat diarrhea, diabetes, and emaciation.

lithic (lith′ik). 1. Pertaining to calculus. 2. Pertaining to lithium.

lithicosis (lith″ĭ-ko′sis) [Gr. *lithikos* made of stone]. Pneumoconiosis.

lithium (lith′e-um) [Gr. *lithos* stone]. A white metal; atomic number, 3; atomic weight, 6.939; symbol, Li; its oxide, lithia, Li_2O, is alkaline; its salts are solvents of uric acid to a certain extent in the test tube: based on this, it was formerly erroneously thought to be indicated in gout and rheumatic conditions. **l. benzoate,** a salt, $C_6H_5.CO.O.Li$, in a white powder or in scales. **l. bromide,** a white, deliquescent, slightly bitter granular powder, $LiBr.H_2O$: used as a central nervous system depressant. **l. cacodylate,** a salt, $(CH_3)_2AsOLi$: used like sodium cacodylate. **l. caffeine sulfonate,** a salt used in gout and rheumatism: strongly commended as a diuretic. **l. carbonate,** a white, powdery salt, Li_2CO_3; normal lithium carbonate: useful in urinary and calculous disorders. **l. citrate,** a white, crystalline powder, $C_6H_5O_7Li_3 + 4H_2O$: used like the carbonate. **l. citrate, effervescent,** effervescent citrate of lithium: the ordinary citrate, 10 parts; common sugar, milk sugar, and tartaric acid, each, 20 parts; sodium bicarbonate, 20 parts. **l. dithiosalicylate.** 1. An amorphous salt, used in the treatment of gout and rheumatism. 2. A yellow salt of one of the nine dithiosalicylic acids. **l. diuretin,** diuretin in which the sodium is replaced by lithium; double salicylate of theobromine and lithium: diuretic. **l. formate,** a salt in colorless needles, $HCOOLi + H_2O$: used in gout and rheumatism. **l. glycerophosphate,** a white powder, $C_3H_5(OH)_2.PO_2(OLi)_2$: a nerve tonic and antilithic. **l. hippurate,** a gout remedy. **l. iodate,** a salt, $LiIO_3$, used in gouty and renal disorders. **l. iodide,** a white crystalline body, LiI, in deliquescent prisms. **l. phenolsulfonate,** white crystals of lithium sulfocarbolate, $OH.C_6H_4.SO_2.OLi$: used in gonorrhea. **l. salicylate,** a white, crystalline powder, $OH.-C_6H_4.COOLi$: used in rheumatism. **l. salolophosphite,** the lithium salt of salol-orthophosphorous acid, $C_6H_5.CO.O.C_6H_4.O.PO(OH)OLi$. It is a white, crystalline compound, used in influenza and gout. **l. sozoiodolate,** an antiseptic agent, lithium diiodoparaphenolsulfonic acid, $OH.C_6H_2I_2.SO_2OLi$, in glancing white or yellowish plates. **l. sulfocyanate,** a white, crystalline powder, LiCNS. **l. sulfoichthyolate,** a tarry substance: antirheumatic. **l. theobromine salicylate,** a white, diuretic salt.

litho- (lith′o) [Gr. *lithos* stone]. Combining form denoting relationship to stone or to a calculus.

lithocenosis (lith″o-se-no′sis) [*litho-* + Gr. *kenōsis* evacuation]. The removal from the bladder of the fragments of calculi that have been crushed.

lithoclast (lith′o-klast) [*litho-* + Gr. *klan* to crush]. A lithotrite, or stone-crushing forceps, of various forms.

lithoclysmia (lith″o-kliz′me-ah) [*litho-* + Gr. *klysma* clyster]. Treatment of calculus by injecting solvent liquids into the bladder.

lithocystotomy (lith″o-sis-tot′o-me) [*litho-* + Gr. *kystis* bladder + *temnein* to cut]. A cutting operation for removing a stone from the bladder.

lithodialysis (lith″o-di-al′ĭ-sis) [*litho-* + Gr. *dialyein* to dissolve]. 1. The solution of calculi in the bladder by injected solvents. 2. The crushing of a calculus in the bladder.

lithogenesis (lith″o-jen′e-sis) [*litho-* + Gr. *gennan* to produce]. The formation of calculi.

lithogenous (lith-oj′e-nus). Producing or causing the formation of calculi.

lithokelyphopedion (lith″o-kel″ĭ-fo-pe′de-on) [*litho-* + Gr. *kelyphos* sheath + *paidion* child]. A lithopedion in which both the fetus and the membranes are petrified.

lithokelyphos (lith″o-kel′ĭ-fos) [*litho-* + Gr. *kelyphos* sheath]. A dead fetus in which the fetal membranes are calcified.

lithokonion (lith″o-ko′ne-on) [*litho-* + Gr. *konios* dusty]. An instrument for pulverizing calculi in the bladder.

litholabe (lith′o-lab) [*litho-* + Gr. *lambanein* to hold]. An instrument for holding a vesical calculus in the operation for its removal.

litholapaxy (lith-ol′ah-pak″se) [*litho-* + Gr. *lapaxis* evacuation]. The crushing of a calculus in the bladder, followed at once by the washing out of the fragments. **Bigelow's l.,** the crushing of a stone by a special kind of lithotrite and the removal of the fragments by another apparatus.

lithology (lith-ol′o-je) [*litho-* + *-logy*]. The sum of what is known regarding calculi and their treatment.

litholysis (lith-ol′ĭ-sis) [*litho-* + Gr. *lysis* dissolution]. The solution of calculi in the bladder.

litholyte (lith′o-lit) [*litho-* + Gr. *lysis* dissolution]. An instrument used in injecting solvents of calculi into the bladder.

lithometer (lith-om′e-ter) [*litho-* + Gr. *metron* measure]. An instrument for measuring calculi.

lithometra (lith-o-me′trah) [*litho-* + Gr. *mētra* uterus]. Ossification of the uterus.

lithomoscus (lith-o-mos′kus) [*litho-* + Gr. *moschos* calf]. Lithopedion in cattle.

lithomyl (lith′o-mil) [*litho-* + Gr. *mylē* mill]. An instrument for crushing a stone in the bladder.

lithonephria (lith″o-nef′re-ah) [*litho-* + Gr. *nephros* kidney]. Any disease condition due to the presence of calculi in the kidney.

lithonephritis (lith″o-ne-fri′tis) [*litho-* + *nephritis*]. Inflammation of the kidney due to irritation of calculi.

lithonephrotomy (lith″o-ne-frot′o-me) [*litho-* + Gr. *nephros* kidney + *tomē* a cutting]. The operative removal of a renal calculus.

lithontriptic (lith″on-trip′tik). Lithotriptic.

lithopedion (lith″o-pe′de-on) [L. *lithopaedium;* from Gr. *lithos* stone + *paidion* child]. A dead fetus that has become stony or petrified.

Lithopedion (Arey).

lithophone (lith′o-fōn) [*litho-* + Gr. *phōnē* sound]. A device for indicating the presence of a calculus by the sound which the latter emits when struck.

lithoscope (lith′o-skōp) [*litho-* + Gr. *skopein* to examine]. An instrument for examining calculi in the bladder.

lithosis (lith-o′sis) [*litho-* + *-osis*]. A form of pneumoconiosis due to the inhalation of stone dust; stone grinders' disease.

lithotome (lith′o-tōm). A knife for performing lithotomy.

lithotomist (lith-ot′o-mist). One who performs a lithotomy.

lithotomy (lith-ot′o-me) [*litho-* + Gr. *tomē* a cutting]. Incision of a duct or organ, especially of the bladder, for removal of stone. **bilateral l.,** one performed by a transverse incision across the perineum. **high l.,** suprapubic l. **lateral l.,** one in which the cut is before the rectum and to one side of the raphe. **marian l., median l.,** one made on the raphe of the perineum before the anus. **mediolateral l.,** a combination of the median and lateral operations. **perineal l.,** that in which the incision is made in the perineum. **prerectal l.,** marian l. **rectal l., rectovesical l.,** one performed by an incision within the dilated rectum. **suprapubic l.,** one performed by an incision above the pubes. **vaginal l., vesicovaginal l.,** one performed by an incision within the vagina.

lithotony (lith-ot′o-ne) [*litho-* + Gr. *teinein* to stretch]. The creation of an artificial vesical fistula which is dilated to allow the extraction of a stone.

lithotresis (lith″o-tre′sis) [*litho-* + Gr. *trēsis* a boring]. The drilling or boring of holes in a calculus.

lithotripsy (lith′o-trip″se) [*litho-* + Gr. *tribein* to rub]. The crushing of a calculus within the bladder.

lithotriptic (lith″o-trip′tik). Pertaining to or producing lithotripsy.

lithotriptor (lith′o-trip″tor). An instrument for crushing calculi in the bladder.

lithotriptoscope (lith″o-trip′to-skōp). An instrument for performing lithotriptoscopy.

lithotriptoscopy (lith″o-trip-tos′ko-pe) [*litho-* + Gr. *tripsis* a crushing + *skopein* to examine]. The crushing of a vesical calculus under direct visual control.

lithotrite (lith′o-trīt) [*litho-* + Gr. *tribein* to rub]. An instrument for crushing a stone in the bladder.

lithotrity (lith-ot′rĭ-te). The crushing of a vesical calculus within the bladder by means of the lithotrite.

lithous (lith′us) [Gr. *lithos* stone]. Pertaining to or of the nature of a calculus.

lithoxiduria (lith″ok-sĭ-du′re-ah) [*litho-* + *oxide* + Gr. *ouron* urine + *-ia*]. The existence of xanthic oxide in the urine.

lithuresis (lith″u-re′sis) [*litho-* + Gr. *ourēsis* urination]. The passage of gravel through the urethra with the urine.

lithureteria (lith″u-re-te′re-ah) [*litho-* + Gr. *ourētēr* ureter]. Calculous disease of the ureter.

lithuria (lith-u′re-ah) [*litho-* + Gr. *ouron* urine + *-ia*]. Excess of uric acid or of urates in the urine.

litmocidin (lit″mo-si′din). An antibiotic substance obtained from *Proactinomyces cyaneus.* It is an anthocyanidine derivative and is bacteriostatic and bactericidal for cocci, *Vibrio comma* and tubercle bacilli.

litmus (lit′mus). A blue pigment prepared from *Roccella tinctoria* and other lichens: used as a test for acidity and alkalinity. It has a pH range of 4.5 to 8.3. See *azolitmin.*

Litomosoides carinii (lit″o-mo-soi′dēz kah-rin′-e-e). A filarial worm found in the pleural and peritoneal cavities of the cotton rat, *Sigmodon hispidus.*

litre (le′ter) [Fr.]. Liter.

Litten's sign (lit′enz) [Moritz *Litten,* German physician, 1845–1907]. See under *sign.*

litter (lit′er). 1. A movable couch for transporting the sick or wounded. 2. The offspring produced at one birth by a multiparous animal.

Little's disease (lit′elz) [William John *Little,* English physician, 1810–1894]. See under *disease.*

Littre's colotomy, glands, hernia, etc. (le-trāz′) [Alexis *Littre,* French surgeon, 1658–1726]. See under the nouns.

littritis (lit-tri′tis). Inflammation of the urethral (Littre's) glands.

Litzmann's obliquity (litz′manz) [Karl Konrad Theodor *Litzmann,* German gynecologist, 1815–1890]. See under *obliquity.*

livedo (lĭ-ve′do) [L.]. A discolored spot or patch on the skin, commonly due to passive congestion. **l. annula′ris, l. racemo′sa,** l. reticularis. **l. reticula′ris,** a peripheral vascular condition characterized by a reddish blue netlike mottling of the skin of the extremities. Called also *asphyxia reticularis, livedo annularis* and *livedo racemosa.* **l. reticula′ris idiopath′ica,** a permanent mottling of the skin occurring on exposure of the skin to cold. **l. reticula′ris symptomat′ica,** mottling of the skin due to some demonstrable cause. **l. telangiectat′ica,** permanent mottling of the skin due to anomaly of the capillaries of the skin.

livedoid (liv′e-doid). Resembling livedo; a term applied to a form of dermatitis.

liver (liv′er) [L. *jecur;* Gr. *hēpar*]. 1. A large gland of a dark-red color situated in the upper part of the abdomen on the right side. Called also *hepar* [N A]. It is dome-shaped from fitting in under the diaphragm, it has a double blood supply from the hepatic artery and the portal vein, it produces bile, it converts most sugars into glycogen which it stores, and it is essential to life. 2. The same gland of certain animals sometimes used as food or from which pharmaceutical products are prepared. **albuminoid l., amyloid l.,** a liver which is the seat of an albuminoid or amyloid degeneration. **biliary cirrhotic l.,** one in which the bile ducts are clogged and distended, the substance of the organ being inflamed. **brimstone l.,** an enlarged liver of a deep-yellow color, seen in some cases of congenital syphilis. **bronze l.,** the bronze-colored liver of malarial poisoning. **cardiac l.** See *stasis cirrhosis,* under *cirrhosis.* **cirrhotic l.,** one that is the site of a chronic inflammation, the bile ducts being distended. **degraded l.,** a human liver divided into many lobes, like that of the gorilla. **fatty l.,** one affected with fatty degeneration and infiltration. **feuerstein l.** (Ger. *fire-stone* liver), brimstone l. **floating l.,** wandering l. **foamy l.,** a liver seen post mortem, marked by the presence of numerous gas bubbles. **frosted l.,** perihepatitis chronica hyperplastica. **hobnail l.,** a liver whose surface is marked by nail-like points from atrophic cirrhosis. **icing l.,** perihepatitis chronica hyperplastica. **infantile l.** See *biliary cirrhosis of children,* under *cirrhosis.* **iron l.,** the condition of the liver in hepatic siderosis. **lardaceous l.,** amyloid l. **nutmeg l.,** one presenting a mottled appearance when cut. **pigmented l.,** one stained with blood pigments: usually a result of malaria and melanemia. **sago l.,** one affected with amyloid degeneration, the acini resembling boiled sago grains. **stasis l.** See *stasis cirrhosis,* under *cirrhosis.* **sugar-icing l.,** perihepatitis chronica hyperplastica. **tropical l.,** a condition of the unacclimated natives of the temperate zone residing in the tropics, marked by acute congestion of the liver and due to the effect of heat, excess of food and alcohol, and lack of exercise. **wandering l.,** a displaced and movable liver. **waxy l.,** albuminoid l.

livetin (li′vĕ-tin). A protein found along with lecithin in yolk of egg.

Livi's index (le′vēz) [Rudolfo *Livi,* Italian physician, 1856–1920]. See under *index.*

livid (liv′id) [L. *lividus,* lead-colored]. Discolored, as from the effects of contusion or congestion; black and blue.

lividity (lĭ-vid′ĭ-te) [L. *lividitas*]. The quality of being livid; discoloration, as of dependent parts, by the gravitation of the blood. **postmortem l.,** livor mortis.

Livierato's sign, test (le″ve-er-at′ōz) [Panagino *Livierato,* Italian physician, 1860–1936]. See under *sign* and *tests.*

livor (li′vor), pl. *livo′res* [L.]. Discoloration. **l. mor′tis,** discoloration appearing on dependent parts of the body after death, as a result of cessation of circulation, stagnation of blood, and settling of the blood by gravity.

lixiviation (liks″iv-e-a′shun) [L. *lixivia* lye]. The separation of soluble from insoluble matter by dissolving out the soluble matter and drawing off the solution.

lixivium (liks-iv′e-um) [L.]. Any alkaline filtrate obtained by leaching ashes or other similar powdered substance; lye.

Lizars' line, operation (li′zarz) [John *Lizars,* Edinburgh surgeon, 1794–1860]. See under *line* and *operation.*

L.K.Q.C.P.I. Abbreviation for *Licentiate of the King and Queen's College of Physicians of Ireland.*

L.L.L. Abbreviation for *left lower lobe* (of the lung).

L.M. Abbreviation for *Licentiate in Midwifery,* and *linguomesial.*

L.M.A. Abbreviation for *left mento-anterior* position of the fetus.

L.M.P. Abbreviation for *left mentoposterior* position of the fetus and *last menstrual period.*

L.M.R.C.P. Abbreviation for *Licentiate in Midwifery of the Royal College of Physicians.*

L.M.S. Abbreviation for *Licentiate in Medicine and Surgery.*

L.M.S.S.A. Abbreviation for *Licentiate in Medicine and Surgery of the Society of Apothecaries.*

L.M.T. Abbreviation for *left mentotransverse* position of the fetus.

L.O. Abbreviation for *linguo-occlusal.*

L.O.A. Abbreviation for *left occipito-anterior* position of the fetus.

Loa (lo′ah) [a native word in Angola, West Africa]. A genus of filarial roundworms. **L. lo′a,** a threadlike worm of West Africa, 1–2 inches long, which inhabits the subcutaneous connective tissue of the body, which it traverses freely. It is seen especially about the orbit and even under the conjunctiva. It causes itching and occasionally edematous swellings (Calabar swellings). Flies of the genus *Chrysops* are probably the intermediate hosts and vectors. It was formerly known as *Filaria loa.*

load (lōd). The quantity of a measurable entity borne, by an object or organism, such as the work (*work l.*) required of an individual, or the body content, as of water, salt, or heat, especially as it varies from normal. **negative l.,** an abnormally diminished amount, as of the body content of water, salt, or heat. **occlusal l.,** the total force exerted on the teeth through the occlusal surfaces during mastication. **positive l.,** an abnormally increased amount, as of the body content of water, salt, or heat. **work l.,** the amount of work required to be done by an individual.

loaiasis (lo″ah-i′ah-sis). The state of being infected with nematodes of the genus Loa.

loasis (lo′ah-sis). Loaiasis.

lobar (lo′ber). Of or pertaining to a lobe.

Lobaria islandica (lo-ba′re-ah is-land′ĭ-kah). *Lichen islandicus.*

lobate (lo′bāt) [L. *lobatus*]. Provided with lobes, or disposed in lobes.

lobe (lōb) [L. *lobus;* Gr. *lobos*]. 1. A more or less well-defined portion of any organ, especially of the brain and glands. Lobes are demarcated by fissures, sulci, connective tissue, and by their shape. 2. One of the main divisions of the crown of a tooth. **anterior l. of hypophysis, anterior l. of pituitary body,** lobus anterior hypophyseos. **appendicular l.,** an abnormal tongue-shaped downward depression of a portion of the right lobe of the liver. **azygos l.,** a small accessory or anomalous lobe situated at the apex of the right lung. **caudate l. of cerebrum,** insula. **caudate l. of liver,** lobus caudatus. **l's of cerebrum,** lobi cerebri. **crescentic l. of cerebellum, inferior,** lobulus semilunaris inferior. **crescentic l. of cerebellum, superior,** lobulus semilunaris superior. **cuneate l.,** cuneus. **digastric l.,** lobulus biventer. **frontal l.,** the anterior portion of the pallium. See *lobus frontalis.* **lateral l's of prostate gland.** See *lobus prostatae* [*dexter et sinister*]. **limbic l.,** gyrus fornicatus. **linguiform l.,** Riedel's l. **l's of liver,** lobuli hepatis. **l. of liver, left,** lobus hepatis sinister. **l. of liver, right,** lobus hepatis dexter. **l's of mammary gland,** lobi glandulae mammariae. **median l. of prostate,** l. medius prostatae. **occipital l.,** the posterior portion of the cerebral hemisphere. See *lobus occipitalis.* **olfactory l.,** lobus olfactorius. **optic l's,** corpora quadrigemina. **parietal l.,** the upper central lobe of the pallium. See *lobus parietalis.* **piriform l.,** the lateral exposed portion of the olfactory cerebral cortex in lower mammals. **posterior l. of hypophysis,** lobus posterior hypophyseos. **prefrontal l.,** the part of the frontal lobe of the brain anterior to the ascending convolution. **l's of prostate.** See *lobus prostatae* [*dexter et sinister*]. **pyramidal l. of thyroid gland,** lobus pyramidalis glandulae thyroideae. **quadrangular l. of cerebellum,** lobulus quadrangularis cerebelli. **quadrate l. of cerebral hemisphere,** precuneus. **quadrate l. of liver,** lobus quadratus hepatis. **renal l's,** lobi renales. **Riedel's l.,** a tongue-shaped portion of liver substance attached to the right lobe. **semilunar l., inferior,** lobulus semilunaris inferior. **semilunar l., superior,** lobulus semilunaris superior. **spigelian l.,** lobus caudatus. **temporal l.,** the lower lateral lobe of the cerebral hemisphere. See *lobus temporalis.* **temporosphenoidal l. of cerebral hemisphere,** lobus temporalis. **l's of thymus.** See *lobus thymi* [*dexter et sinister*]. **l's of thyroid gland.** See *lobus glandulae thyroideae* [*dexter et sinister*]. **vagal l.,** visceral l. **vermiform l.,** vermis cerebelli. **visceral l.,** the visceral sensory area of fishes.

lobectomy (lo-bek'to-me) [Gr. *lobos* lobe + *ektomē* excision]. Excision of a lobe, as of the thyroid, liver, brain, or lung.

lobeline (lob'e-lin). An alkaloid, alpha-lobeline, $C_6H_5.CHOH.CH_2.C_5NH_8(CH_3).CH_2.CO.C_6H_5$, respiratory stimulant: claimed to be a powerful resuscitant in respiratory failure, collapse, or shock.

lobengulism (lo-ben'gu-lizm). A disorder characterized by development of subcutaneous fat and with decrease of the sexual function.

lobi (lo'bi) [L.]. Plural of *lobus.*

lobite (lo'bīt). Limited to a definite lobe.

lobitis (lo-bi'tis). Inflammation of a lobe, especially of a lobe of the lung.

lobocyte (lo'bo-sīt) [Gr. *lobos* lobe + *-cyte*]. A granulocyte with a segmented nucleus.

lobopod (lo'bo-pod"). Lobopodium.

lobopodium (lo"bo-po'de-um), pl. *lobopo'dia* [Gr. *lobos* lobe + *pous* foot]. A pseudopodium which is broad to cylindrical and round at the tip.

lobostomy (lo-bos'to-me) [Gr. *lobos* lobe + *stoma* opening]. The operation of performing external drainage of a lobe of the lung.

lobotomy (lo-bot'o-me). Incision into a lobe. In psychosurgery, surgical incision of all the fibers of the lobe. **frontal l., prefrontal l.,** an operation in which, through holes drilled in the skull, the white matter of the frontal lobe is incised with a leukotome passed through a cannula. **transorbital l.,** lobotomy performed by cutting through the bony orbit.

Lobstein's cancer, disease, ganglion, etc. (lōb'stīnz) [Johann Friedrich Georg Christian Martin *Lobstein,* surgeon in Strasbourg, 1777–1835]. See under the nouns.

lobular (lob'u-lar) [L. *lobularis*]. Of or pertaining to a lobule.

lobulated (lob'u-lāt"ed). Made up of or divided into lobules.

lobule (lob'ūl). A small lobe. See *lobulus.* **anterior l. of pituitary body,** lobus anterior hypophyseos. **l. of auricle,** lobulus auriculae. **biventral l.,** lobulus biventer. **central l. of cerebellum,** lobulus centralis cerebelli. **cortical l's of kidney,** lobuli corticales renis. **l's of epididymis,** lobuli epididymidis. **falciform l.,** cuneus. **fusiform l.,** polus temporalis. **hepatic l's,** lobuli hepatis. **l's of lung,** segmenta bronchopulmonalia. **l's of mammary gland,** lobuli glandulae mammariae. **paracentral l.,** lobulus paracentralis. **parietal l., inferior,** lobulus parietalis inferior. **parietal l., superior,** lobulus parietalis superior. **pulmonary l's,** segmenta bronchopulmonalia. **quadrangular l. of cerebellum,** lobulus quadrangularis cerebelli. **semilunar l., inferior,** lobulus semilunaris inferior. **semilunar l., superior,** lobulus semilunaris superior. **l's of testis,** lobuli testis. **l's of thymus,** lobuli thymi. **l's of thyroid gland,** lobuli glandulae thyroideae.

lobulette (lob"u-let') [Fr.]. 1. A minute lobule. 2. Any one of the primary divisions of a lobule.

lobuli (lob'u-li) [L.]. Plural of *lobulus.*

lobulose (lob'u-lōs). Divided into lobules.

lobulous (lob'u-lus). Lobulose.

lobulus (lob'u-lus), pl. *lob'uli* [L., dim. of *lobus*]. A small lobe; used in anatomical nomenclature as a general term to designate a small lobe or one of the primary divisions of a lobe. Called also *lobule.* **l. auric'ulae** [N A, B N A], the inferior, dependent part of the auricle below the antitragus, which contains fibrous and fatty tissue but no cartilage. Called also *lobule of auricle.* **l. biven'ter** [N A, B N A], a lobule on the inferior surface of the hemisphere of the cerebellum situated between the tonsilla of the cerebellum and the inferior semilunar lobule. Called also *biventral lobule.* **l. centra'lis cerebel'li** [N A, B N A], the portion of the vermis between the lingula and the culmen, resting on the anterior medullary velum. Called also *central lobule of cerebellum.* **lob'uli cortica'les re'nis** [N A, B N A], more or less distinctly marked small polygonal areas on the surface of a kidney. Each area corresponds to a medullary ray together with its attached renal corpuscles and tubules. Called also *cortical lobules of kidney.* **lob'uli epididym'idis** [N A, B N A], the wedge-shaped parts of the head of the epididymis, each comprising a single efferent ductule of the testis. Called also *lobules of epididymis.* **lob'uli glan'dulae mamma'riae** [N A], the smaller subdivisions that make up a lobe of the mammary gland, each drained by a single branch of a lactiferous duct. Called also *lobuli mammae* [B N A], and *lobules of mammary gland.* **lob'uli glan'dulae thyroi'deae** [N A], irregular areas on the surface of the thyroid gland produced by entrance into the gland of fibrous trabeculae from the sheath. Called also *lobules of thyroid gland.* **lob'uli hep'atis** [N A, B N A], the small vascular units comprising the substance of the liver. Called also *hepatic lobules.* **lob'uli mam'mae** [B N A], lobuli glandulae mammariae. **l. paracentra'lis** [N A, B N A], a lobe on the medial surface of the cerebral hemisphere, continuous with the precentral and postcentral gyri of the frontal and parietal lobes. It is limited below by the cingulate sulcus. Called also *paracentral lobule.* **l. parieta'lis infe'rior** [N A, B N A], the lobule that forms the posterior part of the lateral portion of the parietal lobe of the cerebrum. It lies below the intraparietal sulcus, above the posterior ramus of the lateral cerebral fissure, and back of the postcentral sulcus. It includes the supramarginal and the angular gyri. Called also *inferior parietal lobule.* **l. parieta'lis supe'rior** [N A, B N A], the posterior part of the upper portion of the parietal lobe of the brain. It lies back of the postcentral sulcus, in front of the parietooccipital fissure, and above the intraparietal sulcus. Called also *superior parietal lobule.* **lob'uli pulmo'num** [B N A], segmenta bronchopulmonalia. **l. quadrangula'ris cerebel'li** [N A, B N A], the part of the hemisphere of the cerebellum continuous with the culmen and declive of the vermis. Sometimes also used to refer to only that part of the hemisphere continuous with the culmen. Called also *quadrangular lobule of cerebellum.* **l. semiluna'ris infe'rior** [N A, B N A], that part of the hemisphere of the cerebellum continuous with the tuber vermis. Called crus II in comparative anatomy. Called also *inferior semilunar lobule.* **l. semiluna'ris supe'rior** [N A, B N A], that part of the hemisphere of the cerebellum continuous with the folium vermis. Called crus I in comparative anatomy. Called also *superior semilunar lobule.* **l. sim'plex** [N A], that part of the cerebellar hemisphere which is continuous with the declive of the vermis. **lob'uli tes'tis** [N A, B N A], the pyramidal subdivisions of the testicular substance, each with its base against the albuginea and its apex at the mediastinum, and composed largely of tubuli seminiferi. Called also *lobules of testis.* **lob'uli thy'mi** [N A, B N A], the smaller subdivisions of the lobes of the thymus gland, separated by fibrous trabeculae. Called also *lobules of thymus.*

lobus (lo'bus), pl. *lo'bi* [L.]. A more or less well defined portion of any organ; used in anatomical nomenclature as a general term to designate such subdivisions, especially of the brain, lungs, and various glands, demarcated by fissures, sulci, or connective tissue septa. Called also *lobe.* **l. anterior hypophys'eos** [N A, B N A], the anterior lobe of the hypophysis cerebri, which arises from the buccal epithelium in the embryo. See discussion under *pituitary gland.* **l. cauda'tus** [N A], **l. cauda'tus [Spige'li]** [B N A], a small lobe of the liver bounded on the right by the inferior vena cava, which separates it from the right lobe, and on the left by the attachment of the gastrohepatic ligament, which separates it from the left lobe. Called also *caudate lobe.* **lo'bi cer'ebri** [N A, B N A], the well defined areas of the pallium, demarcated by fissures, sulci, and arbitrary lines, including the frontal, temporal, parietal, and occipital lobes. Called also *lobes of cerebrum.* **l. fronta'lis** [N A, B N A], the anterior portion of the pallium, extending from the frontal pole of the cerebral hemisphere to the sulcus centralis. Called also *frontal lobe.* **lo'bi glan'dulae mamma'riae** [N A], the major subdivisions of the secreting portion of the mammary gland, each drained by a single lactiferous duct. Called also *lobi mammae* [B N A], and *lobes of mammary gland.* **l. glan'dulae thyroi'deae [dex'ter et sinis'ter]** [N A], either of the lobes (right or left) of the thyroid gland, closely applied to either side of the trachea, cricoid cartilage, and thyroid cartilage. Called also *lobe of thyroid gland.* **l. hep'atis dex'ter** [N A, B N A], the largest of the four lobes of the liver. Anteriorly, it is separated from the left lobe by the falciform ligament. Posteroinferiorly, it is separated from the caudate lobe by the inferior vena cava and from the quadrate lobe by the gallbladder. Used in the broad sense, the term includes the caudate and quadrate lobes. Called also *right lobe of liver.* **l. hep'atis sinis'ter** [N A, B N A], the smaller of the two main lobes of the liver. Anteriorly, it is separated from the right lobe by the falciform ligament. Posteroinferiorly, it is separated from the caudate and quadrate lobes by the attachment of the gastrohepatic ligament and the ligamentum teres. Called also *left lobe of liver.* **l. infe'rior pulmo'nis** [N A, B N A], the inferior lobe of either lung. **lo'bi mam'mae** [B N A], lobi glandulae mammariae. **l. me'dius prosta'tae** [N A, B N A], a normal enlargement of the isthmus of the prostate that sometimes occurs. Called also *median lobe of prostate.* **l. me'dius pulmo'nis dex'tri** [N A, B N A], the middle lobe of the right lung. **l. occipita'lis** [N A, B N A], the posterior portion of the cerebral hemisphere, extending from the posterior pole to the parieto-occipital fissure. Called also *occipital lobe.* **l. olfacto'rius** [B N A], a structure on the lower surface of the frontal lobe of the brain which in man is somewhat rudimentary. It consists of the olfactory bulb, tract, and trigone. Omitted in N A. **l. parieta'lis** [N A, B N A], the upper central lobe of the pallium, separated from the temporal lobe below and the frontal lobe in front by the posterior and ascending branches, respectively, of the lateral cerebral fissure, and from the occipital lobe behind by the parieto-occipital fissure. Called also *parietal lobe.* **lo'bi placen'tae,** distinct areas on the uterine surface of the placenta, demarcated by the connective tissue septa. **l. poste'rior hypophys'eos** [N A, B N A], the posterior lobe of the hypophysis cerebri, which originates in the embryo as an evagination from the floor of the diencephalon. See discussion under *pituitary gland.* **l. prosta'tae [dex'ter et sinis'ter]** [N A, B N A], either of the paired halves (right and left) of the prostate, separated by a more or less distinct median sulcus. Called also *lobe of prostate.* **l. pyramida'lis glan'dulae thyroi'deae** [N A], an occasional third lobe of the thyroid gland which extends upward from the isthmus across the thyroid cartilage to the hyoid bone; it is the remains of the thyroid stalk of the fetus. Called also *pyramidal lobe of thyroid gland.* **l. quadra'tus hep'atis** [N A, B N A], a small lobe of the liver bounded on the right by the gallbladder, which separates it from the right lobe, and on the left by the ligamentum teres, which separates it from the left lobe. Called also *quadrate lobe of liver.* **lo'bi rena'les** [N A, B N A], the units of the kidney, each consisting of a pyramid and its surrounding cortical substance; the division of the kidney into lobes is more distinctly marked in some animals and in infants than in adult man. Called also *renal lobes.* **l. spige'lii,** l. caudatus. **l. supe'rior pulmo'nis** [N A, B N A], the superior lobe of either lung. **l. tempora'lis** [N A, B N A], the lower lateral lobe of the cerebral hemisphere, lying below the posterior ramus of the lateral cerebral fissure, lateral to the collateral fissure, and merging behind with the occipital lobe. Called also *temporal lobe.* **l. thy'mi [dex'ter et sinis'ter]** [N A, B N A], either of the two chief parts (right or left) of the thymus, which meet in the midline. Called also *lobe of thymus.* **l. va'gi,** visceral lobe.

local (lo'kal) [L. *localis*]. Restricted to or pertaining to one spot or part; not general.

localization (lo″kal-i-za'shun). 1. The determination of the site or place of any process or lesion. 2. Restriction to a circumscribed or limited area. 3. Prelocalization. **cerebral l.,** the determination of the situation of the various centers of the brain; also the limitation of the various cerebral faculties to a particular center or organ of the brain. **elective l.,** selective l. **germinal l.,** the location on a blastoderm of prospective organs. See *fate map,* under *map.* **selective l.,** the tendency of a microorganism to infect a specific variety of tissue.

localized (lo'kal-īzd). Not general; restricted to a limited region or to one or more spots.

localizer (lo'kal-īz″er). An instrument for locating solid particles in the eyeball by means of the roentgen ray.

locator (lo'ka-ter). An instrument or apparatus by which the location of an object is determined. **Berman-Moorhead l.,** an instrument for locating metallic fragments embedded in body tissues. **electroacoustic l.,** an apparatus which amplifies into an audible click the contact of the probe with a solid object: used in locating foreign objects within the body.

Loc. dol. Abbreviation for L. *lo'co dolen'ti,* to the painful spot.

lochia (lo'ke-ah) [Gr. *lochia*]. The vaginal discharge that takes place during the first week or two after childbirth. **l. al'ba,** the final vaginal discharge after childbirth, when the amount of blood is decreased and the leukocytes are increased. **l. cruen'ta,** l. rubra. **l. purulen'ta,** l. alba. **l. ru'bra,** the vaginal discharge of almost pure blood immediately after childbirth. **l. sanguinolen'ta,** the thick, maroon-colored vaginal discharge occurring a few days after childbirth.

lochial (lo'ke-al). Pertaining to the lochia.

lochiocolpos (lo″ke-o-kol'pos) [*lochia* + Gr. *kolpos* vagina]. Distention of the vagina by retained lochia.

lochiocyte (lo'ke-o-sīt″) [*lochia* + *-cyte*]. One of the characteristic decidual cells of the lochia.

lochiometra (lo″ke-o-me'trah) [*lochia* + Gr. *mētra* uterus]. Distention of the uterus by retained lochia.

lochiometritis (lo″ke-o-me-tri'tis) [*lochia* + *metritis*]. Puerperal metritis.

lochiopyra (lo″ke-op'ĭ-rah) [*lochia* + Gr. *pyr* fever]. Puerperal fever.

lochiorrhagia (lo″ke-o-ra'je-ah) [*lochia* + Gr. *rhēgnynai* to burst forth]. Lochiorrhea.

lochiorrhea (lo″ke-o-re'ah) [*lochia* + Gr. *rhoia* flow]. An abnormally profuse discharge of lochia.

lochioschesis (lo″ke-os'ke-sis) [*lochia* + Gr. *schesis* retention]. Retention of the lochia.

lochiostasis (lo″ke-os'tah-sis) [*lochia* + Gr. *stasis* halt]. Retention of the lochia.

lochometritis (lo″ko-me-tri'tis) [Gr. *lochos* childbirth + *metritis*]. Puerperal metritis.

lochoperitonitis (lo″ko-per″ĭ-to-ni'tis) [Gr. *lochos* childbirth + *peritonitis*]. Puerperal peritonitis.

loci (lo'si) [L.]. Plural of *locus.*

Locke's solution (loks) [Frank Spiller *Locke*, British physician]. See under *solution*.

lockjaw (lok′jaw). 1. Tetanus. 2. Trismus.

Lockwood's ligament, sign (lok′woodz) [Charles Barrett *Lockwood*, English surgeon, 1858–1914]. See under *ligament* and *sign*.

loco (lo′ko) [Sp. "insane"]. 1. A name of various leguminous plants of the genera *Astragalus*, *Hosackia*, *Sophora*, and *Oxytropis:* poisonous to horses, cattle, and sheep in certain arid regions because of the selenium they contain. 2. Locoism. 3. An animal affected with locoism. **blue l.,** *Astragalus diphysus.*

locoism (lo′ko-izm). A disease of horses, cattle, and sheep ascribed to poisoning by loco. Called also *loco* disease and *loco poisoning.*

locomotion (lo″ko-mo′shun) [L. *locus* place + *movere* to move]. Movement from one place to another. **brachial l.,** brachiation. **quadruped l.,** walking upon all fours: the only mode possible in certain extreme cases of tuberculosis of the spinal column.

locomotive (lo″ko-mo′tiv). Pertaining to locomotion.

locomotor (lo″ko-mo′tor). Of or pertaining to locomotion.

locomotorial (lo″ko-mo-to′re-al). Pertaining to the locomotorium.

locomotorium (lo″ko-mo-to′re-um). The motive apparatus of the body.

locomotory (lo″ko-mo′tor-e). Pertaining to locomotion.

locular (lok′u-lar). Pertaining to a loculus.

loculate (lok′u-lāt). Divided into loculi.

loculi (lok′u-li) [L.]. Plural of *loculus.*

loculus (lok′u-lus), pl. *loc′uli* [L.]. 1. A small space or cavity. 2. A local enlargement of the uterus in some mammals, containing an embryo.

locum (lo′kum) [L.]. Place. **l. ten′ens, l. ten′ent,** a practitioner who temporarily takes the place of another.

locus (lo′kus), pl. *lo′ci* [L.]. Place. In genetics, the specific site of a gene in a chromosome. **l. ceru′leus** [N A], a pigmented eminence in the superior angle of the floor of the fourth ventricle. **l. cine′reus, l. ferrugin′eus,** l. ceruleus. **l. mino′ris resisten′tiae,** a site of lessened resistance; that organ or part which is more liable to be affected by exposure to any moribific influence. **l. ni′ger,** substantia nigra. **l. perfora′tus an′ticus,** substantia perforata anterior. **l. perfora′tus pos′ticus,** substantia perforata posterior. **l. ru′ber,** nucleus ruber.

Loefflerella (lef″ler-el′ah). Former name of a genus of microorganisms, now called Malleomyces.

loemology (le-mol′o-je) [Gr. *loimos* plague + *-logy*]. Lemology.

loempe (lem′pe). Beriberi.

Loeschia (lēsh′e-ah). The name given by Chatton and Lalung-Bonnaire in 1912 to the parasitic amebae having no contractile vacuoles. See *Entamoeba.* **L. co′li,** *Entamoeba coli.* **L. gingiva′lis,** *Entamoeba gingivalis.* **L. histolyt′ica,** *Entamoeba histolytica.*

loeschiasis (lēsh-i′ah-sis). Amebiasis.

Loevit's cells (le′fits) [Moritz *Loevit*, Prague pathologist, 1851–1918]. Erythroblasts.

Loewi's reaction, symptom, test (la′vēz) [Otto *Loewi*, German pharmacologist in the United States, 1873–1961; co-winner in 1936, with Sir Henry Hallett Dale, of the Nobel prize for physiology and medicine, for their work on the chemical transmission of nerve impulses]. See under *tests.*

Löffler's blood serum, stain, etc. (lef′lerz) [Friederich August Johannes *Löffler*, German bacteriologist, 1852–1915]. See under the nouns.

Löffler's eosinophilia, syndrome (lef′lerz) [W. *Löffler*, Swiss physician]. See under *syndrome.*

löffleria (lef-le′re-ah) [F. A. J. *Löffler*]. A disease in which the diphtheria bacillus is present without the ordinary symptoms of diphtheria.

logadectomy (log″ah-dek′to-me) [Gr. *logades* the whites of the eyes + *ektomē* excision]. Excision of a portion of the conjunctiva.

logaditis (log″ah-di′tis) [Gr. *logades* the whites of the eyes + *-itis*]. Inflammation of the sclera.

logadoblennorrhea (log″ah-do-blen″o-re′ah) [Gr. *logades* the whites of the eyes + *blennorrhea*]. Egyptian conjunctivitis (C. Graefe).

logagnosia (log″ag-no′ze-ah) [*logo-* + *a* neg. + Gr. *gnōsis* knowledge]. Aphasia, alogia, or other central word defect.

logagraphia (log″ah-graf′e-ah) [*logo-* + *a* neg. + Gr. *graphein* to write]. Inability to express ideas in writing.

logamnesia (log″am-ne′ze-ah) [*logo-* + Gr. *amnēsia* forgetfulness]. Sensory aphasia.

logaphasia (log″ah-fa′ze-ah) [*logo-* + *aphasia*]. Motor aphasia.

logasthenia (log″as-the′ne-ah) [*logo-* + *asthenia*]. Disturbance of that faculty of the mind which deals with the comprehension of speech.

logistics (lo-jis′tiks) [Fr. *logis* lodging]. The branch of military science that deals with quartering, transport and supply of troops. **military l.,** deals with the mobilization and coordination of personnel, and supplies, casualty evacuation, etc.

logo- (log′o) [Gr. *logos* word]. Combining form denoting relationship to words or speech.

logoclonia (log″o-klon′e-ah). Logoklony.

logogram (log′o-gram). The graphic record of the symptoms and signs exhibited by a specific patient, charted by means of the logoscope.

logoklony (log′o-klon″e) [*logo-* + Gr. *klonos* tumult]. Spasmodic repetition of the end syllables of words.

logokophosis (log″o-ko-fo′sis) [*logo-* + Gr. *kōphōsis* deafness]. Word deafness; inability to comprehend spoken language.

logomania (log″o-ma′ne-ah) [*logo-* + Gr. *mania* madness]. 1. Overtalkativeness. 2. Aphasia.

logoneurosis (log″o-nu-ro′sis) [*logo-* + *neurosis*]. Any neurosis with disorder of the speech.

logopathy (log-op′ah-the) [*logo-* + Gr. *pathos* illness]. Any disorder of speech arising from derangement of the central nervous system.

logopedia (log″o-pe′de-ah). Logopedics.

logopedics (log-o-pe′diks) [*logo-* + ortho*pedics*]. The science dealing with the study and treatment of speech defects.

logoplegia (log″o-ple′je-ah) [*logo-* + Gr. *plēgē* stroke]. 1. Any paralysis of the speech organs. 2. Inability to speak, while words are remembered.

logorrhea (log″o-re′ah) [*logo-* + Gr. *rhoia* flow]. Excessive or abnormal volubility.

logoscope (log′o-skōp) [Gr. *logos* a thought, idea, or word + *skopein* to regard or view). A device, in slide-rule form, designed to facilitate identification of the diseases in which certain signs and symptoms occur.

logoscopy (lo-gos′ko-pe). The use of a logoscope for determining the differential diagnostic possibilities in a case exhibiting certain signs and symptoms.

logospasm (log′o-spazm) [*logo-* + Gr. *spasmos* spasm]. The spasmodic utterance of words.

-logy [Gr. *logos* word, reason]. Word termination meaning the science or study of, or a treatise on, the subject designated by the stem to which it is affixed.

Löhlein's diameter (la′līnz) [Hermann *Löhlein*, German gynecologist, 1847–1901]. See under *diameter.*

Lohnstein's saccharimeter (lōn′stīnz) [Theodor *Lohnstein*, German physician, 1866–1918]. See under *saccharimeter.*

lo-hon (lo-han′). A Chinese plant the dried fruit of which is used as a food flavoring agent.

loiasis (lo-i′ah-sis). Infection with *Loa loa*.

loimic (loi′mik) [Gr. *loimos* plague]. Lemic.

loimographia (loi″mo-gra′fe-ah) [Gr. *loimos* plague + *graphein* to write]. Lemography.

loimology (loi-mol′o-je). Lemology.

loin (loin). The part of the back between the thorax and the pelvis. Called also *lumbus* [N A].

loliism (lo′le-izm). Lolism.

lolism (lo′lizm). Poisoning by seeds of *Lolium temulentum,* or poisonous darnel.

lomadera (lo″mah-de′rah). A variety of Texas cattle fever seen in Venezuela.

Lombardi's sign (lom-bar′dēz) [Antonio *Lombardi,* physician in Naples]. See under *sign.*

lombriz (lom′briz). A hemorrhagic septicemia of sheep.

lomotil (lo′mo-til). Trade mark for preparations of diphenoxylate hydrochloride.

Lonchocarpus (lon″ko-kar′pus). A genus of leguminous tropical trees and shrubs which furnish rotenone.

Long's coefficient, formula (longz) [John Harper *Long,* American physician, 1856–1927]. See under *formula.*

longevity (lon-jev′ĭ-te) [L. *longus* long + *aevum* age]. The condition or quality of being long lived.

longilineal (lon″jĭ-lin′e-al). Built on long, narrow lines; dolichomorphic.

longimanous (lon″jĭ-man′us) [L. *longus* long + *manus* hand]. Having long hands.

longipedate (lon″jĭ-pe′dāt) [L. *longus* long + *pes* foot]. Having long feet.

longiradiate (lon″jĭ-ra′de-āt). Having long radiations; a term applied to certain neuroglia cells.

longissimus (lon-jis′ĭ-mus) [L.]. Longest.

longitudinal (lon″jĭ-tu′dĭ-nal) [L. *longitudo* length]. Lengthwise; parallel to the long axis of the body.

longitudinalis (lon″jĭ-tu″dĭ-na′lis) [L.]. Lengthwise; in official anatomical nomenclature it designates a structure that is parallel to the long axis of the body or an organ.

longitypical (lon″jĭ-tip′ĭ-kal). Longilineal.

Longmire operation (long′mīr) [William P. *Longmire,* surgeon in Los Angeles, born 1913]. See under *operation.*

longsightedness (long-sīt′ed-nes). Hyperopia.

longus (long′gus) [L.]. Long.

Loomis' mixture (loo′mis) [Alfred L. *Loomis,* physician in New York, 1831–1895]. See under *mixture.*

loop (lo͞op). A turn or sharp curve in a cordlike structure. See also *ansa.* **archoplasmic l.,** pseudochromosome. **capillary l's,** minute endothelial tubes that carry blood in the papillae of the skin. **Gerdy's interauricular l.,** a small muscular bundle in the interatrial septum of the heart. **Henle's l.,** a U-shaped turn in the medullary portion of a renal tubule, with a descending limb from the proximal convoluted tubule and an ascending limb to the distal convoluted tubule. See also *kidney.* **l. of hypoglossal nerve,** ansa cervicalis. **Hyrtl's l.,** an occasional looplike anastomosis between the right and left hypoglossal nerves in the geniohyoid muscle. **lenticular l.,** ansa lenticularis. **Meyer's l.,** a loop formed by passage of the neurons of the geniculate bundle around the ventricle of the temporal lobe. **peduncular l.,** ansa peduncularis. **platinum l.,** a loop of platinum or other suitable wire mounted in a handle for use in transferring microorganisms to other culture media. **l's of spinal nerves,** ansae nervorum spinalium. **Stoerck's l.,** the primitive loop in the embryonic uriniferous tubule which develops into a Henle loop and a portion of the proximal convoluted tubule. **subclavian l.,** ansa subclavia. **ventricular l.,** the early, U-shaped loop of the embryonic heart. **l. of Vieussens,** ansa subclavia.

loopful (lo͞op′ful). The quantity of liquid that can be held within the loop of platinum wire used in transferring microorganisms to other culture media.

Loosia dobrogiensis (loo′se-ah dob″ro-je-en′sis). *Metagonimus yokogawai.*

L.O.P. Abbreviation for *left occipitoposterior* position of the fetus.

lophius (lo′fe-us) [Gr. *lophos* ridge]. A ridge between two furrows on the ventricular surface of the cerebrum.

lophodont (lof′o-dont) [Gr. *lophos* ridge + *odous* tooth]. Having cheek teeth on which the cusps have become connected to form ridges.

Lophophora (lo-fof′o-rah). A genus of Mexican cacti. **L. william′sii,** a species which is the source of several alkaloids which have been used in medicine.

lophophorine (lo-fof′o-rin). A poisonous alkaloid, $C_{13}H_{17}NO_3$, from *Anhalonium lewinii,* having effects similar to those of mezcaline.

Lophophyton gallinarum (lo″fo-fi′ton gal″ĭ-na′rum). A variety of Achorion which causes comb disease in fowls.

lophophytosis (lo-fof″ĭ-to′sis). Comb disease.

Lophotrichea (lo″fo-trik′e-ah). A group of bacteria, including those forms which have a tuft of cilia at one pole.

lophotrichous (lo-fot′rĭ-kus) [Gr. *lophos* ridge, tuft + *thrix* hair]. Having a tuft of flagella at one end: applied to a bacterial cell.

Lorain type (lo-rān′) [Paul *Lorain,* Paris physician, 1827–1875]. Hypophysial infantilism.

lordoma (lor-do′mah). Lordosis.

lordoscoliosis (lor″do-sko″le-o′sis) [*lordosis* + *scoliosis*]. Lordosis complicated with scoliosis.

lordosis (lor-do′sis) [Gr. *lordōsis*]. An abnormally increased concavity in the curvature of the lumbar spine as viewed from the side.

lordotic (lor-dot′ik). Pertaining to or characterized by lordosis.

Lorenz's operation, osteotomy, sign (lo′rents-ez) [Adolf *Lorenz,* Austrian surgeon, 1854–1946]. See under the nouns.

Loreta's operation (lo-re′tahz) [Pietro *Loreta,* Italian surgeon, 1831–1889]. See under *operation.*

lorfan (lor′fan). Trade mark for preparations of levallorphan.

Loring's ophthalmoscope (lor′ingz) [Edward Greely *Loring,* American oculist, 1837–1888]. See under *ophthalmoscope.*

Lossen's rule (los′enz) [Herman Friedrich *Lossen,* Heidelberg surgeon, 1842–1909]. See under *rule.*

L.O.T. Abbreviation for *left occipitotransverse* position of the fetus.

Lot. Abbreviation for L. *lo′tio,* lotion.

lotahiston (lo″tah-his′ton). A histon found in the spermatozoa of the frog.

lotase (lo′tās). An enzyme from *Lotus arabicus,* which splits lotusin into lotoflavine, hydrocyanic acid, and dextrose.

lotio (lo′she-o) [L.]. Lotion. **l. adstrin′gens,** a mixture of sulfuric acid, alcohol, and oil of turpentine. **l. al′ba, l. sulfura′ta,** white lotion.

lotion (lo′shun) [L. *lotio*]. A liquid preparation used for washing; a wash. **A.B.C. l.,** a lotion of carbolic and boracic acids. **Abercrombie's l.,** an infusion of tobacco. **benzyl benzoate l.,** a watery solution of benzyl benzoate, triethanolamine, and oleic acid: scabicide. **calamine l.,** a preparation of calamine with zinc oxide, glycerin, bentonite magma, and calcium hydroxide solution. **calamine l., phenolated,** a mixture of calamine lotion and liquefied phenol: used topically as a protective. **evaporating l.,** a lotion of lead acetate dissolved in dilute alcohol. **Goulard's l.,** a solution of lead acetate and lead monoxide in water: applied topically as an astringent. **Granville's l.,** a lotion composed of stronger water of ammonia, spirit of camphor, and spirit of rosemary. **Hardy's l.**, a lotion containing corrosive sublimate dissolved in alcohol, zinc sulfate, lead acetate, and water. **white l.**, a preparation of zinc sulfate, sulfurated potash, and purified water: used as an astringent.

lotoflavine (lo″to-fla′vin). A yellow substance produced by the hydrolysis of lotusin.

lotusate (lo′tŭ-sāt). Trade mark for a preparation of talbutal.

louchettes (loo-shets′) [Fr.]. A kind of goggles worn for the correction of strabismus.

Louis's angle, law (loo-ēz′) [Pierre Charles Alexandre *Louis*, French physician, 1787–1872; the founder of medical statistics]. See *angulus sterni*, and under *law*.

loupe (lo͞op) [Fr.]. A convex lens for magnifying or for concentrating light upon an object. **corneal l.**, a magnifying lens, properly mounted, for examining the cornea of the eye.

louse (lows) [L. *pediculus*]. A general name for various parasitic insects; the true lice, which infest mammals, belong to the suborder *Anoplura*. Those which are parasitic upon man are *Pediculus humanus* var. *capitis*, or head louse; *P. humanus* var. *corporis*, the body or clothes louse; and *Phthirus pubis*, or crab louse, which lives in the hair upon the pubes and in the eyelashes and eyebrows. The causal organisms of typhus fever, relapsing fever, trench fever, and possibly plague are transmitted by the bite of lice. **biting l.**, Mallophaga. **body l.**, *Pediculus humanus* var. *corporis*. **chicken l.**, *Dermanyssus*. **clothes l.**, *Pediculus humanus* var. *corporis*. **crab l.**, *Phthirus pubis*. **goat l.**, *Lignognathus stenopis*. **head l.**, *Pediculus humanus* var. *capitis*. **horse l.**, *Trichodectes pilosus*. **pubic l.**, *Phthirus pubis*. **sucking l.**, *Anoplura*.

lousicide (lows′ĭ-sid). Pediculicide.

loutrotherapy (lu″tro-ther′ah-pe) [Gr. *loutron* bath + *therapeia* treatment]. The therapeutical use of baths, especially carbonated baths.

Lowe's disease (lōz) [Charles Upton *Lowe*, American pediatrician, born 1921]. Oculocerebrorenal syndrome.

Löwe's ring, test (la′vez) [Karl Friedrich *Löwe*, German optician, born 1874]. See under *ring* and *tests*.

Löwenberg's canal, forceps (la′ven-bergz) [Benjamin Benno *Löwenberg*, otologist in Vienna and Paris, born 1836]. See under *canal* and *forceps*.

Löwenstein's medium (la′ven-stīnz) [Ernest *Löwenstein*, Vienna pathologist, born 1878]. See under *culture medium*.

Löwenthal's reaction, tract (la′ven-talz) [Wilhelm *Löwenthal*, German physician, 1850–1894]. See under *reaction* and *tract*.

Lower's rings, tubercle (lo′erz) [Richard *Lower*, English anatomist, 1631–1691]. See under *ring* and *tubercle*.

Löwitt's bodies or **lymphocytes** (la′vits) [Moritz *Löwitt*, German physician, 1851–1918]. Lymphogonia.

Lowman balance board (lo′man) [Charles LeRoy *Lowman*, American orthopedic surgeon, born 1879]. An isosceles triangle board on which the patient walks with feet in supination: for correction of flatfeet.

Lowy's test (lo′ēz) [Otto *Lowy*, American pathologist, born 1879]. See under *tests*.

loxarthron (loks-ar′thron) [Gr. *loxos* oblique + *arthron* joint]. An oblique deformity of a joint without luxation.

loxarthrosis (loks″ar-thro′sis). Loxarthron.

loxia (lok′se-ah). Torticollis.

loxic (lok′sik). Twisted.

loxophthalmus (loks″of-thal′mus) [Gr. *loxos* oblique + *ophthalmos* eye]. Strabismus.

loxoscelism (loks-os′sĕ-lizm). A morbid condition resulting from the bite of the brown spider, *Loxosceles reclusa*, beginning with a painful erythematous vesicle and progressing to a gangrenous slough of the affected area; first recognized in South America, a few cases have been diagnosed in North America. **viscerocutaneous l.**, a sometimes fatal condition resulting from the bite of the brown spider, with fever and hematuria occurring, in addition to the local reaction.

loxotic (lok-sot′ik) [Gr. *loxos* oblique]. Slanting.

loxotomy (lok-sot′o-me) [Gr. *loxos* oblique + *temnein* to cut]. Oblique amputation.

Loxotrema ovatum (lok″so-tre′mah o-va′tum). *Metagonimus yokogawai.*

lozenge (loz′enj) [Fr.]. A form of medicated troche.

L.P. Abbreviation for *linguopulpal.*

L.P.F. Abbreviation for *leukocytosis-promoting factor.*

lpf. Abbreviation for *low power field.*

L.R.C.P. Abbreviation for *Licentiate of the Royal College of Physicians.*

L.R.C.P.&S.I. Abbreviation for *Licentiate of the Royal College of Physicians and Surgeons, Ireland.*

L.R.C.S. Abbreviation for *Licentiate of the Royal College of Surgeons.*

L.R.C.S.E. Abbreviation for *Licentiate of the Royal College of Surgeons, Edinburgh.*

L.S.A. Abbreviation for *left sacro-anterior* position of the fetus, and *Licentiate of Society of Apothecaries.*

L.Sc.A. Abbreviation for *left scapulo-anterior* position of the fetus.

L.Sc.P. Abbreviation for *left scapuloposterior* position of the fetus.

L.S.D. Abbreviation for *lysergic acid diethylamide*, a hallucinogenic compound derived from ergot; used experimentally in the study of mental disorders. The substance has also been found to be antagonistic to serotonin in its action on smooth muscle.

L.S.P. Abbreviation for *left sacroposterior* position of the fetus.

L.S.T. Abbreviation for *left sacrotransverse* position of the fetus.

LTH. Abbreviation for *luteotropic hormone* (lactogenic hormone).

Lu. Chemical symbol for *lutetium.*

luargol (lu-ar′gol) [*lues* + *argol*]. An orange-colored powder, bromo-argento-ammoniated arseno-benzene: used like arsphenamine in the treatment of syphilis and trypanosomiasis. Called also *102.*

Lubarsch's crystals (loo′barsh-ez) [Otto *Lubarsch*, German pathologist, 1863–1933]. See under *crystal.*

lubb (lub). A syllable used to represent the first sound of the heart in auscultation: it is a dull, slightly prolonged low sound. See *dupp.*

lubb-dupp (lub-dup′). Syllables used to represent the combination of the first and second heart sounds. See *lubb* and *dupp.*

Luc's operation (luks) [Henri *Luc*, French laryngologist, 1855–1925]. Caldwell-Luc operation.

Lucae's probe (loo′kāz) [August Johann Constanz *Lucae*, otologist in Berlin, 1835–1911]. See under *probe.*

Lucaena glauca (lu-ke′nah glaw′kah). A South American plant: its seed is said to destroy the hair of animals that eat it, to abolish completely the sexual appetite, and to cause remarkable fatness. The bark and root are used as emmenagogues. It is known as wild tamarind and jambul.

Lucas' sign (loo′kas) [Richard Clement *Lucas*, English physician, 1846–1915]. Enlargement of the abdomen in rickets.

Lucas-Championnière's disease (le-kah′ shaw″pe-on-e-airz′) [Just Marie Marcellin *Lucas-Championnière*, French surgeon, 1843–1913]. Pseudomembranous bronchitis.

Lucatello's sign (loo″kah-tel′ōz) [Luigi *Lucatello*, Italian physician, 1863–1926]. See under *sign.*

Luciani's triad (loo″che-an′ēz) [Luigi *Luciani*, Italian physiologist, 1842–1919]. See under *triad*.

lucid (lu′sid) [L. *lucidus* clear]. Clear; not obscure; as, *lucid* interval.

lucidification (lu-sid″ĭ-fi-ka′shun) [L. *lucidus* clear + *facere* to make]. The clearing up of the protoplasm of cells.

lucidity (lu-sid′ĭ-te). The quality or state of having a clear mind; clearness of the mind.

lucidusculine (lu″sĭ-dus′ku-lin). A crystalline alkaloid, $C_{24}H_{37}O_4N$, from *Aconitum lucidusculum*.

luciferase (lu-sif′er-ās) [L. *lux* light + *ferre* to bear + *-ase*]. An enzyme, of which there are many forms, that catalyzes the bioluminescent reaction in certain animals capable of luminescence.

luciferin (lu-sif′er-in). A compound, of which there are many forms, which is present in certain animals capable of bioluminescence and which, when acted upon by luciferase, produces light.

lucifugal (lu-sif′u-gal) [L. *lux* light + *fugere* to flee from]. Avoiding, or being repelled by, bright light.

Lucilia (lu-sil′e-ah). A genus of flies which have a blue or green metallic iridescence. **L. cae′sar,** the common "gold-fly" or "sheep maggot," which infests sheep; its larvae have been found in the intestine and in myiasis of the skin. **L. cupri′na,** the sheep maggot fly of Australia. **L. illus′tris,** a species sometimes found in the wool of sheep. **L. no′bilis,** a species that has been found in the external meatus. **L. regi′na,** a species that has been found in wounds. **L. serica′ta,** a sheep maggot fly of the British Isles which lays its eggs in wounds of sheep and in soiled wool. The larvae have been introduced into infected wounds to facilitate healing.

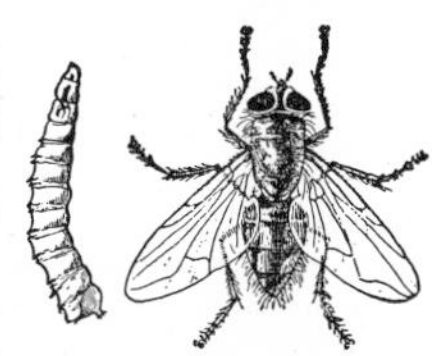
Larva and adult of Lucilia caesar.

lucipetal (lu-sip′ĭ-tal) [L. *lux* light + *petere* to seek]. Seeking, or being attracted to, bright light.

lucium (lu′se-um). A supposed chemical element discovered in 1896, later found to be a mixture of rare earth metals.

Lücke's test (lik′ez) [George Albert *Lücke*, German surgeon, 1829–1894]. See under *tests*.

lückenschädel (lik′en-sha″del) [Ger.]. A condition marked by defective calcification of the skull bones, combined with meningocele or encephalocele.

lucotherapy (lu″ko-ther′ah-pe) [L. *lux* light + *therapy*]. The treatment of disease by rays of light.

Ludloff's sign (lood′lawfs) [Karl *Ludloff*, surgeon in Breslau, born 1864]. See under *sign*.

Ludwig's angina (lood′vigz) [Wilhelm Friedrich von *Ludwig*, German surgeon, 1790–1865]. See under *angina*.

Ludwig's angle (lood′vigz) [Daniel *Ludwig*, German anatomist, 1625–1680]. See under *angle*.

Ludwig's ganglion (lood′vigz) [Karl Friedrich Wilhelm *Ludwig*, eminent German physiologist, 1816–1895, one of the greatest teachers of physiology of all time]. See under *ganglion*.

Luer's syringe (lu′erz) [German instrument maker in Paris, died 1883]. See under *syringe*.

lues (lu′ēz) [L. "a plague"]. Syphilis. **l. hep′atis,** syphilis of the liver. **l. nervo′sa,** syphilis with marked nervous lesions. **l. tar′da,** late syphilis. **l. vene′rea,** syphilis.

luetic (lu-et′ik). Syphilitic.

luetin (lu′ĕ-tin). An extract of a killed culture of several strains of *Treponema pallidum:* used in the skin test for syphilis. See *Noguchi's luetin reaction*, under *reaction*.

luetism (lu′ĕ-tizm). An attenuated form of syphilis not reactive to tests.

luette (lu-et′) [Fr.]. Uvula. **Lieutaud's l.,** uvula vesicae.

Lugol's caustic, solution (loo-golz′) [Jean Georg Antoine *Lugol*, physician in Paris, 1786–1851]. See under *caustic* and *solution*.

luic (lu′ik). Syphilitic.

L.U.L. Abbreviation for *left upper lobe* (of lungs).

lullamin (lul′lah-min). Trade mark for a preparation of methapyrilene.

lumbago (lum-ba′go) [L. *lumbus* loin]. Pain in the lumbar region. **ischemic l.,** pain in the back due to vascular causes.

lumbar (lum′ber). Pertaining to the loins.

lumbarization (lum″ber-i-za′shun). A condition in which the first segment of the sacrum is not fused with the second, so that there is one additional articulated vertebra and the sacrum consists of only four segments.

lumbo-abdominal (lum″bo-ab-dom′ĭ-nal). Pertaining to the loins and abdomen.

lumbocolostomy (lum″bo-ko-los′to-me) [L. *lumbus* loin + *colostomy*]. The operation of forming a permanent opening into the colon by an incision through the lumbar region.

lumbocolotomy (lum″bo-ko-lot′o-me) [L. *lumbus* loin + *colotomy*]. An incision into the colon through the loin.

lumbocostal (lum″bo-kos′tal) [L. *lumbus* loin + *costa* rib]. Pertaining to the loin and ribs.

lumbocrural (lum″bo-kroo′ral). Pertaining to or affecting the lumbar and crural regions.

lumbodorsal (lum″bo-dor′sal). Pertaining to the lumbar and dorsal regions.

lumbodynia (lum″bo-din′e-ah) [L. *lumbus* loin + Gr. *odynē* pain]. Lumbago.

lumbo-iliac (lum″bo-il′e-ak). Pertaining to the loin and ilium.

lumbosacral (lum″bo-sa′kral). Pertaining to the loins and sacrum.

lumbrici (lum-bri′se) [L.]. Plural of *lumbricus*.

lumbricide (lum′brĭ-sīd) [*lumbricus* + L. *caedere* to kill]. An agent which destroys lumbrici.

lumbricin (lum′brĭ-sin). A hemolytic substance extracted from earthworms.

lumbricoid (lum′brĭ-koid) [*lumbricus* + Gr. *eidos* form]. Resembling the earthworm; designating the ascaris, or round intestinal worm.

lumbricosis (lum″brĭ-ko′sis). The condition of being infected with lumbrici.

Lumbricus (lum-bri′kus) [L. "earthworm"]. A genus of annelids, including the earthworm, *L. terres′tris*, which may act as the host of *Metastrongylus elongatus* and thus transmit swine influenza.

lumbricus (lum-bri′kus), pl. *lumbri′ci* [L.]. 1. The ascaris, or round intestinal worm. 2. An earthworm.

lumbus (lum′bus) [L.]. [N A, B N A] The part of the back between the thorax and the pelvis. Called also *loin*.

lumen (lu′men), pl. *lu′mina* [L. "light"]. 1. The cavity or channel within a tube or tubular organ. 2. The unit of light flux: it is the flux emitted in a unit solid angle by a uniform point source of one international candle. Called also *meter candle*. **residual l.,** the remains of Rathke's pouch located between the pars distalis and pars intermedia of the hypophysis.

lumichrome (lu′mĭ-krōm). A product of the irradiation decomposition of riboflavin: it is 6,7-dimethyl-alloxazine.

lumiflavin (lu″mĭ-fla′vin). A product of the luminiferous decomposition of riboflavin: it is 6,7,9-trimethyl iso-alloxazine.

luminal (lu′mĭ-nal). 1. Pertaining to the lumen of a tubular structure. 2. Trade mark for preparations of phenobarbital.

luminescence (lu″mĭ-nes′ens). The property of giving off light without showing a corresponding degree of heat.

luminiferous (lu″mĭ-nif′er-us) [L. *lumen* light +

ferre to bear]. Conveying light or propagating those vibrations which constitute light.

luminophore (lu′mĭ-no-fōr) [L. *lumen* light + Gr. *phoros* bearing]. A chemical group which gives the property of luminescence to organic compounds.

luminous (lu′mĭ-nus). Emitting or reflecting light; glowing with light.

lumps (lumps). Hypopteronosis cystica.

Lumsden's center (lumz′denz) [Thomas William *Lumsden*, British physician, 1874–1953]. Pneumotaxic center.

lunacy (lu′nah-se) [L. *luna* moon]. Insanity; formerly supposed to be sometimes due to or affected by the influence of the moon.

lunar (lu′nar) [L. *lunaris; luna* moon, also silver]. 1. Pertaining to the moon. 2. Pertaining to or containing silver.

lunare (lu-na′re). The lunate bone (os lunatum [N A]).

lunate (lu′nāt) [L. *luna* moon]. Moon-shaped, or crescentic. See *os lunatum.*

lunatic (lu′nah-tik) [L. *lunaticus;* from *luna* moon]. A mentally deranged person.

lunatism (lu′nah-tizm) [L. *luna* moon]. 1. A disease varying with the lunar changes. 2. Sleep walking during moonlight.

lunatomalacia (lu-na″to-mah-la′she-ah). Osteochondrosis of the semilunar (carpal lunate) bone. See *Kienbock's disease,* under *disease.*

Lundvall's blood crisis (loond′valz) [Halvar *Lundvall*, Swedish neurologist]. See under *crisis.*

lung (lung) [L. *pulmo;* Gr. *pneumōn* or *pleumōn*]. The organ of respiration; called also *pulmo* [N A, B N A]. Either one of the pair of organs that effect the aeration of the blood. The lungs occupy the lateral cavities of the chest, and are separated from each other by the heart and mediastinal structures. The right lung is composed of superior, middle, and inferior lobes, and the left, of superior and inferior lobes. Each lobe is subdivided into two to six bronchopulmonary segments which are separated by connective tissue septa. Pulmonary disorders may be confined to, or localized in, one or more of these segments. Each lung consists of an external serous coat (the visceral layer of the pleura), subserous areolar tissue, and the lung parenchyma. The latter is made up of lobules, which are bound together by connective tissue. A primary lobule consists of a bronchiole and infundibulum, or air passage, communicating with many air cells, each air cell being surrounded by a network of capillary blood vessels. **cardiac l.,** engorgement of the lung with blood due to mitral stenosis or left ventricular failure. **coal-miner's l.,** anthracosis. **drowned l.,** atelectasis or massive collapse of the lung. **farmer's l.,** a morbid condition caused by inhalation of moldy hay dust, characterized by breathlessness with cyanosis or with a dry cough, anorexia, and weight loss. **fibroid l.,** a lung affected with chronic interstitial pneumonia. **honeycomb l.,** a lung containing numerous small pus-filled cavities. **iron l.,** a popular name for the Drinker respirator. **masons' l.,** a lung affected with pneumoconiosis due to the inhalation of lime, gypsum, etc. **miners' l.,** anthracosis. **trench l.,** a condition observed in the trenches in World War I, characterized by attacks of rapid breathing. **wet l.,** accumulation of fluid in the lungs after injury or operation. **white l.,** white pneumonia.

lungmotor (lung′mo-tor). An apparatus for forcing air or air and oxygen into the lungs in cases of asphyxia.

lunula (lu′nu-lah), pl. *lu′nulae* [L., dim. of *luna* moon]. A small crescentic or moon-shaped area. **lunulae of aortic valves,** lunulae valvularum aortae. **l. of nail,** l. unguis. **lunulae of pulmonary trunk valves,** lunulae valvularum semilunarium. **l. of scapula,** incisura scapulae. **lunulae of semilunar valves of aorta,** lunulae valvularum aortae. **l. un′guis** [N A, B N A], the crescentic white area at the base of the nail on a finger or toe. Called also *l. of nail.* **lu′nulae valvula′rum aor′tae** [N A], small thinned areas in the cusps of the valve of the aorta, one located on each side of the nodule of each cusp, between the free margin and the most peripheral segment of the cusp. Called also *lunulae of aortic valves.* **lu′nulae valvula′rum semiluna′rium** [N A], small thinned areas in the cusps of the valve of the pulmonary trunk, one located on each side of the nodule of each cusp, between the free margin and the most peripheral segment of the cusp. Called also *lunulae of semilunar valves.* **lu′nulae valvula′rum semiluna′rium aor′tae** [B N A], lunulae valvularum aortae. **lu′nulae valvula′rum semiluna′rium arte′riae pulmona′lis** [B N A], lunulae valvularum semilunarium.

lunulae (lu′nu-le) [L.]. Plural of *lunula.*

lupeose (lu′pe-ōs). A tetrasaccharide from the seeds of lupines.

lupetazin (lu-pet′ah-zin). Dimethylpiperazin, a white, crystalline powder, $HN(CH_2.CHCH_3)_2NH$: used in gout and rheumatism.

lupia (lu′pe-ah). An old term for encysted tumor of the eyelids (Himley).

lupiform (lu′pĭ-form) [L. *lupus* + *forma* form]. 1. Resembling lupus. 2. Resembling a wen.

lupinosis (lu-pĭ-no′sis). A morbid condition resulting from ingestion of the seeds of lupines. Cf. *lathyrism.*

lupinotoxin (lu″pĭ-no-tok′sin). A poisonous substance thought to be present in lupines.

lupoid (lu′poid). 1. Lupiform. 2. A lupiform disease of the skin, described by Boeck, and ascribed to an acid-fast bacillus. See *Boeck's sarcoid,* under *sarcoid.*

lupoma (lu-po′mah) [*lupus* + *-oma*]. The nodosity whence lupus is developed.

lupous (lu′pus) [L. *luposus*]. Pertaining to or of the nature of lupus.

lupulin (lu′pu-lin) [L. *lupulinum; lupulus* hop]. A yellow, resinous powder from hops: sedative and stomachic.

lupulon (lu′pu-lon). An antibiotic obtained from hops, said to be active against tubercle bacilli and against certain fungi.

lupulus (lu′pu-lus) [L.]. Hops.

lupus (lu′pus) [L. "wolf" or "pike"]. A name originally given to a destructive type of skin condition, implying "a local degeneration, strumous in its origin, essentially chronic in its character, and 'attended with more or less hypertrophy, with absorption, and with ulceration'. As one or other of these characters is most marked, . . . a special name [is applied]," e.g. lupus erythematosus, lupus tuberculosus. Although the term is frequently used alone to designate lupus vulgaris, without a modifier it has no specific meaning. **l. erythemato′des,** l. erythematosus, discoid. **l. erythemato′sus.** See *l. erythematosus, discoid,* and *l. erythematosus, systemic.* **l. erythemato′sus, discoid, l. erythemato′sus discoi′des,** a superficial inflammation of the skin marked by disklike patches with raised reddish edges and depressed centers, and covered with scales or crusts. These fall off, leaving dull white cicatrices. Called also *l. erythematodes.* **l. erythemato′sus dissemina′tus,** l. erythematosus, systemic. **l. erythemato′sus, systemic,** a morbid condition, ranging from mild to fulminating, associated with visceral lesions and characterized by skin eruptions, prolonged fever, and other constitutional symptoms. L.E. cells are also characteristically found in the tissues, bone marrow, and blood. **l. liv′ido,** a condition characterized by persistent livid lesions on the extremities, allied to Raynaud's disease. **l. per′nio,** Boeck's sarcoid. **l. tuberculo′sus,** a variety characterized by the formation of more or less typical tubercles. **l. tu′midus,** a form marked by subcutaneous infiltration and doughy swelling. **l. verruco′sus, l. vo′rax,** l. vulgaris. **l. vulga′ris,** a tuberculous

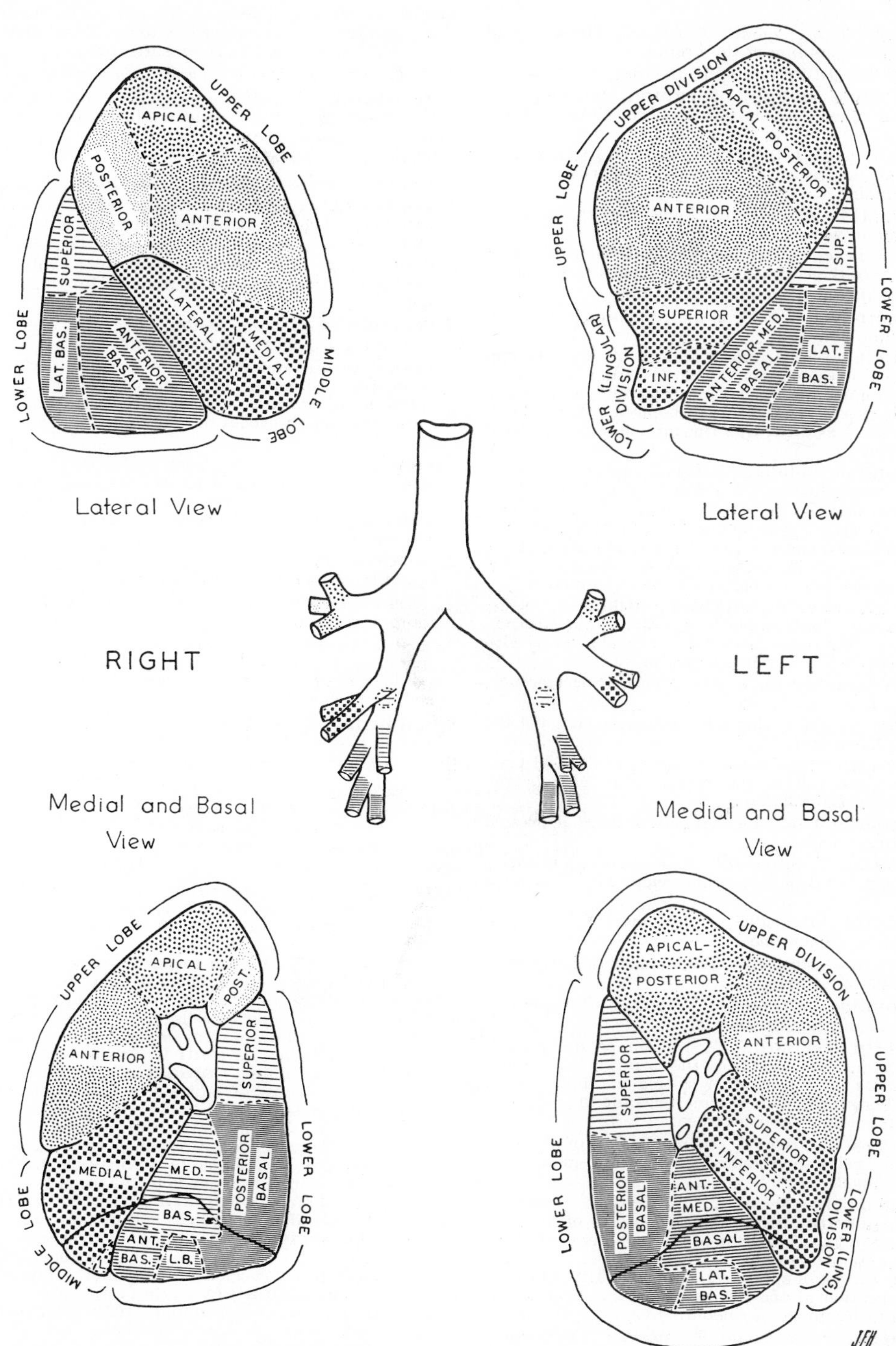

PULMONARY SEGMENTS

Tracheobronchial branching correlated with subdivision of the lungs. Each bronchus is marked the same as the segment it branches out to supply, and should be designated by the same name. The terminology used is that suggested by Jackson and Huber (Diseases of the Chest, volume 9, 1943).

disease of the skin and mucous membranes, marked by the formation of brownish nodules in the corium.

lura (lu′ra) [L. "mouth of a bag"]. The orifice of the infundibulum of the brain.

lural (lu′ral). Pertaining to the lura.

Luschka's crypts, foramen, gland, etc. (lush′kahz) [Hubert von *Luschka*, German anatomist, 1820–1875]. See under the nouns.

lusus (lu′sus) [L.]. A game, sport. **l. natu′rae,** a sport or freak of nature, a minor congenital anomaly.

lute (lūt) [L. *lutum* mud]. A paste for covering the joints of vessels.

luteal (lu′te-al). Pertaining to or having the properties of the corpus luteum or its active principle.

lutecium (lu-te′she-um). Lutetium.

luteectomy (lu″te-ek′to-me). Excision of the corpus luteum.

lutein (lu′te-in) [L. *luteus* yellow]. 1. A yellow pigment, or lipochrome, $C_{48}H_{56}O_2$, from the corpus luteum, from fat cells, and from the yolk of eggs. It is closely related to xanthophyll. 2. Any lipochrome. **serum l.,** a lipochrome found in blood serum.

luteinic (lu″te-in′ik). 1. Pertaining to lutein or to the corpus luteum. 2. Pertaining to luteinization.

luteinization (lu″te-in″i-za′shun). The process taking place in the follicle cells of graafian follicles which have matured and discharged their egg: the cells become hypertrophied and assume a yellow color, the follicles becoming corpora lutea.

Lutembacher's complex, disease, syndrome (loo′tem-bak″erz) [René *Lutembacher*, French physician, born 1884]. Mitral stenosis with defect of the interauricular septum.

luteohormone (lu″te-o-hor′mōn). Progesterone.

luteoid (lu′te-oid) [*luteum* + Gr. *eidos* form]. A substance simulating the hormone activity of the corpus luteum.

luteoma (lu″te-o′mah). A neoplasm derived from the lutein cells of the ovary. Called also *xanthofibroma thecocellulare.*

luteose (lu′te-ōs). A neutral polysaccharide present in luteic acid.

lutetium (lu-te′she-um). The chemical element, atomic number 71, atomic weight 174.97, symbol Lu.

lutocylol (lu″to-si′lol). Trade mark for preparations of ethisterone.

lutrexin (lu-trek′sin). Trade mark for a preparation of lututrin.

lutromone (lu′tro-mōn). Trade mark for a preparation of progesterone.

lututrin (loo′tu-trin). A protein or polypeptide substance obtained from the corpus luteum of sow ovaries by a process of salting out followed by dialysis: used as a uterine relaxant in treatment of functional dysmenorrhea.

lux (luks) [L. "light"]. The metric unit of illumination, being one lumen per square meter. Cf. *foot-candle.*

luxatio (luks-a′she-o) [L.]. Dislocation. **l. cox′ae congen′ita,** congenital dislocation of the hip. **l. erec′ta,** dislocation of the shoulder so that the arm stands straight up above the head. **l. imperfec′ta,** a sprain. **l. perinea′lis,** a form of dislocation of the hip in which the head of the femur lies in the perineum.

luxation (luks-a′shun) [L. *luxatio*]. Dislocation. **Malgaigne's l.,** pulled elbow.

luxuriant (luk-su′re-ant). Growing freely or excessively.

luxus (luks′us) [L.]. Excess. See under *consumption* and *heart.*

Luys' body, nucleus (lu-ēz′) [Jules Bernard *Luys*, French physician, 1828–1898]. The subthalamic nucleus.

Luys' segregator, separator (lu-ēz′) [Georges *Luys*, French physician, 1870–1953]. See under *segregator.*

luz (looz) [Hebrew]. A bone, located in the spinal column, from which, according to the Talmudists, the body is restored at the resurrection.

L.V.H. Abbreviation for *left ventricular hypertrophy.*

lycanthropy (li-kan′thro-pe) [Gr. *lykos* wolf + *anthrōpos* man]. A delusion in which the patient believes himself a wolf.

lycine (li′sin). Betaine.

lycomania (li″ko-ma′ne-ah). Lycanthropy.

lycopene (li′ko-pēn). The red-colored carotinoid pigment, $C_{40}H_{56}$, of tomatoes and various berries and fruits.

Lycoperdon (li″ko-per′don) [Gr. *lykos* wolf + *perdesthai* to break wind]. A genus of fungi; puffballs.

Lycopodium (li″ko-po′de-um) [Gr. *lykos* wolf + *pous* foot]. A genus of club-mosses.

lycopodium (li″ko-po′de-um). A light dry powder formed by the yellow, inflammable sporules of *L. clavatum, L. saururus,* and other species, used as a dusting and absorbent powder, and as a coating for pills.

Lycopus (li′ko-pus) [Gr. *lykos* wolf + *pous* foot]. A genus of nonaromatic mints; the bugle-weed, formerly used in medicine. **L. europae′us,** the bitter bugle-weed of Europe. **L. virgin′icus,** the sweet bugle-weed.

lycorexia (li″ko-rek′se-ah) [Gr. *lykos* wolf + *orexis* appetite]. Ravenous, wolfish hunger.

Lycosa tarentula (li-ko′sah tah-ren′tu-lah). The European tarantula.

lye (li). An alkaline percolate from wood ashes; lixivium. To the public lye generally means a crude mixture of sodium hydroxide with some sodium carbonate, known as household lye.

lygophilia (li″go-fil′e-ah) [Gr. *lygē* twilight + *philein* to love]. Abnormal longing for dark places.

lying-in (li″ing-in′). 1. Puerperal. 2. The puerperium.

Lymnaea (lim-ne′ah). A genus of snails, several species of which act as invertebrate hosts for various flukes, such as *Fasciola hepatica.*

lymph-. See *lympho-.*

lymph (limf) [L. *lympha* water]. 1. A transparent, slightly yellow liquid of alkaline reaction, found in the lymphatic vessels. Called also *lympha* [N A, B N A]. It is occasionally of a light-rose color from the presence of red blood corpuscles, and is often opalescent from particles of fat. Under the microscope lymph is seen to consist of a liquid portion (*liquor lymphae*) and of cells, most of which are lymphocytes. 2. Any clear, watery fluid resembling true lymph. **animal l.,** vaccine or other lymph from an animal. **aplastic l.,** lymph that contains an excess of leukocytes and does not tend to become organized. Called also *corpuscular l.* **bovine l.,** vaccine lymph from the cow. **calf l.,** lymph for vaccination obtained from calves. **corpuscular l.,** aplastic l. **croupous l.,** inflammatory lymph that tends to the formation of a false membrane. **euplastic l., fibrinous l.,** that which tends to coagulate and become organized. **glycerinated l.,** vaccine virus mixed with glycerin in order to destroy any bacteria. **humanized l.,** vaccine virus from the human subject. **inflammatory l.,** the lymph produced by inflammation, as in a wound. **intercellular l.,** lymph occupying the intercellular spaces of tissues. **intravascular l.,** the lymph of the lymph vessels. **Koch's l.** See *tuberculin.* **plastic l.** 1. That from which embryonic tissue is formed. 2. Inflammatory lymph that has a tendency to become organized. **tissue l.,** lymph derived from the tissues and not from the blood. **vaccine l.,** the serous exudate from the vesicles of cowpox.

lympha (lim′fah) [L. "water"]. [N A, B N A] The fluid found in the lymphatic vessels. See *lymph.*

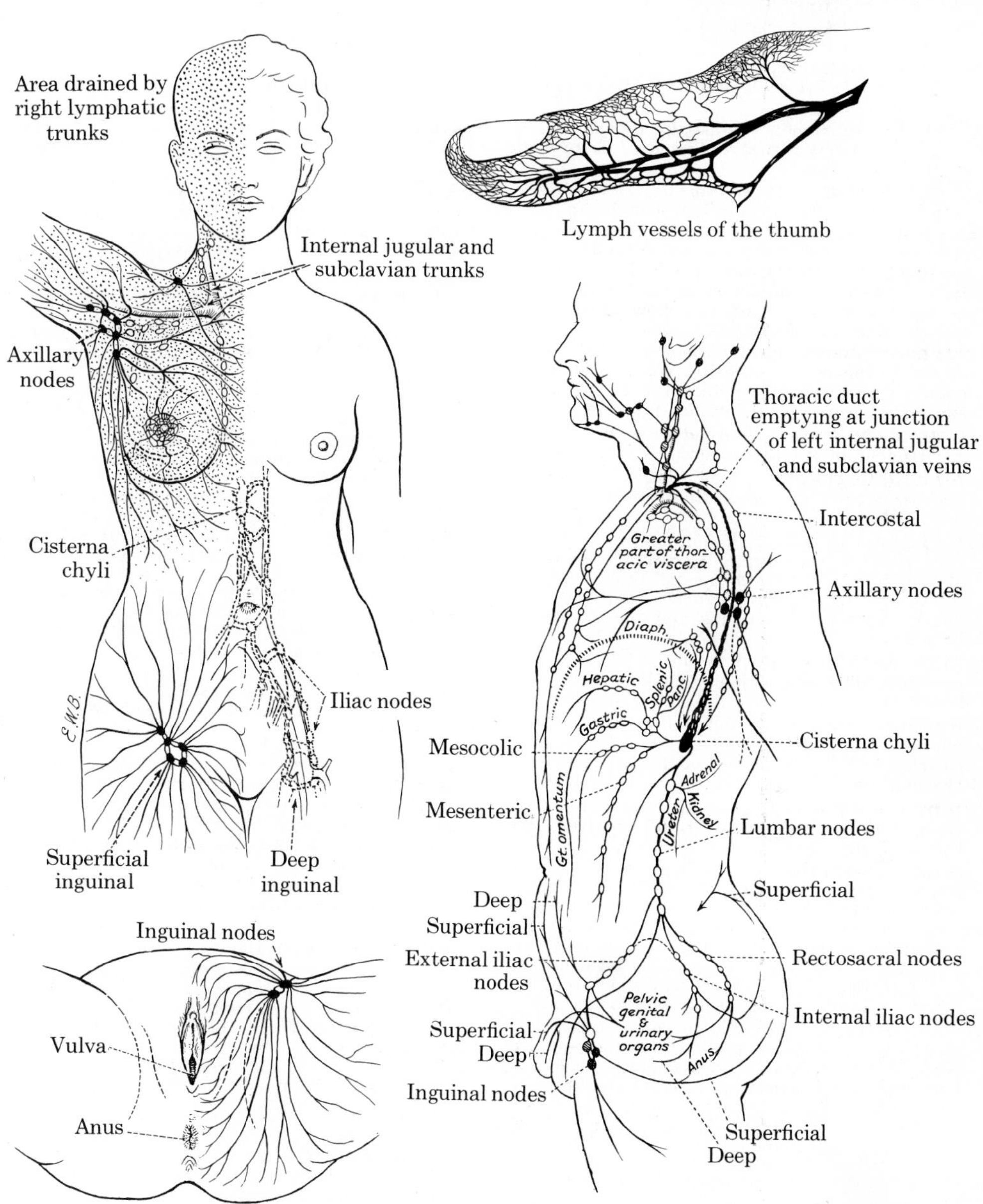

DIAGRAMMATIC REPRESENTATION OF LYMPHATIC DRAINAGE OF VARIOUS PARTS OF THE BODY

lymphaden (lim′fah-den) [*lymph-* + Gr. *adēn* gland]. A lymph node.

lymphadenectasis (lim-fad″e-nek′tah-sis) [*lymph-* + Gr. *adēn* gland + *ektasis* distention]. Enlargement of a lymph node.

lymphadenectomy (lim-fad″e-nek′to-me) [*lymphaden* + Gr. *ektomē* excision]. Surgical excision of a lymph node.

lymphadenhypertrophy (lim-fad″en-hi-per′-tro-fe) [*lymphaden* + *hypertrophy*]. Hypertrophy of a lymph node.

lymphadenia (lim″fah-de′ne-ah) [*lymphaden* + *-ia*]. Hypertrophy of the lymph nodes. **l. os′sea,** multiple myeloma.

lymphadenism (lim-fad′e-nizm). The disease condition that accompanies lymphadenoma.

lymphadenitis (lim-fad″e-ni′tis) [*lymph-* + Gr. *adēn* gland + *-itis*]. Inflammation of lymph nodes. **caseous l., paratuberculous l.,** inflammation of the lymph nodes associated with tuberculosis of some other part, but showing no tubercle bacilli in the lymphatics.

lymphadenocyst (lim-fad′e-no-sist″). A degenerated lymph node caused by occlusion of its incoming lymph vessels. By dilatation of the lymph sinuses it becomes a fine-meshed network.

lymphadenogram (lim-fad′e-no-gram″). A roentgenogram of lymph nodes.

lymphadenography (lim-fad″e-nog′rah-fe). Roentgenographic visualization of the lymph nodes.

lymphadenoid (lim-fad′e-noid) [*lymph-* + Gr. *adēn* gland + *eidos* form]. Resembling the tissue of lymph nodes. Lymphadenoid tissue includes the spleen, bone marrow, tonsils, and the lymphatic tissue of the organs and mucous membranes.

lymphadenoleukopoiesis (lim-fad″e-no-lu″ko-poi-e′sis). The production of leukocytes by the lymphadenoid tissue.

lymphadenoma (lim″fad-e-no′mah). Hyperplasia of the lymphadenoid tissue; lymphoma. **malignant l.,** lymphosarcoma. **multiple l.,** Hodgkin's disease.

lymphadenomatosis (lim-fad″e-no-mah-to′sis). Lymphomatosis. **general l. of bones,** Kahler's disease.

lymphadenopathy (lim-fad″e-nop′ah-the) [*lymphaden* + Gr. *pathos* disease]. Disease of the lymph nodes. **giant follicular l.,** one of the malignant lymphomas, so called because its microscopic appearance is characterized by multiple, proliferative, follicle-like nodules which disturb the normal architecture of the lymph nodes. Called also *giant follicular lymphoma* and *Brill-Symmers disease.*

lymphadenosis (lim-fad″e-no′sis) [*lymphaden* + *-osis*]. Hypertrophy or proliferation of lymphoid tissue. **acute l.,** infectious mononucleosis. **l. aleucae′mica parasita′ria,** Rhodesian fever. **aleukemic l.,** a disease marked by diffuse generalized hyperplasia of the lymphadenoid system (lymph glands, spleen, bone marrow, tonsils, and other lymphatic tissues), but without leukemia. See *lymphosarcoma.* **leukemic l.,** lymphatic leukemia.

lymphadenovarix (lim-fad″e-no-va′riks). Enlargement of the lymph nodes from the pressure of dilated lymph vessels.

lymphagogue (lim′fah-gog). An agent which promotes the production of lymph.

lymphangeitis (lim″fan-je-i′tis). Lymphangitis.

lymphangial (lim-fan′je-al). Pertaining to a lymphatic vessel.

lymphangiectasis (lim-fan″je-ek′tah-sis) [*lymph-* + Gr. *angeion* vessel + *ektasis* distention]. Dilatation of the lymphatic vessels.

lymphangiectatic (lim-fan″je-ek-tat′ik). Pertaining to or marked by lymphangiectasis.

lymphangiectodes (lim-fan″je-ek-to′dēz). Lymphangioma circumscriptum.

lymphangiectomy (lim-fan″je-ek′to-me). Excision of a lymphatic vessel.

lymphangiitis (lim-fan″je-i′tis). Lymphangitis.

lymphangioadenography (lym-fan″je-o-ad″e-nog′rah-fe). Lymphography.

lymphangioendothelioblastoma (lim-fan″je-o-en″do-the″le-o-blas-to′mah). A tumor composed of endothelial cells which tend to form lymph vessels.

lymphangioendothelioma (lim-fan″je-o-en″-do-the-le-o′mah). Endothelioma arising from lymph vessels or lymph spaces—the ordinary variety of endothelioma. Called also *lymphendothelioma.*

lymphangiofibroma (lim-fan″je-o-fi-bro′mah). Fibroma with lymphangiomatous tissue.

lymphangiogram (lim-fan″je-o-gram). A roentgenogram of the lymphatic vessels.

lymphangiography (lim-fan″je-og′rah-fe). Roentgenography of the lymphatic vessels following the injection of contrast medium.

lymphangioitis (lim-fan″je-o-i′tis). Lymphangitis. **l. farcimino′sa bo′vis,** cattle farcy.

lymphangiology (lim-fan″je-ol′o-je) [*lymph-* + Gr. *angeion* vessel + *-logy*]. The branch of anatomy relating to the lymphatic vessels.

lymphangioma (lim-fan″je-o′mah). A tumor composed of new-formed lymph spaces and channels. **l. capsula′re varico′sum,** lymphangioma circumscriptum. **l. caverno′sum,** dilatation of the lymphatic vessels resulting in cavities filled with lymph. **l. circumscrip′tum,** a skin disease of early life marked by the development of yellow vesicles connected with the lymphatic vessels. **cystic l., l. cys′ticum,** a cystic growth occurring almost exclusively in the neck or groin and more commonly in children than in adults, and thought to originate from some anomaly in development of the primitive lymphatic spaces. The symptoms are largely the result of compression of adjoining structures by the mass. **fissural l.,** simple or cavernous lymphangiomas at the site of fetal fissures. **l. sim′plex,** dilatation of a lymph vessel over a circumscribed area. **l. tubero′sum mul′tiplex,** a skin disease marked by the development of groups of papules or tubercles resembling and believed to be lymphangioma. **l. xanthelasmoi′deum,** lymphangioma circumscriptum marked by formation on the skin of yellow or brownish patches.

lymphangiophlebitis (lim-fan″je-o-fle-bi′tis). Inflammation of the lymph vessels and veins.

lymphangioplasty (lim-fan′je-o-plas″te) [*lymph-* + Gr. *angeion* vessel + *plassein* to form]. Operative restoration or replacement of lymph vessels that have been destroyed; subcutaneous introduction in an extremity of silk or nylon threads or of celloidin strips, as a means of increasing lymphatic drainage of the part, especially of the arm after radical mastectomy.

lymphangiosarcoma (lim-fan″je-o-sar-ko′-mah). Lymphangioma blended with sarcoma.

lymphangiotomy (lim-fan″je-ot′o-me) [*lymph-* + Gr. *angeion* vessel + *temnein* to cut]. Dissection of the lymphatic vessels.

lymphangitis (lim″fan-ji′tis). Inflammation of a lymphatic vessel or vessels. **l. carcinomato′sa,** proliferating inflammation of the lymphatic vessels of the peritoneum, associated with peritoneal tumors. **l. epizoot′ica,** a chronic contagious disease of horses caused by a yeast fungus, *Cryptococcus* (*Blastomyces*) *farciminosus,* and marked by purulent inflammation of the subcutaneous lymphatic vessels and of the regional lymph glands. Called also *pseudofarcy, blastomycosis farciminosus, saccharomycosis, cryptococcus farcy, lymphosporidiosis, African glanders, Japanese glanders, Japanese farcy, Neapolitan farcy.* **l. ulcero′sa pseudofarcino′sa,** a disease of horses resembling glanders, and due to a bacillus closely resembling the glanders bacillus. Called also *pseudoglanders.*

lymphatic (lim-fat′ik) [L. *lymphaticus*]. 1. Pertaining to or containing lymph; by extension, the term is sometimes used alone to designate a lymphatic vessel. 2. Of a sluggish or phlegmatic temperament.

lymphaticostomy (lim-fat″ĭ-kos′to-me) [*lymphatic* + Gr. *stomoun* to provide with an opening, or mouth]. The operation of making a permanent opening into a lymphatic duct, such as the thoracic duct: done for peritonitis.

lymphatism (lim′fah-tizm). 1. The lymphatic temperament; a slow or sluggish habit. 2. A morbid state due to excessive production or growth of lymphoid tissues, resulting in impaired development and lowered vitality. Called also *lymphotoxemia*, *lymphoidotoxemia*, and *status lymphaticus*.

lymphatitis (lim″fah-ti′tis). Inflammation of some part of the lymphatic system.

lymphatology (lim″fah-tol′o-je). The study of the lymph and lymphatic system.

lymphatolysin (lim″fah-tol′ĭ-sin). A lysin which acts on lymphatic tissue.

lymphatolysis (lim″fah-tol′ĭ-sis) [*lymphatic* + Gr. *lysis* dissolution]. The destruction or solution of lymphatic tissue.

lymphatolytic (lim″fah-to-lit′ik) [*lymphatic* + Gr. *lysis* dissolution]. Destroying lymphatic tissue.

lymphatome (lim′fah-tōm). Lymphotome.

lymphectasia (lim″fek-ta′ze-ah) [*lymph-* + Gr. *ektasis* distention]. Distention with lymph.

lymphedema (lim″fe-de′mah) [*lymph-* + *edema*]. Swelling of subcutaneous tissues due to the presence of excessive lymph fluid. **congenital l.,** Milroy's disease; a congenital and sometimes hereditary form of lymphedema. **l. prae′cox, primary l.,** a disease primarily of young females, characterized by puffiness and swelling of the lower limbs.

lymphemia (lim-fe′me-ah) [*lymph-* + Gr. *haima* blood + *-ia*]. The presence of an undue number of lymphocytes or their forerunners in the blood; lymphatic leukemia.

lymphendothelioma (lim″fen-do-the″le-o′-mah). Lymphangioendothelioma.

lymphenteritis (lim″fen-ter-i′tis). Enteritis with serous infiltration.

lymphepithelioma (limf″ep-ĭ-the″le-o′mah). Lymphoepithelioma.

lympherythrocyte (limf″e-rith′ro-sīt). Anerythrocyte.

lymphization (lim″fi-za′shun). The formation of lymph.

lymphnoditis (limf″no-di′tis). Inflammation of a lymph node.

lympho-, lymph- (lim′fo, limf) [L. *lympha* water]. Combining form denoting relationship to lymph.

lymphoadenoma (lim″fo-ad″e-no′mah). A benign neoplasm of the uterus, involving the interstitial lymph tissue and the glandular structures.

lymphoblast (lim′fo-blast) [*lympho-* + Gr. *blastos* germ]. A lymphocyte in its germinative stage; a developing lymphocyte. Such cells are found in the blood in acute lymphatic leukemia.

lymphoblasthemia (lim″fo-blast-he′me-ah). Lymphoblastosis.

lymphoblastic (lim″fo-blas′tik). Pertaining to a lymphoblast; producing lymphocytes.

lymphoblastoma (lim″fo-blas-to′mah). A form of malignant lymphoma in which the predominant cell is morphologically similar to the lymphoblast and contains a fine nuclear chromatin structure with one or more nucleoli. Called also *lymphoblastic lymphoma*.

lymphoblastomatosis (lim″fo-blas″to-mah-to′-sis). The condition produced by the presence of lymphoblastomas.

lymphoblastomatous (lim″fo-blas-to′mah-tus). Of the nature of or characterized by lymphoblastoma.

lymphoblastomid (lim″fo-blas-to′mid). Any specific cutaneous lesion of lymphoblastoma.

lymphoblastosis (lim″fo-blas-to′sis). Excess of lymphoblasts in the blood. **acute benign l.,** infectious mononucleosis.

lymphocele (lim′fo-sēl) [*lympho-* + Gr. *kēlē* tumor]. A tumor containing lymph.

lymphocerastism (lim″fo-se-ras′tizm) [*lympho-* + Gr. *kerastos* mixed]. The formation of lymphoid cells.

lymphocinesia (lim″fo-si-ne′ze-ah) [*lympho-* + Gr. *kinēsis* motion]. Lymphokinesis.

lymphococcus (lim″fo-kok′us). A diplococcus isolated from the lymph in elephantiasis.

lymphocyst (lim′fo-sist). Lymphocele.

lymphocystosis (lim″fo-sis-to′sis). The formation of cysts containing lymph.

lymphocyte (lim′fo-sīt) [*lympho-* + *-cyte*]. 1. A variety of white blood corpuscle which arises in the reticular tissue of the lymph glands. The nucleus is single and is surrounded by protoplasm which is generally described as nongranular. Two varieties are described: (*a*) the small lymphocytes (*small mononuclear leukocytes* or *microlymphocytes*), which are about the size of a red corpuscle and constitute from 22 to 25 per cent of the white corpuscles; (*b*) the large lymphocytes (*macrolymphocytes* or *lymphoblasts*), which are probably lymphocytes in their grown stage, are two or three times larger than the small lymphocytes and contain a larger proportion of protoplasm. They form about 1 per cent of the white corpuscles. 2. A lymph corpuscle. **Rieder's l.,** a lymphocyte having a nucleus which is lobed and twisted: seen in chronic lymphemia.

lymphocythemia (lim″fo-si-the′me-ah) [*lymphocyte* + Gr. *haima* blood + *-ia*]. Excess of lymphocytes in the blood.

lymphocytic (lim″fo-sit′ik). Pertaining to lymphocytes.

lymphocytoblast (lim″fo-si′to-blast). Lymphoblast.

lymphocytoma (lim″fo-si-to′mah) [*lymphocyte* + *-oma*]. A form of malignant lymphoma in which the predominant cell is the mature-type lymphocyte. Called also *lymphocytic lymphoma*.

lymphocytomatosis (lim″fo-si″to-mah-to′sis). The condition produced by the presence of lymphocytomas.

lymphocytomatous (lim″fo-si-to′mah-tus). Of the nature of or characterized by lymphocytoma.

lymphocytopenia (lim″fo-si″to-pe′ne-ah). Reduction in the number of lymphocytes in the blood.

lymphocytopoiesis (lim″fo-si″to-poi-e′sis) [*lymphocyte* + Gr. *poiein* to make]. The development of lymphocytes.

lymphocytopoietic (lim″fo-si″to-poi-et′ik). Pertaining to or characterized by lymphocytopoiesis.

lymphocytorrhexis (lim″fo-si″to-rek′sis). The rupturing or bursting of lymphocytes.

lymphocytosis (lim″fo-si-to′sis). Excess of normal lymphocytes in the blood or in any effusion. **acute infectious l.,** a disease of children characterized by an excess of normal small lymphocytes in the blood.

lymphocytotic (lim″fo-si-tot′ik). Pertaining to lymphocytosis.

lymphocytotoxin (lim″fo-si″to-tok′sin). A toxin that has a specific destructive action on lymphocytes.

Lymphocytozoon (lim″fo-si″to-zo′on) [*lymphocyte* + Gr. *zōon* animal]. A genus of ameboid bodies, species of which are found in leukocytes. **L. coba′yae,** Kurloff's bodies. **L. pal′lidum,** Ross's bodies.

lymphodermia (lim″fo-der′me-ah) [*lympho-* + Gr. *derma* skin]. Any disease of the lymphatics of the skin. **l. pernicio′sa,** enlargement of the glands due to leukocythemia.

lymphoduct (lim′fo-dukt). A lymphatic vessel.

lymphoepithelioma (lim″fo-ep″ĭ-the″le-o′mah). A tumor arising from modified epithelium overlying lymphoid tissue of the nasopharynx.

lymphoerythrocyte (lim″fo-e-rith′ro-sīt). Anerythrocyte.

lymphoganglin (lim″fo-gang′glin). A hypothetical hormone from lymph glands.

lymphogenesis (lim″fo-jen′e-sis). The production of lymph.

lymphogenous (lim-foj′e-nus) [*lympho-* + Gr. *gennan* to produce]. 1. Producing lymph. 2. Produced from lymph or in the lymphatics.

lymphoglandula (lim″fo-glan′du-lah), pl. *lymphoglan′dulae* [B N A]. Lymph node. See *nodus lymphaticus* [N A], under *nodus*.

lymphogonia (lim″fo-go′ne-ah) [*lympho-* + Gr. *gonos* generation]. Large lymphocytes with a large nucleus, little chromatin, and nongranular protoplasm. They are the mother cells of small lymphocytes and are seen in lymphatic leukemia.

lymphogram (lim′fo-gram). A roentgenogram of the lymphatic vessels and lymph nodes.

lymphogranuloma (lim″fo-gran″u-lo′mah). Hodgkin's disease. **l. benig′num,** Boeck's sarcoid. **l. inguina′le,** venereal l. **Schaumann's benign l.,** Boeck's sarcoid. **venereal l., l. vene′reum,** a specific venereal disease caused by a virus closely related to those causing psittacosis, ornithosis, and pneumonitis. It may lead to nondestructive elephantiasis of the labia and clitoris, or of the penis and scrotum, and to the development of rectal stenosis or strictures. Called also *lymphogranuloma inguinale, lymphopathia venereum, poradenitis nostras, Frei's disease, Nicolas-Favre disease, fifth venereal disease, climatic bubo, tropical bubo.*

lymphogranulomatosis (lim″fo-gran″u-lo-mah-to′sis). Infectious granuloma of the lymphatic system: used by continental writers as a synonym for Hodgkin's disease. **benign l.,** Schaumann's name for sarcoidosis. **l. cu′tis,** the cutaneous manifestation of Hodgkin's disease. **l. inguina′lis,** venereal lymphogranuloma. **l. malig′na,** Hodgkin's disease.

lymphography (lim-fog′rah-fe). Roentgenography of the lymphatic channels and lymph nodes, following injection of radiopaque material in a lymphatic vessel.

lymphoid (lim′foid) [*lymph* + Gr. *eidos* form]. Resembling lymph.

lymphoidectomy (lim″foi-dek′to-me). Excision of lymphoid tissue, such as adenoids and tonsils.

lymphoididity (lim″foi-did′ĭ-te). The condition of exhibiting lymphoid characteristics.

lymphoidocyte (lim-foi′do-sīt). An embryonic cell, the primordial mother cell of all the types of blood cells; hemocytoblast.

lymphoidotoxemia (lim-foi″do-tok-se′me-ah). Lymphatism (def. 2).

lymphokentric (lim″fo-ken′trik) [*lympho-* + Gr. *kentron* a stimulant]. Stimulating the formation of lymphoid cells. Cf. *myelokentric.*

lymphokinesis (lim″fo-ki-ne′sis) [*lympho-* + Gr. *kinēsis* movement]. 1. The movement of the endolymph in the semicircular canals. 2. The circulation of lymph in the body.

lympholeukocyte (lim″fo-lu′ko-sīt). A large mononuclear leukocyte.

lymphology (lim-fol′o-je) [*lympho-* + *-logy*]. The scientific study of the lymphatic system.

lymphoma (lim-fo′mah). A general term applied to any neoplastic disorder of the lymphoid tissue, including, with others, *Hodgkin's disease* and *reticulum cell sarcoma.* Called also *malignant lymphoma.* **clasmocytic l.,** reticulum cell sarcoma. **giant follicular l.,** giant follicular lymphadenopathy. **lymphoblastic l.,** lymphoblastoma. **lymphocytic l.,** lymphocytoma.

lymphomatoid (lim-fo′mah-toid). Resembling lymphoma.

lymphomatosis (lim″fo-mah-to′sis). The development of multiple lymphomas in various parts of the body; a form of leukosis involving chiefly the lymphocytes. **avian l., l. of fowl,** a group of diseases of chickens marked by formation of lymphomatous tumors of varying sizes in the visceral organs, or by lymphoid cell infiltration of various organs, including nerves. Certain forms are transmissible. The number of white blood cells in the circulating blood may be increased. *neural l.,* a disease of fowl marked by paralysis of the neck, wings or legs, due to infiltration of nerves by lymphoid cells. Called also *range paralysis, fowl paralysis,* and *neurolymphomatosis gallinarum. ocular l.,* a condition marked by infiltration of the iris by lymphoid cells. *osteopetrotic l.,* a condition marked by thickening of the diaphyses of the long bones, associated with visceral lymphomatosis. Called also *osteopetrosis gallinarum. visceral l.,* a condition marked by involvement of the parenchymal organs either diffusely or with the formation of definite tumors. **l. granulomato′sa,** Hodgkin's disease.

lymphomatous (lim-fo′mah-tus). Pertaining to or of the nature of lymphoma.

lymphomegaloblast (lim″fo-meg′ah-lo-blast). A megaloblast without hemoglobin.

lymphomonocyte (lim″fo-mon′o-sīt). A large uninuclear leukocyte.

lymphomyelocyte (lim″fo-mi′ĕ-lo-sīt). A myeloblast.

lymphomyeloma (lim″fo-mi-ĕ-lo′mah). Plasma cell myeloma.

lymphomyxoma (lim″fo-mik-so′mah). Any benign growth consisting of adenoid tissue.

lymphonodi (lim″fo-no′di). Plural of *lymphonodus.*

lymphonodus (lim″fo-no′dus), pl. *lymphono′di* [*lympho-* + L. *nodis* a knot]. N A alternative for *nodus lymphaticus.*

lymphopathia (lim″fo-path′e-ah). Lymphopathy. **l. vene′reum,** venereal lymphogranuloma.

lymphopathy (lim-fop′ah-the) [*lympho-* + Gr. *pathos* disease]. Any disease of the lymphatic system. **ataxic l.,** a sudden swelling of the lymph nodes sometimes accompanying the pain crises of locomotor ataxia.

lymphopenia (lim-fo-pe′ne-ah) [*lymphocyte* + Gr. *penia* poverty]. Decrease in the proportion of lymphocytes in the blood.

lymphoplasm (lim′fo-plazm). Spongioplasm.

lymphoplasmia (lim″fo-plaz′me-ah). A condition of the red blood corpuscles in which they contain no hemoglobin.

lymphoplasty (lim′fo-plas″te). Lymphangioplasty.

lymphopoiesis (lim″fo-poi-e′sis) [*lympho-* + Gr. *poiein* to make]. 1. The development of lymphatic tissue. 2. Lymphocytopoiesis.

lymphopoietic (lim″fo-poi-et′ik). Pertaining to, characterized by, or causing lymphopoiesis.

lymphoproliferative (lim″fo-pro-lif″er-a′tiv). Pertaining to or characterized by proliferation of lymphoid tissue. See *lymphoproliferative syndrome,* under *syndrome.*

lymphoprotease (lim″fo-pro′te-ās). A protein-splitting ferment existing in the lymphocytes.

lymphoreticulosis (lim″fo-re-tik″u-lo′sis). Proliferation of the reticuloendothelial cells of the lymph glands. **benign l.,** cat-scratch disease.

lymphorrhage (lim′fo-rij). An accumulation of lymphocytes in a muscle.

lymphorrhagia (lim″fo-ra′je-ah) [*lympho-* + Gr. *rhegnynai* to break out]. Lymphorrhea.

lymphorrhea (lim″fo-re′ah) [*lympho-* + Gr. *rhoia* flow]. A flow of lymph from cut or ruptured lymph vessels.

lymphorrhoid (limf′o-roid). A localized dilatation of a perianal lymph channel, resembling a hemorrhoid: sometimes occurring in lymphogranuloma venereum.

lymphosarcoleukemia (lim″fo-sar″ko-lu-ke′-me-ah). Lymphosarcoma cell leukemia.

lymphosarcoma (lim″fo-sar-ko′mah). A general term applied to malignant neoplastic disorders of lymphoid tissue, but not including Hodgkin's disease. See *lymphoma.* **Kundrat's l.,** a form of lymphosarcoma which rapidly extends to adjacent glands, but shows no tendency to invade neighboring organs. The blood shows anemia with neutrophil leukocytosis and decrease of lymphocytes.

lymphosarcomatosis (lim″fo-sar″ko-mah-to′-sis). A condition characterized by the presence of multiple lesions of lymphosarcoma.

lymphosporidiosis (lim″fo-spo-rid″e-o′sis). Lymphangitis epizootica.

lymphostasis (lim-fos′tah-sis) [*lympho-* + Gr. *stasis* standing]. Stoppage of the lymph flow.

lymphotaxis (lim″fo-tak′sis) [*lymphocyte* + Gr. *taxis* arrangement]. The property of attracting or repulsing lymphocytes.

lymphotism (lim′fo-tizm). A disordered state associated with the development of adenoid tissue.

lymphotome (lim′fo-tōm) [*lympho-* + Gr. *tomē* a cut]. An instrument for excising adenoids.

lymphotomy (lim-fot′o-me) [*lympho-* + Gr. *temnein* to cut]. The anatomy of the lymphatic system.

lymphotoxemia (lim″fo-tok-se′me-ah). Toxemia due to excess of lymphoid material or lymphoid tissue, as in rickets, exophthalmic goiter, enlarged thymus, etc.

lymphotoxin (lim″fo-tok′sin). A toxin contained in lymph glands or acting on lymph cells.

lymphotrophy (lim-fot′ro-fe) [*lympho-* + Gr. *trephein* to nourish]. The attractive energy of cells for lymph.

lymphous (lim′fus). Pertaining to or containing lymph.

lymphuria (lim-fu′re-ah). The presence of lymph in the urine.

lymph-vascular (limf-vas′ku-lar). Pertaining to or containing lymphatic vessels.

Lynchia maura (lin′ke-ah maw′rah). *Pseudolynchia maura.*

Lynen (li′nen), Feodor. German biochemist, born 1911; co-winner, with Konrad Bloch, of the Nobel prize for medicine and physiology in 1964, for investigations in biosynthesis of fatty acids and cholesterol.

lynoral (lin′or-al). Trade mark for a preparation of ethinyl estradiol.

lyo- (li′o) [Gr. *lyein* to dissolve]. Combining form meaning dissolved.

lyochrome (li′o-krōm) [*lyo-* + Gr. *chrōma* color]. Flavin.

lyoenzyme (li′o-en-zim). An enzyme which is dissolved in the cell protoplasm. Cf. *desmoenzyme.*

lyogel (li′o-jel) [*lyo-* + *gel*]. A gel containing much liquid.

Lyon method, test (li′on) [B. B. Vincent *Lyon*, American physician, 1880–1953]. Meltzer-Lyon test. See under *tests.*

Lyon-Horgan operation (li′on-hor′gan) [James Alexander *Lyon*, American physician, 1882–1955; Edmund *Horgan*, American physician, born 1884]. See under *operation.*

lyophil (li′o-fil). A lyophilic substance; a material that readily goes into solution.

lyophile (li′o-fil). 1. Lyophil. 2. Lyophilic.

lyophilic (li″o-fil′ik) [*lyo-* + Gr. *philein* to love]. Having an affinity for solution; designating a colloid system in which the solvent and the dispersed particles mutually attract each other and which is quite stable.

lyophilization (li-of″ĭ-li-za′shun). The creation of a stable preparation of a biological substance (blood plasma, serum, etc.), by rapid freezing and dehydration of the frozen product under high vacuum.

lyophobe (li′o-fōb) [*lyo-* + *phobia*]. A lyophobic substance; a material that does not readily go into or tends to separate out from solution.

lyophobic (li″o-fo′bik) [*lyo-* + Gr. *phobein* to fear]. Not having an affinity for solution; designating a colloid system in which no attraction exists between the solvent and the dispersed particles and which is unstable.

lyosol (li′o-sol). A sol in which the dispersion medium is a liquid.

lyosorption (li″o-sorp′shun). The selective adsorption of the solvent portion of a solution.

lyotropic (li″o-trop′ik) [*lyo-* + Gr. *tropos* a turning]. Entering easily into solution; readily soluble.

lypemania (li″pe-ma′ne-ah) [Gr. *lypē* grief + *mania* madness]. A state of morbid depression.

lyperophrenia (li″per-o-fre′ne-ah) [Gr. *lypēros* distressing + *phrēn* mind]. Melancholia.

Lyperosia irritans (li″per-o′se-ah ir′ĭ-tans). *Hematobium serrata.*

Lyponyssus (li″po-nis′us). A genus of mites which sometimes attack man. *L. baco′ti* live normally on rats and *L. bur′sae* on birds.

lypothymia (li″po-thi′me-ah) [Gr. *lypē* grief + *thymos* mind]. A depressed state of mind.

lyra (li′rah) [L., Gr. "a stringed instrument resembling the lute"]. A name applied to certain anatomical structures because of their fancied resemblance to a lute. **l. Da′vidis,** commissura fornicis. **l. u′teri, l. uteri′na,** plicae palmatae. **l. vagi′nae,** the vaginal rugae.

lyre (lir). Lyra. **l. of David,** commissura fornicis. **l. of uterus,** plicae palmatae. **l. of vagina,** the vaginal rugae.

lysate (li′sāt). 1. The material formed by the lysis of cells. 2. A medicinal preparation obtained from an animal organ by means of artificial digestion.

lysatin (lis′ah-tin). A basic principle or leukomaine, $C_6H_{13}N_3O_2$, derivable from casein.

lysatinin (lis-at′ĭ-nin). A mixture of lysine and arginine.

lyse (līz). 1. To cause or produce disintegration of a compound, substance, or cell. 2. To undergo lysis.

lysemia (li-se′me-ah) [Gr. *lysis* dissolution + *haima* blood + *-ia*]. Disintegration of the blood.

lysidin (lis′ĭ-din). A red, crystalline body; methylglyoxalidin, $CH_2.NH.C(CH_3){:}N.CH_2$; also its yellowish or pinkish, soapy, 50 per cent solution: used as a solvent for uric acid. **l. bitartrate,** a soluble, white, crystalline powder, of one third the solvent power of pure lysidin.

lysimeter (li-sim′e-ter) [Gr. *lysis* dissolution + *metron* measure]. An apparatus for determining the solubilities of substances.

lysin (li′sin) [Gr. *lyein* to dissolve]. An antibody, an alpha lysin, which has the power of causing dissolution of cells. The term includes hemolysin, bacteriolysin, cytolysin, etc. **beta l.,** a naturally occurring and relatively thermostabile bactericidal serum constituent of certain animals that is not inactivated by a temperature of 56–60°C. for 30–40 minutes. **Dubos' l.,** tyrothricin. **immune l.,** a cytolytic antibody which mediates the lysis of a cellular antigen by complement.

lysine (li′sin). An amino acid, $NH_2(CH_2)_4.CH(NH_2).COOH$ (Ellinger, 1900), or α-ϵ-diaminocaproic acid, first isolated from casein (Drechsel, 1889): essential for, optimal growth in infants and for maintenance of nitrogen equilibrium in human adults. It is a hydrolytic cleavage product of protein either by digestion or by boiling with hydrochloric acid.

lysinogen (li-sin′o-jen) [*lysin* + Gr. *gennan* to produce]. A substance having the power of producing lysins.

lysinogenesis (li″sin-o-jen′e-sis). The production or formation of lysins.

lysinosis (lis″ĭ-no′sis) [Gr. *lyein* to dissolve + *is, inos* fiber + *-osis*]. Lung disease due to inhaling cotton fibers, as in mills.

lysis (li′sis) [Gr. "dissolution; a loosing, setting free, releasing"]. 1. Destruction, as of cells by a specific lysin. 2. Decomposition, as of a chemical compound by a specific agent. 3. Loosening of an organ from adhesions. 4. The gradual abatement of the symptoms of a disease. **hot-cold l.,** a lysis that occurs only if the material is incubated as usual and then allowed to stand overnight at room temperature.

lyso- (li′so) [Gr. *lysis* dissolution]. A combining form, indicating lysis or dissolution.

lysobacteria (li″so-bak-te′re-ah). Bacteria which are able to dissolve other bacteria, both alive and dead.

lysocephalin (li″so-sef′ah-lin). A cephalin from which the unsaturated fatty acid radical has been removed as by the action of cobra venom.

lysocythin (li″so-si′thin). A substance formed by combination between an animal poison and the body tissues and having a cytolytic action.

lysogen (li′so-jen) [*lysin* + Gr. *gennan* to produce]. A substance or body which produces a lysin.

lysogenesis (li″so-jen′e-sis). 1. The production of lysis or lysins. 2. Lysogenicity.

lysogenic (li-so-jen′ik) [*lysin* + Gr. *gennan* to produce]. 1. Producing lysins or causing lysis. 2. Pertaining to lysogenicity.

lysogenicity (li″so-je-nis′ĭ-te) [*lyso-* + Gr. *gennan* to produce + *-ity* condition]. 1. The ability to produce lysins or cause lysis. 2. The potentiality of a bacterium to produce phage. 3. Symbiosis of a bacterium with a phage.

lysogeny (li-soj′e-ne). Lysogenicity.

lysokinase (li″so-ki′nās). A general term for substances of the fibrinolytic system that activate the plasma proactivators.

lysolecithin (li″so-les′ĭ-thin). A lecithin from which the unsaturated fatty acid radical has been removed as by the action of cobra venom. It has strongly hemolytic properties.

lysophosphatide (li″so-fos′fah-tīd). A phosphate from which one molecule of fatty acid has been split off by the action of cobra venom.

lysosome (li′so-sōm) [*lyso-* + Gr. *sōma* body]. One of the minute bodies seen with the electron microscope in many types of cells, containing various enzymes, mainly hydrolytic. Injury to the cell is followed by release of the enzymes into the cell.

lysotype (li′so-tīp) [*lyso-* + *type*]. 1. The type of a microorganism as determined by its reactions to specific phages. 2. A taxonomic subdivision of bacteria based on their reactions to specific phages, or a formula expressing the reactions on which such a subdivision is based.

lysozym (li′so-zīm). Lysozyme.

lysozyme (li′so-zīm) [Gr. *lysis* dissolution + *zymē* leaven]. A crystalline, basic protein, which is present in saliva, tears, egg white, and many animal fluids and which functions as an antibacterial enzyme, especially effective in lysing *Micrococcus lysodeikticus.*

lyssa (lis′ah) [Gr. "frenzy"; "*the worm* under the tongue of dogs, removed because of the belief that it caused rabies"]. 1. Rabies. 2. Septum linguae.

lyssic (lis′ik). Pertaining to rabies, or to hydrophobia.

lysso- (lis′o) [Gr. *lyssa* frenzy]. Combining form denoting relationship to rabies, or hydrophobia.

lyssodexis (lis″o-dek′sis) [*lysso-* + Gr. *dexis* a bite]. The bite of a rabid dog.

lyssoid (lis′oid) [*lysso-* + Gr. *eidos* form]. Resembling rabies.

lyssophobia (lis″o-fo′be-ah) [*lysso-* + *phobia*]. Morbid dread of rabies, with symptoms simulating those of that disease: hydrophobophobia.

Lyster bag, tube (lis′ter) [William J. L. *Lyster*, U. S. Army surgeon, 1869–1947]. See under *bag* and *tube.*

lyterian (li-te′re-an). Indicative of the approach of lysis.

lytic (lit′ik). 1. Pertaining to lysis or to a lysin. 2. Producing lysis.

lytta (lit′ah). Hydrophobia.

lyxose (lik′sōs). A pentose isomeric with ribose, $CH_2OH.(CHOH)_3.CHO$.

lyze (līz). Lyse.

M

M. 1. Abbreviation for *Micrococcus, mil, mille,* thousand; *misce,* mix; *mistura,* mixture; *macerare,* macerate; *meter, minim, muscle, myopia, manipulus,* handful, and *mucoid* colony (see under *colony*); also symbol for *strength of pole.* 2. Symbol for *molar* (solution); the expressions M/10, M/100, etc., denote the strength of a solution in comparison with the molar, as tenth molar, hundredth molar, etc.

m. Abbreviation for *meta-* and *meter.*

μ. Mu, the twelfth letter of the Greek alphabet; symbol for *micron.* See also *mu.*

M.A. Abbreviation for *mental age, meter angle,* and *Master of Arts.*

Ma. Symbol for *masurium.*

ma. Abbreviation for *milliampere.*

M.A.B. British abbreviation for *Metropolitan Asylums Board.*

M.A.C. Abbreviation for *maximum allowable concentration* (of poisons encountered in industry, etc.).

Mac. Abbreviation for L. *macerare,* macerate.

macabuhay (mak″ah-boo-hi′). A plant of the Philippines, *Menispermum crispum:* febrifuge and emetic.

Macaca (mah-kak′ah). A genus of monkeys containing many species. **M. mulat′ta,** a species of monkeys widely used in physiological research.

macaja, macaya (mah-kah′yah). A fixed oil obtained from the fruit of *Acrocomia sclerocarpa.*

macalline (mah-kal′in). An alkaloid from macallo, a tree of Yucatan: used like quinine.

McArthur's method (mak-ar′thurz) [Louis Linn *McArthur*, Chicago surgeon, 1858–1934]. See under *method.*

McBurney's incision, point (mak-ber′nēz) [Charles *McBurney*, New York surgeon, 1845–1914]. See under *incision* and *point.*

McCarthy's reflex (mah-kar′thēz) [Daniel J. *McCarthy*, American neurologist, 1874–1958]. See under *reflex.*

McClintock's sign (mah-klin′toks) [Alfred Henry *McClintock*, Irish physician, 1822–1881]. See under *sign.*

MacConkey's agar, bouillon (mah-kon′kēz) [Alfred Theodore *MacConkey*, English bacteriologist, 1861–1931]. See under *agar* and *bouillon.*

McDowell's operation (mak-dow′elz) [Ephraim *McDowell*, American surgeon, 1771–1830]. See under *operation.*

mace (mās) [L. *macis*]. The dried aril or envelop of the fruit of the nutmeg tree, *Myristica fragrans.* The volatile oil contains macene, and is used as a flavoring agent.

maceration (mas″er-a′shun) [L. *maceratio*]. The softening of a solid by soaking. In obstetrics, the degenerative changes with discoloration and softening of tissues, and eventual disintegration, of a fetus retained in the uterus after its death.

macerative (mas′er-a″tiv). Characterized by maceration.

Macewen's operation, triangle, etc. (mak-u′enz) [Sir William *Macewen*, surgeon in Glasgow, 1848–1924]. See under the nouns.

McGinn-White sign (mak-gin′ hwit) [Sylvester *McGinn*, American cardiologist, born 1904; Paul D. *White*, American cardiologist, born 1886]. See under *sign*.

McGraw's ligature (mak-grawz′) [Theodore A. *McGraw*, surgeon in Detroit, Michigan, 1839–1921]. See under *ligature*.

Machaon (mak′ah-on). The older of two brothers, the younger being Podalirius, who were the sons of Æsculapius and, according to legend, were the chief medical officers attached to the Greek forces during the Trojan war.

Mache unit (mah′keh) [Heinrich *Mache*, Austrian physicist, born 1876]. See under *unit*.

machine (mah-shēn′) [L. *machina*]. A contrivance or apparatus for the production, conversion, or transmission of some form of energy or force. **Holtz m.,** an apparatus for developing static electricity.

machlosyne (mak″lo-si′ne) [Gr. *machlosynē*]. Lewdness or wantonness, especially in the female; nymphomania.

macho (mah′cho). The tubercle type of dermal leishmaniasis.

machonnement (mah-shōn-maw′) [Fr.]. A chewing motion of the jaws.

machromin (mak-ro′min). A yellow substance formed by reducing maclurin with zinc and sulfuric acid. It turns blue when oxidized.

Macht's test (makts) [David I. *Macht*, American pharmacologist, born 1882]. See under *tests*.

macies (ma′she-ēz) [L.]. Wasting.

macintosh (mak′in-tosh) [Charles *Macintosh*, Scottish chemist, 1766–1843, the inventor]. Cloth made waterproof by treating with a solution of India-rubber: used for surgical dressings.

macis (ma′sis) [L.]. Mace.

Mackenrodt's operation (mahk′en-rōts) [Alwin Karl *Mackenrodt*, German gynecologist, 1859–1925]. See under *operation*.

Mackenzie's disease (mah-ken′zēz) [Sir James *Mackenzie*, Scottish physician, 1853–1925]. See *x-disease*, under *disease*.

Mackenzie's syndrome (mah-ken′zēz) [Sir Stephen *Mackenzie*, London physician, 1844–1909]. See under *syndrome*.

Maclagan's thymol turbidity test (mak-lahg′anz) [Noel Francis *Maclagan*, English pathologist]. See *thymol turbidity test*, under *tests*.

McLean's formula, index (mak-lānz′) [Franklin C. *McLean*, American pathologist, born 1888]. See under *formula*.

MacLean-Maxwell disease (mak-lān′ maks′-wel) [Charles Murray *MacLean*, physician in West Africa; James Laidlaw *Maxwell*, English physician in Formosa]. See under *disease*.

Macleod (mak-lowd′), John James Rickard. Scottish physiologist, 1876–1935; co-winner, with Sir Frederick Grant Banting, of the Nobel prize for medicine and physiology in 1923.

MacLeod's rheumatism (mak-lowdz′) [Roderick *MacLeod*, Scottish physician, 1795–1852]. See under *rheumatism*.

MacMunn's test (mak-munz′) [Charles Alexander *MacMunn*, British pathologist, 1852–1911]. See under *tests*.

McPheeters' treatment (mak-fe′terz) [Herman Oscar *McPheeters*, American surgeon, born 1891]. See under *treatment*.

MacQuarrie's test (mah-kwor′ēz) [F. W. *MacQuarrie*, American psychologist]. See under *tests*.

Macracanthorhynchus (mak″rah-kan″tho-ring′kus). A genus of parasites of the class Acanthocephala. **M. hirudina′ceus,** a species parasitic in swine in the United States.

macradenous (mak-rad′e-nus) [*macro-* + Gr. *adēn* gland]. Having large glands.

macrencephalia (mak-ren″se-fa′le-ah) [*macro-* + Gr. *enkephalos* brain + *-ia*]. Overgrowth of the brain.

macrencephaly (mak″ren-sef′ah-le). Macrencephalia.

macro- (mak′ro) [Gr. *makros* large, or long]. Combining form meaning large, or abnormal size or length.

macrobacterium (mak″ro-bak-te′re-um). A large bacterium.

Macrobdella (mak″ro-del′ah). A genus of leeches. **M. deco′ra,** a species widely distributed in United States and Canada.

macrobiota (mak″ro-bi-o′tah). The macroscopic living organisms of a region; the combined macroflora and macrofauna of a region.

macrobiotic (mak″ro-bi-ot′ik). Pertaining to the macrobiota, or to macroscopic living organisms.

macroblast (mak′ro-blast) [*macro-* + Gr. *blastos* germ]. An abnormally large nucleated red blood cell; a large young normoblast; a megaloblast. **m. of Naegeli,** proerythroblast.

macroblepharia (mak″ro-blĕ-fa′re-ah) [*macro-* + Gr. *blepharon* eyelid]. Abnormal largeness of the eyelid.

macrobrachia (mak″ro-bra′ke-ah) [*macro-* + Gr. *brachiōn* arm]. Abnormal size or length of the arms.

macrocardius (mak″ro-kar′de-us) [*macro-* + Gr. *kardia* heart]. A fetal monster with an extremely large heart.

macrocephalia (mak″ro-se-fa′le-ah) [*macro-* + Gr *kephalē* head + *-ia*]. Excessive size of the head.

macrocephalic (mak″ro-se-fal′ik). Macrocephalous.

macrocephalous (mak″ro-sef′ah-lus). Having an excessively large head.

macrocephaly (mak″ro-sef′ah-le). Macrocephalia.

macrocheilia (mak″ro-ki′le-ah) [*macro-* + Gr. *cheilos* lip + *-ia*]. Excessive size of the lips.

macrocheiria (mak″ro-ki′re-ah) [*macro-* + Gr. *cheir* hand + *-ia*]. Excessive size of the hands.

macrochemical (mak″ro-kem′e-kal). Pertaining to macrochemistry.

macrochemistry (mak″ro-kem′is-tre) [*macro-* + *chemistry*]. Chemistry in which the reactions may be seen with the naked eye. Cf. *microchemistry*.

macrochilia (mak″ro-ki′le-ah). Macrocheilia.

macrochiria (mak″ro-ki′re-ah). Macrocheiria.

macroclitoris (mak″ro-klit′o-ris). Hypertrophy of the clitoris.

macrocnemia (mak″rok-ne′me-ah) [*macro-* + Gr. *knēmē* shin + *-ia*]. Abnormal size of the legs below the knee.

macrococcus (mak″ro-kok′us) [*macro-* + Gr. *kokkos* berry]. A bacterial coccus of the largest recognized type.

macrocolon (mak″ro-ko′lon). Excessive size of the colon.

macrocoly (mak″ro-ko′le). Macrocolon.

macroconidium (mak″ro-ko-nid′e-um), pl. *macroconidia* [*macro-* + *conidium*]. A large-sized conidium.

macrocornea (mak″ro-kor′ne-ah) [*macro-* + *cornea*]. Unusually large size of the cornea.

macrocrania (mak″ro-kra′ne-ah). Abnormal increase in the size of the skull, the facial area being disproportionately small in comparison.

macrocyst (mak′ro-sist) [*macro-* + *cyst*]. A large cyst.

macrocytase (mak″ro-si′tās). A cytase formed by the macrocytes, and capable of causing destruction of animal cells. Cf. *microcytase*.

macrocyte (mak′ro-sīt) [*macro-* + *-cyte*]. An abnormally large erythrocyte, i.e., one from 10 to 12 microns in diameter. Cf. *megalocyte* and *gigantocyte*.

macrocythemia (mak″ro-si-the′me-ah) [*macrocyte* + Gr. *haima* blood + *-ia*]. A condition in which the erythrocytes are larger than normal. **hyperchromatic m.,** macrocythemia in which the macrocytes are abnormally rich in hemoglobin; called also *macrocytic hyperchromatism*.

macrocytosis (mak″ro-si-to′sis). Macrocythemia.

macrodactylia (mak″ro-dak-til′e-ah). Macrodactyly.

macrodactyly (mak″ro-dak′tĭ-le) [*macro-* + Gr. *daktylos* finger]. Abnormal largeness of the fingers and toes.

macrodont (mak′ro-dont). Macrodontic.

macrodontia (mak-ro-don′she-ah) [*macro-* + Gr. *odous* tooth]. Abnormal increase in size of the teeth. It may affect a single tooth, or all of them (*generalized macrodontia*), and be true or only relative.

macrodontic (mak″ro-don′tik). Pertaining to or characterized by macrodontia.

macrodontism (mak″ro-don′tizm). Macrodontia.

macrodystrophia (mak″ro-dis-tro′fe-ah) [*macro-* + *dys-* + *trophē* nutrition]. Overgrowth of a part. **m. lipomato′sa progres′siva,** partial gigantism associated with tumor-like overgrowth of adipose tissue.

macroerythroblast (mak″ro-e-rith′ro-blast). A very large nucleated red blood corpuscle.

macroesthesia (mak″ro-es-the′ze-ah) [*macro-* + Gr. *aisthēsis* perception + *-ia*]. A sensory impression that all things are larger than they really are.

macrofauna (mak″ro-faw′nah). The animal life, visible to the naked eye, which is present in or characteristic of a special location.

macroflora (mak″ro-flo′rah). The plant life, visible to the naked eye, which is present in or characteristic of a special location.

macrogamete (mak″ro-gam′et) [*macro-* + Gr. *gametē* wife]. The female form of the malarial parasite which, fertilized by a flagellum in the mosquito, becomes an ookinete and goes through the exogenous cycle of development. See *gamete*.

macrogametocyte (mak″ro-gah-me′to-sīt) [*macro-* + Gr. *gametē* wife + *-cyte*]. The female form of the malarial parasite which, transferred from man to the mosquito, becomes a macrogamete.

macrogammaglobulin (mak″ro-gam″ah-glob′u-lin). A gamma globulin of extremely high molecular weight.

macrogammaglobulinemia (mak″ro-gam″ah-glob″u-lĭ-ne′me-ah). Presence in the blood of gamma globulins of extremely high molecular weight.

macrogamy (mak-rog′ah-me). Conjugation or fusion between adult protozoan individuals.

macrogastria (mak″ro-gas′tre-ah) [*macro-* + Gr. *gastēr* stomach + *-ia*]. Dilatation of the stomach.

macrogenesy (mak″ro-jen′e-se) [*macro-* + Gr. *genesis* production]. Gigantism.

macrogenitosomia (mak″ro-jen″ĭ-to-so′me-ah) [*macro-* + *genito-* + Gr. *sōma* body + *-ia*]. Excessive bodily development, with unusual enlargement of the genital organs. **m. prae′cox,** excessive bodily development, with marked enlargement of the genital organs, occurring at an unusually early age.

macrogingivae (mak″ro-jin-ji′ve). Fibromatosis gingivae.

macroglia (mak-rog′le-ah). Astroglia.

macroglobulin (mak″ro-glob′u-lin). A globulin of high molecular weight, in the 1,000,000 category, with sedimentation constants of 19S, as determined by ultracentrifugation; observed in the blood in a number of diseases, but mainly in various proliferative disturbances affecting the lymphoid plasma cell and reticuloendothelial systems.

macroglobulinemia (mak″ro-glob″u-lĭ-ne′me-ah) [*macroglobulin* + Gr. *haima* blood + *-ia*]. A condition characterized by increase in macroglobulins in the blood. **Waldenström's m.,** a form of macroglobulinemia first described by J. Waldenström, observed particularly in males past age 50, associated generally with adenopathy, hepatomegaly, splenomegaly, hemorrhagic phenomena, anemia, and lymphocytosis of the bone marrow.

macroglossia (mak″ro-glos′e-ah) [*macro-* + Gr. *glōssa* tongue + *-ia*]. Excessive size of the tongue.

macrognathia (mak″ro-na′the-ah) [*macro-* + Gr. *gnathos* jaw + *-ia*]. Enlargement of the jaw.

macrogonite (mak″ro-go′nīt). A large gonite.

macrographia (mak″ro-gra′fe-ah). Macrography.

macrography (mak-rog′rah-fe) [*macro-* + Gr. *graphein* to write]. The formation in writing of letters that are larger than the normal writing of the individual.

macrogyria (mak″ro-ji′re-ah) [*macro-* + *gyrus*]. Moderate reduction in the number of sulci of the cerebrum, sometimes with increase in the brain substance, resulting in excessive size of the gyri.

macrolabia (mak″ro-la′be-ah) [*macro-* + L. *labium* lip]. Macrocheilia.

macrolecithal (mak″ro-les′ĭ-thal) [*macro-* + Gr. *lekithos* yolk]. Having a large amount of yolk.

macroleukoblast (mak″ro-lu′ko-blast). A large leukoblast.

macrolymphocyte (mak″ro-lim′fo-sīt). A large lymphocyte.

macrolymphocytosis (mak-ro-lim″fo-si-to′sis). The formation of macrolymphocytes.

macromania (mak″ro-ma′ne-ah) [*macro-* + Gr. *mania* madness]. 1. Delusive belief that external objects or one's own members are larger than they really are. 2. Megalomania; delusions of grandeur.

macromastia (mak″ro-mas′te-ah) [*macro-* + Gr. *mastos* breast + *-ia*]. Oversize of the breasts or mammae.

macromazia (mak″ro-ma′ze-ah) [*macro-* + Gr. *mazos* breast + *-ia*]. Macromastia.

macromelia (mak″ro-me′le-ah). Enlargement of one or more members. **m. paraesthet′ica,** a sensation occurring in the initial form of acromegaly as well as in the formes frustes of hyperpituitarism in which the patient feels as if the head were growing larger and the extremities longer.

macromelus (mak-rom′e-lus) [*macro-* + Gr. *melos* limb]. A fetus with abnormally large or long limbs.

macromere (mak′ro-mēr) [*macro-* + Gr. *meros* part]. One of the large blastomeres formed by unequal cleavage of a fertilized ovum, located in the vegetal hemisphere and dividing less rapidly than the micromeres of the animal hemisphere.

macromerozoite (mak″ro-mer-o-zo′īt). A large merozoite.

macromethod (mak′ro-meth″od). A chemical method in which the substance to be analyzed is used in customary (not minute) quantity. Cf. *micromethod*.

macromimia (mak″ro-mim′e-ah). Excessive or exaggerated mimicry.

macromolecular (mak″ro-mo-lek′u-lar). Having large molecules.

Macromonas (mak″ro-mo′nas). A genus of microorganisms of the family Thiobacteriaceae, suborder Pseudomonadineae, order Pseudomonadales, occurring as colorless, cylindrical to bean-shaped bacteria characterized chiefly by the presence of calcium carbonate inclusions. It includes two species, *M. bipuncta′ta* and *M. mo′bilis*.

macromonocyte (mak″ro-mon′o-sīt). A very large monocyte.

macromyeloblast (mak″ro-mi′ĕ-lo-blast). A large myeloblast.

macronormoblast (mak″ro-nor′mo-blast). A very large nucleated red blood corpuscle; macroblast.

macronormochromoblast (mak″ro-nor″mo-kro′mo-blast). A macronormoblast.

macronormocyte (mak″ro-nor′mo-sīt). A giant red blood corpuscle.

macronucleus (mak″ro-nu′kle-us) [*macro-* + *nucleus*]. In ciliate protozoa, the larger of two types of nucleus in each cell, which is required for vegetative but not for sexual reproduction. Called also *trophic nucleus* or *trophonucleus*. Cf. *micronucleus*, def. 1.

macronychia (mak″ro-nik′e-ah) [*macro-* + Gr. *onyx* nail + *-ia*]. Abnormal length of the finger nails.

macropathology (mak″ro-pah-thol′o-je) [*macro-* + *pathology*]. The nonmicroscopical pathologic account of any disease or organ.

macrophage (mak′ro-fāj) [*macro-* + Gr. *phagein* to eat]. Metchnikoff's name for a large mononuclear wandering phagocytic cell which originates in the tissues. **fixed m.,** a quiescent phagocyte, such as the histiocyte of loose connective tissue or those lining the sinuses of the liver, spleen, lymph glands, and bone marrow. **free m.,** an ameboid phagocyte present at the site of inflammation; called also *polyblast* and *inflammatory macrophage*. **inflammatory m.,** free m.

macrophagocyte (mak″ro-fag′o-sīt). A phagocyte of relatively large size.

macrophagus (mak-krof′ah-gus). Macrophage.

macrophallus (mak″ro-fal′us) [*macro-* + Gr. *phallos* penis]. Abnormal largeness of the penis.

macrophotograph (mak″ro-fo′to-graf) [*macro-* + *photograph*]. An enlarged photograph.

macrophthalmia (mak″rof-thal′me-ah) [*macro-* + Gr. *ophthalmos* eye + *-ia*]. Abnormal enlargement of the eyeball.

macrophthalmous (mak″rof-thal′mus). Having abnormally large eyes.

macropia (mah-kro′pe-ah) [*macro-* + Gr. *ōps* eye]. Macropsia.

macroplasia (mak″ro-pla′ze-ah) [*macro-* + Gr. *plasis* forming + *-ia*]. Excessive growth of a part or tissue.

macroplastia (mak″ro-plas′te-ah). Macroplasia.

macropodia (mak″ro-po′de-ah) [*macro-* + Gr. *pous* foot + *-ia*]. Excessive size of the feet.

macropolycyte (mak″ro-pol′e-sit). A hypersegmented polymorphonuclear leukocyte of greater than normal size. Cf. *polycyte*.

macropromyelocyte (mak″ro-pro-mi′ĕ-lo-sīt). A very large promyelocyte.

macroprosopia (mak″ro-pro-so′pe-ah) [*macro-* + Gr. *prosōpon* face + *-ia*]. Excessive size of the face.

macropsia (mah-krop′se-ah) [*macro-* + Gr. *opsis* vision + *-ia*]. A disturbance of vision in which objects are seen as larger than they actually are.

macrorhinia (mak″ro-rin′e-ah) [*macro-* + Gr. *rhis* nose + *-ia*]. Excessive size of the nose.

macroscelia (mak″ro-se′le-ah) [*macro-* + Gr. *skelos* leg + *-ia*]. Excessive size of the legs.

macroscopic (mak″ro-skop′ik) [*macro-* + Gr. *skopein* to examine]. Visible with the unaided eye or without the microscope.

macroscopical (mak″ro-skop′e-kal). 1. Pertaining to macroscopy. 2. Macroscopic.

macroscopy (mah-kros′ko-pe). Examination with the naked eye.

macrosigma (mak″ro-sig′mah). Macrosigmoid.

macrosigmoid (mak″ro-sig′moid) [*macro-* + *sigmoid*]. Abnormal enlargement of the sigmoid.

macrosis (mah-kro′sis) [*macro-* + *-osis*]. Increase in size.

macrosmatic (mak″ros-mat′ik) [*macro-* + Gr. *osmasthai* to smell]. Having the sense of smell strongly or acutely developed.

macrosomatia (mak″ro-so-ma′she-ah) [*macro-* + Gr. *sōma* body]. Great bodily size. **m. adipo′sa congen′ita,** an obese type of premature development probably dependent on hyperfunction of the adrenal cortex.

macrosomia (mak″ro-so′me-ah). Macrosomatia.

macrosplanchnic (mak″ro-splank′nik) [*macro-* + Gr. *splanchnon* viscus]. Having large viscera: a term applied to that type of body constitution in which the horizontal diameters are excessively developed as compared with the vertical ones. Cf. *microsplanchnic* and *pyknic*.

macrospore (mak′ro-spōr) [*macro-* + Gr. *sporos* seed]. An unusually large spore.

macrostereognosia (mak″ro-ste″re-o-no′se-ah) [*macro-* + Gr. *stereos* solid + *gnōsis* knowledge + *-ia*]. Abnormality of perception in which objects felt seem larger than they really are.

Macrostoma mesnili (mak-ros′to-mah mes-ni′le). *Chilomastix mesnili.*

macrostomia (mak″ro-sto′me-ah) [*macro-* + Gr. *stoma* mouth + *-ia*]. Greatly exaggerated width of the mouth, resulting from failure of union of the maxillary and mandibular processes, with extension of the oral orifice to the ear. The defect may be unilateral or bilateral.

macrostructural (mak″ro-struk′tūr-al). Pertaining to gross structure.

macrotia (mak-ro′she-ah) [*macro-* + Gr. *ous* ear]. Abnormal enlargement of the pinna of the ear.

macrotome (mak′ro-tōm) [*macro-* + Gr. *tomē* cut]. An apparatus for cutting large sections of tissue for anatomical study.

macrotooth (mak′ro-tōōth), pl. *macroteeth*. An abnormally large tooth.

macrotys (mak-ro′tis). Cimicifuga.

macula (mak′u-lah), pl. *mac′ulae* [L.]. 1. A stain or spot; used in anatomical nomenclature as a general term to designate an area distinguishable by color or otherwise from its surroundings. 2. A discolored spot on the skin that is not elevated above the surface; applied also to a fairly well pronounced opacity of the cornea, appreciated as a gray spot in daylight. **acoustic maculae, mac′ulae acus′ticae** [B N A]. See *m. sacculi* and *m. utriculi*. **m. acus′tica sac′culi** [B N A], m. sacculi. **m. acus′tica utric′uli** [B N A], m. utriculi. **mac′ulae al′bidae,** white spots sometimes seen after death on the serous layer of the peritoneum. **mac′ulae atroph′icae,** white patches resembling scars formed on the skin by atrophy. **mac′ulae caeru′leae,** bluish patches on the skin sometimes seen in pediculosis. **cerebral m.,** tache cérébrale. **m. commu′nis,** a thickened area on the wall of the otic vesicle which divides into the macula sacculi and macula utriculi. **m. cor′neae,** a circumscribed opacity of the cornea. **mac′ulae cribro′sae** [N A, B N A]. See *m. cribrosa inferior*, *m. cribrosa media*, and *m. cribrosa superior*. **m. cribro′sa infe′rior** [N A, B N A], the perforated area on the wall of the vestibule through which branches of the vestibulocochlear nerve pass to the posterior semicircular canal. **m. cribro′sa me′dia** [N A, B N A], the perforated area on the vestibular wall through which branches of the vestibulocochlear nerve pass to the sacculus. **m. cribro′sa supe′rior** [N A, B N A], the perforated area on the vestibular wall through which branches of the vestibulocochlear nerve pass to the utricle and to the anterior and lateral semicircular canals. **m. den′sa,** a zone composed of heavily nucleated cells, located in the distal renal tubule where it makes contact with the vascular pole of the glomerulus, and closely associated anatomically with the juxtaglomerular cells of the afferent arteriole. **false m.,** the extramacular point on the retina of a squinting eye which receives the same light stimulus as the macula of the fixing eye. **m. fla′va laryn′gis** [B N A], a yellowish nodule visible at one end of a vocal cord. Omitted in N A. **m. fla′va ret′inae,** m. retinae. **m. follic′uli,** the point on the surface of a vesicular ovarian follicle where rupture occurs. **m. germinati′va,** germinal area. **m. gonorrhoe′ica,** the red inflamed orifice of the duct of Bartholin's gland in gonorrheal vulvitis. Called also *Saenger's m.* **mac′ulae lac′teae,** maculae albidae. **m. lu′tea ret′inae** [B N A], m. retinae. **maculae of**

membranous labyrinth. See *m. sacculi* and *m. utriculi.* **Mongolian maculae,** Mongolian spots. **m. ret′inae,** an irregular yellowish depression on the retina, about 3 degrees wide, lateral to and slightly below the optic disk; it is the site of absorption of short wavelengths of light, and it is thought that its variation in size, shape, and coloring may be related to variant types of color vision. Called also *m. lutea retinae* [B N A]. **Robert's m.,** a mass of coloring matter seen in the red corpuscles when blood is treated with dilute tannic acid solution. **m. sac′culi** [N A], a thickening in the wall of the saccule where the epithelium contains hair cells that receive and transmit vestibular impulses. Called also *m. acustica sacculi* [B N A]. **Saenger's m.,** m. gonorrhoeica. **m. sola′ris,** a freckle. **mac′ulae tendin′eae,** maculae albidae. **m. utric′uli** [N A], a thickening in the wall of the utricle where the epithelium contains hair cells that receive and transmit vestibular impulses. Called also *m. acustica utriculi* [B N A].

maculae (mak′u-le) [L.]. Plural of *macula.*

macular (mak′u-lar). Pertaining to or characterized by the presence of maculae.

maculate (mak′u-lāt) [L. *maculatus* spotted]. Spotted or blotched.

maculation (mak″u-la′shun) [L. *macula* spot]. The condition of being spotted; the formation of spots or macules. **pernicious m.,** a coarse dark-violet maculation seen in severe forms of tropical malaria.

macule (mak′ūl). A macula

maculocerebral (mak″u-lo-ser′e-bral). Pertaining to the macula retinae and the brain.

maculopapular (mak″u-lo-pap′u-lar). Both macular and papular.

maculopapule (mak″u-lo-pap′ūl). A lesion resembling both a macule and a papule.

MacWilliam's test (mak-wil′yamz) [John Alexander *MacWilliam,* British physician, 1857–1937]. See under *tests.*

mad (mad). 1. Affected with madness. 2. Affected with rabies; rabid.

madarosis (mad″ah-ro′sis) [Gr. *madaros* bald]. Loss of the eyelashes or eyebrows (Galen).

madder (mad′er). The root of *Rubia tinctoria,* affording a red dye.

Maddox prism, rod (mad′oks) [Ernest Edmund *Maddox,* English ophthalmologist, 1860–1933]. See under *prism* and *rod.*

madefaction (mad″e-fak′shun) [L. *madefacere* to moisten]. The act of moistening or making wet.

Madelung's deformity, disease, neck, operation, sign [Otto Wilhelm *Madelung,* surgeon in Strasbourg, 1846–1926]. See under the nouns.

madescent (mah-des′ent) [L. *madescere* to become moist]. Slightly moist.

madidans (mad′ĭ-dans). Moist, wet.

Madurella (mad″u-rel′ah). The type of organisms found in mycetoma which have septate mycelia.

maduromycosis (mah-du″ro-mi-ko′sis). A chronic disease caused by a variety of fungi, affecting the foot, hands, legs and other parts including the internal organs. The most common form is that of the foot, known as *Madura foot.* Following infection through a penetrating wound, the deep tissues become necrosed, sinuses form and there is marked swelling of the feet, in which nodules and vesicles develop. The parts become filled with sinuses, which discharge pus and penetrate into the bone. The pus contains granules, red, black, or yellow in color, which are masses of the fungus that is the cause of the disease.

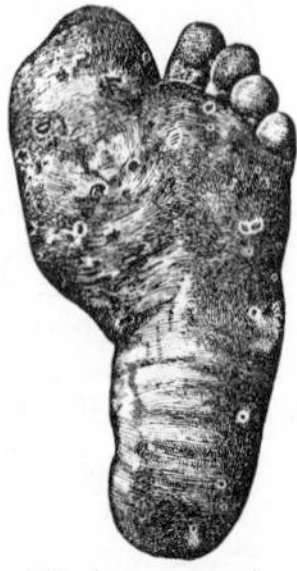

Maduromycosis.

mafenide (maf′en-īd). Chemical name: α-amino-p-toluenesulfonamide: used in the topical treatment of superficial infections.

Mag. Abbreviation for L. *mag′nus,* large.

mageiric (mah-ji′rik) [Gr. *mageirikos* relating to cookery]. Pertaining to cookery or dietetics.

magenblase (mah″gen-blah′zĕ) [Ger. "stomach bubble"]. In the radiogram of the stomach, a dark area above the light shadow of the opaque meal, marking a collection of gas in the upper part of the stomach.

Magendie's foramen, law, solution, spaces (ma-jen′dēz) [François *Magendie,* French physiologist, 1783–1855; the pioneer of experimental physiology in France]. See under the nouns.

magenstrasse (mah″gen-stras′sĕ) [Ger. "stomach street"]. A portion of the lesser curvature of the stomach which exhibits longitudinal furrows; along this "street" propulsion of the gastric contents is effected.

magenta (mah-jen′tah). Basic fuchsin. **acid m.,** acid fuchsin. **basic m.,** basic fuchsin.

magersucht (mah′ger-sookt) [Ger.]. Pathologic leanness.

maggot (mag′ot). A soft-bodied larva of an insect, especially a form living in decaying flesh. The living maggots of the bluebottle fly (*Lucilia sericata* and *Phormia regina*) have been used in the treatment of osteomyelitis and other suppurative infections in order to clear away dead tissue and promote healing, this latter effect being due to the allantoin in the secretions of the maggots. **Congo floor m.,** Auchmeromyia. **rat-tail m.,** a maggot of a hover-fly of the genera *Tubipra* and *Helophilus;* they cause intestinal and nasal myiasis. **sheep m.,** the maggot of *Lucilia sericata* which invades the tissue of sheep in the British Isles and elsewhere.

magistery (maj′is-ter″e) [L. *magisterium; magister* master]. A precipitate; any subtle or masterly preparation.

magistral (maj′is-tral) [L. *magister* master]. Pertaining to a master: applied to medicines that are prepared in accordance with a physician's prescription.

Magitot's disease (mazh″ĭ-tōz′) [Emile *Magitot,* French dentist, 1833–1897]. See under *disease.*

magma (mag′mah) [Gr. *massein* to knead]. 1. A suspension of finely divided material in a small amount of water. 2. A thin, paste-like substance composed of organic material. **bentonite m.,** a preparation of bentonite and purified water: used as a suspending agent. **bismuth m.,** a suspension of bismuth hydroxide and bismuth subcarbonate in water: antidiarrheic. **magnesia m.,** a suspension of 7 to 8.5 per cent of magnesium hydroxide: used as a laxative and antacid. **m. reticula′re,** a mesenchymal reticulum within the early chorionic sac.

magnacort (mag′nah-kort). Trade mark for a preparation of hydrocortamate.

Magnan's movement, sign (mag′nanz) [Valentin Jacques Joseph *Magnan,* alienist in Paris, 1835–1916]. See under *movement* and *sign.*

magnesemia (mag″nēs-e′me-ah). The presence of magnesium in the blood.

magnesia (mag-ne′ze-ah) [the name of a district in ancient Lydia]. Magnesium oxide. **m. al′ba,** magnesium carbonate. **m. calcina′ta,** magnesium oxide. **m. carbonata′da,** magnesium carbonate. **m. us′ta,** magnesium oxide.

magnesic (mag-ne′sik). Relating to or containing magnesium or one of its compounds.

magnesiemia (mag″ne-se-e′me-ah). Magnesemia.

magnesite (mag-ne′sīt). Native magnesium carbonate, $MgCO_3$: used like plaster of paris in splints and dressings.

magnesium (mag-ne′ze-um), gen. *magne′sii* [L.]. A white, metallic element; symbol, Mg; atomic number, 12; atomic weight, 24.312; specific gravity, 1.74. It is essential in nutrition, deficiency producing trophic disturbances, nutritive failure and increased irritability of the nervous system such as tetany, vasodilation and death in convulsions. **m. benzoate,** a white, crystalline powder, $(C_6H_5.CO_2)_2Mg.3H_2O$, which has been used in gout and rheumatism. **m. bromide,** colorless deliquescent crystals, $MgBr_2.6H_2O$. **m. carbonate,** a basic hydrated magnesium carbonate containing the equivalent of 40 to 43.5 per cent of magnesium oxide: used as an antacid. **m. chloride,** colorless transparent crystals, $MgCl_2.6H_2O$: formerly used as a laxative. **m. hydroxide,** a bulky white powder, $Mg(OH)_2$: used as a laxative and gastric antacid. **m. lactate,** a colorless crystalline salt, $(CH_3.CHOH.CO_2)_2Mg + 3H_2O$: aperient. **m. oxide,** a bulky (*light m. oxide*) or relatively dense (*heavy m. oxide*) white powder, containing, after ignition, at least 96 per cent of MgO: used as a gastric antacid. **m. peroxide,** MgO_2: a white powder, insoluble in water, but gradually decomposed with the liberation of oxygen. **m. phosphate, dibasic,** a salt, $MgHPO_4.3H_2O$: mild saline laxative. **m. phosphate, tribasic,** a salt, $Mg_3(PO_4)_2.5H_2O$: used as a gastric antacid. **m. salicylate,** a colorless or slightly reddish, efflorescent, crystalline powder, $Mg[C_6H_4(OH)CO_2]_2$: intestinal antiseptic. **m. stearate,** a compound of magnesium with varying proportions of stearic and palmitic acids: used as a dusting powder. **m. sulfate,** a white, crystalline salt, $MgSO_4.7H_2O$: active saline cathartic. **m. sulfate, exsiccated,** hydrated magnesium sulfate the weight of which has been reduced 25 per cent by drying at 100°C.: aperient. **m. trisilicate,** a compound of magnesium oxide and silicon dioxide with varying proportions of water: used as a gastric antacid.

magnet (mag′net) [L. *magnes;* Gr. *magnēs* magnet]. A lodestone; native iron oxide that attracts iron; also a bar of steel or iron that attracts iron and has magnetic polarity. **Grüning's m.,** one made up of a number of steel rods: used in removing metal particles from the eye. **Haab's m.,** a powerful magnet for extracting foreign metallic bodies from the eye. **Hirschberg's m.,** an electromagnet for removing particles of iron from the eye. **horseshoe m.,** a magnet shaped like the letter U. **permanent m.,** one with permanent magnetic qualities. **temporary m.,** a substance that possesses magnetic properties only during the passage of an electric current or when a permanent magnet is near it.

magnetic (mag-net′ik). Pertaining to, derived from, or having the properties of, a magnet.

magnetism (mag′ne-tizm). Magnetic attraction or repulsion. **animal m.,** a hypothetical nervous power which can be projected to another person for curative or other purposes.

magnetization (mag″net-i-za′shun). The act or process of rendering an object or substance magnetic.

magnetoconstriction (mag-ne″to-kon-strik′shun). A change in the dimensions of a body produced by the application of a magnetic field.

magneto-electricity (mag-ne″to-e″lek-tris′ĭ-te). Electricity induced by means of a magnet.

magneto-induction (mag-ne″to-in-duk′shun). Magnetic induction.

magnetology (mag″ne-tol′o-je). That branch of physics which treats of magnetics.

magnetometer (mag″ne-tom′e-ter) [*magnetic* + Gr. *metron* measure]. An apparatus for measuring magnetic forces.

magneton (mag′ne-ton). An ultimate elemental magnetic particle.

magnetotherapy (mag-ne″to-ther′ah-pe). The treatment of disease by magnets or by magnetism.

magnetron (mag′ne-tron). An electric vacuum tube for generating extremely short electromagnetic waves (microwaves).

magnetropism (mag-net′ro-pizm) [*magnet* + Gr. *tropē* a turn, turning]. A growth response in a non-motile organism under the influence of a magnet.

magnification (mag″nĭ-fi-ka′shun) [L. *magnificatio; magnus* great + *facere* to make]. Apparent increase in size under the microscope.

magnify (mag′nĭ-fi) [L. *magnus* great + *facere* to make]. To cause to appear larger than is natural by the use of lenses or suitable mirrors.

magniscope (mag′nĭ-skōp). A variety of chromophotograph.

Magnolia (mag-no′le-ah) [after Pierre *Magnol,* 1638–1715]. A genus of magnoliaceous trees.

magnolia (mag-no′le-ah). The bitter aromatic bark of *Magnolia acuminata, M. glauca,* and *M. tripetala:* diaphoretic and antifebrile.

magnum (mag′num) [L.]. Great.

mahamari (mah″hah-mah′re). The native name for a form of plague occurring in the southern slopes of the Himalayas.

Maher's disease (ma′herz) [J. J. E. *Maher,* New York physician, 1857–1931]. Paracolpitis.

Mahler's sign (mah′lerz) [Richard A. *Mahler,* German obstetrician]. See under *sign.*

ma huang (mah hoo-ang′). The native name for a Chinese variety of *Ephedra vulgaris.*

maidism (ma′ĭ-dizm) [L. *mais* maize]. Poisoning by damaged maize; pellagra.

maidismus (ma″ĭ-diz′mus). Maidism.

Maier's sinus (mi′erz) [Rudolf *Maier,* German physician, 1824–1888]. See under *sinus.*

maieusiomania (mi-u″se-o-ma′ne-ah) [Gr. *maieusis* childbirth + *mania*]. Puerperal mania.

maieusiophobia (mi-u″se-o-fo′be-ah) [Gr. *maieusis* childbirth + *phobia*]. Morbid dread of childbirth.

maieutic (mi-u′tik) [Gr. *maieutikos* of or for midwifery]. 1. Obstetrical. 2. A rubber bag attached over the end of a catheter for dilating the uterine cervix.

maieutics (mi-u′tiks) [Gr. *maieutikē* midwifery]. Obstetrics.

maim (mām). 1. To disable by a wound; to dismember by violence. 2. A dismemberment or disablement effected by violence.

Maimonides (mi-mon′ĭ-dēz) (1135–1204). Rabbi Moses ben Maimon, called the greatest Jew after Moses, a native of Spain who later practiced medicine in Morocco and Egypt. A prayer attributed to him is considered to rank beside the oath of Hippocrates as an ethical guide to the medical profession.

main (mān) [Fr.]. Hand. **m. d'accoucheur** (mān″dak-oo-shuhr′), obstetrician's hand. **m. de tranchées** (mān″dŭ-tran-sha′), trench hand. **m. en crochet** (ma″nong-kro-sha′), a permanently flexed condition of the third and fourth fingers. **m. en griffe** (ma″nong-grif′), claw-hand. **m. en lorgnette** (ma″nong-lor-nyet′), opera-glass hand. **m. en pince** (ma″nong-pins′), cleft hand. **m. en singe** (ma″nong-sēnzh′), monkey hand. **m. en squelette** (ma″nong-skel-et′), skeleton hand. **m. fourché** (mān″-foor-sha′), cleft hand. **m. succulente** (mān″-suk-u-lent′). See *Marinesco's succulent hand.*

Mainini test (mi-ne′ne). See *Galli Mainini,* and under *tests.*

maise (māz) [L. *mais* maize]. Indian corn; a cereal grain, the seed of *Zea mays.*

maisin (ma′zin). A protein found in the seeds of maize.

maisonneuve (ma″zo-nev′). Maisonneuve's urethrotome.

Maisonneuve's bandage, urethrotome (ma″zo-nevz′) [Jules Germain François *Maisonneuve,* French surgeon, 1809–1897]. See under the nouns.

Maissiat's band (ma″se-ahz′) [Jacques Henri *Maissiat,* French anatomist, 1805–1878]. See under *band.*

Maixner's cirrhosis (mīks′nerz) [Emmerich *Maixner*, Prague physician, 1847–1920]. A form of portal cirrhosis with copious gastric and intestinal hemorrhage, enlargement of the spleen, ascites, and diarrhea.

maizenate (ma′zen-āt). Any salt of maizenic acid.

Majocchi's disease, purpura (mah-yok′ēz) [Domenico *Majocchi*, Italian physician, 1849–1929]. Purpura annularis telangiectodes.

make (māk). The closure and completion of an electric circuit.

Makins' murmur (ma′kinz) [Sir George Henry *Makins*, British surgeon, 1853–1933]. See under *murmur*.

makro- (mak′ro). For words thus beginning, see those beginning *macro-*.

mal (mahl) [Fr.; L. *malum* ill]. Disease. **m. de abajo,** Peruvian name for uterine cancer or syphilis. **m. d'aviateur,** aviators' disease. **m. de Boeck,** Boeck's sarcoid. **m. de caderas,** a disease of horses, mules, and dogs in South America which is characterized by weakness, especially of the hind quarters, and a staggering, swinging gait. It is caused by *Trypanosoma equinum* which is probably transmitted by tabanid flies. **m. de Cayenne,** elephantiasis. **m. de coit,** dourine. **m. comitial,** epilepsy. **m. d'engasgo,** entalação. **m. d'estomac,** ancylostomiasis. **grand m.** See *epilepsy*. **m. de la rosa,** pellagra. **m. de los pintos,** pinta. **m. de Meleda,** symmetrical keratosis of the palms and soles associated with an ichthyotic thickening of the wrists and ankles, occurring endemically in the island of Meleda. **m. de mer,** sea-sickness. **m. perforant,** perforating ulcer of the foot. **m. perforant palatin,** perforating ulcer of the roof of the mouth. **petit m.** See *epilepsy*. **m. de quebracho,** paaj. **m. de siete dias,** seven-day disease. **m. del sole,** pellagra. **m. de Zousfana,** a disease of horses in Algeria; probably a form of surra.

mala (ma′lah) [L.]. The cheek or cheek bone.

malabsorption (mal″ab-sorp′shun). Disorder of normal nutritive absorption; disordered anabolism.

Malacarne's pyramid, space (mal″ah-kar′nāz) [Michele Vincenzo Giacintos *Malacarne*, Italian surgeon, 1744–1816]. See under *pyramid* and *space*.

malacia (mah-la′she-ah) [Gr. *malakia*]. 1. The morbid softening or softness of a part or tissue. 2. Craving for highly spiced food and dishes, as pickles, salads, mustard, etc. **metaplastic m.,** osteitis fibrosa cystica. **myeloplastic m.,** osteogenesis imperfecta. **porotic m.,** softening accompanied by proliferation of connective tissue. **m. traumat′ica,** Kienböck's disease (def. 2.).

malacic (mah-la′sik). Marked by malacia or morbid softness.

malaco- (mal′ah-ko) [Gr. *malakos* soft]. Combining form meaning a condition of abnormal softness.

malacoma (mal″ah-ko′mah) [*malaco-* + *-oma*]. A morbidly soft part or spot.

malacopathia (mal″ah-ko-path′e-ah) [*malaco-* + Gr. *pathos* disease]. Köhler's disease.

malacoplakia (mal″ah-ko-pla′ke-ah) [*malaco-* + Gr. *plax* plaque]. The formation of soft patches on the mucous membrane of a hollow organ. **m. vesi′cae,** a soft, yellowish, fungus-like growth on the mucous membrane of the bladder and ureters.

malacosarcosis (mal″ah-ko-sar-ko′sis) [*malaco-* + Gr. *sarx* flesh]. Softness of muscular tissue.

malacosis (mal″ah-ko′sis). Malacia.

malacosteon (mal″ah-kos′te-on) [*malaco-* + Gr. *osteon* bone]. Osteomalacia.

malacotic (mal″ah-kot′ik). Inclined to malacia; soft: said of teeth.

malacotomy (mal″ah-kot′o-me) [*malaco-* + Gr. *tomē* a cutting]. Incision of the abdominal wall.

malactic (mah-lak′tik). 1. Softening, emollient. 2. An emollient medicine.

maladie (mal″ah-de′) [Fr.]. A disease. **m. bleue,** morbus caeruleus. **m. bronzée** (braw-za′). 1. Epidemic hemoglobinuria. 2. Addison's disease. **m. de Carré** (duh kah-ra′), canine distemper. **m. de coit** (duh kwah′), dourine. **m. cystique** (sis-tēk′), cystic degeneration of the breast. **m. des jambes** (da-zhamb′), a disease of rice growers in Louisiana, probably beriberi. **m. de plongeurs** (duh-plon-zher′), inflammation and ulceration in divers in the Mediterranean caused by the stings of sea anemones. **m. de Roger,** Roger's disease. **m. du sommeil** (du-so-ma′e), sleeping sickness. **m. de Woillez** (duh woy-ya′), Woillez's disease.

maladjustment (mal″ad-just′ment). In psychiatry, defective adaptation to environment, marked by anxiety, depression, and irritability.

malady (mal′ah-de) [Fr. *maladie*]. Any disease or illness.

malagma (mah-lag′mah) [Gr.]. An emollient or cataplasm.

malaise (mal-āz′) [Fr.]. A vague feeling of bodily discomfort.

malakoplakia (mal″ah-ko-pla′ke-ah). Malacoplakia.

malalignment (mal″ah-līn′ment). Displacement out of line, especially displacement of the teeth from their normal relation to the line of the dental arch.

malalinement (mal″ah-līn′ment). Malalignment.

malanders (mal′an-derz). A scab variety of eczema above the forefoot and about the knee of a horse. Called also *mallenders* and *callenders*.

malar (ma′lar) [L. *mala* cheek]. Pertaining to the cheek or cheek bone.

malaria (mah-la′re-ah) [It. "bad air"]. An infectious febrile disease caused by protozoa of the genus *Plasmodium* which are transmitted by the bites of infected mosquitoes of the genus *Anopheles*. The disease is characterized by attacks of chills, fever, and sweating, occurring at intervals which depend on the time required for development of a new generation of parasites in the body. After recovery from the acute attack, the disease has a tendency to become chronic, with occasional relapses. **algid m.,** falciparum malaria with coldness of the skin and prostration due to involvement of the vessels of the gastrointestinal tract. **bovine m.,** Texas fever. **cerebral m.,** falciparum malaria with delirium or coma, as a result of localization of parasites in the brain. **cold m.,** algid m. **m. comato′sa,** cerebral malaria characterized by coma. **estivoautumnal m.,** falciparum m. **falciparum m.,** the most serious form of malaria, caused by *Plasmodium falciparum*, characterized by severe constitutional symptoms and sometimes causing death. **hemolytic m.,** blackwater fever. **hemorrhagic m.,** falciparum malaria in which hemorrhage is a prominent symptom. **induced m.,** malaria that is purposely produced by introduction of the causative parasites, as sometimes used in treating neurosyphilis. **ovale m.,** a mild disease caused by infection with *Plasmodium ovale*, usually characterized by a few regularly recurring tertian febrile paroxysms, beginning with a feeling of chilliness or cold shivers rather than the rigors typical of vivax malaria, and tending to end in spontaneous recovery. **pernicious m.,** falciparum m. **quartan m.,** that in which the febrile paroxysms occur every fourth day, counting the day of occurrence as the first day; caused by *Plasmodium malariae*, which requires 72 hours for completion of each asexual cycle in the erythrocyte. **quotidian m.,** that in which the febrile paroxysms occur daily. **tertian m.,** that in which the febrile paroxysms occur every third day, counting the day of occurrence as the first day. **therapeutic m.,** induced m. **vivax m.,** malaria caused by *Plasmodium vivax*, the form most common, mildest, and most likely to recur; the febrile paroxysms commonly occur every other day (tertian m.), but may occur daily (quotidian m.), if there are two broods of parasites segmenting on alternate days.

malariacidal (mah-la″re-ah-si′dal). Destructive to malarial plasmodia; plasmodicidal.

malarial (mah-la′re-al). Pertaining or due to malaria.

malarialization (mah-la″re-al-i-za′shun). Treatment by the production of malaria in a patient.

malarialize (mah-la′re-al-īz). To infect with malaria, especially to inject malarial organisms into the body for the treatment of dementia paralytica.

malariated (mah-la′re-āt-ed). Affected with malaria.

malariatherapy (mah-la″re-ah-ther′ah-pe). Malariotherapy.

malariologist (mah-la″re-ol′o-jist). A person versed in or engaged in the study of malaria.

malariology (mah-la″re-ol′o-je) [*malaria* + *-logy*]. The study of malaria.

malariometry (mah-la″re-om′e-tre). The employment of quantitative methods in the study of malaria.

malariotherapy (mah-la″re-o-ther′ah-pe). Treatment of general paralysis or paresis by infecting the patient with the parasite of tertian malaria.

malarious (mah-la′re-us). Pertaining to or marked by the presence of malaria.

malaris (mah-la′ris) [L.]. Malar.

Malassez's disease, rests (mal″ah-sāz′) [Louis Charles *Malassez*, physiologist in Paris, 1842–1910]. See under *disease* and *rest*.

Malassezia (mal″ah-se′ze-ah) [Louis Charles *Malassez*]. A genus of fungi. **M. fur′fur,** a species sometimes causing a noninflammatory infection of the skin. Called also *M. macfadyani*, *M. tropica*, and *Microsporon furfur*.

Malassezia (de Rivas).

malassimilation (mal″ah-sim″ĭ-la′shun) [L. *malus* ill + *assimilatio* a rendering like]. Imperfect, faulty, or disordered assimilation.

malate (ma′lāt). Any salt of malic acid.

malaxate (mal′aks-āt). To knead, as in making pills.

malaxation (mal″ak-sa′shun) [Gr. *malaxis* a softening]. An act of kneading.

malcoeur (mal-ker′). Ancylostomiasis.

maldigestion (mal″di-jes′chun). Impaired digestion.

male (māl). 1. An organism of the sex that begets young or that produces spermatozoa. 2. Masculine.

malemission (mal″e-mish′un). Failure of the semen to be discharged from the urinary meatus in coitus.

Malerba's test (mah-ler′bahz) [Pasquale *Malerba*, Italian physician, 1849–1917]. See under *tests*.

maleruption (mal″e-rup′shun). Faulty eruption of a tooth, so that it is out of its normal position.

malformation (mal″for-ma′shun) [L. *malus* evil + *formatio* a forming]. Defective or abnormal formation; deformity.

malfunction (mal-funk′shun). Dysfunction.

Malgaigne's amputation, fossa, hernia, hook, pads (mal-gānz′) [Joseph François *Malgaigne*, French surgeon, 1806–1865]. See under the nouns.

maliasmus (mal″e-as′mus). Glanders, or farcy.

malignancy (mah-lig′nan-se) [L. *malignare* to act maliciously]. A tendency to progress in virulence; the quality of being malignant.

malignant (mah-lig′nant) [L. *malignans* acting maliciously]. Tending to become progressively worse and to result in death.

malignogram (mah-lig′no-gram). A systematic arrangement of numerical values assigned to the various factors in cases of carcinoma.

mali-mali (mah″le-mah′le). A form of palmus, or jumping disease, endemic in the Philippines.

malingerer (mah-ling′ger-er) [Fr. *malingre* sickly]. An individual who is guilty of malingering.

malingering (mah-ling′ger-ing). The willful, deliberate, and fraudulent feigning or exaggeration of the symptoms of illness or injury, done for the purpose of a consciously desired end.

malinterdigitation (mal″in-ter-dij″ĭ-ta′shun). Failure of interdigitation of parts which are normally so related.

Mall's formula (mahlz) [Franklin Paine *Mall*, Baltimore anatomist, 1862–1917]. See under *formula*.

malleability (mal″e-ah-bil′ĭ-te). The quality of being malleable.

malleable (mal′e-ah-b′l) [L. *malleare* to hammer]. Susceptible of being beaten out into a thin plate.

mallease (mal′e-ās). A neutralized and filtered solution of glanders bacilli used in testing for glanders.

malleation (mal″e-a′shun) [L. *malleare* to hammer]. Sharp and swift muscular twitching of the hands.

mallein (mal′e-in) [L. *malleus* glanders]. A fluid from cultures of the glanders bacillus or an extract of the bacillus: used in the diagnosis of glanders, since, when injected into an animal affected with glanders, it causes a rise of temperature.

malleinization (mal″e-in″i-za′shun). Inoculation with mallein.

malleoidosis (mal″e-oi-do′sis). Melioidosis.

malleo-incudal (mal″e-o-ing′ku-dal). Pertaining to the malleus and incus.

malleolar (mal-e′o-lar). Pertaining to a malleolus.

malleoli (mal-le′o-li) [L.]. Plural of *malleolus*.

malleolus (mal-le′o-lus), pl. *malle′oli* [L., dim. of *malleus* hammer]. A rounded process, such as the protuberance on either side of the ankle joint. **external m., m. exter′nus,** m. lateralis. **m. fib′ulae, fibular m.,** m. lateralis fibulae. **inner m., internal m., m. inter′nus,** m. medialis. **lateral m.,** m. lateralis. **lateral m. of fibula,** m. lateralis fibulae. **m. latera′lis** [N A, B N A], the rounded protuberance on the lateral surface of the ankle joint, produced by the m. lateralis fibulae. **m. latera′lis fib′ulae** [N A, B N A], the process at the outer side of the lower end of the fibula, forming, with the malleolus medialis tibiae, the mortise in which the talus articulates. Called also *lateral m. of fibula*. **medial m.,** m. medialis. **medial m. of tibia,** m. medialis tibiae. **m. media′lis** [N A, B N A], the rounded protuberance on the medial surface of the ankle joint, produced by the m. medialis tibiae. **m. media′lis tib′iae** [N A, B N A], the process at the inner side of the lower end of the tibia, forming, with the malleolus lateralis fibulae, the mortise in which the talus articulates. Called also *medial m. of tibia*. **outer m.,** m. lateralis. **radial m., m. radia′lis,** processus styloideus radii. **m. tib′iae, tibial m.,** m. medialis tibiae. **ulnar m., m. ulna′ris,** processus styloideus ulnae.

Malleomyces (mal″e-o-mi′sēz) [L. *malleus* glanders + Gr. *mykēs* fungus]. A name formerly given a genus of schizomycetes (order Eubacteriales). **M. mal′lei,** *Actinobacillus mallei*. **M. pseudomal′lei, M. whitmo′ri,** *Pseudomonas pseudomallei*.

malleotomy (mal″e-ot′o-me) [*malleus* + Gr. *tomē*

a cutting]. 1. The operation of dividing the malleus in cases of ankylosis of the ossicles of the middle ear. 2. The operation of separating the malleoli by dividing the ligaments which hold them together.

malleus (mal′e-us) [L. "hammer"]. 1. [N A, B N A] The largest of the auditory ossicles, and the one attached to the membrana tympani. Its club-shaped head articulates with the incus. Called also *hammer*. 2. Glanders.

mallochorion (mal″o-ko′re-on) [Gr. *mallos* wool + *chorion*]. The primitive mammalian chorion; so called from its villi.

Mallophaga (mal-of′ah-gah) [Gr. *mallos* wool + *phagein* to eat]. An order of biting lice, the bird lice, which feed on the feathers and hair of birds and which may attack man.

Mallory's bodies, stain (mal′o-rēz) [Frank Burr *Mallory*, pathologist in Boston, 1862–1941]. See under *body* and *stain*.

mallotoxin (mal″o-tok′sin). Rottlerin.

mallow (mal′o) [L. *malva*]. Any plant of the genus *Malva*. The flowers and leaves of *M. sylvestris* and *M. rotundifolia* are demulcent.

malnutrition (mal″nu-trish′un). Any disorder of nutrition.

malocclusion (mal-ŏ-kloo′zhun). Such contact of the maxillary and mandibular teeth as will interfere with the highest efficiency during the excursive movements of the jaw that are essential to mastication, graded by Angle into four classes, depending on the degree of abnormality of the relationship (see table). **close-bite m.** See *close bite*, under *bite*. **open-bite m.** See *open bite*, under *bite*.

Angle's Classification of Malocclusion

Class I. Normal mesiodistal relation of the dental arches with contracted and undeveloped maxillary arches especially in the anterior portion in which teeth often assume varied forms of individual malocclusion.

Class II. The lower dental arch is distal to the upper on one or both lateral halves.
- Division 1. Bilaterally distal with protruding upper incisors.
- Division 2. Bilaterally distal with retruding upper incisors.
- Subdivision, unilaterally distal with retruding upper incisors.

Class III. The lower dental arch is mesial to the upper on one or both lateral halves with protruding lower incisors.
- Division. Bilaterally mesial with protruding lower incisors.
- Subdivision. Unilaterally mesial with protruding lower incisors.

Class IV. The occlusal relations of the dental arches present the peculiar condition of being in distal occlusion upon one lateral half, and in mesial occlusion upon the other half of the mouth.

malonal (mal′o-nal). Barbital.

malonyl (mal′o-nil). The divalent radical, $OCCH_2CO$.

maloplasty (ma′lo-plas″te) [L. *mala* cheek + Gr. *plassein* to form]. Plastic surgery upon the cheek.

malpighian bodies, corpuscles (mal-pig′ĭ-an) [Marcello *Malpighi*, Italian anatomist, 1628–1694]. See *corpuscula renis* and *folliculi lymphatici lienales*.

malposed (mal-pōzd′). Not in the normal position.

malposition (mal″po-zish′un) [L. *malus* bad + *positio* placement]. Abnormal or anomalous position.

malpractice (mal-prak′tis) [L. *mal* bad + *practice*]. Improper or injurious practice; unskillful and faulty medical or surgical treatment.

malpraxis (mal-prak′sis). Malpractice.

malpresentation (mal″prez-en-ta′shun). A faulty or abnormal fetal presentation.

malrotation (mal″ro-ta′shun). Abnormal or pathologic rotation, as of the spinal column.

malt (mawlt) [L. *maltum*]. Grain, for the most part barley, which has been soaked, made to germinate, and then dried: it contains dextrin, maltose, and diastase. It is nutritive and digestant, aiding in the digestion of starchy foods, and is used in tuberculosis, cholera infantum, and other wasting diseases.

maltase (mawl′tās). An enzyme, widely distributed in the animal and vegetable world, which catalyzes the hydrolysis of maltose into dextrose.

malthusian law (mal-thu′se-an) [Rev. T. R. *Malthus*, English economist, 1766–1834]. See under *law*.

maltobiose (mawl″to-bi′ōs). Maltose.

maltodextrin (mawl″to-deks′trin). A dextrin convertible into maltose.

maltoflavin (mawl″to-fla′vin). A flavin or lyochrome malt.

maltol (mawl′tol). A compound, 3-hydroxy-2-methyl-4-pyrone, $CH.CH:CO.C(OH):C(CH_3)$ (ring closed through O).

maltosazone (mawl″to-sa′zōn). The phenylosazone of maltose. It is a yellow crystalline substance formed by treating maltose with phenyl hydrazine and acetic acid. The crystals melt at 205°C. and may be used in identifying maltose.

maltose (mawl′tōs). A white crystalline disaccharide formed when starch is hydrolyzed by amylase.

maltoside (mawl′to-sīd). A compound homologous with a glucoside, but in which the sugar is maltose instead of glucose.

maltosuria (mawl″to-su′re-ah). The presence of maltose in the urine.

maltum (mal′tum) [L.]. Malt.

malturned (mal-turnd′). Turned abnormally: said of teeth twisted on their central axes.

malum (ma′lum) [L.]. Evil or disease. **m. artic′ulorum seni′lis**, a painful, degenerative state of a joint, occurring as a result of aging. **m. cox′ae**, hip joint disease. **m. cox′ae seni′lis**, osteoarthritis of the hip joint. **m. malan′num** ["evil year disease"], the name given during the middle ages to a carbunculus or gangrenous eruption affecting the jaws of man or animals: possibly anthrax or glanders. **m. per′forans pe′dis**, perforating ulcer of the foot. **m. seni′le**, a variety of osteoarthritis peculiar to aged persons. See *morbus coxae senilis*. **m. vene′reum**, syphilis. **m. vertebra′le suboccipita′le**, tuberculosis of the atlas and axis.

malunion (mal-ūn′yon). Union of the fragments of a fractured bone in a faulty position.

Malva (mal′vah) [L.]. See *mallow*.

Maly's test (mah′lēz) [Richard Leo *Maly*, Austrian chemist, 1839–1894]. See under *tests*.

M.A.M. Abbreviation for *milliampere minute*.

M + Am. Compound myopic astigmatism.

mamanpian (mah-mahn″pe-ahn′) [Fr. *maman* mother + *pian* yaw]. Mother yaw.

mamelon (mam′ĕ-lon) [Fr. "nipple"]. 1. One of three tubercles sometimes present on the cutting edge of an incisor tooth. 2. The nipple-like elevation in the umbilicus, considered to be the remains of the solid lower part of the umbilical cord which contained the umbilical arteries and urachus.

mamelonated (mam′ĕ-lon-āt″ed). Mamillated.

mamelonation (mam″ĕ-lo-na′shun). Mamillation.

mamilla (mah-mil′lah), pl. *mamil′lae* [L., dim. of *mamma*, a breast, teat]. 1. The nipple. 2. Any nipple-like structure.

mamillae (mah-mil′le) [L.]. Plural of *mamilla*.

mamillary (mam′ĭ-ler″e) [L. *mamilla*, dim. of *mamma*, a breast, teat]. Pertaining to or resembling a nipple.

mamillated (mam″il-lāt′ed). Having nipple-like projections.

mamillation (mam″il-la′shun). 1. The condition of being mamillated. 2. A nipple-like elevation or projection.

mamilliform (mah-mil′lĭ-form) [*mamilla* + L. *forma* form]. Shaped like a nipple.

manilliplasty (mah-mil′lĭ-plas″te). Theleplasty.

mamillitis (mam″il-li′tis) [manilla + *-itis*]. Inflammation of the nipple.

mamma (mam′mah), pl. *mam′mae* [L.]. [N A, B N A] The modified cutaneous, glandular structure on the anterior aspect of the thorax that contains, in the female, the elements that secrete milk for nourishment of the young. **mam′mae accesso′riae [femini′nae et masculi′nae]** [N A], **accessory mammae,** mammary glands present in excess of the normal number, generally found along the line of the embryonic mammary crest. Called also *accessory mammary glands.* **m. areola′ta,** a condition of the breast in which there is bulging of the areola of the nipple. **m. masculi′na** [N A], the rudimentary mammary gland of the male. Called also *m. virilis* [B N A]. **supernumerary mammae,** mammae accessoriae [femininae et masculinae]. **m. vir′ilis** [B N A], m. masculina.

mammae (mam′me) [L.]. Plural of *mamma.*

mammal (mam′al). An individual belonging to the Mammalia.

mammalgia (mam-mal′je-ah). Mastalgia.

Mammalia (mah-ma′le-ah). A division of vertebrate animals, including all that possess hair and suckle their young.

mammalogy (mah-mal′o-je) [*mammal* + *-logy*]. The study of mammals.

mammaplasty (mam′mah-plas″te). Mammoplasty.

mammary (mam′er-e) [L. *mammarius*]. Pertaining to the mamma, or breast.

mammectomy (mam-mek′to-me) [*mamma* + Gr. *ektomē* excision]. Excision of the breast.

mammiform (mam′ĭ-form) [*mamma* + L. *forma* form]. Shaped like the mamma, or breast.

mammilla (mah-mil′lah). Mamilla.

Mammillaria (mam″mil-la′re-ah). Anhalonium.

mammillary (mam′mil-ler″e). Mamillary.

mammillated (mam′mil-lāt″ed). Mamillated.

mammillation (mam″mil-la′shun). Mamillation.

mammilliform (mah-mil′lĭ-form). Mamilliform.

mammillitis (mam″mil-li′tis). Mamillitis.

mammiplasia (mam″mĭ-pla′ze-ah). Mammoplasia.

mammiplasty (mam′mĭ-plas″te). Mammoplasty.

mammitis (mam-i′tis). Mastitis.

mammo- (mam′mo) [Gr. *mammē*, Gr., L. *mamma* the mother's breast]. Combining form denoting relationship to the breast, or mammary gland. See also words beginning *masto-* and *mazo-*.

mammogen (mam′o-jen). A hormone of the anterior pituitary: *m. I* stimulates growth of the ducts; *m. II* stimulates growth of the lobules of the mammary gland.

mammogram (mam′o-gram). A roentgenogram of the breast.

mammography (mam-og′rah-fe). Roentgenography of the mammary gland.

mammoplasia (mam″mo-pla′ze-ah) [*mammo-* + Gr. *plasis* formation + *-ia*]. The development of breast tissue. **adolescent m.,** the development of breast tissue at adolescence, applied especially to the development and later regression which occurs in males under the influence of pituitary and, later, testicular androgens.

mammoplasty (mam′mo-plas″te) [*mammo-* + Gr. *plassein* to shape, form]. Plastic reconstruction of the breast. **augmentation m.,** plastic reconstruction of the breast, with increase of its volume by insertion of a prosthetic material.

mammose (mam-mōs′) [L. *mammosus*]. 1. Having large breasts, or mammae. 2. Mamillated.

mammotomy (mam-mot′o-me). Mastotomy.

mammotropic (mam-mo-trop′ik) [*mammo-* + Gr. *tropikos* inclined]. Having affinity for or a stimulating effect on the mammary gland.

mammotropin (mam-mot′ro-pin). The lactogenic hormone, prolactin.

Man. Abbreviation for L. *manip′ulus*, a handful.

manaca (man′ah-kah). The Brazilian plant, *Brunfelsia* (*Franciscea*) *hopeana:* used in the treatment of gout and rheumatism.

manchette (man-chet′) [Fr. "a cuff"]. A temporary band around the neck of a spermatozoon.

manchineel (man″kĭ-nēl′). The *Hippomane mancinella*, a tree of tropical America. It abounds in a caustic poisonous sap or juice.

mancinism (man′si-nizm) [L. *mancus* crippled]. Left-handedness.

mandama (man-dam′ah). The native name for phrynoderma.

Mandel's test (man′delz) [John Alfred *Mandel*, physiologic chemist in New York, 1865–1929]. See under *tests.*

Mandelbaum's reaction (man′del-bawmz) [Maier *Mandelbaum*, German physician, born 1881]. See under *reaction.*

mandible (man′dĭ-b′l). The bone of the lower jaw. See *mandibula.*

mandibula (man-dib′u-lah), pl. *mandib′ulae* [L.]. [N A, B N A] The horseshoe-shaped bone forming the lower jaw; the largest and strongest bone of the face, presenting a body and a pair of rami, which articulate with the skull at the temporomandibular joints. Called also *mandible.*

mandibulae (man-dib′u-le) [L.]. Plural of *mandibula.*

mandibular (man-dib′u-lar). Pertaining to the lower jaw bone, or mandible.

mandibulopharyngeal (man-dib″u-lo-fah-rin′je-al). Pertaining to the mandible and the pharynx.

Mandl's solution (man′dlz) [Louis *Mandl*, Hungarian physician in Paris, 1812–1881]. See under *solution.*

Mandragora (man-drag′o-rah) [L.]. A genus of solanaceous plants. *M. officina′lis*, the true or oriental mandrake, has the general properties of belladonna, and was formerly used as a narcotic and sedative.

mandrake (man′drāk). See *Mandragora.*

mandrel (man′drel). The shaft on which a dental tool is held in the dental handpiece, for rotation by the dental engine.

mandril (man′dril). Mandrel.

mandrin (man′drin). A stilet or guide for a catheter.

manducation (man″du-ka′shun) [L. *manducatio*]. The mastication or chewing of food.

manducatory (man-du′kah-to-re). Pertaining to, or adapted to, manducation.

maneuver (mah-noo′ver). Any dextrous proceeding; applied especially to procedures employed by the obstetrician in manual delivery of an infant. **Bracht's m.,** for breech presentation: as soon as the inferior angle of the scapula appears, the body is rotated around the mother's symphysis so that the child's back comes to rest on the mother's abdomen. **Credé's m.** See under *method.* **DeLee's m.,** an obstetrical method of changing a face presentation to a brow presentation. **Heiberg-Esmarch m.,** a pushing forward by the

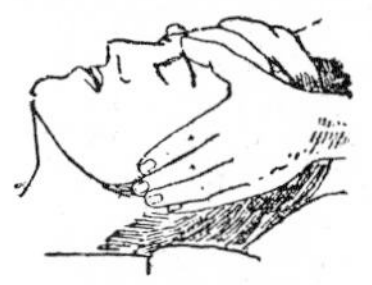
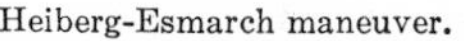

Heiberg-Esmarch maneuver.

Kappeler's maneuver.

anesthetist of the patient's lower jaw in order to prevent the tongue from slipping backward. **Hodge m.,** pressing up on the sinciput of the baby during the labor pains, to increase flexion and thus assist rotation. **Hoguet's m.,** drawing of the sac from beneath deep epigastric vessels in hernioplasty. **Hueter's m.,** when introducing a stomach tube the physician should press the patient's tongue downward and forward with his left forefinger. **Jendrassik's m.,** a procedure for emphasizing the patellar reflex: the patient hooks his hands together by the flexed fingers and pulls apart as hard as he can. **Kappeler's m.,** a drawing forward of the patient's lower jaw by the anesthetist. **Leopold's m's,** four maneuvers in palpating the abdomen for ascertaining the position and presentation of the fetus. **Massini's m.,** in forceps delivery, the blades are reversed, their front directed to the face; the head is flexed by sweeping their handles to the corresponding side, mobilized, rotated so as to bring the occiput posteriorly into a diagonal of the inlet, and then drawn down into the pelvis. **Mauriceau m.,** a method of delivering the after-coming head in cases of breech presentation. **Müller's m.,** an inspiratory effort with a closed glottis after expiration, used during fluoroscopic examination to cause a negative intrathoracic pressure with engorgement of intrathoracic vascular structures, which is helpful in recognizing esophageal varices, and distinguishing vascular from nonvascular structures. **Müller-Hillis m.,** procedures for ascertaining the relation between the size of the fetal head and the pelvis of the mother. **Munro Kerr m.,** a maneuver for ascertaining the proportion between the head of the fetus and the pelvis of the mother. **Nägeli's m.,** pushing upward of the patient's head with one hand under the occiput and the other under the jaw, for cure of nosebleed. **Pajot's m.,** for forceps traction along axis of superior strait; one hand over the lock of the forceps pulls downward towards the floor, while the other hand applies horizontal traction. **Pinard's m.,** a method of bringing down the foot in breech extraction. **Prague m.,** a method in breech presentation of engaging the head by bringing down the breech and making traction on the head with the finger which is hooked over the nape of the neck. **Ritgen m.,** delivery of the child's head by lifting the head upward and forward through the vulva, between pains, by pressing with the tips of the fingers upon the perineum behind the anus. **Saxtorph's m.,** Pajot's m. **Scanzoni m.,** a method of forceps rotation of the fetal head in the posterior position of the occiput. **Schatz's m.,** an obstetrical method of changing a face presentation into a brow presentation. **Schreiber's m.,** rubbing of the inner side of the upper part of the thigh while testing for patellar reflex. **Valsalva's m.,** increase of intrapulmonic pressure by forcible exhalation against the closed glottis. **Van Hoorn's m.,** a maneuver like the Prague maneuver, with the addition of pressure on the baby's forehead from outside. **Wigand's m.,** external version accomplished by pushing the baby's head up with one hand and its buttocks down with the other.

manganese (man′gah-nēs) [L. *manganum, manganesium*]. A metal resembling iron; symbol, Mn; atomic number, 25; atomic weight, 54.938; specific gravity, 7.2. **m. butyrate,** a red powder, $(CH_3CH_2CH_2COO)_2Mn$: used in treatment of some skin diseases. **m. citrate,** $Mn_3(C_6H_5O_7)_2$: used in making solution of iron peptonate and manganese. **m. dioxide,** the black oxide of manganese, MnO_2: a strong oxidizing agent. **m. glycerophosphate,** a white or pinkish white powder, $C_3H_7MnO_6P$: claimed to have value as a hematinic and nerve tonic. **m. hypophosphite,** a pink granular or crystalline powder, $Mn(HP_2O_2)_2.H_2O$: claimed to be a hematinic. **m. sulfate,** a salt, $MnSO_4 + 4H_2O$: used in veterinary medicine as a cathartic and in combination with chloral hydrate as a narcotic and general anesthetic.

manganic (man-gan′ik). Pertaining to manganese as a trivalent element.

manganism (man′gah-nizm). A toxic condition occurring in persons who work with manganese.

manganous (man′gah-nus). Pertaining to manganese as a divalent element.

manganum (man′gah-num) [L.]. Manganese.

mange (mānj). A communicable disease of domestic animals, due to itch mites of the family Sarcoptidae. **demodectic m., follicular m.,** an intractable form of mange in dogs due to the presence of *Demodex folliculorum* in the hair follicles. **Texas m.,** grain itch.

Mangoldt's epithelial grafting (mahn′gōlts) [Heinrich von *Mangoldt*, Dresden surgeon, 1860–1909]. The covering of wounds and granulating areas with epithelial tissue cut from the epidermis with a razor.

mangosteen (man′gos-tēn). The pericarp of the fruit of *Garcinia mangostana:* astringent.

mangostin (man′gos-tin). A yellow, crystalline pigment, $C_{23}H_{24}O_6$, from mangosteen rind.

mania (ma′ne-ah) [Gr. "madness"]. 1. A phase of mental disorder characterized by an expansive emotional state, elation, hyperirritability, overtalkativeness or flight of ideas, and increased motor activity; specifically, the manic type of manic-depressive psychosis. 2. As a combining form, it signifies obsessive preoccupation with something, as in *dipsomania, erotomania, oniomania,* etc. **acute hallucinatory m.,** Ganser's syndrome. **akinetic m.,** marked emotional exaltation with decreased psychomotor activity. **m. à po′tu,** delirium tremens. **Bell's m.,** acute maniacal excitement, often leading to death from exhaustion. **dancing m.,** a mental disorder characterized by uncontrolled dancing. **doubting m.,** folie de doute. **epileptic m.,** mania with attacks of violence following, preceding, or replacing an epileptic attack. **hysterical m.,** mania as one of the concomitants of a hysterical condition. **m. mi′tis,** the mildest form of mania. **periodical m.,** a condition in which maniacal attacks of varying duration follow one another at more or less regular intervals. **puerperal m.,** the manic reaction which sometimes follows childbirth. **Ray's m.,** so-called moral insanity. **reasoning m.,** simple mania with active but perverted ideation. **religious m.,** mania with abnormal or perverted religious impulses. **m. secan′di,** undue haste to perform unnecessary surgical operations. **transitory m.,** severe frenzied mania the attacks of which are of short duration. **unproductive m.,** a condition in which the behavior is that of mania, but the patient's thinking and speech are repressed.

maniac (ma′ne-ak) [L. *maniacus*]. One who is affected with mania.

maniacal (mah-ni′ah-kal). Affected with mania.

maniaphobia (ma″ne-ah-fo′be-ah). Fear of insanity.

manic (ma′nik). Pertaining to or affected with mania.

manifold (man′ĭ-fold). Omasum.

manigraphy (mah-nig′rah-fe) [Gr. *mania* madness + *graphein* to write]. Description of insanity in its various forms.

manikin (man′ĭ-kin). A model of the body, with movable members and parts, used to illustrate anatomy, or for the practice of nursing or certain surgical procedures, such as the removal of foreign bodies by bronchoscopy.

maniloquism (mah-nil′o-kwizm) [L. *manus* hand + *loqui* speak]. Dactylology.

maniluvium (man″ĭ-lu′ve-um). A hand bath.

Manip. Abbreviation for L. *manip′ulus*, a handful.

maniphalanx (man″ĭ-fa′lanks) [L. *manus* hand + *phalanx*]. A phalanx of the hand.

manipulation (mah-nip″u-la′shun) [L. *manip-*

ulare to handle]. Skilful or dextrous treatment by the hand. In physical therapy, the forceful passive movement of a joint beyond its active limit of motion. **conjoined m.,** manipulation with both hands.

manipulus (mah-nip′u-lus) [L.]. Handful.

Mann's sign (manz) [John Dixon *Mann*, English physician, 1840–1912]. See under *sign*.

Mann-Bollman fistula (man-bol′man) [Frank Charles *Mann*, American physiologist and surgeon, 1887–1962; Jesse L. *Bollman*, American physiologist, born 1896]. See under *fistula*.

Mann-Williamson ulcer (man′ wil′yam-son) [Frank C. *Mann;* Carl S. *Williamson*, American surgeon, 1896–1952]. See under *ulcer*.

manna (man′ah) [L.]. Mannitol.

Mannaberg's sign (man′ah-bergz) [Julius *Mannaberg*, physician in Vienna, born 1860]. See under *sign*.

mannan (man′an). A hard, white, insoluble polysaccharide, $(C_6H_{10}O_5)_n$, which yields mannose on hydrolysis. It is found in the vegetable ivory nut, *Phytelephas macrocarpa*, and other plants.

mannerism (man′er-izm). A stereotyped movement or habit differing from the usual.

manninositose (man″ĭ-no-si′tōs). A mannite and inosite compound developed in tubercle bacilli.

manninotriose (man″ĭ-no-tri′ōs). A trisaccharide, $C_{18}H_{32}O_{16}$, from ash manna, which on hydrolysis yields two molecules of galactose and one of glucose.

mannitan (man′ĭ-tan). A modified form of mannitol, having an internal ring formation in the molecule and which tends to revert to mannitol.

mannite (man′īt). Mannitol.

mannitol (man′ĭ-tol). A sugar, $HOCH_2(CHOH)_4$-CH_2OH, widely distributed in nature, particularly in the fungi: used in a diagnostic test of kidney function. **m. hexanitrate,** a compound formed by the nitration of mannitol; used as a vasodilator, mainly in urinary insufficiency.

mannitose (man′ĭ-tōs). Mannose.

Mannkopf's sign (mahn′kopfs) [Emil Wilhelm *Mannkopf*, German physician, 1836–1918]. See under *sign*.

mannocarolose (man″o-kar′o-lōs). A polysaccharide made up of mannose units and formed by the growth of *Penicillium charlesii* on culture media containing glucose.

mannohydrazone (man″o-hi′drah-zōn). The phenylhydrazone of mannose. It consists of colorless platelike crystals which melt at 195°C. and may be used in identifying mannose.

mannoketoheptose (man″o-ke″to-hep′tōs). A natural sugar, $CH_2OH.CO(CHOH)_4.CH_2OH$, found in *Persea gratissima*.

mannopyranose (man″o-pi′rah-nōs). Mannose.

mannosan (man′o-san). Mannan.

mannose (man′ōs). A monosaccharide, $CH_2OH.$-$(CHOH)_4.CHO$; an aldehyde sugar produced by the oxidation of mannitol; similar to dextrose in general properties and conveniently prepared by hydrolyzing the vegetable ivory nut.

mannosidostreptomycin (man″o-si″do-strep″-to-mi′sin). A compound of the elements of streptomycin joined glycosidically to *d*-mannose.

mannosocellulose (man-o″so-sel′u-lōs). A variety of cellulose from coffee; it is changed by hydrolysis into mannose and dextrose.

Manoiloff's (Manoilov's) reaction (man-oi′-lofs) [E. O. *Manoiloff*, Russian physician]. See under *reaction*.

manometer (mah-nom′e-ter) [Gr. *manos* thin + *metron* measure]. An instrument for measuring the pressure or tension of liquids or gases, as the blood, etc. **König's m.,** an apparatus by which the notes of a musical instrument connected with it produce variations in the appearance of a flame, and thus indicate the character of the vibrations.

manometric (man″o-met′rik). 1. Pertaining to or ascertained by the manometer. 2. Varying with the pressure.

manoptoscope (man-op′to-skōp) [L. *manus* hand + Gr. *optos* seen + *skopein* to examine]. An apparatus for detecting ocular dominance.

manoscopy (man-os′ko-pe). The measurement of the density of gases.

Man. pr. Abbreviation for L. *ma′ne pri′mo*, early in the morning.

manquea (mahn-ka′ah). An infectious disease of young cattle in South America, caused by a minute oval bacillus. It is marked by the formation of abscesses upon the legs.

mansa (man′sah). The root or rhizome of *Houttuynia californica:* used as a tonic in dysentery and malaria.

Manson's disease, pyosis, solution (man′-sonz) [Sir Patrick *Manson*, British physician, 1844–1922]. See under *pyosis* and *solution*.

Mansonella ozzardi (man″so-nel′ah o-zar′de). A filaroid nematode parasite found in the mesentery and visceral fat of man in Panama, Yucatan, and neighboring islands.

mansonelliasis (man″so-nel-i′ah-sis). Infection with *Mansonella ozzardi*.

Mansonia (man-so′ne-ah). A genus of mosquitoes, several species of which transmit *Wuchereria bancrofti*. Some species of this genus may also transmit viruses such as those causing equine encephalomyelitis.

Mansonoides (man-so-noi′dēz). A subgenus of *Mansonia*.

mantle (man′t'l). An enveloping structure or layer. **brain m.,** pallium. **myoepicardial m.,** a layer of visceral mesoderm in the early embryo, surrounding the endocardial tube and developing into the myocardium and epicardium. **nail m.,** the nail fold.

Mantoux's reaction, test (man-to͞oz′) [Charles *Mantoux*, French physician, 1877–1947]. See under *tests*.

manual (man′u-al) [L. *manualis; manus* hand]. Of or pertaining to the hand; performed by the hand or hands.

manubria (mah-nu′bre-ah) [L.]. Plural of *manubrium*.

manubrium (mah-nu′bre-um), pl. *manu′bria* [L.]. A handle-like structure or part; often used alone to designate the manubrium sterni. **m. mal′lei** [N A, B N A], **m. of malleus,** the largest process of the malleus, which is attached to the inner surface of the tympanic membrane and has the tendon of the tensor tympani muscle attached to it. **m. ster′ni** [N A, B N A], **m. of sternum,** the cranial portion of the sternum, which articulates with the clavicles and the first two pairs of ribs.

manudynamometer (man″u-di″nah-mom′e-ter) [L. *manus* hand + Gr. *dynamis* force + *metron* measure]. An apparatus for measuring the force of the thrust of an instrument.

manus (ma′nus), pl. *ma′nus* [L.]. [N A, B N A] The distal portion of the arm, or hand, including the carpus, metacarpus, and fingers. **m. ca′va,** a hand deformed by a deep hollowing of the palm. **m. exten′sa,** backward deviation of the hand. **m. flex′a,** forward deviation of the hand. **m. pla′na,** flattening of the arch formed normally by the proximal row of the carpal bones; flat hand. **m. superexten′sa,** manus extensa. **m. val′ga,** clubhand marked by deflection of the hand toward the ulnar side; Madelung's deformity. **m. va′ra,** clubhand marked by deflection of the hand to the radial side.

manustupration (man″u-stu-pra′shun) [L. *manustupratio*]. Masturbation.

manyplies (men′ĭ-plīz″). Omasum.

Manz's disease, glands (mahnts′ez) [Wilhelm *Manz*, German ophthalmologist, 1833–1911]. See *retinitis proliferans*, and under *gland*.

manzanita (man″zah-ne′ta) [Sp., dim. of *manzana*

apple]. A small shrub or tree of the genus *Arctostaphylos*, found in the western part of the United States.

Manzullo's test (man-zul′ōz) [Alfredo *Manzullo*]. See *tellurite test*, under *tests*.

map (map′). A two-dimensional graphic representation of arrangement in space. **fate m.,** a plan of a blastula or early gastrula stage of an embryo showing areas of prospective significance in normal development.

mapharsen (mah-far′sen). Trade mark for a preparation of oxophenarsine hydrochloride.

maqui (mah′kwe). A liliaceous shrub of South America: its berries afford an antifebrile wine.

Marañón's reaction, sign, syndrome (mar-ahn′yonz) [Gregorio *Marañón*, Spanish physician, 1887–1960]. See under *sign* and *syndrome*.

Maranta (mah-ran′tah) [after B. *Maranta*, physician in Venosa, died 1554]. A genus of tropical herbs: the roots of several species afford arrowroot.

marantic (mah-ran′tik) [Gr. *marantikos* wasting away]. Pertaining to or of the nature of marasmus.

marasmatic (mar″az-mat′ik). Marasmic.

marasmic (mah-raz′mik). Pertaining to or characterized by marasmus.

marasmoid (mah-raz′moid) [Gr. *marasmos* a dying away + *eidos* form]. Resembling marasmus.

marasmus (mah-raz′mus) [Gr. *marasmos* a dying away]. Progressive wasting and emaciation, especially such a wasting in infants when there is no obvious or ascertainable cause. It is also called *infantile atrophy*, *athrepsia*, *pedatrophy*, and *decomposition* (Finkelstein), *m. infantilis*, and *m. lactantium*. **chlorotic m.,** periarteritis nodosa. **enzootic m.,** a condition of malnutrition in domestic animals due to a deficiency of one or more of the trace elements, especially cobalt and copper. It is variously known as *bush sickness* in New Zealand, *Denmark wasting disease* in Australia, *lechsucht* in Holland, *nakuruitis* in Kenya, *pine* in Scotland and *salt sickness* in Florida.

marble (mar′bl) [L. *marmor*]. Native crystalline calcium carbonate occurring as a rock.

marbleization (mar″bel-i-za′shun). The state of being veined like marble.

marc (mark) [Fr.]. The residue left after maceration of a substance, such as that remaining after the pressing of grapes for wine or olives for their oil, or the maceration of substances used in the preparation of various drugs.

Marchand's adrenals (mar′shandz) [Felix *Marchand*, German pathologist, 1846–1928]. Accessory adrenals in the broad ligament.

marche à petits pas (marsh-ah-pte′pah) [Fr.]. A gait in which the patient takes very short steps: seen in cerebral arteriosclerotic rigidity.

Marchi's globules, reaction, tract, etc. (mar′kēz) [Vittorio *Marchi*, Italian physician, 1851–1908]. See under the nouns.

Marchiafava-Bignami disease (mar″ke-ah-fah′vah-bēn-yah′me) [Ettore *Marchiafava*, Italian pathologist, 1847–1916; Amico *Bignami*, Italian pathologist, 1862–1929]. Degeneration of the corpus callosum.

Marchiafava-Micheli disease, syndrome (mar″ke-ah-fah′vah-me-ka′le) [Ettore *Marchiafava;* F. *Micheli*, Italian clinician]. See under *syndrome.*

marcid (mar′sid) [L. *marcere* to waste away]. Wasting away.

marcov (mar′kov) [L. *marcere* to waste away]. Marasmus.

Marcus Gunn (mar′kus gun). See *Gunn*.

Maréchal's test (mar″a-shalz′) [Louis Eugène *Maréchal*, French physician]. See under *tests*.

marennin (mah-ren′in). A green pigment from the oysters of Marennes, in France; derived from the chlorophyll of a microorganism that infests them.

mareo (mar-a′o) [Sp. "vexation"]. Seasickness. **m. de la Cordillera,** mountain sickness.

Marey's law (mar-ēz′) [Étienne Jules *Marey*, French physiologist, 1830–1904]. See under *law*.

marezine (mar′ē-zēn). Trade mark for a preparation of cyclizine hydrochloride.

Marfan's disease, method of puncture, sign, syndrome (mar-fahnz′) [Bernard-Jean Antonin *Marfan*, French pediatrician, 1858–1942]. See under the nouns.

margarid (mar′gar-id). Pearl-like.

margarine (mar′jar-in) [Gr. *margaron* pearl]. 1. A food product containing 80 per cent of fat, manufactured primarily from refined cottonseed and soybean oils—sources of vitamin E and essential fatty acids, and fortified to supply a minimum of 15,000 U.S.P. units of vitamin A per pound. 2. A (theoretical) trimargarate of propenyl.

margaritoma (mar″gar-ĭ-to′mah). Cholesteatoma.

margarone (mar′gar-on). Palmitone.

Margaropus annulatus (mar-gar′o-pus an″u-la′tus). *Boophilus annulatus*.

margin (mar′jin). An edge or border, such as the border of an organ or other anatomic structure. Called also *margo* [N A]. **alveolar m. of mandible,** arcus alveolaris mandibulae. **alveolar m. of maxilla,** arcus alveolaris maxillae. **axillary m. of scapula,** margo lateralis scapulae. **cartilaginous m. of acetabulum,** labrum acetabulare. **ciliary m. of iris,** margo ciliaris iridis. **convex m. of testis,** margo arterior testis. **coronal m. of frontal bone,** margo parietalis ossis frontalis. **coronal m. of parietal bone,** margo frontalis ossis parietalis. **crenate m. of spleen, cristate m. of spleen,** margo superior lienis. **dentate m.,** pectinate line. **falciform m. of fascia lata, falciform m. of saphenus hiatus,** margo falciformis hiatus saphenus. **falciform m. of white line of pelvic fascia,** arcus tendineus fasciae pelvis. **m. of fibula, anterior,** margo anterior fibulae. **m. of fibula, posterior,** margo posterior fibulae. **fibular m. of foot,** margo lateralis pedis. **m. of foot, fibular, m. of foot, lateral,** margo lateralis pedis. **m. of foot, medial,** margo medialis pedis. **free m. of eyelid,** the conjunctival-lined portion of each eyelid, about 2 mm. broad, overlying the eyeball; the anterior border of each bears the eyelashes, and the posterior border is closely applied to the eyeball. **free m. of nail,** margo liber unguis. **free m. of ovary,** margo liber ovarii. **frontal m. of great wing of sphenoid bone,** margo frontalis alae majoris. **frontal m. of parietal bone,** margo frontalis ossis parietalis. **gingival m., gum m.,** the border of the gingiva surrounding, but unattached to, the substance of the teeth. **m. of humerus, lateral,** margo lateralis humeri. **m. of humerus, medial,** margo medialis humeri. **infraorbital m. of maxilla,** margo infraorbitalis maxillae. **infraorbital m. of orbit,** margo infraorbitalis orbitae. **interosseous m. of fibula,** margo interosseus fibulae. **interosseous m. of tibia,** margo interosseus tibiae. **m. of kidney, lateral,** margo lateralis renis. **m. of kidney, medial,** margo medialis renis. **lacrimal m. of maxilla,** margo lacrimalis maxillae. **lambdoid m. of occipital bone,** margo lambdoideus squamae occipitalis. **lambdoid m. of parietal bone,** margo occipitalis ossis parietalis. **m. of lung, anterior,** margo anterior pulmonis. **m. of lung, inferior,** margo inferior pulmonis. **malar m.,** margo zygomaticus alae majoris. **mamillary m.,** margo mastoideus squamae occipitalis. **mastoid m. of occipital bone,** margo mastoideus squamae occipitalis. **mastoid m. of parietal bone,** angulus mastoideus ossis parietalis. **mesovarial m. of ovary,** margo mesovaricus ovarii. **m. of nail, free,** margo liber unguis. **m. of nail, hidden,** margo occultus unguis. **m. of nail, lateral,** margo lateralis unguis. **nasal m. of frontal bone,** margo nasalis ossis frontalis. **obtuse m. of spleen,** margo inferior lienis. **occipital m. of parietal bone,** margo occipitalis ossis parietalis. **occipital m. of temporal bone,** margo occipitalis ossis temporalis. **m. of pancreas, superior,** margo superior lienis. **parietal m. of frontal bone,** margo parietalis ossis frontalis. **parietal m. of great wing of sphenoid bone,** margo parietalis alae majoris. **parietal m. of occipital bone,** margo lambdoideus squamae occipitalis. **parietal m. of parietal bone,** margo sagittalis ossis parietalis. **parietal m. of temporal bone,** margo parietalis ossis temporalis. **m. of parietal bone, anterior, m. of parietal bone, frontal,** margo frontalis ossis parietalis. **m. of parietal bone, sagittal, m. of parietal bone, superior,** margo sagittalis ossis parietalis. **parieto-frontal m. of great wing of sphenoid bone,** margo frontalis alae majoris. **pupillary m. of iris,** margo pupillaris iridis. **radial m's of fingers,** facies laterales digitorum manus. **radial m. of forearm,** margo lateralis antebrachii. **m. of radius, dorsal,** margo posterior radii. **sagittal m. of parietal bone,** margo sagittalis ossis parietalis. **m. of scapula, anterior,** margo lateralis scapulae. **m. of scapula, external,** margo lateralis scapulae. **m. of scapula, lateral,** margo lateralis scapulae. **m. of scapula, superior,** margo superior scapulae. **sphenoidal m. of parietal bone,** angulus sphenoidalis ossis parietalis. **sphenoidal m. of temporal bone,** margo sphenoidalis ossis temporalis. **sphenotemporal m. of parietal bone,** margo squamosus ossis parietalis. **m. of spleen, anterior, m. of spleen, superior,** margo superior lienis. **squamous m. of great wing of sphenoid bone,** margo squamosus alae majoris. **squamous m. of parietal bone,** margo squamosus ossis parietalis. **straight m. of testis,** margo posterior testis. **supraorbital m. of frontal bone,** margo supraorbitalis ossis frontalis. **supraorbital m. of orbit,** margo supraorbitalis orbitae. **m. of suprarenal gland, inferior,** facies renalis glandulae suprarenalis. **m. of suprarenal gland, medial,** margo medialis glandulae suprarenalis. **m. of suprarenal gland, superior,** margo superior glandulae suprarenalis. **temporal m. of parietal bone,** margo squamosus ossis parietalis. **m. of testis, anterior, m. of testis, external,** margo anterior testis. **m. of testis, internal, m. of testis, posterior,** margo posterior testis. **m. of tibia, anterior,** margo anterior tibiae. **m. of tibia, medial,** margo medialis tibiae. **tibial m. of foot,** margo medialis pedis. **m. of tongue, m. of tongue, lateral,** margo linguae. **m. of ulna, anterior,** margo anterior ulnae. **m. of ulna, dorsal, m. of ulna, posterior,** margo posterior ulnae. **ulnar m's of fingers,** facies mediales digitorum manus. **ulnar m. of forearm,** margo medialis antebrachii. **m. of uterus, lateral,** margo uteri [dexter et sinister]. **vertebral m. of scapula,** margo medialis scapulae. **volar m. of radius,** margo anterior radii. **volar m. of ulna,** margo anterior ulnae. **zygomatic m. of great wing of sphenoid bone,** margo zygomaticus alae majoris.

marginal (mar′jĭ-nal) [L. *marginalis; margo* margin]. Pertaining to a margin or border.

margination (mar-jĭ-na′shun). Adhesion of leukocytes to the blood vessel walls in the early stages of inflammation.

margines (mar′jĭ-nēz) [L.]. Plural of *margo.*

marginoplasty (mar-jin′o-plas-te) [L. *margo* margin + Gr. *plassein* to mold]. Surgical renewal of a border, as of the eyelid.

margo (mar′go), pl. *mar′gines* [L.]. An edge or border; used in anatomical nomenclature as a general term to designate the edge of a structure. Called also *margin.* **m. alveola′ris.** See *arcus alveolaris mandibulae* and *arcus alveolaris maxillae.* **m. ante′rior fib′ulae** [N A], the anterolateral border of the body of the fibula. Called also *crista anterior fibulae* [B N A], and *anterior crest of fibula.* **m. ante′rior hep′atis** [B N A], m. inferior hepatis. **m. ante′rior lie′nis** [B N A], m. superior lienis. **m. ante′rior pancrea′tis** [N A, B N A], the anterior margin of the pancreas, which bounds the anterior and inferior surfaces. Called also *anterior border of pancreas.* **m. ante′rior pulmo′nis** [N A, B N A], the ventral border of either lung, which descends from behind the sternum, a little to the left of the midline, and curves laterally to meet the inferior margin. Called also *anterior margin of lung.* **m. ante′rior ra′dii** [N A], the edge of the radius that runs obliquely between the radial tuberosity and the styloid process. Called also *m. volaris radii* [B N A], and *anterior border of radius.* **m. ante′rior tes′tis** [N A, B N A], the rounded free border of the testis. Called also *anterior margin of testis.* **m. ante′rior tib′iae** [N A], the prominent anteromedial margin of the body of the tibia, separating the medial and lateral surfaces. Called also *crista anterior tibiae* [B N A], and *anterior border of tibia.* **m. ante′rior ul′nae** [N A], the volar border of the ulna, separating the medial and posterior surfaces. Called also *m. volaris ulnae* [B N A], and *anterior margin of ulna.* **m. axilla′ris scap′ulae** [B N A], m. lateralis scapulae. **m. cilia′ris i′ridis** [N A, B N A], the outer border of the iris, where it is continuous with the ciliary body. Called also *ciliary margin of iris.* **m. dex′ter cor′dis** [N A], the curved right margin of the heart, which runs from the apex toward the right, marking the junction of the sternocostal and diaphragmatic surfaces of the heart. The inferior portion, especially, tends to be a sharp edge. Called also *right border of heart.* **m. dorsa′lis ra′dii** [B N A], m. posterior radii. **m. dorsa′lis ul′nae** [B N A], m. posterior ulnae. **m. falcifor′mis fas′ciae la′tae** [B N A], m. falciformis hiatus saphenus. **m. falcifor′mis hia′tus saphe′nus** [N A], the lateral margin of the saphenous hiatus. Called also *m. falciformis fasciae latae* [B N A], and *falciform margin of saphenous hiatus.* **m. fibula′ris pe′dis,** N A alternative for *m. lateralis pedis.* **m. fronta′lis a′lae mag′nae** [B N A], m. frontalis alae majoris. **m. fronta′lis a′lae majo′ris** [N A], a roughened area on the great wing of the sphenoid bone where it articulates with the frontal bone. It is situated at the upper lateral margin of the orbital surface of the great wing where this meets the cerebral and temporal surfaces. Called also *m. frontalis alae magnae* [B N A], and *frontal margin of great wing of sphenoid bone.* **m. fronta′lis os′sis parie-ta′lis** [N A, B N A], the edge of the parietal bone that articulates with the frontal bone along the coronal suture. Called also *frontal margin of parietal bone.* **m. infe′rior hep′atis** [N A], the anteroinferior edge of the liver, separating the anterior and the visceral surface. Called also *m. anterior hepatis* [B N A], and *inferior border of liver.* **m. infe′rior lie′nis** [N A], a straight margin of the spleen somewhat less prominent than the superior margin, separating the renal surface from the diaphragmatic surface. Called also *m. posterior lienis* [B N A], and *inferior border of spleen.* **m. infe′rior pancrea′tis** [N A], the inferior margin of the pancreas, which bounds the inferior and posterior surfaces. Called also *m. posterior pancreatis* [B N A]. **m. infe′rior pulmo′nis** [N A, B N A], the border of the lung that extends in a curve behind the sixth costal cartilage, the upper margin of the eighth rib in the axillary line, the ninth or tenth rib in the scapular line, and passes medially to the eleventh costovertebral joint. Called also *inferior margin of lung.* **m. infraglenoida′lis tib′iae** [B N A]. Omitted in N A. **m. infraorbita′lis maxil′lae** [N A, B N A], the short rounded edge of the maxilla where the orbital surface becomes continuous with the anterior surface. Called also *infraorbital margin of maxilla.* **m. infraorbita'lis or'bitae** [N A, B N A], the inferior edge of the entrance to the orbit, formed by the infraorbital process of the zygomatic bone and the infraorbital margin of the maxilla. Called also *infraorbital margin of orbit.* **m. interos'seus fib'ulae** [N A], a prominent ridge medial to the anterior border of the fibula, connected with a similar ridge on the tibia by a strong, wide fibrous sheet, the interosseous membrane. Called also *crista interossea fibulae* [B N A], and *interosseous border of fibula.* **m. interos'seus ra'dii** [N A], the prominent medial border of the radius, connected with a similar ridge on the ulna by a strong, wide fibrous sheet, the interosseous membrane. Called also *crista interossea radii* [B N A], and *interosseous border of radius.* **m. interos'seus tib'iae** [N A], the prominent lateral border of the body of the tibia, which separates the posterior and lateral surfaces and gives attachment to the interosseous membrane. Called also *crista interossea tibiae* [B N A], and *interosseous border of tibia.* **m. interos'seus ul'nae** [N A], the prominent lateral border of the ulna, connected with a similar ridge on the radius by the interosseous membrane. Called also *crista interossea ulnae* [B N A], and *interosseous border of ulna.* **m. lacrima'lis maxil'lae** [N A, B N A], the posterior border of the frontal process of the maxilla where it articulates with the lacrimal bone. Called also *lacrimal border of maxilla.* **m. lambdoi'deus squa'mae occipita'lis** [N A, B N A], the edge of the occipital bone that extends from the lateral angle to the superior angle, articulating with the parietal bone to help form the lambdoid suture. Called also *lambdoid margin of occipital bone.* **m. latera'lis antebra'chii** [N A], the lateral, or radial, border of the forearm. **mar'gines latera'les digito'rum pe'dis** [B N A], facies laterales digitorum pedis. **m. latera'lis hu'meri** [N A, B N A], the edge of the humerus that extends from posteroinferior part of the greater tubercle to the lateral epicondyle. Called also *lateral border of humerus.* **m. latera'lis [lin'guae]** [B N A], m. linguae. **m. latera'lis pe'dis** [N A], the lateral, or fibular, border of the foot. **m. latera'lis re'nis** [N A, B N A], the convex narrow border of the kidney. Called also *lateral margin of kidney.* **m. latera'lis scap'ulae** [N A], the thick edge of the scapula, extending from the inferior margin of the glenoid cavity to the inferior angle. Called also *m. axillaris scapulae* [B N A], and *lateral border of scapula.* **m. latera'lis un'guis** [N A, B N A], the edge on either side of the nail. Called also *lateral margin of nail.* **m. latera'lis u'teri** [B N A], m. uteri [dexter et sinister]. **m. li'ber ova'rii** [N A, B N A], the broad, convex border of the ovary, opposite the mesovarial margin. Called also *free margin of ovary.* **m. li'ber un'guis** [N A, B N A], the distal, free edge of the nail. **m. lin'guae** [N A], the lateral border of the body of the tongue. Called also *m. lateralis linguae* [B N A], and *margin of tongue.* **m. mastoi'deus squa'mae occipita'lis** [N A, B N A], the edge of the occipital bone that extends from the jugular process to the lateral angle, articulating with the part of the temporal bone that bears the mastoid process. Called also *mastoid margin of occipital bone.* **m. media'lis antebra'chii** [N A], the medial, or ulnar, border of the forearm. **mar'gines media'les digito'rum pe'dis** [B N A], facies mediales digitorum pedis. **m. media'lis glan'dulae suprarena'lis** [N A, B N A], the medial border, which with the superior border divides the anterior from the posterior surface. Called also *medial margin of suprarenal gland.* **m. media'lis hu'meri** [N A, B N A], the edge of the humerus that begins at the lesser tubercle above and continues downward to the medial epicondyle. Called also *medial border of humerus.* **m. media'lis pe'dis** [N A], the medial, or tibial, border of the foot. **m. media'lis re'nis** [N A, B N A], the concave border of the kidney, which contains the hilus. Called also *medial margin of kidney.* **m. media'lis scap'ulae** [N A], the thin edge of the scapula extending from the superior to the inferior angle. Called also *m. vertebralis scapulae* [B N A], and *vertebral border of scapula.* **m. media'lis tib'iae** [N A, B N A], the border that extends between the medial condyle and medial malleolus of the tibia, separating the medial and posterior surfaces. Called also *medial border of tibia.* **m. mesova'ricus ova'rii** [N A, B N A], the border of the ovary that is attached to the broad ligament by means of the mesovarium. Called also *mesovarial margin of ovary.* **m. nasa'lis os'sis fronta'lis** [N A, B N A], the articular surface, on each nasal part of the frontal bone, that articulates with the nasal bones and with the frontal processes of the maxilla. Called also *nasal margin of frontal bone.* **m. na'si** [B N A]. Omitted in N A. **m. occipita'lis os'sis parieta'lis** [N A, B N A], the edge of the parietal bone that articulates with the occipital bone at the lambdoid suture. Called also *occipital margin of parietal bone.* **m. occipita'lis os'sis tempora'lis** [N A, B N A], the border of the petrous part of the temporal bone that articulates with the occipital bone along the occipitomastoid suture. Called also *occipital margin of temporal bone.* **m. occul'tus un'guis** [N A, B N A], the proximal, buried edge of the nail. **m. palpe'brae.** See *free margin of eyelid.* **m. parieta'lis a'lae majo'ris** [N A], the superior extremity of the squamous margin of the great wing of the sphenoid bone where it articulates with the parietal bone. Called also *angulus parietalis ossis sphenoidalis* [B N A], and *parietal margin of great wing of sphenoid bone.* **m. parieta'lis os'sis fronta'lis** [N A, B N A], the posterior border of the frontal bone, semicircular in shape, which articulates with the parietal bones. Called also *parietal margin of frontal bone.* **m. parieta'lis os'sis tempora'lis** [N A], the superior border of the squamous part of the temporal bone where it articulates with the parietal bone. Called also *m. parietalis squamae temporalis* [B N A], and *parietal margin of temporal bone.* **m. parieta'lis squa'mae tempora'lis** [B N A], m. parietalis ossis temporalis. **m. pe'dis latera'lis** [B N A], m. lateralis pedis. **m. pe'dis media'lis** [B N A], m. medialis pedis. **m. poste'rior fib'ulae** [N A], the posterolateral margin of the body of the fibula. Called also *crista lateralis fibulae* [B N A], and *posterior border of fibula.* **m. poste'rior lie'nis** [B N A], m. inferior lienis. **m. poste'rior pancrea'tis** [B N A], m. inferior pancreatis. **m. poste'rior ra'dii** [N A], the edge of the radius that extends from the posterior part of the radial tuberosity to the middle tubercle. Called also *m. dorsalis radii* [B N A], and *posterior border of radius.* **m. poste'rior tes'tis** [N A, B N A], the border of the testis that is attached to the epididymis and the lower end of the ductus deferens. Called also *posterior margin of testis.* **m. poste'rior ul'nae** [N A], the dorsal border of the ulna, separating the posterior and medial surfaces. Called also *m. dorsalis ulnae* [B N A], and *posterior margin of ulna.* **m. pupilla'ris i'ridis** [N A, B N A], the inner edge of the iris, surrounding the pupil. Called also *pupillary margin of iris.* **m. radia'lis antebra'chii,** N A alternative for *m. lateralis antebrachii.* **m. radia'lis antibra'chii** [B N A], m. lateralis antebrachii. **mar'gines radia'les digito'rum ma'nus** [B N A], facies laterales digitorum manus. **m. radia'lis hu'meri,** the lateral border of the humerus. **m. sagitta'lis os'sis parieta'lis** [N A, B N A], the edge of the parietal bone that articulates with the other parietal bone along the sagittal suture. Called also *sagittal margin of parietal bone.* **m. sphenoida'lis os'sis tempora'lis** [N A], the anterior border of the temporal bone, articulating with the great wing of the sphenoid bone. Called also *m. sphenoidalis squamae temporalis* [B N A], and *sphenoidal margin of temporal bone.* **m. sphenoida'lis squa'mae tempora'lis**

[B N A], m. sphenoidalis ossis temporalis. **m. squamo'sus a'lae mag'nae** [B N A], m. squamosus alae majoris. **m. squamo'sus a'lae majo'ris** [N A], the border of the great wing of the sphenoid bone that articulates with the squama of the temporal bone. Called also *m. squamosus alae magnae* [B N A], and *squamous margin of great wing of sphenoid bone.* **m. squamo'sus os'sis parieta'lis** [N A, B N A], the inferior edge of the parietal bone, which articulates with the sphenoid and temporal bones along the squamous suture. Called also *squamous margin of parietal bone.* **m. supe'rior glan'dulae suprarena'lis** [N A, B N A], the superior border of the suprarenal gland, which with the medial border divides the anterior from the posterior surface. **m. supe'rior lie'nis** [N A], a somewhat sharp, convex line, sometimes serrated, between the gastric and diaphragmatic surfaces of the spleen. Called also *m. anterior lienis* [B N A], and *superior border of spleen.* **m. supe'rior pancrea'tis** [N A, B N A], the superior border of the pancreas, which bounds the anterior and posterior surfaces. **m. supe'rior scap'ulae** [N A, B N A], the thin, short edge of the scapula, extending from the superior angle to the coracoid process. Called also *superior border of scapula.* **m. supraorbita'lis or'bitae** [N A, B N A], the superior edge of the entrance to the orbit, formed by the supraorbital margin of the frontal bone. **m. supraorbita'lis os'sis fronta'lis** [N A, B N A], the anteroinferior edge of the frontal bone, bending down laterally to the zygomatic bone and medially to the frontal process of the maxilla. It marks the junction between the squama and the orbital portion of the bone. **m. tibia'lis pe'dis,** N A alternative for *m. medialis pedis.* **m. ulna'ris antebra'chii,** N A alternative for *m. medialis antebrachii.* **m. ulna'ris antibra'chii** [B N A], m. medialis antebrachii. **mar'gines ulna'res digito'rum ma'nus** [B N A], facies mediales digitorum manus. **m. ulna'ris hu'meri,** the medial border of the humerus. **m. u'teri** [dex'ter et sinis'ter] [N A], either border of the uterus (right and left) at which the surfaces of the urinary bladder and intestines are in contact, and at the upper portion of which the uterine tube is attached. Called also *m. lateralis uteri* [B N A], and *lateral margin of uterus.* **m. vertebra'lis scap'ulae** [B N A], m. medialis scapulae. **m. vola'ris ra'dii** [B N A], m. anterior radii. **m. vola'ris ul'nae** [B N A], m. anterior ulnae. **m. zygomat'icus a'lae mag'nae** [B N A], m. zygomaticus alae majoris. **m. zygomat'icus a'lae majo'ris** [N A], the border on the great wing of the sphenoid bone that separates its temporal and orbital surfaces and articulates with the zygomatic bone. Called also *m. zygomaticus alae magnae* [B N A], and *zygomatic margin of great wing of sphenoid bone.*

margosate (mar-go-sāt). A salt of margosic acid. The margosates have antiprotozoal action and are used in syphilis.

mariahuana, mariajuana (mah-re-ah-wah'-nah). Marihuana.

Marie's disease, hypertrophy, sign (mah-rēz') [Pierre *Marie,* French physician, 1853–1940]. See under the nouns.

Marie-Strümpell disease (mah-re' strim'pel) [Pierre *Marie;* Adolf von *Strümpell,* physician in Leipzig, 1853–1925]. Spondylitis ankylopoietica.

mariguana (mar″ĭ-hwah'nah). Marihuana.

marihuana (mar″ĭ-hwan'ah) [Portuguese]. The leaves and flowering tops of *Cannabis sativa,* a habit-forming, intoxicating agent, usually employed in cigarets by addicts and inhaled as smoke.

marijuana (mar″ĭ-hwah'nah). Marihuana.

Marinesco's succulent hand, sign (mar″ĭ-nes'kōz) [Georges *Marinesco,* Roumanian neurologist, 1863–1938]. See under *hand.*

marinobufagin (mar″ĭ-no-bu'fah-jin). A cardiac poison, $C_{24}H_{32}O_5$, from the skin of the toad, *Bufo marinus.*

marinotherapy (mar″ĭ-no-ther'ah-pe). Treatment by residence at the seashore.

Mariotte's experiment, law, spot (mar″e-ots') [Edme *Mariotte,* French physicist, 1620–1684]. See under the nouns.

mariposia (mar″ĭ-po'ze-ah) [L. *mare* the sea + Gr. *posis* drinking + *-ia*]. Thalassoposia.

marisca (mah-ris'kah), pl. *maris'cae* [L. *marisca* a large fig]. A hemorrhoid.

mariscal (mah-ris'kal). Hemorrhoidal.

marital (mar'ĭ-tal). 1. Of or pertaining to a husband. 2. Of or pertaining to marriage.

maritonucleus (mar″ĭ-to-nu'kle-us) [L. *maritus* married + *nucleus*]. The nucleus of the ovum after the sperm cell has entered it.

Marjolin's ulcer (mar″zho-lanz') [Jean Nicolas *Marjolin,* 1780–1850]. See under *ulcer.*

mark (mark). A spot or blemish. **mother's m.,** nevus. **mulberry m.,** nevus morus. **Pohl's m.,** a limited thinning of the shaft of a hair, usually accompanied by interruption of the medulla; it has the same significance as Beau's line on the nail. **port-wine m.,** nevus flammeus. **raspberry m., strawberry m.,** hemangioma simplex.

Markee test (mar-ke') [J. E. *Markee,* American anatomist, born 1904]. See under *tests.*

marking (mark'ing). A conspicuous line or spot visible on a surface. **Fontana's m's,** minute transverse folds seen on a divided nerve trunk.

Marlow's test (mar'lōz) [Frank W. *Marlow,* Syracuse ophthalmologist, born 1858]. See under *tests.*

marma (mar'mah). The ancient Indian name for a place or region of vital importance in the body which, if injured, results in serious consequences or death.

Marmo's method (mar'mōz) [Serafino *Marmo,* Italian obstetrician]. See under *method.*

marmoration (mar″mo-ra'shun) [L. *marmor* marble]. Marbelization.

marmoreal (mar-mo're-al). Resembling marble. See *Albers-Schönberg bones,* under *bone.*

marmot (mar'mot). The tarbagan; a large furbearing rodent, *Arctomys bobac;* it is a natural reservoir for the plague which is transmitted by a flea, *Ceratophyllus silantiewi.* **small m.** See *Spermophilus.*

marplan (mar'plan). Trade mark for a preparation of isocarboxazid.

Marriott's method (mar'e-ots) [William McKim *Marriott,* American physician, 1885–1936]. See under *method.*

marrow (mar'o). The soft material that fills the cavities of the bones. See *medulla ossium.* **black m.,** a pigmented marrow seen in the melanosis of old horses. **bone m.,** medulla ossium. **bone m., red,** medulla ossium rubra. **bone m., yellow,** medulla ossium flava. **depressed m.,** bone marrow exhibiting decreased functional activity. **fat m.,** medulla ossium flava. **gelatinous m.,** bone marrow that has lost its blood cells and its fat and has acquired a gelatinous appearance. **red m.,** medulla ossium rubra. **spinal m.,** medulla spinalis. **yellow m.,** medulla ossium flava.

marrowbrain (mar'o-brān). The myelencephalon.

mars (marz) [L.]. Iron.

Marsden's paste (marz'denz) [Alexander *Marsden,* London surgeon, 1832–1902]. See under *paste.*

Marsh's disease (marsh'ez) [Sir Henry *Marsh,* Irish physician, 1790–1860]. Exophthalmic goiter.

Marsh's test (marsh'ez) [James *Marsh,* English chemist, 1789–1846]. See under *tests.*

Marshall's fold, vein (mar'shalz) [John *Marshall,* English anatomist, 1818–1891]. See *vestigial* *fold*, under *fold*, and *Marshall's oblique vein*, under *vein*.

Marshall Hall's disease, facies, etc. [*Marshall Hall*, English physician, 1790–1857]. See under the nouns.

marsupia (mar-su′pe-ah) [L.]. Plural of *marsupium*.

marsupial (mar-su′pe-al) [L. *marsupium* a pouch]. One of a class of mammals characterized by the possession of an abdominal pouch in which the young are carried for some time after birth.

marsupialization (mar-su″pe-al-i-za′shun) [L. *marsupium* pouch]. The creation of a pouch; applied especially to surgical exposure of a cyst by resection of the anterior portion of the wall and the overlying skin, and suture of the cut edges of the remaining cyst wall to the adjacent skin layers.

marsupium (mar-su′pe-um), pl. *marsu′pia* [L. "a pouch"]. The scrotum. **marsu′pia patella′ris,** plicae alares.

martial (mar′shal) [L. *martialis; mars* iron]. Containing iron: ferruginous.

Martin's bandage, disease, operation, etc. (mar′tinz) [Henry Austin *Martin*, American surgeon, 1824–1884]. See under the nouns.

Martin's tube (mar′tinz) [August *Martin*, gynecologist in Berlin, 1847–1933]. See under *tube*.

Martinotti's cell (mar″tĭ-not′ēz) [Giovanni *Martinotti*, Bologna pathologist, 1857–1928]. See under *cell*.

Ma.S. Abbreviation for *milliampere-second*.

maschaladenitis (mas″kal-ad″e-ni′tis) [Gr. *maschalē* armpit + *adēn* gland + *-itis*]. Inflammation of the glands of the axilla.

maschalephidrosis (mas″kal-ef″ĭ-dro′sis) [Gr. *maschalē* armpit + *ephidrōsis* excessive sweating]. Excessive sweating in the armpits.

maschaliatry (mas-kal″e-at′re) [Gr. *maschalē* armpit + *iatreia* treatment]. Medication by inunction into the armpit.

maschaloncus (mas″kal-ong′kus). A tumor of the axilla.

masculation (mas″ku-la′shun). The development of male characteristics.

masculine (mas′ku-lin) [L. *masculinus*]. Pertaining to the male sex, or possessing qualities normally characteristic of the male.

masculinity (mas″ku-lin′ĭ-te). The possession of normal masculine qualities.

masculinization (mas″ku-lin-i-za′shun). The induction or development of male secondary sex characters in the female.

masculinize (mas′ku-lin-īz″). To produce male characteristics (virilism) in a female.

masculinovoblastoma (mas″ku-lin-o″vo-blas-to′mah). A tumor of the ovary resembling adrenal cortical tissue, and causing masculinization of the patient.

masculonucleus (mas″ku-lo-nu′kle-us). Arsenoblast.

maser (ma′zer) [*m*icrowave *a*mplification by *s*timulated *e*mission of *r*adiation]. A device which produces an extremely intense, small, and nearly non-divergent beam of monochromatic radiation in the microwave region with all waves in phase.

mask (mask) [Fr. *masque*]. 1. To cover or conceal. In audiometry, to obscure or diminish a sound by the presence of another sound of different frequency. 2. An appliance for shading, protecting, or medicating the face. **BLB m.,** an oxygen-breathing mask for use by aviators. It has a combined inspiratory and expiratory valve and a bag for rebreathing (Boothby, Lovelace, Bulbulian). **Curschmann's m.,** a mask for inhaling turpentine vapors. **death m.,** a plaster cast of the face of a dead person. **ecchymotic m.,** cyanotic discoloration of the head and neck as a result of traumatic asphyxia. **Esmarch's m.,** a frame of metal over which strips of gauze are stretched: used for administering ether or chloroform by inhalation. **Hutchinson's m.,** a sensation as if the skin of the face were compressed by a mask; often a symptom of tabes dorsalis. **Julliard's m.,** a mask for administering ether. **Kuhn's m.,** a mask to be worn over the nose and mouth, which, by obstructing the respiration, produces artificial hyperemia of the pulmonary tissues. It is used in treating pulmonary tuberculosis. **luetic m.,** a brownish, blotchy pigmentation over the forehead, temples, and cheeks, sometimes seen in persons with tertiary syphilis. **meter m.,** an oxygen-breathing mask for aviators. **Mikulicz's m.,** a mask for covering the surgeon's nose and mouth while operating. It consists of a wire frame covered with gauze. **Ombrédanne's m.,** a form of mask for ether administration. **Parkinson's m.,** a fixed masklike expression with infrequent winking, characteristic of Parkinson's disease. **m. of pregnancy,** brown pigmentation of the forehead, cheeks, and nose: sometimes seen in pregnant women. **Schimmelbusch's m.,** a mask for chloroform administration. **tabetic m.,** Hutchinson's m. **tropical m.,** chloasma bronzinum. **Tuttle's m.,** a wire frame covered with gauze to go over the face of a surgeon while operating.

masochism (mas′o-kizm) [Leopold von Sacher-*Masoch*, an Austrian novelist, 1836–1895]. A form of sexual perversion in which cruel treatment gives sexual gratification to the recipient.

masochist (mas′o-kist). One who is given to masochism.

Mas. pil. Abbreviation for L. *mas′sa pilula′rum*, pill mass.

mass (mas) [L. *massa*]. 1. A lump or body made up of cohering particles. See also *massa*. 2. A cohesive mixture suitable for being made up into pills. 3. That characteristic of matter which gives it inertia. The mass of a hypothetical atom of atomic weight 1.000 (a dalton) is 1.648×10^{-24} Gm., and the mass of any other atom may be found by multiplying this number by the atomic weight of the atom. **achromatic m.,** the non-staining portion of the karyokinetic figure. **appendix m.,** a palpable mass in the right iliac fossa or right loin in appendicitis. **blue m.,** mercury m. **body cell m.,** the total weight of the cells of the body, including the cell nucleus, cytoplasm, water, salt, protein, and surrounding membrane, but excluding extracellular water and extracellular solids such as collagen, elastin, and bone matrix, constituting in essence the total mass of oxygen-utilizing, carbohydrate-burning, and energy-exchanging cells of the body; regarded as proportional to total exchangeable potassium in the body. **electronic m.,** the mass of a negative electron when moving at moderate velocity. It is 8.999×10^{-28} Gm. **ferrous carbonate m.,** a soft, dark greenish gray substance containing 36–41 per cent of ferrous carbonate: formerly used in anemia. **fibrillar m. of Flemming,** spongioplasm, def. 1. **inner cell m.,** the cell cluster at the animal pole of a blastocyst from which the embryo proper develops. **intermediate m.,** adhesio interthalamica. **intermediate cell m.,** nephrotome. **lateral m. of atlas,** massa lateralis atlantis. **lateral m's of ethmoid bone.** See *labyrinthus ethmoidalis*. **lateral m. of sacrum,** pars lateralis ossis sacri. **lateral m. of vertebrae,** pediculus arcus vertebrae. **lean body m.,** that part of the body including all its components except neutral storage lipid; in essence, the fat-free mass of the body. **mercury m.,** a mixture of mercury oleate, mercury, honey, glycerin, glycyrrhiza, and althea, containing 31–35 per cent of mercury. Called also *massa hydrargyri, blue mass*, and *blue pill*. **pill m., pilular m.,** a drug mass of the proper consistency for being made into pills. **Priestley's m.,** a green or brownish substance sometimes seen upon the canine and incisor teeth, caused by a chromogenic microorganism. **Schultze's granular m's,**

collections of granular material, consisting largely of broken-down blood platelets, formed in the blood. **Stent's m.,** a plastic resinous material which sets into a very hard substance; used in dentistry for making impressions of the mouth, or in surgery for making molds for keeping grafts in place. **tigroid m's,** Nissl's bodies. **Vallet's m.,** ferrous carbonate m. **ventrolateral m.,** that portion of the primitive lateral mass of the embryo from which are developed the abdominal, thoracic, and anterior cervical muscles.

massa (mas′sah), pl. *mas′sae* [L.]. A lump or body of cohering material; used in anatomical nomenclature as a general term to designate a cohesive accumulation of tissue. Called also *mass.* **m. copa′ibae,** copaiba solidified by the addition of magnesia. **m. fer′ri carbona′tis,** ferrous carbonate mass. **m. hydrar′gyri,** mercury mass. **m. innomina′ta,** paradidymis. **m. interme′dia** [B N A], adhesio interthalamica. **m. latera′lis atlan′tis** [N A, B N A], the thickened lateral portion of the atlas to which the arches are attached and which bears the articulating surfaces. Called also *lateral mass of atlas.* **mas′sae latera′les os′sis ethmoida′lis.** See *labyrinthus ethmoidalis.* **m. latera′lis os′sis sa′cri,** pars lateralis ossis sacri. **m. latera′lis ver′tebrae,** pediculus arcus vertebrae. **m. mol′lis,** adhesio interthalamica.

massae (mas′se) [L.]. Plural of *massa.*

massage (mah-sahzh′) [Fr.; Gr. *massein* to knead]. The systematic therapeutical friction, stroking, and kneading of the body. **auditory m.,** massage of the drum membrane. **Cederschiöld's m.,** massage by making rhythmic pressure over the parts. **douche m.,** massage combined with the application of a douche. **electrovibratory m.,** massage by means of an electric vibrator. **hydropneumatic m.,** massage by means of air forced through a tube at the end of which is a chamber containing water, the water chamber being applied to the part to be massaged. **inspiratory m.,** indirect massage of the liver by means of diaphragmatic breathing. **tremolo m.,** a variety of mechanical massage. **vapoaural m.,** a vapor and massage treatment of the ear. **vapopulmonary m.,** a massage and vapor treatment for the lungs. **vapor m.,** treatment of a cavity by a medicated and nebulized vapor under interrupted pressure. **vibratory m.,** massage by rapidly repeated light percussion with a vibrating hammer or sound.

Masselon's spectacles (mas″ĕ-lawz′) [Miche Julien *Masselon*, French ophthalmologist, 1844–1917]. See under *spectacles.*

Masset's test (mas-āz′) [Alfred Auguste *Masset*, French physician, born 1870]. See under *tests.*

masseter (mas-se′ter) [Gr. *masētēr* chewer]. See *musculus masseter.*

masseteric (mas″e-ter′ik). Pertaining to the masseter muscle.

masseur (mah-ser′) [Fr.]. 1. A man who performs massage. 2. An instrument for performing massage.

masseuse (mah-suhz′) [Fr.]. A woman who performs massage.

massicot (mas′ĭ-kot). Lead monoxide, PbO.

Massini's maneuver (mah-se′nēz). See under *maneuver.*

massive (mas′iv). Having a solid bulky form; heavy; in a mass; complete.

massodent (mas′o-dent). An instrument for performing massage of the gums.

Massol's bacillus (mah-solz′) [Léon *Massol*, Swiss bacteriologist, 1837–1909]. *Lactobacillus bulgaricus.*

massor (mas′or). Masseur.

massotherapy (mas″o-ther′ah-pe) [Gr. *massein* to knead + *therapy*]. The treatment of disease by massage.

mast-. See *masto-.*

mastadenitis (mas″tad-e-ni′tis) [*mast-* + Gr. *adēn* gland + *-itis*]. Inflammation of the mammary gland.

mastadenoma (mas″tad-e-no′mah) [*mast-* + Gr. *adēn* gland + *-oma*]. Tumor of the breast.

mastalgia (mas-tal′je-ah) [*mast-* + *-algia*]. Pain in the mammary gland.

mastatrophia (mas″tah-tro′fe-ah). Mastatrophy.

mastatrophy (mas-tat′ro-fe) [*mast-* + *atrophy*]. Atrophy of the mammary gland.

mastauxe (mas-tawk′se) [*mast-* + Gr. *auxē* increase]. Enlargement of the breast.

mastectomy (mas-tek′to-me) [*mast-* + Gr. *ektomē* excision]. Excision of the breast; mammectomy.

Master "2-step" exercise test (mas′ter) [Arthur M. *Master*, American physician, born 1895]. See under *tests.*

masthelcosis (mas″thel-ko′sis) [*mast-* + Gr. *helkōsis* ulceration]. Ulceration of the breast or mammary gland.

mastic (mas′tik) [L. *mastiche;* Gr. *mastichē*]. A resin obtained from *Pistacia lentiscus*, a tree of the Mediterranean region: styptic, stimulant, and stomachic, and used in microscopy and dentistry.

mastication (mas″tĭ-ka′shun) [L. *masticare* to chew]. The chewing of food.

masticatory (mas′tĭ-kah-to″re). 1. Subserving or pertaining to mastication; affecting the muscles of mastication. 2. A remedy to be chewed but not swallowed.

mastiche (mas′tĭ-kĕ) [L.]. Mastic.

Mastigophora (mas″tĭ-gof′o-rah) [Gr. *mastix* whip + *pherein* to bear]. A class of protozoan organisms comprising those which have from one to four flagella. Several species are occasionally found as parasites within the hollow organs of the body.

mastigote (mas′tĭ-gōt). Any organism of the class *Mastigophora.*

mastitis (mas-ti′tis) [*mast-* + *-itis*]. Inflammation of the mammary gland, or breast. **m. carcino′sa,** carcinoma mastitoides. **chronic cystic m.,** a disease of the breast characterized by cyst formation which gives a nodular feel to the organ, and by tenderness and pain. **gargantuan m.,** pathologic enlargement of the breasts to a tremendous size. **glandular m.,** parenchymatous m. **interstitial m.,** inflammation of the stroma of the mammary gland. **m. neonato′rum,** a general term applied to an abnormal condition of the breast of the newborn, such as hypertrophy, engorgement and secretion, or inflammation, with or without suppuration. **parenchymatous m.,** inflammation of the secreting elements of the mammary gland. **periductal m.,** inflammation of tissues about the ducts of the mammary gland, caused by escape into the stroma of secretion resulting from abnormal hormonal stimulation of the gland. **phlegmonous m.,** inflammation of the breast leading to abscess formation. **plasma cell m.,** a morbid condition of the breast characterized by infiltration of the breast stroma with plasma cells and proliferation of the cells lining the ducts, thought by some to be the end-stage of mammary duct ectasia. **puerperal m.,** a common form of mastitis occurring after delivery. **retromammary m., submammary m.,** paramastitis. **stagnation m.,** a local engorgement affecting one or more lobules of the breast and forming a painful lump on the organ. It occurs during early lactation. Called also *caked breast.* **suppurative m.,** pyogenic infection of the breast.

masto-, mast- (mas′to, mast) [Gr. *mastos* breast]. Combining form denoting relationship to the breast. See also words beginning *mammo.*

mastocarcinoma (mas″to-kar″sĭ-no′mah) [*masto-* + *carcinoma*]. Carcinoma of the breast.

mastoccipital (mas″tok-sip′ĭ-tal). Masto-occipital.

mastochondroma (mas″to-kon-dro′mah) [*masto-* + *chondroma*]. A chondroma, or cartilaginous tumor, of the breast.

mastochondrosis (mas″to-kon-dro′sis). Mastochondroma.

mastocyte (mas′to-sīt) [Ger. *Mast* food + *-cyte*]. A mast cell.

mastocytoma (mas″to-si-to′mah). A neoplasm containing mastocytes.

mastocytosis (mas″to-si-to′sis). Urticaria pigmentosa.

mastodynia (mas″to-din′e-ah) [*masto-* + Gr. *odynē* pain]. Pain in the breast.

mastogram (mas′to-gram). A roentgenogram of the breast.

mastography (mas-tog′rah-fe) [*masto-* + Gr. *graphein* to write]. Roentgenography of the breast.

mastoid (mas′toid) [Gr. *mastos* breast + *eidos* form]. 1. Nipple shaped. 2. The mastoid process of the temporal bone; sometimes called the mastoid bone. 3. Pertaining to the mastoid process.

mastoidal (mas-toi′dal). Pertaining to the mastoid process of the temporal bone.

mastoidale (mas″toi-da′le). The lowest point of the mastoid process.

mastoidalgia (mas″toi-dal′je-ah) [*mastoid* + *-algia*]. Pain in the mastoid region.

mastoidea (mas-toi′de-ah). The mastoid portion of the temporal bone.

mastoidectomy (mas″toid-ek′to-me) [*mastoid* + Gr. *ektomē* excision]. Excision of the mastoid cells or the mastoid process of the temporal bone.

mastoideocentesis (mas-toi″de-o-sen-te′sis) [*mastoid* + Gr. *kentēsis* puncture]. Paracentesis of the mastoid cells.

mastoideum (mas-toi′de-um). The mastoid portion of the temporal bone.

mastoiditis (mas″toid-i′tis). Inflammation of the mastoid antrum and cells. **Bezold's m.,** a form in which the pus has escaped into the digastric groove and the head of the sternocleidomastoid muscle. **m. exter′na,** inflammation of the periosteum of the mastoid process. **m. inter′na,** inflammation of the cells of the mastoid. **sclerosing m.,** mastoiditis attended with hardening and condensation of the bone. **silent m.,** a progressive destructive mastoiditis with mild systemic and local manifestations.

mastoidotomy (mas″toid-ot′o-me) [*mastoid* + Gr. *temnein* to cut]. Surgical incision of the mastoid process of the temporal bone.

mastoidotympanectomy (mas-toi″do-tim″pah-nek′to-me). Radical mastoidectomy.

mastologist (mas-tol′o-jist). An expert in mastology.

mastology (mas-tol′o-je) [*masto-* + *-logy*]. The science or study of the mammary gland, or breast.

mastomenia (mas″to-me′ne-ah) [*masto-* + Gr. *mēniaia* the menses]. Vicarious menstruation from the breast.

mastoncus (mas-tong′kus) [*masto-* + Gr. *onkos* bulk]. A tumor of the breast or mammary gland.

masto-occipital (mas″to-ok-sip′ĭ-tal). Pertaining to the mastoid process and the occipital bone.

mastoparietal (mas″to-pah-ri′ĕ-tal) [*mastoid* + *parietal*]. Pertaining to the mastoid process and the parietal bone.

mastopathia (mas″to-path′e-ah). Mastopathy. **m. cys′tica,** a morbid condition of the mammary gland, with the formation of cysts.

mastopathy (mas-top′ah-the) [*masto-* + Gr. *pathos* disease]. Disease of the mammary gland. **cystic m.,** mastopathia cystica.

mastopexy (mas′to-pek-se) [*masto-* + Gr. *pēxis* fixation]. The surgical fixation of a pendulous breast.

mastoplasia (mas″to-pla′ze-ah). Mammoplasia.

mastoplastia (mas″to-plas′te-ah) [*masto-* + Gr. *plassein* to form]. Hyperplasia of breast tissue.

mastoplasty (mas′to-plas″te). Mammoplasty.

mastoptosis (mas″to-to′sis) [*masto-* + Gr. *ptōsis* fall]. Pendulous breasts.

mastorrhagia (mas″to-ra′je-ah) [*masto-* + Gr. *rhegnynai* to burst forth]. Hemorrhage from the mammary gland.

mastoscirrhus (mas″to-skir′us) [*masto-* + Gr. *skirros* hardness]. Hardening, or scirrhus, of the mammary gland.

mastosis (mas-to′sis), pl. *masto′ses* [*mast-* + *-osis*]. A general term for pathologic changes in the breast of a degenerative and productive type characterized by the presence of painful nodular tumefactions.

mastosquamous (mas-to-skwa′mus). Pertaining to or affecting the mastoid and squama.

mastostomy (mas-tos′to-me) [*masto-* + Gr. *stomoun* to provide with an opening, or mouth]. Incision of the breast with drainage.

mastotic (mas-tot′ik). Characterized by mastosis.

mastotomy (mas-tot′o-me) [*masto-* + Gr. *tomē* a cutting]. Surgical incision of a mamma.

masturbation (mas″tur-ba′shun) [L. *manus* hand + *stuprare* to rape]. Production of orgasm by self-manipulation of the genitals.

masurium (mah-su′re-um). A former name of the element technetium.

Matas' band, operation (mat′as) [Rudolph *Matas*, surgeon in New Orleans, 1860–1957]. See under *band*, and *endo-aneurysmorrhaphy*.

matching (mach′ing). Comparison for the purpose of selecting objects having similar or identical characteristics. **m. of blood,** the procedure of comparing the blood of a contemplated donor with that of the patient (recipient) to ascertain whether their bloods belong to the same group. **cross m.,** determination of the compatibility of the blood of a donor and that of a recipient before transfusion by placing red cells of the donor in the recipient's serum and red cells of the recipient in the donor's serum. Absence of agglutination indicates that the two blood specimens belong to the same group and are compatible.

maté (mah-ta′) [Spanish American]. The dried leaves of *Ilex paraguayensis*, used like tea: diuretic and diaphoretic.

Mátéfy reaction, test (mah-ta′fe) [Ladislaus *Mátéfy*, Hungarian physician, born 1889]. See under *tests*.

mater (ma′ter) [L.]. Mother. **dura m.** ["hard mother"]. See *dura* mater. **pia m.** ["tender mother"]. See *pia mater*.

materia (mah-te′re-ah), pl. *mate′riae* [L.]. Matter, or substance. See also *materies*. **m. al′ba,** whitish deposits on the teeth, composed of mucus and epithelial cells containing molds and bacteria. **m. den′tica,** that branch of study which deals with medicinal substances used in the practice of dentistry. **m. med′ica,** that branch of medical study which deals with drugs, their sources, preparations, and uses. **M. Med′ica Pu′ra,** Hahnemann's work giving the result of his provings of sixty-one drugs. It forms the basis of the homeopathic materia medica. **m. pec′cans,** materies peccans.

material (mah-te′re-al). Substance or elements from which a concept may be formulated, or an object constructed. **base m.,** any substance that may be used in making the base for an artificial denture, such as acrylic resin, metal, polystyrene, shellac, vulcanite, etc. **impression m.,** any substance that may be used in making an impression of the teeth and other structures of the mouth, such as plaster of paris, alginates, rubber compounds, etc.

materies (mah-te′re-ēz) [L.]. Substance. See also *materia*. **m. mor′bi** [L. "substance of disease"], the element or principle which causes a disease. **m. pec′cans** [L. "offending substance"], the principle that causes the pathologic changes occurring in disease.

maternal (mah-ter′nal) [L. *maternus; mater* mother]. Pertaining to the mother.

metron measure]. An instrument for detecting and measuring refractive errors of the dioptric mediums.

mediastina (me″de-as-ti′nah) [L.]. Plural of *mediastinum.*

mediastinal (me″de-as-ti′nal) [L. *mediastinalis*]. Of or pertaining to the mediastinum.

mediastinitis (me″de-as″tĭ-ni′tis). Inflammation of the mediastinum. **fibrinous m.,** an exuberant inflammatory sclerogenic process of infectious, rheumatic, hemorrhagic, or undetermined origin, which may be associated with fibrous pericarditis and with inflammatory fibrous masses in other parts of the body; it is often accompanied by obstruction of mediastinal structures, especially the superior vena cava, and, less often, the tracheobronchial tree, the esophagus, and other structures. **indurative m.,** fibrinous m.

mediastinogram (me″de-as-ti′no-gram). A roentgenogram of the mediastinum.

mediastinography (me″de-as″tĭ-nog′rah-fe). Roentgenography of the mediastinum.

mediastinopericarditis (me″de-as″tĭ-no-per″ĭ-kar-di′tis). Inflammation of the mediastinum and the pericardium.

mediastinoscopy (me″de-as″tĭ-nos′ko-pe). Examination of the mediastinum by means of a tubular instrument permitting direct inspection of the tissues in the area.

mediastinotomy (me″de-as″ti-not′o-me) [*mediastinum* + Gr. *tomē* a cutting]. The operation of cutting into the mediastinum. Performed from the front, it is *anterior* or *cervical m.;* from the back, *posterior* or *dorsal m.*

mediastinum (me″de-as-ti′num), pl. *mediasti′na* [L.]. 1. A median septum or partition. 2. [N A] The mass of tissues and organs separating the two lungs, between the sternum in front and the vertebral column behind, and from the thoracic inlet above to the diaphragm below. It contains the heart and its large vessels, the trachea, esophagus, thymus, lymph nodes, and other structures and tissues, and is divided into anterior, middle, posterior, and superior regions. Called also *septum mediastinale* [B N A]. **anterior m., m. ante′rius** [N A], the division of the mediastinum bounded behind by the pericardium, in front by the sternum, and on each side by the pleura. It contains loose areolar tissue, lymphatic vessels, the internal thoracic vessels of the left side, and the origins of the sternohyoid, sternothyroid, and triangularis sterni muscles. Called also *cavum mediastinale anterius* [B N A]. **m. cerebel′li,** falx cerebelli. **m. cer′ebri,** falx cerebri. **m. me′dium** [N A], **middle m.,** the division of the mediastinum containing the heart enclosed in its pericardium, the ascending aorta, the superior vena cava, the bifurcation of the trachea, the pulmonary arteries and veins, the phrenic nerves, a large portion of the roots of the lungs, and the arch of the azygos vein. **posterior m., m. poste′rius** [N A], the division of the mediastinum bounded behind by the vertebral column, in front by the pericardium, and on each side by the pleurae. It contains the descending aorta, the greater and lesser azygos veins, the superior intercostal vein, the thoracic duct, the esophagus, the vagus nerves, and the great splanchnic nerves. Called also *cavum mediastinale posterius* [B N A]. **superior m., m. supe′rius** [N A], the division of the mediastinum extending from the pericardium to the root of the neck, and containing the esophagus and the trachea behind, the thymus or its remains in front, and the great vessels related to the heart and pericardium in between. **m. tes′tis** [N A], the partial septum of the testis, formed near its posterior border by fibrous tissue which is continuous with the tunica albuginea.

mediastinus (me″de-as-ti′nus) [L.]. An assistant physician or surgeon.

mediate (me′de-āt). Indirect; accomplished by the aid of an intervening medium.

mediation (me″de-a′shun). The action of interposing or serving as an intermediary. **chemical m.,** the conception that when a sympathetic nerve impulse arrives at a smooth muscle cell it liberates a chemical (i.e., adrenin) from the cell, which initiates the cell response.

mediator (me′de-a″tor). An object or substance by which something is mediated, such as (1) a structure of the nervous system that transmits impulses eliciting a specific response, or (2) a chemical substance (transmitter substance) that induces activity in an excitable tissue, such as nerve or muscle.

medicable (med′ĭ-kah-bl). Subject to treatment with reasonable expectation of cure.

medical (med′ĭ-kal). Pertaining to medicine or to the treatment of diseases.

medicament (med′ĭ-kah-ment) [L. *medicamentum*]. A medicinal substance or agent.

medicamentarius (med″ĭ-kah-men-ta′re-us) [L.]. Apothecary.

medicamentosus (med″ĭ-kah-men-to′sus) [L.]. Medicamentous.

medicamentous (med″ĭ-kah-men′tus). Pertaining to, used in, or caused by a drug or drugs.

medicaster (med′ĭ-kas″ter). A pretender to medical skill; a charlatan or quack.

medicate (med′ĭ-kāt) [L. *medicatus*]. To impregnate or imbue with a medicinal substance.

medication (med″ĭ-ka′shun) [L. *medicatio*]. 1. Impregnation with a medicine. 2. The administration of remedies. **conservative m.,** treatment aimed to build up the vital powers of the patient. **dialytic m.,** treatment by the internal use of artificial mineral waters, i.e., dilute aqueous solutions of salts. **hypodermatic m.,** the introduction of remedial agents beneath the skin. **ionic m.,** the application of medicines by cataphoresis, the ions of the drugs passing from one pole of the battery to the other through the body. **sublingual m.,** the administration of medicine in powdered form by placing it beneath the tongue. **substitutive m.,** medication for the purpose of causing an acute nonspecific inflammation to overcome a specific one. **transduodenal m.,** the administration of medicine through a duodenal tube into the intestines without soiling the stomach.

medicator (med′ĭ-ka″tor). An instrument for carrying medicines into a cavity of the body; an applicator.

medicephalic (me″de-se-fal′ik). Median cephalic. See under *vein.*

medicerebellar (me″de-ser″e-bel′ar). Middle cerebellar.

medicerebral (me″de-ser′e-bral). Middle cerebral.

medicinal (me-dis′ĭ-nal) [L. *medicinalis*]. 1. Having healing qualities. 2. Pertaining to a medicine or to healing.

medicine (med′ĭ-sin) [L. *medicina*]. 1. Any drug or remedy. 2. The art or science of healing diseases; especially the healing of diseases by the administration of internal remedies. **air m., aviation m.,** that branch of medicine which has to do with the physiological, medical, psychological, and epidemiological problems involved in present-day flying. **clinical m.** 1. The study of disease at the bedside by demonstrations on the living patient. 2. The last two years of the usual curriculum in a medical college. **compound m.,** a medicine containing a mixture of several drugs. **domestic m.,** the home treatment of disorders without the advice of a physician. **dosimetric m.,** the practice of administering medicines by an exact and determinate system of doses. **environmental m.,** that which considers inanimate as well as animate pathogenic agents in the environment. **experimental m.,** study of the science of healing diseases based on experimentation in animals. **forensic m.,** the application of medical knowledge to questions of law; medical jurisprudence; called also *legal m.* **galenic m.,** an absolute system of practice based upon the teachings of Galen. **geriatric m.,** geriatrics. **group m.,** the practice of medicine by a group of physicians who are associated together for the cooperative diagnosis and treatment of patients. **hermetic m.,** spagyric m. **holistic m.,** a system of medicine which considers man as an integrated whole, or as a functioning unit. **Indian m.,** a North American form of quackery alleged to be derived from the aboriginals. **internal m.,** that branch of medicine dealing especially with the diagnosis and medical treatment of diseases and disorders of the internal structures of the human body. **legal m.,** forensic m. **mental m.,** psychiatry. **neo-hippocratic m.,** neo-hippocratism. **patent m.,** vernacular term for a nostrum advertised to the public. It is generally of secret composition. **patented m.,** a remedy the manufacture of which is protected by letters patent. **physical m.,** the employment of physical means in the diagnosis and treatment of disease. It includes the use of heat, cold, water, light, electricity, manipulation, massage, exercise and mechanical devices. **pre-clinical m.** 1. Medical practice devoted to keeping the well well and preventing or postponing the development of clinical conditions in the near sick. 2. The first two years of the usual curriculum in a medical college. **preventive m.,** that branch of study and practice which aims at the prevention of disease. **proprietary m.,** a drug or remedy to which the manufacturing pharmaceutical house has exclusive (proprietary) rights, and which is marketed usually under a name that is registered as a trade mark. **psychologic m.,** medicine in its relation to mental diseases. **psychosomatic m.,** a system of medicine which aims at discovering the exact nature of the relationship of the emotions and bodily function, affirming the principle that the mind and body are one; the simultaneous application of physiologic and psychologic technics in the study and treatment of illness. **rational m.,** practice of medicine based upon actual knowledge: opposed to *empiricism.* **social m.,** phases of preventive medicine and the care of the sick which concern the community as a whole or large groups of persons rather than the individual. **socialized m.,** the practice of medicine under a system in which there is community responsibility for the care of the sick rather than individual responsibility of patient to doctor and doctor to patient. **space m.,** that branch of aviation medicine concerned solely with conditions to be encountered by man in space. **spagyric m.,** the obsolete, semialchemistic system of practice established by Paracelsus (1493–1541). **state m.,** a system of medical care in which the government assumes responsibility for the prevention of disease and the care of the sick. **static m.,** practice of medicine based on the varying relations of administration of food, excretion, and body weight. **suggestive m.,** treatment of disease by hypnotic suggestion. **tropical m.,** medical science as applied to diseases ordinarily occurring only in hot, or tropical, countries. **veterinary m.,** the treatment of the diseases of animals.

medicinerea (med″ĭ-sĭ-ne′re-ah) [L. *medius* middle + *cinerea* ashen]. The gray matter of the lenticula and the claustrum.

medicisterna (med″ĭ-sis-ter′nah). The cisterna venae magnae cerebri.

medicochirurgic (med″ĭ-ko-ki-rur′jik). Pertaining to medicine and surgery.

medicodental (med″ĭ-ko-den′tal). Pertaining to both medicine and dentistry.

medicolegal (med″ĭ-ko-le′gal). Pertaining to medicine and law, or to forensic medicine.

medicomechanical (med″ĭ-ko-me-kan′ĭ-kal). Both medicinal and mechanical.

medicommissure (me″dĭ-kom′ĭ-sūr). The middle commissure, or commissura media.

medicophysical (med″ĭ-ko-fiz′ĭ-kal). Both medical and physical.

medicophysics (med″ĭ-ko-fiz′iks). Physics as applied to medicine; medical physics.

medicopsychological (med″ĭ-ko-si″ko-loj′ĭ-kal). Pertaining to medicopsychology.

medicopsychology (med″ĭ-ko-si-kol′o-je). The science of medicine in its relations with the mind or with mental diseases.

medicornu (me″dĭ-kor′nu). Cornu inferius ventriculi lateralis.

medicothorax (med″ĭ-ko-tho′raks). Artificial pneumothorax in which medicated vapor is introduced.

medicotopographical (med″ĭ-ko-to″po-graf′ĭ-kal). Pertaining to topography in its relation to disease.

medicozoological (med″ĭ-ko-zo-o-loj′ĭ-kal). Pertaining to zoology in its relation to medicine.

medicus (med′ĭ-kus), pl. *med′ici* [L.]. Physician.

medidural (me″dĭ-du′ral). Pertaining to the central part of the dura mater.

medifrontal (me″dĭ-fron′tal). Median and also frontal; pertaining to the middle of the forehead.

Medin's disease (ma′dēnz) [Oskar *Medin*, Swedish physician, 1874–1928]. Epidemic poliomyelitis.

mediocarpal (me″de-o-kar′pal). Midcarpal.

medioccipital (me″de-ok-sip′ĭ-tal). Midoccipital.

mediocommissure (me″de-o-kom′ĭ-sūr). Medicommissure.

mediolateral (me″do-o-lat′er-al) [L. *medius* middle + *lateralis* lateral]. Pertaining to the middle and to one side.

medionecrosis (me″de-o-ne-kro′sis). Necrosis of the tunica media of a blood vessel, often leading to its rupture.

mediopontine (me″de-o-pon′tin) [L. *medius* middle + *pons* bridge]. Pertaining to the center of the pons.

mediotarsal (me″de-o-tar′sal) [L. *medius* middle + *tarsus*]. Pertaining to the middle of the tarsus.

medipeduncle (me″de-pe′dunk-'l). Pedunculus cerebellaris medius.

mediscalenus (me″de-skah-le′nus). Musculus scalenus medius.

medisect (me′dĭ-sekt) [L. *medius* middle + *secare* to cut]. To divide or dissect medially.

medisylvian (me″dĭ-sil′ve-an). Pertaining to the middle portion of the fissure of Sylvius.

meditemporal (me″dĭ-tem′po-ral). Pertaining to the middle portion of the temporal lobe of the brain.

meditullium (me″dĭ-tul′le-um) [L. "midland"]. 1. Centrum semiovale. 2. Corpus medullare cerebelli. 3. Substantia alba.

medium (me′de-um), pl. *mediums* or *me′dia* [L. "middle"]. 1. Means. 2. A substance which transmits impulses. 3. A substance used in the culture of bacteria. See *culture medium*, under C. **Bruns's glucose m.,** a mixture of distilled water, glucose, glycerin, and camphorated spirit, used for mounting fresh tissue specimens. **clearing m.,** a substance used for rendering histologic specimens transparent. **contrast m.,** a radiopaque substance used to facilitate roentgen visualization of internal structures of the body. **culture m.,** a substance used to support the growth of microorganisms or other cells. See *culture medium*, under C. **dioptric media,** refracting media. **disperse m., dispersion m., dispersive m.,** the continuous or external portion of a colloid system in which the particles of the disperse phase are distributed. It is analogous to the solvent in a true solution. **nutrient m.,** a culture medium to which certain nutrient materials have been added. **refracting media,** the transparent tissues and fluids in the eye through which light rays pass and by which they are refracted and brought to a focus on the retina; the structures include the cornea, aqueous humor, crystalline lens, and vitreous body. **separating m.,** any substance which facilitates separation, such as a coating used upon a surface which serves to prevent adherence to it of another surface; used in dentistry on impressions to facilitate removal of the cast. **Wickersheimer's m.** See under *fluid.*

medius (me'de-us) [L.]. In the middle; in official anatomical nomenclature, used in reference to a structure lying between two other structures that are anterior and posterior, superior and inferior, or internal and external in position.

medomin (med'o-min). Trade mark for a preparation of heptabarbital.

medorrhea (med"o-re'ah) [Gr. *mēdea* genitals + *rhoia* flow]. A urethral discharge.

medrol (med'rol). Trade mark for preparations of methylprednisolone.

medroxyprogesterone (med-rok"se-pro-jes'-ter-ōn). Chemical name: 6α-methyl-17α-acetoxy-progesterone: used as a progestational agent.

medulla (me-dul'lah), pl. *medul'lae* [L.]. The middle, inmost part; used as a general term in anatomical nomenclature to designate the inmost portion of an organ or structure. Called also *marrow.* **adrenal m.,** m. glandulae suprarenalis. **m. of bone,** m. ossium. **dorsal m., m. dorsa'lis,** m. spinalis. **m. glan'dulae suprarena'lis** [N A], the inner, reddish brown, soft part of the suprarenal gland. Called also *substantia medullae glandulae suprarenalis* [B N A], and *adrenal medulla.* **m. of kidney,** m. renis. **m. of lymph node,** m. nodi lymphatici. **m. neph'rica,** m. renis. **m. no'di lymphat'ici** [N A], the central part of a lymph node, comprising cords and sinuses. Called also *substantia medullaris lymphoglandulae* [B N A], and *m. of lymph node.* **m. oblonga'ta** [N A, B N A], the truncated cone of nervous tissue continuous above with the pons and below with the spinal cord. It lies ventral to the cerebellum and its posterior surface forms the floor of the fourth ventricle. **m. os'sium** [B N A], the soft material filling the cavities of the bones; made up of a meshwork of connective tissue containing branching connective tissue corpuscles, the meshes being filled with marrow cells, which consist variously of fat cells, large nucleated cells or myelocytes, and giant cells called megakaryocytes. Called also *bone marrow.* **m. os'sium fla'va** [N A, B N A], ordinary bone marrow of the kind in which the fat cells predominate. Called also *yellow bone marrow.* **m. os'sium ru'bra** [N A, B N A], marrow of developing bone, of the ribs, vertebrae, and many of the smaller bones, which is regarded as having an important hematopoietic function. Called also *red bone marrow.* **m. re'nis** [N A], the inner part of the substance of the kidney, composed chiefly of collecting elements, organized grossly into pyramids. Called also *substantia medullaris renis* [B N A], and *m. of kidney.* **spinal m., m. spina'lis** [N A, B N A], that part of the central nervous system which is lodged in the vertebral canal, extending from the foramen magnum to about the level of the third lumbar vertebra. Called also *spinal cord.* **suprarenal m., m. of suprarenal gland,** m. glandulae suprarenalis.

medullae (me-dul'e) [L.]. Plural of *medulla.*

medullary (med'u-lār"e) [L. *medullaris*]. Pertaining to the marrow or to any medulla; resembling marrow.

medullated (med'u-lāt"ed). Containing or covered by a medullary substance; equipped with myelin sheaths.

medullation (med"u-la'shun). The formation of a medulla or marrow; especially the formation of the medullary sheath around a nerve fiber.

medullectomy (med"u-lek'to-me) [L. *medulla* marrow + Gr. *ektomē* excision]. Excision and excochleation of the medulla of an organ, as of the adrenal gland.

medulliadrenal (me-dul"ĭ-ad-re'nal). Medullo-adrenal.

medullispinal (me-dul"ĭ-spi'nal) [L. *medulla* marrow + *spinalis* spinal]. Pertaining to the spinal cord.

medullitis (med"u-li'tis). 1. Osteomyelitis. 2. Myelitis.

medullization (med"u-li-za'shun). The enlargement of the haversian canals in rarefying osteitis, followed by their conversion into marrow channels; also the replacement of bone by marrow cells.

medullo-adrenal (me-dul"o-ad-re'nal). Pertaining to the adrenal medulla.

medullo-arthritis (me-dul"o-ar-thri'tis) [L. *medulla* marrow + *arthritis*]. Inflammation of the marrow spaces of the articular extremities of bones.

medulloblast (me-dul'o-blast). An undifferentiated cell of the medullary tube which may develop into either a neuroblast or a spongioblast.

medulloblastoma (me-dul"o-blas-to'mah). A cerebellar tumor composed of undifferentiated preneuroglial cells.

medullocell (me-dul'o-sel) [L. *medulla* marrow + *cell*]. Myelocyte.

medulloculture (me-dul'o-kul"tūr) [L. *medulla* marrow + *culture*]. A bacterial culture of bone marrow.

medullo-encephalic (me-dul"o-en"se-fal'ik). Myelo-encephalic.

medullo-epithelioma (me-dul"o-ep"ĭ-the"le-o'-mah). A tumor composed largely of primitive retina epithelium and of neuro-epithelium.

medulloid (med'u-loid) [*medulla* + Gr. *eidos* form]. An adrenergic substance with a hormonal activity simulating that of the adrenal medulla.

medullosis (med"u-lo'sis). Myelocytosis.

medullosuprarenoma (me-dul"o-su"prah-re-no'mah). A tumor derived from the medulla of the adrenal gland.

medullotherapy (me-dul"o-ther'ah-pe). Pasteur's preventive treatment of rabies with spinal cords.

medusocongestin (me-du"so-kon-jes'tin). A toxic substance derived from the tentacles of the jelly fish, *Rhizostoma cuvieri*, which, when injected into laboratory animals, causes intense congestion of the splanchnic vessels; believed to be identical with congestin.

mega- (meg'ah) [Gr. *megas* big, great]. Combining form designating great size; used in naming units of measurement to indicate a quantity one million (10^6) times the unit designated by the root with which it is combined. See also words beginning *megalo-*.

megabacterium (meg"ah-bak-te're-um) [*mega-* + *bacterium*]. A bacterium of large size.

megabladder (meg"ah-blad'er). A condition marked by permanent overdistention of the bladder.

megacardia (meg"ah-kar'de-ah) [*mega-* + Gr. *kardia* heart]. Cardiomegaly.

megacaryoblast (meg"ah-kar'e-o-blast). Megakaryoblast.

megacaryocyte (meg"ah-kar'e-o-sīt). Megakaryocyte.

megacecum (meg"ah-se'kum) [*mega-* + *cecum*]. A cecum which is abnormally large.

megacephalic (meg"ah-se-fal'ik). Megalocephaly.

megacephalous (meg"ah-sef'ah-lus). Megalocephalic.

megacephaly (meg"ah-sef'ah-le). Megalocephaly.

megacholedochus (meg"ah-ko-led'o-kus). Abnormal dilatation of the common bile duct.

megacoccus (meg"ah-kok'us), pl. *megacoc'ci* [*mega-* + Gr. *kokkos* berry]. A spherical microorganism of large size.

megacolon (meg"ah-ko'lon). Abnormally large

colon, due to dilatation and hypertrophy. The condition is usually one of childhood. Called also *giant colon, congenital idiopathic dilatation of colon*, and *Hirschsprung's disease*. **m. congen′itum,** congenital dilatation of the colon.

megacurie (meg″ah-ku′re). A unit of radioactivity, being one million (10^6) curies. Abbreviated Mc.

megacycle (meg′ah-si″k'l). A unit of one million (10^6) cycles, e.g. 1,000,000 cycles per second: applied to the frequency of electromagnetic waves. Abbreviated Mc.

megadolichocolon (meg″ah-dol″ĭ-ko-ko′lon). A condition in which the colon is abnormally long and dilated.

megadont (meg′ah-dont) [*mega-* + Gr. *odous* tooth]. Having a dental index above 44.

megadontia (meg″ah-don′she-ah). Macrodontia.

megadontic (meg″ah-don′tik). Macrodontic.

megadontism (meg″ah-don′tizm). The state of having abnormally large teeth, or a dental index above 44.

megaduodenum (meg″ah-du″o-de′num). Abnormally large size of the duodenum.

megadyne (meg′ah-dīn″) [*mega-* + *dyne*]. A million (10^6) dynes.

mega-esophagus (meg″ah-e-sof′ah-gus). Dilatation and muscular hypertrophy of the esophagus above a constricted distal segment. See *achalasia*.

megagamete (meg″ah-gam′ēt). Macrogamete.

megakaryoblast (meg″ah-kar′e-o-blast). An immature megakaryocyte.

megakaryoblastoma (meg″ah-kar″e-o-blas-to′mah). A tumor of the megakaryoblast, a name that has been applied to Hodgkin's disease.

megakaryocyte (meg″ah-kar′e-o-sīt) [*mega-* + Gr. *karyon* nucleus + *-cyte*]. The giant cell of bone marrow; it is a large cell with a greatly lobulated nucleus, and is generally supposed to give rise to blood platelets.

megakaryocytosis (meg″ah-kar″e-o-si-to′sis). The presence of megakaryocytes in the blood.

megakaryophthisis (meg″ah-kar″e-o-thi′sis) [*megakaryocyte* + Gr. *phthisis* wasting]. Deficiency of megakaryocytes in the marrow.

megalakria (meg″ah-lak′re-ah) [*megalo-* + Gr. *akron* extremity]. Acromegaly.

megalecithal (meg″ah-les′ĭ-thal) [*mega-* + Gr. *lekithos* yolk). Containing a large amount of yolk.

megalencephalon (meg″al-en-sef′ah-lon) [*megalo-* + Gr. *enkephalos* brain]. An abnormally large brain.

megalencephaly (meg″al-en-sef′ah-le). Macrencephaly.

megalerythema (meg″al-er″ĭ-the′mah). Erythema with swelling of the part; a term sometimes applied to erythema infectiosum because of the large erythematous patches characteristic of that disease.

megalgia (meg-al′je-ah) [Gr. *megas* large + *-algia*]. Severe pain, as in muscular rheumatism.

megalo- (meg′ah-lo) [Gr. *megaleios* magnificent]. Combining form designating great size. See also words beginning *mega-*.

megaloblast (meg′ah-lo-blast″) [*megalo-* + Gr. *blastos* germ]. An erythroblast or primitive red blood corpuscle of large size, i.e., more than 11 μ in diameter. It consists of a homogeneous cytoplasm with a relatively large nucleus with granular chromatin. Megaloblasts are found in the blood in pernicious anemia and are the predominant type of nucleated red cells in the bone marrow of patients with pernicious anemia during relapse. They have been called *ichthyoid cells* because they resemble the red blood cells of fishes. Cf. *erythroblast*. **m. of Sabin,** proerythroblast.

megalobulbus (meg″ah-lo-bul′bus). Enlargement of the duodenal cap in the roentgenogram.

megalocardia (meg″ah-lo-kar′de-ah) [*megalo-* + Gr. *kardia* heart]. Cardiomegaly.

megalocaryocyte (meg″ah-lo-kar′e-o-sīt). Megakaryocyte.

megalocephalia (meg″ah-lo-se-fa′le-ah). Megalocephaly.

megalocephalic (meg″ah-lo-se-fal′ik). Pertaining to or characterized by megalocephaly.

megalocephaly (meg″ah-lo-sef′ah-le) [*megalo-* + Gr. *kephalē* head]. 1. Unusually large size of the head. 2. Progressive enlargement of the bones of the head, face, and neck; leontiasis ossea.

megaloceros (meg″ah-los′ĕ-rus) [*megalo-* + *keras* horn]. A fetal monster having projections from the forehead resembling horns.

megalocheiria (meg″ah-lo-ki′re-ah) [*megalo-* + Gr. *cheir* hand + *-ia*]. Abnormal largeness of the hands.

megaloclitoris (meg″ah-lo-kli′to-ris). Hypertrophy of the clitoris.

megalocoly (meg″ah-lok′o-le). Megacolon.

megalocornea (meg″ah-lo-kor′ne-ah) [*megalo-* + *cornea*]. A developmental anomaly of the cornea, which is of abnormal size at birth and continues to grow, sometimes reaching a diameter of 14 or 15 mm. in the adult.

megalocystis (meg″ah-lo-sis′tis) [*megalo-* + Gr. *kystis* bladder]. An abnormally enlarged bladder.

megalocyte (meg′ah-lo-sīt″) [*megalo-* + *-cyte*]. An extremely large erythrocyte, i.e., one measuring 12 to 25 microns in diameter. Cf. *gigantocyte*.

megalocytosis (meg″ah-lo-si-to′sis). Macrocytosis.

megalodactylia (meg″ah-lo-dak-til′e-ah) [*megalo-* + Gr. *daktylos* finger + *-ia*]. Abnormal largeness of fingers or toes.

megalodactylism (meg″ah-lo-dak′tĭ-lizm). Megalodactylia.

megalodactylous (meg″ah-lo-dak′tĭ-lus). Exhibiting megalodactylia.

megalodactyly (meg″ah-lo-dak′tĭ-le). Megalodactylia.

megalodontia (meg″ah-lo-don′she-ah). Macrodontia.

megalo-enteron (meg″ah-lo-en′ter-on) [*megalo-* + Gr. *enteron* intestine]. Enteromegaly.

megalo-erythema (meg″ah-lo-er″ĭ-the′mah). Megalerythema.

megalo-esophagus (meg″ah-lo-e-sof′ah-gus). Mega-esophagus.

megalogastria (meg″ah-lo-gas′tre-ah) [*megalo-* + Gr. *gastēr* stomach + *-ia*]. Enlargement or abnormally large size of the stomach.

megaloglossia (meg″ah-lo-glos′e-ah) [*megalo-* + Gr. *glōssa* tongue + *-ia*]. Macroglossia.

megalographia (meg″ah-lo-gra′fe-ah). Macrographia.

megalohepatia (meg″ah-lo-he-pat′e-ah) [*megalo-* + Gr. *hēpar* liver + *-ia*]. Enlargement of the liver.

megalokaryocyte (meg″ah-lo-kar′e-o-sit″). Megakaryocyte.

megalomania (meg″ah-lo-ma′ne-ah) [*megalo-* + Gr. *mania* madness]. Delusion of grandeur; unreasonable conviction of one's own extreme greatness, goodness, or power.

megalomaniac (meg″ah-lo-ma′ne-ak). An individual exhibiting megalomania.

megalomelia (meg″ah-lo-me′le-ah) [*megalo-* + Gr. *melos* limb + *-ia*]. Abnormal largeness of the limbs.

megalonychosis (meg″al-on″ĭ-ko′sis) [*megalo-* + Gr. *onyx* nail + *-ia*]. Hypertrophy of the nails and their matrices.

megalopenis (meg″ah-lo-pe′nis). Excessive size of the penis.

megalophthalmos (meg″ah-lof-thal′mos) [*megalo-* + Gr. *ophthalmos* eye]. Abnormally large size of the eyes.

megalophthalmus (meg″ah-lof-thal′mus). Megalophthalmos.

megalopia (meg″ah-lo′pe-ah) [*megalo-* + Gr. *ōps* + *-ia*]. Abnormal enlargement of the eyes.

megaloplastocyte (meg″ah-lo-plas′to-sīt″) [*megalo-* + *plastocyte*]. A blood platelet larger than normal.

megalopodia (meg″ah-lo-po′de-ah) [*megalo-* + Gr. *pous* foot + *-ia*]. Excessive size of the feet.

megalopsia (meg″ah-lop′se-ah) [*megalo-* + Gr. *opsis* vision + *-ia*]. Macropsia.

Megalopyge (meg″ah-lop′ĭ-je). A genus of moths (flannel moths) the caterpillars of which cause a dermatitis in persons who come in contact with them.

megaloscope (meg′ah-lo-skōp″) [*megalo-* + Gr. *skopein* to examine]. A large magnifying lens; a magnifying speculum or mirror.

megalosplanchnic (meg″ah-lo-splank′nik). Having the abdominal portion of the body relatively larger than the thoracic.

megalosplenia (meg″ah-lo-sple′ne-ah) [*megalo-* + Gr. *splen* spleen + *-ia*]. Enlargement of the spleen; splenomegaly.

megalospore (meg′ah-lo-spōr″). 1. A macrospore. 2. A megalosporon.

Megalosporon (meg″ah-los′po-ron) [*megalo-* + Gr. *sporos* seed]. The large-spored division of the trichophyton fungi. **M. ec′tothrix,** the form found outside or on the surface of the hair shaft. **M. en′dothrix,** the form found inside of the hair shaft.

megalosporon (meg″ah-los′po-ron), pl. *megalos′pora.* An organism of the genus Megalosporon.

megalosyndactyly (meg″ah-lo-sin-dak′tĭ-le) [*megalo-* + *syndactyly*]. A condition in which the digits are very large and more or less completely grown together.

megalothymus (meg″ah-lo-thi′mus). An enlarged thymus.

megalo-ureter (meg″ah-lo-u-re′ter) [*megalo-* + *ureter*]. Enlargement of the caliber of the ureter.

megamerozoite (meg″ah-mer″o-zo′īt). A large merozoite.

meganucleus (meg″ah-nu′kle-us). Macronucleus.

megaphonia (meg″ah-fo′ne-ah) [*mega-* + Gr. *phōnē* voice]. Loudness of the voice.

megaprosopous (meg″ah-pros′o-pus) [*mega-* + Gr. *prosōpon* face]. Having a large face.

megarectosigmoid (meg″ah-rek″to-sig′moid). Enormous dilatation of the rectum and sigmoid.

megarectum (meg-ah-rek′tum). A greatly dilated rectum.

Megarhinus (meg″ah-ri′nus). A genus of large, showy, but harmless mosquitoes of tropical and subtropical countries.

Megaselia (meg″ah-se′le-ah). A genus of flies the larvae of which may cause intestinal myiasis.

megaseme (meg′ah-sēm) [*mega-* + Gr. *sēma* sign]. Having an orbital index of 89 or more.

megasigmoid (meg″ah-sig′moid) [*mega-* + *sigmoid*]. An enormously dilated sigmoid.

megasoma (meg″ah-so′mah) [*mega-* + Gr. *sōma* body]. Great size and stature, not amounting to gigantism.

megasome (meg′ah-sōm). Macrosome.

megaspore (meg′ah-spōr). Macrospore.

Megastoma (meg-as′to-mah) [*mega-* + Gr. *stoma* mouth]. *Giardia intestinalis.*

Megatrichophyton (meg″ah-tri″ko-fi′ton). A parasitic fungus, species of which have been isolated from lesions in man and domestic animals.

megaunit (meg′ah-u″nit). A quantity one million (10^6) times that of a standard unit.

megavolt (meg′ah-vōlt) [*mega-* + *volt*]. A million (10^6) volts.

megimide (meg′ĭ-mīd). Trade mark for a preparation of bemegride.

Méglin's point (ma-glanz′) [J. A. *Méglin,* French physician, 1756–1824]. See under *point.*

megohm (meg′ōm) [*mega-* + *ohm*]. A million (10^6) ohms.

megophthalmos (meg-of-thal′mos) [*mega-* + Gr. *ophthalmos* eye]. Buphthalmos.

megoxycyte (meg-ok′sĭ-sīt) [*mega-* + *oxyphil* + *-cyte*]. A large oxyphil cell; a coarsely granular eosinophil leukocyte.

megoxyphil (meg-ok′sĭ-fil) [*mega-* + Gr. *oxys* acid + *philein* to love]. An eosinophil leukocyte containing large granules.

megrim (me′grim). Migraine.

meibomian cyst, gland (mi-bo′me-an) [Heinrich *Meibom,* German anatomist, 1638–1700]. See under *cyst* and *gland.*

meibomianitis (mi-bo″me-ah-ni′tis). Inflammation of the meibomian glands.

meibomitis (mi″bo-mi′tis). Meibomianitis.

Meige's disease (mehzh′ez) [Henri *Meige,* French physician, 1866–1940]. Milroy's disease.

Meigs's capillaries, test (meg′zes) [Arthur V. *Meigs,* Philadelphia physician, 1850–1912]. See under *capillary* and *tests.*

Meigs's syndrome (meg′zes) [Joe Vincent *Meigs,* American surgeon, 1892–1963]. See under *syndrome.*

Meinicke reaction, test (mi′nĭ-ke) [Ernst *Meinicke,* German physician, born 1878]. See under *tests.*

meio- (mi′o) [Gr. *meioun* to make smaller, to lessen]. Combining form denoting relation to decrease in size or number. See also words beginning *mio-.*

meiogenic (mi″o-jen′ik) [Gr. *meiosis* + *gennan* to produce]. Promoting or causing meiosis.

meiosis (mi-o′sis) [Gr. *meiōsis* diminution]. A special method of cell division, occurring in maturation of the sex cells, by means of which each daughter nucleus receives half the number of chromosomes characteristic of the somatic cells of the species. See illustration (p. 890).

meiotic (mi-ot′ik). Pertaining to, characteristic of, or characterized by meiosis.

Meisen mixture (mi′sen) [Valdemar *Meisen,* Danish surgeon, 1878–1934]. See under *mixture.*

Meissner's corpuscles, plexus, etc. (mis′nerz) [Georg *Meissner,* German physiologist, 1829–1905]. See under the nouns.

mel (mel) [L.]. 1. Honey; a saccharine substance deposited by the honey bee, *Apis mellifica.* Clarified honey is chiefly a mixture of levulose and glucose: it is used as a food, as an excipient, and as an application to aphthae. 2. A compound of honey with some medicinal agent.

melagra (mel-ag′rah) [Gr. *melos* limb + *agra* seizure]. Muscular pain in the extremities.

melalgia (mel-al′je-ah) [Gr. *melos* limb + *-algia*]. Neuralgic pain in the limbs.

melancholia (mel″an-ko′le-ah) [*melano-* + Gr. *cholē* bile + *-ia*]. A depressed and unhappy emotional state with abnormal inhibition of mental and bodily activity. **acute m.,** an acute form of melancholia marked, in addition to the usual symptoms, by loss of appetite, emaciation, insomnia, and subnormal temperature. **affective m.,** melancholia corresponding to the depressive phase of manic-depressive insanity. **m. agita′ta, agitated m.,** melancholia with constant motion and signs of great emotional excitement. **m. atton′ita,** stuporous m. **m. with delirium,** melancholia with distressing delusions and hallucinations. **flatuous m.,** that which is characterized by gases in the alimentary canal. **m. hypochondri′aca,** extreme hypochondriasis. **involution m.,** melancholia developing in advanced life during senile involution. **recurrent m.,** a condition in which attacks of melancholia follow one another at more or less regular intervals. **m. religio′sa,** the delusion of one's own personal damnation. **m. simplex,** a mild form with neither delusions nor great excitement. **stuporous m.,** a form in which the patient lies motionless and silent, with

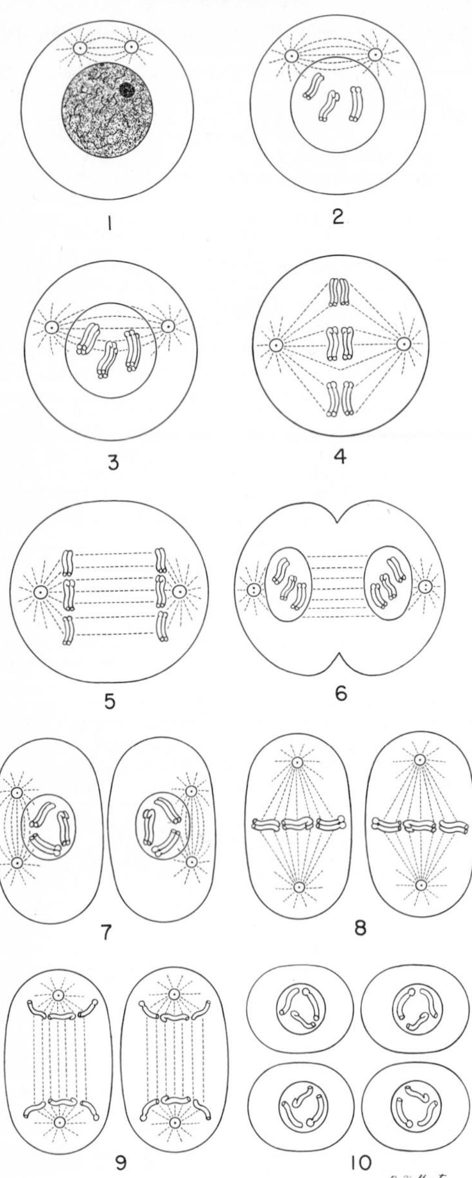

Meiosis shown as occurring in a cell of a hypothetical animal with a diploid chromosome number of six (haploid number three); one pair of chromosomes is short, one pair is long and hooked, and one pair is long and knobbed. *1*, Early prophase of the first meiotic division: chromosomes begin to appear. *2*, Synapsis: the pairing of the homologous chromosomes. *3*, Apparent doubling of the synapsed chromosomes to form groups of four identical chromosomes, tetrads. *4*, Metaphase of the first meiotic division, with the tetrads lined up at the equator of the spindle. *5*, Anaphase of the first meiotic division: the chromosomes migrating toward the poles. *6*, Telophase of the first meiotic division. *7*, Prophase of the second meiotic division. *8*, Metaphase of the second meiotic division. *9*, Anaphase of the second meiotic division. *10*, Mature gametes, each of which contains only one of each kind of chromosome. (Villee.)

fixed eyes and indifference to surroundings; there are sometimes hallucinations.

melancholiac (mel″an-ko′le-ak). 1. Affected with melancholia. 2. A person affected with melancholia.

melanedema (mel″an-e-de′mah) [*melano-* + Gr. *oidēma* swelling]. Anthracosis.

melanemesis (mel″an-em′e-sis) [*melano-* + Gr. *emein* to vomit]. Black vomit.

melanemia (mel″an-e′me-ah) [*melano-* + Gr. *haima* blood + *-ia*]. The presence of black, pigmentary masses in the blood; hemachromatosis. The condition is seen chiefly in pernicious anemia.

melanephidrosis (mel″an-ef″ĭ-dro′sis) [*melano-* + Gr. *ephidrōsis* excessive sweating]. The discharge of black sweat.

mélangeur (ma″lan-zher′) [Fr. "mixer"]. An instrument for drawing and diluting specimens of blood for examination.

melanicterus (mel″an-ik′ter-us). Winckel's disease.

melanidrosis (mel″an-ĭ-dro′sis) [*melano-* + Gr. *hidrōs* sweat]. Melanephidrosis.

melaniferous (mel″an-if′er-us) [*melanin* + L. *ferre* to bear]. Containing melanin or other black pigment.

melanin (mel′ah-nin) [Gr. *melas* black]. The dark amorphous pigment of the skin, hair, and various tumors, of the choroid coat of the eye and the substantia nigra of the brain. It is produced by polymerization of oxidation products of tyrosine and dihydroxyphenyl compounds, and contains carbon, hydrogen, nitrogen, oxygen, and often sulfur. **artificial m., factitious m.,** a compound that resembles melanin, and is formed when a protein is heated in strong hydrochloric acid. Called also *melanoid*.

melanism (mel′ah-nizm). Excessive pigmentation or blackening of the integuments or tissues; melanosis. **metallic m.,** argyrosis.

melanistic (mel″ah-nis′tik). Characterized by melanism.

melano- (mel′ah-no) [Gr. *melas* black]. Combining form meaning black, or denoting relation to melanin.

melanoameloblastoma (mel″ah-no-ah-mel″o-blas-to′mah). Ameloblastoma exhibiting bluish black discoloration because of the presence of melanin granules.

melanoblast (mĕ-lan′o-blast) [*melano-* + Gr. *blastos* germ]. A cell originating from the neural crest that differentiates into a melanocyte.

melanoblastoma (mel″ah-no-blas-to′mah). A tumor made up of melanoblasts.

melanoblastosis (mel″ah-no-blas-to′sis). A condition characterized by the presence of melanoblasts.

melanocancroid (mel″ah-no-kang′kroid). A strongly pigmented epithelial tumor.

melanocarcinoma (mel″ah-no-kar″sĭ-no′mah) [*melano-* + *carcinoma*]. A melanoma attributed to epithelial origin.

melanochroous (mel″ah-nok′ro-us) [*melano-* + Gr. *chrōs* complexion]. Having a dark complexion.

melanocomous (mel″ah-nok′o-mus) [*melano-* + Gr. *komē* hair]. Having black hair.

melanocyte (mĕ-lan′o-sit). The cell responsible for the synthesis of melanin; melanocytes constitute 5 per cent of the cells of the epidermis, with keratinocytes constituting the other 95 per cent of its binary cell system.

melanoderm (mel′ah-no-derm). A person belonging to one of the black races.

melanoderma (mel″ah-no-der′mah) [*melano-* + Gr. *derma* skin]. An increased amount of melanin in the skin, due either to an increase in the production of melanin by the melanocytes normally present or to an increase in the number of melanocytes, with production of hyperpigmented patches. **m. cachectico′rum,** a form seen in certain systemic disorders, as malarial fever, syphilis, cancer, tuberculosis, etc. **parasitic m.,** vagabonds' disease. **senile m.,** pigmentation of the skin in the aged.

melanodermatitis (mel″ah-no-der″mah-ti′tis). Dermatitis associated with an increased deposit of melanin in the skin. **m. tox′ica lichenoi′des,** a condition occurring in persons exposed to tar and subsequently to sunlight; marked by pruritus and the appearance of lichenoid papules, hyperpigmentation, and telangiectasia.

melanodermic (mel″ah-no-der′mik). Having a dark skin.

melano-epithelioma (mel″ah-no-ep″ĭ-the-le-o′mah). An epithelioma containing melanin.

melanoflocculation (mel″ah-no-flok″u-la′shun). A flocculation test for malaria, performed with a melanin antigen. See *Henry's test*, under *tests*.

melanogen (mĕ-lan′o-jen) [*melanin* + Gr. *gennan* to produce]. A colorless chromogen, convertible into melanin, which may occur in the urine in certain diseases.

melanogenesis (mel″ah-no-jen′e-sis). The production of melanin.

melanogenic (mel″ah-no-jen′ik). Causing the production of melanin.

melanoglossia (mel″ah-no-glos′e-ah) [*melano-* + Gr. *glōssa* tongue]. Black tongue.

melanoid (mel′ah-noid) [*melano-* + Gr. *eidos* form]. 1. Resembling melanin; of a dark color. 2. A material resembling melanin.

Melanoides (mel″ah-noi′dēz). A genus of snails, species of which are intermediate hosts of *Paragonimus.*

melanoidin (mel″ah-noi′din). A melanin obtained from the albumins.

Melanolestes (mel″ah-no-les′tēz). A genus of insects. **m. pic′ipes,** the "black corsair" or "kissing bug"; its bite much resembles the sting of a wasp, but it is often much more serious.

melanoleukoderma (mel″ah-no-lu″ko-der′mah) [*melano-* + Gr. *leukos* white + *derma* skin]. A mottled appearance of the skin. **m. col′li,** a mottled appearance of the skin of the neck and adjacent regions, seen as a rare manifestation of syphilis. Called also *venereal collar* and *collar of Venus.*

melanoma (mel″ah-no′mah) [*melano-* + *-oma*]. A tumor made up of melanin-pigmented cells. **malignant m.,** a malignant tumor, usually developing from a nevus and consisting of black masses of cells with a marked tendency to metastasis. **subungual m.,** melanotic whitlow.

melanomatosis (mel″ah-no″mah-to′sis). The formation of melanomas in various parts of the body.

melanonychia (mel″ah-no-nik′e-ah) [*melano-* + Gr. *onyx* nail + *-ia*]. Blackening of the nail by melanin pigmentation.

melanopathy (mel″ah-nop′ah-the) [*melano-* + Gr. *pathos* illness]. Any disease characterized by abnormal pigmentation of the skin or tissues.

melanophore (mel′ah-no-fōr) [*melano-* + Gr. *phoros* bearing]. A pigment cell containing melanin, especially such a cell in fishes, amphibians, and reptiles.

melanophorin (mel″ah-nof′o-rin). A principle which is thought to stimulate melanophores.

melanoplakia (mel″ah-no-pla′ke-ah) [*melano-* + Gr. *plax* plate + *-ia*]. The formation of pigmented patches on the mucous membrane of the mouth in certain diseases, as stomatitis, jaundice, etc.

melanoprecipitation (mel″ah-no-pre-sip″ĭ-ta′shun). The precipitation of melanin pigment: used as a test for malaria.

melanorrhagia (mel″ah-no-ra′je-ah) [*melano-* + Gr. *rhēgnynai* to burst forth]. The free and frequent discharge of feces darkened with blood pigments.

melanorrhea (mel″ah-no-re′ah) [*melano-* + Gr. *rhoia* flow]. Melanorrhagia.

melanosarcoma (mel″ah-no-sar-ko′mah) [*melano-* + *sarcoma*]. A melanoma derived from mesoblastic tissue.

melanosarcomatosis (mel″ah-no-sar-ko″mah-to′sis). The development of melanosarcomas.

melanoscirrhus (mel″ah-no-skir′us) [*melano-* + *scirrhus*]. Melanocarcinoma.

melanosed (mel′ah-nōsd). Blackened; affected with melanosis.

melanosis (mel″ah-no′sis) [*melano-* + *-osis*]. 1. Melanism; a condition characterized by abnormal pigmentary deposits. 2. Disorder of pigment metabolism. **m. co′li,** a condition in which the mucous membrane of the colon is pigmented with melanin. **m. lenticula′ris progressi′va,** xeroderma pigmentosum. **Riehl's m.,** a pigmentary affection of the skin marked by itching, reddening, desquamation, and a spotty brown pigmentation particularly on the forehead, malar region and the sides of the neck. **m. scle′rae,** congenital violet flecks in the sclera (Schmidt-Rimpler). **tar m.,** a diffuse mottled pigmentation of the skin due to heated tar and pitch.

melanosity (mel″ah-nos′ĭ-te). Swarthiness of complexion.

melanotic (mel″ah-not′ik). Pertaining to or characterized by melanosis.

melanotrichia (mel″ah-no-trik′e-ah) [*melano-* + Gr. *thrix* hair + *-ia*]. Abnormal hyperpigmentation of the hair. **m. lin′guae,** black tongue.

melanotrichous (mel″ah-not′rĭ-kus). Melanocomous.

melanotropic (mel″ah-no-trop′ik) [*melanin* + Gr. *tropikos* turning]. Having an affinity for melanin; influencing the deposit of melanin.

melanous (mel′ah-nus) [Gr. *melas* black]. Having a dark or swarthy complexion.

melanthin (mel-an′thin). An amorphous and poisonous glycoside, or saponin, $C_{20}H_{33}O_7$, from the seeds of *Nigella sativa.*

melanuresis (mel″an-u-re′sis). Melanuria.

melanuria (mel″an-u′re-ah) [*melano-* + Gr. *ouron* urine + *-ia*]. The excretion of darkly stained urine or of urine which turns dark on standing.

melanuric (mel″an-u′rik). Pertaining to or marked by melanuria.

melanurin (mel″an-u′rin). A black substance from morbid urine in certain rare cases.

melasicterus (mel″as-ik′ter-us). Winckel's disease.

melasma (mĕ-laz′mah) [Gr. *melas* black]. A disease characterized by dark pigmentation of the skin. **m. addiso′nii,** Addison's disease, **m. gravida′rum,** discoloration of the skin in pregnant women. **m. suprarena′le,** Addison's disease. **m. universa′le,** discoloration of nearly the entire surface of the body.

Meleda disease (mĕ′la-dah) [*Meleda*, a small island off the Dalmatian coast, where the condition is prevalent, because of intermarriage within the small population]. Familial hyperkeratosis palmaris et plantaris.

melena (mel′ĕ-nah) [Gr. *melaina*, feminine of Gr. *melas* black]. 1. The passage of dark, pitchy, and grumous stools stained with blood pigments or with altered blood. 2. Black vomit. **m. neonato′rum,** melena of the newborn, due to the extravasation of blood into the alimentary canal. **m. spu′ria,** melena in nurslings in which the blood comes from the fissured nipple of the nurse. **m. ve′ra,** true melena.

melenemesis (mel″en-em′e-sis) [Gr. *melaina* black + *emesis* vomiting]. Black vomit.

melenic (mĕ-le′nik). Marked by melena.

meletin (mel′ĕ-tin). Quercetin.

melezitose (mĕ-lez′ĭ-tōs). A trisaccharide, $C_{18}H_{32}O_{16}$, from manna, from the sap of poplars and conifers, which on hydrolysis yields glucose and turanose.

meli- (mel′ĭ) [Gr. *meli* honey]. Combining form meaning sweet, or denoting a relationship to honey.

melibiase (mel″ĭ-bi′ās). An enzyme which catalyzes the hydrolysis of melibiose to sucrose and galactose.

melibiose (mel″ĭ-bi′ōs). A disaccharide, beta-glucose 6-α-galactoside, $C_6H_{22}O_{11}$, obtained from molasses and from Australian manna. On hydrolysis it yields galactose and dextrose.

melicera, meliceris (mel″ĭ-se′rah, mel″ĭ-se′ris) [Gr. *meli* honey + *kēros* wax]. 1. A cyst filled with honey-like substance. 2. Viscid, syrupy.

melicitose (mĕ-lis′ĭ-tōs). Melezitose.

melilotoxin (mel″ĭ-lo-tok′sin). Dicoumarin.

melioidosis (me″le-oi-do′sis) [Gr. *melis* a distemper of asses + *eidos* resemblance]. A glanders-like disease of rodents, transmissible to man, occurring in India, the Malay States, and Indo-China, and caused by *Malleomyces pseudomallei.* Formerly called *Whitmore's disease.*

Melissa (mĕ-lis′ah) [Gr. "bee"]. A genus of labiate plants. The tops and leaves of *M. officinalis,* lemon-balm, containing tannin and an essential oil, are a cooling stimulant and diaphoretic.

melissophobia (mĕ-lis″o-fo′be-ah) [Gr. *melissa* bee + *phobia*]. An abnormal dread of bees and other stinging insects.

melissotherapy (mĕ-lis″o-ther′ah-pe) [Gr. *melissa* bee + *therapeia* medical treatment]. Treatment with bee venom.

melitagra (mel′ĭ-tag′rah, me-lit′ah-grah) [*meli-* + Gr. *agra* seizure]. Eczema with honeycomb crusts.

melitemia (mel″ĭ-te′me-ah) [*meli-* + Gr. *haima* blood + *-ia*]. Hyperglycemia.

melitensis (mel′ĭ-ten′sis). Brucellosis.

melitis (mĕ-li′tis) [Gr. *mēlon* cheek + *-itis*]. Inflammation of the cheek.

melitococcosis (mel″ĭ-to-kok-ko′sis). Brucellosis.

melitococcus (mel-ĭ-to-kok′us). *Brucella melitensis.*

melitoptyalism (mel″ĭ-to-ti′ah-lizm) [*meli-* + Gr. *ptyalon* saliva + *-ism*]. The secretion of saliva containing glucose.

melitoptyalon (mel″ĭ-to-ti′ah-lon). Glucose occurring in the saliva.

melitose (mel′ĭ-tōs). A crystalline sugar from Australian manna, sugar beets and cotton seed. It is a trisaccharide, $C_{18}H_{32}O_{16} + 5H_2O$, and yields on hydrolysis dextrose, fructose, and galactose. Called also *raffinose* and *melitriose.*

melitriose (mĕ-lit′ri-ōs). Melitose.

Melittangium (mel″ĭ-tan′je-um) [*meli-* + Gr. *angeion* vessel]. A genus of bacteria occurring in manure.

melituria (mel″ĭ-tu′re-ah) [*meli-* + Gr. *ouron* urine + *-ia*]. The presence of any sugar in the urine. **m. inosi′ta,** inosituria.

melituric (mel″ĭ-tu′rik). Pertaining to or affected with melituria.

melizitose (mĕ-liz′ĭ-tōs). Melezitose.

mellaril (mel′lah-ril). Trade mark for preparations of thioridazine hydrochloride.

mellitum (mĕ-li′tum), pl. *melli′ti* [L.]. A preparation made with honey.

mellituria (mel″ĭ-tu′re-ah). Melituria.

melodidymus (mel″o-did′ĭ-mus) [Gr. *melos* limb + *didymos* twin]. An individual with a supernumerary limb.

melodiotherapy (mĕ-lo″de-o-ther′ah-pe). Musicotherapy.

melomania (mel″o-ma′ne-ah) [Gr. *melos* song + *mania* madness]. Obsessive fondness for music.

melomaniac (mel″o-ma′ne-ak). An individual exhibiting melomania.

melomelus (mĕ-lom′e-lus) [Gr. *melos* limb + *melos* limb]. A fetal monster with both normal limbs and rudimentary supernumerary limbs.

meloncus (mĕ-long′kus) [Gr. *mēlon* cheek + *onkus* bulk]. Tumor of the cheek.

melonoplasty (mĕ-lon′o-plas″te). Meloplasty, def. 1.

Melophagus (mĕ-lof′ah-gus). A genus of wingless insects of the family Hippoboscidae. **M. ovi′nus,** the common sheep tick or ked of sheep.

meloplasty (mel′o-plas″te). 1. [Gr. *mēlon* cheek + *plassein* to form]. Plastic surgery of the cheek. 2. [Gr. *melos* limb + *plassein* to form]. Plastic surgery of the extremities.

melorheostosis (mel″o-re″os-to′sis) [Gr. *melos* limb + *rhein* to flow + *osteon* bone]. A form of osteosclerosis or hyperostosis extending in a linear track through one of the long bones of an extremity, and consisting of proliferated ivory-like new bone. Called also *m. leri.* See *rheostosis.*

melosalgia (mel″o-sal′je-ah) [Gr. *melos* limb + *-algia*]. Pain in the lower limbs.

meloschisis (mĕ-los′kĭ-sis). Macrostomia.

melotia (mĕ-lo′she-ah) [Gr. *mēlon* cheek + *ous* ear + *-ia*]. A developmental anomaly characterized by displacement of the ear onto the cheek.

Melotte's metal (mel-ots′) [George W. *Melotte,* American dentist, 1835–1915]. See under *metal.*

melotus (mĕ-lo′tus). An individual exhibiting melotia.

Meltzer's law, method, treatment (melt′serz) [Samuel J. *Meltzer,* American physiologist, 1851–1920]. See under the nouns.

Meltzer-Lyon method, test (melt′ser li′on) [S. J. *Meltzer;* B. B. Vincent *Lyon,* Philadelphia physician, 1880–1953]. See under *tests.*

member (mem′ber) [L. *membrum*]. 1. A part of the body distinct from the rest in function or position. 2. An outlying part or limb.

memberment (mem′ber-ment). The manner of arrangement of parts in a body.

membrana (mem-brah′nah), pl. *membra′nae* [L.]. A thin skin; used in anatomical nomenclature as a general term to designate a thin layer of tissue covering a surface or dividing a space or organ. Called also *membrane.* **m. abdom′inis,** peritoneum. **m. adamanti′na,** cuticula dentis. **m. adventi′tia.** 1. Tunica adventitia. 2. Decidua capsularis. 3. A membrane not normal to the part, as the membrane of a cicatrix. **m. agni′na,** the amnion. **m. atlantooccipita′lis ante′rior** [N A, B N A], a single mid-line ligamentous structure that passes from the anterior arch of the atlas to the anterior margin of the foramen magnum, and corresponds in position with the anterior longitudinal ligament of the vertebral column. Called also *anterior atlanto-occipital membrane.* **m. atlantooccipita′lis poste′rior** [N A, B N A], a single mid-line ligamentous structure that passes from the posterior arch of the atlas to the posterior margin of the foramen magnum, and corresponds in position with the ligamenta flava. Called also *posterior atlantooccipital membrane.* **m. basa′lis duc′tus semicircula′ris** [N A], the basement membrane underlying the epithelium of a semicircular duct. Called also *basal membrane of semicircular duct.* **m. basila′ris duc′tus cochlea′ris,** lamina basilaris ductus cochlearis. **m. cadu′ca.** See *membranae deciduae.* **m. capsula′ris,** capsula articularis. **m. choriocapilla′ris,** lamina choriocapillaris. **membra′nae decid′uae** [N A, B N A], the mucous lining of the uterus, which is thrown off after parturition. See under *decidua.* Called also *deciduous membranes.* **m. eb′oris of Kölliker,** dentinum. **m. elas′tica laryn′gis** [B N A], m. fibroelastica laryngis. **m. epipapilla′ris,** an abnormal fibrous membrane on the optic disk. **m. fibroelas′tica laryn′gis** [N A], the fibroelastic layer beneath the mucous coat of the larynx, comprising the quadrangular membrane and the conus elasticus. Called also *m. elastica laryngis* [B N A], and *fibroelastic membrane of larynx.* **m. fibro′sa cap′sulae articula′ris** [N A] the outer of the two layers of the articular capsule of a synovial joint, composed of dense white fibrous tissue. Called also *stratum fibrosum capsulae articularis* [B N A], and *fibrous membrane of articular capsule.* **m. flac′cida,** pars flaccida membranae tympani. **m. fus′ca,** lamina fusca sclerae. **m. germina-ti′va,** blastoderm. **m. granulo′sa,** cumulus oophorus. **m. granulo′sa exter′na,** the external granular layer of the retina. **m. granulo′sa inter′na,** the internal granular layer of the retina. **m. hyaloi'dea** [B N A], m. vitrea. **m. hyothyreoi'dea** [B N A], m. thyrohyoidea. **m. intercosta'lis exter'na** [N A], any of the aponeurotic bands parallel with, and perhaps replacing, the fibers of the external intercostal muscles in the spaces between the costal cartilages, from the ventral tips of the ribs medially to the sternum. Called also *ligamenta intercostalia externa* [B N A], and *external intercostal membrane.* **m. intercosta'lis inter'na** [N A], any of the aponeurotic bands parallel with, and perhaps replacing, the fibers of the internal intercostal muscles in the spaces between the ribs, from the angles of the ribs medially to the vertebral column. Called also *ligamenta intercostalia interna* [B N A], and *internal intercostal membrane.* **m. interos'sea antebra'chii** [N A], **m. interos'sea antibra'chii** [B N A], a thin fibrous sheet that connects the bodies of the radius and ulna, passing from the interosseous margin of the radius to that of the ulna. Called also *interosseous membrane of forearm.* **m. interos'sea cru'ris** [N A, B N A], a thin aponeurotic lamina attached to the interosseous margins of the tibia and fibula, deficient for a short distance at the proximal end of the bones. It separates the muscles on the anterior and posterior parts of the leg. Called also *interosseous membrane of leg.* **m. lim'itans.** 1. One of the limiting membranes of the retina. 2. The limiting membrane of glia fibrils and perivascular feet separating the neural parenchyma from the pia and blood vessels. **m. muco'sa na'si** [B N A], tunica mucosa nasi. **m. muco'sa ves'icae fel'leae,** tunica mucosa vexicae felleae. **m. nic'titans.** 1. Plica semilunaris conjunctivae. 2. Nictitating membrane. **m. obturato'ria** [N A, B N A], a strong membrane that fills the obturator foramen except superiorly at the obturator groove, where a deficiency is left, the obturator canal. Called also *obturator membrane.* **m. obturato'ria [stape'dis]** [B N A], m. stapedis. **m. obtura'trix,** m. obturatoria. **m. orbita'lis musculo'sa,** a system of smooth muscles deep in the orbit. **m. perine'i,** N A alternative for *fascia diaphragmatis urogenitalis inferior.* **m. pituito'sa,** tunica mucosa nasi. **m. pro'pria,** lamina propria mucosae. **m. pro'pria duc'tus semicircula'ris** [N A], the outer, loose, connective tissue layer of a semicircular duct. Called also *proper membrane of semicircular duct.* **m. pupilla'ris** [N A, B N A], a mesodermal layer attached to the rim or front of the iris during embryonic development, sometimes persisting in the adult. Called also *pupillary membrane.* **m. quadrangula'ris** [N A], the upper part of the fibroelastic membrane of the larynx. Called also *quadrangular membrane.* **m. reticula'ris duc'tus cochlea'ris** [N A], **m. reticula'ta,** a netlike membrane over the spiral organ; the free ends of the outer hair cells pass through its apertures. Called also *reticular membrane.* **m. ruyschia'na,** lamina choriocapillaris. **m. saccifor'mis,** the synovial membrane of the inferior radioulnar articulation. **m. sero'sa.** 1. Tunica serosa. 2. The chorion. **m. seroti'na,** decidua basalis. **m. spira'lis duc'tus cochlea'ris** [N A], the fibrous outer zone of the lamina basilaris ductus cochlearis. **m. stape'dis** [N A], a membrane filling the arch formed by the crura and base of the stapes. Called also *m. obturatoria* [*stapedis*] [B N A], and *stapedial membrane.* **m. statoconio'rum macula'rum** [N A], the gelatinous membrane surmounting the maculae, containing the statoconia, and having special sensory hairs projecting into it. Called also *statoconic membrane of maculae.* **m. ster'ni** [N A, B N A], the thick fibrous membrane that envelopes the sternum. It is formed by the intermingling of fibers of the radiate sternocostal ligaments, the periosteum, and the tendinous origin of the pectoralis major. Called also *sternal membrane.* **m. succin'gens,** the pleura. **m. suprapleura'lis** [N A], the strengthened portion of the endothoracic fascia attached to the inner part of the first rib and the transverse process of the seventh cervical vertebra. Called also *suprapleural membrane.* **m. synovia'lis cap'sulae articula'ris** [N A], the inner of the two layers of the articular capsule of a synovial joint; composed of loose connective tissue and having a free smooth surface that lines the joint cavity. Called also *stratum synoviale capsulae articularis* [B N A], and *synovial membrane of articular capsule.* **m. tecto'ria** [N A, B N A], a strong fibrous band connected cranially with the basilar part of the occipital bone and caudally with the dorsal surface of the bodies of the second and third cervical vertebrae. It is actually the cranial prolongation of the deeper portion of the posterior longitudinal ligament of the vertebral column. Called also *tectorial membrane.* **m. tecto'ria duc'tus cochlea'ris** [N A], a delicate gelatinous mass resting on the spiral organ and connected with the hairs of the hair cells. Called also *tectorial membrane of cochlear duct.* **m. ten'sa,** pars tensa membranae tympani. **m. thyrohyoi'dea** [N A], a broad fibroelastic sheet attached above to the upper margin of the posterior surface of the hyoid bone and below to the upper border of the thyroid cartilage. Called also *m. hyothyreoidea* [B N A], and *thyrohyoid membrane.* **m. tym'pani** [N A, B N A], the obliquely placed, thin membranous partition between the external acoustic meatus and the tympanic cavity. The greater portion, the pars tensa, is attached by a fibrocartilaginous ring to the tympanic plate of the temporal bone; the much smaller, triangular portion, the pars flaccida, is situated anterosuperiorly between the two mallear folds. Called also *tympanic membrane.* **m. tym'pani secunda'ria** [N A, B N A], the membrane that closes in the fenestra cochlearis. Called also *secondary tympanic membrane.* **m. versic'olor of Fielding,** tapetum. **m. vestibula'ris [Reiss'neri]** [B N A], paries vestibularis ductus cochlearis. **m. vi'brans,** pars tensa membranae tympani. **m. vitelli'na,** vitelline membrane. **m. vit'rea** [N A], a delicate boundary layer investing the vitreous body of the eye. Called also *m. hyaloidea* [B N A], and *vitreous membrane.*

membranaceous (mem″brah-na'shus) [L. *membranaceus*]. Of the nature of a membrane.

membranae (mem-brah'ne) [L.]. Plural of *membrana.*

membranate (mem'brah-nāt). Having the character of a membrane.

membrane (mem'brān). A thin layer of tissue which covers a surface or divides a space or organ. See also *membrana.* **abdominal m.,** peritoneum. **accidental m.,** false m. **adamantine m.,** cuticula dentis. **adventitious m.,** a membrane not normal to the part, as the membrane of a cicatrix. **alveolodental m.,** periodontium. **anal m.,** the membrane that closes the anal end of the embryonic gut. **animal m.,** a thin membranous diaphragm, as of bladder: used as a dialyzer. **aponeurotic m.,** aponeurosis. **arachnoid m.,** arachnoidea. **Ascherson's m.,** the covering of casein enclosing the milk globules. **asphyxial m.,** hyaline m. (def. 3); so called because of its interference with gaseous exchange in the lungs. **atlantooccipital m., anterior,** membrana atlantooccipitalis anterior. **atlantooccipital m., posterior,** membrana atlantooccipitalis posterior. **Baer's m.,** chromicized pig's bladder, used as a dressing over cut bone surfaces. **basal m. of semicircular duct** membrana basalis ductus semicircularis. **basement m.,** the delicate, noncellular layer underlying the epithelium of mucous membranes and secreting glands. **basilar m. of cochlear duct,** lamina basilaris ductus cochlearis. **Bichat's m.,** Henle's fenestrated m. **birth m's,** the amnion and placenta. **Bowman's m.,** lamina limitans anterior corneae. **Bruch's m.** 1. Lamina basalis choroideae. 2. Musculus dilator pupillae. 3. Stratum pigmenti bulbi oculi. **Brunn's m.,**

the epithelium of the olfactory region of the nose. **bucconasal m.,** oronasal m. **buccopharyngeal m.,** fascia pharyngobasilaris. **capsular m.,** capsula articularis. **capsulopupillary m.,** membrana pupillaris. **Cargile m.,** prepared ox peritoneum used for covering surfaces from which the peritoneum has been removed, as a means of preventing the formation of adhesions. **cell m.,** the condensed protoplasm which forms the enveloping capsule of a cell. **chorio-allantoic m.,** chorio-allantois. **cloacal m.,** the exposed wall of the cloaca, formed by the outer and inner germ layers. **cobalt aurate m.,** gold-beaters' skin saturated with cobalt chloride and gold chloride and water, with oil of cassia: used as an application for causing granulation in wounds. **complex m.,** a membrane made up of several layers differing in structure. **compound m.,** a membrane, like that of the tympanum, made up of two distinct layers. **Corti's m.,** membrana tectoria ductus cochlearis. **costocoracoid m.,** fascia clavipectoralis. **cribriform m.,** fascia cribrosa. **cricothyroid m., cricovocal m.,** conus elasticus laryngis. **croupous m.,** a false membrane formed in true croup. **cyclitic m.,** a false membrane which sometimes covers the vitreous body in cyclitis. **Debove's m.,** the delicate layer between the epithelium and the tunica propria of the bronchial, tracheal, and intestinal mucous membranes. **decidual m's, deciduous m's,** membranae deciduae. **Demours' m.,** lamina limitans posterior corneae. **dentinoenamel m.,** a continuous thin membrane laid down by ameloblasts adjoining the basement membrane separating them from the dentin in an early developing tooth. **Descemet's m.,** lamina limitans posterior corneae. **diphtheritic m.,** a false membrane characteristic of diphtheria and resulting from coagulation necrosis. **drum m.,** membrana tympani. **Duddell's m.,** lamina limitans posterior corneae. **egg m.,** the investment surrounding the ovum or egg: if derived from the ovum, it is called *primary;* if from the follicle cells, it is *secondary;* if from the oviduct, it is *tertiary.* **elastic m.,** a variety of membrane composed largely of elastic fibers. **elastic m., external,** a fenestrated elastic membrane that constitutes the innermost component of the tunica adventitia of arteries. **elastic m., internal,** a fenestrated elastic membrane that constitutes the outermost component of the tunica intima of arteries. **enamel m.** 1. Cuticula dentis. 2. The inner layer of cells within the enamel organ of the dental germ in the fetus. **endoneural m.,** neurilemma. **exocoelomic m.,** Heuser's m. **false m.,** a morbid pellicle or skinlike layer resembling an organized and living membrane, but made up of coagulated fibrin with bacteria and leukocytes, such as may be formed on mucous membranes in diphtheria. **fenestrated m.,** one of the multiply perforated elastic plates of the tunica intima and tunica media of arteries. **fertilization m.,** a strong membrane formed around the fertilized ovum in some species of animals by adhesion of part of the contents of the cortical granules to the inner surface of the vitalline membrane. **fetal m's,** the membranous structures that serve to protect the embryo and provide for its nutrition, respiration, and excretion: they are the yolk sac (umbilical vesicle), allantois, amnion, chorion, decidua, and placenta. **fibroelastic m. of larynx,** membrana fibroelastica laryngis. **fibrous m. of articular capsule,** membrana fibrosa capsulae articularis. **Fielding's m.,** tapetum. **germinal m.,** blastoderm. **glassy m.** 1. The basement membrane of a vesicular ovarian follicle which in cross section appears as a distinct brilliant line. Called also *m. of Slavianski.* 2. Lamina basalis choroideae. **gradocol m's,** thin membranes used in ultrafiltration; made of collodion or other similar substances, they are graded as to porosity. **ground m.,** inophragma. **Haller's m.,** lamina vasculosa choroideae. **Hannover's intermediate m.,** enamel m. **haptogen m.,** the membrane of protein matter formerly believed to enclose milk globules. **Harris' m's,** congenital anomalous membranes or bands extending from the region of the gallbladder and under surface of the liver to the pylorus and duodenum. **Henle's m.,** lamina basalis choroideae. **Henle's elastic m.,** a fenestrated layer between the outer and middle tunics of certain arteries. **Henle's fenestrated m.,** a subendothelial fibroelastic fenestrated layer in the tunica intima of an artery. **Heuser's m.,** a delicate sac within the blastocyst that presumably represents a provisional yolk sac. Called also *exocoelomic membrane.* **homogeneous m.,** a membrane covering the placental villi. **Hovius' m.,** the entochoroidea. **Huxley's m.,** the cellular membrane of the root sheath and proximal end of a hair. **hyaline m.** 1. The membrane between the outer root sheath and the inner fibrous layer of a hair follicle. 2. Basement membrane. 3. A layer of eosinophilic hyaline material lining the alveoli, alveolar ducts, and bronchioles, found at autopsy in infants who have died of idiopathic respiratory distress of the newborn. Called also *asphyxial membrane* and *vernix membrane.* **hyaloid m.,** membrana vitrea. **hymenal m.,** hymen. **hyoglossal m.,** a fibrous lamina connecting the under surface of the tongue with the hyoid bone. **hyothyroid m.,** membrana thyrohyoidea. **intercostal m., external,** membrana intercostalis externa. **intercostal m., internal,** membrana intercostalis interna. **interosseous m., radioulnar, interosseous m. of forearm,** membrana interossea antebrachii. **interosseous m. of leg,** membrana interossea cruris. **interpubic m.,** discus interpubicus. **interspinal m's.** See *ligamentum interspinale.* **intersutural m.,** the pericranium lying between the cerebral sutures. **ivory m.,** dentinum. **Jackson's m.,** a delicate curtain or web of adhesions (regarded by some as a sheet of peritoneum) sometimes seen covering the cecum and producing obstruction of the bowel and a clinical condition, called membranous pericolitis, characterized by a series of definite symptoms. **Jacob's m.,** bacillary layer. **keratogenous m.,** matrix unguis. **Kölliker's m.,** membrana reticularis ductus cochlearis. **Krause's m.,** a membrane, seen as a dark line on longitudinal section, serving to limit the sarcomeres of striated muscle. Called also *Amici's disk, intermediate disk, thin disk, Z band* or *disk, Dobie's line,* and *telophragma.* **ligamentous m.,** membrana tectoria. **limiting m.,** a membrane which constitutes the border of some tissue or structure. **limiting m., external.** 1. A thin fenestrated sheet in the retina, through which extend the visual rods and cones. 2. A membrane investing the external surface of the embryonic neural tube. **limiting m., internal.** 1. The innermost layer of the retina. 2. A membrane lining the internal surface of the embryonic neural tube. **Mauthner's m.,** Mauthner's sheath. **meconic m.,** a layer within the fetal rectum. **medullary m.,** endosteum. **mucocutaneous m.,** a membrane that is partly mucous and partly cutaneous, like that of the tympanum. **mucous m.,** tunica mucosa. **mucous m., proper,** lamina propria mucosae. **mucous m. of colon,** tunica mucosa coli. **mucous m. of esophagus,** tunica mucosa esophagi. **mucous m. of gallbladder,** tunica mucosa vesicae felleae. **mucous m. of mouth,** tunica mucosa oris. **mucous m. of pharynx,** tunica mucosa pharyngis. **mucous m. of rectum,** tunica mucosa intestini recti. **mucous m. of small intestine,** tunica mucosa intestini tenuis. **mucous m. of stomach,** tunica mucosa ventriculi. **mucous m. of tongue,** tunica mucosa linguae. **mucous m. of ureter,** tunica mucosa ureteris. **mucous m. of urinary bladder,** tunica mucosa vesicae urinariae. **Nasmyth's m.,** cuticula dentis. **nictitating m.,** a transparent fold of skin lying deep to the other eyelids at the mesial side, which may be drawn over the front of the eyeball; the so-called third eyelid, found in reptiles and birds generally and in many mammals. **nuclear m.,** the outer layer of the nucleoplasm. **oblique m. of forearm,** chorda obliqua membranae interosseae antebrachii. **obturator m.,** membrana obturatoria. **obturator m. of atlas, anterior,** membrana atlantooccipitalis anterior. **obturator m. of atlas, posterior,** membrana atlantooccipitalis posterior. **obturator m. of larynx,** membrana thyrohyoidea. **occipitoaxial m., long,** membrana tectoria. **olfactory m.,** the olfactory portion of the mucous membrane lining the nasal fossa. **oral m.,** fascia pharyngobasilaris. **oronasal m.,** a thin epithelial plate separating the nasal pits from the oral cavity of the embryo. **otolithic m.,** membrana statoconiorum macularum. **ovular m.,** vitelline m. **palatine m.,** the membrane covering the roof of the mouth. **pericolic m., pericolonic m.,** a membrane passing from the serosa of the abdominal wall to the colon. Cf. *Jackson's membrane, Treves' fold,* etc. **peridental m.,** periodontium. **perineal m.,** fascia diaphragmatis urogenitalis inferior. **periodontal m.,** periodontium. **periorbital m.,** periorbita. **pharyngeal m., pharyngobasilar m.,** fascia pharyngobasilaris. **pituitary m. of nose,** tunica mucosa nasi. **placental m.,** the semipermeable membrane which separates the fetal from the maternal blood in the placenta. It is composed of fetal vascular endothelium, cytotrophoblast, and syncytium, and it becomes thinner as pregnancy progresses. **plasma m.,** the hypothetical membrane surrounding or enveloping a cell; the superficial layer of the protoplasm of a cell. See *ectoplasm.* **pleuropericardial m.,** a membrane in the embryo separating the heart and the lung sac. **pleuroperitoneal m.,** a membrane in the embryo separating the pleural cavity from the peritoneal cavity and developing into a part of the diaphragm. **proligerous m.,** cumulus oophorus. **proper m. of semicircular duct,** membrana propia ductus semicircularis. **prophylactic m.,** pyophylactic m. **pseudoserous m.,** a membrane resembling serous membrane, but differing from it in structure. **pupillary m.,** membrana pupillaris. **purpurogenous m.,** the pigment epithelium of the eye. **pyogenic m.,** a membrane which produces pus. **pyophylactic m.,** a fibrinous membrane lining a pus cavity and tending to prevent reabsorption of injurious materials. **Ranvier's m.,** Rénaut's layer. **Reichert's m.,** lamina limitans anterior corneae. **Reissner's m.,** paries vestibularis ductus cochlearis. **reticular m., reticulated m.,** membrana reticularis ductus cochlearis. **Ruysch's m., ruyschian m,** lamina choriocapillaris. **Scarpa's m.,** membrana tympani secundaria. **schneiderian m.,** tunica mucosa nasi. **Schwann's m.,** neurilemma. **semipermeable m.,** a membrane which permits the passage of a solvent, such as water, but prevents the passage of the dissolved substance or solute. **serous m.,** tunica serosa. **shell m.,** a double fibrous layer lining the shell of the egg of some animals, such as birds. **Shrapnell's m.,** pars flaccida membranae tympani. **m. of Slavianski,** glassy m., def. 1. **spiral m. of cochlear duct,** membrana spiralis ductus cochlearis. **spore m.,** sporocyst, def. 2. **stapedial m.,** membrana stapedis. **statoconic m. of maculae,** membrana statoconiorum macularum. **sternal m., m. of sternum,** membrana sterni. **striated m.,** zona pellucida. **subenamel m.,** a membrane said to exist between the enamel of a tooth and the enamel pulp. **subepithelial m.,** basement membrane. **submucous m.,** tela submucosa. **submucous m. of stomach,** tela submucosa ventriculi. **suprapleural m.,** membrana suprapleuralis. **synaptic m.,** the layer separating the neuroplasm of an axon from that of the body of the nerve cell with which it makes synapsis. **synovial m. of articular capsule,** membrana synovialis capsulae articularis. **tarsal m.,** septum orbitale. **tectorial m.,** membrana tectoria. **tectorial m. of cochlear duct,** membrana tectoria ductus cochlearis. **tendinous m.,** aponeurosis. **Tenon's m.** See *vaginae bulbi.* **thyreohyoid m.,** membrana thyrohyoidea. **Traube's m.,** a film of potassium formed at the plane of contact of the two liquids, when a solution of potassium ferrocyanide is brought into contact with a solution of a copper salt. **tympanic m.,** the membrane separating the middle from the external ear. See *membrana tympani.* **tympanic m., secondary,** membrana tympani secundaria. **undulating m.,** a protoplasmic membrane running like a fin along the body of certain protozoa. **vascular m. of viscera,** tela submucosa. **vernix m.,** hyaline m. (def. 3); so called because it was originally thought to be the result of aspiration of vernix by the fetus *in utero.* **vestibular m. of cochlear duct,** paries vestibularis ductus cochlearis. **virginal m.,** hymen. **vitelline m.,** the external cytoplasmic envelope of the ovum. **vitreous m.** 1. Membrana vitrea. 2. Lamina basalis choroidea. 3. Lamina limitans posterior. 4. Hyaline membrane, def. 1. **Volkmann's m.,** a thin, yellowish membrane, studded with miliary tubercles, lining the fibrous wall of a tubercular abscess. **Wachendorf's m.** 1. Membrana pupillaris. 2. The membrane investing a cell. **yolk m.,** vitelline m. **Zinn's m.,** zonula ciliaris.

membranelle (mem″brah-nel′). A small membrane composed of cilia, seen in ciliate organisms.

membraniform (mem-bra′nĭ-form). Resembling a membrane.

membranin (mem′brah-nin). 1. A protein making up the lens capsule and Descemet's membrane. 2. The cellulose of yeast cells.

membranocartilaginous (mem″brah-no-kar″tĭ-laj′ĭ-nus). 1. Developed in both membrane and cartilage. 2. Partly cartilaginous and partly membranous.

membranoid (mem′brah-noid). Resembling a membrane.

membranous (mem′brah-nus) [L. *membranosus*]. Pertaining to or of the nature of a membrane.

membrum (mem′brum), pl *mem′bra* [L.]. A limb, or member of the body; used in anatomical nomenclature as a general term to designate one of the limbs, that is, the upper (arm, forearm, hand), or lower (thigh, leg, foot). Called also *extremitas* (pl. *extremitates*) [B N A]. **m. infe′rius** [N A], the lower limb of the body (thigh, leg, and foot). Called also *extremitas inferior* [B N A]. **m. mulie′bre,** clitoris. **m. supe′rius** [N A], the upper limb of the body (arm, forearm, and hand). Called also *extremitas superior* [B N A]. **m. viri′le,** penis.

memory (mem′o-re) [L. *memoria*]. That mental faculty by which sensations, impressions, and ideas are recalled. **affect m.,** the memory of a psychic trauma. **anterograde m.,** a memory serviceable for events long past, but not able to acquire new recollections. **coast m.,** tropical amnesia. **eye m.,** visual memory. **kinesthetic m.,** the memory of movements in the limbs and other parts of the body. **visual m.,** memory for visual impressions.

menacme (me-nak′me) [Gr. *mēn* month + *akmē* top]. 1. The height of menstrual activity. 2. That period of a woman's life which is marked by menstrual activity.

menadiol (men″ah-di′ol). Chemical name: 2-methyl-1,4-naphthohydroquinone, a vitamin K analogue. **m. sodium diphosphate,** the hexahydrate of the tetrasodium salt of 2-methyl-1,4-naphthalenediol diphosphate: used to promote the formation of prothrombin.

menadione (men″ah-di′ōn). Chemical name: 2-methyl-1,4-naphthoquinone: used as a prothrombinogenic vitamin.

menalgia (men-al′je-ah) [Gr. *mēn* month + *-algia*]. Pain accompanying menstruation.

menaphthone (men-af′thōn). Menadione.

menarche (me-nar′ke) [Gr. *mēn* month + *archē* beginning]. The establishment or beginning of the menstrual function.

menarchial (mĕ-nar′ke-al). Pertaining to or characterized by the establishment of the menstrual function (menarche).

mendacity (men-das′ĭ-te). A tendency to make false statements; lying.

Mendel's law (men′delz) [Gregor Johann *Mendel*, 1822–1884, Austrian monk and naturalist]. See under *law*.

Mendel's reflex [Kurt *Mendel*, German neurologist, born 1874]. See under *reflex*.

Mendel's test [Felix *Mendel*, German physician, 1862–1912]. See *Mantoux test*, under *tests*.

Mendel-Bechterew reflex [Kurt *Mendel;* V. M. von *Bechterew*, Russian neurologist, 1857–1927]. Mendel's reflex.

Mendeléeff's law, test (men″dĕ-la′efs) [Dimitri Ivanovich *Mendeléeff*, Russian chemist, 1834–1907]. See *periodic law*, under *law*, and under *tests*.

mendelevium (men″dĕ-le′ve-um) [Dimitri Ivanovich *Mendeléeff*]. The chemical element of atomic number 101, atomic weight 256, symbol Md, originally discovered in debris from a thermonuclear explosion in 1952.

mendelian (men-de′le-an). Named for Gregor Johann *Mendel*. See *Mendel's law*, under *law*.

mendelism (men′del-izm). See *Mendel's law*, under *law*.

Mendelsohn's test (men′del-sōnz) [Martin *Mendelsohn*, German physician, 1860–1930]. See under *tests*.

menelipsis (men″ĕ-lip′sis). Menolipsis.

menelkosis (men″el-ko′sis) [Gr. *mēn* month + *helkōsis* ulceration]. Vicarious menstruation from an ulcer.

Menetrier's disease (men″ĕ-tre-ārz′) [Pierre *Menetrier*, French physician, 1859–1935]. Giant hypertrophic gastritis.

menformon (men′for-mon). Trade mark for a preparation of estrone.

Menge's operation, pessary (meng′gez) [Karl *Menge*, Heidelberg gynecologist, born 1864]. See under *operation* and *pessary*.

menhidrosis (men″hid-ro′sis) [Gr. *mēn* month + *hidrōs* sweat]. A form of vicarious menstruation consisting of monthly discharge of sweat, sometimes bloody.

menidrosis (men″id-ro′sis). Menhidrosis.

Meniere's disease, syndrome (men″e-ārz′) [Prosper *Meniere*, French physician, 1799–1862]. See under *syndrome*.

meningeal (mĕ-nin′je-al). Of or pertaining to the meninges.

meningematoma (mĕ-nin″jem-ah-to′mah). Hematoma of the dura mater.

meningeocortical (mĕ-nin″je-o-kor′tĭ-kal). Of or pertaining to the meninges and cortex of the brain.

meningeoma (mĕ-nin″je-o′mah). Meningioma.

meningeorrhaphy (mĕ-nin″je-or′ah-fe) [Gr. *mēninx* membrane + *rhaphē* suture]. Suture of membranes: especially suture of the spinal cord, in which the sutures pass through the membranes only.

meninges (mĕ-nin′jēz) [Gr., pl. of *mēninx* membrane]. [N A, B N A] The three membranes that envelop the brain and spinal cord: the dura mater, pia mater, and arachnoid.

meninghematoma (mĕ-ninj″hem-ah-to′mah). Meningematoma.

meningina (men″in-ji′nah). Pia-arachnoid.

meninginitis (men″in-jin-i′tis). Inflammation of the meningina; leptomeningitis.

meningioma (mĕ-nin″je-o′mah) [*meninges* + *-oma* tumor]. A hard, slow-growing vascular tumor which occurs mainly along the meningeal vessels and superior longitudinal sinus, invading the dura and skull and leading to erosion and thinning of the skull. **angioblastic m.**, angioblastoma.

meningiomatosis (mĕ-nin″je-o″mah-to′sis). A condition characterized by the formation of multiple meningiomas.

meningism (mĕ-nin′jizm). 1. A condition due to pain in the meningeocortical region of the brain, marked by excitation, followed by depression of the cortex, with vomiting, constipation, and thermic disorders. 2. A hysterical simulation of meningitis.

meningismus (men″in-jis′mus). Meningism.

meningitic (men″in-jit′ik). Pertaining to or of the nature of meningitis.

meningitides (men″in-jit′ĭ-dēz). Plural of *meningitis*.

meningitis (men″in-ji′tis), pl. *meningit′ides* [Gr. *mēninx* membrane + *-itis*]. Inflammation of the meninges. When it affects the dura mater, the disease is termed *pachymeningitis;* when the arachnoid and pia mater are involved, it is called *leptomeningitis*, or meningitis proper. **acute aseptic m.**, lymphocytic choriomeningitis. **African m.**, sleeping sickness. **alcoholic m.**, a form associated with the excessive use of alcoholic drinks. **aseptic m.**, a meningitis with characteristic symptoms and spinal fluid changes but in which no causative agent can be demonstrated. **m. of the base, basilar m.**, that which affects the meninges at the base of the brain. **benign lymphocytic m.**, lymphocytic choriomeningitis. **cerebral m.**, inflammation of the meninges of the brain. **cerebrospinal m.**, an inflammation of the membranes of the brain and spinal cord. It may be caused by many different organisms. **epidemic cerebrospinal m.**, an acute infectious disease attended by seropurulent inflammation of the membranes of the brain and spinal cord, and due to infection by the *Neisseria meningitidis*. The disease appears usually in epidemics, and the symptoms are those of acute cerebral and spinal meningitis, in addition to which there is usually an eruption of erythematous, herpetic, or hemorrhagic spots upon the skin. Called also *cerebrospinal fever*. **epizootic cerebrospinal m.**, a disease of horses, frequently occurring in epidemics, and characterized by dysphagia, unsteady gait, delirium, and muscular contractions. **external m.**, pachymeningitis externa. **gummatous m.**, meningitis during the third stage of syphilis in which there are many small gummata in the membranes. **internal m.**, pachymeningitis interna. **lymphocytic m.**, meningitis in which there is an excess of lymphocytes in the cerebrospinal fluid. See *lymphocytic choriomeningitis*, under *choriomeningitis*. **meningococcic m.**, epidemic cerebrospinal m. **metastatic m.**, that which is due to the transmission of the affection from a remote part. **mumps m.**, an aseptic meningitis secondary to mumps. **m. necrotox′ica reacti′va**, a condition marked by areas of focal cerebral softening with symptoms and signs of meningeal irritation suggesting primary inflammatory changes of the cerebral cortex. **occlusive m.**, leptomeningitis of children which leads to the closure of the foramen of Magendie. **m. ossif′icans**, ossification of the cerebral meninges. **otitic m.**, a form that sometimes complicates an attack of otitis. **parameningococcus m.**, meningitis caused by parameningococcus. **posterior m.**, meningitis of the cerebellar region. **purulent m.**, that which is suppurative. **Quincke's m.**, acute serous meningitis. **septicemic m.**, that which is due to septic blood poisoning. **m. sero′sa**, serous m. **m. sero′sa circumscrip′ta**, meningitis giving rise to cystic accumulations of serous fluid which cause symptoms of tumors. **m. sero′sa circumscrip′ta cys′tica**, chronic meningitis with cyst formation. **serous m.**, meningitis with serous exudation into the ventricles and subarachnoid spaces and slight to moderate changes in the spinal fluid. **simple m.,** that in which there is an exudate of fibrin and serum. **spinal m.,** inflammation of the meninges of the spinal cord. *Acute spinal m.* is attended with fever, pain in the back and limbs, radiating along the peripheral nerves, rigidity of the muscles, dyspnea, retention of urine, and paralyses. In *chronic spinal m.* there are pains in the back and along the courses of nerves, hyperesthesia, paralysis, and atrophy of muscles. **sterile m.,** meningitis in which there is no infection, i.e., meningitis caused by injection of air or of serum. **m. sympath'ica,** a condition of the cerebrospinal fluid caused by inflammation in the neighborhood of the meninges. It is marked by increase in the pressure of the fluid and increase in its albumin and cellular content. The fluid is sterile and there may be symptoms of meningitis (Plant and Schottmüller). **torula m., torular m.,** cryptococcosis encephalitis usually secondary to infection in some other part. **traumatic m.,** that due to traumatism or injury. **tubercular m., tuberculous m.,** a severe meningitis in children resulting from the spread of a tuberculous infection. It is frequently marked by bulging of the fontanels from intracranial pressure (acute hydrocephalus).

meningitophobia (men″in-jit″o-fo'be-ah) [*meningitis* + *phobia*]. A condition simulating meningitis, but due to fear of that disease.

meningo- (mĕ-ning'go) [Gr. *mēninx* membrane]. Combining form denoting relationship to the membranes covering the brain and/or spinal cord, or to other membrane.

meningo-arteritis (mĕ-ning″go-ar″ter-i'tis). Inflammation of the meningeal arteries.

meningoblastoma (mĕ-ning″go-blas-to'mah). A melanoblastoma of the cerebral meninges.

meningocele (mĕ-ning'go-sēl) [*meningo-* + Gr. *kēlē* hernia]. Hernial protrusion of the meninges through a defect in the skull (*cranial m.*) or vertebral column (*spinal m.*).

meningocephalitis (mĕ-ning″go-sef″ah-li'tis). Meningoencephalitis.

meningocerebritis (mĕ-ning″go-ser″e-bri'tis) [*meningo-* + *cerebritis*]. Meningoencephalitis.

meningococcemia (mĕ-ning″go-kok-se'me-ah). Invasion of the blood stream by meningococci. **acute fulminating m.,** Waterhouse-Friderichsen syndrome.

meningococci (mĕ-ning″go-kok'si). Plural of *meningococcus.*

meningococcidal (mĕ-ning″go-kok-si'dal) [*meningococcus* + L. *caedere* to kill]. Destroying meningococci.

meningococcin (mĕ-ning″go-kok'sin). An antigenic material precipitated from saline suspensions of the meningococcus by means of alcohol. It is applied as a skin test (intradermal) in the detection of meningococcus carriers.

meningococcosis (mĕ-ning″go-kok-ko'sis). Infection caused by meningococci.

meningococcus (mĕ-ning″go-kok'us), pl. *meningococ'ci* [*meningo-* + Gr. *kokkos* berry]. A microorganism of the species *Neisseria meningitidis.*

meningocortical (mĕ-ning″go-kor'tĭ-kal). Pertaining to or affecting the meninges and cortex of the brain.

meningocyte (mĕ-ning'go-sīt). A histiocyte of the meninges.

meningoencephalitis (mĕ-ning″go-en-sef″ah-li'tis) [*meningo-* + Gr. *enkephalos* brain + *-itis*]. Inflammation of the brain and meninges. **chronic m., syphilitic m.,** dementia paralytica.

meningoencephalocele (mĕ-ning″go-en-sef'ah-lo-sēl) [*meningo-* + Gr. *enkephalos* brain + *kēlē* hernia]. Hernial protrusion of the meninges and brain substance through a defect in the skull.

meningoencephalomyelitis (mĕ-ning″go-en-sef″ah-lo-mi″ĕ-li'tis) [*meningo-* + Gr. *enkephalos* brain + *myelos* marrow + *-itis*]. Inflammation of the meninges, brain, and spinal cord.

meningoencephalopathy (mĕ-ning″go-en-sef″-ah-lop'ah-the). Non-inflammatory disease of the cerebral meninges and the brain.

meningoexothelioma (mĕ-ning″go-ek″so-the″-le-o'mah). A tumor of the exothelium of the cerebral meninges.

meningofibroblastoma (mĕ-ning″go-fi″bro-blas-to'mah). Meningioma.

meningoma (men″in-go'mah). Meningioma.

meningomalacia (mĕ-ning″go-mah-la'she-ah) [*meningo-* + Gr. *malakia* softness]. Softening of a membrane.

meningomyelitis (mĕ-ning″go-mi″ĕ-li'tis) [*meningo-* + Gr. *myelos* marrow + *-itis*]. Inflammation of the spinal cord and its membranes.

meningomyelocele (mĕ-ning″go-mi-el'o-sēl) [*meningo-* + Gr. *myelos* marrow + *kēlē* hernia]. Hernial protrusion of a part of the meninges and substance of the spinal cord through a defect in the vertebral column.

meningomyeloradiculitis (mĕ-ning″go-mi″ĕ-lo-rah-dik″u-li'tis). Inflammation of the meninges, spinal cord, and roots of the spinal nerves.

meningomyelorrhaphy (mĕ-ning″go-mi″ĕ-lor'-ah-fe) [*meningo-* + Gr. *myelos* marrow + *rhaphē* suture]. Suture of the spinal cord and meninges.

meningo-osteophlebitis (mĕ-ning″go-os″te-o-fle-bi'tis) [*meningo-* + Gr. *osteon* bone + *phleps* vein + *-itis*]. Periostitis with inflammation of the veins of a bone.

meningopathy (men″in-gop'ah-the) [*meningo-* + Gr. *pathos* disease]. Any disease of the meninges.

meningopneumonitis (mĕ-ning″go-nu-mo-ni'-tis). A virus disease produced in experimental animals by the injection of the virus of psittacosis and marked by acute meningitis and pneumonitis.

meningorachidian (mĕ-ning″go-rah-kid'e-an) [*meningo-* + Gr. *rhachis* spine]. Pertaining to the spinal cord and its membranes.

meningoradicular (mĕ-ning″go-rah-dik'u-lar) [*meningo-* + L. *radix* root]. Pertaining to the meninges and the roots of the cranial and spinal nerves.

meningoradiculitis (mĕ-ning″go-rah-dik″u-li'-tis). Inflammation of the meninges and roots of the spinal nerves.

meningorecurrence (mĕ-ning″go-re-kur'ens). Syphilitic meningitis induced in a syphilitic patient by antisyphilitic treatment.

meningorrhagia (mĕ-ning″go-ra'je-ah) [*meningo-* + Gr. *rhēgnynai* to break]. Hemorrhage from the cerebral or spinal membranes.

meningorrhea (mĕ-ning″go-re'ah) [*meningo-* + Gr. *rhoia* flow]. Effusion of blood between or upon the meninges.

meningosis (men″in-go'sis). The membranous attachment of bones to each other.

meningothelioma (mĕ-ning″go-the″le-o'mah). Meningioma.

meningotyphoid (mĕ-ning″go-ti'foid). Typhoid fever with prominent meningeal symptoms.

meningovascular (mĕ-ning″go-vas'ku-lar). Pertaining to the blood vessels of the meninges.

meninguria (men″in-gu're-ah) [*meningo-* + Gr. *ouron* urine + *-ia*]. The occurrence of membranous shreds in the urine.

meninx (me'ninks), pl. *menin'ges* [Gr. *mēninx* membrane]. A membrane; especially one of the three membranes enveloping the brain and spinal cord. **m. fibro'sa,** the dura mater. **m. sero'sa,** the arachnoid. **m. ten'uis,** the pia-arachnoid. **m. vasculo'sa,** the pia mater.

meniscectomy (men″ĭ-sek'to-me). Excision of a meniscus of the knee joint.

menischesis (men″ĭ-ske'sis). Menoschesis.

meniscitis (men″ĭ-si'tis). Inflammation of a meniscus of the knee joint.

meniscocyte (mĕ-nis'ko-sīt) [Gr. *mēniskos* crescent + *-cyte*]. A crescent-shaped or sickle-shaped red blood cell.

meniscocytosis (mĕ-nis″ko-si-to′sis). The presence of meniscocytes in the blood. See *sickle cell anemia*, under *anemia*.

meniscus (mĕ-nis′kus), pl. *menis′ci* [L.; Gr. *mēniskos* crescent]. 1. A crescent-shaped structure, such as the surface of a liquid column, as in a pipet or buret, made concave or convex by the influence of capillarity. Often used alone to designate one of the crescent-shaped disks of fibrocartilage attached to the superior articular surface of the tibia. **m. of acromioclavicular joint,** discus articularis articulationis acromioclavicularis. **articular m., m. articula′ris** [N A, B N A], a pad, commonly a wedge-shaped crescent of fibrocartilage or dense fibrous tissue, found in some synovial joints; one side forms a marginal attachment at the articular capsule and the other two sides extend into the joint, ending in a free edge. **converging m.,** positive m. **diverging m.,** negative m. **m. of inferior radioulnar joint,** discus articularis articulationis radioulnaris distalis. **joint m.,** articular m. **lateral m. of knee joint, m. latera′lis articulatio′nis ge′nus** [N A], a crescent-shaped disk of fibrocartilage, but nearly circular in form, attached to the lateral margin of the superior articular surface of the tibia. Called also *m. lateralis articulationis genu* [B N A]. **medial m. of knee joint, m. media′lis articulatio′nis ge′nus** [N A], a crescent-shaped disk of fibrocartilage attached to the medial margin of the superior articular surface of the tibia. Called also *m. medialis articulationis genu* [B N A]. **negative m.,** a convexoconcave lens. **positive m.,** a concavoconvex lens. **m. of sternoclavicular joint,** discus articularis articulationis sternoclavicularis. **tactile menisci, menis′ci tac′tus** [N A], small, cup-shaped, tactile nerve endings within the skin, many of which are formed by branches of a single nerve fiber. **m. of temporomaxillary joint,** discus articularis articulationis temporomandibularis.

menispermine (men″ĭ-sper′min). A crystalline alkaloid, $C_{18}H_{24}N_2O_2$, from *Anamirta paniculata*.

Menispermum (men″ĭ-sper′mum) [Gr. *mēnē* moon + *sperma* seed]. A genus of plants. The rhizome and roots of *M. canadense*, moonseed or yellow parilla, are tonic and alterative.

meno- (men′o) [Gr. *mēn* month; *mēniaia* the menses]. A combining form denoting relationship to the menses.

menolipsis (men″o-lip′sis) [*meno-* + Gr. *leipsis* failing]. Cessation of menstruation.

menometastasis (men″o-mĕ-tas′tah-sis). Vicarious menstruation.

menometrorrhagia (men″o-met″ro-ra′je-ah). Excessive uterine bleeding occurring at irregular intervals, the period of flow being of greater than usual duration.

menopausal (men″o-paw′zal). Pertaining to or associated with the menopause.

menopause (men′o-pawz) [*meno-* + Gr. *pausis* cessation]. Cessation of menstruation in the human female, occurring usually between the age of 46 and 50. **artificial m.,** cessation of menstruation produced by artificial means, such as surgical operation or irradiation.

menophania (men″o-fa′ne-ah) [*meno-* + Gr. *phainesthai* to appear]. The appearance of the menses at puberty.

menoplania (men″o-pla′ne-ah) [*meno-* + Gr. *planē* deviation]. Metastasis or aberration of the menses; vicarious menstruation.

menorrhagia (men″o-ra′je-ah) [*meno-* + Gr. *rhēgnynai* to burst forth]. Excessive uterine bleeding occurring at regular intervals, the period of flow being of greater than usual duration.

menorrhalgia (men″o-ral′je-ah) [*menorrhea* + *-algia*]. Distress associated with menstruation, including premenstrual tension, pelvic vascular congestion, and dysmenorrhea.

menorrhea (men″o-re′ah) [*meno-* + Gr. *rhoia* flow]. 1. The normal discharge of the menses. 2. Too free or profuse menstruation.

menorrheal (men″o-re′al). Pertaining to menorrhea.

menoschesis (men″o-ske′sis) [*meno-* + Gr. *schesis* retention]. Suppression of the menses.

menosepsis (men″o-sep′sis) [*meno-* + Gr. *sēpsis* decay]. Septic poisoning from retained menses.

menostasia (men″o-sta′ze-ah). Menostasis.

menostasis (men-os′tah-sis) [*meno-* + Gr. *stasis* halt]. 1. Suppression of the menses. 2. Cessation of menstruation; menopause.

menostaxis (men″o-stak′sis) [*meno-* + Gr. *staxis* dripping]. A prolonged period of menstruation due to necrosis of the endometrium.

menotoxic (men″o-tok′sik). 1. Caused by the toxic influence of retained menses. 2. Pertaining to menotoxin.

menotoxin (men″o-tok′sin). A toxic substance in the blood and body fluids of women during the menstrual period.

menoxenia (men″ok-se′ne-ah) [*meno-* + Gr. *xenos* strange]. Abnormal menstruation.

menses (men′sēz) [L., pl. of *mensis* month]. The monthly flow of blood from the genital tract of women. See *menstruation*.

menstrual (men′stroo-al) [L. *menstrualis*]. Pertaining to the menses.

menstruant (men′stroo-ant). A person who is menstruating or is capable of menstruating.

menstruate (men′stroo-āt) [L. *menstruare*]. To discharge blood from the genital tract at monthly intervals.

menstruation (men″stroo-a′shun). The cyclic, physiologic uterine bleeding which normally recurs, usually at approximately four-week intervals, in the absence of pregnancy during the reproductive period of the female of the human and a few other species of primates. **anovular m., anovulatory m.,** periodic uterine bleeding without preceding ovulation. **delayed m.,** menstruation the first appearance of which is delayed beyond the sixteenth year. **difficult m.,** dysmenorrhea. **infrequent m.,** menstruation occurring less frequently than normal. **nonovulational m.,** anovular m. **profuse m.,** menstruation marked by excessive flow. **regurgitant m.,** a back flow through the tubes by which epithelial cells and other materials may be discharged through the ostium and deposited on the ovary and adjacent organs, as in endometrioma. **retrograde m.,** regurgitant m. **scanty m.,** menstruation marked by abnormally small flow. **supplementary m.,** menstrual discharge from the uterus and also from some other part. **suppressed m.,** failure of the menstrual flow to appear. **vicarious m.,** blood loss from an extragenital source at the time a menstrual period is normally expected; thought to result from generally increased capillary permeability related to the menstrual cycle.

menstruous (men′stroo-us). Pertaining to menstruation.

menstruum (men′stroo-um) [L. *menstruus* menstruous: it was long believed that the menstrual fluid had a peculiar solvent quality]. A solvent medium. **Pitkin m.,** a medium for the administration of heparin, consisting of a mixture of gelatin, dextrose, glacial acetic acid, and water.

mensual (men′su-al) [L. *mensis* month]. Monthly.

mensuration (men″su-ra′shun) [L. *mensuratio; mensura* measure]. The act or process of measuring.

mentagra (men-tah′grah) [L. *mentum* chin + It. *agra* rough]. Sycosis.

mentagrophyton (men″tah-grof′ĭ-ton) [L. *mentagra* sycosis + Gr. *phyton* plant]. The fungus *Microsporon mentagrophytes*, the cause of sycosis.

mental (men′tal). 1. [L. *mens* mind]. Pertaining to the mind. 2. [L. *mentum* chin]. Pertaining to the chin.

mentalia (men-ta′le-ah). Psychalia.

mentalis (men-ta′lis) [L.]. Relating to the chin.

mentality (men-tal′ĭ-te). The mental power or activity.

Mentha (men′thah) [L.]. A genus of labiate plants: the mints. **M. piperi′ta,** peppermint. **M. pule′gium,** true pennyroyal. **M. vir′idis,** spearmint: a carminative and aromatic stimulant.

menthol (men′thol). An alcohol, 3-p-menthanol, obtained from diverse mint oils or prepared synthetically: used as a local antipruritic.

menthyl (men′thil). The monovalent radical, $C_{10}H_{18}$.

menticide (men′tĭ-sīd) [L. *mens* mind + *caedere* to kill]. Destruction of the mind of an individual by synthetic injection of the thoughts and words of a powerful tyrant or dictator, by means of drugs, narcohypnosis, brain surgery, or distorted psychiatric procedures.

mentimeter (men-tim′e-ter) [L. *mens* mind + Gr. *metron* measure]. A method or means of measuring mental capacity.

mentism (men′tizm). A condition marked by the formation of vivid involuntary mental images.

mento-anterior (men″to-an-te′re-or) [L. *mentum* chin + *anterior* before]. See under *position.*

mentolabial (men″to-la′be-al). Pertaining to the chin and lip.

mentoposterior (men″to-pos-te′re-or) [L. *mentum* chin + *posterior*]. See under *position.*

mentotransverse (men″to-trans-vers′) [L. *mentum* chin + *transverse*]. See under *position.*

mentula (men′tu-lah) [L.]. Penis.

mentulagra (men″tu-lag′rah) [L. *mentula* penis + Gr. *agra* seizure]. 1. Priapism. 2. Chordee.

mentulate (men′tu-lāt). Having a large penis.

mentulomania (men″tu-lo-ma′ne-ah) [L. *mentula* penis + *mania*]. Masturbation.

mentum (men′tum) [L.]. [N A, B N A] The chin.

Menyanthes (men″e-an′thēz) [perhaps from Gr. *mēn* month + *anthos* flower]. A genus of gentianaceous plants. *M. trifoliata,* or buckbean, is a bitter tonic.

meonine (me′o-nīn). Trade mark for a preparation of methionine.

mepacrine (mep′ah-krin). Atabrine.

mepazine (mep′ah-zēn). Chemical name: 10-[(1-methyl-3-piperidyl)methyl]phenothiazine: used as a sedative in psychoses and severe neuroses.

mepenzolate (me-pen′zo-lāt). Chemical name: 1-methyl-3-piperidyl benzilate: used in parasympathetic blockade, and as an antispasmodic.

meperidine (mĕ-per′ĭ-dēn). Chemical name: ethyl-1-methyl-4-phenylpiperidine-4-carboxylate: used as a narcotic analgesic.

mephenamine (mĕ-fen′ah-mēn). Orphenadrine.

mephenesin (mĕ-fen′ĕ-sin). Chemical name: 3-o-toloxy-1,2-propanediol: used as a relaxant for skeletal muscle.

mephenoxalone (mef″en-ok′sah-lōn). Chemical name: 5-(o-methoxymethyl)-2-oxazolidinone: used as an antianxiety and calming agent.

mephentermine (mĕ-fen′ter-mēn). Chemical name: N,α,α-trimethylphenethylamine: used as a sympathomimetic and as a pressor substance.

mephitibiosis (mĕ-fit″ĭ-bi-o′sis) [L. *mephitis* foul exhalation + Gr. *bios* life]. The capacity of certain bacteria to grow better under increased carbon dioxide tension.

mephitibiotic (mĕ-fit″ĭ-bi-ot′ik). Pertaining to or characterized by mephitibiosis.

mephitic (mĕ-fit′ik) [L. *mephiticus; mephitis* foul exhalation]. Emitting a foul odor.

mephitis (mĕ-fi′tis) [L.]. A foul exhalation.

mephobarbital (mef″o-bar′bĭ-tal). Chemical name: 5-ethyl-1-methyl-5-phenylbarbituric acid: used as an anticonvulsant with a slight hypnotic action.

mephyton (mef′ĭ-ton). Trade mark for preparations of vitamin K_1. See *phytonadione.*

meprane (me′prān). Trade mark for preparations of promethestrol.

meprobamate (mĕ-pro′bah-māt). Chemical name: 2-methyl-2-n-propyl-1,3-propanediol dicarbamate: used as a tranquilizer.

meprylcaine (mep′ril-kān). Chemical name: 2-methyl-2-propylaminopropyl benzoate: used as a local anesthetic.

mepyramine (me-pir′ah-mēn). Pyrilamine.

mepyrapone (mĕ-pi′rah-pōn). Chemical name: 2-methyl-1,2-di-3-pyridyl-1-propanone: used in diagnosis of pituitary function, and to inhibit production of cortisol by adrenals and induce compensatory increase in secretion of adrenocorticotropic hormone by the anterior pituitary.

mEq. Abbreviation for *milliequivalent.*

meralgia (me-ral′je-ah) [Gr. *mēros* thigh + *-algia*]. Pain in the thigh. **m. paresthet′ica,** a disease marked by paresthesia and disturbance of sensation in the outer surface of the thigh, in the region supplied by the external cutaneous femoral nerve. The paresthesia consists of burning, tingling, stabbing pains of considerable severity, or possibly only of a feeling of numbness. The sensory disturbances vary from slight hyperesthesia to total anesthesia. Called also *Bernhardt's disturbance of sensation.*

meralluride (mer-al′lu-rīd). A mixture of methoxyhydroxymercuripropylsuccinylurea and theophylline in approximately molecular proportions: used as a diuretic.

merbromin (mer-bro′min). Chemical name: dibromohydroxymercurifluorescein disodium salt: used as an antibacterial.

mercaptan (mer-kap′tan) [L. *mercurium captans* seizing or combining with mercury]. An alcohol in which hydroxyl oxygen is replaced by sulfur; a thio-alcohol.

mercaptide (mer-kap′tid). A compound derived from a mercaptan, with a metal replacing the sulfur hydrogen radical.

mercaptol (mer-kap′tol). A compound formed from a ketone by introducing two thio-alkyl groups in place of the bivalent oxygen.

mercaptomerin (mer″kap-tom′er-in). Chemical name: N-[3-(carboxymethylthiomercuri)-2-methoxypropyl]-α-camphoramate: used as a diuretic.

mercaptopurine (mer-kap″to-pu′rēn). Chemical name: 6-purinethiol: used as a neoplastic suppressant.

Mercier's bar, valve (mer-se-āz′) [Louis Auguste *Mercier,* French urologist, 1811–1882]. Interureteric ridge.

mercocresols (mer″ko-kre′solz). A combination of cresol derivatives and an organic mercury, used for its germicidal, fungicidal, and bacteriostatic properties.

mercodinone (mer″ko-di′nōn). Trade mark for a preparation of dihydroxodeinone.

mercuhydrin (mer″ku-hi′drin). Trade mark for preparations of meralluride.

mercupurin (mer-ku′pu-rin). Former name of mercuzanthin.

mercuramide (mer-kūr′ah-mid). Mersalyl.

mercurammonium (mer-ku″rah-mo′ne-um). A precipitate produced when ammonium hydroxide is added to a solution of a mercuric salt. **m. chloride,** ammoniated mercury.

mercurial (mer-ku′re-al) [L. *mercurialis*]. 1. Pertaining to mercury. 2. A preparation of mercury.

Mercurialis (mer-ku″re-a′lis). A genus of plants of Europe. *M. an′nua* and *M. peren′nis* have alterative properties.

mercurialism (mer-ku′re-al-izm). Chronic poisoning from misuse of mercury; hydrargyrism.

mercurialization (mer-ku″re-al-i-za′shun). The act or process of putting under the influence of mercury.

mercurialized (mer-ku′re-al-īzd). Treated with mercury; containing mercury.

mercuric (mer-ku′ric). Pertaining to mercury as a bivalent element. **m. benzoate,** a white, crystalline, tasteless salt, $(C_6H_5.CO.O)_2Hg + H_2O$, for intramuscular injection in the treatment of syphilis. **m. chloride,** mercury bichloride. **m. cyanide,** a very poisonous salt, $Hg(CN)_2$; is colorless; to be used subcutaneously, with great caution, in the treatment of syphilis. **m. iodide, red,** mercury biniodide, HgI_2: used as an antibacterial agent. **m. oxide, yellow,** a yellow to orange-yellow, heavy, impalpable powder, HgO, used as a local antibacterial agent. **m oxycyanide,** a white crystalline powder, $Hg(CN)_2.HgO$: antiseptic and antisyphilitic. **m. salicylate,** a white, tasteless powder, $(OH.C_6H_4.CO_2)_2Hg$, insoluble in water and alcohol. **m. sulfide,** a brilliant scarlet powder, HgS. Called also *vermilion* or *cinnabar*.

Mercurio's position (mer-koo′re-ōz) [Geronimo Scipione *Mercurio*, Italian accoucheur, 1550–1595]. See under *position.*

mercurochrome (mer-ku′ro-krōm). Trade mark for preparations of merbromin.

mercurophylline (mer″ku-ro-fil′lin). The sodium salt of N-[3-(hydroxymercuri)-2-methoxypropyl]-camphoric acid: used as a diuretic.

mercurous (mer′ku-rus). Pertaining to mercury as a monovalent element. **m. chloride,** a white odorless, tasteless, heavy powder, HgCl; used in pills or tablets as a cathartic, or, combined in an ointment, as a local antibacterial agent. **m. iodide, yellow,** a bright yellow insoluble amorphous powder, HgI: it has been used in the treatment of syphilis.

mercury (mer′ku-re) [L. *mercurius,* or *hydrargyrum*]. A metallic element, liquid at ordinary temperatures; quicksilver. Its symbol is Hg; atomic number, 80; atomic weight, 200.59; specific gravity, 13.546. It is insoluble in ordinary solvents, being only partially soluble in boiling hydrochloric acid. It may be dissolved, however, in nitric acid. Mercury forms two sets of classes of compounds—*mercurous,* in which a single atom of mercury combines with a monovalent radical, and *mercuric,* in which a single atom of mercury combines with a bivalent radical. Mercury and its salts have been employed therapeutically as purgatives; as alteratives in chronic inflammations; as antisyphilitics, intestinal antiseptics, disinfectants, and astringents. They are absorbed by the skin and mucous membranes, causing chronic mercurial poisoning, or hydrargyrism. The mercuric salts are more soluble and irritant than the mercurous. See also under *mercuric* and *mercurous.* **ammoniated m.,** an anti-infective compound, $HgNH_2Cl$, occurring in white, pulverulent pieces or as a white amorphous powder. **m. bichloride,** an extremely poisonous compound, $HgCl_2$, occurring as odorless, heavy, colorless crystals, as crystalline masses, or as a white powder: used as an antibacterial agent. **m. chloride, mild,** mercurous chloride. **French m.,** *Mercurialis annua.* **m. oleate,** a mixture of yellow mercuric oxide and oleic acid: applied locally in parasitic skin diseases. **m. perchloride,** m. bichloride. **m. salicylate,** a basic salt, $Hg.C_6H_3(OH).$-COOH, containing 54 to 59 per cent of mercury. **m. with chalk,** metallic mercury rubbed up with chalk and honey until the particles are very small.

mercuzanthin (mer″ku-zan′thin). Trade mark for a preparation of mercurophylline.

mere (mēr) [Gr. *meros* part]. Any one of the parts into which the substance of a zygote of a cell sometimes divides. Meres in their turn develop into blasts.

merergasia (mer-er-ga′se-ah). See *merergastic.*

merergastic (mer″er-gas′tik) [Gr. *meros* part + *ergon* work]. Meyer's term for "part disorders," the simplest type of disorder of psychic function, characterized by emotional instability and anxiety (psychoneuroses or neuroses). Cf. *holergastic.*

merethoxylline (mer″ĕ-thok′sil-lēn). Chemical name: dehydro-2-[N-(3′-hydroxymercuri-2′-methoxyethoxy) propylcarbamyl]-phenoxyacetic acid: used as a diuretic.

meridian (mĕ-rid′e-an). An imaginary line on the surface of a spherical body. See also *meridianus.* **m. of cornea,** an imaginary line marking the intersection with its surface of an anteroposterior plane passing through the apex of the cornea. **m's of eyeball,** meridiani bulbi oculi.

meridiani (mĕ-rid″e-a′ni) [L.]. Plural of *meridianus.*

meridianus (mĕ-rid″e-a′nus), pl. *meridia′ni* [L., from *medius* middle + *dies* day]. An imaginary line on the surface of a spherical body, marking the intersection with the surface of a plane passing through its axis. Called also *meridian.* **meridia′ni bul′bi oc′uli** [N A, B N A], imaginary lines encircling the eyeball, marking the intersection with its surface of planes passing through its anteroposterior axis. Called also *meridians of eyeball.*

meridional (mĕ-rid′e-o-nal). Pertaining to a meridian or made along a meridian; as, *meridional* section.

merisis (mer′ĭ-sis). Growth in size due to cell division.

merism (mer′izm) [Gr. *meros* a part]. The repetition of parts in an organism so as to form a regular pattern.

merispore (mer′ĭ-spōr) [Gr. *meros* part + *sporos* seed]. A spore produced by the division of another spore.

meristem (mer′ĭ-stem) [Gr. *merizein* to divide]. The undifferentiated embryonic tissue of plants.

meristematic (mer″ĭ-stĕ-mat′ik). Pertaining to or composed of meristem.

meristic (mer-is′tik) [Gr. *meristikos* fit for dividing]. Pertaining to or possessing merism; symmetrical; having symmetrically arranged parts.

meristiform (mĕ-ris′tĭ-form) [Gr. *meristos* divided + L. *forma* form]. A tetrad of cocci. See under *tetrad.*

meristoma (mer″ĭ-sto′mah) [*meristem* + *-oma*]. A tumor of meristem.

Merkel's corpuscles, ganglia, touch cells (mer′kelz) [Friedrich Siegismund *Merkel,* German anatomist, 1845–1919]. See under the nouns.

Merkel's filtrum, muscle (mer′kelz) [Karl Ludwig *Merkel,* German anatomist, 1812–1876]. See under *filtrum* and *muscle.*

Mermithidae (mer-mith′ĭ-de). A systematic family of Nematoda; the land hair worms.

mero- (mer′o) [Gr. *meros* part]. Combining form meaning part.

meroacrania (mer″o-ah-kra′ne-ah) [*mero-* + *a* neg. + Gr. *kranion* skull]. Congenital absence of part of the cranium.

meroblastic (mer″o-blas′tik) [*mero-* + Gr. *blastos* germ]. Undergoing cleavage in which only part of the ovum participates; partially dividing.

merocele (me′ro-sēl) [Gr. *mēros* thigh + *kēlē* hernia]. Femoral hernia.

merocoxalgia (me″ro-kok-sal′je-ah) [Gr. *mēros* thigh + L. *coxa* hip + *-algia*]. Pain in the thigh and hip.

merocrine (mer′o-krīn) [*mero-* + Gr. *krinein* to separate]. Partly secreting: noting that type of glandular secretion in which the secreting cell remains intact throughout the process of formation and discharge of the secretory products; as in the salivary and pancreatic glands. Cf. *apocrine* and *holocrine.*

merocyte (mer′o-sīt) [*mero-* + *-cyte*]. Supernumerary sperm nucleus in the ovum in cases of polyspermy.

merodiastolic (mer″o-di-ah-stol′ik) [*mero-* + *diastole*]. Pertaining to a part of the diastole.

mero-ergasia (mer″o-er-ga′se-ah). See *merergastic.*

merogamy (mĕ-rog′ah-me). Microgamy.

merogastrula (mer″o-gas′troo-lah). The gastrula of a meroblastic ovum.

merogenesis (mer″o-jen′e-sis) [*mero-* + Gr. *genesis* production]. Cleavage of an ovum.

merogenetic (mer″o-je-net′ik). Pertaining to merogenesis.

merogenic (mer″o-jen′ik). Pertaining to or producing segmentation.

merogonic (mer″o-gon′ik). Pertaining to or resulting from merogony.

merogony (mĕ-rog′o-ne) [*mero-* + Gr. *gonos* procreation]. The development of a portion only of an ovum. See *andromerogony* and *gynomerogony.* **diploid m.,** development of a portion of an ovum containing the fused male and female pronuclei. **parthenogenetic m.,** development, as a result of artificial stimulation, of a part of an ovum containing the nucleus.

merology (mĕ-rol′o-je) [*mero-* + *-logy*]. That part of anatomy which deals with elementary tissues.

meromicrosomia (mer″o-mi″kro-so′me-ah) [*mero-* + *microsomia*]. Unusual smallness of some part of the body.

meromorphosis (mer″o-mor-fo′sis) [*mero-* + Gr. *morphōsis* a shaping, bringing into shape]. Incomplete restoration or regeneration of a lost part.

meromyarial (mer″o-mi-a′re-al). Designating a type of nematode musculature in which there are only a few muscle cells in a given area, the cells being platymyarial in type.

meronecrobiosis (me″ro-nek″ro-bi-o′sis). Meronecrosis.

meronecrosis (me″ro-ne-kro′sis) [*mero-* + *necrosis*]. Cellular necrosis.

meroparesthesia (me″ro-par″es-the′ze-ah) [*mero-* + *paresthesia*]. Alteration of the tactile sense in the extremities.

meropia (mĕ-ro′pe-ah) [*mero-* + Gr. *ōps* vision + *-ia*]. Partial blindness.

merorachischisis (me″ro-rah-kis′kĭ-sis) [*mero-* + Gr. *rhachis* spine + *schisis* fissure]. Fissure of a part of the spinal cord.

meroscope (me′ro-skōp). An instrument for performing meroscopy.

meroscopy (mĕ-ros′ko-pe) [*mero-* + Gr. *skopein* to examine]. Fractional auscultation of the heart; dissociated auscultation of various parts of the cardiac cycle.

merosmia (mĕ-ros′me-ah) [*mero-* + Gr. *osmē* smell + *-ia*]. A disorder of the sense of smell in which certain odors are not perceived.

merostotic (mer″os-tot′ik) [*mero-* + L. *os* bone]. Pertaining to or affecting only a part of a bone.

merosystolic (me″ro-sis-tol′ik) [*mero-* + Gr. *systolē* systole]. Pertaining to a part of the systole.

merotomy (mĕ-rot′o-me) [*mero-* + Gr. *temnein* to cut]. Division into segments.

merozoite (mer″o-zo′īt) [*mero-* + Gr. *zōon* animal]. One of the young forms derived from the splitting up of the schizont in the human cycle of the malarial plasmodium. It is released into the circulating blood and attacks new erythrocytes.

merphene (mer′fēn). Trade mark for preparations of phenylmercuric nitrate.

mersalyl (mer′sah-lil). Chemical name: O-{[3-(hydroxymercuri)-2-methoxypropyl]carbamyl} phenoxyacetic acid: used as a diuretic.

Merseburg triad (mār′zeh-boorg) [*Merseburg*, a town in Germany]. See under *triad.*

merthiolate (mer-thi′o-lāt). Trade mark for preparations of thimerosal.

Merulius (mĕ-roo′le-us). A genus of fungi. **M. lac′rimans,** the fungus of the dry-rot of wood; inhaled in dust, it becomes parasitic, causing a persistent and sometimes fatal catarrh and bronchitis.

Méry's glands (ma-rēz′) [Jean *Méry*, anatomist in Paris, 1645–1722]. Cowper's glands.

merycism (mer′ĭ-sizm) [Gr. *mērykismos* chewing the cud]. The regurgitation of food from the stomach and chewing it again; rumination.

merycismus (mer″ĭ-siz′mus). Merycism.

Merzbacher-Pelizaeus disease (merz′bak-er-pa″le-zi′us) [Ludwig *Merzbacher*, in Buenos Aires, born 1875; Friedrich *Pelizaeus*, German neurologist, born 1850]. Familial centrolobar sclerosis.

mesad (me′sad). Toward the median line or plane.

mesal (me′sal) [Gr. *mesos* middle]. Pertaining to the median line or plane.

mesameboid (mes″ah-me′boid) [*meso-* + Gr. *amoibē* change + *eidos* shape]. Hemocytoblast.

mesangium (mes-an′je-um). The thin membrane which helps to support the capillary loops in a renal glomerulus.

mesaortitis (mes″a-or-ti′tis) [*meso-* + *aortitis*]. Inflammation of the middle coat of the aorta.

mesaraic (mes″ah-ra′ik) [*meso-* + Gr. *mesaraion* the mesentery]. Mesenteric.

mesarteritis (mes″ar-ter-i′tis) [*meso-* + Gr. *artēria* artery + *-itis*]. Inflammation of the middle coat of an artery. **Mönckeberg's m.,** Mönckeberg's sclerosis.

mesaticephalic (mes-at″ĭ-se-fal′ik) [Gr. *mesatos* medium + *kephalē* head]. Mesocephalic.

mesatikerkic (mes-at″ĭ-ker′kik) [Gr. *mesatos* medium + *kerkis* the radius of the arm]. Having a radiohumeral index of 75–80.

mesatipellic (mes-at″ĭ-pel′ik) [Gr. *mesatos* medium + *pella* bowl]. Having a pelvic index between 90 and 95.

mesatipelvic (mes-at″ĭ-pel′vik). Mesatipellic.

mescal (mes-kahl′) [Mex.]. The fermented juice of *Agave americana* and other Mexican species of that genus.

mescaline (mes′kah-lin). A poisonous alkaloid, 3,4,5-trimethoxy phenyl ethylamine, $(CH_3.O)_3$-$C_6H_2.CH_2.CH_2.NH_2$, in the form of a colorless alkaline oil from *Lophophora williamsii.* It produces an intoxication with delusions of color and music.

mescalism (mes′kah-lizm). Intoxication caused by mescal buttons or mescaline.

mesectic (mes-ek′tik) [*mes-* + Gr. *echein* to hold]. Taking up a medium or average amount of oxygen. If at an oxygen pressure of 40 mm. the blood will take up oxygen to the extent of 70–79 per cent, it is said to be mesectic. Cf. *mionectic* and *pleonectic.*

mesectoblast (mes-ek′to-blast). Ectomesoblast.

mesectoderm (mes-ek′to-derm). Migratory cells, derived from the neural crest of the head, that contribute to the formation of the meninges and become pigment cells.

mesencephal (mes-en′se-fal). Mesencephalon.

mesencephalic (mes-en″se-fal′ik). Pertaining to the mesencephalon.

mesencephalitis (mes″en-sef″ah-li′tis). Inflammation of the mesencephalon.

mesencephalohypophyseal (mes″en-sef″ah-lo-hi-po-fiz′e-al). Pertaining to the mesencephalon and the pituitary body (hypophysis).

mesencephalon (mes″en-sef′ah-lon) [*meso-* + Gr. *enkephalos* brain]. 1. [N A, B N A] The part of the central nervous system developed from the middle of the three primary divisions of the embryonic neural tube; it comprises the tectum and the cerebral peduncle, which includes the tegmentum, substantia nigra, and basis pedunculi. Called also *midbrain.* 2. The middle of the three primary divisions of the neural axis of the embryo, between the prosencephalon and the rhombencephalon.

mesencephalotomy (mes″en-sef″ah-lot′o-me) [*mesencephalon* + Gr. *tomē* a cutting]. Surgical production of lesions in the midbrain, especially in the pain-conducting pathways for the relief of intractable pain.

mesenchyma (mes-eng′kĭ-mah) [*meso-* + Gr. *enchyma* infusion]. The meshwork of embryonic connective tissue in the mesoderm from which are formed the connective tissues of the body, and also the blood vessels and lymphatic vessels.

mesenchymal (mes-eng′kĭ-mal). Pertaining to the mesenchyma.

mesenchyme (mes′eng-kīm). Mesenchyma.

mesenchymoma (mes″en-ki-mo′mah). A mixed mesenchymal tumor composed of two or more cellular elements not commonly associated, not counting fibrous tissue as one of the elements.

mesenterectomy (mes″en-ter-ek′to-me) [*mesentery* + Gr. *ektomē* excision]. Resection of the mesentery or of a mesenteric lesion.

mesenteric (mes″en-ter′ik) [Gr. *mesenterikos*]. Pertaining to the mesentery.

mesenteriolum (mes-en″ter-i′o-lum). A small mesentery. **m. appen′dicis vermifor′mis, m. proces′sus vermifor′mis** [B N A], mesoappendix.

mesenteriopexy (mes″en-ter′e-o-pek″se) [*mesentery* + Gr. *pēxis* fixation]. The operation of fixing or attaching a torn mesentery.

mesenteriorrhaphy (mes″en-ter″e-or′ah-fe) [*mesentery* + Gr. *rhaphē* suture]. Suture of the mesentery.

mesenteriplication (mes″en-ter″e-pli-ka′shun) [*mesentery* + L. *plicare* to fold]. The operation of shortening the mesentery by making a tuck in it.

mesenteritis (mes″en-ter-i′tis). Inflammation of the mesentery. **retractile m.,** inflammation of the mesentery producing thickening, sclerosis, and retraction, and occasionally resulting in distortion of intestinal loops.

mesenterium (mes″en-te′re-um). [N A, B N A] The peritoneal fold attaching the small intestine to the posterior abdominal wall. Called also *mesentery*. **m. commu′ne** [B N A], **m. dorsa′le commu′ne** [N A], the primitive embryonic mesentery, a double-layered median partition formed by association of the splanchnic mesoderm with the entoderm, extending from the roof of the coelom toward the midventral wall, and dividing the coelom into halves; it contains the primitive gut, and encloses the heart, lungs, and liver as they develop.

mesenteron (mes-en′ter-on) [*meso-* + Gr. *enteron* intestine]. The midgut.

mesentery (mes′en-ter″e). A membranous fold attaching various organs to the body wall. Commonly used with specific reference to the peritoneal fold attaching the small intestine to the dorsal body wall. Called also *mesenterium*. **m. of ascending part of colon,** mesocolon ascendens. **caval m.,** a ridge, at the right of the embryonic mesogastrium, in which develops a hepatic segment of the inferior vena cava. **common m., common m., dorsal,** mesenterium dorsale commune. **m. of descending part of colon,** mesocolon descendens. **dorsal m.,** mesenterium dorsale commune. **primitive m.,** the double-layered partition formed in the early embryo. See *mesenterium dorsale commune*. **m. of rectum,** mesorectum. **m. of sigmoid colon,** mesocolon sigmoideum. **m. of transverse part of colon,** mesocolon transversum. **ventral m.,** the embryonic mesentery attaching the duodenal region of the early intestine to the ventral body wall. **m. of vermiform appendix,** mesoappendix.

mesentoderm (mes-en′to-derm). The inner layer of an amphibian gastrula not yet separated into mesoderm and entoderm.

mesentomere (mes-en′to-mēr). A blastomere not yet divided into mesomeres and entomeres.

mesentorrhaphy (mes″en-tor′ah-fe) [*mesentery* + Gr. *rhaphē* suture]. The operation of suturing the mesentery.

mesepithelium (mes″ep-ĭ-the′le-um). Mesothelium.

mesiad (me′ze-ad). Toward the middle; mesad.

mesial (me′ze-al). Situated in the middle; median; nearer the middle line of the body or nearer the center line of the dental arch.

mesially (me′ze-al″e). Toward the median line.

mesien (me′ze-en). Pertaining to the mesion.

mesiobuccal (me″ze-o-buk′kal). Pertaining to or formed by the mesial and buccal surfaces of a tooth, or the mesial and buccal walls of a tooth cavity.

mesiobucco-occlusal (me″ze-o-buk″ko-ŏ-kloo′zal). Pertaining to or formed by the mesial, buccal, and occlusal surfaces of a tooth.

mesiobuccopulpal (me″ze-o-buk″ko-pul′pal). Pertaining to or formed by the mesial, buccal, and pulpal walls of a tooth cavity.

mesiocervical (me″ze-o-ser′vĭ-kal). 1. Pertaining to the mesial surface of the neck of a tooth. 2. Mesiogingival.

mesioclination (me″ze-o-kli-na′shun). Deviation of a tooth from the vertical, in the direction of the tooth next mesial to it in the dental arch.

mesioclusion (me″ze-o-kloo′zhun). Anteroclusion, the teeth of the mandibular arch being mesial to their opposite numbers in the maxillary arch.

mesiodens (me′ze-o-denz), pl. *mesioden′tes*. A small supernumerary tooth with a cone-shaped crown and a short root, occurring singly or paired, and generally situated between the maxillary central incisors.

mesiodentes (me″ze-o-den′tēz). Plural of *mesiodens*.

mesiodistal (me″ze-o-dis′tal). Pertaining to the mesial and distal surfaces of a tooth.

mesiogingival (me″ze-o-jin′jĭ-val). Pertaining to or formed by the mesial and gingival walls of a tooth cavity.

mesioincisodistal (me″ze-o-in-si″so-dis′tal). Pertaining to the mesial, incisal, and distal surfaces of an anterior tooth.

mesiolabial (me″ze-o-la′be-al). Pertaining to or formed by the mesial and labial surfaces of a tooth, or the mesial and labial walls of a tooth cavity.

mesiolabioincisal (me″ze-o-la″be-o-in-si′zal). Pertaining to or formed by the mesial, labial, and incisal surfaces of a tooth.

mesiolingual (me″ze-o-ling′gwal). Pertaining to or formed by the mesial and lingual surfaces of a tooth, or the mesial and lingual walls of a tooth cavity.

mesiolinguoincisal (me″ze-o-ling″gwo-in-si′zal). Pertaining to or formed by the mesial, lingual, and incisal surfaces of a tooth.

mesiolinguo-occlusal (me″ze-o-ling″gwo-ŏ-kloo′zal). Pertaining to or formed by the mesial, lingual, and occlusal surfaces of a tooth.

mesiolinguopulpal (me″ze-o-ling″gwo-pul′pal). Pertaining to or formed by the mesial, lingual, and pulpal walls of a tooth cavity.

mesion (me′se-on) [Gr. *mesos* middle]. The plane that divides the body into right and left symmetric halves.

mesio-occlusal (me″ze-o-ŏ-kloo′zal). Pertaining to or formed by the mesial and occlusal surfaces of a tooth, or the mesial and occlusal walls of a tooth cavity.

mesio-occlusion (me″ze-o-ŏ-kloo′zhun). Mesioclusion.

mesio-occlusodistal (me″ze-o-ŏ-kloo″so-dis′tal). Pertaining to the mesial, occlusal, and distal surfaces of a posterior tooth.

mesiopulpal (me″ze-o-pul′pal). Pertaining to

or formed by the mesial and pulpal walls of a tooth cavity.

mesiopulpolabial (me″ze-o-pul″po-la′be-al). Pertaining to or formed by the mesial, pulpal, and labial walls of a tooth cavity.

mesiopulpolingual (me″ze-o-pul″po-ling′gwal). Pertaining to or formed by the mesial, pulpal, and lingual walls of a tooth cavity.

mesioversion (me″ze-o-ver′zhun). The condition of a tooth which is nearer than normal to the median line of the face along the dental arch.

mesiris (mes-i′ris) [*meso-* + *iris*]. The middle layer of the iris.

mesitylene (mes-it′ĭ-lēn). Symmetric trimethylbenzene, $C_6H_3(CH_3)_3$, from coal tar.

mesmerism (mes′mer-izm) [after Franz A. *Mesmer*, 1733–1815]. The use of animal magnetism and hypnotism as practiced by Mesmer.

mesmeromania (mes″mer-o-ma′ne-ah) [*mesmerism* + Gr. *mania* madness]. Insane devotion to mesmerism.

meso- (mes′o) [Gr. *mesos* middle]. 1. A prefix signifying "middle," either situated in the middle or intermediate. 2. In chemistry, a prefix signifying inactive or without effect on polarized light.

meso-aortitis (mes″o-a″or-ti′tis). Inflammation of the middle coat of the aorta. **m. syphilit′ica,** inflammation of the middle coat of the aorta due to syphilis.

mesoappendicitis (mes″o-ah-pen″dĭ-si′tis). Inflammation of the mesoappendix.

mesoappendix (mes″o-ah-pen′diks) [*meso-* + *appendix*]. [N A] The peritoneal fold attaching the appendix to the mesentery of the ileum. Called also *mesenteriolum processus vermiformis* [B N A].

mesoarial (mes″o-a′re-al). Pertaining to the mesovarium.

mesoarium (mes″o-a′re-um). Mesovarium.

mesobacteria (mes″o-bak-te′re-ah). Plural of *mesobacterium*.

mesobacterium (mes″o-bak-te′re-um), pl. *mesobacteria*. A rod-shaped microorganism of medium size.

mesobilin (mes″o-bi′lin). A compound, $C_{33}H_{42}O_6N_4$, occurring in the urine.

mesobilirubin (mes″o-bil″ĭ-roo′bin). A compound, $C_{33}H_{44}O_6N_4$, formed by the reduction of bilirubin.

mesobilirubinogen (mes″o-bil″ĭ-roo-bin′o-jen). A reduced form of bilirubin, formed in the intestine, which on oxidation forms stercobilin.

mesobiliviolin (mes″o-bil″ĭ-vi′o-lin). An oxidation product of mesobilirubinogen and of stercobilinogen.

mesoblast (mes′o-blast) [*meso-* + Gr. *blastos* germ]. Mesoderm, especially in the early stages.

mesoblastema (mes″o-blas-te′mah). The cells composing the mesoblast.

mesoblastic (mes″o-blas′tik). Pertaining to or derived from the mesoblast.

mesobronchitis (mes″o-brong-ki′tis) [*meso-* + *bronchitis*]. Inflammation of the middle coat of the bronchi.

mesocardia (mes″o-kar′de-ah) [*meso-* + Gr. *kardia* heart]. Atypical location of the heart in the middle line of the thorax.

mesocardium (mes″o-kar′de-um) [*meso-* + Gr. *kardia* heart]. 1. That part of the embryonic mesentery which connects the embryonic heart with the body wall in front and the foregut behind. 2. Myocardium. **arterial m.,** that part of the pericardium which, in the form of a tube, encloses the aorta and pulmonary artery. **dorsal m.,** the temporary dorsal mesentery of the heart in the embryo; its site is represented by the transverse sinus of the pericardium. **lateral m.,** pulmonary ridge. **venous m.,** that part of the pericardium which, in the form of a tube, encloses the venae cavae and pulmonary veins. **ventral m.,** a mesentery attaching the heart to the ventral body wall; it is scarcely represented in human development.

mesocarpal (mes′o-kar′pal). Midcarpal.

mesocecal (mes″o-se′kal). Pertaining to the mesocecum.

mesocecum (mes″o-se′kum) [*meso-* + *cecum*]. The peritoneal fold which gives attachment to the cecum.

mesocele (mes′o-sēl) [*meso-* + Gr. *koilia* hollow]. The aqueduct of Sylvius.

mesocephalic (mes″o-se-fal′ik). 1. Pertaining to the mesocephalon. 2. Having a cephalic index between 76.0 and 80.9.

mesocephalon (mes″o-sef′ah-lon). Mesencephalon.

mesochondrium (mes″o-kon′dre-um) [*meso-* + Gr. *chondros* cartilage]. The matrix in which are embedded the cellular elements of hyaline cartilage.

mesochoroidea (mes″o-ko-roi′de-ah). The middle coat of the choroid.

mesococci (mes″o-kok′si). Plural of *mesococcus*.

mesococcus (mes″o-kok′us), pl. *mesococ′ci*. A spherical microorganism of medium size.

mesocoelia (mes″o-se′le-ah). The aqueduct of Sylvius.

mesocolic (mes″o-kol′ik). Pertaining to the mesocolon.

mesocolon (mes″o-ko′lon) [*meso-* + Gr. *kolon* colon]. [N A, B N A] The process of peritoneum by which the colon is attached to the posterior abdominal wall. It is divided into an ascending, transverse, descending, and sigmoid or pelvic portions, according to the segment of the colon to which it gives attachment. **m. ascen′dens** [N A, B N A], **ascending m.,** the peritoneum attaching the ascending colon to the posterior abdominal wall, usually obliterated when the ascending colon becomes retroperitoneal. **m. descen′dens** [N A, B N A], **descending m.,** the peritoneum attaching the descending colon to the posterior abdominal wall, usually obliterated when the descending colon becomes retroperitoneal. **iliac m.,** m. sigmoideum. **left m.,** m. descendens. **pelvic m.,** m. sigmoideum. **right m.,** m. ascendens. **sigmoid m., m. sigmoi′deum** [N A, B N A], the peritoneum attaching the sigmoid colon to the posterior abdominal wall. Called also *pelvic m.* **transverse m., m. transver′sum** [N A, B N A], the peritoneum attaching the transverse colon to the posterior abdominal wall.

mesocolopexy (mes″o-ko′lo-pek″se) [*mesocolon* + Gr. *pēxis* fixation]. Mesocoloplication.

mesocoloplication (mes″o-ko″lo-pli-ka′shun) [*mesocolon* + *plication*]. The operation of folding and suturing the mesocolon to limit the mobility of the bowel.

mesocord (mes′o-kord). An umbilical cord adherent to the placenta by a connecting fold of the amnion; more correctly, the connecting fold itself.

mesocornea (mes″o-kor′ne-ah). The substantia propria of the cornea.

mesocranic (mes″o-kra′nik). Having a cranial index between 75.0 and 79.9.

mesocuneiform (mes″o-ku′ne-ĭ-form). The middle cuneiform bone.

mesocyst (mes′o-sist) [*meso-* + Gr. *kystis* bladder]. The layer of peritoneum attaching the gallbladder to the liver.

mesocyte (mes′o-sit) [*meso-* + *-cyte*]. Mesolymphocyte.

mesocytoma (mes″o-si-to′mah) [*mesocyte* + *-oma*]. A connective tissue tumor; a sarcoma.

mesodens (mes′o-dens). Mesiodens.

mesoderm (mes′o-derm) [*meso-* + Gr. *derma* skin]. The middle layer of the three primary germ layers of the embryo, lying between the ectoderm and the entoderm. From it are derived the connective tissue, bone and cartilage, the muscles, the blood and blood vessels, lymphatics and lymphoid organs, the notochord, the epithelium of pleura, pericardium, peritoneum, kidney and sex organs. Cf. *ectoderm* and *entoderm*. **extraembryonic m.,** that located outside the embryo and belonging to fetal accessory organs. **gastral m.,** that infolded with the entoderm during gastrulation. **head m.,** loose mesoderm, cranial to the somites. **lateral m.,** the lateral sheets of mesoderm within which the embryonic coelom arises. **paraxial m.,** that lying alongside the notochord and neural tube. **peristomal m.,** that derived from the ventral lip of the blastopore or from the primitive streak. **somatic m.,** the outer of the two layers into which the mesoderm divides. **splanchnic m.,** the inner of the two layers into which the mesoderm divides.

mesodermal (mes″o-der′mal). Pertaining to or derived from the mesoderm.

mesodermic (mes″o-der′mik). Pertaining to the mesoderm.

mesodermopath (mes″o-der′mo-path) [*mesoderm* + Gr. *pathos* disease]. A person who is constitutionally susceptible to diseases of the tissues derived from embryonic mesoderm, such as heart and kidneys, arteries and veins, joints and muscles.

mesodesma (mes″o-des′mah) [*meso-* + Gr. *desma* band]. The broad ligament of the uterus.

mesodiastolic (mes″o-di″ah-stol′ik) [*meso-* + *diastole*]. Pertaining to the middle of the diastole.

mesodmitis (mes″od-mi′tis) [Gr. *mesodmē* something built between + *-itis*]. Mediastinitis.

mesodont (mes′o-dont) [*meso-* + Gr. *odous* tooth]. Having a dental index between 42 and 44.

mesodontic (mes″o-don′tik). Having medium sized teeth.

mesodontism (mes″o-don′tizm). The state of having medium sized teeth, or a dental index between 42 and 44.

mesoduodenal (mes″o-du″o-de′nal). Pertaining to the mesoduodenum.

mesoduodenum (mes″o-du″o-de′num) [*meso-* + *duodenum*]. The mesenteric fold which in early fetal life encloses the duodenum.

meso-epididymis (mes″o-ep″ĭ-did′ĭ-mis). A fold of tunica vaginalis that sometimes connects the epididymis with the testicle.

meso-esophagus (mes″o-e-sof′ah-gus). The portion of the primitive mesentery which encloses the developing esophagus.

mesogaster (mes″o-gas′ter) [*meso-* + Gr. *gastēr* belly]. Mesogastrium.

mesogastric (mes″o-gas′trik). Pertaining to the mesogastrium.

mesogastrium (mes″o-gas′tre-um) [*meso-* + Gr. *gastēr* belly]. The portion of the primitive mesentery which encloses the stomach, and from which the greater omentum is developed.

mesoglea (mes″o-gle′ah) [*meso-* + Gr. *gloia* glue]. A structureless jelly located between the ectoderm and entoderm of coelenterates and held to be the homologue of mesoderm in higher animals.

mesoglia (mes-og′le-ah). 1. Microglia. 2. Oligodendroglia.

mesoglioma (mes″o-gli-o′mah). A tumor of the mesoglia.

mesogluteal (mes″o-gloo′te-al). Pertaining to the gluteus medius muscle.

mesogluteus (mes″o-gloo′te-us). The gluteus medius muscle.

mesognathic (mes″og-na′thik). Mesognathous.

mesognathion (mes″og-na′the-on) [*meso-* + Gr. *gnathos* jaw]. The lateral center of ossification in the os incisivum for the lateral incisor tooth.

mesognathous (mes-og′nah-thus). Having a gnathic index between 98 and 103.

Mesogonimus (mes″o-gon′ĭ-mus). A genus of flukes. See *Paragonimus*. **M. heteroph′yes,** *Heterophyes heterophyes*.

mesohemin (mes″o-he′min). A reduced form of hemin, $C_{34}H_{36}O_4N_4FeCl$.

mesohyloma (mes″o-hi-lo′mah) [*meso-* + Gr. *hylē* matter + *-oma*]. A tumor developed from the mesothelium.

mesohypoblast (mes″o-hi′po-blast). Mesentoderm.

meso-ileum (mes″o-il′e-um). The mesentery of the ileum.

mesojejunum (mes″o-je-ju′num). The mesentery of the jejunum.

mesolecithal (mes″o-les′ĭ-thal) [*meso-* + Gr. *lekithos* yolk]. Possessing a moderate amount of yolk.

mesolepidoma (mes″o-lep″ĭ-do′mah) [*meso-* + Gr. *lepis* scale + *-oma*]. A tumor made up of tissue derived from the persistent embryonic mesothelium. **atypic m.,** carcinoma of a genitourinary organ or of a serous membrane. **typical m.,** adenoma of a genitourinary organ or of a serous membrane.

mesolobus (mes-ol′o-bus) [*meso-* + Gr. *lobos* lobe]. The corpus callosum.

mesology (mes-ol′o-je). Ecology.

mesolymphocyte (mes″o-lim′fo-sit) [*meso-* + *lymphocyte*]. A medium sized lymphocyte.

mesomelic (mes″o-mel′ik) [*meso-* + Gr. *melus* limb]. Pertaining to the midportion of the arm or leg.

mesomere (mes′o-mēr) [*meso-* + Gr. *meros* part]. 1. A blastomere of size intermediate between a macromere and a micromere. 2. A midzone of the mesoderm between the epimere and hypomere.

mesomeric (mes″o-mer′ik). Exhibiting mesomerism.

mesomerism (mes-om′er-izm). The existence of organic chemical structures differing only in the position of electrons, rather than atoms. For example, the two Kekulé structures for benzene. Such a molecule does not possess one electronic structure part of the time and another structure the rest of the time; the actual electronic state of the molecule is at all times intermediate to the two extremes.

mesometritis (mes″o-me-tri′tis) [*meso-* + Gr. *mētra* uterus + *-itis*]. Inflammation of the middle layer of the uterus, or myometrium.

mesometrium (mes″o-me′tre-um) [*meso-* + Gr. *mētra* uterus]. 1. [N A, B N A] The portion of the broad ligament below the mesovarium, composed of the layers of peritoneum that separate to enclose the uterus. 2. The tunica muscularis uteri, or myometrium.

mesomorph (mes′o-morf) [Gr. *morphē* form]. An individual exhibiting mesomorphy.

mesomorphic (mes″o-mor′fik). Pertaining to or characterized by mesomorphy.

mesomorphy (mes′o-mor″fe) [*meso-* + Gr. *morphē* form]. A type of body build in which tissues derived from the mesoderm predominate. There is relative preponderance of muscle, bone, and connective tissue, usually with heavy, hard physique of rectangular outline.

mesomucinase (mes″o-mu′sĭ-nās). A testicular mucinolytic enzyme which is essential for fertilization.

mesomula (mes-om′u-lah). An early stage of the embryo, when it consists of an epithelial ectoderm and entoderm inclosing a mass of mesenchyma.

meson (mes′on) [Gr. *mesos* middle]. 1. Mesion. 2. A sub-atomic, short-lived particle of a mass less than that of a proton but more than that of an electron, carrying either a positive or a negative electric charge.

mesonasal (mes″o-na′zal). Situated in the middle of the nose.

mesonephric (mes″o-nef′rik). Pertaining to the mesonephros.

mesonephroi (mes″o-nef′roi). Plural of *mesonephros*.

mesonephroma (mes″o-ne-fro′mah). A tumor of the ovary arising from the mesonephros or primitive kidney.

mesonephron (mes″o-nef′ron). Mesonephros.

mesonephros (mes″o-nef′ros), pl. *mesoneph′roi* [*meso-* + Gr. *nephros* kidney]. [N A] The excretory organ of the embryo, arising caudad to the pronephros and using its duct. The mesonephros consists of a long tube in the lower part of the body cavity, running parallel with the spinal axis and joined at right angles by a row of twisting tubes. Called also *corpus Wolffi* [B N A], and *wolffian body*.

mesoneuritis (mes″o-nu-ri′tis) [*meso-* + Gr. *neuron* nerve + *-itis*]. 1. Inflammation of the substance of a nerve. 2. Inflammation of the lymphatics of a nerve. **nodular m.,** inflammatory hyperplasia of the connective tissue of a nerve, resulting in nodular thickenings upon its surface.

meso-omentum (mes″o-o-men′tum). The fold by which the omentum is attached to the abdominal wall.

meso-ontomorph (mes″o-on′to-morf) [*meso-* + Gr. *ōn* being + *morphē* form]. A person of stocky build having a tendency toward hypothyroidism.

mesopallium (mes″o-pal′e-um) [*meso-* + L. *pallium* cloak]. That portion of the pallium showing stratification and organization that is transitional between the archipallium and neopallium. It includes the pyriform and entorrhinal cortex of the hippocampal gyrus, the perirhinal cortex of the temporal pole and insula, and the cortex of the subcallosal, cingulate, and retrosplenial gyri.

mesopexy (mes′o-pek″se). Mesenteriopexy.

mesophile (mes′o-fīl). An organism which grows best at temperatures between 20 and 55°C.

mesophilic (mes″o-fil′ik) [*meso-* + Gr. *philein* to love]. Fond of moderate temperature: said of bacteria which develop best at temperatures between 20 and 55°C. Cf. *psychrophilic* and *thermophilic.*

mesophlebitis (mes″o-fle-bi′tis). Inflammation of the middle coat of a vein.

mesophragma (mes″o-frag′mah) [*meso-* + Gr. *phragmos* a fencing in]. A name given to Hensen's line. Cf. *inophragma* and *telophragma.*

mesophryon (mes-of′re-on) [*meso-* + Gr. *ophrys* eyebrow]. The glabella or its central point.

mesophyll (mes′o-fil) [*meso-* + Gr. *phyllon* leaf]. The tissue of the inner part of a leaf.

mesopin (mes′o-pin). A proprietary brand of homatropine methylbromide.

mesopneumon (mes″o-nu′mon) [*meso-* + Gr. *pneumon* lung]. The union of the two layers of the pleura at the hilus of the lung.

mesopneumonium (mes″o-nu-mo′ne-um). Mesopneumon.

mesoporphyrin (mes″o-por′fĭ-rin). A crystalline iron-free porphyrin, $C_{34}H_{38}O_4N_4$, from hematin obtained by a process of reduction.

mesoprosopic (mes″o-pro-sop′ik) [*meso-* + Gr. *prosōpon* face]. Having a face of moderate width.

mesopsychic (mes″o-si′kik). Pertaining to the middle period of mental development.

mesopulmonum (mes″o-pul-mo′num). The portion of the embryonic mesentery which encloses the laterally expanding lung.

mesorachischisis (mes″o-rah-kis′kĭ-sis) [*meso-* + *rachischisis*]. Partial rachischisis; partial fissure of the spinal cord.

mesorchial (mes-or′ke-al). Pertaining to the mesorchium.

mesorchium (mes-or′ke-um) [*meso-* + Gr. *orchis* testis]. [N A, B N A] The portion of the primitive mesentery that encloses the fetal testis, represented in the adult by a fold between the testis and epididymis.

mesorectum (mes″o-rek′tum) [*meso-* + *rectum*]. [B N A] The fold of peritoneum connecting the upper portion of the rectum with the sacrum. Omitted in N A.

mesoretina (mes″o-ret′ĭ-nah) [*meso-* + *retina*]. The middle layer of the retina.

mesoropter (mes″o-rop′ter) [*meso-* + Gr. *horos* boundary + Gr. *optēr* observer]. The normal position of the eyes with their muscles at rest.

mesorrhaphy (mes-or′ah-fe). Mesenteriorrhaphy.

mesorrhine (mes′o-rīn) [*meso-* + Gr. *rhis* nose]. Having a nasal index between 48 and 53.

mesosalpinx (mes″o-sal′pinks) [*meso-* + Gr. *salpinx* tube]. [N A, B N A] The part of the broad ligament of the uterus above the mesovarium, composed of layers that enclose the uterine tube.

mesoscapula (mes″o-skap′u-lah). Spina scapula.

mesoseme (mes′o-sēm) [*meso-* + Gr. *sēma* sign]. Having an orbital index between 83 and 89.

mesosigmoid (mes″o-sig′moid). The peritoneal fold by which the sigmoid flexure is attached.

mesosigmoiditis (mes″o-sig″moi-di′tis). Inflammation of the mesosigmoid.

mesosigmoidopexy (mes″o-sig-moi′do-pek″se) [*mesosigmoid* + Gr. *pēxis* fixation]. The operation of shortening or fixing the mesosigmoid in cases of prolapse of the rectum.

mesoskelic (mes″o-skel′ik) [*meso-* + Gr. *skelos* leg]. Having legs of normal length.

mesosoma (mes″o-so′mah) [*meso-* + Gr. *sōma* body]. Medium stature.

mesosomatous (mes″o-so′mah-tus). Having medium stature.

mesostaphyline (mes″o-staf′ĭ-līn). Having a palatal index between 80.0 and 84.9.

mesostate (mes′o-stāt) [*meso-* + Gr. *histanai* to stand]. Any product of metabolism which represents an intermediate stage in the formation of another product.

mesostenium (mes″o-ste′ne-um). Mesenterium.

mesosternum (mes″o-ster′num) [*meso-* + Gr. *sternon* sternum]. The corpus sterni.

mesostroma (mes″o-stro′mah). The embryonic fibrillar tissue analogous to the vitreous, which develops into Bowman's and Descemet's membranes.

mesosyphilis (mes″o-sif′ĭ-lis). Secondary syphilis.

mesosystolic (mes″o-sis-tol′ik) [*meso-* + Gr. *systolē* systole]. Pertaining to the middle of the systole.

mesotarsal (mes″o-tar′sal). Midtarsal.

mesotendineum (mes″o-ten-din′e-um) [N A]. The delicate connective tissue sheath attaching a tendon to its fibrous sheath.

mesotendon (mes″o-ten′don). Mesotendineum.

mesotenon (mes″o-ten′on). Mesotendineum.

mesothelial (mes″o-the′le-al). Pertaining to the mesothelium.

mesothelioma (mes″o-the″le-o′mah). A tumor developed from mesothelial tissue.

mesothelium (mes″o-the′le-um) [*meso-* + *epithelium*]. [N A] The layer of flat cells, derived from the mesoderm, which lines the coelom or body cavity of the embryo. In the adult it forms the simple squamous-celled layer of the epithelium which covers the surface of all true serous membranes (peritoneum, pericardium, pleura).

mesothenar (mes-oth′e-nar) [*meso-* + Gr. *thenar* palm]. Musculus adductor pollicis.

mesothorium (mes″o-tho′re-um). A disintegration product of thorium, intermediate between thorium and radiothorium and isotopic with radium. It has radioactive properties and has been used in the treatment of cancer.

mesotron (mes′o-tron). Meson, def. 2.

mesotropic (mes″o-trop′ik). Situated in the middle of a cavity, as the abdomen.

mesoturbinal, mesoturbinate (mes″o-ter′bĭ-nal, mes″o-ter′bĭ-nāt). The middle turbinal bone.

meso-uranic (mes″o-u-ran′ik). Mesuranic.

mesovarium (mes″o-va′re-um). [N A, B N A] The portion of the broad ligament of the uterus between the mesometrium and mesosalpinx, which is drawn out to enclose and hold the ovary in place.

mestinon (mes′tĭ-non). Trade mark for preparations of pyridostigmine.

mesuranic (mes″u-ran′ik) [*meso-* + Gr. *ouranos* palate]. Having a maxillo-alveolar index between 110.0 and 114.9.

met (met). A unit of measurement of heat production by the body: the metabolic heat produced by a resting-sitting subject, being 50 kilogram calories per square meter of body surface per hour.

meta- (met′ah) [Gr. *meta* after, beyond, over]. A prefix indicating (1) change, transformation, or exchange; (2) after or next; (3) the 1,3 position in derivatives of benzene.

meta-arthritic (met″ah-ar-thrit′ik). Occurring as a consequence or result of arthritis.

metabasis (mĕ-tab′ah-sis) [*meta-* + Gr. *bainein* to go]. 1. A change from one disease to another. 2. Metastasis, or change in the site of a morbid process from one region of the body to another.

metabiosis (met″ah-bi-o′sis) [*meta-* + Gr. *biōsis* way of life]. The dependence of one organism upon another for its existence; commensalism.

metabolic (met″ah-bol′ik). Pertaining to or of the nature of metabolism.

metabolimeter (met″ah-bo-lim′e-ter) [*metabolism* + Gr. *metron* measure]. An apparatus for measuring basal metabolism.

metabolimetry (met″ah-bo-lim′e-tre). The measurement of basal metabolism.

metabolin (mĕ-tab′o-lin). Metabolite.

metabolism (mĕ-tab′o-lizm) [Gr. *metaballein* to turn about, change, alter]. The sum of all the physical and chemical processes by which living organized substance is produced and maintained (*substance m., constructive m.*, or anabolism), and also the transformation by which energy is made available for the uses of the organism (*energy m., destructive m.*, or catabolism). **ammonotelic m.,** that in which ammonia is the final product of nitrogen metabolism. **basal m.,** the minimal energy expended for the maintenance of respiration, circulation, peristalsis, muscle tonus, body temperature, glandular activity, and the other vegetative functions of the body. The rate of basal metabolism (basal metabolic rate) is measured by means of a calorimeter, in a subject at absolute rest, 14 to 18 hours after eating, and is expressed in calories per hour per square meter of body surface. **constructive m.,** anabolism. **destructive m.,** catabolism. **endogenous m.,** metabolism of the proteins of the body tissues. **energy m.,** the metabolic process by which energy is released; catabolism. **excess m. of exercise,** the amount by which the oxygen consumed or the carbon dioxide eliminated during exercise and recovery exceeds the corresponding amounts during sleep. **exogenous m.,** metabolism of ingested protein. **substance m.,** the metabolic process by which living organized substance is produced; anabolism. **ureotelic m.,** that in which urea is the final product of nitrogen metabolism. **uricotelic m.,** that in which uric acid is the final product of nitrogen metabolism.

metabolite (mĕ-tab′o-līt). Any substance produced by metabolism or by a metabolic process. **essential m.,** a necessary constituent of normal metabolic processes.

metabolizable (mĕ-tab′o-līz″ah-b′l). Capable of being transformed by metabolism.

metabolodispersion (mĕ-tab″o-lo-dis-per′zhun). The degree of dispersion of the colloids present in the body.

metabology (met″ah-bol′o-je). The study of metabolism and metabolic processes.

metabolology (met″ah-bo-lol′o-je). Metabology.

metabolon (mĕ-tab′o-lon). A form of matter having only a temporary existence, formed during conversion of one material to another.

metabolor (met″ah-bo′lor). An instrument for measuring the basal metabolic rate.

metabutethamine (met″ah-bu-teth′ah-min). Chemical name: 2-isobutylaminoethyl m-aminobenzoate acid: used as a local anesthetic.

metabutoxycaine (met″ah-bu-tok′se-kān). Chemical name: 2′-diethylaminoethyl-3-amino-2-butoxybenzoate: used as a local anesthetic.

metacarcinogen (met″ah-kar-sin′o-jen). An agent which tends to make a simple growth malignant.

metacarpal (met″ah-kar′pal). 1. Pertaining to the metacarpus. 2. A bone of the metacarpus.

metacarpectomy (met″ah-kar-pek′to-me). Excision or resection of a metacarpal bone.

metacarpophalangeal (met″ah-kar″po-fah-lan′je-al). Pertaining to the metacarpus and phalanges.

metacarpus (met″ah-kar′pus) [*meta-* + Gr. *karpos* wrist]. [N A, B N A] The part of the hand between the wrist and the fingers, its skeleton being five cylindric bones (metacarpals) extending from the carpus to the phalanges.

metacasein (met″ah-ka′se-in). An intermediate product formed in the conversion of caseinogen into casein by the action of pancreatic juice.

metacele (met′ah-sēl). Metacoele.

metacercaria (met″ah-ser-ka′re-ah), pl. *metacerca′riae*. The encysted resting or maturing stage of a trematode parasite in the tissues of an intermediate host (mollusks, aquatic arthropods, fishes, or amphibia). The metacercaria may be the infective or transfer stage to man and other animals.

metacercariae (met″ah-ser-ka′re-e). Plural of *metacercaria*.

metacetone (met-as′ĕ-tōn). Propion.

metachemical (met″ah-kem′ĭ-kal). Beyond the bounds of chemistry.

metachromasia (met″ah-kro-ma′ze-ah) [*meta-* + Gr. *chrōma* color]. 1. A condition in which tissues do not stain true with a given stain. 2. Staining in which the same stain colors different tissues in different tints. 3. The change of color produced by staining.

metachromatic (met″ah-kro-mat′ik) [*meta-* + Gr. *chrōmatikos* relating to color]. Staining differently with the same dye, said of tissues in which different elements take on different colors when a certain dye is applied. By extension, said of dyes by which different tissues are stained differently.

metachromatin (met″ah-kro′mah-tin). The basophil element in chromatin.

metachromatism (met″ah-kro′mah-tizm). Metachromasia.

metachromatophil (met″ah-kro-mat′o-fil). A cell which does not stain in the usual manner with a given stain.

metachromia (met″ah-kro′me-ah). Metachromasia.

metachromic (met″ah-kro′mik). Metachromatic.

metachromophil (met-ah-kro′mo-fil) [*meta-* + Gr. *chrōma* color + *philein* to love]. Staining in an abnormal manner with a given stain.

metachromophile (met″ah-kro′mo-fil). Metachromophil.

metachromosome (met″ah-kro′mo-sōm). One of two small chromosomes which conjugate only in the last phase of the spermatocyte division.

metachronous (mĕ-tak′ro-nus) [*meta-* + Gr. *chronos* time]. Occurring at different times.

metachrosis (met″ah-kro′sis) [*meta-* + Gr. *chrōsis* coloring]. Change of color in animals.

metachysis (mĕ-tak′ĭ-sis) [*meta-* + Gr. *chysis* effusion]. The transfusion of blood.

metacinesis (met″ah-si-ne′sis) [*meta-* + Gr. *kinēsis* motion]. The separation of daughter stars (asters) from each other in mitosis.

metacoele (met′ah-sēl) [*meta-* + Gr. *koilia* hollow]. 1. That cavity of the metencephalon which, with the epicoele, makes up the fourth ventricle. 2. Metacoeloma.

metacoeloma (met″ah-se-lo′mah). That part of the embryonic coelom which develops into the pleuroperitoneal cavity.

metacone (met′ah-kōn) [*meta-* + Gr. *kōnos* cone]. The distobuccal cusp of an upper molar tooth.

metaconid (met″ah-kon′id). The mesiolingual cusp of a lower molar tooth.

metaconule (met″ah-kon′ūl). The distal intermediate cusp of an upper molar tooth.

metacortandracin (met″ah-kor-tan′drah-sin). Prednisone.

metacortandralone (met″ah-kor-tan′drah-lōn). Prednisolone.

metacresol (met″ah-kre′sol). One of the three isomeric forms of cresol, and the most strongly antiseptic of the group. **m. acetate,** a compound that has been used in fungus infections. **m. purple, m. sulfonphthalein,** a triphenylmethane compound which is a brilliant indicator, being red at pH 1.2, blue at pH 2.8, yellow at pH 7.4, and purple at pH 9.0.

metacryptozoite (met″ah-krip″to-zo′īt). A cryptozoite of a generation subsequent to the cryptozoite.

metacyesis (met″ah-si-e′sis) [*meta-* + Gr. *kyēsis* pregnancy]. Extra-uterine pregnancy.

metaduodenum (met″ah-du″o-de′num). The portion of the duodenum distal to the duodenal papilla, developed embryonically from the midgut.

metadysentery (met″ah-dis′en-ter″e). A chronic colitis characterized by recurrent attacks of diarrhea, which are occasionally dysenteric for short periods of time: due to the so-called metadysentery group of bacteria.

metagaster (met″ah-gas′ter) [*meta-* + Gr. *gastēr* belly]. The permanent intestinal canal of the embryo.

metagastrula (met″ah-gas′troo-lah) [*meta-* + *gastrula*]. A gastrula with a cleavage differing from that of the standard type.

metagelatin (met″ah-jel′ah-tin). A substance produced by treating gelatin with oxalic acid.

metagenesis (met″ah-jen′e-sis) [*meta-* + *genesis*]. Alternation of generations; alternation in regular sequence of asexual with sexual methods of reproduction in the same species.

metagglutinin (met″ah-gloo′tĭ-nin). An agglutinin present in an agglutinative serum which acts on organisms that are closely related to the specific antigen and in a lower dilution. Called also *partial agglutinin* and *minor agglutinin.*

metaglobulin (met″ah-glob′u-lin). A fibrogenous substance occurring in cell protoplasm; fibrinogen.

metagonimiasis (met″ah-go″nĭ-mi′ah-sis). Infestation with Metagonimus.

Metagonimus (met″ah-gon′ĭ-mus) [*meta-* + Gr. *gonimos* productive]. A genus of trematodes. **M. ova′tus, M. yokoga′wai,** an intestinal trematode found in the small intestine of man and mammals in Japan, China, Dutch East Indies, Balkans, and Palestine.

metagranulocyte (met″ah-gran′u-lo-sīt). Progranulocyte.

metagrippal (met″ah-grip′al). Occurring as an after-result of influenza.

metahemoglobin (met″ah-he″mo-glo′bin). Methemoglobin.

meta-icteric (met″ah-ik-ter′ik). Occurring after jaundice.

meta-infective (met″ah-in-fek′tiv). Occurring after an infection; a term applied to a febrile state occurring during convalescence from an infectious disease.

metakinesis (met″ah-ki-ne′sis). 1. Metacinesis. 2. Lloyd Morgan's term for the hypothetical property possessed by all types of life of being endowed with something which is not consciousness, but which has the potentiality of developing into consciousness. 3. Metaphase.

metal (met″l) [L. *metallum;* Gr. *metallon*]. Any element marked by luster, malleability, ductility, and conductivity of electricity and heat. **alkali m.,** one of a group of monovalent metals including lithium, sodium, potassium, rubidium and cesium. **Babbitt m.,** an alloy of tin, copper, and antimony: sometimes used in dentistry. **bell m.,** an alloy of copper and tin. **cliche m.,** a fusible alloy containing tin, lead, antimony, and bismuth: sometimes used in dentistry. **colloidal m.,** a colloidal solution of a metal. See *electrosol.* **d'Arcet's m.,** an alloy of lead, bismuth and tin: used in dentistry. **fusible m.,** an alloy that melts at a relatively low temperature, as at or around the boiling point of water. Bismuth, lead and tin are usually the principal constituents. **Melotte's m.,** a rather soft alloy consisting of bismuth, lead, and tin: sometimes used in dentistry. **Wood's m.,** a metal used in making casts of blood vessels: bismuth, 50 per cent; lead, 25 per cent; tin, 12.5 per cent; cadmium, 12.5 per cent.

metalbumin (met-al-bu′min) [*meta-* + *albumin*]. Pseudomucin.

metaldehyde (met-al′de-hīd). A crystalline body, a polymer of acetaldehyde, $(CH_3.CHO)_3$: antiseptic.

metallaxis (met″ah-lak′sis) [Gr. "exchange," "interchange"]. The transformation or building over of an organ by pathologic processes.

metallergy (met-al′er-je). A condition in which an allergic state, produced by specific sensitization, predisposes the organism to react to other antigens with the same clinical manifestations as the original reaction.

metallesthesia (met″al-es-the′ze-ah) [*metal* + Gr. *aisthēsis* perception + *-ia*]. The recognition of metals by the sense of touch.

metallic (me-tal′ik). Pertaining to or made of metal.

metallization (met″′l-i-za′shun). Impregnation with metals.

metallized (met″l-īzd). Treated with metals.

metallocyanide (me-tal″o-si′ah-nīd). A compound of cyanogen with a metal.

metalloid (met″l-oid) [*metal* + Gr. *eidos* form]. 1. Any nonmetallic element. 2. Any metallic element that has not all the characters of a typical metal. 3. Resembling a metal.

metallophobia (me-tal″o-fo′be-ah) [*metal* + *phobia*]. Morbid fear of metals and metal objects.

metalloplastic (me-tal″o-plas′tik). Pertaining to the plastic use of metals.

metalloporphyrin (me-tal″o-por′fĭ-rin). A combination of a metal with porphyrin. For example, heme (iron) and turacin (copper).

metalloscopy (met″′l-os′ko-pe) [*metal* + Gr. *skopein* to examine]. Observation of the effects of applying metal to the body.

metallotherapy (me-tal″o-ther′ah-pe) [*metal* + Gr. *therapeuein* to heal]. The treatment of disease by applying metals to the integument.

metallurgy (met″l-ur″je) [*metal* + Gr. *ergon* work]. The science and art of using metals.

metal-sol (met″l-sol″). A colloidal solution of a metal. Such solutions have properties similar to those of enzymes, and are therefore sometimes called *inorganic enzymes.*

metaluetic (met″ah-lu-et′ik). Metasyphilitic.

metamer (met′ah-mer). A compound exhibiting, or capable of exhibiting, metamerism.

metamere (met′ah-mēr) [*meta-* + Gr. *meros* part]. One of a series of homologous segments of the body of an animal.

metameric (met″ah-mer′ik). Pertaining to or characterized by metamerism.

metamerism (me-tam′er-ism). 1. A type of structural isomerism in which different radicals of the same chemical type are attached to the same polyvalent element and yet give rise to compounds possessing identical molecular formulas. For example, diethylamine, $(C_2H_5)_2NH$, and methyl propylamine, $CH_3NHC_3H_7$. The term metamerism is seldom used, such compounds being called simply structural isomers of the same chemical type. 2. Arrangement into metameres by the serial repetition of a structural pattern.

metamine (met′ah-mēn). Trade mark for preparations of trolnitrate.

metamorphopsia (met″ah-mor-fop′se-ah) [*meta-* + Gr. *morphē* form + *opsis* sight]. A disturbance of vision in which objects are seen as distorted in shape. **m. va′rians,** metamorphopsia in which the outline of the object seems to change as it is being viewed.

metamorphosis (met″ah-mor′fo-sis) [*meta-* + Gr. *morphōsis* a shaping, bringing into shape]. Change of shape or structure; particularly a transition from one developmental stage to another, as in insects. **fatty m.,** any normal or pathologic transformation of fat, including fatty infiltration and fatty degeneration. **ovulational m.,** the developmental changes which occur during ovulation. **platelet m.** See *viscous m.* **retrograde m., retrogressive m.,** a degeneration: more often a retrograde metabolic change. **revisionary m.** See *cataplasia.* **m. sexua′lis parano′ica,** the delusion that one has changed sex. **structural m.** See *viscous m.* **tissue m.,** any change in tissues, either normal or pathologic. **viscous m.,** a series of progressive, irreversible structural alterations that platelets undergo during the process of coagulation, and which are dependent on the presence of divalent metallic ions. Called also *structural m.* and *platelet m.*

metamorphotic (met″ah-mor-fot′ik). Pertaining to or characterized by metamorphosis.

metamucil (met″ah-mu′sil). Trade mark for a preparation of psyllium hydrophilic mucilloid.

metamyelocyte (met″ah-mi-el′o-sīt). A polymorphonuclear leukocyte in which the nuclear element is a single fragment no longer containing a definite nucleolus. Called also *juvenile cell.*

metandren (mĕ-tan′dren). Trade mark for preparations of methyltestosterone.

metanephrogenic (met″ah-nef″ro-jen′ik) [*meta-* + Gr. *nephros* kidney + *gennan* to produce]. Capable of giving rise to the metanephros.

metanephroi (met″ah-nef′roi). Plural of *metanephros.*

metanephron (met″ah-nef′ron). Metanephros.

metanephros (met″ah-nef′ros), pl. *metaneph′roi* [*meta-* + Gr. *nephros,* kidney]. The permanent embryonic kidney, which develops later than and caudal to the mesonephros, from the mesonephric duct and nephrogenic cord.

metaneutrophil (met″ah-nu′tro-fil) [*meta-* + *neutrophil*]. Staining abnormally with neutral stains.

metanucleus (met″ah-nu′kle-us) [*meta-* + *nucleus*]. The egg nucleus during the maturative period.

metapeptone (met″ah-pep′tōn) [*meta-* + *peptone*]. A digestive product between dyspeptone and parapeptone.

metaphase (met′ah-fāz) [*meta-* + *phase*]. The middle stage of mitosis during which the lengthwise separation of the chromosomes in the equatorial plate occurs. See *mitosis.*

metaphen (met′ah-fen). Trade mark for preparations of nitromersol.

metaphrenia (met″ah-fre′ne-ah) [*meta-* + Gr. *phrēn* mind]. The mental condition in which the interests are withdrawn from the family or group and directed to personal gain or aggrandisement.

metaphrenon (met″ah-fre′non) [Gr. "the part behind the midriff"]. The back, especially the region about the kidneys.

metaphyseal (met″ah-fiz′e-al). Pertaining to or of the nature of a metaphysis.

metaphyses (me-taf′ĭ-sēz). Plural of *metaphysis.*

metaphysial (met″ah-fiz′e-al). Metaphyseal.

metaphysis (me-taf′ĭ-sis), pl. *metaph′yses* [*meta-* + Gr. *phyein* to grow]. The wider part at the extremity of the shaft of a long bone, adjacent to the epiphyseal disc. During development it contains the growth zone and consists of spongy bone; in the adult it is continuous with the epiphysis.

metaphysitis (met″ah-fis-i′tis). Inflammation of the metaphysis of a long bone.

metaplasia (met″ah-pla′ze-ah) [*meta-* + Gr. *plassein* to form]. The change in the type of adult cells in a tissue to a form which is not normal for that tissue. **myeloid m., agnogenic,** a condition characterized by foci of extramedullary hematopoiesis, particularly in the spleen, and by immature red and white cells in the peripheral blood and mild to moderate anemia; it is grouped by some hematologists with the myeloproliferative disorders. **m. of pulp,** a state of the pulp tissue of a tooth in which it has deteriorated from its power of dentin formation to the condition of connective tissue.

metaplasis (met-ap′lah-sis). The stage in which the organism has attained completed growth.

metaplasm (met′ah-plazm) [*meta-* + Gr. *plasma* something formed]. Deutoplasm.

metaplastic (met″ah-plas′tik). 1. Pertaining to or characterized by metaplasia. 2. Formed by or of the nature of metaplasm.

metaplex (met′ah-pleks). Metaplexus.

metaplexus (met″ah-plek′sus). The choroid plexus of the fourth ventricle.

metapneumonic (met″ah-nu-mon′ik) [*meta-* + *pneumonia*]. Succeeding or following pneumonia.

metapodialia (met″ah-po″de-a′le-ah) [*meta-* + Gr. *pous* foot]. A collective term for the bones of the metacarpus and metatarsus.

metapophysis (met″ah-pof′ĭ-sis) [*meta-* + *apophysis*]. The mamillary process on the superior articular or prearticular processes of certain vertebrae.

metapore (met′ah-pōr). The foramen of Magendie.

metaprotein (met″ah-pro′te-in). A product of the action of an acid (*acid m.*) or alkali (*alkali m.*) on a protein, resulting in a compound soluble in very weak acids and alkalis, but insoluble in neutral fluids.

metapsyche (met″ah-si′ke) [*meta-* + Gr. *psychē* soul]. The metencephalon.

metapsychics (met″ah-si′kiks) [*meta-* + Gr. *psychē* soul]. The science which deals with psychic phenomena that are beyond the realm of consciousness; parapsychology.

metapsychology (met″ah-si-kol′o-je). Psychology which regards mental processes from the dynamic, topographical, and economic points of view.

metaptosis (met″ah-to′sis) [*meta-* + Gr. *ptōsis* falling]. Metastasis.

metapyretic (met″ah-pi-ret′ik) [*meta-* + Gr. *pyretos* fever]. Performed or occurring after the advent (after the decline) of septic fever.

metaraminol (met″ah-ram′ĭ-nol). Chemical name: l-m-hydroxynorephedrine: used as a sympathomimetic and pressor agent.

metargon (met-ar′gon). A name given an isotope of argon, atomic weight 38.

metarteriole (met″ar-te′re-ōl). A precapillary.

metarubricyte (met″ah-roo′brĭ-sīt). A red cell containing a pyknotic, contracted nucleus, the last stage in erythrocyte development. Called also *orthochromatophilic normoblast.*

metasomatome (met″ah-so′mah-tōm). One of the constrictions between successive protovertebrae.

metastable (met′ah-sta″b'l). Maintaining stability under changing conditions by continuous adjustment of the counterbalancing factors.

metastases (mĕ-tas′tah-sēz). Plural of *metastasis* (def. 2).

metastasis (mĕ-tas′tah-sis) [*meta-* + Gr. *stasis* stand]. 1. The transfer of disease from one organ or part to another not directly connected with it. It may be due either to the transfer of pathogenic microorganisms (e.g., tubercle bacilli) or to transfer of cells, as in malignant tumors. 2. Pl. *metastases.* A growth of pathogenic microorganisms or of abnormal cells distant from the site primarily involved by the morbid process. **biochemical m.,** the transportation from the point of production and the deposition in previously normal tissues of abnormal or pathologically produced biochemical substances which bring about immunological or other changes in the tissues. **calcareous m.,** the formation of bone salts in the kidneys and elsewhere in softening of bone. **contact m.,** transfer from one surface to another with which the former is in contact. **crossed m.,** passage of material from the venous to the arterial circulation without going through the lungs. **direct m.,** metastasis in the direction of the blood or lymph stream. **implantation m.,** metastasis brought about by transfer of tumor cells by fluid and their implantation in a distant location. **paradoxic m., retrograde m.,** metastasis taking place in a direction opposite to that of the blood stream. **transplantation m.,** metastasis from one tissue to another.

metastasize (me-tas′tah-sīz). To form new foci of disease in a distant part by metastasis.

metastatic (met″ah-stat′ik). Pertaining to or of the nature of metastasis.

metasternum (met″ah-ster′num) [*meta-* + Gr. *sternon* sternum]. Processus xiphoideus.

Metastrongylus (met″ah-stron′jĭ-lus). A genus of nematodes of the family Strongylidae. *M. a′pri*, a species found in the lungs of hogs.

metasynapsis (met″ah-sĭ-nap′sis). End-to-end union of the chromosomes in synapsis.

metasyncrisis (met″ah-sin′krĭ-sis). The elimination of waste or morbid matter.

metasyndesis (met″ah-sin-de′sis). Metasynapsis.

metasyphilis (met″ah-sif′ĭ-lis) [*meta-* + *syphilis*]. 1. Congenital syphilis with general degeneration but without syphilids. 2. Parasyphilis.

metasyphilitic (met″ah-sif″ĭ-lit′ik). 1. Following or resulting from syphilis. 2. Pertaining to hereditary syphilis.

metatarsal (met″ah-tar′sal). 1. Pertaining to the metatarsus. 2. A bone of the metatarsus.

metatarsalgia (met″ah-tar-sal′je-ah) [*meta-* + Gr. *tarsos* tarsus + *-algia*]. Pain in the metatarsus due to osteochondrosis of the heads of the metatarsal bones: called also *Morton's disease*, *Morton's foot*, *Morton's neuralgia*, and *Morton's toe*.

metatarsectomy (met″ah-tar-sek′to-me). Excision or resection of the metatarsus.

metatarsophalangeal (met″ah-tar″so-fah-lan′je-al). Pertaining to the metatarsus and the phalanges of the toes.

metatarsus (met″ah-tar′sus) [*meta-* + Gr. *tarsos* tarsus]. [N A, B N A] The part of the foot between the tarsus and the toes, its skeleton being the five long bones (the metatarsals) extending from the tarsus to the phalanges. **m. adductoca′vus,** a deformity of the foot in which metatarsus adductus is associated with pes cavus. **m. adducto-va′rus,** a deformity of the foot in which metatarsus adductus is associated with metatarsus varus. **m. adduc′tus,** a congenital deformity of the foot in which the fore part of the foot deviates toward the midline. **m. atav′icus,** abnormal shortness of the first metatarsal bone. **m. la′tus,** a broadened foot due to spreading of the anterior part of the foot resulting from separation of the heads of the metatarsal bones from each other: called also *broad foot* and *spread foot*. **m. pri′mus va′rus,** angulation of the first metatarsal bone toward the midline of the body, producing an angle sometimes of 20 degrees, or more between its base and that of the second metatarsal bone. **m. va′rus,** a congenital deformity of the foot in which its inner border is off the ground with the sole turned inward, the patient walking on the outer border of the foot.

metatela (met″ah-tel′ah). The tela choroidea of the fourth ventricle.

metathalamus (met″ah-thal′ah-mus). [N A, B N A] The part of the thalamencephalon composed of the medial and lateral geniculate bodies.

metathesis (me-tath′e-sis) [*meta-* + Gr. *thesis* placement]. 1. The artificial transfer of a morbid process. 2. A chemical reaction in which an element or radical in one compound exchanges places with another element or radical in another compound.

metathetic (met″ah-thet′ik). Pertaining to or of the nature of metathesis.

metathrombin (met″ah-throm′bin) [*meta-* + *thrombin*]. The inactive combination of thrombin and antithrombin.

metatroph (met′ah-trōf). A metatrophic organism.

metatrophia (met-ah-tro′fe-ah). 1. Atrophy from malnutrition. 2. A change in diet.

metatrophic (met-ah-trof′ik). Utilizing organic matter for food.

metatrophy (met-at′ro-fe) [*meta-* + Gr. *trophē* nutrition]. 1. The state of being metatrophic; metatrophic nutrition. 2. Metatrophia.

metatuberculosis (met″ah-tu-ber″ku-lo′sis). A condition in which the patient shows tuberculous reactions without specific tuberculous lesions.

metatypic (met″ah-tip′ik). Metatypical.

metatypical (met″ah-tip′e-kal). Composed of the elements of the tissue on which it develops, but having those elements arranged in an atypical manner: said of tumors.

metavanadate (met″ah-van′ah-dāt). Any salt of metavanadic acid. **sodium m.,** a highly poisonous salt.

metaxenia (met″ah-ze′ne-ah). An improper term for ectogony.

metaxeny (me-tak′sĕ-ne). Metoxeny.

Metazoa (met″ah-zo′ah) [*meta-* + Gr. *zōon* animal]. That division of the animal kingdom which embraces all multicellular animals whose cells become differentiated to form tissues. It includes all animals except the protozoa.

metazoal (met″ah-zo′al). 1. Belonging to the Metazoa. 2. Caused by metazoa.

metazoan (met″ah-zo′an). 1. Metazoal. 2. Metazoon.

metazonal (met″ah-zo′nal). Situated after or below a sclerozone.

metazoon (met″ah-zo′on), *pl. metazo′a.* An individual of the Metazoa.

Metchnikoff theory (mech′nĭ-kof) [Elie *Metchnikoff* (I. *Mechnikov*), a Russian zoologist in Paris, 1845–1916; discoverer of phagocytes and phagocytosis, co-winner, with Paul Ehrlich, of the Nobel prize for medicine and physiology in 1908]. See under *theory*.

metecious (me-te′shus) [*meta-* + Gr. *oikos* house]. Heterecious.

metencephal (met-en′se-fal). The metencephalon.

metencephalic (met-en″se-fal′ik). Pertaining to the metencephalon.

metencephalon (met″en-sef′ah-lon) [*meta-* + Gr. *enkephalos* brain]. 1. [N A, B N A] The part of the central nervous system developed from the anterior part of the posterior primary brain vesicle comprising the pons and the cerebellum. 2. The anterior of the two brain vesicles formed by specialization of the rhombencephalon in the developing embryo.

metencephalospinal (met″en-sef″ah-lo-spi′nal]. Pertaining to the metencephalon (cerebellum) and the spinal cord.

meteorism (me′te-er-izm) [Gr. *meteōrizein* to raise

up]. Tympanites; the presence of gas in the abdomen or intestine.

meteorology (me′te-er-ol′o-je) [Gr. *meteōros* high in the air + *-logy*]. The science of the atmosphere and its phenomena; the science of the weather.

meteoropathology (me″te-er-o-pah-thol′o-je). The pathology of conditions caused by atmospheric conditions.

meteoropathy (me″te-er-op′ah-the) [Gr. *meteōros* high in the air + *pathos* disease]. Any disorder due to conditions of climate.

meteorophobia (me″te-er-o-fo′be-ah) [*meteor* + *phobia*]. Morbid fear of meteors.

meteororesistant (me″te-er-o-re-zis′tant). Comparatively insensitive to weather conditions.

meteorosensitive (me″te-er-o-sen′si-tiv). Abnormally sensitive to weather conditions.

meteorotropic (me″te-er-o-trop′ik). Responding to influence by meteorological factors; pertaining to or characterized by meteorotropism.

meteorotropism (me″te-er-ot′ro-pizm). The response to influence by meteorological factors noted in certain biological events, such as sudden death, attacks of angina, joint pain, insomnia, and traffic accidents.

metepencephalon (met″ep-en-sef′ah-lon) [*meta-* + *epi-* + Gr. *enkephalos* brain]. Myelencephalon.

meter (me′ter) [Gr. *metron* measure; Fr. *mètre*]. 1. The basic unit of linear measure in the metric system, equivalent approximately to 39.37 inches; formerly established as the length of a bar of an alloy of platinum and iridium preserved in a vault at the International Bureau of Weights and Measures, near Paris. Although its dimension is unchanged, it is now defined in terms of the wavelength of a certain line in the spectrum of krypton. 2. An apparatus devised to measure the quantity of anything passing through it, such as of a gas, amperes of electric current, etc. **dosage m.,** dosimeter. **flicker m.,** flicker photometer. **hot wire m.,** an apparatus for measuring the amperage in high frequency circuits. **light m.,** an instrument for measuring light in foot candles.

-meter [Gr. *metron* measure]. Word termination designating relationship to measurement, or denoting especially an instrument used in measuring.

metergasis (met″er-ga′sis) [*meta-* + Gr. *ergon* work]. Change of function.

metestrum (met-es′trum). Metestrus.

metestrus (met-es′trus) [*meta-* + L. *oestrus*]. The period of subsiding follicular function following estrus in female mammals.

methacholine (meth″ah-ko′lēn). Chemical name: acetyl-β-methylcholine: used as a parasympathomimetic, and vasodilator.

methadone (meth′ah-don). Chemical name: 6-dimethylamino-4,4-diphenyl-3-heptanone: used as a narcotic analgesic.

methallenestril (meth″al-lĕ-nes′tril). A nonsteroid estrogenic compound, α,α-dimethyl-β-ethyl-6-methoxy-2-naphthalenepropionic acid.

methamphetamine (meth″am-fet′ah-mēn). Chemical name: N,α-dimethylphenethylamine: used as a sympathomimetic, a central nervous system stimulant, and as a pressor substance.

methandriol (meth-an′dre-ol). Chemical name: 17α-methyl-5-androstene-3β,17β-diol: used as an anabolic stimulant.

methandrostenolone (meth-an″dro-sten′o-lōn). Chemical name: Δ^1-17α-methyltestosterone: used as an anabolic hormone.

methane (meth′ān). Marsh gas, CH_4, a colorless, odorless, inflammable gas, produced by the decomposition of organic matter.

Methanobacterium (meth″ah-no-bak-te′re-um). A genus of microorganisms of the family Spirillaceae, suborder Pseudomonadineae, order Pseudomonadales, made up of long, slightly curved, slender rods with rounded ends, containing deeply staining granules. It includes four species, *C. flaves′cens*, *C. ful′vus*, *C. ochra′ceus*, and *C. vulga′ris*.

Methanococcus (meth″ah-no-kok′kus). A genus of microorganisms of the family Micrococcaceae, order Eubacteriales, made up of gram-variable spherical cells which are chemoheterotrophic and saprophytic.

methanol (meth′ah-nol). A clear, colorless, flammable liquid, with characteristic odor, CH_3OH; miscible with alcohol, ether, and water.

methanolysis (meth″ah-nol′ĭ-sis). Alcoholysis of methyl alcohol.

Methanomonadaceae (meth″ah-no-mo″nah-da′se-e). A family of Schizomycetes (order Pseudomonadales, suborder Pseudomonadineae), found in soil and water, and deriving energy from oxidation of simple carbon compounds. It includes three genera, *Carboxydomonas*, *Hydrogenomonas*, and *Methanomonas*.

Methanomonas (meth″ah-no-mo′nas). A genus of microorganisms of the family Methanomonadaceae, suborder Pseudomonadineae, order Pseudomonadales, occurring as monotrichous cells obtaining energy from the oxidation of methane to CO_2 and H_2O. The type species is *M. methan′ica*.

methantheline (meth-an′thĕ-lin). Chemical name: β-diethylaminoethyl-9-xanthenecarboxylate: used in parasympathetic blockade, and to depress gastric activity.

methapyrilene (meth″ah-pir′-ĭ-lēn). Chemical name: 2-[(β-dimethylaminoethyl)-2-thenylamino]-pyridine: used as an antihistaminic.

metharbital (meth-ar′bĭ-tal). Chemical name: 5,5-diethyl-1-methylbarbituric acid: used as a central depressant with anticonvulsant action.

methdilazine (meth-di′lah-zēn). Chemical name: 10-(1-methyl-3-pyrrolidylmethyl)phenothiazine: used as an antihistaminic.

methectic (mĕ-thek′tik) [Gr. *methektikos* participating]. Noting participation of the various strata of intelligence.

methedrine (meth′ĕ-drin). Trade mark for preparations of methamphetamine.

methemalbumin (met″hem-al-bu′min). A compound formed by binding of albumin with two moles of heme, occurring only when the serum has been depleted of unsaturated haptoglobin.

metheme (met′hēm). Hematin.

methemoglobin (met″he″mo-glo′bin). A compound formed from hemoglobin by oxidation of the ferrous to the ferric state with essentially ionic bonds.

methemoglobinemia (met″he-mo-glo″bi-ne′me-ah) [*methemoglobin* + Gr. *haima* blood + *-ia*]. The presence of methemoglobin in the blood.

methemoglobinuria (met″he-mo-glo-bi-nu′re-ah) [*methemoglobin* + Gr. *ouron* urine + *-ia*]. The occurrence of methemoglobin in the urine.

methenamine (meth″en-am′in). Chemical name: hexamethylenetetramine: used as a urinary antibacterial. **m. mandelate,** a salt of methenamine and mandelic acid, $C_6H_{12}N_4.C_8H_8O_3$: used in infections of the urinary tract. **m. tetraiodide,** a red powder, $(CH_2)_6N_4I_4$, which breaks down in the intestinal tract to hexamethylene and iodides: for use where iodides are indicated.

methene (meth′ēn). Methylene.

methenyl (meth′ĕ-nil). Formyl.

methergine (meth′er-jin). Trade mark for preparations of methylergonovine.

methexenyl (meth-ek′sē-nyl). Hexobarbital.

methicillin (meth″ĭ-sil″lin). Dimethoxyphenyl penicillin.

methilepsia (meth″il-ep′se-ah). Methomania.

methimazole (meth-im′ah-zōl). Chemical name: 1-methyl-2-mercaptoimidazole: used as a thyroid inhibitor.

methiodal (meth-i′o-dal). Chemical name: monoiodomethanesulfonic acid: used as a radiopaque medium for roentgenography of the urinary tract.

methionine (mĕ-thi′o-nin). A sulfur-bearing amino acid, 2-amino-4-methylthiobutyric acid, essential for optimal growth in infants and nitrogen equilibrium in human adults: used as a dietary supplement with lipotropic action.

methium (meth′e-um). Trade mark for preparations of hexamethonium.

methocarbamol (meth″o-kar′bah-mol). Chemical name: 2-hydroxy-3-o-methoxyphenoxypropyl carbamate: used as a skeletal muscle relaxant.

method (meth′ud) [Gr. *methodos*]. The manner of performing any act or operation. See also under *maneuver, stains, tests, treatment*, etc. **Abbott's m.,** treatment of scoliosis by lateral pulling and counterpulling on the spinal column by means of wide bandages and pads until the deformity is overcorrected, and then applying a plaster jacket to produce pressure, counter-pressure, and fixation of the spine in its corrected position. **A. B. C. (alum, blood, clay) m.,** a method of deodorizing and precipitating sludge by the addition of alum, charcoal (or some other material), and clay to the raw sewage. **absorption m.,** the separate addition to agglutinative serums of the various bacteria in the group to remove separately the partial agglutinins. **aceto-acetic acid, m. for.** See *Folin and Hart's m., Scott and Wilson's m., Van Slyke* and *Palmer's m.* **acetone, m's for.** See *Folin's m.* (1), *Folin and Hart's m., Messinger and Huppert's m., Shaffer and Marriott's m., Scott and Wilson's m.* **Achard-Castaigne m.,** the methylene blue test. **acid hematin m.** (*for hemoglobin*): Dilute the blood in tenth normal HCl and compare the color with a standard hematin solution or glass standards. **Addis's m.,** a quantitative method for counting the total number of casts in a 24-hour specimen of urine. **Adelmann's m.,** forcible flexion of an extremity to control arterial hemorrhage. **adrenaline, m. for.** See *Folin, Cannon, and Denis' m.* **Ahlfeld's m.,** hand disinfection with hot water and alcohol. **albumin in urine, m's for.** See *Esbach's m., Folin's m., Folin and Denis' m.* (1), *Folin's gravimetric m., Kwilecki's m., life insurance m., Sherer's m.* **alkali reserve, m's for.** See *Fridericia's m., Marriott's m., Van Slyke and Cullen's m.*, and *Van Slyke and Fitz's m.* **allantoin, m's for.** See *Folin's m.* (15), *Plimmer and Skelton's m., Wiechowski and Handorsky's m.* **Altmann-Gersh m.,** a method of preparing tissue for histological study by freeze drying. **amino-acid nitrogen, m. for.** See *nitrogen, m. for.* **ammonia nitrogen, m's for.** See *nitrogen, ammonia, m's for.* **anaerobic m's.** See *Buchner's m., Esbach's m., Hauser's m., Liborious' m., McIntosh and Fildes' m., Roux's m., Wright's m.* **Arnold and Gunning's m.** (*for total nitrogen*): A modified form of the Kjeldahl process for urine. **Aronson's m.,** volatilizing formaldehyde gas from the solid polymer, trioxymethylene, by heat. **Askenstedt's m.** (Parker's modification) (*for indican*): Precipitate the urine with solid mercuric chloride; oxidize the indican to indigo with Obermeyer's reagent; shake out with chloroform and compare the blue color with a standard solution of indigo. **Austin and Van Slyke's m.** (*for chlorides in whole blood*): Lake the blood with distilled water, precipitate the proteins with picric acid, and then proceed as in McLean and Van Slyke's method for chlorides in oxalated plasma. **Autenrieth and Funk's m.** (*for cholesterol*): Boil the blood or serum to saponify the fats. Extract with chloroform and evaporate the chloroform. Make a Liebermann-Burchard test on the residue and compare it with a standard solution of cholesterol. **autoclave m.** See *Clark-Collip m.* (2). **Baccelli's m.** 1. Treatment of tetanus by injections of carbolic acid. 2. Treatment of aneurysm by introduction of a watchspring into the sac by means of a trocar. **Baer's m.,** prevention of the reforming of adhesions by the injection of sterilized oil into an ankylosed joint. **Bang's m.** 1. Estimation of the quantities of the sugar, albumin, urea, etc., in the blood by examination of a few drops only, collected on blotting paper. 2. (*for dextrose*): To an excess of the boiling reagent (an alkaline solution of copper thiocyanate) add the urine and titrate the excess of copper thiocyanate with hydroxylamine sulfate. 3. (*a micromethod for dextrose*): Boil the urine with an excess of the reagent ($KHCO_3$, 160 Gm.; K_2CO_3, 100 Gm.; KCl, 66 Gm.; $CuSO_4.5H_2O$, 4.4 Gm.; and water to 1 liter) and titrate excess of CuCl with a solution of iodine, using starch as an indicator. **Barèty's m.,** an extension method for treating hip disease and fracture of the thigh. **Bastianelli's m.,** sterilization of the skin of the patient previous to operation with a 1:1000 benzine solution of iodine, followed by a 50 per cent tincture of iodine. **Bence Jones protein, m. for.** See *Folin and Denis' m.* (2). **Benedict's m.** 1. (*for dextrose*): Titrate the sugar in the urine with the following reagent: $CuSO_4$ (crystals), 18 Gm.; Na_2CO_3 (crystals), 200 Gm.; sodium citrate, 200 Gm.; potassium thiocyanate, 125 Gm.; potassium ferrocyanide, 5 per cent solution, 5 cc.; water to make 1 liter. 2. (*for total sulfur*): Add the reagent (crystallized copper nitrate, 200 Gm.; sodium chlorate, 50 Gm.; water to make 1 liter) to the urine and evaporate to dryness, ignite, take up in dilute hydrochloric acid, precipitate with $BaCl_2$, filter, dry, and weigh. 3. (*for urea*): The urea is hydrolyzed to ammonium carbonate by heating with $KHSO_4$ and $ZnSO_4$, made alkaline, distilled into standard sulfuric acid, and the excess acid titrated. 4. (*for uric acid in blood*): The same as *Benedict and Franke's m. for uric acid in urine.* **Benedict and Denis' m.** (*for total sulfur*): Mix the urine with the reagent [$Cu(NO_3)_2$, 25 Gm.; NaCl, 25 Gm.; NH_4NO_3, 10 Gm.; and water 100 cc.] and evaporate to dryness, ignite, dissolve in 10 per cent hydrochloric acid and test for inorganic sulfates by Folin's method (6) (q.v.). **Benedict and Franke's m.** (*for uric acid in urine*): To the diluted urine is added sodium cyanide and the arsenophosphotungstic acid reagent. The blue color produced is compared with a standard uric acid solution. **Benedict and Hitchcock's m.** (*for uric acid*): Precipitate the uric acid with an ammoniacal silver-magnesium solution (3 per cent silver lactate solution, 70 cc.; magnesia mixture, 30 cc.; concentrated ammonium hydroxide, 100 cc.). Dissolve the precipitate with potassium cyanide, add the uric acid reagent (boil 100 Gm. of sodium tungstate and 80 cc. of 85 per cent phosphoric acid in 750 cc. of water for two hours and make up to 1 liter) and sodium carbonate solution. Compare in colorimeter with a known uric acid standard. **Benedict and Leche's m.** (*for inorganic phosphate in blood*): The method is the same as that of Fiske and SubbaRow except that the reducing agent is a hydroquinone-sulfite mixture instead of amino-naphthol-sulfonic acid. **Benedict and Murlin's m.** (*for amino-acid nitrogen by formol titration*): Add phosphotungstic acid to the urine to precipitate ammonia and other basic substances, neutralize to litmus, add solution of formaldehyde, and titrate with tenth normal sodium hydroxide. **Benedict and Osterberg's m.** (*for sugar in normal urine*): Treat the urine with picric acid, sodium carbonate, and acetone. Compare the red color produced with a standard solution of sugar. **Benedict and Theis' m.** 1. (*for lipoid phosphorus*): Oxidize the lipoid phosphorus to phosphoric acid with a mixture of concentrated nitric and sulfuric acids and then proceed as with inorganic phosphates. 2. (*for phenols in blood*): To 10 cc. of blood filtrate add 1 cc. of 1 per cent gum acacia solution, 1 cc. of 50 per cent sodium acetate solution, 1 cc. of the diazotized nitroaniline reagent, mix and after one minute add 2 cc. of a 20 per cent sodium carbonate solution. Compare the orange color with a standard phenol solution containing 0.025 mg. of phenol in 10 cc. **Bergeim's m.** (*for indole in feces*): Make the feces alkaline and distil off phenols. Make distillate acid with H_2SO_4 and redistil to leave NH_3 in residue. To the second distillate add beta-naphtha-quinone sodium monosulfonate and alkali. Extract the blue color with chloroform and compare it with that of a standard solution of indole similarly treated. **Berger's m.,** suture of transverse fracture of the patella. **Bergonié's m.,** reduction of fat by the use of general faradization. **Bertrand's m.** (*for glucose*): Boil the urine with alkaline copper sulfate solution, filter, dissolve the precipitate in an acid solution of ferric sulfate, and titrate with potassium permanganate. **beta-hydroxy-butyric acid, m's for.** See *Black's m.* and *Van Slyke and Palmer's m.* **Bethea's m.** See under *sign.* **Beuttner's m.,** removal of the adnexa uteri, but with preservation of a portion of the ovaries and transverse cuneiform excision of the fundus uteri. **bile pigments, m's for.** See *Meulengracht's m., Wallace and Diamond's m.* **Bivine's m.,** treatment of strychnine poisoning by administration of chloral hydrate. **Black's m.** (*for beta-hydroxy-butyric acid*): Evaporate the urine to a small volume, acidify, add plaster of paris to form a coarse meal, extract the beta-hydroxy-butyric acid with ether in a Soxhlet apparatus, evaporate to dryness, take up in water, and determine the amount by a polariscope. **Bloor's m.** 1. (*for lipoid phosphorus*). See *Benedict and Theis' m.* 2. (*for cholesterol*): Extract the cholesterol from whole blood with hot alcohol-ether. Dry, extract with chloroform and determine by the Liebermann reaction. **Bloor, Pelkan, and Allen's m.** (*for fatty acids and cholesterol*): Extract the lipoids by an alcohol-ether mixture, saponify, extract the cholesterol with chloroform and the soaps with hot alcohol. The cholesterol is then determined colorimetrically and the fatty acids nephelometrically. **Bock and Benedict's m.** (*for total nitrogen*): It is similar to Folin and Farmer's method, except that the ammonia is distilled instead of aerated over into the acid. **Bogg's m.** (*for protein in milk*): This is a modification of Esbach's method for protein in urine. The protein is precipitated with Bogg's reagent instead of with picric acid. **Bonnaire's m.,** induction of labor by digital dilation of the cervix. **Bouchon's m.,** treatment of wounds by the application of formaldehyde followed by irrigation with Javel solution. **Brandt's m.,** deep massage of the fallopian tubes for expression of the pus in pyosalpinx. **Brauer's m.,** production of artificial pneumothorax by the injection of nitrogen for the treatment of tuberculosis of the lung. **Brazilian m.,** treatment of aneurysms by continuous electric current. **Breslau's m.,** volatilizing formaldehyde from dilute (8 per cent) solutions to prevent polymerization. **brine flotation m.** (*for concentration of ova*): Rub up a portion of the stool in a saturated solution of sodium chloride. Let it stand for a time and collect the ova from the surface. **Brunn's m.** See *Breslau's m.* **Buchner's m.,** a method for the anaerobic cultivation of bacteria in which an alkaline solution of pyrogallol is placed in the container and this removes the oxygen by absorption. **Bülau's m.,** treatment of empyema by means of continuous drainage with a special apparatus. **Byrd-Dew m.,** a method of starting artificial respiration in asphyxia of the newborn. **calcium, m's for.** See *Clark and Collip's m., Corley and Denis' m., Lyman's m., McCrudden's m.,* and *Shohl and Pedley's m.* **carbon dioxide, m. for.** See *Van Slyke and Cullen's m.* (1). **Carrel's m.** 1. A method of end-to-end suture of blood vessels. 2. Dakin-Carrel m. 3. A method of determining when to make secondary closure of wounds. A loop of material is taken from the wound, spread on a slide, stained, and the number of bacteria counted. **casein, m. for.** Saturate the milk with magnesium sulfate, filter, wash, determine the nitrogen by the Kjeldahl method, and multiply the result by 6.37. See also *Hart's m.* **cathartic m.,** a method of treating psychoneuroses by enabling the patient, through properly directed questions, to bring to full consciousness the vague and unformed dread from which he has been suffering. **Cathelin's m.,** introduction of anesthetics into the epidural space through the sacrococcygeal ligament. **Chandler's m.** (*for fibrinogen*): Precipitate the fibrinogen with calcium chloride, centrifugalize and determine the nitrogen in the clot. **Chaput's m.,** treatment of osteomyelitis by scraping the cavity and inserting fat taken from the thigh or abdomen. **Chick-Martin m.,** testing the germidical value of disinfectants, for water supplies: it is applied in the presence of 3 per cent of human feces and for a fixed period of thirty minutes. **chlorides, m's for.** See *Austin and Van Slyke's m., Dehn and Clark's m., McLean and Van Slyke's m., Mohr's m., Volhard and Arnold's m., Volhard and Harvey's m.,* and *Whitehorn's m.* **cholesterol, m's for.** See *Bloor's m.* (2), and *Myers and Wardell's m.* **Christiansen's m.** (*for Mett tubes*): Thin-walled glass tubes with an internal diameter of 1 to 2 mm. are filled with egg white, placed in water at 85 C., and allowed to stay until cool. **Ciaccio's m.,** treatment of tissue for the purpose of rendering visible the intracellular lipoids. They are fixed with acid chromate solution and stained with sudan III. **Ciniselli's m.,** galvanopuncture of aneurysms. **Clark-Collip m.** 1. (*for calcium in serum*): Dilute the serum and add ammonium oxalate. Wash the precipitate, dissolve with sulfuric acid, and titrate with potassium permanganate. 2. (*for urea in blood*): To 5 cc. of blood filtrate add 1 cc. of NH_4Cl and heat in autoclave at 150 C. for ten minutes. Make alkaline, distil into acid, and titrate, using methyl red as indicator. **Claudius' m.,** sterilization of catgut by placing in a 1 per cent solution of iodine potassium iodide solution for a week. **Clausen's m.** 1. (*for lactic acid in blood*): Remove the glucose by adding copper sulfate and calcium hydroxide, filter, and proceed with filtrate as in Clausen's method for lactic acid in urine. 2. (*for lactic acid in urine*): Extract the lactic acid from the urine with ether, convert it into acetaldehyde by treatment with sulfuric acid, add sodium bisulfite, and titrate with standard iodine solution. **closed-plaster m.,** treatment of wounds, compound fractures, and osteomyelitis by enclosing the limb in an immobilizing plaster cast. See *Orr* and *Trueta* under *treatment.* **cold iron m.** See *Percy cautery,* under *cautery.* **Corley and Denis m.** (*for calcium in tissues*): If there is only a small amount of organic material it may be removed by washing, aided by nitric acid. With more organic material, add 5 volumes of tenth normal sodium hydroxide and heat in autoclave at 180 C. for two hours. Precipitate as oxalate, dissolve in sulfuric acid, and titrate with potassium permanganate. **Corri's m.** (*for lactic acid in tissues*): Precipitate the protein with $HgCl_2$, remove the mercury from the filtrate with H_2S, determine lactic acid by Clausen's method. **creatine, m's for.** See *Folin's m.* (7,8), *Folin, Benedict, and Myers' m., Folin and Wu's m.* (1,2), *Meyer's m.* **creatinine, m's for.** See *Folin's m.* (9), *Folin and Wu's m.* (1,2), *Shaffer's m.* **Credé's m.** 1. Method of expressing the placenta by resting the hand on the fundus uteri and gently rubbing until the placenta is loosened; then expelling it by firmly squeezing the fundus. 2. The placing of a drop of 2 per cent solution of silver nitrate in each eye of a newborn child for the prevention of ophthalmia neonatorum. **cubicle m.,** the treatment of patients with contagious disease by placing each patient in one of the cubicle-like compartments into which the ward is divided. **cup plate m.** See *ring test,* under *tests.* **Dakin-Carrel m.,** treatment of wounds by irrigation with surgical solution of chlorinated soda (Dakin's fluid). See *Carrel treatment,* under *treatment.* **Dare's m.** (*for estimation of hemoglobin*): Compare the color of the blood in a thin layer with a standard color scale. **Defer's m.,** treatment of hydrocele by evacuation and cauterization of the sac with silver nitrate. **Dehn and Clark's m.** (*for chlorides*): Oxidize any interfering organic matter with sodium peroxide and then proceed with Volhard and Arnold's method. **Delbastaille's m.,** injection of tumors with osmic acid. **Delore's m.,** manual osteoclasis for correcting genu valgum. **Demme's m.,** treatment of hydrocele by injection of iodine. **Denis' m.** (*for magnesium in serum*): Remove the calcium by the Clark-Collip method, precipitate as magnesium ammonium phosphate, dissolve the precipitate in tenth normal HCl, reduce it with amino-naphthol-sulfonic acid, and compare the blue color with a standard solution of ammonium magnesium phosphate in 0.1 per cent HCl. **Denis and Leche's m.** (*for total sulfate*): Add acid and autoclave to decompose protein, then precipitate with barium chloride, dry, and weigh. **diacetic acid, m's for.** See *Folin and Hart's m.*, *Scott and Wilson's m.*, *Van Slyke and Palmer's m.* **direct m.,** in ophthalmoscopy, that in which the ophthalmoscope is held close to the eye examined and an erect virtual image is obtained of the fungus. **direct aeration m.** (*for urea in blood*). See *Myers' m.* **direct centrifugal flotation m.,** Lane m. **Domagk's m.** (*for demonstration of reticulo-endothelial cells*): A culture of gram-positive staphylococci in physiologic salt solution is injected into the femoral vein of a rat which is then killed in fifteen to thirty minutes. In formalin-fixed sections stained by cresyl violet or by Gram's stain followed by alum-carmine, Kupffer's cells and other cells of the reticulo-endothelial system stand out strikingly. **Dubois's m.,** a method of psychotherapy involving explanation to the patient of his condition and the securing of the patient's cooperation in his treatment. **Duke's m.** See *bleeding time*, under *time*. **Duncan's m.,** autotherapy. **Eggleston's m.,** administration of digitalis in large doses frequently repeated, producing rapid digitalization. **Eicken's m.,** examination of the hypopharynx, with the cricoid cartilage drawn forward. **Ellinger's m.** (*for indican*): Precipitate the urine with basic lead acetate and filter. To the filtrate add Obermayer's reagent. Shake out the indigo with chloroform, evaporate off the chloroform, and titrate the residue with potassium permanganate. **Epstein's m.** (*for dextrose*): A modification of the Lewis and Benedict method, making it possible to make the test with very little blood. **Esbach's m.** (*for albumin in urine*): Precipitate the protein with picric acid, let precipitate settle in a graduated tube, and read the result. **ethereal sulfates, m's for.** See *sulfates, ethereal, m's for.* **Fichera's m.** See *Fichera treatment*, under *treatment.* **Fishberg's m.,** one for determining specific gravity of the urine. **Fiske's m.** (*for total fixed base*): Removed phosphates with ferric chloride, convert fixed bases into sulfates by heating in H_2SO_4, ignite, take up in water, precipitate sulfates as benzidine sulfate, and titrate with alkali. **Fiske and SubbaRow's m.** 1. (*for acid-soluble phosphorus in blood*): Destroy organic matter by heating with sulfuric and nitric acids, precipitate the phosphates as magnesium ammonium phosphate, and reduce the precipitate with amino-naphthol-sulfonic acid. Compare the blue color with a standard phosphate solution. 2. (*for inorganic phosphates*): The phosphates are precipitated as ammonium phosphomolybdate. This is then reduced by amino-naphthol-sulfonic acid and the blue color compared colorimetrically with a standard solution. **fixed base, m. for.** See *Fiske's m.* **flash m.,** a method of pasteurizing milk whereby the milk is brought up to a temperature of 178 F. and chilled at once. Cf. *holding m.* **flotation m.,** Fulleborn's m. **Folin's m.** 1. (*for acetone*): Aerate the acetone from the urine over into an alkaline hypo-iodite solution of known strength. The acetone is thus changed to iodoform and the excess of iodine is titrated with a standard thiosulfate solution, using starch as an indicator. 2. (*for acetone*): Micromethod. Aerate the acetone over into a solution of sodium bisulfite and then determine the amount of nephelometric comparison with a standard acetone solution using Scott and Wilson's reagent. 3. (*for amino-acids in blood*): Make 10 cc. of protein-free blood filtrate slightly alkaline to phenolphthalein. Add 2 cc. of beta-naphtha-quinone solution and place in the dark. The next day add 2 cc. of acetic acid-acetate solution and 2 cc. of 4 per cent thiosulfate solution. Dilute to 25 cc. and compare the blue color with a standard amino-acid solution similarly treated. 4. (*for amino-acid nitrogen in blood*): Treat the urine with permutit to remove the ammonia and then with beta-naphtha-quinone sulfonic acid. The red color is compared with a standard amino-acid solution. 5. (*for ammonia nitrogen*): Sodium carbonate is added to the urine to free the ammonia, which is aerated into standard acid and titrated. 6. (*for blood sugar*): To 2 cc. of neutral protein-free blood filtrate, add 2 cc. of the Folin copper solution and heat in boiling water bath ten minutes. Cool and add 2 cc. of acid molybdate reagent. Dilute to 25 cc. mark and compare the blue color with a standard glucose solution similarly treated. 7. (*for creatine*): Precipitate the proteins of the blood with picric acid and filter. To the filtrate add sodium hydroxide and compare color with a standard solution of creatine. 8. (*for creatine in urine*): Change creatine into creatinine by heating at 90 C. for three hours in the presence of third normal HCl. Determine creatinine by picric acid and alkali and deduct the preformed creatinine. 9. (*for creatinine in urine*): To the urine add picric acid and sodium hydroxide and compare the red color with a half normal solution of potassium bichromate. 10. (*for ethereal sulfates*): Remove the inorganic sulfates with barium chloride and then the conjugated sulfates after hydrolyzing with boiling dilute hydrochloric acid. 11. (*for inorganic sulfates*): Acidify the urine with hydrochloric acid, precipitate with barium chloride, filter, dry, ignite, and weigh. 12. (*for protein in urine*): Add acetic acid and heat, wash, dry, and weigh the precipitate. 13. (*for total acidity*): Add potassium oxalate to the urine to precipitate the calcium which should otherwise precipitate at the neutral point, and titrate with tenth normal sodium hydroxide, using phenolphthalein as an indicator. 14. (*for total sulfates*): Boil the urine for thirty minutes with dilute hydrochloric acid, precipitate with barium chloride, filter, dry, ignite, and weigh. 15. (*for urea and allantoin*): Decompose the urea by heating with magnesium chloride and hydrochloric acid, distil off the ammonia, and titrate. **Folin's gravimetric m.** (*for protein in urine*): Precipitate the protein by heat and acetic acid; centrifugalize, wash, dry, and weigh the precipitate. **Folin and Bell's m.** (*for ammonia in urine*). See *permutit m.* **Folin-Benedict and Myers' m.** (*for creatine in urine*): To 20 cc. of urine add 20 cc. of normal HCl and autoclave at 120 C. for one-half hour. Neutralize, add picric acid and alkali, and compare the color with a standard solution of potassium bichromate. **Folin and Berglund's m.** (*for sugar in normal urine*): Remove interfering substances by shaking the urine with Lloyd's alkaloidal reagent and then proceed as in the Folin-Wu method. **Folin, Cannon, and Denis' m.** (*for epinephrine*): Add Folin's uric acid phosphotungstic reagent and sodium carbonate to the unknown and estimate amount by comparison of blue color with a standard uric acid solution similarly treated. **Folin and Denis' m.** 1. (*for albumin*): Precipitate the albumin with sulfosalicylic acid and compare the turbidity with that of a standard protein solution. 2. (*for Bence Jones protein*): Coagulate the Bence Jones protein at 60 C., centrifugalize, wash precipitate with 50 per cent alcohol, dry, and weigh. 3. (*for nitrogen in urine*): Destroy the organic matter in the diluted urine with the phosphoric-sulfuric acid-copper sulfate mixture, add Nessler's reagent, and compare it with a standard ammonia solution. 4. (*for nonprotein nitrogen*): It is much the same as Folin and Wu's method except that the proteins are removed with methyl alcohol and zinc chloride. The alcohol is boiled off and the nitrogen changed into ammonia and nesslerized in the usual way. 5. (*for phenols*): Precipitate interfering substances by adding acid silver lactate solution and colloidal iron. To 20 cc. of the filtrate add 5 cc. of the phosphotungstic phosphomolybdic acid reagent and 15 cc. of a saturated solution of sodium carbonate and compare the blue color, etc. 6. (*for urea*): The same as the method of Folin and Pettibone except that the urine is diluted twenty to one hundred times to prevent sugar from interfering with the test. 7. (*for uric acid in blood*): Remove the proteins by boiling acetic acid and then proceed with Benedict and Hitchcock's method. **Folin and Farmer's m.** (*for total nitrogen*): A modified microchemical Kjeldahl method for urine. Decompose the nitrogenous bodies with sulfuric acid as usual, add alkali, aerate the ammonia over into standard acid, nesslerize, and compare with a standard solution of ammonium sulfate. **Folin and Flander's m.** (*for hippuric acid*): 100 cc. of the urine is evaporated to dryness with 10 cc. of 5 per cent sodium hydroxide. Hydrolyze the residue with nitric acid, shake out the benzoic acid with chloroform, and titrate it with tenth normal sodium alcoholate, using phenolphthalein as indicator. **Folin and Hart's m.** (*for acetone and diacetic acid*): Determine the acetone by Folin's method, then heat the urine with hydrochloric acid to change diacetic acid to acetone, and determine again. **Folin and Macallum's m.** (*for ammonia nitrogen*): To the urine add potassium carbonate and potassium oxalate, aerate the ammonia over into standard acid, nesslerize, and compare with a standard solution of ammonium sulfate. **Folin, McEllroy, and Peck's m.** (*for dextrose in urine*): Mix 5 cc. of an acidified 5.9 per cent copper sulfate solution, 1 cc. of 20 per cent sodium carbonate solution and then add 4 to 5 Gm. of phosphate-thiocyanate mixture. Heat and add enough urine to produce a sudden turbidity after not more than five seconds of boiling; 25 mg. of glucose will reduce the 5 cc. of copper solution. **Folin and Peck's m.** (*for dextrose*): To the boiling copper solution of Folin and McEllroy run in urine until the color changes from green to yellow. **Folin and Pettibone's m.** (*for urea*): Microchemical. The urea is decomposed by heating with potassium acetate and acetic acid, the ammonia is liberated by sodium hydroxide, aerated over into standard acid, and nesslerized. **Folin and Shaffer's m.** (*for uric acid*): Phosphates and certain organic substances are first precipitated by an acetic acid solution of ammonium sulfate and uranium acetate. The uric acid is then precipitated as ammonium urate and the amount determined by titration with potassium permanganate. **Folin and Wright's m.** (*for nitrogen in urine*): A simplified macro-Kjeldahl method in which the digestion is brought about by a mixture of phosphoric and sulfuric acids aided by ferric chloride, and the liberated ammonia is distilled without the use of a condenser. **Folin and Wu's m.** 1. (*for creatinine*): The color produced by the unknown (protein-free blood filtrate or urine) in an alkaline solution of picric acid is compared in a colorimeter with the color produced by a known solution of creatinine or with a standard solution of potassium bichromate. 2. (*for creatine plus creatinine*): The creatine of a protein-free blood filtrate is changed to creatinine by heating with dilute HCl in an autoclave and the creatinine thus produced together with the preformed is determined colorimetrically after adding an alkaline picrate solution. 3. (*for glucose*): The protein-free blood filtrate is boiled with a dilute alkaline copper tartrate solution, the cuprous oxide is dissolved by adding a phosphomolybdic-phosphoric acid solution, and the blue color produced is compared with the color from sugar solutions of known strength. 4. (*nonprotein nitrogen*): The total nonprotein nitrogen in the protein-free blood filtrate is determined by setting free the nitrogen as ammonia by the Kjeldahl process, nesslerizing this ammonia, and comparing with a standard. 5. (*for protein-free blood filtrate*): Lake the blood with distilled water, add sodium tungstate and sulfuric acid, and filter. 6. (*for urea*): Change the urea to ammonia by means of urease, and nesslerize. 7. (*for uric acid*): Uric acid is precipitated from the protein-free blood filtrate or from urine by silver lactate, treated with phosphotungstic acid and the blue color compared with the color produced by known amounts of uric acid. **Folin and Youngburg's m.** (*for urea in urine*): The ammonia is removed from the urine by permutit, the urea is changed to ammonium carbonate by urease, and nesslerized directly. **Forlanini-Morelli m.,** treatment of empyema by systematic induction of pneumothorax, continuous aspiration drainage combined with irrigation, and the use of an airtight pneumatic jacket drainage tube. **m's for (volatilizing) formaldehyde gas.** See *Aronson's m., Breslau's m., Brunn's m., lime m., Schlossmann's m., Trillat's m.* **formol titration, m's of.** See *Benedict and Murlin's method, Malfatti's method,* and *Sörensen's method.* **Freiburg m.** Same as *twilight sleep.* See under *sleep.* **Frey and Gigon's m.** (*for amino-acid nitrogen*): A modified form of Sörensen's method in that the ammonia is aspirated off after adding the barium hydroxide. **Fridericia's m.** (*for alveolar carbon dioxide tension*): The carbon dioxide is absorbed into a solution of potassium hydroxide and the decrease in volume read in percentage in a special apparatus. **Fulleborn's m.** (*for filaria in stools*): Grind 1 Gm. of stool and mix with 20 cc. of a saturated solution of sodium chloride. Allow to stand one hour or more, then float coverglasses on the surface and transfer them, without draining, to slides. **Gabastou's hydraulic m.,** treatment of retention of the placenta by filling it with saline solution injected through the umbilical cord. **gasometric m.** (*for urea*). See *Stehle's m.* **Gerota's m.,** injection of the lymphatics with a dye, such as prussian blue, which is soluble in chloroform or ether, but not in water. **Given's m.** (*for peptic activity*): Varying amounts of diluted gastric juice are added to a series of tubes containing pea globulin, the mixtures are incubated, and the amount of digestion noted. **glucose (dextrose), m's for.** See *Bang's m., Benedict's m., Benedict and Osterberg's m., Bertrand's m., Folin's m., Folin and Berglund's m., Folin, McEllroy, and Peck's m., Folin and Peck's m., Folin and Wu's m.* (3), *Hagedorn and Jensen's m., life insurance m.* (2), *Peter's m., Power and Wilder's m., Summer's m.* **gold number m.** See *Lange's test,* under *tests.* **Gram's m.** See under *staining.* **Greenwald's m.** (*for nonprotein nitrogen*): The proteins are precipitated by trichloracetic acid; the filtrate is decomposed by sulfuric acid as in the Kjeldahl method; the ammonia is distilled off and the amount titrated with tenth normal sodium hydroxide. **Greenwald and Lewman's m.** (*for titratable alkali of blood*): The protein of the blood is precipitated with an excess of picric acid. Both the free and the total picric acid in the filtrate are then determined. The difference represents the picric acid which is combined with the bases of the blood. **Griffith's m.** (*for hippuric acid*): Extract the hippuric acid with ether. Distil off the ether and destroy urea in the residue with sodium hypobromite solution. Determine the nitrogen in the residue by the Kjeldahl method. **Gross's m.** (*for tryptic activity*): Add increasing amounts of a trypsin solution to a series of tubes of pure, fat-free casein which have been heated to 40 C. Incubate at 40 C. for fifteen minutes. Test by adding a few drops of acetic acid (dilute) to each tube. A precipitate on acidification indicates that digestion is incomplete or lacking; no precipitate indicates digestion. **Grossich's m.,** the use of tincture of iodine as an antiseptic in surgical operations. **Hagedorn and Jensen's m.** (*for sugar in blood*): Precipitate the protein with zinc hydroxide. Heat the filtrate with potassium ferricyanide solution and determine the amount of ferricyanide reduced by adding an iodide solution and titrating the iodine set free with sodium thiosulfate. **Hall's m.** (*for total purine nitrogen*): Remove phosphates by means of magnesia mixture and precipitate the purine bodies in a specially graduated tube by means of silver nitrate and ammonium hydroxide. After twenty-four hours read the volume of the purine precipitate. **Ham-**

ilton's m. (in postpartum hemorrhage): Compress the uterus between a fist in the vagina and a hand pressing down the abdominal wall. **Hammerschlag's m.** (*for specific gravity of blood*): Prepare a mixture of benzene and chloroform of about 1.050 specific gravity. Into this let fall a drop of blood and add benzene or chloroform until the drop neither rises nor sinks. Then take the specific gravity of the mixture. **Harrison's m.** (*for dilating the cervix*): A manual method by inserting the fingers progressively into the cervix. **Hart's m.** (*for casein in milk*): Precipitate the casein from the diluted milk, filter, wash, redissolve in excess of tenth normal potassium hydroxide, and titrate remaining alkali with tenth normal HCl. The difference is casein. **Heintz's m.** (*for uric acid*): Precipitate the urine by adding hydrochloric acid, filter off the crystals, wash, dry, and weigh. **hemoglobin, m. for.** See *acid hematin m.* **Henderson and Palmer's m.** (*for hydrogen ion concentration*): The reaction of the urine is estimated by matching colors produced by certain indicators in the urine and in solutions of known hydrogen ion concentration. **Henriques and Sörensen's m.** (*for amino-acid nitrogen by solution of formaldehyde titration*). See *Sörensen's m.* **Herter-Foster m.** (*for indole in feces, modified by Bergeim*): Make the feces alkaline and distil. Make the distillate acid and distil again. To the second distillate add beta-naphtha-quinone sodium monosulfonate and alkali. Extract the blue color with chloroform and compare it with a standard solution of indole containing 0.1 mg. of indole per cubic centimeter. **Heublein m.,** treatment of cancer by low voltage doses of roentgen ray over the entire body given for from ten to twenty hours out of the twenty-four and continued for a period of several days. **hippuric acid, m's for.** See *Folin and Flander's m.*, *Griffith's m.*, and *Roaf's m.* **Hirschberg's m.,** measurement of the deviation of a strabismic eye by observing the reflection of a candle from the cornea. **Hodgen's m.,** treatment of traumatic tetanus by large doses of Fowler's solution. **holding m.,** a method of pasteurizing milk whereby the milk is heated to 65 C. and kept at that temperature for thirty to forty-five minutes. Cf. *flash m.* **Howell's m.** (*for clotting time of blood*): Place 5 cc. of blood in a 21-mm. test tube with suitable precautions. Tilt the tube every two minutes and note time of clotting. **Hung's m.,** a method of floating feces on a slide for the detection of helminth eggs. **Hunt's m.** (*for the activity of thyroid products*): Mice on a cracker diet are fed varying amounts of the thyroid product for ten days. They are then injected with 0.4 mg. of acetonitril per gram of body weight. If the product is active the treated mice usually live, whereas untreated mice are killed in two hours by 1.2 mg. per gram of body weight. **Hunter and Given's m.** (*for uric acid and purine bases*): Precipitate and decompose the precipitate as in the Krueger-Schmidt method. Determine the uric acid in an aliquot part and in the remainder destroy the uric acid by oxidation and determine the purine bases as in the Krueger-Schmidt method. **hydrogen ion concentration, m's for.** See *Henderson and Palmer's m.*, and *Levy, Rowntree, and Marriott's m.* **India ink m.** See under *tests.* **indican, m's for.** See *Askenstedt's m.*, *Ellinger's m.* **indole, m's for.** See *Bergeim's m.*, *Herter and Foster's m.* **inorganic sulfates, m's for.** See *sulfates, inorganic, m's for.* **iron, m's for.** See *Walker's m.*, and *Wolter's m.* **Irving's m.** (*in occipitoposterior presentation*): Manual rotation of the head to a mentoposterior presentation. **Issayeff's m.,** intraperitoneal injection of saline solution twenty-four hours previous to an abdominal operation: done to promote local leukocytosis. **Japanese m.,** a method for fixing paraffin sections to glass slides with the use of Mayer's albumin **Kaiserling's m.,** a procedure for preserving the natural colors in museum preparations, employing formaldehyde and potassium acetate. **Karr's m.** (*for urea in blood*): Change the urea to ammonium carbonate by means of urease, nesslerize directly, and compare the color with that of a standard urea solution similarly treated. **Kendall's m.** (*for iodine in thyroid tissue*): Oxidize the organic matter by fusion in KNO_3 and strong KOH. Acidify, oxidize with bromine, add an excess of KI, and titrate the liberated iodine with sodium thiosulfate. **Kenny m.** See under *treatment.* **Kirstein's m.,** direct inspection of the larynx by pushing the head far back and depressing the tongue. **Kjeldahl's m.** (1883), a method of determining the amount of nitrogen in an organic compound. It consists in heating the material to be analyzed with strong sulfuric acid. The nitrogen is thereby converted to ammonia, which is distilled off and caught in tenth normal solution of sulfuric acid. By titration the amount of ammonia is determined, and from this the amount of nitrogen is estimated. **Kluge's m.,** induction of premature labor by dilatation of the cervix by specially prepared sponges. **Koch and McMeekin's m.** (*for total nitrogen*): Destroy organic matter with sulfuric acid and hydrogen peroxide and nesslerize the resulting solution directly. **Korotkoff's m.,** the auscultatory method of determining blood pressure. **Kramer and Gittleman's m.** (*for sodium in serum*): Dry and ash the serum. Take it up in 0.1 per cent HCl and make slightly alkaline with KOH. Precipitate with the pyroantimonate reagent and alcohol, dissolve precipitate in strong HCl, add potassium iodide, and titrate with sodium thiosulfate. **Kramer and Tisdall's m.** 1. (*for potassium in serum*): Precipitate with sodium cobaltinitrite reagent, treat precipitate with acid permanganate solution, then with sodium oxalate, and titrate with standard permanganate. 2. (*for calcium in serum*): Precipitate the calcium as oxalate. Wash, dissolve and titrate with potassium permanganate. **Kristeller's m.,** a method of expressing the fetus in labor. The fetal head should be in the vulva and the abdomen must be sufficiently relaxed so that the assistant may grasp the fundus. The grip on the fundus is made by the fingers of the two hands parallel behind and the thumb in front, the line of force being in the direction of the axis of the inlet. The expression should be done in one or two sustained efforts. **Krogh's m.** (*for urea*): The urea is oxidized by sodium hypobromite to carbon dioxide and nitrogen in an alkaline solution which absorbs the carbon dioxide. The remaining nitrogen is then measured. **Krönig's m.,** sterilization of catgut by heating for an hour in cumol at 165 C. **Krueger and Schmidt's m.** (*for uric acid and purine bases*): Precipitate the uric acid with copper sulfate, decompose the precipitate with sodium sulfite, acidify, concentrate, and let uric acid crystals separate. Determine the nitrogen in them by the Kjeldahl method. Reprecipitate the purine bases with copper sulfate, filter, wash and determine the nitrogen in the precipitate by the Kjeldahl method. **Kwilecki's m.** (*for albumin*): 10 drops of a 10 per cent solution of ferric chloride are added to the urine before proceeding with the regular method of Esbach. **Laborde's m.,** the making of rhythmical traction movements on the tongue in order to stimulate the respiratory center in asphyxiation. **lactalbumin, m. for,** remove casein from the milk with magnesium sulfate, add Alman's reagent to the filtrate, determine the nitrogen in the precipitate with the Kjeldahl method, and multiply the result by 6.37. **Lane m.,** a method of diagnosing hookworm infection by centrifugation of 1 ml. of washed feces mixed with brine, the tube being covered with a cover slip on which the eggs can be counted. Called also *direct centrifugal flotation method*, or *D.C.F.* **Lashmet and Newburgh m.,** one for determining specific gravity of urine. **Leipert's m.** (*for iodine in blood*): Destroy organic matter with chromic-sulfuric acid. Reduce iodic acid to free iodine with arsenous acid, distil off the iodine and titrate. **Leroux's m.,** treatment of placenta praevia by tamponade of the vagina. **Levy, Rowntree, and Marriott's**

m. (*for hydrogen ion concentration of blood*): Dialyze the blood through a collodion tube against neutral physiologic salt solution; then match the color produced by phenolsulfonphthalein in the dialysate and in solution of known hydrogen ion concentration. **Lewis and Benedict's m.** (*for dextrose*): The proteins of the blood are precipitated by means of picric acid, sodium carbonate is added, and the color of the picramic acid solution is compared with that of a standard glucose solution. **Lewisohn's m.,** a method of indirect transfusion by adding sodium citrate to the blood. **life insurance m.** 1. (*for albumin in urine*): The clarified urine is treated with sulfosalicylic acid and the turbidity is compared with permanent turbidity standards. 2. (*for glucose in urine*): Add picric acid and alkali and compare the red color with permanent sugar standards made by mixing varying amounts of ferric chloride and cobalt chloride in dilute HCl. **lime m.,** a method of generating or volatilizing formaldehyde gas. Forty per cent formaldehyde, containing 10 per cent of sulfuric acid, is poured over quicklime in a suitable container. One and a half to 2 pounds of lime should be used for each pint of the solution. **Lindemann's m.** (*for transfusion*): One needle cannula is placed in the arm of the donor and one in the arm of the patient. Syringes are filled from the donor and emptied into the recipient through the cannulas. **Lorthiore's m.,** radical cure of hernia by dissection and extirpation of the sac without opening the inguinal canal. **Lyman's m.** (*for calcium*): Precipitate the calcium from the protein-free blood filtrate or from urine as calcium oxalate, redissolve in dilute acid and reprecipitate as calcium ricinate, and determine the amount nephelometrically. **Lyon's m.** See *Meltzer-Lyon test*, under *tests*. **McArthur's m.,** enteroclysis through a catheter placed in the common bile duct after operations on the gallbladder. **McCrudden's m.** (*for calcium and magnesium*): Make 200 cc. of urine faintly acid to litmus, add 10 cc. of concentrated hydrochloric acid, precipitate with oxalic acid, filter, ignite, and weigh as calcium oxide, or filter and titrate the precipitate with potassium permanganate. This gives the calcium. For the magnesium, add to the filtrate from the calcium, nitric acid, evaporate to dryness, and heat until the residue fuses. Take up in water, add sodium acid phosphate and ammonia, filter, wash, ignite, and weigh as the pyrophosphate. **McIntosh and Fildes' m.,** a portion of platinized or palladinized asbestos is placed in the anaerobic jar and hydrogen gas is introduced until no oxygen remains, the oxygen having been removed by uniting with the hydrogen under the catalytic influence of the platinum black. **Maclachlan m.,** a method of conditioning liquid sludge by the application of sulfur dioxide gas. **McLean and Van Slyke's m.** (*for chlorides*): Precipitate the chlorides from oxalated plasma with an excess of silver nitrate and titrate the excess with potassium iodide and starch. **magnesium, m's for.** See *Denis' m.* and *McCrudden's m.* **Malfatti's m.** (*for ammonia nitrogen by solution of formaldehyde titration*): Add potassium oxalate to the urine and make neutral to phenolphthalein with tenth normal sodium hydroxide; add the neutral solution of formaldehyde and titrate again. **Marfan's m.,** puncture of the pericardium in which the trocar is passed just below the xiphoid cartilage in the middle line, directed obliquely from below upward, passing for 2 cm. along the posterior surface of the sternum. It is then directed somewhat obliquely backward, passing into the gap in the sternal insertion of the diaphragm, entering the pericardium at its base. **Marmo's m.,** a method of producing artificial respiration in asphyxiated infants; the surgeon holds the infant suspended with his hands in its axillae, raises it, and then suddenly lets it drop a foot or two, which will produce inspiration; expiration is then produced by pressure of the hands against the chest wall. **Marriott's m.** (*for alkali reserve*): The patient rebreathes the air in a bag until its carbon dioxide tension is virtually that of venous blood. This air is then bubbled through a standard bicarbonate solution until the solution is saturated and the color produced is compared with standard color tubes. **Marshall's m.** (*for urea*): The urea is changed into ammonium carbonate by the enzyme urease and the ammonia titrated with tenth normal hydrochloric acid, using methyl orange, as indicator. **Meltzer's m.,** insufflation through an endotracheal tube of air containing an anesthetic vapor; employed in thoracic surgery. **Meltzer-Lyon m.** See *Meltzer-Lyon test*, under *tests*. **Messinger and Huppert's m.** (*for acetone*): The same as the method of Folin and Hart except that the acetone is distilled instead of aspirated. **Mett's m.** (*for peptic activity*). See *Nirenstein and Schiff's m.* **Meulengracht's m.** (*for bile pigment in serum*): The serum is diluted until the yellow color corresponds to that of a standard potassium bichromate solution. **Meyer's m.** (*for creatine*): A modification of Folin and Benedict's method in that the creatine is changed into creatinine after adding hydrochloric acid by digesting in an autoclave. **Miles' acid m.,** a method of treating sewage by the fumes of burning sulfur. **Minkowski's m.** Same as *Naunyn-Minkowski m.* **Moerner-Sjöqvist m.** See *Sjöqvist m.* **Mohr's m.** (*for chlorides*): Oxidize interfering organic matter by igniting with potassium nitrate. To the solution of the ash add potassium chromate and titrate with standard silver nitrate until the red silver chromate appears. **Mojon's m.,** injection of cold water to which acids have been added through the umbilical vein into the placenta with a view to facilitating its detachment from the uterus after birth. **Monias and Shapiro's m.,** convert the indican into indigolignon and compare with a standard. **Montel m.,** a method of treating leprosy by the use of a 1 per cent solution of methylene blue and the Wandremer vaccine. **Morelli m.** See *Forlanini-Morelli m.* **Morison's (Rutherford) m.,** a method of treating wounds which consists of a thorough opening up and mechanical cleansing of the wound, sponging of it with alcohol, and the application to the raw surface of a thin layer of a paste consisting of 1 part of bismuth subnitrate, 2 parts of iodoform, and enough liquid paraffin to make a soft paste. This paste is known as bismuth iodoform paraffin paste, or in vernacular in the British Isles as bipp or B.I.P. The wound is then sutured without drainage. **Müller's m.,** Deventer's m. **Murphy m.** 1. Suture of an artery by invaginating the ends over a cylinder in two pieces which can be removed. 2. Continuous proctoclysis; the continuous administration per rectum of salt solution, drop by drop, with the patient in the Fowler position: used in infections of the peritoneum. Called also *Murphy drip*. 3. See *Murphy treatment*, under *treatment*. **Myers' m.** (*for urea in blood*): Change the urea to ammonium carbonate by the action of urease, aerate off the ammonia into an acid solution, and nesslerize. **Myers and Wardell's m.** (*for cholesterol*): Dry the blood on plaster of paris and extract the cholesterol with chloroform. Add acetic anhydride and sulfuric acid and compare the color with that of a standard solution of cholesterol similarly treated. **Nägeli's m.** See *Nägeli's treatment*, under *treatment*. **Naunyn-Minkowski m.,** palpation of the kidney after first dilating the colon with gas. **Neumann's m.,** local anesthesia for surgery on the ear by the subperiosteal injection of a solution of cocaine and epinephrine. **Nikiforoff's m.,** a method of fixing blood films by placing them for from five to fifteen minutes in absolute alcohol, pure ether, or equal parts of alcohol and ether. **Nimeh's m.,** a method of determining the size of liver and spleen, based on measurements made on flat films of the hepatic and splenic regions taken separately without any preparation or after retroperitoneal insufflation of carbon dioxide gas. **Nirenstein and Schiff's m.** (*for peptic activity*): Mett's tubes are placed in the solution to be tested and incubated for twenty-four hours. The length of the column digested at each end is then determined. **nitrogen, amino acid, m's for.** See *Benedict and Murlin's m.*, *Folin's m.* (4), *Frey and Gignon's m.*, *Sörensen's m.*, and *Van Slyke's m.* **nitrogen, ammonia, m's for.** See *Folin's m.* (5), *Folin and Macallum's m.*, *Malfatti's m.*, and *permutit m.* **nitrogen, nonprotein, m's for.** See *Folin and Denis' m.* (4), *Folin and Wu's m.* (4), and *Greenwald's m.* **nitrogen, purine, m. for.** See *Hall's m.* **nitrogen, total, m's for.** See *Arnold and Gunning's m.*, *Bock and Benedict's m.*, *Folin and Denis' m.*, *Folin and Farmer's m.*, *Folin and Wright's m.*, *Koch and McMeekin's m.*, *Taylor and Hulton's m.* **Oberst's m.,** local anesthesia produced by injecting saline solution or distilled water into the subcutaneous connective tissue. **Ogata's m.,** a method of stimulating respiration by stroking the chest. **Olshausen's m.,** a method of operating for umbilical hernia by reduction without opening the sac, and then suturing the skin. **Orsi-Brocco m.,** palpatory percussion of the heart. **Osborne and Folin's m.** (*for total sulfur in urine*): Destroy the organic matter in the concentrated urine and oxidize the sulfur by fusing with sodium peroxide. Precipitate with barium chloride, wash, dry, ignite, and weigh. **Pachon's m.,** cardiography with the patient lying on the left side. **Pajot's m.,** decapitation of the fetus with Pajot's hook. **panoptic m.** See *Giemsa's staining method*, in *stains and staining methods, table of.* **Parker's m.** (*for indican*). See *Askenstedt's m.* **Pasteur's m.** 1. (*For Bacillus anthracis*). A method of attenuating bacteria by growing them at a temperature higher than body temperature, usually 42 to 43 C. 2. (*For the preparation of rabies vaccine*). The spinal cords of rabbits infected with rabies (fixed virus) are removed aseptically, dried and emulsified. **Pavlov's m.,** study of the changes in the salivary reflex produced by psychic influence. **Payr's m.** 1. The use of absorbable cylinders of magnesium for performing suture of blood vessels. 2. Transplantation of blood vessels so that they hang free in the ventricle of the brain in order to absorb the fluid in hydrocephalus. **Percy m.** See under *cautery.* **permutit m.** (*for ammonia in urine*): Add permutit to the urine and shake for five minutes. Wash the permutit ammonia compound several times, add sodium hydroxide, and nesslerize. Compare the color with a standard solution of ammonium sulfate. **Perthes' m.,** continuous aspiration of a pleuritic exudate by means of a drainage tube which passes into an airtight receiving vessel which is exhausted by water power. **Peter's m.** (*for dextrose*): Boil the unknown in an excess of the reagent, filter off the reduced copper, and titrate the filtrate with potassium iodide and standard thiosulfate solution. **Pfiffner and Myers' m.** (*for guanidine in blood*): A colorimetric method by the use of an alkaline nitroprusside-ferricyanide reagent. **Plimmer and Skelton's m.** (*for allantoin*): Determine the urea and allantoin by Folin's method (15), and the urea alone by Marshall's urease method. The difference is allantoin. **potassium, m's for.** See *Kramer and Tisdall's m.*, def. 1. **Power and Wilder's m.** (*for glucose in urine*): Remove interfering substances with mercuric sulfate. To the filtrate add alkaline ferricyanide; heat for ten minutes, cool, and add KI and an acid zinc sulfate solution. Titrate the liberated iodine with standard thiosulfate solution. **probit m.,** a method of calculating a 50 per cent end-point by interpolation, as in plotting the probit of percentage death against the logarithm of the dose to determine the median lethal dose. **Prochownick's m.,** artificial respiration for asphyxia of the newborn by compression of the child's chest while his head is allowed to hang backward. **protein in urine, m's for.** See *albumin in urine, m's for.* **protein-free blood filtrate, m's for.** See *Folin's m.* (4), *Folin and Denis' m.* (5), and *Folin and Wu's m.* (5). **Purdy's m.,** the use of the centrifuge for the determination of the quantity of albumin, chlorides, sulfates, etc. **purine bodies, m's for.** See *Hunter and Given's m.*, *Krueger and Schmidt's m.*, *Salkowski's m.*, *Salkowski and Arnstein's m.*, and *Welker's m.* **purine, nitrogen, m. for.** See *nitrogen, purine, m. for.* **Puzo's m.,** early rupture of the membranes in cases of placenta praevia. **quellung m.** See *Neufeld's test*, under *tests.* **Raiziss and Dubin's m.** (*for ethereal and inorganic sulfates*): Oxidize the urine by Benedict's method, precipitate the sulfate with benzidine hydrochloride, as in the method of Rosenheim and Drummond, and titrate with tenth normal potassium permanganate. **Reclus' m.,** the induction of local anesthesia by cocaine. **Reed and Muench m.,** a method of calculating a 50 per cent end-point by interpolation, as in plotting the logarithm of the dose against the logarithm of accumulated deaths to determine the median lethal dose. **Rehfuss' m.,** after an Ewald test meal a tube is passed into the stomach and small quantities of the stomach contents are removed at fifteen-minute intervals and examined. **Reichert's m.** (*for crystallizing oxyhemoglobin*): Add to the blood (defibrinated, laked, or whole) 1 to 5 per cent of ammonium oxalate crystals and examine under the microscope. **rhythm m.,** a method of preventing conception by restricting coitus to the so-called safe period, avoiding the days just before and after the expected time of ovulation. **Ribera's m.,** the induction of anemia in the legs by compressing the waist with an elastic spica. **Roaf's m.** (*for the preparation of hippuric acid*): Add 125 Gm. of ammonium sulfate and 7.5 Gm. of concentrated sulfuric acid to 500 cc. of urine of a horse. Hippuric acid will crystallize out. **Rosenheim and Drummond's m.** (*for ethereal and inorganic sulfates*): Precipitate the sulfates with benzidine hydrochloride and titrate the acid in the benzidine sulfate with tenth normal potassium hydroxide. **Ruhemann's uricometer m.** (*for uric acid*): Urine is added in a specially graduated tube to a mixture of carbon bisulfide and iodine solution until the carbon bisulfide is decolorized. **Sahli's m.** (*for estimation of hemoglobin*): Convert the hemoglobin into acid hematin by adding HCl and compare the color with a standard color scale. **Salkowski's m.** (*for purine bodies and uric acid*): Precipitate as silver magnesium salts, decompose the precipitate with hydrogen sulfide, precipitate uric acid by means of sulfuric acid, and the purine bodies as silver salts. **Salkowski and Arnstein's m.** (*for purines*): Precipitate the urine with magnesia mixture and to the filtrate add 3 per cent ammoniacal silver nitrate solution. Wash the precipitate and determine the nitrogen in it by the Kjeldahl method. The uric acid nitrogen is separately determined and deducted. **Salkowski-Autenrieth and Barth's m.** (*for oxalic acid*): Precipitate the oxalic acid by means of calcium chloride. Dissolve the precipitate in hydrochloric acid, extract the oxalic acid with ether, and reprecipitate it as calcium oxalate. **Scherer's m.** (*for proteins*): Precipitate the protein by boiling with dilute acetic acid, wash, dry, and weigh. **Schlösser's m.** See *Schlösser's treatment*, under *treatment.* **Schlossmann's m.,** to prevent polymerization, 10 per cent of glycerin is added to formaldehyde before it is volatilized by heat. **Schüller's m.,** a method of performing artificial respiration by rhythmic raisings of the thorax by means of the fingers hooked under the ribs. **Schultze's m.,** a method of resuscitating an infant in asphyxia neonatorum. **Schuman's m.,** a manual method for the rotation of the head in obstetrics. **Schwartz's m.,** multiple ligation for varicose veins. **Scott and Wilson's m.** (*for acetone and diacetic acid*): Distil the acetone into an alkaline solution of basic mercuric cyanide, filter, and titrate the precipitate with potassium thiocyanate. **Shaffer's m.** (*for creatinine*): Folin's method adapted to very dilute solutions. **Shaffer and Marriott's m.** (*for acetone bodies*): Precipitate the urine with basic lead acetate and ammonia. Distil off the acetone (acetone and diacetic acid). Oxidize the residue with potassium bichromate and distil again (beta-hydroxybutyric acid). Titrate the distillates with standard iodine and thiosulfate solutions. **Shohl and Pedley's m.** (*for calcium in urine*): Oxidize the urine with ammonium persulfate, precipitate the calcium as oxalate, add H_2SO_4 to the precipitate, and titrate with potassium permanganate. **Sjöqvist's m.,** quantitative estimation of the urea in the urine by means of a baryta mixture. **Smellie's m.,** delivery of the after-coming head with the body of the child resting on the forearm of the obstetrician. **sodium, m. for.** See *Kramer and Gittleman's m.* **Sörensen's m.** (*for amino acids by solution of formaldehyde titration*): Titrate the urine for total acidity using phenolphthalein as indicator, add fresh solution of formaldehyde (15 cc. of formalin, 30 cc. of water, and sufficient sodium to make it faintly alkaline to phenolphthalein), and titrate again. **Souligoux-Morestin m.,** the use of ether lavage of the peritoneal cavity in acute infections of the abdominal and pelvic viscera. **specific gravity, m. for.** See *Hammerschlag's m.* **Stammer's m.** (*for glucose in blood*): Precipitate blood proteins by boiling with acid sodium sulfate and treatment with dialyzed iron. In a test tube place 20 cc. of blood filtrate, 2 drops of a 20 per cent solution of sodium hydroxide and 1 cc. of a 0.0075 per cent solution of methylene blue. Boil until the blue color is discharged. The length of time required indicates the amount of sugar present. Time is counted from the beginning of vigorous boiling: thirty-seven seconds indicates 0.3 per cent sugar; sixty seconds, 0.225 per cent; one minute twenty-five seconds, 0.175 per cent; one minute fifty-five seconds, 0.125 per cent; and two minutes forty-five seconds, 0.075 per cent. **Stehle's m.** (*for urea*): Decompose the urea in a Van Slyke pipet by sodium hypobromite and measure the nitrogen. **Steinach's m.** See *Steinach's operation*, under *operation*. **Stockholm and Koch's m.** (*for total sulfur in biological material*): The material is disintegrated by heating in strong sodium hydroxide, then oxidized with 30 per cent H_2O_2, and then with nitric acid, and bromine. Precipitate the sulfuric acid with barium, wash, dry, ignite, and weigh. **sulfates, ethereal, m's for.** See *Folin's m.* (10), *Raiziss and Dubin's m.*, and *Rosenheim and Drummond's m.* **sulfates, inorganic, m's for.** See *Folin's m.* (11), *Raiziss and Dubin's m.*, and *Rosenheim and Drummond's m.* **sulfur, total, m's for.** See *Benedict's m.* (2), *Benedict and Denis' m.*, *Denis and Leche's m.*, *Folin's m.*, *Osborne and Folin's m.*, and *Stockholm and Koch's m.* **Sumner's m.** (*for sugar in urine*): Heat 1 cc. of urine and 3 cc. of Sumner's dinitrosalicylic acid reagent, dilute to 25 cc. and compare the color with that of a standard sugar solution similarly treated. **Taylor and Hulton's m.** (*for total nitrogen*): Similar to Folin and Farmer's method except that small amounts of sulfuric acid are used and the ammonia is nesslerized in the original tube without being aerated over into acid. **Thézac-Porsmeur m.,** heliotherapy of suppurating wounds by concentrating the sun's rays on the part by means of a large double convex lens mounted on a cylinder of canvas three feet long. **thyroid activity, m. for.** See *Hunt's m.* **Tisdall's m.** (*for phenols in urine*): Extract the phenolic substances from the urine with ether and then shake them from the ether with 10 per cent NaOH. Neutralize and proceed as in the Folin and Denis method. **total acidity, m. for.** See *Folin's m.* (13). **total fixed base, m. for.** See *Fiske's m.* **total nitrogen, m. for.** See *nitrogen, total, m. for.* **total sulfur, m. for.** See *sulfur, total, m. for.* **toxin-antitoxin m.** See *Behring's m.* **Tracy and Welker's m.** (*for deproteinizing urine*): A method depending on the use of aluminum hydroxide cream. **Trillat's m.,** volatilization of formaldehyde in an autoclave under pressure to prevent polymerization. **tryptic activity, m. for.** See *Gross's m.* **Tswett's m.,** chromatography. **Tuffier's m.** See *spinal anesthesia* (1), under *anesthesia.* **turbidity m.** (*for albumin*): See *Folin and Denis' m.* (1). **uranium acetate m.** (*for phosphorus*): Add sodium acetate and acetic acid to the urine, heat to boiling, and titrate with a special uranium acetate solution. **urea, m's for.** See *Benedict's m.* (3), *Clark-Collip m.* (2), *Folin and Denis' m.* (6), *Folin and Pettibone's m.*, *Folin and Wu's m.* (6), *Folin and Youngsburg's m.*, *Karr's m.*, *Krogh's m.*, *Marshall's m.*, *Myers' m.*, *Stehle's m.*, and *Van Slyke and Cullen's m.* (2). **urease m.** See *Marshall's m.* and *Van Slyke and Cullen's m.* (2). **uric acid, m's for.** See *Benedict's m.* (4), *Benedict and Franke's m.*, *Benedict and Hitchcock's m.*, *Folin and Denis' m.* (7), *Folin and Shaffer's m.*, *Folin and Wu's m.* (7), *Heintz's m.*, *Hunter and Given's m.*, *Krueger and Schmidt's m.*, *Ruhemann's m.*, and *Salkowski's m.* **van Gehuchten's m.,** fixing of a histologic tissue in a mixture of glacial acetic acid 10 parts, chloroform 30 parts, and alcohol 60 parts. **Van Slyke's m.** (*for amino-nitrogen*): The unknown is treated with nitrous acid in a special apparatus and the nitrogen liberated is measured. **Van Slyke and Cullen's m.** 1. (*for the carbon dioxide in blood*, or *for the alkali reserve of blood*): Freshly prepared oxalated plasma is brought into equilibrium with the carbon dioxide of expired air, acid is then added to a measured amount of the blood, the carbon dioxide is pumped out, and measured. 2. (*for urea*): The urea is changed into ammonium carbonate by means of the enzyme urease, the ammonia is aerated over into standard acid, and the excess titrated. **Van Slyke and Fitz's m.** (*for alkali reserve*): Collect the urine for a two-hour period between meals and note amount and determine the ammonia and the titratable acid by Folin's methods. The plasma carbon dioxide capacity (C) may be calculated from the formula

$$C = 80 - 5\sqrt{\frac{D}{W}}$$

where D = rate of excretion per twenty-four hours, and W = body weight in kilograms. **Van Slyke and Meyer's m.** (*for amino-acid nitrogen*): Precipitate the proteins of the blood by means of alcohol and then proceed by Van Slyke's nitrous acid method. **Van Slyke and Palmer's m.** (*for organic acids in urine*): Remove carbonates and phosphates and titrate with acid from the turning point for phenolphthalein to the turning point for tropeolin OO. **Volhard and Arnold's m.** (*for chlorides*): Acidify the urine with nitric acid and add a known amount of silver nitrate. Titrate excess of silver nitrate with ammonium sulfocyanate, using ferric thiocyanate as indicator. **Volhard and Fahr m.,** one for determining specific gravity of urine. **Volhard and Harvey's m.** (*for chlorides*): Similar to the method of Volhard and Arnold except the silver chloride is not filtered out, the excess of silver nitrate being titrated in the original mixture. **von Fürth and Charnass' m.** (*for lactic acid in blood*): Remove the glucose and convert the lactic acid into acetaldehyde by permanganate. Combine the aldehyde with sodium bisulfite and determine the bound sulfite iodometrically. **Walker's m.** (*for iron in foods*): Ignite sample, cool, and dissolve in dilute HNO_3. Filter, oxidize, filtrate with H_2O_2, add potassium thiocyanate and compare color with standard iron solution, similarly treated. **Wallace and Diamond's m.** (*for urobilinogen*): Add Ehrlich's aldehyde reagent to a series of dilutions of the urine, note the highest dilution which shows a faint pink coloration, and express the result in terms of this dilution. **Wardrop's m.,** treatment of erectile tumors by the application of potassa fusa. **Watson's m.** (*for the induction of labor*): The successive administration of castor oil, quinine and pituitrin. **Weber's m.** (*for guanidine*): A colorimetric method based on the reaction of guanidine with an alkaline nitroprusside-ferricyanide reagent. **Welcher's m.,** determination of the total blood volume by bleeding and then washing out the blood vessels. **Welker's m.** (*for purine bodies*): Remove the phosphates with magnesia mixture, then precipitate the purine bodies with silver nitrate and ammonium hydroxide. Determine nitrogen in the precipitate by Kjeldahl's method. **Welker and Marsh's m.** (*for clarifying milk*): A method using aluminum hydroxide. **Whitehorn's m.** (*for chlorides in blood*): To the protein-free blood filtrate add nitric acid, then heat, and add an excess of silver nitrate. Titrate excess silver with thiocyanate, using ferric ammonium sulfate as indicator. **Wiechowski and Handorsky's m.** (*for allantoin*): Precipitate the urine with phosphotungstic acid, with lead acetate, and with silver acetate to remove chlorides, ammonia, and basic substances. Then add sodium acetate and 0.5 per cent mercuric acetate to precipitate the allantoin, which may be weighed, submitted to a Kjeldahl, or titrated with ammonium thiocyanate. **Wintrobe and Landsberg m.** (*for the sedimentation rate of red blood corpuscles*): Determine the amount of sedimentation after one hour, then centrifuge and measure the volume of the packed red cells. Correct the first reading by the second by means of a table. **Wolter's m.** (*for iron*): Add nitric acid to urine, evaporate to dryness, ignite, oxidize the iron with hydrogen peroxide, add potassium iodide and starch, and titrate excess of iodine with one-hundredth normal thiosulfate. **Wong's m.** (*for iron in hemoglobin*): Separate the iron in the cold by sulfuric acid and potassium persulfate. Remove the proteins and determine the iron colorimetrically by the thiocyanate reaction. **Wright's m.** 1. Treatment of wounds by irrigating first with hypertonic salt solution and then with isotonic salt solution. Vaccines may be used as adjuvants. Finally the wound is closed. 2. (*for determining the bactericidal power of blood*): To fixed amounts of the patient's serum are added decreasing amounts of the culture to be tested, incubated for twenty-four hours and then planted in nutrient bouillon. The largest number of bacteria that a constant quantity of serum is able to kill measures its bactericidal power. **Wright's modification of Buchner's m.**, the alkaline solution of pyrogallol is absorbed into the absorbent cotton stopper of the test tube, which is then pushed down far enough to permit the insertion of a rubber stopper. **Wyeth's m.**, treatment of angiomas by the injection of boiling water. **Ziehl-Neelsen's m.** See *stains, table of.* **Zsigmondy's gold number m.** See *Lange's test*, under *tests.*

methodism (meth′od-izm). The system of the Methodist school of medicine.

Methodist (meth′od-ist). 1. An ancient sect or school, which based the practice of medicine on a few simple rules and theories. This school, influenced by Asclepiades, was founded (c. 50 B.C.) by Themison of Laodicea. The Methodists believed that disease is caused either by a narrowing of the internal pores of the body (*status strictus*) or by their excessive relaxation (*status laxus*). Such extreme simplification of the nature of disease is discernible as late as the 18th century, for example, in the so-called Brunonian system (John Brown, 1735–1788). 2. A believer in or practitioner of the Methodist theory of medicine.

methodology (meth″od-ol′o-je). The science of method; the science which deals with the principles of procedure in research and study.

methohexital (meth″o-hek′sĭ-tal). Chemical name: α-dl-1-methyl-5-allyl-5-(l-methyl-2-pentynyl)barbituric acid: used as an intravenous general anesthetic.

methomania (meth″o-ma′ne-ah) [Gr. *methē* drunkenness + *mania* madness). Insanity caused by the habitual misuse of alcoholic drinks.

methopromazine (meth″o-pro′mah-zēn). Methoxypromazine.

methotrexate (meth-o′trek-sāt). Chemical name: 4-amino-10-methylfolic acid: used as a neoplastic suppressant.

methoxamine (meth-ok′sah-mēn). Chemical name: α-(1-aminoethyl)-2,5-dimethoxybenzyl alcohol: used as a sympathomimetic and pressor agent.

methoxsalen (meth-ok′sah-len). Chemical name: δ-lactone of 3-(6-hydroxy-7-methoxybenzofuranyl)acrylic acid: used in conjunction with exposure to ultraviolet light in treatment of idiopathic vitiligo.

methoxy-cyclopenteno-phenanthrene (meth-ok″se-si″klo-pen″tĕ-no-fe-nan′thrēn). A carcinogenic substance.

methoxyflurane (meth-ok″se-floo′rān). Chemical name: halogenated ethyl methyl ether: used as a general anesthetic administered by inhalation.

methoxyl (meth-ok′sil). The chemical group, $CH_3.O—$.

methoxyphenamine (meth-ok″se-fen′ah-mēn). Chemical name: 2-(o-methoxyphenyl)isopropylmethylamine: used as a sympathomimetic drug with predominant bronchodilator action.

methoxypromazine (meth-ok″se-pro′mah-zēn). Chemical name: 2-methoxy-10-(3′-dimethylaminopropyl)phenothiazine: used as a tranquilizer.

methscopolamine (meth″sko-pol′ah-min). Chemical name: epoxytropine tropate: used in parasympathetic blockade.

methsuximide (meth-suk′sĭ-mīd). Chemical name: N,2-dimethyl-2-phenylsuccinimide: used as an anticonvulsant to treat petit mal and psychomotor epilepsy.

methyl (meth′il) [Gr. *methy* wine + *hylē* wood]. The chemical group or radical $CH_3—$, sometimes abbreviated Me. **m. amylketone,** a volatile oil, $C_3H_{11}.CO.CH_3$, found in oil of cloves. **m. anthranilate,** a volatile oil, methyl ortho-aminobenzoate, $NH_2.C_6H_4.CO.O.CH_3$, the odoriferous constituent or neroli oil, bergamot, jasmine, and other essential oils. **m. benzine,** toluene. **m. chloride,** the hydrochloric acid ester of methyl alcohol, CH_3Cl. It is a gas which converted into a liquid by pressure is a valuable local anesthetic when used as a spray. **m. cyanide,** acetonitril. **m. ditannin,** tannoform. **m. ether,** a colorless, anesthetic gas, $(CH_3)_2O$. **m. ethyl-maleicimid,** a substituted pyrrole, $C_2H_5(C.CO)_2$-$(NH)CH_3$, obtained from hemoglobin and from chlorophyl. **m. ethyl-pyrrole,** a substituted pyrrole, $CH_3(C.CH)_2(NH)C_2H_5$, obtained from, and probably a constituent of, bilirubin. **m. eugenol,** a volatile oil, $C_3H_5.C_6H_3(OCH_3)_2$, found in oil of bay. **m. heptenone,** a volatile oil, CH_3CO-$(CH_2)_4CH_3$, found in lemon-grass oil. **m. hydride,** methane. **m. hydroxy-furfurol,** the furfural, $CH_3.C{:}CH.C(OH){:}C.CHO$, produced from the hexose in Molisch's test and which produces the color. **m. iodide,** a colorless or brownish liquid, CH_3I: local anesthetic. **m. methacrylate,** a plastic material sometimes used in surgical procedures and in dentistry. **m. salicylate,** natural or synthetic wintergreen oil, used as a topical application to inflamed joints. **m. sulfonate,** a crystalline, noncaustic, and nonpoisonous antiseptic. **m. telluride,** a gas, $(CH_3)_2Te$, of penetrating odor found in excreta of animals after feeding with telluric and tellurious acids.

methylal (meth′ĭ-lal). Formal, a colorless liquid, $CH_2(OMe)_2$, used as a hypnotic and anesthetic and like formaldehyde in certain chemical reactions.

methylamine (meth″il-am′in). A gaseous ptomaine $CH_3.NH_2$, from decaying fish and from comma-bacillus cultures.

methylantipyrine (meth″il-an″te-pi′rin). Tolypyrine. **m. salicylate,** tolysal.

methylarsinate (meth″il-ar′si-nāt). A salt of methylarsinic acid.

methylate (meth′ĭ-lāt). A compound of methyl alcohol and a base.

methylated (meth′ĭ-lāt-ed). Containing or combined with methyl alcohol.

methylation (meth″ĭ-la′shun). Treatment with methyl.

methylaurin (meth-il-aw′rin). A substance, $C_{23}H_{16}O_3$, derivable from rosalic acid.

methylbenzethonium (meth″il-ben″zĕ-tho′ne-um). Chemical name: benzyldimethyl{2-[2-(p-1,1,3,3-tetramethyl-butylcresoxy) ethoxy]ethyl} ammonium: used as a local anti-infective.

methylcellulose (meth″il-sel′u-lōs). A methyl ester of cellulose: used as a bulk laxative and as a suspending agent for drugs. **hydroxypropyl m.,** the propylene glycol ether of methylcellulose, in which both hydroxypropyl and methyl groups are attached to the anhydroglucose rings of cellulose by ether linkages: used as a suspending agent for drugs.

methylchloroformate (meth″il-klo″ro-for′māt). A lacrimatory gas, $ClCOOCH_3$: used as a warning agent in fumigations with hydro-cyanic acid.

methylcreosol (meth″il-kre′o-sol). A phenol, $C_9H_{12}O_2$, obtainable from wood tar creosote.

methylcytosine (meth″il-si′to-sin). A pyrimidine occurring in deoxyribonucleic acid.

methyldichlorarsin (meth″il-di″klor-ar′sin). A lethal and vesicating war gas, CH_3AsCl_2.

methylene (meth′ĭ-lēn). The bivalent hydrocarbon radical, CH_2. **m. bichloride.** 1. See *m. chloride.* 2. A mixture of methyl alcohol and chloroform: formerly used as an anesthetic agent. **m. chloride, m. dichloride,** a volatile anesthetic liquid, CH_2Cl_2, resembling chloroform: formerly used as an anesthetic in minor operations.

methylenophil (meth″ĭ-len′o-fil). 1. An element easily stainable with methylene blue. 2. Methylenophilous.

methylenophilous (meth″il-en-of′ĭ-lus) [*methylene* + Gr. *philein* to love]. Stainable with methylene blue.

methylergonovine (meth″il-er″go-no′vin). Chemical name: N-[α-(hydroxymethyl)propyl]-d-lysergamide: used as an oxytoxic.

methylglucamine (meth″il-gloo′kah-mīn). A compound prepared from D-glucose and methylamine, used in the synthesis of pharmaceuticals. **m. diatrizoate,** the N-methylglucamine salt of 3,5-diacetamido-2,4,6-triiodobenzoic acid, used as a contrast medium for roentgenography.

methylglyoxalase (meth″il-gli-oks′ah-lās). An enzyme which catalyzes the change of methylglyoxal to lactic acid.

methylglyoxalidin (meth″il-gli″oks-al′ĭ-din). Lysidin.

methylgranatonine (meth″il-grah-nat′o-nin). Pseudopelletierine.

methylguanidine (meth″il-gwan′ĭ-din). A poisonous ptomaine, $NH.C(NH)_2NH.CH_3$, from spoiled fish, etc.

methylhexaneamine (meth″il-heks-ān′ah-min). Chemical name: 1,3-dimethylamylamine: used as an inhalant to relieve nasal congestion.

methylhydantoin (meth″il-hi-dan′to-in). A crystalline compound, $CH_3.N.CO.NH.CO.CH_2$ (N and CH_2 joined by a bond), found in fresh meat, and formed by the decomposition of creatine.

methylhydrocupreine (meth″il-hi″dro-ku-pre′-in). Hydroquinine.

methylic (me-thil′ik). Containing methyl.

methylindol (meth″il-in′dol). Skatol.

methyllaurotetanine (meth″il-law″ro-tet′ah-nin). An alkaloid, $C_{20}H_{23}O_4N$, from *Litsea citrata.*

methylmelubrin (meth″il-mel′u-brin). Dipyrone.

methylmercaptan (meth″il-mer-kap′tan). A gas, methyl hydrosulfide, $CH_3.SH$, formed in the intestines by the decomposition of proteins; said to impart to the urine the odor noticed after eating asparagus.

methylmorphine (meth″il-mor′fēn). Codeine.

methylparaben (meth″il-par′ah-ben). Chemical name: methyl p-hydroxybenzoate: used as a preservative for drug solutions in 0.05 to 0.2 per cent concentrations.

methylparafynol (meth″il-par″ah-fi′nol). Chemical name: 3-methyl-1-pentyn-3-ol: used as a hypnotic and sedative.

methylphenidate (meth″il-fen′ĭ-dāt). Chemical name: methyl α-phenyl-2-piperidineacetate: used as a mild psychomotor stimulant.

methylphenyl levulosazone (meth″il-fen′-il lev″u-lo′sa-zōn). The methyl-phenyl-osazone of levulose, $CH_2OH(CHOH)_4C[:N.N(CH_3).C_6H_5]$.-$CHCH.NHN(CH_3).C_6H_5$:, homologous with glucosazone.

methylphenylhydrazine (meth″il-fe″nil-hi′-drah-zin). A reagent, $C_6H_5N(CH_3)NH_2$, by which ketoses can be distinguished from aldoses, as the former yield osazones, the latter, hydrazones.

methylprednisolone (meth″il-pred′nĭ-so-lōn). Chemical name: 11β,17α,21-trihydroxy-6α-methyl-1,4-pregnadiene-3,20-dione, having an anti-inflammatory action similar to that of prednisolone.

methylpurine (meth″il-pu′rin). See under *purine.*

methylpyridine (meth″il-pi′ri-din). A basic substance, $C_5H_4(CH_3)N$, oxidized in the body to pyridine-carboxylic acid. **m. sulfocyanate,** a crystalline, noncaustic, and nonpoisonous antiseptic.

methylquinoline (meth″il-kwin′o-lin). An oily basic substance, $C_9H_6N.CH_3$, from the secretion of the skunk.

methylrosaniline chloride (meth″il-ro-zan′i-lin klo′rīd). A faintly odorous compound, $C_{25}H_{30}ClN_3$, occurring as a dark green powder or as glistening greenish pieces with a metallic luster; soluble in alcohol, chloroform, glycerin, and water: used as a dye and in medicine as an anthelmintic and anti-infective. Called also *crystal violet, gentian violet,* and *methyl violet.*

methyltestosterone (meth″il-tes-tos′ter-ōn). An androgenic compound, 17-methyl-4-androstene-17(β)-ol-3-one.

methyltheobromine (meth″il-the″o-bro′mēn). Caffeine.

methylthionine chloride (meth″il-thi′o-nin). Methylene blue.

methylthiouracil (meth″il-thi″o-u′rah-sil). Chemical name: 6-methyl-2-thiouracil: used as a thyroid inhibitor.

methyluramine (meth″il-u-ram′in). Methylguanidine.

methylxanthine (meth″il-zan′thin). Heteroxanthine.

methyprylon (meth″ĭ-pri′lon). Chemical name: 3,3-diethyl-5-methyl-2,4-piperidinedione: used as a sedative and hypnotic.

meticortelone (met″ĭ-kor′tĕ-lōn). Trade mark for preparations of prednisolone.

meticorten (met″ĭ-kor′ten). Trade mark for a preparation of prednisone.

metmyoglobin (met-mi″o-glo′bin). A compound formed from myoglobin by oxidation of the ferrous to the ferric state with essentially ionic bonds.

metodontiasis (met″o-don-ti′ah-sis) [Gr. *meta* beyond, over + *odous* tooth]. 1. Permanent dentition. 2. Imperfect development of the teeth.

metoestrum (met-es′trum). Metestrus.

metoestrus (met-es′trus). Metestrus.

metol (me′tol). Trade mark for a photographic developer, *N*-methyl-*p*-aminophenol sulfate, $CH_3NHC_6H_4OH.H_2SO_4$, which sometimes is the cause of a dermatitis in those who use it.

metonymy (me-ton′ĭ-me) [*meta-* + Gr. *onyma* name]. Disorder of thinking in which the patient uses, instead of the correct term, a poor approximation to it.

metopagus (me-top′ah-gus). Metopopagus.

metopantralgia (met″o-pan-tral′je-ah) [Gr. *metōpon* forehead + *antron* cave + *-algia*]. Pain in the frontal sinuses.

metopantritis (met″o-pan-tri′tis). Inflammation of the frontal sinuses.

metopic (me-top′ik). Pertaining to the forehead; frontal.

metopion (me-to′pe-on). Glabella.

metopirone (met″o-pi′rōn). Trade mark for preparations of mepyrapone.

metopism (met′o-pizm). The persistence of the frontal suture.

metopo- (met′o-po) [Gr. *metōpon* forehead]. Combining form denoting relationship to the forehead.

metopodynia (met″o-po-din′e-ah) [*metopo-* + Gr. *odynē* pain). Frontal headache.

metopon (met-o′pon). 1. [Gr. *metōpon* forehead]. The anterior metopic lobule of the brain. 2. A morphine derivative, methyldihydromorphinone hydrochloride, used to relieve the pain of cancer.

metopopagus (met″o-pop′ah-gus) [*metopo-* + Gr. *pagos* thing fixed]. A craniopagus in which the fusion is in the region of the forehead.

metopoplasty (me-top′o-plas″te) [*metopo-* + Gr. *plassein* to form]. Plastic surgery of the forehead.

metoposcopy (met″o-pos′ko-pe) [*metopo-* + Gr. *skopein* to examine]. The analysis of character based on shape of the forehead.

Metorchis (met-or′kis) [*meta-* + Gr. *orchis* testicle]. A genus of flukes. *M. trunca′tus* is found in seals, deer, and cats.

metoxenous (met″ok-se′nus) [*meta-* + Gr. *xenos* host]. Requiring two hosts for the full cycle of existence: said of certain parasites.

metoxeny (met-ok′sĕ-ne). The condition of being metoxenous.

metra (me′trah) [Gr. *metra* womb]. The uterus, or womb.

metra-. See *metro-*.

metraderm (me′trah-derm) [*metra-* + Gr. *derma* skin]. The external opening of the uterus in some tapeworms (Dibothriocephalidae).

metralgia (me-tral′je-ah) [*metra-* + *-algia*]. Pain in the uterus.

metranoikter (me″trah-no-ik′ter). An instrument for dilating the uterine cervix, consisting of two blades which are forcibly spread by the action of a spring.

metratome (me′trah-tōm). Hysterotome.

metratomy (me-trat′o-me). Hysterotomy.

metratonia (me″trah-to′ne-ah) [*metra-* + Gr. *atonia* atony]. Uterine atony.

metratrophia (me″trah-tro′fe-ah) [*metra-* + Gr. *atrophia* atrophy]. Uterine atrophy.

metrazol (met′rah-zol). Trade mark for preparations of pentylenetetrazol.

metre (me′ter). Meter.

metrechoscopy (met″re-kos′ko-pe) [Gr. *metron* measure + *ēchō* sound + *skopein* to examine]. Combined mensuration, auscultation, and inspection.

metrectasia (me″trek-ta′se-ah) [*metra-* + Gr. *ektasis* extension]. Dilatation of the nonpregnant uterus.

metrectomy (me-trek′to-me) [*metra-* + Gr. *ektomē* excision]. The surgical removal of the uterus; hysterectomy.

metrectopia (me-trek-to′pe-ah) [*metra-* + Gr. *ektopos* displaced + *-ia*]. Uterine displacement.

metreurynter (me″troo-rin′ter) [*metra-* + Gr. *eurynein* to stretch]. An inflatable bag for dilating the cervical canal of the uterus.

metreurysis (me-troo′ri-sis). Dilatation of the uterine cervix with the metreurynter.

metria (me′tre-ah). Any inflammatory condition during the puerperium.

metric (met′rik) [Gr. *metron* measure]. 1. Pertaining to measures or measurement. 2. Having the meter as a basis.

metriocephalic (met″re-o-se-fal′ik) [Gr. *metrios* moderate + *kephalē* head]. Having a skull with a vertical index between 72 and 77.

metritis (me-tri′tis) [*metra-* + *-itis*]. Inflammation of the uterus. Several varieties are named, according to the part of the organ affected—cervical, corporeal, interstitial, and parenchymatous. **m. dis′secans, dissecting m.,** metritis characterized by the passage of fragments or large masses of the necrotic uterine wall. **puerperal m.,** infection of the uterus of the puerperal woman.

metro-, metra- (me′tro, me′trah) [Gr. *metra* uterus]. Combining form denoting relationship to the uterus. See also *hystero-*, and words beginning therewith.

metrocampsis (me″tro-kamp′sis) [*metro-* + Gr. *kampsis* bending]. Uterine flexion.

metrocarcinoma (me″tro-kar″sĭ-no′mah). Uterine carcinoma.

metrocele (me′tro-sēl) [*metro-* + Gr. *kēlē* hernia]. Hernia of the uterus.

metrocolpocele (me″tro-kol′po-sēl) [*metro-* + Gr. *kolpos* vagina + *kēlē* hernia]. Hernia of the uterus into the vagina.

metrocyte (me′tro-sīt) [Gr. *mētēr* mother + *-cyte*]. 1. A mother cell. 2. A large uninuclear cell containing hemoglobin: supposed to be the mother cell of the red corpuscles of the blood.

metrodynia (me″tro-din′e-ah) [*metro-* + Gr. *odynē* pain]. Pain in the uterus.

metro-endometritis (me″tro-en″do-me-tri′tis). Combined inflammation of the uterus and its mucous membranes.

metrofibroma (me″tro-fi-bro′mah) [*metro-* + *fibroma*]. Fibroma of the uterus.

metrogenous (me-troj′e-nus). Derived from the uterus.

metrogonorrhea (met″ro-gon-o-re′ah). Gonorrhea of the uterus.

metrography (me-trog′rah-fe) Hysterography.

metrology (me-trol′o-je) [Gr. *metron* measure + *-logy*]. The science which deals with measurement.

metromalacoma (me″tro-mal-ah-ko′mah) [*metro-* + Gr. *malakos* soft]. Abnormal softening of the uterus.

metromalacosis (me″tro-mal″ah-ko′sis). Metromalacoma.

metromania (me″tro-ma′ne-ah). 1. [*metro-* + Gr. *mania* madness]. Nymphomania. 2. [Gr. *metron* measure + *mania* madness]. A mania for writing verse.

metromenorrhagia (me″tro-men″o-ra′je-ah). Menorrhagia.

metronoscope (me-tron′o-skōp). An instrument for giving exercises in rhythmic reading to correct poorly coordinated ocular movements.

metropathia (me″tro-path′e-ah). Metropathy. **m. haemorrha′gica,** essential uterine hemorrhage.

metropathic (me-tro-path′ik). Pertaining to or characterized by uterine disorder.

metropathy (me-trop′ah-the) [*metro-* + Gr. *pathos* suffering]. Any uterine disease or disorder.

metroperitoneal (me″tro-per″ĭ-to-ne′al). Pertaining to the uterus and peritoneum, or communicating with the uterine and peritoneal cavities, as a metroperitoneal fistula.

metroperitonitis (me″tro-per″ĭ-to-ni′tis) [*metro-* + *peritonitis*]. Inflammation of the peritoneum about the uterus, or peritonitis resulting from infection after metritis.

metrophlebitis (me″tro-fle-bi′tis) [*metro-* + Gr. *phleps* vein + *-itis*]. Inflammation of the veins of the uterus.

metropine (met′ro-pin). Trade mark for preparations of methyl atropine nitrate.

metropolis (me-trop′o-lis) [Gr. *mētropolis* mother-state, as opposed to her colonies]. The area in which a particular organism commonly occurs.

metroptosis (me″tro-to′sis) [*metro-* + Gr. *ptōsis* falling]. Falling, or prolapse of the uterus.

metrorrhagia (me″tro-ra′je-ah) [*metro-* + Gr. *rhēgnynai* to burst out]. Uterine bleeding, usually of normal amount, occurring at completely irregular intervals, the period of flow sometimes being prolonged. **m. myopath'ica,** uterine hemorrhage due to insufficient contraction of uterine muscles after parturition.

metrorrhea (me"tro-re'ah) [*metro-* + Gr. *rhoia* flow]. A free or abnormal uterine discharge.

metrorrhexis (me"tro-rek'sis) [*metro-* + Gr. *rhēxis* rupture]. Rupture of the uterus.

metrosalpingitis (me"tro-sal"pin-ji'tis) [*metro-* + Gr. *salpinx* tube + *-itis*]. Inflammation of the uterus and oviducts.

metrosalpingography (me"tro-sal"ping-gog'-rah-fe). Hysterosalpingography.

metroscope (me'tro-skōp). Hysteroscope.

metrostasis (me-tros'tah-sis) [Gr. *metron* measure + *stasis* a setting]. A state in which the length of a muscle fiber is relatively fixed, and at which length it contracts and relaxes.

metrostaxis (me"tro-stak'sis) [*metro-* + Gr. *staxis* a dripping]. A slight but persistent escape of blood from the uterus.

metrostenosis (me"tro-ste-no'sis) [*metro-* + Gr. *stenosis* contraction]. Contraction or stenosis of the cavity of the uterus.

metrotherapy (met"ro-ther'ah-pe) [Gr. *metron* measure + *therapeia* treatment]. Treatment by measurement, i.e., by demonstrating to the patient his improvement by means of accurate measurements of the increase in the voluntary movements of an impaired joint.

metrotome (me'tro-tōm). Hysterotome.

metrotomy (me-trot'o-me). Hysterotomy.

metrotoxin (me"tro-tok'sin). A substance from the pregnant uterus which is thought to exert an inhibitory action on the ovarian function.

metrotubography (me"tro-tu-bog'rah-fe). Hysterosalpingography.

metro-urethrotome (me"tro-u-re'thro-tōm) [Gr. *metron* measure + *urethrotome*]. A urethrotome with a device which regulates the amount of cutting.

-metry (Gr. *metrein* to measure]. Word termination meaning the act of measuring, or the measurement of, the object measured being indicated by the word stem to which it is affixed, as *hemoglobinometry*.

M. et sig. Abbreviation for L. *mi'sce et sig'na*, mix and write a label.

Mett's test (mets) [Emil Ludwig Paul *Mett*, German physician of the 19th century]. See under *tests*.

metubine (mĕ-tu'bin). Trade mark for a preparation of dimethyl tubocurarine.

metycaine (met'ĭ-kān). Trade mark for preparations of piperocaine.

Meulengracht's diet, method (moi'len-grakts) [Einar *Meulengracht*, Danish internist, born 1887]. See under *diet* and *method*.

Mev. Abbreviation for *million electron volts;* the equivalent of 3.82 $\times$ 10^{-14} gram calories, or 1.6 $\times$ 10^{-6} ergs.

Meyer's disease (mi'erz) [Hans Wilhelm *Meyer*, Danish physician, 1824–1898]. Adenoid vegetations of the pharynx.

Meyer's line, organ (mi'erz) [Georg Hermann v. *Meyer*, anatomist in Zürich, 1815–1892]. See under *line* and *organ*.

Meyer's solution (mi'erz) [Willy *Meyer*, American surgeon, 1854–1932]. See under *solution*.

Meyer's theory (mi'erz) [Adolf *Meyer*, Baltimore psychiatrist, 1866–1950]. See under *theory*.

Meyerhof (mi'er-hof"), Otto Fritz. German physiologist, 1884–1951, noted for his work on the metabolism of muscles; co-winner, with Archibald Vivian Hill, of the Nobel prize for medicine and physiology in 1922.

Meynert's bundle, commissure, fasciculus (mi'nerts) [Theodor Herman *Meynert*, professor of neurology and psychiatry at Vienna, 1833–1892]. See under the nouns.

Meynet's nodes (ma-nāz') [Paul Claude Hyacinthe *Meynet*, French physician, 1831–1892). See under *node*.

mezereon (me-ze're-on). Mezereum.

mezereum (me-ze're-um) [L.]. The plant *Daphne mezereum*, a shrub of Europe. Its bark is diaphoretic, diuretic, and stimulant.

mezzo-aortitis (mez"o-a"or-ti'tis). Meso-aortitis.

Mf. Abbreviation for *Microfilaria*.

μf. Abbreviation for *microfarad*.

M. flac. Abbreviation for L. *membra'na flac'cida* (pars flaccida membranae tympani [N A]).

M. ft. Abbreviation for L. *mistu'ra fi'at*, let a mixture be made.

M.G. Abbreviation for *mesiogingival*.

Mg. Chemical symbol for *magnesium*.

mg. Abbreviation for *milligram*.

mγ. Abbreviation for *milligamma* (millimicrogram, or nanogram).

μg. Abbreviation for *microgram*.

μγ. Abbreviation for *microgamma* (micromicrogram, or picogram).

$MgCl_2$. Magnesium chloride.

MgO. Magnesium oxide.

$MgSO_4$. Magnesium sulfate.

M.H.D. Abbreviation for *minimum hemolytic dose*.

mHg. Symbol for *millimeters of mercury*.

mho (mo). The unit of electric conductivity.

miana (mi-an'ah). A relapsing fever in Persia.

miasm (mi'azm). Miasma.

miasma (mi-az'mah) [Gr. "defilement, pollution"]. A supposed noxious emanation from the soil or earth, alleged to be the cause of diseases endemic in certain areas, such as malaria, before the true cause became known. See *tellurism*.

miasmatic (mi"az-mat'ik). Pertaining to miasma.

Mibelli's disease (me-bel'ēz) [Vittorio *Mibelli*, Italian dermatologist, 1860–1910]. Porokeratosis.

mic. pan. Abbreviation for L. *mi'ca pa'nis*, bread crumb.

mica (mi'kah) [L.]. A crumb or grain; a small particle. **m. pa'nis,** bread crumb.

mication (mi-ka'shun). Any quick motion, such as winking.

micella (mi-sel'ah). See *micelle*.

micelle (mi-sel'). 1. A hypothetical vital unit of living matter, visible or invisible, made up of one or more molecules, and having the power of growth and division. See also *biophore*. Similar terms which have been used in various theories are: *bioplast, bioblast, chondria, gemma, gemmule, idioblast, idiosome, microzyme, pangen, physiologic unit, plastidule, protomere, somacule, tagmata*. 2. A supermolecular colloid particle, most often a packet of chain molecules in parallel arrangement.

Michaelis's rhomboid (me-ka'lēz) [Gustav A. *Michaelis*, Kiel gynecologist, 1798–1848]. See under *rhomboid*.

Michel's clamps (me-shelz') [Paul *Michel*, French surgeon, late 19th century]. See under *clamp*.

micr-. See *micro-*.

micra (mi'krah). Plural of *micron*.

micracoustic (mi"krah-kōōs'tik) [*micr-* + Gr. *akoustikos* acoustic]. 1. Rendering very faint sounds audible. 2. An instrument which renders faint sounds audible.

micranatomy (mi"kran-at'o-me) [*micro-* + *anatomy*]. Microscopical anatomy; histology.

micrangiopathy (mi"kran-je-op'ah-the). Microangiopathy.

micrangium (mi-kran'je-um). A capillary.

micranthine (mi-kran'thin). A crystalline alkaloid, $C_{36}H_{32}N_2O_6$, from *Daphnandra micrantha*.

micrencephalia (mi"kren-se-fa'le-ah). Micrencephaly.

micrencephalon (mi″kren-sef′ah-lon) [*micr-* + Gr. *enkephalos* brain]. 1. A small brain. 2. The cerebellum.

micrencephalous (mi″kren-sef′ah-lus). Having a small brain.

micrencephaly (mi″kren-sef′ah-le) [*micr-* + Gr. *enkephalos* brain]. Abnormal smallness of the brain.

micrergy (mi′krer-je). Micrurgy.

micro- (mi′kro) [Gr. *mikros* small]. Combining form designating small size; used in naming units of measurement to indicate one-millionth (10^{-6}) of the unit designated by the root with which it is combined.

microabscess (mi″kro-ab′ses). A minute abscess, visible only under a microscope. **Pautrier m.,** a collection of hyperchromatic mononuclear cells within the epidermis, characterizing malignant lymphoma of the skin, particularly mycosis fungoides.

microadenopathy (mi″kro-ad″e-nop′ah-the) [*micro-* + Gr. *adēn* gland + *pathos* disease]. Disease of the small lymphatics.

microaerobion (mi″kro-a″er-o′be-on). A microaerophilic organism.

microaerophile (mi″kro-a′er-o-fīl). A microaerophilic microorganism.

microaerophilic (mi″kro-a′er-o-fil″ik) [*micro-* + *aero-* + Gr. *philein* to love]. Growing best in only a small amount of atmospheric oxygen: said of bacteria.

microaerophilous (mi″kro-a″er-of′ĭ-lus). Microaerophilic.

microaerotonometer (mi″kro-a″er-o-to-nom′e-ter). An instrument for measuring volume of gases in the blood.

microanalysis (mi″kro-ah-nal′ĭ-sis) [*micro-* + *analysis*]. The chemical analysis of minute quantities of material.

microanatomy (mi″kro-ah-nat′o-me). Histology, especially organology.

microaneurysm (mi″kro-an′u-rizm). A minute aneurysm, visible only under the microscope.

microangiopathic (mi″kro-an″je-o-path′ik). Pertaining to or characterized by microangiopathy.

microangiopathy (mi″kro-an″je-op′ah-the) [*micro-* + Gr. *angeion* vessel + *pathos* disease]. Disease of the small blood vessels. **thrombotic m.,** a condition characterized by fever, hemolytic anemia, thrombocytopenic purpura, and neurological disturbances, occlusion of small blood vessels being widespread and eosinophilic thrombi a dominant pathological feature.

microangioscopy (mi″kro-an″je-os′ko-pe). Capillaroscopy.

microbacillary (mi″kro-bas′ĭ-lār″e). Bacterial.

microbacteria (mi″kro-bak-te′re-ah) [L.]. Plural of *microbacterium*.

Microbacterium (mi″kro-bak-te′re-um). A genus of microorganisms of the family Corynebacteriaceae, order Eubacteriales, made up of gram-positive rods found in dairy products and characterized by relatively high resistance to heat.

microbacterium (mi″kro-bak-te′re-um), pl. *microbacte′ria* [L.]. 1. An organism belonging to the genus Microbacterium. 2. A microorganism.

microbalance (mi′kro-bal″ans). A balance for measuring minute changes in weight.

microbe (mi′krōb) [*micro-* + Gr. *bios* life]. A minute living organism, a microphyte or microzoon; applied especially to those minute forms of life which are capable of causing disease in animals, including bacteria, protozoa, and fungi.

microbemia (mi″kro-be′me-ah). Microbiemia.

microbial (mi-kro′be-al). Pertaining to or caused by microbes.

microbian (mi-kro′be-an). 1. Pertaining to or of the nature of a microbe. 2. A microbe.

microbic (mi-kro′bik). Of or pertaining to microbes.

microbicidal (mi-kro″bĭ-si′dal) [*microbe* + L. *caedere* to kill]. Destructive to microbes.

microbicide (mi-kro′bĭ-sid) [*microbe* + L. *caedere* to kill]. An agent that destroys microbes.

microbid (mi′kro-bid). Any skin lesion due to allergy to a microorganism or its products.

microbiemia (mi″kro-bi-e′me-ah). The presence of microbes in the blood; bacillemia.

microbioassay (mi″kro-bi″o-as′a). Determination of the active power of a nutrient or other factor by noting its effect upon the growth of a microorganism, as compared with the effect of a standard preparation.

microbiohemia (mi″kro-bi″o-he′me-ah) [*micro-* + Gr. *bios* life + *haima* blood]. A disease condition resulting from the presence of microbes in the blood.

microbiological (mi″kro-bi″o-loj′ĭ-kal). Pertaining to microbiology.

microbiologist (mi″kro-bi-ol′o-jist). One expert and learned in microbiology.

microbiology (mi″kro-bi-ol′o-je) [*micro-* + Gr. *bios* life + *-logy*]. The science which deals with the study of microorganisms, including bacteria, molds, and pathogenic protozoa. As generally employed the term is synonymous with bacteriology.

microbion (mi-kro′be-on). Microbes.

microbionation (mi-kro″bĭ-o-na′shun). Bacterination.

microbiophobia (mi-kro″bĭ-o-fo′be-ah) [*microbe* + *phobia*]. A morbid dread of microbes.

microbiophotometer (mi″kro-bi″o-fo-tom′e-ter). An apparatus for measuring the growth of bacterial cultures by recording their increasing turbidity.

microbioscope (mi″kro-bi′o-skōp) [*micro-* + Gr. *bios* life + *skopein* to examine]. A microscope for examining microbes or for studying living tissue.

microbiota (mi″kro-bi-o′tah). The microscopic living organisms of a region; the combined microflora and microfauna of a region.

microbiotic (mi″kro-bi-ot′ik). Pertaining to the microbiota, or to microscopic living organisms.

microbism (mi′kro-bizm). Infection with microbes. **latent m.,** the presence in the body of inactive organisms which only await favorable conditions to become active.

microbivorous (mi″kro-biv′o-rus) [*microbe* + L. *vorare* to devour]. Devouring or dissolving bacteria; bacteriophagic.

microblast (mi′kro-blast) [*micro-* + Gr. *blastos* germ]. An erythroblast of small size, i.e., 5 μ or less in diameter. Cf. *erythroblast.*

microblepharia (mi″kro-ble-fa′re-ah) [*micro-* + Gr. *blepharon* eyelid + *-ia*]. Abnormal smallness of the eyelids.

microblepharon (mi″kro-blef′ah-ron). An abnormally small eyelid.

microbrachia (mi″kro-bra′ke-ah) [*micro-* + Gr. *brachiōn* arm]. Abnormal smallness of the arms.

microbrachius (mi″kro-bra′ke-us) [*micro-* + Gr. *brachiōn* arm]. A fetus with preternaturally small arms.

microbrenner (mi″kro-bren′er) [*micro-* + Ger. *Brenner* burner]. A needle-pointed electric cautery.

microby (mi′kro-be). Microbiology.

microcalorie (mi″kro-kal′o-re). The heat required to raise 1 cc. of distilled water from 0 to 1°C.

microcalory (mi″kro-kal′o-re). Microcalorie.

microcardia (mi″kro-kar′de-ah) [*micro-* + Gr. *kardia* heart]. Smallness of the heart.

microcardius (mi″kro-kar′de-us). An individual with an abnormally small heart.

microcaulia (mi″kro-kaw′le-ah) [*micro-* + Gr. *kaulos* penis]. Abnormal smallness of the penis.

microcentrum (mi″kro-sen′trum) [*micro-* + Gr. *kentron* center]. Centrosome.

microcephalia (mi″kro-se-fa′le-ah). Microcephaly.

microcephalic (mi″kro-se-fal′ik). Pertaining to or exhibiting microcephalia.

microcephalism (mi″kro-sef′ah-lizm). Microcephalia.

microcephalous (mi″kro-sef′ah-lus). Microcephalic.

microcephalus (mi″kro-sef′ah-lus). An idiot or fetus with a very small head.

microcephaly (mi″kro-sef′ah-le). [*micro-* + Gr. *kephalē* head]. Abnormal smallness of the head.

microcheilia (mi″kro-ki′le-ah) [*micro-* + Gr. *cheilos* lip]. Abnormal smallness of the lips.

microcheiria (mi″kro-ki′re-ah) [*micro-* + Gr. *cheir* hand + *-ia*]. Abnormal smallness of the hands, as a result of hypoplasia of all the skeletal elements.

microchemical (mi″kro-kem′ĭ-kal). Pertaining to microchemistry.

microchemistry (mi″kro-kem′is-tre) [*micro-* + *chemistry*]. Minute chemical investigation; chemistry which deals with minute quantities (a few milligrams) of substances, using apparatus of small size.

microcinematography (mi″kro-sin″e-mah-tog′-rah-fe). The making of moving picture photographs of microscopic subjects.

microclimate (mi″kro-kli′mit). The immediate climatic environment, as that of a vector insect.

microclyster (mi″kro-klis′ter) [*micro-* + *clyster*]. A rectal injection of a small amount of substance.

microcnemia (mi″kro-ne′me-ah) [*micro-* + Gr. *knēmē* tibia). Abnormal shortness of the lower leg.

Micrococcaceae (mi″kro-kok-ka′se-e). A family of Schizomycetes (order Eubacteriales), made up of spherical cells dividing primarily in two or three planes, and sometimes remaining in contact after division. It includes six genera, *Gaff′kya, Methanococ′cus, Micrococ′cus, Peptococ′cus, Sarci′na,* and *Staphylococ′cus.*

Micrococcus (mi″kro-kok′us). A genus of microorganisms of the family Micrococcaceae, order Eubacteriales, spherical, gram-positive cells, usually occurring in irregular masses, saprophytic and nonpathogenic forms found in soil, water, etc. Sixteen species have been recognized.

micrococcus (mi″kro-kok′us). 1. An organism of the genus *Micrococcus.* 2. A spherical microorganism of extremely small size.

microcolon (mi″kro-ko′lon). An abnormally small colon.

microcolony (mi′kro-kol″o-ne). A microscopical colony of bacteria.

microcolorimeter (mi″kro-kol″o-rim′e-ter). A colorimeter for use with small quantities of blood.

microconidium (mi″kro-ko-nid′e-um). The smaller form of conidium or exospore of certain of the higher parasitic fungi.

microcoria (mi″kro-ko′re-ah) [*micro-* + Gr. *korē* pupil]. Smallness of the pupil.

microcornea (mi″kro-kor′ne-ah) [*micro-* + *cornea*]. Unusual smallness of the cornea.

microcosmic (mi″kro-koz′mik) [*micro-* + Gr. *kosmos* world]. Pertaining to or derived from the human body (man was formerly spoken of as the *microcosm,* or little world; that is, as an epitome of the universe).

microcoulomb (mi″kro-koo′lom). A unit of quantity of current electricity, being one one-millionth (10^{-6}) of a coulomb. Abbreviated μcoul.

microcoustic (mi″kro-koo′stik) [*micro-* + Gr. *akouein* to hear]. 1. Rendering feeble sounds audible. 2. An apparatus for such purpose.

microcrania (mi″kro-kra′ne-ah). Abnormal smallness of the skull, the cranial cavity being reduced in all diameters, and the facial area being disproportionately large in comparison.

microcrith (mi′kro-krith) [*micro-* + *crith*]. The weight of one atom of hydrogen.

microcrystal (mi′kro-kris″tal). An extremely minute crystal.

microcrystalline (mi″kro-kris′tal-īn) [*micro-* + *crystalline*]. Made up of minute crystals.

microcurie (mi″kro-ku′re). A unit of radioactivity, being one one-millionth (10^{-6}) curie, or the quantity of radioactive material in which the number of nuclear disintegrations is 3.7×10^4 per second. Abbreviated μc.

microcurie-hour (mi′kro-ku″re-owr″). A unit of dose equivalent to that obtained by exposure for one hour to radioactive material disintegrating at the rate of 3.7×10^4 atoms per second. Abbreviated μc-hr.

Microcyclus (mi″kro-si′klus). A genus of microorganisms of the family Spirillaceae, suborder Pseudomonadineae, order Pseudomonadales, made up of non-motile small, slightly curved rods which during growth form a closed ring. The type species is *M. aqua′ticus.*

microcyst (mi′kro-sist) [*micro-* + Gr. *kystis* sac, bladder]. A very small cyst.

microcystometer (mi″kro-sis-tom′e-ter). A small portable cystometer.

microcytase (mi″kro-si′tās). A cytase formed by microphages and capable of dissolving bacteria. See *macrocytase.*

microcyte (mi′kro-sīt) [*micro-* + *-cyte*]. An abnormally small erythrocyte, i.e., one 5 microns or less in diameter.

microcythemia (mi″kro-si-the′me-ah) [*microcyte* + Gr. *haima* blood + *-ia*]. A condition in which the erythrocytes are smaller than normal.

microcytosis (mi″kro-si-to′sis). Microcythemia.

microdactylia (mi″kro-dak-til′e-ah). Microdactyly.

microdactyly (mi″kro-dak′tĭ-le) [*micro-* + Gr. *daktylos* finger]. Abnormal smallness of the digits.

microdentism (mi″kro-den′tizm). Microdontia.

microdetermination (mi″kro-de-ter″mĭ-na′-shun). A chemical examination in which minute quantities of the substance to be examined are used.

microdissection (mi″kro-di-sek′shun). Dissection of tissue or cells under the microscope.

microdont (mi′kro-dont) [*micro-* + Gr. *odous* tooth]. Having a dental index below 42.

microdontia (mi″kro-don′she-ah). Abnormal smallness of the teeth. It may affect a single tooth, or all of them (*generalized m.*), and be true or only relative.

microdontic (mi″kro-don′tik). Pertaining to or characterized by microdontia.

microdontism (mi″kro-don′tizm). Microdontia.

microdosage (mi′kro-do″sij). Dosage in small quantities.

microdose (mi′kro-dōs). A very small dose.

microecosystem (mi″kro-e″ko-sis′tem). A miniature ecological system, occurring naturally or produced in the laboratory for experimental purposes.

microencephaly (mi″kro-en-sef′ah-le). Micrencephaly.

microerythrocyte (mi″kro-e-rith′ro-sīt). Microcyte.

micro-estimation (mi″kro-es″tĭ-ma′shun). Microdetermination.

microfarad (mi″kro-far′ad). A unit of electrical capacity, being one one-millionth of a farad (10^{-6} f.). Abbreviated μf.

microfauna (mi″kro-faw′nah). The animal life, visible only under the microscope, which is present in or characteristic of a special location.

microfibril (mi″kro-fi′bril). An extremely small fibril.

microfilaria (mi″kro-fi-la′re-ah). The prelarval stage of Filarioidea in the blood of man and in the tissues of the vector. This term is sometimes used as a genus name and is then spelled with a capital M. **m. bancrof′ti,** the microfilaria of *Wuchereria bancrofti.* **m. streptocer′ca** is the larval form of *Onchocerca volvulus* and is found in cutaneous lesions of the natives of the Gold Coast.

microfilm (mi′kro-film). 1. A trade term for 16- or 35-millimeter film to be used in high-speed automatic machines for the photographic reproduction, in greatly reduced size, of books, documents, forms, or other record files. 2. To photographically reproduce, in greatly reduced size, on film specially designed for the purpose.

microflora (mi″kro-flo′rah). The plant life, visible only under the microscope, which is present in or characteristic of a special location.

microgamete (mi″kro-gam′ēt) [*micro-* + Gr. *gametēs* spouse]. The male gamete of the malarial plasmodium. See under *gamete.*

microgametocyte (mi″kro-gah-me′to-sīt) [*micro-* + Gr. *gametēs* spouse + *-cyte*]. The male gametocyte.

microgamma (mi″kro-gam′mah). Picogram.

microgamy (mi-krog′ah-me). Conjugation or fusion when the gametes are smaller than the somatic cells.

microgastria (mi″kro-gas′tre-ah) [*micro-* + Gr. *gastēr* stomach + *-ia*]. Congenital smallness of the stomach.

microgenesis (mi″kro-jen′e-sis) [*micro-* + Gr. *genesis* production]. Abnormally small development of a part.

microgenia (mi″kro-je′ne-ah) [*micro-* + Gr. *geneion* chin]. Abnormal smallness of the chin.

microgenitalism (mi″kro-jen′ĭ-tal-izm) [*micro-* + *genitalism*]. Smallness of the external genitals.

microglia (mi-krog′le-ah). That type of nerve tissue which consists of small interstitial cells, probably of mesodermal origin. The cells are of various forms and may have slender branched processes. They are migratory and act as phagocytes to waste products of nerve tissue. Called also *Hortega cell, compound granular corpuscle, gitter cell.*

microgliacyte (mi-krog′le-ah-sīt). Microgliocyte.

microgliocyte (mi-krog′le-o-sīt) [*microglia* + *-cyte*]. The early cell which develops into a microglia cell.

microgliomatosis (mi″kro-gli″o-mah-to′sis). A condition characterized by the formation of tumors containing microglia.

microglossia (mi″kro-glos′e-ah) [*micro-* + Gr. *glōssa* tongue + *-ia*]. Undersize of the tongue.

micrognathia (mi″kro-na′the-ah) [*micro-* + Gr. *gnathos* jaw + *-ia*]. Unusual or undue smallness of the lower jaw, with recession of the chin.

microgonioscope (mi″kro-go′ne-o-skōp) [*micro-* + Gr. *gōnia* angle + *skopein* to examine]. An instrument for observing and measuring small angles: used in examining the eye in glaucoma.

microgonite (mi″kro-gon′īt). A small gonite.

microgram (mi′kro-gram). A unit of mass (weight) of the metric system, being one one-millionth of a gram (10^{-6} Gm.), or one one-thousandth of a milligram (10^{-3} mg.). Abbreviated μg. or mcg.

micrograph (mi′kro-graf). 1. An instrument for recording extremely minute movements. It acts by making a greatly magnified record on a photographic film of the minute motions of a diaphragm. 2. The photograph of a minute object or specimen (tissue, etc.) as seen through a microscope. **electron m.,** the photograph of an object through an electron microscope.

micrographia (mi″kro-gra′fe-ah) [*micro-* + Gr. *graphein* to write]. A reduction in the size of the lettering of the writer in comparison with his normal writing.

micrography (mi-krog′rah-fe) [*micro-* + Gr. *graphein* to write]. 1. An account of microscopical objects. 2. The writing of very small letters. 3. Examination with the microscope.

microgyria (mi″kro-jir′e-ah) [*micro-* + Gr. *gyros* + *-ia*]. Polymicrogyria.

microgyrus (mi″kro-ji′rus), pl. *microgy′ri* [*micro-* + *gyrus*]. An abnormally small, malformed convolution of the brain.

microhematocrit (mi″kro-he-mat′o-krit). The rapid determination of packed cell volume of erythrocytes of an extremely small quantity of blood, by use of a capillary tube and a high speed centrifuge.

microhepatia (mi″kro-he-pat′e-ah) [*micro-* + Gr. *hēpar* liver]. Smallness of the liver.

microhistology (mi″kro-his-tol′o-je) [*micro-* + *histology*]. Microscopical histology.

microhm (mi′krōm) [*micro-* + *ohm*]. One millionth part of an ohm.

microincineration (mi″kro-in-sin″er-a′shun). The incineration of minute specimens of tissue or other substance, for identification from the ash of the elements composing it.

microkinematography (mi″kro-kin″e-mah-tog′rah-fe) [*micro-* + Gr. *kinēma* movement + *graphein* to write]. The making of moving pictures of microscopical objects.

microlecithal (mi″kro-les′ĭ-thal) [*micro-* + Gr. *lekithos* yolk]. Having a small amount of yolk.

microlentia (mi″kro-len′she-ah). Microphakia.

microlesion (mi″kro-le′zhun). A minute lesion.

microleukoblast (mi″kro-lu′ko-blast). Myeloblast.

microliter (mi′kro-le″ter) [Fr. *microlitre; micro-* + *liter*]. A thousandth part of a milliliter or a millionth part of a liter. Usually abbreviated μl.

microlith (mi′kro-lith) [*micro-* + Gr. *lithos* stone]. A minute concretion or calculus.

microlithiasis (mi″kro-lĭ-thi′ah-sis) [*micro-* + *lithiasis*]. The formation of minute concretions in an organ. **m. alveola′ris pulmo′num, pulmonary alveolar m.,** a condition simulating pulmonary tuberculosis, with deposition in the alveoli of the lungs of minute calculi, which appear roentgenographically as fine, sandlike mottling.

micrology (mi-krol′o-je) [*micro-* + *-logy*]. The science dealing with the preparation and handling of minute objects for microscopical study.

microlymphoidocyte (mi″kro-lim-foi′do-sīt). A small, nongranular, immature lymphoidocyte.

micromandible (mi″kro-man′dĭ-b′l). Extreme smallness of the mandible.

micromania (mi″kro-ma′ne-ah) [*micro-* + Gr. *mania* madness]. A delusional belief that one's own body has become reduced in size or his personality reduced in importance.

micromanipulator (mi″kro-mah-nip′u-la″tor). An attachment to a microscope for manipulating tiny instruments used in examination and dissection of minute objects under the microscope.

micromastia (mi″kro-mas′te-ah). Micromazia.

micromazia (mi″kro-ma′ze-ah) [*micro-* + Gr. *mazos* breast]. Abnormal smallness of the mamma.

micromegalopsia (mi″kro-meg″ah-lop′se-ah) [*micro-* + Gr. *megas* large + *opsis* vision]. The condition in which objects appear too small or too large or too small and too large by turns.

micromegaly (mi″kro-meg′ah-le) [*micro-* + Gr. *megas* great]. Progeria.

micromelia (mi″kro-me′le-ah) [*micro-* + Gr. *melos* limb + *-ia*]. A developmental anomaly characterized by abnormal smallness or shortness of the limbs.

micromelus (mi-krom′e-lus). An individual exhibiting micromelia.

micromere (mi′kro-mēr) [*micro-* + Gr. *meros* part]. One of the small blastomeres formed by unequal cleavage of a fertilized ovum, located in the animal hemisphere and dividing more rapidly than the macromeres of the vegetal hemisphere.

micrometabolism (mi″kro-mĕ-tab′o-lism). Metabolism as studied through the ultramicroscopic particles of the serum and body cells.

micrometeorology (mi″kro-me″te-er-ol′o-je). That branch of meteorology dealing with the effects on living organisms of the extra-organic aspects of the physical environment within a few inches of the surface of the earth.

micrometer (mi-krom′e-ter) [*micro-* + Gr. *metron* measure]. An instrument for measuring objects seen through the microscope. **diffraction m.,** halometer. **eyepiece m.,** a micrometer that is used in connection with the eyepiece of a microscope. **filar m.,** an eyepiece micrometer in which the micrometer screw acts upon a slide carrying a movable wire: one revolution of the screw moves the wire 1 mm. across the field. **ocular m.,** eyepiece m. **stage m.,** a micrometer fastened to the stage of a microscope.

micrometer (mi′kro-me″ter). Micron.

micromethod (mi″kro-meth′od). Any technique involving use of exceedingly small quantities of material.

micrometry (mi-krom′e-tre). The measurement of microscopic objects.

micromicro- (mi″kro-mi′kro). A prefix used in naming units of measurement to indicate one-millionth of one-millionth (10^{-12}) of the unit designated by the root with which it is combined. Now being supplanted by the prefix *pico-*.

micromicrocurie (mi″kro-mi″kro-ku′re). One-millionth (10^{-6}) microcurie, or 10^{-12} curie. Abbreviated $\mu\mu$c. Called also *picocurie.*

micromicrogram (mi″kro-mi′kro-gram). One-millionth (10^{-6}) microgram, or 10^{-12} gram. Abbreviated $\mu\mu$g or $\mu\gamma$. Called also *picogram.*

micromicron (mi-kro-mi′kron). A unit of linear measure in the metric system, being 10^{-6} micron, 10^{-9} millimeter, or 10^{-12} meter. Abbreviated $\mu\mu$.

micromilligram (mi″kro-mil′lĭ-gram). A unit of mass (weight) in the metric system, being 10^{-6} milligram, or 10^{-9} gram. Abbreviated μmg. Called also *nanogram.*

micromillimeter (mi″kro-mil′lĭ-me″ter). A unit of linear measure in the metric system, being 10^{-6} millimeter. Abbreviated μmm.

Micromonospora (mi″kro-mo-nos′po-rah) [*micro-* + Gr. *monos* single + *sporos* seed]. A genus of microorganisms of the family Streptomycetaceae, order Actinomycetales, made up of saprophytic forms occurring in soil and water.

micromonosporin (mi″kro-mo-nos′po-rin). An antibiotic substance produced by cultures of Micromonospora, which is active against gram-positive bacteria.

micromotoscope (mi″kro-mo′to-skōp) [*micro-* + L. *motio* motion + Gr. *skopein* to examine]. A device for photographing microscopical objects and showing their movements.

Micromyces (mi-krom′ĭ-sēz) [*micro-* + Gr. *mykēs* fungus]. Streptothrix.

micromyelia (mi″kro-mi-e′le-ah) [*micro-* + Gr. *myelos* marrow + *-ia*]. Abnormal smallness of the spinal cord.

micromyeloblast (mi″kro-mi′ĕ-lo-blast). A small, immature myelocyte, observed in micromyeloblastic leukemia.

micromyelolymphocyte (mi″kro-mi″ĕ-lo-lim′-fo-sīt). Micromyeloblast.

micron (mi′kron), pl. *mi′crons, mi′cra* [Gr. *mikros* small]. 1. A unit of linear measure in the metric system, being 10^{-3} millimeter, or 10^{-6} meter. Abbreviated μ. 2. Microne.

microne (mi′krōn) [Gr. *mikros* small]. A mass of extremely small size; a colloid particle varying in size from 10^{-3} to 10^{-5} cm., visible only with a microscope. Cf. *amicrone* and *submicrone.*

microneedle (mi″kro-ne′dl). A fine glass needle for use in micrurgy.

micronize (mi′kro-nīz) [Gr. *micron* a small thing]. To reduce to a fine powder; to reduce to particles of a micron in diameter.

micronodular (mi″kro-nod′u-lar). Marked by the presence of small nodules.

micronucleus (mi″kro-nu′kle-us) [*micro-* + *nucleus*]. 1. In ciliate protozoa, the smaller of two types of nucleus in each cell, which is required for sexual but not for vegetative reproduction. Cf. *macronucleus.* 2. A small nucleus. 3. The nucleolus.

micronychia (mi″kro-nik′e-ah) [*micr-* + Gr. *onyx* nail]. Abnormal smallness of the nails of fingers or toes.

micronychosis (mi″kro-nik-o′sis). Micronychia.

micro-orchidia (mi″kro-or-kid′e-ah). Microrchidia.

microorganic (mi″kro-or-gan′ik). Pertaining to a microorganism.

microorganism (mi″kro-or′gan-izm) [*micro-* + *organism*]. A minute living organism, usually microscopic. Those of medical interest are bacteria, spiral organisms, rickettsiae, viruses, molds, and yeasts.

microorganismal (mi″kro-or″gan-iz′mal). Pertaining to microorganisms.

microparasite (mi″kro-par′ah-sīt). A parasitic microorganism.

micropathology (mi″kro-pah-thol′o-je) [*micro-* + *pathology*]. 1. The sum of what is known regarding minute pathologic changes. 2. The pathology of diseases caused by microorganisms.

micropenis (mi″kro-pe′nis). Abnormal smallness of the penis.

microphage (mi′kro-fāj) [*micro-* + Gr. *phagein* to eat]. A phagocyte of small size; an actively motile, neutrophilic leukocyte which causes phagocytosis of the bacteria of acute affections.

microphagocyte (mi″kro-fag′o-sīt) [*micro-* + *phagocyte*]. A phagocyte of the smaller type.

microphagus (mi-krof′ah-gus). Microphage.

microphakia (mi″kro-fa′ke-ah) [*micro-* + Gr. *phakos* lens + *-ia*]. Abnormal smallness of the crystalline lens.

microphallus (mi″kro-fal′us) [*micro-* + Gr. *phallos* penis]. Abnormal smallness of the penis.

microphilic (mi″kro-fil′ik) [*micro-* + Gr. *philein* to love]. Growing best in the presence of very small amounts of carbon dioxide or oxygen.

microphobia (mi″kro-fo′be-ah) [*micro-* + *phobia*]. 1. Morbid dread of small objects. 2. Insane dread of microbes.

microphonia (mi″kro-fo′ne-ah) [*micro-* + Gr. *phōnē* voice + *-ia*]. Marked weakness of the voice.

microphonograph (mi″kro-fo′no-graf) [*micro-* + Gr. *phōnē* voice + *graphein* to record]. An instrument which magnifies and records delicate sounds: it is used in training the deaf to speak.

microphonoscope (mi″kro-fo′no-skōp) [*micro-* + Gr. *phōnē* voice + *skopein* to examine]. A binaural stethoscope having a membrane in the chest-piece which accentuates the sound.

microphotograph (mi″kro-fo′to-graf) [*micro-* + *photograph*]. A photograph of small size. Cf. *photomicrograph.*

microphthalmia (mi″krof-thal′me-ah) [*micro-* + Gr. *ophthalmos* eye + *-ia*]. Abnormal smallness of the eyes.

microphthalmoscope (mi″krof-thal′mo-skōp). An instrument for performing fundus microscopy.

microphthalmus (mi″krof-thal′mus). 1. Microphthalmia. 2. A person with abnormally small eyes.

microphysics (mi″kro-fiz′iks) [*micro-* + *physics*]. The science which deals with the ultimate structure of matter, i.e., with molecules, atoms, and electrons.

microphyte (mi′kro-fīt) [*micro-* + Gr. *phyton* plant]. A microscopic vegetable organism.

microphytic (mi″kro-fit′ik). Pertaining to or caused by microphytes.

micropia (mi-kro′pe-ah). Micropsia.

microplania (mi″kro-pla′ne-ah) [*micro-* + L. *planum*, a flat surface]. A condition in which the horizontal diameter of erythrocytes is decreased.

microplasia (mi″kro-pla′ze-ah) [*micro-* + Gr. *plassein* to form]. Dwarfism.

microplastocyte (mi″kro-plas′to-sīt) [*micro-* + *plastocyte*]. An undersized blood platelet.

microplethysmography (mi″kro-pleth″is-mog′rah-fe) [*micro-* + Gr. *plēthysmos* increase + *graphein* to record]. The recording of minute changes in the size of a part as produced by the circulation of blood in it, the instrument showing a deflection of 10 to 20 divisions for a volume change of 20 mm.: used in detection of patent ductus arteriosus and coarctation of the aorta.

micropodia (mi″kro-po′de-ah) [*micro-* + Gr. *pous* foot]. Abnormal smallness of the feet.

micropolariscope (mi″kro-po-lar′ĭ-skōp). A microscope with a polariscope attached.

micropolygyria (mi″kro-pol″e-ji′re-ah). Polymicrogyria.

microprecipitation (mi″kro-pre-sip″ĭ-ta′shun). Precipitation with a minute amount (½ to 1 drop) of reagent observed under the microscope.

micropredation (mi″kro-pre-da′shun). The derivation by an organism of elements essential for its existence from larger organisms of other species which it does not destroy.

micropredator (mi″kro-pred′ah-tor) [*micro-* + L. *praedator* a plunderer, pillager]. An organism that derives elements essential for its existence from other species of organisms, larger than itself, without causing their destruction.

microprojection (mi″kro-pro-jek′shun) [*micro-* + *projection*]. The throwing of the image of a microscopic object on a screen.

microprosopus (mi″kro-pro-so′pus) [*micro-* + Gr. *prosōpon* face]. A fetus with a small or undeveloped face.

microprotein (mi″kro-pro′te-in). The albuminous element of a bacillus.

micropsia (mi-krop′se-ah) [*micro-* + Gr. *opsis* vision + *-ia*]. A condition in which objects are seen as smaller than they actually are.

micropsychia (mi″krop-si′ke-ah) [*micro-* + Gr. *psychē* soul + *-ia*]. Feebleness of mind.

microptic (mi-krop′tik). Pertaining to or affected with micropsia.

micropus (mi-kro′pus) [*micro-* + Gr. *pous* foot]. A person with abnormally small feet.

micropyle (mi′kro-pīl) [*micro-* + Gr. *pylē* gate]. An opening through which the spermatozoon enters the ovum of certain species of animals.

microradiogram (mi″kro-ra′de-o-gram). A picture produced by microradiography.

microradiography (mi″kro-ra″de-og′rah-fe) [*micro-* + *radiography*]. A process by which an x-ray shadow image (radiograph) of a small or very thin object is produced on fine-grained photographic film under conditions which permit subsequent microscopic examination or enlargement of the radiograph at linear magnifications of up to several hundred and with a resolution approaching the resolving power of the photographic emulsion (about 1000 lines per millimeter).

microrchidia (mi″kror-kid′e-ah) [*micro-* + Gr. *orchis* testicle + *-ia*]. Abnormal smallness of the testicle.

microrefractometer (mi″kro-re″frak-tom′e-ter). A refractometer for the discovery of variations in the minute structure of blood corpuscles.

microrespirometer (mi″kro-res″pĭ-rom′e-ter). An apparatus for investigating the oxygen utilization of isolated tissues.

microrhinia (mi″kro-rin′e-ah) [*micro-* + Gr. *rhis* nose]. Abnormal smallness of the nose.

microroentgen (mi″kro-rent′gen) [*micro-* + *roentgen*]. One millionth of a roentgen. Abbreviated μr.

microscelous (mi-kros′kĕ-lus) [*micro-* + Gr. *skelos* leg]. Short legged.

microscler (mi′kro-sklēr). Dolichomorphic.

microscope (mi′kro-skōp) [*micro-* + Gr. *skopein* to view]. An instrument which is used to obtain an enlarged image of small objects and reveal details of structure not otherwise distinguishable. **beta ray m.**, one which reveals emission of beta particles from a microscopic specimen by means of a scintillator. **binocular m.**, a microscope which has two eyepieces, making possible simultaneous viewing with both eyes. **capillary m.**, an instrument for giving an enlarged image of capillaries, often used for viewing the capillaries of the nail bed. **centrifuge m.**, a microscope built into a high-speed centrifuge, by which a magnified image of a specimen undergoing centrifugal force may be produced. **comparison m.**, an instrument which permits simultaneous viewing of parts of images of two separate specimens, involving two microscopes bridged together with a comparison eyepiece, or one microscope with two body tubes and lens systems. **compound m.**, one that consists of two lens systems, one above the other, in which the image formed by the system nearer the object (objective) is further magnified by the system nearer the eye (eyepiece). **corneal m.**, a specially designed instrument with lens of high magnifying power, for observing minute changes in the cornea and iris. **darkfield m.**, one with a central stop in the condenser, permitting diversion of the light rays and illumination of the object from the side, so that the details appear light against a dark background. **electron m.**, one in which an electron beam, instead of light, forms an image for viewing on a fluorescent screen, or for photography. **epic m.** See *epimicroscope.* **fluorescence m.**, one in which light of one wavelength is used to illuminate the specimen, and the image seen is due to light of longer wavelength, re-emitted by the specimen. **Greenough m.**, a binocular, biobjective, stereoscopic instrument giving a low-power erect image. **infrared m.**, one in which radiation of 800 mμ or longer wavelength is used as the image-forming energy. **integrating m.**, one in which a special mechanical stage permits recording of the sizes of the components of the specimen. **interference m.**, a microscope for observing the same kind of refractile detail as that observed with the phase microscope, but utilizing two separate beams of light which are sent through the specimen and combined with each other in the image plane. **ion m.**, an electron microscope modified to use ions (e.g., of lithium), instead of electrons. **light m.**, one in which the specimen is viewed under ordinary illumination. **opaque m.**, one with vertical illumination or with the condenser built around the objective (epimicroscope) for viewing opaque specimens. **operating m.**, a specially designed instrument employed in the performance of delicate surgical procedures, as in operations on the middle ear, or on small blood vessels of the heart. **oto-m.** See *oto-microscope.* **phase m., phase-contrast m.**, a microscope which alters the phase relationships of the light passing through and that passing around the object, the contrast permitting visualization of the object without the necessity for staining or other special preparation. **photon m.**, light m. **polarizing m.**, one equipped with a polarizer, analyzer, and means for measurement of the alteration of the polarized light by the specimen. **polarizing m., rectified**, a polarizing microscope corrected for depolarization from curved lens surfaces so that full apertures can be used. **reflecting m.**, one which utilizes mirrors instead of lenses to form the image. **Rheinberg m.**, a

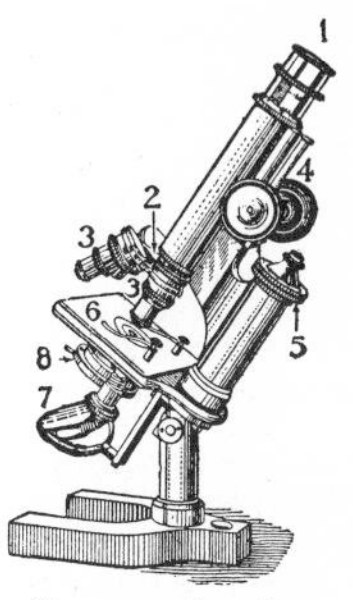

Compound microscope: 1, Eyepiece; 2, rotating nosepiece, carrying three objectives (3); 4, rack and pinion for coarse adjustment; 5, graduated head of screw for fine adjustment; 6, stage; 7, illuminating mirror; 8, condenser.

darkfield microscope in which the condenser is modified by having a colored instead of an opaque stop, with the annulus in a complementary color. **schlieren m.,** one in which light is deviated by the insertion of one or two diaphragms in the optical system, to reveal differences in refractive index in a specimen. **simple m.,** one which consists of a single lens; a magnifying glass. **slit lamp m.,** a corneal microscope with a special attachment that permits examination of the endothelium on the posterior surface of the cornea. **stereoscopic m.,** a binocular biobjective microscope, or a binocular monobjective microscope modified to give a three-dimensional view of the specimen. **stroboscopic m.,** one which utilizes flashing illumination, permitting analysis of motion in the specimen. **trinocular m.,** a binocular microscope with a third eyepiece tube for photomicrography or other use. **ultra-m.** See *ultramicroscope.* **ultrasonic m.,** one which utilizes the reflection of ultrasonic or mechanical vibration to reveal the detail of the specimen. **ultraviolet m.,** a microscope which utilizes reflecting optics or quartz and other ultraviolet-transmitting lenses, with radiation of less than 400 mμ wavelength as the image-forming energy. **x-ray m.,** one in which a beam of x-rays is used instead of light, the image usually being reproduced on film.

microscopic (mi″kro-skop′ik). Of extremely small size; visible only by the aid of the microscope.

microscopical (mi″kro-skop′e-k'l). 1. Pertaining to microscopy. 2. Microscopic.

microscopist (mi-kros′ko-pist). A person skilled in using the microscope.

microscopy (mi-kros′ko-pe) [*micro-* + Gr. *skopein* to examine]. Examination under or observation by means of the microscope. **clinical m.,** employment of the microscope in making clinical diagnoses. **fundus m.,** examination of the fundus of the eye with an instrument which combines a corneal microscope with an ophthalmoscope. **television m.,** projection on a television screen of the image obtained by use of a flying spot, or scanning, microscope, or by use of a television camera over a microscope.

microsecond (mi′kro-sek″und). One millionth of a second. Abbreviated μsec.

microsection (mi″kro-sek′shun). An extremely thin section for examination with the microscope.

microseme (mi′kro-sēm) [*micro-* + Gr. *sēma* sign]. Having an orbital index of 83 or less.

Microsiphonales (mi″kro-si″fo-na′lēz). Trichomycetes.

microslide (mi′kro-slīd). The slide on which objects for microscopical examination are mounted.

microsmatic (mi″kros-mat′ik) [*micro-* + Gr. *osmasthai* to smell]. Having the sense of smell, but of relatively feeble development.

microsoma (mi″kro-so′mah) [*micro-* + Gr. *sōma* body]. A very low but not dwarfish stature.

microsomatia (mi″kro-so-ma′she-ah). Microsomia.

microsome (mi′kro-sōm) [*micro-* + Gr. *sōma* body]. One of the finely granular elements of protoplasm.

microsomia (mi″kro-so′me-ah) [*micro-* + Gr. *sōma* body + *-ia*]. An undersized state of the body. **m. feta′lis,** abnormally small size of the fetus.

microspectroscope (mi″kro-spek′tro-skōp) [*micro-* + *spectroscope*]. A spectroscope to be used in connection with a microscope for the examination of the spectra of microscopical objects.

microsphere (mi-kro-sfēr′). Centrosome.

microspherocyte (mi″kro-sfe′ro-sīt). An erythrocyte whose diameter is less than normal but whose thickness is increased, so it more closely resembles a small sphere.

microspherocytosis (mi″kro-sfe″ro-si-to′sis). The presence in the blood of an excessive number of microspherocytes, observed in hemolytic jaundice.

microsphygmia (mi-kro-sfig′me-ah) [*micro-* + Gr. *sphygmos* pulse + *-ia*]. That condition of the pulse in which it is perceived with difficulty by the finger.

microsphygmy (mi″kro-sfig′me). Microsphygmia.

microsphyxia (mi″kro-sfik′se-ah). Microsphygmia.

Microspira (mi″kro-spi′rah) [*micro-* + Gr. *speira* coil]. A genus name used in early classifications for a group of small, spiral-shaped microorganisms.

Microspironema (mi″kro-spi″ro-ne′mah) [*micro-* + Gr. *speira* coil + *nema* thread]. A genus name proposed by Stiles and Pfender (1905) for organisms now included in the genus *Treponema.* **M. pal′lidum,** *Treponema pallidum.*

microsplanchnic (mi″kro-splank′nik). Having the abdominal portion of the body relatively smaller than the thoracic: a term applied to a type of bodily constitution in which the vertical diameters are excessively developed as compared with the horizontal ones.

microsplanchnous (mi″kro-splank′nus). Microsplanchnic.

microsplenia (mi″kro-sple′ne-ah) [*micro-* + Gr. *splēn* spleen + *-ia*]. Smallness of the spleen.

microsplenic (mi″kro-sple′nik). Marked by smallness of the spleen.

microsporia (mi″kro-spo′re-ah). Gruby's disease.

microsporid (mi-kros′po-rid). A skin eruption ascribed to allergy toward Microsporum.

Microsporidia (mi″kro-spo-rid′e-a) [*micro-* + *sporidium*]. An order of sporidia having small spores and usually one polar capsule. See *Nosema.*

Microsporon (mi″kro-spo′ron). Microsporum.

microsporosis (mi″kro-spo-ro′sis). A ringworm infection caused by one of the fungi of the Microsporum group. **m. cap′itis,** tinea tonsurans.

Microsporum (mi″kro-spo′rum) [*micro-* + Gr. *sporos* seed]. A genus of small-spored ringworm fungi which cause various diseases of the skin and hair. **M. audoui′ni,** the most common cause of ringworm of the scalp in many parts of the United States. **M. ca′nis,** a common cause of ringworm in cats and dogs; often transmitted to children. **M. feli′neum,** *M. canis.* **M. ful′vum,** *M. gypseum.* **M. fur′fur,** *Malassezia furfur.* **M. gyp′seum,** a species commonly found in the soil, with epidemiological qualities similar to those of *M. canis.* **M. lano′sum,** *M. canis.* Other species recognized as pathogenic, but which have not been isolated from man, include *M. cook′ei, M. distor′tum,* and *M. na′num.*

microstat (mi′kro-stat). The stage and finder of a microscope.

microstethoscope (mi″kro-steth′o-skōp) [*micro-* + *stethoscope*]. A form of stethoscope said to be constructed upon the principles of a telephone.

microsthenic (mi″kro-sthen′ik) [*micro-* + Gr. *sthenos* strength]. Having feeble muscular power.

microstomia (mi″kro-sto′me-ah) [*micro-* + Gr. *stoma* mouth + *-ia*]. A congenital defect in which the mouth is unusually small.

microsurgery (mi′kro-ser″jer-e). Dissection of minute structures under the microscope by means of a micromanipulator.

microsyringe (mi″kro-sēr′inj). A syringe fitted with a screw-thread micrometer head for the accurate control of minute measurements.

Microtatobiotes (mi″kro-ta″to-bi-o′tēz) [Gr. *mikrotatos* smallest + *biōtes* one must live]. A class made up of the smallest of the living things, characterized by a dependence on other living organisms for their growth and multiplication. It includes two orders, *Rickettsiales* and *Virales.*

microtechnic (mi″kro-tek′nik). Micrology.

microthelia (mi″kro-the′le-ah) [*micro-* + Gr. *thēlē* nipple + *-ia*]. Unusual smallness of the nipples.

microthrombosis (mi″kro-throm-bo′sis). Presence of many small thrombi in the capillaries and other small blood vessels of various organs of the body.

microthrombus (mi″kro-throm′bus), pl. *microthrom′bi* [*micro-* + Gr. *thrombos* clot]. A small thrombus located in a capillary or other small blood vessel.

microtia (mi-kro′she-ah) [*micro-* + Gr. *ous* ear + *-ia*]. Gross hypoplasia or aplasia of the pinna of the ear, with a blind or absent external auditory meatus.

microtome (mi′kro-tōm) [*micro-* + Gr. *tomē* a cut]. An instrument for cutting thin slices of tissue for microscopical study. **freezing m.,** a microtome for cutting frozen sections. **rocking m.,** a microtome in which the specimen is held in the end of a lever which passes up and down over a stationary knife. **rotary m.,** one in which a wheel action is translated into a back-and-forth movement of the specimen being sectioned. **sliding m.,** one in which the specimen being sectioned is made to slide on a tract.

microtomy (mi-krot′o-me) [*micro-* + Gr. *temnein* to cut]. The cutting of thin sections.

microtonometer (mi″kro-to-nom′e-ter). A small tonometer for measuring the oxygen and carbon dioxide tension in arterial blood.

microtransfusion (mi″kro-trans-fu′shun). Introduction into the circulation of a small quantity of blood of another individual, as sometimes occurs with transplacental passage of a small amount of fetal blood into the maternal circulation.

microtrauma (mi″kro-traw′mah). A slight trauma or lesion; a microscopic lesion.

Microtrombidium akamushi (mi″kro-trombid′e-um ak″ah-moo′she). *Trombicula akamushi.*

Microtus (mi-kro′tus) [*micro-* + Gr. *ous*, *ōtos*, ear]. A genus of mice-like animals. The smaller species are called voles. See *voles* and *vole bacillus.* **M. montebel′li,** the field vole.

microtus (mi-kro′tus). An individual exhibiting microtia.

micro-unit (mi′kro-u″nit). One-millionth (10^{-6}) of a standard unit. Abbreviated μU.

microviscosimeter (mi″kro-vis″ko-sim′e-ter). A viscosimeter for measuring the viscosity of blood plasma, using a small quantity of blood.

microvivisection (mi″kro-viv″ĭ-sek′shun). Microdissection.

microvolt (mi′kro-volt) [*micro-* + *volt*]. One millionth of a volt. Abbreviated μv.

microvoltometer (mi″kro-vōl-tom′e-ter). An instrument for detecting minute changes of electric potential in the body.

microvolumetry (mi″kro-vol-u′me-tre). Vierordt's term for the counting of the cells of any body fluid.

microwatt (mi′kro-wat) [*micro-* + *watt*]. One millionth of a watt. Abbreviated μw.

microwave (mi′kro-wāv). An electromagnetic wave of very high frequency and of short wave length, considered by various authors as ranging between 1 millimeter and 1 meter, or between 1 centimeter and 1 meter.

microxycyte (mi-krok′sĭ-sīt) [*micro-* + Gr. *oxys* sharp, acid + *-cyte*]. Any finely granular oxyphil cell.

microxyphil (mi-krok′sĭ-fil). Microxycyte.

microzoa (mi″kro-zo′ah). Plural of *microzoon.*

microzoaria (mi″kro-zo-a′re-ah) [*micro-* + Gr. *zōon* animal]. A general term for all microorganisms.

microzoon (mi″kro-zo′on), pl. *microzo′a* [*micro-* + Gr. *zōon* animal]. A microscopic animal organism.

microzyme (mi′kro-zīm) [*micro-* + Gr. *zymē* leaven]. See *micelle.*

micrurgic (mi-krur′jik). Pertaining to micrurgy.

micrurgy (mi′krur-je) [*micro-* + Gr. *ergon* work]. Micromanipulative technic in the field of a microscope. See *micromanipulator.*

Micrurus (mi-kroo′rus). A genus of poisonous snakes. *M. euryxan′thus* is the coral snake. *M. ful′vius* is the harlequin snake.

miction (mik′shun). Urination.

micturate (mik′tu-rāt). Urinate.

micturition (mik″tu-rish′un) [L. *micturire* to urinate]. The passage of urine.

M.I.D. Abbreviation for *mesioincisal distal* and for *minimum infective dose.*

midaxilla (mid″ak-sil′ah). The center of the axilla.

midbody (mid′bod-e). A body or a mass of granules developed in the equatorial region of the spindle during the anaphase of mitosis.

midbrain (mid′brān). Mesencephalon.

midcarpal (mid-kar′pal). Between the two rows of bones of the carpus.

Middeldorpf's splint, triangle (mid″l-dorpfs) [Albrecht Theodore *Middeldorpf*, Breslau surgeon, 1824–1868]. See under *triangle.*

middlepiece (mid″l-pēs). 1. The part of a horse between the fore and hind quarters. 2. The portion of a spermatozoon between its head and flagellum.

midfrontal (mid-fron′tal). Pertaining to the middle of the forehead.

midge (mij). A small dipterous insect. See also *mite.* **owl m.,** Phlebotomus.

midget (mij′et). A normal dwarf; an individual who is undersized but is perfectly formed.

midgetism (mij′ĕ-tizm). The condition of being a midget.

midgracile (mid-gras′il). Median and gracile: noting the median gracile sulcus.

midgut (mid′gut). A region in the developing embryo between the foregut and the hindgut, opening into the yolk sac.

midicel (mid′ĭ-sel). Trade mark for preparations of sulfamethoxypyridazine.

midoccipital (mid″ok-sip′ĭ-tal). Pertaining to or located in the middle of the occiput.

midpain (mid′pān). Intermenstrual pain.

midperiphery (mid″pĕ-rif′er-e). The middle zone of the retina.

midpiece (mid′pēs). The precipitated globulin fraction in complement splitting.

midplane (mid′plān). The narrow pelvic plane.

midriff (mid′rif). The diaphragm.

midsection (mid-sek′shun). A cut through the middle of any organ.

midsternum (mid-ster′num). Mesosternum.

midtarsal (mid-tar′sal). Between the two rows of bones of the tarsus.

midtegmentum (mid″teg-men′tum). The median or central part of the tegmentum.

midventricle (mid-ven′trĭ-k'l). The cavity of the midbrain or mesencephalon.

midwife (mid′wif). A woman who assists in childbirth.

midwifery (mid′wi-fer-e). Obstetrics.

Mierzejewski effect (mēr″ze-yef′ske) [Johann Lucian *Mierzejewski*, Russian neurologist and psychiatrist, 1839–1908]. See under *effect.*

Miescher's corpuscles, tubes (me′sherz) [Johann Friedrich *Miescher*, Swiss pathologist, 1811–1887]. See under *corpuscle* and *tubule.*

Miescheria (me-she′re-ah) [J. F. *Miescher*]. A genus of sarcosporidia. *M. mu′ris* infests the muscles and livers of domestic and other animals, and has been found in human subjects, producing what are called Miescher's tubules.

migraine (mi′grān, mē′grān) [Fr., from Gr. *hemikrania* an affection of half of the head]. A syndrome characterized by periodic headaches, often one sided, and accompanied by nausea, vomiting, and various sensory disturbances. **abdominal m.,** migraine in which abdominal symptoms (nausea and vomiting) are prominent. **fulgurating m.,** violent migraine developing abruptly. **ophthal-**

mic m., migraine accompanied by amblyopia or other visual disturbance. **ophthalmoplegic m.,** periodic migraine followed by ophthalmoplegia.

migraineur (me″grān-er′) [Fr.]. A person who suffers from migraine.

migrainoid (mi′grah-noid) [*migraine* + Gr. *eidos* form]. Resembling migraine.

migrainous (mi′gra-nus). Resembling, or of the nature of migraine.

migrateur (me″grah-ter′) [Fr.]. A person with an obsession to wander.

migration (mi-gra′shun) [L. *migratio*]. 1. An apparently spontaneous change of place. 2. The movement of leukocytes through the walls of the vessels. **anodic m.,** the migration of a negatively charged particle toward the positive pole in an electrical field. **cathodic m.,** the migration of a positively charged particle toward the negative pole in an electric field. **external m.,** the passage of an ovum from the ovary to the oviduct of the opposite side without passing through the uterus. **internal m.,** the passing of an ovum from an ovary into the uterus in the normal way, followed by its entry into the opposite oviduct. **m. of leukocytes,** the passage of white corpuscles through the wall of a vessel. **m. of ovum,** the passage of the ovum into the uterine tube after its discharge from the ovary. **transperitoneal m.,** external migration.

Migula's classification (me′goo-lahz) [Walter *Migula*, German naturalist, born 1863]. A classification of bacteria drawn up by Migula in 1900.

mikedimide (mi-ked′ĭ-mīd). Trade mark for a preparation of bemegride.

mikro-. For words beginning thus, see those beginning *micro-*.

Mikulicz's cells, disease, drain, operation (mik′u-lich″ez) [Johann von *Mikulicz*-Radecki, Polish surgeon, 1850–1905]. See under the nouns.

mil (mil). Contraction of *milliliter*.

milammeter (mil-am′e-ter). Milliammeter.

mildew (mil′du). A parasitic fungus of many species, or the condition caused by the growth of such a fungus on vegetable or other material.

Miles' operation (mīlz) [William Ernest *Miles*, British surgeon, 1869–1947]. Abdominoperineal excision of the rectum for carcinoma.

milfoil (mil′foil). Yarrow. See *Achillea*.

milia (mil′e-ah) [L.]. Plural of *milium*.

Milian's erythema, sign, syndrome (mēl-yahz′) [Gaston *Milian*, French dermatologist, 1871–1945]. See under *erythema* and *sign*.

miliaria (mil″e-a′re-ah) [L. *milium* millet]. A syndrome of cutaneous changes associated with sweat retention and extravasation of sweat occurring at different levels in the skin. **m. al′ba,** miliaria in which the sweat escapes in the stratum corneum, producing non-inflammatory vesicles which, because of the thickness of the layer covering them, appear white. **m. crystalli′na,** miliaria in which the sweat escapes in the stratum corneum, producing non-inflammatory vesicles which, because of the thinness of the layer covering them, have the appearance of clear droplets. **m. profun′da,** miliaria in which the sweat escapes into the upper dermis, producing non-pruritic, non-inflammatory flesh-colored papules which change in size with the sweating response of the patient; usually occurring only as a late sequel to recurrent severe generalized miliaria rubra, and, when extensive, leading to heat intolerance, as in tropical anhidrotic asthenia. **m. pustulo′sa,** miliaria occurring as a complication of a preceding dermatitis, with escape of sweat into the epidermis and a leukocyte response, producing pruritic erythematous pustules. **m. ru′bra,** a condition resulting from obstruction to the ducts of the sweat glands caused by prolonged maceration of the skin surface; the sweat escapes into the epidermis, producing pruritic erythematous papulovesicles. The severity of the symptoms fluctuates with the heat load of the individual.

miliary (mil′e-a-re) [L. *miliaris* like a millet seed]. 1. Resembling a millet seed. 2. Characterized by the formation of lesions resembling millet seeds.

milibis (mil′ĭ-bis). Trade mark for preparations of glycobiarsol.

milieu (me-lyuh′) [Fr.]. Surroundings: environment. **m. exterieur** (me-lyuk′ eks-ta″re-ur′), the external environment. **m. interieur** (me-lyuh′ an-ta″re-ur′), [Fr. "interior environment"], Claude Bernard's term for the blood and lymph which bathe the cells of the body.

milium (mil′e-um), pl. *mil′ia* [L. "millet seed"]. A small whitish nodule in the skin, especially of the face. Milia are usually retention cysts of sebaceous glands or hair follicles. **colloid m.,** a small yellowish papule in the corium of the skin which is the seat of a colloid degeneration.

milk (milk) [L. *lac*]. The fluid secretion of the mammary gland forming the natural food of young mammals. **acidophilus m.,** milk fermented with cultures of *Lactobacillus acidophilus:* used in gastro-intestinal disorders to modify the bacterial flora of the intestinal tract. **adapted m.,** milk especially modified so as to adapt it to the child's digestive capacity. **after-m.,** the stripping, or last milk taken at any one milking. **albumin m.,** Finkelstein's specially prepared milk, poor in lactose and salts and rich in casein and fat. **arsphenamine m.,** the milk from a goat that has received injection of arsphenamine: used in treating syphilis in children. **m. of asafetida,** emulsion of asafetida. **m. of bismuth,** a 6 per cent suspension of basic bismuth carbonate. **bitter m.,** milk that is bitter in taste when first drawn because of bitter herbs in the feed or has become bitter later from the growth of certain microorganisms. **blue m.,** milk made blue in color by the action of bacteria, usually *Pseudomonas syncyanea.* **Budd m., buddeized m.,** milk sterilized by adding hydrogen dioxide and heating, so as to decompose the dioxide and liberate the oxygen. **cancer m.,** a viscid opaque granular fluid which may be scraped from the surface of a carcinoma which has undergone fatty degeneration. **casein m.,** a prepared milk containing very little salts and sugars and a large amount of fat and casein. **certified m.,** milk whose purity is certified by a committee of physicians or a medical milk commission. **citric acid m.,** milk prepared by adding 4 Gm. of dehydrated citric acid to a quart of milk. **condensed m.,** milk which has been partly evaporated and sweetened with sugar. **diabetic m.,** milk containing a small percentage of lactose. **dialyzed m.,** milk from which the sugar has been abstracted by being passed by dialysis through a parchment membrane. **fat m.,** a modified milk that contains as much or more fat than human milk. **fore-m.** 1. The first milk taken at any one milking. 2. Colostrum. **fortified m.,** milk made more nutritious by the addition of cream or white of egg. **homogenized m.,** milk so treated that the fats become intimately combined with the general body of the milk: the emulsified particles of fat are made so minute that the cream does not separate. **hydrochloric acid m.,** acid milk prepared by adding 5 cc. of tenth normal hydrochloric acid to 100 cc. of cow's milk. **m. of iron,** water which contains freshly precipitated ferric phosphate. **laboratory m.,** milk prepared according to a special formula. **lemon juice m.,** acid milk prepared by adding $\frac{3}{4}$ oz. (22 cc.) of lemon juice to 1 quart of cow's milk. **litmus m.,** a nutrient in which litmus is used as an indicator in bacteriology. **m. of magnesia,** magnesia magma. **metallized m.,** milk in which metals (copper, iron, magnesium) are dissolved: used to produce regeneration of hemoglobin. **modified m.,** milk in which the constituents have been made to correspond in amount to the composition of human milk. **perhydrase m.,** milk to which hydrogen dioxide has been added. **protein m.,** a modified milk preparation having a relatively low content of carbohydrate and fat and a relatively high protein content. **red m.,** milk made red by blood, eating of madder root, or the growth of *Erythrobacillus prodigiosus* or other microorganisms. **ropy m.,** milk which has become viscid so that it can be drawn out into threads. It is usually caused by the growth of *Alcaligenes viscosus* and is eaten as a delicacy in Norway. **salvarsan m.,** arsphenamine milk. **Schloss m.,** a modified milk containing the same proportion of salts and fat as human milk. **skimmed m.,** milk from which the cream has been removed. **soft curd m.,** milk the curd of which has been rendered soft and homogeneous by boiling, by the addition of cream or by the addition of sodium citrate. **sour m.,** milk containing lactic acid, produced by the action of lactic acid bacteria. **m. of sulfur,** precipitated sulfur. **uterine m.,** a white milky substance between the villi of the placenta of the gravid uterus. **uviol m.,** milk sterilized by the action of ultraviolet rays. **vegetable m.,** synthetic milk made out of vegetables. **vinegar m.,** acid milk prepared by adding vinegar to cow's milk. **virgin's m.,** lac virginale. **vitamin D m.,** cow's milk to which vitamin D has been added either by direct addition, by exposure to ultraviolet light, or by feeding irradiated yeast to the cows. **witch's m.,** milk secreted in the breast of the newborn child. **yeast m.,** milk from cows which have been fed on irradiated yeast: it has antirachitic potency.

milking (milk′ing). The pressing out of the contents of a tubular part, such as the urethra, by running the finger along it.

milk-leg (milk′leg). Phlegmasia alba dolens.

Milkman's syndrome (milk′manz) [Louis Arthur *Milkman*, American roentgenologist, 1895–1951]. See under *syndrome.*

milkpox (milk′poks). Variola minor.

milk sick (milk′sik). Poisoning by white snake root, *Eupatorium urticaefolium.*

Millar's asthma (mil′arz) [John *Millar*, British physician, 1735–1801]. See under *asthma.*

Millard's test (mil′ards) [Henry B. *Millard*, American physician, 1832–1893]. See under *tests.*

Millard-Gubler paralysis, syndrome (me-yar′-goob′ler) [August L. J. *Millard*, French physician, 1830–1915; Adolph *Gubler*, French physician, 1821–1879]. The superior type of hemiplegia alternans.

Miller-Abbott tube [T. Grier *Miller*, Philadelphia physician, born 1886; W. Osler *Abbott*, Philadelphia physician, 1902–1943]. See under *tube.*

milli- (mil′ĭ) [Fr. *mille* thousand]. A prefix used in naming units of measurement to indicate one one-thousandth (10^{-3}) of the unit designated by the root with which it is combined.

milliammeter (mil″le-am′e-ter). An ammeter which registers a current in milliamperes.

milliampere (mil″le-am′pēr) [Fr.]. One-thousandth part of an ampere.

milliampere-minute (mil″le-am″pēr-min′ut). A unit of electrical quantity equivalent to that delivered by one milliampere in one minute.

milliamperemeter (mil″le-am-pēr′me-ter). Milliammeter.

millibar (mil′ĭ-bar). One-thousandth part of a bar.

millicoulomb (mil″ĭ-koo′lom). A unit of quantity of current electricity, being one one-thousandth (10^{-3}) of a coulomb. Abbreviated mcoul.

millicurie (mil″ĭ-ku′re). A unit of radioactivity, being one one-thousandth (10^{-3}) curie, or the quantity of radioactive material in which the number of nuclear disintegrations is 3.7×10^7 per second. Abbreviated mc.

millicurie-hour (mil″ĭ-ku′re-owr″). A unit of dose equivalent to that obtained by exposure for one hour to radioactive material disintegrating at the rate of 3.7×10^7 atoms per second. Abbreviated mc.-hr.

milliequivalent (mil″le-e-kwiv′ah-lent). The number of grams of a solute contained in one milliliter of a normal solution. Abbreviated mEq.

milligamma (mil″ĭ-gam′mah). Nanogram. Abbreviated mγ.

milligram (mil′ĭ-gram) [*milli-* + *gram*]. A unit of mass (weight) in the metric system, being 10^{-3} gram, or the equivalent of 0.015432 grains. Abbreviated mg.

Millikan rays (mil′ĭ-kan) [Robert Andrews *Millikan*, American physicist, 1868–1953]. Cosmic rays.

millilambert (mil″ĭ-lam′bert). One thousandth of a lambert.

milliliter (mil′ĭ-le″ter) [*milli-* + *liter*]. A unit of capacity in the metric system, being 10^{-3} liter, or the equivalent of 0.033815 of a fluid ounce. Abbreviated ml.

millimeter (mil′ĭ-me-ter). A unit of linear measure of the metric system, being one one-thousandth (10^{-3}) meter, or about 0.03937 inch. Abbreviated mm.

millimicro- (mil″ĭ-mi′kro). A prefix used in naming units of measurement to indicate one-thousandth of one-millionth (10^{-9}) of the unit designated by the root with which it is combined; now being supplanted by the prefix *nano-*.

millimicrocurie (mil″ĭ-mi″kro-ku′re). One-thousandth (10^{-3}) microcurie, or 10^{-9} curie. Abbreviated mμc. Called also *nanocurie.*

millimicrogram (mil″ĭ-mi′kro-gram). One-thousandth (10^{-3}) microgram, or 10^{-9} gram. Abbreviated mμg or mγ. Called also *nanogram.*

millimicron (mil″ĭ-mi′kron). A unit of linear measure in the metric system, being 10^{-3} micron, 10^{-6} millimeter, or 10^{-9} meter. Abbreviated mμ or mmm.

millimole (mil′ĭ-mōl). One-thousandth part of a mole (def. 3). Abbreviated mM.

millimu (mil′ĭ-mu). Millimicron.

milling-in (mil′ing-in). The correction of disharmonies of occlusion of natural or artificial teeth by modification of their occlusal surfaces by abrasives while they are rubbed together in the mouth or on the articulator.

millinormal (mil″ĭ-nor′mal). Having a concentration one-thousandth of normal.

millions (mil′yunz). A name applied to various small fish that devour mosquito larvae. See *Lebistes reticulatus.*

milliosmole (mil″ĭ-os′mōl). One thousandth of an osmole.

milliphot (mil′e-fot). The practical unit of illumination being 0.001 phot and approximately one foot candle.

millirad (mil′ĭ-rad). A unit of absorbed radiation dose, 10^{-3} rad. Abbreviated mrad.

milliroentgen (mil′ĭ-rent″gen). A unit of dose equal to one-thousandth (10^{-3}) roentgen. Abbreviated mr.

millisecond (mil″e-sek′ond). One one-thousandth of a second. Abbreviated msec.

milliunit (mil′ĭ-u″nit). One-thousandth (10^{-3}) of a standard unit. Abbreviated mU.

millivolt (mil′e-vōlt). One one-thousandth of a volt. Abbreviated mv.

Millon's reagent, test (mil′onz) [Auguste N. E. *Millon*, French chemist, 1812–1867]. See under *reagent* and *tests.*

Mills's disease (milz) [Charles K. *Mills*, Philadelphia neurologist, 1845–1931]. Ascending hemiplegia.

Mills-Reincke phenomenon (milz-rīn′kĕ) [Hiram F. *Mills*, American engineer; J. J. *Reincke*, German physician]. See under *phenomenon.*

milontin (mi-lon′tin). Trade mark for preparations of phensuximide.

milpath (mil′path). Trade mark for a preparation of meprobamate and tridihexethyl chloride.

milphae (mil′fe) [Gr. *milphai*]. The falling of the hair of the eyelids.

milphosis (mil-fo′sis) [Gr. *milphōsis*]. Milphae.

Milroy's disease (mil′roys) [William Forsyth *Milroy*, American physician, 1855–1942]. See under *disease*.

Milton's disease, urticaria (mil′tonz) [John Laws *Milton*, dermatologist in London, 1820–1898]. Giant urticaria.

miltown (mil′town). Trade mark for a preparation of meprobamate.

milt-sickness (milt′sik-nes). Splenic disease in cattle.

milzbrand (milts′brahnt) [Ger.]. Anthrax.

mimesis (mi-me′sis) [Gr. *mimēsis* imitation]. The simulation of one disease by another.

mimetic (mi-met′ik) [Gr. *mimētikos*]. Marked by simulation of another disease.

mimic (mim′ik). Mimetic.

mimmation (mi-ma′shun). The habitual insertion of the "m" sound in speech in places where it does not belong.

mimosis (mi-mo′sis). Mimesis.

min. Abbreviation for L. *min′imum*, a minim.

Minamata disease (min″ah-mah′tah) [*Minamata* Bay, Japan]. See under *disease*.

mincard (min′kard). Trade mark for a preparation of aminometradine.

mind (mīnd) [L. *mens;* Gr. *psychē*]. The faculty, or function of the brain, by which an individual becomes aware of his surroundings and of their distribution in space and time, and by which he experiences feelings, emotions, and desires, and is able to attend, to remember, to reason, and to decide.

Mindererus, spirit of (min-der-e′rus) [Raymund *Minderer*, German physician, 1570(?)–1621]. Solution of ammonium acetate.

mineral (min′er-al) [L. *minerale*]. A nonorganic homogeneous substance. **crystal m.,** fused potassium nitrate. **kermes m.,** antimony oxysulfide. **turpeth m.,** yellow subsulfate of mercury.

mineralization (min″er-al-i-za′shun). The addition of mineral matter to the body.

mineralocorticoid (min″er-al-o-kor′tĭ-koid). A corticoid particularly effective in causing the retention of sodium and the loss of potassium.

mingin (min′jin). A nitrogenous compound, $C_{13}H_{18}N_2O_2$, found in small amounts in the urine.

minify (min′ĭ-fi) [L. *minus* less]. To render less; to diminish. The opposite of magnify.

minim (min′im) [L. *minimum* least]. A unit of capacity (liquid measure), being one-sixtieth part of a fluid dram, or the equivalent of 0.0616 milliliter.

minima (min′ĭ-mah) [L.]. Plural of *minimum*.

minimal (min′ĭ-mal) [L. *minimus* least]. The smallest or least; the smallest possible.

minimum (min′ĭ-mum), pl. *min′ima* [L. "smallest"]. The smallest amount or lowest limit. **m. audib′ile,** auditory threshold. **m. cognoscib′ile,** the threshold of visual recognition of complicated shapes or contours. **m. legib′ile,** the threshold of visible recognition of form, as of test letters or numbers. **light m.,** the minimum intensity of light which is visually perceptible in completely darkened surroundings: called also *liminal value*. **m. sensib′ile,** threshold of consciousness. **m. separab′ile,** the least distance that two objects may be apart and still be distinguished as two. **m. visib′ile,** light m.

Minin light (min′in) [A. V. *Minin*, Russian surgeon]. See under *light*.

minium (min′e-um) [L.]. Lead tetroxide, Pb_3O_4: red lead.

Minkowski's figure, method (min-kov′skēz) [Oskar *Minkowski*, Lithuanian physician in Wiesbaden, 1858–1931]. See under *figure* and *method*.

Minkowski-Chauffard syndrome (min-kov′ske-sho-far′). Hemolytic jaundice.

Minor's disease, sign (me′norz) [Lazar Salomovitsch *Minor*, Russian neurologist, born 1855]. See under the nouns.

Minot-Murphy diet, treatment (mi′nut-mur′fe) [George R. *Minot*, American physician, 1885–1950, and William Parry *Murphy*, American physician, born 1892, co-winners, with George Hoyt Whipple, of the Nobel prize for medicine and physiology in 1934, for their work on pernicious anemia]. See under *treatment*.

minstra (min-strah′) [Ital.]. A liqueur, or cordial, prepared at Soresina, Italy.

mint (mint). See *Mentha*. **horse m.** See *Monarda*. **wild m.,** a fragrant North American plant, *Mentha canadensis*, resembling pennyroyal in its odor and other properties.

minuthesis (min-u′the-sis) [Gr. *minuthēsis* a wasting]. A decrease in the psychophysical sensitivity of a sense organ due to continuous stimulation of that organ; fatigue.

M.I.O. Abbreviation for *minimal identifiable odor*.

mio- (mi′o) [Gr. *meiōn* less]. Combining form meaning less.

miocardia (mi″o-kar′de-ah) [*mio-* + Gr. *kardia* heart]. The contraction of the heart; systole.

miodidymus (mi″o-did′ĭ-mus) [*mio-* + Gr. *didymos* twin]. A fetus with two heads joined at the occiputs.

miolecithal (mi″o-les′ĭ-thal) [*mio-* + Gr. *lekithos* yolk]. Containing little yolk.

mionectic (mi″o-nek′tik) [Gr. *meionektikos* disposed to take too little]. Taking up less than the average amount of oxygen, i.e., less than 70 per cent. Cf. *mesectic* and *pleonectic*.

miophone (mi′o-fōn) [*mio-* + Gr. *phōnē* sound]. A microphone for testing the muscles.

mioplasmia (mi″o-plaz′me-ah) [*mio-* + Gr. *plasma* plasma]. Abnormal decrease in the amount of plasma in the blood.

miopragia (mi″o-pra′je-ah) [*mio-* + Gr. *prassein* to perform]. Decreased functional activity.

miopus (mi′o-pus) [*mio-* + Gr. *ōps* face]. A fetal monster with two fused heads, one face being rudimentary.

miosis (mi-o′sis) [Gr. *meiōsis* diminution]. 1. Excessive contraction of the pupil. 2. Meiosis. 3. That stage of disease during which the intensity of the symptoms diminishes. **irritative m.,** spastic miosis. **paralytic m.,** miosis due to paralysis of the dilator of the iris. **spastic m.,** miosis due to spasm of the sphincter pupillae. **spinal m.,** miosis occurring in spinal diseases.

miosphygmia (mi″o-sfig′me-ah) [*mio-* + Gr. *sphygmos* pulse]. A condition in which the pulse beats are fewer than the heart beats.

miostagmin (mi″o-stag′min) [*mio-* + Gr. *stagma* drop]. A hypothetical substance in the blood serum of infected animals which will combine with antigen to lower the surface tension of the mixture.

miotic (mi-ot′ik). 1. Pertaining to, characterized by, or producing miosis. 2. An agent that causes the pupil to contract. 3. Meiotic.

miotin (mi′o-tin). The chief avidin-uncombinable biotin vitamer in urine and other biological materials. (Dean Burk.) Cf. *tiotin* and *vitamer*.

miracidium (mi-rah-sid′e-um), pl. *miracid′ia* [Gr. *meirakidion* a boy, lad, stripling]. The free swimming larva of a trematode which emerges from an egg and penetrates the body of a snail host, where it develops into a sporocyst.

mire (mēr) [Fr.; L. *mirari* to look at]. One of the figures on the arm of an ophthalmometer whose images are reflected on the cornea. The measurement of their variations measures the amount of corneal astigmatism.

mirror (mir′or) [Fr. *miroir*]. A polished surface that reflects light or creates visible images of objects in front of it. **concave m.,** one with a concave reflecting surface. **convex m.,** one with a convex reflecting surface. **dental m.,** mouth m. **frontal m., head m.,** a circular mirror strapped to the head: used especially in connection with the laryngoscope or rhinoscope. **Glatzel m.**, a flat plate of cold metal held horizontally below and in front of the nose. The patch of moisture deposited on its polished surface indicates the functional patency of the two sides of the nose. **mouth m.**, a small mirror used by dentists. **nasographic m.**, Glatzel m. **plane m.**, one with a flat reflecting surface. **van Helmont's m.**, the central tendon of the diaphragm.

miryachit (mir-e′ah-chit) [Russ.]. A variety of palmus, or jumping disease, prevalent in Siberia.

mis-action (mis-ak′shun). Any accidental act, lapse of memory, or slip of the tongue, attributed to lack of normal repression of the ego, as in sleep or fatigue.

misandria (mis-an′dre-ah) [*miso-* + Gr. *anēr* man]. Morbid dislike of men.

misanthropia (mis″an-thro′pe-ah) [*miso-* + Gr. *anthrōpos* man + *-ia*]. Hatred of mankind.

misce (mis′e) [L.]. Mix.

miscegenation (mis″e-je-na′shun) [L. *miscere* to mix + *genus* race]. The intermarriage or union of persons of different races, or the procreation of persons of mixed race.

miscible (mis′ĭ-b′l). Susceptible of being mixed.

miserere mei (miz″er-a′re ma′e) [L. "have mercy on me"]. Volvulus or intestinal colic.

miso- (mis′o) [Gr. *misos* hatred felt against]. Combining form meaning hatred of.

misocainia (mis″o-ki′ne-ah) [*miso-* + Gr. *kainos* new]. Hatred of anything new or strange.

misogamy (mis-og′ah-me) [*miso-* + Gr. *gamos* marriage]. Morbid aversion to marriage.

misogyny (mis-oj′ĭ-ne) [*miso-* + Gr. *gynē* woman]. Aversion to women.

misologia (mis″o-lo′je-ah) [*miso-* + Gr. *logos* word]. 1. Morbid dread of conversation. 2. Morbid dread of mental application.

misoneism (mis″o-ne′izm) [*miso-* + Gr. *neos* new]. Morbid dislike of new things or new ideas.

misopedia (mis″o-pe′de-ah) [*miso-* + Gr. *pais* child + *-ia*]. Morbid aversion to children.

misopedy (mis-op′ĕ-de). Misopedia.

missexual (mis-seks′u-al). Pertaining to an abnormal sexual balance, on the theory that every person is a mixture of male and female elements in varying degrees.

mist. Abbreviation for L. *mistu′ra*, a mixture.

mistura (mis-tu′rah) [L.]. Mixture. **m. ammoni′aci**, mixture or milk of ammonia. **m. amyg′dalae**, mixture or milk of almonds. **m. asafoet′idae**, mixture or milk of asafetida. **m. campho′rae aromat′ica**, Parish's mixture: compound tincture of lavender 25, sugar 35, camphor water to make 100. **m. chlorofor′mi**, chloroform mixture: anodyne and stimulant. **m. copa′ibae compos′ita**, the compound mixture of copaiba. **m. cre′tae**, chalk mixture: used as an antacid. **m. fer′ri aromat′ica**, aromatic iron mixture. **m. fer′ri compos′ita**, compound mixture of iron. **m. fer′ri et ammo′niae aceta′tis.** See *liquor ferri*, etc. **m. glycyrrhi′zae compos′ita**, compound mixture of licorice; brown mixture. **m. guai′aci**, mixture or emulsion of the resin of guaiacum. **m. magne′siae et asafoet′idae**, milk of magnesia and asafetida. **m. o′lei ric′ini**, castor oil mixture. **m. oleobalsam′ica**, alcoholic solution of balsam of Peru with aromatic oils and flavoring: used as a local stimulant. **m. pectora′lis**, expectorant mixture; ammonium carbonate 1.75 per cent, fluid extract of senega and squill each 3.5 per cent, camphorated tincture of opium 17.5 per cent, water and syrup of tolu. **m. potas′sii citra′tis**, mixture of the citrate of potassium. **m. rhe′i et so′dae**, mixture of rhubarb and soda. **m. scammo′nii**, mixture of scammony. **m. sen′nae compos′ita**, compound mixture of senna. **m. spir′itus vi′ni gal′lici**, mixture of brandy; contains 4 fl.oz. each of brandy and cinnamon water, ½ oz. sugar, yolk of two eggs. **m. splenet′ica**, Gadberry's mixture: quinine sulfate, 4.2; potassium nitrate and ferrous sulfate, each, 1.4; nitric acid, 1.4; water to make 100. It is tonic and antiperiodic.

Mit. Abbreviation for L. *mit′te*, send.

mitagglutinin (mit″ah-gloo′tĭ-nin). Coagglutinin.

mitapsis (mit-ap′sis) [*mito-* + Gr. *hapsis* joining]. The fusion of the chromatin granules in the final stage of cell conjugation.

Mitchell's disease, skin, treatment (mich′elz) [Silas Weir *Mitchell*, Philadelphia neurologist, 1829–1914]. See under the nouns.

mitchella (mich-el′ah) [John *Mitchell*, American botanist, 18th century]. The plant *Mitchella repens*, squaw vine, partridge berry, of the U.S. and Canada: formerly used as a uterine tonic.

mite (mīt). Any member of the order Acarina except the ticks (Ixodidae). The mites are minute animals, related to the spiders, and are parasitic on man and domestic animals, producing various irritations of the skin (acariasis). Mites important in human and veterinary medicine are *Sarcoptes, Psoroptes, Demodex, Trombicula, Eutrombicula, Dermanyssus, Liponyssus, Pneumonyssus, Acarapis, Glyciphagus, Neochogastia, Notroedres, Tetranychus, Pediculoides, Tyroglyphus, Chorioptes, Otodectes*, and *Cnemidocoptes*. **auricular m.** See *Otodectes*. **bird m., chicken m.** See *Dermanyssus*. **copra m.**, *Tyroglyphus longior*. **deplum-ing m.**, *Cnemidocoptes gallinae*. **face m.**, *Demodex folliculorum*. **flour m.** See *Tyroglyphus*. **follicle m.** See *Demodex*. **food m.**, *Glyciphagus domesticus*. **fowl m.** See *Dermanyssus*. **hair follicle m.**, *Demodex folliculorum*. **harvest m.** See *chigger*. **itch m.** See *Sarcoptes*. **kedani m.**, *Trombicula akamushi*. **louse m.** See *Pediculoides*. **mange m.** See *Sarcoptes*. **meal m.** See *Tyroglyphus*. **mower's m.** See *chigger*. **onion m.**, *Acarus rhyzoglypticus hyacinthi*. **poultry m.** See *Dermanyssus*. **rat m.** See *Liponyssus*. **red m.** See *chigger*. **scab m.** See *Psoroptes*. **snout m.**, *Bdella cardinalis*. **spinning m.**, *Bryobia praetiosa*. **straw m.** See *Pediculoides*. **tropical rat m.**, *Liponyssus bacoti*.

mitella (mi-tel′ah) [L.]. An arm sling.

mithridatism (mith″rĭ-da′tizm) [after *Mithridates*, king of Pontus, who took poisons so as to become immunized against them]. The acquisition of immunity to the effects of a poison by ingestion of gradually increasing amounts of it.

miticidal (mi″tĭ-si′dal). Destructive to mites.

miticide (mi′tĭ-sīd). An agent that is destructive to mites.

mitigate (mit′ĭ-gāt) [L. *mitigare* to soften]. To moderate; to render milder.

mitis (mi′tis) [L.]. Mild.

mito- (mi′to) [Gr. *mitos* thread]. Combining form meaning threadlike, or denoting relationship to a thread.

mitochondria (mi″to-kon′dre-ah). Plural of *mitochondrion.*

mitochondrion (mi″to-kon′dre-on), pl. *mitochon′dria* [*mito-* + Gr. *chondrion* granule]. A filamentous or granular component (organelle) of cytoplasm, the principal site of oxidative reactions by which the energy in foodstuff is made available for endergonic processes which occur in the cell.

mitogenesia (mi″to-je-ne′se-ah). Production or formation by mitosis.

mitogenesis (mi″to-jen′e-sis) [*mitosis* + Gr. *genesis* production]. The production, or causation, of mitosis in a cell.

mitogenetic (mi″to-je-net′ik). Pertaining to or characterized by mitogenesis.

mitogenic (mi″to-jen′ik). Causing or inducing mitosis.

mitokinetic (mit″o-ki-net′ik) [*mito-* + Gr. *kinēsis* motion]. A term applied to the force existing in the kinoplasm of a cell which produces the achromatic spindle in karyokinesis.

mitome (mi′tōm). A thready network of the protoplasm of a cell; the more solid portion of cell protoplasm.

mitoplasm (mit′o-plazm) [*mito-* + Gr. *plassein* to form]. The chromatic substance of a cell nucleus.

mitoschisis (mĭ-tos′kĭ-sis) [*mito-* + Gr. *schisis* split]. Karyokinesis.

mitoses (mi-to′sēz). Plural of *mitosis.*

mitosin (mit′o-sin). A hormone producing mitosis or follicular maturation.

mitosis (mi-to′sis), pl. *mito′ses* [*mito-* + *-osis*]. A method of indirect division of a cell, consisting of a complex of various processes, by means of which the two daughter nuclei normally receive identical complements of the number of chromosomes characteristic of the somatic cells of the species. Mitosis is divided into four phases. 1. *Prophase:* Formation of a duplicate spireme; disappearance of nuclear membrane; breaking up of spireme into chromosomes; appearance of the achromatic spindle; formation of polar bodies. 2. *Metaphase:* Arrangement of chromosomes in equatorial plane of central spindle to form the monaster. Chromosomes separate into exactly similar halves. 3. *Anaphase:* The two groups of daughter chromosomes separate and move along the fibers of the central spindle, each toward one of the asters, forming the diaster. 4. *Telophase:* The daughter chromosomes resolve themselves into a reticulum and the daughter nuclei are formed; the cytoplasm divides, forming two complete daughter cells. **heterotypic m.,** mitosis in which the halves of bivalent chromosomes move away from each other toward the poles, as occurs in the first, or reductional, division of meiosis. **homeotypic m.,** the ordinary type of cell division in mitosis, as occurs also in the second, or equational, division of meiosis. **multicentric m.,** pluripolar m. **pathologic m.,** atypical, asymmetrical mitosis indicative of malignancy. **pluripolar m.,** cell division that results in the formation of more than two daughter cells.

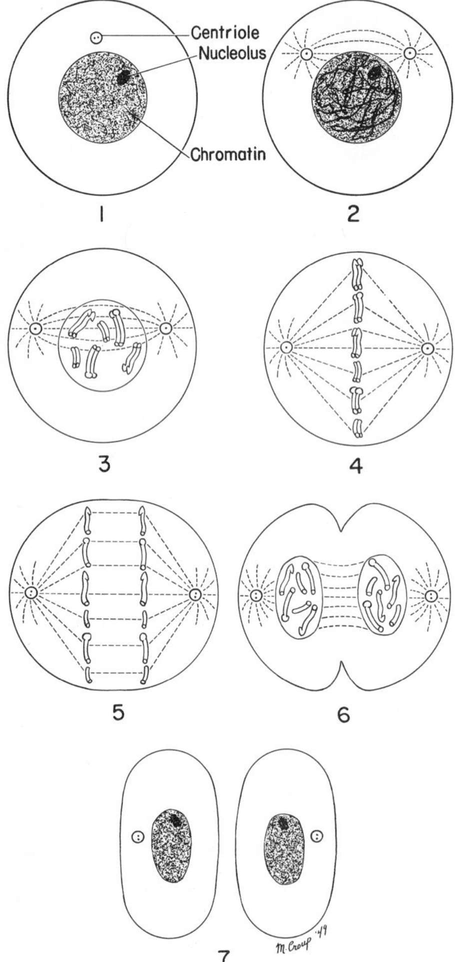

Mitosis shown as occurring in a cell of a hypothetical animal with a diploid chromosome number of six (haploid number three); one pair of chromosomes is short, one pair is long and hooked, and one pair is long and knobbed. *1,* Resting stage. *2,* Early prophase: centriole divided and chromosomes appearing. *3,* Later prophase: centrioles at poles, chromosomes shortened and visibly doubled. *4,* Metaphase: chromosomes arranged on equator of spindle. *5,* Anaphase: chromosomes migrating toward poles. *6,* Telophase: nuclear membranes formed; chromosomes elongating; cytoplasmic divisions beginning. *7,* Daughter cells: resting phase. (Villee.)

mitosome (mit′o-sōm) [*mito-* + Gr. *sōma* body]. A body formed from the spindle fibers of the preceding mitosis; a spindle remnant.

mitotic (mi-tot′ik). Pertaining to mitosis, or karyokinesis.

mitral (mi′tral). 1. Shaped somewhat like a miter. 2. Pertaining to the mitral or bicuspid valve.

mitralism (mi′tral-izm). A tendency toward the development of mitral lesions in the heart.

mitralization (mi″tral-i-za′shun). Straightening of the left border and prominence of the pulmonary salient of the cardiac shadow, a configuration commonly seen roentgenographically in mitral stenosis.

mitro-arterial (mi″tro-ar-te′re-al). Pertaining to or affecting the mitral valve and the arteries.

mittelschmerz (mit′el-shmārts) [Ger. *mittel* mid, middle, + *schmerz* pain, suffering]. Intermenstrual pain.

mittor (mit′or) [L. *mittere* to send]. Any one of the terminals of a neuron which give off the impulse or stimulus to the ceptors of the adjoining neuron. See *neuromittor.*

Mitt. sang. Abbreviation for L. *mit′te san′guinem,* bleed.

mixed (mikst). Affecting various parts at once; showing two or more different characteristics.

mixer (miks′er). A receptacle for diluting a drop of blood preparatory to counting the corpuscles.

mixoscopia (miks″o-sko′pe-ah) [Gr. *mixis* intercourse + *skopein* to examine]. Sexual perversion in which gratification is obtained by the sight of others engaged in sexual intercourse.

mixoscopy (miks-os′ko-pe). Mixoscopia.

Mixter. See *Paul-Mixter.*

mixture (miks′tūr) [L. *mixtura, mistura*]. A combination of different drugs or ingredients, as a fluid resulting from mixing a fluid with other fluids, or with solids, or a suspension of a solid in a liquid. See also under *mistura.* **A.C.E. m.,** an anesthetic mixture of 1 part alcohol, 2 parts chloroform, and 3 parts ether. **Agazotti's m.,** a mixture of oxygen and carbon dioxide: formerly used for aviation sickness. **Aldrich m.,** a 1 per cent aqueous solution of gentian violet for the treatment of burns. **alkali-blood m.,** defibrinated blood 1 part, normal solution of potassium hydroxide 1 part. **antifoaming m.,** saponify spermaceti in an alcoholic solution of sodium hydroxide (2 per cent), and recrystallize the acetyl alcohol from ethyl alcohol. **Baccelli's m.,** a mixture containing quinine sulfate, 3 Gm.; tartaric acid, 3 Gm.; sodium arsenate, 0.05 Gm.; water, 300 cc.: used in malarial fevers. **Bagot's m.,** a local anesthetic mixture of cocaine hydrochloride and spartein sulfate, in boiled water. **baryta m.,** one volume of a saturated solution of barium nitrate and two volumes of a saturated solution of barium hydroxide mixed. **Basham's m.,** liquor ferri et ammonii acetatis. **Bertram's m.,** a mixture of sodium acetate, sulfate, phosphate, and chloride plus a small quantity of iodophenol: used for intravenous injection. **Bestucheff's m.,** ethereal tincture of ferric chloride. **Biedert's cream m.,** a food for young infants, containing cream, water, and milk sugar. **Bonain's m.,** a mixture of phenol, cocaine, and menthol for anesthetizing the tympanic membrane in paracentesis. **brown m.,** mistura glycyrrhizae composita. **Carrel's m.,** a preparation for holding in place grafts on an ulcerated surface, consisting of 18 parts of paraffin melting at 52 C., 6 parts of paraffin melting at 20 C., 2 parts of beeswax, and 1 part of castor oil. **Castellani's m.,** a mixture for treating frambesia, containing tartar emetic, sodium salicylate, potassium iodide, sodium bicarbonate, and water. **C.-E. m.** See *E.-C. m.* **Chabaud's m.,** a fixative mixture containing alcohol, phenol, formalin, and acetic acid. **chalk m.,** prepared chalk, with bentonite magma, cinnamon water, and saccharin sodium: used as an antacid. **Chapman's m.,** a preparation for gonorrhea containing copaiba and spirit of nitrous ether, tincture of opium, compound tincture of lavender, mucilage of acacia, and water. **Coley's m.** See under *fluid.* **Cowgill's salt m.,** sodium chloride, magnesium citrate, KH_2PO_4, $CaHPO_4.2H_2O$, potassium chloride, ferric citrate, potassium iodide. **Dorsey's m.,** magnesium sulfate 5 oz., dilute sulfuric acid 1 dram, oil of cinnamon 5 min., water to make 8 oz. **E.-C. m.,** ether modified by chloroform, usually in the proportion of 16 parts of ether to 1 of chloroform: it secures some of the advantages of chloroform and yet possesses the safety of pure ether. Called also *mitigated ether.* **ECO m.,** 1 cc. ethyl esters of hydnocarpus oil, 1 Gm. camphor, 1 cc. creosote, 25 cc. olive oil: used intramuscularly in leprosy. **Elzholz's m.,** a solution of eosin in glycerin and water: used in leukocyte estimation. **Erlenmeyer's m.,** a mixture of equal parts of the bromides of sodium, potassium, and ammonium. **expectorant m.** See *mistura pectoralis.* **freezing m.,** a mixture for producing artificial cold. **Gadberry's m.,** mistura splenetica. **Glegg's m.,** a mixture of 3 parts liquid paraffin and 1 part of hard paraffin, flavored with rose, applied to the mucosa of the nose and nasopharynx in colds. **Gregory's m.,** Gregory's powder. **Griffith's m.,** compound mixture of iron. **Gunning's m.,** a mixture used in estimating the nitrogen in the urine: consisting of 15 cc. of concentrated sulfuric acid, 10 Gm. of potassium sulfate, and 0.5 Gm. of copper sulfate. **Hermann's m.,** 3 cc. of chloroform, 2 cc. of oil of eucalyptus, and 40 cc. of castor oil. This is divided into two doses and given at hour intervals for intestinal parasites. **Hope's m.,** mistura camphorae acida: an antidysenteric preparation. **Huenefeld's m.,** acetic acid 2, distilled water 1, oil of turpentine, absolute alcohol, chloroform 100 of each. **kaolin m. with pectin,** a preparation containing kaolin, pectin, powdered tragacanth, benzoic acid, saccharin sodium, glycerin, and peppermint oil in purified water: used as an antacid and demulcent. **Karr's salt m.,** sodium chloride, 10; calcium lactate, 4; magnesium citrate, 4; ferric citrate, 1; Lugol's solution, a few drops. **Loomis' m.,** a diarrhea mixture containing oil of sassafras, tincture of opium, tincture of rhubarb, tincture of gambir, and compound tincture of lavender. **magnesia m.,** a mixture of magnesium sulfate, ammonium chloride, distilled water, and concentrated ammonium hydroxide. **Mayer's glycerin-albumin m.,** a mixture of equal parts of white of egg and glycerin, with a little camphor or phenol, for affixing paraffin sections to slides. **Meisen m.,** a 50 per cent solution of dextrose for chemical obliteration of varicose veins. **Mencière's m.,** a mixture of iodoform, guaiacol, eucalyptol, and Peruvian balsam in alcohol and ether: used as a wound dressing. **M.S. m.,** an anesthetic mixture containing 57 parts of ether and 43 parts of chloroform. **N.C.I. m.** See *N.C.I. powder,* under *powder.* **neutral m.,** liquor potassi citratis. **oleobalsamic m.** See *mistura oleobalsamica.* **Osborne and Mendel's salt m.,** $CaCO_3$, 134.8; $MgCO_3$, 24.2; Na_2CO_3, 34.2; KI, 0.02; K_2CO_3, 141.3; H_3PO_4, 103.2; HCl, 53.4; $MnSO_4$, 0.079; H_2SO_4, 9.2; citric acid + H_2O, 111.1; iron citrate + $1\frac{1}{2}H_2O$, 6.34; sodium fluoride, 0.248; $KAl(SO_4)_2$, 0.0245. **Parrish's camphor m.,** mistura camphorae aromatica. **pectoral m.,** mistura pectoralis. **phosphate-carbonate-thiocyanate m.,** powder in a mortar 200 Gm. $Na_2HPO_4.12H_2O$, sprinkle over it 50 Gm. of sodium thiocyanate (or 60 Gm. of potassium thiocyanate), and stir to a uniform semiliquid paste. Add 120 Gm. of monohydrated sodium carbonate (or 110 Gm. of anhydrous carbonate) and mix to a rather fluffy, granular powder. **phosphoric-sulfuric acid-copper sulfate m.,** mix 50 cc. of 5 per cent copper sulfate solution with 300 cc. of 85 per cent phosphoric acid and then add 100 cc. of concentrated sulfuric acid. **racemic m.,** racemate. **Ringer's m.** See under *solution.* **spleen m.,** mistura splenetica. **Squibb's rhubarb m.,** compound rhubarb mixture, N.F. **Startin's m.,** a mixture composed of 4 drachms of magnesium sulfate, 1 drachm of iron sulfate, 4 drachms of syrup of ginger, 3 oz. of dilute sulfuric acid, and enough water to make 3 oz. **T.A. m.** See *toxin-antitoxin.* **Tellyesniczky's m.** See *Tellyesniczky's fluid,* under *fluid.* **Thielmann's m.,** a diarrhea mixture containing 1 fl.oz. of wine of opium, $1\frac{1}{2}$ fl.oz. of tincture of valerian, $\frac{1}{2}$ fl.oz. of ether, 60 minims of oil of peppermint, 15 minims of fluid extract of ipecac, and enough alcohol to make 4 fl.oz. **Townsend's m.,** a mixture of 1 grain of red mercuric oxide, 300 grains of potassium iodide, 2 fl.oz. of syrup of orange peel, 2 fluidrachms of compound tincture of cardamom, and water. **toxin-antitoxin m.** See *toxin-antitoxin.* **triple dye-soap m.,** equal parts of triple dye and soap solution (sapo molis diluted with three parts of water), used as a pliable coagulum for burns. **Velpeau's diarrhea m.,** tincture of opium 42, camphor 4, and compound tincture of gambir to make 100. **Vienna m.,** chloroform 1 part, ether 3 parts. **Vincent's m.** 1. Stearin, paraffin, and petrolatum in the proportion of 1–2–2: used for paraffining tubes used in blood transfusion. 2. A powder composed of an intimate mixture of sodium hypochlorite and boric acid: used as a wound dressing. **Wachsmuth's m.,** an anesthetic mixture of 5 parts of chloroform with 1 part of turpentine.

Miyagawanella (mi″yah-ga″wah-nel′lah) [Yoneji *Miyagawa,* Japanese bacteriologist, born 1885]. A genus of the family Chlamydiaceae, order Rickettsiales, occurring as 12 species making up the psittacosis–lymphogranuloma venereum group of virus-like agents. **M. bo′vis,** a species found in the feces of normal calves. **M. broncho-pneumo′niae,** the etiological agent of mouse pneumonitis. **M. fe′lis,** the etiological agent of feline pneumonitis. **M. illi′nii,** an etiological agent of viral pneumonia. **M. louisia′nae,** the etiological agent of Louisiana pneumonitis. **M. lymphogranulomato′sis,** the etiologic agent of the human disease variously known as lymphogranuloma venereum, lymphogranuloma inguinale, climatic bubo, and esthiomene. **M. opos′sumi,** a species causing paralysis in opossums. **M. ornitho′sis,** the etiological agent of ornithosis. **M. o′vis,** a species causing abortion in sheep. **M. pe′coris,** a species which is the cause of sporadic encephalomyelitis in cattle. **M. pneumo′niae,** an etiological agent of viral pneumonia in man. **M. psit′taci,** the etiological agent of psittacosis (parrot fever) in man and psittacine birds.

M.K.S. Abbreviation for *meter-kilogram-second* system, a system of measurements in which the units are based on the meter as the unit of length, the kilogram as the unit of mass, and the second as the unit of time.

M.L. Abbreviation for *Licentiate in Medicine*, *mesiolingual*, and *midline*.

ml. Abbreviation for *milliliter*.

M.L.A. Abbreviation for L. *mento-laeva anterior* (left mento anterior) position of the fetus, and for *Medical Library Association*.

M.La. Abbreviation for *mesiolabial*.

M. La.I. Abbreviation for *mesiolabioincisal*.

M.L.D. Abbreviation for *minimum lethal dose*.

M.L.I. Abbreviation for *mesiolinguoincisal*.

M.L.O. Abbreviation for *mesiolinguo-occlusal*.

M.L.P. Abbreviation for L. *mento-laeva posterior* (left mento posterior) position of the fetus, and *mesiolinguopulpal*.

M.L.T. Abbreviation for L. *mento-laeva transversa* (left mento transverse) position of the fetus.

M.M. Abbreviation for *mucous membranes*.

mM. Abbreviation for *millimole*.

mm. Abbreviation for *millimeter*, and for *muscles*.

mmm. Abbreviation for *millimicron*.

mm.p.p. Abbreviation for *millimeters partial pressure* (partial pressure expressed in millimeters of mercury).

mμ. Abbreviation for *millimicron*.

mμc. Abbreviation for *millimicrocurie* (nanocurie).

mμg. Abbreviation for *millimicrogram* (nanogram).

μμ. Abbreviation for *micromicron*.

μμc. Abbreviation for *micromicrocurie* (picocurie).

μμg. Abbreviation for *micromicrogram* (picogram).

Mn. Chemical symbol for *manganese*.

mN. Abbreviation for *millinormal*.

M'Naghten rule (mik-naw'ten) [from *M'Naghten*, a person who in 1843 was acquitted by a British court of murder on the ground of insanity]. See under *rule*.

mnemic (ne'mik). Mnemonic.

mnemism (ne'mizm). Mnemic theory.

mnemonic (ne-mon'ik) [Gr. *mnēmonikos* pertaining to memory]. Pertaining to, characterized by, or promoting recollection, or memory.

mnemonics (ne-mon'iks). The cultivation or improvement of memory by special methods or techniques.

mnemotechnics (ne″mo-tek'niks). Mnemonics.

M.O. Abbreviation for *Medical Officer*, and *mesio-occlusal*.

Mo. Chemical symbol for *molybdenum*.

mobility (mo-bil'ĭ-te) [L. *mobilitas*]. Susceptibility of being moved.

mobilization (mo″bĭ-li-za'shun). The process of making a fixed or ankylosed part movable. **stapes m.,** surgical correction of immobility of the stapes, in treatment of deafness.

mobilometer (mo″bil-om'e-ter). An instrument for measuring the consistency of liquids such as oil, cream, liquid foods, etc.

Möbius' disease, sign (me'be-us) [Paul Julius *Möbius*, German neurologist, 1853–1907]. See under the nouns.

moccasin (mok'ah-sin). The venomous snake, *Agkistrodon piscivorus* or water moccasin.

mocezuelo (mo″se-zwa'lo) [Mexican]. Trismus neonatorum.

mock-knee (mok'ne). A large swelling on the knees of horses and cattle, caused usually by repeated injury.

mock-up (mok'up). A full-sized model of an apparatus or other equipment constructed out of substitute materials, used in instruction or for study and improvement of design.

M.O.D. Abbreviation for *mesio-occlusodistal*.

modality (mo-dal'ĭ-te). 1. A homeopathic term signifying a condition which modifies drug action; a condition under which symptoms develop, becoming better or worse. 2. A method of application of, or the employment of, any therapeutic agent; limited usually to physical agents. 3. A specific sensory entity, such as taste.

mode (mōd). In statistics, the value or item in a variations curve which shows the maximum frequency of occurrence.

moderil (mod'er-il). Trade mark for a preparation of rescinnamine.

modification (mod″ĭ-fi-ka'shun). The process or result of changing the form or characteristics of an object or substance. **racemic m.** See *racemate*.

modioliform (mo″de-o'lĭ-form). Shaped like the hub of a wheel.

modiolus (mo-di'o-lus) [L. "nave," "hub"]. [N A, B N A] The central pillar or columella of the cochlea.

Mod. praesc. Abbreviation for L. *mo'do praescrip'to*, in the way directed.

modulation (mod″u-la'shun) [L. *modulare* to measure]. The normal capacity of cell adaptability to its environment.

modulator (mod″u-la'tor). A specific inductor that brings out characteristics peculiar to a definite region.

modumate (mod'u-māt). Trade mark for a preparation of arginine and glutamic acid.

modus (mo'dus) [L.]. Manner; method. **m. operan'di,** the method of performing an operation or action.

Moe plate (mo) [John H. *Moe*, American surgeon, born 1905]. See under *plate*.

Moeller's glossitis (me'lerz) [Julius Otto L. *Moeller*, German surgeon, 1819–1887]. See under *glossitis*.

Moeller's itch (me'lerz) [C. P. *Moeller*, Danish dermatologist, 1845–1917]. Norwegian scabies.

Moeller's reaction (me'lerz) [Alfred *Moeller*, German bacteriologist, born 1868]. See under *reaction*.

Moeller-Barlow disease (me'ler-bar'lo) [J. O. L. *Moeller;* Sir Thomas *Barlow*, London physician, 1845–1945]. See under *disease*.

Moenckeberg (menk'ĕ-berg). See *Mönckeberg*.

Moentjang tina. The Malay term in the Netherlands East Indies for intoxication caused by the use in food of oil obtained from the fruit of *Hernanda sonora*. Ordinarily the oil is used only in lamps.

Moerner-Sjöqvist method, test (mer'ner-syek'vist) [Carl Thore *Moerner*, Swedish physician, 1864–1917; John August *Sjöqvist*, Swedish physician, 1863–1934]. See *Sjöqvist method*, under *method*.

mogi- (moj'e) [Gr. *mogis* with difficulty]. A combining form meaning difficult, or with difficulty.

mogiarthria (moj-e-ar'thre-ah) [*mogi-* + Gr. *arthron* joint + *-ia*]. A form of dysarthria in which there is defective coordination of the muscles involved.

mogigraphia (moj-e-gra'fe-ah) [*mogi-* + Gr. *graphein* to write]. Writers' cramp.

mogilalia (moj-e-la'le-ah) [*mogi-* + *lalia* chatter]. Difficulty in speech; stuttering.

mogiphonia (moj-e-fo'ne-ah) [*mogi-* + Gr. *phōnē* voice]. Difficulty in making vocal sounds.

M.O.H. Abbreviation for *Medical Officer of Health*.

Mohr's test (mōrz) [Francis *Mohr*, American pharmaceutical chemist]. See under *tests*.

Mohrenheim's fossa (mo'ren-hīmz) [Baron Joseph Jacob Freiherr von *Mohrenheim*, Austrian surgeon, died 1799]. See under *fossa*.

moiety (moi'ĕ-te) [Fr. *moitié*, from L. *medietas*, *medius*, middle]. Any equal part; a half; also any part or portion. **carbohydrate m.,** the nonnitrogenous residue of the amino acids resulting from deamination.

moist (moist). Somewhat wet; damp.

Mojon's method (mo'e-onz) [Benedetto *Mojon*, professor of anatomy and physiology at Genoa, 19th century]. See under *method*.

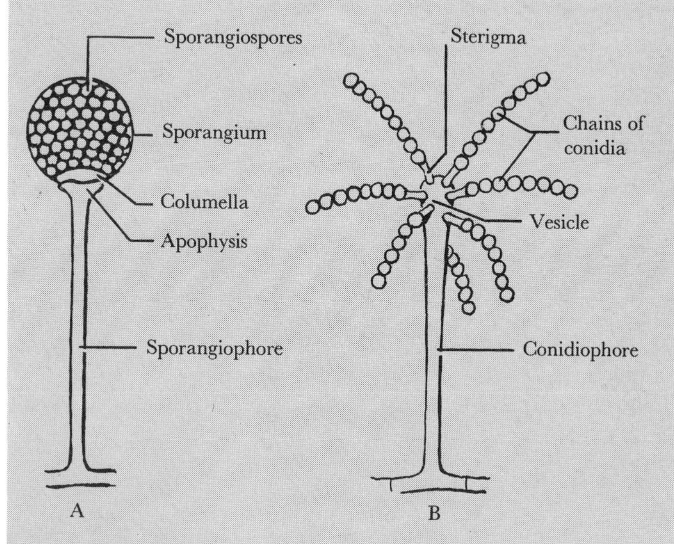

Fruiting bodies of Rhizopus (A) and Aspergillus (B). (Carpenter: Microbiology.)

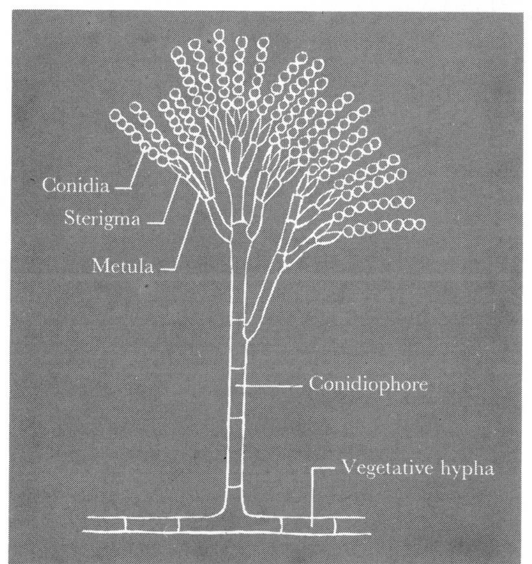

Drawing of Penicillium, showing the brush-like appearance of the parallel chains of conidia characteristic of this genus. (Carpenter: Microbiology.)

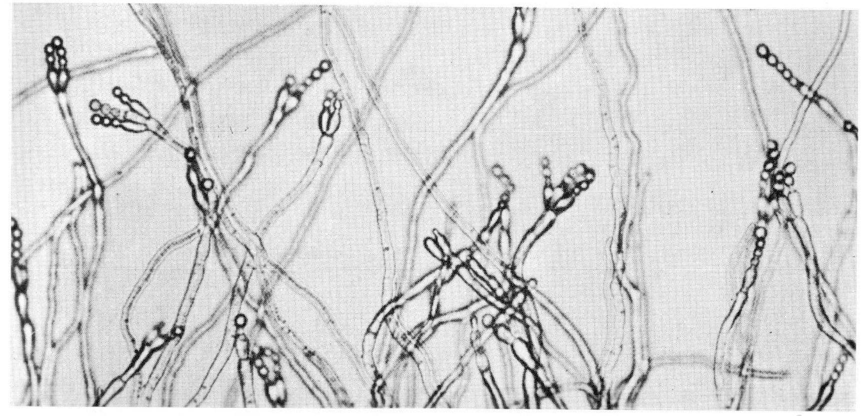

Photomicrograph of a Penicillium, showing twisted, branching hyphae and a few chains of conidia. (Courtesy of The Abbott Laboratories, North Chicago, Ill.)

CHARACTERISTIC STRUCTURES OF COMMON MOLDS

mol (mol). Mole, def. 3.

molality (mo-lal′ĭ-te). The number of moles of a solute per kilogram of pure solvent. Cf. *molarity.*

molar (mo′lar). 1. [L. *moles* mass.] Pertaining to a mass; not molecular. 2. [L. *molaris* to do with grinding]. Adapted for grinding. See under *tooth.* 3. Pertaining to a mole. **impacted m.,** a molar tooth that is prevented from erupting, or from taking its place in normal occlusion. **Moon's m's.** See under *tooth.* **mulberry m.,** a molar tooth with irregular crown, the enamel apparently consisting of an agglomerate mass of globules; seen in congenital syphilis. **sixth-year m.,** one of the permanent first molar teeth, so called because they erupt at the age of 6 (or 7) years. **twelfth-year m.,** one of the permanent second molar teeth, so called because they erupt at the age of 12 (11 to 13) years.

molariform (mo-lar′ĭ-form). Shaped like a molar tooth.

molarity (mol-ar′ĭ-te). The number of moles of a solute per liter of solution. Cf. *molality.*

molasquit (mo-las′kit). A horse and cattle food prepared from molasses and the bagasse from sugar mills.

molasses (mo-las′ez) [L. *mellaceus* like honey]. A thick, sweet syrup, the residue left after crystallization of sugar; treacle; syrupus fuscus. **sugar-house m.,** that which is left after the refining of sugar. **West India m.,** a variety obtained in making raw sugar.

mold (mōld). 1. Any one of a large group of minute parasitic and saprophytic fungi which cause mold or moldiness; also the deposit or growth produced by such fungi. The common molds are *Mucor, Penicillium, Rhizopus,* or *Aspergillus.* 2. A form in which an object is given shape, or cast. **white m.,** white or slightly woolly patches which form on the surface of meat in cold storage due to the growth of a fungus, *Sporotrichum carnis.*

molding (mōld′ing). The creation of shape, or fashioning of an object. **border m.,** the shaping of an impression material by the manipulation or action of the tissues and structures adjacent to the edge of the material. **compression m.,** the pressing or squeezing together of a plastic material to form a shape in a mold. **injection m.,** the fashioning of an object by forcing a plastic material into a closed mold through appropriate openings. **tissue m.,** border m.

mole (mōl) [L. *moles* a shapeless mass]. 1. A fleshy mass or tumor formed in the uterus by the degeneration or abortive development of an ovum. 2. A nevus; the term is also used to designate a pigmented fleshy growth, and is applied loosely to any blemish of the skin. 3. That amount of a chemical compound whose mass in grams is equivalent to its formula mass. **blood m.,** a mass in the uterus which is made up of blood clots, the placenta, and fetal membranes retained after abortion. **Breus' m.,** a malformation of the ovum consisting of tuberous subchorional hematoma of the decidua. Called also *hematomole.* **cystic m.,** hydatid m. **false m.,** an intra-uterine mass formed from a polyp or tumor. **fleshy m.** 1. A blood mole which has assumed a fleshlike appearance. 2. One formed by a dead ovum in the uterus. **hairy m.,** hairy nevus. **hydatid m., hydatidiform m.,** a mole formed by the proliferation of the chorionic villi, resulting in a mass of cysts that resembles a bunch of grapes. Called also *vesicular m.* **invasive m., malignant m.,** chorioadenoma. **pigmented m.,** nevus pigmentosus. **stone m.,** a mole which has undergone a calcareous degeneration. **true m.,** a mole which represents the degenerated ovum itself. **tubal m.,** the mass of blood clot and chorionic villi found after death of the embryo in a tubal pregnancy. **vesicular m.,** hydatid m.

molecular (mo-lek′u-lar). Of, pertaining to, or composed of, molecules.

molecule (mol′ĕ-kūl) [L. *molecula* little mass]. A very small mass of matter; an aggregation of atoms; specifically, a chemical combination of two or more atoms which form a specific chemical substance. To break up the molecule into its constituent atoms is to change its character. The number of atoms in a molecule varies with the compound. **diatomic m.,** one containing two atoms. **hexatomic m.,** one containing six atoms. **monatomic m.,** one which consists of a single atom. **nonpolar m.,** a molecule in which the electrical potential is symmetrically distributed over the molecule. **polar m.,** a molecule in which the electrical potential is not symmetrically distributed. **tetratomic m.,** a molecule made up of four atoms. **triatomic m.,** one composed of three atoms.

molilalia (mol″ĭ-la′le-ah). Mogilalia.

molimen (mo-li′men), pl. *molim′ina* [L. "effort"]. A natural and normal effort made for the performance of any function; especially the monthly effort to establish the menstrual flow.

Molisch's test (mol′ish-ez) [Hans *Molisch,* chemist in Vienna, 1856–1937]. See under *tests.*

Moll's glands (molz) [Jacob Antonius *Moll,* Dutch oculist, 1832–1914]. The ciliary glands, the small modified sudoriferous glands of the eyelids.

mollescuse (mol-les′kūs) [L. *mollis* soft]. Softening.

Möllgaard treatment (mel′gahrd) [Holger *Möllgaard,* Danish veterinarian]. Treatment of tuberculosis with sanocrysin and convalescent serum. Cf. *sanocrysin.*

mollin (mol′in). A glycerinated soft soap with excess of fats: used as a vehicle for medicines to be applied externally.

mollities (mo-lish′e-ēz) [L.]. Softness; abnormal softening. **m. os′sium,** osteomalacia. **m. un′guium,** abnormal softness of the nails.

mollusc (mol′usk). Any member of the phylum Mollusca.

Mollusca (mol-lus′kah) [L. *molluscus* soft]. A phylum of animals containing snails, slugs, mussels, oysters, clams, etc.

molluscacidal (mol-lusk″ah-si′dal). Destructive to snails and other molluscs.

molluscacide (mol-lusk′ah-sīd). An agent that will destroy snails and other molluscs.

molluscicide (mol-lus′sĭ-sīd). Molluscacide.

molluscous (mol-lus′kus). Pertaining to molluscum.

molluscum (mol-lus′kum) [L. "soft"]. The name of various skin diseases characterized by the formation of soft rounded cutaneous tumors. **cholesterinic m.,** essential xanthoma. **m. contagio′sum, m. epithelia′le,** a skin disease caused by a virus and marked by the formation of firm, rounded skin tubercles containing a semifluid caseous matter or solid masses made up of fat, epidermis, and peculiar capsulated bodies (*m. corpuscles*). The tubercles appear usually upon the face, are very chronic in their course, and are without general symptoms. **m. fibro′sum, m. pen′dulum, m. sim′plex,** diseases marked by the development of multiple fibromas of the skin, which often form pendulous growths. They arise from the corium or the subcutaneous tissue. **m. lipomato′des,** essential xanthoma. **m. seba′ceum, m. variolifor′mis,** molluscum contagiosum. **m. verruco′sum,** a late stage of molluscum contagiosum in which the growths have become wartlike masses.

mollusk (mol′usk). Mollusc.

Moloney test (mo-lo′ne) [Peter J. *Moloney,* Canadian immunochemist, born 1891]. See under *tests.*

molting (mōlt′ing). Ecdysis.

molugram (mol′u-gram). A gram-molecule.

Mol. wt. Abbreviation for *molecular weight.*

molybdate (mo-lib′dāt). Any salt of molybdic acid: some are used as tests.

molybdenosis (mo-lib″dĕ-no′sis). Chronic molybdenum poisoning.

molybdenum (mo-lib′dĕ-num) [Gr. *molybdos* lead]. A hard, silvery-white, metallic element; symbol, Mo; atomic number, 42; atomic weight, 95.94; specific gravity, 10.2.

molybdic (mo-lib′dik). Containing molybdenum as a hexad element.

molybdous (mo-lib′dus). Containing molybdenum as a tetrad element.

molysmophobia (mol″is-mo-fo′be-ah) [Gr. *molysma* stain + *phobia*]. Mysophobia; fear of contamination.

Momburg's belt (mom′burgz) [Friedrich *Momburg*, German surgeon, born 1870]. See under *belt*.

momentum (mo-men′tum) [L.]. The quantity of motion; the product of mass by velocity.

monacid (mon-as′id). Containing one atom of hydrogen that is replaceable by a base: said of a salt or of an alcohol.

monad (mon′ad) [Gr. *monas* a unit]. 1. A single-celled protozoon or a single-celled coccus. 2. A univalent radical or element. 3. In miosis, one member of a tetrad.

monadin (mon′ah-din). Any microorganism or species belonging to the Monadina.

Monadina (mon″ah-di′nah). A group of rhizopod animal endoparasites; sometimes found in feces and sputum, but not known to have any pathogenic influence.

Monakow's bundle, fasciculus, tract (mon-ah′kovz) [Constantin von *Monakow*, neurologist in Zurich, 1853–1930]. Prepyramidal tract. **M's theory.** See *diaschisis*.

Monaldi's drainage (mo-nal′dēz) [V. *Monaldi*, Italian physician]. See under *drainage*.

monamide (mon-am′id). An amide which contains only one amide group.

monamine (mon-am′in). An amine which contains only one amine group.

monaminuria (mon″am-ĭ-nu′re-ah). The presence of a monamine in the urine.

monangle (mon′ang-g'l). Having only one angle; Black's term for a dental instrument having only one angulation in the shank connecting the handle, or shaft, with the working portion of the instrument, known as the blade, or nib.

monarthric (mon-ar′thrik). Pertaining to or affecting a single joint.

monarthritis (mon″ar-thri′tis) [*mono-* + *arthritis*]. Inflammation of a single joint. **m. defor′mans,** arthritis deformans of a single joint.

monarticular (mon″ar-tik′u-lar). Monarthric.

Monas (mo′nas) [Gr. *monas* monad]. A genus of minute, solitary, free-swimming, protozoan organisms. *M. lens* is found in sputum.

monaster (mon-as′ter) [*mono-* + Gr. *astēr* star]. The single star-shaped figure at the end of the prophase in mitosis.

monathetosis (mon″ath-e-to′sis) [*mono-* + *athetosis*]. Athetosis of one part of the body.

monatomic (mon″ah-tom′ik) [*mono-* + Gr. *atomos* indivisible]. 1. Univalent. 2. Monobasic.

monauchenos (mon-awk′ĕ-nus). A dicephalic monster with one neck.

monaural (mon-aw′ral). Pertaining to one ear.

monavalent (mon-av′ah-lent). Monovalent.

monavitaminosis (mon″ah-vi″tah-min-o′sis). A deficiency disease in which only one vitamin is lacking in the diet.

monaxon (mon-ak′son) [*mono-* + Gr. *axōn* axis]. A neuron possessing only one axon.

monaxonic (mon″ak-son′ik). Having one axon.

Mönckeberg's arteriosclerosis, calcification, degeneration, sclerosis (menk′ĕ-bergz) [Johann Georg *Mönckeberg*, pathologist at Bonn, 1878–1925]. See under *arteriosclerosis*.

Mondeville (mon″dĕ-ve′yuh), Henri de (1260–1320). A distinguished French surgeon—surgeon to Philip the Fair and Louis X, who wrote a surgical text (the first French one) containing many observations (e.g., on wound healing) that were far ahead of the times.

Mondonesi reflex (mon″do-na′ze) [Filippo *Mondonesi*, Italian physician]. See under *reflex*.

Mondor's disease (mon′dorz) [Henri *Mondor*, French surgeon, 1885–1962]. See under *disease*.

moner (mo′ner). A non-nucleated mass of protoplasm.

Monera (mo-ne′rah) [Gr. *monērēs* single]. A name previously given a supposed group of protozoal organisms of the simplest form, microorganisms without true nuclei, plastids, or sexual reproduction.

monerula (mo-ner′u-lah), pl. *moner′ulae* [Gr. *monērēs* single]. An impregnated ovum with as yet no cleavage nucleus.

monesia (mo-ne′ze-ah) [L.]. An extract from monesia bark, the product of *Chrysophyllum glyciphloeum*, a tree of Brazil: astringent and stomachic.

monesthetic (mon″es-thet′ik) [Gr. *monos* single + *aisthēsis* perception]. Pertaining to or affecting a single sense or sensation.

monestrous (mon-es′trus). Completing only one estrous cycle in each sexual season.

Monge's disease (mon′gez) [Carlos *Monge*, pathologist in Lima, Peru]. See under *disease*.

mongolian (mon-go′le-an). Pertaining to, resembling, or belonging to the Mongols. See *mongoloid*.

mongolism (mon′go-lizm). A condition characterized by a small, anteroposteriorly flattened skull, short, flat-bridged nose, epicanthus, short phalanges, and widened space between the first and second digits of hands and feet, with moderate to severe mental retardation, and associated with a chromosomal abnormality.

mongoloid (mon′go-loid) [*Mongol* + Gr. *eidos* like]. 1. Pertaining to or resembling the Mongols, one of the chief ethnological divisions of the Asiatic peoples. See *mongolism*. 2. An individual with characteristics resembling the Mongols.

Moniezia (mon″ĭ-e′ze-ah). A genus of tapeworms of cattle, goats and sheep.

monilated (mon′il-āt″ed). Moniliform.

monilethricosis (mo-nil″e-thrik-o′sis). Monilethrix.

monilethrix (mo-nil′e-thriks) [L. *monile* necklace + Gr. *thrix* hair]. A disease condition in which the hairs exhibit beadlike enlargements and become brittle.

Monilia (mo-nil′e-ah) [L. *monile* necklace]. The former name for a genus of fungi now called Candida.

monilial (mo-nil′e-al). Pertaining to or caused by Monilia (Candida).

moniliasis (mon-ĭ-li′ah-sis). An infection caused by Monilia (Candida); candidiasis.

moniliform (mo-nil′ĭ-form) [L. *monile* necklace + *forma* form]. Shaped like a necklace or string of beads.

Moniliformis (mo-nil″ĭ-for′mis). A genus of acanthocephalous nematodes. *M. monilifor′mis* is a parasite of rats, mice, and dogs, and a facultative parasite in man.

moniliid (mo-nil′e-id). Any allergic skin eruption due to cutaneous moniliasis.

moniliosis (mo-nil″e-o′sis). Moniliasis.

monitor (mon′ĭ-tor) [L. "one who reminds," from *monere* to remind, admonish]. 1. To constantly check on a state or condition, as to constantly check on the vital signs of a patient under anesthesia and undergoing surgery, or to determine the amount received by a person exposed to radiation. 2. An apparatus which automatically records such physiological signs as respiration, pulse, and blood pressure in an anesthetized patient or one undergoing surgical or other procedures.

monium (mo′ne-um) [Gr. *monos* single]. A name

given an earth metal discovered in 1898, later found to be a mixture of rare earth metals.

Moniz (mo′nēz), Antonio Egas. Portuguese neurosurgeon, 1874–1955, noted for the development of cerebral angiography and the introduction of prefrontal lobotomy; co-winner, with Walter Rudolf Hess, of the Nobel prize for medicine and physiology in 1949.

monkey paw (mon′ke-paw). A condition in which the thumb lies in adduction and extension and cannot be opposed so as to touch the tips of the other fingers, occurring in lesion of the median nerve.

Monneret's pulse (mon-rāz′) [Jules Auguste Eduard *Monneret*, physician in Paris, 1810–1868]. See under *pulse*.

mono- (mon′o) [Gr. *monos* single]. Combining form denoting one or single; limited to one part; in chemistry, combined with one atom.

mono-aminodiphosphatide (mon″o-am″ĭ-no-di-fos′fah-tīd). A phosphatide containing 1 atom of nitrogen and 2 of phosphorus to the molecule.

mono-aminomonophosphatide (mon″o-am″-ĭ-no-mon″o-fos′fah-tīd). A phosphatide containing 1 atom of nitrogen and 1 of phosphorus to the molecule.

mono-anesthesia (mon″o-an″es-the′ze-ah) [*mono-* + *anesthesia*]. Anesthesia of a single part or organ.

mono-articular (mon″o-ar-tik′u-lar). Monarthric.

monobacillary (mon″o-bas′ĭ-lār″e). Caused by or containing a single species of bacillus.

monobacterial (mon″o-bak-te′re-al). Monobacillary.

monobasic (mon″o-ba′sik) [*mono-* + Gr. *basis* base]. Having but one base; a term applied to an acid having only one replaceable atom of hydrogen and therefore yielding only one series of salts, as HCl.

monobenzone (mon″o-ben′zōn). Chemical name: p-benzyloxyphenol: used as a hypopigmenting agent.

monoblast (mon′o-blast) [*mono-* + Gr. *blastos* germ]. The cell which is the precursor of the mature monocyte.

monoblastoma (mon″o-blas-to′mah). A neoplasm containing monoblasts and monocytes.

monoblepsia (mon″o-blep′se-ah) [*mono-* + Gr. *blepsis* sight + *-ia*]. 1. A condition of the vision in which it is more distinct when only one eye is used. 2. A variety of color blindness in which only one color is perceived.

monobrachia (mon″o-bra′ke-ah) [*mono-* + Gr. *brachion* arm + *-ia*]. A developmental anomaly characterized by the presence of a single arm.

monobrachius (mon″o-bra′ke-us). An individual exhibiting monobrachia.

monobromated (mon″o-bro′māt-ed) [L. *monobromatus*]. Having a single atom of bromine in each molecule.

monobromophenol (mon″o-bro″mo-fe′nol). A violet-colored liquid, $OH.C_6H_4Br$, of penetrating odor, soluble in water, alcohol, and ether, and used as an external antiseptic, especially in erysipelas, in 3 to 6 per cent ointment.

monobulia (mon″o-bu′le-ah) [*mono-* + Gr. *boulē* will + *-ia*]. An abnormally concentrated wishing on one thing only.

monocalcic (mon″o-kal′sik). Containing one atom of calcium in the molecule.

monocardian (mon-o-kar′de-an) [*mono-* + Gr. *kardia* heart]. Possessing a heart with a single atrium and ventricle.

monocelled (mon′o-seld) [*mono-* + *cell*]. Unicellular; consisting of a single cell.

monocephalus (mon″o-sef′ah-lus) [*mono-* + Gr. *kephalē* head]. A fetal monster with one head but with some duplication of its parts. **m. tet′rapus dibra′chius,** a fetal monster with one head, two arms, and partial or complete duplication of the pelvis, with four legs, the pair belonging to one member often being fused in a single limb. **m. tri′pus dibra′chius,** a fetal monster with one head, two arms, and partial duplication of the pelvis, with a median third leg or leg rudiment.

monochlorothymol (mon″o-klo″ro-thi′mol). Chlorothymol.

monochord (mon′o-kord) [*mono-* + Gr. *chordē* cord]. An instrument for testing upper tone audition. It consists of a long steel or silver wire fastened at the ends and having an intermediate movable clamp. The tone is produced by longitudinal friction. Called also *Schultze's monochord.*

monochorea (mon″o-ko-re′ah) [*mono-* + *chorea*]. Chorea affecting but one part.

monochorionic (mon″o-ko″re-on′ik) [*mono-* + *chorionic*]. Having one common chorion: said of true twins.

monochroic (mon″o-kro′ik) [*mono-* + Gr. *chroa* color]. Having only one color.

monochromasy (mon″o-kro′mah-se). Blindness to all colors but one: color blindness, in which all colors are seen as one color.

monochromat (mon″o-kro′mat). A person totally color blind.

monochromatic (mon″o-kro-mat′ik) [*mono-* + Gr. *chrōma* color]. 1. Existing in or having only one color. 2. Pertaining to or characterized by perception of a single color band in the spectrum. 3. Staining with only one dye at a time. Cf. *polychromatic.*

monochromatophil (mon″o-kro-mat′o-fil) [*mono-* + Gr. *chrōma* color + *philein* to love]. 1. Stainable with only one kind of stain. 2. Any cell or other element that will take only one stain.

monochromator (mon″o-kro′mah-tor). A device designed for selective transmission of homogeneous radiant energy.

monochromophilic (mon″o-kro″mo-fil′ik). Stainable with only one kind of stain.

monoclinic (mon″o-klin′ik) [*mono-* + Gr. *klinein* to incline]. A term applied to crystals in which the vertical axis is inclined to one lateral axis, but is at right angles to the other.

monococcus (mon″o-kok′us), pl. *monococ′ci* [*mono-* + Gr. *kokkos* berry]. A coccus neither double nor formed into groups, pairs, or chains.

monocontaminated (mon″o-kon-tam′ĭ-nāt″ed). Infected by a single species of microorganism, or by a single type of contaminating agent.

monocontamination (mon″o-kon-tam″ĭ-na′-shun). Experimental infection of a previously germ-free animal by a single infectious agent.

monocorditis (mon″o-kōr-di′tis). Inflammation of one vocal cord.

monocranius (mon″o-kra′ne-us) [*mono-* + Gr. *kranion* cranium]. Monocephalus.

monocrotic (mon″o-krot′ik). Characterized by monocrotism.

monocrotism (mo-nok′ro-tizm) [*mono-* + Gr. *krotos* beat]. The quality in a pulse wave of having neither a normal elastic elevation nor a dicrotic or tricrotic one.

monocular (mon-ok′u-lar) [*mono-* + L. *oculus* eye]. 1. Pertaining to or having but one eye. 2. Having but one eyepiece, as in a microscope.

monoculus (mon-ok′u-lus) [*mono-* + L. *oculus* eye]. 1. A bandage for but one eye. 2. A cyclops.

monocyclic (mon″o-si′klik). Pertaining to one cycle. In chemistry, having an atomic structure containing only one ring.

monocyesis (mon″o-si-e′sis) [*mono-* + Gr. *kyēsis* pregnancy]. Pregnancy with a single fetus.

Monocystis (mon″o-sis′tis) [*mono-* + Gr. *kystis* sac, bladder]. A genus of gregarines, species of which are parasitic in the seminal vesicles of the earthworm. **M. epithelia′lis,** Pfeiffer's name for the protozoan bodies found by him in the cells of the skin.

monocytangina (mon″o-sīt-an′jin-ah). Infectious mononucleosis.

monocyte (mon′o-sīt) [*mono-* + *-cyte*]. A large leukocyte, 9 to 12 μ in diameter, with an oval or indented, pale nucleus and having more protoplasm than a lymphocyte; a large hyaline leukocyte. Such cells were formerly called large mononuclear leukocytes and transitional leukocytes.

monocytic (mon″o-sit′ik). Characterized by or of the nature of monocytes.

monocytoid (mon″o-si′toid). Resembling a monocyte.

monocytopenia (mon″o-si″to-pe′ne-ah) [*monocyte* + Gr. *penia* poverty]. Abnormal decrease in the proportion of monocytes in the blood.

monocytopoiesis (mon″o-si″to-poi-e′sis) [*monocyte* + Gr. *poiein* to make]. The formation of monocytes.

monocytosis (mon″o-si-to′sis). Increase in the proportion of monocytes in the blood.

monodactylia (mon″o-dak-til′e-ah) [*mono-* + Gr. *daktylos* finger + *-ia*]. A developmental anomaly characterized by the presence of only one digit on a hand or foot.

monodactylism (mon-o-dak′til-izm). Monodactylia.

monodactyly (mon″o-dak′tĭ-le). Monodactylia.

monodal (mon-o′dal) [*mono-* + Gr. *hodos* road]. Having connection with one terminal of a resonator or of a grounded solenoid, so that the patient is a capacitor for entrance and exit of high frequency currents.

monodermoma (mon″o-der-mo′mah). A tumor that has developed from one germinal layer.

monodiplopia (mon″o-dĭ-plo′pe-ah) [*mono-* + Gr. *diploos* double + *ōps* eye + *-ia*]. Double vision in either eye alone.

Monodontus (mon″o-don′tus). A genus of tapeworms of cattle and sheep and other ruminants.

monodral (mon′o-dral). Trade mark for preparations of penthienate.

monoerg (mon′o-erg). An antiserum which reacts with its homologous antigen only.

monofilm (mon′o-film). A monomolecular layer of protein transferred to a prepared plate.

monogametic (mon″o-gah-met′ik) [*mono-* + *gamete*]. Having only one kind of gametes with respect to the sex chromosomes.

monogamy (mo-nog′ah-me) [*mono-* + Gr. *gamos* marriage]. Marriage to a single spouse.

monoganglial (mon″o-gang′gle-al). Affecting a single ganglion.

monogastric (mon″o-gas′trik) [*mono-* + Gr. *gastēr* stomach]. Having but one belly or stomach.

monogen (mon′o-jen). 1. A univalent chemical element which combines in only one proportion. 2. An antiserum produced by the use of one antigen.

monogenesis (mon″o-jen′e-sis) [*mono-* + Gr. *genesis* production]. 1. Nonsexual reproduction. 2. The production of only male or female offspring. 3. The theory that all things develop from a single cell.

monogenous (mo-noj′e-nus) [*mono-* + Gr. *gennan* to produce]. Produced or formed asexually, as by fission.

monogerminal (mon″o-jer′mĭ-nal). Developed from one ovum: said of twin fetuses occupying a single chorionic sac.

monogonium (mon″o-go′ne-um), pl. *monogo′nia*. Any one of the asexual forms of the malarial parasite as it occurs in the blood. These forms produce the febrile attacks.

monogony (mo-nog′o-ne) [*mono-* + Gr. *gonē* seed]. Asexual reproduction.

monograph (mon′o-graf) [*mono-* + Gr. *graphein* to write]. An essay or treatise on one subject.

monohemerous (mon″o-hem′er-us) [*mono-* + Gr. *hēmera* day]. Lasting only one day.

monohybrid (mon″o-hi′brid). The offspring of parents differing in one character.

monohydrated (mon″o-hi′drāt-ed). United with a single molecule of water or of hydroxyl.

monohydric (mon″o-hi′drik). Containing one atom of replaceable hydrogen.

monoideism (mon″o-i-de′izm) [Gr. *monos* single + *idea* idea + *-ism*]. Morbid preoccupation with a single idea.

monoinfection (mon″o-in-fek′shun). Infection with a single kind of organism.

monoiodotyrosine (mon″o-i-o″do-ti′ro-sēn). One of the thyroid hormones: an organic iodine-containing compound liberated from thyroglobulin by hydrolysis, and thought to be formed by the iodination of tyrosine.

monoketoheptose (mon″o-ke″to-hep′tōs). A natural sugar, $CH_2OH.CO(CHOH)_4.CH_2OH$, found in *Persea gratissima*.

monolayer (mon″o-la′er). Pertaining to or consisting of a single layer, such as a monolayer sheet of cells in cultures used in studies of viruses.

monolene (mon′o-lēn). A clear white, oily hydrocarbon.

monolepsis (mon″o-lep′sis) [*mono-* + Gr. *lēpsis* a taking]. The transmission to the offspring of the characters of one parent, to the exclusion of those of the other.

monolocular (mon″o-lok′u-lar) [*mono-* + L. *loculus* cell]. Having but one cell or cavity.

monomania (mon″o-ma′ne-ah) [*mono-* + Gr. *mania* madness]. Insanity on a single subject or class of subjects. **emotional m.,** monomania with respect to one or a few related emotions. **intellectual m.,** a monomania with respect to one or a few related delusions.

monomastigote (mon″o-mas′tĭ-gōt) [*mono-* + Gr. *mastix* lash]. Having a single flagellum.

monomaxillary (mon″o-mak′sĭ-ler″e). Affecting one jaw.

monomelic (mon″o-mel′ik) [*mono-* + Gr. *melos* limb]. Affecting one limb.

monomer (mon′o-mer). A simple molecule of a compound of relatively low molecular weight. **fibrin m.,** the material resulting from the action of thrombin on fibrinogen, which then polymerizes to form fibrin.

monomeric (mon″o-mer′ik) [*mono-* + Gr. *meros* part]. Pertaining to, made up of, or affecting, a single segment.

monometallic (mon″o-me-tal′ik). Having one atom of a metal in the molecule.

monomethylxanthine (mon″o-meth″il-zan′-thin). Heteroxanthine.

monomicrobic (mon″o-mi-kro′bik). Characterized by the presence of a single species of microbe.

monomolecular (mon″o-mo-lek′u-lar). Pertaining to or involving one molecule.

monomoria (mon″o-mo′re-ah) [*mono-* + Gr. *mōria* silliness, folly]. Monomania.

monomorphic (mon″o-mor′fik) [*mono-* + Gr. *morphē* form]. Existing in only one form; maintaining the same form throughout all stages of development.

monomorphism (mon″o-mor′fizm). The quality or condition of being monomorphic.

monomphalus (mon-om′fah-lus) [*mono-* + Gr. *omphalos* navel]. A double monster joined at the navel.

monomyoplegia (mon″o-mi′o-ple′je-ah) [*mono-* + Gr. *mys* muscle + *plēgē* stroke]. Paralysis restricted to a single muscle.

monomyositis (mon″o-mi″o-si′tis) [*mono-* + *myositis*]. A myositis of the biceps muscle occurring periodically.

Mononchus (mon-ong′kus). A genus of nematodes found in urine of inhabitants in the Canal Zone.

mononephrous (mon″o-nef′rus) [*mono-* + Gr. *nephros* kidney]. Affecting one kidney only.

mononeural (mon″o-nu′ral). Pertaining to or receiving branches from a single nerve.

mononeuric (mon″o-nu′rik) [*mono-* + Gr. *neuron* nerve]. Having only one neuron.

mononeuritis (mon″o-nu-ri′tis) [*mono-* + Gr. *neuron* nerve + *-itis*]. Inflammation of a single nerve. **m. mul′tiplex,** simultaneous inflammation of several nerves remote from one another.

mononoea (mon″o-ne′ah) [*mono-* + Gr. *nous* mind]. Mental concentration on a single subject.

monont (mon′ont). Schizont.

mononuclear (mon″o-nu′kle-ar) [*mono-* + *nucleus*]. 1. Having but one nucleus; uninuclear. 2. A cell having a single nucleus, especially a monocyte of the blood or tissues.

mononucleate (mon″o-nu′kle-āt). Having a single nucleus.

mononucleosis (mon″o-nu″kle-o′sis). The presence of an abnormally large number of mononuclear leukocytes (monocytes) in the blood. **infectious m.,** an acute infectious disease characterized by a sudden onset and acute course, with fever and inflammatory swelling of the lymph nodes, especially those of the cervical region. There is a moderate leukocytosis due almost entirely to abnormal mononuclear cells and sometimes there are severe faucial lesions. Three clinical types are recognized: 1, glandular or Pfeiffer's type; 2, anginose type (monocytic angina); 3, febrile type. Called also *glandular fever, acute benign lymphoblastosis, acute lymphadenosis, monocytic angina,* and *acute infectious adenitis.*

mononucleotide (mon″o-nu′kle-o-tīd). A product obtained by the digestion or hydrolytic decomposition of nucleic acid. It is a compound of phosphoric acid and a glucoside or a pentoside. These latter are combinations of dextrose or a pentose (ribose) with one of the following bases: guanine, adenine, cytosine, or uracil.

mono-osteitic (mon″o-os″te-it′ik). Denoting a type of osteitis which affects a single bone.

monoparesis (mon″o-par′e-sis) [*mono-* + Gr. *paresis* slackening of strength, paralysis]. Paresis of a single part.

monoparesthesia (mon″o-par″es-the′ze-ah) [*mono-* + *paresthesia*]. Paresthesia of a single part or limb.

monopathophobia (mon″o-path″o-fo′be-ah). Dread of some definite disease.

monopathy (mo-nop′ah-the) [*mono-* + Gr. *pathos* disease]. A disease affecting a single part.

monopenia (mon″o-pe′ne-ah). Monocytopenia.

monophagia (mon″o-fa′je-ah) [*mono-* + Gr. *phagein* to eat + *-ia*]. 1. Desire for one kind of food only. 2. The eating of only one meal a day.

monophagism (mo-nof′ah-jizm). Monophagia.

monophasia (mon″o-fa′ze-ah) [*mono-* + Gr. *phasis* speaking]. Aphasia with ability to utter but one word or phrase.

monophasic (mon″o-fa′zik). Exhibiting only one phase or variation. Cf. *diphasic, triphasic.*

monophobia (mon″o-fo′be-ah) [*mono-* + *phobia*]. Morbid dread of being left alone.

monophthalmus (mon″of-thal′mus) [*mono-* + Gr. *ophthalmos* eye]. A cyclops.

monophyletic (mon″o-fi-let′ik) [*mono-* + Gr. *phylē* tribe]. Arising or descended from a single cell type.

monophyletism (mon″o-fi′lĕ-tizm). Monophyletic theory.

monophyletist (mon″o-fi′lĕ-tist). An adherent of the monophyletic theory, as in blood origin.

monophyodont (mon″o-fi′o-dont) [*mono-* + Gr. *phyein* to grow + *odous* tooth]. Having only one set of teeth, and those permanent.

monopia (mon-o′pe-ah) [*mono-* + Gr. *ops* eye + *-ia*]. Cyclopia.

monoplasmatic (mon″o-plaz-mat′ik) [*mono-* + Gr. *plasma* plasm]. Made up of a single substance.

monoplast (mon′o-plast) [*mono-* + Gr. *plastos* formed]. A single constituent cell.

monoplegia (mon″o-ple′je-ah) [*mono-* + Gr. *plēgē* stroke]. Paralysis of but a single part. Different varieties are distinguished according to the part affected or to the site of the lesion producing the disease; as, brachial, facial, central, peripheral, etc.

monoplegic (mon″o-ple′jik). Pertaining to or characterized by monoplegia.

monopodia (mon″o-po′de-ah) [*mono-* + Gr. *pous* foot + *-ia*]. A type of symmelia characterized by the presence of one median foot.

monopodial (mon″o-po′de-al). Pertaining to or characterized by monopodia; having a single median foot.

monopolar (mon′o-po″lar). Monoterminal.

monops (mon′ops) [*mono-* + Gr. *ōps* eye]. A fetus having but a single eye.

monopsychosis (mon″o-si-ko′sis). Monomania.

Monopsyllus (mon″o-sil′us) [*mono-* + Gr. *psylla* flea]. A genus of fleas. **M. ani′sus,** the common rat flea of Japan and North China.

monoptychial (mon″o-ti′ke-al) [*mono-* + Gr. *ptychē* fold]. Arranged in a single layer: said of glands whose cells are arranged on the basement membrane in a single layer. Cf. *polyptychial.*

monopus (mon′o-pus) [*mono-* + Gr. *pous* foot]. A fetus having but a single foot or leg.

monorchia (mon-or′ke-ah). Monorchism.

monorchid (mon-or′kid). An individual exhibiting monorchism.

monorchidic (mon″or-kid′ik) [*mono-* + Gr. *orchis* testicle]. Pertaining to or characterized by monorchism; having but one descended testicle.

monorchidism (mon-or′kid-izm). Monorchism.

monorchis (mon-or′kis). Monorchid.

monorchism (mon′or-kizm). The condition of having only one testis in the scrotum.

Monorchotrema (mon-or″ko-tre′mah) [*mono-* + Gr. *orchis* testicle + *trēma* aperture]. A genus of heterophyid flukes found in Japan and Formosa and characterized by having only a single testis. They have as invertebrate host an operculate snail (Melania), and as first vertebrate host an edible fish.

monorecidive (mon″o-res″ĭ-dēv′). Recurrence of chancre at the site of an apparently cured chancre: called also *chancre redux, recurrent chancre,* and *sclerosis redux.*

monorhinic (mon″o-rin′ik). Pertaining to or possessing one nasal cavity.

monosaccharide (mon″o-sak′ah-rīd). A simple sugar; a carbohydrate which cannot be decomposed by hydrolysis. The monosaccharides are colorless crystalline substances, with a sweet taste and have the same general formula CH_2O. They are classified according to the number of carbon atoms in the chain into diose ($C_2H_4O_2$), triose ($C_3H_6O_3$), tetrose ($C_4H_8O_4$), pentose ($C_5H_{10}O_5$), hexose ($C_6H_{12}O_6$), and heptose ($C_7H_{14}O_7$). Those containing an aldehyde group are termed *aldoses;* those with a ketone group *ketoses.*

monosaccharose (mon″o-sak′ah-rōs). Monosaccharide.

monoscenism (mon″o-se′nizm). The going over and over again of some event in one's past life.

monose (mon′ōs). 1. A monosaccharide. 2. A hypothetical sugar containing only one oxygen atom.

monosexual (mon″o-seks′u-al). Showing the traits of one sex only.

monoside (mon′o-sīd). A glycoside which has one sugar molecule attached to its aglycone.

monosomatic (mon″o-so-mat′ik). Pertaining to or affecting a single individual.

monosome (mon′o-sōm). 1. The unpaired sex chromosome. 2. The monosomic chromosome in an aneuploid complement.

monosomian (mon″o-so′me-an) [*mono-* + Gr. *sōma* body]. A double fetus with only one body.

monosomic (mon″o-so′mik). Pertaining to or characterized by monosomy.

monosomy (mon′o-so″me). The absence of one chromosome from the complement of an otherwise diploid cell (2n-1).

monospasm (mon′o-spazm) [*mono-* + *spasm*]. Spasm of a single limb or part. Different varieties are distinguished according to the part affected or to the site of the causal lesion; as, brachial, facial, lateral, peripheral, etc.

monospermy (mon′o-sper″me) [*mono-* + Gr. *sperma* seed]. Fertilization in which only one spermatozoon enters the ovum.

Monosporium (mon″o-spo′re-um). A genus of fungi. **M. apiosper′mum,** a fungus that is one of the causative organisms of maduromycosis.

Monostoma (mon″o-sto′mah) [Gr. *monos* single + *stoma* mouth]. A genus of trematode worms. One species occurs in the crystalline lens.

monostomidosis (mon″o-sto″mĭ-do′sis). Infestation with Monostoma.

Monostomum (mon″o-sto′mum). Monostoma.

monostotic (mon″os-tot′ik) [*mono-* + Gr. *osteon* bone]. Pertaining to or affecting a single bone.

monostratal (mon″o-stra′tal). Pertaining to a single layer or stratum.

monostratified (mon″o-strat′ĭ-fīd). Disposed in a single layer or stratum.

monosubstituted (mon″o-sub′stĭ-tūt″ed). Having only one atom in the molecule replaced.

monosymptom (mon″o-simp′tom) [*mono-* + *symptom*]. A symptom occurring singly.

monosymptomatic (mon″o-simp″to-mat′ik). Expressed by a single symptom.

monosynaptic (mon″o-sĭ-nap′tik). Pertaining to or relayed through only one synapse.

monosyphilid, monosyphilide (mon″o-sif′ĭ-lid) [*mono-* + *syphilid*]. Showing only a single syphilitic lesion.

monoterminal (mon″o-ter′mĭ-nal). The use of one terminal only in giving treatments, the ground acting as the second terminal.

monotheamin (mon″o-the′ah-min). Trade mark for preparations of theophylline monoethanolamine.

monothermia (mon″o-ther′me-ah) [*mono-* + Gr. *thermē* heat]. A condition in which the temperature of the body remains the same throughout the day.

monothetic (mon″o-thet′ik). Based on a single principle.

monotic (mon-o′tik) [*mono-* + Gr. *ous* ear]. Affecting, pertaining to, or possessing a single ear.

monotocous (mo-not′o-kus) [*mono-* + Gr. *tokos* birth]. Giving birth to but one offspring at a time.

Monotremata (mon″o-tre′mah-tah). The lowest order of mammals, including animals which lay eggs similar to those of reptiles, and nourish their young by a mammary gland which has no nipple, in a shallow pouch developed only during lactation.

monotreme (mon′o-trēm). A member of the order Monotremata.

Monotricha (mo-not′rĭ-kah). A group of bacteria including those forms which have one polar flagellum.

monotrichic (mon″o-trik′ik). Monotrichous.

monotrichous (mon-ot′rĭ-kus) [*mono-* + Gr. *thrix* hair]. Having a single polar flagellum: applied to a bacterial cell.

monotropic (mon″o-trop′ik) [*mono-* + Gr. *tropos* a turning]. Affecting only one particular species of bacterium or one variety of tissue. Cf. *polytropic.*

monoureid (mon″o-u′re-id). See *ureid.*

monovalent (mon″o-va′lent). 1. Having a valency or potency of one. 2. Capable of binding one complement only: said of an amboceptor.

monovular (mon-ov′u-lar). Pertaining to or derived from a single ovum.

monovulatory (mon-ov′u-lah-to″re). Ordinarily discharging only one ovum in one ovarian cycle.

monoxenic (mon″o-zen′ik) [*mono-* + Gr. *xenos* a guest-friend, stranger]. Associated with a single species of microorganisms; said of otherwise germ-free animals contaminated by a single type of organism.

monoxenous (mo-nok′se-nus). Requiring only one host in order to complete the life cycle: said of parasitic organisms. Cf. *heteroxenous.*

monoxeny (mo-nok′se-ne) [*mono-* + Gr. *xenos* host]. The quality or condition of being monoxenous.

monoxide (mon-ok′sīd). An oxide containing but one atom of oxygen; vernacularly applied to carbon monoxide.

monozygotic (mon″o-zi-got′ik). Pertaining to or derived from one zygote.

Monro's bursa, foramen, gland, line, etc. (mon-roz′) [Alexander *Monro* (Secundus), Scottish anatomist and surgeon, 1733–1817]. See under the nouns.

Monro-Richter line (mon-ro′ rik′ter) [Alexander *Monro;* August Gottlieb *Richter,* surgeon in Göttingen, 1742–1812]. See under *line.*

mons (monz), pl. *mon′tes* [L. "mountain"]. An elevation, or eminence. **m. pu′bis** [N A, B N A], the rounded fleshy prominence over the symphysis pubis. **m. ure′teris,** a papilla-like elevation of the mucosa of the bladder at its junction with the ureter. **m. ven′eris,** m. pubis.

Monsonia (mon-so′ne-ah). A genus of African and Asiatic geraniaceous plants. Some of the species are used in medicine as astringents.

monster (mon′ster) [L. *monstrum*]. An infant born with an anomaly so pronounced that it interferes with the general or local development of the body. **acardiac m.,** acardius. **acraniate m.,** a fetus lacking cranium and a brain as such. **autositic m.,** one capable of independent life, the circulation of which supplies nutrition to a parasitic monster. **celosomian m.,** a celosomus. **compound m.,** one which shows some duplication of body parts. **cyclopic m.,** a cyclops. **diaxial m.,** one which shows duplication of the body axis. **double m.,** one arising from a single ovum but with duplication or doubling of head, trunk, or limbs. See *teras.* **emmenic m.,** an infant that menstruates. **endocymic m.,** one which is retained in the uterus and forms the basis of a dermoid tumor. **Gila m.,** a venomous lizard, *Heloderma horridum,* of Mexico and the southwestern part of the United States. **hair m.,** one with a heavy hair-coat. **monoaxial m.,** a monster which has a single body axis. **parasitic m.,** an imperfect fetus unable to exist alone and attached to or deriving its nutrition from the circulation of another, more perfectly developed fetus. **polysomatous m.,** a monster consisting of multiple components, each of which shows some of the characteristics of a separate individual. **single m.,** one with a single body but with a defect, malformation or displacement, or enlargement or duplication of an organ. See *monstrum.* **sirenoform m.,** a sympus. **triplet m.,** a monster with triplication of body parts. **twin m.,** double m.

monstra (mon′strah) [L.]. Plural of *monstrum.*

monstricide (mon′strĭ-sīd) [*monster* + L. *caedere* to kill]. Destruction of a fetal monster.

monstriparity (mon″strĭ-par′ĭ-te) [*monster* + L. *parere* to give birth to]. The act of giving birth to a monster.

monstrosity (mon-stros′ĭ-te) [L. *monstrositas*]. 1. Great congenital deformity. 2. A monster or teratism.

monstrum (mon′strum), pl. *mon′stra* [L.]. A fetal monster. **m. abun′dans,** m. per excessum. **m. defic′iens,** m. per defectum. **m. per defec′tum,** a single monster in which all or part of an organ is missing. **m. per exces′sum,** a single monster in which an organ is enlarged or duplicated. **m. per fab'ricam alie'nam,** a single monster in which an organ is wrongly formed or displaced. **m. sirenofor'me,** a sympus.

Monteggia's dislocation, fracture (mon-tej'ahz) [Giovanni Battista *Monteggia*, Italian surgeon, 1762–1815]. See under *dislocation* and *fracture.*

Montgomery's glands (mont-gom'er-ēz) [William Fetherstone *Montgomery*, Irish obstetrician, 1797–1859]. See under *gland.*

monticulus (mon-tik'u-lus), pl. *montic'uli* [L.]. A small eminence. **m. cerebel'li,** the projecting or central part of the superior vermis. Omitted in N A.

mood (mo͞od). A mental state or emotion due to an unconscious tendency which gives character to conscious impressions. **impure m.,** a mood which is directed to some object, such as hate, fear, suspicion and anger. **pure m.,** a mood which is not directed toward an object, such as anxiety, depression, or happiness.

Moon's molars, teeth (mo͞onz) [Henry *Moon*, 19th century English surgeon]. See under *tooth.*

Moore's fracture (moorz) [Edward Mott *Moore*, American surgeon, 1814–1902]. See under *fracture.*

Moore's syndrome (moorz) [Matthew T. *Moore*, American neuropsychiatrist, born 1901]. Abdominal epilepsy.

Moore's test (moorz) [John *Moore*, English physician of the 19th century]. See under *tests.*

Mooren's ulcer (moor'enz) [Albert *Mooren*, German oculist, 1828–1899]. See under *ulcer.*

Moorhead foreign body locator (moor'hed) [John J. *Moorhead*, New York surgeon, born 1874]. Berman-Moorhead locator.

Moots's rule (mo͞ots) [Charles W. *Moots*, American physician, 1869–1933]. See under *rule.*

morament (mōr-am'ent). A feebleminded person without moral sense; a low-grade moron.

moramentia (mōr″ah-men'she-ah). The condition of being feebleminded and without moral sense.

Morand's disease, foot, foramen, spur (mor-ahnz') [Sauveur François *Morand*, French surgeon, 1697–1773]. See under the nouns.

Morax-Axenfeld conjunctivitis, diplococcus (mōr'aks ak'sen-felt″) [Victor *Morax*, ophthalmologist in Paris, 1866–1935; Theodor *Axenfeld*, German ophthalmologist, 1867–1930]. See under *conjunctivitis*, and *Haemophilus duplex.*

Moraxella (mo″rak-sel'lah) [Victor *Morax*]. A genus of microorganisms of the family Brucellaceae, order Eubacteriales, made up of gram-negative, non-motile, short, rod-shaped cells occasionally occurring singly, and found as parasites and pathogens in warm-blooded animals. **M. bo'vis,** an organism found in acute conjunctivitis in cattle. **M. lacuna'ta,** *Haemophilus duplex.* **M. liquefa'ciens,** a variant of *M. lacunata* (*Haemophilus duplex*), also found associated with conjunctivitis in man.

morbid (mor'bid) [L. *morbidus* sick]. Pertaining to or affected with disease; diseased.

morbidity (mor-bid'ĭ-te). 1. The condition of being diseased or morbid. 2. The sick rate; the ratio of sick to well persons in a community.

morbidostatic (mor″bĭ-do-stat'ik). Checking morbidity; inhibiting the progression of morbid changes, or disease.

morbific (mor-bif'ik) [L. *morbificus; morbus* sickness + *facere* to make]. Causing disease.

morbigenous (mor-bij'e-nus). Producing disease.

morbilli (mor-bil'i) [L.]. Measles.

morbilliform (mor-bil'ĭ-form) [L. *morbilli* measles + *forma* shape]. Like measles; resembling measles or the eruption of measles.

morbillous (mor-bil'us). Pertaining to measles.

morbus (mor'bus) [L.]. Disease. **m. addiso'nii,** Addison's disease. **m. apoplectifor'mis,** Meniere's disease. **m. asthen'icus,** asthenia universalis. **m. bright'ii,** Bright's disease. **m. britan'nicus,** fireman's cramp. **m. cadu'cus,** epilepsy. **m. caeru'leus,** the cyanotic group of congenital heart disease, with persisting venous-arterial shunt. **m. comitia'lis,** epilepsy. **m. cox'ae seni'lis,** the hip joint disease of aged people. **m. coxa'rius,** hip joint disease. **m. divin'us,** epilepsy. **m. dormiti'vus,** sleeping sickness. **m. ele'phas,** elephantiasis. **m. gal'licus,** syphilis. **m. hemorrhag'icus neonato'rum,** hemorrhagic disease of the newborn. **m. hercu'leus.** 1. Elephantiasis. 2. Epilepsy. **m. maculo'sus werlho'fii,** idiopathic thrombocytopenic purpura. **m. medico'rum,** a morbid propensity to consult physicians for trifling ailments. **m. mise'riae,** any disease due to want and neglect. **m. mor'sus mu'ris,** rat-bite fever. **m. nau'ticus, m. navit'icus,** seasickness. **m. ni'ger,** melena. **m. pediculo'sus,** lousiness. **m. re'gius,** jaundice. **m. sa'cer,** epilepsy. **m. seni'lis,** arthritis deformans. **m. strangulato'rius,** diphtheria. **m. vagabon'dus,** vagabond's disease. **m. virgin'eus,** chlorosis. **m. vul'pis,** alopecia. **m. werlhofii** [Werlhof's disease], idiopathic thrombocytopenic purpura.

M.O.R.C. Abbreviation for *Medical Officers Reserve Corps.*

morcellation (mor″sel-a'shun) [Fr. *morcellement*]. The division of a tumor or of a fetal monster, followed by its removal piecemeal.

morcellement (mor″sel-maw'). Morcellation.

mordant (mor'dant) [L. *mordere* to bite]. 1. A substance capable of combining with a stain or dye; the chief mordants are alum, aniline, oil, and phenol. 2. To subject to the action of a mordant preliminary to staining.

Mor. dict. Abbreviation for L. *mo're dic'to*, in the manner directed.

Morel delirium, ear, syndrome (mo'rel) [Benoît Augustin *Morel*, French alienist, 1809–1873]. See under the nouns.

Morel-Kraepelin disease (mo-rel' kra'pĕ-lin) [B. A. *Morel;* Emil *Kraepelin*, German psychiatrist, 1856–1926]. Dementia praecox.

Morelli's reaction (mo-rel'ēz) [F. *Morelli*, Italian physician, died 1918]. See under *reaction.*

mores (mo'rēz) [L., pl. of *mos*, "manners"]. The traditions and habits which are generally regarded as conducive to social welfare.

Moreschi's phenomenon (mo-res'kēz) [Carlo *Moreschi*, Italian pathologist, 1876–1921]. Bordet-Gengou phenomenon or fixation of complement.

Morestin's method, operation (mor″es-taz') [Hippolyte *Morestin*, French surgeon, 1869–1919]. See under *operation.*

Moretti's test (mo-ret'ēz) [E. *Moretti*, physician in Milan]. See under *tests.*

Morgagni's cartilage, caruncle, etc. (mor-gahn'yēz) [Giovanni Battista *Morgagni*, Italian anatomist and pathologist, 1682–1771; professor at Padua, and the founder of pathological anatomy, whose superb clinicopathological reports were published in 1761 under the title *De sedibus et causis morborum* ("The Seats and Causes of Disease")]. See under the nouns.

Morgan (mor'gan), Thomas Hunt. American biologist, 1866–1945, noted for his discoveries concerning the hereditary functions of the chromosomes; winner of the Nobel prize for medicine in 1933.

Morgan's bacillus (mor'ganz) [Harry de Reimer *Morgan*, British physician, died 1931]. *Proteus morganii.*

morgue (morg) [Fr.]. A place where dead bodies may be temporarily kept, for identification or until claimed for burial.

moria (mo're-ah) [Gr. *mōria* folly]. Dementia or fatuity. In psychiatry, a morbid tendency to joke.

moribund (mor'ĭ-bund) [L. *moribundus*]. In a dying state.

Moringa (mo-rin'gah). A genus of plants. **M. pterygosper'ma,** an East Indian plant, called sajina, which yields benoil.

morioplasty (mo′re-o-plas″te) [Gr. *morion* piece + *plassein* to form]. The surgical restoration of lost parts.

Morison's method, paste, pouch (mor′ĭ-sunz) [James Rutherford *Morison*, British surgeon, 1853–1939]. See under the nouns.

Moritz reaction, test (mo′rits) [Friedrich Heinrich Ludwig *Moritz*, German physician, 1861–1938]. Rivalta's reaction.

Mörner's test (mer′nerz) [K. A. H. *Mörner*, Stockholm chemist, 1855–1917]. See under *tests*.

mornidine (mor′nĭ-dēn). Trade mark for preparations of pipamazine.

Moro's reaction, reflex, test (mo′rōz) [E. *Moro*, pediatrist in Heidelberg, 1874–1951]. See under *reaction* and *reflex*.

morococcus (mo-ro-kok′us) [L. *morus* mulberry + *coccus*]. A form of coccus or microbial mass from the eczematous skin.

moron (mo′ron) [Gr. *mōros* stupid]. A feebleminded person whose mental age is between eight and twelve years. Cf. *idiot* and *imbecile*.

moronism (mo′ron-izm). Moronity.

moronity (mo-ron′ĭ-te). The condition of being a moron.

morosis (mo-ro′sis). Moronity.

-morph [Gr. *morphē* form]. Word termination denoting relationship to form or shape, such as an individual possessing a certain form, indicated by the preceding root, as *mesomorph*.

morphallactic (mor″fal-lak′tik). Pertaining to or characterized by morphallaxis.

morphallaxis (mor″fah-lak′sis) [Gr. *morphē* form + *allaxis* exchange]. The renewal of a lost tissue or part by reorganization of the remaining part of the body of an animal.

morphea (mor-fe′ah) [Gr. *morphē* form]. A skin disease marked by the formation of pinkish patches or bands, bordered by a purplish areola. The lesions are firm, but not hard, and are usually elevated or depressed. They may atrophy and disappear, leaving cicatrix-like marks. The disease is probably a trophoneurosis. Called also *localized scleroderma* and *Addison's keloid*. **acroteric m.,** a form specially affecting the extremities. **m. al′ba,** morphea in which there is little pigmentation. **m. atro′phica,** morphea in which the patches are atrophied. **m. flam′mea,** naevus vascularis. **m. gutta′ta,** white-spot disease. **herpetiform m.,** morphea in which the lesions are disposed as in herpes. **m. linea′ris,** morphea arranged in lines or bands. **m. ni′gra,** morphea with pigmented lesions.

morphia (mor′fe-ah). Morphine.

morphina (mor-fi′nah), pl. and gen. *morphi′nae* [L.]. Morphine.

morphine (mor′fēn) [L. *morphina, morphinum*]. The principal and most active alkaloid of opium, $C_{17}H_{19}NO_3+H_2O$, occurring in the form of colorless, shining crystals, having a bitter taste and an alkaline reaction. Used as a narcotic analgesic. **dimethyl m.,** thebaine. **m. hydrochloride,** a white, crystalline substance, $C_{17}H_{19}NO_3HCl + 3H_2O$. **m. sulfate,** a white, crystalline substance, $(C_{17}H_{19}NO_3)_2.H_2SO_4 + 5H_2O$.

morphinic (mor-fin′ik). Pertaining to morphine.

morphinism (mor′fin-izm). A morbid state due to the habitual misuse of morphine; also the morphine habit.

morphinist (mor′fin-ist). A morphine addict.

morphinistic (mor″fi-nis′tik). Pertaining to or characteristic of morphinism.

morphinium (mor-fin′e-um) [L.]. Morphine. **m. chloride,** morphine chloride. **m. sulfate,** morphine sulfate.

morphinization (mor″fin-i-za′shun). Subjection to the influence of morphine.

morphinomania (mor″fin-o-ma′ne-ah). 1. A morbid and habitual craving for morphine. 2. Insanity due to the misuse of morphine.

morphiomania (mor″fe-o-ma′ne-ah). Morphinomania.

morphiometry (mor″fe-om′e-tre) [*morphine* + Gr. *metron* measure]. The measurement of the amount or proportion of morphine in a drug or preparation.

morphium (mor′fe-um). Morphine.

morpho- (mor′fo) [Gr. *morphē* form]. Combining form denoting relationship to form.

morphodifferentiation (mor″fo-dif″er-en″she-a′shun). The arrangement of formative cells in the development of tissues or organs, which leads to production of the ultimate shape of the structure.

morphoea (mor-fe′ah). Morphea.

morphogenesia (mor″fo-jĕ-ne′se-ah). Morphogenesis.

morphogenesis (mor″fo-jen′e-sis) [Gr. *morphē* form + *gennan* to produce]. The evolution and development of form, as the development of the shape of a particular organ or part of the body, or the development undergone by individuals who attain the type to which the majority of the individuals of the species approximate.

morphogenetic (mor″fo-je-net′ik). Producing growth; producing form or shape.

morphogeny (mor-foj′e-ne). Morphogenesis.

morphography (mor-fog′rah-fe) [*morpho-* + Gr. *graphein* to write]. A description of organized beings, with special reference to their forms and structure.

morphological (mor″fo-loj′ĭ-kal). Pertaining to morphology.

morphology (mor-fol′o-je) [*morpho-* + *-logy*]. The science of the forms and structure of organized beings.

morpholysis (mor-fol′ĭ-sis) [*morpho-* + Gr. *lysis* dissolution]. Destruction of form.

morphometry (mor-fom′e-tre) [*morpho-* + Gr. *metron* measure]. The measurement of the forms of organisms.

morphon (mor′fon) [Gr. *morphōn* forming]. An individual organism or structural unit.

morphophyly (mor-fof′ĭ-le) [*morpho-* + Gr. *phylon* tribe]. The branch of phylogenesis dealing with the evolutionary development of form.

morphophysics (mor″fo-fiz′iks). The study of the physical and chemical causes of development.

morphoplasm (mor′fo-plazm) [*morpho-* + Gr. *plasma* anything formed]. The substance of the cellular reticulum.

morphosis (mor-fo′sis) [Gr. *morphōsis* a shaping, bringing into shape]. The process of formation of a part or organ.

morphotic (mor-fot′ik). Pertaining to morphosis or formation: concerned in a formative process.

-morphous [Gr. *morphē* form, shape]. Word termination indicating the manner of shape or form.

morpio, morpion (mor′pe-o, mor′pe-on), pl. *morpio′nes* [L.]. The crab louse, *Phthirus pubis*.

Morquio's disease (mor-ke′ōz) [Louis *Morquio*, pediatrician in Montevideo, 1867–1935]. Eccentro-osteochondrodysplasia.

morrhua (mor′u-ah) [L.]. The codfish, *Gadus morrhua*, which furnishes cod liver oil.

morrhuate (mor′u-āt). A salt of morrhuic acid.

morrhuin (mor′u-in) [L. *morrhua* codfish]. A thick, oily ptomaine, $C_{19}H_{27}N_3$, from some samples of cod liver oil.

Morris's appendix, point (mor′is) [Robert T. *Morris*, New York surgeon, 1857–1945]. See under *appendix* and *point*.

Morrison crown (mor′rĭ-son) [William Newton *Morrison*, American dentist, 1842–1896]. See under *crown*.

mors (morz) [L.]. Death. **m. thy′mica,** sudden death allegedly occurring in thymic asthma and status lymphaticus.

morsal (mor′sal) [L. *morsus* bite]. Taking part in mastication; a term applied to the masticating surface of a bicuspid or molar.

Mor. sol. Abbreviation for L. *mo're sol'ito,* in the usual way.

morsulus (mor'su-lus) [L., dim. of *morsus* bite]. A troche.

morsus (mor'sus) [L.]. Bite; sting. **m. diab'oli,** the fimbriae at the ovarian extremity of an oviduct. **m. huma'nus,** a bite by a human being.

mortal (mor'tal) [L. *mortalis*]. 1. Subject to death, or destined to die. 2. Fatal; causing or terminating in death.

mortality (mor-tal'ĭ-te). 1. The quality of being mortal. 2. The death rate; the ratio of total number of deaths to the total number of population. The mortality rate of a disease is the ratio of the number of deaths from a given disease to the total number of cases of that disease. 3. In life insurance, the ratio of deaths that take place to expected deaths. **actual m.,** the number of deaths in 1,000,000 insured lives, over a period of 100 years. **annual actual m.,** the number of deaths per 1000 insured lives. **perinatal m.,** the death rate of infants about the time of birth, often considered as including stillbirths and deaths in the first week of life. **tabular m.,** the expected death rate per 1000 insured persons as shown in the mortality table.

mortalogram (mor-tal'o-gram). A graphic presentation, in grid form, of crude and age-standardized mortality rates and the numerical distribution of deaths for a given cause according to the time period, age, and sex, and the median age at death.

mortar (mor'tar) [L. *mortarium*]. A bell-shaped or urn-shaped vessel of glass, iron, porcelain, or other material, in which drugs are beaten, crushed, or ground with a pestle.

mortician (mor-tish'an) [L. *mors* death]. An undertaker; a person trained to care for the dead.

mortification (mor"tĭ-fi-ka'shun). Gangrene or sphacelus; molar death.

mortinatality (mor"tĭ-na-tal'ĭ-te) [L. *mors* death + *natus* birth]. Natimortality.

mortisemblant (mor"tĭ-sem'blant). Apparently dead.

Morton's cough (mor'tunz) [Richard *Morton,* English physician, 1637–1698]. See under *cough.*

Morton's current (mor'tunz) [William James *Morton,* American neurologist, 1846–1920]. See under *current.*

Morton's disease, foot, neuralgia, toe (mor'tunz) [Thomas George *Morton,* Philadelphia surgeon, 1835–1903]. Metatarsalgia.

mortuary (mor'tu-a"re) [L. *mortuarium* tomb]. 1. Pertaining to death. 2. A place where dead bodies are kept until burial or cremation.

morula (mor'u-lah) [L. *morus* mulberry]. The solid mass of blastomeres formed by cleavage of a fertilized ovum, filling all the space occupied by the ovum before cleavage.

morular (mor'u-lar). 1. Pertaining to a morula. 2. Resembling a mulberry.

morulation (mor"u-la'shun). The process of formation of the morula.

moruloid (mor'u-loid) [L. *morus* mulberry + Gr. *eidos* form]. 1. Shaped like a mulberry. 2. A bacterial colony in the form of a mulberry-like mass.

Morus (mo'rus). A genus of the family Urticaceae which contains the mulberry. **M. ni'gra,** the black mulberry from which mori succus is obtained. **M. tincto'ria,** yellow-wood, which contains maclurin.

Morvan's chorea, disease (mor'vanz) [Augustin Marie de Lannitis *Morvan,* French physician, 1819–1897]. See under *chorea* and *disease.*

morvin (mor'vin). Mallein.

mosaic (mo-za'ik) [Gr. *mouseion;* L. *opus musivum*]. A pattern made of numerous small pieces fitted together. (1) *Genetics:* the occurrence in an individual of two or more cell populations derived from a single zygote, each population having a different chromosome complement. (2) *Embryology:* the condition in the fertilized eggs of some species, such as the sea urchin, whereby the cells of early stages have developed cytoplasm which determines the parts that are to develop. (3) *Plant pathology:* a virus disease characterized by mottling of the foliage.

mosaicism (mo-sa'ĭ-sizm). In genetics, the presence in an individual of cells of differing chromosomal constitution.

Moschcowitz's operation (mos'ko-witz) [Alexis V. *Moschcowitz,* American surgeon, 1865–1933]. See under *operation.*

Moschcowitz's test (mos'ko-witz) [Eli *Moschcowitz,* American physician, born 1879]. See under *tests.*

Moser's serum (mo'zerz) [Paul *Moser,* pediatrician in Vienna, 1865–1924]. See under *serum.*

Mosetig-Moorhof bone wax (mōs-et'ig-mōr'-hof) [Albert von *Mosetig-Moorhof,* German surgeon, 1838–1907]. See under *wax.*

Mosler's diabetes (mos'lerz) [Karl Friedrich *Mosler,* German physician, 1831–1911]. See under *diabetes.*

mosquito (mos-ke'to), pl. *mosquitoes* [Sp. "little fly"]. 1. A popular name for gnatlike, blood-sucking and venomous insects of the family Culicidae and of various genera, chiefly *Culex, Aedes, Anopheles, Mansonia, Haemagogus, Psorophora, Theobaldia* and *Chagasia.* 2. An apparatus for drawing blood from a vessel in sterile condition. **anautogenous m.,** a mosquito that requires a blood meal in the adult stage for the production of viable eggs. **arygamous m.,** a mosquito that requires large or outdoor spaces for breeding. **autogenous m.,** a mosquito that can produce viable eggs without a blood meal. **house m.** See *Culex pipiens* and *C. quinquefasciatus.* **steyogamous m.,** a mosquito that can breed in captivity in limited spaces. **tiger m.,** *Aedes aegypti.*

mosquitocidal (mos-ke"to-si'dal). Destructive to mosquitoes.

mosquitocide (mos-ke'to-sīd) [*mosquito* + L. *caedere* to kill]. An agent that is destructive to mosquitoes.

moss (mos). 1. Any plant or species of the cryptogamic order *Musci.* 2. Material composed of or derived from a plant of the cryptogamic order *Musci.* **Ceylon m.,** a seaweed, *Gracilaria lichenoides:* one of the sources of agar. **Irish m., pearl m., salt rock m.,** chondrus.

Moss's classification (mos'ez) [William Lorenzo *Moss,* American physician, born 1876]. A classification of blood types in which they are designated by roman numerals I to IV, corresponding with types AB, A, B, and O, respectively, in the international, or Landsteiner, classification.

Mosso's ergograph, sphygmomanometer (mos'ōz) [Angelo *Mosso,* Italian physiologist, 1846–1910]. See under the nouns.

Most's bath (mōsts) [August *Most,* German surgeon, born 1867]. See under *bath.*

Moszkowicz's operation (mos'ko-wiks) [Ludwig *Moszkowicz,* Austrian surgeon, 1873–1945]. See under *operation.*

Motais' operation (mo-tāz') [Ernst *Motais,* French ophthalmologist, 1845–1913]. See under *operation.*

motarium (mo-ta're-um) [L.]. Lint.

moth (mawth). 1. A night-flying lepidopterous insect. 2. Chloasma. **brown-tail m.,** *Euproctis chrysorrhoea.* **flannel m.** See *Megalopyge.* **io m.,** *Automeris io.* **tussock m.,** *Hemerocampa leucostigma.*

mother (muth'er) [L. *mater*]. The female parent. **Colles' m.,** the apparently normal mother of a syphilitic child. **m. of vinegar,** *Acetobacter aceti.*

motile (mo'til). Having a spontaneous but not conscious or volitional movement.

motility (mo-til'ĭ-te). The ability to move spontaneously.

motoceptor (mo′to-sep″tor). Any muscle sense receptor.

motofacient (mo″to-fa′shent). Producing motion; a term applied to that phase of muscular activity by which the muscle produces actual motion, in contradistinction to the *nonmotofacient* phase in which the muscle is contracting without producing motion.

motoneuron (mo″to-nu′ron). A neuron possessing a motor function; a motor neuron.

motor (mo′tor) [L.]. 1. A muscle, nerve, or center that effects or produces movement. 2. Producing or subserving motion. **m. oc′uli,** the third cranial nerve. **plastic m.,** the tissues of an amputation stump used to secure motion in an artificial limb.

motorgraphic (mo″tor-graf′ik). Kinetographic.

motorial (mo-to′re-al). Pertaining to motion or to a motorium.

motoricity (mo″tor-is′ĭ-te). The faculty of performing movement; power of movement.

motorium (mo-to′re-um) [L.]. 1. A motor center. 2. The motor apparatus of the body. 3. In psychology, the mental functions that direct purposeful activities. **m. commu′ne,** the common center of motor influences in the brain.

motorius (mo-to′re-us) [L.]. A motor nerve.

motormeter (mo″tor-me′ter). A device for recording the mechanical movements of the stomach.

motorogerminative (mo″tor-o-jer′mĭ-na-tiv). Developing into the muscles: said of portions of the mesoderm.

motorpathy (mo-tor′pah-the) [*motor* + Gr. *pathos* disease]. Treatment of disease by gymnastics.

Mott's law (motz) [Sir Frederick Walker *Mott*, English neurologist, 1853–1926]. See under *law*.

mottling (mot′ling). A condition of spotting with patches of color.

mouche (mo͞osh), pl. *mouches* [Fr.]. A speck, or fly. **mouches volantes** (mo͞osh vo-lahnt′), muscae volitantes.

moulage (moo-lahzh′) [Fr. "molding"]. The making of molds or models in wax or plaster, as of a structure or a lesion; also such a mold or model.

mould (mōld). See *mold*.

moulding (mōld′ing). The shaping of the child's head in adjustment to the size and shape of the birth canal.

mounding (mownd′ing). The rising in a lump of a wasting muscle when struck.

mounting (mownt′ing). 1. The preparation of specimens and slides for study. The chief mediums used in mounting large specimens are alcohol and glycerin jelly; for microscopical objects on a slide, Canada balsam and glycerin. 2. Attachment, in the laboratory, of the maxillary and/or mandibular cast to an articulator.

mouse (mows). 1. A small rodent belonging to the genus Mus, frequently used as an experimental animal. 2. A small weight, or movable structure. **C.F.W. m.** (cancer-*f*ree *w*hite mouse), one of a strain of mice bred for use in cancer research laboratories. **joint m.,** one of the portions of the fringes in the synovial membrane of joints in osteoarthritis which are changed into cartilage and become free in the joints. **peritoneal m.,** a free body in the peritoneal cavity, probably representing a small mass of omentum or epiploic appendage which has twisted off and become coated with fibrin, and sometimes appearing as a soft density on the roentgenogram. **pleural m.,** a fibrous foreign body sometimes seen by x-ray of the chest in pleurisy.

mouth (mowth) [L. *os, oris*]. An opening or aperture. Specifically, the anterior or proximal opening of the alimentary canal, which is bounded anteriorly by the lips and which contains the tongue and teeth. **Ceylon sore m.,** sprue. **dry m.** See *Sjögren's syndrome*, under *syndrome*. **glass-blowers' m.,** swelling of the parotid gland in glass-blowers. **parrot m.,** retraction of the lower jaw in the horse. **rubber sore m.,** soreness in the mouth due to the vulcanite, helcolite or other similar material in the dental plate. **tapir m.,** a condition in which the mouth has something of the appearance of that of a tapir, the orbicular oris muscle being atrophied, and the lips thickened and separated; seen in fascioscapulohumeral muscular atrophy. **trench m.,** necrotizing ulcerative gingivitis. **white m.** See *thrush*.

movement (mo͞ov′ment). 1. An act of moving; motion. 2. An act of defecation. **active m.,** a movement produced by the person's own muscles. **ameboid m.,** the movement of an ameba or leukocyte by the protrusion of a pseudopodium, or a movement similar to it. **angular m.,** a movement which changes the angle between two bones. **associated m.,** a movement of parts which act together, as of the eyes. **automatic m.,** a movement originating within the organism, but not by an act of the will. **Bennett m.,** the anterolateral shift in the position of the condyle on the working side in lateral excursion of the mandible in mastication. **border tissue m's,** movements produced by action of the muscles and other tissues adjoining the borders of a denture. **brownian m., Brownian-Zsigmondy m., brunonian m.,** the dancing motion of minute particles suspended in a liquid. **choreic m's, choreiform m's,** irregular, jerky movements of muscles or groups of muscles. **ciliary m.,** the lashing motion of cilia occurring in certain of the tissues. **circus m.** 1. A peculiar circular gait; an involuntary rolling or tumbling movement, the result of lesions of the brain and basal nerve centers. 2. A circular movement of the excitatory wave in the auricle of the heart, each circular movement being interrupted by a gap between its beginning and its ending, so that only a portion of the impulses are conducted to the ventricle. This is the mechanism of auricular fibrillation. (Sir Thomas Lewis.) **communicated m.,** one produced by a force acting from without. **contralateral associated m.,** a movement on the paralyzed side in hemiplegia associated with active movement of the corresponding part on the unaffected side. **dystonic m.,** a large slow, amplified athetoid movement. **elastic m.,** a movement due to the return of a stretched fiber to its natural length. **excessive m.,** hyperkinesis. **excursive m's,** those movements performed by the mandible in mastication. See *lateral, protrusive,* and *retrusive excursion,* under *excursion*. **fetal m.,** that of a fetus in the uterus, sometimes observable as early as the twelfth week of gestation. **forced m.,** a movement caused by an injury to a motor center or a conducting path. **Frenkel's m's,** a series of movements of precision to be performed by ataxic patients for the purpose of restoring lost coordination. **hinge m.,** movement occurring in a single plane, as that occurring in opening or closing of the mouth. **index m.,** a movement of the cephalic part of a body about the fixed caudal part. **intermediary m's,** all movements of which the mandible is capable between the extreme lateral, protrusive, and retrusive positions. **jaw m.,** mandibular m. **lateral m.,** movement to one side. **Magnan's m.,** forward and backward movement of the tongue when it is drawn out, observed in dementia paralytica. **mandibular m.,** any movement of which the mandible is capable. **mandibular m., free,** any unhampered movement of the mandible. **mandibular m's, functional,** those movements of the mandible which occur in the performance of some function, as mastication, swallowing, articulation of vocal sounds, and yawning. **masticatory m's,** those movements of the mandible occurring in the mastication of food. **molecular m.,** brownian m. **morphogenetic m.,** a flowing of cell groups concerned with the formation of germ layers or of organ primordia. **nucleopetal m.,** the movement of a male pronucleus toward the female pronucleus in the fertilized ovum. **opening m.,** that movement of the mandible by which the distance between the anterior teeth of the mandible and maxilla is increased. **passive m.,** any movement of the body effected by a force entirely outside of the organism. **pendular m., pendulum m.,** one of the movements of the intestine in digestion, consisting of a gentle swinging to and fro of the different loops. These movements are ascribed to rhythmical contractions of the longitudinal muscles. **reflex m.,** an involuntary movement provoked by a remote external stimulus acting through a nerve center. **rolling m.,** the rolling of an animal on its long axis. **scissors m.,** a movement of the pupillary reflex resembling the opening and shutting of scissors: indicative of irregular astigmatism. **spontaneous m.,** one which is originated within the organism. **Swedish m.** See under *gymnastics.* **synkinetic m's,** minor, unconscious movements that accompany major voluntary movements, such as the facial contortions in severe exertion.

moxa (mok′sah) [Japanese]. A tuft of soft, combustible substance to be burned upon the skin.

moxibustion (mok″sĭ-bus′chun). The burning of a moxa upon the skin.

Moynihan's test (moin′yanz) [Berkeley George *Moynihan* (Lord Moynihan), British surgeon, 1865–1936]. See under *tests.*

M.P. Abbreviation for *mesiopulpal.*

mp. Abbreviation for *melting point.*

M.P.D. Abbreviation for *maximum permissible dose,* that amount of ionizing radiation that, in the light of current knowledge, is not expected to lead to bodily injury.

M.P.L. Abbreviation for *mesiopulpolingual.*

M.P.La. Abbreviation for *mesiopulpolabial.*

M.P.U. Abbreviations for *Medical Practitioners Union* (British).

mr. Abbreviation for *milliroentgen.*

μr. Abbreviation for *microroentgen.*

M.R.A.C.P. Abbreviation for *Member of Royal Australasian College of Physicians.*

M.R.C. Abbreviation for *Medical Reserve Corps.*

M.R.C.P. Abbreviation for *Member of the Royal College of Physicians.*

M.R.C.P.E. Abbreviation for *Member of the Royal College of Physicians of Edinburgh.*

M.R.C.P. (Glasg.). Abbreviation for *Member of the Royal College of Physicians and Surgeons of Glasgow* qua *Physician.*

M.R.C.P.I. Abbreviation for *Member of the Royal College of Physicians of Ireland.*

M.R.C.S. Abbreviation for *Member of the Royal College of Surgeons.*

M.R.C.S.E. Abbreviation for *Member of the Royal College of Surgeons of Edinburgh.*

M.R.C.S.I. Abbreviation for *Member of the Royal College of Surgeons of Ireland.*

M.R.C.V.S. Abbreviation for *Member of the Royal College of Veterinary Surgeons.*

M.R.D. Abbreviation for *minimum reacting dose.*

M.S. Abbreviation for *Master of Surgery.*

msec. Abbreviation for *millisecond.*

μsec. Abbreviation for *microsecond.*

MSH. Abbreviation for *melanocyte-stimulating hormone.*

M.S.L. Abbreviation for *midsternal line.*

M.T. Abbreviation for *Medical Technologist,* and *membrana tympani.*

M.T.R. Abbreviation for *Meinicke turbidity reaction.* See *Meinicke test,* under *tests.*

MT6. Thiomerin.

MTU. Methylthiouracil.

M.u. Abbreviation for *Mache unit.*

mU. Abbreviation for *milliunit.*

m.u. Abbreviation for *mouse unit.*

μU. Abbreviation for *microunit.*

mu (mu). The twelfth letter of the Greek alphabet, μ. In micrometry, a micron.

Muc. Abbreviation for L. *mucila′go,* mucilage.

mucase (mu′kās). An enzyme that catalyzes the hydrolysis of mucin; a mucopolysaccharidase.

mucedin (mu′sĕ-din). An amorphous protein derivable from gluten.

Much's granules, reaction (mooks) [Hans Christian R. *Much,* German physician, 1880–1932]. See under *granule* and *reaction.*

Much-Holzmann reaction (mook-holts′man) [Hans *Much;* V. *Holzmann,* German physician]. See under *reaction.*

mucicarmine (mu″sĭ-kar′min). A specific stain for mucin consisting of carmine, aluminum chloride, and distilled water.

mucidin (mu′sĭ-din). A solution of the mucus of red snails: it is bactericidal, but not antitoxic.

muciferous (mu-sif′er-us) [*mucus* + L. *ferre* to bear]. Secreting mucus.

mucification (mu″sĭ-fi-ka′shun). The mucous producing changes in the vaginal epithelium of laboratory animals during the progestational stage of the ovarian cycle.

muciform (mu′sĭ-form) [*mucus* + L. *forma* form]. Resembling mucus.

mucigen (mu′sĭ-jen) [*mucus* + Gr. *gennan* to produce]. A substance found in the epithelial cells that secrete mucus: it is convertible into mucin and mucus.

mucigenous (mu-sij′e-nus). Producing mucus.

mucigogue (mu′sĭ-gog) [*mucus* + Gr. *agōgos* leading]. 1. Stimulating the secretion of mucus. 2. An agent which stimulates the secretion of mucus.

mucilage (mu′sĭ-lij) [L. *mucilago*]. 1. An artificial viscid paste of gum or dextrin: used in pharmacy as a vehicle or excipient, or in therapy as a demulcent. 2. A naturally formed viscid principle in a plant, consisting of a gum dissolved in the juices of the plant. **acacia m.,** a preparation of acacia and benzoic acid in purified water, used as a suspending agent for drugs. **chondrus m., Irish moss m.,** a preparation of chondrus or chondrus extract in water. **tragacanth m.,** a preparation of tragacanth, benzoic acid, and glycerin in distilled water.

mucilaginous (mu″sĭ-laj′ĭ-nus). Of the nature of mucilage; slimy and adhesive.

mucilago (mu″sĭ-lah′go) [L.]. Mucilage. **m. aca′ciae,** acacia mucilage. **m. chon′dri,** chondrus mucilage. **m. tragacan′thae,** tragacanth mucilage.

mucilloid (mu′sil-loid). A preparation of a mucilaginous substance. **psyllium hydrophilic m.,** a powdered preparation of the mucilaginous portion of blond psyllium seeds (*Plantago ovata*), used in treatment of constipation.

mucin (mu′sin). A mucopolysaccharide or glycoprotein, the chief constituent of mucus. **gastric m.,** a substance derived from the lining of hog stomachs: sometimes used for its protective and lubricating action in the treatment of peptic ulcer.

mucinemia (mu″sin-e′me-ah) [*mucin* + Gr. *haima* blood + *-ia*]. The presence of mucin in the blood.

mucinoblast (mu-sin′o-blast) [*mucin* + Gr. *blastos* germ]. The progenitor of a mucous cell.

mucinogen (mu-sin′o-jen) [*mucin* + Gr. *gennan* to produce]. A precursor of mucin.

mucinoid (mu′sĭ-noid) [*mucin* + Gr. *eidos* form]. 1. Resembling mucin. 2. Mucoid, def. 2.

mucinolytic (mu″sĭ-no-lit′ik) [*mucin* + Gr. *lysis* dissolution]. Dissolving or splitting up mucin.

mucinosis (mu″sĭ-no′sis). A condition characterized by abnormal deposits of mucin in the skin, appearing as infiltrations, papules, or nodules. Associated with hypothyroidism, it has long been known as myxedema, but it may also occur in the absence of thyroid disorder (e.g., lichen myxedematosus). **follicular m.,** a disease of unknown cause, characterized clinically by plaques of folliculopapules and histologically by mucinosis of the pilosebaceous unit; alopecia is usually evident. **papular m.,** lichen myxedematosus.

mucinous (mu′sĭ-nus). Resembling or marked by the formation of mucin.

mucinuria (mu″sin-u′re-ah) [*mucin* + Gr. *ouron* urine + *-ia*]. The occurrence of mucin in the urine.

muciparous (mu-sip′ah-rus) [*mucus* + L. *parere* to produce]. Secreting mucus.

mucitis (mu-si′tis). Inflammation of the mucous membrane.

Muck's reaction, test (mooks) [Otto *Muck*, physician in Essen, 1871–1942]. See under *tests*.

mucocartilage (mu″ko-kar′tĭ-lij). A soft cartilage the cells of which are in a mucus-like matrix.

mucocele (mu′ko-sēl) [*mucus* + Gr. *kēlē* tumor]. 1. Dilatation of a cavity with accumulated mucous secretion. 2. A mucous polyp. **suppurating m.,** a mucocele whose contents are purulent.

mucoclasis (mu-kok′lah-sis) [*mucus* + Gr. *klasis* a breaking]. Destruction of the mucous lining of any organ, e.g., the gallbladder with the thermocautery.

mucocolitis (mu″ko-ko-li′tis). Mucous colitis.

mucocolpos (mu″ko-kol′pos) [*mucus* + Gr. *kolpos* vagina]. Accumulation of mucus in the vaginal canal.

mucocutaneous (mu″ko-ku-ta′ne-us) [*mucus* + *cutaneous*]. Pertaining to or affecting the mucous membrane and the skin.

mucocyte (mu′ko-sīt). An oligodendroglia cell whose cytoplasm has undergone mucoid degeneration.

mucoderm (mu′ko-derm). Lamina propria mucosae.

mucodermal (mu″ko-der′mal). 1. Pertaining to mucoderm. 2. Pertaining to the skin and mucous membrane.

muco-enteritis (mu″ko-en-ter-i′tis). Acute catarrhal enteritis.

mucofibrous (mu″ko-fi′brus). Composed of mucus and fibrous tissue.

mucoflocculent (mu″ko-flok′u-lent). Containing threads of mucus.

mucoglobulin (mu″ko-glob′u-lin). Any one of the class of proteins to which plastin belongs.

mucoid (mu′koid). 1. Resembling mucus. 2. Any one of a group of mucus-like conjugated proteins of animal origin. The mucoids differ from mucins in solubility. They are precipitated by acetic acid. They include colloid and ovomucoid. Called also *mucinoid.*

mucoitin sulfate (mu-ko′ĭ-tin). A sulfur-containing polysaccharide from gastric mucin and from the cornea of the eye.

mucolysine (mu-kol′ĭ-sin) [*mucus* + Gr. *lysis* dissolution]. A lysine which is capable of causing dissolution of mucus.

mucolytic (mu″ko-lit′ik). Destroying or dissolving mucus.

mucomembranous (mu″ko-mem′brah-nus). Pertaining to or composed of mucous membrane.

mucoperiosteal (mu″ko-per″e-os′te-al). Consisting of mucous membrane and periosteum.

mucoperiosteum (mu″ko-per″e-os′te-um). Periosteum having a mucous surface, as in parts of the auditory apparatus.

mucopolysaccharidase (mu″ko-pol″e-sak′ah-ri-dās). An enzyme that catalyzes the hydrolysis of mucopolysaccharides.

mucopolysaccharide (mu″ko-pol″e-sak′ah-rīd). A group of polysaccharides which contains hexosamine, which may or may not be combined with protein and which, dispersed in water, form many of the mucins.

mucoprotein (mu″ko-pro′te-in). Any one of a series of amino compounds of undetermined action.

mucopurulent (mu″ko-pu′roo-lent). Containing both mucus and pus.

mucopus (mu′ko-pus) [*mucus* + *pus*]. Mucus which has the appearance of pus on account of the presence of leukocytes.

Mucor (mu′kor) [L.]. A genus of fungi forming delicate, white tubular filaments and spherical, black sporangia. **M. corym′bifer,** *Lichtheimia corymbifera.* **M. muce′do,** a nonpathogenic species from feces or other nitrogenous substances. It produces a fatal disease in bees, and has twice been found as a parasite in man in cases of mycosis. **M. pusil′lus,** a species resembling *M. rhizopodiformis*, from moist bread. It is pathogenic for rabbits and is occasionally found in cases of otomycosis in man. **M. racemo′sus,** a mold from diseased pineapples; it sometimes causes intestinal inflammation. **M. ramo′sus,** an extremely virulent pathogenic species from white bread and from the ear in otomycosis. **M. rhizopodifor′mis,** a pathogenic organism which has been found in white bread and in the mouth in cases of hyperkeratosis. In rabbits it causes a fatal mycosis of the spleen, kidneys, bone marrow, etc.

Mucoraceae (mu″ko-ra′se-e). A family of the order Phycomycetes in which the thallus is not segmented and ramified.

mucoriferous (mu″kor-if′er-us) [L. *mucor* mold + *ferre* to carry]. Covered with mold.

mucorin (mu′ko-rin). An albuminous substance from certain molds.

mucormycosis (mu″kor-mi-ko′sis). A mycosis due to fungus of the genus *Mucor.* It is usually a pulmonary infection but metastatic abscesses may form in various organs.

mucosa (mu-ko′sah) [L. "mucus"]. A mucous membrane, or tunica mucosa.

mucosal (mu-ko′sal). Pertaining to the mucous membrane.

mucosanguineous (mu″ko-sang-gwin′e-us). Composed of mucus and blood.

mucosedative (mu″ko-sed′ah-tiv). Soothing to the mucous surfaces.

mucoserous (mu″ko-se′rus). Pertaining to or producing both mucus and serum.

mucosin (mu-ko′sin). A form of mucin peculiar to the more tenacious varieties of mucus, as that of the nasal and uterine cavities.

mucositis (mu″ko-si′tis). Inflammation of a mucous membrane. **m. necrot′icans agranulocyt′ica,** necrotic inflammation of mucous membranes associated with agranulocytosis.

mucosocutaneous (mu-ko″so-ku-ta′ne-us). Pertaining to a mucous membrane and the skin.

mucostatic (mu″ko-stat′ik). Arresting the secretion of mucus.

mucous (mu′kus) [L. *mucosus*]. Pertaining to or resembling mucus; also secreting mucus.

mucoviscidosis (mu″ko-vis″ĭ-do′sis). Cystic fibrosis of the pancreas (q.v. under *fibrosis*); so called because of the abnormally viscous mucoid secretions observed in the disease.

mucro (mu′kro), pl. *mucro′nes* [L. "a sharp point"]. The pointed end of a part or organ. **m. ba′seos cartilag′inis arytaenoi′deae,** the vocal process. **m. cor′dis,** the apex of the heart. **m. ster′ni,** the xiphoid process.

mucronate (mu′kro-nāt) [L. *mucro* a sharp point]. Having a spinelike tip or end.

mucroniform (mu-kron′ĭ-form). Spinelike.

Mucuna (mu-ku′nah) [Brazilian]. A genus of leguminous plants of the family Fabaceae. *M. pru′riens*, cowitch or cowage, bears easily detached hairs which may cause unbearable itching. *M. u′rens* is the source of seeds which have been used as a substitute for calabar bean.

mucus (mu′kus) [L.]. The free slime of the mucous membranes, composed of secretion of the glands, along with various inorganic salts, desquamated cells, and leukocytes; listed as an official term in B N A, it was omitted in N A.

Muellerius (mil-ler′e-us). A genus of lung-worms.

M. capilla'ris, a species of lung-worms that is parasitic in sheep and goats.

muffle (muf'f'l). A part of a furnace, usually removable or replaceable, in which material may be placed for processing, without exposing it to the direct action of the fire.

muguet (moo-gwa') [Fr.]. Thrush (1st def.).

muhinyo (mu-hin'yo). A fever endemic in Uganda, similar to brucellosis.

mular (mu'lar) [L. *mulus* mule]. Pertaining to mules. The term has been applied to certain lesions of verruga peruana in man which resemble the characteristic lesions of this disease in mules.

mulatto (mu-lat'o) [Sp. "of mixed breed," from *mulo* mule]. A person one of whose parents is white and the other Negro.

mulberry (mul'ber-e). Any tree of the genus *Morus*. From the juice of the fruit a syrup is made which is used as a drink in fevers.

Mulder's angle (mul'derz) [Johannes *Mulder*, Dutch anatomist, 1769–1810]. See under *angle*.

Mulder's test (mul'derz) [Gerard Jan *Mulder*, Dutch chemist, 1802–1880]. See under *tests*.

Mules's operation (mūlz) [Philip Henry *Mules*, English oculist, 1843–1905]. See under *operation*.

muliebria (mu″le-eb're-ah) [L.]. The female generative organs.

muliebrity (mu″le-eb'rĭ-te) [L. *muliebritas*]. 1. Womanly quality; the sum of the characteristics typical of the female sex. 2. The assumption of female qualities by the male.

mull (mul). A variety of thin, soft muslin, used in surgery. **plaster m.,** a sheet of mull coated with gutta-percha.

Muller (mul'er), Hermann Joseph. American biologist, born 1890, noted for his research on genes; winner of the Nobel prize for physiology in 1946.

Müller (mil'er), Paul. Swiss chemist, born 1900, noted for synthesis of D.D.T. and discovery of its insecticidal properties; winner of the Nobel prize for medicine in 1948.

muller (mul'er). A kind of pestle, flat at the bottom: used for grinding drugs upon a slab of similar material.

Müller's canal, capsule, duct, experiment, etc. (mil'erz) [Johannes Peter *Müller*, German physiologist, 1801–1858; one of the most distinguished physiologists of Germany and the founder of scientific medicine in Germany]. See under the nouns.

Müller's fiber, muscle, trigone (mil'erz) [Heinrich *Müller*, German anatomist, 1820–1864]. See under the nouns.

Müller's fluid, liquid (mil'erz) [Hermann Franz *Müller*, German histologist, 1866–1898]. See under *fluid*.

Müller's reaction, test [Rudolf *Müller*, Vienna dermatologist, 1877–1934]. See under *tests* (3).

Müller's sign [Friedrich von *Müller*, Munich physician, 1858–1941]. See under *sign*.

Müller's test [Edward *Müller*, German physician, 1876–1928]. See under *tests* (1) and (2).

Müller-Haeckel law (mil'ler hek″l) [Fritz *Müller*, German naturalist, 1821–1897; Ernst Heinrich *Haeckel*, German biologist, 1834–1919]. Biogenetic law. See under *law*.

Müller-Jochmann test [Edward *Müller;* George *Jochmann*, Berlin physician, 1874–1915]. See under *tests*.

müllerian (mil-e're-an). Named for Johannes Peter *Müller*, as müllerian duct.

müllerianoma (mil-e″re-ah-no'mah). A tumor developed from the duct of Müller.

müllerianosis (mil-e″re-ah-no'sis). Endometriosis.

mulleriosis (mul-er″e-o'sis). Blair Bell's term for adenomyosis or endometriosis.

multi- (mul'ti) [L. *multus* many, much]. Combining form signifying many or much.

multiallelic (mul″te-ah-lel'ik). Pertaining to or occupied by many different genes affecting the same or different hereditary characters.

multi-articular (mul″te-ar-tik'u-lar). Pertaining to or affecting many joints.

multibacillary (mul″tĭ-bas'ĭ-la″re). Pertaining to or made up of a number of bacilli.

multicapsular (mul″tĭ-kap'su-lar). Having many capsules.

multicell (mul'tĭ-sel). Any organ made up of many cells; any group of functionally active cells.

multicellular (mul″tĭ-sel'u-lar) [*multi-* + L. *cellula* cell]. 1. Composed of many cells. 2. Containing many hollow spaces.

multicentric (mul″tĭ-sen'trik) [*multi-* + *center*]. Having many centers, or points of origin.

multicentricity (mul″tĭ-sen-tris'ĭ-te). The state or quality of being multicentric.

Multiceps (mul'tĭ-seps). A genus of tapeworms, the bladder worms of which are found in herbivorous animals and the adult forms in carnivorous animals. **M. mul'ticeps** in the adult stage is parasitic in dogs. Its larval stage (*Coenurus cerebralis*) develops in the central nervous system of goats and sheep and occasionally in man and is productive of staggers in sheep. **M. seria'lis** is parasitic in dogs, its larval stage developing in rabbits, squirrels, and other rodents.

multicontaminated (mul″tĭ-kon-tam'ĭ-nāt″ed). Infected by several different species of microorganisms, or by several different contaminating agents.

multicuspidate (mul″tĭ-kus'pĭ-dāt) [*multi-* + L. *cuspis* point]. Having many cusps.

multidentate (mul″tĭ-den'tāt). Having many teeth or many indentations.

multifactorial (mul″tĭ-fak-to're-al). 1. Of or pertaining to, or arising through the action of many factors. 2. In genetics, arising as the result of the interaction of several genes.

multifamilial (mul″tĭ-fah-mil'e-al). Affecting the several successive generations of a family.

multifid (mul'tĭ-fid). Cleft into many parts.

multifidus (mul-tif'ĭ-dus) [L., from *multus* many + *findere* to split]. Cleft into many parts.

multifocal (mul″tĭ-fo'kal). Arising from or pertaining to many foci.

multiform (mul'tĭ-form). Occurring in several forms; polymorphous.

multiganglionic (mul″tĭ-gang″gle-on'ik). Pertaining to, affecting, or possessing many ganglia.

multigesta (mul″tĭ-jes'tah). Multigravida.

multiglandular (mul″tĭ-glan'du-lar). Pluriglandular.

multigravida (mul″tĭ-grav'ĭ-dah) [*multi-* + L. *gravida* pregnant]. A woman pregnant for the third (or more) time. Also written Gravida III (IV, V, etc.). **grand m.,** a woman who has had six or more previous pregnancies.

multihallucalism (mul″tĭ-hal'ŭ-kal-izm) [*multi-* + L. *hallux, hallucis*, great toe + *-ism*]. A developmental anomaly characterized by the presence of more than one great toe on one foot.

multihallucism (mul″tĭ-hal'u-sizm). Multihallucalism.

multi-infection (mul″tĭ-in-fek'shun). Infection with several varieties of organisms.

multilobar (mul″tĭ-lo'bar). Having numerous lobes.

multilobular (mul″tĭ-lob'u-lar) [*multi-* + L. *lobulus* lobule]. Having many lobules.

multilocular (mul″tĭ-lok'u-lar) [*multi-* + L. *loculus* cell]. Having many cells or compartments.

multimammae (mul″tĭ-mam'e) [*multi-* + L. *mamma* breast]. The condition of having more than two breasts.

multinodular (mul″tĭ-nod'u-lar). Composed of many nodules.

multinucleate (mul″tĭ-nu'kle-āt) [*multi-* + *nucleus*]. Having several nuclei.

multipara (mul-tip′ah-rah) [*multi-* + L. *parere* to bring forth, produce]. A woman who has had two or more pregnancies which resulted in viable offspring, whether or not the offspring were alive at birth. Also written Para II, III, IV, etc. **grand m.,** a woman who has had seven or more pregnancies which resulted in viable offspring.

multiparity (mul″tĭ-par′ĭ-te). 1. The condition of being a multipara. 2. The production of several offspring in one gestation.

multiparous (mul-tip′ah-rus). 1. Having had two or more pregnancies which resulted in viable offspring. 2. Producing several ova or offspring at one time.

multipartial (mul″tĭ-par′shal). Made from several strains of the same organism: said of serums.

multiple (mul′tĭ-p′l) [L. *multiplex*]. Manifold; occurring in various parts of the body at once.

multiplicitas (mul″te-plis′ĭ-tas). A multiplication; a developmental anomaly characterized by the presence of an abnormal multiplicity of organs, or of a specific organ. **m. cor′dis,** a developmental anomaly characterized by the presence of a number of separate hearts.

multipolar (mul″tĭ-po′lar) [*multi-* + L. *polus* pole]. Having more than two poles or processes.

multipollicalism (mul″tĭ-pol′ĭ-kal-izm) [*multi-* + L. *pollex, pollicis* thumb + *-ism*]. A developmental anomaly characterized by the presence of more than one thumb on one hand.

multirooted (mul″tĭ-ro͞ot′ed). Having many roots; said of molar teeth.

multisensitivity (mul″tĭ-sen″sĭ-tiv′ĭ-te). The condition of being sensitive (allergic) to more than one antigen.

multisynaptic (mul″te-sĭ-nap′tik). Polysynaptic.

multiterminal (mul″tĭ-ter′mĭ-nal). Having several sets of terminals so that several electrodes may be used.

multituberculate (mul″tĭ-tu-ber′ku-lāt). Having many tubercles.

multivalent (mul″tĭ-va′lent) [*multi-* + L. *valere* to have value]. 1. Having the power of combining with three or more univalent atoms. 2. Active against several strains of an organism.

muma (mu′mah). Myositis purulenta tropica.

mummification (mum″ĭ-fi-ka′shun). Conversion into a state resembling that of a mummy, such as occurs in dry gangrene, or the shriveling and drying up of a dead fetus.

mummying (mum′e-ing). A form of physical restraint in which the entire body is enclosed in a sheet or blanket, leaving only the head exposed.

mumps (mumps). A contagious febrile disease caused by a virus, and marked by inflammation and swelling of the parotid gland and sometimes of the pancreas, ovaries or testicles. After an incubation period of about three weeks the symptoms appear with fever, headache, and pain beneath the ear. Soon there develops a tense, painful swelling in the parotid region, which interferes with mastication and swallowing and renders both actions painful. After a period of a few days to a week the symptoms gradually disappear. Sometimes the submaxillary and other salivary glands are involved, and occasionally the testicles, mammae, or the labia majora become swollen. One attack generally confers immunity from another. **iodine m.,** swelling of the salivary and lacrimal glands as a toxic reaction to iodine therapy. **metastatic m.,** involvement of other glands or organs of the body occurring in association with mumps. **single m.,** that which affects only one of the parotid glands.

Münchmeyer's disease (minch′mi-erz) [Ernst *Münchmeyer*, German physician, 1846–1880]. See under *disease.*

Mundinus (mun-di′nus) [It. *Mondino* de Luzzi] (?1275–1326). An Italian physician and anatomist —"the restorer of anatomy." His *Anothomia* (1316) was the first text devoted to human anatomy and, although not illustrated, it was greatly esteemed for some two hundred years.

munity (mu′nĭ-te). The state of being susceptible to infection.

Munk's disease (munks) [Fritz *Munk*, Berlin internist, born 1879]. Lipid nephrosis.

Munro's point (mun-rōz′) [John Cummings *Munro*, Boston surgeon, 1858–1910]. See under *point.*

mural (mu′ral) [L. *muralis*, from *murus* wall]. Pertaining to or occurring in the wall of a cavity.

Murchison's pill (mur′chĭ-sunz) [Charles *Murchison*, English physician, 1830–1879]. See under *pill.*

murel (mu′rel). Trade mark for preparations of valethamate bromide.

Murex (mu′reks). A genus of mollusks. **M. purpu′rea,** a gastropodous mollusk of the Mediterranean that furnished an ancient purple dye: from it a homeopathic remedy, used in uterine diseases, is prepared.

murexide (mu-rek′sīd) [L. *murex* purple sea snail]. Ammonium purpurate, $C_8H_4O_6N_5.NH_4.H_2O$, a brownish-red powder formerly used as a dye.

murexin (mu-rek′sin) [L. *murex, muricis* the purple fish or pointed rock + *-ine*, suffix for chemical compounds]. A neurotoxic substance derived from the median zone of the hypobranchial gland of gastropods of the genus *Murex;* identified as β-[imidazolyl-(4)]-acrylcholine, and believed to be the same as purpurin.

muriate (mu′re-āt) [L. *muria* brine]. An obsolete synonym of chloride.

muriatic (mu″re-at′ik) [L. *muriaticus; muria* brine]. Derived from common salt.

Murimyces (mu″re-mi′sēz). A name proposed for the pleuropneumonia-like organisms isolated from rats.

murine (mu′rin) [L. *mus, muris* mouse]. Pertaining to or affecting mice or rats.

murmekiasmosis amphilaphes (mur″me-ki″as-mo′sis am-fil′ah-fēz) [Gr. *myrmēkiasmos* outbreak of warts on the body; Gr. *amphilaphēs* spreading]. A disease of the tropics, consisting of cutaneous warts marked by extremely rapid growth, spreading to the whole side of the face and neck.

murmur (mur′mur) [L.]. A gentle blowing auscultatory sound. **accidental m.,** one due to some temporary and unimportant circumstance. **amphoric m.,** a respiratory murmur having an amphoric character. **anemic m.,** one observed in anemia. **aneurysmal m.,** a vascular murmur caused by an aneurysm. **aortic m.,** a sound indicative of disease of the aortic valves. **apex m.,** one heard over the apex of the heart. **arterial m.,** a murmur in an artery, sometimes aneurysmal and sometimes hemic. **attrition m.,** the sound produced by the friction of the pericardial surfaces in some cases of pericarditis. **Austin Flint m.,** Flint m. **bellows m.,** the bruit de souffle, a puffing systolic heart sound. **blood m.,** one due to an abnormal, and commonly an anemic condition of the blood. Called also *hemic m.* **brain m.,** a systolic murmur chiefly heard in the temporal region, and principally in cases of rickets. **Bright's m.,** bruit de cuir neuf. **bronchial m.,** one heard over the large bronchi resembling a laryngeal respiratory murmur. **cardiac m.,** any adventitious sound heard over the region of the heart. **cardiopulmonary m., cardiorespiratory m.,** a murmur caused by the impact of the heart against the lung: sometimes also due to physical and histologic changes in the substance of the lung. **crescendo m.,** a heart murmur marked by a progressively rising pitch, a progressively increasing force, and a sudden termination: it is heard in mitral stenosis. **deglutition m.,** one heard over the esophagus during the act of swallowing. **diastolic m.,** one occurring with and after the second sound of the heart. Heard at the apex, it is a sign of mitral ob-

A TABLE OF ENDOCARDIAL MURMURS

TIME OF OCCURRENCE	SITE OF GREATEST INTENSITY	DIRECTION OF TRANSMISSION	SEAT OF LESION	NATURE OF LESION
Systolic.	At cardiac apex.	Along left fifth and sixth ribs—in left axilla—in the back, at inferior angle of left scapula.	Mitral orifice.	Incompetency—Regurgitation.
Systolic.	At junction of right second costal cartilage with sternum.	To junction of right clavicle with sternum—in course of right carotid.	Aortic orifice.	Narrowing—Obstruction.
Systolic.	At ensiform cartilage.	Feebly transmitted.	Tricuspid orifice.	Incompetency—Regurgitation.
Systolic.	At left second intercostal space, close to sternum.	Feebly transmitted.	Pulmonary orifice.	Narrowing—Obstruction.
Diastolic.	At junction of right second costal cartilage with sternum.	To midsternum—in course of sternum.	Aortic orifice.	Incompetency—Regurgitation.
Diastolic.	At left second intercostal space, close to sternum.	In course of sternum.	Pulmonary orifice.	Incompetency—Regurgitation.
(Diastolic) presystolic.	Over body of heart.	To apex of heart.	Mitral orifice.	Narrowing—Obstruction.
(Diastolic) presystolic.	At ensiform cartilage.	Feebly transmitted.	Tricuspid orifice.	Narrowing—Obstruction.

struction; at the base of the heart, it is due to aortic regurgitation; more rarely to pulmonary regurgitation. **direct m.,** one due to a roughened endocardium and contracted valvular orifice. Called also *obstructive m.* **Duroziez's m.,** a double murmur in the femoral or other large peripheral artery, due to aortic insufficiency. **dynamic m.,** one caused by irregular pulsation of the heart. **endocardial m.,** an abnormal sound produced within the cavity of the heart. **Eustace Smith's m.,** a venous hum heard over the manubrium when the patient's head is stretched backward in bronchial stenosis. **exocardial m.,** a cardiac murmur produced outside of the heart's cavities. **expiratory m.,** a soft buzzing sound heard on expiration and caused by the current of air passing through the bronchi. **Fisher's m.,** a systolic murmur heard over the anterior fontanel or in the temporal region in rickets. **Flint's m.,** a loud presystolic murmur at the apex in aortic regurgitation. **Fraentzel m.,** one louder at the beginning and the end of diastole than during the midperiod: heard in mitral stenosis. **friction m.,** one due to the rubbing together of two serous surfaces. **functional m.,** a cardiac murmur due to anemia or to excited action of the heart. **Gibson m.,** a long rumbling sound occupying most of systole and diastole, usually localized in the second left interspace near the sternum, and pathognomonic of patent ductus arteriosus. **Graham Steell m.,** one caused by relative pulmonary insufficiency; it is a soft diastolic murmur heard in the pulmonary area in the third left intercostal space near the border of the sternum and thence propagated down the sternum. **heart m.,** cardiac m. **hemic m.,** blood m. **hour-glass m.,** a murmur which is characterized by two periods of maximum loudness joined by a period of decreased loudness. **humming-top m.,** venous hum. **indirect m.,** one that is caused by the reversal of the direction of the blood current. **inorganic m.,** any murmur not due to a valvular or other lesion. **inspiratory m.,** the murmur heard over the lungs during inspiration. **lapping m.,** a cardiac murmur resembling the sound of a cat lapping milk, heard in rupture of the aorta. **machinery m.,** a continuous loud, rough heart murmur heard in the second left space in case of patent ductus arteriosus. **Makins' m.,** a reproduction in the heart of the systolic murmur heard over a wounded artery. **metallic m.,** a metallic musical sound heard over the lungs during inspiration. **mitral m.,** one due to disease of the mitral valve. **muscle m.,** one heard over a muscle in a state of contraction. **musical m.,** a cardiac murmur with a musical quality. **nun's m.,** bruit de diable. **obstructive m.,** direct m. **organic m.,** one due to a structural change in the heart, in a vessel, or in the lung substance. **Parrot's m.,** a soft murmur heard instead of the cardiac sound in asystole. **pericardial m.,** a murmur produced in the pericardial sac. **pleuropericardial m.,** a pleural friction sound heard in the pericardial region and resembling a pericardial murmur. **prediastolic m.,** one occurring just before and with the diastole. Heard at the apex, it is due to mitral obstruction; at the base of the heart, to aortic regurgitation; more rarely, to pulmonary regurgitation. **presystolic m.,** one occurring just before the systole, from mitral or tricuspid obstruction. **pulmonic m.,** one due to disease of the valves of the pulmonary artery. **reduplication m.,** a heart murmur in which the mitral and tricuspid first sound or the aortic and pulmonary second sounds are heard separately. **regurgitant m.,** a murmur due to regurgitation of blood through a dilated valvular orifice. **respiratory m.,** one heard on auscultation over the normal lung during respiration. **Roger's m.,** bruit de Roger. **sea-gull m.,** a musical murmur resembling the call of a sea gull, frequently heard in aortic insufficiency, and attributed specifically to eversion or retroversion of the right anterior aortic cusp. **seesaw m.,** to-and-fro m. **spontaneous m.,** a cardiac murmur heard over a wide extent, and chiefly due to aortic valvular insufficiency. **Steell's m.,** Graham Steell m. **stenosal m.,** a sound produced in an artery by artificial pressure or by a stenosis. **subclavicular m.,** a sound sometimes produced in the subclavian artery during systole, and due to a stenosis: mostly a symptom of tuberculous disease. **systolic m.,** one at the systole: due to mitral, aortic, tricuspid, or pulmonary obstruction. **to-and-fro m.,** a pericardial murmur occurring with both systole and diastole. **Traube's m.,** gallop rhythm. **tricuspid m.,** a murmur caused by disease of the tricuspid valves. **vascular m.,** a murmur heard over a blood vessel. **venous m.,** a murmur heard over a vein. **vesicular m.,** the murmur of normal breathing. **water-wheel m.,** bruit de moulin.

Murphy (mur′fe), William Parry. American physician, born in 1892, co-winner, with George Richards Minot and George Hoyt Whipple, of the Nobel prize for medicine and physiology in 1934, for their work on anemia.

Murphy button, method, sign, test, treatment (mur′fe) [John Benjamin *Murphy*, Chicago surgeon, 1857–1916]. See under the nouns.

murrain (mur′in). Any destructive cattle plague.

Murri's disease, law (moor′ēz) [Augusto *Murri*, Italian clinician, 1841–1932]. See under *disease* and *law*.

murrina (moo-re′nah). A form of trypanosomiasis among mules and horses in the Canal Zone (Darling, 1911). It is thought to be caused by the *Trypanosoma hippicum*, and is marked by anemia, weakness, emaciation and edema, conjunctivitis, pyrexia, and some posterior paralyses.

Mus (mus) [L. "mouse"]. A genus of rats and mice. **M. alexandri'nus,** the Egyptian or roof rat. **M. decuma'nus,** *M. norvegicus.* **M. mus'-culus,** the common house mouse. **M. norve'-gicus,** the brown or barn rat. **M. rat'tus,** the English black rat.

Musca (mus'kah) [L. "fly"]. A genus of flies of the family Muscidae which have their mouth parts adapted for suction only. **M. autumna'lis,** the common housefly of Europe. **M. bra'va,** a South American fly which is probably instrumental in transmitting mal de Caderas. **M. domes'tica,** the common housefly. It may act as a mechanical carrier of the micoorganisms of typhoid fever, cholera, dysentery, plague, anthrax, tetanus, trachoma, leprosy, and encephalitis, and of pyogenic bacteria. The larvae may cause myiasis. **M. lute'ola.** See *Auchmeromyia.* **M. vomito'ria,** *Calliphora vomitoria.*

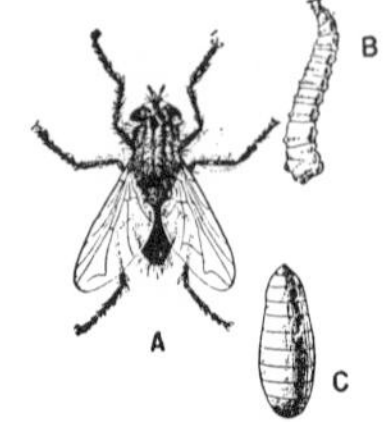

Musca domestica: A Fly; B, larva; C, pupa.

musca (mus'kah), pl. *mus'cae* [L.]. A fly. **mus'-cae hispan'icae,** cantharides. **mus'cae volitan'tes** [L. "flitting flies"], specks seen floating before the eyes.

muscacide (mus'kah-sīd) [L. *musca* fly + *caedere* to kill]. 1. Destructive to flies. 2. Any agent which destroys flies.

muscae (mus'ke) [L.]. Plural of *musca.*

muscardine (mus'kar-din). A disease of silkworms caused by *Botrytis bassiana.*

muscarine (mus'kah-rin) [L. *muscarius* pertaining to flies]. A deadly alkaloid, $CH_3.CH_2.CHOH.$-$CH(CHO)N(CH_3)_3OH$, from various mushrooms, as the fly-agaric, *Agaricus muscarius,* and also from rotten fish.

muscarinism (mus'kar-in-izm). Poisoning by muscarine.

muscegenetic (mus"e-je-net'ik). Giving rise to muscae volitantes.

muscicide (mus'ĭ-sīd). Muscacide.

Muscidae (mus'ĭ-de). A family of flies of the order Diptera. It includes the following genera: *Fannia, Glossina, Musca, Muscina* and *Stomoxys.*

Muscina (mŭ-si'nah). The nonbiting stable-fly which breeds in dung. It is closely related to the housefly and it also frequents dwellings.

muscle (mus'el). An organ which by contraction produces the movements of an animal organism. Called also *musculus* [N A]. Muscles are of two varieties: *striated,* or *striped,* including all the muscles in which contraction is voluntary and the heart muscle; *unstriated, smooth,* or *organic,* including all the involuntary muscles except the heart, such as the muscular layer of the intestines, bladder, blood vessels, etc. Striated muscles are covered with a thin layer of connective tissue (*epimysium*) from which septa (*perimysium*) pass, dividing the muscle into bundles of fibers, or *fasciculi.* Each fasciculus contains a number of parallel fibers separated by connective tissue septa (*endomysium*). Each fiber consists of sarcoplasm which is cross striated or composed of alternate light and dark portions (whence the name *striated muscle*); each contains embedded in it the *myofibrils* and each is surrounded by *sarcolemma.* Smooth muscles are composed of elongated, spindle-shaped, nucleated cells arranged parallel to one another and to the long axis of the muscle and these cells are often grouped into bundles of varying size. The muscles, bundles, and cells are inclosed in an indifferent connective tissue material much as is found in striated muscles. **abdominal m's,** musculi abdominis. **abductor m. of fifth digit of foot,** musculus abductor digiti minimi pedis. **abductor m. of fifth digit of hand,** musculus abductor digiti minimi manus. **abductor m. of great toe,** musculus abductor hallucis. **abductor m. of little finger,** musculus abductor digiti minimi manus. **abductor m. of little toe,** musculus abductor digiti minimi pedis. **abductor m. of thumb, long,** musculus abductor pollicis longus. **abductor m. of thumb, short,** musculus abductor pollicis brevis. **adductor m., great,** musculus adductor magnus. **adductor m., long,** musculus adductor longus. **adductor m., short,** musculus adductor brevis. **adductor m., smallest,** musculus adductor minimus. **adductor m. of great toe,** musculus adductor hallucis. **adductor m. of thumb,** musculus adductor pollicis. **Aeby's m.,** musculus depressor labii inferioris. **agonistic m.,** a muscle opposed in action by another muscle, called the antagonist. **Albinus' m.** 1. Musculus risorius. 2. Musculus scalenus medius. **anconeus m.,** musculus anconeus. **anconeus m., external,** caput laterale musculi tricipitis brachii. **anconeus m., internal,** caput mediale musculi tricipitis brachii. **anconeus m., lateral,** caput laterale musculi tricipitis brachii. **anconeus m., medial,** caput mediale musculi tricipitis brachii. **anconeus m., short,** caput laterale musculi tricipitis brachii. **antagonistic m.,** a muscle that counteracts the action of another muscle. **antigravity m's,** those muscles that by their tone resist the constant pull of gravity in the maintenance of normal posture. **m. of antitragus,** musculus antitragicus. **appendicular m.,** one of the muscles of a limb. **arrector m's of hair,** musculi arrectores pilorum. **articular m.,** a muscle that has one end attached to the synovial capsule of a joint. Called also *musculus articularis.* **articular m. of elbow,** musculus articularis cubiti. **articular m. of knee,** musculus articularis genus. **aryepiglottic m.,** musculus aryepiglotticus. **arytenoid m., oblique,** musculus arytenoideus obliquus. **arytenoid m., transverse,** musculus arytenoideus transversus. **m's of auditory ossicles,** musculi ossiculorum auditus. **auricular m., anterior,** musculus auricularis anterior. **auricular m., posterior,** musculus auricularis posterior. **auricular m., superior,** musculus auricularis superior. **Bell's m.,** the muscular strands between the ureteric orifices and the uvula, bounding the trigone of the urinary bladder. **biceps m. of arm,** musculus biceps brachii. **biceps m. of thigh,** musculus biceps femoris. **bipennate m.,** musculus bipennatus. **Bowman's m.,** musculus ciliaris. **brachial m.,** musculus brachialis. **brachioradial m.,** musculus brachioradialis. **bronchoesophageal m.,** musculus bronchoesophageus. **Brücke's m.,** the longitudinal fibers of the ciliary muscle. **buccinator m.,** musculus buccinator. **buccopharyngeal m.,** pars buccopharyngea musculi constrictoris pharyngis superioris. **bulbocavernous m.,** musculus bulbospongiosus. **canine m.,** musculus levator anguli oris. **cardiac m.,** the muscle of the heart, composed of striated muscle fibers. **Casser's m.,** ligamentum mallei anterius. **ceratocricoid m.,** musculus ceratocricoideus. **ceratopharyngeal m.,** pars ceratopharyngea musculi constrictoris pharyngis medii. **Chassaignac's axillary m.,** an occasional fascicle of muscle tissue extending from the lower edge of the latissimus dorsi across the hollow of the axilla to the brachial fascia or to the lower border of the pectoralis minor. **m's of chest,** musculi thoracis. **chin m.,** musculus mentalis. **chondroglossus m.,** musculus chondroglossus. **chondropharyngeal m.,** pars chondropharyngea musculi constrictoris pharyngis medii. **ciliary m.,** musculus ciliaris. **coccygeal m's,** those connected with the coccyx, including the musculus coccygeus, musculus sacrococcygeus dorsalis, and musculus

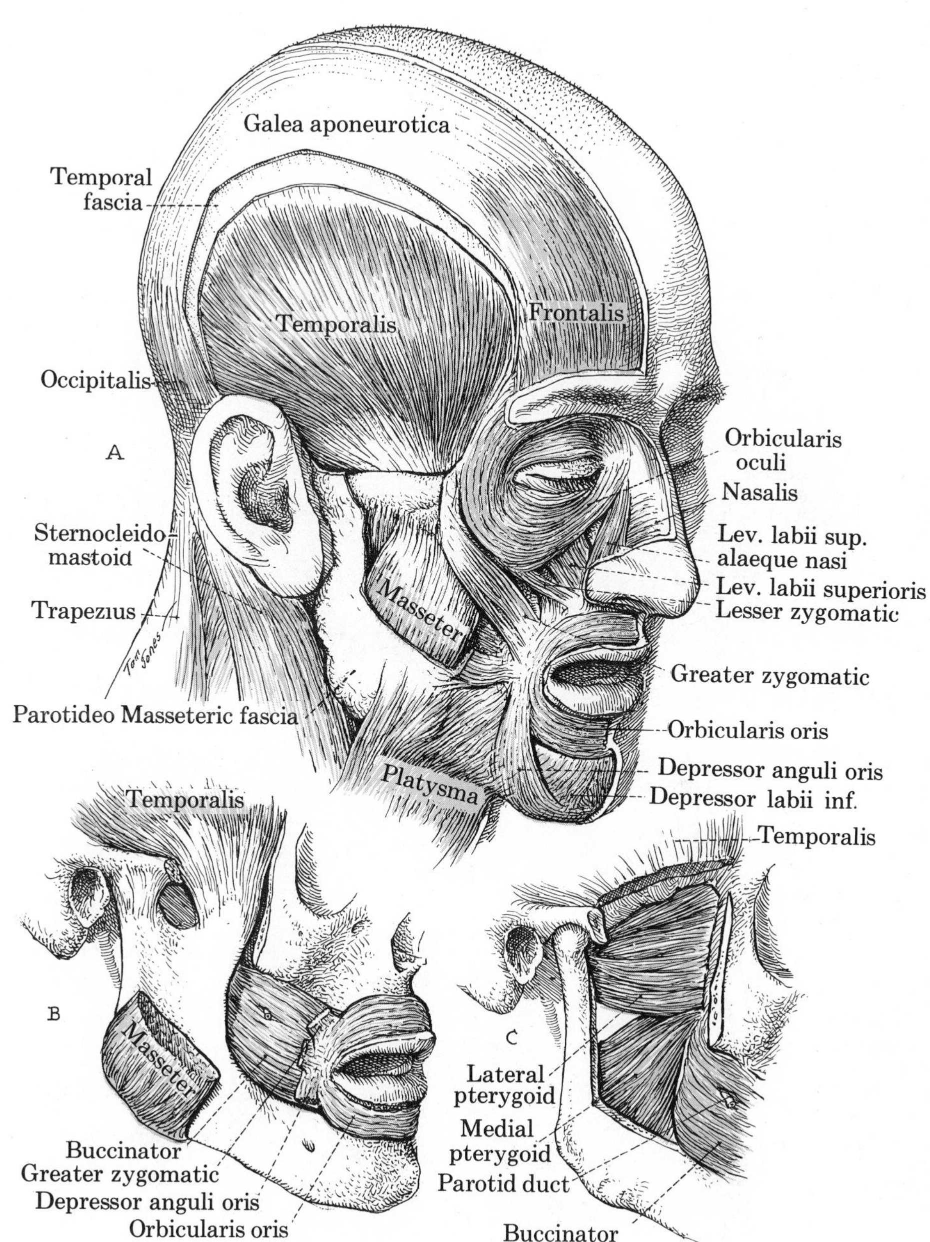

MUSCLES OF THE HEAD AND FACE

A, muscles of face and scalp, showing insertion of platysma; B, buccinator and orbicularis oris; C, pterygoid muscles. (Jones and Shepard.)

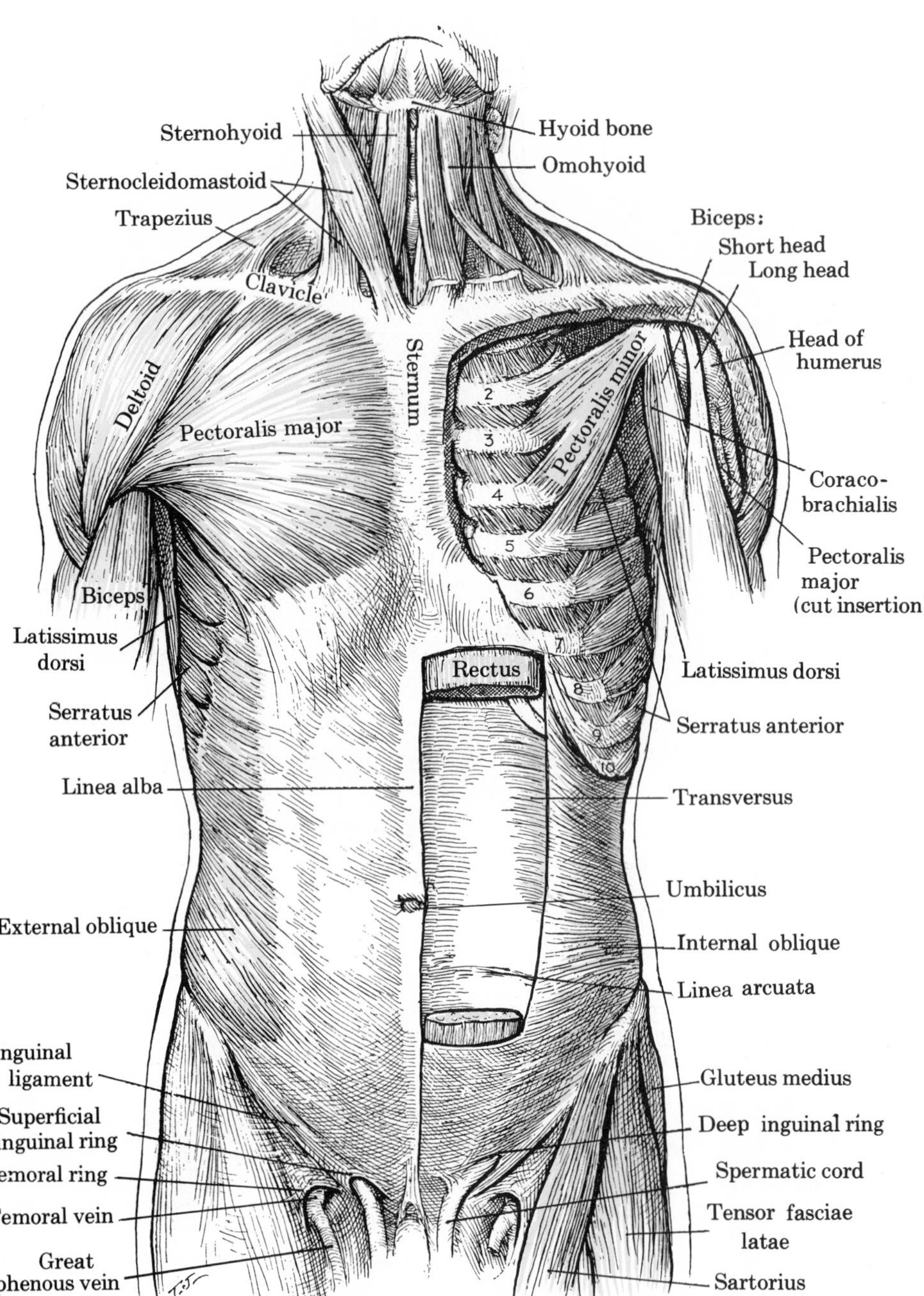

MUSCLES OF TRUNK, ANTERIOR VIEW

The left sternocleidomastoid, pectoralis major, external oblique, and a portion of the deltoid have been removed to show underlying muscles. A portion of the rectus abdominis has been cut away to expose the posterior part of its sheath. (Jones and Shepard.)

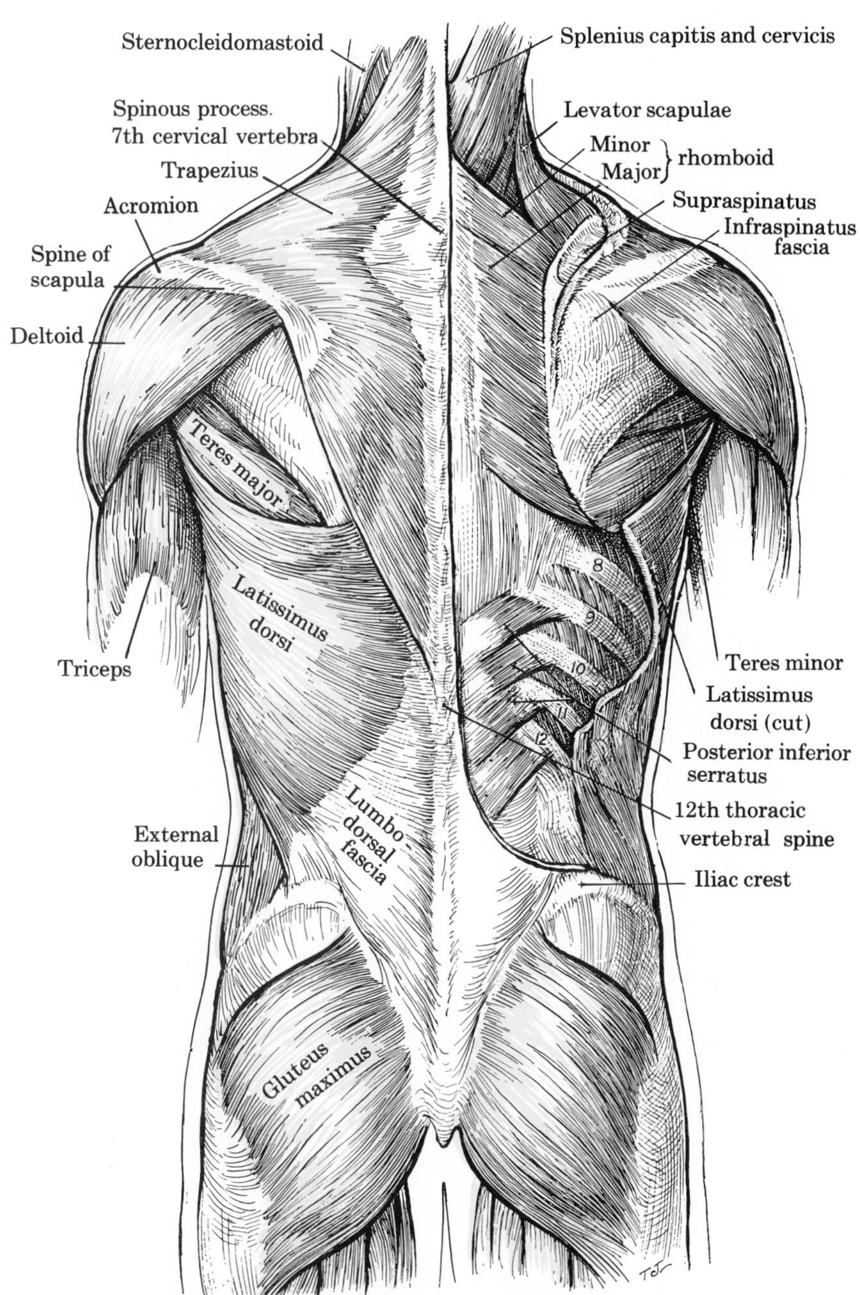

MUSCLES OF TRUNK, POSTERIOR VIEW

The latissimus dorsi and trapezius on the right side have been cut away to expose the underlying muscles. (Jones and Shepard.)

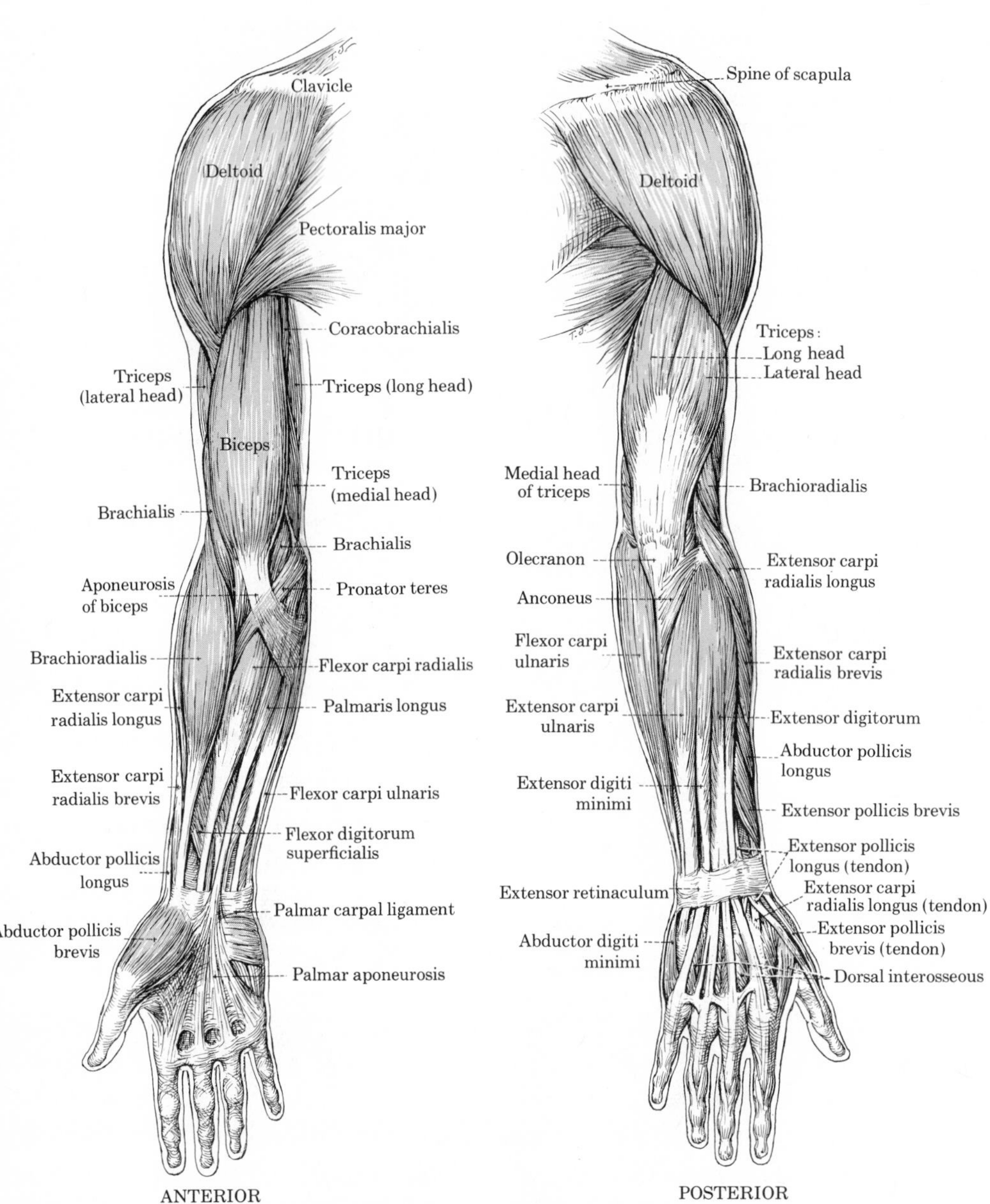

SUPERFICIAL MUSCLES OF RIGHT UPPER EXTREMITY

(Jones and Shepard)

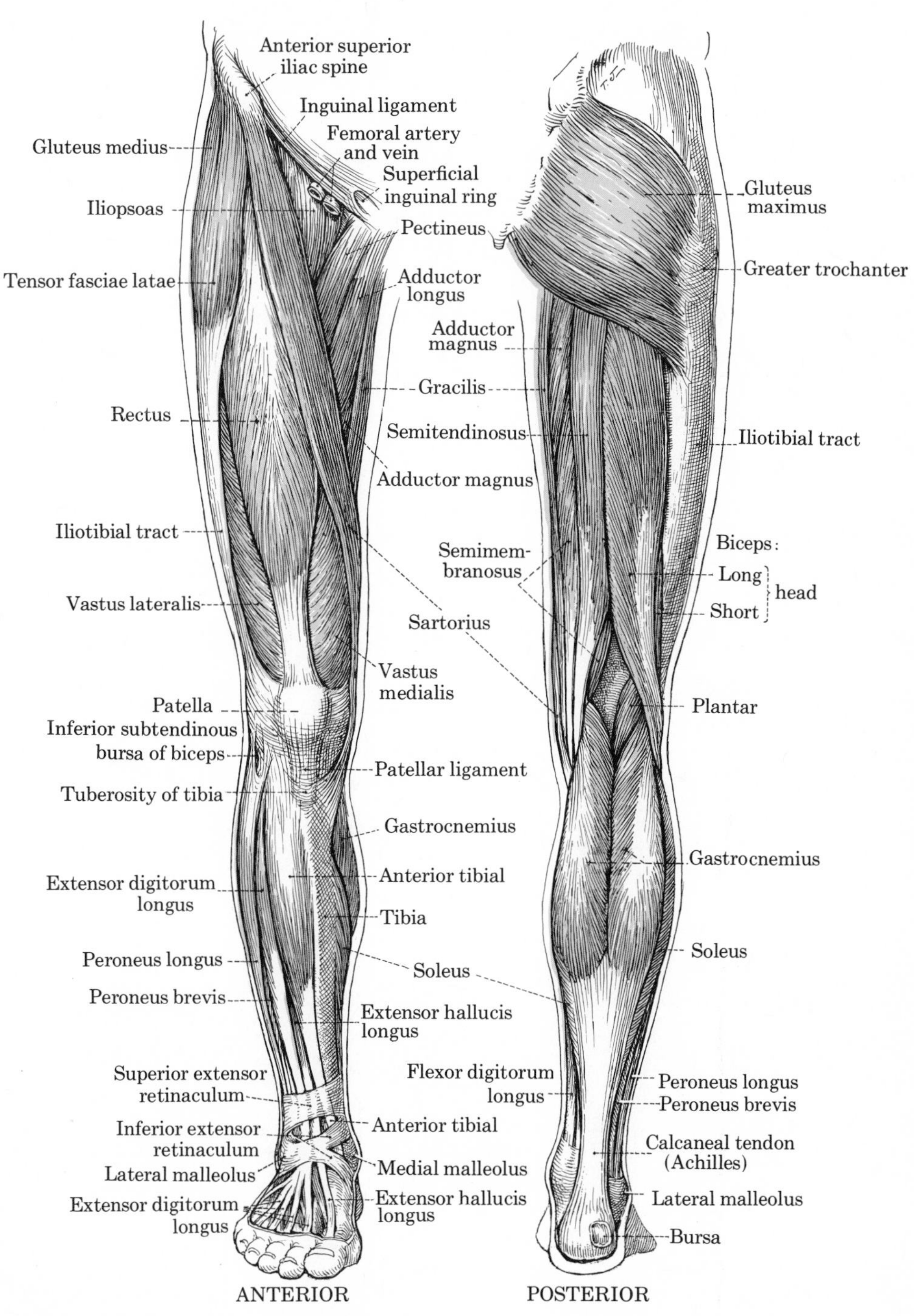

SUPERFICIAL MUSCLES OF RIGHT LOWER EXTREMITY

(Jones and Shepard)

sacrococcygeus ventralis. **compressor m. of naris,** pars transversa musculi nasalis. **constrictor m. of pharynx, inferior,** musculus constrictor pharyngis inferior. **constrictor m. of pharynx, middle,** musculus constrictor pharyngis medius. **constrictor m. of pharynx, superior,** musculus constrictor pharyngis superior. **coracobrachial m.,** musculus coracobrachialis. **corrugator m., superciliary,** musculus corrugator supercilii. **Crampton's m.,** the anterior portion of the ciliary muscle in birds. **cremaster m.,** musculus cremaster. **cricoarytenoid m., lateral,** musculus cricoarytenoideus lateralis. **cricoarytenoid m., posterior,** musculus cricoarytenoideus posterior. **cricopharyngeal m.,** pars cricopharyngea musculi constrictoris pharyngis inferioris. **cricothyroid m.,** musculus cricothyroideus. **cutaneous m.,** striated muscle that inserts into the skin. Called also *musculus cutaneus*. **dartos m. of scrotum,** tunica dartos. **deltoid m.,** musculus deltoideus. **depressor m., superciliary,** musculus depressor supercilii. **depressor m. of angle of mouth,** musculus depressor anguli oris. **depressor m. of lower lip,** musculus depressor labii inferioris. **depressor m. of septum of nose,** musculus depressor septi nasi. **diaphragmatic m.,** diaphragma. **digastric m.,** musculus digastricus. **dilator m. of nose,** pars alaris musculi nasalis. **dilator m. of pupil,** musculus dilator pupillae. **epicranial m.,** musculus epicranius. **epimeric m.,** a muscle derived from an epimere and innervated by a posterior ramus of a spinal nerve. **epitrochleoanconeus m.,** musculus epitrochleoanconaeus. **erector m. of penis,** musculus ischiocavernosus. **erector m. of spine,** musculus erector spinae. **eustachian m.,** musculus tensor tympani. **extensor m. of digits, common, extensor m. of fingers,** musculus extensor digitorum. **extensor m. of fifth digit, proper,** musculus extensor digiti minimi. **extensor m. of great toe, long,** musculus extensor hallucis longus. **extensor m. of great toe, short,** musculus extensor hallucis brevis. **extensor m. of index finger,** musculus extensor indicis. **extensor m. of little finger,** musculus extensor digiti minimi. **extensor m. of thumb, long,** musculus extensor pollicis longus. **extensor m. of thumb, short,** musculus extensor pollicis brevis. **extensor m. of toes, long,** musculus extensor digitorum longus pedis. **extensor m. of toes, short,** musculus extensor digitorum brevis. **extensor m. of wrist, radial, long,** musculus extensor carpi radialis longus. **extensor m. of wrist, radial, short,** musculus extensor carpi radialis brevis. **extensor m. of wrist, ulnar,** musculus extensor carpi ulnaris. **extraocular m's,** musculi bulbi. **extrinsic m.,** a muscle whose origin is not in the same limb or part in which it is inserted. **m's of eye,** musculi bulbi. **m's of fauces,** musculi palati et faucium. **femoral m.,** musculus vastus intermedius. **fibular m., long,** musculus peroneus longus. **fibular m., short,** musculus peroneus brevis. **fibular m., third,** musculus peroneus tertius. **fixation m's, fixator m's,** accessory muscles that serve to steady a part. **fixator m. of base of stapes,** musculus fixator baseos stapedis. **flexor m., accessory,** musculus quadratus plantae. **flexor m. of fifth digit of foot, short,** musculus flexor digiti minimi brevis pedis. **flexor m. of fifth digit of hand, short,** musculus flexor digiti minimi brevis manus. **flexor m. of fingers, deep,** musculus flexor digitorum profundus. **flexor m. of fingers, superficial,** musculus flexor digitorum superficialis. **flexor m. of great toe, long,** musculus flexor hallucis longus. **flexor m. of great toe, short,** musculus flexor hallucis brevis. **flexor m. of little finger, short,** musculus flexor digiti minimi brevis manus. **flexor m. of little toe, short,** musculus flexor digiti minimi brevis pedis. **flexor m. of thumb, long,** musculus flexor pollicis longus. **flexor m. of thumb, short,** musculus flexor pollicis brevis. **flexor m. of toes, long,** musculus flexor digitorum longus. **flexor m. of toes, short,** musculus flexor digitorum brevis. **flexor m. of wrist, radial,** musculus flexor carpi radialis. **flexor m. of wrist, ulnar,** musculus flexor carpi ulnaris. **Folius' m.,** ligamentum mallei laterale. **frontal m.,** venter frontalis musculi occipitofrontalis. **fusiform m.,** a spindle-shaped muscle. See *musculus fusiformis*. **gastrocnemius m.,** musculus gastrocnemius. **gastrocnemius m., internal,** caput mediale musculi gastrocnemii. **gastrocnemius m., lateral,** caput laterale musculi gastrocnemii. **gastrocnemius m., medial,** caput mediale musculi gastrocnemii. **Gavard's m.,** the oblique muscular elements of the stomach wall. **gemellus m., inferior,** musculus gemellus inferior. **gemellus m., superior,** musculus gemellus superior. **genioglossus m.,** musculus genioglossus. **geniohyoid m.,** musculus geniohyoideus. **glossopalatine m.,** musculus palatoglossus. **glossopharyngeal m.,** pars glossopharyngea musculi constrictoris pharyngis superioris. **gluteal m., greatest,** musculus gluteus maximus. **gluteal m., least,** musculus gluteus minimus. **gluteal m., middle,** musculus gluteus medius. **gracilis m.,** musculus gracilis. **great m., intermediate,** musculus vastus intermedius. **great m., lateral,** musculus vastus lateralis. **great m., medial,** musculus vastus medialis. **Guthrie's m.,** musculus sphincter urethrae. **hamstring m's,** the muscles of the back of the thigh, including the biceps femoris, the semitendinosus, and the semimembranosus. **m. of helix, larger,** musculus helicis major. **m. of helix, smaller,** musculus helicis minor. **Hilton's m.,** musculus aryepiglotticus. **Horner's m.,** pars lacrimalis musculi orbicularis oculi. **Houston's m.,** fibers of the bulbocavernosus muscle compressing the dorsal vein of the penis. **hyoglossus m.,** musculus hyoglossus. **m's of hyoid bone.** See *musculi infrahyoidei* and *musculi suprahyoidei*. **hypaxial m's,** musculus longus capitis, musculus longus colli, the vertebral portion of the diaphragm, and musculus sacrococcygeus anterior. Called also *subvertebral m's*. **hypomeric m.,** a muscle derived from a hypomere and innervated by an anterior ramus of a spinal nerve. **iliac m.,** musculus iliacus. **iliococcygeal m.,** musculus iliococcygeus. **iliocostal m.,** musculus iliocostalis. **iliocostal m. of back,** musculus iliocostalis thoracis. **iliocostal m. of loins,** musculus iliocostalis lumborum. **iliocostal m. of neck,** musculus iliocostalis cervicis. **iliocostal m. of thorax,** musculus iliocostalis thoracis. **iliopsoas m.,** musculus iliopsoas. **incisive m's of lower lip,** musculi incisivi labii inferioris. **incisive m's of upper lip,** musculi incisivi labii superioris. **m. of incisure of helix,** musculus incisurae helicis. **m's of inferior extremity,** musculi membri inferioris. **infrahyoid m's,** musculi infrahyoidei. **infraspinous m.,** musculus infraspinatus. **inspiratory m's,** the muscles that act in inspiration, such as the diaphragm, and the intercostal and pectoral muscles. **intercostal m's, external,** musculi intercostales externi. **intercostal m's, innermost,** musculi intercostales intimi. **intercostal m's, internal,** musculi intercostales interni. **interfoveolar m.,** ligamentum interfoveolare. **interosseous m's, palmar,** musculi interossei palmares. **interosseous m's, plantar,** musculi interossei plantares. **interosseous m's, volar,** musculi interossei palmares. **interosseous m's of foot, dorsal,** musculi interossei dorsales pedis. **interosseous m's of hand, dorsal,** musculi interossei dorsales manus. **interspinal m's,** musculi interspinales. **intertransverse m's,** musculi intertransversarii. **intertransverse m's, anterior,** musculi intertransversarii thoracis. **intertransverse**

m's of loins, lateral, musculi intertransversarii laterales lumborum. **intertransverse m's of loins, medial,** musculi intertransversarii mediales lumborum. **intertransverse m's of neck, anterior,** musculi intertransversarii anteriores cervicis. **intertransverse m's of neck, posterior,** musculi intertransversarii posteriores cervicis. **intertransverse m's of thorax,** musculi intertransversarii thoracis. **intraauricular m's,** the stapedius and tensor tympani muscles. **intrinsic m.,** a muscle whose origin and insertion are both in the same limb or part. **involuntary m.,** a muscle that is not under the control of the will; such muscles are, for the most part, composed of nonstriated fibers. **iridic m's,** the muscles controlling the iris. **ischiocavernous m.,** musculus ischiocavernosus. **Jarjavay's m.,** a muscle described by Jarjavay as arising from the ramus of the ischium and inserting in the constrictor muscle of the vagina, which acts to depress the urethra. **joint m.,** musculus articularis. **Jung's m.,** musculus pyramidalis auriculae. **Koyter's m.,** musculus corrugator supercilii. **Landström's m.,** minute muscle fibers in the fascia around and behind the eyeball, attached in front to the anterior orbital fascia and eyelids. **Langer's m.,** muscular fibers from the insertion of the pectoralis major muscle over the bicipital groove to the insertion of the latissimus dorsi. **latissimus dorsi m.,** musculus latissimus dorsi. **levator m. of angle of mouth,** musculus levator anguli oris. **levator ani m.,** musculus levator ani. **levator m. of palatine velum,** musculus levator veli palatini. **levator m. of prostate,** musculus levator prostatae. **levator m's of ribs,** musculi levatores costarum. **levator m's of ribs, long,** musculi levatores costarum longi. **levator m's of ribs, short,** musculi levatores costarum breves. **levator m. of scapula,** musculus levator scapulae. **levator m. of thyroid gland,** musculus levator glandulae thyroideae. **levator m. of upper eyelid,** musculus levator palpebrae superioris. **levator m. of upper lip,** musculus levator labii superioris. **long m. of head,** musculus longus capitis. **long m. of neck,** musculus longus colli. **longissimus m.,** musculus longissimus. **longissimus m. of back,** musculus longissimus thoracis. **longissimus m. of head,** musculus longissimus capitis. **longissimus m. of neck,** musculus longissimus cervicis. **longissimus m. of thorax,** musculus longissimus thoracis. **longitudinal m. of tongue, inferior,** musculus longitudinalis inferior linguae. **longitudinal m. of tongue, superior,** musculus longitudinalis superior linguae. **m's of lower extremity,** musculi membri inferioris. **lumbrical m's of foot,** musculi lumbricales pedis. **lumbrical m's of hand,** musculi lumbricales manus. **Luschka's m's,** the uterosacral ligaments, which contain muscular tissue. **masseter m.,** musculus masseter. **Merkel's m.,** musculus ceratocricoideus. **mesothenar m.,** musculus adductor pollicis. **Müller's m.,** the circular fibers of the ciliary muscle. **multifidus m.,** musculus multifidus. **mylohyoid m.,** musculus mylohyoideus. **mylopharyngeal m.,** pars mylopharyngea musculi constrictoris pharyngis superioris. **nasal m.,** musculus nasalis. **nonstriated m.,** a type of muscle without transverse striations upon its constituent fibers; such muscles are in almost every case involuntary. **oblique m. of abdomen, external,** musculus obliquus externus abdominis. **oblique m. of abdomen, internal,** musculus obliquus internus abdominis. **oblique m. of auricle,** musculus obliquus auriculae. **oblique m. of eyeball, inferior,** musculus obliquus inferior bulbi. **oblique m. of eyeball, superior,** musculus obliquus superior bulbi. **oblique m. of head, inferior,** musculus obliquus capitis inferior. **oblique m. of head, superior,** musculus obliquus capitis superior. **obturator m., external,** musculus obturatorius externus. **obturator m., internal,** musculus obturatorius internus. **occipital m.,** venter occipitalis musculi occipitofrontalis. **occipitofrontal m.,** musculus occipitofrontalis. **Ochsner's m.,** Ochsner's ring. **ocular m's,** musculi bulbi. **Oddi's m.,** musculus sphincter ductus choledochi, or the combination of this with musculus sphincter ampullae hepatopancreaticae when the ampulla is present. **omohyoid m.,** musculus omohyoideus. **opposing m. of little finger,** musculus opponens digiti minimi. **opposing m. of thumb,** musculus opponens pollicis. **orbicular m.,** a muscle that encircles a body opening, such as the eye or mouth. Called also *musculus orbicularis.* **orbicular m. of eye,** musculus orbicularis oculi. **orbicular m. of mouth,** musculus orbicularis oris. **orbital m.,** musculus orbitalis. **organic m.,** visceral m. **m's of palate and fauces,** musculi palati et faucium. **palatoglossus m.,** musculus palatoglossus. **palatopharyngeal m.,** musculus palatopharyngeus. **palmar m., long,** musculus palmaris longus. **palmar m., short,** musculus palmaris brevis. **papillary m's,** musculi papillares. **papillary m. of left ventricle, anterior,** musculus papillaris anterior ventriculi sinistri. **papillary m. of left ventricle, posterior,** musculus papillaris posterior ventriculi sinistri. **papillary m. of right ventricle, anterior,** musculus papillaris anterior ventriculi dextri. **papillary m. of right ventricle, posterior,** musculus papillaris posterior ventriculi dextri. **papillary m's of right ventricle, septal,** musculi papillares septales ventriculi dextri. **pectinate m's,** musculi pectinati. **pectineal m.,** musculus pectineus. **pectoral m., greater,** musculus pectoralis major. **pectoral m., smaller,** musculus pectoralis minor. **penniform m.,** musculus unipennatus. **m's of perineum,** musculi perinei. **peroneal m., long,** musculus peroneus longus. **peroneal m., short,** musculus peroneus brevis. **peroneal m., third,** musculus peroneus tertius. **pharyngopalatine m.,** musculus palatopharyngeus. **Phillips' m.,** a muscular slip from the radial collateral ligament of the wrist and the styloid process of the radius to the phalanges. **piriform m.,** musculus piriformis. **plantar m.,** musculus plantaris. **pleuroesophageal m.,** musculus pleuroesophageus. **popliteal m.,** musculus popliteus. **postaxial m.,** a muscle on the dorsal side of an extremity. **preaxial m.,** a muscle on the ventral side of an extremity. **procerus m.,** musculus procerus. **pronator m., quadrate,** musculus pronator quadratus. **pronator m., round,** musculus pronator teres. **psoas m., greater,** musculus psoas major. **psoas m., smaller,** musculus psoas minor. **pterygoid m., external,** musculus pterygoideus lateralis. **pterygoid m., internal,** musculus pterygoideus medialis. **pterygoid m., lateral,** musculus pterygoideus lateralis. **pterygoid m., medial,** musculus pterygoideus medialis. **pterygopharyngeal m.,** pars pterygopharyngea musculi constrictoris pharyngis superioris. **pubicoperitoneal m.,** ligamentum interfoveolare. **pubococcygeal m.,** musculus pubococcygeus. **puboprostatic m.,** musculus puboprostaticus. **puborectal m.,** musculus puborectalis. **pubovaginal m.,** musculus pubovaginalis. **pubovesical m.,** musculus pubovesicalis. **pyramidal m.,** musculus pyramidalis. **pyramidal m. of auricle,** musculus pyramidalis auriculae. **quadrate m. of loins,** musculus quadratus lumborum. **quadrate m. of lower lip,** musculus depressor labii inferioris. **quadrate m. of sole,** musculus quadratus plantae. **quadrate m. of thigh,** musculus quadratus femoris. **quadrate m. of upper lip,** musculus levator labii superioris. **quadriceps m. of thigh,** musculus quadriceps femoris. **rectococcygeus m.,** musculus rectococcygeus. **rectourethral m.,** musculus rectourethralis. **recto-uterine m.,** musculus rectouterinus. **rectovesical m.,** musculus rectovesicalis. **red m.,** the darker-colored muscle tissue of some mammals, composed of fibers rich in sarcoplasm but with only faint cross-striping. **Reisseisen's m.,** the smooth muscle fibers of the smallest bronchi. **rhomboid m., greater,** musculus rhomboideus major. **rhomboid m., lesser,** musculus rhomboideus minor. **ribbon m's,** musculi infrahyoidei. **rider's m's,** the adductor muscles of the thigh. **Riolan's m.** 1. Ciliary bundle of pars palpebralis musculi orbicularis oculi. 2. Musculus cremaster. **risorius m.,** musculus risorius. **rotator m's,** musculi rotatores. **rotator m's, long,** musculi rotatores longi. **rotator m's, short,** musculi rotatores breves. **rotator m's of back,** musculi rotatores thoracis. **rotator m's of loins,** musculi rotatores lumborum. **rotator m's of neck,** musculi rotatores cervicis. **rotator m's of thorax,** musculi rotatores thoracis. **Rouget's m.,** the circular portion of the ciliary muscle. **Ruysch's m.,** the muscular tissue of the fundus uteri. **sacrococcygeal m., anterior,** musculus sacrococcygeus ventralis. **sacrococcygeal m., dorsal,** musculus sacrococcygeus dorsalis. **sacrococcygeal m., posterior,** musculus sacrococcygeus dorsalis. **sacrococcygeal m., ventral,** musculus sacrococcygeus ventralis. **sacrospinal m.,** musculus erector spinae. **salpingopharyngeal m.,** musculus salpingopharyngeus. **Santorini's m.,** musculus risorius. **Santorini's m's, circular,** the nonstriated fibers that encircle the urethra beneath the sphincter urethrae. **sartorius m.,** musculus sartorius. **scalene m., anterior,** musculus scalenus anterior. **scalene m., middle,** musculus scalenus medius. **scalene m., posterior,** musculus scalenus posterior. **scalene m., smallest,** musculus scalenus minimus. **semimembranous m.,** musculus semimembranosus. **semispinal m.,** musculus semispinalis. **semispinal m. of back,** musculus semispinalis thoracis. **semispinal m. of head,** musculus semispinalis capitis. **semispinal m. of neck,** musculus semispinalis cervicis. **semispinal m. of thorax,** musculus semispinalis thoracis. **semitendinous m.,** musculus semitendinosus. **serratus m., anterior,** musculus serratus anterior. **serratus m., posterior, inferior,** musculus serratus posterior inferior. **serratus m., posterior, superior,** musculus serratus posterior superior. **skeletal m's,** striated muscles that are attached to bones and typically cross at least one joint. Called also *musculi skeleti*. **smooth m.,** nonstriated, involuntary muscle. **soleus m.,** musculus soleus. **somatic m's,** musculi skeleti. **sphincter m.,** musculus sphincter. **sphincter m. of anus, external,** musculus sphincter ani externus. **sphincter m. of anus, internal,** musculus sphincter ani internus. **sphincter m. of bile duct,** musculus sphincter ductus choledochi. **sphincter m. of hepatopancreatic ampulla,** musculus sphincter ampullae hepatopancreaticae. **sphincter m. of membranous urethra,** musculus sphincter urethrae. **sphincter m. of pupil,** musculus sphincter pupillae. **sphincter m. of pylorus,** musculus sphincter pylori. **sphincter m. of urethra,** musculus sphincter urethrae. **sphincter m. of urinary bladder,** musculus sphincter vesicae urinariae. **spinal m.,** musculus spinalis. **spinal m. of back,** musculus spinalis thoracis. **spinal m. of head,** musculus spinalis capitis. **spinal m. of neck,** musculus spinalis cervicis. **spinal m. of thorax,** musculus spinalis thoracis. **splenius m. of head,** musculus splenius capitis. **splenius m. of neck,** musculus splenius cervicis. **stapedius m.,** musculus stapedius. **sternal m.,** musculus sternalis. **sternocleidomastoid m.,** musculus sternocleidomastoideus. **sternohyoid m.,** musculus sternohyoideus. **sternothyroid m.,** musculus sternothyroideus. **straight m. of abdomen,** musculus rectus abdominis. **straight m. of eyeball, inferior,** musculus rectus inferior bulbi. **straight m. of eyeball, lateral,** musculus rectus lateralis bulbi. **straight m. of eyeball, medial,** musculus rectus medialis bulbi. **straight m. of eyeball, superior,** musculus rectus superior bulbi. **straight m. of head, anterior,** musculus rectus capitis anterior. **straight m. of head, lateral,** musculus rectus capitis lateralis. **straight m. of head, posterior, greater,** musculus rectus capitis posterior major. **straight m. of head, posterior, smaller,** musculus rectus capitis posterior minor. **straight m. of thigh,** musculus rectus femoris. **striated m., striped m.,** any muscle whose fibers are divided by transverse bands into striations; such muscles are voluntary. **styloglossus m.,** musculus styloglossus. **stylohyoid m.,** musculus stylohyoideus. **stylopharyngeus m.,** musculus stylopharyngeus. **subclavius m.,** musculus subclavius. **subcostal m's,** musculi subcostales. **subscapular m.,** musculus subscapularis. **subvertebral m's,** hypaxial m's. **supinator m.,** musculus supinator. **suprahyoid m's,** musculi suprahyoidei. **supraspinous m.,** musculus supraspinatus. **suspensory m. of duodenum,** musculus suspensorius duodeni. **synergic m's, synergistic m's,** muscles that assist one another in action. **tarsal m., inferior,** musculus tarsalis inferior. **tarsal m., superior,** musculus tarsalis superior. **temporal m.,** musculus temporalis. **temporoparietal m.,** musculus temporoparietalis. **tensor m. of fascia lata,** musculus tensor fasciae latae. **tensor m. of palatine velum,** musculus tensor veli palatini. **tensor m. of tympanum,** musculus tensor tympani. **teres major m.,** musculus teres major. **teres minor m.,** musculus teres minor. **thenar m's,** the abductor and flexor muscles of the thumb. **thyroarytenoid m.,** musculus thyroarytenoideus. **thyroepiglottic m.,** musculus thyroepiglotticus. **thyrohyoid m.,** musculus thyrohyoideus. **thyropharyngeal m.,** pars thyropharyngea musculi constrictoris pharyngis inferioris. **tibial m., anterior,** musculus tibialis anterior. **tibial m., posterior,** musculus tibialis posterior. **m's of tongue,** musculi linguae. **tracheal m.,** musculus trachealis. **trachelomastoid m.,** musculus longissimus capitis. **m. of tragus,** musculus tragicus. **transverse m. of abdomen,** musculus transversus abdominis. **transverse m. of auricle,** musculus transversus auriculae. **transverse m. of chin,** musculus transversus menti. **transverse m. of nape,** musculus transversus nuchae. **transverse m. of perineum, deep,** musculus transversus perinei profundus. **transverse m. of perineum, superficial,** musculus transversus perinei superficialis. **transverse m. of thorax,** musculus transversus thoracis. **transverse m. of tongue,** musculus transversus linguae. **transversospinal m.,** musculus transversospinalis. **trapezius m.,** musculus trapezius. **m. of Treitz,** musculus suspensorius duodeni. **triangular m.,** musculus depressor anguli oris. **triceps m. of arm,** musculus triceps brachii. **triceps m. of calf,** musculus triceps surae. **unipennate m.,** musculus unipennatus. **unstriated m.,** nonstriated m. **m's of upper extremity,** musculi membri superioris. **m. of uvula,** musculus uvulae. **veratrinized m.** (Kölliker, 1856), frog muscle treated with veratrin, which on stimulation gives a double-summited curve, a normal period of shortening being followed by brief relaxation, and a second, slower contraction being followed by prolonged relaxation. **vertical m. of tongue,** musculus verticalis linguae. **vestigial m.,** a muscle that is rudimentary in man but well developed in some other mammals. **visceral m.,** muscle fibers associated chiefly with the hollow viscera and largely of splanchnic mesodermal origin; except for the striated fibers in the wall of the heart, they are smooth-muscle fibers bound together by reticular fibers. **vocal** m., musculus vocalis. **voluntary m.,** any muscle that normally is under the control of the will; such muscles are nearly always composed of striated fibers. **white m.,** the paler-colored muscle tissue of some mammals, composed of fibers with little sarcoplasm and prominent cross-striping. **Wilson's m.,** musculus sphincter urethrae. **yoked m's,** muscles that normally act simultaneously and equally, as in moving the eyes. **zygomatic m., zygomatic m., greater,** musculus zygomaticus major. **zygomatic m., lesser,** musculus zygomaticus minor.

musculamine (mus″ku-lam′in). A base isolated from hydrolyzed calf's muscle. It is the same as spermine.

muscular (mus′ku-lar) [L. *muscularis*]. 1. Pertaining to a muscle. 2. Having well-developed muscles.

muscularis (mus″ku-la′ris) [L.]. Relating to muscles, specifically a muscular coat. See *tunica muscularis.*

muscularity (mus″ku-lar′ĭ-te). The condition or quality of being muscular.

muscularize (mus′ku-lar-īz). To change into muscle tissue.

musculation (mus″ku-la′shun). 1. The muscular system or apparatus. 2. The muscular activity or work.

musculature (mus′ku-lah-tūr). The muscular apparatus of the body, or of any part of it.

musculi (mus′ku-li) [L.]. Plural of *musculus.*

musculin (mus′ku-lin). A globulin or protein contained in muscle tissue. It is characterized by its low coagulation temperature—47°C.

musculocutaneous (mus″ku-lo-ku-ta′ne-us). Pertaining to or supplying both muscles and skin.

musculodermic (mus″ku-lo-der′mik). Musculocutaneous.

musculo-elastic (mus″ku-lo-e-las′tik). Composed of muscular and elastic tissue.

musculo-intestinal (mus″ku-lo-in-tes′tĭ-nal). Pertaining to the muscles and the intestines.

musculomembranous (mus″ku-lo-mem′brah-nus) [L. *musculus* muscle + *membrana* membrane]. Both muscular and membranous.

Musculomyces (mus″ku-lo-mi′sēz). A name proposed for the pleuropneumonia-like bacteria found in mice.

musculophrenic (mus″ku-lo-fren′ik) [*muscular* + *phrenic*]. Pertaining to or supplying both the muscles and the diaphragm.

musculoprecipitin (mus″ku-lo-pre-sip′ĭ-tin). Any one of a series of precipitins used in distinguishing various kinds of meat.

musculorachidian (mus″ku-lo-rah-kid′e-an). Pertaining to the spinal muscles.

musculoskeletal (mus″ku-lo-skel′ĕ-tal). Pertaining to or comprising the skeleton and the muscles; as musculoskeletal system.

musculospiral (mus″ku-lo-spi′ral) [L. *musculus* muscle + *spira* coil]. Pertaining to muscles and having a spiral direction.

musculospiralis (mus″ku-lo-spi-ra′lis). The radial nerve.

musculotegumentary (mus″ku-lo-teg″u-men′tar-e). Pertaining to muscle and the integument.

musculotendinous (mus″ku-lo-ten′dĭ-nus). Pertaining to or composed of muscle and tendon.

musculotonic (mus″ku-lo-ton′ik). Pertaining to muscular contractility.

musculotropic (mus″ku-lo-trop′ik). Having a special affinity for or exerting its principal effect upon muscular tissue.

musculus (mus′ku-lus), pl. *mus′culi* [L., dim. of *mus* mouse, because of a fancied resemblance to a mouse of a muscle moving under the skin]. [N A, B N A] An organ which by its contraction and relaxation produces movements of certain organs or of the entire animal organism. See also *muscle.* For names and description of specific muscles see *Table of Musculi.*

TABLE OF MUSCULI

Descriptions of muscles are given on N A terms, and include anglicized names of specific muscles. B N A terms, when different, are cross referred to names used in Nomina Anatomica.

mus′culi abdo′minis [N A, B N A], the muscles of the abdomen.

m. abduc′tor dig′iti min′imi ma′nus [N A], abductor muscle of little finger: *origin,* pisiform bone, flexor carpi ulnaris tendon; *insertion,* medial surface of base of proximal phalanx of little finger; *innervation,* ulnar; *action,* abducts little finger.

m. abduc′tor dig′iti min′imi pe′dis [N A], abductor muscle of little toe: *origin,* medial and lateral tubercles of calcaneus, plantar fascia; *insertion,* lateral surface of base of proximal phalanx of little toe; *innervation,* superficial branch of lateral plantar; *action,* abducts little toe.

m. abduc′tor dig′iti quin′ti ma′nus [B N A], m. abductor digiti minimi manus.

m. abduc′tor dig′iti quin′ti pe′dis [B N A], m. abductor digiti minimi pedis.

m. abduc′tor hal′lucis [N A, B N A], abductor muscle of great toe: *origin,* medial tubercle of calcaneus, plantar fascia; *insertion,* medial surface of base of proximal phalanx of great toe; *innervation,* medial plantar; *action,* abducts, flexes great toe.

m. abduc′tor pol′licis bre′vis [N A, B N A], short abductor muscle of thumb: *origin,* navicular, ridge of trapezium, transverse carpal ligament; *insertion,* lateral surface of base of proximal phalanx of thumb; *innervation,* median; *action,* abducts thumb.

m. abduc′tor pol′licis lon′gus [N A, B N A], long abductor muscle of thumb: *origin,* posterior surfaces of radius and ulna; *insertion,* radial side of base of first metacarpal bone; *innervation,* posterior interosseous; *action,* abducts, extends thumb.

m. adduc′tor bre′vis [N A, B N A], short adductor muscle: *origin,* outer surface of inferior ramus of pubis; *insertion,* upper part of linea aspera of femur; *innervation,* obturator; *action,* adducts, rotates, flexes thigh.

m. adduc′tor hal′lucis [N A, B N A], adductor muscle of great toe (2 heads): *origin,* CAPUT OBLIQUUM—bases of second, third, and fourth metatarsals, and sheath of peroneus longus, CAPUT TRANSVERSUM—capsules of metatarsophalangeal joints of three lateral toes; *insertion,* lateral side of base of proximal phalanx of great toe; *innervation,* lateral plantar; *action,* adducts great toe.

m. adduc′tor lon′gus [N A, B N A], long adductor muscle: *origin,* crest and symphysis of pubis; *insertion,* linea aspera of femur; *innervation,* obturator; *action,* adducts, rotates, flexes thigh.

m. adduc′tor mag′nus [N A, B N A], great adductor muscle (2 parts): *origin,* DEEP PART—inferior ramus of pubis, ramus of ischium, SUPERFICIAL PART—ischial tuberosity; *insertion,* DEEP PART—linea aspera of femur, SUPERFICIAL PART—adductor tubercle of femur; *innervation,* DEEP PART—obturator, SUPERFICIAL PART—sciatic; *action,* DEEP PART—adducts thigh, SUPERFICIAL PART—extends thigh.

m. adduc′tor min′imus [B N A], a name given the anterior portion of the adductor magnus muscle; *insertion,* ischium, body and ramus of pubis; *innervation,* obturator and sciatic; *action,* adducts thigh. Called also *smallest adductor muscle.* Omitted in N A.

m. adduc′tor pol′licis [N A, B N A], adductor muscle of thumb (2 heads): *origin,* CAPUT OBLIQUUM—sheath of flexor carpi radialis, anterior carpal ligament, capitate bone, and bases of second and third metacarpals, CAPUT TRANSVERSUM—lower two-thirds of anterior surface of third metacarpal; *insertion*, medial surface of base of proximal phalanx of thumb; *innervation*, ulnar; *action*, adducts, opposes thumb.

m. ancone'us [N A], anconeus muscle: *origin*, back of lateral epicondyle of humerus; *insertion*, olecranon and posterior surface of ulna; *innervation*, radial; *action*, extends forearm.

m. antitrag'icus [N A, B N A], antitragus muscle: *origin*, outer part of antitragus; *insertion*, caudate process of helix and anthelix; *innervation*, temporal and posterior auricular.

mus'culi arrecto'res pilo'rum [N A, B N A], arrector muscles of hairs: *origin*, papillary layer of skin; *insertion*, hair follicles; *innervation*, sympathetic; *action*, elevate hairs of skin.

m. articula'ris [N A, B N A], a muscle that is attached at one end to the synovial capsule of a joint. Called also *articular muscle*.

m. articula'ris cu'biti [N A], a few fibers of the deep surface of the triceps brachii that insert into the posterior ligament and synovial membrane of the elbow joint. Called also *articular muscle of elbow*.

m. articula'ris ge'nu [B N A], m. articularis genus.

m. articula'ris ge'nus [N A], articular muscle of knee: *origin*, distal fourth of anterior surface of shaft of femur; *insertion*, synovial membrane of knee joint; *innervation*, femoral; *action*, lifts capsule of knee joint.

m. aryepiglot'ticus [N A, B N A], a name given to an inconstant fascicle of the oblique arytenoid muscle, originating from the apex of the arytenoid cartilage and inserting on the lateral margin of the epiglottis.

m. arytaenoi'deus obli'quus [B N A], m. arytenoideus obliquus.

m. arytaenoi'deus transver'sus [B N A], m. arytenoideus transversus.

m. arytenoi'deus obli'quus [N A], oblique arytenoid muscle: *origin*, dorsal aspect of muscular process of arytenoid cartilage; *insertion*, apex of opposite arytenoid cartilage; *innervation*, recurrent laryngeal; *action*, closes inlet of larynx.

m. arytenoi'deus transver'sus [N A], transverse arytenoid muscle: *origin*, dorsal aspect of muscular process of arytenoid cartilage; *insertion*, continuous with thyroarytenoid, apex of opposite cartilage; *innervation*, recurrent laryngeal; *action*, approximates arytenoid cartilages.

m. auricula'ris ante'rior [N A, B N A], anterior auricular muscle: *origin*, superficial temporal fascia; *insertion*, cartilage of ear; *innervation*, facial; *action*, draws the pinna forward.

m. auricula'ris poste'rior [N A, B N A], posterior auricular muscle: *origin*, mastoid process; *insertion*, cartilage of ear; *innervation*, facial; *action*, draws pinna backward.

m. auricula'ris supe'rior [N A, B N A], superior auricular muscle: *origin*, galea aponeurotica; *insertion*, cartilage of ear; *innervation*, facial; *action*, raises pinna.

m. bi'ceps bra'chii [N A, B N A], biceps muscle of arm (2 heads): *origin*, CAPUT LONGUM—upper border of glenoid cavity, CAPUT BREVE—apex of coracoid process; *insertion*, radial tuberosity and deep fascia of forearm; *innervation*, musculocutaneous; *action*, flexes forearm, supinates hand.

m. bi'ceps fem'oris [N A, B N A], biceps muscle of thigh (2 heads): *origin*, CAPUT LONGUM—ischial tuberosity, CAPUT BREVE—linea aspera of femur; *insertion*, head of fibula, lateral condyle of tibia; *innervation*, CAPUT LONGUM—tibial, CAPUT BREVE—peroneal, popliteal; *action*, flexes leg, extends thigh.

m. bipenna'tus [N A, B N A], a muscle in which the fibers approach the tendon of insertion from a wide area and are inserted through a large segment of its circumference. Called also *bipennate muscle*.

m. brachia'lis [N A, B N A], brachial muscle: *origin*, anterior surface of humerus; *insertion*, coronoid process of ulna; *innervation*, radial, musculocutaneous; *action*, flexes forearm.

m. brachioradia'lis [N A, B N A], brachioradial muscle: *origin*, lateral supracondyloid ridge of humerus; *insertion*, lower end of radius; *innervation*, radial; *action*, flexes forearm.

m. bronchoesophage'us [N A], a name given fasciculi of muscle arising from the wall of the left bronchus, reinforcing muscles of the esophagus. Called also *bronchoesophageal muscle*.

m. bronchooesophage'us [B N A], m. bronchoesophageus.

m. buccina'tor [N A, B N A], buccinator muscle: *origin*, buccinator ridge of mandible, alveolar process of maxilla, pterygomandibular ligament; *insertion*, orbicularis oris at angle of mouth; *innervation*, buccal branch of facial; *action*, compresses cheek and retracts angle of the mouth.

m. buccopharyn'geus [B N A], pars buccopharyngea musculi constrictoris pharyngis superioris.

mus'culi bul'bi [N A, B N A], the six voluntary muscles that move the eyeball, including the superior, inferior, middle, and lateral rectus, and the superior and inferior oblique muscles. Called also *extraocular muscles*.

m. bulbocaverno'sus [B N A], m. bulbospongiosus.

m. bulbospongio'sus [N A], bulbocavernous muscle: *origin*, central point of perineum, median raphe of bulb; *insertion*, fascia of penis (clitoris); *innervation*, pudendal; *action*, constricts bulbous urethra (urethra).

m. cani'nus [B N A], m. levator anguli oris.

mus'culi cap'itis [N A, B N A], the muscles of the head.

m. ceratocricoi'deus [N A, B N A], a name given a fasciculus of muscle fibers arising from the cricoid cartilage and inserted on the inferior cornu of the thyroid cartilage. Called also *ceratocricoid muscle*.

m. ceratopharyn'geus [B N A], pars ceratopharyngea musculi constrictoris pharyngis medii.

m. chondroglos'sus [N A, B N A], chondroglossus muscle: *origin*, inner side and base of lesser cornu of hyoid bone; *insertion*, substance of tongue; *innervation*, hypoglossal; *action*, depresses, retracts tongue.

m. chondropharyn'geus [B N A], pars chondropharyngea musculi constrictoris pharyngis medii.

m. cilia'ris [N A, B N A], ciliary muscle: *origin*, LONGITUDINAL DIVISION (Brücke's muscles)—junction of cornea and sclera, CIRCULAR DIVISION (Müller's muscle)—sphincter of ciliary body; *insertion*, outer layers of choroid and ciliary processes; *innervation*, short ciliary; *action*, affects shape of lens in visual accommodation.

mus'culi coccyg'ei [N A, B N A], the muscles acting upon the coccyx, including the coccygeal and the dorsal and ventral sacrococcygeal muscles.

m. coccyg'eus [N A, B N A], coccygeal muscle: *origin*, ischial spine and lesser sacrosciatic ligament; *insertion*, lateral border of lower sacrum, upper coccyx; *innervation*, third and fourth sacral; *action*, supports and raises coccyx.

mus'culi col'li [N A, B N A], the muscles of the neck, including the sternocleidomastoid and the longus colli, and the suprahyoid, infrahyoid, and scalene muscles.

m. compres'sor na'ris, pars transversa musculi nasalis.

m. constric'tor pharyn'gis infe'rior [N A, B N A], inferior constrictor muscle of pharynx: *origin*, under surfaces of cricoid and thyroid cartilages; *insertion*, median raphe of posterior wall of pharynx; *innervation*, glossopharyngeal, pharyngeal plexus, and external and recurrent laryngeal; *action*, constricts pharynx.

m. constric'tor pharyn'gis me'dius [N A, B N A], middle constrictor muscle of pharynx: *origin*, cornua of hyoid and stylohyoid ligament; *insertion*, median raphe of posterior wall of pharynx; *innervation*, pharyngeal plexus of vagus and glossopharyngeal; *action*, constricts pharynx.

m. constric'tor pharyn'gis supe'rior [N A, B N A], superior constrictor muscle of pharynx: *origin*, medial pterygoid plate, pterygomandibular raphe, mylohyoid ridge of mandible, and mucous membrane of floor of mouth; *insertion*, median raphe of posterior wall of pharynx; *innervation*, pharyngeal plexus of vagus; *action*, constricts pharynx.

m. coracobrachia'lis [N A, B N A], coracobrachial muscle: *origin*, coracoid process of scapula; *insertion*, medial surface of shaft of humerus; *innervation*, musculocutaneous; *action*, flexes, adducts arm.

m. corruga'tor supercil'ii [N A], superciliary corrugator muscle: *origin*, medial end of superciliary arch; *insertion*, skin of eyebrow; *innervation*, facial; *action*, draws eyebrow downward and medially.

m. cremas'ter [N A, B N A], cremaster muscle: *origin*, inferior margin of internal oblique muscle of abdomen; *insertion*, pubic tubercle; *innervation*, genital branch of genitofemoral; *action*, elevates testis.

m. cricoarytaenoi'deus latera'lis [B N A], m. cricoarytenoideus lateralis.

m. cricoarytaenoi'deus poste'rior [B N A], m. cricoarytenoideus posterior.

m. cricoarytenoi'deus latera'lis [N A], lateral cricoarytenoid muscle: *origin*, lateral surface of cricoid cartilage; *insertion*, muscular process of arytenoid cartilage; *innervation*, recurrent laryngeal; *action*, approximates vocal folds.

m. cricoarytenoi'deus poste'rior [N A], posterior cricoarytenoid muscle: *origin*, back of cricoid cartilage; *insertion*, muscular process of arytenoid cartilage; *innervation*, recurrent laryngeal; *action*, separates vocal folds.

m. cricopharyn'geus [B N A], pars cricopharyngea musculi constrictoris pharyngis inferioris.

m. cricothyreoi'deus [B N A], m. cricothyroideus.

m. cricothyroi'deus [N A], cricothyroid muscle: *origin*, front and side of cricoid cartilage; *insertion*, lamina of thyroid cartilage; *innervation*, superior laryngeal; *action*, tenses vocal folds.

m. cuta'neus [N A, B N A], striated muscle that inserts into the skin. Called also *cutaneous muscle*.

m. deltoi'deus [N A, B N A], deltoid muscle: *origin*, clavicle, acromion, spine of scapula; *insertion*, deltoid tuberosity of humerus; *innervation*, axillary; *action*, abducts, flexes, extends arm.

m. depres'sor an'guli o'ris [N A], depressor muscle of angle of mouth: *origin*, lower border of mandible; *insertion*, angle of mouth; *innervation*, facial; *action*, pulls down angle of mouth.

m. depres'sor la'bii inferio'ris [N A], depressor muscle of lower lip: *origin*, anterior portion of lower border of mandible; *insertion*, orbicularis oris and skin of lower lip; *innervation*, facial; *action*, depresses lower lip.

m. depres'sor sep'ti na'si [N A, B N A], depressor muscle of nasal septum: *origin*, incisor fossa of maxilla; *insertion*, ala and septum of nose; *innervation*, facial; *action*, contracts nostril and depresses ala.

m. depres'sor supercil'ii [N A], a name given a few fibers of the orbital part of the orbicularis oculi muscle that are inserted in the eyebrow, which they depress.

m. digas'tricus [N A, B N A], digastric muscle: *origin*, VENTER ANTERIOR—digastric fossa on inner surface of lower border of mandible near symphysis, VENTER POSTERIOR—mastoid notch of temporal bone; *insertion*, intermediate tendon on hyoid bone; *innervation*, VENTER ANTERIOR—mylohyoid, VENTER POSTERIOR—digastric branch of facial; *action*, elevates hyoid bone, lowers jaw.

m. dila'tor na'ris, pars alaris musculi nasalis.

m. dila'tor pupil'lae [N A], a name given fibers extending radially from the sphincter pupillae to the ciliary margin; *innervation*, sympathetic; *action*, dilates iris. Called also *dilator muscle of pupil*.

mus'culi dor'si [N A, B N A], the muscles of the back. Called also *dorsal muscles*.

m. epicra'nius [N A, B N A], a name given the muscular covering of the scalp, including the occipitofrontalis and temporoparietalis muscles, and the galea aponeurotica.

m. epitrochleoanconae'us [B N A], an occasional band of fibers originating at the back of the internal condyle of the humerus and inserting on the inner side of the olecranon process, innervated by a branch of the ulnar nerve, and representing the adductor of the olecranon of lower animals. Called also *epitrochleoanconeus muscle*. Omitted in N A.

m. erec'tor spi'nae [N A], a name given the fibers of the more superficial of the deep muscles of the back, originating from the sacrum, spines of the lumbar and the eleventh and twelfth thoracic vertebrae, and the iliac crest, which split and insert as the iliocostalis, longissimus, and spinalis muscles (q.v.).

m. exten'sor car'pi radia'lis bre'vis [N A, B N A], short radial extensor muscle of wrist: *origin*, lateral epicondyle of humerus, *insertion*, base of third metacarpal bone; *innervation*, radial; *action*, extends and abducts wrist joint.

m. exten'sor car'pi radia'lis lon'gus [N A, B N A], long radial extensor muscle of wrist: *origin*, lateral supracondyloid ridge of humerus; *insertion*, base of second metacarpal bone; *innervation*, radial; *action*, extends and abducts wrist joint.

m. exten'sor car'pi ulna'ris [N A, B N A], ulnar extensor muscle of wrist (2 heads): *origin*, CAPUT HUMERALE—lateral epicondyle of humerus, CAPUT ULNARE—dorsal border of ulna; *insertion*, base of fifth metacarpal bone; *innervation*, deep radial; *action*, extends and adducts wrist joint.

m. exten'sor dig'iti min'imi [N A], extensor muscle of little finger: *origin*, common extensor tendon; *insertion*, tendon of extensor digitorum to little finger; *innervation*, deep radial; *action*, extends little finger.

m. exten'sor dig'iti quin'ti pro'prius [B N A], m. extensor digiti minimi.

m. exten'sor digito'rum [N A], extensor muscle of fingers: *origin*, lateral epicondyle of humerus; *insertion*, common extensor tendon of each finger; *innervation*, deep radial; *action*, extends wrist joint and phalanges.

m. exten'sor digito'rum bre'vis [N A, B N A], short extensor muscle of toes: *origin*, dorsal surface of calcaneus; *insertion*, extensor tendons of first, second, third, fourth toes; *innervation*, deep peroneal; *action*, extends toes.

m. exten'sor digito'rum commu'nis [B N A], m. extensor digitorum.

m. exten'sor digito'rum lon'gus [N A, B N A], long extensor muscle of toes: *origin*, anterior surface of fibula, lateral condyle of tibia, interosseous membrane; *insertion*, common extensor tendon of four lateral toes: *innervation*, deep peroneal; *action*, extends toes.

m. exten'sor hal'lucis bre'vis [N A, B N A], a name given the portion of the extensor digitorum brevis muscle that goes to the great toe. Called also *short extensor muscle of great toe*.

m. exten'sor hal'lucis lon'gus [N A, B N A], long extensor muscle of great toe: *origin*, front of fibula and interosseous membrane; *insertion*, dorsal surface of base of distal phalanx of great toe; *innervation*, deep peroneal; *action*, dorsiflexes ankle joint, extends great toe.

m. exten'sor in'dicis [N A], extensor muscle of index finger: *origin*, dorsal surface of body of ulna, interosseous membrane; *insertion*, common extensor tendon of index finger; *innervation*, deep radial; *action*, extends index finger.

m. exten'sor in'dicis pro'prius [B N A], m. extensor indicis.

m. exten'sor pol'licis bre'vis [N A, B N A], short extensor muscle of thumb: *origin*, dorsal surface of radius and interosseous membrane; *insertion*, dorsal surface of proximal phalanx of thumb; *innervation*, deep radial; *action*, extends thumb.

m. exten'sor pol'licis lon'gus [N A, B N A], long extensor muscle of thumb: *origin*, dorsal surface of ulna and interosseous membrane; *insertion*, dorsal surface of distal phalanx of thumb; *innervation*, deep radial; *action*, extends, abducts thumb.

mus'culi extremita'tis inferio'ris [B N A], musculi membri inferioris.

mus'culi extremita'tis superio'ris [B N A], musculi membri superioris.

m. fibula'ris bre'vis, N A alternative for *m. peroneus brevis.*

m. fibula'ris lon'gus, N A alternative for *m. peroneus longus.*

m. fibula'ris ter'tius, N A alternative for *m. peroneus tertius.*

m. fixa'tor ba'seos stape'dis [B N A], fibers attaching the base of the stapes. Omitted in N A.

m. flex'or accesso'rius, N A alternative for *m. quadratus plantae.*

m. flex'or car'pi radia'lis [N A, B N A], radial flexor muscle of wrist: *origin*, medial epicondyle of humerus; *insertion*, base of second metacarpal; *innervation*, median; *action*, flexes and abducts wrist joint.

m. flex'or car'pi ulna'ris [N A, B N A], ulnar flexor muscle of wrist (2 heads): *origin*, CAPUT HUMERALE—medial epicondyle of humerus, CAPUT ULNARE—olecranon, ulna, intermuscular septum; *insertion*, pisiform, hamulus of hamate, proximal end of fifth metacarpal; *innervation*, ulnar; *action*, flexes and adducts wrist joint.

m. flex'or dig'iti min'imi bre'vis ma'nus [N A], short flexor muscle of little finger: *origin*, hamulus of hamate bone, transverse carpal ligament; *insertion*, medial side of proximal phalanx of little finger; *innervation*, ulnar; *action*, flexes little finger.

m. flex'or dig'iti min'imi bre'vis pe'dis [N A], short flexor muscle of little toe: *origin*, base of fifth metatarsal, plantar fascia; *insertion*, lateral surface of base of proximal phalanx of little toe; *innervation*, lateral plantar; *action*, flexes little toe.

m. flex'or dig'iti quin'ti bre'vis ma'nus [B N A], m. flexor digiti minimi brevis manus.

m. flex'or dig'iti quin'ti bre'vis pe'dis [B N A], m. flexor digiti minimi brevis pedis.

m. flex'or digito'rum bre'vis [N A, B N A], short flexor muscle of toes: *origin*, medial tuberosity of calcaneus, plantar fascia; *insertion*, middle phalanges of four lateral toes; *innervation*, medial plantar; *action*, flexes toes.

m. flex'or digito'rum lon'gus [N A, B N A], long flexor muscle of toes: *origin*, posterior surface of shaft of tibia; *insertion*, distal phalanges of four lateral toes; *innervation*, posterior tibial; *action*, flexes toes and extends foot.

m. flex'or digito'rum profun'dus [N A, B N A], deep flexor muscle of fingers: *origin*, shaft of ulna, coronoid process; *insertion*, distal phalanges of fingers; *innervation*, ulnar and anterior interosseous; *action*, flexes distal phalanges.

m. flex'or digito'rum subli'mis [B N A], m. flexor digitorum superficialis.

m. flex'or digito'rum superficia'lis [N A], superficial flexor muscle of fingers (2 heads): *origin*, CAPUT HUMEROULNARE—medial epicondyle of humerus, coronoid process of ulna, CAPUT RADIALE—oblique line of radius, anterior border; *insertion*, middle phalanges of fingers; *innervation*, median; *action*, flexes middle phalanges.

m. flex'or hal'lucis bre'vis [N A, B N A], short flexor muscle of great toe: *origin*, under surface of cuboid, lateral cuneiform; *insertion*, base of proximal phalanx of great toe; *innervation*, lateral and medial plantar; *action*, flexes great toe.

m. flex'or hal'lucis lon'gus [N A, B N A], long flexor muscle of great toe: *origin*, posterior surface of fibula; *insertion*, base of distal phalanx of great toe; *innervation*, posterior tibial; *action*, flexes great toe.

m. flex'or pol'licis bre'vis [N A, B N A], short flexor muscle of thumb: *origin*, transverse carpal ligament, ridge of trapezium; *insertion*, base of proximal phalanx of thumb; *innervation*, median, ulnar; *action*, flexes and adducts thumb.

m. flex'or pol'licis lon'gus [N A, B N A], long flexor muscle of thumb: *origin*, anterior surface of radius and coronoid process of ulna; *insertion*, base of distal phalanx of thumb; *innervation*, anterior interosseous; *action*, flexes thumb.

m. fronta'lis [B N A], venter frontalis musculi occipitofrontalis.

m. fusifor'mis [N A, B N A], a spindle-shaped muscle in which the fibers are approximately parallel to the long axis of the muscle but converge upon a tendon at either end. Called also *fusiform muscle.*

m. gastrocne'mius [N A, B N A], gastrocnemius muscle (2 heads): *origin*, CAPUT MEDIALE—popliteal surface of femur, upper part of medial condyle, and capsule of knee, CAPUT LATERALE—lateral condyle and capsule of knee; *insertion*, aponeurosis unites with tendon of soleus to form calcaneal tendon (Achilles tendon); *innervation*, tibial; *action*, plantar flexes ankle joint, flexes knee joint.

m. gemel'lus infe'rior [N A, B N A], inferior gemellus muscle: *origin*, tuberosity of ischium; *insertion*, greater trochanter of femur; *innervation*, sacral plexus; *action*, rotates thigh laterally.

m. gemel'lus supe'rior [N A, B N A], superior gemellus muscle: *origin*, spine of ischium; *insertion*, greater trochanter of femur; *innervation*, sacral plexus; *action*, rotates thigh laterally.

m. genioglos'sus [N A, B N A], genioglossus muscle: *origin*, mental spine of mandible; *insertion*, hyoid bone and under surface of tongue; *innervation*, hypoglossal; *action*, protrudes and depresses tongue.

m. geniohyoi'deus [N A, B N A], geniohyoid muscle: *origin*, mental spine of mandible; *insertion*, body of hyoid bone; *innervation*, a branch of first cervical nerve through hypoglossal; *action*, elevates, draws hyoid forward.

m. glossopalati'nus [B N A], m. palatoglossus.

m. glossopharyn'geus [B N A], pars glossopharyngea musculi constrictoris pharyngis superioris.

m. glu'teus max'imus [N A], greatest gluteal muscle: *origin*, lateral surface of ilium, dorsal surface of sacrum and coccyx, sacrotuberous ligament; *insertion*, iliotibial band of fascia lata, gluteal tuberosity of femur; *innervation*, inferior gluteal; *action*, extends, abducts, and rotates thigh outward.

m. glu'teus me'dius [N A], middle gluteal muscle: *origin*, lateral surface of ilium between anterior and posterior gluteal lines; *insertion*, greater trochanter of femur; *innervation*, superior gluteal; *action*, abducts thigh.

m. glu'teus min'imus [N A], least gluteal muscle: *origin*, lateral surface of ilium between anterior and inferior gluteal lines; *insertion*, greater trochanter of femur; *innervation*, superior gluteal; *action*, abducts, medially rotates thigh.

m. gra'cilis [N A, B N A], gracilis muscle: *origin*, inferior ramus of pubis; *insertion*, medial surface of body of tibia; *innervation*, obturator; *action*, adducts thigh, flexes knee joint.

m. hel'icis ma'jor [N A, B N A], larger muscle of helix: *origin*, spine of helix; *insertion*, anterior border of helix; *innervation*, auriculotemporal and posterior auricular; *action*, tenses skin of auditory canal.

m. hel'icis mi'nor [N A, B N A], smaller muscle of helix: *origin*, anterior rim of helix; *insertion*, concha; *innervation*, temporal, posterior auricular.

m. hyoglos'sus [N A, B N A], hyoglossus muscle: *origin*, body and greater cornu of hyoid bone; *insertion*, side of tongue; *innervation*, hypoglossal; *action*, depresses and retracts tongue.

m. ili'acus [N A, B N A], iliac muscle: *origin*, iliac fossa and base of sacrum; *insertion*, lesser trochanter of femur; *innervation*, femoral; *action*, flexes thigh, trunk on extremity.

m. iliococcyg'eus [N A], a name given the posterior portion of the levator ani which originates as far forward as the obturator canal and inserts on the side of the coccyx and the anococcygeal body; *innervation*, third and fourth sacral; *action*, helps support pelvic viscera and resist increases in intra-abdominal pressure. Called also *iliococcygeal muscle*.

m. iliocosta'lis [N A, B N A], the lateral division of m. erector spinae, which includes the *m. iliocostalis cervicis, m. iliocostalis thoracis*, and *m. iliocostalis lumborum*. Called also *iliocostal muscle*.

m. iliocosta'lis cer'vicis [N A, B N A], iliocostal muscle of neck: *origin*, angles of third, fourth, fifth, and sixth ribs; *insertion*, transverse processes of fourth, fifth, and sixth cervical vertebrae; *innervation*, branches of cervical; *action*, extends cervical spine.

m. iliocosta'lis dor'si [B N A], m. iliocostalis thoracis.

m. iliocosta'lis lumbo'rum [N A, B N A], iliocostal muscle of loins: *origin*, iliac crest; *insertion*, angles of lower six or seven ribs; *innervation*, branches of thoracic and lumbar; *action*, extends lumbar spine.

m. iliocosta'lis thora'cis [N A], iliocostal muscle of thorax: *origin*, upper borders of angles of six lower ribs; *insertion*, angles of six upper ribs and transverse process of seventh cervical vertebra; *innervation*, branches of thoracic; *action*, keeps dorsal spine erect.

m. iliopso'as [N A, B N A], a compound muscle consisting of iliacus and psoas major.

mus'culi inci'sivi la'bii inferio'ris [B N A], small bundles of muscle fibers, one arising from the incisive fossa of the mandible on either side and passing laterally to the angle of the mouth. Called also *incisive muscles of inferior lip*. Omitted in N A.

mus'culi inci'sivi la'bii superio'ris [B N A], small bundles of muscle fibers, one arising from the incisive fossa of the maxilla on either side and passing laterally to the angle of the mouth. Called also *incisive muscles of superior lip*. Omitted in N A.

m. incisu'rae hel'icis [N A], an inconstant muscle slip continuing forward from the m. tragicus to bridge the incisure of the cartilaginous meatus. Called also *muscle of incisure of helix*.

m. incisu'rae hel'icis [Santori'ni] [B N A], m. incisurae helicis.

mus'culi infrahyoi'dei [N A], the muscles that anchor the hyoid bone to the sternum, clavicle, and scapula, including the sternohyoid, omohyoid, sternothyroid, and thyrohyoid muscles.

m. infraspina'tus [N A, B N A], infraspinous muscle: *origin*, infraspinous fossa of scapula; *insertion*, greater tubercle of humerus; *innervation*, suprascapular; *action*, rotates humerus laterally.

mus'culi intercosta'les exter'ni [N A, B N A], external intercostal muscles (11 on each side): *origin*, inferior border of rib; *insertion*, superior border of rib below; *innervation*, intercostal; *action*, draw ribs together in respiration and expulsive movements.

mus'culi intercosta'les inter'ni [N A, B N A], internal intercostal muscles (11 on each side): *origin*, inferior border of rib and costal cartilage; *insertion*, superior border of rib and costal cartilage below; *innervation*, intercostal; *action*, draw ribs together in respiration and expulsive movements.

mus'culi intercosta'les in'timi [N A], the layer of muscle fibers separated from the internal intercostal muscles by the intercostal nerves. Called also *innermost intercostal muscles*.

mus'culi interos'sei dorsa'les ma'nus [N A, B N A], dorsal interosseous muscles of hand (4): *origin*, by two heads from adjacent sides of metacarpal bones; *insertion*, extensor tendons of second, third, and fourth fingers; *innervation*, ulnar; *action*, abduct, flex proximal phalanges.

mus'culi interos'sei dorsa'les pe'dis [N A, B N A], dorsal interosseous muscles of foot (4): *origin*, surfaces of adjacent metatarsal bones; *insertion*, extensor tendons of second, third, and fourth toes; *innervation*, lateral plantar; *action*, abduct, flex toes.

mus'culi interos'sei palma'res [N A], palmar interosseous muscles (3): *origin*, sides of second, fourth, and fifth metacarpal bones; *insertion*, extensor tendons of second, fourth, and fifth fingers; *innervation*, ulnar; *action*, adduct, flex proximal phalanges.

mus'culi interos'sei planta'res [N A, B N A], plantar interosseous muscles (3): *origin*, medial surface of third, fourth, and fifth metatarsal bones; *insertion*, extensor tendons of third, fourth, and fifth toes; *innervation*, lateral plantar; *action*, adduct, flex toes.

mus'culi interos'sei vola'res [B N A], musculi interossei palmares.

mus'culi interspina'les [N A, B N A], short bands of muscle fibers between spinous processes of contiguous vertebrae, including the *musculi interspinales cervicis, musculi interspinales thoracis*, and *musculi interspinales lumborum*. Called also *interspinal muscles*.

mus'culi interspina'les cer'vicis [N A], paired bands of muscle fibers extending between spinous processes of contiguous cervical vertebrae, innervated by spinal nerves, and acting to extend the vertebral column. Called also *interspinal muscles of neck*.

mus'culi interspina'les lumbo'rum [N A], paired bands of muscle fibers extending between spinous processes of contiguous lumbar vertebrae, innervated by spinal nerves, and acting to extend the vertebral column. Called also *interspinal muscles of loins*.

mus'culi interspina'les thora'cis [N A], paired bands of muscle fibers extending between spinous processes of contiguous thoracic vertebrae, innervated by spinal nerves, and acting to extend the vertebral column. Called also *interspinal muscles of thorax*.

mus'culi intertransversa'rii [N A, B N A], small muscles passing between the transverse processes of contiguous vertebrae, including the lateral and medial intertransverse muscles of the loins, the intertransverse muscles of the thorax, and the anterior and posterior intertransverse muscles of the neck.

mus'culi intertransversa'rii anterio'res [B N A], musculi intertransversarii thoracis.

mus'culi intertransversa'rii anterio'res cer'vicis [N A], small muscles passing between the anterior tubercles of adjacent cervical vertebrae, innervated by spinal nerves, and acting to bend the vertebral column laterally. Called also *anterior intertransverse muscles of neck*.

mus'culi intertransversa'rii latera'les [B N A], musculi intertransversarii laterales lumborum.

mus'culi intertransversa'rii latera'les lumbo'rum [N A], small muscles passing between the transverse processes of adjacent lumbar vertebrae, innervated by spinal nerves, and acting to bend the vertebral column laterally. Called also *lateral intertransverse muscles of loins*.

mus'culi intertransversa'rii media'les [B N A], musculi intertransversarii mediales lumborum.

mus'culi intertransversa'rii media'les lumbo'rum [N A], small muscles passing from the accessory process of one lumbar vertebra to the mamillary process of the contiguous lumbar vertebra, innervated by spinal nerves, and acting to bend the vertebral column laterally. Called also *medial intertransverse muscles of loins.*

mus′culi intertransversa′rii posterio′res [B N A], musculi intertransversarii posteriores cervicis.

mus′culi intertransversa′rii posterio′res cer′vicis [N A], small muscles, divided into medial and lateral parts, passing between the posterior tubercles of adjacent cervical vertebrae, innervated by spinal nerves, and acting to bend the vertebral column laterally. Called also *posterior intertransverse muscles of neck.*

mus′culi intertransversa′rii thora′cis [N A], poorly developed muscle bundles extending between the anterior tubercles of adjacent thoracic vertebrae, innervated by spinal nerves, and acting to bend the vertebral column laterally. Called also *intertransverse muscles of thorax.*

m. ischiocaverno′sus [N A, B N A], ischiocavernous muscle: *origin,* ramus of ischium; *insertion,* crus penis (crus clitoridis); *innervation,* perineal; *action,* maintains erection of penis (clitoris).

mus′culi laryn′gis [N A, B N A], the intrinsic and extrinsic muscles of the larynx.

m. latis′simus dor′si [N A, B N A], latissimus muscle of back: *origin,* spines of thoracic and lumbar vertebrae, lumbodorsal fascia, iliac crest, lower ribs, inferior angle of scapula; *insertion,* crest of intertubercular sulcus of humerus; *innervation,* thoracodorsal; *action,* adducts, extends, and medially rotates humerus.

m. leva′tor an′guli o′ris [N A], levator muscle of angle of mouth: *origin,* canine fossa of maxilla; *insertion,* orbicularis oris and skin at angle of mouth; *innervation,* facial; *action,* raises angle of mouth.

m. leva′tor a′ni [N A, B N A], a name applied collectively to important muscular components of the pelvic diaphragm, including the pubococcygeus (levator prostatae and pubovaginalis), the puborectalis, and the iliococcygeus muscles.

mus′culi levato′res costa′rum [N A, B N A], levator muscles of ribs (12 on each side). Originating from the transverse processes of the seventh cervical and first to eleventh thoracic vertebrae and inserting medial to the angle of a lower rib (see *musculi levatores costarum breves* and *musculi levatores costarum longi*); innervated by intercostal nerves and aiding in elevation of the ribs in respiration.

mus′culi levato′res costa′rum bre′ves [N A, B N A], the levatores costarum muscles of each side that insert medial to the angle of the rib next below the vertebra of origin. Called also *short levator muscles of ribs.*

mus′culi levato′res costa′rum lon′gi [N A, B N A], the lower levatores costarum muscles of each side, which have fascicles extending down to the second rib below the vertebra of origin. Called also *long levator muscles of ribs.*

m. leva′tor glan′dulae thyreoi′deae [B N A], m. levator glandulae thyroideae.

m. leva′tor glan′dulae thyroi′deae [N A], an anomalous muscle sometimes originating on the isthmus or pyramid of the thyroid gland and inserting on the body of the hyoid bone. Called also *levator muscle of thyroid gland.*

m. leva′tor la′bii superio′ris [N A], levator muscle of upper lip: *origin,* lower orbital margin; *insertion,* muscle of upper lip; *innervation,* facial nerve; *action,* raises upper lip.

m. leva′tor la′bii superio′ris alae′que na′si [N A], levator muscle of upper lip and ala of nose: *origin,* nasal process of maxilla; *insertion,* cartilage of ala nasi and upper lip; *innervation,* infraorbital branch of facial; *action,* raises upper lip and dilates nostril.

m. leva′tor palpe′brae superio′ris [N A, B N A], levator muscle of upper eyelid: *origin,* upper border of optic foramen; *insertion,* tarsal plate of upper eyelid; *innervation,* oculomotor; *action,* raises upper lid.

m. leva′tor prosta′tae [N A], a name applied to a part of the anterior portion of the pubococcygeus muscle, which is inserted in the prostate gland and the tendinous center of the perineum; innervated by sacral and pudendal nerves, it supports and compresses the prostate and is involved in control of micturition. Called also *levator muscle of prostate.*

m. leva′tor scap′ulae [N A, B N A], levator muscle of scapula: *origin,* transverse processes of four upper cervical vertebrae; *insertion,* vertebral border of scapula; *innervation,* third and fourth cervical; *action,* raises scapula.

m. leva′tor ve′li palati′ni [N A, B N A], levator muscle of velum palatini: *origin,* apex of petrous portion of temporal bone and cartilaginous auditory tube; *insertion,* aponeurosis of soft palate; *innervation,* pharyngeal plexus of vagus; *action,* raises soft palate.

mus′culi lin′guae [N A, B N A], the extrinsic and intrinsic muscles that move the tongue.

m. longis′simus [N A, B N A], the largest element of the m. erector spinae, which includes the *m. longissimus capitis, m. longissimus cervicis,* and *m. longissimus thoracis.*

m. longis′simus cap′itis [N A, B N A], longissimus muscle of head: *origin,* transverse processes of four or five upper thoracic vertebrae, articular processes of three or four lower cervical vertebrae; *insertion,* mastoid process of temporal bone; *innervation,* branches of cervical; *action,* draws head backward, rotates head.

m. longis′simus cer′vicis [N A, B N A], longissimus muscle of neck: *origin,* transverse processes of four or five upper thoracic vertebrae; *insertion,* transverse processes of second to sixth cervical vertebrae; *innervation,* lower cervical and upper thoracic; *action,* extends cervical vertebrae.

m. longis′simus dor′si [B N A], m. longissimus thoracis.

m. longis′simus thora′cis [N A], longissimus muscle of thorax: *origin,* transverse and articular processes of lumbar vertebrae and lumbodorsal fascia; *insertion,* transverse processes of all thoracic vertebrae, nine or ten lower ribs; *innervation,* lumbar and thoracic; *action,* extends thoracic vertebrae.

m. longitudina′lis infe′rior lin′guae [N A, B N A], inferior longitudinal muscle of tongue: *origin,* under surface of tongue at base; *insertion,* tip of tongue; *innervation,* hypoglossal; *action,* changes shape of tongue in mastication and deglutition.

m. longitudina′lis supe′rior lin′guae [N A, B N A], superior longitudinal muscle of tongue: *origin,* submucosa and septum of tongue; *insertion,* margins of tongue; *innervation,* hypoglossal; *action,* changes shape of tongue in mastication and deglutition.

m. lon′gus cap′itis [N A, B N A], long muscle of head: *origin,* transverse processes of third to sixth cervical vertebrae; *insertion,* basal portion of occipital bone; *innervation,* branches from first, second, and third cervical; *action,* flexes head.

m. lon′gus col′li [N A, B N A], long muscle of neck: *origin,* SUPERIOR OBLIQUE PORTION—transverse processes of third to fifth cervical vertebrae, INFERIOR OBLIQUE PORTION—bodies of first to third thoracic vertebrae, VERTICAL PORTION—bodies of three upper thoracic and three lower cervical vertebrae; *insertion,* SUPERIOR OBLIQUE PORTION—tubercle of anterior arch of atlas, INFERIOR OBLIQUE PORTION—transverse processes of fifth and sixth cervical vertebrae, VERTICAL PORTION—bodies of second to fourth cervical vertebrae; *innervation,* anterior cervical; *action,* flexes and supports cervical vertebrae.

mus′culi lumbrica′les ma′nus [N A, B N A], lumbrical muscles of hand: *origin,* tendons of flexor digitorum profundus; *insertion,* extensor tendons of four lateral fingers; *innervation,* median and ulnar; *action,* flex metacarpophalangeal joint and extend two distal phalanges.

mus′culi lumbrica′les pe′dis [N A, B N A],

lumbrical muscles of foot: *origin*, tendons of flexor digitorum longus; *insertion*, extensor tendons of four lateral toes; *innervation*, medial and lateral plantar; *action*, flex proximal phalanges.

m. masse'ter [N A, B N A], masseter muscle: *origin*, PARS SUPERFICIALIS—zygomatic process of maxilla and lower border of zygomatic arch, PARS PROFUNDA—lower border and medial surface of zygomatic arch; *insertion*, PARS SUPERFICIALIS—angle and ramus of mandible, PARS PROFUNDA—upper half of ramus and lateral surface of coronoid process of mandible; *innervation*, mandibular division of trigeminal; *action*, raises mandible, closes jaws.

mus'culi mem'bri inferio'ris [N A], the muscles acting on the thigh, leg, and foot.

mus'culi mem'bri superio'ris [N A], the muscles acting on the arm, forearm, and hand.

m. menta'lis [N A, B N A], chin muscle: *origin*, incisive fossa of mandible; *insertion*, skin of chin; *innervation*, facial; *action*, wrinkles skin of chin.

m. multif'idus [N A, B N A], multifidus muscle: *origin*, sacrum, sacroiliac ligament, mamillary processes of lumbar, transverse processes of thoracic, and articular processes of cervical vertebrae; *insertion*, spines of contiguous vertebrae above; *innervation*, dorsal branches of spinal nerves; *action*, extends, rotates vertebral column.

m. mylohyoi'deus [N A, B N A], mylohyoid muscle: *origin*, mylohyoid line of mandible; *insertion*, body of hyoid bone and median raphe; *innervation*, mylohyoid branch of trigeminal; *action*, elevates hyoid bone, supports floor of mouth.

m. mylopharyn'geus [B N A], pars mylopharyngea musculi constrictoris pharyngis superioris.

m. nasa'lis [N A, B N A], nasal muscle: *origin*, maxilla; *insertion*, PARS ALARIS—ala of nose, PARS TRANSVERSA—by aponeurotic expansion with fellow of opposite side; *innervation*, facial; *action*, PARS ALARIS—aids in widening nostril, PARS TRANSVERSA—depresses cartilage of nose.

m. obli'quus auric'ulae [N A, B N A], oblique muscle of auricle: *origin*, cranial surface of concha; *insertion*, cranial surface of pinna above concha; *innervation*, posterior auricular and temporal.

m. obli'quus cap'itis infe'rior [N A, B N A], inferior oblique muscle of head: *origin*, spinous process of axis; *insertion*, transverse process of atlas; *innervation*, dorsal branches of spinal nerves; *action*, rotates atlas and head.

m. obli'quus cap'itis supe'rior [N A, B N A], superior oblique muscle of head: *origin*, transverse process of atlas; *insertion*, occipital bone; *innervation*, dorsal branches of spinal nerves; *action*, extends and moves head laterally.

m. obli'quus exter'nus abdom'inis [N A, B N A], external oblique muscle of abdomen: *origin*, lower eight ribs at costal cartilages; *insertion*, crest of ilium, linea alba through rectus sheath; *innervation*, lower intercostal; *action*, flexes and rotates vertebral column, compresses abdominal viscera.

m. obli'quus infe'rior bul'bi [N A], inferior oblique muscle of eyeball: *origin*, orbital plate of maxilla; *insertion*, sclera; *innervation*, oculomotor; *action*, rotates eyeball upward and outward.

m. obli'quus infe'rior oc'uli [B N A], m. obliquus inferior bulbi.

m. obli'quus inter'nus abdom'inis [N A, B N A], internal oblique muscle of abdomen: *origin*, inguinal ligament, iliac crest, lumbar aponeurosis; *insertion*, lower three or four costal cartilages, linea alba, conjoined tendon to pubis; *innervation*, lower intercostal; *action*, flexes and rotates vertebral column, compresses abdominal viscera.

m. obli'quus supe'rior bul'bi [N A], superior oblique muscle of eyeball: *origin*, lesser wing of sphenoid above optic foramen; *insertion*, sclera; *innervation*, trochlear; *action*, rotates eyeball downward and outward.

m. obli'quus supe'rior oc'uli [B N A], m. obliquus superior bulbi.

m. obtura'tor exter'nus [B N A], m. obturatorius externus.

m. obtura'tor inter'nus [B N A], m. obturatorius internus.

m. obturato'rius exter'nus [N A], external obturator muscle: *origin*, pubis, ischium, and superficial surface of obturator membrane; *insertion*, trochanteric fossa of femur; *innervation*, obturator; *action*, rotates thigh laterally.

m. obturato'rius inter'nus [N A], internal obturator muscle: *origin*, pelvic surface of hip bone, margin of obturator foramen, ramus of ischium, inferior ramus of pubis, internal surface of obturator membrane; *insertion*, greater trochanter of femur; *innervation*, first, second, and third sacral; *action*, rotates thigh laterally.

m. occipita'lis [B N A], venter occipitalis musculi occipitofrontalis.

m. occipitofronta'lis [N A], occipitofrontal muscle: *origin*, VENTER FRONTALIS—galea aponeurotica, VENTER OCCIPITALIS—highest nuchal line of occipital bone; *insertion*, VENTER FRONTALIS—skin of eyebrows and root of nose, VENTER OCCIPITALIS—galea aponeurotica; *innervation*, VENTER FRONTALIS—temporal branch of facial, VENTER OCCIPITALIS—posterior auricular branch of facial; *action*, VENTER FRONTALIS—raises eyebrows, VENTER OCCIPITALIS—draws scalp backward.

mus'culi oc'uli [B N A], musculi bulbi.

m. omohyoi'deus [N A, B N A], omohyoid muscle, comprising two bellies (superior and inferior) connected by a central tendon that is bound to the clavicle by a fibrous expansion of the cervical fascia; *origin*, superior border of scapula; *insertion*, lateral border of hyoid bone; *innervation*, upper cervical through ansa hypoglossi; *action*, depresses hyoid bone.

m. oppo'nens dig'iti min'imi [N A], opposing muscle of little finger: *origin*, hamulus of hamate bone, transverse carpal ligament; *insertion*, medial aspect of fifth metacarpal; *innervation*, eighth cervical through ulnar; *action*, rotates, abducts fifth metacarpal.

m. oppo'nens dig'iti quin'ti ma'nus [B N A], m. opponens digiti minimi.

m. oppo'nens dig'iti quin'ti pe'dis [B N A]. Omitted in N A.

m. oppo'nens pol'licis [N A, B N A], opposing muscle of thumb: *origin*, ridge of trapezium, transverse carpal ligament; *insertion*, radial side of first metacarpal; *innervation*, sixth and seventh cervical through median; *action*, flexes and opposes thumb.

m. orbicula'ris [N A, B N A], a muscle that encircles a body opening, such as the eye or mouth. Called also *orbicular muscle.*

m. orbicula'ris oc'uli [N A, B N A], orbicular muscle of eye; the oval sphincter muscle surrounding the eyelids, consisting of three parts: *origin*, PARS ORBITALIS—medial margin of orbit, including frontal process of maxilla, PARS PALPEBRALIS—inner canthus, medial palpebral ligament, PARS LACRIMALIS—posterior lacrimal crest; *insertion*, PARS ORBITALIS—near origin after encircling orbit, PARS PALPEBRALIS—outer canthus, PARS LACRIMALIS—joins palpebral portion; *innervation*, facial; *action*, closes eyelids, wrinkles forehead, compresses lacrimal sac.

m. orbicula'ris o'ris [N A, B N A], orbicular muscle of mouth, comprising a *pars labialis*, fibers restricted to the lips, and a *pars marginalis*, fibers blending with those of adjacent muscles; *innervation*, facial; *action*, protrudes lips.

m. orbita'lis [N A, B N A], orbital muscle: *origin*, orbital periosteum; *insertion*, fascia of interorbital fissure; *innervation*, sympathetic fibers; *action*, protrudes eye.

mus'culi ossiculo'rum audi'tus [N A, B N A], the two muscles of the middle ear, the tensor tympani and the stapedius. Called also *muscles of auditory ossicles.*

mus'culi os'sis hyoi'dei [B N A], muscles of

the hyoid bone. See *musculi infrahyoidei* and *musculi suprahyoidei.*

mus'culi pala'ti et fau'cium [N A, B N A], muscles of palate and fauces, the intrinsic and extrinsic muscles that act upon the soft palate and the adjacent pharyngeal wall.

m. palatoglos'sus [N A], palatoglossus muscle: *origin*, under surface of soft palate; *insertion*, side of tongue; *innervation*, pharyngeal plexus of vagus; *action*, elevates tongue, constricts fauces.

m. palatopharyn'geus [N A], palatopharyngeal muscle: *origin*, soft palate; *insertion*, aponeurosis of pharynx, dorsal border of thyroid cartilage; *innervation*, pharyngeal plexus of vagus; *action*, aids in deglutition.

m. palma'ris bre'vis [N A, B N A], short palmar muscle: *origin*, palmar aponeurosis; *insertion*, skin of medial border of hand; *innervation*, ulnar; *action*, tenses palm of hand.

m. palma'ris lon'gus [N A, B N A], long palmar muscle: *origin*, medial epicondyle of humerus; *insertion*, transverse carpal ligament, palmar aponeurosis; *innervation*, median; *action*, flexes wrist joint.

mus'culi papilla'res [N A, B N A], conical muscular projections from the walls of the cardiac ventricles, attached to the cusps of the atrioventricular valves by the chordae tendineae. There is an anterior and a posterior papillary muscle in each ventricle, as well as a group of small papillary muscles on the septum in the right ventricle. Called also *papillary muscles.*

m. papilla'ris ante'rior ventric'uli dex'tri [N A], the papillary muscle arising from the sternocostal wall of the right ventricle. Called also *anterior papillary muscle of right ventricle.*

m. papilla'ris ante'rior ventric'uli sinis'tri [N A], the papillary muscle arising from the anterior wall of the left ventricle. Called also *anterior papillary muscle of left ventricle.*

m. papilla'ris poste'rior ventric'uli dex'tri [N A], the papillary muscle arising from the diaphragmatic wall of the right ventricle. Called also *posterior papillary muscle of right ventricle.*

m. papilla'ris poste'rior ventric'uli sinis'tri [N A], the papillary muscle arising from the posterior wall of the left ventricle. Called also *posterior papillary muscle of left ventricle.*

mus'culi papilla'res septa'les ventric'uli dex'tri [N A], several small papillary muscles in the right ventricle of the heart, arising from the interventricular septum. Called also *septal papillary muscles of right ventricle.*

mus'culi pectina'ti [N A, B N A], small ridges of muscle fibers projecting from the inner walls of the auricles of the heart and extending in the right atrium from the auricle to the crista terminalis. Called also *pectinate muscles.*

m. pectin'eus [N A, B N A], pectineal muscle: *origin*, iliopectineal line, spine of pubis; *insertion*, femur distal to lesser trochanter; *innervation*, obturator and femoral; *action*, flexes, adducts thigh.

m. pectora'lis ma'jor [N A, B N A], greater pectoral muscle: *origin*, clavicle, sternum, six upper ribs, aponeurosis of obliquus externus abdominis. These origins are reflected in the subdivision of the muscle into clavicular, sternocostal, and abdominal parts; *insertion*, crest of intertubercular groove of humerus; *innervation*, anterior thoracic; *action*, adducts, flexes, medially rotates arm.

m. pectora'lis mi'nor [N A, B N A], smaller pectoral muscle: *origin*, third, fourth, and fifth ribs; *insertion*, coracoid process of scapula; *innervation*, anterior thoracic; *action*, draws shoulder forward and downward.

mus'culi perine'i [N A, B N A], the muscles participating in formation of the perineum.

m. perone'us bre'vis [N A], short peroneal muscle: *origin*, lateral surface of fibula; *insertion*, base of fifth metatarsal bone; *innervation*, superficial peroneal; *action*, abducts, plantar flexes foot.

m. perone'us lon'gus [N A], long peroneal muscle: *origin*, lateral condyle of tibia, lateral surface of fibula; *insertion*, medial cuneiform, first metatarsal; *innervation*, superficial peroneal; *action*, abducts, everts, plantar flexes foot.

m. perone'us ter'tius [N A], third peroneal muscle: *origin*, medial surface of fibula; *insertion*, fifth metatarsal; *innervation*, deep peroneal; *action*, everts, dorsiflexes foot.

m. pharyngopalati'nus [B N A], m. palatopharyngeus.

m. pirifor'mis [N A, B N A], piriform muscle: *origin*, ilium, second to fourth sacral vertebrae; *insertion*, upper border of greater trochanter; *innervation*, first and second sacral; *action*, rotates thigh outward.

m. planta'ris [N A, B N A], plantar muscle: *origin*, lateral condyle of femur; *insertion*, posterior part of calcaneus; *innervation*, tibial; *action*, plantar flexes foot.

m. pleuroesophage'us [N A], a bundle of smooth muscle usually connecting the esophagus with the left mediastinal pleura.

m. pleurooesophage'us [B N A], m. pleuroesophageus.

m. poplite'us [N A, B N A], popliteal muscle: *origin*, lateral condyle of femur; *insertion*, posterior surface of tibia; *innervation*, fourth and fifth lumbar and first sacral; *action*, flexes leg, rotates leg inward.

m. proce'rus [N A, B N A], procerus muscle: *origin*, skin over nose; *insertion*, skin of forehead; *innervation*, facial; *action*, draws down eyebrows.

m. prona'tor quadra'tus [N A, B N A], quadrate pronator muscle: *origin*, anterior surface and border of distal third or fourth of ulna; *insertion*, distal fourth of shaft of radius; *innervation*, anterior interosseous; *action*, pronates hand.

m. prona'tor te'res [N A, B N A], round pronator muscle (2 heads): *origin*, CAPUT HUMERALE —medial epicondyle of humerus, CAPUT ULNARE— coronoid process of ulna; *insertion*, lateral surface of radius; *innervation*, median; *action*, pronates hand.

m. prostat'icus [B N A], substantia muscularis prostatae.

m. pso'as ma'jor [N A, B N A], greater psoas muscle: *origin*, lumbar vertebrae and fascia; *insertion*, lesser trochanter of femur; *innervation*, second and third lumbar; *action*, flexes trunk, flexes and medially rotates thigh.

m. pso'as mi'nor [N A, B N A], smaller psoas muscle: *origin*, last thoracic and first lumbar vertebrae; *insertion*, iliopectineal eminence; *innervation*, first lumbar; *action*, flexes trunk on pelvis.

m. pterygoi'deus exter'nus [B N A], m. pterygoideus lateralis.

m. pterygoi'deus inter'nus [B N A], m. pterygoideus medialis.

m. pterygoi'deus latera'lis [N A], lateral pterygoid muscle (2 heads): *origin*, UPPER HEAD— lateral surface of great wing of sphenoid and infratemporal crest; LOWER HEAD—lateral surface of lateral pterygoid plate; *insertion*, neck of condyle of mandible, temporomandibular joint capsule; *innervation*, mandibular division of trigeminal; *action*, protrudes mandible, opens jaws, moves mandible from side to side.

m. pterygoi'deus media'lis [N A], medial pterygoid muscle: *origin*, lateral pterygoid plate, tuberosity of maxilla; *insertion*, medial surface of ramus and angle of mandible; *innervation*, mandibular division of trigeminal; *action*, closes jaws.

m. pterygopharyn'geus [B N A], pars pterygopharyngea musculi constrictoris pharyngis superioris.

m. pubococcyg'eus [N A], a name applied to the anterior portion of the levator ani, originating in front of the obturator canal; *insertion*, anococcygeal ligament and side of coccyx; *innervation*, third and fourth sacral; *action*, helps support pelvic viscera and resist increases in intraabdominal pressure. Called also *pubococcygeal muscle.*

m. puboprostat'icus [N A], a name applied to smooth muscle fibers contained within the medial puboprostatic ligament, which pass from the prostate anteriorly to the pubis. Called also *puboprostatic muscle.*

m. puborecta'lis [N A], a name applied to a portion of the levator ani having a more lateral origin from the pubic bone, and continuous posteriorly with the corresponding muscle of the opposite side; *innervation*, third and fourth sacral; *action*, helps support pelvic viscera and resist increases in intraabdominal pressure. Called also *puborectal muscle.*

m. pubovagina'lis [N A], a name applied to a part of the anterior portion of the pubococcygeus muscle, which is inserted into the urethra and vagina; innervated by the sacral and pudendal nerves, it is involved in control of micturition. Called also *pubovaginal muscle.*

m. pubovesica'lis [N A, B N A], a name applied to smooth muscle fibers extending from the neck of the urinary bladder to the pubis. Called also *pubovesical muscle.*

m. pyramida'lis [N A, B N A], pyramidal muscle: *origin*, front of pubis, anterior pubic ligament; *insertion*, linea alba; *innervation*, last thoracic; *action*, tenses abdominal wall.

m. pyramida'lis auric'ulae [N A], a prolongation of the fibers of the tragicus to the spina helicis. Called also *pyramidal muscle of auricle.*

m. quadra'tus fem'oris [N A, B N A], quadrate muscle of thigh: *origin*, upper part of external border of tuberosity of ischium; *insertion*, quadrate tubercle of femur; *innervation*, last lumbar and first sacral; *action*, adducts, laterally rotates thigh.

m. quadra'tus la'bii inferio'ris [B N A], m. depressor labii inferioris.

m. quadra'tus la'bii superio'ris [B N A], m. levator labii superioris.

m. quadra'tus lumbo'rum [N A, B N A], quadrate muscle of loins: *origin*, crest of ilium, lumbodorsal fascia, lumbar vertebrae; *insertion*, twelfth rib, transverse processes of four upper lumbar vertebrae; *innervation*, first and second lumbar and twelfth thoracic; *action*, laterally flexes lumbar vertebrae.

m. quadra'tus plan'tae [N A, B N A], quadrate muscle of sole: *origin*, calcaneus and plantar fascia; *insertion*, tendons of flexor digitorum longus; *innervation*, external plantar; *action*, aids in flexing toes.

m. quad'riceps fem'oris [N A, B N A], a name applied collectively to the rectus femoris, vastus intermedius, vastus lateralis, and vastus medialis, inserting by a common tendon that surrounds the patella and ends on the tuberosity of the tibia, and acting to extend the leg upon the thigh. See individual components. Called also *quadriceps muscle of thigh.*

m. rectococcyg'eus [N A, B N A], smooth muscle fibers originating on the anterior surface of the second and third coccygeal vertebrae and inserting on the posterior surface of the rectum, innervated by autonomic nerves, and acting to retract and elevate the rectum. Called also *rectococcygeal muscle.*

m. rectourethra'lis [N A], a band of smooth muscle fibers extending from the perineal flexure of the rectum to the membranous urethra in the male. Called also *rectourethral muscle.*

m. rectouteri'nus [N A, B N A], a band of fibers running between the cervix of the uterus and the rectum, in the rectouterine fold.

m. rectovesica'lis [N A, B N A], a band of fibers in the male, connecting the longitudinal musculature of the rectum with the external muscular coat of the bladder. Called also *rectovesical muscle.*

m. rec'tus abdom'inis [N A, B N A], straight muscle of abdomen: *origin*, pubis; *insertion*, xiphoid process, cartilages of fifth, sixth, and seventh ribs; *innervation*, branches of lower thoracic; *action*, flexes lumbar vertebrae, supports abdomen.

m. rec'tus cap'itis ante'rior [N A, B N A], anterior straight muscle of head: *origin*, lateral mass of atlas; *insertion*, basilar process of occipital bone; *innervation*, first and second cervical; *action*, flexes, supports head.

m. rec'tus cap'itis latera'lis [N A, B N A], lateral straight muscle of head: *origin*, upper surface of transverse process of atlas; *insertion*, jugular process of occipital bone; *innervation*, first and second cervical; *action*, flexes, supports head.

m. rec'tus cap'itis poste'rior ma'jor [N A, B N A], greater posterior straight muscle of head: *origin*, spinous process of axis; *insertion*, occipital bone; *innervation*, suboccipital and greater occipital; *action*, extends head.

m. rec'tus cap'itis poste'rior mi'nor [N A, B N A], smaller posterior straight muscle of head: *origin*, tubercle on dorsal arch of atlas; *insertion*, occipital bone; *innervation*, suboccipital and greater occipital; *action*, extends head.

m. rec'tus fem'oris [N A, B N A], straight muscle of thigh: *origin*, anterior inferior iliac spine, brim of acetabulum; *insertion*, patella, tubercle of tibia; *innervation*, femoral; *action*, extends leg, flexes thigh.

m. rec'tus infe'rior bul'bi [N A], inferior straight muscle of eyeball: *origin*, circumference of optic foramen; *insertion*, under side of sclera; *innervation*, oculomotor; *action*, adducts, rotates eyeball downward and inward.

m. rec'tus infe'rior oc'uli [B N A], m. rectus inferior bulbi.

m. rec'tus latera'lis bul'bi [N A], lateral straight muscle of eyeball: *origin*, outer margin of optic foramen, margin of sphenoidal fissure; *insertion*, outer side of sclera; *innervation*, abducens; *action*, abducts eyeball.

m. rec'tus latera'lis oc'uli [B N A], m. rectus lateralis bulbi.

m. rec'tus media'lis bul'bi [N A], medial straight muscle of eyeball: *origin*, circumference of optic foramen; *insertion*, inner side of sclera; *innervation*, oculomotor; *action*, adducts eyeball.

m. rec'tus media'lis oc'uli [B N A], m. rectus medialis bulbi.

m. rec'tus supe'rior bul'bi [N A], superior straight muscle of eyeball: *origin*, upper border of optic foramen; *insertion*, upper aspect of sclera; *innervation*, oculomotor; *action*, adducts, rotates eyeball upward and inward.

m. rec'tus supe'rior oc'uli [B N A], m. rectus superior bulbi.

m. rhomboi'deus ma'jor [N A, B N A], greater rhomboid muscle: *origin*, spinous processes of second, third, fourth, and fifth thoracic vertebrae; *insertion*, vertebral margin of scapula; *innervation*, dorsal scapular; *action*, retracts, elevates scapula.

m. rhomboi'deus mi'nor [N A, B N A], lesser rhomboid muscle: *origin*, spinous processes of seventh cervical to first thoracic vertebrae, lower part of ligamentum nuchae; *insertion*, vertebral margin of scapula at root of the spine; *innervation*, dorsal scapular; *action*, adducts, elevates scapula.

m. riso'rius [N A, B N A], risorius muscle: *origin*, fascia over masseter; *insertion*, skin at angle of mouth; *innervation*, buccal branch of facial; *action*, draws angle of mouth laterally.

mus'culi rotato'res [N A, B N A], a series of small muscles deep in the groove between the spinous and transverse processes of the vertebrae, including the *musculi rotatores cervicis*, *musculi rotatores thoracis*, and *musculi rotatores lumborum.*

mus'culi rotato'res bre'ves [B N A], a name given the musculi rotatores that insert on the lamina of the vertebra next above the vertebra of origin. Omitted in N A.

mus'culi rotato'res cer'vicis [N A], rotator muscles of neck: *origin*, transverse processes of cervical vertebrae; *insertion*, base of spinous process of suprajacent vertebrae; *innervation,* spinal nerves; *action,* extend vertebral column and rotate it toward the opposite side.

mus'culi rotato'res lon'gi [B N A], a name given the musculi rotatores that cross one or two segments of the vertebral column and insert into the spine of the vertebra next above. Omitted in N A.

mus'culi rotato'res lumbo'rum [N A], rotator muscles of loins: *origin,* transverse processes of lumbar vertebrae; *insertion,* base of spinous process of suprajacent vertebrae; *innervation,* spinal nerves; *action,* extend vertebral column and rotate it toward the opposite side.

mus'culi rotato'res thora'cis [N A], rotator muscles of thorax: *origin,* transverse processes of thoracic vertebrae; *insertion,* base of spinous process of suprajacent vertebrae; *innervation,* spinal nerves; *action,* extend vertebral column and rotate it toward the opposite side.

m. sacrococcyg'eus ante'rior [B N A], m. sacrococcygeus ventralis.

m. sacrococcyg'eus dorsa'lis [N A], a muscular slip passing from the dorsal aspect of the sacrum to the coccyx. Called also *dorsal sacrococcygeal muscle.*

m. sacrococcyg'eus poste'rior [B N A], m. sacrococcygeus dorsalis.

m. sacrococcyg'eus ventra'lis [N A], a musculotendinous slip passing from the lower sacral vertebrae to the coccyx. Called also *ventral sacrococcygeal muscle.*

m. sacrospina'lis [B N A], m. erector spinae.

m. salpingopharyn'geus [N A, B N A], salpingopharyngeal muscle: *origin,* auditory tube near its orifice; *insertion,* posterior part of palatopharyngeus; *innervation,* pharyngeal plexus of vagus; *action,* raises nasopharynx.

m. sarto'rius [N A, B N A], sartorius muscle: *origin,* anterior superior spine of ilium; *insertion,* medial side of proximal end of tibia; *innervation,* femoral; *action,* flexes thigh and leg.

m. scale'nus ante'rior [N A, B N A], anterior scalene muscle: *origin,* transverse processes of third to sixth cervical vertebrae; *insertion,* tubercle of first rib; *innervation,* second to seventh cervical; *action,* raises first rib.

m. scale'nus me'dius [N A, B N A], middle scalene muscle: *origin,* transverse processes of second to sixth cervical vertebrae; *insertion,* first rib; *innervation,* second to seventh cervical; *action,* raises first rib.

m. scale'nus min'imus [N A, B N A], a band occasionally found between the m. scalenus anterior and the m. scalenus medius. Called also *smallest scalene muscle.*

m. scale'nus poste'rior [N A, B N A], posterior scalene muscle: *origin,* tubercles of fourth to sixth cervical vertebrae; *insertion,* second rib; *innervation,* second to seventh cervical; *action,* raises first and second ribs.

m. semimembrano'sus [N A, B N A], semimembranous muscle: *origin,* tuberosity of ischium; *insertion,* medial condyle of tibia; *innervation,* tibial; *action,* flexes leg, extends thigh.

m. semispina'lis [N A, B N A], a muscle composed of fibers extending obliquely from the transverse processes of the vertebrae to the spines, except for the semispinalis capitis; it includes the *m. semispinalis capitis, m. semispinalis cervicis,* and *m. semispinalis thoracis.* Called also *semispinal muscle.*

m. semispina'lis cap'itis [N A, B N A], semispinal muscle of head: *origin,* transverse processes of five or six upper thoracic and four lower cervical vertebrae; *insertion,* occipital bone; *innervation,* suboccipital, greater occipital, and branches of cervical; *action,* extends head.

m. semispina'lis cer'vicis [N A, B N A], semispinal muscle of neck: *origin,* transverse processes of five or six upper thoracic vertebrae; *insertion,* spinous processes of second to fifth cervical vertebrae; *innervation,* branches of cervical; *action,* extends, rotates vertebral column.

m. semispina'lis dor'si [B N A], m. semispinalis thoracis.

m. semispina'lis thora'cis [N A], semispinal muscle of thorax: *origin,* transverse processes of sixth to tenth thoracic vertebrae; *insertion,* spinous processes of two lower cervical and four upper thoracic vertebrae; *innervation,* spinal nerves; *action,* extends, rotates vertebral column.

m. semitendino'sus [N A, B N A], semitendinous muscle: *origin,* tuberosity of ischium; *insertion,* upper and medial surface of tibia; *innervation,* tibial; *action,* flexes leg, extends thigh.

m. serra'tus ante'rior [N A, B N A], anterior serratus muscle: *origin,* eight or nine upper ribs; *insertion,* vertebral border of scapula; *innervation,* long thoracic; *action,* draws scapula forward; rotates scapula to raise shoulder in abduction of arm.

m. serra'tus poste'rior infe'rior [N A, B N A], inferior posterior serratus muscle: *origin,* spines of two lower thoracic and two or three upper lumbar vertebrae; *insertion,* inferior border of four lower ribs; *innervation,* ninth to twelfth thoracic; *action,* lowers ribs in expiration.

m. serra'tus poste'rior supe'rior [N A, B N A], superior posterior serratus muscle: *origin,* ligamentum nuchae, spinous processes of upper thoracic vertebrae; *insertion,* second, third, fourth, and fifth ribs; *innervation,* upper four intercostal; *action,* raises ribs in inspiration.

mus'culi skel'eti [N A, B N A], striated muscles that are attached to bones and typically cross at least one joint. Called also *skeletal muscles.*

m. so'leus [N A, B N A], soleus muscle: *origin,* fibula, popliteal fascia, tibia; *insertion,* calcaneus by tendo calcaneus (tendo Achillis); *innervation,* tibial; *action,* plantar flexes ankle joint.

m. sphinc'ter [N A, B N A], a ringlike muscle that closes a natural orifice. Called also *sphincter.*

m. sphinc'ter ampul'lae hepatopancreat'icae [N A], muscle fibers investing the hepatopancreatic ampulla.

m. sphinc'ter a'ni exter'nus [N A, B N A], external sphincter muscle of anus: *origin,* tip of coccyx and surrounding fascia; *insertion,* tendinous center of perineum; *innervation,* inferior rectal and fourth sacral; *action,* closes anus.

m. sphinc'ter a'ni inter'nus [N A, B N A], a thickening of the circular lamina of the tunica muscularis at the caudal end of the rectum. Called also *internal sphincter muscle of anus.*

m. sphinc'ter duc'tus choledo'chi [N A], an annular sheath of muscle that invests the common bile duct within the wall of the duodenum.

m. sphinc'ter pupil'lae [N A, B N A], sphincter muscle of pupil: circular fibers of the iris, innervated by the oculomotor nerve (parasympathetic), and acting to contract the pupil.

m. sphinc'ter pylo'ri [N A, B N A], a thickening of the middle layer of the stomach musculature around the pylorus. Called also *sphincter muscle of pylorus.*

m. sphinc'ter ure'thrae [N A], sphincter muscle of urethra: *origin,* ramus of pubis; *insertion,* median raphe behind and in front of urethra; *innervation,* pudendal; *action,* compresses urethra.

m. sphinc'ter ure'thrae membrana'ceae [B N A], m. sphincter urethrae.

m. sphinc'ter ves'icae urina'riae [N A], a circular layer of fibers surrounding the internal urethral orifice, innervated by the vesical nerve, and acting to close the internal orifice of the urethra. Called also *sphincter muscle of urinary bladder.*

m. spina'lis [N A, B N A], the medial division of the erector spinae, including the *m. spinalis capitis, m. spinalis cervicis,* and *m. spinalis thoracis.*

m. spina'lis cap'itis [N A, B N A], spinal muscle of head: *origin,* spines of upper thoracic and lower cervical vertebrae; *insertion,* occipital bone; *innervation,* spinal nerves; *action,* extends head.

m. spina'lis cer'vicis [N A, B N A], spinal muscle of neck: *origin*, spinous processes of fifth, sixth, and seventh cervical and two upper thoracic vertebrae; *insertion*, spinous processes of axis and sometimes of second to fourth cervical vertebrae; *innervation*, branches of cervical; *action*, extends vertebral column.

m. spina'lis dor'si [B N A], m. spinalis thoracis.

m. spina'lis thora'cis [N A], spinal muscle of thorax: *origin*, spinous processes of two upper lumbar and two lower thoracic; *insertion*, spines of upper thoracic vertebrae; *innervation*, branches of spinal nerves; *action*, extends vertebral column.

m. sple'nius cap'itis [N A, B N A], splenius muscle of head: *origin*, lower half of ligamentum nuchae, spines of seventh cervical and three upper thoracic vertebrae; *insertion*, occipital bone; *innervation*, middle and lower cervical; *action*, extends, rotates head.

m. sple'nius cer'vicis [N A], splenius muscle of neck: *origin*, spinous processes of third to sixth thoracic vertebrae; *insertion*, transverse processes of two or three upper cervical vertebrae; *innervation*, dorsal branches of lower cervical; *action*, extends, rotates head and neck.

m. stape'dius [N A, B N A], stapedius muscle: *origin*, interior of pyramid of tympanic cavity; *insertion*, posterior surface of neck of stapes; *innervation*, stapedial branch of facial; *action*, dampens stapedial movement.

m. sterna'lis [N A, B N A], a band occasionally found parallel to the sternum on the sternocostal origin of the pectoralis major. Called also *sternal muscle*.

m. sternocleidomastoi'deus [N A, B N A], sternocleidomastoid muscle (2 heads): *origin*, sternum and clavicle; *insertion*, mastoid process and superior nuchal line of occipital bone; *innervation*, spinal accessory and cervical plexus; *action*, flexes vertebral column, rotates head.

m. sternohyoi'deus [N A, B N A], sternohyoid muscle: *origin*, manubrium sterni; *insertion*, body of hyoid bone; *innervation*, upper cervical; *action*, depresses hyoid bone and larynx.

m. sternothyreoi'deus [B N A], m. sternothyroideus.

m. sternothyroi'deus [N A], sternothyroid muscle: *origin*, manubrium sterni; *insertion*, thyroid cartilage; *innervation*, upper cervical; *action*, depresses thyroid cartilage.

m. styloglos'sus [N A, B N A], styloglossus muscle: *origin*, styloid process; *insertion*, margin of tongue; *innervation*, hypoglossal; *action*, raises and retracts tongue.

m. stylohyoi'deus [N A, B N A], stylohyoid muscle: *origin*, styloid process; *insertion*, body of hyoid bone; *innervation*, facial; *action*, draws hyoid and tongue upward.

m. stylopharyn'geus [N A, B N A], stylopharyngeal muscle: *origin*, styloid process; *insertion*, thyroid cartilage and pharyngeal constrictors; *innervation*, pharyngeal plexus, glossopharyngeal; *action*, raises and dilates pharynx.

m. subcla'vius [N A, B N A], subclavius muscle: *origin*, first rib and its cartilage; *insertion*, lower surface of clavicle; *innervation*, fifth and sixth cervical; *action*, depresses lateral end of clavicle.

mus'culi subcosta'les [N A, B N A], subcostal muscles: *origin*, inner surface of ribs; *insertion*, inner surface of first, second, third rib below; *innervation*, intercostal; *action*, raise ribs in inspiration.

m. subscapula'ris [N A, B N A], subscapular muscle: *origin*, subscapular fossa of scapula; *insertion*, lesser tubercle of humerus; *innervation*, subscapular; *action*, rotates humerus medially.

m. supina'tor [N A, B N A], supinator muscle: *origin*, lateral epicondyle of humerus, ulna, elbow joint fascia; *insertion*, radius; *innervation*, deep radial; *action*, supinates hand.

mus'culi suprahyoi'dei [N A], the muscles that attach the hyoid bone to the skull, including the digastric, stylohyoid, mylohyoid, and geniohyoid muscles.

m. supraspina'tus [N A, B N A], supraspinous muscle: *origin*, supraspinous fossa of scapula; *insertion*, greater tuberosity of humerus; *innervation*, suprascapular; *action*, abducts humerus.

m. suspenso'rius duode'ni [N A, B N A], a flat band of smooth muscle originating from the left crus of the diaphragm, and continuous with the muscular coat of the duodenum at its junction with the jejunum. Called also *suspensory muscle of duodenum*.

m. tarsa'lis infe'rior [N A, B N A], inferior tarsal muscle: *origin*, inferior rectus muscle; *insertion*, tarsal plate of lower eyelid; *innervation*, sympathetic; *action*, widens palpebral fissure.

m. tarsa'lis supe'rior [N A, B N A], superior tarsal muscle: *origin*, m. levator palpebrae superioris; *insertion*, tarsal plate of upper eyelid; *innervation*, sympathetic; *action*, widens palpebral fissure.

m. tempora'lis [N A, B N A], temporal muscle: *origin*, temporal fossa and fascia; *insertion*, coronoid process of mandible; *innervation*, mandibular division of trigeminal; *action*, closes jaws.

m. temporoparieta'lis [N A], temporoparietal muscle: *origin*, temporal fascia above ear; *insertion*, galea aponeurotica; *innervation*, temporal branches of facial; *action*, tightens scalp.

m. ten'sor fas'ciae la'tae [N A, B N A], tensor muscle of fascia lata: *origin*, iliac crest; *insertion*, iliotibial band of fascia lata; *innervation*, superior gluteal; *action*, flexes, abducts thigh.

m. ten'sor tym'pani [N A, B N A], tensor muscle of tympanic membrane: *origin*, cartilaginous portion of auditory tube; *insertion*, manubrium of malleus; *innervation*, mandibular division of trigeminal; *action*, tenses tympanic membrane.

m. ten'sor ve'li palati'ni [N A, B N A], tensor muscle of velum palatini: *origin*, scaphoid fossa of sphenoid, wall of auditory tube; *insertion*, aponeurosis of soft palate, horizontal part of palatine bone; *innervation*, mandibular division of trigeminal; *action*, tenses soft palate, opens auditory tube.

m. te'res ma'jor [N A, B N A], teres major muscle: *origin*, inferior angle of scapula; *insertion*, crest of intertubercular sulcus of humerus; *innervation*, subscapular; *action*, adducts, extends, medially rotates arm.

m. te'res mi'nor [N A, B N A], teres minor muscle: *origin*, lateral margin of scapula; *insertion*, greater tuberosity of humerus; *innervation*, axillary; *action*, laterally rotates arm.

mus'culi thora'cis [N A, B N A], the muscles of the thorax.

m. thyreoarytaenoi'deus [exter'nus] [B N A], m. thyroarytenoideus.

m. thyreoepiglot'ticus [B N A], m. thyroepiglotticus.

m. thyreohyoi'deus [B N A], m. thyrohyoideus.

m. thyreopharyn'geus [B N A], pars thyropharyngea musculi constrictoris pharyngis inferioris.

m. thyroarytenoi'deus [N A], thyroarytenoid muscle: *origin*, lamina of thyroid cartilage; *insertion*, muscular process of arytenoid cartilage; *innervation*, recurrent laryngeal; *action*, relaxes, shortens vocal folds.

m. thyroepiglot'ticus [N A], thyroepiglottic muscle: *origin*, lamina of thyroid cartilage; *insertion*, epiglottis; *innervation*, recurrent laryngeal; *action*, closes inlet to larynx.

m. thyrohyoi'deus [N A], thyrohyoid muscle: *origin*, thyroid cartilage; *insertion*, greater cornu of hyoid bone; *innervation*, upper cervical; *action*, raises and changes form of larynx.

m. tibia'lis ante'rior [N A, B N A], anterior tibial muscle: *origin*, tibia, interosseous membrane;

insertion, medial cuneiform and first metatarsal; *innervation*, deep peroneal; *action*, dorsiflexes and inverts foot.

m. tibia'lis poste'rior [N A, B N A], posterior tibial muscle: *origin*, tibia, fibula, interosseous membrane; *insertion*, bases of metatarsals and tarsals, except talus; *innervation*, posterior tibial; *action*, plantar flexes and inverts foot.

m. trachea'lis [N A], a transverse layer of smooth fibers in the dorsal portion of the trachea; *insertion*, tracheal cartilages; *innervation*, autonomic fibers; *action*, lessens caliber of trachea.

m. trag'icus [N A, B N A], a short, flattened vertical band on the lateral surface of the tragus, innervated by the auriculotemporal and posterior auricular nerves.

m. transversospina'lis [N A], a general term including the semispinalis and multifidus muscles and the rotatores.

m. transver'sus abdom'inis [N A, B N A], transverse muscle of abdomen: *origin*, cartilages of six lower ribs, lumbodorsal fascia, iliac crest, inguinal ligament; *insertion*, linea alba through rectus sheath, conjoined tendon to pubis; *innervation*, lower intercostals, iliohypogastric, ilioinguinal; *action*, compresses abdominal viscera.

m. transver'sus auric'ulae [N A, B N A], transverse muscle of auricle: *origin*, cranial surface of pinna; *insertion*, circumference of pinna; *innervation*, great auricular and posterior auricular; *action*, retracts helix.

m. transver'sus lin'guae [N A, B N A], transverse muscle of tongue: *origin*, median septum of tongue; *insertion*, dorsum and margins of tongue; *innervation*, hypoglossal; *action*, changes shape of tongue in mastication and deglutition.

m. transver'sus men'ti [N A, B N A], superficial fibers of the depressor anguli oris which turn back and cross to the opposite side. Called also *transverse muscle of chin*.

m. transver'sus nu'chae [N A, B N A], a small muscle often present, passing from the occipital protuberance to the posterior auricular muscle. It may be either superficial or deep to the trapezius. Called also *transverse muscle of nape*.

m. transver'sus perine'i profun'dus [N A, B N A], deep transverse muscle of perineum: *origin*, inferior ramus of ischium; *insertion*, median raphe of perineum; *innervation*, pudendal; *action*, draws back central point of perineum.

m. transver'sus perine'i superficia'lis [N A, B N A], superficial transverse muscle of perineum: *origin*, tuberosity of ischium; *insertion*, central tendon of perineum; *innervation*, perineal branch of pudendal; *action*, tenses central point of perineum.

m. transver'sus thora'cis [N A, B N A], transverse muscle of thorax: *origin*, mediastinal surface of sternum and of xiphoid process; *insertion*, cartilages of second to sixth ribs; *innervation*, intercostal; *action*, narrows chest.

m. trape'zius [N A, B N A], trapezius muscle: *origin*, occipital bone, ligamentum nuchae, spinous processes of seventh cervical and all thoracic vertebrae; *insertion*, clavicle, acromion, spine of scapula; *innervation*, spinal accessory and cervical plexus; *action*, rotates scapula to raise shoulder in abduction of arm, draws scapula backward.

m. triangula'ris [B N A], m. depressor anguli oris.

m. tri'ceps bra'chii [N A, B N A], triceps muscle of arm (3 heads): *origin*, CAPUT LONGUM—infraglenoid tuberosity of scapula, CAPUT LATERALE—posterior surface of humerus, lateral border of humerus, lateral intermuscular septum, CAPUT MEDIALE—posterior surface of humerus below radial groove, medial border of humerus, medial intermuscular septa; *insertion*, olecranon of ulna; *innervation*, radial; *action*, extends forearm, adducts and extends arm.

m. tri'ceps su'rae [N A, B N A], the gastrocnemius and soleus considered together.

m. unipenna'tus [N A, B N A], a muscle in which the fiber bundles approach the tendon of insertion from only one direction and are inserted through only a small segment of its circumference. Called also *unipennate muscle*.

m. u'vulae [N A, B N A], muscle of uvula: *origin*, posterior nasal spine of palatine bone and aponeurosis of soft palate; *insertion*, uvula; *innervation*, pharyngeal plexus of vagus; *action*, raises uvula.

m. vas'tus interme'dius [N A, B N A], intermediate great muscle: *origin*, anterior and lateral surfaces of femur; *insertion*, patella, common tendon of quadriceps femoris; *innervation*, femoral; *action*, extends leg.

m. vas'tus latera'lis [N A, B N A], lateral great muscle: *origin*, capsule of hip joint, lateral aspect of femur; *insertion*, patella, common tendon of quadriceps femoris; *innervation*, femoral; *action*, extends leg.

m. vas'tus media'lis [N A, B N A], medial great muscle: *origin*, medial aspect of femur; *insertion*, patella, common tendon of quadriceps femoris; *innervation*, femoral; *action*, extends leg.

m. ventricula'ris [B N A], a name applied to fibers of the thyroarytenoideus muscle running into the false vocal cords. Omitted in N A.

m. vertica'lis lin'guae [N A, B N A], vertical muscle of tongue: *origin*, dorsal fascia of tongue; *insertion*, sides and base of tongue; *innervation*, hypoglossus; *action*, changes shape of tongue in mastication and deglutition.

m. vis'cerum [B N A], a term applied to muscle of a body organ. Omitted in N A.

m. voca'lis [N A, B N A], vocal muscle: *origin*, thyroid cartilage; *insertion*, vocal process of arytenoid cartilage; *innervation*, recurrent laryngeal; *action*, shortens vocal folds.

m. zygomat'icus [B N A], m. zygomaticus major.

m. zygomat'icus ma'jor [N A], greater zygomatic muscle: *origin*, zygomatic bone in front of temporal process; *insertion*, angle of mouth; *innervation*, facial; *action*, draws angle of mouth backward and upward.

m. zygomat'icus mi'nor [N A], lesser zygomatic muscle: *origin*, zygomatic bone near maxillary suture; *insertion*, orbicularis oris and levator labii superioris; *innervation*, facial; *action*, draws upper lip upward and outward.

---

mushbite (mush'bīt). The making simultaneously of an impression of both upper and lower teeth and/or associated structures by having the subject bite on a mass of plastic material placed between the jaws. See *wax bite*, under *bite*.

musicogenic (mu″zĭ-ko-jen'ik). Caused or produced by musical sounds.

musicomania (mu″zĭ-ko-ma'ne-ah) [Gr. *mousikē* music + *mania* madness]. Insane fondness for music.

musicotherapy (mu″zĭ-ko-ther'ah-pe) [Gr. *mousikē* music + *therapeia* treatment]. The treatment of disease by music.

musomania (mu″zo-ma'ne-ah). Musicomania.

musophobia (mus″o-fo'be-ah) [L. *mus* mouse + *phobia*]. Morbid fear of mice.

Musset's sign (mu-sāz') [Louis Charles Alfred de *Musset*, French poet, 1810–1857, who died of aortic insufficiency]. See under *sign*.

mussitation (mus″ĭ-ta'shun) [L. *mussitare* to mutter]. The moving of the lips with no utterance of sounds.

Mussy. See *Guéneau de Mussy*.

must (must) [L. *mustum*]. The unfermented juice of grapes.

mustard (mus'tard) [L. *sinapis*]. 1. A plant of the genus Brassica. 2. The ripe seeds of *Brassica nigra* (black mustard) and of *Sinapis* (*Brassica*) *alba* (white mustard). When mustard seeds are crushed and moistened, volatile oils are liberated. These oils give mustard its counterirritant, stimulant, and revulsant properties. **black m., brown m.,** *Brassica nigra.* **nitrogen m's,** a class of chemical compounds homologous with mustard gas, some of which have been used in the treatment of neoplastic disease. **white m., yellow m.,** *Brassica alba.*

mustargen (mus′tar-jen). Trade mark for a preparation of mechlorethamine.

mutacism (mu′tah-sizm). 1. The improper pronunciation of the sounds of mute letters. 2. Mytacism.

mutafacient (mu″tah-fa′shent). Mutagenic.

mutagen (mu′tah-jen) [*muta*tion + *gen*esis]. A chemical or physical agent that induces genetic mutations.

mutagenesis (mu″tah-jen′e-sis) [*muta*tion + *genesis*]. 1. The production of change. 2. The induction of genetic mutation.

mutagenic (mu″tah-jen′ik). 1. Causing change. 2. Inducing genetic mutation.

mutagenicity (mu″tah-je-nis′ĭ-te). The property of being able to induce genetic mutation.

mutant (mu′tant) [L. *mutare* to change]. A sport or variation which breeds true. See *mutation.*

mutarotation (mu″tah-ro-ta′shun). A special type of tautomerism involving either (*a*) the transformation of one optical isomer into another, or (*b*) the transformation of one structural isomer into another (both possessing asymmetric centers and optical activity). With each type the rotatory power of a freshly prepared solution of the compound will change, under a variety of conditions, until an equilibrium value is set up which (unlike in racemization) will not be zero.

mutase (mu′tās) [L. *mutare* to change + *-ase*]. 1. An enzyme that hastens oxidation-reduction reactions. 2. A vegetable food preparation rich in proteins. **aldehyde m.,** an enzyme which catalyzes the Cannizzaro reaction.

mutation (mu-ta′shun) [L. *mutatio,* from *mutare* to change]. 1. A change in form, quality, or some other characteristic. 2. In biology, a permanent transmissible change in the characters of an offspring from those of its parents; also, an individual showing such a change; a sport (De Vries). See *theory of mutation,* under *theory.* **induced m.,** a genetic mutation caused by external factors which are experimentally or accidentally produced. **natural m.,** a genetic mutation occurring without the intervention of any known external factors. **somatic m.,** a genetic mutation occurring in a somatic cell, providing the basis for a mosaic condition.

mutational (mu-ta′shun-al). Pertaining to mutation.

mute (mūt) [L. *mutus*]. 1. Unable to speak. 2. One who cannot speak. **deaf m.,** a person who can neither hear nor speak.

mutilation (mu″tĭ-la′shun) [L. *mutilatio*]. The act of depriving of a limb, member, or important part; deprival of an organ.

Mutisia (mu-tiz′e-ah). A genus of plants. **M. viciaefo′lia,** a composite-flowered plant of South America: used there as a sedative and in various diseases of the heart, respiratory organs, and nervous system.

mutism (mu′tizm) [L. *mutus* unable to speak, inarticulate]. Inability or refusal to speak. **akinetic m.,** a state in which the individual makes no spontaneous movement or sound. **deaf m.,** inability to speak as a result of deafness and never having heard spoken words. **hysterical m.,** hysterical inability to utter words.

muton (mu′ton) [*muta*tion + Gr. *on* neuter ending]. A term used to designate a gene, when specified as the smallest hereditary element that can be altered by mutation. Cf. *cistron* and *recon.*

mutualism (mu′tu-al-izm). Symbiosis in which both populations (or individuals) gain from the association and are unable to survive without it.

mutualist (mu′tu-al-ist). Any organism or species associated with another in a relationship which is beneficial to both.

M.V. Abbreviation for L. *Med′icus Veterina′rius,* veterinary physician.

mv. Abbreviation for *millivolt.*

μv. Abbreviation for *microvolt.*

μw. Abbreviation for *microwatt.*

My. Abbreviation for *myopia.*

my. Abbreviation for *mayer.*

my-. See *myo-.*

Myà's disease (me-āz′) [Giuseppe *Myà,* Italian physician, 1857–1911]. See under *disease.*

myalgia (mi-al′je-ah) [*my-* + *algia*]. Pain in a muscle or muscles. **m. abdom′inis,** pain in the abdominal wall. **m. cap′itis,** pain in the scalp muscles; cephalodynia. **m. cervica′lis,** torticollis. **epidemic m.,** epidemic pleurodynia. **lumbar m.,** lumbago.

myasis (mi-a′sis). Myiasis.

myasthenia (mi″as-the′ne-ah) [*my-* + Gr. *astheneia* weakness]. Muscular debility; any constitutional anomaly of muscle. **angiosclerotic m.,** excessive muscular fatigue due to vascular changes. **m. gas′trica,** weakness and loss of tone in the muscular coats of the stomach; atony of the stomach. **m. gra′vis, m. gra′vis pseudoparalyt′ica,** a syndrome of fatigue and exhaustion of the muscular system marked by progressive paralysis of muscles without sensory disturbance or atrophy. It may affect any muscle of the body, but especially those of the face, lips, tongue, throat, and neck. **m. laryn′gis,** disability of the phonatory laryngeal muscles from overuse.

myasthenic (mi″as-then′ik). Pertaining to or characterized by muscular weakness.

myatonia (mi″ah-to′ne-ah) [*my-* + *a* neg. + Gr. *tonos* tension]. Deficiency or absence of muscular tone. **m. congen′ita,** amyotonia congenita.

myatony (mi-at′o-ne). Myatonia.

myatrophy (mi-at′ro-fe) [*my-* + *atrophy*]. Atrophy of a muscle; muscular atrophy.

myautonomy (mi″aw-ton′o-me) [*my-* + Gr. *autos* self + *nomos* law]. A condition in which muscular contraction aroused by stimulation is so long delayed that it appears to occur independently of the stimulation.

myc-. See *myco-.*

mycelian (mi-se′le-an). Pertaining to mycelium.

mycelioid (mi-se′le-oid). Having the radiate filamentous appearance of mold colonies.

mycelium (mi-se′le-um) [*myc-* + Gr. *hēlos* nail]. The vegetative body of a fungus composed of a mass of filaments called hyphae.

mycete (mi′sēt) [Gr. *mykēs* fungus]. A fungus.

mycethemia (mi″sĕ-the′me-ah) [*myceto-* + Gr. *haima* blood + *-ia*]. The presence of fungi in the blood.

mycetism (mi′sĕ-tizm). Mycetismus.

mycetismus (mi″sĕ-tiz′mus). Poisoning caused by a fungus, as that resulting from ingestion of poisonous mushrooms.

myceto-. See *myco-.*

mycetocyte (mi-se′to-sīt). One of the cells which make up a mycetoma.

mycetogenic, mycetogenous (mi″sĕ-to-jen′ik, mi″sĕ-toj′e-nus) [*myceto-* + Gr. *gennan* to produce]. Caused by fungous growths.

mycetoma (mi″sĕ-to′mah) [*myceto-* + *-oma*]. Maduromycosis. **white m.,** mycetoma in which the granules are colorless or nearly so.

Mycetozoa (mi-se″to-zo′ah) [*myceto-* + Gr. *zōon* animal]. The slime animals; a subclass of Rhizopoda whose members consist of a mass of multinucleated ameboid protoplasm.

mycid (mi′sid). A secondary lesion occurring in some kinds of dermatophytosis.

Myco. Abbreviation for *Mycobacterium.*

myco-, myc-, mycet- [Gr. *mykēs* fungus]. Combining form denoting relationship to fungus.

myco-agglutinin (mi″ko-ah-gloo′tĭ-nin). An agglutinin which has the power of agglutinating the infecting fungi.

mycobacteria (mi″ko-bak-te′re-ah). Plural of *mycobacterium.*

Mycobacteriaceae (mi″ko-bak-te″re-a′se-e). A family of Schizomycetes, order Actinomycetales, made up of spherical to rod-shaped gram-positive, aerobic, mesophilic cells showing no branching on ordinary media, found in soil and dairy products and occurring as parasites in man and other animals. It includes two genera, *Mycobacterium* and *Mycococcus.*

mycobacteriosis (mi″ko-bak-te″re-o′sis). An infection caused by mycobacteria.

Mycobacterium (mi″ko-bak-te′re-um). A genus of microorganisms of the family Myobacteriaceae, order Actinomycetales, occurring as gram-positive slender rods and distinguished by acid-fast staining. **M. a′vium,** the avian type of tubercle bacillus, commonly producing disease in chickens and swine, and only rarely infecting man. Called also *M. tuberculosis* var. *avium.* **M. bo′vis,** the bovine variety of tubercle bacillus, most commonly infecting cattle and acquired by man usually by infected milk, more commonly found in children and producing a hilar pulmonary infection, or a tracheobronchial lymphatic or mesenteric lymphatic infection with tendency to generalization. Called also *M. tuberculosis* var. *bovis.* **M. intracellula′ris,** a group III anonymous mycobacterium associated with chronic pulmonary infection in man. **M. kansas′ii** [of Kansas], a photochromogenic species which is the etiological agent of a tuberculosis-like disease in man. **M. lep′rae,** a species found in enormous numbers in typical aggregates of parallel cells in nasal smears and other pathologic material from human leprosy; considered to be the etiological agent of leprosy, although it has not been cultivated in vitro nor has the disease been reproduced experimentally. **M. lep′rae mu′rium,** the causative agent of rat leprosy, which is transmissible by tissue transplant from rat to rat, but has not been cultivated in vitro; nonpathogenic for man. **M. lucifla′vum,** *M. kansasii.* **M. micro′ti,** an organism infecting voles but not rabbits or fowls; nonpathogenic for man, and used for the preparation of experimental vaccines. **M. paratuberculo′sis,** the causative agent of Johne's disease, a chronic enteritis of cattle; nonpathogenic

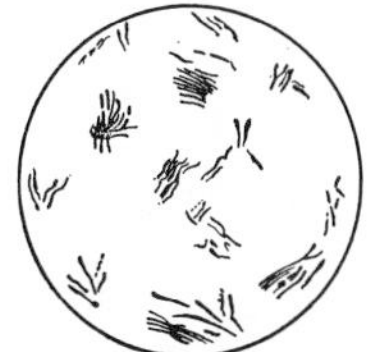

Mycobacterium leprae.

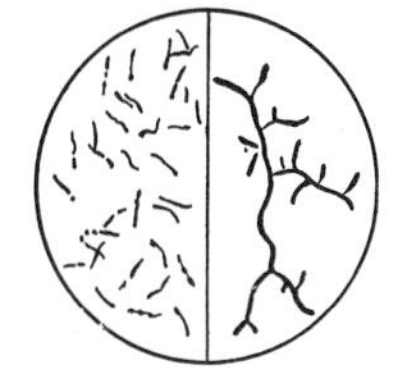

Mycobacterium tuberculosis.

for man. **M. phle′i,** a saprophytic form found on grasses and in soil and water. **M. scrofula′ceum,** an anonymous scotochromogenic mycobacterium, apparently nonpathogenic. **M. smeg′matis,** a parasitic but nonpathogenic mycobacterium found in human smegma. **M. tuberculo′sis,** the causative agent of tuberculosis, most commonly pulmonary, in man. Called also *M. tuberculosis* var. *hominis.* **M. tuberculo′sis** var. **a′vium.** See *M. avium.* **M. tuberculo′sis** var. **bo′vis.** See *M. bovis.* **M. tuberculo′sis** var. **hom′inis.** See *M. tuberculosis.*

mycobacterium (mi″ko-bak-te′re-um), pl. *mycobacte′ria.* 1. An organism of the genus Mycobacterium. 2. A slender, acid-fast microorganism resembling the bacillus which causes tuberculosis. **anonymous mycobacteria,** acid-fast bacteria resembling the tubercle bacilli, found in pulmonary infections, usually of a chronic nature, in man, for which species names have not been established. They are divided into the chromogens and nonchromogens, the former including photochromogens, which produce yellow pigment in the presence of light, and scotochromogens, which produce orange pigment independent of light. The nonchromogens are subdivided into filamentous forms and rapid growers (2–4 days).

Mycocandida (mi″ko-kan′dĭ-dah). Candida.

mycocidin (mi″ko-si′din). An antibiotic substance extracted from a mold (Aspergillaceae): active in vito against *Mycobacterium tuberculosis.*

Mycococcus (mi″ko-kok′kus). A genus of microorganisms of the family Mycobacteriaceae, order Actinomycetales, made up of non–acid-fast, gram-positive, saprophytic rod-shaped microorganisms producing pigments and resembling actinomyces in mode of reproduction; found in soil and water.

Mycoderma (mi″ko-der′mah) [*myco-* + Gr. *derma* skin]. A genus of fungi. **M. ace′ti.** See *Acetobacter.* **M. dermati′tis,** an organism causing a blastomycetic infection in man. **M. immi′te.** See *Coccidioides.*

mycoderma (mi″ko-der′mah) [Gr. *mykos* mucus + *derma* skin]. Mucous membrane.

mycodermatitis (mi″ko-der″mah-ti′tis). Inflammation of a mucous membrane.

mycodermomycosis (mi″ko-der″mo-mi-ko′sis). Moniliasis.

mycodesmoid (mi″ko-des′moid) [*myco-* + Gr. *desmē* bundle + *eidos* form]. A colony of *Micrococcus ascoformans* in the cut end of the spermatic cord after castration in horses.

mycofibroma (mi″ko-fi-bro′mah). Mycodesmoid.

mycogastritis (mi″ko-gas-tri′tis) [Gr. *mykos* mucus + *gastēr* stomach + *-itis*]. Inflammation of the mucous membrane of the stomach.

mycohemia (mi″ko-he′me-ah) [*myco-* + Gr. *haima* blood + *-ia*]. The presence of fungi in the blood.

mycologist (mi-kol′o-jist). A person learned in mycology; a student of mycology.

mycology (mi-kol′o-je) [*myco-* + *-logy*]. The science and study of fungi.

mycomyringitis (mi″ko-mir″in-ji′tis) [*myco-* + L. *myringa* membrana tympani + *-itis*]. Myringomycosis.

Myconostoc (mi″ko-nos′tok). A genus of microorganisms of the family Spirillaceae, suborder Pseudomonadineae, order Pseudomonadales, made up of curved cells occurring singly or in spiral or curved chains and in small gelatinous masses. The type species is *M. gregar′ium.*

myconucleo-albumin (mi″ko-nu″kle-o-al-bu′-min). An offensive and defensive toxin of microbic life.

mycopathology (mi″ko-pah-thol′o-je). The scientific study of the pathologic changes caused by fungi.

mycophage (mi′ko-fāj) [*myco-* + Gr. *phagein* to eat]. A virus which causes the lysis of molds.

mycophylaxin (mi″ko-fi-lak′sin) [*myco-* + *phylaxin*]. Any phylaxin that destroys microbes.

Mycoplana (mi″ko-pla′nah). A genus of microorganisms of the family Pseudomonadaceae, suborder Pseudomonadineae, order Pseudomonadales, occurring as branching cells in soil. It includes two species, *M. bulla′ta* and *M. dimor′pha.*

Mycoplasma (mi″ko-plaz′mah) [*myco-* + Gr. *plasma* anything formed or molded]. A taxonomic name given a genus including the pleuropneumonia-like organisms (PPLO) and separated into 15 species on the basis of source, glucose fermentation, and growth on agar media.

Mycoplasmataceae (mi″ko-plaz″mah-ta′se-e).

A family of Schizomycetes, order Mycoplasmatales, made up of a single genus, *Mycoplasma.*

Mycoplasmatales (mi″ko-plaz″mah-ta′les). An order of Schizomycetes, made up of highly pleomorphic organisms reproducing, according to some investigators, by breaking of the filaments into coccoid elementary bodies. It includes a single family, Mycoplasmataceae.

mycoprecipitin (mi″ko-pre-sip′ĭ-tin) [*myco-* + *precipitin*]. A precipitin which will precipitate extractives of yeast and fungi.

mycoprotein (mi″ko-pro′te-in) [*myco-* + *protein*]. The protein of bacterial cells. When set free in the tissues it may produce some of the effects of the bacteria themselves.

mycoproteination (mi″ko-pro″te-in-a′shun). Inoculation with dead bacterial cells.

mycoproteinization (mi″ko-pro″te-in-i-za′shun). Mycoproteination.

mycopus (mi′ko-pus). Mucus containing pus.

mycorrhiza (mi″ko-ri′zah) [*myco-* + Gr. *rhiza* root]. A peculiar mycelial growth seen on the roots of certain plants, and thought to be concerned with the fixation of nitrogen.

mycose (mi′kōs) [*myc-* + *-ose*]. A sugar from ergot and also from trehala manna, $C_{12}H_{22}O_{11} + 2H_2O$; trehalose.

mycosin (mi′ko-sin). A compound thought to exist in the cell wall of fungi.

mycosis (mi-ko′sis) [*myco-* + *-osis*]. Any disease caused by a fungus. **cutaneous m.,** dermatomycosis. **m. cu′tis chron′ica,** a chronic skin disease caused by a fungus. **m. favo′sa,** favus. **m. framboesioi′des,** yaws. **m. fungoi′des,** a rare chronic skin disease marked by the development upon the face, scalp, and chest of firm, reddish tumors that are painful and have a tendency to spread and ulcerate. The disease leads to cachexia, and usually ends fatally after continuing a number of years. Called also *granuloma fungoides, granuloma sarcomatodes, inflammatory fungoid neoplasm, eczema scrofuloderma,* and *ulcerative scrofuloderma.* **m. interdigita′lis,** dermatophytosis. **m. intestina′lis,** anthrax. **m. leptoth′rica,** a disease of the tonsil and pharynx produced by *Leptothrix buccalis.* **Posadas' m.,** coccidioidal granuloma. **splenic m.,** siderotic splenomegaly.

mycosozin (mi″ko-so′zin) [*myco-* + *sozin*]. Any sozin that destroys microbes.

mycostasis (mi-kos′tah-sis) [*myco-* + Gr. *stasis* stoppage]. Prevention of the growth or multiplication of fungi.

mycostat (mi′ko-stat). An agent which inhibits the growth of fungi.

mycosterol (mi-kos′ter-ol). Zymosterol.

mycotic (mi-kot′ik). Pertaining to a mycosis, or caused by vegetable microorganisms.

mycoticopeptic (mi-kot″ĭ-ko-pep′tik). Both mycotic and peptic.

Mycotoruloides (mi″ko-tor″u-loi′dēz). Candida.

mycotoxicosis (mi″ko-tok″sĭ-ko′sis). 1. Poisoning caused by a fungal or bacterial toxin. 2. Poisoning resulting from ingestion of fungi, such as that caused by the fungus *Claviceps purpurea* (ergot poisoning).

mycotoxin (mi″ko-tok′sin). A fungal or bacterial toxin.

mycotoxinization (mi″ko-tok″sin-i-za′shun). Inoculation with a fungal or bacterial toxin.

mycteric (mik-ter′ik) [Gr. *myktēr* nostril]. Pertaining to the nasal cavities.

mycteroxerosis (mik″ter-o-ze-ro′sis) [Gr. *myktēr* nostril + *xēros* dry]. Dryness of the nostrils.

mydaleine (mi-da′le-in) [Gr. *mydaleos* damp, mouldy]. A poisonous ptomaine from putrefied viscera. Poisoning by it is attended with salivation, dilatation of the pupils, rise of temperature followed by a fall, and arrest of the heart in diastole.

mydatoxine (mi″dah-tok′sin) [Gr. *mydan* to be damp + *toxin*]. A deadly ptomaine, $C_6H_{13}NO_2$, from decaying flesh; also obtained from human intestines kept for a long time at a low temperature.

mydine (mi′din) [Gr. *mydan* to be damp]. A nonpoisonous ptomaine, $C_9H_{11}NO_2$, from viscera of dead bodies, and found also in cultures of the typhoid bacillus.

mydriasis (mid-ri′ah-sis) [Gr.]. Extreme or morbid dilatation of the pupil; dilatation of the pupil as the effect of a drug. **alternating m.,** varying inequality of the pupils, mydriasis occurring first on one side, then on the other. Called also *springing m.* **bounding m.,** alternating mydriasis. **paralytic m.,** that caused by paralysis of the oculomotor nerve. **spasmodic m., spastic m.,** that due to spasm of the dilator of the iris or to overaction of the sympathetic. **spinal m.,** that due to lesion of the ciliospinal center of the spinal cord. **springing m.,** alternating m.

mydriatic (mid″re-at′ik). 1. Dilating the pupil. 2. Any drug that dilates the pupil.

myectomy (mi-ek′to-me) [*my-* + Gr. *ektomē* excision]. Excision of a portion of muscle.

myectopia (mi-ek-to′pe-ah) [Gr. *mys* muscle + *ektopos* displaced + *-ia*]. Displacement of a muscle.

myectopy (mi-ek′to-pe). Myectopia.

myel (mi′el) [Gr. *myelos* marrow]. The spinal cord.

myel-. See *myelo-*.

myelacephalus (mi″el-ah-sef′ah-lus) [*myel-* + *a* neg. + Gr. *kephalē* head]. The lowest grade of acephalous monster, being only slightly above a fetus amorphus.

myelalgia (mi″ĕ-lal′je-ah) [*myel-* + *-algia*]. Pain in the spinal cord.

myelanalosis (mi″el-an″ah-lo′sis) [*myel-* + Gr. *analiskein* to spend, waste + *-osis*]. Wasting of the spinal marrow; tabes dorsalis.

myelapoplexy (mi″el-ap′o-plek-se) [*myel-* + *apoplexy*]. Hemorrhage within the spinal cord.

myelasthenia (mi″el-as-the′ne-ah) [*myel-* + *asthenia*]. Neurasthenia due to some cause which affects the spinal cord.

myelatelia (mi″el-ah-te′le-ah) [*myel-* + Gr. *ateleia* imperfection]. Imperfect development of the spinal cord.

myelatrophy (mi″el-at′ro-fe) [*myel-* + *atrophy*]. Atrophy of the spinal cord.

myelauxe (mi″el-awks′e) [*myel-* + Gr. *auxē* increase]. Morbid increase in size of the spinal cord.

myelemia (mi″ĕ-le′me-ah) [*myel-* + Gr. *haima* blood + *-ia*]. The occurrence of myelocytes or neutrophil leukocytes in the blood; myeloid leukemia, splenomedullary leukemia.

myelencephalitis (mi″ĕ-len-sef″ah-li′tis). Inflammation of the brain and spinal cord.

myelencephalon (mi″ĕ-len-sef′ah-lon) [*myel-* + Gr. *enkephalos* brain]. 1. [N A, B N A] The portion of the central nervous system developed from the posterior part of the rhombencephalon, including the medulla oblongata and the lower part of the fourth ventricle. 2. The posterior of the two brain vesicles formed by specialization of the rhombencephalon in the developing embryo.

myelencephalospinal (mi″ĕ-len-sef″ah-lo-spi′nal). Pertaining to the myelencephalon and spinal cord.

myelencephalous (mi″ĕ-len-sef′ah-lus). Cerebrospinal.

myeleterosis (mi″ĕ-let″er-o′sis) [*myel-* + Gr. *heterōsis* alteration]. Morbid alteration of the spinal cord.

myelic (mi-el′ik) [Gr. *myelos* marrow]. Pertaining to the spinal cord.

myelin (mi′ĕ-lin) [Gr. *myelos* marrow]. 1. The fatlike substance forming a sheath around certain nerve fibers. See *myelin sheath,* under *sheath.* 2.

Any one of a certain group of lipoid substances found in various normal and pathologic tissues and differing from fats in being doubly refractive. 3. A monoaminomonophosphatide found in small quantities in the brain.

myelinated (mi′ĕ-lĭ-nāt″ed). Medullated.

myelination (mi″ĕ-lĭ-na′shun). Myelinization.

myelinic (mi″ĕ-lin′ik). Pertaining to, or of the nature of, myelin.

myelinization (mi″e-lĭ-ni-za′shun). The act of furnishing with or taking on myelin.

myelinoclasis (mi″ĕ-lin-ok′lah-sis) [*myelin* + Gr. *klasis* a breaking]. Destruction of myelin; demyelination. **acute perivascular m.,** postinfection encephalitis.

myelinogenesis (mi″ĕ-lin″o-jen′e-sis). Myelinization.

myelinogenetic (mi″ĕ-lin″o-je-net′ik). Producing myelin; producing myelinization.

myelinogeny (mi″ĕ-lĭ-noj′e-ne) [*myelin* + Gr. *gennan* to produce]. The development of the myelin of nerve fibers; the myelinization of nerve fibers.

myelinolysin (mi″ĕ-lĭ-nol′ĭ-sin) [*myelin* + *lysin*]. A substance in the serum of patients with multiple sclerosis which destroys myelin.

myelinoma (mi″ĕ-lĭ-no′mah). A tumor of the myelin.

myelinopathy (mi″ĕ-lĭ-nop′ah-the). Any disease of the myelin; degeneration of the white matter of the brain.

myelinosis (mi″ĕ-lĭ-no′sis). A form of fatty necrosis in which myelin is formed.

myelitic (mi″ĕ-lit′ik). Pertaining to myelitis.

myelitis (mi″ĕ-li′tis) [Gr. *myelos* marrow + *-itis*]. 1. Inflammation of the bone marrow. See *osteomyelitis*. 2. Inflammation of the spinal cord. See *leukomyelitis*, *poliomyelitis*. The symptoms of myelitis vary with the location of the lesion, and include pain in the back, girdle sensation, hyperesthesia, formication, anesthesia, motor disturbances, paralysis, increase of the reflexes, paralysis of the sphincters, decubitus ulcers, and, in later stages, spasmodic contractions of the paralyzed limbs. **acute m.,** simple myelitis due to exposure, disease, or injury. **apoplectiform m.,** myelitis in which the paralysis comes on suddenly. **ascending m.,** a myelitis that progresses cephalad along the cord. **bulbar m.,** that which involves the oblongata. **cavitary m.,** that which is accompanied by the formation of cavities. **central m.,** inflammation affecting chiefly the gray substance of the cord. **m. cervica′lis,** myelitis affecting the cervical portion of the cord, and marked by muscular atrophy of the arms and spastic paralysis of the legs. **chronic m.,** a slowly progressing form. **compression m.,** a form due to pressure on the cord, as of a tumor. **concussion m.,** a form due to spinal concussion. **cornual m.,** that which affects the horns of gray matter in the cord. **descending m.,** a myelitis that progresses caudad along the cord. **diffuse m.,** inflammation involving large and variously placed sections of the cord. **disseminated m.,** a form with several distinct foci. **focal m.,** myelitis affecting a small area only, or several small areas. **foudroyant m.,** central m. **funicular m.,** myelitis involving the white matter, especially the posterior funiculus; it is characteristic of pernicious anemia. **hemorrhagic m.,** a form associated with hemorrhage. **interstitial m.,** sclerosing m. **neuro-optic m.,** a combined inflammation of the optic nerve and the spinal cord: it is marked by diminution of vision and possibly blindness, flaccid paralysis of the extremities and by sensory and genito-urinary disturbances. Called also *ophthalmoneuromyelitis*. **parenchymatous m.,** a variety in which mainly the proper nerve substance of the myelon is affected. **periependymal m.,** myelitis surrounding the central canal of the cord. **sclerosing m.,** a form characterized by hardening of the cord and overgrowth of the interstitial tissue. Called also *interstitial m.* **systemic m.,** myelitis which affects distinct tracts or systems in the cord. **transverse m.,** a form which extends across the cord. **traumatic m.,** myelitis which follows injury to the cord. **m. vaccin′ia,** myelitis which sometimes follows vaccination.

myelo-, myel- [Gr. *myelos* marrow]. Combining form denoting relationship to marrow, often used in specific reference to the spinal cord.

myeloarchitecture (mi″ĕ-lo-ar′kĭ-tek″tūr). The organization of the nerve tracts in the spinal cord.

myeloblast (mi′ĕ-lo-blast) [*myelo-* + Gr. *blastos* germ]. 1. One of the large mononuclear nongranular cells of bone marrow which develop into myelocytes, and also into erythroblasts, according to some hematologists. 2. One of the cells of the myotome which give rise to muscle tissue.

myeloblastemia (mi″ĕ-lo-blas-te′me-ah) [*myeloblast* + Gr. *haima* blood + *-ia*]. Presence of myeloblasts in the blood.

myeloblastoma (mi″ĕ-lo-blas-to′mah) [*myeloblast* + *-oma*]. A focal malignant tumor, observed in chronic or acute myelogenous leukemia, composed of myeloblasts and lacking green coloration.

myeloblastomatosis (mi″ĕ-lo-blas″to-mah-to′sis). The presence of multiple myeloblastomas.

myeloblastosis (mi″ĕ-lo-blas-to′sis). The presence of an excess of myeloblasts in the blood.

myelobrachium (mi″ĕ-lo-bra′ke-um) [*myelo-* + Gr. *brachiōn* arm]. The inferior tubercle of the cerebellum.

myelocele (mi′ĕ-lo-sēl) [*myelo-* + Gr. *kēlē* hernia]. Hernial protrusion of the substance of the spinal cord through a defect in the bony spinal canal.

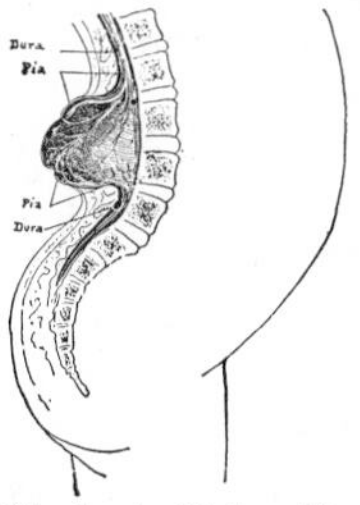

Myelocele (Babcock).

myeloclast (mi′ĕ-lo-klast) [*myelo-* + Gr. *klan* to break]. A cell which splits up myelin sheaths.

myelocoele (mi-el′o-sēl) [*myelo-* + Gr. *koilia* cavity]. The central canal of the spinal cord.

myelocone (mi′ĕ-lo-kōn) [*myelo-* + Gr. *konis* dust]. A fatty matter from the brain.

myelocyst (mi′ĕ-lo-sist) [*myelo-* + *cyst*]. Cysts that are developed from rudimentary medullary canals.

myelocystic (mi″ĕ-lo-sis′tik). Both myeloid and cystic in structure.

myelocystocele (mi″ĕ-lo-sis′to-sēl) [*myelo-* + Gr. *kēlē* hernia]. A cystic protrusion of the substance of the spinal cord through a defect in the bony canal.

myelocystomeningocele (mi″ĕ-lo-sis″to-mening′go-sēl). A cystic protrusion of the substance of the spinal cord, with its meninges, through a defect in the bony spinal canal.

myelocyte (mi′ĕ-lo-sit) [*myelo-* + *-cyte*]. 1. A marrow cell; one of the typical cells of red bone marrow. They are slightly larger than leukocytes, having vesicular nuclei and a cytoplasm containing neutrophil, eosinophil, or basophil granules. From them are developed the granular leukocytes of the blood. Myelocytes occur in the blood in certain forms of leukemia. Myelocytes are divided into three groups, A, B, and C, according to their age and the number of granules in their cytoplasm. Group A is the youngest and has the fewest granules. 2. Any cell of the gray matter of the nervous system.

myelocythemia (mi″ĕ-lo-si-the′me-ah) [*myelocyte* + Gr. *haima* blood + *-ia*]. Excess of myelocytes in the blood.

myelocytic (mi″ĕ-lo-sit′ik). Relating to or of the nature of myelocytes.

myelocytoma (mi″ĕ-lo-si-to′mah). Chronic myelocytic leukemia; myeloma.

myelocytomatosis (mi″ĕ-lo-si″to-mah-to′sis). 1. A form of leukosis in which the myelocytes are chiefly involved. 2. A disease of fowl marked by the presence of tumors composed of myeloid cells. There may also be an increase of immature myeloid cells in the circulating blood.

myelocytosis (mi″ĕ-lo-si-to′sis). The presence of an excessive number of myelocytes in the blood.

myelodiastasis (mi″ĕ-lo-di-as′tah-sis) [*myelo-* + Gr. *diastasis* separation]. Disintegration of the spinal marrow.

myelodysplasia (mi″ĕ-lo-dis-pla′se-ah) [*myelo-* + *dys-* + Gr. *plassein* to form]. Defective development of any part (especially the lower segments) of the spinal cord (Fuchs, 1909).

myelo-encephalic (mi″ĕ-lo-en″se-fal′ik). Pertaining to the spinal cord and the brain.

myelo-encephalitis (mi″ĕ-lo-en-sef″ah-li′tis) [*myelo-* + Gr. *enkephalos* brain + *-itis*]. Inflammation of the spinal cord and brain. **epidemic m.,** acute anterior poliomyelitis. See *poliomyelitis*.

myelofibrosis (mi″ĕ-lo-fi-bro′sis). Replacement of the bone marrow by fibrous tissue, occurring in association with a myeloproliferative disorder or secondary to another, unrelated condition. **osteosclerosis m.,** myelosclerosis, def. 2.

myelofugal (mi″ĕ-lof′u-gal) [*myelo-* + L. *fugare* to flee]. Moving away from the spinal cord.

myeloganglitis (mi″ĕ-lo-gang-gli′tis). A disease with choleraic symptoms attributed to ganglitis of the solar and the hepatic plexus.

myelogenesis (mi″ĕ-lo-jen′e-sis). 1. The development of the nervous system, especially of the brain and cord. 2. The deposition of myelin around the axon.

myelogenic (mi″ĕ-lo-jen′ik). Myelogenous.

myelogenous (mi″ĕ-loj′e-nus) [*myelo-* + Gr. *gennan* to produce]. Produced in the bone marrow.

myelogeny (mi″ĕ-loj′e-ne). The maturation of the myelin sheaths of nerve fibers in the development of the central nervous system.

myelogone (mi′ĕ-lo-gōn). A white blood cell of the myeloid series having a reticulate violaceous nucleus, well-stained nucleolus, and a deep blue rim of cytoplasm.

myelogonic (mi″ĕ-lo-go′nik). Characterized by the presence of myelogones.

myelogonium (mi″ĕ-lo-go′ne-um). Myelogone.

myelogram (mi′ĕ-lo-gram). 1. A roentgenogram of the spinal cord. 2. A graphic representation of the differential count of cells found in a stained preparation of bone marrow.

myelography (mi″ĕ-log′rah-fe) [*myelo-* + Gr. *graphein* to write]. Roentgenography of the spinal cord after injection of a contrast medium. **oxygen m.,** myelography in which oxygen is used as the contrast medium.

myeloid (mi′ĕ-loid) [*myelo-* + Gr. *eidos* form]. 1. Pertaining to, derived from, or resembling bone marrow. 2. Pertaining to the spinal cord. 3. Having the appearance of myelocytes, but not derived from bone marrow.

myeloidin (mi″ĕ-loi′din) [*myelin* + Gr. *eidos* form]. A substance resembling myelin, occurring in the pigmented cells of the retina.

myeloidosis (mi″ĕ-loi-do′sis). The development of myeloid tissue, especially hyperplastic development of such tissue.

myelokentric (mi″ĕ-lo-ken′trik) [*myeloid* + Gr. *kentron* stimulus]. Stimulating the formation of myeloid cells. Cf. *lymphokentric*.

myelolymphangioma (mi″ĕ-lo-lim-fan″je-o′mah). Elephantiasis.

myelolysis (mi″ĕ-lol′ĭ-sis) [*myelin* + Gr. *lysis* dissolution]. The dissolution of myelin.

myelolytic (mi″ĕ-lo-lit′ik). Pertaining to, characterized by, or causing myelolysis.

myeloma (mi″ĕ-lo′mah) [*myelo-* + *-oma*]. 1. A tumor composed of cells of the type normally found in the bone marrow. 2. Any medullary tumor. 3. Giant cell sarcoma. 4. A slow-growing tumor of a tendinous sheath containing myeloplaxes. **giant cell m.,** a tumor of bone marrow containing many giant cells. **multiple m.,** a primary malignant tumor of bone marrow, marked by circumscribed or diffuse tumor-like hyperplasia of the bone marrow, and usually associated with anemia and with Bence Jones protein in the urine. The patient complains of neuralgic pains; later painful swellings appear on the ribs and skull and spontaneous fractures may occur. Called also *Kahler's disease, Huppert's disease, myelopathic albumosuria, Bence Jones albumosuria,* and *lymphadenia ossea*.

myelomalacia (mi″ĕ-lo-mah-la′she-ah) [*myelo-* + Gr. *malakia* softening]. Morbid softening of the spinal cord.

myelomatoid (mi″ĕ-lo′mah-toid). Resembling myeloma.

myelomatosis (mi″ĕ-lo-mah-to′sis). 1. The simultaneous presence of numerous myelomas. 2. Any leukemic disease in which myeloblasts are abundant in the blood.

myelomenia (mi″ĕ-lo-me′ne-ah) [*myelo-* + Gr. *mēn* month]. Menstrual hemorrhage into the spinal cord.

myelomeningitis (mi″ĕ-lo-men″in-ji′tis) [*myelo-* + *meningitis*]. Inflammation of the spinal cord and its membranes.

myelomeningocele (mi″ĕ-lo-me-ning′go-sēl) [*myelo-* + *meningocele*]. Hernial protrusion of the cord and its meninges through a defect in the vertebral canal.

myelomere (mi′ĕ-lo-mēr) [*myelo-* + Gr. *meros* part]. One of the segments, corresponding to a pair of mesoblastic somites, in the brain and spinal cord of the embryo.

myelomonocyte (mi″ĕ-lo-mon′o-sīt). A monocyte that arises from bone marrow.

myelomyces (mi″ĕ-lom′ĭ-sēz) [*myelo-* + Gr. *mykēs* fungus]. Encephaloid cancer.

myelon (mi′ĕ-lon) [Gr. *myelos* marrow]. The spinal cord.

myeloneuritis (mi″ĕ-lo-nu-ri′tis). Inflammation of both spinal cord and peripheral nerves.

myelonic (mi″ĕ-lon′ik). Pertaining to the myelon.

myeloparalysis (mi″ĕ-lo-pah-ral′ĭ-sis) [*myelo-* + *paralysis*]. Spinal paralysis.

myelopathic (mi″ĕ-lo-path′ik). Pertaining to or characterized by myelopathy.

myelopathy (mi″ĕ-lop′ah-the) [*myelo-* + Gr. *pathos* disease]. A general term denoting functional disturbances and/or pathological changes in the brain. The term is often used to designate nonspecific lesions, in contrast to inflammatory lesions (myelitis).

myelopetal (mi″ĕ-lop′ĕ-tal) [*myelo-* + L. *petere* to seek for]. Moving toward the spinal cord.

myelophage (mi′ĕ-lo-fāj) [*myelo-* + Gr. *phagein* to eat]. A macrophage which digests or breaks down myelin.

myelophthisis (mi″ĕ-lof′thĭ-sis) [*myelo-* + Gr. *phthisis* wasting]. 1. Wasting of the spinal cord. 2. Reduction of the cell-forming functions of the bone marrow. See *aleukia haemorrhagica*.

myeloplaque (mi-el′o-plak). Myeloplax.

myeloplast (mi′ĕ-lo-plast) [*myelo-* + Gr. *plastos* formed]. Any leukocyte of the bone marrow.

myeloplax (mi-el′o-plaks) [*myelo-* + Gr. *plax* plate]. Any multinuclear giant cell of the bone marrow. **Robin's m's,** osteoclasts.

myeloplaxoma (mi″ĕ-lo-plak-so′mah) [*myeloplax* + *-oma*]. A tumor containing myeloplaxes.

myeloplegia (mi″ĕ-lo-ple′je-ah) [*myelo-* + Gr. *plēgē* stroke]. Spinal paralysis.

myelopoiesis (mi″ĕ-lo-poi-e′sis) [*myelo-* + Gr. *poiein* to form]. The formation of bone marrow or the cells that arise from it. **ectopic m., extramedullary m.,** the formation of myeloid tissue in unusual situations.

myelopore (mi′ĕ-lo-pōr) [*myelo-* + Gr. *poros* opening]. A canal or opening in the spinal cord.

myeloproliferative (mi″ĕ-lo-pro-lif″er-a′tiv). Pertaining to or characterized by medullary and extramedullary proliferation of bone marrow constituents. See *myeloproliferative syndrome.*

myeloradiculitis (mi″ĕ-lo-rah-dik″u-li′tis) [*myelo-* + L. *radiculus* rootlet + *-itis*]. Inflammation of the spinal cord and the posterior nerve roots.

myeloradiculodysplasia (mi″ĕ-lo-rah-dik″u-lo-dis-pla′ze-ah). Developmental abnormality of the spinal cord and spinal nerve roots.

myeloradiculopathy (mi″ĕ-lo-rah-dik″u-lop′-ah-the). Disease of the spinal cord and spinal nerve roots.

myelorrhagia (mi″ĕ-lo-ra′je-ah) [*myelo-* + Gr. *rhēgnynai* to burst forth]. Spinal hemorrhage.

myelorrhaphy (mi″ĕ-lor′ah-fe) [*myelo-* + Gr. *rhaphē* suture]. Suturation of a severed spinal cord.

myelosarcoma (mi″ĕ-lo-sar-ko′mah). A sarcomatous growth made up of myeloid tissue or bone marrow cells.

myelosarcomatosis (mi″ĕ-lo-sar-ko″mah-to′-sis). Multiple myelosarcoma throughout the body.

myeloschisis (mi″ĕ-los′kĭ-sis) [*myelo-* + Gr. *schisis* cleft]. A developmental anomaly characterized by a cleft spinal cord, owing to failure of the neural plate to form a complete tube.

myelosclerosis (mi″ĕ-lo-skle-ro′sis). 1. Sclerosis of the spinal cord. 2. A condition characterized by obliteration of the normal marrow cavity by the formation of small spicules of bone, the pathogenesis possibly being similar to that of myelofibrosis. Called also *osteosclerosis myelofibrosis.* 3. Myelofibrosis.

myelosis (mi″ĕ-lo′sis). 1. The proliferation of marrow tissue which produces the blood changes of myeloid leukemia; myelocytosis. 2. The formation of a tumor of the spinal cord. 3. Multiple myeloma. **aleukemic m.,** myelosis with low total white count and a normal differential count. **chronic nonleukemic m.,** a condition of hyperplasia of the leukopoietic tissues of the body, which results in no increase in the white cell count, but in the appearance of immature white cells in the peripheral blood. **erythremic m.,** a condition characterized by overgrowth of erythroid and reticuloendothelial cells in bone marrow, with severe, rapidly developing anemia, enlargement of liver and spleen, weakness, fever, and gradual weight loss. **funicular m.,** myelosis marked by degenerative foci in the white substance of the spinal cord. **leukemic m.,** myelosis with a high total white count and with many immature forms. **nonleukemic m.,** aleukemic m. **subleukemic m.,** myelosis with a low total white count and many immature forms.

myelospasm (mi′ĕ-lo-spazm) [*myelo-* + *spasm*]. Spasm of the spinal cord.

myelospongium (mi″ĕ-lo-spon′je-um) [*myelo-* + Gr. *spongos* sponge]. The network from which the neuroglia tissue is developed: it pervades the embryonic neural tube, and is composed of the spongioblasts and their branching processes.

myelosyphilis (mi″ĕ-lo-sif′ĭ-lis). Syphilis of the spinal cord.

myelosyphilosis (mi″ĕ-lo-sif″ĭ-lo′sis). Any syphilitic affection of the spinal cord.

myelosyringosis (mi″ĕ-lo-sir″ing-go′sis) [*myelo-* + Gr. *syrinx* pipe]. Syringomyelia.

myelotherapy (mi″ĕ-lo-ther′ah-pe) [*myelo-* + *therapy*]. The therapeutic use of marrow, or of the substance of the spinal cord.

myelotome (mi-el′o-tōm) [*myelo-* + Gr. *tomē* a cut]. 1. An instrument for making sections of the spinal cord. 2. An instrument used for cutting the spinal cord squarely across in removing the brain in postmortem examinations.

myelotomy (mi″ĕ-lot′o-me). The operation of severing nerve fibers in the spinal cord. **commissural m.,** longitudinal division of the spinal cord, to sever crossing sensory fibers and produce localized analgesia.

myelotoxic (mi″ĕ-lo-tok′sik) [*myelo-* + Gr. *toxikon* poison]. 1. Destructive to bone marrow. 2. Arising from diseased bone marrow.

myelotoxicity (mi″ĕ-lo-toks-is′ĭ-te). The quality of being myelotoxic.

myelotoxicosis (mi″ĕ-lo-tok″sĭ-ko′sis). Disease of the bone marrow caused by a chronic intoxication.

myelotoxin (mi″ĕ-lo-tok′sin). A cytotoxin which causes destruction of the marrow cells.

myenteric (mi″en-ter′ik). Pertaining to the myenteron.

myenteron (mi-en′ter-on) [*my-* + Gr. *enteron* intestine]. The muscular coat of the intestine.

myesthesia (mi″es-the′ze-ah) [*my-* + Gr. *aisthēsis* perception]. Muscle sensibility; sensibility to impressions coming from the muscles.

myiasis (mi′yah-sis) [Gr. *myia* fly + *-iasis*]. A condition caused by infestation of the body by flies. **creeping m.,** larva migrans. **m. dermato′sa,** infection of the skin with the larvae of flies. **m. imagino′sa,** myiasis produced by the imago, or full-grown fly. **intestinal m.,** the presence of living fly larvae in the intestines. **m. larvo′sa,** myiasis produced by larvae or maggots. **m. linea′ris,** larva migrans. **m. musco′sa,** a myiasis produced by the common housefly. **m. oestruo′sa,** one produced by a bot fly or gad fly (*Oestrus*). **traumatic m.,** maggot infestation of wounds or ulcers.

myiocephalon (mi″yo-sef′ah-lon) [Gr. *myia* fly + *kephalē* head]. Projection of the iris through a rent in the cornea.

myiocephalum (mi″yo-sef′ah-lum). Myiocephalon.

myiodesopsia (mi″yo-des-op′se-ah) [Gr. *myiōdes* flylike + *opsis* vision + *-ia*]. The appearance of muscae volitantes.

myiosis (mi-yo′sis). Myiasis.

myitis (mi-i′tis) [*my-* + *-itis*]. Inflammation of a muscle; myositis.

myko-. For words beginning thus, see also those beginning *myco-*.

mykol (mi′kol). An alcohol existing in the bodies of certain bacteria.

myleran (mil′er-an). Trade mark for a preparation of busulfan.

mylohyoid (mi″lo-hi′oid) [Gr. *mylē* mill + *hyoid*]. Pertaining to the molar teeth and hyoid bone.

myo-, my- [Gr. *mys* muscle]. Combining form denoting relationship to muscle.

myo-albumin (mi″o-al-bu′min). An albumin constituting about one per cent of the protein of muscle.

myo-albumose (mi″o-al′bu-mōs). A protein from muscle juice.

myo-architectonic (mi″o-ar″ke-tek-ton′ik) [*myo-* + *architectonic*]. Pertaining to the structure of muscle.

myo-asthenia (mi″o-as-the′ne-ah). Amyosthenia.

myo-atrophy (mi″o-at′ro-fe). Myatrophy.

myoblast (mi′o-blast) [*myo-* + Gr. *blastos* germ]. An embryonic cell which becomes a cell of the muscle fiber.

myoblastic (mi″o-blas′tik). Pertaining to a myoblast.

myoblastoma (mi″o-blas-to′mah). A tumor of striated muscle made up of groups of cells which resemble primitive myoblasts. Called also *myoblastic myoma, myoblastomyoma* and *Abrikossoff's* (*Abrikossov's*) *tumor.*

myoblastomyoma (mi″o-blas″to-mi-o′mah). Myoblastoma.

myobradia (mi″o-bra′de-ah) [*myo-* + Gr. *bradys* slow + *-ia*]. A slow, sluggish reaction of muscle to electric stimulation.

myocardia (mi″o-kar′de-ah) [*myo-* + Gr. *kardia* heart]. Noninflammatory myocardial disease; primary cardiac insufficiency.

myocardiac (mi″o-kar′de-ak). 1. Pertaining to myocardia. 2. Myocardial.

myocardial (mi″o-kar′de-al). Pertaining to the muscular tissue of the heart.

myocardiogram (mi″o-kar′de-o-gram). A tracing made by the myocardiograph.

myocardiograph (mi″o-kar′de-o-graf) [*myo-* + Gr. *kardia* heart + *graphein* to record]. An instrument for making a tracing of the movements of the heart muscles.

myocardiorrhaphy (mi″o-kar″de-or′ah-fe). Suture of wounds of the myocardium.

myocardiosis (mi″o-kar″de-o′sis). Myocardosis.

myocardism (mi″o-kar′dizm). A tendency toward the development of myocardial weakness and degeneration.

myocarditic (mi″o-kar-dit′ik). Pertaining to myocarditis.

myocarditis (mi″o-kar-di′tis) [*myo-* + Gr. *kardia* heart + *-itis*]. Inflammation of the myocardium; inflammation of the muscular walls of the heart. **acute bacterial m.,** acute myocarditis due to bacterial infection. **acute isolated m.,** acute myocarditis due to unknown cause. **chronic m.,** a loose term for any chronic myocardial condition. **fibrous m.,** interstitial m. **Fiedler's m.,** acute isolated myocarditis due to unknown cause. **fragmentation m.,** fragmentation of the myocardium. **idiopathic m.,** Fiedler's m. **indurative m.,** myocarditis causing hardening of the heart muscle. **interstitial m.,** myocarditis affecting chiefly the interstitial fibrous tissue. **parenchymatous m.,** myocarditis affecting chiefly the muscle substance itself. **m. scarlatino′sa,** myocarditis sometimes seen associated with scarlet fever. **toxic m.,** myocarditis due to poisoning by drug or to toxins of infecting organisms reaching the heart through the blood stream.

myocardium (mi″o-kar′de-um) [*myo-* + Gr. *kardia* heart]. [N A, B N A] The middle and thickest layer of the heart wall, composed of cardiac muscle.

myocardosis (mi″o-kar-do′sis). A general term for myocardial disorders which are not inflammatory conditions of the myocardium, but result from hypertension, coronary sclerosis and hyperthyroidism. **Riesman's m.,** degenerative (noninflammatory) fibrotic myocardial disease.

myocele (mi′o-sēl) [*myo-* + Gr. *kēlē* hernia]. Hernia of muscle; protrusion of a muscle through its ruptured sheath.

myocelialgia (mi″o-se″le-al′je-ah) [*myo-* + Gr. *koilia* belly + *-algia*]. Pain in the abdominal muscles.

myocelitis (mi″o-se-li′tis) [*myo-* + Gr. *koilia* belly + *-itis*]. Inflammation of the muscles of the abdomen.

myocellulitis (mi″o-sel″u-li′tis). Myositis conjoined with cellulitis.

myoceptor (mi′o-sep″tor) [*myo-* + L. *capere* to take]. The structure in a muscle fiber that receives the nerve stimulus from the motor end-organ of the nerve.

myocerosis (mi″o-se-ro′sis) [*myo-* + Gr. *kēros* wax]. Waxy degeneration of muscle. **m. angiot′ica haemorrhag′ica,** angiohyalinosis haemorrhagica.

myochorditis (mi″o-kor-di′tis) [*myo-* + Gr. *chordē* cord + *-itis*]. Inflammation of the muscles of the vocal cords.

myochrome (mi′o-krōm) [*myo-* + Gr. *chrōma* color]. Any member of a group of muscle pigments. See *histohematin* and *myohematin.*

myochronoscope (mi″o-kron′o-skōp) [*myo-* + Gr. *chronos* time + *skopein* to examine]. A device for measuring the time required for a motor impulse to become effective.

myochrysine (mi″o-kri′sin). Trade mark for a preparation of gold sodium thiomalate.

myocinesimeter (mi″o-sin″e-sim′e-ter). Myokinesimeter.

myoclonia (mi″o-klo′ne-ah). Any disorder which is characterized by myoclonus. **m. epilep′tica,** myoclonus epilepsy. **m. fibrilla′ris mul′tiplex,** myokymia. **fibrillary m.,** the twitching of the fibrils of a muscle. See *fibrillation.* **infectious m.,** chorea. **pseudoglottic m.,** hiccup.

myoclonic (mi″o-klon′ik). Relating to or marked by myoclonus.

myoclonus (mi-ok′lo-nus) [*myo-* + Gr. *klonos* turmoil]. Shocklike contractions of a portion of a muscle, an entire muscle, or a group of muscles, restricted to one area of the body or appearing synchronously or asynchronously in several areas. **m. mul′tiplex,** paramyoclonus multiplex. **palatal m.,** a condition characterized by a rapid rhythmic, up-and-down movement of one side of the palate, sometimes accompanied by ipsilateral synchronous clonic movements of muscles of the face, tongue, pharynx, and diaphragm. Called also *palatal nystagmus.*

myocoele (mi′o-sēl) [*myo-* + Gr. *koilia* cavity]. The cavity within a myotome.

myocolpitis (mi″o-kol-pi′tis) [*myo-* + Gr. *kolpos* vagina + *-itis*]. Inflammation of the muscular layers of the vaginal wall.

myocomma (mi″o-kom′ah) [*myo-* + Gr. *komma* cut]. 1. A myotome or muscle segment, as in a fish. 2. The septum between two adjacent myotomes.

myocrismus (mi″o-kris′mus) [*myo-* + Gr. *krizein* to creak]. A sound heard on auscultation over a contracting muscle.

myoctonine (mi-ok′to-nin) [*myo-* + Gr. *kteinein* to kill]. A poisonous alkaloid, $C_{36}H_{42}N_2O_{10}$, from *Aconitum lycoctonum.*

myoculator (mi-ok′u-la″tor) [*myo-* + L. *oculus* eye]. An instrument, on the principle of the orthoptoscope, which allows fusion and movement laterally, vertically, and in rotation.

myocyte (mi′o-sīt) [*myo-* + *-cyte*]. 1. A cell of the muscular tissue. 2. The inner contractile layer of the ectoplasm of a protozoon. **Anitschkow's m.,** a cardiac histiocyte found in Aschoff's nodules, having a serrated bar of chromatin in its nucleus.

myocytoma (mi″o-si-to′mah). A tumor made up of myocytes or muscle cells.

myodegeneration (mi″o-de-jen″er-a′shun) [*myo-* + *degeneration*]. Degeneration of muscle.

myodemia (mi″o-de′me-ah) [*myo-* + Gr. *dēmos* fat]. Fatty degeneration of muscle.

myodesopsia (mi″o-des-op′se-ah). Myiodesopsia.

myodiastasis (mi″o-di-as′tah-sis) [*myo-* + Gr. *diastasis* separation]. Separation of a muscle.

myodiopter (mi″o-di-op′ter). The force of ciliary muscle contraction necessary to raise the refraction of the emmetropic eye by 1 diopter from a state of rest.

myodynamic (mi″o-di-nam′ik). Relating to muscular force.

myodynamics (mi″o-di-nam′iks). The physiology of muscular action.

myodynamometer (mi″o-di″nah-mom′e-ter) [*myo-* + Gr. *dynamis* power + *metron* measure]. A device for testing the power of the muscles.

myodynia (mi″o-din′e-ah) [*myo-* + Gr. *odynē* pain]. Pains in a muscle; myalgia. **hysterical m.,** muscular pain or tenderness, generally in the ovarian region, in hysteria.

myodystonia (mi″o-dis-to′ne-ah) [*myo-* + *dys-* + Gr. *tonos* tension + *-ia*]. Disorder of muscular tone.

myodystony (mi″o-dis′to-ne). Myodystonia.

myodystrophia (mi″o-dis-tro′fe-ah). Muscular dystrophy; myotonia atrophica.

myodystrophy (mi″o-dis′tro-fe). Myodystrophia.

myo-edema (mi″o-e-de′mah) [*myo-* + Gr. *oidēma* swelling]. 1. Edema of a muscle. 2. Mounding.

myo-elastic (mi″o-e-las′tik). Composed of elastic fibers associated with smooth muscle cells.

myo-electric (mi″o-e-lek′trik). Pertaining to the electric or electromotive properties of muscle.

myo-endocarditis (mi″o-en″do-kar-di′tis). Combined myocarditis and endocarditis.

myo-epithelial (mi″o-ep″ĭ-the′le-al). Pertaining to or composed of myo-epithelium.

myo-epithelium (mi″o-ep″ĭ-the′le-um) [*myo-* + *epithelium*]. Tissue made up of contractile epithelial cells.

myofascitis (mi″o-fas-i′tis) [*myo-* + *fascitis*]. Inflammation of a muscle and its fascia, particularly of the fascial insertion of muscle to bone.

myofibril (mi″o-fi′bril). A muscle fibril; especially one of the slender threads which can be rendered visible in a muscle fiber by maceration in certain acids. They run parallel with the long axis of the fiber, and presumably represent the contractile elements.

myofibrilla (mi″o-fi-bril′ah), pl. *myofibril′lae*. A myofibril.

myofibrillae (mi″o-fi-bril′e). Plural of *myofibrilla*.

myofibroma (mi″o-fi-bro′mah). A tumor containing both muscular and fibrous elements; a fibroma containing muscular elements.

myofibrosis (mi″o-fi-bro′sis) [*myo-* + L. *fibra* fiber]. Replacement of muscle tissue by fibrous tissue. **m. cor′dis,** myofibrosis of the heart.

myofibrositis (mi″o-fi″bro-si′tis). Inflammation of the perimysium.

myofunctional (mi″o-funk′shun-al). Pertaining to muscular function: a term applied to a method of treating malocclusion by restoring to normal the action of muscle groups related to facial development.

myogelosis (mi″o-je-lo′sis) [*myo-* + L. *gelare* to freeze]. An area of hardening in a muscle, especially in the gluteus muscle.

myogen (mi′o-jen) [*myo-* + Gr. *gennan* to produce]. An albumin-like protein, constituting 10 per cent of the protein of muscle. It is spontaneously coagulable, passing first into soluble myogen fibrin, and then into myosin fibrin. Cf. *myosin*.

myogenesis (mi″o-jen′e-sis). The development of muscle tissue, especially its embryonic development.

myogenetic (mi″o-je-net′ik). Pertaining to myogenesis.

myogenic (mi″o-jen′ik). Giving rise to or forming muscle tissue.

myogenous (mi-oj′e-nus). Originating in muscle tissue.

myoglia (mi-og′le-ah) [*myo-* + Gr. *glia* glue]. A fibrillar substance formed by muscle cells; border fibrils.

myoglobin (mi″o-glo′bin). A ferrous protoporphyrin globin complex, present in sarcoplasm in relatively low concentration, and having a molecular weight one fourth that of hemoglobin and one iron atom per molecule instead of the four found in an atom of hemoglobin. Myoglobin contributes to the color of muscle and acts as a store of oxygen.

myoglobulin (mi″o-glob′u-lin) [*myo-* + *globulin*]. A globulin found in muscle serum.

myoglobulinuria (mi″o-glob″u-lin-u′re-ah). The presence of myoglobulin in the urine.

myognathus (mi-og′nah-thus) [*myo-* + Gr. *gnathos* jaw]. A fetal monster with a supernumerary lower jaw attached to the normally placed lower jaw.

myogram (mi′o-gram) [*myo-* + Gr. *gramma* writing]. The record or tracing made by a myograph.

myograph (mi′o-graf) [*myo-* + Gr. *graphein* to record]. An apparatus for recording the effects of a muscular contraction.

myographic (mi″o-graf′ik). Pertaining to a myograph or to myography.

myography (mi-og′rah-fe) [*myo-* + Gr. *graphein* to record]. 1. The use of the myograph. 2. A description of the muscles. 3. Roentgenography of muscle tissue after injection of an opaque medium.

myohematin (mi″o-hem′ah-tin) [*myo-* + *hematin*]. MacMunn's name for the cytochrome of muscle tissue, an iron-containing catalyst of tissue oxidation. See *cytochrome*.

myohemoglobin (mi″o-he″mo-glo′bin). Myoglobin.

myohemoglobinuria (mi″o-he″mo-glo″bin-u′re-ah). Myoglobinuria.

myohypertrophia (mi″o-hi″per-tro′fe-ah). Muscular hypertrophy. **m. kymoparalyt′ica,** a muscular dystrophy, with paralysis, described by Oppenheim (1914).

myohysterectomy (mi″o-his″ter-ek′to-me). Partial removal of the uterus, the cervix being left in place.

myohysteropexy (mi″o-his′ter-o-pek″se) [*myo-* + Gr. *hystera* uterus + *pēxis* fixation]. An operation for uterine prolapse in which intra-abdominal muscles are utilized to form the support.

myoid (mi′oid) [*myo-* + Gr. *eidos* form]. 1. Resembling or like a muscle. 2. A substance resembling muscle. **cone m.,** the contractile portion of the inner member of the visual cones. **rod m.,** the contractile portion of the inner member of the visual rods.

myoidem (mi-oi′dem). Myo-edema.

myoideum (mi-oi′de-um). Myoid tissue.

myoidism (mi-o-id′izm) [*myo-* + Gr. *idios* own]. Idiomuscular contraction.

myoischemia (mi″o-is-ke′me-ah) [*myo-* + *ischemia*]. Local deficiency of blood supply in muscle.

myokerosis (mi″o-ke-ro′sis) [*myo-* + Gr. *kēros* wax]. Waxy degeneration of muscle tissue.

myokinase (mi″o-kin′ās). A heat-stable protein constituent of skeletal muscle, which activates the yeast hexokinase system, thus making possible the transfer of phosphate from adenosine diphosphate to fructose or glucose.

myokinesimeter (mi″o-kin″e-sim′e-ter) [*myokinesis* + Gr. *metron* measure]. An apparatus for measuring muscular contraction aroused by stimulation by an electric current.

myokinesis (mi″o-ki-ne′sis) [*myo-* + Gr. *kinēsis* motion]. Movement of muscles: especially, displacement of muscle fibers in operation.

myokinetic (mi″o-ki-net′ik). 1. Pertaining to or characterized by myokinesis. 2. Pertaining to the motion or kinetic function of muscle, as contrasted with the myotonic or tonic function.

myokinin (mi″o-kin′in). A base, $C_{11}H_{28}N_2O_3$, found in muscle.

myokymia (mi″o-kim′e-ah) [*myo-* + Gr. *kyma* wave]. Persistent quivering of the muscles (Schultze); called also *myoclonia fibrillaris multiplex*.

myolemma (mi″o-lem′ah) [*myo-* + Gr. *lemma* sheath]. The sarcolemma.

myolin (mi′o-lin). The supposed material of the muscular fibrils.

myolipoma (mi″o-li-po′mah) [*myo-* + Gr. *lipos* fat + *-oma*]. Myoma containing fatty or lipomatous elements.

myologia (mi″o-lo′je-ah). Myology; in N A terminology *myologia* encompasses the nomenclature relating to the muscles and to the bursae and synovial sheaths.

myology (mi-ol′o-je) [*myo-* + Gr. *logos* treatise]. The scientific study of muscles, and the body of knowledge relating thereto.

myolysis (mi-ol′ĭ-sis) [*myo-* + Gr. *lysis* dissolution]. Disintegration or degeneration of muscle tissue. **m. cardiotox′ica,** degeneration of the heart muscle due to systemic intoxication, as in infectious diseases. **nodular m.,** a condition of the tongue characterized by the formation of a nodule composed of degenerated muscle tissue.

myoma (mi-o′mah), pl. *myomas* or *myo′mata* [*myo-* + *-oma*]. A tumor made up of muscular elements. **ball m.,** a true myoma, which is spherical. **m. laevicellula′re,** leiomyoma. **myoblastic m.,** myoblastoma. **m. prae′vium,** a myoma of the uterus which blocks the uterine canal of parturient women. **m. sarcomato′des,** myoma in which the muscle tissue has been transformed into sarcomatous tissue. **m. striocellula′re,** rhabdomyoma. **m. telangiecto′des,** a tumor consisting of a coil of blood vessels surrounded by a network of muscular fibers: angiomyoma.

myomagenesis (mi-o″mah-jen′e-sis). The production or causation of myomas (fibroids).

myomalacia (mi″o-mah-la′she-ah) [*myo-* + Gr. *malakia* softening]. Morbid softening of a muscle. **m. cor′dis,** morbid softening of the muscular substance of the heart.

myomatectomy (mi″o-mah-tek′to-me). Surgical removal of a myoma.

myomatosis (mi″o-mah-to′sis). The formation of multiple myomas.

myomatous (mi-o′mah-tus). Pertaining to or of the nature of a myoma.

myomectomy (mi″o-mek′to-me) [*myoma* + Gr. *ektomē* excision]. 1. Surgical removal of a myoma. 2. Myectomy.

myomelanosis (mi″o-mel″ah-no′sis) [*myo-* + Gr. *melanōsis* blackening]. Melanosis, or black pigmentation of a portion of the muscular substance.

myomere (mi′o-mēr) [*myo-* + Gr. *meros* part]. Myotome, def. 2.

myometer (mi-om′e-ter) [*myo-* + Gr. *metron* measure]. An apparatus for measuring muscle contraction.

myometritis (mi″o-me-tri′tis) [*myo-* + Gr. *mētra* womb + *-itis*]. Inflammation of the muscular substance of the uterus.

myometrium (mi-o-me′tre-um) [*myo-* + Gr. *mētra* uterus]. The smooth muscle coat of the uterus (tunica muscularis uteri [N A]), which forms the main mass of the organ. Accepted by N A as an official alternative term.

myomohysterectomy (mi″o-mo-his″ter-ek′to-me) [*myoma* + Gr. *hystera* uterus + *ektomē* excision]. Surgical removal of a myomatous uterus.

myomotomy (mi″o-mot′o-me). Myomectomy.

myon (mi′on) [Gr. *mys* muscle + *on* neuter ending]. A muscular unit.

myonecrosis (mi″o-ne-kro′sis). Necrosis or death of individual muscle fibers. **clostridial m.,** gas gangrene.

myoneme (mi′o-nēm) [*myo-* + Gr. *nēma* thread]. One of the contractile fibrils in the surface of certain protozoa.

myonephropexy (mi″o-nef′ro-pek-se) [*myo-* + Gr. *nephros* kidney + *pēxis* fixation]. The operation of fixing a movable kidney by suturing it to a strap of muscle tissue.

myoneural (mi″o-nu′ral) [*myo-* + Gr. *neuron* nerve]. Pertaining to both muscle and nerve: said of the nerve terminations in muscles.

myoneuralgia (mi″o-nu-ral′je-ah) [*myo-* + *neuralgia*]. Muscular neuralgia.

myoneurasthenia (mi″o-nu″ras-the′ne-ah) [*myo-* + *neurasthenia*]. The relaxed state of the muscular system in neurasthenia.

myoneure (mi′o-nūr) [*myo-* + Gr. *neuron* nerve]. A nerve cell which supplies a muscle.

myoneurectomy (mi″o-nūr-ek′to-me). Surgical interruption of nerve fibers supplying certain muscles, as section of the internal or external popliteal nerve for relief of intermittent claudication.

myoneuroma (mi″o-nu-ro′mah) [*myo-* + Gr. *neuron* nerve + *-oma*]. A neuroma containing muscular tissue; especially a cyst of the pituitary body containing muscular elements.

myoneurosis (mi″o-nu-ro′sis) [*myo-* + *neurosis*]. Any neurosis of muscle. **colic m., intestinal m.,** mucous colitis.

myonosus (mi-on′o-sus) [*myo-* + Gr. *nosos* disease]. Disease of a muscle.

myonymy (mi-on′ĭ-me) [*myo-* + Gr. *onoma* name]. Nomenclature of the muscles.

myopachynsis (mi″o-pah-kin′sis) [*myo-* + Gr. *pachynsis* thickening]. Hypertrophy of muscle.

myopalmus (mi″o-pal′mus). Muscle twitching.

myoparalysis (mi″o-pah-ral′ĭ-sis) [*myo-* + *paralysis*]. Paralysis of a muscle.

myoparesis (mi″o-par′e-sis). Myoparalysis.

myopathia (mi″o-path′e-ah). Myopathy. **m. cor′dis,** myocardosis. **m. infraspina′ta,** a condition marked by the sudden development of pain in the shoulder with tenderness in the infraspinatus muscle.

myopathic (mi″o-path′ik). Of the nature of a myopathy.

myopathy (mi-op′ah-the) [*myo-* + Gr. *pathos* suffering]. Any disease of a muscle.

myope (mi′ōp) [Gr. *myein* to shut + *ōps* eye]. A near-sighted person; one affected with myopia.

myopericarditis (mi″o-per″ĭ-kar-di′tis). Myocarditis combined with pericarditis.

myoperitonitis (mi″o-per″ĭ-to-ni′tis) [*myo-* + *peritonitis*]. Inflammation of the muscular elements of the peritoneum.

myophage (mi′o-fāj). A phagocyte which destroys the contractile substance of muscle.

myophagism (mi-of′ah-jizm) [*myo-* + Gr. *phagein* to eat]. The atrophy or wasting away of muscular tissue.

myophone (mi′o-fōn) [*myo-* + Gr. *phōnē* voice]. A device which renders audible the sound of a muscular contraction.

myopia (mi-o′pe-ah) [Gr. *myein* to shut + *ōps* eye + *-ia*]. That error of refraction in which rays of light entering the eye parallel to the optic axis are brought to a focus in front of the retina, as a result of the eyeball being too long from front to back. Called also near-sightedness, because the near point is less distant than it is in emmetropia with an equal amplitude of accommodation. **chromic m.,** defective color vision for objects at a distance. **curvature m.,** a form due to changes in the curvature of the refracting surfaces of the eye. **index m., indicial m.,** a form due to abnormal refractivity of the mediums of the eye. **malignant m., pernicious m.,** progressive myopia, associated with grave disease of the choroid and leading to retinal detachment and blindness. **prodromal m.,** a condition in which the patient is able to read without his glasses; sometimes seen in incipient cataract. **progressive m.,** myopia that continues to increase in adult life.

myopic (mi-op′ik). Pertaining to or affected with myopia.

myoplasm (mi′o-plazm) [*myo-* + Gr. *plasma* something formed]. The contractile part of the muscle cell, or myofibril.

myoplastic (mi″o-plas′tik) [*myo-* + Gr. *plassein* to form]. Performed by the plastic use of muscle; said of operations.

myoplasty (mi′o-plas″te). Plastic surgery on muscle; an operation in which portions of partly detached muscle are utilized, especially in the field of defects or deformities.

myopolar (mi″o-po′lar) [*myo-* + *polar*]. Applied to a muscle between the electrodes of a battery.

myoprotein (mi″o-pro′te-in). A protein obtained from muscle tissue.

myoproteose (mi″o-pro′te-ōs). Myo-albumose.

myopsin (mi-op′sin). A proteolytic enzyme occurring along with trypsin in the pancreatic juice.

myopsis (mi-op′sis). Myiodesopsia.

myopsychic (mi″o-si′kik). Pertaining to the muscles and the mind—noting the memory images of muscular activity.

myopsychopathy (mi″o-si-kop′ah-the) [*myo-* + Gr. *psychē* soul + *pathos* disease]. Any neuromuscular affection associated with mental weakness or disorder.

myopsychosis (mi″o-si-ko′sis). Myopsychopathy.

myoreceptor (mi″o-re-sep′tor). A proprioceptor occurring in skeletal muscle, and stimulated by muscle contraction.

myorrhaphy (mi-or′ah-fe) [*myo-* + Gr. *rhaphē* suture]. Suturation of divided muscle.

myorrhexis (mi″o-rek′sis) [*myo-* + Gr. *rhēxis* rupture]. The rupture of a muscle.

myosalgia (mi″o-sal′je-ah). Muscular pain.

myosalpingitis (mi″o-sal″pin-ji′tis) [*myo-* + *salpingitis*]. Inflammation of the muscular tissue of the oviduct.

myosalpinx (mi″o-sal′pinks). The muscular tissue of the oviduct.

myosan (mi′o-san). A denatured and insoluble form of myosin.

myosarcoma (mi″o-sar-ko′mah). Myoma blended with sarcoma.

myoschwannoma (mi″o-shwan-no′mah). Schwannoma.

myosclerosis (mi″o-skle-ro′sis) [*myo-* + Gr. *sklēros* hard]. Hardening or sclerosis of muscle.

myoscope (mi′o-skōp) [*myo-* + Gr. *skopein* to examine]. 1. An instrument for observing muscle contraction. 2. An instrument, on the principle of the orthoptoscope, which allows fusion and movement laterally, vertically, and in rotation.

myoseism (mi′o-sīzm) [*myo-* + Gr. *seismos* shake]. Jerky, irregular muscular contractions.

myoseptum (mi″o-sep′tum). Myocomma.

myoserum (mi″o-se′rum). Muscle juice; the juice expressed from meat.

myosin (mi′o-sin). A globin which is the most abundant protein (68 per cent) in muscle. It is soluble, but on long standing it coagulates into an insoluble protein called *myosin fibrin.* Along with actin (q.v.) it is responsible for the contraction and relaxation of muscle. Cf. *actin* and *actomyosin.* **Furth's m.,** paramyosinogen. **vegetable m.,** a substance resembling myosin, from seeds of various plants.

myosinogen (mi″o-sin′o-jen) [*myosin* + Gr. *gennan* to produce]. Kühne's name for the protein now called *myogen.*

myosinose (mi-os′ĭ-nōs). A proteose produced by the digestion of myosin.

myosinuria (mi″o-sin-u′re-ah) [*myosin* + Gr. *ouron* urine + *-ia*]. The presence of myosin in the urine.

myosis (mi-o′sis). Miosis.

myositic (mi″o-sit′ik). Pertaining to myositis.

myositis (mi″o-si′tis) [*myo-* + *-itis*]. Inflammation of a voluntary muscle. **acute disseminated m.,** primary multiple m. **acute progressive m.,** a rare disease in which the inflammation gradually involves the whole muscular system and ends in death by asphyxia and pneumonia. **epidemic m.,** epidemic pleurodynia. **m. fibro′sa,** a type in which there is a formation of connective tissue within the muscle substance. **m. a frigo′re,** muscular rheumatism resulting from cold or chilling. **infectious m., interstitial m.,** inflammation of the connective and septal elements of muscular tissue. **multiple m.,** dermatomyositis. **m. ossif′icans,** myositis which is characterized by bony deposits or by ossification of muscles. **m. ossif′icans circumscrip′ta,** a form marked by the formation of muscular osteomas, such as riders' bone. **m. ossif′icans progres′siva,** a progressive disease, beginning in early life, in which the muscles are gradually converted into bony tissue. **m. ossif′icans traumat′ica,** myositis ossificans due to injury. **parenchymatous m.,** that which affects the essential substance of a muscle. **primary multiple m.,** an acute febrile disease characterized by edema and inflammation of the skin and muscles in various parts of the body. Called also *pseudotrichinosis.* **progressive ossifying m.,** myositis ossificans progressiva. **m. purulen′ta,** a suppurative and gangrenous type, due to a bacterial infection. **m. purulen′ta trop′ica,** a disease of Samoa and the African tropics, characterized by fever, pain in the limbs, and abscesses in the muscles. **rheumatoid m.,** fibrositis. **m. sero′sa,** muscle inflammation characterized by a serous exudation. **suppurative m.,** inflammation of muscle resulting in muscular abscesses or in diffuse suppuration of muscles. **trichinous m.,** that which is caused by the presence of trichinae.

myospasia (mi″o-spa′ze-ah). Clonic contraction of muscle; paramyoclonus.

myospasm (mi′o-spazm) [*myo-* + Gr. *spasmos* spasm]. Spasm of a muscle.

myospasmia (mi″o-spaz′me-ah). Disease characterized by uncontrollable muscular spasm. See *tic.*

myosteoma (mi-os″te-o′mah) [*myo-* + Gr. *osteon* bone + *-oma*]. A bony tumor in muscle.

myosthenic (mi″os-then′ik) [*myo-* + Gr. *sthenos* strength]. Pertaining to strength of muscle.

myosthenometer (mi″o-sthen-om′e-ter) [*myo-* + Gr. *sthenos* strength + *metron* measure]. An instrument for measuring the power of muscle groups.

myostroma (mi″o-stro′mah) [*myo-* + *stroma*]. The stroma or framework of muscle tissue.

myostromin (mi″o-stro′min). A protein occurring in muscle stroma.

myosuria (mi″o-su′re-ah) [*myo-* + Gr. *ouron* urine + *-ia*]. Myosin in the urine.

myosuture (mi″o-su′tūr) [*myo-* + L. *sutura* sewing]. The suturation of a muscle; myorrhaphy.

myosynizesis (mi″o-sin″i-ze′sis) [*myo-* + Gr. *synizēsis* a sinking down]. Adhesion of muscles.

myotactic (mi″o-tak′tik) [*myo-* + L. *tactus* touch]. Pertaining to the proprioceptive sense of muscles.

myotamponade (mi″o-tam′po-nād). Extrapleural pneumonolysis in which the cavity is packed with a mass of attached muscle.

myotasis (mi-ot′ah-sis) [*myo-* + Gr. *tasis* stretching]. Stretching of muscle.

myotatic (mi″o-tat′ik) [*myo-* + Gr. *teinein* to stretch]. Performed or induced by stretching or extending a muscle.

myotenontoplasty (mi″o-ten-on′to-plas″te). Tenontomyoplasty.

myotenositis (mi″o-ten″o-si′tis) [*myo-* + Gr. *tenōn* tendon + *-itis*]. Inflammation of a muscle and its tendon.

myotenotomy (mi″o-ten-ot′o-me) [*myo-* + *tenotomy*]. Surgical division of the tendon of a muscle.

myotherapy (mi″o-ther′ah-pe) [*myo-* + Gr. *therapeia* treatment]. Treatment by administration of muscle tissue and muscle juice.

myothermic (mi″o-ther′mik) [*myo-* + Gr. *thermē* heat]. Pertaining to temperature changes in muscle produced by its activity.

myotility (mi″o-til′ĭ-te). Muscular contractility.

myotome (mi′o-tōm) [*myo-* + Gr. *tomē* a cut]. 1. An instrument for performing myotomy. 2. The muscle plate or portion of a somite that develops into voluntary muscle. 3. A group of muscles innervated from a single spinal segment.

myotomy (mi-ot′o-me) [*myo-* + Gr. *tomē* a cutting]. The cutting or dissection of muscular tissue or of a muscle.

myotone (mi′o-tōn). Myotonia.

myotonia (mi″o-to′ne-ah) [*myo-* + Gr. *tonos* tension]. Increased muscular irritability and contractility with decreased power of relaxation; tonic spasm of muscle. **m. acquis′ita,** tonic muscular spasm developed after injury or in consequence of disease. Called also *Talma's disease.* **m. atroph′ica,** a rare disease marked by stiffness of the muscles followed in time by atrophy of the muscles of the neck and face, producing hatchet face or tapir mouth. The atrophy extends to the muscles of the trunk and extremities and is associated with cataract. Called also *dystrophia myotonica* and *Deleage's disease.* **m. congen′ita, m. heredita′ria,** a disease, usually congenital and hereditary, characterized by tonic spasm and rigidity of certain muscles when an attempt is made to move them after a period of rest or when mechanically stimulated. The stiffness disappears as the muscles are used. Called also *paramyotonia congenita*. **m. neonato'rum,** tetanism.

myotonic (mi"o-ton'ik). 1. Pertaining to or characterized by myotonia. 2. Pertaining to the tonic function of muscle, as contrasted with the myokinetic or motion function.

myotonoid (mi-ot'o-noid) [*myo-* + Gr. *tonos* tension + *eidos* form]. Resembling myotonia: said of reactions in muscle which are marked by slow contraction or relaxation.

myotonometer (mi"o-to-nom'e-ter) [*myotonia* + Gr. *metron* measure]. An instrument for measuring muscular tonus.

myotonus (mi-ot'o-nus). Tonic spasm of a muscle or of a group of muscles.

myotony (mi-ot'o-ne). Myotonia.

myotrophic (mi'o-tro"fik). 1. Increasing weight of muscle. 2. Pertaining to myotrophy.

myotrophy (mi-ot'ro-fe) [*myo-* + Gr. *trophē* nutrition]. Nutrition of muscle.

myotropic (mi"o-trop'ik) [*myo-* + Gr. *tropos* a turning]. Turned toward or attracted by a muscle.

myovascular (mi"o-vas'ku-lar) [*myo-* + *vascular*]. Pertaining to the muscle and its blood vessels.

myozymase (mi"o-zi'mās). The complex enzyme system involved in muscular contraction.

myrcene (mer'sēn). An essential oil from the oil of bay. It is an olefinic terpene, $C_{10}H_{16}$.

myria- [Gr. *myrios* numberless]. Combining form meaning a great number.

myriachit (mir-e'ah-chit) [Russian]. Gilles de la Tourette's disease.

Myriapoda (mir"e-ap'o-dah) [*myria-* + Gr. *pous* foot]. A class of arthropods, including the millepedes and centipedes.

myriapodiasis (mir"e-ap"o-di'ah-sis). Infestation by one of the Myriapoda or centipedes.

myrica (mir-i'kah). The dried bark of the root of *Myrica cerifera*, bayberry or wax myrtle: used by the eclectics in diarrhea, jaundice, scrofula, etc.

myricin (mir'ĭ-sin) [L. *myrica* myrtle]. 1. A crystallizable principle, $C_{30}H_{61}.C_{16}H_{31}O_2$, from beeswax. 2. A medicinal concentration prepared from *Myrica cerifera*, or wax myrtle; astringent, antiluetic.

myricyl (mir'ĭ-sil). The radical, $C_{30}H_{61}$.

myringa (mĭ-ring'gah) [L.]. The membrana tympani.

myringectomy (mir"in-jek'to-me). Myringodectomy.

myringitis (mir"in-ji'tis) [*myringa* + *-itis*]. Inflammation of the membrana tympani. **bullous m., m. bullo'sa,** a form of viral otitis media in which serous or hemorrhagic blebs appear on the membrana tympani and adjacent wall of the auditory meatus.

myringo- (mĭ-ring'go) [L. *myringa* drum membrane]. Combining form denoting relationship to the membrana tympani.

myringodectomy (mĭ-ring"go-dek'to-me) [*myringo-* + Gr. *ektomē* excision]. Surgical removal of the membrana tympani.

myringodermatitis (mĭ-ring"go-der"mah-ti'tis) [*myringo-* + Gr. *derma* skin]. Inflammation of the outer layer of the membrana tympani, with the formation of blebs.

myringomycosis (mĭ-ring"go-mi-ko'sis) [*myringo-* + Gr. *mykēs* fungus]. Disease of the membrana tympani caused by fungus infection; otomycosis. **m. aspergilli'na,** infection of the membrana tympani by an aspergillus. See *otomycosis*.

myringoplasty (mĭ-ring'go-plas"te) [*myringo-* + Gr. *plassein* to form]. Surgical repair of defects of the membrana tympani.

myringorupture (mĭ-ring"go-rup'chur). Rupture of the membrana tympani.

myringoscope (mĭ-ring'go-skōp) [*myringo-* + Gr. *skopein* to examine]. An instrument for inspecting the membrana tympani.

myringostapediopexy (mĭ-ring"go-stah-pe'de-o-pek"se). Fixation of the pars tensa of the membrana tympani to the head of the stapes.

myringotome (mĭ-ring'go-tōm). A knife for use in operating upon the membrana tympani.

myringotomy (mir"in-got'o-me) [*myringo-* + Gr. *tomē* a cutting]. Surgical incision of the membrana tympani.

myrinx (mi'rinks). Membrana tympani.

Myristica (mĭ-ris'tĭ-kah) [L.; Gr. *myrizein* to anoint]. A genus of trees of tropical countries. *M. fragrans* affords nutmegs and mace.

myristica (mĭ-ris'tĭ-kah). The dried ripe seed of *Myristica fragrans* deprived of its seed coat and arillode and with or within a coating of lime, the source of an aromatic oil: used in several pharmaceutical preparations.

myristicene (mĭ-ris'tĭ-sēn). A fragrant eleopten, $C_{10}H_{14}$, from the volatile oil of nutmeg.

myristicol (mĭ-ris'tĭ-kol). A stearopten, or camphor, $C_{10}H_{16}O$, from the volatile oil of nutmeg.

myristin (mĭ-ris'tin). Myristate of glyceryl, $C_3H_5(C_{14}H_{27}O_2)_3$: found in nutmeg butter, spermaceti, and other fats.

myronate (mi'ro-nāt). Any salt of myronic acid (derivable from black mustard). **potassium m.,** sinigrin.

myrosin (mi'ro-sin). An enzyme found in black mustard seed which decomposes the glycoside sinigrin.

myrrh (mur). The oleo-gum-resin obtained from *Commiphora molmol*, or from other species of Commiphora: used as a protective agent.

myrrholin (mur'o-lin). A mixture of myrrh and fat in equal parts: used as a vehicle for the administration of creosote.

myrtenol (mur'tĕ-nol). A terpene alcohol, $(CH_3)_2C{:}C_6H_7.CH_2OH$, from *Myrtus communis*.

myrtiform (mur'tĭ-form) [L. *myrtiformis; myrtus* myrtle + *forma* shape]. Shaped like the leaf or berry of the myrtle.

myrtillin (mur-til'in). 1. An extractive from the leaves of blueberries. 2. An extractive from the blueberry fruit.

Myrtophyllum (mur"to-fil'um) [Gr. *myrtos* myrtle + *phyllon* leaf]. A genus of protozoan organisms. **M. hep'atis,** a species found in hepatic abscess.

Myrtus (mur'tus) [L.; Gr. *myrtos*]. A genus of myrtaceous trees. **M. commu'nis,** the old world myrtle, a species affording leaves which are antiseptic and astringent.

mysoline (mi'so-lēn). Trade mark for preparations of primidone.

mysophilia (mi"so-fil'e-ah) [Gr. *mysos* uncleanness of body or mind + Gr. *philein* to love]. A form of paraphilia in which there is a lustful attitude toward excretions.

mysophobia (mi"so-fo'be-ah) [Gr. *mysos* uncleanness of body or mind + *phobia*]. Morbid dread of filth or contamination.

mysophobiac (mi"so-fo'be-ak). A person affected with mysophobia.

mysophobic (mi"so-fo'bik). Pertaining to or characterized by mysophobia.

mystin (mis'tin). A milk preservative, consisting of formaldehyde and sodium nitrite.

mytacism (mi'tah-sizm) [Gr. *mytakismos*]. Too free use of *m* sounds in utterance.

mytelase (mi'tĕ-lās). Trade mark for a preparation of ambenonium.

mythomania (mith"o-ma'ne-ah) [Gr. *mythos* myth + *mania* madness]. A morbid propensity to lie or to exaggerate.

mythophobia (mith"o-fo'be-ah) [Gr. *mythos* myth

+ *phobia*]. Morbid fear of myths or of stating an untruth.

mythoplasty (mith′o-plas″te). Hysteria.

mytilite (mit′ĭ-līt). An alcohol from the mussel, *Mytilus edulis*, $C_6H_{12}O_5.2H_2O$. It is isomeric with quercite.

mytilocongestin (mit″ĭ-lo-kon-jes′tin) [Gr. *mytilos* mussel + *congestion*]. A toxic substance derived from mussels of the species *Mytilus edulis* which, when injected in laboratory animals, causes intense congestion of the splanchnic vessels, and hemorrhage.

mytilotoxin (mit″ĭ-lo-tok′sin). A neurotoxic substance derived from mussels of the genus Mytilus. See also *saxitoxin*.

mytilotoxism (mit″ĭ-lo-tok′sizm). Severe and sometimes fatal poisoning that occasionally follows the eating of mussels. Called also *mussel poisoning*.

myurous (mi-u′rus) [Gr. *mys* mouse + *oura* tail]. Gradually tapering like a mouse's tail: said of the pulse when it grows gradually more feeble, and also of certain symptoms.

myxadenitis (miks″ad-e-ni′tis) [*myxo-* + Gr. *adēn* gland + *-itis*]. Inflammation of a mucous gland. **m. labia′lis,** cheilitis glandularis apostematosa.

myxadenoma (miks″ad-e-no′mah) [*myxo-* + *adenoma*]. An epithelial tumor with the structure of a mucous gland.

myxangitis (miks″an-ji′tis) [*myxo-* + Gr. *angeion* vessel + *-itis*]. Inflammation of the ducts of mucous glands.

myxangoitis (miks″an-go-i′tis). Myxangitis.

myxasthenia (miks″as-the-ne′ah) [*myxo-* + Gr. *astheneia* weakness]. Deficiency in the secretion of mucus.

myxedema (mik″se-de′mah) [*myxo-* + Gr. *oidēma* swelling]. A condition characterized by a dry, waxy type of swelling, with abnormal deposits of mucin in the skin (mucinosis), and associated with hypothyroidism. The edema is of the non-pitting type, and the facial changes are strikingly distinctive, with swollen lips and a thickened nose. **congenital m.,** cretinism. **infantile m.,** myxedema beginning during infancy in association with hypothyroidism developing after birth. **operative m.,** myxedema developing subsequent to surgical removal of the thyroid gland. **papular m.,** lichen myxedematosus. **pituitary m.,** myxedema associated with hypothyroidism occurring as a consequence of deficient secretion of thyrotropic hormone by the anterior pituitary gland. **pretibial m.,** a localized myxedema associated with preceding hyperthyroidism and exophthalmos, occurring typically on the anterior (pretibial) surface of the legs, the mucin deposits appearing as both plaques and papules.

myxedematoid (mik″se-dem′ah-toid) [*myxedema* + Gr. *eidos* form]. Resembling myxedema.

myxedematous (mik″se-dem′ah-tus). Pertaining to or characterized by myxedema.

myxemia (mik-se′me-ah) [*myxo-* + Gr. *haima* blood + *-ia*]. Mucinemia.

myxidiocy (miks-id′e-o-se). Myxidiotie.

myxidiotie (miks-id′e-o-te). Myxedema accompanied by defective mental development.

myxiosis (mik″se-o′sis). A discharge of mucus.

myxo- (mik′so) [Gr. *myxa* mucus]. Combining form denoting relationship to mucus, or slime.

myxo-adenoma (mik″so-ad″e-no′mah). Myxadenoma.

Myxobacterales (mik″so-bak-tĕ-ra′lēz). An order of class Schizomycetes, made up of unicellular rods which, in the vegetative state, occur in two characteristic shapes, the cylindrical cells having blunt rounded ends, or tapering toward the tips. The cells multiply by binary, transverse fission, and movement is a universal characteristic. The order includes five families, Archangiaceae, Cytophagaceae, Myxococcaceae, Polyangiaceae, and Sorangiaceae, all occurring as saprophytic soil microorganisms.

myxoblastoma (mik″so-blas-to′mah). A tumor composed of mucous connective tissue cells.

Myxobolus (miks-ob′o-lus). A genus of protozoan parasites infecting fish. **M. cypri′ni,** a protozoan parasite causing the pox disease of carp. **M. pfeif′feri,** a parasite of the fish *Barbus fluviatilis*.

myxochondrofibrosarcoma (mik″so-kon″dro-fi″bro-sar-ko′mah). A tumor containing myxomatous, cartilaginous, fibrous, and sarcomatous elements.

myxochondroma (mik″so-kon-dro′mah). Myxoma blended with chondroma.

myxochondrosarcoma (mik″so-kon″dro-sar-ko′mah). A mixed tumor containing elements of myxoma, cartilage, and connective tissue.

Myxococcaceae (mik″so-kok-ka′se-e). A family of Schizomycetes, order Myxobacterales, made up of saprophytic microorganisms found in soil and decaying organic matter, and including four genera, *Myxococcus*, *Chondrococcus*, *Angiococcus*, and *Sporocytophage*.

Myxococcidium stegomyiae (mik″so-kok-sid′e-um steg″o-mi″i-e). A sporozoon found in the body of the mosquito, *Stegomyia fasciata*.

Myxococcus (mik″so-kok′us) [*myxo-* + *coccus*]. A genus of bacteria of the family Myxococcaceae, found in decaying organic matter.

myxocylindroma (mik″so-sil″in-dro′mah). Cylindroma.

myxocystitis (mik″so-sis-ti′tis) [*myxo-* + *cystitis*]. Inflammation of the mucosa of the bladder.

myxocystoma (mik″so-sis-to′mah). Myxoid cystoma.

myxocyte (mik′so-sīt) [*myxo-* + *cyte*]. One of the characteristic cells of mucous tissue.

myxodermia (mik″so-der′me-ah) [*myxo-* + Gr. *derma* skin + *-ia*]. An acute disease marked by ecchymoses, softening of the skin, and contraction of certain muscles.

myxo-enchondroma (mik″so-en″kon-dro′mah). A chondroma in which some of the elements have undergone mucous degeneration.

myxo-endothelioma (mik″so-en″do-the″le-o′mah). An endothelioma containing myxomatous tissue.

myxofibroma (mik″so-fi-bro′mah). A fibroma containing myxomatous tissue.

myxofibrosarcoma (mik″so-fi″bro-sar-ko′mah). A sarcoma with myxomatous and fibromatous elements.

myxoglioma (mik″so-gli-o′mah). A glioma which has undergone myxomatous degeneration.

myxoglobulosis (mik″so-glob″u-lo′sis) [*myxo-* + *globule* + *-osis*]. A cystic condition of the appendix marked by the presence in the cysts of globoid bodies of mucinous character.

myxoid (mik′soid) [*myxo-* + Gr. *eidos* form]. Resembling mucus.

myxoidedema (mik″soid-e-de′mah). Influenza of a severe type; American grip.

myxoinoma (mik″so-in-o′mah). Myxofibroma.

myxolipoma (mik″so-li-po′mah). Lipomyxoma.

myxoma (mik-so′mah), pl. *myxomas* or *myxo′mata* [*myxo-* + *-oma*]. A tumor composed of mucous tissue. **cystic m.,** one which contains cavities. **enchondromatous m.,** one containing cartilage in the intercellular substance. **erectile m.,** one which contains an excess of vessels, so as to resemble an angioma. **m. fibro′sum,** myxofibroma. **infectious m.,** myxomatosis cuniculi. **lipomatous m.,** lipomyxoma. **odontogenic m.,** an uncommon tumor of the jaw, apparently arising from the mesenchymal portion of the tooth germ, and possibly produced by myxomatous degeneration of an odontogenic fibroma. **m. sarcomato′sum,** myxosarcoma. **vascular m.,** a myxoma containing many blood vessels.

myxomatosis (mik″so-mah-to′sis). 1. A condition marked by the development of multiple myxomas. 2. Myxomatous degeneration. **m. cunic′uli, infectious m.,** an infectious, highly fatal, febrile disease of rabbits caused by a virus, and characterized by edematous swelling of the mucous membranes and the presence of myxoma-like tumors of the skin.

myxomatous (mik-so′mah-tus). Of the nature of a myxoma.

myxomycetes (mik″so-mi-se′tēz) [Gr. pl., from *myxo-* + *mykēs* fungus]. A group of fungus-like organisms, the slime molds, now classified as Myxobacterales.

myxomyoma (mik″so-mi-o′mah). A myoma containing myxomatous tissue.

myxoneuroma (mik″so-nu-ro′mah). Myxoma blended with neuroma.

myxoneurosis (mik″so-nu-ro′sis) [*myxo-* + *neurosis*]. A neurosis characterized by deranged mucous secretion. **intestinal m., m. intestina′lis,** an intestinal neurosis marked by the passage of mucous shreds in the stools.

myxopapilloma (mik″so-pap″ĭ-lo′mah). Myxoma combined with papilloma.

myxopod (mik′so-pod) [*myxo-* + Gr. *pous* foot]. An amebula; the youngest stage of a malarial parasite living within the red blood corpuscles. Some become sporocytes, others gametocytes.

myxopoiesis (mik″so-poi-e′sis) [*myxo-* + Gr. *poiēsis* a making, creation]. The formation of mucus.

myxorrhea (mik″so-re′ah) [*myxo-* + Gr. *rhoia* flow]. A flow of mucus; blennorrhea. **m. intestina′lis,** a flow of mucus from the bowel occurring in nervous individuals under mental strain.

myxosarcoma (mik″so-sar-ko′mah). A sarcoma containing myxomatous tissue.

myxosarcomatous (mik″so-sar-ko′mah-tus). Relating to or affected with myxosarcoma.

myxospore (mik′so-spōr) [*myxo-* + Gr. *sporos* seed]. A spore embedded in a jelly-like mass.

Myxosporidia (mik″so-spo-rid′e-ah) [*myxo-* + *sporidia*]. An order of endoparasitic ameboid sporozoa, many species of which infect insects, fishes, and higher animals. Myxosporidian infection of the human subject is said to occur.

myxovirus (mik″so-vi′rus). A general name for a virus of the influenza, parainfluenza, mumps, Newcastle disease, and related groups characterized by agglutination of chicken erythrocytes; given formal generic status by some, as, for example, in the term *Myxovirus influenzae.*

myzesis (mi-ze′sis) [Gr. *myzan* to suck]. Sucking.

Myzomyia (mi″zo-mi′yah) [Gr. *myzan* to suck + *myia* fly]. A subgenus of anopheline mosquitoes, several species of which act as the carrriers of malarial parasites.

Myzorhynchus (mi″zo-ring′kus) [Gr. *myzan* to suck + *rhynchos* snout]. A subgenus of anopheline mosquitoes, several species of which are the carriers of malarial parasites. *M. barbiros′tris,* a species which transmits malaria and filariasis in the Orient. *M. pal′udis,* an African species. *M. pseudopic′tus,* a European species. *M. sinen′sis,* a Japanese species.

N

N. 1. Chemical symbol for *nitrogen.* This symbol is also used as a prefix to denote combination with the nitrogen atom of organic compounds. 2. Symbol for *normal* (solution); the expressions 2N, N/2 or 0.5N, N/10 or 0.1N, N/50 or 0.02N, N/200 or 0.005N, N/1000 or 0.001N denote the strength of a solution in comparison with the normal, respectively double normal, half-normal, tenth-normal, fiftieth-normal, two-hundredth-normal, and thousandth-normal. 3. Abbreviation for *nasal.*

n. 1. Symbol for index of refraction. 2. A chemical symbol for *normal.*

NA. Abbreviation for *Nomina Anatomica,* the official anatomical terminology approved by the Sixth International Congress of Anatomists at Paris in 1955, with later emendations.

N.A. Abbreviation for *numeric aperture.*

Na. Chemical symbol for *sodium* (L. *natrium*).

$Na_2B_4O_7 + 10H_2O$. Borax.

Naboth's cysts, follicles, glands, ovules (na′bōths) [Martin *Naboth,* a Saxon anatomist, 1675–1721]. See under *follicle.*

nabothian (nah-bo′the-an). Described by or named in honor of Martin *Naboth.* See under *follicle.*

NaBr. Sodium bromide.

NaCl. Sodium chloride.

NaClO. Sodium hypochlorite.

$NaClO_3$. Sodium chlorate.

Na_2CO_3. Sodium carbonate.

$Na_2C_2O_4$. Sodium oxalate.

nacreous (nak′re-us) [Fr. *nacre* mother of pearl]. Having a grayish-white, translucent color, with a pearl-like luster: said of bacterial colonies.

nacton (nak′ton). Trade mark for a preparation of poldine methylsulfate.

N.A.D. Abbreviation for *no appreciable disease.*

naepaine (ne′pān). Chemical name: 2-pentylaminoethyl p-aminobenzoate: used as a local anesthetic.

NaF. Sodium fluoride.

Naffziger's operation, syndrome (naf′zigerz) [Howard Christian *Naffziger,* American surgeon, 1884–1961]. See under *operation* and *syndrome.*

Naga sore (nah′gah) [*Naga,* a region in India]. Tropical ulcer.

nagana (nah-gah′nah). A disease of horses and cattle of Central Africa, due to the presence of the parasite, *Trypanosoma brucei.* The parasite is conveyed to the animals by the bite of the tsetse fly, *Glossina morsitans,* and other species of *Glossina.* Called also *tsetse disease.*

naganol (nag′ah-nol). Suramin sodium.

Nagel's test (nah′gelz) [Willibald *Nagel,* German physiologist, 1870–1911]. See under *tests.*

Nägele's obliquity, pelvis, rule, etc. (na′gĕ-lēz) [Franz Karl *Nägele,* German obstetrician, 1777–1851]. See under the nouns.

Nägeli's maneuver (na′gĕ-lēz) [Otto *Nägeli,* Swiss physician, 1843–1922]. See under *maneuver.*

Nageotte bracelets, cell, radicular nerve (nazh-yot′) [Jean *Nageotte,* Paris histologist, 1866–1948]. See under the nouns.

Nagler effect (nahg′ler) [Joseph *Nagler,* Vienna radiologist]. See under *effect.*

Nagler's reaction, test (nag′lerz) [F. P. O. *Nagler,* British bacteriologist]. See under *reaction.*

$NaHCO_3$. Sodium bicarbonate.

NaH_2PO_4. Monosodium acid phosphate (sodium biphosphate).

Na_2HPO_4. Disodium acid phosphate (sodium phosphate).

nail (nāl). 1. [L. *unguis;* Gr. *onyx*]. The horny cutaneous plate on the dorsal surface of the distal end of a finger or toe. See *unguis*. 2. A rod of metal, bone, or other material used for fixation of the ends or the fragments of fractured bones. **double-edge n's,** malformed finger-nails in which the normal transverse convexity is replaced by a flat plateau, with a deep slope on each side, occurring as a family trait. **eggshell n.,** a finger-nail which has become thin and curved upward at its anterior edge. **fracture n.,** a steel nail used to fasten together the fragments of a broken bone. **hang n.,** a shred of epidermis at one side of a nail. **hippocratic n.** See *hippocratic finger*, under *finger*. **ingrown n.,** a condition caused by aberrant growth of a toe-nail, with its margins pressing against the lateral soft tissues. **Jewett n.,** a nail for internal fixation of a trochanteric fracture: the nail is fastened to a plate for fixing the head and neck of the bone to the shaft. **Küntscher n.,** a tubular metal nail for the intramedullary fixation of fractures. **Neufeld n.,** a device for internal fixation of intertrochanteric fracture of the femur, the V nail section being set at an angle of about 130 degrees to the plate portion. **parrot beak n.,** a curvation of the finger-nail like that of a parrot's beak. **reedy n.,** a finger-nail marked by longitudinal furrows. **Smith-Petersen n.,** a flanged nail for fixing the head of the femur in fracture of the femoral neck. **spoon n.,** depression of the central portion of the finger-nail, with raising of the edges at the sides. **turtle-back n.,** a finger-nail which is greatly distorted, being more convex than normal.

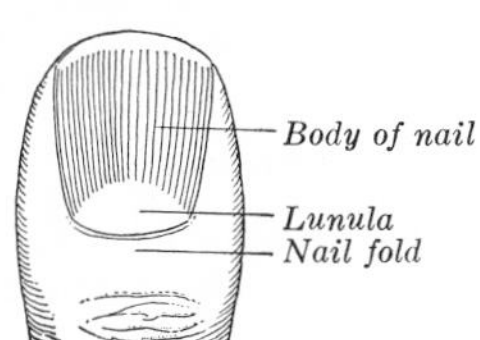

Nail (Hill).

nailing (nāl′ing). The operation of fixing or fastening of a fractured bone with a nail. **intramedullary n., marrow n., medullary n.,** the fixation of a fractured long bone by insertion of a steel nail into the marrow cavity of the bone.

Nairobi disease, eye (ni-ro′be) [*Nairobi*, the capital of Kenya, in East Africa]. See under *disease* and *eye*.

naja (nah′jah) [Arabic]. The cobra di capello, *Naja tripudians*, a venomous snake of India; also a homeopathic preparation of its venom.

nakuruitis (nak″u-roo-i′tis). A form of cobalt deficiency. See *enzootic marasmus*, under *marasmus*.

nalline (nal′lēn). Trade mark for a preparation of nalorphine.

nalorphine (nal-or′fēn). Chemical name: N-allylnormorphine: used as a specific antagonist to excessive doses of narcotic analgesics.

nambi-uvu (nam′be-u′vu). A disease of dogs in Brazil marked by icterus and bleeding from the ear and caused by a blood parasite, *Rangelia vitalii;* called also *bleeding ear* and *blood plague*.

nandhiroba (nand″he-ro′bah). A seed from a tree of South America, having emetic, purgative, and febrifuge properties.

nandrolone (nan′dro-lōn). Chemical name: 19-nor-17β-hydroxy-3-keto-androst-4-ene: used as an anabolic agent.

nanism (na′nizm) [L. *nanus* dwarf]. Dwarfishness; marked undersize. **Paltauf's n.,** nanism associated with lymphatism. **renal n.,** renal infantilism. **senile n.,** progeria. **symptomatic n.,** nanism with defective ossification, dentition, and sexual development.

nanivirus (na″ni-vi′rus) [L. *nanus* dwarf]. A name suggested to include all the very small, ether-resistant ribonucleic acid (RNA) viruses, possessing numerous other common characteristics.

nano- (na′no) [Gr. *nanos;* L. *nanus* dwarf]. Combining form designating small size; used in naming units of measurement to indicate one-billionth of the unit designated by the root with which it is combined (10^{-9}).

nanocephalia (nan″o-se-fa′le-ah). Abnormal smallness of the head.

nanocephalous (na″no-sef′ah-lus) [*nano-* + Gr. *kephalē* head]. Having a small head; pertaining to nanocephalia.

nanocephaly (na″no-sef′ah-le). Nanocephalia.

nanocormia (na″no-kor′me-ah) [*nano-* + Gr. *kormos* trunk + *-ia*]. A developmental anomaly characterized by abnormal smallness of the body, or trunk.

nanocurie (na″no-ku′re). A unit of radioactivity, being 10^{-9} curie, or the quantity of radioactive material in which the number of nuclear disintegrations is 3.7 × 10, or 37, per second. Abbreviated nc. Called also *millimicrocurie.*

nanogram (na′no-gram). A unit of mass (weight) of the metric system, being one one-billionth (10^{-9}) gram. Abbreviated ng. Called also *millimicrogram.*

nanoid (na′noid) [*nano-* + Gr. *eidos* form]. Dwarfish; resembling a dwarf.

nanomelia (na″no-me′le-ah) [*nano-* + Gr. *melos* limb + *-ia*]. A developmental anomaly characterized by abnormal smallness of the limbs.

nanomelous (na-nom′e-lus). Pertaining to or characterized by nanomelia.

nanomelus (na-nom′e-lus). An individual exhibiting nanomelia.

Nanophyes salmincola (na-no′fi-ēz sal-min′ko-lah). *Troglotrema salmincola.*

nanosoma (na″no-so′mah). Nanosomia.

nanosomia (na″no-so′me-ah) [*nano-* + Gr. *sōma* body + *-ia*]. A dwarfish habit of body; nanism.

nanosomus (na-no-so′mus) [*nano-* + Gr. *sōma* body]. A person of dwarfish stature and size; a dwarf.

nanous (na′nus). Dwarfish; stunted.

nanukayami (nah″nu-kah-yah′me). Seven-day fever; a fever with symptoms resembling those of Weil's disease, occurring in Japan, caused by *Leptospira hebdomidis*, the host of which is probably the field vole, *Microtus montebelli.*

nanus (na′nus) [L.; Gr. *nanos*]. A dwarf.

NaOH. Sodium hydroxide.

napelline (na-pel′in) [L. *napellus* aconite]. An analgesic alkaloid, $C_{22}H_{33}O_3N$, from aconite.

napex (na′peks). The region of the scalp just below the occipital protuberance.

naphazoline (naf-az′o-lēn). Chemical name 2-(1-naphthylmethyl)imidazoline: used as a sympathomimetic drug to decongest nasal mucosa.

naphtalin (naf′tah-lin). Naphthalene.

naphtalinum, naphthalinum (naf″tah-li′num, naf″thah-li′num) [L.]. Naphthalene.

naphtha (naf′thah) [L., from Arabic]. A colorless, inflammable oil distilled from petroleum. Same as *benzine.* **n. ace′ti, vinegar n.,** ethyl acetate. **n. vitri′oli,** ether. **wood n.,** methyl alcohol.

naphthalene (naf′thah-lēn) [L. *naphthalinum*]. A silvery, crystalline hydrocarbon, $C_{10}H_8$, from coal tar oil. It is insoluble in cold water, but soluble in hot water, alcohol, ether, chloroform, and benzene. It is used as an antiseptic in diarrhea of typhoid fever, and locally in pruritus, scabies, etc.

naphthalol (naf′thah-lol). Betol.

naphthamine (naf′thah-min). Methenamine.

naphthol (naf′thol). A crystalline, antiseptic substance, $C_{10}H_7.OH$, from coal tar, occurring in two forms, the α (alphanaphthol) and β (betanaphthol). **α-n., alpha-n.** See *alphanaphthol.* **n. aristol,** betanaphthol diiodide. **β-n., beta-n.** See *betanaphthol.*

naphtholate (naf″tho-lāt′). A naphthol compound in which a base takes the place of hydrogen in the hydroxyl.

naphtholism (naf′thol-izm). The toxic condition brought on by the excessive or continued use of naphthol.

naphtholum (naf-tho′lum) [L.]. Naphthol.

naphthoresorcine (naf″tho-re-sor′sin). A principle in transparent crystals derived from naphthol and resorcinol.

naphthyl (naf′thil). The radical, $C_{10}H_7$. **n. alcohol,** naphthol. **n. benzoate,** benzonaphthol. **n. lactate,** lactol. **n. phenol,** naphthol. **n. salicylate,** betol.

naphthylpararosaniline (naf″thil-par″ah-rosan′ĭ-lin). A dye, isamine blue, which has been used experimentally in the treatment of malignant tumors.

naphtol (naf′tol). Naphthol.

napiform (na′pĭ-form) [L. *napus* turnip + *forma* shape]. Having the shape or form of a turnip.

naprapath (nap′rah-path). A person who practices naprapathy.

naprapathy (nah-prap′ah-the) [Bohemian *napravit* to correct + Gr. *pathos* disease]. A system of therapy which attributes all disease to disorder in the ligaments and connective tissue.

naqua (nak′wah). Trade mark for a preparation of trichlormethiazide.

Narath's operation (nah′rats) [Albert *Narath*, Austrian surgeon, 1864–1924]. See under *operation.*

narcism (nar′sizm). Narcissism.

narcissine (nar-sis′in). A crystalline alkaloid, $C_{16}H_{17}NO_4$, from the bulb of *Narcissus pseudonarcissus:* identical with lycorine.

narcissism (nar-sis′izm) [from *Narcissus*, a character in Greek mythology who fell in love with his own image reflected in water]. Sexual excitement through admiration of one's own body; sexual attraction toward oneself.

narcissistic (nar″sĭ-sis′tik). Pertaining to or characterized by narcissism.

narco- (nar′ko) [Gr. *narkē* numbness]. Combining form denoting relationship to stupor or to a stuporous state.

narcoanalysis (nar″ko-ah-nal′ĭ-sis). Psychoanalysis in which the patient is under the influence of a narcotic.

narcoanesthesia (nar″ko-an″es-the′ze-ah) [*narco-* + *anesthesia*]. Anesthesia by the production of a stuporous condition by the hypodermic injection of scopolamine and morphine.

narcodiagnosis (nar″ko-di″ag-no′sis). Narcoanalysis.

narcohypnia (nar″ko-hip′ne-ah) [*narco-* + Gr. *hypnos* sleep + *-ia*]. Numbness felt on waking from sleep.

narcohypnosis (nar″ko-hip-no′sis). Hypnotic suggestions made while the patient is under the influence of some hypnotic drug.

narcolepsy (nar′ko-lep″se) [*narco-* + Gr. *lēpsis* a taking hold, a seizure]. A condition marked by an uncontrollable desire for sleep or by sudden attacks of sleep occurring at intervals. Called also *paroxysmal sleep* and *sleep epilepsy.*

narcoleptic (nar″ko-lep′tik). Pertaining to, characterized by or producing narcolepsy. By extension, sometimes used to denote an individual who exhibits narcolepsy.

narcolysis (nar-kol′ĭ-sis) [*narco-* + Gr. *lysis* dissolution]. Psychoanalysis under light anesthesia.

narcoma (nar-ko′mah). A stuporous state produced by narcotics.

narcomania (nar″ko-ma′ne-ah) [*narco-* + Gr. *mania* madness]. 1. An insane desire for narcotics. 2. Alcoholic insanity.

narcomaniac (nar″ko-ma′ne-ak). One who is affected with narcomania.

narcose (nar′kōs). Stuporous; in a state of stupor.

narcosine (nar′ko-sēn). Noscapine.

narcosis (nar-ko′sis) [Gr. *narkōsis* a benumbing]. A reversible condition characterized by stupor or insensibility. **basal n., basis n.,** narcosis marked by complete unconsciousness and analgesia. **insufflation n.,** insufflation anesthesia. **intravenous n.,** phlebonarcosis. **medullary n.,** spinal cocainization. **Nussbaum's n.,** general narcosis by the use of ether or chloroform after an injection of morphine. **rausch n.** See *rausch.*

narcosomania (nar″ko-so-ma′ne-ah). An insane or pathologic craving for narcosis.

narcostimulant (nar″ko-stim′u-lant). Having both narcotic and stimulant properties.

narcosynthesis (nar″ko-sin′the-sis). Treatment of neuroses by producing with some barbiturate derivative a state of seminarcosis in which the patient recalls his suppressed memories and synthesizes his emotions.

narcotic (nar-kot′ik) [Gr. *narkōtikos* benumbing, deadening]. 1. Pertaining to or producing narcosis. 2. An agent that produces insensibility or stupor.

narcoticism (nar-kot′ĭ-sizm). Narcotism.

narcotico-acrid (nar-kot″ĭ-ko-ak′rid). Both narcotic and acrid.

narcotico-irritant (nar-kot″ĭ-ko-ir′ĭ-tant). Both narcotic and irritant.

narcotile (nar′ko-til). Methylethylene bichloride, a colorless, transparent, and inflammable liquid: used as a general anesthetic.

narcotine (nar′ko-tēn). Noscapine.

narcotism (nar′ko-tizm). 1. Narcosis. 2. Addiction to narcotics.

narcotize (nar′ko-tīz). To put under the influence of a narcotic.

narcous (nar′kus). Narcose.

nardil (nar′dil). Trade mark for a preparation of phenelzine dihydrogen sulfate.

nares (na′rēz) [L., pl. of *na′ris*, q.v.]. [N A, B N A] The external orifices of the nose. Called also *nostrils.*

naris (na′ris), pl. *na′res* [L.]. One of the openings of the nasal cavity. **anterior n., external n.,** either of the external orifices of the nose (nares [N A]). **internal nares.** See *cavum nasi.* **posterior nares,** the openings between the nasal cavity and the nasopharynx (choanae [N A]).

narone (nar′ōn). Trade mark for a preparation of dipyrone.

narry (nar′e). A stomach disease of the Mongols, due to excessive use of alcoholic drinks.

nasal (na′zal) [L. *nasalis*]. Pertaining to the nose.

nasalis (na-za′lis) [L.]. Relating to the nose.

nascent (nas′ent) [L. *nascens*]. 1. Just born; just coming into existence. 2. Just liberated from a chemical combination.

nasio-iniac (na″ze-o-in′e-ak). Pertaining to the nasion and the inion.

nasion (na′ze-on) [L. *nasus* nose]. An anthropometric landmark, the point at which a horizontal line tangential to the highest points on the superior palpebral sulci is intersected by the midsagittal plane.

nasitis (na-zi′tis) [L. *nasus* nose + *-itis*]. Inflammation of the nose.

Nasmyth's membrane (nas′miths) [Alexander *Nasmyth*, Scottish dental surgeon in London, died 1847]. Cuticula dentis.

Na_2SO_4. Disodic sulfate.

$Na_2S_2O_3$. Sodium thiosulfate.

naso- (na′zo) [L. *nasus* nose]. Combining form denoting relationship to the nose.

naso-antral (na″zo-an′tral). Pertaining to the nose and the maxillary antrum.

naso-antritis (na″zo-an-tri′tis). Inflammation of the nose and antrum of Highmore.

nasobronchial (na″zo-brong′ke-al). Pertaining to the nasal cavities and the bronchi.

nasociliary (na″zo-sil′e-a″re). Affecting the eyes, brow, and root of the nose.

nasofrontal (na″zo-fron′tal). Pertaining to the nasal and frontal bones.

nasograph (na′zo-graf). An instrument for measuring the nose.

nasolabial (na″zo-la′be-al) [*naso-* + L. *labium* lip]. Pertaining to the nose and lip.

nasolacrimal (na″zo-lak′rĭ-mal). Pertaining to the nose and lacrimal apparatus.

nasomanometer (na″zo-mah-nom′e-ter). A manometer for measuring intranasal pressure.

nasonnement (na″zon-maw′) [Fr.]. A nasal quality of voice.

naso-oral (na″zo-o′ral). Pertaining to or involving the nose and mouth.

nasopalatine (na″zo-pal′ah-tīn) [*naso-* + *palatine*]. Pertaining to the nose and palate.

nasopharyngeal (na″zo-fah-rin′je-al). Pertaining to the nasopharynx.

nasopharyngitis (na″zo-far″in-ji′tis). Inflammation of the nasopharynx.

nasopharynx (na″zo-far′inks) [*naso-* + *pharynx*]. The part of the pharynx which lies above the level of the soft palate (pars nasalis pharyngis [N A]).

nasorostral (na″zo-ros′tral). Pertaining to the rostrum of the nose.

nasoscope (na′zo-skōp) [*naso-* + Gr. *skopein* to examine]. An electrically lighted instrument for inspecting the nasal cavity.

nasoseptal (na″zo-sep′tal). Pertaining to the nasal septum.

nasoseptitis (na″zo-sep-ti′tis). Inflammation of the nasal septum.

nasosinusitis (na″zo-si″nu-si′tis). Inflammation of the accessory sinuses of the nose.

nasospinale (na″zo-spi-na′le). The point at which a horizontal line tangential to the lower margins of the nasal aperture is intersected by the midsagittal plane.

nasoturbinal (na″zo-tur′bĭ-nal). Pertaining to the nose and turbinate bone.

nasus (na′sus) [L.]. [N A, B N A] The specialized structure of the face that serves as an organ of the sense of smell and as part of the respiratory apparatus. Called also *nose.* **n. exter′nus** [N A, B N A], the part of the nose that protrudes on the face; made up of an osteocartilaginous framework, covered externally by muscles and skin and lined internally by mucous membrane. Called also *external nose.*

natal (na′tal). 1. [L. *natus* birth]. Pertaining to birth. 2. [L. *nates* buttocks]. Pertaining to the buttocks.

natality (na-tal′ĭ-te) [L. *natalis* pertaining to birth]. The birth rate in any community.

nataloin (na-tal′o-in). An aloin, $C_{25}H_{28}O_{11}$, derived from Natal aloes.

nates (na′tēz) [L., pl. of *natis*]. [N A, B N A] The prominences formed by the gluteal muscles on the lower part of the back. Called also *buttocks* and *clunes.*

natimortality (na″te-mor-tal′ĭ-te) [L. *natus* birth + *mortality*]. The proportion of stillbirths to the general birth rate.

National Formulary. See under *formulary.*

natis (na′tis) [L. "rump"]. See *nates.*

native (na′tiv) [L. *nativus*]. Normal to a location; unaltered from its natural state.

natolone (nat′o-lōn). Trade mark for a preparation of pregnenolone.

natremia (nah-tre′me-ah) [L. *natrium* sodium + Gr. *haima* blood + *-ia*]. The presence of sodium in the blood.

natrium (na′tre-um), gen. *na′trii* [L.]. Sodium.

natriuresis (na″tre-u-re′sis) [L. *natrium* sodium + Gr. *ourēsis* a making water]. The excretion of sodium in the urine.

natriuretic (na″tre-u-ret′ik). 1. Pertaining to, characterized by, or promoting natriuresis. 2. An agent that promotes natriuresis.

natron (na′tron). Native sodium carbonate; also soda or sodium hydroxide.

natrum (na′trum). Sodium.

natruresis (nat″roo-re′sis). Natriuresis.

natruretic (nat″roo-ret′ik). Natriuretic.

natuary (nat′u-er″e) [L. *natus* birth]. A ward for women during childbirth.

natural (nat′u-ral) [L. *naturalis,* from *natura* nature]. Neither artificial nor pathologic.

naturetin (nat″u-re′tin). Trade mark for preparations of bendroflumethiazide.

naturopath (na′tūr-o-path). A practitioner of naturopathy.

naturopathic (na″tūr-o-path′ik). Pertaining to naturopathy.

naturopathy (na″tūr-op′ah-the). A drugless system of therapy, making use of physical forces such as air, light, water, heat, massage, etc.

Nauheim treatment (now′hīm) [Bad-*Nauheim,* a town and watering place in Hessen, Germany]. See under *treatment.*

Naumanniella (naw-man″ne-el′lah). A genus of microorganisms of the family Siderocapsaceae, suborder Pseudomonadineae, order Pseudomonadales, occurring as ellipsoidal or rod-shaped cells with rounded ends, found in iron-containing water. It includes five species, *N. catena′ta, N. ellip′tica, N. mi′nor, N. neusto′nica,* and *N. pygmae′a.*

Naunyn-Minkowski method (now′nin-min-kow′ske) [Bernard *Naunyn,* German physician, 1839–1925; Oscar *Minkowski*]. See under *method.*

naupathia (naw-pa′the-ah, naw″pah-the′ah) [Gr. *naus* ship + *pathos* suffering + *-ia*]. Seasickness.

nausea (naw′se-ah) [L.; Gr. *nausia* seasickness]. An unpleasant sensation, vaguely referred to the epigastrium and abdomen, and often culminating in vomiting. **creatic n.,** abnormal aversion to flesh as food. **n. epidem′ica,** a disease observed as an epidemic in Denmark and in England, marked by nausea, vomiting, giddiness and diarrhea. **n. gravida′rum,** the morning sickness of pregnancy. **n. mari′na, n. nava′lis,** seasickness.

nauseant (naw′se-ant). 1. Inducing nausea. 2. An agent which causes nausea.

nauseate (naw′se-āt). To affect with nausea.

nauseous (naw′se-us). Pertaining to or producing nausea.

navel (na′vel). The umbilicus. **blue n.,** hematomphalus. **enamel n.,** an indentation in the outer dental epithelium of a developing tooth, next to the enamel cord.

navicula (nah-vik′u-lah) [L.]. Fossa navicularis.

navicular (nah-vik′u-lar) [L. *navicula* boat]. Boat-shaped.

navicularthritis (nah-vik″u-lar-thri′tis). Inflammation of the navicular joint of the horse's forefoot.

Nb. Chemical symbol for *niobium.*

nc. Abbreviation for *nanocurie.*

N.C.A. Abbreviation for *neurocirculatory asthenia.*

NCI. Abbreviation for *National Cancer Institute.*

Nd. Chemical symbol for *neodymium.*

n_D. Symbol for *refractive index.*

N.D.A. Abbreviation for *National Dental Association.*

NDV. Abbreviation for *Newcastle disease virus.*

Ne. Chemical symbol for *neon.*

nealogy (ne-al′o-je) [Gr. *nealēs* young + *-logy*]. The study of the early infant stages of animals.

near-sight (nēr′sīt). Myopia.

nearsighted (nēr-sīt′ed). Myopic.

nearsightedness (nēr-sīt′ed-nes). Myopia.

nearthrosis (ne″ar-thro′sis) [Gr. *neos* new + *arthron* joint]. 1. A false joint; pseudarthrosis. 2. An artificial joint constructed in the shaft of a bone by a surgical operation.

nebenagglutinin (na″ben-ah-gloo′tĭ-nin) [Ger. *neben* near, beside + *agglutinin*]. Partial agglutinin.

nebenkern (na″ben-kern) [Ger. *neben* near, beside + *kern* kernel, nucleus]. 1. A name given to several structures of the cell, but especially to the paranucleus. 2. A mitochondrial mass that forms the envelope of the axial filament in the flagellum of the spermatozoon.

nebula (neb′u-lah), pl. *neb′ulae* [L. "mist"]. 1. A slight corneal opacity. 2. Cloudiness in urine. 3. An oily preparation for use in an atomizer. **n. epinephri′nae hydrochlor′idi,** epinephrine hydrochloride spray.

nebularine (neb-u-lār′in). An antibiotic substance isolated from the juice of the fungus *Clitocybe nebularis.*

nebulium (ne-bu′le-um) [L. *nebula* mist]. An element that was once thought to exist in the nebulae of astronomical space. It is now known that the light effects attributed to this supposed element are due to oxygen and nitrogen.

nebulization (neb″u-li-za′shun) [L. *nebula* mist]. 1. Conversion into a spray. 2. Treatment by a spray.

nebulizer (neb′u-līz″er). An atomizer; a device for throwing a spray.

Necator (ne-ka′tor) [L. "murderer"]. A genus of nematode parasites. **N. america′nus,** the American hookworm, a nematode parasite, resembling, but shorter and more slender than, *Ancylostoma duodenale.* It is characterized by its buccal cavity containing four plates, four pharyngeal lancets, and a dorsal conic tooth. Infestation by this parasite produces the disease ancylostomiasis. Called also *Ancylostoma americanum* and *Uncinaria americana.* See also *ancylostomiasis.*

necatoriasis (ne-ka″to-ri′ah-sis). The state of being infected with worms of the genus Necator.

neck (nek). A constricted portion, such as the part connecting the head and trunk of the body (collum [N A]), or the constricted part of an organ, as of the uterus (cervix uteri), or other structure (e.g., collum dentis). **anatomical n. of humerus,** collum anatomicum humeri. **n. of ankle bone,** collum tali. **n. of condyloid process of mandible,** collum mandibulae. **dental n.,** collum dentis. **Derbyshire n.,** goiter. **false n. of humerus,** collum chirurgicum humeri. **n. of femur,** collum femoris. **n. of gallbladder,** collum vesicae felleae. **n. of glans penis,** collum glandis penis. **n. of hair follicle,** collum folliculi pili. **n. of humerus,** collum anatomicum humeri. **lateral n. of vertebra,** pediculus arcus vertebrae. **Madelung's n.,** a neck affected with diffuse symmetrical lipoma. **n. of malleus,** collum mallei. **n. of mandible,** collum mandibulae. **Nithsdale n.,** goiter. **n. of pancreas,** a constricted portion marking the junction of the head and body of the pancreas. **n. of radius,** collum radii. **n. of rib,** collum costae. **n. of scapula,** collum scapulae. **surgical n. of humerus,** collum chirurgicum humeri. **n. of talus,** collum tali. **n. of tooth,** the slightly constricted region of union of the crown and root or roots of a tooth. Called also *collum dentis* [N A]. **true n. of humerus,** collum anatomicum humeri. **n. of urinary bladder,** cervix vesicae urinariae. **uterine n., n. of uterus,** cervix uteri. **n. of vertebra, n. of vertebral arch,** pediculus arcus vertebrae. **wry n.,** torticollis.

Anatomical neck
Great tuberosity
Surgical neck

Head of humerus showing the anatomical and the surgical necks. (Christopher.)

necrectomy (nek-rek′to-me) [*necro-* + Gr. *ektomē* excision]. The cutting away of necrosed material.

necremia (nek-re′me-ah) [*necro-* + Gr. *haima* blood + *-ia*]. Loss of vitality of the blood.

necrencephalus (nek″ren-sef′ah-lus) [*necro-* + Gr. *enkephalos* brain]. Softening of the brain.

necro- (nek′ro) [Gr. *nekros* dead]. Combining form denoting relationship to death or to a dead body.

necrobacillosis (nek″ro-bas″ĭ-lo′sis). Infection with Schmorl's bacillus, *Spherophorus necrophorus,* which causes diphtheria with abscesses in cattle, gangrenous dermatitis in horses, and areas of necrosis in hogs and cattle.

necrobiosis (nek″ro-bi-o′sis) [*necro-* + Gr. *biōsis* life]. The physiologic degeneration and death of cells or tissue followed by replacement, such as the constant degeneration and replacement of cells of the epidermis or blood. Cf. *gangrene* and *necrosis.* **n. lipoi′dica,** a condition resembling necrobiosis lipoidica diabeticorum, occasionally seen in nondiabetic patients. **n. lipoi′dica diabetico′rum,** a diabetic dermatosis characterized by a peculiar degeneration of the elastic and connective tissue of the skin, with degenerated collagen occurring in irregular patches, especially in the upper dermis. Called also *Oppenheim-Urbach disease.*

necrobiotic (nek″ro-bi-ot′ik). Pertaining to or characterized by necrobiosis.

necrocytosis (nek″ro-si-to′sis) [*necro-* + Gr. *kytos* cell + *-osis*]. Death and decay of cells.

necrocytotoxin (nek″ro-si″to-tok′sin). A toxin that produces death of cells.

necrogenic (nek″ro-jen′ik) [*necro-* + Gr. *gennan* to produce]. Productive of necrosis or death.

necrogenous (nĕ-kroj′e-nus). Originating or arising from dead matter.

necrohormone (nek″ro-hōr′mōn) [*necro-* + *hormone*]. A substance present in dead cells and tissue extracts which excites cell division in, or kills, living cells.

necrologic (nek″ro-loj′ik). Pertaining to necrology.

necrologist (nĕ-krol′o-jist). An expert in necrology.

necrology (nĕ-krol′o-je) [*necro-* + *-logy*]. The statistics or records of deaths.

necromania (nek″ro-ma′ne-ah) [*necro-* + Gr. *mania* madness]. A morbid or insane preoccupation with death or dead persons.

necrometer (nĕ-krom′e-ter) [*necro-* + Gr. *metron* measure]. An instrument for measuring the organs of the dead body.

necromimesis (nek″ro-mi-me′sis) [*necro-* + Gr. *mimēsis* imitation]. A delusion of being dead, or the feigning of death.

necronectomy (nek″ro-nek′to-me) [*necro-* + Gr. *ektomē* excision]. The excision of necrotic ossicles or of any other necrotic part.

necroparasite (nek″ro-par′ah-sīt) [*necro-* + *parasite*]. An organism which flourishes in dead rather than in living tissue; a saprophyte.

necrophagous (nĕ-krof′ah-gus) [*necro-* + Gr. *phagein* to eat]. Devouring or subsisting on dead bodies.

necrophilia (nek″ro-fil′e-ah). Necrophilism.

necrophilism (nĕ-krof′ĭ-lizm) [*necro-* + Gr. *philein* to love]. Morbid attraction to corpses; sexual intercourse with a dead body.

necrophilous (nĕ-krof′ĭ-lus). 1. Living on dead tissues. 2. Pertaining to or characterized by necrophilism.

necrophily (nĕ-krof′ĭ-le). Necrophilism.

necrophobia (nek″ro-fo′be-ah) [*necro-* + *phobia*]. 1. Morbid fear of death. 2. Morbid dread of dead bodies.

necropneumonia (nek″ro-nu-mo′ne-ah) [*necro-* + Gr. *pneumōn* lung + *-ia*]. Gangrene of the lung.

necropsy (nek′rop-se) [Gr. *nekros* dead + *opsis* view]. Examination of a body after death.

necropyoculture (nek″ro-pi′o-kul″tūr) [Gr. *nekros* dead + *pyon* pus + *culture*]. A pyoculture in which the leukocytes of the pus have been killed.

necrosadism (nek″ro-sa′dism) [Gr. *nekros* dead + *sadism*]. Multilation of a corpse for the purpose of exciting or gratifying sexual feelings.

necroscopy (nĕ-kros′ko-pe) [Gr. *nekros* dead + *skopein* to examine]. Necropsy.

necrose (nek′rōs). To be necrotic or to undergo necrosis.

necroses (nĕ-kro′sēz) [Gr.]. Plural of *necrosis*.

necrosin (nek′ro-sin). A toxic substance liberated by injured cells, which produces the signs of inflammation, central necrosis, lymphatic blockade, injury to vascular endothelium, and swelling of collagen.

necrosis (ne-kro′sis), pl. *necro′ses* [Gr. *nekrōsis* deadness]. Death of tissue, usually as individual cells, groups of cells, or in small localized areas. Cf. *gangrene* and *necrobiosis*. **aseptic n.,** increasing sclerosis and cystic changes in the head of the femur which sometimes follow traumatic dislocation of the hip. A similar condition sometimes develops in the head of the humerus after shoulder dislocation. **Balser's fatty n.,** gangrenous pancreatitis with omental bursitis and disseminated patches of necrosis of the fatty tissues. **caseous n.,** cheesy n. **central n.,** that which affects the central portion of a cell or of a bone or a lobule of the liver. **cheesy n.,** necrosis in which the tissue is soft, dry and cheesy, thus resembling cottage cheese. It is seen mostly in tuberculosis and syphilis. **coagulation n.,** necrosis of a portion of some organ or tissue, with the formation of fibrous infarcts, in which a relatively small part seems to have been deprived of the afflux of blood by the plugging of its vessels with coagula. **colliquative n.,** necrosis in which the necrotic material becomes softened and liquefied. **decubital n.,** a decubitus ulcer. **dry n.,** that in which the necrotic tissue becomes dry. **embolic n.,** coagulation necrosis of an infarct following embolism. **fat n.,** a condition in which the neutral fats in the cells of adipose tissue are split into fatty acids and glycerol; necrosis of the fatty tissue in small white areas. **focal n.,** the presence of small foci of necrosis often seen in the course of an infection. **hyaline n.,** Zenker's degeneration. **icteric n.,** necrosis of the liver in icterus. **labial n. of rabbits,** a fatal necrobacillosis of rabbits that begins in the lower lip and extends down to the thorax. **liquefaction n.,** colliquative n. **medial n.,** medionecrosis. **mercurial n.,** a form due to mercurial poisoning. **moist n.,** that in which the dead tissue becomes wet and soft. **mummification n.,** dry gangrene. **Paget's quiet n.,** a process of local necrosis and sequestrum formation in the superficial layers of the shaft of a long bone with a minimal amount of suppuration around the sequestrum and without sinus formation. **peripheral n.,** necrosis of the peripheral portions of a liver lobule as in puerperal eclampsia. **phosphorus n.,** necrosis of the upper jaw bone due to exposure to the fumes of phosphorus. **pressure n.,** a necrosis due to insufficient local blood supply as in decubitus ulcers. **n. progre′diens,** progressive sloughing. **progressive emphysematous n.,** gas phlegmon. **radium n.,** necrosis of the jaw bone occurring in workers in radium plants. **simple n.,** degeneration of the protoplasm and nucleus of the cells of a tissue without change in the appearance of the tissue. **subcutaneous fat n.,** adiponecrosis subcutanea neonatorum. **superficial n.,** that which affects the outer layers only of a bone. **syphilitic n.,** necrosis caused by syphilis. **total n.,** that which affects all parts of a bone. **n. ustilagin′ea,** dry gangrene from ergot poisoning. **Zenker's n.,** Zenker's degeneration of muscle.

necrospermia (nek″ro-sper′me-ah) [Gr. *nekros* dead + *sperm* + *-ia*]. A condition in which the spermatozoa of the semen are dead or motionless.

necrospermic (nek″ro-sper′mik). Pertaining to or characterized by necrospermia.

necrotic (nĕ-krot′ik). Pertaining to or characterized by necrosis.

necrotizing (nek′ro-tīz″ing). Causing necrosis.

necrotomy (nĕ-krot′o-me) [Gr. *nekros* + *tomē* a cutting]. 1. Dissection of a dead body. 2. The excision of a sequestrum. **osteoplastic n.,** removal of a sequestrum from a bone after first lifting a flap of the bone, which is replaced after the operation.

necrotoxin (nek″ro-tok′sin). A factor or substance, produced by certain staphylococci, which kills tissue cells.

necrozoospermia (nek″ro-zo″o-sper′me-ah). Necrospermia.

Necturus (nek-tu′rus). A genus of salamanders having large external gills: employed in physiologic research.

needle (ne′d′l) [L. *acus*]. 1. A sharp instrument for sewing or puncturing. 2. To puncture with a needle, as in discission of the lens for cataract. **aneurysm n.,** one with a handle, used in ligating blood vessels. **artery n., aspirating n.,** a long, hollow needle for removing fluid from a cavity. **Babcock's n.,** a large hypodermic needle, provided with a stilet, for spinal puncture. **cataract n.,** one used in removing a cataract. **Deschamps' n.,** one with the eye near the point: used in ligation of deep-seated arteries. **dipping n.,** a magnetic needle so hung that it can move freely in a vertical plane. **discission n.,** a special form of cataract needle. **Emmet's n.,** a strong, curved needle set in a handle and having an eye in its point. **exploring n.,** a flattened and grooved needle to be thrust into a part where fluid is believed to exist. **Francke's n.,** a spring needle for evacuating effusions of blood. **Frazier's n.,** a hollow needle for insertion into the lateral ventricles of the brain for continuous drainage. **Hagedorn's n's,** surgical needles which are flat from side to side, and have a straight cutting edge near the point and a large eye. **harelip n.,** a cannula introduced by a trocar through edges of the wound in harelip operation, a figure-of-8 suture being applied over the cannula. **hypodermic n.,** a form of hollow needle used in injecting medicines beneath the skin. **knife n.,** a slender knife with a needle-like point: used in discission of a cataract. **ligature n.,** a slender steel needle having an eye in its curved end, used for passing a ligature underneath an artery. **Reverdin's n.,** a surgeon's needle having an eye which can be opened and closed by means of a slide. **Roser's n.,** a combined aneurysm needle and grooved director. **Silverman n.,** an instrument for taking tissue specimens, consisting of an outer cannula, an obturator, and a split needle with longitudinal grooves in which the tissue is retained when the needle and cannula are withdrawn. **stop n.,** a needle with a shoulder that prevents it from being inserted more than a certain distance. **Strauss' n.,** a hollow needle for aseptic extraction of blood from a vein. **swaged n.,** one permanently attached to the suture material.

Neef's hammer (nāfs) [Christopher Ernst *Neef*, German physician, 1782–1849]. See under *hammer*.

Neelsen (nēl′sen). See *Ziehl-Neelsen*.

neencephalon (ne″en-sef′ah-lon) [Gr. *neos* new + *enkephalos* brain]. The new brain; the cerebral cortex and its dependencies.

NEFA. Abbreviation for *nonesterified fatty acids*.

negatan (neg′ah-tan). Trade mark for a preparation of negatol.

negation (ne-ga′shun). Refusal or denial. See *delusion of negation*.

negative (neg′ah-tiv) [L. *negativus*]. Having a value of less than zero; indicating a lack or absence, as chromatin negative or Wassermann negative; characterized by resistance or opposition.

negativism (neg′ah-tiv-izm). A morbid propensity to do the opposite of what most people would do under similar circumstances, or of what one is told to do or of what one's normal desires would suggest.

negatol (neg′ah-tol). A colloidal product obtained by reacting meta-cresol sulfonic acid with formaldehyde: a parasiticide, germicide, and bacteriostatic, for topical application to the cervix.

negatoscope (neg′ah-to-skōp). An apparatus for showing radiographic negatives.

negatron (neg′ah-tron). The negative electron. See *positron* and *electron.*

Negri bodies (na′gre) [Adelchi *Negri,* Italian physician, 1876–1912]. See under *body.*

Negro's phenomenon, sign (na′grōz) [Camillo *Negro,* Italian neurologist, 1861–1927]. See under *phenomenon* and *sign.*

neighborwise (na′bor-wīz). Descriptive of the plastic behavior of transplanted cells or tissue in a manner appropriate to its new and strange location. Cf. *selfwise.*

Neill-Mooser bodies, reaction [Mather Humphrey *Neill,* American physician, 1882–1930; H. *Mooser,* American physician]. See under *reaction.*

Neisser's coccus, syringe (ni′serz) [Albert Ludwig Siegmund *Neisser,* German physician, 1855–1916]. See *Neisseria gonorrhoeae* and under *syringe.*

Neisser-Doering phenomenon (ni″ser-da′-ring) [Ernst *Neisser,* German physician, born 1863; Hans *Doering,* German physician, born 1871]. See under *phenomenon.*

Neisser-Wechsberg phenomenon (ni″ser-veks′berg) [Max *Neisser,* German physician, born 1863; Friedrich *Wechsberg,* German physician]. Deviation of the complement.

Neisseria (nīs-se′re-ah) [Albert Ludwig Siegmund *Neisser*]. A genus of microorganisms of the family Neisseriaceae, order Eubacteriales; it includes the gonococcus, the several meningococcus types, pigmented forms occasionally associated with meningitis, and a number of saprophytic or parasitic but non-pathogenic species. **N. gonorrhoe′ae,** the specific etiological agent of gonorrhea, occurring typically as pairs of flattened cells usually found intracellularly in heterophils in diagnostic smears of purulent material. **N. meningi′tidis,** a prominent cause of meningitis and the specific etiological agent of meningococcus meningitis, or cerebrospinal fever. It occurs as several serologic types, usually taken to be four, of which IIα or C, depending on the system of nomenclature used, is considered to be the most important pathogen.

Neisseriaceae (nīs-se″re-a′se-e). A family of Schizomycetes (order Eubacteriales), made up of non-motile gram-negative spherical cells occurring in pairs or masses; pigment may or may not be produced, and all known species are parasitic. There are two genera, *Neisseria,* or the aerobic forms, and *Veillonella,* the obligate anaerobic forms.

neisseriology (ni-se″re-ol′o-je). The branch of medicine which deals with gonorrhea and its treatment.

neisserosis (ni″sĕ-ro′sis). Infection caused by *Neisseria.*

nekro-. For words beginning thus, see those beginning *necro-.*

Nélaton's catheter, line, probe, etc. (na-lah-tawz′) [Auguste *Nélaton,* French surgeon, 1807–1873]. See under the nouns.

nelavan (nel′ah-van). The African lethargy, or sleeping disease. See *African trypanosomiasis,* under *trypanosomiasis.*

nem (nem) Acronym for Nahrungs Einheit Milch [Ger. "nutritional unit milk"]. The unit of nutrition in Pirquet's system of feeding, equivalent to the nutritive value of 1 Gm. of breast milk.

N.E.M.A. Abbreviation for *National Eclectic Medical Association.*

nema (ne′mah). Trade mark for a preparation of tetrachloroethylene.

nema (ne′mah) [Gr. *nēma* thread]. A nematode.

nemathelminth (nem″ah-thel′minth) [*nemato-* + Gr. *helmins* worm]. A worm of the phylum Nemathelminthes.

Nemathelminthes (nem″ah-thel-min′thēz). The phylum of helminths, the roundworms, which includes Acanthocephala, Gordiacea, and Nematoda.

nemathelminthiasis (nem″ah-thel″min-thi′ah-sis). Infestation by nematodes or roundworms.

nematicide (nĕ-mat′ĭ-sīd). Nematocide.

nematization (nem″ah-ti-za′shun). Infestation with nematodes or roundworms.

nemato- (nem′ah-to) [Gr. *nēma* thread]. Combining form denoting relationship to a nematode, or to a threadlike structure.

nematoblast (nem′ah-to-blast) [Gr. *nēma* thread + *blastos* germ]. Spermatid.

Nematocera (nem″ah-tos′er-ah) [Gr. *nēma* thread + *keras* horn]. A suborder of *Diptera* characterized by having long antennae and comprising the gnats, mosquitoes, midges, craneflies, gallflies, etc.

nematocide (nem′ah-to-sīd) [*nemato-* + L. *caedere* to kill]. 1. Destructive to nematode worms. 2. An agent which destroys nematodes.

nematocyst (nem′ah-to-sist). A minute stinging structure, found in the cnidoblasts of coelenterates and in certain other species, used for anchorage, for defense, and for the capture of prey.

Nematoda (nem″ah-to′dah) [Gr. *nēma* thread + *eidos* form]. A class of the Nemathelminthes; the roundworms or threadworms. It includes the following important genera: Acanthocheilonema, Ancylostoma, Ascaris, Dioctophyma, Dirofilaria, Dracunculus, Enterobius, Filaria, Gnathostoma, Gongylonema, Haemonchus, Loa, Mansonella, Metastrongylus, Necator, Oesophagostomum, Onchocerca, Physaloptera, Sphacia, Syngamus, Strongyloides, Termidens, Toxacara, Toxascaris, Trichinella, Trichuris, Trichostrongylus, and Wuchereria.

nematode (nem′ah-tōd). An endoparasite or species belonging to the Nematoda.

nematodiasis (nem″ah-to-di′ah-sis). Infestation by a nematode parasite.

Nematodirus (nem″ah-to′di-rus). A genus of nematode parasites found in the duodenum of ruminants.

nematoid (nem′ah-toid). Resembling a thread; pertaining to a nematode parasite.

nematologist (nem″ah-tol′o-jist). A specialist in nematology.

nematology (nem″ah-tol′o-je). The branch of zoology which deals with nematode worms.

nematosis (nem″ah-to′sis). The condition of being infested with nematodes or roundworms.

nematospermia (nem″ah-to-sper′me-ah) [*nemato-* + Gr. *sperma* sperm]. Spermatozoa having elongated tails.

nembutal (nem′bu-tal). Trade mark for preparations of pentobarbital.

nemic (nem′ik). Pertaining to nematodes or roundworms.

Nencki's test (nents′kēz) [Marcellus von *Nencki,* Polish physician, 1847–1901]. See under *tests.*

neo- (ne′o) [Gr. *neos* new]. Combining form meaning new or strange.

neo-antergan (ne′o-an′ter-gan). Trade mark for a preparation of pyrilamine maleate.

neoantimosan (ne″o-an-tim′o-san). Fuadin.

neoarsphenamine (ne″o-ars-fen′ah-mēn). A modified soluble compound of arsphenamine consisting largely of 3,3′-diamino-4,4′-dihydroxyarsenobenzene-methylenesulfoxylate: it is used like arsphenamine, from which it differs in being neutral in reaction, less toxic, and more soluble. Called also *neosalvarsan,* 914, *neodiarsenol* (Canada), *neokharsivan* (England), *novarsenobillon* (France), and *neoarsaminol* (Japan).

neo-arthrosis (ne″o-ar-thro′sis). Nearthrosis.

neobiogenesis (ne″o-bi″o-jen′e-sis) [*neo-* + *biogenesis*]. Biopoiesis.

neoblastic (ne″o-blas′tik) [*neo-* + Gr. *blastos* germ]. Originating in, or of the nature of, new tissue.

neocerebellum (ne″o-ser″e-bel′um) [*neo-* + *cerebellum*]. A term applied originally to the cerebellar hemispheres and later to those parts predominantly supplied by corticopontocerebellar fibers.

neocinchophen (ne″o-sin′ko-fen). Chemical name: ethyl 6-methyl-2-phenylcinchoninate: used as an analgesic.

neocinetic (ne″o-si-net′ik). Neokinetic.

neocortex (ne″o-kor′teks). Neopallium.

neocyte (ne′o-sīt) [*neo-* + *-cyte*]. An immature form of leukocyte.

neocytosis (ne″o-si-to′sis). The presence of neocytes or immature form of leukocytes in the blood.

neodiathermy (ne″o-di′ah-ther″me). Short wave diathermy.

neo-diloderm (ne″o-di′lo-derm). Trade mark for a preparation of dichlorisone containing neomycin sulfate.

neodymium (ne″o-dim′e-um). A rare element of atomic number, 60; atomic weight, 144.24; symbol, Nd.

neo-encephalon (ne″o-en-sef′ah-lon). Neencephalon.

neofetal (ne″o-fe′tal). Pertaining to the transitional period, at the end of two months gestation, between the embryonic and fetal stages of the developing human young.

neofetus (ne″o-fe′tus). The embryo at about the eighth week of intra-uterine life.

neoformation (ne″o-for-ma′shun). A new growth or neoplasm.

neoformative (ne″o-for′mah-tiv). Concerned in the formation of new tissue.

neogala (ne-og′ah-lah) [*neo-* + Gr. *gala* milk]. The first milk developed after childbirth. See also *colostrum.*

neogenesis (ne″o-jen′e-sis) [*neo-* + Gr. *genesis* production]. A form of tissue regeneration that is slower than anagenesis.

neogenetic (ne″o-je-net′ik). Pertaining to neogenesis.

neoglycogenesis (ne″o-gli″ko-jen′e-sis). Glyconeogenesis.

neohetramine (ne″o-he′trah-min). Trade mark for a preparation of thonzylamine hydrochloride.

neo-hippocratism (ne″o-hip-pok′rah-tizm). A school of medicine which trends toward a humanistic view of disease focused on the individual patient and scientific observation by the physician, representing a return to the hippocratic theory and practice, with emphasis on observational and bedside medicine.

neo-hombreol (ne″o-hom′bre-ol). Trade mark for preparations of testosterone propionate.

neohydrin (ne″o-hi′drin). Trade mark for a preparation of chlormerodrin.

neohymen (ne″o-hi′men) [*neo-* + Gr. *hymēn* membrane]. A false membrane.

neo-iopax (ne″o-i′o-paks). Trade mark for a preparation of sodium iodomethamate.

neokinetic (ne″o-ki-net′ik) [*neo-* + Gr. *kinētikos* pertaining to movement]. A term applied to the nervous motor mechanism regulating voluntary muscular control. It is associated with the motor area of cerebral cortex, and receives its name because of the fact that it was developed more recently than the older paleokinetic system. Cf. *paleokinetic.*

neolallia, neolallism (ne″o-lal′e-ah, ne″o-lal′izm). Speech into which many neologisms are incorporated.

neologism (ne-ol′o-jizm) [*neo-* + Gr. *logos* word]. 1. A newly coined word. 2. A meaningless word uttered by a psychotic or delirious patient.

neomembrane (ne″o-mem′brān). A false membrane.

neomin (ne′o-min). Neomycin.

neomorph (ne′o-morf) [*neo-* + Gr. *morphē* form]. A recently acquired part or organ.

neomorphism (ne″o-mor′fizm). The development of new form.

neomycin (ne′o-mi″sin). An antibacterial substance produced by the growth of *Streptomyces fradiae:* used as an intestinal antiseptic, and in treatment of systemic infections caused by gram-negative microorganisms.

neon (ne′on) [Gr. *neos* new]. An inert gaseous element discovered in the air in 1898; symbol, Ne; atomic weight, 20.183; atomic number, 10.

neonatal (ne″o-na′tal) [*neo-* + L. *natus* born]. Pertaining to the first four weeks after birth.

neonate (ne′o-nāt). 1. Newly born. 2. A newborn infant.

neonatologist (ne″o-na-tol′o-jist). A physician whose primary concern is in the specialty of neonatology.

neonatology (ne″o-na-tol′o-je). The art and science of diagnosis and treatment of disorders of the newborn infant.

neopallium (ne″o-pal′le-um) [*neo-* + L. *pallium* cloak]. That portion of the pallium showing stratification and organization characteristic of the most highly evolved type, for example, the termination of the afferent plexus predominantly in layer IV, and well developed overlying and underlying layers. It corresponds to the greater part of the isocortex of Vogt and Brodmann, and, with the archipallium and mesopallium, constitutes the pallium of the cerebral hemispheres.

neopathy (ne-op′ah-the) [*neo-* + Gr. *pathos* disease]. 1. A new disease. 2. A new condition or complication of disease in a patient.

neophilism (ne-of′ĭ-lizm) [*neo-* + Gr. *philein* to love]. Morbid or abnormal love of novelty.

neophobia (ne″o-fo′be-ah) [*neo-* + *phobia*]. Abnormal dread of new things.

neophrenia (ne″o-fre′ne-ah) [*neo-* + Gr. *phrēn* mind]. Mental disorder occurring in early youth.

neoplasia (ne″o-pla′ze-ah). The formation of a neoplasm.

neoplasm (ne′o-plazm) [*neo-* + Gr. *plasma* formation]. Any new and abnormal growth, such as a tumor. **histoid n.,** a neoplasm whose structure resembles that of the tissues in which it is situated. **organoid n.,** a neoplasm whose structure resembles that of some organ of the body.

neoplastic (ne″o-plas′tik). Pertaining to or like a neoplasm.

neoplastigenic (ne″o-plas″tĭ-jen′ik). Tending to produce neoplasms.

neoplasty (ne′o-plas″te) [*neo-* + Gr. *plassein* to mold]. The formation of new parts by plastic methods.

neoquassin (ne″o-kwas′in). A crystalline principle from quassia, $C_{24}H_{34}O_6$. It seems to be a tertiary ammonium base.

Neorickettsia (ne″o-rĭ-ket′se-ah). A genus of the tribe Ehrlichieae, family Rickettsiaceae, order Rickettsiales. It includes a single species, *N. helmin′thoeca,* producing disease in dogs, and found in the intestinal trematode *Nanophyetus salmincola,* which is considered to constitute the reservoir of infection.

Neoschöngastia (ne″o-shān-gas′te-ah). A genus of ticks. **N. america′na,** a species of ticks which attack chickens in the southern United States.

neosin (ne′o-sin). A base, $C_6H_{17}NO_2$, found in muscle.

Neosporidia (ne″o-spo-rid′e-ah) [*neo-* + Gr. *sporos* seed]. A division of sporozoa in which growth and sporulation proceed together and simultaneously.

neostigmine (ne″o-stig′min). Chemical name: (m-hydroxyphenyl)trimethylammonium dimethylcarbamate: used as a cholinergic drug to improve muscle function in myasthenia gravis. **n. bromide,** an odorless white crystalline powder with a bitter taste, $C_{12}H_{19}BrN_2O_2$, with actions very similar to those of physostigmine: used in myasthenia gravis and recommended in a wide variety of conditions. **n. methylsulfate,** a powder, $C_{13}H_{22}N_2O_6S$, similar to neostigmine bromide and used for the same purposes.

neostomy (ne-os′to-me) [*neo-* + Gr. *stoma* mouth]. Surgical creation of an artificial opening into an organ or between two organs.

neostriatum (ne″o-stri-a′tum) [*neo-* + *striatum*]. The later developed portion of the corpus striatum represented by the caudate nucleus and the putamen. Cf. *paleostriatum.*

neo-synephrine (ne″o-sin-ef′rin). Trade mark for preparations of phenylephrine.

neoteny (ne-ot′ĕ-ne) [*neo-* + Gr. *teinein* to extend]. The tendency to remain in the larval state, although gaining sexual maturity.

neothalamus (ne″o-thal′ah-mus) [Gr. *neos* new + *thalamus*]. New thalamus; the phylogenetically new part of the thalamus, i.e., the more lateral, cortical part. Cf. *paleothalamus.*

neothylline (ne″o-thil′lin). Trade mark for preparations of dyphylline.

nepaline (nep′ah-lin). Pseudaconitine.

nepenthic (ne-pen′thik) [Gr. *nēpenthēs* free from sorrow]. Pertaining to or inducing peace and forgetfulness.

nephelo- (nef′ĕ-lo) [Gr. *nephelē* cloud or mist]. Combining form denoting relationship to cloudiness or mistiness.

nephelometer (nef″ĕ-lom′e-ter) [*nephalo-* + Gr. *metron* measure]. An instrument, similar in design to a visual colorimeter, which employs the Tyndall phenomenon for measurement of the concentration of substances in suspension. **photoelectric n.,** one in which photoelectric means of measurement is substituted for the human eye.

nephelometry (nef″ĕ-lom′e-tre) [*nephelo-* + Gr. *metron* measure]. Measurement of the concentration of a suspension by means of a nephelometer.

nephelopia (nef″ĕ-lo′pe-ah) [*nephelo-* + Gr. *ōps* eye + *-ia*]. Defect of vision from cloudiness of the cornea.

nephelopsychosis (nef″ĕ-lo-si-ko′sis) [*nephelo-* + *psychosis*]. An abnormal interest in clouds.

nephr-. See *nephro-.*

nephradenoma (nef″rad-e-no′mah) [*nephr-* + *adenoma*]. Adenoma of the kidney.

nephralgia (nĕ-fral′je-ah) [*nephr-* + *-algia*]. Pain in a kidney. **idiopathic n.,** unexplained pain in the kidney.

nephralgic (nĕ-fral′jik). Pertaining to or characterized by nephralgia.

nephrapostasis (nef″rah-pos′tah-sis) [*nephr-* + Gr. *apostasis* suppuration]. Abscess or suppurative inflammation of a kidney.

nephrasthenia (nef″ras-the′ne-ah) [*nephr-* + *asthenia*]. A condition marked by slight renal symptoms, such as albuminuria and cylindruria.

nephratonia (nef″rah-to′ne-ah) [*nephr-* + *a* neg. + Gr. *tonos* tension + *-ia*]. Atony of the kidney.

nephratony (ne-frat′o-ne). Nephratonia.

nephrauxe (nef-rawk′se) [*nephr-* + Gr. *auxē* increase]. Enlargement of the kidney.

nephrectasia (nef″rek-ta′ze-ah) [*nephr-* + Gr. *ektasis* distention + *-ia*]. Distention of the kidney; sacciform kidney.

nephrectasis (ne-frek′tah-sis). Nephrectasia.

nephrectasy (ne-frek′tah-se). Nephrectasia.

nephrectomize (ne-frek′to-mīz). To deprive of one or both kidneys by surgical removal.

nephrectomy (ne-frek′to-me) [*nephr-* + Gr. *ektomē* excision]. Excision of the kidney. **abdominal n., anterior n.,** nephrectomy through an incision in the abdominal wall. **lumbar n.,** nephrectomy through an incision in the loin. **paraperitoneal n.,** the surgical removal of a kidney by a cut through the side along the false rib. **posterior n.,** lumbar nephrectomy.

nephredema (nef″re-de′mah). Hydronephrosis.

nephrelcosis (nef″rel-ko′sis) [*nephr-* + Gr. *helkōsis* ulceration]. Ulceration of the kidney.

nephremia (ne-fre′me-ah) [*nephr-* + Gr. *haima* blood + *-ia*]. Congestion of the kidney.

nephremphraxis (nef″rem-frak′sis) [*nephr-* + Gr. *emphraxis* obstruction]. Obstruction of the vessels of the kidney.

nephria (nef′re-ah). Bright's disease.

nephric (nef′rik). Pertaining to the kidney.

nephridium (ne-frid′e-um). The excretory organ of the embryo; the embryonic tube whence the kidney is developed.

nephrism (nef′rizm). Cachexia due to kidney disease.

nephritic (ne-frit′ik). 1. Pertaining to or affected with nephritis. 2. Pertaining to the kidneys. 3. A drug or agent useful in kidney disease.

nephritides (ne-frit′ĭ-dēz). Plural of *nephritis,* used as a collective term, to include all types of nephritis.

nephritis (ne-fri′tis), pl. *nephrit′ides* [Gr. *nephros* kidney + *-itis*]. Inflammation of the kidney; a diffuse progressive degenerative or proliferative lesion affecting in varying proportion the renal parenchyma, the interstitial tissue, and the renal vascular system. **acute n.,** suppurative nephritis with a short and severe course, constituting the acute form of Bright's disease. The kidney becomes soft and enlarged, with fatty degeneration of the tubular epithelium and the formation of tube casts. It is attended with pain in the lumbar region, fever, dropsy, frequent and painful urination, with presence of casts and of blood in the urine. **albuminous n.,** nephritis in which albuminuria occurs. **arteriosclerotic n.,** a form of chronic interstitial nephritis in which the arterioles are chiefly involved. **azotemic n.,** nephritis in which nitrogen retention is the important feature; contrasted with hydremic nephritis. **bacterial n.,** nephritis which is caused by microorganisms. **capsular n.,** that which specially affects Bowman's capsules. **n. caseo′sa,** cheesy n. **catarrhal n.,** nephritis in which the pyramids are of a reddish hue, from the plugging of the tubular canals with cells. **cheesy n.,** a chronic suppurative form with caseous deposits. **chloro-azotemic n.,** nephritis in which there is retention of chlorides and urea, but not of water. **chronic n.,** any variety having a relatively slow course. **clostridial n.,** chronic nephritis believed to be due to the presence of clostridia. It is characterized by nervousness, sleeplessness, dyspnea, dyspepsia, and albuminuria. **congenital n.,** nephritis existing at birth, as in congenital syphilis. **croupous n.,** acute n. **degenerative n.,** nephrosis. **desquamative n.,** acute catarrhal nephritis. **diffuse n.,** nephritis in which the inflammatory process involves both parenchyma and stroma of the kidney. **diffuse n., chronic,** interstitial n., chronic. **n. dolo-ro′sa,** a kidney disorder marked by renal pain and characterized by a thickened, adherent renal capsule. **dropsical n.,** renal disease accompanied by dropsy (edema). **exudative n.,** nephritis with exudation of the blood serum. **fibrolipomatous n.,** perinephritis in which the perirenal fat has become enmeshed in the scar. **fibrous n.,** that which specially affects the stroma. **focal n.,** multiple foci of inflammation scattered through the kidney. **glomerular n.,** that which principally affects the glomeruli. **glomerulocapsular n.,** a form which primarily affects the glomeruli and Bowman's capsules. **n. gravida′rum,** nephritis complicating pregnancy. **hemorrhagic n.,** nephritis characterized by hematuria. **hydremic n., hydropigenous n.,** nephritis in which dropsy is the predominating feature; contrasted with azotemic nephritis. **hypogenetic n.,** nephritis due to an unusual strain upon kidneys that are congenitally underdeveloped. **idiopathic n.,** nephritis the cause of which is not discoverable. **indurative n.,** chronic nephritis with atrophy of the secreting parts of the kidney and hypertrophy of the connective tissue stroma. **interstitial n., chronic,** a form resulting from acute nephritis or from alcohol and lead poisoning, or from gout. The kidney becomes small, cystic, nodulated, and adherent to its capsule. The interstitial tissue is increased, and there is thickening of the vessel walls and of the malpighian corpuscles: the heart becomes hypertrophied, and the walls of the small arteries thickened; the malpighian tubules contain hyaline casts. The disease is attended with progressive loss of strength, dyspnea, headache, dyspepsia, diarrhea, and the frequent passage of large quantities of light-colored urine containing albumin and casts. Called also *chronic diffuse n., atrophic kidney, arteriosclerotic kidney, senile kidney, contracted kidney, gouty kidney*, and *granular kidney*. **Lancereaux's n.,** interstitial nephritis of rheumatic origin. **lipomatous n.,** a condition in which the renal parenchyma is replaced by fat: called also *lipomatosis renis, lipoma diffusum renis*. **n. mi'tis,** nephrosis. **parenchymatous n.,** nephritis which specially affects the parenchyma of the kidney. **parenchymatous n., chronic,** nephritis marked by changes similar to those of the acute form, without congestion. The kidney becomes soft and white, and the disease is attended by anemia, dropsy, anasarca, gastrointestinal disorder and dyspnea, with secretion of small amounts of high-colored urine containing albumin and casts. Called also *chronic tubal n., large white kidney*, and *branny kidney*. **pneumococcus n.,** nephritis from infection with pneumococci, occurring usually as a complication of pneumonia or empyema. **n. of pregnancy,** n. gravidarum. **productive n.,** nephritis with the development of serous exudate and hypertrophy of the connective tissue stroma. **n. re'pens,** a condition in which the patient has advanced renal insufficiency and raised blood pressure but without an antecedent history of acute nephritis. **saturnine n.,** a form due to chronic lead poisoning. **scarlatinal n.,** acute nephritis due to scarlet fever. **subacute n.,** parenchymatous n., chronic. **suppurative n.,** a form accompanied by abscess of the kidney. **suppurative n., acute,** is due to septic infection, generally from operations on the genito-urinary tract (then called *surgical kidney*), and marked by the development of multiple abscesses. **suppurative n., chronic,** is caused by infection with the tubercle bacillus. In this disease cavities are found in the kidney, filled with puslike, cheesy masses and tubercle bacilli. **syphilitic n.,** a form of nephritis occurring in patients with tertiary syphilis. **tartrate n.,** acute nephritis produced by the subcutaneous injection of racemic tartaric acid. **transfusion n.,** a nephropathy following blood transfusion from a donor whose blood is incompatible with that of the recipient. **trench n.,** war n. **tubal n., tubular n.,** a variety that affects principally the tubules. **tuberculous n.,** a variety of chronic interstitial nephritis due to the bacillus of tuberculosis. **vascular n.,** nephrosclerosis. **war n.,** an acute diffuse glomerulonephritis affecting soldiers under war conditions.

nephritogenic (ne-frit″o-jen′ik). Giving rise to inflammation of the kidney, or nephritis.

nephro-, nephr- [Gr. *nephros* kidney]. Combining forms denoting relationship to the kidney.

nephro-abdominal (nef″ro-ab-dom′ĭ-nal). Pertaining to the kidney and the abdominal wall.

nephro-angiosclerosis (nef″ro-an″je-o-sklero′sis). Hypertension with renal lesions of arterial origin.

nephroblastoma (nef″ro-blas-to′mah). Wilms' tumor.

nephrocalcinosis (nef″ro-kal″si-no′sis) [*nephro-* + *calcium* + *-osis*]. A condition characterized by precipitation of calcium phosphate in the tubules of the kidney, with resultant renal insufficiency.

nephrocapsectomy (nef″ro-kap-sek′to-me) [*nephro-* + L. *capsula* capsule + Gr. *ektomē* excision]. Excision of the renal capsule; decapsulation of the kidney.

nephrocardiac (nef″ro-kar′de-ak). Pertaining to the kidney and the heart.

nephrocele (nef′ro-sēl) [*nephro-* + Gr. *kēlē* hernia]. Hernial protrusion of a kidney.

nephrocirrhosis (nef″ro-si-ro′sis) [*nephro-* + Gr. *kirrhos* orange yellow]. Granular kidney.

nephrocolic (nef″ro-kol′ik) [*nephro-* + *colic*]. 1. Pertaining to the kidney and the colon. 2. Renal colic.

nephrocolopexy (nef″ro-ko′lo-pek″se) [*nephro-* + Gr. *kolon* colon + *pēxis* fixation]. Operative suspension of the kidney and colon by means of the nephrocolic ligament.

nephrocoloptosis (nef″ro-ko″lop-to′sis) [*nephro-* + Gr. *kolon* colon + *ptōsis* fall]. Downward displacement of the kidney and colon.

nephrocystanastomosis (nef″ro-sist″ah-nas″-to-mo′sis) [*nephro-* + Gr. *kystis* bladder + *anastomōsis* an opening]. The surgical formation of a communication between the kidney and the urinary bladder.

nephrocystitis (nef″ro-sis-ti′tis) [*nephro-* + Gr. *kystis* bladder + *-itis*]. Inflammation of the kidney and bladder.

nephrocystosis (nef″ro-sis-to′sis) [*nephro-* + *cyst* + *-osis*]. Development of cysts in the kidney.

nephro-erysipelas (nef″ro-er″ĭ-sip′ĕ-las). Erysipelas complicated with acute nephritis.

nephrogastric (nef″ro-gas′trik). Pertaining to the kidney and the stomach.

nephrogenic (nef″ro-jen′ik) [*nephro-* + Gr. *gennan* to produce]. Forming kidney tissue.

nephrogenous (ne-froj′e-nus). Originating or arising in the kidney.

nephrogram (nef′ro-gram). A roentgenogram of the kidney.

nephrography (ne-frog′rah-fe) [*nephro-* + Gr. *graphein* to write]. Roentgenography of the kidney.

nephrohemia (nef″ro-he′me-ah) [*nephro-* + Gr. *haima* blood + *-ia*]. Congestion of the kidney.

nephrohydrosis (nef″ro-hi-dro′sis). Hydronephrosis.

nephrohypertrophy (nef″ro-hi-per′tro-fe) [*nephro-* + *hypertrophy*]. Hypertrophy of the kidney.

nephroid (nef′roid) [*nephro-* + Gr. *eidos* form]. Kidney-shaped, or resembling a kidney.

nephrolith (nef′ro-lith) [*nephro-* + Gr. *lithos* stone]. A renal calculus; gravel in a kidney.

nephrolithiasis (nef″ro-lĭ-thi′ah-sis). A condition marked by the presence of renal calculi.

nephrolithotomy (nef″ro-lĭ-thot′o-me) [*nephrolith* + Gr. *tomē* a cutting]. The removal of renal calculi by cutting through the body of the kidney.

nephrologist (ne-frol′o-jist). An expert in nephrology.

nephrology (ne-frol′o-je) [*nephro-* + *-logy*]. Scientific study of the kidney and its diseases.

nephrolysine (ne-frol′ĭ-sin) [*nephro-* + *lysine*]. Nephrotoxin.

nephrolysis (ne-frol′ĭ-sis) [*nephro-* + Gr. *lysis* dissolution]. 1. Solution of kidney substance. 2. The operation of separating the kidney from paranephric adhesions.

nephrolytic (nef″ro-lit′ik). Pertaining to, characterized by, or producing nephrolysis.

nephroma (ne-fro′mah) [*nephr-* + *-oma*]. A tumor of kidney tissue; a tumor of the kidney. **embryonal n.,** embryonal carcinosarcoma.

nephromalacia (nef″ro-mah-la′she-ah) [*nephro-* + Gr. *malakia* softness]. Softening of the kidney.

nephromegaly (nef″ro-meg′ah-le) [*nephro-* + Gr. *megas* great]. Enlargement of the kidney.

nephromere (nef′ro-mēr) [*nephro-* + Gr. *meros* part]. Nephrotome.

nephron (nef′ron) [Gr. *nephros* kidney + *on* neuter ending]. The anatomical and functional unit of the kidney, consisting of the renal corpuscle, the proximal convoluted tubule, the descending and ascending limbs of Henle's loop, the distal convoluted tubule, and the collecting tubule. **lower n.,** the distal part of the nephron, including Henle's loop and the parts distal to it.

nephroncus (nef-rong′kus) [*nephr-* + Gr. *onkos* mass]. Tumor of the kidney.

nephro-omentopexy (nef″ro-o-men′to-pek″se). The operation of grafting the omentum on to the decapsulated ischemic kidney: proposed for the relief of hypertension.

nephroparalysis (nef″ro-pah-ral′ĭ-sis) [*nephro-* + *paralysis*]. Paralysis of the kidney.

nephropathic (nef″ro-path′ik). Pertaining to, characterized by, or producing nephropathy.

nephropathy (ne-frop′ah-the) [*nephro-* + Gr. *pathos* disease]. Disease of the kidneys. **dropsical n.,** hypochloruric n. **hypazoturic n.,** kidney disease with retention of nitrogen. **hypochloruric n.,** kidney disease with sodium chloride retention.

nephropexy (nef′ro-pek″se) [*nephro-* + Gr. *pēxis* fixation]. The fixation or suspension of a floating kidney.

nephrophagiasis (nef″ro-fah-ji′ah-sis) [*nephro-* + Gr. *phagein* to eat]. The devouring of the kidney by certain parasites.

nephrophthisis (ne-frof′thĭ-sis) [*nephro-* + Gr. *phthisis* wasting]. Nephrotuberculosis.

nephropoietic (nef″ro-poi-et′ik) [*nephro-* + Gr. *poiein* to make]. Forming kidney tissue.

nephropoietin (nef″ro-poi-e′tin). A substance thought to exist in the blood serum, in embryonic kidney, and in kidneys undergoing regeneration and to stimulate the formation of kidney tissue.

nephroptosia (nef″rop-to′se-ah). Nephroptosis.

nephroptosis (nef″rop-to′sis) [*nephro-* + Gr. *ptōsis* falling]. Downward displacement of the kidney.

nephropyelitis (nef″ro-pi″ĕ-li′tis) [*nephro-* + *pyelitis*]. Parenchymatous inflammation of the kidney and of its pelvis.

nephropyelolithotomy (nef″ro-pi″ĕ-lo-lĭ-thot′o-me) [*nephro-* + Gr. *pyelos* pelvis + *lithos* stone + *tomē* a cut]. The operation of removing a calculus from the renal pelvis by an incision through the kidney substance.

nephropyeloplasty (nef″ro-pi′ĕ-lo-plas″te) [*nephro-* + Gr. *pyelos* pelvis + *plassein* to form]. Plastic operation on the pelvis of the kidney.

nephropyosis (nef″ro-pi-o′sis) [*nephro-* + Gr. *pyōsis* suppuration]. Suppuration of the kidney.

nephrorosein (nef″ro-ro′ze-in). A urinary pigment identified spectroscopically by its showing an absorption spectrum between the *b* and *F* lines.

nephrorrhagia (nef″ro-ra′je-ah) [*nephro-* + Gr. *rhēgnynai* to burst forth]. Hemorrhage from the kidney.

nephrorrhaphy (nef-ror′ah-fe) [*nephro-* + Gr. *rhaphē* suture]. The operation of suturing the kidney.

nephroscleria (nef″ro-skle′re-ah). Nephrosclerosis.

nephrosclerosis (nef″ro-skle-ro′sis) [*nephro-* + Gr. *sklērōsis* hardening]. Sclerosis or hardening of the kidney; the condition of the kidney seen in renal hypertension (cardiovascular-renal disease). **arteriolar n.,** a form of nephritis characterized by thickening of the arterioles, degeneration of the renal tubules, and fibrotic thickening of the glomeruli (glomerulonephritis), and leading to renal insufficiency. **benign n.,** arteriolar n. which is of slow development. **intercapillary n.,** arteriolar n. **malignant n.,** arteriolar n. in which the patient succumbs in a few months. **senile n.,** a vascular nephritis which is just a part of the arteriosclerosis common in old age.

nephroses (ne-fro′sēz). Plural of *nephrosis.*

nephrosis (ne-fro′sis), pl. *nephro′ses* [*nephr-* + *-osis*]. Any disease of the kidney, especially any disease of the kidneys characterized by purely degenerative lesions of the renal tubules and marked by edema (noninflammatory), albuminuria and decreased serum albumin (the nephrotic syndrome). **acute n.,** a nephrosis marked by scanty urine but with little edema or albuminuria. **amyloid n.,** chronic nephrosis with amyloid degeneration of the median coat of the arteries and the glomerular capillaries; amyloid kidney. **chronic n.,** renal disease characterized by chronic degeneration of the renal epithelium. **Epstein's n.,** a type of chronic tubular nephritis resulting from systemic metabolic disorder, occurring usually in young persons and in women, and frequently associated with hypothyroidism or other endocrine disturbance. **larval n.,** a condition in which the renal lesions are slight and manifested clinically by albuminuria. **lipid n., lipoid n.,** a nephrosis characterized by edema, albuminuria, and changes in the protein and lipoids of the blood and the accumulation of globules of cholesterol esters in the tubular epithelium of the kidney. **lower nephron n.,** a condition of renal insufficiency leading to uremia, due to necrosis of the cells of the lower nephron, blocking the tubular lumens of this region. The condition is seen after severe injuries, especially crushing injury to muscles (*crush syndrome*). **necrotizing n.,** renal disease characterized by necrosis of tubular epithelium of the kidney. **toxic n.,** a nephrosis caused by some toxic agent, most frequently and typically by bichloride of mercury.

nephrospasis (nef″ro-spas′is) [*nephro-* + Gr. *span* to draw]. Movable kidney in which the natural supports of the organ are so weakened that the organ hangs by its pedicle.

nephrosplenopexy (nef″ro-sple′no-pek″se). Surgical fixation of the kidney and the spleen.

nephrostoma (ne-fros′to-mah) [*nephro-* + Gr. *stoma* mouth]. One of the funnel-shaped and ciliated orifices of excretory tubules that open into the coelom in the embryo.

nephrostome (nef′ro-stōm). Nephrostoma.

nephrostomy (ne-fros′to-me) [*nephro-* + Gr. *stomoun* to provide with an opening, or mouth]. The creation of a permanent fistula leading directly into the pelvis of the kidney.

nephrotic (ne-frot′ik). Pertaining to, resembling, or caused by nephrosis.

nephrotome (nef′ro-tōm). One of the segmented divisions of the mesoderm connecting the somite with the lateral plates of unsegmented mesoderm. It is the source of much of the urogenital system. Called also *intermediate cell mass, mesial plate,* or *middle plate.*

nephrotomography (nef″ro-to-mog′rah-fe). Body section roentgenography as applied to the kidney.

nephrotomy (ne-frot′o-me) [*nephro-* + Gr. *tomē* a cutting]. A surgical incision into the kidney. **abdominal n.,** nephrotomy performed through an incision into the abdomen. **lumbar n.,** nephrotomy performed through an incision into the loin.

nephrotoxic (nef″ro-tok′sik). Toxic or destructive to kidney cells.

nephrotoxicity (nef″ro-toks-is′ĭ-te). The quality of being toxic or destructive to kidney cells.

nephrotoxin (nef″ro-tok′sin) [*nephro-* + Gr. *toxikon* poison]. A toxin which has a specific destructive effect on kidney cells.

nephrotresis (nef″ro-tre′sis) [*nephro-* + Gr. *trēsis* boring]. The operation of establishing a fistula into the kidney by stitching the edges of the kidney incision to the parietal muscles.

nephrotropic (nef″ro-trop′ik). Having a special affinity for or exerting its principal effect upon kidney tissue.

nephrotuberculosis (nef″ro-tu-ber″ku-lo′sis) [*nephro-* + *tuberculosis*]. Disease of the kidney due to *Mycobacterium tuberculosis.*

nephrotyphoid (nef″ro-ti′foid). Typhoid fever complicated with acute nephritis.

nephrotyphus (nef″ro-ti′fus) [*nephro-* + *typhus*]. Typhus fever with renal hemorrhage.

nephro-ureterectomy (nef″ro-u″re-ter-ek′to-me) [*nephro-* + *ureterectomy*]. Excision of a kidney and a whole or part of the ureter.

nephro-ureterocystectomy (nef″ro-u-re″ter-o-sis-tek′to-me) [*nephro-* + Gr. *ourētēr* ureter + *kystis* bladder + *ektomē* excision]. Excision of the kidney, ureter, and a portion of the bladder wall.

nephrozymase (nef″ro-zi′mās) [*nephro-* + Gr. *zymē* leven]. An enzyme, like diastase, found in the urine.

nephrozymosis (nef″ro-zi-mo′sis). Zymotic or fermentative disease of the kidney.

nephrydrosis (nef″rĭ-dro′sis) [*nephro-* + Gr. *hydōr* water + *-osis*]. Hydronephrosis.

nephrydrotic (nef″rĭ-drot′ik). Pertaining to nephrydrosis.

nepiology (nep″e-ol′o-je) [Gr. *nēpio* infant + *-logy*]. The department of pediatrics treating of young infants.

neptunium (nep-tu′ne-um) [from planet Neptune]. An element of atomic number 93 and atomic weight 237, occurring in certain earths and obtained by splitting the uranium atom with neutrons. Symbol Np. Neptunium is unstable and changes into plutonium.

Nernst lamp, theory (nernst) [Walter H. *Nernst*, German physicist, 1864–1941]. See under *lamp* and *theory*.

nerol (ne′rol). An essential oil, $(CH_3)_2C{:}CH.CH_2.CH_2.C(CH_3){:}CH.CH_2OH$, from bergamot.

neroli (ner′o-le). An essential oil distilled from orange blossoms.

neropathy (ne-rop′ah-the). That part of the sys tem of weltmerism known as the laying on of hands; manual gerocomia.

nerval (ner′val). Pertaining to a nerve or to the nerves.

nerve (nerv) [L. *nervus;* Gr. *neuron*]. A cordlike structure that conveys impulses between a part of the central nervous system and some other region of the body. Called also *nervus* [N A]. A nerve consists of a connective tissue sheath (epineurium) enclosing bundles (fasciculi) of nerve fibers, each bundle being surrounded by its own sheath of connective tissue (perineurium). Within each such bundle, the individual nerve fibers are separated from each other by interstitial connective tissue (endoneurium). An individual nerve fiber consists of a centrally placed bundle of neurofibrils in a matrix of protoplasm (axoplasm), the entire structure being enclosed in a thin membrane (axolemma). Each nerve fiber is enclosed by a cellular sheath (neurolemma), from which it may or may not be separated by a fatty layer (myelin sheath). **abducens n.,** nervus abducens. **accelerator n's,** the cardiac sympathetic nerves, which, when stimulated, accelerate the action of the heart. **accessory n.,** **accessory n., spinal,** nervus accessorius. **accessory n., vagal,** ramus internus nervi accessorii. **acoustic n.,** nervus vestibulocochlearis. **afferent n.,** any nerve that transmits impulses from the periphery toward the central nervous system. See *sensory n.* **alveolar n., inferior,** nervus alveolaris inferior. **alveolar n's, superior.** See *rami alveolares superiores anteriores nervi infraorbitalis, ramus alveolaris superior medius nervi infraorbitalis,* and *rami alveolares superiores posteriores nervi maxillaris.* **ampullar n., anterior,** nervus ampullaris anterior. **ampullar n., inferior,** nervus ampullaris posterior. **ampullar n., lateral,** nervus ampullaris lateralis. **ampullar n., posterior,** nervus ampullaris posterior. **ampullar n., superior,** nervus ampullaris anterior. **anabolic n.,** any nerve, such as the vagus, the stimulation of which serves to promote the anabolic processes. **Andersch's n.,** nervus tympanicus. **anococcygeal n's,** nervi anococcygei. **Arnold's n.,** ramus auricularis nervi vagi. **n. of arrest,** inhibitory n. **articular n.,** nervus articularis. **association n.,** an occasional branch of the abducens nerve running to the nerve of the pterygoid canal. **auditory n.,** nervus vestibulocochlearis. **auricular n's, anterior,** nervi auriculares anteriores. **auricular n., great,** nervus auricularis magnus. **auricular n., internal,** ramus posterior nervi auricularis magni. **auricular n., posterior,** nervus auricularis posterior. **auricular n. of vagus n.,** ramus auricularis nervi vagi. **auriculotemporal n.,** nervus auriculotemporalis. **autonomic n.** See *autonomic nervous system,* under *system.* **axillary n.,** nervus axillaris. **Bell's n.,** nervus thoracicus longus. **Bock's n.** See *rami pharyngei nervi vagi.* **buccal n., buccinator n.,** nervus buccalis. **calorific n.,** any nerve, stimulation of which causes an increase in body temperature. **cardiac n., cervical, inferior,** nervus cardiacus cervicalis inferior. **cardiac n., cervical, middle,** nervus cardiacus cervicalis medius. **cardiac n., cervical, superior,** nervus cardiacus cervicalis superior. **cardiac n., inferior,** nervus cardiacus cervicalis inferior. **cardiac n., middle,** nervus cardiacus cervicalis medius. **cardiac n., superior,** nervus cardiacus cervicalis superior. **cardiac n's, supreme,** rami cardiaci superiores nervi vagi. **cardiac n's, thoracic,** nervi cardiaci thoracici. **caroticotympanic n's,** nervi caroticotympanici. **carotid n's, external,** nervi carotici externi **carotid n., internal,** nervus caroticus internus. **cavernous n's of clitoris,** nervi cavernosi clitoridis. **cavernous n's of penis,** nervi cavernosi penis. **celiac n's,** rami celiaci nervi vagi. **centrifugal n.,** efferent n. **centripetal n.,** afferent n. **cerebral n's,** nervi craniales. **cervical n's,** the eight pairs of nerves arising from the cervical segments of the spinal cord. See *nervi cervicales* [N A]. **cervical n., descending,** radix inferior ansae cervicalis. **cervical n., transverse,** nervus transversus colli. **chorda tympani n.** See *chorda tympani.* **ciliary n's, long,** nervi ciliares longi. **ciliary n's, short,** nervi ciliares breves. **clunial n's, inferior,** nervi clunium inferiores. **clunial n's, middle,** nervi clunium medii. **clunial n's, superior,** nervi clunium superiores. **coccygeal n.,** either of the thirty-first pair of spinal nerves, arising from the coccygeal segment of the spinal cord. Called also *nervus coccygeus.* **cochlear n.,** pars cochlearis nervi octavi. **n. of Cotunnius,** nervus nasopalatinus. **cranial n's,** the twelve pairs of nerves that are connected with the brain. See *nervi craniales* [N A]. **cranial n., eighth,** nervus vestibulocochlearis. **cranial n., eleventh,** nervus accessorius. **cranial n., fifth,** nervus trigeminus. **cranial n., first.** See *nervi olfactorii.* **cranial n., fourth,** nervus trochlearis. **cranial n., ninth,** nervus glossopharyngeus. **cranial n., second,** nervus opticus. **cranial n., seventh,** nervus facialis. **cranial n., sixth,** nervus abducens. **cranial n., tenth,** nervus vagus. **cranial n., third,** nervus oculomotorius. **cranial n., twelfth,** nervus hypoglossus. **crotaphitic n.,** nervus maxillaris. **cryogenic n.,** frigorific n. **cubital n.,** nervus ulnaris. **cutaneous n.,** nervus cutaneus. **cutaneous n. of abdomen, anterior,** ramus cutaneus anterior [pectoralis et abdominalis] nervorum intercostalium. **cutaneous n. of arm, lateral, inferior,** nervus cutaneus brachii lateralis inferior. **cutaneous n. of arm, lateral, superior,** nervus cutaneus brachii lateralis superior. **cutaneous n. of arm, medial,** nervus cutaneus brachii medialis. **cutaneous n. of arm, posterior,** nervus cutaneus brachii posterior. **cutaneous n. of calf, lateral,** nervus cutaneus surae lateralis. **cutaneous n. of calf, medial,** nervus cutaneus surae medialis. **cutaneous n. of foot, dorsal, intermediate,** nervus cutaneus dor-

Pyramidal cell, cerebral cortex

Bouton terminal
Microglial cell
Nissl bodies
Nucleus
Nucleolus
Oligodendrocyte
Astrocyte

Astrocyte
Oligodendrocyte
Microglial cell

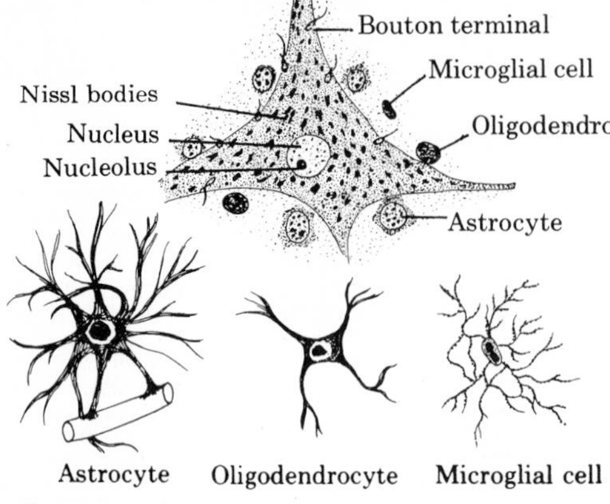

Three types of human neuroglial cell. (King and Showers.)

Perineurium
Perineurial septum
Endoneurium
Single fiber

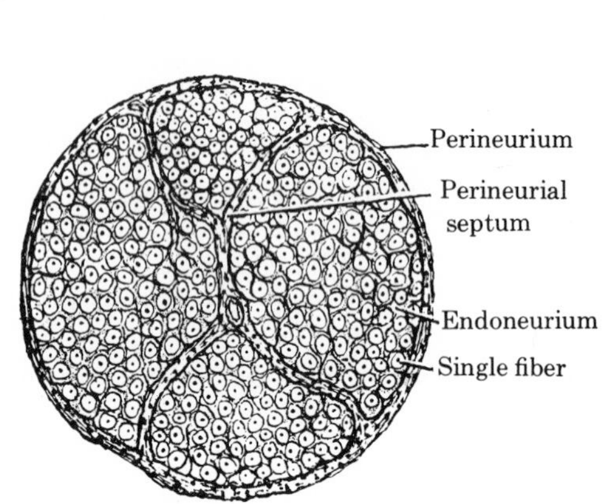

Transverse section of a nerve.

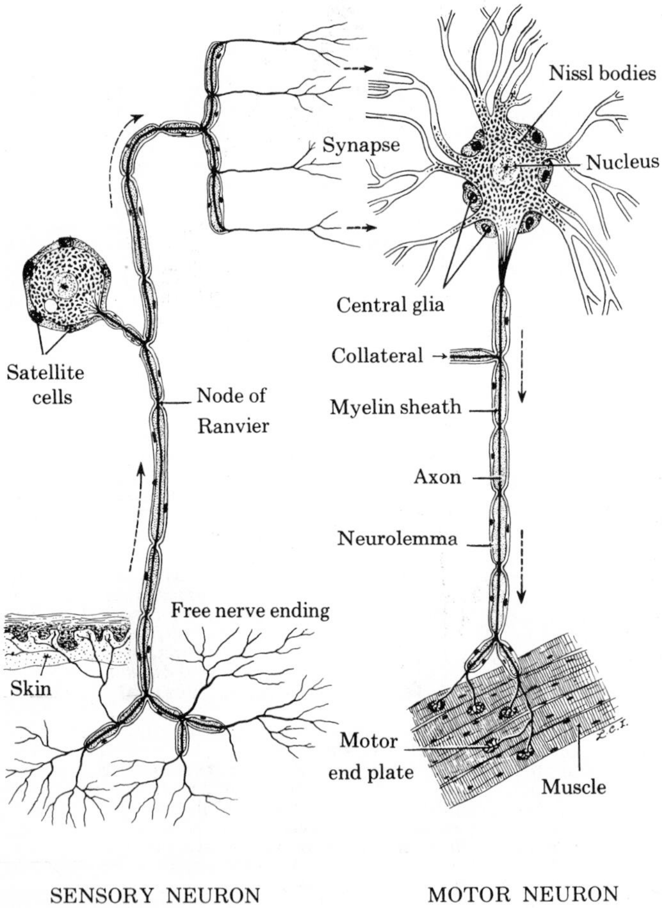

Synapse
Nissl bodies
Nucleus
Central glia
Collateral →
Satellite cells
Node of Ranvier
Myelin sheath
Axon
Neurolemma
Free nerve ending
Skin
Motor end plate
Muscle
SENSORY NEURON
MOTOR NEURON

Diagrammatic representation of two types of neurons. (King and Showers.)

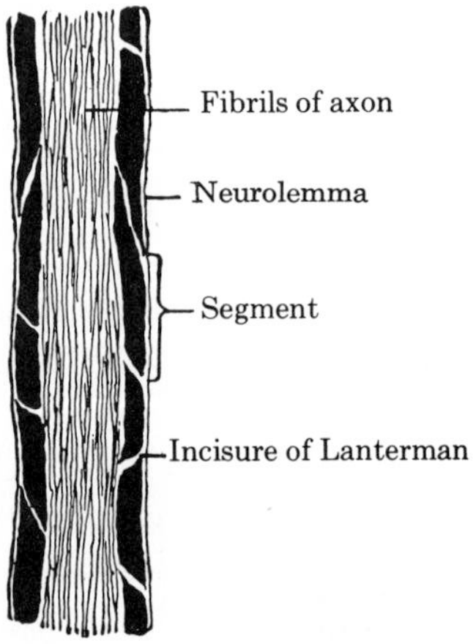

Fibrils of axon
Neurolemma
Segment
Incisure of Lanterman

Longitudinal section of a nerve fiber.

DETAILS OF STRUCTURE OF COMPONENTS OF NERVE TISSUE

salis intermedius pedis. **cutaneous n. of foot, dorsal, lateral,** nervus cutaneus dorsalis lateralis pedis. **cutaneous n. of foot, dorsal, medial,** nervus cutaneus dorsalis medialis pedis. **cutaneous n. of forearm, dorsal,** nervus cutaneus antebrachii posterior. **cutaneous n. of forearm, lateral,** nervus cutaneus antebrachii lateralis. **cutaneous n. of forearm, medial,** nervus cutaneus antebrachii medialis. **cutaneous n. of forearm, posterior,** nervus cutaneus antebrachii posterior. **cutaneous n. of thigh, lateral,** nervus cutaneus femoris lateralis. **cutaneous n. of thigh, posterior,** nervus cutaneus femoris posterior. **Cyon's n.,** a branch of the vagus nerve in the rabbit, stimulation of which results in lowering of the blood pressure. **dental n., inferior,** nervus alveolaris inferior. **depressor n.** 1. Any afferent nerve whose stimulation depresses a motor center. 2. A nerve that lessens the activity of an organ. **diaphragmatic n.,** nervus phrenicus. **digastric n.,** ramus digastricus nervi facialis. **digital n's, dorsal, radial,** nervi digitales dorsales nervi radialis. **digital n's, dorsal, ulnar,** nervi digitales dorsales nervi ulnaris. **digital n's of foot, dorsal,** nervi digitales dorsales pedis. **digital n's of lateral plantar nerve, plantar, common,** nervi digitales plantares communes nervi plantaris lateralis. **digital n's of lateral plantar nerve, plantar, proper,** nervi digitales plantares proprii nervi plantaris lateralis. **digital n's of lateral surface of great toe and of medial surface of second toe, dorsal,** nervi digitales dorsales hallucis lateralis et digiti secundi medialis. **digital n's of medial plantar nerve, plantar, common,** nervi digitales plantares communes nervi plantaris medialis. **digital n's of medial plantar nerve, plantar, proper,** nervi digitales plantares proprii nervi plantaris medialis. **digital n's of median nerve, palmar, common,** nervi digitales palmares communes nervi mediani. **digital n's of median nerve, palmar, proper,** nervi digitales palmares proprii nervi mediani. **digital n's of radial nerve, dorsal,** nervi digitales dorsales nervi radialis. **digital n's of ulnar nerve, dorsal,** nervi digitales dorsales nervi ulnaris. **digital n's of ulnar nerve, palmar, collateral,** nervi digitales palmares proprii nervi ulnaris. **digital n's of ulnar nerve, palmar, common,** nervi digitales palmares communes nervi ulnaris. **digital n's of ulnar nerve, palmar, proper,** nervi digitales palmares proprii nervi ulnaris. **dorsal n. of clitoris,** nervus dorsalis clitoridis. **dorsal n. of penis,** nervus dorsalis penis. **dorsal n. of scapula,** nervus dorsalis scapulae. **efferent n.,** any nerve that carries impulses from the central nervous system toward the periphery. **eighth n.,** nervus vestibulocochlearis. **eleventh n.,** nervus accessorius. **esodic n.,** afferent n. **ethmoidal n., anterior,** nervus ethmoidalis anterior. **ethmoidal n., posterior,** nervus ethmoidalis posterior. **exciter n.,** a nerve that transmits impulses resulting in an increase in functional activity. **excitoreflex n.,** a visceral nerve that produces reflex action. **exodic n.,** efferent n. **n. of external acoustic meatus,** nervus meatus acustici externi. **facial n.,** nervus facialis. **facial n., temporal.** See *rami temporales nervi facialis*. **femoral n.,** nervus femoralis. **fibular n., common,** nervus peroneus communis. **fibular n., deep,** nervus peroneus profundus. **fibular n., superficial,** nervus peroneus superficialis. **fifth n.,** nervus trigeminus. **first n.** See *nervi olfactorii*. **fourth n.,** nervus trochlearis. **frigorific n.,** any nerve, stimulation of which causes a decrease in body temperature. **frontal n.,** nervus frontalis. **furcal n.,** the fourth lumbar nerve, so called because its fibers pass to the lumbar and sacral plexuses. **gangliated n.,** any nerve of the sympathetic nervous system. **gastric n's,** truncus vagalis anterior and truncus vagalis posterior. **genitofemoral n.,** nervus genitofemoralis. **glossopharyngeal n.,** nervus glossopharyngeus. **gluteal n., inferior,** nervus gluteus inferior. **gluteal n's, inferior,** nervi clunium inferiores. **gluteal n's, middle,** nervi clunium medii. **gluteal n., superior,** nervus gluteus superior. **hemorrhoidal n's, inferior,** nervi rectales inferiores. **Hering's n.,** ramus sinus carotici nervi glossopharyngei. **hypogastric n.,** nervus hypogastricus. **hypoglossal n.,** nervus hypoglossus. **hypoglossal n., lesser,** nervus lingualis. **iliohypogastric n.,** nervus iliohypogastricus. **ilioinguinal n.,** nervus ilioinguinalis. **infraoccipital n.,** nervus suboccipitalis. **infraorbital n.,** nervus infraorbitalis. **infratrochlear n.,** nervus infratrochlearis. **inhibitory n.,** a nerve that transmits impulses resulting in a decrease in functional activity. **intercostobrachial n's,** nervi intercostobrachiales. **intermediary n., intermediate n.,** nervus intermedius. **interosseous n. of forearm, anterior,** nervus interosseus antebrachii anterior. **interosseous n. of forearm, posterior,** nervus interosseus antebrachii posterior. **interosseous n. of leg,** nervus interosseus cruris. **ischiadic n.,** nervus ischiadicus. **Jacobson's n.,** nervus tympanicus. **jugular n.,** nervus jugularis. **labial n's, anterior,** nervi labiales anteriores. **labial n's, posterior,** nervi labiales posteriores. **lacrimal n.,** nervus lacrimalis. **n. of Lancisi,** stria longitudinalis medialis corporis callosi. **Langley's n's,** pilomotor n's. **laryngeal n., inferior,** nervus laryngeus inferior. **laryngeal n., recurrent,** nervus laryngeus recurrens. **laryngeal n., superior,** nervus laryngeus superior. **laryngeal n., superior, internal,** ramus internus nervi laryngei. **lingual n.,** nervus lingualis. **longitudinal n. of Lancisi,** stria longitudinalis medialis corporis callosi. **lumbar n's,** the five pairs of nerves arising from the lumbar segments of the spinal cord. See *nervi lumbales*. **lumboinguinal n.,** ramus femoralis nervi genitofemoralis. **mandibular n.,** nervus mandibularis. **masseteric n.,** nervus massetericus. **maxillary n.,** nervus maxillaris. **median n.,** nervus medianus. **meningeal n.,** ramus meningeus nervi vagi. **mental n.,** nervus mentalis. **mixed n.,** a nerve composed of both sensory and motor fibers. **motor n.,** a nerve that contains wholly or chiefly motor fibers. **motor n. of tongue,** nervus hypoglossus. **musculocutaneous n.,** nervus musculocutaneus. **musculocutaneous n., middle,** nervus ilioinguinalis. **musculocutaneous n. of foot,** nervus peroneus superficialis. **musculocutaneous n. of leg,** nervus peroneus profundus. **musculospiral n.,** nervus radialis. **mylohyoid n.,** nervus mylohyoideus. **Nageotte's radicular n.,** the ganglionic portion of a posterior root of a spinal nerve, that is, the region of meeting of the anterior and posterior roots. **nasociliary n.,** nervus nasociliaris. **nasopalatine n.,** nervus nasopalatinus. **ninth n.,** nervus glossopharyngeus. **obturator n.,** nervus obturatorius. **occipital n., greater,** nervus occipitalis major. **occipital n., internal,** nervus occipitalis major. **occipital n., least,** nervus occipitalis tertius. **occipital n., lesser,** nervus occipitalis minor. **oculomotor n.,** nervus oculomotorius. **olfactory n's,** nervi olfactorii. **olfactory n., cerebral,** tractus olfactorius. **ophthalmic n.,** nervus ophthalmicus. **optic n.,** nervus opticus. **pain n.,** a sensory nerve whose function is the conduction of stimuli which produce the sensation of pain. **palatine n., anterior,** nervus palatinus major. **palatine n., greater,** nervus palatinus major. **palatine n's, lesser,** nervi palatini minores. **palatine n., middle.** See *nervi palatini minores*. **palatine n., posterior.** See *nervi palatini minores*. **parotid n's,** rami parotidei nervi auriculotemporalis.

perineal n's, nervi perineales. **peroneal n., common,** nervus peroneus communis. **peroneal n., deep,** nervus peroneus profundus. **peroneal n., superficial,** nervus peroneus superficialis. **petrosal n., deep,** nervus petrosus profundus. **petrosal n., greater,** nervus petrosus major. **petrosal n., lesser,** nervus petrosus minor. **petrosal n., middle, superficial,** nervus petrosus minor. **phrenic n.,** nervus phrenicus. **phrenic n's, accessory,** nervi phrenici accessorii. **phrenicoabdominal n's,** rami phrenicoabdominales nervi phrenici. **pilomotor n's,** the nerves that supply the arrectores pilorum muscles. **plantar n., lateral,** nervus plantaris lateralis. **plantar n., medial,** nervus plantaris medialis. **pneumogastric n.,** nervus vagus. **popliteal n., external,** nervus peroneus communis. **presacral n.,** plexus hypogastricus superior. **pressor n.,** any afferent nerve whose irritation stimulates a vasomotor center and increases intravascular tension. **pterygoid n., external,** nervus pterygoideus lateralis. **pterygoid n., internal,** nervus pterygoideus medialis. **pterygoid n., lateral,** nervus pterygoideus lateralis. **pterygoid n., medial,** nervus pterygoideus medialis. **n. of pterygoid canal,** nervus canalis pterygoidei. **pterygopalatine n's,** nervi pterygopalatini. **pudendal n.,** nervus pudendus. **radial n.,** nervus radialis. **radial n., deep,** ramus profundus nervi radialis. **radial n., superficial,** ramus superficialis nervi radialis. **rectal n's, inferior,** nervi rectales inferiores. **recurrent n.,** nervus laryngeus recurrens. **recurrent n., ophthalmic,** ramus tentorii nervi ophthalmici. **saccular n.,** nervus saccularis. **sacral n's,** the five pairs of nerves arising from the sacral segments of the spinal cord. See *nervi sacrales.* **saphenous n.,** nervus saphenus. **Scarpa's n.,** nervus nasopalatinus. **sciatic n.,** nervus ischiadicus. **sciatic n., small,** nervus cutaneus femoris posterior. **scrotal n's, anterior,** nervi scrotales anteriores. **scrotal n's, posterior,** nervi scrotales posteriores. **second n.,** nervus opticus. **secretory n.,** any efferent nerve whose stimulation increases vascular activity. **sensory n.,** a peripheral nerve that conducts impulses from a sense organ to the spinal cord or brain. **seventh n.,** nervus facialis. **sinus n.,** ramus sinus carotici nervi glossopharyngei. **sixth n.,** nervus abducens. **somatic n's,** the sensory and motor nerves. **spermatic n., external,** ramus genitalis nervi genitofemoralis. **spinal n's,** the thirty-one pairs of nerves arising from the spinal cord. See *nervi spinales.* **splanchnic n's,** the nerves of the blood vessels and viscera. **splanchnic n., greater,** nervus splanchnicus major. **splanchnic n., inferior, splanchnic n., lesser,** nervus splanchnicus minor. **splanchnic n., lowest,** nervus splanchnicus imus. **splanchnic n's, lumbar,** nervi splanchnici lumbales. **splanchnic n's, pelvic,** nervi splanchnici pelvini. **splanchnic n's, sacral,** nervi splanchnici sacrales. **stapedial n., stapedius n.,** nervus stapedius. **stylohyoid n.,** ramus stylohyoideus nervi facialis. **stylopharyngeal n.,** ramus musculi stylopharyngei nervi glossopharyngei. **subclavian n.,** nervus subclavius. **subcostal n.,** nervus subcostalis. **sublingual n.,** nervus sublingualis. **submaxillary n's,** rami glandulares ganglii submandibularis. **suboccipital n.,** nervus suboccipitalis. **subscapular n's,** nervi subscapulares. **sudomotor n's,** the nerves that control sweating. **supraclavicular n's,** nervi supraclaviculares. **supraclavicular n's, anterior,** nervi supraclaviculares mediales. **supraclavicular n's, intermediate,** nervi supraclaviculares intermedii. **supraclavicular n's, medial,** nervi supraclaviculares mediales. **supraclavicular n's, middle,** nervi supraclaviculares intermedii. **supraclavicular n's, posterior,** nervi supraclaviculares laterales. **supraorbital n.,** nervus supraorbitalis. **suprascapular n.,** nervus suprascapularis. **supratrochlear n.,** nervus supratrochlearis. **sural n.,** nervus suralis. **sympathetic n.** 1. Truncus sympatheticus. 2. One of the nerves of the sympathetic nervous system. See *sympathetic system,* under *system.* **temporal n's, deep,** nervi temporales profundus. **temporal n's, subcutaneous,** rami temporales superficiales nervi auriculotemporalis. **n. of tensor tympani,** nervus tensoris tympani. **n. of tensor veli palatini,** nervus tensoris veli palatini. **tenth n.,** nervus vagus. **terminal n's,** nervi terminales. **thermic n., thermogenic n.,** calorific n. **third n.,** nervus oculomotorius. **thoracic n's,** the twelve pairs of spinal nerves arising from the thoracic segments of the spinal cord. See *nervi thoracici.* **thoracic n., long,** nervus thoracicus longus. **thoracodorsal n.,** nervus thoracodorsalis. **tibial n.,** nervus tibialis. **Tiedemann's n.,** a name given a plexus of sympathetic nerve fibrils surrounding the central artery of the retina. **tonsillar n's,** rami tonsillares nervi glossopharyngei. **trigeminal n.,** nervus trigeminus. **trisplanchnic n's,** the nerves of the sympathetic nervous system. **trochlear n.,** nervus trochlearis. **trophic n.,** a nerve that aids in regulating nutrition. **twelfth n.,** nervus hypoglossus. **tympanic n.,** nervus tympanicus. **ulnar n.,** nervus ulnaris. **utricular n.,** nervus utricularis. **utriculoampullar n.,** nervus utriculoampullaris. **vaginal n's,** nervi vaginales. **vagus n.,** nervus vagus. **vascular n.,** nervus vascularis. **vasoconstrictor n.,** a nerve whose stimulation causes contraction of the blood vessels. **vasodilator n.,** a nerve whose stimulation causes dilation of the blood vessels. **vasomotor n.,** any nerve concerned in controlling the caliber of vessels, whether as a vasodilator or a vasoconstrictor. **vasosensory n.,** any nerve supplying sensory fibers to the vessels. **vertebral n.,** nervus vertebralis. **vestibular n.,** pars vestibularis nervi octavi. **vestibulocochlear n.,** nervus vestibulocochlearis. **vidian n.,** nervus canalis pterygoidei. **vidian n., deep,** nervus petrosus profundus. **n. of Willis,** nervus accessorius. **Wrisberg's n.,** nervus intermedius. **zygomatic n.,** nervus zygomaticus. **zygomaticofacial n.,** ramus zygomaticofacialis nervi zygomatici. **zygomaticotemporal n.,** ramus zygomaticotemporalis nervi zygomatici.

nervi (ner′vi) [L.]. Plural of *nervus.*

nervimotility (ner″vĭ-mo-til′ĭ-te). Susceptibility to nervimotion.

nervimotion (ner″vĭ-mo′shun). Motion effected through the agency of a nerve.

nervimotor (ner″vĭ-mo′tor). Pertaining to a motor nerve.

nervimuscular (ner″vĭ-mus′ku-lar). Pertaining to the nerve supply of muscles.

nervomuscular (ner″vo-mus′ku-lar). Nervimuscular.

nervone (ner′vōn). A cerebroside, $C_{48}H_{91}O_8N$, isolated from nerve tissue.

nervosism (ner′vo-sizm). 1. Neurasthenia. 2. The theory that disease is dependent on variations in nerve force.

nervosity (ner-vos′ĭ-te). Morbid nervousness.

nervotabes (ner″vo-ta′bēz). Pseudotabes.

nervous (ner′vus) [L. *nervosus*]. 1. Pertaining to a nerve or to nerves. 2. Unduly excitable.

nervousness (ner′vus-nes). Morbid or undue excitability; a state of excessive irritability, with great mental and physical unrest.

nervus (ner′vus), pl. *ner′vi* [L.]. [N A, B N A] A cordlike structure that conveys impulses between a part of the central nervous system and some other region of the body. See also *nerve.* For names and description of specific nerves, see *Table of Nervi.*

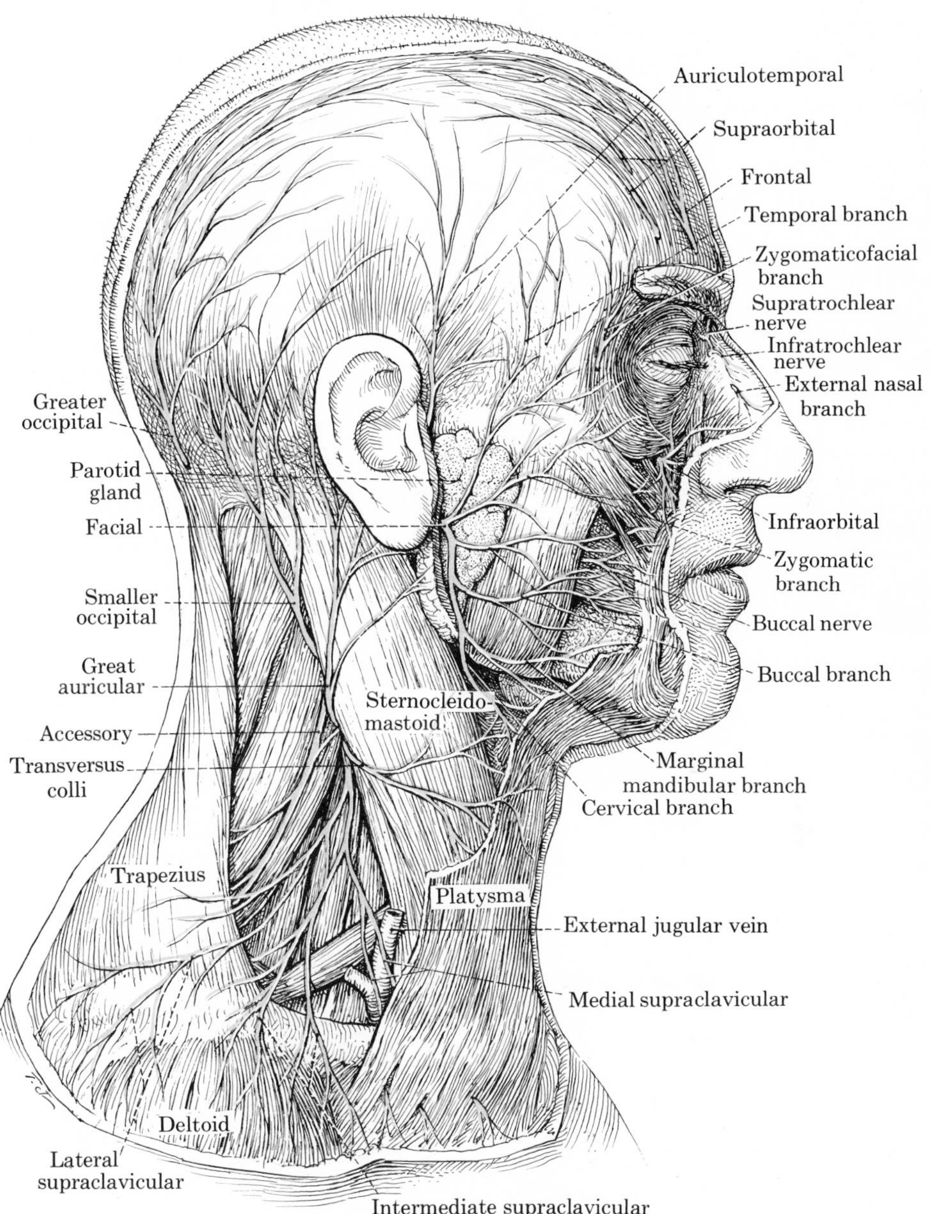

SUPERFICIAL NERVES AND MUSCLES OF HEAD AND NECK

Portions of the parotid gland and platysma muscle are shown cut away. (Jones and Shepard.)

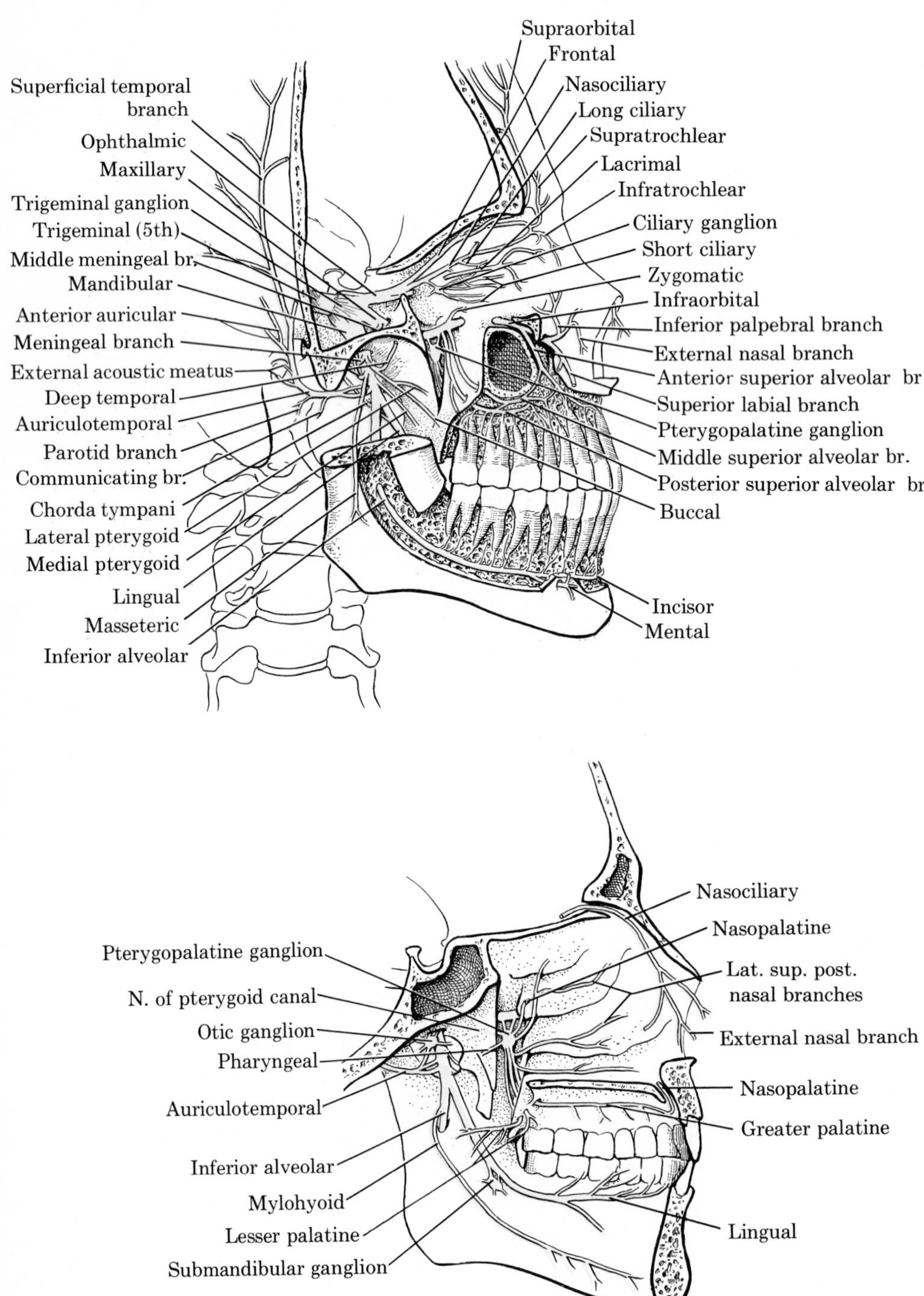

DEEP NERVES SHOWN IN RELATION TO BONES OF FACE

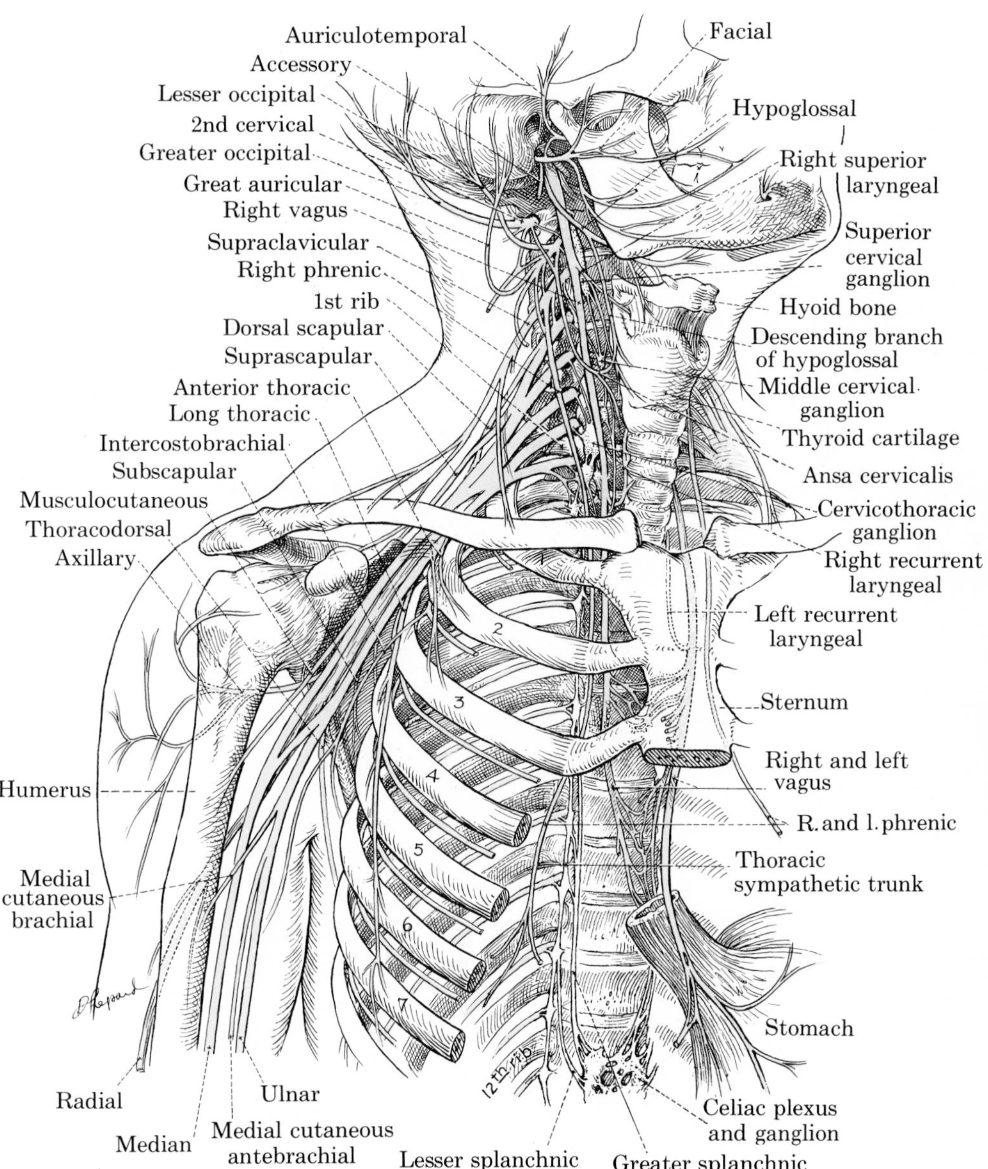

DEEP NERVES OF NECK, AXILLA, AND UPPER THORAX

The sympathetic nerves are uncolored. (Jones and Shepard.)

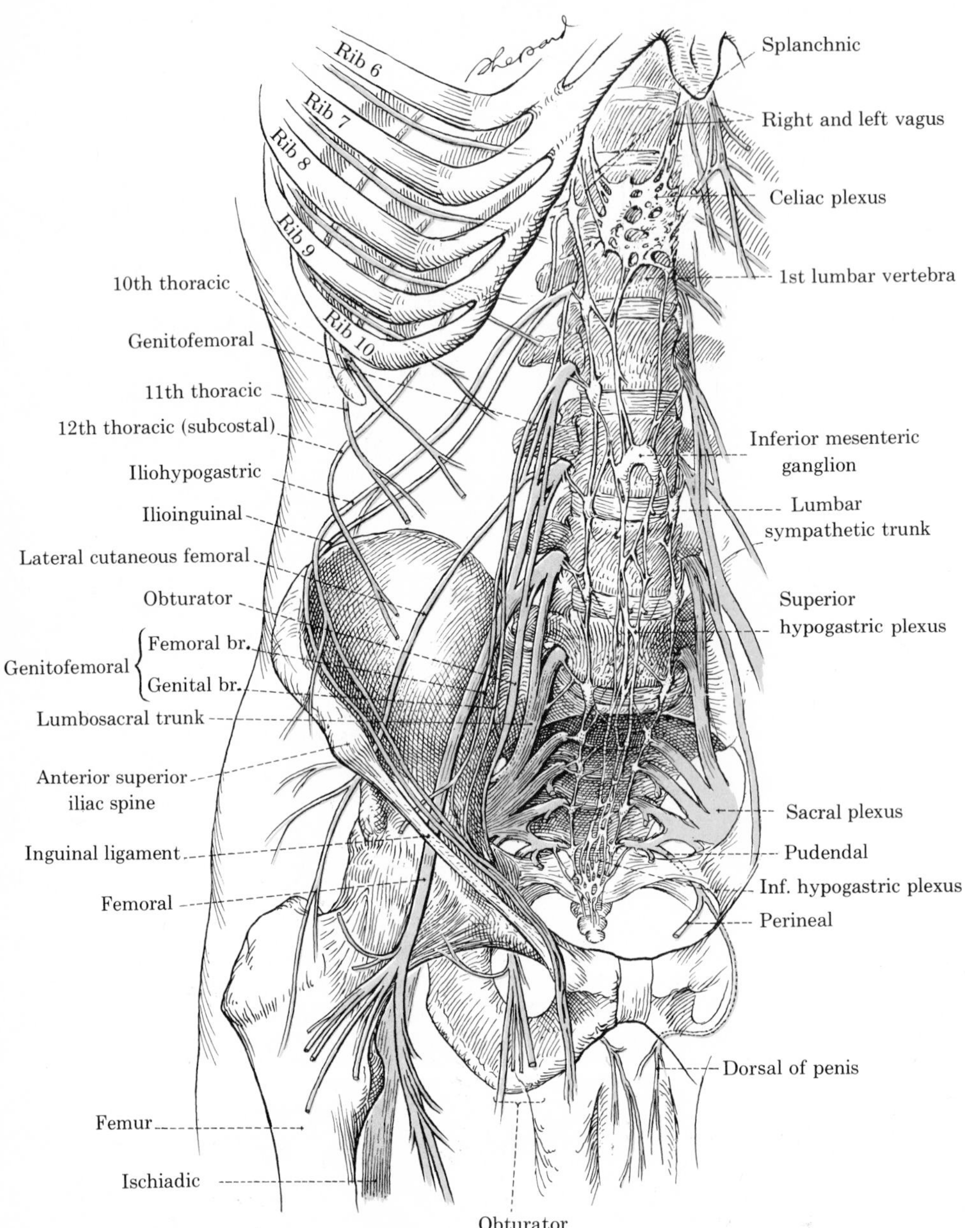

DEEP NERVES OF LOWER TRUNK

The sympathetic nerves are uncolored. (Jones and Shepard.)

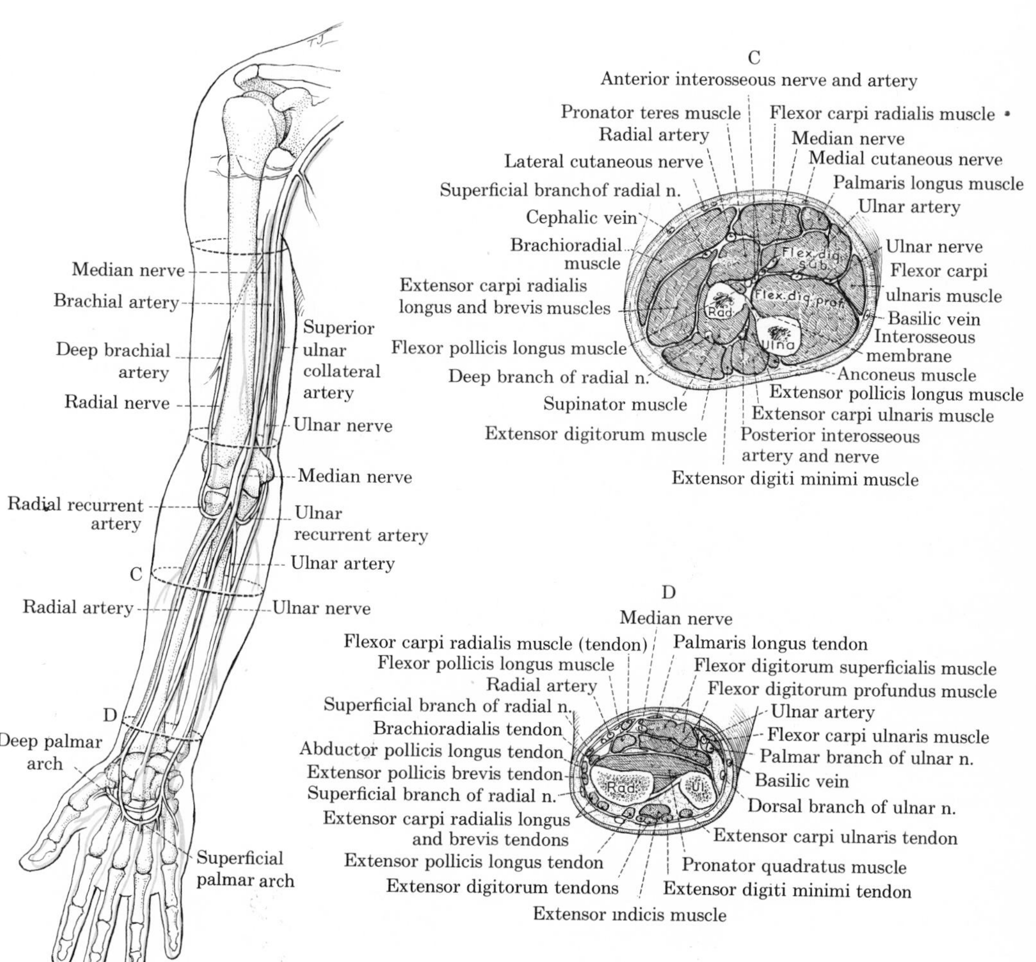

NERVES OF RIGHT UPPER EXTREMITY

Front view shows principal nerves and arteries (uncolored) in relation to the bones. *C* and *D* are cross sections made at levels indicated on drawing at left. (Jones and Shepard.)

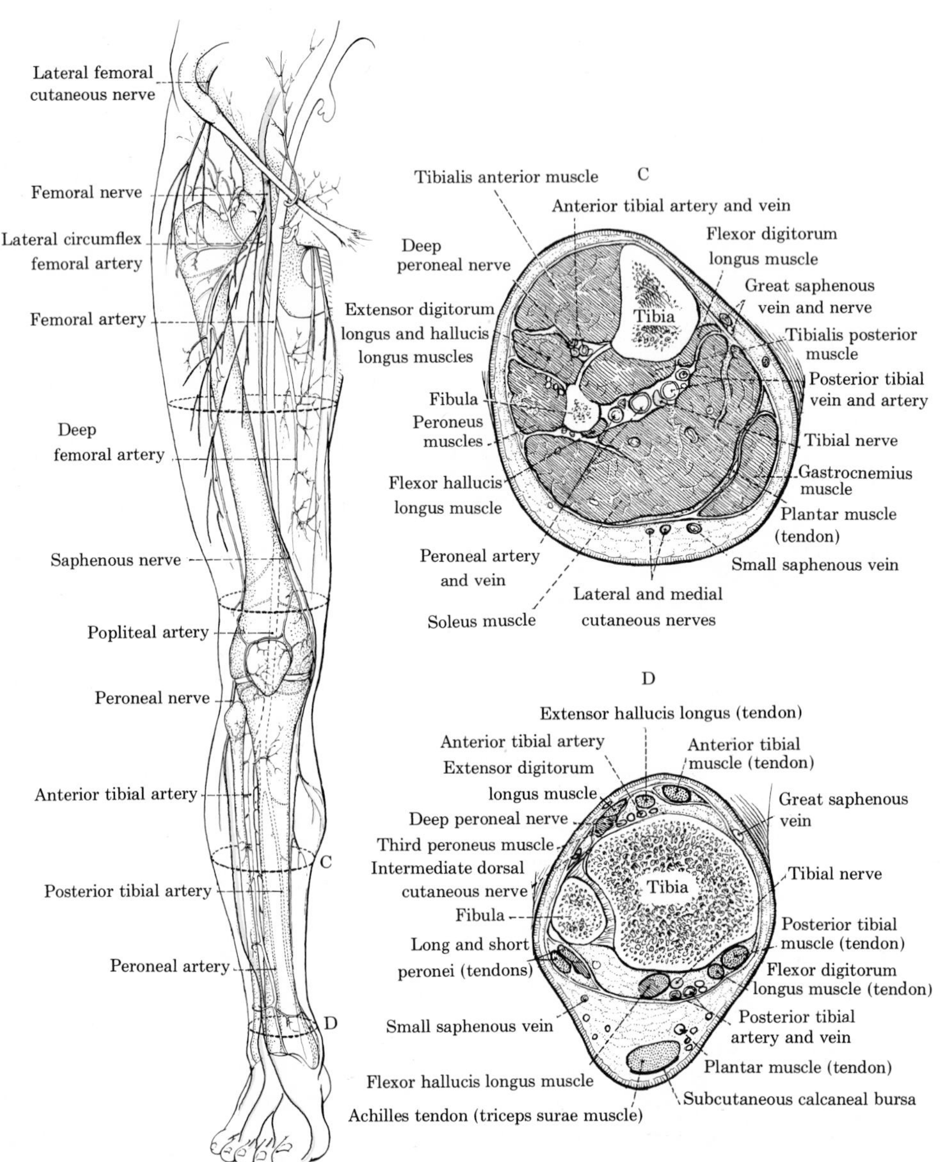

NERVES OF RIGHT LOWER EXTREMITY

Front view shows principal nerves and arteries (uncolored) in relation to the bones. *C* and *D* are cross sections made at levels indicated on drawing at left. (Jones and Shepard.)

TABLE OF NERVI

Descriptions are given on N A terms, and include anglicized names of specific nerves. B N A terms, when different, are cross referred to names used in Nomina Anatomica.

n. ab′ducens [N A, B N A], abducens nerve (6th cranial): *origin*, inferior border of basal surface of pons; *distribution*, lateral rectus muscle of eye; *modality*, motor.

n. accesso′rius [N A, B N A], accessory nerve (11th cranial): *origin*, lateral aspect of first four cervical segments of spinal cord; *distribution*, sternocleidomastoid and trapezius muscles; *modality*, motor.

n. acus′ticus [B N A], n. vestibulocochlearis.

n. alveola′ris infe′rior [N A, B N A], inferior alveolar nerve: *origin*, mandibular division of trigeminal nerve; *branches*, mylohyoid, inferior dental, mental, and inferior gingival nerves; *distribution*—see individual branches, in this table; *modality*, motor and general sensory.

ner′vi alveola′res superio′res [N A, B N A], a term denoting collectively the *rami alveolares superiores anteriores nervi infraorbitalis, ramus alveolaris superior medius nervi infraorbitalis*, and *rami alveolares superiores posteriores nervi maxillaris*. Called also *superior alveolar nerves*.

n. ampulla′ris ante′rior [N A], the branch of the pars vestibularis nervi octavi that innervates the ampulla of the anterior semicircular duct, ending around the hair cells of the ampullary crest. Called also *anterior ampullar nerve*.

n. ampulla′ris infe′rior [B N A], n. ampullaris posterior.

n. ampulla′ris latera′lis [N A, B N A], the branch of the pars vestibularis nervi octavi that innervates the ampulla of the lateral semicircular duct, ending around the hair cells of the ampullary crest. Called also *lateral ampullar nerve*.

n. ampulla′ris poste′rior [N A], the branch of the pars vestibularis nervi octavi that innervates the ampulla of the posterior semicircular duct, ending around the hair cells of the ampullary crest. Called also *posterior ampullar nerve*.

n. ampulla′ris supe′rior [B N A], n. ampullaris anterior.

ner′vi anococcyg′ei [N A, B N A], anococcygeal nerves: *origin*, coccygeal plexus; *distribution*, skin in region of coccyx; *modality*, general sensory.

n. articula′ris [N A, B N A], a peripheral nerve that supplies a joint and its associated structures. Called also *articular nerve*.

ner′vi auricula′res anterio′res [N A, B N A], anterior auricular nerves: *origin*, auriculotemporal nerve; *distribution*, skin of anterosuperior part of external ear; *modality*, general sensory.

n. auricula′ris mag′nus [N A, B N A], great auricular nerve: *origin*, cervical plexus—C2–C3; *branches*, anterior and posterior rami; *distribution*—see individual branches, under *ramus; modality*, general sensory.

n. auricula′ris poste′rior [N A, B N A], posterior auricular nerve: *origin*, facial nerve; *branches*, occipital ramus; *distribution*, auricularis posterior and occipitofrontalis muscles and skin of external acoustic meatus; *modality*, motor and general sensory.

n. auriculotempora′lis [N A, B N A], auriculotemporal nerve: *origin*, mandibular division of trigeminal nerve; *branches*, anterior auricular nerve, nerve of external acoustic meatus, parotid and superficial temporal rami, ramus to tympanic membrane, and communicating ramus with facial nerve; *distribution*—see individual branches, in this table and under *ramus; modality*, general sensory.

n. axilla′ris [N A, B N A], axillary nerve: *origin*, brachial plexus—C5–C6 through posterior cord; *branches*, lateral superior brachial cutaneous nerve and muscular rami; *distribution*, deltoid and teres minor muscles, skin over shoulder; *modality*, motor and general sensory.

n. bucca′lis [N A], buccal nerve: *origin*, mandibular division of trigeminal nerve; *distribution*, skin of mid-cheek, mucosa of floor of mouth; *modality*, general sensory.

n. buccinato′rius [B N A], n. buccalis.

n. cana′lis pterygoi′dei [N A], nerve of pterygoid canal: *origin*, union of deep and major petrosal nerves; *distribution*, pterygopalatine ganglion and branches; *modality*, parasympathetic, sympathetic, and general sensory.

n. cardi′acus cervica′lis infe′rior [N A], inferior cervical cardiac nerve: *origin*, cervicothoracic ganglion; *distribution*, heart via cardiac plexus; *modality*, sympathetic (accelerator) and visceral afferent.

n. cardi′acus cervica′lis me′dius [N A], middle cervical cardiac nerve: *origin*, middle cervical ganglion; *distribution*, heart; *modality*, sympathetic (accelerator) and visceral afferent.

n. cardi′acus cervica′lis supe′rior [N A], superior cervical cardiac nerve: *origin*, superior cervical ganglion; *distribution*, heart; *modality*, sympathetic (accelerator).

n. cardi′acus infe′rior [B N A], n. cardiacus cervicalis inferior.

n. cardi′acus me′dius [B N A], n. cardiacus cervicalis medius.

n. cardi′acus supe′rior [B N A], n. cardiacus cervicalis superior.

ner′vi cardi′aci thora′cici [N A], thoracic cardiac nerves: *origin*, second through fifth thoracic ganglia of sympathetic trunk; *distribution*, heart; *modality*, sympathetic (accelerator) and visceral afferent.

ner′vi caroticotympan′ici [N A], caroticotympanic nerves: *origin*, superior cervical sympathetic ganglion; *branches*, helps form tympanic plexus; *distribution*, tympanic region and parotid gland; *modality*, sympathetic.

n. caroticotympan′icus infe′rior [B N A], **n. caroticotympan′icus supe′rior** [B N A]. See *nervi caroticotympanici*.

ner′vi carot′ici exter′ni [N A, B N A], external carotid nerves: *origin*, superior cervical ganglion; *distribution*, cranial blood vessels and glands via the external carotid plexus; *modality*, sympathetic.

n. carot′icus inter′nus [N A, B N A], internal carotid nerve: *origin*, superior cervical ganglion; *distribution*, cranial blood vessels and glands via internal carotid plexus; *modality*, sympathetic.

ner′vi caverno′si clitor′idis [N A], cavernous nerves of clitoris: *origin*, uterovaginal plexus; *distribution*, erectile tissue of clitoris; *modality*, parasympathetic, sympathetic, and visceral afferent.

n. caverno′sus clitor′idis ma′jor [B N A], **ner′vi caverno′si clitor′idis mino′res** [B N A]. See *nervi cavernosi clitoridis*.

ner′vi caverno′si pe′nis [N A], cavernous nerves of penis: *origin*, prostatic plexus; *distribution*, erectile tissue of penis; *modality*, sympathetic, parasympathetic, and visceral afferent.

n. caverno′sus pe′nis ma′jor [B N A], **ner′vi caverno′si pe′nis mino′res** [B N A]. See *nervi cavernosi penis*.

ner′vi cerebra′les [B N A], nervi craniales.

ner′vi cervica′les [N A, B N A], the eight pairs of nerves that arise from the cervical segments of the spinal cord and, except for the last pair, leave the vertebral column above the correspondingly numbered vertebra. The ventral branches of the upper four, on either side, unite to form the cervical plexus, and those of the lower four contribute most of the brachial plexus. Called also *cervical nerves*.

ner′vi cilia′res bre′ves [N A, B N A], short ciliary nerves: *origin*, ciliary ganglion from oculomotor nerve; *distribution*, smooth muscle of eye; *modality*, parasympathetic, and sympathetic and general sensory from communicating branches with trigeminal nerve.

ner'vi cilia'res lon'gi [N A, B N A], long ciliary nerves: *origin*, nasociliary nerve, from ophthalmic division of trigeminal nerve; *distribution*, intraocular structures; *modality*, general sensory.

ner'vi clu'nium inferio'res [N A, B N A], inferior clunial nerves: *origin*, posterior femoral cutaneous nerve; *distribution*, skin of inferior gluteal region; *modality*, general sensory.

ner'vi clu'nium me'dii [N A, B N A], middle clunial nerves: *origin*, lateral branch of dorsal branch of sacral nerve; *distribution*, skin of middle gluteal region; *modality*, general sensory.

ner'vi clu'nium superio'res [N A, B N A], superior clunial nerves: *origin*, lateral branch of dorsal branch of lumbar nerve; *distribution*, skin of upper gluteal region; *modality*, general sensory.

n. coccyg'eus [N A, B N A], coccygeal nerve: one of the pair of nerves that arise from the coccygeal segment of the spinal cord.

n. coch'leae [B N A], pars cochlearis nervi octavi.

ner'vi crania'les [N A], the twelve pairs of nerves that are connected with the brain, including the nervi olfactorii (I), and the opticus (II), oculomotorius (III), trochlearis (IV), trigeminus (V), abducens (VI), facialis (VII), vestibulocochlearis (VIII), glossopharyngeus (IX), vagus (X), accessorius (XI), and hypoglossus (XII). Called also *nervi cerebrales* [B N A], and *cranial nerves*.

n. cuta'neus [N A, B N A], a peripheral nerve that supplies a region of the skin, many of them not being specifically named. Called also *cutaneous nerve*.

n. cuta'neus antebra'chii latera'lis [N A], lateral cutaneous nerve of forearm: *origin*, musculocutaneous nerve; *distribution*, skin over radial part of forearm; *modality*, general sensory.

n. cuta'neus antebra'chii media'lis [N A], medial cutaneous nerve of forearm: *origin*, brachial plexus—C8–T1 through medial cord; *branches*, anterior and ulnar rami; *distribution*, skin of front, medial, and posteromedial aspects of forearm; *modality*, general sensory.

n. cuta'neus antebra'chii poste'rior [N A], posterior cutaneous nerve of forearm: *origin*, radial nerve; *distribution*, skin of dorsal aspect of lower half of arm and of forearm; *modality*, general sensory.

n. cuta'neus antibra'chii dorsa'lis [B N A], n. cutaneous antebrachii posterior.

n. cuta'neus bra'chii latera'lis infe'rior [N A], inferior lateral cutaneous nerve of arm: *origin*, radial nerve; *distribution*, skin of back of arm; *modality*, general sensory.

n. cuta'neus bra'chii latera'lis supe'rior [N A], lateral superior cutaneous nerve of arm: *origin*, axillary nerve; *distribution*, skin of back of arm; *modality*, general sensory.

n. cuta'neus bra'chii media'lis [N A, B N A], medial cutaneous nerve of arm: *origin*, axillary plexus—T1 through medial cord; *distribution*, skin on medial and posterior aspects of arm; *modality*, general sensory.

n. cuta'neus bra'chii poste'rior [N A, B N A], posterior cutaneous nerve of arm: *origin*, radial nerve; *distribution*, skin on dorsal surface of arm; *modality*, general sensory.

n. cuta'neus col'li [B N A], n. transversus colli.

n. cuta'neus dorsa'lis interme'dius pe'dis [N A, B N A], intermediate dorsal cutaneous nerve of foot: *origin*, superficial peroneal nerve; *branches*, dorsal digital nerves of foot; *distribution*, skin of lateral side of foot and ankle, and adjacent sides of third and fourth, and of fourth and fifth toes; *modality*, general sensory.

n. cuta'neus dorsa'lis latera'lis pe'dis [N A, B N A], lateral dorsal cutaneous nerve of foot: *origin*, sural nerve; *distribution*, adjacent sides of fourth and fifth and lateral side of fifth toe; *modality*, general sensory.

n. cuta'neus dorsa'lis media'lis pe'dis [N A, B N A], medial dorsal cutaneous nerve of foot: *origin*, superficial peroneal nerve; *distribution*, skin of medial side of foot and adjacent sides of second and third toes; *modality*, general sensory.

n. cuta'neus fem'oris latera'lis [N A, B N A], lateral cutaneous nerve of thigh: *origin*, lumbar plexus—L2–L3; *distribution*, skin of lateral and front aspects of thigh; *modality*, general sensory.

n. cuta'neus fem'oris poste'rior [N A, B N A], posterior cutaneous nerve of thigh: *origin*, sacral plexus—S1–S3; *branches*, inferior clunial nerves and perineal rami; *distribution*, skin of inferior gluteal region, back of thigh and leg, and external genitalia; *modality*, general sensory.

n. cuta'neus su'rae latera'lis [N A], lateral cutaneous nerve of calf: *origin*, common peroneal nerve; *branches*, sural nerve; *distribution*, skin of lower dorsal aspect of leg and lateral aspect of foot; *modality*, general sensory.

n. cuta'neus su'rae media'lis [N A, B N A], medial cutaneous nerve of calf: *origin*, tibial nerve; *branches*, sural nerve; *distribution*, skin of lower dorsal aspect of leg and lateral aspect of foot; *modality*, general sensory.

n. depres'sor cor'dis [B N A], a nerve supposedly acting to depress the action of the heart. Omitted in N A.

ner'vi digita'les dorsa'les hal'lucis latera'lis et dig'iti secun'di media'lis [N A, B N A], dorsal digital nerves of lateral surface of great toe and of medial surface of second toe: *origin*, deep peroneal nerve; *distribution*, dorsal interosseous muscles, articulations of ankle and foot, skin of adjacent sides of great and second toes; *modality*, general sensory and motor.

ner'vi digita'les dorsa'les ner'vi radia'lis [N A, B N A], dorsal digital nerves of radial nerve: *origin*, superficial branch of radial nerve; *distribution*, ulnar side of thumb, radial side of second finger, and adjacent sides of second and third, and of third and fourth fingers; *modality*, general sensory.

ner'vi digita'les dorsa'les ner'vi ulna'ris [N A, B N A], dorsal digital nerves of ulnar nerve: *origin*, dorsal branch of ulnar nerve; *distribution*, skin of ulnar sides of third, fourth, and fifth, and of radial sides of fourth and fifth fingers; *modality*, general sensory.

ner'vi digita'les dorsa'les pe'dis [N A, B N A], dorsal digital nerves of foot: *origin*, intermediate dorsal cutaneous nerve; *distribution*, adjacent sides of third and fourth, and of fourth and fifth toes; *modality*, general sensory.

ner'vi digita'les palma'res commu'nes ner'vi media'ni [N A], common palmar digital nerves of median nerve: *origin*, median nerve; *branches*, proper palmar digital nerves; *distribution*—see individual branches, in this table; *modality*, general sensory.

ner'vi digita'les palma'res commu'nes ner'vi ulna'ris [N A], common palmar digital nerves of ulnar nerve: *origin*, superficial branch of palmar branch of ulnar nerve; *branches*, proper palmar digital nerves; *distribution*—see individual branches, in this table; *modality*, general sensory.

ner'vi digita'les palma'res pro'prii ner'vi media'ni [N A], proper palmar digital nerves of median nerve: *origin*, common palmar digital nerves; *distribution*, skin on palmar surface and sides of digits; *modality*, general sensory.

ner'vi digita'les palma'res pro'prii ner'vi ulna'ris [N A], proper palmar digital nerves of ulnar nerve: *origin*, common palmar digital nerves and superficial branch of palmar branch of ulnar nerve; *distribution*, skin of adjacent sides of fourth and fifth fingers; *modality*, general sensory.

ner'vi digita'les planta'res commu'nes ner'vi planta'ris latera'lis [N A, B N A], common plantar digital nerves of lateral plantar nerve: *origin*, superficial branch of lateral plantar nerve; *branches*, proper plantar digital nerves; *distribution*—see individual branches, in this table; *modality*, general sensory.

ner'vi digita'les planta'res commu'nes ner'vi planta'ris media'lis [N A, B N A], common plantar digital nerves of medial plantar nerve: *origin*, medial plantar nerve; *branches*, proper plantar digital nerves; *distribution*—see individual branches, in this table; *modality*, general sensory.

ner'vi digita'les planta'res pro'prii ner'vi planta'ris latera'lis [N A, B N A], proper plantar digital nerves of lateral plantar nerve: *origin*, common plantar digital nerves; *distribution*, lateral plantar surface of foot, and plantar and adjacent surfaces of fourth and fifth toes; *modality*, general sensory.

ner'vi digita'les planta'res pro'prii ner'vi planta'ris media'lis [N A, B N A], proper plantar digital nerves of medial plantar nerve: *origin*, common plantar digital nerves; *distribution*, medial plantar surface of foot and plantar and adjacent surfaces of great and second, and of second and third toes; *modality*, general sensory.

ner'vi digita'les vola'res commu'nes ner'vi media'ni [B N A], nervi digitales palmares communes nervi mediani.

ner'vi digita'les vola'res commu'nes ner'vi ulna'ris [B N A], nervi digitales palmares communes nervi ulnaris.

ner'vi digita'les vola'res pro'prii ner'vi media'ni [B N A], nervi digitales palmares proprii nervi mediani.

ner'vi digita'les vola'res pro'prii ner'vi ulna'ris [B N A], nervi digitales palmares proprii nervi ulnaris.

n. dorsa'lis clitor'idis [N A, B N A], dorsal nerve of clitoris: *origin*, perineal nerves; *distribution*, deep transverse perineal and sphincter urethrae muscles and clitoris; *modality*, general sensory and motor.

n. dorsa'lis pe'nis [N A, B N A], dorsal nerve of penis: *origin*, perineal nerves; *distribution*, deep transverse perineal and sphincter urethrae muscles and skin of penis; *modality*, general sensory and motor.

n. dorsa'lis scap'ulae [N A, B N A], dorsal nerve of scapula: *origin*, brachial plexus—ventral ramus of C5; *distribution*, levator scapulae and rhomboid major and minor muscles; *modality*, motor.

ner'vi erigen'tes, N A alternative for *nervi splanchnici pelvini.*

n. ethmoida'lis ante'rior [N A, B N A], anterior ethmoidal nerve: *origin*, nasociliary nerve, from ophthalmic division of trigeminal nerve; *branches*, internal, external, lateral, and medial rami; *distribution*, mucosa of upper and anterior nasal septum, lateral wall of nasal cavity, skin of lower bridge and tip of nose; *modality*, general sensory.

n. ethmoida'lis poste'rior [N A, B N A], posterior ethmoidal nerve: *origin*, nasociliary nerve, from ophthalmic division of trigeminal nerve; *distribution*, mucosa of posterior ethmoid cells and of sphenoid sinus; *modality*, general sensory.

n. facia'lis [N A, B N A], facial nerve (7th cranial): *origin*, inferior border of pons, between olive and inferior cerebellar peduncle; *branches*, stapedius, greater petrosal, and posterior auricular nerves, parotid plexus, digastric, temporal, zygomatic, buccal, lingual, marginal mandibular, and cervical rami, and a communicating ramus with the tympanic plexus; *distribution*—see individual branches, in this table and under *ramus; modality*, motor, parasympathetic, general sensory, special sensory.

n. femora'lis [N A, B N A], femoral nerve: *origin*, lumbar plexus—L2–L4; *branches*, saphenous nerve, muscular and anterior cutaneous rami; *distribution*—see individual branches, in this table and under *ramus; modality*, general sensory and motor.

n. fibula'ris commu'nis, N A alternative for *n. peroneus communis.*

n. fibula'ris profun'dus, N A alternative for *n. peroneus profundus.*

n. fibula'ris superficia'lis, N A alternative for *n. peroneus superficialis.*

n. fronta'lis [N A, B N A], frontal nerve: *origin*, ophthalmic division of trigeminal nerve; *branches*, supraorbital and supratrochlear nerves; *distribution*—see individual branches, in this table; *modality*, general sensory.

n. genitofemora'lis [N A, B N A], genitofemoral nerve: *origin*, lumbar plexus—L1–L2; *branches*, genital and femoral rami; *distribution*—see individual branches, under *ramus; modality*, general sensory and motor.

n. glossopharyn'geus [N A, B N A], glossopharyngeal nerve (9th cranial): *origin*, several rootlets between the olive and the inferior cerebellar peduncle of the superior part of the medulla oblongata; *branches*, tympanic nerve, pharyngeal, stylopharyngeal, tonsillar, and lingual rami, ramus to the carotid sinus, and a ramus communicating with the auricular ramus of the vagus nerve; *distribution*—see individual branches, in this table and under *ramus; modality*, parasympathetic, general sensory, special sensory, and visceral sensory.

n. glu'teus infe'rior [N A], inferior gluteal nerve; *origin*, sacral plexus—L5–S2; *distribution*, gluteus maximus muscle; *modality*, motor.

n. glu'teus supe'rior [N A], superior gluteal nerve: *origin*, sacral plexus—L4–S1; *distribution*, gluteal muscles; *modality*, motor.

ner'vi haemorrhoida'les inferio'res [B N A], nervi rectales inferiores.

ner'vi haemorrhoida'les me'dii [B N A]. Omitted in N A.

ner'vi haemorrhoida'les superio'res [B N A]. Omitted in N A.

n. hypogas'tricus [dex'ter et sinis'ter] [N A], a nerve trunk situated on either side (right and left), interconnecting the superior and inferior hypogastric plexuses. Called also *hypogastric nerve.*

n. hypoglos'sus [N A, B N A], hypoglossal nerve (12th cranial): *origin*, several rootlets in the anterolateral sulcus between the olive and the pyramid of the medulla oblongata; *branches*, lingual rami; *distribution*, styloglossus, hyoglossus, and genioglossus muscles and intrinsic muscles of the tongue; *modality*, motor.

n. iliohypogas'tricus [N A, B N A], iliohypogastric nerve: *origin*, lumbar plexus—T12; *branches*, lateral and anterior cutaneous rami; *distribution*—see individual branches, under *ramus; modality*, general sensory.

n. ilioinguina'lis [N A, B N A], ilioinguinal nerve: *origin*, lumbar plexus—T12–L1; *branches*, anterior scrotal or labial rami; *distribution*, thigh and anterior scrotal or labial region; *modality*, general sensory.

n. infraorbita'lis [N A, B N A], infraorbital nerve: *origin*, maxillary division of trigeminal nerve; *branches*, middle and anterior superior alveolar, inferior palpebral, internal and external nasal, and superior labial rami; *distribution*—see individual branches, under *ramus; modality*, general sensory.

n. infratrochlea'ris [N A, B N A], infratrochlear nerve: *origin*, nasociliary nerve from ophthalmic division of trigeminal nerve; *branches*, palpebral rami; *distribution*, root and upper bridge of nose, conjunctiva, skin of lower lid, lacrimal duct; *modality*, general sensory.

ner'vi intercostobrachia'les [N A, B N A], intercostobrachial nerves: *origin*, second and third intercostal nerves; *distribution*, skin on back and medial aspect of arm; *modality*, general sensory.

n. interme'dius [N A, B N A], intermediate nerve: a name given a small part of the facial nerve, starting at the inferior border of the pons, between the olive and the inferior cerebellar peduncle, between the remainder of the facial nerve and the vestibulocochlear nerve; *branches*, chorda tympani and greater petrosal nerve; *distribution*, lacrimal, nasal, palatine, submandibular, and sublingual glands, and anterior two-thirds of tongue; *modality*, parasympathetic and special sensory.

n. interos'seus antebra'chii ante'rior [N A], anterior interosseous nerve of forearm: *origin*, median nerve; *distribution*, deep muscles on ventral aspect of forearm; *modality*, motor.

n. interos'seus antebra'chii poste'rior [N A], posterior interosseous nerve of forearm: *origin*, deep branch of radial nerve; *distribution*, abductor pollicis longus and extensors of the thumb and second finger; *modality*, motor.

n. interos'seus [antibra'chii] dorsa'lis [B N A], n. interosseus antebrachii posterior.

n. interos'seus [antibra'chii] vola'ris [B N A], n. interosseus antebrachii anterior.

n. interos'seus cru'ris [N A, B N A], interosseous nerve of leg: *origin*, tibial nerve; *distribution*, inferior tibiofibular joint, interosseous membrane; *modality*, general sensory.

n. ischiad'icus [N A, B N A], sciatic nerve: *origin*, sacral plexus—L4–S3; *branches*, common peroneal and tibial nerves; *distribution*—see individual branches, in this table; *modality*, general sensory and motor.

n. jugula'ris [N A, B N A], jugular nerve: sympathetic fibers originating from the superior cervical ganglion, and distributed to the glossopharyngeal and vagus nerves.

ner'vi labia'les anterio'res [N A, B N A], anterior labial nerves: *origin*, ilioinguinal nerve; *distribution*, skin of anterior labial region; *modality*, general sensory.

ner'vi labia'les posterio'res [N A, B N A], posterior labial nerves: *origin*, perineal nerves; *distribution*, labium majus; *modality*, general sensory.

n. lacrima'lis [N A, B N A], lacrimal nerve: *origin*, ophthalmic division of trigeminal nerve; *distribution*, lacrimal gland, conjunctiva, lateral commissure of eye, and skin of upper eyelid; *modality*, general sensory.

n. laryn'geus infe'rior [N A, B N A], inferior laryngeal nerve: *origin*, recurrent laryngeal nerve; *distribution*, intrinsic muscles of larynx, except cricothyroid; *modality*, motor.

n. laryn'geus recur'rens [N A], recurrent laryngeal nerve: *origin*, vagus nerve; *branches*, inferior laryngeal nerve, tracheal, esophageal, and inferior cardiac rami; *distribution*—see individual branches, in this table and under *ramus; modality*, parasympathetic, visceral afferent, and motor.

n. laryn'geus supe'rior [N A, B N A], superior laryngeal nerve: *origin*, vagus nerve; *branches*, external, internal, and communicating rami; *distribution*—see individual branches, under *ramus; modality*, motor, general sensory, visceral afferent, and parasympathetic.

n. lingua'lis [N A, B N A], lingual nerve: *origin*, mandibular division of trigeminal nerve; *branches*, sublingual nerve, lingual ramus, ramus to the isthmus of the fauces, and rami communicating with the hypoglossal nerve and chorda tympani; *distribution*—see individual branches, in this table and under *ramus; modality*, general sensory.

ner'vi lumba'les [N A, B N A], the five pairs of nerves that arise from the lumbar segments of the spinal cord, each pair leaving the vertebral column below the correspondingly numbered vertebra. The ventral branches of these nerves participate in the formation of the lumbosacral plexus. Called also *lumbar nerves*.

n. mandibula'ris [N A, B N A], mandibular nerve (mandibular division of trigeminal nerve): *origin*, trigeminal ganglion; *branches*, meningeal ramus, masseteric, deep temporal, lateral and medial pterygoid, buccal, auriculotemporal, lingual, and inferior alveolar nerves; *distribution*—see individual branches, in this table and under *ramus; modality*, general sensory and motor.

n. masseter'icus [N A, B N A], masseteric nerve: *origin*, mandibular division of trigeminal nerve; *distribution*, masseter muscle and temporomandibular joint; *modality*, motor and general sensory.

n. masticato'rius [B N A], radix motoria nervi trigemini.

n. maxilla'ris [N A, B N A], maxillary nerve (maxillary division of trigeminal nerve): *origin*, trigeminal ganglion; *branches*, meningeal ramus, zygomatic nerve, posterior superior alveolar rami, infraorbital nerve, pterygopalatine nerves, and the nasopalatine nerve and other branches of pterygopalatine nerves and ganglion; *distribution*—see individual branches, in this table and under *ramus; modality*, general sensory.

n. mea'tus acus'tici exter'ni [N A], nerve of external acoustic meatus: *origin*, auriculotemporal nerve; *branches*, ramus to tympanic membrane; *distribution*, skin lining external acoustic meatus, and tympanic membrane; *modality*, general sensory.

n. mea'tus audito'rii exter'ni [B N A], n. meatus acustici externi.

n. media'nus [N A, B N A], median nerve: *origin*, brachial plexus—C6–T1 through lateral and medial cords; *branches*, anterior interosseous nerve of forearm, common palmar digital nerves, and muscular and palmar rami; *distribution*—see individual branches, in this table and under *ramus; modality*, general sensory.

n. menin'geus [me'dius] [B N A], ramus meningeus [medius] nervi maxillaris.

n. menta'lis [N A, B N A], mental nerve: *origin*, inferior alveolar nerve; *branches*, mental and inferior labial rami; *distibution*, skin of chin, and lower lip; *modality*, general sensory.

n. musculocuta'neus [N A, B N A], musculocutaneous nerve: *origin*, brachial plexus—C5–C7 through lateral cord; *branches*, lateral cutaneous nerve of forearm, and muscular rami; *distribution*, biceps and brachialis muscles, and skin of radial side of forearm; *modality*, general sensory and motor.

n. mylohyoi'deus [N A, B N A], mylohyoid nerve: *origin*, inferior alveolar nerve; *distribution*, mylohyoid muscle, anterior belly of diagastric muscle; *modality*, motor.

n. nasocilia'ris [N A, B N A], nasociliary nerve: *origin*, ophthalmic division of trigeminal nerve; *branches*, long ciliary, posterior ethmoidal, anterior ethmoidal, and infratrochlear nerves; *distribution*—see individual branches, in this table; *modality*, general sensory.

n. nasopalati'nus [N A], nasopalatine nerve: *origin*, pterygopalatine ganglion; *distribution*, mucosa of most of nasal septum and anterior part of hard palate; *modality*, general sensory.

n. obturato'rius [N A, B N A], obturator nerve: *origin*, lumbar plexus—L3–L4; *branches*, anterior and posterior rami; *distribution*—see individual branches, under *ramus; modality*, general sensory and motor.

n. occipita'lis ma'jor [N A, B N A], greater occipital nerve: *origin*, medial branch of dorsal branch of C2; *distribution*, scalp of medial half of back of head, semispinalis capitis muscle; *modality*, general sensory and motor.

n. occipita'lis mi'nor [N A, B N A], lesser occipital nerve: *origin*, spinal cord—C2–C3; *distribution*, scalp of lateral half of back of head; *modality*, general sensory.

n. occipita'lis ter'tius [N A, B N A], third occipital nerve: *origin*, medial branch of dorsal ramus of C3; *distribution*, skin of upper part of back of neck; *modality*, general sensory.

n. octa'vus [L. "eighth nerve"], N A alternative for *n. vestibulocochlearis*.

n. oculomoto'rius [N A, B N A], oculomotor nerve (3rd cranial): *origin*, interpeduncular fossa of mesencephalon; *branches*, superior and inferior rami; *distribution*—see individual branches, under *ramus; modality*, motor, proprioceptive, and parasympathetic.

ner'vi olfacto'rii [N A, B N A], olfactory nerves (1st cranial): *origin*, olfactory bulb; *distribution*, nasal mucosa; *modality*, special sensory.

n. ophthal'micus [N A, B N A], ophthalmic nerve (ophthalmic division of trigeminal nerve): *origin*, trigeminal ganglion; *branches*, tentorial rami, frontal, lacrimal, and nasociliary nerves; *distribution*—see individual branches, in this table and under *ramus; modality*, general sensory.

n. op'ticus [N A, B N A], optic nerve (2nd cranial): *origin*, optic chiasm; *distribution*, retina; *modality*, special sensory.

ner'vi palati'ni [B N A]. See *n. palatinus major* and *nervi palatini minores.*

n. palati'nus ante'rior [B N A], n. palatinus major.

n. palati'nus ma'jor [N A], greater palatine nerve: *origin*, pterygopalatine ganglion; *branches*, posterior inferior lateral nasal nerve; *distribution*, gingiva, mucosa of the soft and hard palate and of the inferior concha; *modality*, general sensory.

n. palati'nus me'dius [B N A]. See *nervi palatini minores.*

ner'vi palati'ni mino'res [N A], lesser palatine nerves: *origin*, pterygopalatine ganglion; *distribution*, soft palate, uvula, and tonsil; *modality*, general sensory.

n. palati'nus poste'rior [B N A]. See *nervi palatini minores.*

ner'vi perinea'les [N A], perineal nerves: *origin*, pudendal nerve; *branches*, posterior scrotal or labial nerves, dorsal nerve of penis or clitoris; *distribution*, muscles of urogenital diaphragm and skin of external genitalia; *modality*, general sensory and motor.

ner'vi perine'i [B N A], nervi perineales.

n. perone'us commu'nis [N A], common peroneal nerve: *origin*, sciatic nerve; *branches*, lateral cutaneous nerve of calf, superficial peroneal, and deep peroneal nerves; *distribution*—see individual branches, in this table; *modality*, general sensory and motor. Called also *n. fibularis communis.*

n. perone'us profun'dus [N A], deep peroneal nerve: *origin*, common peroneal nerve; *branches*, muscular rami, and dorsal digital nerves of lateral surface of great toe and of medial surface of second toe; *distribution*—see individual branches, in this table and under *ramus; modality*, general sensory and motor. Called also *n. fibularis profundus.*

n. perone'us superficia'lis [N A], superficial peroneal nerve: *origin*, common peroneal nerve; *branches*, muscular rami, medial and intermediate dorsal cutaneous nerves; *distribution*—see individual branches, in this table and under *ramus; modality*, general sensory and motor. Called also *n. fibularis superficialis.*

n. petro'sus ma'jor [N A], greater petrosal nerve: *origin*, n. intermedius via geniculate ganglion; *distribution*, lacrimal, nasal, and palatine glands and nasopharynx, via pterygopalatine ganglion and its branches; *modality*, parasympathetic and general sensory.

n. petro'sus mi'nor [N A], lesser petrosal nerve: *origin*, tympanic plexus of glossopharyngeal nerve; *distribution*, otic ganglion and, through communicating branch with auriculotemporal nerve, parotid gland; *modality*, parasympathetic.

n. petro'sus profun'dus [N A, B N A], deep petrosal nerve: *origin*, superior cervical sympathetic ganglion; *distribution*, lacrimal, nasal, and palatine glands via internal carotid plexus, nerve of pterygoid canal, and branches of pterygopalatine ganglion; *modality*, sympathetic.

n. petro'sus superficia'lis ma'jor [B N A], n. petrosus major.

n. petro'sus superficia'lis mi'nor [B N A], n. petrosus minor.

n. phren'icus [N A, B N A], phrenic nerve: *origin*, cervical plexus—C3–C5; *branches*, pericardiac and phrenicoabdominal rami; *distribution*, diaphragm, pericardium; *modality*, general sensory and motor.

ner'vi phren'ici accesso'rii [N A], the contributions of the fifth cervical nerve to the phrenic nerve when the former runs separately from the rest of the phrenic nerve throughout a large part of its course. Called also *accessory phrenic nerves.*

n. planta'ris latera'lis [N A, B N A], lateral plantar nerve: *origin*, tibial nerve; *branches*, muscular, superficial, and deep rami; *distribution*—see individual branches, under *ramus; modality*, general sensory and motor.

n. planta'ris media'lis [N A, B N A], medial plantar nerve: *origin*, tibial nerve; *branches*, common plantar digital nerves and muscular rami; *distribution*—see individual branches, in this table and under *ramus; modality*, general sensory and motor.

n. presacra'lis, N A alternative for *plexus hypogastricus superior.*

n. pterygoi'deus exter'nus [B N A], n. pterygoideus lateralis.

n. pterygoi'deus inter'nus [B N A], n. pterygoideus medialis.

n. pterygoi'deus latera'lis [N A], lateral pterygoid nerve: *origin*, mandibular division of trigeminal nerve; *distribution*, lateral pterygoid muscle; *modality*, motor.

n. pterygoi'deus media'lis [N A], medial pterygoid nerve: *origin*, mandibular division of trigeminal nerve; *distribution*, medial pterygoid muscle; *modality*, motor.

ner'vi pterygopalati'ni [N A], pterygopalatine nerves: *origin*, maxillary division of trigeminal nerve; *branches*, nasopalatine, and greater and lesser palatine nerves, nerve of pterygoid canal, orbital, pharyngeal, posterior superior nasal and posterior inferior nasal rami; *distribution*—see individual branches, in this table and under *ramus; modality*, general sensory.

n. puden'dus [N A, B N A], pudendal nerve: *origin*, sacral plexus—S2–S4; *branches*, inferior rectal and perineal nerves and parasympathetic rami to pelvic viscera; *distribution*—see individual branches; *modality*, general sensory, motor, and parasympathetic.

n. radia'lis [N A, B N A], radial nerve: *origin*, brachial plexus—C6–C8, and sometimes C5 and T1, through posterior cord; *branches*, posterior cutaneous and inferior lateral cutaneous nerves of arm, muscular, deep, and superficial rami; *distribution*—see individual branches, in this table and under *ramus; modality*, general sensory and motor.

ner'vi recta'les inferio'res [N A], inferior rectal nerves: *origin*, pudendal nerve; *distribution*, external anal sphincter, skin around anus, and lining of anal canal; *modality*, general sensory and motor.

n. recur'rens [B N A], n. laryngeus recurrens.

n. saccula'ris [N A, B N A], the branch of the pars vestibularis nervi octavi that innervates the macula of the saccule.

ner'vi sacra'les [N A, B N A], the five pairs of nerves that arise from the sacral segments of the spinal cord; the ventral branches of the first four pairs participate in the formation of the sacral plexus. Called also *sacral nerves.*

n. saphe'nus [N A, B N A], saphenous nerve: *origin*, femoral nerve; *branches*, infrapatellar and medial crural cutaneous rami; *distribution*—see individual branches, under *ramus; modality*, general sensory.

ner'vi scrota'les anterio'res [N A, B N A], anterior scrotal nerves: *origin*, ilioinguinal nerve; *distribution*, skin of anterior scrotal region; *modality*, general sensory.

ner'vi scrota'les posterio'res [N A, B N A], posterior scrotal nerves: *origin*, perineal nerves; *distribution*, skin of scrotum; *modality*, general sensory.

n. spermat'icus exter'nus [B N A], ramus genitalis nervi genitofemoralis.

ner'vi sphenopalati'ni [B N A], nervi pterygopalatini.

ner'vi spina'les [N A, B N A], the thirty-one pairs of nerves that arise from the spinal cord and pass out between the vertebrae, including the eight pairs of cervical, twelve of thoracic, five of lumbar, five of sacral, and one pair of coccygeal nerves. Called also *spinal nerves*.

n. spino′sus [B N A], ramus meningeus nervi mandibularis.

n. splanch′nicus i′mus [N A, B N A], lowest splanchnic nerve: *origin*, last ganglion of sympathetic trunk or lesser splanchnic nerve; *distribution*, renal plexus; *modality*, sympathetic and visceral afferent.

ner′vi splanch′nici lumba′les [N A], lumbar splanchnic nerves: *origin*, lumbar ganglia of sympathetic trunk; *distribution*, celiac, mesenteric, and hypogastric plexuses; *modality*, preganglionic sympathetic and visceral afferent.

n. splanch′nicus ma′jor [N A, B N A], greater splanchnic nerve: *origin*, fifth through tenth thoracic ganglia of sympathetic trunk; *distribution*, celiac ganglion; *modality*, preganglionic sympathetic and visceral afferent.

n. splanch′nicus mi′nor [N A, B N A], lesser splanchnic nerve: *origin*, ninth and tenth thoracic ganglia of sympathetic trunk; *branches*, renal ramus; *distribution*, aorticorenal ganglion; *modality*, preganglionic sympathetic and visceral afferent.

ner′vi splanch′nici pelvi′ni [N A], pelvic splanchnic nerves: *origin*, spinal cord—S2–S4; *distribution*, terminal ganglia in pelvic viscera; *modality*, preganglionic parasympathetic and visceral afferent. Called also *nervi erigentes*.

ner′vi splanch′nici sacra′les [N A], sacral splanchnic nerves: *origin*, sacral part of sympathetic trunk; *distribution*, inferior hypogastric plexus; *modality*, preganglionic sympathetic and visceral afferent.

n. stape′dius [N A, B N A], stapedius nerve: *origin*, facial nerve; *distribution*, stapedius muscle; *modality*, motor.

n. subcla′vius [N A, B N A], subclavian nerve: *origin*, brachial plexus—C5–C6 through superior trunk; *distribution*, subclavius muscle and sternoclavicular joint; *modality*, motor and general sensory.

n. subcosta′lis [N A], subcostal nerve: *origin*, twelfth thoracic nerve; *distribution*, abdominal muscles and skin of lower abdomen and gluteal region; *modality*, general sensory and motor.

n. sublingua′lis [N A, B N A], sublingual nerve: *origin*, lingual nerve; *distribution*, region of sublingual gland; *modality*, general sensory.

n. suboccipita′lis [N A, B N A], suboccipital nerve: *origin*, spinal cord—C1; *distribution*, recti and oblique muscles of neck, etc.; *modality*, motor.

n. subscapula′ris [N A], subscapular nerve: *origin*, brachial plexus—C5 through posterior cord; *distribution*, subscapular and teres major muscles; *modality*, motor.

ner′vi supraclavicula′res [N A, B N A]. See *nervi supraclaviculares intermedii, nervi supraclaviculares laterales,* and *nervi supraclaviculares mediales*.

ner′vi supraclavicula′res anterio′res [B N A], nervi supraclaviculares mediales.

ner′vi supraclavicula′res interme′dii [N A], intermediate supraclavicular nerves: *origin*, cervical plexus—C3–C4; *distribution*, skin over pectoral and deltoid region; *modality*, general sensory.

ner′vi supraclavicula′res latera′les [N A], lateral supraclavicular nerves: *origin*, cervical plexus—C3–C4; *distribution*, skin of superior and posterior parts of shoulder; *modality*, general sensory. Called also *nervi supraclaviculares posteriores*.

ner′vi supraclavicula′res media′les [N A], medial supraclavicular nerves: *origin*, cervical plexus—C3–C4; *distribution*, skin of medial infraclavicular region; *modality*, general sensory.

ner′vi supraclavicula′res me′dii [B N A], nervi supraclaviculares intermedii.

ner′vi supraclavicula′res posterio′res [B N A], accepted by N A as alternative for *nervi supraclaviculares laterales*.

n. supraorbita′lis [N A, B N A], supraorbital nerve: *origin*, frontal nerve, from ophthalmic division of trigeminal nerve; *branches*, lateral and medial rami; *distribution*, skin of upper eyelid, forehead, anterior scalp (to vertex), mucosa of frontal sinus; *modality*, general sensory.

n. suprascapula′ris [N A, B N A], suprascapular nerve: *origin*, brachial plexus—C5–C6 through superior trunk; *distribution*, supraspinatus and infraspinatus muscles and shoulder joint; *modality*, motor and general sensory.

n. supratrochlea′ris [N A, B N A], supratrochlear nerve: *origin*, frontal nerve, from ophthalmic division of trigeminal nerve; *distribution*, medial forehead, root of nose, medial commissure of eye, conjunctiva, and upper lid; *modality*, general sensory.

n. sura′lis [N A, B N A], sural nerve: *origin*, medial and lateral cutaneous nerves of calf; *branches*, lateral dorsal cutaneous nerve and lateral calcaneal rami; *distribution*—see individual branches, in this table and under *ramus; modality*, general sensory.

ner′vi tempora′les profun′di [N A, B N A], deep temporal nerves: *origin*, mandibular division of trigeminal nerve; *distribution*, temporal muscles; *modality*, motor.

n. tempora′lis profun′dus ante′rior [B N A]. Omitted in N A.

n. tempora′lis profun′dus poste′rior [B N A]. Omitted in N A.

n. tenso′ris tym′pani [N A, B N A], nerve of tensor tympani: *origin*, mandibular division of trigeminal nerve via otic ganglion; *distribution*, tensor tympani muscle; *modality*, motor.

n. tenso′ris ve′li palati′ni [N A, B N A], nerve of tensor veli palatini: *origin*, mandibular division of trigeminal nerve via otic ganglion; *distribution*, tensor veli palatini muscle; *modality*, motor.

n. tento′rii [B N A], ramus tentorii nervi ophthalmici.

ner′vi termina′les [N A], nerves usually embedded in the pia mater that overlies the gyri recti on the base of the frontal lobes, and apparently terminating in blood vessels of the nasal mucosa. Called also *terminal nerves*.

ner′vi thoraca′les [B N A], nervi thoracici.

ner′vi thoraca′les anterio′res [B N A]. Omitted in N A.

n. thoraca′lis lon′gus [B N A], n. thoracicus longus.

ner′vi thoraca′les posterio′res [B N A]. Omitted in N A.

ner′vi thora′cici [N A], the twelve pairs of spinal nerves that arise from the thoracic segments of the spinal cord, each pair leaving the vertebral column below the correspondingly numbered vertebra. They innervate the body wall of the thorax and upper abdomen. Called also *thoracic nerves*.

n. thora′cicus lon′gus [N A], long thoracic nerve: *origin*, brachial plexus—ventral rami of C5–C7; *distribution*, serratus anterior muscle; *modality*, motor.

n. thoracodorsa′lis [N A, B N A], thoracodorsal nerve: *origin*, brachial plexus—C7–C8 through posterior cord; *distribution*, latissimus dorsi muscle; *modality*, motor.

n. tibia′lis [N A, B N A], tibial nerve: *origin*, sciatic nerve; *branches*, interosseous nerve of leg, medial cutaneous nerve of calf, sural, and medial and lateral plantar nerves, and muscular and medial calcaneal rami; *distribution*—see individual branches, in this table and under *ramus; modality*, general sensory and motor.

n. transver′sus col′li [N A], transverse nerve of neck: *origin*, cervical plexus—C2–C3; *branches*, superior and inferior rami; *distribution*, see individual branches, under *ramus; modality*, general sensory.

n. trigem′inus [N A, B N A], trigeminal nerve (5th cranial), which emerges from the lateral surface of the pons as a motor and a sensory root, the latter expanding into the trigeminal ganglion, from which the three divisions of the nerve arise. See *n. mandibularis, n. maxillaris,* and *n. ophthalmicus.*

n. trochlea'ris [N A, B N A], trochlear nerve (4th cranial): *origin,* just posterior to inferior colliculus; *distribution,* superior oblique muscle of eyeball; *modality,* motor, proprioceptive.

n. tympan'icus [N A, B N A], tympanic nerve: *origin,* glossopharyngeal nerve; *branches,* helps form tympanic plexus; *distribution,* tympanic cavity, tympanic membrane, mastoid air cells, and auditory tube; *modality,* general sensory and parasympathetic.

n. ulna'ris N A, B N A], ulnar nerve: *origin,* brachial plexus—C7–T1 through medial and lateral cords; *branches,* muscular, palmar cutaneous, dorsal, palmar, superficial, and deep rami; *distribution*—see individual branches, under *ramus; modality,* general sensory and motor.

n. utricula'ris [N A, B N A], the branch of the pars vestibularis nervi octavi that innervates the macula of the utricle.

n. utriculoampulla'ris [N A], a nerve that arises by peripheral division of the vestibular part of the eighth cranial nerve, and supplies the utricle and ampullae of the semicircular ducts. Called also *utriculoampullar nerve.*

ner'vi vagina'les [N A, B N A], vaginal nerves: *origin,* uterovaginal plexus from sacral part of sympathetic trunk and parasympathetic branches from pudendal nerve; *distribution,* vagina; *modality,* sympathetic and parasympathetic.

n. va'gus [N A, B N A], vagus nerve (10th cranial): *origin,* by numerous rootlets in the groove between the olive and the inferior cerebellar peduncle; *branches,* superior and recurrent laryngeal nerves, meningeal, auricular, pharyngeal, bronchial, esophageal, anterior and posterior gastric, hepatic, celiac, and renal rami; *distribution*—see individual branches, in this table and under *ramus; modality,* parasympathetic, visceral afferent, motor, general sensory.

n. vascula'ris [N A], a nerve branch that supplies the adventitia of a blood vessel. Called also *vascular nerve.*

n. vertebra'lis [N A], vertebral nerve: *origin,* cervicothoracic ganglion; *distribution,* posterior fossa of the cranium via the vertebral plexus; *modality,* sympathetic.

ner'vi vesica'les inferio'res plex'us puden'di [B N A]. Omitted in N A.

ner'vi vesica'les inferio'res plex'us vesica'lis [B N A]. Omitted in N A.

ner'vi vesica'les superio'res plex'us vesica'lis [B N A]. Omitted in N A.

n. vestib'uli [B N A], pars vestibularis nervi octavi.

n. vestibulocochlea'ris [N A], vestibulocochlear nerve (8th cranial), which emerges from the brain between the pons and the medulla oblongata, behind the facial nerve. It consists of two sets of fibers, the pars vestibularis nervi octavi and the pars cochlearis nervi octavi, and is connected with the brain by corresponding roots, the radix superior and the radix inferior nervi vestibulocochlearis. Called also *n. acusticus* [B N A], and *n. octavus.*

n. zygomat'icus [N A, B N A], zygomatic nerve: *origin,* maxillary division of trigeminal nerve; *branches,* zygomaticofacial and zygomaticotemporal rami; *distribution*—see individual branches, under *ramus; modality,* general sensory.

---

nesacaine (nes'ah-kān). Trade mark for preparations of chloroprocaine.

nesidiectomy (ne-sid"e-ek'to-me) [Gr. *nēsidion* islet + *ektomē* excision]. Excision of the islands of Langerhans of the pancreas.

nesidioblast (ne-sid'e-o-blast") [Gr. *nēsidion* islet + *blastos* germ]. Any one of the cells that build up the islet cells of the pancreas.

nesidioblastoma (ne-sid"e-o-blas-to'mah). An islet-cell tumor of the pancreas.

nesidioblastosis (ne-sid"e-o-blas-to'sis). Diffuse proliferation of the islet cells of the pancreas.

Nessler's reagent (nes'lerz) [A. *Nessler,* German chemist, 1827–1905]. See under *reagent.*

nesslerization (nes"ler-i-za'shun). Treatment with Nessler's reagent.

nesslerize (nes'ler-iz). To treat with Nessler's reagent.

nest (nest). A small mass of cells foreign to the area in which it is found. **Brunn's epithelial n's,** solid or branched clusters of cells occurring in the healthy ureter. **cancer n's,** masses of concentrically arranged cells seen in cancerous growths. **cell n.,** a mass of closely packed epithelial cells surrounded by a stroma of connective tissue. **swallow's n.,** nidus hirundinis.

nesteostomy (nes"te-os'to-me) [*nestis* + Gr. *stomoun* to provide with an opening, or mouth]. Creation of a permanent opening into the jejunum through the abdominal wall.

nestiatria (nes"te-a'tre-ah). Hunger cure.

nestis (nes'tis) [Gr. *nēstis* fasting]. An old name for the jejunum.

nestitherapy (nes"tĭ-ther'ah-pe). Nestotherapy.

nestotherapy (nes"to-ther'ah-pe) [Gr. *nēstis* fasting + *therapy*]. Hunger cure; the therapeutic use of fasting or of a restricted diet.

net (net). A meshlike structure of interlocking fibers or strands. See also under *network.* **achromatic n.,** the network within the cell which does not stain with dyes. **chromidial n.,** a network of chromatin staining material in the protoplasm of certain cells. It has the properties of active nuclear material. **nerve n.,** a nonsynaptic protoplasmic network of nerve fibers; a form of free nerve fiber ending characteristic of connective tissue, consisting of a network of thin threads. **Trolard's n.,** rete canalis hypoglossi.

Ne tr. s. num. Abbreviation for L. *ne tra'das si'ne num'mo,* do not deliver unless paid.

Nettleship's disease (net"l-ships") [Edward *Nettleship,* London ophthalmologist, 1845–1913]. Urticaria pigmentosa.

network (net'werk). A meshlike structure of interlocking fibers or strands. See also under *net.* **cell n.,** mitoma. **Chiari's n.,** a network of fine fibers which sometimes extend across the interior of the right auricle of the heart from the thebesian and eustachian valves to the crista terminalis. **Gerlach's n.,** an apparent (but not real) interlacement of the dendritic processes of the ganglion cells of the spinal cord. **n. of Gesvelst,** a reticular appearance sometimes seen on the myelin sheath, perhaps artificial. **neurofibrillar n.,** the network formed by the neurofibrils of a nerve cell. **peritarsal n.,** a set of lymphatics in the eyelid. **Purkinje's n.,** a reticulation of immature muscle fibers in the subendocardial tissue of the ventricles of the heart. **subpapillary n.,** the layer of capillaries underlying the skin. **venous n.,** rete venosum.

neu (nu). Neurilemma.

Neubauer's artery, ganglion (noi'bow-erz) [Johann Ernst *Neubauer,* German anatomist, 1742–1777]. See under *artery* and *ganglion.*

Neubauer-Fischer test (noi'bow-er-fish'er) [Otto *Neubauer,* Munich physician, born 1874]. See *glycyltryptophan test,* under *tests.*

Neuber's treatment, tubes (noi'berz) [Gustav Adolf *Neuber,* German surgeon, 1850–1932]. See under the nouns.

Neufeld nail (nu'feld) [Alonzo J. *Neufeld,* American orthopedic surgeon, born 1906]. See under *nail.*

Neufeld's reaction (noi'felts) [Fred *Neufeld,* German bacteriologist, born 1869]. See under *reaction.*

Neumann's cells, sheath (noi′manz) [Ernst *Neumann*, German pathologist, 1834–1918]. See under *cell* and *sheath.*

Neumann's disease [Isador *Neumann*, dermatologist in Vienna, 1832–1906]. Pemphigus vegetans.

Neumann's law [Franz Ernst *Neumann*, German physicist, 1798–1895]. See under *law.*

Neumann's method [Heinrich *Neumann*, otologist in Vienna, 1873–1939]. See under *method.*

neur-. See *neuro-.*

neurad (nu′rad). Toward a neural axis or aspect.

neuradynamia (nu″rah-di-na′me-ah) [*neur-* + *a* neg. + Gr. *dynamis* power]. Neurasthenia.

neuragmia (nu-rag′me-ah) [*neur-* + Gr. *agmos* break]. The tearing of a nerve trunk from its ganglion.

neural (nu′ral) [L. *neuralis;* Gr. *neuron* nerve]. Pertaining to a nerve or to the nerves.

neuralgia (nu-ral′je-ah) [*neur-* + *-algia*]. Paroxysmal pain which extends along the course of one or more nerves. Many varieties of neuralgia are distinguished according to the part affected or to the cause, as brachial, facial, occipital, supraorbital, etc., and anemic, diabetic, gouty, malarial, syphilitic, etc. **alveolar n.,** pain in an alveolus from which the tooth has been extracted. **cardiac n.,** angina pectoris. **cervico-occipital n.,** neuralgia in the upper cervical nerves, especially the posterior division of the second cervical nerve. **cranial n.,** neuralgia along the course of a cranial nerve. **degenerative n.,** that which occurs in persons of advanced age, and is marked by signs of degeneration in the central nervous system. **epileptiform n.,** trifacial n. **n. facia′lis ve′ra,** geniculate n. **Fothergill's n.,** trigeminal n. **geniculate n.,** neuralgia involving the geniculate ganglion which is the sensory mechanism of the facial nerve. The pain is limited to the middle ear and the auditory canal. Called also *geniculate otalgia, Hunt's n.,* and *n. facialis vera.* **glossopharyngeal n.,** neuralgia affecting the petrosal and jugular ganglion of the glossopharyngeal nerve. **hallucinatory n.,** a mental impression of pain without any actual peripheral stimulus. **Hunt's n.,** geniculate n. **idiopathic n.,** neuralgia that is not accompanied by any structural change. **intercostal n.,** neuralgia of the intercostal nerves causing pain in the side. **mammary n.,** neuralgic pain in the breast. **mandibular joint n.,** vertex and occipital pain, otalgia, glossodynia, and pain about the nose and eyes, associated with disturbed function of the temporomandibular joint. **Morton's n.,** metatarsalgia. **nasociliary n.,** pain in the eyes, brow, and root of the nose. **otic n.,** geniculate n. **peripheral n.,** pain along the course of a peripheral sensory nerve. **postherpetic n.,** neuralgia in herpes zoster. **red n.,** erythromelalgia. **reminiscent n.,** a mental impression of neuralgic pain persisting after the actual pain has ceased. **sciatic n.,** sciatica. **segmental n.,** neuralgia restricted to sharply defined areas. **Sluder's n.,** neuralgia of the sphenopalatine ganglion, causing a burning and boring pain in the area of the superior maxilla and a radiation of the pain into the neck and shoulder. **sphenopalatine n.,** Sluder's n. **stump n.,** neuralgia at the site of an amputation. **supra-orbital n.,** neuralgia of the supra-orbital nerve. **symptomatic n.,** neuralgia in which there is slight structural change. **trifacial n., trigeminal n.,** neuralgia due to involvement of the gasserian ganglion and the root and branches of the trigeminal nerve, and marked by pain along the course of the trigeminal nerve. **vidian n.,** neuralgia affecting the vidian nerve. **visceral n.,** neurasthenic pain in the pelvic region.

neuralgic (nu-ral′jik). Pertaining to or of the nature of neuralgia.

neuralgiform (nu-ral′jĭ-form). Like neuralgia.

neuramebimeter (nu″ram-ĕ-bim′e-ter) [*neur-* + Gr. *amoibē* response + *metron* measure]. An instrument for measuring the reaction time of the nerves.

neuranagenesis (nu″ran-ah-jen′e-sis) [*neur-* + Gr. *anagennan* to regenerate]. Regeneration or renewal of nerve tissue.

neurangiosis (nu″ran-je-o′sis) [*neur-* + Gr. *angeion* vessel]. A neurosis of the blood vessels.

neurapophysis (nu″rah-pof′ĭ-sis) [*neur-* + *apophysis*]. The structure forming either side of the neural arch; also the part supposedly homologous with this structure in a so-called cranial vertebra.

neurapraxia (nu″rah-prak′se-ah) [*neur-* + Gr. *apraxia* absence of action]. Nerve injury in which paralysis occurs in the absence of peripheral degeneration. Cf. *axonotmeiis* and *neurotmesis.*

neurarchy (nu′rar-ke) [*neur-* + Gr. *archē* rule]. The control of the cerebrospinal system over the body.

neurarthropathy (nu″rar-throp′ah-the). Neuroarthropathy.

neurasthenia (nu″ras-the′ne-ah) [*neur-* + Gr. *astheneia* debility]. Nervous prostration; a psychoneurosis or nervous exhaustion characterized by abnormal fatigability. The name for a group of symptoms resulting from some functional disorder of the nervous system, with severe depression of the vital forces. It is usually due to prolonged and excessive expenditure of energy, and is marked by tendency to fatigue, lack of energy, pain in the back, loss of memory, insomnia, constipation, loss of appetite, etc. **acoustic n.,** neurasthenia marked by deafness of varying degrees. **adrenal n.,** neurasthenia due to defective or disordered adrenal activity. **angioparalytic n., angiopathic n.,** a condition in neurasthenic patients in which there is a constant sense of the pulse beat. **cardiac n.,** cardioneurosis. **cardiovascular n.,** phrenocardia. **cerebral n.,** a variety characterized by mental and visual disturbances and other head symptoms. **n. cor′dis,** the irregularity of pulse, heart action, and blood pressure frequently seen in neurasthenia. **gastric n.,** a form characterized by functional stomach complications. **n. gra′vis,** a severe form of neurasthenia with great exhaustion on the slightest exertion. **grippal n.,** neurasthenia occurring as a sequel of influenza. **obsessive n.,** psychasthenia. **optic n.,** neurasthenia attended with contraction of the field of vision. **n. prae′cox,** neurasthenia occurring during adolescence. **prostatic n.,** a neurasthenic condition due to prostatic hyperemia and hyperesthesia. **pulsating n.,** angioparalytic n. **n. pu′ra,** true neurasthenia. **sexual n.,** a variety associated with disorders of the sexual function. **spinal n.,** neurasthenia with marked spinal cord symptoms. **traumatic n.,** neurasthenia following shock or injury.

neurastheniac (nu″ras-the′ne-ak). A person suffering from neurasthenia.

neurasthenic (nu″ras-then′ik). Pertaining to or affected with neurasthenia.

neurataxia (nu″rah-tak′se-ah) [*neur-* + *ataxia*]. Neurasthenia.

neurataxy (nu″rah-tak′se). Neurataxia.

neuratrophia (nu″rah-tro′fe-ah) [*neur-* + Gr. *atrophia* atrophy]. Impaired nutrition of the nervous system.

neuratrophic (nu″rah-trof′ik). 1. Characterized by atrophy of the nerves. 2. A person affected with atrophy of the nerves.

neuratrophy (nu-rat′ro-fe). Neuratrophia.

neuraxial (nu-rak′se-al). Pertaining to the neuraxis.

neuraxis (nu-rak′sis) [*neur-* + *axis*]. 1. An axon. 2. The cerebrospinal axis.

neuraxitis (nu″rak-si′tis) [*neur-* + *axis* + *-itis*]. Encephalitis. **epidemic n.,** epidemic encephalitis.

neuraxon (nu-rak′son) [*neur-* + Gr. *axōn* axis]. An axon.

neure (nūr). A nerve cell with all its processes; a neuron.

neurectasia, neurectasis, neurectasy (nu″-rek-ta′ze-ah, nu-rek′tah-sis, nu-rek′tah-se) [*neur-* + Gr. *ektasis* stretching]. The surgical stretching of a nerve.

neurectomy (nu-rek′to-me) [*neur-* + Gr. *ektomē* excision]. The excision of a part of a nerve. **gastric n.**, vagotomy. **opticociliary n.**, excision of the optic and ciliary nerves.

neurectopia (nu″rek-to′pe-ah) [*neur-* + Gr. *ektopos* out of place + *-ia*]. Displacement of a nerve or abnormal situation of a nerve.

neurectopy (nu-rek′to-pe). Neurectopia.

neurenergen (nu-ren′er-jen) [*neur-* + Gr. *energeia* energy + *gennan* to produce]. A substance which, it is supposed, is absorbed by the neurons from the bodily fluids and serves to maintain their energy.

neurenteric (nu″ren-ter′ik) [*neur-* + Gr. *enteron* intestine]. Pertaining to the neural tube and archenteron of the embryo, applied especially to the canal interconnecting them.

neurepithelial (nūr″ep-ĭ-the′le-al). Pertaining to neurepithelium.

neurepithelium (nūr″ep-ĭ-the′le-um). Neuroepithelium.

neurergic (nu-rer′jik) [*neur-* + Gr. *ergon* work]. Pertaining to or dependent on nerve action.

neurexairesis (nūr″ek-si′rĕ-sis). Neurexeresis.

neurexeresis (nūr″ek-ser′ĕ-sis) [*neur-* + Gr. *exairein* to extract]. Operation of tearing out (avulsion) of a nerve.

neurhypnology (nūr″hip-nol′o-je). Neurohypnology.

neuriatry (nu-ri′ah-tre) [*neur-* + Gr. *iatreia* medication]. The treatment of nervous diseases.

neuricity (nu-ris′ĭ-te). The energy peculiar to the nervous system.

neuridin (nu′rĭ-din). Spermine isolated from fresh human brain.

neurilemma (nu″rĭ-lem′mah). Neurolemma.

neurilemmitis (nu″rĭ-lem-mi′tis). Neurolemmitis.

neurilemmoma (nu″rĭ-lem-mo′mah). Neurilemoma.

neurilemoma (nu″rĭ-lĕ-mo′mah) [*neur-* + Gr. *eilēma* a closely adhering sheath + *-oma*]. Arthur Purdy Stout's name for a tumor of a peripheral nerve sheath (neurolemma).

neurility (nu-ril′ĭ-te). The sum of the attributes and functions of nerve tissue.

neurimotility (nu″rĭ-mo-til′ĭ-te). Nervimotility.

neurimotor (nu″rĭ-mo′tor). Nervimotor.

neurine (nu′rin). A poisonous ptomaine, vinyl trimethyl ammonium hydroxide, CH_2.CH:N.-$(CH_3)_3$.OH, found in decaying fish, fungi, and in the brain and in many other normal tissues.

neurinoma (nu″rĭ-no′mah) [*neur-* + Gr. *is* fiber + *-oma*]. A specialized type of fibroma of nerves arising from the endoneurium or from the sheath of Schwann. **malignant n.**, a neurinoma showing characteristics of malignancy.

neurinomatosis (nu″rĭ-no″mah-to′sis). A condition characterized by development of numerous neurinomas.

neurite (nu′rit). An axon.

neuritic (nu-rit′ik). Pertaining to or affected with neuritis.

neuritis (nu-ri′tis) [*neur-* + *-itis*]. Inflammation of a nerve. The condition is attended by pain and tenderness over the nerves, anesthesia and paresthesias, paralysis, wasting, and disappearance of the reflexes. **adventitial n.**, that which affects the sheath of a nerve. **alcoholic n.**, a form due to alcoholism. **ascending n.**, that which progresses centripetally or toward the brain and spinal cord. **axial n.**, inflammation of the central part of a nerve. **central n.**, parenchymatous n. **degenerative n.**, neuritis in which there is degeneration of the proper nerve substance. **descending n.**, that which progresses centrifugally or away from the brain and spinal cord. **diabetic n.**, that which is associated with diabetes. **dietetic n.**, beriberi. **diphtheritic n.**, a form resulting from diphtheria. **disseminated n.**, neuritis affecting multiple nerves. **Eichhorst's n.**, n. fascians. **endemic n.**, beriberi. **facial n.**, Bell's palsy. **fallopian n.**, neuritis of the facial nerve in the fallopian canal. **n. fas′cians**, neuritis in which the lesions of the nerve sheath seem to affect also the interstitial tissue of the muscles. Called also *Eichhorst's n.* **Gombault's n.**, periaxial n. involving segments of a nerve. **interstitial n.**, inflammation of the connective tissue of a nerve trunk. **interstitial hypertrophic n.**, progressive hypertrophic interstitial neuropathy. **intraocular n.**, neuritis of the retinal part of the optic nerve. **jake n.**, Jamaica ginger paralysis. **latent n.**, degeneration of the fibers of a nerve without corresponding clinical phenomena. **lead n.**, n. saturnina. **leprous n.**, a form associated with true leprosy. **Leyden's n.**, lipomatous n. **lipomatous n.**, that in which the nerve fibers are destroyed and a fatty connective tissue takes their place. **lymphatic n.**, mesoneuritis. **malarial n.**, a form due to malarial poisoning. **malarial multiple n.**, inflammation involving many nerves, and associated with malaria. **n. mi′grans, migrating n.**, neuritis affecting first one nerve and then another. **multiple n.**, that which affects simultaneously several symmetrically distributed nerves. It is due to various causes, especially to alcoholic or other poisoning, to diphtheria, pneumonia, and other infectious diseases. See *polyneuritis.* **n. mul′tiplex endem′ica**, beriberi. **n. nodo′sa**, a form characterized by the formation of nodes on the nerves. **optic n.**, inflammation of the optic nerve. It may affect the part of the nerve within the eyeball (*papillitis*) or the portion behind the eyeball (*retrobulbar n.*). **orbital optic n.**, retrobulbar n. **parenchymatous n.**, neuritis affecting principally the medullary substance and axons of the central nervous system (cerebral cortex); called also *central n.* **periaxial n.**, neuritis involving the neural sheath while the axon is preserved. **peripheral n.**, inflammation of the nerve endings or of terminal nerves. **porphyric n.**, neuritis occurring as a manifestation of acute porphyria. **postfebrile n.**, that which mostly follows an attack of severe exanthematous disease. **postocular n.**, retrobulbar n. **pressure n.**, a form due to compression of the nerve. **n. puerpera′lis traumat′ica**, neuritis occurring in parturient women as a result of injury at childbirth. **radicular n.**, neuritis involving the spinal roots of the nerves; radiculitis. **retrobulbar n.**, inflammation in that portion of the optic nerve which is posterior to the eyeball. **rheumatic n.**, a form associated with rheumatic symptoms. **n. saturni′na**, neuritis due to lead poisoning. **sciatic n.**, sciatica. **segmental n., segmentary n.**, inflammation affecting isolated segments of a nerve, the portions separating them being relatively healthy. **senile n.**, a form occurring in aged persons, and affecting chiefly the nerves of the extremities. **sympathetic n.**, that form which involves an opposite nerve without invading a nerve center. **syphilitic n.**, neuritis due to syphilis. **tabetic n.**, neuritis associated with locomotor ataxia. **toxic n.**, that which is due to some poison. **traumatic n.**, that which follows and is caused by an injury.

neuro-, neur- (nu′ro, nūr) [Gr. *neuron* nerve]. Combining form denoting relationship to a nerve or nerves, or to the nervous system.

neuroallergy (nu″ro-al′er-je). Allergy in nervous tissue.

neuroamebiasis (nu″ro-am″e-bi′ah-sis). Neuritis due to amebiasis.

neuroanastomosis (nu″ro-ah-nas″to-mo′sis). The operation of forming an anastomosis of nerves.

neuroanatomy (nu″ro-ah-nat′o-me) [*neuro-* + *anatomy*]. That phase of neurology which is concerned with the anatomy of the nervous system.

neuroappendicopathy (nu″ro-ah-pen″dĭ-kop′-ah-the). Any nervous lesion of the vermiform appendix.

neuroarthritism (nu″ro-ar′thrĭ-tizm). The nervous and gouty diathesis.

neuroarthropathy (nu″ro-ar-throp′ah-the) [*neuro-* + Gr. *arthron* joint + *pathos* disease]. Any disease of joint structures associated with disease of the central nervous system; Charcot's joint.

neurobartonellosis (nu″ro-bar″to-nel-lo′sis). A severe form of Bartonella infection characterized by nervous symptoms.

neurobiology (nu″ro-bi-ol′o-je). The biology of the nervous system.

neurobion (nu″ro-bi′on) [*neuro-* + Gr. *bios* life]. 1. Any one of the delicate granules filling the nerve cells. 2. Any one of the hypothetical ultramicroscopical particles of living matter concerned in the regeneration of nerves.

neurobiotaxis (nu″ro-bi″o-tak′sis) [*neuro-* + *biotaxis*]. The tendency of cell bodies during development to migrate in the direction from which they habitually receive their stimuli.

neuroblast (nu′ro-blast) [*neuro-* + Gr. *blastos* germ]. Any embryonic cell which develops into a nerve cell or neuron; an immature nerve cell.

neuroblastoma (nu″ro-blas-to′mah). A malignant tumor of the nervous system composed chiefly of neuroblasts. Cf. *neurocytoma*. **n. sympathet′icum, n. sympath′icum,** a tumor of sympathetic nerve cell origin located in the adrenals.

neurobrucellosis (nu″ro-broo″sĕ-lo′sis). Brucellosis marked by involvement of the nervous system.

neurocanal (nu″ro-kah-nal′) [*neuro-* + *canal*]. The neural canal.

neurocardiac (nu″ro-kar′de-ak) [*neuro-* + Gr. *kardia* heart]. Pertaining to the nervous system and the heart.

neurocele (nu′ro-sēl). Neurocoele.

neurocentral (nu″ro-sen′tral). Pertaining to the centrum and the two lateral masses of a developing vertebra.

neurocentrum (nu″ro-sen′trum). One of the embryonic vertebral elements from which the spinous processes of the vertebrae develop.

neuroceptor (nu′ro-sep″tor) [*neuro-* + L. *capere* to take]. One of the terminal elements of a dendrite which receives the stimulus from the neuromittor of the adjoining neuron. Called also *ceptor*.

neuroceratin (nu″ro-ser′ah-tin). Neurokeratin.

neurochemism (nu″ro-kem′izm). The state of nervous and chemical equilibrium in the organism.

neurochemistry (nu″ro-kem′is-tre). That phase of neurology which is concerned with the chemistry of the nervous system.

neurochitin (nu″ro-ki′tin) [*neuro-* + Gr. *chitōn* frock, skin, membrane]. The substance that forms the framework support of nerve fibers.

neurochondrite (nu″ro-kon′drīt) [*neuro-* + Gr. *chondros* cartilage]. One of the embryonic cartilaginous elements which develop into the neural arch of a vertebra.

neurochorioretinitis (nu″ro-ko″re-o-ret″ĭ-ni′-tis) [*neuro-* + *chorioretinitis*]. Inflammation of the optic nerve, choroid, and retina.

neurochoroiditis (nu″ro-ko″roid-i′tis). Inflammation of the choroid coat and ciliary nerves.

neurocirculatory (nu″ro-cir′cu-lah-to″re). Pertaining to the nervous and circulatory systems.

neurocladism (nu-rok′lah-dizm) [*neuro-* + Gr. *klados* branch]. The formation of new branches by the process of a neuron; especially the force by which, in regeneration of divided nerves, the newly formed axons of the proximal stump become attracted by the peripheral stump so as to form a bridge between the two ends. Called also *odogenesis*.

neuroclonic (nu″ro-klon′ik) [*neuro-* + Gr. *klonos* spasm]. Characterized by nervous spasms.

neurocoele (nu′ro-sēl) [*neuro-* + Gr. *koilon* hollow]. The neural canal; the cavity or lumen of the embryonic neural tube.

neurocranial (nu″ro-kra′ne-al). Pertaining to the neurocranium.

neurocranium (nu″ro-kra′ne-um). The portion of the cranium which encloses the brain.

neurocrine (nu′ro-krin) [*neuro-* + Gr. *krinein* to secrete]. 1. Denoting an endocrine influence on or by the nerves. 2. Pertaining to neurosecretion.

neurocrinia (nu″ro-krin′e-ah). Endocrine influence on the nerves.

neurocutaneous (nu″ro-ku-ta′ne-us). Pertaining to the nerves and the skin; pertaining to the cutaneous nerves.

neurocyte (nu′ro-sīt) [*neuro-* + *-cyte*]. A nerve cell of any kind; a neuron.

neurocytology (nu″ro-si-tol′o-je). That phase of neurology which is concerned with the cellular components of the nervous system.

neurocytolysin (nu″ro-si-tol′ĭ-sin). A constituent of the venom of certain snakes (rattler, coral, cobra), which lyses nerve cells.

neurocytoma (nu″ro-si-to′mah). 1. A brain tumor consisting of undifferentiated cells of nervous origin, i.e., cells resembling medullary neural epithelium. Called also *neuro-epithelioma* and *medullo-epithelioma*. 2. A round-cell sarcoma of the adrenals, liver, etc. of infants, which is apparently derived from sympathetic formative cells. Called also *neuroblastoma* and *sympathoblastoma*.

neurodealgia (nu-ro″de-al′je-ah) [Gr. *neurōdēs* retina + *-algia*]. Pain in the retina.

neurodeatrophia (nu-ro″de-ah-tro′fe-ah) [Gr. *neurōdēs* retina + *atrophia*]. Retinal atrophy.

neurodegenerative (nu″ro-de-jen′er-a-tiv). Relating to or marked by nervous degeneration.

neurodendrite (nu″ro-den′drīt) [*neuro-* + Gr. *dendritēs* of a tree]. Dendrite.

neurodendron (nu″ro-den′dron). Dendrite.

neuroderm (nu′ro-derm). The neural ectoderm; that portion of the ectoderm which will become the neural tube.

neurodermatitis (nu″ro-der″mah-ti′tis) [*neuro-* + Gr. *derma* skin + *-itis*]. A chronic itching lichenoid eruption on the axillary and pubic regions due to nervous disorder: called also *lichen simplex chronicus* (Vidal), *lichen simplex circumscriptus*, *chronic circumscribed neurodermatitis* (Brocq, Jacquet), *neurodermatitis circumscripta*, and *lichen planus circumscriptus*. **n. dissemina′ta,** atopic eczema.

neurodermatosis (nu″ro-der″mah-to′sis). Dermatoneurosis; any nervous manifestation in the cutaneous structures.

neurodermite (nu″ro-der′mīt). A skin lesion in neurodermatitis.

neurodermitis (nu″ro-der-mi′tis). Neurodermatitis.

neurodiagnosis (nu″ro-di″ag-no′sis) [*neuro-* + *diagnosis*]. The diagnosis of diseases of the nervous system.

neurodin (nu-ro′din). Acetyl para-oxyphenylurethane, $C_6H_4(OCOCH_3)NH.COOC_2H_5$, used as an antineuralgic and antipyretic.

neurodocitis (nu″ro-do-si′tis). Inflammation of nerve roots resulting from compression in osseous or aponeurotic canals outside of the meninges (Sicard).

neurodokon (nu″ro-do′kon). The part of a nerve which lies in the intervertebral foramen or in an osseous canal.

neurodynamic (nu″ro-di-nam′ik) [*neuro-* + Gr. *dynamis* force]. Relating to nervous energy.

neurodynia (nu″ro-din′e-ah) [*neuro-* + Gr. *odynē* pain]. Pain in a nerve or in nerves.

neurodystonia (nu″ro-dis-to′ne-ah). Dystonia with disturbance of visceral innervation.

neuro-electricity (nu″ro-e″lek-tris′ĭ-te). Electric current generated in the nervous system.

neuro-electrotherapeutics (nu″ro-e-lek″tro-ther″ah-pu′tiks). The treatment of nervous diseases by electricity.

neuroencephalomyelopathy (nu″ro-en-sef″-ah-lo-mi″ĕ-lop′ah-the) [*neuro-* + Gr. *enkephalos* brain + *myelos* marrow + *pathos* disease]. Disease involving the brain, spinal cord and nerves. **optic n.,** disease of the brain and spinal cord, with obvious involvement of the optic nerve.

neuroendocrine (nu″ro-en′do-krin). Pertaining to neural and endocrine influence.

neuroenteric (nu″ro-en-ter′ik). Neurenteric.

neuroepidermal (nu″ro-ep″ĭ-der′mal) [*neuro-* + *epidermis*]. Pertaining to or giving origin to the nervous and epidermal tissues.

neuroepithelial (nu″ro-ep″ĭ-the′le-al). Pertaining to or composed of neuroepithelium.

neuroepithelioma (nu″ro-ep″ĭ-the″le-o′mah). Neurocytoma.

neuroepithelium (nu″ro-ep″ĭ-the′le-um) [*neuro-* + *epithelium*]. 1. Simple columnar epithelium made up of cells which are specialized to serve as sensory cells for the reception of external stimuli: such are the sensory cells of the cochlea, vestibule, nasal mucosa, and tongue. 2. The epithelium of the ectoderm, from which the cerebrospinal axis is developed. **n. of ampullary crest, n. cris′tae ampulla′ris** [N A], the specialized epithelium of the ampullary crest, containing receptor cells from some of which sensory hairs project into the cupula. **n. of maculae, n. macula′rum** [N A], the specialized epithelium of the maculae, containing receptor cells from some of which sensory hairs project into the statoconic membrane.

neuroequilibrium (nu″ro-e″kwĭ-lib′re-um). The condition of even tension in the nervous system favorable to a ready response to stimuli.

neurofibril (nu″ro-fi′bril). One of the delicate threads running in every direction through the cytoplasm of the body of a nerve cell and extending into the axon and the dendrites of the cell.

neurofibrilla (nu″ro-fi-bril′ah), pl. *neurofibril′lae.* A neurofibril.

neurofibrillar (nu″ro-fi-bril′ar). Pertaining to neurofibrils.

neurofibroma (nu″ro-fi-bro′mah) [*neuro-* + *fibroma*]. A connective tissue tumor of the nerve fiber fasciculus, formed by proliferation of the perineurium and endoneurium.

neurofibromatosis (nu″ro-fi″bro-mah-to′sis). A familial condition characterized by developmental changes in the nervous system, muscles, bones and skin and marked superficially by the formation of multiple pedunculated soft tumors (neurofibromas) distributed over the entire body associated with areas of pigmentation. Called also *multiple neuroma, neuromatosis,* and *Recklinghausen's disease.*

neurofibrositis (nu″ro-fi″bro-si′tis). Inflammation of nerve filaments; also inflammation of muscle fibers (fibrositis) involving sensory nerve filaments.

neurofixation (nu″ro-fik-sa′shun). Development of syphilis of the nervous system following the successful treatment of a syphilitic skin lesion by one of the arsenical preparations.

neurogangliitis (nu″ro-gang″gle-i′tis). Inflammation of a neuroganglion.

neuroganglion (nu″ro-gang′gle-on). A ganglion, or mass of nervous matter.

neurogastric (nu″ro-gas′trik). Involving the nerves of the stomach.

neurogen (nu′ro-jen). 1. A substance supposed to exist at the synapse and liberate nervous energy. 2. The chemical substance by means of which the primary organizer causes the development of the neural plate.

neurogenesis (nu″ro-jen′e-sis) [*neuro-* + Gr. *genesis* production]. The development of nervous tissue.

neurogenetic (nu″ro-je-net′ik). Pertaining to neurogenesis.

neurogenic (nu″ro-jen′ik) [*neuro-* + Gr. *gennan* to produce]. 1. Forming nervous tissue, or stimulating nervous energy. 2. Originating in the nervous system.

neurogenous (nu-roj′e-nus). Arising in the nervous system; arising from some lesion of the nervous system.

neuroglia (nu-rog′le-ah) [*neuro-* + Gr. *glia* glue]. The supporting structure of nervous tissue (Virchow, 1854). It consists of a fine web of tissue made up of modified ectodermic elements, in which are enclosed peculiar branched cells known as *neuroglia cells* or *glia cells.* The neuroglia cells are of three types: macroglia or astroglia, oligodendroglia, and microglia. Called also *bind web.* **interfascicular n.,** oligodendroglia of white matter along the myelin sheaths.

neuroglial, neurogliar (nu-rog′le-al, nu-rog′-le-ar). Pertaining to the neuroglia.

neurogliocyte (nu-rog′le-o-sīt) [*neuroglia* + *-cyte*]. A neuroglia cell.

neurogliocytoma (nu-rog″le-o-si-to′mah). A tumor composed of neuroglia cells.

neuroglioma (nu″ro-gli-o′mah) [*neuro-* + *glioma*]. Glioma containing nerve cells; a tumor made up of neurogliar tissue. **n. gangliona′re,** a glioma in which ganglion cells are embedded.

neurogliomatosis (nu″ro-gli″o-mah-to′sis). Neurogliosis.

neurogliosis (nu-rog″le-o′sis). A condition marked by diffuse formation of neurogliomas. **n. gangliocellula′ris diffu′sa,** epiloia.

neurogram (nu′ro-gram) [*neuro-* + Gr. *gramma* mark]. Prince's name for residua of past cerebral activities which make up the brain disposition and thus take part in the formation of personality.

neurography (nu-rog′rah-fe) [*neuro-* + Gr. *graphein* to write]. A treatise on or description of the nerves.

neurohematology (nu″ro-he″mah-tol′o-je). The study of blood changes occurring in diseases of the nervous system.

neurohistology (nu″ro-his-tol′o-je). The histology of the nervous system.

neurohormonal (nu″ro-hor′mo-nal). Both neural and hormonal.

neurohormone (nu′ro-hor″mōn). A hormone stimulating the neural mechanism.

neurohumor (nu″ro-hu′mor). A chemical substance formed in a neuron and able to activate a neighboring neuron or muscle.

neurohumoral (nu″ro-hu′mor-al). Pertaining to the qualities possessed by neurohumors.

neurohumoralism (nu″ro-hu′mor-al-izm). The theory that the action of the autonomic nerves on peripheral organs is produced through the medium of chemicals (neurohumors) which are liberated at the endings of activated nerves.

neurohypnologist (nu″ro-hip-nol′o-jist). An expert in neurohypnology.

neurohypnology (nu″ro-hip-nol′o-je) [*neuro-* + Gr. *hypnos* sleep + *-logy*]. The sum of knowledge concerning hypnotic conditions.

neurohypophyseal (nu″ro-hi″po-fiz′e-al). Pertaining to the neurohypophysis.

neurohypophysial (nu″ro-hi″po-fiz′e-al). Neurohypophyseal.

neurohypophysis (nu″ro-hi-pof′ĭ-sis). The pars nervosa or main part of the posterior lobe of the pituitary body. See *hypophysis cerebri.*

neuroid (nu′roid) [*neuro-* + Gr. *eidos* form]. Resembling a nerve.

neuro-induction (nu″ro-in-duk′shun) [*neuro-* + L. *inducere* to persuade]. Mental suggestion.

neuro-inidia (nu″ro-ĭ-nid′e-ah). Deficient nutrition of nerve cells.

neuro-inoma (nu″ro-ĭ-no′mah). Neurofibroma.

neuro-inomatosis (nu″ro-ĭ-no″mah-to′sis) [*neuro-* + Gr. *is* fiber + *-oma*]. Neurofibromatosis.

neurokeratin (nu″ro-ker′ah-tin) [*neuro-* + Gr. *keras* horn]. A variety of keratin said to form the supporting network of the myelin sheath of medullated nerve fibers.

neurokinet (nu″ro-kin′et) [*neuro-* + Gr. *kinein* to move]. An apparatus for stimulating the nerve by percussion.

neurokyme (nu′ro-kīm). A nervous process in general.

neurolabyrinthitis (nu″ro-lab″ĭ-rin-thi′tis). Inflammation of the nervous structures of the labyrinth.

neurolemma (nu″ro-lem′mah). The thin membrane spirally enwrapping the myelin layers of a myelinated nerve fiber or the axon of an unmyelinated nerve fiber.

neurolemmitis (nu″ro-lem-mi′tis). Inflammation of the neurolemma.

neurolemmoma (nu″ro-lem-mo′mah). A tumor of a peripheral nerve sheath. Called also *neurilemoma.*

neuroleptic (nu″ro-lep′tik) [*neuro-* + Gr. *lēpsis* a taking hold]. 1. Producing symptoms resembling those of disorders of the nervous system. 2. A drug or agent which produces symptoms resembling those of disorders of the nervous system.

neurolipomatosis (nu″ro-lĭ-po″mah-to′sus). A condition characterized by the formation of multiple fat deposits, with involvement of the nervous system because of resultant pressure on the nerves. **n. doloro′sa,** adiposis dolorosa.

neurologia (nu″ro-lo′je-ah). Neurology; used in B N A terminology to encompass the nomenclature relating to the organ system (nervous system) concerned with correlation of the adjustments and reactions of an organism to internal and environmental conditions.

neurologist (nu-rol′o-jist). An expert in neurology or in the treatment of disorders of the nervous system.

neurology (nu-rol′o-je) [*neuro-* + *-logy*]. That branch of medical science which deals with the nervous system, both normal and in disease.

neurolues (nu″ro-lu′ēz). Neurosyphilis.

neurolymph (nu′ro-limf). The cerebrospinal fluid.

neurolymphomatosis (nu″ro-lim″fo-mah-to′sis). Lymphoblastic infiltration of a nerve. **n. gallina′rum.** See under *lymphomatosis of fowl.*

neurolysin (nu-rol′ĭ-sin). A cytolysin which has a specific destructive action upon nerve cells.

neurolysis (nu-rol′ĭ-sis) [*neuro-* + Gr. *lysis* dissolution]. 1. Release of a nerve sheath by cutting it longitudinally. 2. The operative breaking up of perineural adhesions. 3. The relief of tension upon a nerve obtained by stretching. 4. Exhaustion of nervous energy. 5. Destruction or dissolution of nerve tissue.

neurolytic (nu″ro-lit′ik). Destructive of nerve substance.

neuroma (nu-ro′mah) [*neuro-* + *-oma*]. A tumor or new growth largely made up of nerve cells and nerve fibers; a tumor growing from a nerve. **amputation n.,** traumatic neuroma occurring after amputation of an extremity or part. **amyelinic n.,** one containing only nonmedullated nerve fibers. **n. cu′tis,** neuroma seated in the skin. **cystic n.,** a false neuroma, or a neuroma which has become cystic. **false n.,** one which does not contain genuine nerve cells. **fascicular n., medullated n.,** a neuroma made up of medullated nerve fibers. **ganglionar n., ganglionated n., ganglionic n.,** one made up of true nerve cells. **malignant n.,** sarcoma of a nerve structure, usually spindle celled. **multiple n.** See *neuromatosis.* **myelinic n.,** one that contains medullated nerve fibers. **nevoid n.,** neuroma telangiectodes. **plexiform n.,** a neuroma made up of contorted nerve trunks. **n. telangiecto′des,** one which contains an excess of blood vessels. **traumatic n.,** an unorganized bulbous or nodular mass of nerve fibers and Schwann cells produced by hyperplasia of nerve fibers and their supporting tissues after accidental or purposeful sectioning of the nerve. **true n.,** a neuroma made up of nerve tissue. **Verneuil's n.,** plexiform n.

neuromalacia (nu″ro-mah-la′she-ah) [*neuro-* + Gr. *malakia* softening]. Morbid softening of the nerves.

neuromalakia (nu″ro-mah-la′ke-ah). Neuromalacia.

neuromast (nu′ro-mast) [*neuro-* + Gr. *mastos* hill]. A nerve hillock; a mass of neuroepithelium constituting a sense organ.

neuromatosis (nu″ro-mah-to′sis). A disease condition characterized by the presence of many neuromas.

neuromatous (nu-rom′ah-tus). Affected with or of the nature of neuroma.

neuromechanism (nu″ro-mek′ah-nizm). The structure and arrangement of the nervous system in relation to function.

neuromelitococcosis (nu″ro-mel″ĭ-to-kok-o′sis). Neurobrucellosis.

neuromere (nu′ro-mēr) [*neuro-* + Gr. *meros* part]. One of the segments of the rhombencephalon; a rhombomere.

neuromimesis (nu″ro-mi-me′sis) [*neuro-* + *mimesis*]. Hysterical simulation of organic disease.

neuromimetic (nu″ro-mi-met′ik). 1. Pertaining to neuromimesis. 2. Resembling nerve impulses: a term applied to agents which stimulate nerve action.

neuromittor (nu″ro-mit′or) [*neuro-* + L. *mittere* to send]. One of the terminal elements at the peripheral end of a neuron which transfers a stimulus to the neuroceptor of the adjoining neuron. Called also *mittor.*

neuromuscular (nu″ro-mus′ku-lar). Neuromyal.

neuromyal (nu″ro-mi′al) [*neuro-* + Gr. *mus* a muscle]. Pertaining to nerves and muscles.

neuromyelitis (nu″ro-mi″ĕ-li′tis) [*neuro-* + Gr. *myelos* marrow + *-itis*]. Inflammation of nervous and medullary or myelonic substance; myelitis attended with neuritis. **n. op′tica,** acute transverse myelitis with optic neuritis.

neuromyic (nu″ro-mi′ik) [*neuro-* + Gr. *mys* muscle]. Neuromuscular.

neuromyon (nu″ro-mi′on) [*neuro-* + Gr. *mys* muscle]. The neural elements in a muscle.

neuromyositis (nu″ro-mi″o-si′tis) [*neuro-* + *myositis*]. Neuritis complicated with myositis.

neuron (nu′ron) [Gr. *neuron* nerve]. 1. A nerve cell with its processes, collaterals, and terminations regarded as a structural unit of the nervous system. See *nerve cell.* 2. An axon. 3. The cerebrospinal axis. **afferent n.,** a neuron which conducts a nervous impulse from a receptor to a center. **bipolar n.,** a neuron having two axons. **central n.,** a neuron which belongs entirely to the central nervous system. **correlation n.,** a neuron which takes part in the function of correlating various stimuli into the appropriate response. See *correlation.* **efferent n.,** a neuron which conducts a nervous impulse from a center to an organ of response. **intercalary n., internuncial n.,** interneuron. **long n.,** an axon. **lower motor n's,** the peripheral neurons whose cell bodies lie in the ventral gray columns of the spinal cord and whose terminations are in the skeletal muscles. Cf. *upper motor n's.* **motor n.,** any neuron possessing a motor function; an efferent neuron conveying motor impulses. See *lower motor n's, peripheral motor n.,* and *upper motor n's.* **multiform n.,** polymorphic n. **peripheral motor n.,** the neuron in a peripheral reflex arc that receives the impulse from an interneuron and transmits it to a voluntary muscle. **peripheral sensory n.,** a neuron forming the first part of a peripheral reflex arc; situated outside the central nervous system, it has a peripheral branch which enters the central nervous system. Together with the interneurons and the peripheral motor neuron it forms a peripheral reflex arc. **polymorphic n.,** a neuron of irregular shape. **postganglionic n's,** neurons whose cell bodies are situated in the autonomic ganglia and whose purpose is to relay impulses beyond the ganglia. **preganglionic n's,** neurons whose cell bodies lie in the central nervous system and whose efferent fibers terminate in the autonomic ganglia. **premotor n.,** a neuron not connected directly with muscle, but serving as a connecting center to command excitation in one or more motor neurons. **projection n.,** one which serves for the transmission of nervous impulses, whether motor or sensory. **pyramidal n.,** pyramidal cell. **sensory n.,** any neuron possessing a sensory function; an afferent neuron conveying sensory impulses. **short n.,** a local process from a nerve cell or brain cell reaching only to a nearby gray mass. **unipolar n.,** a neuron having only one axon. **upper motor n's,** the neurons in the cerebral cortex which conduct impulses from the motor cortex to the motor nuclei of the cerebral nerves or to the ventral gray columns of the spinal cord. Cf. *lower motor n's.*

neuronagenesis (nu″rōn-ah-jen′e-sis) [*neuron* + *a* neg. + Gr. *gennan* to produce]. Lack of development of neurons.

neuronal (nu′ro-nal). Pertaining to a neuron or neurons.

neuronatrophy (nu″ron-at′ro-fe). Southard and Solomon's term for any nervous disease due to sclerosis of neurons.

neurone (nu′rōn). Neuron.

neuronephric (nu″ro-nef′rik). Pertaining to the nervous and renal systems.

neuronevus (nu″ro-ne′vus). Intradermal nevus.

neuronic (nu-ron′ik). Pertaining to or affecting a neuron.

neuronin (nu′ro-nin). The principal protein of the axon of a nerve.

neuronist (nu′ro-nist). An anatomist who considers the nervous system as a mass of neurons.

neuronitis (nu″ro-ni′tis). A term applied by Foster Kennedy to a disorder of unknown origin involving the more proximal part of the peripheral nervous system, characterized by breakdown of nerve fibers, sometimes in association with inflammatory-cell reaction. Currently seldom used, it was in the past one of numerous synonyms used for the Guillain-Barré syndrome.

neuronophage (nu-ron′o-fāj) [*neuron* + Gr. *phagein* to eat]. A phagocyte which destroys nerve cells.

neuronophagia (nu″ron-o-fa′je-ah). The destruction of nerve cells by phagocytic action.

neuronophagy (nu″ron-of′ah-je). Neuronophagia.

neuronosis (nu″ro-no′sis) [*neuron* + Gr. *nosos* disease]. Any disease of nervous origin.

neuronotropic (nu-ron″o-trōp′ik) [*neuron* + Gr. *tropein* to turn]. Having a special affinity for neurons.

neuronymy (nu-ron′ĭ-me) [*neuron* + Gr. *onoma* name]. The systematic naming of the parts of the nervous system.

neuronyxis (nu″ro-nik′sis) [*neuro-* + Gr. *nyxis* puncture]. Surgical puncture of a nerve.

neuro-ophthalmology (nu″ro-of″thal-mol′o-je). That part of ophthalmology dealing especially with portions of the nervous system related to the eye.

neuro-otology (nu″ro-o-tol′o-je). That part of otology dealing especially with portions of the nervous system related to the ear.

neuropapillitis (nu″ro-pap″ĭ-li′tis). Optic neuritis.

neuroparalysis (nu″ro-pah-ral′ĭ-sis). Paralysis due to disease of a nerve or nerves.

neuroparalytic (nu″ro-par″ah-lit′ik). Pertaining to or characterized by neuroparalysis.

neuropath (nu′ro-path). A person with a tendency to neurosis.

neuropathic (nu″ro-path′ik). Pertaining to or characterized by neuropathy.

neuropathogenesis (nu″ro-path″o-jen′e-sis). Development of disease of the nervous system.

neuropathogenicity (nu″ro-path″o-je-nis′ĭ-te). The quality of producing or the ability to produce pathologic changes in nerve tissue.

neuropathology (nu″ro-pah-thol′o-je). The branch of medicine dealing with morphological and other aspects of disease of the nervous system.

neuropathy (nu-rop′ah-the). A general term denoting functional disturbances and/or pathological changes in the peripheral nervous system. The etiology may be known (e.g., *arsenical n., diabetic n., ischemic n., traumatic n.*), or unknown. *Encephalopathy* and *myelopathy* are corresponding terms relating to involvement of the brain and spinal cord, respectively. The term is often used to designate non-specific lesions in the peripheral nervous system, in contrast to inflammatory lesions, for which the term *peripheral neuritis* is generally used. **progressive hypertrophic interstitial n.,** a condition characterized by hyperplasia of the interstitial connective tissue, causing thickening of peripheral nerve trunks and posterior roots, and by sclerosis of the posterior columns of the spinal cord; a slowly progressive familial disease beginning in early life, marked by atrophy of distal parts of the legs, and by diminution of tendon reflexes and of sensation. Called also *Dejerine-Sottas disease.*

neurophage (nu′ro-fāj). Neuronophage.

neuropharmacology (nu″ro-fahr″mah-kol′o-je). That branch of pharmacology dealing especially with the action of drugs upon various parts and elements of the nervous system.

neurophilic (nu″ro-fil′ik). Neurotropic.

neurophonia (nu″ro-fo′ne-ah) [*neuro-* + Gr. *phōnē* voice + *-ia*]. A form of nervous disorder in which the patient utters peculiar cries, sometimes like those of certain animals.

neurophthalmology (nu″rof-thah-mol″o-je) Neuro-ophthalmology.

neurophthisis (nu-rof′thĭ-sis) [*neuro-* + Gr. *phthisis* wasting]. Wasting of nerve tissue.

neurophysiology (nu″ro-fiz″e-ol′o-je) [*neuro-* + *physiology*]. The physiology of the nervous system.

neuropil (nu′ro-pīl) [*neuro-* + Gr. *pilos* felt]. A dense feltwork of interwoven cytoplasmic processes of nerve cells (dendrites and neurites) and of glia cells in the central nervous system and in some parts of the peripheral nervous system.

neuropile (nu′ro-pīl). Neuropil.

neuropilem (nu-ro-pi′lem). Neuropil.

neuroplasm (nu′ro-plazm) [*neuro-* + Gr. *plasma* something formed]. The undifferentiated basophilic protoplasm of a nerve cell.

neuroplasmic (nu″ro-plaz′mik). Of or relating to neuroplasm.

neuroplasty (nu′ro-plas″te) [*neuro-* + Gr. *plassein* to form]. Plastic surgery of a nerve.

neuroplexus (nu″ro-plek′sus). A plexus of nerves.

neuroploca (nu-rop′lo-kah) [*neuro-* + Gr. *plokē* web]. A nerve ganglion.

neuropodia (nu″ro-po′de-ah). Plural of *neuropodium.*

neuropodion (nu″ro-po′de-on). Neuropodium.

neuropodium (nu″ro-po′de-um), pl. *neuropo′dia* [*neuro-* + Gr. *pous* foot]. A bullous termination of an axon in one type of synapse.

neuropore (nu′ro-pōr) [*neuro-* + Gr. *poros* pore]. The open anterior end (foramen anterius) or the posterior end (foramen posterius) of the neural tube of the early embryo. These gradually close as the tube develops.

neuropotential (nu″ro-po-ten′shal). Nerve energy; nerve potential.

neuroprobasia (nu″ro-pro-ba′se-ah) [*neuro-* + Gr. *pro* forward + *basis* walking]. Advance along the nerves; said of the action of certain filtrable viruses.

neuropsychiatrist (nu″ro-si-ki′ah-trist). A physician who specializes in neuropsychiatry.

neuropsychiatry (nu″ro-si-ki′ah-tre). The branch of medicine which includes both neurology and psychiatry.

neuropsychic (nu″ro-si′kik) [*neuro-* + Gr. *psychē* soul]. Pertaining to the nerve center concerned in mental processes.

neuropsychopathy (nu″ro-si-kop′ah-the) [*neuro-* + Gr. *psychē* soul + *pathos* disease]. A disease condition of the nerves and mind.

neuropsychosis (nu″ro-si-ko′sis) [*neuro-* + *psychosis*]. Nervous disease complicated with mental disorder; a psychosis.

neuropyra (nu″ro-pi′rah) [*neuro-* + Gr. *pyr* fever]. Nervous fever.

neuropyretic (nu″ro-pi-ret′ik). Pertaining to nervous fever.

neuroradiology (nu″ro-ra″de-ol′o-je). Radiology of the nervous system.

neurorecidive (nu″ro-res″ĭ-dēv′). Neurorelapse.

neurorecurrence (nu″ro-re-kur′ens). Neurorelapse.

neuroregulation (nu″ro-reg″u-la′shun) [*neuro-* + *regulation*]. The regulation and control of nervous activity.

neurorelapse (nu″ro-re-laps′). A peculiar outburst of neurosyphilis precipitated by insufficient treatment with arsphenamine, and characterized by various nervous symptoms. Called also *neurorecidive* and *neurorecurrence*.

neuroretinitis (nu″ro-ret″ĭ-ni′tis). Inflammation of the optic nerve and retina.

neuroretinopathy (nu″ro-ret″ĭ-nop′ah-the) [*neuro-* + *retina* + Gr. *pathos* disease]. A disease of the optic disk and retina. **hypertensive r.**, swelling of the optic disk and formation of serous and fibrinous precipitates in the retina, occurring in hypertension.

neurorrhaphy (nu-ror′ah-fe) [*neuro-* + Gr. *rhaphē* stitch]. The suturing of a cut nerve.

neurorrheuma (nu″ro-roo′mah) [*neuro-* + Gr. *rheuma* flow]. Nervous energy.

Neurorrhyctes hydrophobiae (nu″ro-rik′tēz hi″dro-fo′be-e). Negri bodies.

neurosal (nu-ro′sal). Pertaining to a neurosis.

neurosarcokleisis (nu″ro-sar″ko-kli′sis) [*neuro-* + Gr. *sarx* flesh + *kleisis* closure]. An operation performed for neuralgia, done by relieving pressure on the affected nerve by partial resection of the bony canal through which it passes, and transplanting the nerve among soft tissues.

neurosarcoma (nu″ro-sar-ko′mah). A sarcoma with neuromatous elements.

neurosclerosis (nu″ro-skle-ro′sis) [*neuro-* + Gr. *sklēros* hard]. The hardening of the substance of a nerve or nerve center.

neurosecretion (nu″ro-se-kre′shun) [*neuro-* + *secretion*]. The secretory activities of nerve cells.

neurosensory (nu″ro-sen′so-re). Pertaining to a sensory nerve.

neuroses (nu-ro′sēz). Plural of *neurosis*.

neurosis (nu-ro′sis), pl. *neuro′ses* [*neur-* + *-osis*]. A disorder of the psychic or mental constitution; in contrast with the psychosis, it is less incapacitating, and in it the personality remains more or less intact. Sometimes called *psychoneurosis*. **accident n.**, a neurosis with hysterical symptoms caused by accident or injury. **anxiety n.**, a form of neurosis characterized by morbid and unjustified dread. **association n.**, a condition in which an abnormal mental experience tends to be reproduced, with all its original mental and physical phenomena, when an idea related to the original experience is brought into the mind. **cardiac n.**, neurocirculatory asthenia. **compensation n.**, the psychoneurotic phenomena developing after an accident in persons who are insured or who believe that by being ill they may increase their chances of receiving compensation. **compulsion n.**, a psychoneurosis marked by an imperative impulse toward some absurd act or speech. **conversion n.**, a neurosis characterized by disorders of the motility, sensation or other organic systems of the body. Called also *conversion hysteria*. **craft n.**, occupation n. **expectation n.**, a neurotic condition in which the expectation of an occurrence induces mental tension, etc. **fatigue n.**, a neurosis due to nerve tire, as neurasthenia or psychasthenia. **fixation n.**, a neurosis based on fixation of the personality at a stage short of complete maturity. **gastric n.**, a disorder of gastric digestion based on disturbance of the nervous system. **homosexual n.**, a paranoid psychosis which is regarded as the result of repressed homosexuality. **intestinal n.**, intestinal indigestion due to disturbance of innervation or of psychic control. **obsessional n.**, a psychoneurosis marked by obsessions which dominate the conduct of the patient. **obsessive-compulsive n.**, a neurosis marked by obsessions and compulsions. **occupation n.**, a neurosis due to the patient's employment. See *copodyskinesia*. **pension n.**, compensation n. **professional n.**, occupation n. **rectal n.**, a rectal disorder due to disturbance of innervation or of psychic control. **regression n.**, fixation neurosis. **sexual n.**, a neurosis of the sexual function. **torsion n.**, dysbasia lordotica progressiva. **transference n.**, hysteria and compulsion neurosis. **traumatic n.**, one which results from an injury. **vegetative n.**, erythredema polyneuropathy. **war n.**, a term referring to a number of conditions, chiefly hysterical conversion phenomena, seen in soldiers.

neurosism (nu′ro-sizm). Neurasthenia.

neuroskeletal (nu″ro-skel′ĕ-tal). Pertaining to the nervous tissues and the skeletal muscular tissue.

neuroskeleton (nu″ro-skel′ĕ-ton) [*neuro-* + Gr. *skeleton* skeleton]. Endoskeleton.

neurosome (nu′ro-sōm) [*neuro-* + Gr. *sōma* body]. 1. The body of a nerve cell. 2. Any one of a set of minute particles in the ground substance of the protoplasm of the neurons.

neurospasm (nu′ro-spazm) [*neuro-* + Gr. *spasmos* spasm]. The nervous twitching of a muscle.

neurosplanchnic (nu″ro-splangk′nik). Pertaining to the cerebrospinal and sympathetic nervous systems.

neurospongioma (nu″ro-spon″je-o′mah). Neuroglioma.

neurospongium (nu″ro-spon′je-um) [*neuro-* + Gr. *spongos* sponge]. 1. The fibrillar component of neurons. 2. A meshwork of nerve fibers, especially the inner reticular layer of the retina.

neurostatus (nu″ro-sta′tus). The state or condition of neural symptoms in a case history.

neurostearic (nu″ro-ste-ar′ik) [*neuro-* + Gr. *stear* fat]. Derived from the fatty elements of the nerve substance.

neurosthenia (nu″ro-sthe′ne-ah) [*neuro-* + Gr. *sthenos* strength + *-ia*]. Great nervous power and excitement.

neurosurgeon (nu″ro-sur′jun). A physician who specializes in neurosurgery.

neurosurgery (nu″ro-sur′jer-e). Surgery of the nervous system.

neurosuture (nu″ro-su′tūr). Neurorrhaphy.

neurosyphilis (nu″ro-sif′ĭ-lis). Syphilis of the

central nervous system. **ectodermogenic n.,** neurosyphilis affecting the substance of the brain, cord or nerves. **meningeal n.,** neurosyphilis affecting chiefly the meninges. **meningovascular n.,** neurosyphilis in which both the meninges and the vessels of the nervous system are involved. **mesodermogenic n.,** neurosyphilis affecting the meninges, blood vessels, and nerve sheaths. **paretic n.,** dementia paralytica. **tabetic n.,** tabes dorsalis.

neurosystemitis (nu″ro-sis″tĕ-mi′tis). Inflammation involving structures of the nervous system. **n. epidem′ica,** encephalitis lethargica.

neurotabes (nu″ro-ta′bēz) [*neuro-* + *tabes*]. Multiple peripheral neuritis with symptoms like those of locomotor ataxia. See *pseudotabes.* **n. diabet′ica,** tabes diabetica.

neurotagma (nu″ro-tag′mah) [*neuro-* + Gr. *tagma* arrangement]. A linear arrangement of the structural elements of a nerve cell.

neurotendinous (nu″ro-ten′dĭ-nus). Pertaining to both nerve and tendon.

neurotension (nu″ro-ten′shun). Neurectasis.

neuroterminal (nu″ro-ter′mĭ-nal). An end-organ of a peripheral nerve.

neurothecitis (nu″ro-the-si′tis) [*neuro-* + Gr. *thēkē* sheath + *-itis*]. Inflammation of a nerve sheath.

neurothele (nu″ro-the′le) [*neuro-* + Gr. *thele* nipple]. A sensory papilla of the corium.

neurothelitis (nu″ro-the-li′tis) [*neurothele* + *-itis*]. Inflammation of a neurothele.

neurotherapeutics (nu″ro-ther″ah-pu′tiks). Neurotherapy.

neurotherapy (nu″ro-ther′ah-pe) [*neuro-* + Gr. *therapeia* treatment]. 1. The treatment of nervous disorders. 2. A term proposed for psychotherapy on the ground that the basis of such treatment is the employment of all sources of nervous activity.

neurothlipsis (nu″ro-thlip′sis) [*neuro-* + Gr. *thlipsis* pressure]. Pressure on a nerve or irritation of a nerve.

neurotic (nu-rot′ik). 1. Pertaining to or affected with a neurosis. 2. Pertaining to the nerves. 3. A nervous person in whom emotions predominate over reason.

neurotica (nu-rot′ĭ-kah). Functional nervous disorders.

neuroticism (nu-rot′ĭ-sizm). A state of perverted or excessive nervous action.

neurotigenic (nu-rot″ĭ-jen′ik). Producing a neurosis.

neurotization (nu″rot-ĭ-za′shun). 1. The regeneration of a nerve after its division. 2. The operation of implanting a nerve into a paralyzed muscle.

neurotmesis (nu″rot-me′sis) [*neuro-* + Gr. *tmēsis* cutting apart]. Nerve injury in which all essential structures have been sundered, despite apparent maintenance of anatomic continuity. Cf. *axonotmesis* and *neurapraxia.*

neurotology (nu″ro-tol′o-je). Neuro-otology.

neurotome (nu′ro-tōm) [*neuro-* + Gr. *tomē* a cut]. 1. A needle-like knife for dissecting the nerves. 2. Neuromere.

neurotomy (nu-rot′o-me) [*neuro-* + Gr. *temnein* to cut]. 1. The dissection or anatomy of the nerves. 2. The surgical cutting of a nerve. **opticociliary n.,** division of the optic and ciliary nerves for prevention of sympathetic ophthalmia. **retrogasserian n.,** division of the posterior root of the gasserian ganglion in treatment of facial neuralgia.

neurotonia (nu″ro-to′ne-ah). Instability of tonus of the vegetative nervous system.

neurotonic (nu″ro-ton′ik) [*neuro-* + *tonic*]. Having a tonic effect upon the nerves.

neurotonogenic (nu-rot″o-no-jen′ik). Producing nerve tonus.

neurotonometer (nu″ro-to-nom′e-ter). An apparatus for measuring minute differences in skin tonus.

neurotony (nu-rot′o-ne) [*neuro-* + Gr. *teinein* to stretch]. The stretching of a nerve, chiefly to relieve pain. Called also *nerve stretching.*

neurotoxia (nu″ro-tok′se-ah). A toxic condition of the nervous system; neurasthenia regarded as an auto-intoxication.

neurotoxic (nu″ro-tok′sik). Poisonous or destructive to nerve tissue.

neurotoxicity (nu″ro-toks-is′ĭ-te). The quality of exerting a destructive or poisonous effect upon nerve tissue.

neurotoxin (nu″ro-tok′sin). A substance that is poisonous or destructive to nerve tissue, especially an exotoxin which is characterized by a marked affinity for nerve tissue and which produces a fatty degeneration in the myelin sheath of peripheral nerves, in the white substance of the brain and spinal cord, and in certain other tissues, such as heart muscle.

neurotrauma (nu″ro-traw′mah) [*neuro-* + *trauma*]. Wounding of a nerve.

neurotripsy (nu″ro-trip′se) [*neuro-* + Gr. *tribein* to rub]. The operation of crushing or bruising a nerve.

neurotrophasthenia (nu″ro-tro″fas-the′ne-ah) [*neuro-* + Gr. *trophē* nutrition + *astheneia* weakness]. Defective nutrition of the nervous system.

neurotrophic (nu″ro-trof′ik). Pertaining to neurotrophy.

neurotrophy (nu-rot′ro-fe) [*neuro-* + Gr. *trophē* nutrition]. The nutrition and maintenance of tissues as regulated by nervous influence.

neurotropic (nu″ro-trop′ik). Having a selective affinity for nervous tissue, or exerting its principal effect on the nervous system.

neurotropism (nu-rot′ro-pizm) [*neuro-* + Gr. *tropē* a turn, turning]. 1. The quality of having a special affinity for nervous tissue. 2. The alleged tendency of regenerating nerve fibers to grow toward specific portions of the periphery.

neurotropy (nu-rot′ro-pe). Neurotropism.

neurotrosis (nu″ro-tro′sis) [*neuro-* + Gr. *trōsis* wound]. Neurotrauma.

neurovaccine (nu″ro-vak′sin). Vaccine virus prepared by growing the virus in the brain of a rabbit.

neurovaricosis (nu″ro-var″ĭ-ko′sis) [*neuro-* + *varicose* + *-osis*]. A varicose state of the fibers of a nerve.

neurovariola (nu″ro-vah-ri′o-lah). Neurovaccine.

neurovascular (nu″ro-vas′ku-lar). Both nervous and vascular.

neurovegetative (nu″ro-vej′ĕ-ta″tiv). Pertaining to the vegetative nervous system.

neurovirulence (nu″ro-vir′u-lens). The competence of an infectious agent to produce pathologic effects on the nervous system.

neurovirulent (nu″ro-vir′u-lent). Capable of producing pathologic effects on the nervous system.

neurovirus (nu″ro-vi′rus). A vaccine virus which has been modified by passing into nervous tissue.

neurovisceral (nu″ro-vis′er-al). Neurosplanchnic.

neurovoltometer (nu″ro-vōl-tom′e-ter). An instrument for measuring the state of a nervous patient's nervousness.

neurula (nu′roo-lah) [*neuro-* + dim. *-ula*]. The early embryo during the development of the neural tube from the neural plate, marking the first appearance of the nervous system; the next stage after the gastrula, and occurring during the fourth week.

neurulation (nu″roo-la′shun). Formation, in the early embryo, of the neural plate, followed by its closure with development of the neural tube.

neururgic (nu-rer′jik) [*neuro-* + Gr. *ergon* work]. Pertaining to nerve action.

neurypnology (nu″rip-nol′o-je). Neurohypnology.

Neusser's granules (noi′serz) [Edmund von *Neusser*, Austrian physician, 1852–1912]. See under *granule.*

neutral (nu′tral) [L. *neutralis; neuter,* neither]. Neither acid nor basic.

neutrality (nu-tral′ĭ-te). The state of being neutral.

neutralize (nu′tral-īz). To render neutral.

neutrapen (nu′trah-pen). Trade mark for a lyophilized preparation of penicillinase.

neutretto (nu-tret′o). A particle similar in mass to a barytron but having no electrical charge.

neutrino (nu-tri′no). A hypothetical elementary particle with an extremely small mass and carrying no electric charge.

neutroclusion (nu″trŏ-kloo′zhun). Malocclusion characterized by normal mesiodistal or normal anteroposterior relation of the mandibular to the maxillary dental arch [A S O]. Generally regarded as identical with class I in Angle's classification of malocclusion.

neutrocyte (nu′tro-sīt). A neutrophil leukocyte. See *neutrophil,* 2nd def.

neutrocytopenia (nu″tro-si″to-pe′ne-ah). Neutropenia.

neutrocytophilia (nu″tro-si″to-fil′e-ah). Neutrophilia.

neutrocytosis (nu″tro-si-to′sis). Neutrophilia.

neutroflavine (nu″tro-fla′vin). Acriflavine.

neutron (nu′tron). An electrically neutral or uncharged particle of matter existing along with protons in the atoms of all elements except the mass 1 isotope of hydrogen.

neutropenia (nu″tro-pe′ne-ah) [*neutrophil* + Gr. *penia* poverty]. A decrease in the number of neutrophilic leukocytes in the blood. See *agranulocytosis.* **chronic n. of childhood,** a condition observed in children in which granulocytopenia, recurrent infections, lymphadenopathy, and hepatosplenomegaly may be present for a considerable time, with subsequent spontaneous remission. **chronic hypoplastic n.,** a syndrome resembling primary splenic neutropenia, but with hypocellular bone marrow. **cyclic n.,** periodic n. **familial n.,** a type of peripheral neutropenia which is familial in occurrence, and is probably transmitted by an autosomal recessive gene. **idiopathic n., malignant n.,** agranulocytosis. **neonatal n., transitory,** a short-lived neutropenia, observed in the newborn, which may be of the isoimmune type. **periodic n.,** a chronic form of neutropenia characterized by its regular, periodic episodic recurrences, and associated with malaise, fever, stomatitis, and various types of infections. **peripheral n.,** decrease in the number of neutrophils in the circulating blood. **primary splenic n.,** a syndrome characterized by splenomegaly and a decrease in the number of neutrophils in the circulating blood, with a normocellular or hyperplastic bone marrow.

neutrophil (nu′tro-fil) [L. *neuter* neither + Gr. *philein* to love]. 1. Stainable by neutral dyes. 2. A cell or structural element, particularly a leukocyte, stainable by neutral dyes; a polymorphonuclear neutrophilic leukocyte. 3. Neither anthropophilic nor zoophilous: said of certain mosquitoes. **filamented n.,** a neutrophil leukocyte which has two or more lobes connected by a filament of chromatin. **giant n.,** macropolycyte. **juvenile n.,** a metamyelocyte. **nonfilamented n.,** a neutrophil whose lobes are connected by thick strands of chromatin. **rod n., stab n.,** a neutrophil leukocyte whose nucleus is not divided into segments.

neutrophilia (nu″tro-fil′e-ah). Increase in the number of neutrophil leukocytes in the blood; neutrophilic leukocytosis. **dysoremos n.,** a condition caused by failure of maturation of granulocytes, with myeloblasts and promyelocytes constituting the dominant elements in the bone marrow.

neutrophilic (nu″tro-fil′ik). Stainable by neutral dyes.

neutrophilopenia (nu″tro-fil″o-pe′ne-ah) [*neutrophil* + Gr. *penia* poverty]. Abnormal decrease in the proportion of neutrophils in the blood.

neutropism (nu′tro-pizm). Neurotropism.

neutrotaxis (nu″tro-tak′sis) [*neutrophil* + Gr. *taxis* arrangement]. The attractive or repellent influence exerted by neutrophil leukocytes.

nevi (ne′vi) [L.]. Plural of *nevus.*

nevocarcinoma (ne″vo-kar″sĭ-no′mah). Carcinoma developing from nevi or moles; melanocarcinoma.

nevoid (ne′void). Resembling a nevus.

nevolipoma (ne″vo-lĭ-po′mah). A nevus containing a large amount of fibrofatty tissue.

nevose (ne′vōs). Having nevi; spotted with nevi.

nevoxantho-endothelioma (ne″vo-zan″tho-en″do-the″le-o′mah). A condition in which groups of yellow-brown papules or nodules occur on the extensor surfaces of the extremities of infants.

Nevskia (nev′ske-ah) [*Neva,* a river in Russia]. A genus of microorganisms of the family Caulobacteraceae, suborder Pseudomonadineae, order Pseudomonadales, occurring as stalked, rod-shaped cells, the long axis of the cell being at right angles to the axis of the stalk. The type species is *N. ramo′sa.*

nevus (ne′vus), pl. *ne′vi* [L. *naevus*]. A circumscribed new growth of the skin of congenital origin; it may be either vascular (due to hypertrophy of blood or lymph vessels) or nonvascular (with epidermal and connective tissue predominating, or even arising from nervous tissue). **amelanotic n.,** one which contains no pigment. **n. ane′micus,** a nevus characterized by the presence of depigmented macules and by a paucity of blood vessels. **n. angiecto′des,** n. vascularis. **n. angiomato′des,** angioelephantiasis. **n. arachnoi′deus, n. araneo′sus,** n. araneus. **n. ara′neus,** a nevus composed of small telangiectases radiating from a central point in fine hairlike branches resembling the legs of a spider. Called also *n. arachnoideus, n. araneosus, arterial n., spider n., stellar n., spider angioma, vascular spider,* and *spider telangiectasis.* **n. avasculo′sus,** n. anemicus. **bathing trunk n.,** nevus affecting the lower portion of the body, or the area usually covered by bathing trunks. **blue n.,** a sharply circumscribed round to oval, papular to nodular solitary growth, usually 2–15 mm. in diameter and blue to black in color, being composed of masses of dermal melanoblasts in the cutis, developing in childhood, and occurring on the face, forearms, or hands. **capillary n.,** one that involves the capillaries of the skin. **n. caverno′sus,** cavernous angioma. **n. cerebellifor′mis,** a large elevated nevus with furrows and sulci producing a surface resembling that of the cerebellum. **compound n.,** an intradermal nevus with accompanying junctional change. **connective-tissue n.,** a rare type of nevus composed of papules or lichenoid nodules of pinhead size or larger, snow-white to brownish in color, and usually occurring on the chest in bands or in zosteriform or systematized patterns. **depigmented n., n. depigmento′sus,** n. anemicus. **dermoepidermal n.,** junctional n. **epithelial nevi,** congenital skin tumors which do not contain melanocytes, ordinarily present at birth or appearing in early childhood, and showing some predilection for the flexor surfaces; they vary widely in appearance, size, and distribution. **fatty n.,** n. lipomatosus. **n. fibro′sus,** one having a fibrous structure. **n. flam′meus,** a diffuse, poorly defined area varying from pink to dark bluish red, involving otherwise normal skin; called also *capillary hemangioma, nevus vinosus*, and *port-wine stain* or *mark*. **fleshy n.,** one in which epidermal and connective tissue predominates and which is elevated to a varying degree above the surface of the surrounding normal skin and contains a varying amount of pigmentation. **n. follicula′ris,** nevus involving the hair follicles, with comedo-like lesions which may become acneform. **n. fusco-caeru′leus ophthalmo-maxilla′ris,** n. of Ota. **hairy n.,** a more or less pigmented nevus of variable size, with hairs growing from its surface. **halo n.,** a nevus surrounded by a ring of depigmentation. **hepatic n.,** hemorrhagic infarct of the liver. **intradermal n.,** one in which the nevus cells occur in nests in the upper part of the corium. **junction n., junctional n.,** one in which the alteration involves the junction of the dermis and epidermis. Called also *dermoepidermal n.* and *marginal n.* **linear n.,** a collection of papillary elevations, occurring in elongated streaks, and due to hypertrophy of the papillary and corneous layers of the skin. **n. lipomato′sus,** one containing much fibrofatty tissue. **n. lymphangiecto′des, lymphatic n., n. lymphat′icus,** a skin growth containing lymph and blood elements intermediate in position between hemangioma and lymphangioma; hemolymphangioma. **marginal n.,** junctional n. **n. mater′nus,** congenital angioma. **melanocytic n.,** the most common tumor of the skin, characteristically developing during infancy and childhood but sometimes not until adult life, and usually benign; they vary in color from light brown to black, and are elevated to a varying degree above the surrounding normal skin. **n. molluscifor′mis,** one forming a protruding fatlike tumor. **n. mo′rus,** a fleshy nevus forming a mulberry-like elevation on the skin. **multiplex n.,** sebaceous n. **n. nervo′sus,** linear n. **n. of Ota, Ota's n.,** dermal melanocytic pigmentation of the side of the face, involving the sclera of the eye, ocular muscle, retrobulbar fat, and sometimes the periosteum of the orbit. **n. papilla′ris,** a papillary pigmented tumor of the skin. **n. papillomato′sus,** one which becomes papillomatous in appearance. **pigmented n., n. pigmento′sus,** melanocytic n. **pilose n., n. pilo′sus,** hairy n. **polyploid n.,** a nevus whose surface is covered with coarse club-tipped excrescences. **n. sanguin′eus,** hemangioma simplex. **sebaceous n.,** a benign sebaceous tumor, with highly differentiated cells, usually found in persons past middle age, and sometimes simulating early basal cell carcinoma. **sebaceous n. of Jadassohn,** a congenital type of tumor of the sebaceous glands, present at birth, and appearing as a single slightly raised, firm yellow plaque on the face or scalp. **n. seba′ceus,** sebaceous n. **spider n.,** n. araneus. **n. spi′lus,** a pigmented macular nevus with a smooth surface. **n. spongio′sus al′bus muco′sae,** a white spongy nevus of a mucous membrane, occurring frequently as a familial condition. **stellar n.,** n. araneus. **strawberry n.,** cavernous angioma. **n. syringocystadeno′sus papillif′erus,** a nevus usually involving the apocrine sweat glands, and with a predilection for the shoulders, axillae, genital and inguinal regions, and scalp; the lesions are rose-red papules of firm consistency, with vesicle-like inclusions filled with clear fluid. **n. u′nius latera′lis,** an epithelial nevus occurring as a transverse band around one side of the trunk. **Unna's n.,** n. flammeus. **vascular n., n. vascula′ris, n. vasculo′sus,** a reddish swelling or patch on the skin due to hypertrophy of the skin capillaries: the term includes nevus flammeus, the elevated strawberry marks, nevus araneus, and cavernous angioma. **n. veno′sus, venous n.,** a complex form of capillary hemangioma occurring most often on the face, and having the deep purple color of port wine. **verrucoid n., n. verruco′sus,** a pigmented, raised nevus, with fine digitate excrescences on its surface. **n. vino′sus,** n. flammeus. **white n.,** amelanotic n.

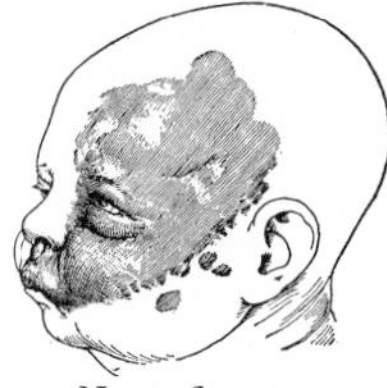

Nevus flammeus. (Homans.)

newborn (nu′born). 1. Recently born. 2. A recently born infant.

newton (nu′ton) [Sir Isaac *Newton*, English mathematician, 1643–1727]. The M.K.S. unit of force; the force which, when acting continuously upon a mass of one kilogram, will impart to it an acceleration of one meter per second per second.

Newton's law, rings (nu′tonz) [Sir Isaac *Newton*]. See under *law* and *ring*.

nexus (nek′sus), pl. *nex′us* [L. "bond"]. A bond, especially one between members of a series or group.

N.F. Abbreviation for *National Formulary*. See under *formulary*.

ng. Abbreviation for *nanogram*.

n'gana (na-gah′nah). Nagana.

NH_3. Ammonia.

NH_4Br. Ammonium bromide.

NH_4Cl. Ammonium chloride.

NH_4CNO. Ammonium cyanate.

$(NH_2)_2CO$. Urea.

$(NH_4)_2CO_3$. Ammonium carbonate.

$(NH_4)HS$. Ammonium hydrosulfide.

N.H.I. Abbreviation for *National Health Insurance*, and *National Heart Institute*.

N.H.M.R.C. Abbreviation for *National Health and Medical Research Council*.

NH_4NO_3. Ammonium nitrate.

$NH_4O.CO.NH_2$. Ammonium carbamate.

N.H.S. Abbreviation for *National Health Service* (British).

$(NH_4)_2.SO_2$. Ammonium sulfate.

Ni. Chemical symbol for *nickel*.

niacin (ni′ah-sin). Nicotinic acid.

niacinamide (ni″ah-sin-am′īd). Nicotinamide.

NIAID. Abbreviation for *National Institute of Allergy and Infectious Diseases*.

nialamide (ni-al′ah-mīd). Chemical name: N-benzyl-β(isonicotinoylhydrazine)-propionamide: a monoamine oxidase inhibitor with antidepressive action used in psychoses.

NIAMD. Abbreviation for *National Institute of Arthritis and Metabolic Diseases*.

niamid (ni′ah-mid). Trade mark for a preparation of nialamide.

niani (ne-an′e). A varioloid of Senegal riflemen.

Nicander (nik-an′der) (3rd century B.C.). A celebrated Greek physician and poet. Two of his works (on toxicology), the *Theriaca* and the *Alexipharmaca*, have survived. He is said to have been the first writer to describe the use of leeches in medicine.

niccolum (nik′o-lum), gen. *nic′coli* [L.]. Nickel.

niche (nich). A defect in an otherwise even surface, especially a depression or recess in the wall of a hollow organ, as seen in the roentgenogram, or such a depression in an organ visible to the naked eye. **Barclay's n.,** a deformity of the cap in the roentgenogram in duodenal ulcer consisting of a small projection. **enamel n.,** either of two depressions between the dental lamina and the developing tooth germ, one pointing distally (*distal enamel n.*) and the other mesially (*mesial enamel n.*). **Haudek's n.,** a budlike prominence on the roentgenographic contour of the stomach caused by the crater of a penetrating gastric ulcer.

NICHHD. Abbreviation for *National Institute of Child Health and Human Development*.

nichrome (nik′krōm). Trade mark for an alloy

of nickel and chromium, having a melting point between that of brass and that of iron, and being very durable because of its resistance to oxidation under heat; widely used for laboratory equipment.

nickel (nik′el) [L. *niccolum*]. A silver-white metallic element: symbol, Ni; specific gravity, 8.9; atomic number, 28; atomic weight, 58.71. **carbonyl n.,** a volatile liquid, $Ni(CO)_4$, used in industry, which may produce serious dyspnea, cyanosis, and cardiac dilatation.

nicking (nik′ing). Localized constrictions in the retinal blood vessels seen in arterial hypertension.

Nicklès' test (ne-klēz′) [François Joseph J. *Nicklès*, a French chemist, 1821–1869]. See under *tests.*

Nicol prism (nik′ol) [William *Nicol*, English physicist, 1768–1851]. See under *prism.*

Nicolaier's bacillus (nik-o′li-erz) [Arthur *Nicolaier*, Berlin physician, born 1862]. *Clostridium tetani.*

Nicolas-Favre disease (ne-ko-lah fav′r) [Joseph *Nicolas;* M. *Favre*, French physicians]. Venereal lymphogranuloma.

Nicollia (nĭ-kol′e-ah) [Charles Jules Henri *Nicolle*, French physician, 1866–1936, noted for his discovery of the role of body lice in the transmission of typhus fever; winner of the Nobel prize for medicine in 1928]. A genus of protozoan blood parasites.

niconyl (ni′ko-nil). Trade mark for a preparation of isoniazid.

Nicotiana (nik″o-she-a′nah) [Jean *Nicot* de Villemain, 1530–1600, who introduced tobacco chewing to Catherine de Medici]. A genus of plants, native to tropical America, from which tobacco is derived.

nicotinamide (nik″o-tin′ah-mīd). The amide of nicotinic acid, a component of the vitamin B complex.

nicotinamidemia (nik″o-tin-am″ĭ-de′me-ah). The presence of nicotinamide in the blood.

nicotine (nik′o-tin) [L. *nicotiana* tobacco]. A colorless, soluble fluid alkaloid, β-pyridyl-α-N-methylpyrrolidine, $C_{10}H_{14}N_2$, with a pyridine-like odor and a burning taste. Nicotine has been prescribed as an antitetanic agent.

nicotinism (nik′o-tin-izm). Poisoning by nicotine.

nicotinolytic (nik″o-tin-o-lit′ik) [*nicotine* + Gr. *lysis* dissolution]. Destroying or suppressing the toxic action of nicotine.

nicotyrine (nik-o′ti-rin). An alkaloid, $C_{10}H_{10}N_2$, from tobacco.

nicoumalone (ni-koo′mah-lōn). Acenocoumarol.

nictation (nik-ta′shun). Nictitation.

nictitation (nik″tĭ-ta′shun) [L. *nictitare* to wink]. The act of winking.

nidal (ni′dal). Pertaining to a nidus.

nidation (ni-da′shun) [L. *nidus* nest]. The implantation of the fertilized ovum (zygote) in the endometrium of the uterus in pregnancy.

nidi (ni′di) [L.]. Plural of *nidus.*

NIDR. Abbreviation for *National Institute of Dental Research.*

nidus (ni′dus), pl. *ni′di* [L. "nest"]. 1. The point of origin or focus of a morbid process. 2. Nucleus, def. 2. **n. a′vis** [B N A], a depression in the cerebellum between the posterior velum and the uvula. Omitted in N A. **n. hirun′dinis,** n. avis.

Niemann's disease, Niemann-Pick disease (ne′man) [Albert *Niemann*, German pediatrician, 1880–1921; Ludwig *Pick*, German physician, born 1868]. See under *disease.*

Niemeyer's pill (ne′mi-erz) [Felix von *Niemeyer*, German physician, 1820–1871]. See under *pill.*

Niewenglowski's ray (nya-ven-glov′ske) [Gaston Henri *Niewenglowski*, French physicist]. See under *ray.*

nifuroxime (ni″fūr-ok′sim). Chemical name: anti-5-nitro-2-furaldehyde oxime: used as a local antibacterial and antiprotozoan agent.

nightshade (nīt′shād). A plant of the genus Solanum. **deadly n.,** belladonna leaf.

NIGMS. Abbreviation for *National Institute of General Medical Sciences.*

nigra (ni′grah) [L. "black"]. The substantia nigra.

nigral (ni′gral). Pertaining to the substantia nigra.

nigricans (ni′grĭ-kans) [L.]. Blackish.

nigrities (ni-grish′e-ēz) [L.]. Blackness. **n. ar′tis,** melasma. **n. lin′guae,** black tongue.

nigrometer (ni-grom′e-ter) [L. *niger* black + Gr. *metron* measure]. An instrument for measuring the intensity of black in black pigments.

nigrosin (ni′gro-sin). An aniline dye, $C_{36}H_{27}N_3$, having a special affinity for ganglion cells, used to stain tissues from the central nervous system for study under the microscope.

nigua (ne′gwah). A Latin American name for *Tunga penetrans.*

NIH. Abbreviation for *National Institutes of Health.*

NIH 204. An antimalarial drug, 9-(2-diamylamino-1-hydroxyethyl-1,2,3,4-tetrahydroxyphenanthrene hydrochloride with effects much like those of atabrine.

nihilism (ni′hil-izm) [L. *nihil* nothing + *-ism*]. A form of delusion in which, to the patient, everything no longer exists. **therapeutic n.,** skepticism regarding the therapeutic value of drugs.

niin (ni′in). A fatty substance thought to be identical with axin.

nikethamide (nik-eth′ah-mīd). Chemical name: N,N-diethylnicotinamide: used as a central nervous system stimulant.

Nikiforoff's method (ne″ke-for′ofs) [Mikhail *Nikiforoff*, Russian dermatologist, born 1858]. See under *method.*

Nikolsky's sign (nĭ-kol′skēz) [Pyotr Vasilyevich *Nikolsky*, Russian dermatologist, born 1855]. See under *sign.*

nilevar (ni′le-var). Trade mark for preparations of norethandrolone.

Nimeh's method (ne′mez) [William *Nimeh*, Lebanese gastroenterologist, born 1898]. See under *method.*

nimetti (nim-et′e). *Simulium griseicollis.*

NIMH. Abbreviation for *National Institute of Mental Health.*

nimiety (nĭ-mi′ĕ-te) [L. *nimis* overmuch + *-ety* state or condition of]. Repletion or excess; as that degree of repletion or excess of water which, beyond satiety, elicits aversion to the ingestion of fluids.

NINDB. Abbreviation for *National Institute of Neurological Diseases and Blindness.*

nine-fourteen (914). Neoarsphenamine.

ninsi (nin′se). The root of *Sium ninsi:* used in Korea and China as a substitute for ginseng.

niobium (ni-o′be-um) [named for *Niobe*, of Greek mythology, who was turned into stone]. The chemical element, atomic number, 41; atomic weight, 92.906; symbol, Nb. It was formerly called *columbium.*

nionate (ni′o-nāt). Trade mark for a preparation of ferrous gluconate.

niperyt (ni′per-it). Pentaerythritol tetranitrate.

niphablepsia (nif″ah-blep′se-ah) [Gr. *nipha* snow + *ablepsia* blindness]. Snow blindness.

niphotyphlosis (nif″o-tif-lo′sis) [Gr. *nipha* snow + *typhlōsis* blindness]. Snow blindness.

nipiology (nip″e-ol′o-je). Nepiology.

nipper (nip′er). An incisor tooth of a horse.

nipple (nip′l). The conic organ which gives outlet to milk from the breast (papilla mammae [N A]), or a similarly shaped structure.

Nippostrongylus (nip″o-stron′jĭ-lus). A genus of hookworms. **N. mu′ris,** a species occurring in rats.

nirvana (nir-van′ah) [*Nirvana*, the Buddhist state of freedom from worldly evils]. A blissful state of freedom from the ills and cares of the world.

Nisbet's chancre (nis′bets) [William *Nisbet*, English physician, 1759–1822]. See under *chancre*.

nisentil (ni′sen-til). Trade mark for a preparation of alphaprodine.

nisin (ni′sin). An antibiotic substance from cultures of lactic acid streptococci: said to be effective against gram-positive organisms, including *Mycobacterium tuberculosis*.

Nissl's bodies, degeneration, method of staining (nis″lz) [Franz *Nissl*, neurologist in Heidelberg, 1860–1919]. See under *body, degeneration*, and *stains, table of*.

nisulfazole (ni-sul′fah-zōl). Trade mark for a preparation of para-nitrosulfathiazole.

nisus (ni′sus) [L.]. An effort, strong tendency, or molimen.

nit (nit). The egg of a louse.

Nitabuch's layer, stria (ne′tah-books) [Raissa *Nitabuch*, German physician of 19th century]. See under *stria*.

nitavirus (ni″tah-vi′rus) [*n*uclear *i*nclusion *t*ype *A*]. A name suggested to include numerous ether-sensitive, probably deoxyribonucleic acid (DNA) viruses in the size range of 100 to 200 mμ, morphologically similar and generally associated with single homogeneous eosinophilic bodies occupying most of the central area of the nucleus of the affected cells, and clearly separated from the marginated chromatin (A-type inclusions).

niter (ni′ter). Nitre.

niton (ni′ton). Radon.

nitragin (ni′trah-jin). A nitrifying bacterial soil ferment from leguminous root tubercles: said to be a valuable fertilizer.

nitramine (ni-tram′in). A nitro derivative of an amine.

nitratase (ni′trah-tās) [*nitr*ate + *-ase*]. A bacterial enzyme catalyzing the reduction of nitrate to nitrite.

nitrate (ni′trāt) [L. *nitratum*]. Any salt of nitric acid.

nitre (ni′ter) [L. *nitrum;* Gr. *nitron*]. Potassium nitrate, or saltpeter. **cubic n.,** sodium nitrate.

nitremia (ni-tre′me-ah). Excess of nitrogen in the blood.

nitretamin (ni-tre′tah-min). Trade mark for preparations of trolnitrate.

nitric (ni′trik). Pertaining to or containing nitrogen, applied especially to compounds containing nitrogen with a higher valence than that contained in the nitrous compounds.

nitridation (ni-trĭ-da′shun). Combination with nitrogen to form a nitride.

nitride (ni′trīd). A binary compound of nitrogen with a metal.

nitrification (ni″trĭ-fi-ka′shun) [*nitric acid* + L. *facere* to make]. The bacterial oxidation of ammonia to nitrite and nitrate in the soil.

nitrifier (ni′trĭ-fi″er). A nitrifying microorganism.

nitrifying (ni′trĭ-fi″ing). Oxidizing nitrites into nitrates: said of certain of the nitrogen bacteria.

nitrilase (ni′tril-ās). An enzyme which catalyzes the decomposition of nitriles.

nitrile (ni′tril). An organic compound containing trivalent nitrogen. Nitriles may be *nitrile bases*, which are tertiary amines, or *acid nitriles*, which may be considered esters of HCN or as acids in which carboxyl is replaced with cyanogen, or as ammonia whose hydrogen atoms have been replaced by a trivalent radical.

nitrite (ni′trīt). Any salt of nitrous acid. The nitrites act as antispasmodics and lessen the arterial tension. The principal medicinal nitrites are those of amyl, ethyl, potassium, and sodium. Glyceryl trinitrate yields nitrite reactions in the body.

nitritoid (ni′trĭ-toid). Resembling a nitrite or the reaction caused by a nitrite.

nitrituria (ni″trĭ-tu′re-ah) [*nitrite* + Gr. *ouron* urine + *-ia*]. The presence of nitrites in the urine.

nitro- (ni′tro). A prefix indicating presence of the group $—NO_2$.

nitro-amine (ni″tro-am′in). Nitramine.

nitro-anisol (ni″tro-an′ĭ-sol). A nitro derivative of anisol, $NO_2.C_6H_4.O.CH_3$.

Nitrobacter (ni″tro-bak′ter) [L. *nitrum* nitre + *bactrum* rod]. A genus of microrganisms of the family Nitrobacteraceae, suborder Pseudomonadineae, order Pseudomonadales, occurring as rod-shaped cells which oxidize nitrites to nitrates. It includes two species, *N. ag′ilis* and *N. winograd′skyi*.

Nitrobacteraceae (ni″tro-bak″te-ra′se-e). A family of Schizomycetes (order Pseudomonadales, suborder Pseudomonadineae), occurring as rod-shaped, ellipsoidal, spherical or spirillar cells, deriving energy exclusively from oxidation of ammonia to nitrite, or of nitrite to nitrate; also known informally as the nitrifying bacteria. It includes seven genera, *Nitrobacter, Nitrocystis, Nitrosococcus, Nitrosocystis, Nitrosogloea, Nitrosomonas*, and *Nitrosospira*.

nitrobacteria (ni″tro-bak-te′re-ah). Plural of *nitrobacterium*.

nitrobacterium (ni″tro-bak-te′re-um), pl. *nitrobacte′ria*. A microorganism which oxidizes ammonia to nitrites.

nitrocellulose (ni″tro-sel′u-lōs). Pyroxylin.

Nitrocystis (ni″tro-sis′tis). A genus of microorganisms of the family Nitrobacteraceae, suborder Pseudomonadineae, order Pseudomonadales, occuring as ellipsoidal or rod-shaped cells, which are embedded in slime to form zoogloea and which oxidize nitrites to nitrates. It includes two species, *N. micropuncta′ta* and *N. sarcinoi′des*.

nitrofurantoin (ni″tro-fu-ran′to-in). Chemical name: N-(5-nitro-2-furfurylidene)-1-aminohydantoin: used as an antibacterial agent in infections of the urinary tract.

nitrofurazone (ni″tro-fu′rah-zōn). Chemical name: 5-nitro-2-furaldehyde semicarbazone: used as a local antibacterial.

nitrogen (ni′tro-jen) [Gr. *nitron* niter + *gennan* to produce]. A colorless, gaseous element found free in the air; symbol, N; specific gravity, 0.9713; atomic number, 7; atomic weight, 14.007. It constitutes part of the atmosphere, forming about four fifths of common air. Chemically, it is almost inert, but forms by combination nitric acid and ammonia. It is a gas unfitted to support respiration; not a poison, but proving fatal if breathed alone, because of the want of oxygen. It is soluble in the blood and body fluids and when released as bubbles of gas by reduction of atmospheric pressure causes serious symptoms. See *compressed air illness*. **alloxuric n.,** nitrogen in the form of alloxur bases. See *purine bases*, under *purine*. **amide n., amino n.,** that portion of the nitrogen in protein that exists in the form of acid amides. **authentic n.,** legitimate nitrogen. **filtrate n.,** nonprotein nitrogen. **illegitimate n.,** that part of administered nitrogen which is not found in the excreta and the retention of which in the organism is not justifiable. **justifiable n.,** legitimate n. **legitimate n.,** that part of administered nitrogen which is used by the organism in building up its own tissues or else is excreted. **n. monoxide,** nitrous oxide. **nomadic n.,** free nitrogen from the air which enters into plant and animal growth. **nonprotein n.,** the nitrogenous constituents of the blood exclusive of the protein bodies. It consists of the nitrogen of urea, uric acid, creatine, creatinine, amino acids, polypeptides, and an undetermined part known as *rest nitrogen*. **n. pentoxide,** a crystalline compound, N_2O_5, or nitric anhydride, which combines with water to form nitric acid. **n. peroxide, n. tetroxide,** a poisonous volatile liquid, N_2O_4, giving off brownish irritant fumes. **rest n.** See *nonprotein n.*

nitrogenase (ni′tro-jen-ās). Azotase.

nitrogenization (ni″tro-jen-i-za′shun). The act of impregnating with nitrogen.

nitrogenous (ni-troj′e-nus). Containing nitrogen.

nitroglycerin (ni-tro-glis′er-in). Glyceryl trinitrate.

nitroglyn (ni′tro-glin). Trade mark for a preparation of glyceryl trinitrate.

nitrol (ni′trol). Trade mark for preparations of glyceryl trinitrate.

nitromannite (ni″tro-man′īt). Mannitol hexanitrate.

nitromersol (ni″tro-mer′sol). Chemical name: 4-nitro-3-hydroxy-mercuri-o-cresol anhydride: used as a local antibacterial.

nitrometer (ni-trom-e′ter) [*nitrogen* + Gr. *metron* measure]. An apparatus for measuring the quantity of nitrogen given off in a reaction.

nitromethane (ni″tro-meth′ān). A nitrated form of methane, which is a powerful explosive.

nitron (ni′tron). The name suggested by Sir W. Ramsay and R. W. Gray for the molecular weight of a radium emanation.

nitronaphthalin (ni″tro-naf′thah-lin). A substance, $C_{10}H_7.NO_2$, whose vapors may cause vesication and opacity of the cornea.

nitrophenol (ni″tro-fe′nol). An indicator, para-nitro-phenylic acid, $C_6H_4(NO_2)OH$, with a pH range of 5 to 7; being colorless at 5 and yellow at 7.

nitropropiol (ni″tro-pro′pe-ol). Orthonitrophenylpropiolic acid, $No_2.C_6H_4.C{:}C.COOH$: used as a test for sugar.

nitroprotein (ni″tro-pro′te-in). A protein made by treating serum protein with nitric acid.

nitroprusside (ni″tro-prus′īd). A salt of nitroprussic acid.

nitrosaccharose (ni″tro-sak′ah-rōs). Nitrated saccharose; an explosive and vasodilator: used like glyceryltrinitrate.

nitrosalol (ni″tro-sal′ol). An ester, $C_6H_4(OH)$-$CO_2.C_6H_4NO_2$, in a yellowish, crystalline powder.

nitrose (ni′trōs). A term used to include nitric and nitrous acids.

nitrosification (ni-tro″sĭ-fi-ka′shun). The oxidation of ammonia into nitrites.

nitrosifying (ni-tro″sĭ-fi′ing). Oxidizing ammonia into nitrites: said of certain nitrogen bacteria.

nitroso- (ni-tro′so). A prefix indicating presence of the group —N:O.

nitrosobacteria (ni-tro″so-bak-te′re-ah). Plural of *nitrosobacterium.*

nitrosobacterium (ni-tro″so-bak-te′re-um), pl. *nitrosobacteria.* A microorganism which oxidizes nitrites to nitrates.

Nitrosococcus (ni″tro-so-kok′us). [L. *nitrosus* full of soda + Gr. *kokkos* berry]. A genus of microorganisms of the family Nitrobacteraceae, suborder Pseudomonadineae, order Pseudomonadales, occurring as large spherical, non-motile cells, which oxidize ammonia to nitrite. The type species is *N. nitro′sus.*

Nitrosocystis (ni-tro″so-sis′tis). A genus of microorganisms of the family Nitrobacteraceae, suborder Pseudomonadineae, order Pseudomonadales, occurring as ellipsoidal or elongated cells which unite in cystlike compact rounded aggregates, and oxidizing ammonia to nitrite. It includes two species, *N. coccoi′des* and *N. javanen′sis.*

Nitrosogloea (ni-tro″so-gle′ah). A genus of microorganisms of the family Nitrobacteraceae, suborder Pseudomonadineae, order Pseudomonadales, occurring as ellipsoidal or rod-shaped bacteria, embedded in slime to form zoogloea, and oxidizing ammonia to nitrite. It includes three species, *M. menbrana′cea, M. merismoi′des,* and *M. schizobacteroi′des.*

nitroso-indol (ni-tro″so-in′dol). A compound which gives a red reaction when indol is treated with sulfuric acid and potassium nitrite.

Nitrosomonas (ni-tro″so-mo′nas) [L. *nitrosus* full of soda + Gr. *monas* unit]. A genus of microorganisms of the family Nitrobacteraceae, suborder Pseudomonadineae, order Pseudomonadales, occurring as non-motile ellipsoidal cells, which oxidize ammonia to nitrite more rapidly than other genera of the family. It includes two species, *N. europae′a* and *N. monocel′la.*

Nitrosospira (ni-tro″so-spi′rah) [L. *nitrosus* full of soda + *spira* coil]. A genus of microorganisms of the family Nitrobacteraceae, suborder Pseudomonadineae, order Pseudomonadales, occurring as spiral-shaped cells which oxidize ammonia to nitrite very slowly. It includes two species, *N. antarc′tica* and *N. brien′sis.*

nitrososubstitution (ni-tro″so-sub″stĭ-tu′shun). The substitution of the radical nitroxyl for some other radical or atom in a compound.

nitro-sugars (ni″tro-shug′erz). A class of substances which have been used as vasodilators.

nitrosyl (ni′tro-sil). The univalent radical NO.

nitrous (ni′trus). Pertaining to nitrogen in its lowest valency. **n. oxide,** a colorless gas, N_2O, having a sweetish taste and a pleasant odor: used as a general anesthetic. Called also *nitrogen monoxide, factitious air,* and *laughing gas.*

nitrovas (ni′tro-vas). Trade mark for a preparation of glyceryl trinitrate.

nitroxyl (ni-trok′sil). The radical NO_2.

nitryl (ni′tril). Nitroxyl.

nivemycin (niv′ĕ-mi′sin). Neomycin.

NK. Abbreviation for *Nomenklatur Kommission,* a committee of the Anatomical Society of Germany which has given supplementary names to the terminology of anatomy.

N.L.N.E. Abbreviation for *National League of Nursing Education.*

Nm. Abbreviation for L. *nux moscha′ta,* nutmeg.

NMRI. Abbreviation for *Naval Medical Research Institute,* part of the National Naval Medical Center.

NMRI 448. A powerful insecticide and insect repellent developed by the Naval Medical Research Institute.

N:N. The azo group.

nn. Abbreviation for L. *nervi* (nerves).

N.N.D. *New and Nonofficial Drugs,* an annual publication of the American Medical Association containing descriptions of agents proposed for use in or on the human body in the prevention, diagnosis, or treatment of disease, which have been evaluated by the Council on Drugs of the A.M.A. Formerly called *New and Nonofficial Remedies.*

N.N.N. medium [Nicolle, Novy, MacNeal]. See under *culture medium.*

NO. Nitric oxide.

N_2O. Nitrogen monoxide (nitrous oxide).

N_2O_3. Nitrogen trioxide.

N_2O_4. Nitrogen peroxide.

N_2O_5. Nitrogen pentoxide.

No. Abbreviation of L. *nu′mero,* "to the number of."

noasthenia (no″as-the′ne-ah) [Gr. *noos* mind + *asthenēs* without strength + *-ia*]. Intellectual or mental weakness.

Nobel prize (no-bel′) [Alfred Bernard *Nobel,* Swedish chemist and engineer, 1833–1896; the inventor of dynamite, under the terms of whose will the prizes were established]. An award usually given annually for outstanding achievement in chemistry, physics, medicine and physiology, literature, and in the interest of world peace. First presented in 1901.

nobelium (no-be′le-um) [Alfred Bernard *Nobel*]. The chemical element of atomic number 102, atomic weight 253, symbol No, obtained in 1958 by bombardment of Cm^{246} with C^{12} ions in a heavy ion linear accelerator.

Noble's position (no'b'lz) [Charles P. *Noble*, American gynecologist, 1863–1935]. See under *position*.

Nocard's bacillus [Edmund Isidore Étienne *Nocard*, French veterinarian, 1850–1903]. *Salmonella typhimurium.*

Nocardia (no-kar'de-ah) [Edmund Isidore Étienne *Nocard*]. A genus of microorganisms of the family Actinomycetaceae, order Actinomycetales, separable into 45 species, of which 3 are pathogenic and the remainder saprophytic forms. **N. asteroi'des,** an acid-fast filamentous microorganism producing pulmonary infection in man simulating tuberculosis. **N. farci'nica,** an acid-fast filamentous microorganism associated with disease in cattle resembling tuberculosis. **N. madu'rae,** a non-acid-fast filamentous microorganism found as the etiologic agent in some cases of Madura foot.

nocardial (no-kar'de-al). Pertaining to or caused by Nocardia.

nocardiasis (no"kar-di'ah-sis). Nocardiosis.

nocardin (no-kar'din). An antibiotic substance from *Nocardia coeliaca;* active against tubercle bacilli.

nocardiosis (no-kar-de-o'sis). Infection with Nocardia.

Nochtia (nok'te-ah). A genus of small nematode worms. **N. noch'ti,** a species of worms found in and apparently causing the production of tumors in the stomachs of Javanese monkeys.

noci- (no'se) [L. *nocere* to injure]. Combining form denoting relation to injury or to a noxious or deleterious agent or influence.

noci-association (no"se-ah-so"se-a'shun). The unconscious discharge of nervous energy under the stimulus of trauma, as in surgical shock.

nociceptive (no"se-sep'tiv) [*noci-* + L. *capere* to receive]. Receiving injury: said of a receptive neuron for painful sensations.

nociceptor (no"se-sep'tor). A receptor which is stimulated by injury; a receptor for pain.

nocifensor (no"se-fen'sor) [*noci-* + L. *fendere* to defend]. Sir Thomas Lewis' name for a system of nerves in the skin and mucous membranes which are concerned with local defense against injury.

noci-influence (no"se-in'floo-ens). Injurious or traumatic influence.

nociperception (no"se-per-sep'shun). The perception by the system of injurious (traumatic) stimuli.

Noct. Abbreviation for L. *noc'te*, at night.

noctalbuminuria (nok"tal-bu"mĭ-nu're-ah) [L. *nox* night + *albuminuria*]. The presence of excessive amounts of albumin in the urine secreted during the night.

noctambulation (nok"tam-bu-la'shun) [L. *noctambulatio; nox* night + *ambulare* to walk]. Sleep walking; somnambulism.

noctambulic (nok"tam-bu'lik). Pertaining to or marked by sleep walking.

noctec (nok'tek). Trade mark for preparations of chloral hydrate.

noctiphobia (nok"te-fo'be-ah) [L. *nox* night + *phobia*]. Morbid dread of night and its darkness and silence.

Noct. maneq. Abbreviation for L. *noc'te mane'que*, at night and in the morning.

nocturia (nok-tu're-ah) [L. *nox* night + Gr. *ouron* urine + *-ia*]. Excessive urination at night.

nocturnal (nok-tur'nal) [L. *nocturnus*]. Pertaining to the night.

nocuity (nok-u'ĭ-te). Injuriousness; harmfulness.

nodal (no'dal). Pertaining to a node, particularly the atrioventricular node.

node (nōd) [L. *nodus* knot]. A swelling or protuberance. See also under *nodule* and *nodus*. **Aschoff's n., n. of Aschoff and Tawara,** nodus atrioventricularis. **atrioventricular n.,** nodus atrioventricularis. **axillary n's,** nodi lymphatici axillares. **Bouchard's n's,** nodules on the second joints of the fingers, believed to be symptomatic of gastrectasis. **buccal lymph n's,** nodi lymphatici buccales. **celiac lymph n's,** nodi lymphatici celiaci. **cervical lymph n's, deep,** nodi lymphatici cervicales profundae. **cervical lymph n's, superficial,** nodi lymphatici cervicales superficiales. **colic lymph n's, left,** nodi lymphatici colici sinistri. **colic lymph n's, middle,** nodi lymphatici colici medii. **colic lymph n's, right,** nodi lymphatici colici dextri. **cubital lymph n's,** nodi lymphatici cubitales. **Delphian n.,** a lymph node encased in the fascia in the midline, just above the thyroid isthmus, so called because it is exposed first at surgery and, if diseased, is indicative of the disease process to be found in the thyroid gland. **Dürck's n's,** granulomatous perivascular infiltrations in the cerebral cortex in trypanosomiasis. **epigastric lymph n's,** nodi lymphatici epigastrici. **Féréol's n's,** subcutaneous nodes sometimes occurring in acute rheumatism. **Flack's n.,** sinoatrial n. **gastric lymph n's, left,** nodi lymphatici gastrici sinistri. **gastric lymph n's, right,** nodi lymphatici gastrici dextri. **gouty n.,** a nodule produced by gouty inflammation. **Haygarth's n's,** joint swellings in arthritis deformans. **Heberden's n's,** small hard nodules, formed usually at the distal interphalangeal articulations of the fingers in interphalangeal osteoarthritis. **hemal n's, hemolymph n's,** hemolymph glands. **Hensen's n.,** primitive knot. **hepatic lymph n's,** nodi lymphatici hepatici. **ileocolic lymph n's,** nodi lymphatici ileocolici. **iliac lymph n's,** nodi lymphatici iliaci. **iliac lymph n's, internal,** nodi lymphatici iliaci interni. **inguinal lymph n's, deep,** nodi lymphatici inguinales profundi. **inguinal lymph n's, superficial,** nodi lymphatici inguinales superficiales. **intercostal lymph n's,** nodi lymphatici intercostales. **Keith's n., Keith-Flack n.,** sinoatrial n. **Koch's n.,** nodus atrioventricularis. **Legendré's n's,** Bouchard's n's. **lumbar lymph n's,** nodi lymphatici lumbales. **lymph n.,** one of the accumulations of lymphatic tissue organized as definite lymphatic organs, varying from 1 to 25 mm. in diameter, situated along the course of lymphatic vessels, and consisting of an outer cortical and an inner medullary part. Called also *nodus lymphaticus* [N A]. **mandibular lymph n's,** nodi lymphatici mandibulares. **mediastinal lymph n's, anterior,** nodi lymphatici mediastinales anteriores. **mediastinal lymph n's, posterior,** nodi lymphatici mediastinales posteriores. **mesenteric lymph n's,** nodi lymphatici mesenterici. **mesenteric lymph n's, inferior,** nodi lymphatici mesenterici inferiores. **Meynet's n's,** nodules in the capsules of joints and in tendons in rheumatic disorders, especially of children. **occipital lymph n's,** nodi lymphatici occipitales. **Osler's n's,** small, raised, swollen tender areas, about the size of a pea, characteristically bluish but sometimes pink or red, and rarely having a blanched center, occurring most commonly in the pads of the fingers or toes, in the thenar or hypothenar eminences, or the soles of the feet; they are practically pathognomonic of subacute bacterial endocarditis. **pancreaticosplenic lymph n's,** nodi lymphatici pancreaticolienales. **parasternal lymph n's,** nodi lymphatici parasternales. **parotid lymph n's, superficial and deep,** nodi lymphatici parotidei superficiales et profundi. **Parrot's n.,** a syphilitic node on the outer table of the skull. See *Parrot's sign*, def. 2. **phrenic lymph n's,** nodi lymphatici phrenici. **piedric n's,** nodes seen on the hair in piedra. **popliteal lymph n's,** nodi lymphatici poplitei. **primitive n.,** primitive knot. **pulmonary lymph n's,** nodi lymphatici pulmonales.

pyloric lymph n's, nodi lymphatici pylorici. **n's of Ranvier,** constrictions occurring on myelinated nerve fibers at regular intervals of about 1 millimeter; at these sites the myelin sheath is absent and the axon is enclosed only by Schwann cell processes. **retroauricular lymph n's,** nodi lymphatici retroauriculares. **retropharyngeal lymph nodes,** nodi lymphatici retropharyngei. **Rosenmüller's n.** 1. Glandula lacrimalis inferior. 2. See *lymphoglandulae subinguinales profundae.* **Rotter's n's,** lymph nodes occasionally found between the pectoralis major and minor muscles which often contain metastases from mammary cancer. **sacral lymph n's,** nodi lymphatici sacrales. **Schmidt's n.,** the medullated interannular segment of a nerve fiber. **sentinel n., signal n.,** an enlarged supraclavicular node which is often the first sign of an abdominal tumor. Called also *Virchow's node* and *Troisier's node.* **singer's n.,** a small white nodule occurring on the vocal cord in chorditis tuberosa. **sinoatrial n.,** a microscopic collection of atypical cardiac muscle fibers at the superior end of the sulcus terminalis, at the junction of the superior vena cava and right atrium. Called also *nodus sinuatrialis* [N A]. The cardiac rhythm normally takes its origin in this node which is, for that reason, also known as the pacemaker of the heart. **submandibular lymph n's,** nodi lymphatici submandibulares. **submental lymph n's,** nodi lymphatici submentales. **syphilitic n.,** a swelling on a bone due to syphilitic periostitis. **n. of Tawara,** nodus atrioventricularis. **teacher's n.,** singer's n. **tibial lymph n's, anterior,** nodi lymphatici tibialis anterior. **tracheal lymph n's,** nodi lymphatici tracheales. **tracheobronchial lymph n's, inferior,** nodi lymphatici tracheobronchiales inferiores. **tracheobronchial lymph n's, superior,** nodi lymphatici tracheobronchiales superiores. **triticeous n.,** cartilago triticea. **Troisier's n., Virchow's n.,** signal n. **vital n.,** a name applied to the respiratory center.

nodose (no'dōs) [L. *nodosus*]. Having nodes or projections.

nodosity (no-dos'ĭ-te) [L. *nodositas*]. 1. The quality or condition of being nodose. 2. A node.

nodular (nod'u-lar). 1. Like a nodule or node. 2. Marked with nodules.

nodulated (nod'u-lāt"ed). Marked with nodules.

nodulation (nod"u-la'shun). The presence of nodules.

nodule (nod'ūl) [L. *nodulus* little knot]. A small boss or node which is solid and can be detected by touch. **accessory thymic n's,** noduli thymici accessorii. **aggregate n's,** Peyer's patches. **Albini's n's,** gray nodules of the size of sago grains, sometimes seen on the free edges of the auriculoventricular valves of infants. They are remains of fetal structures. **n's of aortic valves,** noduli valvularum aortae. **apple jelly n's,** minute translucent nodules of a distinctive yellowish or reddish brown color, visible on diascopic examination of the lesions of lupus vulgaris. **n's of Arantius,** noduli valvularum aortae. **Aschoff's n's,** Aschoff bodies. **Bianchi's n's,** noduli valvularum aortae. **Bohn's n's,** small white or yellow nodules near the midline of the palate in the newborn, which disappear soon after birth. They are small retention cysts arising from mucus glands. **Bouchard's n's.** See under *node.* **cortical n's,** nodules of closely packed lymphocytes in the cortical portion of a lymph gland. **Cruveilhier's n's,** Albini's n's. **Dalen-Fuchs n's,** small nodules in the pigment layer of the choroid in sympathetic ophthalmia. **epicardial n's,** nodules over the vessels of the epicardium, probably due to high pressure. **Fraenkel's n's,** typhus nodules of the cutaneous blood vessels. **Gamna n's,** brown or yellow pigmented nodules seen in the spleen in certain cases of enlargement and called by Gamna *nodules tabac.* **Gandy-Gamna n's,** Gamna n's. **Guatamahri's n's,** nodules on the scalp and face in onchocerciasis. **Hoboken's n's,** dilatations of the outer surface of the umbilical arteries. **Jeanselme's n's,** movable nodules on the limbs near the joints due to syphilis, yaws or other treponemal diseases; called also *juxta-articular n's* and *Steiner's tumors.* **juxta-articular n's,** Jeanselme's n's. **n's of Kerckring,** noduli valvularum aortae. **Koeppe n's,** gelatinous nodules observed at the pupillary border in chronic iridocyclitis. **Koster's n.,** a tubercle composed of one giant cell enclosed by a double layer of cells. **Leishman's n's,** pinkish nodules observed in the nonulcerative keloid-like type of oriental sore. **lentiform n.,** processus lenticularis. **Lutz-Jeanselme n's,** Jeanselme's n's. **lymphatic n's,** a term applied to lymph nodes, as well as to one of the small collections of lymphatic tissue (folliculus lymphaticus [N A]) situated deep to epithelial surfaces, and also to temporary small (about 1 mm. in diameter), dense accumulations of lymphocytes located within the cortex of a lymph node and expressing the cytogenetic and defense functions of the tissue. **lymphatic n's, solitary, of large intestine,** folliculi lymphatici solitarii intestini crassi. **lymphatic n's, solitary, of small intestine,** folliculi lymphatici solitarii intestini tenuis. **lymphatic n's of stomach,** folliculi lymphatici gastrici. **milkers' n's,** hard circumscribed nodules on the hands of persons who milk cows suffering from cowpox. **Morgagni's n's,** corpora arantii. **pearly n.,** one of the nodules of bovine tuberculosis. **primary n.,** a lymph nodule without a germinal center, or apart from a center. **n's of pulmonary trunk valves,** noduli valvularum semilunarium. **pulp n.,** a mass of dentin found in the pulp cavity of a tooth. Called also *denticle* and *pulp stone.* **rheumatic n's,** small round or oval, mostly subcutaneous nodules made up chiefly of a mass of Aschoff bodies and seen in cases of rheumatic fever. **Schmorl's n.,** a nodule seen in roentgenograms of the spine, due to prolapse of a nucleus pulposus into an adjoining vertebra. **secondary n's,** an area of actively proliferating lymphocytes in a lymph nodule; called also *germinal center.* **siderotic n's,** focal fibrotic lesions characterized by the presence of crystals of iron on the degenerated elastic tissue fibers, seen in the spleen in Banti's disease. **singers' n.,** chorditis tuberosa. **n's tabac,** Gamna n's. **teachers' n.,** chorditis tuberosa. **triticeous n.,** cartilago triticea. **typhoid n.,** a mass of macrophages and other necrotic cells observed in the liver in typhoid fever. **typhus n's,** minute nodules in the skin, formed by perivascular infiltration of mononuclear cells in typhus fever. **n. of vermis,** nodulus vermis. **vestigial n.,** darwinian tubercle.

noduli (nod'u-li) [L.]. Plural of *nodulus.*

nodulous (nod'u-lus). Nodose.

nodulus (nod'u-lus), pl. *nod'uli* [L., dim. of *nodus*]. A small knot; used in anatomical nomenclature as a general term to designate a comparatively minute collection of tissue. **nod'uli aggrega'ti proces'sus vermifor'mis** [B N A], folliculi lymphatici aggregati appendicis vermiformis. **n. cerebel'li,** n. vermis. **n. intercarot'icus,** glomus caroticum. **n. lymphat'icus** [B N A], folliculus lymphaticus. **nod'uli lymphat'ici aggrega'ti [Peyer'i],** folliculi lymphatici aggregati. **nod'uli lymphat'ici bronchia'les** [B N A], lymph nodules situated in the lining of the bronchi. Omitted in N A. **nod'uli lymphat'ici conjunctiva'les** [B N A], lymph nodules situated in the conjunctiva. Omitted in N A. **nod'uli lymphat'ici gas'trici** [B N A], folliculi lymphatici gastrici. **nod'uli lymphat'ici laryn'gei** [B N A], folliculi lymphatici laryngei. **nod'uli lymphat'ici liena'les [Malpig'hii]** [B N A], folliculi lymphatici lienales. **nod'uli lymphat'ici rec'ti** [B N A], folliculi lymphatici recti. **nod'uli lymphat'ici solita'-**

rii intesti′ni cras′si [B N A], folliculi lymphatici solitarii intestini crassi. **nod′uli lymphat′ici solita′rii intesti′ni ten′uis** [B N A], folliculi lymphatici solitarii intestini tenuis. **nod′uli lymphat′ici tuba′rii tu′bae auditi′vae** [B N A], lymphatic follicles about the pharyngeal end and internally along the median wall of the auditory tube. Called also *Gerlach's tonsil.* Omitted in N A. **nod′uli lymphat′ici vagina′les** [B N A], small collections of lymphatic tissue deep to the epithelial surface of the vagina. Omitted in N A. **nod′uli lymphat′ici vesica′les** [B N A], collections of lymphatic tissue in the lining of the urinary bladder. Omitted in N A. **nod′uli thy′mici accesso′rii** [N A], portions of thymus tissue that have been detached from the stalk and left behind in the caudal migration of the gland in embryonic development. Called also *accessory thymic nodules.* **nod′uli valvula′rum aor′tae** [N A], small fibrous tubercles, one at the center of the free margin of each of the three cusps of the valve of the aorta. Called also *noduli valvularum semilunarium* [*Arantii*] [B N A]. **nod′uli valvula′rum semiluna′rium** [N A], small fibrous tubercles, one at the center of the free margin of each of the three cusps of the valve of the pulmonary trunk. Called also *noduli valvularum semilunarium* [*ventriculi dextri*] [B N A]. **nod′uli valvula′rum semiluna′rium [Aran′tii]** [B N A], noduli valvularum aortae. **nod′uli valvula′rum semiluna′rium [ventric′uli dex′tri]** [B N A], noduli valvularum semilunarium. **n. ver′mis** [N A, B N A], the part of the vermis of the cerebellum, on the ventral surface, where the inferior medullary velum attaches.

nodus (no′dus), pl. *no′di* [L.]. A knot; used in anatomical nomenclature as a general term to designate a small mass of tissue. **n. atrioventricula′ris** [N A], a microscopic collection of specialized cardiac muscle fibers, located beneath the endocardium of the right atrium, and continuous with atrial muscle fibers and with the atrioventricular bundle; it is similar to but somewhat smaller than the nodus sinuatrialis. Called also *atrioventricular node.* **no′di cer′ebri.** See *pons.* **n. cor′dis.** See *trigona fibrosa.* **n. curso′rius,** a point in the corpus striatum of some animals, as the rabbit, stimulation of which causes the animal to rush forward. **n. lymphat′icus** [N A], one of the accumulations of lymphatic tissue interposed throughout the lymphatic system. See *lymph node.* Called also *lymphoglandula* [B N A], and *lymphonodus.* **no′di lymphat′ici apica′les** [N A]. See *nodi lymphatici axillares.* **no′di lymphat′ici axilla′res** [N A], the lymph nodes of the axilla, which receive lymph from the arm and the thoracic wall. They comprise five groups: the apical nodes (nodi lymphatici apicales), lying medial to the axillary vein; the central (nodi lymphatici centrales), near the base of the axilla; the lateral (nodi lymphatici laterales), behind the axillary vein; the pectoral (nodi lymphatici pectorales), along the lateral thoracic veins; and the subscapular (nodi lymphatici subscapulares), along the subscapular vein. Called also *lymphoglandulae axillares* [B N A], and *axillary lymph nodes.* **no′di lymphat′ici bronchopulmona′les** [N A], nodes embedded in and receiving lymph from the root of the lung. Called also *bronchopulmonary lymph nodes.* **no′di lymphat′ici bucca′les** [N A], a variable number of lymph nodes lying on a line between the angle of the mandible and the angle of the mouth. Called also *lymphoglandulae faciales profundae* [B N A], and *buccal lymph nodes.* **no′di lymphat′ici celi′aci** [N A], a few nodes along the celiac trunk, which receive lymph from the stomach, spleen, duodenum, liver, and pancreas. Called also *lymphoglandulae coeliacae* [B N A], and *celiac lymph nodes.* **no′di lymphat′ici centra′les** [N A]. See *nodi lymphatici axillares.* **no′di lymphat′ici cervica′les profun′dae** [N A], the 15 to 30 nodes that lie along the course of the carotid artery and internal jugular vein, including the jugulodigastric, lingual, and juguloomohyoid nodes. They receive lymph from both superficial and deep structures. Called also *lymphoglandulae cervicales profundae superiores* [B N A], and *deep cervical lymph nodes.* **no′di lymphat′ici cervica′les superficia′les** [N A], nodes along the external jugular vein which receive lymph from the entire cervical skin surface. Called also *lymphoglandulae cervicales superficiales* [B N A], and *superficial cervical lymph nodes.* **no′di lymphat′ici col′ici dex′tri** [N A], nodes accompanying the right colic vessels and receiving lymph from the adjacent region. Called also *right colic lymph nodes.* **no′di lymphat′ici col′ici me′dii** [N A], nodes accompanying the middle colic vessels and receiving lymph from the adjacent region. Called also *middle colic lymph nodes.* **no′di lymphat′ici col′ici sinis′tri** [N A], nodes situated along the left colic vessels and receiving lymph drained from the adjacent region. Called also *left colic lymph nodes.* **no′di lymphat′ici cubita′les** [N A], a few lymph nodes situated in the deep part of the elbow. Called also *cubital lymph nodes.* **no′di lymphat′ici epigas′trici** [N A], lymph nodes along the deep epigastric vessels, receiving lymph from the lower abdominal wall. Called also *lymphoglandulae epigastricae* [B N A], and *epigastric lymph nodes.* **no′di lymphat′ici gas′trici dex′tri** [N A], a few nodes along the right gastric artery that receive lymph from the stomach, spleen, duodenum, liver, and pancreas. Called also *lymphoglandulae gastricae inferiores* [B N A], and *right gastric lymph nodes.* **no′di lymphat′ici gas′trici sinis′tri** [N A], a few nodes along the left gastric artery that receive lymph from the stomach, spleen, duodenum, liver, and pancreas. Called also *lymphoglandulae gastricae superiores* [B N A], and *left gastric lymph nodes.* **no′di lymphat′ici hepat′ici** [N A], a few nodes along the common hepatic artery that receive lymph from the stomach, spleen, duodenum, liver, and pancreas. Called also *lymphoglandulae hepaticae* [B N A], and *hepatic lymph nodes.* **no′di lymphat′ici ileocol′ici** [N A], nodes in the region of the ileocolic junction, draining adjacent structures. Called also *ileocolic lymph nodes.* **no′di lymphat′ici ili′aci** [N A], nodes located along the aorta and the common and external iliac arteries, receiving lymph from the pelvic viscera. Called also *lymphoglandulae iliacae* [B N A], and *iliac lymph nodes.* **no′di lymphat′ici ili′aci inter′ni** [N A], nodes grouped around the origins of the branches of the internal iliac vessels, receiving lymph from the regions supplied by these various branches. Called also *lymphoglandulae hypogastricae* [B N A], and *internal iliac lymph nodes.* **no′di lymphat′ici inguina′les profun′di** [N A], nodes deep to the fascia lata along the femoral vein, receiving lymph from adjacent areas. Called also *lymphoglandulae subinguinales profundae* [B N A], and *deep inguinal lymph nodes.* **no′di lymphat′ici inguina′les superficia′les** [N A], nodes in the subcutaneous tissue inferior to the inguinal ligament. Called also *lymphoglandulae subinguinales superficiales* [B N A], and *superficial inguinal lymph nodes.* **no′di lymphat′ici intercosta′les** [N A], lymph nodes in the back of the thorax, along the intercostal vessels. Called also *lymphoglandulae intercostales* [B N A], and *intercostal lymph nodes.* **n. lymphat′icus jugulodigas′tricus** [N A], one of the deep cervical lymph nodes lying on the internal jugular vein at the level of the greater cornu of the hyoid bone. **n. lymphat′icus juguloomohyoi′deus** [N A], one of the deep cervical lymph nodes lying on the internal jugular vein just above the tendon of the omohyoid muscle. **no′di lymphat′ici latera′les** [N A]. See *nodi lymphatici axillares.* **no′di lymphat′ici lingua′les** [N A], deep cervical lymph nodes receiving afferent vessels from the tongue. Called also *lymphoglandulae* *linguales* [B N A]. **no'di lymphat'ici lumba'les** [N A], a chain of nodes alongside the lower abdominal aorta, receiving most of the lymph from the abdominal structures. Called also *lymphoglandulae lumbales* [B N A], and *lumbar lymph nodes.* **no'di lymphat'ici mandibula'res** [N A], nodes near the angle of the mandible, into which lymph from some of the superficial tissues of the head and neck is drained. Called also *mandibular lymph nodes.* **no'di lymphat'ici mediastina'les anterio'res** [N A], nodes along the great vessels of the superior mediastinum and on the anterior part of the diaphragm, receiving lymph from adjacent structures. Called also *lymphoglandulae mediastinales anteriores* [B N A], and *anterior mediastinal lymph nodes.* **no'di lymphat'ici mediastina'les posterio'res** [N A], 8 to 10 nodes along the thoracic aorta, receiving lymph from the mediastinal structures. Called also *lymphoglandulae mediastinales posteriores* [B N A], and *posterior mediastinal lymph nodes.* **no'di lymphat'ici mesenter'ici** [N A], nodes that lie at the root of the mesentery, receiving lymph from parts of the small intestine, cecum, appendix, and large intestine. Called also *lymphoglandulae mesentericae* [B N A], and *mesenteric lymph nodes.* **no'di lymphat'ici mesenter'ici inferio'res** [N A], nodes situated along the inferior mesenteric vessels and receiving lymph from the adjacent region. Called also *inferior mesenteric lymph nodes.* **no'di lymphat'ici occipita'les** [N A], several small nodes near the occipital insertion of the semispinalis capitis muscle. Called also *lymphoglandulae occipitales* [B N A], and *occipital lymph nodes.* **no'di lymphat'ici pancreaticolienа'les** [N A], a few nodes along the splenic artery that receive lymph from the stomach, spleen, duodenum, liver, and pancreas. Called also *lymphoglandulae pancreaticolienales* [B N A], and *pancreaticosplenic lymph nodes.* **no'di lymphat'ici parasterna'les** [N A], nodes located along the course of the internal thoracic artery, which drain the mammary gland, abdominal wall, and diaphragm. Called also *lymphoglandulae sternales* [B N A], and *parasternal lymph nodes.* **no'di lymphat'ici parotide'i superficia'les et profun'di** [N A], a dozen or so nodes in the substance of the parotid gland, through which lymph drains from the adjacent area. Called also *lymphoglandulae parotideae* [B N A]. **no'di lymphat'ici pectora'les** [N A]. See *nodi lymphatici axillares.* **no'di lymphat'ici phren'ici** [N A], several nodes on the thoracic surface of the diaphragm, receiving lymph from the intercostal spaces, pericardium, diaphragm, and liver. Called also *phrenic lymph nodes.* **no'di lymphat'ici poplite'i** [N A], a few nodes deep to the fascia around the popliteal vessels, through which lymph drains from nearby areas. Called also *lymphoglandulae poplitea* [B N A], and *popliteal lymph nodes.* **no'di lymphat'ici pulmona'les** [N A], nodes located along the larger bronchi within the lung substance, through which lymph from the lung drains. Called also *lymphoglandulae pulmonales* [B N A], and *pulmonary lymph nodes.* **no'di lymphat'ici pylo'rici** [N A], nodes that lie in front of the head of the pancreas, receiving lymph from the pyloric part of the stomach, the adjacent part of the duodenum, and part of the inferior portion of the body of the stomach. Called also *pyloric lymph nodes.* **no'di lymphat'ici retroauricula'res** [N A], two small nodes on the insertion of the sternocleidomastoid muscle. Called also *lymphoglandulae auriculares posteriores* [B N A], and *retroauricular lymph nodes.* **no'di lymphat'ici retropharyn'gei** [N A], nodes deep in the neck behind the pharynx, receiving lymph from some of the deeper structures of the head and neck. Called also *retropharyngeal lymph nodes.* **no'di lymphat'ici sacra'les** [N A], nodes located in the hollow of the sacrum, receiving lymph from the pelvic, perineal, and gluteal regions. Called also *lymphoglandulae sacrales* [B N A], and *sacral lymph nodes.* **no'di lymphat'ici submandibula'res** [N A], three to six nodes alongside the submandibular gland, through which lymph drains from the adjacent skin and mucous membrane. Called also *lymphoglandulae submaxillares* [B N A], and *submandibular lymph nodes.* **no'di lymphat'ici submenta'les** [N A], nodes under the chin into which the lymph from some of the superficial tissues of the head and neck is drained. Called also *submental lymph nodes.* **no'di lymphat'ici subscapula'res** [N A]. See *nodi lymphatici axillares.* **no'di lymphat'ici tibia'lis ante'rior** [N A], lymph nodes occasionally occurring along the anterior tibial vessels. Called also *lymphoglandulae tibialis anterior* [B N A], and *anterior tibial lymph nodes.* **no'di lymphat'ici trachea'les** [N A], nodes along each side of the trachea, receiving lymph from the trachea, esophagus, and tracheobronchial nodes. Called also *lymphoglandulae tracheales* [B N A], and *tracheal lymph nodes.* **no'di lymphat'ici tracheobronchia'les inferio'res** [N A], nodes in the angle of the bifurcation of the trachea, receiving lymph from adjacent structures. Called also *inferior tracheobronchial lymph nodes.* **no'di lymphat'ici tracheobronchia'les superio'res** [N A], nodes between the trachea and the bronchus on either side, receiving lymph from the adjacent structures. Called also *superior tracheobronchial lymph nodes.* **n. sinuatria'lis** [N A], a microscopic collection of atypical cardiac muscle fibers at the superior end of the sulcus terminalis, at the junction of the superior vena cava and the right atrium. See *sinoatrial node.*

noematachograph (no-e″mah-tak′o-graf) [Gr. *noēma* thought + *tachys* swift + *graphein* to write]. A device for registering the time required in a mental operation.

noematachometer (no-e″mah-tah-kom′e-ter) [Gr. *noēma* thought + *tachys* swift + *metron* measure]. A device for measuring the time required in a mental operation.

noematic (no″e-mat′ik). Pertaining to thought or the operation of the mind.

noesis (no-e′sis) [Gr. *noēsis* thought]. The operation of the intellect; cognition.

noetic (no-et′ik). Pertaining to the intellect or to cognition.

noeud (nuh) [Fr.]. Knot, or node. **n. vital** (nuh ve-tal′) ["vital node"], the respiratory center.

Noguchi's test (no-goo′chēz) [Hideyo *Noguchi*, Japanese pathologist in New York, 1876–1928]. See under *tests.*

Noguchia (no-goo′che-ah) [Hideyo *Noguchi*]. A genus of microorganisms of the family Brucellaceae, order Eubacteriales, made up of small, gram-negative rods, motile by means of peritrichous flagella, and found in the conjunctiva of man and animals having a follicular type of disease. **N. cuni′culi,** an organism that is said to be the cause of conjunctival folliculosis in rabbits. **N. granulo′sis,** an organism which at one time was thought to be the etiologic agent of trachoma. **N. si′miae,** an organism that is said to be the cause of conjunctival folliculosis in monkeys.

noli-me-tangere (no″li-me-tan′jer-e) [L. "touch me not"]. A term believed to have been originally applied by the Romans to the ulcerative form of lupus, because of the unfortunate effects of certain types of treatment; frequently applied to different types of destructive lesions of the skin.

noludar (nol′u-dar). Trade mark for preparations of methyprylon.

noma (no′mah) [Gr. *nomē* a spreading]. Gangrenous stomatitis. **n. puden′di, n. vul′vae,** ulceration of the pudendum of young children.

nomadic (no-mad′ik). Wandering; unsettled; free.

nomen (no′men), pl. *no′mina* [L.]. Name. **No′mina Anatom′ica** [L. "anatomical names"], the official body of anatomical nomenclature, applied especially to that revised by the International

Anatomical Nomenclature Committee appointed by the Fifth International Congress of Anatomists held at Oxford in 1950, and approved by the Sixth and Seventh International Congresses of Anatomists held in Paris, 1955, and New York, 1960. Abbreviated N A. **Basle No′mina Anatom′ica,** the official body of anatomical nomenclature prepared in 1895 by a group of German anatomists with some help from anatomists in other countries. Abbreviated B N A.

nomenclature (no′men-kla″tūr) [L. *nomen* name + *calare* to call]. Terminology; especially a classified system of names. See *Nomina Anatomica*, under *nomen*. **binomial n.,** the Linnean system of designating plants and animals by two latinized words signifying the genus and species.

nomina (no′mĭ-nah) [L.]. Plural of *nomen*.

nomo- (no′mo) [Gr. *nomos* law]. Combining form denoting relationship to usage or law.

nomogenesis (no″mo-jen′e-sis) [*nomo-* + Gr. *genesis* generation]. The theory of evolution according to which the course of evolution is fixed and predetermined by law, no place being left for chance.

nomogram (nom′o-gram) [*nomo-* + Gr. *gramma* mark]. The graphic representation produced in nomography; a chart or diagram on which a number of variables are plotted, forming a computation chart for the solution of complex numerical formulae.

nomography (no-mog′rah-fe) [*nomo-* + Gr. *graphein* to write]. A graphic method by which the relation between any number of variables may be represented graphically on a plane surface, such as a piece of paper.

nomotopic (no″mo-top′ik) [*nomo-* + Gr. *topos* place]. Occurring at a normal place; occurring normally.

nona (no′nah). A condition resembling lethargic encephalitis which appeared in epidemic form in southern Europe in 1889–1890.

nonacosane (non″ah-ko′sān). An aliphatic hydrocarbon, $C_{29}H_{60}$, extracted from plant waxes.

nonadherent (non″ad-he′rent). Not adherent to or connected with adjacent structures.

nonan (no′nan) [L. *nonus* ninth]. Recurring every ninth day, or at intervals of eight days.

nonantigenic (non″an-tĭ-jen′ik). Not producing antibodies; without antigenic effect.

nonapeptide (non″ah-pep′tid). A peptide containing nine amino acids.

non compos mentis (non kom′pos men′tis) [L.]. Not of sound mind.

nonconductor (non″kon-duk′tor). Any substance that does not readily transmit electricity, light, or heat.

nondisjunction (non″dis-junk′shun). Failure of a pair of chromosomes to separate at meiosis, so that both members of the pair are carried to the same daughter nucleus, and the other daughter cell is lacking that particular chromosome.

nonelectrolyte (non″e-lek′tro-līt). A solution that is a nonconductor.

nonhomogeneity (non-ho″mo-je-ne′ĭ-te). The lack of homogeneity; the state of not being homogeneous.

nonigravida (no″ne-grav′ĭ-dah) [L. *nonus* ninth + *gravida* pregnant]. A woman pregnant for the ninth time. Written Gravida IX.

noninfectious (non″in-fek′shus). Not infectious; not able to spread disease.

nonipara (no-nip′ah-rah) [L. *nonus* ninth + *parere* to bring forth, produce]. A woman who has had nine pregnancies which resulted in viable offspring. Written Para IX.

nonmetal (non-met′al). Any chemical element that is not a metal.

Nonne's syndrome (non′ez) [Max *Nonne*, Hamburg neurologist, 1861–1959]. See under *syndrome*.

Nonne-Apelt reaction (non′ĕ-ah′pelt) [Max *Nonne;* F. *Apelt*, German physician]. See under *reaction*.

non-nucleated (non-nu′kle-āt″ed). Without a nucleus.

nonocclusion (non″ŏ-kloo′zhun). Open bite malocclusion.

non-oliguric (non-ol″ĭ-gu′rik). Not pertaining to, characterized by, or conducive to oliguria.

non-oncogenic (non″on-ko-jen′ik). Not giving rise to tumors or causing tumor formation.

nonopaque (non″o-pāk′). Not opaque to the roentgen ray.

nonose (non′ōs) [L. *nonus* ninth]. A carbohydrate containing nine atoms of carbon in the molecule.

nonovalytic (non″o-vah-lit′ik). Not splitting egg albumin.

nonparous (non-par′us). Nulliparous.

nonphotochromogen (non″fo-to-kro′mo-jen). A microorganism which is not conspicuously affected in color by exposure to light; specifically a member of Group III of the so-called "anonymous" or "unclassified" mycobacteria, e.g., Battey bacilli.

nonradiable (non-ra′de-ah-b′l). Impervious to rays, such as roentgen rays, cathode rays, etc.

non repetat. Abbreviation for L. *non repeta′tur*, do not repeat.

nonrotation (non″ro-ta′shun) [*non-* + L. *rotare* to turn]. Failure of rotation of a part to the proper position. **n. of the intestine,** failure of rotation of the intestine during embryonic development, with the result that the small intestine lies on the right side of the abdomen and the large intestine on the left.

non-secretor (non″se-kre′tor). An individual possessing A or B type blood whose saliva and other body secretions do not contain the particular (A or B) substance.

nonseptate (non-sep′tāt). Without a septum or septa.

non-taster (non-tās′ter). An individual incapable of tasting a particular test substance, such as phenylthiocarbamide, used in certain genetic studies.

nonunion (non-ūn′yun). Failure of the ends of a fractured bone to unite.

nonus (no′nus) [L. "ninth"]. The hypoglossal nerve, formerly regarded as the ninth cranial nerve.

nonvalent (non-va′lent) [L. *non* not + *valere* to be able]. Having no chemical valency: not capable of entering into chemical composition: used of argon, helium, and the other inert gases.

nonviable (non-vi′ah-b′l) [L. *non* not + *viable*]. Not capable of living.

nonyl (no′nil). The monovalent radical C_9H_{19}.

nookleptia (no″o-klep′te-ah) [Gr. *nous* mind + *kleptein* to steal]. A morbid belief that one's thoughts are being stolen.

noopsyche (no′o-si″ke) [Gr. *nous* mind + *psychē* soul]. The intellectual processes of the mind. Cf. *thymopsyche*.

Noorden treatment (noor′den) [Carl Harko von *Noorden*, German physician, 1858–1944]. Oatmeal treatment.

noothymopsychic (no″o-thi″mo-si′kik). Pertaining to the intellectual and the affective processes of the mind.

nopalin G (no′pal-in). Bluish eosin. See under *eosin*.

N.O.P.H.N. Abbreviation for *National Organization for Public Health Nursing*.

noradrenalin (nor″ad-ren′ah-lin). Levarterenol.

noramidopyrine (nor-am″ĭ-do-pi′rēn). Dipyrone.

norandrostenolone (nor-an″dro-sten′o-lōn). Nandrolone.

Nordau's disease, nordauism (nor′dowz, nor-dow′izm) [Max Simon *Nordau*, German scientist, 1849–1923]. Degeneracy.

nordefrin (nor′dĕ-frin). Chemical name: dl-1-(3′,

4′-dihydroxyphenyl)-2-amino-1-propanol: used as a sympathomimetic agent.

norepinephrine (nor″ep-ĭ-nef′rin). A hormone secreted by the adrenal medulla in response to splanchnic stimulation, and stored in the chromaffin granules, being released predominantly in response to hypotension. A synthetic compound is used as a sympathomimetic and as a pressor agent.

norethandrolone (nor″eth-an′dro-lōn). Chemical name: 17α-ethyl-17-hydroxy-19-nor-4-androsten-3-one: a synthetic androgen equal to testosterone in anabolic activity, but having less androgenic activity.

norethindrone (nor-eth′in-drōn). Chemical name: 17α-ethinyl-19-nortestosterone, a compound similar in action to progesterone and used as a progestational agent.

nori (no′re). A Japanese culture gelatin.

norisodrine (nor-i′so-drin). Trade mark for preparations of isoproterenol.

norleucine (nor-lu′sin). An amino acid, alpha-amino normal caproic acid, $CH_3.(CH_2)_3.CH(NH_2).COOH$, extracted from the leucine fraction of the decomposition of the proteins of nervous tissue (Abderhalden and Weil, 1913).

norlutin (nor-lu′tin). Trade mark for a preparation of norethindrone.

norm (norm) [L. *norma* rule]. A fixed or ideal standard.

norma (nor′mah) [L.]. A line established to define the aspects of the cranium. **n. ante′rior,** norma frontalis. **n. basila′ris,** the outline of the inferior aspect of the skull. **n. facia′lis,** norma frontalis. **n. fronta′lis,** the outline of the skull viewed from the front. **n. infe′rior,** norma basilaris. **n. latera′lis,** the outline of the skull seen from either side. **n. occipita′lis,** the outline of the skull seen from behind. **n. poste′rior,** norma occipitalis. **n. sagitta′lis,** the outline of a sagittal section through the skull. **n. supe′rior,** normal verticalis. **n. tempora′lis,** norma lateralis. **n. ventra′lis,** the outline of the inferior aspect of the skull. **n. vertica′lis,** the outline of a vertical section of the skull.

normal (nor′mal) [L. *norma* rule]. 1. Agreeing with the regular and established type. 2. In chemistry, (*a*) denoting a solution containing in each 1000 cc. 1 gram equivalent weight of the active substance; (*b*) denoting aliphatic hydrocarbons in which no carbon atom is combined with more than two other carbon atoms; (*c*) denoting salts formed from acids and bases in such a way that no acidic hydrogen of the acid remains nor any of the basic hydroxyl of the base. 3. In bacteriology, not immunized or otherwise bacteriologically treated.

normalization (nor″mal-i-za′shun). The process of bringing or restoring to the normal standard.

normergic (norm-er′jik) [*norm-* + Gr. *ergon* work]. Reacting in a normal manner.

normo- (nor′mo) [L. *norma* rule]. Combining form meaning conforming to the rule; normal or usual.

normoblast (nor′mo-blast) [*normo-* + Gr. *blastos* germ]. A late stage in the development of a red blood corpuscle characterized by a pyknotic nucleus and abundant hemoglobin in the cytoplasm. **intermediate n.,** polychromatophilic erythroblast. **orthochromatophilic n.,** metarubricyte. **polychromatophilic n.,** polychromatophilic erythroblast.

normoblastic (nor″mo-blas′tik). Relating to or having the character of a normoblast.

normoblastosis (nor″mo-blas-to′sis). Excessive production of normoblasts by the bone marrow.

normocalcemia (nor″mo-kal-se′me-ah). A normal level of calcium in the blood.

normocalcemic (nor″mo-kal-se′mik). Pertaining to or characterized by normocalcemia.

normocapnia (nor″mo-kap′ne-ah). A normal level of carbon dioxide in the blood.

normocapnic (nor″mo-kap′nik). Pertaining to or characterized by normocapnia.

normocholesterolemia (nor″mo-ko-les″ter-ol-e′me-ah). A normal level of cholesterol in the blood.

normocholesterolemic (nor″mo-ko-les″ter-ol-e′mik). Pertaining to, characterized by, or tending to produce a normal level of cholesterol in the blood.

normochromasia (nor″mo-kro-ma′ze-ah) [*normo-* + Gr. *chrōma* color]. 1. A normal staining reaction in a cell or tissue. 2. Normal color of the red blood corpuscles.

normochromia (nor″mo-kro′me-ah). Normal color of the red blood corpuscles.

normochromic (nor″mo-kro′mik). Having a normal color; having a normal hemoglobin content.

normochromocyte (nor″mo-kro′mo-sīt). A red blood corpuscle having the normal amount of hemoglobin.

normocrinic (nor″mo-krin′ik). Pertaining to normal secretion or to normal endocrine action.

normocyte (nor′mo-sīt) [*normo-* + *-cyte*]. An erythrocyte that is normal in size, shape and color.

normocytic (nor″mo-sit′ik). Relating to or having the character of a normocyte.

normocytin (nor″mo-si′tin). Trade mark for preparations of concentrated crystalline vitamin B_{12}. See *cyanocobalamin.*

normocytosis (nor″mo-si-to′sis). A normal state of the blood in respect to the erythrocytes.

normoerythrocyte (nor″mo-e-rith′ro-sīt). Normocyte.

normoglycemia (nor″mo-gli-se′me-ah). The state of having the level of sugar in the blood within the normal range.

normoglycemic (nor″mo-gli-se′mik). Pertaining to, characterized by, or conducive to normoglycemia.

normolineal (nor″mo-lin′e-al). Built on normal lines.

normomastic (nor″mo-mas′tik). See *Kafka's test,* under *tests.*

normonormocytosis (nor″mo-nor″mo-si-to′sis). Isonormocytosis.

normo-orthocytosis (nor″mo-or″tho-si-to′sis) [*normo-* + Gr. *orthos* correct + *-cyte* + *-osis*]. A condition of the blood leukocytes in which the total number is increased, but the proportion between the different varieties remains normal.

normoproteinemia (nor″mo-pro″te-in-e′me-ah) [*normo-* + *protein* + Gr. *haima* blood + *-ia*]. Normal protein content of the blood.

normoproteinia (nor″mo-pro″te-in′e-ah). Normal protein status of the body.

normosexual (nor″mo-seks′u-al). Having normal sexuality.

normoskeocytosis (nor″mo-ske″o-si-to′sis) [*normo-* + Gr. *skaios* left + *-cyte* + *-osis*]. A condition of the leukocytes of the blood in which the number is normal, but many immature forms (deviation to the left) are present.

normosthenuria (nor″mo-sthen-u′re-ah) [*normo-* + Gr. *sthenos* strength + *ouron* urine + *-ia*]. 1. The secretion of urine of normal specific gravity. 2. Normally active urination.

normotension (nor″mo-ten′shun). Normal tone, tension, or pressure.

normotensive (nor″mo-ten′siv). 1. Characterized by normal tone, tension, or pressure, as by normal blood pressure. 2. A person with normal blood pressure.

normothermia (nor″mo-ther′me-ah) [*normo-* + Gr. *thermē* heat + *-ia*]. A normal state of temperature, especially (*a*) normal body temperature (98.6°F.), or (*b*) that state of normal environmental temperature at which there is neither stimulation nor depression of the activity of the body cells (Herrmann).

normothermic (nor″mo-ther′mik). Pertaining to

or characterized by normal temperature; neither hyperthermic nor hypothermic.

normotonia (nor″mo-to′ne-ah). Normal tone or tension.

normotonic (nor″mo-ton′ik). Pertaining to or characterized by normotonia.

normotopia (nor″mo-to′pe-ah) [*normo-* + Gr. *topos* place + *-ia*]. Normal location.

normotopic (nor″mo-top′ik). Normally located.

normotrophic (nor″mo-trof′ik). Of normal development; not exhibiting either hypertrophy or hypotrophy.

normouricemia (nor″mo-u″rĭ-se′me-ah). A normal value of uric acid in the blood.

normouricemic (nor″mo-u″rĭ-se′mik). Pertaining to or characterized by normouricemia.

normouricuria (nor″mo-u″rĭ-ku′re-ah). A normal amount of uric acid in the urine.

normouricuric (nor″mo-u″rĭ-ku′rik). Pertaining to or characterized by normouricuria.

normovolemia (nor″mo-vo-le′me-ah) [*normo-* + *volume* + Gr. *haima* blood + *-ia*]. Normal blood volume.

normovolemic (nor″mo-vo-le′mik). Pertaining to or characterized by normovolemia; having a normal volume of circulating fluid (plasma) in the body.

norodin (nor′o-din). Trade mark for a preparation of methamphetamine hydrochloride.

Norris's corpuscles (nor′is-ez) [Richard *Norris*, English physician, 1831–1916]. See under *corpuscle*.

norsulfazole (nor-sul′fah-zōl). Sulfathiazole.

nortropinon (nor-tro′pĭ-non). A solid, fusible ketone, $C_6H_{11}NO$, derived from tropin.

nosazontology (nos-az″on-tol′o-je). Nosetiology.

noscapine (nos′kah-pēn). An alkaloid, 1-α-narcotine, present in opium in an amount varying from 3 to 10 per cent: used as non-addictive antitussive.

nose (nōz) [L. *nasus;* Gr. *rhis*]. The specialized structure of the face that serves as an organ of the sense of smell, and as part of the respiratory apparatus, acting as a filter and warmer of the inspired air. Called also *nasus* [N A]. **brandy n.,** rosacea. **cleft n.,** a developmental anomaly resulting from incomplete union of the paired nasal primordia. **external n.,** nasus externus. **hammer n.,** rhinophyma. **potato n.,** rhinophyma. **saddle n., saddle-back n., sway-back n.,** a nose with a sunken bridge.

nosebrain (nōz′brān). Rhinencephalon.

nosegay (nōz′ga). A name applied to an anatomical structure resembling a small bunch of flowers. **Riolan's n.,** the group of muscles that take their origin from the styloid process of the temporal bone.

Nosema (no-se′mah). A genus of Microsporidia. *N. a′pis* causes the nosema disease of bees. *N. bom′bycis* causes the disease pébrine in silkworms.

nosema (no-se′mah), pl. *nose′mas* or *nosem′ata* [Gr. *nosēma* a sickness]. Any illness or disease.

nosematosis (no-se″mah-to′sis). Infestation with *Nosema.*

nosencephalus (no″sen-sef′ah-lus) [*noso-* + Gr. *enkephalos* brain]. A fetus with a defective cranium and brain.

nosepiece (nōz′pēs). The portion of a microscope nearest to the stage, which bears the objective or objectives, constructed so as to permit change of the objective without disturbing the focus of the instrument. **quick-change n.,** one bearing a single objective, which may be quickly attached to or removed from a microscope. **rotating n.,** one bearing more than one objective, designed to permit the one selected to be rotated into place, with its axis coincident with the optical axis of the microscope.

nosetiology (nos″e-te-ol′o-je) [*noso-* + Gr. *aitia* cause + *-logy*]. The study of the causation of disease.

noso- (nos′o) [Gr. *nosos* disease]. Combining form denoting relationship to disease.

nosochthonography (nos″ok-tho-nog′rah-fe) [*noso* + Gr. *chthōn* land + *graphein* to write]. The geography of epidemic or other diseases; the study of the geographical distribution of diseases; nosogeography.

nosocomial (nos″o-ko′me-al). Pertaining to a hospital or an infirmary.

nosocomium (nos″o-ko′me-um) [Gr. *nosokomeion*, from *nosos* disease + *komeion* to take care of]. A hospital or an infirmary.

nosode (nos′ōd). Any disease product used as a remedy.

nosogenesis (nos″o-jen′e-sis). Nosogeny.

nosogenic (nos″o-jen′ik). Causing disease.

nosogeny (no-soj′e-ne) [*noso-* + Gr. *gennan* to produce]. Pathogenesis.

nosogeography (nos″o-je-og′rah-fe) [*noso-* + Gr. *gē* earth + *graphein* to write]. Nosochthonography.

nosographer (no-sog′rah-fer). A writer of nosography.

nosography (no-sog′rah-fe) [*noso-* + Gr. *graphein* to write]. A written account or description of diseases.

nosohemia (nos″o-he′me-ah) [*noso-* + Gr. *haima* blood + *-ia*]. Blood disease.

noso-intoxication (nos″o-in-tok″sĭ-ka′shun). Intoxication by the harmful products of disease.

nosologic (nos″o-loj′ik). Pertaining to the classification of disease.

nosological (nos″o-loj′e-kal). Pertaining to nosology.

nosology (no-sol′o-je) [*noso-* + *-logy*]. The science of the classification of diseases.

nosomania (nos″o-ma′ne-ah) [*noso-* + Gr. *mania* madness]. The insane and incorrect belief of a patient that he has some special disease.

nosometry (no-som′e-tre) [*noso-* + Gr. *metron* measure]. The measurement of the morbidity rate.

nosomycosis (nos″o-mi-ko′sis) [*noso-* + Gr. *mykēs* fungus]. A disease caused by a parasitic fungus.

nosonomy (no-son′o-me) [*noso-* + Gr. *nomos* law]. The classification of diseases.

nosoparasite (nos″o-par′ah-sīt) [*noso-* + *parasite*]. An organism found in conjunction with a disease which it is able to modify, but not to produce.

nosophilia (nos″o-fil′e-ah) [*noso-* + Gr. *philein* to love]. A morbid desire to be sick.

nosophobe (nos′o-fōb). A person who has an abnormal fear of some particular disease, such as cancer, venereal disease, appendicitis, etc.

nosophobia (nos″o-fo′be-ah) [*noso-* + *phobia*]. Morbid dread of sickness or of any special disease.

nosophyte (nos′o-fīt) [*noso-* + Gr. *phyton* plant]. A pathogenic plant microorganism.

nosopoietic (nos″o-poi-et′ik) [*noso-* + Gr. *poiein* to make]. Causing or producing disease.

Nosopsyllus (nos″o-sil′us) [*noso-* + Gr. *psylla* flea]. A genus of fleas. **N. fascia′tus** is the common rat flea of North America and Europe. It is a vector of murine typhus and probably of plague. Formerly called *Ceratophyllus fasciatus.*

nosotaxy (nos′o-tak″se) [*noso-* + Gr. *taxis* arrangement]. The classification of disease.

nosotherapy (nos″o-ther′ah-pe). The treatment of one disease by means of another, as in malaria therapy.

nosotoxic (nos″o-tok′sik). Producing nosotoxicosis.

nosotoxicity (nos″o-tok-sis′ĭ-te). The quality of being nosotoxic.

nosotoxicosis (nos″o-tok″sĭ-ko′sis) [*noso-* + *toxicosis*]. Any disease due to or associated with poisoning.

nosotoxin (nos″o-tok′sin) [*noso-* + *toxin*]. Any toxin causing or associated with disease.

nosotrophy (no-sot′ro-fe) [*noso-* + Gr. *trophē* nourishment]. The care and nursing of the sick.

nosotropic (no″so-trop′ik) [*noso-* + Gr. *tropos* a turning]. Directed against or opposed to a disease.

nostalgia (nos-tal′je-ah) [Gr. *nostein* to return home + *-algia*]. Homesickness; longing to return home or to one's native land.

nostology (nos-tol′o-je) [Gr. *nostein* to return home + *-logy*]. Gerontology.

nostomania (nos″to-ma′ne-ah) [Gr. *nostein* to return home + *mania* madness]. Intense or insane nostalgia.

nostril (nos′tril). One of the external orifices of the nose (nares [N A]).

nostrum (nos′trum) [L.]. A quack, patent, or secret remedy.

nostyn (nos′tin). Trade mark for a preparation of ectylurea.

notal (no′tal) [Gr. *nōton* back]. Pertaining to the back; dorsal.

notalgia (no-tal′je-ah) [Gr. *nōton* back + *-algia*]. Pain in the back.

notalysin (no-tal′ĭ-sin). An antibiotic substance which causes lysis of *Staphylococcus aureus.*

notancephalia (no″tan-se-fa′le-ah) [Gr. *nōton* + *an* neg. + *kephalē* head + *-ia*]. Congenital absence of the back of the skull.

notanencephalia (no″tan-en-se-fa′le-ah) [Gr. *nōton* back + *an* neg. + *enkephalos* brain + *-ia*]. Absence of the cerebellum.

N.O.T.B. Abbreviation for *National Ophthalmic Treatment Board* (British).

notch (noch). An indentation or depression; especially one on the edge of a bone or other organ. See also *incisura.* **acetabular n.,** incisura acetabuli. **aortic n.,** dicrotic n. **auricular n.,** incisura anterior auris. **cardiac n. of left lung,** incisura cardiaca pulmonis sinistri. **cardiac n. of stomach,** incisura cardiaca ventriculi. **cerebellar n., anterior,** incisura cerebelli anterior. **cerebellar n., posterior,** incisura cerebelli posterior. **clavicular n. of sternum,** incisura clavicularis sterni. **coracoid n.,** incisura scapulae. **costal n's of sternum,** incisurae costales sterni. **cotyloid n.,** incisura acetabuli. **craniofacial n.,** an opening in the bony partition between the orbital and nasal cavities. **dicrotic n.,** the depression on the sphygmogram, separating the primary from the dicrotic elevation of a dicrotic pulse wave, and caused by closure of the aortic valves; called also *aortic notch.* **ethmoidal n. of frontal bone,** incisura ethmoidalis ossis frontalis. **fibular n.,** incisura fibularis tibiae. **frontal n.,** incisura frontalis. **n. of gallbladder,** fossa vesicae felleae. **gastric n.,** incisura angularis ventriculi. **iliosciatic n.,** incisura ischiadica major. **interarytenoid n.,** incisura interarytenoidea laryngis. **interclavicular n.,** incisura jugularis sterni. **interclavicular n. of occipital bone,** incisura jugularis ossis occipitalis. **interclavicular n. of temporal bone,** incisura jugularis ossis temporalis. **intercondylar n. of femur,** fossa intercondylaris femoris. **interlobar n.,** incisura ligamenti teretis. **intertragic n.,** incisura intertragica. **intervertebral n.** See *incisura vertebralis inferior* and *incisura vertebralis superior.* **ischiatic n., greater,** incisura ischiadica major. **ischiatic n., lesser,** incisura ischiadica minor. **jugular n. of occipital bone,** incisura jugularis ossis occipitalis. **jugular n. of sternum,** incisura jugularis sterni. **jugular n. of temporal bone,** incisura jugularis ossis temporalis. **lacrimal n. of maxilla,** incisura lacrimalis maxillae. **n. of ligamentum teres,** incisura ligamenti teretis. **mandibular n.,** incisura mandibulae. **marsupial n.,** incisura cerebelli posterior. **mastoid n.** 1. Incisura mastoidea ossis temporalis. 2. Fossa digastrica. **nasal n. of maxilla,** incisura nasalis maxillae **palatine n.,** fissura pterygoidea. **palatine n. of palatine bone,** incisura sphenopalatina ossis palatini. **pancreatic n.,** incisura pancreatis. **parietal n. of temporal bone,** incisura parietalis ossis temporalis. **parotid n.,** the notch between the ramus of the mandible and the mastoid process of the temporal bone. **popliteal n.,** fossa intercondylaris femoris. **preoccipital n.,** a notch on the lower edge of the external surface of a cerebral hemisphere, between the occipital and temporal lobes. **presternal n.,** incisura jugularis sterni. **pterygoid n.,** fissura pterygoidea. **radial n.,** incisura radialis ulnae. **rivinian n., n. of Rivinus,** incisura tympanica. **sacrosciatic n., greater,** incisura ischiadica major. **sacrosciatic n., lesser,** incisura ischiadica minor. **scapular n.,** incisura scapulae. **sciatic n., greater,** incisura ischiadica major. **sciatic n., lesser,** incisura ischiadica minor. **semilunar n. of mandible,** incisura mandibulae. **semilunar n. of scapula,** incisura scapulae. **Sibson's n.,** an inward bend of the left upward limit of precordial dullness in acute pericardial effusion. **sigmoid n.,** incisura mandibulae. **sphenopalatine n. of palatine bone,** incisura sphenopalatina ossis palatini. **sternal n.,** incisura jugularis sterni. **supraorbital n.** 1. Incisura supraorbitalis. 2. Incisura frontalis. **suprascapular n.,** incisura scapulae. **suprasternal n.,** incisura jugularis sterni. **tentorial n.,** incisura tentorii cerebelli. **thyroid n., inferior,** incisura thyroidea inferior. **thyroid n., superior,** incisura thyroidea superior. **trigeminal n.,** a notch in the superior border of the petrosal portion of the temporal bone, near the apex, for transmission of the trigeminal nerve. **trochlear n. of ulna,** incisura trochlearis ulnae. **tympanic n.,** incisura tympanica. **ulnar n. of radius,** incisura ulnaris radii. **umbilical n.,** incisura ligamenti teretis. **vertebral n., inferior,** incisura vertebralis superior. **vertebral n., superior,** incisura vertebralis superior.

notencephalocele (no″ten-se-fal′o-sēl) [*noto-* + Gr. *enkephalos* brain + *kēlē* hernia]. Hernial protrusion of the brain from the back of the head.

notencephalus (no″ten-sef′ah-lus) [*noto-* + Gr. *enkephalos* brain]. A fetal monster affected with notencephalocele.

Nothnagel's bodies, sign, test (nōt′nah-gelz) [Carl Wilhelm Hermann *Nothnagel*, German physician, 1841–1905]. See under the nouns.

notifiable (no′tĭ-fi″ah-b'l). That should be made known: said of diseases that are required to be made known to the board of health.

noto- (no′to) [Gr. *nōton* back]. Combining form denoting relationship to the back.

notochord (no′to-kord) [*noto-* + Gr. *chordē* cord]. The rod-shaped body, composed of cells derived from the mesoblast, below the primitive groove of the embryo, defining the primitive axis of the body. Called also *chorda dorsalis.*

notochordoma (no″to-kor-do′mah). Chordoma.

Notoedres (no″to-ed′rēz). A genus of mites. **N. ca′ti,** an itch mite which causes a very persistent and often fatal mange in cats; it also infests domestic rabbits, and may temporarily infest man.

notogenesis (no″to-jen′e-sis) [*noto-* + Gr. *gennan* to produce]. The development of the notochord.

notomelus (no-tom′e-lus) [*noto-* + Gr. *melos* limb]. A fetus with accessory limbs on the back.

notomyelitis (no″to-mi″ĕ-li′tis) [*noto-* + *myelitis*]. Inflammation of the spinal cord.

not-self (not′self). A term used by Burnet and Fenner to denote antigen constituents foreign to the organism (*self*), which are eliminated through antibodies.

noumenal (nu′me-nal). Pertaining to the noumenon; pertaining to rational intuition independent of sensory perception.

noumenon (nu′me-non) [Gr. *nooumenon* a thing

thought]. An object of intuition by the understanding independent of sensory perception.

nousic (noo′sik) [Gr. *nous* mind]. Pertaining to or affecting cerebration or the intellectual powers.

novaldin (no-val′din). Trade mark for preparations of dipyrone.

novobiocin (no″vo-bi′o-sin). An antibacterial substance produced by the growth of various species of streptomyces.

novocain (no′vo-kān). Trade mark for preparations of procaine hydrochloride.

novoscope (no′vo-skōp) [L. *novus* new + *scope*]. Fornai's instrument for auscultatory percussion.

novrad (nov′rad). Trade mark for preparations of levopropoxyphene.

Novy's bacillus (no′vēz) [Frederick George *Novy*, American bacteriologist, 1864–1957]. *Clostridium novyi.* **N's rat disease,** a filtrable virus disease discovered by Novy in his stock of experimental rats.

Novy-MacNeal blood agar [F. G. *Novy;* Ward J. *MacNeal*, American pathologist, 1881–1946]. See under *agar.*

noxa (nok′sah), pl. *nox′ae* [L. "harm"]. An injurious agent, act, or influence.

noxious (nok′shus) [L. *noxius*]. Hurtful; not wholesome; pernicious.

Np. Chemical symbol for *neptunium.*

NPN. Abbreviation for *nonprotein nitrogen.*

N.R.C. Abbreviation for *normal retinal correspondence.*

N.S.D.P. Abbreviation for *National Society of Denture Prosthetists.*

N.T.P. Abbreviation for *normal temperature and pressure.*

nubecula (nu-bek′u-lah) [L., dim. of *nubes* cloud]. 1. A slight cloudiness of the cornea or of the urine. 2. Statoconia.

nubility (nu-bil′ĭ-te) [L. *nubilitas;* from *nubere* to marry]. Marriageableness; fitness to marry: used of the female.

nucha (nu′kah) [L.]. [N A] The back, nape, or scruff of the neck.

nuchal (nu′kal). Pertaining to the nucha.

nucin (nu′sin) [L. *nux, nucis,* nut]. Juglandic acid.

nucis (nu′sis) [L.]. Genitive of *nux.*

Nuck's canal, diverticulum, gland, hydrocele (nuks) [Anton *Nuck*, Dutch anatomist, 1650–1692]. See under the nouns.

nuclear (nu′kle-ar). Pertaining to a nucleus.

nuclease (nu′kle-ās). An enzyme or a group of enzymes which split nucleic acid into mononucleotides and other products. They are present as digestive enzymes in the intestinal tract and as autolytic enzymes in many cells. Similar enzymes are found in bacterial cultures. **purine n.,** an enzyme which causes the hydrolysis of purine nucleotides so as to liberate the purine base. It has been found in the pancreas.

nucleated (nu′kle-āt″ed) [L. *nucleatus*]. Having a nucleus or nuclei.

nuclei (nu′kle-i) [L.]. Plural of *nucleus.*

nucleicacidase (nu″kle-ik-as′ĭ-dās). An enzyme which splits nucleic acid into nucleotides.

nucleide (nu′kle-īd). Any compound of nucleic acid with a metallic element.

nucleiform (nu′kle-ĭ-form). Shaped like a nucleus.

nuclein (nu′kle-in). A decomposition product of nucleoprotein intermediate between native nucleoprotein and nucleic acid (F. Miescher, 1874). It is a colorless, amorphous compound, soluble in dilute alkalis, but insoluble in dilute acids. The nucleins consists of nucleic acid and bases which vary in the different nucleins. Yeast nuclein yields two purines, adenine and guanine, and two pyrimidins, cytosin and uracil. The nucleins include *cell nucleins* or *true nucleins,* which split up into protein and nucleic acids; *pseudonucleins* and *paranucleins,* or *nucleoalbumins.* The nuclein of various glands is sometimes given therapeutically. **n. animal,** an animal into whose blood a certain amount of nuclein has been injected. **n. bases,** the bases formed by the chemical decomposition of nuclein. **yeast n.,** a nuclein extracted from the cells of the yeast (Saccharomyces) which differs somewhat from that obtained from the thymus gland.

nucleinase (nu′kle-in-ās). Nuclease.

nucleinotherapy (nu-kle″ĭ-no-ther′ah-pe). Treatment with sodium nucleinate, e.g., in paralysis agitans.

nucleoalbumin (nu″kle-o-al-bu′min). A conjugated protein which differs from nucleoproteins by containing paranucleic acid, which forms no xanthine bodies. Called also *paranuclein* and *pseudonuclein.*

nucleoalbuminuria (nu″kle-o-al-bu″mĭ-nu′reah). The presence of nucleoalbumin in the urine.

nucleoalbumose (nu″kle-o-al′bu-mōs). Nucleoalbumin which has been partly hydrolyzed; it has been found in the urine of osteomalacia.

nucleoanalysis (nu″kle-o-ah-nal′ĭ-sis). Analysis of the blood in relation to the nucleated leukocytes.

nucleoanalytic (nu″kle-o-an″ah-lit′ik). Pertaining to or based on nucleoanalysis.

nucleochylema (nu″kle-o-ki-le′mah) [*nucleus* + Gr. *chylos* juice]. The ground substance of the nucleus of a cell as distinguished from that of the cytoplasm.

nucleochyme (nu′kle-o-kīm) [*nucleus* + Gr. *chymos* juice]. Karyenchyma.

nucleocytoplasmic (nu″kle-o-si″to-plaz′mik). Pertaining to the nucleus and the cytoplasm of cells.

nucleofugal (nu″kle-of′u-gal) [*nucleus* + L. *fugere* to flee]. Moving away from a nucleus.

nucleoglucoprotein (nu″kle-o-gloo″ko-pro′tein). A combination of a nucleoprotein with a carbohydrate.

nucleohistone (nu″kle-o-his′tōn). A nucleoprotein found in the nuclei of the spermatozoa of various animals, the avian erythrocyte, and somatic cells in general.

nucleohyaloplasm (nu″kle-o-hi-al′o-plazm). Linin.

nucleoid (nu′kle-oid). 1. Resembling a nucleus. 2. A nucleus-like body sometimes seen in the center of an erythrocyte. **Ladovski's n.,** the attraction sphere.

nucleokeratin (nu″kle-o-ker′ah-tin). A variety of keratin found in the nervous system.

nucleol (nu′kle-ol). A protein forming soluble compounds with metallic salts.

nucleolar (nu-kle′o-lar). Pertaining to a nucleolus.

nucleoliform (nu″kle-ol′ĭ-form). Resembling a nucleolus.

nucleolin (nu-kle′o-lin). The substance composing the nucleolus of a cell.

nucleolinus (nu″kle-o-li′nus). A deeply staining granule in the nucleolus.

nucleoloid (nu′kle-o-loid). Resembling a nucleolus.

nucleololus (nu″kle-ol′o-lus). A minute spot within the nucleolus.

nucleolonema (nu″kle-o″lo-ne′mah) [*nucleolus* + Gr. *nēma* thread]. A network of strands formed by organization of a finely granular substance, perhaps containing ribonucleic acid, in the nucleolus of a cell.

nucleoloneme (nu″kle-o′lo-nēm). Nucleolonema.

nucleolonucleus (nu″kle-o-lo-nu′kle-us). A nucleololus.

nucleolus (nu-kle′o-lus), pl. *nucle′oli* [L., dim. of *nucleus*]. A round achromatic body within the nucleus of a cell. Called also *plasmosome.* **chromatin n., false n., nucleinic n.,** karyosome. **secondary n.,** a mass sometimes seen near a nucleolus, and looking like a separated portion of the latter.

nucleomicrosome (nu″kle-o-mi′kro-sōm) [*nucleus* + Gr. *mikros* small + *sōma* body]. Any one of the minute segments of a chromatin fiber.

nucleomitophobia (nu″kle-o-mi″to-fo′be-ah). Morbid fear of an atomic explosion.

nucleon (nu′kle-on). 1. A particle of the atomic nucleus, a proton or a neutron. 2. Phosphocarnic acid.

nucleonic (nu″kle-on′ik). Pertaining to a nucleus. Consisting of compounds of one or more protein molecules with nucleic acid.

nucleonics (nu″kle-on′iks). The study of atomic nuclei and their reactions; nuclear physics.

nucleopetal (nu″kle-op′e-tal) [*nucleus* + L. *petere* to seek]. Moving toward a nucleus.

Nucleophaga (nu″kle-of′ah-gah) [*nucleus* + Gr. *phagein* to eat]. An organism which is parasitic in amebas, destroying the nucleus of the latter.

nucleophilic (nu″kle-o-fil′ik). Having an affinity for nuclei.

nucleophosphatase (nu″kle-o-fos′fah-tās). Nucleotidase.

nucleoplasm (nu′kle-o-plazm) [*nucleus* + *plasma*]. The protoplasm composing the nucleus of a cell; karyoplasm.

nucleoprotamine (nu″kle-o-pro-tam′in). A compound of protamine and nucleic acid found chiefly in fish sperm.

nucleoproteid (nu″kle-o-pro′te-id). Nucleoprotein.

nucleoprotein (nu″kle-o-pro′te-in). A substance composed of a simple basic protein, usually a histone or protamine, combined with a nucleic acid. **deoxyribose n.,** deoxyribose nucleic acid. **ribose n.,** ribose nucleic acid.

nucleopurine (nu″kle-o-pu′rin). Aminopurine.

nucleoreticulum (nu″kle-o-re-tik′u-lum) [*nucleus* + *reticulum*]. Any intranuclear network.

nucleose (nu′kle-ōs). Any albumose of the class to which the vegetable nucleoalbumins belong. The nucleoses are foods, and are also antiseptic, bactericidal, phagocytic, and diuretic.

nucleosidase (nu″kle-o′si-dās). An enzyme which catalyzes the splitting of nucleosides. The nucleosidases are adenosin-hydrolase, guanosin-hydrolase, inosin-hydrolase, and xanthosin-hydrolase.

nucleoside (nu′kle-o-sīd). One of the glycosidic compounds into which a nucleotide is split by the action of nucleotidase or by chemical means. It is a combination of a sugar (a hexose or pentose) with a purine or a pyrimidine base.

nucleosin (nu′kle-o-sin). Thymin.

nucleosis (nu″kle-o′sis). Nuclear proliferation; abnormal increase in the production of nuclei, such as occurs in the subsarcolemmal nuclei of muscle following injury.

nucleospindle (nu″kle-o-spin′d'l). The spindle-shaped body in mitosis.

nucleotherapy (nu″kle-o-ther′ah-pe) [*nuclein* + *therapy*]. The treatment of disease with nucleins.

nucleotidase (nu″kle-ot′ĭ-dās). An enzyme which splits nucleotides into nucleosides and phosphoric acid; called also *phosphonuclease* and *nucleophosphatase.*

nucleotide (nu′kle-o-tīd). One of the compounds into which nucleic acid is split by the action of nuclease. See *mononucleotide.* **diphosphopyridine n.,** a co-enzyme widely found in nature and involved in numerous enzymatic reactions, the dinucleotide of nicotinamide and of adenine: the products of hydrolysis are 1 molecule of adenine, 1 molecule of nicotinamide, 2 molecules of *d*-ribose, and 2 molecules of phosphoric acid. Called also *codehydrogenase I, co-enzyme I, CoI, cozymase, dihydroco-enzyme I,* and *DPN.* **triphosphopyridine n.,** a co-enzyme required for a limited number of reactions, and similar to diphosphopyridine nucleotide, except for the inclusion of three phosphate units. Called also *co-enzyme II, codehydrogenase II, coferment, CoII, TPN,* and *Warburg's co-enzyme.*

nucleotoxin (nu″kle-o-tok′sin). A toxin from cell nuclei; also any toxin which affects the cell nuclei.

nucleus (nu′kle-us), pl. *nu′clei* [L., dim. of *nux* nut]. 1. A spheroid body within a cell, consisting of a number of characteristic organelles visible with the optical microscope, a thin nuclear membrane, nucleoli, irregular granules of chromatin and linin, and a diffuse karyoplasm. 2. [N A, B N A] A general term used to designate a group of nerve cells ordinarily located within the central nervous system and bearing a direct relationship to the fibers of a particular nerve. 3. In chemistry, the combination of atoms forming the central element or basic framework of the molecule of a specific compound or class of compounds. **abducens n., n. of abducens nerve, n. abducen′tis,** n. nervi abducentis. **accessory n. of auditory nerve.** See *nuclei cochleares, ventralis et dorsalis.* **accessory cuneate n.,** n. cuneatus accessorius. **n. accom′bens.** See *nuclei nervi vestibulocochlearis.* **nuclei of acoustic nerve,** nuclei nervi vestibulocochlearis. **n. acus′ticus.** See *nuclei nervi vestibulocochlearis.* **n. acus′ticus, infe′rior et latera′lis.** See *nuclei cochleares, ventralis et dorsalis.* **n. acus′ticus supe′rior,** the superior vestibular nucleus. See *nuclei vestibulares.* **n. a′lae cine′reae** [B N A], n. dorsalis nervi vagi. **ambiguous n.,** n. ambiguus. **ambiguous n. of Quain,** n. nervi hypoglossi. **n. ambig′uus** [N A, B N A], the nucleus of origin of motor fibers of the vagus, glossopharyngeal, and accessory nerves that supply the striated muscles of the larynx and pharynx. It consists of an intermittent cell column in the middle of the lateral funiculus of the medulla oblongata, between the caudal end of the medulla and the point of exit of the glossopharyngeal nerve. **n. amyg′dalae** [B N A], corpus amygdaloideum. **n. amygdalifor′mis of J. Stilling,** n. subthalamicus. **amygdaloid n.,** corpus amygdaloideum. **n. angula′ris, Bechterew′i,** the superior vestibular nucleus. See *nuclei vestibulares.* **n. ante′rior thal′ami** [N A, B N A], **anterior n. of thalamus,** a nuclear mass located in the anterior part of the thalamus, separated from the remainder of the thalamus by the diverging limbs of the internal medullary lamina. **nu′clei arcifor′mes,** nuclei arcuati. **arcuate nuclei of medulla oblongata, nu′clei arcua′ti** [N A, B N A], small, irregular areas of gray substance found on the ventromedial aspect of the pyramid of the medulla oblongata. **n. of atom, atomic n.,** the central core of an atom, constituting almost all of its mass but only a small part of its volume, and containing an excess of electricity, the exact amount depending on the atomic number of the element. **auditory nuclei.** See *nuclei cochleares, ventralis et dorsalis,* and *nuclei vestibularis.* **nuclei of auditory nerve,** nuclei nervi vestibulocochlearis. **n. of auditory nerve, accessory.** See *nuclei cochleares, ventralis et dorsalis.* **Balbiani's n.,** yolk n. **basal n.** 1. Nucleus olivaris. 2. [Pl.]. The corpus striatum, amygdaloid body, and claustrum. See also *basal ganglia.* **n. basa′lis,** n. olivaris. **Bechterew's n.,** the superior vestibular nucleus. See *nuclei vestibulares.* **Béclard's n.,** a vascular lentil-shaped center of ossification seen in the cartilage of the lower epiphysis of the femur during the latter part of fetal life. **Blumenau's n.,** the lateral portion of the cuneate nucleus. **n. of Burdach's column,** n. cuneatus. **caudal n.,** n. nervi oculomotorii. **caudate n., n. cauda′tus** [N A, B N A], a long horseshoe-shaped mass of gray substance which forms part of the corpus striatum and is closely related to the lateral ventricle throughout its entire extent. It consists of a head, body, and tail. **central n. of thalamus, n. centra′lis thal′ami** [N A], a collection of cells lying close to the wall of the third ventricle, between the medial and the posterior ventral nuclei of the thalamus, medial to and partially embedded in the internal medullary lamina. Called also *centrum medianum.* **n.**

cerebel'li, n. dentatus cerebelli. **cervical n.,** a nucleus in the spinal cord opposite the origin of the third and fourth cervical nerves. **cholane n.,** a combination of atoms forming the basis of the specific compound, found in the bile acids, the sterols, in toad poisons, in digitalis, strophanthus, ouabain, and other heart aglycones, in the sex hormones, and in some carcinogenic hydrocarbons. **n. cine'reum,** gray n. **Clark's n., n. of Clark's column,** n. thoracicus. **cleavage n.,** segmentation n. **cochlear n., dorsal.** See *nuclei cochleares, ventralis et dorsalis.* **cochlear n., ventral.** See *nuclei cochleares, ventralis et dorsalis.* **nu'clei cochlea'res, ventra'lis et dorsa'lis** [N A], the nuclei of termination of the sensory fibers of the pars cochlearis nervi octavi, which enter the brain through the inferior root of the nerve. The nuclei are found at the junction between the medulla oblongata and pons, partly encircling the inferior cerebellar peduncle. A dorsal and a ventral cochlear nucleus are distinguished at the dorsal and ventral borders of the restiform body. Called also *nuclei nervi cochlearis* [B N A]. **nuclei of cochlear nerve,** nuclei cochlearis, ventralis et dorsalis. **n. collic'uli inferio'ris** [N A, B N A], the large oval-shaped group of nerve cell bodies that makes up most of the substance of the inferior colliculus. Called also *n. of inferior colliculus.* **conjugation n.,** fertilization n. **n. cor'poris genicula'ti latera'lis** [N A, B N A], the group of nerve cell bodies located within the lateral geniculate body. Called also *n. of lateral geniculate body.* **n. cor'poris genicula'ti media'lis** [N A, B N A], the group of nerve cell bodies located within the medial geniculate body. Called also *n. of medial geniculate body.* **nu'clei cor'poris mamilla'ris** [N A, B N A], three masses of cells in the mamillary body, some of the fibers from which form the mamillothalamic fasciculus. Called also *nuclei of mamillary body.* **nuclei of cranial nerves,** nuclei nervorum cranialium. **cuneate n.,** n. cuneatus. **cuneate n., accessory, cuneate n., lateral,** n. cuneatus accessorius. **n. cunea'tus** [N A], a nucleus in the medulla oblongata at the rostral end of the fasciculus cuneatus, in which the fibers of this fasciculus synapse. Called also *n. funiculi cuneati* [B N A], and *cuneate n.* **n. cunea'tus accesso'rius** [N A], a group of nerve cells lying lateral to the nucleus cuneatus and giving rise to external arcuate fibers that reach the cerebellum through the inferior cerebellar peduncle. Called also *accessory cuneate n.* and *lateral cuneate n.* **Darkschewitsch's n.,** a collection of cells at the point of transition between the third ventricle and aqueduct, which is said to contribute fibers to the medial longitudinal fasciculus. **Deiters' n.,** the lateral vestibular nucleus. See *nuclei vestibulares.* **dental n.,** pulpa dentis. **dentate n. of cerebellum, n. denta'tus cerebel'li** [N A, B N A], a large nucleus embedded within the hemisphere of the cerebellum just lateral to the emboliform nucleus; from it fibers of the brachium conjunctivum arise. **n. denta'tus par'tis commissura'lis,** n. dorsalis corporis trapezoidei. **diploid n.,** a cell nucleus containing the number of chromosomes typical of the somatic cells of the particular species. **dorsal n. of Clark, n. dorsa'lis,** n. thoracicus. **dorsal n. of glossopharyngeal nerve,** n. dorsalis nervi glossopharyngei. **dorsal n. of trapezoid body,** n. dorsalis corporis trapezoidei. **dorsal n. of vagus nerve,** n. dorsalis nervi vagi. **n. dorsa'lis [Stillin'gi, Clark'ii]** [B N A], n. thoracicus. **n. dorsa'lis cor'poris trapezoi'dei** [N A], a group of nerve cell bodies dorsolateral to the trapezoid body. It receives cochlear fibers and contributes to the formation of the trapezoid body and lateral lemniscus. Called also *n. olivaris superior* [B N A]. **n. dorsa'lis ner'vi glossopharyn'gei** [N A], the nucleus of origin of the parasympathetic fibers of the glossopharyngeal nerve. It lies rostral to the dorsal nucleus of the vagus nerve, in the dorsal part of the brain stem at the junction of the medulla oblongata and the pons. Called also *dorsal n. of glossopharyngeal nerve.* **n. dorsa'lis ner'vi va'gi** [N A], the nucleus of origin of the parasympathetic fibers of the vagus nerve, situated just dorsal or dorsolateral to the nucleus intercalatus. Called also *n. alae cinereae* [B N A], and *dorsal n. of vagus nerve.* **dorsomedial n. of hypothalamus, n. dorsomedia'lis hypothal'ami** [N A], the dorsal one of two main groups of nerve cell bodies found in the middle, tuberal region of the hypothalamus. **Duval's n.,** a collection of multipolar ganglion cells situated ventrolaterally from the hypoglossal nucleus in the medulla oblongata. **Edinger's n.** 1. Westphal's nucleus. 2. A collection of nerve cells at the beginning of the sylvian aqueduct in the third ventricle. **emboliform n., n. embolifor'mis cerebel'li** [N A, B N A], a small mass between the dentate nucleus and the globose nucleus. **end nuclei,** terminal nuclei. **n. of facial nerve,** n. nervi facialis. **fastigial n., n. fasti'gii** [N A, B N A], a flat mass of gray matter in the cerebellum over the roof of the fourth ventricle, medial to the globose nucleus. **fertilization n.,** the nucleus produced by fusion of the male and female pronuclei in the fertilized ovum. Called also *synkaryon.* **fibrous n. of tongue,** septum linguae. **free n.,** a cell nucleus from which the other elements of the cell have disappeared. **n. funic'uli cunea'ti** [B N A], n. cuneatus. **n. funic'uli gra'cilis** [B N A], n. gracilis. **gametic n.,** the gonad of sarcodina. **n. gelatino'sus,** n. pulposus disci intervertebralis. **germ n., germinal n.,** pronucleus. **gingival n.,** a part of the cerebellum in the third and fourth months of fetal life. **globose n., n. globo'sus cerebel'li** [N A, B N A], a mass of gray matter in the cerebellum between the emboliform nucleus and the fastigial nucleus. **n. of glossopharyngeal nerve, dorsal,** n. dorsalis nervi glossopharyngei. **n. of Goll's column,** n. gracilis. **gonad n.,** the reproductive nucleus of a cell, as distinguished from the trophonucleus. **n. gra'cilis** [N A], a nucleus in the medulla oblongata at the rostral end of the fasciculus gracilis, in which the fibers of the fasciculus gracilis synapse. Called also *n. funiculi gracilis* [B N A]. **gray n.,** substantia grisea medullae spinalis. **n. of habenula, n. haben'ulae** [N A, B N A], **habenular n.,** the group of nerve cell bodies within the habenula. **haploid n.,** a cell nucleus containing half of the number of chromosomes typical of the somatic cells of a particular species. **hypoglossal n., n. of hypoglossal nerve,** n. nervi hypoglossi. **hypothalamic n., n. hypothalam'icus** [B N A], n. subthalamicus. **n. of hypothalamus, dorsomedial,** n. dorsomedialis hypothalami. **n. of hypothalamus, posterior,** n. posterior hypothalami. **n. of inferior colliculus,** n. colliculi inferioris. **n. intercala'tus** [N A], a group of nerve cells between the dorsal nucleus of the vagus nerve and the nucleus of the hypoglossal nerve. Called also *Staderini's n.* **n. of internal geniculate body,** n. corporis geniculati medialis. **interpeduncular n., n. interpeduncula'ris** [N A], a nucleus situated between the cerebral peduncles which receives the habenulopeduncular tract. **intralaminar nuclei of thalamus, nu'clei intralamina'res thal'ami** [N A], groups of nerve cell bodies found within the lamina separating the major thalamic nuclei. **intraventricular n. of corpus striatum,** n. caudatus. **Kaiser's nuclei,** longitudinal motor nuclei in the cervical and lumbar enlargements of the cord, between the intermediolateral column and the median column. **Klein-Gumprecht nuclei,** unstainable nuclei seen in degenerating lymphocytes in leukemia. **Kölliker's n.,** substantia intermedia centralis medullae spinalis. **large cell n.,** n. ambiguus. **large cell auditory n.,** the lateral vestibular nucleus. See *nuclei vestibulares.* **laryngeal n.,** the nucleus of origin of the nerve fibers going to the larynx. **n. of lateral geniculate body,** n. corporis geniculati lateralis. **n. of lateral lemniscus,** n. lemnisci lateralis. **n. latera'lis medul'lae oblonga'tae** [N A], a nucleus in the reticular substance of the medulla oblongata, dorsolateral to the olive. **n. latera'lis thal'ami** [N A, B N A], a nuclear mass lying between the internal medullary lamina and the internal capsule, commonly divided into a larger ventral part and a smaller dorsal part. **Laurer's n.,** the lateral vestibular nucleus. See *nuclei vestibulares.* **n. lemnis'ci latera'lis** [N A, B N A], a collection of nerve cells in the rostral part of the lateral lemniscus. Called also *n. of lateral lemniscus.* **n. of lens,** n. lentis. **lenticular n., lentiform n.,** n. lentiformis. **n. lentifor'mis** [N A, B N A], the part of the corpus striatum comprising the putamen and globus pallidus. It lies just lateral to the internal capsule. **n. len'tis** [N A, B N A], the harder internal part of the lens of the eye. **n. of Luys.** 1. Hypophysis cerebri. 2. Nucleus subthalamicus. **n. magnocellula'ris,** the lateral vestibular nucleus. See *nuclei vestibulares.* **nuclei of mamillary body,** nuclei corporis mamillaris. **n. of medial geniculate body,** n. corporis geniculati medialis. **n. media'lis thal'ami** [N A, B N A], a nuclear mass lying between the midline of the thalamus and the internal medullary lamina. Called also *medial n. of thalamus.* **n. medulla'ris cerebel'li, medullary n. of cerebellum,** corpus medullare cerebelli. **merocyte n.,** merocyte. **mesencephalic n.,** Spitzka's n. **n. of mesencephalic tract of trigeminal nerve,** n. tractus mesencephalicus nervi trigemini. **Monakow's n.,** the lateral part of the cuneate nucleus. **motion n.,** kinetoplast. **motor n.,** any collection of cells of the central nervous system giving origin to motor fibers of a nerve. **motor n. of trigeminal nerve, n. moto'rius ner'vi trigem'ini** [N A], the nucelus of origin of the motor fibers of the trigeminal nerve, located in the middle of the pons, in the dorsal part, just medial to the fibers of the trigeminal nerve. See also *n. sensorius superior nervi trigemini.* **nerve n.,** a collection of cells in the nervous system directly related to a peripheral nerve. **n. ner'vi abducen'tis** [N A, B N A], the nucleus of origin of the abducens nerve, a gray mass within the caudal part of the pons, near the floor of the fourth ventricle. Called also *n. of abducens nerve.* **nu'clei ner'vi acus'tici** [B N A], nuclei nervi vestibulocochlearis. **nu'clei nervo'rum cerebra'lium** [B N A], nuclei nervorum cranialium. **nu'clei ner'vi cochlea'ris** [B N A], nuclei cochleares, ventralis et dorsalis. **nu'clei nervo'rum crania'lium** [N A], groups of nerve cells in the central nervous system that are directly related to the cranial nerves. Called also *nuclei of cranial nerves.* **n. ner'vi facia'lis** [N A, B N A], the nucleus of origin of the motor fibers of the facial nerve. These fibers innervate the muscles of facial expression. Called also *n. of facial nerve.* **n. ner'vi facia'lis of Arnold,** colliculus facialis. **n. ner'vi hypoglos'si** [N A, B N A], the nucleus of origin of the hypoglossal nerve, situated in the medulla oblongata just anterolateral to the central canal and the caudal part of the fourth ventricle. Called also *n. of hypoglossal nerve.* **n. ner'vi oculomoto'rii** [N A, B N A], the nucleus of origin of the fibers of the oculomotor nerve, situated in the tegmentum of the mesencephalon just dorsomedial to the medial longitudinal fasciculus; one of its several variously named subdivisions gives rise to parasympathetic fibers of this nerve. Called also *n. of oculomotor nerve.* **n. ner'vi pneumogas'trici,** flocculus. **nu'clei ner'vi trigem'ini.** See *n. motorius nervi trigemini* and *n. sensorius superior nervi trigemini.* **n. ner'vi trochlea'ris** [N A, B N A], the nucleus of origin of the motor fibers of the trochlear nerve. It lies on the dorsal side of the medial longitudinal fasciculus toward the caudal end of the mesencephalon. Called also *n. of trochlear nerve.* **nu'clei ner'vi vestibula'ris** [B N A], nuclei vestibulares. **nu'clei ner'vi vestibulocochlea'ris** [N A], the nuclei of termination of the sensory fibers of the vestibular and cochlear divisions of the eighth cranial nerve. Called also *nuclei nervi acustici* [B N A], and *vestibulocochlear nuclei.* **nutrition n.,** macronucleus. **n. of oculomotor nerve,** n. nervi oculomotorii. **n. oliva'ris** [N A], a folded band of gray substance enclosing a white core (hilus nuclei olivaris), and producing the elevation on the medulla oblongata known as the olive. Called also *n. olivaris inferior* [B N A], and *olivary n.* **n. oliva'ris accesso'rius dorsa'lis** [N A, B N A], the band of gray substance that lies dorsal to the olivary nucleus. Called also *dorsal accessory olivary n.* **n. oliva'ris accesso'rius media'lis** [N A, B N A], the band of gray substance that lies medial to the olivary nucleus. Called also *medial accessory olivary n.* **n. oliva'ris infe'rior** [B N A], n. olivaris. **n. oliva'ris supe'rior** [B N A], n. dorsalis corporis trapezoidei. **olivary n.** 1. Nucleus olivaris. 2. Oliva. **olivary n., accessory, olivary n., dorsal accessory,** n. olivaris accessorius dorsalis. **olivary n., inferior,** n. olivaris. **olivary n., medial accessory,** n. olivaris accessorius medialis. **olivary n., superior,** n. dorsalis corporis trapezoidei. **n. of origin,** any collection of nerve cells giving origin to the fibers, or a part of the fibers, of a peripheral nerve. **nuclei of origin of cranial nerves, nu'clei ori'ginis nervo'rum cerebra'lium** [B N A], **nu'clei ori'ginis nervo'rum crania'lium** [N A], groups of nerve cells in the central nervous system, the axons of which exit as the efferent fibers of various cranial nerves. **Pander's n.,** a lentil-shaped mass of gray matter between the tegmental nucleus and the corresponding corpus albicans, beneath the optic thalamus. **paraventricular n. of hypothalamus, n. paraventricula'ris hypothal'ami** [N A], a group of nerve cell bodies in the anterior or supraoptic part of the hypothalamus. **Perlia's n.,** an oculomotor center situated in the cinerea below the aqueduct of Sylvius. **phenanthrene n.,** cholane n. **Piorry's n.,** an area of dullness to percussion on the back over the liver. **polymorphic n.,** a cell nucleus that assumes an irregular form or splits up into more or less completely separated lobes, such as the nuclei in the polymorphonuclear leukocytes. **pontine nuclei, nu'clei pon'tis** [N A, B N A], groups of nerve cell bodies within the pars basilaris of the pons upon which the corticopontine fibers synapse, and which in turn contribute axons to the middle

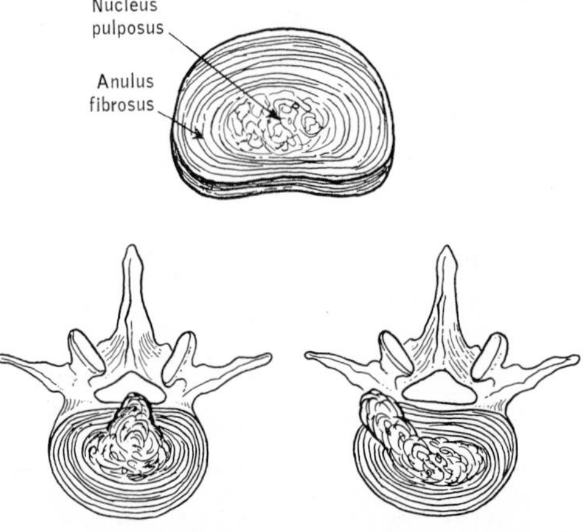

Nucleus pulposus. (Finneson.) *Upper:* normal intervertebral disk. *Lower:* intervertebral disks with central (*left*) and lateral (*right*) herniation of the nucleus pulposus.

cerebellar peduncle. **n. poste′rior hypothal′ami** [N A], a group of nerve cell bodies in the posterior, mamillary part of the hypothalamus, above the nucleus of the mamillary body. Called also *posterior n. of hypothalamus.* **n. pulpo′sus dis′ci intervertebra′lis** [N A, B N A], **pulpy n.,** a semifluid mass of fine white and elastic fibers that forms the central portion of an intervertebral disk. It has been regarded as the persistent remains of the embryonic notochord. **pyramidal n.,** n. olivaris accessorius medialis. **n. radi′cis descenden′tis ner′vi trigem′ini** [B N A], n. tractus mesencephalicus nervi trigemini. **red n.,** n. ruber. **reproductive n.,** micronucleus, def. 1. **reticular n., lateral,** n. lateralis. **n. reticula′ris tegmen′ti,** n. ruber. **ring nuclei, ringed nuclei,** ringlike nuclei observed in the polymorphonuclear leukocytes in the stools of patients with bacillary dysentery. **Roller's n.,** a collection of cells near the hilus of the olivary nucleus. **Roller's central n.,** a nucleus in the medulla oblongata, near the raphe and between the posterior longitudinal fasciculus and the lemniscus. **n. of roof of cerebellum,** n. fastigii. **n. ru′ber** [N A, B N A], an oval mass of gray matter (pink in fresh specimens) located in the anterior part of the tegmentum and extending into the posterior part of the subthalamic region. It receives fibers mainly from the superior cerebellar peduncle. Called also *red n.* **sacral n.,** a mass of gray substance in the spinal cord opposite the origin of the second and third sacral nerves. **n. of Sappey,** n. ruber. **Schwalbe's n.,** the medial vestibular nucleus. See *nuclei vestibulares.* **Schwann's n.,** the nucleus of a cell of Schwann. **segmentation n.,** the fertilization nucleus after cleavage has begun. **n. senso′rius infe′rior ner′vi trigem′ini,** n. tractus spinalis nervi trigemini. **n. senso′rius supe′rior ner′vi trigem′ini** [N A], the nucleus of termination of afferent fibers of the trigeminal nerve which carry impulses causing sensations of touch and pressure, located in the middle of the pons in the dorsal part, just lateral to the fibers of the trigeminal nerve. **sensory n.,** the nucleus of termination of the afferent (sensory) fibers of a peripheral nerve. **sensory n. of trigeminal nerve, lower,** n. tractus spinalis nervi trigemini. **sensory n. of trigeminal nerve, superior,** n. sensorius superior nervi trigemini. **shadow n.,** a cell nucleus that does not stain and appears as a faint shadow under the microscope. **Siemerling's n.,** one of the anterior group of oculomotor nuclei in the cinerea under the aqueduct of Sylvius. **n. of solitary tract,** n. tractus solitarii. **somatic n.,** macronucleus. **sperm n.,** the male pronucleus. **spherical n.,** n. globosus. **n. of spinal tract of trigeminal nerve,** n. tractus spinalis nervi trigemini. **Spitzka's n.,** one of a group of oculomotor nuclei in the cinerea below the aqueduct of Sylvius. **Staderini's n.,** n. intercalatus. **Stilling's n.** 1. Nucleus nervi hypoglossi. 2. Nucleus thoracicus. 3. Nucleus ruber. **Stilling's sacral n.,** sacral n. **striate n.,** corpus striatum. **subependymal n.,** the internal nucleus of the auditory nerve. **subthalamic n., n. subthalam′icus** [N A], a biconvex mass of gray matter on the medial side of the junction of the internal capsule and the basis pedunculi, forming a part of the descending pathway from the corpus striatum. Called also *n. hypothalamicus* and *corpus Luysi* [B N A]. **superior n.,** the superior vestibular nucleus. See *nuclei vestibulares.* **supraoptic n. of hypothalamus, n. supraop′ticus hypothal′ami** [N A], a group of closely packed nerve cell bodies overlying the beginning of the optic tract. **n. taeniaefor′mis,** corpus amygdaloideum. **n. tec′ti,** n. fastigii. **tegmental n.** 1. Nucleus fastigii. 2. Nucleus ruber. **n. tegmen′ti.** 1. Nucleus fastigii. 2. (Pl.) [N A, B N A] Various groups of nerve cell bodies situated within the tegmentum of the pons and mesencephalon. Called also *nuclei of tegmentum.* **terminal nuclei, nu′clei termina′les** [B N A], **nu′clei terminatio′nis nervo′rum crania′lium** [N A], **nuclei of termination of cranial nerves,** groups of nerve cells within the central nervous system upon which the axons of primary afferent neurons of various cranial nerves synapse. **n. of thalamus, anterior,** n. anterior thalami. **nuclei of thalamus, intralaminar,** nuclei intralaminares thalami. **n. of thalamus, lateral,** n. lateralis thalami. **n. of thalamus, medial,** n. medialis thalami. **n. thorac′icus** [N A], a group of cells in the posterior gray column of the spinal cord, running longitudinally from the seventh and eighth cervical masses to the level of the second lumbar nerve. Called also *n. dorsalis* [*Stillingi, Clarkii*] [B N A]. **n. trac′tus mesencephal′icus ner′vi trigem′ini** [N A], a nucleus situated in the lateral wall of the rostral portion of the fourth ventricle and the lateral part of the gray matter surrounding the cerebral aqueduct. It contains the cells of origin of the fibers of the mesencephalic tract of the trigeminal nerve and is the only place where the cell bodies of primary sensory neurons are found within the central nervous system. Called also *n. radicis descendentis nervi trigemini* [B N A], and *n. of mesencephalic tract of trigeminal nerve.* **n. trac′tus solita′rii** [N A, B N A], the nucleus of termination of the visceral afferent fibers of the facial, glossopharyngeal, and vagus nerves, which are in the tractus solitarius. It surrounds the tractus solitarius, and is joined, at the caudal end, with its fellow of the opposite side. Called also *n. of solitary tract.* **n. trac′tus spina′lis ner′vi trigem′ini** [N A, B N A], the part of the gelatinous substance of the spinal cord in the upper cervical segments, and its continuation into the medulla oblongata to a midpontine level, in which the fibers of the spinal tract of the trigeminal nerve synapse. Called also *n. of spinal tract of trigeminal nerve.* **triangular n.,** n. cuneatus. **nuclei of trigeminal nerve.** See *n. motorius nervi trigemini, n. sensorius superior nervi trigemini,* and *n. tractus spinalis nervi trigemini.* **n. of trochlear nerve,** n. nervi trochlearis. **trophic n.,** macronucleus. **tuberal nuclei, nu′clei tubera′les** [N A], **nu′clei tu′beres.** See *n. dorsomedialis hypothalami* and *n. ventromedialis hypothalami.* **vagoglossopharyngeal n.,** n. ambiguus. **n. of vagus nerve, dorsal,** n. dorsalis nervi vagi. **ventral n. of thalamus,** n. ventralis thalami. **ventral n. of thalamus, anterior,** n. ventralis thalami anterior. **ventral n. of thalamus, intermediate,** n. ventralis thalami intermedius. **ventral n. of thalamus, posterior,** n. ventralis thalami posterior. **ventral n. of trapezoid body,** n. ventralis corporis trapezoidei. **n. ventra′lis cor′poris trapezoi′dei** [N A], a group of nerve cell bodies intermingled with the fibers of the trapezoid body. They contribute fibers to the lateral lemniscus. Called also *ventral n. of trapezoid body.* **n. ventra′lis thal′ami** [N A], the ventral part of the lateral nucleus of the thalamus. **n. ventra′lis thal′ami ante′rior** [N A], the anterior part of the ventral nucleus of the thalamus, which receives fibers from the globus pallidus and sends other fibers back to the corpus striatum. **n. ventra′lis thal′ami interme′dius** [N A], the intermediate part of the ventral nucleus of the thalamus, which receives fibers from the superior cerebellar peduncle and sends fibers to the motor cortex and to the premotor cortex of the frontal lobe. **n. ventra′lis thal′ami poste′rior** [N A], the posterior part of the ventral nucleus of the thalamus, which is the site of termination of the main ascending sensory pathways. **ventromedial n. of hypothalamus, n. ventromedia′lis hypothal′ami** [N A], the ventral one of two main groups of nerve cell bodies found in the middle, tuberal region of the hypothalamus. **vesicular n.,** a form of cell nucleus the membrane of which stains deeply, while the central part is rather pale. **vestibular nuclei, nu'clei vestibula'res** [N A], the four cellular masses in the floor of the fourth ventricle, the superior, lateral, medial, and inferior vestibular nuclei, in which the short ascending and longer descending branches of the pars vestibularis nervi octavi terminate. Called also *nuclei nervi vestibularis* [B N A]. **vestibulocochlear nuclei,** nuclei nervi vestibulocochlearis. **Voit's n.,** a cerebellar nucleus accessory to the corpus dentatum. **Westphal's n.,** a group of relatively small nerve cells in the rostral part of the nucleus of the oculomotor nerve. **white n.,** hilus nuclei olivaris. **yolk n.,** a special area of the cytoplasm of an ovum in which the synthetic activities leading to the accumulation of food supplies in the oocyte are apparently initiated. Called also *vitelline body, Balbiani's body,* and *Balbiani's n.* **zygote n.,** fertilization n.

nuclide (nu'klīd). A species of atom characterized by the charge, mass, number, and quantum state of its nucleus, and capable of existing for a measurable lifetime (generally greater than 10^{-10} sec.). Thus nuclear isomers are separate nuclides, but promptly decaying excited nuclear states and unstable intermediates in nuclear reactions are not so considered.

nudomania (nu″do-ma'ne-ah) [L. *nudus* unclothed, bare + Gr. *mania* madness]. An abnormal devotion to going naked.

nudophobia (nu″do-fo'be-ah) [L. *nudus* unclothed, bare + Gr. *phobos* fear + *-ia*]. An abnormal aversion to being unclothed.

Nuel's space (ne-elz') [Jean Pierre *Nuel*, Belgian oculist, 1847–1920]. See under *space.*

Nuhn's glands (noonz) [Anton *Nuhn*, German anatomist, 1814–1889]. See under *gland.*

nullipara (nul-lip'ah-rah) [L. *nullus* none + *parere* to bring forth, produce]. A woman who has never borne a viable child. Also written Para 0.

nulliparity (nul″ĭ-par'ĭ-te). The condition or fact of being nulliparous.

nulliparous (nul-lip'ah-rus). Having never given birth to a viable infant.

nullisomatic (nul″ĭ-so-mat'ik). Lacking one pair of chromosomes.

number (num'ber). A symbol, as a figure or word, expressive of a certain value or of a specified quantity determined by count. **acetyl n.,** the number of milligrams of KOH necessary to neutralize the acetic acid saponified from 1 gram of acetylated fat. It represents the extent to which hydroxyl groups are present. **acid n.,** the number of milligrams of potassium hydroxide necessary to neutralize the free fatty acids in 1 gram of fat. It represents a measure of the amount of free fatty acids in the fat. **atomic n.,** the whole number representing the number of units of positive charge on the nucleus of an atom. **Avogadro's n.,** the number of particles, real or imaginary, of the type specified by the chemical formula of a certain substance in one gram mole of the substance; the value currently assigned to the number is 6.02246×10^{23}. **Brinell hardness n.,** an expression of the hardness of a substance determined by use of the Brinell tester. **Hehner n.,** the percentage of fatty acids not volatile with steam, obtainable from a fat. **Hittorf n.,** the portion of the current conducted by an ion in electrolysis; called also *transport n.* **Hübl n.,** iodine n. **hydrogen n.,** the amount of hydrogen that fats can take up. It represents the amount of unsaturated fatty acids present. **iodine n.,** the amount of iodine which 1 gram of the fat can take up. It indicates the amount of unsaturated fatty acids present in the fat. **isotopic n.,** the number which added to twice the atomic number gives the atomic weight. **Knoop hardness n.,** an expression of the hardness (indentation) of a material determined by use of a special indenting tool. **Loschmidt's n.** 1. Avogadro's number. 2. The number of molecules per unit volume of an ideal gas at 0°C. and normal pressure. **mass n.,** the whole number nearest to the atomic weight of an element or isotope. **polar n.,** the number of valences (positive or negative) possessed by an atom in any particular compound. **Polenske n.,** the number of cubic centimeters of tenth normal KOH required to neutralize the insoluble, volatile fatty acids from 5 Gm. of the fat. **Reichert-Meissl n.,** the number of cubic centimeters of tenth normal KOH required to neutralize the soluble volatile fatty acids distilled from 5 Gm. of fat after it has been saponified with KOH and then made acid with H_3PO_4 or H_2SO_4. **Reynold's n.,** the velocity of flow of a fluid multiplied by the diameter of the vessel and divided by the kinematic viscosity of the circulating fluid. **saponification n.,** the number of milligrams of potassium hydroxide required to neutralize the fatty acids in 1 gram of a fat or oil. It indicates the average size of the fatty acid molecules or the amount of the lower fatty acids present. **thiocyanogen n.,** the amount of thiocyanogen absorbed by a fat or oil. **transport n.,** Hittorf number. **wave n.,** in light waves the reciprocal of the wavelength expressed as a fraction of a centimeter.

numbness (num'nes). A paresthesia of touch insensibility in a part.

nummiform (num'ĭ-form) [L. *nummus* coin + *forma* form]. Shaped like a coin or round disk.

nummular (num'u-lar) [L. *nummularis*]. 1. Coin shaped. 2. Made up of round, flat disks. 3. Piled, like coins, in a rouleau.

nummulation (num″u-la'shun). The assumption of a nummular form.

numorphan (nu-mor'fan). Trade mark for preparations of oxymorphone hydrochloride.

nunnation (nun-a'shun) [Heb. *nun* letter N]. The too frequent use of *n* sounds, or the nasalizing of sounds or words.

nupercaine (nu'per-kān). Trade mark for preparations of dibucaine.

nuptiality (nup-shal'ĭ-te) [L. *nuptus* married]. The proportion of marriages to the population.

nurse (nurs). A person who takes care of the sick, wounded, or enfeebled, especially one who makes a profession of it. **charge n.,** a nurse who is in charge of a hospital ward. **child's n.,** a nurse who has the care of an infant or young child. **community n., district n.,** the name given in Great Britain to a visiting nurse, from the fact that such a nurse was placed in charge of each one of the districts into which the city or community was divided. **dry n.,** a baby's nurse who does not suckle the baby. **general duty n.,** a nurse who is prepared to do any sort of nursing duty. **graduate n.,** a nurse who is a graduate of a nursing school. **head n.,** a nurse who heads the nursing staff of a hospital. **hospital n.,** a nurse who serves in a hospital ward. **monthly n.,** a nurse who attends confinement cases. **practical n.,** a nurse who has had practical experience in nursing but is not a graduate of a nursing school. **private n.,** a nurse who attends an individual patient. **private duty n.,** a nurse who does not belong to the hospital staff, but is prepared to care for an individual patient in the hospital. **probationer n.,** a person who has entered a school of nursing and is under observation to determine her fitness for the nursing profession. **public health n.,** a graduate nurse employed in a community to safeguard the health of its people. She gives care to the sick in their homes, promotes health by teaching families how to keep well, and assists in the prevention of disease. **Queen's n.,** in Great Britain, a district nurse who has been trained at or in accordance with the regulations of the Queen Victoria Jubilee Institute for Nurses. **registered n.,** a graduate nurse who has been registered and licensed to practice by a State Board of Nurse Examiners or other state authority. Such a nurse is legally entitled to place the letters R.N. after her name. **school n.,** a trained nurse whose duties are to visit the elementary public schools and supplement the work of the physician in medical inspection of schools. **scrub n.,** a scrubbed-up operating-room nurse, wearing sterile gloves, who hands instruments to the operating surgeon. **special n.** 1. A private nurse. 2. A nurse who specializes in a particular class of cases. **student n.,** a woman who is a student in a hospital school of nursing. **trained n.,** a nurse who has been trained in and graduated from a nursing school. **visiting n.,** a trained nurse, employed by an association whose duties consist in visiting and caring for the sick poor in their homes. **wet n.,** a woman who suckles the infants of others.

nursery (nur′ser-e). The department in a hospital where newborn infants are cared for. **day n.,** an institution devoted to the care of young children during the day.

Nussbaum's bracelet, narcosis (no͞os′-bowmz) [Johann Nepomuk von *Nussbaum*, German surgeon, 1829–1890]. See under *bracelet* and *narcosis*.

Nussbaum's experiment (no͞os′bowmz) [Moritz *Nussbaum*, German histologist, 1850–1915]. See under *experiment*.

nut (nut) [L. *nux;* Gr. *karyon*]. A seed element, as of various trees, usually enclosed in a coating of variable hardness. **betel n.,** areca.

nutation (nu-ta′shun) [L. *nutatio*]. The act of nodding; a to-and-fro movement.

nutatory (nu′tah-tor″e) [L. *nutare* to keep nodding, to sway]. Nodding.

nutrescin (nu-tres′in). A substance supposed to be split off from the bioplasm molecule and to supply the nutrition of the cell.

nutriceptor (nu″trĭ-sep′tor). A receptor or side chain which combines with nutritive matter to serve the nutrition of a cell.

nutrient (nu′tre-ent) [L. *nutriens*]. 1. Nourishing; affording nutriment. 2. A substance which affects the nutritive or metabolic processes of the body. **secondary n.,** a substance which stimulates the intestinal microflora to synthesize other nutrients.

nutrilite (nu′trĭ-līt). Any organic substance which in minute amounts is important in the nutrition of a microorganism.

nutriment (nu′trĭ-ment) [L. *nutrimentum*]. Nourishment; nutritious material.

nutriology (nu″tre-ol′o-je). The science of nutrition; the study of foods and their use in diet and therapy.

nutrition (nu-trish′un) [L. *nutritio*]. 1. The process of assimilating food. 2. Nutriment. **adequate n., optimal n.** See under *diet*.

nutritional (nu-trish′un-al). Relating to or affecting nutrition.

nutritionist (nu-trish′un-ist). A person who specializes in food and nutrition.

nutritious (nu-trish′us) [L. *nutritius*]. Affording nourishment.

nutritive (nu′trĭ-tiv). Pertaining to nutrition.

nutritorium (nu″trĭ-to′re-um) [L. *nutritorius* nourishing]. The apparatus of nutrition in the body.

nutriture (nu′trĭ-tūr″). The status of the body in relation to nutrition, generally or in regard to a specific nutrient, such as protein.

nutrix (nu′triks). A wet nurse.

nutrose (nu′trōs). Neutral casein sodium; a dry food preparation of milk for the use of invalids.

Nuttallia (nŭ-tal′e-ah) [George H. F. *Nuttall*, biologist, Cambridge University, 1862–1937]. Small protozoan parasites found in the red blood corpuscles of horse and dogs. **N. e′qui,** a species causing hemoglobinuric fever of horses in South Africa. It is probably transmitted by the tick, *Rhinicephalus everti*. Called also *Babesia equi* and *B. caballi*. **N. gibso′ni,** a species found in dogs.

nuttalliosus (nŭ-tal″e-o′sis). Infection with Nuttallia.

nux (nuks), gen. *nu′cis* [L.]. Nut. **n. moscha′ta,** myristica. **n. vom′ica,** the dried ripe seed of *Strychnos nux-vomica*, containing not less than 1.15 per cent of strychnine: used as a tincture, extract, or fluidextract, for its bitter tonic properties.

Nv. Abbreviation for *naked vision*.

nyacyne (ni′ah-sīn). Neomycin.

nyad (ni′ad). The nymph form of certain arthropods.

nyctalbuminuria (nik″tal-bu″mĭ-nu′re-ah). Noctalbuminuria.

nyctalgia (nik-tal′je-ah) [*nycto-* + *-algia*]. Pain that occurs in sleep only.

nyctalope (nik′tah-lōp). A person affected with nyctalopia.

nyctalopia (nik″tah-lo′pe-ah) [Gr. *nyktalōps*]. 1. Night blindness (Galen); failure or imperfection of vision at night or in a dim light, with good vision only on bright days (Heberden, 1767). 2. Less correctly, day blindness (Hippocrates), or hemeralopia, a condition in which the patient sees better in an obscure light than in bright sunlight.

nyctaphonia (nik″tah-fo′ne-ah) [*nycto-* + *aphonia*]. Loss of voice during the night.

nycterine (nik′ter-in) [Gr. *nykterinos* by night]. 1. Occurring at night. 2. Obscure.

nycterohemeral (nik″ter-o-hem′er-al). Nyctohemeral.

nycto- (nik′to) [Gr. *nyx* night]. Combining form denoting relationship to night or to darkness.

nyctohemeral (nik″to-hem′er-al) [*nycto-* + Gr. *hēmera* day]. Pertaining to both night and day.

nyctophilia (nik″to-fil′e-ah) [*nycto-* + Gr. *philein* to love]. Abnormal preference for night over day.

nyctophobia (nik″to-fo′be-ah) [*nycto-* + Gr. *phobein* to be affrighted by]. Morbid dread of darkness.

nyctophonia (nik″to-fo′ne-ah) [*nycto-* + Gr. *phōnē* voice]. Loss of voice during the day but not at night.

Nyctotherus (nik-toth′er-us) [Gr. "one who hunts at night"]. A genus of infusorian microparasites. *N. africa′nus* was found in large numbers in the cecum of a case of sleeping sickness. *N. cordifor′mis* occurs in the rectums of frogs and tadpoles. *N. fa′ba* has been found in the diarrheal discharges of the human subject. *N. gigan′tus*, a large species found in the intestines of a man in Germany. *N. ova′lis* occurs in the intestines of cockroaches.

nyctotyphlosis (nik″to-tif-lo′sis) [*nycto-* + Gr. *typhlōsis* blindness]. Nyctalopia.

nycturia (nik-tu′re-ah) [*nycto-* + Gr. *ouron* urine + *-ia*]. Frequent urination during the night, especially the passage of more urine at night than during the day.

N.Y.D. Abbreviation for *not yet diagnosed*.

nydrazid (ni′dra-zid). Trade mark for preparations of isoniazid.

Nylander's test (ni′lan-derz) [Claes Wilhelm Gabriel *Nylander*, Swedish chemist, 1835–1907]. See under *tests*.

nylidrin (nil′ĭ-drin). Chemical name: p-hydroxy-N-(1-methyl-3-phenylpropyl)norephedrine: used as a peripheral vasodilator.

nylon (ni′lon). A synthetic polymerized plastic which in fiber form is used as suture material.

nymph (nimf) [Gr. *nymphē* a bride]. A stage in the life cycle of certain arthropods, as the ticks, between the larva and the adult. A nymph resembles the adult in appearance.

nympha (nim′fah), pl. *nym′phae* [L.; Gr. *nymphē*]. Labium minus pudendi. **n. of Krause,** clitoris.

nymphae (nim′fe) [L.]. Plural of *nympha*.

nymphectomy (nim-fek′to-me) [*nympha* + Gr. *ektomē* excision]. Excision of the nymphae.

nymphitis (nim-fi′tis). Inflammation of the nymphae.

nympho- (nim′fo) [L. *nympha:* Gr. *nymphē*]. Combining form denoting relationship to the nymphae, or labia minora.

nymphocaruncular (nim″fo-kah-rung′ku-lar). Pertaining to the labia minora and the caruncula hymenalis.

nymphohymeneal (nim″fo-hi″mĕ-ne′al). Pertaining to the labia minora and the hymen.

nympholepsy (nim′fo-lep″se) [*nympho-* + Gr. *lēpsis* seizure]. Ecstatic frenzy; morbid exaltation.

nymphomania (nim″fo-ma′ne-ah) [*nympho-* + Gr. *mania* madness]. Exaggerated sexual desire in a female.

nymphomaniac (nim″fo-ma′ne-ak). 1. Affected with nymphomania. 2. One who is affected with nymphomania.

nymphoncus (nim-fong′kus) [*nympho-* + Gr. *onkos* mass, bulk]. Swelling of the nymphae.

nymphotomy (nim-fot′o-me) [*nympho-* + Gr. *tomē* a cutting]. Surgical incision of the nymphae or clitoris.

Nyssorhynchus (nis″o-ring′kus) [Gr. *nyssa* prick + *rhynchos* snout]. A genus of anopheline mosquitoes, several species of which act as carriers of the malarial parasite in tropical America.

nystagmic (nis-tag′mik). Pertaining to or characterized by nystagmus.

nystagmiform (nis-tag′mĭ-form). Nystagmoid.

nystagmograph (nis-tag′mo-graf) [*nystagmus* + Gr. *graphein* to write]. An instrument for recording the movements of the eyeball in nystagmus.

nystagmoid (nis-tag′moid). Resembling nystagmus.

nystagmus (nis-tag′mus) [Gr. *nystagmos* drowsiness, from *nystazein* to nod]. An involuntary rapid movement of the eyeball, which may be horizontal, vertical, rotatory, or mixed, i.e., of two varieties. **aural n.,** nystagmus due to disturbances in the labyrinth: the eye movement is jerky. **caloric n.** See *Bárány's sign.* **Cheyne's n.,** a peculiar rhythmical eye movement resembling Cheyne-Stokes respiration in its rhythm. **darkness n.,** darkness tremor. **disjunctive n.,** nystagmus in which the eyes swing toward and away from each other. **dissociated n.,** nystagmus in which the movements in the two eyes are dissimilar. **end-position n.,** nystagmus occurring at extremes of gaze. **fixation n.,** nystagmus which appears only on gazing fixedly at an object. **head n.,** an oscillatory motion of the head of an animal which occurs when it is rotated. **jerking n.,** rhythmical n. **labyrinthine n.,** vestibular n. **latent n.,** nystagmus which occurs only when one eye is covered. **lateral n.,** nystagmus in which the movement of the eyes is from side to side. **miner's n.,** an occupation neurosis of the eyes peculiar to miners. **ocular n.,** nystagmus due to eye disease. **optokinetic n.,** nystagmus induced by looking at a moving object. **oscillating n.,** undulatory n. **paretic n.,** a false nystagmus occurring when there is a weakness of the ocular muscles. **pendular n.,** undulatory n. **railroad n.,** optokinetic n. **resilient n.,** rhythmical n. **retraction n.,** a backward retraction of the eyeball occurring on attempted movement of the eye; a sign of cerebral tumor. **rhythmical n.,** nystagmus which consists of a slow movement in one direction, followed by a rapid return movement in the opposite direction. Called also *resilient n.* and *jerking n.* **rotatory n.,** nystagmus in which the movement is about the visual axis. **undulatory n.,** one which consists of to-and-fro movements of equal velocity. Called also *vibratory n.* and *oscillating n.* **unilateral n.,** nystagmus manifest in only one eye. **vertical n.,** an up-and-down movement of the eyes. **vestibular n.,** nystagmus due to vestibular disturbance. **vibratory n.,** undulatory n. **visual n.,** nystagmus characterized by smooth pendulum-like movement.

nystagmus-myoclonus (nis-tag′mus-mi-ok′lo-nus). A rare congenital condition in which there is nystagmus together with abnormal involuntary movements of the extremities and trunk.

nystatin (nis′tah-tin). An antibiotic substance produced by the growth of *Streptomyces noursei:* used in treatment of infections caused by *Candida albicans.*

nystaxis (nis-tak′sis) [Gr.]. Nystagmus.

Nysten's law (ne-stahz′) [Pierre Hubert *Nysten,* French pediatrician, 1774–1817]. See under *law.*

nyxis (nik′sis) [Gr. "pricking"]. Puncture, or paracentesis.

O

O. 1. Chemical symbol for *oxygen.* 2. Abbreviation for L. *oculus,* eye; *octarius,* pint; *opening.*

O. A symbol for the nonmotile strain of an organism. Cf. *H.*

o-. An abbreviation for *ortho-.*

O_2. 1. Symbol for the diatomic gas, oxygen. 2. Symbol for *both eyes.*

O_3. Symbol for *ozone.*

oak (ōk). A cupuliferous tree of the genus *Quercus.* The bark of all species contains a large proportion of tannin. **dyers' o.,** *Quercus lusitanica* affords nutgall. **poison o.,** *Rhus toxicodendron.*

oakum (o′kum). Prepared fiber from old ropes: formerly used in making surgical dressings.

oarialgia (o″a-re-al′je-ah) [Gr. *ōarion* little egg + *-algia*]. Pain in the ovary; ovarialgia.

oaric (o-a′rik) [Gr. *ōarion* little egg]. Pertaining to the ovary; ovarian.

oario-. For words beginning thus, see those beginning *ovario-.*

oarium (o-a′re-um), pl. *oa′ria* [L.; Gr. *ōarion* little egg]. An ovary.

oasis (o-a′sis), pl. *oa′ses* [Gr. "a fertile islet in a desert"]. An island or spot of healthy tissue in a diseased area.

oath (ōth). A solemn declaration or affirmation. **o. of Hippocrates, hippocratic o.** See under *Hippocrates.*

OB. Abbreviation for *obstetrics.*

ob- [L. *ob* against]. Prefix signifying against, in front of, etc.

obcecation (ob″se-ka′shun). Incomplete blindness.

obdormition (ob″dor-mish′un) [L. *obdormitio*]. Numbness and anesthesia of a part resulting from pressure on a nerve.

obducent (ob-du′sent) [L. *obducere* to draw over, to cover]. Serving as a cover; covering.

obduction (ob-duk′shun) [L. *obductio*]. A medicolegal autopsy.

O'Beirne's sphincter, tube (o-birnz′) [James *O'Beirne,* Irish surgeon, 1786–1862]. See under *sphincter* and *tube.*

obeliac (o-be′le-ak). Pertaining to the obelion.

obeliad (o-be′le-ad). Toward the obelion.

obelion (o-be′le-on) [*dim.* of Gr. *obelos* a spit]. A point on the sagittal suture where it is crossed by a line which connects the parietal foramina.

Ober's operation, sign, test (o′berz) [Frank R. *Ober,* Boston orthopedic surgeon, born 1881]. See under *operation* and *tests.*

Obermayer's test (o′ber-mi″erz) [Fritz *Ober-*

mayer, physiologic chemist in Vienna, 1861–1925]. See under *tests.*

Obermeier's spirillum (o′ber-mi″erz) [Otto Hugo Franz *Obermeier*, German physician, 1843–1873]. *Borrelia recurrentis.*

Obermüller's test (o′ber-mil-erz) [Kuno *Obermüller*, German physician, born 1861]. See under *tests.*

Oberst's method, operation (o′bersts) [Maximilian *Oberst*, German surgeon, 1849–1925]. See under *method* and *operation.*

Obersteiner-Redlich area, zone (o′ber-sti″-ner-red′likh) [Heinrich *Obersteiner*, Austrian neurologist, 1847–1922; Emil *Redlich*, Austrian neurologist, 1866–1930]. See under *area.*

obese (o-bēs′) [L. *obesus*]. Excessively fat.

obesitas (o-be′sĭ-tas) [L.]. Obesity.

obesity (o-bēs′ĭ-te) [L. *obesitas*]. An increase in body weight beyond the limitation of skeletal and physical requirement, as the result of an excessive accumulation of fat in the body. **alimentary o.,** exogenous obesity. **endogenous o.,** obesity due to metabolic (endocrine) abnormalities. **exogenous o.,** obesity due to overeating. **hyperinsulinar o.,** obesity due to overactivity of insulin secretion, associated with hypoglycemia and increased appetite. **hyperinterrenal o.,** obesity associated with hyperfunction of the adrenal cortex. **hyperplasmic o.,** obesity due to increase in the body protoplasm, as distinguished from that due to accumulation of fat and water. **hypogonad o.,** obesity associated with hypofunction of the gonads. **hypoplasmic o.,** obesity due to increase of fat and water and marked by decrease of the body protoplasm. **hypothyroid o.,** obesity due to hypothyroidism. **simple o.,** exogenous o.

obesogenous (o-bēs-oj′e-nus). Producing or causing obesity.

obex (o′beks) [L. "barrier"]. [N A, B N A] The thickening of the ependyma at the caudal angle of the roof of the fourth ventricle.

obfuscation (ob″fus-ka′shun) [L. *obfuscatio* a darkening]. The act of rendering or process of becoming obscure; a darkening.

objective (ob-jek′tiv) [L. *objectivus*]. 1. Perceptible to the external senses. 2. A result for whose achievement an effort is made. 3. The lens or system of lenses in a microscope (or telescope) that is nearest to the object under examination. **achromatic o.,** a microscope objective in which the chromatic aberration is corrected for light of two wavelengths and the spherical aberration is corrected for that of one wavelength. **apochromatic o.,** a microscope objective in which the chromatic aberration is corrected for light of three wavelengths and the spherical aberration is corrected for that of two. **dry o.,** a microscope objective designed to be used without a liquid between its tip and the cover glass over the specimen. **fluorite o.,** a microscope objective in which some of the lenses are made from fluorite instead of glass. **immersion o.,** a microscope objective designed to have its tip and the cover glass over the specimen connected by a liquid instead of by air. The liquid may be water (water immersion) or a specially prepared oil (oil immersion). **semiapochromatic o.,** a microscope objective in which the correction of chromatic and spherical aberrations is between those of the achromatic and apochromatic objectives.

obligate (ob′lĭ-gāt) [L. *obligatus*]. Necessary; compulsory; not facultative.

oblique (ob-lēk′, ob-līk′) [L. *obliquus*]. Slanting; inclined; between a horizontal and a perpendicular direction.

obliquimeter (ob″lĭ-kwim′e-ter) [*oblique* + Gr. *metron* measure]. An instrument for measuring the obliquity of the pelvic brim.

obliquity (ob-lik′wĭ-te). The state of being oblique, or slanting. **Litzmann's o.,** inclination of the fetal head so that the posterior parietal bone presents to the parturient canal. **Nägele's o.,** the position of the fetal head in which the anterior parietal bone presents to the parturient canal, the biparietal diameter being oblique in relation to the brim of the pelvis. **o. of pelvis,** inclination of the pelvis. **Roederer's o.,** the position of the fetal head with the occiput presenting at the brim of the pelvis.

obliquus (ob-li′kwus) [L.]. Oblique.

obliteration (ob-lit″er-a′shun) [L. *obliteratio*]. Complete removal, whether by disease and degeneration or by a surgical operation. **cortical o.,** cortical achromia; a condition in which the cerebral cortex is marked by areas in which the ganglion cells have disappeared.

oblongatal (ob″long-ga′tal). Pertaining to the medulla oblongata.

obmutescence (ob″mu-tes′ens) [L. *obmutescere* to be dumb]. Loss of voice.

obnubilation (ob-nu″bĭ-la′shun). A clouded state of the mind.

O'Brien akinesia (o-bri′en) [Cecil Starling *O'Brien*, American ophthalmologist, born 1889]. See under *akinesia.*

observerscope (ob-zer′ver-skōp). A form of endoscope with two branches, enabling two persons to inspect the same spot at the same time.

obsession (ob-sesh′un) [L. *obsessio*]. Preoccupation with an idea which morbidly dominates the mind constantly, suggesting irrational action.

obsessive (ob-ses′siv). Pertaining to or characterized by obsession.

obsessive-compulsive (ob-ses″siv-kom-pul′-siv). Marked by compulsion to repetitively perform certain acts, or carry out certain rituals.

obsidional (ob-sid′e-o-nal) [L. *obsidium* siege]. Occurring in trench warfare.

obsolescence (ob″so-les′ens) [L. *obsolescere* to grow old]. The cessation or the beginning of the cessation of any physiologic process.

obsolete (ob′so-lēt) [L. *obsoletus*, from *obsolere* to go out of use]. Indistinct; faded; gone out of use.

obstetric, obstetrical (ob-stet′rik, ob-stet′re-kal) [L. *obstetricius*]. Pertaining to obstetrics.

obstetrician (ob″stĕ-trish′un) [L. *obstetrix* midwife]. One who practices obstetrics.

obstetrics (ob-stet′riks) [L. *obstetricia*]. That branch of surgery which deals with the management of pregnancy, labor, and the puerperium.

obstipation (ob″stĭ-pa′shun) [L. *obstipatio*]. Intractable constipation.

obstruction (ob-struk′shun) [L. *obstructio*]. 1. The act of blocking or clogging. 2. The state or condition of being clogged. **aortic o.,** adhesion or thickening of the cusps of the aortic valves, obstructing the flow of blood from the left ventricle into the aorta. **false colonic o.** See *Ogilvie's syndrome*, under *syndrome.* **intestinal o.,** any hindrance to the passage of the intestinal contents.

obstruent (ob′stroo-ent) [L. *obstruens*]. 1. Causing obstruction or blocking. 2. Any agent or agency that causes obstruction.

obtund (ob-tund′) [L. *obtundere*]. To render dull or blunt; to render less acute.

obtundent (ob-tun′dent) [L. *obtundens*]. 1. Having the power to dull sensibility or to soothe pain. 2. A soothing or partially anesthetic medicine.

obturation (ob″tu-ra′shun). The act of closing or occluding; a form of intestinal obstruction.

obturator (ob′tu-ra″tor) [L.]. A disk or plate, natural or artificial, which closes an opening, such as a prosthetic appliance used to close a congenital or acquired opening in the palate. **Cripps's o.,** an instrument for closing a gastric fistula.

obtuse (ob-tūs′) [L. *obtusus*]. 1. Blunt; dull. 2. Having a dull intellect.

obtusion (ob-tu′zhun) [L. *obtusio*]. Morbid bluntness or dullness of sensibility.

O.C. Abbreviation for *occlusocervical.*

occalcarine (ok-kal′kar-īn). Occipitocalcarine.

occipital (ok-sip′ĭ-tal) [L. *occipitalis*]. Pertaining to the occiput.

occipitalis (ok-sip″ĭ-ta′lis) [L.]. The posterior part of the occipitofrontalis muscle.

occipitalization (ok-sip″ĭ-tal-i-za′shun). Synostosis of the atlas with the occipital bone.

occipito-anterior (ok-sip″ĭ-to-an-te′re-or). Having the occiput directed forward (designating the position of the fetus in relation to the maternal pelvis).

occipito-atloid (ok-sip″ĭ-to-at′loid). Pertaining to the occipital bone and the atlas.

occipito-axoid (ok-sip′ĭ-to-ak′soid). Pertaining to the occipital bone and the axis.

occipitobasilar (ok-sip″ĭ-to-bas′ĭ-ler). Pertaining to the occiput and the base of the skull.

occipitobregmatic (ok-sip″ĭ-to-breg-mat′ik). Pertaining to the occiput and the bregma.

occipitocalcarine (ok-sip″ĭ-to-kal′kar-īn). Both occipital and calcarine.

occipitocervical (ok-sip″ĭ-to-ser′vĭ-kal). Pertaining to the occiput and neck.

occipitofacial (ok-sip″ĭ-to-fa′shal). Pertaining to the occiput and the face.

occipitofrontal (ok-sip″ĭ-to-fron′tal). Pertaining to the occiput and the forehead.

occipitomastoid (ok-sip″ĭ-to-mas′toid). Pertaining to the occipital bone and the mastoid process.

occipitomental (ok-sip″ĭ-to-men′tal). Pertaining to the occiput and the chin.

occipitoparietal (ok-sip″ĭ-to-pah-ri′e-tal). Pertaining to the occipital bones or lobes.

occipitoposterior (ok-sip″ĭ-to-pos-te′re-or). Having the occiput directed toward the back, or turned toward the sacrum (designating the position of the fetus in relation to the maternal pelvis).

occipitotemporal (ok-sip″ĭ-to-tem′po-ral). Pertaining to the occipital and the temporal bones.

occipitothalamic (ok-sip″ĭ-to-thah-lam′ik). Pertaining to the occipital lobe and thalamus.

occiput (ok′sĭ-put) [L.]. [N A, B N A] The back part of the head. Called also *o. cra′nii* and *o. of cranium.*

occlude (ŏ-klōōd′). To fit close together; to close tight, as to bring the mandibular teeth into contact with the teeth in the maxilla.

occlusal (ŏ-kloo′zal). Pertaining to closure; applied to the masticating surfaces of the premolar and molar teeth, or to the contacting surfaces of opposing occlusion rims, or designating a position toward the hypothetical plane passing between the mandibular and maxillary teeth when the jaws are brought into approximation.

occlusion (ŏ-kloo′zhun) [L. *occlusio*]. 1. The act of closure or state of being closed. 2. A state of molecular adhesion between a precipitate and a soluble substance or between a gas and a metal. 3. The relation of the maxillary and mandibular teeth when in functional contact during activity of the mandible. **abnormal o.,** malocclusion. **afunctional o.,** malocclusion which prevents mastication. **anatomic o.,** occlusion in which all the teeth are present and occlude normally according to the anatomical standard. **anterior o.,** anteroclusion. **balanced o.,** that in which the occlusal contact of the teeth on the working side of the jaw is accompanied by the harmonious contact of the teeth of the opposite (balancing) side. The occlusion of artificial teeth may be *mechanically balanced,* as on an articulator, without reference to physiologic considerations, or *physiologically balanced,* functioning in harmony with the temporomandibular joint and the neuromuscular system. **buccal o.,** the position of a posterior tooth when it is outside (buccal to) the line of occlusion. **capsular o.,** surgical closure of the perinephric capsule for the relief of floating kidney. **central o.,** centric o. **centric o.,** occlusion of the teeth when the jaws are closed and the mandible is in centric relation to the maxilla. **coronary o.,** obstruction to the flow of blood through an artery of the heart as the result of spasm of the vessel or the presence of a thrombus. **distal o.,** the position of a lower tooth when it is distal to its opposite number in the maxilla. **eccentric o.,** occlusion of the teeth when the lower jaw has moved from the centric position. **edge-to-edge o.,** occlusion in which the anterior maxillary and mandibular teeth meet along their incisal edges when the mandile is in centric position. **end-to-end o.,** edge-to-edge o. **enteromesenteric o.,** obstruction of blood vessels both of the mesentery and in the wall of the intestine. **functional o.,** such contact of the maxillary and mandibular teeth as will provide the highest efficiency in the centric position and during all excursive movements of the jaw that are essential to mastication, without producing trauma. **hyperfunctional o.,** traumatic o. **ideal o.,** normal o. **labial o.,** the position of an anterior tooth when it is outside (labial to) the line of occlusion. **lateral o.,** the occlusion of the teeth when the lower jaw is moved to the right or left of centric position. **lingual o.,** the position of a tooth when it is inside (lingual to) the line of occlusion. **mesial o.,** the position of a lower tooth when it is mesial to its opposite number in the maxilla. **neutral o.,** normal o. **normal o.,** the meeting of the teeth when they are in the normal lateral and anteroposterior position and relationship. **pathogenic o.,** an occlusal relationship that is capable of producing pathologic changes in the supporting tissues. **physiologic o.,** occlusion which is in harmony with the functioning of the temporomandibular joint and the neuromuscular system. **posterior o.,** posteroclusion. **postnormal o.,** distal o. **prenormal o.,** mesial o. **protrusive o.,** anteroclusion. **o. of pupil,** closure of the opening in the iris of the eye by formation of an opaque membrane. **retrusive o.,** posteroclusion. **traumagenic o.,** traumatogenic o. **traumatic o.,** occlusion in which the contact relation of the masticatory surfaces of the teeth is directly the result of trauma. **traumatogenic o.,** occlusion which, under biting pressure, produces injury to the periodontal tissues. **working o.,** the contact made between the teeth on the side toward which the mandible is moved.

occlusive (ŏ-kloo′siv). Pertaining to or effecting occlusion.

occlusocervical (ŏ-kloo″so-ser′vĭ-kal). Pertaining to the occlusal surface and the neck of a tooth.

occlusometer (ok″loo-som′e-ter). Gnathodynamometer.

occluso-rehabilitation (ŏ-kloo″zo-re″hah-bil″ĭ-ta′shun). The employment of procedures designed to restore the dentition to an optimal functional relationship.

occult (ŏ-kult′) [L. *occultus*]. Obscure; concealed from observation; difficult to be understood.

ocellus (o-sel′us) [L., dim. of *oculus* eye]. 1. A small simple eye in insects and other invertebrates. 2. One of the elements of a compound eye. 3. A roundish, eyelike patch of color.

Ochlerotatus (ok″ler-o-ta′tus). A genus of mosquitoes, species of which are regarded as transmitters of African horse sickness.

ochlesis (ok-le′sis) [Gr. *ochlēsis* crowding]. Any disease due to overcrowding.

ochlophobia (ok″lo-fo′be-ah) [Gr. *ochlos* crowd + *phobia*]. Morbid fear of crowds.

Ochoa (o-cho′ah), Severo. United States physician and biochemist, born 1905; co-winner, with Arthur Kornberg, of the Nobel prize in medicine and physiology for 1959, for work in the discovery of enzymes for producing nucleic acids artificially.

Ochrobium (o-kro′be-um). A genus of microorganisms of the family Siderocapsaceae, suborder Pseudomonadineae, order Pseudomonadales, occurring as ellipsoidal to rod-shaped cells partially surrounded by a marginal thickening heavily impregnated with iron, and contained in a delicate, transparent capsule. The type species is *O. tec'tum.*

ochrodermatosis (o″kro-der″mah-to′sis). A condition marked by yellowness of the skin.

ochrodermia (o″kro-der′me-ah) [Gr. *ōchros* pale, wan, especially pale yellow + *derma* skin + *-ia*]. Yellowness or paleness of the skin.

ochrometer (o-krom′e-ter) [Gr. *ōchros* paleness + *metron* measure]. An instrument for measuring the capillary blood pressure by registering the force necessary to compress a finger by a rubber balloon until blanching of the skin occurs.

Ochromyia (o″kro-mi′yah). A genus of flies. **O. anthropoph′aga,** a species of flies of Senegal whose larva, the cayor worm, attacks man.

ochronosis (o″kro-no′sis) [Gr. *ōchros* yellow + *nosos* disease]. A peculiar discoloration of certain tissues of the body, caused by the deposit of alkapton bodies as the result of a metabolic disorder. **exogenous o.,** ochronosis allegedly resulting from exposure to some noxious substance in the internal environment, such as phenol, trinitrophenol, or benzene derivatives. **ocular o.,** a condition characterized by symmetrical, semilunar or V-shaped accumulations of brown or gray pigment in the sclera, midway between the margin of the cornea and the inner or outer canthus. The eyelids and conjunctivae may also be affected.

ochronosus (o″kro-no′sus). Ochronosis.

ochronotic (o″kro-not′ik). Pertaining to, characterized by, or caused by ochronosis.

Ochsner's ring, solution, treatment (oks′nerz) [Albert John *Ochsner*, surgeon in Chicago, 1858–1925]. See under the nouns.

Ocimum (os′ĭ-mum). A genus of herbs. **O. ca′num,** a labiate herb of tropical America, from which a homeopathic preparation is derived.

octa- (ok′tah) [Gr. *oktō*, L. *octo* eight]. Combining form meaning eight.

octacosane (ok″tah-ko′sān). An aliphatic hydrocarbon, $C_{29}H_{60}$, extracted from plant waxes.

octacosanol (ok″tah-ko-sa′nol). A solid white alcohol, $C_{28}H_{57}OH$, from wheat oil and from the cuticular wax of apples.

octad (ok′tad). Any octavalent chemical element.

octadecanol (ok″tah-dek′ah-nol). An optically active alcohol, $C_{18}H_{35}OH$, from *Mycobacterium leprae.*

octamethyl pyrophosphoramide (ok″tah-meth′il pir″o-fos-for′ah-mid). A chemical compound used as a plant insecticide, which has a powerful antagonism to peripheral cholinesterase, and has been found effective in treatment of myasthenia gravis.

octamylose (ok-tam′ĭ-lōs). A crystalline amylose, $(C_6H_{10}O_5)_8$.

octan (ok′tan) [L. *octo* eight]. Recurring every eighth day, or at intervals of seven days.

octane (ok′tān). An oily hydrocarbon, $CH_3(CH_2)_6$-CH_3, occurring in petroleum.

octapeptide (ok″tah-pep′tid). A peptide which on hydrolysis yields eight amino acids.

octaploid (ok′tah-ploid). 1. Pertaining to or characterized by octaploidy. 2. An individual or cell having eight sets of chromosomes.

octaploidy (ok′tah-ploi″de). The state of having eight sets of chromosomes (8n).

octarius (ok-ta′re-us) [L.; from *octo* eight]. A pint; the eighth part of a gallon.

octavalent (ok-tav′ah-lent) [L. *octo* eight + *valens* able]. Having a valency of eight.

octet (ok′tet). A group of eight identical or similar objects or entities, as the group of eight electrons in the outer shell of an atomic nucleus.

octigravida (ok″tĭ-grav′ĭ-dah) [L. *octo* eight + *gravida* pregnant]. A woman pregnant for the eighth time. Also written Gravida VIII.

octin (ok′tin). Trade mark for preparations of isometheptene.

octipara (ok-tip′ah-rah) [L. *octo* eight + *parere* to bring forth, produce]. A woman who has had eight pregnancies which resulted in viable offspring. Also written Para VIII.

octofollin (ok″to-fol′in). Benzestrol.

Octomitus (ok-tom′ĭ-tus). A genus of minute flagellate protozoa. **O. hom′inis,** a species found in the human intestine.

Octomyces (ok″to-mi′sēz). A genus of fungi. **O. etien′nei,** a species of yeastlike fungi isolated from a severe pleuropulmonary infection.

octoroon (ok″to-rōōn′). The offspring of a white person and a quadroon.

octose (ok′tōs) [L. *octo* eight]. A monosaccharide having the formula $C_8H_{16}O_8$.

ocular (ok′u-lar) [L. *ocularis; oculus* eye]. 1. Pertaining to the eye. 2. The lens or system of lenses in a microscope (or telescope) that is nearest to the eye of the user. See *eyepiece.*

oculentum (ok″u-len′tum), pl. *oculen′ta.* An eye ointment.

oculi (ok′u-li) [L.]. Plural of *oculus.*

oculist (ok′u-list). An old term for ophthalmologist.

oculistics (ok″u-lis′tiks). The treatment of diseases of the eye.

oculo- (ok′u-lo) [L. *oculus* eye]. Combining form denoting relationship to the eye.

oculocephalogyric (ok″u-lo-sef″ah-lo-ji′rik). Pertaining to the movements of the head in connection with vision.

oculofacial (ok″u-lo-fa′she-al). Pertaining to the eyes and the face.

oculogyration (ok″u-lo-ji-ra′shun). Movement of the eye about the anteroposterior axis.

oculogyria (ok″u-lo-ji′re-ah). A condition characterized by oculogyration.

oculogyric (ok″u-lo-ji′rik) [*oculo-* + L. *gyrus* a turn]. Pertaining to, characterized by, or causing oculogyria.

oculometroscope (ok″u-lo-met′ro-skōp). An instrument for performing retinoscopy in which the trial lenses are rotated before the eyes without effort on the part of the examiner.

oculomotor (ok″u-lo-mo′tor) [*oculo-* + L. *motor* mover]. Pertaining to the movements of the eye.

oculomotorius (ok″u-lo-mo-to′re-us) [L.]. The oculomotor nerve.

oculomycosis (ok″u-lo-mi-ko′sis) [*oculo-* + *mycosis*]. Any eye disease caused by a fungus.

oculonasal (ok″u-lo-na′zal). Pertaining to the eye and the nose.

oculopathy (ok″u-lop′ah-the) [*oculo-* + Gr. *pathos* disease]. Any morbid condition of the eyes. **pituitarigenic o.,** abnormality of the eye caused by secretions of the pituitary gland.

oculopupillary (ok″u-lo-pu′pĭ-lār-e). Pertaining to the pupil of the eye.

oculoreaction (ok″u-lo-re-ak′shun). The ophthalmic reaction.

oculospinal (ok″u-lo-spi′nal). Pertaining to the eye and the spinal cord.

oculozygomatic (ok″u-lo-zi″go-mat′ik). Pertaining to the eye and the zygoma.

oculus (ok′u-lus), pl. *oc′uli* [L.]. [N A, B N A] The organ of vision. See *eye.*

ocyodinic (o″se-o-din′ik) [Gr. *ōkys* swift + *ōdis* labor]. Oxytocic.

ocytocic (o″se-to′sik). Oxytocic.

O.D. Abbreviation for *Doctor of Optometry.* L. *oc′ulus dex′ter*, right eye, and *outside diameter.*

od (od) [Gr. *hodos* pathway]. The influence supposedly exerted upon the nervous system by mesmerism.

O.D.A. Abbreviation for L. *occipito-dextra anterior* (right occipito-anterior) position of the fetus.

odaxesmus (o″dak-sez′mus) [Gr. *odaxēsmos* an itching]. 1. The biting of the tongue or cheek in an epileptic fit. 2. Odontocnesis.

odaxetic (o″dak-set′ik) [Gr. *odaxētikos*]. Causing a biting or itching sensation.

Oddi's sphincter (od′ēz) [Ruggero *Oddi,* Italian physician of 19th century]. See under *sphincter.*

odditis (od-di′tis). Inflammation of the sphincter of Oddi.

odogenesis (od″o-jen′e-sis) [Gr. *hodos* pathway + *genesis* formation]. Neurocladism.

odon-eki (o″don-ek′e) [Japanese "icteric pestilence"]. A disease resembling spirochetal jaundice.

odontagra (o″don-ta′grah) [*odonto-* + Gr. *agra* seizure]. Gouty pain in a tooth.

odontalgia (o-don-tal′je-ah) [*odonto-* + *-algia*]. Pain in a tooth. **phantom o.,** alveolar neuralgia.

odontalgic (o-don-tal′jik). Pertaining to or characterized by toothache.

odontatrophia (o-don″tah-tro′fe-ah) [*odonto-* + Gr. *atrophia* atrophy]. Atrophy of the teeth.

odontectomy (o″don-tek′to-me) [*odonto-* + Gr. *ektomē* excision]. Excision of an erupted tooth, or of an unerupted or impacted tooth.

odonterism (o-don′ter-izm) [*odonto-* + Gr. *erismos* quarrel]. Chattering of the teeth.

odontexesis (o″don-teks′e-sis) [*odonto-* + Gr. *xesis* scraping]. The removal of dental calculus and polishing of the teeth.

odonthemodia (o-dont″he-mo′de-ah) [*odonto-* + Gr. *haimōdia* state of having the teeth on edge]. Great sensitiveness of the teeth.

odontiasis (o″don-ti′ah-sis) [*odonto-* + *-iasis*]. Eruption of the teeth, or any disorder caused thereby.

odontiatria (o-don″te-at′re-ah) [*odonto-* + Gr. *iatreia* treatment]. Dentistry.

odontic (o-don′tik) [Gr. *odous* tooth]. Pertaining to the teeth.

odontinoid (o-don′tĭ-noid) [*odonto-* + Gr. *eidos* form]. 1. Resembling tooth substance. 2. A tumor composed of tooth substance.

odontitis (o″don-ti′tis). Inflammation of a tooth.

odonto- (o-don′to) [Gr. *odous* tooth]. Combining form denoting relationship to a tooth or to the teeth.

odontoblast (o-don′to-blast) [*odonto-* + Gr. *blastos* germ]. One of the columnar connective tissue cells which form the outer surface of the dental pulp adjacent to the dentin.

odontoblastoma (o-don″to-blas-to′mah). A tumor made up of odontoblasts.

odontobothrion (o-don″to-both′re-on) [*odonto-* + Gr. *bothrion* a small trench]. An alveolar crypt.

odontobothritis (o-don″to-both-ri′tis). Inflammation of the alveolar process.

odontocele (o-don′to-sēl) [*odonto-* + Gr. *kēlē* hernia]. A dental cyst.

odontoceramic (o-don″to-sĕ-ram′ik). Pertaining to porcelain teeth, or to dental ceramics.

odontoceramotechny (o-don″to-sĕ-ram′o-tek″-ne) [*odonto-* + Gr. *keramos* potter's clay + *technē* art]. The art of making porcelain teeth; dental ceramics.

odontocia (o″don-to′se-ah). Softening of the teeth.

odontoclamis (o-don″to-kla′mis) [*odonto-* + Gr. *klamys* cloak]. Dental operculum.

odontoclasis (o″don-tok′lah-sis) [*odonto-* + Gr. *klasis* fracture]. Fracture of a tooth.

odontoclast (o-don′to-klast) [*odonto-* + Gr. *klan* break]. A multinucleated giant cell (osteoclast), found associated with absorption of the roots of a deciduous tooth.

odontocnesis (o-don″tok-ne′sis) [*odonto-* + Gr. *knēsis* itching]. Itching of the gums.

odontodynia (o-don″to-din′e-ah) [*odonto-* + Gr. *odynē* pain]. Odontalgia.

odontogen (o-don′to-jen) [*odonto-* + Gr. *gennan* to produce]. The substance which develops into the dentin of the teeth.

odontogenesis (o-don″to-jen′e-sis) [*odonto-* + Gr. *genesis* production]. The origin and histogenesis of the teeth. **o. imperfec′ta,** dentinogenesis imperfecta.

odontogenetic (o-don″to-je-net′ik). Pertaining to odontogenesis.

odontogenic (o-don″to-jen′ik). 1. Forming teeth. 2. Arising in tissues which give origin to the teeth.

odontogenous (o″don-toj′e-nus). Arising or originating in the teeth, or a dental condition.

odontogeny (o″don-toj′e-ne). Odontogenesis.

odontoglyph (o-don′to-glif) [*odonto-* + Gr. *glyphein* to carve]. An instrument used for scraping the teeth, or for carving artificial teeth.

odontogram (o-don′to-gram) [*odonto-* + Gr. *gramma* mark]. The tracing made by an odontograph.

odontograph (o-don′to-graf) [*odonto-* + Gr. *graphein* to write]. An instrument for recording the unevenness of surface of tooth enamel.

odontography (o″don-tog′rah-fe) [*odonto-* + Gr. *graphein* to write]. 1. A description of the teeth. 2. The use of the odontograph.

odontohyperesthesia (o-don″to-hi″per-es-the′-ze-ah) [*odonto-* + *hyperesthesia*]. Excessive sensitivity of a tooth.

odontoiatria (o-don″to-i-at′re-ah) [*odonto-* + Gr. *iatreia* cure]. Dentistry.

odontoid (o-don′toid) [*odonto-* + Gr. *eidos* form]. Toothlike; resembling a tooth.

odontolith (o-don′to-lith) [*odonto-* + Gr. *lithos* stone]. Dental calculus.

odontolithiasis (o-don″to-lĭ-thi′ah-sis). A condition marked by the presence of calculous deposits on the teeth.

odontologist (o″don-tol′o-jist). A dentist.

odontology (o″don-tol′o-je) [*odonto-* + *-logy*]. 1. The sum of knowledge regarding the teeth. 2. Dentistry.

odontoloxia (o-don″to-lok′se-ah) [*odonto-* + Gr. *loxos* slanting + *-ia*]. Irregularity of the teeth.

odontoloxy (o″don-tol′ok-se). Odontoloxia.

odontolysis (o-don-tol′ĭ-sis) [*odonto-* + Gr. *lysis* dissolution]. The resorption of dental tissue.

odontoma (o-don-to′mah) [*odonto-* + Gr. *-ōma* tumor]. 1. An exostosis on a tooth. 2. Any tumor of odontogenic origin; customarily used to designate a composite odontoma, q.v. **o. adamanti′num,** ameloblastic o. **ameloblastic o.,** an odontogenic neoplasm characterized by simultaneous occurrence of ameloblastoma and a composite odontoma. **composite o.,** an odontogenic tumor in which both the epithelial and mesenchymal cells exhibit complete differentiation; this results in the formation, by functional ameloblasts and odontoblasts, of enamel and dentin which are usually laid down in an abnormal pattern because of failure of the odontogenic cells to reach a normal state of morphodifferentiation. **composite o., complex,** a composite odontoma in which the calcified dental tissues occur in an irregular mass, and there is no morphologic similarity to even rudimentary teeth. **composite o., compound,** a composite odontoma in which the enamel and dentin are laid down so that the structure bears a superficial anatomic resemblance to normal teeth. **coronal o., coronary o.,** one attacking the crown of a tooth, or one formed at the time when the crown of the tooth was developing. **embryoplastic o.,** a soft odontoma formed in the period that precedes the formation of the dental tissues. **fibrous o.,** an odontoma containing fibrillar elements. **follicular o.,** a dentigerous cyst. **mixed o.,** an odontogenic neoplasm containing different elements of the tooth structure. **odontoplastic o.,** one formed at the time when the dentin and enamel of the tooth were developing. **radicular o.,** one attacking the root of a tooth, or one formed at the time when the root of the tooth was developing.

odontonecrosis (o-don″to-ne-kro′sis) [*odonto-* + *necrosis*]. Massive decay of a tooth.

odontoneuralgia (o-don″to-nu-ral′je-ah) [*odonto-* + *neuralgia*]. **1.** Neuralgia from disease of the teeth. 2. Neuralgic pain in the teeth.

odontonomy (o″don-ton′o-me) [*odonto-* + Gr. *onoma* name]. Dental nomenclature.

odontoparallaxis (o-don″to-par″ah-lak′sis) [*odonto-* + Gr. *parallaxis* alteration]. Irregularity of the teeth.

odontopathy (o″don-top′ah-the) [*odonto-* + Gr. *pathos* illness]. Any disease of the teeth.

odontoperiosteum (o-don″to-per″e-os′te-um). Periodontal membrane.

odontophobia (o-don″to-fo′be-ah) [*odonto-* + Gr. *phobein* to be affrighted by]. A morbid fear associated with teeth, as that aroused by the sight of teeth, or abnormal dread of dental operations.

odontoplast (o-don′to-plast). Odontoblast.

odontoplasty (o-don′to-plas″te) [*odonto-* + Gr. *plassein* to form]. Orthodontics.

odontoplerosis (o-don″to-ple-ro′sis) [*odonto-* + Gr. *plērōsis* filling]. The operation of filling a tooth cavity.

odontoprisis (o-don″to-pri′sis) [*odonto-* + Gr. *prisis* sawing]. Bruxism.

odontoptosis (o-don″top-to′sis) [*odonto-* + Gr. *ptōsis* falling]. Loss or shedding of teeth.

odontoradiograph (o-don″to-ra′de-o-graf). A roentgenogram of a tooth or of the teeth.

odontorrhagia (o-don″to-ra′je-ah) [*odonto-* + Gr. *rhēgnynai* to burst forth]. Hemorrhage following extraction of a tooth.

odontorthosis (o-don″tor-tho′sis) [*odonto-* + Gr. *orthōsis* a making straight]. Orthodontics.

odontoschism (o-don′to-skizm) [*odonto-* + Gr. *schisma* cleft]. Fissure of a tooth.

odontoscope (o-don′to-skōp) [*odonto-* + Gr. *skopein* to examine]. A mouth mirror used in examination of the teeth.

odontoscopy (o″don-tos′ko-pe). The taking of prints of the cutting edges of the teeth, used as a method of personal identification.

odontoseisis (o-don″to-si′sis) [*odonto-* + Gr. *seisis* a shaking]. Looseness of the teeth.

odontosis (o″don-to′sis) [Gr. *odous* tooth]. The formation or eruption of the teeth.

odontosteophyte (o″don-tos′te-o-fīt) [*odonto-* + Gr. *osteon* bone + *phyton* plant]. A bony outgrowth on the surface of a tooth.

odontotechny (o-don′to-tek″ne) [*odonto-* + Gr. *technē* art]. Dentistry.

odontotheca (o-don″to-the′kah) [*odonto-* + Gr. *thēkē* case]. The dental sac.

odontotherapy (o-don″to-ther′ah-pe) [*odonto-* + Gr. *therapeia* cure]. The treatment of diseased teeth.

odontotomy (o″don-tot′o-me) [*odonto-* + Gr. *tomē* a cutting]. The operation of cutting into a tooth, especially incision into an occlusal groove.

odontotripsis (o-don″to-trip′sis) [*odonto-* + Gr. *tripsis* rubbing]. Wearing away of the teeth.

odontotrypy (o″don-tot′rĭ-pe) [*odonto-* + Gr. *trypan* to bore]. The boring or drilling of a tooth.

odor (o′dor) [L.]. A volatile emanation that is perceived by the sense of smell. **butcher shop o.,** a smell like that of a butcher shop given off by yellow fever patients. **empyreumatic o.,** a smoky odor. **minimal identifiable o.,** the lowest concentration of a substance in air, or in another medium, which still permits its identification by the sense of smell.

odoratism (o″dor-a′tizm). A morbid condition produced in experimental animals by diets containing the sweet pea (*Lathyrus odoratus*) or its active principle. See *osteolathyrism*.

odoriferous (o″dor-if′er-us) [*odor* + L. *ferre* to bear]. Fragrant; emitting an odor.

odorimeter (o″dor-im′e-ter). An instrument for performing odorimetry.

odorimetry (o″dor-im′e-tre). The measurement of olfactory stimuli.

odoriphore (o-dor′ĭ-fōr). Osmophore.

odorivector (o″dor-ĭ-vek′tor). A substance which gives off an odor.

odorography (o″dor-og′rah-fe) [*odor* + Gr. *graphein* to write]. A description of odors.

O.D.P. Abbreviation for L. *occipito-dextra posterior* (right occipitoposterior) position of the fetus.

O.D.T. Abbreviation for L. *occipito-dextra transversa* (right occipitotransverse) position of the fetus.

O'Dwyer's tubes (o-dwi′erz) [Joseph P. *O'Dwyer,* American otolaryngologist, 1841–1898]. See under *tube.*

odynacusis (o″din-ah-ku′sis) [*odyno-* + Gr. *akousis* hearing]. Painful hearing.

-odynia (o-din′e-ah) [Gr. *odynē* pain]. A word ending meaning pain.

odyno- (o-din′o) [Gr. *odynē* pain]. Combining form meaning pain.

odynolysis (o″din-ol′ĭ-sis) [*odyno-* + Gr. *lysis* solution]. Relief of pain.

odynometer (o″din-om′e-ter) [*odyno-* + Gr. *metron* measure]. An instrument for measuring pain.

odynophagia (od″ĭ-no-fa′je-ah) [*odyno-* + Gr. *phagein* to eat]. Pain on deglutition.

odynophobia (od″ĭ-no-fo′be-ah) [*odyno-* + *phobia*]. A morbid dread of pain.

odynopoeia (o″din-o-pe′ah) [*odyno-* + Gr. *poiein* to make]. The induction of labor pains.

odynphagia (o″din-fa′je-ah). Odynophagia.

oe-. For other words beginning thus, see also those beginning with *e-*.

Oecactah (e-kak′tah). A midge in Cuba which enters the nasal passages, ears, etc.

oedipism (ed′ĭ-pizm) [see *Oedipus complex*]. Edipism.

Oedipus complex (ed′ĭ-pus) [*Oedipus* Tyrannus, a character in Greek tragedy who, raised by a foster parent, killed his actual father in a quarrel, and subsequently married his mother. Later, when he discovered the true relationship, he blinded himself (edipism)]. See under *complex.*

Oehl's layer (elz) [Eusebio *Oehl,* Italian anatomist, 1827–1903]. The stratum lucidum.

Oehler's symptom (e′lerz) [Johannes *Oehler,* German physician, born 1879]. See under *symptom.*

oenanthol (e-nan′thol). Heptoic aldehyde, CH_3-$(CH_2)_5CHO$.

oersted (er′sted) [Hans Christian *Oersted,* Danish physicist, 1777–1851]. The unit of magnetizing force: its symbol is *H.*

Oertel's treatment (er′telz) [Max J. *Oertel,* physician in Munich, 1835–1897]. See under *treatment.*

oese (e′ze) [Ger. "loop"]. A platinum wire and loop with a glass handle; used in bacteriological culture experiments.

oesophagostomiasis (e-sof″ah-go-sto-mi′ah-sis). Infestation with Œsophagostomum.

Œsophagostomum (e-sof″ah-gos′to-mum) [*œsophagus* + Gr. *stoma* mouth]. A genus of nematode worms of the family Strongylidae, parasitic in the intestines of various animals. The larvae often encyst in the intestinal wall, while the adults are mostly free in the lumen. **Œ. apios′tomum,** a parasite which forms tumors in the large intestine of monkeys and occasionally of man in Africa and the Philippines. **Œ. brevicau′dum** occurs in pigs. **Œ. brump′ti,** a parasite commonly present in monkeys in Africa and occasionally found in man. **Œ. columbia′num,** the nodular worm, infects sheep and goats in the southern United States. **Œ. denta′tum** is found in the pig. **Œ. infla'tum,** one found in cattle. **Œ. longicau'dum** is parasitic in pigs. **Œ. radia'tum** occurs in cattle. **Œ. stephanos'tomum,** a species, normally parasitic in gorillas, which has been found in man in Brazil.

Oestreicher's reaction (est'ri-kerz) [A. *Oestreicher*]. Xanthydrol reaction.

oestriasis (es-tri'ah-sis). Infection with larvae of flies of the genus Oestrus.

Oestridae (es'trĭ-de). The family of the "bot," "heel" or "warble" flies. They are very hairy diptera with rudimentary mouth parts and with the antennae inserted into round pits. The family includes the following genera: *Gasterophilus, Oestrus, Hypoderma, Dermatobia, Rhinoestrus* and *Cuterebra.*

oestrin (es'trin). Estrin.

oestrone (es'trōn). Estrone.

oestrous (es'trus). Estrous.

oestrual (es'troo-al). Estrual.

oestrum (es'trum). Estrus.

oestrus (es'trus). Estrus.

Oestrus (es'trus) [Gr. *oistros* gadfly]. A genus of bot flies. **O. hom'inis,** a bot fly whose larvae sometimes infest the human body. **O. o'vis,** a species of bot fly whose larvae infest nasal cavities and sinuses of sheep: they may cause ocular myiasis in man.

Of. Abbreviation for *official.*

official (ŏ-fish'al) [L. *officialis; officium* duty]. Recognized by the current U. S. Pharmacopeia or National Formulary, and meeting the standards established by the respective authority.

officinal (ŏ-fis'ĭ-nal) [L. *officinalis; officina* shop]. Regularly kept for sale in the shops of druggists.

Ogata's method (o-gah'tahz) [M. *Ogata*, Japanese physician]. See under *method.*

ogive (o'jīv). An S-shaped curve; a term used in biometry.

ogo (o'go). Gangosa.

Ogston's line, operation (og'stonz) [Alexander *Ogston*, Scottish surgeon, 1844–1929]. See under *line* and *operation.*

Ogston-Luc operation (og'ston-luk') [Alexander *Ogston;* Henry *Luc*, French laryngologist, 1855–1925]. See under *operation.*

Oguchi's disease (o-goo'chēz) [Chuta *Oguchi*, Japanese ophthalmologist, born 1875]. A form of congenital night blindness occurring in Japan.

OH. Symbol for the hydroxyl ion in solution; a hydroxide.

Ohara's disease (o-hah'rahz) [Hachiro *Ohara*, Japanese physician]. See under *disease.*

ohm (ōm) [George S. *Ohm*, German physicist, 1787–1854]. The unit of electrical resistance in the M.K.S. system of measurement, being equivalent to that of a column of mercury one square millimeter in cross section and one hundred and six centimeters long.

ohmammeter (ōm'am-me"ter). An ohmmeter and ammeter combined.

ohmmeter (ōm'me-ter). An instrument for measuring electric resistance in ohms.

ohne Hauch (o'nah-houkh) [Ger. "without breath"]. See *O*, and also see *H.*

oicomania (oi-ko-ma'ne-ah). Ecomania.

Oidiomycetes (o-id"e-o-mi-se'tēz). A group of fungi characterized by having mycelial threads in their cultures.

oidiomycetic (o-id"e-o-mi-set'ik). Pertaining to or caused by a fungus of the Oidiomycetes.

oidiomycosis (o-id"e-o-mi-ko'sis) [*oidium* + Gr. *mykēs* fungus]. Candidiasis.

oidiomycotic (o-id"e-o-mi-kot'ik). Pertaining to oidiomycosis.

Oidium (o-id'e-um) [dim. of Gr. *ōon* egg]. The former name for a genus of fungi now called *Candida.*

oikofugic (oi"ko-fu'jik) [Gr. *oikos* house + L. *fugere* to flee]. Marked by an impulse for wandering or leaving home.

oikoid (oi'koid). Ecoid.

oikology (oi-kol'o-je) [Gr. *oikos* house + *-logy*]. The science of houses and homes, considered especially in respect to their sanitary conditions.

oikomania (oi"ko-ma'ne-ah). Ecomania.

oikophobia (oi"ko-fo'be-ah) [Gr. *oikos* house + *phobia*]. Morbid aversion to home surroundings (A. Verga, 1882).

oikosite (oi'ko-sīt). Ecosite.

oil (oil) [L. *o'leum*]. 1. An unctuous, combustible substance which is liquid, or easily liquefiable, on warming, and is soluble in ether but insoluble in water. Such substances, depending on their origin, are classified as animal, mineral, or vegetable oils. Depending on their behavior on heating, they are classified as volatile or fixed. 2. A fat that is liquid at room temperature. **allspice o.,** pimenta o. **almond o.,** a preparation of the fixed oil obtained from the kernels of varieties of *Prunus amygdalus:* used as an emollient, and in the mixing of prescriptions. **almond o., bitter,** the volatile oil obtained from the dried ripe kernels of *Prunus amygdalus* or from other kernels containing amygdalin. **almond o., expressed.** See *almond o.* **almond o., sweet.** See *almond o.* **anise o.,** a volatile oil distilled from the dried, ripe fruit of *Pimpinella anisum* or of *Illicium verum:* used as a flavoring agent for drugs, and as a carminative. **apricot kernel o.,** persic o. **arachis o.,** peanut o. **bay o.,** myrcia o. **Benne o.,** sesame o. **bergamot o.,** a volatile oil obtained by expression from the rind of the fresh fruit of *Citrus bergamia:* used as a perfuming agent. **betula o.,** methyl salicylate. **bhilawanol o.,** a fluid obtained from the nut of a tree, *Semecarpus anacardium* (ral tree, bella gutta tree), in India, used by native washermen for marking laundry, and the cause of dhobie itch. **birch o., sweet,** methyl salicylate. **birch tar o., rectified,** the pyroligneous oil obtained by the dry distillation of the bark and wood of *Betula pendula* and other species of *Betula*, and rectified by steam distillation. **cade o.,** juniper tar. **o. of cajuput,** a volatile oil from *Melaleuca leucadendron.* **camphorated o.,** camphor liniment. **caraway o.,** a volatile oil distilled from the dried ripe fruit of *Carum carvi*, yielding at least 50 per cent by volume of carvone. **cardamom o.,** a volatile oil distilled from the seed of *Elettaria cardamomum:* used as a flavoring agent for pharmaceuticals. **cassia o.,** cinnamon o. **castor o.,** a fixed oil obtained from the seed of *Ricinus communis:* used as a cathartic. **castor o., aromatic,** a mixture of cinnamon, clove, and castor oils, with saccharin, vanillin, coumarin, and alcohol. **cedar o.,** a volatile oil from cedar wood, used as a clearing agent in microscopical technics; the thicker fraction is used as the immersion medium with oil-immersion objectives. **chaulmoogra o.,** a fixed oil expressed from the ripe seeds of a tree of southern Asia (*Taraktogenos kurzii*), which has been used in the treatment of leprosy; ethyl esters of the fatty acids obtained from this oil are now so used. **chenopodium o.,** a volatile oil obtained by steam distillation of fresh overground parts of the flowering and fruiting plant of *Chenopodium ambrosiodes*, containing 65 per cent of ascaridole, an active anthelmintic principle. **chloriodized o.,** an iodine monochloride addition product of vegetable oil: used as a radiopaque medium in roentgenography of the uterus and uterine tubes, and of the bronchi. **cinnamon o.,** a volatile oil distilled with steam from the leaves and twigs of *Cinnamomum cassia;* used as a flavoring agent for pharmaceuticals. **clove o.,** a volatile oil distilled with steam from the dried flowerbuds of *Eugenia caryophyllus:* used as a dental obtundant, and to relieve nausea and stimulate the appetite. **coconut o.,** the fixed oil obtained by expression or extraction from the kernels of seeds of *Cocos nucifera.* **cod liver o.,** the partially destearinated fixed oil obtained from fresh livers of *Gadus morrhua:* used as a source of vitamin A and vitamin D. **cod liver o., non-destearinated,** the entire fixed oil obtained from fresh livers of *Gadus morrhua* and other species of the family Gadidae. **o. of copaiba,** a volatile oil derived from copaiba. **coriander o.,** a volatile oil distilled with steam from the dried ripe fruit of *Coriandrum sativum:* used as a flavoring agent. **corn o.,** a refined fixed oil obtained from the embryo of *Zea mays:* used as a solvent for drugs. **cottonseed o.,** a refined fixed oil obtained from the seeds of cultivated plants of various varieties of *Gossypium hirsutum:* used as a solvent for drugs. **croton o.,** the thick, fixed oil of the seeds of *Croton tiglium,* an Asiatic plant, a drastic purgative and counterirritant, unsafe for human use. **o. of dill,** an oil distilled from the dried ripe fruits of *Anethum graveolens.* **distilled o.,** volatile o. **drying o.,** a type of fixed oil which thickens and hardens on exposure to the air, especially when spread out in a thin layer, being converted to a solid by absorption of oxygen. **empyreumatic o.,** a volatile oil formed by the destructive distillation of organic material. **essential o.,** volatile o. **ethereal o.** 1. A compound of ether with heavy oil of wine. 2. A volatile oil. **eucalyptus o.,** a volatile oil distilled with steam from the fresh leaf of *Eucalyptus globulus:* used as a flavoring agent. **expressed o., fatty o.,** fixed o. **fennel o.,** a volatile oil distilled with steam from the dried ripe fruit of *Faeniculum vulgare:* used as a flavoring agent for pharmaceuticals. **fixed o.,** an oil which does not evaporate on warming. Such oils, consisting of a mixture of fatty acids and their esters, are classified as solid (chiefly stearin), semisolid (chiefly palmitin), and liquid (chiefly olein). Fixed oils are also classified as *drying, semidrying,* and *non-drying,* depending on their tendency to solidify when exposed, in a thin film, to air. Called also *expressed o.* and *fatty o.* **flaxseed o.,** linseed o. **gaultheria o.,** methyl salicylate. **gingilli o.,** sesame o. **Haarlem o.,** juniper tar. **halibut liver o.,** a fixed oil obtained from fresh or suitably preserved livers of halibut species of the genus *Hippoglossus* Linné: used as a source of vitamin A. **heavy o.,** an oily product obtained by the action of sulfuric acid on alcohol. **hydnocarpus o.,** an oil obtained from species of Hydnocarpus, which resembles chaulmoogra oil in physical and chemical properties and is used in the same way (including the use of its ethyl esters) in the treatment of leprosy. **iodized o.,** an iodine addition product of vegetable oil: used as radiopaque medium in roentgenography of the uterus and uterine tubes. **juniper o.,** a volatile oil distilled with steam from the dried ripe fruit of *Juniperus communis.* **lavender o.,** a volatile oil distilled with steam from the fresh flowering tops of *Lavandula officinalis:* used as a perfuming agent. **lavender flowers o.,** lavender o. **lemon o.,** the volatile oil obtained by expression from the fresh peel of the fruit of *Citrus limon:* used as a flavoring agent. **linseed o.,** the fixed oil obtained from the dried ripe seed of *Linum usitatissimum.* **linseed o., raw,** linseed o. **o. of male fern,** a fixed oil from the root of the male fern. **mineral o., light white,** light liquid petrolatum. **mineral o., white,** liquid petrolatum. **mirbane o.,** nitrobenzene. **o. of mustard,** an oil derived from species of Brassica, a name variously applied to a volatile oil from the seeds of black mustard or of Chinese mustard, or to a fixed oil expressed from mustard seeds. **myrcia o.,** a volatile oil distilled from the leaves of *Pimenta racemosa:* used as a perfuming agent. **myristica o.,** the volatile oil distilled with steam from the dried kernels of the ripe seed of *Myristica fragrans,* used as a flavoring agent in pharmaceutical preparations. **neroli o.,** orange flower o. **nutmeg o.,** myristica o. **olive o.,** the fixed oil obtained from the ripe fruit of *Olea europaea:* used as an emollient. **orange o.,** the volatile oil obtained by expression from the fresh peel of the ripe fruit of *Citrus sinensis:* used as a flavoring agent in pharmaceuticals. **orange o., bitter,** a volatile oil obtained by expression from the fresh peel of the fruit of *Citrus aurantium.* **orange o., sweet,** orange o. **orange flower o.,** a volatile oil distilled from the fresh flowers of *Citrus aurantium.* **o. of Palma Christi,** castor o. **peach kernel o.,** persic o. **peanut o.,** the refined fixed oil obtained from the seed kernels of one or more of the cultivated varieties of *Arachis hypogaea:* used as a solvent for drugs administered by injection. **peppermint o.,** the volatile oil distilled with steam from the fresh overground parts of the flowering plant of *Mentha piperita.* **persic o.,** an oil expressed from the kernels of varieties of *Prunus armeniaca:* used as a vehicle for dispensing drugs. **pimenta o.,** the volatile oil distilled from the fruit of *Pimenta officinalis:* used as a flavoring agent for drugs. **pine o.,** the volatile oil obtained by steam distillation of the wood of *Pinus palustris* and of other species of Pinus: used as a deodorant and disinfectant. **pine needle o., dwarf,** the volatile oil distilled with steam from the fresh leaf of the dwarf pine, *Pinus mugo,* used as a perfume or flavoring agent. **ricinus o.,** castor o. **rose o.,** the volatile oil distilled with steam from the fresh flowers of *Rosa gallica,* or other species: used as a perfuming agent. **rosemary o.,** the volatile oil distilled with steam from the fresh flowering tops of *Rosmarinus officinalis:* used as a flavoring or perfuming agent. **safflower o.,** an oily liquid extracted from the seeds of the safflower, *Carthamus tinctorius:* used as a dietary supplement in the management of hypercholesterolemia. **sandalwood o.,** santal o. **santal o.,** a pale yellow, somewhat viscid, oily liquid with characteristic odor and taste of sandalwood, distilled with steam from the dried heartwood of *Santalum album* Linné. **sassafras o.,** the volatile oil distilled with steam from the root of *Sassafras albidum:* used as a flavoring agent for liquid pharmaceutical preparations. **sesame o.,** the refined fixed oil obtained from the seed of one or more cultivated varieties of *Sesamum indicum:* used as a solvent for drugs administered by intramuscular injection. **spearmint o.,** the volatile oil distilled with steam from the fresh overground parts of *Mentha spicata* or *Mentha cardiaca.* **o. of spike,** a volatile oil obtained from a broad-leaved variety of lavender, *Lavandula latifolia,* growing wild in Europe. **o. of spruce,** a volatile oil obtained from the hemlock, or hemlock spruce, sometimes used in veterinary liniments. **sweet o.,** olive o. **tangan-tangan o.,** castor o. **tar o., rectified,** the volatile oil from pine tar rectified by steam distillation. **teel o.,** sesame o. **theobroma o.,** the fat obtained from the roasted seed of *Theobroma cacao:* used as a base in suppositories. **thyme o.,** the volatile oil distilled from the flowering plant of *Thymus vulgaris:* used as a flavoring agent for drugs. **turpentine o.,** the volatile oil distilled from an oleoresin obtained from *Pinus palustris* and other species of Pinus: used as a local irritant. **turpentine o., rectified,** turpentine oil rectified by use of sodium hydroxide, for internal use. **volatile o.,** an oil which evaporates readily. The volatile oils occur in aromatic plants, to which they give odor and other characteristics. Most volatile oils consist of a mixture of two or more terpenes or of a mixture of an eleopten with a stearopten. Called also *distilled o., essential o.,* and *ethereal o.* **wheat-germ o.,** oil derived from the germ of wheat kernels: it is rich in vitamin E. **wintergreen o.,** methyl salicylate. **wormseed o., American,** chenopodium o.

oil breakfast. Two hundred cc. of olive oil (*Volhard's*) or 100–200 cc. of a 2 per cent solution of oleic acid in olive oil (*Boldiref's breakfast*), given in the early morning, fasting. In one half to one hour the stomach contents are drawn off. The oil breakfast having caused the duodenal contents to regurgitate into the stomach, the removed stomach contents contain pancreatic juice from the duodenum.

oinomania (oi″no-ma′ne-ah). Enomania.

ointment (oint′ment) [L. *unguentum*]. A semisolid preparation for external application to the body, and usually containing a medicinal substance. **ammoniated mercury o.,** a preparation of ammoniated mercury, liquid petrolatum, and white ointment, containing 4.5 to 5.5 per cent NH_2Cl: used as a local anti-infective. **anthralin o.,** a preparation of anthralin in white petrolatum: used as a local irritant. **bacitracin o.,** a preparation of bacitracin, liquid petrolatum, and white petrolatum, containing 500 U.S.P. units per gram: local antibiotic. **belladonna o.,** a preparation of pilular belladonna extract and diluted alcohol in yellow ointment: used locally as an analgetic. **benzocaine o.,** ethyl aminobenzoate o. **benzoic and salicylic acid o.,** a preparation of benzoic acid and salicylic acid in a water-soluble base (polyethylene glycol ointment), used topically as an antifungal agent. **blue o.,** mercurial o., mild. **boric acid o.,** a preparation of finely powdered boric acid and liquid petrolatum in white ointment: used as an antibacterial. **calamine o.,** a preparation containing calamine, yellow fat, wool fat, and petrolatum: used as an astringent, protective application. **calomel o.,** mercurous chloride o., mild. **carbolic acid o.,** phenol o. **chloramphenicol ophthalmic o.,** a semisolid preparation containing 1 mg. of chloramphenicol per gram: used topically about the eyes. **chrysarobin o.,** a preparation of chrysarobin, chloroform, and white ointment: used in local treatment of psoriatic lesions. **coal tar o.,** a preparation of coal tar, polysorbate 80, and zinc oxide paste. **Credé's o.,** one containing collargol, water, white wax, and benzoinated lard: used in septicemia, pyemia, boils, carbuncles, etc. **diachylon o.,** a mixture of white petrolatum and lead acetate. **epinephrine bitartrate o.,** a preparation of epinephrine bitartrate, purified water, and hydrophilic petrolatum. **ethyl aminobenzoate o.,** a preparation of finely powdered ethyl aminobenzoate in white ointment: local anesthetic. **hydrocortisone acetate o.,** an ointment containing hydrocortisone acetate, for topical use. **hydrophilic o.,** a preparation containing a mixture of ointment bases which are removable by water. **ichthammol o.,** a preparation of ichthammol in wool fat and petrolatum: used as a local antibacterial and irritant to the skin. **iodine o.,** a preparation of iodine, potassium iodide, glycerin, wool fat, yellow wax, and petrolatum, containing 6.5–7.5 per cent of iodine: antibacterial and irritant. **Löwenstein's o.,** an ointment prepared from a detoxicated unfiltered culture of diphtheria bacilli containing toxoid and killed bacteria: formerly used by inunction in attempted immunization against diphtheria. Called also *dermotubin*. **menthol o., compound,** a preparation of menthol, methyl salicylate, white wax, and hydrous wool fat: local irritant. **mercurial o., diluted,** mercurial o., mild. **mercurial o., mild,** a preparation of mercury and mercury oleate, in solid bases, containing between 9 and 11 per cent mercury. Used as a local parasiticide. **mercurial o., strong,** a preparation of mercury, mercury oleate, wool fat, white wax, and white petrolatum, containing 47.5–52.5 per cent of mercury: parasiticide. **mercuric oxide o., yellow,** a mixture of finely powdered yellow mercuric oxide, liquid petrolatum, and white ointment, containing 0.9–1.1 per cent of mercuric oxide. **mercurous chloride o., mild,** a preparation of mild mercurous chloride, hydrous wool fat, and white petrolatum, containing 28.5–31.5 per cent of mercurous chloride. **mercury bichloride o.,** a preparation of mercury bichloride, $HgCl_2$, dissolved in boiling water and incorporated in white petrolatum: used as an antibacterial in ophthalmic practice. **neomycin sulfate o.,** an ointment containing 3.5 mg. of neomycin base per gram. **nitrofurazone o.,** a mixture of nitrofurazone and polyethylene glycols 1540, 4000, and 300, each 100 gm. of which contains 190–210 mg. of nitrofurazone. **Pagenstecher's o.,** ointment of yellow oxide of mercury: used in eye diseases. **penicillin o.,** a preparation of calcium penicillin, crystalline penicillin, or procaine penicillin in a suitable ointment base, with or without incorporation of a suitable anesthetic. **Peruvian balsam and ichthammol o.,** a preparation of castor oil, Peruvian balsam, ichthammol, and petrolatum: sometimes prescribed in chiropody. **phenol o.,** a preparation of phenol, glycerin, and white ointment, containing 1.8–2.2 per cent of phenol: antipruritic. **phenol and salicylic acid o.,** a preparation of liquefied phenol, salicylic acid, hydrogenated oil, and rose water ointment: used in chiropody. **pine tar o.,** a preparation of pine tar, yellow wax, and yellow ointment: local antibacterial. **polyethylene glycol o.,** a mixture of polyethylene glycol 4000 and polyethylene glycol 400. **resorcinol o., compound,** a preparation of resorcinol, zinc oxide, bismuth subnitrate, juniper tar, yellow wax, petrolatum, wool fat, and glycerin: local irritant, antibacterial, and antifungal. **rose water o.,** a preparation of spermaceti, white wax, expressed almond or persic oil, sodium borate, rose water, purified water, and rose oil. **rose water o., petrolatum,** an ointment prepared with spermaceti, white wax, liquid petrolatum, sodium borate, rose water, purified water, and rose oil. **scarlet red o.,** a preparation of scarlet red, olive oil, wool fat, and petrolatum: applied locally as a protective agent. **simple o.,** white o. **sulfacetamide sodium o.,** an ointment containing 9.5–10 per cent of sulfacetamide sodium. **sulfur o.,** a mixture of precipitated sulfur, liquid petrolatum, and white ointment: used as a scabicide. **tannic acid o., compound,** a preparation of menthol, camphor, tannic acid, glycerin, hydrogenated oil, and white petrolatum: used in chiropody. **tar o., compound,** a preparation of rectified tar oil, benzoin tincture, zinc oxide, yellow wax, lard, and cottonseed oil: used locally as an antibacterial and irritant. **thimerosal o.,** a preparation of thimerosal, purified water, cholesterol, wool fat, white wax, stearyl alcohol, and white petrolatum: antibacterial. **undecylenic acid o., compound.** 1. A preparation of undecylenic acid, zinc undecylenate, and polyethylene glycol ointment: antifungal. 2. A preparation of clove and cinnamon oils, salicylic acid, undecylenic acid, benzoic acid, and white petrolatum: used in chiropody. **Wertheim's o.,** a combination of ammoniated mercury, bismuth, and glycerin ointment: for application in chloasma. **white o.,** an oleaginous ointment base prepared from white wax and white petrolatum. **white precipitate o.,** mercury o., ammoniated. **Whitfield's o.,** benzoic and salicylic acid o. **yellow o.,** a mixture of yellow wax and petrolatum: used as an ointment base for drugs. **zinc o.,** zinc oxide o. **zinc oxide o.,** a preparation of zinc oxide and liquid petrolatum in white ointment, used topically as an astringent and protective.

oite (o′it). The female form of a bacterium. Cf. *gonite*.

Oken's body (o′kenz) [Lorenz *Oken*, German physiologist, 1779–1851]. The mesonephros.

O.L. Abbreviation for L. *oc′ulus lae′vus*, left eye.

Ol. Abbreviation for L. *o′leum*, oil.

-ol. Suffix indicating that the substance is an alcohol or a phenol, i.e., a hydroxyl derivative of a hydrocarbon.

O.L.A. Abbreviation for L. *occipito-laeva anterior* (left occipito-anterior) position of the fetus.

olea (o′le-ah) [L.]. 1. Olive. 2. Plural of *oleum*.

oleaginous (o″le-aj′ĭ-nus) [L. *oleaginus*]. Oily; greasy; unctuous.

oleander (o″le-an′der). An evergreen apocynaceous shrub, *Nerium odorum*, a poisonous cardiac tonic, diuretic, and aperient.

oleandomycin (o″le-an′do-mi″sin). An antibacterial substance elaborated by the growth of *Streptomyces antibioticus:* used chiefly in treatment of infections by gram-positive organisms.

oleandrin (o″le-an′drin). 1. A cardiac glycoside, $C_{30}H_{46}O_8$, from oleander, composed of digitalose and digitaligenin. 2. An alkaloid from oleander: therapeutically active.

oleandrism (o″le-an′drizm). Poisoning by oleander.

oleanol (o-le′ah-nol). A white solid alcohol, $C_{18}H_{35}OH$, from the liver oils of fish.

olease (o′le-ās). An enzyme from olive oil which produces rancidity and discoloration of the oil.

oleaster (o″le-as′ter). 1. The true wild olive, *Olea oleaster.* 2. Any plant of the genus *Elaeagnus.*

oleate (o′le-āt). 1. Any salt of oleic acid. 2. [L. *oleatum*]. A solution of a chemical substance or drug in oleic acid, used as an ointment.

olecranal (o-lek′rah-nal). Pertaining to the olecranon.

olecranarthritis (o-lek″ran-ar-thri′tis) [*olecranon* + *arthritis*]. Inflammation of the elbow joint.

olecranarthrocace (o-lek″ran-ar-throk′ah-se) [*olecranon* + Gr. *arthron* joint + *kakē* badness]. Tuberculosis of the elbow joint.

olecranarthropathy (o-lek″ran-ar-throp′ah-the) [*olecranon* + Gr. *arthron* joint + *pathos* disease]. Disease of the elbow joint.

olecranoid (o-lek′rah-noid). Resembling the olecranon.

olecranon (o-lek′rah-non) [Gr. *ōlekranon*]. [N A, B N A] The proximal bony projection of the ulna at the elbow, its anterior surface forming part of the trochlear notch.

olefin (o′le-fin) [*oleo-* + L. *facere* to make]. An unsaturated aliphatic hydrocarbon.

olein (o′le-in). An oleate (especially the trioleate) of glyceryl, $C_3H_5[CH_3(CH_2)_7CH{:}CH(CH_2)_7CO.O]_3$; found in various fixed oils and fats. It is a colorless, oily liquid, insoluble in water but freely soluble in ether and alcohol.

olenitis (o-len-i′tis). Inflammation of the elbow joint.

oleo- (o′le-o) [L. *oleum* oil]. Combining form denoting relationship to oil.

oleo-arthrosis (o″le-o-ar-thro′sis) [*oleo-* + Gr. *arthron* joint + *-osis*]. Therapeutic injection of oil into a joint.

oleochrysotherapy (o″le-o-kris″o-ther′ah-pe) [*oleo-* + Gr. *chrysos* gold + *therapy*]. Therapeutic administration of gold salts in oily suspensions.

oleocreosote (o″le-o-kre′o-sōt). The oleic acid ester of creosote.

oleodipalmitin (o″le-o-di-pal′mĭ-tin). A fat found in soya bean oil, butter, cocoa fat, etc.

oleodistearin (o″le-o-di-ste′ah-rin). A fat found in the seeds of the Indian mango, *Mangifera indica.*

oleogranuloma (o″le-o-gran″u-lo′mah). Paraffinoma.

oleoguaiacol (o″le-o-gwi′ah-kol). The oleic acid ester of guaiacol.

oleo-infusion (o″le-o-in-fu′zhun). A preparation made by infusing a drug in oil.

oleoma (o″le-o′mah) [*oleo-* + *-oma*]. Paraffinoma.

oleomargarine (o″le-o-mar′jah-rin). Margarine.

oleometer (o″le-om′e-ter) [*oleo-* + Gr. *metron* measure]. An instrument for testing the purity of oil.

oleonucleoprotein (o″le-o-nu″kle-o-pro′te-in). The caseinogen and fat of milk regarded as forming one complex substance.

oleopalmitate (o″le-o-pal′mĭ-tāt). An oleate and a palmitate of the same base.

oleoperitoneography (o″le-o-per″ĭ-to-ne-og′rah-fe). Roentgenography of the peritoneum following the injection of iodized oil.

oleoresin (o″le-o-rez′in) [L. *oleoresina*]. 1. Any natural combination of a resin and a volatile oil such as exudes from pines and other plants. 2. A compound prepared by exhausting a drug by percolation with a volatile solvent, such as acetone, alcohol, or ether, and evaporating the solvent. **aspidium o.,** a thick dark green liquid, extracted from aspidium, yielding not less than 24 per cent of crude filicin. **capsicum o.,** the extract from capsicum obtained by percolation, with either acetone or ether as the menstruum: used as an irritant and carminative.

oleoresina (o″le-o-re-zi′nah), pl. *oleoresi′nae* [L.]. Oleoresin.

oleosaccharum (o″le-o-sak′ah-rum). Eleosaccharum.

oleostearate (o″le-o-ste′ar-āt). An oleate and a stearate of the same base.

oleosus (o″le-o′sus) [L.]. Oily; greasy.

oleotherapy (o″le-o-ther′ah-pe) [*oleo-* + *therapy*]. Treatment with oil, particularly treatment by the injection of oil.

oleothorax (o″le-o-tho′raks) [*oleo-* + *thorax*]. Intrapleural injection of oil in order to compress the lung in pulmonary tuberculosis.

oleotine (o″le-o′tīn). A peptonized fat: for use as a butter substitute.

oleovitamin (o″le-o-vi′tah-min). A preparation of fish liver oil containing vitamin A or vitamins A and D. **o. A,** an oily preparation containing the natural or synthetic form of vitamin A. **o. D, synthetic,** a solution of calciferol or of activated 7-dehydrocholesterol in an edible vegetable oil: used as an antirachitic vitamin. **o. D₂,** calciferol. **o. D₃,** 7-dehydrocholesterol, activated.

oleum (o′le-um), gen. *o′lei,* pl. *o′lea* [L.]. Oil. **o. aethe′reum,** ethereal oil. **o. amyg′dalae ama′rae,** bitter almond oil. **o. amyg′dalae expres′sum,** almond oil. **o. ane′thi,** oil of dill. **o. arach′idis,** peanut oil. **o. auran′tii,** orange oil. **o. auran′tii ama′ri,** bitter orange oil. **o. auran′tii flo′ris,** orange flower oil. **o. bergamot′tae,** bergamot oil. **o. bet′ulae empyreumat′icum rectifica′tum,** rectified birch tar oil. **o. cardamo′mi,** cardamom oil. **o. ca′ri,** caraway oil. **o. caryophyl′li,** clove oil. **o. chaulmoo′grae,** chaulmoogra oil. **o. chenopo′dii,** chenopodium oil. **o. co′cois,** coconut oil. **o. eucalyp′ti,** eucalyptus oil. **o. gossyp′ii sem′inis,** cottonseed oil. **o. hippoglos′si,** halibut liver oil. **o. jec′oris asel′li,** cod liver oil. **o. junip′eri,** juniper oil. **o. junip′eri empyreumat′icum,** juniper tar. **o. li′ni,** linseed oil. **o. may′dis,** corn oil. **o. men′thae piperi′tae,** peppermint oil. **o. mor′rhuae,** cod liver oil. **o. myr′ciae,** myrcia oil. **o. pi′cis li′quidae rectifica′tum,** rectified tar oil. **o. pi′cis rectifica′tum,** rectified tar oil. **o. pimen′tae,** pimenta oil. **o. pi′ni,** pine oil. **o. pi′ni pumilio′nis,** dwarf pine needle oil. **o. ric′ini,** castor oil. **o. ric′ini aromat′icum,** aromatic castor oil. **o. rosmari′ni,** rosemary oil. **o. rus′ci,** rectified birch tar oil. **o. san′tali,** santal oil. **o. ses′ami,** sesame oil. **o. terebin′thinae,** turpentine oil. **o. terebin′thinae rectifica′tum,** rectified turpentine oil. **o. thy′mi,** thyme oil. **o. tig′lii,** croton oil.

olfact (ol′fakt). A unit of odor, the *minimum perceptible odor,* being the minimum concentration of a substance in solution which can be perceived by a large number of normal individuals, expressed in terms of grams per liter.

olfactie (ol-fak′te). A term applied by Zwaardemaker to a unit of the distance of withdrawal of the tube of his olfactometer at which an odorous substance was recognized, representing the exposed surface area of the odorous or solution-impregnated substance of which the cylinders were made.

olfaction (ol-fak′shun) [L. *olfacere* to smell]. The act of smelling; the sense of smell.

olfactism (ol-fak′tizm). A sensation of smell produced by other than olfactory stimuli.

olfactology (ol″fak-tol′o-je). The science of the sense of smell.

olfactometer (ol″fak-tom′e-ter) [L. *olfactus* smell + *metrum* measure]. An apparatus for testing the sensitiveness of the nose to odors.

olfactometry (ol″fak-tom′e-tre). The study of the sense of smell.

olfactophobia (ol-fak″to-fo′be-ah). Morbid aversion to odors.

olfactory (ol-fak′to-re) [L. *olfacere* to smell]. Pertaining to olfaction, or the sense of smell.

olfactus (ol-fak′tus). A unit of acuity of smell.

olfacty (ol-fak′te). Olfactie.

oligakisuria (ol″ĭ-gak″ĭ-su′re-ah) [Gr. *oligakis* few times + *ouron* urine + *-ia*]. A condition in which urination occurs at long intervals.

oligemia (ol″ĭ-ge′me-ah) [*oligo-* + Gr. *haima* blood + *-ia*]. Deficiency in the volume of the blood.

oligemic (ol″ĭ-ge′mik). Pertaining to or characterized by oligemia.

oligergasia (ol″ig-er-ga′se-ah). An oligergastic disorder; a mental disorder based on intellectual inadequacy or feeblemindedness.

oligergastic (ol″ig-er-gas′tik) [*oligo-* + Gr. *ergon* work]. Meyer's term for psychic disorders based on brain deficiency from lack of development.

olighydria (ol″ig-hid′re-ah). Oligidria.

oligidria (ol″ig-id′re-ah) [*oligo-* + Gr. *hidrōs* sweat + *-ia*]. A deficiency in the secretion of the sweat.

oligo- (ol′ĭ-go) [Gr. *oligos* little]. Combining form meaning little, scanty, or few.

oligoamnios (ol″ĭ-go-am′ne-os) [*oligo-* + *amnios*]. Oligohydramnios.

oligoblast (ol′ĭ-go-blast). A primitive oligodendrocyte.

oligocardia (ol″ĭ-go-kar′de-ah) [*oligo-* + Gr. *kardia* heart]. Bradycardia.

oligocholia (ol″ĭ-go-ko′le-ah) [*oligo-* + Gr. *cholē* bile + *-ia*]. A lack or deficiency of the bile.

oligochromasia (ol″ĭ-go-kro-ma′se-ah). Hypochromasia.

oligochromemia (ol″ĭ-go-kro-me′me-ah) [*oligo-* + Gr. *chrōma* color + *haima* blood + *-ia*]. Insufficiency of hemoglobin in the blood.

oligochylia (ol″ĭ-go-ki′le-ah) [*oligo-* + Gr. *chylos* chyle + *-ia*]. Deficiency of chyle.

oligochymia (ol″ĭ-go-ki′me-ah) [*oligo-* + Gr. *chymos* juice + *-ia*]. Deficiency of chyme.

oligocystic (ol″ĭ-go-sis′tik) [*oligo-* + Gr. *kystis* sac, bladder]. Containing only a few cysts.

oligocythemia (ol″ĭ-go-si-the′me-ah) [*oligo-* + *-cyte* + Gr. *haima* blood + *-ia*]. Deficiency in the cellular elements of the blood.

oligocythemic (ol″ĭ-go-si-them′ik). Relating to or affected with oligocythemia.

oligocytosis (ol″ĭ-go-si-to′sis). Oligocythemia.

oligodactylia (ol″ĭ-go-dak-til′e-ah) [*oligo-* + Gr. *daktylos* finger + *-ia*]. A developmental anomaly characterized by a smaller than usual number of fingers or toes.

oligodendria (ol″ĭ-go-den′dre-ah). Oligodendroglia.

oligodendroblastoma (ol″ĭ-go-den″dro-blas-to′mah). A tumor made up of young oligodendroglia cells.

oligodendrocyte (ol″ĭ-go-den′dro-sīt) [*oligodendro*glia + *-cyte*]. An oligodendroglia cell.

oligodendroglia (ol″ĭ-go-den-drog′le-ah) [*oligo-* + Gr. *dendron* dendron + *neuroglia*]. Tissue composed of non-neural cells of ectodermal origin forming part of the adventitial structure of the central nervous system. Their vinelike prolongations form an incomplete investment for the myelin sheaths in the white matter, and with microglia they form the perineuronal satellites in the gray matter.

oligodendroglioma (ol″ĭ-go-den″dro-gli-o′mah). A tumor made up of oligodendroglia.

oligodipsia (ol″ĭ-go-dip′se-ah) [*oligo-* + Gr. *dipsa* thirst + *-ia*]. Abnormally diminished thirst.

oligodontia (ol″ĭ-go-don′she-ah) [*oligo-* + Gr. *odous* tooth]. Presence of less than the normal number of teeth, some of them being congenitally absent.

oligodynamic (ol″ĭ-go-di-nam′ik) [*oligo-* + Gr. *dynamis* power]. Active in very minute quantities.

oligo-erythrocythemia (ol″ĭ-go-e-rith″ro-si-the′me-ah) [*oligo-* + *erythrocyte* + Gr. *haima* blood + *-ia*]. Deficiency of coloring matter in the red blood corpuscles; also deficiency of red blood corpuscles.

oligogalactia (ol″ĭ-go-gah-lak′she-ah) [*oligo-* + Gr. *gala* milk + *-ia*]. Deficient secretion of milk.

oligogenic (ol″e-go-jen′ik) [*oligo-* + *gene*]. Produced by a few genes at most: used in reference to certain hereditary characters.

oligogenics (ol″ĭ-go-jen′iks) [*oligo-* + Gr. *gennan* to produce]. Limitation of the number of offspring; birth control.

oligoglia (ol″ĭ-gog′le-ah). Oligodendroglia.

oligoglobulia (ol″ĭ-go-glo-bu′le-ah). Oligocythemia.

oligohemia (ol″ĭ-go-he′me-ah). Oligemia.

oligohydramnios (ol″ĭ-go-hi-dram′ne-os) [*oligo-* + Gr. *hydōr* water + *amnion*]. The presence of less than 300 cc. of amniotic fluid at term.

oligohydruria (ol″ĭ-go-hi-droo′re-ah) [*oligo-* + Gr. *hydōr* water + *ouron* urine + *-ia*]. Abnormally high concentration of the urine.

oligohypermenorrhea (ol″ĭ-go-hi″per-men″o-re′ah). Infrequent menstruation with excessive menstrual flow.

oligohypomenorrhea (ol″ĭ-go-hi″po-men″o-re′-ah). Infrequent menstruation with diminished menstrual flow.

oligolecithal (ol″ĭ-go-les′ĭ-thal) [*oligo-* + Gr. *lekithos* yolk]. Possessing only a little yolk.

oligoleukocythemia (ol″ĭ-go-lu″ko-si-the′me-ah) [*oligo-* + *leukocyte* + Gr. *haima* blood + *-ia*]. Leukopenia.

oligoleukocytosis (ol″ĭ-go-lu″ko-si-to′sis). Leukopenia.

oligomania (ol″ĭ-go-ma′ne-ah) [*oligo-* + Gr. *mania* madness]. Insanity on a few subjects; impairment of a few of the mental faculties.

oligomastigate (ol″ĭ-go-mas′tĭ-gāt) [*oligo-* + Gr. *mastix* lash]. Having only two flagella.

oligomenorrhea (ol″ĭ-go-men″o-re′ah) [*oligo-* + Gr. *mēn* month + *rhoia* flow]. Abnormally infrequent or scanty menstruation.

oligometallic (ol″ĭ-go-me-tal′ik). Containing only small quantities of metals.

oligomorphic (ol″ĭ-go-mor′fik) [*oligo-* + Gr. *morphē* form]. Passing through only a few forms of growth: said of microorganisms.

oligonatality (ol″ĭ-go-na-tal′ĭ-te) [*oligo-* + L. *natus* birth]. Scanty birth rate.

oligonecrospermia (ol″ĭ-go-nek″ro-sper′me-ah) [*oligo-* + Gr. *nekros* dead + *sperma* sperm + *-ia*]. A condition of the spermatic fluid in which there is diminution of the number of spermatozoa, some of which are dead.

oligonitrophilic (ol″ĭ-go-ni″tro-fil′ik) [*oligo-* + *nitrogen* + Gr. *philein* to love]. Absorbing nitrogen from the air and from media containing combined nitrogen.

oligo-ovulation (ol″ĭ-go-ov″u-la′shun). Maturation and discharge of fewer than the normal number of ova from the ovaries.

oligopepsia (ol″ĭ-go-pep′se-ah) [*oligo-* + Gr. *pepsis* digestion + *-ia*]. Feeble digestion.

oligophosphaturia (ol″ĭ-go-fos″fah-tu′re-ah). Deficiency in the excretion of phosphates in the urine.

oligophrenia (ol″ĭ-go-fre′ne-ah) [*oligo-* + Gr. *phrēn* mind + *-ia*]. Defective mental development. **phenylpyruvic o., o. phenylpyru′vica,** a hereditary mental deficiency characterized by the excretion of phenylpyruvic acid in the urine (phenylketonuria or phenylpyruvicaciduria).

oligoplasmia (ol″ĭ-go-plaz′me-ah) [*oligo-* + Gr. *plasma* thing formed + *-ia*]. A deficient quantity of plasma in the blood.

oligoplastic (ol″ĭ-go-plas′tik). Deficient in plasm.

oligopnea (ol″ĭ-gop-ne′ah) [*oligo-* + Gr. *pnoia* breath]. Retarded breathing.

oligoposia (ol″ĭ-go-po′ze-ah) [*oligo-* + Gr. *posis* drinking + *-ia*]. Abnormally diminished ingestion of fluids.

oligoposy (ol″ĭ-gop′o-se). Oligoposia.

oligopsychia (ol″ĭ-go-si′ke-ah) [*oligo-* + Gr. *psychē* soul]. Mental weakness.

oligoptyalism (ol″ĭ-go-ti′al-izm) [*oligo-* + Gr. *ptyalon* saliva + *-ism*]. Diminished secretion of saliva.

oligopyrene, oligopyrous (ol″ĭ-go-pi′rēn, ol″ĭ-go-pi′rus) [*oligo-* + Gr. *pyrēn* stone of fruit]. Deficient in nuclear or chromatin material.

oligoria (ol″ĭ-go′re-ah) [Gr. *oligōria* contempt, negligence]. A form of melancholia (Snell).

oligosaccharide (ol″ĭ-go-sak′ah-rīd). A carbohydrate which on hydrolysis yields two to ten monosaccharides.

oligosialia (ol″ĭ-go-si-a′le-ah) [*oligo-* + Gr. *sialon* saliva + *-ia*]. Pathologically diminished secretion of saliva.

oligosideremia (ol″ĭ-go-sid″er-e′mia) [*oligo-* + Gr. *sidēros* iron + *haima* blood + *-ia*]. Reduction of iron in the blood.

oligospermatism (ol″ĭ-go-sper′mah-tizm). Oligospermia.

oligospermia (ol″ĭ-go-sper′me-ah) [*oligo-* + Gr. *sperma* seed + *-ia*]. Deficiency in the number of spermatozoa in the semen.

oligosporidia (ol″ĭ-go-spo-rid′e-ah). A suborder of protozoan microorganisms, or coccidia, forming spores which divide, each one producing several sickle-shaped reproductive bodies. Some are pathogenic.

oligotrichia (ol″ĭ-go-trik′e-ah) [*oligo-* + Gr. *thrix* hair + *-ia*]. Congenital thinness of the growth of hair.

oligotrichosis (ol″ĭ-go-trĭ-ko′sis). Oligotrichia.

oligotrophia (ol″ĭ-go-tro′fe-ah) [*oligo-* + Gr. *trophē* nourishment + *-ia*]. A state of poor (insufficient) nutrition.

oligotrophic (ol″ĭ-go-trof′ik). Pertaining to, characterized by, or conducive to poor (insufficient) nutrition.

oligotrophy (ol″ĭ-got′ro-fe). Oligotrophia.

oligozoospermatism (ol″ĭ-go-zo″o-sper′mah-tizm). Oligospermia.

oligozoospermia (ol″ĭ-go-zo″o-sper′me-ah). Oligospermia.

oliguresis (ol″ĭ-gu-re′sis). Oliguria.

oliguria (ol″ĭ-gu′re-ah) [*oligo-* + Gr. *ouron* urine + *-ia*]. Secretion of a diminished amount of urine in relation to the fluid intake.

oliguric (ol″ĭ-gu′rik). Pertaining to or characterized by oliguria.

olisthe (o-lis′the). Olisthy.

olisthy (o-lis′the) [Gr. *olisthanein* to slip]. A slipping, as the slipping of the bones of a joint from their normal relation in the joint.

oliva (o-li′vah), pl. *oli′vae* [L.]. [N A, B N A] A rounded elevation, lateral to the upper part of each pyramid of the medulla oblongata. It is produced by an irregular mass of gray substance, the olivary nucleus, located just beneath its surface. Called also *olive* and *inferior olive*. **o. cerebella′ris,** nucleus dentatus cerebelli.

olivae (o-li′ve) [L.]. Plural of *oliva*.

olivary (ol′ĭ-ver″e) [L. *olivarius*]. Shaped like an olive.

olive (ol′iv) [L. *oliva*]. 1. The tree *Olea europaea*, and its fruit. The latter affords a fixed oil (*olive oil, sweet oil*), which consists chiefly of olein and palmitin, and is employed as a food, as a mild laxative, and as an application to wounds, bruises, etc. 2. A rounded elevation, lateral to the upper part of each pyramid of the medulla oblongata. See *oliva*. **inferior o.,** oliva. **spurge o.,** mezereon. **superior o.,** nucleus dorsalis corporis trapezoidei.

Oliver's sign (ol′ĭ-verz) [William Silver *Oliver*, English physician, 1836–1908]. See under *sign*.

Oliver's test (ol′ĭ-verz) [George *Oliver*, English physician, 1841–1915]. See under *tests*.

Oliver-Cardarelli sign (ol′ĭ-ver-kar″dah-rel′e) [William Silver *Oliver*, English physician, 1836–1908; Antonio *Cardarelli*, Italian physician, 1831–1926]. See under *sign*.

olivifugal (ol″ĭ-vif′u-gal) [*olive* + L. *fugere* to flee]. Moving or conducting away from the oliva.

olivipetal (ol″ĭ-vip′e-tal) [*olive* + L. *petere* to seek]. Passing or conducting toward the oliva.

olivopontocerebellar (ol″ĭ-vo-pon″to-ser″e-bel′ar). Pertaining to the olivae, the middle peduncles, and the cortex of the cerebellum.

Ollier's disease, law, layer (ol″e-āz′) [Léopold Louis Xavier Edouard *Ollier*, a French surgeon, 1830–1901]. See under the nouns.

Ol. oliv. Abbreviation for L. *o′leum oli′vae*, olive oil.

olophonia (ol″lo-fo′ne-ah) [Gr. *oloos* destroyed, lost + *phōnē* voice + *-ia*]. Defective speech due to malformed vocal organs.

O.L.P. Abbreviation for L. *occipito-laeva posterior* (left occipitoposterior) position of the fetus.

Ol. res. Abbreviation for *oleoresin*.

Olshausen's method, operation (ols′how-zenz) [Robert von *Olshausen*, obstetrician in Berlin, 1835–1915]. See under the nouns.

Olshevsky tube (ol-shev′ske) [Dimitry E. *Olshevsky*, American physician, born 1900]. See under *tube*.

O.L.T. Abbreviation for L. *occipito-laeva transversa* (left occipitotransverse) position of the fetus.

o.m. Abbreviation for L. *om′ni ma′ne*, every morning.

-oma [Gr. *-ōma*, perhaps adapted from *onkōma*, a swelling]. Word termination meaning tumor or neoplasm, of the part indicated by the stem to which it is attached.

omacephalus (o″mah-sef′ah-lus) [Gr. *ōmos* shoulder + *a* neg. + *kephalē* head]. A monster fetus with deficient head and no upper extremities.

omagra (o-ma′grah) [Gr. *ōmos* shoulder + *agra* seizure]. Gout in the shoulder.

omalgia (o-mal′je-ah) [Gr. *ōmos* shoulder + *-algia*]. Pain in the shoulder.

omarthritis (o″mar-thri′tis) [Gr. *ōmos* shoulder + *arthron* joint + *-itis*]. Inflammation of the shoulder joint.

omasitis (o″mah-si′tis). Inflammation of the omasum.

omasum (o-ma′sum) [L.]. The third division of the stomach of ruminant animals. Called also *manifold, manyplies*, and *psalterium*.

Ombrédanne's mask, operation (ahm-bra-danz′) [Louis *Ombrédanne*, Paris surgeon, 1871–1956]. See under *mask* and *operation*.

ombrophobia (om″bro-fo′be-ah) [Gr. *ombros* rain + *phobia*]. Fear of rain.

ombrophore (om′bro-fōr) [Gr. *ombros* rain + *phoros* bearer]. An apparatus for applying a douche bath of water containing carbon dioxide.

omega (o′me-gah). The twenty-fourth, and final, letter of the Greek alphabet, Ω or ω. **o. melan-cho′licum,** a folding of the skin between the eyebrows like the Greek letter omega; a sign of melancholia.

omeire (o-mi′re). A native drink of southwest Africa, made by permitting milk to ferment.

omenta (o-men′tah) [L.]. Plural of *omentum*.

omental (o-men′tal). Pertaining to the omentum.

omentectomy (o″men-tek′to-me) [*omentum* + Gr. *ektomē* excision]. Excision of a portion of the omentum.

omentitis (o″men-ti′tis). Inflammation of the omentum.

omentofixation (o-men″to-fiks-a′shun). Omentopexy.

omentopexy (o-men′to-pek″se) [*omentum* + Gr. *pēxis* fixation]. In general, an operation which fastens the omentum to some other tissue, and especially one which uses a part of the omentum as a circulatory bridge either to lessen congestion, as in the Talma operation for relief of the portal circulation, or to supply more vascular nutrition as to the heart in coronary disease.

omentoplasty (o-men′to-plas″te) [*omentum* + Gr. *plassein* to form]. The use of omental grafts.

omentorrhaphy (o″men-tor′ah-fe) [*omentum* + Gr. *rhaphē* suture]. The operation of suturing the omentum.

omentosplenopexy (o-men″to-sple′no-pek″se). Combined omentopexy and splenopexy.

omentotomy (o″men-tot′o-me) [*omentum* + Gr. *temnein* to cut]. Incision of the omentum.

omentovolvulus (o-men″to-vol′vu-lus). Volvulus of the omentum.

omentulum (o-men′tu-lum). The lesser omentum.

omentum (o-men′tum), pl. *omen′ta* [L. "fat skin"]. A fold of peritoneum extending from the stomach to adjacent organs in the abdominal cavity. **colic o., gastrocolic o.,** o. majus. **gastrohepatic o.,** o. minus. **gastrosplenic o.,** ligamentum gastrolienale. **greater o.,** o. majus. **Haller's colic o.,** a process from the greater omentum, which sometimes in fetal life becomes attached to the testis, and may be included in an inguinal hernia. **lesser o.** 1. Ligamentum hepatogastricum. 2. Omentum minus. **o. ma′jus** [N A, B N A], a prominent peritoneal fold suspended from the greater curvature of the stomach and passing inferiorly a variable distance in front of the intestines. It is attached to the anterior surface of the transverse colon. Called also *greater o.* **o. mi′nus** [N A, B N A], a peritoneal fold joining the lesser curvature of the stomach and the first part of the duodenum to the porta hepatis. Called also *lesser o.* **pancreaticosplenic o.,** a fold of peritoneum connecting the tail of the pancreas and the visceral surface of the spleen. **splenogastric o.,** ligamentum gastrolienale.

omentumectomy (o-men″tum-ek′to-me) [*omentum* + Gr. *ektomē* excision]. Excision of the omentum.

omitis (o-mi′tis) [*omo-* + *-itis*]. Inflammation of the shoulder.

ommatidium (om″ah-tid′e-um) [Gr. *omma* the eye]. One of the elongated units of a compound eye of an arthropod.

Omn. bih. Abbreviation for L. *om′ni biho′ra,* every two hours.

Omn. hor. Abbreviation for L. *om′ni ho′ra,* every hour.

omnipotence (om-nip′o-tence). The state of being all-powerful. **o. of thought,** the deluded belief of a patient that his thoughts and wishes are all powerful and will be fulfilled as soon as he expresses them.

omnivorous (om-niv′o-rus) [L. *omnis* all + *vorare* to eat]. Subsisting upon food of every kind.

Omn. noct. Abbreviation for L. *om′ni noc′te,* every night.

omo- [Gr. *ōmos* shoulder]. Combining form denoting relationship to the shoulder.

omocephalus (o″mo-sef′ah-lus) [*omo-* + Gr. *kephalē* head]. A fetus with no arms and an incomplete head.

omoclavicular (o″mo-klah-vik′u-lar). Pertaining to the shoulder and the clavicle.

omodynia (o″mo-din′e-ah) [*omo-* + Gr. *odynē* pain]. Pain in the shoulder.

omohyoid (o″mo-hi′oid). Pertaining to the shoulder and the hyoid bone.

omophagia (o″mo-fa′je-ah) [Gr. *ōmos* raw + *phagein* to eat]. The eating of raw food.

omoplata (o″mo-plat′ah) [Gr. *ōmoplatē* the shoulder-blade]. The scapula.

omosternum (o″mo-ster′num). The interarticular cartilage at the joint between the sternum and clavicle.

omotocia (om″o-to′se-ah) [Gr. *ōmotokia* miscarriage]. Premature delivery.

OMPA. Abbreviation for *octamethyl pyrophosphoramide.*

omphalectomy (om″fah-lek′to-me) [*omphalo-* + Gr. *ektomē* excision]. Excision of the navel.

omphalelcosis (om″fal-el-ko′sis) [*omphalo-* + Gr. *helkōsis* ulceration]. Ulceration of the umbilicus.

omphalic (om-fal′ik) [Gr. *omphalikos*]. Pertaining to the umbilicus.

omphalitis (om″fah-li′tis) [*omphalo-* + *-itis*]. Inflammation of the umbilicus.

omphalo- (om′fah-lo) [Gr. *omphalos* the navel]. Combining form denoting relationship to the umbilicus.

omphalo-angiopagous (om″fah-lo-an″je-op′ah-gus) [*omphalo-* + Gr. *angeion* vessel + *pagos* thing fixed]. Joined by the vessels of the umbilical cords: said of enzygotic twins.

omphalocele (om′fal-o-sēl) [*omphalo-* + Gr. *kēlē* hernia]. Protrusion, at birth, of part of the intestine through a large defect in the abdominal wall at the umbilicus, the protruding bowel being covered only by a thin transparent membrane composed of amnion and peritoneum.

omphalochorion (om″fah-lo-ko′re-on). The structure formed by fusion of the yolk sac with the chorion; a choriovitelline placenta.

omphalodidymus (om″fah-lo-did′ĭ-mus) [*omphalo-* + Gr. *didymos* twin]. Gastrodidymus.

omphalogenesis (om″fah-lo-jen′e-sis) [*omphalo-* + Gr. *genesis* formation]. Development of the umbilicus or yolk sac in the embryo.

omphaloma (om″fah-lo′mah) [*omphalo-* + *-oma*]. A tumor of the umbilicus.

omphalomesaraic (om″fah-lo-mes-ah-ra′ik). Omphalomesenteric.

omphalomesenteric (om″fah-lo-mes″en-ter′ik). Pertaining to the umbilicus and mesentery.

omphaloncus (om″fah-long′kus) [*omphalo-* + Gr. *onkos* mass, bulk]. A tumor or swelling of the umbilicus.

omphalopagus (om″fah-lop′ah-gus) [*omphalo-* + Gr. *pagos* thing fixed]. Monomphalus.

omphalophlebitis (om″fah-lo-fle-bi′tis) [*omphalo-* + Gr. *phleps* vein + *-itis*]. 1. Inflammation of the umbilical veins. 2. Navel ill; a condition of markedly suppurative lesions in young animals, due to infection through the umbilicus.

omphaloproptosis (om″fah-lo-pro-to′sis) [*omphalo-* + Gr. *pro* forward + *ptōsis* falling]. Prolapse of the umbilical cord.

omphalorrhagia (om″fah-lo-ra′je-ah) [*omphalo-* + Gr. *rhēgnynai* to burst forth]. Hemorrhage from the umbilicus.

omphalorrhea (om″fah-lo-re′ah) [*omphalo-* + Gr. *rhoia* flow]. An effusion of lymph at the navel.

omphalorrhexis (om″fah-lo-rek′sis) [*omphalo-* + Gr. *rhēxis* rupture]. Rupture of the umbilicus.

omphalosite (om′fah-lo-sīt) [*omphalo-* + Gr. *sitos* food]. A monster fetus with no heart, which dies when the umbilical cord is cut. See *acardius.*

omphalosotor (om″fah-lo-so′tor) [*omphalo-* + Gr. *sōtēr* preserver]. An instrument for replacing the prolapsed umbilical cord in childbirth.

omphalospinous (om″fah-lo-spi′nus) [*omphalo-* + *spinous*]. Pertaining to the umbilicus and the anterior spine of the ileum.

omphalotaxis (om″fah-lo-tak′sis) [*omphalo-* +

Gr. *taxis* arrangement]. Replacement of the prolapsed umbilical cord.

omphalotomy (om″fah-lot′o-me) [*omphalo-* + Gr. *tomē* a cutting]. The cutting of the umbilical cord.

omphalotribe (om′fah-lo-trīb). An instrument for crushing the umbilical cord.

omphalotripsy (om″fah-lo-trip′se) [*omphalo-* + Gr. *tribein* to crush]. The separation of the umbilical cord by a crushing operation.

omphalus (om′fah-lus) [Gr. *omphalos*]. The umbilicus.

Om. quar. hor. Abbreviation for L. *om′ni quadran′te ho′ra*, every quarter of an hour.

omunono (om″u-no′no). Yaws.

o.n. Abbreviation for L. *om′ni noc′te*, every night.

onanism (o′nan-izm) [*Onan*, son of Judah]. Masturbation; more correctly, withdrawal of the penis before orgasm.

onaye (o-nah′ye). An exceedingly virulent poison from the seeds of *Strophanthus hispidus*.

Onchocerca (ong″ko-ser′kah) [Gr. *onkos* barb + *kerkos* tail]. A genus of filarial worms. The adults live and breed in the subcutaneous, fibroid nodules; the young (the microfilariae) are carried by the lymph and are found chiefly in the skin and the eyes. **O. caecu′tiens,** *O. volvulus*. **O. cervica′lis** is found in the cervical ligament of horses and mules. **O. gibso′ni** infests the subcutaneous tissues of cattle and zebra, producing nodular swellings on the flanks, knees, and shoulders. **O. vol′vulus,** a species that causes subcutaneous nodules on the heads of natives in tropical Africa, Mexico and Central America. It also causes punctate keratitis and loss of vision (blinding filarial disease). It is transmitted by bites of flies of the genus *Simulium* in Africa and by members of *Eusimulium* in Mexico and Central America. The disease is known locally as coast erysipelas.

onchocerciasis (ong″ko-ser-ki′ah-sis). The state of being infected with worms of the genus Onchocerca.

onchocercosis (ong″ko-ser-ko′sis). Onchocerciasis.

Onciola (on-si′o-lah). A genus of acanthocephalous parasites. **O. ca′nis,** a species found in the intestines of dogs in Texas and Nebraska.

onco- (ong′ko) [Gr. *onkos* mass, bulk]. Combining form denoting relationship to a tumor, swelling, or mass.

Oncocerca (ong″ko-ser′kah). Onchocerca.

oncocytoma (ong″ko-si-to′ma) [*oncocyte* + *-oma*]. An oxyphilic granular cell adenoma of the parotid gland.

oncogenesis (ong″ko-jen′e-sis) [*onco-* + Gr. *genesis* production, generation]. The production or causation of tumors.

oncogenetic (ong″ko-je-net′ik). Pertaining to or characterized by oncogenesis.

oncogenic (on″ko-jen′ik). Giving rise to tumors or causing tumor formation.

oncogenicity (ong″ko-je-nis′ĭ-te). The quality or property of being able to cause tumor formation.

oncogenous (ong-koj′e-nus). Arising in or originating from a tumor.

oncograph (ong′ko-graf) [*onco-* + Gr. *graphein* to record]. A recording device attached to the oncometer.

oncography (ong-kog′rah-fe). The graphic recording of the outlines of organs.

oncoides (ong-koi′dēz) [*onco-* + Gr. *eidos* form]. Turgid swelling; intumescence.

oncology (ong-kol′o-je) [*onco-* + *-logy*]. The sum of knowledge concerning tumors; the study of tumors.

oncolysis (ong-kol′ĭ-sis) [*onco-* + Gr. *lysis* dissolution]. The lysis or destruction of tumor cells.

oncolytic (ong″ko-lit′ik). Pertaining to, characterized by, or causing oncolysis.

oncoma (ong-ko′mah) [Gr. *onkōma*]. A swelling; tumor.

Oncomelania (ong″ko-mĕ-la′ne-ah). A genus of snails species of which transmit Japanese schistosomiasis in China.

oncometer (ong-kom′e-ter) [*onco-* + Gr. *metron* measure]. An instrument for measuring variations in the size of various organs or parts of the body, as of the kidney or spleen.

oncometric (ong″ko-met′rik). Pertaining to the oncometer or to oncometry.

oncometry (ong-kom′e-tre). The measurement of variations in the size of viscera.

oncosis (ong-ko′sis) [*onco-* + *-osis*]. A morbid condition characterized by the development of tumors.

oncosphere (ong′ko-sfēr) [Gr. *onkos* barb + *sphaira* sphere]. The larva of the tapeworm in the spherical stage, enclosed in a thick, ciliated membrane and armed with six hooks. It may be found in the feces.

oncotherapy (ong″ko-ther′ah-pe) [*onco-* + *therapy*]. The treatment of tumors.

oncothlipsis (ong″ko-thlip′sis) [*onco-* + Gr. *thlipsis* pressure]. Pressure caused by a tumor.

oncotic (ong-kot′ik). Pertaining to, caused by, or marked by, swelling.

oncotomy (ong-kot′o-me) [*onco-* + Gr. *temnein* to cut]. The incision of a tumor, abscess, or swelling.

oncotropic (ong″ko-trop′ik) [*onco-* + Gr. *tropos* a turning]. Having a special affinity or attraction for tumor cells.

ondometer (on-dom′e-ter). An apparatus for measuring the frequency of the oscillations in high frequency currents.

-one. A suffix used in chemistry to indicate quinquivalent nitrogen.

oneiric (on-i′rik). Pertaining to or characterized by dreaming.

oneirism (o-ni′rizm). A dreamlike waking hallucination; cerebral automatism, as in a dream prolonged into the waking state.

oneiro- (o-ni′ro) [Gr. *oneiros* dream]. Combining form denoting relationship to a dream.

oneiroanalysis (o-ni″ro-ah-nal′ĭ-sis). The exploration of the conscious and unconscious personality through the interpretation of pharmacologically induced dreams.

oneirodynia (o-ni″ro-din′e-ah) [*oneiro-* + Gr. *odynē* pain]. Nightmare.

oneirogenic (o″ni-ro-jen′ik). Producing a dreamlike state; capable of causing dreams.

oneirogmus (o-ni-rog′mus) [Gr. *oneirōgmos* an effusion during sleep]. Emission of semen accompanying dreams.

oneiroid (o′ni-roid). Resembling a dream.

oneirology (o″ni-rol′o-je) [*oneiro-* + *-logy*]. The science of dreams.

oneirophrenia (o-ni″ro-fre′ne-ah) [*oneiro-* + Gr. *phrēn* mind + *-ia*]. Meduna's term for a form of schizophrenia characterized by disturbances of the sensorium (illusions, confusions, disorientation), amnesia, stupor, and hallucinations.

oneiroscopy (o″ni-ros′ko-pe) [Gr. *oneiroskopilsos* of the interpretation of dreams]. Analysis of dreams for the purpose of diagnosing the patient's mental state.

oniomania (o″ne-o-ma′ne-ah) [Gr. *ōnios* for sale + *mania* madness]. A morbid desire to make purchases.

oniric (o-ni′rik). Oneiric.

onirogenic (o″ni-ro-jen′ik). Oneirogenic.

oniroid (o′ni-roid). Oneiroid.

onium (o′ne-um). A term applied to a cation in which nitrogen has its maximum covalency, as in the ammonium ion NH_4^+. The compounds include betaines, cholines, and amine oxides.

onkinocele (on-kin′o-sēl) [Gr. *onkos* swelling + *is* fiber + *kēlē* hernia, tumor]. A swollen condition of a tendon sheath.

onobaio (o″no-ba′yo). A powerful arrow poison

from Obok, in Africa. It has a depressant action on the heart.

onomatology (on″o-mah-tol′o-je) [Gr. *onoma* name + *-logy*]. The science of names and nomenclature.

onomatomania (on″o-mat″o-ma′ne-ah) [Gr. *onoma* name + *mania* madness]. Mental derangement with regard to words or names, marked by persistent dwelling on some particular word, by perplexed effort to recall some word, by attaching some special significance to certain words, or by showing disgust for certain words (Charcot and Magnan, 1885).

onomatophobia (on″o-mat″o-fo′be-ah) [Gr. *onoma* name + *phobia*]. Morbid dread of hearing a certain name or word.

onomatopoiesis (on″o-mat″o-poi-e′sis) [Gr. *onoma* name + *poiein* to make]. The formation of meaningless words by the insane.

Ontjom. The fermented product of peanut press cake, made by the natives of Java and Sumatra. Occasionally this product causes poisoning of which one sign is jaundice.

ontogenesis (on″to-jen′e-sis). Ontogeny.

ontogenetic (on″to-je-net′ik). Ontogenic.

ontogenic (on″to-jen′ik). Pertaining to ontogeny.

ontogeny (on-toj′e-ne) [Gr. *ōn* existing + *gennan* to produce]. The complete developmental history of the individual organism. Cf. *phylogeny.*

onyalai, onyalia (o″ne-al′a-e, o″ne-a′le-ah). A nutritional disorder occurring among the blacks in various parts of Africa, and marked by the formation, on the palatal and buccal mucous membrane, of blebs containing semicoagulated blood and without signs of constitutional disorder. It is a form of thrombopenic purpura.

onych- (on′ik). See *onycho-.*

onychalgia (on″ĭ-kal′je-ah) [*onych-* + *-algia*]. Pain in the nails; painful nails.

onychatrophia (o″nik-ah-tro′fe-ah) [*onych-* + *a* neg. + Gr. *trophē* nutrition + *-ia*]. Atrophy of a nail or of the nails.

onychatrophy (on″ik-at′ro-fe). Onychatrophia.

onychauxis (on″ĭ-kawk′sis) [*onych-* + Gr. *auxein* to increase]. Overgrowth of the nails.

onychectomy (on″ĭ-kek′to-me) [*onych-* + Gr. *ektomē* excision]. Excision of a nail or nail bed.

onychexallaxis (on″ĭ-kek″sah-lak′sis) [*onych-* + Gr. *exallaxis* alteration]. Degeneration of the nails.

onychia (o-nik′e-ah) [*onych-* + *-ia*]. Inflammation of the matrix of the nail resulting in loss of the nail. See *paronychia.* **o. latera′lis,** paronychia. **o. malig′na,** onychia with fetid ulceration and loss of the nail. **o. parasit′ica,** onychomycosis. **o. periungua′lis,** paronychia. **o. sic′ca,** syphilitic inflammation of the nail matrix in which the nail becomes thick and brittle.

onychitis (on″ĭ-ki′tis) [*onych-* + *-itis*]. Inflammation of the matrix of a nail.

onycho-, onych- (on′ĭ-ko, on′ik) [Gr. *onyx* nail]. Combining form denoting relationship to the nails.

onychoclasis (on″ĭ-kok′lah-sis) [*onycho-* + Gr. *klasis* breaking]. Breaking of the nail.

onychocryptosis (on″ĭ-ko-krip-to′sis) [*onycho-* + Gr. *kryptein* to conceal]. Ingrowing toenail.

onychodynia (on″ĭ-ko-din′e-ah). Onychalgia.

onychogenic (on″ĭ-ko-jen′ik) [*onycho-* + Gr. *gennan* to produce]. Producing or forming nail substance.

onychogram (o-nik′o-gram). A tracing made by the onychograph.

onychograph (o-nik′o-graf) [*onycho-* + Gr. *graphein* to write]. An instrument for observing and recording the nail pulse and capillary circulation.

onychogryphosis (on″ĭ-ko-grĭ-fo′sis). Onychogryposis.

onychogryposis (on″ĭ-ko-grĭ-po′sis) [*onycho-* + Gr. *grypōsis* a crooking, hooking]. A deformed overgrowth of the nails; hooked or incurved state of the nails.

onychohelcosis (on″ĭ-ko-hel-ko′sis) [*onycho-* + Gr. *helkōsis* ulceration]. Ulceration of the nail.

onychoid (on′ĭ-koid) [*onycho-* + Gr. *eidos* form]. Resembling a fingernail.

onycholysis (on″ĭ-kol′ĭ-sis) [*onycho-* + Gr. *lysis* dissolution]. Loosening or separation of a nail from its nail bed.

onychoma (on″ĭ-ko′mah) [*onycho-* + *-oma*]. A tumor of the nail or nail bed.

onychomadesis (on″ĭ-ko-mah-de′sis) [*onycho-* + Gr. *madēsis* loss of hair]. Complete loss of the nails.

onychomalacia (on″ĭ-ko-mah-la′she-ah) [*onycho-* + Gr. *malakia* softness]. Softening of the fingernail.

onychomycosis (on″ĭ-ko-mi-ko′sis) [*onycho-* + Gr. *mykēs* fungus + *-osis*]. A disease of the nails of the fingers and toes caused by *Epidermophyton floccosum,* by several species of *Trichophyton* and by *Candida albicans.* The nails become opaque, white, thickened, friable, and brittle. Called also *tinea unguium, ringworm of the nails, onychosis trichophytina.*

onychonosus (on″ĭ-kon′o-sus) [*onycho-* + Gr. *nosos* disease]. Disease of the nails.

onychopacity (on″ĭ-ko-pas′ĭ-te). Leukonychia.

onychopathic (on″ĭ-ko-path′ik). Pertaining to onychopathy or any disease of the nails.

onychopathology (on″ĭ-ko-pah-thol′o-je) [*onycho-* + *pathology*]. The pathology of diseases of the nails.

onychopathy (on″ĭ-kop′ah-the) [*onycho-* + Gr. *pathos* disease]. Disease of the nails.

onychophagia (on″ĭ-ko-fa′je-ah). Onychophagy.

onychophagist (on″ĭ-kof′ah-jist). One who habitually bites the fingernails.

onychophagy (on″ĭ-kof′ah-je) [*onycho-* + Gr. *phagein* to eat]. The morbid habit of biting the nails.

onychophyma (on″ĭ-ko-fi′mah) [*onycho-* + Gr. *phyma* growth]. Thickening or enlargement of the nail.

onychophysis (on″ĭ-ko-fi′sis) [*onycho-* + Gr. *phyein* to grow]. A horny growth beneath the toenails.

onychoptosis (on″ĭ-kop-to′sis) [*onycho-* + Gr. *ptōsis* falling]. Falling off of the nails.

onychorrhexis (on″ĭ-ko-rek′sis). Spontaneous splitting and brittleness of the nail.

onychoschizia (on″ĭ-ko-skiz′e-ah) [*onycho-* + Gr. *schizein* to divide + *-ia*]. Loosening of the nail from its bed.

onychosis (on″ĭ-ko′sis) [*onycho-* + *-osis*]. Disease or deformity of a nail or of the nails.

onychotillomania (on″ĭ-ko-til″o-ma′ne-ah). Neurotic picking at the nails.

onychotomy (on″ĭ-kot′o-me) [*onycho-* + Gr. *tomē* a cutting]. Incision of a nail.

onychotrophy (on″ĭ-kot′ro-fe) [*onycho-* + Gr. *trophē* nutrition]. Nutrition of the nails.

onym (on′im) [Gr. *onyma* name]. A technical name or term.

onyx (on′iks) [Gr. "nail"]. 1. A nail of a finger or toe. 2. A variety of hypopyon.

onyxis (o-nik′sis). Ingrowing nail.

onyxitis (on″ik-si′tis) [*onyx* + *-itis*]. Onychitis.

oo- [Gr. *ōon* an egg]. Combining form denoting relationship to an egg or ovum. See also words beginning *ovo-.*

ooblast (o′o-blast) [*oo-* + Gr. *blastos* germ]. The cell from which an ovum is developed.

oocenter (o″o-sen′ter). Ovocenter.

oocephalus (o″o-sef′ah-lus) [*oo-* + Gr. *kephalē* head]. An individual characterized by an egg-shaped head.

oocinesia (o″o-sĭ-ne′ze-ah). Ookinesis.

oocinete (o″o-sin′ēt). Ookinete.

oocyan (o″o-si′an). A blue-green pigment from the shells of birds' eggs; it is a dehydro bilirubin.

oocyanin (o″o-si′ah-nin) [*oo-* + Gr. *kyanos* blue]. A bluish coloring matter from birds' eggs.

oocyesis (o″o-si-e′sis) [*oo-* + Gr. *kyēsis* pregnancy]. Ovarian pregnancy.

oocyst (o′o-sist) [*oo-* + Gr. *kystis* sac, bladder]. The encysted or encapsulated ookinete in the wall of a mosquito's stomach.

oocytase (o″o-si′tās). An enzyme having a destructive effect on ovarian cells.

oocyte (o′o-sīt) [*oo-* + *-cyte*]. A growing or full-grown oogonial cell that has not yet completed its maturation process. **primary o.,** one growing, fully grown, or entering into the first maturative division. **secondary o.,** one in the period between the first and second maturative division.

oocytin (o″o-si′tin). A substance obtained from spermatozoa, leukocytes, and red blood cells which will cause the formation of fertilization membranes in ova.

oodeocele (o-o′de-o-sēl) [Gr. *ōoeidēs* egg-shaped + *kēlē* hernia]. Obturator hernia.

oogenesis (o″o-jen′e-sis) [*oo-* + Gr. *genesis* production]. The origin and development of the ovum.

oogenetic (o″o-je-net′ik). Pertaining to oogenesis.

oogenic (o″o-jen′ik). Producing ova.

oogonium (o″o-go′ne-um) [*oo-* + Gr. *gonē* generation]. The primordial cell from which the ovarian egg arises, at any stage of its growth to become a primary oocyte.

ookinesis (o″o-kĭ-ne′sis) [*oo-* + Gr. *kinēsis* motion]. The mitotic movements of the egg during maturation and fertilization.

ookinete (o″o-kĭ-nēt′). The fertilized form of the malarial parasite in the body of a mosquito. It is formed by fertilization of a macrogamete by a microgamete and develops into an oocyst.

oolemma (o″o-lem′ah) [*oo-* + Gr. *lemma* sheath]. The limiting membrane of the ovum; the zona pellucida.

oophagia (o″o-fa′je-ah). Oophagy.

oophagy (o-of′ah-je) [Gr. *ōophagein* to eat eggs]. The eating of eggs.

oophor-. See *oophoro-*.

oophoralgia (o″of-or-al′je-ah) [*oophor-* + *-algia*]. Pain in an ovary.

oophorectomize (o″of-o-rek′to-mīz). To deprive of the ovaries by surgical removal.

oophorectomy (o″of-o-rek′to-me) [*oophor-* + Gr. *ektomē* excision]. The removal or destruction of an ovary or ovaries.

oophoritis (o″of-o-ri′tis) [*oophor-* + *-itis*]. Inflammation of an ovary. **o. parotide′a,** oophoritis occurring in association with infection by the virus causing mumps. **o. sero′sa,** edema of the ovary.

oophoro-, oophor- (o-of′or-o, o′o-fōr) [Gr. *ōophoros* bearing eggs]. Combining form denoting relationship to the ovary.

oophorocystectomy (o-of″o-ro-sis-tek′to-me) [*oophoro-* + *cyst* + Gr. *ektomē* excision]. Excision of an ovarian cyst.

oophorocystosis (o-of″o-ro-sis-to′sis) [*oophoro-* + *cyst* + *-osis*]. The formation of an ovarian cyst.

oophorogenous (o-of″o-roj′e-nus). Derived from the ovary.

oophorohysterectomy (o-of″o-ro-his″ter-ek′to-me) [*oophoro-* + Gr. *hystera* uterus + *ektomē* excision]. Surgical removal of the uterus and ovaries.

oophoroma (o-of″o-ro′mah). A malignant tumor of the ovary. **o. follicula′re,** Brenner tumor.

oophoron (o-of′o-ron) [Gr. *ōon* egg + *pherein* to bear]. An ovary (ovarium [N A]).

oophoropathy (o-of″o-rop′ah-the) [*oophoro-* + Gr. *pathos* disease]. Any disease of the ovaries.

oophoropeliopexy (o-of″o-ro-pe′le-o-pek″se) [*oophoro-* + Gr. *pellis* pelvis + *pēxis* fixation]. Adnexopexy.

oophoropexy (o-of′o-ro-pek″se) [*oophoro-* + Gr. *pēxis* fixation]. Adnexopexy.

oophoroplasty (o-of′o-ro-plas″te). Plastic operation on the ovary.

oophororrhaphy (o-of″o-ror′ah-fe) [*oophoro-* + Gr. *rhaphē* suture]. The stitching of an ovary to the pelvic wall.

oophorosalpingectomy (o-of″o-ro-sal″pin-jek′to-me) [*oophoro-* + Gr. *salpinx* tube + *ektomē* excision]. Surgical removal of an ovary and oviduct.

oophorosalpingitis (o-of″o-ro-sal″pin-ji′tis). Salpingo-oophoritis.

oophorostomy (o-of″o-ros′to-me) [*oophoro-* + Gr. *stomoun* to provide with an opening, or mouth]. The making of an opening into an ovarian cyst for drainage purposes.

oophorotomy (o-of″o-rot′o-me) [*oophoro-* + Gr. *tomē* a cutting]. Incision of the ovary.

oophorrhagia (o-of″o-ra′je-ah) [*oophoro-* + Gr. *rhēgnynai* to burst forth]. Severe hemorrhage from an ovulatory site.

oophyte (o′o-fīt) [*oo-* + Gr. *phyton* plant]. The sexual stage of mosses, ferns, etc.

ooplasm (o′o-plazm). The cytoplasm of the egg.

ooporphyrin (o″o-por′fir-in). Protoporphyrin contained in egg shells.

oorhodein (o″o-ro′de-in) [*oo-* + Gr. *rhodon* rose]. A red coloring matter from birds' eggs.

oosome (o′o-sōm) [*oo-* + Gr. *sōma* body]. A cytoplasmic body in the ovum which passes into the germ cells.

oosperm (o′o-sperm) [*oo-* + Gr. *sperma* seed]. The recently fertilized ovum.

Oospora (o-os′po-rah) [*oo-* + Gr. *sporos* seed]. A genus of fungi. **O. catena′ta, O. frag′ilis,** species which have been isolated from black tongue. **O. lac′tis,** a species found on the surface of milk, cheese, etc., and forming a white mold. **O. tozen′ri,** a species cultivated from black mycetoma. It produces a brown or dark color in cultures and may be responsible for the black color of the lesions in man.

oosporangium (o″o-spo-ran′je-um). The female element in the sexual formation of oospores.

oospore (o′o-spōr) [*oo-* + *spore*]. A spore formed by the conjugation of two sexually differentiated elements.

oosporosis (o″o-spo-ro′sis). Infection by an oospore; e.g., in chronic bronchitis.

ootheca (o″o-the′kah) [*oo-* + Gr. *thēkē* case]. 1. An egg case, such as is found in some lower animals. 2. An ovary.

oothecalgia (o″o-the-kal′je-ah). Ovarialgia.

ootheco- [Gr. *ōon* egg + *thēkē* case]. For words beginning thus see those beginning *oophoro-* and *ovario-*.

oothectomy (o″o-thek′to-me). Oophorectomy.

ootherapy (o″o-ther′ah-pe). Ovotherapy.

ootid (o′o-tid). A ripe ovum; one of four cells derived from the two consecutive divisions of the primary oocyte, and corresponding to the spermatids derived from division of the primary spermatocyte.

ootype (o′o-tīp) [*oo-* + Gr. *typos* impression]. In some trematodes, a dilated portion of the uterus into which the oviduct opens and where the ovum is fertilized, provided with the yolk, and invested with a shell.

ooxanthine (o″o-zan′thin) [*oo-* + Gr. *xanthos* yellow]. A yellow pigment found in egg shells.

oozooid (o″o-zo′oid) [*oo-* + Gr. *zōo-eidēs* like an animal]. An individual which is developed from an ovum, that is, as a result of sexual reproduction.

opacification (o-pas″ĭ-fi-ka′shun). The development of opacity, as of the cornea or lens.

opacity (o-pas′ĭ-te) [L. *opacitas*]. 1. The condition of being opaque. 2. An opaque spot or area. **Caspar's ring o.,** a ring-shaped opacity of the cornea caused by contusion.

opacol (o-pa′kol). Tetra-iodophthalein sodium.

opalescent (o″pal-es′ent). Showing various colors like an opal.

opalescin (o″pal-es′in). An albuminoid derivable from milk: its solutions are opalescent.

opalgia (o-pal′je-ah) [Gr. *ōps* face + *-algia*]. Facial neuralgia.

Opalina (o″pah-li′nah). A genus of parasitic infusoria. **O. rana′rum,** a species found in the rectum of the frog.

opaline (o′pah-lēn) [L. *opalus* opal]. Having the appearance of an opal.

opalisin (o-pal′ĭ-sin). An opalescent protein, obtainable from human milk.

opaque (o-pāk′) [L. *opacus*]. Impervious to light rays, or by extension to roentgen rays or other electromagnetic vibrations; neither transparent nor translucent.

OPD. Abbreviation for *outpatient department.*

opeidoscope (o-pi′do-skōp) [Gr. *ops* a voice + *eidos* form + *skopein* to examine]. An apparatus for studying the vibrations of the voice by means of light reflected from a mirror.

open (o′pen). 1. Exposed to the air; attended with exposure to the air; not covered by unbroken skin. 2. So interrupted (as a circuit) that an electric current cannot pass. 3. Not obstructed or closed.

opening (o′pen-ing). An aperture, or space. See also *ostium.* **o. in adductor magnus muscle,** hiatus tendineus. **aortic o. in diaphragm,** hiatus aorticus. **o. of aqueduct of cochlea, external,** apertura externa canaliculi cochleae. **o. of bladder,** ostium urethrae internum. **cardiac o.,** ostium cardiacum. **cutaneous o. of male urethra,** ostium urethrae externum masculinae. **duodenal o. of stomach,** pylorus. **esophageal o. in diaphragm,** hiatus esophageus. **o. of Hunter's canal, inferior,** hiatus tendineus. **ileocecal o.,** ostium ileocecale. **o. to lesser sac of peritoneum,** foramen epiploicum. **o. for lesser superficial petrosal nerve,** apertura superior canaliculi tympanici. **nasal o. of facial skeleton,** apertura piriformis. **orbital o., o. of orbital cavity, anterior,** aditus orbitae. **ovarian o. of uterine tube,** ostium abdominale tubae uterinae. **o. of pelvis, inferior,** apertura pelvis inferior. **o. of pelvis, superior,** apertura pelvis superior. **pharyngeal o. of auditory tube,** ostium pharyngeum tubae auditivae. **piriform o.,** apertura piriformis. **pyloric o.,** ostium pyloricum. **o. of sacral canal, inferior,** hiatus sacralis. **saphenous o.,** hiatus saphenus. **semilunar o. of ethmoid bone,** hiatus semilunaris ossis ethmoidalis. **o. for smaller superficial petrosal nerve,** apertura superior canaliculi tympanici. **o. of sphenoidal sinus,** apertura sinus sphenoidalis. **o. of stomach, anterior,** pylorus. **tendinous o.,** hiatus tendineus. **thoracic o., inferior, thoracic o., lower,** apertura thoracis inferior. **thoracic o., superior, thoracic o., upper,** apertura thoracis superior. **o. for tympanic branch of glossopharyngeal nerve,** apertura inferior canaliculi tympanici. **o. of tympanic canal, superior,** apertura superior canaliculi tympanici. **uterine o. of uterine tube,** ostium uterinum tubae uterinae. **o. for vena cava,** foramen venae cavae. **o. of vermiform appendix,** ostium appendicis vermiformis. **vesicourethral o.,** ostium urethrae internum.

operable (op′er-ah-b′l). Possible of being operated upon with reasonable hope of improvement.

operation (op″er-a′shun) [L. *operatio*]. 1. Any act performed with instruments or by the hands of a surgeon. 2. Any act performed or effect produced, such as the specific effect of any agent employed in therapy. **Abbe's o.** 1. A lateral intestinal anastomosis made with rings of catgut. 2. Division of an esophageal stricture by string friction. 3. Intracranial resection of the second and third divisions of the fifth nerve for tic douloureux. **Abernethy's o.,** an operation for ligation of the external iliac artery, with a curved incision running from a point one inch within and above the anterior superior spine to a point one and a half inches above and outside of the center of Poupart's ligament. **Adams' o.** 1. Subcutaneous intracapsular division of the neck of the femur for ankylosis of the hip. 2. Subcutaneous division of the palmar fascia at various points for Dupuytren's contracture. 3. Excision of a wedge-shaped piece from the eyelid for relief of ectropion. 4. Operation of crushing the projecting portion of a deflected nasal septum with forceps and inserting a splint. 5. Advancement of the round ligaments. **Adelmann's o.,** disarticulation of a finger with the attached head of the metacarpal bone. **Albee's o.** 1. Operation for ankylosis of the hip, consisting of cutting off the upper surface of the head of the femur and freshening a corresponding point on the acetabulum, and permitting the two freshened surfaces to rest in contact. 2. Transplantation of a portion of the tibia into the split spinous processes of the vertebrae for tuberculous spondylitis. **Albee-Delbet o.,** an operation for fracture of the neck of the femur, done by drilling a hole through the trochanter and the neck and head of the femur and inserting a bone peg in this hole. **Albert's o.,** excision of the knee to secure ankylosis for the cure of flail joint. **Aldrich's o.** (for reversible sterilization), bury the fimbriated end of the oviduct in the broad ligament. **Alexander's o.** 1. [William *Alexander*]. The shortening of the round ligaments of the uterus for displacement of that organ. 2. [William *Alexander*]. Ligation of the vertebral arteries for the cure or relief of epilepsy. 3. [Samuel *Alexander*]. Prostatectomy by median suprapubic and median perineal incisions. **Alexander-Adams o.,** Alexander's o., def. 1. **Allarton's o.,** median lithotomy. **Allingham's o.** 1. [Herbert William *Allingham*]. Inguinal colotomy by an incision parallel with and one-half inch above Poupart's ligament. 2. [William *Allingham*]. Excision of the rectum by an incision into the ischiorectal fossae, about the rectum, and extending backward to the coccyx. **Alouette's o.** See under *amputation.* **Ammon's o.** 1. Blepharoplasty by a flap from the cheek. 2. Dacryocystotomy. 3. For epicanthus: resection of a spindle-shaped piece of skin over the bridge of the nose, undermining the flaps of the epicanthal fold and closing with sutures. **Amussat's o.,** lumbar colotomy by an incision across the outer border of the quadratus lumborum. **Anagnostakis' o.,** an operation for entropion; also an operation for trichiasis. **Anderson's o.,** longitudinal splitting of a tendon followed by sliding along of the cut surfaces to produce lengthening of the tendon. **Andrews' o.** 1. An operation for inguinal hernia by the use of an imbricating or an overlapping suture. 2. An operation for hydrocele, including complete eversion of the lining without the use of stitches. **Anel's o.** 1. Ligation of an artery close to an aneurysm and on the cardiac side. 2. Dilatation of the lacrimal duct with a probe, followed by an astringent injection. **Annandale's o.** 1. The removal of the condyles of the femur for genu valgum. 2. The fixation of displaced cartilages of the knee joint by stitches. **Antyllus' o.,** the ligation of an artery on both sides of an aneurysm, followed by evacuation of the contents through an incision. **Appolito's o.,** enterorrhaphy by a right-angled continuous suture. **Arlt's o.,** any one of several operations on the eye and the eyelid. **Arlt-Jaesche o.,** the transplantation of the ciliary bulbs from the edge of the lid for the cure of distichiasis. **Armsby's o.,** an operation for inguinal hernia, consisting of invagination of the sac and the introduction of a single thread, as a seton, through the sac and the inguinal canal. **Asch's o.,** an operation for the correction of deflection of the nasal septum, consisting of making a crucial incision over the deflection, taking up the segments, reducing the deflection, and inserting a tube to keep the segments in place. **Babcock's o.**, extirpation of the saphenous vein by inserting an acorn-tipped probe and drawing out the vein: for varicose veins. **Baccelli's o.**, introduction of a wire thread into the sac of an aneurysm. **Badal's o.**, laceration of the infratrochlear nerve for the pain of glaucoma. **Baldwin's o.**, formation of an artificial vagina by transplantation of a piece of the ileum between the bladder and the rectum. **Baldy's o., Baldy-Webster o.**, Webster's o. **Ball's o.** 1. Cure of inguinal hernia by an obliteration of the sac, which is partially dissected out and then twisted around its own axis; the fundus is then cut off and the stump made fast in the ring. 2. A special method of iliac colotomy by incision in the left linea semilunaris, the gut being secured by clamps above and below the site for the artificial anus until after suturing and opening the bowel. 3. Cutting of the sensory nerve trunks of the anus for the relief of pruritus ani. **Bardenheuer's o.**, ligation of the innominate artery by partial bony resection through transverse and vertical incisions. **Barkan's o.**, goniotomy. **Barker's o.** 1. An excision of the hip joint by an anterior cut. 2. A special method of excising the astragalus by an incision extending from just above the external malleolus forward and inward to the dorsum of the foot. **Barraquer's o.**, phacoerysis. **Barton's o.**, an operation for ankylosis consisting of sawing through the bone and removing a V-shaped piece. **Barwell's o.**, a method of osteotomy for genu valgum by division of the upper end of the tibia below and the lower end of the tibia above their respective epiphyses. **Basset's o.**, a method of dissecting the inguinal glands in operation for cancer of the vulva. **Bassini's o.**, a method for the radical cure of inguinal hernia. **Bates' o.**, the division of a urethral stricture from within outward by means of a special form of urethrotome. **Battle's o.**, an appendix operation in which temporary displacement of the rectus is done. **Baum's o.**, the stretching of the facial nerve by an incision below the ear. **Baynton's o.**, application of adhesive straps and a bandage to indolent leg ulcers. **Beatson's o.**, ovariotomy in cases of inoperable cancer of the breast, on the theory that lack of the internal secretion of the ovary will produce atrophy of the tumor. **Beer's o.**, a flap method for cataract. **Belfield's o.**, vasotomy. **Belmas' o.**, introduction of gold-beaters' skin into the neck of an inguinal hernia. **Bennett's o.**, operation for varicocele by partial excision of the pampiniform plexus, followed by suture of the divided ends of the plexus. **Bent's o.**, a form of shoulder excision with flap taken from the deltoid region. **Bergenhem's o.**, surgical implantation of the ureter into the rectum. **Berger's o.**, interscapulothoracic amputation. **Best's o.**, subcutaneous suture of the abdominal ring for hernia. **Bevan's o.**, an operation for undescended testicle, by which the testicle is brought down permanently into the scrotum. **Beyea's o.**, gastroplication. **Bier's o.** See under *amputation*. **Bigelow's o.**, litholapaxy or rapid lithotrity. **Billroth's o.** 1. Pylorectomy performed through a transverse incision. 2. Pylorogastrectomy with anterior gastroenterostomy. 3. Excision of the tongue by making a transverse incision below the symphysis of the jaw and joining it by two incisions, one on each side, parallel to the body of the mandible, with preliminary ligation of the lingual arteries. **Bircher's o.**, suturing together a portion of the anterior and posterior walls of a dilated stomach in order to reduce its size. **Bissell's o.**, excision of a section of the round and the broad ligaments for uterine retroversion. **Blalock-Taussig o.**, the anastomosis of the subclavian artery to the pulmonary artery in order to shunt some of the systemic circulation into the pulmonary circulation: performed in cases of congenital pulmonary stenosis. **Blaskovics o.**, for epicanthus: resection of a semilunar piece of skin from the canthal fold nearer to the side of the nose than the canthus, followed by closure with black silk sutures. **Boari's o.**, transplantation of the vasa deferentia so that they will empty into the urethra. **Bobb's o.**, cholecystotomy for the removal of gallstones. **Bobroff's o.** 1. An osteoplastic operation for spina bifida. 2. Excision of the lining membrane of a cyst of the liver, followed by closure of abdomen without drainage. **Bogue's o.**, multiple ligation of the veins with catgut in varicocele. **Böhm's o.**, tenotomy of an ocular muscle for strabismus. **Bonzel's o.**, iridodialysis performed with a hook inserted through a corneal incision. **Borthen's o.**, iridotasis. **Bose's o.**, a method of performing tracheotomy. **Bottini's o.**, the operation of making a channel through the prostate with the galvanocautery for the cure of prostatic enlargement. **Brailey's o.**, stretching of the supratrochlear nerve to relieve pain in glaucoma. **Brasdor's o.**, distal ligation for aneurysm. **Brauer's o.**, cardiolysis; removal of several ribs (usually 3) and costal cartilages on the left side over the pericardium for the relief of adherent pericarditis. **Brenner's o.**, a modification of Bassini's operation in which the abdominal muscles are sutured to the cremaster muscle. **Brewer's o.**, closure of wounds of arteries by application of a special rubber plaster. **Brophy's o.**, an operation for cleft palate. **Brunschwig's o.**, pancreatoduodenectomy. **Bryant's o.**, lumbar colotomy by an oblique incision between the lowest rib and the crest of the ilium. **Buck's o.**, cuneiform excision of the patella and the ends of tibia and fibula. **Burckhardt's o.**, incision into a retropharyngeal abscess from the outside of the neck. **(von) Burow's o.**, plastic operation for removal of tumors without scars. **Buzzi's o.**, the creation of an artificial pupil by a needle passed through the cornea. **Caldwell-Luc o.**, the operation of opening into the antrum of Highmore by way of an incision into the supradental fossa opposite the second molar tooth. **Callisen's o.**, lumbar colotomy by a vertical incision. **Calot's o.**, forcible reduction of gibbus by stretching under narcosis. **Carnochan's o.** 1. The ligation of a large artery for elephantiasis. 2. Removal of Meckel's ganglion and a considerable part of the fifth nerve for neuralgia; incision is made below the orbit, and the ganglion is reached by trephination through the maxillary antrum. **Carpue's o.**, the Indian method of rhinoplasty. **Carter's o.** 1. Formation of an artificial pupil by making a small opening in the cornea and doing an iridotomy. 2. Construction of an artificial bridge of the nose by transplanting a piece of bone from the rib. **Cassel's o.**, excision of exostoses of the ear through the external auditory meatus by means of a gouge. **celsian o.** 1. Perineal lithotomy. 2. Embryotomy by decapitation. 3. Excision of epithelioma of the lip by a V-shaped incision. 4. Circular amputation. **Chaput's o.**, an operation for artificial anus and for intestinal anastomosis. **Cheever's o.**, complete tonsillectomy through the neck. **Cheyne's o.**, a radical cure of femoral hernia by covering the orifice with a flap of the pectineus muscle. **Chiazzi's o.**, epiplopexy. **Chiene's o.** 1. The removal of a wedge from the inner condyle of the femur for the cure of knock knee. 2. Exposure of the retropharyngeal space by lateral cervical incision along the posterior border of the sternocleidomastoid. **Chopart's o.** 1. See under *amputation*. 2. A plastic operation on the lip. **Civiale's o.** 1. Mediobilateral lithotomy. 2. Lithotrity. **Clark's o.**, a plastic operation for urethral fistula. **Coakley's o.**, an operation for disease of the frontal sinus by incising through the cheek, removing the anterior wall, and curetting away the mucous membrane. **Cock's o.**, urethrotomy by a cut along the median line of the perineum. **Codivilla's o.**, an operation for pseudarthrosis by surrounding the pseudarthrosis with thin osteoperiosteal plates taken from the internal face of the tibia. **Colonna's o.**, a reconstruction operation for intracapsular fracture of the femoral neck. **Cooper's o.**, a method of tying the external iliac artery in a cut parallel with Poupart's ligament and 1 inch above it. **Corradi's o.,** Moore-Corradi o. **cosmetic o.,** one intended to effect the removal of a deformity. **Cotte's o.,** removal of the presacral nerve. **Cotting's o.,** operation for ingrowing toe-nail, consisting in cutting off the side of the toe down to and including the ingrowing edge of the nail. **Crile and Matas's o.,** production of regional anesthesia by intraneural infiltration. **Cripp's o.,** a method of colotomy in the iliac region. **Critchett's o.,** excision of the anterior part of the eyeball. **Cushing's o.** 1. Exposure of the gasserian ganglion and three divisions of the fifth nerve by the direct infra-arterial route. 2. A method of performing ureterorrhaphy without support. **Czerny's o.,** a method for the radical cure of inguinal hernia. **Dallas' o.,** an operation for the obliteration of the canal of an inguinal or femoral hernia by the mechanical incitement of an inflammation. **Dana's o.,** resection of the posterior roots of the spinal nerves to relieve pain, athetosis, spastic paralysis, etc. **Davat's o.,** cure of varicocele by compressing the veins by acufilopressure. **Daviel's o.,** extraction of cataract through a corneal incision without cutting the iris. **Davies-Colley o.,** the removal of a wedge of bone from the outer side of the tarsus for the correction of talipes. **de Grandmont's o.,** an operation for ptosis of the lid. **Delorme's o.** 1. Fowler's operation. 2. Decortication of the heart in adhesive pericarditis; pericardiectomy. **Delpech's o.,** ligation of the axillary artery between the pectoralis major and deltoid muscles. **Del Toro's o.,** destruction of the apex of a conical cornea by a white-hot knife. **Denans' o.,** the joining of a divided intestine over metallic cylinders. **Denonvilliers' o.,** plastic correction of a defective ala nasi by transferring a triangular flap from the side of the nose. **Dieffenbach's o.** 1. Amputation at the hip by a circular incision, with application of an elastic ligature, followed by removal of the ligature, securing of the vessels, and the making of an incision on the outer aspect from a point two inches above the great trochanter to the circular incision. 2. Plastic closure of triangular defects by displacing a quadrangular flap toward one side of the triangle. **Dittel's o.,** the enucleation of the lateral lobes of an enlarged prostate through an external incision. **Doléris' o.,** for retrodeviation of the uterus by shortening the round ligaments and fixing them on either side by an opening in the rectus muscle just above the spine of the ilium. **Doppler's o.,** bisection of, or injection of phenol into the tissues around, the sympathetic nerve leading to the gonads with the object of increasing hormone production and producing sexual rejuvenation. Called also *sympathicodiaphtheresis.* **Dowell's o.,** the radical cure of hernia by thrusting the fundus of the sac into its neck and suturing it there. **Doyen's o.,** eversion of the sac for the relief of hydrocele. **Drummond-Morison o.,** an operation for ascites done by opening the abdomen, scrubbing the peritoneum of the liver and spleen and the corresponding part of the parietal peritoneum, suturing the omentum across the abdominal wall. **Dudley's o.,** posterior sagittal incision of the cervix for the relief of dysmenorrhea and sterility. **Dührssen's o.,** vaginofixation of the uterus. **Duplay's o.,** a designation for several plastic operations upon the congenitally deformed penis (epispadias and hypospadias). **Dupuy-Dutemps o.,** blepharoplasty of the lower lid with tissue from the opposing lid. **Dupuytren's o.** See under *amputation.* **Edebohls' o.,** decapsulation of the kidney for Bright's disease. **Ekehorn's o.,** rectopexy by means of a single percutaneous suture. **Elliot's o.,** a method of trephining the sclerocornea for the relief of increased tension in glaucoma. **Ely's o.,** skin grafting performed on the granulating surfaces in chronic suppurative otitis media. **Emmet's o.** 1. A method of repairing a lacerated perineum. 2. Trachelorrhaphy, or suturation of the edges of a lacerated cervix uteri. 3. Artificially formed vesicovaginal fistula to secure drainage of the bladder in cystitis. **equilibrating o.,** tenotomy of the direct antagonist of a paralyzed eye muscle. **Esser's o.,** epithelial inlay. **Estes' o.,** implantation of an ovary into a uterine cornu: performed for sterility. **Estlander's o.,** the resection of one or more ribs in empyema so as to allow the chest wall to collapse and close the abnormal cavity. **Eversbusch's o.,** an operation for ptosis. **Falk-Shukuris o.,** hysterectomy by a transverse fundal incision which includes cornual excision. **Farabeuf's o.,** ischiopubiotomy. **Fergusson's o.,** an operation for excising the maxilla. **Finney's o.,** a method of performing gastroduodenostomy. **Flajani's o.,** iridodialysis performed with a needle thrust through the cornea. **flap o.** See under *amputation.* **Förster's o.** 1. The operation of cutting intradurally the seventh, eighth, and ninth dorsal nerve roots on both sides in locomotor ataxia. 2. An operation to produce rapid artificial ripening of cataract (1884). **Förster-Penfield o.,** total excision of the scar tissue along with the epileptogenic cortical area in traumatic epilepsy. **Fothergill o.,** an operation for uterine prolapse by fixation of the cardinal ligaments. **Fowler's o.,** decortication of the lung in empyema in order to allow the lung tissue to expand and fill the pleural space; pleurectomy. **Franco's o.,** suprapubic cystotomy. **Frank's o.,** a method of performing gastrostomy by forming a valve out of a cone of the stomach and suturing it to the incision in the chest wall and inserting a tube. **Franke's o.,** removal of the intercostal nerves for the visceral crises of tabes. **Frazier-Spiller o.,** division of the sensory root of the gasserian ganglion for relief of trigeminal neuralgia. **Fredet-Ramstedt o.,** the operation for congenital stenosis of the pylorus by incising the thickened serosa and muscularis down to the mucosa. **Freund's o.** 1. Laparohysterectomy. 2. Chondrotomy for congenital funnel breast. **Freyer's o.,** a method of performing suprapubic enucleation of the hypertrophied prostate. **Friedrich's o.,** pleuropneumonolysis. **Frommel's o.,** shortening of the uterosacral ligaments for retrodeviation. **Frost-Lang o.,** insertion of a gold ball to take the place of an enucleated eyeball. **Fukala's o.,** removal of the lens of the eye for marked myopia. **Gant's o.,** a division of the shaft of the femur below the lesser trochanter for ankylosis of the hip joint. **Gaza's o.,** section or division of the rami communicantes; ramisection. **Gersuny's o.,** an operation for incontinence of feces, done by loosening the rectum from its adhesions, twisting three fourths of a turn on its long axis, and then suturing it in place. The name is also applied to a similar operation on the female urethra for incontinence of urine. **Gifford's o.** 1. Delimiting keratotomy. 2. Destruction of the lacrimal sac by instilling trichloracetic acid into it. **Gigli's o.,** lateral section of the os pubis for difficult labor. **Gill's o.,** an operation for drop foot or pes equinus done by inserting a wedge of bone in order to limit plantar flexion. **Gillespie's o.,** excision of the wrist by a lengthwise dorsal incision between the extensor communis and extensor medii digiti. **Gilliam's o.,** an operation for retroversion of the uterus by drawing a loop of each round ligament through the abdominal wall and fixing the loops to the abdominal fascia. **Gillies' o.,** operation for ectropion by forming the skin of the eyelids by an epithelial flap. **Goffe's o.,** an operation for vaginal cystocele. **Gonin's o.,** treatment of retinal detachment by thermocautery of the fissure in the retina performed through an opening in the sclera. **Gottschalk's o.,** shortening of the uterosacral ligaments by the vaginal route. **Graber-Duvernay o.,** the operation of boring minute channels through the bone to the center of the head of the femur with the object of modifying the circulation within the bone in chronic arthritis. **Grant's o.,** excision of tumors of the lip by removing a square block of tissue containing the tumor, and then making oblique incisions extending down and out from each angle of the wound. The triangular flaps thus formed are drawn toward the center and sutured. **Gritti's o.** See under *amputation.* **Grossmann's o.,** treatment of retinal detachment by aspiration of the subretinal fluid and the slow injection of warm salt solution into the vitreous. **Gussenbauer's o.,** the cutting of an esophageal stricture through an opening above the stricture. **Guyon's o.** See under *amputation.* **Hagner's o.,** drainage of gonorrheal epididymitis through an incision into the epididymis. **Hahn's o.,** Loreta's o., def. 1. **Halpin's o.,** extirpation of the lacrimal gland by a curved incision through the middle of the eyebrow. **Halsted's o.,** a modification of Bassini's operation. **Hancock's o.** See under *amputation.* **Hartley-Krause o.,** excision of the gasserian ganglion and its roots to relieve facial neuralgia. **Haynes's o.,** the operation of draining the cisterna magna for acute suppurative meningitis. **Heath's o.,** division of the ascending rami of the lower jaw with a saw for ankylosis: performed within the mouth. **Heaton's o.,** an operation for inguinal hernia. **Hegar's o.,** perineorrhaphy by denuding a triangular area on the center of the posterior wall of the vagina and suturing from above downward. **Heine's o.,** cyclodialysis in glaucoma. **Heineke's o.,** operation for cancer of the rectum by a T-shaped incision. **Heineke-Mikulicz o.,** enlargement of the pyloric opening by an incision through its walls in a direction parallel to the long axis of the stomach, and closure of this by suture at right angles to the original incision. **Heisrath's o.,** excision of the tarsal folds for trachoma. **Heller's o.,** cardiomyotomy. **Herbert's o.,** displacement of a wedge-shaped flap of sclera in order to form a filtering cicatrix in glaucoma. **Hey's o.** See under *amputation.* **Hibb's o.,** an operation for Pott's disease by fracturing the spinous processes of the vertebrae and pressing the tip of each downward to rest in the denuded area caused by the fracture of its elbow below. **Hochenegg's o.,** an operation for rectal cancer. **Hoffa-Lorenz o.,** Lorenz's o. **Holmes's o.,** a method of excising the os calcis by an incision along its upper border and at the outer border of the foot to the calcaneocuboid joint, and another across the sole, the peroneal tendons being divided. **Holth's o.,** excision of the sclera by punch operation. **Horsley's o.,** excision of an area of motor cortex for relief of athetoid and convulsive movements of an upper extremity. **Hotchkiss' o.,** operation for epithelioma of the cheek, with resection of part of the mandible and maxilla and plastic restoration of the defect from the tongue and side of the neck. **Hufnagel o.,** surgical reconstruction of the aortic valve for correction of aortic insufficiency. **Huggins' o.,** castration performed for cancer of the prostate. **Huguier's o.,** right lateral or lumbar colotomy. **Hunter's o.,** ligation of an artery in the proximal side of an aneurysm and at a distance from it. **Indian o.,** the formation of an artificial nose by a flap from the forehead, with its pedicle at the root of the nose. **interval o.,** an operation performed during the interval between two attacks of a disease such as appendicitis. **Italian o.,** the formation of an artificial nose by a flap from the arm, to which it remains attached until union has taken place. Called also *tagliacotian o.* **Jaboulay's o.,** interpelviabdominal amputation. **Jacobaeus o.,** the treatment of pleural adhesions by thoracoscopy and cauterization. **Jansen's o.,** operation for disease of the frontal sinus by removing the lower wall and a part of the anterior wall and curetting away the mucous membrane. **Jarvis' o.,** removal of the hypertrophied portion of the lower turbinated bone with a special wire snare écraseur. **Jelks's o.,** for stricture of rectum, done by incising the fibrous tissue around the rectum through incisions on each side of the anus. **Jonnesco's o.,** sympathectomy. **Kader's o., Kader-Senn o.,** gastrostomy by which the feeding tube is introduced through a valvelike flap which closes on withdrawal of the tube. **Keegan's o.,** a modification of the Indian operation for forming an artificial nose: the flap is taken mainly from one side of the forehead. **Keen's o.,** omphalectomy. **Kehr's o.,** removal of the gallbladder and cystic duct with drainage of the hepatic duct. **Kehrer's o.,** an operation for depressed nipple, consisting of excision of a piece of the surrounding skin so as to set up cicatricial contraction. **Kelly's o.** 1. (Howard A.). Fixation of the uterus to the abdominal wall for the correction of retroposition. 2. Arytenoidopexy. **Key's o.,** the lateral operation of lithotomy done with a straight staff. **Killian's o.,** excision of the anterior wall of the frontal sinus, removal of the diseased tissue, and formation of a permanent communication with the nose. **King's o.,** arytenoidopexy. **Kirmisson's o.,** transplantation of the Achilles tendon to the peroneus longus muscle in clubfoot. **Kirschner's o.,** treatment of hemorrhage from the spleen by suturing the rupture and covering it with omentum. **Knapp's o.,** for cataract, by a peripheral opening in the capsule behind the iris, without iridectomy. **Kocher's o.** 1. A method of excising the ankle joint by a cut below the outer malleolus, division of the peroneal tendons, removal of the diseased tissues, and suturation of the divided tendons. 2. A method of removing the thyroid gland by one median incision and two lateral ones, the latter being carried upward almost to the angle of the jaw. 3. A method of reducing a subcoracoid dislocation of the humerus. 4. Excision of the tongue through an incision extending from the symphysis of the jaw to the hyoid bone and thence to the mastoid process. 5. A method of mobilizing the duodenum. 6. A method of pylorectomy. **Kocks's o.,** shortening of the base of the broad ligament by the vaginal route for uterine retroversion or prolapse. **Kolomnin's o.,** cauterization of the diseased tissues in hip joint disease by ignipuncture. **Kondoleon o.,** treatment of elephantiasis by the removal of strips of subcutaneous tissue. **König's o.,** operation for congenital dislocation of hip by reducing the dislocation and forming an edge on the upper border of the acetabulum by an osteoperiosteal flap from the ilium. **Körte-Ballance o.,** anastomosis of the facial and hypoglossal nerves. **Kortzeborn's o.,** an operation to relieve ape hand due to median nerve paralysis. The extensor tendons of the thumb are lengthened and the thumb is tied to the ulnar side of the hand by means of a strip of fascia. **Kraske's o.,** removal of the coccyx and of a part of the sacrum for access to a carcinomatous rectum. **Krause's o.,** extradural excision of the gasserian ganglion for trigeminal neuralgia. **Krimer's o.,** uranoplasty in which mucoperiosteal flaps from each side of the palatal cleft are sutured together at the median line. **Krönlein's o.** 1. Exposure of the third branch of the trigeminal nerve for facial neuralgia. 2. Resection of the outer wall of the orbit for the removal of an orbital tumor without excising the eye. **Kuhnt's o.,** an operation for disease of the frontal sinus by removing the anterior wall of the sinus and curetting away the mucous membrane. **Küster's o.,** an operation for draining the pus in mastoiditis by exposing the attic, antrum, and tympanum. **Labbe's o.,** gastrotomy in which a parietal incision is made along the margin of the lowest left rib. **Lagrange's o.,** sclerecto-iridectomy. **Lancereaux's o.,** treatment of aneurysm of the aorta by subcutaneous injections of gelatin. **Landolt's o.,** the formation of a lower eyelid from materials taken from the upper lid. **Lane's o.,** the operation of dividing the ileum near the cecum, closing the portion attached to the cecum and anastomosing the other end with the upper part of the rectum or lower part of the sigmoid, thus eliminating the colon from taking any part in the fecal current. **Lane-Lannelongue o.,** removal of portions of bone from the skull for cerebral decompression. **Lange's o.,** artificial tendon transplantation with strands of silk. See *silk implantation,* under *implantation.* **Lannelongue's o.,** a designation of various methods of craniotomy in cases of microcephalus, etc. **Lanz's o.,** an operation for elephantiasis of the leg in which the strips of fascia lata are inserted into an opening made in the femur. **Laroyenne's o.,** puncture of Douglas' pouch to secure drainage in pelvic suppuration. **Larrey's o.** See under *amputation.* **Latzko's o.,** a method of cesarean section. See under *section.* **Lauren's o.,** a plastic operation for closure of a cicatricial opening following mastoid operation. **Le Fort's o.,** the operation of uniting the anterior and posterior vaginal walls along the middle line for the repair of prolapse of the uterus. **Lennander's o.,** removal of the inguinal glands, including those in the pelvis, as far as the bifurcation of the aorta. **Leriche's o.,** periarterial sympathectomy. **Lexer's o.,** removal of the gasserian ganglion. **Lisfranc's o.** See under *amputation.* **Liston's o.,** an operation for excision of the upper jaw. **Littre's o.,** a method of inguinal colotomy. The sigmoid flexure is opened on the left side, in a cut parallel to Poupart's ligament and half an inch above it. **Lizar's o.,** excision of the upper jaw by a curved incision extending from the angle of the mouth to the malar bone. **Longmire o.,** anastomosis of one of the intrahepatic biliary ducts to the jejunum after partial resection of the left lobe of the liver, performed in treatment of extensive obstruction of the common bile duct or of the hepatic duct. **Longuet's o.,** extraserous transplantation of the testicle for varicocele and hydrocele. **Lorenz's o.,** for congenital dislocation of the hip, consisting in reduction of the dislocation, and keeping the head of the femur fixed against the rudimentary acetabulum until a socket is formed. **Loreta's o.** 1. Gastrotomy with divulsion of either orifice of the stomach for stenosis. 2. The insertion of a wire into an aneurysm, followed by electrolysis. **Lossen's o.,** removal of the second division of the fifth nerve by a method in which the masseter is not divided. **Luc's o.,** Caldwell-Luc o. **Ludloff's o.,** oblique osteotomy of the first metatarsal bone for the correction of hallux valgus. **Lund's o.,** removal of the astragalus for the correction of talipes. **Lyon-Horgan's o.,** the operation of severing and ligating the superior and inferior thyroid arteries on both sides for the relief of angina pectoris. **McArthur's o.,** catheterization of the common bile duct for making effusions into the duodenum. **McBurney's o.,** an operation for the radical cure of inguinal hernia: the sac is exposed, ligated, and cut off at the internal ring; the skin is turned in and stitched to the underlying tendinous and ligamentous structures. **McDowell's o.,** the removal of an ovarian cyst or of an ovary by abdominal section. **Macewen's o.** 1. The scarification of the interior of an aneurysmal sac with a needle. 2. Supracondyloid division of the femur from within for genu valgum. 3. An operation for the radical cure of hernia by closing the internal ring by a pad made of the hernial sac. **McGill's o.,** suprapubic prostatectomy. **Mackenrodt's o.,** vaginal fixation of the round ligaments for retrodisplacement of the uterus. **Madelung's o.,** lumbar colotomy in which the distal end of the colon is detached, and then closed by invagination and by two rows of stitches. **Madlener o.,** a method of sterilization in the female, in which the middle portion of the fallopian tube is crushed with a clamp, which is then replaced with a ligature of nonabsorbable material. **magnet o.,** removal of a fragment of steel or iron from the eyeball by means of a powerful magnet. **major o.,** a surgical procedure which involves the risk of life. **Makka's o.,** an operation for ectopia of the bladder in which the cecum is utilized as a bladder and the appendix as a ureter. **Manchester o.,** Fothergill o. **Marian's o.,** a perineal median operation for stone in the bladder. **Marshall-Marchetti o.,** an operation for the correction of stress incontinence, the anterior portion of the urethra, vesical neck, and bladder being sutured to the posterior surface of the pubic bone. **Martin's o.,** any of several operations: 1. For vaginal hysterectomy; 2, for lacerated perineum; 3, for radical cure of hydrocele. **Marwedel's o.,** a method of gastrotomy similar to Witzel's operation. **mastoid o.,** mastoidotomy. **Matas' o.,** endoaneurysmorrhaphy. **Maydl's o.** 1. Colostomy in which the colon is exposed and drawn out of the wound, being kept in place until adhesions have been formed by means of a glass rod placed beneath it. 2. Insertion of the ureters into the rectum for exstrophy of the bladder. **Mayo's o.** 1. Excision of more or less of the pyloric end of the stomach, followed by closure of the proximal end of the duodenum and the making of an independent posterior gastrojejunostomy. 2. For radical cure of umbilical hernia by excision of the hernial mass and overlapping the abdominal aponeuroses transversely and suturing them. 3. Subcutaneous treatment of varicose veins with a blunt curet. **Meller's o.,** an operation for excision of the tear sac. **Menge's o.,** an operation for sterilization done by drawing out the fallopian tubes through the inguinal canal and resecting them. **Mercier's o.,** prostatectomy. **mika o.,** the making of a permanent fistula in the bulbous urethra for the purpose of preventing or avoiding procreation. **Mikulicz's o.** 1. Removal of the sternocleidomastoid muscle for torticollis. 2. Heineke-Mikulicz operation. 3. Tarsectomy in which the heel, os calcis, and astragalus are removed, the articular surfaces of the tibia, fibula, cuboid, and scaphoid are sawn away, and the foot brought into line with the leg. Called also *Wladimiroff's o.* 4. By anterior gastrotomy a dilating instrument is introduced into the esophagus, which is stretched up to 6 cm. 5. Enterectomy in stages; exteriorization of section of intestine to be resected; resection of protruding loop; conversion of artificial anus into fecal fistula; closure of fecal fistula. **Miles' o.,** abdominoperineal excision of the rectum for carcinoma. **Mingazzini-Förster o.,** Förster's o. **minor o.,** a surgical operation which is not serious in its extent or severity. **Moore's o.,** introduction of a coil of small wire into the sac of an aortic aneurysm to effect coagulation. **Moore-Corradi o.,** Moore's operation in which a strong galvanic current is passed through the wire. **Morestin's o.,** disarticulation of the knee with intracondyloid division of the femur. **Morischi's o.,** circumcision of the leg for varicose veins. **Moschcowitz's o.,** a femoral hernia operation by the inguinal route. **Motais's o.,** an operation for ptosis, consisting of transplanting the middle portion of the tendon of the superior rectus muscle of the eyeball into the upper lid. **Mules' o.,** evisceration of the eyeball, with insertion of an artificial vitreous. **Müller's o.** 1. A method of vaginal hysterectomy: the uterus is split into lateral halves, which are brought down in succession and removed. 2. Cesarean section in which the uterus is lifted out of the abdomen and then opened. 3. Resection of the sclera for detachment of the retina. **Naffziger's o.,** excision of the superior and lateral walls of the orbit for exophthalmos. **Narath's o.,** fixing of the omentum to the subcutaneous tissue of the abdominal wall in order to establish collateral circulation in portal obstruction. **Nebinger-Praun o.,** an operation for disease of the frontal sinus. **Nélaton's o.,** excision of the shoulder joint by a transverse incision. **Neuber's o.,** the operation of filling a cavity in bone with skin flaps taken from the sides of the wound. **Northcott o.,** the use of the electrolytic galvanic current on the blood stream with the object of stimulating the endothelium to increased output of sex stimulating hormones. **Ober's o.,** cutting or division of a joint capsule. **Oberst's o.,** an operation for ascites in which a flap of skin from the abdomen is buried so that the end projects into the abdomen, thus providing drainage. **Ogston's o.** 1. Removal of the inner condyle of the femur for knock knee. 2. Excision of the wedge of the tarsus for the purpose of restoring the arch in flatfoot. **Ogston-Luc o.,** an operation for frontal sinus disease, the incision being made from the edge of the orbit, the sinus being opened on the outer side of the median line. **Olshausen's o.,** the operation of fixing or suturing the uterus to the abdominal wall for the cure of retroversion. Called also *Koeberle's o.* **Ombrédanne's o.** 1. An operation for hypospadias. 2. Transscrotal orchipexy. **open o.,** an operation in which the parts operated on are exposed to the air. **Ord's o.,** an operation for breaking up fresh adhesions in joints. **Paci's o.,** modification of Lorenz's bloodless operation for congenital dislocation of the hip. **palliative o.,** one which aims simply to relieve untoward symptoms. **Panas' o.** 1. Linear proctotomy. 2. The attachment of the upper eyelid to the occipitofrontalis muscle for ptosis. **Pancoast's o.,** cutting of the trigeminal nerve at the foramen ovale. **Péan's o.** 1. Vaginal hysterectomy bit by bit. 2. Laparotomy for uterine fibroids. 3. Hip joint amputation in which the vessels are ligated as the operation goes on. **Petersen's o.,** a modification of high lithotomy. **Phelps' o.,** for talipes: an open and direct incision through the sole and inner side of the foot. **Phemister o.,** use of an onlay graft of cancellous bone without internal fixation, for treatment of a stable but ununited fracture. **Physick's o.,** the removal of a circular piece of the iris by means of a cutting forceps. **Pirogoff's o.** 1. See under *amputation.* 2. An operation for hernia by inserting a bag of gold-beaters' skin into the sac and allowing it to remain. **Pitts' o.,** the stretching of the inferior dental nerve in an incision within the mouth, along the inner border of the ascending ramus of the lower jaw. **plastic o.,** one in which the shape of a part or the character of its covering is altered by transplantation of tissue, etc. **Politzer's o.** 1. The creation of an artificial opening in the membrana tympani by incision and galvanocautery. 2. Division of the anterior ligament of the malleus. **Pollock's o.,** amputation at the knee joint by a long anterior and short posterior flap, the patella being left. **Polya's o.,** implantation of the end of the stomach into the side of the jejunum: for duodenal ulcer. **Pomeroy's o.,** a method of sterilization in the female, in which the fallopian tube is picked up about two inches from the uterine cornua, a chronic catgut ligature tied around the loop without crushing it, and the tied loop is then resected. **Poncet's o.** 1. Lengthening of the Achilles tendon for talipes equinus. 2. Perineotomy. 3. Perineal urethrostomy. **Porro's o.,** cesarean hysterectomy. **Porro-Veit o.,** cesarean section by Porro's method, in which the stump is ligated and returned to its place. **Potts-Smith-Gibson o.,** anastomosis between the aorta and the pulmonary artery in congenital pulmonary stenosis. **Power's o.,** removal of a corneal leukoma, followed by the insertion of a rabbit's cornea. **Pozzi's o.,** the operation of creating and suturing an artificial bilateral laceration of the cervix uteri for the relief of anteflexion. **Pribram's o.,** thermo-electrocoagulation of the gallbladder. **Puusepp's o.,** splitting of the central canal of the spinal cord for the treatment of syringomyelia. **Quaglino's o.,** sclerotomy done with a small knife and a spatula. **Quénu's o.,** quenuthoracoplasty. **Quénu-Mayo o.,** excision of the rectum, together with the neighboring lymph glands, for cancer. **radical o.,** one involving extensive tissue, which is intended to extirpate the disease completely. **Ramsden's o.,** the tying of the subclavian arteries at a point ½ inch above the clavicle in a transverse cut 3 inches long in the posterior triangle of the neck. **Ramstedt's o.,** Fredet-Ramstedt o. **Ransohoff's o.,** the making of several cross incisions of the pleura for empyema. **Recamier's o.,** curettement of the uterus. **Reclus' o.,** making of an artificial anus in the iliac region in cancer of the rectum. **Regnoli's o.,** excision of the tongue through a median opening below the lower jaw, reaching from the chin to the hyoid bone. **Reverdin's o.,** a process of skin grafting. **Ridell's o.,** excision of the anterior and inferior walls of the frontal sinus for chronic inflammation. **Rigaud's o.,** a plastic operation for urethral fistula: a square flap is taken from below the fistula, turned over it, and reinforced by flaps from each side. **Robert's o.,** a method of correcting a deflected nasal septum. The deflection is corrected by manipulation in a linear incision, after which a steel pin is introduced to hold the septum in place. **Robinson's o.,** section of the veins between two ligatures for varicose veins. **Rodman's o.,** a method of excising the breast with wide dissection of the lymphatics for cancer. **Rose's o.,** removal of the gasserian ganglion; gasserectomy. **Rouge's o.,** a method of opening the nasal sinuses by freeing the upper lip and the nasal cartilages from the maxilla. **Routier's o.,** a method of operating for Dupuytren's contracture. **Routte's o.,** venoperitoneostomy; the operation of suturing the saphenous vein so that it will open into the peritoneal cavity, so as to drain that cavity in cases of ascites with cirrhosis of the liver. **Roux's o.,** cutting of the maxilla in the middle line in the operation for removal of the tongue. **Rovsing's o.,** an operation for gastrocoloptosis. **Ruggi's o.,** gastrojejunostomy, with a double opening between the jejunum and stomach. **Rydygier's o.,** a method for excision of the rectum in which the bowel is reached by dividing the sacrum and turning it back; the portion turned back is replaced after the operation. **Saemisch's o.,** transfixion of the cornea and of the base of the ulcer for the cure of hypopyon. **Saenger's o.,** cesarean section in which the uterus is taken out through a long abdominal cut before the fetus is removed. **Sayre's o.,** the application of a plaster-of-paris jacket in the treatment of spondylitis and Pott's disease. **Scanzoni's o.,** double application of the forceps blades for the delivery of an occiput posterior position. **Scarpa's o.,** the tying of the femoral artery in Scarpa's triangle. **Schauta's o.,** extended vaginal hysterectomy for cancer of the cervix uteri. **Schauta-Wertheim o.,** Wertheim-Schauta o. **Schede's o.** 1. Resection of the thorax for chronic empyema. 2. An operation for varicose veins of the leg: done by a circular incision, rolling one cuff up and another down, so as to reach and remove the varices. 3. Excision of the necrosed part of a bone, all dead bone and diseased tissue being scraped away, and the cavity permitted to fill with blood clot, the latter being kept moist and aseptic with a cover of gauze and rubber tissue, and eventually becoming organized. **Schiassi's o.** 1. Formation of a collateral circulation for the portal blood by making an omental anastomosis. 2. Treatment of varicose veins of the leg by injecting into the vein an aqueous solution of iodine to produce adhesion of the internal surfaces of the veins. **Schlatter's o.,** total excision of the stomach for cancer. **Schmalz's o.,** the introduction of a thread into the lacrimal duct for the cure of stricture. **Schönbein's o.,** staphyloplasty in which a flap of mucous membrane from the posterior wall of the pharynx is stitched to the velum palati, shutting off the nose from the mouth. **Schröder's o.** 1. A method of colporrhaphy. 2. A method of trachelorrhaphy. 3. Removal of the uterus by celiotomy. 4. Excision of the mucous membrane of the cervix uteri for chronic endometritis. **Schuchardt's o.,** paravaginal hysterectomy. **Schwartze's o.,** the opening of the mastoid cells with a hammer and chisel in disease of the middle ear. **Sédillot's o.** 1. A method of staphylorrhaphy. 2. A flap operation for restoring the upper lip. 3. A method of ligating the innominate artery. 4. Embolectomy for pulmonary embolism. **Semb's o.,** extrafascial apicolysis for pulmonary tuberculosis. **Senn's o.,** intestinal anastomosis by lateral approximation and the use of bone plates. **shelf o.,** a reconstructive arthroplasty. **shelving o.,** König's o. **Siebold's o.,** hebotomy. **Simon's o.** 1. [John *Simon.*] Repair of lacerated perineum by suturing the vaginal mucous membrane first and the cutaneous surface afterward. 2. [Gustav *Simon.*] Colpocleisis. Called also *Marckwald's operation.* **Sistrunk o.,** a surgical procedure for removal of thyroglossal cysts and sinuses. **Sluder's o.,** removal of the tonsil along with its capsule. **Smith's o.** 1. The crushing of hemorrhoids by means of clamps, and subsequent application of the Paquelin cautery. 2. Extraction of an immature cataract with an intact capsule. **Socin's o.,** enucleation of a goitrous or thyroidal tumor from the healthy part of the gland to avoid cachexia strumipriva. **Sonneberg's o.,** excision of the inferior maxillary nerve by deep dissection beneath the angle of the jaw. **Sotteau's o.,** the closure of the inguinal canal for hernia by a double fold of the scrotum. **Spinelli's o.,** the operation of splitting the anterior wall of the prolapsed uterus, reversing the organ, and restoring it to the correct position. **Spivack's o.** 1. A method of gastrostomy in which a tube, with a valve at its base, is formed from a flap of the anterior stomach wall. 2. A method of cystostomy on the same principle as 1. **Ssabanejew-Frank o.,** Frank's o. **Stacke's o.,** the removal of the mastoid and the contents of the tympanum, so that the antrum, attic, tympanum, and meatus form a single cavity. **Steinach o.,** ligation of the vas deferens with resection of a portion of the vas; done with a view of rejuvenating the patient by causing atrophy of the spermatogenic apparatus and proliferation of the interstitial tissue of the testicle, thus increasing the patient's output of gonadal hormone. **Stoffel's o.,** resection of a part of the bundles of a nerve trunk supplying a group of muscles affected by spastic paralysis. **Stokes's o.,** Gritti-Stokes amputation. **Stromeyer-Little o.,** operation for abscess of the liver; the pus is located by a cannula and the abscess opened by a knife following the cannula as a guide. **Sturmdorf's o.,** conical excision of the diseased endocervix. **subcutaneous o.,** an operation on a part without opening the skin over it. **Surmay's o.,** jejunostomy. **Syme's o.** 1. See under *amputation.* 2. A method of external urethrotomy. **tagliacotian o.,** Italian o. **Tait's o.,** operation for lacerated perineum: the laceration is closed by two flaps taken from either side. **Talma's o.,** the operation of forming artificial adhesions between the liver and spleen and the omentum and abdominal wall in cases of ascites due to cirrhosis of the liver. **Talma-Morison o.,** omentopexy. **Tansini's o.** 1. Amputation of the breast with all the skin over it, the denuded area being covered by a flap from the back. 2. A method of removing a cyst of the liver. 3. A method of gastric resection. **Taussig's o.,** excision of the central portion of the uterine tube, the severed end of the distal segment being buried in the broad ligament, and the round ligament being anchored over the uterine wound. **Teale's o.** See under *amputation.* **Terrillon's o.,** excision of hydatids by constriction with elastic ligatures. **Textor's o.,** excision of the knee joint by means of a transverse curved anterior cut. **Thiersch's o.,** removal of skin grafts by means of a razor. **Thomas' o.,** removal of the fetus by an opening in the abdominal wall and in the vagina without wounding the uterus. **Torek o.** 1. An operation for undescended testicle. 2. An operation for the excision of the thoracic part of the esophagus. **Toti's o.,** dacryocystorhinostomy. **Touroff's o.,** transpleural ligation of the subclavian artery. **Trendelenburg's o.** 1. Excision of varicose veins. 2. Ligation of the great saphenous vein for varicose veins. 3. Synchondroseotomy. **Treves' o.,** operation for Pott's disease by opening the abscess through the loin, irrigating and curetting the sac, and scraping away dead bone. **Tuffier's o.** 1. Vaginal hysterectomy in which the broad ligaments are treated by angiotripsy without ligation. 2. Apicolysis. **van Buren's o.,** the treatment of prolapsus ani with the Paquelin cautery. **van Hook's o.,** uretero-ureterostomy. **Verhoeff's o.,** posterior sclerotomy followed by electrolytic punctures, for detachment of the retina. **Vermale's o.,** amputation by double-flap transfixion. **Verneuil's o.,** iliac colotomy by a nearly vertical cut: the exposed gut is pinned to the edges of the wound and stitched there, after which the protruding knuckle of the bowel is cut off. **Vicq d'Azyr's o.,** cricothyroid laryngotomy. **Vidal's o.,** subcutaneous ligation of the veins for varicocele. **Volkmann's o.,** incision of the tunica vaginalis for hydrocele. **von Bergmann's o.,** incision of the tunica vaginalis, with removal of its parietal layer, performed for hydrocele. **von Graefe's o.,** removal of the cataractous lens by a scleral cut, with laceration of the capsule and iridectomy. **von Hacker's o.,** an operation for balanitic hypospadias. **Voronoff's o.,** transplantation into man of the testes of an anthropoid ape. **Wagner's o.,** osteoplastic resection of the skull. **Walthardt's o.,** an operation for sterilizing the female in which the oviduct is crushed and ligated in two quite separate places. **Wardrop's o.,** distal ligation of an artery for aneurysm. **Water's o.,** a form of supravaginal extraperitoneal cesarean section. **Watkins' o.,** an operation for prolapse and procidentia uteri in which the bladder is separated from the anterior wall of the uterus so that the uterus is left in a position to support the entire bladder. **Webster's o.,** for retrodisplacement of the uterus: the round ligaments are passed through the perforated broad ligaments and fixed to the back of the uterus. **Weir's o.,** appendicostomy. **Wertheim's o.** 1. Radical hysterectomy; an operation for cancer of the uterus in which there is removed with the uterus as much of the parametrial tissue as possible and a wide margin of the vagina. 2. A modification of Watkins' operation for uterine prolapse in which the bladder is stitched to the posterior wall of the uterus at the level of the internal os; in closing the vaginal wound a portion of the anterior uterine wall is left exposed in the vagina. **Wertheim-Schauta o.,** an operation for cystocele, consisting in the interposition of the uterus between the base of the bladder and the anterior vaginal wall. **Wheelhouse's o.,** a method of perineal section for impermeable stricture of the urethra by cutting the stricture on a fine staff passed through it. **Whipple's o.,** radical excision of the ampulla of Vater. **White's o.,** castration for hypertrophy of the prostate. **Whitehead's o.** 1. Treatment of hemorrhoids by excision. 2. Removal of the tongue with scissors, the operation being performed within the mouth. **Whitman's o.** 1. An operation for arthroplasty of the hip joint. 2. A method of astragalectomy. **Wieting's o.,** anastomosis of the femoral vein to the femoral artery for the relief of arteriosclerotic gangrene. **Wilms' o.,** resection of the ribs so as to produce depression of the chest wall and compression of the lungs thereby: done in tuberculosis of the lungs. **Winiwarter's o.,** cholecystenterostomy. **Witzel's o.,** gastrotomy by drawing a cone of the stomach wall through a thoracic incision, and inserting a tube which is buried in the stomach wall by sutures. The stomach cone is replaced and the wound sutured. **Wladimiroff's o.,** Mikulicz's o., def. 3. **Wölfler's o.,** the formation of a permanent opening between the stomach and lower part of the duodenum in cases of obstructed pylorus. **Wood's o.** 1. Closure of exstrophy of the bladder by a flap of skin cut from the abdominal wall and turned over so that the cutaneous surface forms the inner wall of the bladder. 2. The closure of a hernial canal by subcutaneous sutures through the tendinous tissues surrounding it. **Wützer's o.,** a process for the radical cure of inguinal hernia by stopping up the hernial canal by invaginating the scrotum. **Wyeth's o.,** amputation at the hip joint, hemorrhage being controlled by an elastic cord or tube fastened above large needles which transfix the tissues on each side of the articulation. **Wylie's o.** 1. Operation of shortening the round ligaments for the relief of uterine retroflexion, done by folding the ligaments on themselves and suturing. 2. An operation for appendicitis by pulling aside the rectus, incising its posterior sheath, and making a small incision through the peritoneum. **Yankauer's o.,** curettement of the bony end of the eustachian tube for the purpose of shutting off infection from the nasopharynx and thereby curing chronic suppuration of the middle ear. **Young's o.** 1. Partial prostatectomy by punch. 2. Total excision of the seminal vesicles and partial excision of the ejaculatory ducts by a suprapubic T-shaped incision. **Ziegler's o.,** V-shaped iridectomy for forming artificial pupil.

operative (op′er-a″tiv) [L. *operativus*]. 1. Pertaining to an operation. 2. Effective; not inert.

opercula (o-per′ku-lah) [L.]. Plural of *operculum.*

opercular (o-per′ku-lar). Pertaining to an operculum.

operculum (o-per′ku-lum), pl. *oper′cula* [L.]. 1. A lid or covering structure, such as the mucus plug obstructing the cervix of the gravid uterus in various animals. 2. [B N A]. See *operculum frontale, o. frontoparietale,* and *o. temporale.* **cartilaginous o.,** discus articularis articulationis temporomandibularis. **dental o.,** the hood of gingival tissue overlying the crown of an erupting tooth. **frontal o., o. fronta′le** [N A], the part of the frontal lobe of the cerebrum rostral to the ascending branch of the lateral cerebral sulcus, covering over a part of the insula. Called also *pars frontalis operculi* [B N A]. **frontoparietal o., o. frontoparieta′le** [N A], the part of the frontal and parietal lobes occipital to the ascending branch of the lateral cerebral sulcus, covering over a part of the insula. Called also *pars parietalis operculi* [B N A]. **oper′cula in′sulae,** the folds of the pallium covering the insula. See *o. frontale, o. frontoparietale,* and *o. temporale.* **occipital o.,** a part of the occipital lobe of the brain separated from the main portion by the ape fissure. **temporal o., o. tempora′le** [N A], the part of the temporal lobe that covers over a part of the insula. Called also *pars temporalis operculi* [B N A]. **trophoblastic o.,** the plug of trophoblast that helps close the gap in the endometrium made by the implanting blastocyst.

operon (op′er-on) [L. *opera* exertion + Gr. *on* neuter ending]. A system of adjacent genes on a chromosome of which one, the operator gene, interacts with the level of repressor in the cell and thereby controls the activity of the remaining structural genes of the system.

ophiasis (o-fi′ah-sis) [Gr.]. Baldness in one or more winding streaks across the head.

Ophidia (o-fid′e-ah) [Gr. *ophidion* serpent]. A suborder of Reptilia which embraces the snakes.

ophidiasis (o″fĭ-di′ah-sis). Ophidism.

ophidic (o-fid′ik). Pertaining to, caused by, or derived from snakes.

ophidiophilia (o-fid″e-o-fil′e-ah) [Gr. *ophidion* serpent + *philein* to love]. Morbid fondness for snakes.

ophidiophobia (o-fid″e-o-fo′be-ah) [Gr. *ophidion* serpent + *phobia*]. A morbid dread of snakes.

ophidism (o′fĭ-dizm). Poisoning by snake venom.

Ophiophagus elaps (o″fe-of′ah-gus e′laps). The largest variety of Indian cobra.

ophiotoxemia (o″fe-o-tok-se′me-ah) [Gr. *ophis* snake + *toxemia*]. Poisoning by snake venom.

ophitoxemia (o″fe-tok-se′me-ah). Ophiotoxemia.

ophritis (of-ri′tis). Ophryitis.

ophryitis (of″re-i′tis) [Gr. *ophrys* eyebrow + *-itis*]. Dermatitis in the eyebrow region.

ophryon (of′re-on) [Gr. *ophrys* eyebrow + *on* neuter ending]. The middle point of the transverse supra-orbital line.

ophryosis (of″re-o′sis) [Gr. *ophrys* eyebrow]. Spasm of the eyebrow.

ophthaine (of′thān). Trade mark for a preparation of proparacaine hydrochloride.

ophthalm-. See *ophthalmo-.*

ophthalmagra (of″thal-mag′rah) [*ophthalm-* + Gr. *agra* seizure]. Sudden pain in the eye.

ophthalmalgia (of″thal-mal′je-ah) [*ophthal-* + *-algia*]. Pain in the eye.

ophthalmatrophia (of″thal-mah-tro′fe-ah) [*ophthalm-* + Gr. *atrophia* atrophy]. Atrophy of the eye.

ophthalmectomy (of″thal-mek′to-me) [*ophthalm-* + Gr. *ektomē* excision]. The surgical removal of an eye; enucleation of the eyeball.

ophthalmencephalon (of″thal-men-sef′ah-lon) [*ophthalm-* + Gr. *enkephalos* brain]. The retina, optic nerve, and visual apparatus of the brain.

ophthalmia (of-thal′me-ah) [Gr., from *ophthalmos* eye]. Severe inflammation of the eye or of the conjunctiva. **actinic ray o.,** electric o. **catarrhal o.,** a severe form of simple conjunctivitis. **caterpillar o.,** o. nodosa. **o. eczemato′sa,** phlyctenulosis. **Egyptian o.,** trachoma. **electric o.,** conjunctivitis due to the effect of bright electric light, especially that of a welding arc. **flash o.,** electric o. **gonorrheal o.,** acute and severe purulent conjunctivitis due to gonorrheal infection. **granular o.,** an acute and severe form of purulent conjunctivitis. **jequirity o.,** a form due to poisoning by jequirity. **metastatic o.,** choroiditus due to metastasis or to pyemia. **migratory o.,** sympathetic ophthalmia. **mucous o.,** catarrhal o. **o. neonato′rum,** gonorrheal conjunctivitis in the newborn. **neuroparalytic o.,** keratitis due to lesion of branches of the fifth nerve or of the gasserian ganglion. **o. nivia′lis,** snow blindness. **o. nodo′sa,** inflammation of the conjunctiva produced by caterpillar hairs, and marked by the formation of a round, gray swelling where each hair is embedded. **periodic o.,** a form of uveitis affecting horses. **phlyctenular o.,** a form of conjunctivitis and keratitis with vesicles on the epithelium. **purulent o.,** a form with a purulent discharge, commonly due to gonorrheal infection. **scrofulous o.,** phlyctenular conjunctivitis. **spring o.,** a variety chiefly prevailing in the spring of the year. **strumous o.,** phlyctenular keratitis. **sympathetic o.,** a granulomatous lesion of the eye characterized chiefly by its tendency to involve the uveal tissue of both eyes. **transferred o.,** sympathetic o. **ultraviolet ray o.,** electric o. **varicose o.,** a variety associated with varicosity of the veins of the conjunctiva. **war o.,** trachoma.

ophthalmiac (of-thal′me-ak). A person affected with ophthalmia.

ophthalmiatrics (of″thal-me-at′riks) [*ophthalm-* + Gr. *iatrikē* surgery, medicine]. The treatment of eye diseases.

ophthalmic (of-thal′mik) [Gr. *ophthalmikos*]. Pertaining to the eye.

ophthalmin (of-thal′min). 1. The virus of purulent ophthalmia. 2. A name proposed for vitamin A.

ophthalmitic (of″thal-mit′ik). Pertaining to ophthalmitis.

ophthalmitis (of″thal-mi′tis) [*ophthalm-* + *-itis*]. Inflammation of the eye.

ophthalmo-, ophthalm- [Gr. *ophthalmos* eye]. Combining form denoting relationship to the eye.

ophthalmoblennorrhea (of-thal″mo-blen″o-re′ah) [*ophthalmo-* + Gr. *blenna* mucus + *rhoia* flow]. Gonorrheal or purulent ophthalmia.

ophthalmocarcinoma (of-thal″mo-kar″sĭ-no′mah). Carcinoma of the eyeball.

ophthalmocele (of-thal′mo-sēl) [*ophthalmo-* + Gr. *kēlē* hernia, tumor]. Exophthalmos.

ophthalmocopia (of-thal″mo-ko′pe-ah) [*ophthalmo-* + Gr. *kopos* weariness]. Asthenopia, or eyestrain; fatigue of the eyes.

ophthalmodesmitis (of-thal″mo-dez-mi′tis) [*ophthalmo-* + Gr. *desmos* ligament + *-itis*]. Inflammation of the ocular tendons.

ophthalmodiagnosis (of-thal″mo-di″ag-no′sis). Diagnosis by the aid of the ophthalmic reaction.

ophthalmodiaphanoscope (of-thal″mo-di-ah-fan′o-skōp) [*ophthalmo-* + *diaphanoscope*]. An instrument for examining the back of the eye (retina) by transillumination through the buccal cavity.

ophthalmodiastimeter (of-thal″mo-di″as-tim′-e-ter) [*ophthalmo-* + Gr. *diastēma* interval + *metron* measure]. An instrument for determining the proper distance at which to place lenses for the two eyes.

ophthalmodonesis (of-thal″mo-do-ne′sis) [*ophthalmo-* + Gr. *donēsis* trembling]. A trembling motion of the eyes.

ophthalmodynamometer (of-thal″mo-di″nah-mom′e-ter). 1. An instrument for measuring the blood pressure in the retinal artery. 2. An instrument for determining the near point of convergence.

ophthalmodynamometry (of-thal″mo-di″nah-mom′e-tre). Determination of the blood pressure in the retinal artery.

ophthalmodynia (of-thal″mo-din′e-ah) [*ophthalmo-* + Gr. *odynē* pain]. Pain in the eye.

ophthalmo-eikonometer (of-thal″mo-i″ko-nom′e-ter). An instrument used to determine both the refraction of the eye and the relative size and shape of the ocular images.

ophthalmofundoscope (of-thal″mo-fun′do-skōp). An apparatus for observing the fundus of the eye.

ophthalmograph (of-thal′mo-graf) [*ophthalmo-* + Gr. *graphein* to write]. An instrument for photographing the movements of the eye during reading.

ophthalmography (of″thal-mog′rah-fe) [*ophthalmo-* + Gr. *graphein* to write]. Description of the eyes.

ophthalmogyric (of-thal″mo-ji′rik) [*ophthalmo-* + Gr. *gyros* circle]. Oculogyric.

ophthalmoleukoscope (of-thal″mo-lu′ko-skōp) [*ophthalmo-* + Gr. *leukos* white + *skopein* to examine]. An apparatus for testing color perception by means of colors produced by polarized light.

ophthalmolith (of-thal′mo-lith) [*ophthalmo-* + Gr. *lithos* stone]. A lacrimal calculus.

ophthalmologic (of″thal-mo-loj′ik). Pertaining to ophthalmology.

ophthalmologist (of″thal-mol′o-jist). An expert in ophthalmology.

ophthalmology (of″thal-mol′o-je) [*ophthalmo-* + *-logy*]. The sum of knowledge concerning the eye and its diseases.

ophthalmomalacia (of-thal″mo-mah-la′she-ah) [*ophthalamo-* + Gr. *malakia* softness]. Abnormal softness and shrinkage of the eye, with less than the normal tension; essential phthisis of the eye.

ophthalmometer (of″thal-mom′e-ter) [*ophthalmo-* + Gr. *metron* measure]. Any instrument for measuring the eye, especially one for determining its refractive powers and defects by measuring the size of the images reflected from the cornea and lens. Called also *Javel's o.*

ophthalmometroscope (of-thal″mo-met′ro-skōp). An ophthalmoscope with an attachment for measuring the refraction of the eye.

ophthalmometry (of″thal-mom′e-tre). Determination of the refractive powers and defects of the eye.

ophthalmomycosis (of-thal″mo-mi-ko′sis) [*ophthalmo-* + Gr. *mykēs* fungus + *-osis*]. Any disease of the eye caused by a fungus.

ophthalmomyiasis (of-thal″mo-mi′yah-sis) [*ophthalmo-* + Gr. *myia* a fly + *-sis*]. Infection of the eye by the larvae of the fly *Oestrus ovis.*

ophthalmomyitis (of-thal″mo-mi-i′tis) [*ophthalmo-* + Gr. *mys* muscles + *-itis*]. Inflammation of the muscles that move the eyeball.

ophthalmomyositis (of-thal″mo-mi″o-si′tis). Inflammation of the eye muscles.

ophthalmomyotomy (of-thal″mo-mi-ot′o-me) [*ophthalmo-* + *myotomy*]. Surgical division of the muscles of the eye.

ophthalmoneuritis (of-thal″mo-nu-ri′tis). Inflammation of the ophthalmic nerve.

ophthalmoneuromyelitis (of-thal″mo-nu″ro-mi-ĕ-li′tis). Neuro-optic myelitis.

ophthalmopathy (of″thal-mop′ah-the) [*ophthalmo-* + Gr. *pathos* disease]. Any disease of the eye. **external o.,** any affection of the eyelids, cornea, conjunctiva, or eye muscles. **internal o.,** any affection of the deep or more essential parts of the eye.

ophthalmophacometer (of-thal″mo-fa-kom′e-ter) [*ophthalmo-* + Gr. *phakos* lens + *metron* measure]. A kind of ophthalmometer for measuring the two surfaces of the lens and the posterior surface of the cornea.

ophthalmophantom (of-thal″mo-fan′tom). 1. A model of the eye used in demonstration. 2. An apparatus for holding animals' eyes for operation.

ophthalmophlebotomy (of-thal″mo-fle-bot′o-me) [*ophthalmo-* + *phlebotomy*]. Phlebotomy to relieve congestion of the conjunctival veins.

ophthalmophthisis (of″thal-mof′thĭ-sis) [*ophthalmo-* + Gr. *phthisis* wasting]. Ophthalmomalacia.

ophthalmoplasty (of-thal′mo-plas″te) [*ophthalmo-* + Gr. *plassein* to mold]. Plastic surgery of the eye or of its appendages.

ophthalmoplegia (of-thal″mo-ple′je-ah) [*ophthalmo-* + Gr. *plēgē* stroke + *-ia*]. Paralysis of the eye muscles. **basal o.,** ophthalmoplegia due to a lesion at the base of the brain. **exophthalmic o.,** hyperophthalmopathic syndrome. **o. exter′na,** paralysis of the external ocular muscles. **fascicular o.,** ophthalmoplegia due to lesion in the pons varolii. **infectious o.,** encephalitis lethargica. **o. inter′na,** paralysis of the iris and ciliary apparatus. **nuclear o.,** that which is due to some lesion of the nuclei of the motor nerves of the eye. **orbital o.,** ophthalmoplegia due to lesion in the orbit. **Parinaud's o.,** paralysis of the external rectus muscle of one eye, together with spasm of the internal rectus of the other. **o. partia′lis,** paralysis of either one or two of the muscles of the eye. **o. progressi′va,** gradual paralysis affecting first one eye muscle and then another. **Sauvineau's o.,** paralysis of the internal rectus of one eye and spasm of the external rectus of the other. **o. tota′lis,** that which affects both the extrinsic and the intrinsic muscular apparatus of the eye.

ophthalmoplegic (of-thal″mo-ple′jik). Pertaining to ophthalmoplegia.

ophthalmoptosis (of-thal″mop-to′sis) [*ophthalmo-* + Gr. *ptōsis* fall]. Exophthalmos.

ophthalmoreaction (of-thal″mo-re-ak′shun). See *ophthalmic reaction*, under *reaction.*

ophthalmorrhagia (of-thal″mo-ra′je-ah) [*ophthalmo-* + Gr. *rhēgnynai* to burst forth]. Hemorrhage from the eye.

ophthalmorrhea (of-thal″mo-re′ah) [*ophthalmo-* + Gr. *rhoia* flow]. Oozing of blood from the eye.

ophthalmorrhexis (of-thal″mo-rek′sis) [*ophthalmo-* + Gr. *rhēxis* rupture]. Rupture of the eyeball.

ophthalmoscope (of-thal′mo-skōp) [*ophthalmo-* + Gr. *skopein* to examine]. A perforated mirror used in inspecting the interior of the eye. **ghost o.,** a form in which a portion of the reflected rays are deflected by a mirror. **Loring's o.,** an ophthalmoscope with tilting mirror, complete disk of lenses, and supplemental quadrant of lenses.

ophthalmoscopy (of-thal-mos′ko-pe). The examination of the interior of the eye with the ophthalmoscope. **direct o.,** the observation of an upright or erect mirrored image of the interior of the eye. **indirect o.,** the observation of an inverted image of the interior of the eye. **medical o.,** that which is performed for diagnostic purposes. **metric o.,** that which is performed for the measurement of refraction.

ophthalmostasis (of″thal-mos′tah-sis) [*ophthal-*

mo- + Gr. *stasis* standing]. Fixation of the eye with the ophthalmostat.

ophthalmostat (of-thal′mo-stat) [*ophthalmo-* + Gr. *histanai* to halt]. An instrument for holding the eye steady during operation.

ophthalmostatometer (of-thal″mo-stah-tom′e-ter) [*ophthalmo-* + Gr. *histanai* to halt + *metron* measure]. An instrument for determining the degree of protrusion of the eyeball.

ophthalmosteresis (of-thal″mo-ste-re′sis) [*ophthalmo-* + Gr. *steresis* privation, loss]. Loss of an eye.

ophthalmosynchysis (of-thal″mo-sin′kĭ-sis) [*ophthalmo-* + Gr. *synchysis* a mixing]. Effusion into the eye.

ophthalmothermometer (of-thal″mo-ther-mom′e-ter) [*ophthalmo-* + *thermometer*]. An apparatus for recording the temperature of the eye.

ophthalmotomy (of″thal-mot′o-me) [*ophthalmo-* + Gr. *temnein* to cut]. The operation of incising the eyeball.

ophthalmotonometer (of-thal″mo-to-nom′e-ter) [*ophthalmo-* + Gr. *tonos* tension + *metron* measure]. An instrument used in measuring the intra-ocular tension.

ophthalmotonometry (of-thal″mo-to-nom′e-tre). The measurement of the intra-ocular tension.

ophthalmotoxin (of-thal″mo-tok′sin) [*ophthalmo-* + *toxin*]. 1. A toxin formed on injection of emulsion of the ciliary body. 2. A toxin acting on the eye.

ophthalmotrope (of-thal′mo-trōp) [*ophthalmo-* + Gr. *trepein* to turn]. A mechanical eye that moves like a real eye, used for demonstrating the action of the ocular muscles.

ophthalmotropometer (of-thal″mo-tro-pom′e-ter) [*ophthalmo-* + Gr. *tropos* a turning + *metron* measure]. An instrument for measuring eye movements.

ophthalmovascular (of-thal″mo-vas′ku-lar). Pertaining to the blood vessels of the eye.

ophthalmoxerosis (of-thal″mo-ze-ro′sis). Xerophthalmia.

ophthalmoxyster (of-thal″moks-is′ter) [*ophthalmo-* + Gr. *xystēr* scraper]. An instrument for scraping the conjunctiva.

opian (o′pe-an). Noscapine.

opianine (o-pi′ah-nin). Noscapine.

opiate (o′pe-āt). A remedy containing or derived from opium; also any drug that induces sleep.

Opie paradox (o′pe) [Eugene L. *Opie*, American pathologist, born 1873]. See under *paradox*.

opilação (o″pil-ah-sah′o) [Port.]. A form of trypanosomiasis occurring in Brazil. See *Chagas' disease*, under *disease*.

opilation (o″pĭ-la′shun). Opilação.

opiomania (o″pe-o-ma′ne-ah) [*opium* + Gr. *mania* madness]. An insane craving for opium.

opiomaniac (o″pe-o-ma′ne-ak). A person affected with opiomania.

opiophagism, opiophagy (o″pe-of′ah-jizm, o-pe-of′ah-je) [*opium* + Gr. *phagein* to eat]. The habitual use or eating of opium.

Opisocrostis (o″pĭ-so-kros′tis). A genus of fleas. **O. bru′neri,** a squirrel flea said to be a vector of sylvatic plague.

opisthenar (o-pis′the-nar) [*opistho-* + Gr. *thenar* palm of the hand]. The dorsum of the hand.

opisthencephalon (o-pis″then-sef′ah-lon) [*opistho-* + Gr. *enkephalos* brain]. The cerebellum.

opisthiobasial (o-pis″the-o-ba′se-al). Pertaining to or connecting the opisthion and basion.

opisthion (o-pis′the-on) [Gr. *opisthion* rear]. The midpoint of the lower border of the foramen magnum.

opisthionasial (o-pis″the-o-na′ze-al). Connecting the opisthion and nasion.

opistho- (o-pis′tho) [Gr. *opisthen* behind, at the back]. Combining form meaning backward or denoting relationship to the back.

opisthogenia (o-pis″tho-je′ne-ah). Defective development of the jaws following ankylosis of the jaw.

opisthognathism (o″pis-tho′nah-thizm). The condition of having receding jaws.

opisthoporeia (o-pis″tho-po-ri′ah) [*opistho-* + Gr. *poreia* walk]. Involuntary walking backward.

opisthorchiasis (o″pis-thor-ki′ah-sis). A diseased condition of the liver due to the presence of flukes of the genus *Opisthorchis*.

Opisthorchis (o″pis-thor′kis) [*opistho-* + Gr. *orchis* testicle]. A genus of trematodes or flukes characterized by having the testicles near the posterior end of the body. **O. felin′eus,** the Siberian liver fluke found in the liver of cats, dogs, pigs and man. Infection takes place through eating fish (*Leuciscus rutilis* and *Idus melanotus*). **O. nover′ca,** the Indian liver fluke, found very commonly in the pariah dogs and also in man. **O. sinen′sis,** *Clonorchis sinensis.* **O. viverri′ni,** a species found in Siam in the civet cat and sometimes in man.

opisthorchosis (o″pis-thor-ko′sis). Infestation with any species of Opisthorchis.

opisthotic (o″pis-thot′ik) [*opistho-* + Gr. *ous* ear]. Situated behind the ear.

opisthotonoid (o″pis-thot′o-noid). Resembling opisthotonos.

opisthotonos (o″pis-thot′o-nos) [*opistho-* + Gr. *tonos* tension]. A form of tetanic spasm in which

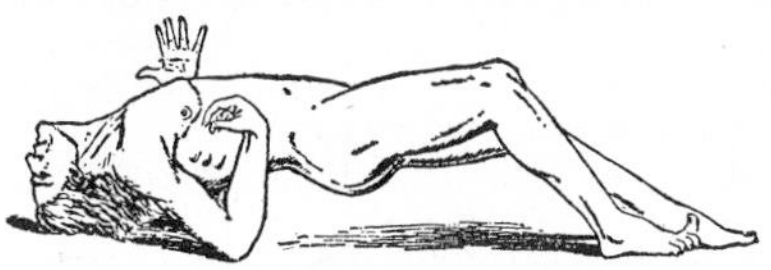

Opisthotonos (Littré).

the head and the heels are bent backward and the body bowed forward. **o. feta′lis,** an exaggerated deflection attitude of the fetus during parturition, which may persist during the neonatal period, but which gradually gives way to a more normal posture.

opisthotonus (o″pis-thot′o-nus). Opisthotonos.

Opitz's disease (o′pitz) [Hans *Opitz*, German pediatrician, born 1888]. Thrombophlebitic splenomegaly.

opium (o′pe-um) [L.; Gr. *opion*]. Air-dried milky exudate obtained by incising the unripe capsules of *Papaver somniferum*, yielding not less than 9.5 per cent of anhydrous morphine. Called also *crude o.* and *gum o.* Various principles and derivatives of opium are used for their narcotic and analgesic effects. **crude o.** See *opium.* **denarcotized o., o. deodora′tum, deodorized o.,** opium freed from certain nauseating constituents by extraction with purified petroleum benzin. **granulated o., o. granula′tum,** opium reduced to a coarse powder. **gum o.** See *opium.* **lettuce o.,** the bitter, inspissated juice of various species of lettuce, formerly used for mild hypnotic and sedative action. **powdered o., o. pulvera′tum,** opium reduced to a very fine powder.

opiumism (o′pe-um-izm). The habitual misuse of opium or its consequences.

opobalsamum (o″po-bal′sah-mum) [Gr. *opos* juice + *balsamon* balsam]. The true balm of Gilead, or Mecca balsam, produced by *Balsamodendron gileadense* or *B. opobalsamum.*

opocephalus (o″po-sef′ah-lus) [Gr. *ōps* face + *kephalē* head]. A monster with the ears fused, one orbit, no mouth, and no nose.

opodidymus (o″po-did′ĭ-mus) [Gr. *ōps* face + *didymos* twin]. A fetus with two fused heads and with the sense organs partly fused.

opodymus (o-pod′ĭ-mus). Opodidymus.

opossum (o-pos′um). A marsupial animal, species

of which (*Didelphis*) in South America are reservoirs of *Trypanosoma cruzi*.

opotherapy (o″po-ther′ah-pe) [Gr. *opos* juice + *therapeia* treatment]. 1. Treatment by juices. 2. Organotherapy; treatment of disease by the administration of extract from animals' organs.

Oppenheim's disease, sign, syndrome (op′en-hīmz) [Hermann *Oppenheim*, neurologist in Berlin, 1858–1919]. See under *disease* and *sign*.

Oppenheim-Urbach disease (op′en-hīm-ur′-bahkh) [Maurice *Oppenheim*, Chicago dermatologist, 1876–1949; Erich *Urbach*, Philadelphia dermatologist, 1893–1946]. Necrobiosis lipoidica diabeticorum.

Oppenheimer treatment (op′en-hi-mer) [Isaac *Oppenheimer*, New York physician, 1855–1928]. See under *treatment*.

oppilation (op″ĭ-la′shun) [L. *oppilatio*]. Constipation.

oppilative (op′ĭ-la″tiv). Closing the pores; also constipating.

opponens (o-po′nenz) [L.]. Opposing.

oppositipolar (o-poz″ĭ-ti-po′lar). Having two poles on opposite sides of a cell.

opsialgia (op″se-al′je-ah) [Gr. *ōps* face + *-algia*]. Facial neuralgia.

opsigenes (op-sij′e-nēz) [Gr. *opsigenēs*]. Late born: a term sometimes applied to the wisdom teeth.

opsinogen (op-sin′o-jen). A substance (antigen) with the power to induce the formation of opsonins in the body.

opsinogenous (op″sin-oj′e-nus). Able to form opsonins.

opsiometer (op″se-om′e-ter) [Gr. *opsis* vision + *metron* measure]. Optometer.

opsiuria (op″se-u′re-ah) [Gr. *opse* late + *ouron* urine + *-ia*]. The condition in which more urine is excreted during fasting than during digestion.

opsoclonia (op″so-klo′ne-ah). A condition characterized by strabismus and jerking nystagmoid movements of the eye: observed in cases of acute anterior poliomyelitis.

opsogen (op′so-jen). Opsinogen.

opsomania (op″so-ma′ne-ah) [Gr. *opson* dainty + *mania* madness]. A craving for some special food.

opsomenorrhea (op″so-men″o-re′ah) [Gr. *opse* late + *menorrhea*]. Delayed menstruation.

opsone (op′sōn). Opsonin.

opsonic (op-son′ik). Pertaining to opsonins.

opsoniferous (op″so-nif′er-us). Bearing opsonin.

opsonification (op-son″ĭ-fi-ka′shun). The rendering of bacteria and other cells subject to phagocytosis.

opsonify (op-son′ĭ-fi). To subject to opsonification.

opsonin (op-so′nin) [Gr. *opsōnein* to buy victuals]. An antibody which renders bacteria and other cells susceptible to phagocytosis. **immune o.,** an antibody which sensitizes a particulate antigen to phagocytosis, following combination with the homologous antigen in vivo or in vitro.

opsonist (op′so-nist). One who is expert in opsonic technic.

opsonization (op″so-ni-za′shun). Opsonification.

opsonize (op′so-nīz). Opsonify.

opsonocytophagic (op″so-no-si″to-fa′jik). Noting the phagocytic activity of blood in the presence of serum opsonins and homologous leukocytes.

opsonogen (op-son′o-jen). Opsinogen.

opsonoid (op′so-noid). An opsonin in which the opsonophoric or active element has been destroyed.

opsonology (op″so-nol′o-je). The study of opsonins and opsonic action.

opsonometry (op″so-nom′e-tre). The measurement of the amount of opsonin present.

opsonophilia (op″so-no-fil′e-ah) [*opsonin* + Gr. *philein* to love]. Affinity for opsonins.

opsonophilic (op″so-no-fil′ik). Having an affinity for opsonins.

opsonophoric (op″so-no-for′ik). Bearing opsonin; the term applied to that group of an opsonin which acts on the bacterium or other cell to render it subject to phagocytosis.

opsonotherapy (op″so-no-ther′ah-pe). Treatment by the use of bacterial vaccines to increase the opsonic action of the blood.

optesthesia (op″tes-the′ze-ah). Visual sensibility; ability to perceive visual stimuli.

optic (op′tik) [Gr. *optikos* of or for sight]. Pertaining to the eye.

optical (op′tĭ-kal) [L. *opticus;* Gr. *optikos*]. Pertaining to or subserving vision.

optician (op-tish′an). An expert in opticianry.

opticianry (op-tish′an-re). The science, craft, and art of optics as applied to the translation, filling, and adapting of ophthalmic prescriptions, products, and accessories.

opticist (op′tĭ-sist). An expert in the science of optics.

opticociliary (op″tĭ-ko-sil′e-a-re). Pertaining to the optic and ciliary nerves.

opticocinerea (op″tĭ-ko-sĭ-ne′re-ah) [*optic* + *cinerea*]. The gray matter of the optic tract.

opticokinetic (op″tĭ-ko-ki-net′ik). Pertaining to movement of the eyes.

opticonasion (op″tĭ-ko-na′se-on). The distance from the posterior edge of the optic foramen to the nasion.

opticopupillary (op″tĭ-ko-pu′pĭ-ler-e). Pertaining to the optic nerve and the pupil.

optics (op′tiks) [Gr. *optikos* of or for sight]. The science which treats of light and of vision.

optimal (op′tĭ-mal). The best; the most favorable.

optimeter (op-tim′e-ter). Optometer.

optimum (op′tĭ-mum) [L. "best"]. 1. That condition of surroundings which is conducive to the most favorable activity or function. 2. Pirquet's term for the amount of food most desirable under given circumstances.

optist (op′tist). A person skilled in optometry.

opto- (op′to) [Gr. *optos* seen]. Combining form meaning visible, or denoting relationship to vision or sight.

optoblast (op′to-blast) [*opto-* + Gr. *blastos* germ]. One of the large ganglion cells of the retina.

optogram (op′to-gram) [*opto-* + Gr. *gramma* mark]. The retinal image formed by the bleaching of the visual purple under the influence of light.

optomeninx (op″to-me′ningks) [*opto-* + Gr. *mēninx* membrane]. The retina.

optometer (op-tom′e-ter) [*opto-* + Gr. *metron* measure]. A device for measuring the power and range of vision.

optometrist (op-tom′e-trist). An expert in optometry.

optometry (op-tom′e-tre). Measurement of the powers of vision and the adaptation of prisms or lenses for the aid thereof, utilizing any means other than drugs.

optomyometer (op″to-mi-om′e-ter) [*opto-* + Gr. *mys* muscle + *metron* measure]. A device used in measuring the power of the ocular muscles.

optophone (op′to-fōn) [*opto-* + Gr. *phōne* voice]. An instrument by means of which light and darkness are made discernible to the blind through their sense of hearing, the light waves being transformed into sound waves.

optostriate (op″to-stri′āt). Pertaining to the thalamus opticus and the corpus striatum.

optotype (op′to-tīp) [*opto-* + *type*]. The test types used by an oculist.

Opuntia (o-pun′she-ah). A genus of cacti. *O. vulgaris*, the prickly pear, is used as a remedy in homeopathic practice.

opzyme (op′zīm). An extract from tumors, endocrine glands or other organs containing the specific proteins of the organs.

ora[1] (o′rah), pl. *o′rae* [L.]. An edge or margin. **o. serra′ta ret′inae** [N A, B N A], the irregular anterior margin of the pars optica of the retina, lying internal and slightly posterior to the junction of the choroid and the ciliary body.

ora[2] (o′rah) [L.]. Plural of *os*, mouth.

orabilex (or″ah-bi′leks). Trade mark for a preparation of bunamiodyl.

orad (o′rad) [L. *os, oris* mouth + *ad* toward]. Toward the mouth.

orae (o′re) [L.]. Plural of *ora*, edge.

oral (o′ral) [L. *oralis*]. Pertaining to the mouth.

orale (o-ra′le). The point of the end of the incisive suture on the inner surface of the alveolar process.

oralogy (o-ral′o-je) [L. *oralis* pertaining to the mouth + *-logy*]. The practice of medical and dental cooperation for health; health dentistry; mouth science.

orange (or′anj) [L. *aurantium*]. **1.** The rutaceous tree, *Citrus aurantium*, and its yellow, edible fruit (*aurantii fructus*). There are two varieties, *bitter orange* (*aurantii amara*) and *sweet orange* (*aurantii dulcis*). The peel of the two varieties is used in making various pharmaceutical preparations. 2. A substance which may be used as a dye or reagent. **acridine o.,** tetramethyl-acridine, $CH[N(CH_3)_2\text{-}C_6H_3]_2N$. **ethyl o.,** an indicator with a pH range of 2–4. **o. G,** an acid azo dye used as a cytoplasmic stain, $C_6H_5.N{:}N.C_{10}H_4(SO_2.ONa)_2.OH$. **gold o.,** helianthin. **o. III,** helianthin. **o. IV,** tropeolin OO. **methyl-o., Poirrier's o.,** helianthin. **o. N,** tropeolin OO. **naphthol o.,** tropeolin OOO. **victoria o.,** a salt of dinitrocresol used in histology as a stain. **wool o.,** orange G.

orangutan (o-rang′oo-tan″) [Malayan *orang* a human being + *utan* (hutan) wild]. One of the anthropoid apes, of the family Pongidae, frequently used for laboratory studies because it is susceptible to some of the same diseases as man.

oranixon (or″ah-nik′son). Trade mark for a preparation of mephenesin.

orb (orb) [L. *orbis* circle, disk]. A sphere; the eyeball.

Orbeli effect, phenomenon (or-ba′le) [L. A. *Orbeli*, Russian scientist, 1881–1958]. See under *phenomenon*.

orbicular (or-bik′u-lar) [L. *orbicularis*]. Circular, or rounded.

orbiculare (or-bik″u-la′re) [L.]. The orbicular bone; an ossicle of the ear that usually becomes attached to the incus at the head of its long process.

orbiculus (or-bik′u-lus), pl. *orbic′uli* [L., dim. of *orbis*]. A small circle, or disk. **o. cilia′ris** [N A, B N A], the thin part of the ciliary body extending between its crown and the ora serrata retinae. Called also *ciliary disk*.

orbit (or′bit). The bony cavity that contains the eyeball. See *orbita*.

orbita (or′bĭ-tah), pl. *or′bitae* [L. "mark of a wheel"]. [N A, B N A] The bony cavity that contains the eyeball and its associated muscles, vessels, and nerves; the ethmoidal, frontal, lacrimal, nasal, palatine, sphenoidal, and zygomatic bones, and the maxilla contribute to its formation.

orbitae (or′bĭ-te) [L.]. Plural of *orbita*.

orbital (or′bĭ-tal) [L. *orbitalis*]. Pertaining to the orbit.

orbitale (or″bĭ-ta′le). An anthropometric landmark, the lowest point on the inferior margin of the orbit.

orbitalis (or″bĭ-ta′lis) [L.]. Pertaining to the orbit.

orbitonasal (or″bĭ-to-na′zal). Pertaining to the orbit and the nose.

orbitonometer (or″bĭ-to-nom′e-ter). An instrument for measurement of the backward displacement of the eyeball produced by a given pressure exerted against its anterior aspect.

orbitonometry (or″bĭ-to-nom′e-tre). The measurement of the backward displacement of the eyeball under varying pressures.

orbitopagus (or″bĭ-top′ah-gus) [*orbit* + Gr. *pagos* thing fixed]. A twin monster composed of a small fetus attached to the orbit of the autosite.

orbitostat (or′bĭ-to-stat). An instrument for measuring the axis of the orbit.

orbitotemporal (or″bĭ-to-tem′po-ral). Pertaining to the orbital and temporal regions.

orbitotomy (or″bĭ-tot′o-me) [*orbit* + Gr. *temnein* to cut]. The operation of incising or opening into the orbit through the orbital margin.

orcein (or-se′in). A brown coloring matter, $C_{28}H_{24}N_2O_7$, derived from orcin and soluble in alcohol: used as a specific stain for elastic tissue.

orchectomy (or-kek′to-me). Orchiectomy.

orchella (or-shel′ah). A histologic stain composed of 5 cc. of acetic acid and 40 cc. each of alcohol and water, colored to a dark red with archil from which excess of ammonia has been driven off.

orchi-. See *orchio-*.

orchialgia (or″ke-al′je-ah) [*orchi-* + *-algia*]. Pain in a testicle.

orchic (or′kik). Orchidic.

orchichorea (or″ke-ko-re′ah) [*orchi-* + *chorea*]. A twitching or jerking movement of a testis.

orchidalgia (or″kĭ-dal′je-ah). Orchialgia.

orchidectomy (or″kĭ-dek′to-me). Orchiectomy.

orchidic (or-kid′ik). Pertaining to the testes.

orchiditis (or″kĭ-di′tis). Orchitis.

orchido- (or′kĭ-do) [Gr. *orchidion*, dim. of *orchis*]. See *orchio-*.

orchidocelioplasty (or″kĭ-do-se′le-o-plas″te) [*orchido-* + Gr. *koilia* belly + *plassein* to form]. The operation of transplanting an undescended testis to the abdominal cavity.

orchido-epididymectomy (or″kĭ-do-ep″ĭ-did″ĭ-mek′to-me) [*orchido-* + *epididymis* + Gr. *ektomē* excision]. The operation of excising the testis and epididymis.

orchidoncus (or″kĭ-dong′kus) [*orchido-* + Gr. *onkos* tumor]. A tumor of a testis.

orchidopathy (or″kĭ-dop′ah-the). Orchiopathy.

orchidopexy (or′kĭ-do-pek″se). Orchiopexy.

orchidoplasty (or′kĭ-do-plas″te). Orchioplasty.

orchidoptosis (or″kĭ-dop-to′sis) [*orchido-* + Gr. *ptōsis* falling]. Falling of the testis: a condition due to varicocele or relaxation of the scrotum.

orchidorrhaphy (or″kĭ-dor′ah-fe). Orchiopexy.

orchidotherapy (or″kĭ-do-ther′ah-pe) [*orchido-* + Gr. *therapeia* treatment]. Use of testicular extract in treating diseases.

orchidotomy (or″kĭ-dot′o-me) [*orchido-* + Gr. *tomē* a cutting]. Incision and drainage of a testis.

orchiectomy (or″ke-ek′to-me) [*orchio-* + Gr. *ektomē* excision]. Excision of one or both testes.

orchiencephaloma (or″ke-en-sef″ah-lo′mah) [*orchio-* + *encephaloma*]. Encephaloma of the testis.

orchiepididymitis (or″ke-ep″ĭ-did″ĭ-mi′tis) [*orchio-* + *epididymis* + *-itis*]. Inflammation of a testis and an epididymis.

orchilytic (or″kĭ-lit′ik) [*orchio-* + Gr. *lytikos* dissolving]. Destroying testicular tissue.

orchio-, orchi-, orchido- (or′ke-o, or′ke, or′kĭ-do) [Gr. *orchis* testis]. Combining form denoting relationship to the testes.

orchiocatabasis (or″ke-o-kah-tab′ah-sis) [*orchio-* + Gr. *katabasis* descent]. The descent of the testes.

orchiocele (or′ke-o-sēl) [*orchio-* + Gr. *kēlē* hernia]. 1. Hernial protrusion of a testis. 2. Scrotal hernia. 3. Tumor of a testis.

orchiococcus (or″ke-o-kok′us) [*orchio-* + Gr. *kokkos* berry]. A diplococcus from gonorrheal orchitis.

orchiodynia (or″ke-o-din′e-ah). Orchialgia.

orchiomyeloma (or″ke-o-mi″ĕ-lo′mah) [*orchio-* + *myeloma*]. Myeloma of the testis.

orchioncus (or″ke-ong′kus) [*orchio-* + Gr. *onkos* mass, tumor]. Tumor of the testis.

orchioneuralgia (or″ke-o-nu-ral′je-ah) [*orchio-* + *neuralgia*]. Pain in the testis.

orchiopathy (or″ke-op′ah-the) [*orchio-* + Gr. *pathos* disease]. Any disease of the testis.

orchiopexy (or″ke-o-pek′se) [*orchio-* + Gr. *pēxis* fixation]. Surgical fixation in the scrotum of an undescended testis.

orchioplasty (or′ke-o-plas″te) [*orchio-* + Gr. *plassein* to form]. Plastic surgery of the testis.

orchiorrhaphy (or″ke-or′ah-fe) [*orchio-* + Gr. *rhaphē* suture]. Orchiopexy.

orchioscheocele (or″ke-os′ke-o-sēl) [*orchio-* + Gr. *oscheon* scrotum + *kēlē* hernia]. Scrotal tumor with scrotal hernia.

orchioscirrhus (or″ke-o-skir′us) [*orchio-* + Gr. *skirrhos* hard]. Hardening of the testis.

orchiotomy (or″ke-ot′o-me). Orchidotomy.

Orchis (or′kis). The typical genus of orchidaceous plants. *O. mas′cula* affords salep: various species are medicinal.

orchis (or′kis) [Gr.]. The testis.

orchitic (or-kit′ik). 1. Orchidic. 2. Pertaining to or caused by orchitis.

orchitis (or-ki′tis) [*orchio-* + *-itis*]. Inflammation of a testis. The disease is marked by pain, swelling, and a feeling of weight. It may occur idiopathically, but is usually due to gonorrhea, syphilis, filarial disease, or tuberculosis. **metastatic o.,** an infection brought to the testis by the blood stream, as in mumps. **o. parotid′ea,** orchitis occurring before, or as the only manifestation of, mumps. **o. variolo′sa,** orchitis occurring in smallpox.

orchitolytic (or″kĭ-to-lit′ik). Orchilytic.

orchotomy (or-kot′o-me). Orchidotomy.

Ord's operation [William Miller *Ord*, English surgeon, 1834–1902]. See under *operation.*

order (or′der) [L. *ordo* a line, row, or series]. A taxonomic category subordinate to a class and superior to a family (or suborder).

orderly (or′der-le). A male attendant in a hospital who does general work, attending especially to the preoperative preparation (shaving, catheterizing, etc.) of male patients.

ordinate (or′dĭ-nāt). One of the lines used as a base of reference in graphs. See *abscissa.*

ordure (or′dūr). Excrement.

oreoselinum (o″re-o-se-li′num) [L.]. An umbelliferous plant of the old world, *Peucedanum oreoselinum:* used in homeopathic practice.

oretic (o-ret′ik). Trade mark for a preparation of hydrochlorothiazide.

oreton (or′e-ton). Trade mark for preparations of testosterone.

orexia (o-rek′se-ah) [Gr. *orexis*]. Appetite.

orexigenic (o-rek″sĭ-jen′ik) [Gr. *orexis* appetite + *gennan* to produce]. Increasing or stimulating the appetite.

oreximania (o-rek″sĭ-ma′ne-ah) [Gr. *orexis* appetite + *mania* madness]. Enormous increase in appetite and food intake due to fear of becoming thin.

orf. 1. A contagious pustular dermatitis of sheep, caused by a virus and communicable to man. 2. Ecthyma contagiosum.

Orfila museum (or″fĭ-lah′). A museum of anatomy at the Medical School of Paris, founded by Mathieu Joseph Bonaventure *Orfila* (1787–1853).

organ (or′gan) [L. *organum:* Gr. *organon*]. A somewhat independent part of the body that performs a special function. See *organum* [N A]. **absorbent o.,** vascular granulation tissue interposed between the enamel epithelium of a growing permanent tooth and the dentin of the deciduous tooth that the former is replacing. **accessory o's of eye,** structures accessory to the eye, including the ocular muscles and fascia, and the eyebrows, eyelids, conjunctiva, and lacrimal apparatus (organa oculi accessoria [N A]). **acoustic o.,** organum spirale. **Berlese's o.,** an organ in the female bedbug which receives the spermatozoa during copulation. **Bidder's o.,** an anterior portion, ovarian in character, of the gonad of male toads. **cell o.,** a structural part of a cell having some definite function in its life or reproduction, as a nucleus or a centrosome. **cement o.,** the embryonic tissue that develops into the cement layer of the tooth. **Chievitz's o.,** an embryonic outgrowth behind the parotid gland which may merge into the latter or may disappear. **o. of Corti,** organum spirale. **digestive o's,** those concerned with the ingestion, digestion, and assimilation of food (apparatus digestorius [N A]). **enamel o.,** a process of epithelium forming a cap over a dental papilla and developing into the enamel. **endocrine o's,** the endocrine glands. **essential o. of thalamus,** some portion of the thalamus, possibly the medial nucleus, which functions as an integrating center in animals with little or no cerebral cortex and functioning in a more or less similar manner in higher forms. **genital o's,** the various internal and external organs that are concerned with reproduction (organa genitalia [N A]). **genital o's, external,** the pudendum and clitoris in the female (partes genitales femininae externae [N A]) and the scrotum and penis in the male (partes genitales masculinae externae [N A]). **genital o's, female,** the various organs in the female that are concerned with reproduction. See *organa genitalia feminina.* **genital o's, male,** the various organs in the male that are concerned with reproduction. See *organa genitalia masculina.* **o. of Giraldès,** paradidymis. **Golgi tendon o.,** a mechanoreceptor found in tendons of mammalian muscles; arranged in series with the muscle, it is sensitive to mechanical distortion induced by either passive stretch of the tendon or isometric contraction of the muscle and thus signals muscle tension, being the receptor responsible for the lengthening reaction, or clasp-knife reflex. **gustatory o.,** the organ concerned with the perception of taste. See *organum gustus* [N A]. **Jacobson's o.,** organum vomeronasale. **lateral line o's,** sense organs in the skin of fishes and amphibians, being intermediate in type between organs of touch and hearing. **Marchand's o.,** accessory adrenal bodies in the broad ligament. **o's of mastication,** the masticatory system. **Meyer's o.,** an area of circumvallate papillae on either side of the posterior part of the tongue. **olfactory o.,** the organ concerned with the perception of odors. See *organum olfactus* [N A]. **parenchymal o., parenchymatous o.,** organon parenchymatosum. **primitive fat o.,** interscapular gland. **pyloric gland o.,** the pyloric portion of the stomach combined with Brunner's gland area of the duodenum. **reproductive o's,** those concerned with reproduction. See *organa genitalia,* under *organum.* **reproductive o's, female,** organa genitalia feminina. See under *organum.* **reproductive o's, male,** organa genitalia masculina. See under *organum.* **o. of Rosenmüller,** epoophoron. **rudimentary o.** 1. A primordium. 2. An imperfectly or incompletely developed organ. **o. of Ruffini,** brushes of Ruffini. **segmental o.,** the pronephros, mesonephros, and metanephros together. **sense o's, sensory o's,** organa sensuum. See under *organum.* **o. of shock, shock o.,** the organ which reacts in anaphylactic shock. **o's of special sense,** organa sensuum. See under *organum.* **spiral o.,** organum spirale. **target o.,** the organ that is affected by a particular hormone. **terminal o.,** the organ situated at either end of a reflex neural arc. **urinary o's,** the organs that are concerned with the production and excretion of urine (organa uropoietica). **vestibulocochlear o's,** those structures outside the central nervous system which are concerned with vestibular and auditory function. See *organum vestibulocochleare* [N A]. **vestigial o.,** an undeveloped organ that either in the embryo or in some more or less remote ancestor was well developed and functional. **visual o.,** organum visus. **vomeronasal o.,** organum vomeronasale. **Weber's o.,** utriculus prostaticus. **o's of Zuckerkandl,** large paraganglia (chromaffin tissue) found in late fetal life and a short time after birth at the origin of the inferior mesenteric artery.

organa (or'gah-nah). Plural of *organum* [L.] and *organon* [Gr.].

organacidia (or"gan-ah-sid'e-ah). The presence of an organic acid, especially in the stomach.

organella (or"gan-el'ah), pl. *organel'lae* [L.]. Organelle.

organelle (or"gan-el'). 1. A specific particle of organized living substance present in practically all cells, including mitochondria, the Golgi complex, ergastoplasm, lysosomes, ribosomes, centrioles, and the cell center. 2. One of the minute organs of protozoa concerned with such functions as locomotion, metabolism, or the like.

organic (or-gan'ik) [L. *organicus;* Gr. *organikos*]. 1. Pertaining to an organ or the organs. 2. Having an organized structure. 3. Arising from an organism. 4. Pertaining to substances derived from living organisms.

organicism (or-gan'ĭ-sizm). 1. The theory that all symptoms are due to organic disease. 2. The theory that each of the various organs of the body has its own special constitution.

organicist (or-gan'ĭ-sist). One who believes that the symptoms of disease are due to organic changes.

organism (or'gan-izm). Any organized body of living economy; an individual animal or plant. **blue pus o.,** *Pseudomonas aeruginosa.* **Donovan o.,** *Donovania granulomatis.* **nitrifying o's,** those nitrogen bacteria which are capable of oxidizing nitrites to nitrates. **nitrosifying o's,** those nitrogen bacteria which are capable of oxidizing ammonia to nitrites. **pus o's,** organisms that stimulate the formation of pus, such as staphylococci and streptococci. **Rickett's o.,** an organism of the genus Rickettsia. **Siegel's o.,** a coccus-like organism from the blood and tissues of a calf affected with vaccinia; called by Siegel *Cytorrhyctes cocci.* **Vincent's o's,** *Fusobacterium plauti vincenti* and *Borrelia vincenti.* **vinegar o.,** *Acetobacter aceti.*

organization (or"gan-i-za'shun). 1. The process of organizing or of becoming organized. 2. The replacement of blood clots by fibrous tissue. 3. An organized body, group, or structure.

organize (or'gan-iz). To provide with an organic structure; to form into organs.

organizer (or'gan-iz"er). A part of an embryo which so influences some other part as to bring about and direct its histological and morphological differentiation. Parts developing as a result of induction, and inducing in their turn are classified as organizers of the second grade, third grade, and so on. **primary o.,** the dorsal lip region of the blastopore. **secondary o.,** one of second grade, such as the optic cup, which exerts influence on the lens. **tertiary o.,** one of third grade, such as the tympanic ring, which exerts influence on the tympanic membrane.

organo- (or'gah-no) [Gr. *organon* organ]. Combining form denoting relationship to an organ.

organocalie (or"gah-no-ka'le). Elective localization.

organofaction (or"gah-no-fak'shun). The formation and development of an organ.

organoferric (or"gah-no-fer'ik). Containing iron and some organic compound.

organogel (or-gan'o-jel). A gel in which an organic liquid takes the place of water.

organogen (or-gan'o-jen). Any one of the chemical elements—carbon, hydrogen, oxygen, nitrogen, sulfur, phosphorus, and chlorine—characteristic of organic substances.

organogenesis (or"gah-no-jen'e-sis) [*organo-* + Gr. *genesis* generation]. The development or growth of organs.

organogenetic (or"gah-no-je-net'ik). Pertaining to organogenesis.

organogenic (or"gah-no-jen'ik). Originating in an organ.

organogeny (or"gah-noj'e-ne). Organogenesis.

organography (or-gah-nog'rah-fe) [*organo-* + Gr. *graphein* to write]. 1. A description of the organs of a living body. 2. The roentgenologic visualization of the organs of the body.

organoid (or'gan-oid) [*organ* + Gr. *eidos* form]. 1. Resembling an organ. 2. A structure which resembles an organ. **cytoplasmic o's,** structures present in all cells which are probably able to divide and thus perpetuate themselves, in contrast to lifeless cell inclusions. Organoids include mitochondria, fibrils, Golgi apparatus, and centrosomes.

organoleptic (or"gah-no-lep'tik) [*organo-* + Gr. *lambanein* to seize]. 1. Making an impression on an organ of special sense. 2. Capable of receiving a sense impression.

organology (or-gah-nol'o-je) [*organo-* + *-logy*]. The sum of what is known regarding the organs of the body.

organoma (or-gah-no'mah). A tumor composed of organs or definite portions of an organ, or characterized by the presence in it of definite organs, as a dermoid cyst.

organometallic (or-gah-no-me-tal'ik). Consisting of a metal in combination with an organic radical.

organon (or'gah-non), pl. *or'gana* [Gr.]. [B N A] A somewhat independent part of the body that performs a special function. See *organum.* **o. audi'tus** [B N A], organum vestibulocochleare. **or'gana genita'lia** [B N A]. See under *organum.* **or'gana genita'lia mulie'bria** [B N A]. See *organa genitalia feminina,* under *organum.* **or'gana genita'lia viril'ia** [B N A]. See *organa genitalia masculina,* under *organum.* **o. gus'tus** [B N A], organum gustus. **or'gana oc'uli accesso'ria** [B N A]. See under *organum.* **o. olfac'tus** [B N A], organum olfactus. **o. parenchymato'sum** [B N A], a parenchymatous organ. Omitted in N A. **or'gana sen'suum** [B N A]. See under *organum.* **o. spira'le [Cor'tii]** [B N A], organum spirale. **or'gana uropoët'ica** [B N A]. See *organa uropoietica,* under *organum.* **o. vi'sus** [B N A], organum visus. **o. vomeronasa'le [Jacobso'ni]** [B N A], organum vomeronasale.

organonomy (or"gah-non'o-me) [*organo-* + Gr. *nomos* law]. The laws of organic life and of living organisms.

organonymy (or"gah-non'ĭ-me) [*organo-* + Gr. *onyma* name]. The nomenclature of the bodily organs.

organopathy (or"gah-nop'ah-the) [*organo-* + Gr. *pathos* disease]. 1. Organic disease. 2. Organotherapy.

organopexia (or"gah-no-pek'se-ah). Organopexy.

organopexil (or"gah-no-pek'sil). A method of enucleating fibroid growths.

organopexy (or'gah-no-pek"se) [*organo-* + Gr. *pēxis* fixation]. The surgical fixation of an organ, especially of the uterus after excision of a myoma.

organophilic (or"gah-no-fil'ik) [*organo-* + Gr. *philein* to love]. Having an affinity for certain organs or tissues of the body.

organophilism (or-gah-nof'ĭ-lizm). The state or quality of being organophilic.

organoscopy (or-gah-nos'ko-pe) [*organo-* + Gr. *skopein* to examine]. Examination of the abdominal viscera by means of a cystoscope inserted through an epigastric incision.

organotaxis (or″gah-no-tak′sis) [*organo-* + Gr. *taxis* arrangement]. A tendency to elective migration to some particular organ.

organotherapy (or″gah-no-ther′ah-pe) [*organo-* + Gr. *therapeia* therapy]. The treatment of disease by the administration of animal organs or their extracts. See *opotherapy*. **heterologous o.,** organotherapy with substances that have no relation to the diseased organ of the patient. **homologous o.,** organotherapy by extractives of the organs of animals corresponding to the diseased organ of the patient.

organotrope (or-gan′o-trōp). An organotropic element or agent.

organotrophic (or″gah-no-trof′ik). Relating to the nutrition of organs of the body.

organotropic (or″gah-no-trop′ik). Pertaining to or characterized by organotropism.

organotropism (or-gan-ot′ro-pizm) [*organo-* + Gr. *tropē* a turning]. The special affinity of chemical compounds or of pathogenic agents for particular tissues or organs of the body.

organotropy (or″gan-ot′ro-pe). Organotropism.

organule (or′gan-ūl). An end-organ of sensory receptors, such as a taste bud.

organum (or′gah-num), pl. *or′gana* [L.]. [N A] A somewhat independent part of the body that performs a special function; it is composed of various tissues, one of which is primary and is arranged according to a characteristic structural plan. Called also *organ*, and *organon* [B N A]. **or′gana genita′lia** [N A, B N A], the various internal and external organs that are concerned with reproduction. **or′gana genita′lia femini′na** [N A], the various organs in the female that are concerned with reproduction, including the ovary, uterine tube, uterus, vagina, labia, and clitoris. Called also *organa genitalia muliebria* [B N A], and *female genital organs*. **or′gana genita′lia masculi′na** [N A], the various organs in the male that are concerned with reproduction, including the testis, epididymis, ductus deferens, seminal vesicle, ejaculatory duct, prostate, bulbourethral gland, and penis. Called also *organa genitalia virilia* [B N A], and *male genital organs*. **o. gus′tus** [N A], the organ of taste, comprising the taste buds, most of which are found within the epithelial covering of the tongue. Called also *organon gustus* [B N A], and *gustatory organ*. **or′gana oc′uli accesso′ria** [N A], the accessory organs of the eye, including the ocular muscles and fascia, and the eyebrows, eyelids, conjunctiva, and lacrimal apparatus. **o. olfac′tus** [N A], the specialized structures subserving the function of the sense of smell, including the olfactory region of the nasal mucosa and the olfactory glands. Called also *organon olfactus* [B N A], and *olfactory organ*. **or′gana sen′suum** [N A], organs that receive stimuli which give rise to sensations. They consist of nerve cells and sensory nerve endings that may be highly specialized. They include the visual, vestibulocochlear, olfactory, and gustatory organs. Called also *sense organs*. **o. spira′le** [N A], the organ, lying against the basilar membrane in the cochlear duct, that contains the special sensory receptors for hearing. It consists of neuroepithelial hair cells and several types of supporting cells. Called also *organon spirale* [*Cortii*] [B N A], and *spiral organ*. **or′gana uropoët′ica** [N A]. See *organa uropoietica*. **or′gana uropoiet′ica,** the organs concerned with the production and excretion of urine, including the kidneys, ureters, bladder, and urethra. Called also *urinary organs*. **o. vestibulocochlea′re** [N A], a collective term in official anatomical nomenclature applied to those structures outside the central nervous system that are concerned with balance and hearing, and comprising the internal, middle, and external ear. Called also *organon auditus* [B N A], and *vestibulocochlear organ*. **o. vi′sus** [N A], a collective term in official anatomical nomenclature applied to those structures outside the central nervous system that are concerned with vision, comprising the eyeball and its fibrous, vascular, and internal tunics, and the accessory organs of the eye. Called also *organon visus* [B N A], and *organ of vision*. **o. vomeronasa′le** [N A], a short rudimentary canal just above the vomeronasal cartilage, opening in the side of the nasal septum and passing from there blindly upward and backward. Called also *organon vomeronasale* [*Jacobsoni*] [B N A], and *vomeronasal organ*.

orgasm (or′gazm) [Gr. *orgasmos* swelling, or *organ* to swell, to be lustful]. The crisis of sexual excitement.

Oribasius (or″ĭ-ba′se-us) (325–403 A.D.). A famous physician and medical writer who became physician to the Emperor Julian. His *magnum opus* was an encyclopedia of medicine in seventy volumes, of which only some seventeen survive; these are invaluable for they contain extracts from the works of many important physicians of antiquity (e.g., Dioscorides, Galen, Antyllus).

orientation (o″re-en-ta′shun) [L. *oriens* arising]. The determination of the east point; hence, the determination of one's position with respect to space and time.

orientomycin (o-re-en″to-mi′sin). Cycloserine.

orifice (or′ĭ-fis) [L. *orificium*]. 1. The entrance or outlet of any body cavity. 2. Any foramen, meatus, or opening. See also *ostium*. **abdominal o. of uterine tube,** ostium abdominale tubae uterinae. **aortic o.,** the opening of the aorta in the left ventricle of the heart. **o. of aqueduct of vestibule, external,** apertura externa aqueductus vestibuli. **atrioventricular o., auriculoventricular o.** See *ostia atrioventricularia* [*dextrum et sinistrum*]. **canal o.,** root canal o. **cardiac o.,** ostium cardiacum. **duodenal o. of stomach,** pylorus. **epiploic o.,** foramen epiploicum. **hymenal o.,** ostium vaginae. **o. of male urethra, external,** ostium urethrae externum masculinae. **o. of maxillary sinus,** hiatus maxillaris. **mitral o.,** ostium arteriosum cordis. **pharyngeal o.,** ostium pharyngeum tubae. **pilosebaceous o's,** the openings of the hair follicles, giving egress to the secretion of the sebaceous glands whose ducts open into the follicles. **pulmonary o.,** the opening of the pulmonary artery in the right ventricle of the heart. **o. of pulp canal,** foramen apicis dentis. **root canal o.,** an opening in the floor of the pulp chamber of a tooth, leading into a root canal. **o. of ureter,** ostium ureteris. **o. of urethra, internal,** ostium urethrae internum. **o. of uterus, external,** ostium uteri. **vesicourethral o.,** ostium urethrae internum.

orificia (or″ĭ-fish′e-ah) [L.]. Plural of *orificium*.

orificial (or″ĭ-fish′al). Pertaining to an orifice.

orificialist (or″ĭ-fish′al-ist). One who treats disease by dilating or otherwise operating upon the external orifices of the body.

orificium (or″ĭ-fish′e-um), pl. *orific′ia* [L.]. [B N A] An opening; especially the entrance or outlet of any body cavity. Called *ostium* [N A]. **o. exter′num isth′mi, o. exter′num u′teri** [B N A], ostium uteri. **o. hy′menis,** ostium vaginae. **o. inter′num isth′mi, o. inter′num u′teri** [B N A], the internal orifice of the cervix uteri, opening into the cavity of the uterus. Omitted in N A. **o. ure′teris** [B N A], ostium ureteris. **o. ure′thrae exter′num mulie′bris** [B N A], ostium urethrae externum feminina. **o. ure′thrae exter′num vir′ilis** [B N A], ostium urethrae externum masculinae. **o. ure′thrae inter′num** [B N A], ostium urethrae internum. **o. vagi′nae** [B N A], ostium vaginae.

Origanum (o-rig′ah-num) [L.; Gr. *origanon*]. A genus of labiate plants. *O. vulga′re,* wild marjoram, affords a stimulant volatile oil, used mainly in veterinary practice and in liniments. *O. majora′na,* sweet marjoram, affords a similar oil.

origin (or′ĭ-jin) [L. *origo* beginning]. The source or beginning of anything, especially the more fixed end or attachment of a muscle, as distinguished from its insertion, or the site of the beginning of a peripheral nerve in the central nervous system.

orinase (or'ĭ-nās). Trade mark for a preparation of tolbutamide.

orinotherapy (o-ri″no-ther'ah-pe) [Gr. *oreinos* pertaining to mountains + *therapeia* treatment]. Treatment by living in high, mountainous regions.

orismology (or″iz-mol'o-ge). Horismology.

ornithine (or'nĭ-thin). An amino acid, alpha-delta-diamino-valerianic acid, $NH_2(CH_2)_3.CH(NH_2).CO_2H$, obtained from arginine by splitting off urea. On decomposition it gives rise to putrescine, and with urea it forms arginine.

Ornithodoros (or″nĭ-thod'o-ros) [Gr. *ornis, ornithos* bird + *doros* bag]. A genus of argasid ticks, many species of which are the reservoirs and vectors of the spirochetes (*Borrelia*) of relapsing fevers. The chief vectors are: *O. as'perus* of Asia; *O. errat'ius* of Spain and North Africa; *O. gur'neyi* of Australia; *O. herm'si* of western United States; *O. mouba'ta,* the tampan tick of South Africa; *O. par'keri* of western United States; *O. ru'dis* of Central and South America; *O. savign'yi* of Africa, Arabia, and India; *O. tala'je* of the tropics of North and South America; *O. tartakov'skyi* in Russia; *O. tholaza'ni* in Turkestan, Syria, and Palestine; *O. turica'ta* in Mexico, Texas, Arizona, Colorado, and California. **O. coria'ceus,** the pajaroello of California which is greatly feared because of its bite. It is not known to transmit disease.

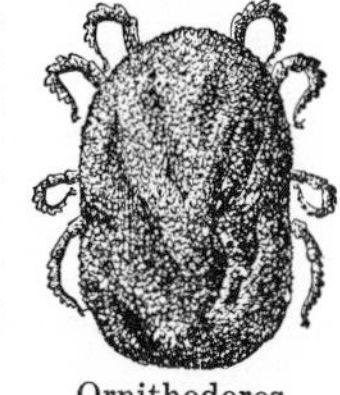
Ornithodoros moubata (after Chandler).

ornithosis (or″nĭ-tho'sis) [Gr. *ornis, ornithos* bird + *-osis*]. A virus disease of birds and domestic fowl, which is transmissible to man, causing chills and fever, headache, photophobia, anorexia, sore throat, nausea, and vomiting; originally called psittacosis because it was first observed in psittacine birds.

oro- (o'ro). 1. [L. *os, oris* mouth]. Combining form denoting relationship to the mouth. 2. [Gr. *oros* the watery part of the blood (serum), or whey]. See *orrho.*

orodiagnosis (or″o-di″ag-no'sis). Serum diagnosis.

oro-immunity (o″ro-ĭ-mu'nĭ-te) [*oro-*(2) + *immunity*]. Passive immunity.

orokinase (o″ro-kin'ās) [*oro-*(1) + *kinase*]. A kinase produced by the buccal glands of certain animals which converts inactive ptyalin into active ptyalin.

orolingual (o″ro-ling'gwal) [*oro-*(1) + L. *lingua* tongue]. Pertaining to the mouth and tongue.

oromaxillary (o″ro-mak'sĭ-ler″e). Pertaining to the mouth and the maxillary region.

oromeningitis (or″o-men″in-ji'tis). Orrhomeningitis.

oronasal (o″ro-na'zal) [*oro-*(1) + L. *nasus* nose]. Pertaining to the mouth and nose.

orophagin (o-rof'ah-jin). A hormone from the anterior pituitary having an influence on fat metabolism.

oropharynx (o″ro-far'inks) [*oro-*(1) + *pharynx*]. That division of the pharynx which lies between the soft palate and the upper edge of the epiglottis (pars oralis pharyngis).

orophysin (or-of'ĭ-sin). The name applied by Magistris to the ketogenic principle of the anterior pituitary.

Oropsylla (o″ro-sil'ah). A genus of fleas. **O. idahoen'sis,** a rodent flea of the western United States, implicated in the transmission of sylvatic plague. **O. silantiew'i,** a flea of the Manchuria marmot or tarbagan, capable of transmitting plague.

orosin (or'o-sin) [Gr. *oros* the watery part of the blood]. The coagulable protein composing the colloidal matrix of cells, tissues and blood plasma.

orotherapy (o″ro-ther'ah-pe) [*oro-*(2) + Gr. *therapeia* treatment]. 1. Whey cure; the treatment of disease by administering whey. 2. Serotherapy.

Oroya fever (o-ro'yah) [*Oroya,* a region in Peru]. Carrión's disease.

orphenadrine (or-fen'ah-drēn). Chemical name: N,N-dimethyl-2-(o-methyl-α-phenylbenzyloxy)-ethylamine: used as an antihistaminic, antitremor and antispasmodic agent for relaxation of skeletal muscle spasm and tremor.

Orr method, technic, treatment [Hiram Winnett *Orr,* American orthopedic surgeon, 1877–1956]. See under *treatment.*

orrho- (or'o) [Gr. *orrhos* serum]. Combining form denoting relationship to serum.

orrhodiagnosis (or″o-di″ag-no'sis). Serum diagnosis.

orrho-immunity (or″o-ĭ-mu'nĭ-te) [*orrho-* + *immunity*]. Passive immunity.

orrhology (or-ol'o-je) [*orrho-* + *-logy*]. The scientific study of serums; serology.

orrhomeningitis (or″o-men″in-ji'tis) [*orrho-* + *meningitis*]. Inflammation of a serous membrane.

orrhoreaction (or″o-re-ak'shun) [*orrho-* + *reaction*]. Seroreaction.

orrhorrhea (or-o-re'ah) [*orrho-* + Gr. *rhoia* flow]. A watery or serous discharge.

orrhotherapeutic (or″o-ther″ah-pu'tik). Pertaining to or of the nature of orrhotherapy.

orrhotherapy (or″o-ther'ah-pe) [*orrho-* + *therapy*]. The therapeutic use of serums.

orris (or'is). The rhizome or root of Florentine iris, *I'ris florenti'na;* used in dentrifices, perfumes, etc.

Orsi-Grocco method (or″se-grok'o) [Francesco *Orsi,* 1828–1890; Pietro *Grocco,* 1857–1916, Italian physicians]. Palpatory percussion of the heart.

orthergasia (or″ther-ga'ze-ah) [*ortho-* + Gr. *ergon* work]. A condition of normal functioning and adjustment.

orthesis (or-the'sis). A brace or other orthopedic device which is applied to the body in the treatment of physical impairment or disability.

orthetics (or-thet'iks). Orthotics.

orthetist (or'thĕ-tist). Orthotist.

ortho- (or'tho) [Gr. *orthos* straight]. Combining form meaning straight, normal, correct, etc. In chemistry, this prefix indicates an isomer; also a cyclic derivative which has two substituents in adjacent positions.

ortho-acid (or″tho-as'id). An acid containing as many hydroxyl groups as the valence of the acidulous element.

ortho-arteriotony (or″tho-ar-te″re-ot'o-ne) [*ortho-* + Gr. *artēria* artery + *tonos* tension]. Normal arterial pressure.

orthobiosis (or″tho-bi-o'sis) [*ortho-* + Gr. *biōsis* way of life]. Proper living; living in accordance with all the laws of health.

orthocephalic (or″tho-se-fal'ik) [Gr. *orthos* straight + *kephalē* head]. Having a head with a vertical index of 70.1 to 75.

orthocephalous (or″tho-sef'ah-lus). Orthocephalic.

orthochorea (or″tho-ko-re'ah) [*ortho-* + *chorea*]. Choreic movements in the erect posture.

orthochromatic (or″tho-kro-mat'ik). 1. Normally colored or stained. 2. Denoting a photographic emulsion sensitive to all colors except red.

orthochromia (or″tho-kro'me-ah) [*ortho-* + Gr. *chrōma* color + *-ia*]. Normal hemoglobin content of the erythrocytes.

orthochromophil (or″tho-kro'mo-fil) [*ortho-* + Gr. *chrōma* color + *philein* to love]. Staining normally with neutral stains.

orthocrasia (or″tho-kra'se-ah) [*ortho-* + Gr. *krasis* a mixing + *-ia*]. A state in which the body reacts normally to ingested or injected drugs, proteins, etc.

orthocresol (or″tho-kre′sol). One of the three isomeric forms of cresol.

orthocytosis (or″tho-si-to′sis) [*ortho-* + *-cyte* + *-osis*]. Presence of mature cells only in the blood.

orthodactylous (or″tho-dak′tĭ-lus) [*ortho-* + Gr. *daktylos* finger]. Having straight digits.

orthodentin (or″tho-den′tin) [*ortho-* + *dentin*]. Straight-tubed dentin, as seen in the teeth of mammals.

orthodiagram (or″tho-di′ah-gram). The print or record made by an orthodiagraph; the silhouette of an organ as traced in orthodiascopy.

orthodiagraph (or″tho-di′ah-graf) [*ortho-* + Gr. *dia* through + *graphein* to write]. A radiographic apparatus for recording accurately the form and size of structures inside the body, doing away with the distortion of the ordinary roentgen-ray plate.

orthodiagraphy (or″tho-di-ag′rah-fe). The use of the orthodiagraph.

orthodiascope (or″tho-di′ah-skōp). An instrument for orthodiascopy.

orthodiascopy (or″tho-di-as′ko-pe). Undistorted fluoroscopy: especially the direct tracing of the silhouette of an organ (e.g., the heart) as projected on a fluoroscopic screen.

orthodichlorobenzene (or″tho-di-klo″ro-ben′-zēn). An insecticide, $C_6H_4Cl_2$, used as a spray.

orthodigita (or″tho-dij′ĭ-tah) [*ortho-* + L. *digitus* finger or toe]. The art of correcting deformities of the toes and fingers.

orthodontia (or″tho-don′she-ah). Orthodontics.

orthodontic (or″tho-don′tik). Pertaining to the proper positioning and relationship of the teeth.

orthodontics (or″tho-don′tiks) [*ortho-* + Gr. *odous* tooth]. That branch of dentistry which deals with the prevention and correction of irregularities of the teeth and malocclusion, and with associated facial problems. **corrective o.,** that phase of orthodontics which is concerned with the reduction or elimination of an existing malocclusion and its attendant sequelae. **interceptive o.,** that phase of orthodontics which is concerned with elimination of a condition which might lead to the development of malocclusion. **preventive o.,** that phase of orthodontics which is concerned with preservation of the integrity of what appears to be normal occlusion.

orthodontist (or″tho-don′tist). A dentist who specializes in orthodontics.

orthodontology (or″tho-don-tol′o-je). Orthodontics.

orthodromic (or″tho-drom′ik) [Gr. *orthodromein* to run straight forward]. Conducting impulses in the normal direction: said of nerve fibers. Cf. *antidromic.*

orthogenesis (or″tho-jen′e-sis) [*ortho-* + *genesis*]. 1. Progressive evolution in a given direction, in contrast with variations in several directions. 2. The theory that the course of evolution is fixed and predetermined; monogenesis.

orthogenics (or″tho-jen′iks) [*ortho-* + Gr. *genikos* sexual]. Eugenics.

orthoglycemic (or″tho-gli-se′mik) [*ortho-* + Gr. *glykys* sweet + *haima* blood]. Having the normal amount of sugar in the blood.

orthognathia (or″thog-nath′e-ah). The science dealing with the cause and treatment of malposition of the bones of the jaw.

orthognathic (or″thog-na′thik). 1. Pertaining to orthognathia. 2. Orthognathous.

orthognathous (or-thog′nah-thus) [*ortho-* + Gr. *gnathos* jaw]. Having a gnathic index of less than 98.

orthograde (or′tho-grād) [*ortho-* + L. *gradi* to walk]. Characterized by walking with the body upright: applied to bipeds.

ortholiposis (or″tho-lĭ-po′sis) [*ortho-* + *liposis*]. The normal proportion of liposin in the serum of the blood.

orthomelic (or″tho-me′lik) [*ortho-* + Gr. *melos* limb]. Correcting deformities of the limbs.

orthometer (or-thom′e-ter) [*ortho-* + Gr. *metron* measure]. An instrument for finding the relative protrusion of the two eyeballs.

orthomorphia (or″tho-mor′fe-ah) [*ortho-* + Gr. *morphē* form]. The surgical and mechanical correction of deformities.

orthoneutrophil (or″tho-nu′tro-fil). Orthochromophil.

orthopaedic (or″tho-pe′dik). Orthopedic.

orthopaedics (or″tho-pe′diks). Orthopedics.

orthopedic (or″tho-pe′dik) [*ortho-* + Gr. *pais* child]. Pertaining to the correction of deformities; pertaining to orthopedics.

orthopedics (or″tho-pe′diks) [*ortho-* + Gr. *pais* child]. That branch of surgery which is specially concerned with the preservation and restoration of the function of the skeletal system, its articulations and associated structures. **dental o.,** orthodontics. **dentofacial o.,** the correction of malformations of the face and jaws.

orthopedist (or″tho-pe′dist). An orthopedic surgeon.

orthopercussion (or″tho-per-kush′un) [*ortho-* + *percussion*]. Percussion in which the distal phalanx of the pleximeter finger is held perpendicularly to the chest wall.

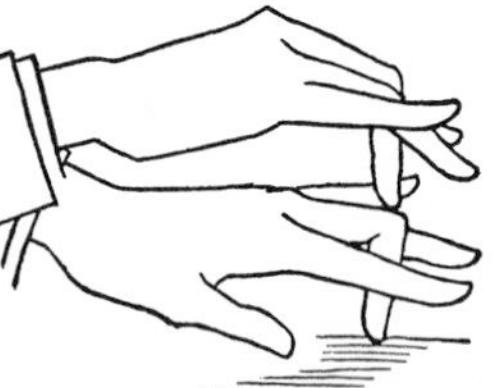

Orthopercussion (Külbs).

orthophenanthrolene (or″tho-fe-nan′thro-lēn). A white powder, $C_{12}H_8N_2.H_2O$, used as an indicator.

orthophenolase (or″tho-fe′nol-ās). An enzyme in sweet potatoes which oxidizes catechol and orthocresol.

orthophony (or-thof′o-ne) [*ortho-* + Gr. *phōnē* voice]. The direct and correct production of sound.

orthophoria (or″tho-fo′re-ah) [*ortho-* + Gr. *pherein* to bear + *-ia*]. The normal or proper placement of organs, especially the condition in which the visual axes remain parallel after the visual fusional stimuli have been more or less eliminated. **asthenic o.,** general weakness of the eye muscles.

orthophoric (or″tho-for′ik). Pertaining to or marked by orthophoria.

orthophosphate (or″tho-fos′fāt). A salt of orthophosphoric acid; a compound of the type M_3PO_4.

orthophrenia (or″tho-fre′ne-ah) [*ortho-* + Gr. *phrēn* mind + *-ia*]. The condition of normal mental reactivity in social relations.

orthopia (or-tho′pe-ah). The prevention or correction of strabismus.

orthoplastocyte (or″tho-plas′to-sīt) [*ortho-* + *plastocyte*]. A normal blood platelet.

orthoplessimeter (or″tho-ple-sim′e-ter). An instrument to take the place of the pleximeter finger in orthopercussion.

orthopnea (or″thop-ne′ah) [*ortho-* + Gr. *pnoia* breath]. Inability to breathe except in an upright position.

orthopneic (or″thop-ne′ik). Pertaining to or marked by orthopnea.

orthopod (or′tho-pod). Orthopedist.

orthopraxis (or″tho-prak′sis). Orthopraxy.

orthopraxy (or′tho-prak-se) [*ortho-* + Gr. *prassein* to make]. The mechanical correction of deformities.

orthopsychiatry (or″tho-si-ki′ah-tre) [*ortho-* + *psychiatry*]. That branch of psychiatry which deals with mental and emotional development, embracing child psychiatry and mental hygiene.

Orthoptera (or-thop′ter-ah) [*ortho-* + Gr. *pteron* wing]. An order of biting insects which do not undergo metamorphosis. They include the grasshoppers, locusts, crickets, and cockroaches.

orthoptic (or-thop′tik) [*ortho-* + Gr. *optikos* of or for sight]. Correcting obliquity of one or both visual axes.

orthoptics (or-thop′tiks). A technique of eye exercises designed to correct the visual axes of eyes not properly coordinated for binocular vision.

orthoptist (or-thop′tist). An expert in orthoptics.

orthoptoscope (or-thop′to-skōp) [*ortho-* + Gr. *op-* to see + *skopein* to examine]. An instrument for orthoptic or exercise treatment in anomalies of the ocular muscles.

orthorhombic (or″tho-rom′bik). Having three unequal axes intersected at right angles.

orthoroentgenography (or″tho-rent″gen-og′rah-fe). Orthodiagraphy.

orthoscope (or′tho-skōp) [*ortho-* + Gr. *skopein* to examine]. An apparatus which neutralizes the corneal refraction by means of a layer of water: it is used in examining the eye.

orthoscopic (or″tho-skop′ik). Affording a correct and undistorted view.

orthoscopy (or-thos′ko-pe). Examination of the eye by means of the orthoscope.

orthosis (or-tho′sis) [Gr. *orthōsis* guiding, a making straight]. 1. The straightening of a distorted part. 2. Orthesis.

orthoskiagraph (or″tho-ski′ah-graf). Orthodiagraph.

orthoskiagraphy (or″tho-ski-ag′rah-fe). Orthodiagraphy.

orthostatic (or″tho-stat′ik) [*ortho-* + Gr. *statikos* causing to stand]. Pertaining to or caused by standing erect.

orthostatism (or′tho-stat″izm). An erect standing position of the body.

orthostereoscope (or″tho-ste′re-o-skōp). An apparatus for stereoscopic radiography.

orthosympathetic (or″tho-sim″pah-thet′ik). A term applied to the sympathetic (thoracolumbar) division of the autonomic nervous system as contrasted with the parasympathetic (craniosacral) division.

orthotast (or′tho-tast) [*ortho-* + Gr. *tassein* to arrange]. An apparatus for straightening curvatures of bones.

orthoterion (or″tho-te′re-on) [Gr. *orthōtēr* one who sets straight]. A device for use in straightening crooked limbs.

orthotherapy (or″tho-ther′ah-pe) [*ortho-* + *therapy*]. Treatment of disorders by correction of posture.

orthotic (or-thot′ik). 1. Pertaining to or promoting the straightening of a deformed or distorted part. 2. Orthostatic.

orthotics (or-thot′iks). The field of knowledge relating to orthopedic appliances and their use.

orthotist (or′tho-tist). An individual skilled in orthotics and practicing its application in individual cases.

ortho-tolueno-azo-beta-naphthol. A poisonous dye used in processing citrus fruits.

orthotonos (or-thot′o-nos) [*ortho-* + Gr. *tonos* tension]. Tetanic fixation of the head, body, and limbs in a rigid straight line.

orthotonus (or-thot′o-nus). Orthotonos.

orthotopic (or″tho-top′ik) [*ortho-* + Gr. *topos* place]. Occurring at the normal place or upon the proper part of the body.

orthotyphoid (or″tho-ti′foid). Normal typhoid fever as distinguished from paratyphoid.

orthoxine (or-thok′sēn). Trade mark for preparations of methoxyphenamine.

orthropsia (or-throp′se-ah) [Gr. *orthros* the time just about daybreak + *opsis* vision]. The ability of the human eye to see better during dawn or twilight than in bright sunlight.

orthuria (or-thu′re-ah) [*ortho-* + Gr. *ouron* urine + *-ia*]. Normal frequency of urination.

Oryza (o-ri′zah) [L.; Gr. *oryza* rice]. A genus of cereal plants. *O. sativa* produces rice.

oryzenin (o-ri′zĕ-nin) [Gr. *oryza* rice]. 1. An extractive from rice bran. 2. A glutelin from rice.

Os. Chemical symbol for *osmium.*

o.s. Abbreviation for L. *oc′ulus sinis′ter,* left eye.

os[1] (os), gen. *o′ris,* pl. *o′ra* [L. "an opening, or mouth"]. [N A, B N A] The anterior or proximal opening of the digestive apparatus. See *mouth.* **o. exter′num u′teri,** ostium uteri. **o. inter′num u′teri,** orificium internum uteri. **o. tin′cae,** ostium uteri. **o. of uterus, external,** ostium uteri. **o. of uterus, internal,** orificium internum uteri.

os[2] (os), gen. *os′sis,* pl. *os′sa* [L.]. Bone; used in anatomical nomenclature as a general term which is combined with the appropriate adjective to designate a specific type of bony structure or a specific segment of the skeleton. **o. acetab′uli,** acetabulum. **o. acromia′le,** a movable joint between the spine of the scapula and the epiphysis of the acromion. **o. acromia′le seconda′rium,** a round structure appearing in the roentgenogram just above the tuberosity of the humerus. **o. basila′re** [B N A], a term applied to the sphenoid and occipital bones. Omitted in N A. **o. bre′ve** [N A, B N A], a bone whose main dimensions are approximately equal. Called also *short bone.* **o. cal′cis.** N A alternative for *calcaneus.* **o. capita′tum** [N A, B N A], the bone in the distal row of carpal bones lying between the trapezoid and hamate bones. Called also *capitate bone.* **o. carpa′le dista′le pri′mum,** o. trapezium. **o. carpa′le dista′le quar′tum,** o. hamatum. **o. carpa′le dista′le secun′dum,** o. trapezoideum. **o. carpa′le dista′le ter′tium,** o. capitatum. **os′sa car′pi** [N A, B N A], the eight bones of the wrist (carpus), including the o. capitatum, o. hamatum, o. lunatum, o. pisiforme, o. scaphoideum, o. trapezium, o. trapezoideum, and o. triquetrum. Called also *carpal bones.* **o. centra′le** [N A, B N A], an accessory bone sometimes found on the back of the carpus. Called also *central bone.* **o. centra′le tar′si,** o. naviculare. **o. coc′cygis** [N A, B N A], the small bone caudad to the sacrum in man, formed by union of four (sometimes five or three) rudimentary vertebrae, and forming the caudal extremity of the vertebral column. Called also *coccygeal bone,* and *coccyx.* **o. coro′nae,** the small pastern bone of the horse. **o. costa′le** [N A, B N A], a rib bone. **o. cox′ae** [N A, B N A], the hip bone, which comprises the ilium, ischium, and pubis. **os′sa cra′nii** [N A], the bones of the cranium, or skull, including the occipital, sphenoidal, temporal, parietal, frontal, ethmoidal, lacrimal, and nasal bones, the concha nasalis, and vomer. **o. cuboi′deum** [N A, B N A], a bone on the lateral side of the tarsus between the calcaneus and the fourth and fifth metatarsal bones. Called also *cuboid bone.* **o. cuneifor′me interme′dium** [N A], the intermediate and smallest of the three wedge-shaped tarsal bones located medial to the cuboid and between the navicular and the first three metatarsal bones. Called also *o. cuneiforme secundum* [B N A], and *intermediate cuneiform bone.* **o. cuneifor′me latera′le** [N A], the most lateral of the three wedge-shaped tarsal bones located medial to the cuboid and between the navicular and the first three metatarsal bones. Called also *o. cuneiforme tertium* [B N A], and *lateral cuneiform bone.* **o. cuneifor′me media′le** [N A], the medial and largest of the three wedge-shaped tarsal bones located medial to the cuboid and between the navicular and the first three metatarsal bones. Called also *o. cuneiforme primum* [B N A], and *medial cuneiform bone.* **o. cuneifor′me pri′mum** [B N A], o. cuneiforme mediale. **o. cuneifor′me secun′dum**

[B N A], o. cuneiforme intermedium. **o. cuneifor'me ter'tium** [B N A], o. cuneiforme laterale. **os'sa digito'rum ma'nus** [N A], the 14 bones that compose the skeleton of the fingers. Called also *phalanges digitorum manus* [B N A], and *phalanges of fingers*. **os'sa digito'rum pe'dis** [N A], the 14 bones that compose the skeleton of the toes. Called also *phalanges digitorum pedis* [B N A], and *phalanges of toes*. **o. epitympan'icum,** a bone of very early fetal life which becomes the posterior portion of the squama that aids in forming the mastoid cells. **o. ethmoida'le** [N A, B N A], the sievelike bone that forms a roof for the nasal fossae and part of the floor of the anterior fossa of the skull. Called also *ethmoid bone*. **os'sa extremita'tis inferio'ris** [B N A], the bones of the lower limb (ossa membri inferioris [N A]). **os'sa extremita'tis superio'ris** [B N A], the bones of the upper limb (ossa membri superioris (N A]). **os'sa fa'ciei** [N A, B N A], the bones that constitute the facial part of the skull, including the maxilla, palatine bone, zygomatic bone, mandible, and hyoid bone. Called also *facial bones*. **o. fronta'le** [N A, B N A], a single bone that closes the front part of the cranial cavity and forms the skeleton of the forehead; it is developed from two halves, the line of separation sometimes persisting in adult life. Called also *frontal bone*. **o. hama'tum** [N A, B N A], the medial bone in the distal row of carpal bones. Called also *hamate bone*. **o. hyoi'deum** [N A, B N A], a horseshoe-shaped bone situated at the base of the tongue, just above the thyroid cartilage. Called also *hyoid bone*. **o. il'ium** [N A, B N A], the expansive superior portion of the hip bone (os coxae); it is a separate bone in early life. Called also *ilium*. **o. in'cae,** o. interparietale. **o. incisi'vum** [N A, B N A], the portion of the maxilla that bears the incisor teeth. Developmentally it is the premaxilla, which in the human subsequently fuses with the maxilla proper to form the adult bone. In most other vertebrates it persists as an independent bone. Called also *incisive bone*. **o. innomina'tum,** o. coxae. **o. intercuneifor'me,** an occasionally occurring bone situated between the medial and intermediate cuneiform bones. **o. interme'dium,** o. lunatum. **o. intermetatar'seum,** an occasionally occurring accessory bone situated between the proximal ends of the first and second metatarsal bones. **o. interparieta'le** [N A, B N A], the part of the squama of the occipital bone that lies superior to the highest nuchal line when this portion remains separate throughout life. Called also *interparietal bone*. **o. is'chii** [N A, B N A], the inferior dorsal portion of the hip bone (os coxae); it is a separate bone in early life. Called also *ischium*. **o. lacrima'le** [N A, B N A], a thin scalelike bone at the anterior part of the medial wall of the orbit, articulating with the frontal and ethmoid bones and the maxilla and inferior nasal concha. Called also *lacrimal bone*. **o. lon'gum** [N A, B N A], a bone whose length exceeds its breadth and thickness. Called also *long bone*. **o. luna'tum** [N A, B N A], the bone in the proximal row of carpal bones lying between the scaphoid and triquetral bones. Called also *lunate bone*. **o. mag'num,** o. capitatum. **o. mastoi'deum,** pars mastoidea ossis temporalis. **os'sa mem'bri inferio'ris** [N A], the bones of the lower limb. Called also *ossa extremitatis inferioris* [B N A]. **os'sa mem'bri superio'ris** [N A], the bones of the upper limb. Called also *ossa extremitatis superioris* [B N A]. **os'sa metacarpa'lia I–V** [N A, B N A], the five cylindric bones of the hand, articulating proximally with bones of the carpus and distally with the proximal phalanges of the fingers; numbered from that articulating with the proximal phalanx of the thumb to the most lateral one, articulating with the proximal phalanx of the little finger. Called also *metacarpal bones*. **o. metacarpa'le III** [N A, B N A], the middle of the metacarpal bones, characterized by the presence of the styloid process at its base. Called also *third metacarpal bone*. **os'sa metatarsa'lia I–V** [N A, B N A], the five bones that extend from the tarsus to the phalanges of the toes, being numbered in the same sequence from the most medial to the most lateral. Called also *metatarsal bones*. **o. multan'gulum ma'jus** [B N A], o. trapezium. **o. multan'gulum mi'nus** [B N A], o. trapezoideum. **o. nasa'le** [N A, B N A], either of the two small, oblong bones that together form the bridge of the nose. Called also *nasal bone*. **o. navicula're** [N A], the ovoid-shaped tarsal bone situated between the talus and the three cuneiform bones. Called also *o. naviculare pedis* [B N A], and *navicular bone*. **o. navicula're ma'nus** [B N A], o. scaphoideum. **o. navicula're pe'dis** [B N A], o. naviculare. **o. navicula're ped'is retarda'tum.** See *Köler's disease*, under *disease*. **o. no'vum,** Orell's name for new bone produced following the subperiosteal implantation of os purum. **o. occipita'le** [N A, B N A], a single trapezoid-shaped bone situated at the posterior and inferior part of the cranium, articulating with the two parietal and two temporal bones, the sphenoid bone, and the atlas. It contains a large opening, the foramen magnum. Called also *occipital bone*. **o. orbicula're.** 1. Processus lenticularis incudis. 2. Os pisiforme. **o. palati'num** [N A, B N A], the irregularly shaped bone forming the posterior part of the hard palate, the lateral wall of the nasal fossa between the medial pterygoid plate and the maxilla, and the posterior part of the floor of the orbit. Called also *palatine bone*. **o. parieta'le** [N A, B N A], one of the two quadrilateral bones forming part of the superior and lateral surfaces of the skull, and joining each other in the midline at the sagittal suture. Called also *parietal bone*. **o. pe'dis,** the coffin bone of the horse. **o. pe'nis,** baculum. **o. perone'um,** a sesamoid bone sometimes formed in the tendon of the peroneus longus muscle. **o. pisifor'me** [N A, B N A], the medial bone of the proximal row of carpal bones. Called also *pisiform bone*. **o. pla'num.** 1. [N A, B N A] A bone whose thickness is slight, sometimes consisting of only a thin layer of compact bone, or two layers with intervening spongy bone and marrow; usually bent or curved, rather than flat. Called also *flat bone*. 2. Lamina orbitalis. **o. pneumat'icum** [N A, B N A], a bone that contains air-filled cavities or sinuses. Called also *pneumatic bone*. **o. pri'api,** baculum. **o. pu'bis** [N A, B N A], the anterior inferior part of the hip bone (os coxae) on either side, articulating with its fellow in the anterior midline at the pubic symphysis; it is a separate bone in early life. Called also *pubic bone* and *pubis*. **o. pu'rum,** Orell's name for bone freed from connective tissue and fat, used for bone grafting. **o. radia'le,** o. scaphoideum. **o. sa'crum** [N A, B N A], the wedge-shaped bone formed usually by five fused vertebrae that are lodged dorsally between the two hip bones (ossa coxae). Called also *sacrum*. **o. scaphoi'deum** [N A], the most lateral bone of the proximal row of carpal bones. Called also *o. naviculare manus* [B N A], and *scaphoid bone*. **o. sedenta'rium,** tuber ischiadicum. **os'sa sesamoi'dea,** a type of short bone occurring mainly in the hands and feet, and found embedded in tendons and joint capsules. Called also *sesamoid bones*. **os'sa sesamoi'dea ma'nus** [N A, B N A], the sesamoid bones of the hand. **os'sa sesamoi'dea pe'dis** [N A, B N A], the sesamoid bones of the foot. **o. sphenoida'le** [N A, B N A], a single irregular, wedge-shaped bone at the base of the skull, forming a part of the floor of the anterior, middle, and posterior cranial fossae. Called also *sphenoid bone*. **o. subtibia'le,** an occasionally occurring bone found over the tip of the medial malleolus. **os'sa suprasterna'lia** [N A, B N A], ossicles occasionally occurring in the ligaments of the sternoclavicular articulation. Called also *suprasternal bones*. **os'sa sutura'rum** [N A, B N A], small irregular bones in the sutures between the bones of the skull. Called also *sutural bones.* **os'sa tarsa'lia,** ossa tarsi. **o. tarsa'le dista'le pri'mum,** o. cuneiforme mediale. **o. tarsa'le dista'le quar'tum,** o. cuboideum. **o. tarsa'le dista'le secun'dum,** o. cuneiforme intermedium. **o. tarsa'le dista'le ter'tium,** o. cuneiforme laterale. **os'sa tar'si** [N A, B N A], the seven bones of the ankle (tarsus), including the calcaneus, o. cuboideum, ossa cuneiformia intermedium, laterale, and mediale, o. naviculare, and talus. Called also *tarsal bones.* **o. tar'si fibula're,** calcaneus. **o. tar'si tibia'le,** talus. **o. tempora'le** [N A, B N A], one of the two irregular bones forming part of the lateral surfaces and base of the skull, and containing the organs of hearing. Called also *temporal bone.* **o. tibia'le exter'num,** a small anomalous bone situated in the angle between the navicular bone and the head of the talus. **o. trape'zium** [N A], the most lateral bone of the distal row of carpal bones. Called also *o. multangulum majus* [B N A], and *trapezium bone.* **o. trapezoi'deum** [N A], the bone in the distal row of carpal bones lying between the trapezium and capitate bones. Called also *o. multangulum minus* [B N A], and *trapezoid bone.* **o. trigo'num tar'si** [N A, B N A], an external tubercle at the back of the talus, sometimes occurring as a separate bone. Called also *triangular bone of tarsus.* **o. trique'trum** [N A, B N A], the bone in the proximal row of carpal bones lying between the lunate and pisiform bones. Called also *triangular bone* and *triquetral bone.* **o. un'guis,** o. lacrimale. **o. vesalia'num pe'dis,** the proximal and external part of the tuberosity of the fifth metatarsal bone. **os'sa Wor'mi,** ossa suturarum. **o. zygomat'icum** [N A, B N A], the quadrangular bone of the cheek, articulating with the frontal bone, the maxilla, the zygomatic process of the temporal bone, and the great wing of the sphenoid bone. Called also *zygomatic bone.*

osazone (o'sa-zōn). Any one of a series of compounds obtained by heating a sugar with phenylhydrazine and acetic acid. See *glucosazone.*

oscedo (os-se'do) [L.]. The act of yawning.

oscheal (os'ke-al) [Gr. *oscheon* scrotum]. Pertaining to the scrotum.

oscheitis (os″ke-i'tis) [*oscheo-* + *-itis*]. Inflammation of the scrotum.

oschelephantiasis (osk″el-ĕ-fan-ti'ah-sis). Elephantiasis of the scrotum.

oscheo- (os'ke-o) [Gr. *oscheon* scrotum]. Combining form denoting relationship to the scrotum.

oscheocele (os'ke-o-sēl) [*oscheo-* + Gr. *kēlē* hernia, tumor]. 1. Tumor or swelling of the scrotum. 2. Scrotal hernia.

oscheohydrocele (os″ke-o-hi'dro-sēl) [*oscheo-* + *hydrocele*]. Hydrocele in the sac of a scrotal hernia.

oscheolith (os'ke-o-lith) [*oscheo-* + Gr. *lithos* stone]. A concretion in the sebaceous glands of the scrotum.

oscheoma (os″ke-o'mah) [*oscheo-* + *-oma*]. A tumor of the scrotum.

oscheoncus (os″ke-ong'kus) [*oscheo-* + Gr. *onkos* mass, bulk]. Oscheoma.

oscheoplasty (os'ke-o-plas″te) [*oscheo-* + Gr. *plassein* to mold]. Plastic surgery of the scrotum.

oschitis (os-ki'tis). Oscheitis.

Oscillaria (os″ĭ-la're-ah). A genus of algae. **O. mala'riae,** Leveran's name for the plasmodium of malaria.

oscillation (os″ĭ-la'shun) [L. *oscillare* to swing]. A backward and forward motion, like a pendulum; also vibration, fluctuation, or variation. **bradykinetic o.,** slow, recurring, choreiform movements seen in epidemic encephalitis.

oscillator (os'ĭ-la″tor). An apparatus for producing oscillations.

oscillo- (os'ĭ-lo) [L. *oscillare* to swing]. Combining form denoting relationship to oscillation.

oscillogram (os'ĭ-lo-gram). The graphic record made by an oscillograph.

oscillograph (os'ĭ-lo-graf) [*oscillo-* + Gr. *graphein* to write]. An instrument for recording electric oscillations. Such an instrument, working on the plan of a string galvanometer, is used in recording the action of the heart.

oscillometer (os″ĭ-lom'e-ter). An instrument for measuring oscillations of any kind, such as changes in the volume of the arteries accompanying the heart beat.

oscillometric (os″ĭ-lo-met'rik). Pertaining to oscillometry or the oscillometer.

oscillometry (os″ĭ-lom'e-tre). The use of the string galvanometer or similar apparatus.

oscillopsia (os″ĭ-lop'se-ah) [*oscillo-* + Gr. *opsis* vision + *-ia*]. Oscillating vision; a condition in which objects seem to move back and forth, to jerk, or to wiggle. It occurs in multiple sclerosis.

oscilloscope (ŏ-sil'o-skōp) [*oscillo-* + Gr. *skopein* to examine]. 1. An instrument which indicates, when electric currents are passed through it, whether they are unidirectional or alternating. 2. An instrument for determining the form of an electric current wave.

Oscillospiraceae (os″sil-lo-spi-ra'se-e). A family of Schizomycetes (order Caryophanales), made up of motile or non-motile cells occurring in filaments of varying lengths each containing a central chromatin body, and found as non-pathogenic parasites in the intestinal tract of vertebrates. It includes a single genus, *Oscillospi'ra.*

oscine (os'in). A substance, $CH_3.N:C_6H_8:CH.O$, obtained on the decomposition of hyoscine.

Oscinis pallipes (os'ĭ-nis pal'ĭ-pēz). A fly that transmits yaws.

oscitate (os'ĭ-tāt). To yawn.

oscitation (os″ĭ-ta'shun) [L. *oscitatio*]. The act of yawning.

osculum (os'ku-lum), pl. *os'cula* [L.]. A small aperture or minute opening.

ose (ōs) [Fr.]. Haloside.

öse (ē'ze) [Ger.]. Oese.

-ose. A suffix indicating that the substance is a carbohydrate.

Osgood's disease, Osgood-Schlatter disease [Robert Bayley *Osgood,* Boston orthopedist, born 1873; Carl *Schlatter,* surgeon in Zurich, 1864–1934]. Osteochondrosis of the tuberosity of the tibia.

-osis. A word termination denoting a process, often a disease or morbid process, and sometimes conveying the meaning of abnormal increase. See also *-sis.*

Osler's disease, nodes, phenomenon, sign (ōs'lerz) [Sir William *Osler,* Canadian-born physician, 1849–1919; successively professor of medicine in McGill University, the University of Pennsylvania, Johns Hopkins University, and the University of Oxford]. See under the nouns.

Osler-Vaquez disease (ōs'ler-vak-āz') [Sir William *Osler;* Louis Henry *Vaquez,* French physician, 1860–1936]. Erythremia.

Oslo breakfast, meal [*Oslo,* Norway]. See under *meal.*

osmate (oz'māt). A salt of osmic acid.

osmatic (oz-mat'ik) [Gr. *osmasthai* to smell]. 1. Pertaining to the sense of smell. 2. Having a sense of smell; applied to a category of animals subdivided further into macrosmatic and microsmatic. Cf. *anosmatic.*

osmazome (oz'mah-zōm) [Gr. *osmē* odor + *zōmos* broth]. A principle derivable from muscular fiber which gives the peculiar flavor and odor to roast meats and gravies.

osmesis (oz-me'sis) [Gr. *osmēsis* smelling]. The act of smelling.

osmesthesia (oz″mes-the'ze-ah) [*osmo-* + Gr. *aisthēsis* perception]. Olfactory sensibility; ability to perceive and distinguish odors.

osmic (oz′mik). Containing osmium.

osmicate (oz′mĭ-kāt). To stain or impregnate with osmic acid.

osmics (oz′miks) [Gr. *osmē* odor]. The pure and applied science relating to the olfactory organs and the sense of smell, and to odoriferous organs and substances.

osmidrosis (oz″mĭ-dro′sis) [*osmo-* + Gr. *hidrōs* sweat]. A condition in which the sweat has an abnormally strong odor.

osmification (oz″mĭ-fi-ka′shun). Treatment with osmium or osmic acid, as in histologic technic.

osmiophilic (oz″me-o-fil′ik) [*osmic* acid + Gr. *philein* to love]. Staining easily with osmium or osmic acid.

osmiophobic (oz″me-o-fo′bik) [*osmic* acid + *phobia*]. Not staining easily with osmium or osmic acid.

osmium (oz′me-um) [Gr. *osmē* odor; so named because of the odor of the vapor, OsO_4, produced by oxidation of the element]. 1. A very hard, gray, and nearly infusible metal; atomic number, 76; atomic weight, 190.2; symbol, Os. See *acid, osmic.* 2. A homeopathic trituration of metallic osmium. **o. tetroxide,** a crystalline compound used for staining histologic preparations.

osmo- (oz′mo). 1. [Gr. *osmē* smell]. Combining form denoting relationship to odors. 2. [Gr. *ōsmos* impulse]. Combining form denoting relationship to an impulse, or to osmosis.

osmoceptor (oz′mo-sep″tor). Osmoreceptor.

osmodysphoria (oz″mo-dis-fo′re-ah) [*osmo-*(1) + *dys-* + Gr. *pherein* to bear]. An intense and abnormal dislike of certain odors.

osmogen (oz′mo-jen) [*osmo-*(2) + Gr. *gennan* to produce]. An embryo ferment, or a substance from which an active ferment is developed.

osmolagnia (oz″mo-lag′ne-ah) [*osmo-*(1) + Gr. *lagneia* lust]. Sexual excitation produced by odor.

osmolality (os″mo-lal′ĭ-te). A property of a solution which depends on the concentration of the solute per unit of solvent.

osmolar (oz-mo′lar). Osmotic.

osmolarity (os″mo-lăr′ĭ-te). A property of a solution which depends on the concentration of the solute per unit of total volume of solution.

osmole (os′mōl). The standard unit of osmotic pressure.

osmology (oz-mol′o-je). 1. [Gr. *osmē* smell + *-logy*]. Osphresiology. 2. [Gr. *ōsmos* impulse + *-logy*]. That branch of physics that treats of osmosis.

osmometer (oz-mom′e-ter). 1. [Gr. *ōsmos* impulse + *metron* measure]. A device for measuring osmotic force. 2. [Gr. *osmē* smell + *metron* measure]. An instrument for measuring the acuteness of the sense of smell.

osmonosology (oz″mo-no-sol′o-je) [*osmo-*(1) + *nosology*]. The study of disorders of the sense of smell.

osmophilic (oz″mo-fil′ik) [*osmo-*(2) + Gr. *philein* to love]. Readily subject to osmosis.

osmophobia (oz″mo-fo′be-ah) [*osmo-*(1) + *phobia*]. Abnormal dread of odors.

osmophore (oz′mo-fōr) [*osmo-*(1) + Gr. *phoros* bearing]. The group of atoms in a molecule of a compound which is responsible for its characteristic odor.

osmoreceptor (oz″mo-re-cep′tor). 1. [*osmo-*(1) + L. *recipere* to receive, accept]. A specialized sensory nerve ending sensitive to stimulation giving rise to the sensation of odors. 2. [*osmo-*(2)]. A specialized sensory nerve ending which is stimulated by changes in osmotic pressure of the surrounding medium.

osmoregulator (oz″mo-reg′u-la″tor). An instrument for regulating the penetrating power of roentgen rays.

osmoscope (oz′mo-skōp) [*osmo-*(1) + Gr. *skopein* to examine]. An apparatus for attachment to the nose for intensifying the sense of smell and enabling the user to make quantitative and qualitative analyses of odor.

osmose (os-mōs). To pass through a membrane by osmosis.

osmosis (os-mo′sis) [Gr. *ōsmos* impulsion]. The passage of pure solvent from the lesser to the greater concentration when two solutions are separated by a membrane which selectively prevents the passage of solute molecules, but is permeable to the solvent.

osmosity (oz-mos′ĭ-te). A measure of the osmotic pressure of a solution, expressed numerically by the molarity.

osmosology (os″mo-sol′o-je). The science of osmosis.

osmotaxis (os″mo-tak′sis) [*osmo-*(2) + Gr. *taxis* arrangement]. The movement of cells as affected by the density of the liquid containing them.

osmotherapy (oz″mo-ther′ah-pe) [*osmo-*(2) + *therapy*]. Treatment by the intravenous injection of hypertonic solutions to produce dehydration.

osmotic (os-mot′ik). Pertaining to or of the nature of osmosis.

osmyl (oz′mil). An odor.

osology (o-sol′o-je). The science of the fluids of the body.

osone (o′sōn). A carbonyl sugar formed by heating an osazone with hydrochloric acid.

osphrencephalon (os″fren-sef′ah-lon) [Gr. *osphrēsis* smell + *enkephalos* brain]. Rhinencephalon.

osphresio- (os-fre′ze-o) [Gr. *osphrēsis* smell]. Combining form denoting relationship to odors.

osphresiolagnia (os-fre″ze-o-lag′ne-ah) [*osphresio-* + Gr. *lagneia* lust]. Erotic stimulation produced by odors.

osphresiolagnic (os-fre″ze-o-lag′nik). 1. Pertaining to or characterized by osphresiolagnia. 2. A person who secures erotic stimulation from odors.

osphresiology (os″fre-ze-ol′o-je) [*osphresio-* + *-logy*]. The sum of knowledge regarding odors and the sense of smell.

osphresiometer (os″fre-ze-om′e-ter) [*osphresio-* + Gr. *metron* measure]. An instrument for measuring the acuteness of the sense of smell.

osphresiophilia (os-fre″ze-o-fil′e-ah) [*osphresio-* + Gr. *philein* to love]. Abnormal interest in odors.

osphresiophobia (os-fre″ze-o-fo′be-ah) [*osphresio-* + *phobia*]. Morbid dislike of odors.

osphresis (os-fre′sis) [Gr. *osphrēsis* smell]. The sense of smell.

osphretic (os-fret′ik). Pertaining to the sense of smell.

osphyalgia (os″fe-al′je-ah) [Gr. *osphys* loin + *-algia*]. Pain in the loins and hips.

osphyarthrosis (os″fe-ar-thro′sis). Inflammation of the hip joint.

osphyitis (os″fe-i′tis) [Gr. *osphys* loin + *-itis*]. Inflammation of the loins.

osphyomyelitis (os″fe-o-mi″ĕ-li′tis) [Gr. *osphys* loin + *myelitis*]. Myelitis of the lumbar region of the cord.

osphyotomy (os″fe-ot′o-me) [Gr. *osphys* loin + *tomē* a cutting]. Surgical incision through the loin.

ossa (os′ah) [L.]. Plural of *os*, bone. See *os*[2].

ossature (os′ah-tūr). The arrangement of bones in the body or in a part.

ossein (os′e-in). The animal matter of bone.

osselet (os′ĕ-let). An exostosis on the inner aspect of a horse's knee or on the lateral aspect of the fetlock.

osseo-albumoid (os″ĕ-o-al′bu-moid). A protein derived from bone after hydration of the collagen.

osseo-aponeurotic (os″e-o-ap″o-nu-rot′ik). Pertaining to bone and the aponeurosis of a muscle.

osseocartilaginous (os″e-o-kar″tĭ-laj′ĭ-nus). Pertaining to or composed of bone and cartilage.

osseofibrous (os″e-o-fi′brus). Made up of fibrous tissue and bone.

osseomucin (os″e-o-mu′sin). The homogeneous ground substance which binds together the collagen and elastic fibrils of bony tissue.

osseomucoid (os″e-o-mu′koid). A mucin existing in bone.

osseosonometer (os″e-o-so-nom′e-ter). An instrument used in osseosonometry.

osseosonometry (os″e-o-so-nom′e-tre) [L. *os, ossa* bone + *sonus* sound + Gr. *metron* measure]. The measurement of the conduction of sound through bone.

osseous (os′e-us) [L. *osseus*]. Of the nature or quality of bone; bony.

ossicle (os′sĭ-k'l) [L. *ossiculum*]. A small bone. **Andernach's o's,** ossa suturarum. **auditory o's,** the malleus, incus, and stapes, of the middle ear. See *ossicula auditus*. **o's of Bertin.** See *concha sphenoidalis*. **epactal o's,** ossa suturarum. **episternal o's,** ossa suprasternalia. **intercalcar o's,** ossa suturarum. **Kerckring's o.,** a small bone of early life which becomes the basilar process of the occipital bone. **Riolan's o's,** small bones occasionally seen in the suture between the mastoid portion of the temporal bone and the occipital bone. **sphenoturbinal o's.** See *concha sphenoidalis*. **wormian o's,** ossa suturarum.

ossicula (ŏ-sik′u-lah) [L.]. Plural of *ossiculum*.

ossiculectomy (os″ĭ-ku-lek′to-me) [*ossiculum* + Gr. *ektomē* excision]. Surgical removal of an ossicle, or of the ossicles, of the ear.

ossiculotomy (os″ĭ-ku-lot′o-me) [*ossiculum* + Gr. *temnein* to cut]. Surgical incision of the bonelets of the ear.

ossiculum (ŏ-sik′u-lum), pl. *ossic′ula* [L.]. A small bone. Called also *ossicle*. **ossic′ula audi′tus** [N A, B N A], the malleus, incus, and stapes, the small bones of the middle ear, which transmit the vibrations from the tympanic membrane to the oval window. Called also *auditory ossicles*.

ossidesmosis (os″ĭ-des-mo′sis). Osteodesmosis.

ossiferous (ŏ-sif′er-us) [L. *os* bone + *ferre* to bear]. Producing bone.

ossific (ŏ-sif′ik) [L. *os* bone + *facere* to make]. Forming or becoming bone.

ossification (os″ĭ-fi-ka′shun) [L. *ossificatio*]. The formation of bone or of a bony substance; the conversion of fibrous tissue or of cartilage into bone or a bony substance. **cartilaginous o.,** ossification that occurs in and replaces cartilage. **endochondral o.,** cartilaginous o. **intramembranous o.,** ossification that occurs in and replaces connective tissue, as occurs in the calvaria and in periosteal bone formation. **metaplastic o.,** the development of bony substance in normally soft structures. **perichondral o.,** that which occurs in a layered manner beneath the perichondrium or, later, the periosteum. **periosteal o.,** a type of intramembranous bone formation.

ossifluence (ŏ-sif′lu-ens). Softening of bony tissue.

ossiform (os′ĭ-form). Resembling bone.

ossifying (os′ĭ-fi″ing). Changing or developing into bone.

ossiphone (os′ĭ-fōn) [L. *os, ossa* bone + Gr. *phōnē* voice]. An apparatus for enabling deaf persons to hear by transmitting the sound from the instrument through the bony structure of the body.

ostalgia (os-tal′je-ah). Ostealgia.

ostarthritis (os″tar-thri′tis). Osteoarthritis.

osteal (os′te-al). Bony; osseous.

ostealbumoid (os″te-al′bu-moid). Osseo-albumoid.

ostealgia (os″te-al′je-ah) [Gr. *osteon* bone + *-algia*]. Pain in a bone or in the bones.

osteameba (os″te-ah-me′bah). A bone corpuscle.

osteanabrosis (os″te-an″ah-bro′sis) [*osteo-* + Gr. *anabrōsis* eating up]. Atrophy of bone.

osteanagenesis (os″te-an″ah-jen′e-sis). Osteoanagenesis.

osteanaphysis (os″te-ah-naf′ĭ-sis) [*osteo-* + Gr. *anaphyein* to reproduce]. Reproduction of bone.

ostearthritis (os″te-ar-thri′tis). Osteoarthritis.

ostearthrotomy (os″te-ar-throt′o-me) [*osteo-* + Gr. *arthron* joint + *temnein* to cut]. Excision of an articular end of a bone.

ostectomy (os-tek′to-me) [*osteo-* + Gr. *ektomē* excision]. The excision of a bone or a portion of a bone.

osteectomy (os″te-ek′to-me). Ostectomy.

osteectopia (os″te-ek-to′pe-ah) [*osteo-* + Gr. *ektopos* out of place + *-ia*]. Displacement of a bone.

osteectopy (os″te-ek′to-pe). Osteectopia.

ostein (os′te-in). Ossein.

osteite (os′te-īt). An independent bony element or center of ossification.

osteitis (os″te-i′tis) [*osteo-* + *-itis*]. Inflammation of a bone, involving the haversian spaces, canals, and their branches, and generally the medullary cavity, and marked by enlargement of the bone, tenderness, and a dull, aching pain. **acute o.,** osteomyelitis, usually of septic origin. **o. albumino′sa,** osteitis with accumulation of a sticky, albuminous liquid. **carious o.,** osteomyelitis. **o. carno′sa,** o. fungosa. **caseous o.,** tuberculous caries of bone. **central o.,** endosteitis. **chronic o.,** central caries or bone abscess; often due to tuberculosis, sometimes syphilitic. **chronic nonsuppurative o.** (Garré), a sclerosing, nonsuppurative thickening of the cortex of a bone, with partial obliteration of the marrow cavity: called also *sclerosing o.* **o. condensans,** condensing o. **o. conden′sans generalisa′ta,** osteopoikilosis. **o. conden′sans il′ii,** a condition marked by an area of dense sclerosis on the iliac side of the sacroiliac joint. **condensing o.,** osteitis with hard deposits of earthy salts in the affected bone. Called also *formative o.* and *sclerosing o.* **cortical o.,** periostitis. **o. defor′mans,** rarefying osteitis leading to bowing of the long bones and deformation of the flat bones. **o. fibro′sa cys′tica,** rarefying osteitis with fibrous degeneration and formation of cysts, and with the presence of fibrous nodules on the affected bones: it is due to hyperfunction of the parathyroid gland. Called also *Albright's disease*. **o. fibro′sa cys′tica generalisa′ta,** a disease characterized by defective ossification of bones which leads to thickening, weakening, and deformity, the bone tissue being replaced by cellular fibrous tissue. It is due to a tumor of one or more of the parathyroid glands. Called also *Recklinghausen's disease* and *parathyroid osteitis*. When it occurs in children it has been termed *osteodystrophia juvenilis*. **o. fibro′sa localisa′ta,** localized fibrous degeneration with weakening and deformity of a bone, as of the patella. **o. fibro′sa osteoplas′tica,** o. fibrosa cystica. **formative o.,** condensing o. **o. fragil′itans,** osteogenesis imperfecta. **o. fungo′sa,** chronic osteitis in which the haversian canals are dilated and filled with granulation tissue. **Garré's o.,** chronic nonsuppurative o. **o. granulo′sa,** o. fungosa. **gummatous o.,** a chronic form associated with syphilis. **necrotic o.,** osteomyelitis. **o. ossif′icans,** condensing o. **parathyroid o.,** o. fibrosa cystica generalisata. **productive o.,** condensing o. **o. pu′bis.** 1. Sclerosis of the pubic bones, in the region of the symphysis, usually observed as an incidental finding in roentgenography of the pelvis. 2. A symptom-producing inflammatory condition of the pubic bones in the region of the symphysis, which may be associated with surgical procedures on pelvic structures or with pregnancy, infection of the urinary tract, degenerative changes, rheumatic disease, or other conditions. **rarefying o.,** a bone disease in which the inorganic matter is lessened and the hard bone becomes cancellated. **sarcomatous o.,** myelomatosis. **sclerosing o.** 1. Chronic nonsuppurative osteitis. 2. Condensing osteitis. **secondary hyperplastic o.,** hypertrophic pulmonary osteoarthropathy. **o. tuberculo'sa cys'tica, o. tuberculo'sa mul'tiplex cystoi'des,** a manifestation of sarcoidosis marked by nonsequestrating spina ventosa with cystlike alteration of the long bones. **vascular o.,** rarefying osteitis in which the spaces formed become occupied by blood vessels.

ostembryon (os-tem'bre-on) [*osteo-* + Gr. *embryon* fetus]. Ossification of a fetus.

ostemia (os-te'me-ah) [*osteo-* + Gr. *haima* blood + *-ia*]. Morbid congestion of blood in a bone.

ostempyesis (os"tem-pi-e'sis) [*osteo-* + Gr. *empyēsis* suppuration]. Suppuration within a bone.

osteo- (os'te-o) [Gr. *osteon* bone]. Combining form denoting relationship to a bone or to the bones.

osteoacusis (os"te-o-ah-ku'sis) [*osteo-* + Gr. *akousis* hearing]. Bone conduction.

osteoanagenesis (os"te-o-an'ah-jen'e-sis) [*osteo-* + Gr. *anagenesis*]. Regeneration of bone.

osteoanesthesia (os"te-o-an"es-the'ze-ah). Insensitiveness of bone.

osteoaneurysm (os"te-o-an'u-rizm). Aneurysm in a bone.

osteoarthritis (os"te-o-ar-thri'tis) [*osteo-* + Gr. *arthron* joint + *-itis*]. Chronic multiple degenerative joint disease. See also *hypertrophic arthritis*, under *arthritis*. **o. defor'mans, endemic o.,** a condition endemic in portions of Russia, marked by thickening of the joints and softening of the articular ends of bones. **hyperplastic o.,** hypertrophic pneumic osteoarthropathy. **interphalangeal o.,** a localized form of arthritis involving the finger joints, characterized by degenerative changes with intermittent inflammatory episodes and leading eventually to deformities and ankyloses.

osteoarthropathy (os"te-o-ar-throp'ah-the) [*osteo-* + *arthropathy*]. Any disease of the joints and bones. **hypertrophic pneumic o., hypertrophic pulmonary o.,** symmetrical osteitis of the four limbs, chiefly localized to the phalanges and the terminal epiphyses of the long bones of the forearm and leg, sometimes extending to the proximal ends of the limbs and the flat bones, and accompanied by a dorsal kyphosis and some affection of the joints. It is often secondary to chronic conditions of the lungs and heart. Called also *osteo-arthropathie hypertrophiante pneumique, toxicogenic osteoperiostitis ossificans*, and *Bamberger-Marie disease*. **pulmonary o.,** hypertrophic pneumic o.

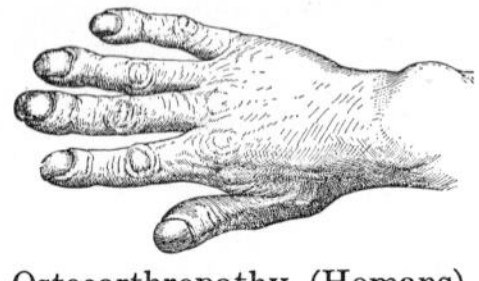
Osteoarthropathy (Homans).

osteoarthrosis (os"te-o-ar-thro'sis). Chronic arthritis of noninflammatory character.

osteoarthrotomy (os"te-o-ar-throt'o-me). Ostearthrotomy.

osteoarticular (os"te-o-ar-tik'u-lar). Pertaining to or affecting bones and joints.

osteoblast (os'te-o-blast) [*osteo-* + Gr. *blastos* germ]. A cell which arises from a fibroblast and which, as it matures, is associated with the production of bone.

osteoblastic (os"te-o-blas'tik). Pertaining to or composed of osteoblasts.

osteoblastoma (os"te-o-blas-to'mah) [*osteoblast* + *-oma*]. A tumor, the cells of which tend to differentiate into bone cells. The term includes osteoma and osteosarcoma.

osteocachectic (os"te-o-kah-kek'tik). Pertaining to or characterized by osteocachexia.

osteocachexia (os"te-o-kah-kek'se-ah). Cachexia due to chronic bone disease; also chronic disease of bone.

osteocamp (os'te-o-kamp). An instrument for bending the femur straight following osteotomy.

osteocampsia (os"te-o-kamp'se-ah) [*osteo-* + Gr. *kamptein* to bend]. Curvature or bending of a bone.

osteocampsis (os"te-o-kamp'sis). Osteocampsia.

osteocarcinoma (os"te-o-kar"sĭ-no'mah). 1. Osteoma combined with carcinoma. 2. Carcinoma of a bone.

osteocartilaginous (os"te-o-kar"tĭ-laj'ĭ-nus). Pertaining to or composed of bone and cartilage.

osteocele (os'te-o-sēl) [*osteo-* + Gr. *kēlē* tumor]. 1. Bony tumor of the testis or scrotum. 2. A hernia containing bone.

osteocementum (os"te-o-se-men'tum). The hard bonelike tissue of the secondary cementum.

osteocephaloma (os"te-o-sef"ah-lo'mah) [*osteo-* + *encephaloma*]. An encephaloid tumor of a bone.

osteochondral (os"te-o-kon'dral). Pertaining to bone and cartilage; pertaining to a bone and its articular cartilage.

osteochondritis (os"te-o-kon-dri'tis) [*osteo-* + Gr. *chondros* cartilage + *-itis*]. Inflammation of both bone and cartilage. **o. defor'mans juveni'lis,** osteochondrosis of capitular epiphysis. **o. defor'mans juveni'lis dor'si,** osteochondrosis of vertebrae. **o. dis'secans,** osteochondritis resulting in the splitting of pieces of cartilage into the joint, particularly the knee joint or shoulder joint. **o. ischiopu'bica,** a condition observed in the roentgenogram, consisting of granular looking bodies at the junction of the ischium and os pubis in children. **juvenile deforming metatarsophalangeal o.,** osteochondrosis of the navicular (tarsal scaphoid). **o. necrot'icans,** a condition marked by necrosis and solution of continuity in the cartilage of the sesamoid bone of the great toe.

osteochondrodystrophia (os"te-o-kon"dro-distro'fe-ah). Osteochondrodystrophy. **o. defor'mans,** eccentro-osteochondrodysplasia.

osteochondrodystrophy (os"te-o-kon"dro-dys'tro-fe). A disorder of bone and cartilage formation, including lipochondrodystrophy and eccentro-osteochondrodysplasia.

osteochondrofibroma (os"te-o-kon"dro-fi-bro'mah). A tumor containing the elements of osteoma, chondroma, and fibroma.

osteochondrolysis (os"te-o-kon-drol'ĭ-sis). Osteochondritis dissecans.

osteochondroma (os"te-o-kon-dro'mah) [*osteo-* + Gr. *chondros* cartilage + *-oma*]. Osteoma blended with chondroma; a tumor that is partly bone and partly cartilaginous.

osteochondromatosis (os"te-o-kon"dro-mah-to'sis). A condition marked by the presence of multiple osteochondromas. **synovial o.,** a rare condition in which cartilage bodies are formed in the synovial membrane of the joints, tendon sheaths, or bursae, later undergoing secondary calcification and ossification; some of the bodies may become detached and remain as viable, growing structures in the synovial spaces.

osteochondropathia (os"te-o-kon"dro-path'e-ah). Osteochondropathy. **o. cretinoi'dea,** Läwen-Roth syndrome.

osteochondropathy (os"te-o-kon-drop'ah-the) [*osteo-* + Gr. *chondros* cartilage + *pathos* disease]. Any morbid condition affecting both bone and cartilage, or marked by abnormal enchondral ossification. **polyglucose (dextran) sulfate-induced o.,** an experimentally produced disorder of enchondral ossification characterized by a deficient formation of bone matrix in the metaphyses of long bones.

osteochondrophyte (os"te-o-kon'dro-fīt) [*osteo-* + Gr. *chondros* cartilage + *phyton* growth]. A growth made up of cartilaginous and bony tissue.

osteochondrosarcoma (os"te-o-kon"dro-sar-ko'mah). Sarcoma blended with osteoma and chondroma.

osteochondrosis (os"te-o-kon-dro'sis). A disease of one or more of the growth or ossification centers in children which begins as a degeneration or necrosis followed by regeneration or recalcification. It may affect (1) the CALCANEUS (os calcis), a condition sometimes called *apophysitis;* (2) the CAPITULAR EPIPHYSIS (head) OF THE FEMUR, a condition known as *Legg-Calvé-Perthes disease, Perthes disease, Waldenström's disease, osteochondritis coxae juvenilis, coxa plana,* and *pseudocoxalgia;* (3) the ILIUM; (4) the LUNATE (SEMILUNAR) BONE, known as *Kienböck's disease;* (5) HEAD OF THE SECOND METATARSAL BONE, known as *Freiberg's infraction;* (6) the NAVICULAR (TARSAL SCAPHOID), known as *Köhler's tarsal scaphoiditis;* (7) the TUBEROSITY OF THE TIBIA, called *Osgood's disease, Osgood-Schlatter disease, Schlatter's disease;* (8) the VERTEBRAE, called *Scheuermann's disease, juvenile kyphosis, vertebral osteochondritis, vertebral epiphysitis,* and *kyphosis dorsalis juvenilis.* **o. defor'mans tib'iae,** tibia vara.

osteochondrous (os″te-o-kon′drus) [*osteo-* + Gr. *chondros* cartilage]. Composed of bone and cartilage.

osteoclasia (os″te-o-kla′ze-ah) [*osteo-* + Gr. *klasis* a breaking + *-ia*]. The absorption and destruction of bony tissue.

osteoclasis (os-te-ok′lah-sis) [*osteo-* + Gr. *klasis* a breaking]. The surgical fracture or refracture of bones.

osteoclast (os′te-o-klast) [*osteo-* + Gr. *klan* to break]. 1. An instrument for use in the surgical fracture or refracture of bones. 2. A large multinuclear cell associated with the absorption and removal of bone. **Collin's o.,** an osteoclast for fracturing a bone at any desired point. **Rizzoli's o.,** an osteoclast consisting of a rod on which are two sliding padded rings, and between these a padded plate that can be screwed down upon the part, thus fracturing the bone.

osteoclastic (os″te-o-klas′tik). Pertaining to or of the nature of an osteoclast; destructive to bone.

osteoclastoma (os″te-o-klas-to′mah). A tumor the cells of which are giant cells analogous to osteoclasts; malignant myeloid sarcoma.

osteoclasty (os′te-o-klas″te). Osteoclasis.

osteocomma (os″te-o-kom′ah) [*osteo-* + Gr. *komma* fragment]. Any one of the pieces or members of a series of bony structures, as a vertebra.

osteocope (os′te-o-kōp) [*osteo-* + Gr. *kopos* pain]. A severe pain in a bone or in the bones: generally a symptom of syphilitic bone disease.

osteocopic (os″te-o-kop′ik). Pertaining to or characterized by osteocope.

osteocranium (os″te-o-kra′ne-um) [*osteo-* + Gr. *kranion* cranium]. The fetal cranium during its stage of ossification.

osteocystoma (os″te-o-sis-to′mah) [*osteo-* + *cystoma*]. A cystic tumor in a bone.

osteocyte (os″te-o-sīt). An osteoblast that has become embedded within the bone matrix, occupying a flat oval cavity (lacuna) and sending, through apertures in its walls, thin cytoplasmic processes which directly connect with other osteocytes in developing bone.

osteodentin (os″te-o-den′tin) [*osteo-* + *dentin*]. Dentin that resembles bone: seen in the teeth of certain fish and pathologically in other lower species, and in man, being produced by rapid formation of secondary dentin, with entrapment of cells.

osteodentoma (os″te-o-den-to′mah). An odontoma composed of bone and dentin.

osteodermatous (os″te-o-der′mah-tus). Marked by ossifications in the skin.

osteodermia (os″te-o-der′me-ah) [*osteo-* + Gr. *derma* skin + *-ia*]. A condition characterized by bony deposits in the skin.

osteodesmosis (os″te-o-des-mo′sis) [*osteo-* + Gr. *desmos* tendon]. 1. The formation of bone and tendon. 2. Ossification of tendon.

osteodiastasis (os″te-o-di-as′tah-sis) [*osteo-* + Gr. *diastasis* separation]. The separation of a bone or of two bones.

osteodynia (os″te-o-din′e-ah) [*osteo-* + Gr. *odynē* pain]. Pain in a bone.

osteodystrophia (os″te-o-dis-tro′fe-ah). Osteodystrophy. **o. cys′tica,** osteitis fibrosa cystica. **o. fibro′sa,** osteitis fibrosa cystica. **o. juveni′lis,** osteitis fibrosa cystica generalisata.

osteodystrophy (os″te-o-dis′tro-fe). Defective bone formation. **renal o.,** a condition resulting from chronic disease of the kidneys, in which serum calcium is dissipated and serum phosphorus elevated, with hyperactivity of the parathyroid glands resulting in deossification of previously normally mineralized bone; the skeletal changes depend on the severity of the condition, and the age at which it develops.

osteo-ectomy (os″te-o-ek′to-me). Ostectomy.

osteo-encephaloma (os″te-o-en-sef″ah-lo′mah) [*osteo-* + Gr. *enkephalos* brain + *-oma*]. Encephaloid tumor of bone.

osteo-enchondroma (os″te-o-en″kon-dro′mah). Osteochondroma.

osteo-epiphysis (os″te-o-e-pif′ĭ-sis) [*osteo-* + *epiphysis*]. Any bony epiphysis.

osteofibrochondrosarcoma (os″te-o-fi″bro-kon″dro-sar-ko′mah). A tumor containing bony, fibrous, cartilaginous, and muscle tissue.

osteofibroma (os″te-o-fi-bro′mah) [*osteo-* + *fibroma*]. A tumor containing both osseous and fibrous elements.

osteofibromatosis (os″te-o-fi″bro-mah-to′sis). A condition of multiple osteofibroma formation. **cystic o.,** Jaffe-Lichtenstein disease.

osteogen (os′te-o-jen) [*osteo-* + Gr. *gennan* to produce]. The substance composing the inner layer of the periosteum, from which bone is formed.

osteogenesis (os″te-o-jen′e-sis) [*osteo-* + Gr. *gennan* to produce]. Formation of bone; the development of the bones. **o. imperfec′ta,** an inherited condition in which the bones are abnormally brittle, and subject to fractures. In *o. imperfec′ta congen′ita* the fractures occur in intra-uterine life and the child is born with deformities. In *o. imperfec′ta tar′da* the fractures occur when the child begins to walk. The condition is usually attended by blue coloration of the sclera of the eyes (Lobstein's disease or syndrome) and sometimes also by otosclerotic deafness (Van der Hoeve's syndrome). Called also *fragilitas ossium, brittle bones, osteopsathyrosis,* and *hypoplasia of the mesenchyme.* **o. imperfec′ta cys′tica,** a disorder in which the marrow spaces contain myxomatous fibroid tissue, the x-ray showing cystic changes.

osteogenetic (os″te-o-je-net′ik). Forming bone; concerned in bone formation.

osteogenic (os″te-o-jen′ik) [*osteo-* + Gr. *gennan* to produce]. Derived from or composed of any tissue which is concerned in the growth or repair of bone.

osteogenous (os″te-oj′e-nus). Osteogenic.

osteogeny (os″te-oj′e-ne). Osteogenesis.

osteogram (os′te-o-gram). A semidiagram of the spine used as a record sheet for the charting of osteopathic lesions.

osteography (os″te-og′rah-fe) [*osteo-* + Gr. *graphein* to write]. A description of the bones.

osteohalisteresis (os″te-o-hah-lis″ter-e′sis) [*osteo-* + Gr. *hals* salt + *sterein* to deprive]. Loss or deficiency of the mineral elements of bones.

osteohemachromatosis (os″te-o-hem″ah-kro″mah-to′sis) [*osteo-* + Gr. *haima* blood + *chrōma* color + *-osis*]. A disease of animals marked by discoloration of the bone by blood pigment.

osteohydatidosis (os″te-o-hi″dah-tid-o′sis). Hydatidosis of bone.

osteoid (os′te-oid) [*osteo-* + Gr. *eidos* form]. 1. Resembling bone. 2. The organic matrix of bone; young bone which has not undergone calcification.

osteoid-osteoma (os″te-oid-os″te-o′mah). Jaffe's name for a benign osteoblastic tumor composed of osteoid and atypical bone.

osteolathyrism (os″te-o-lath′ĭ-rizm). A skeletal disorder produced in animals, by diets containing the sweet pea (*Lathyrus odoratus*) or its active principle, β(γL-glutamyl) aminopropionitrile, or other aminonitriles. Characterized, in rats, by hernias, dissecting aortic aneurysms, lameness of the hind legs, exostoses, and kyphoscoliosis and other skeletal deformities, apparently as the result of defective aging of collagen tissue.

osteolipochondroma (os″te-o-lĭ-po″kon-dro′-mah). Chondroma with bony and fatty elements.

osteolipoma (os″te-o-lĭ-po′mah). A lipoma containing osseous elements.

osteologia (os″te-o-lo′je-ah). Osteology; in N A terminology it encompasses the nomenclature relating to the bones.

osteology (os″te-ol′o-je) [*osteo-* + Gr. *logos* treatise]. The scientific study of the bones; applied also to the body of knowledge relating to the bones.

osteolysis (os″te-ol′ĭ-sis) [*osteo-* + Gr. *lysis* dissolution]. Dissolution of bone; applied especially to the removal or loss of the calcium of bone.

osteolytic (os″te-o-lit′ik). Relating to, characterized by, or promoting osteolysis.

osteoma (os″te-o′mah) [*osteo-* + *-oma*]. A tumor composed of bone tissue; a hard tumor of bonelike structure developing on a bone (*homoplastic o.*) and sometimes on other structures (*heteroplastic o.*). **cavalryman's o.,** osteoma at the insertion of the adductor femoris longus muscle. **compact o.,** o. durum. **o. denta′le,** a dental exostosis. **o. du′rum, o. ebur′neum,** a tumor made up of hard bony tissue. **o. medulla′re,** an osteoma containing marrow spaces. **osteoid o.,** a benign tumor of spongy bone occurring in the bones of the extremities and vertebrae in young persons. **o. sarcomato′sum,** osteosarcoma. **o. spongio′sum,** osteoma containing cancellated bone.

osteomalacia (os″te-o-mah-la′she-ah) [*osteo-* + Gr. *malakia* softness]. A condition marked by softening of the bones, with pain, tenderness, muscular weakness, anorexia, and loss of weight, resulting from deficiency of vitamin D or of calcium and phosphosphorus. **bovine o.,** aphosphorosis. **infantile o., juvenile o.,** late rickets. **puerperal o.,** osteomalacia occurring as a consequence of exhaustion of skeletal stores of calcium and phosphorus by repeated pregnancies and lactation. **renal tubular o.,** osteomalacia occurring as a consequence of acidosis and hypercalciuria, resulting from inability to produce an acid urine or ammonia because of deficient activity of the renal tubules. **senile o.,** softening of bones in old age due to vitamin deficiency.

osteomalacic (os″te-o-mah-la′sik). Pertaining to or characterized by osteomalacia.

osteomalacosis (os″te-o-mal″ah-ko′sis). Osteomalacia.

osteomatoid (os″te-o′mah-toid). Resembling an osteoma.

osteomatosis (os″te-o-mah-to′sis). The multiple formation of osteomas.

osteomere (os′te-o-mēr) [*osteo-* + Gr. *meros* part]. One of a series of similar bony structures, such as the vertebrae.

osteometry (os″te-om′e-tre) [*osteo-* + Gr. *metron* measure]. The measurement of bones.

osteomiosis (os″te-o-mi-o′sis) [*osteo-* + Gr. *meiōsis* diminution]. Disintegration of bone.

osteomyelitic (os″te-o-mi″ĕ-lit′ik). Marked by or characteristic of osteomyelitis.

osteomyelitis (os″te-o-mi″ĕ-li′tis) [*osteo-* + Gr. *myelos* marrow]. Inflammation of bone caused by a pyogenic organism. It may remain localized or it may spread through the bone to involve the marrow, cortex, cancellous tissue and periosteum. **conchiolin o.,** a condition seen in the workers in mother of pearl and probably due to the inhaled dust being deposited in the bone marrow. Cf. *coniosis.* **Garré's o.,** chronic sclerosing, nonsuppurative osteitis which appears in the roentgenogram as a spindle-shaped thickening of the bone. **hemorrhagic o.,** osteitis fibrosa cystica. **malignant o.,** myelomatosis. **typhoid o.,** osteomyelitis occurring as a concurrent or greatly delayed sequel of typhoid fever. **o. variolo′sa,** osteomyelitis due to, or occurring as a complication of, smallpox.

osteomyelodysplasia (os″te-o-mi″ĕ-lo-dis-pla′-se-ah) [*osteo-* + Gr. *myelos* marrow + *dys-* + *plassein* to form]. A condition characterized by thinning of the osseous tissue of bones, increase in size of the marrow cavities and attended with leukopenia and fever.

osteomyelography (os″te-o-mi″ĕ-log′rah-fe). Roentgen visualization of bone marrow.

osteon (os′te-on) [*osteo-* + Gr. *on* neuter ending]. The basic unit of structure of compact bone, comprising a haversian canal and its concentrically arranged lamellae, of which there may be 4 to 20, each 3 to 7 microns thick, in a single (haversian) system; such units are directed mainly in the long axis of the bone.

osteoncus (os″te-ong′kus) [*osteo-* + Gr. *onkos* mass]. Tumor of a bone.

osteone (os′te-ōn). Osteon.

osteonecrosis (os″te-o-ne-kro′sis) [*osteo-* + Gr. *nekrōsis* death]. Death, or necrosis, of bone.

osteoneuralgia (os″te-o-nu-ral′je-ah) [*osteo-* + *neuralgia*]. Neuralgia of a bone.

osteonosus (os″te-on′o-sus) [*osteo-* + Gr. *nosos* disease]. Disease of bone.

osteo-odontoma (os″te-o-o″don-to′mah). Ameloblastic odontoma.

osteopath (os′te-o-path). A practitioner of osteopathy.

osteopathia (os″te-o-path′e-ah). Any disease of a bone. Called also *osteopathy.* **o. conden′sans,** osteosclerosis myelofibrosis. **o. conden′sans dissemina′ta, o. conden′sans generalisa′ta,** osteopoikilosis. **o. haemorrha′gica infan′tum,** Möller-Barlow disease. **o. hyperostot′ica congen′ita,** melorheostosis. **o. stria′ta,** an abnormality apparent only on roentgen examination, and occurring only in cancellous bone; it is characterized by multiple condensations beginning at the epiphyseal line and extending into the diaphysis.

osteopathic (os″te-o-path′ik). Pertaining to osteopathy.

osteopathology (os″te-o-pah-thol′o-je). Any disease of bone.

osteopathy (os″te-op′ah-the) [*osteo-* + Gr. *pathos* disease]. 1. Any disease of a bone. 2. A system of therapy founded by Andrew Taylor Still (1828–1917) and based on the theory that the body is capable of making its own remedies against disease and other toxic conditions when it is in normal structural relationship and has favorable environmental conditions and adequate nutrition. It utilizes generally accepted physical, medicinal, and surgical methods of diagnosis and therapy, while placing chief emphasis on the importance of normal body mechanics and manipulative methods of detecting and correcting faulty structure. **alimentary o.,** hunger o. **disseminated condensing o.,** osteopoikilosis. **hunger o.,** disturbances of the skeletal system observed in famine areas, characterized by a reduction in the amount of normally calcified bone, and attributed to dietary deficiencies and associated hormonal dysfunction. **myelogenic o.,** any bone disease that is due to the impaired relation between the medullary and osseous tissues.

osteopecilia (os″te-o-pĕ-sil′e-ah) [*osteo-* + Gr. *poikilia* spottedness]. Osteosclerosis fragilis generalisata.

osteopedion (os″te-o-pe′de-on) [*osteo-* + Gr. *paidion* child]. Lithopedion.

osteoperiosteal (os″te-o-per″ĭ-os′te-al). Pertaining to bone and its periosteum.

osteoperiostitis (os″te-o-per″ĭ-os-ti′tis) [*osteo-* + *periostitis*]. Inflammation of a bone and its periosteum. **alveolodental o.,** periodontitis.

osteopetrosis (os″te-o-pe-tro′sis) [*osteo-* + Gr. *petra* stone + *-osis*]. A condition in which there are bandlike areas of condensed bone at the epiphyseal lines of long bones and condensation of the edges of smaller bones. Called also *marble bones, ivory bones, Albers-Schönberg disease.* **o. gallina′rum.** See under *lymphomatosis of fowl.*

osteophage (os′te-o-fāj) [*osteo-* + Gr. *phagein* to eat]. Osteoclast.

osteophagia (os″te-o-fa′je-ah) [*osteo-* + Gr. *phagein* to eat]. The eating of bone due to a craving for phosphorus.

osteophlebitis (os″te-o-fle-bi′tis) [*osteo-* + Gr. *phleps* vein + *-itis*]. Inflammation of the veins of a bone.

osteophone (os′te-o-fōn″) [*osteo-* + Gr. *phōnē* voice]. Audiphone.

osteophony (os″te-of′o-ne) [*osteo-* + Gr. *phōnē* voice]. The conduction of sounds by bone; bone conduction.

osteophore (os′te-o-fōr) [*osteo-* + Gr. *pherein* to carry]. A bone-crushing forceps.

osteophyma (os″te-o-fi′mah) [*osteo-* + Gr. *phyma* growth]. A tumor or outgrowth of a bone.

osteophyte (os′te-o-fit) [*osteo-* + Gr. *phyton* plant]. A bony excrescence or osseous outgrowth.

osteophytosis (os″te-o-fi-to′sis). A condition characterized by the formation of osteophytes.

osteoplaque (os′te-o-plak). A layer of bone.

osteoplast (os′te-o-plast) [*osteo-* + Gr. *plastos* formed]. Osteoblast.

osteoplastic (os″te-o-plas′tik). 1. Osteogenic. 2. Pertaining to osteoplasty.

osteoplastica (os″te-o-plas′tĭ-kah). Osteitis fibrosa cystica.

osteoplasty (os′te-o-plas″te) [*osteo-* + Gr. *plassein* to form]. Plastic surgery of the bones.

osteopoikilosis (os″te-o-poi″kĭ-lo′sis) [*osteo-* + Gr. *poikilos* mottled]. A condition characterized by the presence of multiple sclerotic foci in the ends of long bones and scattered stippling in round and flat bones; usually without symptoms and diagnosed fortuitously by x-ray examination.

osteopoikilotic (os″te-o-poi″kĭ-lot′ik). Pertaining to or characterized by osteopoikilosis.

osteoporosis (os″te-o-po-ro′sis) [*osteo-* + Gr. *poros* passage + *-osis*]. Abnormal rarefaction of bone due to failure of the osteoblasts to lay down bone matrix. **adipose o.,** osteoporosis in which the enlarged spaces are filled with fat. **o. circumscrip′ta cra′nii,** demineralization of the bones of the skull, characteristic of the destructive or osteolytic phase of Paget's disease. **o. of disuse,** decrease in bone substance as a result of lack of re-formation of laminae in the absence of functional stress which ordinarily leads to their replacement in new stress lines. **post-traumatic o.,** loss of bone substance following an injury in which there is damage to a nerve, sometimes due to an increased blood supply caused by the neurogenic insult, or to disuse secondary to pain.

osteoporotic (os″te-o-po-rot′ik). Pertaining to or characterized by osteoporosis.

osteopsathyrosis (os″te-op-sath″ĭ-ro′sis) [*osteo-* + Gr. *psathyros* friable]. Osteogenesis imperfecta.

osteoradionecrosis (os″te-o-ra″de-o-ne-kro′sis). Necrosis of bone following irradiation.

osteorrhagia (os″te-o-ra′je-ah) [*osteo-* + Gr. *rhēgnynai* to burst out]. Hemorrhage from bone.

osteorrhaphy (os″te-or′ah-fe) [*osteo-* + Gr. *rhaphē* suture]. The suturing or wiring of bones.

osteosarcoma (os″te-o-sar-ko′mah) [*osteo-* + *sarcoma*]. A sarcoma of bone, or a sarcoma containing osseous tissue.

osteosarcomatous (os″te-o-sar-ko′mah-tus). Of the nature of osteosarcoma.

osteosclerosis (os″te-o-skle-ro′sis) [*osteo-* + Gr. *sklērōsis* hardening]. The hardening or abnormal denseness of bone; eburnation; osteitis ossificans. **o. congen′ita,** achondroplasia. **o. frag′ilis,** osteopetrosis. **o. frag′ilis generalisa′ta,** osteopoikilosis. **o. myelofibrosis,** myelofibrosis, def. 2.

osteosclerotic (os″te-o-skle-rot′ik). Pertaining to or characterized by osteosclerosis.

osteoscope (os′te-o-skōp) [*osteo-* + Gr. *skopein* to examine]. An instrument for testing a roentgen ray apparatus by examining a standard preparation of the bones of the forearm.

osteoseptum (os″te-o-sep′tum) [*osteo-* + *septum*]. The bony part of the nasal septum.

osteosis (os″te-o′sis). The formation of bony tissue, especially the infiltration of connective tissue with bone. **o. cu′tis,** a condition in which bone-containing nodules form on the skin. **o. ebur′nisans monomel′ica,** melorheostosis. **parathyroid o.,** osteitis fibrosa cystica.

osteospongioma (os″te-o-spon″je-o′mah) [*osteo-* + Gr. *spongos* sponge + *-oma*]. A spongy tumor of bone.

osteosteatoma (os″te-o-ste″ah-to′mah) [*osteo-* + Gr. *steatōma* sebaceous tumor]. A suet-like tumor with bony elements.

osteostixis (os″te-o-stik′sis) [*osteo-* + Gr. *stixis* puncture]. Surgical puncture of a bone.

osteosuture (os′te-o-su-tūr) [*osteo-* + L. *sutura* suture]. Osteorrhaphy.

osteosynovitis (os″te-o-sin″o-vi′tis). Synovitis together with osteitis of the neighboring bones.

osteosynthesis (os″te-o-sin′the-sis) [*osteo-* + Gr. *synthesis* a putting together]. Surgical fastening of the ends of a fractured bone by sutures, rings, plates, or other mechanical means.

osteotabes (os″te-o-ta′bēz) [*osteo-* + L. *tabes* wasting]. A disease, chiefly of infants, in which the cells of the bone marrow are destroyed and the marrow disappears.

osteotelangiectasia (os″te-o-tĕ-lan″je-ek-ta′se-ah) [*osteo-* + *telangiectasia*]. A sarcoma of bone containing dilated capillaries.

osteothrombophlebitis (os″te-o-throm″bo-fle-bi′tis). Inflammation extended through intact bone by a progressive thrombophlebitis of small venules, such as sometimes occurs in the mastoid bone.

osteothrombosis (os″te-o-throm-bo′sis) [*osteo-* + *thrombosis*]. Thrombosis of the veins of a bone.

osteotome (os′te-o-tōm) [*osteo-* + Gr. *tomē* a cut]. A knife or chisel for cutting bone.

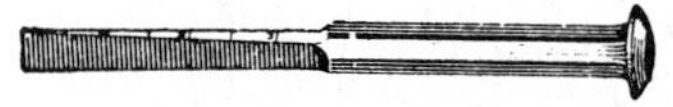

Osteotome (DaCosta).

osteotomoclasia (os″te-o-to″mo-kla′se-ah). Osteotomoclasis.

osteotomoclasis (os″te-o-to-mok′lah-sis) [*osteo-* + Gr. *tomos* section + *klasis* breaking]. Correction of curvature of bone by partial division with the osteotome, followed by forcible fracture.

osteotomy (os″te-ot′o-me) [*osteo-* + Gr. *temnein* to cut]. The surgical cutting of a bone. **block o.,** osteotomy in which a rhomboidal section of the femur is removed. **cuneiform o.,** the removal of a wedge of bone. **cup-and-ball o.,** osteotomy in which the distal fragment is pointed and the proximal fragment is recessed. **hinge o.,** curvilinear cutting of a bone. **linear o.,** the sawing or linear cutting of a bone. **Lorenz's o.,** osteotomy of the neck of the femur by a V-shaped cutting of the femur so as to prevent displacement of the shaft. **Macewen's o.,** supracondylar cuneiform section of the femur for genu valgum. **pelvic o.,** pubeotomy. **subtrochanteric o.,** Gant's operation. **transtrochanteric o.,** division of the femur through the lesser trochanter for deformity about the hip joint.

osteotribe, osteotrite (os′te-o-trīb, os′te-o-trīt)

[osteo- + Gr. *tribein* to rub]. An instrument for rasping carious bone.

osteotrophy (os″te-ot′ro-fe) [*osteo-* + Gr. *trophē* nutrition]. Nutrition of bone.

osteotylus (os″te-ot′ĭ-lus) [*osteo-* + Gr. *tylos* callus]. The callus enclosing the end of a broken bone.

osteotympanic (os″te-o-tim-pan′ik). Craniotympanic.

Ostertagia (os″ter-ta′je-ah) [Robert von *Ostertag*, German veterinarian, 1864–1940]. A genus of filiform nematode parasites found mostly in cysts on the wall of the abomasum of cattle.

osthexia, osthexy (os-thek′se-ah, os′thek-se) [Gr. *osteon* bone + *hexis* condition]. Abnormal ossification.

ostia (os′te-ah) [L.]. Plural of *ostium.*

ostial (os′te-al). Pertaining to an ostium.

ostiary (os′te-a-re) [L. *ostiarius* pertaining to a door]. Pertaining to an orifice.

Ostiolum medioplexus (os″te-o′lum me″de-o-plek′sus). A distome fluke parasitic in the lungs of frogs.

ostitis (os-ti′tis). Osteitis.

ostium (os′te-um), pl. *os′tia* [L.]. A door, or opening; used in anatomical nomenclature as a general term to designate an opening into a tubular organ, or between two distinct body cavities. Called also *orificium* [B N A], *orifice,* and *opening.* **o. abdomina′le tu′bae uteri′nae** [N A, B N A], the funnel-shaped opening by which the uterine tube communicates with the pelvic cavity. It is usually closely applied to the surface of the ovary. Called also *abdominal orifice of uterine tube.* **o. aor′tae** [N A], the opening between the left ventricle and the aorta. **o. appen′dicis vermifor′mis** [N A], the orifice between the vermiform appendix and the cecum. Called also *opening of vermiform appendix.* **o. arterio′sum cor′dis** [B N A], a term applied to the opening between the left atrium and the left ventricle (ostium atrioventriculare sinistrum [N A]). **os′tia atrioventricula′ria [dex′trum et sinis′trum]** [N A], the openings between the atria and ventricles of the heart, guarded by the atrioventricular valves. Called also *o. arteriosum cordis* [B N A] (between the chambers on the left), and *o. venosum cordis* [B N A] (between those on the right). **o. cardi′acum** [N A], the orifice between the esophagus and the cardiac part of the stomach. Called also *cardiac opening.* **o. ileoceca′le** [N A], **o. ileocaecocol′icum,** the orifice between the ileum and cecum. Called also *ileocecal opening.* **o. inter′num u′teri,** o. uterinum tubae uterinae. **o. pharyn′geum tu′bae auditi′vae** [N A, B N A], the pharyngeal opening of the auditory tube. **o. pri′mum,** an opening in the lowest aspect of the septum primum of the embryonic heart, posteriorly, in the neighborhood of the atrioventricular valve. **o. pylo′ricum** [N A], the orifice between the stomach and the duodenum. Called also *pyloric opening.* **o. secun′dum,** an opening high in the septum primum of the embryonic heart, approximately where the foramen ovale will be later. **sinusoidal o.,** any one of the openings of the veins of Vieussens in the chambers of the heart. **o. trun′ci pulmona′lis** [N A], the opening between the right ventricle (from the conus arteriosus portion) and the pulmonary trunk. Called also *opening of pulmonary trunk.* **o. tympan′icum tu′bae auditi′vae** [N A, B N A], the opening of the auditory tube on the carotid wall of the tympanic cavity. Called also *tympanic opening of auditory tube.* **o. ure′teris** [N A], the opening of the ureter in the bladder. Called also *orificium ureteris* [B N A]. **o. ure′thrae exter′num femini′na** [N A], the opening of the urethra into the vestibule. It is surrounded by a sphincter of striated muscle derived from the bulbocavernosus muscle. Called also *orificium urethrae externum muliebris* [B N A], and *external orifice of female urethra.* **o. ure′thrae exter′num masculi′nae** [N A], the slitlike opening of the urethra on the tip of the glans penis. Called also *orificium urethrae externum virilis* [B N A], and *external orifice of male urethra.* **o. ure′thrae inter′num** [N A], the opening between the bladder and the urethra. Called also *orificium urethrae internum* [B N A], and *internal orifice of urethra.* **o. u′teri** [N A], the opening of the cervix of the uterus into the vagina. Called also *orificium externum uteri* [B N A], and *orifice of uterus.* **o. uteri′num tu′bae uteri′nae** [N A, B N A], the point at which the cavity of the uterine tube becomes continuous with that of the uterus. Called also *uterine orifice of uterine tube.* **o. vagi′nae** [N A], the external orifice of the vagina, situated just posterior to the external urethral orifice. Called also *orificium vaginae* [B N A]. **o. ve′nae cav′ae inferio′ris** [N A], the opening of the inferior vena cava into the right atrium of the heart; it is accompanied by a valve which, in the adult, is usually rudimentary. **o. ve′nae cav′ae superio′ris** [N A], the opening of the superior vena cava into the right atrium of the heart; it is unaccompanied by a valve. **os′tia vena′rum pulmona′lium** [N A], the openings of the pulmonary veins (in the human, usually four) into the left atrium of the heart; they are unaccompanied by valves. **o. veno′sum cor′dis** [B N A], a term applied to the opening between the right atrium and the right ventricle (ostium atrioventriculare dextrum [N A]).

ostosis (os-to′sis). Osteogenesis.

ostraceous (os-tra′shus) [Gr. *ostrakon* shell]. Shaped like or resembling an oyster shell.

ostracosis (os″trah-ko′sis) [Gr. *ostrakon* shell]. Bony change which takes on the consistency of oyster shell.

ostreasterol (os″tre-as′ter-ol). A solid alcohol, $C_{29}H_{48}O$, present in oysters.

ostreotoxismus (os″tre-o-tok-siz′mus) [Gr. *ostreon* oyster + *toxikon* poisoning]. Poisoning caused by the eating of contaminated oysters.

Oswaldocruzia (oz-wal″do-kroo′ze-ah) [G. Oswaldo *Cruz*, Brazilian physician, 1872–1917]. A genus of trichostrongyline parasites inhabiting the lungs and intestines of reptiles and batrachians.

OT. 1. Abbreviation for *old term* in anatomy. 2. Old tuberculin.

ot-. See *oto-.*

otacoustic (o″tah-koo′stik). Aiding the hearing.

otagra (o-tag′rah). Pain in the ear.

otalgia (o-tal′je-ah) [Gr. *ōtalgia*]. Pain in the ear. **o. denta′lis,** reflex pain in the ear due to dental disease. **geniculate o.,** geniculate neuralgia. **o. intermit′tens,** otalgia of an intermittent type. **reflex o.,** otalgia dependent upon some lesion of the buccal cavity or nasopharynx. **secondary o.,** otalgia dependent on inflammation of the geniculate ganglion. **tabetic o.,** otalgia in tabes dorsalis due to degeneration of the nerve of Wrisberg.

otalgic (o-tal′jik). 1. Pertaining to earache. 2. An earache remedy.

Otani's test (o-tah′nēz) [Morisuke *Otani*, Japanese physician]. See under *tests.*

otaphone (o′tah-fōn). Otophone.

OTD. Abbreviation for *organ tolerance dose,* that amount of radiation tolerated by the tissues of a normal organ.

otectomy (o-tek′to-me) [*ot-* + Gr. *ektomē* excision]. Excision of tissues of the internal and middle ear.

othelcosis (ōt″hel-ko′sis) [*ot-* + Gr. *helkōsis* ulceration]. Suppuration of the ear.

othematoma (ōt″he-mah-to′mah) [*ot-* + *hematoma*]. Hematoma auris.

othemorrhea (ōt″hem-o-re′ah) [*ot-* + Gr. *haima* blood + *rhoia* flow]. Hemorrhage from the ear.

othenometer (o″thĕ-nom′e-ter) [Gr. *ōthein* to push + *metron* measure]. An instrument for measuring the variations of the nervous force.

othygroma (ōt″hi-gro′mah) [*ot-* + *hygroma*]. A

condition in which the lobe of the ear is distended with fluid.

otiatric (o″te-at′rik). Pertaining to otiatrics.

otiatrics (o″te-at′riks) [*ot-* + Gr. *iatrikos* healing]. The therapeutics of ear diseases.

otiatry (o-ti′ah-tre). Otiatrics.

otic (o′tik) [Gr. *ōtikos*]. Pertaining to the ear; aural.

oticodinia (o″tĭ-ko-din′e-ah) [Gr. *ōtikos* aural + *dinē* whirl]. Vertigo from ear disease.

oticodinosis (o″tĭ-ko-dĭ-no′sis). Oticodinia.

otiobiosis (o″te-o-bi-o′sis). Otobiosis.

Otiobius (o″te-o′be-us). Otobius.

otitic (o-tit′ik). Pertaining to otitis.

otitis (o-ti′tis) [*ot-* + *-itis*]. Inflammation of the ear, which may be marked by pain, fever, abnormalities of hearing, deafness, tinnitus, and vertigo. **aviation o.,** aero-otitis media. **o. croupo′sa,** that which is associated with the formation of a fibrinous membrane. **o. desquamati′va,** external or medial otitis in which there are overdevelopment and desquamation of the cutaneous or mucous epithelium. **o. diphtherit′ica,** o. crouposa. **o. exter′na,** inflammation of the external ear. **o. exter′na circumscrip′ta,** that which affects a limited area or areas. **o. exter′na diffu′sa,** that which affects the greater part of the meatus. **o. exter′na furunculo′sa,** furuncular o. **furuncular o.,** the formation of furuncles in the external meatus. **o. haemorrha′gica,** that which is caused by or attended with hemorrhage. **o. inter′na,** inflammation of the internal ear. **o. labyrin′thica,** inflammation affecting chiefly the labyrinth. **o. mastoi′dea,** otitis which involves the mastoid spaces. **o. me′dia,** inflammation of the middle ear. **o. media, secretory,** a painless accumulation of mucoid fluid in the middle ear, resulting from obstruction of the eustachian tube, and causing conduction deafness. **o. me′dia catarrha′lis acu′ta,** an acute catarrhal form. **o. me′dia catarrha′lis chron′ica,** a chronic catarrhal form of several subvarieties. **o. me′dia purulen′ta acu′ta,** an acute suppurative form. **o. me′dia purulen′ta chron′ica,** otorrhea. **o. me′dia sclerot′ica,** dry catarrh of the middle ear. **o. me′dia sero′sa,** one marked by a copious serous exudation. **o. me′dia suppurati′va,** suppurative inflammation of the middle ear. **o. me′dia vasomotor′ica,** otitis media of vasomotor origin. **mucosis o., mucosus o.,** otitis media caused by *Streptococcus mucosus*. **o. mycot′ica,** that which is due to parasitic fungi. **parasitic o.,** otoacariasis. **o. sclerot′ica,** that which is marked by hardening of the ear structures.

oto-, ot- [Gr. *ous*, *ōtos* ear]. Combining form denoting relationship to the ear.

otoacariasis (o″to-ak″ah-ri′ah-sis) [*oto-* + *acariasis*]. Infection of the ears of cats, dogs, and domestic rabbits with the mite *Otodectes*. Called also *parasitic otitis.*

otoantritis (o″to-an-tri′tis). Otitis involving the attic of the tympanum and the mastoid antrum.

otobiosis (o″to-bi-o′sis). Infestation by Otobius.

Otobius (o-to′be-us) [*oto-* + Gr. *bios* manner of living]. A genus of argasid ticks, the spinous ear ticks. The nymphs of *O. lagophilus* of rabbits and *O. megnini* of cattle may attack the ears of man.

otoblennorrhea (o″to-blen″o-re′ah) [*oto-* + Gr. *blenna* mucus + *rhoia* flow]. Mucous discharge from the ear.

otocariasis (o″to-kah-ri′ah-sis). Otoacariasis.

otocatarrh (o″to-kah-tar′). Aural catarrh.

Otocentor (o″to-sen′tor). A genus name assigned to ticks formerly classified as *Dermacentor nitens*. **O. ni′tens,** a species of inornate ticks, yellow-brown in color, found on horses and related animals, originally described from Jamaica and Santo Domingo, and found in the United States in southern Texas.

otocephalus (o″to-sef′ah-lus) [*oto-* + Gr. *kephalē* head]. A fetal monster lacking the lower jaw and having ears united below the face.

otocerebritis (o″to-ser″e-bri′tis) [*oto-* + *cerebritis*]. Inflammation of the brain dependent upon disease of the middle ear.

otocleisis (o″to-kli′sis) [*oto-* + Gr. *kleisis* closure]. Closure of the auditory passages.

otoconia (o″to-ko′ne-ah) [*oto-* + Gr. *konis* dust]. A dustlike substance made up of minute six-sided prisms of calcium carbonate arranged in a single layer in the gelatinous film which covers the maculae acusticae of the membranous labyrinth of the inner ear. Called also *otoliths* and *ear dust.*

otoconite (o-tok′o-nīt). Otoconium.

otoconium (o″to-ko′ne-um). Singular of *otoconia.*

otocranial (o″to-kra′ne-al). Pertaining to the otocranium.

otocranium (o″to-kra′ne-um) [*oto-* + Gr. *kranion* skull]. 1. The chamber in the petrous bone that lodges the internal ear. 2. The petromastoid; the auditory portion of the cranium.

otocyst (o′to-sist) [*oto-* + Gr. *kystis* sac, bladder]. 1. The auditory vesicle of the embryo. 2. The auditory sac of some of the lower animals.

Otodectes (o″to-dek′tēz) [*oto-* + Gr. *dēktēs* a biter]. A genus of mites. See *otoacariasis.*

otodynia (o″to-din′e-ah) [*oto-* + Gr. *odynē* pain]. Pain in the ear; earache.

otoencephalitis (o″to-en-sef″ah-li′tis) [*oto-* + *encephalitis*]. Inflammation of the brain due to an extension from an inflamed middle ear.

otoganglion (o″to-gang′gle-on) [*oto-* + Gr. *ganglion* ganglion]. The otic ganglion.

otogenic (o″to-jen′ik). Otogenous.

otogenous (o-toj′e-nus) [*oto-* + Gr. *gennan* to produce]. Originating within the ear.

otography (o-tog′rah-fe) [*oto-* + Gr. *graphein* to write]. A description of the ear.

otohemineurasthenia (o″to-hem″e-nu″ras-the′ne-ah) [*oto-* + *hemi-* + *neurasthenia*]. Nervous defect of hearing in one ear.

otolaryngology (o″to-lar″in-gol′o-je). Otology and laryngology considered as a single specialty.

otolite (o′to-līt). Otolith.

otolith (o′to-lith) [*oto-* + Gr. *lithos* stone]. See *otoconia.*

otolithiasis (o″to-lĭ-thi′ah-sis). The presence of calculi in the ear.

otologic (o″to-loj′ik). Pertaining to otology.

otologist (o-tol′o-jist). A physician versed in otology.

otology (o-tol′o-je) [*oto-* + *-logy*]. The sum of what is known regarding the ear.

otomassage (o″to-mah-sahzh′) [*oto-* + Gr. *massein* to knead]. The massage of the tympanic cavity and ossicles.

otomastoiditis (o″to-mas″toid-i′tis). Mastoiditis combined with otitis.

oto-microscope (o″to-mi′kro-skōp). Trade mark for an operating microscope especially devised to improve visualization of the surgical field in operations on the ear, providing both magnification of the structures and illumination of the area.

otomucormycosis (o″to-mu″kor-mi-ko′sis). Mucormycosis affecting the ear.

otomyasthenia (o″to-mi″as-the′ne-ah) [*oto-* + Gr. *mys* muscle + *astheneia* weakness]. A debilitated state of the ear muscles, interfering with the normal selection and amplification of sounds.

Otomyces (o″to-mi′sēz) [*oto-* + Gr. *mykēs* fungus]. A genus of fungi which infest the ear. **O. hage′ni, O. purpu′reus,** species which have been found in the human ear.

otomycosis (o″to-mi-ko′sis) [*oto-* + Gr. *mykēs* fungus]. Fungus infection of the external auditory meatus and ear canal. It is marked by pruritus and exudative inflammation, and there may be secondary bacterial infection. **o. aspergilli′na,** any ear disease caused by the presence of an aspergillus. See *myringomycosis.*

otomyiasis (o″to-mi′yah-sis). Infestation of the ear by larvae.

otoncus (o-tong′kus). A tumor of the ear.

otonecrectomy (o″to-ne-krek′to-me) [*oto-* + *necrectomy*]. The surgical removal of necrosed tissues from the ear.

otoneuralgia (o″to-nu-ral′je-ah) [*oto-* + *neuralgia*]. Neuralgic pain in the ear.

otoneurasthenia (o″to-nu″ras-the′ne-ah) [*oto-* + *neurasthenia*]. Neurasthenia due to ear disease.

otoneurology (o″to-nu-rol′o-je). Neurotology.

otopathy (o-top′ah-the) [*oto-* + Gr. *pathos* disease]. Any disease of the ear.

otopharyngeal (o″to-fah-rin′je-al). Pertaining to the ear and pharynx.

otophone (o′to-fōn) [*oto-* + Gr. *phōnē* sound]. 1. An external appliance used to aid the hearing. 2. A tube used in the auscultation of the ear.

otopiesis (o″to-pi′e-sis) [*oto-* + Gr. *piesis* pressure]. 1. The sinking in or depression of the membrana tympani. 2. Pressure upon the labyrinth, producing deafness.

otoplasty (o′to-plas″te) [*oto-* + Gr. *plassein* to form]. Plastic surgery of the ear; the surgical correction of ear deformities and defects.

otopolypus (o″to-pol′ĭ-pus) [*oto-* + *polypus*]. A polyp of the ear.

otopyorrhea (o″to-pi″o-re′ah) [*oto-* + Gr. *pyon* pus + *rhein* to flow]. A copious purulent discharge from the ear.

otopyosis (o″to-pi-o′sis) [*oto-* + Gr. *pyōsis* suppuration]. A suppurative disease of the ear.

otor (o′tor). Pertaining to the ear; aural.

otorhinolaryngology (o″to-ri″no-lar″in-gol′o-je) [*oto-* + Gr. *rhis* nose + *larynx* larynx + *-logy*]. The sum of knowledge regarding the ear, nose, and larynx, and their diseases.

otorhinology (o″to-ri-nol′o-je) [*oto-* + Gr. *rhis* nose + *-logy*]. That branch of medicine which treats of the nose and ear and their diseases.

otorrhagia (o″to-ra′je-ah) [*oto-* + Gr. *rhēgnynai* to burst forth]. Hemorrhage from the ear.

otorrhea (o″to-re′ah) [*oto-* + Gr. *rhoia* to flow]. A discharge from the ear, especially a purulent one.

otosalpinx (o″to-sal′pinks) [*oto-* + Gr. *salpinx* trumpet]. The auditory tube (tuba auditiva [N A]).

otosclerectomy (o″to-skle-rek′to-me). Otoscleronectomy.

otoscleronectomy (o″to-skle″ro-nek′to-me) [*oto-* + Gr. *sklēros* hard + *ektomē* excision]. Excision of the ankylosed sound-conducting apparatus of the middle ear.

otosclerosis (o″to-skle-ro′sis) [*oto-* + Gr. *sklērōsis* hardening]. The formation of spongy bone in the capsule of the labyrinth of the ear.

otoscope (o′to-skōp) [*oto-* + Gr. *skopein* to examine]. An instrument for inspecting or for auscultating the ear. **Brunton's o.,** an otoscope lighted by means of a funnel attached to the side. **Siegle's o.,** an otoscope which gives a view of the drum membrane when subjected to condensed or rarefied air. **Toynbee's o.,** a tube for insertion into the ear of the patient and of the observer for the purpose of auscultating the patient's ear during politzerization.

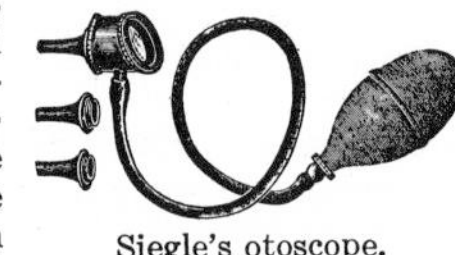

Siegle's otoscope.

otoscopy (o-tos′ko-pe). Examination of the ear by means of the otoscope.

otosis (o-to′sis). A false impression of sounds uttered by others.

otospongiosis (o″to-spon″je-o′sis). Otosclerosis.

otosteal (o-tos′te-al) [*ot-* + Gr. *osteon* bone]. Pertaining to the ear bones.

otosteon (o-tos′te-on) [*ot-* + Gr. *osteon* bone]. 1. An otolith. 2. An auditory ossicle.

ototomy (o-tot′o-me) [*ot-* + Gr. *tomē* a cutting]. The dissection or anatomy of the ear.

ototoxic (o″to-tok′sik). Having a deleterious effect upon the eighth nerve, or upon the organs of hearing and balance.

ototoxicity (o″to-toks-is′ĭ-te). The quality of being poisonous to or of exerting a deleterious effect upon the eighth nerve or upon the organs of hearing and balance.

otrivin (o′trĭ-vin). Trade mark for preparations of xylometazoline hydrochloride.

Ott's test (ots) [Isaac A. *Ott,* American physiologist, 1847–1916]. See under *tests.*

Otto disease, pelvis (ot′o) [Adolph Wilhelm *Otto,* German surgeon, 1786–1845]. See under *disease* and *pelvis.*

O.U. An abbreviation for L. *oc′uli u′nitas,* both eyes together, or *oc′ulus uter′que,* each eye.

ouabain (wah-ba′in). A glycoside obtained from the seeds of *Strophanthus gratus:* used as a cardiotonic.

Oudin current, resonator (or-da′) [Paul *Oudin,* French electrotherapist and roentgenologist, 1851–1923]. See under *current* and *resonator.*

oulectomy (oo-lek′to-me). Ulectomy.

oulitis (oo-li′tis). Ulitis.

oulonitis (oo″lo-ni′tis). Pulpitis.

oulorrhagia (oo″lo-ra′je-ah). Ulorrhagia.

ounce (ouns) [L. *uncia*]. A measure of weight in both the avoirdupois and the apothecaries' system; abbreviation oz. The ounce *avoirdupois* is one sixteenth of a pound, or 437.5 grains (28.3495 Gm.). The *apothecaries'* ounce is one twelfth of a pound, or 480 grains (31.103 Gm.); symbol ℥. **fluid o.,** a unit of capacity (liquid measure) of the apothecaries' system, being 8 fluid drams, or the equivalent of 29.57 ml.

outlay (out′la). A graft applied to the surface of an organ or structure. **epithelial o.,** an epithelial inlay in which the edges of the wound are not completely approximated, permitting new epithelium to grow out around the wound margin. See *inlay, epithelial.*

outlet (out′let). A means by which something escapes. **pelvic o.,** the lower aperture of the pelvis (apertura pelvis inferior [N A]).

outlimb (out′lim). The distal part or segment of an extremity.

outpatient (out′pa-shent). A patient who comes to the hospital, clinic, or dispensary for diagnosis and/or treatment but does not occupy a bed.

outpocketing (out-pok′et-ing). 1. Evagination. 2. Enclosure of the distal end of a pedicle flap within an opening made in the body tissues.

output (out′poot). The yield, or the total of anything produced, as the quantity of metabolic by-products excreted from the body by way of the kidneys, lungs, and skin, usually expressed as quantity per specified unit of time. **cardiac o.,** the effective volume of blood expelled by either ventricle of the heart per unit of time, being equal to the stroke output multiplied by the number of beats per the time unit used in the computation. **energy o.,** the energy a body is able to manifest in work or activity. **stroke o.,** the amount of blood ejected by each ventricle at each beat of the heart. **urinary o.,** the amount of urine secreted by the kidneys.

Ov. Abbreviation for L. *ovum,* egg.

ova (o′vah) [L.]. Plural of *ovum.*

oval (o′val) [L. *ovalis*]. Egg shaped; having the outline of the long section of an egg.

ovalbumin (o″val-bu′min) [L. *ovum* egg + *albumin*]. An albumin obtainable for the whites of eggs.

ovalocytary (o″vah-lo-si′ter-e). Marked by ovalocytosis.

ovalocyte (o′vah-lo-sīt). An elliptical red blood corpuscle.

ovalocytosis (o-val″o-si-to′sis). The presence in the blood of an unusually large number of oval red blood corpuscles.

ovarialgia (o-va″re-al′je-ah). Oophoralgia.

ovarian (o-va′re-an). Pertaining to an ovary or ovaries.

ovariectomy (o″va-re-ek′to-me). Oophorectomy.

ovarin (o′var-in). An ovarian hormone, present in both graafian follicle and corpus luteum, concerned in decidual development.

ovario- (o-va′re-o) [L. *ovarium* ovary]. Combining form denoting relationship to the ovary.

ovariocele (o-va′re-o-sēl) [*ovario-* + Gr. *kēlē* hernia]. Hernial protrusion of an ovary.

ovariocentesis (o-va″re-o-sen-te′sis) [*ovario-* + Gr. *kentēsis* puncture]. Surgical puncture of an ovary.

ovariocyesis (o-va″re-o-si-e′sis) [*ovario-* + Gr. *kyēsis* pregnancy]. Ovarian pregnancy.

ovariodysneuria (o-va″re-o-dis-nu′re-ah) [*ovario-* + *dys-* + Gr. *neuron* nerve + *-ia*]. Neuralgic pain in the ovary.

ovariogenic (o-va″re-o-jen′ik). Arising in the ovary.

ovariohysterectomy (o-va″re-o-his″ter-ek′to-me). Oophorohysterectomy.

ovarioncus (o″va-re-ong′kus) [*ovario-* + Gr. *onkos* mass]. A tumor of the ovary.

ovariopathy (o-va″re-op′ah-the) [*ovario-* + Gr. *pathos* disease]. Ovarian disease.

ovariorrhexis (o-va″re-o-rek′sis) [*ovario-* + Gr. *rhēxis* rupture]. Rupture of an ovary.

ovariosalpingectomy (o-va″re-o-sal″pin-jek′to-me). Surgical removal of an ovary and oviduct.

ovariosteresis (o-va″re-o-ste-re′sis) [*ovario-* + Gr. *sterēsis* loss]. The extirpation of an ovary.

ovariostomy (o″va-re-os′to-me). Oophorostomy.

ovariotestis (o-va″re-o-tes′tis). Ovotestis.

ovariotherapy (o-va″re-o-ther′ah-pe). Ovotherapy.

ovariotomist (o″va-re-ot′o-mist). A surgeon who performs ovariotomy.

ovariotomy (o″va-re-ot′o-me) [*ovario-* + Gr. *tomē* a cutting]. Surgical removal of an ovary, or removal of an ovarian tumor. **abdominal o.,** ovariotomy performed through the abdominal wall. **vaginal o.,** ovariotomy performed through the vagina.

ovariotubal (o-va″re-o-tu′bal). Pertaining to the ovary and uterine tube.

ovariprival (o″vah-rip′rĭ-val). Caused by or due to loss of ovaries.

ovaritis (o″vah-ri′tis). Inflammation of an ovary.

ovarium (o-va′re-um), pl. *ova′ria* [L.]. [N A, B N A] The sexual gland in the female, in which the ova are formed. It is a flat oval body along the lateral wall of the pelvic cavity, attached to the posterior surface of the broad ligament. It consists of stroma and ovarian follicles in various stages of maturation, and is covered by a modified peritoneum. Called also *ovary.* **o. gyra′tum,** superficial fibrosis of the ovary in which the organ becomes transformed into a hard, enlarged mass. **o. masculi′num,** appendix testis.

ovarotherapy (o″vah-ro-ther′ah-pe). Ovotherapy.

ovary (o′vah-re). The sexual gland in the female, in which the ova are formed. See *ovarium.* **adenocystic o.,** an ovary containing numerous small serous cysts. **oyster o′s,** hypertrophied, edematous ovaries sometimes seen in hydatid mole.

ovaserum (o″vah-se′rum). An antiserum found on immunizing with egg albumin.

overbite (o′ver-bīt). That condition in which the incisal ridges of the maxillary anterior teeth extend below the incisal ridges of the mandibular anterior teeth when the jaws are in centric occlusion. **horizontal o.** See *overjet.* **vertical o.** See *overbite.*

overcompensation (o″ver-kom″pen-sa′shun). Excession compensation, thus more or less reversing the effect.

overcorrection (o″ver-ko-rek′shun). The use of too powerful lenses in correcting defect of vision.

overdetermination (o″ver-de-ter″mĭ-na′shun). In psychoanalysis, the unconscious mechanism through which every mental symptom or every element of a dream is determined by more than one association: i.e., every element of the dream or symptom can have many meanings.

overexertion (o″ver-eg-zer′shun). Exertion to the point of exhaustion or overstrain.

overextension (o″ver-eks-ten′shun). Extension beyond the normal limit.

overflapping (o″ver-flap′ping). The placing of a skin flap over an adjacent area or over another flap from which the surface epithelium has been removed.

overflow (o′ver-flo). The continuous escape of a fluid, as of the tears or the urine.

overgrafting (o″ver-graft′ing). The application of a second skin graft over a previously healed graft from which the epithelium has been removed, as a means of reinforcing split thickness grafts.

overgrowth (o′ver-grōth). Excessive growth of a part, due either to increase in size of the constituent cells or to an increase in their number.

overhang (o′ver-hang). The extension, over the margins of a tooth cavity, of an excessive amount of filling material.

overhydration (o″ver-hi-dra′shun). A state of excess fluids in the body.

overjet (o′ver-jet). That condition in which the incisal or buccal cusp ridges of the maxillary teeth extend labially or bucally to the ridges of the mandibular teeth when the jaws are in centric occlusion.

overjut (o′ver-jut). Overjet.

overlay (o′ver-la). An increment; a later addition superimposed upon an already existing mass, state, or condition. **emotional o.,** psychogenic o. **psychogenic o.,** the emotionally determined increment to an existing symptom or disability which has been of an organic or of a physically traumatic origin.

overmaximal (o″ver-mak′sĭ-mal). Over the normal maximum.

overproductivity (o″ver-pro″duk-tiv′ĭ-te). Mental activity, characterized by volubility, psychomotor activity, flights of ideas, incoherence, destructiveness, noisiness, etc.

overreaching (o″ver-rēch′ing). An error of gait in the horse, in which the toe of the hind hoof strikes the heel of the forefoot.

overresponse (o″ver-re-spons′). Abnormally intense response or reaction to a stimulus.

overriding (o″ver-rīd′ing). The slipping of either part of a fractured bone past the other.

overstain (o′ver-stān). To stain a tissue excessively, so that certain elements may be properly stained when the excess of stain is washed out.

overstrain (o′ver-strān). An abnormal degree of fatigue brought about by activity. It is intermediate between fatigue and actual exhaustion.

overstress (o′ver-stres). Excessive activity resulting in overstrain.

overtoe (o′ver-to). Hallux varus in which the great toe overlies its fellows.

overtone (o′ver-tōn). Any one of the tones into which a clang can be resolved other than the lowest or fundamental tone. **psychic o.,** the consciousness of a fringe or halo of associated relations which surrounds every image presented to the mind.

overtransfusion (o″ver-trans-fu′shun). Overloading of the circulation by excessive transfusion of blood or of other fluid.

overventilation (o″ver-ven″tĭ-la′shun). Hyperventilation.

overweight (o′ver-wāt). Obesity.

ovi-. See *ovo-*.

ovi (o′vi) [L.]. Genitive of *ovum*. **o. albu′min** [L.], the white of hens' eggs. **o. vitel′lus** [L.], the yolk of hens' eggs.

oviducal (o′vĭ-du-kal). Pertaining to the oviducts.

oviduct (o′vĭ-dukt) [*ovi-* + L. *ductus* duct]. 1. A passage through which ova leave the maternal organism or pass to an organ which communicates with the exterior of the body. 2. A uterine tube (tuba uterina [N A]).

oviductitis (ov″ĭ-duk-ti′tis). Inflammation of the oviduct in fowls.

oviferous (o-vif′er-us) [*ovi-* + L. *ferre* to bear]. Producing ova.

oviform (o′vĭ-form) [*ovi-* + L. *forma* shape]. Egg-shaped; ovoid.

ovigenesis (o″vĭ-jen′e-sis) [*ovi-* + Gr. *gennan* to produce]. Oogenesis.

ovigenetic (o″vĭ-je-net′ik). Pertaining to ovigenesis (oogenesis).

ovigenic (o″vĭ-jen′ik). Oogenic.

ovigenous (o-vij′e-nus). Oogenic.

ovigerm (o′vĭ-jerm) [*ovi-* + L. *germen* a bud]. A cell which develops into an ovum.

ovigerous (o-vij′er-us) [*ovi-* + L. *gerere* to bear]. Producing or containing ova.

ovination (o″vĭ-na′shun) [L. *ovinus* of a sheep]. Inoculation with the virus of sheep pox.

ovine (o′vīn) [L. *ovinus* of a sheep]. Pertaining to, characteristic of, or derived from sheep.

ovinia (o-vin′e-ah) [L. *ovis* sheep]. A virus disease of sheep resembling and perhaps identical with smallpox; sheep pox; ecthyma contagiosum.

oviparity (o″vĭ-par′ĭ-te). The quality of being oviparous.

oviparous (o-vip′ah-rus) [*ovi-* + L. *parere* to bring forth, produce]. Producing eggs from which the young are hatched outside the body of the maternal organism.

oviposition (o″vĭ-po-zish′un) [*ovi-* + L. *ponere* to place]. The act of laying or depositing eggs.

ovipositor (o″vĭ-pos′ĭ-tor). A specialized organ by means of which many female insects deposit their eggs in various plant structures or in the soil.

ovisac (o′vĭ-sak) [*ovi-* + L. *saccus* bag]. A graafian follicle (folliculi ovarici vesiculosi [N A]).

ovist (o′vist). One who believes that the undeveloped embryo exists preformed in the ovum. Cf. *animalculist.*

ovium (o′ve-um). The mature ovum.

ovo-, ovi- [L. *ovum* egg]. Combining form denoting relationship to an egg, or to ova.

ovocenter (o′vo-sen″ter). The centrosome of the ovum during fertilization.

ovocylin (o″vo-sil′in). Trade mark for a preparation of estradiol.

ovocyte (o′vo-sīt). Oocyte.

ovoflavin (o″vo-fla′vin) [L. *ovum* egg + *flavus* yellow]. Riboflavin derived from eggs.

ovogenesis (o″vo-jen′e-sis). Oogenesis.

ovoglobulin (o″vo-glob′u-lin). The globulin of white of egg.

ovogonium (o″vo-go′ne-um). Oogonium.

ovoid (o′void) [*ovo-* + Gr. *eidos* form]. 1. Egg shaped. 2. A nonflagellated or female malarial microparasite.

ovolysin (o-vol′ĭ-sin) [*ovo-* + *lysin*]. A lysin which acts on egg white.

ovolytic (o″vo-lit′ik). Splitting up egg albumin.

ovomucin (o″vo-mu′sin). A glycoprotein from the white of egg.

ovomucoid (o″vo-mu′koid) [*ovo-* + *mucoid*]. A mucus-like principle derivable from egg white.

ovoplasm (o′vo-plazm) [*ovo-* + Gr. *plasma* anything formed]. The protoplasm of an unfertilized ovum.

Ovoplasma orientale (o″vo-plaz′ma o″re-en-ta′le). *Leishmania tropica.*

ovoprecipitin (o″vo-pre-sip′ĭ-tin). A precipitin specific for the white of egg.

ovoserum (o″vo-se′rum). The serum of an animal into which an egg albumin has been injected. This serum will precipitate the albumin from eggs of the same species as those from which the injection was made.

ovotestis (o″vo-tes′tis). A gonad containing both testicular and ovarian tissue.

ovotherapy (o″vo-ther′ah-pe). Therapeutic use of ovarian extract, especially extract from the corpus luteum.

ovoverdin (o″vo-ver′din) [*ovo-* + Fr. *verd* green]. The green pigment of the chromoprotein of crawfish eggs.

ovovitellin ((o″vo-vi-tel′in). The vitellin of egg yolk.

ovoviviparity (o″vo-viv″ĭ-par′ĭ-te). The quality of being ovoviviparous.

ovoviviparous (o″vo-vi-vip′ah-rus) [*ovo-* + L. *vivus* alive + *parere* to bring forth, produce]. Bearing living young that hatch from eggs inside the body of the maternal organism, the embryo being nourished by food stored in the egg.

ovula (ov′u-lah) [L.]. Plural of *ovulum.*

ovular (o′vu-lar). Pertaining to an ovule or an ovum.

ovulase (o′vu-lās). An enzyme once thought to be present in ova and to stimulate karyokinesis.

ovulation (ov″u-la′shun). The discharge of a mature, unimpregnated ovum from the graafian follicle of the ovary. **amenstrual o.,** that which occurs in the absence of menstrual bleeding. **anestrous o.,** that which occurs in animals unaccompanied by other events of estrus. **paracyclic o.,** supplementary o. **supplementary o.,** an extra ovulation in a particular estrous cycle; called also *paracyclic o.*

ovulatory (ov′u-lah-to″re). Pertaining to ovulation.

ovule (o′vūl) [L. *ovulum*]. 1. The ovum within the graafian follicle. 2. Any small, egglike structure. **graafian o's,** folliculi ovarici vesiculosi. **Naboth's o's,** nabothian follicles. **primitive o., primordial o.,** a rudimentary ovum within the ovary.

ovulogenous (o″vu-loj′e-nus). Producing or developing from an ovule or ovum.

ovulum (ov′u-lum), pl. *ov′ula* [L., dim. of *ovum*]. 1. [B N A] Ovum. 2. Any small, egglike structure. **ov′ula nabo′thi** ["Naboth's ovules"], nabothian follicles.

ovum (o′vum), pl. *o′va*, gen. *o′vi* [L.]. 1. The female reproductive cell which, after fertilization, develops into a new member of the same species (von Baer, 1827); an egg. 2. [N A] A round cell about 0.1 mm. in diameter, produced in the ovary. It consists of protoplasm which contains some yolk,

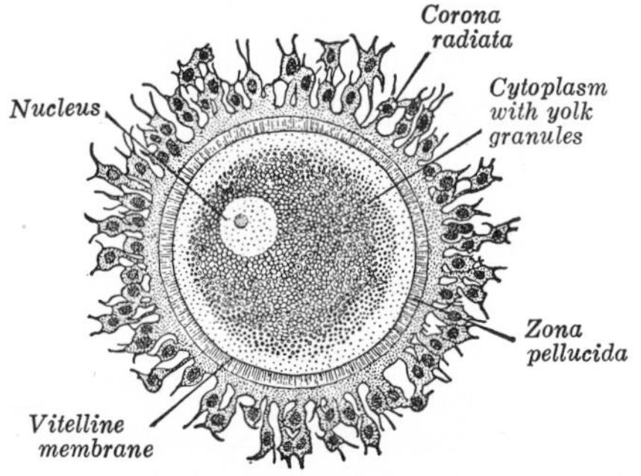

Human ovum (Arey, after Waldeyer).

enclosed by a cell wall consisting of two layers, an outer one (*zona pellucida, zona radiata*) and an inner, thin one (*vitelline membrane*). There is a large nucleus (*germinal vesicle*), within which is a nucleolus (*germinal spot*). By extension, the word is also used to designate any early stage of the developing products of conception, when the embryo itself constitutes a tiny and insignificant part of the whole. **alecithal o.,** one with only a small amount of yolk evenly distributed throughout the protoplasm, as in the ova of mammals and many of the invertebrates. Called also *oligolecithal o.* **blighted o.,** a fertilized ovum in which development has become arrested. **Bryce-Teacher o.,** a human ovum which was thought to be the youngest known ovum at the time of its study in 1908; now known to be a pathological specimen. **centrolecithal o.,** one in which the yolk is centrally located, and surrounded by a peripheral layer of protoplasm, as the ova of arthropods. **cleidoic o.,** one which possesses within itself sufficient nutritive material for the production of a complete embryo and so needs to absorb nothing from its environment except oxygen. For example, a bird's egg. **ectolecithal o.,** one in which the yolk is situated peripherally. **Hertig-Rock ova,** 34 fertilized ova, ranging from 1 to 17 days of age, 21 of which were normal, and 13 abnormal to one degree or another; discovered between 1938 and 1953, they constitute the only series of such early human conceptuses in existence. **holoblastic o.,** one that undergoes total cleavage. **isolecithal o.,** one with little yolk evenly distributed throughout the cytoplasm. **macrolecithal o.,** one with much yolk. **Mateer-Streeter o.,** a fertilized ovum about 18 days old, first described in 1920. **medialecithal o.,** one with a medium amount of yolk. **megalecithal o.,** one with a large amount of yolk. **meroblastic o.,** one that undergoes partial cleavage. **microlecithal o.,** miolecithal o. **Miller o.,** a fertilized ovum 10 or 11 days old, first described in 1913. **miolecithal o.,** one containing little or no yolk. **oligolecithal o.,** alecithal o. **permanent o.,** a mature ovum ready for fertilization. **Peters' o.,** a fertilized ovum about 13 or 14 days old, first described in 1899. **primitive o., primordial o.,** any egg cell which eventually may become an oocyte within the graafian follicle. **telolecithal o.,** one in which the yolk is increasingly concentrated toward one pole.

Owen's lines (o'enz) [Sir Richard *Owen*, English anatomist and paleontologist, 1804–1892]. See under *line*.

ox. Abbreviation for *oxymel*.

oxacid (oks'as-id). Any acid that contains oxygen.

oxaine (ok'sān). Trade mark for a preparation of oxethazine.

oxalate (ok'sah-lāt). A salt of oxalic acid. **ammonium o.,** odorless crystals or white granules, $(NH_4)_2C_2O_4$, formed by evaporation of the product obtained by the reaction of equivalent amounts of ammonia solution and oxalic acid. **balanced o.,** a mixture of ammonium and potassium oxalates in a 3:2 ratio: used as an anticoagulant in the collection of blood for laboratory examination. **potassium o.,** colorless, odorless crystals, $K_2C_2O_4.H_2O$, used extensively as a reagent. **sodium o.,** white, odorless, crystalline powder, $Na_2C_2O_4$, formerly used as an anticoagulant in collection of blood for laboratory examination.

oxalated (ok'sah-lāt"ed). Treated with oxalate solution.

oxalation (ok"sah-la'shun). Treatment with oxalate solution.

oxalemia (ok"sah-le'me-ah) [*oxalate* + Gr. *haima* blood + *-ia*]. The presence of an excess of oxalates in the blood.

oxalism (ok'sal-izm). Poisoning by oxalic acid or an oxalate.

oxalosis (ok"sah-lo'sis). A condition resulting from an inborn error of metabolism, characterized by widely and evenly spread deposits of oxalate crystals in the kidneys, with progressive renal failure, and deposit of the crystals in bones and many other tissues of the body.

oxaluria (ok"sah-lu're-ah). The presence of oxalates in the urine.

oxalyl (ok'sah-lil). The divalent group, $(C:O)_2$, formed from oxalic acid by the loss of two hydroxyl groups.

oxalylurea (ok"sah-lil-u're-ah). 1. Oxaluric acid. 2. Paravanic acid.

oxamide (oks-am'id). The diamide of oxalic acid, $NH_2.CO.CO.NH_2$. It will give the biuret reaction.

oxanamide (oks-an'ah-mīd). Chemical name: 2-ethyl-3-propylglycidamide: used as a tranquilizer.

oxethazaine (oks-eth'ah-zān). Chemical name: N,N-bis-(N-methyl-N-phenyl-t-butyl-acetamido)-β-hydroxyethylamine: used as a gastric mucosal anesthetic, antacid, and demulcent.

oxgall (oks'gawl). See *ox bile extract*, under *extract*.

oxidant (ok'sĭ-dant). The electron acceptor in an oxidation-reduction (redox) reaction.

oxidase (ok'sĭ-dās). A metalloprotein which catalyzes the reduction of molecular oxygen independently of hydrogen peroxide. **amine o.,** an enzyme in animal tissues which oxidizes amines. **amino acid o.,** an enzyme which catalyzes the oxidative removal of alpha amino groups. **ascorbic acid o.,** an enzyme found in squash and other vegetables which catalyzes the oxidation of 1-ascorbic acid to dehydroascorbic acid. **cytochrome o.,** indophenol o. **diamine o.,** an enzyme which catalyzes the change of diamines into the corresponding aldehydes, ammonia, and peroxide. **direct o.,** an oxidase which causes the direct transference of oxygen from the air. **dopa o.** See *dopa-oxidase*. **hypoxanthine o.,** an enzyme which catalyzes the oxidation of hypoxanthine to xanthine. **indirect o.,** an oxidase which acts only with a peroxide. **indophenol o.,** an oxidase present in various tissues and cells; a constituent of the respiratory enzyme; called also *cytochrome o.* **monamine o.,** an enzyme which catalyzes the oxidation of amines into the corresponding aldehydes, ammonia, and hydrogen peroxide. **monophenyl o.,** tyrosinase. **primary o.,** direct o. **tyramine o.,** tyrosinase. **xanthine o.,** an enzyme which catalyzes the oxidation of various purine bases. See *Schardinger's reductase*.

oxidasic (ok"sĭ-da'sik). Of or relating to an oxidase.

oxidation (ok"sĭ-da'shun). The act of oxidizing or state of being oxidized. Chemically it consists in the increase of positive charges on an atom or the loss of negative charges. *Univalent o.* indicates loss of one electron; *divalent o.,* the loss of two electrons. **beta o.** (β-oxidation), oxidation of a fatty acid at the beta carbon atom, the second carbon from the carboxyl group, with the result that the two end carbons are split off as acetic and with the formation of a fatty acid containing two less carbon atoms.

oxide (ok'sīd) [L. *oxidum*]. Any compound of oxygen with an element or radical.

oxidization (ok"sĭ-di-za'shun). Oxidation.

oxidize (ok'sĭ-dīz). To combine or cause to combine with oxygen. See *oxidation*.

oxidoreductase (ok"sĭ-do-re-duk'tās). An enzyme that catalyzes the reversible transfer of electrons from one substance to another (oxidation-reduction, or redox reaction).

oxidosis (ok"sĭ-do'sis). Acidosis.

oxigram (ok'sĭ-gram). Oxyhemogram.

oxim, oxime (ok'sim). Any one of a series of compounds formed by the action of hydroxylamine upon an aldehyde or a ketone.

oximeter (ok-sim'e-ter). A photoelectric device for determining the oxygen saturation of the blood. **ear o.,** an oximeter for attachment to the ear, by which oxygen saturation of the blood flowing through the ear can be determined. **whole blood o.,** an oximeter for determination of oxygen saturation of removed specimens of blood.

oximetry (ok-sim′e-tre). Determination of the oxygen saturation of arterial blood by means of bichromate photoelectric colorimetry.

oxonemia (ok″so-ne′me-ah) [L. *oxone* acetone + Gr. *haima* blood + *-ia*]. Acetonemia.

oxonium (ok-so′ne-um). Containing tetravalent basic oxygen.

oxonuria (ok″so-nu′re-ah). Acetonuria.

oxophenarsine (ok″so-phen-ar′sin). Chemical name: 2-amino-4-arsenosophenol: used as an antitreponemal agent.

oxozone (ok′so-zōn). A hypothetical allotropic form of oxygen, O_4, supposed to be present in ozone.

oxsoralen (oks-sor′ah-len). Trade mark for preparations of methoxsalen.

oxtriphylline (oks-trif′ĭ-lēn). Chemical name: choline theophyllinate: used as a mild diuretic, cardiac stimulant, and a vasodilator and bronchodilator.

oxy- [Gr. *oxys* keen]. Combining form meaning (*a*) sharp, quick, or sour, or (*b*) denoting the presence of oxygen in a compound.

oxyachrestia (ok″se-ah-kres′te-ah) [*oxy-* + *a* neg. + Gr. *chrēsis* use]. A condition of defective supply of glucose to the neurons which is the cause of hypoglycemic coma.

oxyacid (ok′se-as″id). Oxacid.

oxyacoia (ok′se-ah-koi′ah). Oxyecoia.

oxybenzene (ok″se-ben′zēn). Phenol.

oxybiontic (ok″se-bi-on′tik). Aerobic.

oxyblepsia (ok″se-blep′se-ah) [*oxy-* + Gr. *blepsis* vision + *-ia*]. Unusual acuity of vision.

oxybutyria (ok″se-bu-tir′e-ah) [*oxybutyric acid* + Gr. *ouron* urine + *-ia*]. The presence of hydroxybutyric acid in urine.

oxybutyricacidemia (ok″se-bu-tir″ik-as″ĭ-de′me-ah). Oxybutyria.

oxycalorimeter (ok″se-kal-o-rim′e-ter). Benedict's apparatus for determining the caloric value of food by burning a sample in a combustion chamber and measuring the volume of oxygen consumed.

oxycanthine (ok-se-kan′thin). A white alkaloid, $C_{37}H_{40}O_6N_2$, from the root of *Berberis vulgaris*, the barberry: said to paralyze and irritate the brain and spinal cord.

oxycel (ok′sĭ-sel). Trade mark for preparations of oxidized cellulose.

oxycephalia (ok″se-se-fa′le-ah). Oxycephaly.

oxycephalic (ok″se-se-fal′ik). Pertaining to or characterized by oxycephaly.

oxycephalous (ok″se-sef′ah-lus). Oxycephalic.

oxycephaly (ok-se-sef′ah-le) [*oxy-* + Gr. *kephalē* head]. A condition in which the top of the head

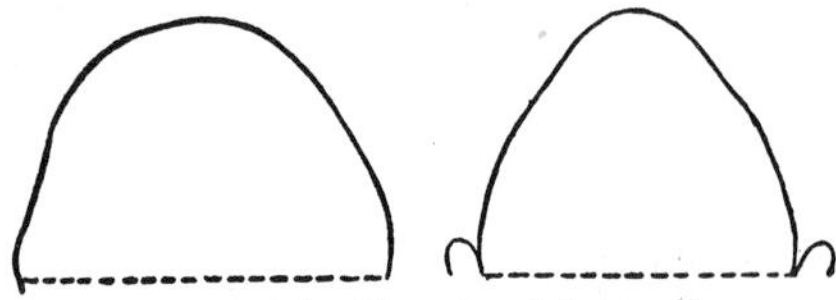

Oxycephaly (Church and Peterson).

is pointed, with a vertical index above 77. Called also *acrocephaly*, *hypsicephaly*, *turricephaly*, *steeple head*, and *tower head*.

oxychloride (ok″se-klo′rīd). An element or radical combined with oxygen and chlorine.

oxycholesterin (ok″se-ko-les′ter-in). Oxycholesterol.

oxycholine (ok″se-ko′lin). Muscarine.

oxychromatic (ok″se-kro-mat′ik) [*oxy-* + Gr. *chrōma* color]. Staining with acid dyes; acidophile.

oxychromatin (ok″se-kro′mah-tin) [*oxy-* + *chromatin*]. That part of the chromatin that stains with acid aniline dyes; called also *lanthanin*.

oxycinesia (ok″se-si-ne′ze-ah) [*oxy-* + Gr. *kinēsis* movement + *-ia*]. Pain on motion.

oxydase (ok′se-dās). Oxidase.

oxydasic (ok″se-da′sik). Oxidasic.

oxydasis (ok″se-da′sis). The oxidizing action produced by an oxidase.

oxydendron (ok″se-den′dron) [*oxy-* + Gr. *dendron* tree]. A homeopathic remedy prepared from the leaves of *Oxydendrum arboreum*, an ericaceous tree of North America.

oxydesis (ok″se-de′sis) [*oxy-* + Gr. *desis* binding]. The acid-binding power expecially of the blood. In the latter it represents the greatest amount of HCl (one hundredth normal) that can be added to oxalated blood without clumping the erythrocytes.

oxydetic (ok″se-det′ik). Pertaining to the acid binding power.

oxydoreductase (ok″se-do-re-duk′tās). One of the enzymes of the zymase system of alcoholic fermentation which rearranges aldehydes. Cf. *mutase*.

oxydum (ok′se-dum) [L.]. Oxides.

oxyecoia (ok″se-e-koi′ah) [*oxy-* + Gr. *akoē* hearing + *-ia*]. Morbid acuteness of the sense of hearing.

oxyesthesia (ok″se-es-the′ze-ah) [*oxy-* + Gr. *aisthesis* perception + *-ia*]. Morbid or abnormal acuteness of the senses. Cf. *hyperesthesia*.

oxyetherotherapy (ok″se-e″ther-o-ther′ah-pe) [*oxy-* + *ether* + Gr. *therapeia* medical treatment]. Treatment by the inhalation of ether vapor which is carried along by a current of oxygen: used in pulmonary infection and in whooping cough.

oxygen (ok′sĭ-jen) [Gr. *oxys* sour + *gennan* to produce]. A gaseous element existing free in the air and in combination in most nonelementary solids, liquids, and gases; atomic number, 8; atomic weight, 15.999; symbol, O. Oxygen exists in three isotopes, with atomic weights of 16, 17 and 18 (heavy oxygen). Oxygen constitutes 20 per cent by weight of the atmospheric air; it is the essential agent in the respiration of plants and animals, and is necessary to support combustion. It forms the characteristic constituent of most acids. It is administered chiefly in pulmonary diseases and anemia, mainly by inhalation. **excess o.,** the quantity of oxygen used over and above the resting requirements of the body. **heavy o.,** an isotope of oxygen of atomic weight 18.

oxygenase (ok′sĭ-je-nās). An enzyme that acts by the direct transference of the molecular oxygen of the air.

oxygenate (ok′sĭ-je-nāt). To saturate with oxygen.

oxygenation (ok′sĭ-je-na′shun). Saturation with oxygen.

oxygenator (ok″sĭ-je-na′tor). A device which mechanically oxygenates venous blood extracorporeally. It is used in combination with one or more pumps for maintaining circulation during open heart surgery, for assisting the circulation in patients seriously ill with heart disease, and for the perfusion of chemotherapeutic agents through isolated vascular beds in the treatment of some localized malignant tumors. **bubble o.,** a device in which pure oxygen is introduced into an extracorporeal reservoir of blood, either directly or through a filter such as porcelain or sintered glass. **disc o.** See *rotating disc o.* **film o.,** a device, encased in a container of oxygen, which makes possible the production of a thin film of blood to facilitate the exchange of gases. See *rotating disc o.* and *screen o.* **membrane o.,** a device, usually consisting of a connected series of flat bags made of semipermeable material, such as cellophane, Teflon, or Silastic, encased in a container of oxygen. The exchange of gases between the blood and oxygen occurs across the membrane.

rotating disc o., a type of film oxygenator in which a series of parallel discs rotate through an extracorporeal pool of venous blood in a container of oxygen; gaseous exchange occurs between the thin film of blood on the exposed surface of the discs and the oxygen in the container. **screen o.**, a type of film oxygenator in which the venous blood is passed over a series of screens in a container of oxygen, gaseous exchange taking place in the thin film of blood produced on the screens.

oxygenic (ok″sĭ-jen′ik). Containing oxygen.

oxygenium (ok″sĭ-jen′e-um). Oxygen.

oxygenize (ok′sĭ-jen-īz). Oxidize.

oxygeusia (ok″sĭ-gu′se-ah) [*oxy-* + Gr. *geusis* taste + *-ia*]. Unusual acuteness of the sense of taste.

oxyhematoporphyrin (ok″se-hem″ah-to-por′fĭ-rin). A pigment sometimes found in the urine, closely allied to hematoporphyrin.

oxyheme (ok′se-hēm). Hematin.

oxyhemochromogen (ok″se-he″mo-kro′mo-jen). Hematin.

oxyhemocyanine (ok″se-he″mo-si′ah-nin). Hemocyanine charged with oxygen.

oxyhemoglobin (ok″se-he″mo-glo′bin). A compound formed from hemoglobin on exposure to atmospheric conditions, with formation of a covalent bond with oxygen and without change of the charge of the ferrous state.

oxyhemoglobinometer (ok″se-he″mo-glo″bin-om′e-ter). An instrument for measuring the oxygen content of the blood.

oxyhemogram (ok″se-he′mo-gram). A graphic record of the oxygen saturation of the blood as determined by use of the oxyhemograph.

oxyhemograph (ok″se-he′mo-graf) [*oxygen* + Gr. *haima* blood + *graphein* to write]. An apparatus for determining the oxygen content of the blood, by photoelectric registration of changes in the spectroscopic properties of hemoglobin.

oxyhydrocephalus (ok″se-hi″dro-sef′ah-lus). Hydrocephalus in which the top of the head assumes a pointed shape.

oxyhyperglycemia (ok″se-hi″per-gli-se′me-ah). A condition in which there is slight glycosuria and an oral glucose tolerance curve which rises about 180–200 mg. per 100 ml. but returns to fasting values $2\frac{1}{2}$ hours after ingestion of the glucose.

oxyiodide (ok″se-i′o-dīd). An element or radical combined with oxygen and iodine; $R{-}I\begin{smallmatrix}\diagup O\\ \diagdown O\end{smallmatrix}$.

oxykrinin (ok-se-krin′in). Secretin.

oxylalia (ok-se-la′le-ah) [*oxy-* + Gr. *lalein* to talk + *-ia*]. Swiftness of speech.

oxyleucotin (ok-se-lu′ko-tin). A compound, $C_{34}H_{32}O_{12}$, from paracoto bark.

oxylone (ok′sĭ-lōn). Trade mark for a preparation of fluorometholone.

oxyluciferin (ok-se-lu-sif′er-in). The product of the oxidation of luciferin by luciferase.

oxymatrine (ok-sim′ah-trin). A crystalline alkaloid, $C_{28}H_{17}O_6N$, resulting from the oxidation of chelidonine.

oxymetholone (ok″se-meth′o-lōn). Chemical name: 2-hydroxymethylene-17α-methyldihydrotestosterone: used as a steroid compound with low androgenic action but high anabolic activity, and in treatment of patients in whom wasting effects from long-standing illness are marked.

oxymetry (ok-sim′e-tre). Oximetry.

oxymorphone (ok″se-mor′fōn). Chemical name: 1-14-hydroxydihydromorphinone: used as a narcotic analgesic.

oxymyoglobin (ok″se-mi″o-glo′bin). A compound formed from myoglobin on exposure to atmospheric conditions, with formation of a covalent bond with oxygen and without change of the charge of the ferrous state.

oxymyohematin (ok″se-mi″o-hem′ah-tin). Oxidized myohematin from muscle.

oxynervon (ok″se-ner′von). A cerebroside isolated from the brain.

oxyneurine (ok″se-nu′rin). Betaine.

oxyneuron (ok″se-nu′ron). A cerebroside supposed to exist in nervous tissue.

oxynitrilase (ok″se-ni′tril-ās). An enzyme which splits mandelonitrite to benzaldehyde and HCN.

oxyntic (oks-in′tik) [Gr. *oxynein* to make acid]. Secreting an acid substance.

oxyopia (ok″se-o′pe-ah) [*oxy-* + Gr. *ōpē* sight + *-ia*]. Acuteness of vision.

oxyopter (ok″se-op′ter) [*oxy-* + Gr. *ōps* vision]. A unit of measurement of visual acuity, being the reciprocal value of the visual angle expressed in degrees. An oxyopter (1 degree) is equivalent to 60 Snellen units (60′) and corresponds to the counting of fingers at 1 meter (De Blaskovics).

oxyosis (ok″se-o′sis) [*oxy-* + *-osis*]. Acidosis.

oxyosmia (ok″se-os′me-ah) [*oxy-* + Gr. *osmē* odor + *-ia*]. Acuteness of the sense of smell.

oxyosphresia (ok″se-os-fre′ze-ah) [*oxy-* + Gr. *osphrēsis* smell + *-ia*]. Unusual acuteness of the sense of smell.

oxyparaplastin (ok″se-par″ah-plas′tin). The oxyphil part of paraplastin.

oxypathia (ok″se-pa′the-ah). 1. Acuteness of sensation. 2. Oxypathy.

oxypathic (ok″se-path′ik). Pertaining to or characterized by oxypathy.

oxypathy (oks-ip′ah-the) [*oxy-* + Gr. *pathos* disease]. Acid poisoning; inability of the body to eliminate unoxidizable acids which injure the organism by uniting with the fixed alkalis of the tissues. The term includes arthritism, lithemia, etc.

oxyperitoneum (ok″se-per″ĭ-to-ne′um). Injection of oxygen into the abdominal cavity.

oxyphenbutazone (ok″se-fen-bu′tah-zōn). Chemical name: 1-(p-hydroxyphenyl)-2-phenyl-4-butyl-3,5-pyrazolidinedione: used as an anti-inflammatory agent, and in treatment of joint diseases.

oxyphencyclimine (ok″se-fen-si′klĭ-mēn). Chemical name: (1-methyl-1,4,5,6-tetrahydro-2-pyrimidyl)methyl-α-cyclohexyl-α-phenylglycolate: used in parasympathetic blockade.

oxyphenisatin (ok″se-fĕ-ni′sah-tin). Chemical name: 3,3bis(4-hydroxyphenyl)oxindole: used as an enema for cleansing the colon.

oxyphenonium (ok″se-fĕ-no′ne-um). Chemical name: diethyl(2-hydroxyethyl)methylammonium-α-phenyl-α-cyclohexylglycolate: used in parasympathetic blockade.

oxyphenylethylamine (ok″se-fen″il-eth″il-am′-in). Tyramine.

oxyphil (ok′se-fil). 1. Oxyphilic. 2. An oxyphilic cell or histologic element.

oxyphilic (ok″se-fil′ik) [*oxy-* + Gr. *philein* to love]. Stainable with an acid dye.

oxyphilous (oks-if′ĭ-lus). Oxyphilic.

oxyphonia (ok″se-fo′ne-ah) [Gr. *oxyphōnia*]. An abnormally sharp quality or pitch of the voice.

oxyphorase (ok′se-for″ās). An oxygen-carrying enzyme.

oxyplasm (ok′se-plazm). The oxyphil part of the cytoplasm.

oxypurinase (ok″se-pu′rĭ-nās). An enzyme which oxidizes oxypurines.

oxypurine (ok″se-pu′rin). A purine containing oxygen. The oxypurines include hypoxanthine or monoxypurine, xanthine or dioxypurine, and uric acid or trioxypurine.

oxyreductase (ok″se-re-duk′tās). An enzyme that, acting with cozymase, produces a Cannizzaro reaction.

oxyrenin (ok″se-re′nin). A term suggested for the hypertensive substance produced by the oxidation of renin E.

oxyrhine (ok′se-rīn) [*oxy-* + Gr. *rhis* nose]. Having a sharp-pointed nose.

oxyrygmia (ok″se-rig′me-ah) [*oxy-* + Gr. *erygmos* eructation]. Acid eructation.

oxysalt (ok′se-sawlt). Any salt of an oxacid.

oxysantonin (ok″se-san′to-nin). A compound formed in the body from ingested santonin.

Oxyspirura (ok″se-spi-roo′rah). A genus of nematode parasites. **O. manso′ni,** a species found beneath the nictitating membrane of chickens and other fowl in Florida, Texas, and Louisiana.

oxyspore (ok′se-spōr) [*oxy-* + Gr. *sporos* spore]. Exotospore.

oxytetracycline (ok″se-tet″rah-si′klēn). An antibiotic substance isolated from the elaboration products of *Streptomyces rimosus* grown on a suitable medium.

oxytocia (ok-se-to′se-ah) [*oxy-* + Gr. *tokos* + *-ia*]. Rapid parturition.

oxytocic (ok-se-to′sik). 1. Pertaining to, characterized by, or promoting oxytocia. 2. An agent that hastens evacuation of the uterus by stimulating contractions of the myometrium.

oxytocin (ok″se-to′sin). One of two hormones formed by the neuronal cells of the hypothalamic nuclei and stored in the posterior lobe of the hypophysis, the other being vasopressin. It stimulates contraction of the uterine musculature, and is used to induce active labor or to cause contraction of the uterus after delivery of the placenta.

oxytoxin (ok″se-tok′sin). Any substance produced by the oxidation of a toxin.

oxytropism (oks-it′ro-pizm) [*oxygen* + Gr. *trepein* to turn]. Response of living cells to the stimulus of oxygen.

oxytuberculin (ok″se-tu-ber′ku-lin). A tuberculin from cultures of an extremely virulent bacillus, modified by oxidation.

oxyuria (ok″se-u′re-ah). Oxyuriasis.

oxyuriasis (ok″se-u-ri′ah-sis). Infection with worms of the genus Oxyuris.

oxyuricide (ok″se-u′rĭ-sīd) [*oxyuris* + L. *caedere* to kill]. An agent that destroys intestinal worms of the genus Oxyuris.

oxyurid (ok-se-u′rid). A seatworm or threadworm; an individual organism of the genus Oxyuris.

oxyurifuge (ok″se-u′rĭ-fūj) [*oxyuris* + L. *fugare* to put to flight]. An agent that promotes the expulsion of intestinal worms of the genus Oxyuris.

oxyuriosis (ok″se-u″re-o′sis). Oxyuriasis.

Oxyuris (ok″se-u′ris) [Gr. *oxys* sharp + *oura* tail]. A genus of nematode, intestinal worms of the family Ascaridae. **O. appendicula′ta, O. diesin′gi** are found in the cockroach (*Periplanea orientalis*). **O. e′qui,** the largest known species of pinworm, found in the horse, mainly in the cecum, colon, and rectum. **O. incogni′ta,** a name given to certain ova found in human stools; possibly *Heterodera radicicola*. **O. vermicula′ris,** *Enterobius vermicularis*.

oz. Abbreviation for *ounce*.

ozena (o-ze′nah) [Gr. *ozaina* a fetid polypus in the nose]. A condition of the nose, of varying etiology, associated with an offensive-smelling discharge. **o. laryn′gis,** a condition of the larynx associated with a foul-smelling discharge resulting from atrophic rhinitis.

ozenous (o′zĕ-nus). Pertaining to or of the nature of ozena.

ozochrotia (o″zo-kro′she-ah) [Gr. *ozē* stench + *chrōs* skin + *-ia*]. Strong odor of the skin.

ozochrotous (o-zok′ro-tus). Having a strong odor of the skin.

ozokerite (o-zo-ke′rīt) [Gr. *ozē* stench + *kēros* wax]. Ceresin.

ozonator (o′zo-nāt″or). An instrument for generating ozone.

ozone (o′zōn) [Gr. *ozē* stench]. An allotropic and more active form of oxygen, O_3: antiseptic and disinfectant. It is formed when oxygen is exposed to the silent discharge of electricity. **o.-ether,** a mixture of ethylic ether, hydrogen peroxide, and alcohol: used as an antiseptic and for whooping cough and diabetes.

ozonide (o′zo-nīd). A compound of an olefin and ozone, the union taking place at the double bond.

ozonize (o′zo-nīz). To impregnate with ozone.

ozonizer (o′zo-nīz″er). An apparatus for applying ozone to wounds, sinuses, etc.

ozonometer (o″zo-nom′e-ter) [*ozone* + Gr. *metron* measure]. An instrument for estimating the ozone in the air.

ozonophore (o-zo′no-fōr) [*ozone* + Gr. *phoros* bearing]. 1. One of the granular elements of cell protoplasm. 2. A red blood corpuscle.

ozonoscope (o-zo′no-skōp) [*ozone* + Gr. *skopein* to examine]. An instrument for studying ozone and its effects.

ozostomia (o″zo-sto′me-ah) [Gr. *ozē* stench + *stoma* mouth + *-ia*]. Foulness of the breath.

P

P. 1. Chemical symbol for *phosphorus*. 2. Abbreviation for *position, presbyopia,* L. *prox′imum* (near), *pugil′lus* (handful), *pulse, pupil,* and L. *pon′dere* (by weight).

P_1. Symbol for *parental generation*.

P_2. Abbreviation for *pulmonic second sound*.

p-. Chemical abbreviation for *para-*.

P.A. Abbreviation for *pulpoaxial*.

Pa. Chemical symbol for *protactinium*.

paaj (pah′aj). A dermatitis caused by contact with the leaves of red quebracho, *Schinopsis lorenzii,* in Argentina. Called also *mal de quebracho*.

Paas's disease (pahz) [H. R. *Paas,* German physician]. See under *disease*.

PAB, PABA. Para-aminobenzoic acid. See under *acid*.

pabular (pab′u-lar). Pertaining to, or of the nature of, pabulum.

pabulin (pab′u-lin). The fatty and albuminous products of digestion which appear in the blood after eating.

pabulum (pab′u-lum) [L.]. Food or aliment.

pacatal (pak′ah-tal). Trade mark for a preparation of mepazine.

pacchionian bodies, depression (pak″e-o′ne-an) [Antonio *Pacchioni,* an Italian anatomist, 1665–1726]. See under *body* and *depression*.

pacemaker (pās′māk-er). An object or substance that influences the rate at which a certain phenomenon occurs; in biological chemistry, a substance whose rate of reaction sets the pace for a series of interrelated reactions. **artificial p.** See *cardiac p., artificial*. **cardiac p.,** the sinoatrial node, so called because of its action in establishing the rate of contraction of the heart muscle. **cardiac p., artificial,** a device designed to stimulate, by electrical impulses, contraction of the heart muscle at a certain rate; used in absence of normal function of the sino-atrial node; it may be connected from the outside or implanted within the body. **p. of heart,** cardiac p. **wandering p.,** a condition in which the site of origin of the impulses controlling the heart rate shifts from the head of the sino-atrial node to a lower part of the node.

pachismus (pah-kiz′mus) [Gr. *pachys* thick]. Thickening.

Pachon's method (pash-awnz′) [Michel Victor *Pachon,* French physiologist, 1867–1938]. See under *method.*

pachulosis (pak-u-lo′sis). Pachylosis.

pachy- (pak′e) [Gr. *pachys* thick, clotted]. Combining form meaning thick.

pachyacria (pak″e-a′kre-ah) [*pachy-* + Gr. *akron* end + *-ia*]. A condition characterized by enlargement of the soft parts of the extremities.

pachyblepharon (pak″e-blef′ah-ron) [*pachy-* + Gr. *blepharon* eyelid]. A thickening of the eyelid, chiefly near the border.

pachyblepharosis (pak″e-blef″ah-ro′sis). Pachyblepharon.

pachycephalia (pak″e-se-fa′le-ah) [*pachy-* + Gr. *kephalē* head + *-ia*]. Abnormal thickness of the bones of the skull.

pachycephalic (pak″e-se-fal′ik). Pertaining to or characterized by pachycephalia.

pachycephalous (pak″e-sef′ah-lus). Pachycephalic.

pachycephaly (pak″e-sef′ah-le). Pachycephalia.

pachycheilia (pak″e-ki′le-ah) [*pachy-* + Gr. *cheilos* lip + *-ia*]. Thickness of the lips.

pachycholia (pak″e-ko′le-ah) [*pachy-* + Gr. *cholē* bile + *-ia*]. Abnormal thickness of the bile.

pachychromatic (pak″e-kro-mat′ik) [*pachy-* + Gr. *chrōma* color]. Having thick chromatin threads.

pachychymia (pak″e-kim′e-ah) [*pachy-* + Gr. *chymos* juice + *-ia*]. Undue thickness of the chyme.

pachycolpismus (pak″e-kol-piz′mus) [*pachy-* + Gr. *kolpos* vagina]. Pachyvaginitis.

pachydactyly (pak″e-dak′tĭ-le) [*pachy-* + Gr. *daktylos* finger]. Abnormal enlargement of the fingers and toes.

pachyderma (pak″e-der′mah) [*pachy-* + Gr. *derma* skin]. Abnormal thickening of the skin. **p. circumscrip′ta, p. laryn′gis,** localized warty epithelial thickenings on the vocal cords. **p. lymphangiectat′ica,** an endematous infiltration and connective tissue hyperplasia of the skin that results from occlusion of the lymphatic channels. **p. verruco′sa,** a condition characterized by papillomatous growths on the vocal cords. **p. vesi′cae,** a dry, thickened condition of the mucous membrane of the bladder.

pachydermatocele (pak″e-der-mat′o-sēl) [*pachy-* + Gr. *derma* skin + *kēlē* tumor]. 1. Plexiform neuroma which attains large dimensions and produces a condition resembling elephantiasis: called also *elephantiasis neuromatosa.* 2. Dermatolysis.

pachydermatosis (pak″e-der″mah-to′sis) [*pachy-* + *dermatosis*]. Chronic pachydermia, or rosacea hypertrophica.

pachydermatous (pak″e-der′mah-tus). Having a thick skin.

pachydermia (pak″e-der′me-ah). Pachyderma.

pachydermic (pak″e-der′mik). Characterized by abnormal thickness of the skin.

pachydermoperiostosis (pak″e-der″mo-per″e-os-to′sis). A thickening of the skin with accentuation of existing folds and the creation of new folds and creases, associated with periostosis. **p. plica′ta,** a familial form of pachydermoperiostosis in which the skin of the face, neck, hands, and feet is thickened and pleated into folds.

pachyemia (pak″e-e′me-ah) [*pachy-* + Gr. *haima* blood + *-ia*]. Thickening of the blood; a thick condition of the blood.

pachyglossia (pak″e-glos′e-ah) [*pachy-* + Gr. *glōssa* tongue + *-ia*]. Abnormal thickness of the tongue.

pachygnathous (pah-kig′nah-thus) [*pachy-* + Gr. *gnathos* jaw]. Having a large jaw.

pachygyria (pak″e-ji′re-ah) [*pachy-* + *gyrus* + *-ia*]. Macrogyria.

pachyhematous (pak″e-hem′ah-tus). Pertaining to or possessing thickened blood.

pachyhemia (pak″e-he′me-ah). Pachyemia.

pachyhymenic (pak″e-hi-men′ik) [*pachy-* + Gr. *hymēn* membrane]. Having an abnormally thick skin.

pachyleptomeningitis (pak″e-lep″to-men″in-ji′tis) [*pachy-* + Gr. *leptos* thin + *mēninx* membrane + *-itis*]. Inflammation of the dura and pia together.

pachylosis (pak″e-lo′sis) [Gr. *pachylos* thick + *-osis*]. A chronic disease in which the skin, particularly that of the legs, becomes dry, and harsh.

pachymenia (pak″e-me′ne-ah) [*pachy-* + Gr. *hymēn* membrane + *-ia*]. A thickening of the skin or of a membrane.

pachymenic (pak″e-men′ik). Having an abnormally thick skin or membrane.

pachymeninges (pak″e-me-nin′jēz). Plural of *pachymeninx.*

pachymeningitis (pak″e-men″in-ji′tis) [*pachy-* + Gr. *mēninx* membrane + *-itis*]. Inflammation of the dura mater. The symptoms of the disease resemble those of meningitis. **cerebral p.,** inflammation of the dura of the brain. **circumscribed p.,** pachymeningitis limited to a definite area of the dura. **external p.,** inflammation of the outer layers of the dura. **hemorrhagic internal p.,** a circumscribed, thickened inflammation of the inner surface of the dura; dural hematoma. **internal p.,** that which affects the inner layer of the dura. **p. intralamella′ris,** intradural abscess. **purulent p.,** abscess on the dura mater. **serous internal p.,** the so-called external hydrocephalus. **spinal p.,** inflammation of the dura of the spinal column. **syphilitic p.,** that which is caused by syphilis.

pachymeningopathy (pak″e-men″in-gop′ah-the) [*pachymeninx* + Gr. *pathos* disease]. Any noninflammatory disease of the dura mater.

pachymeninx (pak″e-me′ninks), pl. *pachymenin′ges* [*pachy-* + Gr. *mēninx* membrane]. The dura mater.

pachymeter (pak-im′e-ter) [*pachy-* + Gr. *metron* measure]. An instrument for measuring the thickness of objects.

pachymucosa (pak″e-mu-ko′sa) [*pachy-* + *mucosa*]. Abnormal thickening of the mucosa. **p. al′ba,** leukoplakia with thickening of the mucous membrane.

pachynema (pak″e-ne′mah) [*pachy-* + Gr. *nēma* thread]. A postsynaptic stage of mitosis in which the chromatin is in the form of thick spireme threads.

pachynesis (pak″e-ne′sis). Thickening and swelling of a chondriosome.

pachynsis (pah-kin′sis) [Gr.]. A thickening; especially, an abnormal thickening.

pachyntic (pah-kin′tik). Pertaining to or characterized by abnormal thickening.

pachyonychia (pak″e-o-nik′e-ah) [*pachy-* + Gr. *onyx* nail + *-ia*]. Thickening of the nails, sometimes congenital.

pachyonyxis (pak″e-o-nik′sis). Pachyonychia.

pachyostosis (pak″e-os-to′sis) [*pachy-* + Gr. *osteon* bone + *-osis*]. A benign form of hypertrophy of the bones; found particularly in aquatic animals.

pachyotia (pak″e-o′she-ah) [*pachy-* + Gr. *ous* ear]. Marked thickness of the ears.

pachypelviperitonitis (pak″e-pel″ve-per″ĭ-to-ni′tis) [*pachy-* + *pelvis* + *peritonitis*]. Pelvic peritonitis with thickening of the affected parts.

pachyperiosteoderma (pak″e-per″e-os″te-o-der′mah). Pachydermoperiostosis.

pachyperiostitis (pak″e-per″e-os-ti′tis). Periostitis of long bones resulting in abnormal thickness of the bones.

pachyperitonitis (pak″e-per″ĭ-to-ni′tis) [*pachy-* + *peritonitis*]. Peritonitis with thickening of the affected membrane.

pachypleuritis (pak″e-ploo-ri′tis) [*pachy-* + *pleuritis*]. Inflammation of the pleura, with thickening.

pachypodous (pah-kip′o-dus) [*pachy-* + Gr. *pous* foot]. Having abnormally thick feet.

pachyrhizid (pak″ir-i′zid). A poisonous glycoside from *Pachyrhizus angulatus*, a plant of various tropical regions.

pachysalpingitis (pak″e-sal″pin-ji′tis) [*pachy-* + Gr. *salpinx* tube + *-itis*]. Chronic interstitial inflammation of the muscular coat of the oviduct producing thickening. Called also *mural salpingitis* and *parenchymatous salpingitis.*

pachysalpingo-oothecitis (pak″e-sal-ping″go-o″o-the-si′tis) [*pachy-* + Gr. *salpinx* tube + *ōon* egg + *thēkē* case + *-itis*]. Chronic parenchymatous inflammation of the ovary and oviduct.

pachysalpingo-ovaritis (pak″e-sal-ping″go-o″-var-i′tis). Pachysalpingo-oothecitis.

pachysomia (pak″e-so′me-ah) [*pachy-* + Gr. *sōma* body]. Abnormal thickening of parts of the body.

pachytene (pak′e-tēn) [Gr. *pachytēs* thickness]. In meiosis, the stage following synapsis in which the homologous chromosome threads shorten, thicken, and intertwine.

pachytrichous (pah-kit′rĭ-kus) [*pachy-* + Gr. *thrix* hair]. Having thick hair.

pachyvaginalitis (pak″e-vaj″ĭ-nal-i′tis) [*pachy-* + *vaginalitis*]. Inflammatory thickening of the tunica vaginalis of the testis.

pachyvaginitis (pak″e-vaj″ĭ-ni′tis) [*pachy-* + *vaginitis*]. Chronic vaginitis with thickening of the vaginal walls. **cystic p.,** emphysematous vaginitis.

pacing (pās′ing). Setting of the pace, or regulation of the rate of. **cardiac p.,** regulation of the rate of contraction of the heart muscle by an artificial cardiac pacemaker.

pacinian corpuscles (pah-sin′e-an) [Filippo *Pacini*, Italian anatomist, 1812–1883]. See under *corpuscle.*

pacinitis (pas″ĭ-ni′tis). Inflammation of the pacinian corpuscles.

pack (pak). 1. Treatment by wrapping a patient in blankets, wet or dry; also the blankets in which a patient is packed. 2. A tampon. **cold p.,** the wrapping of a patient in blankets or sheets dipped in cold water. **Dowling p.,** long thin rolls of absorbent cotton wound around a steel applicator are impregnated with 10 per cent argyrol solution and packed in the recesses of the nose. **dry p.,** the wrapping of a patient in dry, hot blankets. **full p.,** one which encloses the entire body of the patient. **half p.,** a wet-sheet pack applied from the axillae to below the knees. **hot p.,** the wrapping of a patient in hot blankets, wet or dry. **ice p.,** a substitute for the ice-bag, consisting of a folded towel filled with crushed ice. **Mikulicz p.,** a mesh or gutta-percha sac, packed with strips of gauze, placed in a denuded pelvic area to wall off the unperitonealized surfaces. **one sheet p.,** a wet sheet pack in which only one large sheet is used. **partial p.,** a wet pack covering only a portion of the body. **periodontal p.,** a mixture which usually consists of a zinc oxide powder and eugenol liquid, applied to the gingiva around the teeth after surgical periodontal procedures, such as gingivectomy, to protect the tissues during the healing process. **salt p.,** a wet pack done with sheets or blankets wrung out of salt water. **three-quarters p.,** a wet pack extending upward as far as the axillae. **wet p., wet-sheet p.,** the packing of a patient in wet blankets or sheets, hot or cold.

packer (pak′er). An instrument for introducing dressing into the uterus or vagina, or into another body cavity or wound.

packing (pak′ing). 1. The act of filling a wound or cavity with gauze, sponge, or other material. 2. The substance used for filling a cavity. 3. Treatment with the pack.

pad (pad). A cushion-like mass of soft material. **abdominal p.,** a pad for the absorption of discharges from abdominal wounds. **dinner p.,** a pad placed over the stomach before a plaster jacket is applied. The pad is then removed, leaving space under the jacket to take care of expansion of the stomach after eating. **fat p.** 1. Sucking pad. 2. A large pad of fat lying behind and below the patella, between the patellar ligament, the head of the tibia and the femoral condyles: called also *infrapetellar* and *retropatellar fat pad.* **kidney p.,** a pad held in place by a belt for the support of a movable kidney. **knuckle p's,** nodules about the size of a split pea on the dorsal surfaces of the fingers. They are slightly movable and consist of new growths of fibrous tissue. **Malgaigne's p's,** adipose pads in the knee joint immediately above the articular surface of the femur and on either side of the upper end of the patella. **Mikulicz's p.,** a pad composed of folded gauze: used in surgical work. **occlusal p.,** a pad which covers the occlusal surface of a tooth. **periarterial p.** See *juxtaglomerular cells,* under *cell.* **retromolar p.,** a cushion-like mass of tissue situated at the distal termination of the mandibular residual ridge. **sucking p., suctorial p.,** a lobulated mass of fat which occupies the space between the masseter and the external surface of the buccinator. It is well developed in infants. Called also *fatty ball of Bichat, fat pad,* and *corpus adiposum buccae.* **surgical p.,** a rubber sheet for the carrying off of fluids in surgical operations.

Padgett's dermatome (paj′ets) [Earl C. *Padgett*, American surgeon, 1893–1946]. See under *dermatome.*

P. ae. Abbreviation for L. *par′tes aequa′les*, in equal parts.

paed-, paedo-, etc. For other words beginning thus, see those beginning *ped-*, *pedo-*, etc.

Paederus (pe′der-us). A genus of blistering beetles in Brazil, known locally as *podo.*

Pagenstecher's circle, ointment, thread (pah′gen-stek″erz) [Alexander *Pagenstecher*, German ophthalmologist, 1828–1879]. See under the nouns.

Paget's abscess, cell, disease, etc. (paj′ets) [Sir James *Paget*, English surgeon, 1814–1899]. See under the nouns.

pagetoid (paj′ĕ-toid). Resembling Paget's disease.

pagitane (paj′ĭ-tān). Trade mark for a preparation of cycrimine.

pagon (pag′on) [Gr. *pagos* frost]. The plant and animal organisms occurring in ice.

pagoplexia (pa″go-plek′se-ah) [Gr. *pagos* frost + *plēgē* stroke]. Frostbite.

-pagus (pa′gus) [Gr. *pagos* that which is fixed or firmly set]. A word termination denoting a fetal monster composed of symmetrical twins conjoined at the site indicated by the stem to which it is affixed, as *craniopagus, pygopagus, thoracopagus.*

PAH, PAHA. Para-aminohippuric acid. See under *acid.*

Pahvant valley plague (pah′vant) [*Pahvant*, a valley in Utah]. Tularemia.

paidology (pi-dol′o-je) [Gr. *pais* child + *-logy*]. Pedology.

paidonosology (pi″do-no-sol′o-je) [Gr. *pais* child + *nosos* disease + *-logy*]. Pediatrics.

pain (pān) [L. *poena, dolor;* Gr. *algos, odynē*]. A more or less localized sensation of discomfort, distress, or agony, resulting from the stimulation of specialized nerve endings. **bearing-down p.,** a variety of pain in childbirth. **boring p.,** a sensation as of being pierced with a gimlet. Called also *terebrant p.* **Brodie's p.,** pain induced by folding the skin near a joint affected with neuralgia. **central p.,** pain due to a lesion in the central nervous system. **Charcot's p's,** rheumatism of a testicle. **dilating p's,** those of the first stage of labor. **excentric p.,** pain in peripheral organs attributed to lesion of the posterior nerve roots. **expulsive p's,** those of the second stage of labor. **false p's,** ineffective pains which resemble labor pains, but which are not accompanied by effacement and dilatation of the cervix. **fulgurant p's,** intense momentary pains, coming and going with swiftness like that of lightning: they are especially characteristic of tabes dorsalis. Called also *shooting p.* **girdle p.,** a painful sensation as of a cord about the waist. **growing p's,** quasirheumatic pains peculiar to early youth. **heterotopic p.,** referred pain. **homotopic p.,** pain that is felt at the point of injury. **hunger p.,** pain coming on at the time for feeling hunger for the next meal: a symptom of gastric disorder. **ideogenous p.,** pain caused by an erroneous idea; mentally produced pain. **imperative p.,** a persisting painful sensation felt in psychasthenia. **intermenstrual p.,** a pain occurring during the period between the menses, accompanying extrusion of the ovum; mittelschmerz. **jumping p.,** a peculiar pain in joint diseases when the bone is laid bare by ulceration of the cartilage. **labor p's,** the rhythmic pains of increasing severity and frequency, caused by contraction of the uterus at childbirth. **lancinating p.,** a sharp, darting pain. **lightning p's,** the cutting and intense darting pains of locomotor ataxia. See also *fulgurant p's.* **middle p.,** intermenstrual pain. **mind p.,** psychalgia. **osteocopic p.,** osteocope. **parenchymatous p.,** pain at the peripheral end of a nerve. **phantom limb p.,** pain felt as if it were in the patient's limb, although that limb has been amputated. **postprandial p.,** abdominal pain occurring after eating a meal. **premonitory p's,** ineffective uterine contractions before the beginning of true labor. **referred p.,** pain in a part other than that in which the cause that produced it is situated. **root p.,** pain caused by disease of the sensory nerve roots and occurring in the cutaneous areas supplied by the affected roots. **shooting p.,** a fulgurant pain. **soul p.,** psychalgia. **spot p's,** pains which seem like patches on the integument. **starting p's,** pain and muscular spasm in the early stages of sleep. **terebrant p., terebrating p.,** boring pain. **wandering p.,** a pain which repeatedly changes its location.

paint (pānt). 1. A substance which is designed for application to the surface, as of the body, or a tooth. 2. To apply a substance to a specific area as a remedial or protective measure. **Castellani's p.,** a mixture of basic fuchsin, phenol, boric acid, acetone, and resorcinol, used for skin disinfection and in treatment of dermatophytosis, tinea, and other infections.

pair (pār). A combination of two related, similar, or identical entities or objects. **buffer p.,** a buffer system consisting of a weak acid and its salt.

pajaroello (pah-hah-ro-el′yo). *Ornithodoros coriaceus.*

Pajot's hook, law, maneuver, method (pahzh-ōz′) [Charles *Pajot*, French obstetrician, 1816–1896]. See under the nouns.

pakurin (pak′u-rin). An arrow poison derived from the sap of a tree in Colombia: it has a digitalis-like action on the heart.

Pal's stain (pahlz) [Jacob *Pal*, Vienna clinician, 1863–1936]. See *stains, table of.*

pala (pa′lah) [L. "spade"]. A thin, spadelike layer connecting the fimbriae with the cerebrum.

palae-. For words beginning thus, see those beginning *pale-.*

palata (pal-ah′tah) [L.]. Plural of palatum.

palatal (pal′ah-tal). Pertaining to the palate; sometimes used to designate the lingual surface of a maxillary tooth.

palate (pal′at). The partition separating the nasal and oral cavities. See *palatum* [N A]. **artificial p.,** a prosthetic device used to close a cleft palate. **bony p.,** the osseous framework of the hard palate (palatum osseum [N A]). **cleft p.,** a palate having a congenital fissure in the median line. **falling p.,** an abnormally elongated uvula. **gothic p.,** an unusually high and pointed hard palate. **hard p.,** the anterior, rigid portion of the palate. See *palatum durum* [N A]. **pendulous p.,** uvula. **premaxillary p.,** primary p. **primary p.,** that portion of the maxilla contributed by the median nasal processes. **secondary p.,** the palate proper, formed by fusion of the lateral palatine processes. **smoker's p.,** a condition of the palate sometimes occurring in heavy smokers, characterized by prominent mucous glands with inflamed orifices and a diffusely erythematous or wrinkled "cobblestone" surface. **soft p.,** the posterior, fleshy part of the palate. See *palatum molle* [N A].

palategraph (pal′at-graf). Palatograph.

palatiform (pah-lat′ĭ-form) [L. *palatum* palate + *forma* form]. Resembling the palate.

palatine (pal′ah-tīn) [L. *palatinus*]. Pertaining to the palate.

palatinoid (pah-lat′ĭ-noid). A form of vehicle for the administration of volatile or unpalatable medicines.

palatitis (pal-ah-ti′tis). 1. Inflammation of the palate. 2. Lampas.

palato- (pal′ah-to) [L. *palatum* palate]. Combining form denoting relationship to the palate; sometimes used instead of linguo- in terms referring to the lingual surface of maxillary teeth.

palatoglossal (pal″ah-to-glos′al). Pertaining to the palate and tongue.

palatognathous (pal″ah-tog′nah-thus) [*palato-* + Gr. *gnathos* jaw]. Having a congenitally cleft palate.

palatograph (pal′ah-to-graf) [*palato-* + Gr. *graphein* to write]. An instrument to record the movements of the palate in speech.

palatography (pal″ah-tog′rah-fe). The making of graphic records of the movements of the palate in speech.

palatomaxillary (pal″ah-to-mak′sĭ-ler″e). Pertaining to the palate and the maxilla.

palatomyograph (pal″ah-to-mi′o-graf) [*palato-* + Gr. *mys* muscle + *graphein* to write]. An instrument used in registering palatal movements.

palatonasal (pal″ah-to-na′zal) [*palato-* + L. *nasus* nose]. Pertaining to the palate and nose.

palatopharyngeal (pal″ah-to-fah-rin′je-al). Pertaining to the palate and pharynx.

palatoplasty (pal′ah-to-plas″te) [*palato-* + Gr. *plassein* to form]. Plastic reconstruction of the palate, including cleft palate operations.

palatoplegia (pal″ah-to-ple′je-ah) [*palato-* + Gr. *plēgē* stroke]. Paralysis of the palate.

palatoproximal (pal″ah-to-prok′sĭ-mal). Pertaining to the palatal (lingual) and proximal surface of a maxillary tooth.

palatorrhaphy (pal″ah-tor′ah-fe). Staphylorrhaphy.

palatosalpingeus (pal″ah-to-sal-pin′je-us) [*palato-* + Gr. *salpinx* tube]. The tensor veli palatini muscle.

palatoschisis (pal″ah-tos′kĭ-sis) [*palato-* + Gr. *schisis* cleft]. Fissure of the palate.

palatostaphylinus (pal″ah-to-staf″ĭ-li′nus) [*palato-* + Gr. *staphylē* uvula]. A muscular slip going to the uvula.

palato-uvularis (pal″ah-to-u″vu-la′ris) [*palato-* + L. *uvula* uvula]. The uvulae muscle.

palatum (pal-ah′tum), pl. *pala′ta* [L.]. [N A, B N A] The partition separating the nasal and oral cavities, consisting anteriorly of a hard bony part and posteriorly of a soft fleshy part. Called also *palate.* **p. du′rum** [N A, B N A], the anterior part of the palate, characterized by an osseous framework, covered superiorly by mucous membrane of the nasal cavity and, on its oral surface, by mucoperiosteum. Called also *hard palate.* **p. du'rum os'seum** [B N A], p. osseum. **p. fis'sum,** cleft palate. **p. mol'le** [N A, B N A], the fleshy part of the roof of the mouth, extending from the posterior edge of the hard palate; from its free inferior border is a projection of variable length, the uvula. Called also *soft palate.* **p. ogiva'le,** gothic palate. **p. os'seum** [N A], the bony part of the anterior two-thirds of the roof of the mouth, formed by the palatine processes of the maxillae and the horizontal plates of the palatine bones. Called also *p. durum osseum* [B N A], and *bony hard palate.*

paleencephalon (pa″le-en-sef'ah-lon) [*paleo-* + Gr. *enkephalos* brain]. The ancient brain; all of the brain except the cerebral cortex and its dependencies.

paleo- (pa'le-o) [Gr. *palaios* old]. Combining form meaning old.

paleocerebellar (pa″le-o-ser″e-bel'ar). Pertaining to or affecting the paleocerebellum.

paleocerebellum (pal″e-o-ser″e-bel'um) [*paleo-* + *cerebellum*]. A term applied originally to the cerebellar vermis and later to those parts predominantly supplied by spinocerebellar fibers.

paleocinetic (pa″le-o-si-net'ik). Paleokinetic.

paleocortex (pa″le-o-kor'teks). The phylogenetically older portion of the cerebral cortex; the olfactory cortex. Cf. *neocortex.*

paleo-encephalon (pa″le-o-en-sef'ah-lon). Paleencephalon.

paleogenesis (pa″le-o-jen'e-sis). Palingenesis, def. 2.

paleogenetic (pa″le-o-je-net'ik) [*paleo-* + Gr. *gennan* to produce]. Originated in the past; not newly acquired.

paleokinetic (pa″le-o-ki-net'ik) [*paleo-* + Gr. *kinētikos* pertaining to motion]. Old kinetic; a term applied to the nervous motor mechanism concerned in automatic associated movements. It is under the control of the corpus striatum and represents a primitive (that is, early developed) type of motor control. Cf. *neokinetic.*

paleontology (pa″le-on-tol'o-je) [*paleo-* + Gr. *ōn* existing + *-logy*]. The sum of knowledge regarding the early forms of life upon the earth.

paleopallium (pa″le-o-pal'e-um) [*paleo-* + L. *pallium* mantle]. In man, the uncus and adjacent rostral part of the hippocampal gyrus.

paleopathology (pa″le-o-pah-thol'o-je) [*paleo-* + *pathology*]. The study of disease in bodies preserved from ancient times, such as mummies.

paleophrenia (pa″le-o-fre'ne-ah) [*paleo-* + Gr. *phrēn* mind + *-ia*]. A term suggested as a substitute for schizophrenia on the basis that the latter represents a regression to childhood level.

paleopsychology (pa″le-o-si-kol'o-je) [*paleo-* + *psychology*]. The study of mental phenomena which are based on primitive or ancestral mentality.

paleosensation (pa″le-o-sen-sa'shun) [*paleo-* + *sensation*]. The sensation of severe pain and marked variations of temperature, as compared with new sensations such as those of light touch and moderate variations of temperature and the epicritic sensations.

paleostriatal (pa″le-o-stri-a'tal). Pertaining to the paleostriatum.

paleostriatum (pa″le-o-stri-a'tum) [*paleo-* + *striatum*]. The primordial or more early formed portion of the corpus striatum represented by the globus pallidus. Cf. *neostriatum.*

paleothalamus (pa″le-o-thal'ah-mus) [*paleo-* + *thalamus*]. Old thalamus; the phylogenetically older part of the thalamus, i.e., the medial (noncortical) portion of the thalamus.

pali-, palin- (pal'e, pal'in) [Gr. *palin* backward, or again]. Combining form meaning again, often denoting pathologic repetition.

palicinesia (pal″e-si-ne'se-ah). Palikinesia.

palikinesia (pal″e-ki-ne'se-ah) [*pali-* + Gr. *kinēsis* movement]. Pathologic repetition of movements.

palilalia (pal″ĭ-la'le-ah) [*pali-* + Gr. *lalein* to babble]. A condition characterized by the repetition of a phrase or word with increasing rapidity.

palin-. See *pali-*.

palinal (pal'ĭ-nal). Directed or moved backward.

palindromia (pal″in-dro'me-ah) [Gr. *palindromia* a running back]. The recurrence of a disease.

palindromic (pal″in-dro'mik). Returning; recurrent.

palinesthesia (pal″in-es-the'ze-ah) [*palin-* + Gr. *aisthēsis* sensation]. The rapid termination of the anesthetic state and the restoration to consciousness of a person under general anesthesia: it may be induced by the injection of weak hydrochloric acid.

palingenesis (pal″in-jen'e-sis) [*palin-* + Gr. *genesis* birth]. 1. The regeneration or restoration of a lost part. 2. The appearance of ancestral characters in successive generations. Cf. *cenogenesis.*

palingraphia (pal″in-gra'fe-ah) [*palin-* + Gr. *graphein* to write]. Pathologic repetition of letters, words, or parts of words in writing.

palinmnesis (pal″in-ne'sis) [*palin-* + Gr. *-mnēsis* memory]. Memory for past events or experiences.

palinphrasia (pal″in-fra'ze-ah) [*palin-* + Gr. *phrasis* speech + *-ia*]. Pathologic repetition, in speaking, of words or phrases.

paliphrasia (pal″e-fra'ze-ah). Palinphrasia.

palirrhea (pal″ĭ-re'ah) [Gr. *palirrhoia*]. 1. Regurgitation. 2. The recurrence of a discharge.

palistrophia (pal″is-tro'fe-ah) [*pali-* + Gr. *strephein* to turn]. Twisting of the spine upon itself (F. Massa, 1900).

palladium (pah-la'de-um) [L.]. 1. A rare, hard metal resembling platinum; symbol, Pd; specific gravity, 12.16; atomic number, 46; atomic weight, 106.4. It is light in weight and of a neutral color and is used for dentures and orthodontic appliances. 2. A homeopathic preparation of the same metal. **p. chloride,** $PdCl_2$, an agent recommended for use in tuberculosis.

pallanesthesia (pal″an-es-the'ze-ah) [Gr. *pallein* to shake + *anesthesia*]. Loss of vibration senses; insensibility to the vibrations of a tuning fork.

pallescence (pal-les'ens) [L. *pallescere* to grow pale]. Pallor, or paleness; a pale appearance.

pallesthesia (pal″es-the'ze-ah) [Gr. *pallein* to shake + *aisthēsis* perception]. Sensibility to vibrations; the peculiar vibrating sensation felt when a vibrating tuning-fork is placed against a subcutaneous bony prominence of the body. Called also *bone sensibility.*

pallesthetic (pal″es-thet'ik). Pertaining to the vibration sense.

pallhypesthesia (pal″hi-pes-the'ze-ah) [Gr. *pallein* to shake + *hypo* under + *aisthēsis* perception]. Diminished sensibility to vibrations.

pallial (pal'e-al). Pertaining to the pallium.

palliate (pal'e-āt). To reduce the severity of; to relieve.

palliative (pal'e-a″tiv) [L. *palliatus* cloaked]. 1. Affording relief, but not cure. 2. An alleviating medicine.

pallidal (pal'ĭ-dal). Pertaining to the globus pallidus.

pallidectomy (pal″lĭ-dek'to-me). Surgical excision of the globus pallidus or extirpation of it by other means (chemopallidectomy).

pallidin (pal'ĭ-din). A suspension, made from the lung of congenital syphilitics, rich in *Treponema pallidum:* used in cutaneous test for syphilis.

pallidofugal (pal'ĭ-dof'u-gal) [*pallidum* + L. *fugere* to flee]. Conducting impulses away from the globus pallidus.

pallidoidosis (pal″ĭ-doi-do'sis). Rabbit syphilis;

a venereal disease of rabbits caused by *Treponema cuniculi.*

pallidotomy (pal″ĭ-dot′o-me) [*pallidium* + Gr. *tomē* a cutting]. Production of lesions in the globus pallidus for treatment of involuntary movements of extrapyramidal origin.

pallidum (pal′ĭ-dum) [L. "pale"]. The globus pallidus of the brain.

pallium (pal′le-um) [L. "cloak"]. [N A, B N A] The gray matter covering the cerebral hemispheres, characterized by a distinctive layering of the cellular elements. See *cortex cerebri.*

pallor (pal′or) [L.]. Paleness; absence of the skin coloration.

palm (palm) [L. *palma*]. 1. The hollow of the hand. 2. Any tree of the order *Palmaceae.* **handball p.,** contusion of the palm of the hand occurring in handball players. **liver p's,** erythema of the palms of the hands occurring in cirrhosis of the liver.

palma (pal′mah), pl. *pal′mae* [L.]. 1. The palm. 2. The palm tree. **p. ma′nus** [N A], the palm, or flexor surface, of the hand. **pal′mae plica′tae,** the branching folds of the mucosa of the vagina.

palmae (pal′me) [L.]. Plural of *palma.*

palmanesthesia (pal″man-es-the′ze-ah) [Gr. *palmos* vibration + *anesthesia*]. Pallanesthesia.

palmar (pal′mar) [L. *palmaris; palma* palm]. Pertaining to the palm.

palmaris (pal-ma′ris). Palmar; in N A terminology, designating relationship to the palm of the hand.

palmature (pal′mah-tūr) [L. *palma* palm]. A webbed state of the fingers.

palmellin (pal-mel′in). A red pigment from a fresh water alga called *Palmella cruenta.*

palmesthesia (pal″mes-the′ze-ah). Pallesthesia.

palmesthetic (pal″mes-thet′ik). Pertaining to the vibration sense. See *palmesthetic sensibility*, under *sensibility.*

palmic (pal′mik) [Gr. *palmikos*]. 1. Pertaining to palmus, or muscular twitchings. 2. Pertaining to the pulse.

palmin (pal′min). Palmitin.

palmital (pal′mĭ-tal). An aldehyde lipid.

palmitin (pal′mĭ-tin). A crystallizable and saponifiable fat, $C_3H_5(C_{16}H_{31}O_2)_3$, from various fats and oils; glycerol tripalmitate.

palmitone (pal′mĭ-tōn). A crystalline compound, $CH_3(CH_2)_{14}.CO.(CH_2)_{14}.CH_3$, obtained when palmitic acid is distilled with lime.

palmodic (pal-mod′ik). Pertaining to or affected with palmus.

palmoform (pal′mo-form). Guaiaform.

palmoscopy (pal-mos′ko-pe) [Gr. *palmos* vibration + *skopein* to examine]. The observation and study of the heart beat.

palmus (pal′mus) [Gr. *palmos* a quivering motion]. 1. Palpitation. 2. Saltatory spasm.

palograph (pal′o-graf) [Gr. *pallesthai* to oscillate + *graphein* to record]. An instrument for sphygmographic recording in which the impulses are transmitted to a column of mobile fluid in a U-shaped tube, the movements of the liquid surface in the open area of the tube being recorded photographically on a moving sheet of sensitized paper.

palography (pal-og′rah-fe). Sphygmography with the palograph.

palp (palp). A feeler; one of the pointed sense organs attached to the mouth of arthropods.

palpable (pal′pah-b'l). Perceptible by touch.

palpate (pal′pāt) [L. *palpare* to touch]. To examine by the hand; to feel.

palpation (pal-pa′shun) [L. *palpatio*]. The act of feeling with the hand; the application of the fingers with light pressure to the surface of the body for the purpose of determining the consistence of the parts beneath in physical diagnosis. **bimanual p.,** examination with both hands. **light touch p.,** light palpation of the surface of the abdomen and thorax with the tip of a finger for the purpose of finding the outlines of the organs.

palpatometry (pal″pah-tom′e-tre) [*palpation* + Gr. *metron* measure]. Measurement of the amount of pressure that can be borne without causing pain.

palpatopercussion (pal″pah-to-per-kush′un). Palpation combined with percussion.

palpatorium (pal″pah-to′re-um). An instrument for palpating the abdomen to locate tender spots.

palpebra (pal′pe-brah), pl. *pal′pebrae* [L.]. Either of the two movable folds that protect the anterior surface of the eyeball. Called also *eyelid.* **p. infe′rior** [N A, B N A], the lower of the two movable folds protecting the anterior surface of the eyeball. **p. supe′rior** [N A, B N A], the upper of the two movable folds protecting the anterior surface of the eyeball. **p. ter′tius,** nictitating membrane.

palpebrae (pal′pe-bre) [L.]. Plural of *palpebra.*

palpebral (pal′pe-bral) [L. *palpebralis*]. Pertaining to an eyelid.

palpebralis (pal″pe-bra′lis) [L.]. Pertaining to an eyelid.

palpebrate (pal′pe-brāt) [L. *palpebrare* to wink]. 1. To wink. 2. Having eyelids.

palpebration (pal″pe-bra′shun) [L. *palpebratio*]. 1. The act of winking. 2. Abnormally frequent winking.

palpebritis (pal″pe-bri′tis). Blepharitis.

palpitation (pal″pĭ-ta′shun) [L. *palpitatio*]. Unduly rapid action of the heart which is felt by the patient.

palsy (pawl′ze). Paralysis. **Bell's p.,** peripheral facial paralysis due to lesion of the facial nerve and resulting in characteristic distortion of the face. **birth p.** See under *paralysis.* **brachial p.** See under *paralysis.* **bulbar p.** See under *paralysis.* **cerebral p.,** a persisting qualitative motor disorder appearing before the age of three years, due to a non-progressive damage of the brain. **crossed leg p.,** palsy of the peroneal nerve caused by sitting with one leg crossed over the other. **diver's p.,** compressed air illness. **Erb's p.** See under *paralysis.* **Féréol-Graux type of ocular p.,** associated paralysis of the internal rectus muscles of one side and the external rectus of the other. **hammer p.,** a variety caused by hard work with the hammer. **ischemic p.** See under *paralysis.* **Landry's p.** See under *paralysis.* **night p.,** paresthesia of the hands which is worse at night. **printer's p.,** a condition observed in printers due to chronic antimony poisoning, and marked by neuritis with paralysis, pain in the pubes, and papular eruption. **pseudobulbar p.** See under *paralysis.* **scriveners' p.,** writers' cramp. **shaking p.,** paralysis agitans. **Todd's p.** See under *paralysis.* **transverse p.,** crossed paralysis. **wasting p.,** progressive muscular atrophy.

Paltauf's dwarfism, nanism (pahl′towfs) [Arnold *Paltauf*, German physician, 1860–1893]. See under *nanism.*

Paltauf-Sternberg disease [Richard *Paltauf*, Austrian pathologist, 1858–1924; Karl *Sternberg*, Austrian pathologist, 1872–1935]. Lymphogranulomatosis.

paludal (pal′u-dal) [L. *palus* marsh]. Pertaining to or arising from marshes.

paludide (pal′u-did). A cutaneous eruption of malarial origin.

paludism (pal′u-dizm). Malaria.

paludrine (pal′u-drin). Trade mark for a preparation of proguanil hydrochloride.

palustral (pah-lus′tral) [L. *paluster* marshy]. 1. Paludal; pertaining to marshes. 2. Malarial.

pamaquine naphthoate (pam′ah-kwin naf′tho-āt). An antimalarial compound, methylene-bis-β-hydroxynaphthoate of 6-methoxy-8-(1-methyl-4-diethylamino) butylaminoquinoline, discovered in

Germany in 1924. It destroys the gametocyte (sexual forms) of all malarial parasites. Similar compounds are known by various names: *aminoquin; gamefar* (Italy); *plasmocid, plasmocide* (Russia); *plasmoquin, plasmoquine* (British colonies); *quipenyl; praequine, rhodoquine, Fourneau*-710 (France).

pamine (pam′ēn). Trade mark for preparations of methscopolamine.

pamisyl (pam′ĭ-sil). Trade mark for preparations of aminosalicylic acid.

pampiniform (pam-pin′ĭ-form) [L. *pampinus* tendril + *forma* form]. Shaped like a tendril.

pampinocele (pam-pin′o-sēl) [L. *pampinus* tendril + Gr. *kēlē* tumor]. Varicocele.

pamplegia (pam-ple′je-ah) [Gr. *pan* all + *plēgē* stroke]. Total paralysis.

pan- [Gr. *pan* all]. Prefix signifying all.

Panacea (pan″ah-se′ah) [Gr. *Panakeia*]. One of two sisters, the other being Hygeia, who were the daughters of Æsculapius and, according to legend, assisted in the rites and fed the sacred snakes in the early Greek temples of healing.

panacea (pan″ah-se′ah) [Gr. *panakeia*] 1. A universal remedy. 2. An ancient name for a healing herb or its juice.

panagglutinable (pan″ah-gloo′tĭ-nah-b'l). Agglutinable with every type of human blood serum.

panagglutination (pan″ah-gloo″tĭ-na′shun). Agglutination by the serums of all blood groups.

panagglutinin (pan″ah-gloo′tĭ-nin) [*pan-* + *agglutinin*]. An agglutinin which agglutinates the corpuscles of all blood groups.

panangiitis (pan″an-je-i′tis) [*pan-* + Gr. *angeion* vessel + *-itis*]. Inflammation involving all the coats of the vessel. **diffuse necrotizing p.,** a condition with extensive involvement of both arteries and veins, leading to symmetrical gangrene of the lower extremities, and with numerous cutaneous and visceral manifestations.

panariocyte (pan-ar′e-o-sīt). One of the peculiar basket-like cells in carcinoma.

panaris (pan′ah-ris). Paronychia. **analgesic p.,** Morvan's disease.

panaritium (pan″ah-rish′e-um) [L.]. Paronychia. **p. anal′gicum,** Morvan's disease.

panarteritis (pan″ar-tĕ-ri′tis). Periarteritis nodosa.

panarthritis (pan″ar-thri′tis) [*pan-* + Gr. *arthron* joint]. Inflammation of all the joints or of all the structures of a joint.

Panas' operation, solution (pan-ahz′) [Photinos *Panas*, French ophthalmologist, 1832–1903]. See under *operation* and *solution*.

panasthenia (pan″as-the′ne-ah) [*pan-* + *a* neg. + Gr. *sthenos* strength]. A term suggested as a substitute for neurasthenia.

panatrophy (pan-at′ro-fe) [*pan-* + *atrophy*]. Atrophy affecting several parts; general atrophy.

panblastic (pan-blas′tik) [*pan-* + Gr. *blastos* germ]. Pertaining to each of the layers of the blastoderm.

pancarditis (pan″kar-di′tis) [*pan-* + Gr. *kardia* heart]. General inflammation of the heart, involving the pericardium, myocardium, and endocardium.

panchontee (pan-shon-te′). A gum from *Bassia elliptica*, a tree of India: it resembles gutta-percha.

panchrest (pan′krest) [Gr. *panchrēstos* useful for everything]. A panacea, or remedy, for every disease.

panchromatic (pan″kro-mat′ik) [*pan-* + *chromatic*]. Sensitive to all colors: applied to photographic emulsions.

panchromia (pan-kro′me-ah). The condition of staining with various dyes.

Pancoast's drain, operation, suture (pan′kōsts) [Joseph *Pancoast*, American surgeon, 1805–1882]. See under the nouns.

Pancoast's syndrome, tumor [Henry K. *Pancoast*, Philadelphia roentgenologist, 1875–1939]. See under the nouns.

pancolectomy (pan″ko-lek′to-me). Excision of the entire colon with creation of an ileostomy.

pancrealgia (pan″kre-al′je-ah). Pancreatalgia.

pancreas (pan′kre-as), pl. *pan′creata* [Gr. *pan* all + *kreas* flesh]. A large, elongated, racemose gland behind the stomach and in relation with the spleen and the duodenum. Its right extremity, the *head*, is the larger, and directed downward; the left extremity, or *tail*, is transverse, and terminates close to the spleen. The secretion or juice of the pancreas, which passes into the duodenum through the pancreatic duct, is concerned in digestion, and contains a variety of digestive enzymes. An internal secretion, insulin, produced in the beta cells, is concerned with the regulation of carbohydrate metabolism. Glucagon, a glycogenolytic-hyperglycemic factor, is produced in the alpha cells. **aberrant p.,** an exclave of pancreatic tissue occurring as a firm yellow nodule, occurring most commonly in the stomach, duodenum, or jejunum, but encountered also in other sites. **p. accesso′rium** [N A, B N A], **accessory p.,** an inconstant separate part of the head of the pancreas, usually composed of the uncinate process, which has become completely detached. **annular p.,** a developmental anomaly in which the pancreas forms a ring entirely surrounding the duodenum. **Aselli's p.,** an assemblage of lymphatic glands at the root of the mesentery, especially in carnivora. **p. divi′sum,** a developmental anomaly in which the pancreas is present as two separate structures, each with its own duct. **dorsal p.,** an outpocketing from the entodermal lining of the gut on the dorsal wall cephalad to the level of the hepatic diverticulum, which forms much of the pancreas and its functional duct. **lesser p.,** the small, partially detached portion of the pancreas lying dorsad of its head (processus uncinatus pancreatis [N A]). Called also *Willis' p.* and *Winslow's p.* **ventral p.,** an outpocketing from the entodermal lining of the gut on the ventral wall, in the caudal angle between the gut and the hepatic diverticulum, which forms part of the pancreas and the stem of its functional duct. **Willis' p., Winslow's p.,** lesser pancreas.

pancreata (pan′kre-ah-tah). Plural of *pancreas*.

pancreatalgia (pan″kre-ah-tal′je-ah) [*pancreas* + *-algia*]. Pain in the pancreas.

pancreatectomy (pan″kre-ah-tek′to-me) [*pancreas* + Gr. *ektomē* excision]. Surgical removal of all or part of the pancreas.

pancreatemphraxis (pan″kre-at-em-frak′sis) [*pancreas* + Gr. *emphraxis* stoppage]. Congestion or enlargement of the pancreas from obstruction of the pancreatic duct.

pancreathelcosis (pan″kre-ath″el-ko′sis) [*pancreas* + Gr. *helkōsis* ulceration]. Ulceration of the pancreas.

pancreatic (pan″kre-at′ik) [L. *pancreaticus*]. Pertaining to the pancreas.

pancreaticoduodenal (pan″kre-at″ĭ-ko-du″o-de′nal). Pertaining to the pancreas and duodenum.

pancreaticoduodenostomy (pan″kre-at″ĭ-ko-du″o-de-nos′to-me). Surgical anastomosis of the pancreatic duct and the duodenum.

pancreatico-enterostomy (pan″kre-at″ĭ-ko-en″ter-os′to-me). Surgical anastomosis of the pancreatic duct and the intestine.

pancreaticogastrostomy (pan″kre-at″ĭ-ko-gas-tros′to-me). Implantation of the cut end of the pancreas into the wall of the stomach after excision of part of the pancreas.

pancreaticojejunostomy (pan″kre-at″ĭ-ko-je″ju-nos′to-me). Surgical anastomosis of the pancreatic duct and the jejunum.

pancreaticosplenic (pan″kre-at″ĭ-ko-splen′ik). Pertaining to the pancreas and spleen.

pancreatin (pan′kre-ah-tin). A substance obtained from the pancreas of the hog or the ox, which contains amylase, trypsin, and lipase: used as a digestive enzyme.

pancreatism (pan′kre-ah-tizm). Activity of the pancreas.

pancreatitis (pan″kre-ah-ti′tis). Inflammation of the pancreas, with pain and tenderness of the abdomen, tympanites, and vomiting. **acute hemorrhagic p.,** a form due to hemorrhage into the gland. **calcareous p.,** pancreatitis accompanied by the formation of calculi. **centrilobar p.,** pancreatitis located around the branches of the pancreatic duct. **chronic p.,** a condition of fibrosis of the pancreas. **interstitial p.,** one in which there is overgrowth of the inter- and intra-acinar connective tissue and frequently a corresponding atrophy of the glandular tissue. **perilobar p.,** fibrosis of the pancreas surrounding collections of atrophic acini. **purulent p.,** purulent inflammation of the pancreas.

pancreatoduodenectomy (pan″kre-ah-to-du″-o-de-nek′to-me). Excision of the head of the pancreas along with the encircling loop of the duodenum.

pancreatoduodenostomy (pan″kre-ah-to-du″-o-de-nos′to-me). Pancreaticoduodenostomy.

pancreato-enterostomy (pan″kre-ah-to-en″-ter-os′to-me). Pancreatico-enterostomy.

pancreatogenic (pan″kre-ah-to-jen′ik). Pancreatogenous.

pancreatogenous (pan″kre-ah-toj′e-nus). Arising in the pancreas.

pancreatography (pan″kre-ah-tog′rah-fe). Roentgenography of the pancreas performed during surgical exploration, a water-soluble contrast medium being injected into the pancreatic duct and the film being made while the abdomen is open.

pancreatoid (pan-kre′ah-toid). Resembling the pancreas.

pancreatolipase (pan″kre-ah-to-lip′ās). A lipase occurring in the pancreatic juice.

pancreatolith (pan″kre-at′o-lith) [*pancreas* + Gr. *lithos* stone]. A pancreatic calculus.

pancreatolithectomy (pan-kre″ah-to-lĭ-thek′to-me) [*pancreatolith* + Gr. *ektomē* excision]. Excision of a calculus from the pancreas.

pancreatolithotomy (pan-kre″ah-to-lĭ-thot′o-me) [*pancreatolith* + Gr. *tomē* a cutting]. Incision of the pancreas for the removal of a calculus.

pancreatolysis (pan″kre-ah-tol′ĭ-sis). Pancreolysis.

pancreatolytic (pan″kre-ah-to-lit′ik). Pancreolytic.

pancreatomy (pan-kre-at′o-me). Pancreatotomy.

pancreatoncus (pan″kre-ah-ton′kus) [*pancreas* + Gr. *onkos* mass]. A tumor of the pancreas.

pancreatopathy (pan″kre-ah-top′ah-the) [*pancreas* + Gr. *pathos* disease]. Any disease of the pancreas.

pancreatotomy (pan″kre-ah-tot′o-me) [*pancreas* + Gr. *tomē* a cutting]. Incision of the pancreas.

pancreatotropic (pan-kre″ah-to-trop′ik) [*pancreas* + Gr. *tropē* a turning]. Having a special affinity for the pancreas.

pancreatropic (pan″kre-ah-trop′ik). Pancreatotropic.

pancreectomy (pan″kre-ek′to-me). Pancreatectomy.

pancreolithotomy (pan″kre-o-lĭ-thot′o-me). Pancreatolithotomy.

pancreolysis (pan″kre-ol′ĭ-sis) [*pancreas* + Gr. *lysis* dissolution]. Destruction of the pancreatic tissue.

pancreolytic (pan″kre-o-lit′ik). Pertaining to or producing pancreolysis.

pancreopathy (pan″kre-op′ah-the) [*pancreas* + Gr. *pathos* disease]. Any disease of the pancreas.

pancreoprivic (pan″kre-o-priv′ik). Deprived of a pancreas.

pancreotherapy (pan″kre-o-ther′ah-pe). Therapeutic use of pancreas tissue.

pancreotropic (pan″kre-o-trop′ik). Having an affinity for or an influence on the pancreas.

pancreozymin (pan′kre-o-zi″min). A hormone of the duodenal mucosa which stimulates the external secretory activity of the pancreas, especially its production of amylase.

pancytolysis (pan″si-tol′ĭ-sis) [*pan-* + *cyto-* + Gr. *lysis* dissolution]. Lysis of all types of blood cells. **splenogenic p.,** lysis of all types of blood cells by the spleen.

pancytopenia (pan″si-to-pe′ne-ah) [*pan-* + *-cyte* + Gr. *penia* poverty]. Deficiency of all the cell elements of the blood; aplastic anemia.

pancytosis (pan″si-to′sis) [*pan-* + *-cyte* + *-osis*]. Abnormal increase in all the cellular elements of the blood.

pandemic (pan-dem′ik) [*pan-* + Gr. *dēmos* people]. 1. Widely epidemic. 2. A widespread epidemic disease.

pandemicity (pan″dĕ-mis′ĭ-te). The state of being epidemic and widely spread.

Pander's islands, layer, nucleus (pan′derz) [Heinrich Christian von *Pander*, German anatomist, 1794–1865]. See under the nouns.

pandiculation (pan″dik-u-la′shun) [L. *pandiculari* to stretch one's self]. The act of stretching and yawning.

Pandy's reaction, test (pan′dēz) [Kalman *Pandy*, Hungarian neurologist, born 1868]. See under *tests*.

panel (pan′el). A list of names, a number of individuals participating in a specific discussion or activity, especially a list of names of the medical men who are willing to care for insured persons for a stipulated yearly fee under the system of medical insurance carried on by insurance groups under the supervision of the government in Great Britain, or the list of the insured persons assigned as clients to a physician under the British National Health Insurance Act. **personality p.,** a list of the aspects of a person's constitution with reference to his predisposition to particular types of diseases.

panelectroscope (pan″e-lek′tro-skōp). An instrument for examining by electric light the various organs of the body, as the stomach, rectum, urethra, etc.

panendoscope (pan-en′do-skōp). McCarthy's foroblique cystoscope which gives a wide view of the bladder.

panesthesia (pan″es-the′ze-ah) [*pan-* + Gr. *aisthēsis* perception]. The sum of the sensations experienced.

panesthetic (pan″es-thet′ik). Relating to panesthesia.

Paneth's cells (pah′nāts) [Josef *Paneth*, German physician, 1857–1890]. See under *cell*.

pang (pang). A sudden, piercing pain. **breast p.,** angina pectoris. **brow p.,** supraorbital neuralgia, or hemicrania.

pangen (pan′jen) [*pan-* + Gr. *gennan* to produce]. One of the hypothetical units of idioplasm. See *micelle*.

pangenesis (pan-jen′e-sis) [*pan-* + *genesis*]. The doctrine that in reproduction each cell of the parent body is represented by a particle; the hypothesis that all the units or cells of the body reside in the blood as gemmules, multiply by division, and throw off atoms which are transmitted to the offspring, accounting for the hereditary transmission of acquired mental habits and other phenomena of heredity; the theory implying that the whole organism, in the sense of every atom or unit, reproduces itself.

panglossia (pan-glos′e-ah) [Gr. *panglōssia*]. Abnormal or insane garrulity.

panhematopenia (pan-hem″ah-to-pe′ne-ah) [*pan-* + Gr. *haima* blood + *penia* poverty]. Abnormal deficiency of all the cellular elements of the blood. **primary splenic p.,** a form of hypersplenism, of unknown etiology, marked by indiscriminate elimination of all circulating elements of the blood, despite intensive compensatory panmyeloid hyperplasia, so that it actually simulates the condition produced by panmyeloid hypoplasia. Dramatic cure is often effected by splenectomy.

panhematopoietic (pan-hem″ah-to-poi-et′ik) [*pan-* + Gr. *haima* blood + *poietikos* capable of making]. Affecting all the blood-forming factors.

panhemocytophthisis (pan″he-mo-si-tof′thĭ-sis). Degeneration or defective formation of the various cells of the blood.

panhidrosis (pan″hid-ro′sis) [*pan-* + Gr. *hidrōs* sweat]. Perspiration of the whole surface of the body.

panhydrometer (pan″hi-drom′e-ter) [*pan-* + *hydrometer*]. An instrument for ascertaining the specific gravity of any liquid.

panhygrous (pan-hi′grus) [*pan-* + Gr. *hygros* moist]. Moist or damp in all parts.

panhyperemia (pan″hi-per-e′me-ah) [*pan-* + *hyperemia*]. General plethora.

panhypopituitarism (pan-hi″po-pĭ-tu′ĭ-tar-izm). Anterior pituitary insufficiency; Simmonds' disease.

panhysterectomy (pan″his-ter-ek′to-me) [*pan-* + Gr. *hystera* uterus + *ektomē* excision]. Complete extirpation of the uterus and cervix.

panhystero-oophorectomy (pan-his″ter-o-o″-of-o-rek′to-me). Excision of the body of the uterus, cervix, and ovary.

panhysterosalpingectomy (pan-his″ter-o-sal″-pin-jek′to-me). Excision of the body of the uterus, cervix, and uterine tube.

panhysterosalpingo-oophorectomy (pan-his″ter-o-sal″ping-go-o″of-o-rek′to-me). Excision of the uterus, cervix, uterine tube, and ovary.

panic (pan′ik). An extreme and unreasoning fear and anxiety.

panidrosis (pan″id-ro′sis). Panhidrosis.

panighao (pan″e-ga′o). Ground itch.

panimmunity (pan″ĭ-mu′nĭ-te) [*pan-* + *immunity*]. Immunity to several infections. **anachoretic p.** See under *anachoresis*.

panis (pa′nis) [L.]. Bread.

panivorous (pan-iv′o-rus) [L. *panis* bread + *vorare* to devour]. Subsisting or living on bread.

Panizza's plexus (pan-id′zaz) [Bartolomeo *Panizza*, Professor of anatomy at Pavia, 1785–1867]. See under *plexus*.

panki (pan′ke). Keratodermia plantare sulcatum.

panleukopenia (pan″lu-ko-pe′ne-ah). A virus disease of cats, characterized by leukopenia and lymphocytosis and marked by inactivity, refusal of food, diarrhea, and vomiting. Called also *feline agranulocytosis*, *feline enteritis*, *cat distemper*, and *cat plague*.

panmeristic (pan″mer-is′tik) [*pan-* + Gr. *meros* part]. Pertaining to the protoplasm of ova, made up of independent units or pangens.

panmixia (pan-mik′se-ah) [*pan-* + Gr. *mignynai* to mix]. Random mating.

panmycin (pan-mi′sin). Trade mark for preparations of tetracycline.

panmyeloid (pan-mi′ĕ-loid). Pertaining to all the elements of the bone marrow.

panmyelopathia (pan″mi-ĕ-lo-path′e-ah). Panmyelopathy.

panmyelopathy (pan″mi-ĕ-lop′ah-the) [*pan-* + Gr. *myelos* marrow + *pathos* disease]. A pathologic condition of all the elements of the bone marrow.

panmyelophthisis (pan-mi″ĕ-lof′thĭ-sis) [*pan-* + Gr. *myelos* marrow + *phthisis* wasting]. General aplasia of the bone marrow.

panmyelosis (pan″mi-ĕ-lo′sis) [*pan-* + Gr. *myelos* marrow + *-osis*]. Proliferation of all the elements of the bone marrow.

panneuritis (pan″nu-ri′tis) [*pan-* + Gr. *neuron* nerve + *-itis*]. Multiple or general neuritis. **p. epidem′ica,** beriberi.

panniculalgia (pah-nik″u-lal′je-ah). Adiposalgia.

panniculitis (pah-nik″u-li′tis). Inflammation of the panniculus adiposus. **nodular nonsuppurative p.,** a disease marked by the formation of painful nodules in the subcutaneous fatty tissue: called also *Weber-Christian disease*.

panniculus (pah-nik′u-lus), pl. *pannic′uli* [L., dim. of *pannus* cloth]. A layer of membrane. **p. adipo′sus** [N A, B N A], those parts of the subcutaneous tissue which contain especially large amounts of fat. **p. carno′sus,** a thin muscular layer within the superficial fascia of animals with a hairy coat; in man it is represented mainly by the platysma myoides.

pannus (pan′nus) [L. "a piece of cloth"]. 1. Superficial vascularization of the cornea with infiltration of granulation tissue. 2. An inflammatory exudate overlying the lining layer of synovial cells on the inside of a joint, usually occurring in patients with rheumatoid arthritis or related articular rheumatism, and sometimes resulting in fibrous ankylosis of the joint. **allergic p.,** pannus of the cornea as a result of allergy. **p. carate′us,** pinta. **p. carno′sus, p. cras′sus,** pannus of the cornea characterized by extremely dense opacity. **p. degenerati′vus,** a connective-tissue growth between the epithelium of the cornea and Bowman's membrane. **phlyctenular p.,** pannus associated with phlyctenular keratitis, the vascularization running all the way around the periphery of the limbus toward the center. **p. sic′cus,** pannus of the cornea associated with dryness of the cornea and conjunctiva. **p. ten′uis,** pannus of the cornea in which the opacity is very slight. **p. trachomato′sus,** pannus occurring secondarily to trachoma, the small fine branching vessels always appearing at the upper limbus and running down under the epithelium into the cornea.

panodic (pah-nod′ik). Panthodic.

panophobia (pan″o-fo′be-ah). Pantophobia.

panophthalmia (pan″of-thal′me-ah). Panophthalmitis.

panophthalmitis (pan″of-thal-mi′tis) [*pan-* + Gr. *ophthalmos* eye + *-itis*]. Inflammation of all the structures or tissues of the eye.

panoptic (pan-op′tik) [*pan-* + Gr. *optikos* of or for vision]. Rendering everything visible: said of a stain which differentiates all the tissues of a specimen. See *Giemsa's stain*, under *stain*.

panoptosis (pan″op-to′sis) [*pan-* + Gr. *ptōsis* falling]. General ptosis of the abdominal organs.

panosteitis (pan″os-te-i′tis) [*pan-* + Gr. *osteon* bone + *-itis*]. Inflammation of every part of a bone.

panostitis (pan″os-ti′tis). Panosteitis.

panotitis (pan″o-ti′tis) [*pan-* + Gr. *ous* ear + *-itis*]. An inflammation of all the parts or structures of the ear.

panparnit (pan-par′nit). Trade mark for a preparation of caramiphen hydrochloride.

panphobia (pan-fo′be-ah). Pantophobia.

panplegia (pan-ple′je-ah). Pamplegia.

panproctocolectomy (pan-prok″to-ko-lek′to-me). Excision of the entire rectum and colon, with creation of an ileal stoma for elimination of the feces.

Pansch's fissure (pansh′ez) [Adolf *Pansch*, German anatomist, 1841–1887]. See under *fissure*.

pansclerosis (pan″skle-ro′sis) [*pan-* + Gr. *sklērōsis* hardening]. Complete induration of a part or organ.

panseptum (pan-sep′tum). The entire nasal septum, including bony and cartilaginous parts.

pansinuitis (pan″si-nu-i′tis). Pansinusitis.

pansinusectomy (pan″si-nus-ek′to-me). Excision of the diseased membrane of all of the paranasal sinuses of one side.

pansinusitis (pan″si-nus-i′tis) [*pan-* + *sinus* + *-itis*]. Inflammation involving all of the paranasal sinuses.

panspermatism (pan-sper′mah-tizm). Panspermia.

panspermia (pan-sper′me-ah) [*pan-* + Gr. *sperma* seed + *-ia*]. 1. The doctrine that disease germs and bacteria are everywhere present. 2. Biogenesis.

pansphygmograph (pan-sfig′mo-graf) [*pan-* + Gr. *sphygmos* pulse + *graphein* to record]. A device for recording cardiac, pulse, and chest movements at the same time.

pansporoblast (pan-spo′ro-blast) [*pan-* + Gr. *sporos* spore + *blastos* germ]. A mother cell of certain sporozoa, giving rise to two or more sporoblasts, from each of which a single spore is formed.

Panstrongylus (pan-stron′jĭ-lus). A genus of cone-nosed bugs of the family Reduviidae, species of which are vectors of Trypanosoma. **P. genicula′tus,** a species from Panama and northern South America which is a vector of *Trypanosoma cruzi.* **P. infes′tans,** a species which is an important vector of *Trypanosoma cruzi.* **P. megis′tus,** a species in Brazil which is an important vector of *Trypanosoma cruzi.* It frequently bites the face and so is called barbiero by the natives. It was formerly called *Triatoma megista.*

Panstrongylus megistus (female).

pant-. See *panto-.*

pantachromatic (pan″tah-kro-mat′ik) [*pant-* + *achromatic*]. Entirely achromatic.

pantalgia (pan-tal′je-ah) [*pant-* + *-algia*]. Pain over the whole body.

pantamorphia (pan″tah-mor′fe-ah) [*pant-* + Gr. *amorphia* shapelessness]. Complete or general deformity.

pantamorphic (pan″tah-mor′fik). Formless.

pantanencephalia (pan″tan-en″se-fa′le-ah) [*pant-* + *an* neg. + Gr. *enkephalos* brain + *-ia*]. Complete absence of the brain in a fetal monster.

pantankyloblepharon (pan-tang″kĭ-lo-blef′ah-ron) [*pant-* + Gr. *ankylē* noose + *blepharon* lid]. General adhesion of the eyelids to the eyeball and to each other.

pantaphobia (pan″tah-fo′be-ah) [*pant-* + Gr. *aphobia* fearlessness]. Absence of fear.

pantatrophia (pan″tah-tro′fe-ah) [*pant-* + Gr. *atrophia* atrophy]. General or complete malnutrition.

pantatrophy (pan-tat′ro-fe). Pantatrophia.

pantherapist (pan-ther′ah-pist) [*pan-* + Gr. *therapeia* treatment]. A practitioner who is ready to draw his information from any and every source.

panthodic (pan-thod′ik) [*pan-* + Gr. *hodos* way]. Radiating in every direction: said of nervous impulses.

panting (pant′ing). Swift and labored breathing; anhelation.

panto-, pant- [Gr. *pas, pantos* all]. Combining form meaning all, the whole.

pantochromism (pan″to-kro′mizm) [*panto-* + Gr. *chrōma* color]. The phenomenon of existing in two or more differently colored forms.

pantogamy (pan-tog′ah-me) [*panto-* + Gr. *gamos* marriage]. Promiscuous sexual intercourse.

pantograph (pan′to-graf) [*panto-* + Gr. *graphein* to write]. An instrument for recording graphically the contour of the chest.

pantomorphia (pan″to-mor′fe-ah) [*panto-* + Gr. *morphē* form + *-ia*]. General or perfect symmetry.

pantomorphic (pan″to-mor′fik). Able to assume any shape.

pantophobia (pan″to-fo′be-ah) [*panto-* + *phobia*]. Fear of everything; a vague morbid dread of some unknown evil.

pantophobic (pan″to-fo′bik). Characterized by pantophobia.

pantoscopic (pan″to-skop′ik) [*panto-* + Gr. *skopein* to examine]. Adapted to view both near and distant objects: a term applied to bifocal spectacles.

pantosomatous (pan″to-som′ah-tus) [*panto-* + Gr. *soma* body]. Relating to the entire body.

pantothen (pan′to-then). Pantothenic acid.

pantothenate (pan-to′then-āt). A salt of pantothenic acid.

pantothermia (pan″to-ther′me-ah) [*panto-* + Gr. *thermē* heat + *-ia*]. A condition marked by variations of bodily temperature without apparent cause.

pantotropic (pan″to-trop′ik). Pantropic.

pantropic (pan-trop′ik) [*pan-* + Gr. *tropos* a turning]. Having an affinity for many tissues; capable of attacking derivatives of any of the three embryonic layers.

panturbinate (pan-ter′bĭ-nāt). The entire structure of a nasal concha, including bone and soft tissue.

Panum's casein (pah′no͝omz) [Peter Ludwig *Panum*, Danish physiologist, 1820–1885]. Serum globulin.

panus (pa′nus) [L. "swelling"]. A lymphatic gland inflamed but not suppurating.

panzootic (pan″zo-ot′ik) [*pan-* + Gr. *zōon* animal]. Occurring pandemically among animals.

pao-ferro (pah″o-fer′o). The ironwood tree of Brazil. The inner bark is said to have antidiabetic properties.

pap (pap). Any soft food, as bread soaked in milk.

papain (pah′pa-in). A crystalline proteolytic enzyme from the latex of the papaw, *Carica papaya*, which catalyzes the hydrolysis of proteins, proteoses, and peptones to polysaccharides and amino acids. Used chiefly in medicine as a protein digestant.

papainase (pap-a′in-ās). Catheptic enzyme.

Papanicolaou's stain (pap″ah-nik″o-la′o͞oz) [George N. *Papanicolaou*, Greek physician, anatomist, and cytologist in the United States, 1883–1962]. See *table of stains and staining methods.*

papaverine (pah-pav′er-in). An alkaloid, 6,7-dimethoxy-1-veratrylisoquinoline, obtained from opium or prepared synthetically. Used as a smooth muscle relaxant.

papaw (pah-paw′). 1. A large herbaceous plant, *Carica papaya* of Southern United States; also its digestant and anthelmintic fruit. The fruit contains papain and papayotin. 2. Pawpaw; the tree *Asimina triloba*, which has edible fruit.

papaya (pah-pa′yah). The juice of the papaw fruit.

papayotin (pap″a-yo′tin). A digestive ferment from *Carica papaya:* more active than papain.

paper (pa′per). A substance occurring in thin sheets, prepared from wood, rags, or other fibrous substance which has first been reduced to a pulp. **alkanin p.,** filter paper dipped in an alcoholic solution of alkanin: alkalis turn it blue; acids, red. **amboceptor p.,** filter paper saturated with amboceptor serum: used in the Noguchi test for syphilis. **aniline acetate p.,** filter paper dipped into a mixture of aniline, water, and glacial acetic acid, and then dried. **antigen p.,** filter paper saturated with antigen solution: used in the Noguchi test for syphilis. **articulating p.,** carbon paper to be placed between the upper and lower teeth and bitten on, to record the contact relationships of the teeth. **asthma p.,** niter p. **azolitmin p.,** filter paper saturated with a solution of azolitmin. Acids turn it from purple to bright red, alkalis turn it blue. **bibulous p.,** a paper which absorbs water readily. **biuret p.,** filter paper previously dipped in Gies' biuret reagent, dried, and cut into strips. **blue litmus p.** See *litmus p.* **Congo red p.,** wet filter paper with a

0.2 per cent solution of Congo red in water, dry, and cut in strips. **filter p.,** a porous, unsized paper used as a filter. **lacmoid p.,** blotting paper impregnated with lacmoid: used in testing for alkalinity or acidity. **litmus p.,** bibulous paper impregnated with a solution of litmus, dried, and cut into strips. If slightly alkaline the paper is blue, and is used as a test for acids, which turn it red; if slightly acid it is red and alkalis turn it blue. **mustard p.,** charta sinapis. **niter p.,** paper impregnated with potassium nitrate, ignited and used as a moxa or by inhalation in asthma. Called also *saltpeter p.* **occluding p.,** articulating p. **potassium nitrate p.,** niter p. **red litmus p.** See *litmus p.* **saltpeter p.,** niter p. **test p.,** paper that is impregnated with litmus or other indicator. **turmeric p.,** paper dyed yellow with turmeric: alkalis turn it brown. **wax p.,** paper treated with beeswax.

papescent (pah-pes′ent). Having the consistence of pap.

papilla (pah-pil′lah), pl. *papil′lae* [L.]. A small, nipple-shaped projection or elevation; used in anatomical nomenclature as a general term to designate such a structure. **acoustic p.,** organum spirale. **arcuate papillae of tongue,** papillae filiformes. **Bergmeister's p.,** a small mass of neuroglia cells in the center of the embryonic optic disk, surrounding the bulb of the hyaloid artery. **bile p.,** p. duodeni major. **calciform papillae, capitate papillae,** papillae vallatae. **circumvallate papillae,** papillae vallatae. **clavate papillae,** papillae fungiformes. **papil′lae con′icae** [N A, B N A], **conical papillae,** sparsely scattered large elevations on the tongue surface, often considered as a modified type of filiform papillae. **conical papillae of tongue, of Soemmering,** papillae filiformes. **conoid papillae of tongue,** papillae conicae. **papil′lae co′rii** [N A, B N A], **papillae of corium,** small conical masses arranged in rows of double ridges, projecting from the corium up into grooves on the lower surface of the dermis. **corolliform papillae of tongue,** papillae filiformes. **dental p., dentinal p.,** p. dentis. **p. den′tis** [N A, B N A], the small mass of condensed mesenchyme capped by each of the enamel organs. **dermal papillae,** papillae corii. **duodenal p., major,** p. duodeni major. **duodenal p., minor,** p. duodeni minor. **p. duode′ni ma′jor** [N A], a small elevation at the site of the opening of the conjoined common bile duct and the pancreatic duct on the wall of the duodenum. Called also *p. duodeni* [*Santorini*] [B N A], and *major duodenal p.* See also *p. duodeni minor.* **p. duode′ni mi′nor** [N A], a small elevation at the site of the opening of the accessory pancreatic duct on the wall of the duodenum. Called also *minor duodenal p.* **p. duode′ni [Santori′ni]** [B N A], p. duodeni major. **filiform papillae, papil′lae filifor′mes** [N A, B N A], threadlike elevations that cover most of the tongue surface. **papil′lae folia′tae** [N A, B N A], **foliate papillae,** parallel mucosal folds on the margins of the tongue at the junction of its body and root. **fungiform papillae, papil′lae fungifor′mes** [N A, B N A], knoblike projections on the tongue, scattered singly among the filiform papillae. **gingival p.,** the triangular pad of gingiva filling the space between the proximal surfaces of two adjacent teeth. **gustatory papillae,** papillae linguales. **hair p.,** p. pili. **p. inci′siva** [N A, B N A], **incisive p.,** a rounded projection at the anterior end of the raphe of the palate. **interdental p.,** gingival p. **lacrimal p., p. lacrima′lis** [N A], a papilla in the conjunctiva near the medial angle of the eye. **papil′lae lacrima′les** [B N A]. See *p. lacrimalis.* **lenticular papillae, papil′lae lenticula′res** [B N A], a series of papillae of the tongue resembling, but less elevated than, the fungiform papillae. Omitted in N A. **lingual papillae, papil′lae lingua′les** [N A, B N A], the filiform, fungiform, vallate, foliate, and conical papillae of the tongue. **p. mam′mae** [N A, B N A], **mammary p.,** the pigmented projection on the anterior surface of the mammary gland, surrounded by the areola. The lactiferous ducts open onto it. Called also *nipple of breast.* **medial papillae of tongue,** papillae fungiformes. **p. ner′vi op′tici** [B N A], discus nervi optici. **nervous papillae,** the papillae of the skin enclosing special nerve terminations. Cf. *vascular papillae.* **obtuse papillae of tongue,** papillae fungiformes. **optic p.,** discus nervi optici. **palatine p.,** p. incisiva. **parotid p., p. parotide′a** [N A], the small papilla marking the orifice of the parotid duct in the mucous membrane of the cheek. **p. pi′li** [N A, B N A], the mass within the corium upon which each hair bulb rests. Called also *hair p.* **renal papillae, papil′lae rena′les** [N A, B N A], the blunted apices of the renal pyramids, which project into the renal sinus. **p. of Santorini,** p. duodeni major. **simple papillae of tongue,** papillae filiformes. **skin papillae,** papillae corii. **small papillae of tongue,** papillae filiformes. **p. spira′lis,** organum spirale. **sublingual p.,** caruncula sublingualis. **tactile papillae,** corpuscula tactus. **urethral p.,** a slight elevation in the vestibule of the vagina on which is situated the external orifice of the urethra. **papil′lae valla′tae** [N A, B N A], **vallate papillae,** the largest papillae of the tongue, 8 to 12 in number, arranged in the form of a V in front of the sulcus terminalis of the tongue. **vascular papillae,** the papillae of the corium which contain loops of blood vessels. Cf. *nervous papillae.* **p. of Vater,** p. duodeni major. **villous papillae of tongue,** papillae filiformes.

papillae (pah-pil′e) [L.]. Plural of *papilla.*

papillary (pap′ĭ-ler″e). Pertaining to or resembling a papilla, or nipple.

papillate (pap′ĭ-lāt). Marked by nipple-like elevations.

papillectomy (pap″ĭ-lek′to-me) [*papilla* + Gr. *ektomē* excision]. Excision of a papilla; especially removal of one or more engorged papillae from a kidney for the cure of hematuria.

papilledema (pap″ĭ-lĕ-de′mah). Edema of the optic papilla.

papilliferous (pap″ĭ-lif′er-us) [*papilla* + L. *ferre* to bear]. Bearing papillae.

papilliform (pah-pil′ĭ-form) [*papilla* + L. *forma* shape]. Shaped like a papilla.

papillitis (pap″ĭ-li′tis) [*papilla* + *-itis*]. Inflammation of a papilla.

papillo-adenocystoma (pah-pil″o-ad″e-no-sis-to′mah). Papilloma blended with adenoma and cystoma.

papillocarcinoma (pah-pil″o-kar″sĭ-no′mah). 1. A carcinoma in which there are papillary excrescences. 2. A malignant papilloma.

papilloma (pap″ĭ-lo′mah) [*papilla* + *-oma*]. A branching or lobulated benign tumor derived from epithelium. **p. acumina′tum,** condyloma. **p. diffu′sum,** papillomas occurring in numbers on the legs and buttocks. **p. du′rum,** hard p. **hard p.,** one growing from the squamous epithelium. **Hopmann's p.,** Hopmann's polyp. **p. inguina′le trop′icum,** a disease of Colombia marked by the formation of filiform pinkish vegetations in the inguinal region; called also *acanthoma tropicum.* **intracanalicular p.,** a warty, nonmalignant growth within the substance of certain glands, especially of the breast. **intracystic p.,** a papilloma formed within a cystic adenoma. **p. linea′re,** linear ichthyosis. **p. mol′le,** soft p. **p. neuropath′icum, p. neurot′icum,** a papillomatous growth or tumor along the course of a nerve. **rabbit p.,** a virus disease of rabbits marked by the formation of horny warts. **rabbit oral p.,** a virus disease of wild rabbits, characterized by the appearance of nodules on the lower surface of the tongue. **Shope p.,** rabbit p. **soft p.,** one developed from the columnar epithelium. **p. vene'reum,** condyloma. **villous p.** 1. A persistent chorionic villus, usually found in the bladder, sometimes in a renal pelvis. 2. A villous outgrowth from the choroid plexus in a lateral ventricle of the brain. 3. A mammary tumor liable to be confused with villous cancer.

papillomatosis (pap″ĭ-lo″mah-to'sis). The development of a crop of papillomas.

papillomatous (pap″ĭ-lo'mah-tus). Of the nature of a papilloma.

papilloretinitis (pah-pil″o-ret″ĭ-ni'tis). Inflammation of the optic papilla extending to the optic disk and retina.

papillosarcoma (pah-pil″o-sar-ko'mah). A malignant papilloma.

papillosphincterotomy (pap″il-lo-sfingk″ter-ot'o-me). Partial incision of the sphincter of the major duodenal papilla, with preservation of the sphincters of the common bile duct and the pancreatic duct.

Papin's digester (pah-paz') [Denis *Papin,* French physicist, 1647–1714]. An apparatus for subjecting substances to the action of water at a heat greater than the boiling point.

papoid (pap'oid). An enzyme and digestant from papaw fruit. See *papaw.*

Pappenheim's stain (pahp'en-hīmz) [Artur *Pappenheim,* German physician, 1870–1917]. See *stains, table of.*

pappose (pap'pōs). Having a downy surface.

pappus (pap'pus) [L.; Gr. *pappos*]. 1. The first downy growth of the beard. 2. The lanugo.

paprika (pap-re'kah). The fruit of *Capsicum annuum* and a condiment prepared from it: it is rich in vitamin C.

papular (pap'u-lar) [L. *papularis*]. Consisting of, characterized by, or pertaining to a papule.

papulation (pap″u-la'shun). The production of papules.

papule (pap'ūl) [L. *papula*]. A small circumscribed, solid elevation of the skin. **Celsus' p's,** lichen agrius. **dry p.,** the papule of chancre. **moist p., mucous p.,** a syphilitic condyloma. **split p's,** fissured papular syphilides sometimes seen at the corners of the mouth.

papuliferous (pap″u-lif'er-us) [*papule* + L. *ferre* to bear]. Having or covered with papules.

papulo-erythematous (pap″u-lo-er″e-them'ah-tus). Marked by papules on an erythematous surface.

papuloid (pap'u-loid). Resembling a papule.

papulopustular (pap″u-lo-pus'tu-lar). Characterized by the presence of papules and pustules.

papulopustule (pap″u-lo-pus'tūl). A papule which is developing into a pustule.

papulosquamous (pap″u-lo-skwa'mus). Both papular and scaly.

papulovesicular (pap″u-lo-ve-sik'u-lar). Characterized by the presence of papules and vesicles.

papyraceous (pap″ĭ-ra'shus) [L. *papyraceus*]. Like paper; chartaceous.

Paquelin's cautery (pah″kĕ-lanz') [Claude André *Paquelin,* French physician, 1836–1905]. See under *cautery.*

par (par) [L.]. Pair.

Para (par'ah) [L. *parere* to bring forth, to bear]. A woman who has produced living young. Used with numerals to designate the number of pregnancies that have resulted in the birth of viable offspring, as *Para 0* (none—nullipara), *Para 1* (one—unipara), *Para 2* (two—bipara), *Para 3* (three—tripara), *Para 4* (four—quadripara). The number is not indicative of the number of offspring produced in event of a multiple birth.

para- (par'ah) [Gr. *para* beyond]. A prefix meaning beside, beyond, accessory to, apart from, against, etc. In chemistry the prefix indicates the substitution in a derivative of the benzol ring of two atoms linked to opposite carbon atoms in the ring. The abbreviation is *p-.*

para-aceratosis (par″ah-a″ser-ah-to'sis). Parakeratosis.

para-actinomycosis (par″ah-ak″tĭ-no-mi-ko″-sis). Pseudoactinomycosis.

para-agglutinin (par″ah-ah-gloo'tĭ-nin). A partial agglutinin.

para-amidophenetol (par″ah-am″ĭ-do-fen'e-tol). A substance used in preparing pyrantin, $NH_2.C_6H_4.OC_2H_5$.

para-amino-benzene-sulfonamide. Sulfanilamide.

para-aminobenzoate (par″ah-am″ĭ-no-ben'zo-āt). A salt of para-aminobenzoic acid.

para-aminohippurate (par″ah-am″ĭ-no-hip'u-rāt). A salt of para-aminohippuric acid.

para-analgesia (par″ah-an″al-je'ze-ah). Analgesia of the lower part of the body, including the lower limbs.

para-anesthesia (par″ah-an″es-the'ze-ah). Anesthesia of the lower part of the body and of the legs.

para-appendicitis (par″ah-ah-pen″dĭ-si'tis). Inflammation of tissues adjacent to the vermiform appendix.

parabacillus (par″ah-bah-sil'us). See *parabacteria.*

parabacteria (par″ah-bak-te're-ah). Bacteria which have been changed in their immune reactions by growing in contact with other organisms.

parabion (par-ab'e-on). Parabiont.

parabiont (par-ab'e-ont) [*para-* + Gr. *bioun* to live]. One of two or more organisms living in a condition of parabiosis.

parabiosis (par″ah-bi-o'sis) [*para-* + Gr. *biōsis* living]. 1. The union of two individuals, as of joined twins, or by surgical operation. 2. Temporary suppression of conductivity and excitability in a nerve. **dialytic p.,** the circulation of the blood of two animals through a dialyzer, separated by a membrane which permits the removal of harmful material from the recipient's blood and the contribution of essential factors from the donor's blood. **vascular p.,** the crossing of the circulation between two individuals by anastomosis of blood vessels.

parabiotic (par″ah-bi-ot'ik). Pertaining to or characterized by parabiosis.

parablast (par'ah-blast) [*para-* + Gr. *blastos* germ]. That part of the mesoblast from which the blood vessels, lymphatics, etc., are developed.

parablastic (par″ah-blas'tik). Pertaining to the parablast.

parablastoma (par″ah-blas-to'mah) [*parablast* + *-oma*]. Any tumor which is made up of parablastic tissue.

parablepsia (par-ah-blep'se-ah) [*para-* + Gr. *blepsis* vision + *-ia*]. False or perverted vision.

parabolus (pah-rab'o-lus), pl. *parab'oli* [Gr. *parabolos* venturesome]. In medieval medicine, an agent of the church who sought out the indigent sick for care and treatment.

parabulia (par″ah-bu'le-ah) [*para-* + Gr. *boulē* will + *-ia*]. Perversion of the will.

paracanthoma (par″ah-kan-tho'mah). Paracanthosis.

paracanthosis (par″ah-kan-tho'sis) [*para-* + Gr. *akantha* prickle + *-osis*]. A skin cancer or other perversion of growth in the prickle layer of the skin.

paracarbinoxamine (par″ah-kar″bin-ok'sah-min). Carbinoxamine.

paracardiac (par″ah-kar'de-ak). Beside the heart.

paracarmine (par″ah-kar'min). A staining medium consisting of carminic acid, calcium chloride, and alcohol.

paracasein (par″ah-ka'se-in). The chemical product of the action of rennin on casein.

paracele (par'ah-sēl). Paracoele.

paracellulose (par″ah-sel′u-lōs). A kind of cellulose found in the pith of plants.

paracelsian (par″ah-sel′se-an). Pertaining to or named for Paracelsus.

Paracelsus (par-ah-sel′sus) [Philippus Aureolus Theophrastus Bombastus von Hohenheim] (1493–1541). A famous Swiss physician and alchemist; a controversial figure whose alchemical researches led to the introduction of such substances as lead, sulfur, iron, and arsenic into pharmaceutical chemistry. Although he was far ahead of his time in many of his observations (e.g., on metabolic and on occupational diseases), much of his thinking was made obscure by his mystic religiosity.

paracenesthesia (par″ah-se″nes-the′ze-ah) [*para-* + *cenesthesia*]. Any abnormality of the general sense of well being. Cf. *cenesthopathia.*

paracentesis (par″ah-sen-te′sis) [*para-* + Gr. *kentēsis* puncture]. Surgical puncture of a cavity for the aspiration of fluid. **abdominal p., p. abdom′inis,** paracentesis of the abdominal cavity. **p. bul′bi,** puncture of the eyeball. **p. cap′itis,** puncture of the cranium for the removal of effusion in hydrocephalus. **p. cor′dis,** puncture of the heart. **p. oc′uli,** puncture of the eyeball. **p. pericar′dii,** puncture of the pericardial sac. **p. pulmo′nis,** puncture of the lung. **p. thora′cis,** thoracocentesis. **p. tu′nicae vagina′lis,** puncture of the tunica vaginalis. **p. tym′pani,** incision of the tympanic membrane for drainage or irrigation. **p. vesi′cae,** puncture of the bladder wall.

paracentetic (par″ah-sen-tet′ik). Pertaining to or accomplished by paracentesis.

paracentral (par″ah-sen′tral). Near a center.

paracephalus (par″ah-sef′ah-lus) [*para-* + Gr. *kephalē* head]. A fetus with a rudimentary or misshapen head, imperfect sense organs, and defective trunk or limbs.

paracerebellar (par″ah-ser″e-bel′ar). Pertaining to the lateral part of the cerebellum.

paracetaldehyde (par-as″et-al′de-hīd). Paraldehyde.

paracetamol (par-as″et-am′ol). Acetaminophen.

parachloralose (par″ah-klo′ral-ōs). A substance, $C_8H_{12}Cl_3O_6$, in iridescent plates, formed by a combination of dextrose and chloral.

parachloramine (par″ah-klōr′ah-men). Meclizine.

parachlormetaxylenol (par″ah-klor-met″ah-zi′len-ol). A compound, C_8H_9OCl, used in bacterial skin diseases.

parachlorophenol (par″ah-klo″ro-fe′nol). A substance with an unpleasant odor, C_6H_5ClO, obtained by the chlorination of phenol: used as a topical antibacterial agent. **camphorated p.,** a preparation of parachlorophenol and camphor: used in dentistry as a local antibacterial agent.

paracholera (par″ah-kol′er-ah). A disease resembling Asiatic cholera, but caused by an organism other than the *Vibrio cholerae.*

paracholesterin (par″ah-ko-les′ter-in). A form of cholesterin occurring in vegetable tissue.

paracholia (par″ah-ko′le-ah) [*para-* + Gr. *cholē* bile + *-ia*]. Disordered bile secretion.

parachordal (par″ah-kor′dal) [*para-* + Gr. *chordē* cord]. Situated beside the notochord. See *parachordal cartilage,* under *cartilage.*

Parachordodes (par″ah-kor-do′dēz). A genus of Gordiacea. A few cases of infection with this worm have been reported. *P. pustilo′sus,* from Italy. *P. tolosa′nus,* from France and from Italy. *P. viola′ceus,* from Italy, one specimen taken from the throat.

parachroia (par″ah-kroi′ah) [*para-* + Gr. *chroia* color]. Abnormality of coloration.

parachroma (par″ah-kro′mah) [*para-* + Gr. *chrōma* color]. Change in the color of the skin; abnormal coloration of the skin.

parachromatin (par″ah-kro′mah-tin). A chromatophil substance contained in the finer part of the nuclear substance, as in the nucleoplasm of the spindle in karyokinesis.

parachromatism (par″ah-kro′mah-tizm) [*para-* + Gr. *chrōma* color]. Color blindness; incorrect perception of colors.

parachromatopsia (par″ah-kro″mah-top′se-ah) [*para-* + Gr. *chrōma* color + *opsis* vision + *-ia*]. Color blindness.

parachromatosis (par″ah-kro″mah-to′sis). Parachroma.

parachrome (par′ah-krōm). Parachromophoric.

parachromophore (par″ah-kro′mo-fōr) [*para-* + Gr. *chrōma* color + *phoros* bearing]. A bacterium which secretes a pigment and retains it within its own body.

parachromophoric (par″ah-kro″mo-for′ik) [*para-* + *chromophoric*]. Pervertedly chromophoric; secreting coloring matter, but retaining it in the organism.

parachymosin (par″ah-ki-mo′sin) [*para-* + *chymosin*]. The variety of lab ferment found in the human stomach and in that of the pig.

paracinesia (par″ah-si-ne′se-ah). Parakinesia.

paracinesis (par″ah-si-ne′sis). Parakinesia.

paracmastic (par″ak-mas′tik). Pertaining to the paracme.

paracme (par-ak′me) [*para-* + Gr. *akmē* point]. The stage of decline or remission.

paracnemis, paracnemidion (par″ak-ne′mis, par″ak-ne-mid′e-on) [*para-* + Gr. *knēmē* shin]. The fibula.

Paracoccidioides brasiliensis (par″ah-kok-sid″e-oi′dēz brah-sil″e-en′sis). *Blastomyces brasiliensis.*

paracoccidioidomycosis (par″ah-kok-sid″e-oi″do-mi-ko′sis). Infection caused by *Blastomyces* (*Paracoccidioides*) *brasiliensis.* See *South American blastomycosis,* under *blastomycosis.*

paracoele (par″ah-sēl) [*para-* + Gr. *koilos* hollow]. A lateral ventricle of the brain.

paracolitis (par″ah-ko-li′tis). Inflammation of the outer coat of the colon.

Paracolobactrum (par″ah-ko″lo-bak′trum). A genus of microorganisms of the tribe Escherichieae, family Enterobacteriaceae, order Eubacteriales, made up of short rods, characterized by a delayed (3 to 14 days) fermentation of lactose, and which are found in the intestinal tracts of animals, including man, and in surface waters, soil, and grains. It includes four species, *P. aerogenoi′des, P. arizo′nae, P. colifor′me,* and *P. interme′dium.*

paracolpitis (par″ah-kol-pi′tis) [*para-* + Gr. *kolpos* vagina + *-itis*]. Inflammation of the tissues around the vagina.

paracolpium (par″ah-kol′pe-um) [*para-* + Gr. *kolpos* vagina]. The connective and other tissues that surround the vagina.

paracone (par′ah-kōn) [*para-* + Gr. *kōnos* cone]. The mesiobuccal cusp of any upper molar.

paraconid (par″ah-ko′nid). The mesiobuccal cusp of a lower molar.

paracort (par′ah-kort). Trade mark for a preparation of prednisone.

paracortol (par″ah-kor′tol). Trade mark for a preparation of prednisolone.

paracousis (par″ah-koo′sis). Paracusis.

paracoxalgia (par″ah-kok-sal′je-ah). A condition marked by pain simulating that of coxitis.

paracresol (par″ah-kre′sol). 1. One of the three isomeric forms or recognized varieties of cresol. See *cresol.* 2. A patented soluble and nearly odorless preparation of cresol: disinfectant.

paracrisis (par-ak′rĭ-sis) [*para-* + Gr. *krinein* to secrete]. Any disorder of the secretions.

paracrystals (par″ah-kris′tals). Imperfect crystals; such as the "crystals" of tobacco mosaic virus which have only two dimensional symmetry instead of three dimensional.

paracusia (par-ah-ku′se-ah). Paracusis. **p.**

a′cris, intense and incessant acuity of hearing. **p. duplica′ta,** diplacusis. **p. lo′ci,** inability to locate correctly the origin of sounds. **p. willisia′na,** paracusis of Willis.

paracusis (par″ah-ku′sis). Any perversion of the sense of hearing. **p. of Willis,** ability to hear best in a loud din (Thomas Willis, 1672).

paracyesis (par″ah-si-e′sis) [*para-* + Gr. *kyēsis* *pregnancy*]. Extra-uterine pregnancy.

paracystic (par″ah-sis′tik) [*para-* + Gr. *kystis* bladder]. Situated near the bladder.

paracystitis (par″ah-sis-ti′tis) [*para-* + Gr. *kystis* bladder + *-itis*]. Inflammation of the tissues around the bladder.

paracystium (par″ah-sis′te-um) [*para-* + Gr. *kystis* bladder]. The connective and other tissues around the bladder.

paracytic (par″ah-sit′ik) [*para-* + *-cyte*]. Noting cell elements present in the blood or other part of the organism, but enthetic or not normal to it.

paradenitis (par″ad-e-ni′tis) [*para-* + Gr. *adēn* gland + *-itis*]. Inflammation of the tissues around a gland.

paradental (par″ah-den′tal). 1. Having some connection with or relation to the science or practice of dentistry. 2. Periodontal.

paradentitis (par″ah-den-ti′tis). Periodontitis.

paradentium (par″ah-den′she-um). Periodontium.

paradentosis (par″ah-den-to′sis). Periodontosis.

paraderm (par′ah-derm) [*para-* + Gr. *derma* skin]. The part of the vitellus of the ovum that furnishes cells which contribute to the body of the embryo.

paradiabetes (par″ah-di″ah-be′tēz). A condition marked by many of the manifestations of diabetes, but without polyuria or glycosuria.

paradidymal (par″ah-did′ĭ-mal). 1. Pertaining to the paradidymis. 2. Beside the testis.

paradidymis (par″ah-did′ĭ-mis) [*para-* + Gr. *didymos* testis]. [N A, B N A] A body made up of a few convoluted tubules in the anterior part of the spermatic cord, considered to be a remnant of the mesonephros. Called also *organ of Giraldès*, *parepididymis*, and *massa innominata*.

paradimethylaminobenzaldehyde (par″ah-di-meth″il-am″ĭ-no-ben-zal′de-hīd). A substance, $CHO.C_6H_4.N(CH_3)_2$: used in testing for tryptophan or other indole derivative.

paradione (par″ah-di′ōn). Trade mark for preparations of paramethadione.

paradiphenylbiuret (par″ah-di-fen″il-bi′u-ret). A substance, $NH(CO.NH.C_6H_4OH)_2$, transformed into benzoic acid in the body.

paradiphtherial (par″ah-dif-the′re-al). Having a remote or indirect relation to diphtheria.

paradiphtheritic (par″ah-dif″thĕ-rit′ik). Paradiphtherial.

paradipsia (par″ah-dip′se-ah) [*para-* + Gr. *dipsa* thirst + *-ia*]. A perverted appetite for fluids, which are ingested without relation to bodily need.

paradox (par′ah-doks) [Gr. *paradoxos* incredible]. A statement which seems to be, though it may not be, absurd or self-contradictory. **p. of Kretz,** while the injection of an accurately neutralized toxin-antitoxin mixture produces no bad effects in a normal animal, the reverse is the case in an animal that has previously been actively immunized with toxin. **Opie p.,** necrotizing local anaphylaxis sometimes acts as a specific protective mechanism. **Weber's p.,** the elongation of a muscle which has been so stretched that it cannot contract.

paradoxical (par″ah-dok′se-kal). Occurring at variance with the normal rule.

paradysentery (par″ah-dis′en-ter″e). A diarrhea resembling mild dysentery. See *Shigella paradysenteriae.*

para-eccrisis (par″ah-ek′rĭ-sis) [*para-* + Gr. *ekkrisis* excretion]. Disordered secretion or excretion.

para-epilepsy (par″ah-ep′ĭ-lep-se). An epileptic attack consisting only of the aura without convulsions.

para-eponychia (par″ah-ep″o-nik′e-ah). A combination of paronychia and eponychia.

para-equilibrium (par″ah-e″kwĭ-lib′re-um). Vertigo due to disturbance of the vestibular apparatus of the ear.

Par. aff. Abbreviation for L. *pars affec′ta*, the part affected.

paraffin (par′ah-fin) [L. *parum* little + *affinis* akin]. 1. A purified mixture of solid hydrocarbons obtained from petroleum, occurring as an odorless, tasteless, colorless or white, more or less translucent mass. 2. A saturated hydrocarbon of the marsh gas series. **chlorinated p.,** paraffin which has been treated with chlorine. **hard p.,** paraffin which has a high melting point. **liquid p.,** liquid petrolatum. **liquid p., light,** light liquid petrolatum. **pliable p.,** a mixture of paraffin and other ingredients used as a non-absorbent protective dressing for burns and other wounds. **soft p., white,** white petrolatum. **soft p., yellow,** petrolatum.

paraffinoma (par″ah-fĭ-no′mah). A chronic granuloma produced by prolonged continuous exposure to the irritation of paraffin.

parafibrinogen (par″ah-fi-brin′o-jen). A compound resembling fibrin, obtained by repeated precipitation of fibrinogen with salt.

paraflagella (par″ah-flah-jel′lah). Plural of *paraflagellum.*

paraflagellate (par″ah-flaj′ĕ-lāt). Having paraflagella.

paraflagellum (par″ah-flah-jel′um), pl. *paraflagel′la.* A small accessory flagellum.

paraflex (par′ah-fleks). Trade mark for a preparation of chlorzoxazone.

paraflocculus (par″ah-flok′u-lus). Accessory flocculus.

paraformaldehyde (par″ah-for-mal′de-hīd). A white, crystalline polymer of formaldehyde.

parafunction (par′ah-funk″shun). A disordered or perverted function.

parafunctional (par″ah-funk′shun-al). Characterized by perverted or abnormal function.

paragammacism (par″ah-gam′ah-sizm) [*para-* + Gr. *gamma*, the Greek letter G]. The faulty utterance of *g*, *k*, and *ch* sounds.

paraganglia (par″ah-gang′gle-ah). Pleural of *paraganglion.*

paraganglioma (par″ah-gang″gle-o′mah). A tumor of the tissue composing the paraganglia. **medullary p.,** pheochromocytoma. **nonchromaffin p.,** carotid body tumor.

paraganglion (par″ah-gang′gle-on), plural *paragan′glia.* A collection of chromaffin cells, which are derived from neural ectoderm, occurring outside of the adrenal medulla, and found anywhere that sympathetic ganglion cells occur. Most, if not all, of the paraganglia secrete epinephrine (or norepinephrine). The paraganglia [N A] include the corpora paraaortica, glomus carotica, and glomus coccygeum.

paragelatose (par″ah-jel′ah-tōs). A substance obtained by boiling gelatin.

paragenitalis (par″ah-jen″ĭ-ta′lis) [*para-* + L. *genitalis* genital]. 1. In lower vertebrates, the urinary part of the mesonephros, caudal to the genital part. 2. In higher animals, the paradidymis or paraoophoron.

parageusia (par″ah-gu′se-ah) [*para-* + Gr. *geusis* taste + *-ia*]. 1. Perversion of the sense of taste. 2. A bad taste in the mouth.

parageusic (par″ah-gu′sik). Pertaining to or characterized by parageusia.

paragglutination (par″ah-gloo″tĭ-na′shun). Group agglutination.

paraglobulin (par″ah-glob′u-lin). A globulin from blood serum, blood cells, lymph, and various connective tissues. Called also *fibroplastin, fibrinoplastin,* and *serum globulin.*

paraglobulinuria (par″ah-glob″u-lĭ-nu′re-ah) [*paraglobulin* + Gr. *ouron* urine + *-ia*]. The discharge of paraglobulin in the urine.

paraglossa (par″ah-glos′sah) [*para-* + Gr. *glōssa* tongue]. Swelling of the tongue.

paraglossia (par″ah-glos′e-ah) [*para-* + Gr. *glōssa* tongue + *-ia*]. Inflammation of the tissues under the tongue.

paraglossitis (par″ah-glo-si′tis). Paraglossia.

paragnathus (par-ag′nah-thus) [*para-* + Gr. *gnathos* jaw]. 1. A fetal monster with a supernumerary jaw. 2. A parasitic fetus attached laterally to the jaw of the autosite.

paragnosis (par″ag-no′sis) [*para-* + Gr. *gnōsis* knowledge]. Diagnosis, after death, based on contemporaneous accounts of the diseases which affected historical characters.

paragomphosis (par″ah-gom-fo′sis) [*para-* + Gr. *gomphoun* to fasten + *-osis*]. Impaction of the head of the fetus in the pelvic canal.

paragonimiasis (par″ah-gon″ĭ-mi′ah-sis). The state of being infected with flukes of the genus Paragonimus.

Paragonimus (par″ah-gon′ĭ-mus) [*para-* + Gr. *gonimos* having generative power]. A genus of trematode parasites. They have two invertebrate hosts, the first is a mollusk (*Melania*) and the second a crustacean (*Potamon* or *Eriocheir*). **P. kellicot′ti,** a species closely allied to *P. westermani,* found in cats, dogs and hogs in the United States. **P. rin′geri.** Same as *P. westermani.* **P. westerman′i,** the lung fluke, an oval or pear-shaped fluke of a pinkish or reddish-brown color, found in cysts in the lungs and sometimes in the pleura, liver, abdominal cavity, and elsewhere. It causes the disease known as parasitic or oriental hemoptysis. It occurs especially in Asiatic countries, and infests the lower animals as well as man. Called also *Distoma westermani, D. ringeri,* and *D. pulmonale.*

paragonorrheal (par″ah-gon″o-re′al). Having a remote or indirect relation to gonorrhea.

Paragordius (par″ah-gor′de-us). A genus of the Gordiacea. **P. cin′tus,** one case of infection with this worm has been reported from Africa. **P. tricuspida′tus,** in one case in France this worm was extracted from the throat. **P. va′rius,** several cases of infection with this worm have been reported in North America.

paragrammatism (par″ah-gram′ah-tizm). Impairment of speech, with confusion in the use and order of words and grammatical forms.

paragranuloma (par″ah-gran″u-lo′mah). The most benign form of Hodgkin's disease, which is largely confined to the lymph nodes.

paragraphia (par″ah-gra′fe-ah) [*para-* + Gr. *graphein* to write + *-ia*]. A disorder in which the patient makes mistakes in spelling or writes one word in place of another.

parahemoglobin (par″ah-he″mo-glo′bin). A dark form of hemoglobin occurring in crystalline form in the tissue in conditions marked by considerable blood destruction.

parahemophilia (par″ah-he″mo-fil′e-ah). A hemophilia-like condition caused by the congenital absence of blood coagulation factor V. Called also *Owren's disease.*

parahepatic (par″ah-he-pat′ik) [*para-* + Gr. *hēpar* liver]. Beside the liver.

parahepatitis (par″ah-hep″ah-ti′tis). Inflammation of parts around the liver.

paraheredity (par″ah-he-red′ĭ-te). The alleged transmission of characters not from mother cell to daughter cell but through an external medium from affected cell to normal cell.

parahidrosis (par″ah-hid-ro′sis). Paridrosis.

parahormone (par″ah-hor′mōn) [*para-* + *hormone*]. A substance, not a true hormone, which has a hormone-like action in controlling the functioning of some distant organ.

parahypnosis (par″ah-hip-no′sis) [*para-* + Gr. *hypnos* sleep]. Abnormal or perverted sleep.

parahypophysis (par″ah-hi-pof′ĭ-sis). An accessory pituitary body.

para-immunity (par″ah-ĭ-mu′nĭ-te). The immunity manifested by parabacteria.

para-infection (par″ah-in-fek′shun). The condition of being affected with a disease whose symptoms resemble those of an infectious disease, but which is not due to the germs of the infectious disease.

para-infectious (par″ah-in-fek′shus). Due indirectly to infection; due to the conditions produced by infection rather than by the infection itself.

para-influenzal (par″ah-in″floo-en′zal). Due indirectly to influenza; due to the conditions produced by influenza.

para-insulin (par″ah-in′su-lin). A hypothetical substance in tuberculous tissue having an action on the body similar to that of insulin.

parakeratosis (par″ah-ker″ah-to′sis). Any abnormality of the stratum corneum of the skin, especially a condition caused by edema between the cells which prevents the formation of keratin. **p. ostra′cea.** Same as *p. scutularis.* **p. psoriasifor′mis,** a condition characterized by the formation of scabs like those of psoriasis. **p. scutula′ris,** a disease of the scalp marked by the formation of crusts which envelop the hairs and send up incrustations around the hairs. **p. variega′ta,** a disease characterized by a red, scaly eruption in the form of a network enclosing patches of normal skin.

parakinesia (par″ah-ki-ne′se-ah) [*para-* + Gr. *kinēsis* motion + *-ia*]. Perversion of motor function resulting in strange and unnatural movements. In ophthalmology, irregular action of an individual ocular muscle.

parakinetic (par″ah-ki-net′ik). Pertaining to or characterized by parakinesis.

paralalia (par″ah-la′le-ah) [*para-* + Gr. *lalia* speech]. Any disturbance of the faculty of speech, especially the production of a vocal sound different from the one desired, or the substitution in speech of one letter for another. **p. litera′lis,** impairment of the power to utter the sounds of certain letters.

paralambdacism (par″ah-lam′dah-sizm) [*para-* + Gr. *lambdakismos*]. The faulty utterance of *l* sounds, or the substitution of other sounds for *l.*

paralbumin (par″al-bu′min) [*para-* + *albumin*]. An albumin or protein substance found in ovarian cysts.

paraldehyde (par-al′de-hīd). A polymerization product of acetaldehyde, obtained by treatment with a small quantity of sulfuric acid: used as a hypnotic and sedative.

paraldehydism (par-al′de-hīd″izm). A condition produced by excessive use of paraldehyde; paraldehyde poisoning.

paraleprosis (par″ah-lep-ro′sis). Paraleprosy.

paraleprosy (par″ah-lep′ro-se). A mild or aborted form of leprosy.

paralepsy (par′ah-lep″se). Psycholepsy.

paralexia (par″ah-lek′se-ah) [*para-* + *alexia*]. Impairment of the power of reading, marked by the transposition of words and syllables into meaningless combinations.

paralexic (par″ah-lek′sik). Pertaining to or affected with paralexia.

paralgesia (par″al-je′se-ah) [*para-* + Gr. *algesis* sense of pain + *-ia*]. Any condition marked by abnormal and painful sensations; a painful paresthesia.

paralgesic (par″al-je′sik). Pertaining to or affected with paralgesia.

paralgia (par-al′je-ah). Paralgesia.

paralinin (par″ah-li′nin) [*para-* + *linin*]. Karyolymph.

paralipophobia (par″ah-li″po-fo′be-ah) [Gr. *paraleipein* to neglect + *phobos* fear + *-ia*]. Morbid apprehension of neglecting something.

parallactic (par″ah-lak′tik). Pertaining to parallax.

parallagma (par″ah-lag′mah) [Gr.]. Displacement of a bone or of the fragments of a broken bone.

parallax (par′ah-laks) [Gr. "in turn"]. An apparent displacement of an object due to a change in the patient's position. **binocular p.**, the seeming difference in position of an object as seen separately by one eye and then by the other, the head remaining stationary. **crossed p.**, binocular parallax in which the object viewed seems to move away from the open eye. **direct p.**, binocular parallax in which the object viewed seems to move toward the open eye. **heteronymous p.**, crossed p. **homonymous p.**, direct p. **vertical p.**, binocular parallax in which the object seen seems to move vertically.

parallelism (par′ah-lel″izm). The doctrine that mental processes and brain processes run side by side and that they do not interact. See *automatism*.

parallelometer (par″ah-lel-om′e-ter) [*parallel* + Gr. *metron* measure]. An instrument used in artificial denture work to determine the exactness of the parallel relationship of lines and surfaces.

parallergia (par″ah-ler′je-ah). Parallergy.

parallergic (par″ah-ler′jik). Pertaining to or marked by parallergy.

parallergin (par-al′er-jin). An antigen which produces a parallergic reaction.

parallergy (par-al′er-je). A condition in which an allergic state, produced by specific sensitization, predisposes the body to react to other allergens with clinical manifestations that differ from the original reaction.

paralogia (par″ah-lo′je-ah) [*para-* + Gr. *logos* reason + *-ia*]. A disordered state of the reason; impairment of the reasoning power marked by illogical or delusional speech. **thematic p.**, a perversion of the mind in which the patient dwells unduly upon one subject.

paralogism (pah-ral′o-jizm). The use of meaningless or illogical language by the insane.

paralues (par″ah-lu′ēz). Parasyphilis.

paraluetic (par″ah-lu-et′ik). Parasyphilitic.

paralyses (pah-ral′ĭ-sēz). Plural of *paralysis*.

paralysin (pah-ral′ĭ-sin). See *agglutinin*.

paralysis (pah-ral′ĭ-sis), pl. *paral′yses* [*para-* + Gr. *lyein* to loosen]. Loss or impairment of motor function in a part due to lesion of the neural or muscular mechanism; also, by analogy impairment of sensory function (sensory paralysis). In addition to the types named below, paralysis is further distinguished as *traumatic*, *syphilitic*, *toxic*, etc., according to its cause; or as *obturator*, *ulnar*, etc., according to the nerve, part, or muscle specially affected. For other varieties see also under *hemiplegia*, *palsy*, *paraplegia*, and *paresis*. **abducens p.**, lesion of the abducens nerve causing paralysis of the external rectus muscle of the eye with internal strabismus and diplopia on the same side as the lesion. **p. of accommodation**, paralysis of the ciliary muscles so as to prevent accommodation of the eye. **acoustic p.**, nervous deafness. **acute ascending spinal p.**, a rapidly progressing and often fatal ascending paralysis of unknown cause. It begins in the muscles of the feet and gradually ascends to the other muscles of the body. There are no discoverable lesions, and the disease runs its course in two days to four weeks. Called also *Landry's p.* **acute atrophic p.**, the acute anterior poliomyelitis of childhood. **acute infectious p.**, epidemic poliomyelitis. **acute wasting p.**, poliomyelitis. **p. ag′itans**, a disease of late life, progressive in character and marked by masklike facies, a characteristic tremor of resting muscles, a slowing of voluntary movements, a festinating gait, peculiar posture, and weakness of the muscles. There may be excessive sweating and feelings of heat. Called also *Parkinson's disease* and *shaking palsy*. **p. ag′itans, juvenile**, a condition developing in early life, marked by increased muscle tonus with the characteristic attitude and facies of paralysis agitans, due to a progressive degeneration of the globus pallidus. Called also *syndrome of globus pallidus* and *paleostriatal syndrome of Hunt*. **alcoholic p.**, paralysis caused by habitual drunkenness. **alternate p., alternating p.**, alternate hemiplegia. **ambiguo-accessorius p.**, Schmidt's syndrome. **ambiguo-accessorius-hypoglossal p.**, Jackson's syndrome. **ambiguo-hypoglossal p.**, Tapia's syndrome. **ambiguospinothalamic p.**, Avellis' syndrome. **anapeiratic p.**, occupation neurosis. **anesthesia p.**, paralysis following anesthesia. **anterior spinal p.**, anterior poliomyelitis. **arsenical p.**, paralysis due to arsenical poisoning. **ascending p.**, spinal paralysis that progresses cephalad. **association p.**, bulbar p. **asthenic bulbar p.**, myasthenia gravis pseudoparalytica. **astheno-bulbospinal p.**, myasthenia gravis. **atrophic spinal p.**, anterior poliomyelitis. **Avellis's p.** See under *syndrome*. **Bell's p.** See under *palsy*. **bilateral p.**, diplegia; paralysis on both sides. **birth p.**, paralysis due to injury received at birth. **brachial p.**, paralysis of an arm from lesion of the brachial plexus. See *Erb-Duchenne p.* and *Klumpke-Dejerine p.* **brachiofacial p.**, paralysis affecting the face and an arm. **Brown-Séquard's p.** 1. Brown-Séquard's syndrome. 2. A flaccid paralysis seen in disorders of the urinary tract. **bulbar p.**, paralysis due to changes in the motor centers of the oblongata; especially chronic or progressive bulbar paralysis, a chronic, usually fatal, disease, marked by progressive paralysis and atrophy of the muscles of the lips, tongue, mouth, pharynx, and larynx, and due to degeneration of the nerve nuclei of the floor of the fourth ventricle. It is called also *labioglossopharyngeal p.*, *labioglossolaryngeal p.*, and *Duchenne's p.* **bulbospinal p.**, myasthenia gravis. **cage p.**, a condition sometimes seen in captive animals that is said to resemble osteomalacia. **central p.**, any paralysis due to a lesion of the brain or spinal cord. **centrocapsular p.**, that which is due to disease of the internal capsule. **centrocortical p.**, that which is due to disease of the cerebral cortex. **cerebral p.**, any paralysis due to an intracranial lesion. See *cerebral palsy*, under *palsy*. **cerebral, infantile, ataxic p.**, a condition which is dependent upon faulty development of the frontal regions of the brain, is present at birth, affects all extremities and is not definitely progressive; infantile cerebral diataxia. **cerebrocerebellar, diplegic, infantile p.**, a condition developing in infants, affecting all extremities, and due to combined failure of development or destruction of the reciprocating portions of the cerebrum and the cerebellum. **cerebrospinal, hereditary p.** (hemiplegia, diplegia, paraplegia, or tetraplegia) is a hereditary condition which develops usually in early middle life, characterized by gradually developing paralyses which may be manifest in the upper or lower extremities, in the two extremities, or one side, or in all four extremities. **Chastek p.**, progressive ataxia and paralysis in silver foxes due to vitamin deficiency following the substitution of fish for meat in the diet. **chlorotic p.**, paralysis from chlorosis. **circumflex p.**, paralysis of the circumflex nerve. **complete p.**, entire loss of motion, sensation, and function. **compression p.**, paralysis caused by pressure on a nerve, as by a crutch or during sleep. **conjugate p.**, loss of ability to perform some of the ocular parallel movements. **cortical p.**, paralysis dependent upon a lesion of the brain cortex. **creeping p.**, locomotor ataxia. **crossed p., cruciate p.**, paralysis affecting one side of the face and the opposite side of the body. **crural p.**, that which chiefly affects the thigh or thighs. **crutch p.**, paralysis of an arm or of the arms, due to pressure of the crutch in the axilla. **Cruveilhier's p.,** progressive muscular atrophy. **decubitus p.,** paralysis due to pressure on a nerve from lying for a long time in one position. **Dejerine-Klumpke p.,** Klumpke's p. **diphtheric p., diphtheritic p.,** a partial paralysis which often follows diphtheria, chiefly affecting the soft palate and throat muscles. **divers' p.,** paralysis occurring as a result of too rapid reduction of pressure on deep-sea divers. **Duchenne's p.** 1. Bulbar paralysis. 2. Erb-Duchenne paralysis. **Duchenne-Erb p.,** Erb-Duchenne p. **emotional p.,** paralysis with emotional excitement occurring in hysterical subjects. **epidemic infantile p.,** epidemic poliomyelitis. **Erb's p.** 1. Erb-Duchenne paralysis. 2. Syphilitic spastic spinal paralysis. 3. Pseudohypertrophic muscular dystrophy. **Erb-Duchenne p.,** the upper-arm type of brachial paralysis; paralysis of the upper roots of brachial plexus due to destruction of the fifth and sixth cervical roots and characterized by absence of involvement of the small hand muscles. **essential p.,** acute anterior poliomyelitis. **facial p.,** Bell's palsy. **familial periodic p.,** a rare disease marked by recurring attacks of rapidly progressive flaccid paralysis, often associated with a marked fall of serum potassium. It occurs in young people, usually in several members of a family. **Féréol-Graux p.** See under *palsy.* **flaccid p.,** paralysis with loss of tonus of the muscles of the paralyzed part and absence of reflexes. **fowl p.** See under *lymphomatosis of fowl.* **functional p.,** a temporary paralysis which is apparently not caused by a nerve lesion. **p. of gaze,** paralysis due to pathological processes which implicate the supranuclear oculomotor centers and result in either lateral or vertical gaze paralysis. These disturbances may also be due to involvement of the centers for lateral or vertical gaze. **general p., general p. of the insane,** dementia paralytica. **ginger p.,** Jamaica ginger p. **glossolabial p., glossopharyngolabial p.,** bulbar p. **Gubler's p.,** alternate hemiplegia. **histrionic p.,** paralysis of certain muscles of the face, producing a facial expression of some emotion. **hypoglossal p.,** paralysis due to a pathological process affecting the hypoglossal nucleus or the hypoglossal nerve at any point. It may also be due to supranuclear involvement of the cortical nuclear contingent of the pyramidal tract which innervates the opposite half of the tongue. **hysterical p.,** apparent loss of power of movement in a part seen in hysteria, with no apparent causative lesion. **incomplete p.,** partial paralysis or paresis. **Indian bow p.,** paralysis of the thyroarytenoid muscles. **infantile p.** See *poliomyelitis.* **infantile spastic p.,** the cerebral palsy of childhood. **infantile spinal p.,** spinal paralytic poliomyelitis. **intermittent p.,** paralysis due to malaria. **irritative cervical sympathetic p.,** Horner's syndrome. **ischemic p.,** local paralysis due to a stoppage of the circulation, as in certain cases of embolism or thrombosis; called also *Volkmann's ischemic paralysis.* **jake p.,** Jamaica ginger p. **Jamaica ginger p.,** paralysis of the extremities, especially of the legs, following the use of Jamaica ginger as a beverage: called also *jake paralysis, jake neuritis, ginger paralysis, Jamaica ginger polyneuritis.* **juvenile p.,** general paralysis in young persons. **Klumpke's p.,** the lower-arm type of brachial paralysis; atrophic paralysis of the muscles of the arm and hand, from lesion of the eighth cervical and first dorsal nerves. It often occurs in infants delivered by breech extraction. **Kussmaul's p.,** ascending spinal paralysis. **labial p., labioglossolaryngeal p., labioglossopharyngeal p.,** bulbar p. **Landry's p.,** acute ascending spinal p. **laryngeal p.,** paralysis of one of the laryngeal muscles. **lead p.,** paralysis caused by lead poisoning, due to a peripheral neuritis, and marked by wrist drop. **lenticular p.,** that which is due to a lesion of the lenticular nucleus. **lingual p.,** paralysis of the tongue. **Lissauer's p.,** an apoplectiform type of general paresis. **local p.** paralysis of one muscle or of a group of muscles. **masticatory p.,** paralysis of the muscles of mastication. **medullary tegmental p's,** paralyses due to lesions of the medullary tegmentum: they include crossed hemiplegia, Tapia's syndrome, Babinski-Nageotte syndrome, and Cestan-Chenais syndrome. **Millard-Gubler p.** See under *syndrome.* **mimetic p.,** paralysis of the facial muscles. **mixed p.,** combined motor and sensory paralysis. **motor p.,** paralysis of voluntary muscles. **musculospiral p.,** paralysis of the wrist muscles, due to lesion or injury of the musculospiral nerve: sometimes to a toxic influence or to an alcoholic debauch. **myogenic p.,** acute anterior poliomyelitis. **myopathic p.,** paralysis due to disease of the muscle itself. **narcosis p.,** paralysis caused by pressure during anesthesia. **p. notario'rum,** writers' cramp. **nuclear p.,** any paralysis due to a lesion in a nucleus of origin. **obstetric p.,** a birth palsy; paralysis due to injuries received at birth. **ocular p.** See *amaurosis, cycloplegia,* and *ophthalmoplegia.* **oculomotor p.,** paralysis of the oculomotor nerve. **organic p.,** paralysis due to lesion of nerve tissue. **parotitic p.,** paralysis accompanying mumps. **parturient p.,** a form of paralysis following delivery in cows, and thought to be due to poisons formed in the udder. Called also *milk fever.* **periodic p.,** a recurrent paralysis. See also *familial periodic p.* **peripheral p.,** loss of power due to some lesion of the nervous mechanism between the nucleus of origin and the periphery. **peroneal p.,** crossed leg palsy. **phonetic p.,** paralysis of the muscles of speech. **post-diphtheric p.,** diphtheric paralysis. **post-hemiplegic p.,** paralysis occurring after a stroke. **posticus p.,** paralysis of the posterior cricothyroid muscle. **Pott's p.** See under *paraplegia.* **pressure p.,** paralysis, generally temporary, caused by pressure on a nerve trunk. **progressive bulbar p.** See *bulbar p.* **pseudobulbar p.,** a disease affecting especially the facial muscles; simulating bulbar paralysis, but due to supranuclear lesions; supranuclear paralysis. It is marked especially by spasmodic laughing and crying. **pseudohypertrophic muscular p.,** a chronic disease characterized by enlargement without true hypertrophy of the muscles, with paralysis due to disturbance of nutrition, producing atrophy of the muscle fibers with hypertrophy of the connective tissue and fatty infiltration. The disease occurs usually late in childhood, and is marked by various deformities, lordosis, and a peculiar swaying gait with the legs kept wide apart. The paralysis progressively increases, ending in death, which is usually due to respiratory weakness. **psychic p.,** hysterical p. **reflex p.,** one ascribable to peripheral irritation. In some cases secondary changes occur in the spinal cord, and the paralysis ceases to be truly reflex. **segmental p.,** paralysis affecting only a segment of a limb. **sensory p.,** loss of sensation resulting from a morbid process. **serum p.,** peripheral nerve paralysis following administration of serum. **spastic p.,** paralysis marked by rigidity of the muscles and heightened deep muscle reflexes. **spastic spinal p.,** lateral sclerosis of the spinal cord. **spinal p.,** paralysis dependent on a lesion of the spinal cord. See *tabes dorsalis* and *poliomyelitis.* **spinomuscular p.,** paralysis due to lesion of the gray matter of the spinal cord, or the nerves springing therefrom. **spinoneural p.** See under *atrophy.* **supranuclear p.,** paralysis of muscles innervated by the facial nerve, due to lesion of the cortex or of the facial fibers in the corona radiata or capsule. **tick p.,** a progressive ascending flaccid motor paralysis which follows the bite of certain ticks (*Dermacentor*) in children and in domestic animals in Oregon, British Columbia, and other parts of the world. A similar paralysis sometimes follows the bites of species of *Ixodes, Haemaphysalis* and *Rhi-*

picephalus. **Todd's p.**, postepileptic hemiplegia lasting for a few minutes or hours to three or four days, or even longer, after the epileptic attack. **trigeminal p.**, paralysis which involves the trigeminal (fifth) nerve, marked by retraction of the jaw, loss of jaw closing and of rotary motion, and depression of the lower jaw. **p. va′cillans,** chorea. **vasomotor p.**, paralysis of a vasomotor apparatus, resulting in dilatation of blood vessels. **Volkmann's p.**, ischemic p. **waking p.**, a form of hypnogogic helplessness that follows waking, especially in some cases of narcolepsy. **wasting p.**, progressive muscular atrophy. **Weber's p.** See under *syndrome*. **Werdnig-Hoffmann p.**, a type of familial progressive spinal muscular atrophy, beginning in early life and ending fatally in from a few months to four years. **writers' p.**, writers' cramp.

paralysor (par′ah-līz″or). Paralyzer.

paralyssa (par″ah-lis′ah). Rabies occurring in Central and South America caused by the bite of vampire bats.

paralytic (par″ah-lit′ik) [Gr. *paralytikos*]. 1. Affected with or pertaining to paralysis. 2. A person affected with paralysis.

paralytogenic (par″ah-lit″o-jen′ik). Causing paralysis.

paralyzant (par′ah-līz″ant). 1. Causing paralysis. 2. A drug that paralyzes.

paralyze (par′ah-līz). To put into a state of paralysis.

paralyzer (par′ah-līz″er). A substance which hinders or prevents a chemical reaction.

paramagenta (par″ah-mah-jen′tah). Parafuchsin.

paramagnetic (par″ah-mag-net′ik). Characterized by or exhibiting paramagnetism.

paramagnetism (par″ah-mag′ne-tizm) [*para-* + Gr. *magnēs* magnet]. The property of being attracted by a magnet, and of assuming a position parallel to that of a magnetic force.

paramania (par″ah-ma′ne-ah) [*para-* + *mania*]. A condition in which one manifests joy by complaining. Cf. *parathymia*.

paramastigote (par″ah-mas′tĭ-gōt) [*para-* + Gr. *mastix* lash]. Having an accessory flagellum by the side of a larger one.

paramastitis (par″ah-mas-ti′tis) [*para-* + Gr. *mastos* mamma + *-itis*]. Inflammation of the tissues around the mammary gland.

paramastoid (par″ah-mas′toid). Near the mastoid process.

paramastoiditis (par″ah-mas″toid-i′tis). Inflammation of the temporal bone in mastoiditis.

paramecia (par″ah-me′se-ah). Plural of *paramecium*.

paramecin (par″ah-me′sin). An antibiotic compound secreted by a specially developed strain of paramecia; it is destructive to other strains of paramecia.

Paramecium (par″ah-me′se-um) [Gr. *paramēkēs* oblong]. A genus of holotrichous ciliate protozoans of elongated form. Certain strains of this organism have been employed in the protozoan test. See under *tests*. **P. co′li,** *Balantidium coli*.

paramecium (par″ah-me′se-um), pl. *parame′cia*. An organism belonging to the genus Paramecium.

paramedian (par″ah-me′de-an). Paramesial.

paramedical (par″ah-med′ĭ-kal). Having some connection with or relation to the science or practice of medicine; adjunctive to the practice of medicine in the maintenance or restoration of health and normal functioning. The paramedical services include physical, occupational, and speech therapy, and the activity of medical social workers.

paramenia (par″ah-me′ne-ah) [*para-* + Gr. *mēniaia* menses]. Disordered or difficult menstruation.

parameningococcus (par″ah-me-ning″go-kok′us). A microorganism resembling the meningococcus, differing only in its serum reactions.

parameniscitis (par″ah-me-nĭ-si′tis). Inflammation of the parameniscus.

parameniscus (par″ah-me-nis′kus). The structure or area around the menisci (semilunar fibrocartilages) of the knee.

paramesial (par″ah-me′se-al) [*para-* + Gr. *mesos* middle]. Situated near the mesial line.

parameter (par-am′e-ter) [*para-* + Gr. *metron* measure]. An arbitrary constant, the values of which characterize the mathematical expressions into which it enters; e.g., rheobasis and chronaxia as parameters of the excitability of nerves (Lapicque).

paramethadione (par″ah-meth″ah-di′ōn). Chemical name: 3,5-dimethyl-5-ethyloxazolidine-2,4-dione: used as an anticonvulsant in petit mal epilepsy.

paramethasone (par″ah-meth′ah-sōn). Chemical name: 6α-fluoro-16α-methylprednisolone-21-acetate: used as a corticosteroid with anti-inflammatory action.

parametrial (par″ah-me′tre-al). 1. Pertaining to the parametrium. 2. Parametric.

parametric (par″ah-met′rik) [*para-* + Gr. *mētra* uterus]. Situated near the uterus.

parametritic (par″ah-me-trit′ik). Pertaining to parametritis.

parametritis (par″ah-me-tri′tis). Inflammation of the parametrium. **posterior p.**, inflammation of the cellular tissue around the uterosacral ligaments.

parametrium (par″ah-me′tre-um) [*para-* + Gr. *metra* uterus]. [N A, B N A] Loose connective tissue and smooth muscle lying between the two serous layers of the broad ligament, especially near the right and left margins of the uterus, and below, where the two layers diverge.

paramido-acetophenone (par-am″ĭ-do-as″ĕ-to-fe′nōn). $NH_2.C_6H_4.CO.CH_3$: used in Ehrlich's diazo test.

paramimia (par″ah-mim′e-ah) [*para-* + Gr. *mimēsis* imitation]. A condition in which signs are misused in expressing thoughts; the use of wrong or improper gestures in speaking.

paramitome (par″ah-mi′tōm) [*para-* + Gr. *mitos* thread]. Hyaloplasm.

paramnesia (par″am-ne′ze-ah) [*para-* + *amnesia*]. 1. Perversion of memory in which the person believes that he remembers events or circumstances which never happened; called also *retrospective falsification*. 2. A state in which words are remembered, but are used without a comprehension of their meaning.

Paramoeba (par″ah-me′ba). Craigia.

paramolar (par″ah-mo′lar). A supernumerary tooth appearing adjacent to a molar tooth.

Paramonostomum parvum (par″ah-mo-nos′to-mum par′vum). A trematode infecting chicks in North America.

paramorphia (par″ah-mor′fe-ah) [*para-* + Gr. *morphē* form + *-ia*]. Abnormality of form.

paramphistomiasis (par-am″fe-sto-mi′ah-sis). Invasion of the body by trematode parasites of the family Paramphistomidae, namely, *Watsonius watsoni* and *Gastrodiscus hominis*.

Paramphistomum (par″am-fis′to-mum). A genus of flukes. **P. cer′vi,** a species found in the stomach of cattle and sheep in Egypt and also in the United States.

paramucin (par″ah-mu′sin). A colloid substance found in ovarian cysts, which differs from mucin and pseudomucin in the fact that it reduces Fehling's solution before boiling with acid.

paramusia (par″ah-mu′ze-ah) [*para-* + Gr. *mousa* music + *-ia*]. Perversion or partial loss of the power of correct musical expression.

paramycetoma (par″ah-mi″se-to′mah). A mycetoma which causes hypertrophic deformities or destruction of tissues.

paramyelin (par″ah-mi′ĕ-lin). A mono-amino-monophosphatid from brain substance.

paramyoclonus (par″ah-mi-ok′lo-nus) [*para-* + Gr. *mys* muscle + *klonos* turmoil]. A condition characterized by myoclonic contractions of various muscles. **p. mul′tiplex,** a condition occurring more often in males than in females, characterized by sudden shocklike contractions affecting first the proximal muscles of the arms and the shoulder girdle, with any muscles of the limbs and trunk being involved later, and finally involving the face and bulbar muscles.

paramyosinogen (par″ah-mi″o-sin′o-jen) [*para-* + *myosin* + *gennan* to produce]. A protein resembling myosinogen derived from muscle plasm.

paramyotone (par″ah-mi′o-tōn). Paramyotonus.

paramyotonia (par″ah-mi″o-to′ne-ah) [*para-* + Gr. *mys* muscle + *tonos* tension + *-ia*]. A disease marked by tonic spasms due to disorder of muscular tonicity; especially a hereditary and congenital affection. **ataxia p.,** muscular spasm with slight ataxia on attempting to move. **p. congen′ita,** myotonia congenita. **symptomatic p.,** temporary stiffness on starting to walk, seen in paralysis agitans.

paramyotonus (par″ah-mi-ot′o-nus). A condition marked by tonic muscular spasm.

paranagana (par″ah-nah-gah′nah). A disease of horses in central Africa caused by *Trypanosoma congolense.*

paranalgesia (par″an-al-je′se-ah). Analgesia of the lower extremities.

paranea (par″ah-ne′ah). Paranoia.

paranephric (par″ah-nef′rik). 1. Near the kidney. 2. Pertaining to the adrenal gland.

paranephritis (par″ah-ne-fri′tis) [*para-* + Gr. *nephros* kidney + *-itis*]. 1. Inflammation of the paranephros. 2. Inflammation of the connective tissue around and near the kidney. **lipomatous p.,** lipomatous nephritis.

paranephroma (par″ah-ne-fro′mah). A tumor of adrenal tissue.

paranephros (par-ah-nef′ros), pl. *paraneph′roi* [*para-* + Gr. *nephros* kidney]. An adrenal gland.

paranesthesia (par″an-es-the′ze-ah). Para-anesthesia.

paraneural (par″ah-nu′ral) [*para-* + Gr. *neuron* nerve]. Beside or alongside of a nerve.

parangi (pah-ran′je). Ceylonese name for a disease resembling frambesia.

para-nitrosulfathiazole (par″ah-ni″tro-sul″-fah-thi′ah-zōl). Chemical name: p-nitro-N-2-thiazolylbenzenesulfonamide: used as an antibacterial.

paranoia (par″ah-noi′ah) [*para-* + Gr. *nous* mind + *-ia*]. A chronic, slowly progressive mental disorder (personality disorder) characterized by the development of ambitions or suspicions into systematized delusions of persecution and grandeur which are built up in a logical form: the condition is believed to be based on unconscious homosexual conflicts. **acute hallucinatory p.,** paranoia in which hallucinations are combined with the delusions. **alcoholic p.,** a paranoic condition developing in chronic alcoholism. **p. hallucina-to′ria,** acute hallucinatory paranoia. **heboid p.,** the paranoid form of dementia praecox (dementia paranoides), or paranoia with prominent schizoid features. **litigious p.,** paranoia characterized by a tendency to go to law for imaginary causes. **p. origina′ria,** a form of paranoia in children. **querulous p.,** paranoia marked by querulousness. **p. sim′plex,** a form in which the delusions are related to the actual perceptions of the patient.

paranoiac (par″ah-noi′ak). An individual exhibiting paranoia.

paranoic (par″ah-no′ic). Pertaining to or characterized by paranoia.

paranoid (par′ah-noid). Resembling paranoia.

paranoidism (par″ah-noid′izm). A state resembling paranoia.

paranomia (par″ah-no′me-ah) [*para-* + Gr. *onoma* name + *-ia*]. Aphasia characterized by inability to name objects felt (*myotactic p.*) or seen (*visual p.*).

paranormal (par″ah-nor′mal). Not quite normal; slightly abnormal.

paranosic (par″ah-no′sik). Pertaining to paranosis.

paranosis (par″ah-no′sis) [*para-* + Gr. *nosos* disease]. The primary advantage that is to be gained by illness. Cf. *epinosis.*

paranuclear (par″ah-nu′kle-ar). 1. Beside a nucleus. 2. Pertaining to a paranucleus.

paranucleate (par″ah-nu′kle-āt). A salt of paranucleic acid.

paranuclein (par″ah-nu′kle-in). Nucleo-albumin.

paranucleo-albumin (par″ah-nu″kle-o-al-bu′-min). A compound of nucleo-albumin with protein.

paranucleolus (par″ah-nu-kle′o-lus). A small basophil body in the enclosing sac of the nucleus.

paranucleoprotein (par″ah-nu″kle-o-pro′te-in). Any phosphorus-containing protein which, by digestion with acid pepsin, affords soluble peptones and proteoses and an insoluble paranuclein.

paranucleus (par″ah-nu′kle-us) [*para-* + *nucleus*]. A body resembling the nucleus, sometimes seen in the cell protoplasm near the nucleus. Called also *nebenkern.*

para-omphalic (par″ah-om-fal′ik) [*para-* + Gr. *omphalos* navel]. Near the umbilicus.

para-operative (par″ah-op′er-a″tiv). Pertaining to the accessories of an operation, such as care of instruments, asepsis, etc.

para-oral (par″ah-o′ral). Administered by some other route than by the mouth: said of medication.

para-osmia (par″ah-os′me-ah). Parosmia.

para-osteoarthropathy (par″ah-os″te-o-ar-throp′ah-the). Paraplegia with osteo-arthropathy.

parapancreatic (par″ah-pan″kre-at′ik). Situated near the pancreas.

paraparesis (par″ah-par′e-sis) [*para-* + Gr. *paresis* paralysis]. A partial paralysis, especially of the lower extremities.

parapathia (par″ah-path′e-ah). Disorder of emotional content; psychoneurosis.

parapedesis (par″ah-pe-de′sis) [*para-* + Gr. *pēdēsis* a leaping]. Passage of bile pigments into the blood capillaries instead of into the bile capillaries.

parapeptone (par″ah-pep′tōn). Antialbumate.

paraperitoneal (par″ah-per″ĭ-to-ne′al). Near the peritoneum.

parapertussis (par″ah-per-tus′is). A disease resembling pertussis but which is much milder.

parapestis (par″ah-pes′tis). Pestis minor.

paraphasia (par″ah-fa′ze-ah) [*para-* + *aphasia*]. Partial aphasia in which the patient employs wrong words, or uses words in wrong and senseless combinations (*choreic p.*). **central p.,** a partial aphasia due to brain lesion.

paraphasic (par″ah-fa′sik). Characterized by paraphasia.

paraphasis (pah-raf′ah-sis). An evagination of the membranous roof of the telencephalon in front of the velum transversum in certain vertebrate brains.

paraphemia (par″ah-fe′me-ah) [*para-* + Gr. *phēmē* speech + *-ia*]. Aphasia marked by the employment of the wrong words.

paraphenylenediamine (par″ah-fen″il-ēn-di-am′in). An agent, $C_6H_4(NH_2)_2$, whose hydrochloride dyes the hair black, but is liable to cause a dermatitis.

paraphia (par-a′fe-ah) [*para-* + Gr. *haphē* touch + *-ia*]. A perversion of the sense of touch.

paraphilia (par″ah-fil′e-ah) [*para-* + Gr. *philein* to love + *-ia*]. Aberrant sexual activity; expression of the sexual instinct in practices which are socially prohibited or unacceptable or biologically undesirable.

paraphiliac (par″ah-fil′e-ak). 1. Pertaining to paraphilia. 2. An individual exhibiting paraphilia.

paraphimosis (par″ah-fi-mo′sis) [*para-* + Gr. *phimoun* to muzzle + *-osis*]. Retraction of a narrow or inflamed foreskin which cannot be replaced. Called also *capistration.*

paraphobia (par″ah-fo′be-ah) [*para-* + Gr. *phobos* fear + *-ia*]. A mild phobia.

paraphonia (par″ah-fo′ne-ah) [*para-* + Gr. *phōnē* voice + *-ia*]. Morbid alteration of the voice; partial aphonia. **p. pu′berum,** the change in the male voice at the time of puberty.

paraphora (par-af′o-rah) [*para-* + Gr. *pherein* to bear]. A slight mental disorder.

paraphrasia (par″ah-fra′ze-ah) [*para-* + *aphrasia*]. Partial aphrasia; speech defect marked by disorderly arrangement of spoken words.

paraphrenia (par″ah-fre′ne-ah) [*para-* + Gr. *phrēn* mind + *-ia*]. 1. Kraepelin's term for a small group of psychoses now included under the title "paranoid conditions" (American Psychiatric Association classification); true paranoia, in contradistinction to paranoid reactions within the pattern of other psychoses. 2. Paraphrenitis. **p. confab′ulans,** paraphrenia distinguished by falsifications of memory. **p. expan′siva,** paraphrenia marked by delusions of grandeur, exalted mood, and mild excitement. **p. phantas′tica,** paraphrenia with somewhat unsystematized delusions. **p. systemat′ica,** paraphrenia with rigidly systematized delusions of persecution and no intellectual deterioration.

paraphrenic (par″ah-fre′nik). 1. Pertaining to or characterized by paraphrenia. 2. An individual exhibiting paraphrenia.

paraphrenitis (par″ah-fre-ni′tis) [*para-* + Gr. *phrēn* diaphragm + *-itis*]. Inflammation of the diaphragm, or, more correctly, of the parts around it.

paraphronia (par″ah-fro′ne-ah). A condition of abnormal mentality marked by change in disposition and character.

paraphyseal (par″ah-fiz′e-al). Pertaining to the paraphysis.

paraphysis (pah-raf′ĭ-sis) [Gr. "offshoot"). 1. A paraphyseal body; a thin-walled sac, a derivative of the roof plate of the telencephalon. 2. A sterile thread alongside the spore sac or sexual organs of cryptogamous plants.

paraphyte (par′ah-fit) [*para-* + Gr. *phyton* plant]. A proliferation or excrescent vegetation.

paraphyton (par″ah-fi′ton). A vegetable parasite.

parapineal (par″ah-pi′ne-al). Denoting the visual part of the pineal body of certain lizards.

paraplasm (par′ah-plazm) [*para-* + Gr. *plasma* something formed]. 1. Hyaloplasm, def. 1. 2. An abnormal growth.

paraplasmic (par″ah-plaz′mik). Pertaining to paraplasm.

paraplastic (par″ah-plas′tik) [*para-* + Gr. *plassein* to mold]. Exhibiting a perverted formative power; of the nature of a paraplasm.

paraplastin (par″ah-plas′tin). A substance resembling parachromatin in the cytoplasm and nucleus of a cell.

paraplectic (par″ah-plek′tik) [Gr. *paraplēktikos*]. Paraplegic.

paraplegia (par″ah-ple′je-ah) [*para-* + Gr. *plēgē* stroke + *-ia*]. Paralysis of the legs and lower part of the body, both motion and sensation being affected. It is caused by disease or injury of the spine, locomotor ataxia, transverse myelitis, chronic alcoholism, malaria, anemia, and lesion of the brain. **alcoholic p.,** paraplegia due to chronic alcoholism, and probably dependent upon peripheral neuritis. **ataxic p.,** a disease characterized by slowly developing paraplegia and incoordination, with exaggeration of the tendon reflexes, and due to lateral and posterior sclerosis of the spinal cord. **cerebral p.,** that which is due to a bilateral cerebral lesion. **cervical p.,** that which affects especially both arms, due to high spinal pressure. **p. doloro′sa,** a variety attended with severe pains, due to the pressure of neoplasms on the spinal cord and nerves. **flaccid p.** See under *paralysis.* **ideal p.,** a reflex paraplegia due to emotional excitement. **p. infe′rior,** paralysis of both legs. **peripheral p.,** that which is due to pressure on the nerves. **Pott's p.,** that which is due to vertebral caries or spinal tuberculosis. **reflex p.,** paralysis of the lower limbs due to peripheral irritation of the nerve centers. **senile p.,** a form marked by tonic spasm of the paralyzed muscles, with increased reflex irritability. It is usually caused by transverse lesions of the spinal cord or by anterolateral sclerosis. Called also *tetanoid p.* **spastic p.,** senile p. **spastic p., congenital,** spastic p., infantile. **spastic p., infantile,** spastic paralysis occurring in early childhood, and due to injuries in birth, cerebral hemorrhage before birth, or abnormal development of the brain. **spastic p., primary,** a form of spastic paraplegia said to be due to primary degeneration in the pyramidal tracts. **p. supe′rior,** paralysis of both arms. **tetanoid p.,** spastic p. **toxic p.,** paraplegia due to poisons in the blood.

paraplegic (par″ah-plej′ik). Pertaining to or of the nature of paraplegia. By extension, sometimes used to designate an individual affected with paraplegia.

paraplegiform (par″ah-plej′ĭ-form). Resembling paraplegia.

parapleuritis (par″ah-plu-ri′tis) [*para-* + Gr. *pleura* side + *-itis*]. Inflammation in the wall of the chest.

paraplexus (par″ah-plek′sus) [*para-* + *plexus*]. The choroid plexus of the lateral ventricle.

parapneumonia (par″ah-nu-mo′ne-ah). A disease resembling pneumonia clinically.

parapophysis (par″ah-pof′ĭ-sis) [*para-* + *apophysis*]. The lower transverse process of a vertebra (processus transversus vertebrae [N A]), or its homologue.

parapoplexy (par-ap′o-plek″se) [*para-* + *apoplexy*]. A condition resembling apoplexy.

parapraxia (par″ah-prak′se-ah) [*para-* + Gr. *praxis* doing + *-ia*]. 1. Irrational behavior. 2. Inability to perform purposive movements properly.

paraproctitis (par″ah-prok-ti′tis) [*paraproctium* + *-itis*]. Inflammation of the paraproctium.

paraproctium (par″ah-prok′she-um) [*para-* + Gr. *prōktos* anus]. The tissues that surround the rectum and the anus.

paraprostatitis (par″ah-pros″tah-ti′tis). Inflammation of the tissues near the prostate gland.

paraprotein (par″ah-pro′te-in). An abnormal serum globulin identifiable by a unique physical characteristic, such as cold insolubility, high viscosity, or high molecular weight, and by production of a sharp, well defined peak on electrophoresis.

paraproteinemia (par″ah-pro″te-in-e′me-ah). Presence in the blood of a paraprotein, such as a cryoglobulin or a macroglobulin, in amounts not normally observed.

parapsia (par-ap′se-ah). Parapsis.

parapsis (par-ap′sis) [*para-* + Gr. *hapsis* touch]. Perversion of the sense of touch; paraphia.

parapsoriasis (par″ah-so-ri′ah-sis). A name applied by Brocq to a group of maculopapular scaly erythrodermas of slow development. They are marked by persistent red, scaling patches or lichen planus-like lesions, devoid of subjective symptoms, and resistant to treatment. There are three principal forms, the guttate, lichenoid, and patchy. **p. atro′phicans,** p. varioliformis. **p. variolifor′mis,** a skin disease characterized by the sudden appearance of a polymorphous skin eruption composed of macules, papules and occasional vesicles, which may run an acute, subacute or chronic course.

parapsychology (par″ah-si-kol′o-je) [*para-* + *psychology*]. A branch of psychology dealing with those psychical effects and experiences which appear to fall outside the scope of physical law; psychical research.

parapsychosis (par″ah-si-ko′sis). Transitory perversion of the thought function resulting in unnatural and abnormal thinking.

parapyknomorphous (par″ah-pik″no-mor′fus) [*para-* + Gr. *pyknos* compact + *morphē* form]. Neither pyknomorphous nor apyknomorphous, but between the two; staining moderately well: said of certain nerve cells.

parapyramidal (par″ah-pi-ram′ĭ-dal). Beside or near a pyramid.

paraqueduct (par-ak′we-dukt). A lateral extension of the cerebral aqueduct.

pararabin (pah-rar′ah-bin). A carbohydrate residuum identified by Reichardt (1875) and obtained by depriving agar-agar of its nitrogen (Bordet-Zung, 1914).

para-reaction (par″ah-re-ak′shun). Meyer's term for paranoid and schizophrenic states.

pararectal (par″ah-rek′tal). Beside the rectum.

parareducine (par″ah-re-du′sin) [*para-* + *reducin*]. A leukomaine found in the urine.

parareflexia (par″ah-re-flek′se-ah). Any disorder or derangement of the reflexes.

pararenal (par″ah-re′nal). Beside the kidney.

pararhizoclasia (par″ah-ri″zo-kla′se-ah) [*para-* + Gr. *rhiza* root + *klasis* destruction + *-ia*]. Inflammatory destruction of the deep layers of the alveolar process and the periodontal membrane around the roots of a tooth. Cf. *perirhizoclasia.*

pararhotacism (par″ah-ro′tah-sizm) [*para-* + Gr. *rhō* the Greek letter *r*]. Imperfect pronunciation of the sound of the letter *r.*

pararosaniline (par″ah-ro-zan′ĭ-lin). Parafuchsin.

pararrhythmia (par″ah-rith′me-ah). Cardiac arrhythmia in which two separate rhythms are going on at the same time.

pararthria (par-ar′thre-ah) [*para-* + Gr. *arthron* articulation]. Disordered or imperfect utterance of speech.

Parasaccharomyces (par″ah-sak″ah-ro-mi′sēz). A genus of yeastlike fungi, various species of which have been isolated from human lesions. **P. ashfor′di,** *Monilia psilosis.*

parasacral (par″ah-sa′kral). Situated near the sacrum.

parasagittal (par″ah-saj′ĭ-tal). Parallel with the median plane.

parasal (par′ah-sal). Trade mark for preparations of para-aminosalicylic acid.

parasalpingeal (par″ah-sal-pin′je-al). Situated beside or in the wall of the fallopian tube.

parasalpingitis (par″ah-sal″pin-ji′tis) [*para-* + Gr. *salpinx* tube + *-itis*]. Inflammation of the tissues around a fallopian tube.

parascarlatina (par″ah-skar″lah-ti′nah). Exanthema subitum.

parascarlet (par″ah-skar′let). Exanthema subitum.

parasecretion (par″ah-se-kre′shun). Any disorder or derangement of secretion. Also hypersecretion.

parasellar (par″ah-sel′ar). Near or around the sella turcica.

parasexuality (par″ah-seks″u-al′ĭ-te). Perverted sexuality.

parasigmatism (par″ah-sig′mah-tizm) [*para-* + Gr. *sigma* the Greek letter *s*]. Imperfect pronunciation of *s* and *z* sounds.

parasinoidal (par″ah-si-noi′dal) [*para-* + *sinus*]. Situated along the course of a sinus.

Parasita (par″ah-si′tah). An order of nematodes living as parasites in the open cavities or in the tissues of animals, but also capable of free life during part of their existence.

parasite (par′ah-sīt) [Gr. *parasitos*]. 1. A plant or animal which lives upon or within another living organism at whose expense it obtains some advantage without compensation. 2. The smaller, less complete component of asymmetrical conjoined twins, which is attached to and dependent on the autosite. **accidental p.,** an organism which is only occasionally parasitic. **allantoic p.,** a twin embryonic parasite in which the weaker member takes its blood supply from the stronger through its umbilical circulation. **auxiliary p.,** a hyperparasite that helps control a parasite. **celozoic p.,** a parasite which lives in a body cavity. **commensal p.,** a parasite which derives its sustenance from the food of its host. **cytozoic p.,** a parasite which lives in body cells. **diheteroxenic p.,** a parasite which requires two intermediate hosts. **ectophytic p.,** a plant ectoparasite. **ectozoic p.,** an animal ectoparasite. **endophytic p.,** a plant endoparasite. **entozoic p.,** a parasite which lives in the lumen of the intestine. **erratic p.,** a parasite which appears in an organ in which it does not usually live. **estivo-autumnal p.,** *Plasmodium falciparum.* **eurytrophic p.,** an ectoparasite which can feed on various hosts. **facultative p.,** an organism which is usually parasitic upon another but which is capable of independent existence. **hematozoic p.,** a parasite which lives in the blood. **incidental p.,** a parasite in a host which normally it does not inhabit. **intermittent p.,** a parasite which lives in its host only at times, being free living during the interval. **karyozoic p.,** a parasite which lives in cell nuclei. **malarial p.,** *Plasmodium.* **obligatory p.,** a parasite which cannot live apart from its host. **occasional p.,** accidental p. **optimal p.,** facultative p. **pathogenic p.,** a parasite that may cause harmful effects on its host. **periodic p.,** a parasite that resides in its host for short periods. **permanent p.,** a parasite which lives in its host from early life until maturity. **quartan p.,** *Plasmodium malariae.* **specific p.,** one normal to its current host. **sporadic p.,** accidental p. **spurious p.,** an organism which is parasitic on hosts other than man, but which occasionally passes through the human body without causing harm. **stenotrophic p.,** an ectoparasite which can feed on one host only. **temporary p.,** a parasite which lives free of its host during part of its life cycle. **teratoid p.,** a fetal parasite which appears as a tumor-like mass. **tertian p.,** *Plasmodium vivax.* **true p.,** a parasite which derives its sustenance from the tissue of its host.

parasitemia (par″ah-si-te′me-ah). The presence of parasites (especially malarial parasites) in the blood.

parasitic (par″ah-sit′ik) [Gr. *parasitikos*]. Pertaining to or of the nature of a parasite.

parasiticidal (par″ah-sit″ĭ-si′dal). Destructive to parasites.

parasiticide (par″ah-sit′ĭ-sīd) [L. *parasitus* a parasite + *caedere* to kill]. 1. Destructive to parasites. 2. An agent that is destructive to parasites.

parasitifer (par″ah-sit′ĭ-fer) [*parasite* + L. *ferre* to bear]. An organism which serves as the host of a parasite.

parasitiferism (par″ah-si-tif′er-izm). A morbid delusion that one is harboring a parasite.

parasitism (par′ah-sīt″izm). 1. Symbiosis in which one population (or individual) adversely affects the other, but cannot live without it. 2. Infestation with parasites.

parasitization (par″ah-sīt″i-za′shun). Infestation with a parasite.

parasitogenic (par″ah-si″to-jen′ik) [Gr. *parasitos* parasite + *gennan* to produce]. Caused by parasites.

parasitoid (par′ah-si″toid). Resembling a parasite.

parasitologist (par″ah-si-tol′o-jist). An expert in parasitology.

parasitology (par″ah-si-tol′o-je) [Gr. *parasitos* parasite + *-logy*]. The science or study of parasites and parasitism.

parasitophobia (par″ah-si″to-fo′be-ah) [*parasite* + Gr. *phobein* to be affrighted by]. 1. Morbid dread of parasites. 2. Morbid delusion that one is infested with parasites.

parasitosis (par″ah-si-to′sis). Infestation with parasites.

parasitotrope (par″ah-si′to-trōp). Parasitotropic.

parasitotropic (par″ah-si″to-trop′ik) [*parasite* + Gr. *trepein* to turn]. Having special affinity for parasites.

parasitotropism (par″ah-si-tot′ro-pizm). Parasitotropy.

parasitotropy (par″ah-si-tot′ro-pe). The affinity of a drug for infective parasites.

para-smallpox (par″ah-smal′poks). Variola minor.

parasoma (par″ah-so′mah). Paranucleus.

parasomnia (par″ah-som′ne-ah). A state in which there is no response to stimuli, verbal or mental, except that of a reflex nature.

paraspadias (par″ah-spa′de-as) [*para-* + Gr *spadon* a rent]. A developmental anomaly in which the urethra opens upon one side of the penis.

paraspasm (par′ah-spazm) [L. *paraspasmus;* Gr. *paraspasmos*]. Spasm of the corresponding muscles on both sides of the body.

paraspecific (par″ah-spe-sif′ik). Having curative properties in addition to the specific one.

Paraspirillum (par″ah-spi-ril′lum). A genus of microorganisms of the family Spirillaceae, suborder Pseudomonadineae, order Pseudomonadales, made up of spiral or S-shaped cells having a well marked thickening at the middle and tapering toward the ends. The type species is *P. vejdov'skii.*

parasplenic (par″ah-sple′nik). Beside the spleen.

parasteatosis (par″ah-ste″ah-to′sis) [*para-* + Gr. *stear* suet + *-osis*]. Disorder of sebaceous secretions.

parasternal (par″ah-ster′nal) [*para-* + Gr. *sternon* sternum]. Situated beside the sternum.

parasthenia (par″as-the′ne-ah) [*para-* + Gr. *sthenos* strength + *-ia*]. A condition of organic tissue causing it to function at abnormal intervals.

parastruma (par″ah-stroo′mah). A goiter-like enlargement of a parathyroid gland or glands.

parasympathicotonia (par″ah-sim-path″e-ko-to′ne-ah). Vagotonia.

parasympathin (par″ah-sim′pah-thin). A hypothetical product given off when a cranial autonomic nerve is stimulated, and having stimulating action on the parasympathetic nervous system.

parasympatholytic (par″ah-sim″pah-tho-lit′ik) [*parasympathetic* + Gr. *lytikos* dissolving]. 1. Producing effects resembling those of interruption of the parasympathetic nerve supply to a part. 2. An agent that opposes the effects of impulses conveyed by the parasympathetic nerves.

parasympathomimetic (par″ah-sim″pah-tho-mi-met′ik) [*parasympathetic* + Gr. *mimētikos* imitative]. 1. Producing effects resembling those of stimulation of the parasympathetic nerve supply to a part. 2. An agent that produces effects similar to those produced by stimulation of the parasympathetic nerves.

parasynanche (par″ah-sin′an-ke) [Gr. *parasynanchē*]. Inflammation of a parotid gland or of the throat muscles.

parasynapsis (par″ah-sĭ-nap′sis) [*para-* + Gr. *synapsis* conjunction]. The union of chromosomes side by side during miosis. Cf. *telosynapsis.*

parasyndesis (par″ah-sin-de′sis). Parasynapsis.

parasynovitis (par″ah-sin″o-vi′tis) [*para-* + *synovitis*]. Inflammation of the tissues about a synovial sac.

parasyphilis (par″ah-sif′ĭ-lis). A disease condition following and partly due to syphilis, but not itself syphilitic.

parasyphilitic (par″ah-sif″ĭ-lit′ik). Pertaining to a sequel or result of syphilis, but not to syphilis itself.

parasyphilosis (par″ah-sif″ĭ-lo′sis). Parasyphilis.

parasystole (par″ah-sis′to-le) [*para-* + Gr. *systolē* contraction]. An abnormally prolonged interval between the systole and the diastole.

paratarsium (par″ah-tar′se-um) [*para-* + *tarsus*]. The side of the tarsus of the foot.

paratenon (par″ah-ten′ōn) [*para-* + Gr. *tenōn* tendon]. The fatty areolar tissue filling the interstices of the fascial compartment in which a tendon is situated.

paratereseomania (par″ah-ter-e″se-o-ma′ne-ah) [Gr. *paratērēsis* observation + *mania* madness]. A mania for seeing new sights.

paratherapeutic (par″ah-ther″ah-pu′tik). Caused by the treatment of some other disease, as paratherapeutic icterus caused by the therapeutic use of arsphenamine in syphilis.

parathymia (par″ah-thi′me-ah) [*para-* + Gr. *thymos* spirit]. A perverted, contrary, or inappropriate emotional state.

parathyroid (par″ah-thi′roid) [*para-* + *thyroid*]. 1. Situated beside the thyroid gland. 2. Any one of four small glands, disposed as two pairs, near the lateral lobes of the thyroid. Their secretion is concerned chiefly with the metabolism of calcium and phosphorus by the body.

parathyroidal (par″ah-thi-roi′dal). Pertaining to the parathyroids.

parathyroidectomize (par″ah-thi″roid-ek′to-mīz). To deprive of the parathyroid glands by surgical removal.

parathyroidectomy (par″ah-thi″roid-ek′to-me) [*parathyroid* + Gr. *ektomē* excision]. Excision of a parathyroid gland.

parathyroidin (par″ah-thi-roi′din). An extract of the parathyroids.

parathyroidoma (par″ah-thi″roi-do′mah). A tumor arising from or composed of tissue resembling the parathyroids.

parathyropathy (par″ah-thi-rop′ah-the). Any parathyroid disease.

parathyroprival (par″ah-thi″ro-pri′val). Pertaining to or caused by absence of the parathyroid glands.

parathyroprivia (par″ah-thi-ro-pri′ve-ah). The condition resulting from the removal of the parathyroid glands.

parathyroprivic (par″ah-thi″ro-priv′ik). Parathyroprival.

parathyroprivous (par″ah-thi-rop′rĭ-vus). Parathyroprival.

parathyrotoxicosis (par″ah-thi″ro-tok″sĭ-ko′-sis). An acute form of parathyroid intoxication; a morbid condition resulting from overactivity of the parathyroid glands.

parathyrotrophic (par″ah-thi-ro-trof′ik). Parathyrotropic.

parathyrotropic (par″ah-thi-ro-trop′ik). Having an affinity for the parathyroid.

paratoloid, paratoloidin (par″ah-to′loid, par″-ah-to-loi′din). Koch's lymph, or tuberculin.

paratonia (par″ah-to′ne-ah) [*para-* + Gr. *tonos* tension + *-ia*]. A disorder of tone or tension.

paratrachoma (par″ah-trah-ko′mah) [*para-* + *trachoma*]. A conjunctivitis resembling trachoma, caused by the genital inclusion virus. See *inclusion blennorrhea*, under *blennorrhea.*

paratrichosis (par″ah-trĭ-ko′sis) [*para-* + Gr. *trichōsis* hairiness]. Any abnormality in the character or situation of the hair.

paratrimma (par″ah-trim′ah) [*para-* + Gr. *tribein* to rub]. 1. Irritation; chafing. 2. Intertrigo, especially between the nates.

paratripsis (par″ah-trip′sis). 1. Irritation or chafing. 2. Suppression of tissue waste.

paratriptic (par″ah-trip′tik). 1. Pertaining to or preventing waste of body tissue. 2. An agent that prevents the waste of body tissue.

paratrophic (par″ah-trof′ik) [*para-* + Gr. *trophē* nutrition]. Requiring living material or complex protein matter for food.

paratrophy (par-at′ro-fe) [*para-* + Gr. *trophē* nutrition]. 1. Bacterial nutrition in which the growth energy is obtained from the host. 2. Dystrophy.

paratuberculosis (par″ah-tu-ber″ku-lo′sis). Any disease not tuberculous, but flourishing in a tuberculous constitution.

paratuberculous (par″ah-tu-ber′ku-lus). Having an indirect relation to tuberculosis; due to conditions produced by tuberculosis.

paratyphlitis (par″ah-tif-li′tis) [*para-* + Gr. *typhlos* blind + *-itis*]. Inflammation of the postperitoneal tissue of the cecum.

paratyphoid (par″ah-ti′foid). Resembling typhoid fever or the typhoid bacterium.

paratypic (par″ah-tip′ik). Paratypical.

paratypical (par″ah-tip′ĭ-kal). Differing from the type.

para-umbilical (par″ah-um-bil′ĭ-kal). Near the umbilicus.

para-urethra (par″ah-u-re′thrah). An accessory urethral canal.

para-urethral (par″ah-u-re′thral). Near the urethra.

para-urethritis (par″ah-u″re-thri′tis). Inflammation of the tissues near the urethra.

para-uterine (par″ah-u′ter-in). Near the uterus.

paravaccinia (par″ah-vak-sin′e-ah). An eruption of red hemispherical tubercles which sometimes follows vaccination, but which is not vaccinial in nature.

paravaginal (par″ah-vaj′ĭ-nal). Beside or alongside of the vagina.

paravaginitis (par″ah-vaj″ĭ-ni′tis). Inflammation of the tissue about the vagina.

paravariola (par″ah-vah-ri′o-lah). Variola minor.

paravenin (par′ah-ven″in). A venin which has been partially inactivated.

paravenous (par″ah-ve′nus). Beside a vein.

paravertebral (par″ah-ver′te-bral). Beside the vertebral column.

paravitaminosis (par″ah-vi″tah-mĭ-no′sis). A vitamin deficiency disorder with aspecific lesions.

paraxial (par-ak′se-al) [*para-* + *axis*]. Situated alongside an axis.

paraxon (par-ak′son) [*para-* + *axon*]. A collateral branch of a neuraxon or axis-cylinder process.

parazone (par′ah-zōn). One of the white bands alternating with the dark bands (diazones) in the layers of enamel prisms and seen in cross section of a tooth.

parazoon (par″ah-zo′on) [*para-* + Gr. *zōon* animal]. An animal organism parasitic upon or within an animal.

Pardanthus chinensis (par-dan′thus ki-nen′-sis). An iridaceous plant of Asia of high repute as an aperient.

Paré (par-ā′), Ambroise (1510–1590). A French surgeon, the most celebrated surgeon of the Renaissance, who reformed the treatment of gunshot wounds by abolishing cauterization with boiling oil. He also practiced ligation of arteries after amputation, and re-introduced podalic version into obstetrics. His famous aphorism, *Je le pensay, et Dieu le guarit* ("I dressed him and God healed him"), first appeared in 1585, in the fourth edition of his collected works.

parectasia (par″ek-ta′se-ah). Parectasis.

parectasis (par-ek′tah-sis) [*para-* + Gr. *ektasis* extension]. Excessive stretching or distention of a part or organ.

parectropia (par″ek-tro′pe-ah) [*para-* + Gr. *ek* out + *tropos* a turning]. Apraxia.

paredrine (par′ah-drēn). Trade mark for preparations of hydroxyamphetamine.

paregoric (par″ĕ-gor′ik) [Gr. *parēgorikos* consoling]. Camphorated opium tincture.

paregorism (par′ĕ-gor″izm). Opium addiction through the use of paregoric.

pareidolia (par″i-do′le-ah) [*para-* + Gr. *eidōlon* phantom + *-ia*]. An illusion in which visual images are given a fantastic interpretation.

parelectronomic (par″e-lek″tro-nom′ik). Giving no response to electromotive stimuli.

parelectronomy (par″e-lek-tron′o-me) [*para-* + *electric* + Gr. *nomos* law]. A condition in which there is a decrease in strength of an electric current passed through a muscle.

pareleidin (par″el-e′ĭ-din). The keratin of epidermal cells derived from eleidin of the stratum lucidum.

parencephalia (par″en-se-fa′le-ah) [*para-* + Gr. *enkephalos* brain + *-ia*]. Congenital defect of the brain.

parencephalitis (par″en-sef″ah-li′tis). Inflammation of the cerebellum.

parencephalocele (par″en-sef′ah-lo-sēl) [*parencephalon* + Gr. *kēlē* hernia]. Hernial protrusion of the cerebellum.

parencephalon (par″en-sef′ah-lon) [*para-* + Gr. *enkephalos* brain]. The cerebellum.

parencephalous (par″en-sef′ah-lus) [*para-* + Gr. *enkephalos* brain]. Having a congenital deformity of the brain.

parenchyma (par-eng′kĭ-mah) [Gr. "anything poured in beside"]. The essential elements of an organ; used in anatomical nomenclature as a general term to designate the functional elements of an organ, as distinguished from its framework, or stroma. **p. of lens,** substantia lentis. **p. tes′tis** [N A, B N A], **p. of testis,** the seminiferous tubules, which are located within the lobules of the testis.

parenchymal (par-eng′kĭ-mal). Pertaining to or of the nature of parenchyma.

parenchymatitis (par″eng-kim″ah-ti′tis). Inflammation of a parenchyma.

parenchymatous (par″eng-kim′ah-tus). Pertaining to or of the nature of a parenchyma.

parenchymula (par″eng-kim′u-lah). The embryonic stage next succeeding that called the closed blastula.

Parendomyces (par″en-do-mi′sēz). A genus of yeastlike fungi, species of which have been isolated from various lesions of man.

parenogen (par-en′o-jen). Trade mark for a preparation of fibrinogen.

parental (pah-ren′tal). Pertaining to or derived from the parents.

parentalism (pah-ren′tal-izm). In psychiatry, a mental attitude of ownership and domination on the part of a parent toward his child.

parentectomy (par″en-tek′to-me). Removal of a child from the parental environment, as practiced in the treatment of certain asthmatic children.

parenteral (par-en′ter-al) [*para-* + Gr. *enteron* intestine]. Not through the alimentary canal, e.g., by subcutaneous, intramuscular, intrasternal, or intravenous injection.

parepicoele (par-ep′ĭ-sēl). Either of the lateral recesses of the fourth ventricle.

parepididymis (par″ep-ĭ-did′ĭ-mis). Paradidymis.

parepigastric (par″ep-ĭ-gas′trik). Near the epigastrium.

parepithymia (par″ep-ĭ-thim′e-ah) [*para-* + Gr. *epithymia* longing]. Morbid or abnormal desires or appetites; morbid craving.

parergasia (par″er-ga′se-ah) [*para-* + Gr. *ergasia* work]. 1. Kraepelin's term for perverted functioning, such as closing the eyes instead of putting out the tongue. 2. Meyer's term for personality twist reactions such as schizophrenia.

parergastic (par″er-gas′tik) [*para-* + Gr. *ergon* work]. Meyer's term for psychic disorders marked by twist reactions, i.e., incongruities, oddities, mannerisms, or fantastic or passivity projections (schizophrenia and paranoia).

paresis (pah-re′sis, par′e-sis) [Gr. *paresis* relaxation]. 1. Dementia paralytica. 2. Slight or incomplete paralysis. **galloping p.,** an acutely and rapidly progressing paresis. **general p.,** dementia paralytica. **juvenile p.,** a form of general paresis occurring in children as a result of congenital syphilis. **stationary p.,** paresis which has become arrested.

pareso-analgesia (par″e-so-an″al-je′ze-ah). Incomplete paralysis with analgesia.

paresthesia (par″es-the′ze-ah) [*para-* + Gr. *aisthēsis* perception]. Morbid or perverted sensation; an abnormal sensation, as burning, prickling, formication, etc. **Berger's p.,** paresthesia in young persons of one or both lower limbs, accompanied by weakness, but without objective symptoms. **Bernhardt's p.,** numbness, pain on exertion, and hypesthesia of the part of the thigh supplied by the external cutaneous nerve. **visceral p.,** an abnormal sensation referred to some viscus; not a mere excess or defect of a normal visceral sensation.

paresthetic (par″es-thet′ik). Pertaining to or marked by paresthesia.

paretic (pah-ret′ik). Pertaining to or affected with paresis.

pareunia (par-u′ne-ah) [*para-* + Gr. *eunē* couch]. Coitus.

parfocal (par-fo′kal) [L. *par* equal + *focus* hearth]. Retaining correct focus on changing powers in microscopy.

Parham band (pahr′am) [F. W. *Parham,* New Orleans surgeon, 1886–1926]. See under *band.*

parhedonia (par″he-do′ne-ah). Freud's name for the abnormalities of sexuality, such as the obsessive desire to see, to exhibit, or to touch the sexual organs of oneself or another.

parhemoglobin (par″he-mo-glo′bin). A form of hemoglobin insoluble in alcohol.

parhormone (par-hor′mōn). Any metabolic substance of the body which influences the functions of other organs or tissues. For example, carbon dioxide.

parica (par″ĭ-kah′). A narcotic snuff prepared from the seeds of *Piptadenia niops,* a tree of Brazil.

paricine (pah-ris′in). A quinoline alkaloid, $C_{16}H_{18}ON_2$, from the bark of *Cinchona succirubra.*

paridrosis (par″id-ro′sis) [*para-* + Gr. *hidrōsis* perspiration]. Any disorder or perverted state of the perspiration.

paries (pa′re-ez), pl. *pari′etes* [L.]. A wall; used in anatomical nomenclature as a general term to designate the wall of an organ or body cavity. **p. ante′rior vagi′nae** [N A, B N A], the wall of the vagina that is intimately associated with the posterior wall of the bladder and urethra. **p. ante′rior ventric′uli** [N A, B N A], the wall of the stomach that is directed toward the ventral surface of the body. **p. carot′icus ca′vi tym′pani** [N A], the anterior wall of the tympanic cavity, related to the carotid canal in which is lodged the internal carotid artery. **p. exter′nus duc′tus cochlea′ris** [N A], the external wall of the cochlear duct, adjacent to the outer wall of the cochlea. **p. infe′rior or′bitae** [N A, B N A], the inferior wall of the orbit, formed by the orbital surfaces of the maxilla and the zygomatic and palatine bones. Called also *floor of orbit.* **p. jugula′ris ca′vi tym′pani** [N A, B N A], the floor of the tympanic cavity, which is in intimate relation with the jugular fossa, which lodges the bulb of the internal jugular vein. **p. labyrin′thicus ca′vi tym′pani** [N A], the medial wall of the tympanic cavity. **p. latera′lis or′bitae** [N A, B N A], the lateral wall of the orbit, formed by the orbital surfaces of the great wing of the sphenoid bone, the zygomatic bone, and the zygomatic process of the frontal bone. **p. mastoi′deus ca′vi tym′pani** [N A], the posterior wall of the tympanic cavity, related to the mastoid portion of the temporal bone. **p. media′lis or′bitae** [N A, B N A], the medial wall of the orbit, formed by parts of the maxillary, lacrimal, ethmoid, and sphenoid bones. **p. membrana′ceus bron′chi** [N A], that part of the wall of the smaller bronchi where the cartilage is deficient. **p. membrana′ceus ca′vi tym′pani** [N A], the outer, or lateral, wall of the tympanic cavity, formed mainly by the tympanic membrane. **p. membrana′ceus tra′cheae** [N A], the posterior part of the wall of the trachea where the cartilaginous rings are deficient. **p. poste′rior vagi′nae** [N A, B N A], the wall of the vagina that is intimately associated with the anterior wall of the rectum. **p. poste′rior ventric′uli** [N A, B N A], the wall of the stomach that is directed toward the back of the body. **p. supe′rior or′bitae** [N A, B N A], the superior wall of the orbit, formed chiefly by the orbital plate of the frontal bone. Called also *roof of orbit.* **p. tegmenta′lis ca′vi tym′pani** [N A, B N A], the roof of the tympanic cavity, related to part of the petrous portion of the temporal bone. **p. tympan′icus duc′tus cochlea′ris** [N A], the wall of the cochlear duct that separates it from the scala tympani, composed of the osseous spiral laminae and the basilar membrane. Called also *tympanic wall of cochlear duct.* **p. vestibula′ris duc′tus cochlea′ris** [N A], the thin anterior wall of the cochlear duct, which separates it from the scala vestibuli. Called also *membrana vestibularis* [*Reissneri*] [B N A], and *vestibular wall of cochlear duct.*

parietal (pah-ri′ĕ-tal) [L. *parietalis*]. Of or pertaining to the walls of a cavity.

Parietaria (pah-ri″ĕ-ta′re-ah). A genus of plants of the family Urticaceae.

parietes (pah-ri′ĕ-tēz) [L.]. Plural of *paries.*

parietitis (pah-ri″ĕ-ti′tis). Inflammation of the wall of an organ.

parietofrontal (pah-ri″ĕ-to-fron′tal). Pertaining to the parietal and frontal bones, gyri, or fissures.

parietography (pah-ri″ĕ-tog′rah-fe). Roentgenographic visualization of the walls of an organ. **gastric p.,** roentgenographic visualization of the stomach wall by special technique, as a means of detecting early gastric neoplasm.

parieto-occipital (pah-ri″ĕ-to-ok-sip′ĭ-tal). Pertaining to the parietal and occipital bones or lobes.

parietosphenoid (pah-ri″ĕ-to-sfe′noid). Pertaining to the parietal and sphenoid bones.

parietosplanchnic (pah-ri″ĕ-to-splank′nik). Parietovisceral.

parietosquamosal (pah-ri″ĕ-to-skwah-mo′sal). Pertaining to the parietal bone and the squamous portion of the temporal bone.

parietotemporal (pah-ri″ĕ-to-tem′po-ral). Pertaining to the parietal and temporal bones or lobes.

parietovisceral (pah-ri″ĕ-to-vis′er-al). Both parietal and visceral; pertaining to the walls of a cavity and the viscera within it.

Parinaud's conjunctivitis, ophthalmoplegia (pah-rĭ-nōz′) [Henri *Parinaud,* French ophthalmologist, 1844–1905]. See under *conjunctivitis* and *ophthalmoplegia.*

pari passu (pa′re pas′u) [L., "at equal pace"]. Coincidentally with; to the same proportion or degree.

paristhmic (pah-rist′mik). Pertaining to the tonsils.

paristhmion (pah-rist′me-on) [*para-* + Gr. *isthmos* isthmus]. A tonsil.

paristhmitis (par″ist-mi′tis). Tonsillitis.

parity (par′ĭ-te). 1. [L. *parere* to bring forth, produce]. The condition of a woman with respect to her having borne viable offspring. 2. [L. *par* equal]. Equality; close correspondence or similarity.

Park's aneurysm (parks) [Henry *Park*, English surgeon, 1744–1831]. See under *aneurysm.*

Park-Williams bacillus [William Hallock *Park*, American bacteriologist, 1863–1939; Anna Wessels *Williams*, American bacteriologist, 1863–1955]. A strain of *Corynebacterium diphtheriae.*

Parker's fluid (park′erz) [George Howard *Parker*, American zoologist, 1864–1955]. See under *fluid.*

Parker's incision [Willard *Parker*, New York surgeon, 1800–1884]. See under *incision.*

Parkhill screws (park′hil) [Clayton *Parkhill*, American surgeon]. Metal screws for insertion through the tissues into the ends of a fractured bone, the screws being connected with an external clamp (Parkhill bone clamp) to secure external fixation of the fracture.

Parkinson's disease, facies, syndrome (par′kin-sunz) [James *Parkinson*, English physician, 1755–1824]. See under the nouns.

parkinsonian (par″kin-sun′e-an). Pertaining to paralysis agitans.

parkinsonism (par′kin-sun-izm). The chronic condition marked by rigidity characteristic of paralysis agitans, but without the resting tremor. See *Parkinson's syndrome*, under *syndrome.* **postencephalitic p.,** parkinsonism following epidemic encephalitis.

parlodion (par-lo′de-on). Collodion in a shredded form, used as an embedding medium in microscopical technique.

parnate (par′nāt). Trade mark for a preparation of tranylcypromine.

paroccipital (par″ok-sip′ĭ-tal) [*para-* + L. *occiput* occiput]. Near the occipital bone.

parodontal (par″o-don′tal). Situated near or beside a tooth.

parodontid (par″o-don′tid) [*para-* + Gr. *odous* tooth]. A tumor on the gingiva.

parodontitis (par″o-don-ti′tis). Periodontitis.

parodontium (par″o-don′she-um). Periodontium.

parodontopathy (par″o-don-top′ah-the). Periodontopathy.

parodontosis (par″o-don′to-sis). Periodontosis.

parodynia (par″o-din′e-ah) [L. *parere* to bear + Gr. *odynē* pain]. Dystocia, or morbid labor.

paroliva (par-ol′ĭ-vah). An accessory part of the olivary body.

parolivary (par-ol′ĭ-var″e) [*para-* + *olivary*]. Situated near the olivary body.

paromomycin (par′o-mo-mi″sin). A stable antibiotic derived from a strain of Streptomyces and effective against Entamoeba, Salmonella, Shigella, Proteus, Aerobacter and *Escherichia coli.*

paromphalocele (par″om-fal′o-sēl) [*para-* + Gr. *omphalos* navel + *kēlē* hernia]. Hernia situated near the navel.

paroniria (par″o-ni′re-ah) [*para-* + Gr. *oneiros* dream + *-ia*]. Morbid dreaming.

paronychia (par″o-nik′e-ah) [*para-* + Gr. *onyx* nail + *-ia*]. Inflammation involving the folds of tissue surrounding the fingernail. **p. tendino′sa,** septic inflammation of the sheath of the tendon of a finger.

paronychial (par″o-nik′e-al). Of or pertaining to paronychia.

paronychosis (par″o-nĭ-ko′sis). The formation of a nail in some abnormal place.

paroophoric (par″o-o-fo′rik). Pertaining to the paroophoron.

paroophoritis (par″o-of-o-ri′tis). 1. Inflammation of the paroophoron. 2. Inflammation of the tissues about the ovary.

paroophoron (par″o-of′o-ron) [*para-* + Gr. *ōon* egg + *pherein* to bear]. [N A, B N A] An inconstantly present small group of coiled tubules between the layers of the mesosalpinx, being a remnant of the excretory part of the mesonephros.

parophthalmia (par″of-thal′me-ah) [*para-* + Gr. *ophthalmos* eye + *-ia*]. Inflammation of the connective tissue around the eye.

parophthalmoncus (par″of-thal-mong′kus) [*para-* + Gr. *ophthalmos* eye + *onkos* mass]. A tumor situated near the eye.

paropsis (par-op′sis) [*para-* + Gr. *opsis* vision]. Disorder of the sense of vision.

parorchidium (par″or-kid′e-um) [*para-* + Gr. *orchis* testicle]. Misplacement of a testis or testes.

parorchis (par-or′kis). The epididymis.

parorexia (par″o-rek′se-ah) [*para-* + Gr. *orexis* appetite]. Nervous perversion of the appetite, with craving for special articles of diet or for articles that are not suitable for food.

parosmia (par-oz′me-ah) [*para-* + Gr. *osmē* smell]. Any disease or perversion of the sense of smell.

parosphresia (par″os-fre′ze-ah) [*para-* + Gr. *osphrēsis* smelling + *-ia*]. Disorder or perversion of the sense of smell.

parosphresis (par″os-fre′sis). Parosphresia.

parosteal (par-os′te-al). Pertaining to the outer surface of the periosteum.

parosteitis (par″os-te-i′tis) [*para-* + *osteitis*]. Inflammation of the tissues around a bone.

parosteosis (par″os-te-o′sis) [*para-* + Gr. *osteon* bone + *-osis*]. Ossification of the tissues outside of the periosteum.

parostitis (par″os-ti′tis). Parosteitis.

parostosis (par″os-to′sis). Parosteosis.

parotic (pah-rot′ik) [*para-* + Gr. *ous* ear]. Situated or occurring near the ear.

parotid (pah-rot′id) [*para-* + Gr. *ous* ear]. Situated or occurring near the ear.

parotidean (pah-rot″ĭ-de′an). Pertaining to the parotid gland.

parotidectomy (pah-rot″ĭ-dek′to-me) [*parotid* + Gr. *ektomē* excision]. Excision of the parotid gland.

parotiditis (pah-rot″ĭ-di′tis). Parotitis.

parotidoscirrhus (pah-rot″ĭ-do-skir′us) [*parotid* + Gr. *skirrhos* hardness]. Hardening of the parotid gland.

parotidosclerosis (pah-rot″ĭ-do-skle-ro′sis). Sclerosis of the parotid gland.

parotitic (par″o-tit′ik). Pertaining to parotitis.

parotitis (par″o-ti′tis). Inflammation of the parotid gland; mumps. See *mumps.* **celiac p.,** inflammation of the parotid gland after abdominal disease or injury. **epidemic p.,** mumps. **p. phlegmono′sa,** parotitis that goes on to suppuration.

parous (pa′rus) [L. *parere* to bring forth, produce]. Having borne one or more viable offspring.

parovarian (par″o-va′re-an). 1. Situated beside the ovary. 2. Pertaining to the parovarium.

parovariotomy (par″o-va″re-ot′o-me) [*parovarium* + Gr. *tomē* a cutting]. Excision of a parovarian cyst.

parovaritis (par″o-vah-ri′tis). Inflammation of the parovarium.

parovarium (par″o-va′re-um) [*para-* + L. *ovarium* ovary]. Epoophoron.

paroxia (pah-rok′se-ah). Pica.

paroxyl (pah-rok′sil). A proprietary amebacide.

paroxysm (par′ok-sizm) [Gr. *paroxysmos*]. A sudden recurrence or intensification of symptoms.

paroxysmal (par″ok-siz′mal). Recurring in paroxysms.

Parrot's disease, node, sign, ulcer (par-ōz′) [Jules Marie *Parrot*, a French physician, 1839–1883]. See under the nouns.

Parry's disease (pār′ēz) [Caleb Hillier *Parry*,

English physician, 1755–1822]. Exophthalmic goiter.

pars (parz), pl. *par'tes* [L.]. A division or part; used in anatomical nomenclature to designate a particular portion of a larger area, organ, or structure. **p. abdomina'lis esoph'agi** [N A], the part of the esophagus below the diaphragm, joining the stomach. **p. abdomina'lis et pelvi'na systema'tis autonom'ici** [N A], **p. abdomina'lis et pelvi'na systema'tis sympath'ici** [B N A], the portion of the autonomic nervous system arising from the lumbar and sacral parts of the sympathetic trunks and spinal cord. **p. abdomina'lis mus'culi pectora'lis majo'ris** [N A, B N A], the portion of the pectoralis major muscle originating from the aponeurosis of the obliquus externus abdominis. **p. abdomina'lis oesoph'agi** [B N A], p. abdominalis esophagi. **p. abdomina'lis ure'teris** [N A, B N A], that portion of the ureter extending from the kidney to the terminal line of the pelvis. **p. ala'ris mus'culi nasa'lis** [N A, B N A], the part of the nasal muscle that arises from the maxilla below the nose and inserts into the ala nasi. **p. alveola'ris mandib'ulae** [N A, B N A], the superior portion of the body of the mandible, which contains sockets for the teeth. **p. ana'lis rec'ti** [B N A], canalis analis. **p. ante'rior commissu'rae ante-rio'ris cer'ebri** [N A, B N A], the part of the anterior commissure that interconnects the two olfactory bulbs; it is rudimentary in man. **p. ante'rior fa'ciei diaphragmat'icae hep'atis** [N A], the portion of the diaphragmatic surface of the liver that is directed toward the ventral surface of the body. **p. ante'rior hypophys'eos,** lobus anterior hypophyseos. **p. ante'rior lob'uli quadrangula'ris** [B N A], the anterior portion of the quadrangular lobule. Omitted in N A. **p. ante'rior rhinen-ceph'ali** [B N A], the anterior part of the rhinencephalon. Omitted in N A. **p. anula'ris vagi'nae fibro'sae digito'rum ma'nus** [N A], a strong transverse band of fibrous tissue in the vagina fibrosa of the fingers, crossing the flexor tendons at the level of the upper half of the proximal phalanx. **p. anula'ris vagi'nae fibro'sae digito'rum pe'dis** [N A], a fibrous band in the toes resembling those of similar name in the fingers. **p. ascen'dens duode'ni** [N A, B N A], the terminal part of the duodenum, ending at the duodenojejunal flexure. **p. basila'ris fascic'uli pedunculomamilla'ris** [B N A]. Omitted in N A. **p. basila'ris os'sis occipita'lis** [N A, B N A], a quadrilateral plate of the occipital bone that projects superiorly and anteriorly from the foramen magnum. **p. basila'ris pon'tis** [N A, B N A], the part of the pons that connects the cerebrum, cerebellum, and medulla oblongata. It is a broad, transverse band that arches across the ventral surface of the rostral end of the rhombencephalon and on each side narrows to enter the cerebellum as the middle cerebellar peduncle. It comprises longitudinal fibers originating at the cerebral cortex, transverse fibers, and masses of gray matter, the pontine nuclei. **p. bucca'lis hypophys'eos,** an evagination of the ectoderm of the primitive buccal cavity which develops into the anterior lobe of the hypophysis. **p. buccopharyn'gea mus'culi constricto'ris pharyn'gis superio'ris** [N A], the part of the constrictor pharyngis superior muscle arising from the pterygomandibular raphe. Called also *musculus buccopharyngeus* [B N A]. **p. cae'ca oc'uli,** discus nervi optici. **p. cae'ca ret'inae,** the parts of the retina that are not sensitive to light, namely, the pars ciliaris retinae and pars iridica retinae. **p. calcaneocuboi'dea ligamen'ti bifurca'ti** [B N A], ligamentum calcaneocuboideum. **p. calcaneona-vicula'ris ligamen'ti bifurca'ti** [B N A], ligamentum calcaneonaviculare. **p. cardi'aca ventric'uli** [N A, B N A], the part of the stomach immediately adjacent to the esophagus, distinguished only by the presence of the cardiac glands. **p. cartilagin'ea sep'ti na'si** [N A], the plate of cartilage forming the anterior part of the nasal septum. Called also *septum cartilagineum nasi* [B N A], and *cartilaginous part of nasal septum.* **p. cartilagin'ea tu'bae auditi'vae** [N A, B N A], the part of the auditory tube that is chiefly supported by the tubal cartilage. It extends from the pars ossea to the pharyngeal orifice of the auditory tube. **p. caverno'sa ure'thrae vir'ilis** [B N A], p. spongiosa urethrae masculinae. **p. centra'lis ventric'uli latera'lis cer'ebri** [N A, B N A], the part of the lateral ventricle found within the parietal lobe of the cerebrum. It communicates with the anterior, posterior, and inferior horns. **p. cephal'ica et cervica'lis systema'tis autonom'ici** [N A], **p. cephal'ica et cervica'lis systema'tis sympath'ici** [B N A], the portion of the autonomic nervous system arising from the brain and from the cervical portion of the sympathetic trunks. **p. cerato-pharyn'gea mus'culi constricto'ris pharyn'gis me'dii** [N A], the portion of the constrictor pharyngis medius muscle arising from the greater cornu of the hyoid bone. Called also *musculus ceratopharyngeus* [B N A]. **p. cervica'lis esoph'agi** [N A], the part of the esophagus that is located in the cervical region, related anteriorly to the trachea and the recurrent laryngeal nerves, posteriorly to the longus colli muscle and vertebral column, and laterally to the lobes of the thyroid gland and the common carotid arteries. **p. cervica'lis medul'lae spina'lis** [N A, B N A], that part of the spinal cord lodged within the canal of the cervical vertebrae and giving rise to the eight pairs of cervical spinal nerves. **p. cervica'lis oesoph'agi** [B N A], p. cervicalis esophagi. **p. cervica'lis systema'tis sympath'ici** [B N A]. See *p. cephalica et cervicalis systematis autonomici.* **p. chondro-pharyn'gea mus'culi constricto'ris pharyn'gis me'dii** [N A], the portion of the constrictor pharyngis medius muscle arising from the lesser cornu of the hyoid bone. Called also *musculus chondropharyngeus* [B N A]. **p. cilia'ris ret'inae** [N A, B N A], the part of the retina that lies on the posterior surface of the ciliary body. **p. clavicula'ris mus'culi pectora'lis majo'ris** [N A, B N A], the portion of the pectoralis major muscle originating from the clavicle. **p. cochlea'ris ner'vi octa'vi** [N A], the part of the eighth cranial nerve concerned with hearing, consisting of fibers that arise from bipolar cells in the spiral ganglion and have their receptors in the spiral organ of the cochlea. Called also *nervus cochleae* [B N A]. **p. convolu'ta lob'uli cortica'lis re'nis** [N A, B N A], the part of the cortex surrounding the intracortical prolongations of the renal pyramids and composed of convoluted tubules. **par'tes corpo'ris huma'ni** [N A, B N A], the category in anatomical nomenclature embracing the names of the various parts of the human body, from head (caput) to foot (pes). **p. costa'lis diaphrag'matis** [N A, B N A], the part of the respiratory diaphragm arising from the inner surfaces of the ribs and their cartilages. **p. cricopharyn'gea mus'culi constricto'ris pharyn'gis infe-rio'ris** [N A], the portion of the constrictor pharyngis inferior muscle arising from the cricoid cartilage. Called also *musculus cricopharyngeus* [B N A]. **p. crucifor'mis vagi'nae fibro'sae digito'rum ma'nus** [N A], one of the diagonal bundles of the fascia of the fingers which cross each other on the dorsal surface of each digit at the level of the distal end of the proximal phalanx. Called also *ligamenta cruciata digitorum manus* [B N A]. **p. crucifor'mis vagi'nae fibro'sae digito'rum pe'dis** [N A], one of the bundles of fascial fibers in the toes resembling those of similar name in the fingers. Called also *ligamenta cruciata digitorum pedis* [B N A]. **p. cupula'ris reces'sus epitympan'ici** [N A, B N A], the part of the epitympanic recess above the head of the malleus. **p. descen'dens**

duode'ni [N A, B N A], the part of the duodenum between the superior and inferior parts, into which the bile and pancreatic ducts open. **p. dex'tra fa'ciei diaphragmat'icae hep'atis** [N A], the portion of the diaphragmatic surface of the liver that is directed toward the right side of the body. **p. dista'lis lo'bi anterio'ris hypophys'eos.** See *pituitary gland.* **p. dorsa'lis pon'tis** [N A, B N A], the tegmental part of the pons, which resembles the medulla oblongata in structure and is continuous with the tegmentum of the mesencephalon. **p. feta'lis placen'tae** [N A], the part of the placenta derived from the chorionic sac that encloses the embryo, and consisting of a chorionic plate and chorionic villi. Called also *placenta foetalis* [B N A]. **p. flac'cida membra'nae tym'pani** [N A, B N A], the small upper portion of the tympanic membrane, between the mallear folds **p. fronta'lis cap'sulae inter'nae** [B N A], crus anterius capsulae internae. **p. fronta'lis coro'nae radia'tae** [B N A]. Omitted in N A. **p. fronta'lis oper'culi** [B N A], operculum frontale. **p. fronta'lis radiatio'nis corpo'ris callo'si** [B N A], the frontal part of the radiatio corporis callosi, composed of fibers sweeping forward from the genu into the frontal lobe. Omitted in N A. **par'tes genita'les exter'nae mulie'bres** [B N A], partes genitales femininae externae. **par'tes genita'les exter'nae vir'iles** [B N A], partes genitales masculinae externae. **par'tes genita'les femini'nae exter'nae** [N A], the female pudendum and clitoris. Called also *partes genitales externae muliebres* [B N A]. **par'tes genita'les masculi'nae exter'nae** [N A], the scrotum and the penis. Called also *partes genitales externae viriles* [B N A]. **p. gla'bra,** a smooth zone or area, such as the outer smooth zone of the lip appearing early in its embryonic development. **p. glossopharyn'gea mus'culi constricto'ris pharyn'gis superio'ris** [N A], the part of the constrictor pharyngis superior muscle arising from the side of the root of the tongue. **p. gris'ea hypothal'ami** [B N A]. Omitted in N A. **p. horizonta'lis duode'ni** [N A], that part of the duodenum situated between the descending and ascending parts, crossing from right to left ventral to the third lumbar vertebra. Called also *inferior part of duodenum.* **p. horizonta'lis [infe'rior] duode'ni** [B N A], p. horizontalis duodeni. **p. horizonta'lis os'sis palati'ni** [B N A], lamina horizontalis ossis palatini. **p. ili'aca lin'eae termina'lis** [B N A], linea arcuata (def. 1). **p. infe'rior duode'ni** [B N A], p. horizontalis duodeni; accepted by N A as an official alternative for the latter term. **p. infe'rior fos'sae rhomboi'deae** [B N A], a space at the lower part or floor of the fourth ventricle, between the restiform bodies. Omitted in N A. **p. infe'rior gy'ri fronta'lis me'dii** [B N A], the inferior portion of the middle frontal gyrus. Omitted in N A. **p. infe'rior par'tis vestibula'ris ner'vi octa'vi** [N A], the inferior of the branches into which the vestibular part of the eighth cranial nerve divides peripherally; it gives rise to the posterior ampullar and saccular nerves. **p. inflex'a,** the bar of a horse's hoof. **p. infraclavicula'ris plex'us brachia'lis** [N A, B N A], the part of the brachial plexus that lies in the axilla, below the level of the clavicle. In it arise the medial and lateral pectoral, musculocutaneous, medial brachial cutaneous, medial antebrachial cutaneous, median, ulnar, radial, subscapular, thoracodorsal, and axillary nerves. **p. intercartilagin'ea ri'mae glot'tidis** [N A, B N A], the part of the rima glottidis between the arytenoid cartilages. **p. interme'dia fos'sae rhomboi'deae** [B N A], the middle part of the rhomboid fossa. Omitted in N A. **p. interme'dia lo'bi anterio'ris hypophys'eos** [N A]. See *pituitary gland.* **p. intermembrana'cea ri'mae glot'tidis** [N A, B N A], the part of the rima glottidis between the vocal folds. **p. irid'ica ret'inae** [N A], the part of the retina that lies on the posterior surface of the iris. **p. labia'lis mus'culi orbicula'ris o'ris** [N A], the part of the orbicular muscle of the mouth whose fibers are restricted to the lips. **p. lacrima'lis mus'culi orbicula'ris oc'uli** [N A, B N A], the part of the orbicularis oculi muscle that arises from the posterior lacrimal ridge of the lacrimal bone, to become continuous with the palpebral portion. **p. laryn'gea pharyn'gis** [N A, B N A], the portion of the pharynx that lies below the upper edge of the epiglottis and opens into the larynx and esophagus. Called also *laryngopharynx.* **p. latera'lis ar'cus longitudina'lis pe'dis** [N A], that part of the longitudinal arch of the foot formed by the calcaneus, the cuboid bone, and the lateral two metatarsal bones. **p. latera'lis musculo'rum intertransversario'rum posterio'rum cer'vicis** [N A], the lateral part of the posterior intertransverse muscles of the neck. **p. latera'lis os'sis occipita'lis** [N A, B N A], one of the paired parts of the occipital bone which form the lateral boundaries of the foramen magnum, each being prominently characterized by the presence of one of the occipital condyles. **p. latera'lis os'sis sa'cri** [N A, B N A], the part or mass of the sacrum on either side lateral to the dorsal and pelvic sacral foramina. **p. li'bera colum'nae for'nicis** [B N A]. Omitted in N A. **p. lumba'lis diaphrag'matis** [N A, B N A], the portion of the respiratory diaphragm that arises from the lumbar vertebrae, comprising the right and left diaphragmatic crura, the right crus arising from the upper three or four vertebrae, and the left from the upper two or three. **p. lumba'lis medul'lae spina'lis** [N A, B N A], that part of the spinal cord lodged within the lumbar vertebrae and giving rise to the five pairs of lumbar spinal nerves. **p. mamilla'ris hypothal'ami** [B N A]. Omitted in N A. **p. margina'lis mus'culi orbicula'ris o'ris** [N A], the part of the orbicular muscle of the mouth whose fibers blend with those of adjacent muscles. **p. margina'lis sul'ci cin'guli** [B N A], the portion of the cingulate gyrus that turns off at a right angle and is directed toward the dorsal margin of the hemisphere. Omitted in N A. **p. mastoi'dea os'sis tempora'lis** [B N A], the posterior portion of the petrous part of the temporal bone, bounded anteriorly by the external acoustic meatus and articulating superiorly with the parietal bone and posteriorly with the occipital bone. Omitted in N A. **p. media'lis ar'cus longitudina'lis pe'dis** [N A], that part of the longitudinal arch of the foot formed by the calcaneus, talus, and the navicular, cuneiform, and first three tarsal bones. **p. media'lis musculo'rum intertransversario'rum posterio'rum cer'vicis** [N A], the medial part of the posterior intertransverse muscles of the neck. **p. mediastina'lis fa'ciei media'lis pulmo'nis** [N A], the part of the medial surface of each lung that is adjacent to the mediastinum. **p. membrana'cea sep'ti atrio'rum** [B N A], septum atrioventriculare cordis. **p. membrana'cea sep'ti interventricula'ris cor'dis** [N A], the very small, completely membranous area of the interventricular septum of the heart; situated near the root of the aorta, it can be viewed between the opposed margins of the right and posterior semilunar valves of the aorta. Called also *septum membranaceum ventriculorum cordis* [B N A]. **p. membrana'cea sep'ti na'si** [N A], the anterior inferior part of the nasal septum, beneath the cartilaginous part. It is composed of skin and subcutaneous tissues. Called also *septum membranaceum nasi* [B N A]. **p. membrana'cea ure'thrae masculi'nae** [N A], **p. membrana'cea ure'thrae vir'ilis** [B N A], the portion of the male urethra between the pars prostatica and pars spongiosa, and traversing the urogenital diaphragm and the deep perineal space. **p. mo'bilis sep'ti na'si** [N A], the part of the nasal septum at the apex of the nose, formed by skin, subcutaneous tissue, and the greater alar cartilages. Called also *septum mobile nasi* [B N A], and *mobile part of nasal septum.* **p. muscula′ris sep′ti interventricula′ris cor′dis** [N A], the thick muscular partition forming the greater part of the septum between the ventricles of the heart. Called also *septum musculare ventriculorum cordis* [B N A]. **p. mylopharyn′gea mus′culi constricto′ris pharyn′gis superio′ris** [N A], the part of the constrictor pharyngis superior muscle arising from the mylohyoid ridge of the mandible. Called also *musculus mylopharyngeus* [B N A]. **p. nasa′lis os′sis fronta′lis** [N A, B N A], the small, irregularly shaped process that projects downward from the medial part of the squama of the frontal bone to articulate with the nasal bones and the frontal processes of the maxillae. **p. nasa′lis pharyn′gis** [N A, B N A], the part of the pharynx that lies above the level of the soft palate. Called also *nasopharynx.* **p. nervo′sa hypophys′eos,** lobus posterior hypophyseos. **p. obli′qua mus′culi cricothyroi′dei** [N A], the fibers of the cricothyroid muscle that are inserted into the inferior horn, caudal margin, and inner surface of the thyroid cartilage. **p. occipita′lis cap′sulae inter′nae** [B N A], crus posterius capsulae internae. **p. occipita′lis coro′nae radia′tae** [B N A]. Omitted in N A. **p. occipita′lis radiatio′nis corpo′ris callo′si** [B N A], the occipital part of the radiatio corporis callosi, composed of fibers from the splenium bending backward toward the occipital pole. Omitted in N A. **p. opercula′ris gy′ri fronta′lis inferio′ris** [N A, B N A], the part of the inferior frontal lobe adjacent to the parietal lobe and overhanging the insula. **p. op′tica hypothal′ami** [B N A]. Omitted in N A. **p. op′tica ret′inae** [N A, B N A], the part of the retina that contains receptors sensitive to light, extending posteriorly from the ora serrata on the inner surface of the choroid and continuous at the optic disk with the optic nerve; it consists of an outer pigmented stratum and an inner, multilayered cerebral stratum. **p. ora′lis pharyn′gis** [N A, B N A], the division of the pharynx that lies between the soft palate and the upper edge of the epiglottis. Called also *oropharynx.* **p. orbita′lis glan′dulae lacrima′lis** [N A], the main part of the lacrimal gland, limited in front by the orbicularis muscle and the orbital septum. Called also *glandulae lacrimalis superior* [B N A]. **p. orbita′lis gy′ri fronta′lis inferio′ris** [N A, B N A], the part of the inferior frontal gyrus rostral to the anterior branch of the lateral cerebral sulcus. **p. orbita′lis mus′culi orbicula′ris oc′uli** [N A, B N A], the part of the orbicularis oculi muscle that arises from the medial margin of the orbit and surrounds it and the palpebral part of the muscle, inserting near the site of origin. **p. orbita′lis os′sis fronta′lis** [N A, B N A], the horizontally placed part of the frontal bone that forms the greater part of the roof of the orbit and of the floor of the anterior cranial fossa. It is separated from its fellow of the other side by the ethmoid incisure. **p. os′sea sep′ti na′si** [N A], the bony part of the nasal septum, composed posterosuperiorly of the perpendicular plate of the ethmoid bone and posteroinferiorly of the vomer. **p. os′sea tu′bae auditi′vae** [N A, B N A], the part of the auditory tube that lies within the temporal bone, extending from the tympanic orifice to the pars cartilaginea of the auditory tube. **p. palpebra′lis glan′dulae lacrima′lis** [N A], the part of the lacrimal gland that projects laterally into the upper eyelid. Called also *glandula lacrimalis inferior* [B N A]. **p. palpebra′lis mus′culi orbicula′ris oc′uli** [N A, B N A], the part of the orbicularis oculi muscle that is contained in the eyelids, originating from the medial palpebral ligament and inserting in the outer canthus. Called also *palpebral part of orbicularis oculi muscle.* **p. parasympath′ica systema′tis nervo′si autonom′ici** [N A], the craniosacral division of the autonomic nervous system, its preganglionic fibers travelling with cranial nerves III, VII, IX, and X, and with the first three sacral nerves; it innervates the heart, the smooth muscle and glands of the head and neck, and the thoracic, abdominal, and pelvic viscera. Called also *parasympathetic nervous system.* **p. parieta′lis coro′nae radia′tae** [B N A]. Omitted in N A. **p. parieta′lis oper′culi** [B N A], operculum frontoparietale. **p. parieta′lis radiatio′nis cor′poris callo′si** [B N A], the fibers of the radiatio corporis callosi passing into the parietal lobe. Omitted in N A. **p. pelvi′na systema′tis sympath′ici** [B N A]. See *p. abdominalis et pelvina systematis autonomici.* **p. pelvi′na ure′teris** [N A, B N A], the portion of the ureter that extends from the terminal line of the pelvis to the urinary bladder. **p. perpendicula′ris os′sis palati′ni** [B N A], lamina perpendicularis ossis palatini. **p. petro′sa os′sis tempora′lis** [N A, B N A], a pyramid of dense bone located at the base of the cranium; one of the three parts of the temporal bone, it houses the organ of hearing. **p. pla′na cor′poris cilia′ris,** orbiculus ciliaris. **p. plica′ta cor′poris cilia′ris,** corona ciliaris. **p. poste′rior commissu′rae anterio′ris cer′ebri** [N A, B N A], the part of the anterior commissure that interconnects the middle and inferior temporal gyri, the parahippocampal gyri, and the amygdaloid bodies of the two sides. **p. poste′rior fa′ciei diaphragmat′icae hep′atis** [N A], the portion of the diaphragmatic surface of the liver that is directed toward the dorsal surface of the body. Called also *facies posterior hepatis* [B N A]. **p. poste′rior hypophys′eos,** lobus posterior hypophyseos. **p. poste′rior lob′uli quadrangula′ris** [B N A], the posterior portion of the quadrangular lobule. Omitted in N A. **p. poste′rior rhinenceph′ali** [B N A], the posterior portion of the rhinencephalon. Omitted in N A. **p. pri′ma radi′cis ner′vi facia′lis** [B N A], the ascending part of the root of the facial nerve. Omitted in N A. **p. profun′da glan′dulae parot′idis** [N A], that part of the parotid gland located deep to the facial nerve. **p. profun′da mus′culi masse′teris** [N A], the deep portion of the masseter muscle, the fibers of which arise from the medial surface of the zygomatic arch and the fascia over the temporal muscle, and are directed vertically downward. **p. profun′da mus′culi sphinc′teris a′ni exter′ni** [N A], the part of the sphincter ani externus muscle that surrounds the upper part of the anal canal. **p. prostat′ica ure′thrae masculi′nae** [N A], **p. prostat′ica ure′thrae vir′ilis** [B N A], the part of the male urethra that passes through the prostate. **p. pterygopharyn′gea mus′culi constricto′ris pharyn′gis superio′ris** [N A], the part of the constrictor pharyngis superioris muscle arising from the caudal part and hamulus of the medial pterygoid plate. Called also *musculus pterygopharyngeus* [B N A]. **p. pu′bica lin′eae termina′lis** [B N A], the pubic part of the terminal line. Omitted in N A. **p. pylo′rica ventric′uli** [N A, B N A], the caudal one-third of the stomach, consisting of the pyloric antrum and canal, and distinguished by the presence of the pyloric glands. **p. radia′ta lob′uli cortica′lis re′nis** [N A, B N A], any one of the intracortical prolongations of the renal pyramids. Called also *processus Ferreini lobuli corticalis renis* and *pyramid of Ferrein.* **p. rec′ta mus′culi cricothyroi′dei** [N A], the fibers of the cricothyroid muscle that are inserted into the caudal margin of the thyroid cartilage. **p. retrolentifor′mis cap′sulae inter′nae** [N A], that part of the internal capsule resting on the lateral surface of the thalamus behind the lentiform nucleus, and containing the posterior thalamic radiation. **p. sacra′lis lin′eae termina′lis** [B N A], the sacral part of the terminal line. Omitted in N A. **p. secun′da radi′cis ner′vi facia′lis** [B N A], the second portion of the root of the facial nerve. Omitted in N A. **p. spongio'sa ure'thrae masculi'nae** [N A], the portion of the male urethra found within the corpus spongiosum of the penis. Called also *p. cavernosa urethrae virilis* [B N A]. **p. squamo'sa os'sis tempora'lis** [N A], the flat, scalelike, anterior and superior portion of the temporal bone. Called also *squama temporalis* [B N A]. **p. sterna'lis diaphrag'matis** [N A, B N A], the portion of the respiratory diaphragm that arises from the inner aspect of the xiphoid process of the sternum. **p. sterno-costa'lis mus'culi pectora'lis majo'ris** [N A, B N A], the portion of the pectoralis major muscle that originates from the sternum and the ribs. **p. subcuta'nea mus'culi sphinc'teris a'ni exter'ni** [N A], the part of the sphincter ani externus muscle that surrounds the lowermost portion of the anal canal. **p. subfronta'lis sul'ci cin'guli** [B N A], the portion of the cingulate sulcus under the superior frontal gyrus. Omitted in N A. **p. sublenti-for'mis cap'sulae inter'nae** [N A], the part of the internal capsule lying ventral to the back part of the lentiform nucleus, and containing the temporopontile, geniculocalcarine, and auditory radiation fibers. **p. superficia'lis glan'dulae parot'idis** [N A], that part of the parotid gland located superficial to the facial nerve. **p. superficia'lis mus'culi masse'teris** [N A], the superficial portion of the masseter muscle, the fibers of which arise from the anterior part of the zygomatic arch and are directed downward and backward. **p. superficia'lis mus'culi sphinc'teris a'ni exter'ni** [N A], the part of the sphincter ani externus muscle that lies just deep to the pars subcutanea, extending farther toward the rectum. **p. supe'rior duode'ni** [N A, B N A], the part of the duodenum adjacent to the pylorus, forming the superior flexure. **p. supe'rior fa'ciei diaphragmat'icae hep'atis** [N A], the portion of the diaphragmatic surface of the liver that is directed cranially. **p. supe'rior fos'sae rhomboi'deae** [B N A], the superior portion of the rhomboid fossa. Omitted in N A. **p. supe'rior gy'ri fronta'lis me'dii** [B N A], the superior portion of the middle frontal gyrus. Omitted in N A. **p. supe'rior par'tis vestibula'ris ner'vi octa'vi** [N A], the superior of the branches into which the vestibular part of the eighth cranial nerve divides peripherally; it gives rise to the utricular, anterior ampullar, and lateral ampullar nerves. **p. supraclavicula'ris plex'us brachia'lis** [N A, B N A], the part of the brachial plexus lying in the cervical region above the level of the clavicle, in which arise the dorsal scapular, long thoracic, subclavian, and suprascapular nerves. **p. sympath'ica systema'tis nervo'si autonom'ici** [N A], the portion of the autonomic nervous system that arises from the central nervous system by preganglionic neurons with cell bodies situated in the thoracic and the first three lumbar segments of the spinal cord. The fibers enter the sympathetic trunk, either synapsing in ganglia there or passing through to synapse in the ganglia of the autonomic plexuses. The postganglionic fibers innervate cardiac muscle, smooth muscle, and glands of the entire body. Called also *sympathetic nervous system*. **p. tec'ta colum'nae for'nicis** [B N A]. Omitted in N A. **p. tegmenta'lis fascic'uli pedunculo-mamilla'ris** [B N A]. Omitted in N A. **p. tempora'lis coro'nae radia'tae** [B N A]. Omitted in N A. **p. tempora'lis oper'culi** [B N A], operculum temporale. **p. tempora'lis radiatio'nis cor'poris callo'si** [B N A], the fibers of the radiatio corporis callosi passing into the temporal lobe. Omitted in N A. **p. ten'sa membra'nae tym'pani** [N A, B N A], the large lower portion of the tympanic membrane. **p. thoraca'lis esoph'agi** [N A], the middle part of the esophagus, located in the thoracic region, and related anteriorly to the trachea and pericardium and posteriorly to the vertebral column. **p. thoraca'lis medul'lae spina'lis** [B N A], p. thoracica medullae spinalis. **p. thoraca'lis oesoph'agi** [B N A], p. thoracalis esophagi. **p. thoraca'lis systema'tis auto-nom'ici** [N A], **p. thoraca'lis systema'tis sympath'ici** [B N A], the parts of the autonomic nervous system that arise from the thoracic portion of the sympathetic trunks. **p. thora'cica medul'lae spina'lis** [N A], the part of the spinal cord lodged in the canal of the thoracic vertebrae and giving rise to the twelve pairs of thoracic spinal nerves. **p. thyropharyn'gea mus'culi constricto'ris pharyn'gis infe-rio'ris** [N A], the part of the constrictor pharyngis inferior muscle arising from the thyroid cartilage. Called also *musculus thyreopharyngeus* [B N A]. **p. tibiocalca'nea ligamen'ti media'lis** [N A], the middle portion of the superficial fibers of the medial ligament of the ankle joint; attached superiorly to the medial malleolus of the tibia and inferiorly into nearly the entire length of the sustentaculum tali of the calcaneus. Called also *ligamentum calcaneotibiale* [B N A], and *calcaneo-tibial ligament*. **p. tibionavicula'ris liga-men'ti media'lis** [N A], the anterior portion of the superficial fibers of the medial ligament of the ankle joint; attached superiorly to the anterior surface of the medial malleolus of the tibia and inferiorly to the navicular bone and the margin of the calcaneonavicular ligament. Called also *ligamentum tibionaviculare* [B N A], and *tibio-navicular ligament*. **p. tibiotala'ris ante'rior ligamen'ti media'lis** [N A,] the deeper portion of the medial ligament of the ankle joint; attached superiorly to the medial malleolus of the tibia and inferiorly to the medial surface of the talus. Called also *ligamentum talotibiale anterius* [B N A], and *anterior talotibial ligament*. **p. tibiotala'ris poste'rior ligamen'ti media'lis** [N A], the posterior portion of the superficial fibers of the medial ligament of the ankle joint; attached superiorly to the posterior part of the medial malleolus of the tibia and inferiorly to the medial surface of the talus. Called also *ligamentum talotibiale posterius* [B N A], and *posterior talotibial ligament*. **p. transver'sa mus'culi nasa'lis** [N A, B N A], the part of the nasal muscle that arises from the canine eminence of the maxilla and joins by common aponeurosis its fellow of the opposite side. **p. triangula'ris,** operculum frontale. **p. triangula'ris gy'ri fronta'lis inferio'ris** [N A, B N A], the wedge-shaped part of the inferior frontal lobe that lies between the anterior and ascending branches of the lateral cerebral sulcus. **p. tubera'lis lo'bi anterio'ris hypophys'eos** [N A]. See *pituitary gland*. **p. tympan'ica os'sis tempora'lis** [N A, B N A], the part of the temporal bone that forms the anterior and inferior walls and part of the posterior wall of the external auditory meatus. **p. uteri'na placen'tae** [N A], the maternally contributed part of the placenta, derived from the decidua basalis. Called also *placenta uterina* [B N A]. **p. uteri'na tu'bae uteri'nae** [N A, B N A], the proximal part of the uterine tube, located within the wall of the uterus. **p. verte-bra'lis fa'ciei media'lis pulmo'nis** [N A], the part of the medial surface of each lung that is adjacent to the vertebral column. **p. vestib-ula'ris ner'vi octa'vi** [N A], the part of the eighth cranial nerve concerned with equilibration, consisting of fibers that arise from bipolar cells in the vestibular ganglion and divide peripherally into a superior and an inferior part, with receptors in the semicircular canals, utricle, and saccule. Called also *nervus vestibuli* [B N A]. **p. villo'sa,** a villus-covered zone or area, such as the inner villus-covered zone of the lip appearing early in its embryonic development.

parsidol (par'sĭ-dol). Trade mark for a preparation of ethopropazine.

Parsons' disease (par'sunz) [James *Parsons*, English physician, 1705–1770]. Exophthalmic goiter.

part (part) [L. *pars* a portion, piece, share]. A division or portion. For names of other parts of various anatomical structures, see under *pars*. **broad p. of anterior annular ligament of leg,** retinaculum musculorum extensorum pedis superius. **colic p. of omentum,** omentum majus. **condylar p. of occipital bone,** pars lateralis ossis occipitalis. **exoccipital p. of occipital bone,** pars lateralis ossis occipitalis. **jugular p. of occipital bone,** pars lateralis ossis occipitalis. **lambdoidal (lower) p. of anterior annular ligament of leg,** retinaculum musculorum extensorum pedis inferius. **mamillary p. of temporal bone,** pars mastoidea ossis temporalis. **occipital p. of occipital bone,** squama occipitalis. **parietal p. of pelvic fascia,** fascia diaphragmatis pelvis superior. **pectineal p. of inguinal ligament,** ligamentum lacunare. **squamous p. of occipital bone,** squama occipitalis. **sternocostal p. of diaphragm,** pars costalis diaphragmatis. **subphrenic p. of esophagus,** pars abdominalis esophagi. **superior p. of anterior annular ligament of leg,** retinaculum musculorum extensorum pedis superius. **tabular p. of occipital bone,** squama occipitalis. **tendinous p. of epicranius muscle,** galea aponeurotica. **third p. of quadriceps femoris muscle,** musculus adductor minimus. **transverse p. of anterior annular ligament of leg,** retinaculum musculorum extensorum pedis superius. **vaginal p. of cervix,** portio vaginalis cervicis. **vertebral p. of diaphragm,** pars lumbalis diaphragmatis. **visceral p. of pelvic fascia,** fascia endopelvina.

Part. aeq. Abbreviation for L. *par'tes aequa'les*, equal parts.

partal (par'tal). Pertaining to parturition.

partes (par'tēz) [L.]. Plural of *pars*.

parthenogenesis (par″thĕ-no-jen'e-sis) [Gr. *parthenos* virgin + *genesis* production]. Unisexual reproduction; reproduction by the development of an egg without its being fertilized by a spermatozoon, as occurs in certain lower animals. **artificial p.,** the development of an unfertilized ovum initiated by artificial means, such as chemical or mechanical stimulation.

parthenology (par-thĕ-nol'o-je) [Gr. *parthenos* virgin + *-logy*]. The branch of gynecology which has to do with virgins.

parthenophobia (par″thĕ-no-fo'be-ah) [Gr. *parthenos* virgin + *phobein* to be affrighted by]. Morbid dread of girls.

parthenoplasty (par-then'o-plas″te) [Gr. *parthenos* virgin + *plassein* to form]. Production of a spurious virginity by suturing the ruptured hymen.

parthogenesis (par″tho-jen'e-sis). Parthenogenesis.

particle (par'te-k'l) [L. *particula*, dim. of *partus* part]. A tiny mass of material. **alpha p.,** a positively charged particle ejected from the nucleus of a radioactive atom, being a high-speed ionized atom of helium. A stream of these particles constitutes alpha rays. **attraction p.,** a small particle in the center of the attraction sphere. **beta p.,** an electron emitted from an atomic nucleus during beta decay. **colloid p's,** in colloid chemistry the ultimate particles of a disperse phase. In lyophilic colloids the particles are larger than a single molecule, being from 1 to 100 micromicrons in diameter, but not large enough to settle out by gravity; in a lyophobic colloid they may consist of one or more large organic molecules, as of starch or protein. **disperse p's,** the disperse phase of a colloid system; the particles of colloid in a colloid system. **high-velocity p's,** nuclear particles, such as electrons, protons, and deuterons, given high speeds in an accelerator. **lens p's,** fine brown points of pigment on the anterior capsule of the lens, being the vestiges of the capsulopupillary membrane of the fetus. **nuclear p's,** Howell bodies. **X-p.,** a hypothetical particle of matter, believed to arise from the collison of cosmic rays in the upper air. **Zimmermann's elementary p's,** blood platelets.

particulate (par-tik'u-lāt). Composed of separate particles.

partigen (par'tĭ-jen). One of the hypothetical constituents of an antigen, which is considered as a mixture of partigens or partial antigens. See *haptene*.

partimute (par'tĭ-mūt). A deaf-mute.

partimutism (par″tĭ-mu'tizm). Deaf-mutism.

partinium (par-tin'e-um). An alloy of aluminum and tungsten.

parturient (par-tu're-ent) [L. *parturiens*]. Giving birth, or pertaining to childbirth. By extension, sometimes used to designate a woman in labor.

parturifacient (par″tu-re-fa'shent) [L. *parturire* to have the pains of labor + *facere* to cause]. 1. Inducing or facilitating childbirth. 2. A medicine that induces or facilitates childbirth.

parturiometer (par″tu-re-om'e-ter) [L. *parturitio* childbirth + *metrum* measure]. A device used in measuring the expulsive power of the uterus.

parturition (par″tu-rish'un) [L. *parturitio*]. The act or process of giving birth to a child.

partus (par'tus) [L.]. 1. Labor, or childbirth. 2. The young when brought forth. **p. agrippi'nus,** breech delivery. **p. caesa'reus,** delivery by cesarean section. **p. immatu'rus,** premature labor. **p. matu'rus,** labor at full term. **p. precipita'tus,** precipitate labor. **p. prematu'rus,** premature labor. **p. seroti'nus,** delayed labor. **p. sic'cus,** dry labor.

Part. vic. Abbreviation for L. *par'tibus vi'cibus*, in divided doses.

parulis (pah-roo'lis) [*para-* + Gr. *oulon* gum]. A gum-boil or subperiosteal abscess of the gum.

parumbilical (par″um-bil'ĭ-kal). Near the navel.

paruria (par-u're-ah) [*para-* + Gr. *ouron* urine + *-ia*]. Any disorder of the urine or abnormal state of the urine or its discharge.

parvicellular (par″vĭ-sel'u-lar) [L. *parvus* small + *cellula* cell]. Composed of small cells.

Parvobacteriaceae (par″vo-bak-te″re-a'se-e). A name formerly given the family of schizomycetes later called Brucellaceae.

parvoline (par'vo-lin). An amber-colored liquid ptomaine, $C_9H_{13}N$, from decaying fish or horse flesh.

parvule (par'vūl) [L. *parvulus* very small]. A very small pill, pellet, or granule.

PAS, PASA. Para-aminosalicylic acid. See under *acid*.

Pascal's law (pas-kahlz') [Blaise *Pascal*, French scientist, 1623–1662]. See under *law*.

paschachurda (pas-kah-koor'dah). Tashkend ulcer.

Paschen's bodies, corpuscles, granules (pahs'kenz) [Enrique *Paschen*, Hamburg pathologist, 1860–1936]. See under *body*.

Paschutin's degeneration (pas-ku'tinz) [Victor Wassiljewitch *Paschutin*, Russian pathologist, 1845–1901]. See under *degeneration*.

paspalism (pas'pal-izm). Poisoning due to the seeds of a grass, *Paspalum scrobiculatum*, of India.

passage (pas'ij). 1. A channel or meatus. 2. An evacuation of the bowels. 3. Introduction of infectious material into an experimental animal or culture medium, followed by recovery of the infectious agent. 4. The act of moving from one place to another. 5. The introduction of a catheter, probe, or sound, through a natural body orifice. **blind p.,** successive transfer of infection through experimental animals, chick embryo, or tissue culture, when overt lesions of disease are not apparent, at least in the earlier members of the series. **false p.,** an unnatural channel or meatus in a body structure, created by trauma or by disease. **serial p.,** the successive transfer of infection from one experimental animal to another, in series, by the inoculation of tissue, exudate, or other material containing the infectious agent.

Passavant's bar (pas′ah-vants) [Philip Gustav *Passavant*, German surgeon, 1815–1893]. See under *bar*.

Passiflora (pas″ĭ-flo′rah) [L. *passio* passion + *flos* flower]. A genus of twining plants of the warmer parts of America; passion flower. Many species were formerly used medicinally.

passion (pash′un) [L. *passio* suffering]. 1. Pain or suffering. 2. Strong emotion. **ileac p.,** ileus.

passional (pash′un-al). Marked by or exhibiting passion.

passive (pas′iv) [L. *passivus*]. Neither spontaneous nor active; not produced by active efforts.

passivism (pas′ĭ-vizm). Sexual perversion with subjection of the will to another's.

passivity (pas-siv′ĭ-te). A state marked by delusional feelings of being influenced by others or by outside forces or influences.

Past. Abbreviation for *Pasteurella*.

pasta (pas′tah), pl. *pas′tae* [L.]. Paste.

paste (pāst) [L. *pasta*]. A soft, viscid substance. **Alexander's p.,** a paste for treatment of burns, consisting of ichthyol, olive oil, and wool fat. **almond p.,** a magma prepared from bitter almonds. **aluminum p.,** a preparation of aluminum powder, liquid petrolatum, and zinc oxide ointment: used in dressing wounds, and applied topically to skin around an intestinal stoma. **arsenical p.,** a caustic paste containing arsenic. **Beck's p.,** a paste consisting of bismuth subnitrate and sterile petrolatum: injected for the treatment of tuberculous cavities and chronic sinuses. **bipp p.** See *bipp*. **bismuth p.,** Beck's p. **Bougard's p.,** a caustic paste containing mercuric chloride, mercuric sulfide, zinc chloride, arsenic, starch, and flour. **Bourdin's p.,** nitric acid mixed with sublimed sulfur: escharotic. **Brooke's p.,** oleate of mercury, petrolatum, ichthyol, starch, zinc oxide, and salicylic acid, useful in skin diseases. **Canquoin's p.,** zinc chloride mixed with flour and water. **Coster's p.,** a paste of iodine and tar. **Delbet's p.,** a paste for wound dressings, consisting of tincture of iodine, chloroform, and wax. **dermatologic p.,** one made of starch, dextrin, zinc oxide, calcium carbonate, or sulfur, together with glycerin, petrolatum, or a fat, and containing some drug. **dextrinated p.,** a preparation of dextrin, glycerin, and distilled water: used as a vehicle. **Dreuw's p.,** a mixture of ichthyol, purified sulfur, and Lassar's paste. **Dupuytren's p.,** a caustic paste of arsenous anhydride, calomel, and gum. **Esmarch's p.,** a caustic paste made of arsenic, morphine sulfate, calomel, and acacia. **Frère Cosme's p.,** a caustic paste made from arsenic, mercuric sulfide, and burnt sponge. **Ihle's p.,** an ointment containing resorcin, starch, and zinc oxide in soft paraffin. **Landolfi's p.,** a caustic paste containing the chlorides of zinc, antimony, bromine, and gold. **Lassar's p.,** a dressing for erythema, intertrigo, etc., made of petrolatum, zinc oxide, starch, and salicylic acid. **Lassar's betanaphthol p.,** a paste containing betanaphthol, precipitated sulfur, soft soap, and petrolatum. **Leunbach's p.,** a paste for injection into the uterus to produce abortion. Called also *provocol*. **London p.,** a paste containing quicklime and caustic soda. **Marsden's p.,** a mixture of arsenous acid and gum acacia: used as an escharotic. **Morison's p.** See under *method*. **Piffard's p.,** a paste made of copper sulfate, tartrated soda, and caustic soda: used in testing the urine for sugar. **serum p.,** a paste prepared from dried and sterilized blood serum. **sulfuric acid p.,** a mixture of sulfuric acid and powdered saffron: caustic. **Unna's p.,** a paste made of zinc oxide, mucilage of acacia, and glycerin: applied with a brush to eczematous patches. **Veiel p.,** zinc oxide and petrolatum, with boric acid: used for furuncles. **Vienna p.,** a caustic paste of potash and lime. **zinc oxide p.,** a preparation of zinc oxide and starch in white petrolatum, used topically as an astringent. **zipp p.** See *zipp*.

paster (pās′ter). The portion of a bifocal lens ground for near vision.

pastern (pas′tern). The portion of a horse's foot occupied by the first and second phalanges.

Pasteur's effect, fluid, liquid, solution, theory (pas-terz′) [Louis *Pasteur*, French chemist and bacteriologist, 1822–1895, who founded the science of microbiology and developed the technic of vaccination by attenuated virus, and whose discoveries embrace the entire field of microbial activity]. See under *effect, solution*, and *theory*.

Pasteurella (pas″tu-rel′lah) [Louis *Pasteur*]. A genus of microorganisms of the family Brucellaceae, order Eubacteriales, made up of motile or non-motile small, coccoid to rod-shaped, gram-negative cells occurring singly or in pairs, short chains, or groups. **P. anatipes′tifer,** an organism etiologically associated with septicemia in ducklings. **P. haemolyt′ica,** an organism etiologically associated with pneumonia in sheep and cattle. **P. novi′cida,** the etiologic agent for a disease resembling tularemia in guinea pigs, hamsters, and white mice; not known to infect man. **P. pes′tis,** the etiologic agent of plague in man and rats, ground squirrels, and other rodents, transmitted from rat to rat and from rat to man by the rat flea, and from man to man by the human body louse; pathogenic for mice, guinea pigs, and rabbits. **P. pfaf′fii,** the etiologic agent of an epidemic septicemia in canaries, producing a necrotic enteritis. **P. pseudotuberculo′sis,** the etiologic agent of pseudotuberculosis in many animals and birds, and apparently widely distributed in nature. **P. sep′tica,** an organism isolated from cattle, rabbits, and fowls; the etiologic agent of chicken cholera and of a hemorrhagic septicemia in warm-blooded animals. **P. septicae′miae,** an organism isolated from geese, and the cause of a fatal septicemia in young of the species. **P. tularen′sis,** the etiologic agent of tularemia in man, being transmitted from wild animals to man by drinking water, by blood-sucking insects, or by contact.

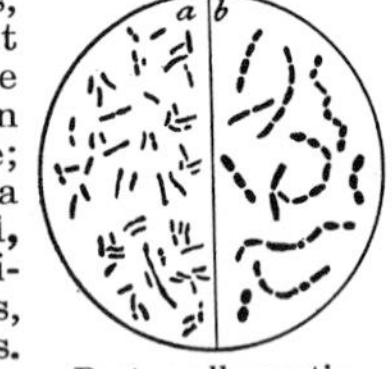

Pasteurella pestis.

Pasteurelleae (pas″ter-el′e-e). A name formerly given a tribe of schizomycetes.

pasteurellosis (pas″ter-el-lo′sis). Infection by microorganisms of the genus Pasteurella.

Pasteuria (pas-tu′re-ah). A genus of microorganisms of the family Pasteuriaceae, order Hyphomicrobiales, made up of pear-shaped, non-motile cells remaining attached in cauliflower-like masses, which are parasitic on fresh-water crustacea. The type species is *P. ramo′sa*.

Pasteuriaceae (pas-tu″re-a′se-e). A family of schizomycetes (order Hyphomicrobiales), made up of spherical or pear-shaped cells, sometimes growing on short stalks in a whorl-like arrangement. It includes two genera, *Blastocaulis* and *Pasteuria*.

pasteurization (pas″tūr-i-za′shun) [Louis *Pasteur*]. The process of heating milk or other substances to a moderate temperature for a definite time, often to 60°C. for thirty minutes. By this heating, pathogenic bacteria are killed and other bacterial development considerably delayed. It is widely used as a sanitary measure in the case of milk.

pasteurizer (pas′tūr-iz″er). An instrument used in effecting pasteurization.

Pastia's lines, sign (pas′te-ahz) [C. *Pastia*, Rumanian physician]. See under *sign*.

pastil (pas′til). Pastille.

pastille (pas-tēl′) [Fr.]. 1. A troche or lozenge.

2. An aromatic mass to be burnt as a fumigant. 3. A small disk of paper coated with platinocyanide of barium or other substance. The green color changes to brown when exposed to the roentgen ray. It is used to estimate the amount of x-ray administered and also to test the intensity of ultraviolet radiation. **Sabouraud's p.,** a small disk of barium platinochloride with acetate of starch and collodion: used to indicate by change of color the strength of roentgen rays.

pastometer (pas-tom′e-ter). An instrument for indicating when milk that is being pasteurized has reached the pasteurization temperature.

pasty (pās′te). Like paste in consistency and color; puffy, pitting, or slightly edematous.

patch (pach) [L. *pittacium;* Gr. *pittakion*]. An area differing from the rest of a surface. **cotton-wool p's,** fleecy-looking white patches observed in ophthalmoscopy, caused by exudates on the retina. **drab-colored p.,** a spot occurring on the liver in various tropical hepatic diseases. **herald p.,** the early eruption in pityriasis rosea, consisting of a solitary patch preceding the general eruption. **Hutchinson's p.,** a reddish or salmon-yellow patch of the cornea in syphilitic keratitis. **mucous p.,** condyloma latum: a lesion characteristic of syphilis. **opaline p.,** a mucous patch of the mouth sometimes seen in syphilis. **Peyer's p's,** oval elevated areas of lymphoid tissue on the mucosa of the small intestine, composed of many lymphoid nodules closely packed together (folliculi lymphatici aggregati [N A]). **salmon p.,** a salmon-colored spot in the cornea in syphilis of that structure. **smokers' p.,** leukoplakia. **white p.,** a white opaque spot on the pericardium or on the capsule of the spleen, due to rubbing against a nodule of a rib in rachitis.

patchouli (pat-shoo′le). A labiate herb of India, *Pogostemon patchouli:* used chiefly in perfumery.

patefaction (pat″e-fak′shun) [L. *patefacere* to lay open]. The act of laying open.

Patein's albumin (pat-anz′) [*Patein,* French physician, died 1928]. See under *albumin.*

patella (pah-tel′lah) [L., dim. of *patera* a shallow dish]. [N A, B N A] A triangular sesamoid bone, about 5 cm. in diameter, situated at the front of the knee in the tendon of insertion of the quadriceps extensor femoris muscle. Called also *knee cap* or *knee pan.* **p. biparti′ta,** a patella that is divided into two parts. **p. cu′biti,** an anomalous sesamoid bone sometimes occurring over the extensor surface of the elbow joint. **floating p.,** a patella that is separated from the condyles by a large effusion in the knee. **p. parti′ta,** a patella that is divided into two or more parts. **slipping p.,** a patella that is easily movable and readily dislocated.

Patella's disease (pah-tel′ahz) [Vincenzo *Patella,* Italian physician, 1856–1928]. Pyloric stenosis in tuberculous patients following fibrous stenosis.

patellapexy (pah-tel′ah-pek″se) [*patella* + Gr. *pēxis* fixation]. The operation of suturing the patella to the lower end of the femur.

patellar (pah-tel′ar) [L. *patellarius*]. Of or pertaining to the patella.

patellectomy (pat″el-lek′to-me) [*patella* + Gr. *ektomē* excision]. Excision or removal of the patella.

patelliform (pah-tel′ĭ-form). Shaped like the patella.

patellofemoral (pah-tel″o-fem′o-ral). Pertaining to the patella and the femur.

patellometer (pat″e-lom′e-ter) [*patella* + Gr. *metron* measure]. An instrument for measuring the patellar reflex.

patency (pa′ten-se) [L. *patens* open]. The condition of being wide open.

patent (pa′tent) [L. *patens*]. 1. Open, unobstructed, or not closed. 2. Apparent, evident.

Paterson's corpuscles, nodules [Robert *Paterson,* Scottish physician, 1814–1889]. Molluscous bodies.

Paterson's syndrome [Donald Rose *Paterson,* laryngologist in Cardiff (Wales), 1863–1939]. Plummer-Vinson syndrome.

path (path). A particular course that is followed, or a route that is ordinarily traversed. In neurology, the set of nerve fibers along which a nervous impulse may move, whether esodic or exodic; particularly the intracranial or intraspinal portion of such a course. See also *pathway.* **condyle p.,** the course followed by the mandibular condyle in the temporomandibular joint during the various movements of the mandible. **copulation p.,** the course taken by the male and female pronuclei as they approach each other in a fertilized ovum. **incisor p.,** the course followed by the incisal edges of the lower anterior teeth in movement of the mandible from the position of normal occlusion to that of edge-to-edge contact. **p. of insertion,** the direction in which a dental prosthesis is inserted in and removed from the mouth, seating and removing its attachments from the abutment teeth. **occlusal p.,** the course followed by the occlusal surfaces of the lower teeth in movements of the mandible.

pathema (pah-the′mah), pl. *pathemas* or *pathem′ata* [Gr. *pathēma* disease]. Any disease state or morbid condition.

pathematology (path″e-mah-tol′o-je) [*pathema* + *-logy*]. 1. Pathology. 2. The science treating of mental affections and of the passions.

pathergasia (path′er-ga″se-ah) [Gr. *pathos* disease + *ergasia* work]. Meyer's term for mental malfunction, implying functional or structural damage and marked by abnormal behavior. **minor p's,** minor somatic disorders and nervousness; minor psychoses or neuroses.

pathergia (pah-ther′je-ah). Pathergy.

pathergic (path′er-jik). Characterized by pathergy.

pathergization (path″er-ji-za′shun). The process of becoming spontaneously or of being made pathergic.

pathergy (path′er-je) [Gr. *pathos* disease + *ergon* work]. 1. A condition in which the application of a stimulus leaves the organism in a state in which it is unduly susceptible to subsequent stimuli of a different kind (Rössle). 2. The condition of being allergic to numerous antigens.

pathetic (pah-thet′ik) [L. *patheticus;* Gr. *pathētikos*]. Pertaining to the feelings.

pathetism (path′e-tizm) [Gr. *pathētos* subject to suffering]. Hypnotism, or mesmerism.

pathfinder (path′fīnd-er). 1. An instrument for locating strictures of the urethra. 2. A dental instrument for tracing the course of root canals. See *smooth broach,* under *broach.*

pathic (path′ik) [L. *pathicus;* Gr. *pathikos*]. One who submits himself or herself to the unnatural sexual desires of another.

pathilon (path′ĭ-lon). Trade mark for preparations of tridihexethyl.

patho- (path′o) [Gr. *pathos* disease]. Combining form denoting relationship to disease.

patho-amine (path″o-am′in). An amine causing disease, or formed as the product of a disease process; a ptomaine.

patho-anatomy (path″o-ah-nat′o-me). Pathologic anatomy.

pathobiology (path″o-bi-ol′o-je). Pathology.

pathobolism (pah-thob′o-lizm) [*patho-* + *metabolism*]. A condition of perverted metabolism of a disease nature.

pathoclisis (path″o-klis′is). A specific elemental sensitivity to specific toxins, or a specific affinity of certain toxins for certain systems of organs.

pathocrine (path′o-krin). Pertaining to pathocrinia.

pathocrinia (path″o-krin′e-ah) [*patho-* + endo*crine*]. Disorder of endocrine function.

pathodixia (path″o-dik′se-ah) [*patho-* + Gr. *deixis* exhibition + *-ia*]. An abnormal tendency to display one's injured or diseased part.

pathodontia (path″o-don′she-ah). Dental pathology.

pathoformic (path″o-for′mik) [*patho-* + L. *forma* form]. Pertaining to the beginning of disease: said of symptoms at the beginning of mental disorder.

pathogen (path′o-jen) [*patho-* + Gr. *gennan* to produce]. Any disease-producing microorganism or material.

pathogenesis (path″o-jen′e-sis) [*patho-* + *genesis*]. The development of morbid conditions or of disease. **drug p.,** the production of symptoms of disease by the use of drugs.

pathogenesy (path″o-jen′e-se). Pathogenesis.

pathogenetic (path″o-je-net′ik). Pertaining to pathogenesis.

pathogenic (path-o-jen′ik). Giving origin to disease or to morbid symptoms.

pathogenicity (path″o-je-nis′ĭ-te). The quality of producing or the ability to produce pathologic changes or disease.

pathogeny (path-oj′e-ne). Pathogenesis.

pathoglycemia (path″o-gli-se′me-ah) [*patho-* + Gr. *glykys* sweet + *haima* blood + *-ia*]. Sugar in the blood (decreased carbohydrate tolerance) as a result of some disease.

pathognomonic (path″og-no-mon′ik) [*patho-* + Gr. *gnōmonikos* fit to give judgment]. Specifically distinctive or characteristic of a disease or pathologic condition; a sign or symptom on which a diagnosis can be made.

pathognomy (path-og′no-me) [*patho-* + Gr. *gnōmē* a means of knowing]. 1. The science of the signs and symptoms of disease. 2. The recognition of the nature of a disease by observation of the unconscious revelation of the feelings and passions of the patient.

pathognostic (path″og-nos′tik). Pathognomonic.

pathography (pah-thog′rah-fe) [*patho-* + Gr. *graphein* to write]. A history or description of disease.

pathoklisis (path″o-klis′is). Pathoclisis.

patholesia (path″o-le′ze-ah). A hysterical condition.

pathologic (path″o-loj′ik). Indicative of or caused by a morbid condition.

pathological (path″o-loj′ĭ-kal). Pertaining to pathology.

pathologico-anatomic (path″o-loj″ĭ-ko-an-ah-tom′ik). Pertaining to pathologic anatomy.

pathologist (pah-thol′o-jist). An expert in pathology.

pathology (pah-thol′o-je) [*patho-* + *-logy*]. That branch of medicine which treats of the essential nature of disease, especially of the structural and functional changes in tissues and organs of the body which cause or are caused by disease. **cellular p.,** that which regards the cells as starting points of the phenomena of disease and that every cell descends from some preexisting cell (Virchow). **clinical p.,** pathology applied to the solution of clinical problems; especially the use of laboratory methods in clinical diagnosis. **comparative p.,** that which institutes comparisons between various diseases of the human body and those of the lower animals. **dental p.,** the science which treats of disease of the teeth. Cf. *oral p.* **exotic p.,** a system of pathology foreign to the country or school in which it has found a lodgment. **experimental p.,** the study of artificially induced disease processes. **external p.,** surgical p. **functional p.,** the study of the changes of function due to morbid tissue changes. **general p.,** that which takes cognizance of pathologic conditions, which may occur in various diseases and in different organs. **geographical p.,** pathology in its geographic and climatic relations. **humoral p.,** the opinion that disease is due to abnormal conditions of the fluids of the body. **internal p.,** medical p. **medical p.,** that which relates to morbid processes which are not accessible to operative intervention. **mental p.,** psychopathology. **oral p.,** the science which treats of disease of the structures of the mouth, especially of the structural and functional changes in them which are caused by or which cause disease. **plant p.,** vegetable p. **solidistic p.,** that opinion which attributes disease to rarefaction or condensation of the solid tissues. **special p.,** the study of the pathology of particular diseases or organs. **surgical p.,** the study of the pathology of such diseases as are accessible to operative intervention. **vegetable p.,** the pathology of plant diseases.

patholysis (pah-thol′ĭ-sis) [*patho-* + Gr. *lysis* dissolution]. The dissolution of disease.

pathomaine (path′o-mān). Any one of the pathogenic cadaveric alkaloids.

pathomania (path-o-ma′ne-ah) [*patho-* + Gr. *mania* madness]. Moral insanity.

pathomeiosis (path″o-mi-o′sis) [*patho-* + Gr. *meiōsis* diminution]. The tendency on the part of a patient to minimize the importance of his disease.

pathometabolism (path″o-me-tab′o-lizm) [*patho-* + *metabolism*]. Metabolism in disease.

pathometer (pah-thom′e-ter). An apparatus for recording the incidence of disease in a given locality.

pathometry (pah-thom′e-tre) [*patho-* + Gr. *metrein* to measure]. Sir Ronald Ross' term for the quantitative study of parasitic invasion and infection in individuals or groups of individuals.

pathomimesis (path″o-mi-me′sis) [*patho-* + Gr. *mimēsis* imitation]. Malingering.

pathomimia (path″o-mim′e-ah). Malingering.

pathomimicry (path″o-mim′ĭ-kre). Malingering.

pathomorphism (path″o-mor′fizm). Perverted or abnormal morphology.

pathomorphology (path″o-mor-fol′o-je). Pathomorphism.

pathoneurosis (path″o-nu-ro′sis). A neurosis which affects bodily functions.

pathonomia (path-o-no′me-ah) [*patho-* + Gr. *nomos* law]. The sum of knowledge regarding the laws of disease.

pathonomy (pah-thon′o-me). Pathonomia.

patho-occlusion (path″o-ŏ-kloo′zhun). Malocclusion.

pathophilia (path″o-fil′e-ah) [*patho-* + Gr. *philein* to love]. The condition in which a patient adapts himself and his mode of life to some chronic affection.

pathophobia (path″o-fo′be-ah) [*patho-* + Gr. *phobein* to be affrighted by]. Morbid dread of disease.

pathophoresis (path″o-fo-re′sis) [*patho-* + Gr. *phoros* bearing]. The transmission of disease.

pathophoric (path″o-for′ik). Pathophorous.

pathophorous (path-of′o-rus). Conveying or transmitting disease.

pathophysiology (path″o-fiz″e-ol′o-je). The physiology of disordered function.

pathopleiosis (path″o-pli-o′sis) [*patho-* + Gr. *pleion* greater]. The tendency on the part of a patient to magnify the importance of his disease.

pathopoiesis (path″o-poi-e′sis) [*patho-* + Gr. *poiēsis* production]. 1. The causation of disease. 2. The tendency of the individual to become diseased.

pathopsychology (path″o-si-kol′o-je) [*patho-* + *psychology*]. The psychology of mental disease.

pathopsychosis (path″o-si-ko′sis). A psychosis which affects bodily functions.

pathoradiography (path″o-ra″de-og′rah-fe). Pathoroentgenography.

pathoroentgenography (path″o-rent″gen-og′rah-fe). The study of pathologic lesions by the roentgenogram.

pathosis (pah-tho′sis) [*patho-* + *-osis*]. A condition of disease; a morbid condition.

pathotropism (pah-thot′ro-pizm) [*patho-* + Gr. *tropos* a turning]. The tendency of drugs to pass to diseased areas.

pathway (path′wa). A path or course, especially a course followed in the attainment of a specific end. In neurology, the nerve structures through which a sensory impression is conducted to the cerebral cortex (*afferent p.*) or through which an impulse passes from the brain to the skeletal musculature (*efferent p.*). See also *path.* **biosynthetic p.,** the sequence of enzymic steps in the process by which a specific end-product is synthesized in a living organism. **internuncial p.,** a correlation tract connecting different centers or neurons within the central nervous system.

-pathy (path′e) [Gr. *pathos* disease]. Word termination denoting a morbid condition, or disease.

patient (pa′shent) [L. *patiens*]. A person who is ill or who is undergoing treatment for disease.

Patrick's sign, test (pat′riks) [Hugh Talbot *Patrick*, neurologist in Chicago, 1860–1938]. See under *tests.*

patrilineal (pat″rĭ-lin′e-al) [L. *pater* father + *linea* line]. Pertaining to the paternal ancestry.

patroclinous (pat″ro-kli′nus) [Gr. *patēr* father + *klinein* to incline]. Inheriting or inherited from the father. Cf. *matroclinous.*

patrogenesis (pat″ro-jen′e-sis) [Gr. *patēr* father + *genesis*]. Androgenesis.

patten (pat′n). A metallic support to be worn under the sound foot in hip joint disease.

pattern (pat′ern). 1. A design to be followed or a device to be used in the construction or fabrication of something. 2. The particular design or arrangement of figures: in psychology, the design or arrangement of ideas and reactions in an individual. **action p.,** the congenital or acquired manner in which certain stimuli produce certain actions in given individuals. **behavior p.,** the general grouping of behavior responses. **muscle p.,** a number of muscles organized in a definite fashion and responding as a whole to a stimulus. **startle p.,** the various phenomena evidenced by an individual in reaction to a sudden, unexpected stimulus. **stimulus p.,** a group of stimuli resulting from a particular situation. **wax p.,** a form created in wax which, when invested and burned out, will produce a mold in which a positive reproduction of a structure can be cast.

patulin (pat′u-lin). An antibiotic substance obtained from *Penicillium patulum*, which has been used in treating the common cold.

patulous (pat′u-lus) [L. *patulus*]. Spreading widely apart; open; distended.

paucibacillary (paw″se-bas′ĭ-ler-e) [L. *paucus* few]. Containing only a few bacilli.

paucine (paw′sin). A yellow, flaky alkaloid, $C_{27}H_{39}N_5O_5.6\frac{1}{2}H_2O$, from the pauco nut, the fruit of *Pentaclethra macrophylla*, an African plant.

Paul of Aegina (e-je′nah) (first half of 7th century). A celebrated Greek medical writer who practiced in Alexandria. Of his writings, only a seven-book compilation on medicine survives, the sixth book of which—on surgery—is of particular interest and importance.

Paul's sign (pawlz) [Constantin Charles Théodore *Paul*, French physician, 1833–1896]. See under *sign.*

Paul's test, treatment (pawlz) [Gustav *Paul*, Austrian physician, 1859–1935]. See under *tests* and *treatment.*

Paul-Bunnell test [J. R. *Paul*, American physician, born 1893; W. W. *Bunnell*, American physician, born 1902]. See under *tests.*

Paul-Mixter tube [Frank Thomas *Paul*, English surgeon, born 1851; Samuel Jason *Mixter*, Boston surgeon, 1855–1926]. See under *tube.*

paulocardia (paw″lo-kar′de-ah) [Gr. *paula* pause + *kardia* heart]. 1. Abnormal prolongation of the period of rest in the cardiac cycle. 2. A subjective sensation of stoppage of the heart beat.

Paulus Aegineta (paw′lus ej″ĭ-ne′tah). See *Paul of Aegina.*

paunch (pawnch). Rumen.

pause (pawz). An interruption, or rest. **compensatory p.,** the prolonged pause following an extrasystole which compensates for the extra beat, so that the total rate of the beat remains constant.

pausimenia (paw″sĭ-me′ne-ah) [Gr. *pausis* pause + *mēniaia* menses]. Menopause.

Pauzat's disease (po-zahz′) [Jean Eugène *Pauzat*, French physician]. Osteoplastic periostitis of the metatarsus.

paveril (pav′er-il). Trade mark for preparations of dioxyline.

pavilion (pah-vil′yun) [L. *papilio* butterfly, tent]. A dilated or flaring expansion at the end of a passage. **p. of the ear,** the auricle. **p. of the oviduct,** the outer, or fimbriated, end of the fallopian tube. **p. of the pelvis,** the upper, flaring portion of the pelvis.

Pavlov's method, stomach (pahv′lovz) [Ivan Petrovich *Pavlov*, Russian physiologist, 1849–1936; winner of the Nobel prize for medicine in 1904]. See under *method* and *stomach.*

pavor (pa′vor) [L.]. Terror. **p. diur′nus** [L. "day terrors"], attacks of fear with tantrums in children occurring during the afternoon nap. **p. noctur′nus** [L. "night terrors"], a kind of nightmare of children.

Pavy's disease (pa′vēz) [Frederick William *Pavy*, English physician, 1829–1911]. Recurrent physiologic albuminuria.

Pawlik's fold, grip, triangle (pahv′liks) [Karel J. *Pawlik*, gynecologist in Prague, 1849–1914]. See under the nouns.

pawpaw (paw′paw). Papaw.

Paxton's disease (paks′tonz) [F. V. *Paxton*, English physician]. Tinea nodosa.

Payr's clamp, disease, method, sign (pīrz) [Erwin *Payr*, German surgeon, 1871–1946]. See under the nouns.

P.B. Abbreviation for *Pharmacopoeia Britannica*, British pharmacopoeia.

Pb. Chemical symbol for *lead* [L. *plumbum*].

P.B.A. Abbreviation for *pulpobuccoaxial.*

$Pb(C_2H_3O_2)_2$. Lead acetate.

$PbCO_3$. Lead carbonate.

$PbCrO_4$. Lead chromate.

PBE. Abbreviation for German *Perlsucht Bacillenemulsion*, a form of tuberculin prepared from a culture of bacilli of bovine tuberculosis.

PBI. Abbreviation for *protein-bound iodine.*

PbI_2. Lead iodide.

$Pb(NO_3)_2$. Lead nitrate.

PBO. Penicillin in beeswax.

PbO. Lead monoxide.

PbO_2. Lead dioxide.

PbS. Lead sulfide.

$PbSO_4$. Lead sulfate.

PBZ. Pyribenzamine.

PC. Phosphocreatine.

P.C. Abbreviation for L. *pon′dus civi′le*, avoirdupois weight.

p.c. Abbreviation for L. *post ci′bum*, after meals.

pc. Abbreviation for *picocurie.*

PcB. Abbreviation for *near point of convergence to the intercentral base line.*

P.Cc. Abbreviation for *periscopic concave.*

PCG. Abbreviation for *phonocardiogram.*

P.C.M.O. Abbreviation of *Principal Colonial Medical Officer.*

P_{CO_2}. Symbol for *carbon dioxide pressure* or *tension.*

pcpt. Abbreviation for *perception.*

Pcs. Abbreviation for *preconscious.*

PCV. Abbreviation for *packed cell volume* (the volume of packed red cells in cubic centimeters per 100 cc. of blood).

P.Cx. Abbreviation for *periscopic convex.*

P.D. Abbreviation for *potential difference, pulpodistal,* and *interpupillary distance.*

Pd. Chemical symbol for *palladium.*

p.d. Abbreviation for *prism diopter, papilla diameter, pupillary distance.*

peak (pēk). The top or upper limit of a graphic tracing or of any variable.

Péan's forceps, operation, position (pa-anz′) [Jules *Péan,* French surgeon, 1830–1898]. See under the nouns.

pearl (perl). 1. A small calcareous concretion from various species of mollusks, formerly regarded as having sovereign curative powers. 2. A small medicated granule, or a glass globule with a single dose of volatile medicine. 3. A rounded mass of tough sputum as seen in the early stages of an attack of bronchial asthma. **Bohn's epithelial p's,** small retention cysts in the mouths of infants. **Elschnig's p's,** cells seen under the iris after cataract extraction. **enamel p.,** enameloma. **epidermic p's, epithelial p's,** rounded concentric masses of epithelial cells found in certain papillomas and epitheliomas. Called also *pearly bodies.* **Epstein's p's,** small, whitish-yellow masses on either side of the raphe of the hard palate of the newborn. **gouty p.,** a sodium urate concretion on the cartilage of the ear in gouty persons. **Laennec's p's,** soft casts of the smaller bronchial tubes expectorated in bronchial asthma.

pearlash (perl′ash). Impure potassium carbonate in crystals.

peat (pēt). Carbonized vegetable matter found in bogs: used in peat baths and as a dry absorbent dressing.

peau (po) [Fr.]. Skin. **p. d'orange** (po″do-rahnj′) [Fr. "orange skin"], a dimpled condition of the skin, resembling that of an orange.

pebble (peb″l). A kind of rock crystal from which lenses are sometimes cut.

pébrine (pa-brēn′) [Fr.]. An infectious disease of silkworms caused by *Nosema bombycis.*

pecazine (pe′kah-zēn). Mepazine.

peccant (pek′ant) [L. *peccans* sinning]. Unhealthy; causing illness or disease.

peccatiphobia (pek″kah-tĭ-fo′be-ah) [L. *peccata,* sins + *phobia*]. Morbid fear of sinning.

pechyagra (pek″e-a′grah) [Gr. *pēchys* forearm + *agra* seizure]. Gout of the elbow.

pecilo- (pe-sil′o). For words beginning thus, see those beginning *poikilo-.*

Pecquet's cistern, duct, reservoir (pek-āz′) [Jean *Pecquet,* French anatomist, 1622–1674]. See *cisterna chyli* and *ductus thoracicus.*

pectase (pek′tās). An enzyme which catalyzes the demethylation of pectin, thus producing pectic acid.

pecten (pek′ten), pl. *pec′tines* [L.]. 1. A comb; applied to certain anatomical structures because of a fancied resemblance to a comb. 2. A name given by Stroud, in 1895, to a narrow zone in the anal canal, bounded above by the pectinate line and possessing a comparatively dense connective tissue matrix with thick muscular and elastic components. 3. A triangular pleated membrane in the eye of birds, extending forward from the optic disk, which it covers, for a variable distance into the vitreous body. **p. os′sis pu′bis** [N A, B N A], the anterior border of the superior ramus of the pubis, beginning at the pubic tubercle and continuing to the iliopubic eminence.

pectenine (pek′tĕ-nin). A poisonous alkaloidal compound from a Mexican cactus, *Cereus pecten.*

pectenitis (pek″tĕ-ni′tis). Inflammation of the pecten of the anus.

pectenosis (pek″tĕ-no′sis). Stenosis of the anal canal caused by a rigid, inelastic ring of tissue of variable width and thickness, between the anal groove and anal crypts, producing pain on defecation, bleeding, and anal irritation.

pectenotomy (pek″tĕ-not′o-me) [*pecten* + Gr. *tomē* a cutting]. Surgical correction of pectenosis by incision of the ring of tissue causing it; internal sphincterotomy.

pectin (pek′tin) [Gr. *pēktos* congealed]. A purified carbohydrate product obtained from the acid extract of the inner portion of the rind of citrus fruits or from apple pomace: used as a protective.

pectinase (pek′tĭ-nās). An enzyme in most plants, which catalyzes the hydrolysis of pectin to sugars and galacturonic acid.

pectinate (pek′tĭ-nāt) [L. *pecten* comb]. Shaped like a comb.

pectineal (pek-tin′e-al) [L. *pecten* comb, pubes]. Pertaining to the os pubis.

pectiniform (pek-tin′ĭ-form) [L. *pecten* comb + *forma* form]. Comb-shaped.

pectization (pek″ti-za′shun) [Gr. *pēktikos* curdling]. Coagulation or gelatinization; a term used in colloidal chemistry.

pectolytic (pek″to-lit′ik) [*pectin* + Gr. *lytikos* dissolving]. Capable of effecting the digestion of pectin.

pectoral (pek′to-ral) [L. *pectoralis*]. 1. Pertaining to the breast or chest. 2. Serviceable in diseases of the chest; bechic.

pectoralgia (pek″to-ral′je-ah) [L. *pectus* breast + *-algia*]. Pain in the breast.

pectoralis (pek″to-ra′lis) [L.]. Pertaining to the breast or chest.

pectoriloquy (pek″to-ril′o-kwe) [L. *pectus* breast + *loqui* to speak]. Transmission of the sound of spoken words through the chest wall. It is indicative of excavation of the lung when heard alone: if it is combined with bronchophony, it indicates consolidation of the lung. **aphonic p.,** the sound of the whispered voice transmitted through a serous, but not through a purulent, exudate within the pleura; Baccelli's sign. **whispered p., whispering p.,** the transmission of the sound of whispered words through the walls of the chest.

pectorophony (pek″to-rof′o-ne) [L. *pectus* breast + Gr. *phōnē* voice]. Exaggeration of the vocal resonance heard on auscultation.

pectose (pek′tōs). A principle in unripe fruits and plants from which pectin is derived.

pectosinase (pek-to′sin-ās). An enzyme which changes pectose into pectin and pectin into various fermentable sugars.

pectous (pek′tus). Pertaining to, composed of, or resembling pectin; having a firm, jelly-like consistence.

pectunculus (pek-tung′ku-lus) [L., dim. of *pecten* comb]. Any one of the series of small longitudinal ridges on the aqueduct of Sylvius.

pectus (pek′tus) [L.]. The breast: the chest or thorax. **p. carina′tum** [L. "keeled breast"], undue prominence of the sternum; called also *chicken breast* and *pigeon breast.* **p. excava′tum** [L. "hollowed breast"], undue depression of the sternum; called also *funnel breast* and *funnel chest.* **p. gallina′tum,** p. carinatum. **p. recurva′tum,** p. excavatum.

pedal (ped′al) [L. *pedalis; pes* foot]. Pertaining to the foot or feet, or to a pes.

pedarthrocace (pe-dar-throk′ah-se) [Gr. *pais* child + *arthrocace*]. Caries of the joints in children.

pedatrophia (pe-dah-tro′fe-ah) [Gr. *pais* child + *atrophia*]. 1. Marasmus. 2. Tabes mesenterica.

pedatrophy (pe-dat′ro-fe). Pedatrophia.

pederast (pe′der-ast). One who practices pederasty.

pederasty (pe′der-as″te) [Gr. *pais* boy + *erastēs* lover]. Sexual intercourse with boys by the anus.

pederosis (pe″der-o′sis). Erotic affection and sexual abuse of children.

pedes (pe′dēz) [L.]. Plural of *pes*.

pedesis (pe-de′sis) [Gr. *pēdēsis* leaping]. The quick darting movement of fine particles of solid matter in a limpid liquid; brownian movement.

pedia- (pe′de-ah) [Gr. *pais, paidos* child]. Combining form denoting relationship to a child. Cf. *pedo-*(1).

pediadontia (pe″de-ah-don′she-ah). Pedodontics.

pediadontist (pe″de-ah-don′tist). Pedodontist.

pediadontology (pe″de-ah-don-tol′o-je). Pedodontics.

pedialgia (ped″e-al′je-ah) [L. *pes* foot + *-algia*]. Neuralgic pain in the foot.

pediatric (pe″de-at′rik). Pertaining to the treatment of disease in children.

pediatrician (pe″de-ah-trish′un). An expert in pediatrics.

pediatrics (pe″de-at′riks) [*pedia-* + Gr. *iatrikē* surgery, medicine]. That branch of medicine which treats of the child and its development and care and of the diseases of children and their treatment.

pediatrist (pe″de-at′rist). Pediatrician.

pediatry (pe′de-at″re). Pediatrics.

pedication (ped″ĭ-ka′shun). Pederasty.

pedicellate, pedicellated (pe-dis′ĭ-lāt, ped′ĭ-sel-āt″ed). Pediculate.

pedicellation (ped″ĭ-sel-la′shun). The development of a pedicle.

pedicle (ped′ĭ-k'l). A footlike or stemlike part, such as a narrow strip by which a graft of tissue remains attached to the donor site. **p. of vertebral arch,** pediculus arcus vertebrae.

pedicled (ped′ĭ-k'ld). Having a pedicle.

pedicterus (pe-dik′ter-us) [*pedo-* + Gr. *ikteros* jaundice]. Jaundice of newborn infants; icterus neonatorum.

pedicular (pe-dik′u-lar) [L. *pedicularis*]. Pertaining to or caused by lice.

pediculate (pe-dik′u-lāt) [L. *pediculatus*]. Provided with a pedicle.

pediculation (pe-dik″u-la′shun) [L. *pediculatio*]. 1. Infestation with lice. 2. The formation of a pedicle.

pediculicide (pe-dik′u-lĭ-sīd) [*pediculus* + L. *caedere* to kill]. 1. Destroying lice. 2. An agent which destroys lice.

Pediculoides (pe-dik″u-loi′dēz). A genus of mites. **P. ventrico′sus,** a small mite of the family Tarsonemidae, found in the straw of various cereals and producing a peculiar urticaroid dermatitis.

pediculophobia (pe-dik″u-lo-fo′be-ah) [*pediculus* + Gr. *phobein* to be affrighted by]. Morbid dread of infestation with lice.

pediculosis (pe-dik″u-lo′sis) [*pediculus* + *-osis*]. Infestation with lice. **p. capillit′ii, p. cap′itis,** infestation of the hair of the head by lice. **p. cor′poris,** infestation of the body by lice. **p. inguina′lis,** infestation of the pubic hairs by lice. **p. palpebra′rum,** infestation of the eyelashes by lice. **p. pu′bis,** infestation by *Phthirus pubis.* **p. vestimen′ti, p. vestimento′rum,** infestation of the clothing by lice.

pediculous (pe-dik′u-lus). Infested with lice.

Pediculus (pe-dik′u-lus). A genus of insects of the order Anoplura, the sucking lice. **P. huma′nus** var. **cap′itis,** the head louse, which may carry typhus fever, favus, and impetigo. **P. huma′nus** var. **cor′poris,** the body louse, which transmits typhus fever, trench fever, relapsing fever, and perhaps other diseases, and causes urticaria and melanoderma. **P. inguina′lis, P. pu′bis,** *Phthirus pubis.*

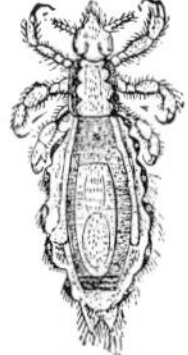

Pediculus humanus *var.* corporis.

Pediculus humanus *var.* capitis.

pediculus (pe-dik′u-lus) pl. *pedic′uli* [L.]. 1. Louse. 2. A footlike or stemlike part. Called also *pedicle.* **p. ar′cus ver′tebrae** [N A], one of the paired parts of the vertebral arch that connect a lamina to the vertebral body. Called also *radix arcus vertebrae* [B N A], and *pedicle of vertebral arch.*

pedicure (ped′ĭ-kūr) [L. *pes* foot + *cura* care]. 1. Professional care and treatment of the feet. 2. A chiropodist, or podiatrist.

pediluvium (ped″ĭ-lu′ve-um) [L. *pes* foot + *luere* to wash]. A foot bath.

Pediococcus (pe″de-o-kok′kus). A genus of microorganisms of the tribe Streptococceae, family Lactobacillaceae, order Eubacteriales, made up of two species, *P. acidilacti′ci* and *P. cerevi′siae,* both saprophytic forms found in fermenting fruit juices.

pediodontia (pe″de-o-don′she-ah). Pedodontics.

pedionalgia (pe″de-o-nal′je-ah) [Gr. *pedion* metatarsus + *-algia* pain]. Pain in the sole of the foot. **p. epidem′ica,** erythredema polyneuropathy.

pediophobia (pe″de-o-fo′be-ah) [Gr. *paidion* child + *phobia* fear]. Morbid dread of infants or of dolls.

pediphalanx (ped″ĭ-fa′lanks) [L. *pes* foot + *phalanx*]. A phalanx of a digit of the foot.

pedistibulum (ped″ĭ-stib′u-lum) [L.]. The stapes.

peditis (pe-di′tis) [L. *pes* foot + *-itis*]. Inflammation of the pedal bone of the horse.

pedo- (pe′do). 1. [Gr. *pais, paidos* child]. Combining form denoting relationship to a child. 2. [L. *pes, pedis* foot]. Combining form denoting relationship to a foot.

pedobaromacrometer (pe″do-bar″o-mah-krom′e-ter) [*pedo-*(1) + Gr. *baros* weight + *makros* long + *metron* measure]. An instrument for measuring and weighing infants.

pedobarometer (pe″do-bah-rom′e-ter) [*pedo-*(1) + Gr. *baros* weight + *metron* measure]. An instrument for weighing infants.

pedodontia (pe″do-don′she-ah). Pedodontics.

pedodontics (pe-do-don′tiks) [*pedo-*(1) + Gr. *odous* tooth]. The department of dentistry which is concerned with the diagnosis and treatment of conditions of the teeth and mouth in children.

pedodontist (pe-do-don′tist). A dentist who specializes in pedodontics.

pedodynamometer (ped″o-di-nah-mom′e-ter) [*pedo-*(2) + *dynamometer*]. An instrument for measuring the strength of a leg.

pedogamy (pe-dog′ah-me) [*pedo-*(1) + Gr. *gamos* marriage]. Endogamy.

pedogenesis (pe″do-jen′e-sis) [*pedo-*(1) + Gr. *genesis* reproduction]. The production of offspring by young or larval forms.

pedograph (ped′o-graf) [*pedo-*(2) + Gr. *graphein* to write]. An imprint on paper of the weight-bearing surface of the foot, surrounded by a pencil-marked contour of the upper foot.

pedologist (pe-dol′o-gist). A specialist in pedology.

pedology (pe-dol′o-je) [*pedo-*(1) + *-logy*]. The systematical study of the life and development of children.

pedometer (pe-dom′e-ter) [*pedo-* + Gr. *metron* measure]. 1. An instrument for measuring infants. 2. An instrument for recording the number of steps taken in walking.

pedomorphic (pe″do-mor′fik). Pertaining to or characterized by pedomorphism.

pedomorphism (pe″do-mor′fizm) [*pedo-*(1) + Gr. *morphē* form + *-ism*]. The retention in the adult organism of highly progressive species of bodily characters which at an earlier stage of evolutionary history were actually only infantile.

pedonosology (pe″do-no-sol′o-je) [*pedo-*(1) + Gr. *nosos* disease + *-logy*]. Pediatrics.

pedopathy (pe-dop′ah-the) [*pedo-*(2) + Gr. *pathos* disease]. Any disease of the foot.

pedophilia (pe″do-fil′e-ah) [*pedo-*(1) + Gr. *philein*

to love]. A morbid interest in children. **p. erot′ica,** sexual perversion toward children.

pedophilic (pe″do-fil′ik). 1. Fond of children. 2. Pertaining to or characterized by pedophilia.

pedophobia (pe″do-fo′be-ah) [*pedo-*(1) + Gr. *phobein* to be affrighted by]. Fear or dread of children.

peduncle (pe-dung′k′l). A stemlike part. Called also *pedunculus.* **cerebellar p., inferior,** pedunculus cerebellaris inferior. **cerebellar p., middle,** pedunculus cerebellaris medius. **cerebellar b., superior,** pedunculus cerebellaris superior. **cerebral p.,** pedunculus cerebri. **p. of flocculus,** pedunculus flocculi. **p. of hypophysis,** infundibulum hypothalami. **olfactory p.,** the constricted portion of the brain which bears the olfactory lobe. **olivary p. of Schwalbe.** See *fibrae arcuatae internae.* **pineal p., p. of pineal body,** habenula. **p. of thalamus, inferior,** pedunculus thalami inferior.

peduncular (pe-dung′ku-lar). Pertaining to a peduncle.

pedunculated (pe-dung′ku-lāt-ed). Provided with a peduncle.

pedunculotomy (pe-dung″ku-lot′o-me) [L. *pedunculus* + Gr. *tomē* a cutting]. Incision of a cerebral peduncle, with division of both pyramidal and non-pyramidal fibers, for relief of the tremor of parkinsonism.

pedunculus (pe-dung′ku-lus) [L.]. A stemlike part. Called also *peduncle.* Applied especially to collections of nerve fibers coursing between different areas in the central nervous system. **p. cerebella′ris infe′rior** [N A], a large bundle of nerve fibers serving to connect the medulla oblongata and spinal cord withthe cerebellum; it courses along the lateral border of the fourth ventricle and turns dorsally into the cerebellum. Called also *corpus restiforme* [B N A], and *inferior cerebellar peduncle.* **p. cerebella′ris me′dius** [N A], a fiber tract originating in the contralateral pontine nuclei and entering the cerebellum. It is continuous with the pons at the line of attachment of the trigeminal nerve. Called also *brachium pontis* [B N A], and *middle cerebellar peduncle.* **p. cerebella′ris supe′rior** [N A], a large fiber bundle extending from each cerebellar hemisphere upward over the pons; it consists of efferent fibers that decussate in the mesencephalon and terminate in the region of the red nucleus and thalamus. Called also *brachium conjunctivum* [*cerebelli*] [B N A], and *superior cerebellar peduncle.* **p. cer′ebri** [N A, B N A], the ventral part of the mesencephalon, comprising the crus cerebri, the substantia nigra, and the tegmentum. Called also *cerebral peduncle.* **p. cor′poris callo′si,** gyrus paraterminalis. **p. cor′poris pinea′lis,** habenula. **p. floc′culi** [N A, B N A], the lateral expansion of the inferior medullary velum toward the flocculus. Called also *peduncle of flocculus.* **p. thal′ami infe′rior** [N A, B N A], fibers passing from the thalamus into the globus pallidus, just medial to the genu of the internal capsule. Called also *inferior peduncle of thalamus.*

peel (pēl) [L. *pilare* to deprive of hair]. The outer rind of a fruit. **lemon p.,** the outer, yellow rind of the fresh ripe fruit of *Citrus limon:* used in preparing lemon oil, lemon syrup, and lemon tincture.

peenash (pe′nash) [India]. Rhinitis due to the presence of insect larvae in the nose.

P.E.G. Abbreviation for *pneumoencephalography.*

peganone (peg′ah-nōn). Trade mark for a preparation of ethotoin.

pegology (pe-gol′o-je) [Gr. *pēgē* fountain + *-logy*]. The study of springs, particularly medicinal or mineral springs.

peinotherapy (pi″no-ther′ah-pe) [Gr. *peina* hunger + *therapeia* cure]. Hunger cure or starvation cure; severe fasting as a means of cure.

pejorative (pe′jo-ra″tiv) [L. *pejor* worse]. Getting worse; unfavorable.

Pekelharing's theory (pa″kel-har′ingz) [Cornelis Adrianus *Pekelharing,* Dutch physiologist, 1848–1922]. See under *theory.*

Pel's crises (pelz) [Pieter Klaases *Pel,* Dutch physician, 1852–1919]. Ocular crises in tabes dorsalis.

Pel-Ebstein disease (pel-eb′stīn) [Pieter Klaases *Pel;* Wilhelm *Ebstein,* German physician, 1836–1912]. See under *disease.*

pelada (pe-la′dah). 1. Alopecia areata. 2. A disease resembling pellagra.

pelade (pel-ad′) [Fr.]. Pelada. **achromic p.,** pelade in which the skin is white and atrophic.

peladic (pe-lad′ik). Pertaining to pelada.

peladophobia (pel″ad-o-fo′be-ah) [*pelade* + Gr. *phobein* to be affrighted by]. Morbid fear of baldness.

pelage (pĕ-lahgh′) [Fr.]. The hairs of the body, limbs, and head collectively.

pelagia (pe-la′je-ah) [L.]. An erysipelatous disease of the hands or face.

pelagic (pe-laj′ik) [Gr. *pelagios* living in the sea]. Pertaining to or inhabiting midocean.

pelagism (pel′ah-jism). Seasickness.

Pelamis (pel′ah-mis). A genus of sea snakes. **P. bico′lor,** a poisonous sea snake of the Indian ocean.

Pelger's nuclear anomaly (pel′gerz) [Karel *Pelger,* Dutch physician, 1885–1931]. See under *anomaly.*

pelidisi (pel″ĭ-de′se) [term coined from L. *pondus decies linearis divisus sidentis* (altitudo) meaning weight ten line divided sitting height]. The unit of Pirquet's index for determining the nutritive condition of children. It is obtained by dividing the cube root of ten times the weight (in grams) by the sitting height (in centimeters). A pelidisi of 94 or less indicates undernutrition; of 95–100, good nutrition, and of 101 or above, overnutrition.

pelidnoma (pel″id-no′mah) [Gr. *pelidnōma* a livid spot]. A discolored spot or patch on the skin.

pelioma (pe″le-o′mah). 1. A livid spot. 2. Peliosis. **p. typho′sum,** a state marked by livid spots on the extremities.

peliosis (pe″le-o′sis) [Gr. *peliōsis* extravasation of blood]. Purpura. **p. rheumat′ica,** purpura rheumatica.

Pelizaeus-Merzbacher. See *Merzbacher-Pelizaeus.*

pella (pel′lah) [L. *pellis* a hide]. Cutis.

pellagra (pel-lag′rah, pel-la′grah) [It. *pelle* skin + *agra* rough]. A clinical deficiency syndrome, manifested in the skin, alimentary tract, and nervous system, and due to a deficiency of niacin, the administration of which reduces or entirely eliminates most of the symptoms. It is marked by a recurring erythema on the portions of the body exposed to light and by subsequent exfoliation of the epidermis. There are weakness and debility, digestive disturbance, spinal pain, convulsions, melancholia, and idiocy. It is called also *Italian leprosy, Lombardy leprosy,* and *maidism.* **monkey p.,** a condition in caged monkeys manifested by loss of appetite, diarrhea, vomiting, emaciation and finally death. It is cured by the administration of nicotinic acid in doses of 2–3 mg. per kilo. **p. sine pellagra,** pellagra in which the characteristic eruption is not present. **typhoid p.,** pellagra characterized by continued high temperature.

pellagragenic (pel-lag″rah-jen′ik). Causing pellagra.

pellagral (pel-lag′ral). Pertaining to pellagra.

pellagramin (pel-lag′rah-min). Nicotinic acid.

pellagraphobia (pel-lag″rah-fo′be-ah). A morbid or unreasonable dread of pellagra.

pellagrazein (pel″lah-gra′ze-in). A poisonous ptomaine from damaged maize, formerly regarded as a probable cause of pellagra.

pellagrin (pel-lag′rin). A person affected with pellagra.

pellagrocein (pel″ah-gro′se-in). Pellagrazein.

pellagroid (pel-lag′roid). A condition resembling pellagra but milder.

pellagrologist (pel″lah-grol′o-jist). One who makes a special study of pellagra.

pellagrology (pel″lah-grol′o-je). The study of pellagra.

pellagrosarium (pel-lag″ro-sa′re-um). A hospital for patients affected with pellagra.

pellagrose (pel-lag′rōs). Pellagrous.

pellagrosis (pel″lag-ro′sis). The dermal syndrome of pellagra characterized by skin pigmentation, eczema and hyperkeratosis.

pellagrous (pel-lag′rus). Affected with or of the nature of pellagra.

pellant (pel′ant) [L. *pellere* to drive]. Depurative.

pellate (pel′āt). To repel or tend to separate.

Pellegrini's disease (pel″a-gre′nēz) [Augusto *Pellegrini*, surgeon in Italy]. See under *disease.*

Pellegrini-Stieda disease (pel″a-gre′ne-ste′-dah) [A. *Pellegrini;* Alfred *Stieda*, German surgeon, born 1869]. See under *disease.*

pellet (pel′et). A small pill or granule, such as a small rod- or ovoid-shaped, sterile mass composed of essentially pure steroid hormones, to be implanted under the skin to provide for their slow absorption, or a small pill made from sucrose and impregnated with a medicine, used in homeopathic practice.

pellicle (pel′ĭ-k′l) [L. *pellicula*]. A thin skin or film, such as a thin film on the surface of a liquid.

pellicula (pel-lik′u-lah) [L., dim. of *pellis* a hide]. Epidermis.

pellicular, pelliculous (pel-lik′u-lar, pel-lik′u-lus). Characterized by a pellicle.

pellitory (pel′ĭ-to″re). Any plant of the genera *Pyrethrum* and *Parietaria.*

pellote (pa-yo′tah). Peyote.

pellucid (pel-lu′sid) [L. *pellucidus*, from *per* through + *lucere* to shine]. Translucent.

pelma (pel′mah) [Gr. "sole"]. The sole of the foot.

pelmatic (pel-mat′ik). Pertaining to the sole of the foot.

pelmatogram (pel-mat′o-gram) [*pelma* + Gr. *gramma* mark]. An impression of the sole of the foot; a footprint.

pelo- (pe′lo) [Gr. *pelos* mud]. Combining form denoting relationship to mud.

Pelodictyon (pe″lo-dik′te-on) [*pelo-* + Gr. *diktyon* net]. A genus of microorganisms of the family Chlorobacteriaceae, suborder Rhodobacteriineae, order Pseudomonadales, occurring as ovoid to rod-shaped cells generally united into large colonies of characteristic shape. It includes three species, *P. aggrega′tum, P. clathratifor′me,* and *P. paralle′lum.*

pelohemia (pe″lo-he′me-ah) [*pelo-* + Gr. *haima* blood + *-ia*]. Undue thickness of the blood.

peloid (pe′loid) [*pelo-* + Gr. *eidos* form]. Resembling mud.

pelology (pe-lol′o-je) [*pelo-* + *-logy*]. The science of mud and similar substances.

Pelonema (pe″lo-ne′mah) [*pelo-* + Gr. *nēma* thread]. A genus of microorganisms of the family Peloplocaceae, order Chlamydobacteriales, made up of long, straight, or spirally twisted, unbranched trichomes, enclosed in an extremely delicate sheath. It includes four species, *P. hyali′num, P. pseudovacuola′tum, P. ten′ue,* and *P. spira′le.*

pelopathy (pe-lop′ah-the). Pelotherapy.

Peloploca (pe″lo-plo′kah) [*pelo-* + Gr. *plokē* anything twisted]. A genus of microorganisms of the family Peloplocaceae, order Chlamydobacteriales, made up of colorless, filamentous, cylindrical cells containing false vacuoles which emit a reddish gleam of light. It includes two species, *P. taenia′ta* and *P. undula′ta.*

Peloplocaceae (pe″lo-plo-ka′se-e). A family of Schizomycetes, order Chlamydobacteriales, made up of long, unbranched filamentous cells usually enclosed in a delicate sheath. It includes two genera, *Pelone′ma* and *Peloplo′ca.*

pelotherapy (pe″lo-ther′ah-pe) [*pelo-* + Gr. *therapeia* cure]. The therapeutic use of earth or mud.

peltate (pel′tāt) [L. *pelta;* Gr. *peltē* shield]. Shield-shaped.

peltation (pel-ta′shun). The protective influence of inoculation with a serum.

pelves (pel′vēs) [L.]. Plural of *pelvis.*

pelvic (pel′vik). Pertaining to the pelvis.

pelvicellulitis (pel″ve-sel″u-li′tis). Pelvic cellulitis.

pelvicephalography (pel″ve-sef″ah-log′rah-fe) [*pelvis* + Gr. *kephalē* head + *graphein* to write]. Roentgenographic measurement of the fetal head and of the birth canal.

pelvicephalometry (pel″ve-sef″ah-lom′e-tre) [*pelvis* + Gr. *kephalē* head + *metron* measure]. Measurement of the diameters of the head of the fetus in relation to those of the mother's pelvis.

pelvicliseometer (pel″ve-kli″se-om′e-ter) [*pelvis* + Gr. *klisis* inclination + *metron* measure]. An instrument for measuring the inclination and the diameters of the pelvis.

pelvifixation (pel″ve-fik-sa′shun). Surgical fixation of a displaced or wandering pelvic organ.

pelvigraph (pel′ve-graf) [*pelvis* + Gr. *graphein* to write]. A recording pelvimeter.

pelvilithotomy (pel″ve-lĭ-thot′o-me). Pelviolithotomy.

pelvimeter (pel-vim′e-ter) [*pelvis* + Gr. *metron* measure]. An instrument for measuring the diameters and capacity of the pelvis.

pelvimetry (pel-vim′e-tre). The measurement of the dimensions and capacity of the pelvis. **combined p.,** pelvimetry in which measurements are made both within and outside the body. **digital p.,** pelvimetry performed with the hands. **external p.,** that in which the measurements are made outside the body. **instrumental p.,** measurement of the pelvis with the pelvimeter. **internal p.,** that in which the measurements are made within the vagina. **manual p.,** that which is performed with the hands.

pelviography (pel″ve-og′rah-fe). Pelviroentgenography.

pelvioileoneocystostomy (pel″ve-o-il″e-o-ne″-o-sis-tos′to-me). Anastomosis of renal pelvis to an isolated segment of the ileum, which is then anastomosed to the urinary bladder.

pelviolithotomy (pel″ve-o-lĭ-thot′o-me). Pyelolithotomy.

pelvioneostomy (pel″ve-o-ne-os′to-me). Ureteroneopyelostomy.

pelvioperitonitis (pel″ve-o-per″ĭ-to-ni′tis). Pelvic peritonitis.

pelvioplasty (pel′ve-o-plas″te). Pyeloplasty.

pelvioradiography (pel″ve-o-ra″de-og′rah-fe). Pelviroentgenography.

pelvioscopy (pel″ve-os′ko-pe) [*pelvis* + Gr. *skopein* to examine]. 1. The inspection or visual examination of the pelvis or pelvic viscera. 2. Pyeloscopy.

pelviostomy (pel″ve-os′to-me). Pyelostomy.

pelviotomy (pel″ve-ot′o-me) [*pelvis* + Gr. *tomē* a cutting]. 1. The cutting of the pelvic bones. 2. Pyelotomy.

pelviperitonitis (pel″ve-per″ĭ-to-ni′tis). Pelvic peritonitis.

pelviradiography (pel″ve-ra″de-og′rah-fe). Pelviroentgenography.

pelvirectal (pel″ve-rek′tal). Pertaining to the pelvis and the rectum.

pelviroentgenography (pel″ve-rent″gen-og′-rah-fe). Roentgenography of the organs of the pelvis.

pelvis (pel′vis), pl. *pel′ves* [L.; Gr. *pyelos* an oblong trough]. [N A, B N A] The lower (caudal) portion of the trunk of the body, bounded anteriorly and laterally by the two hip bones and posteriorly by the sacrum and coccyx. The pelvis is divided by a plane passing through the terminal lines into the *false pelvis* (*p. major* [N A]) above and the *true pelvis* (*p. minor* [N A]) below. The upper boundary of the cavity of the pelvis is known as the *inlet, brim*, or *superior strait of the pelvis.* The true pelvis is limited below by the *inferior strait*, or *outlet*, bounded by the coccyx, the symphysis pubis, and the ischium of either side. The outlet of the pelvis is closed by the coccygeus and levator ani muscles and the perineal fascia, which form the *floor of the pelvis.* The inlet and outlet of the pelvis have each three important diameters —an anteroposterior, a conjugate, and an oblique, the relations of which determine types variously classified by different authors. The term pelvis is applied also to any basin-like structure, such as the renal pelvis (pelvis renalis [N A]). **p. aequabil′iter jus′to ma′jor,** a pelvis that is unusually large, with all its dimensions equally increased. **p. aequabil′iter jus′to mi′nor,** a pelvis that is unusually small, with all its dimensions equally reduced. **android p.,** a pelvis characterized by a wedge-shaped inlet and narrowness of the anterior segment; used also as a general designation of a female pelvis showing characters typical of the pelvis in the male. **p. angus′ta,** a narrow pelvis, or one in which the transverse diameter is abnormally reduced. **anthropoid p.,** a female pelvis characterized by a long anteroposterior diameter of the inlet, which equals or exceeds the transverse diameter. **assimilation p.,** a pelvis in which the transverse processes of the last lumbar vertebra are fused with the sacrum (*high-assimilation p.*—including six vertebral segments), or the last sacral vertebra may fuse with the first coccygeal body (*low-assimilation p.*—including only four vertebral segments). **beaked p.,** one with the pelvic bones laterally compressed and their anterior junction pushed forward. **bony p.,** p. ossea. **brachypellic p.,** an oval type of pelvis, the transverse diameter of the inlet exceeding the anteroposterior diameter by 1 to 3 cm. **contracted p.,** a pelvis in which there is a diminution of 1.5 to 2 cm. in any important diameter. When all dimensions are proportionately diminished it is a *generally contracted pelvis* (*p. aequabiliter justo minor*). **cordate p., cordiform p.,** one that is somewhat heart shaped. **coxalgic p.,** one deformed in consequence of hip joint disease. **Deventer's p.,** a pelvis which is shortened anteroposteriorly. **dolichopellic p.,** an elongated type of pelvis, the anteroposterior diameter of the inlet being greater than the transverse diameter. **dwarf p.,** a small pelvis with the bones united by cartilage. **extrarenal p.** See under *renal p.* **false p.,** p. major. **flat p.,** one in which the anteroposterior dimension is abnormally reduced. **frozen p.,** a condition in which, because of a pathologic process, the fornices of the uterus are filled with a hardened exudate. **funnel-shaped p.,** a female pelvis with a normal inlet, but a greatly narrowed outlet. **giant p.,** p. aequabiliter justo major. **greater p.,** p. major. **gynecoid p.,** a pelvis in which the transverse diameter is placed well ahead of the promontory and the sacrosciatic notch is large; used also as a general designation of a male pelvis showing characters typical of the pelvis in the female. **halisteretic p.,** a pelvis deformed as a result of softening of the bones on account of absorption of their calcium salts. **Hauder's p.,** p. spinosa. **high-assimilation p.** See under *assimilation p.* **India rubber p.,** an osteomalacic pelvis, the bones of which may be stretched. **infantile p.,** a generally contracted pelvis characterized by an oval shape, a high sacrum, and marked inclination of the walls. **inverted p.,** split p. **p. jus′to ma′jor.** See *p. aequabiliter justo major.* **p. jus′to mi′nor.** See *p. aequabiliter justo minor.* **juvenile p.,** infantile p. **Kilian's p.,** one deformed as a result of osteomalacia. **kyphoscoliotic p.,** an irregularly contracted pelvis due to rachitic kyphoscoliosis. **kyphotic p.,** one characterized by increase of the conjugate diameter at the brim, with decrease of the transverse diameter at the outlet. **large p.,** p. major. **lesser p.,** p. minor. **lordotic p.,** one in which the vertebral column has an anterior curvature in the lumbar region. **low-assimilation p.** See under *assimilation p.* **p. ma′jor** [N A, B N A], the part of the pelvis superior to a plane passing through the terminal lines. **malacosteon p.,** rachitic p. **mesatipellic p.,** a round type of pelvis, the transverse diameter of the inlet being the same as or not exceeding the anteroposterior diameter by more than 1 cm. **p. mi′nor** [N A, B N A], the part of the pelvis inferior to a plane passing through the terminal lines. **Nägele's p.,** one so distorted that the conjugate diameter takes an oblique direction. **p. na′na,** dwarf p. **p. nim′is par′va,** p. aequabiliter justo minor. **oblique p.** See *Nägele's p.* **p. obtec′ta,** a kyphotic pelvis in which the vertebral column extends horizontally across the pelvic inlet. **p. os′sea** [N A, B N A], the ring of bone forming the skeleton of the pelvis, supporting the vertebral column and resting upon the inferior members, and composed of the two hip bones anteriorly and laterally, and the sacrum and coccyx posteriorly. Called also *bony pelvis.* **Otto p.,** a pelvis in which the acetabulum is depressed, permitting the head of the femur to protrude intrapelvically. See *arthrokatadysis.* **p. ova′lis,** fossula fenestrae vestibuli. **pithecoid p.,** a term suggested to replace *anthropoid p.* in designating an elongated pelvis. **p. pla′na,** flat p. **platypellic p.,** a flat type of pelvis, the transverse diameter of the inlet exceeding the anteroposterior diameter by 3 cm. or more. **platypelloid p.,** a pelvis characterized by flattening of the pelvic inlet, with a short anteroposterior and a wide transverse diameter. **Prague p.,** spondylolisthetic p. **pseudo-osteomalacic p.,** a deformed pelvis simulating one affected with osteomalacia, but resulting from other causes. **rachitic p.,** one distorted as a result of rickets. **reduced p.,** p. aequabiliter justo minor. **renal p., p. rena′lis** [N A, B N A], the expansion from the upper end of the ureter into which the calices of the kidney open; ordinarily lodged within the renal sinus, under certain conditions, as in a long kidney or obstruction of the ureteropelvic junction, a large part of it may be outside the kidney (*extrarenal p.*).

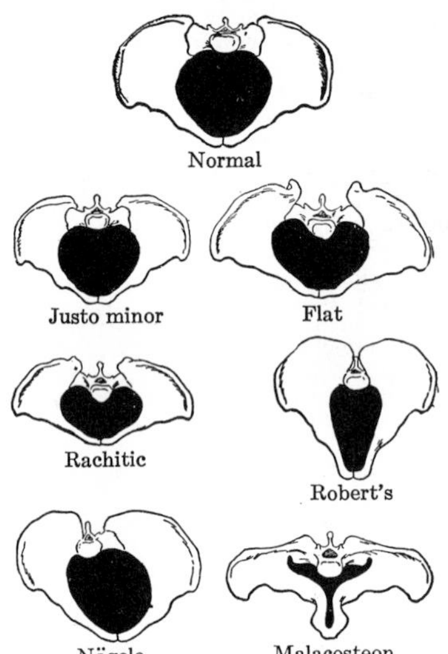

Shapes of various types of pelvic inlet. (Bumm.)

Robert's p., one with a rudimentary sacrum and great reduction of the transverse and oblique diameters. **Rokitansky's p.**, spondylolisthetic p. **rostrate p.**, beaked p. **p. rotun'da**, fossula fenestrae cochleae. **round p.**, one with an inlet of nearly circular outline. **rubber p.**, India rubber p. **scoliotic p.**, one deformed as a result of scoliosis. **simple flat p.**, one with a shortened anteroposterior diameter. **small p.**, p. minor. **spider p.**, a renal pelvis which in the pyelogram shows the calices as narrow, string-like extensions, resembling the legs of a spider. **p. spino'sa**, a rachitic pelvis with the crest of the pubis very sharp. **split p.**, one with a congenital separation at the symphysis pubis. **spondylolisthetic p.**, a pelvis in which the last lumbar vertebra is dislocated in front of the sacrum. Called also *Prague p.* and *Rokitansky's p.* **p. spu'ria**, p. major. **triangular p.**, one with a triangular inlet. **triradiate p.**, beaked p. **true p.**, p. minor. **p. of ureter**, renal p.

pelvisacral (pel″ve-sa'kral). Pertaining to the pelvis and the sacrum.

pelvisacrum (pel-ve-sa'krum). The pelvis and the sacrum together.

pelviscope (pel've-skōp). An apparatus for examining roentgenologically the contours of the pelvis.

pelvisection (pel″ve-sek'shun) [*pelvis* + L. *sectio* a cutting]. A cutting of the pelvis bones, such as pubiotomy and symphysiotomy.

pelvisternum (pel″ve-ster'num). The cartilage of the symphysis pubis.

pelvitherm (pel've-therm) [*pelvis* + Gr. *thermē* heat]. An apparatus for applying heat to the pelvic organs through the vagina.

pelvitomy (pel-vit'o-me) [*pelvis* + Gr. *temnein* to cut]. The operation of cutting the pelvis at any point in order to facilitate delivery.

pelvitrochanterian (pel″ve-tro″kan-te're-an). Relating to the pelvis and the great trochanter of the femur.

pelviureteroradiography (pel″ve-u-re″ter-o-ra″de-og'rah-fe). Roentgenography of the ureter and renal pelvis.

pelvoscopy (pel-vos'ko-pe) [*pelvis* + Gr. *skopein* to examine]. Examination of a pelvis, particularly of the renal pelvis.

pelvospondylitis (pel″vo-spon″dĭ-li'tis). Inflammation of the pelvic portion of the spine. **p. ossif'icans**, rheumatoid spondylitis.

pelyco- (pel'ĭ-ko) [Gr. *pelyx* pelvis]. For words beginning thus, see those beginning *pelvi-* and *pyelo-*.

pemphigoid (pem'fĭ-goid) [Gr. *pemphix* blister + *eidos* form]. 1. Like or resembling pemphigus. 2. A name applied to a group of dermatological syndromes similar to but clearly distinguishable from those of the pemphigus group. **bullous p.**, a chronic, generalized bullous eruption, occurring in elderly adults predominantly, and usually not fatal.

pemphigus (pem'fĭ-gus) [Gr. *pemphix* blister]. A name applied to a distinctive group of diseases characterized by successive crops of bullae which absorb and leave pigmented spots on the skin, the specific type usually being indicated by a modifying term. Frequently used alone to designate pemphigus vulgaris. **p. acu'tus**, a form of bullous skin eruption having a rapid course and associated with severe constitutional symptoms. **benign p.**, bullous pemphigoid. **benign chronic familial p.**, a rare hereditary, chronic pruritic dermatitic process, usually limited to the axillae, groin, and neck. Called also *Hailey-Hailey disease.* **Brazilian p.**, an infectious and contagious disease endemic in Brazil, which is clinically and histologically identical with pemphigus foliaceus. **p. contagio'sus**, an endemic disease of warm regions, such as the Philippines and the tropical East, marked by a vesicular eruption occurring chiefly in the groin and axillae. **p. erythemato'sus**, pemphigus in which the lesions, limited to the face and chest, resemble those of disseminated lupus erythematosus. Called also *Senear-Usher disease* or *syndrome.* **febrile p.**, p. acutus. **p. folia'ceus**, a condition characterized by presence of widespread flaky, slightly exudative lesions, presenting an appearance similar to that of exfoliative dermatitis. **p. gangreno'sus**, dermatitis gangrenosa infantum. **hemorrhagic p., p. hemorrhag'icus**, a condition characterized by the presence of bullae filled with hemorrhagic fluid. **malignant p., p. malig'nus**, p. vulgaris. **p. neonato'rum**, impetigo neonatorum. **South American p.**, Brazilian p. **p. syphilit'icus**, an eruption of bullae associated with syphilis. **p. veg'etans**, a variant of pemphigus vulgaris in which the bullous lesions are replaced by verrucoid hypertrophic vegetative masses. Called also *Neumann's disease.* **p. vulga'ris**, a rare relapsing disease manifested by bullous lesions of mucocutaneous surfaces; invariably fatal if untreated, but remission has been obtained by use of corticosteroid hormones. **wildfire p.**, Brazilian p.

penatin (pen'ah-tin). A toxic antibiotic substance from *Penicillium notatum.*

Pende's sign (pen'dēz) [Nicola *Pende*, Italian physician, born 1880]. See under *sign.*

pendular (pen'du-lar). Having a pendulum-like movement.

pendulous (pen'du-lus) [L. *pendere* to hang]. Hanging loosely; dependent.

penetrance (pen'e-trans) [L. *penetrare* to enter into]. The extent to which a substance is penetrated, or to which an object enters into a substance. In genetics, the expression of the frequency with which a heritable trait is shown in individuals carrying the principal gene or genes conditioning it.

penetrating (pen'e-trāt-ing) [L. *penetrans*]. Piercing; entering deeply.

penetration (pen″e-tra'shun) [L. *penetratio*]. 1. The act of piercing or entering deeply. 2. The focal depth of a lens, or its power of giving a clear definition at various depths.

penetrology (pen″e-trol'o-je). The study of radiant energy.

penetrometer (pen″e-trom'e-ter). 1. An apparatus for measuring the penetrating power and intensity of the roentgen ray. The best known are those of Benoist, Walter, and Wehnelt. 2. An apparatus for registering the resistance of semisolid material to penetration.

penial (pe'ne-al). Pertaining to the penis.

peniaphobia (pe″ne-ah-fo'be-ah) [Gr. *penia* poverty + *phobein* to be affrighted by]. Morbid fear of poverty.

Penic. cam. Abbreviation for L. *penicil'lum cameli'num*, a camel's-hair brush.

penicidin (pen″ĭ-si'din). An antibacterial product isolated from several species of *Penicillium.*

penicillamine (pen″ĭ-sil-am'in). An amino acid obtained from penicillin by treatment with hot mineral acids.

penicilli (pen″ĭ-sil'li) [L.]. Plural of *penicillus.*

penicilliary (pen″ĭ-sil'e-er″e) [L. *penicillium*, dim. of *peniculus* a brush]. Resembling a brush or broom.

penicillin (pen″ĭ-sil'lin). An antibiotic substance extracted from cultures of certain molds of the genus Penicillium that have been grown on special media. **aluminum p.**, the aluminum salt of penicillin extracted from cultures of *Penicillium notatum* or *P. chrysogenum.* **benzathine p. G**, a complex salt of penicillin for oral or parenteral administration. **chloroprocaine p. O**, a combination of 2-chloroprocaine and penicillin O, for intramuscular administration. **dimethoxyphenyl p. sodium**, penicillin synthesized from a fermentation product, effective against many strains of staphylococci that are resistant to other penicillin preparations. **p. G benzhydrylamine**, a form of penicillin suitable for oral administration, 1,1-diphenylmethylamine benzylpenicillinate. **hydralamine phenoxy-**

methyl p., a mixture of penicillin salts for oral administration. **phenoxymethyl p.,** an antibiotic for oral administration, containing a phenoxymethyl group in place of the benzyl group contained in penicillin G. **potassium p. G,** the potassium salt of benzylpenicillinic acid, effective chiefly against gram-positive bacteria. **potassium phenoxymethyl p.,** a preparation of phenoxymethyl penicillin, containing not less than 1,380 U.S.P. penicillin units per milligram. **procaine p. G,** a preparation of procaine benzylpenicillin, with a potency of not less than 900 U.S.P. penicillin units per milligram. **sodium p. G,** a preparation containing not less than 90 per cent of total penicillins. **sodium p. O,** a stable preparation of penicillin for intravenous or intramuscular administration. **p. V,** phenoxymethyl p.

penicillinase (pen″ĭ-sil′ĭ-nās). An enzyme-like substance produced by certain bacteria which antagonizes the antimicrobial action of penicillin: a specially purified preparation obtained by fermentation from cultures of a strain of *Bacillus cereus* is used in treatment of reactions to penicillin.

penicillin-fast (pen″ĭ-sĭl′in-fast). Resistant to the action of penicillin: said of certain strains of bacteria.

penicilliosis (pen′ĭ-sil″e-o′sis). Infection with *Penicillium,* usually a pulmonary infection.

Penicillium (pen″ĭ-sil′e-um) [L. *penicillum* brush, roll]. A genus of molds which develop fruiting organs resembling a broom, or the bones of the hand and fingers. Species which are sometimes found parasitic on man are: *P. bar′bae, P. bouffar′di, P. min′imum, P. montoy′ai.* **P. crusta′ceum,** *P. glau′cum.* **P. glau′cum,** the common bluish-green mold. It is a factor in the ripening of Camembert cheese, making it white, soft, and creamy. **P. nota′tum.** See under *penicillin.* **P. pat′ulum.** See *patulin.* **P. spinulo′sum.** See *spinulosin.*

Penicillium. (de Rivas.)

penicillus (pen″ĭ-sil′us), pl. *penicil′li* [L.]. A structure resembling a brush in appearance. **penicil′li arte′riae liena′lis** [N A, B N A], brushlike groups of arterial branches in the lobules of the spleen.

penile (pe′nil). Pertaining to the penis.

penillamine (pen″il-am′in). An amine derived from penillic acid by the removal of a molecule of carbon dioxide.

penilloaldehyde (pen″ĭ-lo-al′de-hīd). An aldehyde derived from penicillin.

penis (pe′nis) [L.]. [N A, B N A] The male organ of copulation, comprising a root, body, and extremity, or glans penis. The root is attached to the descending portions of the pubic bone by the *crura,* the latter being the extremities of the corpora cavernosa. The body consists of two parallel cylindrical bodies, the *corpora cavernosa,* and beneath them the *corpus spongiosum,* through which the urethra passes. The glans is covered with mucous membrane and ensheathed by the prepuce, or foreskin. **clubbed p.,** a condition in which the penis is curved when erect. **p. mulieb′ris,** clitoris. **p. palma′tus,** webbed p. **p. plas′tica,** Peyronie's disease. **webbed p.,** a penis that is enclosed by the skin of the scrotum. Called also *p. palmatus.*

penischisis (pe-nis′kĭ-sis) [*penis* + Gr. *schisis* splitting]. A fissured state of the penis, such as epispadias, hypospadias, or paraspadias.

penitis (pe-ni′tis). Inflammation of the penis.

penjavar yambi (pen′jah-var yam′be). The hairs of various species of *Polypodium* and *Pyathea;* sometimes prescribed as a styptic and hemostatic.

Penjdeh sore, ulcer (penj′deh) [*Penjdeh,* a town of Turkestan]. Cutaneous leishmaniasis.

Penn sero-flocculation reaction [Harry S. *Penn,* Russian physician and zoologist in the United States, born 1891]. See under *reaction.*

pennate (pen′āt). Penniform.

penniform (pen′ĭ-form) [L. *penna* feather + *forma* form]. Shaped like a feather; looking like a feather.

pennyroyal (pen″e-roi′al). A popular name for various labiate plants, especially *Mentha pulegium (European p.), M. canadensis,* and *Hedeoma pulegioides (American p.).*

pennyweight (pen′e-wāt). A unit of weight in the troy system, being 24 grains, or one twentieth of an ounce.

penology (pe-nol′o-je) [Gr. *poinē* penalty + *-logy*]. The science of punishment; that branch of criminology which deals with the treatment of criminals.

penoscrotal (pe″no-skro′tal). Relating to the penis and the scrotum.

penotherapy (pe″no-ther′ah-pe). The medical examination and regulation of prostitutes in the control of venereal disease.

Penrose drain (pen′rōz) [Charles Bingham *Penrose,* Philadelphia gynecologist, 1862–1925]. See under *drain.*

pent-, penta- [Gr. *pente* five]. Combining form meaning five.

pentabasic (pen″tah-ba′sik). Having five replaceable atoms of hydrogen in the molecule.

pentachlorin (pen″tah-klo′rin). Chlorophenothane.

pentachromic (pen″tah-kro′mik) [*penta-* + Gr. *chrōma* color]. 1. Pertaining to or exhibiting five colors. 2. Able to distinguish only five of the seven colors of the spectrum.

pentacyclic (pen″tah-sik′lik). Having a ring of five atoms in the molecule.

pentad (pen′tad). Any element or radical with a valence of five.

pentadactyl (pen″tah-dak′til) [*penta-* + Gr. *daktylos* finger]. Having five fingers or toes on a hand or a foot.

pentaerythritol (pen″tah-e-rith′rĭ-tol). Chemical name: 2,2-bishydroxymethyl-1,3-propanediol, prepared by treating acetaldehyde with formaldehyde in an aqueous solution of calcium hydroxide: used in synthetic resins and in paints and varnishes. **p. chloral,** petrichloral. **p. tetranitrate,** 2,2-bisdihydroxymethyl-1,3-propanediol tetranitrate: used as a vasodilator.

pentaerythrityl (pen″tah-e-rith′rĭ-til). Pentaerythritol. **p. tetranitrate,** pentaerythritol tetranitrate.

pentaglucose (pen″tah-glu′kōs). Any sugar whose formula contains five atoms of carbon.

pentalogy (pen-tal′o-je). A combination of five elements or factors, such as five concurrent defects or symptoms. **p. of Fallot,** the four defects included in the tetralogy of Fallot, occurring in association with patent foramen ovale or atrial septal defect.

pentamethazene (pen″tah-meth′ah-zēn). Azamethonium.

pentamethylenediamine (pen″tah-meth″il-ēn-di-am′in). Cadaverine.

pentamethylenetetrazol (pen-tah-meth″il-ēn-tet′rah-zol). Pentylenetetrazol.

pentane (pen′tān). An anesthetic liquid hydrocarbon, $CH_3(CH_2)_3CH_3$, obtained by the distillation of petroleum. It is one of the constituents of petroleum ether.

pentapeptide (pen″tah-pep′tid). A polypeptide containing five amino acids.

pentaploid (pen′tah-ploid). 1. Pertaining to or characterized by pentaploidy. 2. An individual or cell having fives sets of chromosomes.

pentaploidy (pen′tah-ploi″de). The state of having five sets of chromosomes (5n).

pentapyrrolidinium (pen″tah-pir-ro″lĭ-din′e-um). Pentolinium.

Pentastoma (pen-tas′to-mah) [*penta-* + Gr. *stoma* mouth]. A genus of endoparasitic, wormlike arthropods. *P. constric′tum* and *P. taenioi′des* occur in the human subject. *P. denticula′tum* is the larva of *Linguatula rhinaria*, occurring in the nose.

pentastomiasis (pen″tah-sto-mi′ah-sis). Infestation with *Pentastoma;* linguatulosis.

pentatomic (pen″tah-tom′ik) [*penta-* + *atom*]. 1. Containing five atoms. 2. Containing five replaceable hydrogen atoms.

Pentatrichomonas (pen″tah-trĭ-kom′o-nas). A genus of intestinal trichomonads marked by having five anterior flagella. **P. ar′din delte′ili,** a flagellate parasite resembling *Trichomonas hominis*, but having five anterior flagella. It seems to be pathogenic for man.

pentatrichomoniasis (pen″tah-trik-o-mo-ni′ah-sis). Infection with Pentatrichomonas.

pentavaccine (pen″tah-vak′sēn) [*penta-* + *vaccine*]. A vaccine containing dead cultures of the bacteria of typhoid, paratyphoid A, paratyphoid B, cholera, and Malta fever.

pentavalent (pen-tav′ah-lent). Having a chemical valency of five; capable of combining with five atoms of hydrogen.

pentdyopent (pent-di′o-pent) [*penta-* + Gr. *dyo* two + *pente* five = 525, referring to the spectroscopic line of the substance]. A substance derived from blood pigment, occurring in the urine in certain diseases.

pentene (pen′tēn). Amylene.

penthienate (pen-thi′ĕ-nāt). Chemical name: diethyl (2-hydroxyethyl) methylammonium α-cyclopentyl-2-thiopheneglycolate: used in parasympathetic blockade.

penthrane (pen′thrān). Trade mark for a preparation of methoxyflurane.

penthrit (pen′thrit). Pentaerythritol tetranitrate.

pentids (pen′tidz). Trade mark for preparations of potassium penicillin G.

pentobarbital (pen″to-bar′bĭ-tal). Chemical name: 5-ethyl-5-(1-methylbutyl)barbituric acid: used as a hypnotic and sedative.

pentobarbitone (pen″to-bar′bĭ-tōn). Pentobarbital.

pentolinium (pen″to-lin′e-um). Chemical name: pentamethylene-1,1′-bis-(1-methylpyrrolidinium): used in ganglionic blockade to reduce blood pressure.

pentolysis (pen-tol′ĭ-sis) [*pentose* + Gr. *lysis* dissolution]. The disintegration of pentose; discovered to be effected by the serum of cancer patients, and suggested as a test for cancer.

pentone (pen′tōn). Valylene.

pentosan (pen′to-san). Any member of a group of pentose polysaccharides having the composition $(C_5H_8O_4)_n$; found in various foods and plant juices. They yield pentose on hydrolysis. **methyl p.,** a pentosan which on hydrolysis yields methyl pentoses.

pentosazon (pen″to-sa′zon). A crystalline compound formed by treating a pentose with phenyl hydrazine, sometimes abnormally occurring in the urine.

pentose (pen′tōs). A monosaccharide containing five carbon atoms in a molecule. **p. nucleotide,** a compound of nucleic acid existing in the nuclei of living cells and in the circulating blood.

pentosemia (pen″to-se′me-ah). The presence of pentose in the blood.

pentosidase (pen-tos′ĭ-dās). An enzyme which hydrolyzes pentoses.

pentoside (pen′to-sid). A compound of a pentose with some other substance. Compounds of pentoses with purine and pyrimidine bases are found in the nucleic acids.

pentosuria (pen″to-su′re-ah) [*pentose* + Gr. *ouron* urine + *-ia*]. The occurrence of pentose in the urine.

pentosuric (pen″to-su′rik). Affected with pentosuria.

pentothal (pen′to-thol). Trade mark for preparations of thiopental.

pentoxide (pen-tok′sīd). An oxide containing five atoms of oxygen in a molecule.

pentritol (pen′trĭ-tol). Trade mark for a preparation of pentaerythritol tetranitrate.

pentylenetetrazol (pen′tĭ-lēn-tet′rah-zol). Chemical name: 6,7,8,9-tetrahydro-5-azepotetrazole: used as a central nervous system stimulant.

pen-vee (pen′ve). Trade mark for preparations of penicillin V. See *penicillin phenoxymethyl.*

Penzoldt's test (pen′zōldz) [Franz *Penzoldt*, physician in Erlangen, 1849–1927]. See under *tests.*

peonin (pe′o-nin). A dye, the amide of pararosolic acid: used as a test for a certain range of hydrogen ion concentration.

peotillomania (pe″o-til″o-ma′ne-ah) [Gr. *peos* penis + *tillein* to pull + *mania* madness]. A ticlike movement consisting in pulling at the penis: called also *pseudomasturbation.*

peotomy (pe-ot′o-me) [Gr. *peos* penis + *temnein* to cut]. Surgical removal of the penis.

pepo (pe′po) [L. "pumpkin"]. Pumpkin seed; the dried ripe seeds of the pumpkin, *Cucurbita pepo:* diuretic and useful against tapeworm.

pepper (pep′er) [L. *piper*]. The dried fruit of *Piper nigrum* and other plants of that genus. **black p.** contains piperine, a volatile oil, and an acrid resin. It is carminative, counterirritant, stimulant, and antiperiodic. **cayenne p.,** capsicum. **water p.** See *Polygonum hydropiper.* **white p.,** a milder form prepared of the ordinary, or black, pepper.

Pepper treatment (pep′er) [William *Pepper*, Philadelphia internist, 1843–1898]. See under *treatment.*

Pepper type [William *Pepper*, Philadelphia physician, 1874–1947]. See under *type.*

peppermint (pep′per-mint). The dried leaves and tops of *Mentha piperita:* used as an oil, spirit, or water extract as a flavored vehicle for drugs.

pepsase (pep′sās). Pepsin considered as an enzyme or nonorganized ferment.

pepsic (pep′sik). Peptic.

pepsin (pep′sin) [L. *pepsinum*, from Gr. *pepsis* digestion]. The proteolytic enzyme of the gastric juice which changes the native proteins of the food into proteoses and peptones (molecular weight not above 1000), by breaking the peptide linkages, particularly those of tyrosine and phenylalanine. It is a crystalline albumin and acts best in the presence of 0.2–0.3 per cent of hydrochloric acid. A preparation obtained from the glandular layer of the fresh stomach of the hog is used therapeutically. **aromatic p.,** a mixture of 10 per cent of pepsin with tartaric acid, sodium chloride, and milk sugar. **Brücke's protein-free p.,** a purified pepsin that contains less nitrogen than crystalline pepsin and that hydrolyzes casein that has already been digested by crystalline pepsin. **ostrich p.,** a pepsin prepared in Argentina from the gizzard of the ostrich or rhea. **saccharated p.,** pepsin mixed with sugar of milk.

pepsinase (pep′sin-ās). One of a class of enzymes which split native proteins to peptides in acid solution.

pepsinate (pep′sin-āt). To treat or charge with pepsin.

pepsinia (pep-sin′e-ah). The secretion of pepsin. It may be normal, excessive (hyperpepsinia), deficient (hypopepsinia), or totally absent (apepsinia).

pepsiniferous (pep″sin-if′er-us) [*pepsin* + L. *ferre* to bear]. Producing or secreting pepsin.

pepsinogen (pep-sin′o-jen) [*pepsin* + Gr. *gennan*

to produce]. A zymogen in or from the gastric cells which is changed into pepsin by hydrochloric acid.

pepsinogenous (pep″sin-oj′e-nus). Producing pepsin.

pepsinum (pep-si′num). Pepsin.

pepsinuria (pep″sĭ-nu′re-ah). The presence of pepsin in the urine.

peptamine (pep-tam′in). Any amine derived from a polypeptide.

peptase (pep′tās). 1. A malt derivative capable of acting on albumin. 2. An enzyme which splits peptides to amino acids.

peptic (pep′tik) [Gr. *peptikos*]. Pertaining to pepsin or to digestion.

peptid (pep′tid). Peptide.

peptidase (pep′tĭ-dās). One of a class of proteolytic enzymes which catalyze the hydrolysis of peptide linkages.

peptide (pep′tid). One of a class of compounds of low molecular weight, yielding two or more amino acids on hydrolysis. Formed by reaction of the NH_2 and COOH groups of adjacent amino acids, they are known as di-, tri-, tetra- [etc.] peptides, depending on the number of amino acids making up the molecule.

peptidolytic (pep″tĭ-do-lit′ik) [*peptide* + Gr. *lytikos* dissolving]. Splitting up peptides.

peptinotoxin (pep″tĭ-no-tok′sin). A poisonous intestinal product of imperfect stomach digestion.

peptization (pep″ti-za′shun). Increase in the degree of dispersion of a colloid solution; the liquefaction of a colloid gel to form a sol.

Peptococcus (pep″to-kok′kus). A genus of microorganisms of the family Micrococcaceae, order Eubacteriales, occurring as spherical, gram-positive, anaerobic forms; some species are saprophytic and others are found in the upper respiratory, gastrointestinal and genitourinary tracts as non-pathogenic parasites.

peptocrinin (pep″to-krin′in). A substance obtained from the mucosa of the intestine having properties like secretin.

peptogaster (pep′to-gas″ter) [Gr. *peptein* to digest + *gastēr* belly]. The alimentary tract.

peptogenic (pep″to-jen′ik) [Gr. *peptein* to digest + *gennan* to produce]. 1. Producing pepsin or peptones. 2. Promoting digestion.

peptogenous (pep-toj′e-nus). Peptogenic.

peptoid (pep′toid). A product of proteolytic digestion, distinguished by not giving the biuret reaction.

peptolysis (pep-tol′ĭ-sis) [*peptone* + Gr. *lysis* dissolution]. The splitting up of peptone.

peptolytic (pep″to-lit′ik). Splitting up peptone.

peptone (pep′tōn) [Gr. *pepton* digesting]. A derived protein, or a mixture of split products, produced by the hydrolysis of a native protein either by an acid or by an enzyme. Peptones are readily soluble in water, are levorotatory, and are not precipitated by heat, by ammonium sulfate, or by the action of alkalis or acids. They include *amphipeptone, antipeptone, hemipeptone,* and *propeptone.* **beef p.,** a peptone made from beef by treating it with extract of pancreas. **casein p.,** a light-brown powder, soluble in water: a nutrient for convalescents. **gelatin p.,** a peptone formed during the digestion of gelatin with pepsin. **glycerin-gelatin p.,** a bacteriologic culture medium. **Höchst's p.,** peptone obtained from silk: used as a test for the presence of peptone-splitting ferments, either by changes in optical activity or by the precipitation of tyrosine. **milk p.,** casein p. **venom p.,** a peptone from snake poison.

peptonemia (pep″to-ne′me-ah) [*peptone* + Gr. *haima* blood + *-ia*]. The presence of peptones in the blood.

peptonic (pep-ton′ik). Pertaining to or containing peptone.

peptonize (pep′to-nīz). The conversion of protein into peptone by enzyme action.

peptonoid (pep′to-noid). Any substance resembling peptone.

peptonuria (pep″to-nu′re-ah) [*peptone* + Gr. *ouron* urine + *-ia*]. The presence of peptones in the urine. See *albumosuria.* **enterogenous p.,** that which is due to disease of the intestine. **hepatogenous p.,** that which is due to disease of the liver. **nephrogenic p.,** that which is due to disease of the kidney. **puerperal p.,** that which occurs during the puerperium. **pyogenic p.,** that which is associated with a suppurative process.

peptophilic (pep″to-fil′ik). Growing in a solution of peptone: said of bacteria.

Peptostreptococcus (pep″to-strep″to-kok′kus). A genus of microorganisms of the tribe Streptococceae, family Lactobacillaceae, order Eubacteriales, made up of obligate anaerobic streptococci occurring as parasitic inhabitants of the intestinal tract, and occasionally found in gangrenous and necrotic lesions probably as secondary invaders. It includes 13 species.

peptotoxin (pep″to-tok′sin). Any toxin or poisonous base developed from a peptone; also a poisonous cadaveric alkaloid or ptomaine occurring in certain peptones and putrefying proteins. **cholera p.,** a poisonous substance resembling a peptone, produced by the cholera bacillus.

peptozym (pep′to-zīm). A substance thought to exist in peptone solutions, and having the power of preventing the coagulation of the blood.

per- [L., *per* through]. 1. A prefix meaning throughout, in space or time, or completely or extremely. 2. A prefix used in chemical terms to denote a large amount or to designate combination of an element in its highest valence.

peracephalus (per″ah-sef′ah-lus) [*per-* + *acephalus*]. A fetal monster with neither head nor arms, and with a defective thorax.

peracetate (per-as′e-tāt). An acetate containing more acetic acid than the ordinary acetate.

peracid (per-as′id). An acid containing more than the usual quantity of oxygen.

peracidity (per″ah-sid′ĭ-te). Excessive acidity.

peracute (per″ah-kūt′) [L. *peracutus*]. Excessively acute or sharp.

perandren (per-an′dren). Trade mark for a preparation of testosterone.

per anum (per a′num) [L.]. Through the anus.

perarticulation (per″ar-tik″u-la′shun) [*per-* + L. *articulatio* joint]. Diarthrosis.

peratodynia (per″at-o-din′e-ah) [Gr. *peran* to pierce + *odynē* pain]. Cardialgia or heartburn.

perazil (per′ah-zil). Trade mark for preparations of chlorcyclizine.

percentile (per-sen′til). 1. Of, pertaining to, or used in percentage. 2. One of 100 equal parts of a series divided in order of their measurable magnitude.

percentual (per-sen′tu-al). Pertaining to percentage; figured on the basis of 100.

percept (per′sept). The object perceived.

perception (per-sep′shun) [L. *perceptio* a gathering together]. The conscious mental registration of a sensory stimulus. **depth p.,** the proper recognition of depth or the relative distances to different objects in space, with ability to orient one's position in relation to them. **extrasensory p.,** knowledge of, or response to, an external thought or objective event not achieved as the result of stimulation of the sense organs. **facial p.** See under *vision.* **stereognostic p.,** the recognition of objects by touch.

perceptive (per-sep′tiv). Pertaining to perception.

perceptivity (per″sep-tiv′ĭ-te). Ability to receive sense impressions.

perceptorium (per″sep-to′re-um). Sensorium.

perchloride (per-klo′rīd). A chloride which contains more chlorine than the ordinary chloride.

perchlormethane (per″klōr-meth′ān). Carbon tetrachloride.

perchlormethylformate (per″klor-meth″il-for′māt). Diphosgene.

percine (per′sin). A protamine from the sperm of yellow perch, *Perca flavescens*.

percolate (per′ko-lāt) [L. *percolare*]. **1.** To strain; to submit to percolation. 2. To trickle slowly through a substance. 3. A liquid that has been submitted to percolation.

percolation (per″ko-la′shun) [L. *percolatio*]. The extraction of the soluble parts of a drug by causing a liquid solvent to flow slowly through it.

percolator (per′ko-la″tor). A vessel used in percolating drugs.

percomorph (per′ko-morf). Pertaining to Percomorphi, an order of fishes whose liver oil is rich in vitamins A and D.

per contiguum (per kon-tig′u-um). In contiguity: arranged in such a way that the edges touch.

per continuum (per kon-tin′u-um). In continuity: without separation or break.

percorten (per-kor′ten). Trade mark for preparations of desoxycorticosterone.

percuss (per-kus′) [L. *percutere*]. To subject to percussion.

percussible (per-kus′ĭ-b'l). Discoverable on percussion.

percussion (per-kush′un) [L. *percussio*]. The act of striking a part with short, sharp blows as an aid in diagnosing the condition of the parts beneath by the sound obtained (Auenbrugger, 1761). **auscultatory p.,** auscultation of the sound produced by percussion. **bimanual p.,** the usual manner of percussion in which the middle finger of the left hand is placed against the body wall and its nail is struck a quick blow with the end of the bent right middle finger. **coin p.** See under *tests*. **comparative p.,** percussion of two or more areas in order to compare the sounds obtained. **deep p.,** percussion in which a firm blow is struck in order to obtain a note from a deep-seated tissue. **direct p.,** immediate percussion. **drop p., drop stroke p.,** percussion in which the hammer is allowed to fall by its own weight on to the pleximeter, the elements considered in the examination being the sound heard, the vibrations felt in the handle of the hammer, and the rebound of the hammer seen. Called also *Lerch's p.* **finger p.,** that in which the fingers of one hand are used as a plexor, and those of the other as a pleximeter. **fist p.,** percussion in which the fist is brought down with a moderate thump over the area to be tested. **Goldscheider's p.** 1. Threshold percussion. 2. Orthopercussion. **immediate p.,** that in which no pleximeter is used. **instrumental p.,** that in which a plexor or hammer is used. **Korányi's p.** See under *auscultation*. **Krönig's p.,** auscultatory percussion over the apexes of the lungs in the diagnosis of tuberculosis. **Lerch's p.,** drop stroke p. **mediate p.,** that in which a pleximeter is employed. **Murphy's p.,** piano p. **palpatory p.,** a combination of palpation and percussion, affording tactile rather than auditory impressions. **paradoxical p.,** resonance of the chest combined with abundant rales as in acute edema of the lungs. **pencil p.,** Plesch's p. **piano p.,** percussion by striking the body by the four fingers one after the other, beginning with the little finger. Called also *Murphy's p.* **Plesch's p.,** percussion within the intercostal spaces to avoid setting the ribs into vibration, the pleximeter finger with the first interphalangeal joint flexed at a right angle. **pleximetric p.,** mediate p. **respiratory p.,** percussion during respiration so as to bring out the difference in the percussion notes of inspiration and expiration. **slapping p.,** percussion made by a slapping blow: used in comparing the resonance. **strip p.,** percussion which starts from above and progresses downward, thus covering a "strip" of the chest wall. **tangential p.,** percussion with the pleximeter placed vertically on the body, the strokes being applied to the pleximeter in a direction parallel with the surface of the skin. **threshold p.,** percussion performed by tapping lightly with the finger upon a glass rod pleximeter, one end of which, fitted with a rubber cap, rests upon an intercostal space, the rod being held at an angle to the surface of the thorax and parallel to the borders of the organ to be delimited. This method confines the percussion vibrations to a very restricted area. Called also *Goldscheider's p.* **topographic p.,** the demarcation and outlining of a dull area by percussion to determine the boundaries of organs or parts of organs.

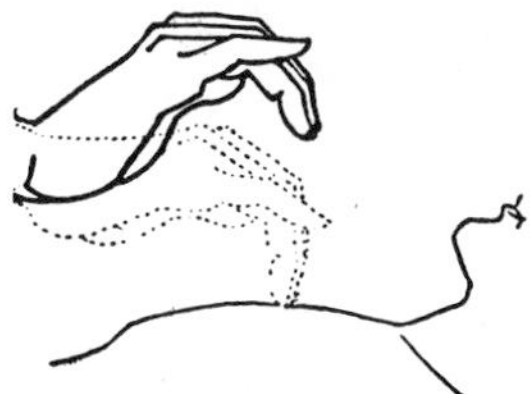
Immediate percussion (Külbs).

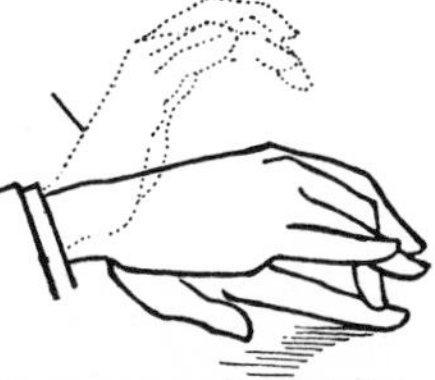
Strong percussion (Külbs).

Weak percussion (Külbs).

percussopunctator (per-kus″o-punk′ta-tor). An instrument for performing multiple acupuncture.

percussor (per-kus′or) [L. "striker"]. An instrument for use in performing percussion.

percutaneous (per″ku-ta′ne-us) [*per-* + L. *cutis*]. Performed through the skin, as injection of radiopaque material in radiological examination, or needle removal of tissue for biopsy.

per cutem [L.]. Through the skin.

percuteur (per″koo-tūr′) [Fr.]. An instrument for therapeutic or diagnostic percussion.

Percy cautery, method (per′se) [James Fulton *Percy*, American surgeon, 1864–1946]. See under *cautery*.

pereirine (per-e′ir-in) [Port. *pereira* brier]. A white alkaloid, $C_{19}H_{24}N_2O$, from the bark of *Geissospermum laeve* (*vellosii*), a tree of tropical America; antiperiodic, antipyretic, and tonic.

perencephaly (per″en-sef′ah-le) [Gr. *pēra* pouch + *enkephalos* brain]. Cystic disease of the brain.

perennial (per-en′ĭ-al) [L. *perennis*, from *per* through + *annus* year]. Lasting through the year or for several years.

perethynol (per-eth′ĭ-nol). A colloidal suspension prepared from fresh horse heart in chlorethylene and alcohol for Vernes' test for syphilis. See *Vernes' test*, under *tests*.

Perez's sign (pa-rāths″) [Jorje *Perez*, Spanish physician, died 1920]. See under *sign*.

perezone (per′e-zon). Pipitzahoic acid.

perfectionism (per-fek′shun-izm). A mental tendency to set up an impossible standard, leading to a feeling of frustration and self-condemnation.

perflation (per-fla′shun) [L. *perflatio*]. **1.** The act of blowing air into a space in order to force secretions or other substances out. 2. A form of natural ventilation in which the air is brought into the room as a result of the movement of natural air currents.

perforans (per′fo-ranz) [L.]. Penetrating: a term applied to various muscles and nerves. **p. gas′seri,** the musculocutaneous nerve. **p. ma′nus,** the flexor digitorum profundus muscle.

perforated (per′fo-rāt″ed) [L. *perforatus*]. Pierced with holes.

perforation (per″fo-ra′shun) [L. *perforare* to pierce through]. 1. The act of boring or piercing through a part. 2. A hole made through a part or substance. **Bezold's p.,** perforation of the inner surface of the mastoid bone.

perforator (per′fo-ra″tor). An instrument for piercing the bones, and especially for perforating the fetal head. **Blot's p.,** an instrument for performing craniotomy in difficult labor.

perforatorium (per″fo-rah-to′re-um). The pointed structure on the head of a spermatozoon; the acrosome.

perfrication (per″fri-ka′shun) [L. *perfricare* to rub]. Rubbing with an ointment or embrocation.

perfrigeration (per-frij″er-a′shun) [*per-* + L. *frigere* to be cold]. Frostbite.

perfusate (per-fu′zāt). A liquid that has been passed over or through something, such as the blood vessels of an organ or part.

perfuse (per-fūz′). To pour over or through.

perfusion (per-fu′zhun). 1. The act of pouring over or through, especially the passage of a fluid through the vessels of a specific organ or body part. 2. A liquid poured over or through something.

perhydride (per-hi′drid). Hydrogen peroxide.

peri- [Gr. *peri* around]. A prefix meaning around.

periacinal (per″e-as′ĭ-nal) [*peri-* + L. *acinus* berry]. Situated around an acinus.

periactin (per″e-ak′tin). Trade mark for preparations of cyproheptadine hydrochloride.

periadenitis (per″e-ad″e-ni′tis) [*peri-* + Gr. *adēn* gland + *-itis*]. Inflammation of the tissues around a gland. **p. muco′sa necrot′ica recur′rens,** a disease of the mouth characterized by the formation of small hard nodules which become ulcerated, the condition tending to recur after healing. Called also *aphthae resistentiae.*

periadventitial (per″e-ad″ven-tish′al). Outside of the adventitia.

perialienitis (per″e-āl″yen-i′tis) [*peri-* + L. *alienus* foreign + *-itis*]. Inflammation around a foreign body, as a biliary concretion.

perianal (per″e-a′nal) [*peri-* + L. *anus* anus]. Located around the anus.

periangiitis (per″e-an″je-i′tis) [*peri-* + Gr. *angeion* vessel + *-itis*]. Inflammation of the tissue around a blood or lymphatic vessel.

periangiocholitis (per″e-an″je-o-ko-li′tis). Inflammation of the tissues around the bile ducts, or interlobar capillaries of the liver.

periangioma (per″e-an-je-o′mah) [*peri-* + Gr. *angeion* vessel + *-oma*]. A tumor which surrounds a blood vessel.

perianth (per′e-anth) [*peri-* + Gr. *anthos* flower]. The floral envelope, including the calyx and corolla.

periaortic (per″e-a-or′tik). Around the aorta.

periaortitis (per″e-a″or-ti′tis). Inflammation of the tissues around the aorta.

periapical (per″e-ap′ĭ-kal) [*peri-* + L. *apex* tip]. Relating to tissues encompassing the apex of a tooth, including periodontal membrane and alveolar bone.

periappendicitis (per″e-ah-pen″dĭ-si′tis) [*peri-* + *appendix* + *-itis*]. Inflammation of the tissues around the vermiform appendix. **p. decidua′lis,** a condition in tubal pregnancy in which, on account of adhesions between the appendix and the fallopian tube, decidual cells are present in the peritoneum of the appendix.

periappendicular (per″e-ap″en-dik′u-lar). Around the appendix vermiformis.

periapt (per′e-apt) [Gr. *periapton* amulet]. A substance worn in the belief that it wards off disease.

periarterial (per″e-ar-te′re-al). Around an artery.

periarteritis (per″e-ar″ter-i′tis) [*peri-* + Gr. *artēria* artery + *-itis*]. Inflammation of the external coats of an artery and of the tissues around the artery. **p. gummo′sa,** accumulation of gummas on the blood vessels in syphilis. **p. nodo′sa,** an inflammatory disease of the coats of the small and medium sized arteries of the body with inflammatory changes around the vessels and marked by symptoms of systemic infection. Called also *polyarteritis, panarteritis* and *necrosing arteritis.*

periarthric (per″e-ar′thrik) [*peri-* + Gr. *arthron* joint]. Around a joint.

periarthritis (per″e-ar-thri′tis). Inflammation of the tissues around a joint.

periarticular (per″e-ar-tik′u-lar) [*peri-* + L. *articulus* joint]. Situated around a joint.

periatrial (per″e-a′tre-al). Around the atrium or auricle of the heart.

periauricular (per″e-aw-rik′u-lar). 1. Around an auricle of the heart. 2. Around the concha of the ear.

periaxial (per″e-ak′se-al) [*peri-* + Gr. *axōn* axis]. Situated around an axis.

periaxillary (per″e-ak′sĭ-ler″e). Situated or occurring around the axilla.

periaxonal (per″e-ak′so-nal) [*peri-* + *axon*]. Occurring around an axon.

periblast (per′ĭ-blast) [*peri-* + Gr. *blastos* germ]. The portion of the blastoderm of telolecithal eggs the cells of which lack complete cell membranes.

periblepsis (per″ĭ-blep′sis) [*peri-* + Gr. *blepsis* looking]. The staring expression of an emotionally or mentally disturbed person.

peribronchial (per″ĭ-brong′ke-al). Situated around a bronchus.

peribronchiolar (per″ĭ-brong-ki′o-lar). Situated around the bronchioles.

peribronchiolitis (per″ĭ-brong″ke-o-li′tis). Inflammation of the tissues around the bronchioles.

peribronchitis (per″ĭ-brong-ki′tis). A form of bronchitis consisting of inflammation of the entire lobe with bronchitis in that portion of the lung and thickening of the peribronchial tissue; subacute bronchopneumonia.

peribulbar (per″ĭ-bul′bar). Surrounding the bulb of the eye.

peribursal (per″ĭ-ber′sal). Surrounding a bursa.

perical (per′ĭ-kal). Mycetoma.

pericanalicular (per″ĭ-kan″ah-lik′u-lar). Occurring around canaliculi.

pericapsular (per″ĭ-kap′su-lar). Surrounding a capsule.

pericardectomy (per″ĭ-kar-dek′to-me). Pericardiectomy.

pericardiac (per″ĭ-kar′de-ak). Pericardial.

pericardial (per″ĭ-kar′de-al). Pertaining to the pericardium.

pericardicentesis (per″ĭ-kar″de-sen-te′sis) [*pericardium* + Gr. *kentēsis* puncture]. The surgical puncture of the pericardium for the purpose of aspirating purulent pericardial effusions.

pericardiectomy (per″ĭ-kar″de-ek′to-me) [*pericardium* + Gr. *ektomē* excision]. Excision of the pericardium.

pericardiocentesis (per″ĭ-kar″de-o-sen-te′sis). Pericardicentesis.

pericardiolysis (per″ĭ-kar″de-ol′ĭ-sis) [*pericardium* + Gr. *lysis* dissolution]. The operation of freeing adhesions between the visceral and parietal pericardium.

pericardiomediastinitis (per″ĭ-kar″de-o-me″de-as-ti-ni′tis). Pericarditis with mediastinitis; inflammation of the pericardium and mediastinum.

pericardiophrenic (per″ĭ-kar″de-o-fren′ik). Pertaining to the pericardium and the diaphragm.

pericardiopleural (per″ĭ-kar″de-o-plu′ral). Pertaining to the pericardium and the pleura.

pericardiorrhaphy (per″ĭ-kar″de-or′ah-fe) [*pericardium* + Gr. *rhaphē* suture]. The operation of suturing a wound in the pericardium.

pericardiostomy (per″ĭ-kar″de-os′to-me) [*pericardium* + Gr. *stoma* mouth]. The operation of making an opening into the pericardium through the chest wall for the drainage of effusions.

pericardiosymphysis (per″ĭ-kar″de-o-sim′fĭ-sis) [*pericardium* + Gr. *symphysis* adhesion]. Adhesion between the visceral and parietal layers of the pericardium.

pericardiotomy (per″ĭ-kar″de-ot′o-me) [*peri-*

cardium + Gr. *temnein* to cut]. Surgical incision of the pericardium.

pericarditic (per″ĭ-kar-dit′ik). Pertaining to pericarditis.

pericarditis (per″ĭ-kar-di′tis) [*pericardium* + *-itis*]. Inflammation of the pericardium. The disease is attended by elevation of temperature, pain in the precordial region, rapid pulse, cough, and dyspnea. The pericardium is covered with fibrinous deposits, giving it a roughened surface, which causes a friction murmur occurring with the heart beats. Later effusion into the sac takes place, producing bulging of the precordia and an area of dullness. **acute fibrinous p.,** inflammation of the pericardium marked by fibrinous exudate on the serous membrane. **adhesive p.,** a condition resulting from the presence of dense fibrous tissue between the pericardium and the heart. There may be complete obliteration of the pericardial cavity (external adhesive pericarditis, concretio pericardii, concretio cordis); or there may be also adhesions extending from the pericardium to the mediastinum (mediastinopericarditis), diaphragm, and chest wall (accretio cordis, accretio pericardii, cardiosymphysis). **bacterial p.,** pericarditis produced by bacterial infection: it may be acute or subacute. **p. calculo′sa,** pericarditis with a calcareous deposit in the pericardium. **p. callo′sa,** a variety of chronic fibrous pericarditis marked by facial cyanosis, edema, and full, tortuous jugular veins, without pulsation and without typical signs of pericarditis. It occurs during childhood. **carcinomatous p.,** that which is associated with malignant disease of the pericardium. **constrictive p.,** inflammation of the pericardium leading to thickening and calcification, resulting in constriction of the heart and restriction of its pulsation. **dry p.,** pericarditis that is not attended with effusion. **p. with effusion,** pericarditis associated with the collection of a serous or purulent exudate in the pericardial cavity. **p. epistenocardi′aca,** the symptom complex of stenocardia, fever, pericarditis, and myocardial insufficiency (Sternberg). **external p.,** that which chiefly affects the outer surface of the pericardium. **p. exter′na et inter′na,** inflammation of the outer and inner surfaces of the pericardium. **fibrous p.,** a chronic pericarditis in which the adhesions become replaced by fibrous bands. **hemorrhagic p.,** that in which there is a bloody exudate. **localized p.,** a form with white or milky spots. **mediastinal p.,** inflammation of the exterior surface of the pericardium and the mediastinal tissue. **p. oblit′erans, obliterating p.,** an adherent pericarditis which leads to the obliteration of the pericardial cavity. **purulent p.,** a form which goes on to pus formation. **rheumatic p.,** rheumatic heart disease. **serofibrinous p.,** a variety attended with a serous fluid effusion containing a little fibrin. **p. sic′ca,** acute fibrinous pericarditis without effusion. **suppurative p.,** purulent p. **syphilitic p.,** syphilis of the pericardium. **tuberculous p.,** a variety caused by tuberculous disease. **uremic p.,** pericarditis occurring as a late complication of uremia. **p. villo′sa,** cor villosum.

pericardium (per″ĭ-kar′de-um) [L.; *peri-* + Gr. *kardia* heart]. [N A, B N A] The fibroserous sac that surrounds the heart, comprising an external layer of dense fibrous tissue (*pericardium fibrosum* [N A]) and an inner serous layer (*pericardium serosum* [N A]). The base of the pericardium is attached to the central tendon of the diaphragm. **adherent p.,** a pericardium that is abnormally connected with the heart by dense fibrous tissue, as in adhesive pericarditis. **bread-and-butter p.,** a pericardium having a thick fibrinous deposit on its inner surface. **calcified p.,** a pericardium containing deposits of lime salts. **cardiac p.,** visceral p. **p. fibro′sum** [N A], **fibrous p.,** the external layer of the pericardium, consisting of dense fibrous tissue. **parietal p.,** the parietal layer (lamina parietalis) of the serous pericardium, which is in contact with the fibrous pericardium. **p. sero′sum** [N A], **serous p.,** the inner serous portion of the pericardium consisting of two layers, the *lamina parietalis*, apposed to the fibrous pericardium, and another layer, the *lamina visceralis*, or epicardium, which is reflected onto the heart to form the outer layer of the heart wall. A potential space (cavum pericardium) exists between the two layers. **shaggy p.,** a pericardium coated with a roughened layer of fibrinous exudate. **visceral p.,** the inner layer (lamina visceralis) of the serous pericardium, which is in contact with the heart. Called also *epicardium*.

pericardosis (per″ĭ-kar-do′sis). Infection of the pericardium.

pericardotomy (per″ĭ-kar-dot′o-me). Pericardiotomy.

pericarp (per′ĭ-karp) [*peri-* + Gr. *karpos* fruit]. The seed vessel or ripened ovary of a flower.

pericaryon (per″ĭ-kar′e-on). Perikaryon.

pericecal (per″ĭ-se′kal). Surrounding the cecum.

pericecitis (per″ĭ-se-si′tis). Inflammation of the tissues around the cecum.

pericellular (per″ĭ-sel′u-lar) [*peri-* + L. *cellula* cell]. Surrounding a cell.

pericemental (per″ĭ-se-men′tal). Pertaining to the pericementum.

pericementitis (per″ĭ-se″men-ti′tis) [*pericementum* + *-itis*]. Periodontitis; inflammation of the pericementum. **apical p.,** apical abscess. **chronic suppurative p.,** pyorrhea alveolaris.

pericementoclasia (per″ĭ-se-men″to-kla′se-ah) [*pericementum* + Gr. *klasis* breaking]. Disintegration of the periodontal membrane (pericementum) and alveolar bone without loss of the overlying gingival tissue. It results in pocket formation. Cf. *pyorrhea alveolaris*.

pericementum (per″ĭ-se-men′tum) [*peri-* + L. *caementum* cement]. The periodontal membrane.

pericentral (per″ĭ-sen′tral). Surrounding a center.

pericephalic (per″ĭ-se-fal′ik). Surrounding the head.

pericerebral (per″ĭ-ser′e-bral). Surrounding the brain.

perichareia (per″ĭ-kah-ri′ah) [Gr.]. Excessive and vehement rejoicing.

pericholangitis (per″ĭ-ko″lan-ji′tis) [*peri-* + Gr. *cholē* bile + *angeion* vessel + *-itis*]. Inflammation of the tissues that surround the bile ducts.

pericholecystitis (per″ĭ-ko″le-sis-ti′tis). Inflammation of the tissues around the gallbladder. **gaseous p.,** emphysematous cholecystitis.

perichondrial (per″ĭ-kon′dre-al). Pertaining to or composed of perichondrium.

perichondritis (per″ĭ-kon-dri′tis). Inflammation of the perichondrium.

perichondrium (per″ĭ-kon′dre-um) [*peri-* + Gr. *chondros* cartilage]. [N A, B N A] The membrane which covers the surface of a cartilage. It is a layer of white, fibrous tissue prolonged over the cartilage from neighboring parts.

perichondroma (per″ĭ-kon-dro′mah). A tumor arising from the perichondrium.

perichord (per′ĭ-kord). The investing sheath of the notochord.

perichordal (per″ĭ-kor′dal) [*peri-* + Gr. *chordē* cord]. Situated around the notochord.

perichorioidal (per″ĭ-ko″re-oi′dal) Perichoroidal.

perichoroidal (per″ĭ-ko-roi′dal). Surrounding the choroid coat.

perichrome (per′ĭ-krōm) [*peri-* + Gr. *chrōma* color]. A nerve cell in which the Nissl bodies are arranged in rows beneath the cell membrane. Cf. *arkyochrome, gyrochrome,* and *stichochrome.*

perichymate (per″ĭ-ki′māt). An enamel prism.

periclasia (per″ĭ-kla′se-ah). Periodontoclasia.

periclaustral (per″ĭ-klaws′tral). Around the claustrum of the brain.

periclor (pār′ĭ-klōr). Trade mark for a preparation of petrichloral.

pericolic (per″ĭ-ko′lik). Around the colon, as pericolic membrane.

pericolitis (per″ĭ-ko-li′tis) [*peri-* + Gr. *kolon* colon + *-itis*]. Inflammation around the colon, especially of the peritoneal coat of the colon. **p. dex′tra,** pericolitis affecting the ascending colon. **membranous p.,** a morbid condition resulting from the presence of Jackson's membrane. **p. sinis′tra,** inflammation of the surrounding connective tissue and peritoneum at the lower part of the descending colon.

pericolonitis (per″ĭ-ko″lon-i′tis). Pericolitis.

pericolpitis (per″ĭ-kol-pi′tis) [*peri-* + Gr. *kolpos* vagina + *-itis*]. Inflammation of the tissues around the vagina.

periconchal (per″ĭ-kong′kal) [*peri-* + Gr. *konchē* a shell-like cavity]. Situated around the concha.

periconchitis (per″ĭ-kong-ki′tis) [*peri-* + Gr. *konchē* a shell-like cavity + *-itis*]. Inflammation of the lining of the orbit.

pericorneal (per″ĭ-kor′ne-al). Surrounding the cornea.

pericoronal (per″ĭ-kor′o-nal). Around the crown of a tooth.

pericoronitis (per″ĭ-kor″o-ni′tis) [*peri-* + L. *corona* crown + *-itis*]. Inflammation of the gingiva surrounding the crown of a partially erupted tooth.

pericoxitis (per″ĭ-kok-si′tis). Inflammation of the tissues about the hip joint.

pericranial (per″ĭ-kra′ne-al). Pertaining to the pericranium.

pericranitis (per″ĭ-kra-ni′tis). Inflammation of the external periosteum of the skull.

pericranium (per″ĭ-kra′ne-um) [*peri-* + Gr. *kranion* cranium]. [N A, B N A] The external periosteum of the skull.

pericystic (per″ĭ-sis′tik). Situated about a cyst.

pericystitis (per″ĭ-sis-ti′tis) [*peri-* + Gr. *kystis* bladder + *-itis*]. Inflammation of the tissues around the bladder.

pericystium (per″ĭ-sis′te-um). The vascular envelope of certain cysts.

pericyte (per′ĭ-sīt) [*peri-* + Gr. *kytos* cell]. One of the peculiar elongated cells with the power of contraction, found spirally wrapped about capillaries outside the basement membrane. Called also *pericyte of Zimmermann* and *Rouget cell.*

pericytial (per″ĭ-si′shal). Situated around a cell.

peridectomy (per″ĭ-dek′to-me). Peritectomy.

perideferentitis (per″ĭ-def″er-en-ti′tis). Inflammation of the tissues surrounding the ductus deferens.

peridendritic (per″ĭ-den-drit′ik). Surrounding the dendrites.

peridens (per″ĭ-dens). A supernumerary tooth appearing elsewhere than in the midline of the dental arch.

peridental (per″ĭ-den′tal). Periodontal.

peridentium (per″ĭ-den′she-um). Periodontium.

periderm (per′ĭ-derm) [*peri-* + Gr. *derma* skin]. 1. The large-celled outer layer of the bilaminar fetal epidermis. In the human it is loosened by the hair which grows beneath it, and generally disappears before birth. Called also *epitrichium.* 2. The cuticle.

peridermal (per″ĭ-der′mal). Pertaining to the periderm; cuticular.

peridesmic (per″ĭ-dez′mik). Around a ligament; pertaining to the peridesmium.

peridesmitis (per″ĭ-dez-mi′tis). Inflammation of the peridesmium.

peridesmium (per″ĭ-dez′me-um) [*peri-* + Gr. *desmion* band]. The areolar membrane which covers the ligaments.

peridiastole (per″ĭ-di-as′to-le) [*peri-* + *diastole*]. The interval between the systole and the diastole.

peridiastolic (per″ĭ-di″ah-stol′ik). Prediastolic.

perididymis (per″ĭ-did′ĭ-mis) [*peri-* + Gr. *didymos* testicle]. The tunica vaginalis testis.

perididymitis (per″ĭ-did″ĭ-mi′tis). Inflammation of the perididymis.

peridiverticulitis (per″ĭ-di″ver-tik″u-li′tis). Inflammation of structures around a diverticulum of the intestine.

peridontoclasia (per″ĭ-don″to-kla′se-ah). Periodontoclasia.

periductal (per″ĭ-duk′tal). Surrounding a duct, particularly a duct of the mammary gland.

periductile (per″ĭ-duk′tīl). Periductal.

periduodenitis (per″ĭ-du″o-de-ni′tis). Inflammation around the duodenum, a condition marked by a deformed duodenum surrounded and fixed by peritoneal adhesions.

peridural (per″ĭ-du′ral). Around or external to the dura mater.

peridurogram (per″ĭ-du′ro-gram). The film obtained in peridurography.

peridurography (per″ĭ-du-rog′rah-fe) [*peri-* + *dura* + Gr. *graphein* to write]. Roentgenography of the spinal canal and interspaces after injection of a contrast medium in the peridural space.

periencephalitis (per″ĭ-en-sef″ah-li′tis) [*peri-* + Gr. *enkephalos* brain + *-itis*]. Inflammation of the surface of the brain; meningitis with cortical encephalitis.

periencephalography (per″e-en-sef″ah-log′rah-fe). Roentgenography of the cerebral meninges.

periencephalomeningitis (per″e-en-sef″ah-lo-men″in-ji′tis) [*peri-* + Gr. *enkephalos* brain + *mēninx* membrane + *-itis*]. Chronic inflammation of the cerebral cortex and meninges: paresis or general paralysis of the insane.

periendothelioma (per″e-en″do-the″le-o′mah). A tumor combining the characteristics of a perithelioma and an endothelioma.

perienteric (per″e-en-ter′ik). Situated around the intestine.

perienteritis (per″e-en″ter-i′tis) [*peri-* + Gr. *enteron* intestine + *-itis*]. Inflammation of the peritoneal coat of the intestine.

perienteron (per″e-en′ter-on) [*peri-* + Gr. *enteron* intestine]. The primitive perivisceral cavity of the embryo.

periependymal (per″e-ep-en′dĭ-mal). Situated around the ependyma.

periepithelioma (per″e-ep″ĭ-the-le-o′mah). A tumor which sometimes affects the suprarenal body, and may lead to a large metastatic growth of the liver.

periesophageal (per″e-e-sof′ah-je-al). Situated around the esophagus.

periesophagitis (per″e-e-sof″ah-ji′tis). Inflammation of the tissues around the esophagus.

perifascicular (per″e-fah-sik′u-lar). Surrounding a fasciculus of nerve or muscle fibers.

perifistular (per″ĭ-fis′tu-lar). Around a fistula.

perifocal (per″ĭ-fo′kal). Around or surrounding a focus, such as a focus of infection.

perifollicular (per″ĭ-fŏ-lik′u-lar). Surrounding a follicle.

perifolliculitis (per″ĭ-fŏ-lik″u-li′tis). Inflammation around the hair follicles. **p. cap′itis absce′dens et suffo′diens,** a suppurating and cicatrizing disease of the scalp marked by numerous fluctuating abscesses, comedones, and scars. **superficial pustular p.,** a staphylococcic perifolliculitis with small pustules at the orifices of the pilosebaceous glands, affecting especially the scalp and the extremities. Called also *Bockhart's impetigo.*

perigangliitis (per″ĭ-gang″gle-i′tis). Inflammation of tissues around a ganglion.

periganglionic (per″ĭ-gang″gle-on′ik). Situated around a ganglion.

perigastric (per″ĭ-gas′trik). Situated around the stomach; pertaining to the peritoneal coat of the stomach.

perigastritis (per″ĭ-gas-tri′tis) [*peri-* + Gr. *gastēr* stomach + *-itis*]. Inflammation of the peritoneal coat of the stomach.

perigemmal (per″ĭ-jem′al). Surrounding a taste bud or other bud.

periglandular (per″ĭ-glan′du-lar). Surrounding a gland or glands.

periglandulitis (per″ĭ-glan″du-li′tis). Inflammation of the tissues about a glandule or glandules.

periglial (per″ĭ-gli′al). Surrounding the glia cells of the brain.

periglossitis (per″ĭ-glŏ-si′tis). Inflammation of the tissues around the tongue.

periglottic (per″ĭ-glot′ik). Situated around the tongue.

periglottis (per″ĭ-glot′is) [*peri-* + Gr. *glōtta* tongue]. The mucous membrane of the tongue.

perihepatic (per″ĭ-he-pat′ik) [*peri-* + Gr. *hēpar* liver]. Situated or occurring about the liver.

perihepatitis (per″ĭ-hep″ah-ti′tis) [*peri-* + Gr. *hēpar* liver + *-itis*]. Inflammation of the peritoneal capsule of the liver and of the tissues around the liver. **p. chron′ica hyperplas′tica,** a disease in which the peritoneal covering of the liver becomes converted into a white mass resembling the icing of a cake. Called *frosted liver, icing liver, sugar-icing liver, zuckergussleber,* etc.

perihernial (per″ĭ-her′ne-al). Situated or occurring around a hernia.

perihysteric (per″ĭ-his-ter′ik) [*peri-* + Gr. *hystera* uterus]. Around the uterus.

peri-insular (per″e-in′su-lar). Surrounding an insula, particularly the island of Reil.

perijejunitis (per″ĭ-je″ju-ni′tis). Inflammation around the jejunum.

perikaryon (per″ĭ-kar′e-on) [*peri-* + Gr. *karyon* nucleus]. The main protoplasmic mass of a cell; the cell body as distinguished from the nucleus and the processes.

perikeratic (per″ĭ-ker-at′ik). Surrounding the cornea.

perikymata (per″ĭ-ki′mah-tah) [pl., *peri-* + Gr. *kyma* wave]. The numerous small transverse ridges on the exposed surface of the enamel of a permanent tooth.

perilabyrinth (per″ĭ-lab′ĭ-rinth). The tissue surrounding the labyrinth of the ear.

perilabyrinthitis (per″ĭ-lab″ĭ-rin-thi′tis). Inflammation of the tissues around the labyrinth.

perilaryngeal (per″ĭ-lah-rin′je-al). Situated around the larynx.

perilaryngitis (per″ĭ-lar″in-ji′tis) [*peri-* + Gr. *larynx* larynx + *-itis*]. Inflammation of the tissues around the larynx.

perilenticular (per″ĭ-len-tik′u-lar). Surrounding the lens of the eye.

periligamentous (per″ĭ-lig″ah-men′tus). Situated around a ligament.

perilobar (per″ĭ-lo′bar). Surrounding a lobe.

perilobulitis (per″ĭ-lob-u-li′tis). Inflammation of the connective tissues surrounding the lobules of the lung.

perilymph (per′ĭ-limf) [*peri-* + L. *lympha* lymph]. The fluid contained within the space separating the membranous from the osseous labyrinth; it is entirely separate from the endolymph. Called also *perilympha* [N A].

perilympha (per″ĭ-lim′fah). [N A, B N A] The perilymph.

perilymphadenitis (per″ĭ-lim″fad-e-ni′tis). Inflammation of the tissues around a lymph gland.

perilymphangeal (per″ĭ-lim-fan′je-al). Located around a lymphatic vessel.

perilymphangitis (per″ĭ-lim″fan-ji′tis). Inflammation of the tissues around a lymphatic vessel.

perilymphatic (per″ĭ-lim-fat′ik). 1. Pertaining to the perilymph. 2. Around a lymphatic vessel.

perimastitis (per″ĭ-mas-ti′tis) [*peri-* + Gr. *mastos* breast + *-itis*]. Inflammation of the connective tissue around the mammary gland.

perimedullary (per″ĭ-med′u-ler″e). Surrounding a medulla, as the medulla oblongata or the marrow of a bone.

perimeningitis (per″ĭ-men″in-ji′tis) [*peri-* + Gr. *mēninx* membrane + *-itis*]. Pachymeningitis.

perimeter (per-im′e-ter) [*peri-* + Gr. *metron* measure]. 1. A line forming the boundary of a plane figure. 2. An apparatus for determining the extent of the peripheral visual field on a curved surface. **bed p.,** an apparatus for determining the limits of peripheral vision in a patient confined to bed. **dental p.,** an instrument for measuring the circumference of a tooth.

perimetric (per″ĭ-met′rik). 1. Pertaining to a perimeter. 2. Around the uterus. 3. Pertaining to the perimetrium.

perimetritic (per″ĭ-me-trit′ik). Pertaining to or characterized by perimetritis.

perimetritis (per″ĭ-me-tri′tis) [*peri-* + Gr. *mētra* uterus + *-itis*]. Inflammation of the perimetrium.

perimetrium (per-ĭ-me′tre-um) [*peri-* + Gr. *mētra* uterus]. The serous coat of the uterus. Accepted by N A as an alternative term for *tunica serosa uteri.*

perimetrosalpingitis (per″ĭ-met″ro-sal″pin-ji′tis). Inflammation of the uterus and uterine tube and of surrounding tissues. **encapsulating p.,** perimetrosalpingitis with formation of a membrane about the organs involved.

perimetry (pĕ-rim′e-tre) [*peri-* + Gr. *metron* measure]. Determination of the extent of the peripheral visual field by use of a perimeter.

perimyelis (per″ĭ-mi′ĕ-lis) [*peri-* + Gr. *myelos* marrow]. Endosteum.

perimyelitis (per″ĭ-mi″ĕ-li′tis). 1. Inflammation of the perimyelis. 2. Spinal meningitis.

perimyelography (per″ĭ-mi″ĕ-log′rah-fe) [*peri-* + Gr. *myelos* marrow + *graphein* to record]. Roentgen-ray examination after injecting iodized oil or other contrast fluid into the subarachnoid space of the spinal cord.

perimylolysis (per″ĭ-mi-lol′ĭ-sis) [*peri-* + Gr. *mylē* mill + *lysis* dissolution]. A slow destruction of the hard tissues of the crown of a tooth.

perimyo-endocarditis (per″ĭ-mi″o-en″do-kar-di′tis). Pericarditis associated with myocarditis and endocarditis.

perimyositis (per″ĭ-mi″o-si′tis). Inflammation of the connective tissue around muscles.

perimysia (per″ĭ-mis′e-ah). Plural of perimysium.

perimysial (per″ĭ-mis′e-al). Pertaining to the perimysium.

perimysiitis (per″ĭ-mis″e-i′tis). Inflammation of the perimysium.

perimysitis (per″ĭ-mis-i′tis). Perimysiitis.

perimysium (per″ĭ-mis′e-um), pl. *perimys′ia* [*peri-* + Gr. *mys* muscle]. [N A, B N A] The connective tissue demarcating a fascicle of skeletal muscle fibers. Called also *internal p.,* or *p. internum.* **external p., p. exter′num,** epimysium. **internal p., p. inter′num,** perimysium.

perinatal (per″ĭ-na′tal) [*peri-* + L. *natus* born]. Pertaining to or occurring in the period shortly before and after birth; in medical statistics generally considered to begin with completion of 28 weeks of gestation and variously defined as ending one to four weeks after birth.

perineal (per″ĭ-ne′al). Pertaining to the perineum.

perineauxesis (per″ĭ-ne-awk-se′sis) [*perineum* + Gr. *auxēsis* increase]. Colpoperineorrhaphy.

perineocele (per″ĭ-ne′o-sēl) [*perineum* + Gr. *kēlē* hernia]. A hernia lying between the rectum and the prostate, or between the rectum and vagina; perineal hernia.

perineocolporectomyomectomy (per″ĭ-ne-o-kol″po-rek″to-mi″o-mek′to-me) [*perineum* + Gr. *kolpos* vagina + *rectum* + *myoma* + Gr. *ektomē* excision]. Removal of a myoma by cutting the perineum, vagina, and rectum.

perineometer (per″ĭ-ne-om′e-ter). An instrument for measuring the strength of contractions of the perivaginal muscles.

perineoplasty (per″ĭ-ne′o-plas″te) [*perineum* + Gr. *plassein* to shape]. Plastic surgery of the perineum.

perineorrhaphy (per″ĭ-ne-or′ah-fe) [*perineum* + Gr. *rhaphē* suture]. Suturation of the perineum, performed for the repair of a laceration.

perineoscrotal (per″ĭ-ne-o-skro′tal). Pertaining to the perineum and scrotum.

perineostomy (per″ĭ-ne-os′to-me) [*perineum* + Gr. *stomoun* to provide with an opening, or mouth]. Urethrostomy through the perineum: called also *Poncet's operation.*

perineosynthesis (per″ĭ-ne″o-sin′the-sis) [*perineum* + Gr. *synthesis* a placing together]. Surgical restoration of a completely lacerated perineum.

perineotomy (per″ĭ-ne-ot′o-me) [*perineum* + Gr. *temnein* to cut]. A surgical incision through the perineum.

perineovaginal (per″ĭ-ne″o-vaj′ĭ-nal). Pertaining to or communicating with the perineum and vagina, as a perineovaginal fistula.

perineovaginorectal (per″ĭ-ne″o-vaj″ĭ-no-rek′-tal). Pertaining to the perineum, vagina, and rectum.

perineovulvar (per″ĭ-ne″o-vul′var). Pertaining to the perineum and the vulva.

perinephrial (per″ĭ-nef′re-al). Pertaining to the perinephrium.

perinephric (per″ĭ-nef′rik). Around the kidney.

perinephritic (per″ĭ-ne-frit′ik). Pertaining to or characterized by perinephritis.

perinephritis (per″ĭ-ne-fri′tis) [*peri-* + Gr. *nephros* kidney + *-itis*]. Inflammation of the perinephrium. It is marked by fever, local pain, and tenderness on pressure.

perinephrium (per″ĭ-nef′re-um) [*peri-* + Gr. *nephros* kidney]. The peritoneal envelope and other tissues around the kidney.

perineum (per″i-ne′um) [Gr. *perineos* the space between the anus and scrotum]. [N A, B N A] The pelvic floor and the associated structures occupying the pelvic outlet. It is bounded anteriorly by the pubic symphysis, laterally by the ischial tuberosities, and posteriorly by the coccyx.

perineural (per″ĭ-nu′ral). Surrounding a nerve or nerves.

perineurial (per″ĭ-nu′re-al). Pertaining to the perineurium.

perineuritic (per″ĭ-nu-rit′ik). Pertaining to or suffering from perineuritis.

perineuritis (per″ĭ-nu-ri′tis). Inflammation of the perineurium.

perineurium (per″ĭ-nu′re-um) [*peri-* + Gr. *neuron* nerve]. The connective tissue sheath surrounding each bundle of fibers (fasciculus) in a peripheral nerve.

perinuclear (per″ĭ-nu′kle-ar). Situated or occurring around a nucleus.

periocular (per″e-ok′u-lar). Situated or occurring around the eye.

period (pe′re-od) [*peri-* + Gr. *hodos* way]. An interval or division of time; the time for the regular recurrence of a phenomenon. **child-bearing p.,** the duration of the reproductive ability in the human female, roughly from puberty to menopause. **ejection p.,** sphygmic p. **gestational p.,** the duration of pregnancy, which in the human female averages about 266 days. **half-life p.** See *half-life.* **incubation p.,** the interval of time required for development; in reference to infectious disease the term is commonly used without qualification to designate the intrinsic incubation period. **incubation p., extrinsic,** the period intervening between acquisition of a pathogenic agent (virus) by a vector and the time when the vector is capable of transmitting the disease. **incubation p., intrinsic,** the period of time between the moment of entrance of the infecting organism into the body and the first appearance of the symptoms of the consequent disease. **intersystolic p.,** the atriocarotid interval. See under *interval.* **isoelectric p.,** the moment in muscular contraction when the electrodes are so related to the contraction wave that no deflection of the galvanometer is produced. **p. of isometric contraction,** presphygmic p. **p. of isometric relaxation,** postsphygmic p. **lag p.,** the time which elapses after a microorganism is introduced into a nutrient medium before reproduction begins. **latency p.** 1. See *latency.* 2. The period between the ages of five and nine or ten which divides the infantile sexuality from the beginning of genital sexuality. 3. The period following convalescence during which the causative organism is still present in the patient. **latent p.,** latency. **menstrual p., monthly p.,** the time of menstruation. **patent p.,** the time during which parasites can be demonstrated in the patient. **postsphygmic p.,** the short interval of ventricular diastole (0.08 second), immediately following the sphygmic period and lasting until the opening of the atrioventricular valves, during which the muscle fibers are relaxing and no blood is entering the ventricles. Called also *period of isometric relaxation.* **prefunctional p.,** a period of differentiation in the fetus, both morphologically and histologically, in preparation for functioning. **prepatent p.,** the time between invasion by the parasite and the demonstration of the parasite in the patient. **presphygmic p.,** the first phase of ventricular systole, being the short period (0.04–0.06 second) immediately following closure of the atrioventricular valves and lasting until opening of the semilunar valves, during which the muscle fibers are contracting against the incompressible mass of fluid filling the ventricles. Called also *period of isometric contraction.* **quarantine p.,** the length of time for any disease which must elapse before a person exposed to the contagion is regarded as incapable of transmitting or acquiring the disease. **reaction p.** 1. The stage of rallying from shock after trauma. 2. Reaction time, the time that elapses between stimulation and the consequent reaction. **refractory p.,** a short period succeeding the time at which a nerve or muscle enters into a condition of functional activity during which the nerve or muscle does not respond to a second stimulus. **safe p.,** the period during the menstrual cycle when conception is considered least likely to occur; it is approximately the ten days after menstruation begins, and the ten days preceding menstruation. **silent p.,** an interval in the course of a disease in which the symptoms become very mild or disappear for a time. **sphygmic p.,** the second phase of ventricular systole, being the period (0.21–0.30 second) intervening between the opening and closing of the semilunar valves, during which the blood is being discharged into the aortic and the pulmonary arteries. Called also *ejection period.* **Wenckebach p.,** an occasional lengthening of the P-R interval in the electrocardiogram, due to an occasional dropped beat in heart block.

periodate (per-i′o-dāt). A salt of periodic acid.

periodic (pe″re-od′ik) [Gr. *periodikos*]. Recurring at regular intervals of time.

periodicity (pe″re-o-dis′ĭ-te). Recurrence at regular intervals of time. In physics, the rate of interruption in an electrical current. **filarial p.,** the periodic recurrence every night of filaria in the blood of a person who has been infected. **lunar p.,** recurrence synchronized with phases of the moon, as the reproductive phenomena in some lower animals. **malarial p.,** the more or less regular recurrence of paroxysms at intervals of one, two, or three days in malaria. See under *malaria*.

periodontal (per″e-o-don′tal) [*peri-* + Gr. *odous* tooth]. Situated or occurring around a tooth; pertaining to the periodontium.

periodontia (per″e-o-don′she-ah). Periodontics.

periodontics (per″e-o-don′tiks) [*peri-* + Gr. *odous* tooth]. That branch of dentistry dealing with the study and treatment of periodontal diseases.

periodontist (per″e-o-don′tist). A dentist who specializes in periodontics.

periodontitis (per″e-o-don-ti′tis) [*peri-* + Gr. *odous* tooth + *-itis*]. Inflammatory reaction of the tissues surrounding a tooth (periodontium). **apical p.,** inflammatory reaction of the tissues surrounding the root of a tooth.

periodontium (per″e-o-don′she-um) [*peri-* + Gr. *odous* tooth]. The tissues investing and supporting the teeth, including the cementum, periodontal membrane, alveolar bone, and gingiva. Anatomically [N A], the term is restricted to the connective tissue interposed between the teeth and their bony sockets. Called also *periosteum alveolare* [B N A].

periodontoclasia (per″e-o-don″to-kla′se-ah) [*peri-* + Gr. *odous* tooth + *klasis* breaking]. A general term sometimes used for any degenerative and destructive disease of the periodontium.

periodontology (per″e-o-don-tol′o-je) [*peri-* + Gr. *odous* tooth + *-logy*]. The scientific study of the periodontium and periodontal diseases.

periodontopathy (per″e-o-don-top′ah-the). A non-inflammatory disorder of the periodontium.

periodontosis (per″e-o-don-to′sis). A degenerative, non-inflammatory condition of the periodontium, originating in one or more of the periodontal structures and characterized by destruction of the tissues.

periomphalic (per″e-om-fal′ik) [*peri-* + Gr. *omphalos* navel]. Around the umbilicus.

perionychia (per″e-o-nik′e-ah). 1. An infected ulceration of the perionychium. 2. Perionychium.

perionychium (per″e-o-nik′e-um) [*peri-* + Gr. *onyx* nail]. The epidermis bordering a nail.

perionyx (per″e-o′niks) [*peri-* + Gr. *onyx* nail]. A relic of the eponychium persisting as a band across the root of the nail, seen in the eighth month of fetal life.

perionyxis (per″e-o-nik′sis) [*peri-* + Gr. *onyx* nail]. Inflammation of the skin surrounding a fingernail or toenail.

perioophoritis (per″e-o-of″o-ri′tis) [*peri-* + Gr. *ōon* egg + *pherein* to bear + *-itis*]. Inflammation of the tissues around the ovary.

perioophorosalpingitis (per″e-o-of″o-ro-sal″-pin-ji′tis) [*peri-* + Gr. *ōon* egg + *pherein* to bear + *salpinx* tube + *-itis*]. Inflammation of the tissues around the ovary and oviduct.

perioothecitis (per-e-o″o-the-si′tis). Perioophoritis.

perioothecosalpingitis (per″e-o″o-the″ko-sal″-pin-ji′tis). Perioophorosalpingitis.

periophthalmia (per″e-of-thal′me-ah). Periophthalmitis.

periophthalmic (per″e-of-thal′mik). Situated around the eye.

periophthalmitis (per″e-o-of″thal-mi′tis). Inflammation of the tissues around the eye.

periople (per′e-o″p'l) [*peri-* + Gr. *hoplē* hoof]. The layer of soft, light-colored horn covering the outer aspect of the hoof in ungulates.

perioptometry (per″e-op-tom′e-tre) [*peri-* + Gr. *optos* visible + *metron* measure]. The measurement of the peripheral acuity of vision or of the limits of the visual field.

perioral (per″e-o′ral) [*peri-* + L. *os* mouth]. Situated or occurring around the mouth.

periorbit (per″e-or′bit). Periorbita.

periorbita (per″e-or′bi-tah) [*peri-* + L. *orbita* orbit]. [N A, B N A] The periosteal covering of the bones forming the orbit, or eye socket.

periorbital (per″e-or′bĭ-tal). Situated around the orbit, or eye socket.

periorbititis (per″e-or″bĭ-ti′tis). Inflammation of the periorbita.

periorchitis (per″e-or-ki′tis) [*peri-* + Gr. *orchis* testis + *-itis*]. Inflammation of the tunica vaginalis testis. **p. adhaesi′va,** a variety in which the two layers of the tunica vaginalis are more or less adherent. **p. purulen′ta,** periorchitis which goes on to pus formation.

periorchium (per″e-or′ke-um). The parietal layer of the tunica vaginalis.

periost (per′e-ost). Periosteum.

periosteal (per″e-os′te-al). Pertaining to the periosteum.

periosteitis (per″e-os″te-i′tis). Periostitis.

periosteodema (per″e-os″te-o-de′mah). Periosteo-edema.

periosteo-edema (per″e-os″te-o-e-de′mah). Edema of the periosteum.

periosteoma (per″e-os-te-o′mah). A morbid bony growth surrounding a bone.

periosteomedullitis (per″e-os″te-o-med″u-li′-tis). Inflammation of the periosteum and bone marrow.

periosteomyelitis (per″e-os″te-o-mi″ĕ-li′tis) [*peri-* + Gr. *osteon* bone + *myelos* marrow + *-itis*]. Inflammation of the entire bone, including periosteum and marrow.

periosteophyte (per″e-os′te-o-fīt) [*periosteum* + Gr. *phyton* growth]. A bony outgrowth on the periosteum.

periosteorrhaphy (per″e-os″te-or′ah-fe) [*periosteum* + Gr. *rhaphē* suture]. The suturing together of the margins of severed periosteum.

periosteosis (per″e-os″te-o′sis). The condition manifested by development of periosteomas.

periosteotome (per″e-os′te-o-tōm). An instrument for cutting the periosteum; also an instrument for separating the periosteum from the bone.

periosteotomy (per″e-os″te-ot′o-me) [*peri-* + Gr. *osteon* bone + *tomē* a cutting]. Surgical incision or slitting of the periosteum.

periosteous (per″e-os′te-us). Pertaining to or of the nature of periosteum.

periosteum (per″e-os′te-um) [*peri-* + Gr. *osteon* bone]. [N A, B N A] A specialized connective tissue covering all bones of the body, and possessing bone-forming potentialities; in adults, it consists of two layers that are not sharply defined, the external layer being a network of dense connective tissue containing blood vessels, and the deep layer composed of more loosely arranged collagenous bundles with spindle-shaped connective tissue cells and a network of thin elastic fibers. **alveolar p., p. alveola′re** [B N A], the connective tissue lining of the tooth sockets. See *periodontium*.

periostitis (per″e-os-ti′tis). Inflammation of the periosteum. The condition is generally chronic, and is marked by tenderness and swelling of the bone and an aching pain. Acute periostitis is due to infection, and is characterized by diffuse suppuration, severe pain, and constitutional symptoms, and usually results in necrosis. **p. albumino′sa, albuminous p.,** a form accompanied by the exudation of a clear, albuminous liquid into a flattened cavity beneath the periosteum; called also *serous abscess* and *periosteal ganglion*. **dental p.,** inflammation of the dental periosteum. **diffuse p.,** a noncircumscribed periostitis of the long bones. **hemorrhagic p.,** a form in which blood is extravasated beneath the periosteum. **p. hyperplas′tica,** hypertrophic pulmonary osteoarthropathy. **p. inter′na cra′nii,** inflammation of the endocranium; external pachymeningitis. **precocious p.,** syphilitic osteoperiostitis occurring as an early symptom.

periostoma (per″e-os-to′mah). Periosteoma.

periostomedullitis (per″e-os″to-med″u-li′tis). Periosteomedullitis.

periostosis (per″e-os-to′sis). The abnormal deposition of periosteal bone.

periostosteitis (per″e-os-tos″te-i′tis). Inflammation involving both bone and its connective tissue covering (periosteum).

periostotome (per″e-os′to-tōm). Periosteotome.

periostotomy (per″e-os-tot′o-me). Periosteotomy.

periotic (per″e-o′tik) [*peri-* + Gr. *ous* ear]. 1. Situated about the ear, especially the internal ear. 2. The petrous and mastoid portions of the temporal bone, at one stage a distinct bone.

periovaritis (per″e-o″vah-ri′tis). Perioophoritis.

periovular (per″e-o′vu-lar). Surrounding an ovum.

peripachymeningitis (per″ĭ-pak″e-men″in-ji′-tis) [*peri-* + Gr. *pachys* thick + *mēninx* membrane + *-itis*]. Inflammation of the substance between the dura and the bony covering of the central nervous system.

peripancreatic (per″ĭ-pan″kre-at′ik). Surrounding the pancreas.

peripancreatitis (per″ĭ-pan″kre-ah-ti′tis) [*peri-* + Gr. *pankreas* pancreas + *-itis*]. Inflammation of tissues around the pancreas.

peripapillary (per″ĭ-pap′ĭ-ler″e). Located around the optic papilla.

peripatetic (per″ĭ-pah-tet′ik) [Gr. *peripatētikos* given to walking about while teaching or disputing]. Walking about.

peripenial (per″ĭ-pe′ne-al). Around the penis.

peripericarditis (per″ĭ-per″ĭ-kar-di′tis). Inflammation around the pericardium producing adhesions of the pericardium to the pleura and chest wall.

periphacitis (per″ĭ-fah-si′tis) [*peri-* + Gr. *phakos* lens + *-itis*]. Inflammation of the capsule of the eye lens.

periphakitis (per″ĭ-fah-ki′tis). Periphacitis.

peripharyngeal (per″ĭ-fah-rin′je-al). Situated around the pharynx.

peripherad (pĕ-rif′er-ad). Toward the periphery.

peripheral (pĕ-rif′er-al). Pertaining to or situated at or near the periphery.

peripheraphose (pĕ-rif′er-ah-fōs). An aphose originating in the peripheral ocular mechanism.

peripheric (per″ĭ-fer′ik). Peripheral.

peripherocentral (pĕ-rif″er-o-sen′tral). Both peripheral and central, but primarily or preponderatingly peripheral.

peripheroceptor (pĕ-rif″er-o-sep′tor). Any one of the receptors at the peripheral ends of the sensory peripheral neuron which receive the stimulus.

peripheromittor (pĕ-rif″er-o-mit′or). A terminal mittor placed in connection with the ceptor of a muscle fiber or gland cell which transmits the impulse to the fiber or cell.

peripheroneural (pĕ-rif″er-o-nu′ral). Pertaining to the nerves situated at the surface of the body.

peripherophose (pĕ-rif′er-o-fōz) [*periphery* + *phose*]. Any phose or subjective sensation of light originating in the peripheral ocular mechanism.

periphery (pĕ-rif′er-e) [Gr. *periphereia*, from *peri* around + *pherein* to bear]. The outward part or surface.

periphlebitic (per″ĭ-fle-bit′ik). Pertaining to periphlebitis.

periphlebitis (per″ĭ-fle-bi′tis) [*peri-* + Gr. *phleps* vein + *-itis*]. Inflammation of the tissues around a vein, or of the external coat of a vein.

periphoria (per″ĭ-fo′re-ah) [*peri-* + Gr. *phoros* bearing + *-ia*]. Cyclophoria.

periphrastic (per″ĭ-fras′tik) [Gr. *periphrastikos*]. Marked by the use of superfluous words and roundabout methods in expressing ideas.

periphrenitis (per″ĭ-fre-ni′tis) [*peri-* + Gr. *phrēn* diaphragm + *-itis*]. Inflammation of the diaphragm and structures around it.

Periplaneta (per″ĭ-plah-ne′tah). A genus of roaches. *P. america′na* is the American cockroach; *P. australa′siae* is the Australian cockroach.

periplasm (per′ĭ-plazm). Periplast.

periplast (per′ĭ-plast) [*peri-* + Gr. *plassein* to mold]. Cytoplasm.

periplastic (per″ĭ-plas′tik). Pertaining to or formed from periplast (cytoplasm).

peripleural (per″ĭ-ploo′ral). Surrounding the pleura.

peripleuritis (per″ĭ-ploo-ri′tis) [*peri-* + *pleura* + *-itis*]. Inflammation of the tissues between the pleura and the chest wall.

periplocin (per″ĭ-plo′sin). A crystallizable glycoside, $C_{36}H_{56}O_{13}$, from *Periploca graeca:* it acts like digitalin as a heart tonic and slower of the pulse.

periplocymarin (per″ĭ-plo-si′mah-rin). A cardiac glycoside, $C_{30}H_{46}O_8$, from the bark of *Periploca graeca.*

periplogenin (per″ĭ-ploj′e-nin). An aglycone sterol derivative, $C_{23}H_{34}O_5$.

peripneumonia (per″ĭ-nu-mo′ne-ah) [*peri-* + Gr. *pneumōn* lung + *-ia*]. Pneumonia; also pleuropneumonia. **p. no′tha,** a variety of acute bronchitis simulating pneumonia.

peripneumonitis (per″ĭ-nu″mo-ni′tis). Peripneumonia.

peripolar (per″ĭ-po′lar). Situated about a pole or the poles.

periportal (per″ĭ-por′tal). Situated around the portal vein.

periproctic (per″ĭ-prok′tik) [*peri-* + Gr. *prōktos* anus]. Situated around the anus.

periproctitis (per″ĭ-prok-ti′tis) [*peri-* + Gr. *prōktos* anus + *-itis*]. Inflammation of the tissues surrounding the rectum and anus.

periprostatic (per″ĭ-pros-tat′ik). Situated about the prostate.

periprostatitis (per″ĭ-pros″tah-ti′tis). Inflammation of the tissues and structures around the prostate gland.

peripyema (per″ĭ-pi-e′mah). Suppuration surrounding a part, as a tooth.

peripylephlebitis (per″ĭ-pi″le-fle-bi′tis) [*peri-* + Gr. *pylē* gate + *phleps* vein + *-itis*]. Inflammation of the tissue about the portal vein.

peripylic (per″ĭ-pi′lik) [*peri-* + Gr. *pylē* gate]. Around the portal vein.

peripyloric (per″ĭ-pi-lor′ik). Around the pylorus.

periradicular (per″ĭ-rah-dik′u-lar). Surrounding a root, especially the root of a tooth.

perirectal (per″ĭ-rek′tal). Around the rectum.

perirectitis (per″ĭ-rek-ti′tis). Periproctitis.

perirenal (per″ĭ-re′nal) [*peri-* + L. *ren* kidney]. Situated around a kidney.

perirhinal (per″ĭ-ri′nal) [*peri-* + Gr. *rhis* nose]. Situated about the nose.

perirhizoclasia (per″ĭ-ri″zo-kla′se-ah) [*peri-* + Gr. *rhiza* root + *klasis* destruction]. Inflammatory destruction of tissues immediately around the root of a tooth, i.e., the pericementum, cementum and superficial layers of the alveolar process. Cf. *pararhizoclasia.*

perisalpingitis (per″ĭ-sal″pin-ji′tis) [*peri-* + Gr. *salpinx* tube + *-itis*]. Inflammation of the tissues and peritoneum around a uterine tube.

perisalpingo-ovaritis (per″ĭ-sal-ping″go-o″-vah-ri′tis]. Inflammation involving the ovary and the tissues around the uterine tube.

perisalpinx (per″ĭ-sal′pinks). The peritoneal cover of the upper border of the uterine tube.

perisclerium (per″ĭ-skle′re-um) [*peri-* + Gr. *sklēros* hard]. Fibrous tissue surrounding ossifying cartilage.

periscopic (per″ĭ-skop′ik) [*peri-* + Gr. *skopein* to examine]. Affording a wide range of vision.

perisigmoiditis (per″ĭ-sig″moid-i′tis). Inflammation of the peritoneal covering of the sigmoid flexure.

perisinuitis (per″ĭ-si″nu-i′tis). Perisinusitis.

perisinuous (per″ĭ-sin′u-us). Situated around a sinus.

perisinusitis (per″ĭ-si″nus-i′tis). Inflammation of the tissues around a sinus.

perispermatitis (per″ĭ-sper″mah-ti′tis). Inflammation of the tissues about the spermatic cord. **p. sero′sa,** encysted hydrocele of the cord.

perisplanchnic (per″ĭ-splank′nik) [*peri-* + Gr. *splanchnon* viscus]. Around a viscus or the viscera.

perisplanchnitis (per″ĭ-splank-ni′tis). Inflammation around the viscera; perivisceritis.

perisplenic (per″ĭ-splen′ik). Occurring around the spleen.

perisplenitis (per″ĭ-sple-ni′tis) [*peri-* + Gr. *splēn* spleen + *-itis*]. Inflammation of the peritoneal coat of the spleen and of the structures around it. **p. cartilagin′ea,** inflammatory overgrowth of the capsule of the spleen, causing a thickening of cartilaginous hardness.

perispondylic (per″ĭ-spon-dil′ik). Around a vertebra.

perispondylitis (per″ĭ-spon″dĭ-li′tis) [*peri-* + Gr. *spondylos* vertebra + *-itis*]. Inflammation of the parts around a vertebra. **Gibney's p.,** a painful condition of the spinal muscles.

Perisporiaceae (per″ĭ-spo″re-a′se-e). A family of the Ascomycetes, including the penicillium and aspergillus molds.

perissad (pĕ-ris′ad). Any element or radical with an odd-numbered valence.

Perissodactyla (pĕ-ris″so-dak′tĭ-lah) [Gr. *perissos* odd + *daktylos* finger]. An order of ungulates having an odd number of toes, including the horse, tapir, and rhinoceros. Cf. *Artiodactyla.*

perissodactylous (pĕ-ris″so-dak′tĭ-lus). Having an odd number of digits on a hand or foot.

peristalsis (per″ĭ-stal′sis) [*peri-* + Gr. *stalsis* contraction]. The wormlike movement by which the alimentary canal or other tubular organs provided with both longitudinal and circular muscle fibers propel their contents. It consists of a wave of contraction passing along the tube. **mass p.,** strong peristaltic movements, which last only a few seconds, but move the intestinal contents from one section of the colon to another. **reversed p.,** that which impels the contents of the intestine cephalad.

peristaltic (per″ĭ-stal′tik). Of the nature of peristalsis.

peristaltin (per″ĭ-stal′tin). A glycoside, $C_{14}H_{18}O_8$, of cascara sagrada.

peristaphyline (per″ĭ-staf′ĭ-lin) [*peri-* + Gr. *staphylē* uvula]. Situated around the uvula.

peristasis (pĕ-ris′tah-sis). Environment.

peristole (pĕ-ris′to-le) [Gr. *peristolē* contracture]. The capacity of the walls of the digestive tract to surround or grasp its contents following the ingestion of food.

peristolic (per″ĭ-stol′ik). Pertaining to peristole.

peristoma (pĕ-ris′to-mah). Peristome.

peristomatous (per″ĭ-stom′ah-tus). Around the mouth.

peristome (per′ĭ-stōm) [*peri-* + Gr. *stoma* mouth]. A groove running from the cytosome in certain protozoa.

peristrumitis (per″ĭ-stroo-mi′tis). Inflammation extending from an inflamed goiter to the surrounding structures.

peristrumous (per″ĭ-stroo′mus). Around or near a goiter.

perisynovial (per″ĭ-sĭ-no′ve-al). Around a synovial structure.

perisyringitis (per″ĭ-sir″in-ji′tis). Inflammation of tissues around ducts of the sweat glands. **p. chron′ica na′si,** granulosis rubra nasi.

perisystole (per″ĭ-sis′to-le) [*peri-* + *systole*]. The pause after the diastole and before the systole.

perisystolic (per″ĭ-sis-tol′ik). Presystolic.

peritectomy (per″ĭ-tek′to-me) [*peri-* + Gr. *ektomē* excision]. Excision of a ring of conjunctiva around and very near the cornea, followed by cauterization of the trench thus made: done for pannus.

peritendineum (per″ĭ-ten-din′e-um). [N A] The connective tissue investing larger tendons and extending as septa between the fibers composing them.

peritendinitis (per″ĭ-ten″dĭ-ni′tis). Inflammation of a tendon sheath. **p. calca′rea,** a painful condition marked by calcareous deposits in tendons and in peritendinous, capsular, and ligamentous tissues. **p. crep′itans,** tendovaginitis crepitans. **p. sero′sa,** ganglion, def. 2.

peritenon (per″ĭ-te′non) [*peri-* + Gr. *tenōn* tendon]. The connective tissue structures associated with a tendon.

peritenoneum (per″ĭ-ten″o-ne′um). The loose connective tissue covering the surface of tendons and ligaments and penetrating inside to separate the substance into bundles.

peritenonitis (per″ĭ-ten″o-ni′tis). Inflammation of a tendon sheath.

peritenontitis (per″ĭ-ten″on-ti′tis). Peritenonitis.

perithecium (per″ĭ-the′se-um) [*peri-* + Gr. *thēkē* case]. A flask-shaped envelope enclosing the fructification of certain fungi and molds.

perithelial (per″ĭ-the′le-al). Pertaining to the perithelium.

perithelioma (per″ĭ-the″le-o′mah). Telangiectatic sarcoma; a tumor of the perithelium; a form of tumor appearing to spring from the adventitia of the blood vessels.

perithelium (per″ĭ-the′le-um) [*peri-* + Gr. *thēlē* nipple]. The layer of connective tissue that surrounds the capillaries and smaller vessels. **Eberth's p.,** a partial layer of cells on the external surface of the capillaries.

perithoracic (per″ĭ-tho-ras′ik). Surrounding the thorax.

perithyreoiditis (per″ĭ-thi″re-oid-i′tis). Perithyroiditis.

perithyroiditis (per″ĭ-thi″roid-i′tis). Inflammation of the capsule of the thyroid body.

peritomist (pĕ-rit′o-mist). One who performs the operation of peritomy.

peritomize (pĕ-rit′o-mīz). To subject to peritomy.

peritomy (pĕ-rit′o-me) [*peri-* + Gr. *temnein* to cut]. 1. Surgical incision of the conjunctiva and subconjunctival tissue about the whole circumference of the cornea. 2. Circumcision.

peritoneal (per″ĭ-to-ne′al). Pertaining to the peritoneum.

peritonealgia (per″ĭ-to″ne-al′je-ah). Pain in the peritoneum.

peritonealize (per″ĭ-to-ne′al-īz). To cover with peritoneum.

peritoneocentesis (per″ĭ-to″ne-o-sen-te′sis) [*peritoneum* + Gr. *kentēsis* puncture]. Puncture of the peritoneal cavity for the purpose of obtaining fluid.

peritoneoclysis (per″ĭ-to″ne-o-kli′sis). Injection of water or nutrient fluids into the peritoneal cavity in anemia or the algid stage of cholera (Sir B. W. Richardson, 1854).

peritoneography (per″ĭ-to-ne-og′rah-fe). Roentgenography of the peritoneum.

peritoneomuscular (per″ĭ-to-ne″o-mus′ku-lar). Pertaining to or composed of peritoneum and muscle.

peritoneopathy (per″ĭ-to-ne-op′ah-the) [*peritoneum* + Gr. *pathos* disease]. Any disease of the peritoneum.

peritoneopericardial (per″ĭ-to-ne″o-per″ĭ-kar′de-al). Pertaining to the peritoneum and pericardium.

peritoneopexy (per″ĭ-to′ne-o-pek″se) [*peritoneum* + Gr. *pēxis* fixation]. Fixation of the uterus by the vaginal route.

peritoneoplasty (per″ĭ-to′ne-o-plas″te) [*peritoneum* + Gr. *plassein* to form]. The operation of covering abraided areas with peritoneum.

peritoneoscope (per″ĭ-to′ne-o-skōp). An instrument for performing peritoneoscopy.

peritoneoscopy (per″ĭ-to″ne-os′ko-pe) [*peritoneum* + Gr. *skopein* to examine]. Examination of the peritoneum by an instrument inserted through the abdominal wall.

peritoneotome (per″ĭ-to-ne′o-tōm). An area of the peritoneum supplied with afferent nerve fibers by a single posterior root.

peritoneotomy (per″ĭ-to″ne-ot′o-me) [*peritoneum* + Gr. *tomē* a cutting]. Incision into the peritoneum.

peritoneum (per″ĭ-to-ne′um) [L.; Gr. *peritonaion*, from *per* around + *teinein* to stretch]. [N A] The serous membrane lining the abdominopelvic walls (*parietal p.*) and investing the viscera (*visceral p.*). It is a strong, colorless membrane with a smooth surface, and forms a closed sac except in the female, in whom it is continuous with the mucous

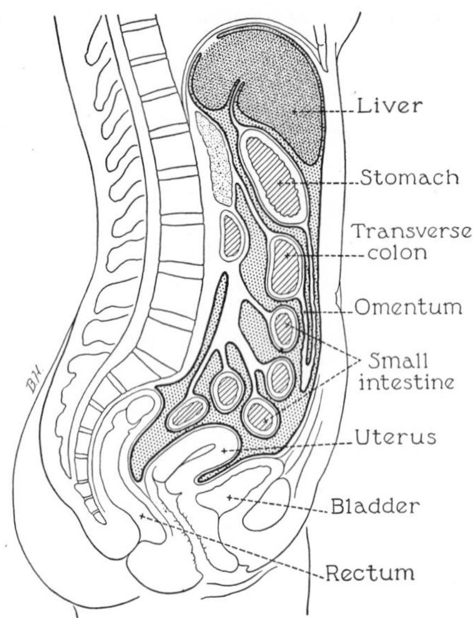

Course of the peritoneum (heavy black line) in a median sagittal section of a female.

membrane of the uterine tubes. **abdominal p.,** p. parietale. **p. of cranium,** pericranium. **intestinal p.,** p. viscerale. **parietal p., p. parieta′le** [N A], the peritoneum that lines the abdominal and pelvic walls and the under surface of the diaphragm. **visceral p., p. viscera′le** [N A], the peritoneum reflected at various places over the viscera, forming a complete covering for the stomach, spleen, liver, ascending portion of the duodenum, jejunum, ileum, transverse colon, sigmoid flexure, upper end of rectum, uterus, and ovaries; it also partially covers the descending and transverse portions of the duodenum, the cecum, ascending and descending colon, the middle part of the rectum, the posterior wall of the bladder, and the upper portion of the vagina. The peritoneum serves to hold the viscera in position by its folds, some of which form the *mesenteries*, connecting portions of the intestine with the posterior abdominal wall; other folds, the *omenta*, are attached to the stomach; and still others form the *ligaments* of the liver, spleen, stomach, kidneys, bladder, and uterus. The potential space between the visceral and the parietal peritoneum is the peritoneal cavity, which consists of the *pelvic peritoneal cavity* below and the *general peritoneal cavity* above. The general peritoneal cavity communicates by the epiploic foramen with the cavity of the greater omentum, which is also known as the *lesser peritoneal cavity*.

peritonism (per′ĭ-to-nizm). A condition of shock simulating peritonitis, but without inflammation of the peritoneum.

peritonitis (per″ĭ-to-ni′tis). Inflammation of the peritoneum; a condition marked by exudations in the peritoneum of serum, fibrin, cells, and pus. It is attended by abdominal pain and tenderness, constipation, vomiting, and moderate fever. **adhesive p.,** that which is characterized by adhesions between adjacent serous surfaces. **p. areno′sa,** chronic peritonitis, characterized by the formation of small sandlike nodules. **autolytic p.,** peritonitis due to autolytic decomposition of a piece of liver in the peritoneal cavity. **bile p., biliary p.,** choleperitoneum. **chemical p.,** peritonitis due to chemical intoxication. **p. chron′ica fibro′sa encap′sulans,** a chronic peritonitis marked by the formation on the intestine of a white coating of fibrous tissue undergoing hyaline degeneration: called also *iced intestine* and *zuckergussdarm*. **circumscribed p.,** that which is limited to a portion of the peritoneum. **p. defor′mans,** chronic peritonitis producing shortening of the mesentery so that the intestines are drawn up in loops toward the spine. **diaphragmatic p.,** that which affects the peritoneal surface of the diaphragm. **diffuse p.,** that which is not limited to a portion of the peritoneum. **p. encap′sulans, encysted p.,** that in which a collection of pus or serum is enclosed by adhesions. **fibrocaseous p.,** tubercular peritonitis with fibrous and caseous degeneration. **gas p.,** peritonitis with the accumulation of gas within the peritoneum. **general p.,** inflammation of the greater part of the peritoneum. **hemorrhagic p.,** that which is attended with hemorrhagic effusion. **localized p.,** circumscribed peritonitis. **pelvic p.,** perimetritis; peritonitis situated in the pelvis. **perforative p.,** that which is due to a perforation in the digestive tract. **puerperal p.,** that which occurs following childbirth. **purulent p.,** peritonitis with the formation of pus. **septic p.,** that which is due to a pyogenic microorganism. **serous p.,** that which is attended by a copious liquid exudation. **silent p.,** acute peritonitis which causes sudden death without betraying its presence by any symptoms. **terminal p.,** primary peritonitis in the late stages of a wasting disease. **traumatic p.,** simple acute peritonitis due to traumatism or injury. **tuberculous p.,** peritonitis caused by the tubercle bacillus.

peritonization (per″ĭ-to-ni-za′shun). The operation of covering an injured surface of an abdominal organ with peritoneum; peritoneoplasty.

peritonize (per′ĭ-to-nīz). To cover with peritoneum.

peritonsillar (per″ĭ-ton′sĭ-lar). Situated near or around a tonsil.

peritonsillitis (per″ĭ-ton″sĭ-li′tis). Inflammation of the peritonsillar tissues.

peritracheal (per″ĭ-tra′ke-al). Situated around the trachea.

peritrate (per′ĭ-trāt). Trade mark for preparations of pentaerythritol tetranitrate.

Peritricha (pe-rit′rĭ-kah) [*peri-* + Gr. *thrix* hair]. A group of bacteria including those forms which have flagella over the entire surface.

peritrichal, peritrichic (pe-rit′rĭ-kal, per″e-trik′ik). Peritrichous.

Peritrichida (per″ĭ-trik′ĭ-dah). An order of Infusoria in which the cilia form a spiral around the mouth.

peritrichous (pĕ-rit′rĭ-kus) [*peri-* + Gr. *thrix* hair]. 1. Having flagella over the entire surface: applied to a bacterial cell. 2. Having cilia around the mouth only: said of Infusoria.

peritrochanteric (per″ĭ-tro″kan-ter′ik). Situated about a trochanter.

perituberculosis (per″ĭ-tu-ber″ku-lo′sis). Paratuberculosis.

perityphlic (per″ĭ-tif′lik) [*peri-* + Gr. *typhlon* cecum]. Around the cecum.

perityphlitis (per″ĭ-tif-li′tis) [*peri-* + Gr. *typhlon* cecum + *-itis*]. Inflammation of the peritoneum surrounding the cecum; appendicitis. **p. actinomycot′ica,** actinomycosis whose principal seat is pericecal.

periumbilical (per″e-um-bil′ĭ-kal). Situated around the umbilicus.

periungual (per″e-ung′gwal). Around the nail.

periureteric (per″e-u″re-ter′ik). About the ureter.

periureteritis (per″e-u″re-ter-i′tis) [*peri-* + Gr. *ourētēr* ureter + *-itis*]. Inflammation of the tissues around a ureter.

periurethral (per″e-u-re′thral). Occurring around the urethra.

periurethritis (per″e-u″re-thri′tis) [*peri-* + Gr. *ourēthra* urethra + *-itis*]. Inflammation of the tissues around the urethra.

periuterine (per″e-u′ter-in). Around the uterus.

periuvular (per″e-u′vu-lar). Around the uvula.

perivaginal (per″ĭ-vaj′ĭ-nal). Around the vagina.

perivaginitis (per″ĭ-vaj″ĭ-ni′tis). Pericolpitis.

perivascular (per″ĭ-vas′ku-lar). Situated around a vessel.

perivasculitis (per″ĭ-vas″ku-li′tis). Inflammation of a perivascular sheath and of the tissues surrounding it.

perivenous (per″ĭ-ve′nus). Around a vein.

perivertebral (per″ĭ-ver′te-bral). Around a vertebra.

perivesical (per″ĭ-ves′ĭ-kal) [*peri-* + L. *vesica* bladder]. Occurring around the bladder.

perivesicular (per″ĭ-ve-sik′u-lar). Around a seminal vesicle.

perivesiculitis (per″ĭ-ve-sik″u-li′tis). Inflammation of tissue around the seminal vesicle.

perivisceral (per″ĭ-vis′er-al). Occurring around a viscus or the viscera.

perivisceritis (per″ĭ-vis″er-i′tis). Inflammation around a viscus or around the viscera.

perivitelline (per″ĭ-vi-tel′in). Situated around a vitellus or yolk.

perixenitis (per″ĭ-zĕ-ni′tis) [*peri-* + Gr. *xenos* strange + *-itis*]. Inflammation occurring around a foreign body in a tissue or organ.

perkeratosis (per″ker-ah-to′sis). Virus X disease of cattle. See *x-disease*, def. 2, under *disease*.

perkinism, perkinsism (per′kin-izm, per′kinsizm) [Elisha *Perkins*, of Norwich, Connecticut, 1741–1799]. An obsolete form of metallotherapy, embracing the therapeutic use of metallic tractors.

perlèche (per-lesh′) [Fr.]. A form of oral moniliasis attacking the labial commissures of children, causing them to lick their lips and resulting in thickening and desquamation of the epithelium.

Perlia's nucleus (per′le-ahz) [Richard *Perlia*, German oculist]. See under *nucleus*.

perlingual (per-ling′gwal) [L. *per* through + *lingua* tongue]. Through the tongue. The term is applied to the administration of medicines which are resorbed from the surface of the tongue.

Perls' bodies, test (perlz) [Max *Perls*, German pathologist, 1843–1881]. See under the nouns.

perlsucht (perl′sookt) [Ger.]. Tuberculosis of the mesentery and peritoneum in cattle.

permanganate (per-man′gah-nāt). Any salt of permanganic acid.

permeability (per″me-ah-bil′ĭ-te). The property or state of being permeable. See also *osmosis*.

permeable (per′me-ah-b′l) [L. *per* through + *meare* to pass]. Not impassable; pervious; that may be traversed.

permease (per′me-ās). A stereospecific membrane transport system. The term was introduced to emphasize the resemblance of these systems in bacteria to enzymes, with respect to kinetics of function and control of formation, but it does not imply either that permeases are enzymes or that they differ from the membrane transport systems of cells other than bacteria.

permeation (per″me-a′shun). The act of spreading through or penetrating a substance, tissue, or organ, as by a disease process, such as cancer.

perna (per′nah). A chlorinated naphthalin, which may cause a serious acne in persons handling it.

pernasal (per-na′sal) [L. *per* through + *nasus* nose]. Performed through the nose.

perneiras (pār-na′ras). Brazilian name for beriberi.

perniciosiform (per-nish″e-o′sĭ-form). Seemingly pernicious, a term applied to a condition which is apparently, but not actually, pernicious or malignant.

pernicious (per-nish′us) [L. *perniciosus*]. Tending to a fatal issue.

pernio (per′ne-o), pl. *pernio′nes* [L.]. Chilblain.

perniosis (per″ne-o′sis). A general term for skin affections caused by cold; the presence of chilblains on various portions of the body.

pero (pe′ro) [L. "a boot"]. The external layer of the olfactory lobe of the brain, giving rise to the olfactory nerves.

pero- (pe′ro) [Gr. *pēros* maimed]. Combining form meaning maimed or deformed.

perobrachius (pe″ro-bra′ke-us) [*pero-* + Gr. *brachiōn* arm]. A fetus with deformed arms.

perocephalus (pe″ro-sef′ah-lus) [*pero-* + Gr. *kephalē* head]. A fetus with a deformed head.

perochirus (pe″ro-ki′rus) [*pero-* + Gr. *cheir* hand]. A fetus with malformed hands.

perocormus (pe″ro-kor′mus) [*pero-* + Gr. *kormos* trunk]. Perosomus.

perodactylus (pe″ro-dak′tĭ-lus) [*pero-* + Gr. *daktylos* finger]. A fetus with deformity of fingers or toes, or both, especially absence of one or more digits.

peromelia (per″o-me′le-ah). Congenital deformity of the limbs.

peromelus (pe-rom′ĕ-lus) [*pero-* + Gr. *melos* limb]. A fetus with malformed limbs.

peronarthrosis (per″o-nar-thro′sis) [Gr. *peronē* anything pointed for piercing or pinning + *arthron* joint]. An articulation in which the surfaces are convex in one direction and concave in the other.

perone (per-o′ne). The fibula.

peroneal (per″o-ne′al). Pertaining to the fibula or to the outer side of the leg.

peroneotibial (per″o-ne″o-tib′e-al). Pertaining to the fibula and tibia.

peronia (pe-ro′ne-ah) [Gr. *pēros* maimed]. A developmental malformation or mutilation.

pero-olfactorius (pe″ro-ol″fak-to′re-us). The outer part of the olfactory bulb.

Per. op. emet. Abbreviation for L. *perac′ta operatio′ne emet′ici*, when the action of the emetic is over.

peropus (pe′ro-pus) [*pero-* + Gr. *pous* foot]. A fetus with malformed legs and feet.

peroral (per-o′ral) [L. *per* through + *os, oris*, the mouth]. Performed through or administered through the mouth.

per os (per os) [L.]. By mouth.

perosis (pĕ-ro′sis). A disease of chicks marked by bone deformities and associated with deficiency of certain dietary factors, such as choline and manganese.

perosomus (pe″ro-so′mus) [*pero-* + Gr. *sōma* body]. A fetal monster with greatly deformed body or trunk.

perosplanchnia (pe″ro-splank′ne-ah) [*pero-* + Gr. *splanchnon* viscus + *-ia*]. A developmental anomaly characterized by malformation of the viscera.

perosseous (per-os′e-us) [L. *per* through + *os* bone]. Transmitted through bone.

perotic (pĕ-rot′ik). Pertaining to or characterized by perosis.

peroxidase (per-ok′sĭ-dās). An enzyme which catalyzes the transfer of oxygen from hydrogen peroxide or an organic peroxide to a suitable substrate and thus brings about oxidation of the substrate. It causes breakdown of peroxide only in the presence of a suitable oxidizable substrate.

peroxide (per-ok′sīd). That oxide of any element which contains more oxygen than any other. More correctly applied to compounds having such linkage as —O—O—; for instance, hydrogen peroxide, H—O—O—H.

peroxydase (per-ok′sĭ-dās). Peroxidase.

peroxydasis (per-ok″sĭ-da′sis). The action produced by peroxidase.

peroxydol (per-ok′sĭ-dol). Sodium perborate.

perphenazine (per-fen′ah-zēn). Chemical name: 2-chloro-10-{3-[4-(2-hydroxyethyl)piperazinyl]-propyl}phenothiazine: used as a tranquilizer and anti-emetic.

perplication (per″pli-ka′shun) [L. *per* through + *plicare* to fold]. The closure of a divided vessel by drawing its bleeding end through an incision in its own wall.

perpolitiones (per″po-lish″e-o′nēz) [L., pl., from *perpolire* to polish thoroughly]. Polishings. **p. ory′zae,** rice polishings.

per primam (per pri′mam) [L.]. See *per primam intentionem.*

per primam intentionem (per pri′mam in-ten″-she-o′nem) [L.]. By first intention. See under *healing.*

per rectum (per rek′tum) [L.]. Through the rectum.

Perrin-Ferraton disease (per′an-fer″ah-ton′) [Maurice *Perrin*, Paris surgeon, 1826–1889; Louis *Ferraton*, French surgeon, born 1860]. Snapping hip.

Perroncito's apparatus, spirals (per″on-se′-tōz) [Aldo *Perroncito*, Italian histologist, 1882–1929]. See under *apparatus.*

persalt (per′sawlt). A salt of a peracid; a salt the acid radical of which has a higher valence than the protosalt.

per saltum (per sal′tum) [L.]. By leaps.

persantin (per-san′tin). Trade mark for preparations of dipyridamole.

per secundam (per se-kun′dam) [L.]. See *per secundam intentionem.*

per secundam intentionem (per se-kun′dam in-ten″she-o′nem) [L.]. By second intention. See under *healing.*

perseveration (per-sev″er-a′shun). Continuance of any activity after cessation of the causative stimulus. **clonic p.,** a condition in which a movement is repeated. **tonic p.,** a condition in which a position is maintained.

persona (per-so′nah) [L. "*mask*"]. Jung's term for the assumed personality which the individual takes on to mask his real individuality.

personalistics (per″sun-al-is′tiks). The study of personality.

personality (per″sŭ-nal′ĭ-te). That which constitutes, distinguishes, and characterizes a person; the total reaction of a person to his environment. **alternating p.,** dual p. **disordered p.,** a condition in which the patient thinks he is some person other than himself. **double p., dual p.,** a state of disordered consciousness in which the subject leads two lives, alternately, in neither of which he is fully aware of the experiences of the other. **multiple p.,** a condition in which the patient seems to have multiple states of consciousness, in none of which he is aware of the experiences in the others. **psychopathic p.,** a constitutional tendency to mental disorder; a type of personality marked by lessened voluntary control and increased emotional response to stimuli. **seclusive p., shut-in p.,** a condition in which the individual habitually responds inadequately to normal social appeal.

perspiratio (per″spĭ-ra′she-o) [L.]. Perspiration. **p. insensib′ilis,** insensible perspiration.

perspiration (per″spĭ-ra′shun) [L. *perspira′re* to breathe through]. 1. Sweating; the functional excretion of sweat. 2. Sweat. **insensible p.,** those gaseous emanations from the body which do not appear in the form of sensible sweat or moisture, such as gaseous productions arising from the lungs in exhalation and from the skin by vaporization. **sensible p.,** perspiration which appears as moisture upon the skin.

perstriction (per-strik′shun). Ligation or compression of a blood vessel for the arrest of hemorrhage.

persulfate (per-sul′fāt). A sulfate which contains more sulfuric acid than the ordinary sulfate.

persulfide (per-sul′fīd). A sulfide which contains more sulfur than the ordinary sulfide.

per tertiam (per ter′she-am) [L.]. See *per tertiam intentionem.*

per tertiam intentionem (per ter′she-am in-ten″she-o′nem) [L.]. By third intention. See under *healing.*

Perthes' disease, incision, method, test (per′tēz) [Georg Clemens *Perthes*, German surgeon, 1869–1927]. See under the nouns.

Pertik's diverticulum (per′tiks) [Otto *Pertik*, Hungarian physician, 1852–1913]. See under *diverticulum.*

per tubam (per tu′bam) [L.]. Through a tube.

pertubation (per″tu-ba′shun). Perflation of the uterine tubes to render them patent.

pertussis (per-tus′is) [L. *per* intensive + *tussis* cough]. Whooping cough.

pertussoid (per-tus′oid) [*pertussis* + Gr. *eidos* form]. 1. Resembling whooping cough. 2. An influenzal cough resembling that of whooping cough.

perücke (per-e′kĕ). An abnormal growth, resembling a malignant tumor, on the antlers of deer when deprived of internal secretion of the testicle.

Perutz reaction (pa′roots) [Alfred *Perutz*, Austrian dermatologist, born 1885]. See under *reaction.*

perversion (per-ver′shun) [L. *per* through + *versio* a turning]. A turning aside from the normal course; a morbid alteration of function which may occur in emotional, intellectual, or volitional fields. In dentistry, impaction of teeth. **sexual p.,** paraphilia.

pervert (per′vert). A perverted person, especially a person who indulges in unnatural sexual acts (*sexual p.*, or *paraphiliac*).

per vias naturales (per vi′as nat″u-ra′lēz) [L.]. By the natural ways.

pervigilium (per″vĭ-jil′e-um) [L.]. Sleeplessness.

pervious (per′ve-us) [L. *pervius*]. Permeable.

pes (pes), pl. *pe′des*, gen. *pe′dis* [L.]. [N A, B N A] The terminal organ of the leg, or lower limb. Used also as a general term to designate a footlike part. **p. abduc′tus,** a deformed foot in which the anterior part is displaced so that it lies laterally to the vertical axis of the leg. **p. accesso′rius,** eminentia collateralis ventriculi lateralis. **p. adduc′tus,** a deformed foot in which the anterior part is displaced so that it lies medially to the vertical axis of the leg. **p. anseri′nus** [L. "goose's foot"], plexus parotideus. **p. ca′vus,** exaggerated height of the longitudinal arch of the foot, present from birth or appearing later because of contractures or disturbed balance of the muscles. **p. cer′ebri,** crus cerebri. **p. corvi′nus** [L. "crow's foot"], a set of wrinkles radiating from the lateral canthus of the eye. **p. febric′itans,** elephantiasis. **p. gi′gas,** macropodia. **p. hippocam′pi** [N A], a formation of two or three elevations on the rostral end of the ventricular surface of the hippocampus. Called also *digitationes hippocampi* [B N A]. **p. hippocam′pi**

ma'jor, hippocampus. **p. hippocam'pi mi'nor,** calcar avis. **p. pedun'culi,** crus cerebri. **p. pla'nus,** a deformed foot in which the position of the bones relative to each other has been altered, with lowering of the longitudinal arch. **p. prona'tus,** a deformed foot in which the outer border of the anterior part is higher than the inner border. **p. supina'tus,** a deformed foot in which the inner border of the anterior part is higher than the outer border. **p. val'gus,** flatfoot.

pessary (pes'ah-re) [L. *pessarium*]. An instrument placed in the vagina to support the uterus or rectum. **cup p.,** a pessary the top of which has a cup-like shape to fit over the os uteri. **diaphragm p.,** a diaphragm for insertion into the vagina as an occlusive contraceptive. **doughnut p.,** an inflated soft rubber pessary shaped like a doughnut. **Emmert-Gellhorn p.,** a hollow stemmed Gellhorn pessary. **Gariel's p.,** a hollow rubber pessary which can be inflated. **Gehrung p.,** a pessary for cystocele, being a Hodge pessary bent on itself so as to form a double horseshoe, one lever being a little shorter than the other. **Gellhorn p.,** a single stem pessary for use in uterine prolapse. **Hodge's p.,** a pessary for retrodeviations of the uterus. **lever p.,** a pessary which acts on the principle of the lever. **Menge's p.,** a ring pessary with a fixed crossbar holding a detachable stem. **ring p.,** a round or ring-shaped pessary.

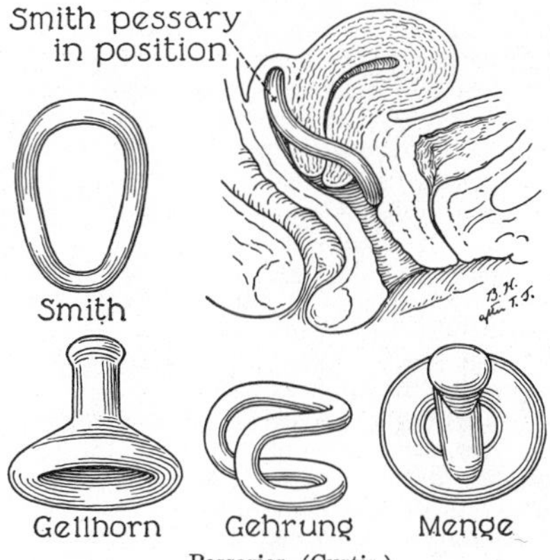

Pessaries. (Curtis.)

Smith's p., a pessary for use in retrodisplacement of the uterus. **stem p.,** a pessary with a stem for introduction into the canal of the cervix uteri. **Thomas p.,** a long, narrow pessary for use in nulliparas. **Zwanck's p.,** a radium carrier which can be fixed in the vault of the vagina.

pessima (pes'ĭ-mah). A skin disease characterized by papules and bordered with inflammatory patches.

pessimism (pes'ĭ-mizm) [L. *pes'simus* worst]. A morbid or insane disposition to put the worst construction upon everything. **therapeutic p.,** a tendency to undervalue the curative properties of drugs.

pessulum, pessum, pessus (pes'u-lum, pes'sum, pes'us) [L.; Gr. *pesson, pessos*]. Pessary.

pest (pest). Plague. **chicken p., fowl p.,** fowl plague. **scratching p.,** Aujeszky's disease. **Siberian p.,** anthrax. **swine p.,** hog cholera.

peste-boba (pes'ta-bo'bah). *Trypanosoma venezuelense.*

pesticemia (pes"tĭ-se'me-ah) [L. *pestis* plague + Gr. *haima* blood + *-ia*]. 1. The presence of plague germs (*Pasteurella pestis*) in the blood. 2. Septicemic plague.

pesticide (pes'tĭ-sīd). A poison used to destroy pests of any sort. The term includes fungicides, herbicides, insecticides, rodenticides, etc.

pestiferous (pes-tif'er-us) [L. *pestiferus; pestis* plague + *ferre* to bear]. Causing or propagating a pestilence.

pestilence (pes'tĭ-lens) [L. *pestilentia*]. Any virulent contagious or infectious epidemic disease; also an epidemic of such a disease.

pestilential (pes"tĭ-len'shal). Of the nature of a pestilence; producing an epidemic disease.

pestis (pes'tis) [L.]. Plague. **p. am'bulans,** ambulatory plague. **p. bovi'na,** cattle plague. **p. bubon'ica,** bubonic plague. **p. equo'rum,** horse sickness. **p. ful'minans, p. ma'jor,** the severe form of bubonic plague. **p. mi'nor,** ambulatory plague. **p. sid'erans,** septicemic plague. **p. variolo'sa,** variola.

pestle (pes'’l) [L. *pestillum*]. An implement for pounding drugs in a mortar.

pestology (pes-tol'o-je). The branch of science concerned with pests.

-petal [L. *petere* to seek]. Word termination meaning directed or moving toward, the point of reference being indicated by the word stem to which it is affixed, as centripetal (toward a center), corticipetal (toward the cortex), etc.

petalo- (pet'ah-lo) [Gr. *petalon* leaf]. Combining form denoting relationship to a leaf.

petalobacteria (pet"ah-lo-bak-te're-ah) [*petalo-* + *bacteria*]. Bacteria which become so aggregated as to form thin pellicles.

petalococcus (pet"ah-lo-kok'us) [*petalo-* + Gr. *kokkos* berry]. Any representative of a group of cocci which becomes so aggregated as to form thin pellicles.

petechia (pe-te'ke-ah), pl. *pete'chiae* [L.]. A small, pinpoint, nonraised, perfectly round, purplish red spot caused by intradermal or submucous hemorrhage, which later turns blue or yellow.

petechial (pe-te'ke-al). Characterized by or of the nature of petechiae.

petechiasis (pe"te-ki'ah-sis). A tendency to the formation of petechiae; a condition marked by petechiae.

Peter (pe'ter) **of Abano** (1250–c. 1316). Physician, philosopher, astrologer; an outstanding professor in the University of Padua whose opinions caused him to be tried for heresy during the Inquisition. His works include the *Conciliator differentiarum* (an attempt to reconcile Arabian and Greek medicine) and *De venenis* (a book on poisons).

Peterman test (pe'ter-man) [Mynie G. *Peterman*, American physician, born 1896]. See under *tests.*

Peters' ovum (pa'terz) [Hubert *Peters*, Budapest gynecologist, 1859–1934]. See under *ovum.*

Petersen's bag (pa'ter-senz) [C. F. *Petersen*, surgeon in Kiel, 1845–1908]. See under *bag.*

pethidine hydrochloride (peth'ĭ-din hi"dro-klo'rīd). Meperidine hydrochloride.

petiolate, petiolated (pet'e-o-lāt, pet'e-o-lāt"-ed). Having a stalk or petiole.

petiole (pet'e-ōl). A stem, stalk, or pedicle. **epiglottic p.,** petiolus epiglottidis.

petioled (pet'e-ōld). Petiolate.

petiolus (pĕ-ti'o-lus) [L., dim. of *pes* foot]. A stem, stalk, or pedicle. **p. epiglot'tidis** [N A, B N A], the pointed lower end of the epiglottic cartilage, which is attached to the back of the thyroid cartilage. Called also *epiglottic petiole.*

Petit's canal, sinus (ptēz) [François Pourfour du *Petit*, French anatomist and surgeon, 1664–1741]. See under *canal* and *sinus.*

Petit's hernia, ligament, triangle (ptēz) [Jean Louis *Petit*, French surgeon, 1674–1750]. See under the nouns.

Petit's law (ptēz) [Alexis Therese *Petit*, French physician, 1791–1820]. See *Dulong and Petit's law*, under *law.*

petit mal (pĕ-te' mahl') [Fr. "little illness"]. A brief blackout of consciousness with only minor rhythmic movements, seen especially in children, recurring daily and accompanied by an alternate dart and dome formation of the electroencephalogram recurring three times per second.

petits maux (pě-te′ mo′) [pl., Fr. "little pains"]. The slight pains preluding the beginning of labor.

Petrén's diet, method, treatment (pa-trenz′) [Karl *Petrén*, Swedish physician, 1869–1927]. See under *diet* and *treatment.*

Pétrequin's ligament (pātr-kanz′) [Joseph Pierre Eléonord *Pétrequin*, Lyons surgeon, 1809–1876]. The anterior thickened portion of the temporomaxillary capsule.

Petri dish, reaction, test (pe′tre) [Julius Richard *Petri*, German bacteriologist, 1852–1921]. See under *dish* and *test.*

petrichloral (pet″rĭ-klo′ral). A derivative of chloral, pentaerythritol chloral, with pharmacological properties similar to those of chloral hydrate: used as a hypnotic and sedative.

petrifaction (pet″rĭ-fak′shun) [L. *petra* stone + *facere* to make]. Conversion into a stonelike substance.

pétrissage (pa″tre-sahzh′) [Fr.]. A kneading action in massage.

petroccipital (pet″rok-sip′ĭ-tal). Petro-occipital.

petrolate (pet′ro-lāt). Petrolatum.

petrolatoma (pet″ro-lah-to′mah). A tumor developing consecutive to injection of liquid petrolatum.

petrolatum (pet″ro-la′tum) [L.]. A purified mixture of semisolid hydrocarbons obtained from petroleum: used as a basis for ointments and as a soothing application to the skin. Called also *yellow soft paraffin* and *petroleum jelly.* **p. al′bum,** white p. **hydrophilic p.,** a mixture of cholesterol, stearyl alcohol, and white wax, in white petrolatum: used as a water-absorbable ointment base. **liquid p.,** a mixture of liquid hydrocarbons obtained from petroleum, with a specific gravity of 0.860–0.905: used as a lubricant laxative: called also *heavy liquid p., white mineral oil,* and *liquid paraffin.* **liquid p., heavy.** See *liquid p.* **liquid p., light,** a mixture of liquid hydrocarbons obtained from petroleum, with a specific gravity of 0.828–0.880: used as a laxative. **p. liq′uidum,** liquid p. **p. liq′uidum le′ve,** liquid p., light. **white p.,** a wholly or nearly decolorized, purified mixture of semisolid hydrocarbons obtained from petroleum: used as an oleaginous ointment base.

petroleum (pě-tro′le-um) [L. *petra* stone + *oleum* oil]. A thick natural oil obtained from wells and springs especially dug in the earth. It consists of a mixture of various hydrocarbons of the paraffin and olefin series. It has been used as an expectorant, diaphoretic, and vermifuge; also in skin diseases, etc.

petrolization (pet″rol-i-za′shun). The spreading of petroleum on water for the purpose of destroying mosquito larvae therein.

petromastoid (pet″ro-mas′toid). 1. Pertaining to the petrous portion of the temporal bone and its mastoid process. 2. The periotic bone.

petro-occipital (pet″ro-ok-sip′ĭ-tal). Pertaining to the petrous and occipital bones.

petropharyngeus (pet″ro-fah-rin′je-us). An occasional muscle arising from the lower surface of the petrous portion of the temporal bone and inserted into the pharynx.

petrosal (pě-tro′sal). Pertaining to the petrous portion of the temporal bone.

petrosalpingostaphylinus (pet″ro-sal-ping″-go-staf″ĭ-li′nus) [Gr. *petra* stone + *salpinx* tube + *staphylē* uvula]. Musculus levator veli palatini.

petrosectomy (pet″ro-sek′to-me) [*petrous* + Gr. *ektomē* excision]. Excision of the cells of the apex of the petrous portion of the temporal bone.

petrositis (pet″ro-si′tis). Inflammation of the petrous portion of the temporal bone.

petrosomastoid (pě-tro″so-mas′toid). Petromastoid.

petrosphenoid (pet″ro-sfe′noid). Pertaining to the sphenoid bone and the petrous portion of the temporal bone.

petrosphere (pet′ro-sfēr). The solid structure of the earth as distinguished from the atmosphere and the aquasphere.

petrosquamosal (pet″ro-skwah-mo′sal). Pertaining to the petrous and squamous portions of temporal bone.

petrosquamous (pet″ro-skwa′mus). Petrosquamosal.

petrostaphylinus (pet″ro-staf″ĭ-li′nus). Musculus levator veli palatini.

petrous (pet′rus) [L. *petrosus*]. Resembling a rock; hard; stony.

petrousitis (pet″rus-i′tis). Petrositis.

Petruschky's litmus whey, spinalgia (pě-trush′kēz) [Johannes *Petruschky*, German bacteriologist, born 1863]. See under *whey* and *spinalgia.*

Pettenkofer's test, theory (pet′en-kof″erz) [Max von *Pettenkofer*, chemist in Munich, 1818–1901]. See under *tests* and *theory.*

pettymorrel (pet″e-mor′rel). Aralia.

Petzetaki's reaction, test (pet″za-tah′kēz). See under *tests.*

peucine (pu′sin) [Gr. *peuke* fir]. Pitch or resin.

peucinous (pu′sĭ-nus). Pertaining to pitch; resinous.

peucyl (pu′sil). An oily liquid hydrocarbon, C_5H_8, from turpentine oil.

pexia (pek′se-ah). Pexis.

pexic (pek′sik) [Gr. *pēxis* fixation]. Having the power of fixing substances: said of tissues.

pexin (pek′sin) [Gr. *pēxis* fixation]. Lab.

pexinogen (pek-sin′o-jen) [*pexin* + Gr. *gennan* to produce]. Renninogen.

pexis (pek′sis) [Gr. *pēxis*]. 1. The fixation of matter by a tissue. 2. Surgical fixation, usually by suturing.

-pexy [Gr. *pēxis* a fixing, putting together]. Word termination meaning fixation.

Peyer's glands, patches (pi′erz) [Johann Conrad *Peyer*, Swiss anatomist, 1653–1712]. See under *gland* and *patch.*

peyote (pa-o′ta). A drug obtained from the Mexican cactus, *Anhalonium:* used by the natives to produce a state of intoxication marked by feelings of ecstasy.

peyotl (pa-o′t'l). Peyote.

Peyronie's disease (pa-ron-ēz′) [François de la *Peyronie*, French surgeon, 1678–1747]. See under *disease.*

Peyrot's thorax (pa-rōz′) [Jean Joseph *Peyrot*, surgeon in Paris, 1843–1918]. See under *thorax.*

Pfannenstiel's incision (pfan′en-stēlz) [Johann *Pfannenstiel*, gynecologist in Breslau, 1862–1909]. See under *incision.*

Pfaundler's reaction (pfound′lerz) [Meinhard von *Pfaundler*, German physician, 1872–1947]. Mandelbaum's reaction. See under *reaction.*

Pfeiffer's bacillus, phenomenon (pfi′ferz) [Richard Friedrich Johann *Pfeiffer*, bacteriologist in Breslau, born 1858]. See under *bacillus* and *phenomenon.*

Pfeiffer's disease, glandular fever (pfi′ferz) [Emil *Pfeiffer*, German physician, 1846–1921]. Infectious mononucleosis.

Pfeifferella (pfi″fer-el′ah) [Richard F. J. *Pfeiffer*]. A genus name formerly given certain bacteria now included in the family Brucellaceae. **P. ana-pes′tifer,** *Pasteurella anapestifer.* **P. mal′lei,** *Actinomyces mallei.*

pferdepest (pfer′dĕ-pest) [Ger.]. Horse sickness.

Pflüger's cords, laws, tubes (pfle′gerz) [Edward Friedrich Wilhelm *Pflüger*, physiologist in Bonn, 1829–1910]. See under *tube* and *law.*

pfropfhebephrenia (pfropf″he-be-fre′ne-ah)

[Ger. *Pfropf* a plug or graft]. Hebephrenia engrafted upon mental deficiency.

pfropfschizophrenia (pfropf″skiz-o-fre′ne-ah). Schizophrenia engrafted upon mental deficiency.

Pfuhl's sign (pfoolz) [Adam *Pfuhl*, German physician 1842–1905]. See under *sign*.

P.G. Abbreviation of *Pharmacopoeia Germanica*, German pharmacopeia.

pg. Abbreviation for *picogram*.

P.G.A. Pteroylglutamic acid (folic acid).

P.H. Abbreviation for *past history*.

Ph. 1. Abbreviation for *Pharmacopeia*. 2. Chemical symbol for *phenyl*.

pH. The symbol commonly used in expressing hydrogen ion concentration, the measure of alkalinity and acidity. It signifies the logarithm of the reciprocal of the hydrogen ion concentration in gram molecules per liter of solution. pH 7 is the neutral point; above 7 alkalinity increases; below 7 acidity increases.

phacitis (fah-si′tis). Phakitis.

phaco- (fak′o) [Gr. *phakos* a lentil, or lentil-shaped object]. Combining form denoting relationship to a lens, as the crystalline lens. See also words beginning *phako-*.

phaco-anaphylaxis (fak″o-an″ah-fi-lak′sis) [*phaco-* + *anaphylaxis*]. Anaphylaxis induced by hypersensitivity to protein of the crystalline lens.

phacocele (fak′o-sēl) [*phaco-* + Gr. *kēlē* hernia]. The escape of the eye lens from its proper place; hernia of the eye lens.

phacocyst (fak′o-sist) [*phaco-* + Gr. *kystis* sac, bladder]. The capsule of the lens (capsula lentis [N A]).

phacocystectomy (fak″o-sis-tek′to-me) [*phacocyst* + Gr. *ektomē* excision]. Excision of a portion of the capsule of the lens for cataract.

phacocystitis (fak″o-sis-ti′tis) [*phacocyst* + *-itis*]. Inflammation of the capsule of the crystalline lens.

phacoerysis (fak″o-er-e′sis) [*phaco-* + Gr. *eryein* to drag away]. Removal of the lens in cataract by means of suction with an instrument known as an erysiphake. Called also *Barraquer's method*.

phacoglaucoma (fak″o-glaw-ko′mah) [*phaco-* + *glaucoma*]. The structural changes in the lens produced by glaucoma.

phacohymenitis (fak″o-hi″men-i′tis) [*phaco-* + Gr. *hymēn* membrane + *-itis*]. Inflammation of the capsule of the crystalline lens.

phacoid (fak′oid) [*phaco-* + Gr. *eidos* form]. Shaped like a lens or a lentil.

phacoiditis (fak″oid-i′tis). Phakitis.

phacoidoscope (fah-koi′do-skōp) [*phaco-* + Gr. *eidos* form + *skopein* to examine]. Phacoscope.

phacolysis (fah-kol′ĭ-sis) [*phaco-* + Gr. *lysis* dissolution]. 1. Discission of the crystalline lens, followed by extraction. 2. Dissolution of the lens of the eye by phacolysin or other antigen.

phacolytic (fak″o-lit′ik). Pertaining to or causing dissolution of the crystalline lens.

phacoma (fah-ko′mah). Phakoma.

phacomalacia (fak″o-mah-la′she-ah) [*phaco-* + Gr. *malakia* softness]. Softening of the lens; a soft cataract.

phacomatosis (fak″o-mah-to′sis). Phakomatosis.

phacometachoresis (fak″o-met″ah-ko-re′sis) [*phaco-* + Gr. *metachōrēsis* displacement]. Displacement of the eye lens.

phacometecesis (fak″o-met″ĕ-se′sis) [*phaco-* + Gr. *metoikēsis* migration]. Phacometachoresis.

phacometer (fah-kom′e-ter) [*phaco-* + Gr. *metron* measure]. An instrument for measuring the refractive power of lenses.

phacopalingenesis (fak″o-pal″in-jen′e-sis) [*phaco-* + Gr. *palin* again + *genesis* production]. Reformation of the crystalline lens.

phacoplanesis (fak″o-plah-ne′sis) [*phaco-* + Gr. *planēsis* wandering]. Wandering lens; preternatural mobility of the eye lens.

phacosclerosis (fak″o-skle-ro′sis) [*phaco-* + Gr. *sklērōsis* hardening]. Hardening of the eye lens; a hard cataract.

phacoscope (fak′o-skōp) [*phaco-* + Gr. *skopein* to examine]. An instrument for viewing accommodative changes of the eye lens of a patient.

phacoscopy (fah-kos′ko-pe). The examination of the eye with a phacoscope.

phacoscotasmus (fak″o-sko-taz′mus) [*phaco-* + Gr. *skotasmos* a clouding]. The clouding of the lens of the eye.

phacotherapy (fak″o-ther′ah-pe) [*phaco-* + Gr. *therapeia* treatment]. Heliotherapy.

phacotoxic (fak″o-tok′sik). Exerting a deleterious effect upon the crystalline lens.

phacozymase (fak″o-zi′mās). An enzyme derived from an aqueous extract of the crystalline lens.

phage (fāj). Bacteriophage.

phagedena (faj″e-de′nah) [Gr. *phagedaina; phagein* to eat]. Rapidly spreading and sloughing ulceration. **sloughing p.,** hospital gangrene. **tropical p.,** cutaneous leishmaniasis.

phagedenic (faj″e-den′ik) [Gr. *phagedainikos*]. Rapidly spreading and eating; like phagedena.

phagedenoma (faj″ĕ-de-no′mah) [Gr. *phagedainōma*]. A phagedenic ulcer.

phagelysis (fāj′li-sis) [*phage* + Gr. *lysis* dissolution]. The destruction or solution of phage; the destructive or solvent action of phage.

phago- (fag′o) [Gr. *phagein* to eat]. Combining form denoting relationship to eating or consumption by ingestion or engulfing.

phagocaryosis (fag″o-kar″e-o′sis). Phagokaryosis.

phagocytable (fag′o-sit″ah-b′l). Capable of being subject to phagocytosis.

phagocyte (fag′o-sīt) [*phago-* + *-cyte*]. Any cell that ingests microorganisms or other cells and foreign particles. In many cases but not always the ingested material is digested within the phagocyte. Phagocytes are either fixed (cells of the reticulo-endothelial system) or free (polymorphonuclear leukocytes, macrophages). The two forms of leukocytes which are phagocytic are monocytes and polymorphonuclear leukocytes. **alveolar p.,** rounded granular phagocytic cells within the alveoli of the lungs, which ingest material brought to them by the air. **educated p.** See under *corpuscle*. **endothelial p.,** endotheliocyte. **globuliferous p.,** one which takes up the blood corpuscles. **melaniferous p.,** one which takes up the blood pigment. **mobile p.,** a free phagocyte. **sessile p.,** a fixed phagocyte.

phagocytic (fag″o-sit′ik). Pertaining to or produced by phagocytes.

phagocytin (fag″o-si′tin). A bactericidal substance contained in neutrophilic leukocytes.

phagocytize (fag′o-sit″iz). To exert a phagocytic action on.

phagocytoblast (fag″o-si′to-blast) [*phagocyte* + Gr. *blastos* germ]. A cell which gives rise to phagocytes.

phagocytolysis (fag″o-si-tol′ĭ-sis) [*phagocyte* + Gr. *lysis* dissolution]. Solution or destruction of phagocytes.

phagocytolytic (fag″o-si″to-lit′ik). Pertaining to phagocytolysis.

phagocytose (fag″o-si′tōs). To envelop and perhaps destroy bacteria and other foreign bodies.

phagocytosis (fag″o-si-to′sis). The engulfing of microorganisms, other cells, and foreign particles by phagocytes. **induced p.,** phagocytosis aided by subjecting bacteria to the action of opsonins in the blood. **spontaneous p.,** phagocytosis of bacteria taking place in an indifferent medium.

phagodynamometer (fag″o-di″nah-mom′e-ter) [*phago-* + Gr. *dynamis* force + *metron* measure]. An apparatus for measuring the force exerted in chewing food.

phagokaryosis (fag″o-kar″e-o′sis) [*phago-* + Gr.

karyon nucleus + *-osis*]. The alleged phagocytic action of the cell nucleus.

phagological (fag″o-loj′e-kal). Pertaining to phage.

phagology (fah-gol′o-je) [*phago-* + *-logy*]. The subject of eating or feeding.

phagolysis (fah-gol′ĭ-sis). Phagocytolysis.

phagolytic (fag″o-lit′ik). Phagocytolytic.

phagomania (fag″o-ma′ne-ah) [*phago-* + Gr. *mania* madness]. An insatiable craving for food, or an obsessive preoccupation with the subject of eating.

phagophobia (fag″o-fo′be-ah) [*phago-* + Gr. *phobein* to be affrighted by]. Morbid fear of eating.

phagopyrosis (fag″o-pi-ro′sis). Pyrosis following eating.

phagotherapy (fag″o-ther′ah-pe) [*phago-* + Gr. *therapeia* treatment]. Treatment by feeding.

phakitis (fa-ki′tis) [Gr. *phakos* lens + *-itis*]. Inflammation of the crystalline lens.

phako- [Gr. *phakos* a lentil, or lentil-shaped object; a spot on the body, a freckle]. For words beginning thus, see also those beginning *phaco-*.

phakoma (fah-ko′mah) [*phaco-* + *-oma*]. 1. An occasional small, grayish white tumor seen microscopically in the retina in tuberous sclerosis. 2. A patch of myelinated nerve fibers seen very infrequently in the retina in neurofibromatosis

phakomatosis (fak″o-mah-to′sis) [Gr. *phakos* mother spot]. Van der Hoeve's term for certain heredofamilial tumorous states characterized by the formation of lenslike masses, such as *phakomatosis Bourneville* (Bourneville's disease, or tuberous sclerosis), and *phakomatosis Recklinghausen* (Recklinghausen's disease, or neurofibromatosis).

phalacrosis (fal″ah-kro′sis) [Gr. *phalakrōsis* baldness]. Alopecia.

phalangeal (fa-lan′je-al). Pertaining to a phalanx.

phalangectomy (fal″an-jek′to-me). 1. Excision of a phalanx of a finger or toe. 2. Amputation of a finger or toe.

phalanges (fa-lan′jēz). Plural of *phalanx*.

phalangette (fal″an-jet′). The distal phalanx of a digit. **drop p.,** dropping of the distal phalanx of a finger and loss of power to extend it when the hand is prone.

phalangitis (fal″an-ji′tis). Inflammation of one or more phalanges.

phalangization (fal″an-ji-za′shun). Surgical separation of the terminal portion of fused digits, without complete extirpation of the connecting web.

phalangophalangeal (fah-lan″go-fah-lan′je-al). Pertaining to two adjoining phalanges of a finger or toe.

phalangosis (fal″an-go′sis). A condition in which the eyelashes grow in rows.

phalanx (fa′lanks), pl. *phalan′ges* [Gr. "a line or array of soldiers"]. 1. Any bone of a finger or toe. 2. Any one of a set of plates disposed in rows which makes up the lamina reticularis. **Deiters' phalanges,** modified cuticular plates forming the ends of sustentacular epithelial cells of the reticular membrane of the organ of Corti. **phalan′ges digito′rum ma′nus** [B N A], the fourteen bones composing the skeleton of the fingers (ossa digitorum manus [N A]). **phalan′ges digito′rum pe′dis** [B N A], the fourteen bones composing the skeleton of the toes (ossa digitorum pedis [N A]). **p. dista′lis digito′rum ma′nus** [N A], any one of the five terminal bones of the fingers, articulating, except in the thumb, with the phalanx media. Called also *p. tertia digitorum manus* [B N A], and *distal p. of fingers*. **p. dista′lis digito′rum pe′dis** [N A], any one of the five terminal bones of the toes, articulating, except in the great toe, with the phalanx media. Called also *p. tertia digitorum pedis* [B N A], and *distal p. of toes*. **p. me′dia digito′rum ma′nus** [N A], any one of the four bones of the fingers (excluding the thumb) situated between the proximal and distal phalanges. Called also *p. secunda digitorum manus* [B N A], and *middle p. of fingers*. **p. me′dia digito′rum pe′dis** [N A], any one of the four bones of the toes (excluding the great toe) situated between the proximal and distal phalanges. Called also *p. secunda digitorum pedis* [B N A], and *middle p. of toes*. **p. pri′ma digito′rum ma′nus** [B N A], p. proximalis digitorum manus. **p. pri′ma digito′rum pe′dis** [B N A], p. proximalis digitorum pedis. **p. proxima′lis digito′rum ma′nus** [N A], any one of the five bones of the fingers that articulate with the metacarpal bones and, except in the thumb, with the phalanx media. Called also *p. prima digitorum manus* [B N A], and *proximal p. of fingers*. **p. proxima′lis digito′rum pe′dis** [N A], any one of the five bones of the toes that articulate with the metatarsal bones and, except in the great toe, with the phalanx media. Called also *p. prima digitorum pedis* [B N A], and *proximal p. of toes*. **p. secun′da digito′rum ma′nus** [B N A], p. media digitorum manus. **p. secun′da digito′rum pe′dis** [B N A], p. media digitorum pedis. **p. ter′tia digito′rum ma′nus** [B N A], p. distalis digitorum manus. **p. ter′tia digito′rum pe′dis** [B N A], p. distalis digitorum pedis. **ungual p. of fingers,** p. distalis digitorum manus. **ungual p. of toes,** p. distalis digitorum pedis.

phallalgia (fal-al′je-ah) [*phallus* + *-algia*]. Pain in the penis.

phallanastrophe (fal″an-as′tro-fe) [*phallus* + Gr. *anastrophē* a turning upward]. Upward distortion of the penis.

phallaneurysm (fal-an′u-rizm) [*phallus* + Gr. *aneurysma* aneurysm]. Aneurysm of the penis.

phallectomy (fal-ek′to-me) [*phallos* + Gr. *ektomē* excision]. Amputation of the penis.

phallic (fal′ik) [Gr. *phallikos*]. Pertaining to the phallus, or penis.

phalliform (fal′ĭ-form) [*phallus* + L. *forma* form]. Shaped like the phallus or penis.

phallin (fal′in). A poisonous hemolytic glycoside from *Amanita phalloides*.

phallitis (fal-i′tis) [*phallus* + *-itis*]. Inflammation of the penis.

phallo- (fal′o) [Gr. *phallos* penis]. Combining form denoting relationship to the penis.

phallocampsis (fal″o-kamp′sis) [*phallo-* + Gr. *kampsis* bending]. Curvature of the penis when erect.

phallocrypsis (fal″o-krip′sis) [*phallo-* + Gr. *krypsis* hiding]. Retraction of the penis.

phallodynia (fal″o-din′e-ah) [*phallo-* + Gr. *odynē* pain]. Pain in the penis.

phalloid (fal′oid) [*phallo-* + Gr. *eidos* form]. Resembling a penis.

phalloncus (fal-ong′kus) [*phallo-* + Gr. *onkos* mass]. A morbid swelling or tumor of the penis.

phalloplasty (fal′o-plas″te) [*phallo-* + Gr. *plassein* to shape]. The plastic surgery of the penis.

phallorrhagia (fal″o-ra′je-ah) [*phallo-* + Gr. *rhēgnynai* to burst forth]. Hemorrhage from the penis.

phallorrhea (fal″o-re′ah) [*phallo-* + Gr. *rhoia* flow]. Gonorrhea in the male.

phallotomy (fal-ot′o-me) [*phallo-* + Gr. *tomē* a cutting]. Incision of the penis.

phallus (fal′us) [Gr. *phallos*]. 1. The penis. 2. The primordium of the penis or clitoris before the definitive organ is established in the developing embryo.

phan (fan) [Gr. *phaneros* visible]. The external manifestation or expression of a physical character.

phanero- (fan′er-o) [Gr. *phaneros* visible]. Combining form meaning visible or apparent.

phanerogam (fan′er-o-gam) [*phanero-* + Gr. *gamos* marriage]. A true seed-bearing plant.

phanerogenetic (fan″er-o-je-net′ik) [*phanero-* +

Gr. *gennan* to produce]. Having a known cause. Cf. *cryptogenetic.*

phanerogenic (fan″er-o-jen′ik). Phanerogenetic.

phaneromania (fan″er-o-ma′ne-ah) [Gr. *phaneros* visible + *mania* madness]. An obsession of abnormal and persistent attention to some exterior growth, as a wart.

phaneroplasm (fan′er-o-plazm) [Gr. *phaneros* visible + *plasm*]. The dispersed globules or rods seen in protoplasm when examined by special dark-field methods.

phaneroscope (fan′er-o-skōp) [Gr. *phaneros* visible + *skopein* to examine]. An instrument for illuminating the skin and rendering it translucent for examination.

phaneroscopy (fan″er-os′ko-pe). The examination of the skin by the phaneroscope.

phanerosis (fan″er-o′sis) [Gr. *phanerōsis*]. The act of becoming visible; the setting free of a substance which has previously been undemonstrable owing to its being held in combination. **fat p.,** conversion in the tissues of invisible fatty substances into fat which can be stained and seen.

phanerosterol (fan″er-os′ter-ol). A sterol of one of the higher plants.

phanerous (fan′er-us). Phanic.

phanic (fan′ik) [Gr. *phainein* to show]. Apparent, visible.

phanodorn (fan′o-dorn). Trade mark for a preparation of cyclobarbital.

phantasia (fan-ta′ze-ah). Phantasy.

phantasm (fan′tazm) [Gr. *phantasma* appearance]. An impression or image not evoked by actual stimuli. Called also *phantom.*

phantasmatology (fan″taz-mah-tol′o-je) [*phantasm* + *-logy*]. The sum of what is known regarding apparitions and phantasms.

phantasmatomoria (fan-taz″mah-to-mo′re-ah) [*phantasm* + Gr. *mōria* folly]. Childishness or dementia with absurd delusions.

phantasmology (fan″taz-mol′o-je). Phantasmatology.

phantasmoscopia (fan″taz-mo-sko′pe-ah) [*phantasm* + Gr. *skopein* to see + *-ia*]. The seeing of insane or delirious phantasms.

phantasy (fan″tah-se) [Gr. *phantasia* imagination; the power by which an object is made apparent to the mind]. A psychic mechanism by which a harsh reality is converted into an imaginary experience that satisfies the patient's subjective demands.

phantom (fan′tom) [Gr. *phantasma* an appearance]. 1. An impression or image not evoked by actual stimuli. 2. A model of the body or of a specific part thereof. In nuclear medicine, a device that simulates the conditions encountered when radioactive material is deposited *in vivo* and permits a quantitative estimation of its effects. **Schultze's p.,** a model of the female pelvis used in the teaching of obstetrics.

phao-. For words beginning thus, see those beginning *pheo-.*

phar., pharm. Abbreviations for *pharmacy, pharmaceutical,* and *pharmacopeia.*

Phar. B. Abbreviation for L. *Pharmaciae Baccalaureus,* Bachelor of Pharmacy.

Phar. C. Abbreviation for *Pharmaceutical Chemist.*

pharcidous (fahr′sĭ-dus) [Gr. *pharkis* wrinkled]. Wrinkled.

Phar. D. Abbreviation for L. *Pharmaciae Doctor,* Doctor of Pharmacy.

Phar. G. Abbreviation for *Graduate in Pharmacy.*

Phar. M. Abbreviation for L. *Pharmaciae Magister,* Master of Pharmacy.

pharmacal (fahr′mah-kal). Pertaining to pharmacy.

pharmaceutic (fahr-mah-su′tik) [Gr. *pharmakeutikos*]. Pertaining to pharmacy or to drugs.

pharmaceutical (fahr″mah-su′tĭ-kal). 1. Pertaining to pharmacy or to drugs. 2. A medicinal drug.

pharmaceutics (fahr″mah-su′tiks). 1. The art of the apothecary. 2. Pharmaceutical preparations.

pharmaceutist (fahr″mah-su′tist). A pharmacist.

pharmacist (fahr′mah-sist). An apothecary or druggist.

pharmaco- (fahr′mah-ko) [Gr. *pharmakon* medicine]. Combining form denoting relationship to a drug or medicine.

pharmacochemistry (fahr″mah-ko-kem′is-tre). Pharmaceutical chemistry.

pharmacodiagnosis (fahr″mah-ko-di″ag-no′sis) [*pharmaco-* + *diagnosis*]. The employment of drugs in the diagnosis of disease.

pharmacodynamic (fahr″mah-ko-di-nam′ik) [*pharmaco-* + Gr. *dynamis* power]. Pertaining to the effects of medicine.

pharmacodynamics (fahr″mah-ko-di-nam′iks). The study of the action of drugs on living organisms.

pharmaco-endocrinology (fahr″mah-ko-en″do-kri-nol′o-je). The study of the influence of drugs on the activity of the ductless glands.

pharmacogenetics (fahr″mah-ko-je-net′iks). The scientific study of the effect of genetic factors on the individual organism's response to drugs.

pharmacognostics (fahr″mah-kog-nos′tiks). Pharmacognosy.

pharmacognosy (fahr″mah-kog′no-se) [*pharmaco-* + Gr. *gnōsis* knowledge]. That branch of pharmacology which deals with the biological, biochemical, and economic features of natural drugs and their constituents.

pharmacography (fahr″mah-kog′rah-fe) [*pharmaco-* + Gr. *graphein* to write]. An account or written description of drugs.

pharmacologist (fahr″mah-kol′o-jist). One who makes a study of drugs.

pharmacology (fahr″mah-kol′o-je) [*pharmaco-* + *-logy*]. The science which deals with the study of drugs in all its aspects.

pharmacomania (fahr″mah-ko-ma′ne-ah) [*pharmaco-* + Gr. *mania* madness]. Uncontrollable desire to take or to administer medicines.

pharmacon (fahr′mah-kon) [Gr. *pharmakon*]. A drug.

pharmaco-oryctology (fahr″mah-ko-or″ik-tol′o-je) [*pharmaco-* + Gr. *oryktos* excavated + *-logy*]. The study of mineral drugs.

pharmacopedia, pharmacopedics (fahr″mah-ko-pe′de-ah, fahr″mah-ko-pe′diks) [*pharmaco-* + Gr. *paideia* instruction]. The science which deals with the properties and preparations of drugs.

pharmacopeia (fahr″mah-ko-pe′ah) [*pharmaco-* + Gr. *poiein* to make]. An authoritative treatise on drugs and their preparations; a book containing a list of products used in medicine, with descriptions, chemical tests for determining identity and purity, and formulas for certain mixtures of these substances. It also generally contains a statement of average dosage. The first United States pharmacopeia was published on December 15, 1820, printed in both Latin and English, and its 272 pages included 217 drugs which were considered worthy of recognition. See *U.S.P.*

pharmacopeial (fahr″mah-ko-pe′al). Pertaining to or recognized by the pharmacopeia.

pharmacophilia (fahr″mah-ko-fil′e-ah) [*pharmaco-* + Gr. *philein* to love]. Morbid fondness for drugs.

pharmacophobia (fahr″mah-ko-fo′be-ah) [*pharmaco-* + Gr. *phobein* to be affrighted by]. Morbid dread of drugs or medicines.

pharmacophore (fahr′mah-ko-fōr″) [*pharmaco-* + Gr. *phoros* bearing]. The group of atoms in a drug molecule which is responsible for the action of the compound.

pharmacopoeia (fahr″mah-ko-pe′ah). Pharmacopeia.

pharmacopsychosis (fahr″mah-ko-si-ko′sis) [*pharmaco-* + *psychosis*]. Southard's term for any one of the group of mental diseases due to alcohol, drugs, or poisons.

pharmacoroentgenography (fahr″mah-ko-rent″gen-og′rah-fe). Roentgen examination of a body organ under the influence of a drug which best facilitates such examination.

pharmacotherapeutics (fahr″mah-ko-ther″ah-pu′tiks) [*pharmaco-* + *therapeutics*]. Study of the uses of drugs in the treatment of disease.

pharmacotherapy (fahr″mah-ko-ther′ah-pe) [*pharmaco-* + Gr. *therapeia* treatment]. The treatment of disease by medicines.

pharmacy (fahr′mah-se) [Gr. *pharmakon* medicine]. 1. The art of preparing, compounding, and dispensing medicines. 2. An apothecary's shop. **chemical p.,** pharmaceutical chemistry. **galenic p.,** the pharmacy of vegetable medicines.

pharyngalgia (far″in-gal′je-ah) [*pharyngo-* + *-algia*]. Pain in the pharynx.

pharyngeal (fah-rin′je-al) [L. *pharyngeus*]. Pertaining to the pharynx.

pharyngectasia (far″in-jek-ta′se-ah). Pharyngocele.

pharyngectomy (far″in-jek′to-me) [*pharyngo-* + Gr. *ektomē* excision]. Surgical removal of a part of the pharynx.

pharyngemphraxis (far″in-jem-frak′sis) [*pharyngo-* + Gr. *emphraxis* stoppage]. Obstruction of the pharynx.

pharyngeus (far-in-je′us) [L.]. Pharyngeal.

pharyngism (far′in-jism). Pharyngismus.

pharyngismus (far″in-jiz′mus). Muscular spasm of the pharynx.

pharyngitic (far″in-jit′ik). Affected with or of the nature of pharyngitis.

pharyngitid (fah-rin′ji-tid). A cutaneous eruption occurring in pharyngitis.

pharyngitis (far″in-ji′tis) [*pharyngo-* + *-itis*]. Inflammation of the pharynx. **acute p.,** inflammation with pain in the throat, especially on swallowing, dryness, followed by moisture of the pharynx, congestion of the mucous membrane and fever. Called also *catarrhal p.* **atrophic p.,** a chronic pharyngitis which leads to wasting of the submucous tissue. **catarrhal p.,** acute p. **chronic p.,** that which results from repeated acute attacks or is due to tuberculosis or syphilis. It is attended with excessive secretion, and in the severe ulcerated varieties by pain and dysphagia. **croupous p.,** membranous p. **diphtheric p.,** diphtheria of the pharynx. **follicular p.,** sore throat with enlargement of the pharyngeal glands. **gangrenous p.,** a form characterized by gangrenous patches. **glandular p.,** follicular p. **granular p.,** a chronic variety in which the mucous membrane becomes granular. **p. herpet′ica,** membranous or aphthous sore throat. A form of acute pharyngitis characterized by the formation of vesicles, which give place to excoriations. **hypertrophic p.,** a chronic form which leads to thickening of the submucous tissues. **p. kerato′sa,** pharyngomycosis. **membranous p.,** pharyngitis with a fibrous exudate leading to the formation of a false membrane. **phlegmonous p.,** acute parenchymatous tonsillitis attended with the formation of abscesses. **p. sic′ca,** an atrophic pharyngitis in which the throat becomes dry. **p. ulcero′sa,** ulcerated or hospital sore throat; pharyngitis with fever, pain, and prostration, and the formation of ulcers covered by a yellow, membrane-like deposit.

pharyngo- (fah-ring′go) [Gr. *pharynx* pharynx]. Combining form denoting relationship to the pharynx.

pharyngo-amygdalitis (fah-ring″go-ah-mig″-dah-li′tis). Inflammation of the pharynx and tonsil.

pharyngocele (fah-ring′go-sēl) [*pharyngo-* + Gr. *kēlē* hernia]. Hernial protrusion of a part of the pharynx; a hernial pouch or other cystic deformity of the pharynx.

pharyngoceratosis (fah-ring″go-ser″ah-to′sis). Pharyngokeratosis.

pharyngoconjunctivitis (fah-ring″go-kon-junk″tĭ-vi′tis). Inflammation involving the pharynx and conjunctiva, the result of a virus infection.

pharyngodynia (fah-ring″go-din′e-ah) [*pharyngo-* + Gr. *odynē* pain]. Pain in the pharynx.

pharyngo-epiglottic (fah-ring″go-ep″ĭ-glot′ik). Pertaining to the pharynx and epiglottis.

pharyngo-epiglottidean (fah-ring″go-ep″ĭ-glŏ-tid′e-an). Pharyngo-epiglottic.

pharyngo-esophageal (fah-ring″go-e-sof′ah-je″al). Pertaining to the pharynx and esophagus.

pharyngoglossal (fah-ring″go-glos′al). Pertaining to the pharynx and the tongue.

pharyngoglossus (fah-ring″go-glos′us). The muscular fibers from the superior constrictor of the pharynx to the tongue.

pharyngokeratosis (fah-ring″go-ker″ah-to′sis). Keratosis of the pharynx.

pharyngolaryngeal (fah-ring″go-lah-rin′je-al). Pertaining to the pharynx and the larynx.

pharyngolaryngitis (fah-ring″go-lar″in-ji′tis) [*pharyngo-* + Gr. *larynx* larynx + *-itis*]. Inflammation of the pharynx and the larynx.

pharyngolith (fah-ring′go-lith) [*pharyngo-* + Gr. *lithos* stone]. A concretion in the walls of the pharynx.

pharyngology (far″ing-gol′o-je) [*pharyngo-* + *-logy*]. The sum of what is known regarding the pharynx.

pharyngolysis (far″ing-gol′ĭ-sis) [*pharyngo-* + Gr. *lysis* dissolution]. Paralysis of the pharynx.

pharyngomaxillary (fah-ring″go-mak′sĭ-ler″e). Pertaining to the pharynx and the jaw.

pharyngomycosis (fah-ring″go-mi-ko′sis) [*pharyngo-* + Gr. *mykēs* fungus + *-osis*]. Any fungus disease of the pharynx.

pharyngonasal (fah-ring″go-na′sal). Pertaining to the pharynx and the nose.

pharyngo-oral (fah-ring″go-o′ral). Pertaining to the pharynx and the mouth.

pharyngopalatine (fah-ring″go-pal′ah-tīn). Pertaining to the pharynx and the palate.

pharyngoparalysis (fah-ring″go-pah-ral′ĭ-sis) [*pharyngo-* + *paralysis*]. Paralysis of the pharyngeal muscles.

pharyngopathy (far″ing-gop′ah-the) [*pharyngo-* + Gr. *pathos* disease]. Disease of the pharynx.

pharyngoperistole (fah-ring″go-pĕ-ris′to-le) [*pharyngo-* + Gr. *peristolē* contracture]. Narrowing of the pharynx.

pharyngoplasty (fah-ring′go-plas″te) [*pharyngo-* + Gr. *plassein* to form]. Plastic operation on the pharynx.

pharyngoplegia (far″ing-go-ple′je-ah) [*pharyngo-* + Gr. *plēgē* stroke]. Paralysis of the muscles of the pharynx.

pharyngorhinitis (fah-ring″go-ri-ni′tis). Inflammation of the nasopharynx.

pharyngorhinoscopy (fah-ring″go-ri-nos′ko-pe). Examination of the nasopharynx and posterior nares with the rhinoscope.

pharyngorrhagia (far″ing-go-ra′je-ah) [*pharyngo-* + Gr. *rhēgnynai* to break forth]. Hemorrhage from the pharynx.

pharyngorrhea (far″ing-go-re′ah) [*pharyngo-* + Gr. *rhoia* flow]. A discharge of mucus from the pharynx.

pharyngosalpingitis (fah-ring″go-sal″pin-ji′-tis). Inflammation of the pharynx and the eustachian tube.

pharyngoscleroma (fah-ring″go-skle-ro′mah). Scleroma of the pharynx.

pharyngoscope (fah-ring′go-skōp) [*pharyngo-* + Gr. *skopein* to examine]. An instrument for inspecting the pharynx.

pharyngoscopy (far″ing-gos′ko-pe). Direct visual examination of the pharynx.

pharyngospasm (fah-ring′go-spazm) [*pharyngo-* + Gr. *spasmos* spasm]. Spasm of the pharyngeal muscles.

pharyngostenosis (fah-ring″go-ste-no′sis) [*pharyngo-* + Gr. *stenōsis* narrowing]. Narrowing of the lumen of the pharynx.

pharyngotherapy (fah-ring″go-ther′ah-pe) [*pharyngo-* + *therapy*]. The treatment of pharyngeal disorders, and especially the irrigation of the nasopharynx in infectious diseases.

pharyngotome (fah-ring′go-tōm). A cutting instrument used in pharyngeal surgery.

pharyngotomy (far″ing-got′o-me) [*pharyngo-* + Gr. *tomē* a cutting]. Surgical incision of the pharynx. **external p.,** pharyngotomy done from the outside. **internal p.,** that which is performed from within the pharynx. **lateral p.,** the opening of the pharynx from one side. **subhyoid p.,** section of the pharynx through the thyrohyoid membrane.

pharyngotonsillitis (fah-ring″go-ton″sĭ-li′tis). Inflammation of the pharynx and the tonsil.

pharyngotyphoid (fah-ring″go-ti′foid). Enteric fever with angina and sore patches on the tonsils.

pharyngoxerosis (fah-ring″go-ze-ro′sis) [*pharyngo-* + Gr. *xērōsis* dryness]. Dryness of the pharynx.

pharynx (far′inks) [Gr.]. [N A, B N A] The musculomembranous sac between the mouth and nares and the esophagus. It is continuous below with the esophagus, and above it communicates with the larynx, mouth, nasal passages, and auditory tubes. The part above the level of the soft palate is the *nasopharynx*, communicating with the posterior nares and the auditory tube. The lower portion consists of two sections—the *oropharynx*, which lies between the soft palate and the upper edge of the epiglottis, and the *laryngopharynx*, which lies below the upper edge of the epiglottis and opens into the larynx and esophagus.

phase (fāz) [Gr. *phasis* an appearance]. 1. The view that a thing presents to the eye. 2. Any one of the varying aspects or stages through which a disease or process may pass. 3. In physical chemistry, any aspect of a substance which is homogeneous in physical state and percentage composition, e.g., ice and steam as phases of water. In heterogeneous chemical systems, phases are separated by surfaces of discontinuity, e.g., oil and water in contact. **alpha p.,** the estrous stage of the ovarian cycle. **apophylactic p.,** negative p. **bacterial p's,** several more or less distinct forms of colony growth which many bacteria manifest under certain conditions. The most important ones are the smooth (S), the rough (R), the mucoid (M), and the gonidial (G). **beta p.,** the progestational stage of the ovarian cycle. **continuous p.,** dispersion medium. **p. of decline,** the stage in the growth of a bacterial culture in which the number of live organisms gradually decreases. **disperse p.,** the internal or discontinuous portion of a colloid system. It is analogous to the solute in a solution. Called also *internal p.* **erythrocytic p.,** that phase in the life cycle of a malarial plasmodium which is lived inside an erythrocyte. **estrin p.,** proliferative stage. **external p.,** dispersion medium. **internal p.,** disperse p. **lag p.,** lag, def. 2. **logarithmic p.,** the stage in the growth of a bacterial culture at which, if the logarithms of their members are plotted against the time, a straight upward line will be formed. **meiotic p.,** that stage in meiosis in which the reduction of the chromosomes occurs. Called also *reduction p.* **motofacient p.** See *motofacient.* **negative p.,** the initial lowering of the antibody content of blood following the injection of corresponding antigen. **nonmotofacient p.** See *motofacient.* **Nonne-Apelt p.** See under *reaction.* **positive p.,** the rise above unity in the opsonic index which follows the negative phase. **postmiotic p.,** the stage following the reduction of the chromosomes in miosis. **premiotic p., prereduction p.,** the stage in miosis which precedes the reduction of the chromosomes. **reduction p.,** miotic p. **stationary p.,** the stage in the growth of a bacterial culture at which multiplication of organisms gradually decreases, the number of bacteria remaining practically constant. **synaptic p.,** synapsis.

phaseolin (fa-se′o-lin). A globulin from the kidney-bean, *Phaseolus vulgaris.*

phaseolunatin (fa″se-o-lu′nah-tin). A bitter glycoside, $C_{10}H_{17}O_6N$, found in the lima bean (*Phaseolus lunatus*).

phasin, phasein (fa′sin). Any one of a group of nitrogenous substances found in seeds, bark, and other plant tissues, which agglutinate red blood corpuscles.

phasmid (faz′mid). One of a pair of caudal chemoreceptors occurring in certain nematodes.

phasmophobia (faz″mo-fo′be-ah) [Gr. *phasma* an apparition + *phobein* to be affrighted by]. Fear of ghosts.

phatnoma (fat-no′mah), pl. *phatnomas* or *phatno′mata* [Gr. *phatnōma*]. A tooth socket.

phatnorrhagia (fat″no-ra′je-ah). Hemorrhage from a tooth socket, or dental alveolus.

Ph.B. Abbreviation for *British Pharmacopoeia.*

Ph.D. Abbreviation for *Doctor of Philosophy.*

phellandral (fĕ-lan′dral). A terpene aldehyde, $(CH_3)_2CH.C_6H_8.CHO$, from *Eucalyptus hemisphloia.*

phellandrene (fĕ-lan′drēn). A liquid hydrocarbon, $C_{10}H_{16}$, occurring in fennel oil, elemi oil, the oil of water hemlock, and Australian eucalyptus.

Phelps' operation (felps) [Abel Mix *Phelps*, surgeon in New York, 1851–1902]. See under *operation.*

phe-mer-nite (fe′mer-nīt). Trade mark for preparations of phenylmercuric nitrate.

phemerol (fe′mer-ol). Trade mark for preparations of benzethonium.

phemitone (fem′ĭ-tōn). Mephobarbital.

phen-. A prefix indicating derivation from benzene.

phenacaine (fen′ah-kān). Chemical name: N,N′-bis(p-ethoxyphenyl)acetamidine: used as a local anesthetic.

phenacemide (fĕ-nas′e-mid). Chemical name: phenacetylurea: used as an anticonvulsant in psychomotor and grand mal epilepsy.

phenacetin (fĕ-nas′e-tin). Acetophenetidin.

phenacetolin (fen″ah-set′o-lin). A red powder, $C_{16}H_{12}O_2$; used as an indicator. It has a pH range of 5 to 6, being yellow at 5 and red at 6.

phenadone (fen′ah-dōn). Methadone.

phenaglycodol (fen″ah-gli′ko-dol). Chemical name: 2-p-chlorophenyl-3-methyl-2,3-butanediol: used as a tranquilizer.

phenakistoscope (fe″nah-kis′to-skōp) [Gr. *phenakistēs* deceiver + *skopein* to examine]. Stroboscope.

phenanthrene (fe-nan′thrēn). A colorless, crystalline hydrocarbon, $(C_6H_4.CH)_2$.

phenanthrolene (fe-nan′thro-lēn). Orthophenanthrolene.

phenate (fe′nāt). A salt formed by union of a base with phenic acid (phenol), a monovalent metal, such as sodium or potassium, replacing the hydrogen of the hydroxyl group.

phenazocine (fĕ-naz′o-sēn). Chemical name: 1,2,3,4,5,6-hexahydro-8-hydroxy-6,11-dimethyl-3-phenethyl-2,6-methano-3-benzazocine: used as an analgesic.

phenelzine (fen′el-zēn). Chemical name: β-phenylethylhydrazine dihydrogen: used as an antidepressant with inhibiting action on monoamine oxidase.

phenergan (fen′er-gan). Trade mark for preparations of promethazine hydrochloride.

phenethicillin (fĕ-neth″ĭ-sil′lin). Phenoxymethyl penicillin.

phenetidin (fe-net′ĭ-din). A substance, the ethyl ester of para-aminophenol, $NH_2.C_6H_4.OC_2H_5$: used in preparing acetophenetidin. It often appears in the urine after the administration of acetophenetidin.

phenetidinuria (fe-net″ĭ-dĭ-nu′re-ah). The presence of phenetidin in the urine.

phenetol (fen′ĕ-tol). Ethyl phenate; an oily liquid, $C_6H_5O.C_2H_5$.

phenformin (fen-for′min). Chemical name: N^1-β-phenethylbiguanide: used orally as a hypoglycemic agent.

phengophobia (fen″go-fo′be-ah) [Gr. *phengos* light + *phobein* to be affrighted by]. Photophobia.

phenicate (fen′ĭ-kāt). To charge with phenic acid, or phenol.

phenidin (fen′ĭ-din). Acetophenetidin.

phenin (fe′nin). Acetophenetidin.

phenindamine (fĕ-nin′dah-min). Chemical name: 2,3,4,9-tetrahydro-2-methyl-9-phenyl-1H-indeno-[2,1-c]pyridine: used as an antihistaminic.

phenindione (fen-in′di-ōn). Chemical name: 2-phenyl-1,3-indandione: used as an anticoagulant by inhibiting synthesis of prothrombin.

pheniramine (fen″ĭ-ram′in). Chemical name: N,N-dimethyl-3-phenyl-3-(2-pyridyl)-propylamine: used as an antihistaminic.

phenmetrazine (fen-met′rah-zēn). Chemical name: 2-phenyl-3-methyltetrahydro-1,4-oxazine: a sympathomimetic agent used to reduce the appetite.

phenobarbital (fe″no-bar′bĭ-tal). Chemical name: 5-ethyl-5-phenylbarbituric acid: used as a hypnotic and sedative.

phenobarbitone (fe″no-bar′bĭ-tōn). Phenobarbital.

phenocopy (fe′no-kop″e) [Gr. *phainein* to show + *copy*]. 1. An individual whose phenotype mimics that of another genotype but whose character is determined by environment and is not hereditary. 2. The simulated trait in a phenocopy individual. 3. The simulation by an individual of traits characteristic of another genotype.

phenodin (fe′no-din) [Gr. *phoinōdēs* blood red]. Hematin.

phenol (fe′nol). 1. An extremely poisonous, colorless, crystalline compound, $C_6H_5.OH$, obtained by the distillation of coal tar, and converted, by the addition of 10 per cent of water, into a clear liquid with a peculiar odor and a burning taste: a powerful antiseptic, disinfectant, and germicide. 2. A generic term for any organic compound containing one or more hydroxyl groups attached to an aromatic or carbon ring. **p. liquefac′tum, liquefied p.,** an aqueous solution of phenol containing not less than 88 per cent of $C_6H_5.OH$. **p. red,** phenolsulfonphthalein. **p. salicylate,** phenyl salicylate.

phenolase (fe′no-lās). A ferment which oxidizes phenols and aromatic amines.

phenolate (fe′no-lāt). 1. To treat with phenol for purposes of sterilization. 2. Phenate.

phenolated (fe′no-lāt″ed). Charged with phenol.

phenolemia (fe″no-le′me-ah). The presence of phenols in the blood.

phenolic (fe-nol′ik). Pertaining to or derived from phenol.

phenolization (fe′nol-i-za′shun). Treatment by subjection to the action of phenol.

phenologist (fe-nol′o-jist). An expert or specialist in phenology.

phenology (fe-nol′o-je) [Gr. *phainesthai* to appear + *-logy*]. A study of the effects of climate upon the life and health of living organisms.

phenololipoid (fe-nol″o-li′poid). A compound of phenol with a lipoid, such as cholesterol with camphor as the connecting link. It is believed to combine the parasitotropic power of phenol and the antitoxic power of cholesterol and yet to be free from the organotropic action of phenol.

phenolphthalein (fe″nol-thal′e-in). Chemical name: 3,3-bis(p-hydroxyphenyl)phthalide: used as a cathartic.

phenolquinine (fe″nol-kwin′in). Quinine phenolate.

phenolsulfonphthalein (fe″nol-sul″fōn-thal′-e-in). Chemical name: 3-3-bis(p-hydroxyphenyl)-2,1,3H-benzoxathiole 1,1-dioxide: used as a test for renal function.

phenoltetrachlorophthalein (fe″nol-tet″rah-klōr″o-thal′e-in). A coal tar derivative, used intravenously in tests of liver function.

phenoltetraiodophthalein (fe″nol-tet″rah-i″o-do-thal′e-in). A coal tar derivative used in cholecystography.

phenoluria (fe″nol-u′re-ah). The presence of phenols in the urine.

phenome (fe′nōm) [Gr. *phainein* to show + *-ōma* mass, abstract entity]. The non–self-reproducing portion of a cell. Cf. *genome.*

phenomenology (fe-nom″e-nol′o-je). The study of phenomena; especially that part of a science, as of psychopathology, which treats of the recognition, classification, and description of the phenomena observed in that science.

phenomenon (fe-nom′e-non), pl. *phenom′ena* [Gr. *phainomenon* thing seen]. Any remarkable appearance; any sign or objective symptom. **abstinence p.** See under *symptom.* **adhesion p.,** Rieckenberg's p. **anaphylactoid p.,** pseudoanaphylaxis. **Anderson's p.,** clumps of red blood cells in the stools of amebic dysentery: seen on microscopic examination. **aqueous-influx p.,** entrance into conjunctival or subconjunctival vessels of clear fluid (aqueous humor), deriving from an aqueous vein during compression of its recipient vessel. Formerly called *glass-rod phenomenon,* because of resemblance of the aqueous-filled vessel to a glass rod. Cf. *blood-influx p.* **arm p.,** Pool's p., def. 2. **p. of Arthus,** a local edema and necrosis following subcutaneous injection of the specific antigen in sensitized rabbits. **Ascher's glass-rod p.,** aqueous-influx p. **Aschner's p.,** slowing of the pulse following pressure on the eyeball: it is indicative of cardiac vagus irritability. **Aubert's p.,** by an optic illusion, when the head is turned toward one side a vertical line appears to incline toward the other side. **Auer's p.,** inflammation or necrosis in the ear of a rabbit that is rubbed with Merck's xylol shortly after the rabbit receives its second injection of horse serum—the rabbit having previously been sensitized and the injection being made into the peritoneal cavity. **Austin Flint p.** See under *murmur.* **autokinetic visible light p.,** the apparent spontaneous movement of a pin-point source of light as seen by certain susceptible persons when they gaze steadily at it in a completely blacked-out room. **Babinski's p.,** extension and spreading in place of flexion of the toes when the sole is excited: it is characteristic of hemiplegia due to a lesion in the pyramidal tract, or of the anterolateral portions of the spinal cord. **Balint's p.,** increased acidity in tissues of patients with peptic ulcer. **Becker's p.,** pulsation of the retinal arteries in exophthalmic goiter. **Bell's p.,** an outward and upward rolling of the eyeball on the attempt to close the eye: it occurs on the affected side in peripheral facial (*Bell's*) paralysis. **Bittorf p.,** in cases of chronic septic endocarditis, blood taken from the lobule of the ear, after massage of the part, contains an increased number of leukocytes and special atypical endothelial cells. These latter are polymorphic, possess elongations and often contain in their protroplasm leukocytes, thrombocytes, and erythrocytes. **blanching p.,** Schultz-Charlton p. **blood-influx p.,** filling of conjunctival or subconjunctival vessels with blood during compression of the recipient vessel of an aqueous vein. This and the aqueous-influx phenomenon, depending on minute pressure differences between blood and aqueous humor, differ in glaucomatous eyes and those with normal intraocular pressure. **Bordet's p.** See *serum test*, under *tests*. **Bordet-Gengou p.** See *fixation of complement*. **brake p.** (of Rieger), the tendency of a muscle to continue or hold itself in its normal resting position. **Bridre-Jonan p.,** the growth stimulation and accelerated multiplication observed in a culture of bacteria when 10 to 20 per cent of immune serum, specific for that organism, is added to the culture medium in which it grows. **chameleon p.,** the assumption of a green color by a potato culture of *Bacillus pyocyaneus* at the point where touched by a platinum wire. **cheek p.,** in meningitis if pressure is exerted on both cheeks just under the zygomas there is reflex upward jerking of both arms with simultaneous bending of both elbows. **Christensen's p.,** when the mandible is protruded, a separation occurs, in the region of the molars, between the surfaces which are in contact in centric occlusion, the degree of separation depending on the downward pitch of the condyle paths. **cogwheel p.,** when a hypertonic muscle is passively stretched it resists, and this resistance sometimes takes the form of an irregular jerkiness; called also *Negro's p.* **Collie p.,** when pure neon is enclosed in a glass tube with a globule of mercury and shaken it glows with a bright, orange-red color, and when the globule rolls it appears to be followed by a flame. **Cushing's p.,** a rise in systemic blood pressure as a result of an increase in intracranial pressure. **Dale p.** See under *reaction*. **Danysz's p.,** decrease of the neutralizing influence of an antitoxin when a toxin is added to it in divided portions instead of all at once. **Debre's p.,** absence of measles rash at the site of injection of convalescent measles serum which has not prevented the appearance of the eruption. **Dejerine-Lichtheim p.,** Lichtheim sign. **dental p.,** thermal and tactile sensations in the gums with toothache, produced by repeated faradic stimulation of hyperesthetic lines on the body (Calligaris). **Denys-Leclef p.,** phagocytosis taking place in a test tube on mixing therein leukocytes, bacteria, and their immune serum. **d'Herelle's p.,** Twort-d'Herelle p. **diaphragm p., diaphragmatic p.,** the movement of the diaphragm as seen through the walls of the body; its variations have a certain diagnostic value. Called also *phrenic phenomenon* and *phrenic wave*. **Donath p.,** blood from a case of paroxysmal hemoglobinuria if cooled to 5°C. outside the body and then warmed to body temperature undergoes hemolysis. **Doppler's p.,** the pitch of a whistle on a rapidly moving body, like a locomotive, is higher when the body is approaching the listener. **Duckworth's p.,** arrest of breathing before stoppage of the heart's action in certain fatal brain affections. **Du Noüy p.,** the addition of sodium oleate to blood serum reduces the surface tension of the serum for a short time only and not permanently. **Eisenberg's p.,** with increasing concentration of the agglutinins added to a bacterial emulsion the absolute absorption by the bacteria rises, while the coefficient of absorption falls. **Erb's p.,** Erb's sign, def. 1. **Erben's p.,** temporary slowness of the pulse on stooping or sitting down: said to characterize certain cases of neurasthenia. **face p., facia'lis p.,** Chvostek's sign. **Fahraeus p.,** erythrocyte sedimentation reaction. **Fick's p.,** a fogging of vision, with the appearance of halos around light, occurring in individuals wearing contact lenses. **finger p.** (in hemiplegia). 1. Extension of all the fingers or of the thumb and index finger, on pressure against the pisiform bone (G. Gordon). 2. Extension and abduction of the fingers, in a fanlike pattern, when the patient attempts to raise the paralyzed arm. **fixation p.,** fixation of the complement. **flicker p.,** a visual phenomenon by which an intermittent light may appear to flicker or to be steady according to the rate of interruption. In studying the visual field the number of flashes per second at which the light just appears to be continuous is called *fusion frequency*. **Friedreich's p.,** the tympanic note of skodaic resonance in pleuritis with effusion varies in pitch during inspiration and expiration, being raised on inspiration. **Galassi's pupillary p.,** Westphal-Piltz p. **Gärtner's p.,** the degree of fulness of the veins of the arm as it is raised to varying heights indicates the degree of pressure in the right auricle. **Gengou-Moreschi p.,** complement fixation test for the differentiation of human from animal blood. **Gerhardt's p.** See under *sign*. **glass-rod p.,** aqueous-influx p. **glass-rod p., negative,** blood-influx p. **Grasset's p., Grasset-Gaussel p.,** inability of a patient to raise both legs at the same time, though he can raise either alone: seen in incomplete organic hemiplegia. **Hamburger p.,** chloride shift. **Hammerschlag's p.,** an abnormal fatigability toward continuous sounds of gradually decreasing intensity. **Hapke's p.,** unusually prominent presentation of the parietal bone of the head of the first one of twins. **Hata p.,** increase in severity of an infectious disease when a small dose of a chemotherapeutical remedy is given. **Hecht p.,** Rumpel-Leede p. **Hektoen p.,** when antigens are introduced into the animal body in allergic states, there may exist an increased range of new antibody production which may include production of antibodies concerned in previous infections and immunizations. **d'Herelle's p.,** Twort-d'Herelle p. **Hering's p.,** a faint murmur heard with the stethoscope over the lower end of the sternum for a short time after death. **hip-flexion p.,** in paraplegia, when the patient attempts to rise from a lying position or when he lies down, he flexes the hip of the paralyzed side. **Hirst's p.,** virus (especially influenza virus) in the allantoic fluid of infected eggs will agglutinate chicken erythrocytes mixed with it. **Hochsinger's p.,** pressure on the inner side of the biceps muscle produces closure of the fist in tetany. **Hoffmann's p.,** increased excitability to electrical stimulation in the sensory nerves: the ulnar nerve is usually employed. **Holmes-Stewart p.,** rebound p. **Houssay p.,** hypoglycemia and marked increase in sensitiveness to insulin produced by hypophysectomy in depancreatized experimental animals. **Huebener-Thomsen-Friedenreich p.,** the *in vivo* or *in vitro* polyagglutinability of red cells by all normal human sera as a result of activation by a bacterial enzyme of a latent "T" receptor common to all erythrocytes. Called also *Thomsen p.* **Hunt's paradoxical p.,** in dystonia musculorum deformans, if the examiner attempts forcible plantar flexion of the foot which is in dorsal spasm there is produced increase of the dorsal spasm, but if the patient is ordered to extend the foot he will perform plantar flexion. **interference p.** 1. The interference of one drug with the therapeutic activity of another drug; especially a sort of drug-fastness toward full therapeutic doses of one drug conferred on a parasite by subtherapeutic doses of another drug. 2. The interference with the virulence of a virus by the simultaneous infection with another and unrelated virus. Called also *preemptive immunity*. **jaw-winking p.,** involuntary movements of a ptotic eyelid associated with movements of the jaw. The eye tends to open as the mouth opens and to close as the mouth closes. **Kienböck's p.,** paradoxical diaphragm contraction; in pyothorax and seropneumothorax the diaphragm on the affected side rises on inspiration and falls on expiration. **Koch's p.,** the sudden collapse of tuberculous animals following the injection of a fresh culture of tubercle bacilli. The exudate that forms contains lymphocytes almost exclusively. **Koebner's p.,** the appearance of lesions of psoriasis at the site of an injury. **Kohnstamm's p.,** after-movement. **Kühne's muscular p.,** Porret's p. **LE p.,** the process by which the LE cell is formed. **Leede-Rumpel p.,** Rumpel-Leede p. **Le Grand-Geblewics p.,** a flickering source of colored light (40–50 per second) when observed indirectly is perceived as a constant white light. **Leichtenstern's p.** See under *sign.* **Lewis' p.,** hydrophagocytosis. **Liesegang's p.,** the peculiar periodic formation of a precipitate in concentric banded rings, waves or spirals, when two electrolytes diffuse into and meet in a colloid gel. **Litten's diaphragm p.,** a movable horizontal depression on the lower part of the sides of the thorax, seen in respiration. **Lust's p.,** abduction with dorsal flexion of the foot on tapping the external popliteal nerve just below the head of the fibula: indicative of spasmophilia. **Metchnikoff's p.,** in Pfeiffer's phenomenon, if the animals are given an intraperitoneal injection of bouillon or other material, twelve hours before the test, lytic phenomena are replaced by phagocytosis. **Mill-Reincke p.,** the mortality from all diseases decreases as a result of water purification. **Moreschi p.,** fixation of complement. **muscle p.,** the tendency of striated muscle to contract in hard lumps upon tapping. **Nasaroff's p.,** gradual decrease in the difference between the rectal temperature before and that after the bath, occurring after repeated cold baths. **Negro's p.,** cogwheel p. **Neisser-Doering p.,** suppression of the normal hemolytic action of human serum due to the presence of some antihemolytic substance; sometimes seen in renal cirrhosis and arteriosclerosis. **Neisser-Wechsberg p.,** deviation of complement. **Neufeld's p.,** the dissolution of pneumococci in a solution of bile salts. **Orbeli p.,** when the response of a nerve-muscle preparation is diminishing because of fatigue, stimulation of the sympathetic increases the height of the contractions. **orbicularis p.,** Westphal-Piltz p. **Osler's p.,** agglutination of the platelets of blood directly after it is withdrawn from the circulation. **palmoplantar p.,** a yellowish discoloration of parts of the palms and soles in typhoid fever. **paradoxical diaphragm p.,** Litten's diaphragm p. **paradoxical p. of dystonia,** Hunt's paradoxical p. **paradoxical pupil p.,** Westphal-Piltz p. **paragglutination p.,** a form of nonspecific agglutination of erythrocytes caused by certain blood sera. It disappears at 37°C. and is often due to bacterial contamination of the serum. **peroneal-nerve p.,** Lust's p. **Pfeiffer's p.,** cholera vibrios, introduced into the peritoneal cavity of a guinea pig that has been immunized against cholera, lose their motility, disintegrate, and pass into solution. The disintegration can be followed under the microscope by removing a portion of the peritoneal contents from time to time. The same result is observed if a bacteriolytic serum (against cholera) is introduced along with the bacteria into the peritoneal cavity of a normal guinea pig. **phrenic p.** 1. Rhythmical spasm of the left half of the diaphragm; seen in tetany. 2. Diaphragmatic phenomenon. **Piltz-Westphal p.,** Westphal-Piltz p. **Pool's p.** 1. Schlesinger's sign. 2. Contraction of the muscles of the arm following the raising of the arm above the head with the forearm extended, so as to cause stretching of the brachial plexus: seen in postoperative tetany. **Porret's p.,** the passage of a continuous current through a living muscle fiber causes an undulation proceeding from the positive toward the negative pole. **prezone p., prozone p.** See *prozone.* **psi p.** [*psyche*], an experience or effect produced without physical agency or intermediation. **Purkinje's p.,** the phenomenon that fields of equal brightness but different color become unequally bright if the intensity of the illumination is decreased. **radial p.,** the involuntary dorsal flexion of the wrist which occurs on palmar flexion of the fingers. **rash extinction p.,** Schultz-Charlton p. **Raynaud's p.,** intermittent attacks of pallor or cyanosis of the extremities, especially of the fingers or toes and sometimes of the ears and nose, brought on by cold or emotion. When the condition is primary, i.e., without any causal disease, it is termed *Raynaud's disease.* **rebound p.,** the tendency for antagonistic muscles to contract spontaneously as soon as stimulation of a group of muscles ceases: when the examiner grasps the patient's wrist and attempts to draw the arm into extension against the patient's resistance and then suddenly releases the wrist the patient's hand rebounds toward his body. A similar rebound occurs in the lower extremity. The phenomenon indicates motor disorder due to cerebellar lesion. Called also *Holmes's p.* **reclotting p.,** thixotropy. **release p.,** the unhampered activity of a lower center when a higher inhibiting control is removed. **Rieckenberg's p.,** when the blood of a mouse cured of a trypanosome infection (or with a chronic infection) is mixed with the same strain of trypanosomes from another mouse, masses of blood platelets adhere to the flagella end of the trypanosomes or may completely cover some of the trypanosomes. **Rieger's p.,** brake p. **Ritter-Rollet p.,** flexion of the foot upon a gentle electric stimulation, and its extension upon energetic stimulation. **Rumpel-Leede p.,** the appearance of minute subcutaneous hemorrhages below the area at which a rubber bandage is applied not too tightly for ten minutes upon the upper arm: characteristic of scarlet fever and hemorrhagic diathesis. **Rust's p.,** in cases of caries or cancer of the upper cervical vertebrae the patient supports his head with his hands when lying down or when rising from a lying position. **Sanarelli p.,** a manifestation of hemorrhagic allergy. A culture of cholera germs injected into the veins of a rabbit produces no symptoms. If, however, the next day an equally innocuous filtrate of proteus or of various other germs is similarly injected the rabbit dies with hemorrhagic lesions of the intestines. **satellite p.,** the more luxuriant development of a microorganism in the neighborhood of a foreign colony, as shown by *Hemophilus influenzae* when contaminated by *Staphylococcus pyogenes* var. *aureus.* **Schellong-Strisower p.,** fall of systolic blood pressure on assuming an erect posture from the lying down position. **Schramm's p.,** visibility with the cystoscope of a whole or part of the posterior urethra: seen in spinal cord disease. **Schüller's p.,** in hemiplegia due to organic lesion, the patient walks sideward more easily to the affected than to the healthy side. **Schültz-Charlton p.,** localized branching of the rash of scarlet fever after intracutaneous injections of serum from normal persons or scarlet fever convalescents; called also *blanching p.* and *rash extinction p.* **second set p.,** the occurrence in a recipient of a more severe immune reaction to the second grafting of tissue from the same donor, because of antibody produced as a result of the first graft. **Sherrington p.,** the response of the hind limb musculature on stimulation of the motor nerve which has previously been degenerated. **shot-silk p.** See under *retina.* **Shwartzman p.,** a severe hemorrhagic reaction with necrosis seen in rabbits which are first injected with 0.25 cc. of typhoid or certain other culture filtrates into the skin of the abdomen and which then twenty-four (eighteen to thirty-two) hours later are injected intravenously with 0.01 cc. of the same filtrate. The injected area turns blue at the center and red at the periphery, the skin is glossy, smooth and edematous, the blood vessels below the surface are ruptured and the numerous leukocytes are dead. **Simonsen p.,** the production of splenic enlargement or of focal lesions in chick embryos by the inoculation of leukocytes from normal chickens. **Sinklers' p.,** in an extremity with spastic paralysis, sharp flexion of the toe may be followed by flexion of the knee and hip. **Solovieff's p.,** phrenic p., def. 1. **Souques' p.,** a phenomenon seen in incomplete hemiplegia, consisting of involuntary extension and separation of the fingers when the arm is raised. Called also *finger p.* **springlike p.,** André-Thomas sign. **staircase p.,** treppe. **Strassmann's phenomena,** phenomena seen in the umbilical cord of the still attached placenta. When the umbilical cord is ligated, the umbilical arteries contract and the umbilical vein remains filled with blood. The slightest tapping upon the fundus uteri will be felt at the lower end of the umbilical cord, and if pressure is applied to the fundus uteri, the umbilical vein becomes distended with blood at its extremity. **Strümpell p.,** dorsiflexion and supination of the foot on active lifting of the extended leg against resistance offered by the examiner. **Theobald Smith's p.,** guinea pigs which have been used for standardizing diphtheria antitoxin and have thus been injected with a small dose of blood serum become highly susceptible to the serum and may die very promptly if given a rather large second dose of the same serum a few weeks later. See *anaphylaxis.* **Thomsen p.,** Huebener-Thomsen-Friedenreich p. **thrombocytobarin p.,** Rieckenberg's p. **toe p.,** dorsal extension of the big toe on stimulation of the sole of the foot: seen in lesions of the pyramidal tract. **tongue p.,** a slight blow upon the tongue produces a contraction with the appearance of deep depressions; seen in tetany. Called also *Schultze's sign* and *tongue test.* **Traube's p.,** a double diastolic and systolic murmur heard at the femoral and other peripheral arteries, as in aortic insufficiency, and sometimes in mitral stenosis. **Trousseau's p.,** spasmodic contractions of muscles provoked by pressure upon the nerves which go to them; seen in tetany, etc. **Twort-d'Herelle p.,** the phenomenon of transmissible bacterial lysis; bacteriophagia; when to a broth culture of typhoid or dysentery bacilli there is added a drop of filtered broth emulsion of the stool from a convalescent typhoid or dysentery patient, complete lysis of the bacterial culture will occur in a few hours. If a drop of this lysed culture is added to another culture of the bacilli lysis will take place exactly as in the first. A drop of this culture will then dissolve a third culture, and so on through hundreds of transfers. d'Herelle attributes this phenomenon to the action of an ultramicroscopic parasite of bacteria which he named the *bacteriophage.* See *bacteriophage.* **Tyndall p.,** the rendering visible of a transverse beam of light through its being broken up by solid particles suspended in a liquid or gas. **Wartenberg's p.,** weakness of the vibration of the upper lid in facial palsy. **Wedensky's p.,** on applying a series of rapidly repeated stimuli to a nerve, the muscle contracts quickly in response to the first stimulus and then fails to respond further; but if the stimuli are applied to the nerve at a slower rate, the muscle responds to all of them. **Westphal's p.** 1. Westphal-Piltz phenomenon. 2. Westphal's sign. **Westphal-Piltz p.,** contraction of the pupil, followed by dilatation, after vigorous closing of the lids; caused by tension of the orbicularis muscle. **Wever-Bray p.,** alternating action potentials in the trunk of the acoustic nerve, corresponding to auditory stimuli impinging on the corresponding cochlea. **Williams' p.,** the tympanic note of skodaic resonance in pleuritis with effusion varies in pitch with the opening and closing of the patient's mouth. **zone p.,** excess of antibody or antigen above their optimal ratio to one another or their optimal concentration often lessens or suppresses the specific activity. See *prozone.*

phenopropazine (fe″no-pro′pah-zēn). Ethopropazine.

phenothiazine (fe″no-thi′ah-zēn). A compound, $C_{12}H_9NS$, prepared by fusing diphenylamine with sulfur: used as a veterinary anthelmintic.

phenotype (fe′no-tīp) [Gr. *phainein* to show + *typos* type]. The outward, visible expression of the hereditary constitution of an organism.

phenotypic (fe″no-tip′ik). Pertaining to or expressive of the phenotype.

phenoxene (fen-ok′sēn). Trade mark for a preparation of chlorphenoxamine.

phenoxy-. A prefix indicating the presence of the group OC_6H_5, composed of phenyl and an atom of oxygen.

phenoxybenzamine (fen-ok″se-ben′zah-mēn). Chemical name: N-(2-chloroethyl)-N-(1-methyl-2-phenoxyethyl)benzylamine: used in adrenergic blockade, to reduce blood pressure, and as a vasodilator.

phenozygous (fe-noz′ĭ-gus) [Gr. *phainein* to show + *zygon* yoke]. Having the cranium much narrower than the face, so that the zygomatic arches are seen when the skull is viewed from above.

phenprocoumon (fen-pro′koo-mon). Chemical name: 3-(1′-phenylpropyl)-4-hydroxycoumarin, an anticoagulant of the coumarin type.

phensuximide (fen-suk′sĭ-mīd). Chemical name: N-methyl-2-phenylsuccinimide: used as an anticonvulsant in petit mal epilepsy.

phentolamine (fen-tol′ah-mēn). Chemical name: 2-(N′-p-tolyl-N′-m-hydroxyphenylaminomethyl)-imidazoline: used as an adrenolytic agent for diagnosis of pheochromocytoma.

phenurone (fen′u-rōn). Trade mark for a preparation of phenacemide.

phenyl (fen′il, fe′nil). The univalent radical, C_6H_5. **p. carbinol,** benzyl alcohol. **p. hydrate, p. hydroxide,** phenol. **p. mercury nitrate,** a compound with high bactericidal power. **p. salicylate,** a compound occurring in fine white crystals, or as a white crystalline powder, $C_{13}H_{10}O_3$: used as an enteric coating for tablets. **p. tertiary butylamine,** a sympathomimetic amine, sometimes used to inhibit the appetite.

phenylalanine (fen″il-al′ah-nīn). A naturally occurring amino acid, $C_6H_5.CH_2CH(NH_2)COOH$, discovered in 1879 by Schulze: essential for optimal growth in infants and for nitrogen equilibrium in human adults.

phenylbutazone (fen″il-bu′tah-zōn). Chemical name: 1,2-diphenyl-4-butyl-3,5-pyrazolidinedione: used as an analgesic and antipyretic.

phenylcarbinol (fen″il-kar′bĭ-nol). Benzyl alcohol.

phenyldimethylpyrazolon (fen″il-di-meth″il-pi-ra′zo-lon). Antipyrine.

phenylene (fe′nĭ-lēn). A divalent radical, $=C_6H_4$.

phenylephrine (fen″il-ef′rin). Chemical name: 1-m-hydroxy-α-(methyl-aminomethyl)benzyl alcohol: used as a sympathomimetic pressor.

phenylic (fe-nil′ik). Pertaining to phenyl.

phenylketonuria (fen″il-ke″to-nu′re-ah). A congenital faulty metabolism of phenylalanine, because of which phenylpyruvic acid appears in the urine. It is often associated with mental defects (phenylpyruvic oligophrenia).

phenylmercuric (fen″il-mer-ku′rik). Denoting a compound containing the radical C_6H_5Hg—, some of which have bacteriostatic and bactericidal properties. **p. nitrate,** a compound of phenol, mercury, and nitric acid, $C_6H_5HgNO_3$; the pharmaceutical preparation, used as a local antibacterial, is a mixture of phenylmercuric nitrate and its hydroxide, containing between 62.75 and 63.50 per cent of mercury.

phenylmethanol (fen″il-meth′ah-nol). Benzyl alcohol.

phenylpropanolamine hydrochloride (fen″-il-pro″pah-nol′am-in hi″dro-klo′rīd). The hydrochloride of racemic-1-phenyl-2-aminopropanol, with actions similar to those of ephedrine. Used by spray or instillation as a bronchodilator and local vasoconstrictor.

phenylpropylmethylamine (fen″il-pro″pil-meth″il-am′ēn). Chemical name: N,β-dimethylphenethylamine: sympathomimetic agent used as a nasal decongestant.

phenylpyruvicaciduria (fen″il-pi-ru″vik-as″ĭ-du′re-a). Phenylketonuria.

phenylthiocarbamide (fen″il-thi″o-kar-bam′-id). A compound

$$C_6H_5\text{—NH—}\underset{\underset{\displaystyle S}{\|}}{C}\text{—NH}_2$$

used either as dry crystals or in a 5 per cent solution, in genetics research, the ability to taste it being determined by presence of a single dominant gene. The compound is intensely bitter to approximately 70 per cent of the population, and nearly tasteless to the rest.

phenyltoloxamine (fen″il-tol-ok′sah-mēn). Chemical name: N,N-dimethyl-2-(α-phenyl-o-tolyloxy)-ethylamine: used as an antihistaminic.

phenylurea (fen″il-u-re′ah). A hypnotic compound, $NH_2CO.NH.C_6H_5$, prepared from urea and aniline.

phenyramidol (fen″ĭ-ram′ĭ-dol). Chemical name: α-(2-pyridylaminomethyl)benzyl alcohol: suggested for use as an analgesic.

phenytoin (fen′ĭ-to-in). Diphenylhydantoin.

pheochrome (fe′o-krōm) [Gr. *phaios* dusky + *chrōma* color]. Staining dark with chromium salts: said of certain embryonic cells; chromaffin.

pheochromoblast (fe″o-kro′mo-blast). Any one of the embryonic structures which develop into pheochrome (chromaffin) cells.

pheochromoblastoma (fe″o-kro″mo-blas-to′-mah). A tumor containing pheochromoblasts; a paraganglioma.

pheochromocyte (fe″o-kro′mo-sīt) [*pheochrome* + Gr. *kytos* hollow vessel]. A chromaffin cell.

pheochromocytoma (fe-o-kro″mo-si-to′mah) [*pheochromocyte* + *-oma*]. A small, well encapsulated lobular, vascular tumor of chromaffin tissue of the adrenal medulla or sympathetic paraganglia, associated with headache, blurred vision, palpitation, and tachycardia.

pheophytin (fe″o-fi′tin) [Gr. *phaios* dusky + *phyton* plant]. A brown pigment derived from chlorophyll by removal of magnesium.

Ph.G. 1. Abbreviation for *Graduate in Pharmacy*. 2. Abbreviation for *Pharmacopoeia germanica*, German pharmacopeia.

phial (fi′al). A vial or small bottle.

phialide (fi′ah-līd) [Gr. *phialis*, dim. of *phialē* a broad flat vessel]. A name given a small stalk arising from the vesicle at the swollen termination of the vegetative mycelium in certain molds.

Phialophora (fi″ah-lof′o-rah). A genus of hyphomycetous fungi. *P. verrucosa* causes a skin lesion resembling blastomycosis. See *chromoblastomycosis*.

philagrypnia (fi″lah-grip′ne-ah) [Gr. *philein* to love + *agrypnia* sleeplessness]. The ability to live with far less than the amount of sleep normally required by most people.

philanthropist (fi-lan′thro-pist). A person who exerts himself for the well-being of his fellow man.

philanthropy (fi-lan′thro-pe) [Gr. *philein* to love + *anthrōpos* man]. Practical benevolence toward mankind.

-philia (fil′e-ah) [Gr. *philein* to regard with affection, to love]. Word termination designating notable or abnormal fondness or attraction for the subject indicated by the stem to which it is affixed.

philiater (fi-li′ah-ter) [Gr. *philos* fond + *iatreia* healing]. A person interested in medical science, particularly a medical student.

Philinos (fĭ-li′nos) **of Cos** (c. 250 B.C.). A Greek physician who was a pupil of Herophilus, and is believed to have been one of the founders of the Empiric school of medicine.

Philip's glands (fil′ips) [Robert William *Philip*, Scottish physician, 1857–1939]. See under *gland*.

phillyrin (fil′ĭ-rin). A crystalline substance, $C_{27}H_{34}O_{11}$, from the leaves and bark of various species of *Phillyrea*. It has antimalarial properties.

philocatalase (fi″lo-kat′ah-lās) [Gr. *philein* to love + *catalase*]. A substance existing in the tissues and serving to protect catalase from the destructive action of anticatalase.

philocytase (fi″lo-si′tās) [Gr. *philein* to love + *cytase*]. Amboceptor.

philoneism (fi-lo′ne-izm) [Gr. *philein* to love + *neos* new]. Abnormal love of novelty.

philopatridomania (fi″lo-pat″rĭ-do-ma′ne-ah) [Gr. *philopatris* loving one's country + *mania* madness]. Uncontrollable desire to return to one's native land.

philothion (fi″lo-thi′on) [Gr. *philein* to love + *theion* sulfur]. Glutathione.

philter (fil′ter). A substance alleged to provoke love or carnal appetite.

philtrum (fil′trum) [Gr. *philtron* love potion]. 1. [N A, B N A] The vertical groove in the median portion of the upper lip, a part of the prolabium. 2. A philter.

Philumenus (fil″u-me′nus) [2nd century A.D.). A Greek physician of the Eclectic school whose works are quoted by Oribasius and Aëtius.

phimosiectomy (fi-mo″se-ek′to-me) [*phimosis* + Gr. *ektomē* excision]. Circumcision for phimosis.

phimosis (fi-mo′sis) [Gr. *phimōsis* a muzzling or closure]. Tightness of the foreskin, so that it cannot be drawn back from over the glans; also the analogous condition in the clitoris. **labial p., oral p.,** atresia of the mouth. **p. vagina′lis,** atresia of the vagina.

phimotic (fi-mot′ik). Pertaining to phimosis.

pHisoHex (fi′so-heks). Trade mark for an emulsion containing hexachlorophene.

phleb-. See *phlebo-*.

phlebalgia (flĕ-bal′je-ah) [*phleb-* + *-algia*]. Neuralgia due to varices within or on the surface of a nerve.

phlebanesthesia (fleb″an-es-the′ze-ah). Phlebonarcosis.

phlebangioma (fleb″an-je-o′mah) [*phleb-* + *angioma*]. A venous aneurysm.

phlebarteriectasia (fleb″ar-te″re-ek-ta′se-ah) [*phleb-* + Gr. *artēria* artery + *ektasis* extension]. General dilatation of veins and arteries.

phlebarteriodialysis (fleb″ar-te″re-o-di-al′ĭ-sis) [*phleb-* + Gr. *artēria* artery + *dialysis* separation]. Arteriovenous aneurysm.

phlebasthenia (fleb″as-the′ne-ah) [*phleb-* + *a* neg. + Gr. *sthenos* strength + *-ia*]. Impairment of the vitality of the walls of blood vessels.

phlebectasia (fleb″ek-ta′ze-ah) [*phleb-* + Gr. *ektasis* dilatation + *-ia*]. A varicosity; a dilatation of a vein. **p. laryn′gis,** permanent dilatation of the veins of the larynx, especially those of the vocal cords.

phlebectasis (fle-bek′tah-sis). Phlebectasia.

phlebectomy (fle-bek′to-me) [*phleb-* + Gr. *ektomē* excision]. Excision of a vein, or of a part of a vein.

phlebectopia (fleb″ek-to′pe-ah) [*phleb-* + Gr. *ektopos* out of place + *-ia*]. Displacement of a vein.

phlebectopy (fle-bek′to-pe). Phlebectopia.

phlebemphraxis (fleb″em-frak′sis) [*phleb-* + Gr. *emphraxis* stoppage]. The stoppage of a vein by a plug or clot.

phlebexairesis (fleb″ek-si′rĕ-sis) [*phleb-* + Gr. *exairesis* a taking out]. Surgical removal of a vein.

phlebin (fleb′in). A pigment supposed to exist in venous blood.

phlebismus (fle-biz′mus). Obstruction and consequent turgescence of veins.

phlebitic (fle-bit′ik). Pertaining to phlebitis.

phlebitis (fle-bi′tis) [*phleb-* + *-itis*]. Inflammation of a vein. The condition is marked by infiltration of the coats of the vein and the formation of a thrombus of coagulated blood. The disease is attended by edema, stiffness, and pain in the affected part, the development of a red cord at the site of the vein, and in the septic variety by pyemic symptoms. **adhesive p.,** a phlebitis which tends to the obliteration of the vein. Called also *plastic p.* and *proliferative p.* **anemic p.,** a form associated with anemia or chlorosis. **blue p.,** phlegmasia cerulea dolens. **chlorotic p.,** anemic p. **gouty p.,** a variety dependent upon the gouty diathesis, often recurrent, and sometimes occlusive. **p. mi′grans, migrating p.,** phlebitis recurring in different parts of the same limb. **p. nodula′ris necrot′isans,** a form in which tuberculous nodules of the skin are formed, becoming necrotic at the center and spreading slowly. **obliterating p., obstructive p.,** phlebitis that permanently closes the lumen of a vein. **plastic p.,** adhesive p. **proliferative p.,** adhesive p. **puerperal p.,** septic inflammation of uterine or other veins following childbirth. **recurrent p.,** that which reappears after periods of disappearance. **septic p.,** that which depends upon a septic process, as in erysipelas, cancer, or tuberculosis. In it the thrombus breaks down and septic emboli are carried to distant parts of the body. Called also *suppurative p.* **sinus p.,** inflammation of a cerebral sinus. **suppurative p.,** septic p.

phlebo-, phleb- (fleb′o, fleb) [Gr. *phleps, phlebos* vein]. Combining form denoting relationship to a vein or veins.

phlebocarcinoma (fleb″o-kar″sĭ-no′mah). Carcinoma of a vein.

phlebocholosis (fleb″o-ko-lo′sis) [*phlebo-* + Gr. *chōlos* maimed]. Disease of veins.

phleboclysis (fle-bok′lĭ-sis) [*phlebo-* + Gr. *klysis* injection]. Injection of a medicinal, nutrient, or other solution into a vein. **drip p., slow p.,** phleboclysis in which the solution is instilled slowly, drop by drop.

phlebogenous (fle-boj′e-nus). Formed in the veins.

phlebogram (fleb′o-gram) [*phlebo-* + Gr. *gramma* a writing]. 1. A tracing of the venous pulse made

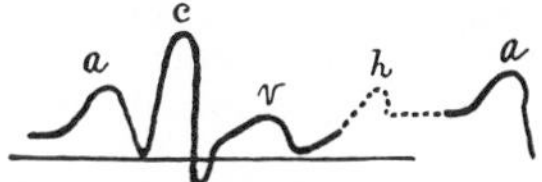

Phlebogram: *a*, Stasis wave due to contraction of the right atrium; *c*, a venous wave due to contraction of the right ventricle; *v*, stasis wave which occurs while the ventricle is filling with blood; *h*, abnormal wave (Norris).

with a phlebograph or sphygmograph. 2. A roentgenogram of the veins of a part.

phlebograph (fleb′o-graf) [*phlebo-* + Gr. *graphein* to write]. An instrument for recording the venous pulse.

phlebography (fle-bog′rah-fe) [*phlebo-* + Gr. *graphein* to write]. 1. A description of the veins. 2. The graphic recording of the venous pulse. 3. Roentgenography of a vein or veins.

phleboid (fleb′oid) [*phlebo-* + Gr. *eidos* form]. Resembling a vein, or composed of veins.

phlebolith (fleb′o-lith) [*phlebo-* + Gr. *lithos* stone]. A calculus or concretion in a vein; a vein stone.

phlebolithiasis (fleb″o-lĭ-thi′ah-sis) [*phlebo-* + *lithiasis*]. A condition characterized by the development of vein stones.

phlebology (fle-bol′o-je) [*phlebo-* + *-logy*]. The department of medicine that has to do with the veins.

phlebomanometer (fleb″o-mah-nom′e-ter) [*phlebo-* + *manometer*]. An instrument for the direct measurement of venous blood pressure (Burch and Winsor).

phlebometritis (fleb″o-me-tri′tis) [*phlebo-* + Gr. *metra* uterus + *-itis*]. Inflammation of the veins of the uterus.

phlebomyomatosis (fleb″o-mi″o-mah-to′sis) [*phlebo-* + *myomatosis*]. A condition in which the muscular fibers of a vein become overgrown, producing thickening of the walls.

phlebonarcosis (fleb″o-nar-ko′sis). Narcosis produced by intravenous injections.

phlebopexy (fleb′o-pek″se) [*phlebo-* + Gr. *pēxis* fixation]. Extraserous transplantation of the testicle, with preservation of the reticulum of veins: done for varicocele.

phlebophlebostomy (fleb″o-fle-bos′to-me) [*phlebo-* + Gr. *phleps* vein + *stomoun* to provide with an opening, or mouth]. Operative anastomosis of vein to vein.

phlebophthalmotomy (fleb″of-thal-mot′o-me) [*phlebo-* + Gr. *ophthalmos* eye + *tomē* a cutting]. Ophthalmophlebotomy.

phlebopiezometry (fleb″o-pi″e-zom′e-tre) [*phlebo-* + Gr. *piesis* pressure + *metron* measure]. Measurement of the venous pressure.

phleboplasty (fleb′o-plas″te) [*phlebo-* + Gr. *plassein* to form]. Plastic operation for the repair of a vein.

phleborrhagia (fleb″o-ra′je-ah) [*phlebo-* + Gr. *rhēgnynai* to burst forth]. Copious hemorrhage from a vein.

phleborrhaphy (fle-bor′ah-fe) [*phlebo-* + Gr. *rhaphē* suture]. The operation of suturing a vein.

phleborrhexis (fleb″o-rek′sis) [*phlebo-* + Gr. *rhēxis* rupture]. Rupture of a vein.

phlebosation (fleb″o-za′shun). Phlebosclerosation.

phlebosclerosation (fleb″o-skle″ro-za′shun) [*phlebo-* + Gr. *sklērōsis* hardening]. Treatment of varicose veins by the induction of artificial sclerosis.

phlebosclerosis (fleb″o-skle-ro′sis) [*phlebo-* + Gr. *sklērōsis* hardening]. A condition characterized by loss of normal elasticity of the veins, with hyperplasia of the middle and inner coats, and fibrous nodular masses protruding into the lumen of the vessel.

phlebosis (fle-bo′sis). Nonseptic inflammation or irritation of a vein.

phlebostasia (fleb″os-ta′ze-ah). Phlebostasis.

phlebostasis (fle-bos′tah-sis) [*phlebo-* + Gr. *stasis* stoppage]. 1. Retardation of the flow of blood in the veins. 2. Temporary abstraction of a portion of the blood from the general circulation by compressing the veins of the extremity.

phlebostenosis (fleb″o-ste-no′sis) [*phlebo-* + Gr. *stenōsis* narrowing]. Stenosis or constriction of a vein.

phlebostrepsis (fleb″o-strep′sis) [*phlebo-* + Gr. *strephein* to turn]. The surgical twisting of a vein.

phlebothrombosis (fleb″o-throm-bo′sis) [*phlebo-* + *thrombosis*]. Presence of a clot in a vein, unassociated with inflammation of the wall of the vein. Cf. *thrombophlebitis.*

phlebotome (fleb′o-tōm). A knife or lancet for use in phlebotomy; a fleam.

phlebotomist (fle-bot′o-mist). One who practices venesection; a bleeder.

phlebotomize (fle-bot′o-miz). To bleed; to take blood from by phlebotomy.

Phlebotomus (fle-bot′o-mus) [*phlebo-* + Gr. *tomos* a cutting]. A genus of biting flies of the family Psychodidae, containing some 60 species, the females of which all suck blood. **P. argen′tipes,** the species which transmits kala-azar in India. **P. chinen′sis,** the species which transmits kala-azar in China. **P. interme′dius,** a species suspected of being a transmitter of leishmaniasis in South America. **P. macedon′icum,** an Italian species. **P. nogu′chi,** a species that transmits *Bartonella bacilliformis*, the organism of Oroya fever. **P. papatas′ii,** the sandfly, a dipterous insect of India and the Mediterranean countries, which conveys by its bite an infection known as *pappataci fever* and *sandfly fever.* **P. ser′genti,** a carrier of Oriental sore. **P. verruca′rum,** a fly abounding in Peru and regarded as the conveyor of the infection of verruga peruana or Oroya fever. **P. vexa′tor,** a species of the United States which is not a disease vector.

Phlebotomus papatasii.

phlebotomy (fle-bot′o-me) [*phlebo-* + Gr. *tomē* a

cutting]. Incision of a vein, as for the letting of blood. **bloodless p.**, phlebostasis, def. 2.

phlebotropism (fle-bot′ro-pizm) [*phlebo-* + Gr. *tropos* a turning]. Selective affinity for the veins.

phlegm (flem) [Gr. *phlegma*]. 1. One of the four humors of the body, according to the obsolete humoral pathology. 2. Morbid or viscid mucus secreted in abnormally large amount, applied especially to such mucus discharged through the mouth.

phlegmasia (fleg-ma′ze-ah) [Gr. "heat, inflammation"]. Inflammation or fever. **p. al′ba do′lens,** phlebitis of the femoral vein, occasionally following parturition and typhoid fever. It is characterized by swelling of the leg, usually without redness. Called also *leukophlegmasia, milk leg,* and *white leg.* **p. al′ba do′lens puerpera′rum,** phlegmasia alba dolens occurring in a woman after childbirth. **cellulitic p.,** swelling and inflammation of the leg after childbirth from infection of the connective tissue. **p. ceru′lea do′lens,** an acute fulminating form of deep venous thrombosis, with pronounced edema of the extremity and severe cyanosis, purpuric areas, and petechiae. Called also *blue phlebitis.* **p. malabar′ica,** elephantiasis. **thrombotic p.,** phlegmasia alba dolens.

phlegmatic (fleg-mat′ik) [Gr. *phlegmatikos*]. Characterized by an excess of the supposed humor called phlegm; hence, heavy, dull, and apathetic.

phlegmon (fleg′mon) [Gr. *phlegmonē*]. Inflammation of the connective tissue, leading to ulceration or abscess. **bronze p.,** a gas phlegmon characterized by bronze colored spots. **diffuse p.,** phlegmona diffusa. **Dupuytren's p.,** phlegmonous suppuration in the anterolateral portion of the neck on one side. **emphysematous p.,** gas gangrene. **gas p.,** gas gangrene. **Holz p.,** a chronic cellulitis of the floor of the mouth and neck. **ligneous p.,** induration of the subcutaneous connective tissue of the neck with little suppuration, fever, or pain, and running a chronic progressive course. Called *Reclus' disease.* **woody p.,** ligneous phlegmon.

phlegmona (fleg′mo-nah). Phlegmon. **p. diffu′sa,** a more or less extensive inflammation of the cutaneous and subcutaneous tissues, with symptoms resembling both deep erysipelas and flat carbuncle, and attended with constitutional symptoms. Called also *phlegmonous cellulitis.*

phlegmonosis (fleg″mo-no′sis). Inflammation or fever.

phlegmonous (fleg′mon-us). Pertaining to or attended by phlegmon.

phlobaphene (flo′bah-fēn) [Gr. *phloios* bark + *baphē* dye]. One of a series of compounds resembling resins and differing from the latter only in that they dissolve in dilute ammonia water. They are derived from tannin by boiling with acids and are characterized by their brown color.

phloem (flo′em) [Gr. *phloios* bark]. In botany that part of the vascular bundle consisting of sieve tubes and their parenchymatous tissue; the last tissue: as distinguished from the *xylem.*

phlogistic (flo-jis′tik) [Gr. *phlogistos*]. Inflammatory.

phlogisticozymoid (flo-jis″tĭ-ko-zi′moid). A hypothetical substance supposed to supply the necessary feeding ground for inflammatory processes.

phlogiston (flo-jis′ton) [Gr. *phlogistos* burnt]. The supposed principle of fire and combustion; a term proposed in 1697 by Stahl, who supposed that combustible substances were compounds of phlogiston and that combustion is due to the phlogiston leaving the other structures of the substance behind.

phlogo- (flo′go) [Gr. *phlogōsis* inflammation]. Combining form denoting relation to inflammation.

phlogocyte (flo′go-sit) [*phlogo-* + *-cyte*]. A cell characteristic of tissue in an inflamed state; a plasma cell.

phlogocytosis (flo″go-si-to′sis). Presence of phlogocytes in the blood.

phlogogen (flo′go-jen). A body that has the power of causing inflammation.

phlogogenic (flo″go-jen′ik) [*phlogo-* + Gr. *gennan* to produce]. Causing inflammation.

phlogogenous (flo-goj′e-nus). Phlogogenic.

phlogosin (flo-go′sin). A crystallizable, nonnitrogenous substance, from cultures of the *Staphylococcus aureus.* Introduced into the eye, it produces an intense suppurative process.

phlogosis (flo-go′sis) [Gr. *phlogōsis*]. 1. Inflammation. 2. Erysipelas.

phlogotherapy (flog″o-ther′ah-pe) [*phlogo-* + Gr. *therapeia* treatment]. Nonspecific therapy. See under *therapy.*

phlogotic (flo-got′ik). Inflammatory.

phlogozelotism (flo″go-zel′o-tism) [*phlogo-* + Gr. *zēlōtēs* zealot]. A perverse habit of ascribing to every disease an inflammatory origin.

phlorhizin (flo-ri′zin) [Gr. *phloios* bark + *rhiza* root]. A bitter glycoside, $C_{21}H_{24}O_{10} + 2H_2O$, from the root bark of apple, cherry, plum, and pear trees. It will cause glycosuria by blocking the tubular reabsorption of glucose.

phlorhizinize (flo-ri′zi-nīz). To bring under the influence of phlorhizin.

phloridzin (flo-rid′zin). Phlorhizin.

phloridzinize (flo-rid′zi-nīz). Phlorhizinize.

phlorizin (flo-ri′zin). Phlorhizin.

phlorol (flo′rol). An oily liquid, $C_6H_5(OC_2H_5)$, derived from creosote. See *phenetol.*

phlorose (flor′ōs). A sugar formed when phlorhizin is boiled with dilute acids; glucose.

phlorrhizin (flo-ri′zin). Phlorhizin.

phloryl (flo′ril). A principle obtainable from creosote.

phloxine (flok′sin). A brick-red acid dye claimed to have a destructive action on cancer cells.

phlycten (flik′ten). Phlyctena.

phlyctena (flik-te′nah), pl. *phlycte′nae* [Gr. *phlyktaina*]. 1. A blister made by a burn. 2. A small, bladder-like pustule containing lymph or a thin ichor, especially such a lesion on the conjunctiva.

phlyctenar (flik′tĕ-nar). Pertaining to or marked by phlyctenae.

phlyctenoid (flik′tĕ-noid) [*phlyctena* + Gr. *eidos* form]. Resembling a phlyctena.

phlyctenosis (flik″tĕ-no′sis) [Gr. *phlyktainōsis*]. Any phlyctenular disease or lesion. **p. strepto′genes,** a disease of the skin due to a streptococcus.

phlyctenotherapy (flik″tĕ-no-ther′ah-pe) [*phlyctenule* + Gr. *therapeia* treatment]. Treatment by the subcutaneous injection of the serum from blisters raised on the patient's own body by applying cantharides.

phlyctenula (flik-ten′u-lah), pl. *phlycten′ulae* [L.]. Phlyctenule.

phlyctenular (flik-ten′u-lar). Associated with the formation of phlyctenules or vesicles, or of prominences that look like vesicles.

phlyctenule (flik′ten-ūl) [L. *phlyctaenulaly;* Gr. *phlyktaina* blister]. A minute vesicle, or an ulcerated nodule of the cornea or of the conjunctiva.

phlyctenulosis (flik″ten-u-lo′sis). The condition marked by the formation of phlyctenules; phlyctenular keratitis. **allergic p.,** phlyctenulosis due to allergy. **tuberculous p.,** phlyctenulosis due to tuberculous allergy.

phlyzacium (fli-za′se-um) [Gr. *phlyzakion,* dim. of *phlyktaina*]. 1. A little pustule. 2. Ecthyma. **p. acu′tum,** ecthyma.

phobia (fo′be-ah) [Gr. *phobos* fear (*phobein* to be affrighted by) + *-ia*]. Any persistent abnormal dread or fear. Used as a word termination designating abnormal or morbid fear of or aversion to the subject indicated by the stem to which it is affixed.

phobic (fo′bik). Of the nature of or pertaining to phobia or morbid fear.

phobophobia (fo-bo-fo′be-ah) [Gr. *phobos* fear + *phobein* to be affrighted by]. A condition in psychasthenia marked by fear of one's own fears.

Phocas' disease (fo-kahz′) [B. G. *Phocas*, French physician]. See under *disease*.

phocomelia (fo″ko-me′le-ah) [Gr. *phōkē* seal + *melos* limb + *-ia*]. A developmental anomaly characterized by absence of the proximal portion of a limb or limbs, the hands or feet being attached to the trunk of the body by a single small, irregularly shaped bone.

Phocomelia in arms and sympodia in legs (Arey).

phocomelus (fo-kom′e-lus) [Gr. *phōkē* seal + *melos* limb]. An individual exhibiting phocomelia.

pholedrine (fo-led′rīn). Veritol.

phon (fōn) [Gr. *phōnē* voice]. A unit of the subjective loudness of a sound.

phon-. See *phono-*.

phonacoscope (fo-nak′o-skōp). The apparatus used in phonacoscopy.

phonacoscopy (fo″nah-kos′ko-pe) [*phon-* + Gr. *skopein* to examine]. Combined auscultation and percussion by means of a bell-shaped resonating chamber containing a percussion hammer, which is held on the anterior thoracic wall while the examiner listens at the back of the thorax.

phonal (fo′nal). Pertaining to the voice.

phonarteriogram (fōn″ar-te′re-o-gram). A tracing or graphic record of arterial sounds obtained in phonarteriography.

phonarteriographic (fōn″ar-te″re-o-graf′ik). Pertaining to phonarteriography or to a phonarteriogram.

phonarteriography (fōn″ar-te″re-og′rah-fe). The recording of arterial sounds by means of a phonocardiograph.

phonasthenia (fōn″as-the′ne-ah) [*phon-* + *asthenia*]. Weakness of the voice; difficult phonation from fatigue.

phonation (fo-na′shun). The utterance of vocal sounds. **subenergetic p.,** hypophonia. **superenergetic p.,** hyperphonia.

phonatory (fo′nah-to″re). Subserving or pertaining to phonation.

phonautograph (fōn-aw′to-graf) [*phon-* + Gr. *autos* self + *graphein* to write]. An apparatus which registers the vibrations of the air caused by the voice.

phoneme (fo′nēm) [Gr. *phōnēma* sound]. An insane hallucination of voices.

phonendoscope (fōn-en′do-skōp) [*phon-* + Gr. *endon* within + *skopein* to examine]. A stethoscope that intensifies auscultatory sounds.

phonendoskiascope (fōn-en″do-ski′ah-skōp). A phonendoscope combined with a fluorescent screen for observing the heart movements at the same time as the heart sounds are heard.

phonetic (fo-net′ik) [Gr. *phonētikos*]. Pertaining to the voice or to articulate sounds.

phonetics (fo-net′iks). The science of vocal sounds.

phoniatrician (fo″ne-ah-trish′an). A person who specializes in treating speech defects.

phoniatrics (fo″ne-at′riks) [*phon-* + Gr. *iatrikē* surgery, medicine]. The treatment of speech defects.

phonic (fo′nik). Pertaining to the voice.

phonism (fo′nizm). A form of synesthesia in which a sensation of hearing is produced by the effect of something seen, felt, tasted, smelt, or thought of.

phono-, phon- (fo′no, fōn) [Gr. *phōnē* voice]. Combining form denoting relationship to sound, often specifically to the sound of the voice.

phono-auscultation (fo″no-aws″kul-ta′shun). Auscultation in which a tuning-fork is placed over the organ to be examined and its vibrations are listened to through a stethoscope placed over the same organ.

phonocardiogram (fo″no-kar′de-o-gram) [*phono-* + Gr. *kardia* heart + *gramma* a writing]. A graphic representation by means of a paper recording of heart sounds obtained by intracardiac phonocatheterization or by acoustic pick-up with a chest microphone.

phonocardiograph (fo″no-kar′de-o-graf). An instrument for recording the sounds of the heart.

phonocardiographic (fo″no-kar″de-o-graf′ik). Pertaining to phonocardiography or to a phonocardiogram.

phonocardiography (fo″no-kar″de-og′rah-fe). The graphic registration of the sounds produced by action of the heart. **intracardiac p.,** the graphic registration of sounds produced by action of the heart by means of a phonocatheter passed into one of the heart chambers.

phonocatheter (fo″no-kath′e-ter). A device similar in appearance to a conventional catheter, with a small sound pick-up in the tip.

phonocatheterization (fo″no-kath″e-ter-i-za′shun). The use of a phonocatheter for the detection of sounds produced by the circulatory system. **intracardiac p.,** the passage of a phonocatheter into a chamber of the heart, for the detection of sounds as an aid in diagnosis of cardiac defects.

phono-electrocardioscope (fo″no-e-lek″tro-kar″de-o-skōp). An instrument incorporating a double beam cathod ray oscilloscope with a fluorescent screen of long afterglow, which permits the simultaneous direct visual recording of two phenomena such as the phonocardiogram and the electrocardiogram, the phonocardiogram and the sphygmogram or the electrocardiogram and the sphygmogram.

phonogram (fo′no-gram) [*phono-* + Gr. *gramma* mark]. A graphic record of a sound, as, for instance, a heart sound.

phonograph (fo′no-graf) [*phono-* + Gr. *graphein* to write]. An instrument for recording and reproducing sounds and speech.

phonology (fo-nol′o-je) [*phono-* + *-logy*]. The science which treats of vocal sounds; phonetics.

phonomania (fon″o-ma′ne-ah) [Gr. *phonē* murder + *mania* madness]. Insanity marked by a tendency to commit murder.

phonomassage (fo″no-mah-sahzh′). The treatment of ear disease by an apparatus which carries more or less of musical vibration into the auditory canal.

phonometer (fo-nom′e-ter) [*phono-* + Gr. *metron* measure]. A device for measuring the intensity of sounds.

phonomyoclonus (fo″no-mi-ok′lo-nus). A condition in which a sound is heard on auscultation over a muscle affected with myoclonus, whether it is at rest or contracting.

phonomyogram (fo″no-mi′o-gram) [*phono-* + Gr. *mys* muscle + *gramma* mark]. A tracing of the sound produced by muscle action.

phonomyography (fo″no-mi-og′rah-fe). The recording of muscle sounds by an oscillograph to which the sounds are transmitted by a microphone placed over the muscle.

phonopathy (fo-nop′ah-the) [*phono-* + Gr. *pathos* disease]. Any disease or disorder of the organs of speech.

phonophobia (fo″no-fo′be-ah) [*phono-* + Gr. *phobein* to be affrighted by]. Morbid dread of sounds or of speaking aloud.

phonophore (fo′no-fōr) [*phono-* + Gr. *pherein* to carry]. 1. An ossicle of the ear. 2. A kind of improved stethoscope, acting on the principle of an ear trumpet, and rendering the sounds more audible.

phonophotography (fo″no-fo-tog′rah-fe) [*phono-* + *photography*]. Photographic recording of the movements of a diaphragm set up by waves of sound.

phonopneumomassage (fo″no-nu″mo-mah-sahzh′) [*phono-* + Gr. *pneuma* air + *massein* to knead]. Air massage of the middle ear.

phonopsia (fo-nop′se-ah) [*phono-* + Gr. *opsis* vision + *-ia*]. A subjective sensation as of seeing colors, caused by the hearing of sounds.

phonoreception (fo″no-re-sep′shun) [Gr. *phōnē* a sound + L. *receptio*, from *recipere* to receive]. The reception of stimuli perceived as sound; the process by which an organism detects vibratory motion, usually of frequencies higher than several vibrations per second, in the surrounding medium.

phonoreceptor (fo″no-re-sep′tor) [*phono-* + *receptor*]. A receptor for sound stimuli.

phonorenogram (fo″no-re′no-gram). A graphic representation by means of a paper recording of pulsations of the renal artery obtained by use of a phonocatheter passed through a ureter into the pelvis of the kidney.

phonoscope (fo′no-skōp) [*phono-* + Gr. *skopein* to examine]. 1. An apparatus for recording photographically the movements of a diaphragm set up by the sounds of the heart. 2. An instrument for auscultatory percussion.

phonoscopy (fo-nos′ko-pe). 1. The delimiting of solid and hollow organs (liver, heart, lungs, etc.) by listening with a stethoscope while percussion is made in the vicinity. 2. The use of the phonoscope.

phonoselectoscope (fo″no-se-lek′to-skōp) [*phono-* + *select* + Gr. *skopein* to examine]. An instrument for auscultation by means of which the lower (normal) range of the pulmonary sounds are eliminated, thus emphasizing the higher-pitched pathologic elements.

phonostethograph (fo″no-steth′o-graf). An instrument by which the chest sounds are amplified, filtered and recorded on a phonograph disk.

phoresis (for′e-sis) [Gr. *phorēsis* a being borne]. The transmission of chemical ions into the tissues by means of an electric current.

phoria (fo′re-ah) [Gr. *pherein* to bear]. Any tendency to deviation of the eyes from the normal. See *cyclophoria, esophoria, exophoria, heterophoria, hyperphoria,* and *hypophoria.*

phoriascope (fo′re-ah-skōp). A prism-refracting instrument for use in orthoptic training.

Phormia (for′me-ah). A genus of flies. **P. regi′na,** a blow fly which causes a cutaneous myiasis of sheep in United States and Canada.

phoroblast (fo′ro-blast) [Gr. *phoros* carrying + *blastos* germ]. Fibroblast.

phorocyte (fo′ro-sīt). A connective tissue cell.

phorocytosis (fo″ro-si-to′sis). Proliferation of connective tissue cells.

phorologist (fo-rol′o-jist). One skilled in tracing the sources of endemic and epidemic diseases.

phorology (fo-rol′o-je) [Gr. *phoros* carrying + *-logy*]. The study of disease carriers.

phorometer (fo-rom′e-ter) [Gr. *pherein* to bear + *metron* measure]. An instrument for ascertaining the degree and kind of heterophoria.

phorometry (fo-rom′e-tre). Use of the phorometer.

phorone (fo′rōn). A yellowish, oily unsaturated ketone, $C_9H_{14}O$, obtained from acetone, camphoric acid, etc.

phoroplast (fo′ro-plast) [Gr. *phoros* carrying + *plastos* formed]. Connective tissue.

phoropter (fo-rop′ter). A phorometer fitted with a battery of cylindrical lenses.

phoroscope (fo′ro-skōp). A fixed trial frame for eye testing, with a head rest which may be fastened to the table or the wall.

phorotone (fo′ro-tōn) [Gr. *phora* motion, movement + *tonos* tension]. An instrument for exercising the muscles of the eye.

phorozoon (fo″ro-zo′on) [Gr. *phoros* fruitful + *zōon* animal]. The asexual stage in the life history of an organism.

phose (fōz) [Gr. *phōs* light]. Any subjective sensation, as of light or color. See *aphose, centraphose, centrophose, chromophose, peripheraphose, peripherophose,* etc.

phosgene (fos′jēn). A suffocating and highly poisonous war gas, carbonyl chloride, $COCl_2$. Called also *CG, collognite* and *D-stoff.*

phosgenic (fos-jen′ik) [Gr. *phōs* light + *gennan* to produce]. Producing light.

phosis (fo′sis). The production of a phose.

phosphagen (fos′fah-jen). A compound, such as phosphocreatine and phosphoarginine, which occurs in tissue and which, when broken down, is the source of high-energy phosphate.

phosphagenic (fos″fah-jen′ik). Producing or forming phosphate.

phosphaljel (fos′fal-jel). Trade mark for a preparation of aluminum phosphate gel.

phosphaminase (fos-fam′ĭ-nās). An enzyme which catalyzes the hydrolysis of amino phosphoric compounds into amines and phosphoric acid.

phosphatase (fos′fah-tās″) [*phosphate* + *-ase*]. An enzyme which hydrolyzes monophosphoric esters, with liberation of inorganic phosphate, found in practically all tissues, body fluids, and cells, including erythrocytes and leukocytes. **acid p.,** a phosphatase active in an acid medium; such enzymes are found in mammalian erythrocytes and yeast (optimal activity at pH 6), prostatic epithelium, spleen, kidney, blood plasma, liver, and pancreas, and in rice bran (optimal activity at pH 5) and taka-diastase (optimal activity at pH 3-4). **alkaline p.,** a phosphatase active in an alkaline medium; such enzymes are found in blood plasma or serum, bone, kidney, mammary gland, spleen, lung, leukocytes, adrenal cortex, and seminiferous tubules (optimal activity at about pH 9.3). **serum p.,** the phosphatase of the blood serum.

phosphate (fos′fāt) [L. *phosphas*]. Any salt of phosphoric acid. **acid p.,** any phosphate in which only one or two of the three replaceable hydrogen atoms are taken up. **alkaline p.,** a phosphate of an alkaline metal, as sodium or potassium. **ammoniomagnesium p.,** a double salt of ammonium and magnesium with orthophosphoric acid, $Mg(NH_4)PO_4.6H_2O$: closely allied to and often associated with triple phosphate. **arginine p.,** phosphoarginine. **calcium p.,** a compound containing calcium and the phosphate radical (PO_4). **creatine p.,** phosphocreatine. **earthy p.,** a phosphate of any one of the alkaline earth metals. **ferric p.,** a yellowish white powder, $FePO_4.4H_2O$, insoluble in water or acetic acid. **ferric p., soluble,** ferric phosphate rendered soluble by the presence of sodium citrate: used as a hematinic. **guanidine p.,** phosphoguanidine. **magnesium p., dibasic,** a salt, $MgHPO_4.3H_2O$: mild saline laxative. **magnesium p., tribasic,** a salt, $Mg_3(PO_4)_2.5H_2O$: used as a gastric antacid. **normal p.,** any phosphate in which all the replaceable hydrogen atoms are replaced. **stellar p.,** calcium phosphate occurring in star-shaped masses of crystals in urinary sediment. **trimagnesium p.,** magnesium p., tribasic. **triorthocresyl p.,** a poisonous compound, $(CH_3C_6H_4.O)PO$, contained in Jamaica ginger and the cause of the paralysis resulting from its ingestion. **triose p.,** phosphotriose. **triple p.,** a calcium, ammonium, and magnesium phosphate, sometimes found in the urine.

phosphated (fos′fāt-ed). Containing phosphates.

phosphatemia (fos″fah-te′me-ah) [*phosphate* + Gr. *haima* blood + *-ia*]. The presence of phosphates in the blood.

phosphatese (fos′fah-tēs). An enzyme (coenzyme) which synthesizes the phosphate esters of carbohydrates.

phosphatic (fos-fat′ik). Pertaining to or containing phosphates.

phosphatide (fos′fah-tid). A fatty acid ester of a phosphorylated polyvalent alcohol. **pro-**

thromboplastic p's, substances having the properties of phospholipids and believed to function as parts of both thromboplastin and antithromboplastin.

phosphatidosis (fos″fah-tĭ-do′sis), pl. *phosphatido′ses* [*phosphatide* + *-osis*]. A lipidosis in which the fatty accumulations are phosphatides.

phosphatidylethanolamine (fos-fat″ĭ-dil-eth″-ah-nol-am′ēn). One of the prothromboplastic phosphatides contained in blood platelets.

phosphatidylserine (fos-fat″ĭ-dil-se′rin). One of the prothromboplastic phosphatides contained in blood platelets.

phosphatine (fos′fah-tin). Any one of a considerable group of phosphorus compounds resembling the phosphates and found in the brain substance.

phosphatometer (fos″fah-tom′e-ter). An instrument for measuring the phosphates of the urine.

phosphatoptosis (fos″fah-top-to′sis) [*phosphate* + Gr. *ptōsis* fall]. The spontaneous precipitation of phosphates from the urine.

phosphaturia (fos″fah-tu′re-ah) [*phosphate* + Gr. *ouron* urine + *-ia*]. 1. A high percentage of phosphates in any given specimen of urine. 2. Ready precipitation of the earthy phosphates from the urine; phosphatoptosis.

phosphene (fos′fēn) [Gr. *phōs* light + *phainein* to show]. A luminous appearance caused by pressing on the eyeball. **accommodation p.,** the streak of light surrounding the visual field seen in the dark after accommodation.

phosphide (fos′fīd). Any binary compound of phosphorus and another element or radical.

phosphin (fos′fin). 1. Hydrogen phosphide, PH_3: a gas and radical. 2. A coal tar dye extremely destructive to infusorial life. It is used as a stain. Called also *Philadelphia yellow.*

phosphite (fos′fīt). Any salt of phosphorous acid.

phosphoarginine (fos″fo-ar′jĭ-nin). An arginine phosphoric acid compound homologous with phosphocreatine but found in invertebrate muscles.

phosphocreatinase (fos″fo-kre-at′ĭ-nās). An enzyme which in the presence of adenosine triphosphate splits phosphocreatine into creatine and phosphoric acid.

phosphocreatine (fos″fo-kre′ah-tin). A creatinine phosphoric acid compound, $(OH)_2PO.NH.C(:NH).N(CH_3).CH_2.COOH$, occurring in muscle metabolism, being broken down into creatine and inorganic phosphorus. It contains a high-energy phosphate bond and has to do with the rephosphorylation of adenylic acid after muscle contraction.

phospho-esterase (fos″fo-es′ter-ās). Phosphatase.

phosphoglobulin (fos″fo-glob′u-lin). Nucleoalbumin.

phosphoglucomutase (fos″fo-gloo″ko-mu′tās). An enzyme which catalyzes the change of the Cori ester into glucose-6-phosphate.

phosphoglucoprotein (fos″fo-gloo″ko-pro′te-in). A phosphorus-containing glucoprotein.

3-phosphoglyceraldehyde (fos″fo-glis″er-al′-de-hīd). A triose phosphate, $CH_2.O.PO(OH)_2.CHOH.CHO$, which results from the splitting of fructose-1,6-diphosphate in muscle metabolism.

phosphoglyceromutase (fos″fo-glis″er-o-mu′-tās). An enzyme which catalyzes the change of 3-phosphoglyceric acid into 2-phosphoglyceric acid.

phosphoguanidine (fos″fo-gwan′ĭ-dēn). A guanidine phosphoric acid compound which on hydrolysis yields low-energy phosphate linkages.

phosphohexoisomerase (fos″fo-hek″so-i-som′-er-ās). An enzyme found in muscle extract which catalyzes an equilibrium between glucose 6-phosphate and fructose 6-phosphate.

phospholecithinase (fos″fo-les′ĭ-thin-ās). An enzyme found in the kidneys and the intestinal mucosa that splits phosphoric acid from lecithin and some other phospholipids.

phospholipid (fos″fo-lip′id). A lipid containing phosphorus which on hydrolysis yields fatty acids, glycerin, and a nitrogenous compound. Lecithin, cephalin, and sphingomyelin are the best known examples.

phospholipidemia (fos″fo-lip″ĭ-de′me-ah). The presence of phospholipid in the blood.

phospholipin (fos″fo-lip′in). Phospholipid.

phosphology (fos-fol′o-je) [*phosphorus* + *-logy*]. The doctrine of the effect of excess or deficiency of oxidizable phosphorus compounds in the bioplasm.

phosphonecrosis (fos″fo-ne-kro′sis). Necrosis of the jaw bone occurring in persons who work with phosphorus: called also *phossy jaw.*

phosphonium (fos-fo′ne-um). The univalent radical, PH_4, forming compounds analogous to those of ammonium.

phosphonuclease (fos″fo-nu′kle-ās). Nucleotidase.

phosphopenia (fos″fo-pe′ne-ah) [*phosphorus* + Gr. *penia* poverty]. Deficiency of phosphorus in the body.

phosphoprotein (fos″fo-pro′te-in). A conjugated protein in which phosphoric acid is esterified with an hydroxy amino acid, especially with serine. To this group belong the vitelline of egg yolk and casein of milk.

phosphoptomaine (fos″fo-to′mān). Any one of a class of toxic compounds found in the blood in phosphorus poisoning.

phosphorated (fos′fo-rāt″ed). Charged or combined with phosphorus.

phosphorenesis (fos″fo-ren′e-sis). Any disease due to excess of calcium phosphate in the body.

phosphorescence (fos″fo-res′ens). The emission of light without appreciable heat; the property of continuing luminous in the dark after exposure to light or other radiation.

phosphorescent (fos″fo-res′ent). Pertaining to or exhibiting phosphorescence.

phosphoretted (fos′fo-ret″ed). Phosphorated.

phosphorhidrosis (fos″fōr-hid-ro′sis) [*phosphorus* + Gr. *hidrōsis* sweating]. The secretion of luminous sweat.

phosphoridrosis (fos″fōr-id-ro′sis). Phosphorhidrosis.

phosphorism (fos′fo-rizm). Chronic phosphorus poisoning.

phosphorized (fos′fo-rīzd). Containing phosphorus.

phosphorolysis (fos″fo-rol′ĭ-sis). The reversible combination and separation of sugar and phosphoric acid brought about by the enzyme phosphorylase in carbohydrate metabolism.

phosphoroscope (fos′fōr-o-skōp). An instrument for measuring phosphorescence.

phosphorpenia (fos″fōr-pe′ne-ah). Phosphopenia.

phosphoruria (fos″fōr-u′re-ah) [*phosphorus* + Gr. *ouron* urine + *-ia*]. The presence of free phosphorus in the urine.

phosphorus (fos′fo-rus) [Gr. *phōs* light + *phorein* to carry]. A nonmetallic, translucent element: poisonous and highly inflammable; symbol, P; atomic number, 15; atomic weight, 30.974. It occurs in three forms—*amorphous, metallic,* and *vitreous.* It is obtainable from bones, urine, and various minerals. The ordinary, or vitreous, phosphorus is the kind used in medicine, and is very inflammable and exceedingly poisonous. Free phosphorus causes a fatty degeneration of the liver and other viscera, and the inhalation of its vapor often leads to necrosis of the lower jaw. Therapeutically, it is used in rickets, osteomalacia, nervous and cerebral disease, scrofula, and tuberculosis; as a genital stimulant in sexual exhaustion, and as a tonic in conditions of exhaustion. **amorphous p.,** a red, amorphous substance, which is not poisonous. **labelled p.,** radioactive p. **metallic p.,** an allotropic form with a metallic luster produced by heating ordinary phosphorus. **ordinary p.,** a waxy solid, which is exceedingly poisonous. **radioactive p.,** an isotope of phosphorus with an atomic mass of 32: used in treating leukemia and allied disorders, and also administered to facilitate the study of phosphorus metabolism, the radioactivity making it possible to trace the element in the body. **red p.,** amorphous p. **rhombohedral p.,** metallic p. **vitreous p.,** ordinary p.

phosphoryl (fos′fōr-il). The trivalent chemical radical ≡P:O.

phosphorylase (fos-fōr′ĭ-lās). An enzyme which, in the presence of inorganic phosphate, is able to catalyze the change of glycogen into glucose-1-phosphate or the Cori ester.

phosphorylation (fos″fōr-ĭ-la′shun). The process of introducing the trivalent PO group into an organic molecule.

phosphorylysis (fos″fo-ril′ĭ-sis). Phosphorolysis.

phospho-sugar (fos″fo-shug′ar). A sugar combined with a phosphate; a hexose phosphate.

phosphotidate (fos′fo-tid-āt). A phospholipid from which choline or colamine has been split off.

phosphotransacetylase (fos″fo-trans″ah-set′ĭ-lās). An enzyme that catalyzes the transfer of an acetyl group between acetylphosphate and acetyl coenzyme A.

phosphotransferase (fos″fo-trans′fer-ās). An enzyme that catalyzes the transfer of a phosphate group. See *kinase* (def. 1).

phosphotriose (fos″fo-tri′ōs). A compound consisting of a 3-carbon sugar combined with a phosphate radical. Two such compounds are formed from hexosediphosphate: 3-phosphoglyceraldehyde and 1-phosphodihydroxyacetone. Called also *triose phosphate.*

phosphuresis (fos″fu-re′sis). The urinary excretion of phosphorus (phosphates).

phosphuret (fos′fu-ret). Phosphide.

phosphuretic (fos″fu-ret′ik). Pertaining to, characterized by, or promoting the urinary excretion of phosphorus (phosphates).

phosphuretted (fos′fu-ret″ed). Phosphorated.

phosphuria (fos-fu′re-ah). Phosphaturia.

phot (fōt). Phote.

phot-. See *photo-.*

photalgia (fo-tal′je-ah) [*phot-* + *-algia*]. Pain, as in the eye, caused by light.

photallochromy (fo-tal′o-kro″me) [*phot-* + Gr. *allos* different + *chrōma* color]. Allotropic change with color alteration due to light, as the change of yellow into red phosphorus.

photaugiaphobia (fo-taw″je-ah-fo′be-ah) [Gr. *phōtaugeia* glare + *phobein* to be affrighted by]. Abnormal intolerance of a glare of light.

phote (fōt) [Gr. *phōs* light]. The C.G.S. unit of illumination, being one lumen per square centimeter.

photechy (fo′tek-e) [*phot-* + Gr. *ēchō* echo]. The power shown by certain substances of becoming radioactive after having been exposed to radiation.

photerythrous (fo″te-rith′rus) [*phot-* + Gr. *erythros* red]. Sensitive to the red rays of the spectrum: said of a form of color blindness in which green is not clearly recognized.

photesthesis (fo″tes-the′sis) [*phot-* + Gr. *aisthēsis* perception]. Sensitiveness to light.

photic (fo′tik). Pertaining to light.

photism (fo′tizm). A visual image; a sensation of color associated with a sensation of hearing, taste, smell, or touch.

photo-, phot- (fo′to, fōt) [Gr. *phōs, phō′tos* light]. Combining form denoting relationship to light.

photoactinic (fo″to-ak-tin′ik). Giving off both luminous and actinic rays.

photoallergic (fo″to-al-ler′jik). Pertaining to or characterized by abnormal sensitivity to light.

photoallergy (fo″to-al′er-je). An allergic type of sensitivity to light.

Photobacterium (fo″to-bak-te′re-um). A genus of microorganisms of the family Pseudomonadaceae, suborder Pseudomonadineae, order Pseudomonadales, occurring usually as coccoid or rod-shaped cells, producing luminescent substances, and found on dead fish and other salt-water animals, and in sea water. It includes four species, *P. fisch′eri, P. har′veyi, P. phospho′reum,* and *P. pieranto′nii.*

photobacterium (fo″to-bak-te′re-um). 1. A bacterium producing luminescent substances. 2. An individual organism of the genus *Photobacterium.*

photobiology (fo″to-bi-ol′o-je) [*photo-* + *biology*]. That department of biology which deals with the effect of light on living organisms.

photobiotic (fo″to-bi-ot′ik) [*photo-* + Gr. *bios* life]. Living in the light only.

photocatalysis (fo″to-kah-tal′ĭ-sis). The promotion or stimulation of a reaction by light.

photocatalyst (fo″to-kat′ah-list). A substance by means of which sunlight is utilized as chlorophyll in the photosynthesis of carbohydrates by green plants.

photocatalytic (fo″to-kat″ah-lit′ik). Promoted or stimulated by light; pertaining to, characterized by, or causing photocatalysis.

photocatalyzer (fo″to-kat′ah-liz″er). Photocatalyst.

photocauterization (fo″to-kaw″ter-i-za′shun) [*photo-* + *cauterization*]. Cauterization by radioactive means, such as radium, roentgen rays, etc.

photocautery (fo″to-kaw′ter-e). 1. Photocauterization. 2. An instrument for producing photocauterization.

photoceptor (fo″to-sep′tor). Photoreceptor.

photochemical (fo″to-kem′e-kal). Pertaining to the chemical properties of light.

photochemistry (fo″to-kem′is-tre) [*photo-* + *chemistry*]. The branch of chemistry which deals with the chemical properties or effects of light rays.

photochromogen (fo″to-kro′mo-jen) [*photo-* + Gr. *chrōma* color + *gennan* to produce]. A microorganism whose pigmentation develops as a result of exposure to light, specifically *Mycobacterium kansasii* (pathogenic for man), which is yellow-orange if grown in the light, and almost colorless if grown in the dark.

photochromogenic (fo″to-kro″mo-jen′ik). Pertaining to or characterized by photochromogenicity.

photochromogenicity (fo″to-kro″mo-je-nis′ĭ-te). The property of forming pigment consequent to light exposure; induction occurs within a few minutes in the shorter wavelengths of visible light, pigmentation then occurring within 24 hours if conditions permit continued growth.

photocinetic (fo″to-si-net′ik). Photokinetic.

photocoagulation (fo″to-ko-ag″u-la′shun). Condensation of protein material by the controlled use of light rays, used especially in treatment of retinal detachment, bleeding from retinal vessels, or of intraocular tumor masses.

photocutaneous (fo″to-ku-ta′ne-us). Relating to skin manifestations in the production of which light is an important factor.

photodermatism (fo″to-der′mah-tizm) [*photo-* + Gr. *derma* skin]. The sensitiveness of the epithelial cells of the skin to light.

photodermatitis (fo″to-der″mah-ti′tis). An abnormal state of the skin in which light is an important causative factor.

photodermatosis (fo″to-der″mah-to′sis). A morbid condition which is produced in the skin by exposure to light.

photodermia (fo″to-der′me-ah). Skin lesions produced by light.

photodromy (fo-tod′ro-me) [*photo-* + Gr. *dromos* running]. The phenomenon of moving toward (*positive p.*) or away from (*negative p.*) light; as in the case of particles in suspension.

photodynamic (fo″to-di-nam′ik) [*photo-* + Gr. *dynamis* power]. Powerful in the light: said of the action exerted by fluorescent substances in the light.

photodynamics (fo″to-di-nam′iks). The science of the activating effects of light.

photodynia (fo″to-din′e-ah) [*photo-* + Gr. *odynē* pain]. Photalgia.

photodysphoria (fo″to-dis-fo′re-ah) [*photo-* + Gr. *dysphoria* distress]. Intolerance of light; photophobia.

photoelectric (fo″to-e-lek′trik). Pertaining to the electric effects of light or other radiation.

photoelectron (fo″to-e-lek′tron). An electron emitted from a metallic surface when the latter is illuminated with light, especially with light of short wavelength.

photoelement (fo″to-el′e-ment). A galvanic element which is decomposed under the influence of light and produces photoelectricity.

photoerythema (fo″to-er″ĭ-the′mah). Erythema due to exposure to light.

photoesthetic (fo″to-es-thet′ik) [*photo-* + Gr. *aisthēsis* perception]. Pertaining to or having the sensation of light.

photofluorogram (fo″to-floo-or′o-gram). The film produced in photofluorography.

photofluorography (fo″to-floo″or-og′rah-fe). The photographic recording of fluoroscopic images on small films, using a fast lens: a procedure used in mass roentgenography of the chest. Called also *fluororoentgenography*, and sometimes *abreuography*, in honor of Manoel de Abreu, Brazilian physician, who discovered the technique.

photofluoroscope (fo″to-floo-or′o-skōp). A form of fluoroscope used in making either observations or photographs by means of roentgen rays.

photogastroscope (fo″to-gas′tro-skōp) [*photo-* + Gr. *gastēr* stomach + *skopein* to examine]. An apparatus for photographing the interior of the stomach.

photogen (fo′to-jen) [*photo-* + Gr. *gennan* to produce]. A substance supposed to exist in photogenic bacteria and to be the cause of their luminescence.

photogene (fo′to-jēn). After-image.

photogenesis (fo″to-jen′e-sis) [*photo-* + *genesis*]. The production of phosphorescence, or the emission of light, by living organisms, such as bacteria.

photogenic (fo″to-jen′ik). Produced by light or producing light.

photogenous (fo-toj′e-nus). Photogenic.

photogram (fo′to-gram) [*photo-* + Gr. *gramma* mark]. The photographic record of a physiologic experiment.

photohalide (fo″to-hal′īd). Any halogen salt that is sensitive to light.

photohematachometer (fo″to-hem″ah-tah-kom′e-ter) [*photo-* + Gr. *haima* blood + *tachys* swift + *metron* measure]. A device for making a photographic record of the speed of the blood current.

photohenric (fo″to-hen′rik) [*photo-* + *henry*]. Noting a change in inductive capacity due to the action of light.

photohmic (fo-to′mik). Noting a change in electric resistance produced by light.

photo-inactivation (fo″to-in-ak″tĭ-va′shun). Inactivation of complement by light.

photokinetic (fo″to-ki-net′ik) [*photo-* + Gr. *kinētikos* pertaining to motion]. Moving in response to the stimulus of light.

photokymograph (fo″to-ki′mo-graf). A camera with a moving film for recording movements as of the string in a string galvanometer. Called also a recording camera.

photolethal (fo″to-le′thal). Pertaining to the lethal or destructive action of light.

photology (fo-tol′o-je) [*photo-* + *-logy*]. The branch of physics which treats of light.

photoluminescence (fo″to-lu″mĭ-nes′ens). The quality of being luminescent after being acted upon by light.

photolysis (fo-tol′ĭ-sis). 1. Chemical decomposition by the action of light. 2. Lysis or solution of cells under the influence of light.

photolyte (fo′to-līt) [*photo-* + Gr. *lyein* to dissolve]. Any substance decomposable by the action of light.

photolytic (fo″to-lit′ik). Decomposed by light or radiant energy.

photoma (fo-to′mah). A flash of light sparks or color with no objective basis.

photomagnetism (fo″to-mag′nĕ-tizm). Magnetism induced by the action of light.

photomania (fo″to-ma′ne-ah) [*photo-* + Gr. *mania* madness]. Maniacal symptoms developed under the influence of light.

photometer (fo-tom′e-ter) [*photo-* + Gr. *metron* measure]. A device for measuring the intensity of light. **flicker p.,** an instrument in which the frequency of a flickering light can be controlled, for use in performing the flicker test. Called also *flicker meter*. **Förster's p.,** photoptometer.

photomethemoglobin (fo″to-met-he″mo-glo′-bin). A compound formed by the action of light on methemoglobin.

photometry (fo-tom′e-tre) [*photo-* + Gr. *metron* measure]. 1. The measurement of light. 2. The reactions of an organism to varying intensities of light. **flicker p.** See *flicker test*, under *tests*.

photomicrograph (fo″to-mi′kro-graf) [*photo-* + Gr. *mikros* small + *graphein* to record]. The photograph of a minute object as seen under the light microscope, produced by ordinary photographic methods.

photomicrography (fo″to-mi-krog′rah-fe). The production of photomicrographs.

photomicroscope (fo″to-mi′kro-skōp). A microscope and camera combined for making photomicrographs.

photomicroscopy (fo″to-mi-kros′ko-pe). Photography of enlarged pictures of minute objects with the photomicroscope.

photomorphism, photomorphosis (fo″to-mor′fizm, fo″to-mor-fo′sis) [*photo-* + Gr. *morphē* form]. The structural effects in organisms due to light.

photon (fo′ton). A particle (quantum) of electromagnetic radiation.

photoncia (fo-ton′se-ah) [*photo-* + Gr. *onkos* mass]. Swelling due to the action of light.

photone (fo′tōn). A visualization or hallucination of light.

photonosus (fo-ton′o-sus) [*photo-* + Gr. *nosos* disease]. Any disease due to excess of light.

photo-ophthalmia (fo″to-of-thal′me-ah) [*photo-* + *ophthalmia*]. Ophthalmia caused by intense light, such as electric light, rays of welding arc, or reflection from snow (ophthalmia nivialis). **flash p.,** ophthalmia produced by exposure to a welding arc.

photopathy (fo-top′ah-the) [*photo-* + Gr. *pathos* affection]. 1. A pathologic effect produced by light. 2. The attractive or repulsive influence of light upon organisms.

photoperceptive (fo″to-per-sep′tiv) [*photo-* + *perceptive*]. Able to perceive light.

photoperiodicity (fo″to-pe″re-o-dis′ĭ-te). The regularly recurring changes in the relation of light and darkness in various areas of the world, noted in the annual passage of the earth about the sun; applied also to rhythm of certain biological phenomena as determined by those changes.

photoperiodism (fo″to-pe′re-od-izm). The physiologic response of animals and plants to variations of light and darkness.

photopharmacology (fo″to-far″mah-kol′o-je) [*photo-* + *pharmacology*]. The study of the effects of light and other radiations on drugs and on their pharmacological action.

photophilic (fo″to-fil′ik) [*photo-* + Gr. *philein* to love]. Loving light; fond of light.

photophobia (fo″to-fo′be-ah) [*photo-* + Gr. *phobein* to be affrighted by]. Abnormal intolerance of light.

photophobic (fo″to-fo′bik). Pertaining to or characterized by photophobia.

photophone (fo′to-fōn) [*photo-* + Gr. *phōnē* voice]. An instrument for producing sound by the action of waves of light.

photophore (fo′to-fōr) [*photo-* + Gr. *phoros* bearing]. A light-bearing instrument for examination of the nose or larynx.

photophthalmia (fo″tof-thal′me-ah). Photo-ophthalmia.

photopia (fo-to′pe-ah) [*photo-* + Gr. *ōpē* sight + *-ia*]. Day vision. See also *light adaptation.*

photopic (fo-top′ik). Pertaining to vision in the light: said of the eye which has become light-adapted.

photoproduct (fo′to-prod″ukt). A substance synthesized in the body by the action of light.

photopsia (fo-top′se-ah) [*photo-* + Gr. *opsis* vision + *-ia*]. An appearance as of sparks or flashes due to retinal disease.

photopsy (fo-top′se). Photopsia.

photoptarmosis (fo″to-tar-mo′sis) [*photo-* + Gr. *ptarmos* sneezing + *-osis*]. Sneezing caused by the influence of light.

photoptometer (fo″top-tom′e-ter) [*photo-* + Gr. *optos* seen + *metron* measure]. A device for testing the acuity of vision by determining the smallest amount of light that will render an object just visible.

photoptometry (fo″top-tom′e-tre). Measurement of light perception.

photoradiometer (fo″to-ra″de-om′e-ter). An apparatus for measuring the quantity of roentgen rays penetrating any given surface.

photoreaction (fo″to-re-ak′shun). A chemical reaction produced by the influence of light.

photoreception (fo″to-re-sep′shun) [Gr. *phōs* light + L. *receptio*, from *recipere* to receive]. The process of detecting radiant energy, usually of wavelengths between 3900 and 7700 Å, being the range of visible light.

photoreceptive (fo″to-re-sep′tiv). Sensitive to stimulation by light.

photoreceptor (fo″to-re-sep′tor) [*photo-* + *receptor*]. A nerve end-organ or receptor which is sensitive to light.

photoscan (fo′to-skan). A two-dimensional representation (map) of the gamma rays emitted by a radioisotope, revealing its varying concentration in a body tissue, differing only from a scintiscan in that the printout mechanism is a light source exposing a photographic film.

photoscanner (fo″to-skan′ner). The system of equipment used in the making of a photoscan.

photoscope (fo′to-skōp) [*photo-* + Gr. *skopein* to examine]. A kind of fluoroscope.

photoscopy (fo-tos′ko-pe) [*photo-* + Gr. *skopein* to examine]. Skiascopy.

photosensitive (fo″to-sen′sĭ-tiv). Sensitive to light.

photosensitization (fo″to-sen″sĭ-ti-za′shun). Sensitization to light.

photosensitize (fo″to-sen′sĭ-tīz) [*photo-* + *sensitize*]. To sensitize a substance or an organism to the influence of light.

photostable (fo′to-sta″b'l). Unchanged by the influence of light.

photostethoscope (fo″to-steth′o-skōp). A lamp which transforms sounds amplified by a microphone into pulsations of light: used for recording the heart beats of the fetus.

photosynthesis (fo″to-sin′the-sis) [*photo-* + Gr. *synthesis* putting together]. A chemical combination caused by the action of light; specifically the formation of carbohydrates from carbon dioxide and water in the chlorophyll tissue of plants under the influence of light. Cf. *chemosynthesis.*

phototaxis (fo″to-tak′sis) [*photo-* + Gr. *taxis* arrangement]. The movement of cells and microorganisms under the influence of light.

phototherapy (fo″to-ther′ah-pe) [*photo-* + *therapy*]. The treatment of disease by the influence of light, especially by variously concentrated light rays.

photothermal (fo″to-ther′mal). Pertaining to the heat produced by radiant energy.

photothermy (fo′to-ther″me) [*photo-* + Gr. *thermē* heat]. The heat effects produced by radiant energy.

phototimer (fo″to-tīm′er). A timer used in photography to give a desired interval for exposure.

phototonus (fo-tot′o-nus) [*photo-* + Gr. *tonos* tension]. An irritable state of protoplasm due to the influence of light.

phototoxic (fo″to-tok′sik). Pertaining to a deleterious effect produced or promoted by exposure to light.

phototoxis (fo″to-tok′sis) [*photo-* + *toxis*]. Any injury due to overexposure to light or other radiation.

phototrophic (fo″to-trof′ik) [*photo-* + Gr. *trophē* nourishment]. Utilizing light in metabolism, as in certain green plants and bacteria.

phototropic (fo″to-trop′ik). Exhibiting phototropism.

phototropism (fo-tot′ro-pizm) [*photo-* + Gr. *tropos* a turning]. 1. The tendency of an organism to turn or move toward (*positive p.*) or away from (*negative p.*) light. 2. Change of color produced in a substance by the action of light.

phototurbidometric (fo″to-tur-bid″o-met′rik). Pertaining to the determination of the turbidity of a solution by colorimetric methods: used in study of the activity of various enzymes.

photovoltic (fo″to-vol′tik) [*photo-* + *voltic*]. A term applied to electromotive force due to light.

photoxylin (fo-tok′sĭ-lin) [*photo-* + Gr. *xylon* wood]. A kind of pyroxylin prepared from wood pulp: used in preparing a collodion, and employed in microscopy and minor surgery.

photronreflectometer (fo″tron-re″flek-tom′e-ter). An apparatus for measuring turbidity in precipitation reactions.

photuria (fo-tu′re-ah) [*photo-* + Gr. *ouron* urine + *-ia*]. The excretion of urine having a luminous appearance.

Phoxinus (fok′sĭ-nus). A genus of minnows. **P. lae′vis,** a minnow used to demonstrate the presence of chromatophore-stimulating hormone. When an extract of posterior pituitary is injected into the minnow, a red coloration appears at the point of attachment of the thoracic, abdominal, and anal fins.

Phragmidiothrix (frag-mid′e-o-thriks). A genus of microorganisms of the family Crenotrichaceae, order Chlamydobacteriales, made up of small disk-shaped cells occurring in attached trichomes which are articulated and unbranched, and are enclosed in extremely delicate, colorless sheaths with no deposits of iron or magnesium compounds. The type species is *P. multisepta′ta.*

phragmoplast (frag′mo-plast) [Gr. *phragmos* inclosure + *plastos* formed]. The barrel-shaped spindle within which the midbody forms in mitosis.

phren (fren) [Gr. *phrēn*]. 1. The diaphragm. 2. The mind, as seat of the intellect, or the heart, as seat of the passions.

phren- (fren) [Gr. *phrēn*]. Combining form denoting relationship to the diaphragm or to the mind.

phrenalgia (fre-nal′je-ah) [*phren-* + *-algia*]. 1. Psychalgia. 2. Pain in the diaphragm.

phrenasthenia (fren″as-the′ne-ah) [*phren-* + Gr. *astheneia* weakness]. Feebleness of mind.

phrenectomy (fre-nek′to-me). Phrenicectomy.

phrenemphraxis (fren″em-frak′sis) [*phrenic* nerve + Gr. *emphraxis* stoppage]. The operation of crushing the phrenic nerve.

phrenetic (fre-net′ik). 1. Maniacal. 2. A maniac.

phrenic (fren′ik) [L. *phrenicus;* Gr. *phrēn* mind; diaphragm]. 1. Pertaining to the mind. 2. Pertaining to the diaphragm.

phrenicectomized (fren″ĭ-sek′to-mīzd). Having the phrenic nerve excised or resected.

phrenicectomy (fren″ĭ-sek′to-me) [*phrenic* nerve + Gr. *ektomē* excision]. Resection of the phrenic nerve.

phreniclasia, phreniclasis (fren″ĭ-kla′se-ah, fren″ĭ-kla′sis) [*phrenic* nerve + Gr. *klasis* crushing]. Crushing of the phrenic nerve with a clamp.

phrenico-exairesis (fren″ĭ-ko-ek-si′re-sis). Phrenico-exeresis.

phrenico-exeresis (fren″ĭ-ko-ek-ser′e-sis) [*phrenic* nerve + Gr. *exairesis* a taking out]. Avulsion of the phrenic nerve.

phreniconeurectomy (fren″ĭ-ko-nu-rek′to-me) [*phrenic* + Gr. *neuron* nerve + *ektomē* excision]. Excision of a whole or a portion of the phrenic nerve; phrenicectomy.

phrenicotomy (fren″ĭ-kot′o-me) [*phrenic* nerve + Gr. *tomē* a cutting]. Surgical division of the phrenic nerve and its accessory for the purpose of causing one-sided paralysis of the diaphragm, which then becomes pushed up by the viscera so as to compress a diseased lung.

phrenicotripsy (fren″ĭ-ko-trip′se) [*phrenic* nerve + Gr. *tripsis* a crushing]. Crushing of the phrenic nerve; phrenemphraxis.

phrenitis (fre-ni′tis) [*phren-* + *-itis*]. 1. Inflammation of the brain. 2. Delirium or frenzy. 3. Inflammation of the diaphragm.

phrenoblabia (fren″o-bla′be-ah) [*phren-* + Gr. *blabē* hurt]. Mental disorder.

phrenocardia (fren″o-kar′de-ah) [*phren-* + Gr. *kardia* heart]. A psychic condition characterized by pain in the cardiac region, respiratory disorders, and cardiac palpitation. Called also *triad of Herz, cardiasthenia,* and *cardiovascular neurasthenia.*

phrenocolic (fren″o-kol′ik). Connecting the diaphragm and colon.

phrenocolopexy (fren″o-ko′lo-pek-se) [*phren-* + Gr. *kolon* colon + *pēxis* fixation]. The operation of anchoring the prolapsed colon to the diaphragm.

phrenodynia (fren″o-din′e-ah) [*phren-* + Gr. *odynē* pain). Pain in the diaphragm.

phrenogastric (fren″o-gas′trik). Pertaining to the diaphragm and the stomach.

phrenoglottic (fren″o-glot′ik). Pertaining to the diaphragm and the glottis.

phrenograph (fren′o-graf) [*phren-* + Gr. *graphein* to write]. An apparatus for recording the movements of the diaphragm.

phrenohepatic (fren″o-he-pat′ik) [*phren-* + Gr. *hēpar* liver]. Pertaining to the diaphragm and the liver.

phrenologist (fre-nol′o-jist). A person who practices phrenology.

phrenology (fre-nol′o-je) [*phren-* + *-logy*]. The study of the mind and character from the shape of the skull.

phrenopathic (fren″o-path′ik). Psychopathic.

phrenopathy (fre-nop′ah-the) [*phren-* + Gr. *pathos* disease]. Any mental disease or disorder.

phrenopericarditis (fren″o-per″ĭ-kar-di′tis) [*phren-* + *pericarditis*]. A condition in which the apex of the heart is attached to the diaphragm by adhesions.

phrenoplegia (fren″o-ple′je-ah) [*phren-* + Gr. *plēgē* stroke]. 1. A sudden attack of mental disorder. 2. Loss or paralysis of the mental faculties. 3. Paralysis of the diaphragm.

phrenoptosis (fren″op-to′sis) [*phren-* + Gr. *ptōsis* falling]. Downward displacement of the diaphragm.

phrenosin (fren′o-sin). A galactoside, probably $C_{48}H_{93}O_9N$ (Levene), obtained from brain substance. It yields on hydrolysis galactose, sphingosine, and phrenosinic acid.

phrenospasm (fren′o-spazm) [*phren-* + *spasm*]. 1. Spasm of the diaphragm. 2. Cardiospasm.

phrenosplenic (fren″o-splen′ik). Connecting the diaphragm and the spleen.

phrenosterol (fren″o-ste′rol). A sterol from brain substance.

phrenotropic (fren″o-trop′ik) [*phreno-* + Gr. *tropē* a turn, turning]. Exerting its principal effect upon the mind.

phrictopathic (frik″to-path′ik) [Gr. *phriktos* producing a shudder + *pathos* disease]. Causing a shudder: a term applied to a peculiar sensation caused by irritating a hysterical anesthetic area during recovery.

phronema (fro-ne′mah) [Gr. *phronēma* mind]. That portion of the cortex of the brain which is occupied by thought centers or association centers.

phronetal (fro-ne′tal). Pertaining to thought.

phrynin (fri′nin). A poisonous substance obtainable from the skin and secretions of various toads. Its properties resemble those of digitalin.

phrynoderma (frin″o-der′mah) [Gr. *phrynē* toad + *derma* skin]. A papular dry skin eruption, frequently accompanied by mild neuritic and eye symptoms, seen in East Indian laborers fed on a diet of maize meal: probably due to vitamin A deficiency. Also called *toadskin.*

phrynolysine (fri-nol′ĭ-sin) [Gr. *phrynē* toad + *lysis* dissolution]. The lysine or toxin from toad venom.

phthalate (thal′āt). A salt of phthalic acid.

phthalein (thal′e-in). Any one of a series of coloring matters formed by the condensation of phthalic anhydride with the phenols. Some of them have a purgative action. See *phenolphthalein.* **alpha-naphthol p.,** an indicator used in the determination of hydrogen ion concentration. It has a pH range of 9.3–10.5. **orthocresol p.,** an indicator used in the determination of hydrogen ion concentration. It has a pH range of 8.2–9.8.

phthaleinometer (thal″e-in-om′e-ter). An instrument for use in performing phenolsulfonphthalein tests.

phthalin (thal′in). Any one of a series of colorless compounds formed by reduction of phthalein.

phthalylsulfacetamide (thal″il-sul″fah-set′ahmid). Chemical name: 4′-(acetylsulfamoyl)phthalanilic acid: used as an intestinal anti-infective.

phthalylsulfathiazole (thal″il-sul″fah-thi′ah-zōl). Chemical name: 4′-(2-thiazolylsulfamoyl)-phthalanilic acid: used as an intestinal anti-infective.

phthalylsulfonazole (thal″il-sul-fon′ah-zōl). Phthalylsulfacetamide.

phthersigenic (ther″si-jen′ik). Causing the destruction of the stock in which they appear; a term applied to the form of mental defect characterized by deterioration or devolution.

phthinode (thin′ōd). A person with a predisposition to phthisis.

phthinoid (thi′noid). Resembling phthisis; consumptive; tuberculous.

phthiocerol (thi″o-se′rol). An alcohol, $C_{35}H_{72}O_3$, isolated from the wax of human tubercle bacilli.

phthiriasis (thir-i′ah-sis) [Gr. *phtheiriasis,* from *phtheir* louse]. Infestation with lice. See *pediculosis.* **p. inguina′lis, pubic p.,** infestation of pubic hairs with lice of the species *Phthirus pubis.*

phthiriophobia (thir″e-o-fo′be-ah) [Gr. *phtheir* louse + *phobia*]. Morbid dread of lice.

Phthirus (thir′us) [Gr. *phtheir* louse]. A genus of insects of the order Anoplura. **P. pu′bis,** the species which infests the hair of the pubic region and which is sometimes found in the eyebrows and eyelashes.

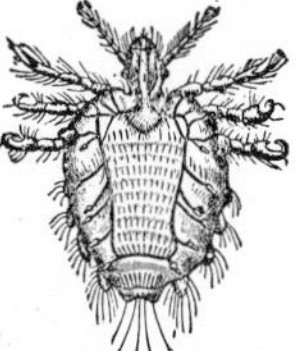

Phthirus pubis.

phthisic (tiz′ik) [Gr. *phthisikos*]. 1. Affected with phthisis. 2. A popular name for asthma.

phthisical (tiz′e-kal). Affected with phthisis, or of the nature of phthisis.

phthisicky (tiz′e-ke). Affected with asthma.

phthisiogenesis (tiz″e-o-jen′e-sis). The development of phthisis.

phthisiogenetic (tiz″e-o-je-net′ik). Causing, or pertaining to the causation of, phthisis.

phthisiogenic (tiz″e-o-jen′ik). Phthisiogenetic.

phthisiologist (tiz″e-ol′o-jist). A physician who specializes in pulmonary tuberculosis.

phthisiology (tiz″e-ol′o-je) [*phthisis* + *-logy*]. The sum of knowledge relating to pulmonary tuberculosis.

phthisiomania (tiz″e-o-ma′ne-ah) [*phthisis* + Gr. *mania* madness]. A morbid and mistaken belief that one has consumption.

phthisiophobia (tiz″e-o-fo′be-ah) [*phthisis* + Gr. *phobein* to be affrighted by]. Morbid dread of phthisis.

phthisiotherapeutical (tiz″e-o-ther″ah-pu′te-kal). Of or relating to the treatment of phthisis.

phthisiotherapeutics (tis″e-o-ther″ah-pu′tiks). Phthisiotherapy.

phthisiotherapeutist, phthisiotherapist (tiz″e-o-ther″ah-pu′tist, tiz″e-o-ther′ah-pist). One who makes a specialty of the treatment of phthisis.

phthisiotherapy (tiz″e-o-ther′ah-pe) [*phthisis* + *therapy*]. The treatment of phthisis.

phthisis (ti′sis) [Gr. *phthisis*, from *phthiein* to decay]. 1. A wasting away of the body or a part of the body. 2. Pulmonary tuberculosis. **abdominal p.,** tuberculosis of the intestines and mesenteric glands. **bacillary p.,** that due to the bacillus of tuberculosis. **black p.,** anthracosis. **p. bul′bi,** shrinkage and wasting of the eyeball. **colliers′ p.,** a form of interstitial pneumonia seen in colliers, and due to the inhalation of particles of coal dust. **p. cor′neae,** the shriveling and disappearance of the cornea after suppurative keratitis. **diabetic p.,** caseous bronchopneumonia in diabetic patients. **dorsal p.,** Pott's disease. **essential p.** (of the eye), ophthalmomalacia. **fibroid p.** 1. Chronic phthisis in which fibrous tissue is developed in the lung. 2. Interstitial pneumonia. **flax dressers′ p.,** a form of pneumoconiosis occurring in flax dressers. **glandular p.,** tuberculosis of the lymphatic glands. **grinders′ p.,** a combination of tuberculosis and silicosis of the lungs occurring among grinders in the cutlery trade and due to the inhalation of the steel dust. **hepatic p.,** tuberculosis of the liver. **laryngeal p.,** tuberculosis of the larynx. **Mediterranean p.,** brucellosis. **miner′s p.,** anthracosis. **p. nodo′sa,** miliary tubercle. **nonbacillary p.,** any pseudotuberculosis not due to a bacillus. **ocular p.,** ophthalmomalacia. **p. pancreat′ica,** a wasted condition associated with disease of the pancreas. **p. phlegmat′ica,** tuberculous disease without loss of flesh. **potters′ p.,** a combination of tuberculosis and silicosis of the lungs in potters due to inhalation of dust. **pulmonary p.,** tuberculosis of the lung. **p. rena′lis,** tuberculosis of the kidney. **stone cutters′ p.,** pulmonary disease of stone cutters due to the inhalation of particles of stone. **p. ventric′uli,** atrophy of the mucous membrane of the stomach and alimentary canal.

phyco- (fi′ko) [Gr. *phykos* seaweed]. Combining form denoting relationship to seaweed.

phycochrome (fi′ko-krōm) [*phyco-* + Gr. *chrōma* color]. 1. A blue-green pigment from various fresh-water algae of the simplest type. 2. Any plant or species of algae of the class Phycochromophyceae.

phycochromoprotein (fi″ko-kro″mo-pro′te-in). A colored, conjugated protein, with respiratory function, found in various seaweeds.

phycocyan (fi″ko-si′an). A blue chromoprotein found in seaweeds.

phycoerythrin (fi″ko-er′ĭ-thrin). A red chromoprotein found in seaweeds.

phycology (fi-kol′o-je) [*phyco-* + *-logy*]. The scientific study of algae.

Phycomycetes (fi″ko-mi-se′tēz) [*phyco-* + Gr. *mykēs* fungus]. An order of fungi in which reproduction takes place by union of equal gametes.

phygogalactic (fi″go-gah-lak′tik) [Gr. *pheugein* to avoid + *gala* milk]. Checking the secretion of milk; galactophygous.

phylacagogic (fi-lak″ah-goj′ik) [Gr. *phylakē* a guarding + *agōgos* leading]. Inducing the formation of phylaxins or protective antibodies.

phylactic (fi-lak′tik) [Gr. *phylaktikos* preservative]. Serving to protect; pertaining to or producing phylaxis.

phylactotransfusion (fi-lak″to-trans-fu′zhun). Immunotransfusion.

phylaxin (fi-lak′sin) [Gr. *phylax* guard]. Any substance that protects against infection and its consequences. There are two classes of phylaxins. The first, or *mycophylaxins*, act by destroying the microorganisms themselves; the second, or *toxophylaxins*, destroy or neutralize the poisonous products of the bacteria.

phylaxiology (fi-lak″se-ol′o-je) [Gr. *phylaxis* a guarding + *-logy*]. The study and practice of phylaxis or protection against infection.

phylaxis (fi-lak′sis) [Gr. "a guarding"] Protection against infection; the bodily defense against infection.

phyletic (fi-let′ik). Pertaining to a phylum, or to phylogeny.

Phyllanthus (fil-lan′thus). A genus of plants. **P. eng′leri,** a plant of northern Rhodesia known as suicide plant: when the bark or root is smoked it causes death.

phyllo- (fil′o) [Gr. *phyllon* leaf]. Combining form denoting relationship to leaves.

phyllochlorin (fil″o-klo′rin). A compound of chlorophyll and protein.

phyllode (fil′ode) [Gr. *phyllon* leaf + *eidos* form]. Resembling a leaf; a term applied to tumors which on section show a lobulated, leaflike appearance.

phyllo-erythrin (fil″o-er′ĭ-thrin). A derivative of chlorophyll formed in the intestinal canal of ruminant animals and found also in their bile.

phylloporphyrin (fil″o-por′fĭ-rin). A compound, $C_{32}H_{34}N_4O_2$, from chlorophyll, very similar to hematoporphyrin.

phyllopyrrole (fil″o-pir′ol). Trimethylethylpyrrole, $(CH_3)_3C_4(NH)C_2H_5$, from bile pigments.

phylloquinone (fil″o-kwin′ōn). Phytonadione.

phylloxanthine (fil″o-san′thin). A compound formed together with phyllocyanic acid by treating chlorophyll with hydrochloric acid.

phylobiology (fi″lo-bi-ol′o-je) [Gr. *phylon* tribe + *biology*]. The application of scientific methods in the field of human behavior.

phylogenesis (fi″lo-jen′e-sis). Phylogeny.

phylogenetic (fi″lo-je-net′ik). Phylogenic.

phylogenic (fi-lo-jen′ik). Pertaining to phylogeny.

phylogeny (fi-loj′e-ne) [Gr. *phylon* tribe + *genesis* generation]. The complete developmental history of a race or group of animals. Cf. *ontogeny.*

phylum (fi′lum), pl. *phy′la* [L.; Gr. *phylon* race]. A primary or main division of the animal or of the vegetable kingdom, including organisms which are assumed to have a common ancestry.

phyma (fi′mah), pl. *phy′mata* [Gr. "a growth"]. Any skin tumor or cutaneous tubercle; especially, a circumscribed swelling on the skin, larger than a tubercle, and produced by exudation into the subcutaneous tissue or the corium.

phymata (fi′mah-tah) [Gr.]. Plural of *phyma.*

phymatiasis (fi″mah-ti′ah-sis). Tuberculosis.

phymatiosis (fi″mat-e-o′sis). Tuberculosis.

phymatoid (fi′mah-toid) [Gr. *phyma* a growth + *eidos* form]. Resembling a tumor or phyma.

phymatology (fi″mah-tol′o-je) [Gr. *phyma* a growth + *-logy*]. The study of tumors.

phymatorhusin (fi″mah-to-roo′sin) [Gr. *phyma* a growth + *rhysis* flow]. A dark pigment from hair and melanotic tumors. It is a form of melanin.

phymatorrhysin (fi″mah-to-ris′in). Phymatorhusin.

phymatosis (fi″mah-to′sis). A condition characterized by the presence of phymata.

physalides (fi-sal′ĭ-dēz). Plural of *physalis*.

physaliferous (fis″ah-lif′er-us) [*physalis* + L. *ferre* to bear]. Physaliphorous.

physaliform (fi-sal′ĭ-form) [*physalis* + L. *forma* shape]. Resembling bubbles.

physaliphore (fi-sal′ĭ-fōr) [*physalis* + Gr. *phorein* to carry]. 1. A globular cavity in certain brood cells of cancers. 2. More correctly, the cell itself which contains such a cavity. Cf. *physalis*.

physaliphorous (fis″ah-lif′o-rus) [*physalis* + Gr. *phoros* bearing]. Containing bubbles or vacuoles.

physalis (fis′ah-lis), pl. *physal′ides* [Gr. *physallis* bubble]. 1. A large brood cell from a cancer. 2. A spherical cavity found in certain cells, such as the large brood cells of cancers or the giant cells of sarcoma.

physallization (fis″al-i-za′shun) [Gr. *physallis* bubble]. The formation of a permanent froth when a liquid is shaken together with a gas.

Physaloptera (fis″ah-lop′ter-ah) [Gr. *physallis* bubble + *pteron* wing]. A genus of nematode worms of the family Strongylidae found in the stomach and intestines of man and other vertebrates. **P. caucas′ica** occurs in Russia. **P. mor′dens,** a round worm not uncommon in Negroes in East Africa. **P. ra′ra,** a species found in the stomach of dogs. **P. trunca′ta,** a species found in the proventriculus of chickens and pheasants.

physalopteriasis (fis″ah-lop-ter-i′ah-sis). Infection with Physaloptera.

physconia (fis-ko′ne-ah) [Gr. *physkōn* pot-belly + *-ia*]. Swelling of the abdomen.

physeal (fiz′e-al). Pertaining to growth, or to the segment of tubular bone which is concerned mainly with growth (the physis).

physiatrician (fiz″e-ah-trish′an). Physiatrist.

physiatrics (fiz″e-at′riks) [*physio-* + Gr. *iatrikē* surgery, medicine]. The diagnosis and treatment of disease with the aid of physical agents, such as light, heat, cold, water, and electricity, or with mechanical apparatus.

physiatrist (fiz″e-at′rist). A physician who specializes in physiatrics.

physiatry (fiz′e-at″re). Physiatrics.

physic (fiz′ik) [Gr. *physikos* natural]. 1. The art of medicine and of therapeutics. 2. A medicine, especially a cathartic.

physical (fiz′e-kal) [Gr. *physikos*]. Pertaining to nature or to the body.

physician (fĭ-zish′un). An authorized practitioner of medicine. **attending p.,** a physician who attends a hospital at stated times to visit the patients and give directions as to their treatment. **resident p.,** a graduate and licensed physician resident in a hospital.

Physick's operation, pouches, etc. (fiz′iks) [Philip Syng *Physick*, American surgeon, 1768–1837]. See under the nouns.

physicochemical (fiz″ĭ-ko-kem′e-kal). Pertaining to physics and chemistry.

physicogenic (fiz″ĭ-ko-jen′ik). Due to physical causes; of physical origin, as opposed to *psychogenic*.

physicotherapeutics, physicotherapy (fiz″-ĭ-ko-ther″ah-pu′tiks, fiz″ĭ-ko-ther′ah-pe). Physical therapy.

physics (fiz′iks) [Gr. *physis* nature]. The science of the laws and phenomena of nature, but especially of the forces and general properties of matter.

physicum (fiz′ĭ-kum). A preliminary examination in German universities leading to a doctor's degree.

physinosis (fiz″ĭ-no′sis) [*physio-* + Gr. *nosos* disease]. Any disease due to physical agents.

physio- (fiz′e-o) [Gr. *physis* nature]. Combining form denoting relationship to nature or to physiology.

physiochemical (fiz″e-o-kem′e-kal). Pertaining to physiologic chemistry.

physiochemistry (fiz″e-o-kem′is-tre). Physiologic chemistry.

physiocracy (fiz″e-ok′rah-se) [*physio-* + Gr. *kratein* to rule]. The passive tendency in therapeutics which permits nature to take its course with little interference by man. Cf. *anthropocracy*.

physiogenesis (fiz″e-o-jen′e-sis). Embryology.

physiognomy (fiz″e-og′no-me) [*physio-* + Gr. *gnōmōn* a judge]. 1. The determination of mental or moral character and qualities by the face. 2. The countenance, or face. 3. The facial expression and appearance as a means of diagnosis.

physiognosis (fiz″e-og-no′sis) [*physio-* + Gr. *gnōsis* knowledge]. Diagnosis by means of the facial expression or appearance.

physiologic (fiz″e-o-loj′ik). Normal; not pathologic.

physiological (fiz″e-o-loj′ĭ-kal). Pertaining to physiology.

physiologico-anatomical (fiz″e-o-loj″e-ko-an″-ah-tom′e-kal). Pertaining to physiology and anatomy.

physiologist (fiz″e-ol′o-jist). A specialist in the study of physiology.

physiology (fiz″e-ol′o-je) [*physio-* + *-logy*]. The science which treats of the functions of the living organism and its parts. **animal p.,** the physiology of animals. **comparative p.,** a study of organ functions in various types of animals, vertebrate and invertebrate, in an effort to find fundamental relations in the physiology of members of the entire animal kingdom. **general p.,** the science of the general laws of life and functional activity. **hominal p.,** the physiology of human beings. **morbid p., pathologic p.,** the study of disordered function or of function in diseased tissues. **special p.,** the physiology of particular organs. **vegetable p.,** the physiology of plants.

physiolysis (fiz″e-ol′ĭ-sis) [*physio-* + Gr. *lysis* dissolution]. Natural dissolution and disintegration of tissue.

physiomedical (fiz″e-o-med′ĭ-kal). Of or relating to physiomedicalism.

physiomedicalism (fiz″e-o-med′ĭ-kal-izm) [*physio-* + *medicalism*]. A system of medical treatment in which only plant remedies are used, excluding those which are poisonous.

physiometry (fiz″e-om′e-tre) [*physio-* + Gr. *metron* measure]. Measurement of the physiologic functions of the body by serologic and physiologic methods.

physioneurosis (fiz″e-o-nu-ro′sis). A true neurosis as distinguished from a psychoneurosis.

physionomy (fiz″e-on′o-me) [*physio-* + Gr. *nomos* law]. The science of the laws of nature.

physiopathic (fiz″e-o-path′ik) [*physio-* + Gr. *pathos* disease]. Babinski's term for the nonpsychopathic functional nervous disorders.

physiopathologic (fiz″e-o-path″o-loj′ik). Pertaining to both the physiologic and pathologic conditions.

physiopathology (fiz″e-o-pah-thol′o-je) [*physio-* + *pathology*]. The science of functions in disease, or as modified by disease.

physiophyly (fiz″e-of′ĭ-le) [*physio-* + Gr. *phylon* tribe]. The evolution of bodily functions.

physiopsychic (fiz″e-o-si′kik) [*physio-* + Gr. *psychē* soul]. Relating to both body and mind.

physiopyrexia (fiz″e-o-pi-rek′se-ah). Artificial fever.

physiosis (fiz″e-o′sis) [Gr. *physioun* to puff up]. Distention of the abdomen with flatus.

physiotherapeutist (fiz″e-o-ther″ah-pu′tist). Physiotherapist.

physiotherapist (fiz″e-o-ther′ah-pist). A qualified practitioner of physical therapy.

physiotherapy (fiz″e-o-ther′ah-pe) [*physio-* + Gr. *therapeia* cure]. Physical therapy.

physique (fĭ-zēk′). Bodily structure, organization, and development.

physis (fi′sis) [Gr. *phyein* to generate]. The segment of tubular bone which is concerned mainly with growth. It consists of four zones, all related to chondrogenesis: zone of resting cartilage, zone of proliferating cartilage, zone of vacuolization, and zone of calcification.

physo- (fi′so) [Gr. *physa* air]. Combining form denoting relationship to air or gas.

physocele (fi′so-sēl) [*physo-* + Gr. *kēlē* tumor]. 1. A tumor filled with gas. 2. A hernial sac filled with gas.

Physocephalus (fi″so-sef′ah-lus). A genus of worms. **P. sexala′tus,** a species of thick, nonbursate worms found in the stomach of pigs.

physocephaly (fi″so-sef′ah-le) [*physo-* + Gr. *kephalē* head]. Emphysematous swelling of the head.

physohematometra (fi″so-hem″ah-to-me′trah) [*physo-* + Gr. *haima* blood + *metra* uterus]. The presence of gas and blood within the uterus.

physohydrometra (fi″so-hi″dro-me′trah) [*physo-* + Gr. *hydōr* water + *metra* uterus]. The presence of gas and fluid within the uterus.

physometra (fi″so-me′trah) [*physo-* + Gr. *metra* uterus]. Air or gas in the uterine cavity.

physopyosalpinx (fi″so-pi″o-sal′pinks) [*physo-* + Gr. *pyon* pus + *salpinx* tube]. Presence of pus and gas in the uterine tube.

Physostigma (fi″so-stig′mah) [*physo-* + Gr. *stigma* stigma]. A genus of tropical leguminous plants. The poisonous seed of *P. venenosum*, Calabar bean, a climbing plant of Africa, contains the alkaloids, physostigmine and calabarine.

physostigmine (fi″so-stig′min). An alkaloid usually obtained from the dried ripe seed of *Physostigma venenosum:* used as a cholinesterase inhibitor, and a miotic.

physostigminism (fi″so-stig′min-izm). Poisoning by physostigmine.

phytagglutinin (fi″tah-gloo′tĭ-nin). A phytotoxin which has the power of agglutinating red blood corpuscles.

phytalbumin (fi″tal-bu′min) [*phyto-* + *albumin*]. Vegetable albumin.

phytalbumose (fi-tal′bu-mōs) [*phyto-* + *albumose*]. An albumose of vegetable origin.

phytate (fi′tāt). A salt of phytic acid.

phytid (fi′tid). Any skin lesion due to dermatophytosis.

phyto- (fi′to) [Gr. *phyton* plant]. Combining form denoting relationship to a plant or plants.

phyto-anaphylactogen (fi″to-an″ah-fi-lak′to-jen). Phytosensitinogen.

phytobezoar (fi″to-be′zōr) [*phyto-* + *bezoar*]. A gastric concretion composed of vegetable matter such as skins, seeds, and the fibers of fruit and vegetables.

phytochemistry (fi″to-kem′is-tre) [*phyto-* + *chemistry*]. The study of plant chemistry, including the chemical processes that take place in plants, the nature of plant chemicals, and the various applications of such chemicals to science and industry.

phytochinin (fi″to-kin′in). A substance isolated from the leaves of certain grasses: said to have an effect on carbohydrate metabolism resembling that of insulin.

phytocholesterol (fi″to-ko-les′ter-ol). Phytosterol.

phytochrome (fi′to-krōm) [*phyto-* + Gr. *chrōma* color]. A plant chromoprotein.

phytodemic (fi″to-dem′ik) [*phyto-* + *epidemic*]. An epidemic attack of any disease of plants.

phytodetritus (fi″to-de-tri′tus). Detritus produced by the disintegration and decomposition of vegetable organisms.

phytogenesis (fi″to-jen′e-sis) [*phyto-* + Gr. *genesis* generation]. The origin and development of plants.

phytogenetic, phytogenic (fi″to-je-net′ik, fi″-to-jen′ik). Phytogenous.

phytogenous (fi-toj′e-nus) [*phyto-* + Gr. *gennan* to produce]. Derived from a plant, or caused by a vegetable growth.

phytoglobulin (fi″to-glob′u-lin) [*phyto-* + *globulin*]. Vegetable globulin.

phytohemagglutinin (fi″to-hem″ah-gloo′tĭ-nin). A hemagglutinin of plant origin.

phytohormone (fi″to-hor′mōn) [*phyto-* + *hormone*]. A plant hormone.

phytoid (fi′toid) [*phyto-* + Gr. *eidos* form]. Resembling a plant.

phytol (fi′tol). An unsaturated aliphatic alcohol, 3,7,11,15-tetramethyl-hexadecen-2-ol-l, $CH_3[CH(CH_3)(CH_2)_3]_3C(CH_3):CH.CH_2OH$. It is related to xanthophyll, to the carotenoids and to vitamin A and it exists in chlorophyll as an ester.

phytomelin (fi″to-mel′in). Rutin.

phytomenadione (fi″to-men″ah-di′ōn). Phytonadione.

phytomitogen (fi″to-mi′to-jen). A name proposed for a factor of vegetable origin that stimulates cell division.

Phytomonas (fi-tom′o-nas). A genus of bacteria that produce pathologic necroses in plants.

phytonadione (fi″to-nah-di′ōn). Chemical name: 2-methyl-3-phytyl-1,4-naphthoquinone: used as prothrombogenic agent.

phytone (fi′tōn). A peptone made from plant protein.

phytonosis (fi-ton′o-sis) [*phyto-* + Gr. *nosos* disease]. Any morbid condition due to a plant.

phytoparasite (fi″to-par′ah-sīt) [*phyto-* + *parasite*]. Any parasitic vegetable organism or species.

phytopathogenic (fi″to-path″o-jen′ik). Producing disease in plants.

phytopathology (fi″to-pah-thol′o-je) [*phyto-* + *pathology*]. 1. The study of plant diseases and their control. 2. The pathology of morbid conditions caused by schizomycetes and other vegetable parasites.

phytopathy (fi-top′ah-the) [*phyto-* + Gr. *pathos* disease]. Any disease of plants.

phytophagous (fi-tof′ah-gus) [*phyto-* + Gr. *phagein* to eat]. Eating vegetable food.

phytopharmacology (fi″to-fahr″mah-kol′o-je) [*phyto-* + *pharmacology*]. The study of the effect of drugs on plant growth.

phytophotodermatitis (fi″to-fo″to-der″mah-ti′-tis). A morbid condition of the skin resulting from the combined exposure to certain plants and then to light.

phytoplankton (fi″to-plank′ton) [*phyto-* + Gr. *planktos* wandering]. The minute plant (vegetable) organisms which, with those of the animal kingdom, make up the plankton of natural waters.

phytoplasm (fi′to-plazm) [*phyto-* + Gr. *plasma* thing formed]. Vegetable protoplasm.

phytoprecipitin (fi″to-pre-sip′ĭ-tin). A precipitin produced by immunization with protein substances of plant origin.

phytosensitinogen (fi″to-sen″sĭ-tin′o-jen) [*phyto-* + *sensitinogen*]. A protein substance of vegetable origin capable of inducing anaphylaxis; called also *phyto-anaphylactogen.*

phytosis (fi-to′sis) [*phyto-* + *-osis*]. Any disease of bacterial origin.

phytosterin (fi-tos′ter-in) [*phyto-* + Gr. *stear* fat]. Phytosterol.

phytosterol (fi″to-ste′rol). A plant sterol.

phytosterolin (fi″to-ste′rol-in). A glucosidic union of a sterol and glucose.

phytotherapy (fi″to-ther′ah-pe) [*phyto-* + Gr. *therapeia* treatment]. Treatment by use of plants.

phytotoxic (fi″to-tok′sik). 1. Pertaining to a phytotoxin. 2. Inhibiting the growth of plants.

phytotoxin (fi″to-tok′sin). An exotoxin produced by certain species of higher plants, notably *Abrus precatorius* (abrin), *Ricinus communis* (ricin), *Croton tiglium* (crotin), and *Robinia pseudacacia* (robin). Phytotoxins are resistant to proteolytic digestion, and are effective when taken by mouth.

phytotrichobezoar (fi″to-tri″ko-be′zōr) [*phyto-* + Gr. *thrix* hair + *bezoar*]. A bezoar composed of both plant fibers and hair.

phytovitellin (fi″to-vi-tel′in). Vitellin of vegetable origin.

phytoxylin (fi-tok′sĭ-lin) [*phyto-* + Gr. *xylon* wood]. A substance resembling pyroxylin: used in preparing celloidin sections.

P.I. Abbreviation for *International Protocol* (*Protocol Internationale*), and *protamine insulin.*

pia (pi′ah) [L.]. Tender; soft. **p. ma′ter.** See *pia mater*, infra.

pia-arachnitis (pi″ah-ar″ak-ni′tis). Inflammation of the pia-arachnoid; leptomeningitis.

pia-arachnoid (pi″ah-ah-rak′noid) [*pia* + *arachnoid*]. The pia and arachnoid considered together as one organ; arachnopia.

pia-glia (pi″ah-gli′ah). A membrane formed by the fusion of the pia mater and the marginal glia, and constituting one of the layers of the pia-arachnoid.

pial (pi′al). Pertaining to the pia mater.

pialyn (pi′ah-lin) [Gr. *piar* fat + *lyein* to loosen]. See *lipase.*

pia mater (pi′ah ma′ter) [L. "tender mother"]. The innermost of the three membranes (meninges) covering the brain and spinal cord, investing them closely and extending into the depths of the fissures and sulci. **p. m. enceph′ali** [N A, B N A], the pia mater covering the brain, very thin over the cerebral cortex, and thicker over the brain stem; the blood vessels for the brain ramify within it and, as they enter the brain, are accompanied for a short distance by a pial sheath. **p. m. spina′lis** [N A, B N A], the pia mater covering the spinal cord.

piamatral (pi″ah-ma′tral). Pial.

pian (pe-ahn′) [Fr.]. Yaws. **p. bois,** a disease similar to yaws, seen in the forest region of Guiana. It is marked by circumscribed swellings on the skin of the legs, on which ulcers form. There are enlargement of the inguinal glands and pains in the legs. **hemorrhagic p.,** verruga peruana.

piantic (pe-an′tik) [Gr. *piantikos* fattening]. Fattened for slaughter; a term applied to bacteria which are descended from sensitized parents and thus are more than ordinarily subject to agglutination or lysis.

piantication (pe-an″tĭ-ka′shun). The process of making subcultures from a culture of a particular strain of bacteria. The bacteria of the subcultures are more than ordinarily sensitive.

piarachnitis (pi″ar-ak-ni′tis). Pia-arachnitis.

piarachnoid (pi″ar-ak′noid). Pia-arachnoid.

piarhemia (pi″ar-he′me-ah) [Gr. *piar* fat + *haima* blood + *-ia*]. The presence of fat in the blood; lipemia.

piastrinemia (pi-as″trĭ-ne′me-ah) [It. *piastre* coin + Gr. *haima* blood + *-ia*]. Thrombocythemia.

Piazza's reaction, test (pe-aht′sahz). See under *tests.*

pica (pi′kah) [L.]. A craving for unnatural articles of food; a depraved appetite, such as is seen in hysteria and in pregnancy.

piceous (pi′se-us) [L. *piceis*]. Of the nature of pitch.

Pick's cell, disease [Ludwig *Pick*, Berlin physician, born 1868]. See under *cell*, and *Niemann-Pick disease*, under *disease.*

Pick's disease (piks) [Arnold *Pick*, Prague psychiatrist, 1851–1924]. See *lobar atrophy*, under *atrophy.*

Pick's disease, liniment [Filipp Josef *Pick*, Prague dermatologist, 1834–1910]. See *erythromelia*, and under *liniment.*

Pick's disease, syndrome [Friedel *Pick*, Prague physician, 1867–1926]. See under *disease*, def. 3, and under *syndrome.*

Pickrell spray, method (pik′rel) [Kenneth Le Roy *Pickrell*, American physician, born 1910]. A solution of 3.5 sulfathiazine in 6 per cent triethanolamine for spraying on burned areas.

Pickwickian syndrome (pik-wik′e-an) [from the description of the fat boy in Dickens' *Pickwick Papers*]. See under *syndrome.*

pico- (pi′ko) [It. *pico* small]. Combining form used in naming units of measurement to indicate one-trillionth of the unit designated by the root with which it is combined (10^{-12}).

picocurie (pi″ko-ku′re). A unit of radioactivity, being 10^{-12} curie, or that quantity of radioactive material in which the number of nuclear disintegrations is 3.7×10^{-2}, or 0.037, per second. Abbreviated pc. Called also *micromicrocurie* (abbreviated $\mu\mu$c).

picogram (pi′ko-gram). A unit of mass (weight) of the metric system, being 10^{-12} gram. Abbreviated pg. Called also *micromicrogram* (abbreviated $\mu\mu$g.).

picopicogram (pi″ko-pi′ko-gram). A unit of mass (weight) of the metric system, being 10^{-12} picogram, or 10^{-24} gram. Abbreviated ppg.

picornavirus (pi-kor″nah-vi′rus). A name applied to one of the extremely small ether-resistant ribonucleic acid viruses, the group comprising the enteroviruses and the coryzaviruses.

picrate (pik′rāt). Any salt of picric acid.

picrin (pik′rin) [Gr. *pikros* bitter]. A bitter substance from *Digitalis purpurea.*

picro- (pik′ro) [Gr. *pikros* bitter]. Combining form meaning bitter.

picrocarmine (pik″ro-kar′min). A stain prepared from picric acid and carmine and used in microscopy. It consists of a mixture of carmine, ammonia, and distilled water, to which is added an aqueous solution of picric acid.

picrogeusia (pik″ro-gu′se-ah) [*picro-* + Gr. *geusis* taste + *-ia*]. A pathologic bitter taste.

picrol (pik′rol). Potassium diiodoresorcin monosulfonate, $(OH)_2.C_6HI_2.SO_2OK$, a colorless and odorless, bitter, antiseptic powder: used as a wound dressing like iodoform.

picronigrosin (pik″ro-ni-gro′sin). A solution of picric acid and nigrosin in alcohol: used as a stain.

picropodophyllin (pik″ro-pod″o-fil′in). A crystalline principle from *Podophyllum peltatum:* medicinally active. It is said to be obtainable from podophyllotoxin also.

picropyrine (pik″ro-pi′rin). A substance, in inflammable yellow needles, derived from picric acid and antipyrine.

Picrorrhiza (pik″ro-ri′zah) [*picro-* + Gr. *rhiza* root]. A genus of herbs. The rhizome of *P. kuerva* is tonic and antiperiodic.

picrosaccharometer (pi″kro-sak″ah-rom′e-ter). An instrument used in estimating diabetic sugar.

picrosclerotine (pik″ro-skle′ro-tin). A poisonous alkaloid occurring in ergot of rye.

picrotoxin (pik″ro-tok′sin). An active principle obtained from the seed of *Anamirta cocculus*: used as a central nervous system stimulant.

picrotoxinism (pik″ro-tok′sĭ-nizm). Poisoning by picrotoxin.

pictograph (pik′to-graf). A chart of silhouette pictures used for testing acuteness of vision of children.

piedra (pe-a′drah) [Sp.]. A fungus disease of the hair in which the shafts are marked by the presence of hard gritty nodules. **black p.,** a fungus disease that affects the hairs of the scalp, occurs in tropical regions, and is caused by *Piedraia hortai.*

p. nos′tras, piedra of the beard. **white p.** affects the beard and mustache, is caused by *Trichosporon bigelii*, and occurs in temperate regions as well as the tropics.

Piedraia (pi″e-dri′ah). A genus of fungi of the family Endomycetales, several species of which are parasitic on hair, forming small black adherent nodules.

pier (pēr). A natural tooth or root which helps support a partial denture elsewhere than at its termination.

Piersol's point (pēr′solz) [George Arthur *Piersol*, Philadelphia anatomist, 1856–1924]. See under *point*.

piesesthesia (pi-e″zes-the′ze-ah) [Gr. *piesis* pressure + *aisthēsis* perception]. Pressure sensibility; the sense by which pressure stimuli are felt.

piesimeter (pi″e-sim′e-ter) [Gr. *piesis* pressure + *metron* measure]. An instrument for testing the sensitiveness of the skin to pressure. **Hale's p.,** a glass tube inserted into an artery for the purpose of ascertaining the blood pressure by the height to which the blood rises in the tube.

piezallochromy (pi″e-zal′o-kro-me) [Gr. *piesis* pressure + *allochromy*]. Change of color of a substance caused by crushing.

piezesthesia (pi″e-zes-the′ze-ah). Piesesthesia.

piezocardiogram (pi-e″zo-kar′de-o-gram). A graphic tracing of the changes in pressure caused by pulsation of the heart against the esophageal wall, recorded through the esophagus.

piezochemistry (pi-e′zo-kem″is-tre) [Gr. *piesis* pressure + *chemistry*]. That branch of chemistry which deals with the effect of pressure on chemical phenomena.

piezometer (pi″e-zom′e-ter) [Gr. *piezein* to press + *metron* measure]. 1. Piesimeter. 2. Orbitonometer.

piezotherapy (pi-e″zo-ther′ah-pe). Artificial pneumothorax.

pigment (pig′ment) [L. *pigmentum* paint]. 1. Any dye or paint; a paintlike medicinal preparation to be applied to the skin. 2. Any normal or abnormal coloring matter of the body. **autochthonous p.,** endogenous p. **bile p.,** any one of the coloring matters of the bile; they are bilirubin, biliverdin, bilifuscin, biliprasin, choleprasin, bilihumin, and bilicyanin. **blood p.,** any one of the pigments derived from hemoglobin; they are hematin, hematoidin, hemosiderin, hematoporphyrin, methemoglobin, and hemofuscin. **ceroid p.,** a coarsely globular, yellow, waxlike pigment found in the cirrhotic livers of rats kept on a low protein, low fat diet. **endogenous p.,** a pigment produced by the body's own metabolism. **exogenous p., extraneous p.,** a pigment which enters the body from without. **hematogenous p.,** any pigment derived from the blood or from the blood pigment. **hepatogenous p.,** bile pigment formed by disintegration of hemoglobin in the liver. **Lake's p.,** a mixture of lactic acid, formaldehyde solution, phenol, and water, suggested for relief of pain in laryngeal tuberculosis. **lipochrome p.,** lipochrome. **malarial p.,** a pigment formed by the malarial parasite from the pigment of the blood and deposited largely in the spleen and liver. **melanotic p.,** melanin. **metabolic p.,** any pigment produced by the metabolic actions of cells. **respiratory p's,** substances, such as hemoglobin, which take part in the oxidation processes of the animal body. **wear and tear p's,** lipochromes.

pigmentary (pig′men-ta″re). Pertaining to or of the nature of a pigment.

pigmentation (pig″men-ta′shun). The deposition of coloring matter; the coloration or discoloration of a part by a pigment. **carotinoid p.,** aurantiasis. **cervicofacial p.,** Riehl's melanosis. **extraneous p., extrogenous p.,** pigmentation caused by coloring matter introduced from outside of the body. **hematogenous p.,** pigmentation produced by the accumulation of hemoglobin derivatives such as hematoidin or hemosiderin. **malarial p.,** a pigmentation due to the accumulation, especially in the spleen and liver, of the dark-brown pigment liberated by those red blood cells which are destroyed by malarial parasites. **vagabonds' p.,** pigmentation of the skin due to lice.

pigmented (pig′ment-ed). Stained by deposit of pigment.

pigmentogenesis (pig″men-to-jen′e-sis) [*pigment* + *genesis*]. The production of pigment.

pigmentogenic (pig″men-to-jen′ik). Inducing the formation or deposit of pigment.

pigmentolysin (pig″men-tol′ĭ-sin). A lysin causing destruction of pigment.

pigmentolysis (pig″men-tol′ĭ-sis) [*pigment* + Gr. *lysis* dissolution]. Destruction of pigment.

pigmentophage (pig-men′to-fāj) [*pigment* + Gr. *phagein* to eat]. Any pigment-devouring cell, especially such a cell of the hair. Called also *chromophage.*

pigmentophore (pig-men′to-fōr). A cell which transports pigment.

pigmentum (pig-men′tum) [L.]. Pigment. **p. ni′grum,** the dark coloring matter which covers the internal surface of the choroid coat of the eye.

Pignet's formula (pēn-yāz′) [Maurice-Charles-Joseph *Pignet*, French physician, born 1871]. See under *formula.*

pigritis (pi-gri′tis) [L. *piger* slow]. Sluggishness and inactivity of spirit from alcoholism.

piitis (pi-i′tis). Inflammation of the pia mater.

Pil. Abbreviation of L. *pilula*, pill, or *pil′ulae*, pills.

pila (pi′lah), pl. *pi′lae* [L.]. A pillar, or pillar-like structure, such as a trabecula of spongy bone.

pilae (pi′le) [L.]. Plural of *pila.*

pilar, pilary (pi′lar, pil′a-re) [L. *pilaris*]. Pertaining to the hair.

pilaster (pi-las′ter). A ridge or fluting. **p. of Broca,** linea aspera femoris.

pilation (pi-la′shun) [L. *pilatio*]. A capillary fracture.

Pilcher bag (pil′cher) [Lewis Stephen *Pilcher*, Brooklyn surgeon, 1845–1934]. See under *bag.*

pile (pil). 1. [L. *pila* pillar]. An aggregation of similar elements for generating electricity. In nucleonics, a chain-reacting fission device for producing slow neutrons and for the preparation of radioactive isotopes. 2. [L. *pila* a ball]. A hemorrhoid. **esophageal p.,** a bleeding varix in the esophagus. **muscular p.,** layers of muscular tissue so arranged as to generate an electric current. **prostatic p.,** enlarged prostate attended by hemorrhage. **sentinel p.,** a hemorrhoid-like thickening of the mucous membrane at the lower end of a fissure of the anus. **thermo-electric p.,** a set of slender metallic bars which, on exposure to heat, generates a current of electricity that moves an index and is made to register delicate changes of temperature. **voltaic p.,** a battery for current electricity made up of a series of metallic disks.

pileous (pi′le-us). Hairy.

pileum (pi′le-um). Pileus.

pileus (pi′le-us) [L. "a close fitting felt cap"]. 1. One of the cerebellar hemispheres. 2. The membrane which sometimes covers a child's head at birth. **p. ventric′uli,** the proximal portion of the duodenum, starting at the pyloric canal and terminating 4–5 cm. distally. Called also *pars superior duodeni, duodenal bulb, duodenal cap, pyloric cap*, and *bishop's cap.*

pili (pi′li) [L.]. Plural of *pilus.*

piliation (pi″le-a′shun) [L. *pilus* hair]. The formation and production of hair.

pilimictio (pi″lĭ-mik′she-o). Pilimiction.

pilimiction (pi″lĭ-mik′shun) [L. *pilus* hair + *mictio* micturition]. Passing of urine containing hair or hairlike threads of mucus.

pilin (pi′lin). A structure resembling spongiopilin.

pill (pil) [L. *pilula*]. A small globular or oval medicated mass to be swallowed. **A. B. S. p.,** a laxative pill, containing aloin, extract of belladonna, and strychnine. **Addison's p.,** a pill of calomel, digitalis, and squill. **Aitken's p.,** a pill containing reduced iron, quinine sulfate, strychnine, and arsenic trioxide. **aloin, belladonna, cascara and podophyllum p.,** a preparation of cascara sagrada, aloin, podophyllum resin, belladonna extract, ginger oleoresin, glycyrrhiza, and liquid glucose in pill form: used as a cathartic. **Asiatic p.,** one containing arsenous acid and black pepper. **Baillie's p.,** Guy's p. **Barker's postpartum p.,** a laxative pill containing colocynth, hyoscyamus, nux vomica, aloes, ipecac, and podophyllum. **Becquerel's p's,** pills containing quinine sulfate, extract of digitalis, and colchicum seed. **Belloste's p.,** a pill containing mercury, white honey, aloes, black pepper, rhubarb, and scammony. **Blanchard's p.,** a pill of iodide of iron. **Blaud's p's,** ferrous carbonate p's. **blue p.,** a pill containing mercury. **Boisragon p's,** powdered scammony, mild mercurous chloride, compound extract of colocynth, aloes, and oil of caraway. **chalybeate p's,** ferrous carbonate p's. **Chapman's p.,** a pill of mastic and purified aloes, powdered ipecac, oil of peppermint or fennel. **cochia p.,** an actively cathartic pill of various composition, often aloetic. **Cole's p.,** a pill containing jalap, mass of mercury, purified aloes, and antimony and potassium tartrate. **compound cathartic p.,** a pill of colocynth, calomel, jalap, and gamboge. **Debout's p.,** a pill for migraine, made of extract of colchicum and quinine sulfate, and powdered digitalis. **dinner p.,** a pill to be taken with the meals. **enteric p.,** one coated with a substance, such as salol, which will not dissolve in the stomach. **ferrous carbonate p's,** pills containing ferrous sulfate, potassium carbonate, sucrose, tragacanth, althea, glycerin, water: used as a hematinic. **ferruginous p's,** ferrous carbonate p's. **Fothergill's p.,** a pill of calomel, squill, and digitalis. **Francis' triplex p.,** a pill of aloes, mercury, and scammony. **Gregory's dinner p.,** a pill of aloes, ipecac and rhubarb. **Gross's p.,** quinine sulfate, strychnine, morphine sulfate, arsenic trioxide, extract of aconite leaves. **Guy's p.,** a pill composed of digitalis, squill, extract of hyoscyamus, and blue mass. **Haën's p's,** pills composed of aloes, scammony, resin of jalap, powdered ginger, and soap. **Hall's p.,** a pill containing licorice extract, powdered soap, and molasses. **Heim's p's,** 1. Pills of ipecac, digitalis, opium, and extract helenium. 2. Pills of gamboge, digitalis, squill, antimony, and extract of Pimpinella. **Hinkle's p.,** aloin, belladonna, cascara, and podophyllum p. **Hooper's p's,** pills of aloes and myrrh. **Janeway's p's,** compound pill of aloes and podophyllin. **Keyser's p.,** protoacetate of mercury and manna. **Lady Webster's p.,** a dinner pill of aloes and mastic. **lapactic p.,** a commercial pill containing aloin, strychnine, and belladonna. **Lartigue's p's,** pills containing compound extract of colchicum and extract of digitalis: used in gout. **Meglin's p's,** pills for headache containing extract of hyoscyamus, extract of valerian, and zinc oxide. **Murchison's p.,** a pill for dropsy containing blue mass, digitalis, and squill. **Niemeyer's p's.** 1. A pill of quinine, digitalis, and opium. 2. Addison's pill. **Rufus' p.,** a pill of aloes and myrrh. **triplex p.,** a pill of aloes, mercurial mass, and resin of podophyllum: purgative and cholagogue. **Twining's p.,** a pill of calomel, blue mass, and ipecac: used in the treatment of dysentery. **vegetable cathartic p.,** a pill of colcynth, jalap, hyoscyamus, leptandra, and resin of podophyllum.

pillar (pil′ar) [L. *pila*]. A supporting structure, usually occurring in pairs. **p. of Corti's organ.** See *pillar cells,* under *cell.* **p's of diaphragm.** See *pars lumbalis diaphragmatis.* **p. of fauces, anterior,** arcus palatoglossus. **p. of fauces, posterior,** arcus palatopharyngeus. **p. of fornix, anterior,** columna fornicis. **p. of fornix, posterior,** crus fornicis. **p's of soft palate,** arcus palatini. **Uskow's p's,** two folds of the embryo attached to the dorsolateral portion of the body wall. From these pillars and the septum transversum the diaphragm is formed.

pillet (pil′et). A little pill, or pellet.

pilleus (pil′e-us). Pileus.

pillion (pil-yon′). A temporary replacement for an amputated leg.

pilo- (pi′lo) [L. *pilus* hair]. Combining form denoting relationship to hair, resembling or composed of hair.

pilobezoar (pi″lo-be′zōr). Trichobezoar.

pilocarpine (pi″lo-kar′pin). An alkaloid from leaves of *Pilocarpus microphyllus.* Uses: 1. cholinergic; 2. miotic.

Pilocarpus (pi″lo-kar′pus) [Gr. *pilos* wool or hair wrought into felt + Gr. *karpos* fruit]. A genus of rutaceous shrubs of tropical America.

pilocystic (pi″lo-sis′tik) [*pilo-* + *cystic*]. Hollow, or cystlike, and containing hairs: used of certain dermoid tumors.

pilocytic (pi″lo-si′tik). Composed of fiber-shaped cells.

pilo-erection (pi″lo-e-rek′shun) [*pilo-* + *erection*]. Erection of the hair.

pilojection (pi″lo-jek′shun) [*pilo* + L. *jacere* to throw]. The introduction of one or more hairs into the sac of an aneurysm by means of a pneumatic gun, to furnish the nucleus for a blood clot inside the sac; used in the treatment of intracranial saccular aneurysms.

pilology (pi-lol′o-je) [*pilo-* + *-logy*]. The study of the hair.

pilomotor (pi″lo-mo′tor) [*pilo-* + L. *motor* mover]. Causing movements of the hair.

pilonidal (pi″lo-ni′dal) [*pilo-* + L. *nidus* nest]. Having hairs for a nidus. See under *cyst* and *fistula.*

pilose (pi′lōs) [L. *pilosus*]. Hairy; covered with hair.

pilosebaceous (pi″lo-se-ba′shus). Pertaining to the hair follicles and sebaceous glands.

pilosis (pi-lo′sis) [*pilo-* + *-osis*]. Excessive or abnormal growth of hair.

pilosity (pi-los′ĭ-te). Hairiness.

pilous (pi′lus). Pilose.

Piltz's reflex, sign (pilts′ez) [Jan *Piltz,* Polish neurologist, 1870–1930]. See *attention reflex,* under *reflex.*

Piltz-Westphal phenomenon (pilts-vest′fahl) [Jan *Piltz;* A. K. O. *Westphal,* German neurologist, 1863–1941]. See *Westphal-Piltz phenomenon,* under *phenomenon.*

pilula (pil′u-lah), pl. *pil′ulae* [L.]. Pill.

pilular (pil′u-lar). Resembling or pertaining to a pill.

pilule (pil′ūl) [L. *pilula*]. A small pill, or pellet.

pilus (pi′lus), pl. *pi′li* [L.]. [N A, B N A] One of the filamentous appendages of the skin, consisting of modified epidermal tissue. See *hair.* **p. annula′tus** [pl. *pi′li annula′ti*), ringed hair. **p. cunicula′tus** (pl. *pi′li cunicula′ti*), burrowing hair. **p. incarna′tus** (pl. *pi′li incarna′ti*), ingrown hair. **p. incarna′tus recur′vus** [pl. *pi′li incarna′ti recur′vi*), ingrown hair that has repenetrated the skin after growing from the hair follicle. **pi′li multigem′ini,** multiple hairs growing from the same follicle, as a result of deep division of its base, producing, in effect, a cluster of separate papillae. **p. tor′tus** (pl. *pi′li tor′ti*), twisted hair.

pimelitis (pim″ĕ-li′tis) [*pimelo-* + *-itis*]. Inflammation of the adipose tissue.

pimelo- (pim′ĕ-lo) [Gr. *pimelē* fat]. Combining form denoting relationship to fat.

pimeloma (pim″ĕ-lo′mah) [*pimelo-* + *-oma*]. A fatty tumor; lipoma.

pimelopterygium (pim″ĕ-lo-ter-ij′e-um) [*pim-*

elo- + Gr. *pterygion* wing]. A fatty outgrowth upon the conjunctiva.

pimelorrhea (pim″ĕ-lo-re′ah) [*pimelo-* + Gr. *rhoia* flow]. Diarrhea with fat in the stools.

pimelorthopnea (pim″el-or″thop-ne′ah) [*pimelo-* + *orthopnea*]. Difficulty in breathing while lying down, due to excessive fatness.

pimelosis (pim″ĕ-lo′sis) [*pimelo-* + *-osis*]. 1. Conversion into fat. 2. Fatness, or obesity.

pimeluria (pim″el-u′re-ah) [*pimelo-* + Gr. *ouron* urine + *-ia*]. The presence of fat in the urine.

Pimenta (pĭ-men′tah) [Sp. "allspice"]. A genus of myrtaceous trees and shrubs of warm regions. The dried fruit of *P. officinalis* (*Eugenia pimenta*), a tree of tropical America, is allspice: aromatic, stimulant, and carminative.

piminodine (pi-min′o-dēn). Chemical name: ethyl-4-phenyl-1[3-(phenylamino)propyl]piperidine-4-carboxylate: used as a narcotic analgesic.

Pimpinella (pim″pĭ-nel′ah) [L.]. A genus of umbelliferous plants. The roots of *P. magna* and *P. saxifrago*, Burnet saxifrage, are tonic, diuretic, emmenagogue, and carminative.

pimpinellin (pim″pĭ-nel′in). A bitter, crystallizable principle, seen in colorless needles, from the root of *Pimpinella saxifraga*.

pimple (pim′p'l). A papule or pustule.

pin (pin). 1. A long slender metal rod for the fixation of the ends of fractured bones. 2. In dentistry, a peg or dowel by means of which an artificial crown is fixed to the root of a tooth. **Steinmann's p.**, a metal rod for the internal fixation of fractures. See *nail extension*, under *extension*.

pinacyanole (pin″ah-si′ah-nōl). An aniline dye, $C_{25}H_{25}N_2I$, used for sensitizing photographic plates for red: used also as a tissue stain.

Pinard's sign (pe-nahrz′) [Adolphe *Pinard*, French obstetrician, 1844–1934]. See under *sign*.

pince-ciseaux (pans″se-zo′) [Fr. "forceps-scissors"]. A cutting forceps used in iridotomy.

pincement (pans-maw′) [Fr.]. The pinching of the flesh in massage.

pincers (pin′serz). 1. Forceps. 2. The median deciduous incisor teeth in the horse.

pinch (pinch). To press together firmly in a limited area, as between the fingers or the points of a forceps, or the injury produced by such pressure. **devil's p's**, unexplained, but benign, purpura observed in women.

pine (pīn) [L. *pinus*]. 1. The name of many coniferous trees, chiefly of the genus *Pinus*. The pines afford turpentine, volatile oils, rosin, pitch, tar, etc. 2. Enzootic marasmus. **white p.**, the dried inner bark of *Pinus strobus*, used as an ingredient in compound white pine syrup.

pineal (pin′e-al) [L. *pinealis; pinea* pine cone]. 1. Shaped like a pine cone. 2. Pertaining to the pineal body.

pinealectomy (pin″e-al-ek′to-me) [*pineal* body + Gr. *exktomē* excision]. Excision of the pineal body.

pinealism (pin′e-al-izm). The condition due to derangement of the secretion of the pineal body.

pinealoblastoma (pin-e″ah-lo-blas-to′mah). Pinealoma.

pinealoma (pin″e-ah-lo′mah). A tumor of the pineal gland.

pinealopathy (pin″e-ah-lop′ah-the). Any disease of the pineal gland.

Pinel's system (pe-nelz′) [Philippe *Pinel*, alienist in Paris, 1745–1826]. See under *system*.

pinene (pi′nēn). A terpene, $(CH_3)_2.C.C_6H_7.CH_3$, found in turpentine and many essential oils.

pineoblastoma (pin″e-o-blas-to′mah). A tumor containing embryonic pineal gland cells.

pinguecula (ping-gwek′u-lah) [L. *pinguis* fat]. A yellowish spot of proliferation on the bulbar conjunctiva near the sclerocorneal junction, usually on the nasal side: seen in elderly people. Called also *palpebral blotch*. Recognized in B N A as an official term for an occasionally occurring feature, but omitted in N A.

piniform (pin′ĭ-form) [L. *pinea* pine cone + *forma* form]. Conical or cone shaped.

pining (pīn′ing). A condition of malnutrition in cattle and sheep in Scotland due to deficiency of potassium, cobalt, and iron in the vegetation.

pink-eye (pink′i). An epidemic, contagious conjunctivitis.

Pinkus' disease (pin′koos) [Felix *Pinkus*, German dermatologist, born 1868]. Lichen nitidus.

pinna (pin′nah) [L. "wing"]. The projecting part of the ear lying outside of the head (auricula [N A]). See *ear*.

pinnaglobin (pin″ah-glo′bin). A brown respiratory pigment found in *Pinna squamosa*, which contains manganese instead of iron.

pinnal (pin′al). Pertaining to the pinna.

pinocarveol (pi″no-kar′ve-ol). A terpene alcohol, $(CH_3)_2C{:}C_6H_7(OH){:}CH_2$, from *Eucalyptus globulus*.

pinocyte (pin′o-sīt). A cell (macrophage) which absorbs and digests tissue fluids.

pinocytosis (pi″no-si-to′sis) [Gr. *pinein* to drink + *kytos* cell + *-osis*]. The absorption of liquids by cells; especially the phenomenon in which minute incuppings or invaginations are formed in the surface of leukocytes, which close to form fluid-filled vacuoles.

pinocytotic (pi″no-si-tot′ik). Pertaining to or characterized by pinocytosis.

pinosome (pi′no-sōm) [Gr. *pinein* to drink + *sōma* body]. A small, fluid-filled vacuole occurring in the cytoplasm of a cell following the breakdown of the canal-like intrusions formed during pinocytosis.

Pinoyella (pi″no-yel′ah). A genus of fungi. **P. sim′ii**, a fungus of the trichophyton group which produces a transmissible disease of the glabrous skin of monkeys.

Pins' sign, syndrome [Emil *Pins*, Vienna physician, 1845–1913]. See under *sign*.

pint (pīnt). A measure of capacity (liquid measure), being 16 fluidounces, or the equivalent of 473.17 milliliters; symbol O (L. *octarius*), or abbreviated pt. The imperial pint is equal to 20 fluidounces.

pinta (pēn′tah) [Sp. "painted"]. A form of treponematosis, being a chronic dyschromic dermatosis endemic in certain parts of tropical America and characterized by the presence on the skin of colored spots, which may be white, coffee colored, blue, red, or violet. It is caused by *Treponema carateum* (the Wassermann reaction is usually positive), and is believed to be transmitted usually by direct person-to-person contact. Results of penicillin therapy are said to be excellent. Called also *mal del pinto, carate, azul, boussarole, tina, lota, empeines*, or *spotted sickness*.

pintado (pēn-tah′do). A person affected with pinta.

pintid (pin′tid). One of the flat erythematous skin lesions constituting the spreading eruption occurring in the second stage of pinta.

pinto (pēn′to). Pinta.

pinus (pi′nus) [L.]. The pineal gland.

pinworm (pin′werm). *Enterobius vermicularis*.

pio- (pi′o) [Gr. *piōn* fat]. Combining form denoting relationship to fat.

pio-epithelium (pi″o-ep″ĭ-the′le-um) [*pio-* + *epithelium*]. Epithelium in which fatty matter is deposited.

pionemia (pi″o-ne′me-ah) [Gr. *pion* fat + *haima* blood + *-ia*]. The presence of fat or oil in the blood; lipemia.

Piophila (pi-of′ĭ-lah). A genus of flies. **P. ca′sei**, the fly whose larvae are the "cheese skippers" and a common cause of intestinal myiasis.

Piorkowski's medium (pe″or-kov′skēz) [Max *Piorkowski*, German bacteriologist, born 1859]. See under *medium*.

piorthopnea (pi″or-thop-ne′ah) [*pio-* + Gr. *orthos*

upright + *pnoia* breath]. Dyspnea when lying down, due to obesity.

pioscope (pi′o-skōp) [*pio-* + Gr. *skopein* to examine]. An instrument for estimating the fat content of milk by comparing its color with the six shades painted on the instrument.

Piotrowski's sign (pe″o-trov′skēz) [Alexander *Piotrowski*, neurologist in Berlin, born in 1878]. See under *sign*.

pipamazine (pi-pam′ah-zēn). Chemical name: 10-[3-(4-carbamoylpiperidino)propyl]-2-chlorphenothiazine: used as an anti-emetic.

pipanol (pip′ah-nol). Trade mark for a preparation of trihexyphenidyl.

pipenzolate (pi-pen′zo-lāt). Chemical name: N-ethyl-3-piperidyl benzilate: used in parasympathetic blockade.

Piper (pi′per) [L. "pepper"]. A genus of plants producing kava-kava, betel, cubeb, matico, and pepper.

piperazine (pi-per′ah-zēn). A compound, $C_4H_{10}N_2$, prepared by the action of alcoholic ammonia on ethylene chloride, or by other methods. Various of its salts are used as anthelmintics. **p. calcium edathamil,** a compound, $C_{14}H_{24}CaN_4O_8.2H_2O$, prepared by the reaction of edathamil with calcium carbonate and piperazine: used in pinworm and roundworm infections. **p. citrate,** a compound, $3C_4H_{10}N_2.2C_6H_8O_7$, formed by reaction of an excess of piperazine hexahydrate with citric acid: used in treatment of pinworm and roundworm infections. **p. hexahydrate,** a crystalline compound, $C_4H_{10}N_2.6H_2O$. **p. tartrate,** a compound, $C_8H_{16}N_2O_6$, formed by the reaction of an excess of piperazine hexahydrate with tartaric acid: used as an anthelmintic.

piperidione (pi″per-ĭ-di′ōn). Dihyprylone.

piperidolate (pi″per-id′o-lāt). Chemical name: 1-ethyl-3-piperidyl diphenylacetate: used in parasympathetic blockade.

piperine (pi′per-in) [L. *piperinum*]. A crystallizable, slightly soluble alkaloid, $C_5H_{10}N.CO.(CH)_3CH.C_6H_3.O_2.CH_2$, from *Piper nigrum:* antiperiodic.

piperism (pi′per-izm) [L. *piper* pepper]. Poisoning by pepper.

piperocaine (pi′per-o-kān). Chemical name: 3-(2-methylpiperidino)propyl benzoate: used as a local anesthetic.

piperonal (pi-per′o-nal). Heliotropin.

pipet (pi-pet′) [Fr. *pipette*]. 1. A glass tube used in handling small quantities of liquid or gas. 2. To dispense fluid or gas by means of a pipet.

pipethanate (pi-peth′ah-nāt). Chemical name: 2-(1-piperidino)ethyl benzilate: used in parasympathetic blockade.

pipette (pi-pet′) [Fr.]. Pipet.

pipitzahoac (pi-pit″zah-ho-ak′) [Mex.]. The root and rhizome of *Perezia adnata*, *P. fruticosa*, and other Mexican plants: cathartic.

pipizan (pi′pĭ-zan). Trade mark for a preparation of piperazine.

pipradrol (pi′prah-dol). Chemical name: α,α-diphenyl-2-piperidinemethanol: used as a central nervous system stimulant.

piptal (pip′tal). Trade mark for preparations of pipenzolate methylbromide.

piqûre (pe-koor′) [Fr.]. Puncture, especially Claude Bernard's diabetic puncture.

piriform (pir′ĭ-form) [L. *pirum* a pear + *forma* shape]. Pear-shaped.

piroblue (pi′ro-bloo). A preparation of a dye combined with sodium cholate: used in the treatment of piroplasmosis.

Pirogoff's amputation, angle, operation (pir″o-gofs′) [Nikolai Ivanovich *Pirogoff*, Russian surgeon, 1810–1881]. See under the nouns.

Piroplasma (pi″ro-plaz′mah) [L. *pirum* pear + Gr. *plasma* something formed]. A name formerly given to a genus of protozoan parasites found in the red blood cells of animals. Now called Babesia. See also *Nuttalia* and *Theileria*.

piroplasmosis (pi″ro-plaz-mo′sis). Infection with piroplasma (*Babesia*). See also *Babesia* and *babesiosis*. **bovine p.** See *Texas fever*, under *fever*. **canine p.,** infection in dogs caused by *Babesia canis*, and marked by jaundice.

Pirquet's reaction (per-kāz′) [Clemens Freiherr von *Pirquet*, Austrian pediatrician, 1874–1929]. See *cutaneous reaction*, under *reaction*.

pis (pe) [Fr.]. Urination. **p. en deux temps** (pe″zaw-dah′taw), installment emptying of the bladder, as in diverticulum or vesical hernia.

piscicide (pis′ĭ-sīd). A substance poisonous to fish.

Piscidia (pĭ-sid′e-ah) [L. *piscis* fish + *caedere* to kill]. A genus of leguminous trees. The bark of *P. erythrina*, Jamaica dogwood, is a mild anodyne.

piscidin (pĭ-si′din). A neutral principle from *Piscidia erythrina:* anodyne and antispasmodic.

piscina (pĭ-si′nah) [L.]. A bathtub.

pisiform (pi′sĭ-form) [L. *pisum* pea + *forma* shape]. Resembling a pea in shape and size.

pisiformis (pi″sĭ-for′mis) [L.]. Pisiform.

Piskacek's sign (pis′kach-eks) [Ludwig *Piskacek*, Hungarian obstetrician, 1854–1932]. See under *sign*.

pit (pit). 1. A hollow fovea or indentation. 2. A pockmark. 3. To indent, or to become indented, by pressure. **anal p.,** the proctodeum. **arm p.,** the axillary fossa. **auditory p.,** a distinct depression appearing in each auditory placode, marking the beginning of the embryonic development of the internal ear. **basilar p.,** a pit in the crown of an incisor tooth above its neck. **chrome p's,** deep ulcers in the skin caused by contact with chromium. **costal p.,** fovea costalis inferior. **ear p.,** a slight depression in front of the helix and above the tragus, sometimes leading to a congenital preauricular cyst or fistula. **gastric p's,** foveolae gastricae. **Gaul's p's,** depressions in the corneal epithelium seen in neuroparalytic keratitis. **Herbert's p's,** cicatricial remains of limbal follicles in trachoma. **lens p.,** a pitlike depression in the ectoderm of the fetal head where the lens is developed. **nasal p.,** olfactory p. **olfactory p.,** the primordium of a nasal cavity. **postanal p.,** coccygeal foveola. **primitive p.,** a depression at the cranial end of the primitive groove; it may open into a neurenteric canal. **pterygoid p.,** fovea pterygoidea. **p. of the stomach,** the epigastrium or scrobiculus cordis.

pitch (pich) [L. *pix*]. 1. A dark, lustrous, more or less viscous residue from the distillation of tar and other substances. 2. Natural asphalt of various kinds. 3. The quality of sound dependent on the frequency of vibration of the waves producing it. **black p.,** an inflammable substance which is obtainable from the tar of various species of pine. **Burgundy p.,** an aromatic, oily resin from *Abies* (or *Picea*) *excelsa*, the Norway spruce of Europe: much used in plasters. **Canada p.,** a resin from *Tsuga canadensis*, the hemlock tree: useful in plasters, etc. **Jew's p.,** bitumen. **liquid p.,** ordinary wood tar. **mineral p.,** bitumen. **naval p.,** black p. **Trinidad p.,** asphalt from Trinidad, British West Indies.

pitchblende (pich′blend). A black mineral containing uranium oxide. From it are obtained radium and polonium.

Pitfield's sign (pit′fēldz) [Robert L. *Pitfield*, American physician, 1870–1942]. See under *sign*.

pith (pith). To pierce in the spinal cord or brain. See *pithing*.

pithecoid (pith′e-koid) [Gr. *pithēkos* ape + *eidos* form]. Apelike.

pithiatic (pith″e-at′ik). Curable by persuasion.

pithiatism (pith-i′ah-tizm) [Gr. *peithein* to persuade + *iatos* curable]. 1. A condition which is caused by suggestion and which renders the patient subject to persuasion. 2. The cure of nervous and mental disorders by persuasion.

pithiatric (pith″e-at′rik). Pertaining to persuasion as a means of treatment; capable of being cured by persuasion and suggestion.

pithiatry (pith-i′ah-tre). Medical treatment by persuasion or suggestion.

pithing (pith′ing). Destruction of the brain and spinal cord by thrusting a blunt needle into the spinal canal and cranium: done on animals to destroy sensibility preparatory to experimenting on their living tissues.

pithode (pi′thōd) [Gr. *pithos* wine cask + *eidos* form]. The nuclear barrel figure formed in mitosis.

pitocin (pĭ-to′sin). Trade mark for a solution of oxytocin for injection.

pitometer (pĭ-tom′e-ter). An instrument for measuring the flow of water in pipes.

PITR. Abbreviation for *plasma iron turnover rate.*

Pitres' sections, sign (pe-tres′) [Jean Albert *Pitres*, physician in Bordeaux, 1848–1927]. See under *section* and *sign.*

pitressin (pĭ-tres′sin). Trade mark for a solution of vasopressin for injection.

pitting (pit′ting). The formation of a small depression. The term is applied also to the removal from erythrocytes, by the spleen, of certain structures, such as iron granules, without destruction of the cells.

pituicyte (pĭ-tu′ĭ-sit) [*pituitary* + *-cyte*]. The dominant and distinctive fusiform cell composing most of the pars nervosa of the pituitary body.

pituita (pĭ-tu′ĭ-tah) [L.]. A glutinous mucus.

pituitarigenic (pĭ-tu″ĭ-tăr″ĭ-jen′ik) [*pituitary* + *gennan* to produce]. Produced by secretions of the pituitary gland.

pituitarism (pĭ-tu′ĭ-tar-izm). Disorder of pituitary function.

pituitarium (pĭ-tu′ĭ-ta′re-um) [L.]. Pituitary. **p. ante′rius,** anterior pituitary. **p. poste′rius,** posterior pituitary. **p. to′tum,** whole pituitary.

pituitary (pĭ-tu′ĭ-tăr″e). 1. Pertaining to or secreting a mucus or phlegm. 2. Pertaining to the hypophysis cerebri (pituitary gland). 3. A preparation of some part of the pituitary gland of domesticated animals that are used as food for human consumption: used therapeutically. **anterior p.,** a preparation of the dried, partially defatted, powdered anterior lobe of the pituitary gland of hogs, sheep, or cattle. **posterior p.,** a preparation of the dried, partially defatted, powdered posterior lobe of the pituitary gland of domesticated animals. **whole p.,** a preparation of the dried, partially defatted, powdered whole pituitary gland of domesticated animals.

pituitectomy (pĭ-tu″ĭ-tek′to-me). Excision of the pituitary gland.

pituitotrope (pĭ-tu′ĭ-to-trōp). A person exhibiting pituitotropism.

pituitotropic (pĭ-tu″ĭ-to-trop′ik). Pertaining to or marked by pituitotropism.

pituitotropism (pĭ-tu″ĭ-to-tro′pism) [*pituitary* + Gr. *tropos* a turning]. Pituitary constitution; a constitution in which the pituitary gland has an abnormally marked influence.

pituitous (pĭ-tu′ĭ-tus) [L. *pituitosus*]. Pertaining to mucus or characterized by its secretion.

pituitrin (pĭ-tu′ĭ-trin). A proprietary brand of posterior pituitary injection.

pituitrism (pĭ-tu′ĭ-trizm). Disorder of pituitary function.

piturine (pit′u-rin). An alkaloid, $C_{12}H_{16}N_2$, from *Duboisia hopwoodii*. It is the same as nicotine.

pityriasic (pit″ĭ-ri-as′ik). Pertaining to or affected with pityriasis.

pityriasis (pit″ĭ-ri′ah-sis) [Gr. *pityron* bran + *-iasis*]. A name applied to a group of skin diseases characterized by the formation of branny scales, specific types usually being indicated by a modifying term. **p. al′ba,** erythema streptogenes. **p. amianta′cea,** tinea amiantacea. **p. cap′itis,** p. sicca. **p. circina′ta,** a noncontagious skin disease with reddish, scaly patches, moderate fever, and usually a short and favorable course. **p. circina′ta et margina′ta,** a form caused by infestation with parasites. **p. furfura′cea,** p. sicca. **Gibert's p.,** p. rosea. **Hebra's p.,** dermatitis exfoliativa. **p. lichenoi′des,** a variety of parapsoriasis. **p. lichenoi′des et variolifor′mis acu′ta,** parapsoriasis varioliformis. **p. lin′guae,** geographic tongue. **p. pila′ris,** keratosis pilaris. **p. ro′sea,** a dermatosis characterized by papulosquamous eruptions on the back, legs, arms, and thighs. The lesions are pinkish oval patches covered with crinkled dry epidermis, and are arranged with the long axes parallel to the lines of the skin; called also *Gibert's disease* and *herpes tonsurans maculosus.* **p. ru′bra,** dermatitis exfoliativa. **p. ru′bra pila′ris,** a rare chronic inflammatory disease of the skin, characterized by the presence of fine acuminate, horny, follicular papules, and appearing in children or adults. It begins usually with severe seborrhea of the scalp and seborrheic dermatitis of the face, and is associated with striking keratoderma of palms and soles. Called also *Devergie's disease* and *lichen ruber acuminatus.* **p. sic′ca,** seborrhea of the scalp, with desquamation of dry branny scales (dandruff). **p. sim′plex,** a common skin condition, with desquamation of dry branny scales. **p. steatoi′des,** a scurfy condition of the scalp of a moist or greasy form. **p. versic′olor,** tinea versicolor.

pityroid (pit′ĭ-roid) [Gr. *pityron* bran + *eidos* form]. Furfuraceous or branny.

Pityrosporon (pit″ĭ-ros′po-ron). A genus of fungi which are yeastlike and produce no mycelium. **P. orbic′ulare,** a species which is a customary resident of normal skin, but is capable of causing disease (tinea versicolor) in susceptible hosts. **P. ova′le,** a lipid-dependent species which is abundant in sebaceous areas, such as the skin of the face and scalp, but is not known to be pathogenic.

Pityrosporum (pit″ĭ-ros′po-rum). Pityrosporon.

pivot (piv′ut). A dowel, or post; also used in dentistry to designate the point of rotation for a removable partial denture.

pix (piks), gen. *pi′cis* [L.]. Pitch. **p. burgun′dica,** Burgundy pitch. **p. ca′di,** juniper tar. **p. canaden′sis,** Canada pitch. **p. carbo′nis,** coal tar. **p. carbo′nis praepara′ta,** prepared coal tar. **p. junip′eri,** juniper tar. **p. liq′uida,** pine tar. **p. liq′uida oxyce′dri,** juniper tar. **p. liq′uida pi′ni,** pine tar. **p. lithan′thracis,** coal tar. **p. pi′ni,** pine tar.

PK. Abbreviation for *psychokinesis.*

PKU. Abbreviation for *phenylketonuria.*

P.L. Abbreviation for *light perception,* and *pulpolingual.*

P.L.A. Abbreviation for *pulpolinguoaxial.*

P. La. Abbreviation for *pulpolabial.*

placebo (plah-se′bo) [L. "I will please"]. An inactive substance or preparation, formerly given to please or gratify a patient, now also used in controlled studies to determine the efficacy of medicinal substances.

placenta (plah-sen′tah), pl. *placentas* or *placentae* [L. "a flat cake"]. 1. Any cakelike mass. 2. The cakelike organ within the uterus which establishes communication between the mother and child by means of the umbilical cord; listed in anatomical nomenclature [N A, B N A] it consists of a uterine and a fetal portion. The chorion, superficial, or fetal, portion, is surfaced by a smooth, shining membrane continuous with the sheath of the cord (*amnion*). The deep, or uterine, portion is divided by deep sulci into lobes of irregular outline and extent (the *cotyledons*). Over the maternal surface of the placenta is stretched a delicate, transparent membrane of fetal origin. Around the periphery of the placenta is a large vein (the *marginal sinus*), which returns a part of the maternal blood from the organ. Placentas vary in weight, size, thickness, form, and consistency. At term it weighs about 500 Gm., the proportion to weight of child being about 1 to 6, but sometimes, under certain pathological conditions, reaching 1 to 3. It is usually 1.5–2 cm. thick, and 15–18 cm. in diameter. **accessory p.,** a portion of placental tissue distinct from the main placenta. **p. accre'ta,** abnormal adherence of part or all of the placenta to the uterine wall, with partial or complete absence of the decidua basalis, especially of the spongiosum layer. **adherent p.,** one which adheres closely to the uterine wall. **annular p.,** one which extends around the interior of the uterus like a ring or belt. **battledore p.,** one with marginal insertion of the cord. **bidiscoidal p.,** one consisting of two separate discoidal masses, as in the macaques. **bilobate p., bilobed p.,** a placenta consisting of two lobes. **p. biparti'ta, bipartite p.,** bilobate p. **chorioallantoic p.,** one in which both the chorionic and allantoic membranes are significant components. **choriovitelline p.,** one in which the yolk sac becomes an intermediary in the fetal-maternal relationship. **p. circumvalla'ta, circumvallate p.,** a placenta in which a ringed infarct is raised from the surface and the attached membranes are doubled back over the edge of the placenta. **cirsoid p., p. cirsoi'des,** a placenta, the vessels of which appear to be varicose. **deciduous p.,** one that is cast off after delivery. **p. diffu'sa,** a placenta in which placental tissue is distributed over the chorionic membrane, as in swine. **p. dimidia'ta, dimidiate p.,** bilobate p. **discoid p., p. discoi'dea,** a disc-shaped placenta. **duplex p.,** bilobate p. **endotheliochorial p.,** one in which syncytial trophoblast embeds maternal vessels bared to their endothelial lining. **epitheliochorial p.,** one in which the uterine lining is not eroded but merely lies in apposition. **p. febri'lis,** the enlarged spleen seen in malaria. **p. fenestra'ta,** one which has spots where placental tissue is lacking. **fetal p., p. foeta'lis** [B N A], pars fetalis placentae. **fundal p.,** one which is attached to the fundus of the uterus in the normal manner. **furcate p.,** lobed p. **hemochorial p.,** one in which maternal blood comes in direct contact with the chorion. **hemoendothelial p.,** one in which maternal blood comes in contact with the endothelium of chorionic vessels. **horseshoe p.,** a crescentic form of placenta sometimes occurring in twin pregnancy. **incarcerated p.,** a placenta retained by irregular uterine contractions. **p. incre'ta,** placenta accreta with penetration of the uterine wall. **labyrinthine p.,** one in which maternal blood courses in channeled trophoblast. **lobed p.,** one that is more or less subdivided into lobes. **p. margina'lis, p. margina'ta,** a placenta which is surrounded by an unusual margin of elevated infarcted tissue. **maternal p.,** pars uterina placentae. **p. membrana'cea,** a placenta which is abnormally thin and spread out over a large area of the uterine wall. **multilobate p., multilobed p., p. multiparti'ta,** a placenta consisting of more than three lobes. **p. nappifor'mis,** p. circumvallata. **nondeciduous p.,** one in which the maternal component is not cast off after delivery. **p. obsole'ta,** one of two opposed placentas which have no vascular anastomosis. **panduriform p., p. panduri-for'mis,** a placenta composed of two halves side by side, resembling a violin in shape. **p. percre'ta,** placenta accreta with invasion of the uterine wall to its serosal layer, sometimes resulting in rupture of the uterus. **p. prae'via,** a placenta which develops in the lower uterine segment, in the zone of dilatation, so that it covers or adjoins the internal os. **p. prae'via centra'lis,** placenta praevia in which the placenta entirely covers the internal os. Called also *complete, total,* or *central placenta previa.* **p. prae'via margina'lis,** placenta praevia in which the placenta is just palpable at the margin of the os. Called also *lateral* or *marginal placenta previa.* **p. prae'via partia'lis,** placenta praevia in which the internal os is partially covered. Called also *incomplete* or *partial placenta previa.* **p. pre'via,** p. praevia. **p. reflex'a,** one in which the margin is thickened, appearing to turn back on itself. **p. renifor'mis,** a kidney-shaped placenta. **retained p.,** one which is either adherent or incarcerated by irregular uterine contractions, and which in consequence fails to be expelled after childbirth. **Schultze's p.,** a placenta which is expelled with the central part ahead of the periphery. **p. spu'ria,** an accessory portion having no blood vessel attachment to the main placenta. **stone p.,** a placenta that contains a great amount of calcareous deposits. **p. succenturia'ta, succenturiate p.,** an accessory portion attached to the main placenta by an artery and vein. **syndesmochorial p.,** one in which the lining epithelium of the uterus is the only maternal tissue eroded. **p. trilo'ba, trilobate p.,** a placenta having three lobes. **p. triparti'ta, tripartite p.,** trilobate p. **p. trip'lex,** trilobate p. **p. truffée,** a placenta containing small, dark-red infarcts. **p. uteri'na** [B N A], **uterine p.,** pars uterina placentae. **velamentous p.,** one in which the umbilical cord is attached on the adjoining membranes. **villous p.,** one characterized by the presence of bushy villi which are outgrowths of the chorion. **yolk-sac p.,** choriovitelline p. **zonary p., zonular p.** 1. Annular placenta. 2. A belt-shaped placenta, as occurs in carnivores.

placental (plah-sen'tal). Pertaining to the placenta.

Placentalia (pla"sen-ta'le-ah). A division of mammals whose embryos are nourished through a placenta. It includes all mammals except marsupials and monotremes.

placentation (plas"en-ta'shun). The manner of formation and attachment of the placenta.

placentin (plah-sen'tin). A defatted desiccation product of beef placenta.

placentitis (plas"en-ti'tis). Inflammation of the placenta.

placentocytotoxin (plah-sen"to-si"to-tok'sin). A substance that has a poisonous action on placental cells.

placentogenesis (plah-sen"to-jen'e-sis) [*placenta* + *genesis*]. The origin and development of the placenta.

placentography (plas"en-tog'rah-fe). Radiological visualization of the placenta after the injection of a contrast medium. **indirect p.,** roentgenographic measurement of the space between the placenta and the presenting head of the fetus, for the recognition of placenta previa.

placentoid (plah-sen'toid). Resembling the placenta.

placentologist (plas"en-tol'o-jist). A specialist in placentology.

placentology (plas"en-tol'o-je). The scientific study of the development, structure, and functioning of the placenta. **comparative p.,** the scientific study of the development, structure, and functioning of the placenta in different species of animals.

placentolysin (plas"en-tol'ĭ-sin) [*placenta* + Gr. *lysis* dissolution]. A lysin formed in the serum of an animal into which have been injected placenta cells from another animal. It is destructive to the placenta of animals of the species from which the cells were originally taken.

placentoma (plas"en-to'mah). A neoplasm derived from a portion of the placenta retained after an abortion.

placentopathy (plas"en-top'ah-the). Any disease of the placenta.

placentotherapy (plah-sen"to-ther'ah-pe) [*placenta* + Gr. *therapeia* treatment]. The therapeutic use of preparations of the placenta.

Placido's disk (plah-si′dōz) [A. *Placido*, Portuguese oculist]. See under *disk*.

placidyl (plas′ĭ-dil). Trade mark for a preparation of ethchlorvynol.

placode (plak′ōd) [Gr. *plax* plate + *eidos* form]. A platelike structure, especially a thickened plate of ectoderm in the early embryo, from which a sense organ develops. **auditory p.,** a thickened epidermal plate located midway alongside the hind brain in the early embryo, from which the internal ear ultimately develops. **dorsolateral p's,** a series of placodes giving rise to the acoustic and lateral line organs. **epibranchial p's,** a series of placodes located dorsal to the branchial grooves that contribute to adjacent cerebral ganglia. **lens p.,** a thickened area of ectoderm directly overlying the optic vesicle in the early embryo, from which the lens develops. **olfactory p.,** an oval area of thickened ectoderm on either ventrolateral surface of the head of the early embryo, constituting the first indication of the olfactory organ.

placuntitis (pla″kun-ti′tis) [Gr. *plakous* flat cake + *-itis*]. Inflammation of the placenta.

placuntoma (pla″kun-to′mah) [Gr. *plakous* flat cake + *-oma*]. Placentoma.

pladaroma (plad″ah-ro′mah). Pladarosis.

pladarosis (plad″ah-ro′sis) [Gr. *pladaros* damp + *-osis*]. A soft or flaccid tumor of the eyelid.

plagiocephalic (pla″je-o-se-fal′ik). Characterized by plagiocephaly.

plagiocephalism (pla″je-o-sef′ah-lism). Plagiocephaly.

plagiocephaly (pla″je-o-sef′ah-le) [Gr. *plagios* oblique + *kephalē* head]. An unsymmetrical and twisted condition of the head, resulting from irregular closure of the cranial sutures.

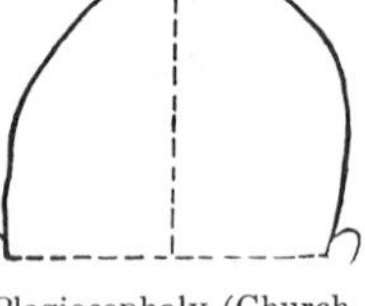

Plagiocephaly (Church and Peterson).

plague (plāg) [L. *plaga, pestis;* Gr. *plēgē* stroke]. An acute febrile, infectious disease with a high fatality rate, caused by *Pasteurella pestis;* it begins with fever and chills, quickly followed by great prostration similar to that of the typhoid state, and frequently attended with dilirium, headache, vomiting, and diarrhea. It is primarily a disease of rats and other rodents and is transmitted to man from infected rodents by the bite of fleas of several genera, or communicated from patient to patient. Called also *pest* and *oriental plague.* See also *bubonic plague, pneumonic plague,* and *septicemic plague.* **ambulatory p.,** a mild form of bubonic plague, with little or no toxemia. **black p.,** hemorrhagic p. **blood p.,** nambi-uvu. **bubonic p., p. bubon′ica,** plague which is marked by swelling of the lymph nodes, forming buboes in the femoral, inguinal, axillary, and cervical regions. The severe form, with septicemia producing petechial hemorrhages, is known as *black death, pestis fulminans,* and *pestis major.* **canine p.,** black tongue of dogs. **cat p.,** panleukopenia. **cattle p.,** a viral disease of cattle, which sometimes affects sheep and goats, marked by fever and croupous diphtheritic lesions of the intestinal tract. Called also *pestis bovina, rinderpest,* and *contagious typhus of cattle.* **cellulocutaneous p.,** plague marked by inflammation and necrosis of the skin and subcutaneous tissues and often associated with involvement of the lymph nodes. **defervescing p.,** a form which ends by a crisis. **fowl p.,** a viral disease of domestic fowls occurring in northern Italy, Germany, and France. Called also *chickenpest* and *fowl pest.* **glandular p.,** bubonic p. **hemorrhagic p.,** a severe form of plague with hemorrhages into the mucous membrane and the skin. **hog p.,** hog cholera. **larval p.,** ambulatory p. **lung p.,** pleuropneumonia, def. 2. **Nebraska-Kansas p.,** Borna disease. **Pahvant Valley p.,** tularemia. **pneumonic p.,** plague in which there is extensive involvement of the lungs, and the sputum is loaded with the causative organisms. **premonitory p.,** a mild form which sometimes foreruns the typical endemic variety. **reindeer p.,** an epidemic disease among the reindeer of Lapland, which kills thousands of calves and young animals. The cadavers show emphysematous edema. **rodent p.,** plague affecting rodents. **septicemic p.,** plague in which there is massive invasion of the blood stream, resulting in death before the appearance of buboes or of pulmonic manifestations. **Siberian p.,** anthrax. **siderating p.,** septicemic p. **Stuttgart dog p.,** Stuttgart disease. **swine p.,** pasteurellosis occurring in swine. **sylvatic p.,** plague of the woods, as for example, the plague widely spread and still spreading among the ground squirrels and other wild rodents of the western U.S.A. **tarabagan p.,** tarabagania tchuma. **Vanin p.,** parangi. **white p.,** tuberculosis.

plakins (pla′kinz). Substances similar to leukins that can be extracted from blood platelets.

Planck's constant, theory (planks) [Max *Planck,* German physicist, 1858–1947]. See under *constant,* and *quantum theory,* under *theory.*

plane (plān) [L. *planus*]. 1. A flat surface determined by the position of three points in space. 2. A specified level, as the plane of anesthesia. **Addison's p's,** a series of planes used as landmarks in the topography of the thorax and abdomen. **Aeby's p.,** one passing through the nasion and basion, perpendicular to the median plane of the cranium. **auricular p. of sacral bone,** facies auricularis ossis sacri. **auriculo-infraorbital p.,** Frankfort horizontal p. **axial p.,** one parallel with the long axis of a solid body, such as a tooth. **axiobuccolingual p.,** one parallel with the long axis of a posterior tooth and passing through its buccal and lingual surfaces. **axiolabiolingual p.,** one parallel with the long axis of an anterior tooth and passing through its labial and lingual surfaces. **axiomesiodistal p.,** one parallel with the long axis of a tooth and passing through its mesial and distal surfaces. **Baer's p.,** one passing through the upper border of the zygomatic arches. **base p.,** an imaginary plane upon which is estimated the retention of an artificial denture. **bite p.,** occlusal p. **Blumenbach's p.,** a plane determined by the base of a skull from which the lower jaw has been removed. **Bolton-nasion p.,** nasion-postcondylare p. **Broadbent-Bolton p.,** nasion-

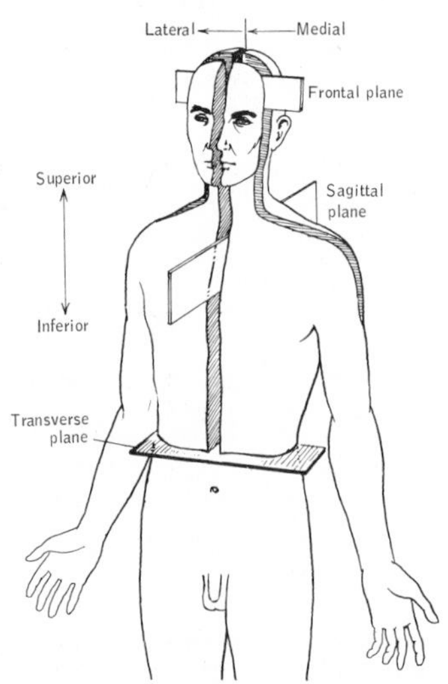

Planes of the body. (Davenport.) Anterior view, in the anatomical position, with standard planes of reference shown by cleavages.

postcondylare p. **Broca's p.**, visual p. **buccolingual p.**, one passing through the buccal and lingual surfaces of a posterior tooth. **coronal p.**, frontal p. **cove p.**, a wave in an electrocardiogram, being an inverted wave preceded and followed by a slight elevation. **datum p.**, a given plane from which craniometric measurements are made. **Daubenton's p.**, one passing through the opisthion and the lower edges of the orbits. **eye-ear p.**, Frankfort horizontal p. **facial p's**, various planes determined by certain landmarks of the face, such as the Frankfort horizontal plane, and the orbital plane. **Frankfort horizontal p.**, a horizontal plane represented in profile by a line between the lowest point on the margin of the orbit and the highest point on the margin of the auditory meatus. **frontal p.**, any plane passing longitudinally through the body from side to side, at right angles to the median plane, and dividing the body into front and back parts. So called because such a plane roughly parallels the frontal suture of the skull. **guide p.** 1. Any plane that guides movement. 2. The plane developed in the occlusal surfaces of the occlusion rims, to position the mandible in centric relation. **Hensen's p.**, one passing through the center of a series of sarcous elements of a muscle fibril. **Hodge's p's**, a series of planes running parallel with the pelvic inlet, the first parallel being in the inlet, the second parallel touching the arch of the pubis and striking the lower part of the second sacral vertebra, the third cutting the spines of the ischia, and the fourth passing through the tip of the coccyx. **horizontal p.**, any plane passing through the body, at right angles to both the median and the frontal plane, and dividing the body into upper and

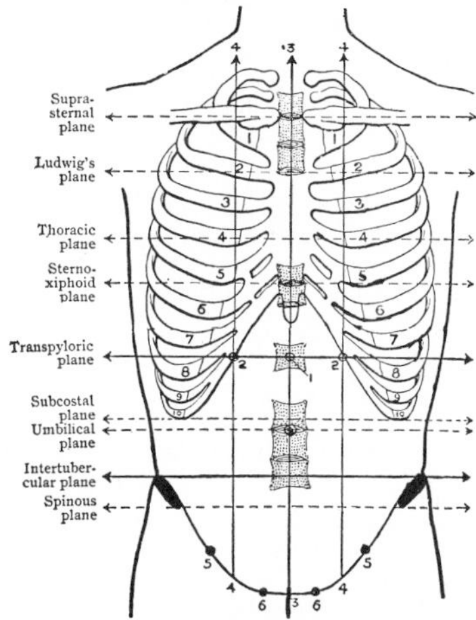

Planes of the trunk. (Rawling.)

lower parts; in dentistry, a plane passing through a tooth at right angles to its long axis. Called also *transverse p.* **interparietal p. of occipital bone**, planum occipitale. **intertubercular p.**, a horizontal plane transecting the trunk at the level of the tubercle of the iliac crest. **labiolingual p.**, one passing through the labial and lingual surfaces of an anterior tooth. **Listing's p.**, a transverse vertical plane perpendicular to the anteroposterior axis of the eye, and containing the center of motion of the eyes; in it lie the transverse and vertical axes of ocular rotation. **Ludwig's p.**, a horizontal plane transecting the trunk at about the level of the joint between the fourth and fifth thoracic vertebrae. **Meckel's p.**, one passing through the auricular and alveolar points. **median p.**, an imaginary plane passing longitudinally through the body from front to back and dividing it into right and left halves. **mesiodistal p.**, one passing through the mesial and distal surfaces of a tooth. **midpelvic p.**, narrow pelvic p. **midsagittal p.**, one passing vertically through the midline of the body, dividing it into right and left halves. **Morton's p.**, one passing through the most projecting points of the parietal and occipital protuberances. **nasion-postcondylare p.**, one passing at right angles to the midsagittal plane, and determined in profile by a line connecting the nasion and postcondylare. **nuchal p. of occipital bone**, planum nuchale. **occipital p.**, planum occipitale. **occlusal p.**, **p. of occlusion**, the hypothetical horizontal plane formed by the contacting surfaces of the upper and lower teeth when the jaws are closed. **orbital p.** 1. planum orbitale. 2. Visual plane. **orbital p. of frontal bone**, pars orbitalis ossis frontalis. **parasagittal p.**, a sagittal plane not passing through the exact midline of the body. **pelvic p.**, one determined by certain landmarks of the innominate bone. **pelvic p., narrow**, an ovoid plane passing through the apex of the pubic arch, the spines of the ischia, and the end of the sacrum. **pelvic p., wide**, an irregularly ovoid plane passing from the middle of the pubis to the junction of the second and third sacral vertebrae, at about the center of the excavation of the pelvis. **pelvic p. of outlet**, a plane passing through the arch of the pubis, the rami of the pubis, the ischial tuberosities, and the tip of the coccyx. See *pelvic outlet.* **popliteal p. of femur**, facies poplitea femoris. **p's of reference**, planes which are referred to as a guide to the location of specific anatomical sites, or of other planes. **p. of regard**, one passing through the center of rotation and the point of fixation in the eye. **sagittal p.**, a vertical plane that passes through the body parallel to the sagittal suture and divides the body into left and right portions. **semicircular p. of frontal bone**, facies temporalis ossis frontalis. **semicircular p. of parietal bone**, planum temporale. **semicircular p. of squama temporalis**, facies temporalis partis squamosae ossis temporalis. **spinous p.**, a horizontal plane transecting the trunk at the level of the anterior superior iliac spine. **sternal p.**, planum sternale. **sternoxiphoid p.**, a horizontal plane transecting the trunk at about the level of the xiphisternal joint. **subcostal p.**, a horizontal plane transecting the trunk at the level of the lower margin of the tenth rib. **suprasternal p.**, a horizontal plane transecting the trunk at the level of the jugular notch. **temporal p.**, planum temporale. **thoracic p.**, a horizontal plane transecting the trunk at about the level of the fourth intercostal space. **tooth p.**, any hypothetical plane passing through a tooth. **transpyloric p.**, a horizontal plane transecting the trunk at about the level of the eighth intercostal space. **transverse p.**, one passing horizontally through the body, at right angles to both the sagittal and the frontal plane, and dividing the body into upper and lower portions. **umbilical p.**, a horizontal plane transecting the trunk at the level of the umbilicus. **vertical p.**, any plane of the body perpendicular to the horizon. **visual p.**, one passing through the visual axes of the two eyes.

planigram (pla'nĭ-gram). A roentgenogram of a structure at a selected level, made by body section roentgenography.

planigraphy (plah-nig'rah-fe). Body section roentgenography.

planimeter (pla-nim'e-ter) [L. *planus* plane + Gr. *metron* measure]. An instrument used in measuring the area of surfaces.

planithorax (plan"ĭ-tho'raks). A diagram of the front and back of the chest.

plankton (plank'ton) [Gr. *planktos* wandering]. A collective name for the minute free-floating organisms which live in practically all natural waters.

planocellular (pla"no-sel'u-lar). Made up of flat cells.

planoconcave (pla"no-kon'kāv). Flat on one side and concave on the other.

planoconvex (pla″no-kon′veks). Flat on one side and convex on the other.

planocyte (pla′no-sit) [Gr. *planē* wandering + *-cyte*]. A wandering cell.

planography (plah-nog′rah-fe). Body section roentgenography.

Planorbis (plan-or′bis). A genus of snails. Several species act as intermediate hosts for *Schistosoma mansoni; P. boissyi,* in Egypt; *P. guadelupensis,* in Venezuela; *P. olivaceus,* in Brazil.

planotopokinesia (pla″no-top″o-ki-ne′ze-ah) [Gr. *planē* wandering + *topos* place + *kinēsis* movement]. Disturbance of the power of orientation in space.

planta (plan′tah), pl. *plan′tae* [L.]. [N A, B N A] The under surface (sole) of the foot.

plantaginis semen (plan-taj′ĭ-nis se′men) [L.]. Psyllium seed.

Plantago (plan-ta′go). A genus of herbs of the family Plantaginaceae, including three species, *P. in′dica, P. ova′ta,* and *P. psyllium,* whose seeds are used as a cathartic. A preparation of the separated mucilaginous outer layers of the seeds of *P. ovata* (*Plantago ovata coating*) is used in simple constipation resulting from lack of sufficient bulk in the intestine.

plantalgia (plan-tal′je-ah) [L. *planta* sole + *-algia*]. A painful condition of the sole of the foot.

plantar (plan′tar). Pertaining to the sole of the foot.

plantaris (plan-tah′ris) [L.]. Plantar; in official anatomical nomenclature, designating relationship to the sole of the foot.

plantation (plan-ta′shun) [L. *plantare* to plant]. The insertion or application of tissue, such as a tooth, or of other material, in or on the human body. It includes *implantation,* the insertion of similar or other material within the body tissues, as of an artificial or natural tooth into a new socket, or of a therapeutic agent or device; *replantation,* return of body tissue to its original site, as reinsertion of a tooth into the socket from which it was dislodged; and *transplantation,* the insertion or application of tissue derived from another individual, or from a different site in the same individual.

plantigrade (plan′tĭ-grād) [L. *planta* sole + *gradi* to walk]. Characterized by walking on the full sole of the foot, applied to animals whose entire sole touches the ground, such as the bear and man.

plantose (plan′tōs). A nutritive albumin from rape seeds.

planula (plan′u-lah). 1. The embryo in the stage when it consists of the two primary germ layers (ectoderm and entoderm) only. 2. A larval coelenterate. **invaginate p.,** the gastrula.

planum (pla′num), pl. *pla′na* [L.]. A flat surface, determined by the position of three points in space. Called also *plane.* Used in anatomical nomenclature [B N A] to designate a more or less flat surface of a bone or other structure. **p. nucha′le** [B N A], the outer surface of the occipital bone between the foramen magnum and the superior nuchal line. Called also *nuchal plane.* Omitted in N A. **p. occipita′le** [B N A], the outer surface of the occipital bone above the superior nuchal line. Called also *occipital plane.* Omitted in N A. **p. orbita′le** [B N A], a plane passing through the two orbital points and perpendicular to the Frankfort horizontal plane. Called also *orbital plane.* Omitted in N A. **p. poplit′eum fem′oris** [B N A], facies poplitea femoris. **p. semiluna′tum,** the rounded end of a crista in a semicircular canal. **p. sterna′le** [B N A], the anterior surface of the sternum. Called also *sternal plane.* Omitted in N A. **p. tempora′le** [B N A], the depressed area on the side of the skull below the inferior temporal line. Called also *temporal plane.* Omitted in N A.

planuria (pla-nu′re-ah) [Gr. *planasthai* to wander + *ouron* urine + *-ia*]. The voiding of urine from an abnormal place.

plaque (plak) [Fr.]. 1. Any patch or flat area. 2. A blood platelet. **bacterial p.,** a collection of bacteria growing in a deposit of material on the surface of a tooth, which may cause a carious lesion. **bacteriophage p.,** a cleared area in a bacterial culture, produced by bacteriophage that has been applied to it. **blood p.,** a blood platelet. **dental p.,** a deposit of material on the surface of a tooth, which may serve as a medium for growth of bacteria or as a nucleus for the formation of a dental calculus. **fibromyelinic p's,** areas of overgrowth of medullated fibers and sheaths in areas of incomplete arteriosclerotic necrosis in the cerebral cortex. **Lichtheim p's,** areas of degeneration in the cerebral white matter that are seen in pernicious anemia. **mucous p., p. muqueuse′,** condyloma latum. **opaline p.,** the gray plaque of secondary syphilis. **Peyer's p's,** Peyer's patches. **Redlich-Fisher miliary p's,** thickened, dark colored areas in the neuroglia reticulum of the brain, seen in cases of senile psychoses. **senile p's,** areas of incomplete necrosis in the senile cerebral cortex. **talc p's,** opaque material visible roentgenographically on pleural surfaces in talc miners and processors.

plaquenil (pla′kwĕ-nil). Trade mark for a preparation of hydroxychloroquine.

plasis (pla′sis). The causal component in vital adaptation.

plasm (plazm). Plasma. **germ p.,** Weismann's term for the reproductive and hereditary substance of individuals which is passed on from the germ cell in which an individual originates in direct continuity to the germ cells of succeeding generations. By it new individuals are produced and hereditary characters are transmitted. Cf. *somatoplasm.*

plasma (plaz′mah) [Gr. "anything formed or molded"]. 1. The fluid portion of the blood in which the corpuscles are suspended. *Plasma* is to be distinguished from *serum,* which is plasma from which the fibrinogen has been separated in the process of clotting. See *blood plasma,* under *blood.* 2. The lymph deprived of its corpuscles or cells. 3. A glycerite of starch used in preparing ointments. 4. Cytoplasm or protoplasm. **albumose p.,** blood plasma extracted after the injection of albumoses. **antihemophilic human p.,** normal human plasma that has been processed promptly to preserve the antihemophilic properties of original blood: used for temporary correction of bleeding tendency in hemophilia. **blood p.,** the liquid portion of the blood in which the corpuscles are suspended. Plasma is obtained from whole blood by removing the corpuscles by centrifuging or by sedimentation. It contains all the chemical constituents of whole blood except hemoglobin. **citrated p.,** blood plasma treated with sodium citrate, which prevents clotting. **muscle p.,** a liquid expressible from muscular tissue. It clots spontaneously and is sometimes injected subcutaneously as a restorative and stimulant. **normal human p.,** sterile plasma obtained by pooling approximately equal amounts of the liquid portion of citrated whole blood from eight or more adult humans, used as a blood volume replenisher. **oxalate p.,** blood plasma to which 1 per cent of ammonium oxalate has been added, to prevent clotting. **peptone p.,** albumose p. **salt p.,** blood plasma to which a neutral salt has been added to prevent clotting. **true p.,** blood plasma drawn direct from the blood without any change in its gas content.

plasmablast (plaz′mah-blast) [*plasma* + Gr. *blastos* germ]. The mother cell of plasmacytes; hemocytoblast.

plasmacule (plaz′mah-kūl). A minute refractive particle present in blood plasma. See *hemoconia.*

plasmacyte (plaz′mah-sīt) [*plasma* + *-cyte*]. Plasma cell.

plasmacytoma (plaz″mah-si-to′mah) [*plasmacyte*

+ *-oma*]. A neoplasm composed of plasma cells; a plasma cell type of multiple myeloma.

plasmacytosis (plaz″mah-si-to′sis). The presence of plasma cells in the blood.

plasmagene (plaz′mah-jēn) [cyto*plasm* + *gene*]. A self-reproducing copy of a nuclear gene persisting in the cytoplasm of a cell.

plasmahaut (plaz′mah-howt) [Ger.]. The superficial layer of the protoplasm of a cell.

plasmalemma (plaz″mah-lem′ah) [*plasma* + Gr. *lemma* husk]. A thin peripheral layer of the ectoplasma in a fertilized egg.

plasmalogen (plaz-mal′o-jen). A term applied to a member of a group of phospholipids, present in platelets, that liberate higher fatty aldehydes on hydrolysis, and may be related to the specialized function of platelets in blood coagulation.

plasmameba (plaz″mah-me′bah). A sporozoan parasite found in the blood plasma in dengue and thought to cause that disease.

plasmapheresis (plaz″mah-fĕ-re′sis) [*plasma* + Gr. *aphairesis* removal]. The removal of blood, separation of plasma by centrifugation, and reinjection of the packed cells suspended in citrate-saline or other suitable medium; used as a means of obtaining plasma without waste of erythrocytes, and also in treatment of certain pathological conditions, such as macroglobulinemic syndromes.

plasmarrhexis (plaz″mah-rek′sis) [*plasma* + Gr. *rhēxis* rupture]. Dissolution of the cytoplasm.

plasmase (plaz′mās). Fibrin ferment.

plasmasome (plaz′mah-sōm) [*plasma* + Gr. *sōma* body]. A leukocyte granule.

plasmatherapy (plaz″mah-ther′ah-pe). The therapeutic use of blood plasma.

plasmatic (plaz-mat′ik). Pertaining to or of the nature of the plasma.

plasmatogamy (plaz″mah-tog′ah-me) [*plasma* + Gr. *gamos* marriage]. Union of cells in which the nucleus of each cell is preserved.

plasmatorrhexis (plaz″mah-to-rek′sis) [*plasma* + Gr. *rhēxis* rupture]. The bursting of a cell due to the pressure exerted from within.

plasmatosis (plaz″mah-to′sis). The liquefaction of the substance of a cell.

plasmeba (plaz-me′bah). Plasmameba.

plasmexhidrosis (plaz″meks-hi-dro′sis) [*plasma* + Gr. *ex* out + *hidrōs* sweat]. The exudation of plasma from the blood vessels.

plasmic (plaz′mik). 1. Plasmatic. 2. Rich in protoplasm.

plasmid (plaz′mid) [*plasm* + *id*]. A generic term for all types of intracellular inclusions that can be considered as having genetic functions, including bioblasts, endosymbionts, plasmagenes, plastids, viruses, etc.

plasmin (plaz′min). The active portion of the fibrinolytic or clot-lysing system, a proteolytic enzyme with a high specificity for fibrin, with the particular ability to dissolve formed fibrin clots but also having a similar effect on other plasma proteins and clotting factors.

plasminogen (plaz-min′o-jen). The inactive precursor of plasmin. Called also *profibrinolysin.*

plasmo- (plaz′mo) [Gr. *plasma* anything formed]. Combining form denoting relationship to plasma, or to the substance of a cell.

plasmochin naphthoate (plaz′mo-kin naf′tho-āt). A proprietary brand of pamaquine naphthoate.

plasmocyte (plaz′mo-sit) [*plasmo-* + *-cyte*]. A mononuclear cell of bone marrow.

plasmodesma (plaz″mo-dez′mah) [Gr. *plasma* plasm + *desmos* band]. The protoplasmic material which binds adjacent cells together in plants (Studnička).

plasmodia (plaz-mo′de-ah). Plural of *plasmodium.*

plasmodial (plaz-mo′de-al). Pertaining to plasmodia.

plasmodiblast (plaz-mo′dĭ-blast). Trophoblast.

plasmodicidal (plaz″mo-dĭ-si′dal) [*plasmodia* + L. *caedere* to kill]. Destructive to plasmodia.

plasmodicide (plaz-mo′dĭ-sīd). An agent which is destructive to plasmodia.

Plasmodidae (plaz-mo′dĭ-de). A family of the Hemosporidia containing three genera: *Plasmodium, Haemoproteus,* and *Proteosoma.*

Plasmodiophora brassicae (plaz″mo-di-of′o-rah bras′ĭ-ke). A rhizopod organism which causes a disease of cabbages and other cruciferous plants, called *fingers and toes* or *stump root.*

plasmoditrophoblast (plaz-mo″di-trof′o-blast). Plasmotrophoblast.

Plasmodium (plaz-mo′de-um). A genus of the Plasmodidae, parasitic in red blood corpuscles; the malarial parasites. **P. bo′vis,** a species found in cattle. **P. brasilia′num,** a species found in monkeys in South America. It is much like *P. malariae.* **P. ca′nis,** a species found in dogs in India. **P. capistra′ni, P. catheme′rium,** forms which cause malaria in birds. **P. cynomol′gi,** a species causing malaria in monkeys of the genus *Macacus.* **P. danilews′kyi,** a species found in birds in Italy, India, and Africa. It is of interest because Ross first traced the development in the mosquito with this parasite. **P. du′rae,** a species pathogenic for turkeys. **P. e′qui,** a species found in the horse. **P. falcip′arum,** the species which causes estivo-autumnal malaria in man. It is characterized by the "signet-ring" forms of trophozoites and the "crescent" form of the gametes. **P. gallina′ceum,** one of the numerous plasmodia of avian malaria. **P. in′ui,** a species pathogenic for monkeys (*Macacus*). **P. knowle′si,** a species causing malaria in monkeys. **P. ko′chi,** a species pathogenic for chimpanzees and for monkeys. **P. loph′urae,** a species recovered from a Borneo fireback pheasant, *Lophura igniti igniti* (Shaw and Nodd) and pathogenic for the domestic fowl. **P. mala′riae,** the species which causes quartan malaria in man. The parasite as seen in the blood of man is an irregular mass of protoplasm which may show ameboid activity. It passes part of its life cycle in the blood of man and part in the body of the mosquito. **P. ova′le,** a species found in the Congo and adjacent regions, causing tertian malaria. **P. pith′eci,** a species found in the orang-utan and in chimpanzees. It resembles *P. vivax* except that man is not susceptible. **P. pleurodyn′iae,** a name given to certain inclusion bodies found in the red blood cells in cases of epidemic diaphragmatic pleurodynia. **P. relic′tum,** a form causing malaria in birds. **P. relic′tum** var. **matuti′num,** an organism isolated from the robin, which is morphologically similar to *P. relictum* but biologically very different. It possesses strict quotidian periodicity and a high degree of synchronism of segmentation, being found daily about 9 a.m. **P. richeno′wi,** a species found in anthropoid apes. **P. schwet′zi,** a species found in chimpanzees. **P. ten′ue,** a species from cases of malaria in India distinguished by its tenuity and ameboid activity. **P. vas′sali,** a species found in the squirrel. **P. vi′vax,** the species which causes the benign tertian form of malaria in the patient and Schüffner's dots in a parasitized red blood cell. **P. vi′vax minu′ta,** a species differing from *P. vivax* in being smaller and in having only four to ten merozoites.

plasmodium (plaz-mo′de-um), pl. *plasmo′dia* [*plasmo-* + Gr. *eidos* form]. 1. A parasite of the genus *Plasmodium.* 2. A multinucleate continuous mass of protoplasm. 3. Syncytium, def. 2. **exoerythrocytic p.,** a malarial parasite outside a red blood corpuscle. **placental p.,** syncytium, def. 2.

Plasmodromata (plaz″mo-dro′mah-tah). A class of protozoa distinguished by the nucleus not being divided into a vegetative and a reproductive portion.

plasmogamy (plaz-mog′ah-me) [*plasmo-* + Gr. *gamos* marriage]. Cytoplasmic fusion of cells.

plasmogen (plaz′mo-jen) [*plasmo-* + Gr. *gennan* to produce]. The essential part of protoplasm; bioplasm.

plasmology (plaz-mol′o-je) [*plasmo-* + *-logy*]. The study of the most minute particles or ultimate corpuscles of living matter.

plasmolysis (plaz-mol′ĭ-sis) [*plasmo-* + Gr. *lysis* dissolution]. Contraction or shrinking of the protoplasm of a cell due to the loss of water by osmotic action.

plasmolytic (plaz″mo-lit′ik). Tending toward, pertaining to, or characterized by plasmolysis.

plasmolyzability (plaz″mo-līz″ah-bil′ĭ-te). The power of undergoing plasmolysis.

plasmolyzable (plaz″mo-līz′ah-b'l). Capable of undergoing plasmolysis.

plasmolyze (plaz′mo-līz). To subject to plasmolysis.

plasmoma (plaz-mo′mah). 1. A mass of plasma cells resembling a tumor. 2. A tumor made up of plasma cells.

plasmon (plaz′mon). The hereditary factors of the egg cytoplasm. Cf. *genome.*

plasmoptysis (plaz-mop′tĭ-sis) [*plasmo-* + Gr. *ptyein* to spit]. Escape of protoplasm from a cell through a ruptured cell wall.

plasmorrhexis (plaz″mo-rek′sis) [*plasmo-* + Gr. *rhēxis* splitting]. Erythrocytorrhexis.

plasmoschisis (plaz-mos′kĭ-sis) [*plasmo-* + Gr. *schisis* fission]. The splitting of protoplasm into fragments.

plasmosin (plaz′mo-sin). A protein constituent of cytoplasm.

plasmosome (plaz′mo-sōm) [*plasmo-* + Gr. *sōma* body]. 1. The true nucleolus of a cell (Ogata, 1883). 2. See *Altmann's granules.*

plasmosphere (plaz′mo-sfēr). Perisphere.

plasmotomy (plaz-mot′o-me) [*plasmo-* + Gr. *temnein* to cut]. Reproduction by the separation from the mother cell of smaller masses of protoplasm, each containing several nuclei.

plasmotrophoblast (plaz″mo-trof′o-blast) [*plasmo-* + *trophoblast*]. The external syncytial layer of trophoblast.

plasmotropic (plaz″mo-trop′ik). Pertaining to or causing plasmotropism.

plasmotropism (plaz-mot′ro-pizm) [Gr. *plasma* plasm + *tropos* a turning]. Solution or destruction of erythrocytes in the liver, spleen, or marrow, as contrasted with their destruction in the circulation.

plasmozyme (plaz′mo-zīm) [*plasmo-* + Gr. *zymē* leaven]. Thrombogen.

plasome (plaz′ōm) [Gr. *plassein* to form]. The hypothetical unit of living protoplasm. See *micelle.*

plasson (plas′on) [Gr. *plassōn* forming]. The protoplasm of a cytode, or non-nucleated cell.

-plast [Gr. *plastos* formed]. A word termination denoting any primitive living cell.

plastein (plas′te-in). The protein synthesized by pepsin from the peptic digestion products of protein.

plaster (plas′ter) [L. *emplastrum*]. 1. A mixture of materials which hardens on aging, used for immobilizing or making impressions of body parts, such as *dental plaster*, or *plaster of paris.* 2. A fabric or other backing material spread with a mixture containing a medicinal agent, to be applied to the surface of the body, such as *mustard plaster.* **adhesive p.,** fabric spread with a mixture having pressure-sensitive adhesive properties, the whole having high tensile strength: used for the application of dressings and sometimes to produce immobilization. **adhesive p., sterile,** adhesive plaster, the adhesive surface of which is covered by strips of a protective material of equal width, and which is sterilized after packaging. **belladonna p.,** a mixture of extract of belladonna root and adhesive plaster mass spread evenly on suitable backing material: used as an anodyne application. **p. of cantharidin,** a mixture of cantharidin and other ingredients, formerly applied to the skin as a blistering agent. **capsicum p.,** a rubefacient plaster made of oleoresin of capsicum and rubber plaster. **dental p.,** a gypsum preparation used for the making of impressions of structures of the mouth. **diachylon p.,** lead p. **lead p.,** a plaster containing lead oxide, olive oil, lard, and water, triturated and boiled, formerly used for applying to slight wounds and bruises and in preparation of other plasters. Called also *diachylon p.* **mercurial p.,** a plaster containing mercury, oleate of mercury, hydrous wool fat, and lead plaster. **mustard p.,** a uniform mixture of powdered black mustard and a solution of a suitable adhesive, spread on a suitable backing material: used as a local irritant. **opium p.,** a plaster containing extract of opium, water, and adhesive plaster: used as an anodyne application. **p. of paris,** native calcium sulfate dihydrate, with about three fourths of the water of crystallization driven off, and reduced to a fine powder; the addition of water produces a porous mass that has been used extensively in making casts and bandages to support or immobilize body parts, and in dentistry for taking dental impressions. **resin p., rosin p.,** a plaster containing rosin, lead plaster, and yellow wax. **salicylic acid p.,** a uniform mixture of 10 to 40 per cent salicylic acid in a suitable base, spread on paper, cloth, or other material: used as a keratolytic. **soap p.,** a discutient plaster made of dried soap and lead plaster.

plasthetics (plas-thet′iks). Synthesized resins and plastic products.

plastic (plas′tik) [L. *plasticus;* Gr. *plastikos*]. 1. Tending to build up tissues or to restore a lost part. 2. Conformable; capable of being molded. 3. A substance produced by chemical condensation or by polymerization. 4. Material that can be molded.

plasticity (plas-tis′ĭ-te). 1. The quality of being plastic or conformable. 2. The ability of early embryonic cells to alter in conformity with the immediate environment.

plastics (plas′tiks). 1. Plastic surgery. 2. Plastic materials used in surgery or dentistry.

plastid (plas′tid) [Gr. *plastos* formed]. 1. Any elementary constructive unit, as a cell. 2. Any specialized organ of the cell other than the nucleus and centrosome, such as chloroplast or amyloplast. **red p.,** erythroplast.

plastidogenetic (plas-tid″o-je-net′ik). Producing plastids or cells.

plastidule (plas′tĭ-dūl). Biophore.

plastin (plas′tin). 1. Linin. 2. Spongioplasm.

plastiosome (plas′te-o-sōm). Mitochondria.

plastochondria (plas″to-kon′dre-ah). Granular mitochondria.

plastocont (plas′to-kont). Chondrioconte.

plastocyte (plas′to-sīt) [Gr. *plastos* formed + *-cyte*]. A blood platelet.

plastocytemia (plas″to-si-te′me-ah). Plastocytosis.

plastocytopenia (plas″to-si″to-pe′ne-ah) [*plastocyte* + Gr. *penia* poverty]. Decrease in the number of blood platelets below normal.

plastocytosis (plas″to-si-to′sis). Abnormal increase in the number of blood platelets.

plastodynamia (plas″to-di-na′me-ah) [Gr. *plastos* formed + *dynamis* power]. Power or ability to develop.

plastogamy (plas-tog′ah-me) [Gr. *plastos* formed matter + *gamos* marriage]. Conjugation in protozoa, in which the protoplasm of two or more individuals undergoes amalgamation, the nuclei remaining separate. See *karyogamy* and *plasmatogamy.*

plastogel (plas′to-jel). A gel possessing great plasticity.

plastokont (plas′to-kont). Chondrioconte.

plastomere (plas′to-mēr). Cytomere.

plastosome (plas′to-sōm) [Gr. *plastos* formed + *sōma* body]. One of the stainable granules or threads of the protoplasm. See *chondriosome.*

plastron (plas′tron) [Fr. "breast-plate"]. The sternum and costal cartilages.

-plasty (plas′te) [Gr. *plassein* to form, mold, shape]. Word termination meaning the shaping or the surgical formation of.

plate (plāt) [Gr. *platē*]. 1. A flat structure or layer, such as a thin layer of bone. See also *lamina, layer,* etc. 2. A dental plate. Sometimes, by extension, incorrectly used to designate a complete denture. **alar p.,** lamina alaris. **anal p.,** anal membrane. **approximation p.,** a disk of bone or other material used in intestinal surgery. **auditory p.,** the bony roof of the auditory meatus. **axial p.,** the primitive streak of the embryo. **basal p.** 1. Lamina basalis. 2. The fused parachordal cartilages, precursors of the occipital bone. 3. The portion of the decidua basalis that becomes an integral part of the placenta. **base p.** See *baseplate.* **bite p.** See *biteplate.* **blood p's,** blood platelets. **bone p.,** an approximation plate of bone. **cardiogenic p.,** an area of splanchnic mesoderm, cephalad of the embryo, from which the heart will arise. **cell p.,** a thickening midway of the mitotic spindle in plants that forms a dividing septum between the future daughter cells. **chorionic p.,** the main fetal portion of the placenta that gives rise to chorionic villi. **clinoid p.,** the portion of the sphenoid bone behind the sella turcica. **collecting p.,** the electronegative element of a galvanic battery, where the hydrogen and other decomposition products collect. **cortical p.,** the outer superficial portion of the alveolar process. **cough p.,** a plate of culture medium on which a patient with a respiratory infection coughs. **p. of cranial bone, inner,** lamina interna ossis cranii. **p. of cranial bone, outer,** lamina externa ossis cranii. **cribriform p.,** fascia cribrosa. **cribriform p. of brain,** substantia perforata anterior. **cribriform p. of ethmoid bone,** lamina cribrosa ossis ethmoidalis. **cutis p.,** dermatome. **deck p.,** roof p. **dental p.,** a plate of acrylic resin, metal, or other material, which is fitted to the shape of the mouth and serves for the support of artificial teeth. **dermomyotome p.,** the portion of the embryonic somite remaining after migration of the sclerotomic tissue. **die p.,** a plate of metal containing dies for forming the cusps in shell crowns. **dorsal p.,** roof p. **dorsolateral p.,** lamina alaris. **end p.** See *end-plate.* **epiphyseal p.,** the thin plate of cartilage between the epiphysis and the newly forming tissue (metaphysis) of a growing long bone. **equatorial p.,** the platelike collection of chromosomes at the equator of the spindle in karyokinesis. **ethmovomerine p.,** the central part of the ethmoid bone in the fetus. **floor p.,** the unpaired ventral longitudinal zone of the neural tube, forming the floor of that tube. Called also *ventral plate* and *bodenplatte.* **foot p.,** the flat portion of the stapes. **frontal p.,** a fetal plate of cartilage between the sides of the ethmoid cartilage and the sphenoid bone. **frontonasal p.,** a fetal plate from which the external nose is developed. **generating p.,** the electropositive element of a galvanic battery. **gray p.,** lamina terminalis. **growth p.,** the area between the epiphysis and diaphysis of long bones, within which growth in length occurs. **horizontal p. of palatine bone,** lamina horizontalis ossis palatini. **Kühne's terminal p's,** the motor end-plates of nerves in the muscle spindles. **Lane p's,** steel plates with holes for screws: used in fixing the fragments of a fractured bone. **lateral mesoblastic p.,** the thickened portion of either side of the mesoblast. **lingual p.,** a major partial denture connector formed as a lingual bar extended to cover the cingula of the lower anterior teeth. **medullary p.,** neural p. **middle p.,** nephrotome. **Moe p.,** a stainless steel plate for internal fixation of intertrochanteric fractures of the femur. **motor p.,** end-plate. **muscle p.,** myotome. **nail p.** 1. Stratum corneum unguis. 2. Stratum germinativum unguis. **nephrotome p.,** nephrotome. **neural p.,** the thickened plate of ectoderm in the embryo from which the neural tube develops. **notochordal p.,** head process. **oral p.,** pharyngeal membrane. **orbital p. of ethmoid bone,** lamina orbitalis ossis ethmoidalis. **palate p.,** that part of the palatine bone which forms a lateral half of the roof of the mouth. **paper p.,** lamina papyracea. **parachordal p.,** basal p., def. 2. **parietal p.,** a thin lamina of the ethmoid bone that forms part of the nasal septum. **perforated p., anterior,** substantia perforata anterior. **perforated p., posterior,** substantia perforata posterior. **perpendicular p. of ethmoid bone,** lamina perpendicularis ossis ethmoidalis. **Petri p.,** a Petri dish containing a nutrient medium ready for inoculation with the microorganism to be cultured. **pharyngeal p.,** pharyngeal membrane. **polar p's, pole p's,** platelike bodies at the end of the spindle in certain forms of mitosis. **pour p.,** a bacterial culture poured into a Petri dish from a test tube in which the medium has been inoculated. **prechordal p., prochordal p.,** thickened entoderm, cephalad of the notochord, that combines with ectoderm to become the pharyngeal membrane. **pterygoid p., external,** lamina lateralis processus pterygoidei. **pterygoid p., internal,** lamina medialis processus pterygoidei. **pterygoid p., lateral,** lamina lateralis processus pterygoidei. **pterygoid p., medial,** lamina medialis processus pterygoidei. **quadrigeminal p.,** lamina tecti mesencephali. **retaining p.,** an appliance used in orthodontics. **reticular p.,** a form of nerve ending in the ciliary body consisting of very fine reticulations of granular nerve fiber. **roof p.,** the unpaired dorsal longitudinal zone of the neural tube, forming the roof of that tube. Called also *deck plate, dorsal plate,* and *deckplatte.* **segmental p.,** a plate of mesoblast on either side of the notochord at the posterior end of the embryo, from which the mesoblastic segments are formed. **Senn's bone p's,** plates of decalcified bone, used in approximating and suturing a divided intestine. **sole p.,** a mass of protoplasm in which motor nerve endings are embedded. **Soyka's p's,** containers, resembling Petri dishes, with depressions in the lower plate, used in making bacterial cultures. **spiral p.,** lamina spiralis ossea. **spring p.,** a dental plate held in place by the elasticity of the material which abuts against natural teeth. **streak p.,** a plate of solid culture medium in which the infectious material is inoculated in streaks across the surface. **subgerminal p.,** a sheet of protoplasm forming the floor of the segmentation cavity of the ovum. **suction p.,** a dental plate held in place in the mouth by suction beneath it. **tarsal p's.** See *tarsus superior palpebrae* and *tarsus inferior palpebrae.* **terminal p.,** lamina terminalis hypothalami. **trial p.** See *baseplate.* **tympanic p.,** a bony plate which forms the floor and sides of the meatus acusticus internus. **urethral p.,** an entodermal plate that gives rise to the terminal portion of the cavernous urethra. **vascular foot p.,** sucker foot. **ventral p.,** floor p. **ventrolateral p.,** lamina basalis. **vertical p. of palatine bone,** lamina perpendicularis ossis palatini. **wing p.,** lamina alaris.

plateau (plah-to′). An elevated and level area. **tibial p.,** either of the bony surfaces of the tibia, internal and external, closest to the condyles of the femur. **ventricular p.,** a level part of the intraventricular curve of blood pressure corresponding to the contraction of the ventricle.

platelet (plāt′let). A circular or oval disk, 2–3 μ in diameter, found in the blood of all mammals, which is concerned in coagulation of the blood and in contraction of the clot, and hence in hemostasis and thrombosis. They average about 250,000 per cu.mm. of blood. **giant p's,** large masses of blood platelets or megakaryocytes that stain like blood platelets: seen in myelogenous leukemia and polycythemia.

platiculture (plat′ĭ-kul″tūr). Plate culture.

platinectomy (plat″ĭ-nek′to-me) [Fr. *platine* (for footplate of stapes) + Gr. *ektomē* excision]. Excision of the footplate in surgical mobilization of the stapes, in treatment of hearing loss.

plating (plāt′ing). 1. The act of applying bacterial culture mediums to glass plates; the cultivation of bacteria on plates. 2. The application of plates to fractured bones for the purpose of holding the fragments in place.

platinic (plah-tin′ik). Containing platinum in its higher valency.

platinode (plat′ĭ-nōd) [*platinum* + Gr. *hodos* way]. The collecting plate of an electric battery.

platinogold (plat′ĭ-no-gold). Gold-plated platinum foil: used for dental fillings.

platinosis (plat″ĭ-no′sis) [*platinum* + *-osis*]. A morbid condition resulting from exposure to soluble platinum salts, with involvement of the upper respiratory tract and allergic manifestations of the skin.

platinous (plat′ĭ-nus). Containing platinum in its lower valency.

platinum (plat′ĭ-num) [L.]. A heavy, soft, whitish metal, resembling tin: symbol, Pt; atomic number, 78; atomic weight, 195.09; specific gravity, 21.37. It also occurs as a black powder (*p. black*) and a spongy substance (*spongy p.*). Metallic platinum is insoluble except in nitrohydrochloric acid, and is fusible only at very high temperatures; it is therefore used in the manufacture of chemical apparatus. Platinum black and spongy platinum have a strong affinity for oxygen, and act as powerful oxidizing and catalytic agents. **p. chloride,** platinic tetrachloride, a poisonous substance, $PCl_4.5H_2O$: used as a chemical reagent and in syphilis.

platy- (plat′e) [Gr. *platys* broad]. Combining form meaning broad or flat.

platybasia (plat″e-ba′se-ah) [*platy-* + Gr. *basis* base (of the skull) + *-ia*]. Basilar impression. See under *impression.*

platycelous (plat″e-se′lus) [*platy-* + Gr. *koilos* hollow]. Having vertebrae flat in front, or cephalad, and concave caudad.

platycephalic (plat″e-se-fal′ik) [*platy-* + Gr. *kephalē* head]. Wide headed; having a breadth-height index of less than 70.

platycephalous (plat″e-sef′ah-lus). Platycephalic.

platycephaly (plat″e-sef′ah-le). The state of being platycephalic.

platycnemia (plat″ik-ne′me-ah). Compression of the tibia from side to side.

platycnemic (plat″ik-ne′mik) [*platy-* + Gr. *knēmē* leg]. Having the tibia compressed from side to side.

platycoria (plat″e-ko′re-ah) [*platy-* + Gr. *korē* pupil]. A dilated condition of the pupil.

platycrania (plat″e-kra′ne-ah) [*platy-* + Gr. *kranion* skull + *-ia*]. Artificial flattening of the skull.

platycyte (plat′e-sīt) [*platy-* + *-cyte*]. A variety of epithelioid cell found in tubercle nodules, intermediate between a leukocyte and a giant cell.

platyglossal (plat″e-glos′al) [*platy-* + Gr. *glōssa* tongue]. Having a broad, flat tongue.

platyhelminth (plat″e-hel′minth). One of the Platyhelminthes.

Platyhelminthes (plat″e-hel-min′thēz) [*platy-* + Gr. *helmins* worm]. A phylum of flatworms. It includes the Turbellaria, Nemertea, Trematoda, Cestodaria, and Cestoda.

platyhieric (plat″e-hi-er′ik) [*platy-* + Gr. *hieron* sacrum]. Having a wide sacrum; having a sacral index exceeding 100.

platyknemia (plat″ik-ne′me-ah). Platycnemia.

platymeria (plat″e-me′re-ah). The condition of being platymeric.

platymeric (plat″e-me′rik) [*platy-* + Gr. *meros* thigh]. Having a femur that is excessively compressed from before backwards.

platymorphic (plat″e-mōr′fik) [*platy-* + Gr. *morphē* form]. Having a shallow or presbyopic eye.

platymyarian (plat″e-mi-a′re-an) [*platy-* + Gr. *mys* muscle]. Having all muscle cells lying next to the subcuticula, their sarcoplasm being uncovered on three sides next to the body cavity: said of the muscle arrangement in certain nematodes.

platymyoid (plat″e-mi′oid) [*platy-* + Gr. *mys* muscle + *eidos* form]. Having the contractile stratum arranged in an even lamina: applied to certain muscle cells.

platyonychia (plat″e-o-nik′e-ah) [*platy-* + Gr. *onyx* nail + *-ia*]. Abnormal flatness and broadness of the nails.

platyopia (plat″e-o′pe-ah) [*platy-* + Gr. *ōps* face + *-ia*]. Broadness across the face.

platyopic (plat″e-op′ik). Marked by platyopia; marked by a broad face.

platypellic (plat″e-pel′ik) [*platy-* + Gr. *pella* bowl]. Having a wide pelvis, i.e., a pelvic index below 90.

platypelloid (plat″e-pel′oid). Platypellic.

platyphylline (plat″e-fil′in). An alkaloid, $C_{18}H_{27}O_5N$, from *Senecio platyphyllus.*

platypodia (plat″e-po′de-ah) [*platy-* + Gr. *pous* foot + *-ia*]. Abnormal flatness of the foot; flatfoot.

Platyrrhina (plat″ĭ-ri′nah) [*platy-* + Gr. *rhis* nose]. A superfamily of the order Primates (suborder Anthropoidea), characterized by a broad nasal septum and often a prehensile tail, and including the New World monkeys.

platyrrhine (plat′e-rīn) [*platy-* + Gr. *rhis* nose]. Having a broad nose; having a nasal index exceeding 53.

platysma (plah-tiz′mah) [Gr.]. [N A, B N A] A platelike muscle that originates from the fascia of the cervical region and inserts in the mandible and the skin around the mouth. It is innervated by the cervical branch of the facial nerve, and acts to wrinkle the skin of the neck and to depress the jaw.

platysmal (plah-tiz′mal). Pertaining to the platysma.

platyspondylia (plat″e-spon-dil′e-ah). Platyspondylisis.

platyspondylisis (plat″e-spon-dil′ĭ-sis) [*platy-* + Gr. *spondylos* vertebra]. Congenital flattening of the vertebral bodies.

platystaphyline (plat″e-staf′ĭ-līn) [*platy-* + Gr. *staphylē* palate]. Having a broad, flat palate.

platystencephalia (plat″e-sten″se-fa′le-ah) [Gr. *platystatos* widest + *enkephalos* brain + *-ia*]. A form of dolichocephalism in which the occiput is very wide and pentagonal, the jaws prognathic: observed among South Africans.

platystencephalic (plat″e-sten-se-fal′ik). Exhibiting or pertaining to platystencephalia.

platystencephalism (plat″e-sten-sef′ah-lizm). Platystencephalia.

platystencephaly (plat″e-sten-sef′ah-le). Platystencephalia.

platytrope (plat′e-trōp) [*platy-* + Gr. *trepein* to turn]. Either of two symmetrical parts on opposite sides of the body; a lateral homologue.

Plaut's angina, ulcer (plowts) [Hugo Karl *Plaut,* German physician, 1858–1928]. Vincent's angina. See under *angina.*

Playfair's treatment (pla′fārz) [William Smoult *Playfair,* British physician, 1836–1903]. See under *treatment.*

plectron (plek′tron) [Gr. *plēktron* anything to

strike with]. The hammer form assumed by certain bacilli during sporulation.

plectrum (plek′trum) [L., from Gr. *plēktron* anything to strike with]. 1. The uvula. 2. The malleus. 3. The styloid process of the temporal bone.

pledget (plej′et). A small compress or tuft, as of wool or lint.

plegaphonia (pleg″ah-fo′ne-ah) [Gr. *plēgē* stroke + *aphonia*]. Auscultation of the chest during percussion over the larynx or trachea in cases in which the patient cannot or is not allowed to speak. The vibrations produced by the percussion take the place of those of the vocal cords.

-plegia (ple′je-ah) [Gr. *plēgē* a blow, stroke]. Word termination meaning paralysis, or a stroke.

Plehn's granules (plānz) [Albert *Plehn*, German physician, 1861–1935]. See under *granule*.

pleiades (pli′ah-dēz) [in Greek mythology, seven daughters of Atlas who were placed by Zeus among the stars and form part of the constellation Taurus]. A mass of enlarged lymph nodes.

pleiochloruria (pli″o-klo-roo′re-ah). An excess of chlorides in the urine.

pleiochromia (pli″o-kro′me-ah) [Gr. *pleiōn* more + *chrōma* color + *-ia*]. Increased coloration; especially increased secretion of bile pigments.

pleionexia ((pli″o-nek′se-ah). Pleonexia.

pleiotropia (pli″o-tro′pe-ah). Pleiotropy.

pleiotropic (pli″o-trop′ik). Pertaining to or characterized by pleiotropy.

pleiotropy (pli-ot′ro-pe) [Gr. *pleiōn* more + *tropē* a turning]. 1. The quality of having affinity for several different types of tissue, representing derivatives of the different primary germ layers. 2. In genetics, the quality of a gene to manifest itself in a multiplicity of ways.

plektron (plek′tron) [Gr.]. Plectron.

Plenck's solution (plenks) [Josef J. von *Plenck*, Vienna physician, 1738–1807]. See under *solution*.

pleniloquence (ple-nil′o-kwens) [L. *plenus* full + *loqui* to talk]. Abnormal talkativeness.

pleo- (ple′o) [Gr. *pleōn* more]. Combining form meaning more.

pleocaryocyte (ple″o-kar′e-o-sīt). Pleokaryocyte.

pleochroic (ple″o-kro′ik) [*pleo-* + Gr. *chroia* color]. Pleochromatic.

pleochroism (ple-ok′ro-izm). The condition of being pleochromatic.

pleochromatic (ple″o-kro-mat′ik) [*pleo-* + Gr. *chrōma* color]. Exhibiting different colors under different circumstances.

pleochromatism (ple″o-kro′mah-tizm) [*pleo-* + Gr. *chrōma* color]. The property possessed by some crystals of transmitting one color in one position and the complementary color in a position at right angles to the first.

pleochromocytoma (ple″o-kro″mo-si-to′mah) [*pleo-* + Gr. *chrōma* color + *-cyte* + *-oma*]. A tumor composed of cells of various colors.

pleocytosis (ple″o-si-to′sis). Increase of lymphocytes in the cerebrospinal fluid, as in syphilitic disease of the central nervous system.

pleokaryocyte (ple″o-kar′e-o-sīt). A large nucleated cell found in cachectic disease such as cancer and tuberculosis.

pleomastia (ple″o-mas′te-ah) [*pleo-* + Gr. *mastos* breast + *-ia*]. The condition of having several breasts or nipples.

pleomastic (ple″o-mas′tik). Pertaining to or characterized by pleomastia.

pleomazia (ple″o-ma′ze-ah) [*pleo-* + Gr. *mazos* breast + *-ia*]. Pleomastia.

pleomorphic (ple″o-mor′fik) [*pleo-* + Gr. *morphē* form]. Occurring in various distinct forms.

pleomorphism (ple″o-mor′fism). The assumption of various distinct forms by a single organism or species; also the property of crystallizing in two or more forms.

pleomorphous (ple″o-mor′fus). Pleomorphic.

pleonasm (ple′o-nazm) [Gr. *pleonasmos* exaggeration]. An excess in the number of parts.

pleonectic (ple″o-nek′tik) [Gr. *pleonexia* greediness]. Taking up more than the average amount of oxygen: a term applied to blood which at a pressure of 40 mm. will take up more than 79 per cent of oxygen. Cf. *mesectic* and *mionektic*.

pleonexia (ple″o-nek′se-ah) [Gr. "greediness"]. 1. Morbid desire for acquisition; morbid greediness. 2. The condition in which the circulating hemoglobin holds more firmly than normal to its oxygen and consequently gives off to the tissues less oxygen than normal.

pleonexy (ple″o-nek′se). Pleonexia.

pleonosteosis (ple″on-os″te-o′sis) [*pleo-* + Gr. *osteon* bone + *-osis*]. Abnormally increased ossification; premature and excessive ossification.

pleonotia (ple″o-no′she-ah) [*pleo-* + Gr. *ous* ear]. A developmental anomaly characterized by the presence of a supernumerary ear located on the neck.

pleoptics (ple-op′tiks) [*pleo-* + Gr. *optikos* of or for sight]. A technique of eye exercises designed to develop fuller vision of an amblyopic eye and assure proper binocular cooperation.

plerocercoid (ple″ro-ser′koid) [Gr. *plēroun* to complete + *kerkos* tail + *eidos* form]. The wormlike completed larval stage of cestode tapeworms, found in the tissues of vertebrates and invertebrates.

plerosis (ple-ro′sis). The restoration of lost tissue, as after illness.

Plesch's percussion, test (plesh′ez) [Johann *Plesch*, German physician in England, born 1878]. See under *percussion* and *tests*.

plesiomorphism (ple″se-o-mor′fizm) [Gr. *plesios* near + *morphē* form]. Similarity in form.

plesiomorphous (ple″se-o-mor′fus). Pertaining to or characterized by plesiomorphism.

plessesthesia (ples″es-the′ze-ah) [Gr. *plēssein* to strike + *aisthēsis* perception]. Palpatory percussion; percussion with one hand against a palpating finger of the other hand.

plessigraph (ples′ĭ-graf) [Gr. *plessein* to strike + *graphein* to write]. A form of pleximeter designed to enable the user to mark out the limits of an area.

plessimeter (ples-sim′e-ter). Pleximeter.

plessimetric (ples″ĭ-met′rik). Pleximetric.

plessor (ples′or). Plexor.

plethora (pleth′o-rah) [L.; Gr. *plēthōrē* fullness, satiety]. A condition marked by vascular turgescence, excess of blood, and fullness of pulse. It is attended with a feeling of tension in the head, a florid complexion, and a liability to nosebleed. **p. apocop′tica,** plethora following amputation in which there is little loss of blood. **p. hydrae′mica,** increase in amount of blood due to increase in the watery element alone.

plethoric (ple-thor′ik). Pertaining to or characterized by plethora.

plethysmogram (ple-thiz′mo-gram). A tracing made by the plethysmograph.

plethysmograph (ple-thiz′mo-graf) [Gr. *plēthysmos* increase + *graphein* to write]. An instrument for determining and registering variations in the size of an organ, part, or limb and in the amount of blood present or passing through it for recording variations in the size of parts and in the blood supply. **finger p.,** a plethysmograph which registers the change in volume taking place in a single finger. **Franck's p.,** a plethysmograph consisting of an upright glass jar into which the hand and wrist are inserted. **jerkin p.,** a double-layered garment resembling a jerkin, filled with air at slightly positive pressure, used to monitor changes in pressure produced by movements of the chest wall in respiration. **Mosso's p.,** a plethysmograph consisting of a glass tube filled with warm water into which the hand and forearm are placed. The changes in the water level, caused by the changes in volume of the limb, are graphically recorded.

plethysmography (pleth″iz-mog′rah-fe). The recording of the changes in the size of a part as modified by the circulation of the blood in it.

plethysmometer (pleth″iz-mom′e-ter). An instrument for detecting swelling of an artery or vein.

plethysmometry (pleth″iz-mom′e-tre). The measurement of the fullness of a hollow organ, as an artery or vein.

pleur-. See *pleuro-*.

pleura (ploor′ah), pl. *pleur′ae* [Gr. "rib," "side"]. [N A, B N A] The serous membrane investing the lungs and lining the thoracic cavity, completely enclosing a potential space known as the pleural cavity. There are two pleurae, right and left, entirely distinct from each other. The pleura is moistened with a serous secretion which facilitates

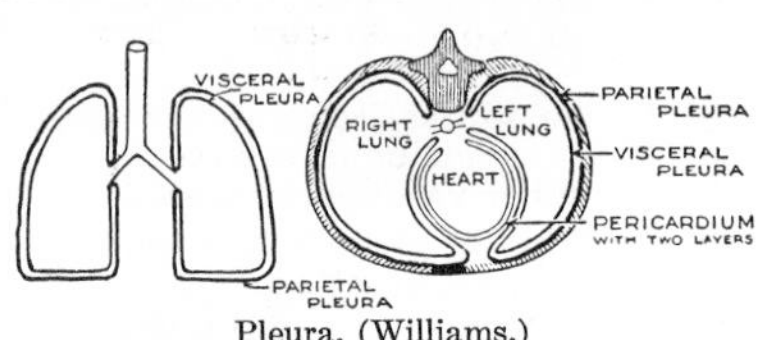

Pleura. (Williams.)

the movements of the lungs in the chest. **cervical p.,** cupula pleurae. **costal p., p. costa′lis** [N A, B N A], the part of the parietal pleura lining the rib cage. **diaphragmatic p., p. diaphragmat′ica** [N A, B N A], the part of the parietal pleura covering the diaphragm. **mediastinal p., p. mediastina′lis** [N A, B N A], a continuation of each pleura, medially, over the lateral face of the mediastinum and the structures within it. **parietal p., p. parieta′lis** [N A, B N A], the portion of the pleura lining the walls of the thoracic cavity. **pericardiac p., p. pericardi′aca** [B N A], the portion of the mediastinal pleura covering the pericardium and firmly attached to it. **p. pulmona′lis** [N A, B N A], **pulmonary p.,** the portion of the pleura investing the lungs and lining their fissures, completely separating the different lobes. **visceral p.,** p. pulmonalis.

pleuracentesis (ploor″ah-sen-te′sis). Pleurocentesis.

pleuracotomy (ploor″ah-kot′o-me) [*pleura* + Gr. *tomē* a cutting]. Incision into the pleural cavity.

pleurae (ploor′e) [L.]. Plural of *pleura*.

pleural (ploor′al). Pertaining to the pleura.

pleuralgia (ploor-al′je-ah) [*pleur-* + *-algia*]. Pain in the pleura, or in the side.

pleuralgic (ploor-al′jik). Pertaining to or affected with pleuralgia.

pleuramnion (ploor-am′ne-on). An amnion that develops by a process of folding of the somatopleure.

pleurapophysis (ploor″ah-pof′ĭ-sis) [*pleur-* + *apophysis*]. A rib, or its homologue; a rib considered as part of a vertebra.

pleurectomy (ploor-ek′to-me) [*pleur-* + Gr. *ektomē* excision]. Excision of a portion of the pleura. See *Fowler's operation*, under *operation*.

pleurisy (ploor′ĭ-se) [Gr. *pleuritis*]. Inflammation of the pleura, with exudation into its cavity and upon its surface. It may occur as either an acute or a chronic process. In acute pleurisy the pleura becomes reddened, then covered with an exudate of lymph, fibrin, and cellular elements (the *dry* stage); the disease may progress to the second stage, in which a copious exudation of serum occurs (stage of *liquid effusion*). The inflamed surfaces of the pleura tend to become united by adhesions, which are usually permanent. The symptoms are a stitch in the side, a chill, followed by fever and a dry cough. As effusion occurs there is an onset of dyspnea and a diminution of pain. The patient lies on the affected side. **acute p.,** a form marked by sharp, stabbing pain, fever, friction fremitus, and to-and-fro friction sounds. **adhesive p.,** dry p. **blocked p.,** pleurisy in which the exudate is imprisoned in a pocket so that it cannot be aspirated. **cholesterol p.,** accumulation of cholesterol-containing fluid in the pleural cavity. **chronic p.,** a dry serofibrinous, or purulent form, which is long continued. **chyliform p., chyloid p.,** a form in which the effused fluid has a milky appearance. **chylous p.,** pleurisy in which the effusion consists of a turbid milky fluid, with sometimes a high percentage of fat. **circumscribed p.,** pleurisy in which the inflammation is limited to a portion of the pleura. **costal p.,** inflammation of the pleura which lines the walls of the thorax. **diaphragmatic p.,** a variety limited to parts near the diaphragm. **diffuse p.,** pleurisy in which the inflammation involves the entire surface of the pleura. **double p.,** inflammation involving the pleurae of both lungs. **dry p.,** a variety with comparatively dry fibrinous exudate, usually chronic. **encysted p.,** a form with adhesions which circumscribe the effused material. **epidemic p.,** epidemic pleurodynia. **exudative p.,** pleurisy with effusion. **fibrinous p.,** the dry and plastic varieties. **hemorrhagic p.,** a variety in which there is a bloody exudate. **humid p.,** bronchitis. **ichorous p.,** empyema with a thin, offensive pus. **indurative p.,** pleurisy marked by thickening and hardening of the pleura. **interlobular p.,** a variety enclosed between the lobules of the lung. **latent p.,** a form attended with but little pain or inconvenience. **mediastinal p.,** a variety that affects the pleural folds about the mediastinum. **metapneumonic p.,** pleurisy characterized by a thick pus and the presence of the pneumonia diplococcus. **plastic p.,** a form characterized by the deposition of a soft, semisolid exudate in a layer. **primary p.,** a form not consequent upon pneumonia or any other disease; generally due to injury or exposure. **proliferating p.,** plastic p. **pulmonary p.,** inflammation of the pleura which covers the lungs. **pulsating p.,** a form in which the heart's action conveys a perceptible throbbing to the effused fluid. **purulent p.,** empyema. **sacculated p.,** pleurisy characterized by an adhesion pocket filled with fluid. **secondary p.,** any pleurisy consequent upon an attack of some other disease. **serofibrinous p.,** one with a watery exudate which contains flocculi, some fibrin being also deposited. **serous p.,** a form characterized by free exudation of serum. **single p.,** pleurisy involving only one lung. **suppurative p.,** empyema. **typhoid p.,** pleurisy with symptoms of severe prostration. **visceral p.,** pulmonary p. **wet p., p. with effusion,** pleurisy marked by serous exudation.

pleuritic (ploor-it′ik). Pertaining to or of the nature of pleurisy.

pleuritis (ploor-i′tis). Pleurisy.

pleuritogenous (ploor″ĭ-toj′e-nus). Causing pleurisy.

pleuro- (ploor′o) [Gr. *pleura* rib, side]. Combining form denoting relationship to the pleura, to the side, or to a rib.

pleurobronchitis (ploor″o-brong-ki′tis). Pleurisy and bronchitis combined.

pleurocele (ploor′o-sēl) [*pleuro-* + Gr. *kēlē* hernia]. Hernia of lung tissue or of pleura.

pleurocentesis (ploor″o-sen-te′sis) [*pleuro-* + Gr. *kentēsis* puncture]. Thoracocentesis.

pleurocentrum (ploor″o-sen′trum) [*pleuro-* + Gr. *kentron* center]. The lateral element of the vertebral column.

pleurocholecystitis (ploor″o-ko″le-sis-ti′tis) [*pleuro-* + *cholecystitis*]. Inflammation of the pleura and the gallbladder.

pleuroclysis (ploor-ok′lĭ-sis) [*pleuro-* + Gr. *klysis* washing]. Injection of fluids into the pleural cavity; the flushing out of a pleural cavity.

pleurocutaneous (ploor″o-ku-ta′ne-us). Pertaining to the pleura and the skin.

pleurodont (ploor′o-dont) [*pleur-* + Gr. *odous* tooth]. Having teeth attached by one side on the inner surface of the jaw elements.

pleurodynia (ploor″o-din′e-ah) [*pleuro-* + Gr. *odynē* pain]. Paroxysmal pain in the intercostal muscles. It is a form of muscular rheumatism (fibrositis). **epidemic p., epidemic diaphragmatic p.,** an epidemic disease marked by a sudden attack of pain in the chest or epigastrium, fever of brief duration, and a tendency to recrudescence on the third day; called also *devil's grip, epidemic myalgia, epidemic myositis* and *Bornholm disease.*

pleurogenic (ploor″o-jen′ik). Pleurogenous.

pleurogenous (ploor-oj′e-nus) [*pleuro-* + Gr. *gennan* to produce]. Originating in the pleura.

pleurography (ploor-og′rah-fe) [*pleuro-* + Gr. *graphein* to write]. Roentgenographic examination of the pleural cavity.

pleurohepatitis (ploor″o-hep″ah-ti′tis) [*pleuro-* + Gr. *hēpar* liver + *-itis*]. Hepatitis with inflammation of a portion of the pleura near the liver.

pleurolith (ploor′o-lith) [*pleuro-* + Gr. *lithos* stone]. A concretion found in the pleura.

pleurolysis (ploor-ol′ĭ-sis) [*pleuro-* + Gr. *lysis* dissolution]. Pneumonolysis.

pleuromelus (ploor″o-me′lus) [*pleuro-* + Gr. *melos* limb]. An individual with a supernumerary limb arising laterally from the thorax.

pleuroparietopexy (ploor″o-pah-ri′ĕ-to-pek″se) [*pleuro-* + *parietal* + Gr. *pēxis* fixation]. The operation of fixing the visceral pleura to the parietal pleura, thus binding the lung to the chest wall.

pleuropericardial (ploor″o-per-ĭ-kar′de-al). Pertaining to both the pleura and the pericardium.

pleuropericarditis (ploor″o-per″ĭ-kar-di′tis). Inflammation involving both the pleura and the pericardium.

pleuroperitoneal (ploor″o-per″ĭ-to-ne′al). Pertaining to both the pleura and the peritoneum, or communicating with both the pleural and the peritoneal cavity, as a pleuroperitoneal fistula.

pleuroperitoneum (ploor″o-per″ĭ-to-ne′um). The pleura and peritoneum considered together.

pleuropneumonia (ploor″o-nu-mo′ne-ah). 1. Pleurisy complicated with pneumonia. 2. A contagious or infectious pneumonia of cattle, combined with pleurisy, caused by *Asterococcus mycoides.* Called also *pleuropneumonia contagiosa bovum* and *lung plague.*

pleuropneumonia-like (ploor″o-nu-mo′nyah-lik). A term applied to a group of filtrable microorganisms similar to the causative agent of bovine pleuropneumonia. Such organisms have been isolated from sheep and goats (contagious agalactia), dogs, rats and mice, and also in humans.

pleuropneumonolysis (ploor″o-nu″mo-nol′ĭ-sis) [*pleuro-* + Gr. *pneumōn* lung + *lysis* destruction]. Removal of the ribs from one side in order to produce collapse of the affected lung for unilateral tuberculosis.

pleuropulmonary (ploor″o-pul′mo-ner″e). Pertaining to the pleura and lungs.

pleurorrhea (ploor″o-re′ah) [*pleuro-* + Gr. *rhoia* flow]. A pleural or pleuritic effusion.

pleuroscopy (ploor-os′ko-pe) [*pleuro-* + Gr. *skopein* to examine]. Examination of the pleural cavity through an incision in the chest wall.

pleurosoma (ploor″o-so′mah). Pleurosomus.

pleurosomus (ploor″o-so′mus) [*pleuro-* + Gr. *sōma* body]. A fetus with protrusion of the intestine and imperfect development of the arm of one side.

pleurothoracopleurectomy (ploor″o-tho″rah-ko-ploor-ek′to-me). An operation comprising the sequence of pleurotomy, thoracoplasty, and pleurectomy.

pleurothotonos (ploor″o-thot′o-nos) [Gr. *pleurothen* from the side + *tonos* tension]. Tetanic bending of the body to one side.

pleurothotonus (ploor″o-thot′o-nus). Pleurothotonos.

pleurotin (ploor-o′tin). An antibiotic substance obtained from the mushroom *Pleurotus griseus;* said to be effective against staphylococcus (of boils) and tubercle bacillus.

pleurotome (ploor′o-tōm). An area of the lung supplied with afferent nerve fibers by a single posterior spinal root.

pleurotomy (ploor-ot′o-me) [*pleuro-* + Gr. *tomē* a cutting]. Surgical incision of the pleura.

pleurotyphoid (ploor″o-ti′foid). Acute pleurisy followed by and complicated with typhoid fever.

pleurovisceral (ploor″o-vis′er-al). Pertaining to the pleura and the viscera.

plexal (plek′sal). Pertaining to a plexus.

plexalgia (pleks-al′je-ah) [Gr. *plēxis* stroke + *-algia*]. A condition seen in troops after long exposure. It is marked by pains in various parts of the body, fatigue, excitability, and insomnia.

plexiform (plek′sĭ-form) [L. *plexus* plait + *forma* form]. Resembling a plexus or network.

pleximeter (pleks-im′e-ter) [Gr. *plexis* stroke + *metron* measure]. 1. A plate to be struck in mediate percussion. 2. A glass plate used to show the condition of the skin under pressure.

pleximetric (plek″sĭ-met′rik). Pertaining to or performed by a pleximeter.

pleximetry (pleks-im′e-tre). The use of the pleximeter.

plexitis (plek-si′tis). Inflammation of a nerve plexus.

plexometer (pleks-om′e-ter). Pleximeter.

plexor (plek′sor). A hammer used in performing percussion.

plexus (plek′sus), pl. *plexus* or *plexuses* [L. "braid"]. A network or tangle; used in anatomical nomenclature as a general term to designate a network of lymphatic vessels, nerves, or veins. **accessory p.,** that part of the stroma plexus which lies immediately beneath the anterior limiting membrane of the cornea. **annular p.,** a plexus of nerve fibers encircling the corneal margin. **anserine p., p. anseri′nus,** p. parotideus nervi facialis. **p. anseri′nus ner′vi media′ni,** bundles of fibers passing from the vestibulocochlear nerve to the median nerve. **aortic p., abdominal,** p. aorticus abdominalis. **aortic p., thoracic,** p. aorticus thoracicus. **p. aor′ticus** [B N A], a network of lymphatic vessels about the aorta. Omitted in N A. **p. aor′ticus abdomina′lis** [N A, B N A], an unpaired subdivision of the celiac plexus, situated on the lower part of the abdominal aorta, and anastomosing with the hypogastric plexus. Called also *abdominal aortic p.* **p. aor′ticus thoraca′lis** [B N A], **p. aor′ticus thora′cicus** [N A], a nerve plexus around the thoracic aorta, continuous with the celiac plexus; formed by branches of the thoracic sympathetic trunk and vagus nerve, and distributing sympathetic, parasympathetic, and visceral afferent fibers via branches accompanying the thoracic aorta. Called also *thoracic aortic p.* **areolar p.,** p. venosus areolaris. **p. arte′riae cer′ebri anterio′ris** [B N A], a plexus of sympathetic fibers accompanying the anterior cerebral artery. Omitted in N A. **p. arte′riae cer′ebri me′diae** [B N A], a plexus of sympathetic fibers accompanying the middle cerebral artery. Omitted in N A. **p. arte′riae chorioi′deae** [B N A], a nerve plexus accompanying the choroid artery. Omitted in N A. **p. arte′riae ovar′icae** [B N A], p. ovaricus. **arteriosonervous p.,** p. cavernosus. **p. articula′ris,** a small venous plexus near the outer aspect of the temporomandibular articulation. **Auerbach's p.,** p. myentericus. **p. auricula′ris poste′rior** [B N A], a sympathetic nerve plexus on the posterior auricular artery. Omitted in N A. **autonomic p's, p.**

autonom'ici [N A], extensive networks of nerve fibers and cell bodies associated with the autonomic nervous system; found particularly in the thorax, abdomen, and pelvis, and containing visceral afferent fibers, in addition to the sympathetic and parasympathetic components. Called also *p. sympathici* [B N A]. **p. axilla'ris** [B N A], a plexus of lymph vessels and nodes in the axilla. Omitted in N A. **axillary p.** 1. Plexus axillaris. 2. Plexus brachialis. **basilar p., p. basila'ris** [N A, B N A], a venous plexus of the dura mater situated over the basilar part of the occipital bone and the posterior portion of the body of the sphenoid, extending from the cavernous sinus to the foramen magnum, and communicating with other dural sinuses. **biliary p.,** a network of bile ducts said to be sometimes observable in the liver. **brachial p., p. brachia'lis** [N A, B N A], a plexus originating from the ventral branches of the last four cervical and the first thoracic spinal nerves, and giving off the dorsal scapular, long thoracic, subclavius, suprascapular, medial and lateral pectoral, medial brachial cutaneous, medial antebrachial cutaneous, median, ulnar, radial, subscapular, thoracodorsal, and axillary nerves. **cardiac p.,** p. cardiacus. **cardiac p., anterior,** superficial cardiac p. **cardiac p., deep,** the larger part of the cardiac plexus, situated between the aortic arch and the tracheal bifurcation. **cardiac p., great,** deep cardiac p. **cardiac p., superficial,** the part of the cardiac plexus that lies beneath the aortic arch to the right of the ligamentum arteriosum. **p. cardi'acus** [N A, B N A], the plexus around the base of the heart, beneath and behind the arch of the aorta, formed by cardiac branches from the vagus nerves and the sympathetic trunks and ganglia, and made up of sympathetic, parasympathetic, and visceral afferent fibers that innervate the heart. **p. cardi'acus profun'dus,** the deep cardiac plexus. **p. cardi'acus superficia'lis,** the superficial cardiac plexus. **p. carot'icus commu'nis** [N A, B N A], a nerve plexus on the common carotid artery, formed by branches of the internal and external carotid plexuses and the cervical sympathetic ganglia, and supplying sympathetic fibers to the head and neck via branches accompanying the cranial blood vessels. Called also *common carotid p.* **p. carot'icus exter'nus** [N A, B N A], a nerve plexus located around the external carotid artery, formed by the external carotid nerve, and supplying sympathetic fibers to the head and neck via branches accompanying the cranial blood vessels. Called also *external carotid p.* **p. carot'icus inter'nus** [N A, B N A], a nerve plexus on the internal carotid artery, formed by the internal carotid nerve and supplying sympathetic fibers to the head and neck via various cranial nerves. Called also *internal carotid p.* and *carotid p.* **carotid p.,** p. caroticus internus. **carotid p., common,** p. caroticus communis. **carotid p., external,** p. caroticus externus. **carotid p., internal,** p. caroticus internus. **p. caverno'sus** [B N A], a plexus of sympathetic fibers about the cavernous sinus of the dura mater. Omitted in N A. **p. caverno'sus clitor'idis** [B N A], a plexus of nerve fibers at the root of the clitoris, derived from the vesical plexus and supplying the corpora cavernosa clitoridis. Omitted in N A. **p. caverno'si concha'rum** [N A, B N A], numerous venous plexuses in the thick mucous membrane of the nasal conchae. Called also *cavernous p's of conchae.* **p. caverno'sus pe'nis** [B N A], a plexus of nerve fibers at the root of the penis, derived from the vesical plexus and supplying the corpora cavernosa penis. Omitted in N A. **cavernous p.,** p. cavernosus. **cavernous p. of clitoris,** p. cavernosus clitoridis. **cavernous p's of conchae,** p. cavernosi concharum. **cavernous p. of penis,** p. cavernosus penis. **celiac p.** 1. Plexus celiacus. 2. Plexus coeliacus (def. 2). **p. celi'acus** [N A], the upper portion of the prevertebral plexus in the abdominopelvic region, specifically the unpaired portion of the plexus that surrounds the celiac trunk. Called also *solar plexus* and formerly sometimes called the *abdominal brain.* **cervical p.,** p. cervicalis. **cervical p., posterior,** a plexus in the posterior cervical region, formed by dorsal rami of the first three spinal nerves. **p. cervica'lis** [N A, B N A], a nerve plexus formed by the ventral branches of the upper four cervical nerves, and giving off the ansa cervicalis, lesser occipital, greater auricular, transverse cervical, phrenic, accessory phrenic, and supraclavicular nerves. **p. cervicobrachia'lis,** the cervical and brachial plexuses together. **p. chorioi'deus ventric'uli latera'lis** [B N A], p. choroideus ventriculi lateralis. **p. chorioi'deus ventric'uli quar'ti** [B N A], p. choroideus ventriculi quarti. **p. chorioi'deus ventric'uli ter'tii** [B N A], p. choroideus ventriculi tertii. **choroid p., inferior, choroid p. of fourth ventricle,** p. choroideus ventriculi quarti. **choroid p. of lateral ventricle,** p. choroideus ventriculi lateralis. **choroid p. of third ventricle,** p. choroideus ventriculi tertii. **p. choroi'deus ventric'uli latera'lis** [N A], a vascular, fringelike fold of the pia mater in the floor of the pars centralis and the roof of the inferior horn of the lateral ventricle; probably concerned with production of the cerebrospinal fluid. Called also *choroid p. of lateral ventricle.* **p. choroi'deus ventric'uli quar'ti** [N A], a vascular fringelike fold of the pia mater in the roof of the posterior part of the fourth ventricle; probably concerned with production of the cerebrospinal fluid. Called also *choroid p. of fourth ventricle.* **p. choroi'deus ventric'uli ter'tii** [N A], a vascular, fringelike fold of the pia mater in the roof of the third ventricle; probably concerned with production of the cerebrospinal fluid. Called also *choroid p. of third ventricle.* **coccygeal p., p. coccyg'eus** [N A, B N A], a small plexus formed by the ventral branches of the coccygeal and the fifth sacral nerve, and a communication from the fourth sacral nerve, and giving off the anococcygeal nerves. **p. coeli'acus** [B N A]. 1. Plexus celiacus. 2. A plexus made up of lymphatic vessels and the superior mesenteric lymph nodes and the celiac lymph nodes behind the stomach, duodenum, and pancreas. Omitted in N A. **colic p., left,** the part of the inferior mesenteric plexus that corresponds to the left colic artery. **colic p., middle,** the part of the superior mesenteric plexus that corresponds to the middle colic artery. **colic p., right,** the part of the superior mesenteric plexus that corresponds to the right colic artery. **p. corona'rius cor'dis ante'rior** [B N A], a plexus of sympathetic nerve fibers anterior to the heart. Omitted in N A. **p. corona'rius cor'dis poste'rior** [B N A], a plexus of sympathetic nerve fibers posterior to the heart. Omitted in N A. **coronary p., gastric,** p. gastrici. **coronary p. of heart, anterior,** p. coronarius cordis anterior. **coronary p. of heart, posterior,** p. coronarius cordis posterior. **coronary p. of stomach, superior,** p. gastrici. **crural p.,** p. femoralis. **Cruveilhier's p.** 1. Posterior cervical plexus. 2. A form of angioma made up of a knot of varicose veins. **cystic p.,** a nerve plexus near the gallbladder. **deferential p., p. deferentia'lis** [N A, B N A], the subdivision of the inferior hypogastric plexus that supplies the ductus deferens. **dental p., inferior,** p. dentalis inferior. **dental p., superior,** p. dentalis superior. **p. denta'lis infe'rior** [N A, B N A], a plexus of fibers from the inferior alveolar nerve, situated around the roots of the lower teeth. Called also *inferior dental p.* **p. denta'lis supe'rior** [N A, B N A], a plexus of fibers from the superior alveolar nerves, situated around the roots of the upper teeth. Called also *superior dental p.* **diaphragmatic p.,** p. phrenicus. **dorsal p., ulnar,** a plexus formed by veins from the little finger and from the third and fourth interdigital clefts. **enteric p., p. enter'icus** [N A], a plexus of autonomic nerve fibers within the wall of the digestive tube, and made up of the submucosal, myenteric, and subserosal plexuses; it contains visceral afferent fibers, sympathetic postganglionic fibers, parasympathetic preganglionic and postganglionic fibers, and parasympathetic postganglionic cell bodies. **epigastric p.,** p. celiacus. **esophageal p., p. esophage'us** [N A], a nerve plexus encircling the esophagus, formed by branches of the left and right vagi and sympathetic trunks, and supplying sympathetic, parasympathetic, and visceral sensory innervation to the esophagus. **Exner's p.,** a layer of nerve fibers near the surface of the cerebral cortex. **facial p., p. of facial artery,** p. maxillaris externus. **femoral p., p. femora'lis** [N A, B N A], a subdivision of the celiac portion of the prevertebral plexuses, surrounding the femoral artery. **fundamental p.,** deep stroma p. **p. ganglio'sus cilia'ris** [B N A], a network of nerve fibers about the ciliary body. Omitted in N A. **gastric p's, p. gas'trici** [N A], subdivisions of the celiac portion of the prevertebral plexuses, in proximity with and supplying fibers to the stomach. **p. gas'tricus ante'rior** [B N A]. See *rami gastrici anteriores nervi vagi.* **p. gas'tricus infe'rior** [B N A], a plexus of nerve fibers on the greater curvature of the stomach. **p. gas'tricus poste'rior** [B N A]. See *rami gastrici posteriores nervi vagi.* **p. gas'tricus supe'rior** [B N A], a plexus of nerve fibers on the lesser curvature of the stomach. **gastroepiploic p., left,** a nerve plexus near the greater curvature of the stomach. **p. gu'lae,** p. esophageus. **p. haemorrhoida'lis** [B N A], p. venosus rectalis. **p. haemorrhoida'lis me'dius** [B N A]. See *p. rectales medii.* **p. haemorrhoida'lis supe'rior** [B N A], p. rectalis superior. **Haller's p.,** laryngeal p. **Heller's p.,** an arterial network in the submucosa of the intestine. **hemorrhoidal p.,** p. venosus rectalis. **hemorrhoidal p., middle.** See *p. rectales medii.* **hemorrhoidal p., superior,** p. rectalis superior. **hepatic p., p. hepat'icus** [N A, B N A], a subdivision of the celiac portion of the prevertebral plexuses close to and innervating the liver. **Hovius' p.,** a venous plexus in the ciliary region connected with the sinus venosus sclerae. **hypogastric p.,** the hypogastric portion of the prevertebral plexuses. See *p. hypogastricus inferior* and *p. hypogastricus superior.* **hypogastric p., inferior,** p. hypogastricus inferior. **hypogastric p., superior,** p. hypogastricus superior. **p. hypogas'tricus** [B N A]. 1. See *p. hypogastricus inferior* and *p. hypogastricus superior.* 2. A plexus of lymphatic vessels in the hypogastric region. Omitted in N A. **p. hypogas'tricus infe'rior** [N A], the lower part of the hypogastric portion of the prevertebral plexuses, located deep in the pelvis. Called also *inferior hypogastric p.* and *pelvic p.* **p. hypogas'tricus supe'rior** [N A], the upper part of the hypogastric portion of the prevertebral plexuses, located just anterior to the sacrum. Called also *superior hypogastric p.* and *presacral nerve.* **ileocolic p.,** the part of the superior mesenteric plexus that corresponds to the ileocolic artery. **iliac p's, p. ili'aci** [N A], subdivisions of the celiac portion of the prevertebral plexuses, accompanying the common iliac arteries. **p. ili'acus exter'nus** [B N A], a lymphatic plexus situated about the external iliac vessels. Omitted in N A. **infraorbital p.,** a nerve plexus situated deep to the levator labii superioris muscle. **inguinal p., p. inguina'lis** [B N A], a lymphatic plexus situated near the end of the long saphenous vein and along the femoral artery and vein in the iliopectineal fossa. Omitted in N A. **intercavernous p.,** a network of channels connecting the two cavernous sinuses across both the roof and the floor of the pituitary fossa. **intermesenteric p.,** p. intermesentericus. **intermesenteric p., lumboaortic,** p. aorticus abdominalis. **p. intermesenter'icus** [N A], the part of the celiac portion of the prevertebral plexuses that is located around the aorta, between the celiac trunk and the superior mesenteric artery. **p. of internal carotid vein,** p. venosus caroticus internus. **interradial p.,** Baillarger's lines. **intestinal p., submucous,** p. submucosus. **intramural p.,** an autonomous neuromuscular system within the bladder wall that is capable of functioning when the transmission of impulses from the central nervous system is no longer a possibility. **intrascleral p.,** a network of vessels in the sclera, receiving junctional branches from the sinus venosus sclerae. **ischiadic p.,** p. sacralis. **Jacobson's p.,** p. tympanicus. **jugular p., p. jugula'ris** [B N A], a plexus of lymphatic vessels along the internal jugular vein. Omitted in N A. **laryngeal p.,** a nerve plexus on the outer surface of the inferior constrictor of the pharynx, made up of fibers from the sympathetic and external laryngeal nerves. **lateral p.,** p. choroideus ventriculi lateralis. **Leber's p.,** Hovius' p. **lienal p., p. liena'lis** [N A, B N A], a subdivision of the celiac portion of the prevertebral plexuses, in proximity with and innervating the spleen. Called also *splenic p.* **lingual p., p. lingua'lis** [B N A], a nerve plexus around the lingual artery. Omitted in N A. **p. lumba'lis.** 1. [N A, B N A] A plexus originating from the ventral branches of the twelfth thoracic and the first four lumbar nerves, and giving off the iliohypogastric, ilioinguinal, genitofemoral, lateral femoral cutaneous, obturator, and femoral nerves. 2. [B N A] A lymphatic plexus in the lumbar region. Omitted in N A. **lumbar p.,** p. lumbalis. **lumbosacral p., p. lumbosacra'lis** [N A, B N A], a term applied to the lumbar and sacral nerve plexuses together, because of their continuous nature. **lymphatic p., p. lymphat'icus** [N A, B N A], an interconnecting network of lymph vessels. **p. mamma'rius** [B N A], a plexus of lymph vessels along the internal mammary artery. Omitted in N A. **p. mamma'rius inter'nus** [B N A], a nerve plexus deep in the mammary gland. Omitted in N A. **p. maxilla'ris exter'nus** [B N A], a nerve plexus accompanying the external maxillary artery. Omitted in N A. **p. maxilla'ris inter'nus** [B N A], a nerve plexus accompanying the internal maxillary artery. Omitted in N A. **maxillary p.** See *p. maxillaris externus* and *p. maxillaris internus.* **mediastinal p., subpleural,** a network of arteries situated beneath the mediastinal pleura. **Meissner's p.,** p. submucosus. **p. menin'geus** [B N A], a nerve plexus accompanying the meningeal artery. Omitted in N A. **mesenteric p., inferior,** p. mesentericus inferior. **mesenteric p., superior,** p. mesentericus superior. **p. mesenter'icus infe'rior** [N A, B N A], a subdivision of the celiac portion of the prevertebral plexuses, surrounding the inferior mesenteric artery. Called also *inferior mesenteric p.* **p. mesenter'icus supe'rior** [N A, B N A], a subdivision of the celiac portion of the prevertebral plexuses, surrounding the superior mesenteric artery. **molecular p.,** Exner's p. **myenteric p., p. myenter'icus** [N A, B N A], that part of the enteric plexus within the tunica muscularis. **nasopalatine p.,** a nerve plexus near the incisor foramen. **nerve p.,** a plexus made up of intermingled nerve fibers. **nervoprotoplasmic p's,** three systems of nerve elements contained in the three principal cortical layers of the brain substance. **p. nervo'rum spina'lium** [N A, B N A], a plexus formed by the intermingling of the fibers of two or more spinal nerves, such as the brachial or lumbosacral plexus. Called also *p. of spinal nerves.* **nervous p.,** a plexus made up of intermingled nerve fibers. **occipital p., p. occipita'lis** [B N A], a nerve plexus around the occipital artery. Omitted in N A. **p. oesophage'us ante'rior** [B N A]. See *p. esophageus.* **p. oesophage'us poste'rior** [B N A]. See *p. esophageus.* **ophthalmic p., p. ophthal'micus** [B N A], a nerve plexus situated around the ophthalmic artery and the optic nerve. Omitted in N A. **ovarian p., p. ova'ricus**

[N A], a subdivision of the celiac portion of the prevertebral plexuses, in proximity with and innervating an ovary. Called also *p. arteriae ovaricae* [B N A]. **pampiniform p., p. pampinifor′mis** [N A, B N A]. 1. In the male, a plexus of veins from the testicle and the epididymis, constituting part of the spermatic cord. 2. In the female, a plexus of ovarian veins in the broad ligament. **pancreatic p., p. pancreat′icus** [N A], a subdivision of the celiac portion of the prevertebral plexuses, in proximity with and innervating the pancreas. **Panizza's p's,** two plexuses of the lymph vessels in the lateral fossae of the frenum of the prepuce. **parotid p. of facial nerve, p. parotide′us ner′vi facia′lis** [N A, B N A], a plexus formed by anastomosis of the terminal branches of the temporal, zygomatic, buccal, marginal mandibular, and cervical rami of the facial nerve, arising in the parotid gland. **patellar p.,** a plexus of nerve fibers supplying the region in front of the knee. **pelvic p.,** p. hypogastricus inferior. **p. pelvi′nus,** N A alternative for *p. hypogastricus inferior.* **periarterial p., p. periarteria′lis** [N A], a network of autonomic and sensory nerve fibers in the adventitia of an artery, some of which are following the course of the artery to reach and innervate other structures and some of which innervate the artery itself. **pericorneal p.,** anastomosing branches of the anterior conjunctival arteries, arranged in a superficial conjunctival and a deep episcleral layer about the cornea. **pharyngeal p.,** p. pharyngeus. **pharyngeal p. of vagus nerve,** p. pharyngeus nervi vagi. **p. pharyn′geus** [N A, B N A], a venous plexus posterolateral to the pharynx, formed by the pharyngeal veins, communicating with the pterygoid venous plexus, and draining into the internal jugular vein. **p. pharyn′geus ascen′dens** [B N A], a nerve plexus about the ascending pharyngeal artery. Omitted in N A. **p. pharyn′geus ner′vi va′gi** [N A, B N A], a plexus formed by fibers from branches of the vagus and glossopharyngeal nerves and the autonomic chain, supplying motor, general sensory, and sympathetic innervation to the muscles and mucosa of the pharynx and soft palate, except for the tensor veli palatini muscle. Called also *pharyngeal p. of vagus nerve.* **phrenic p., p. phren′icus** [B N A], a nerve plexus that sends filaments to the diaphragm and the suprarenal capsules. Omitted in N A. **polymorphic p.,** the most deep-seated of the four plexuses of the cerebral cortical substance. **popliteal p., p. poplite′us** [B N A], a plexus of nerve fibers surrounding the popliteal artery. Omitted in N A. **presacral p.,** p. venosus sacralis. **prevertebral p's,** nerve plexuses situated in the thorax, abdomen, and pelvis, anterior to the vertebral column, consisting of visceral afferent fibers, preganglionic parasympathetic fibers, preganglionic and postganglionic sympathetic fibers, and ganglia formed by sympathetic postganglionic cell bodies. In the thorax, the cardiac and pulmonary plexuses, supplying the heart and lungs, are continuous. In the abdominopelvic region, what is essentially one large plexus is divided into an upper, or celiac, portion and a lower, or hypogastric (pelvic), portion. These are in turn subdivided and named according to the organs which they are close to and which they innervate, or according to the arteries which they accompany. **prostatic p.** 1. Plexus prostaticus. 2. Plexus venosus prostaticus. **prostaticovesical p.,** the plexus venosus vesicalis in the male. **p. prostat′icus** [N A, B N A], a subdivision of the inferior hypogastric plexus that supplies fibers to the prostate and adjacent organs. **pterygoid p., p. pterygoi′deus** [N A, B N A], a network of veins corresponding to the second and third parts of the maxillary artery; situated on the lateral surface of the medial pterygoid muscle and on both surfaces of the lateral pterygoid muscle, and draining into the facial vein. **pudendal p.** 1. Nervus pudendus. 2. Plexus venosus prostaticus. **p. pudenda′lis** [B N A], p. venosus prostaticus. **pudendocaudal p.,** the coccygeal and pudendal nerve plexuses together. **p. puden′dus** [B N A], nervus pudendus. **p. pulmona′lis** [N A, B N A], a nerve plexus encircling the root of the lung, formed by branches of the vagus nerve and the sympathetic trunk, and giving sympathetic and parasympathetic innervation to the lung. Called also *pulmonary p.* **p. pulmona′lis ante′rior** [B N A], the portion of the pulmonary plexus in front of the root of the lung. See *p. pulmonalis.* **p. pulmona′lis poste′rior** [B N A], the portion of the pulmonary plexus behind the root of the lung. See *p. pulmonalis.* **pulmonary p.,** p. pulmonalis. **pulmonary p., anterior,** p. pulmonalis anterior. **pulmonary p., posterior,** p. pulmonalis posterior. **pyloric p.,** a nerve plexus that supplies the region of the pylorus. **Ranvier's p.,** accessory p. **p. of Raschkow,** a delicate plexus of nervous fibers beneath the odontoblasts in the dental papilla during the formation of dentin. **rectal p's, inferior,** p. rectales inferiores. **rectal p's, middle,** p. rectales medii. **rectal p., superior,** p. rectalis superior. **p. recta′les inferio′res** [N A], subdivisions of the inferior hypogastric plexus, in proximity with and innervating the lower part of the rectum. Called also *inferior rectal p's.* **p. recta′les me′dii** [N A], subdivisions of the inferior hypogastric plexus, in proximity with and supplying fibers to the rectum. Called also *p. haemorrhoidalis medius* [B N A], and *middle rectal p.* **p. recta′lis supe′rior** [N A], a subdivision of the celiac portion of the prevertebral plexuses, in proximity with and innervating the upper part of the rectum. Called also *p. haemorrhoidalis superior* [B N A], and *superior rectal p.* **Remak's p.,** p. submucosus. **renal p., p. rena′lis** [N A, B N A], a subdivision of the celiac portion of the prevertebral plexuses, in proximity with and innervating a kidney. **sacral p.** 1. Plexus sacralis. 2. Plexus venosus sacralis. **sacral p., anterior,** p. venosus sacralis. **sacral lymphatic p.,** p. sacralis medius. **p. sacra′lis** [N A, B N A], a plexus arising from the ventral branches of the last two lumbar and first four sacral nerves, and giving off the superior and inferior gluteal, posterior femoral cutaneous, ischiadic, and pudendal nerves. **p. sacra′lis ante′rior** [B N A], p. venosus sacralis. **p. sacra′lis me′dius** [B N A], a fine network of lymphatic vessels in the hollow of the sacrum. Omitted in N A. **Santorini's p.** 1. Plexus prostaticus. 2. Plexus venosus prostaticus. **Sappey's subareolar p.,** a lymphatic plexus situated beneath the areola of the nipple. **solar p.,** p. celiacus. **spermatic p.** 1. Plexus testicularis. 2. Plexus pampiniformis. **p. spermat′icus** [B N A], p. testicularis. **sphenoid p.,** the upper portion of the internal carotid plexus. **p. of spinal nerves,** p. nervorum spinalium. **splenic p.,** p. lienalis. **Stenson's p.,** the venous network around the parotid duct. **stroma p.,** a network formed by ramifications of nerve fibrils within the substantia propria of the cornea. **stroma p., deep,** the more deeply seated portion of the stroma plexus. **sub-basal p.,** the superficial stroma plexus. **subclavian p., p. subcla′vius** [N A, B N A], a sympathetic plexus on the subclavian artery, arising from the cervicothoracic ganglion, and contributing fibers to the internal thoracic artery and the phrenic nerve. **submolecular p.,** a plexus of the cerebral cortex lying just within Exner's plexus. **submucosal p., p. submuco′sus** [N A, B N A], **submucous p.,** the part of the enteric plexus that is situated deep to the tunica mucosa. **subpleural mediastinal p.,** an arterial plexus beneath the mediastinal pleura. **subsartorial p.,** a nerve plexus at the posterior border of the sartorius muscle, formed by fibers from the obturator, long saphenous, and internal cutaneous nerves. **subserosal p., p. subsero′sus** [N A], the part of the enteric plexus situated deep to the tunica serosa. **subtrapezius p.,** a nerve plexus which is situated deep to the trapezius muscle. **supraradial p.,** Bechterew's layer. **suprarenal p., p. suprarena'lis** [N A, B N A], a subdivision of the celic portion of the prevertebral plexuses, in proximity with and supplying fibers to a suprarenal (adrenal) gland. **p. sympath'ici** [B N A], p. autonomici. **p. tempora'lis superficia'lis** [B N A], a plexus of nerve fibers about the superficial temporal artery. Omitted in N A. **testicular p., p. testicula'ris** [N A], a subdivision of the celiac portion of the prevertebral plexuses, accompanying the spermatic artery to a testis. Called also *p. spermaticus* [B N A]. **p. thyreoi'deus im'par** [B N A], p. thyroideus impar. **p. thyreoi'deus infe'rior** [B N A], a nerve plexus accompanying the inferior thyroid artery and supplying fibers to the larynx, pharynx, and thyroid region. Omitted in N A. **p. thyreoi'deus supe'rior** [B N A], a nerve plexus accompanying the superior thyroid artery and supplying fibers to the larynx, pharynx, and thyroid region. Omitted in N A. **thyroid p., inferior,** p. thyreoideus inferior. **thyroid p., superior,** p. thyreoideus superior. **thyroid p., unpaired,** p. thyroideus impar. **p. thyroi'deus im'par** [N A], a venous plexus investing the surface of the thyroid gland. **tonsillar p.,** a nerve plexus supplying fibers to the fauces, tonsil, and soft palate. **Trolard's p.,** p. venosus canalis hypoglossi. **tympanic p., p. tympan'icus** [N A], **p. tympan'icus [Jacobso'ni]** [B N A], a nerve plexus in the middle ear on the promontory, formed by the tympanic and caroticotympanic nerves. It sends sensory fibers to the middle ear, tympanic membrane, and auditory tube, and sympathetic fibers to the parotid gland. It also contains parasympathetic fibers destined for the parotid gland. **ureteric p., p. ureter'icus** [N A], a subdivision of the celiac portion of the prevertebral plexuses, in proximity with and innervating a ureter. **uterine p.** 1. The part of the uterovaginal plexus that supplies the cervix and lower part of the uterus. 2. Plexus venosus uterinus. **uterovaginal p., p. uterovagina'lis.** 1. [N A, B N A] The subdivision of the inferior hypogastric plexus that supplies fibers to the uterus, ovary, vagina, urethra, and the erectile tissue of the vestibule. 2. [B N A] See *p. venosus uterinus* and *p. venosus vaginalis.* **vaginal p.** 1. The part of the uterovaginal plexus that supplies nerve fibers to the walls of the vagina. 2. Plexus venosus vaginalis. **vascular p.,** p. vasculosus. **vascular p., coccygeal,** glomus coccygeum. **p. vascu'losus** [N A, B N A], a network of intercommunicating blood vessels. Called also *vascular plexus.* **p. veno'sus** [N A, B N A], a network of interconnecting veins. Called also *venous p.* **p. veno'sus areola'ris** [N A], a venous plexus in the areola around the nipple, formed by branches of the internal thoracic veins and draining into the lateral thoracic vein. Called also *p. venosus mamillae* [B N A], and *areolar venous p.* **p. veno'sus cana'lis hypoglos'si** [N A], a venous plexus surrounding the hypoglossal nerve in its canal, and connecting the occipital sinus with the vertebral vein and with the longitudinal vertebral venous sinuses. Called also *rete canalis hypoglossi* [B N A], and *venous p. of hypoglossal canal.* **p. veno'sus carot'icus inter'nus** [N A, B N A], a venous plexus around the petrosal portion of the internal carotid artery, through which the cavernous sinus communicates with the internal jugular vein. Called also *p. of internal carotid vein.* **p. veno'sus foram'inis ova'lis** [N A], a venous plexus that connects the cavernous sinus through the foramen ovale with the pterygoid plexus and the pharyngeal plexus. Called also *rete foraminis ovalis* [B N A], and *venous p. of foramen ovale.* **p. veno'sus mamil'lae** [B N A], p. venosus areolaris. **p. veno'sus prostat'icus** [N A], a venous plexus around the prostate gland, receiving the deep dorsal vein of the penis and draining through the vesical plexus and the prostatic veins. Called also *p. pudendalis* [B N A], and *prostatic venous p.* **p. veno'sus recta'lis** [N A], a venous plexus that surrounds the lower part of the rectum and drains into the rectal veins; a source of collateral portal circulation in event of hepatic obstruction. Called also *p. haemorrhoidalis* [B N A], and *rectal venous p.* **p. veno'sus sacra'lis** [N A], the plexus on the pelvic surface of the sacrum that receives the sacral intervertebral veins, anastomoses with neighboring lumbar and pelvic veins, and drains into the middle and lateral sacral veins. Called also *p. sacralis anterior* [B N A], and *sacral venous p.* **p. veno'sus suboccipita'lis** [N A], that part of the external vertebral plexus which lies on and in the suboccipital triangle, receives the occipital veins of the scalp, and drains into the subclavian vein. Called also *suboccipital venous p.* **p. veno'sus uteri'nus** [N A], the venous plexus around the uterus, draining into the internal iliac veins by way of the uterine veins. Called also *uterine p.* **p. veno'sus vagina'lis** [N A], a venous plexus in the walls of the vagina, which drains into the internal iliac veins by way of the internal pudendal veins. Called also *vaginal p.* **p. veno'si vertebra'les anterio'res** [B N A], plexuses of veins on the anterior aspect of the vertebral column. See *p. venosi vertebrales externi [anterior et posterior].* **p. veno'si vertebra'les exter'ni** [B N A], plexuses of veins ramifying external to the bodies of the vertebrae. See *p. venosi vertebrales externi [anterior et posterior].* **p. veno'si vertebra'les exter'ni [ante'rior et poste'rior]** [N A], venous plexuses situated on the anterior aspect of the bodies of the vertebrae and on the posterior aspect of the vertebral arches, spines, and transverse processes. Called also *external vertebral p's [anterior and posterior].* **p. veno'si vertebra'les inter'ni** [B N A], plexuses of venous sinuses ramifying external to the dura mater, within the vertebral canal. See *p. venosi vertebrales interni [anterior et posterior].* **p. veno'si vertebra'les inter'ni [ante'rior et poste'rior]** [N A], networks of venous sinuses communicating freely within the vertebral foramina and ramifying externally to the dura mater, anterior and posterior to the spinal cord. Called also *internal vertebral p's [anterior and posterior].* **p. veno'si vertebra'les posterio'res** [B N A], plexuses of veins on the posterior aspect of the vertebral column. See *p. venosi vertebrales externi [anterior et posterior].* **p. veno'sus vesica'lis** [N A], a venous plexus surrounding the upper part of the urethra and the neck of the bladder, communicating with the vaginal plexus in the female and with the prostatic plexus in the male. Called also *vesical venous p.* **venous p.,** a network of interconnecting veins (p. venosus [N A]). **venous p., areolar,** p. venous areolaris. **venous p., hemorrhoidal,** p. venous rectalis. **venous p., prostatic,** p. venosus prostaticus. **venous p., rectal,** p. venosus rectalis. **venous p., sacral,** p. venosus sacralis. **venous p., suboccipital,** p. venosus suboccipitalis. **venous p., uterine,** p. venosus uterinus. **venous p., vaginal,** p. venosus vaginalis. **venous p., vesical,** p. venosus vesicalis. **venous p. of foot, dorsal,** rete venosum dorsale pedis. **venous p. of foramen ovale,** p. venosus foraminis ovalis. **venous p. of hand, dorsal,** rete venosum dorsale manus. **venous p. of hypoglossal canal,** p. venosus canalis hypoglossi. **vertebral p.** 1. A plexus of nerves related to the vertebral artery. See *p. vertebralis.* 2. A plexus of veins related to the vertebral column. See terms beginning *p. venosi vertebrales.* **vertebral p's, internal.** See *p. venosi vertebrales interni [anterior et posterior].* **vertebral p's, external.** See *p. venosi vertebrales externi [anterior et posterior].* **p. vertebra'lis** [N A, B N A], a nerve plexus around the vertebral artery, formed by the vertebral nerve and giving sympathetic innervation to the posterior cranial fossa via cranial nerves. Called also *vertebral p.* **vesical p.** 1. Plexus vesicale. 2. Plexus venosus vesicalis. **p. vesica'le** [N A], the subdivision of the inferior hypogastric plexus that supplies sympathetic fibers to the urinary bladder and adjacent structures. Called also *p. vesicalis* [B N A]. **p. vesica'lis** [B N A]. 1. Plexus venosus vesicalis. 2. Plexus vesicale. **vesicoprostatic p.,** the plexus venosus vesicalis in the male. **vidian p.,** nervus canalis pterygoidei.

-plexy (plek'se) [Gr. *plēxis* a stroke]. Word termination meaning a stroke, or seizure.

plica (pli'kah), pl. *pli'cae* [L.]. A fold. Used in anatomical nomenclature to designate a ridge or fold, as of peritoneum or other membrane. **pli'cae adipo'sae pleu'rae** [B N A], folds of fat in the pleura. Omitted in N A. **pli'cae ala'res** [N A, B N A], a pair of folds of the synovial membrane of the knee joint; attached to the medial and lateral margins of the articular surface of the patella, they pass posteriorly, converge, and become continuous with the infrapatellar synovial fold. Called also *alar folds.* **pli'cae ampulla'res tu'bae uteri'nae** [B N A], the folds of the mucous coat lining the ampulla of the uterine tube. Omitted in N A. **p. aryepiglot'tica** [N A, B N A], a fold of mucous membrane extending on each side between the lateral border of the epiglottis and the summit of the arytenoid cartilage. Called also *aryepiglottic fold.* **p. axilla'ris ante'rior** [N A, B N A], the fold of skin forming the anterior boundary of the axilla. **p. axilla'ris poste'rior** [N A, B N A], the fold of skin forming the posterior boundary of the axilla. **p. caeca'lis** [B N A]. See *plicae cecales.* **pli'cae ceca'les** [N A], peritoneal folds on either side of the retrocecal recess, which may connect the cecum to the abdominal wall. Called also *cecal folds.* **p. ceca'lis vascula'ris** [N A], the fold of peritoneum that covers the anterior cecal vessels, forming the superior ileocecal recess. Called also *vascular cecal fold.* **p. chor'dae tym'pani** [N A], a fold in the mucous membrane of the tympanic cavity overlying the chorda tympani nerve. **pli'cae cilia'res** [N A, B N A], low ridges in the furrows between the ciliary processes. Called also *ciliary folds.* **pli'cae circula'res** [N A], **pli'cae circula'res [Kerk'ringi]** [B N A], **pli'cae conniven'tes,** the permanent transverse folds of the small intestine, involving both the mucosa and submucosa. Called also *circular folds.* **p. cor'dae utero-inguina'lis,** ligamentum teres uteri. **p. duodena'lis infe'rior** [N A], a thin fold of peritoneum that bounds the inferior duodenal recess. Called also *p. duodenomesocolica* [B N A], and *inferior duodenal fold.* **p. duodena'lis supe'rior** [N A], a fold of peritoneum covering the inferior mesenteric vein and the ascending branch of the left colic artery. Called also *p. duodenojejunalis* [B N A], and *superior duodenal fold.* **p. duodenojejuna'lis** [B N A], p. duodenalis superior; accepted as an official alternative by N A. **p. duodenomesocol'ica** [B N A], p. duodenalis inferior; accepted as an official alternative by N A. **p. epigas'trica** [B N A], p. umbilicalis lateralis, def. 1. **p. epigas'trica peritonae'i** [B N A], p. umbilicalis lateralis, def. 2. **epiglottic p.,** a fold of mucous membrane between the tongue and the epiglottis. **p. fimbria'ta** [N A, B N A], the lobulated fold running backward and outward from the anterior extremity of the frenulum of the tongue. Called also *fimbriated fold.* **pli'cae gas'tricae** [N A], the series of folds in the mucous membrane of the stomach; they are oriented chiefly longitudinally and partially disappear when the stomach is distended. Called also *gastric folds.* **p. gastropancreat'ica** [B N A]. See *plicae gastropancreaticae.* **pli'cae gastropancreat'icae** [N A], two folds of peritoneum, one covering the left gastric artery, the other the common hepatic artery, between the pancreas and the lesser curvature of the stomach. Called also *gastropancreatic folds.* **p. glossoepiglot'tica latera'lis** [B N A], either of two folds of mucous membrane extending, one on either side, between the base of the tongue and the epiglottis. Omitted in N A. **p. glossoepiglot'tica media'na** [B N A], a single fold of mucous membrane between the two lateral glossoepiglottic folds, connecting the base of the tongue and the epiglottis. Omitted in N A. **p. hypogas'trica,** p. umbilicalis medialis. **p. ileocaeca'lis** [B N A], **p. ileoceca'lis** [N A], a fold of peritoneum at the left border of the cecum, extending from the ileum above to the appendix below. Called also *ileocecal fold.* **p. in'cudis** [N A, B N A], a variable fold in the tunica mucosa of the tympanic cavity, passing from the roof of the cavity to the body and short crus of the incus. Called also *incudal fold.* **p. interdigita'lis,** the free border of the web connecting the bases of adjoining digits. **p. interureter'ica** [N A], a fold of mucous membrane passing between the two ureteric orifices. Called also *p. ureterica* [B N A], and *interureteric fold.* **pli'cae i'ridis** [N A, B N A], the numerous minute folds on the posterior surface of the iris. Called also *iridial folds.* **pli'cae isth'micae tu'bae uteri'nae** [B N A], a fold of peritoneum at the junction of the uterine tube and uterus. Omitted in N A. **p. lacrima'lis** [N A], **p. lacrima'lis [Has'neri]** [B N A], a fold of mucous membrane at the lower opening of the nasolacrimal duct. Called also *lacrimal fold.* **p. longitudina'lis duode'ni** [N A, B N A], a more or less distinct elevation on the medial wall of the descending part of the duodenum. Called also *longitudinal fold of duodenum.* **p. luna'ta,** p. semilunaris conjunctivae. **p. mallea'ris ante'rior membra'nae tym'pani** [N A], the fold in the tympanic membrane that extends anteriorly from the mallear prominence to help separate the pars tensa from the pars flaccida. Called also *p. malleolaris anterior membranae tympani* [B N A], and *anterior mallear fold of tympanic membrane.* **p. mallea'ris ante'rior tu'nicae muco'sae ca'vi ty'mpani** [N A], a fold in the tunica mucosa of the tympanic cavity, reflected from the tympanic membrane over the anterior process and ligament of the malleus and part of the chorda tympani nerve. Called also *p. malleolaris anterior tunicae mucosae cavi tympani* [B N A], and *anterior mallear fold of mucous coat of tympanic cavity.* **p. mallea'ris poste'rior membra'nae tym'pani** [N A], the fold in the tympanic membrane that extends posteriorly from the mallear prominence to help separate the pars tensa from the pars flaccida. Called also *p. malleolaris posterior membranae tympani* [B N A], and *posterior mallear fold of tympanic membrane.* **p. mallea'ris poste'rior tu'nicae muco'sae ca'vi tym'pani** [N A], a fold of the tunica mucosa of the tympanic cavity, extending from the manubrium of the malleus to the posterior wall of the cavity. Called also *p. malleolaris posterior tunicae mucosae cavi tympani* [B N A], and *posterior mallear fold of mucous coat of tympanic cavity.* **p. malleola'ris ante'rior membra'nae tym'pani** [B N A], p. mallearis anterior membranae tympani. **p. malleola'ris ante'rior tu'nicae muco'sae tympan'icae** [B N A], p. mallearis anterior tunicae mucosae cavi tympani. **p. malleola'ris poste'rior membra'nae tym'pani** [B N A], p. mallearis posterior membranae tympani. **p. malleola'ris poste'rior tu'nicae muco'sae tympan'icae** [B N A], p. mallearis posterior tunicae mucosae cavi tympani. **p. membra'nae tym'pani exter'na ante'rior,** p. mallearis anterior membranae tympani. **p. membra'nae tym'pani exter'na poste'rior,** p. mallearis posterior membranae tympani. **p. muco'sa** [B N A], a fold of mucous membrane. Omitted in N A. **p. ner'vi laryn'gei** [B N A], a fold of mucous membrane in the larynx, overlying the laryngeal nerve. Omitted in N A. **pli'cae palati'nae transver'sae** [N A, B N A], four to six transverse ridges on the anterior part of the hard palate. Called also *transverse palatine ridges.* **pli'cae palma'tae** [N A, B N A], a system of folds on the anterior and posterior walls of the cervical canal of the uterus, consisting of a median longitudinal ridge and shorter elevations extending laterally and upward. Called also *palmate folds.* **p. palpebronasa'lis** [N A], a vertical fold of skin on either side of the nose, covering the medial canthus of the eye. See *epicanthus.* **p. paraduodena'lis** [N A], an occasionally found peritoneal fold containing a branch of the left colic artery. Called also *paraduodenal fold.* **p. polon'ica,** a matted state of the hair, as the result of being covered with crusts and vermin. **p. pubovesica'lis** [B N A], a fold of peritoneum between the pubis and bladder. Omitted in N A. **p. rec'ti.** See *plicae transversales recti.* **p. rectouteri'na** [N A], **p. rectouteri'na [Doug'lasi]** [B N A], a crescentic fold of peritoneum extending from the rectum to the base of the broad ligament on either side, forming the rectouterine pouch. Called also *rectouterine fold.* **p. salpingopalati'na** [N A, B N A], the mucosal fold passing caudally from the auditory tube to the lateral pharyngeal wall. Called also *salpingopalatine fold.* **p. salpingopharyn'gea** [N A, B N A], a mucosal fold passing caudally from the posterior lip of the pharyngeal orifice of the auditory tube to the lateral pharyngeal wall. Called also *salpingopharyngeal fold.* **p. semiluna'ris** [N A], a curved fold interconnecting the palatoglossal and palatopharyngeal arches and forming the upper boundary of the supratonsillar fossa. Called also *semilunar fold.* **pli'cae semiluna'res co'li** [N A, B N A], crescentic folds in the wall of the large intestine, projecting into the lumen between the haustra. Called also *semilunar folds of colon.* **p. semiluna'ris conjuncti'vae** [N A, B N A], a fold of mucous membrane at the medial angle of the eye. Called also *semilunar fold of conjunctiva.* **p. sero'sa** [B N A], a fold of serous membrane. Omitted in N A. **p. sigmoi'dea co'li.** See *plicae semilunares coli.* **p. spira'lis** [N A], a spirally arranged elevation in the mucosa of the first part of the cystic duct. Called also *valvula spiralis [Heisteri]* [B N A], and *spiral fold.* **p. stape'dis** [N A, B N A], a mucosal fold that passes from the posterior wall of the tympanic cavity along the tympanic membrane and surrounds the stapes. Called also *stapedial fold.* **p. sublingua'lis** [N A, B N A], the elevation on the floor of the mouth under the tongue, covering part of the sublingual gland and containing its excretory ducts. Called also *sublingual fold.* **p. synovia'lis** [N A, B N A], an extension of the synovial membrane from its free inner surface into the joint cavity. Called also *synovial fold.* **p. synovia'lis infrapatella'ris** [N A], **p. synovia'lis patella'ris** [B N A], a large process of synovial membrane, containing some fat, which projects into the knee joint; attached to the infrapatellar adipose body, it passes posteriorly and superiorly to the intercondylar fossa of the femur. Called also *infrapatellar synovial fold.* **pli'cae transversa'les rec'ti** [N A, B N A], three permanent transverse folds in the rectum, involving the tunica mucosa and tela submucosa, and the circular layer of the tunica muscularis. Called also *transverse folds of rectum.* **p. triangula'ris** [N A, B N A], a fold of mucous membrane extending backward from the palatoglossal arch and covering the anteroinferior part of the palatine tonsil. Called also *triangular fold.* **pli'cae tuba'riae tu'bae uteri'nae** [N A, B N A], the folds of the mucous lining of the uterine tube, which are high and complex in the ampulla. Called also *tubal folds of uterine tube.* **pli'cae tu'nicae muco'sae ves'icae fel'leae** [N A, B N A], the folds in the mucosa of the gallbladder that bound the polygonal spaces, giving the interior a honeycombed appearance. **p. umbilica'lis latera'lis.** 1. [N A] A laterally placed indistinct line on either side of the inferior part of the anterior abdominal wall, overlying the inferior epigastric vessels. Called also *p. epigastrica* [B N A], and *lateral umbilical fold.* 2. [N A] The fold of peritoneum covering the inferior epigastric vessels. Called also *plica epigastrica peritonaei* [B N A]. 3. [B N A] Plica umbilicalis medialis. **p. umbilica'lis me'dia** [B N A], p. umbilicalis mediana. **p. umbilica'lis media'lis** [N A], the fold of peritoneum that covers the obliterated umbilical artery. Called also *p. umbilicalis lateralis* [B N A], and *medial umbilical fold.* **p. umbilica'lis media'na** [N A], the fold of peritoneum that covers the median umbilical ligament. Called also *p. umbilicalis media* [B N A], and *median umbilical fold.* **p. ura'chi,** p. umbilicalis mediana. **p. ureter'ica** [B N A], p. interureterica. **pli'cae vagi'nae,** rugae vaginales. **p. ve'nae ca'vae sinis'trae** [N A], a fold of visceral pericardium enclosing the remnant of the embryonic left anterior cardinal vein. Called also *ligamentum venae cavae sinistrae* [B N A]. **p. ventricula'ris** [B N A], p. vestibularis. **p. vesica'lis transver'sa** [N A, B N A], a transverse fold of the peritoneum extending from the bladder onto the pelvic wall when the bladder is empty. Called also *transverse vesical fold.* **p. vestibula'ris** [N A], a fold of mucous membrane in the larynx, separating the ventricle from the vestibule. Called also *false vocal cord* and *vestibular fold.* **pli'cae villo'sae ventric'uli** [N A, B N A], a fine network of furrows, marking off areas of the stomach. Called also *villous folds of stomach.* **p. voca'lis** [N A, B N A], a fold of mucous membrane in the larynx, forming the inferior boundary of the ventricle, the vocalis muscle being situated deep to it. Called also *true vocal cord* and *vocal fold.*

plicadentin (pli″kah-den′tin) [*plica* + *dentin*]. A modification of the dentin in which the fibers diverge in many lines from the central pulp cavity of the tooth.

plicate (pli′kāt) [L. *plicatus*]. Plaited or folded.

plication (pli-ka′shun). A folding; also the operation of taking tucks in a muscle for shortening it, or in the walls of a hollow organ in order to reduce its size.

plicidentin (pli″sĭ-den′tin). Dentin formed in complex foldings, as seen in the teeth of reptiles and certain fish.

plicotomy (pli-kot′o-me) [*plica* + Gr. *tomē* a cutting]. Surgical division of the posterior fold of the tympanic membrane.

pliers (pli′erz). Small tong-jawed pincers for bending metals or holding small objects. Various forms are much used in dental work. **Allen's root p.,** an instrument for removing fragments of bone broken off from tooth roots or from the alveolar process in extraction of teeth.

Plimmer's bodies, salt (plim′erz) [Henry George *Plimmer*, English zoologist, 1857–1918]. See under *body* and *salt.*

plint (plint). Plinth.

plinth (plinth). A padded table for a patient to sit or lie on while performing therapeutic exercises.

plocach (plo′kāk). Sheep cholera.

-ploid (ploid). Word termination denoting (1—adjective) condition in regard to degree of multiplication of chromosome sets in the karyotype, or (2—noun) an individual or cell having chromosome sets of the particular degree of multiplication in the karyotype indicated by the root to which it is added.

ploidy (ploi′de) [from Gr. suffix *ploos* in *diploos*, etc; actually from poly*ploidy*]. The status of the chromosome set in the karyotype. Used also as a word termination denoting the condition in regard to the degree of multiplication of chromosome sets, as aneuploidy, diploidy, haploidy, etc.

plombage (plom-bahzh′) [Fr., "sealing, stopping"]. The surgical filling of an empty space in the body with inert material, as the filling of part of the chest with methyl methacrylate balls.

plombierung (plom-bēr′ung) [Ger. "plugging"]. 1. The operation of plugging defects in bone, such as osteomyelitis, with preparations of iodoform. 2. Plombage.

plotolysin (plo″to-li′sin). The hemotoxic fraction of plototoxin.

plotospasmin (plo″to-spaz′min). The neurotoxic fraction of plototoxin.

plototoxin (plo″to-tok′sin). A toxic substance derived from the catfish, *Plotosus lineatus*, said to be composed of a hemotoxic fraction (plotolysin) and a neurotoxic fraction (plotospasmin).

plug (plug). A lumpy mass, which closes or obstructs an opening. **copulation p.**, vaginal p. **Corner's p.**, a piece of omentum inserted into a duodenal perforation as a temporary measure in cases which cannot be operated on at the time. **Dittrich's p's**, yellowish or gray caseous masses, of varying size, consisting of granular debris, fat globules, fatty acid crystals, and bacteria frequently found in the sputum, or expectorated alone, in cases of putrid bronchitis or bronchiectasis. **Ecker's p.**, a plug of cells in the primitive mouth of the gastrula. **epithelial p.**, a mass of ectodermal cells that temporarily closes the external naris of the fetus. **Imlach's fat p.**, a mass of fatty tissue sometimes found at the mesial angle of the external inguinal ring. **mucous p.**, a plug formed by secretions of the mucous glands of the cervix uteri and closing the cervical canal during pregnancy. **Traube's p's**, Dittrich's p's. **vaginal p.**, a plug consisting of a mass of coagulated sperm which forms in the vagina of animals after coitus: called also *bouchon vaginal* and *copulation p.* **yolk p.**, the mass of yolk cells protruding from the blastopore of amphibians at the end of gastrulation.

Plugge's test (plug′ēz) [Pieter Cornelis *Plugge*, Dutch biochemist, 1847–1897]. See under *tests.*

plugger (plug′er). A dental instrument used for packing, condensing, and compacting filling material into a tooth cavity. **amalgam p.**, an instrument for condensing amalgam in a tooth cavity. **automatic p.**, one which operates by means of a spring, by attachment to a dental engine, or by a pneumatic or electronic device. **back-action p.**, one having a bent shank so that the direction of the force applied is toward the operator. **electromagnetic p.**, one which is activated by an electromagnet. **foil p.**, one for condensing foil in a tooth cavity. **foot p.**, one having a long, angled, foot-shaped nib. **gold p.**, an instrument for condensing gold in a tooth cavity. **reverse p.**, back-action p.

plumbage (ploom-bahzh′). Plombage.

plumbagin (plum-ba′jin). An irritant substance, 5-hydroxy 2-methyl 1,4-naphthoquinone, $CH_3.C_{10}H_4(:O)_2.OH$, obtained from various species of *Plumbago*, which has been used as an abortifacient.

plumbago (plum-ba′go). See *graphite.*

plumbi (plum′bi) [L.]. Genitive of *plumbum*, lead. **p. ace′tas**, lead acetate. **p. carbo′nas**, lead carbonate. **p. chlo′ridum**, lead chloride. **p. io′didum**, lead iodide. **p. monox′idum**, lead monoxide. **p. ni′tras**, lead nitrate. **p. ox′idum**, lead monoxide. **p. tan′nas**, lead tannate.

plumbic (plum′bik) [L. *plumbicus* leaden]. Pertaining to or containing lead.

plumbism (plum′bizm). A chronic form of poisoning produced by the absorption of lead or one of the salts of lead.

plumbotherapy (plum″bo-ther′ah-pe) [L. *plumbum* lead + *therapy*]. Lead treatment; lead cure.

plumbum (plum′bum), gen. *plum′bi* [L.]. Lead.

Plummer's disease (plum′erz) [Henry S. *Plummer*, American physician, 1874–1937]. See under *disease.*

Plummer-Vinson syndrome (plum′er-vin′son) [Henry S. *Plummer;* Porter P. *Vinson*, American surgeon, born 1890]. See under *syndrome.*

plumose (plu′mōs) [L. *plumosus*, Fr. *pluma* feather]. Feathery; resembling a feather.

plumula (plum′u-lah). A set of delicate crossfurrows on the upper wall of the aqueduct of Sylvius.

pluri- (ploor′ĭ) [L. *plus* more]. Combining form meaning several or more.

pluriceptor (ploor″ĭ-sep′tor) [*pluri-* + L. *capere* to take]. A receptor which has more than two complementophil groups.

pluricordonal (ploor″ĭ-kor′do-nal). See under *cell.*

pluricytopenia (ploor″ĭ-si″to-pe′ne-ah). Deficiency of all the cellular elements of the blood; aplastic anemia.

pluridyscrinia (ploor″ĭ-dis-krin′e-ah) [*pluri-* + *dyscrinia*]. Coincident disorder of several endocrine organs.

pluriglandular (ploor″ĭ-glan′du-lar). Pertaining to, derived from, or affecting several glands.

plurigravida (ploor″ĭ-grav′ĭ-dah) [*pluri-* + L. *gravida* pregnant]. A woman pregnant for the third time or more.

plurilocular (ploor″ĭ-lok′u-lar). Multilocular.

plurimenorrhea (ploor″ĭ-men″o-re′ah). Increased frequency of menstrual periods.

plurinatality (ploor″ĭ-na-tal′ĭ-te). Large birth rate.

plurinuclear (ploor″ĭ-nu′kle-ar) [*pluri-* + *nucleus*]. Having several nuclei.

pluriorificial (ploor″e-or″ĭ-fish′al) [*pluri-* + L. *orificium* orifice]. Pertaining to or affecting several orifices of the body.

pluripara (ploo-rip′ah-rah) [*pluri-* + L. *parere* to bear]. Multipara.

pluriparity (ploor″ĭ-par′ĭ-te). The fact or condition of having borne several children.

pluripolar (ploor″ĭ-po′lar). Having several poles, said of ganglion cells, etc.

pluripotent (ploo-rip′o-tent). Pluripotential.

pluripotential (ploor″ĭ-po-ten′shal). Pertaining to or characterized by pluripotentiality.

pluripotentiality (ploor″ĭ-po-ten″she-al′ĭ-te) [*pluri-* + L. *potentia* power]. Possession of the power of developing or acting in any one of several possible ways.

pluriresistant (ploor″ĭ-re-zis′tant). Resistant to several drugs: said especially of syphilis which does not respond to arsphenamine, bismuth, and mercury.

pluritissular (ploor″ĭ-tis′u-lar). Composed of several tissues.

plutomania (ploo″to-ma′ne-ah) [Gr. *ploutos* riches + *mania* madness]. Delusion that one is wealthy; morbid preoccupation with thoughts of riches.

plutonium (ploo-to′ne-um) [named from the planet *Pluto*]. An element of atomic number 94, atomic weight 242, obtained by splitting the uranium atom, which changes into neptunium and then into plutonium. Symbol Pu.

P.M. Abbreviation for *pulpomesial.*

Pm. Chemical symbol for *promethium.*

PMA. An expression of the prevalence of gingivitis in large groups of persons, *P* representing the papillary portion of the gingiva, *M* the marginal portion, and *A* the attached portion.

P.M.B. Abbreviation for *polymorphonuclear basophil leukocytes.*

P.M.E. Abbreviation for *polymorphonuclear eosinophil leukocytes.*

P.M.I. Abbreviation for *point of maximal impulse.*

P.M.N. Abbreviation for *polymorphonuclear neutrophil leukocytes.*

P.N. Abbreviation for *percussion note.*

pnein (ne′in). A hypothetical substance supposed to be present in the tissues and to act as an accelerator of the oxidizing activities of the tissues.

pneo- (ne′o) [Gr. *pnein* to breathe]. Combining form denoting relationship to the breath, or to breathing.

pneodynamics (ne″o-di-nam′iks) [*pneo-* + *dynamics*]. The dynamics of respiration.

pneogaster (ne′o-gas″ter) [*pneo-* + Gr. *gastēr* the belly]. The respiratory tract of the embryo.

pneogram (ne′o-gram). The tracing obtained by use of the pneograph.

pneograph (ne′o-graf) [*pneo-* + Gr. *graphein* to write]. A device for registering the movements of the chest wall in respiration.

pneometer (ne-om′e-ter) [*pneo-* + Gr. *metron* measure]. A device for measuring the air passing into and out of the lungs in respiration.

pneoscope (ne′o-skōp) [*pneo-* + Gr. *skopein* to examine]. A device for determining movements of the chest wall in respiration.

pneuma- (nu′mah). See *pneumato-*.

pneumal (nu′mal). Pertaining to the lungs.

pneumarthrogram (nu-mar′thro-gram) [*pneumo-* + Gr. *arthron* joint + *gamma* that which is written]. A roentgenogram of a joint after it has been injected with air.

pneumarthrography (nu″mar-throg′rah-fe). Roentgenography of a joint after it has been injected with air.

pneumarthrosis (nu″mar-thro′sis) [*pneumo-* + Gr. *arthron* joint + *-osis*]. 1. The presence of gas or air in a joint. 2. The inflation of a joint with air or gas for the purpose of aiding roentgenographical examination.

pneumascope (nu′mah-skōp). Pneumoscope.

pneumascos (nu-mas′kos) [*pneuma-* + Gr. *askos* sac]. Pneumoperitoneum.

pneumathemia (nu″mah-the′me-ah) [*pneumo-* + Gr. *haima* blood + *-ia*]. The presence of air or gas in the blood vessels; aeremia.

pneumatic (nu-mat′ik) [L. *pneumaticus;* Gr. *pneumatikos*]. Of or pertaining to air or respiration.

pneumatics (nu-mat′iks). The science which deals with the physical properties of gases.

pneumatinuria (nu″mah-tĭ-nu′re-ah). Pneumaturia.

pneumatism (nu′mah-tizm). The doctrine of the Pneumatist school or sect of ancient medicine.

Pneumatist (nu′mah-tist). 1. A school or sect of ancient medicine, founded by Athenaeus of Attalia, and based on the action and constitution of the *pneuma*, or vital air, which passed from the lungs into the heart and arteries and was then disseminated throughout the body. Among other members of this school were Agathinus of Sparta, Archigenes of Apamea, Aretaeus of Cappadocia, and Antyllus. 2. A believer in or practitioner of the Pneumatist theory of medicine.

pneumatization (nu″mah-ti-za′shun). The formation of pneumatic cells or cavities in tissue, especially such formation in the temporal bone.

pneumatized (nu′mah-tīzd). Filled with air; containing pneumatic cells.

pneumato-, pneuma- (nu′mah-to, nu′mah) [Gr. *pneuma, pneumatos* air]. Combining form denoting relationship to air or gas, or to respiration.

pneumatocardia (nu″mah-to-kar′de-ah) [*pneumato-* + Gr. *kardia* heart]. The presence of air in the heart.

pneumatocele (nu-mat′o-sēl) [*pneumato-* + Gr. *kēlē* hernia]. 1. Hernial protrusion of the lung tissue. 2. A tumor or sac containing gas; especially, a gaseous swelling of the scrotum. **p. cra′nii,** gaseous tumors beneath the scalp after fracture of the skull which communicates with the paranasal sinuses. **intracranial p.,** pneumocephalus.

pneumatocephalus (nu″mah-to-sef′ah-lus). Pneumocephalus.

pneumatodyspnea (nu″mah-to-disp′ne-ah) [*pneumato-* + *dyspnea*]. Difficulty in breathing due to emphysema.

pneumatogram (nu-mat′o-gram). Pneogram.

pneumatograph (nu-mat′o-graf). Pneograph.

pneumatology (nu″mah-tol′o-je) [*pneumato-* + *-logy*]. The sum of what is known regarding gases and air and their therapeutical and other properties.

pneumatometer (nu″mah-tom′e-ter) [*pneumato-* + Gr. *metron* measure]. A form of spirometer, or instrument for measuring the air inspired and expired.

pneumatometry (nu″mah-tom′e-tre). The measurement of the air inspired and expired.

pneumatophore (nu-mat′o-fōr) [*pneumato-* + Gr. *phoros* bearing]. An apparatus consisting of a bag with a tube and mouthpiece, which may be attached to the body. The bag contains oxygen, to be breathed by the wearer in rescue work in mines, etc.

pneumatorhachis (nu″mah-tor′ah-kis) [*pneumato-* + Gr. *rhachis* spine]. The presence of gas in the vertebral canal.

pneumatoscope (nu-mat′o-skōp) [*pneumato-* + Gr. *skopein* to examine]. 1. A device for determining the absence or presence of pus in the air cells of the mastoid process of the temporal bone. 2. An instrument devised by Gabritschewsky for auscultating the percussion of the thorax from the mouth.

pneumatosis (nu″mah-to′sis) [Gr. *pneumatōsis*]. The presence of air or gas in an abnormal situation in the body. **p. cystoi′des intestina′lis, p. cystoi′des intestino′rum,** a condition characterized by the presence of thin-walled, gas-containing cysts in the wall of the intestines; the lesions may be subserosal or submucosal. **p. intestina′les,** p. cystoides intestinalis. **p. pul′monum,** pulmonary emphysema.

pneumatotherapy (nu″mah-to-ther′ah-pe) [*pneumato-* + *therapy*]. The treatment of disease by rarefied or condensed air. **cerebral p.,** injection of pure oxygen into the subarachnoid space: used in treatment of psychoses.

pneumatothorax (nu″mah-to-tho′raks) [*pneumato-* + *thorax*]. Pneumothorax.

pneumaturia (nu″mah-tu′re-ah) [*pneumato-* + Gr. *ouron* urine + *-ia*]. Passage of urine charged with air or gas.

pneumatype (nu′mah-tīp) [*pneuma-* + Gr. *typos* type]. A breath picture; a deposition of moisture upon a glass surface from the exhaled air: used in the diagnosis of nasal obstructions.

pneumectomy (nu-mek′to-me) [Gr. *pneumōn* lung + *ektomē* excision]. The excision of lung tissue.

pneumencephalography (nūm″en-sef″ah-log′rah-fe). Pneumoencephalography.

pneumo-, pneumono- (nu′mo, nu′mo-no) [Gr. *pneumōn* lung]. Combining form denoting relationship to the lungs. *Pneumo-* is also used as a combining form to denote relationship to air or to the breath.

pneumoalveolography (nu″mo-al″ve-o-log′rah-fe). Roentgenography of the alveoli of the lungs.

pneumoamnios (nu″mo-am′ne-os). The presence of gas in the amniotic fluid.

pneumoangiography (nu″mo-an″je-og′rah-fe). Roentgenography of the blood vessels of the lungs.

pneumoarthrography (nu″mo-ar-throg′rah-fe). Roentgenography of a joint after the injection of air or gas as a contrast medium.

pneumobacillin (nu″mo-bah-sil′in). A poisonous substance extracted from the pneumobacillus.

pneumobacillus (nu″mo-bah-sil′us) [*pneumo-* + *bacillus*]. A name given the microorganism causing pneumonia. **Friedländer's p.,** *Klebsiella pneumoniae.*

pneumobronchotomy (nu″mo-brong-kot′o-me). Incision of the lungs and bronchi.

pneumobulbar (nu″mo-bul′bar). Pertaining to the lungs and to the medulla oblongata.

pneumobulbous (nu″mo-bul′bus). Pneumobulbar.

pneumocardial (nu″mo-kar′de-al). Pertaining to the lungs and the heart.

pneumocele (nu′mo-sēl) [*pneumo-* + Gr. *kēlē* tumor]. Pneumatocele.

pneumocentesis (nu″mo-sen-te′sis) [*pneumo-* + Gr. *kentēsis* puncture]. Surgical puncture of a lung for the purpose of draining a collection of fluid.

pneumocephalon (nu″mo-sef′ah-lon). Pneumocephalus. **p. artificia′le,** treatment by insufflation of air into the cranial cavity.

pneumocephalus (nu″mo-sef′ah-lus) [Gr. *pneuma* air + *kephalē* head]. The presence of air in the intracranial cavity; intracranial pneumatocele.

pneumochirurgia (nu″mo-ki-rur′je-ah) [*pneumo-* + Gr. *cheirourgia* a working by hand]. Surgery of the lungs.

pneumocholecystitis (nu″mo-ko″le-sis-ti′tis). Emphysematous cholecystitis.

pneumochysis (nu-mok′ĭ-sis). Pulmonary edema, or serous infiltration of the lung.

pneumococcal (nu″mo-kok′al). Pertaining to or caused by pneumococci.

pneumococcemia (nu″mo-kok-se′me-ah). The presence of pneumococci in the blood.

pneumococcic (nu″mo-kok′sik). Pertaining to or caused by pneumococci.

pneumococcidal (nu″mo-kok-si′dal). Destroying pneumococci.

pneumococcolysis (nu″mo-kok-kol′ĭ-sis) [*pneumococcus* + Gr. *lysis* dissolution]. Destruction of pneumococci.

pneumococcosis (nu″mo-kok-ko′sis). Infection with pneumococci.

pneumococcosuria (nu″mo-kok″o-su′re-ah). The presence in the urine of pneumococci or of pneumococcus polysaccharide.

pneumococcus (nu″mo-kok′us) [*pneumo-* + Gr. *kokkos* berry]. *Diplococcus pneumoniae.*

pneumocolon (nu″mo-ko′lon) [*pneumo-* + *colon*]. 1. The presence of air in the colon. 2. Inflation of the colon with air as an aid to diagnosis.

pneumoconiosis (nu″mo-ko″ne-o′sis) [*pneumo-* + Gr. *konis* dust]. A chronic fibrous reaction in the lungs to the inhalation of dust. It is attended by fibroid induration and pigmentation. See *aluminosis, anthracosis, asbestosis, byssinosis, chalicosis, ptilosis, siderosis, silicosis,* and *tabacosis.* **p. siderot′ica,** siderosis.

pneumocrania (nu″mo-kra′ne-ah). Pneumocephalus.

pneumocystography (nu″mo-sis-tog′rah-fe). Cystography following the injection of air into the bladder.

pneumocystotomography (nu″mo-sis″to-to-mog′rah-fe). Body section roentgenography after inflation of the bladder with air.

pneumoderma (nu″mo-der′mah) [*pneumo-* + Gr. *derma* skin]. Subcutaneous emphysema; air beneath the skin.

pneumodograph (nu-mod′o-graf) [*pneumo-* + Gr. *hodos* way + *graphein* to write]. An apparatus for registering the degree of respiratory nasal efficiency.

pneumodynamics (nu″mo-di-nam′iks) [*pneumo-* + Gr. *dynamis* force]. The dynamics of the respiratory process; the study of the forces exerted in the act of breathing.

pneumoempyema (nu″mo-em″pi-e′mah). Empyema marked by the presence of gas.

pneumoencephalitis (nu″mo-en-sef″ah-li′tis). Newcastle disease.

pneumoencephalogram (nu″mo-en-sef′ah-lo-gram). The roentgenogram obtained by pneumoencephalography.

pneumoencephalography (nu″mo-en-sef″ah-log′rah-fe). The making of x-ray films of the head after injection into the subarachnoid space of air or gas, permitting visualization of the cerebral cortex and ventricles.

pneumoencephalomyelogram (nu″mo-en-sef″ah-lo-mi-el′o-gram). The roentgenogram obtained by pneumoencephalomyelography.

pneumoencephalomyelography (nu″mo-en-sef″ah-lo-mi″e-log′rah-fe). The making of x-ray films of the brain and spinal cord after injection into the subarachnoid space of air or gas.

pneumoencephalos (nu″mo-en-sef′ah-los) [*pneumo-* + Gr. *enkephalos* brain]. The presence of air or gas in the brain.

pneumoenteritis (nu″mo-en″ter-i′tis) [*pneumo-* + Gr. *enteron* intestine + *-itis*]. Inflammation of the lung and intestine. **p. of calves,** scours.

pneumoerysipelas (nu″mo-er″ĭ-sip′e-las). Erysipelas complicated with pneumonia.

pneumofasciogram (nu″mo-fas′e-o-gram). A roentgenogram of tissue after injection of air into the fascial spaces.

pneumogalactocele (nu″mo-gah-lak′to-sēl) [*pneumo-* + Gr. *gala* milk + *kēlē* tumor]. A tumor containing gas and milk.

pneumogastric (nu″mo-gas′trik) [*pneumo-* + Gr. *gastēr* stomach]. Pertaining to the lungs and stomach.

pneumogastrography (nu″mo-gas-trog′rah-fe) *pneumo-* + *gastrography*]. Roentgenography of the stomach after the injection of air.

pneumogastroscopy (nu″mo-gas-tros′ko-pe). Endoscopic examination of the stomach after injection of air.

pneumogram (nu′mo-gram). 1. The tracing or graphic record of respiratory movements. 2. A roentgenogram made after the injection of air into the part.

pneumograph (nu′mo-graf) [*pneumo-* + Gr. *graphein* to write]. An instrument for registering the respiratory movements.

pneumography (nu-mog′rah-fe) [*pneumo-* + Gr. *graphein* to write]. 1. An anatomical description of the lungs. 2. Graphic recording of the respiratory movements. 3. Roentgenography of a part after injection of oxygen. **cerebral p.,** roentgenography of the brain after the injection of oxygen; pneumoventriculography. **retroperitoneal p.,** roentgenography of the abdominal organs after retroperitoneal injection of air or oxygen.

pneumohemia (nu″mo-he′me-ah) [*pneumo-* + Gr. *haima* blood + *-ia*]. The presence of air or gas in the blood vessels.

pneumohemopericardium (nu″mo-he″mo-per″ĭ-kar′de-um) [*pneumo-* + Gr. *haima* blood + *pericardium*]. The collection of air or gas and blood in the pericardial cavity.

pneumohemothorax (nu″mo-he″mo-tho′raks) [*pneumo-* + Gr. *haima* blood + *thōrax* chest]. The presence of air or gas and blood in the pleural cavity.

pneumohydrometra (nu″mo-hi″dro-me′trah) [*pneumo-* + Gr. *hydōr* water + *mētra* uterus]. A collection of gas and fluid in the uterine cavity.

pneumohydropericardium (nu″mo-hi″dro-per″ĭ-kar′de-um) [*pneumo-* + Gr. *hydōr* water + *pericardium*]. A collection of air or gas and fluid in the pericardial cavity.

pneumohydrothorax (nu″mo-hi″dro-tho′raks) [*pneumo-* + Gr. *hydōr* water + *thōrax* chest]. A collection of air or gas and fluid in the pleural cavity.

pneumohypoderma (nu″mo-hi″po-der′mah) [*pneumo-* + Gr. *hypo* under + *derma* skin]. The presence of air or gas in the subcutaneous tissues.

pneumokidney (nu′mo-kid″ne) [*pneumo-* + *kidney*]. The presence of gas in the kidney pelvis.

pneumokoniosis (nu″mo-ko″ne-o′sis). Pneumoconiosis.

pneumolith (nu′mo-lith) [*pneumo-* + Gr. *lithos* stone]. A pulmonary calculus or concretion.

pneumolithiasis (nu″mo-lĭ-thi′ah-sis). The presence of concretions in the lungs.

pneumology (nu-mol′o-je) [*pneumo-* + *-logy*]. The study of disease of the air passages.

pneumolysis (nu-mol′ĭ-sis). Pneumonolysis.

pneumomalacia (nu″mo-mah-la′she-ah) [*pneumo-* + Gr. *malakia* softness]. Morbid softening of lung tissue.

pneumomassage (nu″mo-mah-sahzh′) [*pneumo-* + *massage*]. Air massage of the tympanum by the alternate compression and rarefaction of the air in the external auditory canal.

pneumomediastinogram (nu″mo-me″de-as-ti′-no-gram). The film produced by pneumomediastinography.

pneumomediastinography (nu″mo-me″de-as″tĭ-nog′rah-fe). Roentgenography of the mediastinum after injection of gas or air.

pneumomediastinum (nu″mo-me″de-as-ti′-num) [*pneumo-* + *mediastinum*]. The presence of air or gas in the mediastinum, sometimes deliberately introduced as an aid to examination and diagnosis.

pneumomelanosis (nu″mo-mel″ah-no′sis) [*pneumo-* + *melanosis*]. The blackening of the lung tissue by inhaled coal dust.

pneumometer (nu-mom′e-ter). Pneumatometer.

pneumomycosis (nu″mo-mi-ko′sis) [*pneumo-* + *mycosis*]. Any fungus disease of the lungs.

pneumomyelography (nu″mo-mi″ĕ-log′rah-fe) [*pneumo-* + Gr. *myelos* marrow + *graphein* to write]. The roentgen-ray examination after the injection of air or gas into the spinal canal.

pneumonectasia (nu″mon-ek-ta′ze-ah). Pneumonectasis.

pneumonectasis (nu″mo-nek′tah-sis) [*pneumo-* + Gr. *ektasis* extension]. Emphysema of the lungs.

pneumonectomy (nu″mo-nek′to-me). The excision of lung tissue. **total p.,** surgical excision of an entire lung.

pneumonedema (nu″mo-ne-de′mah) [*pneumo-* + *edema*]. Edema of the lungs.

pneumonemia (nu″mo-ne′me-ah) [*pneumo-* + Gr. *haima* blood + *-ia*]. Congestion of the lungs.

pneumonere (nu′mo-nēr). One of the end-buds which cap the primitive bronchi.

pneumonia (nu-mo′ne-ah) [Gr. *pneumōnia*]. Inflammation of the lungs; especially the disease known as croupous or lobar pneumonia. See *lobar p.* **abortive p.,** a form with a short and favorable course. **acute p.,** lobar p. **p. al′ba,** white p. **alcoholic p.,** the lobar pneumonia of drunkards. **anthrax p.,** anthrax of the lung. **apex p., apical p.,** croupous pneumonia limited to the apex of the lung. **p. apostemato′sa,** suppurative p. **aspiration p.,** pneumonia due to the entrance of foreign matter, such as food particles, into the respiratory passages (bronchi). **atypical p.,** a pulmonary virus disease with symptoms resembling those of pneumonia. It has been called *acute interstitial pneumonia, acute pneumonitis, acute influenzal pneumonia, atypical bronchopneumonia,* and *virus pneumonia.* **bilious p.,** lobar pneumonia attended with jaundice. **bronchial p.,** bronchopneumonia. **brooder p.,** a pneumonic disease (aspergillosis) of chicks acquired from moldy grain or straw. **Buhl's desquamative p.,** caseous pneumonia in which the exudate is composed chiefly of desquamated alveolar epithelium. **caseous p.,** cheesy p. **cat p.,** a lung disease of cats due probably to a virus of the psittacosis. **catarrhal p.,** bronchopneumonia. **central p.,** lobar pneumonia beginning in the interior of a lobe of the lung. **cerebral p.,** a pneumonia usually apical and having severe head symptoms. **cheesy p.,** a pneumonia, usually tuberculous, in which the alveoli become filled with necrosed cells and the cut surface looks like cheese. **chronic p.,** a long-continuing form, usually fibrous. **congenital aspiration p.,** idiopathic respiratory distress of newborn. **contagious p. of horses,** a condition that may follow equine influenza, characterized by high fever, pneumonia, and necrosis of the lungs. **contusion p.,** a pneumonia following an injury. **core p.,** central p. **Corrigan's p.,** Kaufman's p. **croupous p.,** lobar p. **deglutition p.,** pneumonia from the entrance of food into the lungs. **dermal p.,** a condition produced by injection of virulent pneumococci into the skin of rabbits. **Desnos' p.,** massive pneumonia; splenopneumonia. **desquamative p.,** chronic lobar pneumonia with hardening of the fibrous exudate and proliferation of the interstitial tissue and epithelium of the lung. Called also *parenchymatous p.* and *primary indurative p.* **p. dis′secans,** pneumonia interlobularis purulenta. **double p.,** that which affects both lungs. **embolic p.,** pneumonia due to embolism of a blood vessel or vessels of the lungs. **ephemeral p.,** that in which the signs of pneumonia disappear after two days. Called also *congestion of the lungs.* **ether p.,** pneumonia occurring after anesthesia by ether. **fibrinous p.,** lobar p. **fibrous p.,** a form characterized by an increase of the interstitial and somatic elements. **fibrous p., chronic,** interstitial p. **Friedländer's p., Friedländer's bacillus p.,** an acute specific infectious disease characterized by massive mucoid inflammatory exudates in a lobe of the lung, and caused by *Klebsiella pneumoniae.* **gangrenous p.,** gangrene of the lung. **hypostatic p.,** a pneumonia due to dorsal decubitus in weak or aged persons. **indurative p.,** desquamative p. **infective p. of goats,** a fatal disease of goats in South Africa. **influenzal p.,** pneumonia in which the influenza bacillus is a secondary invader. **inhalation p.** 1. Aspiration pneumonia. 2. Bronchopneumonia due to the inhalation of irritating vapors. **p. interlobula′ris purulen′ta,** pneumonia in which the lobules are separated from one another. **interstitial p.,** a chronic form of pneumonia with increase of the interstitial tissue and decrease of the proper lung tissue, with induration. Called also *cirrhosis of the lung* and *fibroid phthisis.* **interstitial plasma cell p.,** a pulmonary disease of infants in which cellular detritus containing plasma cells appears in the lung tissue. **Kaufman's p.,** acute interstitial pneumonia, a rare fatal form of pneumonia in young infants. **larval p.,** an attack presenting the initial symptoms of the disease only. **lipid p., lipoid p.,** a pneumonia-like reaction of the lung tissue to the aspiration of oils: called also *oil p., oil-aspiration p.,* and *pneumonolipoidosis.* **lobar p.,** an acute febrile disease produced by the *Diplococcus pneumoniae,* and marked by inflammation of one or more lobes of the lung, together with consolidation. It is attended with chill, followed by sudden elevation of temperature, dyspnea, rapid breathing, pain in the side, and cough, with blood-stained expectoration. The symptoms abate after a week. It usually begins in the lower lobe, the lung being at first intensely congested (*stage of congestion* or *engorgement*), and afterward becoming red and solid from accumulation of exudate and blood cells in the alveoli (*red hepatization*), and later gray (*gray hepatization*), from degeneration of the exudates, which are finally absorbed. Called also *croupous p., fibrinous p., lung fever,* and *pneumonic fever.* **lobular p.,** bronchopneumonia. **Löffler's p.,** Löffler's syndrome. **Louisiana p.,** a form of pneumonia encountered in Louisiana, caused by the virus, *Miyagawanella louisianae.* **p. malleo′sa,** pneumonia caused by or associated with glanders. **massive p.,** lobar pneumonia with solidification of the air cells, bronchi, or even an entire lung. **metastatic p.,** suppurative pneumonia due to metastasis in pyemia. **migratory p.,** pneumonia gradually involving one lobe of the lung after another. **Montana progressive p.,** jagziekte. **oil-aspiration p.,** lipid p. **parenchymatous p.,** desquamative p. **plague p.,** pneumonic plague. **pleuritic p.,** pleuropneumonia. **pleurogenetic p., pleurogenic p.,** that which is secondary to pleural disease. **pneumococcal p.,** lobar p. **primary atypical p.,** atypical p. **pseudopleuritic p.,** Desnos' p. **purulent p.,** a form characterized by the formation of pus. **Riesman's p.,** a peculiar form of chronic bronchopneumonia. **secondary p.,** inflammation of the lungs coming on as a complication of an infectious disease. **septic p.,** a form due to septic poison, and often lobular. **stable p.,** epizootic pleuropneumonia in horses. **Stoll's p.,** pneumonia with gastrohepatic complications. **streptococcus p.,** an epidemic type of pneumonia caused by the *Streptococcus haemolyticus.* **stripe p.,** a type in which the affected part takes the form of an upright stripe. **superficial p.,** a form which affects only the parts near the pleura. **suppurative p.,** pneumonia with formation of abscesses in the lungs. **terminal p.,** pneumonia developing during some other disease and hastening a fatal termination. **toxemic p.,** infection of the system with pneumococci without marked lung involvement. **traumatic p.,** inflammation of the lung following a wound of the lung or chest. **tularemic p.,** a pneumonic disease specific for tularemia. **typhoid p.,** an asthenic form of pneumonia with typhoid symptoms. **unresolved p.,** pneumonia in which the lung signs fail to clear up within a week or ten days after crisis. **vagus p.,** pneumonia due to injury of the pneumogastric nerve. **virus p.,** atypical p. **wandering p.,** migratory p. **white p.,** indurative syphilitic pneumonia of the newborn; infantile syphilitic pneumonia with a white, fatty degeneration of the lung. Called also *pneumonia alba.* **woolsorters' p.,** anthrax p.

pneumonic (nu-mon′ik) [Gr. *pneumonikos*]. Pertaining to the lung or to pneumonia.

pneumonitis (nu″mo-ni′tis) [Gr. *pneumōn* lung + *-itis*]. A condition of localized acute inflammation of the lung without gross toxemia; benign pneumonia. **acute interstitial p.,** atypical pneumonia. **feline p.,** a fatal pneumonitis with conjunctivitis in cats, caused by *Miyagawanella felis.* **mouse p.,** a bronchopneumonia of laboratory mice caused by *Miyagawanella bronchopneumoniae.*

pneumono-. See *pneumo-.*

pneumonocele (nu-mon′o-sēl). Pneumatocele.

pneumonocentesis (nu-mo″no-sen-te′sis). Pneumocentesis; the operation of puncturing a lung for aspiration.

pneumonochirurgia (nu-mo″no-ki-rur′je-ah). Surgery of the lung.

pneumonocirrhosis (nu-mo″no-si-ro′sis) [Gr. *pneumōn* lung + *cirrhosis*]. Cirrhosis, or hardening, of a lung.

pneumonococcus (nu″mo-no-kok′us). Pneumococcus.

pneumonoconiosis (nu-mo″no-ko-ne-o′sis). Pneumoconiosis.

pneumonocyte (nu-mon′o-sit). The characteristic cell of the lung, assumed to be of endodermal origin.

pneumonoenteritis (nu-mo″no-en″ter-i′tis). Pneumoenteritis.

pneumonoerysipelas (nu-mo″no-er″ĭ-sip′e-las). Pneumoerysipelas.

pneumonograph (nu-mon′o-graf). A roentgenogram of the lungs.

pneumonography (nu″mo-nog′rah-fe) [*pneumono-* + Gr. *graphein* to write]. Roentgenography of the lungs.

pneumonokoniosis (nu-mo″no-ko′ne-o′sis). Pneumoconiosis.

pneumonolipoidosis (nu-mo″no-lip″oi-do′sis) [*pneumono-* + Gr. *lipos* fat + *-osis*]. See *lipoid pneumonia,* under *pneumonia.*

pneumonolysis (nu″mo-nol′ĭ-sis) [*pneumono-* + Gr. *lysis* dissolution]. The operation of stripping the pleura from the fascia of the thoracic wall in order to allow the lung to collapse; called also *extrapleural p.* and *pleurolysis.* In *intrapleural p.* the lung is freed by separating the parietal from the visceral pleura.

pneumonomelanosis (nu-mo″no-mel″ah-no′sis) [*pneumono-* + Gr. *melas* black + *-osis*]. Melanosis of the lung tissue.

pneumonometer (nu″mo-nom′e-ter) [*pneumono-* + Gr. *metron* measure]. A form of spirometer.

pneumonomoniliasis (nu-mo″no-mo″nĭ-li′ah-sis). Moniliasis of the lungs.

pneumonomycosis (nu-mo″no-mi-ko′sis). Pneumomycosis.

pneumonopaludism (nu-mo″no-pal′u-dizm). Pneumopaludism.

pneumonoparesis (nu-mo″no-pah-re′sis). Pneumoparesis.

pneumonopathy (nu″mo-nop′ah-the) [*pneumono-* + Gr. *pathos* disease]. Any disease of the lung. **eosinophilic p.,** Löffler's syndrome.

pneumonopexy (nu-mo′no-pek″se). Pneumopexy.

pneumonophthisis (nu″mon-of-thi′sis). Pulmonary tuberculosis.

pneumonopleuritis (nu-mo″no-ploo-ri′tis). Pneumopleuritis.

pneumonorrhagia (nu-mo″no-ra′je-ah). Pneumorrhagia.

pneumonorrhaphy (nu″mo-nor′ah-fe) [*pneumono-* + Gr. *rhaphē* suture]. Suture of the lung.

pneumonosis (nu″mo-no′sis) [*pneumo-* + Gr. *nosos* disease]. Any lung disease.

pneumonotherapy (nu-mo″no-ther′ah-pe). Treatment of disease of the lung.

pneumonotomy (nu″mo-not′o-me) [*pneumono-* + Gr. *tomē* a cutting]. Surgical incision of the lung.

pneumonyssus (nu″mo-nis′us). A mite found in the lungs of monkeys.

pneumo-oxygenator (nu″mo-ok′sĭ-je-na″tor). An apparatus for long-continued administration of large quantities of oxygen.

pneumopaludism (nu″mo-pal′u-dizm) [*pneumo-* + L. *palus* swamp]. Disease of the lungs of malarial origin.

pneumoparesis (nu″mo-pah-re′sis) [*pneumo-* + *paresis*]. A lung disease marked by progressive congestion and infiltration of the vesicles of the lung.

pneumopathy (nu-mop′ah-the). Pneumonopathy.

pneumopericardium (nu″mo-per″ĭ-kar′de-um) [*pneumo-* + *pericardium*]. The presence of air or gas in the cavity of the pericardium.

pneumoperitoneal (nu″mo-per″ĭ-to-ne′al). Pertaining to or characterized by pneumoperitoneum.

pneumoperitoneum (nu″mo-per″ĭ-to-ne′um) [*pneumo-* + *peritoneum*]. The presence of gas or air in the peritoneal cavity, sometimes deliberately introduced as an aid to examination and diagnosis (*diagnostic p.*).

pneumoperitonitis (nu″mo-per″ĭ-to-ni′tis) [*pneumo-* + *peritonitis*]. Peritonitis with the accumulation of air or gas in the peritoneal cavity.

pneumopexy (nu′mo-pek″se) [*pneumo-* + Gr. *pēxis* fixation]. Surgical fixation of the lung to the thoracic wall.

pneumophagia (nu″mo-fa′je-ah) [*pneumo-* + Gr. *phagein* to eat + *-ia*]. Aerophagy.

pneumophone (nu′mo-fōn) [*pneumo-* + Gr. *phōnē* voice]. An instrument for measuring pressure in the middle ear.

pneumophonia (nu″mo-fo′ne-ah). A form of dysphonia characterized by a breathy voice.

pneumopleuritis (nu″mo-ploo-ri′tis). Inflammation of the lungs and pleura.

pneumopleuroparietopexy (nu″mo-ploor″o-pah-ri′ĕ-to-pek″se) [*pneumo-* + *pleura* + *parieto-* + Gr. *pēxis* fixation]. The operation of suturing the lung with its parietal pleura to the margin of a thoracic wound.

pneumoprecordium (nu″mo-pre-kor′de-um). The presence of air in the precordial space.

pneumopreperitoneum (nu″mo-pre-per″ĭ-to-ne′um). The presence of air or gas in the preperitoneal space, sometimes deliberately introduced as an aid to examination and diagnosis.

pneumoprotein (nu″mo-pro′te-in). A principle derived from the pneumococcus by the action of glycerin and water.

pneumopyelography (nu″mo-pi″ĕ-log′rah-fe) [*pneumo-* + Gr. *pyelos* pelvis + *graphein* to write]. Pyelography in which oxygen or air, instead of an opaque solution, is injected into the kidney pelvis.

pneumopyopericardium (nu″mo-pi″o-per″ĭ-kar′de-um) [*pneumo-* + Gr. *pyon* pus + *pericardium*]. The presence of air or gas and pus in the pericardium.

pneumopyothorax (nu″mo-pi″o-tho′raks) [*pneumo-* + Gr. *pyon* pus + *thōrax* thorax]. The presence of air and pus in the pleural cavity.

pneumorachicentesis (nu″mo-ra″ke-sen-te′sis) [*pneumo-* + Gr. *rhachis* spine + *kentēsis* puncture]. The introduction of air or gas into the spinal canal as a contrast medium for roentgen examination.

pneumorachis (nu″mo-ra′kis) [*pneumo-* + Gr. *rhachis* spine]. 1. The presence of a gaseous collection in the spinal cord. 2. The injection of gas into the spinal canal for the facilitation of roentgenological examination.

pneumoradiography (nu″mo-ra″de-og′rah-fe) [*pneumo-* + *radiography*]. Radiography of a part following the injection of air or oxygen, as in pneumoperitoneum.

pneumoresection (nu″mo-re-sek′shun). Removal of a portion of the lung.

pneumoretroperitoneum (nu″mo-re″tro-per″ĭ-to-ne′um). The presence of air or gas in the retroperitoneal space.

pneumoroentgenogram (nu″mo-rent-gen′o-gram). A roentgenogram of a part after the injection of air or gas into it.

pneumoroentgenography (nu″mo-rent″gen-og′rah-fe). Roentgenography of a part into which air or gas has been injected.

pneumorrhagia (nu″mo-ra′je-ah) [*pneumo-* + Gr. *rhēgnynai* to burst forth]. 1. Hemorrhage from the lungs. 2. Pulmonary apoplexy.

pneumoscope (nu′mo-skōp). Pneoscope.

pneumosepticemia (nu″mo-sep″tĭ-se′me-ah). Influenzal pneumonia of an extreme and fatal form.

pneumoserosa (nu″mo-se-ro′sah). Injection of air into a joint cavity for roentgenoscopy.

pneumoserothorax (nu″mo-se″ro-tho′raks) [*pneumo-* + *serum* + Gr. *thōrax* thorax]. The presence of gas and serum in the thoracic cavity.

pneumosilicosis (nu″mo-sil″ĭ-ko′sis). The deposition of silica-bearing particles of foreign matter in the lungs.

pneumotachygraph (nu″mo-tak′e-graf) [*pneumo-* + Gr. *tachys* swift + *graphein* to write]. An instrument for recording the velocity of the respired air.

pneumotherapy (nu″mo-ther′ah-pe). 1. Pneumatotherapy. 2. The treatment of diseases of the lungs.

pneumothermomassage (nu″mo-ther″mo-mah-sahzh′) [*pneumo-* + Gr. *thermē* heat + *massage*]. The application to the body of hot condensed air that has been medicated.

pneumothorax (nu″mo-tho′raks) [*pneumo-* + Gr. *thōrax* thorax]. An accumulation of air or gas in the pleural cavity, which may occur spontaneously or as a result of trauma or a pathological process, or be introduced deliberately. See *artificial p.* and *diagnostic p.* **artificial p.,** pneumothorax induced intentionally by artificial means, employed for the purpose of immobilizing the lung in treatment of pulmonary tuberculosis. Cf. *Forlanini treatment,* under *treatment.* **clicking p.,** pneumothorax in which the patient is conscious of a clicking sound synchronous with the heart beat. **extrapleural p.,** production of collapse of the lung by formation of an air pocket by stripping the pleural layers from the inner surface of the ribs and intercostal muscle sheaths. **induced p.,** artificial p. **insatiable p.,** artificial pneumothorax in which the injected air unaccountably disappears. **open p.,** pneumothorax communicating with a lung. **spontaneous p.,** pneumothorax without known cause. **therapeutic p.,** artificial p. **valvular p.,** pneumothorax in which an aperture in the pleura has a valvelike action.

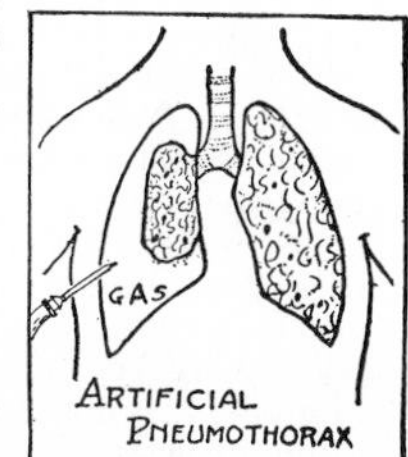

pneumotomography (nu″mo-to-mog′rah-fe). Body section radiography after injection of air or other gas into the region or organ being visualized roentgenographically.

pneumotomy (nu-mot′o-me). Pneumonotomy.

pneumotoxin (nu″mo-tok′sin). A toxin produced by the bacteria of pneumonia, and thought to be the cause of the symptoms of lobar pneumonia.

pneumotropic (nu″mo-trop′ik). 1. Having a selective affinity for pulmonary tissue; exerting its principal effect upon the lungs. 2. Having a selective affinity for pneumococci.

pneumotropism (nu-mot′ro-pizm). The predilection of an agent or organism for lung tissue.

pneumotympanum (nu″mo-tim′pah-num). Air in the middle ear.

pneumotyphoid (nu″mo-ti′foid). Typhoid with unusual localization of the lesions in the lungs.

pneumotyphus (nu″mo-ti′fus). Pneumonia concurrent with typhoid fever.

pneumouria (nu″mo-u′re-ah). Pneumaturia.

pneumoventricle (nu″mo-ven′trĭ-k'l). Pneumoventriculi.

pneumoventriculi (nu″mo-ven-trik′u-li) [*pneumo-* + L. *ventriculus* ventricle]. Presence of air in the cerebral ventricles.

pneumoventriculography (nu″mo-ven-trik″u-log′rah-fe). Roentgenography of the cerebral ventricles after the injection of air or gas.

pneusis (nu′sis) [Gr. *pneusis* a blowing]. 1. Respiration. 2. Anhelation.

pneusometer (nu-som′e-ter) [*pneusis* + Gr. *metron* measure]. A spirometer.

pnigophobia (ni″go-fo′be-ah) [Gr. *pnigos* choking + *phobein* to be affrighted by]. Abnormal dread of choking.

P.O. Abbreviation for L. *per os,* by mouth, orally.

Po. Chemical symbol for *polonium.*

pO_2. Symbol for *oxygen pressure* (*tension*).

Pocill. Abbreviation for L. *pocil′lum,* a small cup.

pock (pok). A pustule, especially one of the lesions of smallpox.

pocket (pok′et). A saclike space or cavity, such as an abnormal extension of a gingival sulcus (*periodontal pocket*). **absolute p.,** a dental condition in which the deepening of the gingival sulcus entails migration of the epithelial attachment along the root and destruction of the periodontal membrane. It may be either gingival or infrabony. **complex p.,** a spiral type of periodontal pocket involving more than one surface of the tooth, but communicating with the gingival margin only along the surface at which it originates. **compound p.,** a periodontal pocket involving more than one tooth surface, and communicating with the gum margin along each of the involved surfaces. **gingival p.,** a periodontal pocket in which the bottom is coronal to the level of the underlying alveolar bone. **infrabony p.,** a periodontal pocket, in which the bottom is attached to the tooth in an area apical to the level of the adjacent alveolar bone. **intra-alveolar p.,** infrabony p. **intrabony p.,** infrabony p. **periodontal p.,** a gingival sulcus pathologically deepened by periodontal disease. **relative p.,**

a dental condition in which the deepening of the gingival sulcus results primarily from an increase in bulk of the gingiva, without apical migration of the epithelial attachment or appreciable destruction of the underlying tissues. **simple p.,** a periodontal pocket involving only one tooth surface. **subcrestal p.,** infrabony p. **supracrestal p., supragingival p.,** gingival p. **p's of Zahn,** shallow pockets with miniature leaflets, resembling cusps of the semilunar valve, produced in the endocardium of the left ventricle by the regurgitant aortic stream; observed in syphilitic aortitis.

Pocul. Abbreviation for L. *poc'ulum*, cup.

poculum (pok'u-lum) [L.]. Cup. **p. Diog'enis** ["Diogenes' cup"], the concave palm of the hand.

pod-. See *podo-*.

podagra (po-dag'rah) [*pod-* + Gr. *agra* seizure]. Gouty pain in the great toe.

podagral (pod'ah-gral). Pertaining to or characterized by podagra.

podagric (po-dag'rik). Podagral.

podagrous (pod'ah-grus). Podagral.

podalgia (po-dal'je-ah) [*pod-* + *-algia*]. Pain in the foot, as from gout or rheumatism.

podalic (po-dal'ik) [Gr. *pous* foot]. Accomplished by means of the feet, as podalic version.

Podalirius (po"dah-lir'e-us). The younger of two brothers, the older being Machaon, who were the sons of Æsculapius and, according to legend, the chief medical officers attached to the Greek forces during the Trojan war.

podarthritis (pod"ar-thri'tis) [*pod-* + *arthritis*]. Inflammation of the joints of the feet.

podasteroid (pod-as'ter-oid) [*pod-* + Gr. *astēr* star + *eidos* form]. Having a stellate foot or pedicle.

podedema (pod"e-de'mah). Edema of the feet.

podelkoma (pod"el-ko'mah) [*pod-* + Gr. *helkōma* ulcer]. Mycetoma of the foot.

podencephalus (pod"en-sef'ah-lus) [*pod-* + Gr. *enkephalos* brain]. A fetal monster the brain of which, without cranium, hangs by a pedicle.

podia (po'de-ah) [L.]. Plural of *podium*.

podiatrist (po-di'ah-trist). An individual who practices podiatry.

podiatry (po-di'ah-tre) [Gr. *pous* foot + *iatreia* healing]. The diagnosis and treatment of disorders of the feet.

podium (po'de-um), pl. *po'dia* [L.]. A footlike projection; a sucker foot. See under *foot*.

podo-, pod- [Gr. *pous, podos* foot]. Combining form denoting relationship to the foot.

podobromidrosis (pod"o-brom"id-ro'sis) [*podo-* + Gr. *brōmos* stench + *hidrōs* sweat]. Fetid perspiration of the feet.

pododerm (pod'o-derm) [*podo-* + Gr. *derma* skin]. That portion of the skin which is continued downward within the horn capsule of the hoof of an animal.

pododynamometer (pod"o-di"nah-mom'e-ter). A device for determining the strength of the leg muscles.

pododynia (pod"o-din'e-ah) [*podo-* + Gr. *odynē* pain]. Neuralgic pain of the heel and sole; burning pain without redness in the sole of the foot.

podogram (pod'o-gram) [*podo-* + Gr. *gramma* mark]. A print of, or an outline tracing of, the sole of the foot.

podograph (pod'o-graf) [*podo-* + Gr. *graphein* to write]. The instrument used in the making of a podogram.

podology (po-dol'o-je) [*podo-* + *-logy*]. The study of the feet.

podophyllin (pod"o-fil'in). Podophyllum resin.

podophyllous (po-dof'ĭ-lus) [*podo-* + Gr. *phyllon* leaf]. Designating the tissues which constitute the sensitive wall of the hoofs of animals.

Podophyllum (pod"o-fil'um) [*podo-* + Gr. *phyllon* leaf]. A genus of berberidaceous plants.

podophyllum (pod"o-fil'um). The dried rhizome and roots of *Podophyllum peltatum*, yielding a resin used as a caustic agent for certain skin tumors.

podotrochilitis (pod"o-tro-kĭ-li'tis) [*podo-* + Gr. *trochilea* pulley + *-itis*]. Inflammation of the navicular bone of the horse's foot.

poecil-. For words beginning thus, see those beginning *poikil-*.

Poehl's test (pelz) [Alexander Vasilyevich von *Poehl*, Russian chemist, 1850–1908]. See under *tests*.

pogoniasis (po"go-ni'ah-sis) [Gr. *pōgōn* beard + *-iasis*]. 1. Excessive growth of a beard. 2. The growth of a beard upon a woman.

pogonion (po-go'ne-on) [Gr., dim. of *pōgōn* beard]. The most anterior point of the chin in the middle line.

pOH. A symbol used in expressing the hydroxyl concentration (alkalinity) of a solution.

Pohl's test [Julius *Pohl*, German pharmacologist, born 1861]. See under *tests*.

poikilergasia (poi"kil-er-ga'se-ah) [*poikilo-* + Gr. *ergasia* work]. Meyer's term for psychopathic constitution.

poikilionia (poi-kil"e-o'ne-ah) [*poikilo-* + *ion*]. Variation in the ionic concentration (inorganic content) of the blood.

poikilo- (poi'kĭ-lo) [Gr. *poikilos* varied]. Combining form meaning varied or irregular.

poikiloblast (poi'kĭ-lo-blast) [*poikilo-* + Gr. *blastos* germ]. An abnormally shaped erythroblast.

poikilocarynosis (poi"kĭ-lo-kar"ĭ-no'sis) [*poikilo-* + Gr. *karyon* nucleus + *-osis*]. Darier's term for the formation of various types and arrangements of cells which occurs in Bowen's disease.

poikilocyte (poi'kĭ-lo-sīt) [*poikilo-* + *-cyte*]. An erythrocyte showing abnormal variation in shape.

poikilocythemia (poi-kil"o-si-the'me-ah). Poikilocytosis.

poikilocytosis (poi"kĭ-lo-si-to'sis) [*poikilocyte* + *-osis*]. Presence in the blood of erythrocytes showing abnormal variation in shape.

poikilodentosis (poi"kĭ-lo-den-to'sis) [*poikilo-* + L. *dens* tooth + *-osis*]. A mottled condition of the teeth.

poikiloderma (poi"kĭ-lo-der'mah). A condition characterized by pigmentary and atrophic changes in the skin, giving it a mottled appearance. **p. atroph'icans vascula're** (Jacobi), a rare, slowly progressive atrophic disorder, usually of early adult life, which resembles radiodermatitis, with telangiectasia, atrophy, and mottled pigmentation of the skin. **Civatte's p.,** simple reticular pigmentation of the face, neck, and upper chest, occurring symmetrically; sometimes the result of sensitivity to sunlight or to chemicals or cosmetics. **p. congenita'le,** Thomson's disease.

poikilodermatomyositis (poi"kĭ-lo-der"mah-to-mi"o-si'tis). Poikiloderma atrophicans vasculare.

poikilonymy (poi"kĭ-lon'ĭ-me) [*poikilo-* + Gr. *onoma* name]. The mingling of names or terms from different systems of nomenclature.

poikilopicria (poi"kĭ-lo-pik're-ah) [*poikilo-* + Gr. *pikros* bitter + *-ia*]. Variation in the concentrations of the anions of the blood with resultant loss of acid-base equilibrium.

poikiloplastocyte (poi"kĭ-lo-plas'to-sīt) [*poikilo-* + *plastocyte*]. An irregularly shaped blood platelet.

poikiloploid (poi'kĭ-lo-ploid). 1. Pertaining to or characterized by poikiloploidy. 2. An individual having different cells with varying numbers of chromosomes.

poikiloploidy (poi'kĭ-lo-ploi"de). The state of having varying numbers of chromosomes in different cells.

poikilosmosis (poi″kil-os-mo′sis). The adjustment, by a cell, tissue, organ, or organism, of the osmotic pressure (or tonicity) of its fluid milieu to the tonicity of the surrounding medium.

poikilosmotic (poi″kil-os-mot′ik). Having an internal osmotic pressure which may vary over a wide range, depending on the osmotic pressure of the external medium.

poikilotherm (poi-kil′o-therm). An animal that exhibits poikilothermy; a so-called cold-blooded animal.

poikilothermic (poi″kĭ-lo-ther′mik). Pertaining to or characterized by poikilothermy.

poikilothermism (poi″kĭ-lo-ther′mizm). Poikilothermy.

poikilothermy (poi″kĭ-lo-ther′me) [*poikilo-* + Gr. *thermē* heat]. 1. The exhibition of body temperature which varies with the environmental temperature. 2. The ability of organisms to adapt themselves to variations in the temperature of their environment.

poikilothrombocyte (poi-kil″o-throm′bo-sit) [*poikilo-* + *thrombocyte*]. A blood platelet of abnormal shape.

poikilothymia (poi″kĭ-lo-thi′me-ah) [*poikilo-* + Gr. *thymos* spirit]. A mental condition characterized by abnormal variations of mood.

point (point) [L. *punctum*]. 1. A small area or spot; the sharp end of an object. 2. To approach the surface, like the pus of an abscess, at a definite spot or place. **p. of an abscess,** the place at which the pus comes nearest to the surface. **Addison's p.,** the midpoint of the epigastric region. **alveolar p.,** prosthion. **apophysiary p.** 1. Subnasal point. 2. See *Trousseau's apophysiary points.* **auricular p.,** the center of the opening of the external auditory meatus. **Barker's p.,** a point $1\frac{1}{4}$ inches above and $1\frac{1}{4}$ inches behind the middle external auditory meatus, the proper spot to apply the trephine in abscess of the temporosphenoid lobe. **Boas' p.,** a tender area to the left of the twelfth thoracic vertebra in patients with gastric ulcer. **boiling p.,** the temperature at which a liquid will boil; at sea level water boils at 100°C., or 212°F. **boiling p., normal,** the temperature at which a liquid boils at one atmosphere pressure. **Bolton p.,** the upper part of the notch in the shadow cast by the occipital bone in the x-ray of the lateral aspect of the skull. **Brewer's p.,** the point of the costovertebral angle, tenderness over which points to kidney infection. **Broadbent's registration p.,** a cephalometric landmark, being the midpoint on a perpendicular line from the center of the sella turcica to the Bolton plane. **Broca's p.,** auricular p. **Canon's p.,** in the roentgenogram after a barium meal, a point or ring of contraction at the mid-third of the colon, marking a division of the latter into two separate neurologic units of extrinsic innervation. **Capuron's p's, Capuron's cardinal p's,** four points within the pelvic inlet—the two sacro-iliac articulations and the two iliopectineal eminences. **cardinal p's.** 1. Principal points; points on the optic axis which include the nodal points, the principal foci, and the optic center; may include conjugate focal points of object and image (Fording). 2. Capuron's points. **Chauffard's p.,** a point of tenderness in gallbladder disease, situated under the right clavicle. **Clado's p.,** a point of special tenderness in appendicitis, situated at the intersection of the right semilunar line by the interspinal line at the external border of the rectus abdominis muscle. **cold p.,** any point on the surface at which hot bodies are not felt to be hot. **cold rigor p.,** that point of cold temperature at which the activity of a cell ceases. **conjugate p's,** conjugate foci. **contact p.** See under *area.* **convenience p.,** a groove or depression cut in the wall of a cavity in such a way as to retain the first piece of the gold placed for its filling. **p. of convergence,** the point nearest to the patient to which both eyes can converge on an object moved up toward them. **Cope's p.,** a point of maximum tenderness on the abdomen in appendicitis, being the middle of the line joining the umbilicus and the anterior superior spine of the right ilium. **corresponding p's,** points upon the two retinae whose impressions unite to produce a single perception. **Cova's p.,** a point at the apex of the costolumbar angle which is tender on pressure in cases of pyelitis of pregnancy. **craniometric p.,** any one of a numerous set of points of reference assumed for use in craniometry. **critical p.** 1. The temperature at or above which a gas can no longer be liquefied by pressure alone. 2. The temperature above which a substance can no longer be retained in liquid form by pressure. **deaf p.,** one of certain points near the ear where a vibrating tuning-fork cannot be heard. **de Mussy's p.,** a point, exceedingly painful on pressure on the line of the left border of the sternum, at the level of the end of the tenth rib: it is a symptom of diaphragmatic pleurisy. **Desjardins' p.,** a point on the abdomen 5 to 7 cm. from the navel, on a line to the right axilla: it lies over the head of the pancreas. **dew p.,** the temperature of the atmosphere at which the moisture begins to be deposited as dew. **p. of direction.** See under *position.* **disparate p's,** points on the retina which are not paired exactly. Cf. *corresponding p's.* **p. of dispersion,** in optics, the virtual focus. **p. of divergence,** the conjugate focus from which the light proceeds. **dorsal p.,** a point, tender on pressure, situated between the spinous processes of the vertebrae at the border of the right scapula at the level of the fourth and fifth intercostal spaces at a distance of about 2 or 3 centimeters from the middle line. It is found in hepatic colic. Called also *Pauly's p.* **p's douloureux** (pwă doo-loo-ruh′) [Fr.], Valleix's p's. **p. of election,** that point at which any particular surgical operation is done by preference. **Erb's p.,** a point two or three centimeters above the clavicle and without the posterior border of the sternomastoid, at the level of the transverse process of the sixth cervical vertebra; stimulation here contracts various arm muscles. **eye p.** 1. An eye spot or ocellus. 2. The bright circle seen at the crossing point or nearest the approximation of the rays above the microscopical ocular. **far p.,** the remotest point at which an object is clearly seen when the eye is at rest. **fixation p.,** the point or object on which the vision is fixed. **focal p.** See *focus,* and under *cardinal p.* **freezing p.,** the temperature at which a liquid begins to freeze: that of water is 0°C., or 32°F. **fusing p.,** melting point. **glenoid p.,** the center of the glenoid cavity of the maxilla. **Gray's p.,** a point on the abdomen $1\frac{1}{2}$ inches below and to the right of the umbilicus, corresponding to the point at which the terminal branch of the eleventh dorsal nerve emerges on the abdominal wall. **Guéneau de Mussy's p.** See *de Mussy's p.* **Hallé's p.,** a point on the surface of the abdomen corresponding to the point where the ureter crosses the pelvic brim. It is the point of intersection between a horizontal line connecting the anterior superior iliac spines and a vertical line projected upward from the pubic spine. **Hartmann's p.,** the point on the large intestine where the sigmoid artery meets the superior rectal branch. **hot p.,** any point on the surface at which cold bodies are not felt to be cold. **hystero-epileptogenous p., hysterogenic p.,** a point on which, if pressure be made, a hysteric or hystero-epileptic attack may be produced. **ice p.,** the temperature of equilibrium between ice and air-saturated water under one atmosphere pressure. **identical p's,** the corresponding points on the retinae of the two eyes. **p. of incidence.** See *refraction.* **isoelectric p.,** the pH of a solution at which a dipolar ion does not migrate in an electric field. **isoionic p.,** the pH of a solution at which the number of cations equals the number of anions, solutes other than water and other ions being absent; presence of these factors will cause the isoelectric point and isoionic point to differ. **jugal**

p., the point of the angle formed by the masseteric and maxillary edges of the malar bone. **jugomaxillary p.,** the point at the anteroinferior angle of the malar bone. **Keen's p.,** a point for puncture of the lateral ventricles: 3 cm. above and 3 cm. behind the external auditory meatus. **Kienböck-Adamson p's,** points and lines to be marked on the scalp to indicate the locations for the application of x-ray epilation for tinea capitis. **Kocher's p.,** a point for puncture of the lateral ventricles: 2.5 cm. from the midline, 3.5 cm. in front of the bregma. **Kümmell's p.,** a tender point in chronic appendicitis; it is 1 to 2 cm. below and slightly to the right of the navel. **lacrimal p's,** the puncta lacrimalia; the outlets of the lacrimal canaliculi. **Lanz's p.,** a point which indicates the position of the vermiform appendix. It is situated on a line connecting the two anterior superior iliac spines one third of the distance from the right spine. **Lavitas p's,** three points of tenderness on the abdomen in appendicitis. **leak p.,** the point of sugar concentration in the blood (180 mg. per 100 cc. in the normal) at which the kidney will secrete sugar. **Lenzmann's p.,** a point which is tender on pressure in appendicitis: situated on a line joining the two anterior iliac spines, 5 to 6 cm. from the right spine, about 2 cm. below McBurney's point. **Lian's p.,** a point at the junction of the outer and middle thirds of a line joining the umbilicus and the left anterior superior iliac spine, the point of election for paracentesis of the abdomen. See *Munro's p.* **Lothlissen's p.,** a point 2 inches below McBurney's point at right angles to the spinoumbilical line: a point of tenderness in appendicitis. **McBurney's p.,** the point of special tenderness in acute appendicitis, situated about 2 inches from the right anterior superior spine of the ilium, on a line between this spine and the umbilicus. It corresponds with the normal position of the appendix. **McEwen's p.,** a point above the inner canthus of the eye which is tender in acute frontal sinusitis. **Mackenzie's p.,** a point of tenderness in gallbladder disease in the upper segment of the rectus muscle. **malar p.,** a point on the external tubercle of the malar bone. **marginal p's,** anaplasma marginale. **p. of maximal impulse,** the point on the chest where is felt the impulse of the left ventricle proximal to the apex of the heart: normally it is felt in the fifth costal interspace inside the left mamillary line; abbreviated P.M.I. **maximum occipital p.,** the point in the occipital bone situated furthest from the glabella. **Méglin's p.,** a point located where the palatine nerve emerges from the great palatine foramen. **melting p.,** the temperature in degrees at which a solid becomes liquefied by heat. **mental p.,** pogonion. **metopic p.,** metopion. **Morris' p.,** a point of special tenderness in chronic appendicitis, situated about 2 inches from the navel in a line running thence to the anterior superior iliac spine. **motor p.** 1. The point at which a motor nerve enters a muscle. 2. The point wherever, if galvanic stimulation be applied, it will cause contraction of a corresponding muscle. **Munro's p.,** a point midway between the umbilicus and the left anterior iliac spine: usually selected as the point for performing abdominal puncture. See *Lian's p.* **Mussy's p.** See *de Mussy's p.* **nasal p.,** nasion. **near p.,** the nearest point at which the eye can distinctly perceive an object; the nearest point of clear vision. **near p., absolute,** the near point for either eye alone with accommodation relaxed. **near p., relative,** the near point for both eyes with the employment of accommodation. **nodal p's,** one of two points on the axis of an optical system so situated that a ray falling on one will produce a parallel ray emerging through the other. **occipital p.** 1. The posterior point on the occipital bone. 2. The pointed posterior end of the occipital lobe of the brain. **ossification p.,** the center of ossification in bone. **Pagniello's p.,** a point painful on light pressure when a finger is drawn over the ninth left costal interspace in malarial subjects. **painful p's,** Valleix's p's. **Pauly's p.,** dorsal p. **phrenic-pressure p.,** a point along the phrenic nerve between the sternocleidomastoid and the scalenus anticus on the right side: pressure on the point suggests gallbladder disease. **Piersol's p.,** a point indicating the location of the vesical orifice. **pour p.,** the temperature at which a liquid just begins to flow. **preauricular p.,** a point on the posterior root of the zygomatic arch just in front of the auricular point. **pressure p.,** a point of extreme sensibility to pressure. **pressure-arresting p.,** a point at which pressure arrests spasm. **pressure-exciting p.,** a point at which pressure produces spasm. **principal p's,** cardinal p's, def. 1. **Ramond's p.,** a point of tenderness in gallbladder disease between the heads of the sternocleidomastoid muscle. **reflection p.,** the point from which a ray of light is reflected. **refraction p.,** the point at which a ray of light is refracted. **p. of regard,** the point at which the eye is directly looking. **retromandibular tender p.,** a point behind the superior extremity of the inferior maxilla below the lobule of the ear and in front of the mastoid process. Pressure on this point elicits extreme pain in meningitis. **Robson's p.,** the point of greatest tenderness in gallbladder inflammation, situated opposite the junction of the middle and lower third of a line drawn from the right nipple to the umbilicus. **Rolando's p's,** the points at the upper and lower ends of the fissure of Rolando. **spinal p.,** subnasal p. **stereo-identical p's,** points in space outside of the region within which fusion of double images occurs. **subnasal p.,** the central point of the root of the anterior nasal spine. **subtemporal p.,** the point where the sphenotemporal suture and infratemporal crest intersect. **p. of Sudeck,** the portion of the rectum between the last sigmoid artery and the bifurcation of the superior hemorrhoidal artery; the former belief that ligation of the latter below this point would lead to gangrene of the rectum has not been borne out by clinical experience. **supra-auricular p.,** a point at the root of the zygoma directly above the auricular point. **supraclavicular p.,** a point above the clavicle and outside of the sternomastoid where the application of a stimulus causes contraction of the biceps brachii, deltoideus, brachialis, and brachioradialis muscles. **supranasal p.,** ophryon. **supra-orbital p.** 1. The ophryon. 2. In neuralgia, a tender spot just above the supra-orbital notch. **sylvian p.,** a point on the surface of the skull from 29 to 32 millimeters behind the external angular process. **thermal death p.,** the degree of heat required to kill a given microorganism in a stated length of time. **trigger p.,** a particular spot on the body on which pressure or other stimulus will give rise to specific sensations or symptoms. **Trousseau's apophysiary p's,** points sensitive to pressure along the dorsal and lumbar vertebrae in certain cases of neuralgia. **vaccine p.,** a piece of bone or quill, one end of which is coated with vaccine lymph. **Valleix's p's,** tender points on the course of certain nerves in neuralgia. **vital p.,** a point in the medulla oblongata, at the respiratory center, puncture of which causes immediate death. **Vogt's p., Vogt-Hueter p.,** a point of the intersection of a horizontal line, two finger-breadths above the zygoma, with a vertical line a thumb-breadth behind the ascending sphenofrontal process; here trephination may be performed in traumatic meningeal hemorrhage. **Voillemier's p.,** a point on the linea alba 6.5 cm. below the line which joins the anterior superior iliac spinous processes; here the bladder may be punctured in obese or edematous patients. **Ziemssen's motor p's,** the places of entrance of motor nerves into muscles: they are points of election in the therapeutical application of electricity to muscles.

pointillage (pwahn″te-yahzh′) [Fr.]. Massage with the points of the fingers.

Poirier's glands, line (pwah-re-āz′) [Paul *Poirier*, surgeon in Paris, 1853–1907]. See under *gland* and *line*.

poise (poiz; Fr. pwahz) [J. M. *Poiseuille*]. The unit of viscosity of a liquid, being number of grams per centimeter per second. The commonly used unit is the *centipoise*, or one one-hundredth of a poise.

Poiseuille's law, space (pwah-zuh′yez) [Jean Marie *Poiseuille*, physiologist in Paris, 1799–1869]. See under *law* and *space*.

poison (poi′zn) [L. *potio* draft; *toxicum;* Gr. *toxikon*]. Any substance which, when ingested, inhaled or absorbed, or when applied to, injected into, or developed within the body, in relatively small amounts, by its chemical action may cause damage to structure or disturbance of function. **acrid p.,** one which produces irritation or inflammation, as the mineral acids, oxalic acid, the caustic alkalis, antimony, arsenic, barium, the salts of copper, some of the compounds of lead, silver nitrate, the salts of zinc, iodine, cantharides, phosphorus, etc. **acronarcotic p., acrosedative p.,** poisons which produce sometimes irritation, sometimes narcotism (or sedation) or both together. They are chiefly derived from the vegetable kingdom. Stramonium and belladonna are examples of the acronarcotic and aconite is an example of the acrosedative poisons. **arrow p.,** a preparation of plant alkaloids used on their arrows by members of certain savage tribes. **clam p.,** a toxic substance obtained from poisonous clams. See *saxitoxin.* **corrosive p.,** any poison which acts by directly destroying tissue. **fatigue p.,** fatigue toxin. **fugu p.,** tetraodontoxin. **gonyaulax p.,** a toxic substance produced by certain members of the dinoflagellate genus, *Gonyaulax.* See also *saxitoxin.* **hemotropic p.,** a poison which has a special affinity for erythrocytes. **irritant p.,** acrid p. **microbial p.,** a toxic substance produced by a microorganism. **mitotic p.,** a toxic principle that interferes with cell division. **muscle p.,** one that interferes with normal action or functioning of muscle. **mussel p.,** mytilotoxin. **narcotic p's,** poisons causing stupor or delirium, as opium, hyoscyamus, etc. **paralytic shellfish p.,** mytilotoxin. **protein p.,** a highly active toxic principle derived from protein and believed to be a constituent of every true protein. **puffer p.,** tetraodontoxin. **sedative p's,** those which directly reduce the vital powers, as hydrocyanic acid, potassium cyanide, hydrogen sulfide, and other of the poisonous gases. **toot p.,** a poison from *Coriaria sarmentosa*, a plant of New Zealand. **vascular p.,** a poison which acts by affecting the blood pressure. **whelk p.,** a toxic substance which is localized in the salivary gland of whelks, members of the mollusk family, Buccinidae; its principal ingredient is believed to be tetramine.

poisoning (poi′zun-ing). The morbid condition produced by a poison. **akee p.,** an acute, often fatal, illness occurring in Jamaica, marked by vomiting and collapse, and caused by eating the unsound fruit of the akee tree, *Blighia sapida.* **blood p.,** septicemia. **bongkrek p.** See under *intoxication.* **broom p.,** poisoning caused by eating broom, *Cyticus scoparius*, which contains both sparteine and cysticine. **carbon disulfide p.,** a condition occurring in workers in rubber and viscose products caused by carbon disulfide and marked by weakness, sleeplessness, visual impairment, gastric ulcer and paralysis. **carbon monoxide p.,** poisoning due to the inhalation of carbon monoxide and the resulting change of oxyhemoglobin to carbon monoxide hemoglobin. **cheese p.,** tyrotoxicosis. **corncockle p.,** githagism. **dural p.,** poisoning in aircraft workers caused by the magnesium in the aluminum-magnesium alloy (duralumin) used in airplanes. **elasmobranch p.,** a form of ichthyosarcotoxism produced by the ingestion of certain toxic sharks and skates. **food p.,** acute illness caused by food which is inherently poisonous or more commonly an acute gastroenteritis due to food contaminated with certain bacteria, especially of the salmonella group. See *sitotoxism, allantiasis, botulism, bromatotoxism,* and *meat poisoning.* **forage p.,** a disease of domestic animals, especially of horses, resulting from ingestion of moldy or fermented food, or from an encephalomyelitic infection. **fugu p.,** tetraodontoxism. **gossypol p.,** poisoning from eating cottonseed cake. **gymnothorax p.,** a form of ichthyosarcotoxism produced by ingestion of certain moray eels of the genus *Gymnothorax.* **lead p.,** plumbism. **loco p.,** locoism. **meat p.,** acute, often severe gastroenteritis, caused by *Salmonella enteritidis*, staphylococcus or streptococcus, or some similar organism. **milk p.,** trembles. **mussel p.,** mytilotoxism. **O_2 p.** See *hyperventilation.* **puffer p.,** tetraodontoxism. **Renghas p.,** an itching type of contact dermatitis in the Netherlands East Indies, caused by contact with the sap or wood of various trees. **salmon p.,** a hemorrhagic enteritis in dogs caused by infestation with the trematode, *Troglotrema salmincola* which is acquired by eating salmon. **saturnine p.,** plumbism. **sausage p.** See *allantiasis* and *botulism.* **scombroid p.,** a histamine-like form of ichthyosarcotoxism produced by the ingestion of inadequately preserved scombroid or tuna-like fishes in certain tropical regions. **selenium p.,** a form of poisoning of livestock of the North Central Great Plains region of the United States due to the feeding on plants which have absorbed selenium from the soil and characterized by cirrhosis of the liver, anemia, loss of hair, erosions of long bones, emaciation. **shellfish p.,** mytilotoxism. **tetrachlorethane p.,** a form of poisoning in munition workers caused by inhalation of fumes of tetrachlorethane, and marked by toxic jaundice, headache, anorexia, and gastrointestinal disturbance. **tetraodon p.,** tetraodontoxism. **T.N.T. p.,** trinitrotoluene p. **tobacco p.,** tabacosis. **trinitrotoluene p.,** a form of poisoning in munition workers, characterized by dermatitis, gastritis with abdominal pain, vomiting, constipation, flatulence, and blood changes. **whelk p.,** a form of intoxication resulting from the ingestion of whelks, members of the mollusk family Buccinidae. See also under *poison.*

poitrinaire (pwah″tre-nār′) [Fr.]. A patient with a chronic disease of the chest.

polar (po′lar) [L. *polaris, polus;* Gr. *polos*]. Of, or pertaining to, a pole.

polaramine (po-lar′ah-mēn). Trade mark for preparations of dexchlorpheniramine maleate.

polarimeter (po″lar-im′e-ter) [*polar* + Gr. *metron* measure]. A device for measuring the rotation of polarized light; a polariscope.

polarimetry (po″lar-im′e-tre). Measurement of the rotation of polarized light.

polariscope (po-lar′ĭ-skōp) [*polar* + Gr. *skopein* to examine]. An instrument for the measurement of polarized light.

polariscopic (po″lar-ĭ-skop′ik). Pertaining to the polariscope or to polariscopy.

polariscopy (po″lar-is′ko-pe). The science of polarized light and the use of the polariscope.

polaristrobometer (po-lar″is-tro-bom′e-ter). A form of polarimeter used for delicate analyses.

polarity (po-lar′ĭ-te). 1. The fact or condition of having poles. 2. The exhibition of opposite effects at the two extremities. 3. The presence of an axial gradient and exhibition by a nerve of both anelectrotonus and catelectrotonus. **dynamic p.,** the specialization of a nerve cell with reference to the flow of impulses.

polarization (po″lar-i-za′shun). 1. The production of that condition in light by virtue of which its vibrations take place all in one plane or else in circles and ellipses. 2. The accumulation of bubbles of hydrogen gas on the negative plate of a galvanic battery, so that the generation of electricity is impeded. **circular p.,** that polarization which causes the vibrations all to take place in circles. **elliptical p.,** that which causes the vibrations to move in ellipses. **plane p.,** the production of such a polarization that the light vibrations are all in one plane. **rotatory p.,** that which rotates the plane in which the vibrations take place.

polarize (po′lar-iz). 1. To endue with polarity. 2. To put into a state of polarization.

polarizer (po′lar-iz″er). An appliance for polarizing light.

polarogram (po-lar′o-gram). The curve of current voltage obtained in polarography.

polarography (po″lar-og′rah-fe). The photographic recording of the current-voltage curve produced in electroanalysis by means of a dropping mercury cathode.

polaroid (po′lar-oid). A commercial film containing oriented crystals used as a substitute for Nicol prisms and for reducing glare through lenses and windshields.

poldine (pol′dēn). Chemical name: 2-benziloxymethyl-1,1-dimethylpyrrolidinium: used in parasympathetic blockade, and to reduce acid formation in the stomach.

pole (pōl) [L. *polus;* Gr. *polos*]. 1. Either extremity of an axis, as of the fetal ellipse, or of an organ of the body. Called also *polus* or *extremitas.* 2. Either one of two points which have opposite physical qualities (electric or other). **animal p.,** the site of an ovum to which the nucleus is approximated, and from which the polar bodies pinch off. **anterior p. of eyeball,** polus anterior bulbi oculi. **anterior p. of lens,** polus anterior lentis. **antigerminal p.,** vegetal p. **cephalic p.,** the end of the fetal ellipse at which the head of the fetus is situated. **frontal p. of hemisphere of cerebrum,** polus frontalis hemispherii cerebri. **germinal p.,** animal p. **inferior p. of kidney,** extremitas inferior renis. **inferior p. of testis,** extremitas inferior testis. **negative p.,** cathode. **nutritive p.,** vegetal p. **occipital p. of hemisphere of cerebrum,** polus occipitalis hemispherii cerebri. **pelvic p.,** the end of the fetal ellipse at which the breech of the fetus is situated. **positive p.,** anode. **posterior p. of eyeball,** polus posterior bulbi oculi. **posterior p. of lens,** polus posterior lentis. **temporal p. of hemisphere of cerebrum,** polus temporalis hemispherii cerebri. **twin p.,** that part of a spiral-fibered nerve cell from which both the straight and spiral fibers spring. **upper p. of kidney,** extremitas superior renis. **upper p. of testis,** extremitas superior testis. **vegetal p.,** that pole of an ovum at which the greater amount of food yolk is deposited. **vegetative p., vitelline p.,** vegetal p.

Polemonium (pol″e-mo′ne-um). A genus of herbs; Greek valerian. Some species are said to have medicinal properties, and to be expectorant and diaphoretic.

polemophthalmia (pol″em-of-thal′me-ah) [Gr. *polemos* war + *ophthalmia*]. Military ophthalmia; ophthalmia affecting soldiers.

policeman (po-lēs′man). A glass rod with a piece of rubber tubing on one end, used as a stirring rod in chemical analysis.

policlinic (pol″e-klin′ik) [Gr. *polis* city + *klinē* bed]. A city hospital, infirmary, or clinic. Cf. *polyclinic.*

poliencephalitis (pol″e-en-sef″ah-li′tis). Polioencephalitis.

poliencephalomyelitis (pol″e-en-sef″ah-lo-mi″ĕ-li′tis). Inflammatory disease of the gray matter of the brain and spinal cord.

polio (po′le-o). Poliomyelitis.

polio- (po′le-o) [Gr. *polios* gray]. Combining form denoting relationship to the gray matter of the nervous system.

poliocidal (po″le-o-si′dal). Neutralizing the virus of epidemic poliomyelitis.

polioclastic (po″le-o-klas′tik) [*polio-* + Gr. *klastos* breaking]. Destroying the gray matter of the nervous system: a term applied to the viruses of poliomyelitis, epidemic encephalitis, and rabies.

polioencephalitis (po″le-o-en-sef″ah-li′tis) [*polio-* + *encephalitis*]. 1. Inflammatory disease of the gray substance of the brain. 2. Cerebral poliomyelitis. **p. acu′ta haemorrha′gica,** p. haemorrhagica superior. **p. acu′ta infan′tum,** an acute variety seen in children under six years of age, and marked by fever, vomiting, and convulsions. It is usually followed by permanent paralysis of the limbs which were affected with convulsions. **acute bulbar p.,** acute bulbar palsy. **p. haemorrha′gica supe′rior,** an inflammatory hemorrhagic type of encephalitis, with lesions about the cerebral aqueduct, occurring mainly, but not always, in chronic alcoholism. It is marked by paralysis of the eye muscles, a reeling gait and disturbances of consciousness: called also *encephalopathia alcoholica* and *Wernicke's encephalopathy.* **inferior p.,** bulbar paralysis. **posterior p.,** inflammation of the gray matter of the posterior part of the fourth ventricle. **superior hemorrhagic p.,** p. haemorrhagica superior.

polioencephalomeningomyelitis (po″le-o-en-sef″ah-lo-mĕ-nin″go-mi″ĕ-li′tis). Inflammation of the gray matter of the brain and spinal cord and of the meninges covering it.

polioencephalomyelitis (po″le-o-en-sef″ah-lo-mi″ĕ-li′tis). Poliencephalomyelitis.

polioencephalopathy (po″le-o-en-sef″ah-lop′ah-the) [*polio-* + Gr. *enkephalos* brain + *pathos* disease]. Disease of the gray matter of the brain.

polioencephalotropic (po″le-o-en-sef″ah-lo-trop′ik). Having a special affinity for the gray substance of the brain.

poliomyelencephalitis (po″le-o-mi″el-en-sef″ah-li′tis) [*polio-* + Gr. *myelos* marrow + *enkephalos* brain + *-itis*]. Poliomyelitis combined with polioencephalitis.

poliomyeliticidal (po″le-o-mi″ĕ-li′tĭ-si″dal). Having the power of destroying poliomyelitis virus.

poliomyelitis (po″le-o-mi″ĕ-li′tis) [*polio-* + Gr. *myelos* marrow + *-itis*]. A common, acute viral disease characterized clinically by fever, sore throat, headache, and vomiting, often with stiffness of the neck and back. In the *minor illness* these may represent the only symptoms the patient has. The *major illness,* which may or may not be preceded by the minor illness, is characterized by involvement of the central nervous system, stiff neck, pleocytosis in the spinal fluid, and perhaps paralysis. There may be subsequent atrophy of groups of muscles, ending in contraction and permanent deformity. Called also *polio, acute anterior poliomyelitis, infantile paralysis,* and *Heine-Medin disease.* See also *poliovirus.* **acute anterior p.** See *poliomyelitis.* **anterior p.,** inflammation of the anterior horns of the gray substance of the spinal cord. **ascending p.,** a paralytic affection which is first manifested in the legs and rapidly ascends cephalad. **bulbar p.,** a serious form of poliomyelitis in which the medulla oblongata is affected, and in which there may be dysfunction of the swallowing mechanism, and respiratory and circulatory distress. **cerebral p.,** poliomyelitis in which the areas most likely to be involved are the brain stem and the motor cortex. Called also *polioencephalitis.* **endemic p.,** poliomyelitis occurring sporadically or in a small number of cases, particularly during periods of warm weather, in most countries throughout the world. **epidemic p.,** poliomyelitis occurring in epidemic form. **mouse p.,** a disease of mice with encephalomyelitis as its prominent symptom, caused by the virus known as *poliovirus muris.* **post-inoculation p.,** acute poliomyelitis appearing within three weeks after some type of inoculation. **post-tonsil-**

lectomy **p.**, acute poliomyelitis appearing within a short time after tonsillectomy. **post-vaccinal p.**, acute poliomyelitis appearing within three weeks after some type of vaccination. **spinal paralytic p.**, the classic form of acute anterior poliomyelitis, in which the appearance of flaccid paralysis, usually of one or more limbs, makes the diagnosis quite definite. **p. su′um,** Teschen disease.

poliomyeloencephalitis (po″le-o-mi″ĕ-lo-en-sef″ah-li′tis) [*polio-* + Gr. *myelos* marrow + *enkephalos* brain + *-itis*]. Poliencephalomyelitis.

poliomyelopathy (po″le-o-mi″ĕ-lop′ah-the) [*polio-* + Gr. *myelos* marrow + *pathos* disease]. Any disease primarily affecting the gray matter of the spinal cord; chronic poliomyelitis.

polioneuromere (po″le-o-nu′ro-mēr) [*polio-* + Gr. *neuron* nerve + *meros* part]. One of the primitive segments of the gray matter of the spinal cord.

polioplasm (pol′e-o-plazm) [*polio-* + Gr. *plasma* something formed]. The internal, granular protoplasm proper of a cell.

poliosis (pol″e-o′sis). Premature grayness of the hair. **p. eccen′trica,** whiteness of the hair in irregularly placed patches in partial albinism.

poliothrix (pol′e-o-thriks) [*polio-* + Gr. *thrix* hair]. Graying of the hair.

poliovirus (po″le-o-vi′rus). The etiologic agent of poliomyelitis, separable, on the basis of specificity of neutralizing antibody, into three serotypes, designated types 1, 2, and 3. Over the years, type 1 has been responsible for about 85 per cent of all paralytic poliomyelitis and for most epidemics, and type 3 for about 10 per cent of paralytic poliomyelitis and for occasional epidemics. Type 2, over the years, has been responsible for only about 5 per cent of paralytic poliomyelitis, and only recently have epidemics caused by this type been recognized in Central America and in Asia. **p. mu′ris,** the etiologic agent of mouse poliomyelitis.

polishing (pol′ish-ing). 1. The creation of a smooth and glossy finish on a surface, as of a denture. 2. [Pl.]. Material obtained by abrasion of a solid, such as that (*rice polishings*, a rich source of vitamin B) produced by the milling of rice.

polisography (pol″e-sog′rah-fe) [Gr. *polys* many + *isos* same + *graphein* to write]. Roentgenography in which several exposures are made in the same film.

Politzer's bag, cone, speculum, test, etc. (pol′it-zerz) [Adam *Politzer*, Hungarian otologist, 1835–1920]. See under the nouns.

politzerization (pol″it-zer-i-za′shun) [Adam *Politzer*]. Inflation of the middle ear by means of a Politzer bag. **negative p.,** suction of secretion from a cavity by means of a Politzer bag.

polkissen (pōl-kis′en) [Ger. "pole cushion"]. Juxtaglomerular cells.

poll (pōl). The back part of the head, especially that of an animal.

pollakicoprosis (pol-lak″ĭ-kop-ro′sis) [Gr. *pollakis* often + *koprōsis* defecation]. Unduly frequent evacuation of feces.

pollakidipsia (pol″ah-kĭ-dip′se-ah) [Gr. *pollakis* often + *dipsa* thirst + *-ia*]. A condition characterized by abnormally frequent occurrence of the sensation of thirst.

pollakisuria (pol″ah-kĭ-su′re-ah). Pollakiuria.

pollakiuria (pol″ah-ke-u′re-ah) [Gr. *pollakis* often + *ouron* urine + *-ia*]. Unduly frequent passage of the urine.

pollantin (pol-lan′tin). An antitoxin derived from the blood of horses by inoculating them with the toxin of the pollen of certain plants: used in hay fever (Dunbar and Weichardt, 1903).

pollen (pol′en). The mass of microspores (male fertilizing elements) of flowering plants.

pollenarium (pol″ĕ-na′re-um). A building or room for the collection and storing of pollens.

pollenogenic (pol″ĕ-no-jen′ik) [*pollen* + Gr. *gennan* to produce]. Caused by the pollen of plants.

pollenosis (pol″ĕ-no′sis). Pollinosis.

pollex (pol′eks), pl. *pol′lices* [L.]. [N A, B N A] The first digit of the hand, or thumb. **p. exten′sus,** backward deviation of the thumb. **p. flex′us,** permanent flexion of the thumb. **p. val′gus,** deviation of the thumb toward the ulnar side. **p. va′rus,** deviation of the thumb toward the radial side.

pollicization (pol″is-i-za′shun) [L. *pollex* thumb]. The replacement or rehabilitation of a thumb; especially surgical construction of a thumb from a portion of the index finger.

pollinosis (pol″ĭ-no′sis). The allergic reaction in the body to the air-borne pollen of plants, resulting in the seasonal type of hay fever or rose cold. See *hay fever*, under *fever*.

Pollitzer's disease (pol′it-zerz) [Sigmund *Pollitzer*, New York dermatologist, 1859–1937]. Hidrosadenitis destruens suppurativa.

pollodic (pol-lo′dik) [Gr. *polloi* many + *hodos* way]. Panthodic.

pollopas (pol′o-pas). A glass which is more penetrable than flint glass to ultraviolet and infrared rays.

pollution (pŏ-lu′shun) [L. *pollutio*]. 1. The act of defiling or making impure. 2. The discharge of semen without coition. **diurnal p., p. nim′iae,** spermatorrhea. **nocturnal p.,** the discharge of semen during sleep. **self-p., voluntary p.,** masturbation.

polocyte (po′lo-sīt) [Gr. *polos* pole + *-cyte*]. See *polar body*, under *body*.

polonium (po-lo′ne-um) [L. *Polonia* Poland]. A rare metal resembling bismuth, discovered in 1898 in pitchblende; atomic number, 84; atomic weight, 210; symbol, Po. It is radioactive, but less so than radium.

poloxalkol (pol-ok′sal-kol). A pharmacologically inert oxyalkylene polymer, used as a fecal softener.

poltophagy (pol-tof′ah-je) [Gr. *poltos* porridge + *phagein* to eat]. Thorough chewing of the food so that it becomes reduced to a porridge-like mass.

polus (po′lus), pl. *po′li* [L.]. Either extremity of an axis. Used in anatomical nomenclature to designate the extremity of an organ. Called also *pole.* **p. ante′rior bul′bi oc′uli** [N A, B N A], the center of the anterior curvature of the eyeball. Called also *anterior pole of eyeball.* **p. ante′rior len′tis** [N A, B N A], the central point of the anterior surface of the lens. Called also *anterior pole of lens.* **p. fronta′lis hemisphe′rii cer′ebri** [N A], the most prominent part of the anterior end of each hemisphere of the brain. Called also *frontal pole of hemisphere of cerebrum.* **p. occipita′lis hemisphe′rii cer′ebri** [N A], the most posterior prominence of the occipital lobe of the cerebral hemisphere. Called also *occipital pole of hemisphere of cerebrum.* **p. poste′rior bul′bi oc′uli** [N A, B N A], the center of the posterior curvature of the eyeball. Called also *posterior pole of eyeball.* **p. poste′rior len′tis** [N A, B N A], the central point of the posterior surface of the lens. Called also *posterior pole of lens.* **p. tempora′lis hemisphe′rii cer′ebri** [N A], the prominent anterior end of the temporal lobe of the brain. Called also *temporal pole of hemisphere of cerebrum.*

poly (pol′e). A polymorphonuclear leukocyte.

poly- [Gr. *polys* many]. Combining form meaning many or much.

Polya's operation (pōl′yahz) [Jenö (Eugene) *Polya*, Budapest surgeon, 1876–1944]. See under *operation*.

polyacid (pol″e-as′id). Capable of saturating several molecules of an acid radical: said of a base or basic radical.

polyacoustic (pol″e-ah-kōōs′tik) [*poly-* + Gr. *akoustikos* relating to hearing]. Increasing or intensifying sound.

polyadenia (pol″e-ah-de′ne-ah) [*poly-* + Gr. *adēn* gland + *-ia*]. Pseudoleukemia.

polyadenitis (pol″e-ad″e-ni′tis) [*poly-* + Gr. *adēn* gland + *-itis*]. Inflammation of several or many glands. **malignant p.,** bubonic plague.

polyadenoma (pol″e-ad″e-no′mah). Adenoma of many glands.

polyadenomatosis (pol″e-ad″e-no-mah-to′sis). Multiple adenomas in a part.

polyadenopathy (pol″e-ad″e-nop′ah-the). Any disease affecting several glands at once.

polyadenosis (pol″e-ad″e-no′sis). Disorder of several glands, particularly of several endocrine glands.

polyadenous (pol″e-ad′e-nus) [*poly-* + Gr. *adēn* gland]. Having or affecting many glands.

polyagglutinability (pol″e-ah-gloo″tĭ-nah-bil′ĭ-te). The susceptibility to agglutination by a number of agents not necessarily corresponding to the antigenic structure of the agglutinogen.

polyalcoholism (pol″e-al′ko-hol-izm). Intoxication or poisoning by a mixture of different alcohols.

polyalgesia (pol″e-al-je′se-ah) [*poly-* + Gr. *algēsis* sense of pain + *-ia*]. A condition in which a single pin-prick feels as if several had been made.

polyandry (pol″e-an′dre) [*poly-* + Gr. *aner* man]. 1. The concurrent marriage of a woman to more than one man, as practiced by certain primitive peoples. 2. Union of two or more male pronuclei with a female pronucleus, resulting in polyploidy of the zygote.

Polyangiaceae (pol″e-an″je-a′se-e). A systematic family of schizomycetes, order Myxobacterales, made up of saprophytic microorganisms found in soil and decaying organic matter, and including four genera, *Chondromy′ces, Podan′gium, Polyan′gium,* and *Synan′gium.*

polyangiitis (pol″e-an″je-i′tis). Inflammation involving multiple blood or lymph vessels.

polyarteritis (pol″e-ar″ter-i′tis) [*poly-* + Gr. *artēria* artery + *-itis*]. Inflammation of several arteries at the same time. See *periarteritis nodosa.*

polyarthric (pol″e-ar′thrik) [*poly-* + Gr. *arthron* joint]. Pertaining to or affecting many joints.

polyarthritis (pol″e-ar-thri′tis) [*poly-* + Gr. *arthron* joint + *-itis*]. An inflammation of several joints together. **chronic villous p.,** chronic inflammation of the synovial membrane of several joints. **p. des′truens,** proliferative arthritis. **infectious p. of rats,** an infectious disease of rats in Java marked by arthritis and swelling of the legs. **p. rheumat′ica acu′ta,** rheumatic fever. **tuberculous p.,** pulmonary osteo-arthropathy. **vertebral p.,** disease of the intervertebral substance without caries of the bodies of the vertebrae.

polyarticular (pol″e-ar-tik′u-lar) [*poly-* + L. *articulus* joint]. Affecting many joints.

polyase (pol′e-ās). An enzyme which catalyzes the hydrolysis of polysaccharides.

polyatomic (pol″e-ah-tom′ik) [*poly-* + Gr. *atomon* atom]. 1. Composed of several atoms. 2. Having more than two hydroxyl groups.

polyauxotroph (pol″e-awk′so-trōf) [*poly-* + Gr. *auxein* to increase + *trophē* nourishment]. An organism, especially a mutant, which requires multiple growth factors.

polyauxotrophic (pol″e-awk″so-trōf′ik). Requiring multiple growth factors; used especially with reference to a single mutation that causes a multiple requirement.

polyavitaminosis (pol″e-a-vi″tah-min-o′sis) [*poly-* + *avitaminosis*]. A deficiency disease in which more than one vitamin is lacking in the diet.

polyaxon (pol″e-ak′son) [*poly-* + Gr. *axōn* axis]. A nerve cell from the horizontal dendrites of which four or more axons or branches are given off.

polyaxonic (pol″e-ak-son′ik). Having several axons.

polyazin (pol″e-az′in). An organic chemical compound whose molecules contain atoms two or more of which are nitrogen.

polybasic (pol″e-ba′sik) [*poly-* + Gr. *basis* base]. 1. Noting any acid which has several hydrogen atoms replaceable by a base. 2. Noting any salt of a polybasic acid formed by replacing some or all of its hydrogen atoms by a base.

polyblast (pol′e-blast) [*poly-* + Gr. *blastos* germ]. Maximow's name for the mononuclear exudate cells in inflamed tissues. According to him they arise from the wandering cells of the tissues and from hypertrophied nongranular leukocytes which have left the blood stream.

polyblennia (pol″e-blen′e-ah) [*poly-* + Gr. *blenna* mucus + *-ia*]. The secretion of an excessive quantity of mucus.

polybrene (pol′e-brēn). Trade mark for a preparation of hexadimethrine bromide.

polycardia (pol″e-kar′de-ah) [*poly-* + Gr. *kardia* heart]. Tachycardia.

polycellular (pol″e-sel′u-lar). Multicellular.

polycentric (pol″e-sen′trik). Having many centers.

polyceptor (pol″e-sep′tor) [*poly-* + *ceptor*]. An amboceptor which is capable of binding a number of different complements.

polycheiria (pol″e-ki′re-ah) [*poly-* + Gr. *cheir* hand + *-ia*]. The condition of having more than two hands.

polychemotherapy (pol″e-ke″mo-ther′ah-pe). Treatment by the simultaneous administration of several chemotherapeutic agents.

polychloruria (pol″e-klo-roo′re-ah). An increased excretion of chlorine in the urine.

polycholia (pol″e-ko′le-ah) [*poly-* + Gr. *cholē* bile + *-ia*]. Excessive flow or secretion of bile.

polychondritis (pol″e-kon-dri′tis). Inflammation involving many cartilages of the body. **chronic atrophic p., p. chron′ica atro′phicans,** relapsing p. **relapsing p.,** an acquired disease of unknown etiology, chiefly involving various cartilages of the body, and showing both chronicity and a tendency to recurrence.

polychondropathia (pol″e-kon″dro-path′e-ah). Relapsing polychondritis.

polychondropathy (pol″e-kon-drop′ah-the). Relapsing polychondritis.

polychrest (pol′e-krest) [*poly-* + Gr. *chrēstos* useful]. 1. Useful in many conditions. 2. A remedy useful in many diseases.

polychromasia (pol″e-kro-ma′ze-ah). 1. Variation in the hemoglobin content of the erythrocytes of the blood. 2. Polychromatophilia.

polychromate (pol″e-kro′māt). A person who can distinguish many colors.

polychromatia (pol″e-kro-ma′she-ah). Polychromatophilia.

polychromatic (pol″e-kro-mat′ik) [*poly-* + Gr. *chrōma* color]. Exhibiting many colors.

polychromatocyte (pol″e-kro-mat′o-sīt). A cell that is stainable with various stains or colors.

polychromatocytosis (pol″e-kro″mah-to-si-to′sis). Polychromatophilia.

polychromatophil (pol″e-kro-mat′o-fil) [*poly-* + Gr. *chrōma* color + *philein* to love]. A cell or other element that is stainable with various stains or colors.

polychromatophilia (pol″e-kro″mah-to-fil′e-ah). 1. The quality of being stainable with various stains or tints; affinity for all sorts of stains. 2. A condition in which the erythrocytes, on staining, show various shades of blue combined with tinges of pink.

polychromatophilic (pol″e-kro″mah-to-fil′ik). Pertaining to or characterized by polychromatophilia.

polychromatosis (pol″e-kro″mah-to′sis). An excess of abnormally staining erythrocytes in the blood. See *polychromatophilia,* def. 2.

polychromemia (pol″e-kro-me′me-ah) [*poly-* + Gr. *chrōma* color + *haima* blood + *-ia*]. Increase in the coloring matter of the blood.

polychromia (pol″e-kro′me-ah) [*poly-* + Gr. *chrōma* color + *-ia*]. Increased or abnormal pigment formation.

polychromic (pol″e-kro′mik). Pertaining to or exhibiting many colors.

polychromophil (pol″e-kro′mo-fil). Polychromatophil.

polychromophilia (pol″e-kro-mo-fil′e-ah). Polychromatophilia.

polychylia (pol″e-ki′le-ah) [*poly-* + Gr. *chylos* chyle + *-ia*]. Excessive production of chyle.

polyclinic (pol″e-klin′ik) [*poly-* + Gr. *klinē* bed]. A hospital and school where diseases and injuries of all kinds are studied and treated clinically.

polyclonia (pol″e-klo′ne-ah) [*poly-* + Gr. *klonos* clonus + *-ia*]. A disease marked by many clonic spasms, resembling tic and chorea, but distinct from either.

polycopria (pol″e-kop′re-ah) [*poly-* + Gr. *kopros* filth + *-ia*]. Excessive formation of feces.

polycoria (pol″e-ko′re-ah). 1. [*poly-* + Gr. *korē* pupil + *-ia*]. The existence of more than one pupil in an eye. 2. [*poly-* + Gr. *koros* surfeit + *-ia*]. The deposit of reserve material in an organ or tissue so as to produce enlargement. **p. spu′ria,** a condition in which the iris contains several openings or holes. **p. ve′ra,** the existence in the eye of several pupils, each with its own sphincter.

polycrotic (pol″e-krot′ik) [*poly-* + Gr. *krotos* beat]. Having several secondary waves to each pulse beat.

polycrotism (pol-ik′ro-tizm). The fact or quality of being polycrotic.

polycyclic (pol″e-si′klik) [*poly-* + Gr. *kyklos* ring]. Containing more than one ring or cycle (frequency).

polycycline (pol″e-si′klēn). Trade mark for preparations of tetracycline hydrochloride.

polycyesis (pol″e-si-e′sis) [*poly-* + Gr. *kyēsis* pregnancy]. Multiple pregnancy.

polycystic (pol″e-sis′tik) [*poly-* + Gr. *kystis* cyst]. Containing or made up of many cysts.

polycystoma (pol″e-sis-to′mah). A condition in which a part, especially the breast, is riddled with cysts.

polycyte (pol′e-sīt) [*poly* + Gr. *kytos* cell]. A hypersegmented polymorphonuclear leukocyte of normal size. Cf. *macropolycyte*.

polycythemia (pol″e-si-the′me-ah) [*poly-* + Gr. *kytos* cell + *haima* blood + *-ia*]. Excess in the number of red corpuscles in the blood. **p. hyperton′ica,** a condition marked by an abnormal increase in the number of red corpuscles, without enlargement of the spleen, but with hypertrophy of the heart and increased blood pressure. Called also *Gaisböck's disease.* **myelopathic p., primary p.,** p. vera. **relative p.,** relative excess in the number of red corpuscles resulting from loss of the fluid portion of the blood. **p. ru′bra,** p. vera. **secondary p.,** any absolute increase in the total red cell mass other than polycythemia vera, such as that occurring in association with congenital heart disease, pulmonary abnormalities, and diseases of the kidneys, both neoplastic and non-neoplastic. **splenomegalic p.,** p. vera. **stress p.,** stress erythrocytosis. **p. ve′ra,** a familial disease of unknown etiology, characterized by a striking absolute increase in red cell mass and total blood volume, associated frequently with splenomegaly, leukocytosis, thrombocytosis, and signs of bone marrow hyperactivity; the concurrent changes in the blood leukocytes and platelets, in addition to the hematologic complications, have suggested a relationship to myelocytic leukemia, and the disease has, by some, been grouped with the myeloproliferative disorders. Called also *erythremia, erythrocythemia, p. rubra, splenomegalic polycythemia, myelopathic polycythemia, erythrocytosis megalosplenica, Osler's disease, Vaquez's disease,* and *Vaquez-Osler disease.*

polycytosis (pol″e-si-to′sis) [*poly-* + *-cyte* + *-osis*]. Abnormal increase in erythrocytes and leukocytes in the blood, the plasma being reduced in volume.

polydactylia (pol″e-dak-til′e-ah) [*poly-* + Gr. *daktylos* finger + *-ia*]. A developmental anomaly characterized by the presence of supernumerary digits (fingers or toes) on the hands or feet.

polydactylism (pol-e-dak′til-izm). Polydactylia.

polydactyly (pol″e-dak′tĭ-le). Polydactylia.

polydentia (pol″e-den′she-ah). Polyodontia.

polydipsia (pol″e-dip′se-ah) [*poly-* + Gr. *dipsa* thirst + *-ia*]. Excessive thirst persisting for long periods of time. **p. ebrio′ria,** a craving for intoxicant liquors.

polydispersoid (pol″e-dis-per′soid). A colloid in which the disperse phase consists of particles having different degrees of dispersion.

polydyscrinia (pol″e-dis-krin′e-ah). Pluridyscrinia.

polydysplasia (pol″e-dis-pla′ze-ah) [*poly-* + *dysplasia*]. Faulty development in several types of tissue or several organs or systems. **hereditary ectodermal p.,** hereditary ectodermal dysplasia.

polydysspondylism (pol″e-dis-spon′dĭ-lizm). Malformation of several vertebrae, associated with dwarfed stature, low intelligence, and malformation of the sella turcica.

polyelectrolyte (pol″e-e-lek′tro-līt). An electrolyte of high molecular weight.

polyembryony (pol″e-em-bri′o-ne) [*poly-* + *embryo*]. The production of two or more embryos from the same ovum or seed.

polyemia (pol″e-e′me-ah) [*poly-* + Gr. *haima* blood + *-ia*]. Excess in the quantity or amount of blood in the body. **p. aquo′sa,** excess in the volume of the blood due to the drinking of much water. **p. hyperalbumino′sa,** an excess of albumin in the blood plasma. **p. polycythaem′ica,** an absolute increase in the number of red corpuscles in the blood. **p. sero′sa,** excess in the amount of blood serum, sometimes due to the injection of serum into the blood vessels.

polyene (pol-e′ēn). A chemical compound in which there are several conjugated double bonds.

polyerg (pol′e-erg) [*poly-* + Gr. *ergon* work]. A monogenic antiserum which reacts with heterologous antigens.

polyergic (pol″e-er′jik). Able to act in several different ways.

polyesthesia (pol″e-es-the′ze-ah) [*poly-* + Gr. *aisthēsis* perception + *-ia*]. A condition in which a single object seems to be felt in several different places.

polyesthetic (pol″e-es-thet′ik). Pertaining to or affecting several senses or sensations.

polyestrous (pol″e-es′trus). Completing two or more estrus cycles in each sexual season.

polyethylene (pol″e-eth′ĭ-lēn). Polymerized ethylene, $(CH_2{-}CH_2)_n$, a synthetic plastic material, forms of which have been used in reparative surgery. **p. glycol 400,** a clear, colorless, viscous liquid, a condensation polymer of ethylene oxide and water, represented by the formula $H(OCH_2\text{-}CH_2)_nOH$, in which n varies from 8 to 10: used as a water-soluble ointment base. **p. glycol 4000,** a condensation polymer of ethylene and water respresented by the same formula as polyethylene glycol 400, except that n varies from 70 to 85: also used as a water-soluble ointment base.

polyfolliculinic (pol″e-fo-lik″u-lin′ik). Marked by extensive secretion of folliculin.

Polygala (po-lig′ah-lah) [*poly-* + Gr. *gala* milk]. A genus of plants (milkworts) of many species. See *Senega.*

polygalactia (pol″e-gah-lak′she-ah) [*poly-* + Gr. *gala* milk]. An excessive secretion of milk.

polygalin (po-lig′ah-lin). A bitter substance, one of the active principles of senega (*Polygala senega*). Called also polygalic acid.

polygamy (po-lig′ah-me) [*poly-* + Gr. *gamos* marriage]. The concurrent marriage of a woman or man to more than one mate.

polyganglionic (pol″e-gang″gle-on′ik) [*poly-* + Gr. *ganglion* ganglion]. 1. Having or pertaining to several or many ganglia. 2. Affecting several lymphatic glands.

polygastria (pol″e-gas′tre-ah) [*poly-* + Gr. *gastēr* stomach]. Excessive secretion of gastric juice.

polygen (pol′e-jen). 1. An element which is able to combine in two or more proportions. 2. An antiserum which has been produced by the use of more than one antigen.

polygenic (pol″e-jēn′ik) [*poly-* + *gene*]. Pertaining to or influenced by several different genes.

polyglandular (pol″e-glan′du-lar). Pertaining to or affecting several different glands.

polyglobulia (pol″e-glo-bu′le-ah). Polycythemia.

polyglobulism (pol″e-glob′u-lizm). Polycythemia.

polygnathus (po-lig′nah-thus) [*poly-* + Gr. *gnathos* jaw]. A fetal monster in which a parasitic twin is attached to the jaw of the autosite.

Polygonatum (pol″e-go-na′tum) [*poly-* + Gr. *gony* knee]. A genus of liliaceous plants called Solomon's seal. Several of the species are tonic, vulnerary, diuretic, and purgative: in a considerable dose they are cardiant poisons.

polygram (pol′e-gram). A tracing made by a polygraph.

polygraph (pol′e-graf) [*poly-* + Gr. *graphein* to write]. An instrument for simultaneously recording several mechanical or electrical impulses, such as respiratory movements, pulse wave, blood pressure, and the psychogalvanic reflex. Such phenomena reveal emotional reactions which are of use in detecting deception.

polygyny (po-lij′ĭ-ne) [*poly-* + Gr. *gynē* woman]. 1. The concurrent marriage of a man to more than one woman, as practiced by certain primitive peoples. 2. Union of two or more female pronuclei with a male pronucleus, resulting in polyploidy of the zygote.

polygyria (pol″e-ji′re-ah) [*poly-* + Gr. *gyros* gyrus + *-ia*]. A condition in which there is more than the normal number of convolutions in the brain.

polyhedral (pol″e-he′dral) [*poly-* + Gr. *hedra* seat, base]. Having many faces or sides.

polyhexose (pol″e-hek′sōs). Polysaccharide.

polyhidrosis (pol″e-hid-ro′sis) [*poly-* + Gr. *hidrōs* sweat + *-osis*]. 1. Excess in the secretion of sweat. 2. Miliary fever, or sweating sickness.

polyhybrid (pol″e-hi′brid). A hybrid whose parents differ from each other in more than three characters.

polyhydramnios (pol″e-hi-dram′ne-os) [*poly-* + Gr. *hydōr* water + *amnion* amnion]. The presence of more than 2000 ml. of amniotic fluid at term.

polyhydric (pol″e-hi′drik). Containing more than two hyroxyl groups.

polyhydruria (pol″e-hi-droo′re-ah) [*poly-* + Gr. *hydōr* water + *ouron* urine + *-ia*]. Abnormal dilution of the urine.

polyhypermenorrhea (pol″e-hi″per-men″o-re′ah) [*poly-* + Gr. *hyper* over + *menorrhea*]. Frequent menstruation with abnormally profuse discharge.

polyhypomenorrhea (pol″e-hi″po-men″o-re′ah) [*poly-* + Gr. *hypo* under + *menorrhea*]. Frequent menstruation with deficient amount of discharge.

polyidrosis (pol″e-id-ro′sis). Polyhidrosis.

polyinfection (pol″e-in-fek′shun) [*poly-* + *infection*]. Infection with more than one organism.

polykaryocyte (pol″e-kar′e-o-sīt) [*poly-* + Gr. *karyon* nucleus + *-cyte*]. A giant cell containing several nuclei.

polykol (pol′e-kol). Trade mark for preparations of poloxalkol.

polylecithal (pol″e-les′ĭ-thal) [*poly-* + Gr. *lekithos* yolk]. Megalecithal.

polyleptic (pol″e-lep′tik) [*poly-* + Gr. *lambanein* to seize]. Having many remissions and exacerbations.

polylogia (pol″e-lo′je-ah) [*poly-* + Gr. *logos* word]. Much talking due to mental disorder.

polymastia (pol″e-mas′te-ah) [*poly-* + Gr. *mastos* breast]. The presence of more than two mammae, or breasts.

Polymastigina (pol″e-mas″tĭ-gi′nah). An order of the Flagellata the members of which possess three to eight flagella. It includes the trichomonads and Giardia.

polymastigote (pol″e-mas′tĭ-gōt) [*poly-* + Gr. *mastix* lash]. Having several flagella.

polymazia (pol″e-ma′ze-ah). Polymastia.

polymelia (pol″e-me′le-ah) [*poly-* + Gr. *melos* limb + *-ia*]. A developmental anomaly characterized by the presence of supernumerary limbs.

polymelus (po-lim′e-lus). An individual exhibiting polymelia.

polymenia (pol″e-me′ne-ah). Polymenorrhea.

polymenorrhea (pol″e-men″o-re′ah) [*poly-* + *menorrhea*]. Abnormally frequent menstruation.

polymer (pol′ĭ-mer) [*poly-* + Gr. *meros* part]. A compound, usually of high molecular weight, formed by the combination of simpler molecules. **addition p.,** a compound formed by the repeated combination of smaller molecules (monomers) without the formation of any other products (e.g., polyethylene). **condensation p.,** a compound formed by the repeated reaction of smaller molecules, involving at the same time the elimination of water or other simple compound (e.g., nylon).

polymeria (pol″ĭ-me′re-ah) [*poly-* + Gr. *meros* part + *-ia*]. A developmental anomaly characterized by the presence of supernumerary parts or organs of the body.

polymeric (pol″ĭ-mer′ik). Exhibiting the characteristics of a polymer.

polymerid (po-lim′er-id). A polymer.

polymerism (po-lim′er-izm). The phenomenon, or process, which results in the formation of a polymer.

polymerization (pol″ĭ-mer″ĭ-za′shun). The act or process of forming a compound, usually of high molecular weight, by the combination of simpler molecules.

polymerize (pol′ĭ-mer-īz). To subject to or to undergo polymerization.

polymetacarpia (pol″e-met″ah-kar′pe-ah) [*poly-* + *metacarpus* + *-ia*]. Presence of more than the normal number of metacarpal bones.

polymetatarsia (pol″e-met″ah-tar′se-ah) [*poly-* + *metatarsus* + -ia]. Presence of more than the normal number of metatarsal bones.

polymicrobial (pol″e-mi-kro′be-al) [*poly-* + *microbe*]. Characterized by the presence of several species of microorganisms.

polymicrobic (pol″e-mi-kro′bik). Polymicrobial.

polymicrogyria (pol″e-mi″kro-ji′re-ah) [*poly-* + Gr. *mikros* small + *gyros* convolution + *-ia*]. A malformation of the brain characterized by development of numerous small convolutions (microgyri).

polymicrolipomatosis (pol″e-mi″kro-lip″o-mah-to′sis) [*poly-* + Gr. *mikros* small + *lipomatosis*]. The presence in the subcutaneous tissue of numerous small fatty tumors.

polymicrotome (pol″e-mi′kro-tōm) [*poly-* + *microtome*]. A microtome which cuts several sections at once.

polymitus (po-lim′ĭ-tus) [*poly-* + Gr. *mitos* thread]. An animal microorganism, or stage, of various forms, provided with threadlike filaments or with buds, or both. Forms of polymitus have been observed within the Gymnosporidia, the blood parasites of birds, and of human malaria. The nature and functions are undetermined.

Polymnia (po-lim′ne-ah) [Gr.; one of the nine

Muses]. A genus of composite-flowered plants. *P. uvedalia*, leafcup or bearsfoot, is anthelmintic, alterative, and antispasmodic.

polymorph (pol′e-morf). A polymorphonuclear leukocyte.

polymorphic (pol″e-mor′fik) [*poly-* + Gr. *morphē* form]. Occurring in several or many forms; appearing in different forms at different stages of development.

polymorphism (pol″e-mor′fizm) [*poly-* + Gr. *morphē* form]. The quality or character of being polymorphic.

polymorphocellular (pol″e-mor″fo-sel′u-lar) [*poly-* + Gr. *morphē* form + L. *cellula* cell]. Having cells of many forms.

polymorphocyte (pol″e-mor′fo-sīt). A cell with a polymorphous nucleus.

polymorphonuclear (pol″e-mor″fo-nu′kle-ar) [*poly-* + Gr. *morphē* form + *nucleus*]. 1. Having a nucleus deeply lobed or so divided that it appears to be multiple. 2. A polymorphonuclear leukocyte. **filament p.,** one whose nuclear segments are joined by the filaments. **nonfilament p.,** one whose nuclear segments are joined by wide bands.

polymorphous (pol″e-mor′fus). Polymorphic. **p. perverse,** a term applied to infantile sexual impulses which have not become repressed into normal mature sexuality, but appear as sexual perversions or the bases of neuroses.

polymyalgia (pol″e-mi-al′je-ah). Myalgia affecting several muscles.

polymyarian (pol″e-mi-a′re-an) [*poly-* + Gr. *mys* muscle]. Having many muscle cells in each quadrant of a cross section, the cells being coelomyarian in type: said of the muscle arrangement in certain nematodes.

polymyoclonus (pol″e-mi-ok′lo-nus) [*poly-* + Gr. *mys* muscle + *klonos* clonus]. 1. A fine or minute muscular tremor. 2. Polyclonia.

polymyopathy (pol″e-mi-op′ah-the). Disease affecting several muscles simultaneously.

polymyositis (pol″e-mi″o-si′tis) [*poly-* + Gr. *mys* muscle + *-itis*]. Inflammation of several or many muscles at once. It is attended by pain, tension, edema, deformity, insomnia, and sweats. **p. haemorrha′gica,** inflammation of muscles associated with edema, dermatitis, and the presence of hemorrhages into and between the muscles. **trichinous p.,** trichinosis.

polymyxin (pol″e-mik′sin). A generic term used to designate a number of antibiotic substances derived from strains of the soil bacterium, *Bacillus polymyxa*, which are differentiated by affixing different letters of the alphabet. **p. B,** the least toxic of the polymyxins: the sulfate is used in treatment of various infections.

polynesic (pol″e-ne′sik) [*poly-* + Gr. *nēsos* island]. Multiple and insular; occurring in many foci.

polyneural (pol″e-nu′ral) [*poly-* + Gr. *neuron* nerve]. Pertaining to or supplied by several nerves.

polyneuralgia (pol″e-nu-ral′je-ah). Neuralgia of several nerves.

polyneuric (pol″e-nu′rik). Polyneural.

polyneuritic (pol″e-nu-rit′ik). Pertaining to or affected with polyneuritis.

polyneuritis (pol″e-nu-ri′tis) [*poly-* + Gr. *neuron* nerve + *-itis*]. Inflammation of many nerves at once; multiple peripheral neuritis. **acute febrile p., acute infectious p.,** a disease beginning with febrile symptoms and followed by suddenly developing widespread bilateral paralysis of the face, trunk, and proximal segments of the limbs. **anemic p.,** polyneuritis seen in subacute combined degeneration of the spinal cord which occurs in pernicious anemia. **p. cerebra′lis menierifor′mis,** symptoms of cochlear, vestibular, facial, and trigeminal nerve irritation occurring in the early period of syphilis. Also called *Frankl-Hochwart's disease.* **endemic p.,** beriberi. **p. gallina′rum,** a form of polyneuritis seen in fowls after feeding with peeled grain. **Guillain-Barré p.** See under *syndrome.* **Jamaica ginger p.** See under *paralysis.* **p. potato′rum,** a chronic neuritis resulting from the excessive use of alcoholic stimulants. Called also *alcoholic neuritis* and *pseudotabes.* **uveoparotitic p.,** uveoparotid fever.

polyneuromyositis (pol″e-nu″ro-mi″ĕ-li′tis). Inflammation involving several muscles, with loss of reflexes, sensory loss, and paresthesias.

polyneuropathy (pol″e-nu-rop′ah-the) [*poly-* + Gr. *neuron* nerve + *pathos* disease]. A disease which involves several nerves. **erythredema p.** See *erythredema polyneuropathy.*

polyneuroradiculitis (pol″e-nu″ro-rah-dik″u-li′tis) [*poly-* + Gr. *neuron* nerve + L. *radix* root + *-itis*]. Inflammation of the spinal ganglia, the nerve roots, and the peripheral nerves.

polynuclear (pol″e-nu′kle-ar). 1. Pertaining to or having several nuclei. 2. Polymorphonuclear.

polynucleated (pol″e-nu′kle-āt″ed). Polynuclear.

polynucleolar (pol″e-nu-kle′o-lar). Having several nucleoli.

polynucleosis (pol″e-nu″kle-o′sis). The presence of a large number of polynuclear cells in the blood or in an exudate.

polynucleotidase (pol″e-nu″kle-o′ti-dās). An enzyme or a group of enzymes which catalyze the depolymerization of nucleic acids of high molecular weight to form mononucleotides.

polynucleotide (pol″e-nu′kle-o-tīd). A nucleotide made up of four mononucleotides. It is a nucleic acid.

polyodontia (pol″e-o-don′she-ah) [*poly-* + Gr. *odous* tooth]. The presence of supernumerary teeth.

polyonychia (pol″e-o-nik′e-ah) [*poly-* + Gr. *onyx* nail + *-ia*]. The occurrence of supernumerary nails.

polyopia, polyopsia (pol″e-o′pe-ah, pol″e-op′se-ah) [*poly-* + Gr. *opsis* vision + *-ia*]. The condition in which one object appears as two or more objects. **binocular p.,** diplopia. **p. monophthal′mica,** a condition in which an object looked at by one eye appears double.

polyopy (pol′e-o″pe). Polyopia.

polyorchidism (pol″e-or′kĭ-dizm). A developmental anomaly characterized by the presence of more than two testes.

polyorchis (pol″e-or′kis) [*poly-* + Gr. *orchis* testis]. A person with more than two testes.

polyorchism (pol″e-or′kizm). Polyorchidism.

polyorrhomeningitis (pol″e-or″o-men″in-ji′tis). Polyorrhymenitis.

polyorrhymenitis (pol″e-or″hi-mĕ-ni′tis) [*poly-* + Gr. *orrhos* serum + *hymēn* membrane + *-itis*]. Malignant inflammation of serous membranes; Concato's disease.

polyorrhymenosis (pol″e-or″hi-mĕ-no′sis). Polyorrhymenitis.

polyostotic (pol″e-os-tot′ik) [*poly-* + L. *os* bone]. Pertaining to or affecting many bones.

polyotia (pol″e-o′she-ah) [*poly-* + Gr. *ous* ear]. The condition of having more than two ears.

polyovulatory (pol″e-ov′u-lah-to″re). Ordinarily discharging several ova in one ovarian cycle.

polyp (pol′ip) [Gr. *polypous* a morbid excrescence]. A morbid excrescence, or protruding growth, from mucous membrane; classically applied to a growth on the mucous membrane of the nose, the term is now applied to such protrusions from any mucous membrane. **adenomatous p.,** one which has undergone malignant degeneration. **cardiac p.,** a ball thrombus attached by a pedicle to the inside of the heart. **fibrinous p.,** an intrauterine polyp made up of fibrin from retained blood. It may grow from portions of an ovum or from a thrombus at the placental site. **gelatinous p.,** myxoma. **gum p.,** a small pedunculated growth on the gingiva. **Hopmann's p.,** a mass produced by papillary hypertrophy of the nasal mucosa, having something of the appearance of a papilloma. **hydatid p.,** polypus cysticus.

polypapilloma (pol″e-pap″ĭ-lo′mah) [*poly-* + *papilloma*]. Yaws.

polyparasitism (pol″e-par′ah-si-tizm). Infestation by more than one variety of parasite.

polyparesis (pol″e-par′e-sis) [*poly-* + Gr. *paresis* slackening]. Dementia paralytica.

polypathia (pol″e-path′e-ah) [*poly-* + Gr. *pathos* disease + *-ia*]. The presence of several diseases at once.

polypectomy (pol″ĭ-pek′to-me) [*polyp* + Gr. *ektomē* excision]. Surgical removal of a polyp.

polypeptidase (pol″e-pep′tĭ-dās). An enzyme which catalyzes the hydrolysis of polypeptides.

polypeptide (pol″e-pep′tid) [*poly-* + *peptide*]. A peptide which on hydrolysis yields more than two amino acids; called tripeptides, tetrapeptides, etc., according to the number of amino acids contained.

polypeptidemia (pol″e-pep″tĭ-de′me-ah) [*polypeptide* + Gr. *haima* blood + *-ia*]. The presence of polypeptides in the blood.

polypeptidorrhachia (pol″e-pep″tĭ-do-ra′ke-ah) [*polypeptide* + Gr. *rhachis* spine + *-ia*]. The presence of polypeptides in the spinal fluid.

polyperiostitis (pol″e-per″e-os-ti′tis). Inflammation of the periosteum. **p. hyperesthet′ica,** a chronic disease of the periosteum attended by extreme hyperesthesia of the skin and soft parts.

polyphagia (pol″e-fa′je-ah) [*poly-* + Gr. *phagein* to eat]. 1. Excessive or voracious eating. Cf. *bulimia*. 2. Omnivorousness; craving for all kinds of food.

polyphalangia (pol″e-fah-lan′je-ah). Side-by-side duplication of one or more of the phalanges of a digit.

polyphalangism (pol″e-fah-lan′jizm). Polyphalangia.

polypharmaceutic (pol″e-fahr″mah-su′tik). Pertaining to several drugs, especially to the administration of several drugs together.

polypharmacy (pol″e-fahr′mah-se) [*poly-* + Gr. *pharmakon* drug]. 1. The administration of many drugs together. 2. The administration of excessive medication.

polyphase (pol′e-fāz) [*poly-* + *phase*]. Having several phases; containing colloids of several types.

polyphenoloxidase (pol″e-fe″nol-ok′sĭ-dās). An oxidizing enzyme which oxidizes phenols and their amino compounds, but not tyrosine.

polyphobia (pol″e-fo′be-ah) [*poly-* + Gr. *phobein* to be affrighted by]. Morbid dread or fear of many things.

polyphrasia (pol″e-fra′ze-ah) [*poly-* + Gr. *phrasis* speech]. Morbid or insane volubility or loquacity; verbigeration.

polyphyletic (pol″e-fi-let′ik) [*poly-* + Gr. *phylē* tribe]. Arising or descending from more than one cell type.

polyphyletism (pol″e-fi′lĕ-tizm). Polyphyletic theory.

polyphyletist (pol″e-fi′lĕ-tist). An adherent of the polyphyletic theory, as in blood origin.

polyphyodont (pol″e-fi′o-dont) [*poly-* + Gr. *phyein* to produce + *odous* tooth]. Developing several sets of teeth successively throughout life.

polypi (pol′ĭ-pi) [L.]. Plural of *polypus*.

polypiform (po-lip′ĭ-form). Resembling a polyp.

polypionia (pol″e-pi-o′ne-ah) [*poly-* + Gr. *piōn* fat + *-ia*]. Obesity.

polyplasmia (pol″e-plaz′me-ah) [*poly-* + *plasma* + *-ia*]. Excessive fluidity of, or excess of, plasma in the blood.

polyplastic (pol″e-plas′tik) [*poly-* + Gr. *plastos* molded]. 1. Containing many structural or constituent elements. 2. Undergoing many changes of form.

polyplastocytosis (pol″e-plas″to-si-to′sis). Abnormal increase in the number of blood platelets.

Polyplax (pol′e-plaks). A sucking louse of rats and mice. *P. miacan′thus*, a form found infrequently on rats; *P. serra′tus*, a louse of rabbits which transmits tularemia; and *P. spinulo′sa*, the common louse of rats.

polyplegia (pol″e-ple′je-ah) [*poly-* + Gr. *plēgē* stroke + *-ia*]. Simultaneous paralysis of several muscles.

polypleurodiaphragmotomy (pol″e-ploo″ro-di″ah-fram-ot′o-me) [*poly-* + Gr. *pleura* rib + *diaphragm* + *tomē* a cutting]. The operation of resecting several ribs and cutting through the diaphragm for access to the convex aspect of the liver.

polyploid (pol′e-ploid) [*poly-* + ha*ploid*]. 1. Having more than two full sets of homologous chromosomes. There may be three (triploid), four (tetraploid), five (pentaploid), six (hexaploid), seven (heptaploid), eight (octaploid), etc. 2. An individual or cell having more than two full sets of homologous chromosomes.

polyploidy (pol′e-ploi″de). The state of having more than two full sets of homologous chromosomes.

polypnea (pol″ip-ne′ah) [*poly-* + Gr. *pnoia* respiration]. A condition in which the rate of respiration is increased.

polypodia (pol″e-po′de-ah) [*poly-* + Gr. *pous* foot]. The presence of supernumerary feet.

polypoid (pol′e-poid) [*polyp* + Gr. *eidos* form]. Resembling a polyp.

polypoidosis (pol″e-poi-do′sis). A condition of multiple polypoid carcinomas; diffuse adenomatosis.

polyporin (pol-ip′o-rin). An antibiotic substance from species of Polyporus, which is active (lytic) for cultures of typhoid and staphylococci.

polyporous (pol-ip′o-rus). Having many pores.

Polyporus (pol-ip′o-rus) [*poly-* + Gr. *poros* pore]. A genus of mushrooms, containing many species. See *agaric*.

polyposia (pol″e-po′ze-ah) [*poly-* + Gr. *posis* + *-ia*]. Ingestion of abnormally increased amounts of fluids for long periods of time.

polyposis (pol″e-po′sis). The development of multiple polyps on a part. **p. gas′trica,** the presence of multiple polyps on the gastric mucosa. **p. intestina′lis,** a condition in which polyps occur in the intestine and rectum. **p. ventric′uli,** p. gastrica.

polypotome (po-lip′o-tōm). A cutting instrument for removing polyps.

polypotrite (po-lip′o-trīt) [*polyp* + L. *terere* to crush]. An instrument for crushing polyps.

polypous (pol′e-pus). Of the nature of a polyp; polyp-like.

polypragmasy (pol″e-prag′mah-se) [*poly-* + Gr. *pragma* a doing]. Polypharmacy.

polyptychial (pol″e-ti′ke-al) [*poly-* + Gr. *ptychē* fold]. Arranged in several layers: said of glands whose cells are arranged on the basement membrane in several layers.

polypus (pol′ĭ-pus), pl. *pol′ypi* [L.; Gr. *polypous*]. A polyp. **p. angiomato′des,** a polyp rich in blood vessels. **p. carno′sus,** a sarcoma. **p. cys′ticus,** a polyp in which the fibrous network is coarse, thus simulating or actually producing cysts. **p. hydatido′sus,** p. cysticus. **p. telangiecto′des,** a polyp which contains many dilated blood vessels.

polyradiculitis (pol″e-rah-dik″u-li′tis) [*poly-* + L. *radix* root + *-itis*]. Inflammation of the nerve roots.

polyradiculoneuritis (pol″e-rah-dik″u-lo-nu-ri′tis) [*poly-* + L. *radix* root + Gr. *neuron* nerve + *-itis*]. Acute infectious polyneuritis which involves the peripheral nerves, the spinal nerve roots and the spinal cord. See *Guillain-Barré syndrome*, under *syndrome*.

polyradiotherapy (pol″e-ra″de-o-ther′ah-pe). Treatment with several forms of radiant energy.

polyrrhea (pol″e-re′ah) [*poly-* + Gr. *rhoia* flow]. A copious fluid discharge.

polysaccharide (pol″e-sak′ah-rīd). A carbohydrate which on hydrolysis yields more than ten monosaccharides. **bacterial p's,** polysaccharides that are found in bacteria and especially in bacterial capsules. **gastric p.,** the mucopolysaccharide found in gastric mucus. **immune p's,** polysaccharides which can function as specific antigens, such as capsular substances. **pneumococcus p.,** a polysaccharide derived from the capsule of a pneumococcus: that of Type III pneumococcus consists of equimolecular amounts of glucose and glucuronic acid; that of Type VIII, the same components but in the ratio of 7:2; that of Type XIV, 1 part of N-acetylglucosamine to 3 parts of galactose. **specific p's,** soluble polysaccharides obtained from various microorganisms which in high dilution precipitate specifically the antisera to the corresponding organisms.

polysaccharose (pol″e-sak′ah-rōs). Polysaccharide.

polysarcia (pol″e-sar′se-ah) [*poly-* + Gr. *sarx* flesh]. Corpulence or obesity. **p. cor′dis,** cor adiposum.

polysarcous (pol″e-sar′kus). Corpulent; obese; affected with polysarcia.

polyscelia (pol″e-se′le-ah) [*poly-* + Gr. *skelos* leg + *-ia*]. A developmental anomaly characterized by the presence of more than two legs.

polyscelus (pŏ-lis′ĕ-lus) [*poly-* + Gr. *skelos* leg]. An individual exhibiting polyscelia.

polyscope (pol′e-skōp) [*poly-* + Gr. *skopein* to examine]. Diaphanoscope.

polyserositis (pol″e-se-ro-si′tis). General inflammation of serous membranes with serous effusion.

polysialia (pol″e-si-a′le-ah) [*poly-* + Gr. *sialon* saliva + *-ia*]. Ptyalism.

polysinuitis (pol″e-sin″u-i′tis). Polysinusitis.

polysinusectomy (pol″e-si″nus-ek′to-me). Excision of the diseased membrane of several of the paranasal sinuses.

polysinusitis (pol″e-si-nus-i′tis) [*poly-* + *sinusitis*]. Inflammation of several sinuses at once.

polysolve (pol′e-solv). Polysolveol.

polysomatic (pol″e-so-mat′ik). Characterized by or pertaining to polysomaty.

polysomaty (pol″e-so′mah-te) [*poly-* + chromo*some*]. The state of having reduplicated chromatin in the nucleus. The term is applied both to the condition of increase in chromosome number resulting from a previous endomitotic cycle (endopolyploidy, def. 3) and to increase in the amount of chromatin per chromosome (polyteny).

polysomia (pol″e-so′me-ah) [*poly-* + Gr. *sōma* body + *-ia*]. A doubling or tripling of the body of a fetus.

polysomus (pol″e-so′mus) [*poly-* + Gr. *sōma* body]. A fetal monster exhibiting polysomia.

polysomy (pol″e-so′me) [*poly-* + chromo*some*]. An excess of a particular chromosome.

polysorbate 80 (pol″e-sor′bāt). An oleate ester of sorbitol and its anhydride condensed with polymers of ethylene oxide, consisting of approximately 20 oxyethylene units: used as a surfactant agent.

polyspermia (pol″e-sper′me-ah) [*poly-* + Gr. *sperma* seed + *-ia*]. 1. Excessive secretion of semen. 2. Polyspermy.

polyspermism (pol″e-sper′mizm). Polyspermia.

polyspermy (pol″e-sper′me). Fertilization of an ovum by more than one spermatozoon. **pathological p.,** entrance of more than one spermatozoon in an ovum when entrance of only one is the rule; development is abnormal and the embryo is not viable. **physiological p.,** entrance of more than one spermatozoon in an ovum, occurring normally in certain species, but with only one spermatozoon participating fully in the development of the embryo.

polystat (pol′e-stat) [*poly-* + *stat*]. An instrument by which the ordinary street current can be transformed so as to furnish galvanic, faradic, and sinusoidal currents.

polystichia (pol″e-stik′e-ah) [*poly-* + Gr. *stichos* row + *-ia*]. The presence of two or more rows of eyelashes upon a lid.

polystyrene (pol″e-sti′rēn). The resin produced by polymerization of styrene, a clear resin of the thermoplastic type, used to a limited extent in the construction of denture bases.

polysuspensoid (pol″e-sus-pen′soid). A suspensoid in which the particles are of different degrees of dispersion.

polysynaptic (pol″e-sĭ-nap′tik). Pertaining to or relayed through two or more synapses.

polysynovitis (pol″e-si″no-vi′tis) [*poly-* + *synovitis*]. General inflammation of the synovial membranes.

polysyphilide (pol″e-sif′ĭ-lid). Characterized by many syphilitic lesions.

polytendinitis (pol″e-ten″dĭ-ni′tis). Inflammation affecting several tendons.

polytendinobursitis (pol″e-ten″dĭ-no-bur-si′tis). Associated bursitis and tendinitis in several parts of the body.

polytene (pol′e-tēn) [*poly-* + Gr. *tainia* (L. *taenia*) band]. Composed of or containing many strands of chromatin (chromonemata).

polyteny (pol″e-te′ne). Reduplication of chromonemata in the chromosome without separation into distinct daughter chromosomes.

polythelia (pol″e-the′le-ah) [*poly-* + Gr. *thēlē* nipple + *-ia*]. A developmental anomaly characterized by the presence of supernumerary nipples.

polythelism (pol″e-the′lizm). Polythelia.

polythene (pol′e-thēn). Generic term for polymers of ethylene used as plastics. Cf. *polyethylene.*

polytocous (po-lit′o-kus) [*poly-* + Gr. *tokos* birth]. Giving birth to several offspring at one time.

polytrichia (pol″e-trik′e-ah) [*poly-* + Gr. *thrix* hair]. Excessive growth or development of the hair; hypertrichosis.

polytrichosis (pol″e-tri-ko′sis). Polytrichia.

Polytrichum (po-lit′rĭ-kum) [*poly-* + Gr. *thrix* hair]. A genus of mosses. *P. juniperi′num,* haircap, or juniper moss, is diuretic.

polytrophia (pol″e-tro′fe-ah) [*poly-* + Gr. *trophē* nourishment]. Excessive nutrition.

polytrophic (pol″e-trof′ik). Pertaining to or characterized by polytrophia.

polytrophy (po-lit′ro-fe). Polytrophia.

polytropic (pol″e-trop′ik) [*poly-* + Gr. *tropē* a turning]. Affecting many kinds of bacteria or many varieties of tissue. Cf. *monotropic.*

polytropous (po-lit′ro-pus). Polytropic.

polyunguia (pol″e-ung′gwe-ah). Polyonychia.

polyuria (pol″e-u′re-ah) [*poly-* + Gr. *ouron* urine + *-ia*]. The passage of a large volume of urine in a given period.

polyvalent (po-liv′ah-lent). Having more than one valency.

polyvinyl (pol″e-vi′nil). A polymerization product containing the vinyl group.

polyvinylacetate (pol″e-vi″nil-as′e-tāt). A light- and heat-stable resin formed by the polymerization of vinyl acetate.

polyvinylbenzene (pol″e-vi″nil-ben′zēn). Polystyrene.

polyvinylchloride (pol″e-vi″nil-klōr′īd). A substance formed by the polymerization of vinyl chloride; a tasteless, odorless, clear hard resin, which changes color on exposure to ultraviolet light or heat.

polyvinylpyrrolidone (pol″e-vi″nil-pir-rol′ĭ-dōn). A polymerization product occurring as a faintly yellow solid resembling albumin, but not giving the same reactions as albumin. Sometimes used as a plasma volume expander.

pomade (po-mād′). Pomatum.

pomatum (po-ma′tum) [L., from *pomum* apple]. An ointment, especially one for the hair.

pomegranate (pum-gran′et) [L. *pomum granatum* grained apple]. The punicaceous tree, *Punica granatum,* and its fruit. The root bark and the bark of the tree contain pelletierine, isopelletierine, and punicotannic acid, and are useful teniacides, especially for tapeworm. The rind of the fruit is actively astringent.

pomphoid (pom′foid) [Gr. *pomphos* a wheal + *eidos* form]. Wheal-like.

pompholygometer (pom″fo-le-gom′e-ter) [*pompholyx* + Gr. *metron* measure]. An instrument for detecting or measuring bubbles.

pompholyhemia (pom″fo-le-he′me-ah) [*pompholyx* + Gr. *haima* blood + *-ia*]. The presence of bubbles of gas in the blood, as in decompression sickness.

pompholyx (pom′fo-liks) [Gr. "bubble"]. A dermatosis characterized by small, deep-seated (sagolike) vesicles on the palms and soles and between the digits.

pomphus (pom′fus) [L.; Gr. *pomphos*]. A wheal or blister.

pomum (po′mum) [L.]. Apple. **p. ada′mi** ["Adam's apple"], the prominence on the throat caused by the thyroid cartilage; prominentia laryngea.

ponceau B. Biebrich scarlet. **p. 3 B,** scarlet red.

Poncet's disease, operation (pahw-sāz′) [Antonin *Poncet,* French surgeon, 1849–1913]. See under *disease* and *operation.*

Pond. Abbreviation for L. *pon′dere,* by weight.

ponderable (pon′der-ah-b'l) [L. *ponderabilis; pondus* weight]. Having weight.

ponderal (pon′der-al) [L. *pondus,* weight]. Pertaining to weight.

pondostatural (pon″do-stat′u-ral). Pertaining to weight and stature.

Ponfick's shadows (pon′fiks) [Emil *Ponfick,* German pathologist, 1844–1913]. See *phantom corpuscles,* under *corpuscle.*

Pongamia (pon-ga′me-ah) [Malay *pongam*]. A genus of leguminous East Indian trees. *P. gla′bra* affords a fixed oil.

pono- (po′no) [Gr. *ponos* hard work, toil, bodily exertion; the consequences of toil, distress, suffering, pain]. Combining form denoting relationship to hard work or to pain.

ponograph (po′no-graf) [*pono-* + Gr. *graphein* to write]. An instrument for estimating and recording sensitiveness to pain.

ponopalmosis (po″no-pal-mo′sis) [*pono-* + Gr. *palmos* palpitation]. Palpitation on effort; Sir Clifford Albutt's term for soldier's heart or neurocirculatory asthenia.

ponophobia (po″no-fo′be-ah) [*pono-* + Gr. *phobein* to be affrighted by]. 1. Abnormal dread of pain. 2. Dread of work; morbid laziness.

ponos (po′nos). Infantile kala-azar.

pons (ponz), pl. *pon′tes,* gen. *pon′tis* [L. "*bridge*"]. 1. Any slip of tissue connecting two parts of an organ. 2. [N A, B N A] That part of the central nervous system lying between the medulla oblongata and the mesencephalon, ventral to the cerebellum, and consisting of a pars dorsalis and a pars basilaris. **p. cerebel′li,** pons [N A]. **p. hep′atis,** an occasional projection of fibers partially bridging the longitudinal fissure of the liver. **p. tari′ni,** substantia perforata posterior. **p. varo′lii,** pons [N A].

pons-oblongata (ponz″ob-lon-ga′tah). The pons and medulla oblongata considered together.

pontibrachium (pon″te-bra′ke-um). Pedunculus cerebellaris medius.

pontic (pon′tik) [L. *pons, pontis* bridge]. The portion of a bridge which substitutes for an absent tooth, both esthetically and functionally; it usually, but not necessarily, occupies the space formerly filled by a natural tooth.

ponticular (pon-tik′u-lar). Pertaining to the ponticulus or propons.

ponticulus (pon-tik′u-lus), pl. *pontic′uli* [L., dim. of *pons* bridge]. Propons. **p. auric′ulae,** a point on the eminentia cochleae where the retrahens aurem is attached. **p. hep′atis,** the isthmus which joins the spigelian lobe to the right lobe of the liver. **p. promonto′rii,** a ridge on the median wall of the tympanic cavity connecting the promontory with the pyramid.

pontile (pon′tēl). Pertaining to the pons.

pontimeter (pon-tim′e-ter) [L. *pons, pontis* bridge + Gr. *metron* measure]. An instrument for measuring the bony bridge in mastoid operations.

pontine (pon′tēn). Pertaining to the pons; pontile.

pontobulbia (pon″to-bul′be-ah). A condition in which cavities exist in the pons and medulla oblongata.

pontocaine (pon′to-kān). Trade mark for preparations of tetracaine.

pontocerebellar (pon″to-ser″e-bel′ar). Pertaining to the pons and the cerebellum.

pontoon (pon-to͞on′) [Fr. *ponton;* L. *ponto* boat]. A loop or knuckle of the small intestine.

pool (po͞ol). 1. A common reservoir on which to draw. 2. An accumulation, as of blood in any part of the body due to retardation of the venous circulation. **abdominal p.,** the blood within the abdomen, much increased in shock. **metabolic p.,** the entire mass of labile and reactive substances in the body, to which and from which innumerable substances continuously pass.

Pool's phenomenon (po͞olz) [Eugene Hillhouse *Pool,* New York surgeon, 1874–1949]. See under *phenomenon.*

popin (pop′in). A glycoside of unknown origin which is used in Barbados for amebic dysentery.

poples (pop′lez) [L. "ham"]. [N A, B N A] The posterior surface of the knee.

popliteal (pop-lit′e-al; pop″lĭ-te′al) [L. *poples* ham]. Pertaining to the posterior surface of the knee.

population (pop″u-la′shun) [L. *populatio*]. 1. The individuals collectively constituting a certain category or inhabiting a specified geographic area. 2. A contiguously distributed grouping of a single community that is characterized by both genetic and cultural continuity through several generations. **C3 p.,** a general category constituted by those individuals who are deficient mentally or physically.

populi (pop′u-li) [L.]. Genitive of *populus* poplar. **p. gem′ma,** poplar bud.

Populus (pop′u-lus) [L.]. A genus of salicaceous trees; the poplars, aspens, and cottonwoods. The bark is tonic, containing populin and salicin, and the leaf buds of some species, as *P. candicans* or *P. balsamifera,* called balm of Gilead, afford a variety of tacamahac. These buds are stimulant, tonic, and vulnerary.

poradenia (pōr″ah-de′ne-ah). Poradenitis.

poradenitis (pōr″ad-e-ni′tis) [Gr. *poros* pore + *adēn* gland + *-itis*]. A disease of the iliac glands characterized by the formation of small abscesses. **p. nos′tras, subacute inguinal p., p. vene′rea,** lymphogranuloma venereum.

poradenolymphitis (por-ad″e-no-lim-fi′tis). Lymphogranuloma venereum.

porcelain (por′sĕ-lan). A fused mixture of kaolin, felspar, quartz, and other substances, used in the making of artificial teeth, jacket crowns, facings, and veneers.

porcelaneous (por″sĕ-la′ne-us). Pertaining to or resembling porcelain.

porcine (por′sin) [L. *porcus* hog]. Pertaining to, characteristic of, or derived from swine.

pore (pōr) [L. *porus;* Gr. *poros*]. A small opening. Called also *porus* [N A]. **acoustic p., osseous,**

external, porus acusticus externus osseus. **acoustic p., osseous, internal,** porus acusticus internus osseus. **biliary p.,** ductus choledochus. **birth p.,** metraderm. **cranionasal p.,** foramen cecum ossis frontalis. **Galen's p.,** canalis inguinalis. **gustatory p.,** porus gustatorius. **interalveolar p's, p's of Kohn,** openings in the interalveolar septa of the lungs. **sweat p., p. of sweat duct,** porus sudoriferus. **taste p.,** porus gustatorius.

porencephalia (po″ren-se-fa′le-ah) [Gr. *poros* pore + *enkephalos* brain + *-ia*]. 1. The presence of cysts or cavities in the brain cortex communicating by a "pore" with the arachnoid space (Heschl, 1850). 2. The presence of cavities in the brain developed in fetal life or early infancy, whether or not they communicate with the arachnoid space. The cavities are usually the residues of destructive lesions (*encephaloclastic p.*), but sometimes are the result of maldevelopment (*schizencephalic p.*).

porencephalic (po″ren-se-fal′ik). Pertaining to or characterized by porencephalia.

porencephalitis (po″ren-sef″ah-li′tis). Porencephalia associated with an inflammatory process, such as polioencephalitis.

porencephalous (po″ren-sef′ah-lus). Porencephalic.

porencephaly (po″ren-sef′ah-le). Porencephalia.

Porges-Meier test [Otto *Porges*, Vienna physician, born 1879; Georg *Meier*, German serologist, born 1875]. See under *tests.*

Porges-Pollatschek test [Otto *Porges;* Otto *Pollatschek*, Vienna physicians]. See under *tests.*

Porges-Salomon test [Otto *Porges;* Hugo *Salomon*]. See under *tests.*

pori (po′ri) [L.]. Plural of *porus.*

poriomania (po″re-o-ma′ne-ah) [Gr. *poreia* walking + *mania* madness]. An impulsive tendency to wander away from home; ambulatory automatism.

porion (po′re-on) [Gr. *poros* pore + *-on* neuter ending]. A cephalometric landmark, being the midpoint on the upper edge of the porus acusticus externus, situated about 5 mm. above the superior margin of the cutaneous external auditory meatus.

pornographomania (por″no-graf″o-ma′ne-ah) [Gr. *pornographos* writing of harlots + *mania*]. Morbid impulse toward obscene writing.

pornolagnia (por″no-lag′ne-ah) [Gr. *pornē* prostitute + *lagneia* lust]. A perverted sexual interest in prostitutes.

porocele (po′ro-sēl) [Gr. *pōros* callus + *kēlē* hernia]. Scrotal hernia with thickening and hardening of the coverings of the testes.

porocephaliasis (po″ro-sef″ah-li′ah-sis). Infection with parasites of the genus Porocephalus.

porocephalosis (po″ro-sef″ah-lo′sis). Porocephaliasis.

Porocephalus (po″ro-sef′ah-lus) [Gr. *poros* pore + *kephalē* head]. A genus of wormlike arthropods of the order Linguatulida, which are parasitic in man and animals. **P. armilla′tus,** the adult is found in the lungs and trachea of the python (*P. sebae* and *P. regius*); the larval forms are found in the organs of monkeys, lions, and occasionally in man. Called also *Armillifer armillatus.* **P. clava′tus,** a species parasitic in man. **P. constric′tus,** a larval form infesting the mesentery. **P. denticula′tus,** the larva of *Linguatula rhinaria.*

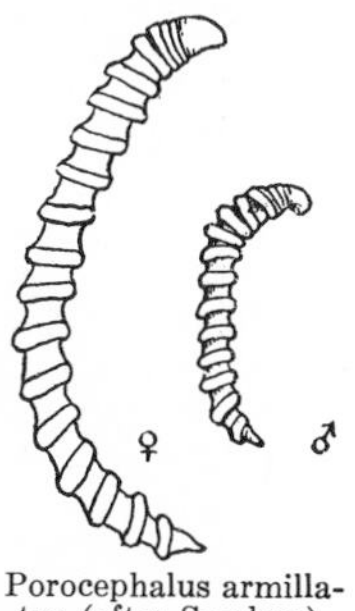

♀ ♂

Porocephalus armillatus (after Sambon).

porokeratosis (po″ro-ker″ah-to′sis) [Gr. *poros* pore + *keratosis*]. A skin disease characterized by hypertrophy of the stratum corneum about the ducts of the sweat glands, followed by its centrifugal and progressive atrophy. Called also *p. excen′trica.*

poroma (po-ro′mah) [Gr. *pōrōma* callus]. An inflammatory induration.

poropathy (po-rop′ah-the). An alleged system of healing in which medicines are supposed to reach the diseased organs through the pores of the skin.

poroplastic (po″ro-plas′tik). Both porous and plastic.

porosis (po-ro′sis). 1. [Gr. *pōrōsis* callosity]. Poroma. 2. The formation of the callus in the repair of a fractured bone. 3. [Gr. *pōros* pore]. Cavity formation. **cerebral p.,** a condition in which there are cavities in the brain substance; porencephaly.

porosity (po-ros′ĭ-te). 1. The condition of being porous. 2. A pore.

porotic (po-rot′ik). Pertaining to or characterized by porosis favoring the growth of connective tissue.

porotomy (po-rot′o-me) [Gr. *poros* pore + *tomē* a cutting]. Meatotomy.

porous (po′rus). Penetrated by pores and open spaces.

porphin (por′fin). The fundamental ring structure of four linked pyrrole nuclei around which porphyrins, hemin, and chlorophyll are built.

porphobilin (por″fo-bi′lin). A dark brown non-porphyrin pigment of unknown chemical structure.

porphobilinogen (por″fo-bi-lin′o-jen). The Ehrlich aldehyde–reacting chromogen which is an intermediary product in the biosynthesis of heme; not in evidence under normal circumstances, it characteristically appears in the urine in acute porphyria.

porphobilinogenuria (por″fo-bi-lin″o-jen-u′re-ah). The excretion of urine containing porphobilinogen.

porphyran (por′fĭ-ran). A combination of a porphyrin with a metal; a metalloporphyrin.

porphyria (por-fi′re-ah). A disturbance of porphyrin metabolism, characterized by marked increase in formation and excretion of porphyrins or their precursors. **p. cuta′nea tar′da heredita′ria,** a familial or genetic abnormality of porphyrin metabolism in which cutaneous manifestations are in the foreground of the clinical picture. **p. cuta′nea tar′da symptomat′ica,** a cutaneous form of porphyria which is not believed to be hereditary. **p. erythropoiet′ica,** a form of porphyria in which the excessive porphyrin formation takes place in certain of the bone marrow normoblasts. This disease is characterized by cutaneous photosensitivity and often by hemolytic anemia and splenomegaly; in contrast to the hepatic cutaneous porphyria group, the onset is usually at a very early age. **p. hepat′ica,** porphyria which represents a disturbance of hepatic function; one of the two major categories, which embraces all forms of porphyria except porphyria erythropoietica. **p. variega′ta, variegate p.,** a form of porphyria, common in South Africa, which may, in the same individual or in members of the same family, present either with acute abdominal or nervous manifestations or with photosensitivity of the skin and cutaneous lesions on the exposed surfaces.

porphyrin (por′fĭ-rin). Any one of a group of iron-free or magnesium-free pyrrole derivatives which occur universally in protoplasm. They form the basis of the respiratory pigments of animals and plants. The porphyrins are protoporphyrin, mesoporphyrin, hematoporphyrin, deuteroporphyrin, etioporphyrin, coproporphyrin, uroporphyrin, rhodoporphyrin, pyrroporphyrin, pyrroetioporphyrin, chlorophyllin and chlorophyll.

porphyrine (por′fĭ-rin). An alkaloid, $C_{21}H_{25}N_3O_2$, from the bark of *Alstonia constricta.*

porphyrinemia (por″fĭ-rin-e′me-ah). The presence of porphyrin in the blood.

porphyrinogen (por″fĭ-rin′o-jen). A reduced,

colorless non-fluorescing compound, fully hydrogenated and readily giving rise to the corresponding porphyrin by oxidation.

porphyrinuria (por″fĭ-rĭ-nu′re-ah) [*porphyrin* + Gr. *ouron* urine + *-ia*]. The presence in the urine of porphyrin (coproporphyrin or uroporphyrin) in excess of the normal amount.

porphyrism (por′fĭ-rizm). Porphyria.

porphyrization (por″fĭ-ri-za′shun). Pulverization; reduction to a powder: so called because sometimes performed on a porphyry tablet.

porphyropsin (por″fĭ-rop′sin). A purple pigment in the retinal rods of certain fresh-water fishes.

porphyrosine (por-fi′ro-sin). An alkaloid from *Alstonia constricta.*

porphyroxine (por″fĭ-rok′sin). An opium alkaloid, $C_{19}H_{23}O_4N$.

porphyruria (por″fir-u′re-ah). Porphyrinuria.

porphyryl (por′fĭ-ril). A name for hemin from which iron has been removed.

porrigo (por′rĭ-go) [L. "I stretch out, or extend"]. A term formerly applied to spreading lesions, such as tinea capitis, or other diseases of the scalp. **p. decal′vans,** alopecia areata. **p. favo′sa,** favus. **p. fur′furans,** tinea tonsurans. **p. larva′lis,** eczema with impetigo of the scalp. **p. lupino′sa, p. porrigoph′yta, p. scutula′ta,** favus.

Porro's operation (por′ōz) [Eduardo *Porro*, obstetrician in Milan, 1842–1902]. Cesarean hysterectomy.

porta (por′tah), pl. *por′tae* [L.]. An entrance or portal; used in anatomical nomenclature to designate an opening, especially the site of entrance to an organ of the blood vessels and other structures supplying or draining it. **p. hep′atis** [N A, B N A], the transverse fissure on the visceral surface of the liver where the portal vein and hepatic artery enter and the hepatic ducts leave. Called also *hepatic portal.* **p. labyrin′thi,** fenestra cochleae. **p. lie′nis,** hilus lienis. **p. of lung,** hilus pulmonis. **p. omen′ti, p. of omentum,** foramen epiploicum. **p. pulmo′nis,** hilus pulmonis. **p. re′nis,** hilus renalis. **p. of spleen,** hilus lienis.

portacaval (por″tah-ka′val). Pertaining to or connecting the portal vein and the vena cava.

portacid (port-as′id). A dropper for the local application of an acid.

portal (por′tal). 1. An entrance or gateway. 2. Pertaining to a porta, or entrance, especially to the porta hepatis. **p. of entry,** the pathway by which bacteria or other pathogenic agents gain entry to the body. **hepatic p.,** porta hepatis. **intestinal p., anterior,** the region of opening of the embryonic foregut into the yolk sac or unclosed midgut. **intestinal p., posterior,** the region of opening of the embryonic hindgut into the yolk sac or unclosed midgut.

portcaustic (port-kaws′tik) [Fr. *porte-caustique*]. A handle for holding a caustic substance.

porte-acid (port-as′id). Portacid.

porte-aiguille (port″a-gēl′) [Fr.]. A surgeon's needle holder.

porte-caustique (port″ko-stēk′). Portcaustic.

porte-ligature (port-lig′ah-tūr). Portligature.

porte-meche (port-mesh′) [Fr.]. A probe or director with a fork at one end for pushing a tent into a wound or fistula.

porte-noeud (port-ned′) [Fr. "knot-carrier"]. An instrument for applying a ligature to the pedicle of a tumor.

porte-polisher (pōrt-pol′ish-er). A hand instrument constructed to hold a wooden point, to be used in a dental engine for applying polishing paste to and burnishing teeth.

Porter's sign (por′terz) [William Henry *Porter*, Dublin physician, 1790–1861]. Tracheal tugging.

Porter's test (por′terz) [William Henry *Porter*, New York physician, 1853–1933]. See under *tests.*

portio (por′she-o), pl. *portio′nes* [L.]. A part, or division; used in anatomical nomenclature as a general term to designate a particular portion of another organ or structure. **p. du′ra pa′ris sep′timi,** nervus facialis (formerly considered as forming one nerve with the portio mollis paris septimi). **p. interme′dia ner′vi acus′tici,** nervus intermedius. **p. ma′jor ner′vi trigem′ini** [B N A], radix sensoria nervi trigemini. **p. mi′nor ner′vi trigem′ini** [B N A], radix motoria nervi trigemini. **p. mol′lis pa′ris sep′timi,** nervus vestibulocochlearis (formerly considered as forming one nerve with the portio dura paris septimi). **p. supravagina′lis cer′vicis** [N A, B N A], the part of the cervix uteri that does not protrude into the vagina. **p. vagina′lis cer′vicis** [N A, B N A], the part of the cervix uteri that protrudes into the vagina.

portiones (por″she-o′nēz) [L.]. Plural of *portio.*

portiplex, portiplexus (por′tĭ-pleks, por″tĭ-plek′sus). The plexus which joins the two lateral choroid plexuses, passing through the foramen of Monro.

portligature (port-lig′ah-tūr). An instrument for applying a ligature to a deeply situated part.

portogram (por′to-gram). A roentgenogram of the portal vein.

portography (por-tog′rah-fe). Roentgenography of the portal vein after injection of opaque material. **portal p.,** portography after injection of opaque material into the superior mesenteric vein or one of its branches after laparotomy has been performed. **splenic p.,** portography after percutaneous injection into the substance of the spleen, usually through the ninth intercostal space in the midaxillary line, of opaque material, which passes immediately into the splenic vein and then into the portal vein, permitting visualization of those two vessels.

portovenogram (por″to-ve′no-gram). Portogram.

portovenography (por″to-ve-nog′rah-fe). Portography.

porus (po′rus), pl. *po′ri* [L.; Gr. *poros* passage]. A small cavity, or opening; used in anatomical nomenclature as a general term to designate certain openings in the body. Called also *pore.* **p. acus′ticus exter′nus** [N A, B N A], the outer end of the external acoustic meatus. **p. acus′ticus exter′nus os′seus** [N A, B N A], the outer end of the bony external acoustic meatus in the tympanic portion of the temporal bone. **p. acus′ticus inter′nus** [N A, B N A], the opening of the internal acoustic meatus. **p. acus′ticus inter′nus os′seus** [N A, B N A], the opening into the internal acoustic meatus, found on the posteromedial portion of the internal surface of the petrous part of the temporal bone. **p. gale′ni,** canalis inguinalis. **p. gustato′rius** [N A], the small opening of a taste bud onto the surface of the tongue. Called also *gustatory pore.* **p. op′ticus,** the opening in the sclera for passage of the optic nerve. **p. sudorif′erus** [N A, B N A], the opening of the duct of the sweat gland on the surface of the skin. Called also *pore of sweat duct.*

Posadas-Wernicke disease [Alejandro *Posadas*, Argentine parasitologist, 1870–1902; Robert Wernicke, Argentine pathologist of 19th century]. Coccidioidomycosis.

posed (pōsd). Placed. In dentistry, a term applied to the position of a tooth. **normally p., regularly p.,** in normal position. Cf. *malposed.*

-posia (po′ze-ah) [Gr. *posis* drinking + *-ia*]. Word termination denoting relationship to drinking, or to intake of fluids.

posiomania (po″se-o-ma′ne-ah) [Gr. *posis* drinking + *mania* madness]. Dipsomania.

position (po-zish′un) [L. *positio*]. 1. The placement of body members, as a particular position assumed by the patient to achieve comfort in certain conditions, or the particular arrangement of body parts to facilitate the performance of certain diagnostic or therapeutic procedures. 2. In obstetrics, the situation of the child in the pelvis, determined and described by the relation of a given arbitrary point (point of direction) in the presenting part to the periphery of the pelvic planes. For the various possible positions see the table (from Greenhill-DeLee, Principles and Practice of Obstetrics). **Adams' p.,** patient stands with heels together, well stretched, bends body forward from hips; head and arms hanging forward. **Albert's p.,** a semirecumbent position of the patient for roentgenography as a means of determining the diameters of the superior strait of the pelvis. **anatomical p.,** the position of the human body, standing erect, with the palms of the hands turned forward; used as the position of reference in description of site or direction of various structures or parts as established in official anatomical nomenclature. **Bonner's p.,** flexion, abduction, and outward rotation of the thigh in coxitis. **Bozeman's p.,** the patient is strapped to supports in the knee-elbow position. **Brickner p.,** a position for treating shoulder disability, secured by tying the patient's wrist to the head of the bed with his arm supported on a pillow and raising the head of the bed. Thus traction with abduction and external rotation is obtained. **Casselberry's p.,** a prone position of the patient employed after intubation so that the patient may swallow without danger of fluid entering the tube. **coiled p.,** the attitude of a patient on his side with legs drawn up to the body. **decubitus p.,** the position of an individual lying on a horizontal surface, designated, according to the portion of the body resting on the surface, *dorsal decubitus* (lying on the back), *left lateral decubitus* (on the left side), *right lateral decubitus* (on the right side), or *ventral decubitus* (on the stomach). **Depage's p.,** a prone position with the pelvis elevated to form the apex of an inverted V, while the trunk and lower limbs form the branches of the V. **dorsal p.,** the posture of a person lying on his back. Called also *supine p.* **dorsal elevated p.,** position of patient lying on the back, with shoulders and head elevated: employed in digital examination of genitals. **dorsal inertia p.,** the position of a patient on his back and tending to slide down in bed: observed in conditions of great inertia. **dorsal recumbent p.,** position of patient on back, with lower limbs flexed and rotated outward: used in vaginal examination, application of obstetrical forceps, etc. **dorsal rigid p.,** position on the back with the legs drawn up to the body. **dorsosacral p.,** lithotomy p. **Duncan's p.,** the position of the placenta, with its margin presenting at the os for delivery. **Edebohls' p.,** a dorsal position, the knees and thighs drawn up, legs flexed on the thighs, and thighs flexed on the belly, the hips raised, and the thighs adducted. Called also *Simon's p.* **Elliot's p.,** position of a patient on the operating table with lower chest elevated by placing a support under the small of the back: used in operations on the gallbladder. **emprosthotonos p.,** emprosthotonos. **English p.,** the patient on the left side, the right thigh and knee drawn up. Called also *left lateral recumbent p.* and *obstetrical p.* **Fowler's p.,** the position in which the head of the patient's bed is raised 18 or 20 inches above the level. **fronto-anterior p.,** a position of the fetus in cephalic presentation in labor, with its brow directed toward the right (R.F.A.) or left (L.F.A.) anterior quadrant of the maternal pelvis. **frontoposterior p.,** a position of the fetus in cephalic presentation in labor, with its brow directed toward the right (R.F.P.) or left (L.F.P.) posterior quadrant of the maternal pelvis. **frontotransverse p.,** a position of the fetus in cephalic presentation in labor, with its brow directed toward the right (R.F.T.) or left (L.F.T.) iliac fossa of the maternal pelvis. **genucubital p.,** knee-chest p. **genupectoral p.,** the position of the patient resting on his knees and chest, the arms crossed above the head. **hinge p.,** the position of the condyle in the temporomandibular joint from which an opening by hinge movement is possible beyond the amplitude of rest position. **horizontal p.,** the position of a person lying on his back with limbs and feet extended. **hornpipe p.,** a position of the patient with the arms flexed and elevated, so they cross the face as in the start of the hornpipe dance: a position advocated for use in operations for portal hypertension, or procedures on other organs in the upper abdomen. **jackknife p.,** position of patient on back, with the shoulders elevated, legs flexed on thighs, and thighs at right angles to the abdomen: used in passing the urethral sound. **Jones' p.,** acute flexion of the forearm for the treatment of fracture of the internal condyle of the humerus. **Jonge's p.,** a position for labor in slightly contracted pelvis: it is an exaggerated lithotomy position with legs extended. **knee-chest p.,** the position of the patient on his knees and elbows, the head on his hands. **knee-elbow p.,** knee-chest p. **kneeling-squatting p.,** squatting position with the knees bent and pressed against the abdomen while the body is held erect. **Kraske's p.,** the patient lies prone on the table with buttocks raised on a kidney elevator. **lateral recumbent p.,** English p. **lithotomy p.,** the patient on the back, legs flexed on the thighs, thighs flexed on the belly, and abducted. Called also *dorsosacral p.* **mento-anterior p.,** a position of the fetus in cephalic presentation in labor, with its chin directed toward the right (R.M.A.) or left (L.M.A.) anterior quadrant of the maternal pelvis. **mentoposterior p.,** a position of the fetus in cephalic presentation in labor, with its chin directed toward the right (R.M.P.) or left (L.M.P.) posterior quadrant of the maternal pelvis. **mentotransverse p.,** a position of the fetus in cephalic presentation in labor, with its chin directed toward the right (R.M.T.) or left (L.M.T.) iliac fossa of the maternal pelvis. **Mercurio's p.,** a position

POSITIONS OF THE CHILD IN UTERO IN VARIOUS PRESENTATIONS

CEPHALIC PRESENTATIONS

1. Vertex—occiput, the point of direction

Left occipito-anterior	L.O.A.
Left occipitotransverse	L.O.T.
Right occipitoposterior	R.O.P.
Right occipitotransverse	R.O.T.
Right occipito-anterior	R.O.A.
Left occipitoposterior	L.O.P.

2. Face—chin, the point of direction

Right mentoposterior	R.M.P.
Left mento-anterior	L.M.A.
Right mentotransverse	R.M.T.
Right mento-anterior	R.M.A.
Left mentotransverse	L.M.T.
Left mentoposterior	L.M.P.

3. Brow—the point of direction

Right frontoposterior	R.F.P.
Left fronto-anterior	L.F.A.
Right frontotransverse	R.F.T.
Right fronto-anterior	R.F.A.
Left frontotransverse	L.F.T.
Left frontoposterior	L.F.P.

BREECH OR PELVIC PRESENTATIONS

1. Complete Breech—sacrum, the point of direction (feet crossed and thighs flexed on abdomen)

Left sacro-anterior	L.S.A.
Left sacrotransverse	L.S.T.
Right sacroposterior	R.S.P.
Right sacro-anterior	R.S.A.
Right sacrotransverse	R.S.T.
Left sacroposterior	L.S.P.

2. Incomplete breech—sacrum, the point of direction. Same designations as above, adding the qualifications footling, knee, etc.

TRANSVERSE OR TORSO PRESENTATIONS

Shoulder—scapula, the point of direction

Left scapulo-anterior	L.Sc.A.	Back anterior positions
Right scapulo-anterior	R.Sc.A.	
Right scapuloposterior	R.Sc.P.	Back posterior positions
Left scapuloposterior	L.Sc.P.	

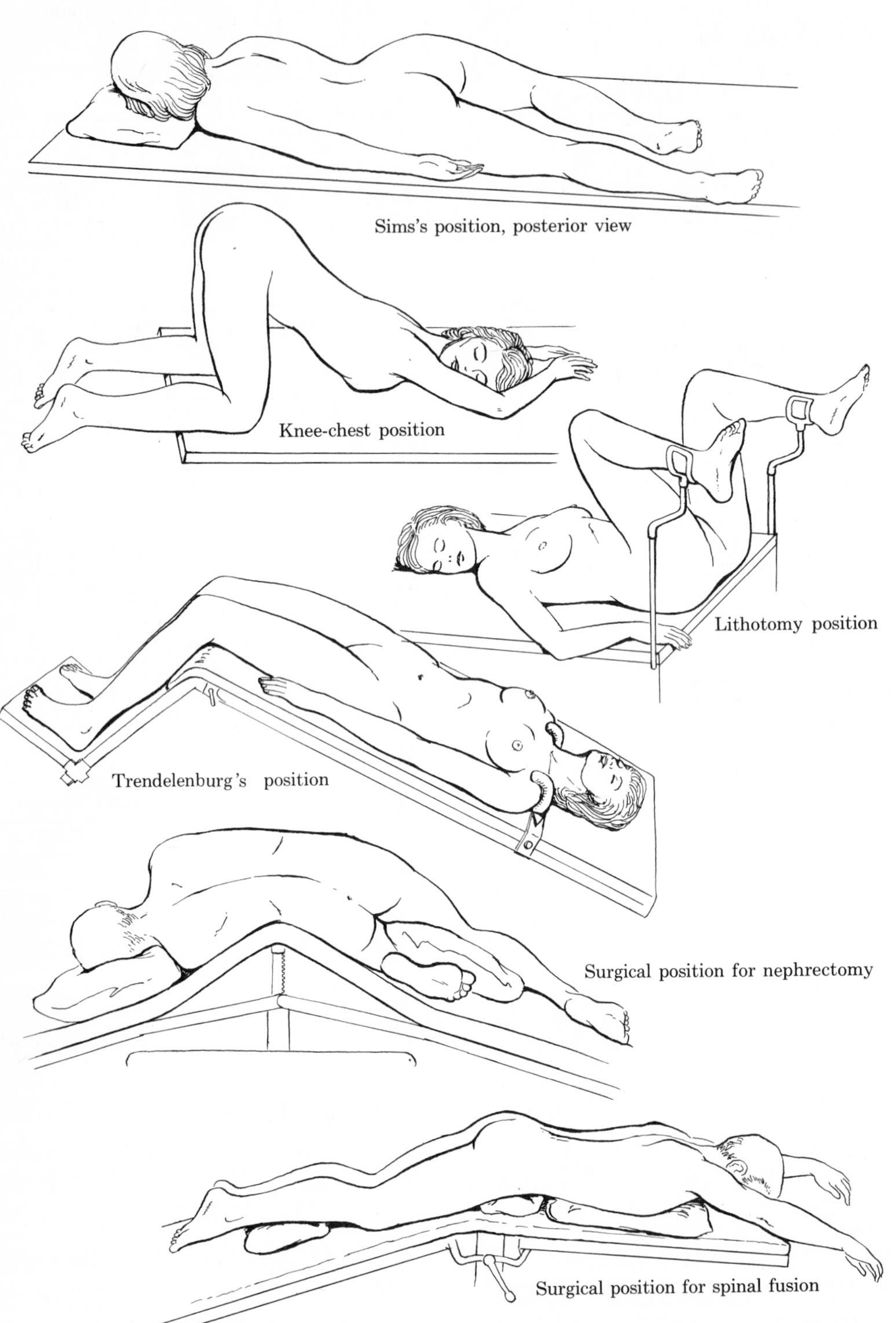

VARIOUS POSITIONS USED IN EXAMINATION OR TREATMENT

similar to Walcher's position. **Noble's p.,** position of the patient standing up, leaning forward and supporting the upper body on the arms: used in examining the kidney. **obstetrical p.,** English p. **occipito-anterior p.,** a position of the fetus in cephalic presentation in labor, with its occiput directed toward the right (R.O.A.) or left (L.O.A.) anterior quadrant of the maternal pelvis. **occipitoposterior p.,** a position of the fetus in cephalic presentation in labor, with its occiput directed toward the right (R.O.P.) or left (L.O.P.) posterior quadrant of the maternal pelvis. **occipitosacral p.,** a position of the fetus in cephalic presentation in labor, with the occiput presenting directly behind, or rotated squarely into the hollow of the sacrum. **occipitotransverse p.,** a position of the fetus in cephalic presentation in labor, with its occiput directed toward the right (R.O.T.) or left (L.O.T.) iliac fossa of the maternal pelvis. **opisthotonos p.,** opisthotonos. **orthopnea p.,** the patient sitting up straight with hands or elbows on the arm of the chair. See *orthopnea*. **orthotonos p.,** orthotonos. **Péan's p.,** a position for operating in which the operator sits between the patient's legs, which rest in hollow supports or hang down over the operator's thighs. The operator sits in a high chair with the patient lying on a low table, so that he can bend over the abdomen and look into the peritoneal cavity. **Proetz p.,** the patient lying on his back on a table with his head hanging over the end and hyperextended so that a line from the chin to the external auditory meatus is vertical. **prone p.,** patient lying face down. **rest p.,** the position passively assumed by the mandible when its musculature is relaxed, in the upright standing or sitting position, with eyes focused to distance. **Robson's p.,** the patient lying on the back with a sand-bag under the hollow of the back: used in surgery on the biliary tract. **Rose's p.,** the patient on his back with head hanging over the end of the table in full extension so as to enable the patient to "bleed" over the margins of the inverted upper incisors. **sacro-anterior p.,** a position of the fetus in breech presentation in labor, with its sacrum directed toward the right (R.S.A.) or left (L.S.A.) anterior quadrant of the maternal pelvis. **sacroposterior p.,** a position of the fetus in breech presentation in labor, with its sacrum directed toward the right (R.S.P.) or left (L.S.P.) posterior quadrant of the maternal pelvis. **sacrotransverse p.,** a position of the fetus in breech presentation in labor, with its sacrum directed toward the right (R.S.T.) or left (L.S.T.) iliac fossa of the maternal pelvis. **Samuel's p.,** the patient lying on her back with thighs flexed and knees flexed, the legs being grasped by the patient's hands. This position is said to widen the pelvic outlet and to render labor pains less intense: it is recommended for difficult labor after the head has reached the floor of the pelvis. **scapulo-anterior p.,** a position of the fetus in transverse presentation in labor, with its head to the right (R.Sc.A.) or left (L.Sc.A.) of the maternal pelvis, and its back anterior. **scapuloposterior p.,** a position of the fetus in transverse presentation in labor, with its head to the right (R.Sc.P.) or left (L.Sc.P.) of the maternal pelvis, and its back posterior. **Scultetus' p.,** patient lying on an inclined plane with head downward. **semiprone p.,** Sims' p. **semireclining p.,** a partly reclining position seen in heart disease, asthma, and pleural effusion. **shoe-and-stocking p.,** a position in which the limb of one side is crossed upon the other. **Simon's p.,** Edebohls' p. **Sims's p.,** patient on the left side and the chest, the right knee and thigh drawn up, the left arm along the back. Called also *semiprone p.* **Stern's p.,** the patient supine with the head lowered over the end of the table, the murmur of tricuspid insufficiency being heard more distinctly. **supine p.,** dorsal p. **Trendelenburg's p.,** the patient on the back on a plane inclined 30 to 40 degrees, the legs and feet hanging over the end of the table. **Valentine's p.,** the patient supine and the hips flexed by means of a double inclined plane: used in irrigating the urethra. **Walcher's p.,** the patient on the back, with the hips at the edge of the table and the legs hanging down. **Wolfenden's p.,** a position of the patient with the head hanging over the side of the bed.

positive (poz′ĭ-tiv) [L. *positivus*]. Having a value greater than zero; indicating existence or presence, as chromatin positive or Wassermann positive; characterized by affirmation or cooperation.

positrocephalogram (pos″ĭ-tro-sef′ah-lo-gram″) [*positron* + Gr. *kephalos* head + *gramma* a mark]. A record produced by the emission of positrons by isotopes of arsenic administered to facilitate localization of brain tumors.

positron (pos′ĭ-tron). The positive electron, a particle having the mass of the electron but with a positive electric charge; a free positive electron.

Posner's reaction, test (pōs′nerz) [Carl *Posner*, Berlin urologist, 1854–1929]. See under *tests*.

posologic (po″so-loj′ik). Pertaining to doses.

posology (po-sol′o-je) [Gr. *posos* how much + *-logy*]. The science of dosage, or a system of dosage.

Possum (pos′um) [*P*atient-*O*perated *S*elector *M*echanism]. A machine designed for the disabled by which, when breathed into in the correct manner, the individual can operate the telephone, ring bells, turn on the television, switch off a light, type a letter, or perform any of a number of other functions by no movement other than that involved in respiration.

post- (pōst) [L. *post* after]. A prefix signifying after or behind.

postabortal (pōst-ah-bor′tal). Occurring after abortion.

postaccessual (pōst-ak-sesh′u-al). Occurring after a paroxysm.

postacetabular (pōst″as-e-tab′u-lar). Behind the acetabulum.

postacidotic (pōst″as-ĭ-dot′ik). Occurring after the cessation of acidosis.

postadolescence (pōst″ad-o-les′ens). The period following adolescence.

postadolescent (pōst″ad-o-les′ent). 1. Pertaining to or occurring in the period following adolescence. 2. A young adult.

postalbumin (pōst″al-bu′min). A serum protein which has an electrophoretic mobility between albumin and alpha-globulin at pH 8.6.

postanal (pōst-a′nal). Situated behind the anus.

postanesthetic (pōst″an-es-thet′ik). After anesthesia.

postapoplectic (pōst″ap-o-plek′tik). Occurring after an attack of apoplexy.

postaurale (pōst″aw-ra′le). An anthropometric landmark, the most posterior point on the helix of the ear.

postaxial (pōst-ak′se-al). Situated behind an axis. In anatomical usage, postaxial refers to the medial (ulnar) aspect of the upper limb, and the lateral (fibular) aspect of the lower limb.

postbrachial (pōst-bra′ke-al). On the posterior part of the upper arm.

postbrachium (pōst-bra′ke-um). Brachium colliculi inferioris.

postbuccal (pōst-buk′al). Behind the buccal region.

postbulbar (pōst-bul′bar). Situated behind or distal to a bulb as behind the medulla oblongata, or distal to the pileus ventriculi (duodenal bulb).

postcardiotomy (pōst-kar″de-ot′o-me). Occurring after or as a consequence of incision (open surgery) of the heart.

postcava (pōst-ka′vah). The vena cava inferior.

postcaval (pōst-ka′val). Pertaining to the postcava.

postcecal (pōst-se′kal). Situated behind the cecum.

postcentral (pōst-sen′tral). Situated or occurring behind a center.

postcentralis (pōst″sen-tra′lis). The postcentral fissure.

postcerebellar (pōst″ser-e-bel′ar). In the posterior part of the cerebellum.

postcerebral (pōst-ser′e-bral). Behind the cerebrum.

postcesarean (pōst″se-za′re-an). Following cesarean operation.

postcibal (pōst-si′bal) [*post-* + L. *cibum* food]. Occurring after ingestion of food.

post cibum (pōst si′bum) [L.]. After meals (after food).

postcisterna (pōst″sis-ter′nah). The cisterna magna.

postclavicular (pōst″klah-vik′u-lar) [*post-* + *clavicle*]. Situated or occurring behind the clavicle.

postclimacteric (pōst″kli-mak-ter′ik). 1. Occurring after the climacteric. 2. Postmenopausal.

post coitum (pōst ko-i′tum). After coitus.

postcommissure (pōst″kom′ĭ-sūr). The posterior commissure of the brain.

postcondylar (pōst-kon′dĭ-lar). Behind a condyle.

postcondylare (pōst″kon-dĭ-lah′re). The highest point of the curvature behind the occipital condyle.

postconnubial (pōst″kŏ-nu′be-al) [*post-* + L. *connubium* marriage]. Occurring after marriage.

postconvulsive (pōst″kon-vul′siv). Occurring after a convulsion.

postcordial (pōst-kor′de-al). Back of the heart.

postcornu (pōst-kor′nu). Cornu posterius ventriculi lateralis.

postcranial (pōst-kra′ne-al). Situated posterior or inferior to the cranium, or head.

postcribrum (pōst-kri′brum). Substantia perforata posterior.

postcubital (pōst-ku′bĭ-tal). On the dorsal side of the forearm.

postcyclodialysis (pōst-si″klo-di-al′ĭ-sis). Occurring after or as a consequence of cyclodialysis.

postdevelopmental (pōst″de-vel″op-men′tal). Occurring after the period of development.

postdiastolic (pōst″di-as-tol′ik). Occurring after or following the diastole.

postdicrotic (pōst″di-krot′ik). Occurring after the dicrotic elevation of the sphygmogram.

postdigestive (pōst″di-jes′tiv). After digestion.

postdiphtheric (pōst″dif-ther′ik). Occurring after or as a consequence of diphtheria.

postdiphtheritic (pōst″dif-ther-it′ik). Postdiphtheric.

postdormital (pōst-dor′mĭ-tal). Pertaining to or occurring during the postdormitum.

postdormitum (pōst-dor′mĭ-tum). The period of increasing consciousness interposed between sound sleep and wakening.

postdural (pōst-du′ral). Behind the dura mater.

postembryonic (pōst″em-bre-on′ik) [*post-* + Gr. *embryon* embryo]. Occurring after the embryonic stage.

postencephalitic (pōst″en-sef″ah-lit′ik). Occurring after or as a consequence of encephalitis.

postencephalitis (pōst″en-sef″ah-li′tis). The condition which sometimes remains after recovery from epidemic encephalitis, marked by abnormal behavior.

postepileptic (pōst″ep-ĭ-lep′tik). Occurring after or as a consequence of an epileptic attack.

posteriad (pos-te′re-ad). Toward the posterior surface of the body.

posterior (pos-te′re-or). Situated in back of, or in the back part of, or affecting the back part of an organ; in official anatomical nomenclature, used in reference to the back or dorsal surface of the body.

postero- (pos′ter-o) [L. *posterus* behind] Combining form denoting relationship to the posterior part.

posteroanterior (pos″ter-o-an-te′re-or). From back to front, or from the posterior (dorsal) to the anterior (ventral) surface. In roentgenology, denoting direction of the beam from the x-ray source to the beam exit surface.

posteroclusion (pos″ter-o-kloo′zhun). A malrelation of the dental arches in which the mandibular arch is in a posterior position in relation to the maxillary arch.

postero-external (pos″ter-o-eks-ter′nal). Situated on the outer side of a posterior aspect.

postero-inferior (pos″ter-o-in-fe′re-or). Posterior and inferior.

postero-internal (pos″ter-o-in-ter′nal). Situated within and toward the back.

posterolateral (pos″ter-o-lat′er-al). Situated behind and to one side.

posteromedial (pos″ter-o-me′de-al). Situated toward the middle of the back.

posteromedian (pos″ter-o-me′de-an). Situated on the midline of the back.

posteroparietal (pos″ter-o-pah-ri′ĕ-tal). Situated at the back part of the parietal bone.

posterosuperior (pos″ter-o-su-pe′re-or). Situated behind and above.

posterotemporal (pos″ter-o-tem′po-ral). Situated at the back part of the temporal bone.

posterula (pos-ter′u-lah) [L.]. The space between the nasal conchae and the posterior nares.

postesophageal (pōst″e-sof″ah-je′al). Situated behind the esophagus.

postethmoid (pōst-eth′moid). Behind the ethmoid bone.

postexed (pōs-tekst′). Bent backward.

postexion (pōs-teks′yun). Posterior flexion.

postfebrile (pōst-feb′ril). Occurring after or as the result of a fever.

postganglionic (pōst″gang-gle-on′ik). Situated posterior or distal to a ganglion.

postgeminum (pōst-jem′ĭ-num). Colliculus inferior lamina tecti.

postgeniculatum (pōst″je-nik″u-la′tum). Corpus geniculatum mediale.

postgeniculum (pōst″je-nik′u-lum). Corpus geniculatum mediale.

postglenoid (pōst-gle′noid). Situated behind the glenoid fossa.

postglomerular (pōst″glo-mer′u-lar). Located or occurring distal to a glomerulus of the kidney.

postgrippal (pōst-grip′al). Occurring after grippe or influenza.

posthemiplegic (pōst″hem-ĭ-ple′jik). Occurring after or as a consequence of hemiplegia.

posthemorrhage (pōst-hem′o-rāj). Secondary hemorrhage.

posthemorrhagic (pōst-hem″o-raj′ik). Occurring after hemorrhage.

posthepatic (pōst″he-pat′ik). Situated behind the liver.

posthepatitic (pōst″hep-ah-tit′ik). Occurring after or as a consequence of hepatitis.

postherpetic (pōst″her-pet′ik). Occurring after or as a consequence of herpes.

posthetomy (pos-thet′o-me) [Gr. *posthē* foreskin + *tomē* a cutting]. Circumcision.

posthioplasty (pos′the-o-plas″te) [Gr. *posthē* foreskin + *plastos* formed]. Plastic surgery of the prepuce.

posthippocampal (pōst″hip-o-kam′pal). Behind the hippocampus.

posthitis (pos-thi′tis) [Gr. *posthē* foreskin + *-itis*]. Inflammation of the prepuce.

postholith (pos′tho-lith) [Gr. *posthē* foreskin + *lithos* stone]. A preputial concretion or calculus.

posthumous (pos′tu-mus) [L. *postumus* coming

after]. Occurring after death; born after the father's death.

posthyoid (pōst-hi'oid). Situated or occurring behind the hyoid bone.

posthypnotic (pōst″hip-not'ik). Succeeding the hypnotic state.

posthypoglycemic (pōst-hi″po-gli-se'mik). Occurring after or as a consequence of hypoglycemia.

posthypophysis (pōst″hi-pof'ĭ-sis). The posterior part of the hypophysis or pituitary body.

posthypoxic (pōst″hĭ-pok'sik). Occurring after or as a consequence of hypoxia.

postictal (pōst-ik'tal). Following a stroke or seizure, such as an acute epileptic attack.

posticus (pos-ti'kus) [L.]. Posterior.

postinfluenzal (pōst″in-flu-en'zal). Occurring after influenza.

postinsula (pōst-in'su-lah). The posterior part of the insula.

postischial (pōst-is'ke-al). Situated behind the ischium.

postligation (pōst″li-ga'shun). Occurring after or as a consequence of ligation of a blood vessel.

postmalarial (pōst″mah-la're-al). Occurring after malaria.

postmastectomy (pōst″mas-tek'to-me). Occurring after or as a consequence of mastectomy.

postmastoid (pōst-mas'toid). Situated behind the mastoid process of the temporal bone.

postmature (pōst″ma-tūr). Overly developed.

postmaturity (pōst″mah-tu'rĭ-te). Overdevelopment; the condition of a postmature infant.

postmaximal (pōst-mak'sĭ-mal). After a maximum.

postmeatal (pōst″me-a'tal). Behind a meatus.

postmedian (pōst-me'de-an) [*post-* + L. *medius* middle]. Situated or occurring behind a median line or plane.

postmediastinal (pōst″me-de-as'tĭ-nal). Behind the mediastinum: pertaining to the posterior mediastinum.

postmediastinum (pōst″me-de-as-ti'num). Cavum mediastinale posterius.

postmeiotic (pōst″mi-ot'ik) [*post-* + Gr. *meioun* to decrease]. Occurring after or pertaining to the time following meiosis.

postmenopausal (pōst″men-o-paw'zal). Occurring after the menopause.

postmenstrua (pōst-men'stroo-ah). The period immediately following cessation of menstrual flow.

postmesenteric (pōst″mes-en-ter'ik). Behind or in the posterior part of the mesentery.

postminimus (pōst-min'ĭ-mus), pl. *postmin'imi* [*post-* + L. *minimus* small]. Digitus postminimus.

postmiotic (pōst″mi-ot'ik). Postmeiotic.

postmitotic (pōst″mi-tot'ik). Pertaining to the time following or occurring after mitosis.

postmortal (pōst-mor'tal). Occurring after death.

post mortem (pōst mor'tem) [L.]. After death.

postmortem (pōst-mor'tem). Occurring or performed after death; pertaining to the period after death.

postnarial (pōst-na're-al). Pertaining to the posterior nares.

postnaris (pōst-na'ris). The posterior naris.

postnasal (pōst-na'zal) [*post-* + L. *nasus* nose]. Situated or occurring behind the nose.

postnatal (pōst-na'tal). Occurring after birth.

postnecrotic (pōst″ne-krot'ik). After death of a part.

postneuritic (pōst″nu-rit'ik). Occurring after neuritis.

postnodular (pōst-nod'u-lar). Behind the nodulus.

postoblongata (pōst″ob-long-ga'tah). The part of the medulla oblongata below the pons.

postocular (pōst-ok'u-lar) [*post-* + L. *oculus* eye]. Situated or occurring behind the eye.

postolivary (pōst-ol'ĭ-va″re). Behind the olivary body.

postoperative (pōst-op'er-a″tiv). Occurring after a surgical operation.

postoral (pōst-o'ral) [*post-* + L. *os* mouth]. Behind the mouth.

postorbital (pōst-or'bĭ-tal). Behind the orbit.

postpalatine (pōst-pal'ah-tin). Behind the palate, or behind the palatine bone.

postpallium (pōst-pal'e-um). The portion of the cortex of the cerebrum posterior to the sulcus centralis.

postpaludal (pōst-pal'u-dal). Postmalarial.

postparalytic (pōst″par-ah-lit'ik). Following an attack of paralysis.

post partum (pōst par'tum) [L.]. After childbirth, or after delivery.

postpartum (pōst-par'tum). Occurring after childbirth, or after delivery.

postpeduncle (pōst-pe'dung-k'l). The posterior peduncle of the cerebellum.

postperforatum (pōst″per-fo-ra'tum). Substantia perforata posterior.

postpharyngeal (pōst-fah-rin'je-al). Situated or occurring behind the pharynx.

postpituitary (pōst-pĭ-tu'ĭ-ta-re). Pertaining to the posterior lobe of the pituitary body.

postpneumonic (pōst″nu-mon'ik). Following pneumonia.

postponent (pōst-po'nent) [*post-* + L. *ponere* to place]. Having a more or less delayed recurrence.

postpontile (pōst-pon'til) [*post-* + L. *pons* bridge]. Situated or occurring behind the pons.

postprandial (pōst-pran'de-al). Occurring after dinner, or after a meal.

postpuberal (pōst-pu'ber-al). Occurring in or pertaining to the period following puberty.

postpubertal (pōst-pu'ber-tal). Postpuberal.

postpuberty (pōst-pu'ber-te). The period following puberty.

postpubescence (pōst″pu-bes'ens). Postpuberty.

postpubescent (pōst″pu-bes'ent). Postpuberal.

postpycnotic (pōst″pik-not'ik). Occurring after the stage of pyknosis.

postpyramid (pōst-pir'ah-mid). 1. One of the posterior pyramids of the cerebellum. 2. The funiculus gracilis of the oblongata.

postpyramidal (pōst″pi-ram'ĭ-dal). Situated or occurring behind the pyramidal tract.

postradiation (pōst″ra-de-a'shun). Following and caused by excessive exposure to roentgen rays or radium.

postramus (pōst-ra'mus) [*post-* + L. *ramus* branch]. The horizontal branch of the stem of the arbor vitae of the cerebellum.

postrolandic (pōst″ro-lan'dik). Situated behind the fissure of Rolando (sulcus centralis).

postsacral (pōst-sa'kral). Behind or below the sacrum.

postscapular (pōst-skap'u-lar). Behind the scapula.

postscarlatinal (pōst″skar-lah-ti'nal). Occurring after or as a consequence of scarlatina.

Post sing. sed. liq. Abbreviation for L. *post sin'gulas se'des liq'uidas*, after every loose stool.

postsphenoid (pōst-sfe'noid). The basisphenoid, pterygoid, and alisphenoid bones together; separate bones in infancy they usually become united with the sphenoid.

postsphygmic (pōst-sfig'mik). Occurring after the pulse wave. See under *period.*

postsplenectomy (pōst″sple-nek'to-me). Occurring after or as a consequence of splenectomy.

postsplenic (pōst-splen'ik). Behind the spleen.

poststertorous (pōst-ster'tor-us). Occurring after stertor has begun in anesthesia.

postsylvian (pōst-sil've-an). Behind the sylvian fissure (sulcus lateralis).

postsynaptic (pōst″sĭ-nap′tik). Situated distal to a synapse, or occurring after the synapse is crossed.

postsyphilitic (pōst″sif-ĭ-lit′ik). Occurring after or as a consequence of syphilis.

post-tarsal (pōst-tar′sal). Behind the tarsus.

post-tibial (pōst-tib′e-al). Behind the tibia.

post-traumatic (pōst″traw-mat′ik). Occurring after injury.

post-tussis (pōst-tus′is) [L.]. After coughing.

post-typhoid (pōst-ti′foid). Occurring after typhoid.

postulate (pos′tu-lāt) [L. *postulatum* demanded]. Anything assumed or taken for granted. **Ehrlich's p.** See *Ehrlich's side-chain theory*, under *theory*. **Koch's p's,** a statement of the kind of experimental evidence required to establish the etiologic relationship of a given microorganism to a given disease. The conditions included are (1) the microorganism must be observed in every case of the disease; (2) it must be isolated and grown in pure culture; (3) the pure culture must, when inoculated into a susceptible animal, reproduce the disease; and (4) the microorganism must be observed in, and recovered from, the experimentally diseased animal.

postural (pos′tu-ral). Pertaining to posture or position.

posture (pos′tūr) [L. *postura*]. The attitude of the body. **Drosin's p's,** three postures for eliciting tenderness in appendicitis.

postuterine (pōst-u′ter-in). Situated behind the uterus.

postvaccinal (pōst-vak′sĭ-nal). Occurring after or as a consequence of vaccination for smallpox.

postvaccinial (pōst″vak-sin′e-al). Occurring after or as a consequence of vaccinia.

postvermis (pōst-ver′mis). The inferior vermis of the cerebellum.

postvital (pōst-vi′tal). See *postvital staining*, under *staining*.

postzygotic (pōst″zi-got′ik). Occurring, or determined by events occurring, after union of the gametes, that is, after conception, or formation of the zygote.

Pot. Abbreviation for *potion* and L. *potas′sa*.

potable (po′tah-b'l) [L. *potabilis*]. Fit to drink; drinkable.

Potain's apparatus, disease, sign, solution, syndrome (po-tānz′) [Pierre Carl Edouard *Potain*, French physician, 1825–1901]. See under the nouns.

potamophobia (pot″ah-mo-fo′be-ah) [Gr. *potamos* river + *phobein* to be affrighted by]. A morbid dread of rivers or of streams and lakes.

potash (pot′ash). Impure potassium carbonate. **caustic p.,** potassium hydroxide. **sulfurated p.,** a mixture of potassium polysulfides and potassium thiosulfate, containing 12.8 per cent of sulfur in combination as sulfide.

potassa (po-tas′ah) [L.]. Potassium hydroxide. **p. caus′tica,** potassium hydroxide. **p. sulfura′ta,** sulfurated potash.

potassemia (pot″ah-se′me-ah) [*potassa* + Gr. *haima* blood + *-ia*]. The presence of an abnormally large amount of potassium in the blood.

potassic (po-tas′ik). Containing potash.

potassiocupric (po-tas″e-o-ku′prik). Containing potassium and copper in its divalent form.

potassiomercuric (po-tas″e-o-mer-ku′rik). Containing potassium and mercury in its divalent form. **p. iodide,** potassium mercuric oxide.

potassium (po-tas′e-um) [L.]. A metallic element of the alkali group, many of whose salts are used in medicine. It is a soft, silver-white metal, melting at 58°F.; atomic number, 19; atomic weight, 39.102; specific gravity, 0.87; symbol, K (kalium). **p. acetate,** a compound, $CH_3.COOK$: used as a systemic and urinary alkalizer. **p. alum.** See *alum*. **p. antimonyltartrate,** antimony potassium tartrate. See under *antimony*. **p. arsenite,** a compound formed by the interaction of arsenic trioxide and potassium hydroxide. **p. bicarbonate,** a transparent, crystalline salt, $KHCO_3$: used as a gastric antacid and an electrolyte replenisher. **p. bichromate,** an orange-red, crystalline salt, $K_2Cr_2O_7$: a caustic poison, used as a preservative for tissues. **p. bismuth tartrate,** bismuth potassium tartrate. See under *bismuth*. **p. bitartrate,** a white, crystalline salt, KOOCCH(OH)CH(OH)COOH: diuretic, cathartic, and refrigerant. **p. bromide,** a colorless, crystalline body, KBr: used as a sedative and antiepileptic. **p. carbonate,** a white, crystalline or granular salt, K_2CO_3: used chiefly in pharmaceutical and chemical manufacturing procedures. **p. chlorate,** an explosive, white, crystalline salt, $KClO_3$: used in diseases of the mouth and throat, also for hemorrhoids and proctitis. **p. chloride,** a white crystalline compound, KCl, used as a reagent and in the prophylaxis and treatment of potassium deficiency. **p. citrate,** a white, granular powder, $C_6H_5K_3O_7 + H_2O$: used as a diuretic, expectorant, and sudorific. **p. cyanide,** an extremely poisonous white solid or powder, KCN. **p. dichromate,** p. bichromate. **p. ferricyanide,** deep-red crystals, $K_3Fe(CN)_6$, used in a delicate test for ferrous salts. **p. glycerophosphate,** a white, vitreous substance, $K_2C_3H_5(OH)_2PO_4$. **p. guaiacolsulfonate,** a white crystalline powder, $C_7H_7KO_5S$: sometimes used in treatment of bronchitis. **p. hydroxide,** a white, crystalline compound, KOH, with powerful alkaline and caustic properties. **p. hypophosphite,** a white, crystalline salt, KH_2PO_2: formerly used in the treatment of tuberculosis. **p. iodate,** a salt, KIO_3, formerly used in diseases of the mucous membranes. **p. iodide,** a colorless, transparent body, KI: used as a source of iodine and as an expectorant. **p. mercuric iodide,** a complex, K_2HgI_4, containing about 25.5 per cent of mercury: used as a germicide, and as an ingredient of various reagents. **p. nitrate,** a white, crystalline salt, KNO_3: used as a diuretic. **p. nitrite,** a compound, KNO_2: sometimes used in place of sodium nitrite. **p. osmate,** a red, crystalline powder, $K_2OsO_4.2H_2O$. **p. permanganate,** a dark purple, crystalline salt, $KMnO_4$: used as a local anti-infective and oxidant. **p. phosphate,** a salt, K_2HPO_4: mild laxative and diuretic. **p. silicate,** soluble glass, $K_2Si_2O_3$: sometimes used like plaster of paris in making rigid dressings. **p. sodium tartrate,** a mild saline cathartic, $C_4H_4KNaO_6.4H_2O$. **p. sulfate,** a compound, K_2SO_4, with an extremely irritant action on stomach and intestines. **p. sulfite,** a white, crystalline salt, $K_2SO_3 + 2H_2O$: mild laxative and diuretic. **p. sulfocyanate,** p. thiocyanate. **p. tartrate,** $K_2C_4H_4O_6 + \frac{1}{2}H_2O$: diuretic, diaphoretic, and cathartic. **p. tellurate,** a salt in white crystals, K_2TeO: formerly used in tuberculosis. **p. thiocyanate,** a colorless, crystalline salt, KSCN, used as a reagent and as a vasodilator.

potator (po′tah-tor) [L.]. A drinker. **p. stren′uus,** a heavy drinker.

potency (po′ten-se) [L. *potentia* power]. Power; especially (1) the ability of the male to perform sexual intercourse; (2) the power of a medicinal agent to produce the desired effects; (3) the ability of an embryonic part to develop and complete its destiny. **prospective p.,** the total developmental possibilities of which an embryonic part is capable. **reactive p.** See *competence*.

potentia (po-ten′she-ah) [L.]. Power. **p. coeun′di** ["power of coming together"], the ability to perform the sexual act. **p. concipien′di,** the ability to conceive. **p. generan′di,** the ability to procreate.

potential (po-ten′shal) [L. *potentia* power]. 1. Existing and ready for action, but not yet active. 2. Electric tension or pressure, as measured by the capacity of producing electric effects in bodies of a different state of electrization. When bodies of different potentials are brought into communication, a current is set up between them; if they are of the same potential, no current passes between them. **action p.,** the electrical activity developed in a muscle, nerve or the central nervous system during activity. **after-p.** See under *spike.* **bio-electric p.,** the varying electric potential which accompanies all biochemical processes, as manifested in the electrocardiogram and the electroencephalogram. **caries-producing p.,** decalcification p. **decalcification p.,** the amount of acid produced by oral bacteria from a unit amount of foodstuff, multiplied by the number of such units adhering to the teeth after ingestion of the particular food. **demarcation p.,** the difference in electrical potential between the intact longitudinal surface and the injured end of a muscle or nerve. **membrane p.,** the electric potential which exists on the two sides of a membrane or across the wall of a cell. **morphogenetic p.,** the degree of strength or ability of an embryonic part to develop into a specific structure.

potentialization, potentiation (po-ten″she-al-i-za′shun, po-ten″she-a′shun). 1. The preparation of the various homeopathic potencies. 2. The combined action of two drugs, being greater than the sum of the effects of each used alone.

potentiometer (po-ten″she-om′e-ter). An instrument for the accurate measuring of voltage.

potio (po′she-o) [L.]. Potion.

potion (po′shun) [L. *po′tio* draft]. A draft; a large dose of liquid medicine. **Rivière's p.,** an effervescing drink produced by combining a solution of citric acid with one of sodium or potassium bicarbonate. **Todd's p.,** tincture of canella, 5; brandy, 40; syrup, 30, and water, 75.

potocytosis (po″to-si-to′sis) [Gr. *potos* drinking + *kytos* cell + *-osis*]. The hypothetical action of cells passing fluids through themselves from one place to another.

potomania (po″to-ma′ne-ah) [Gr. *potos* drinking + *mania* madness]. 1. An abnormal desire to drink. 2. Delirium tremens.

Pott's aneurysm, caries, curvature, disease, fracture, gangrene, paralysis, tumor, etc. (pots) [Percivall *Pott*, English surgeon, 1713–1788]. See under the nouns.

Pottenger's sign (pot′en-jerz) [F. M. *Pottenger*, American physician, born 1869]. See under *sign.*

Potter treatment (pot′er) [Caryl A. *Potter*, American physician, 1886–1933]. See under *treatment.*

Potter version (pot′er) [Irving W. *Potter*, American obstetrician, 1868–1956]. See under *version.*

Potts-Smith-Gibson operation [Willis J. *Potts*, Chicago surgeon, born 1895; Sidney *Smith*, Chicago surgeon, born 1912; Stanley *Gibson*, Chicago pediatrician, born 1883]. See under *operation.*

potus (po′tus) [L. "drink"]. A potion. **p. imperia′lis,** imperial drink, a solution of ½ oz. of cream of tartar in 3 pts. of water, sweetened, and flavored with lemon peel.

pouch (powch). A pocket-like space, cavity, or sac, as of the peritoneum. **abdominovesical p.,** the pouch formed by reflection of the peritoneum from the anterior abdominal wall to the distended bladder. **anterior p. of Tröltsch,** recessus membranae tympani anterior. **branchial p.,** pharyngeal p. **Broca's p.,** a pear-shaped sac in the labium majus, its large extremity directed downward and backward, and its smaller one upward, forward, and outward toward the opening of the inguinal canal; composed of elastic fibers, and containing connective tissue and fat. Called also *pudendal sac.* **craniobuccal p., craniopharyngeal p.,** Rathke's p. **p. of Douglas,** excavatio rectouterina. **enterocoelic p.,** a diverticulum of the enteron of the embryo. **guttural p's,** large mucous sacs in the horse, which are ventral diverticula of the eustachian tube, situated between the base of the cranium and the atlas dorsally and the pharynx ventrally. **Hartmann's p.,** an abnormal sacculation of the neck of the gallbladder. **Heidenhain p.,** an isolated part of the stomach, the vagal fibers of which have been interrupted: used in the experimental study of gastric physiology. **ileocecal p.,** a peritoneal pouch at the ileocecal junction. **laryngeal p.,** sacculus laryngis. **Morison's p.,** a pouch of peritoneum below the liver and to the right of the right kidney. **neurobuccal p.,** Rathke's p. **obturator p.,** paravesical p. **paracystic p.,** the lateral part of the excavatio vesicouterina. **pararectal p.,** the lateral part of the excavatio rectouterina. **paravesical p.,** the lateral part of the uteroabdominal pouch, beside the bladder and in which the obturator canal opens. Called also *obturator p.* **Pavlov p.,** an isolated part of the stomach with the nervous connections still intact: used in the experimental study of gastric physiology. **pharyngeal p.,** a lateral diverticulum of the pharynx that meets a corresponding groove in the ectoderm, forming a closing plate that may rupture and complete the gill slit condition observed in lower vertebrates. **Physick's p's,** inflamed sacculations between the rectal valves, with mucous discharge. **posterior p. of Tröltsch,** recessus membranae tympani posterior. **Prussak's p.** See under *space.* **Rathke's p.,** a diverticulum from the embryonic buccal cavity, from which the anterior lobe of the pituitary gland is developed. Called also *craniobuccal p.* and *neurobuccal p.* **recto-uterine p., rectovaginal p.,** excavatio rectouterina. **rectovesical p.,** excavatio rectovesicalis. **Seessel's p.,** a transient outpouching of the embryonic pharynx rostrad of the pharyngeal membrane and caudal to Rathke's pouch. **utero-abdominal p.,** the compartment of the pelvic cavity anterior to the uterus and broad ligaments. **uterovesical p., vesico-uterine p.,** excavatio vesicouterina. **visceral p.,** pharyngeal p. **Willis' p.,** omentum minus.

poudrage (poo-drahzh′) [Fr.]. Powdering. **pleural p.,** the blowing of an irritating powder on the surfaces of the pleura to promote adhesion.

Poulet's disease (poo-lāz′) [Alfred *Poulet*, French physician, 1848–1888]. Rheumatic osteoperiostitis.

poultice (pōl′tis) [L. *puls* pap; Gr. *kataplasma*]. A soft, moist, pultaceous mass applied hot to the surface of a part for the purpose of supplying heat and moisture. **pus p.,** a mass of pus retained in a wound as a sort of natural dressing.

pound (pownd) [L. *pondus* weight; *libra* pound]. A unit of mass (weight) of both the avoirdupois and the apothecaries' system. The avoirdupois pound contains 16 ounces, or 7000 grains, and is the equivalent of 453.592 Gm. The apothecaries' pound contains 12 ounces, or 5760 grains, and is the equivalent of 373.242 Gm. Abbreviated lb.

Poupart's ligament, line, etc. (poo-parts′) [François *Poupart*, French anatomist, 1616–1708]. See under *ligament, line,* etc.

poverty (pov′er-te). The absence or scarcity of requisite substance or elements. **emotional p.,** diminution in the normal emotional qualities of the mind, such as love, sympathy, honor, etc. **p. of movement,** the relative immobility and stationariness of position seen in subjects of shaking palsy; akinesia.

povidone-iodine (po′vĭ-dōn i′o-dīn). A complex produced by reacting iodine with the polymer polyvinylpyrrolidone: used as a mild anti-infective agent.

powder (pow′der) [L. *pulvis*]. A substance made up of an aggregation of small particles obtained by the grinding or trituration of a solid drug. See *pulvis.* **bleaching p.,** chlorinated lime, originally used as a bleach. **p. of chalk, aromatic,** a preparation of chalk, cinnamon, myristica, clove, cardamom, and sucrose: antacid, stimulant, and astringent. **p. of chalk, aromatic, with opium,** aromatic powder of chalk containing 2.5 per cent of powdered opium. **chalk p., com-**

pound, a powder containing prepared chalk, finely powdered acacia, and sucrose: antacid, used in treatment of diarrhea. **chiniofon p.,** chiniofon. **Dover's p.,** ipecac and opium p. **dusting p.,** a fine powder used as a substitute for talc. **dusting p., absorbable,** an absorbable powder prepared by processing cornstarch, and containing not more than 2 per cent of magnesium oxide: used for dusting surgeons' rubber gloves and other applications for which talc is used in the hospital. **effervescent p's, compound,** a combination of sodium carbonate, potassium sodium tartrate, and tartaric acid: used as a cathartic. **glycyrrhiza p., compound,** senna p., compound. **Goa p.,** a bitter, brownish yellow to umber brown powder deposited in irregular interspaces of the wood of *Andira araroba*, a large leguminous tree common in Brazil. **gray p.,** mercury with chalk. **Gregory's p.,** p. of rhubarb, compound. **impalpable p.,** a powder so fine that its particles cannot be felt as distinct bodies. **insect p.,** any powder destructive to insects. **iodochlorhydroxyquin p., compound,** a preparation of iodochlorhydroxyquin, boric acid, lactic acid, zinc stearate, and lactose: used topically as an anti-infective in the vaginal tract. **ipecac and opium p.,** a pale brown powder prepared by triturating 100 Gm. of finely powdered ipecac, 100 Gm. of powdered opium, and 800 Gm. of coarsely powdered lactose to a very fine, uniform powder: formerly widely used as a sedative and diaphoretic. **p. of jalap, compound,** a mixture of jalap and potassium bitartrate, formerly used in treatment of dropsy. **Jesuit's p.,** powdered cinchona. **licorice p., compound, p. of liquorice, compound,** senna p., compound. **p. of rhubarb, compound,** a preparation of rhubarb, ginger, and magnesium oxide: formerly used as a laxative antacid. **Seidlitz p's,** effervescent p's, compound. **senna p., compound,** a weak or dusky yellow powder prepared from fennel oil, finely powdered sucrose, powdered senna, powdered glycyrrhiza, and washed sulfur: laxative. **Sippy p. No. 1,** sodium bicarbonate and calcium carbonate p. **Sippy p. No. 2,** sodium bicarbonate and magnesium oxide p. **sodium bicarbonate and calcium carbonate p.,** a mixture of precipitated calcium carbonate and sodium bicarbonate: antacid; widely used in treatment of peptic ulcer in combination with sodium bicarbonate and magnesium oxide powder. **sodium bicarbonate and magnesium oxide p.,** a mixture of magnesium oxide and sodium carbonate: antacid and laxative. **p. of tragacanth, compound,** a mixture of finely powdered tragacanth, acacia, starch, and sucrose: demulcent. **zinc sulfate p., compound,** a preparation of salicylic acid, zinc sulfate, phenol, eucalyptol, menthol, thymol, and boric acid: antiseptic.

power (pow′er) [L. *posse* to have power]. Capability; potency; the ability to act. **candle p.,** the numerical expression, in international candles, of the luminous intensity of a light source. **carbon dioxide-combining p., CO_2-combining p.,** ability of the blood plasma to combine with carbon dioxide; indicative of the alkali reserve and a measure of the acid-base equilibrium of the blood. Normal values are between 50 and 70 per cent. **resolving p.,** the ability of the eye or of a lens to make small objects that are close together, separately visible; thus revealing the structure of an object.

pox (poks). A term applied to an eruptive disease; sometimes used as a vulgar name for syphilis. **brick p.,** a form of swine erysipelas. **camel p.,** a virus disease of camels. **canary p.,** a virus disease of canaries. **carp p.,** an epizootic form of fish pox occurring in European carp. **cotton p.,** variola minor. **cow p.,** a mild eruptive skin disease of milk cows, usually limited to the udder and teats, and caused by vaccinia virus. **fish p.,** a hyperplastic epidermal disease of viral origin occurring in fresh-water and marine fish. **fowl p.,** a virus disease of chickens, turkeys, and other birds, with wartlike nodules occurring on the unfeathered parts of the head and legs. **glass p.,** variola minor. **goat p.,** a highly infectious disease of goats, less severe than sheep pox, and caused by a virus thought to be similar to the vaccinia virus. **horse p.,** an infectious pustular disease of horses, caused by an epitheliotropic virus. **Kaffir p., milk p.,** variola minor. **monkey p.,** a mild disease resembling smallpox, occurring in laboratory monkeys and caused by a virus related to that causing smallpox. **mouse p.,** ectromelia. **rabbit p.,** an acute disease of laboratory rabbits, caused by a virus closely related to that causing vaccinia. **Samoa p., Sanaga p.,** variola minor. **sheep p.,** a highly infectious and sometimes fatal disease in sheep, caused by a virus similar to that causing vaccinia in cows. **swine p.,** an acute infectious virus disease of swine, with skin lesions resembling those of pox in other animals. **water p.,** ground itch. **wet p.,** a disease resembling fowl pox, with lesions occurring in the mouth and frequently causing death by suffocation. **white p.,** variola minor.

poxvirus (poks-vi′rus). One of a group of morphologically similar and immunologically related agents, including the viruses of vaccinia and variola and those producing pox disease in lower animals.

Pozzi's operation, syndrome (pod′zēz) [Samuel Jean *Pozzi*, gynecologist in Paris, 1846–1918]. See under *operation* and *syndrome.*

P.P. Abbreviation for L. *punc′tum prox′imum*, near point of accommodation.

P.p.a. Abbreviation for L. *phi′ala pri′us agita′ta*, the bottle having first been shaken.

P.P.D. Abbreviation for *purified protein derivative* (*tuberculin*). See under *tuberculin.*

ppg. Abbreviation for *picopicogram.*

PPLO. Abbreviation for *pleuropneumonia-like organisms.*

ppm. Abbreviation for *parts per million.*

Ppt. Abbreviation for *precipitate* and *prepared.*

P.Q. Abbreviation for *permeability quotient.*

P.R. Abbreviation for L. *punc′tum remo′tum*, far point of accommodation.

Pr. 1. Abbreviation for *presbyopia* and *prism.* 2. Chemical symbol for *praseodymium.*

practice (prak′tis) [Gr. *praktikē*]. The utilization of one's knowledge in a particular profession, the practice of medicine being the exercise of one's knowledge in the practical recognition and treatment of disease. **contract p.,** the treatment of the members of a specified group for a lump sum, or at so much per member. **group p.** See under *medicine.* **panel p.** See under *panel.*

practitioner (prak-tish′un-er). One who has complied with the requirements and who is engaged in the practice of medicine.

prae-. For words beginning thus, see also those beginning *pre-.*

praecox (pre′koks) [L.]. Beforetime; early. See *dementia praecox.*

praeputium (pre-pu′she-um) [L.]. Preputium. **p. clitor′idis** [B N A], preputium clitoridis. **p. pe′nis** [B N A], preputium penis.

praevia, praevius (pre′ve-a, pre′ve-us) [L.]. In front of, in the way.

pragmatagnosia (prag″mat-ag-no′ze-ah) [Gr. *pragma* object + *agnōsia* absence of recognition]. Inability to recognize formerly known objects.

pragmatamnesia (prag″mat-am-ne′ze-ah) [Gr. *pragma* object + *amnesia* forgetfulness]. Loss of power of remembering the appearance of objects.

pragmatic (prag-mat′ik). Pertaining to pragmatism; dealing with practical aspects.

pragmatism (prag′mah-tizm). The doctrine that the whole meaning of a conception lies in its practical consequences.

pramoxine (pram-ok′sēn). Chemical name: 4-[3-

(p-butoxyphenoxy)propyl]morpholine: used as a local anesthetic.

prandial (pran′de-al) [L. *prandium* breakfast]. Pertaining to a meal, especially dinner.

pranone (pra′nōn). Trade mark for a preparation of ethisterone.

prantal (pran′tal). Trade mark for preparations of diphemanil.

praseodymium (pra″se-o-dim′e-um). A rare earth element; atomic number, 59; atomic weight, 140.907; symbol, Pr.

P. rat. aetat. Abbreviation for L. *pro ratio′ne aeta′tis*, in proportion to age.

pratique (prah-tek′) [Fr.]. A certificate which releases an incoming vessel from quarantine. It is given by the quarantine officer to the master, and when presented to the collector of the port admits the boat to entry.

Pratt's symptom, test (prats) [Joseph Hersey *Pratt*, American physician, 1872–1956]. See under *symptom* and *tests*.

Prausnitz-Küstner reaction, test (prows′-nits-kist′ner) [Carl *Prausnitz*, German hygienist, born 1876; Heinz *Küstner*, German gynecologist, born 1897]. See under *reaction*.

Pravaz's syringe (prah-vahz′) [Charles Gabriel *Pravaz*, French physician in Lyons, 1791–1853]. See under *syringe*.

Praxagoras (prak-sag′o-ras) **of Cos** (c. 340 B.C.). A Greek physician who succeeded Diocles as leader of the Dogmatists. He was apparently the first Greek physician to recognize the difference between arteries and veins, and to comment on the pulse.

praxiology (prak″se-ol′o-je) [Gr. *praxis* action + *-logy*]. The study of conduct.

praxis (prak′sis) [Gr. "action"]. The doing or performance of action: Edinger's term for the execution of pallial impulses. Cf. *gnosis*.

pre- [L. *prae* before]. Prefix signifying before.

preadult (pre″ah-dult′). Prior to adult life.

preagonal (pre-ag′o-nal). Preceding the death agony.

preagonic (pre″ah-gon′ik). Preagonal.

prealbumin (pre″al-bu′min). One of a group of serum proteins which have an electrophoretic mobility slightly faster than albumin at pH 8.6.

prealbuminuric (pre″al-bu″mĭ-nu′rik). Occurring before albuminuria sets in.

preanal (pre-a′nal). In front of the anus.

preanesthesia (pre″an-es-the′ze-ah). Preliminary anesthesia; light anesthesia or narcosis induced by medication as a preliminary to administration of a general anesthetic.

preanesthetic (pre″an-es-thet′ik). 1. Pertaining to or inducing preanesthesia. 2. An agent that induces preanesthesia.

preantiseptic (pre″an-tĭ-sep′tik). Pertaining to the time before the discovery of antisepsis.

preaortic (pre″a-or′tik). In front of the aorta.

preaseptic (pre″a-sep′tik). Pertaining to the time before aseptic surgery was practiced.

preataxic (pre″ah-tak′sik). Occurring before or preceding ataxia.

preaurale (pre″aw-ra′le). A cephalometric landmark, the point at which a straight line from the postaurale, perpendicular to the long axis of the auricle, meets the base of the auricle.

preauricular (pre″aw-rik′u-lar). Situated in front of the ear.

preaxial (pre-ak′se-al). Situated or occurring before an axis. In anatomical usage, preaxial refers to the lateral (radial) aspect of the upper limb, and the medial (tibial) aspect of the lower limb.

prebacillary (pre-bas′ĭ-ler″e). Occurring before the entrance of bacilli into the system, or before they become discoverable.

prebacteriological (pre″bak-te″re-o-loj′ĭ-kal). Before the development of bacteriology.

prebase (pre′bās). That part of the dorsum of the tongue lying in front of the base.

prebladder (pre-blad′er). An extensive cavity formed in front of the orifice of the bladder within the capsule of the prostate.

prebrachium (pre-bra′ke-um). Brachium colliculi superioris.

precancer (pre′kan-ser). A condition which will eventually become malignant, even when the carcinogenic agent is withdrawn.

precancerosis (pre″kan-ser-o′sis). A precancerous condition; a condition of early cancer.

precancerous (pre-kan′ser-us). Pertaining to an early stage in the development of a cancer.

precapillary (pre-kap′ĭ-ler″e). A vessel lacking complete coats, intermediate between an arteriole and a true capillary. Called also *metarteriole*.

precarcinomatous (pre″kar-sĭ-nom′ah-tus). Preceding the development of carcinoma.

precardiac (pre-kar′de-ak). Situated ventrad from the heart.

precardium (pre-kar′de-um) [*pre-* + Gr. *kardia* heart]. Precordium.

precartilage (pre-kar′tĭ-lij). Embryonic cartilaginous tissue.

precava (pre-ka′vah). The vena cava superior.

precentral (pre-sen′tral). Situated in front of a center.

prechordal (pre-kor′dal). Situated in front of the notochord.

precipitable (pre-sip′ĭ-tah-b'l). Capable of being precipitated.

precipitant (pre-sip′ĭ-tant). A substance which causes a chemical or mechanical precipitation.

precipitate (pre-sip′ĭ-tāt) [L. *praecipitare* to cast down]. 1. To cause a substance in solution to settle down in solid particles. 2. [L. *praecipitatum*]. A deposit made or substance thrown down by precipitation. 3. Occurring with undue rapidity, as precipitate labor. **black p.,** mercurous oxide. **green p.,** copper oxyacetate. **keratic p's.** See under *keratitis punctata*. **red p.,** red mercuric oxide. **sweet p.,** calomel (mild mercurous chloride). **white p.,** ammoniated mercury. **yellow p.,** yellow mercuric oxide.

precipitation (pre-sip″ĭ-ta′shun) [L. *praecipitatio*]. The act or process of precipitating. **group p.,** precipitation of more than one antigen by a precipitin.

precipitin (pre-sip′ĭ-tin). An antibody to soluble antigen that specifically aggregates the macromolecular antigen in vivo or in vitro to give a visible precipitate. **heat p.,** coctoprecipitin.

precipitinogen (pre-sip″ĭ-tin′o-jen). The soluble antigen which stimulates the formation of a precipitin.

precipitinoid (pre-sip′ĭ-tin-oid). A precipitin in which the zymophore group has been changed or lost so that it cannot cause precipitation, although it still retains its affinity for the antigen.

precipitinophoric (pre-sip″ĭ-tin-o-for′ik). Denoting the active precipitating element or group in a precipitin.

precipitogen (pre-sip′ĭ-to-jen). Precipitinogen.

precipitogenoid (pre-sip″ĭ-toj′e-noid). A precipitogen which has lost its power of causing precipitation.

precipitoid (pre-sip′ĭ-toid). Precipitinoid.

precipitophore (pre-sip′ĭ-to-fōr″). The group in a precipitin which causes the actual precipitation.

precipitum (pre-sip′ĭ-tum). The precipitate resulting from the action of a precipitin.

precirrhosis (pre″sir-ro′sis). The early stages of cirrhosis of the liver, preceding the development of swelling, jaundice or hematemesis.

preclavicular (pre″klah-vik′u-lar). In front of the clavicle.

preclinical (pre-klin′ĭ-kal). Before the disease becomes clinically recognizable.

preclival (pre-kli′val). In front of the clivus of the cerebellum.

precocious (pre-ko′shus). Developed more than is usual at a given age.

precocity (pre-kos′ĭ-te). Unusually early development of mental or physical traits.

precognition (pre″kog-nish′un) [*pre-* + *cognition*]. The extrasensory perception of a future event.

precoid (pre′koid). Resembling dementia praecox.

precollagenous (pre″kŏ-laj′ĭ-nus) [*pre-* + *collagen*]. Denoting an incomplete stage in the formation of collagen.

precommissure (pre-kom′ĭ-shūr). The anterior cornu of the lateral ventricle.

preconscious (pre-kon′shus). In Freudian terminology, all the mental processes that are "out of mind" at the time, but can be recalled with little or no effort.

preconvulsant (pre″kon-vul′sant). Preceding the occurrence of convulsions.

preconvulsive (pre″kon-vul′siv). Occurring before the convulsive stage.

precordia (pre-kor′de-ah) [L. *praecordia*]. Precordium.

precordial (pre-kor′de-al). Pertaining to the precordium.

precordialgia (pre″kor-de-al′je-ah) [*precordia* + *-algia*]. Pain in the precordium.

precordium (pre-kor′de-um). The region over the heart or stomach; the epigastrium and lower part of the thorax.

precornu (pre-kor′nu). Cornu anterius ventriculi lateralis.

precostal (pre-kos′tal). In front of the ribs.

precranial (pre-kra′ne-al). In the anterior part of the cranium.

precribrum (pre-kri′brum). Substantia perforata anterior.

precritical (pre-krit′ĭ-kal). Previous to the occurrence of the crisis.

precuneal (pre-ku′ne-al). Situated in front of the cuneus.

precuneate (pre-ku′ne-āt). Pertaining to the precuneus.

precuneus (pre-ku′ne-us) [*pre-* + L. *cuneus* wedge]. [N A] A small, square-shaped convolution on the medial surface of the parietal lobe of the cerebrum, bounded posteriorly by the medial part of the parietooccipital sulcus and anteriorly by the paracentral lobule.

predation (pre-da′shun). The derivation by an organism of elements essential for its existence from organisms of other species which it consumes and destroys.

predator (pred′ah-tor) [L. *praedator* a plunderer, pillager]. An organism that derives elements essential for its existence from organisms of other species, which it consumes and destroys.

predentin (pre-den′tin). The soft fibrillar substance composing the primitive dentin and forming the inner layer of the circumpulpar dentin. Called also *dentinoid.*

prediabetes (pre-di″ah-be′tēz). A state of latent impairment of carbohydrate metabolism, in which the criteria for diabetes mellitus are not all satisfied; sometimes controllable by diet alone.

prediastole (pre″di-as′to-le). The interval immediately preceding the diastole in the cardiac cycle.

prediastolic (pre″di-ah-stol′ik). 1. Pertaining to the beginning of the diastole. 2. Occurring just before the diastole.

predicrotic (pre″di-krot′ik). Occurring before the dicrotic wave of the sphygmogram.

predigestion (pre″di-jes′chun). The partial artificial digestion of food before its ingestion.

predisposing (pre″dis-pōz′ing). Conferring a tendency to disease.

predisposition (pre″dis-po-zish′un) [*pre-* + L. *disponere* to dispose]. A latent susceptibility to disease which may be activated under certain conditions, as by stress.

prednisolone (pred′nĭ-so″lōn). Chemical name: 1,4-pregnadiene-3,20-dione-11β,17α,21-triol: used as an adrenocortical steroid of glucogenic type.

prednisone (pred′nĭ-sōn). Chemical name: 1,4-pregnadiene-17α,21-diol-3,11,20-trione: used as an adrenocortical steroid of glucogenic type.

predormital (pre-dor′mĭ-tal). Pertaining to or occurring in the predormitum.

predormitium (pre″dor-mish′e-um). Predormitum.

predormitum (pre-dor′mĭ-tum). The period of waning consciousness interposed between the waking state and sound slumber.

preeclampsia (pre″e-klamp′se-ah). A toxemia of late pregnancy, characterized by hypertension, albuminuria, and edema.

preelacin (pre-el′ah-sin). A precursor of elacin in the circulating blood.

preepiglottic (pre″ep-ĭ-glot′ik). Situated or occurring in front of the epiglottis.

preeruptive (pre″e-rup′tiv). Preceding eruption.

preflagellate (pre-flaj′ĕ-lāt). Preceding the flagellate state: said of protozoa.

preformation (pre″for-ma′shun). The theory of early physiologists that the fully formed animal or plant exists in a minute form in the germ cell. Opposed to the theory of *epigenesis.* See *animalculist* and *ovist.*

preformationist (pre″for-ma′shun-ist). A believer in the theory of preformation.

prefrontal (pre-fron′tal). 1. Situated in the anterior part of the frontal lobe or region. 2. The central part of the ethmoid bone.

preganglionic (pre″gang-gle-on′ik). Situated anterior or proximal to a ganglion.

pregeminal (pre-jem′ĭ-nal). Pertaining to the pregeminum.

pregeminum (pre-jem′ĭ-num). Colliculus superior laminae tecti.

pregeniculatum (pre″je-nik″u-la′tum). Corpus geniculatum laterale.

pregeniculum (pre″je-nik′u-lum). Corpus geniculatum laterale.

pregenital (pre-jen′ĭ-tal). Pertaining to the early infantile stage of sexual life before the genitals have become the dominant zone.

Pregl's test (pra′g′lz) [Fritz *Pregl*, Austrian chemist, 1869–1930]. See under *tests.*

preglobulin (pre-glob′u-lin). A protein derivable from cytoglobulin by decomposition with acids.

preglomerular (pre″glo-mer′u-lar). Located or occurring proximal to a glomerulus of the kidney.

pregnancy (preg′nan-se) [L. *praegnans* with child]. The condition of having a developing embryo or fetus in the body, after union of an ovum and spermatozoon. In woman duration of pregnancy is about 266 days. Pregnancy is marked by cessation of the menses; nausea on arising in the morning (morning sickness); enlargement of the breasts and pigmentation of the nipples; progressive enlargement of the abdomen. The absolute signs of pregnancy are ballottement, fetal movements, and sounds of the fetal heart. **abdominal p.,** development of the ovum in the abdominal cavity. **afetal p.,** false p. **ampullar p.,** pregnancy in which the ovum has been arrested in the ampulla of the oviduct. **angular p.,** pregnancy in which the fertilized ovum becomes implanted in the angle or cornu of the uterus. **bigeminal p.,** twin p. **broad ligament p.,** development of the fertilized ovum in the broad ligament. **cervical p.,** the development of the ovum within the cervical canal. **combined p.,** simultaneous existence of intra-uterine and extra-uterine pregnancy. **compound p.,** superimposition of an intra-uterine pregnancy on a previously existing extra-uterine pregnancy, generally a lithopedion. **cornual p.,** pregnancy in one of the horns of a bicornate uterus. **ectopic p.,** extra-uterine p. **entopic p.,** normal uterine pregnancy. **exochorial p.,** graviditas exochorialis. **extra-uterine p.,** development of

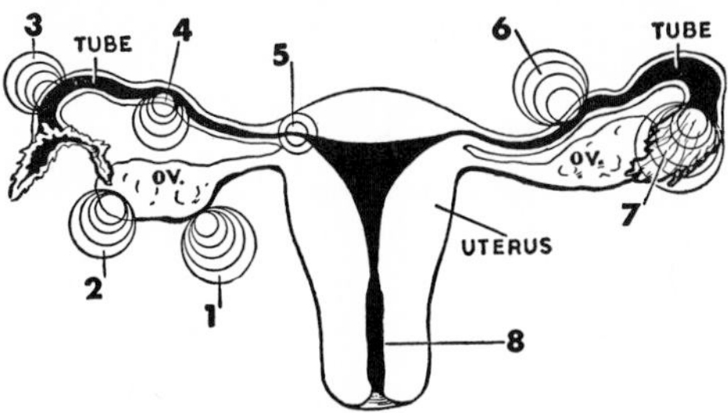

Diagram showing locations of extrauterine (ectopic) pregnancy: (1) primary abdominal; (2) ovarian; (3) ampullar; (4) tubal—rupture into broad ligament; (5) interstitial; (6) tubal—rupture into peritoneal cavity; (7) tubo-ovarian; (8) cervical (Greenhill).

the ovum outside of the cavity of the uterus. **fallopian p.,** tubal p. **false p.,** absence of the menses and presence of other signs of pregnancy, without occurrence of conception and development of an embryo. **gemellary p.,** twin p. **heterotopic p.,** combined p. **hydatid p.,** that which is accompanied with the formation of a hydatid mole. **hysteric p.,** symptoms of pregnancy in hysterical women who are not really pregnant. **incomplete p.,** pregnancy which is interrupted prematurely: abortion (up to the 16th week); immature delivery (16th to 28th week), premature delivery (28th to 36th week). **interstitial p.,** gestation in that part of the oviduct which is within the wall of the uterus. **intraligamentary p.,** a pregnancy within the broad ligament. **intramural p.,** interstitial p. **intraperitoneal p.,** pregnancy within the peritoneal cavity. **membranous p.,** pregnancy in

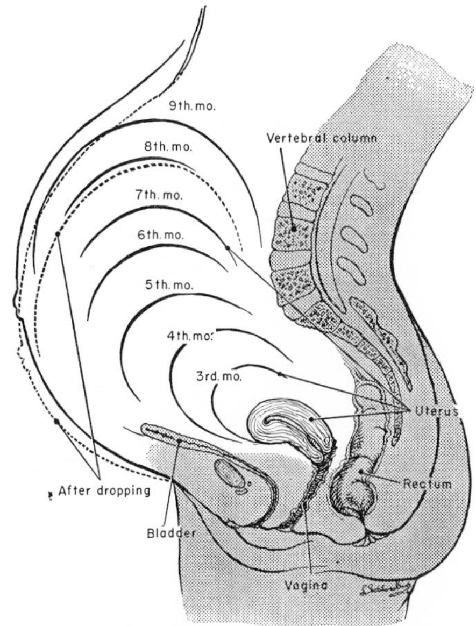

Pregnancy—Uterine levels.

which the fetus has broken through its membranous envelope and lies in contact with the uterine walls. **mesenteric p.,** tuboligamentary p. **molar p.,** conversion of the ovum into a mole. **multiple p.,** pregnancy resulting in the birth of more than one infant; it may be *monovular* (resulting from the fertilization of a single ovum) or *polyovular* (resulting from the fertilization of more than one ovum). When more than two fetuses coexist, they may come from one ovum or be the result of combined monovular and polyovular twinning. **mural p.,** interstitial p. **nervous p.,** hysteric p. **ovarian p.,** pregnancy occurring within an ovary. **ovario-abdominal p.,** a pregnancy which begins ovarian, but afterward becomes abdominal. **oviducal p.,** tubal p. **parietal p.,** interstitial p. **phantom p.,** an abdominal enlargement in hysterical women simulating pregnancy. **plural p.,** pregnancy with more than one fetus. **prolonged p.,** pregnancy continuing beyond the normal duration. **pseudo-intraligamentary p.,** an extra-uterine pregnancy in which a sac has been formed in such a way as to simulate an intraligamentary pregnancy. **sarcofetal p.,** pregnancy with both a fetus and a mole. **sarcohysteric p.,** false pregnancy due to a mole. **spurious p.,** false p. **stump p.,** pregnancy at the stump remaining after a pelvic operation. **tubal p.,** pregnancy within an oviduct. **tubo-abdominal p.,** one occurring partly in the fimbriated end of the oviduct and partly in the abdominal cavity. **tuboligamentary p.,** a pregnancy partly in the tube and partly in the broad ligament. **tubo-ovarian p.,** one occurring partly in the ovary and partly in the oviduct. **tubo-uterine p.,** gestation partly within the uterus and partly in an oviduct. **twin p.,** gestation with development of two fetuses. **utero-abdominal p.,** pregnancy with one fetus in the uterus and another in the abdominal cavity. **utero-ovarian p.,** pregnancy with one fetus in the uterus and another in the ovary. **uterotubal p.,** tubo-uterine pregnancy.

pregnant (preg′nant) [L. *praegnans*]. With child; gravid.

pregnene (preg′nēn). A crystalline unsaturated steroid with one double bond and three methyl groups, $C_{21}H_{34}$, Δ^4-pregnene forms the nucleus of the corpus luteum principle, progesterone.

pregneninolone (preg-nēn-in′o-lōn). Ethisterone.

pregnenolone (preg-nēn′o-lōn). Chemical name: 3-hydroxy-5-pregnen-20-one: used as an antiarthritic.

pregonium (pre-go′ne-um). A recess on the lower edge of the body of the mandible in advance of the angle.

pregranular (pre-gran′u-lar). Occurring before the granular stage.

pregravidic (pre″grah-vid′ik). Preceding pregnancy.

prehabilitation (pre″hah-bil″ĭ-ta′shun). The re-education and training of handicapped individuals preparatory to being fitted to assume definite jobs in industry.

prehallux (pre-hal′uks). A supernumerary bone of the foot sometimes found growing from the medial border of the scaphoid.

prehemiplegic (pre″hem-ĭ-ple′jik). Forerunning an attack of hemiplegia.

prehensile (pre-hen′sil) [L. *prehendere* to lay hold of]. Adapted for grasping or seizing.

prehension (pre-hen′shun) [L. *prehensio*]. The act of seizing or grasping.

prehepaticus (pre″he-pat′ĭ-kus) [*pre-* + Gr. *hēpar* liver]. A mass of vascular and connective tissue in the embryo which develops into the interstitial tissue of the liver.

prehyoid (pre-hi′oid). In front of the hyoid bone.

prehypertensin (pre″hi-per-ten′sin). Hypertensinogen.

prehypophyseal (pre″hi-po-fiz′e-al). Pertaining to or derived from the anterior lobe of the pituitary gland (lobus anterior hypophyseos [N A]).

prehypophysial (pre″hi-po-fiz′e-al). Prehypophyseal.

prehypophysis (pre″hi-pof′ĭ-sis). The anterior lobe of the pituitary gland (lobus anterior hypophyseos [N A]).

preictal (pre-ik′tal) [*pre-* + L. *ictus* stroke]. Occurring before a stroke or an attack, such as an acute epileptic attack.

preimmunization (pre-im″u-ni-za′shun). Artificial immunization produced in very young infants, as by the BCG vaccine.

preinduction (pre″in-duk′shun). An environmental influence on the germ cells of an individual which does not produce a modification until the third generation of his descendants, i.e., in the grandchildren.

preinsula (pre-in′su-lah). The cephalic portion of the insula.

preinvasive (pre″in-va′siv). Not yet invading other tissues. See *carcinoma in situ.*

preiotation (pre″i-o-ta′shun) [*pre-* + Gr. *iōta*, the Greek letter *i*]. The conversion of the initial sound of *i* into *y*.

Preiser's disease (pri′zerz) [Georg Karl Felix *Preiser*, orthopedic surgeon, Hamburg, Germany, 1879–1913]. See under *disease.*

Preisz-Nocard bacillus (prīs-no-kard′) [Hugo von *Preisz*, Budapest bacteriologist, 1860–1940; E. I. E. *Nocard*]. *Corynebacterium pseudotuberculosis.*

prelacrimal (pre-lak′rĭ-mal). In front of the lacrimal sac.

prelacteal (pre-lak′te-al). Preceding the establishment of milk flow: a term applied to the feeding of a newborn baby with lactose-citrate solution to reduce initial weight loss until breast feeding is fully established.

prelaryngeal (pre″lah-rin′je-al). In front of the larynx.

prelimbic (pre-lim′bik). Situated before a limbus.

prelipoid (pre-li′poid). 1. Preceding or before the lipoid state. 2. A preliminary stage of lipoid substance.

prelocalization (pre″lo-kal-i-za′shun). The localization in the egg or blastomere of materials which will develop into a particular tissue or organ.

prelocomotion (pre″lo-ko-mo′shun). The movements of a child made with the intention of moving from place to place before motor coordination is sufficiently developed to enable it to walk.

preludin (prel′u-din). Trade mark for preparations of phenmetrazine hydrochloride.

prelum (pre′lum) [L.]. Press. **p. abdomina′le,** the squeezing of the abdominal viscera between the diaphragm and the abdominal wall, as in defecation.

premalignant (pre″mah-lig′nant). Preceding the development of malignant characters.

premaniacal (pre″ma-ni′ah-kal). Preceding an attack of mania.

premature (pre-mah-tūr′) [L. *praematurus* early ripe]. 1. Occurring before the proper time. 2. A premature infant.

prematurity (pre″mah-tu′rĭ-te). Underdevelopment; the condition of a premature infant.

premaxilla (pre″mak-sil′ah). Os incisivum [N A]; a separate element derived from the median nasal processes in the embryo, which later fuses with the maxilla.

premaxillary (pre-mak′sĭ-ler″e). 1. Situated in front of the maxilla proper. 2. The intermaxillary bone.

premedical (pre-med′ĭ-kal). Preceding and preparing for the regular medical course of study, as premedical education.

premedicant (pre-med′ĭ-kant). A drug used for premedication.

premedication (pre″med-ĭ-ka′shun). Preliminary medication, particularly internal medication to produce narcosis prior to inhalation anesthesia.

premeiotic (pre″mi-ot′ik) [*pre-* + Gr. *meioun* to decrease]. Occurring before or pertaining to the time preceding meiosis.

premenarchal (pre″mĕ-nar′kal). Pertaining to the period before menstruation is established; occurring prior to the menarche.

premenstrua (pre-men′stroo-ah). Plural of *premenstruum.*

premenstrual (pre-men′stroo-al). Occurring before menstruation.

premenstruum (pre-men′stroo-um), pl. *premenstrua* [L.]. The period immediately preceding occurrence of the menstrual flow.

premitotic (pre″mi-tot′ik). Occurring before or pertaining to the time preceding mitosis.

premolar (pre-mo′lar) [*pre-* + L. *molaris* molar]. Situated in front of the molar teeth. See under *tooth.*

premonitory (pre-mon′ĭ-to-re) [L. *praemonitorius*]. Serving as a warning.

premonocyte (pre-mon′o-sīt). Promonocyte.

premorbid (pre-mor′bid). Occurring before the development of disease.

premortal (pre-mor′tal). Occurring just before death.

premunition (pre″mu-nish′un). 1. Measures taken to secure prevention. 2. Relative immunity; infection immunity; a state of resistance to infection which is established after an acute infection has become chronic and which lasts as long as the infecting organisms remain in the body.

premunitive (pre-mu′nĭ-tiv). Pertaining to or produced by preventive vaccination.

premycosic (pre″mi-ko′sik). Pertaining to a mycotic disease at a stage prior to the maturity of its fungal element.

premyeloblast (pre-mi′ĕ-lo-blast). An early precursor of a myelocyte: it develops first into a myeloblast.

premyelocyte (pre-mi′ĕ-lo-sīt). Promyelocyte.

prenarcosis (pre″nar-ko′sis). Narcosis induced as a preliminary to full general anesthesia or previous to local anesthesia.

prenarcotic (pre″nar-kot′ik). Previous to the occurrence of narcosis.

prenares (pre-na′rēz). The nostrils.

prenasale (pre″na-sa′le). A cephalometric landmark, the most projecting point, in the midsagittal plane, at the tip of the nose.

prenatal (pre-na′tal) [*pre-* + L. *natalis* natal]. Existing or occurring before birth.

preneoplastic (pre″ne-o-plas′tik). Before the development or existence of a tumor.

preoblongata (pre″ob-long-ga′tah). That part of the oblongata which lies between the fourth ventricle and the pons.

preoperative (pre-op′er-a″tiv). Preceding an operation.

preoptic (pre-op′tik). Situated anterior to the optic lobes.

preopticus (pre-op′tĭ-kus) [*pre-* + L. *opticus* optic]. Colliculus superior laminae tecti.

preoral (pre-o′ral) [*pre-* + L. *os* mouth]. Situated in front of the mouth, or cranial to it.

preoxygenation (pre-ok″sĭ-jen-a′shun). The prolonged breathing of oxygen before exposure to low atmospheric pressure at high altitudes, as prophylaxis against decompression sickness.

prepalatal (pre-pal′ah-tal). Situated in front of the palate.

prepallium (pre-pal′e-um). The portion of the cortex of the cerebrum anterior to the sulcus centralis.

preparalytic (pre″par-ah-lit′ik). Preceding the appearance of paralysis.

preparation (prep″ah-ra′shun) [L. *praeparatio*]. 1. The act or process of making ready. 2. A medicine made ready for use. 3. An anatomical or pathologic specimen made ready and preserved for study. **allergenic protein p's,** extracts of various substances such as pollens, foods, dusts, etc., that are used for the diagnosis, prophylaxis and desensitization in allergic cases. **cavity p.,** the removal of carious tissue and the shaping of the cavity in a tooth preliminary to insertion of filling material. **corrosion p.,** an anatomical preparation made by injecting the parts to be retained and eating away the rest of the tissues with some corrosive substance. **Dover's p.,** an ointment of citronella in petroleum jelly for use as a mosquito repellent. **Ehrlich-Hata p.,** arsphenamine. **Hata p.,** arsphenamine. **heart-lung p.,** an animal prepared for the study of the action of the heart muscle. The perfused fluid flows through an unaltered pulmonic circle. **impression p.,** a preparation of bacteria on a slide for examination, made by lightly touching a coverglass to a colony. **klatsch p.,** impression p. **p. 2020,** a synthetic compound that raises the blood pressure by direct action on the blood vessels. It is trimethoxybenzyl-dihydroimidazole hydrochloride.

preparative (pre-par′ah-tiv). Amboceptor.

preparator (prep′ah-ra″tor). Amboceptor.

prepartal (pre-par′tal) [*pre-* + L. *partus* labor]. Occurring before, or just previous to, labor.

prepatellar (pre″pah-tel′ar). Situated in front of the patella.

prepatent (pre-pa′tent). Before becoming apparent or manifest. In malariology the term is applied to the period elapsing between infection and appearance of parasites in blood.

prepeduncle (pre-pe′dung-k′l). The anterior peduncle of the cerebellum.

preperception (pre″per-sep′shun). In psychology, anticipation of a perception.

preperforative (pre-per′fo-ra″tiv). Before the occurrence of perforation.

preperforatum (pre″per-fo-ra′tum). Substantia perforata anterior.

preperitoneal (pre″per-ĭ-to-ne′al). Situated in front of the peritoneum.

prephthisis (pre-thi′sis). The initial stages of pulmonary phthisis.

preplacental (pre″plah-sen′tal). Previous to the formation of the placenta.

preponderance (pre-pon′der-ans) [*pre-* + L. *pondere* to weigh]. The condition of having greater weight, force, or influence. **ventricular p.,** disproportionate development between the ventricles of the heart: diagnosed by the electrocardiograph.

prepontile (pre-pon′tēl). In front of the pons.

prepotency (pre-po′ten-se) [L. *praepotentia*]. Power superior to that of the other parent in transmitting inheritable characters to the offspring.

prepotent (pre-po′tent) [L. *praepotens*]. Having superior force; having greater power than the other parent in transmitting inheritable characters to the offspring.

preprophage (pre-pro′fāj) [*pre-* + *prophage*]. A postulated stage in the life cycle of a temperate bacteriophage, occurring after infection of a bacterium and before establishment of the prophage.

prepuberal (pre-pu′ber-al). Prepubertal.

prepubertal (pre-pu′ber-tal). Occurring before puberty; pertaining to the period of accelerated growth preceding gonadal maturity.

prepuberty (pre-pu′ber-te). The period preceding puberty.

prepubescence (pre″pu-bes′ens). Prepuberty.

prepubescent (pre″pu-bes′ent). Prepuberal.

prepuce (pre′pūs). A covering fold of skin; often used alone to designate the preputium penis. **p. of clitoris,** preputium clitoridis. **p. of penis,** preputium penis.

preputial (pre-pu′shal). Pertaining to the prepuce.

preputiotomy (pre-pu″she-ot′o-me) [*preputium* + Gr. *tomē* a cutting]. Incision of the preputium penis on the dorsum or side of the penis, to relieve the constriction in phimosis.

preputium (pre-pu′she-um). A covering fold of skin, as the preputium penis. **p. clitor′idis** [N A], a fold formed by the union of the labia minora anterior with the clitoris. Called also *prepuce of clitoris*. **p. pe′nis** [N A], the fold of skin covering the glans penis. Called also *prepuce of penis* and *foreskin*.

prepyloric (pre″pi-lor′ik). In front of the pylorus.

prepyramidal (pre″pi-ram′ĭ-dal). Situated in front of the pyramid.

preramus (pre-ra′mus). The vertical branch of the stem of the arbor vitae of the cerebellum.

prerectal (pre-rek′tal). Situated in front of the rectum.

prerenal (pre-re′nal). In front of the kidney.

prereproductive (pre″re-pro-duk′tiv). Pertaining to childhood, or the stage preceding puberty.

preretinal (pre-ret′ĭ-nal). In front of the retina.

presby- (pres′be) [Gr. *presbys* old]. Combining form meaning old or denoting relationship to old age.

presbyacusia (pres″be-ah-ku′se-ah). Presbycusis.

presbyatrics (pres-be-at′riks) [*presby-* + Gr. *iatrikē* surgery, medicine]. Geriatrics.

presbycardia (pres″bĭ-kar′de-ah). Disease of the heart occurring as the result of the aging process, occurring in association with recognizable changes of senescence in the body and in the absence of convincing evidence of other forms of heart disease.

presbycusis (pres″be-ku′sis) [*presby-* + Gr. *akousis* hearing]. A progressive, bilaterally symmetrical perceptive hearing loss occurring with age.

presbyope (pres′be-ōp) [*presby-* + Gr. *ōps* eye]. One who is presbyopic.

presbyophrenia (pres″be-o-fre′ne-ah) [*presby-* + Gr. *phrēn* mind + *-ia*]. A mental condition often seen in old age, consisting of defective memory, loss of sense of location, and confabulation. Called also *Wernicke's syndrome*.

presbyopia (pres″be-o′pe-ah) [*presby-* + Gr. *ōps* eye + *-ia*]. Hyperopia; long sight and impairment of vision due to advancing years or to old age. It is dependent on diminution of the power of accommodation from loss of elasticity of the crystalline lens, causing the near point of distinct vision to be removed farther from the eye.

presbyopic (pres″be-op′ik). Pertaining to presbyopia.

presbysphacelus (pres″be-sfas′ĕ-lus) [*presby-* + Gr. *sphakelos* gangrene]. Senile gangrene.

presbytia (pres-bish′e-ah). Presbyopia.

presbytism (pres′bĭ-tizm). Presbyopia.

prescapula (pre-skap′u-lah). The suprascapular portion of the scapula.

prescapular (pre-skap′u-lar). 1. In front of the scapula. 2. Pertaining to the prescapula.

presclerosis (pre″skle-ro′sis). A state of arterial hypertension preceding arteriosclerosis.

presclerotic (pre″skle-rot′ik). Occurring before sclerosis takes place.

prescribe (pre-skrīb′) [L. *praescribere* to write before]. To designate in writing a remedy for administration.

prescription (pre-skrip′shun) [L. *praescriptio*]. A written direction for the preparation and administration of a remedy. A prescription consists of the heading or *superscription*—that is, the symbol ℞ or the word Recipe, meaning "take"; the *inscription*, which contains the names and quantities of the ingredients; the *subscription*, or directions for compounding; and the *signature*, usually introduced by the sign S. for *sig′na*, "mark," which gives the directions for the patient which are to be marked on the receptacle. **shotgun p.,** an irrational prescription that contains a number of ingredients given with the idea that one or more of them may be effective.

presecretin (pre″se-kre′tin). A substance existing in the mucous membrane of the duodenum from which, by the action of hydrochloric acid, secretin is split off.

presegmenter (pre″seg-men′ter). A full-grown malarial parasite in the stage in which the pigment is accumulated into masses just previous to segmentation.

presenile (pre-se′nil). Pertaining to a condition resembling senility, but occurring in early or middle life.

presenility (pre″se-nil′ĭ-te). Premature old age.

presenium (pre-se′ne-um). The period immediately preceding old age.

present (pre-zent′) [L. *praesentare* to show]. To appear, or to show; as to appear first at the os uteri, said of various parts of the fetus.

presentation (pre″zen-ta′shun) [L. *praesentatio*]. In obstetrics, the presenting part; that portion of the fetus which is touched by the examining finger through the cervix, or, during labor, is bounded by the girdle of resistance. Cf. *position*. **breech p.,** presentation of the buttocks of the fetus in labor. **breech p., complete,** presentation of the buttocks of the fetus in labor, with the feet alongside of the buttocks, the fetus being in the same attitude as in vertex presentation, but with polarity reversed. **breech p., double,** complete breech p. **breech p., frank,** presentation of the buttocks of the fetus in labor, with the legs extended against the trunk and the feet lying against the face. **breech p., incomplete,** presentation of the fetus in labor, with one or both feet or one or both knees of the fetus prolapsed into the maternal vagina. **breech p., single,** frank breech p. **brow p.,** presentation of the fetal brow in labor. **cephalic p.,** presentation of any part of the fetal head in labor, including occiput, brow, and face. **compound p.,** prolapse of an extremity of the fetus (an arm or leg, or both), alongside the head, or of one or both arms alongside a presenting breech, at the beginning of labor. **face p.,** the presentation of the face of the fetus in labor. **footling p.,** presentation of the fetus in labor with one (single footling) or both feet (double footling) prolapsed into the maternal vagina. **funis p.,** presentation of the umbilical cord in labor. **longitudinal p.,** presentation of the cephalic or pelvic end of the fetal ellipse in labor. **oblique p.,** presentation of the fetus in labor with the fetal cylinder oblique to the maternal spine. **parietal p.,** presentation of the parietal portion of the fetal head in labor. **pelvic p.,** breech p. **placental p.,** placenta praevia. **polar p.,** longitudinal p. **shoulder p.,** presentation of the fetal shoulder in labor. **torso p.,** transverse p. **transverse p.,** presentation of the fetus in labor with the long axis of the fetal body crossing the long axis of the maternal body. **trunk p.,** transverse p. **vertex p.,** the presentation of the vertex of the fetal head in labor.

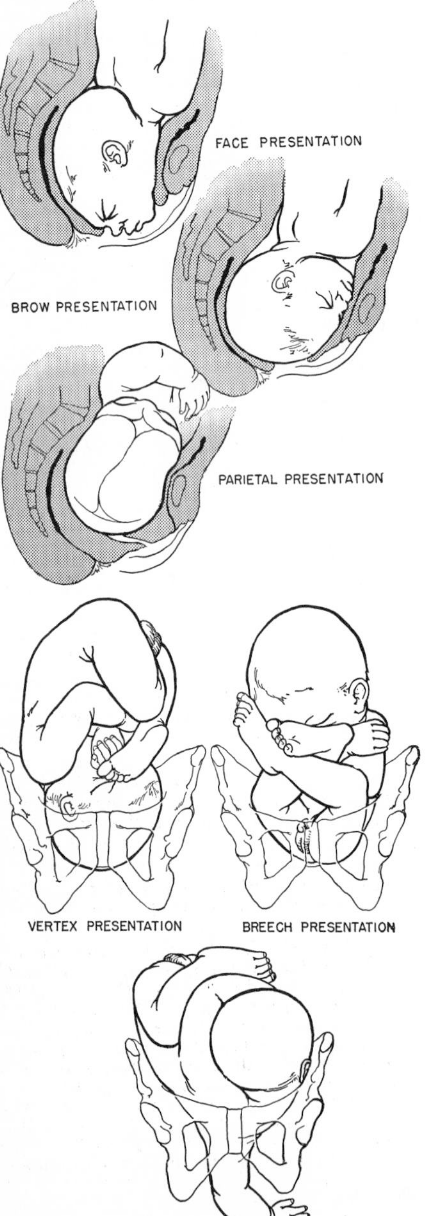

preservative (pre-zer′vah-tiv). "A substance or preparation added to a product for the purpose of destroying or inhibiting the multiplication of microorganisms" (Council on Pharmacy and Chemistry).

presomite (pre-so′mit) [*pre-* + *somite*]. Referring to embryos before the appearance of somites.

prespermatid (pre-sper′mah-tid). A secondary spermatocyte.

presphenoid (pre-sfe′noid). The anterior portion of the body of the sphenoid bone.

presphygmic (pre-sfig′mik). Occurring before the pulse wave. See under *period*.

prespinal (pre-spi′nal). Situated in front of the spine.

prespondylolisthesis (pre-spon″dĭ-lo-lis-the′sis). A congenital defect in the last lumbar vertebra consisting in a bilateral defect in the neural arches at the pedicles.

pressinervoscopy (pres″ĭ-ner-vos′ko-pe). Diagnosis of thoracic and abdominal disease by pressure upon the pneumogastric and sympathetic nerves (A. Pinel).

pressometer (pres-som′e-ter). A manometer for measuring pressure. **Jarcho p.,** an instrument specially designed for measuring pressure during injection of radiopaque material into the uterus in hysterosalpingography.

pressor (pres′or). Tending to increase blood pressure, as a pressor substance.

pressoreceptive (pres″o-re-sep′tiv). Sensitive to stimuli due to vasomotor activity, such as blood pressure.

pressoreceptor (pres″o-re-sep′tor). A receptor or nerve ending sensitive to stimuli of vasomotor activity.

pressosensitive (pres″o-sen′sĭ-tiv). Pressoreceptive.

pressure (presh′ur) [L. *pressura*]. Stress or strain, whether by compression, pull, thrust, or shear.

after p., a sense of pressure which lasts for a short period after removal of the actual pressure. **arterial p.**, the pressure of the blood within the arteries. **atmospheric p.**, the pressure exerted by the atmosphere. It is about 15 pounds to the square inch at the level of the sea. **back p.**, the pressure caused by the damming back of the blood in a heart chamber due to a damaged heart valve and considered to be a factor in causing cardiac dilatation. **biting p.**, occlusal p. **blood p.**, the pressure of the blood on the walls of the arteries, dependent on the energy of the heart action, the elasticity of the walls of the arteries, the resistance in the capillaries, and the volume and viscosity of the blood. The maximum pressure occurs at the time of the systole of the left ventricle of the heart and is termed *maximum* or *systolic* pressure. The minimum pressure is felt at the diastole of the ventricle and is termed *minimum* or *diastolic* pressure. *basic blood pressure* is the pressure exerted on the blood by the contractile walls independently of the additional pressure due to the systolic contraction of the heart. *mean blood pressure* is half of the sum of the systolic and diastolic pressures. *static blood pressure* is the pressure present throughout the circulation when the heart has stopped. **brain p.**, the capillary venous pressure in the brain. **capillary p.**, the blood pressure in the capillaries. **cerebrospinal p.**, the pressure or tension of the cerebrospinal fluid: normally 100–150 mm. as measured by the manometer. **diastolic p.**, arterial pressure during diastole. **Donders' p.**, increase of manometric pressure with the instrument placed on the trachea on opening the chest of a dead body: due to collapse of the lung. **endocardial p.**, pressure of blood within the heart. **intra-abdominal p.**, the pressure of the viscera within the abdomen. **intracranial p.**, the pressure in the space between the skull and the brain, i.e., the pressure of the subarachnoidal fluid. **intraocular p.**, the pressure of the fluids of the eye against the tunics. It is produced by continual renewal of the fluids within the interior of the eye, and is altered in certain pathological conditions. It may be roughly estimated by palpation of the eye or measured, directly or indirectly, with a specially devised instrument, the tonometer. **intrapulmonic p.**, the air pressure within the lungs. **intrathecal p.**, pressure within a sheath; particularly the pressure of the cerebrospinal fluid within the subarachnoid membrane. **intrathoracic p.**, the pressure within the thorax, that is, the pressure in the pleural cavity and mediastinal spaces. **intraventricular p.**, the pressure within the ventricles of the heart. **negative p.**, a pressure less than that of the atmosphere. **occlusal p.**, pressure exerted on the occlusal surfaces of the teeth when the jaws are brought into apposition. **oncotic p.**, the osmotic pressure of colloids in a colloid system. **osmotic p.**, the pressure which brings about diffusion between solutions of different concentration or between a solute and the fluid in which it is dissolved. **osmotic p., effective**, that part of the total osmotic pressure of a solution which governs the tendency of its solvent to pass through a semipermeable bounding membrane or across another boundary. **partial p.**, the pressure exerted by each of the constituents of a mixture of gases. **pulse p.**, the difference between the systolic and diastolic pressures. **solution p.**, the force which tends to bring into solution the molecules of a solid contained in the solvent. **systolic p.**, arterial pressure during systole. **venous p.**, the blood pressure in the veins.

presternum (pre-ster′num). Manubrium sterni.

presubiculum (pre″su-bik′u-lum). The portion of the parahippocampal gyrus between the principal olfactory portion and the subiculum.

presumptive (pre-zump′tiv). Referring to the expected fate of an embryonic part on the basis of established fate mapping.

presuppurative (pre-sup′u-ra″tiv). Occurring before suppuration.

presylvian (pre-sil′ve-an). Pertaining to the anterior or ascending branch of the sylvian fissure (sulcus lateralis).

presymptom (pre-simp′tom). An indication which is a forerunner of the actual symptoms of a condition.

presymptomatic (pre″simp-to-mat′ik). Existing before the appearance of symptoms.

presynaptic (pre″sĭ-nap′tik). Situated proximal to a synapse, or occurring before the synapse is crossed.

presystole (pre-sis′to-le). The interval of time just preceding the systole.

presystolic (pre″sis-tol′ik) [*pre-* + *systole*]. 1. Pertaining to the beginning of the systole. 2. Occurring just before the systole.

pretarsal (pre-tar′sal). Situated in front of the tarsus.

prethyroideal, prethyroidean (pre″thi-roi′de-al, pre″thi-roi-de′an). Situated in front of the thyroid gland or thyroid cartilage.

pretibial (pre-tib′e-al). Situated in front of the tibia.

pretracheal (pre-tra′ke-al). Situated in front of the trachea.

pretuberculosis (pre″tu-ber″ku-lo′sis). Tuberculosis in an incipient and occult stage before any symptoms of the disease have appeared.

pretuberculous (pre″tu-ber′ku-lus). Preceding the development of tubercle.

pretympanic (pre″tim-pan′ik). Situated in front of the tympanum.

preurethritis (pre″u-re-thri′tis). Inflammation of a part of the vulvar follicles before the urethral orifice.

prevalence (prev′ah-lens). The number of cases of a disease in existence at a certain time in a designated area.

preventive (pre-ven′tiv). Serving to avert the occurrence of.

preventorium (pre″ven-to′re-um). An institution where patients are confined for the purpose of checking the systemic spread of disease.

preventriculosis (pre″ven-trik″u-lo′sis) [*pre-* + *ventriculus* stomach + *-osis*]. Closing of the cardiac opening of the stomach due to the action of the esophageal muscular fibers or of the periesophageal diaphragmatic structures. Called also *preventricular stenosis*.

preventriculus (pre″ven-trik′u-lus). The cardiac opening of the stomach (ostium cardiacum ventriculi [N A]).

prevermis (pre-ver′mis). The superior vermis of the cerebellum.

prevertebral (pre-ver′te-bral). Situated in front of a vertebra.

prevertiginous (pre″ver-tij′ĭ-nus). Having the sense of being pushed from behind.

prevesical (pre-ves′ĭ-kal) [*pre-* + L. *vesica* bladder]. Situated in front of the bladder.

previable (pre-vi′ah-b′l). Not yet viable: said of a fetus incapable of extrauterine existence.

previtamin (pre-vi′tah-min). A precursor of a vitamin. **p. H**, carotene.

Prévost's law, sign (pra-vōz′) [Jean Louis *Prévost*, Swiss physician, 1838–1927]. See under *law* and *sign*.

Preyer's reflex, test (pri-erz) [Wilhelm Thierry *Preyer*, German physiologic chemist and physiologist, 1841–1897]. See under *reflex* and *tests*.

prezone (pre′zōn). Prozone.

prezygapophysis (pre″zi-gah-pof′ĭ-sis). Processus articularis superior vertebrarum.

prezygotic (pre-zi-got′ik). Occurring, or determined by events occurring, before union of the gametes, that is, before conception, or formation of the zygote.

prezymogen (pre-zi′mo-jen). A substance existing in the cell which becomes converted into zymogen.

priapism (pri′ah-pizm) [L. *priapismus;* Gr. *priapismos*]. Persistent abnormal erection of the penis, usually without sexual desire. It is seen in diseases and injuries of the spinal cord, and may be caused by vesical calculus and certain injuries to the penis.

priapitis (pri″ah-pi′tis). Inflammation of the penis.

priapus (pri′ah-pus). The penis.

Price-Jones curve, method [Cecil *Price-Jones,* English physician, 1863–1943]. See under *curve.*

Priessnitz bandage, compress (prēs′nitz) [Vincent *Priessnitz,* a Silesian farmer, 1799–1852]. A cold wet compress.

Priestley's mass (prēst′lēz) [Joseph *Priestley,* English naturalist, the discoverer of oxygen, 1733–1804]. See under *mass.*

primal (pri′mal). A hair dye consisting of a solution of para-toluylene-di-amine with neutral sulfites.

primaquine (pri′mah-kwin). Chemical name: 8-(4-amino-1-methylbutylamino)-6-methoxyquinoline: used as an antimalarial agent.

primary (pri′ma-re) [L. *primarius* principal; *primus* first]. First in order; principal.

primate (pri′māt). An individual belonging to the order Primates.

Primates (pri-ma′tēz) [L. *primus* first]. The highest order of mammals, including man, apes, monkeys, and lemurs.

primaverose (pri-mav′er-ōs). A disaccharide, 6-xylosido glucose, $C_{11}H_{20}O_{10}$, from *Primula officinalis.*

primer (prĭm′er). A substance which prepares for or facilitates the action of another. **cavity p.,** a material which is used to increase the ability of resin material to adhere to the cavity wall.

primerite (pri′mer-īt) [L. *primus* first + Gr. *meros* part]. The anterior part of a cephalont. Cf. *deutomerite.*

primidone (pri′mĭ-dōn). Chemical name: 5-ethyldihydro-5-phenyl-4,6(1H5H)-pyrimidinedione: used as an anticonvulsant.

primigravid (pri″mĭ-grav′id). Pregnant for the first time.

primigravida (pri″mĭ-grav′ĭ-dah) [L. *prima* first + *gravida* pregnant]. A woman pregnant for the first time. Also written Gravida I.

primipara (pri-mip′ah-rah), pl. *primip′arae* [L. *prima* first + *parere* to bring forth, produce]. A woman who has had one pregnancy which resulted in a viable child, regardless of whether the child was living at birth, and regardless of whether it was a single or multiple birth. Also written Para I.

primiparity (pri″mĭ-par′ĭ-te). The condition or fact of being a primipara.

primiparous (pri-mip′ah-rus). Bearing or having borne but one child.

primite (pri′mīt). Protomerite.

primitiae (pri-mish′e-e) [L. pl., "first things"]. That part of the amniotic fluid discharged before the fetus is extruded.

primitive (prim′ĭ-tiv) [L. *primitivus*]. First in point of time; existing in a simple form, or showing little evolution.

primordial (pri-mor′de-al) [L. *primordialis*]. Original or primitive; of the simplest and most undeveloped character.

primordium (pri-mor′de-um), pl. *primor′dia* [L. "the beginning"]. The earliest discernible indication during embryonic development of an organ or part. Called also *anlage* or *rudiment.*

primverose (prim′ver-ōs). A disaccharide occurring in zein.

prinadol (prin′ah-dol). Trade mark for a preparation of phenazocine.

princeps (prin′seps) [L.]. Principal; chief.

principle (prin′sĭ-p′l) [L. *principium*]. 1. A chemical component. 2. A substance on which certain of the properties of a drug depend. 3. A law of conduct. **active p.,** any constituent of a drug which helps to confer upon it a medicinal property. **anti-anemia p.,** the constituent in liver and certain other tissues that produces the hematopoietic effect in pernicious anemia. **anti-insulin p.,** glycotropic p. **follicle-stimulating p.,** prolan A. **glycotropic p.,** a substance from the pituitary gland which antagonizes the hypoglycemic action of insulin both in the liver and in the peripheral tissues. **hematinic p.,** anti-anemia principle. **immediate p.,** any one of the more or less complex substances of definite chemical constitution into which a heterogeneous substance can be readily resolved. **luteinizing p.,** prolan B. **p's of medical ethics,** a set of rules adopted by the American Medical Association for the guidance of physicians in their professional relations. **organic p.,** immediate p. **pleasure p.,** the automatic instinct or tendency to avoid pain and secure pleasure. **proximate p.,** immediate p. **reality p.,** the mental activity which develops to control the pleasure principle under the pressure of necessity or the demands of reality. **ultimate p.,** a chemical element.

Pringle's disease (pring′g'lz) [John James *Pringle,* British dermatologist, 1855–1922]. Adenoma sebaceum.

Prinos (pri′nos) [Gr. *prinos* oak]. A genus or subgenus of aquifoliaceous shrubs, commonly assigned to the genus *Ilex* (holly). *P. verticilla′tus,* the black alder, or winterberry, of North America, has a tonic and astringent bark.

priodax (pri′o-daks). Trade mark for a preparation of iodoalphionic acid.

Prior-Finkler spirillum, vibrio (pri′or-fink′-ler). *Vibrio proteus.*

priscoline (pris′ko-lēn). Trade mark for preparations of tolazoline.

prism (prizm) [Gr. *prisma*]. A solid with a triangular or polygonal cross section. A triangular prism splits up a ray of light into its constituent colors, and turns or deflects light rays toward its base. Prisms are used to correct deviations of the eyes, since they alter the apparent situation of objects. **adamantine p's, enamel p's,** prismata adamantina. **Maddox p.,** two prisms with their bases together: used in testing for torsion of the eyeball. **Nicol p.,** two slabs of Iceland spar cemented together and deflecting a ray of light in such a way that it is split in two, one part (the ordinary ray) being totally reflected and the other (polarized ray) passing through. **Risley's p.,** a prism which rotates in a metal frame marked with a scale: used in testing ocular muscles for imbalance.

prisma (priz′mah), pl. *pris′mata* [Gr.]. Prism. **pris′mata adaman′tina** [N A, B N A], the microscopic prisms or columns, arranged perpendicular to the surface, that make up the enamel of the teeth. Called also *enamel prisms.*

prismata (priz′mah-tah). Plural of *prisma.*

prismatic (priz-mat′ik). Shaped like a prism; produced by a prism.

prismoid (priz′moid). Resembling a prism.

prismoptometer (priz″mop-tom′e-ter) [*prism* + *optometer*]. An instrument for testing the eye by means of a revolving prism.

prismosphere (priz′mo-sfēr) [*prism* + *sphere*]. A prism combined with a globular lens.

prisoptometer (priz″op-tom′e-ter). Prismoptometer.

privine (pri′vēn). Trade mark for preparations of naphazoline.

p.r.n. Abbreviation for L. *pro re na′ta,* according as circumstances may require.

pro- [L., Gr. *pro* before]. Prefix signifying before or in front of.

proaccelerin (pro″ak-sel′er-in). Factor V. See under *coagulation factors*.

pro-actinium (pro″ak-tin′e-um). Protactinium.

Proactinomyces (pro″ak-tĭ-no-mi′sēz). A name formerly given a genus of microorganisms.

proactinomycin (pro-ak″tĭ-no-mi′sin). An antibiotic substance from cultures of *Nocardia gardneri*, which acts strongly against gram-positive bacilli.

proactivator (pro-ak′tĭ-va″tor). The precursor of an activator, or a factor that reacts with an enzyme to form an activator; applied to a substance present in plasma (*plasminogen proactivator*), which is absorbed onto fibrin during clotting and which, when activated, will convert plasminogen to plasmin.

proagglutinoid (pro″ah-gloo′tĭ-noid). An agglutinoid that has a stronger affinity for the agglutinogen than has the agglutinin.

proal (pro′al). Characterized by forward movement.

proamnion (pro-am′ne-on). That part of the embryonal area at the front and side of the head which remains without mesoderm for some time.

pro-antithrombin (pro″an-te-throm′bin). A substance present in blood plasm and blood serum which is converted into antithrombin by a reaction with heparin.

proarrhythmic (pro″ah-rith′mik). 1. Tending to produce cardiac arrhythmia. 2. An agent that tends to produce cardiac arrhythmia.

proatlas (pro-at′las). A rudimentary vertebra which in some animals lies in front of the atlas: sometimes seen as an anomaly in man.

proazamine (pro-az′ah-mēn). Promethazine.

proband (pro′band) [Ger.; from L. *probare* to prove]. Propositus.

probang (pro′bang). A flexible rod with a ball, tuft, or sponge at the end: used in diseases of the esophagus or larynx. **ball p.,** a probang with a ball or bulb at the end. **bristle p., horse hair p.,** one with an expansible tuft of bristles or horse hairs at the end. **sponge p.,** one which is tufted with sponge at the end.

pro-banthine (pro-ban-thīn′). Trade mark for preparations of propantheline bromide.

probarbital (pro-bar′bĭ-tal). Chemical name: 5-ethyl-5-isopropylbarbiturate: used as a sedative and hypnotic.

probe (prōb) [L. *proba; probare* to test]. A slender, flexible instrument designed for introduction into a wound or cavity for purposes of exploration. **Amussat's p.,** a probe used in lithotrity. **Anel's p.,** a delicate probe for the lacrimal puncta and canals. **blunt p.,** a probe with a blunt end. **Bowman's p.,** one of a set of probes for use on the nasal ducts. **Brackett's p's,** delicate and flexible probes of silver wire for exploring dental fistulas. **bullet p.,** one used for detecting the presence or determining the location of a bullet. **drum p.,** a probe with an attachment which emits a sound when it comes in contact with a foreign body. **electric p.,** one which on contact with a foreign body completes an electric circuit, so that a sound is made. **eyed p.,** one with a slit for a ligature or tape near one end. **Fluhrer's p.,** an aluminum probe for examining gunshot wounds of the brain. **Girdner's p.,** an electric probe. **lacrimal p.,** one designed for use on the tear passages. **Lente's p.,** a silver probe having a bulb coated with silver nitrate. **Lilienthal's p.,** an apparatus for probing for bullets. It consists of a probe composed of two or four pieces of metal attached to two insulated copper wires which run to a mouth piece composed of two plates, one of copper and one of zinc. These plates are applied to the side of the tongue and the probe inserted in the wound. If the probe touches a bullet, a distinct metallic taste is perceived. **Lucae's p.,** a probe in a hollow handle and operated by a spring, to apply massage in treating catarrhal otitis media. **meerschaum p.,** a probe with a meerschaum tip, which on contact with a leaden bullet becomes darkened. **Nélaton's p.,** a bullet probe with an unglazed porcelain head. **pocket p.,** a dental instrument having a tapered, rodlike blade with a blunt, rounded tip and graduated in millimeters, used to measure the depth and determine the outline of a periodontal pocket. **scissors p.,** a long, delicate pair of scissors that can be used as a probe. **telephonic p.,** electric probe. **uterine p.,** a probe for uterine exploration. **vertebrated p.,** a flexible probe made up of joined links. **wire p.,** a probe of steel wire.

probenecid (pro-ben′e-sid). Chemical name: p-(dipropylsulfamyl)benzoic acid: used as a uricosuric agent.

probit (pro′bit). The normal deviate of the gaussian curve plus 5, the addition being made to avoid the use of negative numbers in the calculation of a 50 per cent end-point by the probit method. See also under *method.*

procainamide (pro-kān′ah-mīd). Chemical name: p-amino-N-(2-diethylaminoethyl)benzamide: used in treatment of cardiac arrhythmia.

procaine (pro′kān). Chemical name: 2-diethylaminoethyl-p-aminobenzoate: used as a local anesthetic.

procallus (pro-kal′us). The granulation tissue formed about the site of fracture of a bone, which develops into callus.

procarboxypeptidase (pro″kar-bok″se-pep′tĭ-dās). The inactive precursor of carboxypeptidase, which is converted to the active enzyme by the action of trypsin.

procatarctic (pro″kah-tark′tik). Predisposing: said of a cause of disease.

procatarxis (pro″kah-tark′sis) [Gr. *prokatarxis* a first beginning]. 1. A predisposing cause. 2. Predisposition. 3. The production of a disease partially as a result of predisposition.

procedure (pro-se′dūr) [L. *procedere*, from *pro* forward + *cedere* move]. A series of steps by which a desired result is accomplished.

procelous (pro-se′lus) [*pro-* + Gr. *koilos* hollow]. Concave on the anterior surface: applied to the vertebrae of certain animals.

procephalic (pro″se-fal′ik) [*pro-* + Gr. *kephalē* head]. Pertaining to the anterior part of the head.

procercoid (pro-ser′koid). One of the larval stages of fish tapeworms.

procerus (pro-se′rus) [L.]. Long; slender.

process (pros′es) [L. *processus*]. 1. A prominence or projection, as of bone. For names of specific anatomical structures, see official Latinized terms under *processus.* 2. A series of operations leading to the achievement of a specific result; used also as a verb to designate subjection to such a series of operations designed to produce desired changes in the original material, or achieve other result. **A.B.C. p.** See under *method.* **accessory p. of sacrum, spurious,** crista sacralis lateralis. **acromial p., acromion p.,** acromion scapulae. **acute p. of helix,** spina helicis. **alar p. of sacrum,** crista sacralis lateralis. **aliform p. of sphenoid bone,** ala minor ossis sphenoidalis. **anconeal p. of ulna,** olecranon. **angular p. of frontal bone, external,** processus zygomaticus ossis frontalis. **articular p. of axis, anterior,** facies articularis anterior axis. **articular p. of coccyx, false,** cornu coccygeum. **articular p. of sacrum, spurious,** crista sacralis intermedia. **ascending p's of vertebrae.** See *processus articularis superior vertebrarum.* **axis-cylinder p.,** axon. **Beccari p.,** a method of garbage disposal involving bacterial fermentation in closed cells. **p. of Blumenbach,** processus uncinatus ossis ethmoidalis. **capitular p.,** the articular process on a vertebra for the head of a rib. **p. of cartilage of nasal septum, posterior,** processus posterior sphenoidalis. **Civinini's p. of external pterygoid plate,** processus pterygospinosus. **condyloid p. of vertebrae, inferior,**

processus articularis inferior vertebrarum. **condyloid p. of vertebrae, superior,** processus articularis superior vertebrarum. **conoid p.,** impressio ligamenti costoclavicularis. **cubital p. of humerus.** See *trochlea humeri* and *capitulum humeri.* **Deiters' p.,** axon. **dental p.,** processus alveolaris maxillae. **dentoid p. of axis,** dens axis. **descending p's of vertebrae.** See *processus articularis inferior vertebrarum.* **ensiform p. of sphenoid bone,** ala minor ossis sphenoidalis. **ensiform p. of sternum,** processus xiphoideus. **epiphyseal p.,** epiphysis. **ethmoidal p. of Macalister,** crista sphenoidalis. **falciform p. of cerebellum,** falx cerebelli. **falciform p. of cerebrum,** falx cerebri. **falciform p. of fascia lata,** margo falciformis hiatus saphenus. **falciform p. of fascia pelvis,** arcus tendineus fasciae pelvis. **falciform p. of rectus abdominis muscle,** falx inguinalis. **floccular p.,** flocculus. **folian p., p. of Folius,** processus anterior mallei. **frontal p., external,** spina nasalis ossis frontalis. **frontonasal p.,** an expansive facial process in the embryo, which develops into the forehead and bridge of the nose. **Gottstein's basal p.,** any attenuated basal process connecting the basilar membrane of the organ of Corti with an outer hair cell. **Gowers' intermediate p.,** the lateral horn of gray substance of the spinal cord. **greater p. of ethmoid bone, hamate p. of ethmoid bone,** processus uncinatus ossis ethmoidalis. **hamular p. of lacrimal bone,** hamulus lacrimalis. **hamular p. of sphenoid bone,** hamulus pterygoideus. **hamular p. of unciform bone,** hamulus ossis hamati. **head p.,** an axial strand of cells in the embryo extending forward from the primitive knot; called also *notochordal plate.* **inframalleolar p. of calcaneus,** trochlea peronealis calcanei. **Ingrassias' p.,** ala minor ossis sphenoidalis. **intercondylar p. of tibia,** eminentia intercondylaris. **internal p. of humerus,** processus supracondylaris humeri. **jugular p. of occipital bone, lateral,** processus paramastoideus ossis occipitalis. **jugular p. of occipital bone, middle,** processus intrajugularis ossis occipitalis. **jugular p. of occipital bone, posterior, of Krause,** processus paramastoideus ossis occipitalis. **lateral p. of calcaneus,** sustentaculum tali. **MacLachlan's p.** See under *method.* **malar p.,** processus zygomaticus maxillae. **mamillary p's of sacrum, oblique.** See *crista sacralis intermedia.* **mamillary p. of temporal bone,** processus mastoideus ossis temporalis. **mandibular p.,** one of the processes formed by bifurcation of the first branchial arch in the embryo, which unites ventrally with its fellow to form the lower jaw. **marginal p. of malar bone,** tuberculum marginale ossis zygomatici. **maxillary p.,** one of the processes formed by bifurcation of the first branchial arch in the embryo, which joins with the ipsilateral median nasal process in the formation of the upper jaw. **mental p.,** protuberantia mentalis. **nasal p., lateral,** one of the two limbs of the horseshoe-shaped elevation bounding a nasal pit in the embryo, which participates in formation of the side and wing of the nose. **nasal p., median,** one of the two limbs of the horseshoe-shaped elevation bounding a nasal pit in the embryo, which participates with the ipsilateral maxillary process in forming half of the upper jaw. **nasal p. of frontal bone,** pars nasalis ossis frontalis. **nasal p. of inferior turbinate bone,** processus lacrimalis conchae nasalis inferioris. **oblique p. of vertebrae, inferior,** processus articularis inferior vertebrarum. **oblique p. of vertebrae, superior,** processus articularis superior vertebrarum. **occipital p. of occipital bone,** pars basilaris ossis occipitalis. **odontoid p. of axis,** dens axis. **olecranon p. of ulna,** olecranon. **olivary p.,** tuberculum sellae turcicae. **palatine p., lateral,** a shelflike projection developing from each maxillary process region of the upper jaw in the embryo, later fusing with each other and with the nasal septum to form the palate. **palatine p., median,** a shelflike projection developing from each median nasal process in the embryo, which participates with its fellow in forming the premaxillary portion of the upper jaw. **palpebral p.,** pars palpebralis glandulae lacrimalis. **paracondyloid p. of occipital bone, paroccipital p. of occipital bone,** processus paramastoideus ossis occipitalis. **petrosal p., anterior,** lingula sphenoidalis. **petrosal p., middle,** processus clinoideus medius. **petrosal p., posterior superior,** processus clinoideus posterior. **Rau's p., ravian p.,** processus anterior mallei. **restiform p. of Henle,** pedunculus cerebellaris inferior. **Riedel's p.,** a strap-shaped process of the liver sometimes developed over the gallbladder in cholelithiasis. **small p. of Soemmering,** tuberculum marginale ossis zygomatici. **spinous p.,** a slender, more or less sharp-pointed projection. See under *spina.* **spinous p. of sacrum, spurious,** crista sacralis mediana. **spinous p. of tibia.** 1. Eminentia intercondylaris. 2. Tuberculum intercondylare mediale. **spinous p. of vertebrae,** processus spinosus vertebrarum. **Stieda's p.,** processus posterior tali. **styloid p. of fibula,** apex capitis fibulae. **sucker p.** See under *foot.* **synovial p.,** plica synovialis. **temporal p. of mandible,** processus coronoideus mandibulae. **Todd's p.** See *fibrae intercrurales.* **Tomes' p.,** a process from an enamel cell, around which calcification occurs. **transverse p. of sacrum,** crista sacralis lateralis. **transverse p. of vertebrae, accessory,** processus accessorius vertebrarum lumbalium. **trochlear p. of calcaneus,** trochlea peronealis calcanei. **unciform p. of scapula,** processus coracoideus scapulae. **uncinate p. of lacrimal bone,** hamulus lacrimalis. **uncinate p. of unciform bone,** hamulus ossis hamati. **ungual p. of third phalanx of foot,** tuberositas phalangis distalis pedis. **vermiform p.,** appendix vermiformis. **vermiform p. of cerebellum,** vermis cerebelli. **xiphoid p. of sphenoid bone,** ala minor ossis sphenoidalis. **zygomatico-orbital p. of maxilla,** processus zygomaticus maxillae.

processus (pro-ses'sus), pl. *processus* [L.]. A prominence or projection; used in anatomical nomenclature as a general term to designate such a mass projecting from a larger structure. Called also *process.* **p. accesso'rii spur'ii,** crista sacralis lateralis. **p. accesso'rius vertebra'rum lumba'lium** [N A, B N A], a small nodule that projects backward from the posterior surface of the transverse process of a lumbar vertebra. It is situated lateral to and below the mamillary process and varies in size. Called also *accessory process of lumbar vertebrae.* **p. ala'ris os'sis ethmoida'lis** [B N A], ala cristae galli. **p. alveola'ris maxil'lae** [N A, B N A], the thick parabolically curved ridge that projects downward and forms the free lower border of the maxilla; it is in front of and lateral to the palatine process and it bears the teeth. Called also *alveolar process of maxilla.* **p. ante'rior mal'lei** [N A], **p. ante'rior mal'lei [Fo'lii]** [B N A], a slender process that arises from the anterior aspect of the neck of the malleus, passes forward and downward to the petrotympanic fissure, and is attached to the petrous portion of the temporal bone by ligamentous fibers. Called also *anterior process of malleus.* **p. articula'res inferio'res vertebra'rum** [B N A]. See *p. articularis inferior vertebrarum.* **p. articula'ris infe'rior vertebra'rum** [N A], a process on either side of the vertebrae, springing from the inferior surface of the arch near the junction of the lamina and pedicle; it bears a surface that faces anteriorly and inferiorly, articulating with the superior articular process of the vertebra below. Called also *inferior articular process of vertebrae.* **p. articula'ris supe'rior os'sis sa'cri** [N A, B N A], either of two processes projecting backward and medialward from the first sacral vertebra at the junctions between the body and the alae; they articulate with the inferior articular processes of the fifth lumbar vertebra. Called also *superior articular process of sacrum.* **p. articula′res superio′res vertebra′rum** [B N A]. See *p. articularis superior vertebrarum.* **p. articula′ris supe′rior vertebra′rum** [N A], a process on either side of the vertebrae, springing from the superior surface of the arch near the junction of the lamina and pedicle; it bears a surface that faces posteriorly and superiorly, articulating with the inferior articular process of the vertebra above. Called also *superior articular process of vertebrae.* **p. bre′vis in′cudis,** ligamentum incudis superius. **p. bre′vis mal′lei,** p. lateralis mallei. **p. cauda′tus hep′atis** [N A, B N A], the right of the two processes seen on the caudate lobe of the liver. Called also *caudate process.* **p. cilia′res** [N A, B N A], about 70 meridionally arranged ridges or folds projecting from the crown of the ciliary body. Called also *ciliary processes.* **p. clinoi′deus ante′rior** [N A, B N A], the bony process found on the medial extremity of the posterior border of the small wing of the sphenoid bone. Called also *anterior clinoid process.* **p. clinoi′deus me′dius** [N A, B N A], either of two small inconstant eminences on the internal surface of the sphenoid bone, one on either side of the anterior part of the hypophyseal fossa. Called also *middle clinoid process.* **p. clinoi′deus poste′rior** [N A, B N A], either of two tubercles found on the superior angle of either side of the dorsum sellae of the sphenoid bone, and giving attachment to the tentorium of the cerebellum. Called also *posterior clinoid process.* **p. cochlearifor′mis** [N A, B N A], a small spoon-shaped plate of bone at the end of the semicanalis tubae auditivae, just above the vestibular window. Called also *cochleariform process.* **p. condyla′ris mandib′ulae** [N A], **p. condyloi′deus mandib′ulae** [B N A], the posterior process on the ramus of the mandible that articulates with the mandibular fossa of the temporal bone. Called also *condylar process of mandible.* **p. coracoi′deus scap′ulae** [N A, B N A], a strong curved process that arises from the upper part of the neck of the scapula and overhangs the shoulder joint. Called also *coracoid process of scapula.* **p. coronoi′deus mandib′ulae** [N A, B N A], the anterior part of the upper end of the ramus of the mandible, to which the temporal muscle is attached. Called also *coronoid process of mandible.* **p. coronoi′deus ul′nae** [N A, B N A], a wide eminence at the proximal end of the ulna, forming the anterior and inferior part of the trochlear incisure. Called also *coronoid process of ulna.* **p. costa′rius ver′tebrae** [N A, B N A], in a cervical vertebra, the part of the transverse process anterior to the transverse foramen. Called also *costal process of vertebra.* **p. e cerebel′lo ad medul′lam,** pedunculus cerebellaris inferior. **p. e cerebel′lo ad pon′tem,** pedunculus cerebellaris medius. **p. e cerebel′lo ad tes′tes,** pedunculus cerebellaris superior. **p. ethmoida′lis con′chae nasa′lis inferio′ris** [N A, B N A], a bony projection above and behind the maxillary process of the inferior nasal concha. Called also *ethmoidal process of inferior nasal concha.* **p. falcifor′mis ligamen′ti sacrotubero′si** [N A, B N A], a prolongation of the sacrotuberal ligament, continuing forward along the inner border of the ramus of the ischium from the point of attachment of the ligament on the tuber of the ischium. Called also *falciform process of sacrotuberal ligament.* **p. Ferrei′ni lob′uli cortica′lis re′nis** [B N A], pars radiata lobuli corticalis renis. **p. fronta′lis maxil′lae** [N A, B N A], a large, strong, irregular process of bone that projects upward from the body of the maxilla, its medial surface forming part of the lateral wall of the nasal cavity. Called also *frontal process of maxilla.* **p. fronta′lis os′sis zygomat′ici** [N A], **p. frontosphenoida′lis os′sis zygomat′ici** [B N A], the strong, upward projecting triangular process of the zygomatic bone lying behind the malar surface and between the orbital and temporal surfaces; it unites above with the zygomatic process of the frontal bone and behind with the great wing of the sphenoid bone. Called also *frontal process of zygomatic bone.* **p. gra′cilis,** p. anterior mallei. **p. of Ingrassias,** ala minor ossis sphenoidalis. **p. intrajugula′ris os′sis occipita′lis** [N A, B N A], a small process that subdivides the jugular notch of the occipital bone into a lateral and a medial part. Called also *intrajugular process of occipital bone.* **p. intrajugula′ris os′sis tempora′lis** [N A, B N A], a small ridge on the petrous part of the temporal bone that separates the jugular notch into a medial and a lateral part, corresponding to similar parts of the jugular notch of the facing occipital bone. Called also *intrajugular process of temporal bone.* **p. jugula′ris os′sis occipita′lis** [N A, B N A], either of two processes on the occipital bone that project laterally from the occipital condyles and form the posterior boundary of the jugular foramen. Called also *jugular process of occipital bone.* **p. lacrima′lis con′chae nasa′lis inferio′ris** [N A, B N A], a process of the inferior nasal concha that articulates with the lacrimal bone. Called also *lacrimal process of inferior nasal concha.* **p. latera′lis mal′lei** [N A, B N A], a small tapered process that projects laterally from the base of the manubrium mallei and, pressing against the tympanic membrane, produces the mallear prominence. Called also *lateral process of malleus.* **p. latera′lis ta′li** [N A, B N A], a large low process on the lateral surface of the talus, articulating with the lateral malleolus. Called also *lateral process of talus.* **p. latera′lis tu′beris calca′nei** [N A, B N A], a rough process projecting downward from the lower lateral portion of the tuber calcanei. Called also *lateral process of tuberosity of calcaneus.* **p. lenticula′ris in′cudis** [N A, B N A], a small oval knob on the medial side of the tip of the long limb of the incus, which articulates with or is ossified to the head of the stapes. Called also *lenticular process of incus.* **p. mamilla′ris vertebra′rum** [N A, B N A], a tubercle on each superior articular process of the lumbar vertebrae. Called also *mamillary process of vertebrae.* **p. margina′lis os′sis zygomat′ici** [B N A], tuberculum marginale ossis zygomatici. **p. mastoi′deus os′sis tempora′lis** [N A, B N A], a conical process projecting forward and downward from the external surface of the petrous part of the temporal bone just posterior to the external acoustic meatus. Called also *mastoid process of temporal bone.* **p. maxilla′ris con′chae nasa′lis inferio′ris** [N A, B N A], a bony process descending from the ethmoid process of the inferior nasal concha. Called also *maxillary process of inferior nasal concha.* **p. media′lis tu′beris calca′nei** [N A, B N A], a rough process projecting downward from the lower medial portion of the tuber calcanei. Called also *medial process of tuberosity of calcaneus.* **p. muscula′ris cartilag′inis arytenoi′deae** [N A], the lateral and posterior lower angular projection of the arytenoid cartilage to which the cricoarytenoid muscles are attached. Called also *muscular process of arytenoid cartilage.* **p. orbita′lis os′sis palati′ni** [N A, B N A], a pyramidal process on the uppermost part of the palatine bone, one surface of it forming the posterior angle of the floor of the orbit. Called also *orbital process of palatine bone.* **p. palati′nus maxil′lae** [N A, B N A], a horizontally arched plate of bone that helps to form the lower part of the maxilla and with its fellow of the opposite side the anterior two-thirds of the hard palate. Called also *palatine process of maxilla.* **p. papilla′ris hep′atis** [N A, B N A], the left of the two processes seen on the caudate lobe of the liver. Called also *papillary process of liver.* **p. para-**

mastoi'deus os'sis occipita'lis [N A, B N A], a process that in man is represented by a tubercle on the under surface of the jugular process. Called also *paramastoid process of occipital bone.* **p. poste'rior sphenoida'lis** [N A], a narrow flat strip of cartilage that extends backward and upward along the groove on the upper margin of the vomer and below the perpendicular plate of the ethmoid bone, from the septal cartilage nearly to the sphenoid bone. Called also *p. sphenoidalis septi cartilaginei* [B N A], and *posterior process of cartilage of nasal septum.* **p. poste'rior ta'li** [N A, B N A], a backward projection from the posterior portion of the talus, divided into two unequal parts by the sulcus tendinis musculi flexoris hallucis longi tali. Called also *posterior process of talus.* **p. pterygoi'deus os'sis sphenoida'lis** [N A, B N A], either of two processes on the sphenoid bone descending from the points of junction of the great wings and body of the bone, and each consisting of a lateral and a medial plate. Called also *pterygoid process of sphenoid bone.* **p. pterygospino'sus** [N A], **p. pterygospino'sus [Civini'ni]** [B N A], a small spine on the posterior edge of the lateral pterygoid plate of the sphenoid bone, giving attachment to the pterygospinous ligament. Called also *pterygospinous process.* **p. pyramida'lis os'sis palati'ni** [N A, B N A], a strong process projecting downward, backward and laterally from the lateral part of the posterior margin of the palatine bone and helping to form the pterygoid fossa. Called also *pyramidal process of palatine bone.* **p. retromandibula'ris glan'dulae parot'idis** [B N A], an irregularly wedge-shaped portion of the parotid gland passing medially behind the ramus of the mandible almost to the wall of the pharynx. Omitted in N A. **p. sphenoida'lis os'sis palati'ni** [N A, B N A], an irregular mass of bone that projects upward and medially from the posterior portion of the superior margin of the perpendicular portion of the palatine bone, and articulates with the body of the sphenoid bone and with the ala vomeris. Called also *sphenoid process of palatine bone.* **p. sphenoida'lis sep'ti cartilagin'ei** [B N A], processus posterior sphenoidalis. **p. spino'sus vertebra'rum** [N A, B N A], a part of the vertebrae projecting backward from the arch, giving attachment to muscles of the back. Called also *spinous process of vertebrae.* **p. styloi'deus fib'ulae,** apex capitis fibulae. **p. styloi'deus os'sis metacarpa'lis III** [N A, B N A], a prominent process projecting proximally from the base of the third metacarpal bone. Called also *styloid process of third metacarpal bone.* **p. styloi'deus os'sis tempora'lis** [N A, B N A], a long spine projecting downward from the inferior surface of the temporal bone just anterior to the stylomastoid foramen, giving attachment to three muscles and two ligaments. Called also *styloid process of temporal bone.* **p. styloi'deus ra'dii** [N A, B N A], a blunt projection from the lateral surface of the distal end of the radius. Called also *styloid process of radius.* **p. styloi'deus ul'nae** [N A, B N A], the medial, non-articular process on the distal extremity of the ulna. Called also *styloid process of ulna.* **p. supracondyla'ris hu'meri** [N A], **p. supracondyloi'deus hu'meri** [B N A], a small inconstant process just proximal to the medial epicondyle of the humerus. Called also *supracondylar process of humerus.* **p. tempora'lis os'sis zygomat'ici** [N A, B N A], the posterior blunt process of the zygomatic bone that articulates with the zygomatic process of the temporal bone. Called also *temporal process of zygomatic bone.* **p. transver'sus vertebra'rum** [N A, B N A], a process on either side of the vertebrae, projecting laterally from the junction between the lamina and the pedicle. Called also *transverse process of vertebrae.* **p. trochlea'ris calca'nei** [B N A], trochlea peronealis calcanei. **p. uncina'tus os'sis ethmoida'lis,** [N A, B N A], a curved plate of bone that extends inferiorly and posteriorly from the anterior part of the ethmoid labyrinth. Called also *uncinate process of ethmoid bone.* **p. uncina'tus pancrea'tis** [N A, B N A], the left and caudal part of the head of the pancreas, which hooks around behind the pancreatic vessels. Called also *uncinate process of pancreas* and *pancreas of Winslow.* **p. vagina'lis os'sis sphenoida'lis** [N A, B N A], a small plate on the inferior surface of the body of the sphenoid bone on either side, running medially from the medial pterygoid plate to articulate with the ala of the vomer and with the sphenoid process of the palatine bone. Called also *vaginal process of sphenoid bone.* **p. vagina'lis peritone'i** [N A], a diverticulum of the peritoneal membrane extending into the inguinal canal, accompanying the round ligament in the female, or the testis in its descent into the scrotum in the male (*processus vaginalis testis*); usually completely obliterated in the female. **p. vermifor'mis** [B N A], appendix vermiformis. **p. voca'lis** [N A, B N A], the process of the arytenoid cartilage to which the vocal ligament is attached. Called also *vocal process.* **p. xiphoi'deus** [N A, B N A], the pointed process of cartilage, supported by a core of bone, connected with the lower end of the body of the sternum. Called also *xiphoid process.* **p. zygomat'icus maxil'lae** [N A, B N A], the rough triangular eminence that articulates with the zygomatic bone and marks the separation of the facies anterior, infratemporalis, and orbitalis. Called also *zygomatic process of maxilla.* **p. zygomat'icus os'sis fronta'lis** [N A, B N A], a thick, strong process of the frontal bone, situated at the lateral end of the supraorbital margin and articulating with the zygomatic bone, and from which the temporal line starts. Called also *zygomatic process of frontal bone.* **p. zygomat'icus os'sis tempora'lis** [N A, B N A], a long, strong process arising from the lower portion of the squamous part of the temporal bone, passing forward from just above the entrance of the external acoustic meatus to join the zygomatic bone and thus forming the zygomatic arch. Called also *zygomatic process of temporal bone.*

procheilon (pro-ki'lon) [*pro-* + Gr. *cheilon* lip + *-on* neuter ending]. The central prominence of the upper border between the skin and the mucous membrane of the upper lip, marking the distal termination of the philtrum (tuberculum labii superioris [N A]).

prochlorpemazine (pro"klōr-pem'ah-zēn). Prochlorperazine.

prochlorperazine (pro"klōr-per'ah-zēn). Chemical name: 2-chloro-10-[3-(1-methyl-4-piperazinyl)-propyl]phenothiazine: used as a tranquilizer and anti-emetic.

prochondral (pro-kon'dral). Occurring previous to the formation of cartilage.

prochordal (pro-kor'dal). In front of the notochord.

prochoresis (pro"ko-re'sis) [Gr. *prochōrēsis* advancement]. The propulsion of food through the pylorus or along the alimentary canal.

prochorion (pro-ko're-on). 1. The thin zona pellucida of the fertilized ovum when it reaches the uterus. 2. The coating of albuminous matter which the ovum receives as it passes along the oviduct.

Prochownick's diet, method (pro-kov'niks) [Ludwig *Prochownick*, German obstetrician, 1851–1923]. See under *diet* and *method.*

prochromatin (pro-kro'mah-tin). The substance composing the true nucleoli; paranuclein.

prochromosome (pro-kro'mo-sōm). A chromosome-like body occurring in resting nuclei.

prochymosin (pro-ki'mo-sin). Renninogen.

procidentia (pro"si-den'she-ah) [L.]. A prolapse, or falling down; especially prolapse of the uterus to such a degree that the cervix protrudes from the vaginal outlet.

procoagulant (pro″ko-ag′u-lant). 1. Tending to favor the occurrence of coagulation. 2. A precursor of a natural substance necessary to coagulation of the blood.

procoelia (pro-se′le-ah) [*pro-* + Gr. *koilia* hollow]. Ventriculus lateralis cerebri.

proconceptive (pro″kon-sep′tiv). 1. Aiding or favoring conception. 2. An agent that facilitates or promotes conception.

proconvertin (pro″kon-ver′tin). Factor VII. See discussion of *coagulation factors*, under *factor*.

procreation (pro″kre-a′shun) [L. *procreatio*]. The entire process of bringing a new individual into the world.

procreative (pro′kre-a″tiv). Concerned in procreation; able to beget.

proct-. See *procto-*.

proctagra (prok′tag-rah, prok-ta′grah) [*proct-* + Gr. *agra* seizure]. Pain in and around the anus.

proctalgia (prok-tal′je-ah) [*proct-* + *-algia*]. Neuralgia of the lower rectum. **p. fu′gax,** a condition characterized by spasmodic high pain in the rectum.

proctatresia (prok″tah-tre′ze-ah) [*proct-* + *a* neg. + Gr. *trēsis* perforation]. Imperforation of the anus.

proctectasia (prok″tek-ta′ze-ah) [*proct-* + Gr. *ektasis* dilatation + *-ia*]. Dilatation of the rectum or of the anus.

proctectomy (prok-tek′to-me) [*proct-* + Gr. *ektomē* excision]. Surgical removal of the rectum.

proctencleisis (prok″ten-kli′sis) [*proct-* + Gr. *enkleiein* to shut in]. Constriction, or stenosis, of the lower rectum.

procteurynter (prok′tu-rin″ter) [*proct-* + Gr. *eurynein* to widen]. A baglike device used in dilating the rectum.

procteurysis (prok-tu′rĭ-sis). Dilatation of the rectum by means of a procteurynter.

proctitis (prok-ti′tis) [*proct-* + *-itis*]. Inflammation of the rectum. **epidemic gangrenous p.,** a disease of the northern part of South America and the Fiji and other islands of the South Pacific Ocean, marked by rapidly spreading ulceration of the anus and lower bowel, with bloody discharges, fever, and great prostration. Called also *bicho* and *carib*.

procto-, proct- (prok′to, prokt) [Gr. *prōktos* anus, hence the hinder parts]. Combining form used to designate relationship to the rectum.

proctocele (prok′to-sēl) [*procto-* + Gr. *kēlē* hernia]. Rectocele.

proctoclysis (prok-tok′lĭ-sis) [*procto-* + Gr. *klysis* a drenching]. The slow injection of large quantities of liquid into the rectum. Called also *Murphy drip*. See *Murphy's method* (2d def.), under *method*.

proctococcypexy (prok″to-kok′sĭ-pek″se) [*procto-* + Gr. *kokkyx* coccyx + *pēxis* fixation]. The fastening of the rectum to the coccyx by sutures.

proctocolectomy (prok″to-ko-lek′to-me). Surgical removal of the rectum and colon.

proctocolitis (prok″to-ko-li′tis). Inflammation of the rectum and colon.

proctocolonoscopy (prok″to-ko″lon-os′ko-pe). Inspection of the interior of the rectum and lower colon.

proctocolpoplasty (prok″to-kol′po-plas″te) [*procto-* + Gr. *kolpos* vagina + *plassein* to form]. Operative closure of a rectovaginal fistula.

proctocystoplasty (prok″to-sis′to-plas″te) [*procto-* + Gr. *kystis* bladder + *plassein* to form]. A plastic operation on the rectum and bladder; operative closure of a rectovesical fistula.

proctocystotomy (prok″to-sis-tot′o-me) [*procto-* + Gr. *kystis* bladder + *tomē* a cutting]. The rectovesical operation for stone in the bladder.

proctodaeum (prok″to-de′um). Proctodeum.

proctodeum (prok″to-de′um) [*proct-* + Gr. *hodaios* pertaining to a way]. An invagination of the ectoderm of the embryo at the point where later the anus is formed.

proctodynia (prok″to-din′e-ah) [*proct-* + Gr. *odynē* pain]. Pain in or about the anus.

procto-elytroplasty (prok″to-el′ĭ-tro-plas″te) [*procto-* + Gr. *elytron* vagina + *plassein* to form]. A plastic operation on the rectum and vagina.

proctogenic (prok″to-jen′ik) [*procto-* + Gr. *gennan* to produce]. Derived from the anus or rectum.

proctologic (prok″to-loj′ik). Pertaining to proctology.

proctologist (prok-tol′o-jist). A practitioner skilled in proctology.

proctology (prok-tol′o-je) [*procto-* + *-logy*]. The branch of medicine treating of the rectum and its diseases.

proctoparalysis (prok″to-pah-ral′ĭ-sis) [*procto-* + *paralysis*]. Paralysis of the muscles of the anus and rectum.

proctoperineoplasty (prok″to-per″ĭ-ne′o-plas″te). Plastic repair of the anus and perineum.

proctoperineorrhaphy (prok″to-per″ĭ-ne-or′ah-fe). Proctoperineoplasty.

proctopexy (prok′to-pek″se) [*procto-* + Gr. *pexis* fixation]. The fixation of the rectum to some other part by suture.

proctophobia (prok″to-fo′be-ah) [*procto-* + Gr. *phobos* fear]. The mental state of apprehension common in persons with rectal disease.

proctoplasty (prok′to-plas″te) [*procto-* + Gr. *plassein* to form]. Plastic surgery of the rectum and anus.

proctoplegia (prok″to-ple′je-ah) [*procto-* + Gr. *plēgē* stroke]. Proctoparalysis.

proctopolypus (prok″to-pol′ĭ-pus) [*procto-* + *polypus*]. Polypus of the rectum.

proctoptoma (prok″top-to′mah). Proctoptosis.

proctoptosis (prok″top-to′sis) [*procto-* + Gr. *ptōsis* fall]. Prolapse of the anus.

proctorrhagia (prok″to-ra′je-ah). Bleeding from the rectum.

proctorrhaphy (prok-tor′ah-fe) [*procto-* + Gr. *rhaphē* seam]. The stitching, or suturation, of the rectum.

proctorrhea (prok″to-re′ah) [*procto-* + Gr. *rhoia* flow]. A mucous discharge from the anus.

proctoscope (prok′to-skōp) [*procto-* + Gr. *skopein* to examine]. A speculum for inspecting the rectum. **Tuttle's p.,** a rectal speculum with an electric light at its extremity and an arrangement for inflating the rectal ampulla.

proctoscopy (prok-tos′ko-pe) [*procto-* + Gr. *skopein* to examine]. Inspection of the rectum with a proctoscope.

proctosigmoidectomy (prok″to-sig″moid-ek′to-me) [*procto-* + *sigmoid* + Gr. *ektomē* excision]. Excision of the anus and sigmoid flexure.

proctosigmoiditis (prok″to-sig″moid-i′tis). Inflammation of the rectum and sigmoid.

proctosigmoidoscopy (prok″to-sig″moi-dos′ko-pe). Examination of the rectum and sigmoid by means of the sigmoidoscope.

proctospasm (prok′to-spazm) [*procto-* + *spasm*]. Spasm of the rectum.

proctostasis (prok-tos′tah-sis) [*procto-* + Gr. *stasis* stoppage]. Constipation due to anesthesia of the rectum to the stimulus of defecation.

proctostat (prok′to-stat). A radium-containing tube for insertion into the rectum.

proctostenosis (prok″to-ste-no′sis) [*procto-* + Gr. *stenōsis* narrowing]. Stricture of the rectum.

proctostomy (prok-tos′to-me) [*procto-* + Gr. *stomoun* to provide with an opening, or mouth]. Surgical creation of a permanent artificial opening into the rectum.

proctotome (prok′to-tōm). A knife for proctotomy.

proctotomy (prok-tot′o-me) [*procto-* + Gr. *tomē* a cutting]. The cutting of an anal or rectal stricture; the opening of an imperforate anus. **external p.,** that done on or near the sphincter. **internal p.,** an incision of the rectum from within above the sphincter.

proctotoreusis (prok″to-to-roo′sis) [*procto-* + Gr. *toreusis* boring]. The making of an artificial anus.

proctotresia (prok-to-tre′se-ah). Proctotoreusis.

proctovalvotomy (prok″to-val-vot′o-me). The operation of cutting the rectal valves.

procumbent (pro-kum′bent). Lying on the face.

procursive (pro-kur′siv) [L. *procursivus*]. Characterized by a tendency to run forward.

procurvation (pro″kur-va′shun) [L. *procurvare* to bend forward]. A bending forward, as of the body.

procyclidine (pro-si′klĭ-dēn). Tricyclamol.

prodigiosin (pro-dij″e-o′sin). An antibiotic dye from *Serratia marcescens*, which has been found active against anthrax and coccidioidomycosis.

prodroma (pro-dro′mah), pl. *prodro′mata* [Gr. *prodromē* a running forward]. Prodrome.

prodromal (pro-dro′mal). Prodromic.

prodromata (pro-dro′mah-tah) [Gr.]. Plural of *prodroma.*

prodrome (pro′drōm) [L. *prodromus;* Gr. *prodromos* forerunning]. A premonitory symptom or precursor; a symptom indicating the onset of a disease.

prodromic (pro-dro′mik). Premonitory; indicating the approach of a disease or other morbid state.

product (prod′ukt). Something produced. **adaptation p.,** reaction substance. **anaphylactic reaction p.,** anaphylactin. **cleavage p.,** a substance formed by the splitting of a compound molecule into simpler molecules. **contact activation p.,** a product of the interaction of blood coagulation factors XII and XI, which functions to activate factor IX during the formation of intrinsic thromboplastin. **fission p.,** an isotope, usually radioactive, of an element in the middle of the periodic table, produced by fission of a heavy element, such as uranium, under bombardment by high energy particles. **intermediate p.,** one which is formed as a step in a definite sequence of events. *intermediate product 1,* a substance postulated as resulting from the interaction of blood coagulation factors IV, VIII, IX, and X, in the formation of intrinsic thromboplastin. *intermediate product 2,* a substance formed by the interaction of intermediate product 1, platelet factor 3, and blood coagulation factor IV, then interacts with factor V to form intrinsic thromboplastin. **spallation p's,** the many different chemical elements produced in small quantities in nuclear fission. **substitution p.,** a chemical product obtained by substituting for one element in a molecule an atom or a radical of some other substance. **Vaughan's split p's,** a protein which has been split up into a poisonous and a nonpoisonous part, the former soluble in the menstruum, the latter not. The former is called the "poison"; the latter, the "residue."

productive (pro-duk′tiv). Producing or forming, especially producing new tissue.

proemial (pro-e′me-al) [L. *prooemium* a prelude]. Introductory; serving as an introduction or indication; prodromal; potentially dangerous.

proencephalon (pro″en-sef′ah-lon). Prosencephalon.

proencephalus (pro″en-sef′ah-lus) [*pro-* + Gr. *enkephalos* brain]. A monster with a part of the brain protruding from a frontal fissure.

proenzyme (pro-en′zīm). Zymogen.

proeotia (pro″e-o′she-ah). Proiotia.

proerythroblast (pro″e-rith′ro-blast). An early red cell precursor characterized by a relatively large nucleus containing nucleoli, well dispersed chromatin, and a thin rim of basophilic cytoplasm. Called also *pronormoblast, macroblast of Naegeli, megaloblast of Sabin, lymphoid hemoblast of Pappenheim, rubriblast,* and *prorubricyte.*

proerythrocyte (pro″e-rith′ro-sīt). A precursor of an erythrocyte. The term is without standing in any scheme of morphological development.

proestrum (pro-es′trum). Proestrus.

proestrus (pro-es′trus) [*pro-* + L. *oestrus*]. The period of heightened follicular activity preceding estrus in female mammals.

Proetz position, treatment (prets) [Arthur W. *Proetz,* American otolaryngologist, born 1888]. See under *position* and *treatment.*

profenamine (pro-fen′ah-mēn). Ethopropazine.

proferment (pro-fer′ment). Zymogen.

professional (pro-fesh′un-al). Pertaining to one's profession or occupation.

Profeta's law (pro-fa′tahz) [Giuseppe *Profeta.* Italian dermatologist, 1840–1910]. See under *law,*

profibrillatory (pro-fib″rĭ-lah-to′re). Tending to produce cardiac fibrillation.

profibrinolysin (pro″fi-brĭ-no-li′sin). The inactive precursor of fibrinolysin; plasminogen.

Profichet's disease, syndrome (pro″fe-shāz′) [Georges Charles *Profichet,* French physician, born 1873]. See under *syndrome.*

profile (pro′fīl). A simple outline of the shape or form of an object, such as the head or face, viewed from the side.

profilograph (pro′fĭ-lo-graf) [*profile* + Gr. *graphein* to draw]. A device for recording the profile of the face.

profilometer (pro″fĭ-lom′e-ter). An apparatus for measuring the profile and outlining it on paper.

Proflagellata (pro″flaj-e-la′tah). Doflein's name for a proposed group to embrace organisms supposed to be transitional from bacteria to flagellates, i.e., the spirochetes.

proflavine (pro-fla′vin). A reddish-brown crystalline powder, 3,6-di-aminoacridinium monohydrogen sulfate, $NH_2.C_6H_4.CH.C_6H_4(NH_2).NH.$-$H_2SO_4$, used in the treatment of infected wounds.

profluvium (pro-floo′ve-um) [L.]. A flowing forth. **p. sem′inis,** a flowing from the vagina of the semen deposited during coitus.

profondometer (pro″fon-dom′e-ter). An apparatus for locating a foreign body by the fluoroscope by obtaining three lines of sight which intersect at the foreign body.

profundus (pro-fun′dus) [L.]. Deep; in official anatomical nomenclature, used to designate a structure situated more deeply than another from the surface of the body.

progamous (prog′ah-mus) [*pro-* + Gr. *gamos* marriage]. Previous to fertilization of the ovum.

progaster (pro′gas-ter) [*pro-* + Gr. *gastēr* stomache]. The archenteron.

progastrin (pro-gas′trin). An inactive precursor of gastrin.

progenia (pro-je′ne-ah) [*pro-* + L. *gena* chin]. Prognathism.

progenital (pro-jen′ĭ-tal). On the external surface of the genitals.

progenitor (pro-jen′ĭ-tor) [L.]. A parent or ancestor.

progeny (proj′e-ne) [L. *progignere* to bring forth]. Offspring, or descendants.

progeria (pro-je′re-ah) [*pro-* + Gr. *gēras* old age + *-ia*]. Premature old age; a form of infantilism marked by small stature, absence of facial and pubic hair, wrinkled skin, gray hair, and the facial appearance, attitude, and manner of old age (Gilford).

progestational (pro″jes-ta′shun-al). A term applied to that phase of the menstrual cycle, just before menstruation, when the corpus luteum is active and the endometrium secreting.

progesteroid (pro-jes′ter-oid). A progesterone-like compound; sometimes used to include progesterone and all other compounds having progestational effects.

progesterone (pro-jes′ter-ōn). The hormone produced by the corpora lutea whose function it is to prepare the uterus for the reception and development of the fertilized ovum by a glandular proliferation of the endometrium.

progestin (pro-jes′tin). The name originally given (Corner and Allen, 1930) to the crude hormone of the corpora lutea. It has since been isolated in pure form and is now known as *progesterone.* The name progestin is used for certain brands of synthetic progesterone.

progestogen (pro-jes′to-jen). A term applied to any substance possessing progestational activity.

progestomimetic (pro-jes″to-mi-met′ik). Having physiologic activity similar to that of progesterone.

proglossis (pro-glos′is) [Gr. *proglōssis*]. The tip of the tongue.

proglottid (pro-glot′id). Proglottis.

proglottis (pro-glot′is), pl. *proglot′tides* [*pro-* + *glottis*]. Any one of the joints of a tapeworm.

prognathic (prog-na′thik). Prognathous.

prognathism (prog′nah-thizm). The condition of being prognathous; marked projection of the jaw.

prognathometer (prog″nah-thom′e-ter) [*prognathous* + Gr. *metron* measure]. An instrument for measuring the form and degree of prognathism.

prognathous (prog′nah-thus) [*pro-* + Gr. *gnathos* jaw]. Having projecting jaws, having a gnathic index above 103.

prognose (prog-nōs). To forecast the course and outcome of a disease.

prognosis (prog-no′sis) [Gr. *prognōsis* foreknowledge]. A forecast as to the probable result of an attack of disease: the prospect as to recovery from a disease as indicated by the nature and symptoms of the case. **dental p.,** an evaluation of the results to be achieved from treatment of certain conditions of the mouth, or from the use of dental prostheses.

prognostic (prog-nos′tik). 1. Affording an indication as to prognosis. 2. A symptom or sign on which a prognosis may be based.

prognosticate (prog-nos′tĭ-kāt). To forecast the probable outcome of an attack of disease.

prognostician (prog″nos-tish′an). One who is skilled in prognosis.

progoitrin (pro-goi′trin). An inactive compound found in the seeds of most plants belonging to the genus Brassica, which liberates goitrin through specific enzymatic hydrolysis.

progonoma (pro″go-no′mah) [Gr. *pro* before + *gonos* sperm + *-oma*]. A tumor due to misplacement of tissue as the result of fetal atavism to a stage which does not occur in the life history of the species, but which does occur in ancestral forms of the species.

progranulocyte (pro-gran′u-lo-sīt). Promyelocyte.

progravid (pro-grav′id) [*pro-* + L. *gravidus* pregnant]. Denoting the phase of the endometrium, under the influence of the corpus luteum, during which it is prepared for pregnancy.

progression (pro-gresh′un). The act of moving or walking forward. **backward p.,** walking backward: an act seen in certain nervous diseases. **cross-legged p.,** a walk in which the toes are turned in and the foot is placed in front of its fellow. **metadromic p.,** one of the sequelae of epidemic encephalitis, consisting in the fact that a person who is barely able to walk may have no difficulty in running.

progressive (pro-gres′iv). Advancing; going forward; of a disease, going from bad to worse.

proguanil (pro-gwan′il). Chemical name: 1-(p-chlorophenyl)-5-isopropylbiguanide: used as an antimalarial.

progynon (pro-jin′on). Trade mark for preparations of estradiol.

pro-invasin (pro″in-va′sin). A precursor of invasin (hyaluronidase). **p. I,** an enzyme in bacteria said to destroy anti-invasin I.

proiomenorrhea (pro″e-o-men″o-re′ah) [Gr. *prōi* early + *menorrhea*]. Early or premature menstruation.

proiosystole (pro″e-o-sis′to-le) [Gr. *prōi* early + systole]. A contraction of the heart occurring before its normal time. See *hysterosystole.*

proiosystolia (pro″e-o-sis-to′le-ah). A condition marked by proiosystoles.

proiotia (pro″e-o′she-ah) [Gr. *prōiotēs* earliness]. Sexual or genital precocity.

projection (pro-jek′shun) [*pro-* + L. *jacere* to throw]. 1. A throwing forward, especially the act of referring impressions made on the sense organs to their proper source, so as to locate correctly the objects producing them. 2. The act of extending or jutting out, or a part that juts out. 3. A mental mechanism by which a repressed complex is disguised by being regarded as belonging to the external world or to someone else. **eccentric p.** See *referred sensation,* under *sensation.* **erroneous p.,** a misjudging of the position of an object, due to weakness of the eye muscles.

projectoscope (pro-jek′to-skōp). An apparatus for throwing pictures on a screen by reflected light.

prokaryocyte (pro-kar′e-o-sīt). An immature erythrocyte intermediate between a karyoblast and a karyocyte.

prokaryosis (pro″kar-e-o′sis) [*pro-* + Gr. *karyon* + *-osis*]. The state of not having a true nucleus, the nuclear material being scattered in the protoplasm of the cell.

prokaryotic (pro″kar-e-ot′ik). Pertaining to or characterized by prokaryosis.

prolabium (pro-la′be-um) [*pro-* + L. *labium* lip]. The prominent central part of the upper lip, in its full thickness, which overlies the premaxilla.

prolactin (pro-lak′tin) [*pro-* + L. *lac* milk]. A proteohormone from the anterior pituitary which stimulates lactation in mammary glands and proliferation of the mucosa of the crop-sac of doves and pigeons. Called also *galactin* and *mammotropin.*

prolamin (pro-lam′in). Any one of a group of proteins found in cereals. They are soluble in alcohol (70–80 per cent), but insoluble in water and absolute alcohol. They are also called *alcohol-soluble proteins.*

prolan (pro′lan). Zondek's term for the gonadotropic principle of human pregnancy urine, responsible for the biologic pregnancy tests. Originally, the response of rodents to pregnancy urine was ascribed to two hormones, *prolan A,* follicle-stimulating, and *prolan B,* luteinizing. It is now known that the gonadotropic principle in human pregnancy is a single entity and differs from the gonadotropic substance of the anterior pituitary. The term prolan has fallen into disuse but is of historic value. See *chorionic gonadotropin.*

prolapse (pro-laps′) [L. *prolapsus; pro* before + *labi* to fall]. The falling down, or sinking, of a part or viscus; procidentia. **anal p., p. of anus,** protrusion of modified anal skin through the anal orifice. **p. of the cord,** premature expulsion of the umbilical cord in labor. **frank p.,** prolapse of the uterus in which the vagina is inverted and hangs from the vulva. **p. of the iris,** protrusion of the iris through a wound in the cornea. **Morgagni's p.,** chronic inflammatory hyperplasia of the mucosa and submucosa of the sacculus laryngis. **rectal p., p. of rectum,** protrusion of the rectal mucous membrane through the anus in varying degree, classified as *incomplete* or *partial* with no displacement of anal sphincter muscle, *complete with displacement* of anal sphincter muscle, *complete with no displacement* of anal muscles but usually with herniation of bowel, and *internal complete* (*concealed*) with

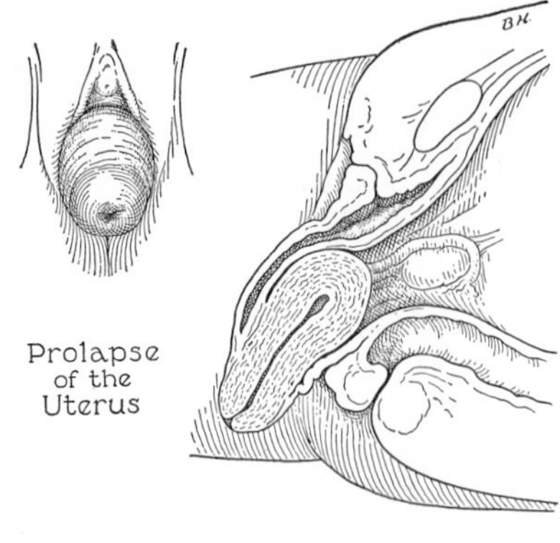

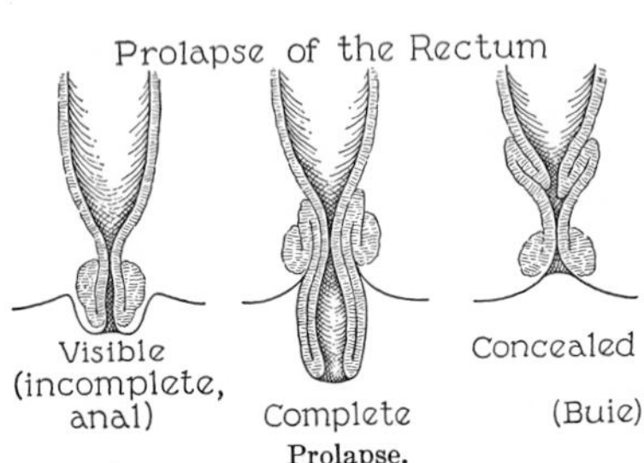

Prolapse.

intussusception of the rectosigmoid and upper portion of the rectum into the lower rectum. **p. of uterus,** protrusion of the uterus through the vaginal orifice.

prolapsus (pro-lap′sus) [L.]. Prolapse. **p. a′ni,** prolapse of the anus. **p. rec′ti,** prolapse of the rectum. **p. u′teri,** prolapse of the uterus.

prolepsis (pro-lep′sis). The return of a paroxysm before the expected time.

proleptic (pro-lep′tik). Occurring prior to the usual time: said of a periodic disease whose paroxysms return at successively shorter intervals.

proleukocyte (pro-lu′ko-sīt). A precursor of a leukocyte; the term is without standing in any current scheme of morphological development.

prolidase (pro′lĭ-dās). An intestinal enzyme which catalyzes the hydrolysis of polypeptidases by loosing the —CO.NH— linkage.

proliferate (pro-lif′er-āt). To grow by the reproduction of similar cells.

proliferation (pro-lif″er-a′shun) [L. *proles* offspring + *ferre* to bear]. The reproduction or multiplication of similar forms, especially of cells and morbid cysts. **fibroplastic p.,** diffuse collagen disease.

proliferative (pro-lif′er-a-tiv). Characterized by proliferation.

proliferous (pro-lif′er-us). Proliferative.

prolific (pro-lif′ik) [L. *prolificus*]. Fruitful; productive.

proligerous (pro-lij′er-us) [L. *proles* offspring + *gerere* to bear]. Producing offspring.

prolinase (pro′lĭ-nās). An intestinal enzyme which catalyzes the hydrolysis of peptides, in which there is no free amino group, by loosing the peptide linkage of proline.

proline (pro′lin). One of the amino acids, 2-pyrrolidine-carboxylic acid, discovered by Fischer in 1901.

prolipin (pro-lip′in). Omnadin.

prolixin (pro-lik′sin). Trade mark for preparations of fluphenazine.

proluton (pro-lu′ton). Trade mark for preparations of progesterone.

promanide (pro′man-id). Promin.

promazine (pro′mah-zēn). Chemical name: 10-(3-dimethylaminopropyl)phenothiazine: used as a tranquilizer.

promegaloblast (pro-meg′ah-lo-blast). A cell developing from a lymphoidocyte and developing into a megaloblast; observed in conditions of abnormal erythropoiesis, of which primary pernicious anemia is an example. Also called *erythrogone.*

promethazine (pro-meth′ah-zēn). Chemical name: 10-(2-dimethylaminopropyl)phenothiazine: used as an antihistaminic.

promethestrol (pro-meth′es-trol). Chemical name: 4,4′-(1,2-diethylethylene)di-o-cresol: used as an estrogenic substance.

promethium (pro-me′the-um). The chemical element of atomic number 61, atomic weight 147, and symbol Pm.

promin (pro′min). Trade mark for a preparation of glucosulfone sodium.

promine (pro′mēn). A substance which is widely distributed in animal cells, characterized by its ability to promote cell division and growth. Cf. *retine.*

prominence (prom′ĭ-nens). A protrusion or projection. For names of specific anatomical structures see under *prominentia.* **Ammon's scleral p.,** a prominence on the globe of the eye of the fetus. **tubal p.,** torus tubarius.

prominentia (prom″ĭ-nen′she-ah), pl. *prominen′tiae* [L.]. A protrusion or projection; used in anatomical nomenclature as a general term for a small protrusion on another structure or part. Called also *prominence.* **p. cana′lis facia′lis** [N A, B N A], an elongated elevation on the medial wall of the tympanic cavity, just below the prominence of the lateral semicircular canal and above and behind the vestibular window. Called also *prominence of facial canal.* **p. cana′lis semicircula′ris latera′lis** [N A, B N A], a large rounded prominence on the upper portion of the medial wall of the tympanic cavity, between the vestibular window and the mastoid antrum and overlying the lateral semicircular canal. Called also *prominence of lateral semicircular canal.* **p. laryn′gea** [N A, B N A], a subcutaneous prominence on the front of the neck produced by the thyroid cartilage of the larynx. Called also *laryngeal prominence* and *Adam's apple.* **p. mallea′ris membra′nae tym′pani** [N A], **p. malleola′ris membra′nae tym′pani** [B N A], a small projection at the upper extremity of the stria mallearis, formed by the lateral process of the malleus. Called also *mallear prominence of tympanic membrane.* **p. spira′lis** [N A, B N A], a prominence on the external wall of the cochlear duct, separating the stria vascularis from the external spiral sulcus. **p. styloi′dea** [N A, B N A], an irregular nodule on the posterior portion of the floor of the tympanic cavity, corresponding to the base of the styloid process. Called also *styloid prominence.*

prominen′tiae (prom″ĭ-nen′she-e). Plural of *prominentia.*

promitosis (pro″mi-to′sis). A simple form of cell division seen in tumor cells, in which the nucleolus or karyosome divides as in mitosis, the rest of the division simulating amitosis.

promonocyte (pro-mon′o-sīt). A cell intermediate in development between the monoblast and monocyte.

promontorium (prom″on-to′re-um), pl. *promonto′ria* [L.]. A projecting eminence or process. **p. fa′ciei,** nasus externus. **p. os′sis sa′cri** [N A, B N A], the prominent anterior border of the pelvic surface of the body of the first sacral vertebra. Called also *promontory of sacrum.* **p. tym′pani** [N A, B N A], the prominence on the medial wall of the tympanic cavity, formed by the first turn of the cochlea. Called also *promontory of tympanic cavity.*

promontory (prom′on-to″re). A projecting eminence or process. For names of specific anatomical structures see under *promontorium.*

promoter (pro-mo′ter). A substance in a catalyst

which increases the rate of activity of the latter. Cf. *protector*.

promoxolane (pro-mok′so-lān). Chemical name: 2,2-diisopropyl-1,3-dioxolane-4-methanol: used as a tranquilizer.

promyelocyte (pro-mi′ĕ-lo-sīt). A cell intermediate in development between a myeloblast and myelocyte, and containing a few, as yet undifferentiated, cytoplasmic granules.

pronate (pro′nāt). To assume or place in a prone position.

pronation (pro-na′shun) [L. *pronatio*]. The act of assuming the prone position, or the state of being prone. Applied to the hand, the act of turning the palm backward (posteriorly) or downward, performed by medial rotation of the forearm. Applied to the foot, a combination of eversion and abduction movements taking place in the tarsal and metatarsal joints and resulting in lowering of the medial margin of the foot, hence of the longitudinal arch.

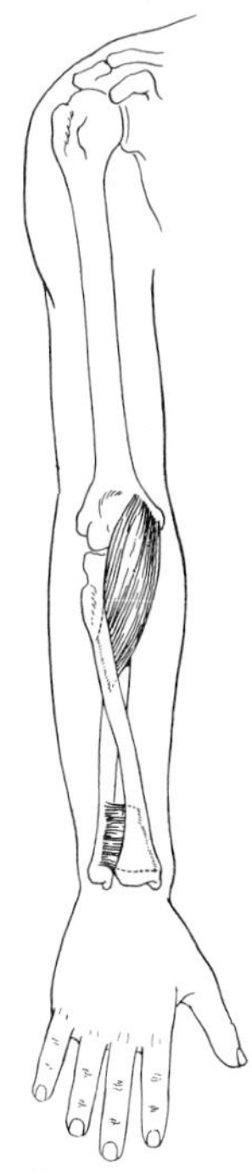

Pronators contracted, forearm and hand pronated. (King and Showers.)

pronatoflexor (pro-na″to-flek′sor). Both pronator and flexor.

pronator (pro-na′tor) [L.]. That which pronates.

pronaus (pro′na-us) [*pro-* + Gr. *naos* temple]. The vestibule of the vagina (vestibulum vaginae [N A]).

prone (prōn) [L. *pronus* inclined forward]. Lying with the face downward. See also *pronation*.

pronephron (pro-nef′ron). Pronephros.

pronephros (pro-nef′ros), pl. *pronephroi* [*pro-* + Gr. *nephros* kidney]. The primordial kidney; a structure developing in the embryo before the mesonephros. Its duct is later used by the mesonephros, which arises caudal to it.

pronestyl (pro-nes′til). Trade mark for preparations of procainamide hydrochloride.

prong (prong). A conical projection, such as a conical root of a tooth.

pronograde (pro′no-grād) [L. *pronus* bent downward + *gradi* to walk]. Characterized by walking with the body approximately horizontal; applied to quadrupeds. Cf. *orthograde*.

pronometer (pro-nom′e-ter). An instrument for measuring the amount of pronation or supination of the forearm.

pronormoblast (pro-nor′mo-blast). Proerythroblast.

prontosil (pron′to-sil). Trade mark for an orange red, crystalline substance, first prepared in 1932, the forerunner of the sulfonamide drugs. **p. al′bum,** sulfanilamide. **p. fla′vum, p. ru′brum,** prontosil. **p. soluble,** neoprontosil.

pronucleus (pro-nu′kle-us). The precursor of a nucleus. **female p.,** the reduced nucleus of the ovum which unites with the male pronucleus in the fertilized ovum to form the cleavage nucleus. **male p.,** the nuclear material of the head of a spermatozoon, after it has penetrated the ovum.

prootic (pro-ot′ik) [*pro-* + Gr. *ous* ear]. Situated in front of the ear.

propagation (prop″ah-ga′shun). Reproduction.

propagative (prop′ah-ga″tiv). Pertaining to or concerned in propagation.

propalinal (pro-pal′ĭ-nal) [*pro-* + Gr. *palin* back]. Having a backward and forward direction or motion.

propancreatitis (pro-pan″kre-ah-ti′tis). Purulent pancreatitis.

propane (pro′pān). A volatile liquid or gaseous hydrocarbon, $CH_3.CH_2.CH_3$, from petroleum.

propanolide (pro-pan′o-līd). Betapropiolactone.

propantheline (pro-pan′thĕ-lēn). Chemical name: (2-hydroxyethyl)diisopropylmethylammonium 9-xanthenecarboxylate: used in parasympathetic blockade.

proparacaine (pro-par′ah-kān). Chemical name: 2-diethylaminoethyl 3-amino-4-propoxybenzoate: used as a local anesthetic.

propedeutic (pro″pe-du′tik). Pertaining to preliminary instruction.

propedeutics (pro″pe-du′tiks) [Gr. *propaideia* preparatory teaching]. Preliminary instruction.

propene (pro′pēn). Propylene.

propenyl (pro-pe′nil). Glyceryl.

Propeomyces (pro″pe-o-mi′sēz). A genus of yeastlike fungi, of the family Eremascaceae, various species of which cause dermal lesions.

propepsin (pro-pep′sin). Pepsinogen.

propeptone (pro-pep′tōn). Hemialbumose.

propeptonuria (pro″pep-to-nu′re-ah). Hemialbumosuria.

properitoneal (pro″per-ĭ-to-ne′al). Situated between the parietal peritoneum and the abdominal wall.

prophage (pro′fāj) [*pro-* + *phage*]. The latent stage of a phage in a lysogenic bacterium.

prophase (pro′fāz). The first stage in mitosis, including all the processes up to the metaphase or separation of the chromosomes. See *mitosis*.

prophenpyridamine (pro″fen-pi-rid′ah-mēn). Pheniramine.

prophylactic (pro″fi-lak′tik) [Gr. *prophylaktikos*]. 1. Tending to ward off disease. 2. An agent that tends to ward off disease.

prophylactodontics (pro″fi-lak″to-don′tiks). Preventive dentistry.

prophylactodontist (pro″fi-lak″to-don′tist). A specialist in preventive dentistry.

prophylaxis (pro″fi-lak′sis) [Gr. *prophylassein* to keep guard before]. The prevention of disease; preventive treatment. **causal p.,** removal of the cause of a disease. **chemical p.,** the use of chemicals in preventing the transmission of disease, especially venereal disease. **collective p.,** the protection of the community from infection. **dental p.,** the use of appropriate procedures and/or techniques to prevent dental and oral disease and malformations. **drug p.,** the use of drugs in the prevention of infection, especially malarial infection. **gametocidal p.,** the use of drugs, such as plasmochin, to destroy the gametocytes of malaria in the people. **individual p.,**

the prevention of infection in an individual. **mechanical p.**, prevention of the transmission of venereal disease by mechanical means (e.g., a condom). **oral p.**, dental p. **serum p.**, prevention of disease by the use of immune serums.

propiodal (pro-pi′o-dal). Chemical name: 2-hydroxytrimethylene-bis-(trimethylammonium) iodide: used as a source of iodine.

propiolactone (pro″pe-o-lak′tōn). Betapropiolactone.

propiomazine (pro″pe-o-ma′zēn). Chemical name: 3-propionyl-10-dimethylaminoisopropylphenothiazine: used to potentiate the sedative action of barbiturates, and as an adjunct to ether anesthesia.

Propionibacteriaceae (pro″pe-on″e-bak-te″re-a′se-e). A family of Schizomycetes (order Eubacteriales), occurring as non-motile, irregularly shaped rods. It includes three genera, *Butyribacterium*, *Propionibacterium*, and *Zymobacterium*.

Propionibacterium (pro″pe-on″e-bak-te′re-um) [*pro-* + Gr. *piōn* fat + *baktērion* little rod]. A genus of microorganisms of the family Propionibacteriaceae, order Eubacteriales, made up of non–spore-forming, anaerobic, gram-positive bacilli found as saprophytes in dairy products.

propionitril (pro″pe-o-ni′tril). Ethyl cyanide.

proplasmacyte (pro-plaz′mah-sīt). Türk's irritation leukocyte.

proplasmin (pro-plaz′min). Plasminogen.

proplex, proplexus (pro′pleks, pro-plek′sus). The choroid plexus of the lateral ventricle of the brain.

propolycyte (pro-pol′e-sīt). Polycyte.

propons (pro′pons) [L. *pro* before + *pons* bridge]. The delicate plates of white substance which pass transversely across the anterior end of the pyramid and just below the pons varolii. Called also *ponticulus*.

propositi (pro-poz′ĭ-ti). Plural of *propositus*.

propositus (pro-poz′ĭ-tus), pl. *propos′iti* [L. *proponere* to put on view]. The original person presenting with a mental or physical disorder and whose case serves as the stimulus for a hereditary or genetic study. Called also *proband*.

propoxycaine (pro-pok′se-kān). Chemical name: 2-diethylaminoethyl 4-amino-2-propoxybenzoate: used as a local anesthetic.

propoxyphene (pro-pok′se-fēn). Dextropropoxyphene.

proprietary (pro-pri′ĕ-ta-re). A proprietary medicine; "any chemical, drug, or similar preparation used in the treatment of diseases, if such article is protected against free competition as to name, product, composition, or process of manufacture by secrecy, patent, trade mark, or copyright, or by any other means."

proprioceptive (pro″pre-o-sep′tiv). Receiving stimulations within the tissues of the body.

proprioceptor (pro″pre-o-sep′tor). Sensory nerve terminals which give information concerning movements and position of the body. They occur chiefly in the muscles, tendons and the labyrinth. See *receptor*, def. 2.

propriodentium (pro″pre-o-den′she-um). The tissues of a tooth.

propriospinal (pro″pre-o-spi′nal). Pertaining wholly to the spinal cord.

proptometer (pro-tom′e-ter) [Gr. *proptōsis* a fall forward + *metron* measure]. An instrument for measuring protrusion; especially, a scale for measuring the degree of exophthalmos.

proptosis (prop-to′sis) [Gr. *proptōsis* a fall forward]. A forward displacement; a projecting. **ocular p.**, bulging of the eyeball; exophthalmos.

propulsion (pro-pul′shun) [*pro-* + L. *pellere* to thrust]. 1. Tendency to fall forward in walking. 2. Festination.

propyl (pro′pil). The univalent chemical radical, C_3H_7 or $CH_3.CH_2.CH_2$.

propylene (prop′ĭ-lēn). A gaseous hydrocarbon, $CH_3.CH{:}CH_2$, of the olefin series, which has anesthetic properties.

propylhexedrine (pro″pil-hek′sĕ-drēn). Chemical name: N,α-dimethyl-2-cyclohexylethylamine: used as an inhalant to decongest nasal mucosa.

propyliodone (pro″pil-i′o-dōn). Chemical name: propyl 3,5-diiodo-4-oxo-1(${}_4$H) pyridineacetate: used as a radiopaque medium in bronchography.

propylparaben (pro″pil-par′ah-ben). Chemical name: propyl p-hydroxybenzoate: used as an antifungal preservative.

propylthiouracil (pro″pil-thi″o-u′rah-sil). Chemical name: 6-propyl-2-thiouracil: used as a thyroid inhibitor.

pro re nata (pro re na′tah) [L.]. According to circumstances. Abbreviated p.r.n.

prorennin (pro-ren′in). Renninogen.

prorrhaphy (pro′rah-fe) [*pro-* + Gr. *rhaphē* suture]. Advancement.

prorsad (pror′sad) [L. *prorsum* forward]. In a forward direction.

prorubricyte (pro-roo′brĭ-sīt). Proerythroblast.

proscillaridin A (pro-sil-ar′ĭ-din). A cardiac glycoside, $C_{30}H_{42}O_8$, that results from the enzymatic splitting of scillaren A. On hydrolysis it yields scillaridin A and rhamnose.

proscolex (pro-sko′leks), pl. *prosco′lices* [Gr. *pro* before + *skōlēx* worm]. The embryonic form of a cestode worm just after leaving the egg.

prosecretin (pro″se-kre′tin). The supposed precursor of secretin, thought to be contained in epithelial cells and to be converted into secretin on hydrolysis with acids.

prosector (pro-sek′tor) [L.]. One who dissects anatomical subjects for demonstration.

prosencephalon (pros″en-sef′ah-lon) [Gr. *prosō* before + *enkephalos* brain]. 1. [N A, B N A] The part of the brain developed from the anterior of the three primary divisions of the embryonic neural tube; it comprises the cerebral hemispheres, diencephalon, hypothalamus, and thalamencephalon. Called also *forebrain*. 2. The most anterior of the three primary divisions of the neural axis of the embryo, which later divides into the telencephalon and the diencephalon.

proserozym, proserozyme (pro-se′ro-zīm). Prothrombin.

proso- (pros′o) [Gr. *prosō* forward]. Combining form meaning forward, or anterior.

prosocele (pros′o-sēl). Prosocoele.

prosocoele (pros′o-sēl) [*proso-* + Gr. *koilia* a hollow]. The foremost cavity of the brain; the ventricular cavity of the prosencephalon.

prosodemic (pros″o-dem′ik) [*proso-* + Gr. *dēmos* people]. Passing from one person to another instead of reaching a large number at once, through some means such as water supply: said of a disease progressing in that way.

prosody (pros′o-de) [Gr. *prosodos* a solemn procession]. The variation in stress, pitch, and rhythm of speech by which different shades of meaning are conveyed.

prosogaster (pros′o-gas″ter) [*proso-* + Gr. *gastēr* stomach]. Foregut.

prosopagnosia (pros″o-pag-no′se-ah) [*prosopo-* + *a* neg. + Gr. *gnōsis* perception + *-ia*]. A variety of visual agnosia characterized by inability to recognize the faces of other people, or even one's own face in a mirror, associated usually with agnosia also for color, objects, and places.

prosopalgia (pros″o-pal′je-ah) [*prosopo-* + *-algia*]. Trigeminal neuralgia.

prosopalgic (pros″o-pal′jik). Pertaining to or affected with prosopalgia (trigeminal neuralgia).

prosopantritis (pros″o-pan-tri′tis) [*prosopo-* + Gr. *antron* cavity + *-itis*]. Inflammation of the frontal sinuses.

prosopectasia (pros″o-pek-ta′ze-ah) [*prosopo-* + Gr. *ektasis* expansion + *-ia*]. Oversize of the face.

prosoplasia (pros″o-pla′se-ah) [*proso-* + Gr. *plassein* to form]. 1. Abnormal differentiation of tissue. 2. Development into a higher state of organization or functionating.

prosopo- (pros′o-po) [Gr. *prosōpon* face]. Combining form denoting relationship to the face.

prosopoanoschisis (pros″o-po-ah-nos′kĭ-sis) [*prosopo-* + Gr. *ana* up + *schisis* cleft]. Oblique facial cleft.

prosopodiaschisis (pros″o-po-di-as′kĭ-sis) [*prosopo-* + Gr. *dia* apart + *schisis* cleft]. An operation for opening all of the paranasal sinuses.

prosopodiplegia (pros″o-po-di-ple′je-ah) [*prosopo-* + Gr. *dis* (*di-*) twice + *plēgē* stroke]. Paralysis of the face and one lower extremity.

prosopodysmorphia (pros″o-po-dis-mor′fe-ah) [*prosopo-* + *dys-* + Gr. *morphē* form + *-ia*]. Facial hemiatrophy.

prosopolepsy (pros′o-po-lep″se) [*prosopo-* + Gr. *lambanein* to take]. The reading of character from the features.

prosoponeuralgia (pros″o-po-nu-ral′je-ah). Pain in the nerves of the face.

prosopopagus (pros″o-pop′ah-gus) [*prosopo-* + Gr. *pagus* thing fixed]. Unequal conjoined twins in which the parasite is attached to the face elsewhere than at the jaw.

prosopopilar, prosopopilary (pros″o-po-pi′lar, -pi′lar-e) [*prosopo-* + L. *pilus* hair]. Marked by abnormal growth of hair on the face.

prosopoplegia (pros″o-po-ple′je-ah) [*prosopo-* + Gr. *plēgē* stroke]. Facial paralysis.

prosopoplegic (pros″o-po-ple′jik). Pertaining to or affected with facial paralysis.

prosoposchisis (pros″o-pos′kĭ-sis) [*prosopo-* + Gr. *schisis* cleft]. Congenital fissure of the face.

prosoposcopy (pros″o-pos′ko-pe) [*prosopo-* + Gr. *skopein* to examine]. The study of the face and especially the changes produced in it by various diseases.

prosopospasm (pros′o-po-spazm) [*prosopo-* + *spasm*]. Spasm of the muscles of the face.

prosoposternodymia (pros″o-po-ster″no-dim′e-ah) [*prosopo-* + Gr. *sternon* sternum + *didymos* twin]. A double fetal monster joined face to face and sternum to sternum.

prosopothoracopagus (pros″o-po-tho″rah-kop′ah-gus) [*prosopo-* + Gr. *thōrax* chest + *pagos* thing fixed]. Conjoined symmetrical twins united in the frontal plane, the fusion extending from the oral region through the thorax.

prospermia (pro-sper′me-ah) [Gr. *pro* before + *sperma* sperm + *-ia*]. Ejaculatio praecox.

prostaglandin (pros″tah-glan′din). A naturally occurring substance, first found in the semen of man and sheep, that causes strong contraction of smooth muscle and dilation of certain vascular beds; subsequently found also in menstrual fluid.

prostata (pros′tah-tah). [N A, B N A] A gland which in the male surrounds the neck of the bladder and part of the urethra. See *prostate*.

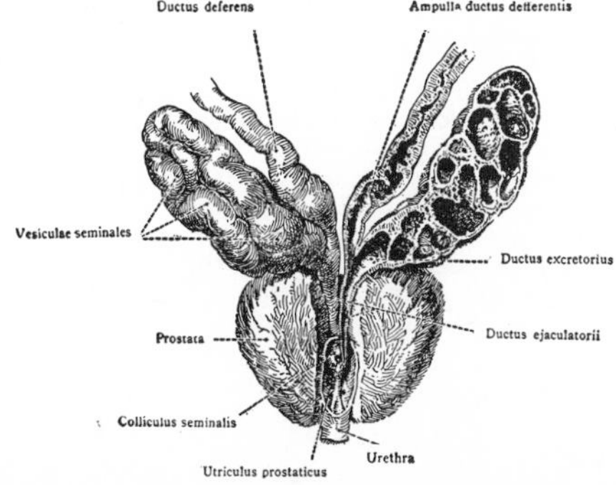

Prostate and seminal vesicles. (Eycleshymer and Jones.)

prostatalgia (pros″tah-tal′je-ah) [*prostate* + *-algia*]. Pain in the prostate gland.

prostatauxe (pros″tah-tawk′se) [*prostate* + Gr. *auxē* increase]. Enlargement of the prostate.

prostate (pros′tāt) [Gr. *prostates* one who stands before, from *pro* before + *histanai* to stand]. A gland which in the male surrounds the neck of the bladder and the urethra. Called also *prostata* [N A]. It consists of a median lobe and two lateral lobes, and is made up partly of glandular matter, the ducts from which empty into the prostatic portion of the urethra, and partly of muscular fibers which encircle the urethra.

prostatectomy (pros″tah-tek′to-me) [*prostate* + *ektomē* excision]. Surgical removal of the prostate or of a part of it. **perineal p.,** removal of the prostate through an incision in the perineum. **retropubic prevesical p.,** removal of the prostate through a suprapubic incision but without entering the urinary bladder. **suprapubic transvesical p.,** removal of the prostate through an incision above the pubis and through the urinary bladder. **transurethral p.** See under *resection*.

prostatelcosis (pros″tat-el-ko′sis) [*prostate* + Gr. *helkōsis* ulceration]. Ulceration of the prostate.

prostateria (pros″tah-te′re-ah). Prostatism.

prostatic (pros-tat′ik). Pertaining to the prostate gland.

prostaticovesical (pros-tat″ĭ-ko-ves′ĭ-kal). Pertaining to the prostate and the bladder.

prostaticovesiculectomy (pros-tat″ĭ-ko-vesik″u-lek′to-me). Excision of the prostate gland and seminal vesicles.

prostatism (pros′tah-tizm). A morbid state of mind and body due to prostatic disease, especially the condition which results from obstruction to urination due to prostatic hypertrophy. **vesical p.,** a condition of retention of the urine resembling that of prostatic disease, but existing in the absence of any affection of the prostate.

prostatisme (pros′tah-tizm). Prostatism. **p. sans prostate,** the symptoms of prostatic obstruction without enlargement of the prostate.

prostatitic (pros″tah-ti′tik). Pertaining to prostatitis.

prostatitis (pros″tah-ti′tis). Inflammation of the prostate gland.

prostatocystitis (pros-ta″to-sis-ti′tis) [*prostate* + Gr. *kystis* bladder + *-itis*]. Inflammation of the neck of the bladder (prostatic urethra) and the bladder cavity.

prostatocystotomy (pros-ta″to-sis-tot′o-me) [*prostate* + Gr. *kystis* bladder + *tomē* a cutting]. Surgical incision of the bladder and prostate.

prostatodynia (pros″tah-to-din′e-ah) [*prostate* + Gr. *odynē* pain]. Pain in the prostate gland.

prostatography (pros″tah-tog′rah-fe). Roentgenography of the prostate.

prostatolith (pros-tat′o-lith). A prostatic calculus.

prostatolithotomy (pros-tat″o-lĭ-thot′o-me). Incision of the prostate for the removal of calculus.

prostatomegaly (pros″tah-to-meg′ah-le) [*prostate* + Gr. *megalē* great]. Hypertrophy of the prostate.

prostatometer (pros″tah-tom′e-ter) [*prostate* + Gr. *metron* measure]. An instrument for measuring the prostate.

prostatomy (pros-tat′o-me). Prostatotomy.

prostatomyomectomy (pros-ta″to-mi″o-mek′to-me) [*prostate* + *myomectomy*]. The surgical removal of a prostatic myoma.

prostatorrhea (pros″tah-to-re′ah) [*prostate* + Gr. *rhoia* flow]. A catarrhal discharge from the prostate.

prostatotomy (pros″tah-tot′o-me) [*prostate* + Gr. *tomē* a cutting]. Surgical incision of the prostate.

prostatotoxin (pros″tah-to-tok′sin). A toxin formed on injection of an extract of the prostate gland: it is destructive to prostatic cells.

prostatovesiculectomy (pros″tah-to-ve-sik″u-lek′to-me). Excision of the prostate and seminal vesicles.

prostatovesiculitis (pros″tah-to-ve-sik″u-li′tis). Inflammation of the prostate and seminal vesicles.

prostaxia (pro-stak′se-ah). A stabilized condition of protein dispersion in the body.

prosternation (pro″ster-na′shun). Camptocormy.

prostheses (pros-the′sēz). Plural of *prosthesis*.

prosthesis (pros′the-sis), pl. *prosthe′ses* [Gr. "a putting to"]. 1. The replacement of an absent part by an artificial substitute. 2. An artificial substitute for a missing part, such as an eye, leg, or denture; the term is also applied to any device by which performance of a natural function is aided or augmented, such as a hearing aid or eyeglasses. **cleft palate p.,** an appliance used to restore integrity of the roof of the mouth in patients with cleft palate. **dental p.,** a replacement for one or more of the teeth or other oral structure, ranging from a single tooth to a complete denture. **maxillofacial p.,** a replacement for parts of the upper jaw or the face missing because of disease or injury. **ocular p.** 1. An artificial substitute for the eyeball. 2. Eyeglasses. **Sauerbruch's p.,** an artificial limb with which the tissues of the stump are used to secure motion. **Vanghetti's p.,** an artificial limb similar to Sauerbruch's prosthesis, designed to be moved by muscles of the stump.

prosthetic (pros-thet′ik). Pertaining to prosthesis.

prosthetics (pros-thet′iks). The art and science of replacing, by artificial means, body parts that may be missing or defective as a result of surgical intervention, trauma, disease, or developmental anomaly. **dental p.,** prosthodontics. **facial p.,** prosthetics concerned only with the replacement of parts of the face.

prosthetist (pros′the-tist). One skilled in the construction or application of prostheses.

prosthion (pros′the-on) [Gr. *prosthios* the foremost + *-on* neuter ending]. The lowest anterior point on the gum between the maxillary central incisors.

prosthodontia (pros″tho-don′she-ah). Prosthodontics.

prosthodontics (pros″tho-don′tiks) [*prosthesis* + Gr. *odous* tooth]. That branch of dental art and science concerned with the construction of artificial appliances designed to replace missing teeth and sometimes other parts of the oral cavity and face.

prosthodontist (pros″tho-don′tist). A dentist who specializes in prosthodontics.

Prosthogonimus (pros″tho-gon′ĭ-mus). A genus of trematode parasites. **P. macror′chis,** a species occurring in chickens, turkeys, pheasants, and other birds.

prostigmin (pro-stig′min). Trade mark for preparations of neostigmine.

prostration (pros-tra′shun) [L. *prostratio*]. Extreme exhaustion or powerlessness. **electric p.,** a condition due to prolonged exposure to electric light, marked by pains in the face, photophobia and pigmentation of the skin. **heat p.,** heat exhaustion. **nervous p.,** neurasthenia.

prot-. See *proto-*.

protactinium (pro″tak-tin′e-um). A chemical element occurring along with radium in pitchblende, carnotite and other minerals. It is one of the radioactive series; atomic weight, 231; atomic number, 91; symbol Pa.

protagon (pro′tah-gon) [*prot-* + Gr. *agein* to lead]. A crystalline mass, $C_{108}H_{360}N_5PO_{35}$, which separates from an alcoholic extract of brain substance on cooling.

protal (pro′tal). Congenital: dating from the origin of life.

protalba (pro-tal′bah). Trade mark for preparations of protoveratrine A.

protalbumose (pro-tal′bu-mōs). Protoproteose.

protaminase (pro-tam′ĭ-nās). An enzyme which splits up protamines.

protamine (pro′tah-min) [*prot-* + *amine*]. 1. Any one of a series of basic proteins of the most simple composition, occurring in the spermatozoa of fish. They are strongly basic and yield large amounts of diamino-acids. 2. An amine or base, $C_{16}H_{32}N_9O_2$, from spermatozoa and from fish spawn.

Protaminobacter (pro″tah-mi″no-bak′ter). A genus of microorganisms of the family Pseudomonadaceae, suborder Pseudomonadineae, order Pseudomonadales, occurring as motile or nonmotile, frequently pigmented cells in soil or water. It includes two species, *P. albofla′vus* and *P. ru′ber*.

protan (pro′tan). An individual exhibiting protanomalopia or protanopia, marked by derangement or loss of the red-green sensory mechanism, with a noticeable shift or shortening of the spectrum and luminancy loss in the long-wave (red) end. Cf. *deutan*.

protandry (prōt-an′dre) [Gr. *prōtos* first + *aner, andros* man]. Hermaphroditism in which the male gonad matures before the female gonad.

protanomalopia (pro″tah-nom″ah-lo′pe-ah) [*prot-* + Gr. *anōmalos* irregular + *ōpē* sight + *-ia*]. A problematic variant of normal color vision, in which none of the constituents for complete chromatic perception are lacking, but a greater than usual proportion of lithium red light to thallium green is required to match a fixed sodium yellow. Sometimes called "red weakness," and viewed as a transitional stage to complete loss of color vision.

protanomalopsia (pro″tah-nom″ah-lop′se-ah). Protanomalopia.

protanomalous (pro″tah-nom′ah-lus). Pertaining to or characterized by protanomalopia.

protanomaly (pro″tah-nom′ah-le). Protanomalopia.

protanope (pro′tah-nōp). An individual exhibiting protanopia.

protanopia (pro″tah-no′pe-ah) [*prot-* + *an-* neg. + Gr. *ōpē* sight + *-ia*]. Defective color vision of the dichromatic type, characterized by retention of the sensory mechanism for two hues only (blue and yellow) of the normal 4-primary quota, and lacking that for red and green and their derivatives, with loss of luminance and shift of brightness and hue curves toward the short-wave end of the spectrum, as in twilight vision. Coined by von Kries (1897) to replace "red blindness." Cf. the correlative terms *deuteranopia*, *tritanopia*, and *tetartanopia*, in which the color vision deficiency is in the second, third, and fourth primary, respectively.

protanopic (pro″tah-nop′ik). Pertaining to or characterized by protanopia.

protanopsia (pro″tah-nop′se-ah). Protanopia.

Protea (pro′te-ah) [L.]. A genus of trees of many species from various wet and warm regions; several species are medicinal.

protean (pro′te-an) [Gr. *Prōteus* a many-formed deity]. 1. Assuming different shapes; changeable in form. 2. An insoluble derivative of protein, being the first product of the action of water, dilute acids, or enzymes.

proteantigen (pro″te-an′tĭ-jen). A protein used by injection as an antigen.

protease (pro′te-ās). A general term for a proteolytic enzyme. See *peptidase*. **fig-tree p.,** a protease found in the sap of various species of fig trees, especially *Ficus carica*, which is able to digest live Ascaris worms.

protectant (pro-tek′tant). Protective.

protectin (pro-tek′tin). 1. Noguchi's term for a substance which develops in blood serum on standing, and having the effect of protecting the blood corpuscles against hemolytic action. 2. Thin paper coated on one side with an adhesive caoutchouc plaster: used in surgery.

protective (pro-tek′tiv) [L. *protegere* to cover over]. 1. Affording defense or immunity. 2. An agent that affords defense against a deleterious influence, such as a substance applied to the skin (*skin p.*) to avoid the effects of the sun's rays (*solar p.*) or other noxious influences.

protector (pro-tek′tor). A substance in a catalyst which prolongs the rate of activity of the latter. Cf. *promoter.*

Proteeae (pro-te′e-e). A taxonomic tribe of the family Enterobacteriaceae, order Eubacteriales, made up of straight, motile, gram-negative rods, which are found primarily in fecal matter and other putrefying material. It includes a single genus, *Proteus.*

proteid (pro′te-id). Protein.

proteidic (pro″te-id′ik). Pertaining to a proteid or proteids.

proteidin (pro′te-ĭ-din). An immunizing bacteriolytic substance developed in the organism by a combination between a bacteriolytic enzyme and any albuminous material. **pyocyanase p.,** the proteidin of *Bacillus pyocyaneus:* used for protective inoculation against diphtheria.

proteidogenous (pro″te-ĭ-doj′e-nus). Giving rise to or producing proteins.

protein (pro′te-in) [Gr. *prōtos* first]. Any one of a group of complex organic nitrogenous compounds, widely distributed in plants and animals and which form the principal constituents of the cell protoplasm. They are essentially combinations of α-amino acids and their derivatives. The following classification has been recommended: 1. *Simple proteins*, or those that yield only α-amino acids or their derivatives on hydrolysis. They are albumins, globulins, glutelins, alcohol-soluble proteins, albuminoids (scleroproteins), histones, and protamines. 2. *Conjugated proteins*, or those that contain the protein molecule united to some other molecule or molecules, the prosthetic group, otherwise than as a salt. They are nucleoproteins, glycoproteins, phosphoproteins, hemoglobins (chromoproteins), lecithoproteins, lipoproteins. 3. *Derived proteins*, or derivatives of the protein molecule formed by hydrolytic changes. They are proteins, metaproteins, coagulated proteins, proteoses, peptones, and peptides. The most important members of this group are albumin, casein, legumin, fibrin, vegetable fibrin, myosin, syntonin, glutin. **alcohol-soluble p.,** prolamine. **bacterial p.,** a protein formed by bacterial activity. **bacterial cellular p.,** a protein that forms part of the substance of a bacterium. **Bence Jones p.,** a low-molecular weight, thermosensitive urinary protein, which is found almost exclusively in multiple myeloma, and the outstanding characteristic of which is its unique property of coagulating on heating at 45–55°C. and of redissolving partially or wholly on boiling. **coagulated p.,** an insoluble form which certain proteins assume when denatured at their isoelectric point by heat, alcohol, ultraviolet rays, or other agents. **compound p.,** a protein which on hydrolysis yields a simple protein and a nonprotein matter. **conjugated p.** See under *protein.* **defensive p.** (Hankin), any protein formed within the body and serving as a protection against disease; any alexin, phylaxin, or sozin. **denatured p.** See *denaturation.* **derived p.** See under *protein.* **floating p.,** a protein which does not constitute part of the tissues, but simply circulates in the body and is then excreted. **halogen p.,** one of a group of protein derivatives produced by the action of free halogen on protein solutions. **Hektoen, Kretschmer, and Welker p.,** a protein found in urine which resembles Bence Jones protein in solubility, but differs in its crystalline form, in its behavior toward heat, and in its precipitin reactions. **immune p's,** proteins formed by the combinations of albuminous matters of the body with the enzymes of pathogenic bacteria. **insoluble p.,** a substance left behind after the other proteins have been extracted from a cell. **iodized p.,** a protein treated with iodine. **maintenance p.,** the smallest amount of protein upon which the normal conditions of the body can be maintained. **native p.,** unchanged animal or vegetable proteins, especially as they occur in foods. **plasma p's,** immune bodies (gamma globulins) used in the prophylaxis of measles. They may be convalescent serum, placental extract or gamma globulins concentrated from normal human plasma. See *gamma globulin*, under *globulin.* **prophylactic measles p.,** an immune substance for prophylaxis against measles. It may be a convalescent serum, and was formerly a placental extract. **prosthetic p's,** proteins adsorbed onto a hypothetical skeleton of myosine which in their impure form resist N/10 hydrochloric acid at 100°C. for 15 minutes and can be precipitated by trichloracetic acid. **protective p.,** defensive protein. **pyocyanic p.,** a substance prepared by treating the *Pseudomonas pyocyaneus* with potassa: used in suppuration. **pyogenic p.,** the protein portion of a bacterium which is the suppuration-producing element of the bacterium. **racemized p.,** protein so changed by chemical or other agents that it loses more or less of its specific characteristics. **serum p.,** any protein found in the serum of the blood. **silver p., mild.** See under *silver.* **silver p., strong.** See under *silver.* **simple p.** See under *protein.* **split p.** See *Vaughan's split product*, under *product.* **synthetic p.,** highly complex polypeptides made in the laboratory. They show most of the characteristics of native protein. **whole p.,** protein which has not been split.

proteinase (pro′te-in-ās). Any enzyme that splits native proteins. **anastrophic p.,** a proteinase which can be inactivated by oxidation and then reactivated by reduction. **clothes-moth p.,** an enzyme found in the intestine of the clothes moth, *Tineola biselliella*, which will digest wool keratin at pH 9.3 after the keratin has been reduced. **ficin p.,** a crystallizable enzyme from the sap of fig trees which digests proteins at pH 4–7 to proteoses. **stasidynic p.,** a proteinase whose activity is unaffected by either oxidation or reduction.

proteinemia (pro″te-in-e′me-ah). An excess of protein in the blood.

proteinic (pro″te-in′ik). Pertaining to protein.

proteinivorous (pro″te-in-iv′o-rus) [*protein* + L. *vorare* to devour]. Subsisting or feeding on protein.

proteinochrome (pro″te-in′o-krōm) [*protein* + Gr. *chrōma* color]. Any one of a series of coloring matters formed by the action of bromine or chlorine on tryptophan.

proteinochromogen (pro″te-in-o-kro′mo-jen). Tryptophan.

proteinogen (pro″te-in′o-jen). Northrop's name for the hypothetical mother substance of all proteins.

proteinogenous (pro″te-in-oj′e-nus). Formed by or from a protein.

proteinogram (pro″te-in′o-gram). A graphic representation of the proteins present in the blood serum.

proteinology (pro″te-in-ol′o-je) [*protein* + *-logy*]. The scientific study of the protein status of the body.

proteinosis (pro″te-in-o′sis). The accumulation of protein in the tissues. **lipid p.,** a disturbance of lipid metabolism marked by yellowish deposits of a lipid-protein mixture on the inner surface of the lips, under the tongue, on the fauces. There may be nodular masses on the face and extremities. Called also *lipoidosis cutis et mucosae* and *Erbach-Wiethe disease.* **tissue p.** See *amyloidosis.*

proteinotherapy (pro-te″in-o-ther′ah-pe). Treatment by the injection of foreign protein.

proteinphobia (pro″te-in-fo′be-ah) [*protein* + Gr. *phobein* to be affrighted by + *-ia*]. Morbid aversion to protein foods.

proteinum pyocyaneum (pro″te-i′num pi″o-sia′ne-um). A derivative from cultures of *Pseudomonas pyocyanea:* used as an application to ulcers.

proteinuria (pro″te-in-u′re-ah) [*protein* + Gr. *ouron* urine + *-ia*]. The presence of protein in the urine. **Bence Jones p.,** the presence in the urine of Bence Jones protein.

proteinuric (pro″te-in-u′rik). Pertaining to proteinuria.

proteoclastic (pro″te-o-klas′tik) [*protein* + Gr. *klasis* breakage]. Splitting up proteins or the protein molecule.

proteocrasic (pro″te-o-kras′ik). Pertaining to proteocrasis.

proteocrasis (pro″te-ok′rah-sis) [*protein* + Gr. *krasis* mixture]. The mixing and fixation of proteins.

Proteoglypha (pro″te-og′lĭ-fah). A group of poisonous snakes that have small stationary fangs which are grooved rather than hollow and so must be held in the wound if the poison is to reach the deeper tissues. Examples are the harlequin snake and the Sonoran coral snake.

proteohormone (pro″te-o-hor′mōn). A hormone that is a peptide or a protein and so is destroyed in the intestinal tract.

proteolipid (pro″te-o-lip′id). A combination of a protein with a lipid, having the solubility characteristics of lipids. Cf. *lipoprotein.*

proteolipin (pro″te-o-li′pin). Proteolipid.

proteolysin (pro″te-ol′ĭ-sin). A specific substance causing proteolysis.

proteolysis (pro″te-ol′ĭ-sis) [*protein* + Gr. *lysis* dissolution]. The hydrolysis of proteins into proteoses, peptones and other products by means of enzymes.

proteolytic (pro″te-o-lit′ik). 1. Pertaining to, characterized by, or promoting proteolysis. 2. An agent that promotes proteolysis.

proteometabolic (pro″te-o-met″ah-bol′ik). Pertaining to proteometabolism.

proteometabolism (pro″te-o-mĕ-tab′o-lism). The metabolism of protein.

proteopectic (pro″te-o-pek-′tik). Proteopexic.

proteopepsis (pro″te-o-pep′sis) [*protein* + Gr. *pepsis* digestion]. The digestion of protein.

proteopeptic (pro″te-o-pep′tik). Digesting protein; pertaining to the digestion of protein.

proteopexic (pro″te-o-pek′sik). Fixing protein within the organism.

proteopexy (pro′te-o-pek″se) [*protein* + Gr. *pēxis* fixation]. The fixation of proteins within the organism.

proteophilic (pro″te-o-fil′ik). Growing best in a protein-rich medium: said of certain bacteria.

proteose (pro′te-ōs) [*protein* + *-ose*]. A secondary protein derivative or a mixture of split products formed by a hydrolytic cleavage of the protein molecule more complete than that which occurs with the primary protein derivatives, but not so complete as that which forms amino-acids. The *primary* proteoses are precipitated by half saturation with ammonium sulfate, the *secondary*, by full saturation.

Proteosoma (pro″te-o-so′mah) [*proteus* + Gr. *sōma* body]. A genus of parasite (microzoon) from the blood of birds; probably concerned in the causation of malarial fever in birds.

proteosomal (pro″te-o-so′mal). Pertaining to or caused by proteosoma.

proteosotherapy (pro″te-o-so-ther′ah-pe). Treatment by the injection of foreign proteose.

proteosuria (pro″te-o-su′re-ah) [*proteose* + Gr. *ouron* urine + *-ia*]. The presence of proteose in the urine; albumosuria.

proteotherapy (pro″te-o-ther′ah-pe). Proteinotherapy.

proteotoxin (pro″te-o-tok′sin). Anaphylatoxin.

proteuria (pro″te-u′re-ah) [*protein* + Gr. *ouron* urine + *-ia*]. Proteinuria.

proteuric (pro″te-u′rik). Proteinuric.

Proteus (pro′te-us) [Gr. *Prōteus* a many-formed deity]. A genus of microorganisms of the tribe Proteeae, family Enterobacteriaceae, order Eubacteriales, made up of gram-negative, generally active motile, rod-shaped bacteria of limited pathogenicity, usually found in fecal and other putrefying material. **P. incon′stans,** a species isolated from patients with gastroenteritis, and also found in urinary tract infections; more than 150 different serotypes have been recognized. **P. mirab′ilis,** a species which is usually saprophytic and occasionally is found as a human pathogen. **P. morga′nii,** an organism found in the intestinal tract and associated with summer diarrhea of infants. **P. rettge′ri,** the causative agent of fowl typhoid and other diarrheal diseases of birds; also isolated from patients with sporadic and epidemic gastroenteritis. **P. vulga′ris,** the type species of Proteus, occurring, often as a secondary invader, in a variety of localized suppurative pathologic processes, and being a common cause of cystitis. It occurs as several serotypes; the X strains agglutinate in antiserum to certain of the rickettsia, X-19 strains in antisera to the typhus group, and X-K in antisera to the tsutsugamushi group, in the Weil-Felix reaction used for diagnostic purposes.

prothesis (proth′e-sis) [Gr. "a placing in public"]. Prosthesis.

prothetic (pro-thet′ik). Prosthetic.

prothipendyl (pro-thi′pen-dil). Chemical name: 4-dimethyl-aminopropyl-pyrido (3,2β)-(1,4)-benzothiazine: used as a tranquilizer.

prothrombase (pro-throm′bās). Thrombogen.

prothrombin (pro-throm′bin) [*pro-* + Gr. *thrombos* clot + *-in* chemical suffix]. A glycoprotein present in the plasma that is converted to thrombin by extrinsic thromboplastin during the second stage of blood coagulation. Called also *coagulation factor II.* **activated p.,** according to the Quick concept, the form of prothrombin which is measured by the Quick one-stage method and which, prior to its conversion, exists in the inactive form.

prothrombinase (pro-throm′bin-āse). Thromboplastin. **extrinsic p.,** extrinsic thromboplastin. **intrinsic p.,** intrinsic thromboplastin.

prothrombinogen (pro″throm-bin′o-jen). Factor VII. See discussion of *coagulation factors,* under *factor.*

prothrombinogenic (pro-throm″bĭ-no-jen′ik). Promoting the production of prothrombin.

prothrombinokinase (pro-throm″bĭ-no-ki′nās). Factor VII. See discussion of *coagulation factors,* under *factor.*

prothrombinopenia (pro-throm″bĭ-no-pe′ne-ah). An abnormally diminished amount of prothrombin in the blood.

prothyl (pro′thil). Protyl.

prothymia (pro-thim′e-ah) [*pro-* + Gr. *thymos* spirit + *-ia*]. Forwardness or alertness of mind and will.

protide (pro′tīd). Protein.

protidemia (pro″tĭ-de′me-ah). Proteinemia.

protidolytic (pro″tid-o-lit′ik). Proteolytic.

protidtemns (pro′tid-temz). A collective name for the products produced by the digestion of proteins, namely, proteoses, peptones, peptides, and amino acids.

protinium (pro-tin′e-um). Protium.

protiodide (pro-ti′o-did). That one of the series of iodides of the same base which contains the smallest amount of iodine.

Protista (pro-tis′tah) [Gr. *prōtista* the very first, from *prōtos* first]. Haeckel's name for a proposed kingdom of organisms including the lowest (unicellular) forms of animals and plants.

protistologist (pro″tis-tol′o-jist). A microbiologist.

protistology (pro″tis-tol′o-je) [*Protista* + *-logy*]. Microbiology.

protium (pro′te-um). The mass one isotope of hydrogen; ordinary hydrogen. See *hydrogen.*

proto-, prot- [Gr. *prōtos* first]. Combining form meaning first.

proto-actinium (pro″to-ak-tin′e-um). Protactinium.

proto-albumose (pro″to-al′bu-mōs). Protalbumose.

protoanemonin (pro″to-ah-nem′o-nin). An antibiotic substance from *Anemone pulsatilla:* it inhibits the growth of *Candida albicans, Escherichia coli* and *Staph. aureus.*

Protobacterieae (pro″to-bak″te-ri′e-e). A tribe of the family Nitrobacteriaceae that obtain their life energy by the oxidation of simple inorganic compounds of carbon or hydrogen.

protobe (pro′tōb). Protobios.

protobiology (pro″to-bi-ol′o-je) [*proto-* + Gr. *bios* life + *-logy*]. The science which deals with the forms of life more minute than bacteria, such as the ultraviruses and bacteriophages.

protobios (pro″to-bi′os) [*proto-* + Gr. *bios* life]. A name proposed by d'Herelle for the bacteriophage (protobios bacteriophagus).

protoblast (pro′to-blast) [*proto-* + Gr. *blastos* germ]. 1. A cell with no cell wall; an embryonic cell. 2. The nucleus of an ovum. 3. A blastomere from which a particular organ or part develops.

protoblastic (pro″to-blas′tik). Pertaining to a protoblast.

protobrochal (pro″to-bro′kal) [*proto-* + Gr. *brochos* mesh]. Denoting the first stage in the development of an ovary.

Protocalliphora (pro″to-kah-lif′o-rah). A genus of flies whose larvae feed on nesting birds.

protocaryon (pro″to-kar′e-on) [*proto-* + Gr. *karyon* nucleus]. A cell nucleus formed of a single karyosome in a network of linin.

protochloride (pro″to-klo′rid). That one of a series of chlorides of the same element which contains the least amount of chlorine.

protochlorophyll (pro″to-klo′ro-fil). A substance in plant tissue which is changed by the action of light into chlorophyll.

protochondrium (pro″to-kon′dre-um) [*proto-* + Gr. *chondros* cartilage]. The basophil substance developed from precartilage which constitutes the intermediate stage in cartilage formation.

protochrome (pro′to-krōm). A substance derived from proteins giving reactions identical with urochrome.

protocol (pro′to-kol). The original notes made on a necropsy, an experiment, or on a case of disease.

protocone (pro′to-kōn) [*proto-* + Gr. *kōnos* cone]. The earliest developed tubercle of a molar tooth.

protocooperation (pro″to-co-op″er-a′shun). Symbiosis in which both populations (or individuals) gain from the association but are able to survive without it.

protocoproporphyria (pro″to-kop″ro-por-fir′e-ah). A term used by Waldenström to indicate a preponderant excretion in the feces of protoporphyrin and coproporphyrin; according to Waldenström, this is synonymous with *porphyria cutanea tarda hereditaria.*

protodiastolic (pro″to-di″ah-stol′ik). Immediately following the second heart sound.

protoduodenitis (pro″to-du″o-de-ni′tis). Inflammation of the protoduodenum.

protoduodenum (pro″to-du-o-de′num). The first or proximal portion of the duodenum, extending from the pylorus to the duodenal papilla, and developed embryonically from the foregut.

proto-elastose (pro″to-e-las′tōs). Hemielastin, a product of the digestion of elastin.

proto-erythrocyte (pro″to-e-rith′ro-sīt). A name once applied to the earliest recognizable precursor of an erythrocyte; currently without standing in any scheme of morphological development.

protofibril (pro″to-fi′bril). The first elongated unit appearing in the process of formation of any type of fiber.

protogala (pro-tog′ah-lah) [*proto-* + Gr. *gala* milk]. Colostrum.

protogaster (pro′to-gas″ter) [*proto-* + Gr. *gastēr* stomach]. Archenteron.

protoglobulose (pro″to-glob′u-lōs). Any albumose produced in the digestion of globulin.

protogonocyte (pro″to-go′no-sīt) [*proto-* + *gonocyte*]. One of the two cells resulting from division of the impregnated ovum of Ascaris.

protogonoplasm (pro″to-go′no-plazm) [*proto-* + Gr. *gonē* seed + *plasma* anything formed or molded]. That part of the extranuclear chromatin of a cell that is concerned in the reproductive energies of the cell. This substance is also called *idiochromidia.*

protogyny (pro-toj′ĭ-ne) [*proto-* + Gr. *gyne* woman]. Hermaphroditism in which the female gonad matures before the male gonad.

protohematoblast (pro″to-hem′ah-to-blast). A name once applied to the earliest recognizable precursor of a blood corpuscle; currently without standing in any scheme of morphological development.

protohemin (pro″to-hem′in). Hemin.

protohydrogen (pro″to-hi′dro-jen). Protium.

protoiodide (pro″to-i′o-dīd). Protiodide.

protokylol (pro″to-ki′lol). Chemical name: α[(α-methyl-3,4-methylenedioxyphenethylamino)methyl]protocatechuyl alcohol: used as a sympathomimetic agent, and as a bronchodilator.

protoleukocyte (pro″to-lu′ko-sīt). A name once applied to the earliest recognizable precursor of a leukocyte; currently without standing in any scheme of morphological development.

protomedicus (pro″to-med′ĭ-kus) [*proto-* + L. *medicus* physician]. A medieval term for physician-in-chief.

protomere (pro′to-mēr). Micelle.

protomerite (pro″to-me′rīt) [*proto-* + Gr. *meros* part]. The anterior portion of certain gregarine protozoa; called also *primite.* Cf. *deutomerite.*

protometer (pro-tom′e-ter) [L. *pro-* + Gr. *metron* measure]. An instrument for measuring the forward protrusion of the eyeball.

protometrocyte (pro″to-me′tro-sīt) [*proto-* + *metrocyte*]. The mother cell of the leukocyte and erythrocyte series of cells.

Protominobacter (pro-tom′ĭ-no-bak″ter). A genus of bacteria containing several species found in soil and water.

protomyosinose (pro″to-mi-o′sĭ-nōs). One of the two albumoses formed in the digestion of myosin.

proton (pro′ton) [Gr. *prōtos* first + *-on* neuter ending]. 1. The primitive rudiment of a part; an anlage. 2. A peptone-like body formed by the hydrolysis of a protamine: a tripeptide. 3. The positive core or nucleus of ordinary hydrogen atom of mass one; the unit of positive electricity being equivalent to the electron in charge and to the hydrogen ion in mass.

protonephron (pro″to-nef′ron). Pronephros.

protonephros (pro″to-nef′ros). Pronephros.

protoneuron (pro″to-nu′ron) [*proto-* + Gr. *neuron* nerve]. 1. The first neuron in a peripheral reflex arc. 2. A unit of the nerve net of low metazoans that lacks polarization.

protonic (pro-ton′ik). Pertaining to a proton or anlage.

protonitrate (pro″to-ni′trāt). That one of several nitrates of the same base which contains the least amount of nitric acid.

protopathic (pro″to-path′ik) [*proto-* + Gr. *pathos* disease]. Primary; idiopathic. See *protopathic sensibility,* under *sensibility.*

protopecten (pro″to-pek′ten). Pectose.

protophyllin (pro″to-fil′in). Chlorophyll hydride, a colorless substance which is changed into chlorophyll by the action of air or carbon dioxide.

Protophyta (pro-tof′ĭ-tah). A group of the vegetable kingdom, including the lowest and simplest plants, such as the bacteria.

protophyte (pro′to-fit) [*proto-* + Gr. *phyton* plant]. Any unicellular plant or vegetable organism.

protopine (pro′to-pin). 1. An alkaloid, $C_{20}H_{19}NO_5$, from *Eschscholtzia californica* and many other plants: anodyne and hypnotic. 2. A poisonous alkaloid from various species of *Dicentra*.

protoplasia (pro-to-pla′se-ah). Primary formation of tissue.

protoplasm (pro′to-plazm) [*proto-* + Gr. *plasma* plasm]. The only known form of matter in which life is manifested. It is a viscid, translucent polyphasic colloid with water as the continuous phase, and it makes up the essential material of all plant and animal cells (Purkinje, 1839). It is composed mainly of proteins, lipins, carbohydrates and inorganic salts. **functional p.,** kinoplasm. **superior p.,** ergastoplasm. **totipotential p.,** protoplasm which has the power of forming all cell organs.

protoplasmatic (pro″to-plaz-mat′ik). Protoplasmic.

protoplasmic (pro″to-plaz′mik). Pertaining to or consisting of protoplasm.

protoplast (pro′to-plast) [*proto-* + Gr. *plastos* formed]. 1. The type or model of some organic being. 2. A cell (Hanstein, 1880). 3. A bacterial or plant cell deprived of its rigid wall, and dependent for its integrity on an isotonic or hypertonic medium.

protoporphyrin (pro″to-por′fĭ-rin). The most important natural porphyrin, $C_{34}H_{34}N_4O_4$, whose iron complex, united with protein, occurs as hemoglobin, myoglobin, catalase, and certain respiratory pigments.

protoporphyrinuria (pro″to-por″fĭ-rin-u′re-ah). The presence of protoporphyrin in the urine.

protoproteose (pro″to-pro′te-ōs). A primary proteose.

protopsis (pro-top′sis). Protrusion of the eye; exophthalmos.

protosalt (pro′to-sawlt). That one of a series of salts of the same base which contains the smallest amount of the substance combining with the base.

protospasm (pro′to-spazm) [*proto-* + Gr. *spasmos* spasm]. A spasm which begins in a limited area and extends to other parts; the earlier and minor spasm of jacksonian epilepsy.

Protospirura (pro″to-spi-roo′rah). A genus of nematode parasites. **P. grac′ilis,** a species found in cats.

protostoma (pro″to-sto′mah). Blastopore.

Protostrongylus (pro″to-stron′jĭ-lus). A genus of lung worms. **P. rufes′cens,** a species that infects sheep, goats, and deer.

protosulfate (pro″to-sul′fāt). That one of several sulfates of the same base which contains the least amount of sulfuric acid.

protosyphilis (pro″to-sif′ĭ-lis). Primary syphilis.

prototoxin (pro″to-tok′sin) [*proto-* + *toxin*]. That portion or constituent of a toxin which has the greatest combining capacity for the antitoxin. See *deuterotoxin*, *hematotoxin*, *tritotoxin*.

prototoxoid (pro″to-tok′soid). Protoxoid.

prototroph (pro′to-trōf) [*proto-* + Gr. *trophē* nourishment]. A prototrophic organism.

prototrophic (pro″to-trof′ik). 1. Having the same growth factor requirements as the ancestral or prototype strain: used of microbial mutants. 2. Deriving food from inorganic substances. Cf. *metatrophic* and *paratrophic*.

prototropy (pro-tot′ro-pe) [*proton* + Gr. *tropē* a turning]. The more usual type of tautomerism, which is the result of a mobile hydrogen ion. For example, acetoacetic ester,

$$CH_3\underset{\underset{O}{\|}}{C}CH_2COOC_2H_5 \rightleftharpoons CH_3\underset{\underset{OH}{|}}{C}{=}CHCOOC_2H_5.$$

prototype (pro′to-tip) [*proto-* + Gr. *typos* type]. The original type or form after which other types or forms are developed.

protoveratrine (pro″to-ver′ah-trēn). A name applied to different alkaloids isolated from *Veratrum album*. **p. A,** one of the alkaloids isolated from *Veratrum album*, protoverine 3-(d)-2-hydroxy-2-methylbutyrate 6,7-diacetate 15-(l)-2-methylbutyrate: used as an antihypertensive. **p. B,** an alkaloid isolated from *Veratrum album* with an action qualitatively similar to that of protoveratrine A, but less potent than the latter; the two are sometimes administered in combination.

protovertebra (pro″to-ver′te-brah). 1. Somite. 2. The caudal half of a somite that forms most of a vertebra.

protoxeoid (pro-tok′se-oid). Protoxoid.

protoxide (pro-tok′sid). That one of a series of oxides of the same metal which contains the smallest amount of oxygen.

protoxoid (pro-tok′soid). Any toxoid which has a greater affinity for the antitoxin than has the toxin. See *toxoid*.

Protozoa (pro″to-zo′ah). The lowest division of the animal kingdom, including unicellular organisms. Protozoa are usually separated in four classes: Sarcodina, having pseudopodia; Mastigophora, having flagella; Sporozoa, having no locomotor organs in the adult stages and reproducing by sporulation; Infusoria, having cilia.

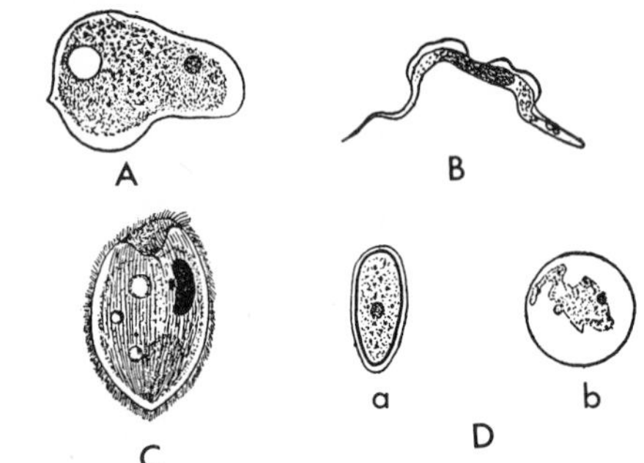

Classes of Protozoa: A, Sarcodina, represented by *Entamoeba histolytica* of amebic dysentery. B, Mastigophora represented by *Trypanosoma gambiense* of African sleeping sickness. C, Infusoria, represented by *Balantidium coli*, causative organism of a certain oriental dysentery (redrawn after Leuckart). D, Sporozoa, represented by (*a*) *Coccidium oviforme* from liver of rabbit, (*b*) *Plasmodium vivax*, of malaria, shown in a red blood corpuscle (all greatly enlarged). (Herms.)

protozoa (pro″to-zo′ah). Plural of *protozoon*.

protozoacide (pro″to-zo′ah-sīd). Destructive to protozoa; an agent destructive to protozoa.

protozo-agglutinin (pro″to-zo″ah-gloo′tĭ-nin). An agglutinin formed in the blood in protozoal infections which has the power of agglutinating the infecting protozoa.

protozoal (pro″to-zo′al). Pertaining to or caused by protozoa.

protozoan (pro″to-zo′an). 1. An organism belonging to the Protozoa. 2. Pertaining to Protozoa.

protozoiasis (pro″to-zo-i′ah-sis). Any disease caused by protozoa.

protozoology (pro″to-zo-ol′o-je). The study of protozoa. **clinical p.,** the study of protozoan parasites causing diseases in animals.

protozoon (pro″to-zo′on), pl. *protozoa* [*proto-* +

Gr. *zōon* animal]. A primitive organism consisting of a single cell; a protozoan.

protozoophage (pro″to-zo′o-fāj) [*protozoa* + Gr. *phagein* to eat]. A cell which has a phagocytic action on protozoa.

protozoosis (pro″to-zo-o′sis). Protozoiasis.

protozootherapy (pro″to-zo″o-ther′ah-pe). The treatment of diseases caused by protozoa, particularly the chemotherapy of such diseases.

protraction (pro-trak′shun) [L. *protrahere* to drag forth from a place]. A facial anomaly in which a cephalometric landmark stands farther forward than usual. **mandibular d.,** a facial anomaly in which the gnathion is anterior to the orbital plane. **maxillary p.,** a facial anomaly in which the subnasion is anterior to the orbital plane.

protractor (pro-trak′tor) [*pro-* + L. *trahere* to draw]. An instrument for extracting bits of bone, bullets, or other foreign material from wounds.

protrusio (pro-troo′ze-o) [L.]. The state of being thrust forward; projection. **p. acetab′uli,** arthrokatadysis.

protrusion (pro-troo′zhun) [L. *protrusi* to push forward]. The state of being thrust forward or laterally, as in masticatory movements of the mandible.

protrypsin (pro-trip′sin). A substance convertible into trypsin and believed by some to be a product of the spleen.

protuberance (pro-tu′ber-ans) [*pro-* + L. *tuber* bulge]. A projecting part, or prominence; an apophysis, process, or swelling. For names of specific anatomical structures not included here, see under *protuberantia*. **p. of chin,** protuberantia mentalis. **laryngeal p.,** prominentia laryngea. **occipital p., transverse,** torus occipitalis. **palatine p.,** torus palatinus. **tubal p.,** torus tubarius.

protuberantia (pro-tu″ber-an′she-ah) [L.]. A projecting part, or prominence. Called also *protuberance*. **p. menta′lis** [N A, B N A], a more or less distinct and triangular prominence on the anterior surface of the body of the mandible, on or near the median line. Called also *mental protuberance*. **p. occipita′lis exter′na** [N A, B N A], a prominence at the center of the outer surface of the squama of the occipital bone which gives attachment to the ligamentum nuchae. Called also *external occipital protuberance*. **p. occipita′lis inter′na** [N A, B N A], the projection of bone at the midpoint of the cruciform eminence, on the internal surface of the squama of the occipital bone, sometimes presenting as a ridge (*crista occipitalis interna* [N A]). Called also *internal occipital protuberance*.

protyl, protyle (pro′til) [*proto-* + Gr. *hylē* matter]. A theoretical substance from which all the chemical elements were formerly supposed to be derived.

provell (pro-vel′). Trade mark for a preparation of protoveratrines A and B.

provera (pro-ver′ah). Trade mark for preparations of medroxyprogesterone acetate.

provertebra (pro-ver′te-brah). Somite.

provirus (pro-vi′rus). A latent stage of an animal virus, equivalent to prophage.

provisional (pro-vizh′un-al). Formed or performed for temporary purposes; temporary.

provitamin (pro-vi′tah-min). A hypothetical precursor of vitamin, especially a substance from which the animal organism can form vitamin. Provitamin A is carotene. Ergosterol has been spoken of as provitamin D.

provocative (pro-vok′ah-tiv). Stimulating the appearance of a sign, reflex, reaction, or therapeutic effect.

Prowazek's bodies (pro-vaht′seks) [Stanislas Josef Mathias von *Prowazek*, zoologist in Hamburg, 1876–1915]. Trachoma bodies.

Prowazek-Greeff bodies (pro-vaht′sek-grāf) [S. J. M. von *Prowazek;* Carl Richard *Greeff*, German ophthalmologist, born 1862]. Trachoma bodies.

Prowazekella (pro-vaht″ze-kel′ah). Prowazekia.

Prowazekia (pro″vaht-zek′e-ah). A genus of flagellate organisms having two nuclei and two flagella. They are found in the feces and urine of man, but are not known to be pathogenic.

proximad (prok′sĭ-mad). Toward the proximal end or in a proximal direction.

proximal (prok′sĭ-mal) [L. *proximus* next]. Nearest; closer to any point of reference: opposed to *distal*.

proximalis (prok″sĭ-ma′lis). Proximal; in official anatomical nomenclature, used to designate proximity to the point of origin or attachment of an organ or part.

proximate (prok′sĭ-māt) [L. *proximatus* drawn near]. Immediate or nearest.

proximo-ataxia (prok″sĭ-mo-ah-tak′se-ah). Ataxia affecting the proximal part of an extremity, as the arm, forearm, thigh, or leg. Cf. *acroataxia*.

proximobuccal (prok″sĭ-mo-buk′al). Pertaining to the proximal and buccal surfaces of a posterior tooth.

proximoceptor (prok″sĭ-mo-sep′tor). Contiguous receptor.

proximolabial (prok″sĭ-mo-la′be-al). Pertaining to the proximal and labial surfaces of an anterior tooth.

proximolingual (prok″sĭ-mo-ling′gwal). Pertaining to the proximal and lingual surfaces of a tooth.

prozonal (pro′zo-nal). 1. Situated before a sclerozone. 2. Pertaining to a prozone.

prozone (pro′zōn) [*pro-* + *zone*]. That portion of the dilution range in which an immune serum of high agglutinin titer fails to agglutinate the homologous bacteria in low dilution. Called also *prezone, prozone phenomenon, zone phenomenon, inhibition zone* and *agglutinoid reaction*.

prozygosis (pro″zi-go′sis). Syncephaly.

prozymogen (pro-zi′mo-jen). Prezymogen.

prual (proo′al). A very violent poison from the root of *Coptosapelta flavescens*.

pruinate (proo′ĭ-nāt) [L. *pruina* hoarfrost]. Having the appearance of being covered with hoarfrost.

Prunella (proo-nel′ah). A genus of labiate plants. *P. vulgaris*, heal-all, is astringent and tonic.

prunin (proo′nin). A concentration prepared from *Prunus serotina:* used in thoracic and nervous diseases.

Prunus (proo′nus) [L. "plum-tree"]. A genus of rosaceous trees and shrubs, including the plums, cherries, and sloes. **P. america′na,** plum. **P. amyg′dala,** almond. **P. domes′tica,** plum. **P. lauro-cer′asus,** cherry laurel. **P. serot′, ina,** wild cherry. **P. spino′sa,** a species of plum and its homeopathic preparation: the sloe, or blackthorn. **P. virginia′na,** the choke-cherry of North America; its bark has sedative qualities and its fruit is highly astringent.

pruriginous (proo-rij″ĭ-nus). Of the nature of or tending to cause prurigo.

prurigo (proo-ri′go) [L. "the itch"]. A chronic skin disease, usually beginning in childhood, and marked by the development of small pale, deep-seated papules and by intense itching. **p. estiva′lis,** a severe relapsing, bullous eruption, occurring in warm weather only. **Besnier's p.,** a form of prurigo associated with asthma, hay fever, and urticaria. **p. fe′rox,** a condition characterized by intense itching, large papules, and swollen lymph glands. **p. mi′tis,** prurigo of a mild type. **p. nodula′ris,** a type of neurodermatitis, with discrete, firm erythematous nodules formed at sites of scratching or irritation of the skin. **p. sim′plex,** a relatively mild form characterized by crops of papules tending to recur in cycles. **summer p.,** p. estivalis. **p. uni-**

versa′lis, prurigo occurring over the entire body.

pruritic (proo-rit′ik). Pertaining to or characterized by pruritus.

pruritogenic (proo″rĭ-to-jen′ik). Capable of causing or tending to cause pruritus.

pruritus (proo-ri′tus) [L. from *prurire* to itch]. Itching. Also used as the name of various conditions characterized by itching, the specific site or type being indicated by a modifying term. **p. a′ni,** intense itching in the anal region. **Duhring's p.,** p. hiemalis. **essential p.,** pruritus occurring idiopathically, without other discoverable abnormality. **p. hiema′lis,** an itching of the skin occurring in cold weather, and unconnected with structural lesions. **p. seni′lis,** an itching in the aged, due to degeneration of the skin. **symptomatic p.,** itching which is associated with and symptomatic of some other disease. **p. vul′vae,** intense itching of the external genitals of the female. See *kraurosis vulvae.*

Prussak's fibers, pouch, space (proo′sahks) [Alexander *Prussak,* Russian otologist, 1839–1897]. See under *fiber* and *space.*

prussiate (prus′e-āt). Cyanide.

PS. Abbreviation for *chloropicrin.*

p.s. Abbreviation for *per second.*

psalis (sa′lis) [Gr. "arch"]. The fornix of the cerebrum (fornix cerebri [N A]).

psalterial (sal-te′re-al). Pertaining to the psalterium.

psalterium (sal-te′re-um) [L.; Gr. *psaltērion* harp]. 1. Commissura fornicis. 2. The omasum.

psammo- (sam′o) [Gr. *psammos* sand]. Combining form denoting relation to sand or to sandlike material.

psammocarcinoma (sam″o-kar″sĭ-no′mah) [*psammo-* + *carcinoma*]. Carcinoma containing calcareous matter.

psammoma (sam-o′mah) [*psammo-* + *-oma*]. A tumor, especially a meningioma, that contains psammoma bodies; formerly sometimes called *Virchow's psammoma.*

psammosarcoma (sam″o-sar-ko′mah) [*psammo-* + *sarcoma*]. A sarcoma containing a sandy deposit.

psammotherapy (sam″o-ther′ah-pe) [*psammo-* + Gr. *therapeia* treatment]. Ammotherapy.

psammous (sam′us). Sandy.

psauoscopy (saw-os′ko-pe) [Gr. *psauein* to touch + *skopein* to examine]. A method of physical examination by passing the ball of the index finger back and forth lightly over the margin of an abnormal area. Over the pathological area the finger seems to encounter greater resistance and the skin seems more tense and less supple.

pselaphesia (sel-ah-fe′ze-ah) [Gr. *psēlaphēsis* touching]. The tactile sense.

psellism (sel′izm) [Gr. *psellisma* stammer]. Stammering or stuttering.

pseud-. See *pseudo-.*

pseudacousis (su″dah-koo′sis) [*pseud-* + Gr. *akousis* hearing]. Pseudacousma.

pseudacousma (su″dah-kōōz′mah) [*pseud-* + Gr. *akousma* thing heard]. A subjective sensation as if sounds were altered in pitch and quality.

pseudacromegaly (su-dak″ro-meg′ah-le). Pseudoacromegaly.

pseudactinomycosis (su-dak″tĭ-no-mi-ko′sis). Pseudoactinomycosis.

pseudagraphia (su″dah-gra′fe-ah). Pseudoagraphia.

pseudalbuminuria (su″dal-bu″mĭ-nu′re-ah). Pseudoalbuminuria.

Pseudamphistomum truncatum (sūd-am-fis′to-mum trun-ka′tum). A fluke found in the bile ducts of cats and dogs in Europe and India: occasionally found in man.

pseudangina (su″dan-ji′nah). Pseudoangina.

pseudankylosis (su″dang-kĭ-lo′sis). Pseudoankylosis.

pseudaphia (su-da′fe-ah) [*pseud-* + Gr. *haphē* touch + *-ia*]. Defect in the power of perceiving touch.

pseudarrhenia (su″dah-re′ne-ah). Female pseudohermaphroditism.

pseudarthritis (su″dar-thri′tis) [*pseud-* + *arthritis*]. A hysterical affection of the joints.

pseudarthrosis (su″dar-thro′sis) [*pseud-* + Gr. *arthrōsis* joint]. A pathologic entity characterized by deossification of a weight-bearing long bone, followed by bending and pathologic fracture, with inability to form normal callus leading to existence of the "false joint" that gives the condition its name.

pseudelminth (su-del′minth) [*pseud-* + Gr. *helmins* worm]. A structure or object that resembles an endoparasitic worm.

pseudencephalus (su″den-sef′ah-lus) [*pseud-* + Gr. *enkephalos* brain]. A fetal monster with a vascular tumor in place of the brain.

pseudesthesia (su″des-the′ze-ah) [*pseud-* + Gr. *aisthēsis* perception]. Any imaginary sensation; a sensation which is felt without any external stimulus, or a sensation which does not correspond to the stimulus that causes it.

pseudinoma (su″dĭ-no′mah) [*pseud-* + *-oma*]. A spurious or phantom tumor.

pseudo-, pseud- [Gr. *pseudēs* false]. Combining form signifying false or spurious.

pseudoacephalus (su″do-a-sef′ah-lus) [*pseudo-* + *acephalus*]. A placental parasitic twin, apparently headless, but with a rudimentary cranium contained in the autosite.

pseudoacromegaly (su″do-ak″ro-meg′ah-le). A condition resembling acromegaly. See *acropachyderma.*

pseudoactinomycosis (su″do-ak″tĭ-no-mi-ko′sis) [*pseudo-* + *actinomycosis*]. A variety of pulmonary phthisis in which the sputum contains crystalline bodies that resemble the grains of actinomycosis; nocardiosis.

pseudoagglutination (su″do-ah-gloo″tĭ-na′shun). Pseudohemagglutination.

pseudoagraphia (su″do-ah-gra′fe-ah). A condition in which the patient can copy writing, but cannot write except in a meaningless and illegible manner.

pseudoalbuminuria (su″do-al″bu-mĭ-nu′re-ah). Adventitious albuminuria.

pseudoalleles (su″do-ah-lēlz′) [*pseudo-* + *allele*]. 1. Genes which are seemingly allelic, but which can eventually be shown to have distinctive loci. 2. Allelic genes which form heterozygotes resembling the wild type rather than either mutant type.

pseudoallelic (su″do-ah-lel′ik). Pertaining to pseudoalleles; seemingly allelic but located at different sites on homologous chromosomes.

pseudo-alopecia (su″do-al″o-pe′she-ah). A condition that resembles but is not true alopecia. **p. area′ta,** loss of hair in spots, resulting from morbid extraction of the hair by the patient.

pseudoalveolar (su″do-al-ve′o-lar). Simulating an alveolar structure.

pseudoanaphylactic (su″do-an″ah-fi-lak′tik). Pertaining to pseudoanaphylaxis.

pseudoanaphylaxis (su″do-an″ah-fi-lak′sis) [*pseudo-* + *anaphylaxis*]. A reaction, the symptoms of which resemble those of the anaphylactic reaction, produced by the injection of serum which has been acted upon by agar, kaolin, starch and other substances, and also by the injection of other nonspecific proteins. See *anaphylactoid.*

pseudoanemia (su″do-ah-ne′me-ah) [*pseudo-* + *anemia*]. Marked pallor with no clinical or hematological evidence of anemia. **p. angiospas′tica,** a form due to vasoconstriction.

pseudoangina (su″do-an-ji′nah) [*pseudo-* + *angina*]. False angina; a syndrome occurring in nervous individuals, marked by precordial pain, fatigue, and lassitude, without evidence of organic disease of the heart. See *angina pectoris vasomotoria.*

pseudoangioma (su″do-an″je-o′mah). A recanalized thrombus of the portal vein.

pseudoankylosis (su″do-ang″kĭ-lo′sis). A false ankylosis.

pseudoanodontia (su″do-an″o-don′she-ah). The condition in which teeth develop but do not erupt.

pseudoantagonist (su″do-an-tag′o-nist). A muscle which by flexing a joint enhances the effect of another muscle crossing that joint to act on a more distant one.

pseudoaphakia (su″do-ah-fa′ke-ah). Membranous cataract.

pseudoapoplexy (su″do-ap′o-plek″se) [*pseudo-* + *apoplexy*]. A condition resembling apoplexy, but without cerebral hemorrhage.

pseudoappendicitis (su″do-ah-pen″dĭ-si′tis). A condition with symptoms simulating appendicitis, sometimes hysterical and sometimes of syphilitic origin, but without affection of the appendix. **p. zooparasit′ica,** a condition in which parasites are present in the vermiform appendix.

pseudoarteriosclerosis (su″do-ar-te″re-o-sklero′sis). A tortuosity of blood vessels which causes pathologic conditions resembling those of arteriosclerosis.

pseudoarthrosis (su″do-ar-thro′sis). Pseudarthrosis.

pseudoasthma (su″do-as′mah), Dyspnea.

pseudoataxia (su″do-ah-tak′se-ah) [*pseudo-* + *ataxia*]. A condition of complete general incoordination in which the patient exhibits incoordination and ataxic symptoms. See *pseudotabes.*

pseudoatheroma (su″do-ath″er-o′mah). A sebaceous cyst.

pseudoathetosis (su″do-ath″e-to′sis). Movements of the fingers elicited when the patient closes his eyes and extends his arms in cases of tabes and combined sclerosis.

pseudoatrophoderma (su″do-at″ro-fo-der′mah). A skin disease with pigmentary lesions resembling those of vitiligo. **p. col′li,** a condition characterized by presence of depigmented glossy lesions on the skin of the neck.

pseudobacillus (su″do-bah-sil′us). An exceedingly small, rodlike poikilocyte, resembling a microorganism.

pseudobacterium (su″do-bak-te′re-um) [*pseudo-* + Gr. *baktērion* stick]. A cell that resembles a bacterium.

pseudobasedow (su″do-bas′e-dow). Basedoid.

pseudoblepsis (su″do-blep′sis) [*pseudo-* + Gr. *blepsis* sight]. A condition in which objects appear different from what they really are.

pseudobulbar (su″do-bul′bar). Apparently, but not really, due to a bulbar lesion.

pseudocartilage (su″do-kar′tĭ-lij). Chondroid tissue.

pseudocartilaginous (su″do-kar″tĭ-laj′ĭ-nus). Composed of a substance resembling cartilage.

pseudocast (su′do-kast). A false cast: a form of urinary sediment resembling true casts, but being an accidental formation, taking the shape of casts by adherence to mucus threads, cotton fibers, etc.

pseudocele (su′do-sēl). Pseudocoele.

pseudocephalocele (su″do-sef′ah-lo-sēl). A hernia of the brain not congenital, but due to disease or injury of the skull.

pseudochalazion (su″do-kah-la′ze-on) [*pseudo-* + *chalazion*]. An eye lesion resembling a chalazion.

pseudochancre (su″do-shang′ker). An indurated lesion resembling or simulating chancre. **p. re′dux,** a gummatous recurrence at the site of a primary syphilitic lesion.

pseudocholecystitis (su″do-ko″le-sis-ti′tis). A syndrome resembling cholecystitis but occurring as an allergic response to eating certain foods.

pseudocholesteatoma (su″do-ko″les-te-ah-to′mah). A mass of cornified epithelial cells resembling cholesteatoma in the tympanic cavity in chronic middle ear inflammation.

pseudochorea (su″do-ko-re′ah) [*pseudo-* + *chorea*]. A condition of complete general incoordination with symptoms like those of chorea.

pseudochromatin (su″do-kro′mah-tin). Paranuclein.

pseudochromesthesia (su″do-kro″mes-the′zeah) [*pseudo-* + Gr. *chrōma* color + *aisthēsis* perception + *-ia*]. A false sensation of color.

pseudochromidrosis (su″do-kro″mid-ro′sis) [*pseudo-* + *chromidrosis*]. Sweating with the presence on the skin of pigment due to the action of bacteria.

pseudochromosome (su″do-kro′mo-sōm). Rodlike Golgi bodies of the spermatocytes.

pseudochylous (su″do-ki′lus). Resembling chyle, but containing no fat.

pseudocide (su′do-sīd) [*pseudo-* + L. *caedere* to kill]. The deliberate taking of measures to harm one's self without wishing to die.

pseudocirrhosis (su″do-si-ro′sis) [*pseudo-* + *cirrhosis*]. Apparent cirrhosis of the liver, often due to pericarditis. **pericarditic p.,** Pick's syndrome.

pseudoclonus (su″do-klo′nus). A short-lived clonic response.

pseudocoarctation (su″do-ko″ark-ta′shun). A condition resembling coarctation, but without compromise of the lumen of the affected structure. **p. of the aorta,** an uncommon congenital anomaly of the arch of the aorta that is embryologically and anatomically similar to coarctation but does not produce occlusion of the vessel.

pseudocoele (su′do-sēl) [*pseudo-* + Gr. *koilia* hollow]. The cavum septi pellucidi.

pseudocolloid (su″do-kol′oid). A mucoid substance sometimes found in ovarian cysts. **p. of lips,** Fordyce's disease.

pseudocoloboma (su″do-kol″o-bo′mah). A line or scar on the iris giving the appearance of a coloboma.

pseudocolony (su″do-kol′o-ne). A small aggregation of crystalline or other materials which sometimes appears on the surface of sterile serum agar or other culture plates, especially after long incubation or drying.

pseudoconjugation (su″do-kon″ju-ga′shun). A stage in certain forms of protozoan development in which the two gametocytes instead of actually undergoing conjugation become enclosed together within one common cyst wall.

pseudocopulation (su″do-kop″u-la′shun). The fertilization of animal ova by the spermatozoa of the male without sexual union. See *amplexus.*

pseudo-corpus luteum (su″do-kor″pus-lu′teum). A maturing graafian follicle which does not rupture but retains its ovum and then becomes luteinized.

pseudocoxalgia (su″do-kok-sal′je-ah). Osteochondritis deformans juvenilis.

pseudocrisis (su-dok′rĭ-sis) [*pseudo-* + Gr. *krisis* crisis]. A false crisis; a sudden but temporary abatement of febrile symptoms.

pseudocroup (su″do-kro͞op′). 1. Laryngismus stridulus. 2. Thymic asthma.

pseudocyesis (su″do-si-e′sis) [*pseudo-* + Gr. *kyēsis* pregnancy]. Spurious or false pregnancy.

pseudocylindroid (su″do-sĭ-lin′droid). A shread of mucin in the urine resembling a cylindroid; sometimes of spermatic origin.

pseudocyst (su′do-sist) [*pseudo-* + *cyst*]. An abnormal or dilated space resembling a cyst. **pancreatic p.,** an accumulation of pancreatic juice in the retroperitoneal space, as a result of necrosis and rupture of a pancreatic duct.

pseudodementia (su″do-de-men′she-ah). An extreme condition of general apathy simulating dementia, but with no actual defect of intelligence.

pseudodextrocardia (su″do-deks″tro-kar′de-ah). A condition in which the heart is displaced to the right, but is not transposed to the right side of body.

pseudodiastolic (su″do-di″ah-stol′ik). Apparently but not truly diastolic.

pseudodiphtheria (su″do-dif-the′re-ah). A sort of diphtheria in which there is developed a false membrane not due to *Corynbacterium diphtheriae.*

pseudodipsia (su″do-dip′se-ah) [*pseudo-* + Gr. *dipsa* thirst + *-ia*]. False thirst.

Pseudodiscus (su″do-dis′kus). A genus of flukes. **P. wat′soni,** a fluke found in the small intestine of man in Africa.

pseudodysentery (su″do-dis′en-ter″e). A condition marked by the symptoms of dysentery, but due to some local irritation and not to the organisms of dysentery.

pseudoedema (su″do-e-de′mah). A puffy state resembling edema.

pseudoembryonic (su″do-em″bre-on′ik). Apparently, but not truly, embryonic.

pseudoemphysema (su″do-em″fi-ze′mah). A condition resembling emphysema, but due to temporary blocking of the bronchial tubes.

pseudoencephalitis (su″do-en-sef″ah-li′tis). A state resembling encephalitis, but due to colliquative diarrhea.

pseudoendometritis (su″do-en″do-me-tri′tis). A condition simulating endometritis, in which there are changes in the blood vessels, hyperplasia of the stroma and glands, and atrophy.

pseudoephedrine (su″do-ĕ-fed′rin). One of the optical isomers of ephedrine, d-ψ-ephedrine, derived from the leaves of *Ephedra distachya:* used as a nasal decongestant.

pseudoepiphysis (su″do-e-pif′ĭ-sis). An accessory bone at the distal and the proximal end of the second metacarpal bone.

pseudoerysipelas (su″do-er″ĭ-sip′e-las). An inflammatory subcutaneous disease resembling erysipelas.

pseudoesthesia (su″do-es-the′ze-ah). Pseudesthesia.

pseudoexophoria (su″do-ek″so-fo′re-ah). An outward tendency of the visual axis excited by diminishing the activity of the accommodative centers.

pseudofarcy (su′do-far″se). Lymphangitis epizootica.

pseudoflagellata (su″do-flaj″ĕ-la′tah). The tertian parasites in one of their stages: probably gametes.

pseudofluctuation (su″do-fluk″tu-a′shun). A tremor resembling fluctuation, such as is sometimes seen on tapping lipomas.

pseudofracture (su″do-frak′tūr). A condition seen in the roentgenogram of a bone as a thickening of the periosteum and formation of new bone over what looks like an incomplete fracture.

pseudofructose (su″do-fruk′tōs). A form of fructose, differing from it in the carbon atom configuration.

pseudoganglion (su″do-gang′gle-on). A thickening of a nerve simulating a ganglion. **Bochdalek's p.** See under *ganglion.* **Cloquet's p.** See under *ganglion.* **Valentin's p.** See under *ganglion.*

pseudogestation (su″do-jes-ta′shun). False pregnancy.

pseudogeusesthesia (su″do-gūs″es-the′ze-ah) [*pseudo-* + Gr. *geusis* taste + *aisthēsis* perception + *-ia*]. A false sensation of taste associated with a sensation of another modality.

pseudogeusia (su″do-gu′se-ah) [*pseudo-* + Gr. *geusis* taste + *-ia*]. A sensation of taste inappropriate to the exciting stimulus or occurring in the absence of a stimulus.

pseudoglanders (su″do-glan′derz). Lymphangitis ulcerosa.

pseudoglaucoma (su″do-glaw-ko′mah). A condition of nonglaucomatous atrophy of the optic nerve with all the ophthalmoscopic characteristics and visual field defects found in true glaucoma.

pseudoglioma (su″do-gli-o′mah). A condition resembling glioma, a membrane being produced back of the lens because of failure of the posterior vascular sheath of the lens to atrophy, or because of its replacement by connective tissue.

pseudoglobulin (su″do-glob′u-lin). One of a class of globulins characterized by being soluble in water in the absence of neutral salts and thus not true globulins (euglobulins). See also under *globulin.*

pseudoglottis (su″do-glot′is). The aperture between the false vocal cords.

pseudoglucosazone (su″do-gloo″ko-sa′zōn). A crystalline substance sometimes developed in normal urine in testing for sugar.

pseudogonococcus (su″do-gon″o-kok′us). A name given to certain microbes capable of producing urethral irritation.

pseudogonorrhea (su″do-gon″o-re′ah). Nonspecific urethritis.

pseudogout (su′do-gowt). An apparently hereditary and familial condition resembling gout, but with crystals of a calcium salt rather than urate crystals in the synovial fluid, leading to calcification and degenerative alterations in cartilage.

pseudographia (su″do-graf′e-ah) [*pseudo-* + Gr. *graphein* to write + *-ia*]. The production of meaningless written symbols.

pseudohallucination (su″do-hah-loo″sĭ-na′-shun). A hallucination brought about by the exercise of memory and imagination.

pseudohaustration (su″do-haw-stra′shun). A false appearance of normal sacculation of the wall of the colon, the roentgenographic appearance being produced by edematous islands of mucosa regularly placed between deep areas of ulceration in the muscle layers.

pseudohemagglutination (su″do-hem″ah-gloo″tĭ-na′shun). A clumping of erythrocytes due to rouleau formation.

pseudohemophilia (su″do-he″mo-fil′e-ah). Angiohemophilia. **p. hepat′ica,** a condition in which the clotting time of the blood is prolonged because of cirrhosis of the liver.

pseudohemoptysis (su″do-he-mop′tĭ-sis). Spitting of blood which comes from some other source than the lungs or bronchial tubes.

pseudohermaphrodism (su″do-her-maf′ro-dizm). Pseudohermaphroditism.

pseudohermaphrodite (su″do-her-maf′ro-dīt). An individual exhibiting pseudohermaphroditism. **female p.,** female intersex. **male p.,** male intersex.

pseudohermaphroditism (su″do-her-maf′ro-dīt-izm). A condition in which the gonads are of one sex but one or more contradictions exist in the morphologic criteria of sex. See also *intersexuality.*

pseudohernia (su″do-her′ne-ah). An inflamed sac or gland simulating strangulated hernia.

pseudoheterotopia (su″do-het″er-o-to′pe-ah). Displacement of gray or white matter of the brain or cord, produced by unskillful manipulation in the autopsy.

pseudohydronephrosis (su″do-hi″dro-ne-fro′-sis). A paranephritic cyst.

pseudohydrophobia (su″do-hi″dro-fo′be-ah). Aujeszky's disease.

pseudohyoscyamine (su″do-hi″o-si′ah-min). An alkaloid, $C_{17}H_{23}NO_3$, from *Duboisia myoporoides:* antispasmodic and sedative.

pseudohypertrichosis (su″do-hi″per-trik-o′sis). Persistence after birth of the fine hair present during fetal life, owing to inability of the skin to throw it off.

pseudohypertrophic (su″do-hi″per-trof′ik). Characterized by apparent, but not real, hypertrophy.

pseudohypertrophy (su″do-hi-per′tro-fe). False hypertrophy; increase of size without true hypertrophy. **muscular p.,** pseudohypertrophic paralysis.

pseudohypoparathyroidism (su″do-hi″po-par″ah-thi′roid-izm). A condition clinically resembling hypoparathyroidism, but caused by failure of response to rather than deficiency of parathyroid hormone.

pseudo-icterus (su″do-ik′ter-us). Pseudojaundice.

pseudo-ileus (su″do-il′e-us). An attack resembling ileus, but due to paralysis of the bowels.

pseudo-influenza (su″do-in″floo-en′zah). An affection resembling influenza, and due to a bacillus resembling, but not identical with, that of true influenza.

pseudo-ion (su″do-i′on). One of the electrically charged particles of a colloidal solution.

pseudo-isochromatic (su″do-i″so-kro-mat′ik). Seemingly of the same color throughout: applied to solutions for testing color blindness, containing two pigments which will be distinguished by the normal eye, but not by the color blind. Cf. *anisochromatic.*

pseudojaundice (su″do-jawn′dis). Skin discoloration caused by blood changes and not due to liver disease.

pseudokeratin (su″do-ker′ah-tin). False keratin, found in the skin and the nervous system.

pseudoleprosy (su″do-lep′ro-se). Punudos.

pseudoleukemia (su″do-lu-ke′me-ah). A term used for a group of conditions resembling one another in showing enlargement of the lymph glands and in characteristics which resemble the conditions present in leukemia, but without leukemic blood findings. The term includes aleukemic lymphadenosis, aleukemic myelosis, Hodgkin's disease, Kundrat's lymphosarcoma, multiple myeloma, and tuberculosis and syphilis of the lymph glands. See *lymphogranulomatosis* and *aleukemic myelosis.* **p. cu′tis,** pseudoleukemia with the development of skin lesions. **p. gastrointestina′lis,** a condition characterized by extensive lymphocytic infiltration of the gastrointestinal tract, without the typical clinical picture of leukemia. **infantile p.,** anemia infantum pseudoleukemica. **p. lymphat′ica,** nonsplenic leukemia, a state associated with Hodgkin's disease and also with lymphomatous tumors of the kidneys and intestines in children. **myelogenous p.,** myelomatosis.

pseudoleukocythemia (su″do-lu″ko-si-the′me-ah). Pseudoleukemia.

pseudolimax (su″do-li′maks). *Iodamoeba buetschlii.*

pseudolipoma (su″do-lĭ-po′mah). Localized edema of neuropathic origin simulating lipoma. It occurs in hysteria and certain lesions of the nervous system. Called also *neuropathic edema.*

pseudolithiasis (su″do-lĭ-thi′ah-sis). A condition with symptoms of spasm resembling gallstone colic.

pseudologia (su″do-lo′je-ah) [*pseudo-* + Gr. *logos* word + *-ia*]. The writing of anonymous letters to people of prominence, to one's self, etc. **p. fantas′tica,** a tendency to tell extravagant and fantastic falsehoods centered about one's self.

pseudolupus (su″do-lu′pus). A disease which closely simulates lupus: believed to be due to the presence of an oidium.

pseudoluxation (su″do-luk-sa′shun). Partial dislocation of a bone.

Pseudolynchia (su″do-linch′e-a). A genus of flies. **P. canarien′sis,** a species of pigeon flies that transmit the organism causing pigeon malaria.

pseudolyssa (su″do-lis′ah). A disease resembling lyssa; lyssophobia.

pseudomalaria (su″do-mah-la′re-ah). A disease resembling malaria in its symptoms, but due to toxic metabolites or ptomaines.

pseudomamma (su″do-mam′ah). A structure resembling a nipple, or even a complete mamma, sometimes found on ovarian dermoids.

pseudomania (su″do-ma′ne-ah) [*pseudo-* + Gr. *mania* madness]. 1. False or pretended mental disorder. 2. Pathologic lying.

pseudomasturbation (su″do-mas″tur-ba′shun). Peotillomania.

pseudomegacolon (su″do-meg′ah-ko″lon). Dilatation of the colon in adults. Cf. *megacolon.*

pseudomelanosis (su″do-mel″ah-no′sis). A staining of the tissue after death with pigments from the blood.

pseudomelia (su″do-me′le-ah) [*pseudo-* + Gr. *melos* limb + *-ia*]. Phantom limb. **p. paraesthet′ica,** the perception of various morbid or perverted sensations as occurring in an absent or paralyzed limb.

pseudomembrane (su″do-mem′brān). A false membrane.

pseudomembranous (su″do-mem′brah-nus). Marked by or pertaining to false membrane.

pseudomeningitis (su″do-men″in-ji′tis). Pial inflammation with symptoms resembling meningitis.

pseudomenstruation (su″do-men″stroo-a′shun). Uterine bleeding which is not attended with endometrial changes of menstruation.

pseudometaplasia (su″do-met″ah-pla′ze-ah). Histologic accommodation.

pseudomethemoglobin (su″do-met-he″mo-glo′bin). Methalbumin.

pseudomicrocephalus (su″do-mi″kro-sef′ah-lus). An individual with a small brain due to the atrophy of one hemisphere, probably acquired secondarily.

pseudomnesia (su″dom-ne′ze-ah) [*pseudo-* + Gr. *mimnēskesthai* to remember]. A condition in which the patient seems to remember things which have never occurred.

Pseudomonadaceae (su″do-mo″nah-da′se-e). A family of microorganisms (order Pseudomonadales, suborder Pseudomonadineae), occurring as elongate straight rods or coccoid cells in soil and fresh or salt water. It includes 12 genera, *Acetobacter, Aeromonas, Alginomonas, Azotomonas, Halobacterium, Mycoplana, Photobacterium, Protaminobacter, Pseudomonas, Xanthomonas, Zoogloea,* and *Zymomonas.*

Pseudomonadales (su″do-mo″nah-da′lēz). An order of class Schizomycetes, made up of straight, curved, or spiral, rigid, rod-shaped, gram-negative microorganisms, rarely occurring in pairs or chains, and including two suborders, *Pseudomonadineae* and *Rhodobacteriineae.*

Pseudomonadineae (su″do-mo″nah-di′ne-e). A suborder of Schizomycetes (order Pseudomonadales), made up of cells of various shapes and sizes, containing unique pigments, soluble in water or organic solvents. It includes seven families, *Caulobacteriaceae, Methanomonadaceae, Nitrobacteraceae, Pseudomonadaceae, Siderocapsaceae, Spirillaceae,* and *Thiobacteriaceae.*

Pseudomonas (su″do-mo′nas). A genus of microorganisms of the family Pseudomonadaceae, suborder Pseudomonadineae, order Pseudomonadales, occurring usually as monotrichous, lophotrichous, or non-motile straight rods. Some of the 149 described species are pathogenic for plants or for warm- and cold-blooded vertebrates. **P. aerugino′sa,** the type species of the genus, and the only one pathogenic for man, made up of microorganisms which produce the blue-green pigment, pyocyanin, which gives the color to "blue pus" observed in certain suppurative infections. **P. eisenber′gii,** a

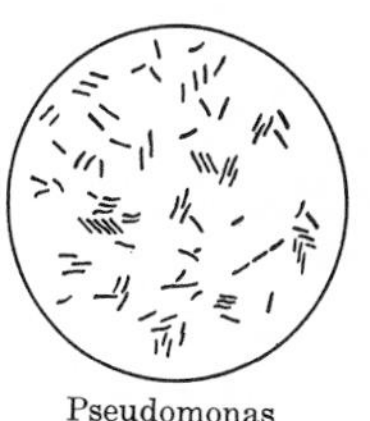

Pseudomonas aeruginosa.

species of non-pathogenic fluorescent microorganisms found in water, which do not liquefy gelatin. **P. fluores'cens,** a species of non-pathogenic fluorescent microorganisms found in feces, sewage, soil, and water, and which liquefy gelatin. **P. non-liquefa'ciens,** *P. eisenbergii.* **P. pseudomal'lei,** the causative agent of melioidosis, a glanders-like infection observed in rodents and occasionally in man. **P. pyocya'nea,** *P. aeruginosa.* **P. reptiliv'ora,** a species which is pathogenic for lizards. **P. sep'tica,** a species which causes a disease of caterpillars. **P. syncya'nea,** a species isolated from blue milk, which produces the blue pigment responsible for its color.

Pseudomonilia (su″do-mo-nil′e-ah). A genus of yeastlike fungi, many species of which have been isolated from blastomycotic lesions in man.

pseudomorphine (su″do-mor′fin). Dehydromorphine.

pseudomotor (su″do-mo′tor). Producing movements which are not normal.

pseudomucin (su″do-mu′sin). A substance resembling mucin found in ovarian cysts.

pseudomycetoma (su″do-mi″se-to′mah). A sarcomatous or epitheliomatous growth, resembling mycetoma but without the typical granules in the discharge.

pseudomycosis sarcinica (su″do-mi-ko′sis sarsin′ĭ-kah). A disease of the lungs believed to be caused by *Sarcina virchowii.*

pseudomyopia (su″do-mi-o′pe-ah). Defective vision, not myopia, which causes the patient to hold objects nearer than normal to the eyes, thus simulating myopia.

pseudomyxoma (su″do-mik-so′mah). A colloid growth developed upon the peritoneum, often secondary to an ovarian dermoid cyst. **p. peritone'i,** the presence in the peritoneal cavity of mucoid matter from a ruptured ovarian cyst or a ruptured mucocele of the appendix; called also *hydrops spurius.*

pseudonarcotic (su″do-nar-kot′ik). Sedative and apparently, but not directly, narcotic.

pseudonarcotism (su″do-nar′ko-tizm). A hysterical condition simulating narcotism.

pseudonavicella (su″do-nav″ĭ-sel′ah) [*pseudo-* + L. *navicella* boat]. A form of spore or stage of growth seen in certain protozoa.

pseudoneoplasm (su″do-ne′o-plazm) [*pseudo-* + *neoplasm*]. 1. A temporary formation resembling a tumor. 2. A phantom tumor.

pseudoneuritis (su″do-nu-ri′tis). A hyperemic condition of the optic papilla, occurring as a congenital anomaly.

pseudoneuroma (su″do-nu-ro′mah) [*pseudo-* + *neuroma*]. A tumor on a nerve simulating a neuroma; false neuroma.

pseudoneuronophagia (su″do-nu-ro″no-fa′jeah). A false appearance of phagocytosis of nerve cells.

pseudonuclein (su″do-nu′kle-in). Paranuclein.

pseudonucleolus (su″do-nu-kle′o-lus) [*pseudo-* + *nucleolus*]. Karyosome.

pseudonystagmus (su″do-nis-tag′mus). Large rhythmic jerking movements of the eye occurring in association with other diseases.

pseudo-obstruction (su″do-ob-struk′shun). A condition simulating obstruction. **intestinal p.,** a condition characterized by constipation, colicky pain, and vomiting, but without evidence of organic obstruction apparent at laparotomy.

pseudo-ochronosis (su″do-o-kro′no-sis). A condition resembling ochronosis, but not caused by a disorder of metabolism.

pseudo-optogram (su″do-op′to-gram). An optogram in which the rods strip off from the illuminated spot and only the cones remain.

pseudo-osteomalacia (su″do-os″te-o-mah-la′she-ah). Rachitic contraction of the pelvis.

pseudo-ovum (su″do-o′vum). A large prominent cell, resembling an ovum, seen in granuloma-cell tumor.

pseudopapilledema (su″do-pap″ĭ-lĕ-de′mah). Anomalous elevation of the optic disk.

pseudoparalysis (su″do-pah-ral′ĭ-sis). False paralysis: apparent loss of muscular power, without true paralysis, marked by defective coordination of movements or by repression of movement on account of pain. **p. ag'itans,** paralysis agitans. **arthritic general p.,** a condition resembling general paralysis, dependent on intracranial atheroma in arthritic persons. **congenital atonic p.,** amyotonia congenita. **Parrot's p., syphilitic p.,** pseudoparalysis of one or more of the extremities in infants caused by syphilitic osteochondritis of the epiphysis.

pseudoparaphrasia (su″do-par″ah-fra′ze-ah). Complete general incoherence in which the patient calls everything by a wrong name.

pseudoparaplegia (su″do-par″ah-ple′je-ah). Paralysis of the lower limbs in which the reflexes are normal.

pseudoparasite (su″do-par′ah-sīt). Any object resembling or mistaken for a parasite.

pseudoparesis (su″do-pah-re′sis). A hysterical or other condition simulating paresis.

pseudopelade (su″do-pe′lād). Alopecia cicatrisata.

pseudopellagra (su″do-pĕ-lag′rah). Pellagra-like symptoms in alcoholics.

pseudopepsin (su″do-pep′sin). A proteolytic enzyme secreted by certain glands of the stomach.

pseudopeptone (su″do-pep′tōn). Ovomucoid.

pseudopericardial (su″do-per″ĭ-kar′de-al). Seemingly, but not actually, arising from the pericardium.

pseudoperitonitis (su″do-per″ĭ-to-ni′tis). Peritonism.

pseudophakia (su″do-fa′ke-ah). Failure of development of the crystalline lens, its place being occupied by tissue of abnormal type. **p. adipo'sa,** a condition in which the crystalline lens is replaced by a mass of fatty tissue. **p. fibro'sa,** replacement of the crystalline lens by a mass of connective tissue that represents hyperplasia of both the anterior and posterior vascular sheaths of the lens.

pseudophlebitis (su″do-fle-bi′tis). Phlegmasia cerulea dolens.

pseudophlegmon (su″do-fleg′mon). A swollen and reddened state of the skin which follows irritative lesions of the nerves. **Hamilton's p.,** a circumscribed swelling which may become red and indurated, but never suppurates.

pseudophotesthesia (su″do-fo″tes-the′ze-ah). The perception of light on receipt of an abnormal stimulus.

pseudophthisis (su-dof′thĭ-sis). A wasting disease not of the nature of tuberculosis.

Pseudophyllidea (su″do-fĭ-lid′e-ah). An order of cestodes in which the scolex has a single terminal or two opposite sucking organs.

pseudoplasm (su′do-plazm). A new growth which disappears spontaneously.

pseudoplegia (su″do-ple′je-ah) [*pseudo-* + Gr. *plēgē* stroke + *-ia*]. Hysterical paralysis or pseudoparalysis.

pseudopneumococcus (su″do-nu″mo-kok′us). A coccus from acute lobar pneumonia much larger than the pneumococcus, and otherwise distinguishable from it.

pseudopneumonia (su″do-nu-mo′ne-ah). A condition marked by the symptoms of pneumonia, but without any lesions in the lungs.

pseudopod (su′do-pod). Pseudopodium.

pseudopodiospore (su″do-po′de-o-spōr) [*pseudopodium* + *spore*]. A spore having pseudopodia like an ameba. Called also *amebula.*

pseudopodium (su″do-po′de-um) [*pseudo-* + Gr. *pous* foot]. A temporary protrusion of the ectosarc of an ameba, serving for purposes of locomotion and for feeding.

pseudopolymelia (su″do-pol″e-mi-e′le-ah). An illusory sensation which may be referred to many extreme portions of the body, including the nose, nipples, and glans penis, as well as the hands and feet. **p. paraesthet′ica,** the perception of various morbid or perverted sensations, referred to various extreme portions of the body.

pseudopolyp (su″do-pol′ip). A hypertrophied tab of mucous membrane resembling a polyp, but caused by ulceration surrounding and sometimes undermining a portion of intact mucosa; frequently observed in chronic inflammatory diseases, such as ulcerative colitis.

pseudopolyposis (su″do-pol″ĭ-po′sis). The occurrence of numbers of pseudopolyps in the colon and rectum, as the result of long-standing inflammation.

pseudoporencephaly (su″do-po″ren-sef′ah-le). A condition resembling porencephaly, but without idiocy or even impairment of the intellect.

pseudopregnancy (su″do-preg′nan-se). 1. False pregnancy. 2. The premenstrual stage of the endometrium: so called because it resembles the endometrium just before implantation of the blastocyst.

pseudoprotein (su″do-pro′te-in). A protein which is lacking in one or more of the essential amino acids, for example, gelatin.

pseudopseudohypoparathyroidism (su″do-su″do-hi″po-par″ah-thi′roid-izm). A condition resembling pseudohypoparathyroidism but characterized by normal levels of calcium and phosphorus in the serum.

pseudopsia (su-dop′se-ah) [*pseudo-* + Gr. *opsis* vision + *-ia*]. False or depraved vision; pseudoblepsia.

pseudopterygium (su″do-ter-ij′e-um). A fold of conjunctiva attached to any part of the cornea, following ulceration of the latter; it resembles true pterygium, but when the fold is separated from its corneal attachment the conjunctiva retracts to its normal position.

pseudoptosis (su″do-to′sis) [*pseudo-* + Gr. *ptōsis* fall]. Decrease in the size of the palpebral aperture.

pseudoptyalism (su″do-ti′al-izm). Accumulation and dribbling of saliva due to dysphagia.

pseudopunicin (su″do-pu′nĭ-sin). Pseudopelletierine.

pseudorabies (su″do-ra′be-ēz). A disease resembling rabies; lyssophobia. **bovine p.,** mad itch.

pseudoreaction (su″do-re-ak′shun). A false or deceptive reaction; a skin reaction in intradermal tests which is not due to the specific protein used in the test but to the protein of the medium employed in producing the toxin.

pseudoreduction (su″do-re-duk′shun). The apparent halving of the chromosome number by synapsis.

pseudoreminiscence (su″do-rem″ĭ-nis′ens). Confabulation.

pseudorheumatism (su″do-roo′mah-tizm). A condition resembling rheumatism, due to some nonrheumatic disease, as gonorrhea.

pseudorickets (su″do-rik′ets). Renal osteodystrophy.

pseudorubella (su″do-roo-bel′ah). Roseola infantum.

pseudoscarlatina (su″do-skar″lah-ti′nah). A febrile condition with an eruption like that of scarlet fever, but due to septic poisoning.

pseudosclerema (su″do-skle-re′mah). Adiponecrosis subcutanea neonatorum.

pseudosclerosis (su″do-skle-ro′sis) [*pseudo-* + Gr. *sklērōsis* hardening]. A condition with the symptoms, but without the lesions of disseminated sclerosis; a form of hepaticolenticular degeneration with lesions more diffuse than those of progressive lenticular degeneration (Wilson's disease). It is marked by tremors, rigidity, emotional disturbance and optic atrophy. Called also *Strümpell-Westphal pseudosclerosis* and *Westphal's pseudosclerosis.* **p. spas′tica,** Jakob's name for a form of pseudosclerosis, occurring in middle life, marked by partial degeneration of the pyramidal and extrapyramidal systems: called *Jakob's disease* and *Jakob-Creutzfeldt disease.*

pseudoscrotum (su″do-skro′tum). A solid partition with a median raphe, resembling the scrotum in the male, obliterating the opening into the vagina in female pseudohermaphrodites.

pseudosmallpox (su″do-smal′poks). Variola minor.

pseudosmia (su-doz′me-ah) [*pseudo-* + Gr. *osmē* odor + *-ia*]. A delusion as to smell.

pseudosolution (su″do-so-lu′shun). Solutions which do not act according to the usual physical laws of solutions. The term is sometimes applied to colloidal solutions.

pseudostoma (su-dos′to-mah) [*pseudo-* + Gr. *stoma* mouth]. An apparent communication between silver-stained endothelial cells.

pseudostrophanthin (su″do-stro-fan′thin). A poisonous glycoside, $C_{40}H_{60}O_{16}.H_2O$, from *Strophanthus hispidus.*

pseudostructure (su″do-struk′chur). Reticular substance.

pseudosyphilis (su″do-sif′ĭ-lis). A condition marked by ulcers and eruption resembling those of syphilis, but yielding to nonspecific treatment.

pseudosyringomyelia (su″do-sĭ-rin″go-mi-e′le-ah). A condition in which there are cavities in the spinal cord caused by maldevelopment, cysts, injuries, etc.

pseudotabes (su″do-ta′bēz) [*pseudo-* + L. *tabes* wasting]. A condition marked by the symptoms of tabes dorsalis, but distinguished from it by its tendency to become completely cured, by tenderness on pressure of muscles, and by absence of Argyll Robertson pupil. Called also *pseudo-ataxia, neurotabes,* and *peripheral tabes.* **p. alcohol′ica,** alcoholic symptoms resembling tabes. **p. arsenico′sa,** arsenical polyneuritis resembling tabes. **diabetic p.,** tabes diabetica. **p. mesenter′ica,** hysterical pseudotabes, chiefly of young women. **papillotonic p.,** Adie's syndrome. **p. peripher′ica,** an acute syphilitic disease involving the nerve roots and the meninges and simulating tabes. **p. pituita′ria,** tabetic symptoms produced by tumors of the hypophysis.

pseudotetanus (su″do-tet′ah-nus). Persistent muscular contractions resembling tetanus but not associated with the presence of *Clostridium tetani.*

pseudotextoma (su″do-teks-to′mah). A neoplasm composed of partially differentiated tissue cells. Cf. *textoma.*

pseudothrill (su′do-thril). A condition that simulates a true thrill.

pseudotoxin (su″do-tok′sin). A poisonous extract from belladonna leaves.

pseudotrachoma (su″do-trah-ko′mah). A disease of the eye and lids resembling trachoma.

pseudotrichiniasis (su″do-trik″ĭ-ni′ah-sis). Pseudotrichinosis.

pseudotrichinosis (su″do-trik″ĭ-no′sis). Dermatomyositis.

pseudotropine (su-dot′ro-pin). A dark-brown, syrupy, liquid base: a decomposition product of tropine.

pseudotubercle (su″do-tu′ber-k'l). A tubercle resembling that of tuberculosis, but not due to the tubercle bacillus.

pseudotuberculoma (su″do-tu-ber″ku-lo′mah). A tumor resembling in structure a tuberculoma. **p. silicot′icum,** a pseudotuberculoma due to the presence in the tissue of silica.

pseudotuberculosis (su″do-tu-ber″ku-lo′sis). Infection by *Pasteurella pseudotuberculosis.* **p. hom′inis streptoth′rica,** a disease of man closely resembling tuberculosis, but due to a streptothrix.

pseudotumor (su″do-tu′mor). Phantom tumor. **p. cer′ebri,** a nontumorous condition which produces the symptoms of tumor of the brain.

pseudotympanites, pseudotympany (su″do-tim″pah-ni′tēz, su″do-tim′pah-ne). False tympanites, as in accordion abdomen.

pseudotyphoid (su″do-ti′foid). Spurious typhoid fever; a disease showing the symptoms of typhoid fever, but without the characteristic lesions of that disease and without typhoid bacilli.

pseudotyphus (su″do-ti′fus). A disease of Sumatra resembling scrub typhus (tsutsugamushi disease).

pseudo-uremia (su″do-u-re′me-ah). Uremia-like symptoms occurring in acute glomerulonephritis and in hypertensive vascular disease (hypertensive encephalopathy).

pseudovacuole (su″do-vak′u-ōl). A round space within certain red blood corpuscles containing an animal microorganism.

pseudovalve (su′do-valv). A peculiar formation on the parietal endocardium of the left ventricle, seen especially in insufficiency of the aortic valves.

pseudovariola (su″do-vah-ri′o-lah). Variola minor.

pseudoventricle (su″do-ven′tre-k'l). The fifth ventricle of the encephalon.

pseudovermicule, pseudovermiculus (su″-do-ver′mĭ-kūl, su″do-ver-mik′u-lus). A stage in the development of the plasmodium of pernicious malaria. It is a gregarine-like body developing in the intestine of the mosquito.

pseudovoice (su′do-vois). The vocal sounds produced under proper training by a person who has lost his larynx.

pseudovomiting (su″do-vom′it-ing). Regurgitation of matter from the stomach.

pseudoxanthine (su″do-zan′thin). 1. A leukomaine, $C_4H_5N_5O$, from muscle tissue. 2. A compound, $C_5H_4N_4O_2$, from uric acid.

pseudoxanthoma (su″do-zan-tho′mah). A disease resembling xanthoma. **p. elas′ticum,** a rare skin disease marked by small papules, individual or confluent, or massed into plaques, thickening of the skin where the lesions exist, and exaggeration of the normal creases and folds of the skin. The histologic features are masses of swollen and degenerated elastic fibers with degeneration of the collagen fibers in the lower and middle layers of the dermis. Called also *elastoma*, *elastosis atrophicans*, and *nevus elasticus*.

pseudozooglea (su″do-zo″o-gle′ah). A clump of bacteria not disintegrating readily in water, arising from imperfect separation or more or less fusion of the components, but not having the degree of compactness and gelatinization seen in zooglea.

p.s.i. Abbreviation for *pounds per square inch.*

psilocin (si′lo-sin). A hallucinogenic substance closely related to psilocybin.

psilocybin (si″lo-si′bin). A hallucinogenic crystalline compound, $C_{13}H_{18(20)}O_3N_2P_2$, possessing indole characteristics, isolated from the mushroom *Psilocybe mexicana* Heim.

psilosis (si-lo′sis) [Gr. *psilōsis* a stripping bare]. 1. Falling out of the hair. 2. Sprue.

psilothron (sil′o-thron) [Gr. *psilōthron* a means for bringing hair off]. A depilatory.

psilotic (si-lo′tik). Pertaining to psilosis.

psittacosis (sit-ah-ko′sis) [Gr. *psittakos* parrot + *-osis*]. A virus disease first observed in parrots and known to be communicated by them to man, but later discovered to exist in other birds and domestic fowl. See *ornithosis.*

psodymus (sod′ĭ-mus) [Gr. *psoa* muscle of the loin + *didymos* twin]. A monster with two heads and bodies, but single at and below the loins.

psoitis (so-i′tis) [Gr. *psoa* muscle of the loin + *-itis*]. Inflammation of a psoas muscle or of its sheath.

psomophagia (so″mo-fa′je-ah) [Gr. *psōmos* morsel + *phagein* to eat]. Thorough chewing of the food.

psomophagy (so-mof′ah-je). Psomophagia.

psora (so′rah) [Gr. *psōra* itch]. 1. Scabies or the itch. 2. Psoriasis. 3. Hahnemann's term for the underlying "itch" constitution which disposes toward or is the cause of all chronic diseases. See *homeopathy.*

psorelcosis (so″rel-ko′sis) [*psora* + Gr. *helkōsis* ulceration]. Ulceration due to scabies.

psorenteria (so″ren-te′re-ah). Abnormal prominence of the closed follicles of the intestine.

psorenteritis (so″ren-ter-i′tis) [*psora* + *enteritis*]. A condition of the bowels peculiar to Asiatic cholera.

psoriasic (so″re-as′ik). Psoriatic.

psoriasiform (so″re-as′ĭ-form). Resembling psoriasis.

psoriasis (so-ri′ah-sis) [Gr. *psōriasis*]. A chronic, recurrent papulosquamous dermatosis, the distinctive lesion being a silvery gray scaling papule or plaque. **p. annula′ris,** psoriasis with lesions occurring in ring-shaped patches. Called also *p. circinata.* **p. arthropath′ica,** a form of psoriasis associated with chronic arthritis. **p. bucca′lis,** a rare form of psoriasis affecting the oral mucosa. **p. circina′ta,** p. annularis. **p. diffu′sa,** a form of psoriasis in which the lesions enlarge and coalesce, to form large scaling plaques. **p. discoi′des,** psoriasis with the lesions occurring in solid, persistent patches. **p. figura′ta,** psoriasis in which the lesions coalesce to form marked patterns. **p. follicula′ris,** psoriasis with small scaly lesions located at the openings of sebaceous and sweat glands. **p. gutta′ta,** psoriasis in which the lesions are small and distinct. **p. gyra′ta,** psoriasis in which the lesions have coalesced to form a serpentine pattern. **p. invetera′ta,** a form with confluent lesions and with thickening and hardening of the skin. **p. lin′guae,** a rare form of psoriasis affecting the mucosa of the tongue. **p. nummula′ris,** psoriasis in which the lesions occur in circular patches, resembling small coins. **p. ostra′cea,** psoriasis in which the lesions form thick, tough patches covered with scales, giving them a resemblance to the outside of an oyster shell. **p. palma′ris et planta′ris,** psoriasis of the palms and soles. **p. puncta′ta,** a variety in which the lesions consist of minute, red, pinhead-shaped papules, often surmounted with pearly scales. **pustular p.,** psoriasis in which the skin is covered with small pustules. **p. rupioi′des,** psoriasis with rupia-like crusts. **p. universa′lis,** psoriasis in which the lesions occur over the entire body.

psoriatic (so″re-at′ik). 1. Pertaining to, affected with, or of the nature of, psoriasis. 2. A person affected with psoriasis.

psoric (so′rik). Pertaining to or affected with scabies.

psorocomium (so″ro-ko′me-ŭm) [Gr. *psōra* itch + *komein* to care for]. A hospital for psoriasis.

psoroid (so′roid). Resembling scabies.

Psorophora (so-rof′o-rah). A genus of large, annoying mosquitoes, the larvae of which prey on the larvae of other kinds of mosquitoes.

psorophthalmia (so″rof-thal′me-ah) [Gr. *psōrophthalmia*]. A form of ulcerative marginal blepharitis.

Psoroptes (so-rop′tēz). A genus of itch mites. **P. bo′vis,** a species which is occasionally the cause of mange in cattle. **P. cunic′uli,** a common external parasite of rabbits, leading to secondary infections that may extend to the inner ear and involve the central nervous system. **P. e′qui,** a species causing skin lesions (psoroptic mange) in horses, especially in areas covered with long hair. **P. o′vis,** a species which causes the most common type of mange in sheep, with intense itching and sometimes general symptoms.

psorosperm (so′ro-sperm) [Gr. *psōros* rough, scabby + *sperma* seed]. Any parasitic myxosporidian animal microorganism.

psorospermia (so″ro-sper′me-ah), pl. *psorosper′miae.* The spore of a psorospermic organism; Rainey's corpuscle.

psorospermial (so″ro-sper′me-al). Of the nature of or pertaining to a psorosperm.

psorospermiasis (so″ro-sper-mi′ah-sis). Psorospermosis.

psorospermic (so″ro-sper′mik). Psorospermial.

psorospermosis (so″ro-sper-mo′sis). A morbid state due to the presence of psorosperms. **p. follicularis,** keratosis follicularis.

psorous (so′rus) [Gr. *psōros*]. Affected with psora, or itch.

P.S.P. Abbreviation for *phenolsulfonphthalein.*

psych-. See *psycho-.*

psychalgalia (si″kal-ga′le-ah). Algopsychalia.

psychalgia (si-kal′je-ah). 1. A pain of mental or hysterical origin, such as neurasthenic headache, clavus hystericus, etc. 2. Pain attending or resulting from a mental operation: called also *mind pain* or *soul pain.*

psychalgic (si-kal′jik). Pertaining to or characterized by psychalgia.

psychalia (si-ka′le-ah). A morbid state of mind in which voices seem to be heard and images to be seen. Called also *mentalia.*

psychanalysis (si-kah-nal′ĭ-sis). Psychoanalysis.

psychanopsia (si-kah-nop′se-ah) [*psych-* + *an* neg. + Gr. *opsis* vision + *-ia*]. Psychic blindness.

psychasthene (si′kas-thēn). A person afflicted with psychasthenia.

psychasthenia (si″kas-the′ne-ah). A functional neurosis marked by stages of pathologic fear or anxiety, obsessions, fixed ideas, tics, feelings of inadequacy, self-accusation, and peculiar feelings of strangeness, unreality, and depersonalization (Janet).

psychasthenic (si″kas-then′ik). Marked by, or characteristic of, psychasthenia.

psychataxia (si″kah-tak′se-ah). A disordered mental condition marked by inability to fix the attention, agitation, etc.

psyche (si′ke) [Gr. *psychē* the organ of thought and judgment]. The human faculty for thought, judgment, and emotion; the mental life, including both conscious and unconscious processes.

psycheclampsia (si″ke-klamp′se-ah). Mania.

psychedelic (si″ke-del′ik). Psychodelic.

psycheism (si′ke-izm). Hypnotism.

psychergograph (si-ker′go-graf) [*psyche* + Gr. *ergon* work + *graphein* to write]. An instrument for recording serial responses to a series of stimuli.

psychiater (si″ke-a′ter). Psychiatrist.

psychiatric (si″ke-at′rik). Pertaining to psychiatry.

psychiatrics (si″ke-at′riks). Psychiatry.

psychiatrist (si-ki′ah-trist). An expert in psychiatry.

psychiatry (si-ki′ah-tre) [*psyche* + Gr. *iatreia* healing]. That branch of medicine which deals with disorders of the psyche.

psychic (si′kik) [Gr. *psychikos*]. Pertaining to the psyche or to the mind; mental.

psychics (si′kiks). Psychology.

psychinosis (si″kĭ-no′sis) [*psyche* + Gr. *nosos* disease]. A functional nervous disease.

psychism (si′kizm). The theory that there is a fluid diffused through all living beings, animating all alike.

psychlampsia (si-klamp′se-ah). Mania.

psycho- (si′ko). Combining form denoting relationship to the psyche, or to the mind.

psychoalgalia (si″ko-al-ga′le-ah). Algopsychalia.

psycho-allergy (si″ko-al′er-je). A condition of sensitization to certain words, ideas, people, and other symbols of emotional patterns.

psychoanaleptic (si″ko-an″ah-lep′tik) [*psycho-* + Gr. *analēpsis* a taking up]. Exerting a stimulating effect upon the mind.

psychoanalysis (si″ko-ah-nal′ĭ-sis). The method of eliciting from patients an idea of their past emotional experiences and the facts of their mental life, in order to discover the mechanism by which a pathologic mental state has been produced, and to furnish hints for psychotherapeutic procedures.

psychoanalyst (si″ko-an′ah-list). A practitioner of psychoanalysis.

psychoanalytic (si″ko-an″ah-lit′ik). Pertaining to psychoanalysis.

psycho-asthenics (si″ko-as-then′iks) [*psycho-* + *a* neg. + Gr. *sthenos* strength]. The study of the feebleminded.

psychoauditory (si″ko-aw′dĭ-to″re). Pertaining to the consciousness and intelligent perception of sound.

psychobacillosis (si″ko-bas″ĭ-lo′sis). Inoculation of bacteria for the treatment of dementia praecox.

psychobiological (si″ko-bi″o-loj′e-kal). Pertaining to the interactions between mind and body in the formation and continuation of the personality.

psychobiology (si″ko-bi-ol′o-je). That branch of biology which considers the interactions between body and mind in the formation and functioning of personality; the scientific study of the personality function.

psychocatharsis (si″ko-kah-thar′sis) [*psycho-* + Gr. *katharsis* purging]. See *catharsis*, def. 2.

psychocentric (si″ko-sen′trik) [*psycho-* + Gr. *kentrikos* of or from a center]. Relating to the concept, or designating, that control of the personality centers in the mind, the subjective system of the individual, as distinguished from the physical organs of the nervous system. Cf. *cerebrocentric.*

psychochemistry (si″ko-kem′is-tre). The application of chemistry to the study of psychology and behavior.

psychochrome (si′ko-krōm) [*psycho-* + Gr. *chrōma* color]. A subjective mental association between any bodily sensation and some particular color.

psychochromesthesia (si″ko-krōm″es-the′ze-ah) [*psycho-* + Gr. *chrōma* color + *aisthēsis* perception + *-ia*]. The condition in which auditory or other nonvisual stimuli produce sensations or associated sensations of color.

psychocoma (si″ko-ko′mah). Melancholic stupor.

psychocortical (si″ko-kor′te-kal). Pertaining to the mind and to the cortex of the brain.

psychodelic (si″ko-del′ik) [*psycho-* + Gr. *dēlos* manifest, evident]. Pertaining to or characterized by freedom from anxiety, and by relaxation, enjoyable perceptual changes, and highly creative thought patterns. By extension, applied to a type of drug which produces these effects.

psychodiagnosis (si″ko-di″ag-no′sis). The use of psychological testing in the diagnosis of disease.

psychodiagnostics (si″ko-di″ag-nos′tiks). Psychodiagnosis.

Psychodidae (si-ko′dĭ-de). A family of flies of the order Diptera, characterized by small size, long legs, and abundant hair on both wings and body.

psychodometer (si″ko-dom′e-ter). An instrument for measuring the time factor in mental activity.

psychodometry (si″ko-dom′e-tre) [*psycho-* + Gr. *hodos* way + *metron* measure]. The measurement of the rate of mental action.

psychodrama (si″ko-dram′ah). The psychiatric technic of having a patient act out conflicting situations of his daily life.

psychodynamics (si″ko-di-nam′iks) [*psycho-* + Gr. *dynamis* power]. The science of mental processes.

psychodysleptic (si″ko-dis-lep′tik) [*psycho-* + Gr. *dys-* bad + *lēpsis* a taking hold]. Inducing a dreamlike or delusional state of mind.

psycho-epilepsy (si″ko-ep″ĭ-lep′se). A functional neurosis with symptoms closely resembling those of true epilepsy.

psychogalvanometer (si″ko-gal″vah-nom′e-ter). A galvanometer for recording the electrical agitations produced by emotional stresses.

psychogenesis (si″ko-jen′e-sis). The development of the mind.

psychogenia (si″ko-je′ne-ah). Any disorder of behavior due to mental conflict, self-consciousness, or embarrassment.

psychogenic (si″ko-jen′ik). Of intrapsychic origin; having an emotional or psychologic origin (in reference to a symptom), as opposed to an organic basis.

psychogenous (si-koj′e-nus). Psychogenic.

psychogeriatrics (si″ko-jer″e-at′riks). Management of the psychologic and psychiatric problems of the aged.

psychognosis (si″kog-no′sis) [*psycho-* + Gr. *gnōsis* knowledge]. Sidis' term for the study which was intended to enable the examiner to gain a complete knowledge of the patient's soul, chiefly by means of hypnosis or hypnoidal states.

psychognostic (si″kog-nos′tik). Pertaining to psychognosis.

psychogogic (si″ko-goj′ik). Increasing intrapsychic tensions and acting as a stimulant.

psychogram (si′ko-gram) [*psycho-* + Gr. *gramma* a writing]. 1. Psychograph. 2. A visual sensation associated with a mental idea as of a certain number which appears visualized when it is thought of.

psychograph (si′ko-graf) [*psycho-* + Gr. *graphein* to write]. 1. A chart for recording graphically the personality traits of an individual. 2. A written description of the mental functioning of an individual.

psychokinesia (si″ko-ki-ne′ze-ah) [*psycho-* + Gr. *kinēsis* motion + *-ia*]. Explosive cerebral action due to defective inhibition.

psychokinesis (si″ko-ki-ne′sis) [*psycho-* + Gr. *kinēsis* motion]. The direct influence of volitional action on a physical object, or the influence of mind on matter without the intermediation of physical force.

psychokym (si′ko-kim). A psychic process conceived physiologically; that something which flows through the central nervous system and which is at the basis of psychic processes.

psycholagny (si′ko-lag″ne) [*psycho-* + Gr. *lagneia* lust]. The experiencing of sexual enjoyment from imagining or thinking of sexual acts.

psycholepsy (si″ko-lep′se) [*psycho-* + Gr. *lēpsis* a taking hold, a seizure]. A condition characterized by sudden changes of mood.

psycholeptic (si″ko-lep′tik) [*psycho-* + Gr. *lēptikos* assimilative]. Exerting a relaxing effect upon the mind.

psychologic, psychological (si″ko-loj′ik, -loj′-e-kal). Pertaining to psychology.

psychology (si-kol′o-je) [*psycho-* + *-logy*]. That branch of science which treats of the mind and mental operations, especially as they are shown in behavior. **abnormal p.,** the study of derangements or deviations of mental functions. **analytic p., analytical p.,** psychology by introspective methods, as opposed to experimental psychology. **animal p.,** the study of the mental activity of animals. **behavioristic p.** See *behaviorism.* **child p.,** the study of the development of the mind of the child. **cognitive p.,** that branch of psychology which deals with the human mind as it receives and interprets impressions from the external world. **comparative p.,** the study of the mental action of animals. **constitutional p.,** the relation of the psychology of the individual to the morphology and physiology of his body. **criminal p.,** the study of the mentality, the motivation, and the social behavior of criminals. **depth p.,** the psychology of the unconscious; psychoanalysis. **dynamic p.,** psychology which stresses the element of energy in mental processes. **experimental p.,** the study of the mind and mental operations by the employment of experimental methods. **genetic p.,** that branch of psychology which deals with the development of mind in the individual and with its evolution in the race. **gestalt p.** See *gestaltism.* **hormic p.,** a psychology which asserts that active striving toward a goal is a fundamental category of psychology (McDougall). **physiologic p.,** psychology which applies the facts taught in neurology to show the relation between the mental and the neural. **social p.,** psychology which treats of the social aspects of mental life.

psychomathematics (si″ko-math″e-mat′iks). Mathematics applied to the study of psychology.

psychometer (si-kom′e-ter). An instrument used in psychometry.

psychometrics (si″ko-met′riks). Psychometry.

psychometry (si-kom′e-tre) [*psycho-* + Gr. *metron* measure]. 1. Measurement of the duration and force of mental operations. 2. The measurement of intelligence.

psychomotor (si″ko-mo′tor). Pertaining to motor effects of cerebral or psychic activity.

psychoneuroses (si″ko-nu-ro′sēz). Plural of *psychoneurosis.*

psychoneurosis (si″ko-nu-ro′sis), pl. *psychoneuroses* [*psycho-* + Gr. *neuron* nerve + *-osis*]. Mental disorder which is of psychogenic origin but presents the essential symptoms of functional nervous disease, as hysteria, neurasthenia, psychasthenia. Cf. *neurosis.* **defense p.,** a psychosis or neurosis whose symptoms are due to the attempt to repress a painful idea. The idea is excluded from the mind, but remains in subconsciousness, where it acts as a cause of disturbance. The term includes hysteria as well as various neuroses and psychoses. **p. mai′dica,** pellagra. **paranoid p.,** a psychoneurosis marked by a delusion on the part of the patient that others are plotting to injure him.

psychonomy (si″kon-o′me) [*psycho-* + Gr. *nomos* law]. The science of the laws of mental activity.

psychonosema (si″ko-no-se′mah) [*psycho-* + Gr. *nosēma* illness]. Any mental disorder.

psychonosis (si″ko-no′sis) [*psycho-* + Gr. *nosos* disease]. Any disease or affection caused by mental or moral agents.

psychoparesis (si″ko-pah-re′sis) [*psycho-* + Gr. *paresis* slackening]. Weakness of mind.

psychopath (si′ko-path). A person who has a psychopathic personality. **sexual p.,** an individual whose sexual behavior is manifestly antisocial and criminal.

psychopathia (si″ko-pa′the-ah). Psychopathy. **p. martia′lis,** mental disease resulting from experiences in war. **p. sexua′lis,** mental disease marked by perversion of the sexual feelings.

psychopathic (si″ko-path′ik). Pertaining to mental disease.

psychopathist (si-kop′ah-thist). An alienist.

psychopathology (si″ko-pah-thol′o-je) [*psycho-* + *pathology*]. The pathology of mental disorders; the branch of medicine which deals with the causes and nature of mental disease.

psychopathosis (si″ko-pah-tho′sis). Southard's term for the condition characteristic of a psychopathic personality.

psychopathy (si-kop′ah-the) [*psycho-* + Gr. *pathos* disease]. A disorder of the psyche, whether or not associated with subnormal intelligence.

psychopharmacology (si″ko-fahr″mah-kol′o-je). The study of the action of drugs on the psychological functions.

psychophonasthenia (si″ko-fōn″as-the′ne-ah) [*psycho-* + Gr. *phōnē* voice + *asthenia*]. A speech difficulty of psychic origin.

psychophylaxis (si″ko-fi-lak′sis). Prophylaxis in mental disease; mental hygiene.

psychophysical (si″ko-fiz′e-kal). Pertaining to

the mind and its relation to physical manifestations.

psychophysics (si″ko-fiz′iks) [*psycho-* + Gr. *physikos* natural]. The science dealing with the quantitative relationships between the characteristics or patterns of physical stimuli and the resultant sensations.

psychophysiology (si″ko-fiz″e-ol′o-je). The physiology of the mental organs or apparatus.

psychoplasm (si′ko-plazm). Protyl.

psychoplegia (si″ko-ple′je-ah) [*psycho-* + Gr. *plēgē* stroke + *-ia*]. A sudden attack of mental weakness.

psychoplegic (si″ko-ple′jik). An agent that lessens cerebral activity or excitability.

psychopneumatology (si″ko-nu″mah-tol′o-je) [*phycho-* + Gr. *pneuma* breath + *-logy*]. The study of the interactions of mind, body, and soul.

psychoprophylactic (si″ko-pro″fi-lak′tik). Pertaining to psychoprophylaxis.

psychoprophylaxis (si″ko-pro″fi-lak′sis). A technique of psychophysical training aimed at the suppression of all painful sensation associated with normal childbirth.

psychoreaction (si″ko-re-ak′shun). Much's reaction.

psychorhythmia (si″ko-rith′me-ah) [*psycho-* + Gr. *rhythmos* rhythm + *-ia*]. A condition in which there is involuntary repetition of the various mental actions.

psychorrhagia (si″ko-ra′je-ah) [Gr.]. The death struggle.

psychorrhea (si″ko-re′ah) [*psycho-* + Gr. *rhoia* flow]. A mental condition characterized by an overabundance of theories and ideas with vitiation of instinct, reason, and common sense, resulting in an incoherent stream of thought.

psychorrhexis (si″ko-rek′sis) [*phycho-* + Gr. *rhēxis* rupture]. A malignant form of anxiety neurosis, marked by perplexity and anguish, sometimes produced by shock.

psychosensorial (si″ko-sen-so′re-al). Psychosensory.

psychosensory (si″ko-sen′so-re). Pertaining to the conscious perception of sensory impulses to the mind and to sensation.

psychoses (si-ko′sēz). Plural of *psychosis*.

psychosexual (si″ko-seks′u-al). Pertaining to the psychic or emotional aspects of the sex instinct.

psychosin (si-ko′sin). A galactoside, $C_{23}H_{45}N_7O$, resulting from the decomposition of phrenosin. On hydrolysis it yields galactose and sphingosine.

psychosis (si-ko′sis), pl. *psycho′ses* [*psych-* + *-osis*]. 1. Formerly, a generic name for any mental disorder. Specifically, the deeper, more far-reaching and prolonged behavior disorders, such as *dementia praecox* and *manic-depressive p.* 2. Any thought process. **affective p.,** a functional emotional psychosis; manic-depressive psychosis. **alcoholic p.,** mental disorder in which excessive use of alcohol is the chief etiologic factor. **Cheyne-Stokes p.,** a condition resembling cardiac asthma, with intense motor agitation, sometimes seen along with the onset of Cheyne-Stokes respiration in chronic heart disease. **circular p.,** properly, the circular type of manic-depressive psychosis, that type in which there is no free interval between the manic and depressive reactions. **depressive p.,** a psychosis characterized by states of mental depression, melancholy, despondency, inadequacy, and feelings of guilt. **drug p.,** a toxic psychosis due to the ingestion of drugs. **epileptic p.,** psychosis occurring in a person suffering from epilepsy. **exhaustion p.,** mental disorder due to some exhausting or depressing occurrence, as an operation. **famine p.,** a mental condition resulting from malnutrition among destitute civilians under conditions of oppression. **febrile p.,** exhaustion delirium. **functional p.,** a psychosis in which organic disease or dysfunction does not play a part. **gestational p.,** a psychosis developing during pregnancy. **idiophrenic p.,** organic p. **infection exhaustion p.,** exhaustion delirium. **involutional p.,** mental disorder occurring in or about the middle years of life, believed to be associated with the climacteric changes, and characterized by agitation, depression, self-condemnatory trends and sometimes by paranoid reactions. **Korsakoff's p.,** a psychosis which is usually based on chronic alcoholism, and which is accompanied by disturbance of orientation, susceptibility to external stimulation and suggestion, falsification of memory, and hallucinations. The signs of polyneuritis (wristdrop, etc.) are usually present. Called also *polyneuritic psychosis, cerebropathia psychica toxaemica,* and *chronic alcoholic delirium.* **manic p.,** a psychosis characterized by marked emotional instability. **manic-depressive p.,** an essentially benign, affective psychosis, chiefly marked by emotional instability, striking mood swings, and a tendency to recurrence. It is seen in the manic, depressed, circular, mixed, perplexed, and stuporous types. **organic p.,** a psychosis due to a lesion of the central nervous system, such as general paresis. **paranoiac p., paranoid p.,** a psychosis in which the patient has delusions that others are plotting to injure him. **periodic p.,** a condition in which intermittent periods of depression or hypomania recur regularly in a seemingly mentally healthy or nearly healthy individual. **polyneuritic p., p. polyneurit′ica,** Korsakoff's p. **prison p.,** any psychosis for which prison environment has been a precipitating factor. **puerperal p.,** any psychotic state occurring during pregnancy or following childbirth. **purpose p.,** a psychotic state motivated by a clear-cut wish, such as a wish to appear insane and therefore irresponsible. **schizoaffective p.,** a psychotic state characterized by mixed schizophrenic and manic-depressive symptoms. **senile p.,** one of the several forms of mental deterioration in old age in which the patient shows a tendency to confabulation, loss of memory of recent events, irritability and assaultiveness. **situational p.,** a transitory mental disorder caused by an unbearable situation over which the patient has no control. **toxic p.,** a psychosis due to the ingestion of toxic agents (e.g., alcohol, opium) into the body, or to presence of toxins within the body. **zoophil p.,** a psychosis marked by abnormal affection for or interest in animals.

psychosolytic (si-ko″so-lit′ik) [*psychosis* + Gr. *lytikos* dissolving]. Tending to relieve or abolish psychotic symptoms.

psychosomatic (si″ko-so-mat′ik) [*psycho-* + Gr. *sōma* body]. Pertaining to the mind-body relationship; having bodily symptoms of a psychic, emotional or mental origin.

psychosomaticist (si″ko-so-mat′ah-sist). One who practices psychosomatic medicine.

psychosomimetic (si-ko″so-mi-met′ik). Psychotomimetic.

psychosurgery (si″ko-ser′jer-e). Brain surgery performed for the relief of mental and psychic symptoms.

psychotechnics (si″ko-tek′niks) [*psycho-* + Gr. *technē* art]. The employment of psychological methods in studying sociological and other problems.

psychotherapeutics (si″ko-ther″ah-pu′tiks). Psychotherapy.

psychotherapy (si-ko-ther′ah-pe) [*psycho-* + Gr. *therapeia* treatment]. Treatment designed to produce a response by mental rather than by physical effects, including the use of suggestion, persuasion, re-education, reassurance, and support, as well as the techniques of hypnosis, abreaction, and psychoanalysis which are employed in the so-called deep psychotherapy.

psychotic (si-kot′ik). Pertaining to, characterized by, or caused by psychosis.

psychotogenic (si-kot″o-jen′ik). Producing a state of psychosis.

psychotomimetic (si-kot″o-mi-met′ik) [*psychosis* + Gr. *mimētikos* imitative]. Pertaining to, characterized by, or producing manifestations resembling those of a psychosis.

psychotonic (si″ko-ton′ik) [*psycho-* + Gr. *tonos* tone]. Exerting an elevating or stimulating effect upon the mind.

psychotropic (si″ko-tro′pik) [*psycho-* + Gr. *tropē* a turning]. Exerting an effect upon the mind; capable of modifying mental activity.

psychro- (si′kro) [Gr. *psychros* cold]. Combining form denoting relationship to cold.

psychro-algia (si″kro-al′je-ah). A painful feeling of cold.

psychro-esthesia (si″kro-es-the′ze-ah) [*psychro-* + Gr. *aisthēsis* perception + *-ia*]. A state in which a part of the body, though warm, seems cold.

psychrolusia (si″kro-loo′se-ah) [*psychro-* + Gr. *louein* to wash]. Bathing in cold water.

psychrometer (si-krom′e-ter) [*psychro-* + Gr. *metron* measure]. An apparatus for measuring atmospheric moisture by the difference in reading of two thermometers, one with a dry bulb and one with a wet bulb. **sling p.,** an instrument in which the thermometers are swung through the air to facilitate evaporation from the wet bulb.

psychrophile (si′kro-fīl). An organism which grows best at temperatures between 15 and 20°C.

psychrophilic (si″kro-fil′ik) [*psychro-* + Gr. *philein* to love]. Fond of cold: said of bacteria which develop best between 15 and 20°C. See also *mesophilic* and *thermophilic*.

psychrophobia (si″kro-fo′be-ah) [*psychro-* + Gr. *phobein* to be affrighted by]. Abnormal dread of cold.

psychrophore (si′kro-fōr) [*psychro-* + Gr. *pherein* to bear]. A double catheter for applying cold to the urethra.

psychrotherapy (si″kro-ther′ah-pe) [*psychro-* + Gr. *therapeia* treatment]. The treatment of disease by the application of cold.

psyctic (sik′tik) [Gr. *psychein* to cool]. Cooling.

psydracium (si-dra′se-um) [Gr. *psydrakion* blister]. An old name for a pustular skin disease.

psyllium (sil′e-um). The plant *Plantago psyllium*, the seed of which is used as a mild laxative.

Pt. Chemical symbol for *platinum*.

pt. Abbreviation for *pint*.

PTA. Abbreviation for *plasma thromboplastin antecedent* (blood coagulation factor XI).

PTAP. A purified diphtheria toxoid precipitated by aluminum phosphate.

ptarmic (tar′mik) [Gr. *ptarmikos* making to sneeze]. Relating to or producing spasmodic sneezing.

ptarmus (tar′mus) [Gr. *ptarmos*]. Spasmodic sneezing.

PTC. Abbreviation for *plasma thromboplastin component* (blood coagulation factor IX), and for *phenylthiocarbamide*.

pteridine (ter′ĭ-din). A nitrogenous base characterizing the pterins.

Pteridophyta (ter″ĭ-dof′ĭ-tah) [Gr. *pteris* fern + *phyton* plant]. A division of the plant kingdom including the ferns.

pteridophyte (ter′ĭ-do-fīt″). One of the Pteridophyta.

pterin (ter′in) [Gr. *pteron* wing]. Any one of a class of nitrogenous compounds first observed in the wings of butterflies. Cf. *xanthopterin*, *uropterin*, *aminopterin*, etc.

pterion (te′re-on) [Gr. *pteron* wing]. A point at the junction of the frontal, parietal, temporal, and great wing of the sphenoid bone; about 3 cm. behind the external angular process of the orbit.

pternalgia (ter-nal′je-ah) [Gr. *pterna* heel + *algos* pain + *-ia*]. Pain in the heel.

pteroylglutamate (ter″o-il-gloo′tah-mate). A salt of pteroylglutamic (folic) acid.

pterygium (tĕ-rij′e-um) [Gr. *pterygion* wing]. A winglike structure, applied especially to a triangular fold of membrane, in the interpalpebral fissure, extending from the conjunctiva to the cornea, being immovably united to the cornea at its apex, firmly attached to the sclera throughout its middle portion, and merged with the conjunctiva at its base. **p. col′li,** a thick fold of skin on the lateral aspect of the neck, extending from the mastoid region to the acromion, producing congenital webbed neck. **p. un′guis,** abnormal extension and adherence of the cuticle over the proximal portion of the nail plate.

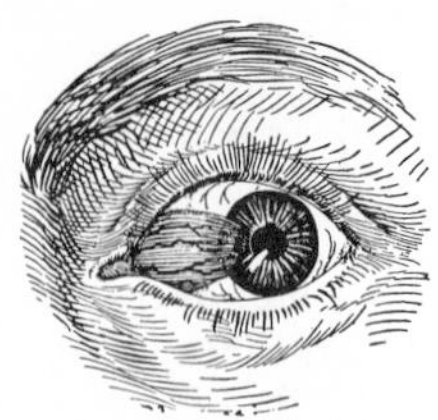

Pterygium (Woolf).

pterygoid (ter′ĭ-goid) [Gr. *pterygōdēs* like a wing]. Shaped like a wing.

pterygomandibular (ter″ĭ-go-man-dib′u-lar). Pertaining to the pterygoid process and the mandible.

pterygomaxillary (ter″ĭ-go-mak′sĭ-ler″e). Pertaining to a pterygoid process and the upper jaw.

pterygopalatine (ter″ĭ-go-pal′ah-tin). Pertaining to a pterygoid process and to the palate bone.

pterygospermin (ter″ĭ-go-sper′min). An antibiotic compound from *Moringa pterygosperma*.

ptilosis (ti-lo′sis) [Gr. *ptilōsis*]. 1. A falling out or loss of the eyelashes. 2. A form of pneumoconiosis caused by inhaling the dust from ostrich feathers.

ptisan (tiz′an) [L. *ptisana;* Gr. *ptisanē*]. Sweetened barley water, or other similar preparation: a decoction or medicinal tea.

P.T.O. Abbreviation for Ger. *Perlsucht Tuberculin Original*, or Klemperer's tuberculin.

ptomaine (to′mān) [Gr. *ptōma* carcass]. Any one of a class of bases formed under the action of bacteria or of metabolism. Some are formed by the decarboxylation of amino acids. Called also *animal alkaloid*, *putrefactive alkaloid*, and *cadaveric alkaloid*.

ptomainemia (to″mān-e′me-ah) [*ptomaine* + Gr. *haima* blood + *-ia*]. The presence of ptomaines in the blood.

ptomainotoxism (to″mān-o-tok′sizm). Poisoning by a ptomaine.

ptomatine (to′mah-tin). Ptomaine.

ptomatopsia (to″mah-top′se-ah) [Gr. *ptōma* corpse + *opsis* vision + *-ia*]. Necropsy.

ptomatopsy (to″mah-top′se). Necropsy.

ptomatropine (to-mat′ro-pin) [*ptomaine* + *atropine*]. A ptomaine from putrid sausages and the viscera of corpses of those dead from typhoid fever. It has effects somewhat like those of atropine.

ptosed (tōst). Affected with ptosis; prolapsed.

ptosis (to′sis) [Gr. *ptōsis* fall]. 1. Prolapse of an organ or part. 2. Drooping of the upper eyelid from paralysis of the third nerve. **abdominal p.,** splanchnoptosis. **p. adipo′sa, false p.,** an apparent ptosis caused by a fold of skin and fat hanging down below the border of the eyelid. **Horner's p.,** moderate ptosis of an eye, with retraction of the eyeball, miosis, and flushing of the affected side of the face, due to lesions of the cervical sympathetic. **p. lipomato′sis,** ptosis produced by lipoma of the eyelid. **morning p.,** waking ptosis. **p. sympath′ica,** ptosis associated with miosis, vasomotor facial paralysis, and diseases of the cervical sympathetic system. **visceral p.,** splanchnoptosis. **waking p.,** temporary paralysis of the upper lid on awakening from sleep.

ptotic (tot′ik). Pertaining to or affected with ptosis.

P.T.R. Abbreviation for Ger. *Perlsucht Tuberculin Rest*, a tuberculin prepared from bovine bacilli in the same manner as Koch's new tuberculin.

PTT. Abbreviation for *partial thromboplastin time* (test).

ptyalagogue (ti-al′ah-gog) [*ptyalo-* + Gr. *agōgos* leading]. Sialagogue.

ptyalectasis (ti″ah-lek′tah-sis) [*ptyalo-* + Gr. *ektasis* distention]. 1. Operative dilatation of a salivary duct. 2. Dilatation of one of the ducts of the salivary glands.

ptyalin (ti′ah-lin) [Gr. *ptyalon* spittle]. An enzyme occurring in the saliva which converts starch into maltose and dextrose.

ptyalinogen (ti″ah-lin′o-jen) [*ptyalin* + Gr. *gennan* to produce]. A hypothetical substance which is supposed to exist in the cells of the salivary glands, and to be intermediary in the formation of ptyalin.

ptyalism (ti′ah-lizm) [Gr. *ptyalismos*]. Excessive secretion of saliva; salivation. **mercurial p.** See *salivation.*

ptyalith (ti′ah-lith) [*ptyalo-* + Gr. *lithos* stone]. A salivary calculus.

ptyalize (ti′ah-līz). To increase or stimulate the secretion of saliva.

ptyalo- (ti′ah-lo) [Gr. *ptyalon* spittle]. Combining form denoting relationship to the saliva.

ptyalocele (ti-al′o-sēl) [*ptyalo-* + Gr. *kēlē* tumor]. A cystic tumor containing saliva. **sublingual p.,** ranula.

ptyalogenic (ti″ah-lo-jen′ik) [*ptyalo-* + Gr. *gennan* to produce]. Formed from or by the action of saliva.

ptyalography (ti″ah-log′rah-fe) [*ptyalo-* + Gr. *graphein* to write]. Sialography.

ptyalolith (ti′ah-lo-lith). Ptyalith.

ptyalolithiasis (ti″ah-lo-lĭ-thi′ah-sis). The presence of salivary calculi.

ptyalolithotomy (ti″ah-lo-lĭ-thot′o-me). Sialolithotomy.

ptyaloreaction (ti″ah-lo-re-ak′shun). A reaction occurring in the saliva. **Zambrini's p.,** a reaction of saliva produced by adding to it a reagent consisting of cochineal carmine, bioxyantroquinone, trioxyantroquinone, tincture of madder, and 75 per cent alcohol. The saliva takes on a color varying from light yellow to dark violet. A light shade indicates poor vital resistance; a dark shade, good vital resistance.

ptyalorrhea (ti″ah-lo-re′ah) [*ptyalo-* + Gr. *rhoia* flow]. An abnormally copious flow of saliva.

ptyalose (ti′ah-lōs). Maltose produced by the action of ptyalin on starch.

ptyocrinous (ti-ok′rĭ-nus) [Gr. *ptyon* a winnowing shovel, or fan + *krinein* to separate]. Elaborating secretion in the form of granules which are eventually extruded: said of unicellular glands, as globlet cells, which secrete in this way. Cf. *diacrinous.*

Pu. Chemical symbol for *plutonium.*

pubarche (pu-bar′ke). The beginning of growth of the pubic hair.

puberal (pu′ber-al) [L. *puber* of marriageable age]. Arrived at the age of puberty.

pubertal (pu′ber-tal). Pertaining to or characteristic of puberty.

pubertas (pu′ber-tas) [L.]. Puberty. **p. prae′cox,** pathologically early sexual maturity.

puberty (pu′ber-te) [L. *pubertas*]. The period intervening between the time of appearance of secondary sex characters and the completion of somatic growth.

pubes (pu′bēz) [L.]. 1. Plural of *pubis.* 2. [N A, B N A] The hair growing over the pubic region.

pubescence (pu-bes′ens). 1. Puberty. 2. Downiness; lanugo.

pubescent (pu-bes′ent) [L. *pubescens* becoming hairy]. 1. Arriving at the age of puberty. 2. Covered with down or lanugo.

pubetrotomy (pu″bĕ-trot′o-me). Section of the os pubis and of the lower abdominal wall.

pubic (pu′bik). Pertaining to the pubes, or pubic bones.

pubioplasty (pu′be-o-plas″te). A plastic operation on the pubes.

pubiotomy (pu″be-ot′o-me) [*pubis* + Gr. *tomē* a cutting]. Surgical separation of the pubic bone lateral to the median line.

pubis (pu′bis), pl. *pu′bes* [L.]. The os pubis.

pubisure (pu′bĭ-sūr). The pubic hair.

pubofemoral (pu″bo-fem′o-ral). Pertaining to the os pubis and femur.

puboprostatic (pu″bo-pros-tat′ik). Pertaining to the os pubis and prostate gland.

pubotibial (pu″bo-tib′e-al). Pertaining to the pubes and tibia.

pubovesical (pu″bo-ves′ĭ-kal). Pertaining to the pubes and bladder.

puces (pu′sēz). Scabies.

pudenda (pu-den′dah) [L.]. Plural of *pudendum.*

pudendagra (pu″den-dag′rah) [*pudenda* + Gr. *agra* seizure]. Pain in the genitals, especially the female genitals.

pudendal (pu-den′dal). Pertaining to the pudenda.

pudendum (pu-den′dum), pl. *puden′da* [L., from *pudere* to be ashamed]. That of which one ought to be ashamed. **female p.,** p. femininum. **p. femini′num** [N A], the mons pubis, labia majora, labia minora, and the vestibule of the vagina. **p. mulie′bre** [B N A], p. femininum.

pudic (pu′dik) [L. *pudicus*]. Pertaining to the pudenda.

puericulture (pu-er′ĭ-kul″tūr) [L. *puer* child + *cultura* culture]. The art of rearing and training children.

puericulturist (pu″er-ĭ-kul′tūr-ist). A specialist in the training of children.

puerile (pu′er-il) [L. *puerilis; puer* child]. Pertaining to childhood or to children; childish.

puerilism (pu′er-il-izm) [L. *puer* child]. A condition in which the patient's mind seems to return to its state when a child.

puerpera (pu-er′per-ah) [L. *puer* child + *parere* to bring forth, to bear]. A woman who has just given birth to an infant.

puerperal (pu-er′per-al) [L. *puerperalis*]. Pertaining to the puerperium.

puerperalism (pu-er′per-al-izm). A disease condition incident to childbirth.

puerperant (pu-er′per-ant). 1. Giving birth. 2. A puerpera.

puerperium (pu″er-pe′re-um) [L.]. The period or state of confinement after labor.

puff (puf). A short, blowing, auscultation sound. **veiled p.,** a faint, muffled pulmonary murmur.

pugil, pugillus (pu′jil, pu-jil′us) [L. *pugillus*]. A handful.

pujos blancos (poo′hōs blahnk′ōs) [Sp. "white straining"]. A Chilean dysentery with white discharges.

Pukall filter (poo′kal) [Wilhelm *Pukall,* German chemist, born 1860]. See under *filter.*

pukateine (pu-kat′e-in). A crystalline alkaloid, $C_{18}H_{17}NO_3$, from *Laurelia novae-zelandiae.*

pulegone (pu′le-gōn). A volatile oil, a menthene, $(CH_3)_2C{:}C_6H_7(O).CH_3$, from pennyroyal oil.

Pulex (pu′leks) [L. "flea"]. A genus of fleas which are parasitic on man and on dogs, cats, and badgers. **P. cheo′pis,** *Xenopsylla cheopis.* **P. duge′si,** a flea found in Mexico which much resembles *P. irritans,* but has a longer rostrum. **P. ir′ritans,** the common flea or human flea, which is parasitic in the skin of man, its bite producing itching. **P. pen′etrans,** the chigo or jigger-flea. See *chigger.* **P. serrat′iceps,** *Ctenocephalus canis.*

pulex (pu′leks), pl. *pu′lices* [L.]. An organism of the genus Pulex; a flea.

Pulheems (pul′hēmz). A system of medical classification for recording the physical and mental status of recruits in the British fighting services, representing: P, physical capacity; U, upper limbs; L, lower limbs; H, hearing (acuity); EE, eyesight (visual acuity); M, mental capacity; S, stability (emotional).

pulicicide (pu-lis′ĭ-sīd) [L. *pulex* flea + *caedere* to kill]. An agent destructive to fleas.

Pulicidae (pu-lis′ĭ-de). A family of the Siphonaptera which includes most of the fleas. Four genera are important to man: *Ctenocephalides, Hoplopsyllus, Pulex,* and *Xenopsylla.*

pulicosis (pu″lĭ-ko′sis). Irritation of the skin caused by the bites of *Pulex irritans.*

pullorin (pul′o-rin). A dissociation product obtained by washing eighteen-hour agar cultures of the organism of bacillary white diarrhea occurring in chickens.

Pullularia (pul″u-la′re-ah). A genus of fungi, species of which have been isolated from pigmented lesions resembling mycetoma.

pullulate (pul′u-lāt). To germinate.

pullulation (pul″u-la′shun) [L. *pullulare* to sprout]. The act or process of budding or of sprouting; germination.

Pulm. Abbreviation for L. *pulment′um,* gruel.

pulmin (pul′min). A plasmin and trypsin inhibitor found in lung tissue from the ox, but not in that from pig, rabbit, mouse, or man.

pulmo (pul′mo), gen. *pulmo′nis,* pl. *pulmo′nes* [L.]. [N A, B N A] The organ of respiration. See *lung.*

pulmo- (pul′mo). Combining form denoting relationship to the lungs. See also words beginning *pulmono-.*

pulmo-aortic (pul″mo-a-or′tik). Pertaining to the lungs and the aorta.

pulmogram (pul′mo-gram). A roentgenogram of the lungs.

pulmolith (pul′mo-lith) [*pulmo-* + Gr. *lithos* stone]. A lung calculus.

pulmometer (pul-mom′e-ter) [*pulmo-* + L. *metrum* measure]. A form of spirometer for measuring the capacity of the lungs for air.

pulmometry (pul-mom′e-tre). The measurement of the lung capacity.

pulmonal (pul′mo-nal). Pulmonary.

pulmonary (pul′mo-ner″e) [L. *pulmonarius*]. Pertaining to the lungs.

pulmonectomy (pul″mo-nek′to-me). Pneumonectomy.

pulmonic (pul-mon′ik). 1. Pertaining to the lungs; pulmonary. 2. Pertaining to the pulmonary artery.

pulmonitis (pul″mo-ni′tis). Inflammation of the lungs; pneumonia.

pulmono- (pul′mo-no). Combining form denoting relationship to the lungs. See also words beginning *pulmo-.*

pulmonohepatic (pul″mo-no-he-pat′ik). Pertaining to or communicating with the lungs and the liver; hepatopulmonary.

pulmonologist (pul″mo-nol′o-jist). An individual who is skilled in pulmonology.

pulmonology (pul″mo-nol′o-je). The science concerned with the anatomy, physiology, and pathology of the lungs.

pulmonoperitoneal (pul″mo-no-per″ĭ-to-ne′al). Pertaining to or communicating with the lungs and the peritoneum.

pulmotor (pul′mo-tor) [*pulmo-* + L. *motor* mover]. An apparatus for producing artificial respiration by forcing oxygen into the lungs, and, when they are distended, sucking out the air.

pulp (pulp) [L. *pulpa* flesh]. Any soft, juicy animal or vegetable tissue, such as that contained within the pulp chamber of a tooth. See *dental pulp.* **coronal p.,** the part of the dental pulp contained in the crown portion of the pulp cavity. **dead p.,** necrotic p. **dental p.,** the richly vascularized and innervated connective tissue contained in the pulp cavity of a tooth, constituting the formative, nutritive, and sensory organ of the dentin. Called also *pulpa dentis* [N A]. **devitalized p.,** necrotic p. **digital p.,** the mass of tissue forming the soft cushion on the palmar or plantar surface of the distal phalanx of a finger or toe. **enamel p.,** stellate reticulum. **exposed p.,** dental pulp which, through trauma or disease, has become exposed to the external environment. **mummified p.,** dental pulp which has undergone caseation necrosis. **necrotic p.,** dental pulp which has been deprived of its blood and nerve supply and is no longer composed of living tissue, as evidenced by its insensitivity to stimulation by electricity, heat, cold, or trauma. **nonvital p.,** necrotic p. **putrescent p.,** a necrotic pulp which has been invaded by putrefactive microorganisms and is characterized by a particularly foul odor. **radicular p.,** the part of the dental pulp contained in the root canal of a tooth. **red p., splenic p.,** the dark, reddish-brown substance which fills up the interspaces of the sinuses of the spleen. Called also *pulpa lienis* [N A]. **tooth p.,** dental p. **vertebral p.,** the soft central portion of an intervertebral disk. **vital p.,** a dental pulp which is characterized by vascularity and sensation. **white p.,** sheaths of lymphatic tissue surrounding the arteries of the spleen. **wood p.,** a purified cellulose prepared from finely shredded wood and used in the manufacture of paper; sometimes used also as an absorbent dressing.

pulpa (pul′pah), pl. *pul′pae* [L. "flesh"]. Pulp. **p. den′tis** [N A, B N A], the richly vascularized and innervated connective tissue contained in the pulp cavity of a tooth. Called also *dental pulp.* **p. lie′nis** [N A, B N A], the dark, reddish-brown substance that fills up the interspaces of the sinuses of the spleen. Called also *red pulp* and *pulp of spleen.*

pulpal (pul′pal). Pertaining to the pulp.

pulpalgia (pul-pal′je-ah). Pain in the pulp of a tooth.

pulpation (pul-pa′shun). Pulpefaction.

pulpectomy (pul-pek′to-me) [*pulp* + Gr. *ektomē* excision]. Extirpation of the pulp from the pulp chamber and root canals of a tooth.

pulpefaction (pul″pĕ-fak′shun) [*pulp* + L. *facere* to make]. Conversion into pulp.

pulpiform (pul′pĭ-form). Resembling pulp.

pulpitides (pul-pit′ĭ-dēz). Plural of *pulpitis;* applied to all types of pulp inflammation collectively.

pulpitis (pul-pi′tis), pl. *pulpit′ides.* Inflammation of the dental pulp. **anachoretic p.,** pulpitis caused by bacteria attracted to the pulp because of local irritation—the "anachoretic effect."

pulpless (pulp′les). Without pulp; having the pulp removed.

pulpoaxial (pul″po-ak′se-al). Pertaining to or formed by the pulpal and axial walls of a tooth cavity.

pulpobuccoaxial (pul″po-buk″ko-ak′se-al). Pertaining to or formed by the pulpal, buccal, and axial walls of a tooth cavity.

pulpodistal (pul″po-dis′tal). Pertaining to or formed by the pulpal and distal walls of a tooth cavity.

pulpodontia (pul″po-don′she-ah). Pulpodontics.

pulpodontics (pul″po-don′tiks). That area of dentistry dealing with the dental pulp.

pulpolabial (pul″po-la′be-al). Pertaining to or formed by the pulpal and labial walls of a tooth cavity.

pulpolingual (pul″po-ling′gwal). Pertaining to or formed by the pulpal and lingual walls of a tooth cavity.

pulpolinguoaxial (pul″po-ling″gwo-ak′se-al). Pertaining to or formed by the pulpal, lingual, and axial walls of a tooth cavity.

pulpomesial (pul″po-me′ze-al). Pertaining to or formed by the pulpal and mesial walls of a tooth cavity.

pulpotomy (pul-pot′o-me) [*pulp* + Gr. *tomē* a cutting]. Surgical excision of the coronal portion of a vital pulp.

pulpy (pul′pe). Soft or pulpaceous.

pulque (pul′ke). A fermented drink made in Mexico and Central America from the juice of agave.

pulsate (pul′sāt). To beat rhythmically, as the heart.

pulsatile (pul′sah-til). Characterized by a rhythmical pulsation.

pulsatilla (pul″sah-til′ah). The ranunculaceous flowering herb *Anemone pulsatilla;* also *A. pratensis.* Formerly employed in a variety of conditions, its use has been largely abandoned.

pulsation (pul-sa′shun) [L. *pulsatio*]. A throb or rhythmical beat, as of the heart. **expansile p.,** a pulsation which is seen or felt to become larger and wider with each impact of the pulse. **suprasternal p.,** arterial pulsation in the region of the suprasternal notch, due to dilatation of the aortic arch or to aneurysm.

pulsator (pul′sa-tor). See *Bragg-Paul pulsator.*

pulse (puls) [L. *pulsus* stroke]. The expansion and contraction of an artery which may be felt with the finger. The pulse is usually felt on the radial artery at the wrist, though it may be felt over the temporal, carotid, ulnar, brachial, femoral, and other arteries. The *pulse rate* or number of pulsations of an artery per minute normally varies from 70 to 72 in men and from 78 to 82 in women. **abdominal p.,** the pulse seen in emaciated persons over the abdominal aorta. **abrupt p.,** a pulse which strikes the finger rapidly; a quick pulse. **allorhythmic p.,** a pulse marked by irregularities in rhythm. **alternating p.,** pulsus alternans. **anacrotic p.,** one in which the ascending limb of the tracing shows an additional wave or notch. **anadicrotic p.,** one in which the ascending limb of the tracing shows two small additional waves or notches. **anatricrotic p.,** one in which the ascending limb of the tracing shows three small additional waves or notches. **arachnoid p.,** a small, feeble, tremulous pulse. **ardent p.,** a pulse which appears to strike the finger at a single point. **auriculovenous p.,** jugular pulsation in which the wave due to the auricle precedes the ventricular contraction. Called also *normal venous p.* and *negative venous p.* **Bamberger's bulbar p.,** a pulsation observable in the bulbus of the jugular vein and synchronous with the systole. It occurs in tricuspid inadequacy. **bigeminal p.,** a pulse in which two beats follow each other in rapid succession, each group of two being separated from the following by a longer interval. **bisferious p.,** pulsus bisferiens. **bulbar p.,** Bamberger's bulbar p. **cannon ball p.,** Corrigan's p. **capillary p.,** Quincke's p. **catacrotic p.,** one in which the descending limb of the tracing shows an additional wave or notch. **catadicrotic p.,** one in which the descending limb of the tracing shows two small additional waves or notches. **catatricrotic p.,** one in which the descending limb of the tracing shows three small additional waves or notches. **centripetal venous p.,** a venous pulse caused by an impulse passed from the arteries through the capillaries and venules into the larger veins. **collapsing p.,** Corrigan's p. **cordy p.,** a tense, firm pulse. **Corrigan's p.,** a jerky pulse with a full expansion, followed by a sudden collapse. It occurs in aortic regurgitation. Called also *water-hammer p.* **coupled p.,** bigeminal p. **decurtate p.,** a pulse which gradually tapers away in strength like the tail of a mouse. **deficient p.,** a pulse marked by an occasional lack of a beat, due to failure of the heart to contract. **dicrotic p.,** one in which the tracing shows two marked expansions in one beat of the artery: seen in decreased arterial tension. **digitalate p.,** bigeminal p. **dropped-beat p.,** intermittent p. **elastic p.,** a full pulse which gives an elastic feeling to the finger. **entoptic p.,** the subjective sensation of seeing in the dark a flash of light at each heart beat. **epigastric p.,** abdominal p. **equal p.,** one in which all of the beats are of the same strength. **febrile p.,** a pulse characteristic of fever. **filiform p.,** thready p. **formicant p.,** a small, nearly imperceptible pulse. **frequent p.,** one which is faster in rate than normal. **full p.,** one with a copious volume of blood. **funic p.,** the arterial tide in the umbilical cord. **gaseous p.,** a very soft, full pulse. **guttural p.,** a pulse felt in the throat. **hard p.,** one which is characterized by very high tension. **hepatic p.,** the pulsations of the liver. **high-tension p.,** one characterized by a gradual impulse, long duration, slow subsidence, and a firm, cordy state of the artery between the beats. **hyperdicrotic p.,** one in which the tracing shows an aortic notch below the base line: a sign of extreme exhaustion. **infrequent p.,** one which is slower in rate than normal. **intermittent p.,** one in which various beats are dropped. **irregular p.,** one in which the beats occur at irregular intervals. **jerky p.,** one in which the artery is suddenly and markedly distended. **jugular p.,** a pulsation felt over the jugular vein. **Kussmaul's p.,** paradoxical p. **labile p.,** a pulse which is normal with the patient resting, but which is increased by sitting, standing or exercise. **locomotive p.,** Corrigan's p. **long p.,** one in which the stroke is markedly prolonged. **low-tension p.,** a pulse with a sudden onset, short duration, and quick decline, and which is easily obliterated by pressure. **Monneret's p.,** a full, slow, and soft pulse characteristic of jaundice. **monocrotic p.,** one in which the tracing shows only one expansion in one beat of the artery. **mouse tail p., myurous p.,** decurtate p. **nail p.,** the pulsation of blood under the nails; usually determined by the onychograph. **negative venous p., normal venous p.,** auriculovenous p. **paradoxical p.,** a pulse that decreases in size during inspiration, such as may occur in some cases of adherent pericardium. **pathologic venous p.,** ventricular venous p. **pistol-shot p.,** a form in which the arteries are subject to sudden distention and collapse. **plateau p.,** a pulse which is slowly rising and sustained. **polycrotic p.,** one in which the tracing shows several secondary pulse waves. **positive venous p.,** ventricular venous p. **pulmonary p.,** the second sound of the heart as heard over the pulmonary valve. **quadrigeminal p.,** one with a pause after every fourth beat. **quick p.** 1. One which strikes the finger smartly and leaves it quickly. Called also *short p.* 2. One with a faster rate than normal. **Quincke's p.,** pulsation in the capillaries which may be detected by a perceptible nail pulse; alternate flushing and blanching of the nails, due to aortic insufficiency. Called also *capillary p.* **radial p.,** that felt over the radial artery. **respiratory p.** 1. A pulsation observed even in health in the superficial cervical veins after rapid exercise. 2. Paradoxical pulse. **retrosternal p.,** a venous pulse perceptible just above the suprasternal notch. **Riegel's p.,** a pulse which is diminished in size during expiration. **running p.,** a pulse with small irregular excursions. **sharp p.,** jerky p. **short p.,** quick p. **sixty-six p.,** a pulse rate of sixty-six per minute; such a pulse is regarded by some as indicative of vagotonia. **slow p.,** one with less than the usual number of pulsations per minute. **soft p.,** a pulse of low tension. **strong p.,** one that is hard or wiry. **tense p.,** a pulse that is hard and full, but without wide excursions. **thready p.,** one that is very fine and scarcely perceptible. **trembling p., tremulous p.,** running p. **tricrotic p.,** one in which the tracing shows three marked expansions in one beat of the artery. **trigeminal p.,** one with a pause after every third beat. **trip-hammer p.,** Corrigan's p. **undulating p.,** a pulse giving the sensation of successive waves. **unequal p.,** a pulse in which some of the beats are strong and others weak. **vagus p.,** a small, slow pulse. **venous p.,** the pulsation which occurs in a vein, usually observed at the right jugular vein just above the sternoclavicular junction. **ventricu-**

lar venous p., jugular pulsation in which the auricular wave disappears or coincides with the period of ventricular systole. Called also *positive venous p.* or *pathologic venous p.* **vermicular p.,** a small rapid pulse giving to the finger a sensation of wormlike movement. **vibrating p.,** jerky p. **water-hammer p.,** Corrigan's p. **wiry p.,** a small, tense pulse.

pulsellum (pul-sel'um) [L.]. A posterior propelling flagellum.

pulsimeter (pul-sim'e-ter) [*pulse* + L. *metrum* measure]. An apparatus for measuring the force of the pulse.

pulsion (pul'shun). A pushing forward, or outward or to either side.

pulsometer (pul-som'e-ter) [*pulse* + L. *metrum* measure]. An apparatus for measuring the rate of flow of the blood.

pulsus (pul'sus), pl. *pul'sus* [L.]. Pulse. **p. abdomina'lis,** abdominal pulse. **p. aequa'lis,** equal pulse. **p. alter'nans,** a pulse in which there is regular alternation of weak and strong beats. **p. bigem'inus,** bigeminal pulse. **p. bifer'iens, p. bisfer'iens,** a dicrotic pulse in which the waves are of nearly equal height. **p. ce'ler,** quick pulse. **p. contrac'tus,** a small, hard pulse. **p. cor'dis,** the pulse felt over the apex of the heart. **p. deb'ilis,** a weak pulse. **p. defic'iens,** deficient pulse. **p. dele'tus,** absence of pulse, seen in aortic aneurysm. **p. dif'ferens,** inequality of the pulse observable at corresponding sites on either side of the body. **p. du'plex,** dicrotic pulse. **p. du'rus,** hard pulse. **p. filifor'mis,** thready pulse. **p. for'micans,** formicant pulse. **p. for'tis,** a strong pulse. **p. fre'quens,** frequent pulse. **p. heterochron'icus,** an arrhythmic pulse. **p. inter'cidens, p. intercur'rens,** a pulse in which there is an extra beat. **p. irregula'ris perpet'uus,** a pulse which is wholly irregular. **p. mag'nus,** a large, full pulse. **p. mag'nus et ce'ler,** a large, full, and rapid pulse. **p. mol'lis,** soft pulse. **p. monoc'rotus,** monocrotic pulse. **p. oppres'sus,** a pulse which appears to be pushing its way through a contracted artery. **p. paradox'us,** paradoxical pulse. **p. par'vus,** small pulse. **p. par'vus et tar'dus,** a small hard pulse which rises and falls slowly. **p. ple'nus,** full pulse. **p. pseudo-intermit'tens,** a pulse showing an occasional intermittence, owing to a feeble contraction of the ventricle. **p. ra'rus,** a slow pulse due to prolongation of the heart's pause. **p. tar'dus,** an abnormally slow pulse due to a prolongation of the systole or diastole. **p. trigem'inus,** trigeminal pulse. **p. undulo'sus,** undulating pulse. **p. vac'uus,** an extremely weak pulse. **p. veno'sus,** venous pulse. **p. vi'brans,** jerky pulse.

pultaceous (pul-ta'shus) [L. *pultaceus*]. Like a pulp or poultice.

pulv. Abbreviation for L. *pulvis* powder.

pulverization (pul″ver-i-za'shun) [L. *pulvis* powder]. The reduction of any substance to powder.

pulverulent (pul-ver'u-lent) [L. *pulverulentus*]. Powdery; dustlike.

pulvinar (pul-vi'nar) [L. "a cushioned seat"]. [N A, B N A] The medial portion of the posterior end of the thalamus, which is prominent and cushion-like and partly overhangs the superior colliculus.

pulvinate (pul'vĭ-nāt) [L. *pulvinus* cushion]. Shaped like a cushion.

pumex (pu'meks) [L. "foam"]. Pumice.

pumice (pum'is). A substance of volcanic origin, consisting chiefly of complex silicates of aluminum, potassium, and sodium: used in dentistry as an abrasive or polishing agent, the effect achieved depending on the particle size.

pump (pump). An apparatus for drawing or forcing fluids or gases. **air p.,** a pump for exhausting or forcing in air. **Alvegniat's p.,** a mercurial air pump: used in measuring the free gaseous constituents of the blood. **blood p.,** a machine used to propel blood through the tubing of extracorporeal circulation devices, especially designed to achieve this without occluding the tubing or causing damage to the blood constituents, particularly the erythrocytes. **breast p.,** a pump for abstracting milk from the breast. **dental p.,** saliva ejector. **Lindbergh p.,** a perfusion pump by means of which an organ removed from the body may be kept alive indefinitely. **saliva p.,** saliva ejector. **stomach p.,** a pump for removing the contents from the stomach. **Woodyatt's p.,** a device for continuous intravenous injection at a constant rate.

puna (poo'nah). Mountain sickness.

punch (punch). 1. An instrument for indenting, perforating, or cutting out a disk of material. 2. An instrument for extracting the root of a tooth. **Ainsworth's p.,** an instrument for punching holes in rubber dam for application to teeth. **Caulk p.,** a cautery punch for the removal of median bar prostatic enlargements. **kidney p.** See *Murphy's test*, under *tests*. **pin p.,** an instrument for piercing the metal plate to receive the pins for fastening artificial teeth. **plate p.,** a tool for cutting out parts of an artificial dental plate.

punched-out (puncht'owt). Having the appearance of substance or tissue having been removed with a punch.

puncta (punk'tah) [L.]. Plural of *punctum*.

punctate (punk'tāt). 1. [L. *punctum* point]. Resembling or marked with points or dots. 2. The fluid obtained by an exploratory puncture.

punctiform (punk'tĭ-form) [L. *punctum* point + *forma* shape]. Like a point; located in a point. In bacteriology, said of very minute colonies.

punctio (punk'she-o) [L.]. The act of puncturing, pricking or dotting.

punctograph (punk'to-graf) [L. *punctum* point + Gr. *graphein* to write]. An instrument for the roentgenographic localization of foreign bodies in the tissues.

punctum (punk'tum), pl. *punc'ta* [L.]. An extremely small spot, or point; used in anatomical nomenclature as a general term to designate an extremely small area, or point of projection. **p. cae'cum,** blind spot. **punc'ta doloro'sa,** painful points in the course of nerves affected with neuralgia. Called also *Valleix's points*. **punc'ta lacrima'lia** [B N A]. See *punctum lacrimale*. **p. lacrima'le** [N A], the opening on the lacrimal papilla of an eyelid, near the medial angle of the eye, through which tears from the lacrimal lake enter the lacrimal canaliculi. **p. lu'teum,** macula lutea. **p. nasa'le infe'rius,** the rhinion. **p. op'timum** [L.], best point. **p. ossificatio'nis,** ossification center. **p. prox'imum** [L.], near point. **punc'ta prurit'ica,** itchy points. **p. remo'tum** [L.], far point. **punc'ta vasculo'sa,** minute red spots marking the cut surface of the white substance of the brain, produced by blood from divided vessels.

punctumeter (punk-tum'e-ter) [L. *punctum* point + *metrum* measure]. An instrument for measuring the range of accommodation.

punctura (punk-tu'rah) [L.]. Puncture. **p. explorato'ria,** exploratory puncture.

puncturatio (punk″tu-ra'she-o) [L.]. The act of puncturing.

puncture (punk'tūr) [L. *punctura*]. 1. An act of piercing. 2. A wound made by a pointed instrument. **Bernard's p.,** puncture on a definite point of the floor of the fourth ventricle causing artificial diabetes. **cisternal p.,** puncture of the cisterna magna through the occipitoatlantoid ligament for the purpose of withdrawing cerebrospinal fluid. **Corning's p.,** lumbar p. **cranial p.,** cisternal p. **diabetic p.,** Bernard's p. **epigastric p.** See *Marfan's method*, under *method*. **exploratory p.,** the piercing of a cavity or tumor and the removal of some portion of the contents for the purpose of examination. **heat**

p., elevation of the temperature of the animal body produced by puncturing the base of the brain. **intracisternal p.,** cisternal p. **Kronecker's p.,** puncture of the inhibitory nerve center of the heart by means of a long fine needle. **lumbar p.,** the tapping of the subarachnoid space in the lumbar region, usually between the third and fourth lumbar vertebrae. **Marfan's epigastric p.** See *Marfan's method,* under *method.* **Quincke's p., spinal p.,** lumbar p. **splenic p.,** puncture of the spleen for the purpose of obtaining a specimen of splenic tissue for laboratory examination. **sternal p.,** removal of bone marrow from the manubrium of the sternum through a spinal puncture needle. **suboccipital p.,** cisternal p. **thecal p.,** puncture of the spinal membranes. **tonsil p.,** puncture into the substance of the tonsil for the purpose of aspirating tissue for examination. **ventricular p.,** puncture of a cerebral ventricle for the purpose of withdrawing fluid.

pungent (pun′jent) [L. *pungens* pricking]. Sharp or biting; somewhat acrid.

puniceous (pu-nish′us). Bright red in color.

punizin (pu′nĭ-zin). A purple dye formed by the action of light and air on a colorless chromogen found in the secretions of *Murex trunculus* and *Purpurea lapillus.*

Puntius (pun′te-us). A genus of fresh-water fish. **P. javan′icus,** a species placed in fresh-water ponds in certain areas of the world, because it eliminates the weeds necessary for the propagation of mosquitoes.

punudos (pu′nu-dos). Pseudoleprosy; a disease of Guatemala resembling leprosy but without the presence of the leprosy bacillus.

P.U.O. Abbreviation for *pyrexia of unknown origin.*

pupa (pu′pah) [L. "a doll"]. The second stage in the development of an insect, between the larva and the imago.

pupal (pu′pal). Pertaining to a pupa.

pupil (pu′pil) [L. *pupilla* girl]. The opening at the center of the iris of the eye for the transmission of light. Called also *pupilla* [N A]. **Argyll Robertson p.,** one which is miotic and which responds to accommodation effort, but not to light. **artificial p.,** one made by iridectomy. **bounding p.,** a pupil which shows alternating dilatation and contraction. **Bumke's p.,** dilatation of the pupil following a psychic stimulus. It does not occur in dementia praecox. **cat's-eye p.,** one with a narrow vertical aperture. **fixed p.,** a pupil which does not react either to light or on convergence, or in accommodation. **Hutchinson's p.,** a condition of the pupils in which one is dilated and the other not. **keyhole p.,** a pupil with a coloboma on one side of the margin. **pinhole p.,** one which is extremely contracted. **skew p's,** a condition in which one of the ocular axes deviates upward and the other downward. **stiff p.,** Argyll Robertson pupil. **tonic p.,** a pupil which responds to accommodation and convergence in a slow, delayed fashion. See *Adie's syndrome,* under *syndrome.*

pupilla (pu-pil′ah) [L. "girl"], pl. *pupil′lae.* [N A, B N A] The opening at the center of the iris of the eye. Called also *pupil.*

pupillary (pu′pĭ-ler-e). Pertaining to the pupil.

pupillatonia (pu″pil-ah-to′ne-ah). Failure of the pupil to react to light.

pupillo- (pu′pĭ-lo) [L. *pupilla* pupil]. Combining form denoting relationship to the pupil.

pupillometer (pu″pĭ-lom′e-ter) [*pupillo-* + L. *metrum* measure]. An instrument for measuring the width or diameter of the pupil.

pupillometry (pu″pil-lom′e-tre). Measurement of the diameter or width of the pupil of the eye.

pupillomotor (pu″pĭ-lo-mo′tor). Pertaining to the movement of the pupil.

pupilloplegia (pu″pĭ-lo-ple′je-ah) [*pupillo-* + Gr. *plēgē* stroke]. Pupillatonia.

pupilloscope (pu-pil′o-skōp). Von Hess's instrument for measuring reactions of the pupil.

pupilloscopy (pu″pĭ-los′ko-pe) [*pupillo-* + Gr. *skopein* to examine]. Skiametry.

pupillostatometer (pu-pil″o-stah-tom′e-ter) [*pupillo-* + Gr. *statos* placed + *metron* measure]. An instrument for measuring the distance between the pupils.

pupillotonia (pu″pĭ-lo-to′ne-ah). Tonic reaction of the pupil. See *Adie's syndrome,* under *syndrome.*

Purdy's method, solution, test (per′dēz) [Charles Wesley *Purdy,* American physician, 1846–1901]. See under the nouns.

pure (pūr) [L. *purus*]. Free from mixture of other matters. A reagent is *chemically pure* when it contains no other chemicals that might interfere with its action.

purgación (poor″gah-se-on′) [Sp.]. A Peruvian term for gonorrhea.

purgation (pur-ga′shun) [L. *purgatio*]. Catharsis; purging effected by a cathartic medicine.

purgative (pur′gah-tiv) [L. *purgativus*]. 1. Cathartic; causing evacuations from the bowels. 2. A cathartic medicine.

purge (purj) [L. *purgare*]. 1. To relieve of fecal matter. 2. A purgative remedy or dose.

puric (pu′rik). 1. Pertaining to pus. 2. Pertaining to purine.

puriform (pu′rĭ-form) [L. *pus* pus + *forma* form]. Resembling pus. The term is applied to the contents of cold abscesses which resemble pus.

purinase (pu′rĭ-nās). An enzyme which brings about changes, such as oxidation and deamination, in purines.

purine (pu′rin) [L. *purum* pure + *urine*]. The heterocyclic compound, $C_5H_4N_4$ or

```
N=C.H
|   |
HC  C—NH
||  ||   >CH
N—C—N
```

a colorless crystalline substance not found in nature but synthesized by chemists. It is the base of the uric acid group of compounds known as *purines* or *purine bases* (purine bodies). **amino p.,** a purine in which one or more amino groups have been substituted. **methyl p's,** alkaloids formed from purines by substituting methyl groups, usually in positions 1, 3, 7. The principal ones are caffeine, theobromine, and theophylline.

purinemia (pu″rĭ-ne′me-ah) [*purine* + Gr. *haima* blood + *-ia*]. The presence of purine bases in the blood.

purinemic (pu″rĭ-ne′mik). Pertaining to or characterized by purinemia.

purinethol (pu′rēn-thol). Trade mark for a preparation of mercaptopurine.

purinolytic (pu″rin-o-lit′ik) [*purine* + Gr. *lytikos* loosing]. Splitting up purines.

purinometer (pu″rin-om′e-ter) [*purine* + Gr. *metron* measure]. An apparatus for estimating the quantity of purine bodies in the urine.

Purkinje's cells, fibers, figures, image, network, phenomenon, vesicle (pur-kin′jēz) [Johannes Evangelista *Purkinje,* Bohemian physiologist, 1787–1869]. See under the nouns.

Purkinje-Sanson's images (pur-kin′je-sah-sōz′) [J. E. *Purkinje;* Louis Joseph *Sanson,* French physician, 1790–1841]. See under *image.*

Purmann's method (poor′manz) [Matthaeus Gottfried *Purmann,* German surgeon, 1648–1721]. Extirpation of the aneurysmal sac in aneurysm.

purodigin (pu″ro-di′jin). Trade mark for a preparation of crystalline digitoxin.

purohepatitis (pu″ro-hep″ah-ti′tis) [*pus* + *hepatitis*]. Suppurative inflammation of the liver.

puromucous (pu″ro-mu′kus). Consisting of or containing pus and mucus; mucopurulent.

puron (pu′ron). A compound, $C_5H_8N_4O_2$, obtained by electrolysis of uric acid.

purple (pur′p′l). 1. A color, between blue and red. 2. A substance of this color used as a dye or indicator. **bromcresol p.,** an indicator, dibromorthocresol sulfonphthalein, used in the determination of hydrogen ion concentration. It has a pH range of 5.2 to 6.8, being yellow at 5.2 and purple at 6.8. **royal p.,** tyrian purple. **Stewart's p.,** 1 grain of iodine in 1 oz. of petrolatum. **tyrian p.,** a dye of the ancients which was obtained from the snails *Murex trunculus* and *Purpurea lapillus.* **visual p.,** rhodopsin.

purpura (pur′pu-rah) [L. "purple"]. A condition characterized by the presence of confluent petechiae or confluent ecchymoses over any part of the body. **p. abdomina′lis,** Henoch's p. **allergic p., anaphylactoid p.,** a form of non-thrombocytopenic purpura caused by increased permeability of the capillaries and associated with one or more allergic symptoms, the basic etiology of which remains unknown. **p. angioneurot′ica,** one of the allergic purpuras, marked by cutaneous hemorrhages, hyperesthesia, and angioneurotic edema. **p. annula′ris telangiecto′des,** a rare purpuric eruption, commonly beginning on the lower extremities and becoming generalized, the original punctate erythematous lesions coalescing to form an annular or serpiginous pattern; involution is gradual, sometimes followed by atrophy and loss of hair in the area. Called also *Majocchi's purpura* or *disease.* **athrombopenic p.,** non-thrombocytopenic p. **brain p.,** cerebral toxic pericapillary hemorrhage. **p. bullo′sa,** pemphigus hemorrhagicus. **p. cachec′tica,** purpura observed in poorly nourished, elderly individuals, with atrophic skin, poor tissue turgor, and depleted subcutaneous fat. **fibrinolytic p., p. fibrinolyt′ica,** purpura secondary to and accompanied by increased fibrinolytic activity of the blood. Called also *p. thrombolytica.* **p. ful′minans,** a form of non-thrombocytopenic purpura, observed mainly in children, usually following an infectious disease such as scarlet fever, and characterized by fever, shock, anemia, sudden and rapidly spreading symmetrical skin hemorrhages of the lower extremities, often associated with extensive extravascular thromboses and gangrene. **p. hemorrha′gica,** idiopathic thrombocytopenic p. **p. hemorrha′gica, hereditary,** p. hemorrhagica resulting from a genetically determined deficiency of the blood platelets. See *Glanzmann's thrombasthenia.* **Henoch's p.,** non-thrombocytopenic purpura characterized by acute visceral symptoms such as vomiting, diarrhea, distention of the abdomen, hematuria, and renal colic. Called also *p. nervosa.* **p. hyperglobuline′mica,** originally used to designate prolonged, repetitive episodes of purpura associated with an increase in gamma globulins; no longer considered a specific entity inasmuch as the clinical and laboratory findings are observed in a variety of hematologic conditions. **idiopathic p.** See *thrombocytopenic p., idiopathic.* **p. iod′ica,** a purpuric eruption usually on the lower extremities, sometimes accompanying the use of iodides. **Landouzy's p.,** a term originally used to designate a form of purpura with grave systemic manifestations. **p. maculo′sa,** acne scorbutica. **Majocchi's p.,** p. annularis telangiectodes. **malignant p.,** cerebrospinal fever. **p. nervo′sa,** Henoch's p. **non-thrombocytopenic p.,** purpura without any decrease in the platelet count of the blood. **orthostatic p.,** purpura due to settling of blood in dependent parts of the body. **p. pulico′sa,** the formation of purplish spots, or *taches bleuâtres,* caused by the bites of fleas (Pulex). **p. rheumat′ica,** non-thrombocytopenic purpura marked by small purpuric spots appearing in crops, by swelling, pain, and tenderness of joints, and frequently by swelling of the hands, feet, or eyelids. Called also *peliosis rheumatica.* **Schönlein's p.,** p. rheumatica. **Schönlein-Henoch p.,** idiopathic purpura in which there may be concomitant articular symptoms (Schönlein's disease) and intestinal symptoms with onset of abdominal pain. Also called *Schönlein-Henoch syndrome.* **p. seni′lis,** a purpuric eruption on the legs of elderly or debilitated persons. **p. sim′plex,** a general designation for non-thrombocytopenic purpura unaccompanied by defined vascular or intravascular abnormalities. **p. sim′plex, hereditary familial,** a form of non-thrombocytopenic purpura occurring in certain families, more common in the female, and frequently associated with rheumatic fever and rheumatoid arthritis, without other evidence of abnormal hemostasis. **p. symptomat′ica,** a purpuric eruption seen in eruptive fevers. **thrombasthenic p.** See *thrombasthenia.* **thrombocytolytic p.,** fibrinolytic p. **thrombocytopenic p.,** any form of purpura in which the platelet count is decreased. It may be either primary (idiopathic) or secondary. **thrombocytopenic p., idiopathic,** thrombocytopenic purpura unassociated with any definable systemic disease; occurring usually in children and young female adults, and characterized by easy bruising and bleeding, with a deficiency of platelets and a prolonged bleeding time. Called also *purpura hemorrhagica, essential thrombocytopenia, morbus maculosus werlhofii,* and *Werlhof's disease.* **thrombocytopenic p., secondary,** thrombocytopenic purpura occurring as a consequence of a hematologic abnormality such as leukemia, or a non-hematologic entity such as congestive splenomegaly, azotemia, or other condition. **thrombocytopenic p., thrombotic,** a disease characterized by thrombocytopenia, hemolytic anemia, bizarre neurological manifestations, azotemia, hypertension, and thromboses of undetermined composition in terminal arterioles and capillaries. The etiology is unknown, but it may be related to a disordered immune mechanism acting directly on the platelets or on the vascular endothelium, or on both concurrently. **p. thrombolyt′ica,** fibrinolytic p. **thrombopenic p.** See *thrombocytopenic p., idiopathic.* **toxic p.,** purpura which sometimes follows the use of certain drugs. **p. ur′ticans,** purpura associated with the formation of wheals and with itching. **p. variolo′sa,** a form of purpura occurring with smallpox. **vesical p.,** a hemorrhagic eruption on the mucous membrane of the bladder, sometimes observed in idiopathic thrombocytopenic purpura.

purpurate (pur′pu-rāt). A salt of purpuric acid.

purpureaglycoside (pur-pu″re-ah-gli′ko-sīd). A cardiac glycoside, $C_{47}H_{74}O_{18}$, from the leaves of *Digitalis purpurea.* **p. C.** See *deslanoside.*

purpuric (pur-pu′rik). Of the nature of, pertaining to, or affected with, purpura.

purpuriferous (pur″pu-rif′er-us) [L. *purpura* purple + *ferre* to bear]. Producing a purple pigment.

purpurin (pur′pu-rin). 1. A neurotoxic substance derived from the median zone of the hypobranchial or purple gland of gastropods of the genera Murex and Purpura, thought to be an ester or a mixture of esters of choline. Purpurin and murexine are believed to be identical. 2. A glycoside from madder root that has been used as a nuclear stain. It is 1,2,4-trihydroxyanthraquinone, $C_6H_4(CO)_2C_6H(OH)_3$. 3. Uroerythrin.

purpurinuria (pur″pu-rin-u′re-ah). The presence of uroerythrin in the urine.

purpuriparous (pur″pu-rip′ah-rus) [L. *purpura* purple + *parere* to produce]. Purpuriferous.

purpurogenous (pur″pu-roj′e-nus) [L. *purpura* purple + Gr. *gennan* to produce]. Producing visual purple.

purr (pur). A low vibratory murmur, or purring sound.

purring (pur′ing). Having a tremulous quality, like the purr of a cat.

purshianin (pur-shi′ah-nin). A brown, oily liquid glycoside from *Rhamnus purshiana:* laxative.

Purtscher's disease (poor′cherz) [Otmar *Purtscher*, Swiss ophthalmologist, 1852–1927]. Traumatic angiopathy of the retina.

puru (poo′roo). The native name in the Malay States for yaws.

purulence (pu′roo-lens) [L. *purulentia*]. The condition or fact of being purulent.

purulency (pu′roo-len″se). Purulence.

purulent (pu′roo-lent) [L. *purulentus*]. Consisting of or containing pus: associated with the formation of or caused by pus.

puruloid (pu′roo-loid). Resembling pus; puriform.

purupuru (poo-roo″poo-roo′). A contagious skin disease endemic in parts of Brazil in which the skin gradually becomes whitened. It is believed to be of microbic origin.

pus (pus), pl. *pu′ra*, gen. *pu′ris* [L.]. A liquid inflammation product made up of cells (leukocytes) and a thin fluid called liquor puris. **anchovy sauce p.,** the brownish pus seen in amebic abscess of the liver. **blue p.,** pus with a bluish tint, produced by *Pseudomonas aeruginosa*. **p. bo′num et laudab′ile,** laudable pus. **burrowing p.,** pus which is not walled off but may extend between fascial planes for considerable distances. **cheesy p.,** thick, nearly solid pus. **curdy p.,** pus mixed with cheesy flakes. **green p.,** pus having a greenish tint. **ichorous p.,** a thin, acrid pus, often having an ill smell, secreted by unhealthy surfaces. **itch p.,** psorinum. **laudable p., p. laudan′dum,** a term once applied to a creamy yellow, inodorous pus, secreted by a healthy granulating surface, and regarded as indicative of less danger than other varieties. **sanious p.,** bloody pus, often ichorous and ill smelling.

Pusey's emulsion (pu′sēz) [William Allen *Pusey*, American dermatologist, 1865–1940]. See under *emulsion*.

pustula (pus′tu-lah), pl. *pus′tulae* [L.]. Pustule. **p. malig′na,** anthrax.

pustulant (pus′tu-lant). 1. An agent that causes pustulation. 2. Causing pustulation.

pustular (pus′tu-lar). Pertaining to or of the nature of a pustule; consisting of pustules.

pustulation (pus″tu-la′shun). The formation of pustules.

pustule (pus′tūl) [L. *pustula*]. A small elevation of the cuticle filled with pus. **compound p.,** one that is made up of more than one chamber. **malignant p.,** anthrax. **postmortem p.,** a pustule resulting from infection in handling a cadaver. **primary p.,** one formed without any previous lesion. **secondary p.,** one which is preceded by a vesicle or papule. **simple p.,** one which consists of a single cavity.

pustuliform (pus′tu-lĭ-form) [L. *pustula* pustule + *forma* shape]. Resembling a pustule.

pustulocrustaceous (pus″tu-lo-krus-ta′shus). Marked by the presence of both pustules and crusts.

pustulosis (pus″tu-lo′sis). A condition marked by an outbreak of pustules. **p. palma′ris,** inflammation of the palm of the hand, with the formation of pustules. **p. vaccinifor′mis acu′ta,** a disease marked by an outbreak of pustules simulating those of vaccinia on the exposed areas in children suffering from infantile eczema.

pustulo-ulcerating (pus″tu-lo-ul′ser-āt″ing). Pustular and ulcerating.

putamen (pu-ta′men) [L. "shell"]. [N A, B N A] The larger and more lateral part of the lentiform nucleus, separated from the globus pallidus by the lateral medullary lamina.

Putnam type (put′nam) [James Jackson *Putnam*, Boston neurologist, 1846–1918]. See under *type*.

putrefaction (pu″trĕ-fak′shun) [L. *putrefactio*]. Enzymic decomposition, especially of proteins, with the production of foul-smelling compounds, such as hydrogen sulfide, ammonia, and mercaptans. Cf. *fermentation*.

putrefactive (pu″trĕ-fak′tiv). Pertaining to or of the nature of putrefaction.

putrefy (pu′trĕ-fi). To decompose, with the production of foul-smelling compounds: a term applied especially to the decomposition of proteins and organic matter.

putrescence (pu-tres′ens). Partial or complete rottenness.

putrescent (pu-tres′ent) [L. *putrescens* decaying]. Rotting; undergoing putrefaction.

putrescine (pu-tres′in). A liquid, poisonous, and ill-smelling ptomaine, $NH_2(CH_2)_4NH_2$, or tetramethylene-diamine, from decaying animal tissues and from cultures of the comma bacillus and the bacteria of the feces. It is produced from the amino acid, ornithin, by the loss of CO_2.

putrid (pu′trid) [L. *putridus*]. Characterized by putrefaction; rotten or corrupt.

putrilage (pu′trĭ-lij) [L. *putrilago*]. Putrescent or putrid matter.

putromaine (pu-tro′mān). Any poison produced by the decomposition of food within the living body.

putty (put′e). A pliable, sticky material. **Horsley's p.** See under *wax*.

Puusepp's operation, reflex (poos′eps) [Lyudvig Martinovich *Puusepp*, Estonian neurosurgeon, 1875–1942]. See under *operation* and *reflex*.

Puzos' method (pu-zōz′) [Nicholas *Puzos*, accoucheur in Paris, 1686–1753]. See under *method*.

PVM. Abbreviation for *pneumonia virus of mice*.

PVP. Abbreviation for *polyvinylpyrrolidone*.

PVP-I. Abbreviation for *povidone-iodine*.

Px. Abbreviation for *pneumothorax*.

pyarthrosis (pi″ar-thro′sis) [Gr. *pyon* pus + *arthron* joint + *-osis*]. Suppuration within a joint cavity; acute suppurative arthritis.

Pycnanthemum (pik-nan′the-mum) [Gr. *pyknos* dense + *anthemon* bloom]. A genus of labiate American plants, called *basil* and *mountain mint:* aromatic and carminative; resembling pennyroyal and spearmint in taste and smell.

pycnemia (pik-ne′me-ah). Pyknemia.

pycno-. For words thus beginning, see those beginning *pykno-*.

pyecchysis (pi-ek′kĭ-sis) [Gr. *pyon* pus + *ek* out + *chein* to pour]. The effusion of purulent matter.

pyel-. See *pyelo-*.

pyelectasia (pi″ĕ-lek-ta′ze-ah). Pyelectasis.

pyelectasis (pi″ĕ-lek′tah-sis) [*pyel-* + Gr. *ektasis* distention]. Dilatation of the renal pelvis.

pyelic (pi-el′ik). Pertaining to the pelvis of the kidney.

pyelitic (pi″ĕ-lit′ik). Pertaining to or affected with pyelitis.

pyelitis (pi″ĕ-li′tis) [*pyel-* + *-itis*]. Inflammation of the pelvis of the kidney. It is attended by pain and tenderness in the loins, irritability of the bladder, remittent fever, bloody or purulent urine, diarrhea, vomiting, and a peculiar pain on flexion of the thigh. **calculous p.,** that which is caused by calculi. **p. cys′tica,** pyelitis with the formation of multiple submucosal cysts. **defloration p.,** pyelitis in women after the first sexual intercourse, as a result of infection following rupture of the hymen. **encrusted p.,** pyelitis with ulcers which are encrusted with urinary salts. **p. glandula′ris,** pyelitis with conversion of transitional mucosal into cylindrical epithelium, with formation of glandular acini. **p. granulo′sa,** pyelitis marked by the presence of exuberant granulations. **p. gravida′rum,** inflammation of the kidney and ureter occurring in pregnancy. **hematogenous p.,** pyelitis in which the infection comes from the blood. **hemorrhagic p.,** that which is attended with hemorrhage. **suppurative p.,** a form with development of pus which causes abscess of the kidney, or pyonephrosis. **urogenous p.,** pyelitis in which the infection comes from the urine.

pyelo-, pyel- (pi′ĕ-lo, pi′el) [Gr. *pyelos* pelvis]. Combining form denoting relationship to the pelvis of the kidney.

pyelocaliectasis (pi″ĕ-lo-kal″e-ek′tah-sis) [*pyelo-* + *calix* + *ektasis* distention]. Dilatation of the kidney pelvis and calices.

pyelocystanastomosis (pi″ĕ-lo-sist″ah-nas″to-mo′sis). Pyelocystostomosis.

pyelocystitis (pi″ĕ-lo-sis-ti′tis) [*pyelo-* + Gr. *kystis* bladder + *-itis*]. Inflammation of the renal pelvis and of the bladder.

pyelocystostomosis (pi″ĕ-lo-sis″to-sto-mo′sis) [*pyelo-* + Gr. *kystis* bladder + ana*stomosis*]. The surgical formation of a communication between the renal pelvis and the bladder.

pyelofluoroscopy (pi″ĕ-lo-floo″o-ros′ko-pe). Examination of the renal pelvis by means of the fluoroscope.

pyelogram (pi′ĕ-lo-gram) [*pyelo-* + Gr. *gramma* mark]. A roentgenogram of the kidney and ureter, especially showing the pelvis of the kidney. **dragon p.,** bizarre forms in the pyelogram seen in polycystic kidney.

pyelograph (pi′ĕ-lo-graf). Pyelogram.

pyelography (pi″ĕ-log′rah-fe) [*pyelo-* + Gr. *graphein* to draw]. Roentgenography of the kidney and ureter after the structures have been filled with a contrast solution. **air p.,** pneumopyelography. **ascending p.,** retrograde p. **p. by elimination,** intravenous p. **excretion p.,** intravenous p. **intravenous p.,** pyelography in which an intravenous injection is made of a contrast medium (iopax, thorotrast, etc.) which passes quickly into the urine. **lateral p.,** pyelography in which the patient lies in lateral position with his questionable side next to the film. **respiration p.,** pyelography with a diphasic film showing the kidney under several phases of the respiratory cycle. **retrograde p.,** pyelography in which the contrast fluid is injected into the renal pelvis through the ureter.

pyeloileocutaneous (pi″ĕ-lo-il″e-o-ku-ta′ne-us). Pertaining to the kidney pelvis, ileum, and skin. See under *anastomosis*.

pyelolithotomy (pi″ĕ-lo-lĭ-thot′o-me) [*pyelo-* + Gr. *lithos* stone + *tomē* a cutting]. The operation of excising a renal calculus from the pelvis of the kidney.

pyelometer (pi″ĕ-lom′e-ter) [*pyelo-* + Gr. *metron* measure]. Pelvimeter.

pyelometry (pi″ĕ-lom′e-tre) [*pyelo-* + Gr. *metron* measure]. 1. Pelvimetry. 2. The measurement by tracings of the waves of contraction and relaxation of the renal pelvis, recorded by changes of pressure through a ureteral catheter.

pyelonephritis (pi″ĕ-lo-ne-fri′tis) [*pyelo-* + Gr. *nephros* kidney + *-itis*]. Inflammation of the kidney and its pelvis. **p. bacillo′sa bo′vum,** an inflammatory purulent or diphtheritic inflammation of the renal pelvis in cows, usually occurring shortly after parturition. It is caused by a bacillus.

pyelonephrosis (pi″ĕ-lo-ne-fro′sis) [*pyelo-* + Gr. *nephros* kidney + *-osis*]. Any disease of the kidney and its pelvis.

pyelopathy (pi″ĕ-lop′ah-the) [*pyelo-* + Gr. *pathos* disease]. Any disease of the renal pelvis.

pyelophlebitis (pi″ĕ-lo-fle-bi′tis) [*pyelo-* + Gr. *phleps* vein + *-itis*]. Inflammation of the veins of the renal pelvis.

pyeloplasty (pi′ĕ-lo-plas″te) [*pyelo-* + Gr. *plassein* to form]. A plastic operation on the pelvis of the kidney.

pyeloplication (pi″ĕ-lo-pli-ka′shun) [*pyelo-* + L. *plica* fold]. Reduction in size of a dilated renal pelvis by infolding its walls by Lembert sutures.

pyeloscopy (pi″ĕ-los′ko-pe) [*pyelo-* + Gr. *skopein* to examine]. Observation of the kidney pelvis under the fluoroscope after intravenous or retrograde injection of a contrast medium.

pyelostomy (pi″ĕ-los′to-me) [*pyelo-* + Gr. *stomoun* to provide with an opening, or mouth]. The operation of forming an opening into the renal pelvis for the purpose of temporarily diverting the urine from the ureter.

pyelotomy (pi″ĕ-lot′o-me) [*pyelo-* + Gr. *tomē* a cutting]. Incision of the pelvis of the kidney.

pyeloureterectasis (pi″ĕ-lo-u-re″ter-ek′tah-sis). Dilatation of a renal pelvis and a ureter.

pyeloureterography (pi″ĕ-lo-u-re″ter-og′rah-fe). Pyelography.

pyeloureterolysis (pi″ĕ-lo-u-re″ter-ol′ĭ-sis) [*pyelo-* + *ureter* + Gr. *lysis* dissolution]. The freeing of fibrous bands or adhesions near the junction of the kidney pelvis and ureter.

pyeloureteroplasty (pi″ĕ-lo-u-re′ter-o-plas″te). Plastic operation on the renal pelvis and ureter.

pyelovenous (pi″ĕ-lo-ve′nus). Pertaining to the kidney pelvis and renal veins.

pyemesis (pi-em′ĕ-sis) [Gr. *pyon* pus + *emesis* vomiting]. Vomiting of purulent matter.

pyemia (pi-e′me-ah) [Gr. *pyon* pus + *haima* blood + *-ia*]. A general septicemia in which secondary foci of suppuration occur and multiple abscesses are formed. The condition is marked by fever, chills, sweating, jaundice, and abscess in various parts of the body. Called also *metastatic infection*. **arterial p.,** a form due to the dissemination of emboli from cardiac thrombosis. **cryptogenic p.,** that in which the source of infection is in a deep tissue. **otogenous p.,** that which originates in disease of the ear. **portal p.,** suppurative pylephlebitis.

pyemic (pi-e′mik). Pertaining to or marked by pyemia.

pyemid (pi-e′mid). Any metastatic skin affection developing in the course of pyemia.

pyencephalus (pi″en-sef′ah-lus) [Gr. *pyon* pus + *enkephalos* brain]. Abscess of the brain.

pyenin (pi′ĕ-nin). Paranuclein.

pyesis (pi-e′sis). Pyosis.

pygal (pi′gal) [Gr. *pygē* rump]. Pertaining to the buttocks.

pygalgia (pi-gal′je-ah) [*pygo-* + *-algia*]. Pain in the buttocks.

pygist (pi′jist) [Gr. *pygē* rump]. A pederast.

pygmalionism (pig-ma′le-on-izm) [*Pygmalion*, a Greek sculptor who fell in love with a statue he had carved]. The falling in love with an object made by the patient himself.

pygmy (pig′me) [Gr. *pygmaios* dwarfish]. A small individual; a dwarf.

pygo- (pi′go) [Gr. *pygē* rump]. Combining form denoting relationship to the buttocks.

pygoamorphus (pi″go-ah-mor′fus). Asymmetrical conjoined twins, in which the parasite, or teratoma, is an amorphous mass attached to the sacral region of the autosite.

pygodidymus (pi″go-did′ĭ-mus) [*pygo-* + Gr. *didymos* twin]. A fetal monster with double hips and pelvis.

pygomelus (pi-gom′ĕ-lus) [*pygo-* + Gr. *melos* limb]. A fetal monster with a supernumerary limb or limbs attached to or near the buttock.

pygopagus (pi-gop′ah-gus) [*pygo-* + Gr. *pagos* thing fixed]. A double monster consiting of two nearly complete individuals joined at the sacrum, so the two components are back to back. **p. parasit′icus,** an asymmetrical double monster in which the parasitic component is attached to the sacral region of the autosite.

pygopagy (pi-gop′ah-je). The condition of being a pygopagus.

pyic (pi′ik). Of or pertaining to pus.

pyin (pi′in) [Gr. *pyon* pus]. An albuminoid mucus-like substance found in pus, and separated from it by adding sodium chloride and filtering.

pyknemia (pik-ne′me-ah) [*pykno-* + Gr. *haima* blood + *-ia*]. Thickening of the blood.

pyknic (pik′nik) [Gr. *pyknos* thick]. Having a short, thick, stocky build.

pykno- (pik′no) [Gr. *pyknos* thick, frequent]. Combining form meaning thick, compact, or frequent.

pyknocardia (pik-no-kar′de-ah) [*pykno-* + Gr. *kardia* heart]. Tachycardia.

pyknocytoma (pik″no-si-to′mah). Oxyphilic granular cell adenoma.

pykno-epilepsy (pik″no-ep′ĭ-lep″se). Petit mal.

pyknohemia (pik″no-he′me-ah). Pyknemia.

pyknolepsy (pik′no-lep″se). Pykno-epilepsy.

pyknometer (pik-nom′e-ter) [*pykno-* + Gr. *metron* measure]. An instrument for determining the specific gravity of body fluids.

pyknometry (pik-nom′e-tre). Measurement by the pyknometer.

pyknomorphic (pik″no-mor′fik). Pyknomorphous.

pyknomorphous (pik″no-mor′fus) [*pykno-* + Gr. *morphē* form]. Having the stainable elements compactly arranged; a term applied to certain nerve cells.

pyknophrasia (pik″no-fra′ze-ah) [*pykno-* + Gr. *phrasis* speech + *-ia*]. Thickness of speech.

pyknoplasson (pik″no-plas′on) [*pykno-* + *plasson*]. The plasson in its unexpanded form. Cf. *chasmatoplasson.*

pyknosis (pik-no′sis) [Gr. *pyknōsis* condensation]. A thickening; especially degeneration of a cell in which the nucleus shrinks in size and the chromatin condenses to a solid, structureless mass or masses.

pyknosphygmia (pik″no-sfig′me-ah) [*pykno-* + Gr. *sphygmos* pulse + *-ia*]. Tachycardia.

pyknotic (pik-not′ik) [Gr. *pyknōtikos*]. 1. Serving to close the pores. 2. Pertaining to pyknosis.

pyle- (pi′le) [Gr. *pylē* gate]. Combining form denoting relationship to the portal vein.

pylemphraxis (pi″lem-frak′sis) [*pyle-* + Gr. *emphraxis* stoppage]. Obstruction of the portal vein.

pylephlebectasis (pi″le-fle-bek′tah-sis) [*pyle-* + Gr. *phleps* vein + *ektasis* dilatation]. Dilatation of the portal vein.

pylephlebitis (pi″le-fle-bi′tis) [*pyle-* + Gr. *phleps* vein + *-itis*]. Inflammation of the portal vein. It usually results from intestinal disease. Suppurative pylephlebitis is marked by symptoms of pyemia. **adhesive p.,** inflammation of the portal vein producing thrombosis; pylethrombosis.

pylethrombophlebitis (pi″le-throm″bo-fle-bi′tis) [*pyle-* + Gr. *thrombos* clot of blood + *phleps* vein + *-itis*]. Thrombosis and inflammation of the portal vein.

pylethrombosis (pi″le-throm-bo′sis). Thrombosis of the portal vein.

pylic (pi′lik) [Gr. *pylē* gate]. Pertaining to the portal vein.

pylometer (pi-lom′e-ter) [Gr. *pylē* gate + *metron* measure]. An instrument for measuring obstruction at the ureteral opening of the bladder.

pylon (pi′lon). A temporary artificial leg.

pyloralgia (pi″lo-ral′je-ah) [*pylorus* + Gr. *algos* pain + *-ia*]. Pain in the region of the pylorus.

pylorectomy (pi″lo-rek′to-me) [*pylorus* + Gr. *ektomē* excision]. Excision of the pylorus; partial gastrectomy.

pyloric (pi-lor′ik). Pertaining to the pylorus.

pyloristenosis (pi-lor″e-ste-no′sis) [*pylorus* + Gr. *stenōsis* narrowing]. Stenosis, or narrowing, of the caliber of the pylorus.

pyloritis (pi″lo-ri′tis). Inflammation of the pylorus.

pyloro- (pi-lo′ro) [Gr. *pylōros*, from *pylē* gate + *ouros* guard]. Combining form denoting relationship to the pylorus.

pylorodilator (pi-lo″ro-di′la-tor). An instrument for dilating the pylorus for pylorospasm or stricture.

pylorodiosis (pi-lo″ro-di-o′sis) [*pyloro-* + Gr. *diōsis* pushing asunder]. The operation of dilating a stricture of the pylorus by the fingers, which are either inserted through a gastrotomy incision (*Loreta's method*) or invaginated in the anterior stomach wall and thrust through the pyloric canal (*Hahn's method*).

pyloroduodenitis (pi-lo″ro-du″o-de-ni′tis). Inflammation of the pyloric and duodenal mucosa.

pylorogastrectomy (pi-lo″ro-gas-trek′to-me). Excision of the pyloric pocket in cases of bilocular stomach; excision of the pyloric portion of the stomach.

pyloromyotomy (pi-lo″ro-mi-ot′o-me). Incision of the longitudinal and circular muscles of the pylorus; Ramstedt's operation.

pyloroplasty (pi-lo′ro-plas″te) [*pyloro-* + Gr. *plassein* to form]. A plastic operation for the repair of a lesion of the pylorus; especially surgical enlargement of the caliber of a strictured pylorus by dividing the strictured portion longitudinally, stretching the pylorus so that the longitudinal cut becomes a horizontal one, and stitching the edges of the wound in its new position.

pyloroptosis (pi″lo-ro-to′sis) [*pyloro-* + Gr. *ptōsis* falling]. Displacement of the pyloric end of the stomach.

pyloroscopy (pi″lo-ros′ko-pe) [*pyloro-* + Gr. *skopein* to examine]. Inspection of the pylorus.

pylorospasm (pi-lo′ro-spazm) [*pyloro-* + Gr. *spasmos* spasm]. Spasm of the pylorus or of the pyloric portion of the stomach. **congenital p.,** spasm of the pylorus in infants due to prenatal conditions. **reflex p.,** pylorospasm due to extragastric conditions.

pylorostenosis (pi-lo″ro-ste-no′sis). Pyloristenosis.

pylorostomy (pi″lo-ros′to-me) [*pyloro-* + Gr. *stomoun* to provide with an opening, or mouth]. The formation of an opening through the abdominal wall into the pyloric end of the stomach for alimentary purposes.

pylorotomy (pi″lo-rot′o-me) [*pyloro-* + Gr. *tomē* a cutting]. Surgical incision of the pylorus; gastromyotomy.

pylorus (pi-lo′rus) [Gr. *pyloros*, from *pylē* gate + *ouros* guard]. [N A, B N A] The distal aperture of the stomach, through which the stomach contents pass into the duodenum; it is surrounded by a fold of mucous membrane enclosing a circular layer of muscle fibers.

pyo- (pi′o) [Gr. *pyon* pus]. Combining form denoting relationship to pus.

pyoarthrosis (pi″o-ar-thro′sis). Pyarthrosis.

pyoblennorrhea (pi″o-blen″o-re′ah). Suppurative blennorrhea.

pyocalix (pi″o-ka′liks). The presence of pus in a calix of the renal pelvis.

pyocele (pi′o-sēl) [*pyo-* + Gr. *kēlē* hernia]. Distention of a cavity or tube with pus due to retention; as an accumulation of pus in the scrotum.

pyocelia (pi″o-se′le-ah) [*pyo-* + Gr. *koilia* cavity]. Pus in the abdominal cavity.

pyocephalus (pi″o-sef′ah-lus) [*pyo-* + Gr. *kephalē* head]. The presence of purulent fluid in the cerebral ventricles.

pyochezia (pi″o-ke′ze-ah) [*pyo-* + Gr. *chezein* to defecate + *-ia*]. Presence of pus in the stools.

pyococcic (pi″o-kok′sik). Pertaining to or produced by pus-forming cocci.

pyococcus (pi″o-kok′us). Any pus-forming coccus.

pyocolpocele (pi″o-kol′po-sēl) [*pyo-* + Gr. *kolpos* vagina + *kēlē* tumor]. A tumor of the vagina containing pus.

pyocolpos (pi″o-kol′pos) [*pyo-* + Gr. *kolpos* vagina]. A collection of pus within the vagina.

pyoculture (pi′o-kul″tūr) [*pyo-* + *culture*]. The comparison of a bacteriologic culture of pus with uncultured pus from the same lesion, as an indication of the resistance of the patient to the infection.

pyocyanase (pi″o-si′ah-nās). An antibacterial substance from cultures of *Pseudomonas aeru-*

ginosa (*pyocyanea*), which is bactericidal for many bacteria and lytic for some (*Vibrio comma*). It is composed of three fractions, one of which is the blue pigment, pyocyanin.

pyocyanic (pi″o-si-an′ik). Pertaining to blue pus, or to *Pseudomonas aeruginosa.*

pyocyanin (pi″o-si′ah-nin) [*pyo-* + Gr. *kyanos* blue + *-in*, a chemical suffix]. A blue-green antibiotic pigment derived from alpha-hydroxyphenazine by methylation.

pyocyanogenic (pi″o-si″ah-no-jen′ik). Producing pyocyanin.

pyocyanosis (pi″o-si″ah-no′sis). Any disease due to infection with *Pseudomonas aeruginosa* (*P. pyocyanea*).

pyocyst (pi′o-sist) [*pyo-* + *cyst*]. A cyst containing pus.

pyocyte (pi′o-sīt) [*pyo-* + *-cyte*]. A pus corpuscle or neutrophilic leukocyte.

pyoderma (pi″o-der′mah) [*pyo-* + Gr. *derma* skin]. Any purulent skin disease. **chancriform p., p. chancrifor′me fa′ciei,** an ulcerated nodular solitary lesion of the face resembling a chancre. **p. facia′le,** a condition characterized by formation of numerous abscesses and cysts on the face, with intense erythema, and sinus tracts linking the deep-seated lesions. Untreated, the lesions persist for months, and leave severe scars. **p. gangreno′sum,** a cutaneous ulcer originating in an operative or traumatic wound, characterized by marked undermining of the border; once regarded as a complication peculiar to ulcerative colitis, it also occurs with other wasting diseases. **p. ulcero′sum tropica′lum,** an infectious skin disease seen in the tropics, marked by the development of vesicles which break, forming superficial circular ulcers. **p. veg′etans,** dermatitis vegetans. **p. verruco′sum, verrucous p.,** chronic pyoderma gangrenosum associated with vegetative outgrowths on the skin.

pyodermatitis (pi″o-der″mah-ti′tis). A purulent inflammation of the skin. **p. veg′etans,** dermatitis vegetans.

pyodermatosis (pi″o-der″mah-to′sis). Any skin disease of pyogenic origin.

pyodermia (pi″o-der′me-ah). Pyoderma.

pyodermitis (pi″o-der-mi′tis). Any pustular skin inflammation. **p. veg′etans,** dermatitis vegetans.

pyofecia (pi″o-fe′se-ah). Pus in the feces.

pyogenesis (pi″o-jen′e-sis) [*pyo-* + Gr. *genesis* production]. The formation of pus.

pyogenic (pi″o-jen′ik). Producing pus.

pyogenin (pi-oj′e-nin). A compound, $C_{63}H_{128}N_2O_{19}$, derived from the body of pus cells.

pyogenous (pi-oj′e-nus). Caused by pus.

pyohemia (pi″o-he′me-ah). Pyemia.

pyohemothorax (pi″o-he″mo-tho′raks) [*pyo-* + Gr. *haima* blood + *thōrax* chest]. A collection of pus and blood in the pleural cavity.

pyoid (pi′oid) [*pyo-* + Gr. *eidos* form]. 1. Resembling pus. 2. A puslike substance from raw or granulating surfaces, but free from bacteria and nontoxic.

pyolabyrinthitis (pi″o-lab″ĭ-rin-thi′tis). Inflammation of the labyrinth of the ear, with suppuration.

pyometra (pi″o-me′trah) [*pyo-* + Gr. *mētra* womb]. An accumulation of pus within the uterus.

pyometritis (pi″o-me-tri′tis). Purulent inflammation of the uterus.

pyometrium (pi″o-me′tre-um). Pyometra.

pyomyositis (pi″o-mi″o-si′tis). Purulent myositis.

pyonephritis (pi″o-ne-fri′tis). Purulent inflammation of the kidney.

pyonephrolithiasis (pi″o-nef″ro-lĭ-thi′ah-sis) [*pyo-* + Gr. *nephros* kidney + *lithos* stone + *-iasis*]. The presence of stones and pus in the kidney.

pyonephrosis (pi″o-ne-fro′sis) [*pyo-* + Gr. *nephros* kidney + *-osis*]. Suppurative destruction of the parenchyma of the kidney, with total or almost complete loss of renal function.

pyonephrotic (pi″o-ne-frot′ik). Pertaining to or characterized by pyonephrosis.

pyonychia (pi″o-nik′e-ah) [*pyo-* + Gr. *onyx* nail + *-ia*]. A pyogenic infection of the nail folds, usually caused by pathogenic staphylococci or streptococci.

pyo-ovarium (pi″o-o-va′re-um). Abscess of an ovary.

pyopericarditis (pi″o-per″ĭ-kar-di′tis). Purulent inflammation of the pericardium.

pyopericardium (pi″o-per″ĭ-kar′de-um). The presence of pus in the pericardial cavity.

pyoperitoneum (pi″o-per″ĭ-to-ne′um) [*pyo-* + *peritoneum*]. Pus in the peritoneal cavity.

pyoperitonitis (pi″o-per″ĭ-to-ni′tis). Purulent inflammation of the peritoneum.

pyophagia (pi″o-fa′je-ah) [*pyo-* + Gr. *phagein* to eat]. The swallowing of pus.

pyophthalmia (pi″of-thal′me-ah). A suppurative condition of the eye.

pyophthalmitis (pi″of-thal-mi′tis). Purulent inflammation of the eye.

pyophylactic (pi″o-fi-lak′tik) [*pyo-* + Gr. *phylaktikos* guarding]. Serving as a defense against purulent infection.

pyophysometra (pi″o-fi″so-me′trah) [*pyo-* + Gr. *physa* air + *mētra* uterus]. A collection of pus and gas in the uterus.

pyoplania (pi″o-pla′ne-ah) [*pyo-* + Gr. *planē* wandering]. Wandering of pus from one part to another.

pyopneumocholecystitis (pi″o-nu″mo-ko″le-sis-ti′tis) [*pyo-* + Gr. *pneuma* air + *cholecyst* + *-itis*]. Distention of the gallbladder with pus and gas.

pyopneumocyst (pi″o-nu′mo-sist) [*pyo-* + Gr. *pneuma* air + *cyst*]. A cyst containing pus and gas.

pyopneumohepatitis (pi″o-nu″mo-hep″ah-ti′tis). Abscess of the liver with pus and gas in the abscess cavity.

pyopneumopericardium (pi″o-nu″mo-per″ĭ-kar′de-um) [*pyo-* + Gr. *pneuma* air + *pericardium*]. The presence of pus and gas in the pericardial cavity.

pyopneumoperitoneum (pi″o-nu″mo-per″ĭ-to-ne′um). The presence of pus and gas in the peritoneal cavity.

pyopneumoperitonitis (pi″o-nu″mo-per″ĭ-to-ni′tis) [*pyo-* + Gr. *pneuma* air + *peritonitis*]. Peritonitis with the presence of pus and gas in the peritoneal cavity.

pyopneumothorax (pi″o-nu″mo-tho′raks) [*pyo-* + Gr. *pneuma* air + *thōrax* chest]. A collection of pus and air or gas in the pleural cavity.

pyopoiesis (pi″o-poi-e′sis) [*pyo-* + Gr. *poiein* to make]. The formation of pus.

pyopoietic (pi″o-poi-et′ik). Producing pus.

pyoptysis (pi-op′tĭ-sis) [*pyo-* + Gr. *ptysis* spitting]. Spitting of purulent matter.

pyopyelectasis (pi″o-pi″ĕ-lek′tah-sis) [*pyo-* + Gr. *pyelos* pelvis + *ektasis* dilatation]. Dilatation of the renal pelvis with purulent fluid.

pyorrhea (pi″o-re′ah) [*pyo-* + Gr. *rhoia* flow]. A discharge of pus. **p. alveola′ris,** a purulent inflammation of the dental periosteum, with progressive necrosis of the alveoli and looseness of the teeth (Fauchard, 1746). Called also *Riggs' disease, gingivitis expulsiva, parodontitis, parodontosis, cementoperiostitis,* and *gingivopericementitis.* **paradental p.,** pyorrhea in which the pockets are deep and the discharge of pus persists in spite of the removal of all local irritation. **Schmutz p.,** paradental p. with a pocket formation around the tooth with pus, caused by unhygienic local conditions.

pyorrheal (pi″o-re′al). Pertaining to or characterized by pyorrhea.

pyorubin (pi″o-roo′bin). A bright-red, water-soluble, non-fluorescent pigment produced by *Pseudomonas aeruginosa*.

pyosalpingitis (pi″o-sal″pin-ji′tis) [*pyo-* + Gr. *salpinx* tube + *-itis*]. Purulent salpingitis.

pyosalpingo-oophoritis (pi″o-sal-ping″go-o″-of-o-ri′tis). Inflammation of the ovary and oviduct, with the formation and accumulation of pus.

pyosalpingo-oothecitis (pi″o-sal-ping″go-o″o-the-si′tis). Pyosalpingo-oophoritis.

pyosalpinx (pi″o-sal′pinks) [*pyo-* + Gr. *salpinx* tube]. A collection of pus in an oviduct.

pyosapremia (pi″o-sap-re′me-ah) [*pyo-* + Gr. *sapros* rotten + *haima* blood + *-ia*]. Infection of the blood with purulent matter.

pyosclerosis (pi″o-skle-ro′sis). An inflammatory, purulent sclerosis.

pyosepticemia (pi″o-sep″tĭ-se′me-ah). Pyemia combined with septicemia.

pyoseroculture (pi″o-se′ro-kul″tūr). A culture made by implanting pus into blood serum.

pyosin (pi′o-sin). A compound, $C_{57}H_{110}N_2O_{15}$, derived from the plasma of pus cells.

pyosis (pi-o′sis). Suppuration. **Corlett's p.,** impetigo contagiosa bullosa. **Manson's p.,** pemphigus contagiosus. **p. palma′ris,** a disease of children in the East Indies marked by the formation on the palms of numerous pustules. **p. trop′ica,** a disease occurring in Ceylon characterized by yellow or blackish lesions on the body, covered with a crust, which on removal leaves a granulating ulcer. Called also *Kurunegala ulcer*.

pyospermia (pi″o-sper′me-ah) [*pyo-* + Gr. *sperma* seed + *-ia*]. Presence of pus in the semen.

pyostatic (pi″o-stat′ik) [*pyo-* + Gr. *statikos* halting]. 1. Arresting suppuration. 2. An agent that arrests the formation of pus.

pyostomatitis (pi″o-sto″mah-ti′tis). Inflammation of the mouth with suppuration. **p. veg′etans,** inflammation of the mouth beginning with minute flat miliary abscesses of uniform size, tending to conglomerate and spreading to involve the whole mouth, the mucosa becoming proliferative, soft, red, folded, and verrucose.

pyotherapy (pi″o-ther′ah-pe) [*pyo-* + Gr. *therapeia* treatment]. Treatment with pus.

pyothorax (pi″o-tho′raks) [*pyo-* + Gr. *thōrax* chest]. An accumulation of pus in the thorax; empyema.

pyotoxinemia (pi″o-tok″sĭ-ne′me-ah) [*pyo-* + *toxin* + Gr. *haima* blood + *-ia*]. Presence in the blood of the toxins of pus-forming organisms.

pyoumbilicus (pi″o-um-bil′ĭ-kus). Infection of the umbilicus in a newborn infant.

pyourachus (pi″o-u′rah-kus). The presence of pus in the urachus.

pyoureter (pi″o-u-re′ter) [*pyo-* + *ureter*]. An accumulation of pus in a ureter.

pyovesiculosis (pi″o-vĕ-sik″u-lo′sis). An accumulation of pus in the seminal vesicles.

pyoxanthine (pi″o-zan′thin). A brownish-red pigment derivable by oxidation from pyocyanin.

pyoxanthose (pi″o-zan′thōs) [*pyo-* + Gr. *xanthos* yellow]. A yellow pigment produced by the oxidation of pyocyanin in blue pus which has been exposed to air.

pyracin (pi′rah-sin). A derivative of pyridoxine.

pyramid (pir′ah-mid) [Gr. *pyramis*]. A pointed or cone-shaped structure or part. Called also *pyramis* [N A]. **p. of cerebellum,** pyramis vermis. **p. of Ferrein,** pars radiata lobuli corticalis renis. **p's of kidney,** pyramides renales. **Lalouette's p.,** lobus pyramidalis glandulae thyroideae. **p. of light,** a triangular reflection seen upon the membrana tympani. **Malacarné's p.,** the posterior end of the pyramid of the vermis. **p's of Malpighi,** pyramides renales. **p. of medulla oblongata,** pyramis medullae oblongatae. **p. of medulla oblongata, anterior,** pyramis medullae oblongatae. **p. of medulla oblongata, posterior,** fasciculus gracilis medullae oblongatae. **olfactory p.,** trigonum olfactorium. **petrous p.,** pars petrosa ossis temporalis. **renal p's,** pyramides renales. **p. of temporal bone,** pars petrosa ossis temporalis. **p. of temporal bone, of Arnold,** pars mastoidea ossis temporalis. **p. of thyroid,** lobus pyramidalis glandulae thyroideae. **p. of tympanum,** eminentia pyramidalis. **p. of vermis,** pyramis vermis. **p. of vestibule,** pyramis vestibuli. **Wistar's p's.** See *concha sphenoidalis*.

pyramidal (pi-ram′ĭ-dal) [L. *pyramidalis*]. Shaped like a pyramid.

pyramidale (pi-ram″ĭ-da′le). Os triquetrum.

pyramidalis (pi-ram″ĭ-da′lis) [L.]. Pyramidal.

pyramides (pi-ram′ĭ-dēz). Plural of *pyramis*.

pyramidotomy (pir″am-ĭ-dot′o-me). Section of the pyramidal tract, performed for relief of postencephalitic hemiparkinsonism.

pyramis (pir′ah-mis), pl. *pyram′ides* [Gr.]. A pointed or cone-shaped structure or part. Called also *pyramid*. **p. cerebel′li,** p. vermis. **pyram′ides Malpig′hii,** pyramides renales. **p. medul′lae oblonga′tae** [N A, B N A], either of two rounded masses, one on either side of the anterior median fissure of the medulla oblongata, composed of motor fibers from the cerebral cortex to the spinal cord and medulla oblongata. Called also *anterior pyramid of medulla oblongata*. **p. os′sis tempora′lis,** pars petrosa ossis temporalis. **pyram′ides rena′les** [N A], **pyram′ides rena′les [Malpig′hii]** [B N A], the conical masses that make up the medullary substance of the kidney. They contain the collecting apparatus and the tubules. Called also *renal pyramids*. **p. ver′mis** [N A, B N A], the part of the vermis of the cerebellum between the tuber vermis and the uvula. Called also *p. cerebelli*. **p. vestib′uli** [N A, B N A], the triangular-shaped anterior end of the vestibular crest. Called also *pyramid of vestibule*.

pyran (pi′ran). 1. A cyclic compound, C_5H_6O, in which the ring consists of 5 carbon atoms and 1 oxygen atom. 2. An antineuralgic and antirheumatic preparation of benzoic acid, salicylic acid, and thymol.

pyranisamine (pi″rah-nis′ah-mēn). Pyrilamine.

pyranose (pi′rah-nōs). A sugar in which the oxygen ring bridges carbon atoms 1 and 5 in the aldoses or carbon atoms 2 and 6 in the ketoses.

pyranyl (pi′ran-il). The radical C_2H_5O, of which pyran is the hydride.

pyrathiazine (pi″rah-thi′ah-zēn). Chemical name: 10-[2-(1-pyrrolidyl)ethyl]-phenothiazine: used as an antihistaminic.

pyrazinamide (pi″rah-zin′ah-mīd). Chemical name: pyrazinoic acid amide: used as a tuberculostatic agent.

pyrazine (pi′rah-zēn). A volatile compound, with the odor of heliotrope.

pyrectic (pi-rek′tik) [Gr. *pyrektikos* feverish]. 1. Pertaining to or of the nature of fever. 2. An agent that induces fever.

pyremia (pi-re′me-ah) [Gr. *pyr* fire + *haima* blood + *-ia*]. The presence of a normal amount of carbonaceous matter in the blood.

pyrene (pi′ren). A polycyclic hydrocarbon, $C_{16}H_{10}$.

pyrenemia (pi″rĕ-ne′me-ah) [Gr. *pyrēn* fruit stone + *haima* blood + *-ia*]. The presence of nucleated red corpuscles in the blood.

pyrenin (pi′rĕ-nin) [Gr. *pyrēn* fruit stone]. Paranuclein.

pyrenoid (pi′rĕ-noid) [Gr. *pyrēn* fruit stone + *eidos* form]. One of the refringent bodies seen in the chromatophores of certain protozoa; amyloplast.

pyrenolysis (pi″rĕ-nol′ĭ-sis) [Gr. *pyrēn* fruit stone + *lysis* solution]. The breaking down of the nucleolus of a cell.

pyretherapy (pi″rĕ-ther′ah-pe) [Gr. *pyr* fever + *therapy*]. Pyretotherapy.

pyrethrolone (pi-reth′ro-lōn). A cyclic ketonic alcohol found in the pyrethrines.

pyrethron (pi′rĕ-thron). A neutral ester from pyrethrum.

pyrethrum (pi-re′thrum) [Gr. *pyrethron*]. 1. Pellitory. 2. An insecticide. **Dalmation p.,** an insecticidal powder obtained from *Chrysanthemum cinerariaefolium*, a perennial herb indigenous to Japan and Yugoslavia. **Persian p.,** an insecticide obtained from *Chrysanthemum occineum* and *C. marschallii*, indigenous to northern Persia and the Caucasus.

pyretic (pi-ret′ik) [Gr. *pyretos* fever]. Pertaining to or of the nature of fever.

pyreticosis (pi-ret″ĭ-ko′sis). Any febrile affection.

pyreto- (pi-ret′o) [Gr. *pyretos* fever]. Combining form denoting relationship to fever.

pyretogen (pi-ret′o-jen). A substance which excites fever.

pyretogenesis (pi″rĕ-to-jen′e-sis) [*pyreto-* + Gr. *genesis* production]. The origin and causation of fever.

pyretogenetic (pi″rĕ-to-je-net′ik). Pertaining to pyretogenesis.

pyretogenic (pi″rĕ-to-jen′ik). Producing fever.

pyretogenin (pi″rĕ-toj′e-nin) [*pyreto-* + Gr. *gennan* to generate]. A base, derivable from certain bacterial cultures: said to produce fever in animals when injected into them.

pyretogenous (pi″rĕ-toj′e-nus). 1. Caused by high body temperature. 2. Pyrogenic.

pyretography (pi″rĕ-tog′rah-fe) [*pyreto-* + Gr. *graphein* to write]. A description of fever.

pyretology (pi″rĕ-tol′o-je) [*pyreto-* + *-logy*]. The sum of what is known regarding fevers; the science of fevers.

pyretolysis (pi″rĕ-tol′ĭ-sis) [*pyreto-* + Gr. *lysis* dissolution]. 1. Reduction of fever. 2. Lysis which is hastened by fever.

Pyretophorus (pi″rĕ-tof′o-rus). A genus of mosquitoes. *P. costa′lis* transmits malaria and filariasis in Africa.

pyretotherapy (pi″rĕ-to-ther′ah-pe) [*pyreto-* + Gr. *therapeia* treatment]. 1. Treatment of a disease by raising the patient's temperature, especially by means of injecting fever-producing vaccines. 2. The treatment of fever.

pyretotyphosis (pi″rĕ-to-ti-fo′sis) [*pyreto-* + Gr. *typhōsis* delirium]. The delirium of fever.

pyrexia (pi-rek′se-ah), pl. *pyrex′iae* [Gr. *pyressein* to be feverish]. A fever, or a febrile condition; abnormal elevation of the body temperature. **Pel-Ebstein p.** See under *symptom*.

pyrexial (pi-rek′se-al). Pertaining to or characterized by pyrexia.

pyrexiogenic (pi-rek″se-o-jen′ik). Pyrogenic.

pyrexiophobia (pi-rek″se-o-fo′be-ah) [*pyrexia* + Gr. *phobein* to be affrighted by]. Morbid fear of fever.

pyrexy (pi′rek-se). Pyrexia.

pyribenzamine (pir″ĭ-ben′zah-mēn). Trade mark for preparations of tripelennamine.

pyridine (pir′ĭ-dēn). 1. A colorless, liquid, basic coal tar derivative, C_5H_5N, derived also from tobacco and various organic matters. 2. Any one of a large group of substances homologous with normal pyridine.

pyridostigmine (pir″ĭ-do-stig′mēn). Chemical name: 3-hydroxy-1-methylpyridinium dimethylcarbamate: used as a cholinesterase inhibitor, in treatment of myasthenia gravis.

pyridoxine (pir″ĭ-dok′sēn). A component of the vitamin B complex, 5-hydroxy-6-methyl-3,4-pyridinedimethanol: sometimes used in treatment of nausea and vomiting of pregnancy, and in irradiation sickness.

pyridoxol (pir″ĭ-dok′sol). Pyridoxine.

pyriform (pir′ĭ-form). Piriform.

pyrilamine (pi-ril′ah-mēn). Chemical name: 2-[(2-dimethylaminoethyl)(p-methoxybenzyl)amino]pyridine: used as an antihistaminic.

pyrimethamine (pi″rĭ-meth′ah-mēn). Chemical name: 2,4-diamino-5(p-chlorophenyl)-6-ethylpyrimidine: used as an antimalarial.

pyrimidine (pi-rim′ĭ-din). An organic compound, a metadiazine, $C_4H_4N_2$, which is the fundamental form of the pyrimidine bases. These are mostly oxy or amino derivatives, for example, 2,6-dioxypyrimidine is uracil, 2-oxy-6-aminopyrimidine is cytosine, and 2,6-dioxy-5-methylpyrimidine is thymine. Some of these are constituents of nucleic acid.

pyrithiamine (pir″ĭ-thi′ah-min). A synthetic compound, $CH_3.C_4N_2H(NH_2).CH_2.C_5NH_3(CH_3).CH_2.CH_2OH$, which by metabolic competition can cause symptoms of thiamine deficiency.

pyrithyldone (pi-rith′il-dōn). A sedative and hypnotic compound, 3,3-diethyl-2,4-dioxotetrahydropyridine.

pyro- (pi′ro) [Gr. *pyr* fire]. Combining form meaning fire or heat, or, in chemistry, produced by heating.

pyroborate (pi-ro-bo′rāt). Any salt of pyroboric acid.

pyrocatechin (pi″ro-kat′ĕ-kin) [*pyro-* + *catechu*]. A crystallizable substance, $C_6H_4(OH)_2$, obtained by distilling catechu, etc. and sometimes found in the urine. It is an antipyretic, and is used like resorcinol. Called also *catechol*.

pyrocatechinuria (pi″ro-kat″ĕ-ki-nu′re-ah) [*pyrocatechin* + Gr. *ouron* urine + *-ia*]. The occurrence of pyrocatechin in the urine.

pyrocatechol (pi″ro-kat′ĕ-kol). Pyrocatechin.

pyrodextrin (pi″ro-deks′trin). A brown substance produced by the action of heat upon starch.

pyrodine (pir′o-din). A crystalline, poisonous compound, acetylphenylhydrazine, $C_6H_5.NH.NH.CO.CH_3$: used as an antipyretic and like chrysarobin in skin diseases.

pyrogen (pi′ro-jen) [*pyro-* + Gr. *gennan* to produce]. A fever-producing substance. **bacterial p.,** a fever-producing agent of bacterial origin; endotoxin. **distilled water p.,** filtrable thermostable products of bacterial activity that accumulate in distilled water and tend to cause a severe rigor when the water is injected.

pyrogenetic (pi″ro-je-net′ik). Pyrogenic.

pyrogenic (pi″ro-jen′ik) [*pyro-* + Gr. *gennan* to produce]. Inducing fever.

pyrogenous (pi-roj′e-nus). Pyretogenous.

pyroglobulin (pi″ro-glob′u-lin) [*pyro-* + *globulin*]. A blood globulin which precipitates from serum on heating.

pyroglobulinemia (pi″ro-glob″u-li-ne′me-ah). Presence in the blood of an abnormal protein constituent which is precipitated by heat: observed in myeloma and lymphosarcoma and sometimes in patients for whom no diagnosis can be established.

pyrojapaconitine (pi″ro-jap″ah-kon′ĭ-tin). An alkaloid, $C_{32}H_{45}NO_2$, formed by heating japaconitine.

pyrolagnia (pi″ro-lag′ne-ah) [*pyro-* + Gr. *lagneia* lust]. Sexual gratification from witnessing or making fires.

pyroligneous (pi″ro-lig′ne-us) [*pyro-* + L. *lignum* wood]. Pertaining to the destructive distillation of wood.

pyrolusite (pi″ro-lu′sit). Manganese dioxide.

pyrolysis (pi-rol′ĭ-sis) [*pyro-* + Gr. *lysis* dissolution]. Decomposition of organic substances under the influence of a rise in temperature.

pyromania (pi″ro-ma′ne-ah) [*pyro-* + Gr. *mania* madness]. Obsessive preoccupation with fires; also incendiarism.

pyrometer (pi-rom′e-ter) [*pyro-* + Gr. *metron* measure]. An instrument for measuring the intensity of heat, especially for degrees of heat which cannot be measured with a mercury thermometer.

pyrone (pi'rōn). A principle, $CO(CH)_4O$, found in opium, from which several other constituents are derived by substitution.

pyronil (pi'ro-nil). Trade mark for a preparation of pyrrobutamine.

pyronine (pi'ro-nin). A dye used in histology. The pyronines are methylated diamine xanthines. **p. B,** a basic dye, the tetra-ethylpyronine chloride, $(C_2H_5)_2N.C_6H_3(O)CH.C_6H_3.N(C_2H_5)_2Cl$. **p. G,** a basic dye, the tetra-methylpyronine chloride, $(CH_3)_2N.C_6H_3(O)CH.C_6H_3N(CH_3)_2Cl$.

pyroninophilia (pi"ro-nin"o-fil'e-ah) [*pyronine* + Gr. *philein* to love]. Increased affinity for pyronine, sometimes observed in plasma and reticuloendothelial cells.

pyronyxis (pi"ro-nik'sis) [*pyro-* + Gr. *nyxis* a pricking]. Ignipuncture.

pyrophobia (pi"ro-fo'be-ah) [*pyro-* + Gr. *phobein* to be affrighted by]. Abnormal dread of fire.

pyrophosphate (pi"ro-fos'fāt). Any salt of pyrophosphoric acid.

Pyroplasma (pi"ro-plaz'mah). Piroplasma.

pyroptothymia (pi"rop-to-thi'me-ah) [*pyro-* + Gr. *ptoein* to frighten + *thymos* spirit + *-ia*]. Insane delusions of being enveloped in flame.

pyropuncture (pi'ro-punk"tūr) [*pyro-* + *puncture*]. Ignipuncture.

pyroscope (pi'ro-skōp) [*pyro-* + Gr. *skopein* to examine]. An instrument for measuring the intensity of heat radiations.

pyrosis (pi-ro'sis) [Gr. *pyrōsis* burning]. Heartburn; a burning sensation in the esophagus and stomach, with sour eructation.

Pyrosoma (pi"ro-so'mah) [*pyro-* + Gr. *sōma* body]. Piroplasma.

pyrotic (pi-rot'ik) [Gr. *pyrōtikos*]. Caustic; burning.

pyrotoxin (pi"ro-tok'sin) [*pyro-* + Gr. *toxikon* poison]. 1. A toxin developed during a fever. 2. A toxic principle obtained from many bacteria; even if ordinarily non-pathogenic, when injected it causes fever and wasting.

pyroxylin (pi-rok'sĭ-lin) [Gr. *pyr* fire + *xylon* wood]. A product of the action of a mixture of nitric and sulfuric acids on cotton, consisting chiefly of cellulose tetranitrate: a necessary ingredient of collodion.

pyrrobutamine (pir"ro-bu'tah-min). Chemical name: 1-[4-(p-chlorophenyl)-3-phenyl-2-butenyl]-pyrrolidine: used as an antihistaminic.

pyrroetioporphyrin (pir"o-e"te-o-por'fĭ-rin). A porphyrin, $C_{30}H_{34}N_4$.

pyrrole (pir'ol). A liquid, basic, cyclic substance, $(CH)_4NH$, obtained in the destructive distillation of various animal substances. **p. tetraiodide,** iodol.

pyrrolidine (pir-rol'ĭ-din). A simple base, tetramethylene imine, $(CH_2)_4NH$, which may be obtained from tobacco or prepared from pyrrole.

pyrrolin (pir'o-lin). An oily liquid, C_4H_6NH, formed by the action of acetic acid and zinc dust on pyrrole.

pyrroporphyrin (pir"o-por'fĭ-rin). A porphyrin, $C_{31}H_{34}O_2N_4$, derived from chlorophyll.

pyruvate (pi'roo-vāt). A salt or ester of pyruvic acid.

pyruvemia (pi"roo-ve'me-ah). A condition characterized by an increased amount of pyruvic acid in the blood.

pyrvinium (pir-vin'e-um). Chemical name: 6-dimethylamino-2-[2-(2,5-dimethyl-1-phenyl-3-pyrryl)vinyl]-1-methylquinolinium: used as an anthelmintic.

Pythagoras (pĭ-thag'o-ras) **of Samos** (5th century B.C.). The famous Greek philosopher whose interest in mathematics is reflected in his concept of "critical days" in disease which, in the Greek medicine of antiquity, was believed to enter a critical phase on certain days of the illness. Similar number lore (e.g., 4 humors, 4 elements, 4 qualities) is also found later in other concepts of disease and medicine (e.g., galenism).

pythogenesis (pi"tho-jen'e-sis) [Gr. *pythein* to rot + *genesis* production]. 1. The origination of a process of decay or decomposition. 2. Generation from filth.

pythogenic (pi"tho-jen'ik) [Gr. *pythein* to rot + *gennan* to produce]. Causing decay or decomposition.

pythogenous (pi-thoj'e-nus). Caused by putrefaction or filth.

pyuria (pi-u're-ah) [Gr. *pyon* pus + *ouron* urine + *-ia*]. The presence of pus in the urine. **miliary p.,** the presence in the urine of miliary bodies consisting of pus cells, blood cells, and epithelium.

PZI. Abbreviation for *protamine zinc insulin.*

Q

Q. Abbreviation for *electric quantity.*

qcepo (ksa'po). The tubercle type of dermal leishmaniasis.

q.d. Abbreviation for L. *qua'que di'e,* every day.

Q fever (Q for *query*). See under *fever.*

q.h. Abbreviation for L. *qua'que ho'ra,* every hour.

q.i.d. Abbreviation for L. *qua'ter in di'e,* four times a day.

q.l. Abbreviation for L. *quan'tum li'bet,* as much as desired.

Q.N.S. Abbreviation for *Queen's Nursing Sister* (of Queen's Institute of District Nursing).

Q.P. Abbreviation for *quanti-Pirquet reaction.* See under *reaction.*

q.p. Abbreviation for L. *quan'tum pla'ceat,* at will.

q.q.h. Abbreviation for L. *qua'que quar'ta ho'ra,* every four hours.

Qq.hor. Abbreviation for L. *qua'que ho'ra,* every hour.

Q.R.Z. Abbreviation for Ger. *Quaddel Reaktion Zeit* (wheal reaction time).

q.s. Abbreviation for L. *quan'tum sa'tis,* sufficient quantity.

q.suff. Abbreviation for L. *quan'tum suf'ficit,* as much as suffices.

qt. Abbreviation for *quart.*

quack (kwak). One who fraudulently misrepresents his ability and experience in the diagnosis and treatment of disease or the effects to be achieved by the treatment he offers.

quackery (kwak'er-e). The fraudulent misrepresentation of one's ability and experience in the diagnosis and treatment of disease or of the effects to be achieved by the treatment offered.

quacksalver (kwak-sal'ver). One claiming special merit for treatment with his medications and salves.

quader (kwa'der) [Ger. "square"]. The precuneus, or quadrate lobule.

quadrangle (kwod'rang-g'l). 1. A figure having four angles, or sides. 2. Black's term for a dental instrument having four angulations in the shank connecting the handle, or shaft, with the working portion of the instrument, known as the blade, or nib.

quadrangular (kwod-rang'gu-lar) [L. *quadri-* four + *angulus* angle]. Having four angles.

quadrant (kwod′rant) [L. *quadrans* quarter]. 1. One quarter of a circle; that portion of the circumference of a circle that subtends an angle of 90 degrees. 2. Any one of four corresponding parts or quarters, as of the abdominal surface or or the ear drum. **Wilder's q.,** an area on the ventral surface of the cerebral crus of a cat.

quadrantal (kwod-ran′tal). Resembling or affecting a quadrant.

quadrantanopia (kwod″rant-ah-no′pe-ah) [L. *quadrans* a fourth part + Gr. *an-* neg. + *ōpē* vision + *-ia*]. Defective vision or blindness in one fourth of the visual field, bounded by a vertical and a horizontal radius.

quadrantanopsia (kwod″ran-tah-nop′se-ah). Quadrantanopia.

quadrat (kwod′rat) [L. *quadratus* squared]. A rectangular, usually square, sample plot used in ecological studies, especially a plot containing 1 square meter. A sample plot of larger area is often called a *major quadrat.*

quadrate (kwod′rāt) [L. *quadratus* squared]. Square or squared; four sided.

quadratipronator (kwod-ra″te-pro-na′tor). Musculus pronator quadratus.

quadratus (kwod-ra′tus) [L.]. Squared; four sided.

quadri- [L. *quattuor* four; in combination, *quadri-*]. A prefix signifying four, or fourfold.

quadribasic (kwod″rĭ-ba′sik). Having four replaceable atoms of hydrogen.

quadriceps (kwod′rĭ-seps) [*quadri-* + L. *caput* head]. Four headed; possessing four heads.

quadricepsplasty (kwod″rĭ-seps′plas-te). Plastic repair of a ruptured quadriceps femoris muscle.

quadriceptor (kwod″rĭ-sep′tor) [*quadri-* + L. *ceptor*]. An intermediary body having four combining groups.

quadricuspid (kwod″rĭ-kus′pid) [*quadri-* + L. *cuspis* point]. 1. Having four cusps: said of a tooth, or of an aortic valve with supernumerary cusps. 2. A tooth with four cusps.

quadridigitate (kwod″rĭ-dij′ĭ-tāt). Tetradactylous.

quadrigemina (kwod″rĭ-jem′ĭ-nah) [L.]. Plural of *quadrigeminum.*

quadrigeminal (kwod″rĭ-jem′ĭ-nal) [L. *quadrigeminus*]. Fourfold, or in four parts; forming a group of four.

quadrigeminum (kwod″rĭ-jem′ĭ-num), pl. *quadrigem′ina* [L.]. Fourfold.

quadrigeminus (kwod″rĭ-jem′ĭ-nus) [L.]. Quadrigeminal.

quadrilateral (kwod″rĭ-lat′er-al) [*quadri-* + L. *latus* side]. 1. Having four sides. 2. A four-sided figure, or postulate. **Celsus' q.,** "Notae vero inflammationis sunt quatuor, rubor et tumor, cum calore et dolore." (The four cardinal symptoms of inflammation, redness, swelling, heat and pain.)

quadrilocular (kwod″rĭ-lok′u-lar) [*quadri-* + L. *loculus* a small space]. Having four cells, cavities, or chambers.

quadripara (kwod-rip′ah-rah) [*quadri-* + L. *parere* to bring forth, produce]. A woman who has had four pregnancies which resulted in viable offspring. Also written Para IV.

quadripartite (kwod″rĭ-par′tīt). Having four parts or divisions.

quadriplegia (kwod″rĭ-ple′je-ah). Paralysis of all four limbs; tetraplegia.

quadripolar (kwod″rĭ-po′lar). Having four poles, as a cell.

quadrisect (kwod′rĭ-sekt) [*quadri-* + L. *secare* to cut]. To cut into four parts.

quadrisection (kwod″rĭ-sek′shun) [*quadri-* + L. *sectio* cut]. Division into four parts.

quadritubercular (kwod″rĭ-tu-ber′ku-lar). Having four tubercles or cusps.

quadriurate (kwod″rĭ-u′rāt) [*quadri-* + *urate*]. Any hyperacid urate, like those of the human urine.

quadrivalent (kwod-riv′ah-lent) [*quadri-* + L. *valere* to be worth]. Having a chemical valence or combining power of four.

quadroon (kwod-rōōn′) [Sp. *cuarterón*]. The offspring of a white person and a mulatto.

quadruped (kwod′roo-ped) [*quadri-* + L. *pes* foot]. 1. Four footed. 2. An animal having four feet.

quadrupl. Abbreviation for L. *quadruplica′to,* four times as much.

quadruplet (kwod′rup-let) [L. *quadrupulus* fourfold]. One of four offspring produced in one gestation period.

Quain's fatty heart (kwānz) [Sir Richard *Quain,* British physician, 1816–1898]. See under *heart.*

quale (kwa′le). The quality of a thing; especially the quality of a sensation or other conscious process.

qualimeter (kwah-lim′e-ter) [L. *qualis* of what sort + *metrum* measure]. An instrument for measuring the hardness of roentgen rays; a penetrometer.

qualitative, qualitive (kwol′ĭ-ta″tiv, kwol′ĭ-tiv) [L. *qualitativus*]. Pertaining to quality.

quanta (kwon′tah) [L.]. Plural of *quantum.*

quantimeter (kwon-tim′e-ter) [L. *quantus* how much + *metrum* measure]. An apparatus for measuring the quantity of roentgen rays generated by a tube.

quantitative (kwon′tĭ-ta-tiv) [L. *quantitativus*]. Pertaining to quantity.

quantitive (kwon′tĭ-tiv). Quantitative.

quantivalence (kwon-tiv′ah-lens) [L. *quantus* how much + *valere* to be worth]. Chemical valence; the atomic or combining power of an element or radical expressed in the number of atoms of hydrogen with which it can combine.

quantivalent (kwon-tiv′ah-lent). Pertaining to or possessing quantivalence.

quantum (kwon′tum), pl. *quan′ta* [L. "as much as"]. A unit of energy under the quantum theory. It is hν, in which h is Planck's constant, 6.55×10^{-27}, and ν is the frequency of vibration with which the energy is associated. See *quantum theory,* under *theory.* **q. of light,** a quantity of light (radiant energy) equivalent to the frequency of the light times 6.55×10^{-27} erg. sec.

quantum libet (kwon′tum li′bet) [L.]. As much as desired.

quantum satis (kwon′tum sat′is). A sufficient quantity.

quantum sufficit (kwon′tum suf′fĭ-sit) [L.]. As much as suffices.

quarantine (kwor′an-tēn) [Ital. *quarantina*]. 1. A period (usually of forty days' duration) of detention of ships or persons coming from infected or suspected ports. 2. The place where persons are detained for inspection. 3. To detain or isolate on account of suspected contagion. 4. Restrictions placed on the entrance to and exit from the place or premises where a case of communicable disease exists.

quart (kwort) [L. *quartus* fourth]. The fourth part of a gallon (946 cc.).

quartan (kwor′tan) [L. *quartanus,* pertaining to the fourth]. 1. Recurring every third (fourth) day. 2. A variety of intermittent fever of which the paroxysms recur on every third day. See *malaria.* **double q.,** a quartan fever of which the recurrences are alternately severe and relatively mild. **triple q.,** a fever in which the paroxysms occur every day because of infection with three different groups of quartan parasites.

quarter (kwor′ter). The part of a horse's hoof lying between the heel and the toe. **false q.,** a cleft in the quarter of a horse's hoof from the top to the bottom. **fifth q.,** the fat, hide, and other less valuable parts of a slaughtered animal.

quartile (kwor'til) [L. *quartus* one fourth]. The middle term of each half of a series of variables.

quartipara (kwor-tip'ah-rah). Quadripara.

quartiparous (kwor-tip'ah-rus). Quadriparous.

quartisect (kwor'tĭ-sekt) [L. *quartus* fourth + *secare* to cut]. To cut into four parts.

quartisternal (kwor"tĭ-ster'nal) [L. *quartus* fourth + *sternum* sternum]. Pertaining to the fourth sternebra, or the bony segment of the sternum opposite the fourth intercostal space.

quartz (kwarts). Silicon dioxide, the principal ingredient of sandstone.

quassation (kwŏ-sa'shun) [L. *quassatio*]. The crushing of drugs, or their reduction to small pieces.

Quassia (kwosh'e-ah) [after *Quassi,* a Negro who used it as a remedy]. A genus of simaroubaceous tropical trees, the wood of which was first used in the 18th century in the treatment of fevers.

Quat., quat. Abbreviation for L. *quat'tuor,* four.

quater in die (kwah'ter in de'a) [L.]. Four times a day.

quaternary (kwah-ter'nah-re) [L. *quaternarius,* from *quattuor* four]. 1. Fourth in order. 2. Containing four elements.

Quatrefages' angle (katr'fazh-ez) [Jean Louis Armand *Quatrefages* de Bréau, French naturalist, 1810–1892]. See under *angle.*

quebrabunda (ka"brah-boon'dah). A tropical disease of horses and swine not unlike beriberi. Called also *straddling disease.*

quebrachitol (ka-brah'chĭ-tol). A sugar, 1-methylinositol, from quebracho, suggested as a sugar substitute in diabetes.

Queckenstedt's phenomenon, sign, test (kwek'en-stets") [Hans *Queckenstedt,* German physician, died 1918]. See under *sign.*

quelicin (kwel'ĭ-sin). Trade mark for a preparation of succinylcholine.

Quénu-Mayo operation (ka'nuh-ma'o) [Eduard André Victor Alfred *Quénu,* French surgeon, 1852–1933; William James *Mayo,* American surgeon, 1861–1939]. Quenuthoracoplasty.

quenuthoracoplasty (kwe"nu-tho'rah-ko-plas"-te). Quenu's operation of dividing the ribs to promote retraction of the chest wall in empyema.

quercetin (kwer'cĕ-tin). The aglycon of rutin and other glycosides, 3, 3', 4', 5, 7-pentahydroxyflavone: used to reduce abnormal capillary fragility. **q.-3-rutinoside,** rutin.

querciform (kwer'sĭ-form). Tannoform made with oak tannin.

Quercus (kwer'kus) [L.]. A genus of trees including the oaks, the source of substances formerly used in medicine.

Quervain's disease (kār'vanz) [Fritz de *Quervain,* Swiss surgeon, 1868–1940]. See under *disease.*

Quest's rule (kwests) [Robert *Quest,* Lemberg pediatrician, born 1874]. See under *rule.*

Quetelet's rule (ket"ĕ-lāz') [Lambert Ad. Jacques *Quetelet,* Brussels mathematician, 1796–1874]. See under *rule.*

Queyrat's erythroplasia (ka-rahz') [Auguste *Queyrat,* French dermatologist, born 1872]. See under *erythroplasia.*

quick (kwik). 1. Rapid. 2. Alive. 3. Pregnant and able to feel the fetal movements.

Quick test (kwik) [Armand J. *Quick,* Milwaukee physician, born 1894]. See under *tests.*

quickening (kwik'en-ing). The first recognizable movements of the fetus in utero, appearing usually from the sixteenth to the eighteenth week of pregnancy.

quigila (kwij'ĭ-lah). An infectious disease resembling leprosy, occurring in Brazil.

quillaia (kwil-la'yah). The dried inner part of the bark of *Quillaja saponaria,* formerly used in medicine for its local irritant action.

Quillaja (kwil-la'yah) [Chilian *quillai*]. A genus of rosaceous trees. *Q. sapona'ria,* a species native to South America, which was first described in 1782.

quinacrine (kwin'ah-krin). Chemical name: 6-chloro-9-(4-diethylamino-1-methylbutylamino)-2-methoxyacridine: used as an antimalarial and anthelmintic.

quinalbarbitone (kwin"al-bar'bĭ-tōn). Secobarbital.

quinamicine (kwin-am'ĭ-sin). An artificial alkaloid, $C_{19}H_{24}N_2O_2$, from quinamine.

Quincke's capillary pulse, disease, puncture, sign (kwink'ez) [Heinrich Irenaeus *Quincke,* physician in Kiel, 1842–1922]. See under the nouns.

quinidine (kwin'ĭ-din). The dextrorotatory isomer of quinine, obtained from various species of *Cinchona* and their hybrids, and from *Remijia pedunculata,* or prepared from quinine: used in treatment of cardiac arrhythmias.

quinine (kwin'in, kwin-ēn', kwi'nīn) [L. *quinina*]. The most important of the many alkaloids of cinchona bark, $C_{20}H_{24}N_2O_2 + 3H_2O$, a white minutely crystalline or amorphous powder, odorless, and having a bitter taste. It is specific in all forms of malaria and is administered in the form of one of its soluble salts. **q. and urea hydrochloride,** a double salt of quinine and urea hydrochloride, $C_{20}H_{24}N_2O_2.HCl.CO(NH_2)_2.HCl.5H_2O$, used in treatment of malaria and in injection treatment of hemorrhoids and varicose veins. **q. bismuth iodide,** a compound of quinine and bismuth iodide used in the treatment of syphilis. **q. bisulfate,** a colorless, crystalline cinchona salt, $C_{20}H_{24}O_2N_2.H_2SO_4 + 7H_2O$. It is much more soluble than the ordinary sulfate. **q. dihydrochloride,** a cinchona alkaloid, $C_{20}H_{24}N_2O_2.HCl$: used intravenously as emergency treatment of severe malarial infections, in cerebral malaria, or when nausea or vomiting precludes oral administration of quinine. **q. ethylcarbonate,** a white crystalline compound, $C_2H_5.O.CO.O.C_{20}H_{23}N_2O$, formed by the action of ethyl chlorocarbonate on quinine: used like quinine. **q. hydrobromide,** a salt, $C_{20}H_{24}O_2N_2.HBr + H_2O$, esteemed for hypodermic administration. **q. hydrochloride,** a white salt, $C_{20}H_{24}O_2N_2.HCl + 2H_2O$, resembling the sulfate in taste and uses. **q. salicylate,** a salt, $C_{20}H_{24}N_2O_2.C_7H_6O_3 + H_2O$, in slender white needles: antipyretic and antirheumatic. **q. sulfate,** a white crystalline salt, $(C_{20}H_{24}N_2O_2)_2.H_2SO_4 + 2H_2O$, more largely used as a remedy than any other of the cinchona alkaloidal salts. **q. tannate,** a yellowish powder: used in whooping cough and diarrhea.

quininism (kwin'ĭ-nizm). Cinchonism.

quininize (kwin'ĭ-nīz). Cinchonize.

quinoid (kwin'oid). Containing the chromatophoric group, $=C\langle{}^{C=C}_{C=C}\rangle C=$.

quinometry (kwĭ-nom'e-tre). The standardization of the alkaloids of quinine.

quinone (kwin'ōn). 1. A substance, $CO(CH.CH)_2CO$, in golden-yellow crystals, obtained by oxidizing quinic acid. 2. Any benzene derivative in which two hydrogen atoms are replaced by two oxygen atoms.

quinovin (kwin-o'vin). A bitter glycoside, $C_{36}H_{56}O_9$, from cinchona.

quinovose (kwin'o-vōs). Isorhodeose.

quinoxin (kwin-ok'sin). Nitrosophenol, $C_6H_4(NO)OH$; a colorless, crystalline substance prepared from the phenols by the action of nitrous acids.

Quinq. Abbreviation for L. *quin'que,* five.

Quinquaud's disease, sign (kang-kōz')

[Charles Emile *Quinquaud*, French physician, 1841–1894]. See under *disease* and *sign*.

quinquecuspid (kwin″kwe-kus′pid) [L. *quinque* five + *cuspis* point]. 1. Having five cusps. 2. A tooth with five cusps.

quinquetubercular (kwin″kwe-tu-ber′ku-lar). Having five tubercles or cusps.

quinquevalent (kwin-kwev′ah-lent) [L. *quinque* five + *valens* able]. 1. Having five different valencies. 2. Pentavalent.

quinquina (kin-ke′nah). Cinchona.

quinsy (kwin′ze) [L. *cynanche* sore throat]. Peritonsillar abscess. **lingual q.**, suppurative inflammation of the lingual tonsil.

Quint. Abbreviation for L. *quin′tus*, fifth.

quintan (kwin′tan) [L. *quintanus* of the fifth]. Recurring every fifth day.

quintessence (kwin-tes′ens) [L. *quintus* fifth + *essentia* essence]. The highly concentrated extract of any substance.

quintipara (kwin-tip′ah-rah) [L. *quintus* fifth + *parere* to bring forth, produce]. A woman who has had five pregnancies which resulted in viable offspring. Also written Para V.

quintisternal (kwin″tĭ-ster′nal) [L. *quintus* fifth + *sternum*]. Noting the fifth bony portion of the sternum, or the part above the ensiform cartilage and adjacent to the fifth intercostal space.

quintuplet (kwin′tup-let) [L. *quintuplex* five-fold]. One of five offspring produced in one gestation period.

quittor (kwit′or). A fistulous sore on the quarters or the coronet of a horse's foot. **simple q.**, local inflammation resulting in a slough, with formation of pus immediately above the hoof. **skin q.**, a very painful ulcer of the skin above the hoof. **subhorny q.**, inflammation beginning at the coronary band and extending beneath the hoof and producing pus formation in the sensitive tissue. **tendinous q.**, a condition in which the inflammation has extended into the tendons of the leg and the ligaments of the joint.

quoad vitam (kwo′ad vi′tam) [L.]. So far as life is concerned.

quotane (kwo′tān). Trade mark for preparations of dimethisoquin hydrochloride.

Quotid. Abbreviation for L. *quotid′ie*, daily.

quotidian (kwo-tid′e-an) [L. *quotidianus* daily]. 1. Recurring every day. 2. A form of intermittent malarial fever with daily recurrent paroxysms. **double q.**, a fever having two daily paroxysms.

quotient (kwo′shent). A number obtained as the result of division. **achievement q.**, a percentage statement of the extent to which a child has progressed in learning in proportion to his ability. **albumin q.**, the amount of albumin in the blood plasma divided by the amount of albumin present in the blood. **Ayala's q.**, a quotient in examination of the cerebrospinal pressure, obtained by dividing the pressure after removal of 10 cc. of cerebrospinal fluid by that registered before such removal, and multiplying by 10. Normal values are 5.5 to 6.5. A result under 5 indicates a small reservoir, as in subarachnoid block; over 7 means a large reservoir, as may be encountered in serous meningitis or hydrocephalus. **caloric q.**, the quotient obtained by dividing the heat evolved (expressed in calories) by the oxygen consumed (expressed in milligrams) in a metabolic process. **D q.**, the ratio of glucose to nitrogen in the urine. **growth q.**, that portion of the entire food energy which is utilized for the purpose of growth. **intelligence q.**, the measure of intelligence obtained by dividing the patient's mental age, as ascertained by the Binet-Simon scale, by his chronological age and multiplying the result by 100. **protein q.**, the number obtained by dividing the quantity of globulin of the blood plasma by the quantity of albumin. **rachidian q.**, Ayala's quotient. **respiratory q.**, the ratio between the volume of carbon dioxide expired and the volume of oxygen inspired in a given time. **spinal q.**, Ayala's q.

q.v. Abbreviation for L. *quan′tum vis*, as much as you please, and for *quod vi′de*, which see.

R

R. Abbreviation for *organic radical* (in chemical formulas), *Rankine* (scale), *Réaumur* (scale), *remotum* (far), *respiration*, *Rickettsia*, *right*, and *Behnken's unit;* also for *roentgen*, *rough* colony (see under *colony*), and *regression coefficient*.

+R. Symbol for *Rinne's test positive*.

−R. Symbol for *Rinne's test negative*.

℞. Symbol for L. *rec′ipe*, take.

r. Former symbol for *roentgen:* now officially replaced by capital R.

Ra. Chemical symbol for *radium*.

Raabe's test (rah′bez) [Gustav *Raabe*, German physician, born 1875]. See under *tests*.

rabbetting (rab′et-ing). Interlocking of the denticulated broken surfaces of a fractured bone.

rabbia (rab′be-ah). Rabies.

rabelaisin (rab″ĕ-la′ĭ-sin). A poisonous glycoside from *Rabelaisia philippinensis*, a plant of the Philippine Islands: a heart stimulant.

rabiate (ra′be-āt). Affected with rabies.

rabic (ra′bik). Pertaining to rabies

rabicidal (ra″be-si′dal). Destructive to the virus which causes rabies.

rabid (rab′id) [L. *rabidus*]. Affected with rabies, or hydrophobia.

rabies (ra′be-ēz) [L. *rabere* to rage]. A specific infectious disease of certain animals, especially dogs and wolves, communicated to man by direct inoculation, as by a bite of an infected animal, and due to a virus. After an incubation period of from one to six months, the disease begins with malaise, depression of spirits, and swelling of the lymphatics in the region of the wound. There are choking and spasmodic catching of the breath, succeeded by increasing tetanic spasms, especially of the muscles of respiration and deglutition, which are increased by attempts to drink water or even by the sight of water. There are usually also fever, mental derangement, vomiting, profuse secretion of a sticky saliva, and albuminuria. The disease is generally fatal, death occurring in from two to five days. The cytoplasmic inclusion bodies in the brain (Negri bodies) are characteristic and diagnostic. Called also *hydrophobia* and *lyssa*. **r. cani′na,** the rabies of dogs. **dumb r.,** rabies in which paralysis is an early, predominant symptom, the animal showing no signs of viciousness or tendency to bite. **r. feli′na,** rabies in cats. **furious r.,** a form in which there is very pronounced excitement. **paralytic r.,** rabies in which paralysis is a marked symptom—usually an ascending spinal paralysis. **sullen r.,** dumb r.

rabietic (ra″be-et′ik). Pertaining to or affected with rabies.

rabific (ra-bif′ik). Causing or producing rabies.

rabiform (ra′bĭ-form). Resembling rabies.

rabigenic (ra″bĭ-jen′ik). Causing rabies.

$RaBr_2$. Radium bromide.

race (rās). 1. An ethnic stock, or division of mankind; in a narrower sense, a national or tribal stock; in a still narrower sense, a genealogic line of descent; a class of persons of a common lineage. 2. A class or breed of animals; a group of individuals having certain characteristics in common, owing to a common inheritance.

racemase (ra′se-mās). An enzyme in various bacteria which catalyzes the racemization of a mixture of dextro- and levo-lactic acid.

racemate (ra′se-māt). An equimolecular mixture of two enantiomorphic isomers, being optically inactive in solution because of the presence of the same number of dextro- and laevo-rotatory molecules. In the solid state it may have the properties of a loosely bound molecular compound. Called also *racemic form, racemic mixture,* or *racemic modification.*

raceme (ra-sēm′) [L. *racemus* a bunch of grapes]. 1. A form of inflorescence in which the individual flowers are borne on stalks which spring from a long central stem. 2. Racemate.

racemic (ra-se′mik). Made up of two enantiomorphic isomers and therefore optically inactive.

racemization (ra″se-mi-za′shun). The transformation of one half of the molecules of an optically active compound into molecules which possess exactly the opposite (mirror-image) configuration, with complete loss of rotatory power because of the statistical balance between equal numbers of dextro- and laevo-rotatory molecules.

racemose (ras′e-mōs) [L. *racemosus*]. Resembling a bunch of grapes on its stalk.

racephedrine (ra-sef′ĕ-drin). The racemic mixture of ephedrine: used as a sympathomimetic.

rachi- (ra′ke). See *rachio-.*

rachial (ra′ke-al). Rachidial.

rachialbuminimeter (ra″ke-al-bu″mĭ-nim′e-ter). An apparatus for measuring the albumin in a specimen of the cerebrospinal fluid.

rachialbuminimetry (ra″ke-al-bu″mĭ-nim′e-tre). The measurement of the amount of albumin in the spinal fluid.

rachialgia (ra″ke-al′je-ah) [*rachi-* + Gr. *algos* pain + *-ia*]. Pain in the vertebral column.

rachianalgesia (ra″ke-an″al-je′ze-ah). Rachianesthesia.

rachianesthesia (ra″ke-an″es-the′ze-ah). Spinal anesthesia; anesthesia produced by the injection of the anesthetic into the spinal canal.

rachicentesis (ra″ke-sen-te′sis) [*rachi-* + Gr. *kentēsis* puncture]. Puncture into the spinal canal.

rachidial (ra-kid′e-al). Pertaining to the spine.

rachidian (ra-kid′e-an). Pertaining to the spine.

rachigraph (ra′ke-graf) [*rachi-* + Gr. *graphein* to write]. An instrument for recording the outlines of the spine and back.

rachilysis (ra-kil′ĭ-sis) [*rachi-* + Gr. *lysis* dissolution]. Mechanical treatment of a curved vertebral column by combined traction and pressure.

rachio-, rachi- (ra′ke-o, ra′ke) [Gr. *rhachis* spine]. Combining form denoting relation to the spine.

rachiocampsis (ra″ke-o-kamp′sis) [*rachio-* + Gr. *kampsis* curve]. Curvature of the spinal column.

rachiocentesis (ra″ke-o-sen-te′sis) [*rachio-* + Gr. *kentēsis* puncture]. Spinal puncture.

rachiochysis (ra″ke-ok′ĭ-sis) [*rachio-* + Gr. *chysis* a pouring]. The effusion of a fluid within the vertebral canal.

rachiocyphosis (ra″ke-o-si-fo′sis). Kyphosis.

rachiodynia (ra″ke-o-din′e-ah) [*rachio-* + Gr. *odynē* pain + *-ia*]. Pain in the spinal column.

rachiokyphosis (ra″ke-o-ki-fo′sis). Kyphosis.

rachiometer (ra″ke-om′e-ter) [*rachio-* + Gr. *metron* measure]. An instrument for measuring curvatures of the vertebral column.

rachiomyelitis (ra″ke-o-mi″ĕ-li′tis) [*rachio-* + Gr. *myelos* marrow + *-itis*]. Inflammation of the spinal cord.

rachiopagus (ra″ke-op′ah-gus) [*rachio-* + Gr. *pagos* thing fixed]. Symmetrical conjoined twins united back to back in the sagittal plane, fusion being limited to the upper trunk and cervical region.

rachioparalysis (ra″ke-o-pah-ral′ĭ-sis). Paralysis of spinal muscles.

rachiopathy (ra″ke-op′ah-the) [*rachio-* + Gr. *pathos* disease]. Any disease of the spine.

rachioplegia (ra″ke-o-ple′je-ah) [*rachio-* + Gr. *plēgē* stroke + *-ia*]. Spinal paralysis.

rachioscoliosis (ra″ke-o-sko″le-o′sis). Lateral curvature of the spine.

rachiotome (ra′ke-o-tōm). An instrument for cutting the vertebrae.

rachiotomy (ra″ke-ot′o-me) [*rachio-* + Gr. *tomē* a cutting]. Incision of a vertebra, or of the vertebral column.

rachipagus (ra-kip′ah-gus) [*rachi-* + Gr. *pagos* thing fixed]. A double fetal monster joined at the vertebral column.

rachiresistance (ra″ke-re-zis′tans). A condition in which the injection of a spinal anesthetic produces little or no effect.

rachiresistant (ra″ke-re-zis′tant). Abnormally insensitive to spinal anesthetics.

rachis (ra′kis) [Gr. *rhachis* spine]. The vertebral column.

rachisagra (ra″kis-ag′rah) [*rachis* + Gr. *agra* seizure]. Pain or gout in the spine.

rachischisis (ra-kis′kĭ-sis) [*rachi-* + Gr. *schisis* cleft]. Congenital fissure of the spinal column. **r. partia′lis,** fissure of the spinal column of limited extent; merorachischisis. **r. poste′rior,** spina bifida. **r. tota′lis,** holorachischisis.

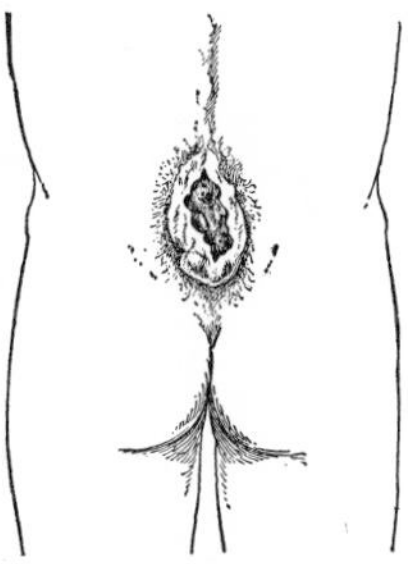

Rachischisis (Babcock).

rachisensibility (ra″ke-sen″sĭ-bil′ĭ-te). The condition of being abnormally sensitive to spinal anesthetics.

rachisensible (ra″ke-sen′sĭ-b′l). Abnormally sensitive to spinal anesthetics.

rachitic (ra-kit′ik). Pertaining to or affected with rickets.

rachitis (ra-ki′tis) [Gr. *rhachitis*]. 1. Rickets. 2. Inflammatory disease of the vertebral column. **r. foeta′lis annula′ris,** the formation before birth of annular thickenings on the long bones. **r. foeta′lis micromel′ica,** deficient longitudinal growth of the bones of the fetus. **r. tar′da,** late rickets.

rachitism (rak′ĭ-tizm). A tendency to rickets.

rachitogenic (rah-kit″o-jen′ik). Causing rickets.

rachitome (rak″ĭ-tōm). A cutting instrument used in opening the spinal canal.

rachitomy (rah-kit′o-me) [*rachi-* + Gr. *tomē* a cutting]. The surgical or anatomical opening of the vertebral canal.

racial (ra′shal). Pertaining to a particular race of mankind.

raclage (rah-klahzh′) [Fr.]. Destruction or removal by rubbing.

raclement (rahkl-mah′). Raclage.

rad.[1] Abbreviation for L. *ra′dix,* root.

rad[2] (rad) [acronym for *radiation absorbed dose*]. a unit of measurement of the absorbed dose of ionizing radiation. It corresponds to an energy transfer of 100 ergs per gram of any absorbing material (including tissues).

radectomy (ra-dek′to-me) [L. *radix* root + Gr. *ektomē* excision]. Excision of a portion of the root of a tooth.

Rademacher's system (rah′dĕ-mah″kerz) [Johann Gottfried *Rademacher,* German physician,

1772–1850]. The belief that there should be a specific remedy for every disease.

radesyge (rah″de-se′gĕ) [Dan. "scab-sickness"]. An ulcerative skin disease formerly prevalent in Scandinavia; also called *Norwegian scabies.*

radia (ra′de-ah). The second stage of a distoma, when it ceases to be a sporocyst and has not yet become a cercaria.

radiability (ra″de-ah-bil′ĭ-te). The property of being readily penetrated by the roentgen or other ray.

radiable (ra′de-ah-b'l). Capable of being examined by the roentgen ray.

radiad (ra′de-ad). Toward the radial side.

radial (ra′de-al) [L. *radialis*]. 1. Pertaining to the radius or to a radius. 2. Radiating; spreading outward from a common center.

radialis (ra″de-a′lis). Radial; in official anatomical nomenclature, designating relationship to the radius.

radian (ra′de-an). In ophthalmometry, an arc whose length equals the radius of its curvature. It is an arc of 57.295 degrees.

radiant (ra′de-ant) [L. *radians*]. 1. Diverging from a common center. 2. Any radioactive substance.

radiate (ra′de-āt) [L. *radiare, radiatus*]. 1. To diverge or spread from a common point. 2. Arranged in a radiating manner.

radiathermy (ra-di″ah-ther′me). Short wave diathermy.

radiatio (ra-de-a′she-o), pl. *radiatio′nes* [L.]. A radiating structure; used in anatomical nomenclature to designate a collection of nerve fibers connecting different portions of the brain. Called also *radiation.* **r. acus′tica** [N A], a fiber tract arising in the medial geniculate nucleus and passing laterally to terminate in the transverse temporal gyri of the temporal lobe. Called also *acoustic radiation.* **r. cor′poris callo′si** [N A, B N A], the fibers of the corpus callosum radiating to all parts of the neopallium. Called also *radiation of corpus callosum.* **r. cor′poris stria′ti** [B N A], the extension of fibers from the thalamus and hypothalamus to the cerebral cortex. Omitted in N A. **r. occipitothalam′ica [Gratiole′ti]** [B N A], r. optica. **r. op′tica** [N A], a fiber tract starting at the lateral geniculate body, passing through the pars retrolentiformis of the internal capsule, and terminating in the striate area on the medial surface of the occipital lobe, on either side of the calcarine sulcus. Called also *r. occipitothalamica* [*Gratioleti*] [B N A], and *optic radiation.* **r. pyramida′lis,** fibers extending from the pyramidal tract to the cortex. **r. striothalam′ica,** a fiber system joining the thalamus and the hypothalamic region.

radiation (ra-de-a′shun) [L. *radiatio*]. 1. Divergence from a common center. 2. A structure made up of divergent elements, as one of the fiber tracts in the brain. For official names of specific structures, see under *radiatio.* 3. Electromagnetic waves, such as those of light, or particulate rays, such as alpha, beta, and gamma rays, given off from some source. **acoustic r., auditory r.,** radiatio acustica. **Cerenkov r.,** energy produced when swiftly travelling electrons pass through a liquid with a speed greater than the speed of light in that liquid. **corpuscular r's,** radiations other than x-rays and γ-rays, such as alpha-, beta-, proton-, neutron-, positron-, and deuteron-rays. **electromagnetic r.** See under *wave.* **r. of Gratiolet,** radiatio optica. **Huldshinsky's r.,** a course of three months' treatment with ultraviolet rays from the quartz-mercury vapor lamp. **interstitial r.,** energy emitted by radium or radon inserted directly into the tissue. **ionizing r.,** high-energy radiation (x-rays and gamma rays) which interacts to produce ion pairs in matter. **irritative r.,** radiation with ultraviolet rays to the point of erythema. **mitogenetic r., mitogenic r.,** specific energy allegedly given off by a cell undergoing mitosis. **occipitothalamic r., optic r.,** radiatio optica. **photochemical r.,** that part of the radiant spectrum which produces chemical changes. **pyramidal r.,** radiatio pyramidalis. **Rollier's r.,** exposure of the body to gradually increasing doses of the ultraviolet rays of the sun. **striothalamic r.,** radiatio striothalamica. **tegmental r.,** fibers radiating laterally from the red nucleus. **thalamic r.,** fibers streaming out through the lateral surface of the thalamus, through the internal capsule to the cerebral cortex. **thalamotemporal r.,** radiatio acustica.

radical (rad′ĭ-kal) [L. *radicalis*]. 1. Directed to the cause; going to the root or source of a morbid process. 2. A group of atoms which enters into and goes out of chemical combination without change, and which forms one of the fundamental constituents of a molecule. **acid r.** 1. The electronegative element which combines with hydrogen to form an acid. 2. All of the acid except the hydroxyl group. **alcohol r.,** all of the alcohol molecule except the hydroxyl group (—OH). **color r.,** chromophore.

radices (rad′ĭ-sēz) [L.]. Plural of *radix.*

radiciform (ra-dis′ĭ-form) [L. *radix* root + *forma* shape]. Shaped like a root; shaped like the root of a tooth.

radicle (rad′ĭ-k'l) [L. *radicula*]. 1. Any one of the smallest branches of a vessel or nerve. 2. Radical, def. 2.

radicotomy (rad″ĭ-kot′o-me). Rhizotomy.

radicula (rah-dik′u-lah) [L.]. Radicle, def. 1.

radiculalgia (rah-dik″u-lal′je-ah). Neuralgia of the nerve roots.

radicular (rah-dik′u-lar). Of or pertaining to a radical or root.

radiculectomy (rah-dik″u-lek′to-me) [L. *radicula* radicle + Gr. *ektomē* excision]. Excision of a rootlet; especially, resection of spinal nerve roots.

radiculitis (rah-dik″u-li′tis) [L. *radicula* radicle + *-itis*]. Inflammation of the root of a spinal nerve, especially of that portion of the root which lies between the spinal cord and the intervertebral canal.

radiculoganglionitis (rah-dik″u-lo-gang″gle-o-ni′tis). Inflammation of the posterior spinal nerve roots and their ganglions.

radiculomedullary (rah-dik″u-lo-med′u-ler″e). Pertaining to or affecting the nerve roots and the spinal cord.

radiculomeningomyelitis (rah-dik″u-lo-me-ning″go-mi″ĕ-li′tis). Inflammation of the nerve roots, the meninges and the spinal cord.

radiculomyelopathy (rah-dik″u-lo-mi″ĕ-lop′ah-the). Disease of the nerve roots and spinal cord.

radiculoneuritis (rah-dik″u-lo-nu-ri′tis). Guillain-Barré syndrome.

radiculoneuropathy (rah-dik″u-lo-nu-rop′ah-the). Disease of the nerve roots and nerve.

radiculopathy (rah-dik″u-lop′ah-the). Disease of the nerve roots.

radiectomy (ra″de-ek′to-me) [L. *radix* root + Gr. *ektomē* excision]. Excision of the root of a tooth.

radiferous (ra-dif′er-us). Containing radium.

radio- (ra′de-o) [L. *radius* ray]. Combining form denoting relationship to radiation; sometimes used with specific reference to the emission of radiant energy, to radium, or to the radius. It is also affixed to the name of a chemical element to designate a radioactive isotope of that particular element, as radiocarbon, radioiodine, etc.

radioactinium (ra″de-o-ak-tin′e-um). A substance formed by the disintegration of actinium.

radioaction (ra″de-o-ak′shun). Radioactivity.

radioactive (ra″de-o-ak′tiv). Having the property of radioactivity.

radioactivity (ra″de-o-ak-tiv′ĭ-te). The quality of emitting or the emission of corpuscular or electromagnetic radiations consequent to nuclear disintegration, a natural property of all chemical elements of atomic number above 83, and possible of induction in all other known elements. **artificial r., induced r.,** radioactivity which has been produced by bombarding an element with high velocity particles.

radioactor (ra″de-o-ak′tor). An apparatus for preparing radium emanation.

radioanaphylaxis (ra″de-o-an″ah-fi-lak′sis). Anaphylactic sensitization to the roentgen ray or other form of radiant energy.

radioautogram (ra″de-o-aw′to-gram). Autoradiogram.

radioautograph (ra″de-o-aw′to-graf). Autoradiogram.

radioautography (ra″de-o-aw-tog′rah-fe). Autoradiography.

radiobe (ra′de-ōb) [*radio-* + Gr. *bios* life]. One of the peculiar microscopical condensations of sterilized bouillon produced by radium, discovered by J. B. Burke, which, by their appearance and the way in which they divide, have suggested the similar phenomena of bacteria.

radiobicipital (ra″de-o-bi-sip′ĭ-tal). Pertaining to the radius and the biceps muscle of the arm.

radiobiologist (ra″de-o-bi-ol′o-jist). One who devotes his studies to radiobiology.

radiobiology (ra″de-o-bi-ol′o-je). That branch of science which is concerned with the effect of light and of ultraviolet and ionizing radiations upon living tissue or organisms.

radiocalcium (ra″de-o-kal′se-um). A radioactive isotope of calcium. Ca^{45}, with a half-life of 180 days, is used as a tracer in the study of calcium metabolism.

radiocarbon (ra″de-o-kar′bon). A radioactive isotope of carbon such as C^{14}, with a half-life of several thousand years, which is the most important of the radioactive tracers.

radiocarcinogenesis (ra″de-o-kar″sĭ-no-jen′e-sis). Cancer formation caused by exposure to radiation.

radiocardiogram (ra″de-o-kar′de-o-gram). The graphic record obtained by radiocardiography.

radiocardiography (ra″de-o-kar″de-og′rah-fe). 1. The technique of recording the concentration of an intravenously injected radioisotope in the chambers of the heart. 2. Rheocardiography. 3. Radioelectrocardiography.

radiocarpal (ra″de-o-kar′pal). Pertaining to the radius and carpus.

radiocarpus (ra″de-o-kar′pus). The flexor carpi radialis muscle.

radiochemistry (ra″de-o-kem′is-tre). The branch of chemistry which treats of radioactive phenomena.

radiochemy (ra″de-o-kem′e). The effects produced by radioactive rays.

radiochroism (ra″de-o-kro′izm) [*radio-* + Gr. *chroa* color]. The capacity of a substance to absorb certain radioactive and roentgen rays.

radiochrometer (ra″de-o-krom′e-ter) [*radio-* + Gr. *chrōma* color + *metron* measure]. An instrument for measuring the penetrating power of roentgen rays according to the Benoist scale.

radiocinematograph (ra″de-o-sin″e-mat′o-graf). An apparatus combining the moving picture camera and the roentgen ray machine, making possible moving pictures of the internal organs.

radiocurable (ra″de-o-kūr′ah-b′l). Curable by radiation therapy.

radiocystitis (ra″de-o-sis-ti′tis). Chronic actinic injury to the urinary bladder following the therapeutic use of roentgen rays or radium.

radiode (ra′de-ōd). An instrument for the therapeutic application of radium.

radiodermatitis (ra″de-o-der-mah-ti′tis). A cutaneous reaction occurring as a result of exposure to excessive quantities of ionizing radiation, such as grenz rays, roentgen or gamma rays, neutrons, or alpha or beta particles.

radiodiagnosis (ra″de-o-di″ag-no′sis). Diagnosis by means of roentgen rays and roentgenograms.

radiodiagnostics (ra″de-o-di″ag-nos′tiks). The art of roentgen-ray diagnosis.

radiodiaphane (ra″de-o-di′ah-fān). An instrument for performing transillumination by means of radium.

radiodigital (ra″de-o-dij′ĭ-tal). Pertaining to the radius and to the fingers.

radiodontics (ra″de-o-don′tiks). That department of dentistry which deals with the taking and interpretation of roentgenograms of the teeth and associated structures.

radiodontist (ra″de-o-don′tist). A dentist who specializes in radiodontics.

radioelectrocardiogram (ra″de-o-e-lek″tro-kar′de-o-gram). The tracing obtained by radioelectrocardiography.

radioelectrocardiograph (ra″de-o-e-lek″tro-kar′de-o-graf). The apparatus used in radioelectrocardiography, consisting of two electrodes which are firmly attached to the skin of the fifth intercostal space, one in each axilla, and a small radiotransmitter carried in a pocket of the subject, to which the electrodes are connected and by which the impulses are beamed to an oscilloscope or a conventional electrocardiograph for recording.

radioelectrocardiography (ra″de-o-e-lek″tro-kar″de-og′rah-fe). The recording of alterations in the electric potential of the heart without direct attachment between the recording apparatus and the subject. The impulses are beamed by radio waves from the subject to a receiver, thereby permitting the tracings to be made during the actual period of exercise close to or at a distance from the recording apparatus.

radio-element (ra″de-o-el′ĕ-ment). Any chemical element having radioactive properties.

radioencephalogram (ra″de-o-en-sef′ah-lo-gram). A curve showing the passage of an injected tracer through the cerebral blood vessels as revealed by an external scintillation counter.

radioencephalography (ra″de-o-en-sef″ah-log′-rah-fe). The recording of changes in the electric potential of the brain without direct attachment between the recording apparatus and the subject, the impulses being beamed by radio waves from the subject to the receiver.

radio-epidermitis (ra″de-o-ep″ĭ-der-mi′tis). Destruction of the epithelial layers of the skin and denudation of the dermis produced by radiation of the skin.

radio-epithelitis (ra″de-o-ep″ĭ-the-li′tis). Destruction of the epithelial cells of an area subjected to irradiation.

radiogen (ra′de-o-jen). Any radioactive substance.

radiogenic (ra″de-o-jen′ik) [*radio-* + Gr. *gennan* to produce]. Produced by roentgen or radium irradiation.

radiogenol (ra″de-o-je′nol). An emulsion of insoluble radioactive minerals, intended for injection into tumors, etc.

radiogold (ra′de-o-gold). A radioactive isotope of gold. Au^{198} has a half-life of 2.7 days, and Au^{199} has a half-life of 3.3 days.

radiogram (ra′de-o-gram). A film or other record produced by the action of actinic rays on a sensitized surface, such as an autoradiogram or a roentgenogram.

radiograph (ra′de-o-graf). Radiogram.

radiography (ra″de-og′rah-fe) [*radio-* + Gr. *graphein* to write]. The making of a record or photograph by means of the action of actinic rays on a sensitized surface. **urine r.,** a technique for measuring the quantity of organic iodide excreted by the kidneys, by comparison of the roentgenographic density of a specimen of urine voided at completion of intravenous urography with that of a calibrated scale.

radiohumeral (ra″de-o-hu′mer-al). Pertaining to the radius and humerus.

radio-immunity (ra″de-o-ĭ-mu′nĭ-te). A condition of decreased sensitivity to radiation sometimes produced by repeated irradiation.

radioiodine (ra″de-o-i′o-dīn). A radioactive isotope of iodine. The most frequently used, I^{131}, produced by the bombardment of tellurium in the cyclotron, has a half-life of 8 days. It is used in the detection of abnormal thyroid function and location of thyroid cancer metastases, and in treatment of toxic goiter.

radioiron (ra″de-o-i′ern). A radioactive isotope of iron. Fe^{55} has a half-life of about 4 years, Fe^{59}, a half-life of 47 days. A mixture of these has been used in study of the blood.

radioisotope (ra″de-o-i′so-tōp). An isotope which is radioactive, produced artificially from the element or from a stable isotope of the element by the action of neutrons, protons, deuterons, or alpha particles in the chain-reacting pile or in the cyclotron. Radioisotopes are used as tracers or indicators by being added to the stable compound under observation, so that the course of the latter in the body (human or animal) can be detected and followed by the radioactivity thus added to it. The stable element so treated is said to be "labeled" or "tagged."

radiokymography (ra″de-o-ki-mog′rah-fe). Roentgen kymography.

radiolead (ra″de-o-led′). Radioactive lead.

radiolesion (ra″de-o-le′zhun). A lesion caused by exposure to radiation.

radiologic, radiological (ra″de-o-loj′ik, ra″de-o-loj′e-kal). Pertaining to radiology.

radiologist (ra″de-ol′o-jist). A physician with special experience in radiology.

radiology (ra″de-ol′o-je). The science of radiant energy and radiant substances; especially that branch of medical science which deals with the use of radiant energy in the diagnosis and treatment of disease.

radiolucency (ra″de-o-lu′sen-se). The property of being radiolucent.

radiolucent (ra-de-o-lu′sent) [*radio-* + L. *lucere* to shine]. Permitting the passage of radiant energy, such as x-rays, yet offering some resistance to it, the representative areas appearing dark on the exposed film.

radiolus (ra-de′o-lus) [L., dim. of *radius* ray]. A probe, staff, or sound.

radiometallography (ra″de-o-met″ah-log′rah-fe). The radiography of metals.

radiometer (ra″de-om′e-ter). 1. An instrument for estimating roentgen-ray quantity. 2. An instrument in which radiant heat and light may be directly converted into mechanical energy. 3. An instrument for measuring radiant energy. **pastille r.,** an apparatus consisting of a color index by means of which the color changes in the pastilles, before and after radiation, may be estimated. **photographic r.,** a radiometer that uses strips of photographic paper which, after exposure and development, are compared with a half-tone color index.

radiomicrometer (ra″de-o-mi-krom′e-ter) [*radio-* + Gr. *mikros* small + *metron* measure]. An instrument for detecting minute changes of radiant energy.

radiomimetic (ra″de-o-mi-met′ik) [*radio-* + Gr. *mimētikos* imitative]. Exerting effects similar to those of ionizing radiation.

radiomuscular (ra″de-o-mus′ku-lar). Going from the radial artery or nerve to the muscles.

radiomutation (ra″de-o-mu-ta′shun). Change in the character of cells caused by exposure to radiation.

radion (ra′de-on). One of the radiant particles thrown off by a radioactive substance.

radionecrosis (ra″de-o-ne-kro′sis). Destruction of tissue or ulceration caused by radiant energy.

radioneuritis (ra″de-o-nu-ri′tis). A form of neuritis resulting from exposure to roentgen rays or other radiant energy.

radionitrogen (ra″de-o-ni′tro-jen). A radioactive substance produced by bombarding boron with alpha rays.

radio-opacity (ra″de-o-o-pas′ĭ-te). Radiopacity.

radiopacity (ra″de-o-pas′ĭ-te). The property of being radiopaque.

radiopalmar (ra″de-o-pal′mar). Pertaining to the radius or radial artery and the palm.

radiopaque (ra″de-o-pāk′) [*radio-* + L. *opacus* dark, obscure]. Not permitting the passage of radiant energy, such as x-rays, the representative areas appearing light or white on the exposed film.

radioparency (ra″de-o-par′en-se). The property of being radioparent.

radioparent (ra″de-o-par′ent). Permitting the passage of roentgen rays.

radiopathology (ra″de-o-pah-thol′o-je). Pathology having to do with the effects of radiation on tissues.

radiopelvimetry (ra″de-o-pel-vim′e-tre). Measurement of the pelvis by roentgen-ray examination.

radiophobia (ra″de-o-fo′be-ah). Morbid anxiety about the damaging effects of x-rays and radium.

radiophosphorus (ra″de-o-fos′fo-rus). A radioactive isotope of phosphorus. P^{32} has a half-life of 14.3 days and has been used as a tracer in studies of tumors and of carbohydrate metabolism, and in the treatment of polycythemia vera, chronic leukemia, and allied diseases.

radiophotography (ra″de-o-fo-tog′rah-fe). Photography of the fluorescent image produced by an x-ray beam.

radiophylaxis (ra″de-o-fi-lak′sis). The modifying effect of a small dose of radiation on the reaction to a large subsequent radiation.

radioplastic (ra″de-o-plas′tik). A term used to designate a method of making a plaster image of an organ, such as the heart, from roentgenoscopic measurements.

radiopotassium (ra″de-o-po-tas′e-um). A radioactive isotope of potassium. K^{42}, with a half-life of 12.4 hours, is used in tracer studies of potassium interchange in the body.

radiopraxis (ra″de-o-prak′sis) [*radio-* + Gr. *praxis* practice]. Use of rays of light, electricity, etc., in treatment of disease.

radiopulmonography (ra″de-o-pul″mo-nog′rah-fe). A rapid method for estimation of ventilation of localized lung areas, based on measurement of variation in intensity of low-voltage x-rays passed through the lungs during breathing.

radioreaction (ra″de-o-re-ak′shun). A bodily reaction, especially a skin reaction, to radiation.

radioreceptor (ra″de-o-re-sep′tor). A receptor for the stimuli which are excited by radiant energy, such as light or heat.

radioresistance (ra″de-o-re-zis′tans). Resistance of matter to irradiation.

radioresistant (ra″de-o-re-zis′tant). Resisting the effects of radiation.

radioresponsive (ra″de-o-re-spon′siv). Reacting favorably to radiation.

radiosclerometer (ra″de-o-skle-rom′e-ter). Penetrometer.

radioscope (ra′de-o-skōp) [*radio-* + Gr. *skopein* to examine]. An instrument for detecting or studying roentgen rays or other forms of radioactivity.

radioscopy (ra″de-os′ko-pe) [*radio-* + Gr. *skopein* to examine]. Fluoroscopy.

radiosensibility (ra″de-o-sen″sĭ-bil′ĭ-te). Sensibility to irradiation.

radiosensitive (ra″de-o-sen′sĭ-tiv). Sensitive to radiant energy, as radium, roentgen ray, or other electric radiations.

radiosensitiveness (ra″de-o-sen′sĭ-tiv-nes). Radiosensibility.

radiosensitivity (ra″de-o-sen″sĭ-tiv′ĭ-te). Radiosensibility.

radiosodium (ra″de-o-so′de-um). A radioactive isotope of sodium. Na^{24} and Na^{22} are used in the study of blood flow, water balance, and peripheral vascular diseases.

radiostereoscopy (ra″de-o-ster″e-os′ko-pe) [*radio-* + Gr. *stereos* solid + *skopein* to examine]. The inspection of the interior organs by means of the roentgen rays.

radiostrontium (ra″de-o-stron′she-um). A radioactive isotope of strontium. Sr^{89} has a half-life of 55 days and has been used in the treatment of bone tumors.

radiosulfur (ra″de-o-sul′fur). A radioactive isotope of sulfur.

radiosurgery (ra″de-o-sur′jer-e). Surgical treatment by the use of radium.

radiotelemetry (ra″de-o-tel-em′e-tre). The determination of measurement of various factors, the specific data being transmitted by radio waves from the object of measurement to the recording apparatus.

radiotellurium (ra″de-o-tel-lu′re-um). Polonium.

radiothanatology (ra″de-o-than″ah-tol′o-je) [*radio-* + Gr. *thanatos* death + *logos* treatise]. The study of the effect of radiant energy on dead tissue.

radiotherapeutics (ra″de-o-ther″ah-pu′tiks). Radiotherapy.

radiotherapist (ra″de-o-ther′ah-pist). A specialist in radiotherapy.

radiotherapy (ra″de-o-ther′ah-pe) [*radio-* + Gr. *therapeia* cure]. The treatment of disease by roentgen rays or other radiant energy.

radiothermitis (ra″de-o-ther-mi′tis). Dermatitis caused by irradiation.

radiothermy (ra″de-o-ther′me) [*radio-* + Gr. *thermē* heat]. 1. Therapeutic use of radiant heat or of heat emanating from radioactive substances. 2. Short wave diathermy.

radiothorium (ra″de-o-tho′re-um). A radioactive isotope of thorium.

radiotomy (ra″de-ot′o-me) [*radio-* + Gr. *tomē* a cutting]. Body section roentgenography.

radiotoxemia (ra″de-o-tok-se′me-ah). Toxemia produced by a radioactive substance, or resulting from radiotherapy.

radiotransparency (ra″de-o-trans-par′en-se). The quality of being pervious to roentgen rays or other forms of radiation.

radiotransparent (ra″de-o-trans-par′ent). Permitting the passage of roentgen rays or of other forms of radiation.

radiotropic (ra″de-o-trop′ik). Influenced by radiation.

radiotropism (ra″de-ot′ro-pizm). A tropism with regard to radiation.

radio-ulnar (ra″de-o-ul′nar). Pertaining to the radius and ulna.

radium (ra′de-um) [so called from its radiant quality]. A rare metal, discovered in 1898 in pitchblende. Metallic radium is unstable in air, the chloride, bromide, sulfate, and carbonate being the salts used. It is a spontaneous source of radiation, and maintains a temperature of from 2 to 5°F. above the surrounding atmosphere. Its atomic number is 88; atomic weight, 226; symbol, Ra. Radium salts emit, besides heat and light, three distinct kinds of radiation, which are distinguished as α-, β-, and γ-rays, and also a radioactive gas called *radium emanation* or *radon*. The γ-rays are similar to roentgen rays, passing through many substances opaque to light. The β-rays are similar to cathode rays, and have less penetrating power than γ-rays. The α-rays have very slight penetrating power. Radium rays have been used in the treatment of lupus, eczema, psoriasis, xanthoma, mycosis fungoides, and other skin diseases; for the removal of papillomas, granulomas, and moles; for palliative treatment in carcinoma and sarcoma, and in myelogenous and lymphatic leukemia.

radiumization (ra″de-um-i-za′shun). Application of radium rays to a part.

radiumologist (ra″de-um-ol′o-jist). A practitioner who specializes in treatment by radium.

radiumology (ra″de-um-ol′o-je). The branch of radiology which deals with radium therapy.

radius (ra′de-us), pl. *ra′dii* [L. "spoke"]. 1. A line radiating from a center, or the circular limit defined by a fixed distance from an established point or center. 2. [N A, B N A] The bone on the outer or thumb side of the forearm. **r. cur′vus,** Madelung's deformity. **dispersion r.,** the extent of insect dispersion. **r. fix′us,** a straight line from the hormion to the inion. **radii of lens, ra′dii len′tis** [N A, B N A], imaginary lines extending from the midpoint of the axis of the lens of the eye to the capsule of the lens.

radix (ra′diks), pl. *radi′ces* [L.]. The lowermost part, or a structure by which something is firmly attached; used in anatomical nomenclature as a general term to designate the lowermost part, or a part by which a structure is anchored, as the portion of a hair, nail, or tooth that is buried in the tissues, or the part of a nerve adjacent to the center to which it is connected. Called also *root.* **r. ante′rior nervo′rum spina′lium** [B N A], r. ventralis nervorum spinalium. **r. ar′cus ver′tebrae** [B N A], pediculus arcus vertebralis. **r. bre′vis gan′glii cilia′ris** [B N A], r. oculomotoria ganglii ciliaris. **r. cochlea′ris ner′vi acus′tici** [B N A], r. inferior nervi vestibulocochlearis. **r. den′tis** [N A, B N A], the portion of a tooth which is covered by cementum, proximal to the neck of the tooth and ordinarily embedded in the dental alveolus. Called also *anatomical root.* **r. descen′dens for′nicis,** fasciculus mamillothalamicus. **r. descen′dens ner′vi trigem′ini** [B N A], tractus mesencephalicus nervi trigemini. **r. dorsa′lis nervo′rum spina′lium** [N A], the posterior, or sensory division of each spinal nerve, arising from the spinal cord and joining with the ventral, or motor, root to form the nerve before it emerges through the intervertebral foramen:

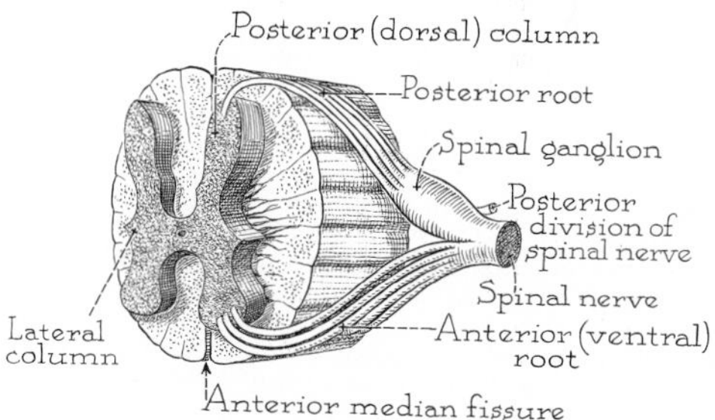

Section of cord showing origin of roots of spinal nerve. (Anson.)

each dorsal root bears a spinal ganglion. Called also *r. posterior nervorum spinalium* [B N A], and *dorsal root of spinal nerves.* **r. facia′lis,** N A alternative for *nervus canalis pterygoidei.* **r. infe′rior an′sae cervica′lis** [N A], a strand of filaments connecting the ansa cervicalis with branches of the second and third cervical nerves. Called also *inferior root of ansa cervicalis.* **r. infe′rior ner′vi vestibulocochlea′ris** [N A], the central continuation of the pars cochlearis nervi octavi from the spiral ganglion, passing dorsal to the inferior cerebellar peduncle to enter the brain. Called also *r. cochlearis nervi acustici* [B N A], and *inferior root of vestibulocochlear nerve.* **r. latera′lis ner′vi media′ni** [N A], the fibers contributed to the median nerve by the lateral cord of the brachial plexus. Called also *lateral root of median nerve.* **r. latera′lis**

trac'tus op'tici [N A, B N A], fibers from the optic tract that enter the lateral geniculate body. Called also *lateral root of optic tract.* **r. lin'guae** [N A, B N A], the portion of the tongue posterior to the sulcus terminalis, being attached below to the hyoid bone, and directed backward as well as upward. Called also *root of tongue.* **r. lon'ga gan'glii cilia'ris** [B N A], ramus communicans nervi nasociliaris cum ganglione ciliari. **r. media'lis ner'vi media'ni** [N A], the fibers contributed to the median nerve by the medial cord of the brachial plexus. Called also *medial root of median nerve.* **r. media'lis trac'tus op'tici** [N A, B N A], fibers from the optic tract that enter the superior colliculus and the pretectal region. Called also *medial root of optic tract.* **r. mesencephal'ica ner'vi trigem'ini,** tractus mesencephalicus nervi trigemini. **r. mesente'rii** [N A, B N A], the line of attachment of the mesentery to the posterior abdominal wall, extending from the duodenojejunal flexure at the left of the second lumbar vertebra diagonally downward to the upper border of the right sacroiliac articulation. Called also *root of mesentery.* **radi'ces mol'les gan'glii cilia'ris.** See *ramus sympathicus ad ganglion ciliare.* **r. moto'ria ner'vi trigem'ini** [N A], the smaller of the two collections of fibers by which the trigeminal nerve arises from the side of the pons, containing proprioceptive as well as motor fibers, and contributing motor fibers to the mandibular nerve. Called also *portio minor nervi trigemini* [B N A], and *motor root of trigeminal nerve.* **r. na'si** [N A, B N A], the upper portion of the nose, which is attached to the frontal bone. Called also *root of nose.* **r. ner'vi facia'lis** [B N A], the root of the facial nerve, consisting of fibers passing from the nucleus of the facial nerve to the facial colliculus, and from there to the ventral surface of the lower portion of the pons. Omitted in N A. **r. ner'vi op'tici,** tractus opticus. **r. oculomoto'ria gan'glii cilia'ris** [N A], a short, thick collection of fibers passing from the inferior branch of the oculomotor nerve to the posterior inferior portion of the ciliary ganglion. Called also *r. brevis ganglii ciliaris* [B N A], and *oculomotor root of ciliary ganglion.* **radi'ces parieta'les ve'nae ca'vae inferio'ris** [B N A], vessels draining blood from the abdominal wall into the inferior vena cava, including the venae lumbales and vena phrenica inferior. Omitted in N A. **r. pe'nis** [N A, B N A], the proximal, attached portion of the penis, consisting of the diverging crura of the corpora cavernosa and the bulb. Called also *root of penis.* **r. pi'li** [N A, B N A], the proximal portion of a hair embedded in the hair follicle. Called also *root of hair.* **r. poste'rior nervo'rum spina'lium** [B N A], r. dorsalis nervorum spinalium. **r. pulmo'nis** [N A, B N A], the attachment of either lung, comprising the structures entering and emerging at the hilus. Called also *root of lung.* **r. senso'ria ner'vi trigem'ini** [N A], the larger of the two collections of fibers by which the trigeminal nerve arises from the side of the pons, containing sensory fibers. It expands into a large flat ganglion (the trigeminal ganglion) which gives rise to the ophthalmic, maxillary, and mandibular nerves. Called also *portio major nervi trigemini* [B N A], and *sensory root of trigeminal nerve.* **r. supe'rior an'sae cervica'lis** [N A], fibers of the first or second cervical nerve, descending in company with the hypoglossal nerve, connecting it and the ansa cervicalis and helping supply the infrahyoid muscles. Called also *ramus descendens nervi hypoglossi* [B N A], and *superior root of ansa cervicalis.* **r. supe'rior ner'vi vestibulocochlea'ris** [N A], the central continuation of the pars vestibularis nervi octavi from the vestibular ganglion, entering the brain just lateral to the intermediate nerve and in front of the inferior cerebellar peduncle. Called also *r. vestibularis nervi acustici* [B N A], and *superior root of vestibulocochlear nerve.* **radi'ces sympath'icae gan'glii cilia'ris** [B N A]. See *ramus sympathicus ad ganglion ciliare.* **r. sympath'ica gan'glii submaxilla'ris** [B N A], ramus sympathicus ad ganglion submandibulare. **r. un'guis** [N A, B N A], the proximal portion of the nail, situated in the sulcus of the matrix of the nail. Called also *root of nail.* **r. ventra'lis nervo'rum spina'lium** [N A], the anterior, or motor, division of each spinal nerve, arising from the spinal cord and joining with the dorsal, or sensory, root to form the nerve before it emerges through the intervertebral foramen. Called also *r. anterior nervorum spinalium* [B N A], and *ventral root of spinal nerves.* **r. vestibula'ris ner'vi acus'tici** [B N A], r. superior nervi vestibulocochlearis. **radi'ces viscera'les ve'nae ca'vae inferio'ris** [B N A], vessels draining blood from the viscera of the abdominal and pelvic cavities to the inferior vena cava, including the venae hepaticae, renales, and suprarenales, the vena spermatica, testicularis, and ovaricus, and the plexus pampiniformis. Omitted in N A.

radon (ra'don). A colorless, gaseous, radioactive element, symbol Rn, atomic weight 222, atomic number 86, obtained by the breaking up of radium. Called also *radium emanation.* Cf. *radium.*

radzyge (rad'zi-gĕ). Radesyge.

raffinase (raf'ĭ-nās). An enzyme which splits up raffinose.

raffinose (raf'ĭ-nōs). Melitose.

rafle (rah'f'l). An eruptive disease of cattle in northern France.

rage (rāj). A state of violent anger. **sham r.,** an outburst of motor activity in a decorticated animal, resembling that manifested in fear and anger; a similar phenomenon may be observed in man in cases of insulin hypoglycemia or carbon monoxide poisoning.

raigan (ra'ĭ-gan). A native Chinese name for dried mushrooms, *Omphalia lapidescens;* anthelmintic.

Raillietina (ri"le-ĕ-ti'nah). A genus of tapeworms, many species of which infect chickens, turkeys and guinea fowl. *R. madagascarien'sis, R. asiat'ica* and *R. celeben'sis* have been reported from man.

raillietiniasis (ri"le-ĕ-tĭ-ni'ah-sis). Infection with a parasite of the genus Raillietina.

Rainey's corpuscles (ra'nēz) [George *Rainey,* English anatomist, 1801–1884]. See under *corpuscle.*

rale (rahl) [Fr. *râle* rattle]. Any abnormal respiratory sound heard in auscultation, and indicating some pathologic condition. Rales are distinguished as *dry* or *moist,* according to the absence or presence of fluid in the air passages, and are classified according to their location as *bronchial, cavernous, laryngeal, pleural, tracheal,* and *vesicular.* **amphoric r.,** a large, musical, and tinkling rale caused by the splashing of fluid in a cavity connected with a bronchus. **atelectatic r.,** a nonpathologic rale which is dissipated by deep breathing or coughing. Such rales are frequently heard in those who breathe feebly and superficially, when on deep inspiration the moist walls of the unexpanded alveoli are suddenly forced apart by the entering air; after a few deep inspirations such rales become lost. These rales are best observed at the margins or borders of the lung and are sometimes known as *marginal* or *border* rales. **border r.,** atelectatic r. **bubbling r.,** a moist rale, finer than a subcrepitant rale, heard in bronchitis, in the resolving stage of croupous pneumonia, and over small cavities. **cavernous r.,** a hollow and metallic rale caused by the alternate expansion and contraction of a pulmonary cavity during respiration. It is heard in the third stage of pulmonary tuberculosis. **clicking r.,** a small, sticky sound heard in inspiration, and caused by the passage of air through softening matter in the smaller bronchi. It occurs in the early stages of pulmonary tuberculosis. **collapse r.,** a fine crepitant rale heard over collapsed lung tissue; also at the base of the healthy lung of a bedridden patient: due to incomplete expansion of the air vesicles. **consonating r.,** a clear, ringing sound produced in bronchial tubes that are surrounded by consolidation tissues: heard in tuberculous pneumonia. **crackling r.,** subcrepitant r. **crepitant r.,** a very fine rale, resembling the sound produced by rubbing a lock of hair between the fingers or by particles of salt thrown on fire. It is heard at the end of inspiration in the early stages of croupous pneumonia. **dry r.,** a rale produced by the presence of viscid secretion in the bronchial tubes or by thickening of the walls of the tubes. It has a whistling, musical, or squeaking quality. Dry rales are heard in asthma and bronchitis. **extrathoracic r.,** a rale produced in the larynx or trachea. **gurgling r.,** a very coarse rale resembling the bursting of large bubbles. They are heard over large cavities that contain fluid, and in the trachea in the death rattle. **guttural r.,** a rale produced in the throat. **Hirtz's r.,** a moist, subcrepitant, metallic rale indicative of tuberculous softening. **r. in'dux,** a crepitant rale heard in the stage of beginning consolidation in pneumonia. **laryngeal r.,** a rale produced in the larynx. **marginal r.,** atelectatic r. **metallic r.,** consonating r. **moist r.,** a rale produced by the presence of liquid in the bronchial tubes. **mucous r., r. muqueux,** a modified subcrepitant rale resembling the sound produced by blowing through a pipe into soapy water. It is caused by the bursting of viscid bubbles in the bronchial tubes: heard in emphysema of lungs. **pleural r.,** a pleural friction sound. **r. redux, r. de retour,** an unequal crackling sound produced by air passing through fluid in a bronchial tube: heard in the resolution stage of pneumonia. **sibilant r.,** a hissing sound resembling that produced by suddenly separating two oiled surfaces. It is produced by the presence of a viscid secretion in the bronchial tubes or by thickening of the walls of the tubes: heard in asthma, bronchitis, and in the beginning of tuberculosis of the lungs. **Skoda's r.,** a bronchial rale heard through consolidated tissue in pneumonia. **sonorous r.,** a small, moist sound resembling the cooing of a dove, produced by the passage of air through mucus in the capillary bronchial tubes: heard in capillary bronchitis and asthma. **subcrepitant r.,** a fine, moist rale heard in conditions that are associated with liquid in the smaller tubes, as in bronchitis, pulmonary edema, and phthisis in the early stages. Called also *crackling r.* **tracheal r.,** a rale produced in the trachea. **vesicular r.,** crepitant r. **whistling r.,** sibilant r.

Ralfe's test (ralfs) [Charles Henry *Ralfe*, English physician, 1842–1896]. See under *tests*.

ramal (ra'mal). Pertaining to a ramus; branching.

Raman effect (ram'an) [Sir Chandnasekhara Venkata *Raman*, Indian physicist, born 1888; winner of the Nobel prize for physics in 1930]. See under *effect*.

ramaninjana (ram″an-in-jah'nah). A form of palmus, or jumping disease, prevailing in Madagascar.

R.A.M.C. Abbreviation for *Royal Army Medical Corps*.

Ramdohr's suture (rahm'dōrz) [Caesar A. von *Ramdohr*, American surgeon, 1855–1912]. See under *suture*.

ramex (ra'meks) [L.]. 1. A hernia. 2. Varicocele.

rami (ra'mi) [L.]. Plural of *ramus*.

Ramibacterium (ra″me-bak-te're-um) [L. *ramus* branch + *bacterium*]. A genus of microorganisms of the tribe Lactobacilleae, family Lactobacillaceae, order Eubacteriales, made up of nonsporulating, anaerobic, gram-positive bacilli found in the intestinal tract and occasionally associated with purulent infections.

ramicotomy (ram″ĭ-kot'o-me) [*ramus* + Gr. *tomē* a cutting]. Ramisection.

ramification (ram″ĭ-fi-ka'shun) [*ramus* + L. *facere* to make]. 1. Distribution in branches. 2. A branch or set of branches. 3. The manner of branching.

ramify (ram'ĭ-fi) [*ramus* + L. *facere* to make]. 1. To branch; to diverge in various directions. 2. To traverse in branches.

ramisection (ram″ĭ-sek'shun) [*ramus* + L. *sectio* a cutting]. The operation of cutting the rami communicantes of the sympathetic (*sympathetic ramisection*): done for the relief of spastic paralysis.

ramisectomy (ram″ĭ-sek'to-me). Ramisection.

ramitis (ram-i'tis) [L. *ramus* branch + *-itis*]. Inflammation of a nerve root.

Rammstedt (rahm'stet). See *Ramstedt*.

ramollissement (rah″mol-ēs-maw') [Fr.]. Softening.

ramollitio (ram″o-lish'e-o) [L.]. Softening. **r. ret'inae,** softening of the retina.

Ramon's flocculation test [Gaston *Ramon*, French bacteriologist]. See under *tests*.

Ramón y Cajal's cells, stain (rah-mōn e kahal'). See *Cajal*, and under *cell* and *stain*.

Ramond's sign (ram-onz') [Louis *Ramond*, French internist, 1879–1952]. See under *sign*.

ramose (ra'mos) [L. *ramus* branch]. Branching; having many branches.

rampart (ram'part). A broad, encircling embankment. **maxillary r.,** a ridge or mound of epithelial cells seen in that portion of the jaw of the embryo which is to become the alveolar border.

Ramsden's ocular (ramz'denz) [Jesse *Ramsden*, English optician, 1735–1800]. See under *eyepiece*.

Ramstedt operation (rahm'stet) [Conrad *Ramstedt*, surgeon in Münster, born 1867]. See *Fredet-Ramstedt operation*, under *operation*.

ramulus (ram'u-lus), pl. *ram'uli* [L., dim. of *ramus*]. A small branch or terminal division; an official term in B N A, but omitted in N A.

ramus (ra'mus), pl. *ra'mi* [L.]. A branch; used in anatomical nomenclature as a general term to designate a smaller structure given off by a larger one, or into which the larger structure, such as a blood vessel or nerve, divides. **r. acetabula'ris arte'riae circumflex'ae fem'oris media'lis** [N A], a branch of the medial circumflex artery of the thigh, distributed to the head of the femur and to the acetabulum. Called also *r. acetabuli arteriae circumflexae femoris medialis* [B N A], and *acetabular branch of medial circumflex femoral artery*. **r. acetabula'ris arte'riae obtura'to'riae** [N A], a branch of the obturator artery that is distributed to the hip joint. Called also *arteria acetabuli* [B N A], and *acetabular branch of obturator artery*. **r. acetab'uli arte'riae circumflex'ae fem'oris media'lis** [B N A], r. acetabularis arteriae circumflexae femoris medialis. **r. acromia'lis arte'riae suprascapula'ris** [N A], a branch of the suprascapular artery distributed to the acromion process. Called also *r. acromialis arteriae transversae scapulae* [B N A], and *acromial branch of suprascapular artery*. **r. acromia'lis arte'riae thoracoacromia'lis** [N A, B N A], a branch of the thoracoacromial artery that is distributed to the deltoid muscle and acromion process. Called also *acromial branch of thoracoacromial artery*. **r. acromia'lis arte'riae transver'sae scap'ulae** [B N A], r. acromialis arteriae suprascapularis. **ra'mi ad pon'tem arte'riae basila'ris** [N A, B N A], branches of the basilar artery that are distributed to the pons and brain stem. Called also *pontine branches of basilar artery*. **ra'mi alveola'res superio'res anterio'res ner'vi infraorbita'lis** [N A, B N A], branches from the infraorbital nerve that innervate the incisor and canine teeth of the upper jaw and help form the superior dental plexus; modality, general sensory. Called also *anterior superior alveolar branches of infraorbital nerve*. **r. alveola'ris supe'rior me'dius ner'vi infraorbita'lis** [N A, B N A], a branch from the infraorbital nerve that innervates the premolar teeth of the upper jaw, helping form the superior dental plexus; modality, general sensory. Called also *middle superior alveolar branch of infraorbital nerve.* **ra′mi alveola′res superio′res posterio′res ner′vi maxilla′ris** [N A], branches from the maxillary nerve that innervate the maxillary sinus and molar teeth of the upper jaw, thus helping form the superior dental plexus; modality, general sensory. Called also *posterior superior alveolar branches of maxillary nerve.* **r. anastomot′icus** [B N A], a structure connecting one nerve to another. See terms beginning *r. communicans.* **r. anastomot′icus arte′riae menin′geae me′diae cum arte′ria lacrima′li** [N A], a branch of the middle meningeal artery that is distributed to the orbit and anastomoses with the recurrent meningeal branch of the lacrimal artery. **r. anastomot′icus gan′glii o′tici cum chor′da tym′pani** [B N A], r. communicans ganglii otici cum chorda tympani. **r. anastomot′icus gan′glii o′tici cum ner′vo auriculotempora′li** [B N A], r. communicans ganglii otici cum nervo auriculotemporali. **r. anastomot′icus gan′glii o′tici cum ner′vo spino′so** [B N A], r. communicans ganglii otici cum ramo meningeo nervi mandibularis. **ra′mi anastomot′ici ner′vi auriculotempora′lis cum ner′vo facia′li** [B N A], rami communicantes nervi auriculotemporalis cum nervo faciali. **r. anastomot′icus ner′vi facia′lis cum ner′vo glossopharyn′geo** [B N A], r. communicans nervi facialis cum nervo glossopharyngeo. **r. anastomot′icus ner′vi facia′lis cum plex′u tympan′ico** [B N A], r. communicans nervi facialis cum plexu tympanico. **r. anastomot′icus ner′vi glossopharyn′gei cum ra′mo auricula′ri ner′vi va′gi** [B N A], r. communicans nervi glossopharyngei cum ramo auriculari nervi vagi. **r. anastomot′icus ner′vi lacrima′lis cum ner′vo zygomat′ico** [B N A], r. communicans nervi lacrimalis cum nervo zygomatico. **ra′mi anastomot′ici ner′vi lingua′lis cum ner′vo hypoglos′so** [B N A], rami communicantes nervi lingualis cum nervo hypoglosso. **r. anastomot′icus ner′vi media′ni cum ner′vo ulna′ri** [B N A], r. communicans nervi mediani cum nervo ulnari. **r. anastomot′icus ner′vi va′gi cum ner′vo glossopharyn′geo** [B N A], r. communicans nervi vagi cum nervo glossopharyngeo. **r. anastomot′icus perona′eus ner′vi peronae′i commu′nis** [B N A], r. communicans peroneus nervi peronei communis. **r. anastomot′icus ulna′ris ner′vi radia′lis** [B N A], r. communicans ulnaris nervi radialis. **ra′mi anterio′res arteria′rum intercosta′lium** [B N A], anterior branches of intercostal arteries. Omitted in N A. **r. ante′rior arte′riae obturato′riae** [N A, B N A], a branch of the obturator artery that passes forward around the medial margin of the obturator foramen, on the obturator membrane, and is distributed to the obturator and adductor muscles. Called also *anterior branch of obturator artery.* **r. ante′rior arte′riae recurren′tis ulna′ris** [N A], a branch of the ulnar recurrent artery that helps supply the pronator teres and brachialis muscles and adjacent skin. Called also *anterior branch of ulnar recurrent artery.* **r. ante′rior arte′riae thyroi′deae superio′ris** [N A], a branch of the superior thyroid artery that helps supply the upper part of the gland, anastomosing with its fellow of the opposite side along the upper border of the isthmus. Called also *anterior branch of superior thyroid artery.* **r. ante′rior ascen′dens fissu′rae cer′ebri latera′lis [Syl′vii]** [B N A], r. ascendens sulci lateralis cerebri. **r. ante′rior horizonta′lis fissu′rae cer′ebri latera′lis [Syl′vii]** [B N A], r. anterior sulci lateralis cerebri. **r. ante′rior ner′vi auricula′ris mag′ni** [N A, B N A], a branch of the greater auricular nerve that is distributed to the skin of the face over the parotid gland; modality, general sensory. Called also *anterior branch of greater auricular nerve.* **ra′mi anterio′res nervo′rum cervica′lium** [B N A], rami ventrales nervorum cervicalium. **r. ante′rior ner′vi coccyg′ei** [B N A], r. ventralis nervi coccygei. **r. ante′rior ner′vi cuta′nei antebrach′ii media′lis** [N A], the branch of the medial cutaneous nerve of the forearm that innervates the skin of the front and medial aspect of the forearm; modality, general sensory. Called also *r. volaris nervi cutanei antibrachii medialis* [B N A], and *anterior branch of medial cutaneous nerve of forearm.* **r. ante′rior ner′vi laryn′gei inferio′ris** [B N A], anterior branch of inferior laryngeal nerve. Omitted in N A. **ra′mi anterio′res nervo′rum lumba′lium** [B N A], rami ventrales nervorum lumbalium. **r. ante′rior ner′vi obturato′rii** [N A, B N A], a branch of the obturator nerve that supplies fibers to the gracilis and the adductor longus and brevis muscles and sometimes to the pectineus, as well as to the skin of the medial side of the thigh and leg; modality, motor and general sensory. Called also *anterior branch of obturator nerve.* **r. ante′rior nervo′rum spina′lium** [B N A], r. ventralis nervorum spinalium. **ra′mi anterio′res nervo′rum thoraca′lium** [B N A], rami ventrales nervorum thoracicorum. **r. ante′rior ramo′rum cutaneo′rum latera′lium [pectora′lium et abdomina′lium] arterio′rum intercosta′lium** [B N A], the anterior branch of the lateral cutaneous branches of the intercostal arteries. Omitted in N A. **r. ante′rior ramo′rum cutaneo′rum latera′lium [pectora′lium et abdomina′lium] nervo′rum intercosta′lium** [B N A], the anterior branch of the lateral cutaneous branches of the intercostal nerve. Omitted in N A. **r. ante′rior sul′ci latera′lis cer′ebri** [N A], a branch of the lateral cerebral sulcus that runs rostrally a short distance into the frontal lobe. Called also *r. anterior horizontalis fissurae cerebri lateralis [Sylvii]* [B N A], and *anterior branch of lateral cerebral sulcus.* **ra′mi arterio′si interlobula′res hep′atis** [B N A], arteriae interlobulares hepatis. **ra′mi articula′res arte′riae ge′nu supre′mae** [B N A], **ra′mi articula′res arte′riae ge′nus descenden′tis** [N A], branches of the descending genicular artery that pass downward in the vastus medialis muscle and help supply the knee joint. Called also *articular branches of descending genicular artery.* **r. ascen′dens arte′riae circumflex′ae fem′oris latera′lis** [N A, B N A], a branch of the lateral circumflex artery of the thigh, running upward along the trochanteric line of the femur and between the gluteus medius and minimus muscles, and anastomosing with branches of the superior gluteal artery. It helps supply the upper thigh muscles. Called also *ascending branch of lateral circumflex femoral artery.* **r. ascen′dens arte′riae circumflex′ae fem′oris media′lis** [N A], a branch of the medial circumflex artery of the thigh, ascending in front of the quadratus femoris muscle to the trochanteric fossa, and there anastomosing with glutteal arteries. Called also *ascending branch of medial circumflex femoral artery.* **r. ascen′dens arte′riae circumflex′ae il′ium profun′dae** [N A], a branch leaving the deep circumflex iliac artery near the anterior superior iliac spine, rising between and distributing to the transversus abdominis and internal oblique muscles. Called also *ascending branch of deep circumflex iliac artery.* **r. ascen′dens arte′riae transver′sae col′li** [B N A], r. superficialis arteriae transversae colli. **r. ascen′dens sul′ci latera′lis cer′ebri** [N A], a branch of the lateral cerebral sulcus that runs superiorly a short distance into the frontal lobe. Called also *r. anterior ascendens fissurae cerebri lateralis [Sylvii]* [B N A], and *ascending branch of lateral cerebral sulcus.* **ra′mi auricula′res anterio′res arte′riae tempora′lis superficia′lis** [N A, B N A], branches of the superficial temporal artery that supply the lateral aspect of the pinna and the external acoustic meatus. Called also *anterior auricular branches of superficial temporal artery.* **r. auricula'ris arte'riae auricula'ris posterio'ris** [N A, B N A], a branch supplying the pinna and adjacent skin. Called also *auricular branch of posterior auricular artery.* **r. auricula'ris arte'riae occipita'lis** [N A, B N A], an inconstant branch of the occipital artery that helps supply the medial aspect of the pinna. Called also *auricular branch of occipital artery.* **r. auricula'ris ner'vi va'gi** [N A, B N A], a branch arising from the superior ganglion of the vagus, innervating the medial surface of the pinna, the floor of the external acoustic meatus, and the adjacent part of the tympanic membrane; modality, general sensory. Called also *auricular branch of vagus nerve.* **ra'mi bronchia'les anterio'res ner'vi va'gi** [B N A]. See *rami bronchiales nervi vagi.* **ra'mi bronchia'les aor'tae thora'cicae** [N A], branches arising from the thoracic aorta to supply the bronchi and lower trachea, and passing along the posterior sides of the bronchi to ramify about the respiratory bronchioles; distributed also to adjacent lymph nodes, pulmonary vessels, and pericardium, and to part of the esophagus. Called also *arteriae bronchiales* [B N A], and *bronchial branches of thoracic aorta.* **ra'mi bronchia'les arte'riae mamma'riae inter'nae** [B N A], rami bronchiales arteriae thoracicae internae. **ra'mi bronchia'les arte'riae thora'cicae inter'nae** [N A], small, variable branches of the internal thoracic artery, with distribution to the bronchi and trachea. Called also *rami bronchiales arteriae mammariae internae* [B N A], and *bronchial branches of internal thoracic artery.* **ra'mi bronchia'les bron'chi** [B N A], a name applied to the first, extrapulmonary divisions of the main bronchi, the eparterial and hyparterial bronchial rami. Omitted in N A. **r. bronchia'lis eparteria'lis** [B N A], a name given to the superior lobar bronchus on the right, which arises above the level of the pulmonary artery. **r. bronchia'les hyparteria'les** [B N A], a name given to the middle and inferior lobar bronchi on the right and the lobar bronchi on the left, all of which arise below the level of the pulmonary artery. **ra'mi bronchia'les ner'vi va'gi** [N A], branches of the vagus that help innervate the bronchi and the pulmonary vessels, participating both anteriorly and posteriorly in the pulmonary plexus; modality, parasympathetic and visceral afferent. **ra'mi bronchia'les posterio'res ner'vi va'gi** [B N A]. See *rami bronchiales nervi vagi.* **ra'mi bronchia'les pulmo'nis** [B N A], a name given intrapulmonary bronchial divisions smaller than the main bronchi and larger than the bronchioles; omitted in N A, which classifies them as lobar and segmental bronchi, and branches (rami) of the latter. **ra'mi bronchia'les segmento'rum** [N A], smaller branches arising from the segmental bronchi. Called also *intrasegmental bronchial branches.* **ra'mi bucca'les ner'vi facia'lis** [N A, B N A], branches of the facial nerve that innervate the zygomatic, levator labii superioris, buccinator, and orbicularis oris muscles; modality, motor and general sensory. Called also *buccal branches of facial nerve.* **ra'mi calca'nei latera'les arte'riae peronae'ae** [B N A], rami calcanei ramorum malleolarium lateralium arteriae peroneae. **ra'mi calca'nei latera'les ner'vi sura'lis** [N A, B N A], branches of the sural nerve innervating the skin on the back of the leg and the lateral side of the foot and heel; modality, general sensory. Called also *lateral calcaneal branches of sural nerve.* **ra'mi calca'nei media'les arte'riae peronae'ae** [B N A], rami calcanei ramorum malleolarium medialium arteriae peroneae. **ra'mi calca'nei media'les ner'vi tibia'lis** [N A, B N A], branches of the tibial nerve supplying the medial side of the heel and of the posterior part of the sole; modality, general sensory. Called also *medial calcaneal branches of tibial nerve.* **ra'mi calca'nei ramo'rum malleola'rium latera'lium arte'riae perone'ae** [N A], branches arising from the lateral malleolar branches of the peroneal artery and distributed to the lateral aspect and back of the heel. Called also *rami calcanei laterales arteriae peronaeae* [B N A], and *calcaneal branches of lateral malleolar branches of peroneal artery.* **ra'mi calca'nei ramo'rum malleola'rium media'lium arte'riae perone'ae** [N A], branches that arise from the medial malleolar branches of the peroneal artery, or sometimes from the posterior tibial artery just proximal to its division, and are distributed to the medial aspect and back of the heel. Called also *rami calcanei mediales arteriae peronaeae* [B N A], and *calcaneal branches of medial malleolar branches of peroneal artery.* **ra'mi capsula'res arte'riae re'nis** [N A, B N A], branches of the renal artery that supply the renal capsule. Called also *capsular branches of renal artery.* **ra'mi cardi'aci inferio'res ner'vi recurren'tis** [B N A], **ra'mi cardi'aci inferio'res ner'vi va'gi** [N A], branches arising in the thorax from the vagus nerves, chiefly the right, and from the recurrent laryngeal nerves close to their origins from the vagus nerves, passing then to the cardiac plexus (intramural cardiac ganglia); modality, parasympathetic and visceral afferent. Called also *inferior cardiac branches of recurrent laryngeal nerve* and *inferior cardiac branches of vagus nerve.* **ra'mi cardi'aci superio'res ner'vi va'gi** [N A, B N A], branches arising from the vagus in the cervical region and passing down to the cardiac plexus (intramural cardiac ganglia); modality, parasympathetic and visceral afferent. Called also *superior cardiac branches of vagus nerve.* **ra'mi caroticotympan'ici arte'riae carot'idis inter'nae** [N A], branches of the internal carotid artery that supply the tympanic cavity. Called also *caroticotympanic branches of internal carotid artery.* **r. car'peus dorsa'lis arte'riae radia'lis** [N A, B N A], a branch of the radial artery that runs medially deep to the extensor tendons, and helps form the dorsal carpal rete. Called also *dorsal carpal branch of radial artery.* **r. car'peus dorsa'lis arte'riae ulna'ris** [N A, B N A], a variable branch of the ulnar artery that runs laterally deep to the tendons of the ulnar muscles of the wrist, helping to form the dorsal carpal rete. Called also *dorsal carpal branch of ulnar artery.* **r. car'peus palma'ris arte'riae radia'lis** [N A], a branch that passes medially behind the flexor tendons on the palmar aspect of the wrist and forms a network with a corresponding branch of the ulnar artery. Called also *r. carpeus volaris arteriae radialis* [B N A], and *palmar carpal branch of radial artery.* **r. car'peus palma'ris arte'riae ulna'ris** [N A], a branch that passes laterally behind the flexor tendons on the palmar aspect of the wrist and forms a network with a corresponding branch of the radial artery. Called also *r. carpeus volaris arteriae ulnaris* [B N A], and *palmar carpal branch of ulnar artery.* **r. car'peus vola'ris arte'riae radia'lis** [B N A], r. carpeus palmaris arteriae radialis. **r. car'peus vola'ris arte'riae ulna'ris** [B N A], r. carpeus palmaris arteriae ulnaris. **ra'mi celi'aci ner'vi va'gi** [N A], branches that arise from both the anterior and posterior vagal trunks and join the celiac plexus; modality, parasympathetic and visceral afferent. Called also *rami coeliaci plexus gastrici posterioris* [B N A], and *celiac branches of vagus nerve.* **ra'mi centra'les arte'riae cer'ebri anterio'ris** [N A], branches of the anterior cerebral artery that ascend into the base of the brain in front of the optic chiasma and are distributed to the hypothalamus, caudate nucleus, and internal capsule. Called also *central branches of anterior cerebral artery.* **ra'mi centra'les arte'riae cer'ebri me'diae** [N A], central branches that pass through the anterior perforated substance, comprising chiefly the rami striati. Called also *central* *branches of medial cerebral artery.* **ra'mi centra'les arte'riae cer'ebri posterio'ris** [N A], branches of the posterior cerebral artery that supply the thalamic area and, by way of the choroid branches, the choroid plexuses of the third and lateral ventricles. Called also *central branches of posterior cerebral artery.* **r. choroi'deus arte'riae cer'ebri posterio'ris** [N A], a branch of the posterior cerebral artery that supplies the choroid plexuses of the third and lateral ventricles. Called also *choroid branch of posterior cerebral artery.* **ra'mi choroi'dei posterio'res arte'riae cer'ebri posterio'ris** [N A], a name applied to the posterior choroidal branches of the posterior cerebral artery when it supplies more than one branch to the choroid plexus. **r. circumflex'us arte'riae corona'riae sinis'trae** [N A, B N A], a branch of the left coronary artery that curves around to the back of the left ventricle in the coronary sulcus, supplying the left ventricle and left atrium. Called also *circumflex branch of left coronary artery.* **r. circumflex'us fib'ulae arte'riae tibia'lis posterio'ris** [N A], a branch of the posterior tibial artery, winding laterally around the neck of the fibula, helping supply the soleus muscle and contributing to the anastomosis around the knee joint. Called also *r. fibularis arteriae tibialis posterioris* [B N A], and *fibular circumflex branch of posterior tibial artery.* **r. clavicula'ris arte'riae thoracoacromia'lis** [N A], a vessel that passes medially to supply the subclavius muscle. Called also *clavicular branch of thoracoacromial artery.* **r. coch'leae arte'riae auditi'vae inter'nae** [B N A], **r. cochlea'ris arte'riae labyrin'thi** [N A], a vessel supplying the cochlea from the labyrinthine artery. Called also *cochlear branch of labyrinthine artery.* **ra'mi coeli'aci plex'us gas'trici posterio'ris** [B N A], rami celiaci nervi vagi. **r. collatera'lis arteria'rum intercosta'lium posterio'rum [III–XI]** [N A], a branch helping supply the thoracic wall, arising from the posterior intercostal arteries near the angle of the rib and running forward in the lower part of the corresponding intercostal space. Called also *collateral branch of posterior intercostal arteries [III–XI].* **r. col'li ner'vi facia'lis** [N A, B N A], a branch of the facial nerve that lies deep to and innervates the platysma muscle; modality, motor. Called also *cervical branch of facial nerve.* **r. commu'nicans.** 1. [N A, B N A] A communicating branch between two nerves. 2. [B N A] A branch connecting two arteries. Omitted in N A. **r. commu'nicans arte'riae perone'ae** [N A], a communicating branch between the peroneal and the posterior tibial arteries, distributed to the interosseous membrane and supramalleolar region. Called also *communicating branch of peroneal artery.* **r. commu'nicans gan'glii cilia'ris cum ner'vo nasocilia'ri** [N A], a branch carrying sensory fibers from the cornea, iris, and ciliary body, and passing through the ciliary ganglion to reach the nasociliary nerve. Called also *communicating branch of ciliary ganglion with nasociliary nerve.* **r. commu'nicans gan'glii o'tici cum chor'da tym'pani** [N A], a small branch that interconnects the otic ganglion and the chorda tympani. Called also *r. anastomoticus ganglii otici cum chorda tympani* [B N A], and *communicating branch of otic ganglion with chorda tympani.* **r. commu'nicans gan'glii o'tici cum ner'vo auriculotempora'li** [N A], a branch carrying postganglionic parasympathetic fibers from the otic ganglion to the auriculotemporal nerve for distribution to the parotid gland. Called also *r. anastomoticus ganglii otici cum nervo auriculotemporali* [B N A], and *communicating branch of otic ganglion with auriculotemporal nerve.* **r. commu'nicans gan'glii o'tici cum ra'mo menin'geo ner'vi mandibula'ris** [N A, B N A], a branch that carries autonomic fibers destined for the meninges from the otic ganglion to the meningeal branch of the mandibular nerve. Called also *r. anastomoticus ganglii otici cum ramo meningeo nervi mandibularis* [B N A], and *communicating branch of otic ganglion with meningeal branch of mandibular nerve.* **ra'mi communican'tes gan'glii submandibula'ris cum ner'vo lingua'li** [N A], **ra'mi communican'tes gan'glii submaxilla'ris cum ner'vo lingua'li** [B N A], branches which interconnect the lingual nerve and the submandibular ganglion, and by which the ganglion is suspended from the nerve. They carry preganglionic fibers that derive from the chorda tympani and synapse in the submandibular ganglion, and postganglionic fibers. Called also *communicating branches of submandibular ganglion with lingual nerve.* **ra'mi communican'tes ner'vi auriculotempora'lis cum ner'vo facia'li** [N A], branches containing sensory fibers from the auriculotemporal nerve that join the facial nerve within the parotid gland, to be distributed with branches of the latter. Called also *rami anastomotici nervi auriculotemporalis cum nervo faciali* [B N A], and *communicating branches of auriculotemporal nerve with facial nerve.* **r. commu'nicans ner'vi facia'lis cum ner'vo glossopharyn'geo** [N A], a branch that interconnects the glossopharyngeal nerve and the facial nerve after emergence of the latter from the stylomastoid foramen. Called also *r. anastomoticus nervi facialis cum nervo glossopharyngeo* [B N A], and *communicating branch of facial nerve with glossopharyngeal nerve.* **r. commu'nicans ner'vi facia'lis cum plex'u tympan'ico** [N A], a branch that interconnects the facial nerve and the tympanic plexus of the glossopharyngeal nerve. Called also *r. anastomoticus nervi facialis cum plexu tympanico* [B N A], and *communicating branch of facial nerve with tympanic plexus.* **r. commu'nicans ner'vi glossopharyn'gei cum ra'mo auricula'ri ner'vi va'gi** [N A], a small branch connecting the glossopharyngeal nerve with the auricular branch of the vagus nerve. Called also *r. anastomoticus nervi glossopharyngei cum ramo auriculari nervi vagi* [B N A], and *communicating branch of glossopharyngeal nerve with auricular branch of vagus nerve.* **r. commu'nicans ner'vi lacrima'lis cum ner'vo zygomat'ico** [N A], a branch that carries parasympathetic postganglionic fibers originating in the pterygopalatine ganglion and destined for the lacrimal gland. Called also *r. anastomoticus nervi lacrimalis cum nervo zygomatico* [B N A], and *communicating branch of lacrimal nerve with zygomatic nerve.* **r. commu'nicans ner'vi laryn'gei recurren'tis cum ra'mo laryn'geo inter'no** [N A], a small branch interconnecting the recurrent laryngeal nerve with the internal branch of the superior laryngeal nerve, behind or in the posterior cricoarytenoid muscle. Called also *communicating branch of recurrent laryngeal nerve with internal laryngeal branch.* **r. commu'nicans ner'vi laryn'gei superio'ris cum ner'vo laryn'geo inferio're** [N A], a small branch interconnecting the internal branch of the superior laryngeal nerve with the inferior laryngeal nerve, behind or in the posterior cricoarytenoid muscle. Called also *r. anastomoticus nervi laryngei superioris cum nervo laryngeo inferiore* [B N A], and *communicating branch of superior laryngeal nerve with inferior laryngeal nerve.* **r. commu'nicans ner'vi lingua'lis cum chor'da tym'pani** [N A], the chorda tympani as it joins the lingual nerve in the infratemporal fossa medial to the lateral pterygoid muscle; modality, parasympathetic and special sensory. Called also *communicating branch of lingual nerve with chorda tympani.* **ra'mi communican'tes ner'vi lingua'lis cum ner'vo hypoglos'so** [N A], plexiform terminal branches interconnecting the lingual and hypoglossal nerves just in front of the hyoglossus muscle. Called also *rami anastomotici nervi lingualis cum nervo hypoglosso* [B N A], and *communicating branches of lingual nerve with hypoglossal nerve.* **r. commu'nicans ner'vi**

media′ni cum ner′vo ulna′ri [N A], a small branch across the flexor digitorum profundus muscle, connecting the median with the ulnar nerve. Called also *r. anastomoticus nervi mediani cum nervo ulnari* [B N A], and *communicating branch of median nerve with ulnar nerve.* **r. commu′nicans ner′vi nasocilia′ris cum ganglio′ne cilia′ri** [N A], a slender branch of the nasociliary nerve passing forward to the ciliary ganglion and entering its posterosuperior portion. Called also *radix longa ganglii ciliaris* [B N A], and *communicating branch of nasociliary nerve with ciliary ganglion.* **ra′mi communi-can′tes nervo′rum spina′lium** [N A], branches connecting spinal nerves with sympathetic ganglia, each spinal nerve receiving a gray communicating ramus, and the thoracic and upper lumbar spinal nerves having in addition a white communicating ramus. Called also *communicating branches of spinal nerves.* **r. commu′nicans ner′vi va′gi cum ner′vo glossopharyn′geo** [N A], a small branch connecting the auricular branch of the vagus nerve with the glossopharyngeal nerve. Called also *r. anastomoticus nervi vagi cum nervo glossopharyngeo* [B N A], and *communicating branch of vagus nerve with glossopharyngeal nerve.* **r. commu′nicans perone′us ner′vi perone′i commu′nis** [N A], a small branch arising from the lateral sural cutaneous nerve and further down joining the medial sural cutaneous to form the sural nerve. Called also *r. anastomoticus peronaeus nervi peronaei communis* [B N A], and *peroneal communicating branch of common peroneal nerve.* **r. commu′nicans ulna′ris ner′vi radia′lis** [N A], a small branch in the hand that interconnects the most medial dorsal digital nerve from the superficial branch of the radial nerve with the adjacent most lateral dorsal digital nerve from the dorsal branch of the ulnar nerve. Called also *r. anastomoticus ulnaris nervi radialis* [B N A], and *ulnar communicating branch of radial nerve.* **ra′mi cortica′les arte′riae cer′ebri ante-rio′ris** [N A], orbital, frontal, and parietal branches of the anterior cerebral artery that supply the cortex of the frontal and parietal lobes. Called also *cortical branches of anterior cerebral artery.* **ra′mi cortica′les arte′riae cer′-ebri me′diae** [N A], orbital, frontal, temporal, and parietal branches from the middle cerebral artery, distributed to the cortex over the insula and the lateral surface of the hemisphere. Called also *cortical branches of middle cerebral artery.* **ra′mi cortica′les arte′riae cer′ebri poste-rio′ris** [N A], temporal, occipital, and parieto-occipital branches from the posterior cerebral artery, distributed to the cortex of the inferior and medial surfaces of the temporal and occipital lobes. Called also *cortical branches of posterior cerebral artery.* **r. costa′lis latera′lis arte′-riae mamma′riae inter′nae** [B N A], **r. costa′lis latera′lis arte′riae thora′cicae inter′nae** [N A], an occasional branch passing inferolaterally behind the ribs, supplying ribs and costal cartilages, and anastomosing with the posterior intercostal arteries. Called also *lateral costal branch of internal thoracic artery.* **r. crico-thyroi′deus arte′riae thyroi′deae supe-rio′ris** [N A], a vessel running medially over the cricothyroid muscle, supplying the cricothyroid ligament, and anastomosing with its fellow of the opposite side. Called also *cricothyroid branch of superior thyroid artery.* **ra′mi cuta′nei ante-rio′res ner′vi femora′lis** [N A, B N A], branches from the femoral nerve that innervate the skin on the front and medial aspect of the thigh and patella; modality, general sensory. Called also *anterior cutaneous branches of femoral nerve.* **r. cuta′neus ante′rior ner′vi ilio-hypogas′trici** [N A, B N A], a branch of the iliohypogastric nerve that runs forward between the internal and external oblique muscles and innervates the skin over the pubis; modality, general sensory. Called also *anterior cutaneous branch of iliohypogastric nerve.* **r. cuta′neus ante′rior [pectora′lis et abdomina′lis] nervo′rum intercosta′lium** [N A, B N A], a branch arising from the intercostal nerves and helping innervate the skin in the anteromedial thoracic and abdominal regions, with medial mammary branches given off in the breast region; modality, general sensory. **ra′mi cuta′nei anterio′res [pectora′les et abdomina′les] ramo′rum anterio′rum arteria′rum in-tercosta′lium** [B N A], anterior cutaneous branches (thoracic and abdominal) of the anterior branches of the intercostal arteries. Omitted in N A. **ra′mi cuta′nei arte′riae mamma′-riae inter′nae** [B N A], cutaneous branches of the internal mammary artery. Omitted in N A. **ra′mi cuta′nei cru′ris media′les ner′vi saphe′ni** [N A, B N A], branches distributed by the saphenous nerve to the skin of the medial aspect of the leg; modality, general sensory. Called also *medial crural cutaneous branches of saphenous nerve.* **r. cuta′neus latera′lis arteria′rum intercosta′lium posterio′rum [III–XI]** [N A], a branch arising from the posterior intercostal arteries, supplying the skin of the anterolateral thoracic wall. The branches of the third through fifth give off small mammary branches. Called also (pl.) *rami cutanei laterales [pectorales et abdominales] ramorum anteriorum arteriarum intercostalium* [B N A], and *lateral cutaneous branch of posterior intercostal arteries [III–XI].* **r. cuta′neus latera′lis ner′vi iliohypo-gas′trici** [N A, B N A], a branch of the iliohypogastric nerve, distributed to the skin over the side of the buttock; modality, general sensory. Called also *lateral cutaneous branch of iliohypogastric nerve.* **r. cuta′neus latera′lis [pecto-ra′lis et abdomina′lis] nervo′rum inter-costa′lium** [N A, B N A], a branch arising from the intercostal nerves, and dividing further into anterior and posterior branches to innervate the skin of the lateral and posterior body wall; modality, general sensory. The branches of the fourth through sixth intercostal nerves give off lateral mammary branches. Called also *lateral cutaneous branch (thoracic and abdominal) of intercostal nerves.* **ra′mi cuta′nei latera′les [pectora′les et abdomina′les] ramo′rum anterio′rum arteria′rum intercosta′lium** [B N A]. See *r. cutaneus lateralis arteriarum intercostalium posteriorum [III–XI].* **r. cuta′-neus latera′lis ra′mi dorsa′lis arteria′-rum intercosta′lium posterio′rum [III–XI]** [N A], a branch arising from the dorsal branch of a posterior intercostal artery, supplying first back muscles and then the skin of the posterolateral aspect of the thorax. The branches of the third through fifth arteries give off small mammary branches. Called also *r. cutaneus lateralis ramorum posteriorum arteriarum intercostalium* [B N A], and *lateral cutaneous branch of dorsal branch of posterior intercostal arteries [III–XI].* **r. cuta′-neus latera′lis ramo′rum dorsa′lium nervo′rum thoracico′rum** [N A], the lateral of the two terminal divisions of the dorsal branch of each thoracic nerve; these innervate the longissimus thoracis and iliocostalis thoracis muscles before becoming superficial laterally to supply skin of the back. Called also *r. cutaneus lateralis ramorum posteriorum nervorum thoracalium* [B N A], and *lateral cutaneous branch of dorsal branches of thoracic nerves.* **r. cuta′neus latera′lis ramo′rum posterio′rum arte-ria′rum intercosta′lium** [B N A], r. cutaneus lateralis ramorum dorsalium arteriarum intercostalium posteriorum [III–XI]. **r. cuta′neus latera′lis ramo′rum posterio′rum nervo′-rum thoraca′lium** [B N A], r. cutaneus lateralis ramorum dorsalium nervorum thoracicorum. **r. cuta′neus media′lis ra′mi dorsa′-lis arteria′rum intercosta′lium poste-rio′rum [III–XI]** [N A], a branch arising from the dorsal branch of a posterior intercostal artery, passing through the more medial of the dorsal muscles, and supplying the skin of the back. Called also *r. cutaneus medialis ramorum poste-*

riorum arteriarum intercostalium [B N A], and *medial cutaneous branch of dorsal branch of posterior intercostal arteries [III–XI]*. **r. cuta′neus media′lis ramo′rum dorsa′lium nervo′rum thoracico′rum** [N A], the medial of the two terminal divisions of the dorsal branch of a thoracic nerve; those of the upper nerves supplying the skin of the back, and those of the lower ones chiefly supplying the erector spinae muscle. Called also *r. cutaneus medialis ramorum posteriorum nervorum thoracalium* [B N A], and *medial cutaneous branch of dorsal branches of thoracic nerves*. **r. cuta′neus media′lis ramo′rum posterio′rum arteria′rum intercosta′lium** [B N A], r. cutaneus medialis rami dorsalis arteriarum intercostalium posteriorum [III–XI]. **r. cuta′neus media′lis ramo′rum posterio′rum nervo′rum thoraca′lium** [B N A], r. cutaneus medialis ramorum dorsalium nervorum thoracicorum. **r. cuta′neus ner′vi obturato′rii** [N A, B N A], a branch arising from the anterior branch of the obturator nerve and innervating the skin of the medial aspect of the thigh and leg; modality, general sensory. Called also *cutaneous branch of obturator nerve*. **r. cuta′neus palma′ris ner′vi ulna′ris** [N A, B N A], a branch innervating the skin of the palm; modality, general sensory. Called also *palmar cutaneous branch of ulnar nerve*. **r. deltoi′deus arte′riae profun′dae bra′chii** [N A, B N A], a branch of the deep brachial artery distributed to the brachialis and deltoid muscles and anastomosing with the posterior circumflex humeral artery. Called also *deltoid branch of deep brachial artery*. **r. deltoi′deus arte′riae thoracoacromia′lis** [N A, B N A], a branch of the thoracoacromial artery descending with the cephalic vein and helping to supply the deltoid and pectoralis major muscles and adjacent skin. Called also *deltoid branch of thoracoacromial artery*. **ra′mi denta′les arte′riae alveola′ris inferio′ris** [N A], branches arising from the inferior alveolar artery in the mandibular canal and supplying the inferior teeth. Called also *dental branches of inferior alveolar artery*. **ra′mi denta′les arteria′rum alveola′rium superio′rum anterio′rum** [N A], branches arising from the anterior superior alveolar arteries and supplying the incisor and canine teeth. Called also *dental branches of anterior superior alveolar arteries*. **ra′mi denta′les arte′riae alveola′ris superio′ris posterio′ris** [N A], branches arising from the posterior superior alveolar artery and supplying the molar and premolar teeth. Called also *dental branches of posterior superior alveolar artery*. **ra′mi denta′les inferio′res plex′us denta′lis inferio′ris** [N A, B N A], branches arising from the inferior dental plexus and supplying the lower teeth; modality, general sensory. Called also *inferior dental branches of inferior dental plexus*. **ra′mi denta′les superio′res plex′us denta′lis superio′ris** [N A, B N A], branches arising from the superior dental plexus and innervating the teeth of the upper jaw; modality, general sensory. Called also *superior dental branches of superior dental plexus*. **r. descen′dens ante′rior arte′riae corona′riae [cor′dis] sinis′trae** [B N A], r. interventricularis anterior arteriae coronariae sinistrae. **r. descen′dens arte′riae circumflex′ae fem′oris latera′lis** [N A, B N A], a branch passing from the lateral circumflex artery (sometimes directly from the deep femoral) to the knee, and supplying the thigh muscles. Called also *descending branch of lateral circumflex femoral artery*. **r. descen′dens arte′riae occipita′lis** [N A, B N A], a branch that arises from the occipital artery on the obliquus capitis superior muscle and divides into superficial and deep branches, supplying the trapezius and deep neck muscles. Called also *descending branch of occipital artery*. **r. descen′dens arte′riae transver′sae col′li** [B N A], r. profundus arteriae transversae colli. **r. descen′dens ner′vi hypoglos′si** [B N A], r. superior ansae cervicalis. **r. descen′dens poste′rior arte′riae corona′riae [cor′dis] dex′trae** [B N A], r. interventricularis posterior arteriae coronariae dextrae. **r. dex′ter arte′riae hepat′icae pro′priae** [N A, B N A], the right of the two branches into which the proper hepatic artery normally divides. It supplies the right lobe of the liver and a branch, the cystic artery, to the gallbladder. Called also *right branch of proper hepatic artery*. **r. dex′ter arte′riae pulmona′lis** [B N A], arteria pulmonalis dextra. **r. digas′tricus ner′vi facia′lis** [N A, B N A], a branch that innervates the posterior belly of the digastric muscle; modality, motor. Called also *digastric branch of facial nerve*. **r. dorsa′lis arteria′rum intercosta′lium posterio′rum [III–XI]** [N A], a branch arising from a posterior intercostal artery, passing backward with the dorsal branch of the corresponding thoracic nerve and dividing into a spinal branch and a medial and a lateral cutaneous branch to supply the posterior thoracic wall. Called also (pl.) *rami posteriores arteriarum intercostalium* [B N A], and *dorsal branch of posterior intercostal arteries*. **ra′mi dorsa′les arte′riae intercosta′lis supre′mae** [N A, B N A], the dorsal branches arising from the first two posterior intercostal arteries, which stem from the highest intercostal artery. Their distribution is similar to that of the other posterior intercostals; see *ramus dorsalis arteriarum intercostalium posteriorum*. Called also *dorsal branches of highest intercostal artery*. **r. dorsa′lis arteria′rum lumba′lium** [N A, B N A], the larger of the two branches into which each lumbar artery (four or five) divides; it supplies lumbar back muscles and gives off a spinal branch. Called also *dorsal branch of lumbar arteries*. **r. dorsa′lis arte′riae subcosta′lis** [N A], a branch supplying back muscles, its distribution being similar to that of the dorsal branches of the lower posterior intercostal arteries. Called also *dorsal branch of subcostal artery*. **ra′mi dorsa′les lin′guae arte′riae lingua′lis** [N A, B N A], branches of the lingual artery arising beneath the hyoglossus muscle and supplying the tonsil and the back of the tongue. Called also *dorsal lingual branches of lingual artery*. **r. dorsa′lis ma′nus ner′vi ulna′ris** [B N A], r. dorsalis nervi ulnaris. **ra′mi dorsa′les nervo′rum cervica′lium** [N A], the dorsal branches of the eight cervical spinal nerves. Called also *rami posteriores nervorum cervicalium* [B N A]. **r. dorsa′lis ner′vi coccyg′ei** [N A], the dorsal branch of the last spinal nerve, which helps innervate the skin over the coccyx. Called also *r. posterior nervi coccygei* [B N A], and *dorsal branch of coccygeal nerve*. **ra′mi dorsa′les nervo′rum lumba′lium** [N A], the dorsal branches of the five lumbar spinal nerves. Called also *rami posteriores nervorum lumbalium* [B N A]. **ra′mi dorsa′les nervo′rum sacra′lium** [N A], the dorsal branches of the five sacral spinal nerves, which emerge from the sacrum through the dorsal sacral foramina. Called also *rami posteriores nervorum sacralium* [B N A]. **r. dorsa′lis nervo′rum spina′lium** [N A], the smaller of the two chief branches into which each spinal nerve divides almost as soon as it emerges from the intervertebral foramen. The dorsal branches supply the skin, muscles, joints, and bone of the dorsal part of the neck and trunk. Commonly each branch divides into a medial and a lateral portion. Called also *r. posterior nervorum spinalium* [B N A], and *dorsal branch of spinal nerves*. **ra′mi dorsa′les nervo′rum thoracico′rum** [N A], the dorsal branches of the twelve thoracic spinal nerves. Called also *rami posteriores nervorum thoracalium* [B N A]. **r. dorsa′lis ner′vi ulna′ris** [N A], a large cutaneous branch that arises from the ulnar nerve and passes down the distal portion of the forearm to the medial side of the back of the hand, where it divides into the three dorsal digital nerves; modality, general sensory. Called also *r. dorsalis manus nervi ulnaris* [B N A], and *dorsal branch of* *ulnar nerve.* **r. dorsa'lis vena'rum intercosta'lium** [B N A], **r. dorsa'lis vena'rum intercosta'lium posterio'rum [IV–XI]** [N A], the dorsal branch of the posterior intercostal veins, corresponding to the dorsal branch of the posterior intercostal arteries. **ra'mi duodena'les arte'riae pancreaticoduodena'lis superio'ris** [N A, B N A], vessels supplying the duodenum. Called also *duodenal branches of superior pancreaticoduodenal artery.* **ra'mi epiplo'ici arte'riae gastroepiplo'icae dex'trae** [N A, B N A], vessels that supply the greater omentum. Called also *epiploic branches of right gastroepiploic artery.* **ra'mi esophage'i aor'tae thora'cicae** [N A], branches, usually two, that arise from the front of the aorta to supply the esophagus. Called also *arteriae oesophageae* [B N A], and *esophageal branches of thoracic aorta.* **ra'mi esophage'i arte'riae gas'tricae sinis'trae** [N A], vessels that supply the esophagus. Called also *esophageal branches of left gastric artery.* **ra'mi esophage'i arte'riae thyroi'deae inferio'ris** [N A], vessels supplying the esophagus. Called also *esophageal branches of inferior thyroid artery.* **ra'mi esophage'i ner'vi laryn'gei recurren'tis** [N A], a branch of the esophageal nerve that helps innervate the esophagus; modality, visceral afferent and general sensory. Called also *esophageal branch of recurrent laryngeal nerve.* **r. exter'nus ner'vi accesso'rii** [N A, B N A], the branch of the eleventh cranial nerve that continues from the spinal roots of the nerve, innervating the sternomastoid and trapezius muscles. Called also *external branch of accessory nerve.* **r. exter'nus ner'vi laryn'gei superio'ris** [N A, B N A], the smaller of the two branches into which the superior laryngeal nerve divides, descending under cover of the sternothyroid muscle and innervating the cricothyroid and the inferior constrictor of the pharynx; modality, motor. Called also *external branch of superior laryngeal nerve.* **r. femora'lis ner'vi genitofemora'lis** [N A], a branch arising by division of the genitofemoral nerve above the inguinal ligament and supplying the skin of the femoral triangle; modality, general sensory. Called also *nervus lumboinguinalis* [B N A], and *femoral branch of genitofemoral nerve.* **r. fibula'ris arte'riae tibia'lis posterio'ris** [B N A], r. circumflexus fibulae arteriae tibialis posterioris. **ra'mi fronta'les arte'riae cer'ebri anterio'ris** [N A], branches of the anterior cerebral artery that supply the cortex of the frontal lobe on the median and superior surfaces and the superior part of the lateral surface. Called also *frontal branches of anterior cerebral artery.* **ra'mi fronta'les arte'riae cer'ebri me'diae** [N A], branches of the middle cerebral artery that supply the cortex of the frontal lobe on the lateral surface. Called also *frontal branches of middle cerebral artery.* **r. fronta'lis arte'riae menin'geae me'diae** [N A], a branch of the middle meningeal artery, lodged in grooves on the sphenoid and parietal bones, and supplying the dura mater of the front of the brain. A part of it is sometimes enclosed in a bony canal. Called also *frontal branch of middle meningeal artery.* **r. fronta'lis arte'riae tempora'lis superficia'lis** [N A, B N A], a tortuous terminal branch that supplies muscles and skin of the forehead and frontal scalp. Called also *frontal branch of superficial temporal artery.* **r. fronta'lis ner'vi fronta'lis** [B N A], the frontal branch of the frontal nerve. Omitted in N A. **ra'mi gas'trici anterio'res ner'vi va'gi** [N A], branches arising from the anterior trunk of the vagus near the cardiac end of the stomach, innervating the anterior aspect of the lesser curvature and the anterior surface of the stomach almost to the pylorus; modality, parasympathetic and visceral afferent. Called also *plexus gastricus anterior* [B N A], and *anterior gastric branches of vagus nerve.* **ra'mi gas'trici ner'vi va'gi** [B N A]. See *rami gastrici anteriores nervi vagi* and *rami gastrici posteriores nervi vagi.* **ra'mi gas'trici posterio'res ner'vi va'gi** [N A], branches arising from the posterior vagal trunk near the cardiac end of the stomach, and innervating the cardiac orifice and fundus, the posterior aspect of the lesser curvature, and the posterior surface of the stomach to the pyloric antrum; modality, parasympathetic and visceral afferent. Called also *plexus gastricus posterior* [B N A], and *posterior gastric branches of vagus nerve.* **r. genita'lis ner'vi genitofemora'lis** [N A], a branch arising from the genitofemoral nerve above the inguinal ligament and descending through the inguinal canal to innervate the cremaster muscle and the skin of the scrotum or of the labium majus, and that of the adjacent area of the thigh; modality, general sensory and motor. Called also *nervus spermaticus externus* [B N A], and *genital branch of genitofemoral nerve.* **ra'mi gingiva'les inferio'res plex'us denta'lis inferio'ris** [N A, B N A], branches originating from the inferior dental plexus and innervating the gingivae of the lower jaw; modality, general sensory. Called also *inferior gingival branches of inferior dental plexus.* **ra'mi gingiva'les superio'res plex'us denta'lis superio'ris** [N A, B N A], branches arising from the superior dental plexus and innervating the gingivae of the upper jaw; modality, general sensory. Called also *superior gingival branches of superior dental plexus.* **ra'mi glandula'res arte'riae facia'lis** [N A], **ra'mi glandula'res arte'riae maxilla'ris exter'nae** [B N A], branches given off to the submandibular gland by the facial artery as it passes over the lateral surface of the gland. Called also *glandular branches of facial artery.* **ra'mi glandula'res arte'riae thyreoi'deae inferio'ris** [B N A], glandular branches of the inferior thyroid artery. Omitted in N A. **ra'mi glandula'res arte'riae thyreoi'deae superio'ris** [B N A], glandular branches of the superior thyroid artery. Omitted in N A. **ra'mi glandula'res gan'glii submandibula'ris** [N A], short branches running from the submandibular ganglion to innervate the submandibular gland, bearing postganglionic parasympathetic (secretory) fibers from this ganglion and sympathetic fibers that are postganglionic from the superior cervical ganglion. Called also *rami submaxillares ganglii submaxillaris* [B N A], and *glandular branches of submandibular ganglion.* **ra'mi hepat'ici ner'vi va'gi** [N A, B N A], branches (sometimes only one) arising from the anterior vagal trunk, contributing to the hepatic plexus, and helping innervate the liver, gallbladder, pancreas, pylorus, and duodenum; modality, parasympathetic and visceral afferent. Called also *hepatic branches of vagus nerve.* **r. hyoi'deus arte'riae lingua'lis** [B N A], r. suprahyoideus arteriae lingualis. **r. hyoi'deus arte'riae thyreoi'deae superio'ris** [B N A], r. infrahyoideus arteriae thyroideae superioris. **r. ili'acus arte'riae iliolumba'lis** [N A, B N A], one of the two branches into which the iliolumbar artery divides in the iliac fossa; it supplies the iliacus muscle and sends a large nutrient branch to the ilium. Called also *iliac branch of iliolumbar artery.* **r. infe'rior arte'riae glu'teae superio'ris** [N A], the lower division of the deep branch of the superior gluteal artery, accompanied by the superior gluteal nerve and helping supply the obturator internus, piriformis, levator ani, and coccygeus muscles, the hip joint, and the ilium. Called also *inferior branch of superior gluteal artery.* **ra'mi inferio'res ner'vi cuta'nei col'li** [B N A], rami inferiores nervi transversi colli. **r. infe'rior ner'vi oculomoto'rii** [N A, B N A], the branch of the oculomotor nerve that innervates the medial and inferior rectus and inferior oblique muscles of the eyeball and, via the ciliary ganglion and short ciliary nerves, the sphincter pupillae and ciliary muscles; modality, motor and parasympathetic. Called also *inferior branch of oculomotor nerve.* **ra'mi inferio'res ner'vi trans-**

ver′si col′li [N A], the more inferior of the branches that arise from the transverse cervical nerve near the anterior border of the sternocleidomastoid muscle, innervating skin and subcutaneous tissue in the anterior cervical region; modality, general sensory. Called also *rami inferiores nervi cutanei colli* [B N A], and *inferior branches of transverse nerve of neck.* **r. infe′rior os′sis is′chii** [B N A], r. ossis ischii. **r. infe′rior os′sis pu′bis** [N A, B N A], **inferior r. of pubis,** the short flattened bar of bone that projects from the body of the pubic bone in a postero-infero-lateral direction to meet the ramus of the ischium. **r. infrahyoi′deus arte′riae thyroi′deae superio′ris** [N A], a vessel running along the inferior border of the hyoid bone, supplying the infrahyoid region, and anastomosing with its fellow of the opposite side. Called also *r. hyoideus arteriae thyreoideae superioris* [B N A], and *infrahyoid branch of superior thyroid artery.* **r. infrapatella′ris ner′vi saphe′ni** [N A, B N A], a branch running inferolaterally from the saphenous nerve, beneath the patella; modality, general sensory. Called also *infrapatellar branch of saphenous nerve.* **ra′mi inguina′les arte′riae femora′lis** [N A, B N A], branches arising from the external pudendal arteries and supplying skin and muscle in the inguinal region. Called also *inguinal branches of femoral artery.* **ra′mi intercosta′les anterio′res arte′riae thora′cicae inter′nae** [N A], **ra′mi intercosta′les arte′riae mamma′riae inter′nae** [B N A], twelve branches, two in each of the upper six intercostal spaces, that supply the intercostal muscles, pectoralis major muscle, and ribs. Within each space both branches run laterally, the upper anastomosing with the posterior intercostal artery, the lower with the collateral branch of that artery. Called also *anterior intercostal branches of internal thoracic artery.* **r. interfunicula′ris,** a branch connecting the two trunks of the sympathetic nervous system. **ra′mi intergangliona′res** [N A], the branches that interconnect the ganglia of the sympathetic trunk. Called also *interganglionic branches.* **r. inter′nus ner′vi accesso′rii** [N A, B N A], the branch that continues from the cranial roots of the nerve, carrying motor fibers that are distributed by branches of the vagus to the soft palate, pharyngeal constrictors, and larynx. Called also *internal branch of accessory nerve.* **r. inter′nus ner′vi laryn′gei superio′ris** [N A, B N A], the larger of the two branches of the superior laryngeal nerve, which innervates the mucosa of the epiglottis, base of the tongue, and larynx; modality, general sensory. Called also *internal branch of superior laryngeal nerve.* **r. interventricula′ris ante′rior arte′riae corona′riae sinis′trae** [N A], the branch of the left coronary artery that runs to the apex of the heart in the anterior interventricular sulcus, supplying the ventricles and most of the interventricular septum. Called also *r. descendens anterior arteriae coronariae [cordis] sinistrae* [B N A], and *anterior interventricular branch of left coronary artery.* **r. interventricula′ris poste′rior arte′riae corona′riae dex′trae** [N A], a branch of the right coronary artery, running toward the apex of the heart in the posterior interventricular sulcus, supplying the diaphragmatic surface of the ventricles and part of the interventricular septum. Called also *r. descendens posterior arteriae coronariae [cordis] dextrae* [B N A], and *posterior interventricular branch of right coronary artery.* **r. of ischium,** r. ossis ischii. **ra′mi isth′mi fau′cium ner′vi lingua′lis** [N A, B N A], branches from the lingual nerve to the isthmus of the fauces; modality, general sensory. **r. of jaw,** r. mandibulae. **ra′mi labia′les anterio′res arte′riae femora′lis** [N A], branches that arise from the external pudendal arteries and supply the labium majus. Called also *arteriae labiales anteriores vulvae* [B N A], and *anterior labial branches of femoral artery.* **ra′mi labia′les inferio′res ner′vi menta′lis** [N A, B N A], branches of the mental nerve that innervate the lower lip; modality, general sensory. Called also *inferior labial branches of mental nerve.* **ra′mi labia′les posterio′res arte′riae puden′dae inter′nae** [N A], two branches arising from the internal pudendal artery in the anterior part of the ischiorectal fossa, helping to supply the ischiocavernosus and bulbospongiosus muscles, and supplying the labium majus and labium minus. Called also *arteriae labiales posteriores vulvae* [B N A], and *posterior labial branches of internal pudendal artery.* **ra′mi labia′les superio′res ner′vi infraorbita′lis** [N A, B N A], branches of the infraorbital nerve that are distributed to mucous membrane of the mouth and skin of the upper lip; modality, general sensory. Called also *superior labial branches of infraorbital nerve.* **ra′mi laryngopharyn′gei gan′glii cervica′lis superio′ris** [N A, B N A], branches from the superior cervical ganglion to the larynx and walls of the pharynx; modality, sympathetic. Called also *laryngopharyngeal branches of superior cervical ganglion.* **r. latera′lis ner′vi supraorbita′lis** [N A], a branch of the supraorbital nerve that innervates skin and subcutaneous tissue of the forehead and scalp laterally as far as the temporal region; modality, general sensory. Called also *lateral branch of supraorbital nerve.* **r. latera′lis ramo′rum dorsa′lium nervo′rum cervica′lium** [N A], the lateral branch that arises from the dorsal branch of each of the eight cervical nerves, supplying adjacent muscles. Called also *r. lateralis ramorum posteriorum nervorum cervicalium* [B N A], and *lateral branch of dorsal branches of cervical nerves.* **r. latera′lis ramo′rum dorsa′lium nervo′rum lumba′lium** [N A], the branch that runs inferolaterally from the dorsal branch of each lumbar nerve, innervating adjacent muscle. The upper of these branches terminally constitute the superior cluneal nerves, supplying skin of the buttock. Called also *r. lateralis ramorum posteriorum nervorum lumbalium* [B N A], and *lateral branch of dorsal branches of lumbar nerves.* **r. latera′lis ramo′rum dorsa′lium nervo′rum sacra′lium** [N A], the lateral branch that arises from the dorsal branch of each of the three upper sacral nerves. Called also *r. lateralis ramorum posteriorum nervorum sacralium* [B N A], and *lateral branch of dorsal branches of sacral nerves.* **r. latera′lis ramo′rum posterio′rum nervo′rum cervica′lium** [B N A], r. lateralis ramorum dorsalium nervorum cervicalium. **r. latera′lis ramo′rum posterio′rum nervo′rum lumba′lium** [B N A], r. lateralis ramorum dorsalium nervorum lumbalium. **r. latera′lis ramo′rum posterio′rum nervo′rum sacra′lium** [B N A], r. lateralis ramorum dorsalium nervorum sacralium. **ra′mi liena′les arte′riae liena′lis** [N A, B N A], the terminal branches of the splenic artery, which follow the trabeculae. Called also *splenic branches of splenic artery.* **ra′mi liena′les plex′us coeli′aci** [B N A], splenic branches of celiac plexus. Omitted in N A. **r. lingua′lis ner′vi facia′lis** [N A], an inconstant branch of the facial nerve sometimes arising together with the stylohyoid branch, and helping to supply the styloglossal and glossopalatine muscles; modality, motor. Called also *lingual branch of facial nerve.* **ra′mi lingua′les ner′vi glossopharyn′gei** [N A, B N A], branches of the glossopharyngeal nerve that innervate the posterior third of the tongue; modality, general and special sensory. Called also *lingual branches of glossopharyngeal nerve.* **ra′mi lingua′les ner′vi hypoglos′si** [N A, B N A], a branch of the hypoglossal nerve that innervates the intrinsic and extrinsic muscles of the tongue; modality, motor. Called also *lingual branches of hypoglossal nerve.* **ra′mi lingua′les ner′vi lingua′lis** [N A, B N A], branches that innervate the anterior two-thirds of the tongue, adjacent areas of the mouth, and the gums; modality, general and special sensory. Called also *lingual branches of lingual nerve.* **r. lumba′lis arte′riae iliolumba′lis** [N A, B N A], a branch that arises from the iliolumbar artery in the iliac fossa and ascends to supply the psoas and quadratus lumborum muscles, sending a spinal branch through the intervertebral foramen just above the sacrum. Called also *lumbar branch of iliolumbar artery.* **ra′mi malleola′res latera′les arte′riae perone′ae** [N A], vessels supplying the lateral aspect of the ankle and giving off calcaneal branches to the lateral aspect and back of the heel. Called also *arteria malleolaris posterior lateralis* [B N A], and *lateral malleolar branches of peroneal artery.* **ra′mi malleola′res media′les arte′riae perone′ae** [N A], vessels supplying the area of the medial malleolus and giving off calcaneal branches to the medial aspect and back of the heel. Called also *arteria malleolaris posterior medialis* [B N A], and *medial malleolar branches of peroneal artery.* **ra′mi mamma′rii arte′riae mamma′riae inter′nae** [B N A], **ra′mi mamma′rii arte′riae thora′cicae inter′nae** [N A], branches arising from the second, third, and fourth perforating branches of the internal thoracic artery and helping to supply the mammary gland. Called also *mammary branches of internal thoracic artery.* **ra′mi mamma′rii exter′ni arte′riae thoraca′lis latera′lis** [B N A], **ra′mi mamma′rii latera′les arte′riae thora′cicae latera′lis** [N A], branches from the lateral thoracic artery that supply the mammary gland. Called also *lateral mammary branches of lateral thoracic artery.* **r. mamma′rii latera′les ramo′rum anterio′rum arteria′rum intercosta′lium** [B N A], lateral mammary branches of anterior branches of intercostal arteries. Omitted in N A. **ra′mi mamma′rii latera′les ramo′rum cutaneo′rum latera′lium nervo′rum intercosta′lium** [N A, B N A], branches given to the lateral part of the mammary gland by lateral cutaneous branches of intercostal nerves; modality, general sensory. Called also *lateral mammary branches of lateral cutaneous branches of intercostal nerves.* **r. mamma′rii media′les arteria′rum intercosta′lium** [B N A], medial mammary branches of the intercostal arteries. Omitted in N A. **ra′mi mamma′rii media′les ramo′rum cutaneo′rum anterio′rum nervo′rum intercosta′lium** [N A, B N A], branches given to the medial part of the mammary gland by anterior cutaneous branches of intercostal nerves; modality, general sensory. Called also *medial mammary branches of anterior cutaneous branches of intercostal nerves.* **ra′mi mamma′rii ra′mi cuta′nei latera′lis arteria′rum intercosta′lium posterio′rum** [N A], branches arising from the lateral cutaneous branches of the third through fifth posterior intercostal arteries and supplying the mammary region. Called also *mammary branches of lateral cutaneous branch of posterior intercostal arteries.* **r. of mandible, r. mandib′ulae** [N A, B N A], a quadrilateral process projecting superiorly from the posterior part of either side of the jaw bone. **r. margina′lis mandib′ulae ner′vi facia′lis** [N A, B N A], a branch of the facial nerve that runs forward from the front of the parotid gland along the border of the mandible, deep to the platysma and depressor anguli oris muscles, supplying the latter and the depressor labii inferioris and mentalis muscles; modality, motor. Called also *marginal mandibular branch of facial nerve.* **ra′mi mastoi′dei arte′riae auricula′ris posterio′ris** [N A, B N A], branches of the stylomastoid artery that supply the mastoid cells. Called also *mastoid branches of posterior auricular artery.* **r. mastoi′deus arte′riae occipita′lis** [N A, B N A], a branch of the occipital artery that enters the cranial cavity through the mastoid foramen and supplies the dura mater, diploe, and mastoid cells. Called also *mastoid branch of occipital artery.* **r. media′lis ner′vi supraorbita′lis** [N A], a branch of the supraorbital nerve innervating skin and subcutaneous tissue of the forehead and scalp as far back as the parietal bone; modality, general sensory. Called also *medial branch of supraorbital nerve.* **r. media′lis ramo′rum dorsa′lium nervo′rum cervica′lium** [N A], the medial branch arising from the dorsal branch of each of the eight cervical nerves, supplying muscle, periosteum, ligaments, and joints; also, except for those of the first, and generally the sixth and seventh cervical nerves, having an eventual cutaneous distribution. Called also *r. medialis ramorum posteriorum nervorum cervicalium* [B N A], and *medial branch of dorsal branches of cervical nerves.* **r. media′lis ramo′rum dorsa′lium nervo′rum lumba′lium** [N A], the medial branch that arises from the dorsal branch of each lumbar nerve, mainly innervating deep muscle, but also helping supply ligaments, periosteum, and joints. Called also *r. medialis ramorum posteriorum nervorum lumbalium* [B N A], and *medial branch of dorsal branches of lumbar nerves.* **r. media′lis ramo′rum dorsa′lium nervo′rum sacra′lium** [N A], the medial branch that arises from the dorsal branch of each of the upper three sacral nerves. Called also *r. medialis ramorum posteriorum nervorum sacralium* [B N A], and *medial branch of dorsal branches of sacral nerves.* **r. media′lis ramo′rum posterio′rum nervo′rum cervica′lium** [B N A], r. medialis ramorum dorsalium nervorum cervicalium. **r. media′lis ramo′rum posterio′rum nervo′rum lumba′lium** [B N A], r. medialis ramorum dorsalium nervorum lumbalium. **r. media′lis ramo′rum posterio′rum nervo′rum sacra′lium** [B N A], r. medialis ramorum dorsalium nervorum sacralium. **ra′mi mediastina′les aor′tae thoraca′lis** [B N A], **ra′mi mediastina′les aor′tae thora′cicae** [N A], small vessels supplying connective tissue and lymph nodes in the posterior mediastinum. Called also *mediastinal branches of thoracic aorta.* **ra′mi mediastina′les arte′riae thora′cicae inter′nae** [N A], branches of the internal thoracic artery that supply areolar tissue, pericardium, lymph nodes, and the thymus, in the anterior and superior mediastina. Called also *arteriae mediastinales anteriores* [B N A], and *mediastinal branches of internal thoracic artery.* **r. membra′nae tym′pani ner′vi auriculotempora′lis** [N A, B N A], a branch given to the tympanic membrane by the nerve of the external acoustic meatus, a branch of the auriculotemporal nerve; modality, general sensory. Called also *branch to tympanic membrane of auriculotemporal nerve.* **r. menin′geus accesso′rius arte′riae menin′geae me′diae** [N A, B N A], a branch arising from the middle meningeal artery, or directly from the maxillary artery, and entering the middle cranial fossa through the foramen ovale to supply the trigeminal ganglion, walls of the cavernous sinus, and neighboring dura mater. Called also *accessory meningeal branch of middle meningeal artery.* **r. menin′geus arte′riae occipita′lis** [N A, B N A], one or more variable branches of the occipital artery that enter the posterior fossa and supply the dura mater. Called also *meningeal branch of occipital artery.* **r. menin′geus arte′riae vertebra′lis** [N A, B N A], a branch arising from the vertebral artery in the foramen magnum, and ramifying in the posterior cranial fossa to supply the dura mater, including the falx cerebelli, and bone. Called also *meningeal branch of vertebral artery.* **r. menin′geus me′dius ner′vi maxilla′ris** [N A], a branch arising from the maxillary nerve in the middle cranial fossa, accompanying the middle meningeal artery, and supplying the dura mater; modality, general sensory. Called also *nervus meningeus [medius]* [B N A], and *middle meningeal branch of maxillary nerve.* **r. menin′geus ner′vi mandibula′ris** [N A], a branch that arises from the trunk of the mandibular nerve, re-enters the cranium through the foramen spinosum, accompanies the middle meningeal artery to supply the dura mater, and also helps innervate the mucous membrane of the mastoid air cells. Called also *nervus spinosus* [B N A], and *meningeal branch of mandibular nerve*. **r. menin'geus nervo'rum spina'lium** [N A, B N A], the small branch of each spinal nerve that re-enters the intervertebral foramen to supply the vertebral column, spinal cord, and associated structures. Called also *meningeal branch of spinal nerves*. **r. menin'geus ner'vi va'gi** [N A, B N A], a branch that arises in the jugular foramen from the superior ganglion of the vagus nerve, innervating dura mater of the posterior cranial fossa. Called also *meningeal branch of vagus nerve*. **ra'mi menta'les ner'vi menta'lis** [N A, B N A], the branches of the mental nerve that innervate the skin of the chin; modality, general sensory. Called also *mental branches of mental nerve*. **r. muscula'ris** [N A, B N A], a branch of a peripheral nerve that supplies muscle, many not being more specifically named. Called also *muscular branch*. **ra'mi muscula'res arte'riae cervica'lis ascenden'tis** [B N A], muscular branches of the ascending cervical artery. Omitted in N A. **ra'mi muscula'res arte'riae femora'lis** [B N A], muscular branches of the femoral artery. Omitted in N A. **r. muscula'res arte'riae ge'nu supre'mae** [B N A], muscular branches of the highest genicular artery. Omitted in N A. **ra'mi muscula'res arte'riae mamma'riae inter'nae** [B N A], muscular branches of the internal mammary artery. Omitted in N A. **ra'mi muscula'res arte'riae ophthal'micae** [B N A], muscular branches of the ophthalmic artery. Omitted in N A. **ra'mi muscula'res arte'riae radia'lis** [B N A], muscular branches of the radial artery. Omitted in N A. **ra'mi muscula'res arte'riae ulna'ris** [B N A], muscular branches of the ulnar artery. Omitted in N A. **ra'mi muscula'res ner'vi axilla'ris** [N A, B N A], branches of the axillary nerve, innervating the deltoid and teres minor muscles; modality, motor. Called also *muscular branches of axillary nerve*. **ra'mi muscula'res ner'vi femora'lis** [N A, B N A], branches of the femoral nerve, innervating the anterior thigh muscles; modality, motor. Called also *muscular branches of femoral nerve*. **ra'mi muscula'res ner'vi fibula'ris profun'di,** N A alternative for *rami musculares nervi peronei profundi*. **ra'mi muscula'res ner'vi fibula'ris superficia'lis,** N A alternative for *rami musculares nervi peronei superficialis*. **ra'mi muscula'res ner'vi iliohypogas'trici** [B N A], muscular branches of iliohypogastric nerve. Omitted in N A. **ra'mi muscula'res ner'vi ilioinguina'lis** [B N A], muscular branches of ilioinguinal nerve. Omitted in N A. **ra'mi muscula'res nervo'rum interCosta'lium** [B N A], muscular branches of the intercostal nerves. Omitted in N A. **ra'mi muscula'res ner'vi ischiad'ici** [B N A], muscular branches of the sciatic nerve. Omitted in N A. **ra'mi muscula'res ner'vi media'ni** [N A, B N A], branches of the median nerve, innervating most of the flexor muscles on the front of the forearm and most of the short muscles of the thumb; modality, motor. Called also *muscular branches of median nerve*. **ra'mi muscula'res ner'vi musculocuta'nei** [N A, B N A], branches of the musculocutaneous nerve that innervate the biceps and brachialis muscles; modality, motor and general sensory. Called also *muscular branches of musculocutaneous nerve*. **ra'mi muscula'res ner'vi obturato'rii** [N A], branches arising from the anterior and posterior rami of the obturator nerve and innervating the adductor muscles of the thigh; modality, motor. Called also *muscular branches of obturator nerve*. **ra'mi muscula'res ner'vi peronae'i commu'nis** [B N A], muscular branches of the common peroneal nerve. Omitted in N A. **ra'mi muscula'res ner'vi perone'i profun'di** [N A], branches from the deep peroneal nerve, innervating the tibialis anterior, extensor hallucis longus, extensor digitorum longus, and peroneus tertius muscles; modality, motor. Called also *muscular branches of deep peroneal nerve*. **ra'mi muscula'res ner'vi perone'i superficia'lis** [N A], branches from the superficial peroneal nerve, innervating the peroneus longus and peroneus brevis muscles; modality, motor. Called also *muscular branches of superficial peroneal nerve*. **ra'mi muscula'res ner'vi radia'lis** [N A, B N A], branches of the radial nerve that innervate the triceps, anconeus, brachioradialis, and extensor carpi radialis muscles; modality, motor. Called also *muscular branches of radial nerve*. **ra'mi muscula'res ner'vi tibia'lis** [N A, B N A], branches arising from the tibial nerve and supplying muscles of the back of the leg; modality, motor. Called also *muscular branches of tibial nerve*. **ra'mi muscula'res ner'vi ulna'ris** [N A, B N A], branches of the ulnar nerve that innervate the flexor carpi ulnaris muscle and the ulnar half of flexor digitorum profundus; modality, motor. Called also *muscular branches of ulnar nerve*. **ra'mi muscula'res plex'us lumba'lis** [B N A], muscular branches of the lumbar plexus. Omitted in N A. **ra'mi muscula'res ramo'rum anterio'rum arteria'rum intercosta'lium** [B N A], muscular branches of anterior branches of intercostal arteries. Omitted in N A. **ra'mi muscula'res ramo'rum posterio'rum arteria'rum intercosta'lium** [B N A], muscular branches of posterior branches of intercostal arteries. Omitted in N A. **r. mus'culi stylopharyn'gei ner'vi glossopharyn'gei** [N A], the branch of the glossopharyngeal nerve supplying the stylopharyngeal muscle; modality, motor. Called also *r. stylopharyngeus nervi glossopharyngei* [B N A], and *stylopharyngeal branch of glossopharyngeal nerve*. **r. mylohyoi'deus arte'riae alveola'ris inferio'ris** [N A, B N A], a branch of the inferior alveolar artery that descends with the mylohyoid nerve in the mylohyoid sulcus to supply the floor of the mouth. Called also *mylohyoid branch of inferior alveolar nerve*. **ra'mi nasa'les anterio'res ner'vi ethmoida'lis anterio'ris** [B N A], rami nasales nervi ethmoidalis anterioris. **ra'mi nasa'lis exter'nus ner'vi ethmoida'lis anterio'ris** [N A, B N A], a branch of the anterior ethmoidal nerve that innervates the skin of the dorsal part of the nose; modality, general sensory. Called also *external nasal branch of anterior ethmoidal nerve*. **ra'mi nasa'les exter'ni ner'vi infraorbita'lis** [N A, B N A], branches of the infraorbital nerve that innervate the skin of the side of the nose; modality, general sensory. Called also *external nasal branches of infraorbital nerve*. **ra'mi nasa'les inter'ni ner'vi ethmoida'lis anterio'ris** [N A, B N A], branches of the anterior ethmoidal nerve which, through medial and lateral branches, innervate the nasal septum and the mucous membrane of the lateral wall of the nasal cavity; modality, general sensory. Called also *internal nasal branches of anterior ethmoidal nerve*. **ra'mi nasa'les inter'ni ner'vi infraorbita'lis** [N A, B N A], branches of the infraorbital nerve that innervate the mobile septum of the nose; modality, general sensory. Called also *internal nasal branches of infraorbital nerve*. **ra'mi nasa'les latera'les ner'vi ethmoida'lis anterio'ris** [N A, B N A], branches arising from the internal nasal branches of the anterior ethmoidal nerve and innervating the mucosa of the lateral wall of the nasal cavity; modality, general sensory. Called also *lateral nasal branches of anterior ethmoidal nerve*. **ra'mi nasa'les media'les ner'vi ethmoida'lis anterio'ris** [N A, B N A], branches arising from the internal nasal branches of the anterior ethmoidal nerve and supplying the nasal septum; modality, general sensory. Called also *medial nasal branches of anterior ethmoidal nerve*. **ra'mi nasa'les ner'vi ethmoida'lis anterio'ris** [N A], the internal and external nasal branches of the anterior ethmoidal nerve, and their subdivisions. Called also *rami nasales anteriores nervi ethmoidalis anterioris* [B N A], and *nasal branches of anterior ethmoidal nerve.* **ra'mi nasa'les posterio'res inferio'res [latera'les] gan'glii pterygopalati'ni** [N A], **ra'mi nasa'les posterio'res inferio'res [latera'les] gan'glii sphenopalati'ni** [B N A], branches arising from the pterygopalatine ganglion, and supplying the middle and inferior nasal meatuses and inferior concha; modality, general sensory. Called also [*lateral*] *inferior posterior nasal branches of pterygopalatine ganglion.* **ra'mi nasa'les posterio'res superio'res [latera'les] gan'glii pterygopalati'ni** [N A], **ra'mi nasa'les posterio'res superio'res [latera'les] gan'glii sphenopalati'ni** [B N A], branches arising from the pterygopalatine ganglion, and supplying the superior and middle nasal conchae; modality, general sensory. Called also [*lateral*] *superior posterior nasal branches of pterygopalatine ganglion.* **ra'mi nasa'les posterio'res superio'res media'les gan'glii pterygopalati'ni** [N A], **ra'mi nasa'les posterio'res superio'res media'les gan'glii sphenopalati'ni** [B N A], branches arising from the pterygopalatine ganglion, and supplying the nasal septum; modality, general sensory. Called also *medial superior posterior nasal branches of pterygopalatine ganglion.* **r. obturato'rius arte'riae epigas'tricae inferio'ris** [N A, B N A], a vessel connecting the pubic branches of the inferior epigastric and the obturator arteries. The obturator artery is sometimes replaced by an accessory obturator artery that arises from the inferior epigastric artery by way of this communication. Called also *obturator branch of inferior epigastric artery.* **r. occipita'lis arte'riae auricula'ris posterio'ris** [N A, B N A], a branch of the posterior auricular artery distributed to the epicranius muscle. Called also *occipital branch of posterior auricular artery.* **ra'mi occipita'les arte'riae cer'ebri posterio'ris** [N A], branches of the posterior cerebral artery that supply the cortex of the occipital lobe. Called also *occipital branches of posterior cerebral artery.* **ra'mi occipita'les arte'riae occipita'lis** [N A, B N A], a medial and a lateral branch of the occipital artery, distributed to the scalp and, through the meningeal branch, to the dura mater. Called also *occipital branches of occipital artery.* **r. occipita'lis ner'vi auricula'ris posterio'ris** [N A, B N A], a branch supplying the occipital belly of the occipitofrontalis muscle; modality, motor. Called also *occipital branch of posterior auricular nerve.* **ra'mi oesophage'i arte'riae gas'tricae sinis'trae** [B N A], rami esophagei arteriae gastricae sinistrae. **ra'mi oesophage'i arte'riae thyreoi'deae inferio'ris** [B N A], rami esophagei arteriae thyroideae inferioris. **ra'mi oesophage'i ner'vi recurren'tis** [B N A], rami esophagei nervi laryngei recurrentis. **ra'mi oesophage'i ner'vi va'gi** [B N A], esophageal branches of vagus nerve. Omitted in N A. **ra'mi orbita'les arte'riae cer'ebri anterio'ris** [N A], branches from the anterior cerebral artery to the cortex of the medial part of the orbital surface of the frontal lobe. Called also *orbital branches of anterior cerebral artery.* **ra'mi orbita'les arte'riae cer'ebri me'diae** [N A], branches from the middle cerebral artery to the cortex of the lateral part of the orbital surface of the frontal lobe. Called also *orbital branches of middle cerebral artery.* **ra'mi orbita'les gan'glii pterygopalati'ni** [N A], **ra'mi orbita'les gan'glii sphenopalati'ni** [B N A], branches passing from the pterygopalatine ganglion through the inferior orbital fissure to supply orbital periosteum, the ethmoidal and sphenoidal sinuses, and the lacrimal gland; modality, general sensory and parasympathetic. Called also *orbital branches of pterygopalatine ganglion.* **r. os'sis is'chii** [N A], the flattened bar of bone that projects from the inferior end of the body of the ischium in an antero-supero-medial direction to meet the inferior ramus of the pubis. It forms part of the border of the obturator foramen. Called also *r. inferior ossis ischii* [B N A], and *r. of ischium.* **r. os'sis pu'bis.** See *r. inferior ossis pubis* and *r. superior ossis pubis.* **r. ova'ricus arte'riae uteri'nae** [N A], **r. ova'rii arte'riae uteri'nae** [B N A], the terminal branch of the uterine artery, which supplies the ovary and anastomoses with the ovarian artery. Called also *ovarian branch of uterine artery.* **r. palma'ris ner'vi media'ni** [N A, B N A], a branch arising from the median nerve in the lower part of the forearm and supplying part of the skin of the palm; modality, general sensory. Called also *palmar branch of median nerve.* **r. palma'ris ner'vi ulna'ris** [N A], a branch that arises from the ulnar nerve in the lower part of the forearm, supplying the cutaneous structures of the medial part of the palm; modality, general sensory. Called also *r. volaris manus nervi ulnaris* [B N A], and *palmar branch of ulnar nerve.* **r. palma'ris profun'dus arte'riae ulna'ris** [N A], a branch that accompanies the deep palmar branch of the ulnar nerve and joins the radial artery to form the deep palmar arch. Called also *r. volaris profundus arteriae ulnaris* [B N A], and *deep palmar branch of ulnar artery.* **r. palma'ris superficia'lis arte'riae radia'lis** [N A], a branch arising from the radial artery in the lower part of the forearm and supplying the thenar eminence. Called also *r. volaris superficialis arteriae radialis* [B N A], and *superficial palmar branch of radial artery.* **ra'mi palpebra'les inferio'res ner'vi infraorbita'lis** [N A, B N A], branches of the infraorbital nerve, supplying the skin and conjunctiva of the lower eyelid; modality, general sensory. Called also *inferior palpebral branches of infraorbital nerve.* **r. palpebra'lis infe'rior ner'vi infratrochlea'ris** [B N A]. See *rami palpebrales nervi infratrochlearis.* **ra'mi palpebra'les ner'vi infratrochlea'ris** [N A], branches of the infratrochlear nerve that help supply the eyelids; modality, general sensory. Called also *palpebral branches of infratrochlear nerve.* **r. palpebra'lis supe'rior ner'vi infratrochlea'ris** [B N A]. See *rami palpebrales nervi infratrochlearis.* **ra'mi pancreat'ici arte'riae liena'lis** [N A, B N A], branches that supply the pancreas, arising from the splenic artery during its tortuous course along the superior border of the body of the pancreas. Called also *pancreatic branches of splenic artery.* **ra'mi pancreat'ici arte'riae pancreaticoduodena'lis superio'ris** [N A, B N A], vessels that help supply the pancreas from its anterior and inferior surfaces. Called also *pancreatic branches of superior pancreaticoduodenal artery.* **ra'mi parieta'les aor'tae abdomina'lis** [B N A], parietal branches of the abdominal aorta. Omitted in N A. **ra'mi parieta'les aor'tae thoraca'lis** [B N A], parietal branches of the thoracic aorta. Omitted in N A. **ra'mi parieta'les arte'riae cer'ebri anterio'ris** [N A], branches of the anterior cerebral artery that supply the cortex of the parietal lobe except on the lower part of the lateral surface. Called also *parietal branches of anterior cerebral artery.* **ra'mi parieta'les arte'riae cer'ebri me'diae** [N A], branches of the middle cerebral artery that supply the cortex of the lower lateral surface of the parietal lobe. Called also *parietal branches of middle cerebral artery.* **ra'mi parieta'les arte'riae hypogas'tricae** [B N A], parietal branches of the hypogastric artery. Omitted in N A. **r. parieta'lis arte'riae menin'geae me'diae** [N A], a vessel that arises in the middle cranial fossa, grooves the temporal and parietal bones, and supplies the posterior dura mater. Called also *parietal branch of middle meningeal artery.* **r. parieta'lis arte'riae tempora'lis superficia'lis** [N A, B N A], the posterior terminal branch of the superficial temporal artery, supplying the auricular muscles and the skin of the scalp in the parietal region. Called also *parietal branch of superficial temporal artery.* **r. parietooccipita'lis arte'riae cer'ebri posterio'ris** [N A], a vessel that supplies the cortex of the medial surface of the hemisphere up to the area of the parietooccipital sulcus. Called also *parietooccipital branch of posterior cerebral artery.* **ra'mi parotide'i arte'riae tempora'lis superficia'lis** [N A, B N A], vessels supplying the parotid gland and the temporomandibular joint. Called also *parotid branches of superficial temporal artery.* **ra'mi parotide'i ner'vi auriculotempora'lis** [N A, B N A], branches that bear postganglionic fibers from the otic ganglion to the parotid gland; modality, parasympathetic. Called also *parotid branches of auriculotemporal nerve.* **ra'mi parotide'i ve'nae facia'lis** [N A], small veins from the substance of the parotid gland which follow the parotid duct and open into the facial vein. Called also *venae parotideae anteriores* [B N A], and *parotid branches of facial vein.* **ra'mi pectora'les arte'riae thoracoacromia'lis** [N A, B N A], branches of the thoracoacromial artery that descend between the pectoralis major and minor muscles, supplying these muscles and the mammary gland. Called also *pectoral branches of thoracoacromial artery.* **ra'mi perforan'tes arte'riae mamma'riae inter'nae** [B N A], rami perforantes arteriae thoracicae internae. **ra'mi perforan'tes arteria'rum metacarpea'rum palma'rium** [N A], **ra'mi perforan'tes arteria'rum metacarpea'rum vola'rium** [B N A], vessels connecting the palmar metacarpal arteries and deep palmar arch with the dorsal metacarpal arteries, between the bases of the metacarpal bones and in the interosseous spaces. Called also *perforating branches of palmar metacarpal arteries.* **ra'mi perforan'tes arteria'rum metatarsea'rum planta'rium** [N A, B N A], vessels connecting the plantar metatarsal arteries with the dorsal metatarsal arteries through the interosseous spaces. Called also *perforating branches of plantar metatarsal arteries.* **r. per'forans arte'riae perone'ae** [N A], a branch passing forward from the peroneal artery where the interosseous membrane and the tibiofibular syndesmosis are continuous, and descending to supply the syndesmosis and the ankle joint. Called also *perforating branch of peroneal artery.* **ra'mi perforan'tes arte'riae thora'cicae inter'nae** [N A, B N A], six branches, one in each of the upper six intercostal spaces, supplying the pectoralis major muscle and adjacent skin; the second, third, and fourth branches give off mammary branches. Called also *rami perforantes arteriae mammariae internae* [B N A], and *perforating branches of internal thoracic artery.* **ra'mi pericardi'aci aor'tae thoraca'lis** [B N A], **ra'mi pericardi'aci aor'tae thora'cicae** [N A], small branches from the aorta distributed to the surface of the pericardium. Called also *pericardiac branches of thoracic aorta.* **r. pericardi'acus ner'vi phren'ici** [N A, B N A], a branch arising from the phrenic or accessory phrenic nerve and supplying the pericardium; modality, general sensory. Called also *pericardiac branch of phrenic nerve.* **ra'mi perinea'les ner'vi cuta'nei fem'oris posterio'ris** [N A, B N A], branches arising from the posterior femoral cutaneous nerve at the lower margin of the gluteus maximus muscle and innervating the skin of the external genitalia; modality, general sensory. Called also *perineal branches of posterior femoral cutaneous nerve.* **r. petro'sus arte'riae menin'geae me'diae** [N A], **r. petro'sus superficia'lis arte'riae menin'geae me'diae** [B N A], a branch that arises in the region of the petrous part of the temporal bone, entering the hiatus for the greater petrosal nerve and anastomosing with the stylomastoid artery. Called also *petrosal branch of middle meningeal artery.* **ra'mi pharyn'gei arte'riae pharyn'geae ascenden'tis** [N A, B N A], irregular vessels supplying the constrictor muscles of the pharynx. Called also *pharyngeal branches of ascending pharyngeal artery.* **ra'mi pharyn'gei arte'riae thyroi'deae inferio'ris** [N A], vessels that supply the pharynx. Called also *pharyngeal branches of inferior thyroid artery.* **ra'mi pharyn'gei ner'vi glossopharyn'gei** [N A, B N A], branches from the glossopharyngeal nerve that innervate the mucous membrane of the oropharynx; modality, general sensory. Called also *pharyngeal branches of glossopharyngeal nerve.* **ra'mi pharyn'gei ner'vi va'gi** [N A, B N A], branches of the vagus nerve that innervate pharyngeal muscles and mucosa; modality, motor and general sensory. Called also *pharyngeal branches of vagus nerve.* **ra'mi phrenicoabdomina'les ner'vi phren'ici** [N A, B N A], branches that arise from the phrenic or accessory phrenic nerve to supply the diaphragm; modality, general sensory and motor. Called also *phrenicoabdominal branches of phrenic nerve.* **r. planta'ris profun'dus arte'riae dorsa'lis pe'dis** [N A, B N A], the main terminal branch of the dorsalis pedis artery, which passes through the first intermetatarsal space to the sole to form the plantar arch. Called also *deep plantar branch of dorsalis pedis artery.* **ra'mi posterio'res arteria'rum intercosta'lium** [B N A]. See *r. dorsalis arteriarum intercostalium posteriorum [III–XI].* **r. poste'rior arte'riae obturato'riae** [N A, B N A], a branch of the obturator artery that passes backward around the lateral margin of the obturator foramen, on the obturator membrane, supplying muscles around the ischial tuberosity and giving off an acetabular branch. Called also *posterior branch of obturator artery.* **r. poste'rior arte'riae recurren'tis ulna'ris** [N A], a branch of the ulnar recurrent artery that runs to the back of the medial epicondyle, supplying the elbow joint and neighboring muscles. Called also *posterior branch of ulnar recurrent artery.* **r. poste'rior arte'riae thyroi'deae superio'ris** [N A], a vessel supplying the posterior part of the thyroid gland. Called also *posterior branch of superior thyroid artery.* **r. poste'rior fissu'rae cer'ebri latera'lis [Syl'vii]** [B N A], r. posterior sulci lateralis cerebri. **r. poste'rior ner'vi auricula'ris mag'ni** [N A, B N A], a branch, formed by division of the great auricular nerve, that innervates the skin over the mastoid process and the back of the external ear; modality, general sensory. Called also *posterior branch of great auricular nerve.* **ra'mi posterio'res nervo'rum cervica'lium** [B N A], rami dorsales nervorum cervicalium. **r. poste'rior ner'vi laryn'gei inferio'ris** [B N A], posterior branch of inferior laryngeal nerve. Omitted in N A. **ra'mi posterio'res nervo'rum lumba'lium** [B N A], rami dorsales nervorum lumbalium. **r. poste'rior ner'vi obturato'rii** [N A, B N A], a branch that descends to innervate the knee joint, giving muscular branches to the obturator externus, adductor magnus, and sometimes the adductor brevis muscle; modality, general sensory and motor. Called also *posterior branch of obturator nerve.* **ra'mi posterio'res nervo'rum sacra'lium** [B N A], rami dorsales nervorum sacralium. **r. poste'rior nervo'rum spina'lium** [B N A], r. dorsalis nervorum spinalium. **ra'mi posterio'res nervo'rum thoraca'lium** [B N A], rami dorsales nervorum thoracicorum. **r. poste'rior ramo'rum cutaneo'rum latera'lium [abdomina'lium et pectora'lium] arteria'rum intercosta'lium** [B N A], posterior branch of (abdominal and thoracic) lateral cutaneous branches of intercostal arteries. Omitted in N A. **r. poste'rior ramo'rum cutaneo'rum latera'lium [abdomina'lium et pectora'lium] nervo'rum intercosta'lium** [B N A], posterior branch of (abdominal and thoracic) lateral cutaneous branches of intercostal nerves. Omitted in N A. **r. poste'rior sul'ci latera'lis cer'ebri** [N A], the part of the lateral cerebral sulcus that runs obliquely posteriorly between the temporal and the parietal lobes. Called also *r. posterior fissurae cerebri lateralis* [*Sylvii*] [B N A], and *posterior branch of lateral cerebral sulcus*. **r. profun'dus arte'riae cervica'lis ascenden'tis** [B N A], deep branch of ascending cervical artery. Omitted in N A. **r. profun'dus arte'riae circumflex'ae fem'oris media'lis** [N A, B N A], a branch ascending toward the trochanteric fossa, and anastomosing with gluteal branches. Called also *deep branch of medial circumflex femoral artery*. **r. profun'dus arte'riae glu'teae superio'ris** [N A], a branch passing forward between the gluteus medius and minimus muscles, and dividing into superior and inferior branches to supply gluteal, obturator internus, piriformis, levator ani, and coccygeus muscles, and the hip joint and ilium. Called also *deep branch of superior gluteal artery*. **r. profun'dus arte'riae planta'ris media'lis** [N A, B N A], a branch of the medial plantar artery that supplies muscles, articulations, and the skin of the anteromedial aspect of the sole, anastomosing with the *medial three plantar metatarsal arteries*. Called also *deep branch of medial plantar artery*. **r. profun'dus arte'riae transver'sae col'li** [N A], a branch of the transverse cervical artery that descends to supply medial and deep back muscles; sometimes replaced by an artery stemming directly from the subclavian artery (arteria scapularis descendens). Called also *r. descendens arteriae transversae colli* [B N A], and *deep branch of transverse cervical artery*. **r. profun'dus ner'vi planta'ris latera'lis** [N A, B N A], the branch of the lateral plantar nerve that accompanies the lateral plantar artery on its medial side and the plantar arch, innervating the interosseous, the second, third, and fourth lumbrical, and the adductor hallucis muscles, and some articulations; modality, general sensory. Called also *deep branch of lateral plantar nerve*. **r. profun'dus ner'vi radia'lis** [N A, B N A], a branch arising from the radial nerve and winding laterally around the radius to the back of the forearm, supplying the supinator, extensor digitorum, extensor digiti minimi, and extensor carpi ulnaris muscles. Its branch, the posterior interosseous nerve, supplies distal forearm muscles and the carpal and intercarpal joints; modality, motor. Called also *deep branch of radial nerve*. **r. profun'dus ner'vi ulna'ris** [N A, B N A], the deep branch that is accompanied by the deep palmar branch of the ulnar artery, rounds the hook of the hamate bone, and follows the deep palmar arch beneath the flexor tendons, innervating wrist articulations and many of the short muscles of the hand; modality, general sensory and motor. Called also *deep branch of ulnar nerve*. **ra'mi pterygoi'dei arte'riae maxilla'ris** [N A], **ra'mi pterygoi'dei arte'riae maxilla'ris inter'nae** [B N A], branches from the maxillary artery that supply the pterygoid muscles. Called also *pterygoid branches of maxillary artery*. **r. pu'bicus arte'riae epigas'tricae inferio'ris** [N A, B N A], a branch that arises from the inferior epigastric artery near the deep inguinal ring and descends on the back of the pubis, anastomosing through an obturator branch with the pubic branch of the obturator artery. Called also *pubic branch of inferior epigastric artery*. **r. pu'bicus arte'riae obturato'riae** [N A, B N A], a branch that ascends on the pelvic surface of the ilium, anastomosing with its fellow of the other side and with the pubic branch of the inferior epigastric artery. Called also *pubic branch of obturator artery*. **r. of pubis.** See *r. inferior ossis pubis* and *r. superior ossis pubis*. **ra'mi pulmona'les plex'us cardi'aci** [B N A], **ra'mi pulmona'les systema'tis autonom'ici** [N A], branches from the sympathetic trunks and cardiac plexus, via the pulmonary plexuses, which accompany the blood vessels and bronchi into the lungs; modality, sympathetic and visceral afferent. Called also *pulmonary branches of autonomic system*. **r. rena'lis ner'vi splanch'nici mino'ris** [N A, B N A], a branch from the lesser splanchnic nerve to the aorticorenal ganglion; modality, sympathetic preganglionic fibers and visceral afferent. Called also *renal branch of lesser splanchnic nerve*. **ra'mi rena'les ner'vi va'gi** [NA], **ra'mi rena'les plex'us coeli'aci** [B N A], branches passing from the vagal trunks by way of the celiac plexus to the kidney; modality, parasympathetic and visceral afferent. Called also *renal branches of vagus nerve*. **r. saphe'nus arte'riae ge'nu supre'mae** [B N A], **r. saphe'nus arte'riae ge'nus descen'dens** [N A], a vessel that accompanies the saphenous nerve between the sartorius and gracilis muscles on the medial side of the knee, supplying the skin and anastomosing with the medial inferior genicular artery. Called also *saphenous branch of descending genicular artery*. **ra'mi scrota'les anterio'res arte'riae femora'lis** [N A], branches arising from the external pudendal arteries and supplying the anterior scrotal region in the male. Called also *arteriae scrotales anteriores* [B N A], and *anterior scrotal branches of femoral artery*. **ra'mi scrota'les posterio'res arte'riae puden'dae inter'nae** [N A], two branches arising from the internal pudendal artery in the anterior part of the ischiorectal fossa, helping to supply the ischiocavernosus and bulbospongiosus muscles, and distributed to the scrotum. Called also *arteriae scrotales posteriores* [B N A], and *posterior scrotal branches of internal pudendal artery*. **r. sinis'ter arte'riae hepat'icae pro'priae** [N A, B N A], a branch of the proper hepatic artery supplying the left lobe of the liver. Called also *left branch of proper hepatic artery*. **r. sinis'ter arte'riae pulmona'lis** [B N A], arteria pulmonalis sinistra. **r. si'nus carot'ici ner'vi glossopharyn'gei** [N A], a branch that supplies the pressoreceptors and chemoreceptors of the carotid sinus and carotid body with visceral afferent fibers. Called also *branch of glossopharyngeal nerve to carotid sinus*. **ra'mi spina'les arte'riae cervica'lis ascenden'tis** [N A, B N A], branches of the ascending cervical artery that help supply the vertebral canal. Called also *spinal branches of ascending cervical artery*. **r. spina'lis arte'riae iliolumba'lis** [B N A], r. spinalis rami lumbalis arteriae iliolumbalis. **ra'mi spina'les arte'riae intercosta'lis supre'mae** [N A, B N A], vessels arising from the dorsal branches of the first two posterior intercostal arteries, entering intervertebral foramina with the corresponding two spinal nerves to help supply vertebrae and the contents of the vertebral canal. Called also *spinal branches of highest intercostal artery*. **r. spina'lis arteria'rum lumba'lium** [N A, B N A], a branch arising from the dorsal branch of the lumbar arteries and entering an intervertebral foramen with the spinal nerve to help supply the vertebral canal. Called also *spinal branch of lumbar arteries*. **ra'mi spina'les arteria'rum sacra'lium latera'lium** [N A], vessels arising from the two lateral sacral arteries and entering the pelvic sacral foramina to supply contents of the vertebral canal. Called also *spinal branches of lateral sacral arteries*. **r. spina'lis arte'riae subcosta'lis** [N A], a spinal branch corresponding to those arising from the dorsal branches of the posterior intercostal arteries; it enters the vertebral canal to help supply the spinal cord, meninges, and vertebrae. Called also *spinal branch of subcostal artery*. **ra'mi spina'les arte'riae vertebra'lis** [N A, B N A], vessels supplying cervical vertebrae, and the spinal cord and membranes in the cervical part of the vertebral canal. Called also *spinal branches of vertebral artery*. **r. spina'lis ra'mi dorsa'lis arteria'rum intercosta'lium posteri'orum [III–XI]** [N A], **r. spina'lis ramo'rum posterio'rum arteria'rum intercosta'lium** [B N A], one of the two branches into which the dorsal branch of a posterior intercostal artery divides, passing through the intervertebral foramen with the corresponding spinal nerve to help supply the contents of the vertebral canal, and the vertebrae. Called also *spinal branch of dorsal branch of posterior intercostal arteries [III–XI]*. **r. spina'lis ra'mi lumba'lis arte'riae iliolumba'lis** [N A], a vessel that arises from the lumbar branch of the iliolumbar artery and passes through the intervertebral foramen between the fifth lumbar vertebra and the sacrum to help supply the vertebral canal. Called also *spinal branch of lumbar branch of iliolumbar artery*. **r. spina'lis vena'rum intercosta'lium** [B N A], **r. spina'lis vena'rum intercosta'lium posterio'rum [IV–XI]** [N A], a vessel, the vena comitans of the arterial spinal branch, that emerges from the vertebral canal and contributes to the dorsal branch of each posterior intercostal vein. Called also *spinal branch of posterior intercostal veins*. **r. stape'dius arte'riae stylomastoi'deae** [N A, B N A], a variable branch from the stylomastoid artery, supplying the stapedius muscle and tendon. Called also *stapedial branch of stylomastoid artery*. **ra'mi sterna'les arte'riae mamma'riae inter'nae** [B N A], **ra'mi sterna'les arte'riae thora'cicae inter'nae** [N A], branches from the internal thoracic artery that supply the sternum and the transversus thoracis muscle. Called also *sternal branches of internal thoracic artery*. **ra'mi sternocleidomastoi'dei arte'riae occipita'lis** [N A], branches of the occipital artery, usually an upper and a lower, that supply the sternocleidomastoid and adjacent muscles. Called also *rami musculares arteriae occipitalis* [B N A], and *sternocleidomastoid branches of occipital artery*. **r. sternocleidomastoi'deus arte'riae thyroi'deae superio'ris** [N A], a branch that arises from the superior thyroid artery, but sometimes directly from the external carotid artery, passing across the carotid sheath to supply the middle portion of the sternocleidomastoid muscle. Called also *sternocleidomastoid branch of superior thyroid artery*. **ra'mi stria'ti arte'riae cer'ebri me'diae** [N A], central branches that supply the basal ganglia, thalamus, and internal capsule. Called also *striate branches of middle cerebral artery*. **r. stylohyoi'deus ner'vi facia'lis** [N A, B N A], a branch that arises from the facial nerve just below the base of the skull to innervate the stylohyoid muscle; modality, motor. Called also *stylohyoid branch of facial nerve*. **r. stylopharyn'geus ner'vi glossopharyn'gei** [B N A], r. musculi stylopharyngei nervi glossopharyngei. **ra'mi submaxilla'res gan'glii submaxilla'ris** [B N A], rami glandulares ganglii submandibularis. **ra'mi subscapula'res arte'riae axilla'ris** [N A, B N A], branches of the axillary artery that supply the subscapularis muscle. Called also *subscapular branches of axillary artery*. **r. superficia'lis arte'riae circumflex'ae fem'oris media'lis** [B N A], the superficial branch of the medial circumflex femoral artery. Omitted in N A. **r. superficia'lis arte'riae glu'teae superio'ris** [N A], a branch of the superior gluteal artery that ramifies to supply the gluteus maximus muscle and overlying skin. Called also *superficial branch of superior gluteal artery*. **r. superficia'lis arte'riae planta'ris media'lis** [N A, B N A], a branch of the medial plantar artery that supplies the medial side of the great toe. Called also *superficial branch of medial plantar artery*. **r. superficia'lis arte'riae transver'sae col'li** [N A], a branch that arises from the transverse cervical artery at the anterior border of the levator scapulae muscle, supplying the levator scapulae, trapezius, and splenius muscles. When there is no deep branch, the superficial branch is the continuation of the transverse cervical called the superficial cervical artery. Called also *r. ascendens arteriae transversae colli* [B N A], and *superficial branch of transverse cervical artery*. **r. superficia'lis ner'vi planta'ris latera'lis** [N A, B N A], a branch that arises from the lateral plantar nerve at the lateral border of the quadratus plantae muscle and passes forward, dividing into a lateral part that innervates skin of the lateral side of the sole and little toe, joints of the toe, and the flexor digiti minimi brevis muscle, and a medial part, a common plantar digital nerve, that gives two proper plantar digital nerves to the adjacent sides of the fourth and fifth toes; modality, general sensory. Called also *superficial branch of lateral plantar nerve*. **r. superficia'lis ner'vi radia'lis** [N A, B N A], the continuation of the radial nerve that accompanies the radial artery in the forearm, winds dorsalward, supplies the lateral side of the back of the hand, and divides into dorsal digital nerves that supply the skin of the dorsal surface and adjacent surfaces of the thumb, index, and middle fingers, and sometimes the radial side of the ring finger; modality, general sensory. Called also *superficial branch of radial nerve*. **r. superficia'lis ner'vi ulna'ris** [N A, B N A], the branch of the ulnar nerve in the hand that supplies the palmaris brevis muscle and divides into a proper palmar digital nerve for the medial side of the little finger, a common palmar digital nerve giving off two proper nerves to supply adjacent sides of the little and fourth fingers, and sometimes palmar digital nerves also for the adjacent sides of the third and fourth fingers; modality, general sensory and motor. Called also *superficial branch of ulnar nerve*. **r. supe'rior arte'riae glu'teae superio'ris** [N A], an upper division of the deep branch of the superior gluteal artery, extending as far as the anterior superior iliac spine and helping supply the gluteus medius, gluteus minimus, and tensor fasciae latae muscles. Called also *superior branch of superior gluteal artery*. **ra'mi superio'res ner'vi cuta'nei col'li** [B N A], rami superiores nervi transversi colli. **r. supe'rior ner'vi oculomoto'rii** [N A, B N A], the upper and smaller of the two branches of the oculomotor nerve, which supplies the superior rectus muscle and, terminally, the levator palpebrae superioris; modality, motor. Called also *superior branch of oculomotor nerve*. **ra'mi superio'res ner'vi transver'si col'li** [N A], the upper of the branches that arise from the transverse cervical nerve near the anterior border of the sternocleidomastoid muscle, innervating skin and subcutaneous tissue in the anterior cervical region; modality, general sensory. Called also *rami superiores nervi cutanei colli* [B N A], and *superior branches of transverse cervical nerve*. **r. supe'rior os'sis is'chii** [B N A], a name formerly given to what is now considered the lower part of the body of the ischium (corpus ossis ischii). Omitted in N A. **r. supe'rior os'sis pu'bis** [N A, B N A], the bar of bone projecting from the body of the pubic bone in a postero-supero-lateral direction to the iliopubic eminence, and forming part of the acetabulum. Called also *superior r. of pubis*. **r. suprahyoi'deus arte'riae lingua'lis** [N A], a branch of the lingual artery that passes along the upper border of the hyoid bone, supplying suprahyoid muscles and anastomosing with its fellow of the other side. Called also *r. hyoideus arteriae lingualis* [B N A], and *suprahyoid branch of lingual artery*. **ra'mi suprarena'les superio'res arte'riae phren'icae inferio'ris** [B N A]. See *arteria suprarenalis superior*. **r. sympath'icus ad gan'glion cilia're** [N A], a branch bearing sympathetic fibers, postganglionic from the superior cervical ganglion and derived from the internal carotid plexus, to the ciliary ganglion, for distribution by the short ciliary nerves to the dilator pupillae, orbitalis, and tarsal muscles, and blood vessels of the eyeball. Called also *radices sympathicae ganglii ciliaris* [B N A], and *sympathetic branch to ciliary ganglion*. **r. sympath'icus ad gan'glion submandibula're** [N A], a branch bearing sympathetic fibers, postganglionic from the superior cervical ganglion and derived from a plexus on the facial artery, to the submandibular ganglion, for distribution to the submandibular gland. Called also *radix sympathica ganglii submaxillaris* [B N A], and *sympathetic branch to submandibular ganglion.* **ra′mi tempora′les arte′riae cer′ebri me′diae** [N A], vessels that supply the cortex of the lateral surface of the temporal lobe, and the temporal pole. Called also *temporal branches of middle cerebral artery.* **ra′mi tempora′les arte′riae cer′ebri posterio′ris** [N A], vessels that supply the cortex of the inferior and medial surfaces of the temporal lobe. Called also *temporal branches of posterior cerebral artery.* **ra′mi tempora′les ner′vi facia′lis** [N A, B N A], terminal branches of the facial nerve that innervate the anterior and superior auricular muscles, the frontal belly of the occipitofrontal muscle, and the orbicularis oculi and corrugator muscles; modality, motor. Called also *temporal branches of facial nerve.* **ra′mi tempora′les superficia′les ner′vi auriculotempora′lis** [N A, B N A], branches to the skin of the scalp in the temporal region; modality, general sensory. Called also *superficial temporal branches of auriculotemporal nerve.* **r. tento′rii ner′vi oph-thal′mici** [N A], a branch that arises from the ophthalmic nerve close to its origin from the trigeminal ganglion, turning back to innervate the dura mater of the tentorium cerebelli and falx cerebri; modality, general sensory. Called also *nervus tentorii* [B N A], and *tentorial branch of ophthalmic nerve.* **ra′mi thy′mici arte′riae thora′cicae inter′nae** [N A], branches distributed to the thymus gland in the anterior mediastinum. Called also *arteriae thymicae* [B N A], and *thymic branches of internal thoracic artery.* **r. thyreohyoi′deus ner′vi hypoglos′si** [B N A], **r. thyrohyoi′deus an′sae cervica′lis** [N A], a branch from the superior root of the ansa cervicalis, innervating the thyrohyoid muscle; modality, motor. Called also *thyrohyoid branch of ansa cervicalis.* **r. tonsilla′ris arte′riae facia′lis** [N A], **r. tonsilla′ris arte′riae maxilla′ris exter′ni** [B N A], a vessel ascending from the facial artery on the pharynx to supply the tonsil and the root of the tongue. Called also *tonsillar branch of facial artery.* **ra′mi tonsilla′res ner′vi glossopharyn′gei** [N A, B N A], branches from the glossopharyngeal nerve that supply the mucosa over the palatine tonsil and the adjacent portion of the soft palate; modality, general sensory. Called also *tonsillar branches of glossopharyngeal nerve.* **ra′mi trachea′les arte′riae thyroi′deae infe-rio′ris** [N A], vessels supplying the trachea. Called also *tracheal branches of inferior thyroid artery.* **ra′mi trachea′les ner′vi laryn′gei recurren′tis** [N A], **ra′mi trachea′les ner′vi recurren′tis** [B N A], branches arising from the recurrent laryngeal nerve and distributed to the tracheal mucosa; modality, general sensory. Called also *tracheal branches of recurrent laryngeal nerve.* **r. transver′sus arte′riae circum-flex′ae fem′oris latera′lis** [N A], a branch that pierces the vastus lateralis muscle, turning around the femur to anastomose with the transverse branch of the medial circumflex femoral artery and with other arteries, deep to the gluteus maximus muscle. Called also *transverse branch of lateral circumflex femoral artery.* **r. transver′sus arte′riae circumflex′ae fem′oris media′lis** [N A], a branch of the medial circumflex artery passing between the quadratus femoris and adductor magnus muscles, supplying them, and then turning around the femur to anastomose with the transverse branch of the lateral circumflex femoral artery and with other arteries, deep to the gluteus maximus muscle. Called also *transverse branch of medial circumflex femoral artery.* **r. tu′bae plex′us tympan′ici [Jacobso′ni]** [B N A], r. tubarius plexus tympanici. **r. tuba′rius arte′riae uteri′nae** [N A, B N A], a branch from the uterine artery that supplies the uterine tube and the round ligament. Called also *tubal branch of uterine artery.* **r. tuba′rius plex′us tympan′ici** [N A], a branch given to the auditory tube from the tympanic plexus; modality, general sensory. Called also *r. tubae plexus tympanici* [*Jacobsoni*] [B N A], and *tubal branch of tympanic plexus.* **r. ulna′ris ner′vi cuta′nei antebra′chii media′lis** [N A], a branch that innervates the skin of the posteromedial and medial aspects of the forearm; modality, general sensory. Called also *ulnar branch of medial antebrachial cutaneous nerve.* **ra′mi ureter′ici arte′riae duc′tus defe-ren′tis** [N A], branches that arise from the artery of the ductus deferens to supply the lower portion of the ureter. Called also *ureteral branches of artery of ductus deferens.* **ra′mi ureter′ici arte′riae ova′ricae** [N A], branches of the ovarian artery that are distributed to the ureter. Called also *ureteral branches of ovarian artery.* **ra′mi ureter′ici arte′riae rena′lis** [N A], branches from the renal artery that supply the upper portion of the ureter. Called also *ureteral branches of renal artery.* **ra′mi ureter′ici arte′riae testicula′ris** [N A], branches from the testicular artery that are distributed to the ureter. Called also *ureteral branches of testicular artery.* **ra′mi ventra′les nervo′rum cervica′lium** [N A], the ventral branches of the cervical spinal nerves, the upper four forming the cervical plexus, and the lower four forming most of the brachial plexus. Called also *rami anteriores nervorum cervicalium* [B N A], and *ventral branches of cervical nerves.* **r. ventra′lis ner′vi coccyg′ei** [N A], the ventral branch of the last spinal nerve, which emerges from the sacral hiatus and helps form the small coccygeal plexus. Called also *r. anterior nervi coccygei* [B N A], and *ventral branch of coccygeal nerve.* **ra′mi ventra′les nervo′rum lumba′lium** [N A], the ventral branches of the five lumbar sacral nerves. The upper four branches form the lumbar plexus, and the fifth and a part of the fourth participate in formation of the sacral plexus. Called also *rami anteriores nervorum lumbalium* [B N A], and *ventral branches of lumbar nerves.* **ra′mi ventra′les nervo′rum sacra′lium** [N A], the ventral branches of the five sacral spinal nerves; the upper four branches emerge from the sacrum through the anterior sacral foramina and help form the sacral plexus; the fifth emerges through the sacral hiatus and participates in formation of the small coccygeal plexus. Called also *rami anteriores nervorum sacralium* [B N A], and *ventral branches of sacral nerves.* **r. ventra′lis nervo′rum spina′lium** [N A], the larger, usually, of the two branches into which each spinal nerve divides almost as soon as it emerges from the intervertebral foramen. The ventral branches supply the ventral and lateral parts of the trunk and all parts of the limbs. Called also *r. anterior nervorum spinalium* [B N A], and *ventral branch of spinal nerves.* **ra′mi ventra′les nervo′rum thoracico′rum** [N A], the ventral branches of the twelve thoracic spinal nerves. The ventral branch of the first thoracic spinal nerve participates in the brachial plexus; those of the second through eleventh are the intercostal nerves; that of the twelfth is the subcostal nerve, which contributes to the lumbar plexus. Called also *rami anteriores nervorum thoracalium* [B N A], and *ventral branches of thoracic nerves.* **ra′mi vestibula′res arte′riae auditi′vae inter′nae** [B N A], **ra′mi vestibula′res arte′riae labyrin′thi** [N A], vessels supplying the vestibule. Called also *vestibular branches of labyrinthine artery.* **ra′mi viscera′les aor′tae abdomina′lis** [B N A], visceral branches of the abdominal aorta. Omitted in N A. **ra′mi viscera′les aor′tae thoraca′lis** [B N A], visceral branches of the thoracic aorta. Omitted in N A. **ra′mi viscera′les arte′riae hypogas′tricae** [B N A], visceral branches of the hypogastric artery. Omitted in N A. **r. vola′ris ma′nus ner′vi ulna′ris** [B N A], r. palmaris nervi ulnaris. **r. vola′ris ner′vi cuta′nei antibrach′ii media′lis** [B N A], r. anterior nervi cutanei antebrachii medialis. **r. vola′ris profun′dus arte′riae ulna′ris** [B N A], r. palmaris profundus arteriae ulnaris. **r. vola′ris superficia′lis arte′riae**

radia'lis [B N A], r. palmaris superficialis arteriae radialis. **ra'mi zygomat'ici ner'vi facia'lis** [N A, B N A], branches that cross the zygomatic bone and innervate the greater zygomatic and orbicularis oculi muscles; modality, motor. Called also *zygomatic branches of facial nerve.* **r. zygomaticofacia'lis ner'vi zygomat'ici** [N A, B N A], a branch that passes from the lateral wall of the orbit, piercing the zygomatic bone to supply overlying skin; modality, general sensory. Called also *zygomaticofacial branch of zygomatic nerve.* **r. zygomaticotempora'lis ner'vi zygomat'ici** [N A, B N A], a branch that passes from the lateral wall of the orbit, piercing the zygomatic bone to innervate skin of the anterior temporal region; modality, general sensory. Called also *zygomaticotemporal branch of zygomatic nerve.*

rancid (ran'sid) [L. *rancidus*]. Having a musty, rank taste or smell; applied to fats that have undergone decomposition, with the liberation of fatty acids.

rancidify (ran-sid'ĭ-fi). To decompose, with the liberation of fatty acids: a term applied especially to the decomposition of fats.

rancidity (ran-sid'ĭ-te). The quality of being rancid.

Randolph's test (ran'dolfs) [Nathaniel Archer *Randolph*, American physician, 1858–1887]. See under *tests.*

range (rānj). The difference between the upper and lower limits of a variable or of a series of values. **r. of accommodation,** the alteration in the refractive state of the eye produced by accommodation. It is the difference in diopters between the refraction by the eye adjusted for its far point and that when adjusted for its near point. Called also *amplitude of accommodation* and *breadth of accommodation.* **r. of audibility.** See under *limit.*

ranine (ra'nīn) [L. *raninus; rana* frog]. 1. Pertaining to a frog. 2. Pertaining to a ranula, or to the lower surface of the tongue.

Ranke's angle (rahn'kēz) [Hans Rudolph *Ranke*, Dutch anatomist, 1849–1887]. See under *angle.*

Ranke's formula, stages (rahn'kēz) [Karl Ernst *Ranke*, Munich internist, 1870–1926]. See under *formula* and *stage.*

rankenangioma (ran"ken-an"je-o'mah) [Ger.]. A racemose or cirsoid aneurysm.

Ransohoff's operation (ran'so-hofs) [Joseph *Ransohoff*, American surgeon, 1853–1921]. See under *operation.*

ranula (ran'u-lah) [L., dim. of *rana* frog]. A cystic tumor beneath the tongue, due to obstruction and dilatation of the sublingual or submaxillary gland or of a mucous gland. **pancreatic r.,** a retention cyst of the pancreatic duct.

ranular (ran'u-lar). Pertaining to or of the nature of ranula.

Ranunculus (rah-nung'ku-lus). A genus of plants, the crowfoots and buttercups, certain species of which are poisonous.

Ranvier's cell, crosses, disks, membrane, nerve, node, etc. (rahn-ve-āz') [Louis Antoine *Ranvier*, French pathologist, 1835–1922]. See under the nouns.

Raoult's law (rah-ōlz') [François Marie *Raoult*, French physicist, 1830–1899]. See under *law.*

raphania (rah-fa'ne-ah) [L. *raphanus;* Gr. *rhaphanos* radish]. A chronic poisoning ascribed to the seeds of wild radish.

raphe (ra'fe) [Gr. *rhaphē*]. A seam; used in anatomical nomenclature as a general term to designate the line of union of the halves of various symmetrical parts. **abdominal r.,** linea alba. **amniotic r.,** the line of junction of the amniotic folds in the amnion of those vertebrates in which it is formed by folding. **r. anococcyg'ea, anococcygeal r.,** ligamentum anococcygeum. **r. chorioi'deae** [B N A]. Omitted in N A. **r. cor'poris callo'si.** See *stria longitudinalis medialis* and *stria longitudinalis lateralis corporis callosi.* **longitudinal r. of tongue,** sulcus medianus linguae. **median r. of neck, posterior,** ligamentum nuchae. **r. of medulla oblongata, r. medul'lae oblonga'tae** [N A, B N A], the line of union of the two halves of the medulla oblongata. **r. pala'ti** [N A, B N A], **palatine r.,** a narrow whitish streak in the midline of the palate, extending from the incisive papilla to the tip of the uvula; it may present as a ridge in front and as a groove posteriorly. **palpebral r., lateral, r. palpebra'lis latera'lis** [N A, B N A], a thin horizontal band of connective tissue extending from the external angle of the rima palpebralis to the lateral margin of the orbit. **r. pe'nis** [N A, B N A], a narrow dark streak or ridge continuous posteriorly with the raphe scroti and extending forward for a variable distance along the midline on the under side of the penis; in the newborn it may extend to the tip of the glans. **r. perine'i** [N A, B N A], **r. of perineum,** a ridge along the median line of the perineum, continuous anteriorly with the raphe scroti and ending posteriorly at the anus. **r. pharyn'gis** [N A, B N A], **r. of pharynx,** a more or less distinct band of connective tissue extending downward from the base of the skull along the posterior wall of the pharynx in the median plane, and giving attachment to the constrictor muscles of the pharynx. **r. of pons, r. pon'tis** [N A, B N A], the line of union of the right and left halves of the pons. **pterygomandibular r., r. pterygomandibula'ris** [N A, B N A], a tendinous line between the buccinator and the constrictor pharyngis superior muscles, from which the middle portions of both muscles originate. **r. scler'ae** [B N A]. Omitted in N A. **r. scro'ti** [N A, B N A], **r. of scrotum,** a ridge along the surface of the scrotum in the median line, dividing it into nearly equal lateral parts. **Stilling's r.,** decussatio pyramidum.

raphidiospore (rah-fid'e-o-spōr). Exotospore.

rapport (rah-port') [Fr.]. A relation of harmony and accord between two persons, especially between patient and physician.

raptus (rap'tus) [L.]. A sudden, violent attack. **r. haemorrha'gicus,** a sudden massive hemorrhage. **r. mani'acus,** a sudden, violent maniacal attack. **r. melanchol'icus,** an attack of frenzy or agitation occurring in a patient with melancholia. **r. nervo'rum,** a sudden, violent attack of nervousness.

rarefaction (rār"ĕ-fak'shun) [L. *rarefactio*]. The condition of being or becoming less dense; diminution in density and weight, but not in volume.

Ras. Abbreviation for L. *rasu'rae,* scrapings or filings.

rasceta (rah-se'tah) [L., pl.]. Transverse markings across the skin of the wrists, on the palmar surface.

Rasch's sign (rahsh'ez) [Hermann *Rasch*, German obstetrician, born 1873]. See under *sign.*

rash (rash). A temporary eruption on the skin, as in urticaria and strophulus; an exanthem. **aniline r.,** a skin inflammation due to aniline poisoning. **antitoxin r.,** a skin eruption frequently following the administration of antitoxin serum. **astacoid r.,** a reddish eruption in smallpox resembling in color the shell of a boiled lobster. **black currant r.,** the peculiar appearance of the skin in xeroderma pigmentosum. **cable r.,** halowax acne. **canker r.,** a popular name for scarlatina. **caterpillar r.,** a local eruption attributed to poisoning by the hairs of caterpillars. **crystal r.,** sudamina. **diaper r.,** a cutaneous reaction in an infant, localized to the area ordinarily covered by the diaper, and due to various primary irritants, such as the feces, or ammonia in decomposed urine, with histopathological changes varying with the causative factor; improperly processed diapers and other contact factors may also be responsible for such irritation. **drug r.,** a rash due to medication. **gum r.,**

strophulus. **heat r.,** miliaria rubra. **hydatid r.,** an urticarial eruption which sometimes follows tapping or rupture of a hydatid cyst. **lily r.,** dermatitis affecting those who pick daffodils and narcissi in early spring. **medicinal r.,** drug r. **mulberry r.,** a peculiar eruption of typhus, looking like that of measles. **nettle r.,** urticaria. **nickel r.,** a rash sometimes occurring in refiners of nickel. **rose r.,** roseola. **serum r.,** the rash that sometimes follows the injection of antitoxic serums. **summer r.,** lichen tropicus. **tonsillotomy r.,** an eruption on the neck and body after tonsillectomy. **tooth r.,** strophulus. **vaccine r.,** a rash that sometimes follows a vaccination. **wandering r.,** geographic tongue. **wildfire r.,** strophulus volaticus.

rasion (ra′zhun) [L. *rasio*]. The grating of drugs with a file.

Rasmussen's aneurysm (ras′mus-ens) [Fritz Waldemar *Rasmussen*, Danish physician, 1834–1881]. See under *aneurysm*.

raspatory (ras′pah-to-re) [L. *raspatorium*]. A file or rasp for surgeon's use; a xyster.

rasura (rah-su′rah) [L., pl.]. Scrapings or filings.

rat (rat). A rodent commonly found about human habitations. Rats not only cause great economic loss, but they are vectors of human disease; they harbor at least eleven different species of intestinal parasites that may be transmitted to man, such as tapeworms, round worms, and trichinae; they are the reservoirs for the infective agents of plague, typhus, Weil's disease and rat-bite fever. **albino r.,** white r. **black r.,** *Mus* (*Rattus*) *rattus*, the English black rat and the one most commonly responsible for transmitting plague to man by means of its flea (*Xenopsylla cheopis*). **brown r.,** *Mus* (*Rattus*) *norvegicus;* also called the barn rat, gray rat, Norway rat, sewer rat, and wharf rat. It is larger than the black rat, has a brownish-gray color, and short ears and tail. **Egyptian r., roof r.,** *Mus alexandrinus*. **white r.,** an albino form of *Mus rattus* or of *Mus norvegicus* which is much used as a laboratory animal. **wood r.,** a rat of the genus *Neotoma*. They are hosts of fleas and ticks.

rate (rāt). An expression of the speed or frequency with which a certain event or circumstance occurs in relation to a certain period of time, a specific population, or some other fixed standard. **attack r.,** the rate at which new cases of a specific disease occur. See *incidence*. **basal metabolic r.,** an expression of the rate at which oxygen is utilized by the body cells in a fasting subject at complete rest. **birth r.,** an expression of the number of births occurring during one year. The *crude birth rate* is the ratio of births to the total population; the *refined birth rate* is the ratio of births to the female population; the *true birth rate* is the ratio of births to the female population of child-bearing age, that is, between the ages of 15 and 45. **case r.,** morbidity r. **case fatality r.,** the number of deaths caused by a specific disease, expressed as a percentage of or otherwise related to the total number of cases of the disease. **circulation r.,** an expression of the amount of blood propelled per minute by the contractions of the left ventricle. **death r.,** the ratio of the total number of deaths in a specified area to the population, generally figured in terms of number of deaths per 1,000, 10,000, or 100,000 of population. The *crude death rate* is the ratio of the number of deaths within a given time (as one year) to the number of people alive at the middle of the period. The *specific death rate* is the proportion of deaths per annum in an age or other specified group of the population per 1,000 of the mean annual number of people in that group. **dose r.,** the amount of any agent administered per unit of time. **erythrocyte sedimentation r.,** an expression of the extent of settling of erythrocytes, per unit time, in a column of fresh citrated or otherwise treated blood, which is a rough measure of abnormal concentrations of fibrinogen and serum globulins that may accompany certain pathological or physiological states, as cancer, tuberculosis, or pregnancy. **fatality r.,** the number of deaths caused by a specific circumstance or disease, expressed as the absolute or relative number of deaths among the individuals encountering the circumstance or having the disease. **growth r.,** an expression of the increase in size of an organic object per unit time, calculations usually being made as to both the absolute and the relative increment. **heart r.,** the number of contractions of the ventricles of the heart per unit of time. It usually corresponds to the pulse rate, but occasionally some of the contractions of the left ventricle fail to produce peripheral pulse waves, so that the rate of the pulse at the wrist is less than that of the heart. **lethality r.,** fatality r. **mendelian r.,** an expression of the numerical relations of the occurrence of distinctly contrasted mendelian characters in succeeding generations of hybrid offspring. **morbidity r.,** the number of cases of a given disease occurring during a specified period per 1,000, 10,000, or 100,000 of population. **mortality r.,** death r. **oocyst r.,** the percentage of wild female mosquitoes found to contain oocysts in the midgut. **parasite r.,** the percentage of persons, in a particular age group or area, in whom parasites, especially malarial parasites, can be found. **pulse r.,** the rate of pulsation noted in a peripheral artery, normally 70 to 72 for men and 78 to 82 for women. **respiration r.,** an expression of the number of movements of the chest, indicative of inspiration and expiration, occurring per minute. **sickness r.,** morbidity r. **spleen r.,** the percentage of persons, in a particular age group or area, in whom the spleen can be palpated. **sporozoite r.,** the percentage of wild female mosquitoes found to contain sporozoites in the glands. **stillbirth r.,** an expression of the relation of the number of stillbirths to the total number of births.

Rathke's pocket, pouch, tumor (rahth′kez) [Martin H. *Rathke*, German anatomist, 1793–1860]. See under *pouch* and *tumor*.

raticide (rat′ĭ-sīd). An agent destructive to rats.

ratin (rat′in). A preparation of living bacteria of the paratyphoid enteritidis group, pathogenic to rats: used as a rat exterminator.

ratio (ra′she-o) [L.]. An expression of the quantity of one substance or entity in relation to that of another. **A-G r., albumin-globulin r.,** the ratio of albumin to globulin in the blood serum, plasma or the urine in various types of renal disease. **birth-death r.,** vital index. **body-weight r.,** body weight in grams divided by stature in centimeters. **cardiothoracic r.,** the ratio of the transverse diameter of the heart to the internal diameter of the chest at its widest point just above the level of the dome of the diaphragm. **cell color r.,** the result obtained by dividing the percentage of red cells by the percentage of hemoglobin. **concentration r.,** the ratio of the average concentration of a solid in the urine to its concentration in the blood. **curative r.,** the fraction of the minimal lethal dose of a drug that is therapeutically effective; called also *therapeutic r.* **D-N r., dextrose-nitrogen r.,** the ratio between the dextrose and the nitrogen of the urine. **G-N r., glucose-nitrogen r.,** D-N r. **hand r.,** the ratio of the length of the hand to its width. **human blood r.,** the proportion of freshly fed mosquitoes that contain human blood. **karyoplasmic r.,** nucleocytoplasmic ratio. **ketogenic-antiketogenic r.,** the proportion between substances that form glucose in the body and those that form fatty acids. **monocyte-lymphocyte r.,** the ratio between the monocytes and the lymphocytes in the blood in tuberculosis: improvement in the disease is associated with decrease of monocytes and increase of lymphocytes. **Moots-McKesson r.,** a blood pressure ratio for operation, namely the pulse pressure divided by the diastolic pressure. The normal range for safety in operations is 25 to 75 per cent, so that a 50 per cent ratio would be ideal. **nucleocytoplasmic r., nucleoplasmic r.,** the ratio of nuclear to cytoplasmic volume. **nutritive r.,** the ratio between the digestible protein and the digestible fats and carbohydrates in a ration in stock feeding. **sex r.,** an expression of the number of females in a population to the number of males, usually stated as the number of females per 100 males. **therapeutic r.,** curative r. **urea excretion r.,** the ratio of the number of milligrams of urea in the urine excreted in one hour to the number of milligrams in 100 cc. of blood: the normal ratio is 50.

ration (ra′shun) [L. *ratio* proportion]. A fixed allowance of food or drink per day or other unit of time. **basal r.,** a ration giving the required energy, but lacking in one or more vitamins.

rational (rash′un-al) [L. *rationalis* reasonable]. Accordant with reason; based upon reasoning and not upon simple experience.

rationale (rash″un-al′) [L.]. A rational exposition of principles; the logical basis of a procedure.

rationalization (rash″un-al-i-za′shun). The mental process by which a plausible explanation (justification) is concocted for ideas or beliefs or activities which one wishes to hold or to do; the real motivation being subconscious or at least obscure.

rat-tails (rat′tālz). A swollen condition of the hair papillae over the flexor tendons of a horse's leg, due to lichen.

Rattus (rat′us). A genus of small rodents; the rats.

Rau's process (row) [Johann J. *Rau* (Ravius), Dutch anatomist, 1658–1719]. See under *process*.

Rauber's layer (row′berz) [August Antinous *Rauber*, German anatomist, 1841–1917]. See under *layer*.

raucedo (raw-se′do) [L.]. Hoarseness.

Rauchfuss' sling, triangle (rowsh′foos) [Charles Andreyevich *Rauchfuss*, physician in Leningrad, 1835–1916]. See under *sling*, and *Grocco's sign*, under *sign*.

rausch (rowsh) [Ger. "intoxication"]. Light general anesthesia with ether only to the point where, if questioned sharply, the patient will not reply. Called also *etherrausch*.

rauschbrand (rowsh′brahnt) [Ger.]. Symptomatic anthrax.

rau-sed (row′sed). Trade mark for a preparation of reserpine.

rauwiloid (row′wĭ-loid). Trade mark for preparations of alseroxylon.

Rauwolfia (raw-wol′fe-ah). A genus of tropical trees and shrubs, many species of which have been used in South America, Africa, and Asia, as a source of arrow poisons. **R. serpenti′na,** a species which is the source of reserpine, widely used in treatment of essential hypertension and certain neuropsychiatric disorders. The dried root is used as a hypotensive agent.

Rauzier's disease (row″ze-āz′) [Georges *Rauzier*, French physician, 1862–1920]. Blue edema.

Ravius' process (ra′ve-us). Rau's process.

ray (ra) [L. *radius* spoke]. A line emanating from a center, as (*a*) a more or less distinct portion of radiant energy (light or heat), proceeding in a specific direction (used in the plural as a general term for any form of radiant energy, whether vibratory or particulate), or (*b*) one of the individual elements at the distal end of the limb of an early embryo, foretelling development of the metacarpal or metatarsal bones and the phalanges of the digits. **actinic r.,** a light ray which produces chemical changes. In general, light rays become more actinic as one passes from the red through the spectrum to the violet and even into the ultraviolet. **alpha r's, α-r's,** high-speed helium nuclei which have been ejected from radioactive substances. Owing to their high velocity (one tenth that of light) their kinetic energy is so great that a single alpha particle produces a microscopic flash of light when it hits a spinthariscope; when it hits another atom (as of nitrogen) it may cause it to disintegrate. **anode r's,** positive r's. **antirachitic r's,** ultraviolet rays between 2700 and 3020 A.U. **astral r.,** one of the rays of an astrosphere. **bactericidal r's,** rays that are destructive to bacteria, i.e., those from 1850 to 2600 A.U. **Becquerel r's,** rays emitted from uranium discovered by Becquerel in 1896. **beta r's, β-r's,** electrons ejected from radioactive substances with velocities which may be as high as 0.98 of the velocity of light. **biotic r.,** mitogenic r's. **Blondlot r's,** n r's. **border r's, borderline r's,** grenz r's. **Bucky's r's,** grenz r's. **caloric r.,** radiant energy which is converted into heat when applied to the body. **canal r's,** positive rays in a vacuum tube; so called from having been first obtained by allowing the discharge from the anode to pass through a perforated (canalized) cathode. **cathode r's,** negative particles of electricity streaming out in a vacuum tube at right angles to the surface of the cathode and away from it irrespective of the position of the anode. They move in a straight line unless deflected by a magnet. By striking on solids they generate roentgen rays. **characteristic r.,** when a metallic surface is exposed to roentgen rays a secondary radiation, called its characteristic ray, is emitted which is nearly homogeneous as to wavelength and is approximately proportional to the reciprocal of the square of the atomic weight of the metal. **chemical r.,** actinic r. **convergent r.,** a ray which is approaching a focus. It may be produced by passage through a convex lens or by reflection from a concave mirror. **cosmic r's,** a form of very penetrating radiations which apparently move through interplanetary space in every direction: called also *Millikan rays, ultra x-rays* and *penetrating radiation of the atmosphere*. **delta r's, δ-r's,** secondary beta rays produced in a gas by the passage of alpha particles. **digital r.,** a digit of the hand or foot and the corresponding portion of the metacarpus or metatarsus, considered as a continuous structural unit. **direct r.,** primary r. **direction r.,** the path of a ray of light from the point of fixation to the retina. **divergent r's,** rays coming from a source nearer than infinity. **Dorno's r's,** the active biological ultraviolet rays, i.e., those below 2890 A.U. **dynamic r's,** rays that are active physically or therapeutically. **erythema-producing r's,** rays that cause erythema, 2050 to 3100 A.U. **Finsen r's.** See under *light*. **gamma r's, γ-r's,** electromagnetic radiation of short wavelengths emitted by the nucleus of an atom during a nuclear reaction. They consist of high energy photons, have no mass and no electric charge, and travel with the speed of light and are usually associated with beta rays. **glass r's,** the rays formed in a roentgen-ray tube by the cathode rays striking the glass wall of the tube, so called to distinguish them from the roentgen rays originating at the anticathode. **Goldstein's r's,** rays formed when roentgen rays pass through some transparent medium. Called also *s r's*. **grenz r's,** very soft roentgen rays having electromagnetic vibrations of wavelength about 2 A.U., lying between the roentgen rays and ultraviolet rays. **Gurvich r's, Gurwisch r's,** mitogenic r's. **H r's,** a stream of hydrogen nuclei. **hard r's,** roentgen rays of short wavelength and great penetrative power. **heat r's.** See *radiant heat*, under *heat*. **hertzian r's,** electromagnetic waves similar to a light wave, but having a greater wavelength. They are the waves used in wireless transmission of signals, speech, etc. **i r's,** an alleged form of radiant emanations allied to n rays, and given off from the brain during certain psychic processes. **indirect r's,** rays formed at the surface of the glass of the tube. **infrared r's,** radiations just beyond the red end of the spectrum: their wavelengths range between 7700 and 500,000 A.U. **infra-roentgen r's,** grenz r's. **intermediate r's,** wavelengths between the ultraviolet and the roentgen rays. **Lenard r's,** cathode rays after they have passed outside the discharge tube. **luminous r's,** the visible rays of the spectrum. **Lyman r's,** electromagnetic vibrations of wavelength between 600 and 12,300 A.U. **medullary r.,** any cortical extension of a bundle of tubules from a malpighian pyramid of the kidney. **Millikan r's,** cosmic r's. **minin r's,** rays generated by passing incandescent light through dark-blue glass. **mitogenetic r's, mitogenic r's,** electromagnetic vibrations claimed to be given off from roots of growing plants, from yeast cultures, and from living beings. **monochromatic r's,** rays characterized by a definite wavelength, as secondary rays. **n r's,** an alleged form of radiation, the identity of which is not well established. Called also *Blondlot r's.* A variety of n rays (called *n' rays*) differ from n rays in diminishing the luminosity of light and of faintly luminous surfaces. **necrobiotic r's,** short ultraviolet rays which kill living cells. **Niewenglowski's r's,** luminous rays given out by substances which have been exposed to the sun. **paracathodic r's,** rays formed by the impaction of cathode rays against a body (the anticathode) in their path. **parallel r's,** rays which come from a source at an infinite distance. Divergent rays may be made parallel by means of a convex lens or a concave mirror. **pigment-producing r's,** rays that cause pigmentation, with a wavelength of 2500–3000 A.U. **polar r.,** astral r. **positive r's,** streams of positively charged atoms traveling at high speed from the anode of a partially evacuated tube under the influence of an applied voltage. **primary r.,** a ray given off directly from a radioactive substance. **roentgen r's,** electromagnetic vibrations of short wavelengths (from 5 A.U. down) or corresponding quanta (wave mechanics) that are produced when electrons moving at high velocity impinge on various substances, especially the heavy metals. They are commonly generated by passing a current of high voltage (from 10,000 volts up) through a Coolidge tube, which see under *tube.* They are able to penetrate most substances to some extent, some much more readily than others, and to affect a photographic plate. These qualities make it possible to use them in taking roentgenograms of various parts of the body thus revealing the presence and position of fractures or foreign bodies or of radiopaque substances that have been purposely introduced. They can also cause certain substances to fluoresce and this makes fluoroscopy possible by which the size, shape and movements of various organs such as the heart, stomach and intestines can be observed. By reason of the high energy of their quanta, they strongly ionize tissue through which they pass by means of the photoelectrons, both primary and secondary, which they liberate. Because of this effect they are used in treating various pathological conditions. Called also *x-rays.* **s. r's,** Goldstein's r's. **Sagnac r's,** secondary beta rays formed when gamma rays are reflected from a metal surface. **scattered r's,** roentgen rays which, during their passage through a substance, have been deviated in direction and modified by an increase in wavelength. **Schumann r's,** rays of wavelengths between 1850 and 1220 A.U. **secondary r.,** rays emitted by the matter on which a beam of roentgen ray impinges. **soft r's,** roentgen rays of long wavelength and little penetrative power. **supersonic r's,** waves with a frequency beyond that of waves which can be perceived by the human ear as sound. **titanium r.,** the radiation produced between metallic electrodes which consist of a tungsten alloy containing titanium. **transition r's,** grenz r's. **ultraviolet r's,** those invisible rays of the spectrum which are beyond the violet rays. They vary in wavelength from approximately 4000 to 2000 A.U. **ultra x-r.,** Millikan rays. **vital r's,** ultraviolet rays, between 2900 and 3200 A.U., which are the rays that act on the body therapeutically. **W r's,** intermediate r's. **x-r's,** the name given by Röntgen to the rays now known as roentgen rays.

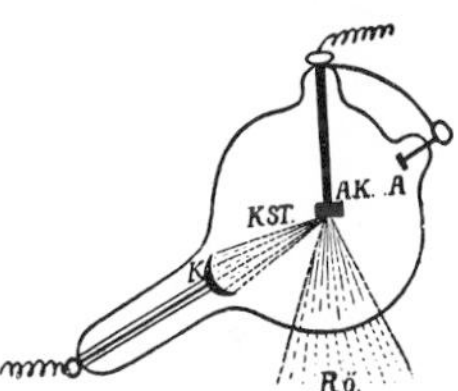

Roentgen ray: *A,* Anode; *K,* cathode; *AK,* anticathode; *KST,* cathode rays; *Rö,* roentgen rays generated and emitted from the tube.

rayage (ra'ij). Dosage of any form of radiant energy.

Rayer's disease (ra-yāz') [Pierre François *Rayer,* French physician, 1793–1867]. Xanthoma.

Raymond type of apoplexy (ra-maw') [Fulgence *Raymond,* French neurologist, 1844–1910]. See under *type.*

Raynaud's disease, gangrene, phenomenon (ra-nōz') [Maurice *Raynaud,* French physician, 1834–1881]. See under the nouns.

Rb. Chemical symbol for *rubidium.*

R.B.C. Abbreviation for *red blood cell* and *red blood [cell] count.*

RBE. Abbreviation for *relative biological effectiveness,* an expression of the effectiveness of other types of radiation in comparison with that of 1 roentgen of gamma or roentgen rays.

R.C.D. Abbreviation for *relative cardiac dullness.*

R.C.O.G. Abbreviation for *Royal College of Obstetricians and Gynaecologists.*

R.C.P. Abbreviation for *Royal College of Physicians.*

R.C.S. Abbreviation for *Royal College of Surgeons.*

R.D. Abbreviation for *reaction of degeneration.*

rd. Abbreviation for *rutherford.*

R.E. Abbreviation for *radium emanation* and *right eye.*

Re. Chemical symbol for *rhenium.*

re- [L.]. Prefix signifying *back, again, contrary,* etc.

reablement (re-a'b'l-ment). Rehabilitation.

react (re-akt'). 1. To respond to a stimulus. 2. To enter into chemical action with.

reactance (re-ak'tans). The weakening of an alternating electric current caused by passage through a coil of wire.

reactant (re-ak'tant). The original substance entering into a chemical reaction.

reaction (re-ak'shun) [*re-* + L. *agere* to act]. 1. Opposite action, or counteraction; the response of a part to stimulation. 2. The phenomena caused by the action of chemical agents; a chemical process in which one substance is transformed into another substance or substances. For specially named reactions not defined here, look under *tests.* 3. In psychology, the mental and/or emotional state that develops in any particular situation. **Abderhalden's r.,** a serum reaction based upon the hypothesis that when a foreign protein gets into the blood the body reacts by elaborating a ferment which causes disintegration of the protein. Such a ferment is called a *protective ferment* (*abwehrfermente*) and is specific for the particular protein which caused its formation. This reaction was first applied to the diagnosis of pregnancy on the principle that in the blood of pregnant women there is present a proteolytic ferment which will cause cleavage of placental albumin and placental peptone. The same principle is applied to the diagnosis of cancer because the blood of cancer patients contains a ferment which digests coagulated cancer protein. Similarly, in dementia praecox, the brain becomes degenerated and furnishes to the blood substances which excite the formation of a ferment capable of decomposing proteins of human brain. This is the *Abderhalden-Fauser reaction.* The same principle has also been applied to the diagnosis of syphilis, tuberculosis, and the acute infections. **Abderhalden-Fauser r.** See under *Abderhalden's r.*

Abelin's r., a reaction for ascertaining the presence of arsphenamine in the urine. **accelerated r.**, a reaction or response which occurs in a shorter time than is usual. **acetic acid r.**, Rivalta's r. **acetonitril r.**, Hunt r. **acid r.** 1. A surplus of hydrogen ions in a solution or a pH below 7. 2. Any test by which an acid reaction is recognized, such as the reddening of blue litmus. **Acree-Rosenheim r.** See under *tests.* **Adamkiewicz's r.** See under *tests.* **adhesion r.**, the adhesion of the erythrocytes to the parasite if the specific antibody is present. Seen especially in protozoal infections. **agglutinoid r.** See *prozone.* **alarm r.**, the total of all nonspecific phenomena elicited by sudden exposure to stimuli which affect large portions of the body and to which the organism is not adapted quantitatively or qualitatively. **aldehyde r.**, Cannizzaro's r. **alkaline r.** 1. A surplus of hydroxyl ions in a solution or a pH of more than 7. 2. Any test by which an alkaline reaction is recognized, such as the bluing of red litmus. **allergic r.**, a reaction, local or general, of the body to contact with a substance to which the subject has an idiosyncrasy. See *allergy* and *cutaneous r.*, def. 2. **Allwörden's r.**, when wool or hair is treated with chlorine water, blister-like droplets form at the edges of the scales. **alpha-naphthol r.** See *Molisch's test*, under *tests.* **amphicrotic r.**, a combination of acid and alkaline properties in the same substance. **amphigenous r., amphoteric r.**, amphicrotic r. **anamnestic r.**, in immunology, a reaction in which antibodies which had previously existed and had disappeared from the blood are redeveloped on the injection of a nonspecific antigen. **anaphylactic r.**, the reaction which occurs in anaphylactic shock. **anaphylactoid r.**, pseudo-anaphylaxis. **anatoxin r.**, an intradermic reaction in which anatoxin is used. **anergastic r.**, a psychosis due to a brain lesion and manifested by impairment of memory and judgment and by fits, palsy and coma. **anserine r.**, goose flesh. **antalgic r.**, a bodily reaction or response having the purpose of avoiding pain. **antigen r. of Debré and Paraf**, a complement fixation reaction for the diagnosis of urinary tuberculosis, using for antigen the patient's urine, for antibody known tuberculosis serum. **antigen-antibody r.**, the specific combination of antigen with homologous antibody by orientation of corresponding fields of polar forces on the surfaces of the reacting substances, with the reversible formation of an antigen-antibody complex through the action of intermolecular forces or secondary valences. **antiglobulin r.**, the agglutination of particles (usually erythrocytes) that have been (1) sensitized by the adsorption of soluble antigen, (2) treated with antibody to that antigen, and (3) treated with antiserum to the serum globulin of the animal species that produced the antibody. **antitryptic r.**, the reaction produced by the blood upon mixtures of trypsin and casein solutions. Such reaction is modified by various disease conditions, such as cancer, tuberculosis; also by the pregnant condition. **Arakawa's r.** See under *reagent.* **arsphenamine r.**, Abelin's r. **Arthus' r.** See under *phenomenon.* **Ascoli's r.**, miostagmin r. **associative r.**, a reaction in which the response is withheld until the idea presented has suggested an associated idea. **Austrian's r.**, an ophthalmic reaction for typhoid fever by the use of an antigen prepared from a mixed culture of a large number of different strains of typhoid bacilli. **axon r., axonal r.**, the series of changes in the ganglion cell (central chromatolysis with displacement of the nucleus) following the severing of its axon. **Bachman r.** See under *tests.* **bacteriolytic r.**, the reaction which brings about specific bacteriolysis. **Bareggi's r.**, the formation in a test tube of an unretracted clot, with but little serum, from the blood of typhoid fever; if the blood is from a patient with tuberculosis, the clot retracts with the separation of much serum. **Bechterew's r.**, in cases of tetany the minimum of electric current needed to arouse muscular contraction needs to be diminished at every interruption or change of density in order to prevent tetanic contraction. **Bence Jones r.**, the precipitation of protein by heat followed by its redissolving on boiling and being precipitated again on cooling. **Besredka's r.**, a complement deviation reaction for tuberculosis. **Beyerinck's r.**, cholera r. **biphasic r.**, a reaction made up of two parts, as flexion followed by extension. **Bittorf's r.**, in renal colic the pain produced by squeezing the testicle or pressing the ovary radiates to the kidney. **biuret r.** See under *tests.* **blanching r.**, Schultz-Charlton r. **Bloch's r.**, dopa r. **Bordet and Gengou r.**, fixation of the complement. **Brieger's cachexia r.**, cachexia r. **Brodie r.**, the extremely sensitive reaction of cats to foreign proteins. Intravenous doses of egg white or blood serum that have no appreciable effect on guinea pigs or rabbits produce marked fall of blood pressure in anesthetized cats. **Brück's nitric acid r.** (*for syphilis*), the precipitate formed when nitric acid is added to syphilitic serum is less soluble in an excess of dilute nitric acid than the precipitate from normal serum. **Buscaino r.** See under *tests.* **cachexia r.**, increase in the antitryptic power of the blood serum seen in malignant disease and other diseases characterized by cachexia. **cadaveric r.**, total loss of electrical response in the affected muscles in familial periodic paralysis. **Calmette's r.**, ophthalmic r. **Cammidge's r.**, pancreatic r. **Cannizzaro's r.**, the reaction which aldehydes undergo when brought in contact with animal tissue; one molecule of the aldehyde is reduced to the corresponding alcohol and another molecule is simultaneously oxidized to the corresponding acid. Cf. *aldehyde mutase.* **carbamino r.**, alpha-amino acids unite with CO_2 in the presence of alkalis or alkaline earths to form salts of carbamino-carboxylic acids. This reaction is used in studying the course of protein digestion. See *formol titration*, under *method.* **Casoni's r.** See *Casoni's intradermal test*, under *tests.* **chain r.**, a nuclear (neutron) reaction which once started will proceed and multiply of its own accord by emitting particles that propagate the reaction in adjacent nuclei. **Chantemesse's r.**, the ophthalmic reaction for typhoid fever. See *ophthalmic r.* **cholera r., cholera red r.**, a red color developing on the addition of concentrated sulfuric acid to a culture of cholera vibrio. **Chopra antimony r.**, dilute the patient's serum with ten volumes of physiological salt solution and add an equal volume of 4 per cent antimony solution. A marked cloudiness indicates kala-azar. **citochol r.** See *Sachs-Witebsky test*, under *tests.* **coagulation r., coagulo r.**, a test for syphilis based on the fact that syphilitic serums inhibit the coagulation of the blood by interference with thrombin production more than do normal serums; called also *Hirschfeld-Klinger r.* **cockade r.** See *Römer's test*, under *tests.* **complement fixation r.** See *fixation of complement.* **complUetic r.**, Wassermann r. **conglobation r.** See *Müller's test*, 3d def., under *tests.* **conglutination r.**, a characteristic clumping reaction obtained by a mixture of conglutinin, bacteria, fresh complement, and a specific immune serum from which the agglutinins have been removed by absorption. See *conglutinin.* **conjunctival r.** ophthalmic r. **consensual r.** 1. Crossed reflex. 2. A reaction that takes place independently of the will. See *consensual.* **contact r.**, an urticarial reaction at the site of contact with a physical agent. **coupled r.**, a series of linked reactions. **cross r.**, a reaction between an antigen and an antibody of closely related though not identical species. **Cushing's thermic r.**, a rise of temperature of one or more degrees following injection of anterior pituitary indicates hypopituitarism. **cutaneous r.** 1. Cutireaction. 2. A reaction produced by applying to an abrasion or by injecting into the skin a solution of a protein or a pollen to which the patient is sensitive. **cutituberculin r.,** Moro's r. **Dale r.,** a test for sensitization in the guinea-pig: a small amount of the antigen added to the fluid in which the excised uterine horn is immersed will cause contraction of the sensitized uterine muscle. **D'Amato's r.** See under *tests.* **Deehan's typhoid r.,** a cutaneous test for typhoid fever. **defense r.** 1. A mental reaction which shuts out from consciousness ideas that are not acceptable to the ego. 2. Conduct that tends to conceal some aspects of one's life from others. **r. of degeneration,** the reaction to electric stimulation of muscles whose nerves have degenerated. It consists of a loss of response to a faradic stimulus in a muscle, and to galvanic and faradic stimulus in a nerve. Galvanic irritability of the muscle is increased. **r. of degeneration, franklinic,** a form of reaction elicited by static electricity and similar to the reaction produced by the faradic current. **delayed-blanch r.,** an unusual, paradoxical reaction to the intradermal injection of acetylcholine or methacholine, associated with atopic disease; characteristically, instead of the usual erythematous wheal and flare, a delayed blanch occurs within the flare 3 to 5 minutes after the injection and persists for 15 to 30 minutes. **depot r.,** a red reaction of the skin around the point of entrance of the needle in the subcutaneous tuberculin test. **dermotuberculin r.,** Pirquet's r. **desmoid r.** (for gastric secretion and motility), a bag of rubber tissue containing methylene blue and iodoform, and tied with a string of soft catgut, is administered to the patient: normal gastric juice will digest the string and liberate the stain, which will appear in the urine after five or six hours. **desmoplastic r.** See *desmoplastic.* **Detre's r.,** a differential reaction between infection with bovine and human tuberculosis, made by simultaneous cutaneous inoculation with a filtrate of human and one of bovine bacilli. Called also *differential cutireaction.* **diazo r.,** Ehrlich's r. **Dick r.** See under *tests.* **digitonin r.,** the formation of a precipitate on treating a sterol, such as cholesterol or ergosterol, with digitonin. **disergastic r.,** a disorder characterized by disorientation, hallucinations, daydreams and fears, due to impaired cerebral circulation and to the resulting reduced nutrition of the brain. **Dochez and Avery's r.** See *precipitin r.,* def. 1. **Donaggio r.,** obstruction of the urine occurring during the period following a surgical operation. **dopa r.,** the reaction by which dopa is changed into melanin under the influence of dopa-oxidase. **Ebbecke's r.,** dermographism. **E-E r.,** Foshay's r. **egg yellow r.,** a yellow foam appearing in Ehrlich's reaction before the addition of ammonia; believed to indicate acute pneumonia. **Ehrlich's diazo r.,** a reaction of a pure pink or red color resulting from the action of diazo-benzenesulfonic acid and ammonia upon certain aromatic substances found in the urine in some conditions. This reaction has diagnostic value in typhoid fever and measles and prognostic value in tuberculosis. **electric r.,** a reaction, such as muscular contraction, caused by the application of electricity to the body. **electronic r.,** a flushing on some part of the body produced by stimulation of the depressor nerve between the third and fourth dorsal spines: used as a test in cancer, syphilis, tuberculosis, etc. (Abrams). **endothermal r., endothermic r.,** a chemical reaction which is accompanied by the absorption of heat; one to which heat must be supplied if it is to proceed. **energonic r.,** a chemical reaction which requires energy for its completion. **epiphanin r.,** a reaction for the determination of antibodies in the blood serum, especially in the serodiagnosis of syphilis. **erythematous-edematous r.,** Foshay's r. **erythremoid r.,** increase in the number of circulating red corpuscles in response to some known stimulus; erythrocytosis. **erythrocyte sedimentation r.** See under *rate.* **erythrophore r.,** a red coloration appearing in certain male fishes after the injection of gonadal hormone. **exergonic r.,** a chemical reaction during and by which energy is released. **r. of exhaustion,** reaction to electric stimulation seen in conditions of exhaustion. In it the reaction normally produced by a certain current can be reproduced only by an increase in the current. **exothermal r., exothermic r.,** a chemical reaction which is accompanied by the evolution of heat. **false positive r.,** a positive reaction to a test for syphilis which is due to some disease other than syphilis. **fatigue r.,** rise of temperature on muscular effort: seen in persons with active tuberculosis. **Fauser r.,** Abderhalden-Fauser r. **Felix-Weil r.,** Weil-Felix r. **Ficker's r.,** the clumping of dead typhoid bacilli by the blood serum of persons affected with typhoid fever. **fixation r.,** fixation of the complement. **flaginac r.,** an indication of the presence of *Bacillus coli* in water, consisting of *fl* or fluorescence in glucose neutral broth, *ag* or acid and gas with lactose, *in* or indol in broth, *ac* or acid and clot in milk. **flocculation r.** See *Sachs-Georgi test,* under *tests.* **Flora's r.** See under *sign.* **Florence's r.** See under *tests.* **focal r.,** the reaction that occurs at or about the site of an infection or the point of an injection. It may be induced by the injection of a specific agent, such as tuberculin, mallein, or a bacterial vaccine, or by the use of nonspecific agents. **formol r.** See *formalin test,* under *tests.* **Fornet's r.,** a reaction for syphilis. The serum of the patient is treated with serum taken from a paretic. If syphilis is present, a flocculent ring will appear at the line of contact of the two serums. **Foshay's r.,** a spreading redness about a slightly elevated central edema developing at the site of the intradermal injection of an antiserum specific for the infection from which the patient is suffering: called also *erythematous-edematous r.* and *E-E reaction.* **Freund's r., Freund-Kaminer r.,** the serum of noncancerous persons destroys cancer cells, while that of cancer patients has no lytic effect. **fright r.,** involuntary contraction of extra-ocular and facial muscles of animals during states of fright and anger. **fuchsinophil r.,** certain substances when stained with fuchsin retain the stain on being treated with picric acid alcohol. **furfurol r.,** a red color produced when furfurol is brought in contact with aniline. **Gangi's r.,** a test of a liquid to determine whether it is a transudate or exudate, utilizing hydrochloric acid. **Gatherman's r.** (for pregnancy), a color reaction for pregnancy, made by adding concentrated sulfuric acid to a degeneration product from the urine. A deep yellow to orange color indicates a positive test. **Gerhardt's r.** See under *tests.* **Ghilarducci's r.,** contraction of the muscles of a limb when the active electrode is placed on a part somewhat removed from them. **Gmellin's r.** See under *tests.* **Goetsch's skin r.,** a test for hyperthyroidism based on local reaction to hypodermic injection of epinephrine. **gold r.** See *Lange's test,* under *tests.* **graft vs. host r.** See *runt disease.* **group r.** See *group agglutination,* under *agglutination.* **Gruber's r., Gruber-Widal r.** (*for typhoid fever*): Dilutions of the patient's serum 1:20, 1:40, and higher, if desired, are made. To each dilution is added an equal volume of a 24-hour bouillon culture of *Salmonella typhosa.* In the *macroscopical method* these mixtures are made in test tubes, are incubated in a water bath at 55 C. for two hours, and then read. The flocculation and precipitation can be seen with the unaided eye or with a hand lens. In the *microscopical method* a small drop of each mixture is mounted as a hanging drop and observed under the microscope. **Gubler's r.,** the formation of a brown color on gradually adding nitrosonitric acid to urine; seen in urobilin jaundice. **Hanganatziu-Deicher r.,** following the parenteral administration of heterogenic serum, human blood serum agglutinates certain heterogenic erythrocytes, particularly those of sheep, horses, hares, and guinea-pigs. **Hecht-Wein-**

berg-Gradwohl modification of the Wassermann r., the natural antisheep amboceptor and the natural hemolytic complement found in the patient's fresh serum are utilized instead of the antisheep-rabbit amboceptor and guinea-pig complement of the regular test. **hemiopic pupillary r.,** reaction in certain cases of hemianopia in which the stimulus of light thrown upon one side of the retina causes the iris to contract, while light thrown on the other side arouses no response. Called also *Wernicke's r.* **hemoclastic r.,** laking of blood due to hemolysis. See *hemoclastic crisis,* under *crisis.* **Henle's r.,** the medullary cells of the adrenals stain dark brown on treatment with chromium salts. **Henry's melanin r.,** add one part of the serum to 4 parts of a formalized suspension of ox choroid melanin, 1:2000. Incubate for three hours, allow to stand thirty minutes and read macroscopically or preferably by using the photometer of Vernes, Bricq and Yvonne. 19–100 degrees is positive for malaria. **Hermann-Perutz r.,** Perutz r. **Herxheimer's r.,** Jarisch-Herxheimer r. **heterophile antibody r.** See *Paul-Bunnell test,* under *tests.* **Hirschberg's r.,** an infectious disease resembling typhoid fever, but not due to organisms of the typhoid group. **Hirschfeld-Klinger r.,** coagulo r. **Hunt r.,** the acetonitrile resistance of white mice is increased by treatment of the mice with blood from a patient with hyperthyroidism. Also called *acetonitrile reaction.* **Ide r.** See under *tests.* **immune r.,** the formation of a papule and areola without the development of a vesicle following smallpox vaccination, indicative of a high degree of immunity. **indophenol r.** See under *tests.* **intracutaneous r., intradermal r.,** a reaction following an injection into the substance of the skin; such a reaction may have diagnostic value as in the Schick test, Dick test, tuberculin, etc. **intracuti r.** See *Frei test,* under *tests.* **Jaffé r.,** creatinine when treated with picric acid in strongly alkaline solution gives an intense red color. **Jarisch-Herxheimer r.,** increase of syphilitic symptoms after administration of antisyphilitic drugs. **Johnin r.,** a reaction like the tuberculin reaction but for the diagnosis of Johne's disease. **Jolly's r.,** failure of response to faradic stimulation in a muscle, the power of voluntary contraction as well as the response to galvanic stimulation being retained. **Keller-Killian r.** (*for 2-desoxy sugars*): dissolve the sugar in glacial acetic acid that contains some ferric chloride, underlay it with concentrated sulfuric acid and the upper layer will take on a deep blue color. **K. H. r.,** a combined complement fixation and hemagglutination reaction used in the diagnosis of glanders. **Kiutsi-Malone r.,** a modification of the Abderhalden test made without the use of dialyzing thimbles, and with the employment of a secret preparation, "ninserin." **Klausner's r.,** the formation of a flocculent precipitate when distilled water is added to fresh blood serum in certain stages of syphilis and other infectious diseases. **Klein r.,** a modification of Freund's reaction for cancer, using for carcinolysis a cell suspension from an adenocarcinoma of the mouse. **Koch's r.,** tuberculin r. **Koler r.,** Adamkiewicz's test. **Konsuloff's r.,** a reaction for the rapid diagnosis of pregnancy by the urine. **Kottmann's r.** See under *tests.* **Krauss' precipitin r.,** an agglutination test for typhoid fever by the use of a mixture of extract of typhoid bacilli and typhoid serum. **Landau's r.** See under *tests.* **Lange's r.** See under *tests.* **lengthening r.,** the elongation of the extensor muscles which permits flexion of a limb. **lentochol r.** See *Sachs-Georgi test,* under *tests.* **leukemic r., leukemoid r.,** a blood picture resembling that of leukemia but characterized by the presence of immature white cells in the blood. **leukocytic r.,** hyperleukocytosis (*positive leukocytoreaction,* if the patient is syphilitic) or leukopenia (*negative leukocytoreaction,* if the patient is not syphilitic), produced by the injection of a bismuth, arsenic or mercury preparation. **Lewis' r.,** the urticaria produced by histamine. See *histamine test,* def. 2, under *tests.* **Lieben's r.** See under *tests.* **Lignières' r.** See under *tests.* **lignin r.,** a color reaction given by wood cellulose, consisting of a yellow color with aniline salts and a red color with a solution of phloroglucinol in concentrated hydrochloric acid. **local r.,** a reaction similar to a focal reaction occurring at the point of injection. **Loeb's r.,** the presence of a glass bead or other irritant causes the formation of a small deciduoma in the uterine mucosa provided corpora lutea are developing normally. **Loewi's r.** See under *tests.* **Löwenthal's r.,** the agglutinative reaction in relapsing fever. **luetin r.,** Noguchi's luetin r. **lymphatic r.,** infectious mononucleosis. **Malmejde r.** See under *tests.* **Malone-Kiutsi r.,** Kiutsi-Malone r. **Maloney r.,** the intradermal injection of diluted diphtheria toxoid as a control in the Schick test. **Mandelbaum's r.,** a test for the detection of typhoid carriers and the differentiation of recent and old cases. **Manoiloff's r., Manoilov's r.** 1. A blood reaction comparing the blood of the parents and of their alleged child for the determination of the paternity of the child. 2. (*for pregnancy*): The serum of a pregnant woman decolorizes to yellow the blue mixture prepared by mixing serum with 2 per cent aqueous solution of theobromine sodio-salicylate colored with nile blue. **Marañón's r.** See under *sign.* **Marchi's r.,** failure of the myelin sheath of a nerve to become discolored when treated with osmic acid. **Meinicke r.** See under *tests.* **Millon's r.** See under *tests.* **miostagmin r., miostagminic r.,** a blood serum test to confirm the diagnosis of malignant tumors, syphilis, typhoid, etc., based on the fact that when the antibodies of a disease and its corresponding antigens are brought together, there is a lowering of the surface tension of the mixture. **Moeller's r.** See *rhinoreaction.* **Molisch's r.** See under *tests.* **Morelli's r.,** a test of pleural fluid to determine whether it is a transudate or exudate, utilizing a saturated aqueous solution of corrosive mercuric chloride. **Moritz r.,** Rivalta's r. **Moritz-Weisz r.** See under *tests.* **Moro's r.,** an eruption of pale or red papules on a cutaneous area after application of an ointment of 5 cc. of old tuberculin and 5 Gm. of anhydrous wool fat. **mouse tail r.,** stiffening of the tail in rats and mice following the administration of a small dose of morphine. **Much's r., Much-Holzmann r.,** inhibition of the hemolytic action of cobra venom on the red blood corpuscles seen in dementia praecox and manic-depressive insanity. Called also *psychoreaction.* **Müller's r.** See *Müller's test,* def. 3, under *tests.* **myasthenic r.,** decrease in faradic excitability of muscle, as in periodic paralysis. **myotonic r.,** an increase in faradic excitability, as in myotonia congenita. **Nadi r.,** the production of a blue color when alpha-naphthol and dimethyl paraphenylene diamine are injected into animals. See *indophenol test.* **Nagler's r.,** the production of turbidity in human blood serum by the addition of the toxin of *Clostridium perfringens* indicates the presence of that organism. **Neill-Mooser r.,** a reaction in laboratory animals produced by inoculation with rickettsiae of murine typhus. The inflammatory exudate of the scrotal swelling contains large mononuclear cells filled with rickettsiae which are intracytoplasmic in position. **Neisser's r.,** a general reaction sometimes following an initial dose of arsphenamine, characterized by transitory increase of headache in cerebral syphilis and of the lightning pains in tabes. **Neufeld's r.,** when pneumococci are mixed with specific immune serum there occurs in addition to agglutination a swelling (quellung) of the peripheral zones of the organisms. **neurotonic r.,** muscular contraction persisting after the stimulus which produced it has ceased. **neutral r.,** a reaction that indicates the absence of both alkaline and acid properties. Accurate neutrality is expressed as pH = 7.0. **ninhydrin r.,** a reaction for the detection of peptone or amino acid in a test for pregnancy. **nitritoid r.** See under *crisis.* **Noguchi's r.** 1. A modification of the Wassermann reaction. This latter Noguchi modifies as follows: (*a*) He prepares the antigen by extracting a lipoid substance from the liver and heart of dogs and cows. (*b*) Instead of using sheep's corpuscles in the hemolytic series, he employs human corpuscles, owing to the fact that a certain percentage of human serums tested produced hemolysis of the sheep's corpuscles. (*c*) In his test, therefore, he obtains the hemolytic amboceptor by immunizing rabbits with washed normal human corpuscles. (*d*) Another important improvement in the technique is the preservation of the specific antigen and the hemolytic amboceptor, which rapidly lose their strength in solution, in a dried form by soaking measured strips of filter paper (0.5 mm. square) with each. 2. A reaction seen in general paralysis and tabes. To 1 cc. of the cerebrospinal fluid is added 0.5 cc. of a solution of 10 per cent butyric acid in normal salt solution. This is heated, and then there is added 0.1 cc. of a 4 per cent sodium hydroxide solution. This is again heated. In about three hours the tube is examined. In tabes and general paralysis a characteristic flocculent precipitate forms, which gradually settles so that after twenty-four hours there is a bulky precipitate at the bottom of the tube, the supernatant fluid being clear. The test indicates an increased amount of globulin in the cerebrospinal fluid. **Noguchi's luetin r.** (1909), a cutaneous reaction for syphilis. A drop of luetin is injected into the skin of the arm. No reaction occurs in a nonsyphilitic person, but in one affected with syphilis there forms, in from six to twenty-four hours, a distinct papule surrounded by a bluish-red halo. See *luetin.* **Nonne-Apelt r.,** 2 cc. of cerebrospinal fluid is mixed with an equal quantity of a neutral saturated solution of ammonium sulfate and compared after three minutes with another tube containing spinal fluid only; if there is no difference or only a faint opalescence the reaction is said to be *negative.* If there is an opalescence or turbidity the reaction is said to be *positive phase 1,* which indicates an excess of globulin in the fluid and points to nervous disorder. A normal fluid treated with heat and acetic acid only becomes turbid and is called *positive phase 2.* **nucleal r.,** upon the addition of fuchsin-sulfonic acid to any solution containing aldehydes, a bluish-red color is produced. **Oestreicher's r.** See *Mulder's test,* under *tests.* **ophthalmic r.,** local reaction of the conjunctiva following instillation into the eye of toxins of typhoid fever and tuberculosis. The reaction is much more severe in persons affected with these diseases than in the healthy or those affected with some other disease. Called also *Calmette's ophthalmoreaction.* **orbicularis r.,** Westphal-Piltz phenomenon. **oxidase r.,** the formation of dark-blue granulations in myeloid cells when treated with alpha-naphthol and dimethyl-paraphenylenediamine. **Pagano's r.,** a tuberculin reaction following application of the tuberculin to the urinary meatus. **pain r.,** dilatation of the pupil on a feeling of pain. **pallidin r.,** a cutaneous reaction for syphilis made by applying pallidin, which is an extract of lung affected with infantile syphilitic pneumonia, to the skin. A positive reaction consists of the development of a slightly raised inflammatory papule surrounded by a zone of erythema. **pancreatic r.** (for ascertaining the presence of pancreatitis or malignant disease of the pancreas), two specimens of urine, one of which is treated with mercuric chloride, are boiled with hydrochloric acid for ten minutes, and after the excess of acid has been neutralized with lead carbonate, are examined by the phenylhydrazine test. A difference in the amount of deposit yielded by the two specimens indicates the presence of pancreatic disease. Called also *Cammidge's r.* **parallergic r.** See *parallergy.* **paraserum r.,** agglutination of strains of typhoid and dysentery bacilli with those of paratyphoid, *Bacillus coli,* mutable cholera, and other infections. **Parish's r.,** an allergic reaction which follows the making of a Schick test. The symptoms appear within a few hours and may be quite severe. **Pasteur's r.,** the inhibiting effect of respiration on fermentation (Warburg). The action of oxygen in diminishing carbohydrate destruction and suppressing or decreasing the accumulation of the products of anaerobic metabolism (Dixon). **paternity r.,** Manoiloff's r. **Paul-Bunnell r.,** the inactivated serum of patients with infectious mononucleosis will agglutinate sheep red corpuscles. **Penn sero-flocculation r.** (*for cancer*): Plasma separated from a small amount of the patient's blood is mixed with a lipoid fraction derived from the liver of a patient who died of cancer. Resulting turbidity constitutes a negative reaction. **percutaneous r.,** Moro's r. **peroxidase r.,** the appearance of deep-blue granules in leukocytes of marrow origin when stained with Goodpasture's stain, distinguishing them from cells of lymphatic origin. **Perutz r.,** a reaction for the serodiagnosis of syphilis. **Petzetaki's r.** See under *tests.* **Pfaundler's r.,** Mandelbaum's r. **Pfeiffer's r.,** a mixture of a culture of cholera spirillum with diluted agglutinating cholera serum is injected into the peritoneal cavity of an animal; if, after twenty-five minutes, some of the mixture is withdrawn, the spirilla will be found to have been killed. **phrenic r.,** lesion of the diaphragm as a result of streptococcal and gonorrheal infection. **Pietrowski's r.,** biuret r. **Pinkerton-Moorer r.,** swelling of the scrotum and formation in the tunica vaginalis of an exudate containing Rickettsia: seen in Mexican typhus. **Pirquet's r.,** a local inflammatory reaction of the skin following inoculation with tuberculin, more marked in tuberculous subjects than in normal ones. Called also *scarification test.* **Porges-Hermann-Perutz r.,** Perutz r. **Porges-Meier r.** See under *tests.* **Prausnitz-Küstner r.,** the production of local hypersensitiveness in man by the intradermal injection of the serum of an allergic person. **precipitin r.** 1. (*For pneumococcus infection of types I, II, III*): Equal volumes of clear urine are mixed with antipneumococcus serums of types I, II, and III, and incubated for an hour. A cloudy to heavy flocculent precipitate indicates a positive reaction. Called also *Dochez and Avery's r.* 2. The specific serologic precipitation reaction of an antigen in solution with its specific antiserum in the presence of electrolytes. **pregnandiol r.,** Gatherman's r. **prozone r.** See *prozone.* **psychogalvanic r.,** variations in the electric current passed through the body when the subject undergoes emotional disturbance of any kind. **puncture r.,** swelling and redness at the point where tuberculin is injected subcutaneously: diagnostic of tuberculosis. **quanti-Pirquet r.,** the Pirquet reaction applied with a view to the amount or activity of the tuberculous infection. **quellung r.** [Ger. "swelling"], Neufeld's r. **questioning r.** See *orienting reflex,* under *reflex.* **recurrent r.** See *revivescence.* **reflex-like r.,** a reaction to physical agents, consisting of urticaria with systemic symptoms such as asthma, dermatoses, etc. **reversible r.,** a chemical reaction which occurs in either direction; a reaction in which the products react to reform the factors of the reaction. **Rieckenberg's r.** See under *phenomenon.* **Rivalta's r.,** a reaction for distinguishing fluids of transudation and exudation, utilizing acetic acid. **Roger's r.,** the existence of albumin in the sputum, indicating tuberculosis. **Rosenbach's r.,** the formation of a deep-red color when concentrated nitric acid containing a small amount of nitrous acid is gradually added to boiling urine, indicative of an increase in the putrefactive processes of the intestine. **Rubino's r.** (*for leprosy*), the inactivated blood serum of leprous individuals when added to a suspension of washed and formalinized sheep erythrocytes causes the latter to agglutinate and to sediment rapidly. The test is correct in about 70 per cent of the cases. **Rumpf's traumatic r.** See *Rumpf's sign* (1st def.), under *sign*. **Russo r.**, a reaction of the urine of typhoid patients on adding 4 drops of a solution of methylene blue to 15 cc. of urine. In the first stage of typhoid the urine becomes light green; at the height of the disease, an emerald color: and during the decline, a bluish color. **Sachs-Georgi r.** See under *tests*. **Sachs-Witebsky r.** See under *tests*. **r. of Salmon and Saxl,** sulfur r. **Schardinger's r.**, a reaction of oxidation or reduction made possible by a simultaneous and compensating reaction of reduction or oxidation. Cf. *Cannizzaro's reaction*. This reaction is used to distinguish between fresh milk and milk which has been heated. The milk is treated with aldehyde and methylene blue or indigo blue; if the milk is fresh the dye is reduced to a colorless compound. **Schick r.** See under *tests*. **Schönbein's r.**, iodine is set free when potassium iodide and sulfate of iron are added to a solution of hydrogen peroxide. **Schultz-Charlton r.**, when scarlet fever antitoxin or scarlet fever convalescent serum is injected into an area of the skin showing a bright red rash, a blanching of the skin at the site of the injection occurs. Serum from scarlet fever patients does not produce this reaction. **Schultz-Dale r.**, a reaction for determining anaphylaxis: smooth muscle fiber freshly extracted from an animal and washed free of serum will react with contraction when brought into contact with suitable antigens. **sedimentation r.**, erythrocyte sedimentation r. **Seifert's r.**, epiphanin r. **Selivanoff r.** (for keto sugars), the fluid is heated in a solution of resorcinol in hydrochloric acid; a red compound is formed. **sero-anaphylactic r.**, an anaphylactic reaction produced by the use of blood serum. **sero-enzyme r.**, Abderhalden's r. **serum r.**, seroreaction. **Sgambati's r.**, a reaction of the urine seen in peritonitis. **shortening r.**, the shortening that succeeds the lengthening reaction when a limb is brought back into the extended position. **Shwartzman r.** See under *phenomenon*. **sigma r.**, a flocculation reaction for the diagnosis of syphilis, being a modification of the Sachs-Georgi reaction in which a series of tests are made to determine which one of the tests produces flocculation. **skin r.**, cutaneous r. **small-drop r.**, miostagmin r. **Smith's r.**, anaphylaxis. **Stammler's r.**, cancer serum when added to a tumor extract clears up the opalescence normal to the extract: normal serums fail to act in this manner. **stemming r.**, resistance in the leg of a standing animal to forward displacement. **Straus's r.**, when material containing virulent glanders bacilli is inoculated into the peritoneal cavity of male guinea-pigs, scrotal lesions develop. **sulfur r.**, a reaction in the urine of cancer patients. **Szent-Györgyi r.**, a deep violet color develops when a 1 per cent solution of ascorbic acid is mixed with a solution of ferrous sulfate; this color disappears on reduction with sodium hyposulfite. **Targowla r.**, a reaction for the presence of syphilis based on the fact that a mixture of normal cerebrospinal fluid with elixir paregoric produces a colloidal suspension, while if the spinal fluid is syphilitic a precipitate is formed. **tendon r.**, a reflex contraction of a muscle induced by a blow on its tendon. **thread r.**, Mandelbaum r. **thrombocytobarin r.**, Rieckenberg's phenomenon. **Tischenko's r.** See *dismutation*. **toxin-antitoxin r.** See *immunoreaction*. **Trambusti's r.**, tuberculin is injected into the skin by a needle inserted parallel to the cutaneous surface. Any reddening within the site of the injection is positive: called also *endodermoreaction*. **Triboulet's r.**, a reaction for the localization of hemorrhages of the digestive tract. **trigger r.** See under *action*. **tryptophan r.**, the appearance of a violet color on the addition of bromine water to filtered gastric contents: said to indicate the presence of gastric cancer. **tuberculin r.** See under *tests*. **tubing r.**, a reaction following the injection of arsphenamine through new rubber tubing. **Ucko's r.**, a modification of Takata-Ara test for liver disease. **uniphasic r.**, a reaction consisting of flexion only. Cf. *biphasic r.* **urochromogen r.** Same as *Moritz-Weisz test*. See under *tests*. **vaccination r.**, the local and systemic reaction to vaccination. **vestibular pupillary r.**, dilatation of the pupils arising from stimulation of the external auditory canal. **Voges-Proskauer r.**, a reaction to detect the presence of acetyl-methyl carbinol and thus to distinguish between the colon group and the aerogenes group of bacteria. **von Brugsch r.**, a blue discoloration of the skin following the intradermal injection of a small amount of a 1 per cent solution of potassium ferrocyanide: used in distinguishing certain types of jaundice. **von Pirquet's r.**, Pirquet's r. **Wassermann r.**, a test for syphilis based on the fixation of complement. **Wassermann r., provocative,** a Wassermann reaction preceded by administration of arsphenamine. This procedure may result in a positive reaction in a patient who had previously given negative results. **Weichbrodt's r.**, three parts of a 1 per cent solution of sublimate solution are added to seven parts of cerebrospinal fluid: cloudiness of the mixture indicates pathologic changes in the fluid, especially syphilis. **Weil-Felix r.**, the diagnostic agglutination of Proteus X bacteria by the blood sera of typhus fever cases due, apparently, to the presence of a common antigen. **Weisz's r.** See *Moritz-Weisz test*, under *tests*. **Weltmann's r.** See under *tests*. **Wernicke's r.**, hemiopic pupillary r. **Widal's r.**, the clumping of typhoid bacilli. See *Gruber-Widal r.* **Wildbolz r.**, a few drops of the patient's own urine are injected intradermically, when a local reaction follows if the patient is tuberculous. **Wolff-Calmette r.**, ophthalmic r. **Wolff-Eisner r.**, ophthalmic r. **xanthoproteic r.** See *Mulder's test*, under *tests*. **xanthydrol r.**, when tissue from a case of uremia is fixed in a solution of xanthydrol in glacial acetic acid, a large deposit of xanthydrol occurs in the tissue. **Zambrini's r.** See under *ptyaloreaction*. **zed r.**, a reaction which appears in infants in cases of starvation after the starvation is relieved: it consists of a slight gain in weight, elevation of temperature, and the appearance of watery stools containing a large number of cells.

reaction-formation (re-ak′shun for-ma′shun). A psychic mechanism by which a patient consciously assumes an attitude which is the reverse of, and a substitute for, a repressed antisocial impulse.

reactivate (re-ak′tĭ-vāt). To make active again; especially the restoring of the activity to immune serum that has had its activity destroyed.

reactivation (re-ak″tĭ-va′shun). The restoration of activity to something that has been inactivated. **r. of serum,** restoration of activity to serum by adding fresh complement. **r. of syphilis,** temporary recrudescence of symptoms that sometimes follows the starting of specific treatment.

reactivity (re″ak-tiv′ĭ-te). The process or property of reacting.

reactrol (re-ak′trol). Trade mark for a preparation of clemizole hydrochloride.

Read's formula (rēdz) [J. Marion *Read*, American physician, born 1889]. See under *formula*.

reading (rēd′ing). Understanding of written or printed symbols representing words. **lip r.**, the understanding of speech through observation of the movement of the lips of the speaker.

reagent (re-a′jent) [*re-* + L. *agere* to act]. 1. A substance employed to produce a chemical reaction. 2. The subject of a psychological experiment, especially one who reacts to a stimulus. **acid molybdate r.**, Folin's acid molybdate r. **Acree-Rosenheim r.**, solution of formaldehyde, 1 part; water, 5000 parts. **Almén's r.**, to 5 grains of tannic acid in 240 cc. of 50 per cent alcohol add 10 cc. of 25 per cent acetic acid.

amino-acid r., a 0.5 per cent solution of the sodium salt of beta-naphthaquinone sulfonate acid freshly prepared. **Anstie's r.,** potassium dichromate 3.33 Gm., concentrated sulfuric acid 250 cc., water to make 500 cc. **Arakawa's r.,** a complicated mixture containing guaiac resin and benzidine for use in testing for peroxidase in milk. If the peroxidase content of breast milk is adequate, the presence of maternal beriberi is excluded. **arsenic-sulfuric acid r.,** Rosenthaler's reagent. **Barfoed's r.** See under *tests*. **Benedict-Hopkins-Cole r.,** 250 cc. of a saturated solution of oxalic acid is added slowly to 10 Gm. of powdered magnesium kept cool. Filter, acidify with acetic acid, and make up to 1 liter. **benzidine r.,** saturate 2 cc. of glacial acetic acid with benzidine and add 1 cc. of 3 per cent hydrogen peroxide. **Bertrand's r.** A. Copper solution: Copper sulfate, 40 Gm., to 1 liter of water. B. Alkaline solution: Rochelle salt, 200 Gm., sodium hydroxide, 150 Gm., to 1 liter of water. C. Iron solution: Ferric sulfate, 50 Gm., sulfuric acid, 200 Gm., to 1 liter of water. D. Permanganate solution: Potassium permanganate, 5 Gm., to 1 liter of water. By heating the alkaline copper solution (made from Solutions A and B) with dextrose, cuprous oxide is formed. This is treated with the ferric sulfate solution, and the ferrous sulfate so formed is titrated with the solution of potassium permanganate. **Bial's r.,** orcinol 1.5 Gm., fuming hydrochloric acid 500 Gm., ferric chloride (10 per cent) 20–30 drops. **biuret r.,** Gies' biuret reagent. **Black's r.,** 5 Gm. of ferric chloride and 0.4 Gm. of ferrous chloride dissolved in 100 cc. of water. **Blum's r.** See under *tests*. **Boas' r.** See under *tests*. **Bogg's r.,** dissolve 25 Gm. of phosphotungstic acid in 125 cc. of water. Dilute 25 cc. of concentrated HCl to 100 cc. Mix the two solutions. **Bohme's r.,** two reagents for use in testing for indol. **Bonchardat's r.,** a general alkaloidal reagent, consisting of 1 per cent of iodine dissolved in a 1 per cent solution of potassium iodide. **Bruecke's r.,** 50 Gm. of KI, 120 Gm. of HgI_2, water up to 1000 cc.: a modification of Meyer's reagent. **Cross and Bevan's r.,** two parts of concentrated hydrochloric acid and 1 part of zinc chloride by weight: used for dissolving cellulose. **Deniges' r.,** the reagent used in Deniges' test for acetone. **diazo r.,** a reagent consisting of two solutions which are mixed just prior to the test in the proportion of 25 cc. of A to 0.75 cc. of B. Solution A: Sulfanilic acid, 1 Gm.; distilled water, 1000 cc. Solution B: Sodium nitrite, 0.5 Gm.; distilled water, 100 cc. **dinitrosalicylic acid r.,** Sumner's r. **Edlefsen's r.,** an alkaline permanganate solution for testing for sugar in the urine. **Ehrlich's diazo r.** Solution A: Dissolve 5 Gm. of sodium nitrite in 1 liter of distilled water. Solution B: Dissolve 5 Gm. of sulfanilic acid and 50 cc. of HCl in 1 liter of distilled water. For use mix 1 part of A with 50 to 100 parts of B. **Erdmann's r.,** a reagent for testing for alkaloids, consisting of nitric and sulfuric acids. **Esbach's r.,** a mixture of a 1 per cent aqueous solution of picric acid and a 2 per cent solution of citric acid; used in quantitative estimation of albumin in urine. **Exton's r.,** dissolve 200 Gm. of $Na_2SO_4 \cdot 10H_2O$ in 800 cc. of water. Cool and add 50 Gm. sulfosalicylic acid and 25 cc. of a 0.4 per cent solution of bromphenol blue. Make up to 1 liter. **Folin's r.,** boil 100 Gm. of sodium tungstate and 80 cc. of 85 per cent orthophosphoric acid in 750 cc. of water for two hours. Cool and dilute 1 liter. **Folin's acid molybdate r.,** dissolve 150 Gm. of sodium molybdate in 300 cc. of water. Filter and add 2 to 3 drops of bromine and shake. Later add 225 cc. of 85 per cent phosphoric acid and 150 cc. of 25 per cent sulfuric acid. Aerate off the bromine, add 75 cc. of 90 per cent acetic acid, and dilute to 1 liter. **Folin's alkaline copper tartrate r.,** dissolve 12 Gm. of sodium tartrate (or 15 Gm. of Rochelle salt), 7 Gm. of anhydrous sodium carbonate, and 20 Gm. of sodium bicarbonate in 600 cc. of water. Dissolve 5 Gm. of copper sulfate in 200 cc. of water. Mix the solutions and dilute to 1 liter. **Folin's sugar r.** Solution A: Dissolve 5 Gm. copper sulfate in 100 cc. of hot water, cool, and add 60 to 70 cc. of glycerin. Solution B: Dissolve 125 Gm. of anhydrous potassium carbonate in 400 cc. of water. Mix 1 part of Solution A and 2 parts of Solution B just before using. **Folin-McEllroy r.,** dissolve 100 Gm. of sodium pyrophosphate, 30 Gm of disodium phosphate, and 50 Gm. of dry sodium carbonate in 1 liter of water. Dissolve 13 Gm. of copper sulfate in 200 cc. of water and pour into the first solution. **formalin-sulfuric acid r.,** Marquis' r. **Fröhde's r.** See under *tests*. **Frohn's r.** See under *tests*. **general r.,** a reagent that indicates the general class of bodies to which a substance belongs. **Gies' biuret r.,** add 25 cc. of a 3 per cent solution of copper sulfate to each liter of 10 per cent potassium hydroxide. **Grignard's r.,** any one of several compounds of magnesium with an organic radical and a halogen. These reagents undergo reactions with many substances producing important products. **Hager's r.,** a reagent for detecting sugar in the urine, consisting of iron ferrocyanide and caustic potash. **Hahn oxine r.,** a 5 per cent solution of hydroxyquinoline in alcohol. **Haines's r.,** copper sulfate, 2; potassium hydroxide, 7.5; glycerin, 15; distilled water, 150. **Ilosvay's r.,** a reagent used as a test for nitrites. It is prepared by treating a mixture of 0.5 Gm. of sulfanilic acid and 150 cc. of dilute acetic acid with 0.1 Gm. of naphthylamine, and then with 20 cc. of boiling water. The sediment produced by this reaction is dissolved in 150 cc. of dilute acetic acid. The suspected substance is heated with this reagent to 80°C., when a red color is formed if nitrites are present. **Izar's r.,** equal parts of linoleic acid and ricinoleic acid. **Lloyd's r.,** a specially fine preparation of fuller's earth obtained by elutriation: used to absorb alkaloids from solutions. **Mandelin's r.** (*for alkaloids*), 1 part of ammonium vanadate in 200 parts of cold concentrated sulfuric acid. **Marme's r.,** a solution of cadmium iodide and potassium iodide for the precipitation of alkaloids. **Marquis' r.,** 2 to 3 drops of formaldehyde solution in 3 cc. of concentrated sulfuric acid. **Mayer's r.** See under *tests*. **Mecke's r.,** 1 part of selenious acid in 200 parts of concentrated sulfuric acid. **Meyer's r.,** phenolphthalein, 0.032; decinormal sodium hydroxide, 21, with enough water to make 100 parts: used in testing for blood, which even in minute quantities gives the solution a purple color. **Millon's r.** (1849). See under *tests*. **Mörner's r.,** a solution of 1 volume of formalin, 45 volumes of distilled water, 55 volumes of concentrated sulfuric acid: used as a test for tyrosine. **Nadi r.,** a mixture of alpha-naphthol and dimethyl paraphenylene diamine, which combine to form indophenol blue from cytochrome C under the influence of cytochrome oxidase. **Nakayama r.,** ferric chloride, 0.4 Gm., concentrated hydrochloric acid, 1 cc., 95 per cent alcohol, 99 cc. **Nessler's r.,** an aqueous solution of 5 per cent of potassium iodide, 2.5 per cent of mercuric chloride, and 16 per cent of potassium hydroxide: used as a test for ammonia. **Noguchi's r.,** butyric acid 10 parts, 0.9 per cent sodium chloride 90 parts. **Nylander's r.** See under *tests*. **Obermayer's r.,** a solution of 2 Gm. of ferric chloride in 1 liter of hydrochloric acid. **Penzoldt's r.** See under *tests*. **Porges-Meier r.** See under *tests*. **Rosenthaler's r.** (*for alkaloids*), 1 part of potassium arsenate in 100 parts of concentrated sulfuric acid. **Sahli's r.,** mix equal parts of a 48 per cent solution of potassium iodide and an 8 per cent solution of potassium iodate. **Schaer's r.** (*for alkaloids*), one volume of 30 per cent pure hydrogen peroxide in 10 volumes of concentrated sulfuric acid. Use while fresh. **Scheibler's r.,** a reagent made by boiling sodium tungstate with half as much phosphoric acid and water, precipitating with barium chloride, dissolving in hot dilute hydrochloric acid, treating with sulfuric acid, and evaporating. **Schiff's r.,** a reagent for testing for the presence of aldehydes, prepared by dissolving 0.25 Gm. of fuchsin in 1000 cc. of water and decolorizing by passing sulfur dioxide into it. In the presence of aldehyde the blue color is restored. **Schweitzer's r.,** a solution of copper hydroxide in ammonia water: used as a solvent for cellulose. **Scott-Wilson r.,** (1) Mercuric cyanide, 5 Gm., (2) sodium hydroxide, 90 Gm., (3) silver nitrate, 1.45 Gm. Dissolve each separately in water and cool. Add (2) to (1), then add (3) with constant stirring. **selenious-sulfuric acid r.,** Mecke's reagent. **Soldaini's r.** See under *tests.* **Sorensen's r.,** an acetate buffer solution for combining with Pardy's test for albumin: 188 Gm. of sodium acetate and 56.5 Gm. of glacial acetic acid brought up to 1000 cc. with distilled water. **Spiegler's r.** See under *tests.* **splenic r.,** any drug or stimulus which causes the spleen to contract. **Stokes' r.,** a solution containing 2 per cent of ferrous sulfate and 3 per cent of tartaric acid. For use add ammonium hydroxide to a small portion until the precipitate redissolves, thus forming ammonium ferrotartrate. **Sumner's r.,** to 10 Gm. crystallized phenol add 22 cc. of 10 per cent NaOH and dilute to 100 cc. To 6.9 Gm. of sodium bisulfite add 69 cc. of the alkaline phenol solution. To this add a solution containing 300 cc. of 4.5 per cent NaOH, 255 Gm. $NaKC_4H_4O_6.4H_2O$, and 880 cc. of 1 per cent dinitrosalicylic acid. **Takata's r.,** the reagent (a mixture of mercuric chloride solution and basic fuchsin solution) used in Takata-Ara test. **Tanret's r.,** for albumin in urine, etc.: mercuric chloride, 1.35 Gm.; potassium iodide, 3.32 Gm.; acetic acid, 20 cc.; distilled water, to make 80 cc.; it gives a white precipitate with albumin. **Triboulet's r.,** bichloride of mercury, 3.5 Gm., acetic acid, 1 cc., water, 100 cc. **trichophytin r.** See under *tests.* **Tsuchiya r.,** an acid alcoholic solution of phosphotungstic acid for detecting small amounts of protein in the urine. **Uffelmann's r.** See under *tests.* **vanadic-sulfuric acid r.,** Mandelin's r. **Weichardt's r.** See *epiphanin reaction.* **Weisz's r.** See *Moritz-Weisz test,* under *tests.* **Wolff's r.,** phosphotungstic acid, 0.3 Gm., concentrated hydrochloric acid, 1 cc., absolute alcohol, 20 cc., distilled water, 200 cc.

reagin (re′ah-jin). An antibody or substance behaving like an antibody in complement fixation and similar reactions. Cf. *atopen.* **atopic r.,** the antibody present in the serum of a naturally hypersensitive person through the agency of which specific hypersensitiveness may be passively conferred on normal persons.

realgar (re″al-gar′) [Arabic *rahj al-ghar* powder of the mine]. Arsenic disulfide, As_2S_2: a pigment.

reamer (re′mer). An instrument used in dentistry for enlarging root canals.

reamputation (re″am-pu-ta′shun). The repeated performance of an amputation.

reattachment (re″ah-tach′ment). 1. The recementing of a dental crown or other prosthesis. 2. The reattachment to the alveolus of a tooth that has been loosened or replanted.

Réaumur's thermometer (ra″o-merz′) [René Antoine Ferschault *Réaumur,* French natural philosopher, 1683–1757]. See under *thermometer.*

rebase (re-bās′). To replace the base material of a denture without changing the occlusal relations of the teeth.

rebound (re′bownd). A reversed response on the withdrawal of a stimulus.

recalcification (re-kal″sĭ-fi-ka′shun). The restoration of lime salts to the bodily tissues.

Récamier's operation (ra″kahm-e-āz′) [Joseph Claude Anselme *Récamier,* French gynecologist, 1774–1852]. Uterine curettage.

recapitulation (re″kah-pit″u-la′shun). Repetition in the individual in its development and growth of the general style of evolutionary development of the species to which it belongs.

receiver (re-sēv′er). 1. A vessel for collecting a gas or a distillate. 2. The portion of an apparatus by which electric energy is converted into signals which may be seen or heard.

receptaculum (re″sep-tak′u-lum), pl. *receptac′ula* [L.]. A receptacle or container; that which serves for receiving or containing something. **r. chy′li,** cisterna chyli. **r. gan′glii petro′si,** fossula petrosa. **r. Pecquet′i,** cisterna chyli.

receptolysin (re″sep-tol′ĭ-sin). A substance which splits up or hydrolyzes receptors or receptor materials.

receptor (re-sep′tor). 1. A hypothetical group in a cell, which has the power of combining with and thus anchoring a haptophore group of a toxin or other substance. Receptors may remain attached to cells or may be cast off into the blood serum. In either case, they retain their combining power and so function as antibodies. See *Ehrlich's side-chain theory,* under *theory.* 2. A sensory nerve terminal which responds to stimuli of various kinds. See *exteroceptive, interoceptive,* and *proprioceptive.* **contact r.,** a sense organ which responds to stimuli from objects in contact with the body. **contiguous r.,** a receptor which must be in direct contact with the stimulant, such as touch and taste. **distance r.,** a sense organ which responds to stimuli from objects remote from the body, as a receptor for the stimuli of hearing, vision, or smell. **dominant r.,** an unknown substance or substances located at the site of action of a drug which by combining with the drug enable it to exert its physiologic action. **r. of the first order,** a receptor which possesses a haptophore group only, and therefore serves only as a connecting link between the toxin and the tissues. This order of receptors includes only the antitoxins. **gustatory r.,** a receptor for the sense of taste; a taste bud. **pressure r.,** a receptor for stimuli of pressure or touch; a touch corpuscle. **r. of the second order,** a receptor which possesses both a haptophore group for anchoring or holding the foreign toxin, and a zymophore group for its digestion. This group includes the agglutinins, the precipitins, and the opsonins. **secondary r's,** unknown substances, other than the dominant receptor, located at points other than the site of action which combine with a drug and so lessen its combination with the dominant receptor and its physiologic activity. **sessile r.,** a receptor which cannot be given off to form an antibody. **r. of the third order,** a receptor which possesses two combining groups only, a haptophore group for combining with the foreign toxin, and a complementophile group which combines with the complement that carries the zymotoxic element. This group includes the lysins. **visual r.,** the layer of rods and cones of the retina.

recess (re′ses). A small empty space or cavity. **accessory r. of elbow,** recessus sacciformis articulationis cubiti. **acetabular r.,** fossa acetabuli. **Arlt's r.,** a small sinus occasionally present in the lower part of the lacrimal sac. **chiasmatic r.,** recessus opticus. **cochlear r. of vestibule,** recessus cochlearis vestibuli. **conarial r.,** recessus pinealis. **costodiaphragmatic r. of pleura,** recessus costodiaphragmaticus pleurae. **costomediastinal r. of pleura,** recessus costomediastinalis pleurae. **duodenal r., inferior,** recessus duodenalis inferior. **duodenal r., superior, duodenojejunal r.,** recessus duodenalis superior. **elliptical r. of vestibule,** recessus ellipticus vestibuli. **epitympanic r.,** recessus epitympanicus. **r. of fourth ventricle, lateral,** recessus lateralis ventriculi quarti. **hepatorenal r.,** recessus hepatorenalis. **Hyrtl's r.,** recessus epitympanicus. **ileocecal r., inferior,** recessus ileocecalis inferior. **ileocecal r., superior,** recessus ileocecalis superior. **infundibular r.,** recessus infundibuli. **infundibuliform r.,** recessus pharyngeus. **r. of infundibulum,** recessus infundibuli. **inter-**

sigmoidal r., recessus intersigmoideus. **laryngopharyngeal r.,** recessus piriformis. **r. of lesser omental cavity,** recessus lienalis. **r. of nasopharynx, lateral,** recessus pharyngeus. **omental r., inferior,** recessus inferior omentalis. **omental r., superior,** recessus superior omentalis. **optic r.,** recessus opticus. **paracolic r's,** sulci paracolici. **paraduodenal r.,** recessus paraduodenalis. **r. of pelvic mesocolon,** recessus intersigmoideus. **pharyngeal r.,** recessus pharyngeus. **pharyngeal r., middle,** bursa pharyngea. **phrenicohepatic r's.** See *recessus subhepatici, recessus subphrenici,* and *recessus hepatorenalis.* **pineal r.,** recessus pinealis. **piriform r.,** recessus piriformis. **pleural r.,** recessus pleuralis. **retrocecal r.,** recessus retrocecalis. **retroduodenal r.,** recessus retroduodenalis. **r. of Rosenmüller,** recessus pharyngeus. **sacciform r. of articulation of elbow,** recessus sacciformis articulationis cubiti. **sacciform r. of distal radioulnar articulation,** recessus sacciformis articulationis radioulnaris distalis. **sphenoethmoidal r.,** recessus sphenoethmoidalis. **sphenoethmoidal r., bony,** recessus sphenoethmoidalis osseus. **spherical r. of vestibule,** r. sphericus vestibuli. **splenic r.,** recessus lienalis. **subhepatic r's,** recessus subhepatici. **subphrenic r's,** recessus subphrenici. **subpopliteal r.,** recessus subpopliteus. **suprapineal r.,** recessus suprapinealis. **supratonsillar r.,** the space above and in front of the tonsils and between the pillars of the fauces. **Tarini's r.,** recessus anterior fossae interpeduncularis. **triangular r.,** recessus triangularis. **r's of Tröltsch.** See *recessus membranae tympani anterior* and *recessus membranae tympani posterior.* **r. of tympanic membrane, anterior,** recessus membranae tympani anterior. **r. of tympanic membrane, posterior,** recessus membranae tympani posterior. **r. of tympanic membrane, superior,** recessus membranae tympani superior. **utricular r.,** utriculus. **r. of vestibule,** recessus sphericus vestibuli.

recession (re-sesh'un) [L. *recedere* to draw back or away]. The act of drawing away. In dentistry, the retraction of the gingival margin and underlying tissue away from the neck of a tooth, resulting in exposure of the cementum.

recessive (re-ses'iv). Tending to recede; not exerting a ruling or controlling influence. In genetics, incapable of expression unless carried by both members of a set of homologous chromosomes.

recessus (re-ses'sus), pl. *reces'sus* [L.]. A small empty space or cavity; used in anatomical nomenclature as a general term to designate such potential spaces. Called also *recess.* **r. ante'rior fos'sae interpeduncula'ris [Tari'ni]** [B N A], the portion of the interpeduncular fossa that passes under the corpora mamillaria. Omitted in N A. **r. chiasma'tis,** r. opticus. **r. cochlea'ris vestib'uli** [N A, B N A], a small depressed area on the medial wall of the vestibule; situated just below the posterior end of the crista vestibuli, and perforated with foramina through which nerve fibers pass to the posterior portion of the ductus cochlearis. Called also *cochlear recess of vestibule.* **r. costodiaphragmat'icus pleu'rae** [N A], the pleural recess situated at the junction of the costal and diaphragmatic pleurae. Called also *sinus phrenicocostalis* [B N A], and *costodiaphragmatic recess of pleura.* **r. costomediastina'lis pleu'rae** [N A], a wedge-shaped space, not completely filled with lung tissue, along the line at which the costal pleura meets the mediastinal pleura in front. Called also *sinus costomediastinalis pleurae* [B N A], and *costomediastinal recess of pleura.* **r. duodena'lis infe'rior** [N A], a pocket in the peritoneum on the left side of the ascending portion of the duodenum, bounded by the inferior duodenal fold. Called also *inferior duodenal recess.* **r. duodena'lis supe'rior** [N A], **r. duodenojejuna'lis** [B N A], a peritoneal pocket behind the superior duodenal fold. Called also *superior duodenal recess.* **r. ellip'ticus vestib'uli** [N A, B N A], an oval depressed area in the roof and medial wall of the vestibule of the inner ear; situated above and behind the crista and pierced by 25 to 30 small foramina through which nerves come from the internal acoustic meatus to the utricle, which occupies the depression. Called also *elliptical recess of vestibule.* **r. epitympan'icus** [N A, B N A], the upper portion of the tympanic cavity, extending above the level of the tympanic membrane and containing the greater part of the incus and the upper half of the malleus. Called also *epitympanic recess.* **r. hepatorena'lis** [N A], a peritoneal pouch between the liver and the kidney. Called also *hepatorenal recess.* **r. ileoceca'lis infe'rior** [N A], a peritoneal pocket situated behind the ileocecal fold, above the vermiform appendix, below the ileum, and medial to the cecum. Called also *inferior ileocecal recess.* **r. ileoceca'lis supe'rior** [N A], a peritoneal pocket situated behind and below the vascular cecal fold, above the ileum and medial to the lower end of the ascending colon. Called also *superior ileocecal recess.* **r. infe'rior omenta'lis** [N A, B N A], the lower portion of the omental bursa, including its extension down into the great omentum. It is bounded in front by the posterior wall of the stomach, and behind by the pancreas, the transverse colon and its mesocolon, the left suprarenal gland, and part of the left kidney. Called also *inferior omental recess.* **r. infundib'uli** [N A, B N A], a funnel-shaped depression in the anterior part of the floor of the third ventricle of the brain, within the infundibulum of the hypophysis. Called also *recess of infundibulum.* **r. intersigmoi'deus** [N A, B N A], a shallow peritoneal pocket running downward and to the left at the base of the sigmoid mesocolon. Called also *intersigmoidal recess.* **r. latera'lis fos'sae rhomboi'dei** [B N A], r. lateralis ventriculi quarti. **r. latera'lis ventric'uli quar'ti** [N A], a narrow, curved prolongation of the cavity of the fourth ventricle, extending laterally onto the dorsal surface of the inferior cerebellar peduncle. Called also *lateral recess of fourth ventricle.* **r. liena'lis** [N A, B N A], an extension of the omental bursa to the left behind the gastrolienal ligament almost to the spleen. Called also *splenic recess.* **r. membra'nae tym'pani ante'rior** [N A, B N A], a pocket in the tympanic membrane formed by the tunica mucosa between the anterior mallear fold and the upper front part of the pars tensa of the membrane, ending blindly above. Called also *anterior recess of tympanic membrane.* **r. membra'nae tym'pani poste'rior** [N A, B N A], a pocket in the tympanic membrane formed by the tunica mucosa between the posterior mallear fold and the upper back part of the pars tensa of the membrane, ending blindly above. Called also *posterior recess of tympanic membrane.* **r. membra'nae tym'pani supe'rior** [N A, B N A], a recess in the tympanic membrane formed by the tunica mucosa between the neck of the malleus and the pars flaccida of the membrane, and ending blindly below. Called also *superior r. of tympanic membrane.* **r. op'ticus** [N A, B N A], a depression in the floor of the third ventricle between the chiasma behind and the lamina terminalis in front. Called also *optic recess.* **r. paracol'ici** [B N A], sulci paracolici. **r. paraduodena'lis** [N A], a pocket occasionally found in the peritoneum behind a fold containing a branch of the left colic artery. Called also *paraduodenal recess.* **r. pharyn'geus** [N A], **r. pharyn'geus [Rosenmül'leri]** [B N A], a wide, slitlike lateral extension in the wall of the nasopharynx, cranial and dorsal to the pharyngeal orifice of the auditory tube. Called also *pharyngeal recess.* **r. phrenicohepat'ici** [B N A]. See *r. subhepatici, r. subphrenici,* and *r. hepatorenalis.* **r. pinea'lis** [N A, B N A], an extension of the third ventricle into the stalk of the pineal body. Called also *pineal recess.* **r. pirifor'mis** [N A, B N A], an elongated fossa in the wall of the laryngeal pharynx caudal to the lateral glossoepiglottic folds. Called also *piriform recess.* **r. pleura'lis** [N A], any one of the spaces where the different portions of the pleura join at an angle and which are never completely filled by lung tissue. Called also *sinus pleurae* [B N A], and *pleural recess.* **r. pneumato-enter'icus,** either of the paired embryonic excavations alongside the dorsal mesogastricum, the right one sometimes persisting as the infracardiac bursa. **r. poste'rior fos'sae interpeduncula'ris [Tari'ni]** [B N A], the portion of the interpeduncular fossa that slightly undermines the anterior margin of the pons. Omitted in N A. **r. pro utric'ulo,** r. ellipticus vestibuli. **r. retroceca'lis** [N A], a peritoneal pocket extending upward behind the cecum and sometimes behind the colon. Called also *retrocecal recess.* **r. retroduodena'lis** [N A], an occasional peritoneal pocket extending behind the horizontal and ascending parts of the duodenum. Called also *retroduodenal recess.* **r. saccifor'mis articulatio'nis cu'biti** [B N A], the distal bulging of the articular capsule of the elbow joint, situated between the incisura radialis ulnae and the circumferentia articularis radii. Omitted in N A. **r. saccifor'mis articulatio'nis radioulna'ris dista'lis** [N A, B N A], a bulging of the synovial membrane of the articular capsule of the distal radioulnar joint, which extends proximally between the radius and ulna beyond the point of their articular surfaces. Called also *sacciform recess of distal radioulnar articulation.* **r. sphenoethmoida'lis** [N A, B N A], a small pocket in the superior meatus of the nasal cavity, above the superior nasal concha, into which the sphenoidal sinus opens. Called also *sphenoethmoidal recess.* **r. sphenoethmoida'lis os'seus** [N A, B N A], a small region in the skull, posterosuperior to the supreme nasal concha and just anterior to the body of the sphenoid bone. The sphenoid sinus opens into it. Called also *bony sphenoethmoidal recess.* **r. spher'icus vestib'uli** [N A], a circular depressed area in the anteroinferior portion of the medial wall of the vestibule of the inner ear. It is pierced by 12 to 15 small foramina through which nerves come from the internal acoustic meatus to the saccule, which occupies the depression. Called also *spherical recess of vestibule.* **r. splenia'lis,** r. lienalis. **r. subhepat'ici** [N A], peritoneal pockets located beneath the liver. Called also *subhepatic recesses.* **r. subphren'ici** [N A], peritoneal pockets located beneath the diaphragm. Called also *subphrenic recesses.* **r. subpoplite'us** [N A], a prolongation of the synovial tendon sheath of the popliteus muscle outside the knee joint into the popliteal space. Called also *bursa musculi poplitei* [B N A], and *subpopliteal recess.* **r. supe'rior omenta'lis** [N A, B N A], a rather long, narrow peritoneal pocket leading from the vestibule upward toward the liver, between the inferior vena cava on the right, the esophagus on the left, the gastrohepatic ligament in front, and the diaphragm behind. Called also *superior omental recess.* **r. suprapinea'lis** [N A, B N A], the posterior extension of the third ventricle above and around the pineal body. Called also *suprapineal recess.* **r. triangula'ris** [B N A], a small triangular recess on the anterior wall of the third ventricle, its base below on the anterior commissure and its sides formed by the converging columns of the fornix. Omitted in N A.

recidivation (re-sid″ĭ-va′shun). 1. The relapse or recurrence of a disease. 2. The repetition of an offense, or crime.

recidivism (re-sid′ĭ-vizm). A tendency to relapse, especially the tendency to return to a life of crime.

recidivist (re-sid′ĭ-vist) [Fr. *récidiviste,* from L. *recidere* to fall back]. One who tends to relapse, especially a person who tends to return to criminal habits after treatment or punishment.

recipe (res′ĭ-pe). 1. [L.]. Take: used at the head of a physician's prescription, and usually indicated by the symbol ℞. 2. A formula for the preparation of a specific combination of ingredients.

recipient (re-sip′e-ent). The person who receives the blood in transfusion. **universal r.,** a person thought to be able to receive blood of any "type" without precipitation or agglutination of the cells.

recipiomotor (re-sip″e-o-mo′tor) [L. *recipere* to receive + *motor* mover]. Pertaining to the reception of motor impressions.

reciprocation (re-sip″ro-ka′shun) [L. *reciprocare* to move backward and forward]. The complementary interaction of two distinct entities. Applied in dentistry to the means by which one part of an appliance is made to counter the effect created by another part, as in a partial denture.

Recklinghausen's canals, disease (rek′ling-how″zenz) [Friedrich Daniel von *Recklinghausen,* German pathologist, 1833–1910]. See under the nouns.

reclination (rek″lĭ-na′shun) [L. *reclinatio*]. One of the operations for cataract: a turning of the lens over into the vitreous.

Reclus' disease (ra-klez′) [Paul *Reclus,* French surgeon, 1847–1914]. See under *disease.*

recombination (re″kom-bĭ-na′shun). The reunion, in the same or a different arrangement, of formerly united elements which have become separated. **bacterial r.,** the Mendelian segregation of marker characters, usually nutritional requirements, in mixed cultures of variant strains of bacteria derived from a common parent strain; studied most extensively with a strain of coliform bacillus designated K-12.

recompression (re″kom-presh′un). The restoration of pressure, especially the return to conditions of normal pressure after exposure to greatly diminished atmospheric pressure.

recon (re′kon) [*re*combination + Gr. *on* neuter ending]. A term used to designate a gene, when specified as a hereditary unit indivisible by genetic recombination. Cf. *cistron* and *muton.*

reconstitution (re″kon-stĭ-tu′shun). 1. The reaggregation of cells, isolated by the breaking up of an organism, into a new whole animal. 2. A type of regeneration in which a new organ forms by the rearrangement of tissues rather than from new formation at an injured surface. 3. The restoration to original form of a substance previously altered for preservation and storage, as the restoration to a liquid state of blood serum or plasma that has been dried and stored.

recontour (re-kon′toor). To give new shape or contour to. In dentistry, to change the contour of a crown or a complete or partial denture.

recrement (rek′re-ment) [L. *recrementum*]. The saliva or other material which, after secretion, is reabsorbed into the blood.

recrementitious (rek″re-men-tish′us). Of the nature of a recrement.

recrudescence (re″kroo-des′ens) [L. *recrudescere* to become sore again]. The recurrence of symptoms after a temporary abatement. See *relapse.* The chief distinction between a recrudescence and a relapse is the time interval, a recrudescence occurring after some days or weeks, a relapse after some weeks or months.

recrudescent (re″kroo-des′ent) [L. *recrudescens*]. Breaking out afresh.

recruitment (re-kro͝ot′ment). The gradual increase to a maximum in a reflex when a stimulus of unaltered intensity is prolonged.

Rect. Abbreviation for L. *rectifica'tus,* rectified.

rectal (rek′tal). Pertaining to the rectum.

rectalgia (rek-tal′je-ah) [*rectum* + *-algia*]. Proctalgia.

rectectomy (rek-tek′to-me) [*rectum* + Gr. *ektomē* excision]. Excision of the rectum.

rectification (rek″tĭ-fi-ka′shun) [L. *rectificatio*].

1. The act of making straight, pure, or correct. 2. Redistillation of a liquid to purify it.

rectified (rek′tĭ-fīd). Refined; made straight.

rectifier (rek′tĭ-fi″er). A device for obtaining a unidirectional current from an alternating current. **thermionic r.,** a rectifier consisting of an electric valve in which the electrons are supplied by a heated electrode.

rectischiac (rek-tis′ke-ak). Pertaining to the rectum and the ischium.

rectitis (rek-ti′tis). Proctitis. **epidemic gangrenous r.** See under *proctitis*.

recto-abdominal (rek″to-ab-dom′ĭ-nal). Pertaining to the rectum and abdomen.

rectocele (rek′to-sēl) [*recto-* + Gr. *kēlē* hernia]. Hernial protrusion of part of the rectum into the vagina. Also called *proctocele*.

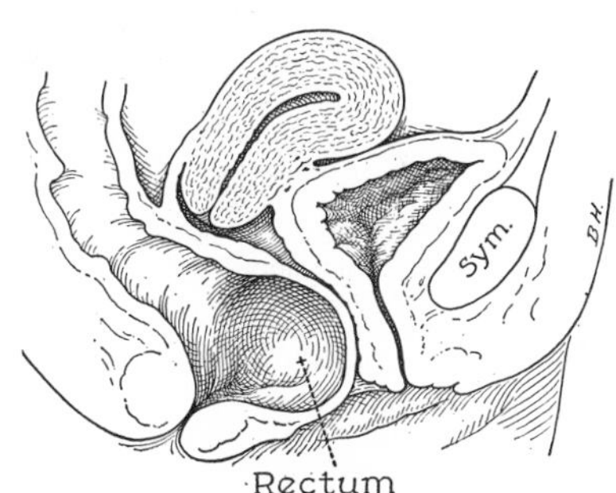

Rectocele.

rectoclysis (rek-tok′lĭ-sis). Proctoclysis.

rectococcygeal (rek″to-kok-sij′e-al). Pertaining to the rectum and the coccyx.

rectococcypexy (rek″to-kok′sĭ-pek-se). Proctococcypexy.

rectocolitis (rek″to-ko-li′tis). Colorectitis.

rectocystotomy (rek″to-sis-tot′o-me). Proctocystotomy.

rectolabial (rek″to-la′be-al). Pertaining to or communicating with the rectum and a labium majus, as a rectolabial fistula.

rectoperineorrhaphy (rek″to-per″ĭ-ne-or′ah-fe). Proctoperineorrhaphy.

rectopexy (rek′to-pek″se). Proctopexy.

rectophobia (rek″to-fo′be-ah) [*rectum* + *phobia*]. A morbid foreboding peculiar to patients with rectal disease.

rectoplasty (rek′to-plas″te). Proctoplasty.

rectorectostomy (rek″to-rek-tos′to-me). Operative formation of an anastomosis between two portions of the rectum.

rectoromanoscope (rek″to-ro-man′o-skōp). A speculum for examining the sigmoid flexure.

rectoromanoscopy (rek″to-ro″mah-nos′ko-pe) [*rectum* + L. *romanum* sigmoid + Gr. *skopein* to examine]. Inspection of the rectum and sigmoid.

rectorrhaphy (rek-tor′ah-fe) [*rectum* + Gr. *rhaphē* suture]. Proctorrhaphy.

rectoscope (rek′to-skōp). Proctoscope.

rectoscopy (rek-tos′ko-pe). Proctoscopy.

rectosigmoid (rek″to-sig′moid). The lower portion of the sigmoid and upper portion of the rectum.

rectosigmoidectomy (rek″to-sig″moid-ek′to-me). Excision of the rectosigmoid.

rectostenosis (rek″to-ste-no′sis). Stenosis, or stricture, of the rectum.

rectostomy (rek-tos′to-me) [*rectum* + Gr. *stomoun* to provide with a mouth, or opening]. The operation of forming a permanent opening into the rectum for the relief of stricture of the rectum.

rectotome (rek′to-tōm). Proctotome.

rectotomy (rek-tot′o-me). Proctotomy.

rectourethral (rek″to-u-re′thral). Pertaining to or communicating with the rectum and urethra, as a rectourethral fistula.

rectouterine (rek″to-u′ter-in). Pertaining to the rectum and uterus.

rectovaginal (rek″to-vaj′ĭ-nal). Pertaining to or communicating with the rectum and vagina, as a rectovaginal fistula.

rectovesical (rek″to-ves′ĭ-kal). Pertaining to or communicating with the rectum and urinary bladder, as a rectovesical fistula.

rectovestibular (rek″to-ves-tib′u-lar). Pertaining to or communicating with the rectum and the vestibule of the vagina, as a rectovestibular fistula.

rectovulvar (rek″to-vul′var). Pertaining to or communicating with the rectum and vulva, as a rectovulvar fistula.

rectum (rek′tum) [L. "straight"]. [N A] The distal portion of the large intestine, beginning anterior to the third sacral vertebra as a continuation of the sigmoid and ending at the anal canal. Called also *intestinum rectum* [B N A].

rectus (rek′tus) [L.]. Straight.

recumbent (re-kum′bent). Lying down.

recuperation (re-ku″per-a′shun) [L. *recuperatio*]. The recovery of health and strength.

recurrence (re-kur′ens) [L. *re-* again + *currere* to run]. The return of symptoms after a remission.

recurrent (re-kur′ent) [L. *recurrens* returning]. 1. Running back, or toward the source. 2. Returning after intermissions.

recurvation (re″kur-va′shun) [L. *recurvatio*]. A backward bending or curvature.

red (red). A red dye or stain. **alizarin r.,** the sodium salt of alizarin monosulfonate. **alizarin r. S, alizarin water-soluble r.,** a dye used as a stain. It is sodium alizarin sulfonate, C_6H_4.-$(CO)_2C_3H(OH)_2.SO_2ONa$. **aniline r.,** basic fuchsin. **bordeaux r.,** cerasin. **bromphenol r.,** an indicator, dibromphenol-sulfonphthalein, $(CH_2Br_2OH)_2C.C_6H_4.SO_2.ONa$. **Caesar r.,** bluish eosin. **carmine r.,** a stain, $C_{11}H_{12}O_7$, derived from carmine. **cerasin r.,** sudan III. **cholera r.** See *cholera red test*. **Congo r.,** an odorless dark red or reddish brown powder, $C_{32}H_{22}N_6Na_2O_6S_2$, which decomposes on exposure to acid fumes: used as a diagnostic aid in amyloidosis. **corallin r.,** the pararosaniline salt of pararosolic acid. **cotton r.,** Congo r. **cotton r. 4 B,** benzopurpurine 4 B. **cresol r.,** an indicator, ortho-cresol-sulfonphthalein, $(CH_3.C_6H_3$.-$OH)_2C.C_6H_4.SO_2.ONa$: used in the determination of the hydrogen ion concentration. It has a pH range of 7.2 to 8.8, being yellow at 7.2 and red at 8.8. **dianil r. 4 C, dianin r. 4 B,** benzopurpurine 4 B. **direct r.,** Congo r. **direct r. 4 B,** benzopurpurine 4 B. **fast r.,** amaranth. **fast r. B** or **P.** cerasin. **indigo r., indoxyl r.,** a coloring matter produced by heating an aqueous solution of indoxyl to 130°C. **magdala r.,** a basic dye used for staining connective tissue. It is a mixture of monoamino- and diamino-naphthosafranins. The diamino compound is $NH_2C_{10}H_5.N_2Cl(C_{10}H_7).C_{10}H_5.NH_2$. **methyl r.,** a dye, para-dimethyl-amino-azo-benzene-ortho-carboxylic acid, $(CH_3)_2N.C_6H_4.N{:}N.C_6H_4.COOH$: used as an indicator in the determination of hydrogen ion concentration and has a pH range of 4.4 to 6, being red at 4.4, and yellow at 6. **nagana r.,** nagarot. **naphthaline r.,** magdala r. **naphthol r.,** amaranth. **neutral r.,** a dye, amino-dimethylamino-toluphenazonium chloride, $(CH_3)_2N.C_6H_3.N_2C_6H_2(CH_3).NH_2HCl$. As an indicator it has a pH range of 6.8 to 8, being red at 6.8 and yellow at 8. **oil r.,** sudan III. **oil r. IV,** scarlet r. **orange r.,** the red oxide of lead, Pb_3O_4: used as a pigment. **phenol r.,** phenolsulfonphthalein. **provisional r.,** a colored lipin obtained from rhodopsin. **scarlet r.,** a red, fat-soluble azo dye, toluyl-azo-toluyl-azo-beta-naphthol, which has a marked power of stimulating the proliferation of epithelial cells.

scarlet r. sulfonate, the sodium salt of azobenzene-disulfonic acid azobeta-naphthol: used the same as scarlet red. **senitol r.,** a dye, C_2H_5.-$NC_9H_6(CH)_3.C_9H_6N(I).C_2H_5$, with a highly selective germicidal action on staphylococci. It is also used to sensitize photographic plates to red rays of light. **sudan r.,** magdala r. **toluylene r.,** the base, the hydrochloride of which is neutral red. **tony r.,** sudan III. **trypan r.,** an acid, azo dye used as a vital stain and as a trypanocidal agent. **visual r.,** porphyropsin. **vital r.,** a dye, disodium disulfonaphthol azotetramethyl triphenyl methane. It is introduced directly into the circulation by venipuncture for the purpose of estimating the volume of the blood in the body by determining the concentration of the dye in the blood plasma. **wool r.,** amaranth.

Red. in pulv. Abbreviation for L. *reduc'tus in pul'verem,* reduced to powder.

redecussate (re″de-kus′āt). To form a secondary decussation.

redia (re′de-ah), pl. *re'diae* [named after F. *Redi,* Italian naturalist, 1626–1698]. The second or third larval stage of certain trematode parasites, which develops in the body of a snail host and gives rise to the next larval stage, the cercaria.

rediae (re′de-e). Plural of *redia.*

redifferentiation (re″dif-er-en″she-a′shun). The return of a dedifferentiated tissue or part to its original or another more or less similar condition.

Redig. in pulv. Abbreviation for L. *rediga'tur in pul'verem,* let it be reduced to powder.

redintegration (red-in″te-gra′shun) [L. *redintegratio*]. 1. The restoration or repair of a lost or damaged part. 2. That type of psychic process in which a part of a complex stimulus provokes the complete reaction that was previously made to the complex stimulus as a whole (Hollingworth).

redislocation (re″dis-lo-ka′shun). Dislocation recurring after reduction.

redisol (red′ĭ-sol). Trade mark for a preparation of crystalline vitamin B_{12}. See *cyanocobalamin.*

Redlich phenomenon (red′likh) [Emil *Redlich,* Austrian neurologist, 1866–1930]. See under *phenomenon.*

Redlich-Obersteiner (red′likh o″ber-sti′ner). See *Obersteiner-Redlich,* and under *area.*

redox (red′oks). In chemistry, mutual reduction and oxidation.

redressement (rĕ-dres-maw′) [Fr.]. 1. A second or repeated dressing. 2. Replacement of a part or correction of a deformity. **r. forcé,** forcible correction of a deformity; especially a procedure for the immediate correction of knock knee.

reducase (re-du′kās). Reductase.

reduce (re-dūs′) [*re-* + L. *ducere* to lead]. 1. To restore to the normal place or relation of parts, as, to *reduce* a fracture. 2. In chemistry, to submit to reduction. 3. To decrease in weight.

reduced (re-dūst′). 1. Returned to the proper place or position, as, a *reduced* fracture. 2. Restored to a metallic form, as, *reduced* iron.

reducible (re-du′sĭ-b′l). Permitting of reduction; capable of being reduced.

reducine (re-du′sin). A leukomaine, $C_{12}H_{24}N_6O_9$, from urochrome.

reductant (re-duk′tant). The electron donor in an oxidation-reduction (redox) reaction.

reductase (re-duk′tās). An enzyme that has a reducing action on chemical compounds; a dehydrogenase. **acetaldehyde r.,** an enzyme that catalyzes the reduction of acetaldehyde to alcohol. It consists of a protein and a prosthetic group, diphosphopyridine nucleotide. **cytochrome r.,** an enzyme that catalyzes the simultaneous oxidation of coenzyme II and the reduction of cytochrome C. **Schardinger's r.,** a reductase in milk which reduces methylene blue, especially in the presence of formaldehyde.

reduction (re-duk′shun) [L. *reductio*]. 1. The correction of a fracture, luxation, or hernia. 2. In chemistry, the subtraction of oxygen from or the addition of hydrogen to a substance, or more generally, the loss of positive charges or the gain of negative charges. **r. of chromosomes,** the passing of the members of a chromosome pair to the daughter cells during meiosis, each daughter cell receiving half the diploid number. **closed r.,** the manipulative reduction of a fracture without incision. **r. en masse,** reduction of a strangulated hernia included in its sac, so that the strangulation is not relieved. **open r.,** reduction of a fracture after incision into the fracture site. **weight r.,** the lessening of one's body weight by a specific regimen which is especially designed for that purpose.

reductone (re-duk′tōn). Glucic acid.

redundant (re-dun′dant). More than necessary.

reduplication (re″du-plĭ-ka′shun) [L. *reduplicatio*]. 1. A doubling back. 2. The recurrence of paroxysms of a double type. 3. A doubling of parts, connected at some point, the extra part being usually a mirror image of the other.

reduviid (re-du′vĭ-id). Belonging to the family Reduviidae.

Reduviidae (re″du-vi′ĭ-de). A family of winged hemipterous insects called cone-nose bugs, kissing bugs, and assassin bugs because they prey on other insects. It includes the genera *Eratyrus, Eutriatoma, Panstrongylus, Rhodnius* and *Triatoma.*

redwater (red′wah-ter). Braxy.

Reed's cells (rēdz) [Dorothy *Reed,* American pathologist]. See under *cell.*

re-education (re″ed-u-ka′shun). The training of a disabled or mentally disordered person in the endeavor to restore some of his lost competence.

Rees's test (rēs′ez) [George Owen *Rees,* English physician, 1813–1889]. See under *tests.*

refect (re-fekt′). To induce refection.

refection (re-fek′shun) [L. *reficere* to restore]. Recovery; repair: applied specifically to the ability of the flora of the cecum of rats to synthesize vitamins of the B group from deficient diets and supply them to the host animal.

refectious (re-fek′shus). Capable of causing, or pertaining to, refection.

refine (re-fin′). To purify or free from foreign matter.

reflected (re-flekt′ed). Turned or bent back. In neurology, caused by nervous transmission to a center, and thence by a motor nerve to the periphery.

reflection (re-flek′shun) [L. *reflexio*]. 1. A turning or bending back; a bending back upon its course. 2. In physics, the turning back of a ray of light, sound, or heat when it strikes against a surface that it does not penetrate. The ray before reflection is known as the *incident ray;* after reflection it is the *reflected ray.*

reflector (re-flek′tor). A device for reflecting light or sound. **dental r.,** a dental mirror.

reflectoscope (re-flek′to-skōp). A form of reflecting lantern.

reflex (re′fleks) [L. *reflexus*]. 1. Reflected. 2. A reflected action or movement; the sum total of any particular involuntary activity. See *reflex arc, reflex act,* and *reflex action.* 3. A reflected image of an object. **abdominal r's,** contractions about the navel on sharp downward friction of the abdominal wall. It indicates that the spinal cord from the eighth to the twelfth dorsal nerve is intact. **abdominocardiac r.,** any reflex in the heart produced by stimulating the abdominal sympathetic. Cf. *Livierato's sign* and *Prevel's sign,* under *sign.* **Abrams' r.,** reflex contraction of the lung following stimulation of the chest wall. **Abrams' heart r.,** contraction of the myocardium, with reduction in the area of cardiac dullness, which results when the skin of the precordial region is irritated. It is observed with the fluoroscope. **accommodation r.,** the coordinated changes that occur when the eye adapts itself for near vision. They are constriction of the pupil, convergence of the eyes, and increased convexity of the lens. **Achilles tendon r.,** triceps surae jerk. **acquired r.,** conditional r. **adductor r.,** on tapping the tendon of the adductor magnus with the thigh in abduction, contraction of the adductors results. **allied r's,** reflexes in which two afferent stimuli use the same common pathway or produce effects on two synergistic muscles. **anal r.,** contraction of the anal sphincter on irritation of the skin of the anus. **ankle r.,** ankle clonus: pressure on the sole with dorsiflexion of the foot causes clonic contraction of the triceps surae muscle. **antagonistic r's,** reflex movements occurring not in the muscle which has been stretched but in its antagonist. **anticus r.,** Piotrowski's sign. **artists' r.,** a specular reflex from the moist surface of the cornea, seen on examination under direct illumination. **Aschner's r.,** oculocardiac r. **attention r. of pupil,** alteration of size in the pupil when the attention is suddenly fixed. Called also *Piltz's r.* **attitudinal r's,** those reflexes having to do with the position of the body. **audito-oculogyric r.,** a turning of both eyes in the direction of a sudden sound. **auditory r.,** any reflex caused by stimulation of the auditory nerve; especially momentary closure of both eyes produced by a sudden sound. **aural r.,** any reflex connected with the auditory apparatus. Aural reflexes of compensation are—(1) Those of the labyrinthine escapement; (2) those of vasomotor compensation; (3) those of tympanic compensation, and (4) those of tubotympanic compensation. **auricle r.,** involuntary movement of the ear produced by auditory stimuli. **auriculocervical nerve r.,** Snellen's r. **auriculopalpebral r.,** Kirsch's r. **auriculopressor r.,** fall in arterial blood pressure (vasoconstriction) caused by fall of pressure in the right auricle and great veins. **axon r.,** a reflex resulting from a stimulus applied to one branch of a nerve which sets up an impulse that moves centrally to the point of division of the nerve where it is reflected down the other branch to the effector organ. **Babinski's r.** (1896), dorsiflexion of the big toe on stimulating the sole of the foot; it occurs in lesions of the pyramidal tract, and indicates organic, as distinguished from hysteric, hemiplegia. Called also *Babinski's toe sign.* **Bainbridge r.,** rise in pressure in, or increased distention of, the large somatic veins causes reflex acceleration of the heart beat. **Barkman's r.,** contraction of the rectus muscle on the same side after stimulation of the skin just below one of the nipples. **basal joint r.,** finger-thumb r. **Bechterew's r.** 1. *Deep.* Passive flexion of the toes and foot in a plantar direction is followed by flexion in a dorsal direction and by flexive movements of the knee and hip. 2. *Hypogastric.* Contraction of the muscles of the lower abdomen on stroking the skin of the inner surface of the thigh. 3. *Pupil.* Dilatation of the pupil on exposure to light: sometimes seen in tabes and general paralysis. 4. Tickling of the mucosa of the nasal cavity with a feather or piece of paper produces contraction of the facial muscles on the same side of the face; called also *nasal r.* **Bechterew-Mendel r.,** tarsophalangeal r. **behavior r.,** conditioned r. **biceps r.,** contractions of the biceps muscle of the arm when its tendon is tapped. This reflex is normal but when greatly increased it indicates the same disease as increased knee jerk. **bladder r.,** urinary r. **Brain's r.,** an extension of the hemiplegic flexed arm when the patient assumes the quadrupedal position: called also *quadrupedal extensor reflex.* **bregmocardiac r.,** pressure upon the bregmatic fontanel slows the action of the heart. **Brissaud's r.,** contraction of the tensor fasciae femoris muscle on tickling the sole. **Brudzinski's r.** See under *sign.* **bulbocavernous r.,** a tap on the dorsum of the penis causes retraction of the bulbocavernous portion. **bulbomimic r.,** in coma from apoplexy, pressure on the eyeball causes contraction of the facial muscles on the side opposite to the lesion; in coma from toxic causes the reflex occurs on both sides. Called also *facial r.* and *Mondonesi's r.* **Capps' r's,** (1) *vasomotor:* collapse, sweating, pallor, fall in blood pressure, due to pleural inflammation, indicate probable recovery; (2) *cardiac:* the same symptoms when greatly intensified indicate probable death. **cardiac r.,** reduction in the size of the area of cardiac dullness following irritation of the skin of the precordial region. **carotid sinus r.,** pressure on the carotid artery at the level of the cricoid cartilage will slow the heart beat, this reflex originating in the wall of the sinus of the internal carotid artery. See *carotid sinus syndrome,* under *syndrome.* **cerebral cortex r.,** Haab's r. **Chaddock r.,** stimulation below the external malleolus produces extension of the great toe: it occurs in lesions of the pyramidal tract. **chain r.,** a series of reflexes, each serving as a stimulus to the next one, representing a complete activity. **chemical r.,** the bodily process produced by the action of a hormone. **chin r.,** a stroke on the lower jaw causes closing of the mouth. **chocked r.,** in skiascopy, absence of movement of the retinal illumination on reaching the point of reversal. **ciliary r.,** the movement of the pupil in accommodation. **ciliospinal r.,** stimulation of the skin of the neck dilates the pupil. **clasp-knife r.,** lengthening reaction. **cochleo-orbicular r., cochleopalpebral r.,** contraction of the orbicularis palpebrarum muscle when a sharp, sudden noise is made close to the ear; does not occur in total deafness from labyrinthine disease. **cochleopapillary r.,** a reaction of the iris (contraction of the pupil followed by dilatation) to a loud sound. **cochleostapedial r.,** the reflex contraction of the stapedius muscle from noises. **concealed r.,** one elicited by a stimulus but concealed by a more dominant reflex elicited by the same stimulus. **conditional r.,** conditioned r. **conditioned r.,** one that does not occur naturally in the animal but that may be developed by regular association of some physiological function with an unrelated outside event, such as a bell or a light. Soon the physiological function starts whenever the outside event occurs (Pavlov, 1911). **conjunctival r.,** closure of the eyelid when the conjunctiva is touched. **consensual r.,** crossed r. **consensual light r.,** stimulation of one eye by light produces a reflex response in the opposite pupil. **contralateral r.,** a reflex of the leg on one side when passive flexion of the leg on the other side is made: seen in tuberculous and epidemic meningitis. **convulsive r.,** one in which several muscles contract convulsively without coordination. **coordinated r.,** one in which several muscles react so as to produce an orderly and useful movement. **corneal r.,** irritation of the cornea closes the lids. Called also *eyelid closure r.* **corneomandibular r., corneopterygoid r.,** movement of the lower jaw toward the side opposite the eye whose cornea is lightly touched, the mouth being open. **coronary r.,** the reflex that controls the caliber of the coronary blood vessels. **cranial r.,** any reflex whose paths are connected directly with the brain. **cremasteric r.,** stimulation of the skin on the front and inner side of the thigh retracts the testis on the same side; shows soundness of cord between first and second lumbar nerves. **crossed r.,** stimulation of one side of the body often causes also a corresponding response on the other side especially in the eye. **cuboidodigital r.,** Mendel's r. **cutaneous pupillary r.,** dilatation of the pupil on pinching the skin of the cheek or neck. **dartos r.,** the patient stands with his feet wide apart and the examiner suddenly applies cold to the perineum; the dartos muscle undergoes vermicular contraction. **Davidson's r.,** a light seen through the pupil when an electric light is held in the mouth. **deep r., deeper r.,** any reflex elicited by irritating a deep structure. **defense r.,** contraction and extension motions in a paralyzed limb produced by plantar flexion of the toes. **delayed r.**, a reflex which occurs some time after the stimulus provoking it has been received. **depressor r.**, a reflex to stimulation resulting in decreased activity of the motor center. **digital r.** See *Hoffmann's sign*, def. 2, under *sign*. **direct r.**, a contraction on the same side as that of the stimulation. **direct light r.**, when a ray of light is thrown upon the retina through the pupil there is immediate contraction of the sphincter iridis, reducing the size of the pupillary aperture. **dorsal r.**, contraction of the back muscles in response to stimulation of the skin along the erector spinae. **dorsocuboidal r.**, Mendel's reflex. **elbow r.**, triceps r. **embrace r.**, Moro's r. **emergency light r.**, excessive stimulation of the retina by light produces contraction of the pupils, closure of the eyelids, and lowering of the eyebrows. **enterogastric r.**, inhibition over the vagus by the stimulation of receptors in the duodenum. **epigastric r.**, contraction of the abdominal muscles caused by stimulating the skin of the epigastrium or over the fifth and sixth intercostal spaces near the axilla. **Erben's r.**, slowing down of the pulse upon bending head and trunk strongly forward, said to indicate vagal excitability. **erector spinae r.**, contraction of the erector spinae muscle on irritation of the skin along its border. **Escherich's r.**, muscular contraction of the lips in the form of a goat's snout produced by irritating the labial mucosa. **esophagosalivary r.**, Roger's r. **ether r.**, the sudden and increased flow of duodenal secretion following the introduction of ether into the duodenum. **external auditory meatus r.**, Kisch's r. **eyeball compression r.**, **eyeball-heart r.**, oculocardiac reflex. **eyelid closure r.** See *corneal r.* and *conjunctival r.* **facial r.**, bulbomimic r. **faucial r.**, irritation of the fauces causes vomiting. **femoral r.**, Remak's r. **finger-thumb r.**, passive flexion of the metacarpophalangeal joint of one of the fingers causes flexion of the basal joint and extension of the terminal joint of the thumb. **flexion r. of leg,** tapping of the tendons of the semimembranosus and semitendinosus muscles causes flexion of the leg. **flexor r., paradoxical,** extension of the great toe or of all the toes when the deep muscles of the calf are pressed upon. **fontanel r.**, Grünfelder's r. **foveolar r.**, the ophthalmoscopic reflex in the form of a dot caused by the foveola. **front-tap r.**, a tap on the skin muscles of the extended leg contracts the gastrocnemius. **fusion r.**, the reflex which tends to merge the images on the two retinas into a single impression. **gag r.**, pharyngeal r. **gastrocolic r.**, a wave of peristalsis in the colon induced by the entrance of food into the empty stomach. **gastro-ileac r.**, opening of the ileocecal valve induced by the presence of food in the stomach. **Gault's cochleopalpebral r.**, cochleopalpebral r. **Geigel's r.**, a reflex in the female corresponding to the cremasteric reflex in the male; i.e., on stroking of the inner anterior aspect of the upper thigh there is a contraction of the muscular fibers at the upper edge of Poupart's ligament. **genital r.**, any reflex irritability due to disorder of the genital organs. **Gifford's r., Gifford-Galassi r.**, contraction of the pupil when an effort is made to close the lids, which are held apart. **gluteal r.**, a stroke over the skin of the buttock contracts the glutei muscles. **Gordon's r.**, flexor r., paradoxical. **grasp r., grasping r.**, a reflex consisting of a grasping motion of the fingers or of the toes in response to stimulation. **Grünfelder's r.**, dorsal flexion of the great toe with a fan-wise spreading of the other toes elicited by continued pressure at the corner of the posterior lateral fontanel: occurs in the presence of disease of the middle ear in children up to the age of five years. **gustolacrimal r.**, an anomalous reflex by which food taken into the mouth tends to stimulate the secretion not only of saliva but also of tears. **Haab's r.**, bilateral pupillary contraction when the patient sits in a darkened room, and without accommodation or convergence directs his attention to a bright object already within the field of vision. Called also *cerebral cortex r.* **heart r.**, Abrams' heart r. **heel-tap r.**, a reflex occurring in disease of the pyramidal tract and consisting of a fanning and plantar flexion of the toes produced by tapping the patient's heel. **hepatojugular r.**, swelling of the jugular vein induced by pressure over the liver. It is indicative of insufficiency of the right heart. **Hering-Breuer r.**, the nervous mechanism which tends to limit the respiratory excursions. Stimuli from the sensory endings in the lungs and perhaps in other parts passing up the vagi tend to limit both inspiration and expiration in ordinary breathing. **Hirschberg's r.**, tickling of the sole at the base of the great toe causes adduction of the foot. **Hoffmann's r.**, a reflex flexion of the thumb when the terminal phalanx of the middle finger is flicked between the fingers of the examiner. **Hughes's r.** See *virile r.*, def. 2. **humoral r.**, chemical r. **hypochondrial r.**, sudden inspiration caused by quick pressure beneath the lower border of the ribs. **ileogastric r.**, when both the ileum and the stomach contain food, the stomach does not empty until the matter in the ileum has passed into the cecum. **inborn r.**, unconditioned r. **indirect r.**, crossed r. **infraspinatus r.**, obtained by tapping a certain spot over the shoulder blade, on a line bisecting the angle formed by the spine of the bone and its inner border; outward rotation of the arm occurs, with simultaneous straightening of the elbow. **inguinal r.**, Geigel's r. **interscapular r.**, a stimulus applied between the scapulae contracts the scapular muscles. Called also *scapular r.* **inverted radial r.**, a flexion of the fingers without movement of the forearm, produced by tapping the lower end of the radius; believed to indicate disease of the fifth cervical segment of the spinal cord. **iris contraction r.**, pupillary r. **irritant vapor r.**, pneocardiac r. **jaw r.**, closure of the mouth caused by a downward blow on the lower jaw while it hangs passively open. It is seen only rarely in health, but is very noticeable in sclerosis of the lateral columns of the cord. **Joffroy's r.**, twitching of the gluteal muscles on pressure against the nates in spastic paralysis. **Juster r.**, extension of the fingers instead of flexion on stimulation of the palm. **juvenile r.**, a glistening white reflex from the smooth surface of the retina in young people. **Kehrer's r., Kisch's r.**, closure of the eye as a result of tactile or thermal stimulation of the deepest part of the external auditory meatus and tympanum. **knee jerk r.**, quadriceps jerk. **Kocher's r.**, contraction of the abdominal muscle on compression of the testicle. **lacrimal r.**, secretion of tears elicited by touching the conjunctiva over the cornea. **laryngeal r.**, irritation of the fauces and larynx causes cough. **laughter r.**, laughter brought on by tickling. **lid r.**, corneal r. **Liddel and Sherrington r.**, stretch r. **light r.** 1. A luminous image reflected from the membrana tympani. 2. A circular spot of light seen reflected from the retina with the retinoscopic mirror. 3. Contraction of the pupil when light falls on the eye. **lip r.**, a reflex movement of the lips of sleeping babies which occurs on tapping near the angle of the mouth. Called also *mouth phenomenon*. **Livierato's r.**, Abrams' heart r. **Lovén r.**, general vasodilatation of an organ when its afferent nerve is stimulated. This secures a maximal supply of blood to the organ, together with a general rise of blood pressure. **lumbar r.**, dorsal r. **lung r.**, reflex dilatation of the subjacent lung tissue from local irritation of the skin, as by cold or continued percussion. It may be sufficient to obscure slight degrees of percussion dullness. **Lust's r.**, abduction of the foot with dorsal flexion on percussion of the external sciatic nerve. **McCarthy's r.**, contraction of the orbicularis oculi muscle on tapping the supraorbital nerve. **McCormac's r.**, percussing the patellar tendon produces adduction of the opposite leg. **Magnus and de Kleijn neck r's,** in children (young) with tuberculous meningitis: extension of both ipsilateral limbs, or one, or part of a limb, and increase of tonus on the side to which the chin is turned when the head is rotated to the side, and flexion with loss of tonus on the side to which occiput points. Essentially it is a sign of *decerebrate rigidity;* it does occur in tuberculous meningitis (about 50 per cent of the cases). **mandibular r.,** jaw jerk r. **Marinesco-Radovici r.,** palm-chin r. **mass r.,** a reflex exhibited by the entire area controlled by the portion of the spinal cord which has been injured. **Mayer's r.,** opposition and adduction of the thumb combined with flexion at the metacarpophalangeal joint and extension at the interphalangeal joint, on downward pressure of the index finger. **Mendel's r., Mendel-Bechterew r.,** percussion of the dorsum of the foot normally causes dorsal flexion of the second to fifth toes; in certain organic nervous conditions it causes plantar flexion of the toes. Called also *Mendel's dorsal r. of foot, cuboidodigital r.,* and *dorsocuboidal r.* **Mondonesi's r.,** bulbomimic r. **Moro embrace r.,** on placing an infant on a table and then forcibly striking the table on either side of the child, the arms are suddenly thrown out in an embrace attitude. **motor r.,** a reflex brought about by stimulation upon the periphery of the motor mechanism. **muscular r.,** a reflex movement due to the stretching of a muscle. **myenteric r.,** contraction of the intestine above and relaxation below a portion of the intestine that is irritated. **myopic r.,** Weiss's r. **myotatic r.,** stretch r. **nasal r.** 1. Irritation of the schneiderian membrane provokes sneezing. 2. See *Bechterew's r.,* def. 4. **nasomental r.,** contraction of the mentalis muscle on tapping the side of the nose with a percussion hammer. **nociceptive r's,** reflexes initiated by painful stimuli. **nostril r.,** reduction of the size of the opening of the naris on the affected side in pulmonary disease. **obliquus r.,** stimulation of the skin below Poupart's ligament contracts a part of the external oblique muscle. **oculocardiac r.,** a slowing of the rhythm of the heart following compression of the eyes. A slowing of from 5 to 13 beats per minute is normal; one of from 13 to 50 or more is exaggerated; one of from 1 to 5 is diminished. If ocular compression produces acceleration of the heart, the reflex is called *inverted.* **oculocephalogyric r.,** the reflex by which the movements of the eye, the head, and the body are directed in the interest of visual attention. **oculopharyngeal r.,** rapid deglutition together with a spontaneous closing of the eyes. **Oppenheim's r.** See under *sign.* **opticofacial winking r.,** closure of the lids when an object is brought suddenly into the field of vision. **orthocardiac r.** See *Livierato's test,* 2d def. **palatal r., palatine r.,** stimulation of the palate causes swallowing. **palm-chin r.,** when the thenar eminence is rapidly and vigorously irritated with a needle, the muscles of the chin on the same side are drawn up. **palmomental r.,** palm-chin r. **paraserum r.,** group agglutination. **patellar r.,** quadriceps jerk. **patello-adductor r.,** crossed adduction of the thigh produced by tapping the quadriceps tendon as in the patellar reflex. **pathologic r.,** one which is not normal, but is the result of a pathologic condition, and may serve as a sign of disease. **pectoral r.,** the arm is placed half way between adduction and abduction and the finger in the muscle tendon near the humerus: a sharp blow on the finger elicits adduction and slight internal rotation. **penile r., penis r.,** bulbocavernous r. **perception r.,** a reflex movement occurring when a perception is formed in consciousness. **pharyngeal r.,** contraction of the constrictor muscle of the pharynx elicited by touching the back of the pharynx. Called also *gag r.* **phasic r.,** an active and coordinated movement occurring as a response to stimulation. **Philippson's r.,** excitation of the knee extensor in one leg induced by inhibition in the knee extensor of the other leg. **pilomotor r.,** the production of goose flesh on stroking the skin; trichographism. **Piltz's r.,** attention r. **plantar r.,** irritation of the sole contracts the toes. **platysmal r.,** the act of nipping the platysma myoides contracts the pupil. **pneocardiac r.,** modification of the cardiac rhythm on injecting irritating vapor into any part of the air passages. **pneopneic r.,** modification of the respiratory rhythm on injecting irritating vapor into any part of the air passages. **postural r.,** a reflex which consists of some assumption of posture. **prepotential r's,** instincts. **pressor r.,** a reflex to stimulation resulting in increased activity of a motor center. **Preyer's r.,** involuntary movements of the ears produced by auditory stimulation. **proprioceptive r.,** a reflex that is initiated by stimuli arising from some function of the reflex mechanism itself. **psychic r.,** a reflex aroused by a stored-up impression of memory, such as the secretion of saliva at the sight or thought of good tasting food. **psychocardiac r.,** increase in the pulse rate on recalling an individual emotional experience. **psychogalvanic r.,** decreased electric resistance of the body as a result of mental or emotional agitation. **pupillary r.,** contraction of the pupil on exposure of the retina to light. **pupillary r., paradoxic,** stimulation of the retina by light dilates the pupil. **Puusepp's r.,** abduction of the little toe on stimulating the posterior external part of the sole of the foot: indicative of lesion of the extrapyramidal and pyramidal tract. **quadrupedal extensor r.,** Brain's r. **radial r.,** flexion of the forearm with sometimes flexion of the fingers as well, following tapping on the lower end of the radius. **rectal r.,** the process by which the accumulation of feces in the rectum excites defecation. **red r.,** a luminous red appearance seen upon the retina. **regional r.,** segmental r. **Remak's r.,** plantar flexion of the first three toes and sometimes of the foot, with extension of the knee on stroking of the upper anterior surface of the thigh: it indicates interruption of the conducting paths of the cord. **reno-renal r.,** a reflex pain or anuria in a sound kidney in cases in which the other kidney is diseased. **resistance r.,** Babinski r. **retrobulbar pupillary r.,** slight dilatation of the pupil which contracts under light stimulation, and then dilates while the light stimulation is still present. **Riddoch's mass r.,** in severe injury of the spinal cord stimulation below the level of the lesion produces flexion reflexes of the lower extremity, evacuation of the bladder, and sweating of the skin below the level of the lesion. **righting r.,** the ability to assume optimal position when there has been a departure from it. **Roger's r.,** salivation on irritation of the esophagus. **Rossolimo's r.,** on tapping the plantar surface of the toes, plantar flexion of the toes occurs when there are lesions of the pyramidal tract. **Ruggeri's r.,** acceleration of the pulse following strong convergence of the eyeballs toward something very close to the eyes: it indicates sympathetic excitability. **scapular r.,** interscapular r. **scapulohumeral r.,** adduction with outward rotation of the humerus produced by percussing along the inner edge of the scapula. **Schaefer's r.,** flexion of the foot and toes on pinching the Achilles tendon at its middle third: seen in organic hemiplegia. **scrotal r.,** a slow, vermicular contraction of the dartos muscle obtained by stroking the perineum or by applying a cold object to it. **segmental r.,** a reflex controlled by a single segment or region of the spinal cord. **senile r.,** a gray reflection from the pupil of aged people due to hardening of the lens. **sexual r.,** the reflex of erection and ejaculation produced by stimulation of the genitals. **shot-silk r.** See *shot-silk retina,* under *retina.* **simple r.,** a reflex involving a single muscle. **skin r.,** a reflex which occurs on stimulation of the skin. **skin pupillary r.,** dilatation of the pupil produced by irritation of the skin of the neck. **Snellen's r.,** unilateral congestion of the ear upon stimulation of the distal end of the divided auriculocervical nerve. **sole r.,** plantar r. **Somagyi's r.,** widening of the pupils on deep inspiration and their contraction on expiration, said to indicate irritable weakness or instability of the cardiac vagus. **spinal r.,** any reflex whose arc is connected with a center in the spinal cord. **startle r.,** jerking movement of a very young infant produced by a loud sound or by other stimuli. **static r.,** the reflex pose and righting of the body. **statotomic r's,** attitudinal r's. **stepping r.,** extension of the hind leg of a dog on pressing the plantar surface of the foot. **Stookey r.,** with the leg semiflexed at the knee, the tendons of the semimembranosus and the semitendinosus muscles are tapped: flexion of the leg results. **stretch r.,** reflex contraction of a muscle in response to passive longitudinal stretching; myotatic reflex. **Strümpell's r.,** leg movement with adduction of the foot produced by stroking the thigh or abdomen. **sucking r.,** sucking movements of the mouth elicited by the touching of an object to an infant's lips. **summation r.,** the combination and reinforcement of two or more nerve impulses in the production of a reflex response. **superficial r.,** any reflex provoked by a superficial stimulation. **supinator longus r.,** tapping of the tendon of the supinator longus produces flexion of the forearm. **supraorbital r.,** McCarthy's r. **suprapatellar r.,** with the leg extended the index finger of the examiner is crooked above the patella and is struck. The result is a kick-back of the patella. **suprapubic r.,** stroking the abdomen above Poupart's ligament causes deviation of the linea alba toward the side that is stroked. **supra-umbilical r.,** epigastric reflex. **swallowing r.,** palatal r. **tapetal light r.,** the glowing of eyes in the dark, just as do the eyes of carnivorous animals. **tarsophalangeal r.,** dorsal flexion of the second and third or second and fifth toes on tapping the dorsum of the foot in the region of the cuboid or external cuneiform bone: said to indicate some central organic lesion of the motor nervous system. **tendon r.,** a deep reflex. **threat r.,** sudden closure of the eyes at a sign of danger. **Throckmorton's r.,** a variation of the Babinski reflex elicited by percussion of the metatarsophalangeal region in the dorsum of the foot. **tibio-adductor r.,** tapping of the tibia on the inner side of the leg results either in homolateral adduction of the leg or crossed adduction from side to side. **toe r.,** strong flexion of the great toe flexes all the muscles of the lower extremity. It is seen in pathologic states in which there is increased knee jerk. **tonic r.,** the passing of an appreciable period of time after the occurrence of a reflex before relaxation; a reflex which maintains the reflex contractions which are the basis of posture and attitude. **trained r.,** conditioned r. **triceps r.,** extension of the forearm on tapping of the triceps tendon at the elbow while the forearm hangs limp at right angles to the arm. **ulnar r.,** tapping of the styloid process of the ulna results in pronation of the hand. **unconditioned r.,** a fixed reflex whose mechanism may be supposed to be inherited as its functioning does not depend on previous experience. Cf. *conditioned r.* **urinary r.,** desire to urinate on accumulation of the urine in the bladder to a certain amount. **vaccinoid r.,** a slight cutaneous reaction to vaccination in a person partially immune to smallpox. **vagus r.,** abnormal sensitiveness to pressure over the course of the vagus nerve seen in a lung affected with tuberculosis. **vascular r.,** constriction of an artery produced by peripheral irritation. **vasopressor r's,** reflexes which arise from stimulation of afferent vagal endings in the right atrium by altered venous pressure and which cause generalized vasoconstriction. **vertebra prominens r.,** pressure upon the last cervical vertebra of an animal reduces the tone of all four limbs. **vesical r.,** desire to urinate produced by moderate distention of the bladder. **virile r.** 1. Bulbocavernous reflex. 2. A reflex in the flaccid penis elicited by pulling upward the foreskin or glans penis, when a sudden downward jerk results. Called also *Hughes's r.* **visceral r.,** that in which the stimulus is set up by some state of an internal organ. **viscerocardiac r.,** reflex alteration in the activity of the heart caused by visceral excitation. **visceromotor r.,** contraction of abdominal muscles due to a stimulus from one of the viscera. **viscerosensory r.,** a region of sensitiveness to pressure on some part of the body due to disease of some internal organ. **viscerotrophic r.,** degeneration of any peripheral tissue as a result of chronic inflammation of any of the viscera. **water-silk r.** See *shot-silk retina,* under *retina.* **Weiss's r.,** a curved reflex seen with the ophthalmoscope on the fundus of the eye to the nasal side of the disk: believed to be indicative of myopia. **Westphal's pupillary r., Westphal-Piltz r.,** contraction of the pupil associated with closure or attempted closure of the eye. **wrist clonus r.,** extreme extension of the hand causes a local jerking movement. **zygomatic r.,** lateral motion of the lower jaw to the percussed side on percussion over the zygoma.

reflexogenic (re-flek″so-jen′ik) [*reflex* + Gr. *gennan* to produce]. Producing or increasing reflex action.

reflexograph (re-flek′so-graf) [*reflex* + Gr. *graphein* to write]. An instrument for graphically recording a reflex.

reflexology (re″flek-sol′o-je). The science or study of reflexes.

reflexometer (re″flek-som′e-ter) [*reflex* + L. *metrum* measure]. An instrument for measuring the force necessary to produce myotatic contraction.

reflexophil (re-flek′so-fil) [*reflex* + Gr. *philein* to love]. Characterized by activity of reflexes.

reflexotherapy (re-flek″so-ther′ah-pe). Treatment by irritation of an area of the body distant from the lesion.

reflux (re′fluks) [*re-* + L. *fluxus* flow]. A backward or return flow. **urethrovesiculo-differential r.,** the passage of a liquid, sperm, or injected substance from the posterior urethra into the genital system.

refract (re-frakt′) [L. *refringere* to break apart]. 1. To cause to deviate. 2. To ascertain errors of ocular refraction.

refracta dosi (re-frak′tah do′si) [L.]. In repeated and divided doses.

refraction (re-frak′shun). 1. The act or process of refracting; specifically the determination of the refractive errors of the eye and their correction by glasses. 2. The deviation of light in passing obliquely from one medium to another of different density. The deviation occurs at the surface of junction of the two mediums which is known as the refracting surface. The ray before refraction is called the *incident ray;* after refraction it is the *refracted ray.* The point of junction of the incident and the refracted ray is known as the *point of incidence.* The angle between the incident ray and a line perpendicular to the refracting surface at the point of incidence is known as the *angle of incidence;* that between the refracted ray and this perpendicular is called the *angle of refraction.* The sine of the angle of incidence divided by the sine of the angle of refraction gives the *relative index of refraction.* **double r.,** that in which the incident ray is divided into two refracted rays, so as to produce a double image. Double refraction is produced by Iceland spar. See *Nicol prism,* under *prism.* **dynamic r.,** the normal accommodation of the eye which is being continually exerted without conscious effort. **ocular r.,** the refraction of light produced by the mediums of the normal eye and resulting in the focusing of images upon the retina. **static r.,** the refraction of the eye when its accommodation is paralyzed.

refractionist (re-frak′shun-ist). One skilled in

determining the refracting power of the eyes and correcting refractive defects.

refractive (re-frak′tiv). Pertaining to or subserving a process of refraction; having the power to refract.

refractivity (re″frak-tiv′ĭ-te). The quality of being refractive; the power or ability to refract.

refractometer (re″frak-tom′e-ter) [*refraction* + Gr. *metron* measure]. 1. An instrument for measuring the refractive power of the eye. 2. An instrument for determining the indexes of refraction of various substances.

refractometry (re″frak-tom′e-tre). The measurement of refractive power with the refractometer.

refractory (re-frak′to-re) [L. *refractorius*]. Not readily yielding to treatment.

refractoscope (re-frak′to-skōp). An apparatus for auscultation of chest sounds so arranged that the listener is able to focus down upon a sound in a manner analogous to focusing a microscope.

refracture (re-frak′chur). The operation of breaking over again a bone which has been fractured and has united with a derfomity.

refrangibility (re-fran″jĭ-bil′ĭ-te). Susceptibility of being refracted; the quality of being refrangible.

refrangible (re-fran′jĭ-b′l). Susceptible of being refracted.

refresh (re-fresh′). To freshen or make raw again; to denude of an epithelial covering.

refresher (re-fresh′er). A course of lectures and clinics designed to refresh the memory and bring the participant up to date.

refrigerant (re-frij′er-ant) [L. *refrigerans*]. 1. Relieving fever and thirst. 2. A cooling remedy. The refrigerants consist of cooling, acidulous drinks and evaporating lotions.

refrigeration (re-frij″er-a′shun) [L. *refrigeratio*]. The application of or exposure to low temperatures.

refringent (re-frin′jent) [L. *refringens*]. Refractive.

Refsum's disease, syndrome (ref′soomz) [Sigvald *Refsum*, Norwegian physician]. See under disease.

refusion (re-fu′shun) [L. *refusio*]. The temporary removal and subsequent return of blood to the circulation.

R.E.G. Abbreviation for *radioencephalogram*.

regel (ra′gel) [Ger.]. Menstruation. **klei′ne r.** ["small menstruation"], a slight bloody discharge from the uterus at the time of ovulation.

regeneration (re-jen″er-a′shun) [*re-* + L. *generare* to produce, bring to life]. The natural renewal of a substance, such as a lost tissue or part. **epimorphic r.,** epimorphosis. **morphallactic r.,** morphallaxis.

regimen (rej′ĭ-men) [L. "guidance"]. A strictly regulated scheme of diet, exercise, or other activity designed to achieve certain ends.

regio (re′je-o), pl. *regio′nes* [L. "a space enclosed by lines"]. A plane area with more or less definite boundaries; used in anatomical nomenclature as a general term to designate certain areas on the surface of the body within certain defined boundaries. **r. abdomina′lis latera′lis** [B N A], r. lateralis abdominis [dextra et sinistra]. **regio′nes abdo′minis** [N A, B N A], the various anatomical regions of the abdomen, including [N A] the hypochondriac, epigastric, lateral, umbilical, inguinal, and pubic regions. **r. acromia′lis** [B N A], the region of the shoulder, overlying the acromion. Omitted in N A. **r. ana′lis** [N A, B N A], the portion of the perineal region surrounding the anus. Called also *anal region*. **r. antebra′chii ante′rior** [N A], the anterior, or palmar, region of the forearm. Called also *regio antibrachii volaris* [B N A]. **r. antebra′chii poste′rior** [N A], **r. antibra′chii dorsa′lis** [B N A], the posterior, or dorsal, region of the forearm. **r. antibra′chii radia′lis** [B N A], the radial aspect of the forearm. Omitted in N A. **r. antibra′chii ulna′ris** [B N A], the ulnar aspect of the forearm. Omitted in N A. **r. antibra′chii vola′ris** [B N A], r. antebrachii anterior. **r. auricula′ris** [B N A], the region of the head on either side, about the ear. Omitted in N A. **r. axilla′ris** [N A, B N A], the region of the chest about the axilla. Called also *axillary region*. **r. bra′chii ante′rior** [N A, B N A], the anterior region of the arm. **r. bra′chii latera′lis** [B N A], the lateral aspect of the arm. Omitted in N A. **r. bra′chii media′lis** [B N A], the medial aspect of the arm. Omitted in N A. **r. bra′chii poste′rior** [N A, B N A], the posterior region of the arm. **r. bucca′lis** [N A, B N A], the region of the cheek. Called also *buccal region*. **r. calca′nea** [N A, B N A], the region about the heel. Called also *calcaneal region*. **regio′nes cap′itis** [N A, B N A], the various anatomical regions of the head, including [N A] the frontal, parietal, occipital, temporal, and infratemporal regions. **r. clavicula′ris** [B N A], the region of the front of the chest, overlying the clavicle. Omitted in N A. **regio′nes col′li** [N A, B N A], the various anatomical regions of the neck, including [N A] the anterior, sternocleidomastoid, lateral, and posterior regions. **r. col′li ante′rior** [N A, B N A], the anteromedial region of the neck. **r. col′li latera′lis** [N A, B N A], the region of the neck lateral to the regio sternocleidomastoidea. Called also *trigonum colli laterale*. **r. col′li poste′rior** [N A, B N A], the posterior region of the neck, between the regio occipitalis above and the regions of the back below. **regio′nes cor′poris** [N A], **regio′nes cor′poris huma′ni** [B N A], the various anatomical areas, or subdivisions, demarcated on the surface of the human body for purpose of topographical description. Called also *regions of body*. **r. costa′lis latera′lis** [B N A], the lateral region of the thorax, or chest, overlying the ribs. Omitted in N A. **r. cox′ae** [B N A], the region of the hip. Omitted in N A. **r. cru′ris ante′rior** [N A, B N A], the anterior region of the leg. Called also *anterior crural region*. **r. cru′ris latera′lis** [B N A], the lateral aspect of the leg. Omitted in N A. **r. cru′ris media′lis** [B N A], the medial aspect of the leg. Omitted in N A. **r. cru′ris poste′rior** [N A, B N A], the posterior region of the leg. Called also *posterior crural region*. **r. cu′biti ante′rior** [N A, B N A], the anterior region about the elbow. Called also *anterior cubital region*. **r. cu′biti latera′lis** [B N A], the lateral aspect of the elbow. Omitted in N A. **r. cu′biti media′lis** [B N A], the medial aspect of the elbow. Omitted in N A. **r. cu′biti poste′rior** [N A, B N A], the posterior or dorsal region about the elbow. Called also *posterior cubital region*. **r. deltoi′dea** [N A, B N A], the region overlying the deltoid muscle. Called also *deltoid region*. **regio′nes digita′les ma′nus** [B N A], the regions of the fingers. Omitted in N A. **regio′nes digita′les pe′dis** [B N A], the regions of the toes. Omitted in N A. **regio′nes dorsa′les digito′rum ma′nus** [B N A], the dorsal aspect of the several fingers. Omitted in N A. **regio′nes dorsa′les digito′rum pe′dis** [B N A], the dorsal aspect of the several toes. Omitted in N A. **r. dorsa′lis ma′nus** [B N A], dorsum manus. **r. dorsa′lis pe′dis** [B N A], dorsum pedis. **regio′nes dor′si** [N A, B N A], the various anatomical regions of the back, including [N A], the vertebral, sacral, scapular, infrascapular, and lumbar regions. **r. epigas′trica** [N A, B N A], the upper middle region of the abdomen, located within the sternal angle. Called also *epigastric region* and *epigastrium*. **regio′nes extremita′tis inferio′ris** [B N A], regiones membri inferioris. **regio′nes extremita′tis superio′ris** [B N A], regiones membri superioris. **regio′nes fa′ciei** [N A, B N A], the various anatomical regions of the face. **r. fem′oris ante′rior** [N A, B N A], the anterior region of the thigh. **r. fem'oris latera'lis** [B N A], the lateral aspect of the thigh. Omitted in N A. **r. fem'oris media'lis** [B N A], the medial aspect of the thigh. Omitted in N A. **r. fem'oris poste'rior** [N A, B N A], the posterior region of the thigh. **r. fronta'lis** [N A, B N A], the region of the head about the frontal bone; the forehead. **r. ge'nu ante'rior** [B N A], r. genus anterior. **r. ge'nu poste'rior** [B N A], r. genus posterior. **r. ge'nus ante'rior** [N A], the anterior region about the knee. Called also *r. genu anterior* [B N A]. **r. ge'nus poste'rior** [N A], the posterior region about the knee. Called also *r. genu posterior* [B N A]. **r. glu'tea** [N A], the region overlying the gluteal muscles. Called also *gluteal region.* **r. hyoi'dea** [B N A], the part of the anterior region of the neck about the hyoid bone. Omitted in N A. **r. hypochondri'aca [dex'tra et sinis'tra]** [N A], the upper lateral region of the abdomen, about the costal cartilages, on either side of the epigastric region. Called also *hypochondriac region.* **r. hypogas'trica** [B N A], the region of the lowest part of the abdomen, including the pubic and inguinal regions. Omitted in N A. **r. infraclavicula'ris** [N A, B N A], the region of the chest just below the clavicle. Called also *infraclavicular region.* **r. inframamma'lis** [B N A], the region of the front of the chest, situated below either mamma and above the lower border of the twelfth rib. Omitted in N A. **r. infraorbita'lis** [N A, B N A], the region beneath the eye, adjacent to the regio nasalis. Called also *infraorbital region.* **r. infrascapula'ris** [N A, B N A], the region of the back below the scapula and lateral to the lower thoracic vertebrae. Called also *infrascapular region.* **r. infratempora'lis** [N A], the region of the head on either side, about the infratemporal fossa. Called also *infratemporal region.* **r. inguina'lis [dex'tra et sinis'tra]** [N A], the region of the abdomen on either side, lateral to the pubic region and about the inguinal canal. Called also *inguinal region.* **r. interscapula'ris** [B N A], the region of the back between the scapulae. Omitted in N A. **r. labia'lis infe'rior** [B N A], the region of the face about the lower lip. Omitted in N A. **r. labia'lis supe'rior** [B N A], the region of the face about the upper lip. Omitted in N A. **r. laryn'gea** [B N A], the part of the anterior region of the neck overlying the larynx. Omitted in N A. **r. latera'lis abdo'minis [dex'tra et sinis'tra]** the region of the abdomen on either side of the umbilical region. Called also *regio abdominalis lateralis* [B N A], and *lateral abdominal region.* **r. lumba'lis** [N A, B N A], the region of the back lying lateral to the lumbar vertebrae. Called also *lumbar region.* **r. malleola'ris latera'lis** [B N A], the region overlying the lateral malleolus. Omitted in N A. **r. malleola'ris media'lis** [B N A], the region overlying the medial malleolus. Omitted in N A. **r. mamma'lis** [N A, B N A], the region of the front of the chest, about the mammary gland. Called also *mammary region.* **r. mastoi'dea** [B N A], the region of the head on either side, about the mastoid process of the temporal bone. Omitted in N A. **r. media'na dor'si** [B N A], r. vertebralis. **regio'nes mem'bri inferio'ris** [N A], the various anatomical regions of the lower limb. Called also *regiones extremitatis inferioris* [B N A]. **regio'nes mem'bri superio'ris** [N A], the various anatomical regions of the upper limb. Called also *regiones extremitatis superioris* [B N A]. **r. menta'lis** [N A, B N A], the region of the chin. Called also *mental region.* **r. mesogas'trica** [B N A], a name given to the middle horizontal region of the abdomen, between the epigastric and hypogastric regions. Omitted in N A. **r. nasa'lis** [N A, B N A], the region of the face about the nose. Called also *nasal region.* **r. nu'chae** [B N A], the part of the posterior region of the neck adjoining the regio lateralis colli. Omitted in N A. **r. occipita'lis** [N A, B N A], the region of the head overlying the occipital bone. Called also *occipital region.* **r. olec'rani** [B N A], the region of the elbow overlying the olecranon. Omitted in N A. **r. olfacto'ria** [N A, B N A], the upper part of the nasal cavity, the mucosa of which contains most of the receptors for the sense of smell. Called also *olfactory region.* **r. ora'lis** [N A, B N A], the region of the face about the mouth. Called also *oral region.* **r. orbita'lis** [N A, B N A], the region of the face about the eye. Called also *ocular* or *orbital region.* **r. palpebra'lis infe'rior** [B N A], the region of the lower eyelid. Omitted in N A. **r. palpebra'lis supe'rior** [B N A], the region of the upper eyelid. Omitted in N A. **r. parieta'lis** [N A, B N A], the region of the head on either side, about the parietal bone. Called also *parietal region.* **r. parotideomasseter'ica** [N A, B N A], the region of the face on either side, about the parotid gland and masseter muscle. Called also *parotideomasseteric region.* **r. patella'ris** [B N A], the region of the knee overlying the patella. Omitted in N A. **regio'nes pecto'ris** [N A, B N A], the various regions of the chest, including [N A] the infraclavicular, mammary, and axillary regions. **r. pecto'ris ante'rior** [B N A], the anterior aspect of the thorax, or chest. Omitted in N A. **r. pecto'ris latera'lis** [B N A], the lateral aspect of the thorax, or chest. Omitted in N A. **r. perinea'lis** [N A, B N A], the region overlying the pelvic outlet, including the anal and urogenital regions. Called also *perineal region.* **regio'nes planta'res digito'rum pe'dis** [B N A], the plantar aspect of the several toes. Omitted in N A. **r. planta'ris pe'dis** [B N A], planta pedis. **r. pu'bica** [N A, B N A], the middle portion of the most inferior region of the abdomen, located below the umbilical region and between the inguinal regions. Called also *pubic region.* **r. pudenda'lis** [B N A], the region of the external genital organs (scrotum or vulva). Omitted in N A. **r. respirato'ria** [N A, B N A], the part of the nasal cavity below the olfactory region. Called also *respiratory region.* **r. retromalleola'ris latera'lis** [B N A], the region back of the lateral malleolus. Omitted in N A. **r. retromalleola'ris media'lis** [B N A], the region back of the medial malleolus. Omitted in N A. **r. sacra'lis** [N A, B N A], the region of the back overlying the sacrum. Called also *sacral region.* **r. scapula'ris** [N A, B N A], the region of the back overlying the scapula. Called also *scapular region.* **r. sterna'lis** [B N A], the region of the front of the chest overlying the sternum. Omitted in N A. **r. sternocleidomastoi'dea** [N A, B N A], the region of the neck overlying the sternocleidomastoid muscle. Called also *sternocleidomastoid region.* **r. subhyoi'dea** [B N A], the part of the anterior region of the neck below the hyoid bone. Omitted in N A. **r. submaxilla'ris** [B N A], trigonum submandibulare. **r. submenta'lis** [B N A], the part of the anterior region of the neck beneath the chin. Omitted in N A. **r. supraorbita'lis** [B N A], the region of the head immediately above the orbit. Omitted in N A. **r. suprascapula'ris** [B N A], the region of the back above the scapula. Omitted in N A. **r. suprasterna'lis** [B N A], the part of the anterior region of the neck above the sternum. Omitted in N A. **r. sura'lis** [B N A], the posterior aspect of the leg, overlying the calf. **r. tempora'lis** [N A, B N A], the region of the head on either side, about the temporal bone. Called also *temporal region.* **r. thyreoi'dea** [B N A], the part of the anterior region of the neck about the thyroid gland. Omitted in N A. **r. trochanter'ica** [B N A], the portion of the lateral region of the thigh overlying the greater trochanter. Omitted in N A. **r. umbilica'lis** [N A, B N A], the region of the abdomen about the umbilicus. Called also *umbilical region.* **regio'nes unguicula'res digito'rum ma'nus** [B N A], the region of the several fingers about the nails. Omitted in N A. **regio'nes unguicula'res digito'rum pe'dis**

[B N A], the region of the several toes about the nails. Omitted in N A. **r. urogenita′lis** [N A, B N A], the portion of the perineal region surrounding the urogenital organs. Called also *urogenital region.* **r. vertebra′lis** [N A], the middle region of the back, overlying the vertebral column. Called also *r. mediana dorsi* [B N A], and *vertebral region.* **regio′nes vola′res digito′rum ma′nus** [B N A], the palmar aspect of the several fingers. Omitted in N A. **r. vola′ris ma′nus** [N A], palma manus. **r. zygomati′ca** [N A, B N A], the region of the face on either side, about the zygomatic bone. Called also *zygomatic region.*

region (re′jun). A plane area with more or less definite boundaries. Called also *regio.* **abdominal r., external, abdominal r., lateral.** See *regio lateralis abdominis [dextra et sinistra].* **r. of accommodation,** the space including all points to which the eye can be adjusted by accommodation. **anal r.,** regio analis. **antebrachial r., anterior,** regio antebrachii anterior. **antebrachial r., posterior,** regio antebrachii posterior. **antebrachial r., radial,** regio antibrachii radialis. **antebrachial r., ulnar,** regio antibrachii ulnaris. **antebrachial r., volar,** regio antebrachii anterior. **anterior r. of neck,** regio colli anterior. **aulic r.,** a region about the aqueduct of Sylvius. **auricular r.,** regio auricularis. **axillary r.,** regio axillaris. **basilar r.,** the base of the skull. **brachial r., anterior,** regio brachii anterior. **Broca's r.** See under *convolution.* **buccal r.,** regio buccalis. **calcaneal r.,** regio calcanea. **ciliary r.,** the part of the eye occupied by the ciliary body and its adjuncts. **clavicular r.,** regio clavicularis. **crural r., anterior,** regio cruris anterior. **crural r., posterior,** regio cruris posterior. **cubital r., anterior,** regio cubiti anterior. **cubital r., posterior,** regio cubiti posterior. **deltoid r.,** regio deltoidea. **dorsal r's of fingers,** regiones dorsales digitorum manus. **dorsal r's of toes,** regiones dorsales digitorum pedis. **dorsal lip r.,** the mesodermal tissue around the dorsal lip of the blastopore; it is the organizer which by induction initiates and controls the early development of the embryo. **ecphylactic r.,** a region of infection that cannot be protected by the defensive agencies of the body on account of the virulence of the infecting agent. **encephalic r.,** alar plate. **epigastric r.,** regio epigastrica. **extrapolar r.,** that region of the body which lies outside the influence of the poles in electrotherapy. **frontal r.,** regio frontalis. **genitourinary r.,** regio urogenitalis. **gluteal r.,** regio glutea. **hyoid r.,** regio hyoidea. **hypochondriac r.** See *regio hypochondriaca [dextra et sinistra].* **hypogastric r.,** regio hypogastrica. **iliac r.** See *regio lateralis abdominis [dextra et sinistra].* **infraclavicular r.,** regio infraclavicularis. **inframammary r.,** regio inframammalis. **infraorbital r.,** regio infraorbitalis. **infrascapular r.,** regio infrascapularis. **infratemporal r.,** regio infratemporalis. **inguinal r.** See *regio inguinalis [dextra et sinistra].* **interscapular r.,** regio interscapularis. **labial r., inferior,** regio labialis inferior. **labial r., superior,** regio labialis superior. **laryngeal r.,** regio laryngea. **lumbar r.,** regio lumbalis. **mammary r.,** regio mammalis. **mastoid r.,** regio mastoidea. **mental r.,** regio mentalis. **motor r.,** the ascending frontal and parietal convolutions of the cerebrum. Called also *rolandic r.* **mylohyoid r.,** the region on the lingual surface of the mandible to which the mylohyoid muscle is attached. **r. of nape,** regio nuchae. **nasal r.,** regio nasalis. **nuchal r.,** regio nuchae. **occipital r.,** regio occipitalis. **ocular r.,** regio orbitalis. **olecranal r.,** regio olecrani. **olfactory r.,** regio olfactoria. **opticostriate r.,** the basal ganglia and the capsule. **oral r.,** regio oralis. **orbital r.,** regio orbitalis. **palpebral r., inferior,** regio palpebralis inferior. **palpebral r., superior,** regio palpebralis superior. **parietal r.,** regio parietalis. **parietotemporal r.,** sensory r. **parotideomasseteric r.,** regio parotideomasseterica. **perineal r.,** regio perinealis. **plantar r's of toes,** regiones plantares digitorum pedis. **posterior r. of neck,** regio colli posterior. **precordial r.,** a part of the anterior surface of the body covering the heart and the pit of the stomach. **prefrontal r.,** the part of the frontal lobe of the cerebrum in front of the precentral fissures. **presumptive r.,** an area of the blastula which has been proved under normal conditions to develop into a specific organ or type of tissue. **pterygomaxillary r.,** the region of the face about the zygoma and the prominences of the lower jaw. **pubic r.,** regio pubica. **respiratory r.,** regio respiratoria. **rolandic r.,** motor r. **sacral r.,** regio sacralis. **scapular r.,** regio scapularis. **sensory r.,** a part of the cerebral cortex on either side of the motor region. Called also *parietotemporal r.* **sternocleidomastoid r.,** regio sternocleidomastoidea. **subauricular r.,** fossa retromandibularis. **subhyoid r.,** regio subhyoidea. **submaxillary r.,** trigonum submandibulare. **submental r.,** regio submentalis. **subthalamic r.,** hypothalamus. **supraclavicular r.,** the region above the clavicle. **supraorbital r.,** regio supraorbitalis. **suprasternal r.,** regio suprasternalis. **temporal r.,** regio temporalis. **thyroid r.,** regio thyreoidea. **trabecular r.,** the region of the embryonic skull from which the sphenoid bone is developed. **umbilical r.,** regio umbilicalis. **urogenital r.,** regio urogenitalis. **vertebral r.,** regio vertebralis. **vestibular r.,** the lowest and the movable portion of the nose. It is lined with stratified epithelium and possesses hairs and sebaceous glands. **volar r's of fingers,** regiones volares digitorum manus. **volar r. of hand,** palma manus. **zygomatic r.,** regio zygomatica.

regional (re′jun-al). Pertaining to a certain region or regions.

regiones (re″je-o′nēz) [L.]. Plural of *regio.*

registrant (rej′is-trant). A nurse who is listed on the books of a registry as available for duty.

registrar (rej′is-trar). 1. An official keeper of records. 2. In British hospitals, a resident specialist who acts as assistant to the chief or attending specialist.

registration (rej″is-tra′shun). The act of recording. In dentistry, the making of a record of the jaw relations present, or of those desired, in order to transfer them to an articulator to facilitate proper construction of a dental prosthesis.

registry (rej′is-tre). 1. An office where a nurse may have her name listed as being available for duty. 2. A central agency for the collection of pathologic material and related clinical, laboratory, x-ray, and other data in a specified field of pathology, so organized that the data can be properly processed and made available for study.

regitine (rej′ĭ-tēn). Trade mark for a preparation of phentolamine.

reglementation (reg″le-men-ta′shun) [Fr.]. Strict control by legal regulation.

regression (re-gresh′un) [L. *regressio* a return]. 1. A return to a former or earlier state. 2. A subsidence of symptoms or of a disease process. 3. In biology, the tendency in successive generations toward mediocrity. See *Galton's law of regression,* under *law.* 4. The turning backward of the libido to an early fixation at infantile levels because of inability to function in terms of reality. **atavistic r.,** a process by which the mind ceases to function at a logical critical level and reverts to a biologically more primitive mode of functioning.

regressive (re-gres′iv). Going back; subsiding; characterized by regression.

regular (reg′u-lar) [L. *regularis; regula* rule]. Normal or conforming to rule; occurring at the proper intervals.

regulation (reg″u-la′shun) [L. *regula* rule]. 1.

The act of adjusting or state of being adjusted to a certain standard. 2. In biology, the adaptation of form or behavior of an organism to changed conditions. 3. The power of a pregastrula stage to form a whole embryo from a part.

Reg. umb. Abbreviation for L. *re'gio umbili'ci,* umbilical region.

regurgitant (re-gur′jĭ-tant) [*re-* + L. *gurgitare* to flood]. Flowing back or in the opposite direction from normal.

regurgitation (re-gur″jĭ-ta′shun) [*re-* + L. *gurgitare* to flood]. A backward flowing, as the casting up of undigested food, or the backward flowing of blood into the heart, or between the chambers of the heart. **aortic r.,** the backflow of blood from the aorta into the left ventricle, owing to imperfect functioning of the aortic semilunar valve. **mitral r.,** the backflow of blood from the left ventricle into the left auricle, owing to imperfect functioning of the mitral valve. **pulmonic r.,** the backflow of blood from the pulmonary artery into the right ventricle, owing to imperfect functioning of the pulmonic semilunar valve.

rehabilitation (re″hah-bil″ĭ-ta′shun). 1. The restoration of normal form and function after injury or illness. 2. The restoration of an ill or injured patient to self-sufficiency or to gainful employment at his highest attainable skill in the shortest possible time.

rehabilitee (re″hah-bil′ĭ-te). The subject of rehabilitation.

rehalation (re″hah-la′shun) [*re-* + L. *halare* to breathe]. Rebreathing.

Rehfuss' test, tube (ra′fus) [Martin E. *Rehfuss,* American physician, 1887–1964]. See under *tests.*

rehydration (re″hi-dra′shun). The restoration of water or of fluid content to a body or to substance which has become dehydrated.

Reichel's chondromatosis, duct (ri′kelz) [Friedrich Paul *Reichel,* German obstetrician, born 1868]. See under *chondromatosis* and *duct.*

Reichert's canal (ri′kerts) [Karl B. *Reichert,* German anatomist, 1811–1884]. Ductus reuniens. **R's cartilages,** cartilaginous bars in the outer side of the embryonic tympanum from which develop the styloid processes, the stylohyoid ligaments and the lesser cornua of the hyoid bone. **R's membrane,** Bowman's membrane. **R's recess,** recessus cochlearis vestibuli. **R's scar,** an area on the fertilized ovum consisting of a fibrinous membrane in place of the decidual tissue. **R's substance,** the posterior portion of the anterior perforated substance.

Reichmann's disease, sign (rīk′manz) [Nikolas *Reichmann,* Warsaw physician, 1851–1918]. See under *disease* and *sign.*

Reichstein (rīk′stīn), Tadeus. Polish chemist in Switzerland, born 1897; co-winner, with E. C. Kendall and P. S. Hench, of the Nobel prize for medicine and physiology in 1950.

Reid's base line (rēdz) [Robert William *Reid,* Scottish anatomist, 1851–1938]. See *base line,* under *line.*

Reid Hunt's reaction, test [*Reid Hunt,* American pharmacologist, 1870–1948]. Acetonitril test.

Reil's ansa, band, insula, line, sulcus (rīlz) [Johann Christian *Reil,* German anatomist, 1759–1813]. See under the nouns.

reimplantation (re″im-plan-ta′shun). Replacement of tissue or a structure, such as a tooth, in the site from which it was previously lost or removed.

reinfection (re″in-fek′shun). A second infection by the same pathogenic agent.

reinforcement (re″in-fors′ment). The increasing of force or strength. **r. of reflex,** the increasing of a reflex response by causing the patient to perform some mental or physical concentration while the reflex is being elicited.

reinnervation (re″in-er-va′shun). The operation of grafting a live nerve to restore the function of a paralyzed muscle.

reinoculation (re″in-ok″u-la′shun). An inoculation that follows a previous one with the same virus.

reintegration (re″in-te-gra′shun). 1. Biological integration. 2. The resumption of normal mental and physical activity after disappearance of the catatonic state, or other psychic disturbance.

reintubation (re″in-tu-ba′shun). Intubation performed a second time.

reinversion (re″in-ver′zhun). Restoration to its normal place of an inverted organ, especially restoration of an inverted uterus.

reinvocation (re″in-vo-ka′shun). Reactivation.

Reisseisen's muscles (ris′ĭ-senz) [François Daniel *Reisseisen,* German anatomist, 1773–1828]. See under *muscle.*

Reissner's canal, corpuscles, membrane (rīs′nerz) [Ernst *Reissner,* German anatomist, 1824–1878]. See under the nouns.

Reiter's disease, syndrome (ri′terz) [Hans *Reiter,* German hygienist, born 1881]. See under *disease.*

reiterature (re-it″er-a-tu′re) [L.]. Repeat or renew, as a prescription.

rejuvenescence (re-ju″vĕ-nes′ens) [*re-* + L. *juvenescere* to become young]. A renewal of youth or of strength and vigor.

relapse (re-laps′) [L. *relapsus*]. The return of a disease after its apparent cessation. Cf. *recrudescence.* **intercurrent r.,** a relapse occurring before the temperature has reached a normal level. **mucocutaneous r.,** the reappearance of infectious lesions of the mucous membranes and skin after the disappearance of the initial secondary lesions of syphilis. **rebound r.,** return of some of the symptoms of a disease on cessation of treatment, applied especially to the relapse of patients with rheumatoid arthritis on withdrawal of cortisone or ACTH (Hench).

relation (re-la′shun) [L. *relatio* a carrying back]. The condition or state of one object or entity when considered in connection with another. **acentric r.,** eccentric jaw r. **buccolingual r.,** the position of a tooth or space in the dental arch in relation to the tongue and the cheek. **centric jaw r.,** the most retruded position of the mandible in respect to the maxilla when the condyles are in the most posterior unstrained position in the glenoid fossae from which lateral movement can be made at any given degree of jaw separation. **dynamic r's,** those existing between two objects or entities when one or both of them are moving or constantly changing. **eccentric jaw r., acquired,** an eccentric relation of the mandible to the maxilla that is assumed in order to bring the teeth into centric occlusion. **jaw r.,** any relation of the mandible to the maxilla, variously designated as centric, eccentric, median, occlusal, protrusive, and the like. **maxillomandibular r.,** jaw r. **median jaw r.,** any relation of the jaws when the mandible is not moved to either side. **median retruded jaw r.,** centric jaw r. **occlusal jaw r.,** the relation of the mandibular teeth to the maxillary teeth when the jaws are in contact; designated, depending on the relative position of the mandibular teeth, as lateral, protrusive, or retrusive. **protrusive jaw r.,** that resulting from protrusion of the mandible. **rest jaw r.,** that maintained when the patient is resting comfortably in the upright position. **ridge r.,** the relation in space of the mandibular ridge to the maxillary ridge. **static r's,** those existing between two objects or entities when neither one of them is moving or changing in any way. **unstrained jaw r.,** that maintained when a state of balanced tonus exists among all the muscles involved, being achieved without undue or unnatural force and causing no undue distortion of the tissues of the temporomandibular joints.

relaxant (re-lak′sant) [L. *relaxare* to loosen]. 1.

Lessening or reducing tension. 2. An agent that lessens tension. **muscle r.,** an agent that specifically aids in reducing muscle tension.

relaxation (re″lak-sa′shun). 1. A lessening of tension. 2. A mitigation of pain. **isometric r.,** relaxation of a muscle without shortening.

relaxin (re-lak′sin). A factor which produces relaxation of the pubic symphysis and dilation of the uterine cervix in certain animal species. A pharmaceutical preparation, extracted from the ovaries of pregnant sows, has been used in treatment of dysmenorrhea and premature labor, and to facilitate labor at term.

releasin (re-le′sin). Trade mark for a preparation of relaxin.

relief (re-lēf′) [L. *relevatio*]. The mitigation or removal of pain or distress.

relieve (re-lēv′) [L. *relevare* to lighten]. To mitigate or remove pain or distress.

reline (re-līn′). To resurface the tissue side of a denture with new base material in order to achieve a more accurate fit.

reluxation (re″luk-sa′shun). Redislocation.

rem (rem) [*r*oentgen-*e*quivalent—*m*an]. The quantity of any ionizing radiation which has the same biological effectiveness as 1 rad of x-rays. 1 rem = 1 rad × RBE (relative biological effectiveness).

Remak's band, fibers, ganglion, plexus, etc. (ra′maks) [Robert *Remak*, German neurologist, 1815–1865]. See under the nouns.

Remak's reflex, sign, type (ra′maks) [Ernest Julius *Remak*, German neurologist, 1849–1911]. See under the nouns.

remedial (re-me′de-al) [L. *remedialis*]. Curative, acting as a remedy.

remedy (rem′ĕ-de) [L. *remedium*]. Anything that cures, palliates, or prevents disease. **ambiotic r.,** an abortifacient. **concordant r's,** a homeopathic term for remedies of similar action, but of dissimilar origin. **Durande's r.,** a remedy formulated for gallstones. **Ehrlich-Hata r.,** arsphenamine. **inimic r's,** a homeopathic term for remedies whose actions are antagonistic. **tissue r's,** the twelve remedies which, according to the biochemical school of homeopathy, form the mineral bases of the body.

Remijia (re-mij′e-ah). A genus of rubiaceous shrubs. *R. peduncula′ta* and *R. purdiea′na* furnish cuprea bark and the derivatives of cupreine.

remineralization (re-min″er-al-i-za′shun). The restoration of mineral elements, as to the human body.

remission (re-mish′un) [L. *remissio*]. A diminution or abatement of the symptoms of a disease; also the period during which such diminution occurs. **Legroux's r's,** long remissions which sometimes occur during the course of pulmonary tuberculosis.

remittence (re-mit′ens). Temporary abatement, without actual cessation, of symptoms.

remittent (re-mit′ent) [L. *remittere* to send back]. Having periods of abatement and of exacerbation.

Remlinger's sign (rem′ling-erz) [R. *Remlinger*, French physician]. See under *sign*.

remnant (rem′nant). Something remaining; a residue. **acroblastic r.,** the peripheral part of the acroblast which recedes into the protoplasm of the spermatid and later disintegrates.

ren (ren), pl. *re′nes*, gen. *re′nis* [L.]. [N A, B N A] One of two glandular bodies in the lumbar region that secrete the urine. See *kidney*. **r. mo′bilis,** movable kidney. **r. ungulifor′mis,** horseshoe kidney.

renal (re′nal) [L. *renalis*]. Pertaining to the kidney.

Renaut's bodies, layer (ren-ōz′) [Joseph Louis *Renaut*, French physician, 1844–1917]. See under the nouns.

renculi (ren′ku-li) [L.]. Plural of *renculus*.

renculus (ren′ku-lus), pl. *ren′culi* [L.]. Reniculus.

Rendu's tremor (ron-duz′) [Henri Jules Louis Marie *Rendu*, French physician, 1844–1902]. See under *tremor*.

Rendu-Osler-Weber disease (ron-duh′-ōs′ler-web′er) [Henri Jules Louis Marie *Rendu;* Sir William *Osler;* Frederick Parkes *Weber*]. See under *disease*.

renes (re′nēz). 1. [L.]. Plural of *ren*. 2. A therapeutic extract of the kidneys of pigs or sheep.

renicapsule (ren′ĭ-kap″sūl) [*ren* + L. *capsula* capsule]. An adrenal gland.

renicardiac (ren″ĭ-kar′de-ak). Pertaining to the kidneys and heart.

reniculi (rĕ-nik′u-li) [L.]. Plural of *reniculus*.

reniculus (rĕ-nik′u-lus), pl. *renic′uli* [L.]. One of the lobules composing the kidney, and consisting of a pyramid and its enclosing cortical substance.

reniform (ren′ĭ-form) [*ren* + L. *forma* form]. Shaped like a kidney.

renin (re′nin). A proteolytic enzyme liberated by ischemia of the kidney or by diminished pulse pressure which changes hypertensinogen into hypertensin.

renipelvic (ren″ĭ-pel′vik). Pertaining to the pelvis of the kidney.

reniportal (ren″ĭ-pōr′tal) [*ren* + L. *porta* gate]. Pertaining to the portal system of the kidneys.

renipuncture (ren″ĭ-punk′tūr) [*ren* + L. *punctura* puncture]. Surgical incision or puncture of the capsule of the kidney: done for relief of albuminuric pain.

rennet (ren′et). An extract of calf's stomach which contains rennin and is used for curdling the milk in cheese making.

rennin (ren′in). The milk-curdling enzyme obtained from the fourth stomach of calves. Called also *chymosin*.

renninogen (rĕ-nin′o-jen). The proenzyme existing in the gastric glands, which, after secretion, is converted into rennin. Called also *prorennin, prochymosin, chymosinogen*, and *pexinogen*.

renninum (rĕ-ni′num). Rennin.

rennogen (ren′o-jen). Renninogen.

renocortical (re″no-kor′tĭ-kal). Pertaining to the cortex of a kidney.

renocutaneous (re″no-ku-ta′ne-us). Pertaining to the kidneys and skin.

renogastric (re″no-gas′trik). Pertaining to the kidney and stomach.

renography (re-nog′rah-fe) [*ren* + Gr. *graphein* to write]. Radiography of the kidney.

reno-intestinal (re″no-in-tes′tĭ-nal). Pertaining to the kidney and intestine.

Rénon-Delille syndrome (ra-naw′ dĕ-lēl′) [Louis *Rénon*, French physician, 1863–1922; Arthur *Delille*, French physician, born 1876]. See under *syndrome*.

renopathy (re-nop′ah-the) [*ren* + Gr. *pathos* disease]. Nephropathy.

renoprival (re″no-pri′val). Pertaining to, characterized by, or resulting from deprivation of kidney function.

renopulmonary (re″no-pul′mo-ner″e). Pertaining to the kidney and lung.

renotrophic (re″no-trof′ik). Having the ability to increase kidney size, due mainly to hypertrophy of the convoluted tubules.

renotropic (re″no-trop′ik). Having a special affinity for kidney tissue.

rentschlerization (rench″ler-i-za′shun) [Harvey C. *Rentschler*, American physicist, 1881–1949]. The process of destroying bacteria by the use of ultraviolet rays of a wavelength of 2537 Angström units.

renunculus (re-nung′ku-lus). Reniculus.

reovirus (re″o-vi′rus) [*r*espiratory and *e*nteric *o*rigin]. One of a subgroup of the ECHO viruses, with ECHO 10 as the prototype strain, and separable into three serotypes.

reoxidation (re-ok″sĭ-da′shun). The act of taking

up oxygen again, as the hemoglobin of the blood.

Rep. Abbreviation for L. *repeta'tur,* let it be repeated.

rep (rep) [roentgen equivalent physical]. An unofficial unit, proposed by H. M. Parker, of amount of radiation of any kind which yields an amount of energy transferred to the tissue equal to that transferred by 1 roentgen of hard x- or γ-radiation (200 Kv. or greater). This amount of energy turns out to be about 93 ergs per gram of water or soft tissue.

repand (re-pand′) [*re-* + L. *pandus* bent]. Wrinkled or wavy: said of bacterial cultures.

repatency (re-pa′ten-se) [*re-* + L. *patens* open]. Reestablishment of the opening in a part or vessel which has been closed.

repellent (re-pel′ent) [L. *repellere* to drive back]. 1. Able to repel or drive off; also an agent so acting, as *insect repellent.* 2. Capable of dispersing a swelling; also an agent or remedy which causes a swelling to disappear.

repeller (re-pel′er). An instrument used in labor of animals to push back the fetus until the head and limbs can be properly placed for normal delivery.

repercolation (re″per-ko-la′shun) [L. *re-* again + *percolare* to filter]. A second or repeated percolation with the same materials.

repercussion (re″per-kush′un) [L. *repercussio* rebound]. 1. The driving in of an eruption or the scattering of a swelling. 2. Ballottement.

repercussive (re″per-kus′iv). 1. Causing, or pertaining to, repercussion. 2. An agent causing repercussion; a repellent.

repetatur (re″pe-ta′tūr) [L.]. Let it be renewed.

replantation (re″plan-ta′shun). The restoration of an organ or other structure to its original site. In dentistry, the reinsertion of a tooth into the alveolus from which it was removed or otherwise lost.

repletion (re-ple′shun) [L. *repletio*]. The condition of being full.

replication (re″pli-ka′shun). 1. A turning back of a part so as to form a duplication. 2. Repetition of an experiment to ensure accuracy.

reposition (re″po-zish′un) [L. *repositio*]. Replacement in the normal position.

repositor (re-poz′ĭ-tor). An instrument used in returning displaced organs to the normal position.

repression (re-presh′un). The thrusting back from consciousness into the unconscious sphere of ideas or perceptions of a disagreeable nature. **coordinate r.,** parallel diminution of the concentrations of the several enzymes of a metabolic pathway, resulting from increases in the level of repressor. **enzyme r.,** interference, usually by the endproduct of a pathway, with synthesis of the enzymes of that pathway. See *corepressor, aporepressor,* and *coordinate repression.* **reactive r.,** a psychosis resulting from repression.

repressor (re-pres′or). A compound that represses the formation of a specific enzyme; the term has been used to refer both to a small molecule (corepressor) that can be added exogenously and to the postulated active repressor (corepressor plus aporepressor).

reproduction (re″pro-duk′shun) [L. *re-* again + *productio* production]. 1. The production of offspring by organized bodies. 2. The creation of a similar object or situation; duplication. **asexual r.,** reproduction without the fusion of sexual cells, as by fission or budding. **cytogenic r.,** reproduction in which the new individual proceeds from a single germ cell or zygote. **sexual r.,** reproduction by the fusion of a female sexual cell with a male sexual cell (*bisexual r., syngamy*) or by the development of an unfertilized egg (*unisexual r., parthenogenesis*). **somatic r.,** reproduction in which the new individual proceeds from a multicellular fragment produced by fission or budding.

reproductive (re″pro-duk′tiv). Subserving or pertaining to the production of offspring.

repullulation (re-pul″u-la′shun) [L. *re-* back + *pullulare* to sprout out]. Renewed growth by sprouting.

repulsion (re-pul′shun) [L. *re-* back + *pellere* to drive]. The act of driving apart or away; a force which tends to drive two bodies apart. It is the opposite of attraction.

RES. Abbreviation for *reticuloendothelial system.*

rescinnamine (re-sin′ah-min). An alkaloid, the 3,4,5-trimethoxycinnamic acid ester of methyl reserpate, which occurs in certain species of Rauwolfia. Used as an antihypertensive and tranquilizer.

resect (re-sekt′). To perform resection.

resectable (re-sek′tah-b′l). Capable of being resected; lending itself to resection.

resection (re-sek′shun) [L. *resectio*]. Excision of a considerable portion of an organ or structure such as bone. **gastric r.,** partial gastrectomy. See under *gastrectomy.* **root r.,** apicoectomy. **submucous r.,** excision of a portion of a deflected nasal septum after first laying back a flap of mucous membrane, which is replaced after the operation. **transurethral r.,** resection of the prostate by means of an instrument passed through the urethra. **wedge r.,** removal of a triangular wedge of tissue, as from the ovary in an operation designed to stimulate ovarian function in patients with Stein-Leventhal syndrome. **window r.,** submucous r.

resectoscope (re-sek′to-skōp). An instrument for transurethral prostatic resection.

resectoscopy (re″sek-tos′ko-pe). Transurethral resection of the prostate.

resene (res′ēn). Any one of a class of resin derivatives.

reserpine (res′er-pēn). An ester alkaloid, 3,4,5-trimethoxybenzoyl methyl reserpate, isolated from the root of certain species of Rauwolfia: used as an antihypertensive and tranquilizer.

reserve (re-zerv′). Something kept in store for future use. **alkali r., alkaline r.,** the amount of buffer compounds in the blood that are capable of neutralizing acids, such as sodium bicarbonate, dipotassium phosphate and proteins. Since the bicarbonates are the most important of these buffers, the term blood bicarbonate is often preferred to alkali reserve. **cardiac r.,** the potential ability of the heart to perform a wide range of work beyond that required under basal conditions, depending on changing demands of various physiological or pathological states.

reservoir (rez′er-vwar). A place or cavity for storage. For anatomical structures serving as a storage space for fluids, see *cisterna* [N A]. **chromatin r.,** karyosome. **r. of infection,** the nonclinical source of infection, such as the alternate host or the passive carrier of a pathogenic organism. **Pecquet's r.,** cisterna chyli. **r. of virus,** the alternate host or the passive carrier of a virus, from which the virus is transmitted to a person who shows clinical signs of infection.

reshaping (re-shāp′ing). A restoration or change of shape, as of a crown, bridge, or denture.

resident (rez′ĭ-dent). A graduate and licensed physician resident in a hospital.

residua (re-zid′u-ah) [L.]. Plural of *residuum.*

residual (re-zid′u-al) [L. *residuus*]. Remaining or left behind.

residue (rez′ĭ-du) [L. *residuum,* from *re-* back + *sidere* to sit]. A remainder; that which remains after the removal of other substances. **cancer r.,** the water-soluble portion of cancer cells left after splitting off the toxic radicals by heating the cancer cells in a 2 per cent solution of sodium hydroxide in absolute alcohol **day r.,** an occurrence or experience from the preceding day which may induce a dream at night. **typhoid r.,** the substance remaining after treating a pure culture of typhoid bacilli with alcohol, ether, and sodium hydroxide: it is used as a remedy and an immunizing agent in typhoid fever.

residuum (re-zid′u-um), pl. *resid′ua* [L.]. A residue or remainder. **gastric r.,** the contents of the stomach during the interdigestive period, as in the morning before eating. **r. ova′rii,** ovarian residue. **r. ru′brum,** desiccated ox blood: used in anemia. **sporal r.,** sporenrest.

resilience (re-zil′e-ens) [L. *resilire* to leap back]. Elasticity; the property of returning to the former shape or size after distortion.

resilient (re-zil′e-ent) [L. *resiliens*]. Elastic; returning to its former shape or size after distortion.

resin (rez′in) [L. *resina*]. 1. A solid or semisolid, amorphous, organic substance, of vegetable origin or produced synthetically. True resins are insoluble in water, but are readily dissolved in alcohol, ether, and volatile oils. 2. Rosin. **acrylic r's,** a class of thermoplastic resins, ethylene derivatives containing a vinyl group, produced by polymerization of acrylic or methacrylic acid or their derivatives: used in the fabrication of medical prostheses and dental restorations and appliances. **activated r.,** self-curing r. **autopolymer r.,** self-curing r. **azure A carbacrylic r.,** azuresin. **carbacrylamine r's,** a mixture of 87.5 per cent of cation exchangers, carbacrylic resin, and potassium carbacrylic resin, with 12.5 per cent of the anion exchanger, polyamine-methylene resin: used to increase fecal excretion of sodium in the treatment of edema. **cold-curing r.,** self-curing r. **copolymer r.,** one that is produced by the concurrent and joint polymerization of two or more different monomers or polymers. **direct filling r.,** a synthetic resin used for direct filling of dental cavities. **heat-curing r.,** one that requires the use of heat to effect its polymerization. **ion exchange r.,** a high molecular weight, insoluble polymer of simple organic compounds with the ability to exchange its attached ions for other ions in the surrounding solution. They are classified as (*a*) *cation* or *anion exchange resins,* depending on which ions the resin exchanges, and (*b*) carboxylic, sulfonic, etc., depending on the nature of the active groups. *Cation exchange resins* are used to restrict sodium absorption in edematous states; *anion exchange resins* are used as antacids in the treatment of ulcers. **podophyllum r.,** resin derived from podophyllum. The pharmaceutical preparation is a mixture of the resins obtained by percolation with alcohol, used as a caustic in treatment of certain papillomas. **polyamine-methylene r.,** a polyethylene polyamine methylene substituted resin of diphenylol dimethylmethane and formaldehyde in basic form, used as a gastric antacid. **quick-cure r.,** self-curing r. **self-curing r.,** any resin which can be polymerized by the addition of an activator and a catalyst without the use of external heat. **styrene r.,** polystyrene. **synthetic r.,** an amorphous, organic, semisolid or solid material produced from simpler compounds by polymerization or condensation. **vinyl r.,** a thermoplastic resin, an ethylene derivative containing the vinyl radical, CH_2:CH—.

resina (re-zi′nah) [L.]. Resin.

resinat (rez′ĭ-nat). Trade mark for preparations of polyamine-methylene resin.

resinoid (rez′ĭ-noid). 1. Resembling a resin. 2. A substance resembling a resin. 3. A dry therapeutic precipitate prepared from a vegetable tincture.

resinotannol (rez″ĭ-no-tan′ol). Any resin alcohol which gives a tannin reaction.

resinous (rez′ĭ-nus) [L. *resinosus*]. Of the nature of a resin.

resistance (re-zis′tans) [L. *resistentia*]. 1. The opposition by a conductor to the passage of an electric current. 2. In psychoanalysis, opposition to the coming into consciousness of repressed material. 3. The natural ability of an individual to ward off the deleterious effects of such noxious agents as poisons, toxins, irritants, or pathogenic microorganisms. See also *immunity.* **acid alcohol r.,** the power of a bacterium to resist the action of acid and alcohol. **essential r.,** the resistance within the cells of a battery to a galvanic current. **external r., extraordinary r.,** the resistance in the part of a circuit outside the battery cells. **hemolytic r.** See *fragility of the blood.* **inductive r.** See *reactance.* **internal r.,** essential r. **peripheral r.,** the resistance to the passage of the blood through the small blood vessels, especially the capillaries. **vital r.,** the resistance of the individual to the untoward effects of infections, fatigue, etc.

resite (res′īt). An insoluble, infusible compound formed by further reaction of resole under heat.

resole (res′ōl). A condensation polymer of an alcohol formed by interaction of phenol and formaldehyde, which is of relatively low molecular weight, thermoplastic, and alcohol soluble.

resolution (rez″o-lu′shun) [L. *resolutum,* from *resolvere* to unbind]. 1. The subsidence of a pathologic state, as the subsidence of an inflammation, or the softening and disappearance of a swelling. 2. The perception as separate of two adjacent objects or points. In microscopy, it is the minimal distance at which two adjacent small objects can be distinguished as separate. The resolving power of an instrument depends on the wavelength of the radiation used and the numerical aperture of the system; it is expressed in microns distance or lines per millimeter.

resolve (re-zolv′) [L. *resolvere*]. 1. To restore to the normal state after some pathologic process. 2. To separate a thing into its component parts.

resolvent (re-zol′vent) [L. *resolvens* dissolving]. 1. Promoting resolution or the dissipation of a pathologic growth. 2. An agent that promotes resolution.

resonance (rez′o-nans) [L. *resonantia*]. 1. The prolongation and intensification of sound produced by the transmission of its vibrations to a cavity, especially a sound elicited by percussion. Decrease of resonance is called *dullness;* absence of resonance, *flatness.* 2. A vocal sound as heard in auscultation. 3. See *mesomerism.* **amphoric r.,** a sound resembling that produced by blowing over the mouth of an empty bottle. **bandbox r.,** the extremely resonant sound elicited by percussion in cases of emphysema of the lungs. **bell-metal r.,** a peculiar sound heard in pneumothorax when a coin placed on the chest wall is struck by another coin. **cough r.,** a peculiar auscultatory sound elicited by coughing. **cracked-pot r.,** a peculiar sound elicited by percussion over a pulmonary cavity that communicates with a bronchus. **hydatid r.,** a peculiar sound heard in the combined auscultation and percussion of a hydatid cyst. **osteal r.,** the sound elicited by percussion over a bony structure. **shoulder-strap r.,** pulmonary resonance in the apex of the lung above the clavicle. **skodaic r.,** increased percussion resonance at the upper part of the chest, with flatness below it. **tympanic r.,** the drumlike reverberation of a cavity full of air. **tympanitic r.,** the peculiar sound elicited by percussing a tympanitic abdomen. **vesicular r.,** the normal pulmonary resonance. **vesiculotympanic r.,** a resonance partly vesicular and partly tympanic. **vocal r.,** the sound of ordinary speech as heard through the chest wall. **whispering r.,** the auscultatory sound of whispered words heard through the chest wall. **wooden r.,** vesiculotympanic r.

resonant (rez′o-nant). Giving a vibrant sound on percussion.

resonator (rez′o-na″ter). An instrument used to intensify sounds. In electricity, an electrical circuit in which oscillations of a certain frequency are set up by oscillations of the same frequency in another circuit. **Oudin r.,** a coil of wire of adjustable number of turns which is designed to be connected to a source of high-frequency current, such as a spark gap and induction coil, for the purpose of applying an effluve to a patient.

resorcin (re-zor′sin). Resorcinol.

resorcinism (re-zor′sĭ-nizm). Chronic poisoning by resorcinol.

resorcinol (re-zor′sĭ-nol). Chemical name: 1,3-benzenediol: used as a local anti-infective.

resorcinolphthalein (re-zor″sĭ-nol-thal′e-in). Fluorescein.

resorcinum (re″zor-si′num). Resorcinol.

resorption (re-sorp′shun) [L. *resorbere* to swallow again]. The loss of substance through physiologic or pathologic means, such as loss of dentin and cementum of a tooth, or of the alveolar process of the mandible or maxilla. **internal r. of teeth,** an unusual form of tooth resorption beginning centrally in a tooth, and apparently initiated by a peculiar inflammatory hyperplasia of the pulp.

respirable (re-spīr′ah-b'l). Suitable for respiration.

respiration (res″pĭ-ra′shun) [L. *respiratio*]. 1. The act or function of breathing; the act by which air is drawn in and expelled from the lungs, including inspiration and expiration. Called also *external r.* 2. Internal respiration. **abdominal r.,** that which is chiefly kept up by the abdominal muscles and the diaphragm. **absent r.,** that in which the respiratory sounds are suppressed. **accelerated r.,** respiration at a rate exceeding 25 per minute. **aerobic r.,** the oxidative transformation of certain substrates into secretory products, the released energy being used in the process of assimilation. **amphoric r.,** that which is characterized by amphoric resonance, or a quality like that of the sound produced by blowing over the mouth of an empty jar. It is heard over phthisical or bronchiectatic cavities, in pneumothorax, in compression of lung from effusion. **anaerobic r.,** a form of respiration in which energy is released from chemical reactions in which free oxygen takes no part. **artificial r.,** that which is maintained by artificial means. Among the various methods of artificial respiration are the following: *Buist's method* is employed in asphyxiation of the newborn, and consists of holding the babe alternately on the stomach and back. *Eve's method:* ". . . the victim is laid face downward on a stretcher and is well wrapped with blankets. His wrists and ankles are lashed to the handles. Then he is hoisted on a trestle or sling and rocking is begun. The first tilt should be head down and steep (50 degrees) and should produce full expiration by the weight of the abdominal contents pressing on the diaphragm. It will also force aortic blood through the coronaries and empty the stomach and lungs of water. Then full inspiration is produced by tilting the foot end down to 50 degrees. The rocking is done a dozen times a minute through an angle of 45 degrees each way." (J.A.M.A.) *Method of Marshall Hall:* Put the body prone, gently press on the back, then removing the back pressure, turn the body on its side and press a little more, repeating this formula sixteen times every minute. It is known as the method of *prone* or *postural respiration*, or "ready method." *Howard method:* Place the body supine, with a cushion under the back, so that the head is lower than the abdomen; the arms are held over the head, forcible pressure is made with both hands inward and upward, over the lower ribs, about sixteen times in a minute. *mouth-to-mouth method:* The rescuer applies his mouth directly to the mouth of the patient and regularly inflates the patient's lungs with his own expired air. *Schafer's method:* Patient prone with forehead on one of his arms: straddle across patient with knees on either side of his hips, and press with both hands firmly upon the back over the lower ribs; then raise your body slowly, at the same time relaxing the pressure with your hands. Repeat this forward and backward movement about every five seconds. *Silvester's method:* Patient supine. The arms are pulled firmly over the head to raise the ribs, and kept there until air ceases to enter the chest. The arms are brought down to the chest, and are pressed against it for a second or so after air ceases to escape. This formula is repeated sixteen times in a minute. **asthmoid r.,** respiration in which expiration is accompanied by a wheezing sound like that of bronchial asthma. **Austin Flint r.,** cavernous r. **Biot's r.,** breathing characterized by irregular periods of apnea alternating with periods in which four or five breaths of identical depth are taken: seen in patients with increased intracranial pressure. **Bouchut's r.,** respiration in which the inspiratory phase is shorter than the expiratory phase: seen in children with bronchopneumonia. **bronchial r.,** tubular r. **bronchocavernous r.,** that which is intermediate in character between bronchial and cavernous. It is heard over a lung cavity with solidified lung tissue adjacent to it. **bronchovesicular r.,** a variety intermediate between the bronchial and vesicular forms. **cavernous r.,** a respiration marked by a peculiar prolonged hollow resonance, usually due to a cavity in the lung. It is heard in the same conditions as amphoric respiration. **cerebral r.,** Corrigan's r. **Cheyne-Stokes r.,** breathing characterized by rhythmic waxing and waning of the depth of respiration, with regularly recurring periods of apnea: seen especially in coma resulting from affection of the nervous centers. **cogwheel r.,** a form with a peculiar jerky inspiration; breathing in which the expiratory and inspiratory sounds are not continuous, but are split into two or more separate sounds. Called also *interrupted r.* **collateral r.,** the entrance of air into alveoli through pulmonary alveolar vents so that a lobule may remain aerated even though its bronchus is obstructed. **controlled diaphragmatic r.,** the intentional use of abdominal respiration for the purpose of limiting the motion of the apices of the lung in tuberculosis or to relieve pressure on the heart. **Corrigan's r.,** a shallow and frequent blowing respiration in a low fever. **costal r.,** that which is performed mainly by the rib muscles. **cutaneous r.,** the exhalation of vapors and absorption of oxygen by the skin. **diaphragmatic r.,** that which is mainly performed by the diaphragm. **diminished r.,** that in which the respiratory sounds are partly suppressed. **divided r.,** respiration marked by a pause between the inspiratory and expiratory sounds: heard on auscultation in emphysema. **electrophrenic r.,** artificial respiration induced by electric stimulation of the phrenic nerve. **external r.,** the exchange of gaseous constituents in the lungs. **fetal r.,** gaseous interchange through the placental barrier. **forced r.,** that which takes in more air than is needed. **granular r.,** a vesicular respiration, giving a sound as if the air were passing through a tube with an uneven surface. **harsh r.,** bronchovesicular r. **indefinite r.,** a respiratory sound so feeble or so confused that it is difficult to assign to it a definite character. **internal r.,** the exchange of gaseous constituents between the body cells and the blood. Called also *tissue r.* **interrupted r.,** that in which the sounds are not continuous. **jerky r.,** cog-wheel r. **Kussmaul's r., Kussmaul Kien r.,** air hunger. See under *hunger.* **labored r.,** that which is performed with difficulty. **meningitic r.,** short and rapid breathing interrupted by pauses of ten to thirty seconds; occurring in healthy persons during sleep it has no important significance, but in meningitis it is regarded as an unfavorable sign. **metamorphosing r.,** bronchocavernous r. **nervous r.,** cerebral r. **paradoxical r.,** respiration in which a lung, or a portion thereof, is deflated during inspiration and inflated during expiration. **periodic r.,** Cheyne-Stokes r. **physiologic r.,** metabolism. **puerile r.,** that in which the breathing sounds are more intense than those of normal adult respiration and resemble those of childhood. **rude r.,** bronchovesicular r. **Seitz's metamorphosing r.,** a variety of bronchial

Place one hand under the patient's chin and the other on top of his head. Lift up on the chin and push down on the top of the head to tilt the head backwards.

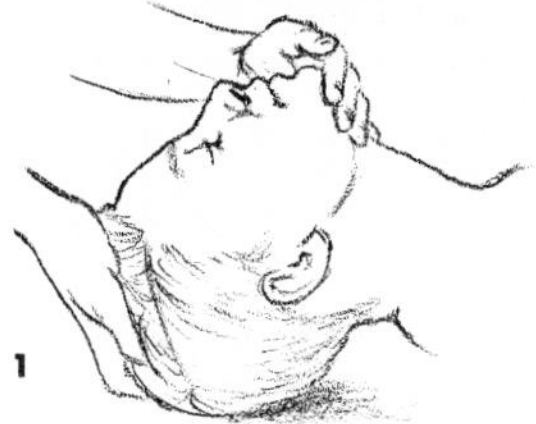

Put the thumb of the hand under the jaw into the patient's mouth; grasp the jaw and pull it forward.

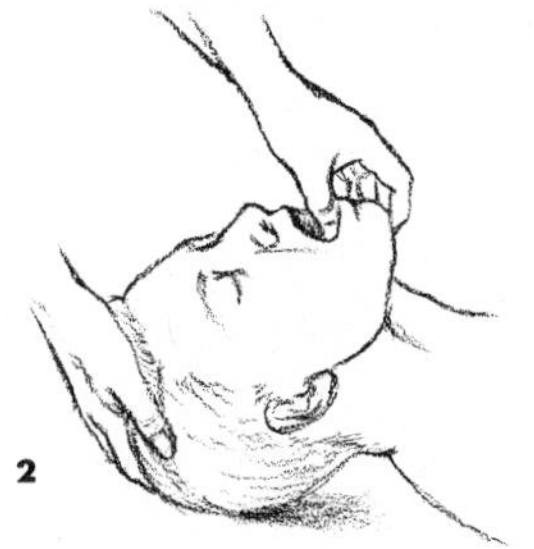

While holding the jaw forward pinch the nostrils closed with the other hand to prevent leakage of air through the nose.

Take a deep breath; place your mouth tightly over the patient's and blow forcefully into his lungs.

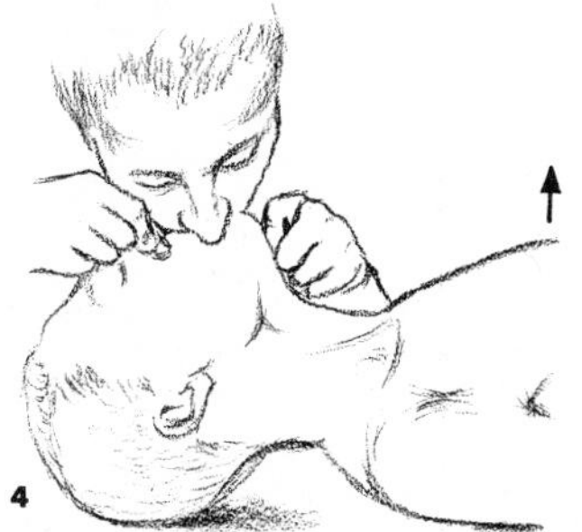

Blowing into the lungs causes the chest to expand. When the chest has expanded adequately remove your mouth from the patient's so that he can exhale.

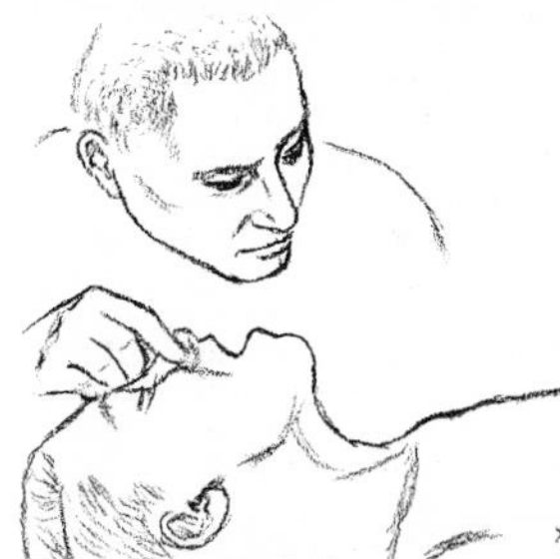

Repeat this sequence of maneuvers every 3 to 4 seconds until other means of ventilation are available.

If you cannot open his mouth blow through his nose. In infants cover both mouth and nose with your mouth. Blow gently into a child's mouth, and in infants use only small puffs from your cheeks.

TECHNIQUE OF ARTIFICIAL RESPIRATION BY MOUTH-TO-MOUTH METHOD

(Nealon)

The patient is placed in a supine position on a rigid support so that there is no give under the patient as pressure is applied. The individual applying the pressure stands or kneels at right angles to the patient. He places the heel of one hand with the heel of the other on top of it on the sternum, just cephalad to the xiphoid process.

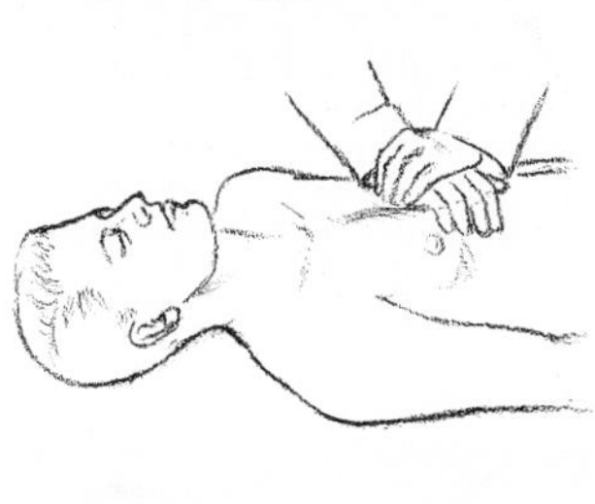

Firm pressure is applied vertically downward about 60 times a minute. At the end of each pressure stroke the hands are relaxed to permit full expansion of the chest. The position of the operator should be such that he can use his body weight while applying the pressure. Sufficient pressure should be exerted to move the sternum 3 or 4 cm. toward the vertebral column.

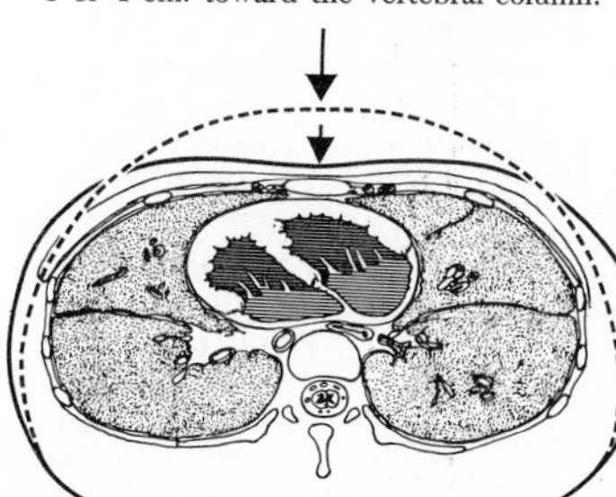

Children up to 10 years of age require the force of only one hand.

Only moderate pressure by the finger tips on the middle third of the sternum should be used on infants.

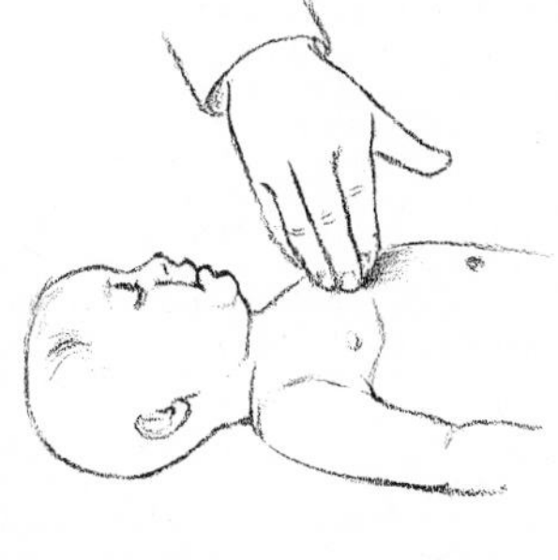

TECHNIQUE OF RESUSCITATION BY CLOSED CHEST CARDIAC MASSAGE

(Kouwenhoven, Jude, and Knickerbocker. J.A.M.A. 173:1064, 1960.)

respiration consisting of an inspiratory murmur, beginning as a tubular bronchial sound and ending as either a cavernous or an amphoric tone. **slow r.,** that in which there are less than twelve respirations in each minute. **stertorous r.,** that which is accompanied by abnormal snoring sounds. **supplementary r.,** puerile r. **suppressed r.,** respiration without any appreciable sound, as may occur in extensive consolidation of the lung, or pleuritic effusion. **thoracic r.,** respiration performed by the intercostal and other thoracic muscles. Cf. *abdominal r.* **tissue r.,** internal r. **transitional r.,** bronchovesicular r. **tubular r.,** that which has high-pitched sounds, not unlike those made by blowing through a tube. It is heard in phthisical and pneumonic consolidation of lung, compression of lung, and sometimes over lung infiltrated with morbid growth. **vesicular r.,** the natural breathing of a sound and healthy adult person. **vesiculocavernous r.,** cavernous respiration with a vesicular quality. It indicates a cavity surrounded by healthy lung tissue. **vicarious r.,** increased action in one lung when that of the other lung is diminished. **wavy r.,** cog-wheel r.

respirator (res′pĭ-ra″tor). An apparatus to qualify the air that is breathed through it, or a device for giving artificial respiration. **cabinet r.,** one which encloses the entire body. **cuirass r.,** an apparatus which is applied only to the chest, either completely surrounding the trunk or applied only to the front of the chest and abdomen. **Drinker r.,** an apparatus for producing artificial respiration over long periods of time, consisting of a metal tank, enclosing the body of the patient, with his head outside, and within which artificial respiration is maintained by alternating negative and positive pressure. Popularly called *iron lung.*

respiratory (re-spi′rah-to″re) [*re-* + L. *spirare* to breathe]. Pertaining to respiration.

respirometer (res″pĭ-rom′e-ter). An instrument for determining the character of the respiratory movements.

response (re-spons′) [L. *respondere* to answer, reply]. An action or movement due to the application of a stimulus. **inverse r.,** the production of inhibitory hormones by the organism in response to the introduction of excessive quantities of a hormone. **recall titer r.,** an increase in specific agglutinins stimulated by a booster injection, as of tetanus toxoid; similar to the nonspecific anamnestic reaction. **reticulocyte r.,** increase in the formation of reticulocytes in response to a bone marrow stimulus, such as that provided by administration of a hematinic agent.

rest (rest). 1. Repose after exertion. 2. A fragment of embryonic tissue that has been retained within the adult organism; called also *embryonal, epithelial,* and *fetal r.* 3. In dentistry, a metallic extension from a removable partial denture which aids in supporting the appliance. **adrenal r.,** an adrenal enclave. **bed r.,** a device for propping patients up in bed. **carbon r.,** the amount of carbon in the deproteinized blood. **constitutional r.,** rest of the whole body or organism as contrasted with rest of a part. **embryonal r., epithelial r., fetal r.** See *rest,* def. 2. **incisal r.,** a metallic extension from a removable partial denture which engages on the incisal surface of an anterior tooth to aid in supporting the appliance. **lingual r.,** a metallic extension from a removable partial denture onto the lingual surface of an anterior tooth to aid in supporting or acting as an indirect retainer for the appliance. **Malassez's r.,** an epithelial remnant of Hertwig's sheath in the periodontal membrane, which sometimes develops into a dental cyst. **occlusal r.,** a metallic extension from a removable partial denture which engages on the occlusal surface of a tooth to aid in supporting the appliance. **precision r.,** one that consists of closely interlocking parts. **suprarenal r.,** adrenal r.

restbacillus (rest″bah-sil′us). Tubercle bacillus after removal of the portions that are soluble in water, a 10 per cent salt solution, alcohol, and ether.

restbite (rest′bit). The occlusion of the teeth when the jaw is at rest.

restenosis (re″stĕ-no′sis). Recurrent stenosis, especially of a valve of the heart, after surgical correction of the primary condition. **false r.,** stenosis recurring after failure to divide either commissure of the cardiac valve beyond the area of incision of the papillary muscles. **true r.,** restenosis occurring after complete opening of one or both of the commissures of the cardiac valve involved.

restibrachium (res″tĭ-bra′ke-um), pl. *restibra′chia* [L. *restis* rope + *brachium* arm]. Pedunculus cerebellaris inferior.

restiform (res′tĭ-form) [L. *restis* rope + *forma* form]. Shaped like a rope.

restim (res′tim) [*r*eticulo*e*ndothelial *s*ystem *stim*ulant]. A biologically derived non-pyrogenic, nontoxic lipid material that has a stimulatory effect on the reticuloendothelial system.

restis (res′tis), pl. *res′tes* [L. "rope"]. Restibrachium.

restitutio (res″tĭ-tu′she-o) [L.]. Restitution. **r. in′tegrum,** complete return to health.

restitution (res″tĭ-tu′shun) [L. *restitutio*]. 1. An active process of restoration. 2. The rotation of the presenting part of the fetus outside of the vagina.

restoration (res″to-ra′shun). 1. Induction of a return to a previous state, such as a return to health, or replacement of a part to its normal position. 2. The partial or complete reconstruction of a body part, or the device used as its replacement. In dentistry, the act of restoring a tooth to its original condition by the filling of a cavity and replacement of lost parts, or the material used in such a procedure. **buccal r.,** the replacement, usually with alloy, gold, or plastic, of the buccal portion of a posterior tooth lost through caries or injury. **prosthetic r.,** the replacement of a lost or absent body part with an artificial structure, or the device or material used for such replacement, such as, in dentistry, an inlay, crown, bridge, or partial or complete denture, or other appliance to replace tissues missing from the mouth.

restorative (re-stŏr′ah-tiv). 1. Promoting a return to health or to consciousness. 2. A remedy that aids in restoring health, vigor, or consciousness.

restraint (re-strānt′). The forcible confinement of a violently psychotic or irrational person. **chemical r.,** the quieting of a violently psychotic or irrational person by means of narcotics.

restropic (res-trop′ik). Acting on the reticuloendothelial system. A stimulating activity is called positive; a depressive one is called negative.

restropin (res′tro-pin). A factor in the blood which stimulates the reticuloendothelial system.

resublimed (re″sub-limd′). Subjected to repeated processes of sublimation.

resultant (re-zul′tant). Any one of the products of a chemical reaction.

resupination (re″su-pĭ-na′shun) [L. *resupinare* to turn on the back]. 1. The act of turning upon the back or dorsum. 2. The position of one lying upon the back.

resurrectionist (rez″ur-rek′shun-ist) [L. *resurgere* to rise again]. One who steals bodies, especially from the grave.

resuscitation (re-sus″ĭ-ta′shun) [L. *resuscitare* to revive]. The restoration to life or consciousness of one apparently dead. **r. of the heart,** the act of restoring heart beat and arterial blood pressure, consisting of (1) restoration of oxygen system to preserve viability of brain (emergency measure done within 3 to 5 minutes), and (2) restoration of coordinated heart beat.

resuscitator (re-sus′ĭ-ta″tor). An apparatus for initiating respiration in cases of asphyxia.

resuture (re-soo′tūr). Secondary suture.

retainer (re-tān′er). An appliance or device for retaining anything in position. In dentistry, an appliance which aids in maintaining in the proper position a tooth whose malposition has been corrected, or helps keep a partial denture in place. **continuous bar r.,** a metal bar, resting on the lingual surfaces of teeth, used to aid in stabilizing the teeth or in retaining a partial denture. **direct r.,** a clasp or attachment applied to an abutment tooth, by which a removable partial denture is maintained in position. **indirect r.,** an attachment which aids the action of a direct retainer by functioning through lever action on the opposite side of the fulcrum line.

retamine (ret′ah-min). An alkaloid, $C_{15}H_{26}N_2O$, from the bark and twigs of *Retama sphaerocarpa*.

retardate (re-tar′dāt). A mentally retarded individual.

retardation (re″tar-da′shun) [L. *retardare* to slow down, impede]. Delay, hindrance. **mental r.,** absence of the normal mental development. **psychomotor r.,** underactivity of both mind and body, especially an unusually slow rate of development. **r. of thought,** delay in thinking in which either the process of thought is set in motion slowly (*initial r.*), or the thought or action once having started is performed slowly (*executive r.*).

retardin (re-tar′din). A hormone from the pancreas which regulates fat metabolism and neutralizes the toxic action of thyroxine.

retching (rech′ing). A strong involuntary effort to vomit.

rete (re′te), pl. *re′tia* [L. "net"]. A net or meshwork; used in anatomical nomenclature as a general term to designate a network of arteries or veins. **acromial r., r. acromia′le** [N A, B N A], a network formed by ramification of the acromial branch of the thoracoacromial artery on the acromion process. **r. arterio′sum** [N A], an anastomotic network formed by arteries just before they become arterioles or capillaries. **articular r.,** a network of anastomosing blood vessels in or around a joint. **articular cubital r., articular r. of elbow,** r. articulare cubiti. **articular r. of knee,** r. articulare genus. **r. articula′re cu′biti** [N A, B N A], an arterial network formed on the posterior aspect of the elbow by the posterior ulnar recurrent, inferior and superior ulnar collateral, and interosseous recurrent arteries. Called also *articular r. of elbow*. **r. articula′re ge′nu** [B N A], **r. articula′re ge′nus** [N A], an extensive arterial rete on the capsule of the knee joint, supplying branches to the contiguous bones and joints. It is formed by the genicular arteries, the termination of the deep femoral artery, the descending branch of the lateral circumflex artery, and the tibial recurrent artery. Called also *articular r. of knee*. **calcaneal r., r. calca′nei, r. calca′neum** [N A, B N A], an arterial rete on the posterior and lower surfaces of the calcaneus, receiving branches from the calcaneal branches of the peroneal artery and the lateral malleolar branches of the peroneal artery. **r. cana′lis hypoglos′si** [B N A], plexus venosus canalis hypoglossi. **carpal r., dorsal,** r. carpi dorsale. **r. car′pi dorsa′le** [N A, B N A], an arterial rete formed by the dorsal radial carpal and dorsal ulnar carpal arteries and giving off the second, third, and fourth dorsal metacarpal arteries to the dorsum of the hand and the second, third, and fourth fingers. Called also *dorsal carpal r.* **dorsal venous r. of foot,** r. venosum dorsale pedis. **dorsal venous r. of hand,** r. venosum dorsale manus. **r. dorsa′le pe′dis** [B N A], an arterial rete on the dorsum of the foot. Omitted in N A. **epidermal r.,** stratum germinativum epidermidis [Malpighii]. **r. foram′inis ova′lis** [B N A], plexus venosus foraminis ovalis. **r. of Haller, r. Halle′ri,** r. testis. **malleolar r., lateral,** r. malleolare laterale. **malleolar r., medial,** r. malleolare mediale. **r. malleola′re latera′le** [N A, B N A], a small arterial rete on the lateral malleolus, formed by the lateral anterior malleolar artery, the perforating branch of the peroneal artery, and the lateral tarsal artery. Called also *lateral malleolar r.* **r. malleola′re media′le** [N A, B N A], a small arterial rete on the medial malleolus, formed by the medial anterior malleolar artery and branches from the posterior tibial artery. Called also *medial malleolar r.* **r. Malpig′hi,** stratum germinativum epidermidis (Malpighii). **r. mira′bile** [N A, B N A], a vascular network formed by division of an artery or a vein into a large number of smaller vessels that subsequently reunite into a single vessel; in the human this occurs only in the arterioles that supply the glomeruli of the kidney. **r. muco′sum,** stratum germinativum epidermidis [Malpighii]. **r. na′si,** a venous plexus in the inferior nasal concha. **r. olec′rani,** r. articulare cubiti. **r. of patella, r. patel′lae** [N A, B N A], a network of arterial branches surrounding the patella, and derived from the various arteries of the knee. **plantar r.,** r. venosum plantare. **r. test′is** [N A], **r. test′is [Halle′ri]** [B N A], a network of channels, formed by the straight seminiferous tubules, traversing the mediastinum testis and draining into the efferent ductules. **r. vasculo′sum** [B N A], a network of anastomosing blood vessels. Omitted in N A. **r. veno′sum** [N A, B N A], an anastomotic network of small veins. **r. veno′sum dorsa′le ma′nus** [N A, B N A], a venous network on the back of the hand, formed by the dorsal metacarpal veins. Called also *dorsal venous r. of hand*. **r. veno′sum dor′sale pe′dis** [N A, B N A], a superficial network of anastomosing veins on the dorsum of the foot proximal to the transverse venous arch, draining into the great and the small saphenous veins. Called also *dorsal venous r. of foot*. **r. veno′sum planta′re** [N A, B N A], a thick venous rete in the subcutaneous tissue of the sole of the foot. Called also *plantar venous r.* **re′tia veno′sa vertebra′rum** [B N A], networks of veins inside the vertebral canal. Omitted in N A.

retention (re-ten′shun) [L. *retentio*, from *retentare* to hold firmly back]. The process of keeping in position, as (*a*) the persistent keeping within the body of matters normally excreted, or (*b*) in dentistry, the maintaining of a dental prosthesis in proper position in the mouth, against all forces that might tend to dislodge it. **direct r.,** maintenance of the position of a removable partial denture in the mouth by means of direct retainers. **indirect r.,** retention in the mouth of a removable partial denture by means of indirect retainers. **surgical r.,** retention in the mouth of a dental prosthesis by means of attachments embedded in the oral tissues. **r. of urine,** accumulation of urine within the bladder because of inability to urinate.

retethelioma (re″te-the-le-o′mah). A reticuloendothelial sarcoma.

retia (re′te-ah) [L.]. Plural of *rete*.

retial (re′te-al). Pertaining to or of the nature of a rete.

reticula (re-tik′u-lah) [L.]. Plural of *reticulum*.

reticular (re-tik′u-lar) [L. *reticularis*]. Pertaining to or resembling a net.

reticulated (re-tik′u-lāt″ed). Reticular.

reticulation (re-tik″u-la′shun) [L. *reticulum* a net]. The formation of, or the presence of, a network. **dust r.,** an early stage of pneumoconiosis, seen especially in coal miners, which may go on to an anthracosilicosis.

reticulemia (re-tik″u-le′me-ah). Presence in the blood of an excessive number of immature red blood cells.

reticulin (re-tik′u-lin). A scleroprotein from the

connective fibers of reticular tissue. **r. M,** an internal secretion produced by the reticuloendothelial system.

reticulitis (re-tik″u-li′tis). Inflammation of the reticulum of a ruminant animal.

reticulocyte (re-tik′u-lo-sit″). A young red blood cell showing a basophilic reticulum under vital staining.

reticulocytogenic (re-tik″u-lo-si″to-jen′ik). Causing the formation of reticulocytes.

reticulocytopenia (re-tik″u-lo-si″to-pe′ne-ah) [*reticulocyte* + Gr. *penia* poverty]. A decrease in the number of reticulocytes of the blood.

reticulocytosis (re-tik″u-lo-si-to′sis). An abnormal increase in the number of reticulocytes.

reticuloendothelial (re-tik″u-lo-en″do-the′le-al). Pertaining to tissues having both reticular and endothelial attributes. See under *system.*

reticuloendothelioma (re-tik″u-lo-en″do-the-le-o′mah). A tumor of the reticuloendothelial system.

reticuloendotheliosis (re-tik″u-lo-en″do-the-le-o′sis). Hyperplasia of reticuloendothelial tissue. **leukemic r.,** leukemia marked by an abundance of monocytes. **systemic aleukemic r.,** Letterer-Siwe disease.

reticuloendothelium (re-tik″u-lo-en″do-the′-le-um). The tissue of the reticuloendothelial system.

reticulohistiocytary (re-tik″u-lo-his″te-o-si′-ter-e). Pertaining to or composed of histiocytes of the reticuloendothelial system.

reticuloma (re-tik″u-lo′mah). A tumor composed of cells of reticuloendothelial origin (monocytes).

reticulopenia (re-tik″u-lo-pe′ne-ah). Reticulocytopenia.

reticuloperithelium (re-tik″u-lo-per″ĭ-the′le-um). Retoperithelium.

reticulopod (re-tik′u-lo-pod). A pseudopod which is threadlike and branching.

reticulopodium (re-tik″u-lo-po′de-um). Reticulopod.

reticulosarcoma (re-tik″u-lo-sar-ko′mah). Reticulum cell sarcoma.

reticulosis (re-tik″u-lo′sis). An abnormal increase in cells derived from or related to reticuloendothelial cells.

reticulothelium (re-tik″u-lo-the′le-um). Retothelium.

reticulum (re-tik′u-lum), pl. *retic′ula* [L., dim. of *rete* net]. 1. A network, especially a protoplasmic network in cells. 2. Reticular tissue. 3. The second division of the stomach of a ruminant animal. **Chiari's r.,** Chiari's network. **Ebner's r.,** a network of cells in the seminiferous tubules. **retic′ula lie′nis,** trabeculae lienis. **stellate r.,** the soft, middle part of the enamel organ of a developing tooth, the cells being separated by an increase in the gelatinous intercellular substance which forces the cells apart without breaking the intercellular connections, giving them a stellate appearance and providing protection later for the enamel-forming cells.

retiform (ret′ĭ-form) [L. *rete* net + *forma* form]. Resembling a network.

retina (ret′ĭ-nah) [L.]. [N A, B N A] The innermost of the three tunics of the eyeball, surrounding the vitreous body and continuous posteriorly with the optic nerve. It is divided into the *pars optica,* which rests upon the choroid, the *pars ciliaris,* which rests upon the ciliary body, and the *pars iridica,* which rests upon the posterior surface of the iris. Grossly, the retina is composed of an outer, pigmented layer (stratum pigmenti) and an inner, transparent layer, the optic part of which is the cerebral stratum (stratum cerebrale). The latter consists of nine layers, named from within outward, as follows: (1) The membrana limitans interna; (2) the nerve fiber layer; (3) the layer of ganglion cells; (4) the inner molecular, or plexiform, layer; (5) the inner nuclear layer;

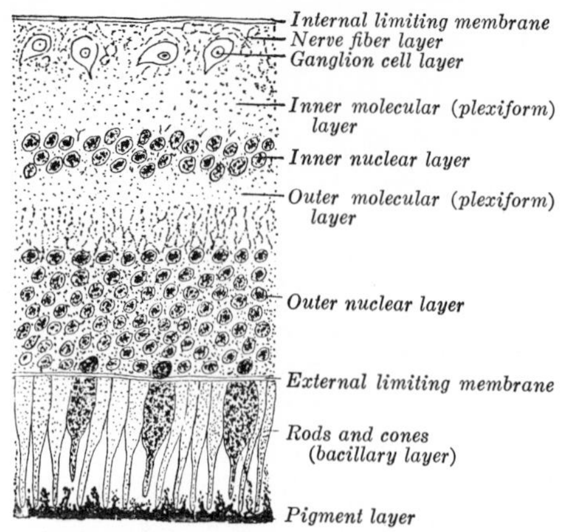

Section of retina of the eye (Hill).

(6) the outer molecular, or plexiform, layer; (7) the outer nuclear layer; (8) the membrana limitans externa; (9) the layer of rods and cones (called also *Jacob's membrane* and *bacillary layer*). The pigmentary layer overlying the optic portion is continued forward over the inner surface of the ciliary body, constituting the *pars ciliaris retinae.* The various layers are connected transversely by fibers of connective tissue (*sustentacular fibers of Müller*). The layer of rods and cones forms the percipient element of the retina and is connected with the nerve fiber layer by nerve fibers which join to form the optic nerve. In the center of the posterior part of the retina is the *macula lutea,* the most sensitive portion of the retina; and in the center of the macula lutea is a depression, the *fovea centralis,* from which the rods are absent. About $\frac{1}{10}$ inch inside the fovea is the point of entrance of the optic nerve and its central artery (*central artery of the retina*). At this point the retina is incomplete and forms the *blind spot.* **coarctate r.,** a funnel-shaped condition of the retina caused by a fluid exudation between the retina and the choroid. **leopard r.,** a retina of a variegated or mottled appearance, due to retinitis pigmentosa. **lower r.,** the lower half of the retina. **nasal r.,** the nasal half of the retina. **physiological r.,** the part of the retina that contains receptors sensitive to light (pars optica retinae [N A]). **shot-silk r.,** an opalescent effect, as of changeable silk, sometimes seen in the retinas of young persons. **temporal r.,** the outer half of the retina. **tigroid r.,** the striped or spotted retina of retinitis pigmentosa. **upper r.,** the upper half of the retina. **watered-silk r.,** shot-silk retina.

retinaculum (ret″ĭ-nak′u-lum), pl. *retinac′ula* [L. "a rope, cable"]. 1. A structure which retains an organ or tissue in place; used in anatomical terminology as a general term to designate such a structure. 2. An instrument or device for holding back tissues during surgery. See *tenaculum.* **r. of arcuate ligament,** r. ligamenti arcuati. **Barry's r.,** any one of a set of filaments within the graafian follicles. **r. cap′sulae articula′ris cox′ae,** one of the longitudinal folds of the cervical portion of the articular capsule of the hip. **caudal r., r. cauda′le** [N A], a fibrous band that extends from the tip of the coccyx to the adjacent skin and thus forms the foveola coccygea. Called also *ligamentum caudale integumenti communis* [B N A]. **r. cos′tae ul′timae,** ligamentum lumbocostale. **retinac′ula cu′tis** [N A, B N A], bands of connective tissue attaching the corium to the subcutaneous tissue. **extensor r. of foot, inferior,** r. musculorum extensorum pedis inferioris. **extensor r. of foot, superior,** r. musculorum extensorum pedis superius. **extensor r. of hand,** r. extensorum manus. **r. extenso′rum ma′nus** [N A], the distal part of the antebrachial fascia, overlying the extensor tendons. Called also *ligamentum carpi dorsale* [B N A], and *extensor r. of hand.* **flexor r. of foot,** r. musculorum flexorum pedis. **flexor r. of hand,** r. flexorum manus. **r. flexo′rum ma′nus** [N A], a heavy fibrous band continuous with the distal part of the antebrachial fascia, completing the carpal canal through which pass the tendons of the flexor muscles of the hand and fingers. Called also *ligamentum carpi transversum* [B N A], and *flexor r. of hand.* **r. of ileocecal valve,** frenulum valvae ileocecalis. **r. ligamen′ti arcua′ti** [B N A], a band of converging fibers passing from the convex lower margin of the arcuate popliteal ligament to the head of the fibula. Omitted in N A. **r. morgag′ni,** frenulum valvae ileocecalis. **r. musculo′rum extenso′rum pe′dis infe′rius** [N A], a thickened band of the fascia cruris passing from each malleolus across the front of the ankle joint, there crossing the other and passing onto the dorsum of the foot. Called also *ligamentum cruciatum cruris* [B N A], and *inferior extensor r. of foot.* **r. musculo′rum extenso′rum pe′dis supe′rius** [N A], the thickened lower portion of the fascia on the front of the leg, attached to the tibia on one side and the fibula on the other, and serving to hold in place the extensor tendons that pass beneath it. Called also *ligamentum transversum cruris* [B N A], and *superior extensor r. of foot.* **r. musculo′rum fibula′rium infe′rius,** N A alternative for *r. musculorum peroneorum inferius.* **r. musculo′rum fibula′rium supe′rius,** N A alternative for *r. musculorum peroneorum superius.* **r. musculo′rum flexo′rum pe′dis** [N A], a strong band of fascia that extends from the medial malleolus down onto the calcaneus. It holds in place the tendons of the tibialis posterior, flexor digitorum, and flexor hallucis muscles as they pass to the sole of the foot, and gives protection to the posterior tibial vessels and tibial nerve. Called also *ligamentum laciniatum* [B N A], and *flexor r. of foot.* **r. musculo′rum peronaeo′rum infe′rius** [B N A], r. musculorum peroneorum inferius. **r. musculo′rum peronaeo′rum supe′rius** [B N A], r. musculorum peroneorum superius. **r. musculo′rum peroneo′rum infe′rius** [N A], a fibrous band that arches over the tendons of the peroneal muscles and holds them in position on the lateral side of the calcaneus. Called also *inferior peroneal r.* **r. musculo′rum peroneo′rum supe′rius** [N A], a fibrous band that arches over the peroneal tendons and helps to hold them in place below and behind the lateral malleolus; it extends from the malleolus downward and backward to the calcaneus. Called also *superior peroneal r.* **r. patel′lae latera′le** [N A, B N A], a fibrous membrane from the tendon of the vastus lateralis muscle, attached to the lateral margin of the patella and then along the side of the patellar ligament, and inserted into the tibia as far distal as the fibular collateral ligament; it also blends with the iliotibial tract of the fascia lata. Called also *lateral patellar r.* **r. patel′lae media′le** [N A, B N A], a fibrous membrane from the tendon of the vastus medialis muscle, attached to the medial margin of the patella and then along the side of the patellar ligament, and inserted into the tibia as far distal as the tibial collateral ligament. Called also *medial patellar r.* **patellar r., lateral,** r. patellae laterale. **patellar r., medial,** r. patellae mediale. **r. ten′dinum,** a tendinous restraining structure, such as an annular ligament. **r. ten′dinum musculo′rum extenso′rum,** r. extensorum manus. **r. ten′dinum musculo′rum extenso′rum infe′rius,** r. musculorum extensorum pedis inferius. **r. ten′dinum musculo′rum extenso′rum supe′rius,** r. musculorum extensorum pedis superius. **r. ten′dinum musculo′rum flexo′rum,** r. flexorum manus. **retinac′ula un′guis** [N A, B N A], structures homologous to the retinacula cutis, attaching the nail to underlying tissue. **Weitbrecht's r.,** retinacular fibers attached to the neck of the femur.

retinal (ret′ĭ-nal). Pertaining to the retina.

retine (ret′ēn). A substance, widely distributed in animal cells, which is characterized by its ability to retard cell division and growth. Cf. *promine.*

retinene (ret′ĭ-nēn). 1. A golden yellow carotinoid pigment in the retina which is formed by the bleaching action of light on rhodopsin. When combined with a protein it is called visual yellow. It is regenerated in the dark to rhodopsin in the presence of vitamin A. 2. The aldehyde of vitamin A which is obtained from fish-liver oils.

retinitis (ret″ĭ-ni′tis). Inflammation of the retina. It is marked by impairment of sight, perversion of vision, edema, and exudation into the retina, and occasionally by hemorrhages into the retina. **actinic r.,** retinitis due to exposure to actinic light rays. **r. albuminu′rica,** that which is associated with kidney disease. **apoplectic r.,** that which is characterized by extravasations of blood within the retina. **central angiospastic r., r. centra′lis sero′sa,** an acute edema of the macula with hypermetropia and recovery. **r. circina′ta, circinate r.,** circinate retinopathy. **Coats's r.,** exudative retinopathy. **diabetic r.,** retinitis occurring in diabetes. **r. discifor′mans,** a degenerative disease of the retina marked by an elevated grayish white mass in the macular region of both eyes. Called also *central disk-shaped retinopathy.* **exudative r.,** exudative retinopathy. **r. gravida′rum,** gravidic r. **gravidic r.,** inflammation of the retina occurring along with the albuminuria of pregnancy. **r. haemorrha′gica,** retinitis marked by profuse retinal hemorrhage. **hypertensive r.,** retinitis occurring in the course of arterial hypertension. **Jacobson's r.,** syphilitic r. **Jensen's r.,** retinochoroiditis juxtapapillaris. **leukemic r.,** a variety seen in leukemia, and marked by hemorrhage and paleness of the retina. Called also *splenic r.* **metastatic r.,** retinitis caused by the location of septic emboli in the retinal vessels. **r. nephrit′ica,** retinal changes associated with nephritis. **r. pigmento′sa,** a disease, frequently hereditary, marked by progressive retinal sclerosis with pigmentation and atrophy. It is attended by contraction of the field of vision and hemeralopia. There are star-shaped deposits of pigment in the retina, and the retinal vessels become obliterated. **r. prolif′erans, proliferating r.,** a condition sometimes resulting from intraocular hemorrhage, with the formation of fibrous tissue bands extending into the vitreous from the surface of the retina; retinal detachment is sometimes a sequel. **r. puncta′ta albes′cens,** a variety characterized by the presence of minute white spots in the fundus. **punctate r.,** a form marked by the presence of a number of white or yellowish spots scattered over the fundus. **renal r.,** r. nephritica. **serous r.,** simple inflammation of the superficial layers of the retina. **solar r.,** retinitis due to excessive exposure to sunlight. **splenic r.,** leukemic r. **r. stella′ta,** a star-shaped figure in the macular area of the retina seen in various conditions. **striate r.,** a form marked by the presence of gray or yellowish streaks just back of the retinal vessels. **suppurative r.,** retinitis due to pyemic infection. **r. syphilit′ica,** retinitis complicating syphilitic iritis. **uremic r.,** retinitis occurring in uremia.

retinoblastoma (ret″ĭ-no-blas-to′mah). A tumor arising from retinal germ cells; glioma of the retina.

retinochoroid (ret″ĭ-no-ko′roid). Pertaining to the retina and the choroid.

retinochoroiditis (ret″ĭ-no-ko-roid-i′tis). Inflammation of the retina and choroid. **r. juxtapapilla′ris,** a condition seen in young healthy subjects marked by a small inflammatory area on the fundus close to the papilla. Called also *Jensen's retinitis* and *Jensen's retinochoroiditis.*

retinocytoma (ret″ĭ-no-si-to′mah). Glioma of the retina.

retinodialysis (ret″ĭ-no-di-al′ĭ-sis) [*retina* + Gr. *dialysis* separation]. Disinsertion of the retina; detachment of the retina at its peripheral insertion.

retinograph (ret′ĭ-no-graf). A photograph of the retina.

retinography (ret″ĭ-nog′rah-fe). Photography of the retina.

retinoid (ret′ĭ-noid). 1. Resembling the retina. 2. [Gr. *rhētinē* resin + *eidos* form]. Resembling a resin.

retinomalacia (ret″ĭ-no-mah-la′she-ah) [*retina* + Gr. *malakos* soft + *-ia*]. Softening of the retina.

retinopapillitis (ret″ĭ-no-pap″ĭ-li′tis). Inflammation of the retina and the optic papilla.

retinopathy (ret″ĭ-nop′ah-the) [*retina* + Gr. *pathos* disease]. Any noninflammatory disease of the retina. **central disk-shaped r.,** retinitis disciformans. **circinate r.,** a condition marked by a circle of white spots enclosing the macular area, leading to complete foveal blindness. Called also *retinitis circinata* or *circinate retinitis.* **exudative r.,** a condition marked by masses of white or yellowish exudate in the posterior part of the fundus oculi, with deposit of cholesterin and blood debris from retinal hemorrhage, and leading to destruction of the macula and blindness. Called also *retinitis hemorrhagica externa, exudative retinitis,* and *Coats's disease.* **leukemic r.,** a condition occurring in leukemia, with paleness of the fundus resulting from infiltration of the retina and choroid with leukocytes, and swelling of the disk with blurring of its margin. **Purtscher's angiopathic r.,** Purtscher's disease.

retinoschisis (ret″ĭ-nos′kĭ-sis) [*retina* + Gr. *schisis* division]. 1. A congenital cleft of the retina. 2. A cleavage of the retinal layers, with the formation of holes, usually occurring on the temporal side of the eye and resulting from degenerative changes associated with age.

retinoscope (ret′ĭ-no-skōp). An instrument for performing retinoscopy.

retinoscopy (ret″ĭ-nos′ko-pe) [*retina* + Gr. *skopein* to examine]. Skiametry.

retinosis (ret″ĭ-no′sis). A general term for degenerative, non-inflammatory conditions of the retina.

retinotoxic (ret″ĭ-no-tok′sik). Exerting a toxic or deleterious effect upon the retina.

retisolution (ret″ĭ-so-lu′shun) [L. *rete* net + *solution*]. Dissolution of the Golgi apparatus.

retispersion (ret″ĭ-sper′shun) [L. *rete* net + *spargere* to throw about]. Migration of the Golgi apparatus from its normal position to the periphery of the cell.

retoperithelium (re″to-per″ĭ-the′le-um) [L. *rete* net + Gr. *peri* around + *thēlē* papilla]. The layer of cells covering a reticular framework.

retort (re-tort′) [L. *retorta* bent back]. A long-necked globular vessel used in distillation.

Retortamonas (re″tor-tam′o-nas) [L. *retortus* bent back + Gr. *monas* unit]. A genus of intestinal flagellates. *R.* (*Embadomonas*) *intestinalis* has been reported from man. Several specimens of this genus have been recorded from the lower animals.

retothel (re′to-thel). Reticuloendothelial.

retothelial (re″to-the′le-al). Pertaining to the retothelium; containing reticulum cells.

retothelioma (re″to-the″le-o′mah). A tumor of retothelium.

retothelium (re″to-the′le-um) [L. *rete* net + Gr. *thēlē* papilla]. The layer of cells covering a reticular tissue.

retractile (re-trak′til) [L. *retractilis*]. Susceptible of being drawn back.

retraction (re-trak′shun) [L. *retractio,* from *re-* back + *trahere* to draw]. The act of drawing back; the condition of being drawn back. **gingival r.,** the apical advancement of the line of attachment of the gingiva on a tooth surface. **mandibular r.,** the condition of the mandible when the gnathion lies posterior to the orbital plane.

retractor (re-trak′tor) [L.]. 1. An instrument for drawing back the edges of a wound. 2. Any retractile muscle. **Emmet's r.,** a self-retaining vaginal speculum. **Moorehead's r.,** a retractor used in dentistry.

retrad (re′trad) [L. *retro* backward]. Toward a posterior or dorsal part.

retrenchment (re-trench′ment). A procedure in plastic surgery consisting in the removal of redundant tissue and the production of cicatricial contraction.

retro- (ret′ro, re′tro) [L. *retro* backward]. Prefix signifying backward, or located behind.

retroaction (ret″ro-ak′shun). Action in a reversed direction.

retroauricular (ret″ro-aw-rik′u-lar). Behind the auricle.

retrobronchial (ret″ro-brong′ke-al). Behind the bronchi.

retrobuccal (ret″ro-buk′al). Pertaining to the back part of the mouth.

retrobulbar (ret″ro-bul′bar) [*retro-* + L. *bulbus* bulb]. Behind the pons or behind the eyeball.

retrocalcaneobursitis (ret″ro-kal-ka″ne-o-bur-si′tis). Achilloburs itis.

retrocardiac (ret″ro-kar′de-ak). Behind the heart.

retrocatheterism (ret″ro-kath′ĕ-ter-izm). Passing of a catheter through a suprapubic opening downward through the urethra to the external meatus.

retrocecal (ret″ro-se′kal). Behind the cecum.

retrocedent (ret″ro-se′dent) [L. *retrocedens* going back]. 1. Going back, or returning. 2. Disappearing from the surface and affecting some interior organ.

retrocervical (ret″ro-ser′ve-kal). Behind the cervix uteri.

retrocession (ret″ro-sesh′un) [L. *retrocessio*]. 1. A going backward; backward displacement; specifically a dropping backward of the entire uterus. 2. The metastasis of a disease from the surface to some interior organ.

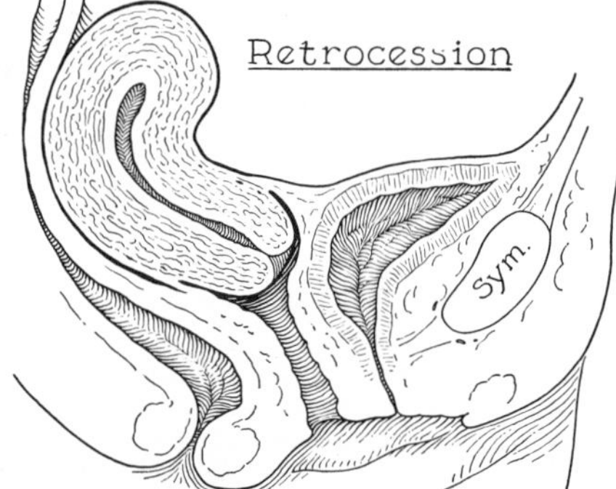

Retrocession of uterus.

retroclavicular (ret″ro-klah-vik′u-lar). Behind the clavicle.

retroclusion (ret″ro-kloo′zhun) [*retro-* + L. *claudere* to close]. Closure of a bleeding artery by means of a pin passed over, behind, and under the vessel.

retrocolic (ret″ro-kol′ik). Behind the colon.

retrocollic (ret″ro-kol′ik). Pertaining to the back of the neck.

retrocollis (ret″ro-kol′is) [*retro-* + L. *collum* neck]. Spasmodic wryneck in which the head is drawn directly backward.

retrocursive (re″tro-kur′siv) [*retro-* + L. *curro* to run]. Marked by stepping backward.

retrodeviation (re″tro-de″ve-a′shun). A general

term inclusive of retroversion, retroflexion, retroposition, etc.

retrodisplacement (re″tro-dis-plās′ment). A backward displacement.

retrodural (ret″ro-du′ral). Behind the dura mater.

retro-esophageal (ret″ro-e-sof″ah-je′al). Behind the esophagus.

retroflexed (ret′ro-flekst) [*retro-* + L. *flexus* bent]. Bent backward; in a state of retroflexion.

retroflexion (ret″ro-flek′shun) [L. *retroflexio*]. The bending of an organ so that its top is turned

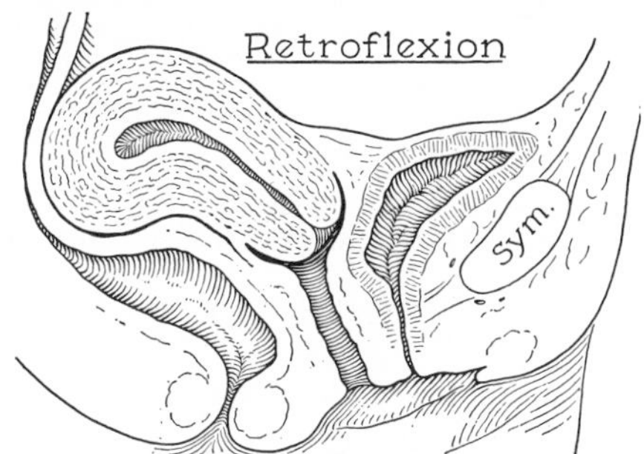

Retroflexion of uterus.

backward: specifically, the bending backward of the body of the uterus upon the cervix.

retrogasserian (ret″ro-gas-se′re-an). Pertaining to the sensory (posterior) root of the trigeminal (gasserian) ganglion.

retrognathia (ret″ro-nath′e-ah) [*retro-* + Gr. *gnathos* jaw + *-ia*]. Position of the jaws back of the frontal plane of the forehead.

retrognathic (ret″ro-nath′ik). Pertaining to or characterized by retrognathia.

retrograde (ret′ro-grād) [*retro-* + L. *gradi* to step]. Going backward; retracing a former course; catabolic.

retrography (re-trog′rah-fe) [*retro-* + Gr. *graphein* to write]. Mirror writing.

retrogression (ret″ro-gresh′un) [*retro-* + L. *gressus* course]. 1. Degeneration. 2. Catabolism.

retroinfection (re″tro-in-fek′shun). Infection of the mother by the fetus in utero.

retroinsular (ret″ro-in′su-lar) [*retro-* + L. *insula* island]. Situated or occurring behind the insula.

retro-iridian (re″tro-i-rid′e-an). Behind the iris.

retrojection (ret″ro-jek′shun) [*retro-* + L. *jacere* to throw]. The washing out of a cavity by an injected fluid.

retrolabyrinthine (re″tro-lab″ĭ-rin′thēn). Behind the labyrinth of the ear.

retrolingual (ret″ro-ling′gwal). Behind the tongue.

retromammary (ret″ro-mam′ar-e). Behind the mammary gland.

retromandibular (re″tro-man-dib′u-lar). Behind the mandible of the lower jaw.

retromastoid (re″tro-mas′toid). Behind the mastoid process.

retromorphosis (re″tro-mor-fo′sis) [*retro-* + Gr. *morphē* form]. Retrograde metamorphosis.

retronasal (ret″ro-na′zal) [*retro-* + L. *nasus* nose]. Behind the nose.

retro-ocular (ret″ro-ok′u-lar) [*retro-* + L. *oculus* eye]. Behind the eye.

retropatellar (ret″ro-pah-tel′ar). Situated behind the patella.

retroperitoneal (re″tro-per″ĭ-to-ne′al). Behind the peritoneum.

retroperitoneum (re″tro-per″ĭ-to-ne′um). The retroperitoneal space.

retroperitonitis (re″tro-per″ĭ-to-ni′tis). Inflammation in the retroperitoneal space.

retropharyngeal (re″tro-fah-rin′je-al) [*retro-* + *pharyngeal*]. Situated or occurring behind the pharynx.

retropharyngitis (re″tro-far″in-ji′tis). Inflammation of the posterior part of the pharynx.

retropharynx (re″tro-far′inks). The posterior part of the pharynx.

retroplacental (re″tro-plah-sen′tal). Behind the placenta.

retroplasia (ret″ro-pla′se-ah) [*retro-* + Gr. *plasis* formation + *-ia*]. Retrograde metaplasia; degeneration of a tissue or cell into a more primitive type.

retropleural (re″tro-plōōr′al). Behind the pleura; posterior to the pleural cavity.

retroposed (re′tro-pōzd) [*retro-* + L. *positus* placed]. Displaced backward.

retroposition (re″tro-po-zish′un). 1. Backward displacement. 2. Reposition.

retropulsion (re″tro-pul′shun) [*retro-* + L. *pellere* to drive]. 1. A driving back, as of the fetal head in labor. 2. A tendency to walk backward, as in some cases of locomotor ataxia. 3. An abnormal gait in which the body is bent backward.

retrorectal (re″tro-rek′tal). Behind the rectum.

retrorsine (ret′ror-sin). A poisonous alkaloid, $C_{18}H_{25}O_6N$, from *Senecio retrorsus*, which may cause a fatal cirrhosis of the liver in horses and cattle that eat the plant.

retrosinus (ret″ro-si′nus). The air cells behind the sigmoid sinus in the mastoid process of the temporal bone.

retrospondylolisthesis (ret″ro-spon″dĭ-lo-lis-the′sis). Sacrolisthesis.

retrostalsis (re″tro-stal′sis). Reversed or backward peristaltic action.

retrosternal (re″tro-ster′nal) [*retro-* + *sternum*]. Situated or occurring behind the sternum.

retrosymphysial (re″tro-sim-fiz′e-al). Behind the symphysis.

retrotarsal (re″tro-tar′sal). Behind the tarsus of the eye.

retro-uterine (re″tro-u′ter-in) [*retro-* + *uterus*]. Behind the uterus.

retrovaccination (re″tro-vak″sĭ-na′shun). The inoculation of a heifer with vaccine virus from a human subject, also vaccination with virus obtained from a cow which has been previously thus inoculated.

retroversioflexion (re″tro-ver″se-o-flek′shun). Retroversion combined with retroflexion.

retroversion (ret″ro-ver′zhun) [L. *retroversio*; *retro* back + *versio* turning]. The tipping of an

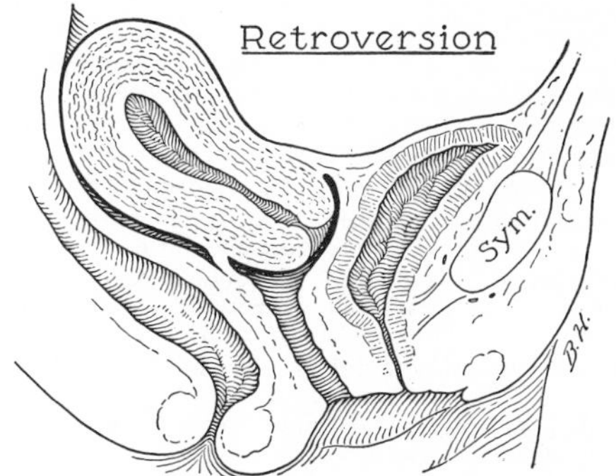

Retroversion of uterus.

entire organ backward. **r. of uterus,** the turning backward of the entire uterus in relation to the pelvic axis.

retroverted (ret″ro-vert′ed). In a condition of retroversion.

retrusion (re-troo′zhun) [L. *re-* back + *trudere* to shove]. 1. The state of being located posterior to the normal position, as malposition of a tooth posteriorly in the line of occlusion. 2. The backward movement or position of the mandible.

Retzius' cavity, fibers, ligament, space, veins, etc. (ret′ze-us) [Anders Adolf *Retzius*, Swedish anatomist, 1796–1860]. See under the nouns.

Retzius' foramen, striae (ret′ze-us) [Magnus Gustav *Retzius*, Swedish anatomist, 1842–1919]. See under *foramen* and *stria*.

reunient (re-ūn′yent) [L. *re-* again + *unire* to unite]. Effecting the union of divided parts.

Reuss's color charts, tables (rois′ez) [August Ritter von *Reuss*, Vienna ophthalmologist, 1841–1924]. Charts with colored letters printed on colored backgrounds: used for testing color vision.

revaccination (re″vak-sĭ-na′shun). A second vaccination.

revellent (re-vel′ent) [L. *re-* back + *vellere* to draw]. Causing revulsion; revulsive.

Reverdin's graft, method, operation (raver-danz′) [Jacques Louis *Reverdin*, surgeon at Geneva, 1842–1908]. See under *graft*.

Reverdin's needle (ra″ver-danz′) [Albert *Reverdin*, Geneva surgeon, 1881–1929]. See under *needle*.

reversal (re-ver′sal). A turning or change in the opposite direction. **r. of gradient,** a changing of direction of the fecal stream due to an area of irritation causing local spasticity of the intestine with higher tonus than that of the proximal area. **sex r.,** a change in characteristics from those typical of one sex to those typical of the other.

reversible (re-ver′sĭ-b'l). Capable of going through a series of changes in either direction, forward or backward, as a reversible chemical reaction.

reversion (re-ver′zhun) [L. *re-* back + *versio* turning]. 1. A returning to a previous condition. 2. In genetics, inheritance from some remote ancestor of a character which has not been manifest for several generations. Cf. *atavism*. **Mantoux r.,** a term suggested to designate the change from the tuberculin-positive to the tuberculin-negative state.

revertose (re-ver′tōs). A disaccharide formed by the action of maltase on very concentrated solutions of glucose.

Revilliod's sign (ra-ve-yōz′) [Léon *Revilliod*, Swiss physician, 1835–1919]. See under *sign*.

revivescence (re″vi-ves′ens) [L. *revivescere* to revive]. 1. The renewal of vital activities. 2. The reappearance of a local (cutaneous) reaction on the subcutaneous administration of tuberculin to a patient who has previously had a diagnostic (cutaneous) tuberculin test. Called also *recurrent reaction*.

revivification (re-viv″ĭ-fi-ka′shun) [L. *re-* again + *vivus* alive + *facere* to make]. The paring or refreshing of diseased surfaces to promote their union.

revolute (rev′o-lūt). Turned back or curled back.

revulsant (re-vul′sant) [L. *revulsans*]. Revulsive.

révulseur (ra″vul-ser′) [Fr.]. An instrument used in the performance of baunscheidtism.

revulsion (re-vul′shun) [L. *revulsio;* from *re-* back + *vellere* to draw]. The drawing of blood from one part to another part, as in counter-irritation.

revulsive (re-vul′siv) [L. *re-* back + *vellere* to draw]. Effecting revulsion.

Reynals' permeability factor. See *Duran-Reynals*, and *hyaluronidase*.

rezipas (rez′ĭ-pas). Trade mark for a preparation of para-aminosalicylic acid.

Rezzonico-Golgi spirals, threads. See under *thread*.

R.F.A. Abbreviation for *right fronto-anterior* position of the fetus.

R.F.N. Abbreviation for *Registered Fever Nurse*.

R.F.P. Abbreviation for *right frontoposterior* position of the fetus.

R.F.P.S.(Glasgow). Abbreviation for *Royal Faculty of Physicians and Surgeons of Glasgow*.

R.F.T. Abbreviation for *right frontotransverse* position of the fetus.

R.G.N. Abbreviation for *Registered General Nurse* (Scotland).

Rh. Chemical symbol for *rhodium*.

rhabditic (rab-dit′ik). Pertaining to Rhabditis.

rhabditiform (rab-dit′ĭ-form). Rhabdoid.

Rhabditis (rab-di′tis) [Gr. *rhabdos* rod]. A genus of minute worms belonging to the class Nematoda, living mostly in damp earth, but occasionally found in man. **R. genita′lis** sometimes occurs in the urinary organs. **R. hom′inis,** a viviparous parasite found in the feces of school children in Korea. **R. intestina′lis** and **R. niel′lyi** also infest the human subject. **R. pel′lio,** a species once found in the vagina.

rhabditoid (rab′dĭ-toid). Rhabdoid.

rhabdium (rab′de-um) [Gr. *rhabdion* a little rod]. A voluntary muscle fiber.

rhabdo- (rab′do) [Gr. *rhabdos* rod]. Combining form meaning rod-shaped or denoting relationship to a rod.

rhabdocyte (rab′do-sīt) [*rhabdo-* + *-cyte*]. Metamyelocyte.

rhabdoid (rab′doid) [Gr. *rhabdo-eides* like a rod, striped looking]. Resembling a rod; rod-shaped.

Rhabdomonas (rab″do-mo′nas) [*rhabdo-* + Gr. *monas* unit]. A genus of microorganisms of the family Thiorhodaceae, suborder Rhodobacteriineae, order Pseudomonadales, made up of irregular long rods or filaments, occurring singly. It includes three species, *R. gra′cilis, R. linsbau′eri,* and *R. ro′sea*.

rhabdomyoblastoma (rab″do-mi″o-blas-to′mah) [*rhabdo-* + Gr. *mys* muscle + *blastos* germ + *-oma*]. A tumor the cells of which tend to differentiate into striated muscle cells.

rhabdomyochondroma (rab″do-mi″o-kon-dro′mah). A mixed chondroma and rhabdomyoma.

rhabdomyolysis (rab″do-mi-ol′ĭ-sis) [*rhabdo-* + Gr. *mys* muscle + *lysis* dissolution]. Disintegration or dissolution of muscle, associated with excretion of myoglobin in the urine.

rhabdomyoma (rab″do-mi-o′mah). A benign tumor derived from striated muscle. Called also *myoma striocellulare*.

rhabdomyomyxoma (rab″do-mi″o-mik-so′mah). A combined myxoma and rhabdomyoma.

rhabdomyosarcoma (rab″do-mi″o-sar-ko′mah). A combined sarcoma and rhabdomyoma.

Rhabdonema (rab″do-ne′mah). Rhabditis.

rhabdophobia (rab″do-fo′be-ah) [*rhabdo-* + Gr. *phobein* to be affrighted by]. Morbid dread of a stick or of a beating.

rhabdosarcoma (rab″do-sar-ko′mah). A sarcoma containing striated muscle fibers. **renal r.,** a renal embryoma in which striated muscle predominates.

rhachi-. For words beginning thus see those beginning *rachi-*.

rhacoma (ra-ko′mah) [Gr. *rhakōma* rags]. 1. An excoriation or rent of the skin. 2. A pendulous scrotum.

rhaebocrania (re″bo-kra′ne-ah) [Gr. *rhaibos* crooked + *kranion* skull + *-ia*]. Torticollis, or wryneck.

rhaeboscelia (re″bo-se′le-ah) [Gr. *rhaibos* crooked + *skelos* leg + *-ia*]. Bowleg, or knock knee.

rhaebosis (re-bo′sis) [Gr. *rhaibos* crooked + *-osis*]. Crookedness of the legs or of any normally straight part.

rhagades (rag′ah-dēz) [pl. of Gr. *rhagas* rent]. Fissures or cracks in the skin, especially such lesions around a body orifice or on regions subjected to frequent movement.

rhagadiform (ra-gad′ĭ-form) [Gr. *rhagas* rent + L. *forma* shape]. Fissured; containing cracks.

-rhage [Gr. *rhēgnynai* to burst forth]. Word termination meaning a breaking or bursting forth, a profuse flow, as hemorrhage.

Rhagio (ra′je-o). A genus of flies some of which are annoying biters.

rhagiocrine (raj′e-o-krīn) [Gr. *rhax* grape + *krinein* to separate]. Denoting colloid vacuoles in the cytoplasm of gland cells that represent a stage in the development of secretory granules.

rhamninose (ram′nĭ-nōs). A trisaccharide which occurs in the glycosides sophorin and xanthorhamnin.

rhamnose (ram′nōs). A methylaldopentose, $C_6H_{12}O_5$, sometimes found in the urine; it is dextrorotatory.

rhamnoside (ram′no-sīd). A glycoside which on hydrolysis yields rhamnose.

rhamnoxanthin (ram″no-zan′thin). Frangulin.

Rhamnus (ram′nus) [L.; Gr. *rhamnos* a kind of prickly shrub]. A genus of rhamnaceous trees and shrubs, often with a purgative bark and fruit. Among them are *R. cathar′tica*, or buckthorn, *R. purshia′na*, and *R. fran′gula*. *R. califor′nica*, California buckthorn or coffee tree, is used in rheumatism. *R. cro′ceus* is a species of buckthorn with edible red fruit, the excessive use of which tinges the skin red.

rhaphania (rah-fa′ne-ah). Raphania.

rhaphe (ra′fe) [Gr. *rhaphē*]. Raphe.

-rhaphy [Gr. *rhaphē* a seam]. Word termination meaning joining in a seam, or suturation.

rhatanine (rat′ah-nin). Surinamine.

rhatany (rat′ah-ne) [Port. *ratanhia*]. Krameria. **Brazilian r.,** *Krameria argentea.* **Peruvian r.,** *Krameria triandra.* **Savanilla r.,** *Krameria ixina.*

Rhazes (ra′zes) (c.860 to c.932 A.D.). A famous Arabian physician (although born in Persia), who was distinguished for his many writings, his treatise on smallpox and measles being particularly outstanding.

R.H.D. Abbreviation for *relative hepatic dullness.*

rhe (re) [Gr. *rheos* current]. The unit of fluidity, being the reciprocal of the unit of velocity or centipoise.

-rhea [Gr. *rhein* to flow, run, gush]. Word termination meaning flow.

rhegma (reg′mah) [Gr. *rhēgma* rent]. A rupture, rent, or fracture.

Rhein's picks (rīnz) [M. L. *Rhein*, American dentist, 1860–1928]. Instruments for opening and enlarging root canals at the apex.

rhembasmus (rem-baz′mus) [Gr. *rhembasmos*]. 1. Mental wandering or distraction. 2. Wavering or morbid indecision.

rhenium (re′ne-um). A chemical element, atomic number 75, atomic weight 186.2, symbol Re.

rheo- (re′o) [Gr. *rheos* current]. Combining form denoting relationship to an electric current, or to a flow, as of fluids.

rheobase (re′o-bās) [*rheo-* + Gr. *basis* step]. The minimum potential of electric current necessary to produce stimulation (L. Lapicque, 1909).

rheobasic (re″o-ba′sik). Pertaining to a rheobase.

rheocardiogram (re″o-kar′de-o-gram). The graphic record obtained by rheocardiography.

rheocardiography (re″o-kar″de-og′rah-fe). The technique of recording the variation, occurring during the course of the cardiac cycle, in the total resistance to the flow of an alternating current sent through the body.

rheocord (re′o-kord) [*rheo-* + Gr. *chordē* chord]. Rheostat.

rheology (re-ol′o-je). The science of the deformation and flow of matter, such as the flow of blood through the heart and blood vessels.

rheometer (re-om′e-ter) [*rheo-* + Gr. *metron* measure]. 1. Galvanometer. 2. An instrument for measuring the velocity of the blood current.

rheonome (re′o-nōm) [*rheo-* + Gr. *nemein* to distribute]. An apparatus for determining the effect of irritation on a nerve.

rheophore (re′o-fōr) [*rheo-* + Gr. *phoros* carrying]. An electrode.

rheoscope (re′o-skōp) [*rheo-* + Gr. *skopein* to examine]. An instrument for detecting the presence of an electric current.

rheostat (re′o-stat) [*rheo-* + Gr. *histanai* to place]. An appliance for regulating the resistance and thus controlling the amount of current entering an electric circuit.

rheostosis (re″os-to′sis) [*rheo-* + *ostosis*]. A condition of hyperostosis marked by the presence of streaks in the bones.

rheotachygraphy (re″o-tah-kig′rah-fe) [*rheo-* + Gr. *tachys* swift + *graphein* to write]. The photographic record of the curve of variation in experiments upon the electromotive action of muscles.

rheotaxis (re″o-tak′sis) [*rheo-* + Gr. *taxis* arrangement]. The orientation of a longitudinal body in a stream of liquid, with its long axis parallel with the direction of fluid flow. **negative r.,** rheotaxis with movement of the organism in the same direction as that of the liquid. **positive r.,** rheotaxis with movement of the organism in the opposite direction to that of the liquid.

rheotome (re′o-tōm) [*rheo-* + Gr. *tomē* a cutting]. A device in a faradic battery for interrupting the current with an adjustable speed control.

rheotrope (re′o-trōp) [Gr. *rheos* current + *trepein* to turn]. An instrument for reversing an electric current.

rheotropism (re-ot′ro-pizm). Rheotaxis.

rhestocythemia (res″to-si-the′me-ah) [Gr. *rhaiein* to break, ruin + *-cyte* + *haima* blood + *-ia*]. The occurrence of broken-down erythrocytes in the blood.

Rheum (re′um). A genus of cathartic polygonaceous plants. See *rhubarb.*

rheum, rheuma (rōōm, roo′mah) [Gr. *rheuma* flux]. Any watery or catarrhal discharge. **epidemic r.,** influenza. **salt r.,** eczema.

rheumapyra (roo″mah-pi′rah) [Gr. *rheuma* flux + *pyr* fire]. Acute rheumatism; rheumatic fever.

rheumarthritis (roo″mar-thri′tis). Rheumatism of the joints.

rheumatalgia (roo″mah-tal′je-ah). Chronic rheumatic pain.

rheumatic (roo-mat′ik) [Gr. *rheumatikos*]. Pertaining to or affected with rheumatism.

rheumaticosis (roo-mat″ĭ-ko′sis). A term suggested to express the general condition seen in the rheumatism of childhood.

rheumatid (roo′mah-tid). Any skin lesion or eruption occurring in rheumatism.

rheumatism (roo′mah-tizm) [L. *rheumatismus;* Gr. *rheumatismos*]. A disease marked by inflammation of the connective tissue structures of the body, especially the muscles and joints, by pain in these parts, by vegetations on the valves of the heart and by the presence of Aschoff bodies in the myocardium and skin. **apoplectic r.,** rheumatism associated with cerebral apoplexy. **articular r., acute,** rheumatic fever. **articular r., chronic.** See *rheumatoid arthritis* and *hypertrophic arthritis*, under *arthritis.* **Besnier's r.,** chronic arthrosynovitis. **cerebral r.,** acute rheumatic fever marked by chorea, delirium, convulsions, and coma. **desert r.,** coccidioidomycosis. **gonorrheal r.,** acute articular rheumatism associated with gonorrheal urethritis, and frequently producing ankylosis of the joints. **r. of the heart,** rheumatism affecting the heart, due to spread of acute articular rheumatism, and producing valvular disease. **Heberden's r.,** rheumatism of the finger joint, marked by the formation of nodosities. **inflammatory r.,** rheumatic fever. **lumbar r.,** lumbago. **MacLeod's capsular r.,** a rheumatoid arthritis with effusion into the synovial capsules, bursae, and sheaths. **muscular r.**, fibrositis. **nodose r.** 1. Articular rheumatism with the formation of nodules in the region of the joints. 2. Arthritis deformans. **osseous r.**, arthritis deformans. **palindromic r.**, a condition in which there are repeated episodes of arthritis and periarthritis without fever and without producing irreversible changes in the joints. **Poncet's r.**, tuberculous rheumatism. **subacute r.**, a mild but protracted form of rheumatism. **tuberculous r.**, an inflammatory state of the joints due to the toxins of tuberculosis. **visceral r.**, that which involves a viscus, more commonly the heart or pericardium.

rheumatismal (roo″mah-tiz′mal). Pertaining to or of the nature of rheumatism.

rheumatocelis (roo″mah-to-ke′lis) [*rheumatic* + Gr. *kēlis* spot]. Purpura rheumatica.

rheumatogenic (roo″mah-to-jen′ik) [*rheumatism* + Gr. *gennan* to produce]. Producing or causing rheumatism.

rheumatoid (roo′mah-toid) [Gr. *rheuma* flux + *eidos* form]. Resembling rheumatism.

rheumatologist (roo″mah-tol′o-jist). A specialist in rheumatic conditions.

rheumatology (roo″mah-tol′o-je). The science of rheumatism.

rheumatopyra (roo″mah-to-pi′rah). Rheumapyra.

rheumatosis (roo″mah-to′sis). Any disorder attributed to rheumatic origin.

rheumic (roo′mik). Pertaining to a rheum or flux.

rhexis (rek′sis) [Gr. *rhēxis* a breaking forth, bursting]. The rupture of an organ or a vessel.

rhigosis (rĭ-go′sis) [Gr. *rhigōsis* a shivering]. The cold sense; the perception of cold.

rhigotic (rĭ-got′ik). Pertaining to rhigosis.

rhin-. See *rhino-*.

rhinal (ri′nal) [Gr. *rhis* nose]. Pertaining to the nose.

rhinalgia (ri-nal′je-ah) [*rhin-* + *-algia*]. Pain in the nose.

rhinallergosis (rīn″al-er-go′sis) [*rhin-* + *allergy* + *-osis*]. Hay fever.

rhinedema (ri″ne-de′mah) [*rhin-* + *edema*]. Edema of the nose; dropsy of the nose.

rhinencephalia (ri″nen-se-fa′le-ah). Rhinocephalia.

rhinencephalon (ri″nen-sef′ah-lon) [*rhin-* + Gr. *enkephalos* brain]. 1. [B N A] A name given the part of the brain that is homologous with the olfactory portions of the brain in lower animals, comprising the structures medial to the rhinal sulcus in the inferior part of the cerebral hemisphere. Omitted in N A. 2. One of the portions of the telencephalon in the early embryo.

rhinencephalus (ri″nen-sef′ah-lus). Rhinocephalus.

rhinenchysis (ri-nen′kĭ-sis) [*rhin-* + Gr. *enchein* to pour in]. Injection of a medicinal fluid into the nose.

rhinesthesia (ri″nes-the′ze-ah) [*rhin-* + Gr. *aisthēsis* perception]. The sense of smell.

rhineurynter (rīn″u-rin′ter) [*rhin-* + Gr. *eurynein* to widen]. A dilatable rubber bag for distending a nostril.

rhinion (rin′e-on) [Gr., dim. of *rhis*]. The lower end of the suture between the nasal bones.

rhinism (ri′nizm). A nasal quality of voice.

rhinitis (ri-ni′tis) [*rhin-* + *-itis*]. Inflammation of the mucous membrane of the nose. **acute catarrhal r.**, coryza, or cold in the head; an acute congestion of the mucous membrane of the nose, marked by dryness, followed by increased mucous secretion from the membrane, impeded respiration through the nose, and some pain. **allergic r., anaphylactic r.**, hay fever. **atrophic r.**, a chronic form marked by wasting of the mucous membrane and the glands. **r. caseo′sa**, rhinitis with a caseous, gelatinous, and fetid discharge. **chronic catarrhal r.**, a form characterized by hypertrophy and later by atrophy of the mucous and submucous tissues. **croupous r.**, fibrinous r. **dyscrinic r.**, rhinitis associated with and dependent on endocrine imbalance. **fibrinous r.**, a form characterized by the development of a false membrane. Called also *croupous r.* **gangrenous r.**, a gangrene-like inflammation of the nasal mucosa. **hypertrophic r.**, a form in which the mucous membrane thickens and swells. **membranous r.**, chronic rhinitis with the formation of a membranous exudate. **pseudomembranous r.**, a form in which the inflamed region is covered with an opaque exudation. **purulent r.**, chronic rhinitis with the formation of pus. **scrofulous r.**, tuberculous rhinitis. **r. sic′ca**, a variety of atrophic rhinitis in which the secretion is entirely absent. **syphilitic r.**, a variety caused by syphilis, and marked by ulceration, caries of the bone, and a fetid discharge. **tuberculous r.**, a variety due to tuberculosis, and attended with ulceration, caries of the bone, and ozena. **vasomotor r.** 1. Mucous secretion from the nose, due to vasomotor neurosis. 2. Hay fever.

rhino-, rhin- [Gr. *rhis* nose]. Combining form denoting relationship to the nose, or a noselike structure.

rhino-anemometer (ri″no-an″ĕ-mom′e-ter) [*rhino-* + *anemometer*]. An apparatus for measuring the air passing through the nose during respiration.

rhino-antritis (ri″no-an-tri′tis) [*rhino-* + *antrum* + *-itis*]. Inflammation of the nasal cavity and the antrum of Highmore.

rhinobyon (ri-no′be-on) [*rhino-* + Gr. *byein* to plug]. A nasal tampon.

rhinocanthectomy (ri″no-kan-thek′to-me). Rhinommectomy.

rhinocele (ri′no-sēl). Rhinocoele.

rhinocephalia (ri″no-se-fa′le-ah) [*rhino-* + Gr. *kephalē* head + *-ia*]. A developmental anomaly characterized by the presence of a proboscis-like nose above eyes partially or completely fused into one.

Rhinocephalus annulatus (ri″no-sef′ah-lus an″u-la′tus). *Boophilus bovis.*

rhinocephalus (ri″no-sef′ah-lus). A fetal monster exhibiting rhinocephalia.

rhinocheiloplasty (ri″no-ki′lo-plas″te) [*rhino-* + Gr. *cheilos* lip + *plassein* to form]. Plastic surgery of the nose and lip.

Rhinocladium (ri″no-kla′de-um). A genus of fungi formerly included under Sporotrichum.

rhinocleisis (ri″no-kli′sis) [*rhino-* + Gr. *kleisis* closure]. Obstruction of the nasal passages.

rhinocoele (ri′no-sēl) [*rhino-* + Gr. *koilia* hollow]. The ventricle of the olfactory lobe of the brain.

rhinodacryolith (ri″no-dak′re-o-lith) [*rhino-* + Gr. *dakryon* tear + *lithos* stone]. A lacrimal concretion in the nasal duct.

rhinoderma (ri″no-der′mah) [*rhino-* + Gr. *derma* skin]. Keratosis pilaris.

rhinodynia (ri″no-din′e-ah) [*rhino-* + Gr. *odynē* pain + *-ia*]. Pain in the nose.

Rhinoestrus (rīn-es′trus). A genus of flies whose larvae occur in the nasal passages of horses in Europe, Asia and Africa: they may deposit larvae in the human eye.

rhinogenous (ri-noj′e-nus) [*rhino-* + Gr. *gennan* to produce]. Arising in the nose.

rhinokyphectomy (ri″no-ki-fek′to-me) [*rhino-* + Gr. *kyphos* hump + *ektomē* excision]. Plastic surgery on the nose for removal of an abnormal hump.

rhinokyphosis (ri″no-ki-fo′sis) [*rhino-* + Gr. *kyphos* hump]. The presence of an abnormal hump in the ridge of the nose.

rhinolalia (ri″no-la′le-ah) [*rhino-* + Gr. *lalia* speech]. A nasal quality of voice due to some disease or defect of the nasal passages. **r. aper′ta,** that which is caused by undue patency of the posterior nares. **r. clau′sa,** that which is due to undue closure of the nasal passages. **open r.,** r. rhinolalia aperta.

rhinolaryngitis (ri″no-lar″in-ji′tis). Inflammation of the mucous membrane of the nose and larynx.

rhinolaryngology (ri″no-lar″in-gol′o-je) [*rhino-* + Gr. *larynx* larynx + *-logy*]. The sum of knowledge concerning the nose and larynx and their diseases.

rhinolith (ri′no-lith) [*rhino-* + Gr. *lithos* stone]. A nasal stone or concretion.

rhinolithiasis (ri″no-lĭ-thi′ah-sis). A condition associated with the formation of rhinoliths.

rhinologist (ri-nol′o-jist). An expert in rhinology.

rhinology (ri-nol′o-je) [*rhino-* + *-logy*]. The sum of knowledge regarding the nose and its diseases.

rhinomanometer (ri″no-mah-nom′e-ter) [*rhino-* + *manometer*]. A manometer for measuring the amount of nasal obstruction.

rhinometaplasty (ri″no-met′ah-plas″te). Rhinoplasty.

rhinometer (ri-nom′e-ter) [*rhino-* + Gr. *metron* measure]. An instrument for measuring the nose or its cavities.

rhinomiosis (ri″no-mi-o′sis) [*rhino-* + Gr. *meiōsis* diminution]. Operative reduction of the size of the nose.

rhinommectomy (ri″nom-mek′to-me) [*rhin-* + Gr. *omma* eye + *ektomē* excision]. Excision of the inner canthus of the eye.

rhinomycosis (ri″no-mi-ko′sis). Fungal infection of the nasal mucosa.

rhinonecrosis (ri″no-ne-kro′sis). Necrosis of the nasal bones.

rhinoneurosis (ri″no-nu-ro′sis). A neurosis or functional disease of the nose.

rhinopathia (ri″no-path′e-ah). Rhinopathy. **r. vasomoto′ria,** hay fever.

rhinopathy (ri-nop′ah-the) [*rhino-* + Gr. *pathos* disease]. Any disease of the nose.

rhinopharyngeal (ri″no-fah-rin′je-al). Nasopharyngeal.

rhinopharyngitis (ri″no-far″in-ji′tis). Inflammation of the nasopharynx. **r. mu′tilans,** gangosa.

rhinopharyngocele (ri″no-fah-ring′go-sēl). A tumor, usually an aerocele, of the nasopharynx.

rhinopharyngolith (ri″no-fah-ring′go-lith) [*rhino-* + Gr. *pharynx* pharynx + *lithos* stone]. Calculus of the nasal pharynx.

rhinopharynx (ri″no-far′inks). Nasopharynx.

rhinophonia (ri″no-fo′ne-ah) [*rhino-* + Gr. *phōnē* voice]. A nasal twang or quality of voice.

rhinophore (ri′no-fōr) [*rhino-* + Gr. *phoros* bearing]. A nasal cannula to facilitate breathing.

rhinophyma (ri″no-fi′mah) [*rhino-* + Gr. *phyma* growth]. A form of rosacea characterized by nodular swelling and congestion of the nose.

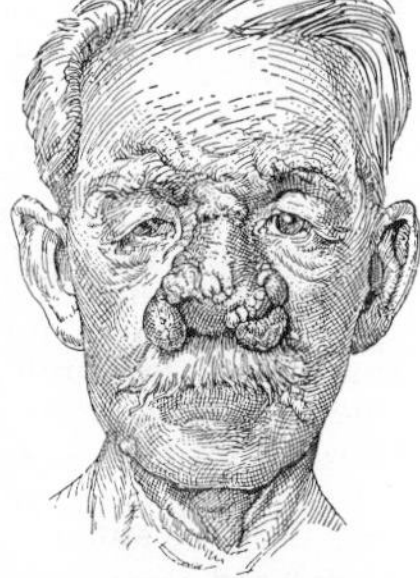
Rhinophyma (Homans).

rhinoplastic (ri″no-plas′tik). Pertaining to rhinoplasty.

rhinoplasty (ri′no-plas″te) [*rhino-* + Gr. *plassein* to form]. The formation of a new nose out of tissue derived from another part. **Carpue's r.,** Indian r. **dactylocostal r.,** the use of tissue from the finger and a costal cartilage in plastic repair of the nose. **English r.,** that in which a nose is formed out of flaps from the cheeks. **Indian r.,** the formation of a nose from a flap taken from the forehead. **Italian r., tagliacotian r.** See *Italian operation*, under *operation*.

rhinopolypus (ri″no-pol′ĭ-pus). A nasal polyp.

rhinoptia (ri-nop′she-ah). Internal strabismus.

rhinoreaction (ri″no-re-ak′shun). The nasal tuberculin reaction; an exudation appearing on the nasal mucous membrane after the application thereto of a solution of tuberculin in patients affected with tuberculosis. Called also *Moeller's reaction.*

rhinorrhagia (ri″no-ra′je-ah) [*rhino-* + Gr. *rhēgnynai* to burst forth]. Nosebleed; epistaxis.

rhinorrhaphy (ri-nor′ah-fe) [*rhino-* + Gr. *rhaphē* suture]. An operation for epicanthus performed by excising a fold of skin from the nose and closing the opening with sutures.

rhinorrhea (ri″no-re′ah) [*rhino-* + Gr. *rhoia* flow]. The free discharge of a thin nasal mucus. **cerebrospinal r.,** discharge of cerebrospinal fluid through the nose.

rhinosalpingitis (ri″no-sal-pin-ji′tis) [*rhino-* + Gr. *salpinx* tube + *-itis*]. Inflammation of the nasal mucosa and the eustachian tube.

rhinoscleroma (ri″no-skle-ro′mah) [*rhino-* + Gr. *sklērōma* a hard swelling]. A granulomatous disease involving the nose and nasopharynx. The growth forms hard patches or nodules, which tend to increase in size and are painful on pressure. The disease occurs in Egypt, Eastern Europe and Central and South America and is ascribed to the presence of the *Klebsiella rhinoscleromatis.*

rhinoscope (ri′no-skōp) [*rhino-* + Gr. *skopein* to examine]. A speculum for use in nasal examinations.

rhinoscopic (ri″no-skop′ik). Pertaining to rhinoscopy.

rhinoscopy (ri-nos′ko-pe). The examination of the nasal passages, either through the anterior nares (*anterior r.*) or through the nasopharynx (*posterior r.*). **median r.,** examination of the nasal cavity and the openings of the ethmoid cells, etc., by means of a long nasal speculum.

rhinosporidiosis (ri″no-spo-rid″e-o′sis). The condition produced by *Rhinosporidium seeberi,* characterized by the development of large pedunculated polyps on the mucosa of the nose, eyes, ears and sometimes on the penis and vagina. It is endemic in India and Ceylon and sporadic in other parts of the world.

Rhinosporidium seeberi (ri″no-spo-rid′e-um se′ber-i). A fungus which causes rhinosporidiosis. Called also *R. kinealyi.*

rhinostegnosis (ri″no-steg-no′sis) [*rhino-* + Gr. *stegnōsis* obstruction]. Obstruction of a nasal passage.

rhinostenosis (ri″no-ste-no′sis). Narrowing of a nasal passage.

rhinotomy (ri-not′o-me) [*rhino-* + Gr. *tomē* a cutting]. Incision into the nose for drainage.

rhinovaccination (ri″no-vak″sĭ-na′shun). The application of vaccine or other immunizing material to the mucous membrane of the nose.

rhinovirus (ri″no-vi′rus). One of a group of viral agents isolated in Salisbury, England, and considered to be etiologically related to the common cold. Several immunological types occur.

rhiotin (ri′o-tin). A biotin vitamin which is active for *Rhizobium* but not for yeast, is avidin-combinable, and stable to acid or neutral autoclaving.

Rhipicephalus (ri″pĭ-sef′ah-lus) [Gr. *rhipis* fan + *kephalē* head]. A genus of cattle ticks, species of which are the agents in transmitting *Babesia* of cattle fever and other disease. **R. appendicula′ris,** the brown tick, transmits the *Theileria parva* of East African Coast fever in cattle and *Rickettsia rickettsii* in man. **R. bur′sa** transmits the *Babesia ovis,* which causes icterohematuria of sheep. **R. capen′sis,** an African species found on cattle and horses. **R. decolora′tus,** a species which is regarded as the transmitter of *Bor-*

relia theileri, boutonneuse fever, Kenya tick fever and possibly Rocky Mountain spotted fever. **R. evert'si,** an African species found on horses and cattle. **R. sanguin'eus,** the brown dog tick, a species found on many domestic animals. It transmits *Rickettsia rickettsii* in man and *Babesia canis*. **R. si'mus,** the black pitted tick, a species which transmits the *Theileria parva* of East African Coast fever.

rhitid-. For words beginning thus, see those beginning rhytid-.

Rhiz. Abbreviation for *Rhizobium*.

rhizagra (ri-zag'rah) [*rhizo-* + Gr. *agra* seizure]. An ancient forceps which was used for extracting roots of teeth.

rhizanesthesia (ri-zan"es-the'ze-ah). Anesthesia produced by injecting a local anesthetic into the cavity of the spinal arachnoid.

rhizo- [Gr. *rhiza* root]. Combining form denoting relationship to a root.

Rhizobiaceae (ri-zo"be-a'se-e). A family of Schizomycetes (order Eubacteriales), made up of rod-shaped, sparsely flagellated cells without endospores. It includes three genera, *Agrobacterium*, *Chromobacterium*, and *Rhizobium*.

Rhizobium (ri-zo'be-um). A genus of microorganisms of the family Rhizobiaceae, order Eubacteriales, made up of gram-negative, rod-shaped symbiotic nitrogen-fixing bacteria, producing nodules on the roots of leguminous plants and fixing free nitrogen in this symbiosis. It includes six species, *R. japo'nicum*, *R. leguminosa'rum*, *R. lupi'ni*, *R. melilo'ti*, *R. phase'oli*, and *R. trifo'lii*.

rhizode (ri'zōd) [Gr. *rhiza* root + *eidos* form]. A submerged multibacillary bulb or rootlike structure extending from the bottom of a colony of microorganisms into the medium, such as a submerged mycelium of Nocardia.

rhizodontropy (ri"zo-don'tro-pe) [*rhizo-* + Gr. *odous* tooth + *tropos* a turn]. The fixation of an artificial crown upon the natural root of a tooth.

Rhizoglyphus (ri-zog'lĭ-fus). A genus of mites. **R. parasit'icus,** the coolie-itch mite, which lives on the ground in India and causes sore feet.

rhizoid (ri'zoid) [*rhizo-* + Gr. *eidos* form]. Rootlike; resembling a root.

rhizoidal (ri-zoi'dal). Rhizoid.

rhizome (ri'zōm) [Gr. *rhizōma* root stem]. The subterraneous root stock of a plant.

rhizomelic (ri-zo-mel'ik) [*rhizo-* + Gr. *melos* limb]. Pertaining to or involving the hip joint and shoulder joint.

rhizomeningomyelitis (ri"zo-mĕ-nin"go-mi"ĕ-li'tis). Radiculomeningomyelitis.

rhizoneure (ri'zo-nūr) [*rhizo-* + Gr. *neuron* nerve]. A nerve cell which forms a nerve root.

rhizoplast (ri'zo-plast) [*rhizo-* + Gr. *plastos* formed]. Axoneme, def. 2.

Rhizopoda (ri-zop'o-dah) [*rhizo-* + Gr. *pous* foot]. A subclass of the Sarcodina, having lobose or reticulate pseudopodia, and including the amebae.

Rhizopus (ri-zo'pus). A genus of the Mucoraceae. **R. equi'nus** has been found in several species of domestic animals. **R. ni'ger, R. ni'gricans,** has been found in mycosis of the nose, ear, tongue, and lungs.

rhizotomist (ri-zot'o-mist). In Greek medicine, a vagrant gatherer of medicinal herbs and simples.

rhizotomy (ri-zot'o-me) [*rhizo-* + Gr. *tomē* a cutting]. Interruption of the roots of spinal nerves within the spinal canal. **anterior r.,** division of the anterior or motor spinal nerve roots: done for relief of essential hypertension. **posterior r.,** division of the posterior or sensory spinal nerve roots: done for relief of intractable pain.

rhodanate (ro'dah-nāt). A salt of thiocyanic acid.

rhodinol (ro'dĭ-nol). Citronellol.

rhodium (ro'de-um) [Gr. *rhodon* rose]. A hard and rare metal of the platinum group; atomic number, 45; atomic weight, 102.905; symbol, Rh.

Rhodnius prolixus (rod'ne-us pro-lik'sus). A South American bug which is capable of transmitting *Trypanosoma cruzi*.

rhodo- (ro'do) [Gr. *rhodon* rose]. Combining form meaning red.

Rhodobacteriineae (ro"do-bak"ter-e-i'ne-e). A suborder of Schizomycetes (order Pseudomonadales), made up of spherical or rod-, vibrio-, or spiral-shaped cells containing bacteriochlorophyll or other green pigments resembling chorophyll, and usually one or more carotenoid pigments. It includes three families, *Athiorhodaceae*, *Chlorobacteriaceae*, and *Thiorhodaceae*.

rhodocyte (ro'do-sīt). Erythrocyte.

rhodogenesis (ro"do-jen'e-sis) [*rhodo-* + Gr. *genesis* production]. The restoration of the purple tint to rhodopsin after it has become bleached by the action of light.

Rhodomicrobium (ro"do-mi-kro'be-um). A genus of microorganisms of the family Hyphomicrobiaceae, order Hyphomicrobiales, made up of ovoid cells connected by filaments, growing in colonies which are salmon pink to orange red. The type species is *R. vanniel'ii*.

rhodophane (ro'do-fān) [*rhodo-* + Gr. *phainein* to show]. A red pigment, or chromophane, from the retinal cones of birds and fishes.

rhodophylactic (ro"do-fi-lak'tik). Tending to preserve or restore the retinal purple; pertaining to rhodophylaxis.

rhodophylaxis (ro"do-fi-lak'sis) [*rhodo-* + Gr. *phylaxis* defense]. The supposed property of the retinal epithelium of protecting and increasing the power of the retinal purple to regain its color after bleaching.

rhodoporphyrin (ro"do-por'fĭ-rin). A porphyrin, $C_{32}H_{34}O_4N_4$, derived from chlorophyll.

Rhodopseudomonas (ro"do-su"do-mo'nas). A genus of microorganisms of the family Athiorhodaceae, suborder Rhodobacteriineae, order Pseudomonadales, occurring as motile, spherical or rod-shaped cells. It includes four species, *R. capsula'ta*, *R. gelatino'sa*, *R. palus'tris*, and *R. spheroi'des*.

rhodopsin (ro-dop'sin) [*rhodo-* + Gr. *opsis* vision]. The visual purple: a photosensitive purple-red chromoprotein in the retinal rods which is bleached to visual yellow by light, thereby producing stimulation of the retinal sensory endings. It is a conjugated protein, the prosthetic group of which is vitamin A.

Rhodospirillum (ro"do-spi-ril'lum). A genus of microorganisms of the family Athiorhodaceae, suborder Rhodobacteriineae, order Pseudomonadales, occurring as motile, spiral-shaped cells. It includes four species, *R. ful'vum*, *R. molischia'num*, *R. photome'tricum*, and *R. ru'brum*.

Rhodothece (ro"do-the'se). A genus of microorganisms of the family Thiorhodaceae, suborder Rhodobacteriineae, order Pseudomonadales, occurring as single spherical cells, each with a wide capsule. The type species is *R. pen'dens*.

rhodotoxin (ro"do-tok'sin). A poisonous compound from the leaves of *Rhododendron hymenanthes*.

rhombencephalon (rom"ben-sef'ah-lon) [Gr. *rhombos* rhomb + *enkephalos* brain]. 1. [N A, B N A] The posterior portion of the brain, or hindbrain, including the medulla oblongata, pons, and cerebellum. 2. The most caudal of the three primary vesicles formed in embryonic development of the brain, which later divides into metencephalon and myelencephalon.

rhombocoele (rom'bo-sēl) [Gr. *rhombos* rhomb + *koilia* cavity]. The terminal distention of the canal of the spinal cord.

rhomboid (rom'boid) [Gr. *rhombos* rhomb + *eidos* form]. Shaped like a rhomb, or kite. **Michaelis's r.,** a diamond-shaped area over the posterior aspect of the pelvis formed by the dimples of the posterior-superior spines of the ilia, the lines formed by the gluteal muscles, and the groove at the end of the spine.

rhonchal, rhonchial (rong′kal, rong′ke-al). Pertaining to, or of the nature of, a ronchus.

rhonchus (rong′kus) [L.; Gr. *rhonchos* a snoring sound]. A rattling in the throat; also a dry, coarse rale in the bronchial tubes, due to a partial obstruction. See *rale.*

Rhopalopsyllus cavicola (ro″pah-lo-sil′us kah-vik′o-lah). The South American cavy flea which transmits *Pasteurella pestis.*

rhotacism (ro′tah-sizm) [Gr. *rhōtakizein* to misuse the letter *r*]. The incorrect use or overuse of *r* sounds; stammering.

rhotanium (ro-ta′ne-um). A gold-palladium alloy said to possess the same physical qualities as platinum.

rhubarb (roo′barb). The dried rhizome and root of *Rheum officinale,* used in fluidextract or aromatic tincture as a cathartic.

Rhuphos (roo′fos). See *Rufus of Ephesus.*

Rhus (rus) [L., gen. *rhois*]. A genus of anacardiaceous trees and shrubs, many of them poisonous. Contact with certain species produces a severe dermatitis. The most important poisonous species are *R. venena′ta,* or poison sumac; *R. toxicoden′dron,* or poison ivy: and *R. diversilo′ba,* or poison oak. Extracts of the leaves and twigs of these plants (rhus extracts, poison ivy extract) have been used in the prophylaxis and treatment of poison ivy dermatitis.

rhyostomaturia (ri″o-sto″mah-tu′re-ah) [Gr. *rhein* to flow + *stoma* mouth + *ouron* urine + *-ia*]. The excretion of urinary elements by the salivary glands.

rhyparia (ri-pa′re-ah) [Gr. "filth"]. Sordes; filth.

rhypophagy (ri-pof′ah-je) [Gr. *rhypos* filth + *phagein* to eat]. The eating of filth.

rhypophobia (ri″po-fo′be-ah) [Gr. *rhypos* filth + *phobein* to be affrighted by]. Morbid dread of filth.

rhythm (rith′m) [L. *rhythmus;* Gr. *rhythmos*]. A measured movement; the recurrence of an action or function at regular intervals. **alpha r.,** a uniform rhythm of waves in the normal electroencephalogram, showing an average frequency of 10 per second. Also called *Berger r.* **auriculoventricular r.,** nodal r. **Berger r.,** alpha r. **beta r.,** a rhythm in the electroencephalogram consisting of waves smaller than those of the alpha rhythm, having a frequency of 25 per second. **cantering r.,** gallop r. **circadian r.,** the regular recurrence in cycles of approximately 24 hours from one stated point to another, as certain biological activities which occur at that interval, regardless of constant darkness or other conditions of illumination. **circus r.,** circus movement or contraction; a movement travelling in circular fashion around a ring of muscle. **coupled r.,** an abnormal relation between the pulse and heart beat in which every other beat of the heart produces no pulse at the wrist. **fetal r.,** embryocardia. **gallop r.,** a cardiac rhythm with an accentuated extra sound, the three heart sounds creating the auscultatory effect of a canter; usually heard only when the heart rate is rapid. **gamma r.,** a rhythm of waves in the electroencephalogram having a frequency of 50 per second. **idioventricular r.,** an automatic rhythm developed in the ventricles of the heart in complete heart block. **nodal r.,** heart rhythm initiated by the auriculoventricular node of the heart. **nyctohemeral r.,** a day and night rhythm. **pendulum r.,** alternation in the rhythm of the heart sounds in which the diastolic sound is equal in time, character, and loudness to the systolic sound, the beat of the heart resembling the tick of a watch. It is indicative of commencing weakness of the heart. **reversed r.,** a condition of cardiac rhythm in which the ventricular beat immediately precedes the auricular beat. **sinus r.,** normal heart rhythm originating in the sinoauricular node. **triple r.,** the cadence produced when three heart sounds recur in successive cardiac cycles. **ventricular r.,** the ventricular contractions which occur in cases of complete heart block.

rhythmeur (rith-mer′). A device for making rhythmic interruptions of the current in a roentgen-ray machine.

rhythmical (rith′me-kal). Characterized by rhythm.

rhythmicity (rith-mis′ĭ-te). A state of rhythmical contraction.

rhythmophone (rith′mo-fōn) [Gr. *rhythmos* rhythm + *phōnē* voice]. An instrument for magnifying the sounds of the heart beat.

rhythmotherapy (rith″mo-ther′ah-pe) [Gr. *rhythmos* rhythm + *therapeia* treatment]. The use of rhythm in treating disease, as the beating of time in treating stammering.

rhytidectomy (rit″ĭ-dek′to-me) [Gr. *rhytis* wrinkle + *ektomē* excision]. Excision of skin for the elimination of wrinkles.

rhytidoplasty (rit′ĭ-do-plas″te). Plastic surgery for the elimination of wrinkles from the skin.

rhytidosis (rit″ĭ-do′sis) [Gr. *rhytidōsis; rhytis* wrinkle]. A wrinkling of the cornea; one of the signs of approaching death.

rib (rib). Any one of the paired bones, twelve on either side, that extend from the thoracic vertebrae toward the median line on the ventral aspect of the trunk. Collectively called *costae* [N A]. **abdominal r's, asternal r's,** false r's. **bicipital r.,** an anomalous rib resulting from fusion of the anterior part of the seventh cervical vertebra with the first thoracic rib. **cervical r.,** a supernumerary rib arising from a cervical vertebra. **false r's,** the lower five ribs on either side, which are not directly attached to the sternum. Called also *costae spuriae.* **floating r's,** the lower two ribs on either side, which ordinarily have no ventral attachment. **slipping r.,** a rib whose attaching cartilage is repeatedly dislocated. **spurious r's,** false r's. **sternal r's,** true r's. **Stiller's r.,** a preternaturally movable tenth rib. **true r's,** the upper seven ribs on either side, which are connected to the sides of the sternum by their costal cartilages. Called also *costae verae* [N A]. **vertebral r's,** floating r's. **vertebrocostal r's,** the upper three false ribs of either side, articulating with the vertebrae and connected by cartilage to the ipsilateral seventh rib. **vertebrosternal r's,** true r's. **Zahn's r's.** See *lines of Zahn.*

Ribbert's theory (rib′erts) [Moritz Wilhelm Hugo *Ribbert,* German pathologist, 1855–1920]. See under *theory.*

ribbon (rib′un). A band-like structure. **r. of Reil,** lemniscus medialis.

Ribera's method (re-ba′rahz) [José *Ribera* y Sans, Spanish surgeon, 1853–1912]. See under *method.*

Ribes's ganglion (rēbz) [François *Ribes,* French surgeon, 1800–1864]. See under *ganglion.*

ribodesose (ri-bo′des-ōs). A sugar occurring in thymonucleic acid.

riboflavin (ri″bo-fla′vin). The heat-stable factor of the vitamin B complex, 6,7-dimethyl-9-[D-1′-ribityl]-isoalloxazin, $C_{17}H_{20}N_4O_6$, formerly called lactoflavin, vitamin B_2, and vitamin G. It occurs in milk, muscle, liver, kidney, eggs, grass, malt, and various algae. Riboflavin promotes the growth of rats, and prevents the occurrence of a nutritional cataract in rats and a specific dermatitis in turkeys. For human beings, 2 to 10 mg. per day seems to be the average dose, although the requirement during pregnancy and lactation is higher.

ribonuclease (ri″bo-nu′kle-ās). An enzyme which catalyzes the depolymerization of ribonucleic acid.

ribopyranose (ri″bo-pi′rah-nōs). Ribose.

ribose (ri′bōs). An aldopentose, $CH_2OH(CHOH)_3$-

CHO. It is found in and characterizes yeast nucleic acid (ribose nucleic acid).

ribosome (ri′bo-sōm). One of the minute granules, seen with the electron microscope, largely nucleic acid in composition, usually attached to the membranes of the endoplasmic reticulum of a cell, and presumably the site of protein synthesis.

R.I.C. Abbreviation for *Royal Institute of Chemistry*.

rice (rīs). The cereal plant, *Oryza sativa;* also its seed or grain. The grain consists mainly of starch, and is used as a food and a dusting powder. **white r.,** rice from which the outer brown coats have been removed. A diet composed too exclusively of white rice is apt to produce beriberi.

Richards (rich′ardz), Dickinson W. United States physician, born 1895; co-winner, with Werner T. O. Forssmann and André F. Cournand, of the Nobel prize for medicine and physiology in 1956, for developing new techniques to measure more precisely lung and heart function.

Richardson's sign (rich′ard-sunz) [Sir Benjamin Ward *Richardson*, London physician, 1828–1896]. See under *sign.*

Richet's aneurysm (re-shāz′) [Didier Dominique Alfred *Richet*, French surgeon, 1816–1891]. A fusiform aneurysm.

Richet's bandage, fascia (re-shāz′) [Charles Robert *Richet*, French physiologist, 1850–1935, noted for his discovery of anaphylaxis; winner of the Nobel prize for medicine and physiology in 1913]. See under *bandage* and *fascia.*

Richter's hernia (rik′terz) [August Gottlieb *Richter*, surgeon in Göttingen, 1742–1812]. See under *hernia.*

Richter-Monro line (rik′ter mon-ro′). See *Monro-Richter*, and under *line.*

ricin (ri′sin). A poisonous substance (phytotoxin) found in the seeds of the castor oil plant (*Ricinus communis*).

ricinism (ri′sĭ-nizm). Intoxication caused by inhalation or ingestion of a poisonous principle of castor bean, producing superficial inflammation of the respiratory mucosa with hemorrhages into the lungs, or edema of the gastrointestinal tract with hemorrhages.

ricinoleated (ri″sin-o′le-āt″ed). Treated with sodium ricinoleate.

Ricinus (ris′ĭ-nus) [L.]. The name of a genus of euphorbiaceous plants. The seeds of *R. commu′nis*, or castor oil plant, are highly poisonous but afford castor oil. The leaves of the castor oil plant are galactagogue.

rickets (rik′ets) [thought to be a corruption of Gr. *rhachitis* a spinal complaint]. A condition caused by deficiency of vitamin D, especially in infancy and childhood, with disturbance of normal ossification. The disease is marked by bending and distortion of the bones under muscular action, by the formation of nodular enlargements on the ends and sides of the bones, by delayed closure of the fontanels, pain in the muscles, sweating of the head, and degeneration of the liver and spleen. Vitamin D and sunlight together with an adequate diet are curative, provided the parathyroid glands are functioning properly. **acute r.,** infantile scurvy. **adult r.,** a disease resembling rickets affecting adults. **beryllium r.,** a form of rickets produced by adding beryllium to an otherwise normal diet. **fat r.,** a form in which the infant is plump and seems well nourished. **fetal r.,** achondroplasia. **glissonian r.,** rickets as described by Glisson. **hemorrhagic r.,** infantile scurvy. **hepatic r.,** a rickets-like condition with cirrhosis of the liver. **late r.,** rickets occurring in older children. **lean r.,** rickets with wasting and progressive emaciation. **renal r.,** a condition characterized by rachitic changes in the skeleton and resulting from dysfunction of the kidneys. See *renal osteodystrophy.* **scurvy r.,** rachitic changes in the skeleton associated with infantile scurvy. **tardy r.,** late r.

Ricketts' organism (rik′ets) [Howard Taylor *Ricketts*, American pathologist, 1871–1910]. See *Rickettsia.*

rickettsemia (rik″ets-e′me-ah). The presence of rickettsiae in the blood.

Rickettsia (rĭ-ket′se-ah) [Howard Taylor *Ricketts*]. A genus of the tribe Rickettsieae, family Rickettsiaceae, order Rickettsiales, made up of small rod-shaped to coccoid, often pleomorphic microorganisms occurring intracytoplasmically or free in the lumen of the gut in lice, fleas, ticks, and mites, by which they are transmitted to man and other animals. The various species are separated into a typhus group, a spotted fever group, a tsutsugamushi group, and a miscellaneous group. **R. akamu′shi,** *R. tsutsugamushi.* **R. ak′ari,** the etiologic agent of rickettsialpox, transmitted by the mite Allodermanyssus from the reservoir of infection in house mice. **R. austra′lis,** the etiologic agent of North Queensland tick typhus, possibly transmitted by Ixodes ticks. **R. cono′rii,** the etiologic agent of boutonneuse fever (Marseilles fever, Mediterranean fever), and possibly also Indian tick typhus, Kenya typhus, South African tick bite fever, and Siberian tick typhus; transmitted by Rhipicephalus and Haemaphysalis ticks. **R. diapor′ica,** *Coxiella burnetii.* **R. moo′seri,** *R. typhi.* **R. murico′la,** *R. typhi.* **R. nippon′ica, R. orienta′lis,** *R. tsutsugamushi.* **R. pedic′uli,** *R. quintana.* **R. prowaze′kii,** the etiologic agent of epidemic, louse-borne, classic or European typhus fever, and the latent infection Brill's disease. **R. quinta′na,** the probable etiologic agent of trench fever, Wolhynian fever, or 5-day fever observed in World Wars I and II, and transmitted by the human body louse. **R. rickett′sii,** the etiologic agent of Rocky Mountain spotted fever, São Paulo typhus, and Tobia fever. Transmitted by Dermacentor, Rhipicephalus, Haemaphysalis, Amblyomma and Ixodes ticks. **R. tsutsuga-mu′shi,** the etiologic agent of scrub typhus of the western Pacific area, tsutsugamushi disease, Japanese river fever, Kedani fever, and rural typhus, transmitted by mites of the genus Trombicula from rodent reservoirs of infection. **R. ty′phi,** the etiologic agent of flea-borne murine typhus. **R. wolhyn′ica,** *R. quintana.*

rickettsia (rĭ-ket′se-ah), pl. *rickett′siae.* An individual organism of the genus *Rickettsia.*

Rickettsiaceae (rĭ-ket″se-a′se-e). A family of the order Rickettsiales, class Microtatobiotes, made up of small rod-shaped, ellipsoidal, coccoid, or diplococcus-shaped, often pleomorphic microorganisms often occurring intracellularly in arthropods, by which they are transmitted to man and other animals, causing disease. It includes three tribes, *Ehrlichieae, Rickettsieae,* and *Wolbachieae.*

rickettsiae (rik-et′se-e). Plural of *rickettsia.*

rickettsial (rĭ-ket′se-al). Caused by rickettsiae.

Rickettsiales (rĭ-ket″se-a′lēz). An order of class Microtatobiotes, made up of small rod-shaped or coccoid, often pleomorphic microorganisms occurring as elementary bodies which are usually intracellular but are occasionally facultatively or exclusively extracellular. Found as parasites in both vertebrates and invertebrates, which may serve as vectors, they may be pathogenic for both man and other animals. The order includes four families, *Anaplasmataceae, Bartonellaceae, Chlamydiaceae,* and *Rickettsiaceae.*

rickettsialpox (rĭ-ket′se-al-poks″). A febrile disease marked by a vesiculopapular eruption, resembling chickenpox clinically and caused by *Rickettsia akari.* Recognized first in New York, the condition is also called Kew Garden fever.

rickettsicidal (rĭ-ket″sĭ-si′dal). Destructive to rickettsiae.

Rickettsieae (rik″et-si′e-e). A tribe of the family Rickettsiaceae, order Rickettsiales, class Microtatobiotes, made up of small pleomorphic, mostly intracellular organisms occurring as parasites in arthropods and causing disease in vertebrate hosts. It includes two genera, *Coxiella* and *Rickettsia.*

Rickettsiella (rĭ-ket″se-el′lah) [*rickettsia* + *-ella* diminutive ending]. A genus of tribe Wolbachieae, family Rickettsiaceae, order Rickettsiales, made up of minute intracellular rickettsia-like organisms, parasitic on the Japanese beetle (*Popillia japonica*) and non-pathogenic for mammals. The type species is *R. popil′liae.*

rickettsiosis (rĭ-ket″se-o′sis). Infection with rickettsiae.

rickettsiostatic (rĭ-ket″se-o-stat′ik). Inhibiting the growth and activity of rickettsiae.

Ricolesia (ri″ko-le′ze-ah) [*Ri*ckettsia + J. D. W. A. *Coles*]. A genus of the family Chlamydiaceae, order Rickettsiales, made up of coccoid organisms, occurring as four species, *R. bo′vis, R. ca′prae, R. conjuncti′vae,* and *R. lestoquar′dii,* producing a keratoconjunctivitis in cattle, goats, fowl, and swine, respectively.

Ricord's chancre (re-korz′) [Philippe *Ricord,* French physician, 1800–1889]. See under *chancre.*

rictal (rik′tal). Pertaining to a fissure.

rictus (rik′tus) [L.]. 1. A fissure or cleft. 2. A gaping, as of the mouth.

Riddoch's reflex (rid′oks) [George *Riddoch,* British neurologist, 1889–1947]. See under *reflex.*

Rideal-Walker coefficient (rid′e-al-waw′ker) [Samuel *Rideal,* English chemist, 1863–1929; J. F. Ainslie *Walker,* English chemist]. Phenol coefficient.

ridge (rij). A projection or projecting structure. See also *crest* and *crista.* **alveolar r., residual,** the bony ridge remaining after disappearance of the alveoli from the alveolar process following removal or loss of the teeth. **alveolar r's of mandible,** juga alveolaria mandibulae. **alveolar r's of maxilla,** juga alveolaria maxillae. **basal r.,** cingulum. **bicipital r., anterior,** crista tuberculi minoris. **bicipital r., external,** crista tuberculi majoris. **bicipital r., internal,** crista tuberculi minoris. **bicipital r., outer, bicipital r., posterior,** crista tuberculi majoris. **buccocervical r.,** a ridge on the buccal surface near the neck of a deciduous molar tooth. **buccogingival r.,** buccocervical r. **bulbar r's,** spiral endocardial thickenings in the bulbus cordis that fuse and form the bulbar septum, separating the bulbus cordis into aortic and pulmonary trunks. **cerebral r's of cranial bones,** juga cerebralia ossis cranii. **deltoid r.,** tuberositas deltoidea humeri. **dental r.,** any linear elevation on the crown of a tooth named according to the surface on which it is located, such as buccal or lingual, or in recognition of some other characteristic. **dermal r's,** cristae cutis. **epicondylic r., lateral,** supracondylar r., lateral. **epicondylic r., medial,** supracondylar r., medial. **epipericardial r.,** a ventral ridge separating the ventral ends of the branchial arches in the embryo from the pericardial swelling. **gastrocnemial r.,** a ridge on the posterior surface of the femur, giving attachment to the gastrocnemius muscle. **genital r.,** the more medial portion of the urogenital ridge, which gives rise to the gonad. **gluteal r. of femur,** tuberositas glutea femoris. **r. of humerus,** tuberositas deltoidea humeri. **incisal r.,** that portion of the crown of an anterior tooth which makes up the actual incisal portion. **interarticular r. of head of rib,** crista capitis costae. **interosseous r. of fibula,** margo interosseus fibulae. **interosseous r. of radius,** margo interosseus radii. **interosseous r. of tibia,** margo interosseus tibiae. **interosseous r. of ulna,** margo interosseus ulnae. **intertrochanteric r.,** crista intertrochanterica. **interureteric r.,** a smooth ridge extending across the bladder from one ureteral opening to the other, produced by a transverse bundle of muscle fibers. **linguocervical r.,** a ridge on the lingual surface near the neck of an anterior tooth. **linguogingival r.,** linguocervical r. **longitudinal r. of hard palate,** raphe palati. **Mall's r.,** pulmonary r. **mammary r.,** a longitudinal epidermal thickening in the embryo from a pectoral part of which the mammary gland develops. **r. of mandibular neck,** a blunt, smooth ridge passing obliquely downward and forward from the mandibular condyle on the medial surface of the mandibular neck and ramus, serving as their buttress. **marginal r's,** rounded borders of the enamel which form the mesial and distal margins of the occlusal surfaces of posterior teeth and of the lingual surfaces of anterior teeth. **mesonephric r.,** the more lateral portion of the urogenital ridge, which gives rise to the mesonephros. **middle r. of femur,** linea pectinea. **milk r.,** mammary r. **mylohyoid r.,** linea mylohyoidea mandibulae. **r. of neck of rib,** crista colli costae. **r. of nose,** agger nasi. **oblique r.** 1. A variable linear elevation obliquely crossing the occlusal surface of a maxillary molar tooth, formed by union of two triangular ridges. 2. Tuberositas masseterica. **oblique r's of scapula,** lineae musculares scapulae. **palatine r's, transverse,** plicae palatinae transversae. **pectoral r.,** crista tuberculi majoris. **pterygoid r.,** crista infratemporalis. **pulmonary r.,** a ridge along the common cardinal vein in the embryo, which develops into the pleuropericardial membrane. **radial r. of wrist,** eminentia carpi radialis. **rough r. of femur,** linea aspera femoris. **semicircular r. of parietal bone, inferior,** linea temporalis inferior ossis parietalis. **semicircular r. of parietal bone, superior,** linea temporalis superior ossis parietalis. **sublingual r.,** frenulum linguae. **superciliary r.,** arcus superciliaris. **supinator r.,** crista musculi supinatoris. **supplemental r.,** an abnormal ridge on the surface of a tooth. **supracondylar r., lateral,** a prominent, curved ridge on the lateral surface of the humerus, giving attachment in front to the brachioradialis and extensor carpi radialis longus muscles. **supracondylar r., medial,** a prominent, curved ridge on the medial surface of the humerus, giving attachment to the brachialis muscle in front and to the medial head of the triceps behind. **supraorbital r.,** arcus superciliaris. **suprarenal r.,** a caudal projection of the dorsal portion of the pleuroperitoneal membrane of the embryo, in which the adrenal cortex develops. **taste r's,** papillae foliatae. **tentorial r.,** a ridge on the upper inner surface of the cranium, to which the tentorium is attached. **transverse r.,** a linear elevation extending transversely across the occlusal surface of a posterior tooth, formed by union of two triangular ridges. **transverse r's of sacrum,** lineae transversae ossis sacri. **transverse r's of vaginal wall,** plicae vaginales. **trapezoid r.,** linea trapezoidea. **triangular r.,** a linear elevation descending from the tip of a cusp toward the central part of the occlusal surface of a posterior tooth. **tubercular r. of sacrum,** crista sacralis mediana. **ulnar r. of wrist,** eminentia carpi ulnaris. **urethral r.,** carina urethralis vaginae. **urogenital r.,** a longitudinal ridge or fold in the embryo, lateral to the root of the mesentery, which later subdivides longitudinally into the mesonephric and the genital ridge. **wolffian r.,** mesonephric r.

ridgel (rid′jel). Ridgling.

ridgling (rij′ling). A man or animal with only one testis.

Ridley's sinus (rid′lēz) [Humphrey *Ridley,* English anatomist, 1653–1708]. See under *sinus.*

Rieckenberg's phenomenon, reaction (re′-ken-bergz). See under *phenomenon.*

Riedel's disease, lobe, struma (re′delz) [Bernhard Moritz Carl Ludwig *Riedel,* surgeon in Jena, 1846–1916]. See under the nouns.

Rieder's cell (re′derz) [Hermann *Rieder,* German roentgenologist, 1858–1932]. See under *cell.*

Riegel's purse, symptom, test meal (re′-gelz) [Franz *Riegel,* German physician, 1843–1904]. See under the nouns.

Riegler's test (rēg′lerz) [Emanuel *Riegler*, German chemist, 1854–1929]. See under *tests*.

Riehl's melanosis (rēlz) [Gustav *Riehl*, Vienna dermatologist, 1855–1943]. See under *melanosis*.

Riesman's myocardosis, pneumonia, sign (rēs′manz) [David *Riesman*, American physician, 1867–1940]. See under the nouns.

Rieux's hernia (re-uhz′) [Léon *Rieux*, French surgeon]. Retrocecal hernia.

R.I.F. Abbreviation for *right iliac fossa*.

Riga's disease (re′gahz) [Antonio *Riga*, Italian physician, 1832–1919]. See under *disease*.

Riga-Fede disease [Antonio *Riga*, Francesco *Fede*, Italian physicians of the nineteenth century]. See under *disease*.

Rigal's suture (re-galz′) [Joseph Jean Antoine *Rigal*, French surgeon, 1797–1865]. See under *suture*.

rigidity (rĭ-jid′ĭ-te) [L. *rigiditas; rigidus* stiff]. Stiffness or inflexibility, chiefly that which is abnormal or morbid. **anatomical r.**, rigidity of the cervix uteri in labor, without pathologic condition of the cervix, so that it dilates to only a limited extent, beyond which uterine contractions are of no avail. **cadaveric r.**, rigor mortis. **cerebellar r.**, stiffness of the body and limbs, due to a lesion of the middle lobe of the cerebellum. **clasp-knife r.**, increased resistance of the extensors (induced by passive flexion of a joint), which suddenly gives way on exertion of further pressure. **cogwheel r.**, rigidity of a muscle which gives way in a series of little jerks when the muscle is passively stretched. **decerebrate r.**, rigid extension of an animal's legs as a result of section of the brain stem in the region of the red nucleus and above Deiters' nucleus. **hemiplegic r.**, rigidity of the paralyzed limbs in hemiplegia. **lead-pipe r.**, the diffuse muscular rigidity seen in paralysis agitans. **muscle r.**, tetanus. **mydriatic r.**, Westphal's pupillary reflex. **pathologic r.**, rigidity of the cervix uteri in labor from some disease. **postmortem r.**, rigor mortis. **spasmodic r.**, rigidity of the cervix uteri due to spasmodic contraction.

rigor (ri′gor) [L.]. 1. A chill. 2. Rigidity. **acid r.**, coagulation of the protein of muscle produced by acids. **heat r.**, rigidity of muscles induced by heat. **r. mor′tis,** the stiffening of a dead body, as a result of depletion of adenosine triphosphate in the muscle fibers. **r. nervo′rum,** tetanus. **r. tre′mens,** paralysis agitans. **water r.**, a condition of rigor in a muscle caused by immersing it in water.

rim (rim). A border, or edge. **bite r.**, occlusion r. **occlusion r.**, a border constructed on temporary or permanent denture bases for the purpose of recording the maxillomandibular relation and for positioning the teeth. **record r.**, occlusion r.

rima (ri′mah), pl. *ri′mae* [L.]. A cleft or crack; used in anatomical nomenclature as a general term to designate such an opening. **r. a′ni, r. clu′nium,** crena ani. **r. cornea′lis** [B N A], the cleft or groove in the scleral margin into which the limbus corneae fits. Omitted in N A. **ri′mae cu′tis,** sulci cutis. **r. glot′tidis** [N A, B N A], the elongated opening between the vocal folds and between the arytenoid cartilages. Called also *fissure of glottis*. **r. glot′tidis cartilagin′ea,** pars intercartilaginea rimae glottidis. **r. glot′tidis membrana′cea,** pars intermembranacea rimae glottidis. **intercartilaginous r.**, pars intercartilaginea rimae glottidis. **intermembranous r.**, pars intermembranacea rimae glottidis. **r. o′ris** [N A, B N A], the longitudinal opening of the mouth, between the lips. Called also *oral fissure*. **r. palpebra′rum** [N A, B N A], the longitudinal opening between the eyelids. Called also *palpebral fissure*. **r. puden′di** [N A, B N A], the cleft between the labia majora in which the urethra and vagina open. Called also *pudendal fissure*. **r. respirato′ria,** pars intercartilaginea rimae glottidis. **r. vestib′uli** [N A, B N A], the space between the right and left vestibular folds of the larynx. **r. voca′lis,** pars intermembranacea rimae glottidis. **r. vul′vae,** r. pudendi.

rimae (ri′me) [L.]. Plural of *rima*.

rimal (ri′mal). Pertaining to a rima.

rimifon (rim′ĭ-fon). Trade mark for a preparation of isoniazid.

rimose (rim′ōs) [L. *rima* crack]. Marked by cracks and fissures.

rimula (rim′u-lah), pl. *rim′ulae* [L.]. A minute fissure, especially of the cord or brain.

rinderpest (rint′er-pest) [Ger. *Rinder* cattle + *pest* plague]. Cattle plague.

rinderseuche (rint″er-zoi′kĕ) [Ger.]. Hemorrhagic septicemia in cattle.

Rindfleisch's cells, folds (rint′flĭsh-ez) [Georg Eduard *Rindfleisch*, German physician, 1836–1908]. See under *cell* and *fold*.

ring (ring) [L. *annulus, circulus, orbiculus*]. 1. Any annular or circular organ or area. For names of specific anatomical structures, see under *anulus*. 2. In chemistry, a collection of atoms united in a continuous or closed chain, or circle. **Abbe's r's,** catgut rings for supporting the ends of intestine which are to be stitched together in intestinal anastomosis. **abdominal r., deep,** anulus inguinalis profundus. **abdominal r., external,** anulus inguinalis superficialis. **abdominal r., internal,** anulus inguinalis profundus. **abdominal r., superficial,** anulus inguinalis superficialis. **Albl's r.**, a ring-shaped shadow observed in a roentgenogram of the skull, caused by an aneurysm of a cerebral artery. **amnion r.**, the attached margin of the amnion about the umbilicus of the fetus. **annular r's,** round or oval opacities surrounding a translucent area in the roentgenogram, indicative of cavitation of the lung in tuberculosis. Called also *pleural rings*. **auricular r.**, the ring surrounding the opening between the auricle and ventricle of the primitive vertebrate heart; represented in the mammalian heart by the auriculoventricular node. **Bandl's r.**, retraction r. **benzene r.** (Kekulé, 1865), the closed hexagon of carbon atoms in benzene (C_6H_6), from which the different benzene compounds are derived by replacement of the hydrogen atoms. **Bickel's r.**, Waldeyer's tonsillar ring. **Braun's r.**, retraction r. **Brokaw r.**, a ring of rubber tubing threaded with catgut strands, used in intestinal anastomosis. **Cabot's r's.** See *Cabot's ring bodies*, under *body*. **Cannon's r.**, a tonic contraction ring often visible in the right half of the transverse colon. **carbocyclic r.**, a chemical ring which includes only carbon atoms. **casting r.**, refractory flask. **ciliary r.**, orbiculus ciliaris. **ciliary r. of iris,** anulus iridis major. **conjunctival r.**, anulus conjunctivae. **constriction r.**, a contracted area of the uterus, allegedly possible at any level, occurring where the resistance of the uterine contents is slight, as over a depression in the contour of the fetal body, or below the presenting part. Cf. *retraction r.* **contact r.**, the wound inflicted at the site of entrance of a bullet on the surface of the body. **contraction r.** See *constriction r.* and *retraction r.* **coronary r.**, coronary cushion. **crural r.**, anulus femoralis. **Döllinger's r.**, an elastic ring around the circumference of the cornea formed by a thickening of Descemet's membrane. **femoral r.**, anulus femoralis. **fibrous r., interpubic,** discus interpubicus. **fibrous r's of heart,** anuli fibrosi cordis. **fibrous r. of intervertebral disc,** anulus fibrosus disci intervertebralis. **Fleischer keratoconus r.**, an incomplete annular pigmented line at the base of the cone in keratoconus. **Fleischer-Strümpell r.**, Kayser-Fleischer r. **furan r.**, a ring containing four atoms of carbon and one of oxygen. **germ r.**, the proliferating marginal zone of the early blastoderm that is about to become the lips of the blastopore. **glaucomatous r.**, a light yellowish ring around the optic disk in glaucoma, indicating atrophy of the choroid. **Gräfenberg's r.,** a flexible ring of silver wire inserted into the uterus to prevent conception. **greater r. of iris,** anulus iridis major. **heterocyclic r.,** a chemical ring which includes atoms of different elements. **homocyclic r.,** a chemical ring in which all the members are atoms of the same element. **infancy r.,** a line of arrested calcification of tooth enamel which is formed at about one year of age. **inguinal r., deep,** anulus inguinalis profundus. **inguinal r., external,** anulus inguinalis superficialis. **inguinal r., internal,** anulus inguinalis profundus. **inguinal r., superficial,** anulus inguinalis superficialis. **isocyclic r.,** homocyclic r. **Kayser-Fleischer r.,** a greenish pigmented ring at the outer margin of the cornea, seen in Westphal's pseudosclerosis. **lesser r. of iris,** anulus iridis minor. **Liesegang r's,** a series of rings formed by the precipitate of a colloid gel by the action of a solution of a salt, as seen in biliary calculi. **Löwe's r.,** a ring in the visual field caused by the macula lutea. **Lower's r's,** anuli fibrosi cordis. **lymphoid r.,** Waldeyer's tonsillar ring. **Maxwell's r.,** a ring resembling Löwe's, but smaller and fainter. **mitro-aortic r.,** a band of muscle fibers surrounding both the mitral and aortic orifices of the heart. **neonatal r.,** a line of demarcation in a tooth, indicating the transition from prenatal to postnatal calcification. **Newton's r's,** colored rings seen on the surface of thin, transparent membranes, as soap-bubbles, due to light wave interference. **Ochsner's r.,** a ring of mucous membrane around the opening of the pancreatic duct. **pleural r's,** annular r's. **pyran r.,** a ring containing five atoms of carbon and one of oxygen. **retraction r.,** a ringlike thickening occurring at the junction of the isthmus and fundus uteri in abnormal or prolonged labor, obstructing expulsion of the fetus. Cf. *constriction r.* **signet r.,** the stage in the life-cycle of a malarial plasmodium in an erythrocyte consisting of a thin ring of protoplasm with a nucleus at one side. **spermatorrheal r.,** a ring worn on the penis to prevent erections. **tendinous r., common,** anulus tendineus communis. **tracheal r's,** cartilagines tracheales. **tympanic r.,** anulus tympanicus. **umbilical r.,** anulus umbilicalis. **vascular r.,** a congenital anomaly of the aortic arch and its tributaries, the vessels forming a ring about the trachea and esophagus, instead of lying anterior to them, and causing varying degrees of compression of those passages. **r. of Vieussens,** limbus fossae ovalis. **Vossius' lenticular r.,** a ring of opacity in the crystalline lens caused by pressure of the pupillary margin against the lens. **Waldeyer's tonsillar r.,** the circular series of lymphoid tissue formed by the lingual, pharyngeal, and faucial tonsils. **Zinn's r.,** anulus tendineus communis.

ring-bone (ring′bōn). A bonelike callus on the pastern bone of a horse, resulting from inflammation. Frequently it extends into the interphalangeal joints, causing lameness. When the joint is not involved, the condition is sometimes called *false ring-bone.* **low r.,** buttress foot.

Ringer's mixture, solution (ring′erz) [Sydney *Ringer,* English physiologist, 1835–1910]. See under *solution.*

ringworm (ring′wurm). A popular name for a group of diseases of the skin of man and domestic animals, marked by the formation of ring-shaped pigmented patches covered with vesicles or scales, and caused by dermatophytes. See also *tinea.* **r. of the beard,** tinea barbae. **black-dot r.,** tinea capitis caused by *Trichophyton violaceum,* with a distinctive appearance resulting from the breaking of the hairs at the scalp surface. **r. of the body,** tinea corporis. **Bowditch Island r., Burmese r., Chinese r.,** tinea imbricata. **crusted r.,** favus. **r. of feet,** tinea pedis. **honeycomb r.,** favus. **hypertrophic r.,** granuloma trichophyticum. **Indian r.,** tinea imbricata. **r. of the nails,** onychomycosis. **oriental r.** 1. Tinea imbricata. 2. Eczema marginatum. **r. of the scalp,** tinea capitis. **Tokelau r.,** tinea imbricata.

Rinne's test (rin′nez) [Heinrich Adolf *Rinne,* German otologist, 1819–1868]. See under *tests.*

Riolan's arch, bones, muscle, nosegay (re″-o-lanz′) [Jean *Riolan,* French physician and physiologist, 1580–1657]. See under the nouns.

riomitsin (ri″o-mit′sin). Oxytetracycline.

Ripault's sign (re-pōz′) [Louis Henry Antoine *Ripault,* French physician, 1807–1856]. See under *sign.*

R.I.P.H. Abbreviation for *Royal Institute of Public Health.*

R.I.P.H.H. Abbreviation for *Royal Institute of Public Health and Hygiene.*

risa (ri′sah). Trade mark for a preparation of radioiodinated serum albumin.

Risley's prism (riz′lēz) [Samuel D. *Risley,* American ophthalmologist, 1845–1920]. See under *prism.*

Risquez's sign (ris-kāz′) [Francisco *Risquez,* Venezuelan pathologist, 1856–1941]. See under *sign.*

ristocetin (ris″to-se′tin). An antibiotic substance produced by the fermentation of *Nocardia lurida:* used in treatment of infections by gram-positive cocci.

risus (ri′sus) [L.]. Laughter. **r. cani′nus, r. sardon′icus,** a grinning expression produced by spasm of the facial muscles.

ritalin (rit′ah-lin). Trade mark for preparations of methylphenidate.

Ritgen maneuver, method (rit′gen) [Ferdinand August Max Franz von *Ritgen,* German gynecologist, 1787–1867]. See under *maneuver.*

Ritter's disease (rit′erz) [Gottfried *Ritter* von Rittersheim, German physician, 1820–1883]. Dermatitis exfoliativa infantum.

Ritter's law, tetanus (rit′erz) [Johann Wilhelm *Ritter,* German physicist, 1776–1810]. See under *law* and *tetanus.*

Ritter-Rollet phenomenon (rit′er-ro-la′) [J. W. *Ritter*]. See under *phenomenon.*

Ritter-Valli law [J. W. *Ritter;* Eusebio *Valli,* Italian physiologist, 1726–1816]. See under *law.*

rivalry (ri′val-re). A state of competition or antagonism. **binocular r., retinal r.,** the apparent alternate displacement of two figures when viewed together, there being no fusion into a continuous picture of the images of the two eyes.

Rivalta's disease (re-val′tahz) [Sebastiano *Rivalta,* Italian veterinary surgeon, 1852–1893]. Actinomycosis.

Rivalta's reaction, test (re-val′tahz) [Fabio *Rivalta,* pathologist in Bologna, born 1863]. See under *reaction.*

Riva-Rocci sphygmomanometer (re″vah-ro′-che) [Scipione *Riva-Rocci,* Italian physician, 1863–1937]. See under *sphygmomanometer.*

Riverius' potion (re-ve′re-us). See *Rivière's potion,* and under *potion.*

Rivière's potion (re″ve-ārz′) [Lazare *Rivière,* French physician, 1589–1655]. See under *potion.*

Riviere's sign (riv-ērz′) [Clive *Riviere,* British physician, 1873–1929]. See under *sign.*

Rivinus's ducts, foramen, gland, membrane, notch (re-ve′nus) [August Quirinus *Rivinus,* anatomist and botanist in Leipzig, 1652–1723]. See under the nouns.

rivulose (riv′u-lōs) [L. *rivus* a brook]. Marked by wavy lines: said of bacterial colonies.

rivus (ri′vus), pl. *ri′vi* [L.]. A brook, or little stream. **r. lacrima′lis** [N A, B N A], the pathway by which the tears reach the lacrimal lake from the excretory ductules of the lacrimal gland.

riziform (riz′ĭ-form). Resembling grains of rice.

RKY. Abbreviation for *roentgen kymography.*

RLF. Abbreviation for *retrolental fibroplasia.*

R.L.L. Abbreviation for *right lower lobe* (of lungs).

R.M. Abbreviation for *respiratory movement.*

R.M.A. Abbreviation for *right mento-anterior* position of the fetus.

R.M.L. Abbreviation for *right middle lobe* (of lungs).

R.M.N. Abbreviation for *Registered Mental Nurse* (England and Wales).

R.M.O. Abbreviation for *Regional Medical Officer* (British).

R.M.P. Abbreviation for *right mentoposterior* position of the fetus.

R.M.T. Abbreviation for *right mentotransverse* position of the fetus.

R.N. Abbreviation for *Registered Nurse.*

Rn. Chemical symbol for *radon.*

RNA (ar′en-a). Ribonucleic acid (q.v. under *acid*). **messenger RNA, soluble RNA, transfer RNA.** See definitions on *ribonucleic acid,* under *acid.*

R.N.M.S. Abbreviation for *Registered Nurse for the Mentally Sub-Normal.*

R.O.A. Abbreviation for *right occipito-anterior* position of the fetus.

roach (rōch). See *Blatta.*

roaring (rōr′ing). A condition in the horse marked by a rough sound on inspiration and sometimes on expiration. It is due to some obstruction in the respiratory tract or to paralysis of the vocal cords.

robalate (ro′bah-lāt). Trade mark for preparations of dihydroxyaluminum aminoacetate.

robaxin (ro-bak′sin). Trade mark for preparations of methocarbamol.

Robbins (rob′binz), Frederick C. American pediatrician, born 1916; co-winner, with John F. Enders and Thomas H. Weller, of the Nobel prize in medicine and physiology for 1954, for the discovery that poliomyelitis viruses multiply in human tissue.

Robert's ligament (ro-bārz′) [Cesar Alphonse *Robert,* French surgeon, 1801–1862]. A fasciculus of fibers from the ligamentum cruciatum posterius genu to the meniscus lateralis.

Robert's pelvis (ro′bārts) [Heinrich Ludwig Ferdinand *Robert,* German gynecologist, 1814–1874]. See under *pelvis.*

Roberts' test (rob′erts) [Sir William *Roberts,* English physician, 1830–1899]. See under *tests.*

Robertson's pupil (rob′ert-sunz). See *Argyll Robertson,* and under *pupil.*

Robertson's sign (rob′ert-sunz) [William Egbert *Robertson,* American physician, 1869–1956]. See under *sign.*

robin (ro′bin). A poisonous substance (phytotoxin) found in the bark of the North American locust tree (*Robinia pseudacacia*).

Robin's myeloplax (ro-baz′) [Charles Philippe *Robin,* French anatomist, 1821–1885]. An osteoclast.

Robinson's circle (rob′in-sunz) [Fred Byron *Robinson,* American anatomist, 1857–1910]. See under *circle.*

Robinson's disease (rob′in-sunz) [Andrew R. *Robinson,* dermatologist in New York, 1845–1924]. See under *disease.*

Robiquet's paste (rob″e-kāz′) [Pierre Jean *Robiquet,* French physician, 1780–1840]. See under *paste.*

Robison ester (ro′bĭ-sun) [Robert *Robison,* British chemist, 1884–1941]. See under *ester.*

roborant (rob′o-rant) [L. *roborans* strengthening]. Conferring strength; strengthening.

Robson (rob′sun). See *Mayo Robson.*

roccal (ro′kal). Trade mark for a preparation of benzalkonium chloride.

rod (rod). A straight, slim mass of substance: specifically, one of the rodlike bodies of the retina. See *retinal r's.* **Corti's r's,** rodlike bodies in a double row (inner and outer rods), having their heads joined and their bases on the basilar membrane widely separated so as to form a spiral tunnel, called the tunnel of Corti. **enamel r's,** the parallel rods or prisms forming the enamel of teeth. They are enclosed in a sheath of organic matter (the enamel rod sheath, or prism sheath) and are embedded in the interprismatic or cement substance. **germinal r.,** a sporozoite. **r's of Heidenhain,** the rodlike cells of the renal tubules. **König's r's,** a series of steel bars each of which gives a note of certain pitch when struck. **Maddox r's,** a set of parallel cylindrical glass rods used in testing for heterophoria. **Meckel's r.,** Meckel's cartilage. **muscle r's,** myofibrillae. **Reichmann's r.,** a short ivory rod with circular grooves and intervening projections: used in auscultatory percussion of the stomach. **retinal r's,** highly specialized cylindrical neuroepithelial cells containing rhodopsin; with the visual cones they form the light-sensitive elements of the retina.

rodenticide (ro-den′tĭ-sīd). 1. Destructive to rodents. 2. Any agent for destroying rodents.

rodentine (ro-den′tīn). Pertaining to a rodent.

Rodman's operation (rod′manz) [William L. *Rodman,* Philadelphia surgeon, 1854–1916]. See under *operation.*

rodonalgia (ro″do-nal′je-ah) [Gr. *rhodon* rose + *-algia*]. Erythromelalgia.

Roederer's obliquity (ra′der-erz) [Johann Georg *Roederer,* German obstetrician, 1727–1763]. See under *obliquity.*

roentgen (rent′gen) [for Wilhelm Conrad *Röntgen,* German physicist, 1845–1923, who discovered roentgen rays in 1895; winner of the Nobel prize in physics for 1901]. The international unit of x- or γ-radiation. It is the quantity of x- or gamma radiation such that the associated corpuscular emission per 0.001293 Gm. of air produces in air ions carrying 1 electrostatic unit of electrical charge of either sign.

roentgenism (rent′gen-izm). 1. The therapeutic application of roentgen rays. 2. The ill effect of the roentgen rays; disease induced by misuse of roentgen rays.

roentgenization (rent″gen-i-za′shun). Exposure or subjection to the action of roentgen rays.

roentgenize (rent′gen-iz). To apply the roentgen rays.

roentgenkater (rent″gen-kah′ter) [Ger.]. Roentgen intoxication.

roentgenkymography (rent″gen-ki-mog′rah-fe). Roentgen kymography.

roentgenocardiogram (rent″gen-o-kar′de-o-gram). A polygraphic tracing of cardiac pulsation made by the roentgen rays.

roentgenocinematography (rent″gen-o-sin″ĕ-mah-tog′rah-fe). Moving picture roentgenography.

roentgenogram (rent-gen′o-gram). A film produced by roentgenography. **cephalometric r.,** a roentgenogram of the full lateral view of the head, for the purposes of making cranial measurements.

roentgenograph (rent′gen-o-graf). Roentgenogram.

roentgenography (rent″gen-og′rah-fe). Photography by means of roentgen rays. Special techniques for roentgenography of different areas of the body have been given specific names, such as angiography, angiocardiography, pneumoencephalography, portography, pyelography, etc. **body section r.,** a special technique to show in detail images of structures lying in a predetermined plane of tissue, while blurring or eliminating detail in images of structures in other planes. Called also *analytical roentgenography* and *sectional roentgenography.* Various mechanisms and methods for such roentgenography have been given various names, such as *laminagraphy, laminography, planigraphy, radiotomy, stratigraphy, tomography,* and *vertigraphy.* **double contrast r.,** mucosal relief roentgenography. **mass r.,** examination by x-rays of the general population or of large groups of the population. **miniature r.,** the taking of miniature x-ray photographs. **miniature r., mass,** the use of miniature x-ray film in mass roentgenography. **mucosal relief r.,** a technique for revealing any abnormality of the intestinal mucosa, involving injection and evacuation of a barium enema, followed by inflation of the intestine with air under light pressure. The light coating of barium on the walls of the inflated intestine in the roentgenogram reveals clearly even small abnormalities. **selective r.,** roentgenography of certain segments of the population, chosen on some specific basis such as symptoms, or some other basis. **serial r.,** the taking of several exposures of a selected area at arbitrary intervals. **spot-film r.,** the making of localized instantaneous roentgenographic exposures during the course of a fluoroscopic examination.

roentgenokymograph (rent″gen-o-ki′mo-graf). An instrument for recording movements of internal structures shown roentgenographically.

roentgenologist (rent″gen-ol′o-jist). A physician who devotes himself to diagnosis and treatment by the roentgen rays.

roentgenology (rent″gen-ol′o-je) [*roentgen rays* + *-logy*]. The branch of radiology which deals with the diagnostic and therapeutic use of roentgen rays.

roentgenolucent (rent″gen-o-lu′sent). Allowing roentgen rays to pass through.

roentgenometer (rent″gen-om′e-ter). A skiameter.

roentgenometry (rent″gen-om′e-tre). 1. Measurement of the penetrating or therapeutic power of the roentgen rays. 2. The direct measurement of structures shown in the roentgenogram without the necessity of correcting for magnification.

roentgenopaque (rent″gen-o-pāk′). Not allowing roentgen rays to pass through.

roentgenoparent (rent″gen-o-par′ent). Visible by means of the roentgen rays.

roentgenoscope (rent-gen′o-skōp). A fluoroscope; an apparatus for examining the body by means of the fluorescent screen excited by the roentgen rays.

roentgenoscopy (rent″gen-os′ko-pe) [*roentgen rays* + Gr. *skopein* to examine]. Examination by means of roentgen rays; fluoroscopy.

roentgenotherapy (rent″gen-o-ther′ah-pe) [*roentgen rays* + Gr. *therapeia* treatment]. Therapeutic use of the roentgen rays.

roeteln (ret′eln) [Ger.]. Rubella.

Roffo's test (rof′ōz) [Angel H. *Roffo*, pathologist, in Buenos Aires, 1882–1947]. See under *tests.*

Roger's disease, reaction, symptom (ro-zhāz′) [Henri Louis *Roger*, French physician, 1809–1891]. See under the nouns.

Roger-Josué test (ro-zha′ zho-zu-a′) [H. L. *Roger;* Otto *Josué*, French physician, born 1869]. See *blister test*, under *tests.*

Rogers' sphygmomanometer (roj′erz) [Oscar H. *Rogers*, American physician, born 1857]. See under *sphygmomanometer.*

Röhl's marginal corpuscles (rālz) [Wilhelm *Röhl*, German physician, 1881–1929]. See under *corpuscle.*

roka (ro′kah). A tree of Arabia and Africa, *Trichilia emetica:* it affords various remedial products.

Rokitansky's disease, tumor, etc. (ro″kĭ-tan′skēz) [Karl Freiherr von *Rokitansky*, pathologist in Vienna, 1804-1878]. See under the nouns.

rolandic (ro-lan′dik). Described by or named in honor of Luigi *Rolando*, Italian anatomist, 1773–1831, as the rolandic *area, convolution, fissure*, etc. See under the nouns.

Rolando (ro-lan′do). See *rolandic.*

rolandometer (ro″lan-dom′e-ter). An instrument for determining the positions of the various fissures of the surface of the brain.

rolicton (ro-lik′ton). Trade mark for a preparation of amisometradine.

rolitetracycline (ro″le-tet″rah-si′klēn). Chemical name: N-(pyrrolidinomethyl) tetracycline, a highly soluble form of tetracycline used for intravenous or intramuscular injection.

roll (rōl). A cylindrical structure. **cotton r.,** a small cylinder of cotton, for use in dentistry. **iliac r.,** a mass shaped like a sausage, located in the left iliac fossa and produced by induration of the walls of th e sigmoid fossa. Called also *sigmoid sausage.* **scleral r.,** the posterior lip of the internal scleral furrow to which the ciliary body is attached.

roller (rōl′er). A cylinder of cotton, linen, or flannel rolled up for surgeons' or dressers' use. **massage r.,** a proprietary apparatus for use in electric massage.

Roller's central nucleus (rol′erz) [Christian Friedrich Wilhelm *Roller*, German neurologist, 1802–1878]. See under *nucleus.*

Rolleston's rule (rol′es-tonz) [Sir Humphrey *Rolleston*, London physician, 1862–1944]. See under *rule.*

Rollet's chancre (ro-lāz′) [Joseph Pierre *Rollet*, French surgeon and syphilographer, 1824–1894]. Mixed chancre.

Rollet's stroma (rol′ets) [Alexander *Rollet*, Austrian physiologist, 1834–1903]. See under *stroma.*

Rollier's treatment (rol-yāz′) [Auguste *Rollier*, Swiss physician, 1874–1954]. See under *treatment.*

Romaña's sign (ro-mahn′yahz) [Cecilio *Romaña*, Brazilian physician]. See under *sign.*

romanopexy (ro-man′o-pek″se) [L. *romanum* the sigmoid + Gr. *pēxis* fixation]. Sigmoidopexy.

romanoscope (ro-man′o-skōp). A speculum for examining the sigmoid flexure.

Romanovsky's (Romanowsky's) method, stain (ro″man-of′skēz) [Dimitri Leonidov *Romanovsky*, Russian physician, 1861–1921]. See under *stain.*

Romberg's disease, sign (rom′bergz) [Moritz Heinrich *Romberg*, physician in Berlin, 1795–1873]. See under *disease* and *sign.*

Romberg-Howship sign, symptom [M. H. *Romberg;* John *Howship*]. See under *sign.*

Romberg-Paessler syndrome [M. H. *Romberg;* H. *Paessler*, German physician]. See under *syndrome.*

rombergism (rom′berg-izm). The tendency of a patient to sway when he closes his eyes while standing still with his feet close together (Romberg's sign), associated with loss of sensory inflow, as in tabes dorsalis.

Römer's experiment, reaction, test (re′merz) [Paul Heinrich *Römer*, hygienist in Greifswald, 1876–1916]. See under *experiment* and *tests.*

romilar (ro′mil-ar). Trade mark for preparations of dextromethorphan hydrobromide.

Rommelaere's law, sign (rom″el-a-erz′) [Guillaume *Rommelaere*, Belgian physician, 1836–1916]. See under *law* and *sign.*

rongeur (raw-zhur′) [Fr. "gnawing, biting"]. See under *forceps.*

Rönne's nasal step (ren′ēz). A steplike defect in the nasal side of the visual field seen in glaucoma.

röntgenography (rent″gen-og′rah-fe). Roentgenography.

roof (roof). A covering structure. **r. of orbit,** paries superior orbitae. **r. of skull,** calvaria. **r. of tympanum,** tegmen tympani.

room (ro͞om). A place in a building enclosed and set apart for occupancy. **delivery r.,** a hospital room to which an obstetrical patient is taken for delivery. **intensive therapy r.,** a hospital unit in which are concentrated special equipment and skilled personnel for seriously ill patients requiring immediate and continuous care and observation. **labor r.,** predelivery room. **operating r.,** a room in a hospital used for surgical operations. **postdelivery r.,** a recovery room for the care of obstetrical patients immediately after delivery. **predelivery r.,** a hospital room where an obstetrical patient remains during the first stage of labor, i.e., from the time the pains begin until she is ready for delivery. **recovery r.,** a hospital unit adjoining operating or delivery rooms, with special equipment and personnel for the care of postoperative or obstetrical patients until they may safely be returned to general duty nursing care in their own room or ward.

rooming-in (ro͞om′ing-in). The practice of keeping a newly born infant in a crib near the mother's bed, instead of in a nursery, during the hospital stay.

root (root). The lowermost part, or a structure by which something is firmly attached. For official names of various anatomical structures, see under *radix.* **anatomical r.,** the portion of a tooth that is covered by cementum. See *radix dentis* [N A]. **r. of ansa cervicalis, inferior,** radix inferior ansae cervicalis. **r. of ansa cervicalis, superior,** radix superior ansae cervicalis. **r. of arch of vertebra,** pediculus arcus vertebrae. **bitter r.,** gentian. **clinical r.,** that portion of a tooth below the clinical crown, being attached to gingiva or alveolus. **r. of clitoris,** crus clitoris. **cochlear r. of acoustic nerve,** radix inferior nervi vestibulocochlearis. **dandelion r.,** taraxacum. **deadly nightshade r.,** belladonna. **facial r.,** radix nervi facialis. **r. of hair,** radix pili. **insane r.,** hyoscyamus. **intermediate r. of olfactory trigone,** stria intermedia trigoni olfactorii. **licorice r.,** glycyrrhiza. **lingual r.,** that root of a mandibular molar tooth which is situated nearest the tongue. **long r. of ciliary ganglion,** ramus communicans nervi nasociliaris cum ganglione ciliari. **r. of lung,** radix pulmonis. **mandrake r.,** podophyllum. **r. of median nerve, lateral,** radix lateralis nervi mediani. **r. of median nerve, medial,** radix medialis nervi mediani. **r. of mesentery,** radix mesenterii. **motor r. of ciliary ganglion,** radix oculomotoria ganglii ciliaris. **motor r. of spinal nerves,** radix ventralis nervorum spinalium. **motor r. of trigeminal nerve,** radix motoria nervi trigemini. **r. of nail,** radix unguis. **r. of nose,** radix nasi. **oculomotor r. of ciliary ganglion,** radix oculomotoria ganglii ciliaris. **olfactory r., internal,** stria medialis trigoni olfactorii. **r. of optic tract, lateral,** radix lateralis tractus optici. **r. of optic tract, medial,** radix medialis tractus optici. **orizaba jalap r.,** ipomea. **orris r.,** orris. **palatine r.,** that root of a maxillary molar tooth which is situated nearest the palate. **r. of penis,** radix penis. **physiological r.,** the portion of a tooth proximal to the gingival crevice, or embedded in the dental alveolus. **puccoon r., red r.,** sanguinaria. **sensory r. of spinal nerves,** radix dorsalis nervorum spinalium. **sensory r. of trigeminal nerve,** radix sensoria nervi trigemini. **short r. of ciliary ganglion,** radix oculomotoria ganglii ciliaris. **r. of spinal nerves, anterior,** radix ventralis nervorum spinalium. **r. of spinal nerves, dorsal, r. of spinal nerves, posterior,** radix dorsalis nervorum spinalium. **r. of spinal nerves, ventral,** radix ventralis nervorum spinalium. **sweet r.,** glycyrrhiza. **r. of tongue,** radix linguae. **r. of tooth,** radix dentis. **vestibular r. of acoustic nerve,** radix superior nervi vestibulocochlearis. **vestibular r. of auditory nerve,** radix superior nervi vestibulocochlearis. **r. of vestibulocochlear nerve, inferior,** radix inferior nervi vestibulocochlearis. **r. of vestibulocochlear nerve, superior,** radix superior nervi vestibulocochlearis.

R.O.P. Abbreviation for *right occipitoposterior* position of the fetus.

Rorschach test (ror′shahk) [Herman *Rorschach,* Swiss psychiatrist, 1884–1922]. See under *tests.*

rosacea (ro-za′se-ah). A chronic disease affecting the skin of the nose, forehead, and cheeks, marked by flushing, followed by red coloration due to dilatation of the capillaries, with appearance of papules and acne-like pustules. Called also *acne erythematosa, acne rosacea.* **r. hypertroph′ica,** rhinophyma.

rosary (ro′zah-re). A structure resembling a string of beads. **rachitic r.,** rachitic beads.

rose (rōz) [L. *rosa*]. Any plant or species of the genus *Rosa.* The flowers of *Ro′sa damasce′na* afford the *oil of r.,* or attar of roses. **r. bengal,** a dye, the dichlor- or the tetrachlorerythrosin, $NaO.(C_6HI_2.O)_2C.C_6H_2Cl_2.COONa$.

Rose's position (ro′zez) [Frank Atcherly *Rose,* British surgeon]. See under *position.*

Rose's tamponade, tetanus (ro′zez) [Edmund *Rose,* German physician, 1836–1914]. See under *tamponade* and *tetanus.*

Rose's test (ro′zez) [Joseph Constantin *Rose,* German physician, 1826–1893]. See under *tests.*

rosein (ro′ze-in). Fuchsin.

Rosenbach's disease (ro′zen-bahks) [Anton Julius Friedrich *Rosenbach,* surgeon in Göttingen, 1842–1923]. Erysipeloid.

Rosenbach's disease, law, sign, test (ro′zen-bahks) [Ottomar *Rosenbach,* physician in Berlin, 1851–1907]. See under the nouns.

Rosenbach's tuberculin (ro′zen-bahks) [F. J. R. *Rosenbach,* German physician, 1843–1923]. See under *tuberculin.*

Rosenheim's enema, sign (ro′zen-hīmz) [Theodor *Rosenheim,* German physician, born 1860]. See under *enema* and *sign.*

Rosenmüller's body, fossa, gland, organ (ro′zen-mil″erz) [Johann Christian *Rosenmüller,* German anatomist, 1771–1820]. See *epoophoron, recessus pharyngeus,* and under *gland.*

Rosenthal's canal (ro′zen-tahlz) [Isidor *Rosenthal,* German physiologist, 1836–1915]. Canalis spiralis modioli.

Rosenthal's test (ro′zen-thahlz) [S. M. *Rosenthal,* American physician, born 1897]. See under *tests.*

Rosenthal's vein (ro′zen-tahlz) [Friedrich Christian *Rosenthal,* German anatomist, 1780–1829]. Vena basalis.

roseola (ro-ze′o-lah) [L.]. Any rose-colored rash; specifically *epidemic r.,* or rubeola. **r. choler′ica,** an eruption sometimes seen in cholera. **epidemic r.,** rubeola. **r. feb′rilis,** a nonpathognomonic erythema occurring in simple and malarial fevers. **idiopathic r.,** roseola occurring independently of any other disease. **r. infan′tilis, r. infan′tum,** exanthema subitum. **symptomatic r.,** roseola occurring as a symptom of some eruptive fever. **syphilitic r.,** an eruption of rose-colored spots in early secondary syphilis. Called also *syphilitic exanthem* and *macular syphilid,* **r. typho′sa,** the eruption of typhoid or typhus fever. **r. vacci′nia,** a rash sometimes occurring after vaccination.

roseolus (ro-ze′o-lus). Of the nature of a roseola, or rash.

Roser's needle, sign (ro′zerz) [Wilhelm *Roser,* German surgeon, 1817–1888]. See under *needle* and *sign.*

roset (ro-zet′). Rosette.

rosette (ro-zet′) [Fr.]. Any structure or formation resembling a rose, such as (*a*) the clusters of polymorphonuclear leukocytes around a globule of lysed nuclear material, as observed in the test for disseminated lupus erythematosus, or (*b*) a figure formed by the chromosomes in an early stage of mitosis (spireme). **r. of Golgi,** sporocyst. **malarial r.,** a stage in the asexual cycle of the malarial plasmodium at which the parasite has attained full growth and is arranged around the periphery of the erythrocyte in the form of small bodies resembling a roset and ready to break up into merozoites.

rosin (roz′in) [L. *resina*]. The resinous substance that remains after the distillation of the oil of turpentine from the fresh pitch of pine wood. It is chiefly abietic acid anhydride, $C_{44}H_{62}O_4$. It is used as an adhesive and stimulant addition to plasters. Called also *colophony*.

Rosin's test [Heinrich *Rosin*, Berlin physician, born 1863]. See under *tests*.

Rosmarinus (ros″mah-ri′nus) [L. "sea-dew"]. A genus of labiate plants. *R. officina′lis*, or common rosemary, affords the fragrant volatile oil of rosemary.

Ross's black spores, cycle (ros′ez) [Sir Ronald *Ross*, British protozoologist, 1857–1932, noted for his demonstration of the life history of the malarial parasite and proof of its transmission by the bite of the female anopheline mosquito; winner of the Nobel prize for medicine in 1902]. See under *spore* and *cycle*.

Ross's bodies (ros′ez) [Edward Halford *Ross*, English pathologist]. See under *body*.

Ross's test (ros′ez) [Hugh Campbell *Ross*, English pathologist, 1875–1926]. See under *tests*.

Rossbach's disease (ros′bahks) [Michael Josef *Rossbach*, German physician, 1842–1899]. Hyperchlorhydria.

Rossel's test (ros-elz′) [Otto *Rossel*, Swiss physician, 1875–1911]. See under *tests*.

Rossiella (ros″e-el′ah) [Sir Ronald *Ross*]. A genus of piroplasma-like organisms parasitic in the blood of certain animals. **R. ros′si,** a species found in the jackal in British East Africa.

Rossolimo's reflex (ros″o-le′mōz) [Gregorij Ivanovitsch *Rossolimo*, Russian neurologist, 1860–1928]. See under *reflex*.

Rostan's asthma (ros-tahz′) [Leon *Rostan*, Paris physician, 1790–1866]. Cardiac asthma.

rostellum (ros-tel′um), pl. *rostel′la* [L. "little beak"]. A small protuberance or beak; especially the fleshy anterior hook-bearing protuberance of the scolex of a tapeworm.

rostrad (ros′trad). 1. Toward a rostrum; situated nearer the rostrum in relation to a specific point of reference. 2. Cephalad.

rostral (ros′tral) [L. *rostralis*, from *rostrum* beak]. 1. Pertaining to or resembling a rostrum; having a rostrum or beak. 2. Rostrad.

rostralis (ros-tra′lis) [L.]. [B N A] Rostral. Omitted in N A.

rostrate (ros′trāt) [L. *rostratus* beaked]. Having a beaklike process.

rostriform (ros′trĭ-form) [L. *rostrum* beak + *forma* form]. Shaped like a beak.

rostrum (ros′trum), pl. *ros′trums* or *ros′tra* [L. "beak"]. A beaklike appendage or part. **r. cor′poris callo′si** [N A, B N A], **r. of corpus callosum,** the anterior and lower end of the corpus callosum. **sphenoidal r., r. sphenoida′le** [N A, B N A], the prominent ridge on the inferior surface of the sphenoid bone that articulates with a deep depression between the wings of the vomer.

R.O.T. Abbreviation for *right occipitotransverse* position of the fetus.

rot (rot). 1. Decay. 2. A disease of sheep, and sometimes of man, caused by *Distoma hepaticum*. **Barcoo r.,** desert sore. **black r.,** a condition sometimes seen in storage eggs, even when kept in a refrigerator. It is caused by *Proteus melanovogenes*. **drosera r.,** inherited phthisis of young children, said by some homeopathists to be curable by drosera. **foot r. of cattle,** a form of necrosis of the foot in cattle caused by infection with *Sphaerophorus necrophorus*. **foot r. of sheep,** a disease of the feet of sheep, marked by decay of the hoof and an offensive discharge. It is caused by *Sphaerophorus necrophorus*, especially on soft, wet pasture. **liver r.,** a disease of sheep and cattle caused by the liver fluke, *Fasciola hepatica*.

rotameter (ro-tam′e-ter). A flow-rate meter of variable area with a rotating float in a tapered tube, used for measuring the gases in administering an anesthetic.

rotary (ro′ter-e). Marked by or produced by rotation.

rotate (ro′tāt). To turn around an axis; to twist.

rotation (ro-ta′shun) [L. *rotatio*, *rotare* to turn]. The process of turning around an axis; movement of a body about its axis, called the *axis of r.* In labor, the turning of the baby's head through 90 degrees so that the long diameter of the head corresponds with the long diameter of the pelvic outlet. It should occur naturally, but if it does not the rotation must be accomplished manually or instrumentally by the obstetrician. See also *maneuver*. In dentistry, the rotation of a malturned tooth in its central axis into a normal position; also malposition of a tooth due to turning around a longitudinal axis. **molecular r.,** the figure obtained by multiplying the specific rotation by the molecular weight and dividing by 100. **specific r.,** the arc through which a substance rotates the plane of polarization.

rotatory (ro″tah-to′re). Occurring in or caused by rotation.

Rotch's sign (roch′es) [Thomas Morgan *Rotch*, physician in Boston, 1848–1914]. See under *sign*.

röteln (ret′eln) [Ger.]. Rubella.

rotenone (ro′te-nōn). A poisonous compound, $C_{23}H_{22}O_6$, from derris root and other roots: used as an insecticide and as a scabicide.

rotexed (ro′tekst). Rotated and bent to one side.

rotexion (ro-tek′shun). Act of rotating and flexing; also the state of being rotated and flexed.

Roth's disease (rōts) [Vladimir Karlovitsch *Roth*, Russian neurologist, 1848–1916]. Meralgia paraesthetica.

Roth's spots, vas aberrans (rōts) [Moritz *Roth*, Swiss physician, 1839–1914]. See under *spot*, and *ductuli aberrantes*.

Roth-Bernhardt disease, syndrome (rōt-bern′hart) [Vladimir K. *Roth*, Russian neurologist, 1848–1916; Martin *Bernhardt*, neurologist in Berlin, 1844–1915]. Meralgia paraesthetica.

rotlauf (rot′lowf) [Ger.]. Swine erysipelas.

Rotter's test (rot′erz) [H. *Rotter*, physician in Budapest]. See under *tests*.

Rottlera (rot′ler-ah). Kamala.

rottlerin (rot′ler-in). A yellowish, crystalline coloring matter, $(C_{11}H_{10}O_3)_3$, from kamala. Called also *mallotoxin*.

rotula (rot′u-lah) [L., dim. of *rota* wheel]. 1. The patella. 2. Any disklike bony process. 3. A troche or lozenge.

rotulad (rot′u-lad). Toward the patella, or the patellar aspect.

rotular (rot′u-lar). Pertaining to the patella.

rotz (rōts) [Ger.]. Glanders in horses.

rouge (ro͞ozh). A fine red powder composed of iron oxide (Fe_2O_3), usually in cake form but sometimes impregnated on paper or cloth; used in dentistry as a polishing agent for restorations of gold and precious metal alloys.

rouget du porc (roo-zha′ du pork′) [Fr.]. Swine erysipelas.

Rouget's bulb (roo-zhāz′) [Antoine D. *Rouget*, French physiologist]. See under *bulb*.

Rouget's cells (roo-zhāz′) [Charles Marie Benjamin *Rouget*, French physiologist, 1824–1904]. See under *cell*.

rough (ruf). Not smooth; having an irregular, uneven surface.

roughage (ruf′ij). Indigestible material such as fibers, cellulose, etc., in the diet.

Rougnon-Heberden disease (roon-yaw′-heb′-er-den) [Nicholas François *Rougnon*, French physician, 1727–1799; William *Heberden*, English physician, 1710–1801]. Angina pectoris.

rouleau (roo-lo′), pl. *rouleaux′* [Fr. "roll"]. A roll of red blood corpuscles like a pile of coins.

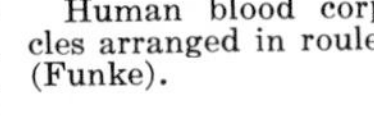
Human blood corpuscles arranged in rouleaux (Funke).

rouleaux (roo-lo′) [Fr.]. Plural of *rouleau.*

roundworm (rownd′-wurm). Ascaris.

roup (ro͞op). An infectious respiratory disease of poultry, marked by formation of a grayish-yellow exudate on the respiratory mucous surfaces; sometimes called *avian diphtheria* and *swelled head.* **nutritional r.,** a condition resembling roup that results from a diet deficient in vitamin A.

Rous's sarcoma, test (rows′es) [Francis Peyton *Rous,* New York pathologist, born 1879]. See under the nouns.

Roussel's sign (roo-selz′) [Theophile *Roussel,* French physician, 1816–1903]. See under *sign.*

Roussy-Dejerine syndrome (roo-se′ deh″zher-ēn′) [Gustav *Roussy,* French pathologist, 1874–1948; Joseph Jules *Dejerine,* French neurologist, 1849–1917]. Thalamic syndrome.

Roussy-Lévy disease (roo-se′ la′ve) [Gustav *Roussy*]. See under *disease.*

Roux's operation (ro͞oz) [Philibert Joseph *Roux,* Paris surgeon, 1780–1854]. See under *operation.*

Roux's serum, spatula (ro͞oz) [Pierre Paul Emile *Roux,* French bacteriologist, 1853–1933]. See under *serum* and *spatula.*

Roux's sign (ro͞oz) [César *Roux,* Swiss surgeon, 1857–1934]. See under *sign.*

Rovighi's sign (ro-vig′ēz) [Alberto *Rovighi,* Bologna physician, 1856–1919]. See under *sign.*

Rovsing's sign (rōv′sings) [Thorkild *Rovsing,* surgeon in Copenhagen, 1862–1927]. See under *sign.*

Rowntree and Geraghty's test (roun′tre; ger′ah-te) [Leonard George *Rowntree,* American physician, born 1883; John T. *Geraghty,* Baltimore physician, 1876–1924]. The phenolsulfonphthalein test.

RPF. Abbreviation for *renal plasma flow.*

rpm. Abbreviation for *revolutions per minute.*

RPS. Abbreviation for *renal pressor substance.*

R.Q. Abbreviation for *respiratory quotient.*

-rrhage, -rrhagia [Gr. *rhegnynai* to burst forth]. Word terminations denoting excessive flow.

-rrhea [Gr. *rhoia* flow]. Word termination denoting flow or discharge.

R.S.A. Abbreviation for *right sacro-anterior* position of the fetus.

R.S.B. Abbreviation for *Regimental Stretcher Bearer.*

R.Sc.A. Abbreviation for *right scapulo-anterior* position of the fetus.

R.S.C.N. Abbreviation for *Registered Sick Children's Nurse.*

R.Sc.P. Abbreviation for *right scapuloposterior* position of the fetus.

R.S.P. Abbreviation for *right sacroposterior* position of the fetus.

R.S.T. Abbreviation for *right sacrotransverse* position of the fetus.

R.T. Abbreviation for *reading test.*

R.U. Abbreviation for *rat unit.*

Ru. Chemical symbol for *ruthenium.*

rubber-dam (rub′er-dam). A sheet of thin latex rubber used by dentists to isolate a tooth from the fluids of the mouth during dental treatment.

rubedo (roo-be′do) [L.]. Blushing or other redness of the skin.

rubefacient (roo″bĕ-fa′shent) [L. *ruber* red + *facere* to make]. 1. Reddening the skin. 2. An agent that reddens the skin by producing active or passive hyperemia.

rubella (roo-bel′ah). 1. An acute exanthematous febrile virus disease with an eruption not unlike that of measles. After an incubation period of from one to three weeks the disease begins with slight fever and catarrhal symptoms, sore throat, pains in the limbs, and the appearance of an eruption of red papules similar to those of measles, but lighter in color, not arranged in crescentic masses, and disappearing without desquamation within a week. Called also *German measles* and *epidemic roseola.* 2. Measles. **r. scarlatino′sa,** fourth disease.

rubeola (roo-be′o-lah) [L. *ruber* red]. 1. Measles. 2. Rubella. **r. scarlatino′sa,** fourth disease.

rubeosis (roo″be-o′sis). Redness, especially reddish discoloration of the skin. **r. i′ridis,** a condition characterized by a new formation of vessels and connective tissue on the surface of the iris, frequently seen in diabetics (*r. i′ridis diabet′ica*). **r. ret′inae,** a name proposed for a condition characterized by formation of new vessels in front of the optic papilla in retinitis proliferans, seen in nondiabetics, as well as in diabetics (*r. ret′inae diabet′ica*).

rubescent (roo-bes′ent) [L. *rubescere* to become red]. Reddish; becoming red.

rubidiol (roo-bid′e-ol). A solution in oil of rubidium and potassium mercuric iodide: used externally as a resolvent.

rubidium (roo-bid′e-um) [L. *rubidus* red]. A rare metallic alkaline element; atomic number, 37; atomic weight, 85.47; symbol, Rb. **r. and ammonium bromide,** a substance, $RbBr + 3NH_4Br$: used like potassium bromide. **r. bromide,** a binary compound, RbBr: used like potassium bromide. **r. chloride,** a substance, RbCl; said to increase the arterial tension. **r. iodide,** a binary compound, RbI, partly soluble in water: valued in treating diseases of the eye, pharynx, and skin. **r. tartrate,** a salt, $RbC_4H_5O_6$: used in cardiac neuroses.

rubiginous, rubiginose (roo-bij′ĭ-nus, roo-bij′ĭ-nōs) [L. *rubigo* rust]. Having a rusty, brownish color: said of sputum.

rubijervine (roo″bĭ-jer′vin). A crystalline alkaloid, $C_{26}H_{43}NO_2.H_2O$, from white hellebore.

rubin (roo′bin). Fuchsin.

Rubin's test (roo′binz) [Isidor Clinton *Rubin,* New York physician, 1883–1958]. See under *tests.*

Rubner's law, test (ro͞ob′nerz) [Max *Rubner,* German physiologist, 1854–1932]. See under *law* and *tests.*

rubor (roo′bor) [L.]. Redness, one of the cardinal signs of inflammation.

rubramin (roo′brah-min). Trade mark for preparations of vitamin B_{12} activity concentrate. See *cyanocobalamin.*

rubriblast (roo′brĭ-blast). Proerythroblast.

rubric (roo′bric). Red; specifically, pertaining to the red nucleus.

rubricyte (roo′brĭ-sit) [L. *rubrum* red + Gr. *kytos* cell]. Polychromatophilic erythroblast.

rubrospinal (roo″bro-spi′nal). Pertaining to the red nucleus and the spinal cord.

rubrum (roo′brum) [L.]. Red. **r. Con′go,** Congo red. **r. scarlati′num,** scarlet red.

Rubus (roo′bus) [L.]. A genus of rosaceous plants, including the blackberries, raspberries, brambles, dewberries, and cloudberries. The root barks of several species of blackberry are tonic and astringent, and have been used in diarrhea. The fruits of *R. idae′us* and *R. strigo′sus,* red raspberries, are used in pharmacy.

Ruck's tuberculin [Karl von *Ruck,* American physician, 1849–1922]. See under *tuberculin.*

ructus (ruk′tus) [L.]. The belching of wind; eructation.

Rudbeckia (rud-bek′e-ah) [O. *Rudbeck,* 1630–1702, and O. *Rudbeck,* Jr., 1660–1740]. A genus of composite-flowered herbs of North America. The cone flower, *R. lacinia'ta*, thimble weed, is diuretic and tonic.

rudiment (roo'dĭ-ment). 1. An organ or part having little or no function but which has functioned at an earlier stage of the same individual or in his ancestors. 2. The first indication of a structure in the course of its development; a primordium. **lens r.**, a thickening of the ectoderm of the sides of the embryonic head, from which the crystalline lens develops. **r. of vaginal process**, vestigium processus vaginalis.

rudimentary (roo″dĭ-men'tah-re). 1. Imperfectly developed. 2. Vestigial.

rudimentum (roo″dĭ-men'tum), pl. *rudimen'ta* [L. "a first beginning"]. 1. [B N A] A vestigial structure. 2. [N A] The first indication of a structure in the course of its development; a primordium. **r. processus vaginalis** [B N A], vestigium processus vaginalis.

rue (roo) [L. *Ruta*]. The rutaceous herb, *Ruta graveolens*. The volatile oil (*oleum rutae*) from the leaves is an irritant poison.

rufescine (roo'fĕ-sin). A substance obtained from a mollusk, *Haliotis rufescens*, which corresponds to the bile pigments in man.

Ruffini's brushes, corpuscles, organs (roo-fe'nēz) [Angelo *Ruffini*, Italian anatomist, 1864–1929]. See under *corpuscle.*

rufiopin (roo″fe-o'pin). A reddish-yellow, crystalline substance, $C_{14}H_8O_4$, derivable from opianic acid, and isomeric with rufigallic acid.

rufous (roo'fus) [L. *rufus* red]. 1. Dull red. 2. Having reddish hair and a ruddy complexion.

Rufus (roo'fus) **of Ephesus** (c. 100 A.D.). A physician and anatomist whose surviving writings are noteworthy, particularly those on anatomy, gout, the pulse, and clinical history taking.

ruga (roo'gah), pl. *ru'gae* [L.]. A ridge, wrinkle, or fold, as of mucous membrane. **r. gas'trica,** r. of stomach. **r. palati'na,** any one of the transverse ridges extending outward on both sides of the raphe of the palate. **r. of stomach,** one of the folds appearing in the mucous membrane of the stomach when the muscular coat contracts. **rugae of vagina, ru'gae vagina'les** [N A, B N A], small transverse folds of the mucous membrane of the vagina extending outward from the columns.

rugae (roo'je) [L.]. Plural of *ruga.*

Ruge-Phillipp test (roo″gah-fil'ip) [Reinhold *Ruge*, German hygienist, 1862–1936; Ernst *Phillipp*, German gynecologist, born 1893]. See under *tests.*

rugine (roo-zhēn'). A raspatory.

rugitus (roo'jĭ-tus) [L. "roaring"]. Rumbling in the intestines.

rugose, rugous (roo'gōs, roo'gus) [L. *rugosus*]. Characterized by wrinkles.

rugosity (roo-gos'ĭ-te) [L. *rugositas*]. 1. The condition of being wrinkled. 2. A fold, wrinkle, or ruga.

Ruhmkorff coil (ro͞om'korf) [Heinrich Daniel *Ruhmkorff*, German electrician, 1823–1887]. See under *coil.*

R.U.L. Abbreviation for *right upper lobe* (of a lung).

rule (ro͞ol) [L. *regula*]. A statement of conditions commonly observed in a given situation, or a statement of a prescribed course of action to obtain a result. **Abegg's r.,** all atoms have the same number of valences. **Anstie's r.,** one used in connection with life insurance examination: the maximum amount of absolute alcohol which can be taken by an adult without injury is $1\frac{1}{2}$ oz. daily. This is equivalent to about 3 oz. of whisky, brandy gin, or rum; about 4 glasses of sherry or other strong wine; to 1 pint of claret, champagne, or other light wine; to 3 glasses of strong ale or porter; or 5 glasses of beer or light ale. **Arey's r.,** the total length of an embryo or fetus in inches, for the first five months, equals the numerical sum of the numbers of lunar months since conception; for the last five lunar months it equals the product of the number of the month multiplied by 2. **Bastedo's r.,** the dose of a drug for a child is obtained by multiplying the adult dose by the child's age in years, adding 3 to the product, and dividing the sum by 30. **Budin's r.,** a bottle-fed baby should not take more than $\frac{1}{10}$ of its own weight of cow's milk per day. **Clark's r.,** the dose of a drug for a child is obtained by multiplying the adult dose by the weight of the child in pounds and dividing the result by 150. **Cowling's r.,** the dose of a drug for a child is obtained by multiplying the adult dose by the age of the child his next birthday and dividing by 24. **delivery date r.,** Nägele's r. **Fried's r.,** the dose of a drug for an infant less than 2 years old is obtained by multiplying the child's age in months by the adult dose and dividing the result by 150. **Gibson's r.,** in pneumonia, if the pulse pressure in millimeters of mercury does not fall below the pulse rate, the prognosis is good; if it does, prognosis is bad. **Goodsall's r.,** an anal fistula with a posterior external opening has its internal opening in the midline posteriorly; a fistula with an anterior external opening has its internal opening radially opposite thereto. **Haase's r.,** the total length of an embryo or fetus in centimeters, for the first five months, equals the square of the number of lunar months since conception; for the last five months it equals the product of the number of the month multiplied by 5. **His' r.,** reckon the duration of pregnancy from the first day of the missed menstruation. **Hudson's lactone r.,** lactones which are dextrorotatory have the lactone ring on the right side, and those which are levorotatory have it on the left side. **Jackson's r.,** after epileptic attacks, simple nervous processes are more quickly recovered from than complex ones. **Liebermeister's r.,** in febrile tachycardia the pulse beats increase at the rate of about eight to every degree centigrade of temperature. **Lossen's r.,** in hemophilia, only women transmit the condition only men inherit it. **M'Naghten r.,** "to establish a defense on the ground of insanity, it must be clearly proved that at the time of committing the act the party accused was laboring under such a defect of reason from disease of the mind as not to know the nature and quality of the act he was doing, or, if he did know it, that he did not know he was doing what was wrong." **Moots's r.,** in anesthesia, the pulse pressure is an indication of cardiac strength and must be high enough to compensate for deficient kidney function. **Nägele's r.** (for predicting day of labor), subtract three months from the first day of the last menstruation and add seven days. **phase r.,** a homogeneous chemical substance of n components is capable of $n + 1$ modifications of phase; e.g., the phases of H_2O are ice, water, and steam. A heterogeneous chemical system of p coexistent phases and c variable components has $p + 2 - c$ degrees of freedom or variations of phase, i.e., the sum of its coexistent phases and its possible changes of phase exceeds the number of its components by 2. **Quest's r.,** if a nursing infant has lost half his normal weight, recovery is unlikely. **Quetelet's r.,** the body weight of an adult ought to be as many kilograms as his body length in centimeters exceeds 100. **Rolleston's r.,** the ideal systolic pressure for an adult is the figure represented by 100 plus half the age in years. The maximal physiologic pressure is 100 plus the age. **Schütz's r., Schütz-Borissov r.,** the amount of substrate decomposed in the same time interval by varying enzyme concentrations is not always proportional to the concentration of the enzyme, but is often proportional to the square root of this quantity. **Spivack's r.,** if the terminal loop of the ileum is attached to the brim of the pelvis the vermiform appendix will be retrocecal or retrocolic in position. **van't Hoff's r.,** the velocity of chemical reactions is increased twofold or more for each rise of 10 degrees C. in temperature. **Young's r.,** the dose of a drug for a child is obtained by multiplying the adult dose by the age in years and dividing the result by the sum of the child's age plus 12.

rumbatron (rum′bah-tron). A high efficiency radio oscillator in which atoms are shattered and which employs electrons as the bombarding particles.

rumen (roo′men). The first stomach of a ruminant, or cud-chewing animal; also called *paunch.*

rumenitis (roo″men-i′tis). Inflammation of the rumen.

rumenotomy (roo″men-ot′o-me) [*rumen* + Gr. *tomē* a cutting]. The operation of cutting into the rumen of an animal for the purpose of removing foreign bodies or impacted food or for evacuating gases.

ruminant (roo′mĭ-nant). 1. Chewing the cud. 2. One of the order of animals which have a stomach with four complete cavities (1, rumen; 2, reticulum; 3, omasum; 4, abomasum), through which the food passes in digestion. The division includes oxen, sheep, goats, deer, and antelopes.

rumination (roo″mĭ-na′shun) [L. *ruminatio*]. 1. The casting up of the food to be chewed a second time, as in cattle. In man, the regurgitation of food after almost every meal, part of it being vomited and the rest swallowed: a condition seen in infants. See *merycism.* 2. Meditation. **obsessive r.,** the constant preoccupation with certain thoughts, with inability to dismiss them from the mind.

ruminative (roo″mĭ-na′tiv). Characterized by rumination; constantly dwelling on certain topics or ideas.

Rummo's disease (room′ōz) [Gaetano *Rummo*, Italian physician, 1853–1917]. Cardioptosis.

Rumpel-Leede phenomenon, sign (room′-pel-la′dĕ) [Theodor *Rumpel*, German physician, 1862–1923; C. *Leede*, German physician, born 1882]. See under *phenomenon.*

Rumpf's symptom (roompfs) [Heinrich Theodor *Rumpf*, German physician, born 1851]. See under *symptom.*

Runeberg's formula, type (roo′nĕ-bergs) [Johan Wilhelm *Runeberg*, Finnish physician, 1843–1918]. See under *formula* and *type.*

Ruphos (roo′fos). See *Rufus of Ephesus.*

rupia (roo′pe-ah) [Gr. *rhypos* filth]. An eruptive disease of the skin in which ill-conditioned bullae or vesicles are formed, which become scabby. It is almost always a manifestation of tertiary syphilis. **r. escharot′ica,** dermatitis gangrenosa infantum.

rupial (roo′pe-al). Pertaining to, resembling, or due to, rupia.

rupioid (roo′pe-oid). Resembling rupia.

rupophobia (roo″po-fo′be-ah). Rhypophobia.

rupture (rup′chur). 1. Forcible tearing or breaking of a part. 2. A hernia. **defense r.,** a breaking down of the body's defense against infection, such as is seen when silica particles inhaled by a worker break down the resistance against tuberculosis.

Rusconi's anus (roos-ko′nēz) [Mauro *Rusconi*, Italian biologist, 1776–1849]. The blastopore.

rushes (rush′ez). Rapid waves of contractile activity progressing from one end of the intestine to the other and serving to transport the intestinal contents. Called also *peristaltic rushes.*

Russell's bodies (rus′elz) [William *Russell*, physician in Edinburgh, 1852–1940]. See under *body.*

Russell effect (rus′el) [W. J. *Russell*, British physicist]. See under *effect.*

Russell's viper (rus′elz) [Patrick *Russell*, Aleppo physician, 1728–1805]. See under *viper.*

Russo's reaction (roo′sōz) [Mario *Russo*, Italian physician]. See under *reaction.*

rust (rust). 1. Iron oxide or hydroxide, forming a reddish deposit on metallic iron where the latter has been exposed to moisture; also a similar deposit on other metals that have been exposed to dampness. 2. A fungous disease of plants characterized by the formation of rust-like spots on them.

Rust's disease, phenomenon (roosts) [Johann Nepomuk *Rust*, German surgeon, 1775–1840]. See under *disease* and *phenomenon.*

rut (rut) [L. *rugitus* roaring]. 1. The period or season of heightened sexual activity in some male mammals that coincides with the season of estrus in the females. 2. Estrus.

rutaecarpine (roo″te-kar′pin). A crystalline alkaloid, $C_{18}H_{13}ON_3$, from *Evodia rutaecarpa.*

ruthenium (roo-the′ne-um). A rare, very hard metallic element; symbol, Ru; atomic weight, 101.07; atomic number, 44.

rutherford (ruth′er-ford) [Ernest *Rutherford*, British physicist, 1871–1937]. The unit representing one million disintegrations of radioactive matter per second. Abbreviated rd.

rutidosis (roo″tĭ-do′sis). Rhytidosis.

rutilism (roo′tĭ-lizm) [L. *rutilis* red, inclining to golden yellow]. Red-headedness.

rutin (roo′tin). A bioflavonoid, 3,3′,4′,5,7-pentahydroxyflavone-3-rutinoside, obtained from buckwheat or other sources: used to reduce capillary fragility.

rutinose (roo′tĭ-nōs). Rhamnosidoglucose, a disaccharide occurring in rutin.

rutoside (roo′to-sīd). Rutin.

Ruysch's membrane, muscle, tube, vein (roish′ez) [Frederic *Ruysch*, Dutch anatomist, 1638–1731]. See under the nouns.

RV. Abbreviation for *residual volume.*

R.V.H. Abbreviation for *right ventricular hypertrophy.*

Ryan's skin test (ri′anz) [A. H. *Ryan*, American physician]. See under *tests.*

Rydygier's operation (rid″ĭ-ge′erz) [Antoni *Rydygier*, Polish surgeon in South America]. See under *operation.*

rye (ri). The cereal plant, *Secale cereale*, and its nutritious seed. **spurred r.** See *ergot.*

Ryle tube (ril) [G. A. *Ryle*, British physician]. See under *tube.*

S

S. 1. Chemical symbol for *sulfur.* 2. Abbreviation for Latin *se'mis* half, *sacral* (in vertebral formulas), *sig'na* mark, *smooth* colony, *sinis'ter* left, *subject, supravergence,* and *Svedberg unit of sedimentation coefficient* (10^{-13} sec.).

σ. Symbol for one-thousandth part of a second.

S.A. Abbreviation for L. *secun'dum ar'tem,* according to art.

Saathoff's test (saht'ofs) [Lübhard *Saathoff,* German physician, 1877–1929]. See under *tests.*

saber-legged (sa'ber-legd). Having the angle of the hock more acute than normal, so that the hind feet stand well under the body: said of horses.

Sabin's vaccine (sa'binz) [Albert Bruce *Sabin,* American virologist, born 1906]. See under *vaccine.*

sabinism (sab'ĭ-nizm). Poisoning by savin.

sabinol (sab'ĭ-nol). A terpene alcohol, $(CH_3)_2$-$CH.C_6H_6(OH)$:CH_2, from *Juniperus sabina.*

Sabouraud's agar (sab'oo-rōz) [Raymond Jacques Adrian *Sabouraud,* French dermatologist, 1864–1938]. See *French proof agar,* under *agar.*

Sabouraudia (sab″oo-ro'de-ah). A proposed subgenus of Trichosporon.

Sabouraudites (sab″oo-ro-di'tēz). A genus name proposed for some species of Microsporon, Trichophyton, etc.

Sabrazés breath-holding test (sah″brah-zeh') [Jean Emile *Sabrazés,* French physician, 1867–1943]. See under *tests.*

sabulous (sab'u-lus) [L. *sabulosus; sabulum* sand]. Gritty or sandy.

sabulum (sab'u-lum) [L. "fine sand"]. Acervulus.

saburra (sah-bur'ah) [L.]. Sordes; foulness of the stomach, mouth, or teeth.

saburral (sah-bur'al) [L. *saburra* sand]. Pertaining to or of the nature of sordes, or of foulness of the stomach.

sac (sak) [L. *saccus;* Gr. *sakkos*]. A pouch; a baglike organ or structure. **abdominal s.,** a serous sac in the embryo which develops into the abdominal cavity. **air s's,** alveoli pulmonum. **allantoic s.,** the dilated portion of the allantois which becomes a part of the placenta in many mammals. **alveolar s's,** sacculi alveolares. **amniotic s.,** amnion. **aneurysmal s.,** the dilated coats of an artery in a sacculated aneurysm. **aortic s.,** the homologue in mammalian embryos of the ventral aorta, from which arise the series of aortic arches. **chorionic s.,** the mammalian chorion. **conjunctival s.,** saccus conjunctivae. **dental s.,** the dense fibrous layer of mesenchyme surrounding the enamel organ and dental papilla. **dural s.,** the process of dura mater at the caudal end of the spinal cord. **embryonic s.,** the blastodermic vesicle. **enamel s.,** the enamel organ during the stage in which its outer layer forms a sac enclosing the whole dental germ. **endolymphatic s.,** saccus endolymphaticus. **epiploic s.,** bursa omentalis. **gestation s.,** the common sac enclosing the embryo in pregnancy. **greater s. of peritoneum,** the peritoneum of the peritoneal cavity proper. **heart s.,** the pericardium. **hernial s.,** the pouch of peritoneum enclosing a herniated loop of intestine. **Hilton's s.,** laryngeal pouch. **lacrimal s.,** saccus lacrimalis. **laryngeal s.,** ventriculus laryngis. **Lower's s's,** sacculated portions of the external jugular vein at exit of the vein from the skull. **omental s.,** bursa omentalis. **pleural s.,** the pleural cavity. **serous s.,** the sac made up of the pleura, pericardium, and peritoneum. **splenic s.,** recessus lienalis. **tear s.,** saccus lacrimalis. **vitelline s.,** yolk s. **yolk s.,** one of the extraembryonic membranes that connects with the midgut; in vertebrates below true mammals it contains a yolk mass.

sacbrood (sak'brōōd). An infectious disease of the larvae of bees, caused by a virus.

saccate (sak'āt) [L. *saccatus*]. 1. Shaped like a sac. 2. Contained in a sac.

saccharascope (sak'ah-rah-skōp) [Gr. *sakcharon* sugar + *skopein* to examine]. A fermentation saccharimeter. See *saccharimeter.*

saccharase (sak'ah-rās). Invertase.

saccharate (sak'ah-rāt). A salt of saccharic acid.

saccharated (sak'ah-rāt″ed) [L. *saccharatus,* from *saccharum* sugar]. Charged with or containing sugar.

saccharephidrosis (sak″ar-ef″ĭ-dro'sis) [Gr. *sakcharon* sugar + *ephidrōsis* sweating]. The discharge of sugar in the sweat.

saccharide (sak'ah-rid). One of a series of carbohydrates, including the sugars. The saccharides are divided into monosaccharides, disaccharides, trisaccharides, and polysaccharides, according to the number of saccharide groups ($C_6H_{10}O_5$) composing them.

sacchariferous (sak″ah-rif'er-us) [L. *saccharum* sugar + *ferre* to bear]. Containing or yielding sugar.

saccharification (sak″ar-ĭ-fi-ka'shun) [L. *saccharum* sugar + *facere* to make]. Conversion into sugar.

saccharimeter (sak″ah-rim'e-ter) [L. *saccharum* sugar + *metrum* measure]. A device for estimating the proportion of sugar in a solution. It is either a polarimeter, indicating the proportion of sugar by the number of degrees through which it rotates the plane of polarization, or a hydrometer, indicating the proportion of sugar by the specific gravity of the solution. **Einhorn's s.,** a form of fermentation saccharimeter. **fermentation s.,** a saccharimeter in the form of a bent graduated tube and closed at one end. The amount of sugar in the urine is indicated by the gas which collects at the closed end when yeast is added to the urine. **Lohnstein's s.,** an instrument for performing a quantitative fermentation test of sugar in the urine.

saccharin (sak'ah-rin). Chemical name: 2,3-dihydro-3-oxobenzisosulfonazole: used as a noncaloric sweetening agent.

saccharine (sak'ah-rīn) [L. *saccharinus*]. Sugary; having a sweet taste.

saccharinol (sah-kar'ĭ-nol). Saccharin.

saccharinum (sak″ah-ri'num). Saccharin.

saccharo- (sak'ah-ro) [L. *saccharum;* Gr. *sakcharon* sugar]. Combining form denoting relationship to sugar.

saccharobiose (sak″ah-ro-bi'ōs). Disaccharose.

saccharocoria (sak″ah-ro-ko're-ah). Abhorrence of sugar.

saccharogalactorrhea (sak″ah-ro-gah-lak″to-re'ah) [*saccharo-* + Gr. *gala* milk + *rhoia* flow]. The secretion of milk containing an excess of sugar.

saccharolytic (sak″ah-ro-lit'ik) [*saccharo-* + Gr. *lysis* dissolution]. Capable of chemically splitting up sugar.

saccharometabolic (sak″ah-ro-met″ah-bol'ik). Pertaining to the metabolism of sugar.

saccharometabolism (sak″ah-ro-mĕ-tab'o-lizm). The metabolism of sugar.

saccharometer (sak″ah-rom'e-ter). Saccharimeter.

Saccharomyces (sak″ah-ro-mi′sēz) [*saccharo-* + Gr. *mykēs* fungus]. A genus of ascomycetous fungi; the yeasts. They are oval or spherical, unicellular organisms which are distinguished by gemmation or budding, the presence of ascospores and absence of mycelial threads. **S. al′bicans,** *Candida albicans.* **S. an′ginae** was found in a case of tonsillitis. **S. apicula′tus,** a species from fermenting fruit; its oval cells are joined at the ends. **Busse's s.,** a form discovered in a patient with degenerated nodules in the bones and internal organs. **S. cant′liei,** a species causing a tropical blastomycosis. **S. capillit′ii,** a species from the scalp, with spherical cells: said to cause alopecia seborrheica. **S. cerevis′iae,** a species with oval or spherical cells, from brewers' yeast: it causes alcoholic fermentation. **S. coprog′enus,** a form from decomposing feces, in short chains of oval or spherical cells. **S. ellipsoi′deus,** a form from wine yeast, forming elliptical cells, solitary or in branching chains: it causes alcoholic fermentation in wines. **S. epider′mica,** *Cryptococcus epidermidis.* **S. exig′uus,** a form in beer yeast: the cells are elliptical and solitary, or in branching chains: it causes late fermentation in beer. **S. galactic′olus,** a species from milk, with oval or elliptical cells: it produces a fermentation in milk. **S. glu′tinis,** a nonpathogenic species from air, potatoes, and the skin in seborrhea; its cells are cylindrical, oval, or spherical: it forms a rosy pigment. **S. granulomato′sus,** a variety producing granulomatous tumors in pigs. **S. guttula′tus,** a species which is able to change glucose into alcohol. It is pathogenic for rats and guinea pigs. **S. hansen′ii,** a species which changes sugars into oxalic acid. **S. hom′inis,** a species occurring in chronic infectious pyemia. It is pathogenic for animals. **S. lemonnie′ri,** a pathogenic fungus found in bronchitis (Sartory and Lasseur, 1915). **S. litho′genes,** a species from the lymph glands of an ox suffering from carcinoma of the liver: pathogenic to animals. **S. mesenter′icus,** a species which causes a fermentation in fruit acids: it is found in fermenting fruits. **S. mycoder′ma,** a species from fermenting liquors and diabetic urine, in which it produces a slight fermentation seen in cylindrical, oval, or elliptical cells, forming branched chains. **S. neofor′mans,** *Cryptococcus neoformans.* **S. pastoria′nus,** a species from fermenting wine and beer. **S. ru′brum,** a Brazilian species causing a parapsoriasic affection (Magalhaes, 1914). **S. subcuta′neus tumefa′ciens,** a species found in a myxoma of the thigh: pathogenic for animals. **S. tumefa′ciens al′bus,** a species discovered in certain cases of pharyngitis, pathogenic for mice, guinea pigs, and rabbits.

Saccharomyces (de Rivas).

saccharomyces (sak″ah-ro-mi′sēz), pl. *saccharomyce′tes.* An organism of the genus Saccharomyces.

Saccharomycetes (sak″ah-ro-mi-se′tēz). A family of Ascomycetes, the members of which are usually unicellular and contain granules and ascospores.

saccharomycetic (sak″ah-ro-mi-set′ik). Pertaining to or due to the presence of yeast fungi.

saccharomycetolysis (sak″ah-ro-mi″se-tol′ĭ-sis) [*saccharomyces* + Gr. *lysis* dissolution]. The splitting up of saccharomyces.

saccharomycosis (sak″ah-ro-mi-ko′sis). 1. Any disease condition due to a yeast fungus. 2. A skin disease in which nodules are seen filled with saccharomycetes.

saccharorrhea (sak″ah-ro-re′ah) [*saccharo-* + Gr. *rhoia* flow]. Glycosuria.

saccharosan (sak′ah-ro-san). A form of anhydrosugar.

saccharose (sak′ah-rōs) [*saccharo-* + *-ose*]. Sucrose.

saccharosuria (sak″ah-ro-su′re-ah) [*saccharose* + Gr. *ouron* urine + *-ia*]. The presence of saccharose in the urine; sucrosuria.

Saccharum (sak′ah-rum). A genus of graminaceous plants. *S. officina′rum,* sugar cane, affords a large part of the commercial supply of sugar.

saccharum (sak′ah-rum) [L.; Gr. *sakcharon*]. Sugar, especially cane sugar, or sucrose. **s. acer′num, s. canaden′se,** maple sugar. **s. lac′tis,** sugar of milk; lactose. **s. us′tum,** caramel.

saccharuria (sak″ah-roo′re-ah) [*saccharo-* + Gr. *ouron* urine + *-ia*]. Glycosuria.

sacciform (sak′sĭ-form) [L. *saccus* sac + *forma* form]. Shaped like a sac or bag.

saccular (sak′u-lar). Shaped like a sac.

sacculated (sak′u-lāt″ed) [L. *sacculatus*]. Characterized by sacculation or by the presence of saccules.

sacculation (sak″u-la′shun). 1. A sacculus, or pouch. 2. The quality of being sacculated, or pursed out with little pouches. **s's of colon,** haustra coli.

saccule (sak′ūl) [L. *sacculus*]. 1. A little bag or sac. 2. See *sacculus.* **air s's, alveolar s's,** sacculi alveolares. **laryngeal s., s. of larynx,** sacculus laryngis.

sacculi (sak′u-li) [L.]. Plural of *sacculus.*

sacculocochlear (sak″u-lo-kok′le-ar). Pertaining to the sacculus and cochlea.

sacculus (sak′u-lus), pl. *sac′culi* [L., dim. of *saccus*]. A little bag or sac; applied in official anatomical nomenclature specifically to the smaller of the two divisions of the membranous labyrinth of the vestibule, which communicates with the cochlear duct by way of the ductus reuniens. Called also *s. proprius, s. rotundus, s. sphaericus, s. vestibularis,* and *saccule.* **sac′culi alveola′res** [N A], the spaces into which the alveolar ducts open distally, and with which the alveoli communicate. Called also *alveolar sacs.* **s. commu′nis,** utriculus. **s. den′tis,** a fibrous sac in the jaw which encloses an unerupted tooth, being connected with the overlying gingiva by the gubernaculum dentis. **s. endolymphat′icus,** saccus endolymphaticus. **s. lacrima′lis,** saccus lacrimalis. **s. laryn′gis** [N A], a diverticulum extending upward from the front of the laryngeal ventricle, between the vestibular fold medially and the thyroarytenoid muscle and thyroid cartilage laterally. Called also *appendix ventriculi laryngis* [B N A], and *laryngeal saccule.* **s. Morgag′nii,** ventriculus laryngis. **s. pro′prius, s. rotun′dus, s. sphae′ricus.** See *sacculus.* **s. ventricula′ris,** s. laryngis. **s. vestibula′ris.** See *sacculus.*

saccus (sak′kus), pl. *sac′ci* [L.; Gr. *sakkos*]. A sac or pouch; used in anatomical nomenclature as a general term to designate a saclike space. **s. conjuncti′vae** [N A], the potential space, lined by conjunctiva, between the eyelids and the eyeball. Called also *conjunctival sac.* **s. endolymphat′icus** [N A, B N A], the blind, flattened cerebral end of the endolymphatic duct. Called also *endolymphatic sac.* **s. lacrima′lis** [N A, B N A], the dilated upper end of the nasolacrimal duct. Called also *lacrimal sac.*

Sachs's disease [Bernard *Sachs,* New York neurologist, 1858–1944]. See *Tay-Sachs disease,* under *disease.*

Sachs's test [Heinrich B. *Sachs,* German gynecologist in the United States, born 1898]. See under *tests.*

Sachs-Georgi test [Hans *Sachs,* German immunologist, 1877–1945; Walter *Georgi,* German bacteriologist, 1889–1920]. See under *tests.*

Sachs-Witebsky test (saks′ wĭ-teb′ske) [Hans *Sachs;* Ernest *Witebsky,* German-born immunologist in the United States, born 1901]. See under *tests.*

Sachsse's solution, test (zahk'sez) [Georg Robert *Sachsse,* German chemist, 1840–1895]. See under *solution* and *tests.*

sacrad (sa'krad). Toward the sacrum, or sacral aspect.

sacral (sa'kral) [L. *sacralis*]. Pertaining to or situated near the sacrum.

sacralgia (sa-kral'je-ah) [*sacrum* + *-algia*]. Pain in the sacrum.

sacralization (sa″kral-i-za'shun). Fusion of the fifth lumbar vertebra to the first segment of the sacrum, so that the sacrum consists of six segments.

sacrarthrogenic (sa″krar-thro-jen'ik) [*sacrum* + Gr. *arthron* joint + *gennan* to produce]. Resulting from disease of a sacral joint.

sacrectomy (sa-krek'to-me) [*sacrum* + Gr. *ektomē* excision]. Excision or resection of the sacrum for cancer of the rectum.

sacriplex (sa'kre-pleks). The sacral plexus.

sacro- (sa'kro) [L. *sacrum* sacred]. Combining form denoting relationship to the sacrum.

sacro-anterior (sa″kro-an-te're-or). Having the sacrum directed forward. See under *position.*

sacrococcygeal (sa″kro-kok-sij'e-al). Pertaining to or located in the region of the sacrum and coccyx.

sacrococcyx (sa″kro-kok'siks). The sacrum and coccyx together.

sacrocoxalgia (sa″kro-koks-al'je-ah). A painful condition of the sacrum and coccyx.

sacrocoxitis (sa″kro-kok-si'tis) [*sacro-* + L. *coxa* hip + *-itis*]. Inflammation of the sacro-iliac joint.

sacrodynia (sa″kro-din'e-ah) [*sacro-* + Gr. *odynē* pain]. Pain in the sacral region.

sacro-iliac (sa″kro-il'e-ak). Pertaining to the sacrum and ilium: noting the joint or articulation between the sacrum and ilium and the ligaments associated therewith.

sacro-iliitis (sa″kro-il″e-i'tis). Inflammation in the sacro-iliac joint.

sacrolisthesis (sa″kro-lis-the'sis). The condition in which the sacrum lies anterior to the fifth lumbar vertebra.

sacrolumbar (sa″kro-lum'bar) [*sacro-* + L. *lumbus* loin]. Pertaining to the sacrum and the loin.

sacroperineal (sa″kro-per″ĭ-ne'al). Pertaining to the sacrum and the perineum.

sacroposterior (sa″kro-pos-te're-or). Having the sacrum directed backward. See under *position.*

sacropromontory (sa″kro-prom'on-to-re). The promontory of the sacrum.

sacrosciatic (sa″kro-si-at'ik). Pertaining to the sacrum and the ischium.

sacrospinal (sa″kro-spi'nal) [*sacro-* + L. *spina* spine]. Pertaining to the sacrum and the spine, or vertebral column.

sacrotomy (sa-krot'o-me) [*sacro-* + Gr. *temnein* to cut]. The operation of cutting out the lower end of the sacrum.

sacrotransverse (sa″kro-trans-vers'). Relating to the direction of the fetal sacrum in breech presentation. See under *position.*

sacro-uterine (sa″kro-u'ter-in). Pertaining to the sacrum and the uterus.

sacrovertebral (sa″kro-ver'te-bral). Pertaining to the sacrum and the vertebral column.

sacrum (sa'krum) [L. "sacred"]. The triangular-shaped bone formed usually by five fused vertebrae that are wedged dorsally between the two hip bones. Called also *os sacrum* [N A]. **assimilation s.** See *assimilation pelvis,* under *pelvis.* **tilted s.,** a condition marked by separation of the sacroiliac joint and forward displacement of the sacrum.

sactosalpinx (sak″to-sal'pinks) [Gr. *saktos* stuffed + *salpinx* tube]. Dilatation of the inflamed uterine tube by retained secretions.

saddle (sad″l). A part or section of the base of a partial denture.

sadism (sad'izm) [Marquis de *Sade,* 1740–1814]. Sexual perversion in which satisfaction is derived from the infliction of cruelty upon another. **anal s.,** the sadistic manifestations of anal erotism, such as aggressiveness, selfishness and stinginess. **oral s.,** a sadistic form of oral erotism manifested by fantasies of chewing, biting, etc.

sadist (sad'ist). A practicer of sadism.

sadistic (sa-dis'tik). Pertaining to sadism.

sadomasochistic (sad″o-maz″o-kis'tik). Characterized by both sadism and masochism.

Saemisch's operation, ulcer (sa'mish-ez) [Edwin Theodor *Saemisch,* ophthalmologist in Bonn, 1833–1909]. See under *operation* and *ulcer.*

Saenger's macula, operation, suture (zeng'-erz) [Max *Saenger,* gynecologist in Prague, 1853–1903]. See under the nouns.

Saenger's reflex, sign (zeng'erz) [Alfred *Saenger,* German neurologist, 1860–1921]. See under *sign.*

saff (saf). Trade mark for a preparation of safflower oil.

safflor (saf'flor). Trade mark for a preparation of safflower oil.

safrene (saf'rēn). A hydrocarbon, $C_{10}H_{16}$, obtained from sassafras.

safrol (saf'rol). An oil, volatile, anodyne substance, the methylene ether of allyl dioxybenzene, from sassafras oil.

safrosin (saf'ro-sin). Bluish eosin.

safu (sah'foo). A disease of the skin seen among the inhabitants of the Turk Islands (South Seas). It may be a form of yaws.

safura (sah-fu'rah). Ancylostomiasis.

sagittal (saj'ĭ-tal) [L. *sagittalis; sagitta* arrow]. 1. Shaped like or resembling an arrow; straight. 2. Situated in the direction of the sagittal suture, said of an anteroposterior plane or section parallel to the long axis of the body.

sagittalis (saj″ĭ-ta'lis). [N A, B N A] Sagittal; situated in the direction of the sagittal suture.

sago (sa'go). A starch mainly derived from the pith of various species of palm, chiefly of the genus *Sagus.*

sagur (sa'gur). An astringent gall formed on certain East Indian tamarisks.

Sahli's desmoid reaction, test, whistle (sah'lēz) [Herman *Sahli,* physician in Bern, 1856–1933]. See under the nouns.

sajina (sah-je'nah). An East Indian plant, *Moringa pterygosperma:* used in rheumatism and dyspepsia.

S.A.L. Abbreviation for L. *secun'dum ar'tis le'ges,* according to the rules of art.

sal (sal) [L.]. Salt. **s. ammoniac,** ammonium chloride. **s. diuret'icum,** potassium acetate. **s. so'da,** sodium carbonate. **s. volat'ile, volat'ilis,** ammonium carbonate.

Sala's cells (sal'ahz) [Luigi *Sala,* Italian zoologist, 1863–1930]. See under *cell.*

salamander (sal″ah-man'der) [Gr. *salamandra* a kind of lizard]. A kind of lizard-like animal. Species of the genus Ambystoma are used in various types of experiments.

salamanderin (sal″ah-man'der-in). A poisonous base from the skin of a species of salamander.

salicylamide (sal″ĭ-sil-am'id). Chemical name: o-hydroxybenzamide: used as an analgesic.

salicylanilide (sal″ĭ-sil-an'ĭ-lid). A compound formed by heating a mixture of salicylic acid, aniline, and phosphorus trichloride.

salicylase (sah-lis'ĭ-lās). An enzyme oxidizing salicylaldehyde into salicylic acid.

salicylate (sal'ĭ-sil″āt). Any salt of salicylic acid. The alkali salicylates are used like salicylic acid in rheumatism.

salicylated (sal'ĭ-sil″āt-ed). Containing or impregnated with salicylic acid.

salicylazosulfapyridine (sal″ĭ-sil″ah-zo-sul″-fah-pir′ĭ-den). Chemical name: 5-[p-(2-pyridylsulfamyl)phenylazo]salicylic acid: used in treatment of chronic ulcerative colitis.

salicylemia (sal″ĭ-sil-e′me-ah) [*salicylate* + Gr. *haima* blood + *-ia*]. The presence of salicylate in the blood.

salicylic (sal″ĭ-sil′ik). Pertaining to the radical salicyl.

salicylide (sal′ĭ-sil″id). Salicylic aldehyde.

salicylism (sal′ĭ-sil″izm). The toxic effects of excessive dosage with salicylic acid or its salts.

salicylize (sal′ĭ-sil″īz). To treat with or bring under the influence of salicylic acid.

salicyltherapy (sal″ĭ-sil-ther′ah-pe). Treatment by salicylic acid or salicylates.

salifiable (sal′ĭ-fi″ah-b'l) [L. *sal* salt + *fieri* to become]. Capable of combining with acids so as to form salts.

salify (sal′ĭ-fi). To convert into a salt.

salimeter (sah-lim′e-ter) [L. *sal* salt + *metrum* measure]. A hydrometer for ascertaining the strength of saline solutions.

saline (sa′līn) [L. *salinus; sal* salt]. Salty; of the nature of a salt; containing a salt or salts.

salinigrin (sal″ĭ-ni′grin). A glycoside, $C_{13}H_{16}O_7$, from the bark of willow.

salinometer (sal″ĭ-nom′e-ter). An instrument (hydrometer) for direct reading of the salt content of a liquid.

saliva (sah-li′vah) [L.]. The clear, alkaline, somewhat viscid secretion from the parotid, submaxillary, sublingual, and smaller mucous glands of the mouth. It serves to moisten and soften the food, keeps the mouth moist, and contains ptyalin, a digestive enzyme which converts starch into maltose. The saliva also contains mucin, serum-albumin, globulin, leukocytes, epithelial debris, and potassium thiocyanate. Certain toxins frequently occur in it. Official in Basle Nomina Anatomica the term was omitted in N A. **chorda s.,** submaxillary saliva produced in response to stimulation of the chorda tympani nerve, less viscid and turbid than that of the unstimulated gland. **ganglionic s.,** saliva obtained by irritating the submaxillary gland. **lingual s.,** the secretion of Ebner's glands and other serous glands of the tongue. **parotid s.,** saliva produced by the parotid gland; thinner and less viscid than the other varieties. **ropy s.,** saliva which is highly viscid. **sublingual s.,** that produced by the sublingual gland, the most viscid of all. **submaxillary s.,** that produced by the submaxillary gland. **sympathetic s.,** submaxillary saliva produced in response to stimulation of its sympathetic nerve supply; more viscid and turbid than that of the unstimulated gland.

salivant (sal′ĭ-vant). Provoking a flow of saliva.

salivary (sal′ĭ-ver-e) [L. *salivarius*]. Pertaining to the saliva.

salivate (sal′ĭ-vāt). To produce an excessive flow of saliva.

salivation (sal″ĭ-va′shun) [L. *salivatio*]. An excessive discharge of saliva; ptyalism.

salivator (sal′ĭ-va″tor). An agent which causes salivation.

salivatory (sal′ĭ-vah-to″re). Causing salivation.

salivin (sal′ĭ-vin). Ptyalin.

salivolithiasis (sah-li″vo-lĭ-thi′ah-sis). Sialolithiasis.

Salk vaccine (sahlk) [Jonas E. *Salk*, American physician, born 1914]. See under *vaccine*.

Salkowski's test (sal-kow′skēz) [Ernst Leopold *Salkowski*, physiologic chemist in Berlin, 1844–1923]. See under *tests*.

sallenders (sal′en-derz). Malanders.

salmiac (sal′me-ak). Ammonium chloride.

salmin (sal′min). A toxic substance derived from the milt of salmon.

Salmon's sign (sam′onz) [Udall J. *Salmon*, New York obstetrician, born 1904]. See under *sign*.

Salmonella (sal″mo-nel′ah) [Daniel Elmer *Salmon*, American pathologist, 1850–1914]. A genus of microorganisms of tribe Salmonelleae, family Enterobacteriaceae, order Eubacteriales, made up of rod-shaped, gram-negative, usually but not invariably motile bacteria set apart from other enteric bacilli by failure to ferment lactose. It includes the typhoid-paratyphoid bacilli and bacteria usually pathogenic for lower animals which are often transmitted to man. The genus is separated into species or serotypes on the basis of O and H antigens, the latter occurring in two phases and identified by antigenic formulae taking the general form: O antigen: phase 1 ⇌ phase 2 in which the O antigens are designated by Roman numerals, the phase 1 antigens by lower case letters, and the phase 2 antigens by Arabic numerals. More than 400 different serotypes have been described. **S. abor′tus e′qui,** a species causing infectious abortion in mares; not found in other animals. **S. abor′tus o′vis,** a species isolated from cases of abortion in sheep. **S. aer′trycke,** *S. typhimurium.* **S. ana′tum,** a species causing keel in ducklings and intestinal disorder in man. **S. choleraesu′is,** a parasite

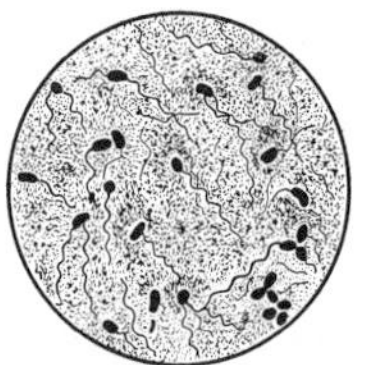

Salmonella choleraesuis.

Salmonella typhosa.

of pigs and an important secondary invader in hog cholera. A member of the suipestifer group that also includes *S. paratyphi C* or Eastern type, the Kunzendorf variety or European type, and the Glässer-Voldagsen type that contains two species, *S. typhisuis* and *S. typhisuis* var. *Voldagsen.* Man is occasionally infected. The antigenic formula is VI,VII:(c):1,5. **S. enterit′idis,** a widely distributed parasite of rodents occurring as a number of serotypes, namely, var. *Danyz*, var. *Chaco*, var. *Essen*, and var. *Jena.* It may produce epidemic diarrheal disease of rodents, and is a common cause of gastroenteritis in man. The antigenic formula is (I),IX,XII:g,m:—. **S. gallina′rum,** the causative agent of fowl typhoid and Moore's infectious leukemia of fowl, with little or no pathogenicity for man. It has the antigenic formula (I),IX,XII:—:— and is notable because only somatic O antigen is present. **S. hirschfel′dii,** *S. paratyphi C.* **S. mor′gani,** *Proteus morgani.* **S. paraty′phi,** *S. paratyphi A.* **S. paraty′phi A,** the etiologic agent of typhoid-like disease in man; usually found in man but occurring occasionally in lower animals. The antigenic formula is (I),II,XII:a:—. **S. paraty′phi B,** the etiologic agent of typhoid-like disease in man, which also produces the acute syndrome of food-poisoning. Occurs in man and in lower animals. The antigenic formula is (I),IV,(V),XII:b:(1,2). **S. paraty′phi C,** the etiologic agent of enteric fevers in Asia, Africa, and southeastern Europe, and an important cause of death in British Guiana; closely related to strains of *S. choleraesuis.* **S. pullo′rum,** the causative agent of bacillary white diarrhea of chickens; serologically identical with *S. gallinarum.* **S. schottmül′leri,** *S. paratyphi B.* **S. sen′dai,** a species causing enteric fever in man. **S. suipes′tifer,** *S. choleraesuis.* **S. ty′phi,** *S. typhosa.* **S. typhimu′rium,** a parasite of rodents, especially mice, and the causative agent of mouse typhoid and of food poisoning in man. The antigenic formula is (I),IV,(V),XII:i:1,2,3. **S. typhisu′is,** a species identical with *S. choleraesuis* except in minor cultural features. **S. typho′sa,** the etiologic agent of typhoid fever, occurring only in man. The antigenic formula is IX,XII(Vi):d—. Strains containing the Vi (virulence) antigen are designated V strains; those that have partially lost Vi antigen, V-W strains; and those that do not contain Vi antigen, W strains. The species is also subdivided into phage types on the basis of susceptibility to empirically numbered bacteriophages.

salmonella (sal″mo-nel′ah), pl. *salmonel′lae.* A microorganism of the genus Salmonella.

salmonellal (sal-mo-nel′al). Caused by salmonellae.

Salmonelleae (sal″mo-nel′e-e). A tribe of the family Enterobacteriaceae, order Eubacteriales, made up of gram-negative rod-shaped organisms which are usually but not invariably motile by means of peritrichous flagella. It includes two genera, *Salmonella* and *Shigella.*

salmonellosis (sal″mo-nel-lo′sis). Infection with salmonellae, especially (1) paratyphoid fever and (2) a form of food poisoning due to certain species of the genus Salmonella. It is caused by the ingestion of food containing the organisms or their products and is marked by violent diarrhea attended by cramps and tenesmus.

salocoll (sal′o-kol). Phenocoll salicylate, $C_2H_5O.C_6H_4.NH.CO.CH_2.NH_2.C_7H_6O_3$, a crystalline salt.

salol (sa′lol). Phenyl salicylate.

Salomon's test (sal′o-monz) [Hugo *Salomon,* German physician in Buenos Aires, 1872–1954]. See under *tests.*

salpingectomy (sal″pin-jek′to-me) [*salpingo-* + Gr. *ektomē* excision]. Surgical removal of the uterine tube.

salpingemphraxis (sal″pin-jem-frak′sis) [*salpingo-* + Gr. *emphraxis* stoppage]. Obstruction of a uterine tube or of the eustachian tube.

salpingian (sal-pin′je-an). Pertaining to the auditory or to the uterine tube.

salpingion (sal-pin′je-on). A point at the apex of the petrous bone on its lower surface.

salpingitic (sal″pin-jit′ik). Pertaining to or characterized by salpingitis.

salpingitis (sal″pin-ji′tis) [*salpingo-* + *-itis* inflammation]. 1. Inflammation of the uterine tube. 2. Inflammation of the auditory tube. **chronic interstitial s.,** inflammation of the uterine tube associated with infiltration of connective tissue and muscle with lymphocytes and plasma cells. **chronic vegetating s.,** inflammation of the uterine tube, with marked hypertrophy of the mucosa. **eustachian s.,** inflammation of the auditory tube. **hemorrhagic s.,** inflammation of the uterine tube associated with rupture of a blood vessel and effusion of blood. **hypertrophic s.,** pachysalpingitis. **s. isth′mica nodo′sa,** a condition marked by nodular thickening of parts of both uterine tubes, most characteristically of the isthmic portion, pathogenically related to adenomyosis of the uterus. **mural s.,** pachysalpingitis. **nodular s.,** inflammation attended with formation of nodules in the wall and mucous lining of the uterine tube. **parenchymatous s.,** pachysalpingitis. **s. prof′luens,** inflammation of the uterine tube, with accumulation in its lumen of fluid that ultimately escapes. **pseudofollicular s.,** inflammation of the uterine tube characterized by agglutination of its walls, causing a formation of saccules. **purulent s.,** inflammation of the uterine tube attended with suppuration. **tuberculous s.,** infection of the uterine tube by the causative organism of tuberculosis.

salpingo- (sal-ping′go) [Gr. *salpinx* tube]. Combining form denoting relationship to a tube, specifically to the auditory or to the uterine tube.

salpingocatheterism (sal-ping″go-kath′e-ter-izm). Catheterization of the auditory tube.

salpingocele (sal-ping′go-sēl) [*salpingo-* + Gr. *kēlē* hernia]. Hernial protrusion of a uterine tube.

salpingocyesis (sal-ping″go-si-e′sis) [*salpingo-* + Gr. *kyēsis* pregnancy]. Ectopic pregnancy, with the fertilized ovum developing in the uterine tube.

salpingography (sal″ping-gog′rah-fe) [*salpingo-* + Gr. *graphein* to write]. Roentgenography of the uterine tubes after the injection of an opaque medium.

salpingolithiasis (sal-ping″go-lĭ-thi′ah-sis). The presence of calcareous deposits in the wall of the uterine tubes.

salpingolysis (sal″ping-gol′ĭ-sis). The separation of adhesions involving the uterine tubes.

salpingo-oophorectomy (sal-ping″go-o″of-o-rek′to-me). Surgical removal of a uterine tube and ovary.

salpingo-oophoritis (sal-ping″go-o″of-o-ri′tis). Inflammation of a uterine tube and ovary.

salpingo-oophorocele (sal-ping″go-o-of′or-o-sēl). Hernia containing a uterine tube and ovary.

salpingo-oothecitis (sal-ping″go-o″o-the-si′tis) [*salpingo-* + Gr. *ōon* egg + *thēkē* case + *-itis*]. Salpingo-oophoritis.

salpingo-oothecocele (sal-ping″go-o″o-the′ko-sēl) [*salpingo-* + Gr. *ōon* egg + *thēkē* case + *kēlē* hernia]. Salpingo-oophorocele.

salpingo-ovariectomy (sal-ping″go-o-va″re-ek′to-me). Salpingo-oophorectomy.

salpingo-ovariotomy (sal-ping″go-o-va″re-ot′o-me). Salpingo-oophorectomy.

salpingoperitonitis (sal-ping″go-per″ĭ-to-ni′tis). Inflammation of the peritoneum covering the uterine tube.

salpingopexy (sal-ping′go-pek″se) [*salpingo-* + Gr. *pēxis* fixation]. The operation of fixing the uterine tube.

salpingopharyngeal (sal-ping″go-fah-rin′je-al). Pertaining to the auditory tube and the pharynx.

salpingoplasty (sal-ping′go-plas″te) [*salpingo-* + Gr. *plassein* to form]. Plastic operation on the uterine tube.

salpingorrhaphy (sal″ping-gor′ah-fe) [*salpingo-* + Gr. *rhaphē* suture]. The stitching of a uterine tube to the ipsilateral ovary after removal of part of the ovary.

salpingoscope (sal-ping′go-skōp) [*salpingo-* + Gr. *skopein* to examine]. An instrument for exploring the nasopharynx and auditory tube.

salpingoscopy (sal″ping-gos′ko-pe). Inspection of the auditory tube.

salpingostaphyline (sal-ping″go-staf′ĭ-lin). Pertaining to the auditory tube and the uvula.

salpingostomatomy (sal-ping″go-sto-mat′o-me) [*salpingo-* + Gr. *stoma* mouth + *tomē* a cutting]. Surgical resection of a portion of the uterine tube, with creation of a new abdominal ostium.

salpingostomatoplasty (sal-ping″go-sto-mat′o-plas″te). Salpingostomatomy.

salpingostomy (sal″ping-gos′to-me) [*salpingo-* + Gr. *stomoun* to provide with an opening or mouth]. 1. Formation of an opening or fistula into a uterine tube for the purpose of drainage. 2. Surgical restoration of the patency of a uterine tube.

salpingotomy (sal″ping-got′o-me) [*salpingo-* + Gr. *tomē* a cutting]. Surgical incision of a uterine tube.

salpinx (sal′pinks) [Gr.]. A tube. **s. auditi′va,** tuba auditiva. **s. uteri′na,** tuba uterina.

salt (sawlt) [L. *sal;* Gr. *hals*]. 1. Sodium chloride, or common salt. 2. Any compound of a base or radical and an acid; any compound of an acid some of whose replaceable hydrogen atoms have been substituted. 3. [pl.]. A saline purgative. See *Epsom s., Glauber's s.,* and *Rochelle s.* **acid s.,** any salt in which the combining power of the acid is not completely exhausted. **baker's s.,** ammonium carbonate: sometimes used in leavening cakes. **basic s.,** any salt with more than the normal proportion of the basic elements. **bile s's,** salts of bile acids that occur normally in the bile. **buffer s.,** a salt, such as sodium bicarbonate and sodium phosphate, in the blood, which is able to absorb acid or alkali without a corresponding change in hydrogen ion concentration. **Carlsbad s.,** a mixture of sodium sulfate, potassium sulfate, sodium chloride, and sodium bicarbonate. **common s.,** sodium chloride, NaCl. **diuretic s.,** potassium acetate, $CH_3.COOK$. **double s.,** any salt in which the hydrogen atoms of the acid have been replaced by two metals. **Epsom s.,** magnesium sulfate. **Everitt's s.,** iron and potassium cyanide. **Gettysburg s.,** a salt compound obtained from the water of a lithic spring at Gettysburg, Pa. **Glauber's s.,** sodium sulfate. **halide s., haloid s.,** any binary compound of a halogen—i.e., of chlorine, iodine, bromine, fluorine. **Homberg's sedative s.,** boracic acid. **Kissingen s's,** an aperient salt from the waters of a spring at Kissingen, Bavaria. **microcosmic s.,** sodium and ammonium phosphate, $NaNH_4HPO_4.4H_2O$. **Monsel's s.,** iron subsulfate: a brown and highly styptic substance. **neural s., normal s.,** any salt which is neither acid nor basic. **pancreatic s.,** a mixture of the pancreatic ferments with common salt: used as a digestant. **peptic s.,** common salt mixed with pepsin: used as a digestant. **Plimmer's s.,** sodium antimony tartrate: used in trypanosome infection. **Preston's s., Rochelle s., Seignette's s.,** potassium sodium tartrate. **smelling s.,** aromatized ammonium carbonate: stimulant and restorative. **Wurster's s's,** the univalent oxidation products of the aromatic p-diamines. They are free radicals which may polymerize in a sufficiently concentrated solution and at low temperatures or in the solid state.

saltation (sal-ta'shun) [L. *saltatio* from *saltare* to jump]. The action of leaping, especially (1) chorea, or the dancing which sometimes accompanies it; (2) in genetics, an abrupt variation in species; a mutation.

saltatorial, saltatoric (sal″tah-to're-al, sal″-tah-to'rik). Saltatory.

saltatory (sal'tah-to″re). Pertaining to or characterized by saltation. See also under *evolution* and *spasm*.

Salter's incremental lines (sawl'terz) [Sir James A. *Salter*, English dentist of the nineteenth century]. See under *line*.

saltpeter (sawlt-pe'ter) [L. *salpetra* or *sal petrae*] Potassium nitrate, KNO_3. **Chile s.,** sodium nitrate.

salt-sensitive (sawlt-sen'sĭ-tĭv). Agglutinating in normal salt solution: said of suspensions of bacteria.

salubrious (sah-lu'bre-us) [L. *salubris*]. Conducive to health; wholesome.

saluresis (sal″u-re'sis) [L. *sal* salt + Gr. *ourēsis* a making water]. The excretion of sodium and chloride ions in the urine.

saluretic (sal″u-ret'ik). 1. Pertaining to, characterized by, or promoting saluresis. 2. An agent that promotes saluresis.

salutarium (sal″u-ta're-um) [L. *salus* health]. A resort for the preservation of health.

salutary (sal'u-ta″re) [L. *salutaris*]. Favorable to the preservation or restoration of health.

salvarsan (sal'var-san). See *arsphenamine*. **s. copper,** a yellowish-red powder, a combination of arsphenamine and copper: suggested by Ehrlich for use in protozoan infections. **silver s.,** silver arsphenamine. **sulfoxylate s.,** a modified arsphenamine.

salve (sav). A thick ointment or cerate. See *ointment*. **Deshler's s.,** compound resin cerate. **Dreuw's s.,** salicylic acid 10, chrysarobin 20, birch tar 20, green soap 25, petrolatum 25. **fetron s.,** a salve composed of from 3 to 5 per cent of the anilide of stearic acid with petrolatum. **scarlet s.,** a synthetic cell proliferant, toluyl-azo-toluyl-azo-beta-naphthol.

Salvia (sal've-ah) [L.]. A genus of labiate plants. The leaves of *S. officinalis*, sage, contain a volatile oil, and are sudorific, carminative, and astringent: used in sore throat and as an application to ulcers, also for the purpose of checking excessive milk secretion. *S. reflexa*, mint weed, sometimes causes poisoning in stock.

salyrgan (sal'er-gan). Trade mark for a preparation of mersalyl.

Salzer's operation, test meal (salz'erz) [Fritz Adolf *Salzer*, surgeon in Utrecht, born 1858]. See under *operation* and *test meal*.

Salzmann's corneal dystrophy (salz'manz) [Maximilian *Salzmann*, German ophthalmologist, 1862–1954]. See under *dystrophy*.

samaderin (sah-mad'er-in). A light-yellow, bitter, crystalline principle from the fruit and bark of *Samadera indica*.

samandaridine (sam″an-dar'ĭ-din). An alkaloid, $C_{20}H_{31}ON$, from the skin of various salamanders: less poisonous than samandarine.

samandarine (sah-man'dah-rin). A poisonous alkaloid, $C_{19}H_{31}O_2N$, from the skin of various salamanders.

samarium (sah-ma're-um). A very rare metallic element; symbol, Sm; atomic number, 62; atomic weight, 150.35.

Sambucus (sam-bu'kus) [L. "the elder-tree"]. A genus of caprifoliaceous trees and shrubs; elder. The flowers were once considered to be diuretic and diaphoretic, and the berries were thought to possess some laxative principles.

sample (sam'p'l) [L. *exemplum* example]. A representative part taken to typify the whole. **random s.,** a representative part so chosen that each item has an equal chance of being selected.

Sampson's cyst (samp'sunz) [John A. *Sampson*, American gynecologist, 1873–1946]. See under *cyst*.

sanative (san'ah-tiv) [L. *sanare* to heal]. Having a tendency to heal; curative.

sanatorium (san″ah-to're-um) [L. *sanatorius* conferring health, from *sanare* to cure]. 1. An establishment for the treatment of sick persons, especially a private hospital for convalescents or those who are not extremely ill. The term is now applied particularly to an establishment for the open-air treatment of tuberculous patients. 2. A health station; a health resort in a hot region.

sanatory (san'ah-to″re) [L. *sanatorius*]. Conducive to health.

Sanctorius (sank-to're-us) [It. Santorio Santorio] (1561–1636). An Italian physician. He was professor of medicine at Padua and devised several instruments of precision (e.g., a clinical thermometer and a pulse clock); he also made quantitative experiments on basal metabolism, and a famous illustration in his most important book, *De statica medicina* (1614), depicts the author in a steel-yard chair—presumably about to weigh himself after a meal.

sand (sand). Material occurring in small, gritty particles. **brain s.,** acervulus. **intestinal s.,** small gritty particles made up of oxides of calcium and phosphorus, bacteria, bile pigment, etc., formed in the intestine.

sandalwood (san'dal-wood) [L. *santalum*]. 1. The fragrant wood of *Santalum album*, white or yellow sandal, and of other trees of the genera *Santalum* and *Fusanus*. 2. The wood of *Pterocarpus santalinus*, a leguminous tree: coloring agent.

sandarac (san'dah-rak) [Gr. *sandarakē*]. A white, transparent resin from *Callitris quadrivalvis*, a tree of Africa: used in dentistry in an alcoholic solution as a separating fluid and as a preservative varnish for plastic casts. Sometimes, by extension, used also as a verb to denote treatment with the solution.

sand crack (sand krak). A crack in a horse's hoof, sometimes causing lameness. When situated on the inside of the hoof it is termed *quarter crack;* when in the fore part of the hoof it is *toe crack.*

Sander's disease (san′derz) [Wilhelm *Sander*, German physician, 1838–1922]. A form of paranoia.

Sanders' disease [Murray *Sanders*, New York bacteriologist, born 1910]. Epidemic keratoconjunctivitis.

Sanders' sign (san′derz) [James *Sanders*, English physician, 1777–1843]. See under *sign*.

sandfly (sand′fli). A name applied to various two-winged flies of the families Heleidae, Simuliidae, and Psychodidae, but especially to flies of the latter family (of the genus Phlebotomus).

sandril (san′dril). Trade mark for preparations of reserpine.

Sandström's bodies (zant-strāmz) [Ivar Victor *Sandström*, Swedish anatomist, 1852–1889]. The parathyroid glands.

Sandwith's bald tongue (sand′withs) [Fleming Mant *Sandwith*, British physician, 1853–1918]. See under *tongue*.

sane (sān) [L. *sanus*]. Of sound mind.

Sänger. See *Saenger*.

sangui- (sang′gwĭ) [L. *sanguis* blood]. Combining form denoting relationship to blood.

sanguicolous (sang-gwik′o-lus) [*sangui-* + L. *colere* to dwell]. Inhabiting or living in the blood.

sanguifacient (sang″gwĭ-fa′shent) [*sangui-* + L. *facere* to make]. Forming blood.

sanguiferous (sang-gwif′er-us) [*sangui-* + L. *ferre* to bear]. Conveying or containing blood.

sanguification (sang″gwĭ-fi-ka′shun) [*sangui-* + L. *facere* to make]. The process of making blood; also conversion into blood.

sanguimotor, sanguimotory (sang″gwĭ-mo′tor, sang″wĭ-mo′tor-e) [*sangui-* + L. *motor* mover]. Pertaining to blood circulation.

sanguinaria (sang″gwĭ-na′re-ah). The dried rhizome of *Sanguinaria canadensis:* used as an ingredient of compound white pine syrup.

sanguine (sang′gwin) [L. *sanguineus; sanguis* blood]. 1. Abounding in blood. 2. Ardent; hopeful.

sanguineous (sang-gwin′e-us). Abounding in blood; pertaining to the blood.

sanguinolent (sang-gwin′o-lent) [L. *sanguinolentus*]. Of a bloody tinge.

sanguinopoietic (sang″gwĭ-no-poi-et′ik). Hematopoietic.

sanguinous (sang′gwĭ-nus). Sanguineous.

sanguirenal (sang″gwĭ-re′nal) [*sangui-* + L. *ren* kidney]. Pertaining to the blood and the kidneys.

sanguis (sang′gwis) [L.]. [N A, B N A] The fluid that circulates through the heart, arteries, capillaries, and veins, carrying nutriment and oxygen to the body cells. See *blood*.

sanguisuction (sang″gwĭ-suk′shun). The abstraction of blood by application of negative pressure.

sanguisuga (sang″gwĭ-su′gah) [*sangui-* + L. *sugere* to suck]. A leech.

sanguivorous (sang-gwiv′o-rus) [*sangui-* + L. *vorare* to eat]. Blood-eating; said of female mosquitoes which prefer blood to other nutrients.

sanicult (san′ĭ-kult). A certain system of quack medicine.

sanies (sa′ne-ēz) [L.]. A fetid, ichorous discharge from a wound or ulcer, containing serum, pus, and blood.

saniopurulent (sa″ne-o-pu′roo-lent). Partly sanious and partly purulent.

sanioserous (sa″ne-o-se′rus). Partly sanious and partly serous.

sanious (sa′ne-us) [L. *saniosus*]. Of the nature of sanies.

sanipractic (san″ĭ-prak′tik). A system of medical practice based on applied prophylactic and therapeutic sanitation.

sanitarian (san″ĭ-ta′re-an). A person who is expert in matters of sanitation and public health.

sanitarium (san″ĭ-ta′re-um) [L.]. An institution for the promotion of health. The word was originally coined to designate the institution established by the Seventh Day Adventists at Battle Creek, Michigan, to distinguish it from institutions providing care for mental or tuberculous patients.

sanitary (san′ĭ-ta″re) [L. *sanitarius*]. Promoting or pertaining to health.

sanitation (san″ĭ-ta′shun) [L. *sanitas* health]. The establishment of environmental conditions favorable to health; assanation.

sanitization (san″ĭ-ti-za′shun). The process of making or the quality of being made sanitary. See *sanitize*.

sanitize (san′ĭ-tiz). To clean and sterilize, as eating or drinking utensils.

sanity (san′ĭ-te) [L. *sanitas* soundness]. Soundness, especially soundness of mind.

Sansom's sign (san′somz) [Arthur Ernest *Sansom*, English physician, 1838–1907]. See under *sign*.

Sanson's images (san′sonz) [Louis Joseph *Sanson*, French physician, 1790–1841]. See *Purkinje-Sanson images*, under *image*.

santalum (san′tah-lum). Sandalwood. **s. rubrum,** the dried heart wood of *Pterocarpus santalinus:* used as a coloring agent.

Santini booming (san-te′ne). A characteristic booming sound heard on percussion over a hydatid cyst.

santonica (san-ton′ĭ-kah) [L.]. The dried flower heads of *Artemisia maritima*.

santonin (san′to-nin). A lactone which may be obtained from the unexpanded flower heads of *Artemisia cina:* used as an anthelmintic.

Santorini's cartilages, duct, muscle, etc. (sahn″to-re′nēz) [Giovanni Domenico *Santorini*, Italian anatomist, 1681–1737]. See under the nouns.

sap (sap). The natural juice of a living organism or tissue. **cell s.,** enchylema. **nuclear s.,** karyolymph.

saphena (sah-fe′nah) [L.; Gr. *saphēnēs* manifest]. Either of two large superficial veins of the leg. See *vena saphena*.

saphenectomy (saf″e-nek′to-me) [*saphena* + Gr. *ektomē* excision]. Excision of a saphenous vein.

saphenous (sah-fe′nus). Pertaining to or associated with a saphena: applied to certain arteries, nerves, veins, etc.

sapid (sap′id) [L. *sapidus*]. Having or imparting an agreeable taste.

sapin (sa′pin). A nontoxic ptomaine, $C_5H_{14}N_2$: isomeric with cadaverine and neuridine.

sapo (sa′po) [L. "soap"]. 1. Soap; a compound of a fatty acid with a suitable base. 2. White castile soap made of soda and olive oil: used in pills, suppositories, plasters, and liniments: detergent. **s. anima′lis,** sapo domesticus. **s. cine′reus** (gray soap, or mercurial salve soap), a soap containing 50 per cent, by weight, of mercury and 5 per cent of benzoinated fat. **s. domes′ticus,** a preparation of a soft soap made of animal fat and soda. **s. du′rus,** hard soap. **s. mol′lis, s. mol′lis medicina′lis,** soft soap. **s. vir′idis,** soft soap.

sapogenin (sah-poj′e-nin). A compound resulting from the decomposition of saponin, $C_{14}H_{22}O_2$.

saponaceous (sa″po-na′shus) [L. *sapo* soap]. Of a soapy quality or nature.

Saponaria (sa″po-na′re-ah). A genus of plants. The root of *S. officinalis*, or soapwort, has alterative properties and was formerly used in skin diseases.

saponatus (sa″po-na′tus) [L.]. Charged or mixed with soap.

saponification (sah-pon″ĭ-fi-ka′shun) [L. *sapo* soap + *facere* to make]. The act or process of converting fats into soaps and glycerol by heating with alkalis. In chemistry, the term now denotes the hydrolysis, of an ester by an alkali, resulting in the production of a free alcohol and an alkali salt of the ester acid.

saponin (sap′o-nin). A group of glycosides, widely distributed in the plant world and characterized by (1) their property of forming a durable foam when their watery solutions are shaken, (2) by their ability to dissolve red blood cells even in high dilutions, and (3) by their having sapogenin as their aglycones. **cholan s's,** a group of saponins that on hydrolysis yield sterol-like compounds. **triterpenoid s's,** a group of saponins that on hydrolysis yield 1,2,7-trimethyl naphthalene.

sapophore (sap′o-for) [L. *sapor* taste + Gr. *phoros* bearing]. The group of atoms in the molecule of a compound that gives the substance its characteristic taste.

sapotalene (sap′o-tal″ēn). A hydrocarbon, 1,2,7-trimethyl-naphthalene, formed by the reduction of sapogenin.

sapotin (sah-po′tin). A white, crystalline glycoside, $C_{29}H_{52}O_{20}$, from the seeds of *Sapota vapotilla.*

Sappey's fibers, ligament, veins (sahp-pāz′) [Marie Philibert Constant *Sappey*, French anatomist, 1810–1896]. See under the nouns.

sapphism (saf′fizm) [*Sappho*, Greek poetess, about 600 B.C.]. Homosexuality between women.

Sappinia diploidea (sah-pin′e-ah dĭ-ploi′de-ah). A genus of coprozoic amebae having a definite cuticle and two similar nuclei. Called also *Amoeba diploidea* and *Vahlkampfia diploidea.*

sapremia (sah-pre′me-ah) [Gr. *sapros* rotten + *haima* blood + *-ia*]. Intoxication due to the presence in the blood of the products of saprophytic and nonpathogenic bacteria. Called also *septic intoxication* and *putrid intoxication.*

sapremic (sah-pre′mik). Pertaining to or characterized by sapremia.

saprin (sa′prin) [Gr. *sapros* rotten]. A ptomaine, $C_5H_{14}N_2$, from decaying visceral substances: not poisonous.

sapro- (sap′ro) [Gr. *sapros* rotten]. Combining form meaning rotten or putrid, or designating relationship to decay or to decaying material.

saprodontia (sap″ro-don′she-ah) [*sapro-* + Gr. *odous* tooth]. Caries of the teeth.

saprogen (sap′ro-jen). Any microorganism capable of causing putrefaction.

saprogenic (sap-ro-jen′ik) [*sapro-* + Gr. *gennan* to produce]. Causing putrefaction.

saprogenous (sap-roj′e-nus). Arising from putrefaction.

Saprolegnia (sap″ro-leg′ne-ah) [*sapro-* + Gr. *legnon* border]. A genus of partially saprophytic, phycomycetous fungi. *S. fe′rax* is destructive to salmon and to various water animals.

saprophilous (sah-prof′ĭ-lus) [*sapro-* + Gr. *philein* to love]. Living upon decaying and dead matter; a term applied mainly to various microorganisms.

saprophyte (sap′ro-fīt) [*sapro-* + Gr. *phyton* plant]. Any vegetable organism, such as a bacterium, living upon dead or decaying organic matter.

saprophytic (sap″ro-fit′ik). Of the nature of or pertaining to a saprophyte; growing on decomposing organic matter.

saprophytism (sap′ro-fi-tizm). The condition of being a saprophyte.

Saprospira (sap″ro-spi′rah) [*sapro-* + Gr. *speira* coil]. A genus of microorganisms of the family Spirochaetaceae, order Spirochaetales, made up of actively motile cells containing spiral protoplasm without evident axial filament and with a definite periplast membrane found free-living in marine ooze. It contains three species, *S. gran′dis, S. lep′ta,* and *S. punc′tum,* the type species being *S. gran′dis.*

saprozoic (sap″ro-zo′ik) [*sapro-* + Gr. *zōon* animal]. Living on dead or lifeless matter.

saprozoite (sap″ro-zo′īt). An animal organism living upon dead or decaying animal matter.

sarapus (sar′ah-pus) [Gr. *sairein* to sweep + *pous* foot]. A person with flat feet.

Sarbó's sign (sar′bōz) [Arthur von *Sarbó*, Budapest neurologist, born 1867]. See under *sign.*

sarcin (sar′sin) [Gr. *sarx* flesh]. 1. Hypoxanthine. 2. Sarcine.

Sarcina (sar-si′nah). A genus of microorganisms of the family Micrococcaceae, order Eubacteriales, occurring as spherical, gram-positive cells in cubical packets of 8 cells, found in soil and water as saprophytes and rarely observed in disease processes.

sarcina (sar′sĭ-nah), pl. *sar′cinae* [L.]. 1. A spherical bacterium occurring predominantly in cubical packets of eight cells as a consequence of failure of daughter cells to separate following cell division in three planes. 2. An organism of the genus *Sarcina.*

sarcinae (sar′sĭ-ne) [L.]. Plural of *sarcina.*

sarcine (sar′sīn) [L. *sarcina* pack]. A cube composed of eight bacterial cells (sarcine of the first power), or of sixty-four cells (sarcine of the second power), produced by the division of sarcinae.

sarcinic (sar-sin′ik). Pertaining to sarcinae.

sarcitis (sar-si′tis) [*sarco-* + *-itis*]. Myositis.

sarco- (sar′ko) [Gr. *sarx, sarkos* flesh]. Combining form denoting relationship to flesh.

sarcoadenoma (sar″ko-ad″e-no′mah). Adenosarcoma.

sarcobiont (sar″ko-bi′ont) [*sarco-* + Gr. *bioun* to live]. An organism that lives on flesh.

Sarcobiot (sar″ko-bi′ot) [*sarco-* + Gr. *bios* life]. A species of fly which deposits its larvae in or near living animal tissue.

sarcoblast (sar′ko-blast) [*sarco-* + Gr. *blastos* germ]. The primitive cell which develops into a muscle cell.

sarcocarcinoma (sar″ko-kar″sĭ-no′mah). Sarcoma and carcinoma combined.

sarcocele (sar′ko-sēl) [*sarco-* + Gr. *kēlē* tumor]. Any fleshy swelling or tumor of the testicle.

sarcocol (sar′ko-kol) [L. *sarcocolla; sarco-* + Gr. *kolla* glue]. A nauseous gum-resin from various African species of *Penaea.*

sarcocyst (sar′ko-sist) [*sarco-* + Gr. *kystis* bladder]. See *Miescher's tubules,* under *tubule.*

sarcocystin (sar″ko-sis′tin). A toxin obtained from the bodies of species of Sarcocystis.

Sarcocystis (sar″ko-sis′tis) [*sarco-* + Gr. *kystis* bladder]. A genus of parasites in animals. *S. bertram′i* is said to have been found in man. *S. blanchar′di* is found in cattle. *S. hue′ti* is found in the seal. *S. kor′tei* is found in monkeys. *S. mischeria′na* is found in the pig. *S. muco′sa* is found in the kangaroo and perhaps in man. *S. mu′ris* is found in rats and perhaps in man. *S. tenel′la* is found in sheep and cattle and in man. *S. tenel′la bu′bali* is found in the meat of Indian buffaloes (*Bu′balus buf′felus*).

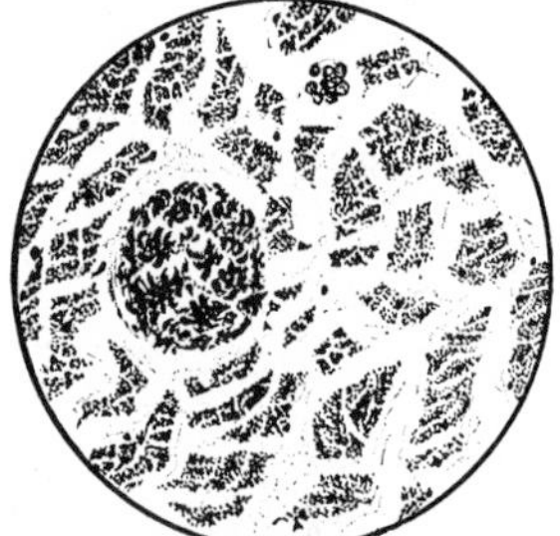

Sarcocystis tenella in heart muscle of cow (de Rivas).

sarcocyte (sar′ko-sīt) [*sarco-* + *-cyte*]. The middle layer of ectoplasm of a protozoan lying between the epicyte and the myocyte.

sarcode (sar′kōd) [*sarco-* + Gr. *eidos* form]. The protoplasm of animal cells.

Sarcodina (sar″ko-di′nah) [Gr. *sarkōdēs* fleshlike]. The lowest class of protozoa in which locomotion and ingestion of food are accomplished by pseudopodia.

sarcoenchondroma (sar″ko-en″kon-dro′mah). Sarcoma combined with enchondroma.

sarcogenic (sar″ko-jen′ik) [*sarco-* + Gr. *gennan* to produce]. Forming flesh.

sarcoglia (sar-kog′le-ah) [*sarco-* + Gr. *glia* glue]. The substance which composes the eminences of Doyen at the entrance of nerves into muscle fibers.

sarcohydrocele (sar″ko-hi′dro-sēl). Sarcocele combined with hydrocele.

sarcoid (sar′koid) [*sarco-* + Gr. *eidos* form]. 1. Resembling flesh; fleshy. 2. A sarcoma-like tumor; a general term applied to a group of skin lesions generally credited with being of tuberculous nature. **s. of Boeck,** a type of multiple benign sarcoid characterized by its superficial nature and showing a predilection for the face, arms, and shoulders. **Darier-Roussy s.,** a type of multiple benign sarcoid, characterized by the large size of its nodules and its subcutaneous location. **multiple benign s.,** a condition marked by the presence of nodules on the skin, caused by proliferation of connective tissue surrounding the blood vessels, the lesions being of a tuberculous nature. Called also *miliary lupoid.* **Roussy-Darier s.,** Darier-Roussy s. **Schaumann's s.,** a form called benign lymphogranulomatosis by Schaumann. **Spiegler-Fendt s.,** a sarcoid in the subcutaneous tissue in the form of a circumscribed cellular mass containing reticulated cells and lymphocytes; probably a solitary lymphocytoma.

sarcoidosis (sar″koi-do′sis). A disorder which may affect any part of the body but most frequently involving the lymph nodes, liver, spleen, lungs, skin, eyes, and small bones of the hands and feet; characterized by the presence in all affected organs or tissues of epithelioid cell tubercles, without caseation, and with little or no round-cell reaction, becoming converted, in the older lesions, into a rather hyaline featureless fibrous tissue. **s. cor′dis,** involvement of the heart in sarcoidosis, with lesions ranging from a few asymptomatic, microscopic granulomas to widespread infiltration of the myocardium by large masses of sarcoid tissue. **muscular s.,** sarcoidosis involving the skeletal muscles, with sarcoid tubercles, interstitial inflammation with fibrosis, and disruption and atrophy of the muscle fibers.

sarcolactate (sar″ko-lak′tāt). Any salt of sarcolactic acid.

sarcolemma (sar″ko-lem′ah) [*sarco-* + Gr. *lemma* husk]. The delicate elastic sheath which invests every striated muscle fiber.

sarcolemmic (sar″ko-lem′ik). Pertaining to or of the nature of sarcolemma.

sarcolemmous (sar″ko-lem′us). Sarcolemmic.

sarcoleukemia (sar″ko-lu-ke′me-ah). Lymphosarcoma cell leukemia.

sarcology (sar-kol′o-je). That branch of anatomy which treats of the soft tissues of the body.

sarcolysis (sar-kol′ĭ-sis) [*sarco-* + Gr. *lysis* dissolution]. Disintegration of the soft tissues; disintegration of flesh.

sarcolyte (sar′ko-lit). 1. A cell concerned in the disintegration of the soft tissues. 2. A disintegrating muscle fiber.

sarcolytic (sar″ko-lit′ik). Pertaining to, characterized by, or causing sarcolysis.

sarcoma (sar-ko′mah), pl. *sarcomas* or *sarco′mata* [*sarco-* + *-oma*]. A tumor made up of a substance like the embryonic connective tissue; tissue composed of closely packed cells embedded in a fibrillar or homogeneous substance. Sarcomas are often highly malignant. See also *chondrosarcoma, fibrosarcoma, lymphosarcoma, melanosarcoma, myxosarcoma, osteosarcoma,* etc. **Abernethy's s.,** a variety of fatty tumor found principally on the trunk. **adipose s.,** one which contains a copious element of fat. **alveolar s.,** a variety having a reticulated fibrous stoma inclosing groups of sarcoma cells, which resemble epithelial cells and are inclosed in alveoli walled with connective tissue. **ameloblastic s.,** the malignant counterpart of ameloblastic fibroma. **angiolithic s.,** psammoma. **botryoid s., s. botryoi′des,** a vaginal sarcoma, observed most frequently in the young infant, occurring as a polypoid, grapelike structure, and involving the upper part of the vagina or the cervix, or both. **chicken s.,** a sarcoma which is found in chickens and which may be of several various cell types. **chloromatous s.,** a round-cell sarcoma of the periosteum of the skull, having a greenish color. **s. col′li u′teri hydro′picum papilla′re,** botryoid s. **cylindromatous s.,** a sarcoma whose substance is traversed by cylinders of myxomatous tissue. **deciduocellular s.,** malignant deciduoma of the uterus. See *syncytioma malignum.* **encephaloid s.,** round cell s. **Ewing's s.** See under *tumor.* **fascial s.,** a sarcoma arising in the fasciae about the joints, especially in the lower extremities (Virchow). **fasciculated s.,** spindle cell s. **fowl s.,** *chicken s.* **fusocellular s.,** spindle cell s. **giant cell s.,** a variety named from its containing large multinucleated cells, or myeloplaxes. **globocellular s.,** round cell s. **Hodgkin's s.,** lymphadenoma with a rapid clinical course and indication of great cell activity. **infective s.,** a growth in the dog of uncertain nature, and attributed to infection. **Jensen's s.,** a malignant tumor in mice transmissible to healthy mice by transplanting a small portion of the tumor. **Kaposi's s.,** multiple soft bluish nodules of the skin with hemorrhages, similar to infectious granulomas, and under certain conditions developing neoplastic characteristics. **leukocytic s.,** leukemia. **lymphatic s.,** lymphosarcoma. **medullary s.,** a soft, bleeding, fungous sarcoma; fungus haematodes. **melanotic s.,** a variety whose substance is pigmented with melanin. **mixed cell s.,** polymorphous s. **multiple hemorrhagic s.,** Kaposi's s. **myelogenic s.,** a sarcoma involving the bone marrow. **myeloid s.,** a variety containing both giant cells and spindle cells. **net cell s.,** a variety of myxosarcoma. **oat cell s., oat-shaped cell s.,** a sarcoma in which the cells are bluntly elongated and contain long oval nuclei. **osteoblastic s.,** an osteogenic sarcoma which produces tissue that resembles bone or cartilage. **osteogenic s.,** a general term for tumors occurring in bone and arising from bone cells of osteogenic tissue. **osteoid s.,** a sarcoma in which bony tissue has developed. **osteolytic s.,** a rarefying tumor of bone composed of very vascular tissue and containing giant cells. **parosteal s.,** a sarcoma situated close to the outer surface of a bone. **polymorphous s.,** a sarcoma containing cells of several varieties. **reticulocytic s., reticuloendothelial s.,** reticulum cell s. **reticulum cell s.,** a form of malignant lymphoma in which the predominant cell is the primitive mesenchymal element, or one which has differentiated into the identifiable reticulum cell. Called also *reticulocytic s., reticuloendothelial s., reticulosarcoma, retothelial s.,* and *clasmocytic lymphoma.* **retothelial s.,** reticulum cell s. **round cell s.,** encephaloid or medullary cancer: a sarcoma with large or small cells resembling leukocytes. **Rous s.,** a peculiar sarcoma-like growth found in some fowls; from it can be obtained a filterable virus which on inoculation into other fowls produces similar growths. **serocystic s.,** a proliferous cyst with intracystic growths. **spindle cell s.,** a form with spindle-shaped cells: a recurrent fibroid or fibroplastic tumor. **withering s.,** mycosis fungoides.

sarcomagenesis (sar″ko-mah-jen′e-sis). The production of sarcoma.

sarcomagenic (sar″ko-mah-jen′ik). Causing sarcoma.

sarcomatoid (sar-ko′mah-toid). Resembling sarcoma.

sarcomatosis (sar″ko-mah-to′sis). A condition characterized by the formation of sarcomas. **s. cu′tis,** the development of sarcomatous growths on the skin. **general s.,** the occurrence of sarcomas in several parts of the body at the same time.

sarcomatous (sar-ko′mah-tus). Pertaining to or of the nature of sarcoma.

sarcomelanin (sar″ko-mel′ah-nin) [*sarco-* + Gr. *melas* black]. The black pigment of melanosarcoma.

sarcomere (sar′ko-mēr) [*sarco-* + Gr. *meros* part]. Any one of the segments into which the lines or membranes of Krause are supposed to divide a muscular fibrilla.

sarcomphalocele (sar″kom-fal′o-sēl) [*sarco-* + Gr. *omphalos* navel + *kēlē* tumor]. A fleshy tumor of the umbilicus.

sarcomyces (sar″ko-mi′sēz) [*sarco-* + Gr. *mykēs* fungus]. A fleshy fungous growth.

Sarcophaga (sar-kof′ah-gah) [*sarco-* + Gr. *phagein* to eat]. A genus of flies of the family Sarcophagidae. The larvae of several species have been found in wounds, ulcers, the nasal passages, and sinuses. *S. carna′ria* causes genitourinary myiasis. Other species are *S. fuscicau′da, S. dux, S. haemorrhoida′lis, S. nificor′nis.*

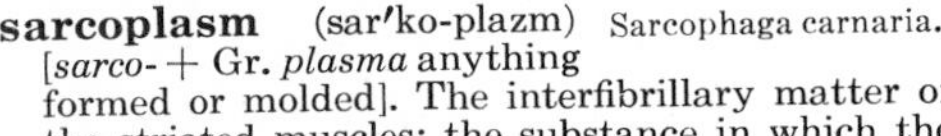

Sarcophaga carnaria.

sarcoplasm (sar′ko-plazm) [*sarco-* + Gr. *plasma* anything formed or molded]. The interfibrillary matter of the striated muscles; the substance in which the fibrillae of the muscle fiber are embedded.

sarcoplasmic (sar″ko-plaz′mik). Composed of or containing sarcoplasm.

sarcoplast (sar′ko-plast) [*sarco-* + Gr. *plastos* formed]. An interstitial cell of a muscle, itself capable of being transformed into a muscle.

sarcopoietic (sar″ko-poi-et′ik) [*sarco-* + Gr. *poiein* to make]. Producing flesh or muscle.

Sarcoptes (sar-kop′tēz) [*sarco-* + Gr. *koptein* to cut]. A genus of acarids, including *S. scabie′i*, or the itch mite which produces scabies in man. See *scabies*. Varieties of *S. scabiei* cause mange of swine, horses, and dogs.

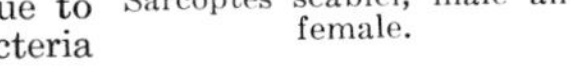

Sarcoptes scabiei, male and female.

sarcoptidosis (sar-kop″tĭ-do′sis). Infestation with Sarcoptes.

sarcosepsis (sar″ko-sep′sis). Sepsis due to the presence of bacteria in the tissues.

sarcosis (sar-ko′sis) [*sarco-* + *-osis*]. 1. The presence of multiple fleshy tumors. 2. Abnormal increase of flesh.

sarcosome (sar′ko-sōm) [*sarco-* + Gr. *sōma* body]. One of the granules, other than mitochondria, located in the sarcoplasm.

Sarcosporidia (sar″ko-spo-rid′e-ah). An order of sporozoan parasites found in the muscles of warm-blooded animals and producing anemia and cachexia.

sarcosporidiasis (sar″ko-spo″rĭ-di′ah-sis). Sarcosporidiosis.

sarcosporidiosis (sar″ko-spo-rid″e-o′sis). The condition of being infected with Sarcosporidia.

sarcosporidium (sar″ko-spo-rid′e-um), pl. *sarcosporid′ia*. An individual organism of the order Sarcosporidia.

sarcostosis (sar″kos-to′sis) [*sarco-* + Gr. *osteon* bone]. Ossification of the fleshy tissues.

sarcostyle (sar′ko-stil) [*sarco-* + Gr. *stylos* column]. 1. A myofibrilla. 2. A bundle of myofibrillae.

sarcotherapeutics (sar″ko-ther″ah-pu′tiks). Treatment of disease by the use of animal extracts.

sarcotherapy (sar″ko-ther′ah-pe). Sarcotherapeutics.

sarcotic (sar-kot′ik) [Gr. *sarkōtikos*]. Promoting the growth of flesh.

sarcotome (sar′ko-tōm). A kind of écraseur worked by a spring.

sarcotripsy (sar′ko-trip″se). Histotripsy.

sarcous (sar′kus). Pertaining to flesh or to muscular tissues.

sardonic (sar-don′ik) [L. *sardonicus;* Gr. *Sardonikos* Sardinian]. Noting a kind of spasmodic or tetanic grin or involuntary smile, the *risus sardonicus:* so called from a plant of Sardinia, probably a *Ranunculus*, or crowfoot, which was believed to produce it.

sarmentocymarin (sar-men″to-si′mah-rin). A cardiac glycoside, $C_{30}H_{46}O_8$, from the seeds of *Strophanthus sarmentosus*. On hydrolysis it yields sarmentogenin and sarmentose.

sarmentogenin (sar″men-toj′e-nin). An aglycone, $C_{23}H_{34}O_5$, from sarmentocymarin. It has been studied as a possible source of cortisone.

sarmentose (sar′men-tōs). A methyl ether of a 2-desoxyhexomethyl sugar from sarmentocymarin.

Sarothamnus (sa″ro-tham′nus) [Gr. *saron* broom + *thamnos* shrub]. A genus of leguminous European shrubs. *S. scopa′rius* is called broom. See *scoparius*.

Sarracenia (sar″ah-se′ne-ah) [Michel *Sarrazin*, Quebec physician and naturalist, 1659–1734]. A genus of polypetalous plants, known as *side-saddle flower* and *pitcher plant*, type of the order Sarraceniaceae. *S. purpu′rea*, the commonest of the pitcher plants of North America. The secretion of the pitcher of this plant is said to contain digestant enzymes. It is a stimulant, diuretic, and aperient.

sarsa (sar′sah), gen. *sar′sae* [L.; Sp. *sarça* briar]. Sarsaparilla.

sarsaparilla (sar″sap-ah-ril′ah) [L.; Sp. "briar vine"]. The dried root of *Smilax aristolochiaefolia:* used as a flavoring agent for drugs.

sartian (sar′shan) [named for the *Sarts*, a people of Central Asia]. Noting an epidemic skin disease of Central Asia, characterized by facial nodules which become converted into scabby ulcers: probably furunculus orientalis.

Sassafras (sas′ah-fras) [L.]. A genus of lauraceous trees. The root bark of *S. variifo′lia*, a tree of North America, is aromatic, stimulant, diaphoretic, and carminative. The volatile oil contains safrene and safrol. It is an antinarcotic and carminative, but is chiefly used as a flavoring agent. The pith of the stems of sassafras (*S. medulla*) affords a mucilage which has been used as a demulcent in bronchial and gastric affections, and as an application in eye diseases.

sat. Abbreviation for *saturated*.

satamul (sah′tah-mool). The *Asparagus sarmentosus*, a medicinal plant of India.

satellite (sat′ĕ-līt) [L. *satelles* companion]. 1. A vein that closely accompanies an artery, such as the brachial. 2. A minor, or attendant, lesion situated near a larger one. 3. A rounded mass connected to the main body of a chromosome by a chromatic filament. **bacterial s.,** a bacterium that grows more vigorously in the immediate vicinity of a colony of some other organism, as *Haemophilus influenzae* near a colony of staphylococci.

satellitosis (sat″ĕ-li-to′sis). Accumulation of glia cells about the ganglion cells of the brain cortex: seen in general paralysis, etc.

satiety (sah-ti′e-ty) [L. *satis* sufficient + *-ety* state or condition of]. Sufficiency, or satisfaction, as full gratification of appetite or thirst, with abolition of the desire to ingest food or liquids.

Satterthwaite's method (sat′er-thwāts) [Thomas Edward *Satterthwaite*, New York physician, 1843–1934]. Artificial respiration produced by alternating pressure and relaxation upon the abdomen.

Sattler's layer (sat′lerz) [Hubert *Sattler*, Austrian ophthalmologist, 1844–1928]. See under *layer.*

saturated (sat′u-rāt″ed). 1. Having all the chemical affinities satisfied. 2. Unable to hold in solution any more of a given substance.

saturation (sat″u-ra′shun) [L. *saturatio*]. 1. The act of saturating or condition of being saturated. 2. In radiotherapy, the delivery of an erythema dose within a short time and then maintaining this effect for some time by additional smaller doses. 3. An effervescing draft or potion.

saturnine (sat′ur-nīn) [L. *saturninus; saturnus* lead]. Pertaining to or produced by lead.

saturnism (sat′ur-nizm) [L. *saturnus* lead]. Chronic lead poisoning; plumbism.

saturnotherapy (sat″ur-no-ther′ah-pe). Lead treatment. See *Bell's treatment*, under *treatment.*

satyriasis (sat″ĭ-ri′ah-sis) [Gr. *satyros* satyr]. Excessive venereal impulse in the male.

satyromania (sat″ĭ-ro-ma′ne-ah) [Gr. *satyros* satyr + *mania* madness]. Satyriasis.

saucer (saw′ser). A rounded, shallow depression. **auditory s.,** a saucer-shaped fold of the embryonic ectoderm which develops into the otocyst.

saucerization (saw″ser-i-za′shun). 1. The shallow, saucer-like depression on the upper surface of a vertebra which has suffered a crush fracture (William Rogers). 2. In wound treatment, the excavation of tissue and laying open of the wound so as to form a shallow shelving depression (G. R. Girdlestone).

Sauer's vaccine (sow′erz) [Louis W. *Sauer*, American pediatrician, born 1885]. See under *vaccine.*

Sauerbruch's cabinet, prosthesis (sow′er-brooks) [Ferdinand *Sauerbruch*, surgeon in Berlin, 1875–1951]. See under *cabinet* and *prosthesis.*

Saundby's test (sawnd′bēz) [Robert *Saundby*, English physician, 1849–1918]. See under *tests.*

Saunders' disease, sign (sawn′derz) [Edward Watt *Saunders*, physician in St. Louis, 1854–1927]. See under *disease* and *sign.*

sauriasis (saw-ri′ah-sis). Ichthyosis.

sauriderma (saw″ri-der′mah) [Gr. *sauros* lizard + *derma* skin]. Ichthyosis hystrix.

sauriosis (saw″re-o′sis) [Gr. *sauros* lizard]. Keratosis follicularis.

sauroid (saw′roid) [Gr. *sauros* lizard + *eidos* form]. Resembling a reptile.

sausarism (saw′sar-izm). A dry or paralyzed condition of the tongue.

Saussure's hygrometer (so-sūrz′) [Horace Bénédict de *Saussure*, Swiss physicist, 1740–1779]. See under *hygrometer.*

Sauvineau's ophthalmoplegia (so″vĭ-nōz′) [Charles *Sauvineau*, French ophthalmologist, born 1862]. See under *ophthalmoplegia.*

Savill's disease (sa′vilz) [Thomas Dixon *Savill*, physician in London, 1856–1910]. See under *disease.*

savin (sav′in) [L. *sabina*]. The evergreen shrub, *Juniperus sabina.* The leaves and tops afford acrid volatile oil, which is used in dysmenorrhea, amenorrhea, gout, and rheumatism, and is used locally as an application to ulcers, condylomas, and carious teeth.

saw (saw). A cutting instrument with a cutting or serrated edge. **Adams' s.,** a small straight saw with a long handle, for osteotomy. **amputating s.,** one for use in performing amputations. **Butcher's s.,** an amputating saw with a blade that can be set at various angles. **chain s.,** one in which the teeth are set upon links, the saw being moved by pulling upon one or the other handle. **crown s.,** a form of trephine. **Farabeuf's s.,** a saw the blade of which can be set at any desired angle. **Gigli's wire s.,** a wire with saw teeth, used in pubiotomy. **hemp s.,** a hempen cord used in cutting soft tissues. **Hey's s.,** a small saw for enlarging orifices in bones. **hole s.,** a trephine. **separating s.,** a saw for separating teeth. **Shrady's s., subcutaneous s.,** a saw for bone work operated through a fenestrated cannula which has been introduced alongside the bone by a trocar.

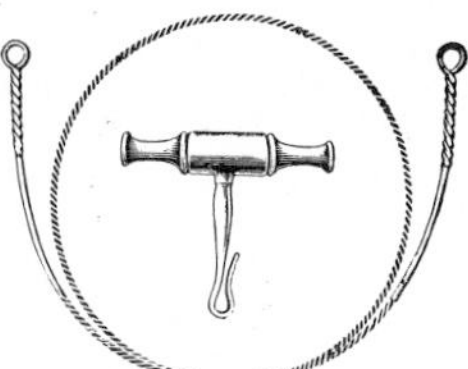

Gigli's wire saw.

saxitoxin (sak″sĭ-tok′sin). A toxic substance obtained from poisonous mussels (*Mytilus*), clams (*Saxidomus*), and plankton (*Gonyaulaux*), said to have a molecular formula of $C_{10}H_{17}N_7O_4.2HCl$.

Sayre's apparatus, bandage, jacket (sa′erz) [Lewis Albert *Sayre*, American surgeon, 1820–1901]. See under the nouns.

Sb. Chemical symbol for *antimony* (L. *stibium*).

$SbCl_3$. Antimony trichloride.

Sb_2O_3. Antimony trioxide.

Sb_2O_5. Antimonic oxide.

Sb_4O_6. Antimonious oxide.

S.C. Abbreviation for *closure of the semilunar valves.*

Sc. Chemical symbol for *scandium.*

s.c. Abbreviation for *subcutaneously.*

scab (skab). 1. The crust of a superficial sore. 2. To become covered with a crust or scab. **crown s.,** a cancerous sore around the corners of the hoof of a horse. **foot s.,** sheep scab. **head s.,** any acariasis of the head, especially the sarcoptic scab of the head of sheep. **sheep s.,** a disease of sheep caused by the mite *Psoroptes communis*, which infests the skin at the base of the hairs. A scab is formed which comes off, bringing the wool along with it. **Transkeian s.,** veldt sore.

scabicide (ska′bĭ-sīd). 1. Destructive to *Sarcoptes scabiei;* used in the treatment of scabies. 2. An agent for destroying *Sarcoptes scabiei.*

scabies (ska′be-ēz) [L., from *scabere* scratch]. A contagious skin disease due to the itch mite, *Sarcoptes scabiei*, which bores beneath the skin, forming cuniculi or burrows. The disease is attended with intense itching, together with the eczema caused by scratching. Called also *the itch* and *psora.* **Boeck's s.,** Norwegian s. **bovine s.,** a disease of cattle resembling sheep scab. **s. crusto′sa,** Norwegian s. **s. feri′na,** acariasis in animals. **Moeller's s.,** Norwegian s. **Norwegian s.,** a rare form associated with an immense number of mites and with marked scales and crusts.

scabieticide (ska″be-et′ĭ-sīd). Scabicide.

scabiophobia (ska″be-o-fo′be-ah) [*scabies* + Gr. *phobein* to be affrighted by]. Morbid fear of scabies.

Scabiosa (ska″be-o′sah) [L.]. A genus of dipsaceous plants called *scabious:* various species are popularly regarded as depuratives of the blood.

scabrities (ska-brish′e-ēz) [L.]. A scaly or rough state of the skin. **s. un′guium,** a thickened and distorted condition of the nails.

scala (ska′lah), pl. *sca′lae* [L. "staircase"]. A stair-like structure, applied especially to various passages of the cochlea. **s. me′dia, s. of Löwenberg,** ductus cochlearis. **s. tym′pani** [N A, B N A], the perilymph-filled part of the cochlea that is continuous with the scala vestibuli at the helicotrema, is separated from other cochlear structures by the spiral lamina and the cochlear duct, and ends blindly near the fenestra cochleae. **s. vestib′uli** [N A, B N A], the perilymph-filled part of the cochlea that begins in the vestibule, is separated from other cochlear structures by the spiral lamina and the cochlear duct, and becomes continuous with the scala tympani at the helicotrema.

scalariform (skah-lar′ĭ-form) [L. *scalaris* like a ladder + *forma* shape]. Resembling the rungs of a ladder.

scald (skawld). 1. A burn caused by a hot liquid or a hot, moist vapor. 2. Scald head.

scale (skāl). 1. [Fr. *écale* shell, husk.] A thin, compacted, platelike structure, as of epithelial cells, on the surface of the body, or shed from the skin. 2. [L. *scala*, usually pl., *scalae*, a series of steps.] A scheme or device by which some property may be evaluated or measured, such as a linear surface bearing marks at regular intervals, representing certain predetermined units. 3. To remove material from a body surface, as incrusted material from the surface of the teeth. **absolute s.,** a temperature scale with zero at the absolute zero of temperature. **Apgar s.** See under *score.* **Baumé s.,** a scale for expressing the specific gravity of fluids. **Benoist's s.,** a scale for denoting the hardness of roentgen rays in terms of the thickness of aluminum necessary to reduce the intensity of the rays to that of the same rays that have been passed through a screen of silver 0.11 mm. thick. **Bloch's s.,** a series of solutions of tincture of benzoin in glycerinated water, employed to determine, by comparison of turbidity, the amount of albumin precipitated in urine or other fluid by heat. **Celsius s.,** a temperature scale with the ice point at 0 and the normal boiling point of water at 100 degrees (100°C.). **centigrade s.,** one in which the interval between two established points is divided into 100 equal units, such as the Celsius scale. **Charrière s.,** a scale for grading the size of urethral sounds and catheters. See *French s.* **Clark's s.,** a scale used in denoting the hardness of water, based on the number of grains of calcium carbonate per imperial gallon. **diaphanometric s.,** a scale used in denoting the transparency of turbid solutions such as are produced in flocculation tests. **Dunfermline s.,** a scheme used in denoting the nutritional status of children: 1, superior condition; 2, passable condition; 3, requiring supervision; 4, requiring medical treatment. **Fahrenheit s.,** a temperature scale with the ice point at 32 and the normal boiling point of water at 212 degrees (212°F.). **French s.,** a scale used for denoting the size of catheters, sounds, and other tubular instruments, each unit being roughly equivalent to 0.33 mm. in diameter, that is, 18 French indicates a diameter of 6 mm. **Gaffky s.,** a scale used in denoting the prognosis in tuberculosis, based on the number of tubercle bacilli in the sputum. **Holzknecht's s.,** a series of colors of gradually differing values, used with Holzknecht's chromoradiometer. **hydrometer s.,** a scale used for expressing the specific gravity of liquids. **Kelvin s.,** an absolute scale on which the unit of measurement corresponds with that of the Celsius (centigrade) scale, and the ice point is at 273.15 degrees (273.15°K.). **Rankine s.,** an absolute scale on which the unit of measurement corresponds with that of the Fahrenheit scale, and the ice point is at 459.67 degrees (459.67°R.). **Réaumur s.,** a temperature scale with the ice point at 0 and the normal boiling point of water at 80 degrees (80°R.). **Sorensen s.,** a scale on which hydrogen ion concentration is expressed in pH. **Tallqvist's s.,** a series of lithographed colors showing the tints of blood of from 10 to 100 per cent of hemoglobin, accompanied by a booklet containing sheets of prepared paper which may be moistened with a drop of blood and hemoglobin determined by comparison of the color with the scale. **temperature s.,** a scale used for expressing the degree of heat, based on absolute zero as a reference point (absolute scale), or with a certain value arbitrarily assigned to such temperatures as the ice point and boiling point of water under certain stipulated conditions, the range between them being divided into a designated number of identical units.

TABLE OF EQUIVALENTS OF CELSIUS (CENTIGRADE) AND FAHRENHEIT TEMPERATURE SCALES

CELSIUS	FAHR.	CELSIUS	FAHR.	CELSIUS	FAHR.
Deg.	Deg.	Deg.	Deg.	Deg.	Deg.
−40	−40.0	9	48.2	57	134.6
−39	−38.2	10	50.0	58	136.4
−38	−36.4	11	51.8	59	138.2
−37	−34.6	12	53.6	60	140.0
−36	−32.8	13	55.4	61	141.8
−35	−31.0	14	57.2	62	143.6
−34	−29.2	15	59.0	63	145.4
−33	−27.4	16	60.8	64	147.2
−32	−25.6	17	62.6	65	149.0
−31	−23.8	18	64.4	66	150.8
−30	−22.0	19	66.2	67	152.6
−29	−20.2	20	68.0	68	154.4
−28	−18.4	21	69.8	69	156.2
−27	−16.6	22	71.6	70	158.0
−26	−14.8	23	73.4	71	159.8
−25	−13.0	24	75.2	72	161.6
−24	−11.2	25	77.0	73	163.4
−23	−9.4	26	78.8	74	165.2
−22	−7.6	27	80.6	75	167.0
−21	−5.8	28	82.4	76	168.8
−20	−4.0	29	84.2	77	170.6
−19	−2.2	30	86.0	78	172.4
−18	−0.4	31	87.8	79	174.2
−17	+1.4	32	89.6	80	176.0
−16	3.2	33	91.4	81	177.8
−15	5.0	34	93.2	82	179.6
−14	6.8	35	95.0	83	181.4
−13	8.6	36	96.8	84	183.2
−12	10.4	37	98.6	85	185.0
−11	12.2	38	100.4	86	186.8
−10	14.0	39	102.2	87	188.6
−9	15.8	40	104.0	88	190.4
−8	17.6	41	105.8	89	192.2
−7	19.4	42	107.6	90	194.0
−6	21.2	43	109.4	91	195.8
−5	23.0	44	111.2	92	197.6
−4	24.8	45	113.0	93	199.4
−3	26.6	46	114.8	94	201.2
−2	28.4	47	116.6	95	203.0
−1	30.2	48	118.4	96	204.8
0	32.0	49	120.2	97	206.6
+1	33.8	50	122.0	98	208.4
2	35.6	51	123.8	99	210.2
3	37.4	52	125.6	100	212.0
4	39.2	53	127.4	101	213.8
5	41.0	54	129.2	102	215.6
6	42.8	55	131.0	103	217.4
7	44.6	56	132.8	104	219.2
8	46.4				

scalene (ska′lēn) [Gr. *skalēnos* uneven]. 1. Unequally three sided. 2. Pertaining to one of the scalenus muscles.

scalenectomy (ska″le-nek′to-me) [*scalenus* + Gr. *ektomē* excision]. The operation of resecting a scalenus muscle.

scalenotomy (ska″le-not′o-me) [*scalenus* + Gr. *tomē* a cutting]. The operation of severing the scaleni muscles close to their insertion on the ribs to restrict respiratory activity of the upper part of the thorax and thus induce apical rest in pulmonary tuberculosis.

scalenus (ska-le′nus) [L.; Gr. *skalēnos*]. Uneven; a name given to various muscles. See *Table of Musculi.*

scaler (ska′ler). A dental instrument used in removing calculus from the surface of the teeth. **chisel s.,** a straight instrument which curves slightly as the blade extends from the shank, the straight cutting edge, at the end of the instrument, being beveled at a 45 degree angle. **curet s.** See *curet.* **deep s.,** a dental instrument designed for use in removal of subgingival calculus. **hoe s.,** one made with different angular relationships of shank and handle, but with the blade bent at a 99 degree angle, and the flattened termination surface beveled at an angle of 45 degrees. **superficial s.,** a dental instrument designed for use in removal of supragingival calculus.

scaling (skāl′ing). Removal of calculous material from the exposed tooth surfaces and that part of the teeth covered by the marginal gingiva.

scall (skawl). 1. Any scaly, or scabby, disease of the skin. 2. Favus of animals. **honeycomb s.,** an eruption consisting of small ulcers separated by raised edges. **milk s.,** crusta lactea.

scalma (skal′mah). A contagious febrile disease of the horse marked by coughing, difficult breathing, fever, weakness, and sometimes pleuritis.

scalp (skalp). That part of the integument of the head which normally is covered with hair.

scalpel (skal′pel) [L. *scalpellum*]. A small, straight knife, usually with a convex edge.

scalpriform (skal′prĭ-form). Shaped like a chisel.

scalprum (skal′prum) [L. "knife"]. 1. A raspatory. 2. A strong knife.

scaly (ska′le) [L. *squamosus*]. 1. Scalelike. 2. Characterized by scales.

scammonia (skah-mo′ne-ah). Scammony.

scammony (skam′o-ne) [L. *scammonium, scammonia*]. The plant *Convolvulus scammonia*, of Asia Minor and Syria. The root affords a gummy and resinous exudate, which is anthelmintic and cathartic. **Mexican s.,** ipomea.

scan (skan). Shortened form of *scintiscan*, q.v.; variously designated, according to the organ under examination, as *brain scan, kidney scan, thyroid scan*, etc.

scandium (skan′de-um). A very rare metallic element; symbol, Sc; atomic number, 21; atomic weight, 44.956.

scanning (skan′ning). 1. The act of examining visually, as a small area or different isolated areas, in detail. 2. A manner of utterance characterized by somewhat regularly recurring pauses. **radioisotope s.,** the production of a two-dimensional picture (scintiscan, or scan), representing the gamma rays emitted by a radioactive isotope concentrated in a specific tissue of the body, such as the brain or thyroid gland.

scanography (skan-og′rah-fe). A method of making radiographs by the use of a narrow slit beneath the tube in such a manner that only a line or sheet of x-rays is employed and the x-ray tube moves over the object so that all the rays of the central beam pass through the part being radiographed at the same angle.

scansion (skan′shun). Scanning.

Scanzoni's maneuver, operation (skan-tso′nē) [Friedrich Wilhelm *Scanzoni*, German obstetrician, 1821–1891]. See under *operation*.

scapha (ska′fah) [L. "a skiff"]. [N A, B N A] The long curved depression which separates the helix from the anthelix. Called also *scaphoid fossa* and *fossa helicis*.

scaphion (ska′fe-on) [Gr. *skaphion* a small bowl or basin]. Basis cranii externa.

scaphocephalia (ska″fo-se-fa′le-ah) [Gr. *skaphē* skiff + *kephalē* head + *-ia*]. A condition in which the skull is abnormally long and narrow, as a result of premature closure of the sagittal suture, with heavy centers of ossification in the line of the suture; usually accompanied by inflammation and atrophy of the optic papillae and by mental retardation.

scaphocephalic (ska″fo-se-fal′ik). Pertaining to or characterized by scaphocephalia.

scaphocephalism (ska″fo-sef′ah-lizm). Scaphocephalia.

scaphocephalous (ska″fo-sef′ah-lus). Scaphocephalic.

scaphocephaly (ska″fo-sef′ah-le). Scaphocephalia.

scaphohydrocephalus (ska″fo-hi″dro-sef′ahlus). Hydrocephalus in which the head assumes a boat-like shape.

scaphohydrocephaly (ska″fo-hi″dro-sef′ah-le). Scaphohydrocephalus.

scaphoid (skaf′oid) [Gr. *skaphē* skiff + *eidos* form]. Shaped like a boat; navicular. Used especially in reference to the most lateral bone in the proximal row of carpal bones (os scaphoideum [N A]). See also *os naviculare*.

scaphoiditis (skaf″oi-di′tis). Inflammation of the scaphoid bone. **tarsal s.,** inflammation involving the navicular (scaphoid) bone of the tarsus.

scaphula (skaf′u-lah) [L., dim. of *scapha*]. Fossa vestibuli vaginae.

scapula (skap′u-lah), pl. *scap′ulae* [L.]. [N A, B N A] The flat, triangular bone in the back of the shoulder. **alar s., s. ala′ta,** winged s. **elevated s.,** congenital elevation of the shoulder blades. **Graves' s.,** scaphoid s. **scaphoid s.,** a scapula in which the vertebral border is more or less concave. **winged s.,** a scapula having a prominent vertebral border.

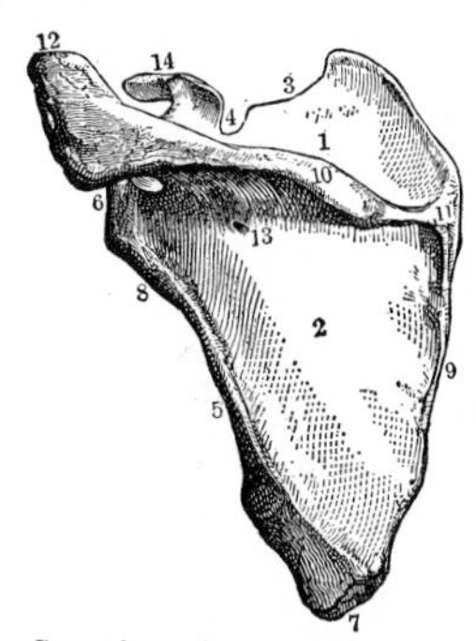

Scapula, dorsal view: 1, Supraspinous fossa; 2, infraspinous fossa; 3, superior margin; 4, scapular (coracoid) notch; 5, lateral margin; 6, glenoid cavity; 7, inferior angle; 8, neck of scapula; 9, medial margin; 10, spine; 11, triangular commencement of the spine, upon which the tendon of the trapezius muscle moves; 12, acromion; 13, arterial foramen; 14, coracoid process (Leidy).

scapulalgia (skap″u-lal′je-ah). Pain in the scapular region.

scapular (skap′u-lar). Of or pertaining to the scapula.

scapulary (skap′u-la″re). A shoulder bandage, like a pair of suspenders or braces, to hold in place a body bandage or girdle.

scapulectomy (skap″u-lek′to-me) [*scapula* + Gr. *ektomē* excision]. The surgical removal of the scapula or a part of it (resection).

scapulo-anterior (skap″u-lo-an-te′re-or). Denoting a position of the fetus in transverse presentation, with the scapula directed anteriorly.

scapuloclavicular (skap″u-lo-klah-vik′u-lar). Pertaining to the scapula and the clavicle.

scapulodynia (skap″u-lo-din′e-ah) [*scapula* + Gr. *odynē* pain + *-ia*]. Pain in the region of the shoulder.

scapulohumeral (skap″u-lo-hu′mer-al). Pertaining to the scapula and the humerus.

scapulopexy (skap′u-lo-pek″se) [*scapula* + Gr. *pēxis* fixation]. Surgical fixation of the scapula.

scapuloposterior (skap″u-lo-pos-te′re-or). Denoting a position of the fetus in transverse presentation, with the scapula directed posteriorly.

scapulothoracic (skap″u-lo-tho-ras′ik). Pertaining to the scapula and the thorax.

scapus (ska′pus), pl. *sca′pi* [L.]. Shaft. **s. pe′nis,** corpus penis. **s. pi′li** [N A, B N A], the major portion of a hair, designating especially the portion that extends beyond the surface of the skin. Called also *hair shaft*.

scar (skar) [Gr. *eschara* the scab or eschar on a wound caused by burning]. A mark remaining after the healing of a wound or other morbid process. By extension applied to other visible manifestations of an earlier event. **Reichert's s.,** an area on the fertilized ovum consisting of a fibrinous membrane in place of the decidual tissue. **shilling s's,** round, superficial scars left after an eruption of rupia. **white s. of ovary,** corpus albicans.

scarf (skarf). A broad strip of fabric. **Mayor's s.,** a triangular bandage for immobilizing the upper limbs.

scarification (skar″ĭ-fi-ka′shun) [L. *scarificatio*, Gr. *skariphismos* a scratching up]. Production in the skin of many small, superficial scratches or punctures, as for the introduction of smallpox vaccine.

scarificator (skar′ĭ-fi-ka″tor). Scarifier.

scarifier (skar″ĭ-fi′er). An instrument bearing many sharp points, used in scarification.

scarlatina (skar″lah-te′nah) [L. "scarlet"]. Scarlet fever. See under *fever*. **s. angino′sa,** a dangerous form with marked throat symptoms. **s. haemorrha′gica,** scarlet fever in which there is extravasation of the blood into skin and mucous membranes. **s. malig′na,** a variety with severe symptoms and great prostration, often fatal; also a form in which the rash disappears suddenly and prematurely. **puerperal s.,** a scarlet rash sometimes seen in puerperal fever. **s. sim'plex,** a mild form attended with but little soreness of the throat.

scarlatinal (skar-lat'ĭ-nal). Pertaining to or due to scarlatina.

scarlatinella (skar-lat"ĭ-nel'ah). Mild apyretic scarlet fever.

scarlatiniform, scarlatinoid (skar"lah-tin'ĭ-form, skar-lat'ĭ-noid). Resembling scarlatina. **metadiphtheritic s.,** an eruption with symptoms resembling those of scarlet fever, sometimes seen in convalescence from diphtheria.

scarlet (skar'let). A bright red tinged with orange or yellow. **Biebrich s., water-soluble,** an azo dye used as a plasma stain, $C_6H_4(SO_2.ONa)$.-$N:N.C_6H_2(SO_2.ONa).N:N.C_{10}H_3.OH$. **s. G,** sudan III. **s. J. Jg,** bluish eosin. **s. R,** scarlet red.

Scarpa's fascia, foramen, membrane, shoe, triangle (skar'pahz) [Antonio *Scarpa*, Italian anatomist and surgeon, 1747–1832]. See under the nouns.

SCAT. Abbreviation for *sheep cell agglutination test*.

Scat. Abbreviation for L. *scat'ula*, a box.

scatacratia (skat"ah-kra'she-ah) [*scato-* + Gr. *akratia* lack of self-control]. Incontinence of the feces.

scatemia (skah-te'me-ah) [*scato-* + Gr. *haima* blood + *-ia*]. Intestinal toxemia.

scato- (skat'o) [Gr. *skōr, skatos* dung]. Combining form denoting relation to dung, or fecal matter. See also words beginning *skato-*.

scatol (ska'tōl). Skatole.

scatologic (skat"o-loj'ik). Pertaining to fecal matter, or to scatology.

scatology (skah-tol'o-je) [*scato-* + *-logy*]. The study of the feces.

scatoma (skah-to'mah) [*scato-* + *-oma*]. Stercoroma.

scatophagy (skah-tof'ah-je) [*scato-* + Gr. *phagein* to eat]. The eating of excrement.

scatophilia (skat"o-fil'e-ah) [*scato-* + Gr. *philein* to love]. A perverted fondness for dung.

scatoscopy (skah-tos'ko-pe) [*scato-* + Gr. *skopein* to examine]. Inspection of the feces.

scatter (skat'er). The diffusion or deviation of roentgen rays produced by a medium through which the rays pass. Backward diffusion is called *back scatter*.

scattergram (skat'er-gram). A graph, representing the results of a statistical study, in which all the findings in a series are represented by disconnected, individual symbols.

scatula (skat'u-lah) [L. "parallelepiped"]. An oblong paper box for powders or pills.

Sc.D. Abbreviation for *Doctor of Science*.

Sc.D.A. Abbreviation for L. *scapulo-dextra anterior* (right scapulo-anterior) position of the fetus.

Sc.D.P. Abbreviation for L. *scapulo-dextra posterior* (right scapuloposterior) position of the fetus.

Scedosporium (se-do-spo're-um). A genus of fungi causing Madura foot.

scelalgia (ske-lal'je-ah) [Gr. *skelos* leg + *algos* pain + *-ia*]. Pain in the leg.

Sceleth treatment (ske'leth) [Charles E. *Sceleth*, Chicago physician, 1873–1942]. See under *treatment*.

scelotyrbe (sel-o-ter'be) [Gr. *skelos* leg + *tyrbē* disorder]. Spastic paralysis of the legs.

Schacher's ganglion (shah'kerz) [Polycarp Gottlieb *Schacher*, German physician, 1674–1737]. The ciliary ganglion.

Schachowa's tube (shah'ko-vahz) [Seraphina *Schachowa*, Russian histologist in Bern, 19th century]. See under *tube*.

Schafer's method (sha'ferz) [Sir Edward Albert Sharpey-*Schafer*, English physiologist, 1850–1935]. See under *respiration, artificial*.

Schäffer's reflex (shef'erz) [Max *Schäffer*, German neurologist, 1852–1923]. See under *reflex*.

Schamberg's disease (sham'bergz) [Jay Frank *Schamberg*, Philadelphia dermatologist, 1870–1934]. See under *disease*.

Schanz's disease, syndrome (shants'ez) [Alfred *Schanz*, German orthopedist, 1868–1931]. See under *disease* and *syndrome*.

Schapiro's sign (shah-pe'rōz) [Heinrich *Schapiro*, Russian physician, 1852–1901]. See under *sign*.

scharlach R (shar'lak). Scarlet red.

Schaudinn's bacillus (shaw-dinz') [Fritz Richard *Schaudinn*, German bacteriologist, 1871–1906]. *Treponema pallidum*.

Schaumann's body, disease (shaw'manz) [Jörgen *Schaumann*, Swedish dermatologist, 1879–1953]. See under the nouns.

Schauta's operation (shaw'tahz) [Friedrich *Schauta*, Vienna gynecologist, 1849–1919]. See under *operation*.

Schede's method, operation, resection (sha'dez) [Max *Schede*, surgeon in Bonn, 1844–1902]. See under *operation*.

Scheele's green (sha'lez, or shēlz) [Karl William *Scheele*, Swedish chemist, 1742–1786]. Copper arsenite.

Scheiner's experiment (shi'nerz) [Christoph *Scheiner*, German mathematician, 1575–1650]. See under *experiment*.

schema (ske'mah) [Gr. *schēma* form, shape]. A plan, outline, or arrangement. **Hamberger's s.,** the external intercostal and the intercartilaginous muscles are inspiratory muscles, the internal intercostal muscles are expiratory.

schematic (ske-mat'ik) [Gr. *schēma* form, shape]. Serving as a diagram or model. See under *eye*.

schematogram (ske-mat'o-gram). A tracing in reduced form of the outline of the body.

schematograph (ske-mat'o-graf). An instrument for making a tracing in reduced form of the outline of the body.

Schenck's disease (shenks) [Benjamin R. *Schenck*, American surgeon, 1842–1920]. Sporotrichosis.

Scherer's test (shār'erz) [Johann Joseph von *Scherer*, German physician, 1814–1869]. See under *tests*.

scherlievo (skār-lya'vo). A contagious disorder formerly prevalent in Illyria and Dalmatia: supposed to have been syphilis.

scheroma (ske-ro'mah). Xerophthalmia.

Scheuermann's disease, kyphosis (shoi'ermanz) [Holger Werfel *Scheuermann*, Danish surgeon, 1877–1960]. Osteochondrosis of the vertebrae.

Schiassi's operation (ske-as'ēz) [B. *Schiassi*, Italian surgeon]. See under *operation*.

Schick's sign, test (shiks) [Béla *Schick*, Hungarian pediatrician in the United States, born 1877]. See under *sign* and *tests*.

Schiefferdecker's disk, theory (she-fer-dek'erz) [Paul *Schiefferdecker*, Bonn anatomist, 1849–1931]. See under *disk* and *theory*.

Schiff's biliary cycle (shifs) [Moritz *Schiff*, German physiologist, 1823–1896]. See under *cycle*.

Schiff's test (shifs) [Hugo *Schiff*, German chemist in Florence, 1834–1915]. See under *tests*.

Schilder's disease, encephalitis (shil'derz) [Paul Ferdinand *Schilder*, Austrian neurologist in the United States, 1886–1940]. Progressive subcortical encephalopathy.

Schiller's test (shil'erz) [Walter *Schiller*, Austrian pathologist in the United States, born 1887]. See under *tests*.

Schilling blood count, hemogram (shil'ing) [Victor *Schilling*, German hematologist, 1883–1960]. See under *count*.

Schilling test (shil'ing) [Robert F. *Schilling*, American hematologist, born 1919]. See under *tests*.

Schimmelbusch's disease, mask (shim′el-boosh″ez) [Curt *Schimmelbusch*, German surgeon, 1860–1895]. See under *disease* and *mask*.

schindylesis (skin″dĭ-le′sis) [Gr. *schindylēsis* a splintering]. A form of articulation in which a thin plate of one bone is received into a cleft in another, as in the articulation of the perpendicular plate of the ethmoid bone with the vomer.

Schinus (ski′nus) [Gr. *schinos* mastic]. A genus of anacardiaceous trees of warm regions. *S. mol′le*, of tropical America (pepper tree), affords a kind of mastic, and is a mild purgative and aromatic.

Schiøtz's tonometer (she-ets′) [Hjalmar *Schiøtz*, Norwegian physician, 1850–1927]. See under *tonometer*.

schistasis (skis′tah-sis). A splitting; specifically, a congenital defect consisting of a split condition of the body, as schistocormia, schistomelia, schistosomia.

schisto- (skis′to) [Gr. *schistos* split]. Combining form meaning split or cleft.

schistocelia (skis″to-se′le-ah). Schistocoelia.

schistocephalus (skis″to-sef′ah-lus) [*schisto-* + Gr. *kephalē* head]. A fetus born with a cleft head.

schistocoelia (skis″to-se′le-ah) [*schisto-* + Gr. *koilia* belly]. Congenital fissure of the abdomen.

schistocormia (skis″to-kor′me-ah) [*schisto-* + Gr. *kormos* trunk + *-ia*]. A developmental anomaly characterized by a cleft condition of the trunk.

schistocormus (skis″to-kor′mus). A fetal monster exhibiting schistocormia.

schistocystis (skis″to-sis′tis) [*schisto-* + Gr. *kystis* bladder]. Fissure of the bladder.

schistocyte (skis′to-sīt). A fragment of a red blood corpuscle, commonly observed in the blood in hemolytic anemias.

schistocytosis (skis″to-si-to′sis). The accumulation of schistocytes in the blood.

schistoglossia (skis″to-glos′e-ah) [*schisto-* + Gr. *glōssa* tongue + *-ia*]. Fissure of the tongue.

schistomelia (skis″to-me′le-ah) [*schisto-* + Gr. *melos* limb + *-ia*]. A developmental anomaly characterized by a cleft condition of a limb.

schistomelus (skis-tom′e-lus). A fetal monster exhibiting schistomelia.

schistometer (skis-tom′e-ter) [*schisto-* + Gr. *metron* measure]. An instrument for measuring the aperture between the vocal cords.

schistoprosopia (skis″to-pro-so′pe-ah) [*schisto-* + Gr. *prosōpon* face + *-ia*]. A developmental anomaly characterized by fissure of the face.

schistoprosopus (skis″to-pros′o-pus). A fetal monster exhibiting schistoprosopia.

schistorachis (skis-tor′ah-kis) [*schisto-* + Gr. *rachis* spine]. Rachischisis.

schistosis (skis-to′sis) [*Schist* a form of slate + *-osis*]. Pneumoconiosis in slate workers.

Schistosoma (skis″to-so′mah) [*schisto-* + Gr. *sōma* body]. A genus of trematode parasites or flukes; the blood flukes. **S. bo′vis,** a species found in the portal system of sheep and oxen in Africa, Mesopotamia, Corsica, Sardinia, and Sicily. **S. haemato′bium,** a common parasite of tropical countries, especially Egypt, occurring in the natives, especially boys from six to ten years of age. It is found in dilatation of the veins, especially the cystic vein, producing irritability of the bladder, hematuria, and dysentery. The parasites enter the body by the alimentary tract, especially in drinking water, or through the skin of persons bathing or wading in infested waters, the invertebrate host being small snails of the genera *Bulinus, Planorbis* and *Physopsis*. Formerly called *Distoma haematobium* and *Bilharzia haematobia*. **S. in′dicum,** a species occurring in cattle, sheep, goats, etc. in India and Rhodesia. **S. intercala′tum,** a species from the Belgian Congo which causes intestinal schistosomiasis. **S. japon′icum,** a species found in Japan, China, and the Philippines, causing schistosomiasis japonica by penetrating the skin of persons in infested waters. The transmitting hosts are snails of the genera *Katayama* and *Oncomelania*. The symptoms of the infection point to the liver and the spleen, consisting of ascites, cachexia, bronchial trouble, and urticarial spots (urticarial fever). **S. manso′ni,** a species very similar to *S. haematobium* except that (1) it is found in the feces instead of the urine, (2) the egg has a spur on the side instead of on the end, and (3) its invertebrate host is the fresh-water snail, *Planorbis*, and probably other genera of snails. **S. mat′theei,** a species found in the portal mesenteric vein of sheep in South America. **S. pathlocop′ticum,** a form pathogenic for mice. The invertebrate host is the snail (*Limnaea*). **S. spinda′le,** a species parasitic in the buffalo and goat in India.

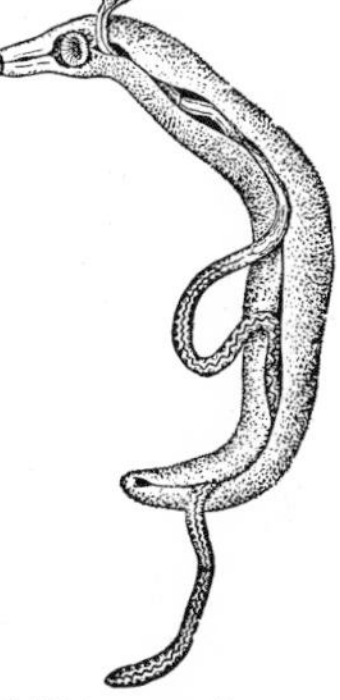

Schistosoma haematobium, male and female (× 6) (Looss).

schistosomacidal (skis″to-so″mah-si′dal). Schistosomicidal.

schistosomacide (skis″to-so′mah-sīd). Schistosomicide.

Schistosomatium (skis″to-so-ma′she-um). A genus of blood flukes allied to Schistosoma. *S. douthitti* is found in the hepatic portal veins of the meadow mouse.

schistosome (skis′to-sōm). An individual of the genus Schistosoma.

schistosomia (skis″to-so′me-ah) [*schisto-* + Gr. *soma* body + *-ia*]. A developmental anomaly characterized by a fissure of the abdomen and lower extremities rudimentary or lacking.

schistosomiasis (skis″to-so-mi′ah-sis). The state of being infected with flukes of the genus Schistosoma. **Asiatic s.,** s. japonica. **cutaneous s.,** a condition resulting from invasion of the skin by schistosome cercaria, marked by prickling sensation and intense itching. **eastern s.,** s. japonica. **hepatic s.,** schistosomiasis with an accumulation of ova of the parasites in the liver tissue. **intestinal s.,** Manson's s. **s. japon′ica,** infection by *Schistosoma japonicum*. Called also *Katayama disease*. **Manson's s., s. manso′ni,** infection with flukes of the species *Schistosoma mansoni*, living principally in the inferior and superior mesenteric veins but migrating into the large and small intestines. **Oriental s.,** s. japonica. **urinary s., vesical s.,** infection with *Schistosoma haematobium*, involving the urinary tract and causing cystitis and hematuria. **visceral s.,** infection with *Schistosoma mansoni*, involving various of the body viscera.

schistosomicidal (skis″to-so″mĭ-si′dal). Destructive to schistosomes.

schistosomicide (skis″to-so′mĭ-sīd). An agent which destroys schistosomes.

Schistosomum (skis″to-so′mum). Schistosoma.

schistosomus (skis″to-so′mus). A fetal monster exhibiting schistosomia.

schistosternia (skis″to-ster′ne-ah) [*schisto-* + *sternum*]. Schistothorax.

schistothorax (skis″to-tho′raks) [*schisto-* + Gr. *thōrax* chest]. A developmental anomaly characterized by fissure of the chest.

schistotrachelus (skis″to-trah-ke′lus) [*schisto-* + *trachēlos* neck]. A fetal monster with fissure of the neck.

schizamnion (skiz-am′ne-on) [Gr. *schizein* to divide + *amnion*]. An amnion formed by cavitation of the inner cell mass.

schizaxon (skiz-ak′sōn). An axon which is divided into two equal, or nearly equal, branches.

schizencephalic (skiz″en-se-fal′ik). Having abnormal clefts in the brain substance.

schizencephaly (skiz″en-sef′ah-le) [Gr. *schizein*

to divide + *enkephalos* brain]. Schizencephalic porencephaly.

schizo- (skiz′o) [Gr. *schizein* to divide]. Combining form meaning divided, or denoting relationship to division.

Schizoblastosporion (skiz″o-blas″to-spo′re-on). A genus of yeastlike fungi of the family Eremascaceae, various species of which have been isolated from onychomycotic lesions.

schizocephalia (skiz″o-se-fa′le-ah). A developmental anomaly characterized by a longitudinal fissure of the head.

schizocyte (skiz′o-sīt). Schistocyte.

schizocytosis (skiz″o-si-to′sis). Schistocytosis.

schizogenesis (skiz″o-jen′e-sis) [*schizo-* + Gr. *genesis* production]. Reproduction by fission.

schizogenous (skiz-oj′e-nus). Reproducing by fission.

schizogony (skiz-og′o-ne) [*schizo-* + Gr. *gonē* seed]. The asexual cycle of sporozoa; particularly the life-cycle of the malarial parasite (*Plasmodium*) in the blood corpuscle of man. Cf. *sporogony.*

schizogyria (skiz″o-ji′re-ah). A condition in which the cerebral convolutions are marked by wedge-shaped cracks.

schizoid (skiz′oid). 1. Resembling schizophrenia: a term applied by Bleuler to the shut-in, unsocial, introspective type of personality and by Kretschmer to the physical type resembling that of persons with dementia praecox, i.e., the asthenic dysplasic type. 2. A person of schizoid personality.

schizoidia (skiz-oi′de-ah). Schizoidism.

schizoidism (skiz′oid-izm). The splitting of the psyche or the personality traits which are characteristic of schizophrenia.

schizomycete (skiz″o-mi-sēt′). Any organism or species belonging to the Schizomycetes.

Schizomycetes (skiz″o-mi-se′tēz) [*schizo-* + Gr. *mykēs* fungus]. A taxonomic class of typically unicellular organisms, considered plants, which commonly multiply by cell division, and which may be free living, saprophytic, parasitic, or even pathogenic, the last causing disease in plants or animals. It includes 10 orders, *Actinomycetales, Beggiatoales, Caryophanales, Chlamydobacteriales, Eubacteriales, Hyphomicrobiales, Mycoplasmatales, Myxobacterales, Pseudomonadales,* and *Spirochaetales.*

schizomycetic (skiz″o-mi-set′ik). Due to the presence of schizomycetes.

schizomycosis (skiz″o-mi-ko′sis). Any disease which is produced by the presence of schizomycetes.

schizont (skiz′ont) [*schizo-* + Gr. *ōn, ontos* being]. The stage in the development of the malarial parasite following the trophozoite whose nucleus divides into many smaller nuclei. This stage is followed by the *segmenter* which consists of segments arranged in rosettes. Called also *monont* and *agamont.*

schizonticide (skiz-on′tĭ-sīd). An agent that destroys schizonts.

schizonychia (skiz″o-nik′e-ah) [*schizo-* + Gr. *onyx* nail + *-ia*]. Splitting of the nails.

schizophasia (skiz″o-fa′ze-ah). The incomprehensible, disordered speech characteristic of schizophrenia.

schizophrenia (skiz″o-fre′ne-ah) [*schizo-* + Gr. *phrēn* mind + *-ia*]. Bleuler's term for dementia praecox which, according to his interpretation, represents a cleavage or fissuration of the mental functions.

schizophreniac (skiz″o-fre′ne-ak). A person affected with schizophrenia.

schizophrenic (skiz″o-fren′ik). Pertaining to or characterized by schizophrenia.

schizophreniform (skiz″o-fren′ĭ-form). Resembling schizophrenia.

schizophrenosis (skiz″o-fre-no′sis). Southard's term for any disease of the dementia praecox group.

schizoprosopia (skiz″o-pro-so′pe-ah). Ununited fissure of the face as in harelip, cleft palate, etc.

Schizosaccharomyces hominis (skiz″o-sak″-ah-ro-mi′sēz hom′ĭ-nis). *Saccharomyces hominis.*

schizosaccharomycosis (skiz″o-sak″ah-ro-mi-ko′sis). A fungus infection caused by *Saccharomyces (Schizosaccharomyces) hominis.* **s. pompholicifor′mis hom′inis,** a dermal mycosis associated with dyshidrosis.

Schizosiphon (skiz″o-si′fon). A genus of nematogenous schizomycetes with flagelliform filaments, slender toward the extremity.

schizosis (skiz-o′sis). Autism.

schizothemia (skiz″o-the′me-ah) [*schizo-* + Gr. *thema* theme + *-ia*]. Interruption of an argument by reminiscences; regarded as hysterical by Breuer and Freud.

schizothemic (skiz″o-the′mik). Pertaining to or characterized by schizothemia.

schizothorax (skiz″o-tho′raks). A fetal monster with a fissure of the chest wall.

schizothymia (skiz″o-thi′me-ah) [*schizo-* + Gr. *thymos* spirit]. Schizoidism.

schizothymic (skiz″o-thi′mik). Pertaining to or characterized by schizothymia.

schizotonia (skiz″o-to′ne-ah) [*schizo-* + Gr. *tonos* tension + *-ia*]. Division of the influx of tone to the muscles, so that, for instance, the flexor groups of the arm become hypertonic, while in the leg the extensors become hypertonic.

schizotrichia (skiz″o-trik′e-ah) [*schizo-* + Gr. *thrix* hair]. Splitting of the hairs at the ends.

schizotropic (skiz″o-trop′ik). Having an affinity for schizonts.

schizotrypanosis, schizotrypanosomiasis (skiz″o-trip″ah-no′sis, skiz″o-trip″ah-no-so-mi′-ah-sis). Chagas' disease.

Schizotrypanum cruzi (skiz″o-trip′ah-num kroo′ze). *Trypanosoma cruzi.*

schizozoite (skiz″o-zo′īt) [*schizo-* + Gr. *zōon* animal]. Merozoite.

schlammfieber (shlahm′fe-ber) [Ger. "slime fever"]. A disease resembling Weil's disease, which prevailed among young persons who worked in the flooded districts near Breslau in the summer of 1891.

Schlange's sign (shlang′ez) [Hans *Schlange*, German surgeon, 1856–1922]. See under *sign.*

Schlatter's disease, operation (shlat′erz) [Carl *Schlatter*, surgeon in Zurich, 1864–1934]. See *osteochondrosis of tuberosity of the tibia* and under *operation.*

Schlemm's canal, ligaments (shlemz) [Friedrich S. *Schlemm*, German anatomist, 1795–1858]. See under *canal* and *ligament.*

Schlesinger's phenomenon, sign (shla′zing-erz) [Hermann *Schlesinger*, Austrian physician, 1868–1934]. See under *sign.*

Schlippe's salt (shlip′ez) [K. F. *Schlippe*, 1799–1867]. Sodium thioantimoniate.

Schloffer's tumor (shlof′erz) [Herman *Schloffer*, surgeon in Prague, 1868–1937]. See under *tumor.*

Schlösser's method, treatment (shles′erz) [Carl *Schlösser*, German oculist, 1857–1925]. See under *treatment.*

Schmidel's anastomosis (shme′delz) [Casimir Christoph *Schmidel*, German anatomist, 1718–1792]. See under *anastomosis.*

Schmidt's fibrinoplastic (shmits) [Eduard Oskar *Schmidt*, German anatomist, 1823–1886]. Serum-globulin.

Schmidt's syndrome (shmits) [Johann Friedrich Moritz *Schmidt*, German laryngologist, 1838–1907]. See under *syndrome.*

Schmidt's test (shmits) [Adolf *Schmidt*, physician in Bonn, 1865–1918]. See under *tests.*

Schmidt-Lanterman incisures (shmit′lahn″-

ter-mahn′) [Henry D. *Schmidt*, American anatomist, 1823–1888; A. J. *Lanterman*, American anatomist at Strassburg, 19th century]. See under *incisure.*

Schmincke tumor (shmin′kĕ) [Alexander *Schmincke*, German pathologist, 1877–1953]. See under *tumor.*

Schmitz bacillus (shmits) [Karl Eitel Friedrich *Schmitz*, German physician, born 1889]. *Shigella ambigua.*

Schmorl's body, disease, furrow, nodule (shmorlz) [Christian G. *Schmorl*, German pathologist, 1861–1932]. See under the nouns.

schmutzdecke (shmoots′dek-ĕ) [Ger.]. The carpet-like layer of bacteria, algae, and other microorganisms which forms on the surface of a slow sand filter and which aids in purifying the water.

Schnabel's caverns (shnab′elz) [Isidor *Schnabel*, Vienna ophthalmologist, 1842–1908]. Caverns or pathologic spaces in the optic nerve in glaucoma.

schnauzkrampf (shnowts′krampf) [Ger.]. A facial grimace resembling pouting.

Schneider's carmine (shni′derz) [Franz Coelestin *Schneider*, German chemist, 1813–1897]. See under *carmine.*

schneiderian membrane (shni-de′re-an) [Conrad Victor *Schneider*, German physician, 1610–1680]. See under *membrane.*

Schoemaker's line (she′mah-kerz) [Jan *Schoemaker*, Dutch surgeon, 1871–1940]. See under *line.*

Schöler's treatment (sha′lerz) [Heinrich Leopold *Schöler*, German ophthalmologist, 1844–1918]. See under *treatment.*

Scholz's disease (shōlts′ez) [Willibald *Scholz*, German neurologist, born 1889]. The familial form of demyelinating encephalopathy.

Schön's theory (shānz) [Wilhelm *Schön*, German ophthalmologist, 1848–1917]. See under *theory.*

Schönbein's reaction, test (shān′bīnz) [Christian Friedrich *Schönbein*, German chemist, 1799–1868]. See under *reaction* and *tests.*

Schönlein's disease, purpura (shān′līnz) [Johann Lukas *Schönlein*, German physician, 1793–1864]. Purpura rheumatica.

Schönlein-Henoch disease, purpura, syndrome (shān′līn-hen′ōk) [J. L. *Schönlein; Edouard Heinrich Henoch*, German pediatrician, 1820–1910]. See under *purpura.*

Schott's treatment (shots) [Theodore *Schott*, physician in Nauheim, 1850–1921]. See under *treatment.*

Schottmüller's disease (shot′mil-erz) [Hugo *Schottmüller*, physician in Hamburg, 1867–1936]. Paratyphoid.

Schreger's bands, lines (shra′gerz) [Bernhard Gottlob *Schreger*, German anatomist, 1766–1825]. See under *band* and *line.*

Schreiber's maneuver (shri′berz) [Julius *Schreiber*, German physician, 1848–1932]. See under *maneuver.*

Schridde's disease, granules (shrid′ez) [Hermann *Schridde*, German pathologist, born 1875]. See under the nouns.

Schröder's operation (shra′derz) [Karl *Schröder*, German gynecologist, 1838–1887]. See under *operation.*

Schröder's test (shra′derz) [Woldemar von *Schröder*, German physician, 1850–1898]. See under *tests.*

Schroeder's disease (shra′derz) [Robert *Schroeder*, German gynecologist, 1884–1959]. See under *disease.*

Schroeder's syndrome (shro′derz) [Henry A. *Schroeder*, St. Louis physician, born 1906]. See under *syndrome.*

Schrön's granule (shrānz) [Otto von *Schrön*, German pathologist in Naples, 1837–1913]. See under *granule.*

Schroth's treatment (shrōts) [Johann *Schroth*, German physician, 1800–1856]. See under *treatment.*

Schrötter's catheter, chorea (shret′erz) [Leopold *Schrötter* von Kristelli, Viennese laryngologist, 1837–1908]. See under the nouns.

Schuchardt's operation (shoo′karts) [Karl August *Schuchardt*, German surgeon, 1856–1901]. Paravaginal hysterectomy.

Schüffner's dots, granules, punctuation (shif′nerz) [Wilhelm *Schüffner*, German pathologist, 1867–1949]. See under *dot.*

Schüle's sign (she′lez) [Heinrich *Schüle*, German psychiatrist, 1839–1916]. See under *sign.*

Schüller's disease, phenomenon, syndrome (shil′erz) [Artur *Schüller*, Vienna neurologist, born 1874]. See under *disease* and *phenomenon.*

Schüller's method (shil′erz) [Karl Heinrich Anton Ludwig Max *Schüller*, surgeon in Berlin, 1843–1907]. See under *method.*

Schüller-Christian disease (shil′er-kris′chan) [Artur *Schüller;* Henry A. *Christian*, American physician, born 1876]. See under *disease.*

Schultz's disease (shoolt′sez) [Werner *Schultz*, German internist, 1878–1947]. Agranulocytosis.

Schultz-Charlton reaction, test (shoolts-charl′ton) [Werner *Schultz;* W. *Charlton*]. See under *reaction.*

Schultze's bundle, cells, tract (shoolt′sez) [Max Johann *Schultze*, German biologist, 1825–1874]. See under the nouns.

Schultze's fold, method (shoolt′sez) [Bernhard Sigismund *Schultze*, German gynecologist, 1827–1919]. See under *fold* and *method.*

Schultze's test (shoolt′sez) [Ernst *Schultze*, Swiss chemist, 1860–1912]. See under *tests.*

Schultze-Chvostek's sign. See *Chvostek's sign*, under *sign.*

Schumm's test (shoomz) [Otto *Schumm*, German chemist, born 1874]. See under *tests.*

Schürmann's test (sher′manz) [Walter *Schürmann*, German serologist, born 1880]. See under *tests.*

Schütz's micrococcus (shitz′ez) [Johann Wilhelm *Schütz*, German veterinarian, 1839–1920]. The organism which causes strangles in horses.

Schwabach's test (shvah′baks) [Dagobert *Schwabach*, otologist in Berlin, 1846–1920]. See under *tests.*

Schwalbe's corpuscles, fissure, foramen, sheath, space, etc. (shvahl′bez) [Gustav Albert *Schwalbe*, German anatomist, 1844–1916]. See under the nouns.

Schwann's sheath, white substance (shvonz) [Theodor *Schwann*, German anatomist and physiologist, 1810–1882; professor of anatomy at Louvain, and the founder of the cell theory]. See under *sheath* and *substance.*

schwannitis (shwon-ni′tis). Schwannosis.

schwannoglioma (shwon″o-gli-o′mah). Schwannoma.

schwannoma (shwon-no′mah). A neoplasm of the white substance of Schwann, i.e., of a nerve sheath.

schwannosis (shwon-no′sis). Hypertrophy of the sheaths of Schwann.

Schwartz's method, test (shvarts′es) [Charles Edouard *Schwartz*, French surgeon, born 1852]. See under *method*, and under *tests*, 1st def.

Schwartze's operation (shvarts′ez) [Hermann *Schwartze*, German otologist, 1837–1910]. See under *operation.*

Schwarz's test (shvarts′ez) 1. [Karl Leonhard Heinrich *Schwarz*, German chemist, 1824–1890]. See under *tests*, def. 1. 2. [Gottwald *Schwarz*, German roentgenologist, 1880–1959]. See under *tests*, def. 2.

Schwediauer's disease (shva′de-ow″erz). See *Swediauer* and under *disease.*

Schweigger-Seidel sheath (shvi′ger-si′del) [Franz *Schweigger-Seidel*, Leipzig physiologist, 1834–1871]. See under *sheath.*

schweinerotlauf (shvi″nĕ-rot′lowf) [Ger.]. Swine erysipelas.

schweineseuche (shvi″nĕ-zoi′ke) [Ger.]. Swine plague.

Schweitzer's reagent (shvīt′serz) [Matthias Eduard *Schweitzer*, German chemist, 1818–1860]. See under *reagent.*

schwelle (shvel′ĕ) [Ger.]. Threshold.

Schweninger's method (shven′in-gerz) [Ernst *Schweninger*, German physician, 1850–1924]. Reduction of obesity by the restriction of fluids in the diet.

scia-. For other words beginning thus, see also those beginning *skia-.*

sciage (se-azh′) [Fr.]. A sawing movement in massage.

scialyscope (si-al′ĭ-skōp). An apparatus for throwing an image of an operation into a darkened room separated from the operating room.

sciatic (si-at′ik) [L. *sciaticus;* Gr. *ischiadikos*]. Pertaining to the ischium.

sciatica (si-at′ĭ-kah) [L.]. Pain along the course of the sciatic nerve, usually a neuritis. It is attended with paresthesia of the thigh and leg, tenderness along the course of the nerve, and sometimes by wasting of the calf muscles. **phlebogenous s.,** sciatica caused by varices of the sciatic vein.

science (si′ens) [L. *scientia* knowledge]. An accumulating body of knowledge, especially that which seeks to establish general laws connecting a number of particular facts. **applied s.,** that concerned with the application of discovered laws to the matters of everyday living. **pure s.,** that concerned solely with the discovery of unknown laws relating to particular facts.

scientist (si′en-tist). One learned in science, especially one active in some particular field of investigation.

scieropia (si-er-o′pe-ah) [Gr. *skieros* shady + *ōps* eye + *-ia*]. Visual defect in which objects appear in a shadow.

scilla (sil′ah) [L.]. Squill.

scillain (sil′ah-in). An amorphous and poisonous glycoside from squill: diuretic.

scillin (sil′in). A yellowish, crystalline glycoside from squill.

scilliroside (sil′ir-o-sīd). A principle from red squill that is poisonous to rodents.

scillism (sil′izm). Poisoning from squill.

scillitic (sil′it-ik). Pertaining to squill.

scillitin (sil′ĭ-tin). One of the active principles of squill.

scintigram (sin′tĭ-gram). Scintiscan.

scintillascope (sin-til′ah-skōp) [L. *scintilla* spark + Gr. *skopein* to examine]. Spinthariscope.

scintillation (sin″tĭ-la′shun) [L. *scintillatio*]. 1. An emission of sparks. 2. A subjective visual sensation, as of seeing sparks. 3. A particle emitted in disintegration of a radioactive element.

scintiscan (sin′tĭ-skan). A two-dimensional representation (map) of the gamma rays emitted by a radioisotope, revealing its varying concentration in a specific tissue of the body, such as the brain, kidney, or thyroid gland.

scintiscanner (sin″tĭ-skan′ner). The system of equipment used in the making of a scintiscan.

sciopody (ski-op′o-de). Unusually large feet, especially in children.

scirrhencanthus (skir″en-kan′thus) [*scirrho-* + Gr. *en* in + *kanthos* canthus]. Scirrhus of the lacrimal gland.

scirrho- (skir′o) [Gr. *skirrhos* hard]. Combining form meaning hard, or denoting relationship to a hard cancer or scirrhus.

scirrhoblepharoncus (skir″o-blef″ah-rong′kus) [*scirrho-* + Gr. *blepharon* eyelid + *onkos* mass]. A scirrhous tumor of the eyelid.

scirrhoid (skir′oid) [*scirrho-* + Gr. *eidos* form]. Resembling a scirrhus.

scirrhoma (skir-ro′mah) [*scirrho-* + *-oma*]. A scirrhus. **s. caminiano′rum,** chimney-sweeper's cancer, or soot cancer.

scirrhophthalmia (skir″of-thal′me-ah) [*scirrho-* + Gr. *ophthalmos* eye + *-ia*]. Scirrhus of the eye.

scirrhosarca (skir″o-sar′kah) [*scirrho-* + Gr. *sarx* flesh]. 1. Scleroderma. 2. Sclerema neonatorum.

scirrhous (skir′us) [L. *scirrhosus*]. Pertaining to or of the nature of a scirrhus.

scirrhus (skir′us) [Gr. *skirrhos*]. A hard cancer with a marked predominance of connective tissue.

scissel (siz′el). Small pieces of metal cut from a plate which is being made into the base of a denture.

scission (sizh′un) [L. *scindere* to split]. Fission; splitting. In chemistry, the splitting of a molecule into two or more simpler molecules.

scissiparity (sis″ĭ-par′ĭ-te) [L. *scindere* to split + *parere* to bring forth]. Reproduction by fission.

scissors (siz′erz). A cutting instrument with two opposed blades. **canalicular s.,** delicate scissors with one of the blades probe pointed: used in slitting the lacrimal canal. **cannula s.,** probe pointed scissors used in slitting a canal lengthwise. **craniotomy s.,** strong *f*-shaped shears for use in opening the fetal head. **de Wecker's s.,** small scissors for operations on the eyeball, in which the blades are operated by pressure on two springs joined at the end like a pair of tweezers. **Liston's s.,** scissors for cutting plaster-of-paris bandages. **Smellie's s.,** short, strong-bladed scissors with external cutting edges: used in craniotomy.

scissura (sĭ-su′rah), pl. *scissu′rae* [L.]. An incisure; a splitting. **s. pilo′rum,** splitting of the hair.

Sc.L.A. Abbreviation for L. *scapulo-laeva anterior* (left scapulo-anterior) position of the fetus.

Sclavo's serum (sklah′vōz) [Achille *Sclavo*, Italian physician, 1861–1930]. See under *serum.*

sclera (skle′rah) [L.; Gr. *skleros* hard]. [N A, B N A] The tough white supporting tunic of the eyeball, covering approximately the posterior five-sixths of its surface, and continuous posteriorly with the external sheath of the optic nerve. **blue s.,** a hereditary condition, transmitted by a dominant gene, and characterized by unusual blue color of the sclera.

scleradenitis (skle″rad-e-ni′tis) [*sclero-* + Gr. *adēn* gland + *-itis*]. Inflammation and hardening of a gland.

scleral (skle′ral). Pertaining to the sclera.

scleratheroma (skle″rath-er-o′mah). Atherosclerosis.

scleratitis (skle″rah-ti′tis). Scleritis.

scleratogenous (skle″rah-toj′e-nus). Sclerogenous.

sclerectasia (skle″rek-ta′ze-ah) [*sclero-* + Gr. *ektasis* extension + *-ia*]. A bulging out of the sclera.

sclerectasis (skle-rek′tah-sis). Sclerectasia.

sclerecto-iridectomy (skle-rek″to-ir″ĭ-dek′to-me). The operation of excision of a portion of the sclera and of the iris for glaucoma. Called also *Lagrange operation.*

sclerecto-iridodialysis (skle-rek″to-ir″ĭ-do-di-al′ĭ-sis). Sclerectomy and iridodialysis.

sclerectome (skle-rek′tōm). An instrument for performing sclerectomy.

sclerectomy (skle-rek′to-me) [*sclero-* + Gr. *ektomē* excision]. 1. Excision of the sclera by scissors (Lagrange's operation), by punch (Holth's operation), or by trephining (Elliot's operation). 2. Removal of the sclerosed parts of the middle ear after otitis media.

scleredema (skle″re-de′mah). Edematous hardening of the skin. **s. adulto′rum, Buschke's**

s., a chronic hardening of the subcutaneous tissues, giving a feeling as if they were infiltrated with wax, and affecting the skin of the head, neck, and trunk, leaving that of the hands and feet unaffected. **s. neonato'rum,** sclerema neonatorum.

sclerema (skle-re'mah). Scleredema. **s. adipo'sum,** s. neonatorum. **s. adulto'rum,** scleredema adultorum. **s. edemato'sum,** scleredema. **s. neonato'rum,** a disease of early infancy, apparently due to hardening of subcutaneous fat and characterized by coldness, hardening, and tightness of the skin, especially that of the feet and legs, with depression of the respiration and pulse.

sclerencephalia (skle"ren-se-fa'le-ah) [*sclero-* + Gr. *enkephalos* brain + *-ia*]. Sclerosis of the brain.

sclerencephaly (skle"ren-sef'ah-le). Sclerencephalia.

sclerenchyma (skle-reng'kĭ-mah). The woody tissue of plants which gives hardness and stiffness in the softer tissues.

sclerenchymatous (skle"reng-kim'ah-tus). Of the nature of sclerenchyma.

sclererythrin (skle-rer'ĭ-thrin) [*sclerotium* + Gr. *erythros* red]. A red coloring matter from ergot.

scleriasis (skle-ri'ah-sis) [Gr. *sklēriasis*]. 1. Scleroderma. 2. A hardened state of an eyelid.

sclerin (skle'rin). Rhinosclerin.

scleriritomy (skle"rĭ-rit'o-me) [*sclera* + *iris* + Gr. *temnein* to cut]. Incision of the sclera and iris in anterior staphyloma.

scleritis (skle-ri'tis) [*sclera* + *-itis*]. Inflammation of the sclera. It may be superficial (*episcleritis*) or deep. The latter form causes bulging and thinning of the sclera. **annular s.,** scleritis occurring in a ring around the limbus of the cornea. **anterior s.,** inflammation of the sclera adjoining the limbus of the cornea. **brawny s.,** scleritis involving the periphery of the cornea. **posterior s.,** scleritis involving the sclera and the underlying retina and choroid.

sclero- (skle'ro) [Gr. *sklēros* hard]. Combining form meaning hard, often used especially to denote relationship to the sclera.

scleroadipose (skle"ro-ad'ĭ-pōs). Composed of fibrous and fatty tissue.

scleroblastema (skle"ro-blas-te'mah) [*sclero-* + *blastema*]. The embryonic tissue which takes part in the formation of bone.

scleroblastemic (skle"ro-blas-tem'ik). Pertaining to the scleroblastema.

sclerocataracta (skle"ro-kat"ah-rak'tah) [*sclero-* + Gr. *katarrhaktēs* waterfall]. A hard cataract.

sclerochoroiditis (skle"ro-ko"roid-i'tis). Inflammation of the sclera and the choroid coat, resulting in atrophy of both coats and protrusion of the former. **s. ante'rior,** involves the anterior portions of the sclera and causes anterior staphyloma. **s. poste'rior,** a condition seen in progressive myopia in which posterior staphyloma occurs in the region of the optic disk.

scleroconjunctival (skle"ro-kon"junk-ti'val). Pertaining to the sclera and conjunctiva.

scleroconjunctivitis (skle"ro-kon-junk"tĭ-vi'tis). Inflammation of the sclera and the conjunctiva.

sclerocornea (skle"ro-kor'ne-ah). The sclera and the cornea considered as forming one organ.

sclerocorneal (skle"ro-kor'ne-al). Pertaining to the sclera and the cornea.

sclerodactylia (skle"ro-dak-til'e-ah) [*sclero-* + Gr. *daktylos* finger + *-ia*]. Localized scleroderma of the digits. **s. annula'ris ainhumoi'des,** a form which sometimes destroys the terminal phalanges.

sclerodactyly (skle"ro-dak'tĭ-le). Sclerodactylia.

scleroderma (skle"ro-der'mah) [*sclero-* + Gr. *derma* skin]. A systemic disease which may involve the connective tissues of any part of the body, including the skin, heart, esophagus, kidney, and lung. The skin may be thickened, hard, and rigid, and pigmented patches may occur. **circumscribed s., s. circumscrip'tum,** localized s. **diffuse s.,** a collagen disease characterized by increase and swelling of collagen fibers, loss or fragmentation of elastic elements, atrophy of rete pegs, deposition of melanin in the basal cells, and retention of calcium. **diffuse symmetrical s.,** diffuse scleroderma with lesions occurring symmetrically on the two sides of the body. **localized s.,** a condition characterized by connective tissue replacement of the skin and sometimes of the subcutaneous tissues, the lesions being superficial and small, or progressing to large plaques which sometimes coalesce. **s. neonato'rum,** sclerema neonatorum.

sclerodermatitis (skle"ro-der"mah-ti'tis) [*sclero-* + Gr. *derma* skin + *-itis*]. Hardening and inflammation of the skin.

sclerodermitis (skle"ro-der-mi'tis). Sclerodermatitis.

sclerodesmia (skle"ro-des'me-ah) [*sclero-* + Gr. *desmos* ligament + *-ia*]. Hardening of ligaments.

sclerogenic (skle"ro-jen'ik). Sclerogenous.

sclerogenous (skle-roj'e-nus) [*sclero-* + Gr. *gennan* to produce]. Producing sclerosis or sclerous tissue.

sclerogummatous (skle"ro-gum'ah-tus). Composed of fibrous and gummatous tissue.

scleroid (skle'roid) [*sclero-* + Gr. *eidos* form]. Having a hard texture.

sclero-iritis (skle"ro-i-ri'tis). Inflammation of the sclera and of the iris.

sclerokeratitis (skle"ro-ker"ah-ti'tis). 1. Inflammation of the sclera and of the cornea. 2. Sclerosing keratitis.

sclerokeratoiritis (skle"ro-ker"ah-to-i-ri'tis). Inflammation of the sclera, cornea, and iris.

sclerokeratosis (skle"ro-ker"ah-to'sis). Sclerokeratitis.

scleroma (skle-ro'mah) [Gr. *sklērōma* induration]. A hardened patch or induration, especially of the nasal or laryngeal tissues. **s. respirato'rium,** rhinoscleroma.

scleromalacia (skle"ro-mah-la'she-ah) [*sclero-* + Gr. *malakia* softness]. 1. Degeneration (softening) of the sclera, occurring in patients with rheumatoid arthritis. Called also *scleromalacia perforans.* 2. Kienbock's name for osteitis deformans.

scleromeninx (skle"ro-me'ninks) [*sclero-* + Gr. *mēninx* membrane]. The dura mater.

scleromere (skle'ro-mēr) [*sclero-* + Gr. *meros* part]. 1. Any segment or metamere of the skeletal system. 2. The caudal half of a sclerotome.

sclerometer (skle-rom'e-ter) [*sclero-* + Gr. *metron* measure]. An instrument for determining the hardness of substances.

scleromucin (skle"ro-mu'sin). A slimy, active principle from ergot.

scleromyxedema (skle"ro-mik"se-de'mah). A variant of lichen myxedematosus which is characterized not only by a generalized eruption of nodules but also by diffuse thickening of the skin.

scleronychia (skle"ro-nik'e-ah) [*sclero-* + Gr. *onyx* nail + *-ia*]. A simultaneous thickening and dryness of the nails.

scleronyxis (skle"ro-nik'sis) [*sclero-* + Gr. *nyxis* puncture]. Surgical puncture of the sclera.

sclero-oophoritis (skle"ro-o-of"o-ri'tis). Sclerosing inflammation of the ovary.

sclero-oothecitis (skle"ro-o"o-the-si'tis). Sclero-oophoritis.

sclero-optic (skle"ro-op'tik). Pertaining to the sclera and the optic nerve.

sclerophthalmia (skle"rof-thal'me-ah) [*sclero-* + Gr. *ophthalmos* eye + *-ia*]. The condition in which, from imperfect differentiation of the sclera and cornea, the former encroaches on the latter, so that only the central part of the cornea remains clear.

scleroplasty (skle′ro-plas″te). Plastic operation on the sclera.

scleroprotein (skle″ro-pro′te-in) [*sclero-* + *protein*]. A simple protein which is characterized by its insolubility, its fibrous structure, and its supportive or protective functions in the body. See *albuminoid*, def. 3.

sclerosal (skle-ro′sal). Sclerous.

sclerosarcoma (skle″ro-sar-ko′mah) [*sclero-* + Gr. *sarkōma* a fleshy excrescence]. A hard, fleshy mass or growth.

sclerose (skle-rōz′). To become sclerotic; to harden.

sclérose en plaques (skla-rōz″ aw-plak′) [Fr.]. Multiple sclerosis.

sclerosed (skle-rōzd′). Affected with sclerosis.

sclerosing (skle-rōz′ing). Causing or undergoing sclerosis.

sclerosis (skle-ro′sis) [Gr. *sklērōsis* hardness]. An induration, or hardening; especially hardening of a part from inflammation and in diseases of the interstitial substance. The term is used chiefly for such a hardening of the nervous system due to hyperplasia of the connective tissue. **Alzheimer's s.,** hyaline degeneration of the smaller cerebral blood vessels, marked by progressive dementia and aphasia; presenile sclerosis. **amyotrophic lateral s.,** a disease marked by a hardening of the lateral columns of the spinal cord with muscular atrophy. It may invade the oblongata and affect the ventral columns also. The disease always ends fatally in from one to three years, death occurring from extension of the hardening to the medulla oblongata. **annular s.,** sclerosis of the spinal cord, forming a band around it. **anterolateral s.,** sclerosis of the ventral and lateral columns of the cord leading to spastic paraplegia. Called also *ventrolateral s.* **arterial s., arteriopapillary s.,** arteriosclerosis. **arteriolar s.,** arteriosclerosis involving the minute arterioles. **benign s.,** a mild type of arterial hypertension. **bone s.,** eburnation. **bulbar s.,** multiple sclerosis involving the medulla oblongata. **cerebellar s.,** multiple sclerosis involving the cerebellum or cerebellar pathways. **cerebral s.,** multiple sclerosis of the brain. **cerebrospinal s.,** multiple sclerosis of the brain and spinal cord. **cervical s.,** multiple sclerosis involving the cervical spinal cord. **s. circumscrip′ta pericar′dii,** maculae albidae. **combined s.,** sclerosis of both the posterior and lateral columns of the cord. **dentinal s.,** regressive alteration in tooth substance with calcification of the dentinal tubules, caused by caries or abrasion or occurring with age, and producing translucent zones (transparent dentin). **diffuse s.,** a form affecting large areas of the brain and cord. **disseminated s.,** multiple sclerosis. **dorsal s.,** multiple sclerosis involving the dorsal spinal cord. **Erb's s.,** primary lateral spinal sclerosis. **familial centrolobar s.,** a rare congenital and familial disease marked by disturbance of speech, incoordination, athetosis, spasticity, intellectual retardation, and psychic peculiarities, due to atrophy of the white matter of the brain: called also *Merzbacher-Pelizaeus disease* and *aplasia axialis extracorticalis congenita.* **focal s.,** multiple s. **hyperplastic s.,** a form of arteriosclerosis seen in small arteries and arterioles as a subintimal thickening of the wall of the vessel. **insular s.,** multiple s. **Krabbe's s.,** diffuse infantile familial cerebral sclerosis, a variety of demyelinating encephalopathy. **lateral s.,** a form seated in the lateral columns of the cord. It occurs either as a *primary* affection, resulting in spastic paraplegia, attended with rigidity of the limbs, increase of the tendon reflexes, and absence of nutritive and sensory disturbance. The disease may also be *secondary* to myelitis, in which there is spastic paraplegia, with sensory and other disturbances. **lobar s.,** presence of narrow, scar-distorted convolutions over a large area (lobe) of the surface of the cerebral hemispheres; seen frequently in cerebral palsy. **Marie's s.,** hereditary form of cerebellar sclerosis. **miliary s.,** sclerosis occurring in minute spots. **Mönckeberg's s.,** Mönckeberg's arteriosclerosis. **multiple s.,** a disease marked by sclerosis occurring in sporadic patches throughout the brain or spinal cord, or both. It is regarded as probably of infective origin. Among its symptoms are weakness, incoordination, strong jerking movements of the legs, and especially of the arms, amenomania or other abnormal mental exaltation, scanning speech, nystagmus, etc. It is not curable, and may last for many years. Called also *Charcot's disease, disseminated s.,* and *insular s.* **nodular s.,** atherosclerosis. **posterior s.,** tabes dorsalis. **posterolateral s.,** Friedreich's ataxia, or, more correctly, the lesion of the posterior and lateral columns of the spinal cord which leads to it. **presenile s.,** Alzheimer's sclerosis. **s. re′dux.** See *monorecidive.* **renal arteriolar s.,** arteriosclerosis involving chiefly the renal arterioles, resulting in contracted kidney. **s. tubero′sa, tuberous s.,** a familial disease characterized pathologically by tumors on the surfaces of the lateral ventricles and sclerotic patches on the surface of the brain and marked clinically by progressive mental deterioration and epileptic convulsions. There may be adenoma sebaceum, congenital tumor of the eye (phacoma) and tumors of the viscera, especially the kidney and heart muscle. Called also *Bourneville's disease* and *epiloia.* **unicellular s.,** the development of bands of fibrous material between the cells of a gland. **vascular s.,** arteriosclerosis. **venous s.,** phlebosclerosis. **s. ventric′uli,** sclerotic gastritis. **ventrolateral s.,** anterolateral s.

scleroskeleton (skle″ro-skel′ĕ-ton) [*sclero-* + *skeleton*]. Those parts of the bony skeleton that are formed by the ossification of ligaments, tendons, or fasciae.

sclerostenosis (skle″ro-ste-no′sis) [Gr. *sklērōs* hard + *stenōsis* narrowing]. Induration or hardening combined with contraction. **s. cuta′nea,** scleroderma.

Sclerostoma (skle-ros′to-mah). A genus of nematode worms. **S. duodena′le,** *Ancylostoma duodenale.* **S. syn′gamus,** *Syngamus trachealis.*

sclerostomy (skle-ros′to-me) [*sclero-* + Gr. *stoma* opening]. The surgical creation of a fistulous opening through the sclera for the relief of glaucoma.

sclerotherapy (skle″ro-ther′ah-pe). The injection of sclerosing solutions in the treatment of hemorrhoids or other varicose veins.

sclerothrix (skle′ro-thriks) [*sclero-* + Gr. *thrix* hair]. Abnormal hardness and dryness of the hair.

sclerotic (skle-rot′ik) [L. *scleroticus;* Gr. *sklērōs* hard]. 1. Hard, or hardening; affected with sclerosis. 2. Sclera.

sclerotica (skle-rot′ĭ-kah) [L.]. Sclera.

scleroticectomy (skle-rot″ĭ-sek′to-me). Sclerectomy.

scleroticochoroiditis (skle-rot″ĭ-ko-ko″roid-i′tis). Sclerochoroiditis.

scleroticonyxis (skle-rot″ĭ-ko-nik′sis). Scleronyxis.

scleroticopuncture (skle-rot″ĭ-ko-punk′tūr). Scleronyxis.

scleroticotomy (skle-rot″ĭ-kot′o-me). Sclerotomy.

sclerotitis (skle″ro-ti′tis). Scleritis.

sclerotium (skle-ro′she-um). The hard, blackish mass formed by certain fungi, such as the ergot of rye.

sclerotome (skle′ro-tōm). 1. An instrument used in the incision of the sclera. 2. The area of a bone innervated from a single spinal segment. 3. One of the paired masses of mesenchymal tissue, separated from the ventromedial part of a somite, which develop into vertebrae and ribs.

sclerotomy (skle-rot′o-me) [*sclero-* + Gr. *tomē* a

cutting]. Surgical incision of the sclera. **anterior s.,** the opening of the anterior chamber of the eye, chiefly done for the relief of glaucoma. **posterior s.,** an opening made into the vitreous through the sclera, as for detached retina or the removal of a foreign body.

sclerotrichia (skle″ro-trik′e-ah) [*sclero-* + Gr. *thrix* hair]. A hard, dry state of the hair.

sclerous (skle′rus). Hard; indurated.

sclerozone (skle′ro-zōn) [*sclero-* + Gr. *zōnē* zone]. Any surface on a bone giving attachment to the muscles from a given myotome.

Sc.L.P. Abbreviation for L. *scapulo-laeva posterior* (left scapuloposterior) position of the fetus.

S.C.M. Abbreviation for *State Certified Midwife.*

scoleciasis (sko-le-si′ah-sis) [*scoleco-* + *-iasis*]. The morbid state due to the presence of larvae of moths or butterflies in the body.

scoleciform (sko-les′ĭ-form). Resembling a scolex.

scolecitis (sko″le-si′tis) [*scoleco-* + *-itis*]. Appendicitis.

scoleco- (sko′le-ko) [Gr. *skōlēx* worm]. Combining form denoting relationship to a worm.

scolecoid (sko′le-koid) [Gr. *skōlekoeidēs* vermiform]. 1. Resembling a worm. 2. Resembling a scolex; hydatid.

scolecoidectomy (sko″le-koi-dek′to-me). Appendectomy.

scolecoiditis (sko″le-koid-i′tis). Appendicitis.

scolecology (sko″le-kol′o-je) [*scoleco-* + *-logy*]. Helminthology.

scolectomy (sko-lek′to-me). Appendectomy.

scoledocostomy (sko-le″do-kos′to-me). Appendicostomy.

scolex (sko′leks), pl. *sco′lices* [Gr. *skōlēx* worm]. The attachment end of a tapeworm, consisting of the head and neck.

scolices (sko′lĭ-sēz). Plural of *scolex.*

scolio- (sko′le-o) [Gr. *skolios* twisted]. Combining form meaning twisted or crooked.

scoliokyphosis (sko″le-o-ki-fo′sis) [*scolio-* + *kyphosis*]. Combined lateral and posterior curvature of the spine.

scoliopathexis (sko″le-o-pah-thek′sis) [*scolio-* + Gr. *pathos* disease]. A perverted state of mind in relation to disease, such as malingering, valetudinarianism, etc.

sciorachitic (sko″le-o-rah-kit′ik). Affected with scoliosis and rickets.

scoliosiometry (sko″le-o-se-om′e-tre) [*scoliosis* + Gr. *metron* measure]. Measurement of curvatures, especially those of the vertebral column.

scoliosis (sko″le-o′sis) [Gr. *skoliōsis* curvation]. An appreciable lateral deviation in the normally

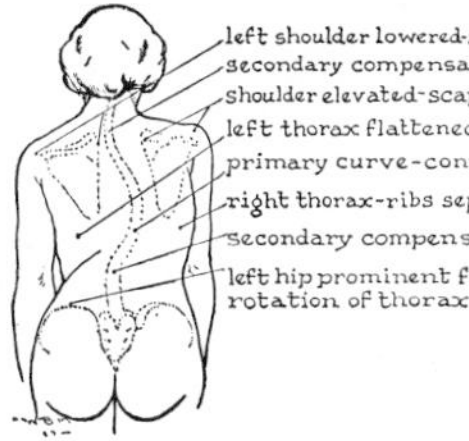

Scoliosis (Babcock).

straight vertical line of the spine. **Brissaud's s.,** sciatic s. **cicatricial s.,** that which is due to a cicatricial contraction following caries or necrosis. **coxitic s.,** scoliosis in the lumbar region caused by hip disease. **empyematic s.,** that which is caused by empyema. **habit s.,** scoliosis due to improper position of the body. **inflammatory s.,** that which is due to vertebral disease. **ischiatic s.,** that which is due to hip disease. **myopathic s.,** that which is due to paralysis of the muscles that support the trunk. **ocular s., ophthalmic s.,** scoliosis attributed to tilting of the head on account of astigmatism. **osteopathic s.,** that which is caused by disease of the vertebrae. **paralytic s.,** lateral curvature of the spinal column. **rachitic s.,** spinal curvature due to rickets. **rheumatic s.,** that which is due to rheumatism of the dorsal muscles. **sciatic s.,** a list of the lumbar part of the spine away from the affected side in sciatica. **static s.,** that which is due to difference in the length of the legs.

scoliosometer (sko″le-o-som′e-ter). An apparatus for measuring curves, especially those of the spinal column.

scoliotic (sko″le-ot′ik) [Gr. *skoliōtos* looking askew]. Pertaining to or characterized by scoliosis.

scoliotone (sko′le-o-tōn). An apparatus for the forcible correction of scoliosis.

Scolopendra (sko″lo-pen′drah) [Gr. *skolops* anything pointed]. A genus of poisonous centipedes. *S. he′ros* and *S. mor′sitans* are American species; *S. gigan′tea* is a tropical species.

scolopsia (sko-lop′se-ah) [Gr. *skolops* anything pointed]. A suture between two bones that allows motion of one on the other.

scombrine (skom′brin). A protamine found in mackerel sperm.

scombrone (skom′bron). A histone from spermatozoa of mackerel.

scoop (skoop). A spoonlike instrument for clearing out cavities. **Mules's s.,** a form of curet used in eye operations.

scoparin (sko-pa′rin). A yellowish, crystalline principle, $C_{22}H_{22}O_{11}$, from the tops of *Cytisus scoparius:* diuretic.

scoparius (sko-pa′re-us). The tops of *Cytisus scoparius,* or broom, a leguminous shrub. They contain the alkaloid sparteine and the principle scoparin. They are diuretic, purgative, and emetic.

-scope (skōp) [Gr. *skopein* to view, examine]. Word termination meaning an instrument for examining.

scopin (sko′pin). A substance formed by the gentle hydrolysis of hyoscine. It is $OH.C_6H_8O.N.CH_3$, and readily changes into oscin.

scopograph (skop′o-graf) [Gr. *skopein* to view + *graphein* to write]. A combined fluoroscope and radiographic unit.

scopola (sko-po′lah). The dried rhizome and larger roots of *Scopolia carniolica.* It contains the same constituents as *Atropa belladonna,* and is used like belladonna, as a sedative and narcotic.

scopolagnia (sko″po-lag′ne-ah) [Gr. *skopein* to view + *lagneia* lust]. Scopophilia.

scopolamine (sko-pol′ah-mēn). An alkaloid derived from Solanaceae, especially *Datura metel* and *Scopola carniolica:* used in parasympathetic blockade and as a central nervous system depressant.

Scopolia (sko-po′le-ah) [Johann Antoni *Scopoli,* physician in Pavia, 1723–1788]. A genus of solanaceous plants. *S. atropoi′des* (*carniolica*), of Europe, and *S. japon′ica* and *S. lu′rida,* of Asia, have properties like those of hyoscyamus and belladonna.

scopometer (sko-pom′e-ter) [Gr. *skopein* to examine + *metron* measure]. An instrument for measuring the turbidity of solutions, i.e., the density of a precipitate.

scopometry (sko-pom′e-tre). Measurement of the optical density of a precipitate to determine the amount of a substance in suspension.

scopomorphinism (sko″po-mor′fin-izm). Addiction to the use of scopolamine and morphine.

scopophilia (sko-po-fil′e-ah) [Gr. *skopein* to view + *philein* to love]. 1. The derivation of sexual pleasure from looking at genital organs (*active s.*). 2. A morbid desire to be seen (*passive s.*).

scopophobia (sko″po-fo′be-ah) [Gr. *skopein* to view + *phobein* to be affrighted by]. A morbid dread of being seen.

scoptolagnia (skop″to-lag′ne-ah). Scopophilia.

scoptophilia (skop″to-fil′e-ah). Scopophilia.

scoptophobia (skop″to-fo′be-ah). Scopophobia.

Scopulariopsis (skop″u-la″re-op′sis). A genus of fungi, species of which have been found in human infections: *S. americana,* in a cutaneous condition resembling blastomycosis; *S. aureus, S. brevicaulis* var. *hominis, S. cinereus,* and *S. minimus,* in onychomycosis; *S. blochi,* in a condition resembling sporotrichosis; and *S. koningi,* in oculomycosis.

scopulariopsosis (skop″u-la″re-op-so′sis). Infection with a fungus of the genus *Scopulariopsis.*

-scopy (skop′e) [Gr. *skopein* to examine]. Word termination meaning the act of examining.

scoracratia (skōr″ah-kra′she-ah) [Gr. *skōr* dung + *akratia* lack of self-control]. The involuntary discharge of feces.

scorbutic (skōr-bu′tik) [L. *scorbuticus*]. Pertaining to or affected with scurvy.

scorbutigenic (skōr-bu″tĭ-jen′ik). Causing scurvy.

scorbutus (skōr-bu′tus) [L.]. Scurvy.

scordinema (skōr″dĭ-ne′mah) [Gr. *skordinēma*]. Yawning and stretching with a feeling of lassitude, occurring as a preliminary symptom of some infectious disease.

score (skōr). A rating, usually expressed numerically, based on achievement or the degree to which certain qualities are present. **Apgar s.,** a numerical expression of the condition of a newborn infant, at 60 seconds after birth, being the sum of points gained on assessment of the heart rate, respiratory effort, muscle tone, reflex irritability, and color. Cf. *recovery s.* **recovery s.,** a number expressing the condition of an infant at various intervals, which should be stipulated, greater than 1 minute after birth, based on the same features assessed by the Apgar score at 60 seconds after birth.

scoretemia (skōr″ĕ-te′me-ah) [Gr. *skōr* dung + *haima* blood + *-ia*]. Autointoxication due to the absorption of putrescent fecal material from the intestine.

scorings (skōr′ingz). Small transverse lines caused by increased density of bone, seen in roentgenograms at the metaphysis of growing bones, and due to temporary cessation of growth.

scorpion (skōr′pe-on). An arthropod of warm countries, having a poisonous sting. More important species are *Buthus quinquestriatus* of Egypt, *Centruroides suffusus* of Mexico, *Euscorpius italicus,* or black scorpion, of Europe and North Africa, and *Tityus serrulatus* of Brazil.

scorpionism (skōr′pe-un-izm). Poisoning by scorpion stings.

scoto- (sko′to) [Gr. *skotos* darkness]. Combining form denoting relationship to darkness.

scotochromogen (sko″to-kro′mo-jen) [*scoto-* + Gr. *chrōma* color + *gennan* to produce]. A microorganism whose pigmentation develops in the dark as well as in the light; specifically a member of Group II of the so-called "unclassified" mycobacteria, but applicable also to many other organisms.

scotochromogenic (sko″to-kro″mo-jen′ik). Pertaining to or characterized by scotochromogenicity.

scotochromogenicity (sko″to-kro″mo-jĕ-nis′ĭ-te). The property of forming pigment in the dark, the coloration occurring irrespective of exposure to light.

scotodinia (sko″to-din′e-ah) [Gr. *skotos* darkness + *dinos* whirl]. Dizziness with blurring of vision and headache.

scotogram, scotograph (sko′to-gram, sko′to-graf) [Gr. *skotos* darkness + *graphein* to write]. 1. Skiagraph. 2. The effect produced upon a photographic plate in the dark by certain substances.

scotographic (sko″to-graf′ik). Affecting a photographic plate in the dark.

scotography (sko-tog′rah-fe). Skiagraphy.

scotoma (sko-to′mah), pl. *scoto′mata* [Gr. *skotōma*]. An area of depressed vision within the visual field, surrounded by an area of less depressed or of normal vision. **absolute s.,** an area within the visual field in which perception of light is entirely lost. **annular s.,** a circular area of depressed vision in the visual field, surrounding the point of fixation. **arcuate s.,** an arc-shaped defect of vision arising in an area near the blind spot, and extending toward it. **aural s., s. au′ris,** loss of ability to perceive auditory stimuli coming from a certain direction. **Bjerrum's s.,** a further development of Seidel's scotoma, the sickle-shaped defect contiguous to the blind spot extending above and below the fixation point and encircling it more or less completely. **central s.,** an area of depressed vision corresponding with the point of fixation and interfering with or entirely abolishing central vision. **centrocecal s.,** a horizontal oval defect in the field of vision situated between and embracing both the point of fixation and the blind spot. **color s.,** an isolated area of depressed or defective vision for color in the visual field. **flittering s.,** teichopsia. **insular s.,** an isolated area of defective or absent vision in the visual field, surrounded on all sides by more nearly normal vision. **motile s's,** positive scotomas occurring as a result of opacities in the vitreous, muscae volitantes being an example of such a defect. **negative s.,** a scotoma which appears as a blank spot or hiatus in the visual field. **paracentral s.,** an area of depressed vision situated near the point of fixation. **peripapillary s.,** an area of depressed vision in the visual field near that corresponding with the optic disk. **peripheral s.,** an area of depressed vision distant from the point of fixation, toward the periphery of the visual field. **physiologic s.,** that area of the visual field corresponding with the optic disk, in which the photosensitive receptors are absent. **positive s.,** one which appears as a dark spot in the visual field. **relative s.,** an area of the visual field in which perception of light is only diminished, or the loss is restricted to light of certain wavelengths. **ring s.,** annular s. **scintillating s.,** teichopsia. **Seidel's s.,** a further development of an arcuate scotoma, which extends at either or both ends, the concavity of the prolongation always being directed toward the fixation point.

scotomagraph (sko-to′mah-graf) [*scotoma* + Gr. *graphein* to write]. An instrument for recording a scotoma.

scotomameter (sko″to-mam′e-ter). A device for measuring scotomata.

scotomatous (sko-tom′ah-tus). Pertaining to or affected with scotoma.

scotometer (sko-tom′e-ter) [*scotoma* + Gr. *metron* measure]. An instrument for diagnosing and measuring scotomata. **Bjerrum's s.,** campimeter.

scotometry (sko-tom′e-tre). The measurement of isolated areas of depressed vision (scotomata) within the visual field.

scotomization (sko″tŏ-mi-za′shun) [*scotoma* + Gr. *-izein* to make into]. The development of scotomata, or blind spots, especially the development of mental "blind spots," the patient attempting to deny existence of everything which conflicts with his ego.

scotophilia (sko″to-fil′e-ah) [*scoto-* + Gr. *philein* to love]. Love of darkness.

scotophobia (sko″to-fo′be-ah) [*scoto-* + Gr. *phobein* to be affrighted by]. Morbid fear of darkness.

scotopia (sko-to′pe-ah) [*scoto-* + Gr. *ōpē* sight + *-ia*]. Night vision. See also *dark adaptation.*

scotopic (sko-top′ik). Pertaining to vision in the dark: said of the eye which has become dark-adapted.

scotoscopy (sko-tos′ko-pe) [*scoto-* + Gr. *skopein* to examine]. Skiascopy.

scototherapy (sko″to-ther′ah-pe) [*scoto-* + Gr. *therapeia* treatment]. Treatment of disease by the complete exclusion of light rays.

scours (skowrz). Diarrhea in newborn animals.

black s., acute dysentery in animals (cattle or swine), intestinal hemorrhage producing a dark color of the feces. **bloody s.**, black scours in swine. **calf s.**, an acute infectious disease of young calves, with severe diarrhea, dehydration, and depression. **white s.**, a disease of calves, lambs, and foals during the first few days after birth, marked by fever and diarrhea, with light-colored, fetid feces. **winter s.**, black scours occurring in cattle when stabled for the winter.

scr. Abbreviation for *scruple*.

scrapie (skra′pe). A disease of the nervous system occurring in sheep and goats, characterized by severe pruritus, debility, and muscular incoordination, and invariably ending fatally. Once considered to be a hereditary disease, it is now thought to be caused by a filterable virus.

scratches (skrach′ez). Eczematous inflammation of the feet of a horse.

screatus (skre-a′tus) [L.]. Paroxysmal hawking and snorting, due to neurosis.

screen (skrēn). A structure resembling a curtain or partition, used as a protection or shield; such a structure used in fluoroscopy; or such a structure on which light rays are projected. **Bjerrum s.**, tangent s. **fluorescent s.** 1. A sheet of cardboard, paper or glass coated with suitable material, which fluoresces visibly, as calcium tungstate, used as an intensifying screen in roentgenography; as the chief part of a fluoroscope; as a substitute for a fluoroscope in a darkened room. 2. A sheet of cardboard, paper or glass coated with anthracene or other fluorescing materials to observe the ultraviolet radiations. **intensifying s.**, a thin sheet of celluloid or other substance coated with a finely divided substance which fluoresces under the influence of roentgen rays and intended to be used in close contact with the emulsion of a photographic plate or film for the purpose of reinforcing the image. **tangent s.**, a large square of black cloth, stretched on a frame, hung from a roller, and having a central mark for fixation: used with a campimeter to map the field of vision. Called also *Bjerrum screen*.

screening (skrēn′ing). Mass examination of the population to detect the existence of a particular disease, as diabetes or tuberculosis. **multiphasic s., multiple s.**, the simultaneous use of multiple laboratory procedures for the detection of various diseases, or pathologic conditions, as anemia, diabetes, heart diseases, hypertension, syphilis, and tuberculosis and other pulmonary diseases.

scribomania (skrib″o-ma′ne-ah). Graphorrhea or graphomania.

scrobiculate (skro-bik′u-lāt) [L. *scrobiculatus*]. Marked with pits or cavities.

scrobiculus (skro-bik′u-lus) [L. "little trench," "pit"]. A small hollow, pit, or cavity. **s. cor′dis** [B N A], fossa epigastrica.

scrofula (skrof′u-lah) [L. "brood sow"]. Tuberculosis of the lymphatic glands, and sometimes of bones and joint surfaces, with slowly suppurating abscesses and fistulous passages, the inflamed structures being subject to a cheesy degeneration. It is essentially a disease of early life.

scrofulid (skrof′u-lid). Scrofuloderma.

scrofulide (skrof′u-līd) [Fr.]. Scrofuloderma.

scrofuloderm (skrof′u-lo-derm). Scrofuloderma.

scrofuloderma (skrof″u-lo-der′mah) [*scrofula* + Gr. *derma* skin]. Any skin affection of tuberculous origin, and marked by irregular superficial ulcers. **s. gummo′sa**, a deep tuberculosis of the skin forming a gumma-like lesion. **papular s.**, lichen scrofulosorum. **pustular s.**, a form in which large or small sluggish pustules of the skin are formed, which, after ulcerating, leave depressed scars. **tuberculous s.**, granuloma; a subcutaneous nodule which degenerates slowly and leads to an indolent fistulous ulcer. **ulcerative s.**, a tuberculous scrofuloderm in its ulcerating stage. **verrucous s.**, tuberculous lupus characterized by necrogenic or other warty growths.

scrofulophyma (skrof″-u-lo-fi′mah) [*scrofula* + Gr. *phyma* growth]. A tuberculous growth of the skin.

scrofulosis (skrof″u-lo′sis). A tendency toward scrofula; the scrofulous diathesis.

scrofulotuberculosis (skrof″u-lo-tu-ber″ku-lo′-sis). Attenuated tuberculosis.

scrofulotuberculous (skrof″u-lo-tu-ber′ku-lus). Characterized by scrofulous tubercles.

scrofulous (skrof′u-lus). Pertaining to or characterized by scrofula.

scrotal (skro′tal). Pertaining to the scrotum.

scrotectomy (skro-tek′to-me) [*scrotum* + Gr. *ektomē* excision]. Excision of a portion of the scrotum.

scrotitis (skro-ti′tis). Inflammation of the scrotum.

scrotocele (skro′to-sēl) [*scrotum* + Gr. *kēlē* hernia]. Scrotal hernia.

scrotoplasty (skro′to-plas″te) [*scrotum* + Gr. *plassein* to form]. Plastic operation on the scrotum.

scrotum (skro′tum) [L. "bag"]. [N A, B N A] The pouch which contains the testes and their accessory organs. It is composed of skin, the dartos, the spermatic, cremasteric and infundibuliform fasciae, and the tunica vaginalis. **s. lapillo′sum**, calcareous atheroma of the scrotum. **lymph s.**, dilatation of the scrotal lymphatics, as in certain cases of filariasis; described by Wong, of Canton, in 1858. **watering-can s.**, a condition in which the under surface of the scrotum and the perineum are marked by multiple sinuses discharging urine: due to neglected stricture of the perineal urethra.

scruple (skroo′p'l) [L. *scrupulus*, dim. of *scrupus* a sharp stone, a worry or anxiety]. 1. A fear of transgression. 2. A unit of mass (weight) of the apothecaries' system, being 20 grains, or the equivalent of 1.296 Gm. Abbreviated scr.; symbol ℈.

scrupulosity (skroo″pu-los′ĭ-te). Morbid sensitiveness in matters of conscience.

scultetus (skul-te′tus) [Johann *Schultes* (called *Scultetus*), German surgeon, 1595–1645]. Scultetus bandage.

scurf (skurf). Dandruff; a branny substance of epidermic origin.

scurvy (skur′ve) [L. *scorbutus*]. A condition due to deficiency of vitamin C in the diet and marked by weakness, anemia, spongy gums, a tendency to mucocutaneous hemorrhages and a brawny induration of the muscles of the calves and legs. It oftenest affects mariners and those who use salted meats and few or no vegetables. The use of fresh potatoes, scurvy grass, and onions as food, and especially the drinking of lime juice, are preventive and remedial measures. **Alpine s., s. of the Alps**, pellagra. **button s.**, a skin disease, formerly endemic in Ireland, characterized by button-like excrescences. **hemorrhagic s.**, infantile scurvy. **infantile s.**, a nutritional disease of infants characterized by the same symptoms as scurvy in adults. Called also *Barlow's disease*, *Moeller's disease*, and *Cheadle's disease*. **land s.**, thrombopenic purpura. **sea s.**, the true scurvy, such as mainly affects mariners.

scute (skūt) [L. *scutum* shield]. 1. Any squama or scalelike structure. 2. The tympanic scute. **tympanic s.**, the bony plate which divides the upper part of the tympanic cavity from the mastoid cells.

scutiform (sku′tĭ-form) [L. *scutum* shield + *forma* form]. Shaped like a shield.

scutular (sku′tu-lar). Marked by scutula, or small, shield-shaped crusts.

scutulum (sku′tu-lum), pl. *scu′tula* [L.]. One of the disklike crusts of favus.

scutum (sku′tum) [L. "shield"]. 1. The tympanic scute. 2. The thyroid cartilage. 3. The patella.

4. A hard chitinous plate on the anterior portion of the dorsal surface of the Ixodidae or true ticks. **s. pec′toris,** the sternum.

scybala (sib′ah-lah). Plural of *scybalum*.

scybalous (sib′ah-lus). Of the nature of or composed of scybala.

scybalum (sib′ah-lum), pl. *scyb′ala* [Gr. *skybalon*]. A dry, hard mass of fecal matter in the intestine.

scyllite (sil′it). A hexose from the liver and kidneys of sharks, skates, etc.

scyllitol (sil′ĭ-tol). A fatty acid formed in the course of development of *Scyllum canicula*, the dog fish.

scymnol (sim′nol). A substance, $C_{27}H_{46}O_5$, allied to cholic acid found in the bile of *Scymnus borealis*, a marine fish of the shark family.

scyphoid (si′foid) [Gr. *skyphos* cup + *eidos* form]. Shaped like a cup.

scythropasmus (si″thro-paz′mus) [Gr. *skythrōpasmos; skythōpazein* to look sullen]. A dull, fatigued expression, regarded as a grave symptom in serious disease.

scytitis (si-ti′tis) [Gr. *skytos* skin + *-itis*]. Dermatitis.

scytoblastema (si″to-blas-te′mah) [Gr. *skytos* skin + *blastēma* sprout]. The rudimentary skin of the embryo.

Scytonema (si″to-ne′mah) [Gr. *skytos* skin + *nēma* thread]. A genus of algae with cylindrical branching filaments.

SD. Abbreviation for *streptodornase*.

S.D. Abbreviation for *skin dose* and *standard deviation*.

S.D.A. Abbreviation for *specific dynamic action* and L. *sacro-dextra anterior* (right sacro-anterior) position of the fetus.

S.D.P. Abbreviation for L. *sacro-dextra posterior* (right sacroposterior) position of the fetus.

S.D.T. Abbreviation for L. *sacro-dextra transversa* (right sacrotransverse) position of the fetus.

S.E. Abbreviation for *standard error*.

Se. Chemical symbol for *selenium*.

seam (sēm). A line of union. **pigment s.,** the portion of the pigmented epithelium of the iris which bends forward around the pupillary border.

searcher (surch′er). A sound used in searching for stone in the bladder: called also *stone searcher*.

seasickness (se′sik-nes). Nausea and malaise caused by the motion of a ship at sea.

seatworm (sēt′werm). *Enterobius vermicularis*.

seaweed (se′wēd). A plant growing in the sea, especially a plant of the class Algae.

sebaceous (se-ba′shus) [L. *sebaceus*]. 1. Pertaining to sebum or suet. 2. Secreting a greasy lubricating substance.

sebastomania (se-bas″to-ma′ne-ah) [Gr. *sebastos* reverenced + *mania* madness]. Religious insanity.

sebiferous (se-bif′er-us) [L. *sebiferus*, from *sebum* suet + *ferre* to bear]. Sebiparous.

Sebileau's bands, hollow (seb″ĭ-lōz′) [Pierre *Sebileau*, French surgeon, 1860–1953]. See under *band* and *hollow*.

sebiparous (se-bip′ah-rus) [L. *sebiparus; sebum* suet + *parere* to produce]. Producing a fatty secretion.

sebocystoma (se″bo-sis-to′mah). A sebaceous cyst.

sebocystomatosis (se″bo-sis″to-mah-to′sis). The presence of numerous sebaceous cysts on the skin.

sebolith (seb′o-lith) [*sebum* + Gr. *lithos* stone]. A concretion formed in a sebaceous gland.

seborrhagia (seb″o-ra′je-ah). Seborrhea.

seborrhea (seb″o-re′ah) [L. *sebum* suet + Gr. *rhoia* flow]. A functional disturbance of the sebaceous glands marked by the occurrence of an excessive discharge of sebum from the glands, forming white or yellowish, greasy scales or cheesy plugs on the body. It is generally attended with itching or burning. **s. adipo′sa,** that in which the secretion is oily, especially occurring about the nose and forehead. Called also *s. oleo′sa*. **s. capillit′ii, s. cap′itis,** alopecia seborrhoeica. **s. ce′rea,** seborrhea with a waxy secretion. **concrete s.,** greasy crusts of the scalp or of the smooth parts. **s. congesti′va,** lupus erythematosus. **s. cor′poris,** a form affecting the trunk; lichen circinatus. **eczematoid s.,** that associated with inflammation of the scalp. **s. facie′i,** a form which affects the face: it may follow smallpox or any of the exanthematous fevers. **s. furfura′cea,** a scaly, dandruffy form of seborrhea sicca. **s. genera′lis,** that which affects the entire surface. **s. ni′gra, s. ni′gricans,** a variety that is characterized by a dark-colored secretion. **s. oleo′sa,** seborrhea adiposa. **s. sic′ca,** seborrheic dermatitis. **s. squa′mo neonato′rum,** ichthyosis sebacea.

seborrheal (seb″o-re′al). Characterized by seborrhea.

seborrheic (seb″o-re′ik). Affected with or of the nature of seborrhea.

seborrheid (seb″o-re′id). A seborrheic eruption.

seborrhoea (seb″o-re′ah). Seborrhea.

seborrhoic (seb″o-ro′ik). Seborrheic.

sebum (se′bum) [L.]. 1. Suet. Cf. *sebum*. 2. The secretion of the sebaceous glands; a thick, semifluid substance composed of fat and epithelial débris from the cells of the malpighian layer. **cutaneous s., s. cuta′neum** [B N A], the fatty secretion of the sebaceous glands. Omitted in N A. **s. palpebra′le** [B N A], the secretion of the tarsal glands. Omitted in N A. **s. praeputia′le,** smegma.

Secale (se-ka′le) [L. "rye"]. A genus of graminaceous plants. **S. cerea′le,** the common rye.

secale cornutum (se-ka′le kor-nu′tum). The name under which ergot was adopted in the first edition of the U.S.P.

secalin (sek′ah-lin). One of the active principles of ergot: said to be identical with trimethylamine, $N(CH_3)_3$.

secalintoxin (sek″ah-lin-tok′sin). A principle obtainable from ergot. It is a compound of secalin with ergochrysin. It is less active than chrysotoxin, and is probably identical with cornutin.

secalose (sek′ah-lōs). A carbohydrate obtainable from rye: when dried, it forms a white, hygroscopic powder, convertible by inversion into levulose.

secernent (se-ser′nent) [L. *secernens* secreting]. 1. Secreting. 2. Any secreting organ or surface.

Sechenoff's center (setsh′en-ofs). See *Setschenow*.

secobarbital (se″ko-bar′bĭ-tal). Chemical name: 5-allyl-5-(1-methylbutyl) barbituric acid: used as a sedative and hypnotic.

secodont (se′ko-dont) [L. *secare* to cut + Gr. *odous* tooth]. Having teeth in which the tubercles of the molars are provided with cutting edges.

seconal (sek′ō-nol). Trade mark for preparations of secobarbital.

secondary (sek′un-der″e) [L. *secundarius; secundus* second]. Second or inferior in order of time, place, or importance.

second intention (sek′und in-ten′shun). See under *healing*.

secreta (se-kre′tah) [L. pl.]. Secretion products.

secretagogue (se-krēt′ah-gog) [*secretion* + Gr. *agōgos* drawing]. 1. Stimulating secretion. 2. An agent that stimulates secretion.

Secrétan's disease (sĕ″kra-tanz′) [Henri *Secrétan*, Swiss physician, 1856–1916]. Severe traumatic edema.

secrete (se-krēt′) [L. *secernere, secretum* to separate]. To separate or elaborate cell products.

secretin (se-kre′tin). 1. A hormone secreted by the mucosa of the duodenum and jejunum when acid chyme enters the intestine. Carried by the blood, it stimulates the secretion of pancreatic juice and bile. 2. A general name for any hormone which stimulates glandular secretion. **gastric s.,** gastrin.

secretinase (se-kre′tĭ-nās). An enzymic substance in blood and other body fluids which inactivates secretin.

secretion (se-kre′shun) [L. *secretio,* from *secernere* to secrete]. 1. The process of elaborating a specific product as a result of the activity of a gland. This activity may range from separating a specific substance of the blood to the elaboration of a new chemical substance. 2. Any substance which is produced by secretion. **antilytic s.,** saliva secreted by the submaxillary gland with nerves intact, as distinguished from that secreted when the nerve is divided. **external s.,** one that is discharged upon the external or internal surface of the body. **internal s.,** a secretion that is not discharged by a duct from the body, but is given off into the blood and lymph, taking an important part in metabolism. Such secretions are furnished by the thyroid, the spleen, the adrenals, the testicles, the pituitary body, etc. Those secretions that excite metabolic processes are hormones, those that depress are chalones or colyones. See *endocrine.* **paralytic s.,** secretion from a gland after paralysis or division of its nerve.

secretodermatosis (se-kre″to-der″mah-to′sis). Any derangement of the secreting functions of the skin.

secretogogue (se-kre′to-gog). Secretagogue.

secreto-inhibitory (se-kre″to-in-hib′ĭ-to″re). Inhibiting secretion.

secretomotor (se-kre″to-mo′tor). Exciting or stimulating secretion: said of nerves.

secretomotory (se-kre″to-mo′tor-e). Secretomotor.

secretor (se-kre′tor). An individual possessing A or B type blood whose saliva and various other body secretions contain the particular (A or B) substance.

secretory (se-kre′to-re). Pertaining to secretion or affecting the secretions.

sectarian (sek-ta′re-an). A practitioner of medicine who "follows a dogma, tenet, or principle based on the authority of its promulgator to the exclusion of demonstration and practice" (Judicial Council A. M. A.).

sectile (sek′til) [L. *sectilis,* from *secare* to cut]. 1. Susceptible of being cut. 2. One of several parts into which a whole is divided.

sectio (sek′she-o), pl. *sectio′nes* [L., from *secare* to cut]. 1. An act of cutting. 2. A segment or subdivision of an organ. Called also *section.* **s. agrippi′na,** cesarean section. **s. al′ta,** suprapubic cystotomy. **s. cadav′eris,** necropsy. **sectio′nes cerebel′li** [N A, B N A], the various anatomical subdivisions of the cerebellum. **sectio′nes corpo′rum quadrigemino′rum** [B N A], the anatomical divisions of the corpora quadrigemina. Omitted in N A. **sectio′nes hypothal′ami** [N A, B N A], the various anatomical subdivisions of the hypothalamus. **sectio′nes isth′mi** [B N A]. See *sectiones mesencephali.* **s. latera′lis,** lateral lithotomy. **s. media′na,** median lithotomy. **sectio′nes medul′lae oblonga′tae** [N A, B N A], the various anatomical subdivisions of the medulla oblongata. **sectio′nes medul′lae spina′lis** [N A, B N A], the various anatomical subdivisions of the spinal cord. **sectio′nes mesencepha′li** [N A], the various anatomical subdivisions of the mesencephalon. **sectio′nes pedun′culi cer′ebri** [B N A], sectiones mesencephali. **sectio′nes pon′tis** [N A, B N A], the various anatomical subdivisions of the pons. **sectio′nes telencepha′li** [N A, B N A], the various anatomical subdivisions of the telencephalon. **sectio′nes thalamencepha′li** [N A, B N A], the various anatomical subdivisions of the thalamencephalon.

section (sek′shun) [L. *sectio*]. 1. An act of cutting. 2. A cut surface. 3. A segment or subdivision of an organ. Called also *sectio* [N A]. **abdominal s.,** laparotomy. **celloidin s.,** a section cut by a microtome from tissue that has been embedded in celloidin. **cesarean s.,** incision through the abdominal and uterine walls for delivery of a fetus, done when birth through the natural passages is impossible or dangerous. The procedure was included (*lex cesarea*) in the codification of Roman law in 715 B.C., as a means of salvaging a fetus, if living, or of providing for its separate burial, in event of the mother's death. **cesarean s., cervical,** cesarean section in which the lower uterine segment is incised, either intraperitoneally or extraperitoneally. **cesarean s., classic, cesarean s., corporeal,** cesarean section in which the upper segment, or corpus, of the uterus is incised. **cesarean s., extraperitoneal,** cesarean section performed without incision of the peritoneum, the peritoneal fold being displaced upward and the bladder being displaced downward or to the midline, the uterus then being opened by an incision in its lower segment. **cesarean s., Latzko's,** extraperitoneal cesarean section with the incision made through one side of the lower segment of the uterus. **cesarean s., low,** cesarean s., cervical. **cesarean s., Porro,** delivery of the fetus through an incision through the abdominal and uterine walls, followed by removal of the uterus. **cesarean s., transperitoneal,** cesarean section performed with an incision through the uterovesical fold of peritoneum. **coronal s.,** a section parallel with the coronal suture, i.e., at right angles to a sagittal section. **frontal s.,** a section parallel with the long axis of the body and at right angles to a sagittal section. It divides the body into a dorsal and ventral part. **frozen s.,** a section cut by a microtome from tissue that has been frozen. **paraffin s.,** a section cut by a microtome from tissue which has been embedded in paraffin. **perineal s.,** external urethrotomy. **Pitres' s's,** a series of six transverse sections made through the brain, as follows: (1) *prefrontal s.,* through the prefrontal lobe; (2) *pediculofrontal s.,* 2 cm. in front of the fissure of Rolando; (3) *frontal s.,* at the level of the ascending frontal convolution; (4) *parietal s.,* through the ascending parietal convolution; (5) *pediculoparietal s.,* 3 cm. behind the fissure of Rolando; (6) *occipital s.,* through the middle of the occipital lobe. **Saemisch's s.,** Saemisch's operation. **sagittal s.,** a section that follows the sagittal suture and runs the entire length of the body, thus dividing the latter into more or less equal right and left halves. **serial s.,** histologic section made in a consecutive order and so arranged for the purpose of microscopical examination. **sigaultian s.,** Sigault's operation. **transverse s.,** one made at right angles to the long axis of a body or structure. **vaginal s.,** incision through the vaginal wall into the abdominal cavity.

sectiones (sek″she-o′nēz) [L.]. Plural of *sectio.*

sector (sek′tor) [L. "cutter"]. The area of a circle included between an arc and the radii bounding it.

sectorial (sek-to′re-al) [L. *sector* cutter]. Cutting.

secundae viae (se-kun′de vi′e) [L. "second passages"]. See under *via.*

secundigravida (se-kun″dĭ-grav′ĭ-dah) [L. *secundus* second + *gravida* pregnant]. A woman pregnant for the second time. Written Gravida II.

secundina (se″kun-di′nah), pl. *secundi′nae* [L., from *secundus* following]. Secundine. **s. cerebri,** the pia-arachnoid. **s. oc′uli,** the middle coat of the choroid. **s. u′teri,** the chorion.

secundinae (se″kun-di′ne) [L.]. Plural of *secundina.*

secundine (se-kun′dīn) [L. *secundina*]. The placenta and membranes expelled after childbirth; the afterbirth.

secundipara (se″kun-dip′ah-rah) [L. *secundus* second + *parere* to bring forth, produce]. A woman who has had two pregnancies which resulted in viable offspring. Written Para II.

secundiparity (se-kun″dĭ-par′ĭ-te). The condition of being a secundipara.

secundiparous (se″kun-dip′ah-rus). Having borne two viable offspring in separate pregnancies.

secundum artem (se-kun′dum ar′tem) [L.]. In an approved or professional manner.

S.E.D. Abbreviation for *skin erythema dose.*

Sed. Abbreviation for L. *se′des,* stool.

sedamyl (sed′ah-mil). Trade mark for a preparation of acetylcarbromal.

sedation (se-da′shun) [L. *sedatio*]. The production of a sedative effect; the act or process of calming.

sedative (sed′ah-tiv) [L. *sedativus*]. 1. Allaying activity and excitement. 2. An agent that allays excitement. **Battley's s.,** a solution made up of extract of opium, boiling water, alcohol, and cold water. **cardiac s.,** one that abates the force of the heart's action. **cerebral s.,** one which principally affects the brain. **gastric s.,** one which soothes or lessens irritability of the stomach. **general s.,** one which affects all the organs and functions. **intestinal s.,** one which diminishes intestinal irritation: in general, they are also gastric sedatives. **nerve trunk s.,** one which acts upon the trunks of the nerves. **nervous s.,** a sedative which acts upon and through the nervous system. The cerebral, spinal and nerve trunk sedatives belong to this class. **respiratory s.,** one which affects especially the respiratory centers and organs. **spinal s.,** any drug which abates the functional or abnormal activity of the spinal cord. **vascular s.,** one which affects the vasomotor activities.

sedentary (sed′en-ter″e) [L. *sedentarius*]. 1. Sitting habitually; of inactive habits. 2. Pertaining to a sitting posture.

Sédillot's operation (sa-de-yōz′) [C. E. *Sédillot,* French surgeon, 1804–1883]. See under *operation.*

sediment (sed′ĭ-ment) [L. *sedimentum*]. A precipitate, especially one that is formed spontaneously. **urinary s.,** the deposit of solid matter left after the urine has been allowed to stand for some time.

sedimentation (sed″ĭ-men-ta′shun). The act of causing the deposit of sediment, especially by the use of a centrifugal machine. **erythrocyte s.,** the sinking of red cells in a volume of drawn blood. See *erythrocyte sedimentation reaction,* under *reaction.*

sedimentator (sed″ĭ-men-ta′tor). A centrifugal machine for separating sediments from the urine.

sedimentin (sed″ĭ-men′tin). A substance in the blood which accelerates sedimentation of the red corpuscles.

sedimentometer (sed″ĭ-men-tom′e-ter). An apparatus for recording the sedimentation rate of blood specimens.

sedopeptose (se″do-pep′tōs). A monosaccharide occurring in plants of the genus *Sedum.*

seed (sēd). 1. The mature ovule of a flowering plant. 2. Semen. 3. A small cylindrical shell of platinum or other suitable material: used in application of radiation therapy. 4. To inoculate a culture medium with microorganisms. **celery s.,** Apium. **larkspur s.,** Delphinium. **plantago s.,** the cleaned, dried, ripe seed of *Plantago psyllium, Plantago indica,* or *Plantago ovata:* used as a cathartic. **radon s.,** a small sealed container for radon, made of platinum, gold, or glass, for insertion into the tissues of the body in the application of radiation therapy.

Seeligmüller's sign (za′lik-mil″erz) [Otto Ludovicus G. A. *Seeligmüller,* German neurologist, 1837–1912]. See under *sign.*

Seessel's pouch, pocket (za′selz) [Albert *Seessel,* American embryologist and neurologist, 1850–1910]. See under *pouch.*

Séglas type (sa-glahz′) [Jules Ernest *Séglas,* French psychiatrist, 1856–1939]. The psychomotor type of paranoia.

segment (seg′ment) [L. *segmentum* a piece cut off]. A portion of a larger body or structure, set off by natural or arbitrarily established boundaries. **bronchopulmonary s.,** one of the smaller divisions of the lobes of the lungs. See *segmenta bronchopulmonalia.* **ceratobranchial s.** See *stylohyoid arch,* under *arch.* **cranial s's,** three segments into which the bones of the cranium may be divided. They are distinguished as the occipital, the parietal, and the frontal. **epibranchial s.** See *stylohyoid arch,* under *arch.* **frontal s.,** the anterior of the three cranial segments. **hypobranchial s.** See *stylohyoid arch,* under *arch.* **interannular s.,** the portion of a nerve fiber between two consecutive nodes of Ranvier. **medullary s.,** a division of the medullary sheath of a nerve fiber between two Schmidt-Lanterman incisures. **mesoblastic s., mesodermal s.,** a somite. **neural s.,** a neuromere. **occipital s.,** the posterior of the three cranial segments. **parietal s.,** the central of the three cranial segments. **pharyngobranchial s.** See *stylohyoid arch,* under *arch.* **primitive s., protovertebral s.,** somite. **pubic s. of the pelvis,** that portion of the floor of the pelvis which is between the symphysis pubis and the anterior wall of the vagina, which latter it includes. **Ranvier's s's,** the portions of the medullary substance of a nerve fiber between Ranvier's nodes. **rivinian s.,** an irregular notch at the upper border of the tympanic sulcus. **rod s.,** the two segments which make up one of the rods of the retina. The *outer rod s.* is the portion presenting a uniform diameter, while the *inner rod s.* has a slightly increased diameter. **sacral s.,** that portion of the floor of the pelvis which lies between the sacrum and the posterior vaginal wall. **Schmidt-Lanterman s.,** medullary s. **spinal s.,** a portion of the spinal cord contained between two imaginary sections, one on each side of a nerve pair. **uterine s.,** one of the portions into which the uterus becomes differentiated early in labor: the upper contractile portion (corpus uteri) which becomes thicker as labor approaches, and the lower non-contractile portion which is thin walled and passive in character.

segmenta (seg-men′tah) [L.]. Plural of *segmentum.*

segmental (seg-men′tal). Pertaining to or forming a segment; undergoing segmentation.

segmentation (seg″men-ta′shun). 1. Division into parts more or less similar, such as somites or metameres. 2. Cleavage. **haustral s.,** the formation of pouches in the wall of the large intestine, by alternating contraction and relaxation of circular muscle fibers. It keeps the intestinal contents plastic and assists in propelling them toward the rectum.

segmenter (seg′ment-er). A young malarial organism in the stage in which it divides into segments in the blood corpuscle. Cf. *schizont.*

segmentum (seg-men′tum), pl. *segmen′ta.* A portion of a larger body or structure. Used in anatomical nomenclature to designate a part of an organ or other structure set off by natural or arbitrarily established boundaries. **segmen′ta bronchopulmona′lia** [N A], the smaller subdivisions of the lobes of the lungs, separated by connective tissue septa and supplied by branches of the respective lobar bronchi. Called also *lobuli pulmonum* [B N A], and *bronchopulmonary segments.* They include: RIGHT LUNG—(*superior lobe*) s. apicale, s. posterius, and s. anterius; (*middle lobe*) s. laterale and s. mediale; (*inferior lobe*) s. apicale (or superius), s. subapicale (or subsuperius), s. basale mediale (or cardiacum), s. basale anterius, s. basale laterale, and s. basale posterius; LEFT LUNG—(*superior lobe*) s. apicoposterius, s. anterius, s. lingulare superius, and s. lingulare inferius; (*inferior lobe*) s. apicale (or superius), s. subapicale (or subsuperius), s. basale mediale (or cardiacum), s. basale anterius, s. basale laterale, and s. basale posterius.

segregation (seg″re-ga′shun). 1. In genetics the separation of the two genes of a pair in the process of maturation so that only one goes to each germ cell. 2. The separation of different elements of a population. 3. The progressive restriction of potencies in the zygote to the various regions of the forming embryo.

segregator (seg′re-ga″tor). An instrument for securing the urine from each kidney separately. **Cathelin's s.,** an appliance inserted into the bladder, separating the cavity into two parts so that the urine from each ureter may be collected separately. **Harris' s.,** an instrument for collecting the urine from each kidney separately. **Luy's s.,** an instrument for collecting the urine from each kidney separately.

Séguin's symptom (sa-ganz′) [Edouard *Séguin*, French alienist, 1812–1880]. See under *symptom*.

Sehrt's clamp, compressor (sārts) [Ernst *Sehrt*, German surgeon, born 1879]. A clamp for compressing the aorta or one for compressing a limb to arrest hemorrhage.

Seidel's scotoma, sign (si′delz) [Erich *Seidel*, German ophthalmologist, born 1882]. See under *scotoma*.

Seidelin bodies (si′dĕ-lin) [Harold *Seidelin*, British physician]. See under *body*.

Seidlitz powder (sīd′litz) [named from a mineral spring in Bohemia]. See under *powder*.

Seignette's salt (sīn-yets′) [Pierre *Seignette*, apothecary in Rochelle, 1660–1719]. Potassium sodium tartrate.

seisesthesia (sīs″es-the′ze-ah). Seismesthesia.

seismesthesia (sīs″mes-the′ze-ah) [Gr. *seismos* a shaking + *aisthēsis* perception + *-ia*]. Tactile perception of vibrations in a liquid or aerial medium.

seismocardiogram (sīz″mo-kar′de-o-gram). The graphic record obtained by seismocardiography.

seismocardiography (sīz″mo-kar″de-og′rah-fe) [Gr. *seismos* a shaking, shock + *kardia* heart + *graphē* representation by means of lines]. The selective recording of cardiac vibrations and beats, giving curves of frequencies between 4 and 5, and between 34 and 40, cycles per second.

seismotherapy (sīz″mo-ther′ah-pe) [Gr. *seismos* a shaking + *therapy*]. The treatment of disease by mechanical vibration.

seizure (se′zhur). 1. The sudden attack or recurrence of a disease. 2. An attack of epilepsy. **audiogenic s.,** a seizure brought on by sound. **cerebral s.,** focal epilepsy. **photogenic s.,** a seizure brought on by light. **psychic s.,** psycholepsy. **psychomotor s.,** psychomotor epilepsy.

sejunction (se-junk′shun). An interruption of the continuity of association complexes which leads to a breaking up of the personality.

sekisanine (sek-is′ah-nin). An alkaloid, $C_{16}H_{19}O_4N$, from *Lycoris radiata*.

selachian (se-la′ke-an). One of a class of vertebrates which includes the sharks and rays.

selene (sĕ-le′ne) [L.; Gr. *selēnē* moon]. A moon-shaped object or structure. **s. un′guium** ["moon of the nails"], the lunula.

selenide (sel′e-nīd). A compound of selenium with an other element or radical.

seleniovanadium (se-le″ne-o-vah-na′de-um). A proprietary selenium preparation recommended for the treatment of cancer.

selenium (se-le′ne-um) [Gr. *selēnē* moon]. A poisonous nonmetallic element resembling sulfur; symbol, Se; atomic number, 34; atomic weight, 78.96. It causes alkali disease in animals that feed on vegetation grown on soils which contain it. **s. sulfide,** the disulfide salt of selenious acid: used as an antiseborrheic.

selenodont (se-le′no-dont) [Gr. *selēnē* moon + *odous* tooth]. Having posterior teeth on which the individual cusps assume a crescentic outline.

Selenomonas (se″le-no-mo′nas). A genus of microorganisms of the family Spirillaceae, suborder Pseudomonadineae, order Pseudomonadales, made up of motile kidney- to crescent-shaped cells with blunt ends. It includes three species, *S. pal′pitans*, *S. ruminan′tium*, and *S. sputi′gena*.

selenoplegia, selenoplexia (se-le″no-ple′je-ah, -plek′se-ah) [Gr. *selēnē* moon + *plēxis* stroke]. A morbid condition once believed to be due to the influence of the moon's rays.

selenosis (se″le-no′sis). Poisoning by selenium.

self (self). An expression used by Burnet and Fenner to denote an animal's own antigenic constituents, in contrast to "not self," denoting foreign antigenic constituents. The "self" constituents are metabolized without antibody formation, whereas the antigens which are "not self" are eliminated through antibodies. It was postulated that there exists some mechanism of "self recognition" which enables the organism to distinguish between "self" and "not self."

self-differentiation (self″dif-er-en″she-a′shun). Perseverance in a course of development by a part, independently of outside influences or changed surroundings.

self-digestion (self″di-jes′chun). Autodigestion.

self-fermentation (self″fer-men-ta′shun). Autolysis.

self-hypnosis (self″hip-no′sis). Hypnosis by autosuggestion.

self-inductance (self″in-duk′tans). The property of an electric circuit which determines, for a given rate of change of current in the circuit, the electromotive force induced in the circuit itself.

self-infection (self″in-fek′shun). Auto-infection.

self-limited (self-lim′it-ed). Limited by its own peculiarities, and not by outside influence: said of a disease that runs a definite limited course.

self-pollution (self″po-lu′shun). Masturbation.

self-suspension (self″sus-pen′shun). The suspension of the body by the head and axillae (*axillocephalic s.*) or by the head (*cephalic s.*) for the purpose of stretching the vertebral column.

selfwise (self′wīz). Developing in a previously determined manner despite transplantation to a new and strange location: said of embryonic cells or tissue. Cf. *neighborwise*.

Selivanoff's (Seliwanow's) test [Feodor Fedorowich *Selivanoff*, Russian chemist, born 1859]. See under *tests*.

sella (sel′ah), pl. *sel′lae* [L.]. A saddle-shaped depression. **s. tur′cica** [N A, B N A], a transverse depression crossing the midline on the superior surface of the body of the sphenoid bone, and containing the hypophysis.

sellae (sel′e) [L.]. Plural of *sella*.

sellanders (sel′an-derz). Malanders.

sellar (sel′ar). Pertaining to the sella turcica.

Sellards' test (sel′ardz) [Andrew Watson *Sellards*, American physician, born 1884]. See under *tests*.

Selter's disease (sel′terz) [Paul *Selter*, German pediatrist, born 1866]. Feer's disease.

Sem. Abbreviation for L. *se′men*, seed.

semantic (se-man′tik). Pertaining to or affecting the meanings or significance of words.

semantics (se-man′tiks) [Gr. *sēmantikos* significant, from *sēma* a sign]. The study of the meanings of words and the rules of their use; the study of the relationship between language and significance.

semasiology (se-ma″se-ol′o-je). Semantics.

Sembs's operation (sāmz) [Carl *Sembs*, Oslo surgeon]. See under *operation*.

semeiography (se″mi-og′rah-fe) [Gr. *sēmeion* sign + *graphein* to write]. A description of the signs or symptoms of disease.

semeiology (se″mi-ol′o-je) [Gr. *sēmeion* sign + *-logy*]. Symptomatology.

semeiotic (se″mi-ot′ik) [Gr. *semeiōtikos*]. 1. Pertaining to the signs or symptoms of disease. 2. Pathognomonic.

semeiotics (se″mi-ot′iks). Symptomatology.

semelincident (sem″el-in′sĭ-dent) [L. *semel* once

+ *incidens* falling upon]. Attacking a person only once.

semelparity (sem″el-par′ĭ-te) [L. *semel* once + *parere* to bear]. The state, in an individual organism, of reproducing only once in a lifetime.

semelparous (sem-el′pah-rus). Pertaining to or characterized by semelparity.

semen (se′men), gen. *sem′inis* [L. "seed"]. 1. Any seed or seedlike fruit. 2. The thick, whitish secretion of the reproductive organs in the male; composed of spermatozoa in their nutrient plasma, secretions from the prostate, seminal vesicles and various other glands, epithelial cells, and minor constituents. **s. cedro′nis,** the seeds of *Simaba cedron* from which cedrin is obtained. **s. con′tra,** santonica.

semenologist (se″mĕ-nol′o-jist). Seminologist.

semenology (se″mĕ-nol′o-je). Seminology.

semenuria (se″mĕ-nu′re-ah). Seminuria.

semi- (sem′e) [L. *semis* half]. A prefix signifying one half.

semiantigen (sem″e-an′tĭ-jen). Half antigen.

semiapochromat (sem″e-ap″o-kro′mat) [*semi-* + *apo-* + *chromat*ic aberration]. Semiapochromatic objective.

semiapochromatic (sem″e-ap″o-kro-mat′ik). See under *objective.*

semicanal (sem″e-kah-nal′). A channel which is open on one side. Called also *semicanalis.* **s. of auditory tube,** semicanalis tubae auditivae. **s. of humerus,** sulcus intertubercularis humeri. **s. of tensor tympani muscle,** semicanalis musculi tensoris tympani.

semicanales (sem″e-kah-na′lēz) [L.]. Plural of *semicanalis.*

semicanalis (sem″e-kah-na′lis), pl. *semicana′les* [L.]. A channel which is open on one side. Called also *semicanal.* **s. mus′culi tenso′ris tym′pani** [N A, B N A], a small canal hidden in the temporal bone, constituting the superior part of the musculotubal canal, and lodging the tensor tympani muscle. Called also *semicanal of tensor tympani muscle.* **s. tu′bae auditi′vae** [N A, B N A], a small canal in the temporal bone, opening on the inferior surface of the skull just posterior and superior to the foramen spinosum. It constitutes the inferior part of the musculotubal canal and lodges the auditory tube. Called also *semicanal of auditory tube.*

semicartilaginous (sem″e-kar″tĭ-laj′ĭ-nus). Partially cartilaginous.

semicoma (sem″e-ko′mah). A mild coma from which the patient may be aroused.

semicomatose (sem″e-ko′mah-tōs). In a condition of semicoma.

semicretin (sem″e-kre′tin). An individual exhibiting semicretinism.

semicretinism (sem″e-kre′tin-izm). A relatively mild form of cretinism; partial cretinism with ability to appreciate the bodily wants and with some knowledge and use of language.

semicrista (sem″e-kris′tah), pl. *semicris′tae* [L.]. A small or rudimentary crest. **s. incisi′va,** crista nasalis maxilla.

Semid. Abbreviation for L. *semidrach′ma,* half a drachm.

semidecussation (sem″e-de″kus-sa′shun). 1. An incomplete crossing of nerve fibers. 2. Decussatio pyramidum.

semidiagrammatic (sem″e-di″ah-grah-mat′ik). Partly diagrammatic; modified so as to illustrate a principle, rather than to serve as an exact copy of nature.

semiflexion (sem″e-flek′shun). The position of a limb midway between flexion and extension.

semifluctuating (sem″e-fluk′chu-āt″ing). Giving a somewhat fluctuating sensation on palpation.

semiglutin (sem″e-gloo′tin). A substance, $C_{55}H_{85}N_{17}O_{22}$, derived from gelatin and resembling a peptone.

Semih. Abbreviation for L. *semiho′ra,* half an hour.

semikon (sem′ĭ-kon). Trade mark for preparations of methapyrilene.

semilunar (sem″e-lu′nar) [L. *semilunaris; semi-* half + *luna* moon]. Resembling a crescent, or half-moon.

semilunare (sem″e-lu-na′re) [L.]. The second bone of the first row of carpal bones, counting from the thumb side (os lunatum [N A]).

semiluxation (sem″e-luk-sa′shun). Subluxation.

semimalignant (sem″e-mah-lig′nant). Somewhat malignant.

semimembranous (sem″e-mem′brah-nus). Made up in part of membrane or fascia.

seminal (sem′ĭ-nal) [L. *seminalis*]. Pertaining to seed or to the semen.

seminarcosis (sem″e-nar-ko′sis). Twilight sleep.

semination (sem″ĭ-na′shun) [L. *seminatio*]. The introduction of semen into the genital tract of the female.

seminiferous (se″mĭ-nif′er-us) [L. *semen* seed + *ferre* to bear]. Producing or conveying semen.

seminologist (se″mĭ-nol′o-jist). A specialist in the study of semen and spermatozoa.

seminology (se″mĭ-nol′o-je). The scientific study of the semen, in relation to the possible causes of infertility in the male.

seminoma (se″mĭ-no′mah) [*semen* + *-oma*]. A dysgerminoma of the testis. **ovarian s.,** a dysgerminoma of an ovary.

seminormal (sem″e-nor′mal). Of one-half the normal or standard strength.

seminose (sem′ĭ-nōs). Mannose.

seminuria (se″mĭ-nu′re-ah) [L. *semen* seed + Gr. *ouron* urine + *-ia*]. The presence of semen in the urine.

semiography (se″me-og′rah-fe). Semeiography.

semiology (se″me-ol′o-je). Symptomatology.

semiorbicular (sem″e-or-bik′u-lar). Semicircular.

semiotic (se″mi-ot′ik). Semeiotic.

semiparasite (sem″e-par′ah-sit). An organism with moderate infectiousness for living tissue, such as the typhoid bacillus and cholera vibrio.

semipenniform (sem″e-pen′ĭ-form). Penniform on one side: said of a muscle the fibers of which are attached to one side of the tendon.

semipermeable (sem″e-per′me-ah-b′l). Permitting the passage of certain molecules and hindering that of others. See under *membrane.*

semiplacenta (sem″e-plah-sen′tah). Strähl's term for a placenta in certain animals in which the fetal and maternal sections of the organ can be separated without tearing.

semiplegia (sem″e-ple′je-ah). Hemiplegia.

semipronation (sem″e-pro-na′shun). 1. The act of bringing to a semiprone position. 2. A semiprone position.

semiprone (sem″e-prōn′) [L. *semis* half + *pronus* prone]. Partly prone. See *Sims's position,* under *position.*

semirecumbent (sem″e-re-kum′bent). Reclining but not completely recumbent.

semis (se′mis) [L.]. Half; abbreviated *ss.*

semisideratio (sem″e-sid″er-a′she-o). Hemiplegia.

semisideration (sem″e-sid″er-a′shun). Hemiplegia.

semisomnus (sem″e-som′nus). Semicoma.

semisopor (sem″e-so′por). Semicoma.

semispeculum (sem″e-spek′u-lum). A blunt gorget shaped like a half-speculum: used in lithotomy.

semistarvation (sem″e-star-va′shun). The so-called hunger cure.

semisulcus (sem″e-sul′kus) [L. *semis* half + *sulcus* furrow]. A channel which, with an adjacent and opposing one, forms a sulcus.

semisupination (sem″e-su″pĭ-na′shun). A position of partial or incomplete supination.

semisupine (sem″e-su′pīn). Partly but not completely supine.

semitendinous (sem″e-ten′dĭ-nus). In part having a tendinous structure.

semitertian (sem″e-ter′shan). Partly tertian and partly quotidian.

semivalent (sem-iv′ah-lent). Having one-half the power which is normal.

Semmelweis (sem′el-vis), Ignaz Philipp (1818–1865). A Hungarian physician, who in Vienna (1847–1849) proved that puerperal fever is a form of septicemia, thus becoming the pioneer of antisepsis in obstetrics. The contagiousness of puerperal fever had been affirmed by Oliver Wendell Holmes of Boston in 1843, and important observations had been made even earlier by Alexander Gordon of Aberdeen and Charles White of Manchester.

Semon's law, sign (se′monz) [Sir Felix *Semon*, German laryngologist in London, 1849–1921]. See under *law* and *sign*.

Semon-Hering hypothesis, theory (za′mon-ha′ring) [Richard Wolfgang *Semon*, German naturalist, 1859–1908; Ewald *Hering*, German physiologist, 1834–1918]. See *mnemic theory*, under *theory*.

semoxydrine (sem-ok′sĭ-drin). Trade mark for a preparation of methamphetamine.

Semple's treatment, vaccine (sem′p'lz) [Sir David *Semple*, British physician, 1856–1937]. See under *treatment* and *vaccine*.

Senear-Usher disease, syndrome (se-nēr′-ush′er) [Francis Eugene *Senear*, Chicago dermatologist, 1889–1958; Barney *Usher*, Canadian dermatologist, born 1899]. Pemphigus erythematosus.

senecifolin (sen″e-sif′o-lin). A poisonous alkaloid, $C_{18}H_{27}O_8N$, of *Senecio*, found in the vascular bundles of the young plant before flowering.

Senecio (sĕ-ne′she-o) [L. "old man"]. A genus of composite-flowered plants: many species were formerly reputed to be tonic and diuretic.

senega (sen′e-gah) [L.]. The root of *Polygala senega*, or seneca snakeroot, a plant of North America. It was formerly used in the later stages of pneumonia, asthma, catarrhal laryngitis, and bronchorrhea, and sometimes in dropsy as a hydragogue.

senegin (sen′e-jin). The active principle of senega; a saponin.

senescence (se-nes′ens) [L. *senescere* to grow old]. The process or condition of growing old. **dental s.**, deterioration of the teeth and other oral structures as a consequence of advancing age or of premature aging processes.

senescent (se-nes′ent). Growing old.

Sengstaken-Blakemore tube (sengz′ta-ken-blāk′mōre) [Robert William *Sengstaken*, American neurosurgeon, born 1923; Arthur H. *Blakemore*, American surgeon, born 1897]. See under *tube*.

senile (se′nīl) [L. *senilis*]. Pertaining to or characteristic of old age.

senilism (se′nil-izm). Premature old age.

senility (se-nil′ĭ-te) [L. *senilitas*]. Old age; feebleness of body and mind associated with old age.

senium (se′ne-um) [L. "the weakness of old age"]. Old age; the period of life marked by the weaknesses and deterioration that may accompany advanced years.

Senn's bone plates, test (senz) [Nicholas *Senn*, American surgeon, 1844–1908]. See under *plate* and *tests*.

senna (sen′ah). The dried leaflets of *Cassia acutifolia:* used in a syrup, fluidextract, or compound powder as a cathartic.

sennatin (sen′ah-tin). An active principle extracted from senna: used subcutaneously as a cathartic.

senopia (se-no′pe-ah) [L. *senium* old age + Gr. *ōpē* sight + *-ia*]. A change in the power of vision of old people by which they return to the sight of their youth.

sensation (sen-sa′shun) [L. *sensatio*]. An impression conveyed by an afferent nerve to the sensorium commune. **articular s.**, the sensation produced by the contact of moving joint surfaces. **cincture s.**, zonesthesia. **common s.** (Gemeingefühl), the general feeling superinduced by the summation of all the bodily sensation (E. H. Weber, 1846). **concomitant s.**, a secondary sensation, developed, without special stimulation, along with a primary sensation. **cutaneous s.**, dermal s. **delayed s.**, a sensation which is not perceived until some time after the application of the stimulation. **dermal s.**, a sensation that arises from a receptor situated in the skin. **epigastric s.**, a peculiar, weak, sinking or anxious feeling localized in the stomach, an organic paresthesia, which may be due to contraction or tonic variation in the esophageal muscles. **external s.**, the effect produced upon the mind by an external object through the medium of the senses. **general s.**, a sensation felt throughout the body. **girdle s.**, zonesthesia. **gnostic s's**, sensations that are perceived by the more recently developed senses, such as those of light touch and the epicritic sensibility to muscle, joint, and tendon vibrations; called also *new sensations*. **internal s.**, a sensation perceptible only to the subject himself, and not connected with any object external to his body. **joint s.**, articular s. **light s.**, the sensation produced when radiant energy of wavelength from 400 to 760 mμ enters a normal eye. **negative s.**, the condition produced by a stimulation below the threshold. **new s's**, gnostic s's. **objective s.**, external s. **palmesthetic s.** See under *sensibility*. **primary s.**, a sensation which is the direct result of the reception of a stimulus. **referred s.**, **reflex s.**, a sensation felt on a place other than the point of application of the stimulus. **skin s.**, dermal s. **strain s.**, a sensation as of a strain or straining. **subjective s.**, internal s. **transferred s.**, referred s. **vascular s.**, the sensation felt when there is a change in vascular tone, as in blushing. **s. of warmth**, the comfortable sensation experienced when the environment is not too cold, also the sensation felt when moderate heat is imparted to the body by radiation or contact.

sense (sens) [L. *sensus; sentire* to think]. A faculty by which the conditions or properties of things are perceived. Hunger, thirst, malaise, and pain are varieties of sense; a sense of equilibrium, of well being (euphoria), and other senses are also distinguished. **acid s.**, that power of the stomach to regulate the secretion of HCl in accordance with the needs of digestion. **chemical s.**, a general sense which causes avoidance reactions in water creatures and residual reactions in man to various irritants, such as onion, pepper, snuff, ammonia, and war gases. **color s.**, the faculty by which various colors are perceived and distinguished. **equilibrium s.**, static s. **form s.**, the ability of the eye to recognize objects as solid. **genesic s.**, the instinct which leads to the act of procreation. **internal s.**, any sense that is normally stimulated from within the body. **kinesthetic s.**, the muscular sense. **labyrinthine s.**, static s. **light s.**, the faculty by which different degrees of brilliancy are distinguished. **muscle s.**, **muscular s.**, the faculty by which muscular movements are perceived. **pain s.**, the sense by which pain is perceived. **posture s.**, a variety of muscular sense by which the position or attitudes of the body or its parts are perceived. **pressure s.**, the faculty by which pressure upon the surface of the body is perceived. **proprioceptive s.**, proprioceptive sensibility. **reproductive s.**, genesic s. **respiratory s.**, besoin de respirer. **seventh s.**, visceral s. **sixth s.**, the general feeling of consciousness of the entire body; cenesthesis. **space s.**, that combination of the senses (chiefly of sight and touch) which gives information as to the relative positions and relations of objects in space. **special s.**, any one of the five senses of seeing, feeling, hearing, taste, and smell. **static s.,** the sense that enables man to maintain an upright position. **stereognostic s.,** the sense by which form and solidity are perceived. **temperature s.,** the faculty by which a person is able to appreciate differences of temperature. **time s.,** the ability to appreciate time intervals, especially in sound and in music. **tone s.,** the power of distinguishing one tone from another. **visceral s.,** the internal and subjective sensations supposed to appertain to the ganglionic portion of the nervous system.

sensibamine (sen-sib′ah-mĭn). A water-soluble alkaloid of ergot, being a complex of ergotamine and ergotaminine.

sensibilatrice (sen″sĭ-be″lah-trēs′). Amboceptor.

sensibiligen (sen″sĭ-bil′ĭ-jen). Sensibilisinogen.

sensibilin (sen″sĭ-bil′in). A substance formed in the body as a reaction against the first injection of a protein in anaphylaxis. Called also *anaphylactic reaction body* and *anaphylactin*.

sensibilisin (sen″sĭ-bil′ĭ-sin). Besredka's term for a specific antibody produced in the blood by a sensitizing injection. The sensitizing injection contains an active element (*sensibilisinogen*), which gives rise in the injected animal to sensibilisin. On injection of the same protein a reaction takes place between the sensibilisin and a third substance present in the protein and called *antisensibilisin*. See *anaphylactic antibody*, under *antibody*.

sensibilisinogen (sen″sĭ-bil″ĭ-sin′o-jen). A substance in proteins which gives rise to a specific antibody, *sensibilisin*, when the protein containing it is injected in an animal.

sensibility (sen″sĭ-bil′ĭ-te) [L. *sensibilitas*]. Susceptibility of feeling; ability to feel or perceive. **bone s.,** pallesthesia. **common s.,** cenesthesia. **cortical s.,** the sensibility controlled by the cerebral cortex which is concerned with the recognition and discrimination of sensory impressions. **deep s.,** the sensibility to pressure and movement which exists after the skin area is made completely anesthetic. **electromuscular s.,** sensibility of muscles to electric stimulation. **epicritic s.,** the sensibility to gentle stimulations which furnishes the means for making fine discriminations of touch and temperature. This sensibility exists in the skin only. **joint s.,** arthresthesia. **mesoblastic s.,** deep s. **pallesthetic s., palmesthetic s.,** pallesthesia. **proprioceptive s.,** the largely ignored and unconscious sense that gives us knowledge of the position and state of muscles, joints, limbs, and other parts. See *proprioceptor*. **protopathic s.,** the sensibility to stimulations of pain and temperature which is low in degree and poorly localized. Such sensibility exists in the skin and in the viscera, and acts as a defensive agency against pathologic changes in the tissues. **recurrent s.,** sensibility exhibited in the anterior root of a spinal nerve when the distal portion is stimulated after division. **somesthetic s.,** proprioceptive sensibility. **splanchnesthetic s.,** the consciousness or sensibility dependent on the splanchnic receptors. **vibratory s.,** pallesthesia.

sensibilization (sen″sĭ-bil-i-za′shun). 1. The act of making more sensitive. 2. Sensitization.

sensibilizer (sen′sĭ-bil-īz″er). Amboceptor.

sensible (sen′sĭ-b′l) [L. *sensibilis*]. Capable of sensation; perceptible to the senses.

sensiferous (sen-sif′er-us) [L. *sensus* sense + *ferre* to carry]. Transmitting sensations.

sensigenous (sen-sij′e-nus) [L. *sensus* sense + Gr. *gennan* to produce]. Producing sensory impulses.

sensimeter (sen-sim′e-ter). An instrument for measuring the degree of sensitiveness of anesthetic and hyperesthetic areas on the body.

sensitin (sen′sĭ-tin). A name suggested for a nonantigenic substance, prepared from a pathogenic agent (virus, bacterium, or fungus), capable of revealing sensitivity of the delayed type evoked by the agent, such as coccidioidin, histoplasmin, and avian and human tuberculin.

sensitinogen (sen″sĭ-tin′o-jen). A general term including all the antigens which have a sensitizing effect on the body or which produce a hypersusceptible condition, such as anaphylactogen, allergen, and sensibilisinogen.

sensitive (sen′sĭ-tiv) [L. *sensitivus*]. Able to receive or respond to stimuli; often used to mean abnormally responsive to stimulation, or responding quickly and acutely.

sensitivity (sen″sĭ-tiv′ĭ-te). The state or quality of being sensitive; often used to denote a state of abnormal responsiveness to stimulation, or of responding quickly and acutely.

sensitization (sen″sĭ-ti-za′shun). 1. The process of rendering a cell sensitive to the action of a complement by subjecting it to the action of a specific amboceptor. 2. Anaphylaxis. 3. The preparation of a tissue or organ by one hormone so that it will respond functionally to the action of another. **active s.,** the sensitization that results from the injection of a dose of antigen into the animal. **mental s.,** in psychiatry, the state in which or the process by which unpleasant situations or emotions become less disturbing. **passive s.,** the sensitization which results when some of the blood of a sensitized animal is injected into a normal animal. **photodynamic s.,** the increased lethal effects of light on microorganisms when certain dyes are present in the solution. **protein s.,** that bodily state in which the individual is sensitive or hypersusceptible to some foreign protein, so that when there is absorption of that protein a typical reaction is set up. **Rh s.,** the process or state of becoming sensitized to the Rh factor as when an Rh-negative woman is pregnant with an Rh-positive fetus.

sensitized (sen′sĭ-tīzd). Rendered sensitive.

sensitizer (sen′sĭ-tīz-er). Amboceptor.

sensitizin (sen″sĭ-ti′zin). Anaphylactogen.

sensitometer (sen″sĭ-tom′e-ter). A set of sensitive photographic plates for testing the penetration of the body by light rays.

sensomobile (sen″so-mo′bil). Moving in response to a stimulus.

sensomobility (sen″so-mo-bil′ĭ-te). The capacity of man or animals for movement in response to a sensory stimulus.

sensomotor (sen″so-mo′tor). Sensorimotor.

sensoparalysis (sen″so-pah-ral′ĭ-sis). Paralysis of the sensory or afferent nerves of a part.

sensorial (sen-so′re-al) [L. *sensorialis*]. Pertaining to the sensorium.

sensoriglandular (sen″so-re-glan′du-lar). Producing glandular activity as one of the consequences of stimulation of the sensory nerves.

sensorimetabolism (sen″so-re-mĕ-tab′o-lizm). The production of some metabolic action as a result of stimulation of the sensory nerves.

sensorimotor (sen″so-re-mo′tor). Both sensory and motor.

sensorimuscular (sen″so-re-mus′ku-lar). Producing reflex muscular action in response to a sensory impression.

sensorium (sen-so′re-um) [L. *sentire* to experience, to feel the force of]. 1. A sensory nerve center. 2. The seat of sensation, located in the brain (*s. commu′ne*); the term is often used to designate the condition of a subject relative to his consciousness or mental clarity.

sensorivascular (sen″so-re-vas′ku-lar). Producing vascular changes as a result of stimulation applied through the sensory nerves.

sensorivasomotor (sen″so-re-vas″o-mo′tor). Sensorivascular.

sensory (sen′so-re) [L. *sensorius*]. Pertaining to or subserving sensation.

sensualism (sen′shu-al-izm) [L. *sensus* sense]. The condition of being dominated by bodily passions.

sentient (sen′she-ent) [L. *sentiens*]. Able to feel; sensitive; having sensation or feeling.

sepal (se′pal). One of the divisions of leaves of the calyx of a flower.

sepaloid (sep′ah-loid). Resembling or shaped like a sepal.

separator (sep′ah-ra″tor) [L.]. A device for effecting a separation. In dentistry, an appliance for forcing adjoining teeth apart.

separatorium (sep″ah-rah-to′re-um). An instrument used in separating the pericranium from the subjacent bone.

sepedogenesis (sep″e-do-jen′e-sis). Sepedonogenesis.

sepedon (sep″e-don′) [Gr. *sēpedōn* rottenness, putrefaction]. A septic condition; putridity.

sepedonogenesis (sep″e-do″no-jen′e-sis) [*sepedon* + Gr. *genesis* production]. The production of septic conditions.

sepia (se′pe-ah) [L.; Gr. *sēpia* cuttle-fish]. The inspissated inky juice of a cuttle-fish, or squid.

sepium (se′pe-um) [L.; Gr. *sēpia* cuttle-fish). The bone of a cuttle-fish, *Sepia officinalis.*

sepsin (sep′sin) [Gr. *sēpsis* decay]. A poisonous, crystallizable ptomaine from decaying yeast and from animal matter.

sepsis (sep′sis) [Gr. *sēpsis* decay]. Poisoning which is caused by the products of a putrefactive process. **s. agranulocyt′ica,** agranulocytosis. **incarcerated s.,** an infection which is latent after the primary lesion has apparently healed, but which may be stirred into activity by a slight trauma. **s. intestina′lis,** poisoning from the eating of contaminated food, such as canned meats, ice cream, sausages, or cheese. **s. len′ta,** a condition produced by infection with the *Streptococcus viridans,* marked by slowly developing symptoms of a low infection ending in chronic endocarditis. **mouse s., murine s.** See under *septicemia.* **oral s.,** a disease condition in the mouth or adjacent parts which may affect the general health through the dissemination of toxins. **puerperal s.,** sepsis occurring after childbirth, due to putrefactive matter absorbed from the parturient canal.

Sepsis violacea (sep′sis vi″o-la′se-ah). The common dung fly, which may be found in houses.

sepsometer (sep-som′e-ter) [Gr. *sēpsis* decay + Gr. *metron* measure]. An instrument for detecting organic matter in the air.

Sept. Abbreviation for L. *sep′tem,* seven.

septa (sep′tah) [L.]. Plural of *septum.*

septal (sep′tal). Pertaining to a septum.

septan (sep′tan) [L. *septem* seven]. Recurring every seventh (sixth) day.

septanose (sep′tah-nōs). A monosaccharide having a seven-numbered ring structure.

septate (sep′tāt). Divided by a septum.

septation (sep-ta′shun). 1. Division into parts by a septum. 2. A septum.

septatome (sep′tah-tōm). Septome.

septavalent (sep″tah-va′lent). Septivalent.

septazine (sep′tah-zin). Proseptasine.

septectomy (sep-tek′to-me) [*septum* + Gr. *ektomē* excision]. Excision of a portion of the nasal septum.

septemia (sep-te′me-ah). Septicemia.

septic (sep′tik) [L. *septicus;* Gr. *sēptikos*]. Produced by or due to putrefaction.

septicemia (sep″tĭ-se′me-ah) [*septic* + Gr. *haima* blood + *-ia*]. Presence in the blood of bacterial toxins. **apoplectiform s. of fowls,** a septicemia of fowls marked by apoplectiform symptoms and caused by the *Streptococcus gallinarum.* **bronchopulmonary s.,** septicemia resulting from the aspiration of infected wound secretions into the trachea in operations on the larynx. **Bruce's s.,** undulant fever. **cryptogenic s.,** septicemia in which the focus of infection is not evident during life. **fowl s.,** a disease of fowls caused by the *Spirillum* (*Vibrio*) *metchnikovii,* marked by diarrhea, hyperemia of the alimentary canal, and the presence of a blood-tinged yellowish liquid in the small intestine. **s. haemorrhag′ica bo′vum,** cornstalk disease. **s. haemorrhag′ica bubalo′rum,** pasteurellosis in buffalo. **s. haemorrhag′ica o′vum,** septicemia pluriformis. **hemorrhagic s.** See *pasteurellosis.* **lymphovenous s.,** infection of the deep cellular planes of the body. **melitensis s.,** brucellosis. **metastasizing s.,** pyemia. **morphine injector's s.,** melioidosis in man. **mouse s.,** an infectious disease of mice, due to *Erysipelothrix* (*Bacillus*) *murisepticus.* **phlebitic s.,** pyemia. **plague s.,** septicemic plague. **s. plurifor′mis,** a hemorrhagic septicemia in sheep due to infection with *Pasteurella oviseptica.* **puerperal s.,** septicemia in which the focus of infection is a lesion of the mucous membrane received during childbirth. **rabbit s.,** pasteurellosis in rabbits. **sputum s.,** a form produced by inoculation of certain of the microorganisms of the sputum. **typhoid s.,** general infection with typhoid bacillus. **vibrio s.,** the deadly septicemia produced by *Vibrio metchnikovii.*

septicemic (sep″tĭ-se′mik). Pertaining to, or of the nature of, septicemia.

septicine (sep′tĭ-sin). A ptomaine, or compound of hexylamine and amylamine, from putrid flesh.

septicophlebitis (sep″tĭ-ko-fle-bi′tis) [*septic* + *phlebitis*]. Inflammation of the veins, due to septic poisoning.

septicopyemia (sep″tĭ-ko-pi-e′me-ah). Septicemia and pyemia combined. **cryptogenic s.,** spontaneous septicopyemia. **metastatic s.,** a form marked by septic deposits in the lungs caused by embolism from putrid thrombi. **spontaneous s.,** a variety developing without obvious cause or from a slight wound of the skin. Called also *cryptogenic s.*

septicopyemic (sep″tĭ-ko-pi-e′mik). Pertaining to septicopyemia.

septicozymoid (sep″tĭ-ko-zi′moid). A hypothetical substance supposed by some to supply the necessary feeding ground for septic processes.

septiferous (sep-tif′er-us) [*septic* + L. *ferre* to carry]. Transmitting septic poisoning.

septigravida (sep″tĭ-grav′ĭ-dah) [L. *septem* seven + *gravida* pregnant]. A woman pregnant for the seventh time. Also written Gravida VII.

septile (sep′tĭl). Of or pertaining to a septum.

septimetritis (sep″tĭ-me-tri′tis) [*septic* + *metritis*]. Septic inflammation of the uterus.

septipara (sep-tip′ah-rah) [L. *septem* seven + *parere* to bring forth, produce]. A woman who has had seven pregnancies which resulted in viable offspring. Also written Para VII.

septivalent (sep″tĭ-va′lent) [L. *septem* seven + *valens* able]. Able to combine with or to replace seven hydrogen atoms.

septomarginal (sep″to-mar′ji-nal). Pertaining to the margin of a septum.

septometer (sep-tom′e-ter). 1. [L. *saeptum* partition + *metrum* measure]. An instrument for measuring the thickness of the nasal septum. 2. [Gr. *sēptos* decayed + *metron* measure]. Sepsometer.

septonasal (sep-to-na′zal). Pertaining to the nasal septum.

septotome (sep′to-tōm). An instrument for operating on the nasal septum.

septotomy (sep-tot′o-me) [*septum* + Gr. *tomē* a cutting]. The operation of incising the nasal septum.

septula (sep′tu-lah) [L.]. Plural of *septulum.*

septulum (sep′tu-lum), pl. *sep′tula* [L., dim. of *septum*]. A small separating wall or partition; used in anatomical nomenclature as a general term to designate such a structure. **sep′tula tes′tis** [N A, B N A], connective tissue lamellae from the inner surface of the tunica albuginea, which unite to form the mediastinum testis.

septum (sep′tum), pl. *sep′ta* [L.]. A dividing wall or partition; used as a general term in anatomical nomenclature. **s. alve′oli.** See *interalveolar s.* and *interradicular s.* **s. atrio′rum cor′dis** [B N A], s. interatriale cordis. **atrioventricular s. of heart, s. atrioventricula′re cor′dis** [N A], the portion of the membranous part of the interventricular septum that is superior to the point where the septal cusp of the right atrioventricular valve attaches to the right side of the septum. It therefore intervenes between the left ventricle and right atrium. Called also *pars membranacea septi atriorum* [B N A]. **s. of auditory tube,** s. canalis musculotubarii. **s. auricula′rum,** s. interatriale cordis. **Bigelow's s.,** a layer of hard, bony tissue in the neck of the femur. **bony s. of eustachian canal,** s. canalis musculotubarii. **bony s. of nose,** s. nasi osseum. **bronchial s., s. bronchia′le,** carina tracheae. **bulbar s.,** a septum, formed by fusion of the bulbar ridges, that divides the bulbus cordis into aortic and pulmonary trunks. **s. bul′bi ure′thrae** [B N A], the fibrous septum dividing the interior of the bulb of the urethra into two approximately equal parts. Omitted in N A. **s. cana′lis musculotuba′rii** [N A, B N A], the thin lamella of bone that divides the musculotubal canal into the semicanals for the tensor tympani muscle and the auditory tube. Called also *s. of musculotubal canal.* **s. cartilagin′eum na′si** [B N A], pars cartilaginea septi nasi. **cervical s., intermediate, s. cervica′le interme′dium** [N A, B N A], an incomplete septum joining the arachnoid and pia mater in the posterior midline along the cervical and thoracic parts of the spinal cord. It is formed by a condensation of the spongy tissue in the subarachnoid space. **clear s.,** s. pellucidum. **cloacal s.,** the advancing wedge of mesoderm that divides the cloaca into rectum and urogenital sinus. Called also *urorectal septum.* **s. of Cloquet,** s. femorale. **s. corpo′rum cavernoso′rum clitor′idis** [N A, B N A], an incomplete fibrous septum between the two lateral halves of the clitoris. **crural s.,** s. femorale. **Douglas' s.,** the septum formed by the union of Rathke's folds, forming the rectum of the fetus. **enamel s.,** enamel cord. **femoral s., s. femora′le** [N A], **s. femora′le [Cloque′ti]** [B N A], the thin fibrous membrane that helps to close the anulus femoralis. It is derived from the fascia transversalis, is perforated for the passage of lymphatic vessels, and is embedded in fat. **s. of frontal sinuses,** s. sinuum frontalium. **gingival s.,** the part of the gingiva interposed between adjoining teeth. **s. glan′dis pe′nis** [N A, B N A], **s. of glans penis,** an incomplete fibrous septum in the median plane of the glans penis, especially below the urethra. **gum s.,** gingival s. **hemal s.,** a structure of lower animals which in man is represented by the linea alba and the transversalis, iliac, and rectovesical fasciae. **interalveolar s.,** one of the partitions of bone separating the alveoli of different teeth (*septa interalveolaria mandibulae* [N A], and *septa interalveolaria maxillae* [N A]). **sep′ta interalveola′ria mandib′ulae** [N A, B N A], the partitions between the tooth sockets in the alveolar part of the mandible. Called also *interalveolar septa of mandible.* **sep′ta interalveola′ria maxil′lae** [N A, B N A], the partitions between the tooth sockets in the alveolar process of the maxilla. Called also *interalveolar septa of maxilla.* **interatrial s. of heart, s. interatria′le cor′dis** [N A], **interauricular s.,** the wall that separates the atria of the heart. Called also *s. atriorum cordis* [B N A]. **interdental s.,** interalveolar s. **intermuscular s. of arm, external,** s. intermusculare brachii laterale. **intermuscular s. of arm, internal,** s. intermusculare brachii mediale. **intermuscular s. of leg, anterior,** s. intermusculare anterius cruris. **intermuscular s. of leg, posterior** s. intermusculare posterius cruris. **intermuscular s. of thigh, external,** s. intermusculare femoris laterale. **intermuscular s. of thigh, medial,** s. intermusculare femoris mediale. **s. intermuscula′re ante′rius cru′ris** [N A], **s. intermuscula′re ante′rius fibula′re** [B N A], a fascial sheet in the leg extending between the extensor digitorum longus and peroneal muscles to the anterior fibular crest. Called also *anterior intermuscular s. of leg.* **s. intermuscula′re bra′chii latera′le** [N A], the fascial sheet extending from the lateral border of the humerus to the under surface of the fascia investing the arm. Called also *s. intermusculare humeri laterale* [B N A], and *lateral intermuscular s. of arm.* **s. intermuscula′re bra′chii media′le** [N A], the fascial sheet extending from the medial border of the humerus to the under surface of the fascia investing the arm. Called also *s. intermusculare humeri mediale* [B N A], and *medial intermuscular s. of arm.* **s. intermuscula′re fem′oris latera′le** [N A, B N A], the fascial sheet in the thigh separating the vastus lateralis muscle from the biceps femoris. Called also *lateral intermuscular s. of thigh.* **s. intermuscula′re fem′oris media′le** [N A, B N A], the fascial sheet in the thigh separating the vastus medialis from the adductor and the pectineus muscles. Called also *medial intermuscular s. of thigh.* **s. intermuscula′re hu′meri latera′le** [B N A], s. intermusculare brachii laterale. **s. intermuscula′re hu′meri media′le** [B N A], s. intermusculare brachii mediale. **s. intermuscula′re poste′rius cru′ris** [N A], **s. intermuscula′re poste′rius fibula′re** [B N A], the fascial sheet extending between the peroneal muscles and soleus to the lateral fibular crest. Called also *posterior intermuscular s. of leg.* **interradicular s., s. interradicula′re,** one of the thin bony partitions separating the crypts of a dental alveolus occupied by the separate roots of a multi-rooted tooth. **interventricular s. of heart, s. interventricula′re cor′dis** [N A], the partition that separates the ventricles of the heart, consisting of a thick muscular portion and a small, completely membranous area. Called also *s. ventriculorum cordis* [B N A]. **s. intra-alveola′rium,** interradicular s. **s. lin′guae** [N A, B N A], **lingual s.,** the median vertical fibrous part of the tongue. **s. longitudina′le,** a sheet of fascia on the anteromedial side of the large blood vessels of the neck, passing diagonally forward and outward to the deep layer of the fascia colli. **s. lu′cidum.** 1. Septum pellucidum. 2. Stratum corneum epidermidis. **mediastinal s., s. mediastina′le** [B N A], mediastinum. **s. membrana′ceum na′si** [B N A], pars membranacea septi nasi. **s. membrana′ceum ventriculo′rum cor′dis** [B N A], pars membranacea septi interventricularis cordis. **membranous s. of nose,** pars membranacea septi nasi. **s. mo′bile na′si** [B N A], **mobile s. of nose,** pars mobilis septi nasi. **s. muscula′re ventriculo′rum cor′dis** [B N A], pars muscularis septi interventricularis cordis. **s. of musculotubal canal,** s. canalis musculotubarii. **nasal s., s. na′si** [N A, B N A], the partition separating the two nasal cavities in the midplane, composed of cartilaginous, membranous, and bony parts. **s. na′si os′seum** [N A, B N A], the bone of the skull interposed between the openings of the nose, consisting primarily of the vomer below and the perpendicular plate of the ethmoid bone above. Called also *bony s. of nose.* **neural s.,** a prolongation, chiefly in the lower vertebrates, of the general investing fascia, extending medially from the surface toward the skeleton; represented in man by the ligamentum nuchae and the supraspinous and interspinous ligaments. **orbital s., s. orbita′le** [N A, B N A], a fibrous membrane anchored to the periorbita along the entire margin of the orbit, extending to the levator palpebrae superioris muscle in the upper lid and to the tarsal plate in the lower lid. Called also *tarsal membrane.* **osseous s. of nose,** s. nasi osseum. **parietal s.,** cuspis posterior valvae atrioventricularis sinistrae. **s. pectinifor'me,** s. penis. **pellucid s., s. pellu'cidum** [N A, B N A], a triangular double membrane separating the anterior horns of the lateral ventricles of the brain; situated in the median plane, it is bounded by the corpus callosum and the body and columns of the fornix. **s. pe'nis** [N A, B N A], the fibrous sheet between the two corpora cavernosa of the penis, formed by union of the tunicae albugineae of the two sides. **pharyngeal s.,** the partition which separates the mouth cavity from the pharynx in the embryo. **placental s.,** tissue, largely trophoblastic, that divides the placenta into cotyledons. **s. pon'tis,** raphe pontis. **posterior median cervical s., s. pos'ticum,** s. cervicale intermedium. **s. pri'mum,** a septum in the embryonic heart, dividing the primitive atrium into right and left chambers. **rectovaginal s., s. rectovagina'le** [N A], a membranous partition between the rectum and the vagina. **rectovesical s., s. rectovesica'le** [N A], a membranous partition separating the rectum from the prostate and urinary bladder. **s. re'nis.** See *columnae renales.* **s. scro'ti** [N A, B N A], **s. of scrotum,** a fibromuscular partition in the median plane, dividing the scrotum into two nearly equal parts. **s. secun'dum,** a septum in the embryonic heart to the right of the septum primum; after birth it fuses with the septum primum to close the foramen ovale. **s. si'nuum fronta'lium** [N A, B N A], a thin lamina of bone, in the lower front part of the frontal bone, that lies more or less in the median plane and separates the frontal sinuses. Called also *s. of frontal sinuses.* **s. si'nuum sphenoida'lium** [N A, B N A], **sphenoidal s., s. of sphenoidal sinuses,** a thin lamina of bone in the body of the sphenoid bone, lying more or less in the median plane and separating the sphenoidal sinuses. **spurious s., s. spu'rium,** a structure formed by union of the two folds, one on either side, guarding the opening of the sinus venosus into the dorsal wall of the right atrium of the heart in the early embryo. **subarachnoidal s.,** s. cervicale intermedium. **septa of testis,** septula testis. **s. of tongue,** s. linguae. **transverse s. of ampulla,** crista ampullaris. **transverse s. of body,** diaphragma. **s. tu'bae,** processus cochleariformis. **urorectal s.,** cloacal s. **s. of ventricles of heart, s. ventriculo'rum cor'dis** [B N A], s. interventriculare cordis.

septuplet (sep'tu-plet) [L. *septuplum* a group of seven]. One of seven offspring produced in one gestation period.

Seq. luce. Abbreviation for L. *sequen'ti lu'ce,* the following day.

sequel (se'kwel). Sequela.

sequela (se-kwe'lah), pl. *seque'lae* [L.]. Any lesion or affection following or caused by an attack of disease.

sequelae (se-kwe'le) [L.]. Plural of *sequela.*

sequester (se-kwes'ter) [L.; Fr. *sequestrer* to shut up illegally]. To detach or separate abnormally a small portion from the whole. See *sequestration* and *sequestrum.*

sequestra (se-kwes'trah) [L.]. Plural of *sequestrum.*

sequestral (se-kwes'tral). Pertaining to or of the nature of a sequestrum.

sequestration (se″kwes-tra'shun) [L. *sequestratio*]. 1. The formation of a sequestrum. 2. The isolation of a patient. 3. A net increase in the quantity of blood within vascular channels, occurring physiologically, with forward flow persisting or not, or produced artificially by the application of tourniquets, for the purpose of reducing hemorrhage. **pulmonary s.,** loss of connection of lung tissue with the bronchial tree and with the pulmonary veins, the tissue receiving its arterial supply from the systemic circulation. The mass may be completely separated anatomically and physiologically from normally connected lung (*extralobar pulmonary s.*) or be in anatomical contiguity with and partly surrounded by normal lung (*intralobar pulmonary s.*).

sequestrectomy (se″kwes-trek'to-me) [*sequestrum* + Gr. *ektomē* excision]. The surgical removal of a sequestrum.

sequestrotomy (se″kwes-trot'o-me) [*sequestrum* + Gr. *tomē* a cutting]. Sequestrectomy.

sequestrum (se-kwes'trum), pl. *seques'tra* [L.]. A piece of dead bone that has become separated during the process of necrosis from the sound bone. **primary s.,** a sequestrum that is entirely detached. **secondary s.,** a sequestrum that is partially detached and may be pushed into place. **tertiary s.,** a sequestrum that is separated by only a slight dividing line and remains in its place.

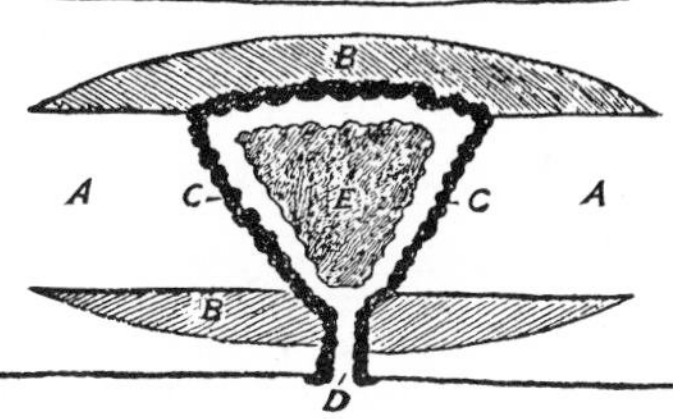

Illustrating the formation of a sequestrum: *A, A,* Sound bone; *B, B,* new bone; *C, C,* granulations lining involucrum; *D,* cloaca; *E,* sequestrum (DaCosta).

sera (se'rah) [L.]. Plural of *serum.*

seralbumin (se″ral-bu'min). Serum albumin; the albumin of the blood.

serangitis (se″ran-ji'tis) [Gr. *sēranx* cavern + *-itis*]. Cavernitis.

serapheresis (se″rah-fĕ-re'sis) [*serum* + Gr. *aphairesis* removal]. The production of serum by permitting the clotting of plasma derived by plasmapheresis.

Serapion (sĕ-ra'pe-on) **of Alexandria** (c. 280 B.C.). A Greek physician who is believed to have been one of the founders of the Empiric school of medicine.

serempion (se-rem'pe-on). A fatal form of measles occurring in the West Indies.

serenium (sĕ-re'ne-um). Trade mark for a preparation of ethoxazene.

Serenoa (ser″e-no'ah) [*Sereno* Watson]. A genus of palms. *S. serrula'ta* is the saw palmetto or sabal of the southern United States. A fluidextract of the berries is diuretic, expectorant, and aphrodisiac: used in diseases of the prostate and bladder.

seretin (ser'e-tin). Carbon tetrachloride.

serfin (ser'fin). Trade mark for a preparation of reserpine.

Sergent's white line (sār-zhawz') [Emile *Sergent,* French physician, 1867–1943]. See under *line.*

serglobulin (ser-glob'u-lin). Paraglobulin.

serial (se're-al). Arranged in or forming a series.

serialograph (se″re-al'o-graf). An apparatus for making series of x-ray pictures.

sericeps (ser'ĭ-seps) [L. *sericus* silken + *caput* head]. A silken baglike bandage used in making traction on the fetal head.

sericin (ser'ĭ-sin). Silk glue or silk gelatin; a protein, $C_{15}H_{25}N_5O_3$, derivable from silk.

sericite (se'rĭ-sīt). A form of mica or muscovite, a complex silicate, causing silicosis.

sericum (ser'ĭ-kum) [L.; Gr. *sērikos* silken]. Silk; a product of various insect larvae, but chiefly of *Bom'byx mo'ri,* the silkworm: used in surgery.

series (sēr'ēz) [L. "row"]. A group or succession of objects or substances arranged in regular order or forming a kind of chain. In electricity, an arrangement of the parts of a circuit by connecting them successively end to end to form a single path for the current. Parts thus arranged are in series. **aliphatic s.,** the compounds having an open chain structure. See *open chain,* under *chain.* **aromatic s.,** the compounds derived from benzene. **fatty s.,** methane and its derivatives and the homologous hydrocarbons. **homologous s.,** a series of compounds each member of which differs from the one preceding it by the radical CH_2.

seriflux (ser'ĭ-fluks) [L. *serum* whey + *fluxus* flow]. A thin, watery discharge.

serioscopy (se"re-os'ko-pe). Roentgenographic visualization of the body in a series of parallel planes by means of multiple exposures. Two or more roentgenograms are taken from different directions. They are laid on each other and moved until the projections of the various planes of the object coincide consecutively.

seriscission (ser"ĭ-sizh'un) [L. *sericum* silk + *scindere* to cut]. The cutting of soft tissues by means of a silken ligature.

sero-albuminous (se"ro-al-bu'mĭ-nus). Containing serum and albumin.

sero-albuminuria (se"ro-al-bu"mĭ-nu're-ah). The presence in the urine of serum albumin.

sero-anaphylaxis (se"ro-an"ah-fi-lak'sis). Anaphylaxis produced by the use of blood serum.

serochrome (se'ro-krōm) [*serum* + Gr. *chrōma* color]. The coloring matter of normal serum.

serocolitis (se"ro-ko-li'tis). Inflammation of the serous surface of the colon.

seroculture (se'ro-kul-tūr). A bacterial culture on blood serum.

serocym (se'ro-sīm). The designation of the fresh normal blood plasma used in Hirschfeld and Klinger's coaguloreaction.

serocystic (se"ro-sis'tik). Made up of serous cysts.

serodermatosis (se"ro-der"mah-to'sis). A skin disease with serous effusion into the skin.

serodiagnosis (se"ro-di"ag-no'sis). Diagnosis made by means of reactions taking place in the blood serum.

sero-enteritis (se"ro-en"ter-i'tis). Inflammation of the serous coat of the intestine.

sero-enzyme (se"ro-en'zīm). An enzyme or ferment existing in the blood serum.

serofibrinous (se"ro-fib'rin-us). Both serous and fibrinous.

serofibrous (se"ro-fi'brus). Pertaining to serous and fibrous surfaces; as, *serofibrous* apposition.

seroflocculation (se"ro-flok"u-la'shun). Flocculation produced in blood serum by an antigen. Cf. *Henry test,* under *tests.*

serofluid (se"ro-floo'id). A serous fluid.

serogastria (se"ro-gas'tre-ah). The presence of blood serum in the stomach.

serogenesis (se"ro-jen'e-sis). 1. The production of a serum. 2. The regular appearance of the natural antibodies during the life of an individual.

seroglobulin (se"ro-glob'u-lin). Serum globulin; the globulin of the blood serum.

seroglycoid (se"ro-gli'koid). A glycoprotein found in serum albumin.

serohemorrhagic (se"ro-hem"o-raj'ik). Characterized by serum and blood.

serohepatitis (se"ro-hep"ah-ti'tis). Inflammation of the peritoneal coat which covers the liver.

sero-immunity (se"ro-ĭ-mu'nĭ-te). Immunity produced by antiserum; passive immunity.

serolactescent (se"ro-lak-tes'ent). Resembling serum and milk.

serolemma (se"ro-lem'ah) [*serous* + Gr. *lemma* sheath]. The membrane from which the serosa or chorion is developed.

serolipase (se"ro-li'pās). Lipase from blood serum.

serologic, serological (se"ro-loj'ik, se"ro-loj'e-kal). Pertaining to serology.

serologist (se-rol'o-jist). One who is an expert in serology.

serology (se-rol'o-je) [*serum* + *-logy*]. The study of antigen-antibody reactions in vitro. **diagnostic s.,** serodiagnosis.

serolysin (se-rol'ĭ-sin). A lysin present in the blood serum.

seroma (sēr-o'mah). A tumor-like collection of serosanguineous fluid in the tissues.

seromembranous (se"ro-mem'brah-nus). Both serous and membranous; composed of serous membrane.

seromucoid (se"ro-mu'koid). Seromucous.

seromucous (se"ro-mu'kus). Partly serous and partly mucous.

seromucus (se"ro-mu'kus). A secretion which is part serum and part mucus.

seromuscular (se"ro-mus'ku-lar). Pertaining to the serous and muscular coats of the intestine.

seromycin (ser'o-mi"sin). Trade mark for preparations of cycloserine.

seronegative (se"ro-neg'ah-tiv). Serologically negative; showing negative results on serological examination.

seronegativity (se"ro-neg"ah-tiv'ĭ-te). The state of being seronegative, or of showing negative results on serological examination.

seroperitoneum (se"ro-per"ĭ-to-ne'um). The presence of free fluid in the peritoneum; ascites.

seropheresis (se"ro-fĕ-re'sis). Serapheresis.

serophysiology (se"ro-fiz"e-ol'o-je). The study of the physiologic mechanism of serum action.

serophyte (se'ro-fīt) [*serum* + Gr. *phyton* plant]. A vegetable microorganism that grows readily in the body fluids.

seroplastic (se"ro-plas'tik). Serofibrinous.

seropneumothorax (se"ro-nu"mo-tho'raks). Pneumothorax with a serous effusion in the pleural cavity.

seropositive (se"ro-poz'ĭ-tiv). Serologically positive; showing positive results on serological examination.

seropositivity (se"ro-poz"ĭ-tiv'ĭ-te). The state of being seropositive, or of showing positive results on serological examination.

seroprognosis (se"ro-prog-no'sis). The prognosis of a disease based on study of its seroreactions.

seroprophylaxis (se"ro-pro"fĭ-lak'sis). The injection of immune serum or convalescent serum for protective purposes.

seropurulent (se"ro-pu'roo-lent). Both serous and purulent.

seropus (se"ro-pus'). Serum mingled with pus.

seroreaction (se"ro-re-ak'shun). A reaction occurring in a serum or as a result of the action of a serum. Cf. *fixation of the complement.* **Klausner's s.** See under *reaction.*

serorelapse (se"ro-re-laps'). A definite rise in serological titer occurring after treatment.

seroresistance (se"ro-re-zis'tans). Failure of the serological titer to fall satisfactorily after treatment.

serosa (se-ro'sah). 1. A serous membrane. 2. The tunica serosa. 3. The chorion.

serosamucin (se-ro"sah-mu'sin). A protein resembling mucin, found in inflammatory ascitic exudates.

serosanguineous (se"ro-sang-gwin'e-us). Pertaining to or containing both serum and blood.

serosaprophyte (se"ro-sap'ro-fīt). A microorganism which thrives in the body fluids only when they have become degenerated.

seroscopy (se-ros'ko-pe) [*serum* + Gr. *skopein* to examine]. Diagnostic examination of serum with the agglutinoscope.

serose (se'rōs). An albumose obtained from serum albumin.

seroserous (se"ro-se'rus). Pertaining to two or more serous membranes.

serositides (se"ro-si'tĭ-dēz). Plural of *serositis.*

serositis (se″ro-si′tis), pl. *serositides* [*serous membrane* + *-itis*]. Inflammation of a serous membrane. **multiple s.,** polyserositis.

serosity (se-ros′ĭ-te). The quality possessed by serous fluids.

serosynovial (se″ro-sĭ-no′ve-al). Both serous and synovial.

serosynovitis (se″ro-sin″o-vi′tis). Synovitis with effusion of serum.

serotherapeutical (se″ro-ther″ah-pu′tĭ-kal). Pertaining to serotherapy.

serotherapist (se″ro-ther′ah-pist). One who treats disease by serotherapy.

serotherapy (se″ro-ther′ah-pe) [*serum* + Gr. *therapeia* treatment]. The treatment of disease by the injection of blood serum from immune individuals, especially immunized animals.

serothorax (se″ro-tho′raks). Hydrothorax.

serotonin (ser″o-to′nin). Chemical name: 3-(2-aminoethyl)-5-indolol; a constituent of blood platelets, enterochromaffin cells, and of other organs: used as an experimental agent to induce vasoconstriction and alter neuronal function.

serotoxin (se″ro-tok′sin). 1. A toxin formed in and from blood serum when the latter is treated with kaolin, barium sulfate, or in other ways. 2. The hypothetical poisonous substance which is formed in the body and responsible for anaphylactic shock.

serotype (se′ro-tīp). 1. The type of a microorganism as determined by the kinds and combinations of constituent antigens present in the cell. 2. A taxonomic subdivision of bacteria based on the kinds and combinations of constituent antigens present in the cell, or a formula expressing the antigenic analysis on which such a subdivision is based. **heterologous s.,** a related but not identical serotype. **homologous s.,** an identical serotype.

serous (se′rus) [L. *serosus*]. 1. Pertaining to or resembling serum. 2. Producing or containing serum, as a serous gland or cyst.

serovaccination (se″ro-vak″sĭ-na′shun). Injection of serum combined with bacterial vaccination to produce passive immunity by the former and active immunity by the latter.

serozyme (se′ro-zīm) [L. *serum* + Gr. *zymē* yeast]. Bordet's name for the prothrombin present in the blood serum.

serpasil (ser′pah-sil). Trade mark for preparations of reserpine.

serpentaria (ser″pen-ta′re-ah) [L. *serpens* snake]. The dried rhizome and roots of *Aristolochia serpentaria*, Virginia snakeroot, and *A. reticulata*, or Texas snakeroot, herbs of North America. Serpentaria is an astringent bitter.

serpiginous (ser-pij′ĭ-nus) [L. *serpere* to creep]. Creeping from part to part.

serpigo (ser-pi′go) [L. *serpere* to creep]. Any creeping eruption; tinea or herpes.

serrated (ser′āt-ed) [L. *serratus*, from *serra* saw]. Having a sawlike edge.

Serratia (ser-ra′she-ah) [named for Serafino *Serrati*, an Italian physicist of the 18th century]. A genus of microorganisms of the tribe Serratieae, family Enterobacteriaceae, order Eubacteriales. It includes five species, *S. in′dica*, *S. kilien′sis*, *S. marces′cens*, *S. piscato′rum*, and *S. plymu′thica*.

Serratieae (ser″ah-ti′e-e). A tribe of the family Enterobacteriaceae, order Eubacteriales, made up of small, gram-negative rods which produce characteristic red pigments and are saprophytic on decaying plant or animal materials. It includes a single genus, *Serratia*.

serration (ser-ra′shun) [L. *serratio*]. A structure or formation with teeth like those of a saw; the condition of being serrated.

serratus (ser-ra′tus) [L.]. Serrated.

serrefine (sār-fēn′) [Fr.]. A small spring forceps for compressing bleeding vessels.

serrenoeud (sār-nud′) [Fr. *serrer* to press + *noeud* knot]. An instrument used in surgery for tightening ligatures.

Serres' angle, glands (sārz) [Antoine Etienne Renaud Augustin *Serres*, French physiologist, 1786–1868]. See under *angle* and *gland*.

serrulate (ser′u-lāt) [L. *serrulatus*]. Marked or bordered with small serrations or projections.

Sertoli's cell, column (ser-to′lēz) [Enrico *Sertoli*, Italian histologist, 1842–1910]. See under *cell* and *column*.

serum (se′rum), pl. *serums* or *se′ra* [L. "whey"]. 1. The clear portion of any animal liquid separated from its more solid elements; especially the clear liquid (*blood s.*) which separates in the clotting of blood from the clot and the corpuscles. 2. Blood serum from animals that have been inoculated with bacteria or their toxins. Such serum, when introduced into the body, produces passive immunization by virtue of the antibodies which it contains. 3. See *blood serum*, under B. **ACS s.,** antireticular cytotoxic s. **active s.,** a serum that contains complement. **allergenic s., allergic s.,** a serum which produces hypersensitiveness (anaphylaxis) to antigen injections. **anallergenic s., anallergic s.,** a serum which does not produce hypersensitiveness (anaphylaxis) to serum injections. **anti-anthrax s.,** a serum prepared by the inoculation of bouillon cultures of virulent anthrax. **antibothropic s.,** serum used to produce immunization against the bites of rattlesnakes. **anticholera s.,** a serum made by injecting horses with killed or (and) live cultures of the *Vibrio cholerae*, or with toxins or with other products of the germs. **anticomplementary s.,** a serum which interferes with or destroys the activity of complement. **anticrotalus s.,** an antivenomous serum which is protective against the poison of the rattlesnake. **antidiphtheric s.** 1. Diphtheria antitoxin. 2. A serum produced by injecting an animal with killed or living diphtheria germs, or with both. It is used therapeutically to inhibit or kill the diphtheria germs rather than to neutralize the diphtheria toxin. **antidysenteric s.,** a serum from horses immunized against the dysentery bacilli or toxins or both. **anti-erysipeloid s.,** serum containing the antibodies of *Erysipelothrix rhusiopathiae*. **antigourmeaux s.,** a serum for the treatment of strangles. **antihepatic s.,** serum of an animal into which has been injected liver matter from another animal. This serum is destructive to the liver of animals of the species from which the injected matter was taken. **antimeningococcus s.,** a polyvalent serum prepared by injecting first an autolysate of the strains and later living cultures (method of Flexner and Jobling). **anti-ophidic s.,** serum which combats the poison of snakes. **antipancreatic s.,** serum of an animal into which has been injected pancreatic extract from another animal. This serum is destructive to the pancreas of animals of the species from which the injected matter was taken. **antipertussis s.,** blood serum from patients convalescent from pertussis. **antipest s.,** antiplague s. **antiphagocytic s.,** a serum which destroys phagocytes. **antiplague s.,** a serum obtained from animals which have been repeatedly injected with killed or living plague germs (*Pfeifferella pestis*), or with both, or with some preparation of the microorganisms. **antiplatelet s.,** a serum that destroys blood platelets by lysis, agglutination, or by other mechanism. **antipneumococcus s. (horse),** a serum obtained from the blood of horses which have been injected with pneumococci of various types. **antipneumococcus s. (rabbit),** serum obtained from blood of rabbits immunized by cultures of pneumococci of any one of the several types. **antireticular cytotoxic s.,** a serum made by inoculating horses with an extract of spleen and bone marrow: said to have, in small doses, a stimulating effect on the reticuloendothelial system, and in large doses a cytotoxic effect on that system. Called also *ACS s.* and *Bogomolets' s.* **anti-sarcomatous s.,** serum from an animal into which sarcoma tissue has been injected: said to be useful to prevent the growth of sarcoma. **anti-scarlatinal s.** See *Dick's s., Dochez' s.,* and *Moser's s.* **anti-snake-bite s.,** antivenomous s. **antispermotoxic s.,** antispermotoxin. **antistaphylococcus s.,** a serum thought to be effective against staphylococcus infection. **antistreptococcus s.,** a serum obtained from the blood of animals which have been injected with killed or living streptococci or with both. It is used in treating various streptococcic infections. **antitetanic s.,** tetanus antitoxin. **antitoxic s.,** a serum which contains antitoxin. **antitubercle s.,** a serum prepared by injecting an animal with killed or with living tubercle germs (*Mycobacterium tuberculosis*) or with both or with a preparation of the germs. **antitularense s.,** Foshay's s. **antityphoid s.,** serum containing antibody to the typhoid bacillus. **antivenomous s.,** a serum used as a remedy for snake bite, prepared from the blood of animals which have been immunized against the venom of serpents; also called *Calmette's s.* See also *antivenin.* **articular s.,** synovia. **artificial s.,** a solution of the salts found in normal blood and in about the same amount. See *Locke's solution* and *Ringer's solution,* under *solution.* **bacteriolytic s.,** a serum which contains the bacteriolysin of a microorganism. **Banzhaf's s.,** a concentrated and purified antipneumococcus serum. **Bardel's s.,** a mixture of sodium chloride, phenol, sodium phosphate, sodium sulfate, and water. **Bargen's s.,** a serum prepared from cultures of an organism from the lesions of chronic ulcerative colitis. **blister s.,** the serous fluid found in a blister, sometimes injected back into the patient in nonspecific protein therapy. **Blondel's s.,** the serum of fresh milk, prepared by filtration after coagulation and neutralization. **blood s.** See *blood serum,* under B. **Bogomolets' s.,** antireticular cytotoxic s. **Bull and Pritchett's s.,** an antitoxic serum for gas-bacillus infection. **Calmette's s.,** antivenomous s. **Cattani's s.,** a mixture of sodium chloride, sodium carbonate, and boiled distilled water: for injection in infectious diseases. **Cheron's s.,** a mixture of crystalline phenol, sodium chloride, sodium phosphate, sodium sulfate, and boiled distilled water: for injection in infectious diseases. **chicken s.,** serum containing antibodies, prepared by the immunization of chickens. **convalescence s., convalescent s., convalescents' s.,** blood serum from a patient who is convalescent from an infectious disease: such a serum is used as a prophylactic injection in such diseases as measles, scarlet fever, whooping cough, etc. **cytotropic s.,** a serum rendering cells ingestible by phagocytes. **despeciated s.,** serum which has lost its species specific qualities, especially bovine blood serum which has been so treated as to be incapable of producing anaphylaxis when injected into human beings. **Dick's s., Dochez' s.,** antitoxic serum for scarlet fever obtained by immunizing horses with the toxin of the streptococcus of scarlet fever. **Dopter's s.,** a serum effective against the parameningococcus. **Dorset-Niles s.,** a serum for immunizing against hog cholera. **Dunbar's s.,** an antitoxin from the pollen of ragweed, goldenrod, rye, etc.; used in the treatment of hay fever. **endotheliolytic s.,** serum which destroys endothelial cells. It is obtained from the blood of animals immunized with endothelial cells. **s. equi'num,** horse s. **Felix Vi s.,** a typhoid antiserum rich in Vi (virulence) antibodies. **Felton's s.,** a concentrated antipneumococcus horse serum. **Flexner's s.,** antimeningococcus s. **foreign s.,** serum from an animal to be injected into one of another species. **Foshay's s.,** a serum for the treatment of tularemia. **gastrotoxic s.,** a serum toxic to the gastric mucous membrane. **glycerin s.,** blood serum which contains 5 per cent of glycerin: used as a culture medium for tubercle bacilli. **heterologous s.** 1. Serum obtained from an animal belonging to a species different from that of the recipient. 2. Serum prepared from an animal immunized by an organism differing from that against which it is to be used. **Hoffmann's s.,** epitheliolysine. **hog cholera s.,** serum obtained from hogs having some immunity, either following recovery from an attack of the disease or as a result of an injection of hog cholera serum, made hyperimmune by intravenous injection, at intervals of three to four weeks, of blood from a hog sick with hog cholera: used both in the prevention and in the cure of hog cholera. **homologous s.** 1. Serum obtained from an animal belonging to the same species as the recipient. 2. Serum prepared from an animal immunized by the same organism against which it is to be used. **horse s.,** serum obtained from the blood of horses. **hyperimmune s.,** a serum unusually rich in antibody, obtained by a vigorous course of active immunization. **immune s.,** a serum containing one or more antibodies; especially one in which the antibody content has been increased by recovery from its specific infection or by injection with its specific antigen. **inactivated s.,** serum which has been heated to 58–60°C. for 30 minutes, to destroy the activity of contained complement. **leukocytogenic s.,** horse serum treated so as to render it stable: said to cause marked migration of leukocytes to the site of injection and used in treating infected wounds. **leukocytolytic s.,** serum that destroys leukocytes; it is from the blood of animals immunized with leukocytes. **leukotoxic s.,** a serum that destroys leukocytes. **Löffler's s.** See *Löffler's blood serum,* under *blood serum.* **lymphatolytic s.,** serum which destroys lymphatic tissues, such as the spleen and lymph glands. **mercurialized s.,** a solution of mercuric chloride in normal horse serum diluted with physiologic salt solution for intravenous or intraspinal injection. **Merz's s.** 1. A preparation containing hamamelis extract in tubes for use in hemorrhoids. 2. Veraserol. **monovalent s.,** antiserum containing antibody to only one strain or species of microorganism or only one kind of antigen. **Moser's s.,** antistreptococcus serum produced by inoculating horses with several kinds of streptococci from the blood of scarlet fever patients. **motile s.,** an immune serum containing flagellar agglutinins. **multipartial s.,** polyvalent s. **muscle s.,** muscle plasma deprived of its myosin. **nephrolytic s., nephrotoxic s.,** a serum having a specific toxic effect on the kidney, produced by immunizing an animal with a brei or emulsion of kidney tissue. **neurolytic s., neurotoxic s.,** a serum having a specific toxic effect on the brain and spinal cord, produced by immunizing an animal with a brei or emulsion of nerve tissue. **normal s.,** serum from a normal untreated animal. **pericardial s.,** liquor pericardii. **petit s.,** a nonsensitizing, nontoxic, but vaccinating substance derived from serum by mixing with 2 parts of 90 per cent alcohol, treating the resulting precipitate with physiologic salt solution, and filtering. Cf. *Vaughan's split products,* under *product.* **plague s.,** antiplague s. **polyvalent s.,** antiserum containing antibody to more than one strain or species of microorganism or to more than one kind of antigen. It is produced by mixing monovalent serums or by immunizing the animal with multiple antigen. **pooled s.,** the mixed serum from a number of individuals. **pregnancy s.,** blood serum taken from pregnant women. **prophylactic s.,** a serum for immunizing against a disease. **Roux's s.,** antidiphtheric s. **salvarsanized s.,** blood serum taken from a patient after an intravenous injection of salvarsan. See *Swift-Ellis method,* under *method.* **Sanarelli's s.,** a serum used in protective inoculation against yellow fever. **Sclavo's s.,** an antiserum for use in human anthrax. **specific s.,** antiserum containing antibody to a specific microorganism or antigen. **streptococcus s.,** antistreptococcus s. **thymotoxic s.,** a serum which has a specific toxic effect on thymus tissue. **thyrolytic s., thyrotoxic s.,** a serum having a specific destructive or toxic effect on thyroid tissue. **yeast s.,** serum from animals which have been given increasing doses of yeast in their food; recommended for use in various infections. **Yersin's s.,** antiplague s.

serumal (se-roo'mal). Pertaining to or formed from serum.

serum-fast (se'rum-fast). Resistant to the destructive effect of serum: said of bacteria.

serumuria (se″rum-u're-ah). Albuminuria.

Serv. Abbreviation for L. *ser'va,* keep, preserve.

Servetus (ser-ve'tus), Michael (1511–1553). A Spanish theologian who also wrote, among other subjects, on geography, astrology, and medicine. His *Christianismi restitutio* (1553) contains the first printed description of the lesser circulation; Servetus was burned at the stake for heresy the same year, and only three copies of the book have survived.

sesame (ses'ah-me) [L. *sesamum;* Gr. *sēsamon*]. The plants *Sesamum indicum* and *S. orientale;* also their oil-bearing seeds. The oil, called oil of benne, is used like olive oil. The seeds are demulcent, and are useful in dysentery.

sesamoid (ses'ah-moid) [L. *sesamoides;* Gr. *sēsamon* sesame + *eidos* form]. Resembling a grain of sesame. See under *bone.*

sesamoiditis (ses″ah-moid-i'tis). Inflammation of the sesamoid bones and surrounding structures of a horse's foot.

sesqui- [L. *sesqui-* a half more]. A prefix meaning one and a half.

sesquibasic (ses″kwe-ba'sik) [*sesqui-* + L. *basis* base]. Formed by the substitution of two atoms of a base for three of the hydrogen atoms of an acid.

sesquibo (ses'kwe-bo) [*sesqui-* + L. *bovinum*]. Pirquet's term for a milk nutriment intermediate between simple and double nutriment. It contains 150 nems. Cf. *dubo* and *sibo.*

sesquicarbonate (ses″kwe-kar'bon-āt). A carbonate in which the carbonic acid radical is united to a base in the proportion of three to two: an archaic term.

sesquichloride (ses″kwe-klo'rīd). A chloride in which the chlorine is united to a base in the proportion of three to two: an archaic term.

sesquih. Abbreviation for L. *sesquiho'ra,* an hour and a half.

sesquihora (ses″kwe-ho'rah) [L.]. An hour and a half.

sesquioxide (ses″kwe-ok'sid). A compound of three parts of oxygen with two of another element.

sesquisalt (ses'kwe-sawlt). A salt containing three parts of an acid with two of a base.

sesquisulfate (ses″kwe-sul'fāt). A sulfate containing three parts of sulfuric acid united with two of another element.

sesquisulfide (ses″kwe-sul'fid). A sulfide containing three parts of sulfur united with two of another element.

sessile (ses'il) [L. *sessilis*]. Attached by a broad base; not pedunculated or stalked.

Sessinia (ses-sin'e-ah). A genus of blistering beetles of certain Pacific islands.

sesunc. Abbreviation for L. *sesun'cia,* an ounce and a half.

setaceous (se-ta'shus) [L. *setaceus; seta* bristle]. Slender and rigid, like a bristle.

Setaria (se-ta're-ah). A genus of filarial nematodes. **S. equi'na,** a species found in the abdominal cavity of the horse. **S. labiatopapillo'sa,** a species found in the peritoneal cavity of cattle.

Setchenow's centers, nuclei (sech'e-nofs) [Ivan Michalovich *Setchenow,* Russian neurologist, 1829–1903, the father of Russian physiology and neurology]. See under *center.*

setiferous (se-tif'er-us) [L. *seta* bristle + *ferre* to bear]. Bearing bristles; covered with bristles.

setigerous (se-tij'er-us) [L. *seta* bristle + *gerere* to carry]. Setiferous.

seton (se'ton) [Fr. *seton;* L. *seta* bristle]. 1. A strip or skein of silk or linen drawn through a wound in the skin to make an issue. 2. The tract or fistula so formed.

Seutin's bandage (su-tanz') [Louis Joseph *Seutin,* Brussels surgeon, 1793–1862]. See under *bandage.*

Sever's disease (se'verz) [James W. *Sever,* Boston orthopedic surgeon, born 1878]. Epiphysitis of the os calcis.

sevum (se'vum) [L.]. Suet.

sewage (su'ij). The matters found in sewers. It consists of the excreta of man and animals, and other waste material from homes and other structures inhabited by man. **activated s.,** sewage mixed with activated sludge. **domestic s.,** sewage from dwellings, business buildings, factories, or institutions. **septic s.,** sewage undergoing anaerobic putrefaction.

sex (seks) [L. *sexus*]. The fundamental distinction, found in most species of animals and plants, based on the type of gametes produced by the individual or the category into which the individual fits on the basis of that criterion; ova, or macrogametes, are produced by the female, and sperm, or microgametes, are produced by the male, the union of these distinctive germ cells being the natural prerequisite for the production of a new individual (sexual reproduction). **chromosomal s.,** the category (male or female) into which an individual is placed, determined by the presence or absence of the Y chromosome in the spermatozoon uniting with the ovum at the time of conception. **genetic s.,** chromosomal s. **gonadal s.,** the sex as determined on the basis of the gonadal tissue present, whether ovarian or testicular. **morphological s.,** that determined on the basis of the morphology of the external genitals. **nuclear s.,** the sex as determined on the basis of the presence or absence of sex chromatin in the somatic cells. **psychological s.,** that determined by the gender role assigned to and played by the growing individual.

sexdigitate (seks-dij'ĭ-tāt) [L. *sex* six + *digitus* digit]. Having six fingers on the hand or six toes on the foot.

sexivalent (sek-siv'ah-lent) [L. *sex* six + *valere* to have power]. Able to combine with or displace six atoms of hydrogen.

sex-limited (seks-lim'it-ed). Affecting one sex only.

sex-linked (seks-linkt'). Transmitted by genes which are located on the sex chromosome.

sexology (seks-ol'o-je). That branch of science which deals with sex and sexual relations from the biological point of view.

sexopathy (seks-op'ah-the). Abnormality of sexual expression.

sextan (seks'tan) [L. *sextanus* of the sixth]. Recurring every sixth day.

sextigravida (seks″tĭ-grav″ĭ-dah) [L. *sextus* sixth + *gravida* pregnant]. A woman pregnant for the sixth time. Also written Gravida VI.

sextipara (seks-tip'ah-rah) [L. *sextus* sixth + *parere* to bring forth, produce]. A woman who has had six pregnancies which resulted in viable offspring. Also written Para VI.

sextuplet (seks'tu-plet) [L. *sextus* sixth]. One of six offspring produced in one gestation period.

sexual (seks'u-al) [L. *sexualis*]. 1. Pertaining to sex. 2. A person considered in his sexual relations. **contrary s.,** a sexual invert.

sexuality (seks″u-al'ĭ-te). 1. The characteristic quality of the male and female reproductive elements. 2. The constitution of an individual in relation to sexual attitudes or activity. **pregenital s.,** the sexuality of early infantile life before object love and the genital zone have become dominant.

Seyderhelm's solution (si′der-helmz) [Richard *Seyderhelm*, Göttingen physician, 1888–1940]. See under *solution.*

S.-G. Abbreviation for *Sachs-Georgi test.*

Sgambati reaction, test (zgahm-bah′te) [O. *Sgambati*, physician in Rome]. See under *reaction.*

S.G.O. Abbreviation for *Surgeon-General's Office.*

SGOT. Abbreviation for *serum glutamic oxaloacetic transaminase.*

SGPT. Abbreviation for *serum glutamic pyruvic transaminase.*

SH. Abbreviation for *serum hepatitis.*

shadocol (shad′ŏ-kol). A proprietary x-ray contrast medium containing sodium tetraiodophenolphthalein.

shadow (shad′o). 1. An attenuated image of an actual object, such as a faded or colorless erythrocyte. 2. A figure or image created by the interruption of light or other rays, such as the representation on a roentgenogram of radiopaque structures. **blood s.,** a phantom corpuscle. **Gumprecht's s.,** a crushed and deformed cell such as is often seen in leukemic lymphadenosis. **heart s.,** the shadow of the heart on a roentgenogram. **Ponfick's s's,** phantom corpuscles. **Purkinje's s's.** See under *figure.*

shadow-casting (shad″o-kast′ing). A technique for increasing the visibility of ultramicroscopic specimens under the microscope by applying a coating of chromium, gold, or other metal.

shadowgram, shadowgraph (shad′o-gram, shad′o-graf). Skiagram.

shadowgraphy (shad′o-graf″e). Skiagraphy.

shaft (shaft). A long slender part, such as the portion of a long bone between the wider ends or extremities. See also *diaphysis* [N A]. **s. of femur,** corpus femoris. **s. of fibula,** corpus fibulae. **hair s.,** scapus pili. **s. of humerus,** corpus humeri. **s. of metacarpal bone,** corpus ossis metacarpalis. **s. of metatarsal bone,** corpus ossis metatarsalis. **s. of penis,** corpus penis. **s. of phalanx of fingers,** corpus phalangis digitorum manus. **s. of phalanx of toes,** corpus phalangis digitorum pedis. **s. of radius,** corpus radii. **s. of rib,** corpus costae. **s. of tibia,** corpus tibiae. **s. of ulna,** corpus ulnae.

shakes (shāks). A popular name for the cold paroxysm of intermittent fever. **hatter's s.,** mercury poisoning among fur hat workers. **spelter s.,** a form of disease seen among brass-founders, characterized by violent chills.

shamanism, shamanismus (sham′ah-nizm), sham″ah-niz′mus). A state of excitement into which certain Dyaks and other people are able to throw themselves for religious purposes.

shank (shangk). A leg, or leglike part.

Sharpey's fibers (shar′pēz) [William *Sharpey*, English anatomist and physiologist, 1802–1880]. See under *fiber.*

shashitsu (shah-shit′soo). Scrub typhus.

sheath (shēth) [L. *vagina;* Gr. *thēkē*]. A tubular structure enclosing or surrounding some organ. **bulbar s.** See *vaginae bulbi.* **carotid s.,** a portion of the cervical fascia enclosing the carotid artery, the internal jugular vein, and the vagus nerve. **caudal s.,** a tubular cytoplasmic structure at the base of the nucleus in the early spermatid. **chordal s.,** notochordal s. **common s. of tendons of peroneal muscles,** vagina synovialis musculorum peroneorum communis. **common s. of testis and spermatic cord,** fascia spermatica interna. **connective tissue s. of Key and Retzius,** a network of elastic fibers extending from the endoneurium of the smaller branches of the peripheral nerves and attaching to the neurolemma. **crural s.,** fascia cruris. **dentinal s.,** the layer of dentin immediately adjacent to a dentinal tubule. **enamel rod s's,** envelopes of organic tissue enclosing the enamel rods. **s's of eyeball,** vaginae bulbi. **fascial s. of prostate,** the sheath, derived from the rectovesical fascia, which surrounds the prostate. **female s.,** vagina. **femoral s.,** canalis femoralis. **fibrous s's of fingers,** vaginae fibrosae digitorum manus. **fibrous s. of optic nerve,** vagina externa nervi optici. **fibrous s. of tendon,** vagina fibrosa tendinis. **fibrous s's of toes,** vaginae fibrosae digitorum pedis. **s. of Henle,** connective tissue s. of Key and Retzius. **s. of Hertwig,** root s., def. 1. **s. of Key and Retzius,** connective tissue s. of Key and Retzius. **lamellar s.,** perineurium. **masculine s.,** utriculus prostaticus. **Mauthner's s.,** axilemma. **medullary s.,** myelin s. **mucous s's,** bursae et vaginae synoviales. **mucous s., intertubercular,** septum intermusculare anterius cruris. **mucous s. of tendon,** vagina synovialis tendinis. **mucous s's of tendons of fingers,** vaginae synoviales digitorum manus. **mucous s's of tendons of toes,** vaginae synoviales digitales pedis. **myelin s.,** the sheath surrounding the axon of some (the myelinated or medullated) nerve fibers, consisting of myelin alternating with the spirally wrapped neurolemma. **Neumann's s.,** dentinal s. **notochordal s.,** an elastic sheath surrounding the notochord. **nucleated s.,** neurolemma. **s's of optic nerve,** vaginae nervi optici. **s. of optic nerve, external,** vagina externa nervi optici. **s. of optic nerve, internal,** vagina interna nervi optici. **perinephric s.,** the sheath of fascia investing the kidney. **perivascular s.,** a lymphatic organ which surrounds some of the blood vessels of the brain. **s. of plantar tendon of long peroneal muscle,** vagina tendinis musculi peronei longi plantaris. **primitive s.,** neurolemma. **prism s's,** enamel rod s's. **s. of rectus abdominis muscle,** vagina musculi recti abdominis. **root s.** 1. An investment of epithelial cells around the unerupted tooth and inside the dental follicle which are derived by budding from the enamel organ. 2. The epithelial portion of the hair follicle. **Ruffini's subsidiary s.,** connective tissue s. of Key and Retzius. **Scarpa's s.,** fascia cremasterica. **Schwalbe's s.,** the thin envelope of an elastic fiber. **s. of Schwann,** neurolemma. **Schweigger-Seidel s.,** a spindle-shaped thickening in the walls of the second portion of the arterial branches forming the penicilli in the spleen. **spiral s.,** a heavily staining filament winding around the axial thread of the middle piece of a spermatozoon. **s. of styloid process,** vagina processus styloidei. **synovial s. of bicipital groove,** vagina synovialis intertubercularis. **synovial s. of tendon,** vagina synovialis tendinis. **synovial s. of tendons of foot,** vaginae synoviales digitales pedis. **tendinous s's of flexor muscles of fingers,** vaginae fibrosae digitorum manus. **tendinous s's of flexor muscles of toes,** vaginae fibrosae digitorum pedis. **tendinous s. of leg,** fascia cruris. **tendinous s. of long peroneal muscle, plantar,** vagina tendinis musculi peronei longi plantaris. **s. of tendon of anterior tibial muscle,** vagina tendinis musculi tibialis anterioris. **s's of tendons of long extensor muscles of toes,** vaginae tendinum musculorum extensoris digitorum pedis longi. **s's of tendons of long flexor muscles of toes,** vaginae tendinum musculorum flexoris digitorum pedis longi. **s. of tendon of posterior tibial muscle,** vagina synovialis tendinis musculi tibialis posterioris.

sheet (shēt). A rectangular piece of cotton or linen for a bed covering. **draw s.,** a folded sheet placed under a patient in bed so that it may be withdrawn without lifting the patient. **drip s.,** a wet sheet from which the water is wrung out and which is then wrapped around a patient standing in a tub of water.

shelf (shelf). A shelflike structure, normal or abnormal, in the body. **Blumer's s.,** a shelflike structure projecting into the rectum as a result of infiltration of Douglas' pouch with inflammatory or neoplastic material. **dental s.,** the shelflike epithelial invagination formed by the dental ridge, beneath which the dental papillae are formed. **mesocolic s.,** the transverse mesocolon and the great omentum taken together. **palatine s.,** palatine process. **rectal s.,** Blumer's s.

shell (shel). A covering or encasement, such as the horny or chitinous covering of an animal. **diffusion s.,** a small sac of semipermeable membrane used in the Abderhalden reaction. **egg s.,** testa ovi.

shellac (shĕ-lak′). A variety of lac from India, produced on various plants by an insect, *Coccus lactis;* sometimes used in dentistry and surgery.

Shenton's line (shen′tonz) [Thomas *Shenton,* English radiologist]. See under *line.*

Shepherd's fracture (shep′ards) [Francis J. *Shepherd,* Canadian surgeon, 1851–1929]. See under *fracture.*

Sherman unit (sher′man) [Henry C. *Sherman,* American biochemist, born 1871]. See under *unit.*

Sherman-Bourquin unit [Henry C. *Sherman;* Ann *Bourquin,* American chemist, born 1897]. See under *unit.*

Sherman-Munsell unit [Henry C. *Sherman;* Hazel E. *Munsell,* American chemist, born 1891]. See under *unit.*

Sherrington's law, solution (sher′ing-tonz) [Sir Charles Scott *Sherrington,* English physiologist, 1857–1952, noted for his work on physiology of the nervous system; co-winner, with Edward Douglas Adrian, of the Nobel prize for physiology and medicine in 1932]. See under *law* and *solution.*

shield (shēld). 1. Any protecting tube. 2. The metal tube that covers the core of soft iron in the primary coil of a faradic battery; by sliding or drawing it the current is intensified or diminished at will. **Buller's s.,** a watch glass fitted over the eye to guard it from gonorrheal or ophthalmic infection. **embryonic s.,** the double-layered disk from which the embryo proper develops. **eye s.,** a shade or covering for the eyes to protect them from light or injury. **nipple s.,** a cover to protect the nipple of a nursing woman. **phallic s.,** a device for the antiseptic protection of the male genitals during surgical operations.

shift (shift). A change of position. **chloride s.,** the exchange of chloride (Cl) and carbonate (HCO_3) between the plasma and the red blood corpuscles which takes place in order to reestablish the equilibrium between carbonate and chloride ions in the plasma and cells. **degenerative blood s.,** a degeneration of the cells of the circulating blood with degeneration of the hematopoietic organ, marked by increase of the degenerative cells and decrease in the total leukocyte count. **s. to the left,** Arneth's term for a preponderance of young neutrophils in the blood picture. **Purkinje s.,** shift of the region of maximum visual intensity in the spectrum from the yellow toward the violet as intensity of illumination diminishes. **regenerative blood s.,** the rapid outpouring of leukocytes of the juvenile and myelocyte type, occurring as the result of an acute stimulus to the bone marrow. **s. to the right,** Arneth's term for a preponderance of older neutrophils in the blood picture.

Shiga's bacillus (she′gahz) [Kiyoshi *Shiga,* Japanese physician, 1870–1957]. *Shigella dysenteriae* type 1.

Shigella (she-gel′ah) [Kiyoshi *Shiga*]. A genus of microorganisms of tribe Salmonelleae, family Enterobacteriaceae, order Eubacteriales, made up of non-motile, rod-shaped, gram-negative bacteria. These microorganisms, which cause dysentery and for that reason are called dysentery bacilli, are separated into the non-mannitol-fermenting and the mannitol-fermenting type; the former make up Group A, and the latter are subdivided into Groups B, C, and D, each group making up a species. See *S. boydii, S. dysenteriae, S. flexneri,* and *S. sonnei.* **S. alkales′cens,** a name given a serologically homogeneous group of microorganisms occasionally causing diarrheal disease in man; culturally and serologically distinct from other Shigella species, they are serologically related to coliform bacilli and are formally classified with them as *Escherichia alkalescens.* **S. ambig′ua,** *S. dysenteriae* type 2. **S. arabinotar′da type A,** a dysentery bacillus identical with *S. dysenteriae* type 3. **S. arabinotar′da type B,** a dysentery bacillus identical with *S. dysenteriae* type 4. **S. boy′dii,** the species name given to Group C dysentery bacilli, the cause of an acute diarrheal disease in man, especially in tropical regions; culturally identical with *S. flexneri* but serologically unrelated, the species includes 15 independent numbered serotypes. **S. ceylonen′sis,** a dysentery-like bacillus, occasionally associated with diarrheal disease in man, and classified with the coliform bacilli as *Escherichia dispar* var. *ceylonensis.* **S. dispar,** a slow lactose-fermenting dysentery bacillus of limited or doubtful pathogenicity; serologically heterogeneous but related to some types of *S. flexneri.* Now formally classified with the coliform bacilli as *Escherichia dispar.* **S. dysente′riae,** the species name given to Group A dysentery bacilli, and separated into numbered serotypes. TYPE 1, the classic Shiga bacillus, which is set apart from other dysentery bacilli by the production of a potent exotoxin, is more common in tropical regions and causes severe dysentery. TYPE 2, the Schmitz bacillus, is a non-mannitol-fermenting organism serologically related to *Escherichia coli* type 0112. Of limited pathogenicity, but occasionally the cause of epidemic diarrheal disease in man, the organism has been found in the chimpanzee but not in other lower animals. The other numbered types include the Large-Sachs group of parashiga bacilli (see *S. parashigae*). **S. etou′sae,** *S. boydii* type 7, Lavington, type T, type 1296/7. **S. flexne′ri,** a species name given to Group B dysentery bacilli, one of the commonest causes of acute diarrheal disease in man, occurring as 8 related serotypes, designated by numbers 1 to 6 and letters X and Y. **S. madampen′sis,** a dysentery-like bacillus, occasionally associated with diarrheal disease in man, and classified with the coliform bacilli as *Escherichia dispar* var. *madampensis.* **S. new′castle,** *S. flexneri* type 6, Boyd 88. **S. paradysente′riae,** *S. flexneri.* **S. parashi′gae,** a name formerly given to a group of non-mannitol-fermenting dysentery bacilli serologically differentiable from the Shiga bacillus (now *S. dysenteriae* type 1); also known as the Large-Sachs group of parashiga bacilli, they are now known as *S. dysenteriae,* types 3 to 7, inclusive. **S. schmit′zii,** *S. dysenteriae* type 2. **S. shi′gae,** *S. dysenteriae* type 1. **S. son′nei,** a species name given to Group D dysentery bacilli, one of the commonest causes of bacillary dysentery in temperate climates; slow (5–14 days) lactose fermenters, the organisms are serologically homogeneous, but two antigens, designated I and II, occur in varying proportions. **S. wake′field,** a species name given a paracolon bacillus.

shigella (she-gel′ah), pl. *shigel′lae.* An individual organism of the genus Shigella.

shigellae (she-gel′e). Plural of shigella.

shigellosis (she″gel-lo′sis). The condition produced by infection with organisms of the genus *Shigella.* See *bacillary dysentery.*

shikimene (shik′ĭ-mēn). Sikimin.

shin (shin). 1. The crest or anterior edge of the tibia. 2. The anterior aspect of the leg below the knee. **bucked s's,** sore s's. **cucumber s.,** a leg with a tibia which is curved with the concavity forward. **saber s.,** a tibia with a marked anterior convexity as seen in hereditary syphilis and in yaws. **sore s's,** periostitis of the large metacarpal or metatarsal bone of the horse.

shingles (shin′g'lz). Herpes zoster.

shiver (shiv′er). 1. A slight chill or tremor. 2. To tremble, as from a chill.

shivering (shiv′er-ing). 1. Involuntary trembling or quivering of the body caused by contraction or twitching of the muscles, a physiologic method of heat production in man and other mammals. 2. A disease of horses characterized by trembling or quivering of various muscles.

shock (shok). A condition of acute peripheral circulatory failure due to derangement of circulatory control or loss of circulating fluid and brought about by injury. It is marked by pallor and clamminess of the skin, decreased blood pressure, feeble rapid pulse, decreased respiration, restlessness, anxiety, and sometimes unconsciousness. **aerial s.,** a neurotic condition in soldiers due to the aerial disturbance produced by bursting shells. The aerial wave compression is believed to affect arterial pressure in the body by causing changes in the atmospheric pressure. **allergic s.,** anaphylactic shock. **anaphylactic s.,** a violent attack of symptoms produced by a second injection of serum or protein and due to anaphylaxis. See *anaphylaxis.* **anaphylactoid s.,** colloidoclasia. **anesthesia s.,** a shocklike condition caused by an overdose of anesthetic. **apoplectic s.,** a stroke of apoplexy. **asthmatic s.,** status asthmaticus. **barium s.,** a hemoclastic shock produced when barium is injected into the veins. **bomb s.,** a condition of dread and loss of emotional equilibrium among children in the British Isles, as a result of repeated bombings. **break s.,** the shock produced by breaking the electric current as it is passing through the body. **cardiac s.,** heart s. **cardiogenic s.,** shock resulting from sudden diminution of cardiac output, as in myocardial infarction. **cerebral s.,** a form of shock sometimes occurring in severe head injury affecting the centers of cardiovascular control. **colloid s.,** pseudoanaphylaxis. **colloidoclastic s.** See *colloidoclasia.* **deferred s., delayed s.,** severe physical or mental disturbance, of which the symptoms occur a considerable time after the injury or mental impression is received. **diastolic s.,** the impulse which strikes the palpating hand at the time of the second heart sound. **electric s.,** the effects produced by the passage of an electric current through any part of the body. **epigastric s.,** the effect of a sudden blow upon the epigastrium. **erethismic s.,** a form of shock in which the patient is excited and restless. **faradic s.,** the effect produced by faradization. **fetal s.,** distress sometimes produced by the movements of the fetus in utero. **gravitation s.,** orthostatic peripheral circulatory failure. **heart s.,** a sudden collapse of the functions of the heart during exertion; often fatal. **hematogenic s.,** shock due to diminished blood volume. **hemoclastic s.,** hemoclastic crisis. **histamine s.,** the reaction, resembling anaphylactic shock, which follows the injection of histamine. **hypnoclastic s.,** interruption of sleep by sudden awakening. **hypoglycemic s.,** insulin s. **insulin s.,** a condition of circulatory insufficiency resulting from overdosage with insulin which causes too sudden reduction of blood sugar. It is marked by tremor, sweating, vertigo, diplopia, convulsions, and collapse. Such a condition produced intentionally has been employed in the treatment of schizophrenia. See *shock therapy,* under *therapy.* **liver s.,** a serious collapse which sometimes follows sudden relief of common bile duct obstruction of long duration. **s. of metabalodispersion,** shock due to a change (usually diminution) in the degree of dispersion of the colloids of the body. **micro s.,** the reaction produced by a preliminary injection of a small amount of a substance, as an antiserum, so that a therapeutic dose will not cause a serious reaction. See *skeptophylaxis.* **neurogenic s.,** shock due to action of the nervous system producing vasodilatation, as in primary shock. **osmotic s.,** the destructive effect on certain viruses of rapid reduction in osmotic pressure produced by dilution of the medium in which they have been living. **paralytic s.,** a sudden paralytic attack. **peptone s.,** protein s. **pleural s.,** a condition sometimes following thoracentesis, and characterized by cyanosis, pallor, dilated pupils, and disturbance of pulse and respiration. **postoperative s.,** a condition of shock following a surgical operation. **postpartum s.,** a condition of shock following childbirth. **primary s.,** a condition of collapse or syncope appearing immediately after injury. **protein s.,** a state of acute intoxication manifested by a chill with fever, spasm of the bronchi, acute emphysema, and vomiting and diarrhea, produced by the intravenous injection of peptone or other substance of protein nature, such as bacterial proteins, animal or vegetable proteins, organic extracts, and the like. **psychic s.,** a shocklike condition produced by strong emotion. **secondary s.,** shock appearing one or more hours after injury; delayed shock. **serum s.** See *serum sickness* and *anaphylactic s.* **shell s.,** a condition of lost nervous control with numerous psychic symptoms, ranging from extreme fear to actual dementia, produced in soldiers under fire by the noise and concussion from bursting shells. **spinal s.,** the loss of spinal reflexes after injury of the spinal cord which appears in the muscles enervated by the cord segments situated below the site of the lesion. **static s.,** the effect produced by the discharge of static electricity. **surgical s.,** shock that occurs during or after surgical operation. **testicular s.,** the effect of a sharp blow upon the testes. **thyroxin s.,** thyrotoxic symptoms produced by overdoses of thyroxin. **torpid s.,** shock in which the patient lies prostrate and immobile. **vasogenic s.,** shock brought about by a substance acting on the vessel walls to produce vascular dilatation.

shoe (shoo). A covering or appliance for the foot. **Charlier's s.,** a horse's shoe which allows the sole and the frog to come to the ground exactly as in the unshod foot. **Scarpa's s.,** a metal brace used in treating talipes equinus by preventing plantar extension of the foot beyond a right angle.

Shope papilloma (shōp) [Richard Edwin *Shope,* American pathologist, born 1902]. See under *papilloma.*

shot-compressor (shot′kom-pres″or). A sort of forceps for compressing split-shot on sutures.

shot-silk phenomenon, reflex, retina. See *shot-silk retina,* under *retina.*

shoulder (shōl′der). The junction of the arm and trunk; also that part of the trunk which is bounded at the back by the scapula. **bull's-eye s.,** a horse's shoulder having on it a loose flabby disk of hyperplastic skin with a central denuded surface. **drop s.,** depression of one shoulder below the level of the other. **frozen s.,** a disability of the shoulder joint due to fibrositis and characterized by limited abduction and rotation of the arm. **knocked-down s.,** separation of or dislocation at the acromioclavicular joint occurring in athletes. **loose s.,** a condition seen in progressive muscular atrophy in which, when attempts to lift the patient by grasping the upper arms at their sides are made, the arms move up but the trunk remains behind. **pegged s.,** a condition in the horse marked by limitation of movement in the shoulder. **stubbed s.,** sprain of the shoulder joint occurring in athletes.

shoulder-blade (shōl′der-blād). The scapula.

shoulder slip (shōl′der slip). Inflammation of shoulder muscles and tendons in the horse.

shower (show′er). A sudden emission or appearance. **erythroblastic s.,** a rapid and marked increase in the nucleated red cells of the blood occurring in pernicious anemia. **uric acid s.,** temporary increase in the uric acid contents of the urine; occurring in the course of a gouty attack.

Shrady's saw (shra′dēz) [George Frederick *Shrady,* New York surgeon, 1837–1907]. See under *saw.*

Shrapnell's membrane (shrap′nelz) [Henry J. *Shrapnell,* English anatomist and Army surgeon, 19th Century]. See under *membrane.*

shunt (shunt). 1. To turn to one side; to divert.

2. A conductor connecting two points in an electric circuit so as to receive a portion of the current of the main circuit. 3. An electric conductor which furnishes a low resistance path for the flow of current. 4. A passage or anastomosis between two natural channels; in surgery, the operation of forming anastomoses between blood vessels to divert the blood from one part of the body to

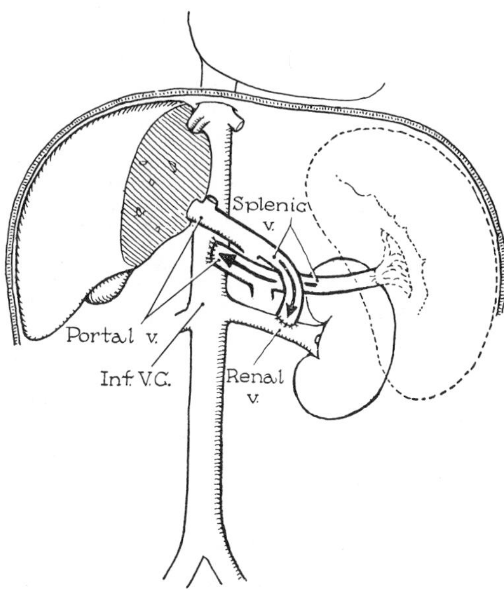

Portal shunts, showing two commonly used types of portal to systemic venous shunt. (Blakemore and Vorhees, Jr.)

another. **portacaval s., postcaval s.,** surgical creation of an anastomosis between the portal and caval veins.

Shwartzman's phenomenon (shwarts'manz) [Gregory *Shwartzman*, New York bacteriologist, born 1896]. See under *phenomenon.*

S.I. Abbreviation for *soluble insulin.*

Si. Chemical symbol for *silicon.*

siagantritis, siagonantritis (si″ag-an-tri'tis, si″ag-on-an-tri'tis) [Gr. *siagōn* jaw bone + *antritis*]. Inflammation of the maxillary sinus.

siagonagra (si″ag-o-nag'rah) [Gr. *siagōn* jaw bone + *agra* seizure]. Pain in the maxilla.

sial-. See *sialo-.*

sialaden (si-al'ah-den) [Gr. *sial-* + Gr. *adēn* gland]. A salivary gland.

sialadenitis (si″al-ad″e-ni'tis). Inflammation of a salivary gland.

sialadenography (si″al-ad″e-nog'rah-fe). Roentgenography of the salivary glands and ducts.

sialadenoncus (si″al-ad″e-nong'kus) [*sialaden* + Gr. *onkos* mass]. A tumor of a salivary gland.

sialagogic (si″ah-lah-goj'ik). Promoting the flow of saliva.

sialagogue (si-al'ah-gog) [*sial-* + Gr. *agōgos* leading]. An agent that promotes the flow of saliva.

sialaporia (si″al-ah-po're-ah) [*sial-* + Gr. *aporia* lack]. Deficiency in the amount of saliva.

sialectasia (si″al-ek-ta'se-ah). Dilatation of a salivary duct.

sialemesis (si″al-em'e-sis) [Gr. *sial-* + Gr. *emesis* vomiting]. The hysteric vomiting of saliva.

sialic (si-al'ik) [Gr. *sialikos*]. Pertaining to the saliva.

sialine (si'ah-līn) [L. *sialinus*]. Pertaining to the saliva.

sialism, sialismus (si'al-izm, si″al-iz'mus) [Gr. *sialismos*]. Salivation.

sialitis (si″ah-li'tis). Inflammation of a salivary gland or duct.

sialo-, sial- (si'ah-lo, si'al) [Gr. *sialon* saliva]. Combining form denoting relationship to saliva or to the salivary glands.

sialoadenectomy (si″ah-lo-ad″e-nek'to-me) [*sialo-* + Gr. *adēn* gland + *ektomē* excision]. Excision of a salivary gland.

sialoadenitis (si″ah-lo-ad″e-ni'tis). Inflammation of a salivary gland.

sialoadenotomy (si″ah-lo-ad″e-not'o-me) [*sialo-* + Gr. *adēn* gland + *tomē* a cutting]. Incision and drainage of a salivary gland.

sialoaerophagy (si″ah-lo-a″er-of'ah-je) [*sialo-* + Gr. *aēr* air + *phagein* to eat]. The swallowing of saliva and air.

sialoangiectasis (si″ah-lo-an″je-ek'tah-sis) [*sialo-* + Gr. *angeion* vessel + *ektasis* distention]. Dilation of the salivary ducts.

sialoangiitis (si″ah-lo-an″je-i'tis). Inflammation of the salivary ducts.

sialoangitis (si″ah-lo-an-ji'tis). Sialoangiitis.

sialocele (si'ah-lo-sēl) [*sialo-* + Gr. *kēlē* tumor]. A salivary cyst or tumor.

sialodochitis (si″ah-lo-do-ki'tis) [*sialo-* + Gr. *dochos* receptacle + *-itis*]. Inflammation of the salivary ducts.

sialodochoplasty (si″ah-lo-do'ko-plas″te) [*sialo-* + Gr. *dochos* receptacle + *plassein* to form]. Plastic operation on the salivary ducts.

sialoductitis (si″ah-lo-duk-ti'tis). Sialoangiitis.

sialogenous (si″ah-loj'e-nus) [*sialo-* + Gr. *gennan* to produce]. Producing saliva.

sialogogic (si″ah-lo-goj'ik). Sialagogic.

sialogogue (si-al'o-gog). Sialagogue.

sialogram (si-al'o-gram) [*sialo-* + Gr. *gramma* a mark]. A roentgenogram obtained by sialography.

sialograph (si-al'o-graf). Sialogram.

sialography (si″ah-log'rah-fe) [*sialo-* + Gr. *graphein* to write]. Roentgen demonstration of the salivary ducts by means of the injection of substances opaque to roentgen rays.

sialolith (si-al'o-lith) [*sialo-* + Gr. *lithos* stone]. A salivary calculus.

sialolithiasis (si″ah-lo-lĭ-thi'ah-sis) [*sialo-* + Gr. *lithiasis* formation of a stone]. The formation of salivary calculi or the condition or infection caused by it.

sialolithotomy (si″ah-lo-lĭ-thot'o-me) [*sialolith* + Gr. *tomē* a cutting]. Incision of a salivary gland or duct for the removal of a calculus.

sialology (si″ah-lol'o-je) [*sialo-* + *-logy*]. The study of the saliva.

sialoma (si″ah-lo'mah). A salivary tumor.

sialophagia (si″ah-lo-fa'je-ah) [*sialo-* + Gr. *phagein* to eat]. The excessive swallowing of saliva.

sialorrhea (si″ah-lo-re'ah) [*sialo-* + Gr. *rhoia* flow]. Salivation. **s. pancreat'ica,** the expectoration of fluid resembling saliva or pancreatic juice, sometimes seen in disease of the pancreas.

sialoschesis (si″ah-los'ke-sis) [*sialo-* + Gr. *schesis* suppression]. Suppression of the salivary secretion.

sialosemeiology (si″ah-lo-se″mi-ol'o-je) [*sialo-* + *semeiology*]. Analysis of the saliva as a means of determining the physiologic status of the patient, especially in regard to metabolic processes.

sialosis (si″ah-lo'sis) [*sial-* + *-osis*]. 1. The flow of saliva. 2. Salivation.

sialostenosis (si″ah-lo-ste-no'sis) [*sialo-* + Gr. *stenos* narrow]. Stenosis, or narrowing, of a salivary duct.

sialosyrinx (si″ah-lo-si'rinks) [*sialo-* + Gr. *syrinx* pipe]. 1. A salivary fistula. 2. A syringe for washing out the salivary ducts, or a drainage tube for the salivary ducts.

sialotic (si″ah-lot'ik). Pertaining to or marked by the flow of saliva.

sialozemia (si″ah-lo-ze'me-ah) [*sialo-* + Gr. *zēmia* loss]. The involuntary flow of saliva.

sib (sib) [Anglo-Saxon *sib* kin]. A blood relative; one of a group of persons all of whom are descendants of a common ancestor. See also *sibling*.

sibbens (sib′enz). A form of treponematosis formerly prevalent in Scotland.

sibilant (sib′ĭ-lant) [L. *sibilans* hissing]. Of a shrill, hissing or whistling character.

sibilus (sib′ĭ-lus) [L.]. A whistling or sibilant rale.

Sibine stimulea (sĭ-bi′nĕ stĭ-mu′le-ah). The saddle-back caterpillar, the irritating hair of which causes a dermatitis.

sibling (sib′ling). Another offspring of the same parents as the person of reference; a brother or sister.

sibo (se′bo). Pirquet's term for a cow's milk nutriment having the same value as human milk (lac *si*mplex *bo*vinum).

sibship (sib′ship). 1. Relationship by blood. 2. In anthropology, a group of persons all of whom are descendants of a common ancestor, commonly used as the basis of study to determine genetic influences.

Sibson's aponeurosis, furrow, groove, notch, vestibule (sib′sunz) [Francis *Sibson*, English physician, 1814–1876]. See under the nouns.

Sicard's treatment (se-karz′) [Jean Athanase *Sicard*, Paris neurologist, 1872–1929]. See under *treatment*.

siccative (sik′ah-tiv) [L. *siccus* dry]. Drying; removing moisture from surrounding objects.

sicchasia (sĭ-ka′ze-ah) [Gr. *sikchasia*]. Nausea.

siccolabile (sik″o-la′bĭl). Altered or destroyed by drying.

siccostabile (sik″o-sta′bĭl). Not altered by drying.

siccus (sik′us) [L.]. Dry.

sick (sik). 1. Not in good health; afflicted by disease. 2. Affected with nausea.

sick bay (sik′ba). Hospital quarters on a naval vessel.

sicklemia (sik-le′me-ah). Sickle cell anemia.

sicklemic (sik-le′mik). Pertaining to or characterized by sicklemia.

sickling (sik′ling). The tendency toward development of sickle cells in the blood.

sickness (sik′nes). A condition or an episode marked by pronounced deviation from the normal healthy state; illness. **aerial s.,** air s. **African s.,** Congo trypanosomiasis. **air s.,** sickness due to change in air pressure and to the movements experienced in an airplane, marked by nausea, salivation and cold sweats. **airplane s.,** air s. **altitude s.,** a condition due to anoxia during high-altitude flying. See *altitude anoxia*, under *anoxia*. **athletes' s.,** weakness, blurred vision, nausea, and headache, following a short period of intense physical exercise, due to hypoglycemia. **aviation s.,** air s. **balloon s.,** a condition similar to mountain sickness occurring in aeronauts. **bay s.,** Haff disease. **black s.,** kala-azar. **Borna s.,** Borna disease. **bush s.,** enzootic marasmus; a disease of herbivorous animals in New Zealand marked by severe anemia and progressive emaciation and due to deficiency of cobalt in the soil and vegetation. **caisson s.,** decompression s. **car s.,** nausea and malaise produced by the motion of trains or automobiles or other vehicles. **cave s.,** a febrile disease of the lungs occurring in persons who were engaged in excavating in an abandoned chalk mine in Arkansas. **compressed-air s.,** decompression s. **decompression s.,** a disorder characterized by joint pains, respiratory manifestations, skin lesions, and neurologic signs, occurring in aviators flying at high altitudes and following rapid reduction of air pressure in persons who have been breathing compressed air in caissons and diving apparatus. **falling s.,** epilepsy. **flying s.,** aeroneurosis. **Gambian horse s.,** a fatal infection of horses and cattle throughout central Africa caused by *Trypanosoma congolense*. **grass s.,** a disorder occurring in western Australia, Queensland, and parts of Brazil, marked by vomiting after meals, and by some attributed to a spirochete in the stomach. Called also *gastric spirochetosis* and *Belyando sprue*. **green s.,** chlorosis. **horse s.,** an infectious disease of horses and mules in South Africa, caused by a virus and marked by serous exudations. Called also *pestis equorum*, *perdesiekte*, *pferdepest*, and *South African pferdesterbe*. **laughing s.,** pseudobulbar paralysis. **milk s.,** an acute disease caused by the ingestion of milk, milk products or the flesh of cattle which have a disease known as trembles. It is marked by weakness, anorexia, vomiting and constipation. See *trembles*. **morning s.,** the nausea of early pregnancy. **motion s.,** sickness caused by motion experienced in any kind of travel, such as sea sickness, train sickness, car sickness, and air sickness. **mountain s.,** a condition resulting from difficulties in adjusting to the diminished partial pressure of oxygen in mountain climbing, especially at altitudes above 12,000 feet. **protein s.,** symptoms, such as eruptions, fever, edema, and pain in the joints, following the injection of foreign proteins into the body. **radiation s.,** ill effects following exposure to radiant energy. **salt s.,** a form of cobalt deficiency; enzootic marasmus. **sea s.,** nausea and malaise caused by the motion of a ship. **serum s.,** a form of anaphylactic or allergic reaction following the injection of foreign serum and marked by urticarial rashes, edema, adenitis, joint pains, high fever, and prostration. Called also *serum disease*. **sleeping s.,** a disease characterized by increasing drowsiness and lethargy, caused by protozoan or microbial infection, such as Congo trypanosomiasis or lethargic encephalitis. **spotted s.,** pinta. **stiff s.,** ephemeral fever in horses. **sweating s.,** miliary fever. **talking s.,** epidemic encephalitis marked by extreme excitement, muscular twitching, and talkativeness. **three-day s.,** ephemeral fever in horses. **veldt s.,** hemoglobinuria of sheep. **vomiting s.,** a fatal disease in Jamaica due to eating damaged akee, the fruit of *Blighia sapida*. **x-ray s.,** a feeling of sickness and acute general symptoms which sometimes follow the application of massive doses of short wave roentgen and radium rays. Called also *radiation sickness*, *roentgenkater*.

Siddall test (sid′al) [A. C. *Siddall*, American physician, born 1897]. See under *tests*.

side (sīd). The lateral (right or left) portion or aspect of the body. **balancing s.,** the segment of a dentition or denture, on the side opposite to that toward which the mandible is moved. **working s.,** the segment of a denture or dentition on the same side as that toward which the mandible is moved.

side-bone (sīd′bōn). A condition of horses marked by ossification of the lateral cartilages of the third phalanx of the foot.

side-effect (sīd′ef-fekt). A consequence other than the one(s) for which an agent or measure is used; sometimes applied to adverse effects produced by a drug, especially on a system other than the one sought to be benefited by its administration.

sideration (sid″er-a′shun) [L. *siderari* to be blasted by a constellation]. 1. Sudden destruction of vital forces. 2. Therapeutical application of electric sparks.

siderinuria (sid″er-ĭ-nu′re-ah) [Gr. *sidēros* iron + *ouron* urine + *-ia*]. Excretion of iron in the urine.

siderism (sid′er-izm). Metallotherapy.

sidero- (sid′er-o) [Gr. *sidēros* iron]. Combining form denoting relationship to iron.

Siderobacter (sid″er-o-bak′ter). A genus of microorganisms of the family Siderocapsaceae, suborder Pseudomonadineae, order Pseudomonadales, occurring as bacilliform cells with rounded ends, singly, in pairs or short chains, or united to form colonies, with iron or manganese compounds in the membranes or on the surfaces of the cells.

It includes five species, *S. bre'vis*, *S. du'plex*, *S. gra'cilis*, *S. la'tus*, and *S. linea'ris.*

Siderocapsa (sid″er-o-kap′sah). A genus of microorganisms of the family Siderocapsaceae, suborder Pseudomonadineae, order Pseudomonadales, occurring as one to many small, ellipsoidal cells embedded in a primary capsule, with iron stored on the surface. It includes six species, *S. botryoi'des*, *S. corona'ta*, *S. eusphae'ra*, *S. ma'jor*, *S. monoe'ca*, and *S. treu'bii.*

Siderocapsaceae (sid″er-o-kap-sa′se-e). A family of microorganisms (order Pseudomonadales, suborder Pseudomonadineae), occurring as spherical, ellipsoidal, or bacilliform cells, frequently embedded in a thick mucilaginous capsule in which there may be deposits of iron or manganese compounds. It includes ten genera, *Ferribacterium*, *Ferrobacillus*, *Naumanniella*, *Ochrobium*, *Siderobacter*, *Siderocapsa*, *Siderococcus*, *Sideromonas*, *Sideronema*, and *Siderosphaera.*

Siderococcus (sid″er-o-kok′kus). A genus of microorganisms of the family Siderocapsaceae, suborder Pseudomonadineae, order Pseudomonadales, occurring as small coccoid cells without a gelatinous capsule. It includes two species, *S. commu'nis* and *S. limoni'ticus.*

siderocyte (sid′er-o-sīt). An erythrocyte containing non-hemoglobin iron.

sideroderma (sid″er-o-der′mah). Bronzed coloration of the skin from disorder of the metabolism of the iron from degenerated hemoglobin.

siderodromophobia (sid″er-o-dro″mo-fo′be-ah) [*sidero-* + Gr. *dromos* way + *phobein* to be affrighted by]. Morbid dread of railway travel.

siderofibrosis (sid″er-o-fi-bro′sis). Fibrosis of the spleen marked by iron-containing deposits.

siderogenous (sid″er-oj′e-nus) [*sidero-* + Gr. *gennan* to produce]. Producing or forming iron.

Sideromonas (sid″er-o-mo′nas). A genus of microorganisms of the family Siderocapsaceae, suborder Pseudomonadineae, order Pseudomonadales, occurring as short coccoid to rod-shaped cells embedded in a large capsule impregnated or completely encrusted with iron or manganese compounds. It includes four species, *S. conferva'rum*, *S. du'plex*, *S. ma'jor*, and *S. vulga'ris.*

Sideronema (sid″er-o-ne′mah). A genus of microorganisms of the family Siderocapsaceae, suborder Pseudomonadineae, order Pseudomonadales, occurring as coccoid cells in short chains, embedded in a gelatinous sheath. The type species is *S. globulife'rum.*

sideropenia (sid″er-o-pe′ne-ah) [*sidero-* + Gr. *penia* poverty]. Iron deficiency; deficiency of iron in the body.

sideropenic (sid″er-o-pe′nik). Pertaining to or characterized by deficiency of iron.

Siderophacus (sid″er-o′fah-kus) [*sidero-* + Gr. *phakos* lentil]. A genus of microorganisms of the family Caulobacteraceae, suborder Pseudomonadineae, order Pseudomonadales, occurring as biconcave or rodlike cells on horn-shaped stalks, in which ferric hydroxide accumulates. The type species is *S. corne'olus.*

siderophil (sid′er-o-fil). 1. Siderophilous. 2. A siderophilous tissue or structure.

siderophilin (si′der-of″ĭ-lin). Transferrin.

siderophilous (sid″er-of′ĭ-lus) [*sidero-* + Gr. *philein* to love]. Having a tendency to absorb iron.

siderophobia (sid″er-o-fo′be-ah). Siderodromophobia.

siderophone (sid′er-o-fōn) [*sidero-* + Gr. *phonē* voice]. An instrument for detecting, by a telephone-like arrangement, the presence of iron splinters in the eyeball.

sideroscope (sid′er-o-skōp) [*sidero-* + Gr. *skopein* to examine]. A magnet or other appliance for determining the presence of metallic iron as a foreign body in the eye.

siderosilicosis (sid″er-o-sil″ĭ-ko′sis). Pneumoconiosis due to the inhalation of iron-ore dust containing silica.

siderosis (sid″er-o′sis). 1. Pneumoconiosis due to the inhalation of iron or other metallic particles. 2. Excess of iron in the blood. 3. The deposit of iron in a tissue. **s. bul′bi,** the deposit of an iron pigment within the eyeball. **s. conjuncti′vae,** rust-colored conjunctivae. **hematogenous s.,** pigmentation with an iron compound derived from the blood. **hepatic s.,** the deposit of an abnormal quantity of iron in the liver. **urinary s.,** presence of hemosiderin granules in the urine. **xenogenous s.,** pigmentation with an iron oxide derived from a foreign body.

Siderosphaera (sid″er-o-sfe′rah). A genus of microorganisms of the family Siderocapsaceae, suborder Pseudomonadineae, order Pseudomonadales, occurring as small coccoid cells, in pairs and embedded in a primary capsule. The type species is *S. conglomera'ta.*

siderotic (sid″er-ot′ik). Pertaining to or characterized by siderosis.

siderous (sid′er-us). Containing iron.

Siebold's operation (se′boltz) [Karl Kaspar von *Siebold*, German surgeon, 1736–1807]. Hebotomy.

Siegert's sign (se′gertz) [Ferdinand *Siegert*, German pediatrician, born 1865]. See under *sign.*

Siegle's otoscope (ze′gelz) [Emil *Siegle*, French aurist in Stuttgart, 1833–1900]. See under *otoscope.*

Siemens' syndrome (se′menz) [Hermann Werner *Siemens*, German dermatologist, born 1891]. Hereditary ectodermal dysplasia.

Siemerling's nucleus (se′mer-lingz) [Ernst *Siemerling*, German neurologist and psychiatrist, 1857–1931]. See under *nucleus.*

Sieur's test (se-erz′) [Célestin *Sieur*, French surgeon, 1860–1955]. See *coin test*, under *tests.*

Sig. Abbreviation for L. *signe'tur*, let it be labeled.

sigaultian (se-go′she-an). Named for Jean René *Sigault*, French obstetrician of the 18th century.

sigh (si) [L. *suspirium*]. An audible and prolonged inspiration, followed by a shortened expiration.

sight (sīt). 1. The act or faculty of vision. 2. A thing seen. **day s.,** nyctalopia, or night blindness. **far s., long s.,** hypermetropia. **near s.,** myopia. **night s.,** hemeralopia, or day blindness. **old s.,** presbyopia. **short s.,** myopia.

sigillative (sij′ĭ-la″tiv) [L. *sigillum* mark]. Tending to cicatrization.

sigma (sig′mah). The eighteenth letter of the Greek alphabet σ, ς, or Σ: used as the symbol for one thousandth of a second, standard deviation, and summation.

sigmasism (sig′mah-sizm). Sigmatism.

sigmatism (sig′mah-tizm). The incorrect, difficult, or too frequent use of the *s* sound.

sigmoid (sig′moid) [L. *sigmoides;* Gr. *sigmoeidēs*]. 1. Shaped like the letter S, or like the Greek sigma (C). 2. The sigmoid flexure.

sigmoidectomy (sig″moid-ek′to-me). Excision of a portion of the sigmoid flexure.

sigmoiditis (sig″moid-i′tis). Inflammation of the sigmoid flexure.

sigmoidopexy (sig-moi′do-pek″se) [*sigmoid* + Gr. *pēxis* fixation]. The operation for rectal prolapse, done by making an incision in the lower abdomen, and pulling the sigmoid until the prolapse disappears, and then stitching the sigmoid to the abdominal wound.

sigmoidoproctostomy (sig-moi″do-prok-tos′to-me). The creation of an artificial opening at the junction of the sigmoid flexure and the rectum.

sigmoidorectostomy (sig-moi″do-rek-tos′to-me). Sigmoidoproctostomy.

sigmoidoscope (sig-moi′do-skōp) [*sigmoid* + Gr. *skopein* to examine]. A speculum for examining the sigmoid flexure.

sigmoidoscopy (sig″moid-os′ko-pe). Inspection of the sigmoid flexure by the aid of a long speculum (sigmoidoscope).

sigmoidosigmoidostomy (sig-moi″do-sig-moid-os′to-me). The operative formation of an anastomosis between two portions of the sigmoid.

sigmoidostomy (sig″moid-os′to-me) [*sigmoid* + Gr. *stomoun* to provide with a mouth, or opening]. The formation of an artificial opening from the surface of the body into the sigmoid flexure.

sigmoidotomy (sig″moid-ot′o-me). Operative incision into the sigmoid.

sigmoidovesical (sig-moi″do-ves′ĭ-kal). Pertaining to or communicating with the sigmoid flexure and the urinary bladder, as a sigmoidovesical fistula.

sigmoscope (sig′mo-skōp). Sigmoidoscope.

sigmoscopy (sig-mos′ko-pe). Sigmoidoscopy.

Sigmund's glands (zig′moonts) [Karl Ludwig *Sigmund*, Austrian physician, 1810–1883]. See under *gland*.

sign (sīn) [L. *signum*]. An indication of the existence of something; any objective evidence of a disease. **Aaron's s.,** a sensation of pain or distress in the epigastric or precordial region on pressure over McBurney's point in appendicitis. **Abadie's s.** 1. Spasm of the levator palpebrae superioris muscle; a sign of exophthalmic goiter. 2. Insensibility of the Achilles tendon to pressure; seen in locomotor ataxia. **abdominocardiac s.** See *Livierato's test*, def. 1. **Abrahams' s.** 1. A sound between dull and flat obtained on percussion over the acromion process in early tuberculosis of the apex of the lung. 2. Acute pain produced in vesical lithiasis when pressure is applied midway between the umbilicus and the ninth right costal cartilage. **accessory s.,** any nonpathognomonic sign of disease. **Ahlfeld's s.,** Hicks's s. **air-cushion s.,** Klemm's s. **Allis' s.,** relaxation of the fascia between the crest of the ilium and the greater trochanter: a sign of fracture of the neck of the femur. **Amoss' s.,** in case of painful flexure of the spine, the patient, when rising to a sitting posture from lying in bed, does so by supporting himself with his hands placed far behind him in the bed. **Andral's s.** See under *decubitus*. **André-Thomas s.,** if during the finger to nose test, the patient is directed to raise his arm over his head and is then suddenly ordered to let it fall to his head, the arm will rebound: seen in disease of the cerebellum. **Anghelescu's s.,** inability to bend the spine while lying on the back so as to rest on the head and heels alone, seen in tuberculosis of the vertebrae. **antecedent s.,** any precursory indication of an attack of disease. **anterior tibial s.,** involuntary extension of the tibialis anterior muscle when the thigh is forcibly flexed on the abdomen: seen in spastic paraplegia. **anticus s.,** Piotrowski's s. **Argyll Robertson pupil s.** See under *pupil*. **Arnoux's s.,** a sign of twin pregnancy, consisting of a peculiar rhythm in the fetal heart beat produced by the action of the two hearts and resembling the sound of the hoofs of a pair of trotting horses. **Arroyo's s.,** asthenocoria. **Ascher's s.,** oculocardiac reflex. **assident s.,** accessory s. **Auenbrugger's s.,** a bulging of the epigastrium, due to extensive pericardial effusion. **Aufrecht's s.,** a feeble breathing sound heard just above the jugular fossa, indicative of tracheal stenosis. **Babés s.,** tenderness over the splenic artery together with muscular rigidity, indicative of aneurysm of the abdominal aorta. **Babinski's s's.** 1. Loss or lessening of the Achilles tendon reflex in sciatica: this distinguishes it from hysteric sciatica. 2. Babinski's reflex. 3. In hemiplegia the contraction of the platysma muscle in the healthy side is more vigorous than on the affected side, as seen in opening the mouth, whistling, blowing, etc. 4. The patient lies on the floor, with arms crossed upon his chest, and then makes an effort to rise to the sitting posture. On the paralyzed side the thigh is flexed upon the pelvis and the heel is lifted from the ground, while on the healthy side the limb does not move. This phenomenon is repeated when the patient resumes the lying posture. It is seen in organic hemiplegia, but not in hysterical hemiplegia. Called also *combined flexion phenomenon*. 5. When the paralyzed forearm is placed in supination it turns over to pronation: seen in organic paralysis. Called also *pronation sign*. **Baccelli's s.,** whisper heard over the chest in patients with pleural effusion. **Baillarger's s.,** inequality of the pupils in paralytic dementia. **Ballance's s.,** resonance of right flank when patient lies on the left side: seen in splenic rupture. **Ballet's s.,** ophthalmoplegia externa, with loss of all voluntary eye movements, the pupil movements and automatic eye movements persisting: seen in exophthalmic goiter and hysteria. **Bamberger's s.** 1. Allochiria. 2. Presence of signs of consolidation at the angle of the scapula, which disappear when the patient leans forward: sign of pericardial effusion. **bandage s.,** the appearance of fine petechiae when a moderately tight bandage is applied to the arm near the elbow: seen in purpura and hemorrhagic states. **Bárány's s.** See under *symptom*. **Bard's s.,** in organic nystagmus the oscillations of the eye increase as the patient's attention follows the finger moved alternately from one side to the other; but in congenital nystagmus the oscillations disappear in like condition. **Baron's s.,** sensitiveness to pressure over the right psoas muscle points to chronic appendicitis. **Barré's s.,** contraction of the iris is retarded in mental deterioration. **Barré's pyramidal s.,** the patient lies face down and the legs are flexed at the knee; he is unable to hold the legs in this vertical position if there is disease of the pyramidal tracts. **Baruch's s.,** resistance of the temperature in the rectum to a bath of 75°F. for fifteen minutes; a sign of typhoid fever. **Bassler's s.,** in chronic appendicitis, a sharp pain is caused by pinching the appendix between the thumb and the iliacus muscle. The procedure is carried out by pressing the tip of the thumb into the abdominal wall midway between the umbilicus and the anterior superior spine of the ilium and then pressing to the right. **Bastedo's s.,** the production of pain and tenderness in the right iliac fossa (at McBurney's point) on inflation of the colon with air by means of a rectal tube: seen in latent or chronic appendicitis. **Bastian-Bruns' s.** See under *law*. **Battle's s.,** discoloration in the line of the posterior auricular artery, the ecchymosis first appearing near the tip of the mastoid process: seen in fracture of the base of the skull. **Baumès' s.,** retrosternal pain as an indication of angina pectoris. **Beccaria's s.,** a painful sense of pulsation in the occiput in pregnancy. **Bechterew's s.** 1. In tabes dorsalis, anesthesia of the popliteal space. 2. Bechterew's reflex. **Becker's s.,** increase of pulsation in the retinal arteries in exophthalmic goiter. **Béclard's s.,** a sign of the maturity of the fetus consisting of a center of ossification in the lower epiphysis of the femur. **Beevor's s.** 1. A sign of functional paralysis consisting in inability of the patient to inhibit the antagonistic muscles. 2. In paralysis of the lower parts of the recti abdominis muscles there is upward excursion of the umbilicus. **Béhier-Hardy s.,** aphonia in the early stages of pulmonary gangrene. **Bell's s.** See under *phenomenon*. **Benzadón's s.,** retraction of the nipple when it is held between the fingers and given a movement of expression at the same time at which the tumor is repelled inwardly with the other fingers. **Berger's s.,** an irregular-shaped or elliptical pupil in the early stages of tabes dorsalis, paralytic dementia, and certain paralyses. **Bespaloff's s.,** in the early stage of measles the ear drum is red and there is nasopharyngeal catarrh. **Bethea's s.,** when the examiner standing back of the patient places his fingers so that the tips rest on the upper surfaces of corresponding ribs high up in the patient's axillae, unilateral impairment of expansion is accurately indicated by the lessened degree of respiratory movement of the ribs on the side affected. **Bezold's s.,** an inflammatory swelling below the apex of the mastoid process; an evidence of mastoiditis. **Biederman's s.,** dark red color (instead of the normal pink) of the anterior pillars of the throat, seen in some syphilitic patients. **Bieg's entotic s.,** when sounds are heard by the patient only when spoken through an ear trumpet, joined by a catheter to the eustachian tube, disease of the malleus or incus is indicated. **Biermer's s.,** the metallic resonance over hydropneumothorax varies in pitch with change of position of the patient. Called also *Biermer's change of note*. **Biernacki's s.,** analgesia of the ulnar nerve in paretic dementia and tabes dorsalis. **Binda's s.,** a sudden movement of the shoulder when the head is passively and sharply turned toward the other side, an early sign of tuberculous meningitis. **Biot's s.** See under *respiration*. **Bird's s.,** a definite zone of dulness with absence of the respiratory sounds in hydatid disease of the lung. **Bjerrum's s.** See under *scotoma*. **Blatin's s.,** hydatid thrill. **Blumberg's s.,** pain on abrupt release of steady pressure over the site of a suspected abdominal lesion indicates peritonitis. Repeated comparison of the pain felt on application and release has prognostic significance: a comparative increase in the release pain indicates advancing peritonitis; a comparative decrease indicates the lesion is subsiding. **Blumer's s.** See under *shelf*. **Boas's s.** 1. Lactic acid in the gastric juice in certain cases of cancer of the stomach. 2. In cholecystitis there is often an area of epicritic hyperesthesia in the lumbar region. **Bolognini's s.,** a sensation of friction observed on alternate pressure with the fingers of both hands on the right and left sides of the belly: an early indication of measles. **Bolt's s.,** in ruptured tubal pregnancy: severe tenderness on lifting the uterine cervix. **Bonnet's s.,** pain on thigh adduction in sciatica. **Bordier-Fränkel s.,** an outward and upward rolling of the eye in peripheral fascial paralysis. **Borsieri's s.,** when the fingernail is drawn along the skin in early stages of scarlet fever, a white line is left which quickly turns red. **Boston's s.,** in exophthalmic goiter, when the eyeball is turned downward there is arrest of descent of the lid, spasm, and continued descent. **Bouchard's s.,** a few drops of Fehling's solution are added to the urine and the mixture is shaken; if pus from the kidney is present, fine bubbles will form which push to the surface the coagulum formed by heating. **Bouillaud's s.** 1. A peculiar tinkling at the right side of the apex beat in hypertrophy of the heart. 2. Permanent retraction of the chest in the precordial region: a sign of adherent pericardium. **Bouveret's s.,** distention of the cecum and right iliac fossa in obstruction of the large intestine. **bowed head s.,** Gould's bowed-head s. **Boyce's s.,** a gurgling sound heard on pressure by the hand on the side of the neck, in diverticulum of the esophagus. **Bozzolo's s.,** a visible pulsation of the arteries within the nostrils: said to indicate aneurysm of the thoracic aorta. **Bragard's s.,** with the knee stiff the lower extremity is flexed at the hip until the patient experiences pain: the foot is then dorsiflexed. Increase of pain points to nerve involvement; no increase of pain indicates muscular involvement. **Branham's s.,** closure of an arteriovenous fistula by digital pressure results in slowing of the pulse, increased diastolic pressure, and disappearance of the cardiac murmur. **Braun-Fernwald s.** (*of pregnancy*), asymmetrical enlargement of the uterus, one side being greater than the other, with a longitudinal line or furrow separating the two. **Braunwald s.,** occurrence of a weak pulse instead of a strong one immediately after a ventricular premature contraction. **Braxton Hicks s.,** Hicks's s. **Brenner's s.,** a metallic rub over the twelfth left rib behind when the patient sits up, heard in perforation of the stomach and caused by bubbles of air collecting between the stomach and the diaphragm. **Brickner's s.,** diminished oculoauricular associated movements seen in impairment of function of the facial nerve. **Brissaud-Marie s.,** hysterical glossolabial hemispasm. **Brittain's s.,** palpation of the lower right abdominal quadrant produces retraction of the right testicle in cases of gangrenous appendicitis. **Broadbent's s.,** a retraction seen on the back, near the eleventh and twelfth ribs, on the left side, due to pericardial adhesion. **Broadbent's inverted s.,** pulsations synchronizing with ventricular systole on the posterior lateral wall of the chest in aneurysm of the left auricle. **Brodie's s.** 1. A black spot on the glans penis: a sign of urinary extravasation into the spongiosum. 2. Brodie's pain. **Brown's dipping crackle s.,** a fine crackling sound heard on placing the stethoscope over the right iliac fossa and dipping suddenly with it: heard in intestinal perforation in typhoid fever. **Brown's gravitation s.,** the area of tenderness in the lower abdomen is marked out. The patient is then turned on the unaffected side. If, in fifteen to thirty minutes, the tenderness has moved one or two inches, or if the tenderness and rigidity should become marked, immediate operation is indicated. **Brown-Séquard's s.** See under *syndrome*. **Brudzinski's s.** 1. In meningitis, when the neck of the patient is bent, flexure movements of the ankle, knee, and hip are produced. 2. In meningitis, when passive flexion of the lower limb on one side is made, a similar movement will be seen in the opposite limb: called also *contralateral sign*. **Brunati's s.,** the appearance of opacities in the cornea during the course of pneumonia or typhoid fever; it points to impending death. **Bruns's s.,** intermittent headache, vertigo, vomiting, etc., on suddenly moving the head in cysticercus disease of the fourth ventricle. **Bryant's s.,** lowering of the axillary folds in dislocation of the shoulder. **Bryson's s.,** lessened power of expansion of the thorax, sometimes noticed in exophthalmic goiter. **Burger's s.,** Garel's s. **Burghart's s.** See under *symptom*. **burning-drops s.,** a sensation as of drops or streams of hot liquid in the abdominal cavity: sometimes observed in perforating gastric ulcer. **Burton's s.,** blue line. **Cantelli's s.,** dissociation between the movements of the head and eyes: as the head is raised the eyes are lowered, and *vice versa*. Called also *doll's eye s.* **Carabelli's s.** See under *tubercle*. **Cardarelli's s.,** transverse pulsation of the laryngotracheal tube in aneurysms and in dilatation of the arch of the aorta. **cardiac s.,** a sign of cancer, consisting of marked diminution in the area of cardiac dulness when the patient is in the recumbent position. Called also *Gordon's s.* **cardiorespiratory s.,** a change in the normal pulse-respiration ratio from 4:1 to 2:1; seen in infantile scurvy. **Carman's s.,** meniscus sign. **Carnett's s.,** the test for demonstrating parietal tenderness consists of palpation during a period in which the patient holds his anterior abdominal muscles as tense as possible. The tense abdominal muscles prevent the examiner's fingers from coming in contact with the underlying viscera and any tenderness that is elicited over them will be parietal in location. Tenderness which is elicited over relaxed muscles may be either parietal or intra-abdominal in origin. Tenderness present with relaxed muscles and absent with tense muscles is due to a subparietal lesion and its cause should be sought inside of the abdomen. Tenderness which is found both when the muscles are relaxed and when they are voluntarily tensed is due to an anterior parietal lesion and its cause should be sought outside of the abdominal cavity. **Castellino's s.,** Cardarelli's s. **Cattaneo's s.,** if, following strong percussion over the spinous processes of the dorsal vertebrae, reddish spots appear directly over the processes, tracheobronchial adenopathy is indicated. **Cejka's s.,** invariability of the cardiac dulness during the different phases of respiration: a sign of adherent pericardium. **Cestan's s.,** Dutemps and Cestan s. **Chaddock's s.,** extension of big toe on irritating the skin in the external malleolar region: seen in lesions of the corticospinal paths. Called also *external malleolar s.* **Chadwick's s.,** Jacquemier's s. **chair s.,** pain passing upward from the anus on sitting down; seen in enterocolitis.

Charcot's s. 1. The raising of the eyebrow in peripheral facial paralysis, and the lowering of the same part in facial contraction. 2. Intermittent limping in arteriosclerosis of the legs and feet. **Charcot-Vigouroux s.,** Vigouroux's s. **Chase's s.,** pain in the cecal region, felt when the examiner's hand is passed quickly and deeply along the transverse colon from left to right, the descending colon being closed by pressing deeply with the other hand. **Chaussier's s.,** pain in the epigastrium preceding eclampsia. **Cheyne-Stokes s.** See under *respiration.* **Chilaiditi s.,** interposition of a loop of bowel between the liver and the diaphragm. **chin-retraction s.,** a sign of the third stage of anesthesia: the chin and larynx move downward during inspiration. **Chvostek's s., Chvostek-Weiss s.,** a spasm of the facial muscles resulting from tapping the muscles or the branches of the facial nerve: seen in tetany. **Clark's s.,** obliteration of hepatic dulness, due to the tympanitic distention of the abdomen. **Claude's hyperkinesis s.,** reflex movements of paretic muscles elicited by painful stimuli. **clavicular s.,** a tumefaction at the inner third of the right clavicle: seen in congenital syphilis. Called also *Higouménakis's s.* **Claybrook's s.,** a sign of rupture of the abdominal viscera, consisting in the transmission of the sounds of the heart beat and of respiration so that they can be heard over the abdomen, the transmission of the sounds being due to the presence of fluid, exudate, or blood. **Cleeman's s.,** creasing of the skin just above the patella, indicative of fracture of the femur with overriding of fragments. **Cloquet's needle s.,** a clean needle is plunged into the biceps muscle; if life is not extinct, it soon oxidizes. **Codman's s.,** in ruptured supraspinatus tendon: the arm can be passively abducted without pain, but when support of the arm is removed and the deltoid contracts suddenly, pain occurs again. **cogwheel s.** See under *phenomenon.* **coin s.** See under *tests.* **Cole's s.,** deformity of the duodenal contour as seen in the roentgenogram, a sign of the presence of duodenal ulcer. **Comby's s.,** whitish patches on the buccal mucosa and the gums: an early sign of measles. **commemorative s.,** any sign of a previous disease. **Comolli's s.,** a sign of scapular fracture consisting in the appearance in the scapular region, shortly after the accident, of a triangular swelling reproducing the shape of the body of the scapula. **complimentary opposition s.,** Grasset, Gaussel, and Hoover s. **contralateral s.,** Brudzinski's s., def. 2. **Coopernail s.,** ecchymosis on the perineum and scrotum or labia: a sign of fracture of the pelvis. **Cope's s.** 1. Tenderness over the appendix on stretching the psoas muscle by extending the thigh. 2. Tenderness elicited by compressing the femoral artery in Scarpa's triangle: in appendicitis. **Cornel's s.,** tenderness over the phrenic nerve pressure point in malaria. **Corrigan's s.** 1. A purple line at the junction of the teeth with the gum in chronic copper poisoning. 2. A peculiar expanding pulsation indicative of aneurysm of the abdominal aorta. See also *Corrigan's pulse*, under *pulse.* 3. Corrigan's respiration. **coughing s.,** Huntington's s. **Couillard's s.,** redness and prominence of the fungiform papillae of the tongue: seen in ascariasis. **Courtois s.,** the comatose patient is placed on his back; flexion of the head on the chest produces in only one region an automatic flexion of the leg on the thigh and the thigh on the abdomen; this movement is strictly unilateral, and on the side on which the anatomic examination revealed a localized lesion of the cerebral centers which had produced the comatose state. **Courvoisier's s.** See under *law.* **Crichton-Browne's s.,** tremor of the outer angles of the eyes and of the labial commissures in the earlier stages of paretic dementia. **Crowe's s.,** engorgement of the retinal vessels on unilateral compression of the jugular vein on the healthy side: seen in sinus thrombosis. **Cruveilhier's s.,** a swelling in the groin is palpated when the patient coughs: in saphenous varix there is felt a tremor as of a jet of water entering and filling the pouch. **Cullen's s.,** discoloration of the skin about the umbilicus, regarded as a sign of ruptured extrauterine pregnancy. A similar discoloration is seen in acute pancreatitis. **Dalrymple's s.,** abnormal wideness of the palpebral opening in exophthalmic goiter. **D'Amato's s.,** in pleural effusion: the location of dulness is altered from the vertebral area in the sitting position to the heart region when the patient assumes a lateral position on the side opposite the effusion. **Damoiseau's s.,** Ellis' line. **Dance's s.,** depression in the right iliac region in intussusception. **Danforth's s.,** shoulder pain on inspiration in ruptured tubal pregnancy. **Davidsohn's s.,** decrease of illumination of the pupil on transillumination with an electric light placed in the mouth: indicates tumor or fluid in the maxillary antrum. **Davis' s.,** an empty state and a yellowish or pale tint of the pulseless arteries; a sign of death. **Dawbarn's s.,** in acute subacromial bursitis, when the arm hangs by the side palpation over the bursa causes pain, but when the arm is abducted this pain disappears. **Dejerine's s.,** aggravation of symptoms of radiculitis produced by coughing, sneezing, and straining at stool. **de la Camp's s.,** relative dulness over and at each side of the fifth and sixth vertebrae in tuberculosis of the bronchial lymph nodes. **Delbet's s.,** in aneurysm of the main artery of a limb, if the nutrition of the part distal to the aneurysm is maintained, although the pulse may have disappeared, the collateral circulation is sufficient. **Delmege's s.,** deltoid flattening, an early sign of phthisis. **Demarquay's s.,** fixation or lowering of the larynx during phonation and deglutition; a sign of syphilis of the trachea. **Demianoff's s.,** a sign that permits the differentiation of pain originating in the sacrolumbalis muscles from lumbar pain of any other origin. The sign is obtained by placing the patient in dorsal decubitus and lifting his extended leg. In the presence of lumbago this produces a pain in the lumbar region which prevents raising the leg high enough to form an angle of 10 degrees, or even less, with the table or bed on which the patient reposes. The pain is due to the stretching of the sacrolumbalis. **de Musset's s.,** rhythmical oscillation of the head caused by pulsations of the carotid arteries: a sign of aortic insufficiency. **de Mussy's s.,** the presence in the left hypochondriac region of a spot intensely painful on pressure: an indication of diaphragmatic pleurisy. **Desault's s.,** a sign of intracapsular fracture of the femur, consisting of alteration of the arc described by rotation of the great trochanter, which normally describes the segment of a circle, but in this fracture rotates only as the apex of the femur as it rotates about its own axis. **d'Espine's s.** 1. In the normal person, on auscultation over the spinous processes, pectoriloquy ceases at the bifurcation of the trachea, and in infants opposite the seventh cervical vertebra. If pectoriloquy is heard lower than this it indicates enlargement of the bronchial lymph nodes. 2. In pulmonary tuberculosis the bronchophony over the spinous processes is heard at a lower level than in health. **Dew's s.,** in diaphragmatic hydatid abscess beneath the right cupola, the area of resonance moves caudally with the patient on hands and knees. **Dewees' s.,** expectoration of tough whitish mucus by pregnant women. **Dixon Mann's s.,** Mann's s. **doll's eye s.** See *Cantelli's s.* and *Widowitz's s.* **Donnelly's s.,** pain on pressure over and below McBurney's point with the right leg extended and adducted in retrocecal appendicitis. **Dorendorf's s.,** fulness of the supraclavicular groove on one side in aneurysm of the aortic arch. **Drummond's s.,** a whiff heard at the open mouth during respiration in cases of aortic aneurysm. **D.T.P. s.** (*distal tingling on percussion*), Tinel's s. **Dubard's s.,** tenderness on pressure over the right pneumogastric nerve in the neck: in appendicitis. **Du Bois's s.**, shortness of the little finger in congenital syphilis. **Duchenne's s.**, the sinking in of the epigastrium on inspiration in paralysis of the diaphragm or in certain cases of hydropericardium. **Duckworth's s.**, seemingly complete stoppage of respiration several hours before stoppage of the heart beat; seen in conditions of intracranial pressure. **duct s.**, a red spot seen at the orifice of Steno's duct in mumps. **Dugas's s.**, inability to place the hand on the shoulder of the other side while the elbow rests on the chest; seen in shoulder dislocation. **Duncan-Bird s.**, Bird's s. **Dupuytren's s.** 1. A crackling sensation on pressure over a sarcomatous bone. 2. In congenital dislocation of the head of the femur there is a free up-and-down movement of the head of the bone. **Duroziez's s.** See under *murmur*. **Dutemps and Cestan s.**, a sign of complete peripheral paralysis: when the patient is asked to look forward, and then attempts to close both eyes slowly, the upper lid on the paralyzed side moves upward a trifle, owing to the action of the levator palpebrae superioris. **Ebstein's s.**, obtuseness of the cardiohepatic angle in large pericardial effusions. **echo s.** 1. A percussion sound resembling an echo which is heard over a hydatid cyst. 2. The repetition of the last word or clause of a sentence, seen in certain brain diseases; echolalia. **Elliot's s.** 1. Induration of the edge of a syphilitic skin lesion. 2. A scotoma extending from the blind spot and made up of numerous points or spots. **Ellis' s.**, the peculiar curved line of dulness discoverable during resorption of a pleuritic exudate. **Ely's s.**, with the patient prone, flexion of the leg on the thigh causes the pelvis to rise from the table: in sacro-iliac disease. **Erb's s.** 1. Increased electric irritability of motor nerves in cases of tetany. 2. Dulness in percussion over the manubrium of the sternum in acromegalia. **Erben's s.** See under *reflex*. **Erb-Westphal s.**, loss of the patellar reflex seen in tabes dorsalis and in some other spinal diseases. **Erichsen's s.**, when the iliac bones are sharply pressed toward each other pain is felt in sacro-iliac disease but not in hip disease. **Erni's s.**, the cavernous tympany developed over an apical cavity that has previously been filled with fluid. Sometimes gently rapping over such a filled cavity with a hard instrument will excite coughing, which will expel the secretion, and thus the cavernous signs are developed. **Escherich's s.**, muscular contraction of the lips in the form of a goat's snout, produced by percussion of the labial mucosa. **ether s.**, a sign of death: 1 or 2 cc. of ether is injected subcutaneously. If the ether spurts back when the needle is withdrawn, death has occurred. Its absorption indicates that life still persists. **Eustace Smith's s.**, Smith's s. **Ewart's s.** 1. Undue prominence of the sternal end of the first rib in certain cases of pericardial effusion. 2. Bronchial breathing and dulness on percussion at the lower angle of the left scapula in pericardial effusion. **Ewing s.**, tenderness at the upper inner angle of the orbit: a sign of obstruction of the outlet of the frontal sinus. **external malleolar s.**, Chaddock's s. **extinction s.**, extinction of the eruption over an area about the size of the palm when normal human serum is injected intracutaneously; characteristic of the eruption of scarlet fever. **fabere s.** See *Patrick's test*, under *tests*. **facial s.**, Chvostek's s. **Faget's s.**, a fall in the pulse rate while the fever remains high or rises; seen in yellow fever. **Fajersztajn's crossed sciatic s.**, in sciatica, when the leg is flexed, the hip can also be flexed, but not if the leg be held straight; flexing sound thigh with leg straight causes pain on affected side. **fan s.**, spreading apart of the toes following the stroking of the sole of the foot with a dull needle. It forms part of the Babinski reflex. **Federici's s.**, on auscultating the abdomen the heart sounds can be heard in cases of intestinal perforation with gas in the peritoneal cavity. **femoral s.**, Cope's s., def. 2. **Filipovitch's s.**, the yellow discoloration of prominent parts of the palms and soles in typhoid fever. **Fischer's s.**, on auscultation over the manubrium with the patient's head bent backward there is sometimes heard, in tuberculosis of the bronchial glands, a murmur due to pressure of the glands on the innominate veins. **Fisher's s.**, a presystolic murmur in certain cases of adherent pericardium. **flag s.**, variation in color of the hair, seen in children recovering from kwashiorkor, when the color is changing from orange back to black. **Flint's s.** See under *murmur*. **flush-tank s.**, the passage of a large amount of urine and the coincident temporary disappearance of a lumbar swelling: a sign of hydronephrosis. **Fodéré's s.**, edema of the lower eyelids in patients with retention of chlorides and urea. **Forchheimer's s.**, the presence of a reddish eruption on the soft palate in rubella. **forearm s.**, Leri's s. **formication s.**, Tinel's s. **Fournier's s.** 1. The sharp delimitation characteristic of a syphilitic skin lesion. 2. Saber shin. **Francke's s.**, deep tenderness over the apex of the lung behind. **Frank's s.**, pseudohemophilia hepatica. **Fränkel's s.**, diminished tonicity of the hip joint muscles in tabes dorsalis. **Frantzel's s.**, the murmur in mitral stenosis is louder at the beginning and at the end of diastole. **Frédéricq's s.**, the presence of a red line on the gums in pulmonary tuberculosis. **Friedreich's s.** 1. Diastolic collapse of the cervical veins due to adherent pericardium. 2. Lowering of the pitch of the percussion note over an area of cavitation during forced inspiration. Called also *Friedreich's change of note*. **Froment's paper s.**, flexion of the distal phalanx of the thumb when a sheet of paper is held between the thumb and index finger; seen in affections of the ulnar nerve. **Fürbringer's s.**, in cases of subphrenic abscess the respiratory movements will be transmitted to a needle inserted into the abscess, which is thus distinguished from abscess above the diaphragm. **Gaénslen's s.**, with the patient on his back on the operating table, the knee and hip of one leg are held in flexed position by the patient, while the other leg, hanging over the edge of the table, is pressed down by the operator to produce hyperextension of the hip: pain occurs on the affected side in lumbosacral disease. **Galeazzi's s.**, in congenital dislocation of the hip: curvature of the spine observed when the patient stands, produced by the shortened leg. **Gangolphe's s.**, a serosanguineous abdominal effusion in strangulated hernia. **Garel's s.**, absence of light perception on the affected side of the antrum of Highmore on electric transillumination; seen in diseases of the antrum of Highmore. **Gauss' s.**, abnormal mobility of the uterus in the first month of pregnancy. **Gerhardt's s.** 1. The absence of laryngeal movements in dyspnea due to aneurysm of the aorta. 2. Change of percussion sound on change of the patient's position; seen in pneumothorax and in pulmonary tuberculosis. Called also *Gerhardt's change of tone*. **Gianelli's s.**, Tournay's s. **Gifford's s.**, inability to evert the upper lid; seen in exophthalmic goiter. **Gilbert's s.**, opsiuria indicative of hepatic cirrhosis. **Glasgow's s.**, a systolic sound in the brachial artery in latent aneurysm of the aorta. **Goggia's s.**, in health, the fibrillary contraction produced by striking and then pinching the brachial biceps extends throughout the whole muscle: in debilitating disease, such as typhoid fever, the contraction is local. **Golden's s.**, paleness of the cervix uteri: regarded as a sign of tubal pregnancy. **Goldstein's s.**, wide space of distance between the great toe and the adjoining toe seen in cretinism and mongolian idiocy. **Goldthwait's s.**, the patient lying supine, his leg is raised by the examiner with one hand, the other hand being placed under the patient's lower back; leverage is then applied to the side of the pelvis. If pain is felt by the patient before the lumbar spine is moved, the lesion is a sprain of the sacroiliac joint. If pain does not appear until after the lumbar spine moves, the lesion is in the sacroiliac or lumbosacral articulation. **Golonbov's s.**, tenderness on percussion over the tibia in chlorosis. **Goodell's s.**, if the cervix uteri is as soft as one's lip the woman is pregnant; if it is as hard as one's nose, she is not. **Gordon's s.** 1. [A. Gordon]. Finger phenomenon. 2. [W. Gordon]. Cardiac sign. **Gould's bowed-head s.**, the bowing of the head in walking to see the ground in any destructive disease of the peripheral portion of the retina: this act brings the image upon the functioning part of the retina. **Gowers' s.**, abrupt intermittent oscillation of the iris under the influence of light: seen in certain stages of tabes dorsalis. **Graefe's s.**, failure of the upper lid to move downward promptly and evenly with the eyeball in looking downward, instead it moves tardily and jerkingly; seen in exophthalmic goiter. **Grancher's s.**, equality of pitch between expiratory and inspiratory murmurs; a sign of obstruction to expiration. **Granger's s.**, if in the radiograph of an infant two years old or less the anterior wall of the lateral sinus is visible, extensive destruction of the mastoid is indicated. **Granström's s.**, marked tortuosity of the retinal arteries, said to occur characteristically in aortic coarctation. **Grasset's s., Grasset-Bychowski s.**, Grasset's phenomenon. **Grasset, Gaussel, and Hoover s.**, when the patient in a recumbent position attempts to lift the paretic limb, there is greater downward pressure on the examiner's hand with the sound limb than is observed in the test with a normal person. **Gray's s.** 1. Tenderness on pressure with the finger $1\frac{1}{2}$ inch-below and to the left of the umbilicus: in appendicitis. 2. Pain in the shoulder in appendicitis. **Greene's s.**, outward displacement of the free cardiac border by the expiratory movement in pleuritic effusion. It is detected by percussion. **Gregory's s.**, Rovsing's s. **Grey-Turner s.**, Turner's s. **Griesinger's s.**, edematous swelling behind the mastoid process; seen in thrombosis of the transverse sinus. **Griesinger-Kussmaul s.**, paradoxical pulse. **Grisolle's s.**, if, on stretching an affected portion of the skin, the papule becomes impalpable to the touch, the eruption is caused by measles; if, on the contrary, the papule can still be felt, the eruption is one of smallpox. **Grocco's s.** 1. A sign of pleural effusion consisting in the presence of a triangular area of dulness (*Grocco's triangle*) on the back, on the side opposite to that on which the effusion is present. Called also *Grocco's triangular dulness.* 2. Acute dilatation of the heart produced by muscular effort in the early stages of exophthalmic goiter. 3. Extension of the liver dulness to the left of the midspinal line, indicating enlargement of the organ. **Grossman's s.**, dilatation of the heart as a sign of early pulmonary tuberculosis. **Gubler's s.**, a swelling on the wrist in lead poisoning. **Guilland's s.**, brisk flexion at the hip and knee joint when the contralateral quadriceps muscle is pinched: a sign of meningeal irritation. **Gunn's s.**, a raising of a ptosed eyelid on opening the mouth and moving the jaw toward the opposite side. **Gunn's crossing s.**, a crossing of an artery over a vein in the fundus of the eye, indicative of essential hypertension. **Günzberg's s.**, a resonant area between the gallbladder and the pylorus with localized borborygmi; seen in duodenal ulcer. **Guttmann's s.**, a humming sound heard over the thyroid in exophthalmic goiter. **Guye's s.**, aprosexia in children with adenoids. **Guyon's s.**, the ballottement and palpation of a floating kidney. **Hahn's s.**, persistent rotation of the head from side to side in cerebellar disease of childhood. **Halban's s.**, increased growth of the fine hair of the face and body during pregnancy. **Hall's s.**, a tracheal diastolic shock felt in aneurysm of the aorta. **halo s.**, a halo effect produced in the roentgenogram of the fetal head between the subcutaneous fat and the cranium; said to be indicative of intrauterine death of the fetus. **Hamman's s.**, a loud crunching, clicking sound, synchronous with the heart beat, heard in mediastinal emphysema. **Hassin's s.**, protrusion and backward drawing of the pinna of the ear seen in lesions of the cervical sympathetic nerves. **Hatchcock's s.**, tenderness on running the finger toward the angle of the jaw in mumps. **Haudek's s.**, a projecting shadow in radiographs of penetrating gastric ulcer, due to settlement of bismuth in pathologic niches of the stomach wall. Called also *Haudek's niche.* **Heberden's s's.** See under *node.* **Hefke-Turner s.**, a widening and change in contour of the normal obturator x-ray shadow, indicative of pathologic condition of the hip joint. Called also *obturator sign.* **Hegar's s.**, softening of the lower segment of the uterus: an indication of pregnancy. **Heilbronner's s.** See under *thigh.* **Heim-Kreysig s.**, a depression of the intercostal spaces occurring along with the cardiac systole in adherent pericarditis. **Helbing's s.**, medialward curving of the Achilles tendon as viewed from behind: seen in flatfoot. **Hellat's s.**, in mastoid suppuration a tuning-fork placed on the diseased area is heard for a shorter time than when placed on any other part. **Hellendall's s.**, Cullen's s. **Hennebert's s.**, in the labyrinthitis of congenital syphilis compression of the air in the external auditory canal produces a rotatory nystagmus to the diseased side; rarefaction of the air in the canal produces a nystagmus to the opposite side. Called also *pneumatic sign* or *test.* **Hernig-Lommel s.**, respiratory arrhythmia. **Hertwig-Magendie s.**, Magendie-Hertwig s. **Hertzel's s.**, if in the normal person the circulation of both legs and one arm is entirely stopped by pneumatic pressure, the blood pressure in the other arm rises about 5 mm. Hg. In arteriosclerosis, however, there is a rise as high as 60 mm. Hg. **Heryng's s.**, an infra-orbital shadow produced by pus in the maxillary antrum and observable by electric illumination of the buccal cavity. **Hicks's s.**, intermittent contraction of the uterus after the third month of pregnancy. **Higouménakis's s.**, clavicular s. **Hirschberg's s.**, internal rotation and adduction of the foot on rubbing the inner lateral side of the foot: seen in disease of the pyramidal tract. **Hochsinger's s.** 1. Indicanuria in the tuberculosis of childhood. 2. Closure of the hand when pressure is applied to the inside of the biceps muscle: seen in tetany. **Hoehne's s.**, absence of uterine contractions during delivery despite repeated injections of hypophyseal preparations, regarded as a sign of rupture of the uterus. **Hoffmann's s.** 1. Increased mechanical irritability of the sensory nerves in tetany. 2. A sudden nipping of the nail of the index, middle, or ring finger produces flexion of the terminal phalanx of the thumb and of the second and third phalanx of some other finger. Called also *digital reflex.* **Hofstätter-Cullen-Hellendall s.**, blueness of the umbilicus due to color of the blood showing through an umbilical hernia. **Holmes's s.**, rebound phenomenon. **Homans' s.**, discomfort behind the knee on forced dorsiflexion of the foot: a sign of thrombosis in the leg. **Hoover's s.** 1. In the normal state or in genuine paralysis, if the patient, lying on a couch, is directed to press the leg against the couch, there will be a lifting movement seen in the other leg. This phenomenon is absent in hysteria and malingering. 2. Movement of the costal margins toward the midline in inspiration, occurring bilaterally in pulmonary emphysema and unilaterally in conditions causing flattening of the diaphragm, such as pleural effusion and pneumothorax. **Hope's s.**, double heart beat in aortic aneurysm. **Horn's s.**, pain produced by traction of the right spermatic cord in acute appendicitis. **Horner's s.**, Spalding's s. **Horsley's s.**, if there is a difference in the temperature in the two axillae, the higher temperature will be on the paralyzed side. **Howship-Romberg s.** See *Romberg-Howship s.* **Huchard's s.** 1. When a change from a standing to a recumbent posture is not followed by a diminution of the pulse rate, it is a sign of arterial hypertension. 2. Paradoxic percussion resonance in pulmonary edema. **Hueter's s.,** the absence of the transmission of osseous vibration in cases of fracture with fibrous material interposed between the fragments. **Human's s.,** chin retraction s. **Huntington's s.,** the patient is recumbent, with his legs hanging over the edge of a table, and is told to cough. If the coughing produces flexion of the thigh and extension of the leg in the paralyzed limb, it indicates lesion in the palliospinal path. **Hutchinson's s's.** 1. Interstitial keratitis and a dull-red discoloration of the cornea in inherited syphilis. 2. See *teeth, Hutchinson's.* 3. Hutchinson's triad: interstitial keratitis, notched teeth, and otitis occurring together in inherited syphilis. **hyperkinesis s.** See *Claude's hyperkinesis s.* **Iliescu's s.,** pressure on the right phrenic nerve in the neck elicits pain in appendicitis. **interossei s.,** Souques's phenomenon. **Itard-Cholewa s.,** anesthesia of the tympanic membrane in otosclerosis. **Jaccoud's s.,** prominence of the aorta in the suprasternal notch: an indication of leukemia. **Jackson's s.** 1. Of cardiac failure: a discrepancy between the pulse rate and that of the heart beat. 2. See *asthmatoid wheeze,* under *wheeze.* 3. Prolongation of the expiratory sound over the affected area in pulmonary tuberculosis. **Jacquemier's s.,** a violet-colored spot on the mucous membrane of the vagina just below the urethral orifice, seen after the fourth week of pregnancy. **Jadelot's s's.** See under *line.* **Jellinek's s.,** the brownish pigmentation which occurs in many cases of hyperthyroidism. **Jendrassik's s.,** paralysis of the extra-ocular muscles in exophthalmic goiter. **Joffroy's s.,** absence of forehead wrinkling in exophthalmic goiter when the patient suddenly turns his eye upward. **Jolly's s.,** the forearm is held in flexion and the shoulder in abduction, and adduction of the arm is impossible: seen in lesions of the seventh cervical segment of the spinal cord. **Jorissenne's s.,** nonacceleration of the pulse on changing from a horizontal to the erect position: a sign of pregnancy. **Josseraud's s.,** a loud metallic sound heard over the pulmonic area in acute pericarditis. **jugular s.,** Queckenstedt's s. **Jürgensen's s.,** delicate crepitation of pleural tubercles sometimes heard in auscultation in acute pneumonic phthisis. **Kanavel's s.,** a point of maximum tenderness in the palm 1 inch proximal to the base of the little finger in infection of tendon sheath. **Kanter's s.,** absence of the fetal movements normally produced by pressure on the fetal head; indicating that the fetus is dead. **Kantor's s.,** a thin stringlike shadow in the roentgenogram of the colon through the filling defect: seen in colitis and regional ileitis. **Karplus' s.,** a modification of the vocal resonance, in which, on auscultation over a pleural effusion, the vowel *u* spoken by the patient is heard as *a.* **Kashida's s.,** spasm of muscles and hyperesthesia produced by applying heat or cold: seen in tetany. **Keen's s.,** increased diameter of the leg at the malleoli in Pott's fracture of the fibula. **Kehr's s.,** severe pain in the left shoulder in some cases of rupture of the spleen. **Kehrer's s.,** deep pressure over the occipital point (corresponding to the point of exit of the greater occipital nerve) produces a severe pain to avoid which the patient jerks his head backward and to the side: seen in brain tumor. **Kellock's s.,** increase of the vibration of the ribs on sharp percussion with the right hand, the left hand being placed firmly on the thorax under the nipple: a sign of pleural effusion. **Kelly's s.,** if the ureter is teased with an artery forceps, it will contract like a snake or worm. **Kennedy's s.,** funic souffle. **Kerandel's s.,** deep hyperesthesia accompanied by pain, often retarded, after some slight blow upon a bony projection of the body: seen in African trypanosomiasis. **Kergaradec's s.,** uterine souffle. **Kernig's s.,** in the dorsal decubitus the patient can easily and completely extend the leg; in the sitting posture or when lying with the thigh flexed upon the abdomen the leg cannot be completely extended: it is a sign of meningitis. **Kerr's s.,** alteration of the texture of the skin below the somatic level in lesions of the spinal cord. **kink s.,** tenderness on a line joining the umbilicus and the center of Poupart's ligament: indicative of ileal kink. **Kleist's s.,** the fingers of the patient's hand when gently elevated by the fingers of the examiner will hook into the examiner's fingers: indicative of frontal and thalamic lesions. **Klemm's s.,** in the roentgenogram in chronic appendicitis there is often an indication of tympanites in the right lower quadrant. **Klippel-Feil s.,** flexion and adduction of the thumb when the patient's flexed fingers are quickly extended by the examiner: indicative of pyramidal tract disease. **Kocher's s.** See under *symptom.* **Koplik's s.,** the appearance of a crop of buccal macules, consisting of small, dark-red spots surrounded by minute white specks; seen in the prodromal stage of measles. **Korânyi's s.,** increase of resonance over the dorsal segment on percussion of the spinal processes of the thoracic vertebrae: occurs in pleural effusion. **Kreysig's s.,** Heim-Kreysig s. **Krisovski's (Krisowski's) s.,** cicatricial lines which radiate from the mouth in inherited syphilis. **Kussmaul's s.** 1. Overfulness of the jugular veins on inspiration, seen in mediastinopericarditis and mediastinal tumor. 2. Air hunger and coma in diabetic coma. 3. Convulsions and coma in stomach disease as a result of toxin absorption. 4. Paradoxical pulse. **Küstner's s.,** a cystic tumor on the median line anterior to the uterus in cases of ovarian dermoids. **Laborde's s.,** Cloquet's needle s. **Ladin's s.,** a sign of pregnancy, consisting in a circular elastic area, which offers a sensation of fluctuation to the examining finger, situated in the median line of the anterior surface of the body of the uterus just above the junction of the body and the cervix. This area increases in size as pregnancy advances. **Laennec's s.,** the occurrence of rounded, gelatinous masses (Laennec's pearls) in the sputum of bronchial asthma. **Lafora's s.,** picking of the nose regarded as an early sign of cerebrospinal meningitis. **Landolfi's s.,** systolic contraction of the pupil and diastolic dilatation, seen in aortic insufficiency. **Landou's s.,** inability to grasp the uterus bimanually in the presence of slight ascites. **Langoria's s.,** relaxation of the extensor muscles of the thigh: a symptom of intracapsular fracture of the femur. **Larcher's s.,** grayish, cloudy discolorations of the conjunctivae that are speedily blackened: a sign of death. **Lasègue's s.** 1. In sciatica, flexion of the thigh upon the hip is painless; and when the knee is bent, such flexion is easily made: this distinguishes the case from hip joint disease. 2. Inability to move the limb when the eyes are closed: in hysterical anesthesia. **Laubry, Routier, and Vanbogaert s.,** inequality of the pulse and a third dull sound in diastole: both indicative of auricular tachycardia. **Laugier's s.,** a condition in which the styloid process of the radius and of the ulna are on the same level: seen in fracture of the lower part of the radius. **Lebhardt's s.,** Jacquemier's s. **leg s.** 1. Schlesinger's s. 2. Neri's s. **Leichtenstern's s.,** in cerebrospinal meningitis, tapping lightly any bone of the extremities causes the patient to wince suddenly. **Lennhoff's s.,** a furrow appearing on deep inspiration below the lowest rib and above an echinococcus cyst of the liver. **Leotta's s.,** the examiner's hand is placed on the patient's right abdominal quadrant and downward pressure is exerted by the fingers. This traction produces pain if the colon is adherent to the liver or gallbladder. **Leri's s.,** passive flexion of the hand and wrist of the affected side in hemiplegia shows no normal flexion at the elbow. **Lesieur's s.,** impaired resonance over the right lower thorax posteriorly, occurring in typhoid fever. **Lesieur-Privey s.,** albuminoreaction. **Leudet's s.,** bruit de Leudet. **Levasseur's s.,** the failure of the scarificator and cupping-glass to draw blood: a sign of death. **Lhermitte's s.,** the development of sudden, transient, electric-like shocks spreading down the body when the patient flexes the head forward: seen in multiple sclerosis, cord degenerations, and cervical cord injuries. **Lian's s.,** echo s. **Libman's s.,** extreme tenderness, but without pain on pressure, of the tips of the mastoid bones. **Lichtheim's s.,** in subcortical aphasia, although patient cannot speak, he is able to indicate with his fingers the number of syllables in the word he is thinking of. **ligature s.,** in hematuria, the development of ecchymoses in the distal part of a limb to which a ligature has been applied. **Linder's s.,** with the patient recumbent or sitting with outstretched legs, passive flexion of the head will cause pain in the leg or the lumbar region in sciatica. **Litten's s.,** diaphragmatic phenomenon. **Livierato's s.,** vasoconstriction when the abdominal sympathetic is irritated by striking the anterior abdomen along the xipho-umbilical line. **Lloyd's s.,** a symptom of renal calculus, consisting of pain in the loin on deep percussion over the kidney, even when pressure causes no pain. **Lockwood's s.,** the patient lies on his back with his head raised on a pillow and his knees drawn up. The surgeon sits near his right side and palpates the right iliac region near McBurney's spot with the three inner fingers of his left hand. If he feels a trickle of flatulence passing his fingers, *and if this can be often repeated after waiting a half to one minute, or a little longer*, the patient has either a chronically inflamed appendix or adhesions near it. **Lombardi's s.,** the appearance of venous varicosities in the region of the spinous processes of the seventh cervical and first three thoracic vertebrae; seen in early pulmonary tuberculosis. Called also *varicose zone of warning*. **Lorenz's s.,** ankylotic rigidity of the spinal column, especially of the thoracic and lumbar segments: sometimes seen in incipient phthisis. **Löwy's s.,** marked dilatation of the pupil on the instillation of epinephrine into the conjunctival sac: seen in pancreatic insufficiency and exophthalmic goiter. **Lucas' s.,** distention of the abdomen in the early stages of rickets. **Lucatello's s.,** the external (axillary) temperature is higher than the oral by 0.2–0.3 degrees in hyperthyroid patients. **Ludloff's s.,** swelling and ecchymosis at the base of Scarpa's triangle together with inability to raise the thigh when in a sitting posture, a sign of traumatic separation of the epiphysis of the greater trochanter. **Lust's s.** See under *phenomenon*. **McBurney's s.,** tenderness at a point midway between the umbilicus and the anterior superior spine of the ilium: indicative of appendicitis. **McClintock's s.,** a pulse rate exceeding 100, an hour or more after childbirth: indicative of postpartum hemorrhage. **Macewen's s.,** on percussion of the skull behind the junction of the frontal, temporal, and parietal bones, there is a more resonant note than normal in internal hydrocephalus and cerebral abscess. **McGinn-White s.,** a Q wave and late inversion of the T wave in Lead 3, low S-T intervals and T waves in Lead 2, and inverted T waves in chest leads V_2 and V_3, the electrocardiographic evidence of right ventricular dilatation due to massive pulmonary embolism, plus the clinical signs of acute cor pulmonale. **McMurray s.,** occurrence of a cartilage click during manipulation of the knee: indicative of menisceal injury. **Madelung's s.,** increased difference between the axillary and rectal temperatures indicates purulent peritonitis. **Magendie's s., Magendie-Hertwig s.,** downward and inward rotation of the homolateral eyeball and upward and outward rotation of the contralateral one. **Magnan's s.** See under *symptom*. **Magnus' s.,** after death the light ligation of a finger causes no visible change in its distal portion. **Mahler's s.,** a steady increase of pulse rate without corresponding elevation of temperature: seen in thrombosis. **Maisonneuve's s.,** marked hyperextensibility of the hand: a symptom of Colles' fracture. **Mann's s.** 1. In exophthalmic goiter the two eyes appear not to be on the same level. 2. Lessened resistance of the scalp to a constant electric current: seen in certain traumatic neuroses. **Mannaberg's s.,** accentuation of the second sound of the heart in abdominal disease, especially appendicitis. **Mannkopf's s., Mannkopf-Rumpf s.,** increase in the frequency of the pulse on pressure over a painful spot: not present in simulated pain. **Marañon's s.,** a vasomotor reaction following stimulation of the skin over the throat; seen in exophthalmic goiter. **Marfan's s.,** a red triangle at the tip of a coated tongue indicates typhoid fever. **Marie's s.,** tremor of the body or extremities in exophthalmic goiter. **Marie-Foix s.,** withdrawal of lower leg on transverse pressure of tarsus or forced flexion of toes, even when the leg is incapable of voluntary movement. **Marinesco's s.,** Marinesco's succulent hand. **Masini's s.,** marked dorsal extension of the fingers and toes in mentally unstable children. **Mastin's s.,** pain in the region of the clavicle in acute appendicitis. **Mathieu's s.,** a splashing sound heard on rapid percussion in the region about the umbilicus in complete intestinal obstruction. **May's s.,** in glaucoma, dilatation of the pupil is produced by instilling a drop of epinephrine in the eye. **Mayo's s.,** relaxation of the muscles controlling the lower jaw, indicative of profound anesthesia. **Mayor's s.,** the sound of the fetal heart beat in pregnancy. **Meltzer's s.** 1. Loss of the normal second sound, heard on auscultation of the heart after swallowing: symptomatic of occlusion or contraction of the lower part of the esophagus. 2. Pain on active flexion of the hip, with the knee extended, while the examiner presses firmly down over McBurney's point: seen in appendicitis. **Mendel's s.,** an area on the epigastrium about the size of a half dollar, tender to percussion: occurring in gastric and duodenal ulcer. **Mendel-Bechterew s.** 1. Bechterew's pupil reflex. 2. Flexion of small toes on percussion with hammer of dorsal surface of cuboid bone: a sign of organic hemiplegia. **meniscus s.,** the radioscopic appearance of a crescentic shadow made by the crater of a gastric ulcer: when the convexity of the crescent points outward the ulcer is on the lesser curvature; when the convexity points downward the ulcer is distal to the angular incisure. **Mennell's s.,** an examining thumb is placed over the posterosuperior spine of the sacrum and then made to slide, first outward and then inward. If on pressure over the former point tenderness is detected, it is due to a sensitive deposit in the structures of the gluteal aspect of the posterosuperior spine. If the tenderness is over the inner point, it is probable that the superior ligaments of the sacral iliac joint are strained and sensitive. If the tenderness is increased by pressure backward on the anterosuperior aspect of the ilium and decreased by pulling forward the crest from behind, this is positive proof that it is caused by the sensitive ligaments. **Meunier's s.,** daily loss of weight in measles, following the incubative stage and preceding the eruptive stage. **Meyer's s.,** formication of the hands and sometimes of the feet, experienced particularly after immersion of the extremities in water; observed in the eruptive stage of scarlet fever but not in other eruptions. **Michelson-Weiss s.,** in otitis media associated with tuberculosis of the lungs the patient is able to hear his own respiratory sounds with his affected ear. **Milian's s.,** in subcutaneous inflammation of the head and face the ears are not involved, but in skin diseases they are. **Minor's s.,** the method of rising from a sitting position characteristic of patient with sciatica; he supports himself on the healthy side, placing one hand on the back, bending the affected leg and balancing on the healthy leg. **Mirchamp's s.,** when a sapid substance, such as vinegar, is applied to the mucous membrane of the tongue, a painful reflex secretion of saliva in the gland about to be affected is indicative of mumps. **Möbius' s.,** inability to keep the eyeballs converged in exophthalmic goiter: due to insufficiency of the internal recti muscles. **Monteverde's s.,** failure of any response to the subcutaneous injection of ammonia: a sign of death. **Moon's s.** See under *tooth*. **Morquio's s.,** the patient lying supine resists all attempts to raise the trunk to a sitting posture until the legs are passively flexed: noticed in epidemic poliomyelitis. **Morris's s.,** deep pressure over Morris's point elicits tenderness of the right lumbar ganglion in appendicitis. **Mortola's s.,** pain on pinching the anterior abdominal wall, the severity of the pain indicating the degree of abdominal inflammation. **Moschcowitz's s.,** a sign of vascular gangrene. On making a circular compression of the base of the limbs by elastic bands, and then, after a few minutes, releasing the pressure, the skin, which has been rendered anemic, will become red. If the limbs are healthy the redness appears with the same intensity and rapidity on each side. On a gangrenous limb there is usually a slower and less extensive hyperemia than on a healthy one. **Mosler's s.,** sternal tenderness in acute myeloblastic anemia. **Müller's s.,** a sign of aortic insufficiency, consisting of pulsation of the uvula and redness of the tonsils and velum palati, occurring synchronously with the action of the heart. **Murat's s.,** in the tuberculous patient there is vibration of the affected side of the chest with a feeling of discomfort when speaking. **Murphy's s.** 1. A sign of gallbladder disease, consisting of inability of the patient to take a deep inspiration when the physician's fingers are hooked up deep beneath the right costal arch, below the hepatic margin. 2. Absence of the ordinary tympanic sound when the lower right abdominal wall is percussed by the four fingers in succession, as in playing the piano: indicates a small amount of exudate in appendicitis. **Musset's s.,** rhythmical jerking movement of the head, seen in cases of aortic aneurysm and aortic insufficiency. **Naunyn's s.,** a sign of cholecystitis, consisting in deep tenderness when, at the end of a full inspiration, the examiner's fingers are thrust upward beneath the costal arch at the outer limit of the right epigastrium. **neck s.,** Brudzinski's s., def. 1. **Negro s.** 1. Exaggerated excursion of the eyeball on the side most severely affected by paralysis when the eyeballs are turned up. 2. Cogwheel phenomenon. **Neri's s.** 1. A sign of organic hemiplegia, consisting in the spontaneous bending of the knee of the affected side as the leg is passively lifted, the patient being in the dorsal position. 2. With the patient standing, forward bending of the trunk will cause flexion of the knee on the affected side in lumbosacral and iliosacral lesions. **niche s.,** Haudek's s. **Nikolsky's s.,** a condition in which the outer layer of the skin is easily rubbed off by slight injury. **Nothnagel's s.,** paralysis of the facial muscles, especially in respect of movements connected with the emotions: observed in cases of tumor of the thalamus. **Ober's s.** See under *tests*. **objective s.,** one that can be seen, heard, or felt by the diagnostician. Called also *physical s.* **obturator s.** 1. Pain on outward pressure on the obturator foramen as a sign of inflammation in the sheath of the obturator nerve probably caused by appendicitis. 2. See *Hefke-Turner s.* **Odienet's s.,** echo s. **Oefelein's s.,** with the patient prone, the muscles of the back are stroked from the seventh to the twelfth thoracic vertebra. In peptic ulcer a unilateral reflex occurs in the muscles of the back. **Oliver's s.,** tracheal tugging: a sign of aneurysm of the aorta. **Oliver-Cardarelli s., Olshausen's s.,** when a tumor is found in young unmarried women lying anterior to the uterus it is likely to be a dermoid cyst. **Onanoff's s.** See under *reflex*. **ophthalmoscopic s.,** as death approaches the blood in the retinal vessels gradually ceases to move and the column of blood splits into fragments. **Oppenheim's s.,** dorsal extension of the big toe on stroking downward the medial side of the tibia: seen in pyramidal tract disease. **Oppolzer's s.,** in serofibrinous pericarditis palpation shows that the seat of the apex beat changes with the posture of the patient. **orange-peel s.,** a sign for distinguishing lipoma: on compressing the tumor between the thumb and forefinger it will be perceived that the skin overlying the mass is irregularly dimpled by the downward traction of the vertical trabeculae; called also *signe de peau d'orange*. **orbicularis s.,** in hemiplegia, inability to close the eye on the paralyzed side without closing the other. **Osiander's s.,** vaginal pulsation, an early sign in pregnancy. **Osler's s.,** small, painful, erythematous swellings in the skin of the hands and feet in malignant endocarditis. **Ott's s.,** a sign of appendicitis consisting of a pulling sensation felt by the patient when lying on the left side. **Pagniello's s.,** intense pain on pressure over the left ninth intercostal space, between the posterior and middle axillary lines: seen in malaria. **palmoplantar s.,** Filipovitch's s. **Parkinson's s.,** an immobile, masklike expression in paralysis agitans. **Parrot's s.** 1. Dilatation of the pupil on pinching the skin of the neck: seen in meningitis. 2. Bony nodes on the outer table of the skull of infants with inherited syphilis, giving it a buttock shape. **Pastia's s.,** transverse lines, usually two or three, in the fold of the elbow in scarlet fever, rose red at first, but later turning dark red or wine colored. They are visible before the appearance of the rash, remain through the eruptive stage, and continue after desquamation. **Patino-Mayer's s.,** a lymphocyte count of over 30 per cent indicates syphilis, in the absence of febrile diseases. **Patrick's s.** See under *tests*. **Paul's s.,** feebleness of the apex beat, with forcible impulse over the rest of the heart: indicative of pericardial adhesions. **Payr's s.,** pain on pressure over the inner side of the foot: an early sign of impending postoperative thrombosis. **Pende's s.,** André-Thomas s. **Perez's s.,** a friction sound heard over the sternum when the patient raises and drops his arms: a sign of mediastinal tumor or of aneurysm of the arch of the aorta. **Pfuhl's s.,** inspiration increases the force of flow in paracentesis in the case of subphrenic abscess, but lessens it in the case of pyopneumothorax. This distinction is lost when the diaphragm is paralyzed. **Pfuhl-Jaffé s.,** in pyopneumothorax the liquid issues from the exploratory puncture or incision with considerable force during inspiration: in true pneumothorax during expiration. **physical s.,** objective s. **piano percussion s.,** Murphy's s., def. 2. **Piltz's s.** 1. Attention reflex. 2. Westphal-Piltz phenomenon. **Pinard's s.,** a sharp pain on pressure over the fundus uteri: after the sixth month of pregnancy this sign is an indication of breech presentation. **Pins' s.,** a sign seen in pericarditis, consisting of disappearance of the symptoms that simulate pleurisy when the patient is in the knee-chest position. **Piotrowski's s.,** percussion of the tibialis muscle produces dorsal flexion and supination of the foot. When this reflex is excessive it indicates organic disease of the central nervous system. Called also *anticus sign* or *reflex*. **Piskacek's s.,** asymmetrical enlargement of the corpus uteri: a sign of pregnancy. **Pitfield's s.** 1. With the patient sitting up, tapping on the back over the suspected area can be felt by the other hand palpating the quadratus lumborum muscle if there is fluid in the pleura. 2. With the patient sitting, one of the quadrati muscles is percussed and the abdominal wall palpated: diminution of the transmitted vibration indicates ascites. **Pitres's s.** 1. Hyperesthesia of the scrotum and testes in tabes dorsalis. 2. Anterior deviation of the sternum in pleuritic effusion. **placental s.,** implantation bleeding. **plumb-line s.,** the estimation in sternal displacement by a plumb-line in the diagnosis of pleuritic effusion. **Plummer's s.,** inability to step up onto a chair or to walk up steps, in toxic goiter. **pneumatic s.,** Henebert's s. **Pool-Schlesinger s.,** Schlesinger's s. **Porter's s.,** Oliver's s. **Potain's s.** 1. Extension of percussion dulness over arch of aorta, in dilatation of the aorta, from the manubrium to the third costal cartilage on the right-hand side. 2. Timbre métallique. **Pottenger's s.** 1. Intercostal muscle rigidity on palpation in pulmonary and pleural inflammatory conditions. 2. Different degrees of resistance on light touch palpation, noted (1) over solid organs when compared with hollow organs; (2) over foci of disease in the lungs and pleura when compared with that over normal organs. **Pratt's s.,** muscular rigidity as a sign of gangrene or necrosis in wounds, and as an indication for operation. **Prehn's s.,** elevation and support of the scrotum will relieve the pain in epididymo-orchitis, but not in torsion of the testicle. **Prevel's s.,** acceleration of the heart beat when a reclining subject changes to the upright position. **Prevost's s.,** conjugate deviation of the head and eyes, the eyes looking toward the affected hemisphere and away from the palsied extremities: seen in hemiplegia. **pronation s.** See *Babinski's s.*, def. 5. **Przewalsky's s.** 1. Swelling over Poupart's ligament produced by glands around the circumflex artery: in appendicitis. 2. Decreased ability to hold up the right leg in appendicitis. **pseudo-Babinski's s.,** in poliomyelitis the Babinski reflex is modified so that only the big toe is extended, because all the foot muscles except the dorsiflexors of the big toe are paralyzed. **pseudo-Graefe's s.,** slow descent of the upper lid on looking down, and quick ascent on looking up: seen in conditions other than exophthalmic goiter. **pyramid s., pyramidal s.,** any sign pointing to disease of the pyramidal tract. **Quant's s.,** a T-shaped depression in the occipital bone, sometimes seen in rickets. **Queckenstedt's s.,** when the veins in the neck are compressed on one or both sides there is a rapid rise in the pressure of the cerebrospinal fluid of healthy persons, and this rise quickly disappears when pressure is taken off the neck. But when there is a block in the vertebral canal the pressure of the cerebrospinal fluid is little or not at all affected by this maneuver. **Quénu-Muret s.,** in aneurysm, the main artery of the limb is compressed and then a puncture is made at the periphery; if blood flows, the collateral circulation is probably established. **Quincke's s.,** a blanching of the finger-nails at each diastole of the heart; seen in aortic insufficiency. **Quinquaud's s.,** trembling of patient's fingers, felt when his fingers, spread apart, are placed vertically in the palm of the examiner's hand: said to be a sign of alcoholism. **radialis s.,** Strumpell's s., def. 2. **Radovici's s.,** palmchin reflex. **Raimiste's s.,** the hand and arm are held upright by the examiner. If the hand is sound, it remains upright on being released; if paretic the hand flexes abruptly at the wrist. **Ramond's s.,** rigidity of the erector spinae muscle indicative of pleurisy with effusion. The rigidity relaxes when the effusion becomes purulent. **Randall's s.,** in a pregnant woman, exaggerated response to immersion of the arm in cold water points to the possibility of the patient developing toxemia. **Rasch's s.,** fluctuation of the liquor amnii obtained as by ballottement in early pregnancy. **Rasin's s.,** Jellinek's s. **Raynaud's s.,** acro-asphyxia. **Reder's s.,** a tender point on the right side above O'Beirne's sphincter: seen in appendicitis. **Reichmann's s.,** the presence in the stomach in the morning before eating of acid food residues; indicates gastrosuccorrhea and stenosis of the pylorus. **Remak's s.** See under *symptom*. **Remlinger's s.,** difficulty in protruding the tongue and the presence of fine tremors in the organ when it is protruded: seen in typhus fever. **Reusner's s.,** increased volume of the pulse in the uterine arteries, perceptible in Douglas' culdesac in the fourth month of pregnancy and later. **Revilliod's s.,** orbicularis s. **Richardson's s.,** the application of a tight fillet to the arm as a test of death: if life be present, the veins on the distal side of the fillet become more or less distended. **Riesman's s.** 1. A bruit heard with the stethoscope over the closed eye in exophthalmic goiter. 2. Softening of the eyeball in diabetic coma. 3. In gallbladder disease: sharp pain on striking the right rectus muscle with the ulnar side of the hand while the patient is holding his breath. **Riess' s.,** on listening over the stomach in some cases of adherent pericardium, the heart sounds are heard loud and metallic in quality. **Rinman's s.,** the appearance in early pregnancy of cordlike radiations proceeding from the nipple. **Ripault's s.,** external pressure upon the eye during life causes only a temporary change in the normal roundness of the pupil; but after death the change so caused may be permanent. **Risquez's s.,** the presence of blood pigment loose in the blood: a sign of malaria. **Ritter-Rollet s.,** flexion of the foot on gentle electric stimulation; extension on energetic stimulation. **Riviere's s.,** an area of change in percussion note denoting a band of increased density across the back at the plane of the spinous processes of the fifth, sixth, and seventh dorsal vertebrae: a sign of pulmonary tuberculosis. **Robertson's s.** 1. The appearance of reddish maculopapules on the upper extremities in myocardial degeneration. 2. Fibrillary contraction of the pectoralis muscle over the cardiac area in approaching death from heart disease. 3. Absence of pupillary dilatation on pressure over alleged painful areas in malingering. 4. Fullness and tension in the patient's flanks, felt by the examiner with the patient supine: in ascites. **Roche's s.,** in torsion of the testis the epididymis cannot be distinguished from the body of the testis, whereas in epididymitis the body of the testis can be felt in the enlarged crescent of the epididymis. **Rockley's s.,** two straight edges are placed vertically at the outer edges of the orbits from the prominence of the malar bone: if depression of the malar bone exists, the difference in the two angles is obvious. **Romaña's s.,** unilateral ophthalmia with palpebral edema, conjunctivitis, and swelling of regional lymph glands as a sign of Chagas' disease. **Romberg's s.,** swaying of the body when standing with the feet close together and the eyes closed, observed in tabes dorsalis. **Romberg-Howship s.,** lancinating pains in the leg indicative of incarcerated obturator hernia. **Rommelaere's s.,** an abnormally small proportion of normal phosphates and of sodium chloride in the urine in cancerous cachexia. **Rosenbach's s.** 1. Absence of the abdominal skin reflex in inflammatory disease of the intestines. 2. Absence of the abdominal skin reflex in pinching the skin of the abdomen on the paralyzed side in hemiplegia. 3. A fine rapid tremor of the closed eyelids in exophthalmic goiter. 4. Inability to close the eyes immediately on command: seen in neurasthenia. **Rosenheim's s.,** a friction sound in the left hypochondrium: a sign of perigastritis. **Roser-Braun s.,** absence of dural pulsation: a sign of cerebral tumor or abscess. **Rossolimo's s.** See under *reflex*. **Rotch's s.,** dulness on percussion of the right fifth intercostal space: a sign of pericardial effusion. **Roth's s.,** percussional dulness between the fifth and sixth costal cartilages. It is due either to tricuspid stenosis and dilatation of the right auricle or to a pericardial effusion. **Rothschild's s.** 1. Preternatural flattening and mobility of the sternal angle: seen in phthisis. 2. Rarefaction of the outer third of the eyebrows in thyroid inadequacy. **Roussel's s.,** sharp pain on light percussion on the subclavicular region, between the clavicle and fourth rib: a sign of incipient tuberculosis. **Roux's s.,** in suppurative appendicitis, palpation of the empty cecum furnishes a soft resistance resembling that given by a wet tube of pasteboard. **Rovighi's s.,** a fremitus felt on percussion and palpation of a superficial hepatic hydatid. **Rovsing's s.,** pressure on the left side over the point corresponding to

McBurney's point will elicit the typical pain at McBurney's point in appendicitis, but not in other abdominal affections. **Ruggeri's s.** See under *reflex*. **Rumpel-Leede s.** See under *phenomenon*. **Rumpf's s.** 1. Alternating fibrillary and tonic contractions after the cessation of strong faradization: seen in traumatic neuroses. Called also *Rumpf's traumatic reaction*. 2. Quickening of the pulse on pressure over a painful point: seen in neurasthenia. **Rust's s.,** in caries or malignant disease of the cervical vertebrae the patient supports his head with his hands while moving the body. **Sabathie's s.,** in aortic disease there is stasis with dilatation of either or both the jugular veins. **Saenger's s.,** a light reflex of the pupil that has ceased returns after a short stay in the dark, in cerebral syphilis, but not in tabes dorsalis. **Salisbury and Melvin's s.,** ophthalmoscopic s. **Salmon's s.,** dilatation of the pupil of one eye in ruptured ectopic pregnancy. **Sanders' s.,** an undulating cardiac impulse, especially at the epigastrium: a sign of pericardial adhesion. **Sansom's s.** 1. Marked increase of the area of dulness in the second and third intercostal spaces, due to pericardial effusion. 2. A rhythmical murmur heard with a stethoscope applied to the lips in aneurysm of the thoracic aorta. **Santoni's s.,** a short booming sound heard with the stethoscope over a portion of a cyst on percussing another portion of the cyst: absent in hydatid cyst. **Sarbó's s.,** analgesia of the peroneal nerve: sometimes noticed in locomotor ataxia. **Sattler's s.,** the seated patient extends and raises his right leg: pressure on the cecum produces severe pain in appendicitis. **Saunders' s.,** on wide opening of the mouth there take place in children associated movements of the hand consisting of opening of the hand and extension and separation of the fingers; called also *mouth-and-hand synkinesia*. **Schapiro's s.,** no slowing of the pulse rate on lying down: indicative of weakness of the heart muscle. **Schepelmann's s.,** in dry pleurisy the pain is increased when the patient bends his body toward the well side, whereas in intercostal neuralgia it is increased by bending toward the affected side. **Schick's s.,** stridor heard on expiration in an infant with tuberculosis of the bronchial glands. **Schlange's s.,** dilatation above and absence of peristalsis below the site of intestinal obstruction. **Schlesinger's s.,** in tetany, if the patient's leg is held at the knee joint and flexed strongly at the hip joint, there will follow within a short time an extensor spasm at the knee joint, with extreme supination of the foot. Called also *leg phenomenon* and *Pool's phenomenon*. **Schüle's s.,** the omega melancholium. **Schultze's s.** 1. Chvostek's sign. 2. Tongue phenomenon. **Seeligmüller's s.,** mydriasis on the side of the face affected with neuralgia. **Séguin's s.** See *Séguin's signal symptom*, under *symptom*. **Seidel's s.** See under *scotoma*. **Seitz's s.,** bronchial inspiration which begins harshly and then becomes faint: indicative of a cavity in the lung. **Semon's s.,** impairment of the mobility of the vocal cords in malignant disease of the larynx. **setting-sun s.,** downward deviation of the eyes, so that each iris appears to "set" beneath the lower lid, with white sclera exposed between it and the upper lid; indicative of intracranial pressure (hemorrhage or meningo-ependymitis) or irritation of the brain stem (as in kernicterus). **Shelly's s.,** a sago-like eruption on the palate and lips in influenza. **Shibley's s.,** in the presence of consolidation of the lung or a collection of fluid in the pleural cavity, all spoken vowels come through the stethoscope to the ear of the examiner as "ah." **Sicar's s.,** a metallic resonance on percussion with two coins on the front of the chest and auscultation at the back, observed in some cases of effusion within the pleura. **Siegert's s.,** in mongolian idiocy the little fingers are short and curved inward. **Sieur's s.** See *coin test*, under *tests*. **Signorelli's s.,** extreme tenderness on pressure on the retromandibular point in meningitis. **Silex's s.,** furrows radiating from the mouth in inherited syphilis. **Simon's s.** 1. [C. E. *Simon*]. Retraction or fixation of the umbilicus during inspiration. 2. [J. *Simon*]. Absence of the usual correlation between the movements of the diaphragm and thorax: seen in beginning meningitis. **Sisto's s.,** constant crying as a sign of congenital syphilis in infancy. **Skeer's s.,** a small circle in the iris, near the pupil, in both eyes; seen in tuberculous meningitis. **Skoda's s.,** a tympanitic sound heard on percussing the chest above a large pleural effusion or above a consolidation in pneumonia. **Smith's s.,** a murmur heard in cases of enlarged bronchial glands on auscultation over the manubrium with the patient's head thrown back. **Snellen's s.,** the bruit heard with a stethoscope over the closed eye in ophthalmic goiter. **Somagyi's s.** See under *reflex*. **somatic s.,** any sign presented by the trunk and limbs rather than by the sensory apparatus. **Soresi's s.,** in supine position with thighs flexed the patient coughs while the examiner presses over the hepatic flexure of the colon: pain at McBurney's point indicates appendicitis. **Soto-Hall s.,** with the patient flat on his back, on flexion of the spine beginning at the neck and going downward, pain will be felt at the site of the lesion in back abnormalities. **Souques' s.** 1. When the patient seated in a chair is suddenly thrown back, the lower extremities do not extend normally or otherwise attempt to counteract the loss of balance. 2. Souques' phenomenon. 3. Decrease in the area of heart dulness in cancerous cachexia. **Spalding's s.,** in the x-ray film of the fetus in utero, overriding of the bones of the vault of the skull indicates death of the fetus. **Spiegelberg's s.,** a feeling like that of friction against wet India rubber, conveyed to the finger by a cervix uteri affected with malignant disease. **spinal s.,** tonic contraction of the spinal muscles on the diseased side in pleurisy. **spine s.,** disinclination to flex the spine anteriorly on account of pain: seen in poliomyelitis. **Squire's s.,** alternate contraction and dilatation of the pupil indicative of basilar meningitis. **stairs s.,** difficulty in descending a stairway in locomotor ataxia. **Steinhardt's s.,** discoloration of the soft palate, progressing from a faded appearance, through a yellow color, to a pinkish color: seen in acquired syphilis. **Stellwag's s.,** retraction of the upper eyelids producing apparent widening of the palpebral opening with which is associated infrequent and incomplete blinking: seen in exophthalmic goiter. **Sterles' s.,** increased pulsation over the cardiac region in intrathoracic tumors. **Sterling-Okuniewski s.,** the patient is unable to put out his tongue when directed to do so: symptomatic of louse-borne typhus fever. **Sternberg's s.,** sensitiveness to palpation of the muscles of the shoulder girdle in pleurisy. **Stewart-Holmes s.,** the patient rests his elbow on the table and the examiner grasps his wrist. The patient then tries to flex the arm against the resistance of the examiner. When the wrist is released, flexion occurs, but is again arrested by the contraction of the triceps. This takes place in normal patients, but in cerebellar disease the flexion of the arm continues without any action on the part of the triceps. **Stiller's s.,** detachment, or loose attachment, of the tenth rib to the costal cartilages; preternatural mobility of fluctuation of the tenth rib in enteroptosis or gastroptosis. **Stocker's s.,** in typhoid fever, if the bed clothes are pulled down, the patient takes no notice; but in tuberculous meningitis the patient resents the interference and immediately draws the clothes up again. **Stokes's s.,** a severe throbbing in the abdomen, at the right of the umbilicus, in acute enteritis. **Straus's s.,** the injection of pilocarpine in facial paralysis due to a central lesion does not cause any difference in the perspiration of the two sides; if the paralysis is of peripheral origin, the secretion of the paralyzed side is markedly affected. **Strauss's s.** 1. Increase of fat following the use of fatty foods in chylous ascites. 2. Blumer's shelf. **string s.** 1. Kantor's sign. 2. The stringing out of tubules, observed on pulling the tissues of an intact testis or one in which there is active spermatogenesis, a phenomenon which is prevented by the fibrosis and hyalinization about the tubules when the testis is atrophic. **Strümpell's s.** 1. Dorsal flexion of the foot when the thigh is drawn up toward the body: seen in spastic paralysis of the lower limb. Called also *tibial phenomenon* and *tibialis sign*. 2. Inability to close the fist without marked dorsal extension of the wrist. Called also *radialis s.* 3. Pronation sign; passive flexion of the forearm caused by pronation: seen in hemiplegia. **Strunsky's s.,** a sign for detecting lesions of the anterior arch of the foot. The examiner grasps the toes and flexes them suddenly. This procedure is painless in the normal foot, but causes pain if there is inflammation of the anterior arch. **Suker's s.,** deficient complementary fixation in lateral eye rotation: seen in exophthalmic goiter. **Sumner's s.,** on gentle palpation of the iliac fossa, a slight increase in tonus of the abdominal muscles indicates appendicitis, stone in the ureter or kidney, or a twisted pedicle of an ovarian cyst. **Tansini's s.,** in cancer at the pylorus the abdomen is shrunken in unless there is metastasis in the bowel below, in which case the abdomen is prominent. **Tarnier's s.,** effacement of the angle between the upper and lower uterine segments in pregnancy; an indication of the inevitable approach of an abortion. **Tay's s.** See *cherry-red spot,* under *spot.* **Tellais' s.,** pigmentation of the eyelid in exophthalmic goiter. **Ten Horn's s.,** if gentle traction in the right spermatic cord causes pain, appendicitis is indicated. **Testivin's s.,** the formation of a collodion-like pellicle on the urine after removing the albumin and treating with acid and then with one third of its volume of ether; said to occur during the incubation of infectious diseases. **Theimich's lip s.,** a protrusion or pouting of the lips elicited by tapping the orbicularis oris muscle. **thermic s.,** Kashida's s. **Thomas' s.** 1. Flexion of the hip joint can be compensated by lordosis. 2. Pinching of the trapezius muscle causes goose flesh above the level of a cord lesion. **Thomayer's s.,** in inflammatory conditions of the peritoneum, the mesentery contracts drawing the intestines over to the right side; therefore when the patient lies on his back, tympany is elicited on the right side, and dulness on the left. The sign distinguishes between inflammatory and noninflammatory ascites. **Thomson's s.,** Pastia's s. **Thornton's s.,** severe pain in the region of the flanks in nephrolithiasis. **thyroid s.,** an injection of thyroid extract retards the pulse and causes a fall in the systolic arterial pressure, while the oculocardiac reflex persists or becomes positive, in persons who have hyperthyroidism. **tibialis s.,** Strümpell's s., def. 1. **Tinel's s.,** a tingling sensation in the distal end of a limb when percussion is made over the site of a divided nerve. It indicates a partial lesion or the beginning regeneration of the nerve. Called also *formication s.* and *distal tingling on percussion* (D.T.P.). **toe s.,** Babinski's plantar reflex. **Toma's s.,** in ascites from peritoneal inflammation when the patient lies on his back percussion on the right side of the abdomen gives tympany; on the left side, dulness. **Tommasi's s.,** a special form of alopecia on the postero-external aspect of the legs, found almost exclusively in adult males who are subjects of the gouty diathesis. **tongue s.** 1. Tapping of the tongue with a sharp instrument produces dimpling: a sign of latent tetany. 2. Remlinger's sign. **Tournay's s.,** unilateral dilatation of the pupil of the abducting eye on extreme lateral fixation. **Traube's s.,** a faint double sound heard in auscultation over the femoral arteries in aortic regurgitation. **Trélat s.,** small yellowish spots in the neighborhood of tuberculous ulcers of the mouth. **Trendelenburg's s.** See under *tests.* **trepidation s.,** patellar clonus. **Tresilian's s.,** a reddish appearance in Stensen's duct in mumps. **Tressder's s.,** assuming the prone position gives relief from pain in appendicitis. **Trimadeau's s.,** if the dilatation above an esophageal stricture is conic, the stricture is fibrous; if cup shaped, the stricture is malignant. **Trimble's s.,** the presence of pigmentary lesions about the mouth, indicative of secondary syphilis. **Troisier's s.,** enlargement of the lymph glands above the clavicle; a sign of intra-abdominal malignant disease or of retrosternal tumor. **Trömner's s.,** Hoffmann's s., def. 2. **Trousseau's s.** 1. A muscular spasm on pressure over large detached arteries or nerves: seen in tetany. 2. Tache cérébrale. 3. Spontaneous peripheral venous thrombosis, suggestive of visceral carcinoma, especially carcinoma of the pancreas. **Turner's s.,** local discoloration of the skin of the loin in acute pancreatitis. **Turyn's s.,** in sciatica, if the patient's great toe is bent dorsally, pain will be felt in the gluteal region. **Uhthoff's s.,** nystagmus occurring in multiple cerebrospinal sclerosis. **Unschuld's s.,** a tendency to cramp in the calves of the legs; an early indication of diabetes. **Uriolla's s.,** the presence in the urine of malarial patients of minute black granules of blood pigment. **Vanzetti's s.,** in sciatica the pelvis is always horizontal in spite of scoliosis, but in other lesions with scoliosis the pelvis is inclined. **Vedder's s's** (*of beriberi*), slight pressure on muscles of calf causes pain; ascertain the presence of anesthesia with a pin over anterior surface of leg; note any changes in patellar reflexes; when patient squats upon heels, note the inability to rise without use of hands. **vein s.,** a bluish cord along the midaxillary line formed by the swollen junction of the thoracic and superficial epigastric vein; seen in tuberculosis of the bronchial glands. **Verco's s.,** subungual striae or dots of hemorrhage on the hands and feet in erythema nodosum. **Vermel's s.,** hypotension with visible pulsations of the temporal artery on the affected side in unilateral headache. **Vigouroux's s.,** diminished electric resistance of the skin in exophthalmic goiter. **Vipond's s.,** generalized adenopathy seen during the incubation period of the exanthematous fevers of childhood. **vital s's,** the pulse, respiration, and temperature. **Volkovitsch's s.,** relaxation and atrophy of the abdominal muscle over the appendix in chronic appendicitis. **Voltolini's s.,** Heryng's s. **von Graefe's s.,** failure of the upper lid to move downward with the eyeball in glancing downward; seen in exophthalmic goiter. **von Wahl's s.** See *Wahl's s.* **Wachenheim-Reder s.,** tenderness on rectal palpation in the right iliac fossa at the ileocecal region indicates appendicitis. **Wahl's s.** 1. Local meteorism, or distention on the proximal side of an obstruction of the bowel. 2. A blowing or scraping sound at the systole, heard over an artery soon after its partial division by an injury. **Wartenberg's s.** 1. A sign of ulnar palsy, consisting of a position of abduction assumed by the little finger. 2. Reduction or absence of the pendulum movements of the arm in walking: seen in patients with cerebellar disease. **Warthin's s.,** exaggerated pulmonary sounds in cases of acute pericarditis. **water-silk s.,** the sensation of silken surfaces sliding over one another when the middle finger is moved back and forth across the inguinal canal, discernible when hernia is present. **Weber's s.,** paralysis of the oculomotor nerve of one side and hemiplegia of the opposite side. **Wegner's s.,** a broadened, discolored appearance of the epiphysial line in infants dying from hereditary syphilis. **Weill's s.,** absence of expansion in the subclavicular region of the affected side in infantile pneumonia. **Weiss's s.,** Chvostek's s. **Wenckebach's s.,** crossing of the profile of the chest in deep inspiration over that of the chest at rest: seen in adherent pericardium. **Wernicke's s.,** hemiopic pupillary reaction. **Westphal's s.,** loss of the knee jerk in locomotor ataxia. **Widmer's s.,** the temperature in the right axilla is distinctly higher than the left; a sign of appendicitis. **Widowitz's s.,** protrusion of the eyeballs and sluggish movements of the eyeballs and eyelids seen in diphtheritic paralysis. Called also *doll's eye s.* **Wilder's s.,** an early sign of exophthalmic goiter consisting in a slight twitch of the eyeball when it changes its movement from adduction to abduction or vice versa. **Williams' s.** 1. A dull tympanitic resonance heard in the second intercostal space in severe pleural effusion. 2. Lessened lung expansion on the affected side; a sign of adherent pericardium. **Williamson's s.,** markedly diminished blood pressure in the leg as compared with that in the arm on the same side, seen in pneumothorax and pleural effusion. **Winterbottom's s.,** enlargement of posterior cervical lymph nodes in African trypanosomiasis. **Wintrich's s.,** a change in the pitch of the percussion note when the mouth is opened and closed; it indicates a cavity in the lung. **Wölfler's s.,** in hour-glass stomach fluids pass quickly, but on subsequent lavage the water contains food and foul matter. **Wolkowitsh's s.,** marked relaxation of the abdominal muscles of the right side in chronic recurrent appendicitis. **Wood's s.,** relaxation of the orbicularis muscle, fixation of the eyeball, and divergent strabismus, indicative of profound anesthesia. **Wreden's s.,** presence of a gelatinous matter in the external auditory meatus in children who are born dead. **Wynter's s.,** absence of the movements of abdominal respiration: seen in acute peritonitis. **Zaufal's s.,** saddle nose. **Zugsmith's s.,** abnormal dulness on percussion in the second interspace for a variable distance on both sides of the sternum, which is encountered in cases of gastric ulcer and carcinoma of the stomach.

signa (sig′nah) [L.]. Mark, or write; abbreviated s. or sig. on prescriptions. See *prescription.*

signature (sig′nah-tūr) [L. *signatura*]. 1. That part of a prescription which gives directions as to the taking of the medicine. See *prescription.* 2. Any characteristic feature of a substance formerly regarded as an indication of its medicinal virtues: thus, the eyelike mark on the flower of the euphrasia was supposed to show its usefulness in eye diseases; the liver-like shape of the leaf of liverwort pointed to its use in hepatic diseases; the yellow color of saffron indicated its use in jaundice.

signaturist (sig′nah-tūr″ist). One who believes in the doctrine of signatures.

signe (sēn) [Fr.]. Sign. **s. de journal** (sēn-dĕ-zhoor-nal′), Froment's paper sign. **s. du lacet** (sēn-du-las-ā′), the appearance of petechia on obstruction of venous return from a part. **s. de peau d'orange** (sēn-dĕ-po-dor-anzh′), orange-peel sign.

Signorelli's sign (sēn-yor-el′ēz) [Angelo *Signorelli*, Italian physician, 1876–1952]. See under *sign.*

Sig. n. pro. Abbreviation for L. *sig′na nom′ine pro′prio*, label with the proper name.

siguatera (sig″wah-ta′rah) [Sp.]. Ciquatera.

sijna (sij′nah). An East Indian bark, used in colics; ecbolic if given in large doses.

sikimi (sik′ĭ-me) [Japanese]. The plant, *Illicium religiosum.*

sikimin (sik′ĭ-min). A poisonous hydrocarbon, $C_{10}H_{16}$, which is found in the leaves of *Illicium religiosum.*

sikimitoxin (sik-im″ĭ-tok′sin). A poisonous substance extracted from sikimi.

silajit (sil′ah-jit). An exudation from rock surfaces during the hot season in certain parts of India: used in Hindoo medicine.

silent (si′lent). Producing no detectible signs or symptoms; noiseless.

silex (si′leks). Silica.

Silex's sign (se′leks-ez) [Paul *Silex*, German ophthalmologist, 1858–1929]. See under *sign.*

silhouettograph (sil″oo-et′o-graf). A photograph of a person's shadow picture (silhouette).

silica (sil′ĭ-kah) [L. *silex* flint]. Silicon dioxide, SiO_2, or silicic anhydride; also its homeopathic preparation.

silicate (sil′ĭ-kāt) [L. *silicus*]. Any salt of silicic acid.

silicatosis (sil″ĭ-kah-to′sis). Pulmonary disease caused by the inhalation of the dust of silicates.

silicea (sĭ-lis′e-ah). A homeopathic preparation of silica.

silicious (sĭ-lish′us). Resembling or containing silica.

silico-anthracosis (sil″ĭ-ko-an″thrah-ko′sis). Silicosis.

silicofluoride (sil″ĭ-ko-floo′o-rīd). A compound of silicon and some other base with fluorine.

silicol (sil′ĭ-kol). An organic silica compound, silicic oxide casein metaphosphate: used in the treatment of tuberculosis.

silicon (sil′ĭ-kon) [L. *silex* flint]. A nonmetallic tetrad element whose dioxide is silica; symbol, Si; atomic number, 14; atomic weight, 28.086. **s. carbide,** a compound produced by the reaction of silicon and carbon at extremely high temperature, used in dentistry as an abrasive agent. **s. fluoride,** a compound whose fumes are sometimes fatal to workers in superphosphate factories.

silicone (sil′ĭ-kōn). Any organic compound in which all or part of the carbon has been replaced by silicon.

silicosiderosis (sil″ĭ-ko-sid″er-o′sis). Pneumoconiosis in which the inhaled dust is that of silicates and iron.

silicosis (sil″ĭ-ko′sis) [L. *silex* flint]. Pneumoconiosis due to the inhalation of the dust of stone, sand, or flint containing silicon dioxide; grinders' disease. Cf. *silicatosis.* **infective s.,** silicotuberculosis.

silicote (sil′ĭ-kōt). Trade mark for preparations of dimethicone.

silicotic (sil″ĭ-kot′ik). Pertaining to or characterized by silicosis.

silicotuberculosis (sil″ĭ-ko-tu-ber″ku-lo′sis). Tuberculous infection of the silicotic lung; infective silicosis.

siliqua (sil′ĭ-kwah) [L.]. Pod, or husk. **s. oli′vae** ["husk of the olive"], the fibers which appear to encircle superficially the inferior olive of the brain. Their outer and inner portions are termed *funiculi siliquae.*

siliquose (sil′ĭ-kwōs). Pertaining to or resembling a pod or husk. See under *cataract* and *desquamation.*

silkosis (sil-ko′sis). A complication sometimes following use of silk sutures, with formation of sinuses from which the sutures may be discharged for months or years.

silkworm-gut (silk′werm-gut). A strand drawn from a silkworm which has been killed when ready to spin its cocoon; used, like catgut, for sutures, but much less pliable than the latter, and not so absorbable.

sillonneur (se-yon-nur′) [Fr.]. A three-bladed scalpel for operations on the eye.

silvatic (sil-vat′ik) [L. *silva* a wood or woods]. Pertaining to or occurring in the woods; as *silvatic plague.*

silver (sil′ver) [L. *argentum*]. A white, soft, malleable, and ductile monad metal; symbol, Ag; atomic number, 47; atomic weight, 107.870. Its compounds are extensively used in medicine, and metallic silver is employed in surgery and in the manufacture of instruments. **s. arsphenamine.** See under *arsphenamine.* **colloidal s.,** a silver preparation in which the silver exists as free ions to only a small extent. See *protein s., mild,* and *protein s., strong.* **s. iodide,** a light-yellowish, binary, powdery compound, AgI: useful in syphilis and in nervous diseases, and also applied locally in cases of conjunctivitis. **s. iodide, colloidal,** silver iodide in solution rendered stable by gelatin: an antiseptic for treating inflammations of mucous membranes. **s.**

nitrate, a compound, $AgNO_3$: used as a caustic and local anti-infective, one important use being in prevention of infection in the eyes of newborn infants. **s. nitrate, toughened,** a compound prepared by fusing silver nitrate with hydrochloric acid, sodium chloride, or potassium nitrate, occurring as white crystalline masses molded into pencils or cones, and containing 94.5 per cent of silver nitrate: a convenient means of applying silver nitrate locally. Called also *lunar caustic, fused silver nitrate,* and *molded silver nitrate.* **s. oxide,** a heavy brownish-black powder, Ag_2O. **s. picrate,** yellow crystals, $C_6H_2(NO_2)_3OAg.H_2O$: used locally in anterior urethritis and in trichomonas and monilia infections of the vagina. **protein s., mild,** a compound of silver with protein, containing 19–23 per cent of silver. **protein s., strong,** a compound of silver and protein containing 7.5–8.5 per cent of silver, an active germicide with a local irritant and astringent effect.

silverskin (sil′ver-skin). The pericarp and germ of grains which are removed in processing, as in polished rice, but which contain the thiamine.

Silvester's method (sil-ves′terz) [Henry Robert *Silvester*, English physician, 1829–1908]. See under *respiration, artificial.*

silvestrene (sil-ves′trēn). A hydrocarbon, $C_{10}H_{16}$, obtainable from European oil of turpentine.

Simaruba (sim″ah-roo′bah). A genus of tropical American trees, several species of which are medicinal. The root bark of *S. ama′ra* is a bitter tonic and astringent.

simesthesia (sim″es-the′ze-ah). Osseous sensibility.

similia similibus curantur (sĭ-mil′e-ah sĭ-mil′ĭ-bus ku-ran′tur) [L. "likes are cured by likes"]. The doctrine, or the brocard expressing it, which lies at the foundation of homeopathy; namely, that a disease is cured by those remedies which produce effects resembling the disease itself.

similimum (sĭ-mil′ĭ-mum) [L. "likest"]. The homeopathic remedy which most exactly reproduces the symptoms of any disease.

Simmonds' disease, syndrome (sim′ondz) [Morris *Simmonds*, physician in Hamburg, 1855–1925]. See under *disease.*

Simon's factor, sign (si′monz) [Charles Edmund *Simon*, Baltimore physician, 1866–1927]. See under *factor* and under *sign*, def. 1.

Simon's operation, sign (si′monz) [John *Simon*, English surgeon, 1824–1876]. See under *operation* and under *sign*, def. 2.

Simon's position, speculum (ze′monz) [Gustav *Simon*, German surgeon, 1824–1876]. See under *position* and *speculum.*

Simonart's thread (se″mo-narz′) [Pierre Joseph Cécilien *Simonart*, Belgian obstetrician, 1817–1847]. See under *thread.*

Simonea folliculorum (sĭ-mo′ne-ah fŏ-lik″u-lo′rum). *Demodex folliculorum.*

Simonelli's test (si″mo-nel′ēz) [F. *Simonelli*, Italian physician]. See under *tests.*

Simons' disease (si′monz) [Arthur *Simons*, Berlin physician, born 1877]. Lipodystrophia progressiva.

Simonsiella (si-mon″se-el′ah). A genus of algae parasitic in the mouths of men and many animals.

simple (sim′p′l) [L. *simplex*]. 1. Neither compound nor complex; single. 2. An old term for any herb with real or supposed medicinal virtues.

simpler (sim′pler). An herb doctor.

Simpson's forceps (simp′sunz) [Sir James Young *Simpson*, Scottish obstetrician, 1811–1870]. See under *forceps.*

Simpson light (simp′sun) [William Speirs *Simpson*, British civil engineer, died 1917]. See under *light.*

Simpson's splint (simp′sunz) [William Kelly *Simpson*, laryngologist in New York, 1855–1914]. See under *splint.*

Sims's position, speculum, etc. (simz) [J. Marion *Sims*, New York gynecologist, 1813–1883]. See under the nouns.

simul (si′mul) [L.]. At the same time as.

simulation (sim″u-la′shun) [L. *simulatio*]. 1. The act of counterfeiting a disease; malingering. 2. The imitation of one disease by another.

Simuliidae (si″mu-le′ĭ-de). A family of flies of the order Diptera, characterized by small size, a humped back, and short stubbed antennae of 10 or 11 segments. It contains approximately 600 species, known variously as black flies, buffalo gnats, or turkey gnats. The females of several species are vicious biters.

Simulium (si-mu′le-um). A genus of flies of the family Simuliidae. They are widely distributed and a great pest at times. *S. arc′ticum* occurs in Alaska. *S. columbaczen′se,* a species in southern Europe which has been known to kill animals. *S. damno′sum* is the intermediate host of *Onchocerca volvulus. S. deco′rum katmai* is a vector of tularemia. *S. griseicol′lis,* the nimetti found in the Sudan. *S. moo′seri* transmits *Onchocerca volvulus* in Mexico. *S. pecua′rum,* the buffalo gnat, a terrible scourge to horses and cattle. *S. venus′tum,* a species widely distributed in North America and Denmark.

sinal (si′nal). Pertaining to a sinus; sinusal.

sinapism (sin′ah-pizm) [L. *sinapismus;* Gr. *sinapismos, sinapisma*]. A plaster or paste of ground mustard seed; a mustard plaster.

sinapized (sin′ah-pizd). Mixed with or containing mustard.

sinaxar (sin′aks-ar). Trade mark for a preparation of styramate.

sincipital (sin-sip′ĭ-tal). Pertaining to the sinciput.

sinciput (sin′sĭ-put) [L.]. [N A, B N A] The anterior and upper part of the head. Called also *bregma.*

sinew (sin′u). The tendon of a muscle. **back s.,** the large flexor tendon at the back of the cannon bone of quadrupeds. Called also *back tendon.* **weeping s.,** an encysted ganglion, chiefly on the back of the hand, containing synovial fluid.

sing. Abbreviation of L. *singulo′rum,* of each.

singoserp (sing′go-serp). Trade mark for preparations of syrosingopine.

singultation (sing″gul-ta′shun). A hiccup.

singultous (sing-gul′tus). Affected with hiccup.

singultus (sing-gul′tus) [L.]. Hiccup. **s. gas′tricus nervo′sus,** hiccup due to a neurotic condition of the stomach.

sinigrin (sin′ĭ-grin). Potassium myronate, $CH_2:CH.CH_2(S.C_6H_{11}O_5)N.CO.SO_2.OK$, a glycoside found in black mustard seed.

sinister (sin-is′ter) [L.]. Left; in official anatomical nomenclature, used to designate the left hand one of two similar structures, or the one situated on the left side of the body.

sinistrad (sin-is′trad). To or toward the left.

sinistral (sin′is-tral) [L. *sinistralis*]. 1. Pertaining to the left side. 2. An individual exhibiting sinistrality.

sinistrality (sin″is-tral′ĭ-te). The preferential use, in voluntary motor acts, of the left member of the major paired organs of the body, as ear, eye, hand, and leg.

sinistraural (sin″is-traw′ral) [L. *sinister* + *auris* ear]. Hearing better with the left ear.

sinistro- (sin′is-tro) [L. *sinister* left]. Combining form meaning left, or denoting relationship to the left side.

sinistrocardia (sin″is-tro-kar′de-ah) [*sinistro-* + Gr. *kardia* heart]. Displacement of the heart to the left.

sinistrocerebral (sin″is-tro-ser′e-bral). Pertaining to or situated in the left cerebral hemisphere.

sinistrocular (sin″is-trok′u-lar) [*sinistro-* + L. *oculus* eye]. Left eyed: having the left eye the master eye.

sinistrocularity (sin″is-trok″u-lar′ĭ-te). The state of having the left eye the master eye.

sinistrogyration (sin″is-tro-ji-ra′shun) [*sinistro-* + L. *gyrus* a turn]. A turning to the left, as a movement of the eye or the plane of polarization.

sinistromanual (sin″is-tro-man′u-al) [*sinistro-* + L. *manus* hand]. Left handed.

sinistropedal (sin″is-trop′ĕ-dal) [*sinistro-* + L. *pes* foot]. Using the left foot in preference to the right.

sinistrophobia (sin″is-tro-fo′be-ah). Morbid dread of things on the left side; also called *levophobia.*

sinistrorse (sin′is-trōrs). Turned to the left.

sinistrose (sin′is-trōs). A levorotatory sugar sometimes found in the urine.

sinistrosis (sin″is-tro′sis) [L. *sinister* unlucky]. A nervous and mental condition, including defects of speech and hearing, occurring in persons who have gone through bombardments in war.

sinistrotorsion (sin″is-tro-tor′shun) [*sinistro-* + L. *torsio* twist]. A twisting toward the left: used mainly of the eye.

sinkaline (sing′kah-lin). Choline.

Sinkler's phenomenon (singk′lerz) [Wharton *Sinkler,* Philadelphia neurologist, 1845–1910]. See under *phenomenon.*

sino-atrial (si″no-a′tre-al). Pertaining to the sinus venosus and the atrium of the heart.

sino-auricular (si″no-aw-rik′u-lar). Sino-atrial.

sinobronchitis (si″no-brong-ki′tis) [*sino-* + Gr. *bronchos* bronchus + *-itis*]. Chronic paranasal sinusitis with recurrent episodes of bronchitis or collapse.

sinography (si-nog′rah-fe) [*sinus* + Gr. *graphein* to write]. Roentgenography of the sinuses.

sinomenine (si-nom′ĕ-nin). A crystalline alkaloid, $C_{19}H_{23}NO_4$, from *Sinomenium diversifolium.*

Si non val. Abbreviation for L. *si non va′leat,* if it is not enough.

sinospiral (si″no-spi′ral). Pertaining to the sinus venosus and having a spiral course: said of certain muscle fibers of the heart.

sinoventricular (si″no-ven-trik′u-lar). Pertaining to the sinus venosus and the ventricle of the heart.

sinter (sin′ter). 1. The calcareous or silicious matter deposited by mineral springs. 2. [Ger.]. To transform into a solid mass by heating without melting.

sintoc (sin′tok). The bark of *Cinnamomum sintoc,* of the East Indies: it resembles cinnamon.

sintrom (sin′trom). Trade mark for a preparation of acenocoumarol.

sinu-atrial (sin″u-a′tre-al). Sino-atrial.

sinu-auricular (sin″u-aw-rik′u-lar). Sino-atrial.

sinuitis (sin″u-i′tis). Sinusitis.

sinuotomy (si″nu-ot′o-me). Sinusotomy.

sinuous (sin′u-us) [L. *sinuosus*]. Bending in and out; winding.

sinus (si′nus), pl. *si′nus* or *sinuses* [L. "a hollow"]. 1. A cavity, or hollow space; used in anatomical nomenclature as a general term to designate such spaces as the dilated channels for venous blood, found chiefly in the cranium, or the air cavities in the cranial bones. 2. An abnormal channel or fistula permitting the escape of pus. **accessory s's of the nose,** s. paranasales. **air s.,** an air-containing space within the substance of a bone. **s. a′lae par′vae,** s. sphenoparietalis. **anal s's, s. ana′les** [N A], furrows, with pouchlike recesses at the lower end, separating the rectal columns. Called also *s. rectales* [B N A]. **s. of anterior chamber,** the narrow space at the edge of the anterior chamber of the eye, between the border of the cornea and the root of the iris. **s. aor′tae** [N A], **s. aor′tae [Valsal′vae]** [B N A], **aortic s.,** the pouchlike dilatations of the aorta, one opposite each of the segments of the semilunar valve. **Arlt's s.,** s. of Maier. **s. arte′riae pulmona′lis,** s. trunci pulmonalis. **articular s. of atlas,** fovea dentis atlantis. **articular s. of atlas, superior,** fovea articularis superior atlantis. **articular s. of axis, anterior,** facies articularis anterior axis. **articular s. of vertebrae, inferior.** See *facies articulares inferiores vertebrarum.* **s. of atlas, anterior,** fovea dentis atlantis. **basilar s.,** plexus basilaris. **s. of Bochdalek,** hiatus pleuroperitonealis. **branchial s.,** a branchial fistula opening on the surface of the body. **Breschet's s.,** s. sphenoparietalis. **s. carot′icus** [N A], **carotid s.,** the dilated portion of the internal carotid artery, situated above the division of the common carotid artery into its two main branches, or sometimes on the terminal portion of the common carotid artery, containing in its wall pressoreceptors that are stimulated by changes in blood pressure. **s. caverno′sus** [N A, B N A], **cavernous s.,** an irregularly shaped venous space in the dura mater at either side of the body of the sphenoid bone, extending from the medial end of the superior orbital fissure in front to the apex of the petrous bone behind. It is continuous with the ophthalmic vein and empties into the petrosal sinuses. The right and left sinuses communicate across the midline and are traversed by numerous trabeculae. **cerebral s.,** one of the ventricles of the brain. **cervical s.,** a temporary depression caudal to the embryonic hyoid arch, containing the succeeding branchial arches. It is overgrown by the hyoid arch and closes off as the cervical vesicle. **circular s., s. circula′ris** [B N A], the venous ring around the hypophysis formed by the two cavernous and the anterior and posterior intercavernous sinuses. Omitted in N A. **s. circula′ris i′ridis,** s. venosus sclerae. **coccygeal s.,** a sinus or fistula situated just over or close to the tip of the coccyx, being the remains of the end of the neurenteric canal. See also *pilonidal s.* **s. coch′leae,** vena canaliculi cochleae. **s. condylo′rum fem′oris,** fossa intercondylaris femoris. **s. corona′rius** [N A, B N A], **coronary s.,** the much-dilated terminal portion of the great cardiac vein, which lies in the coronary sulcus below the base of the heart and empties into the posterior part of the right atrium, below the inferior vena cava. **costal s's of sternum,** incisurae costales sterni. **costodiaphragmatic s.,** recessus costodiaphragmaticus pleurae. **costomediastinal s. of pleura, s. costomediastina′lis pleu′rae** [B N A], recessus costomediastinalis pleurae. **costophrenic s.,** recessus costodiaphragmaticus pleurae. **cranial s's,** s. durae matris. **Cuvier's s's.** See under *duct.* **dermal s.,** a congenital sinus tract extending from the surface of the body, between the bodies of two adjacent lumbar vertebrae, to the spinal canal. **s. du′rae ma′tris** [N A, B N A], large venous channels forming an anastomosing system between the layers of the dura mater encephali. They are devoid of valves, do not collapse when drained, and in some parts contain numerous trabeculae. They drain the cerebral veins and some diploic and meningeal veins into the veins of the neck. Those at the base of the skull also drain most of the blood from the orbit. In some places they communicate with superficial veins by small emissary vessels. Called also *venous s's of dura mater.* **s. epididym′idis** [N A, B N A], **s. of epididymis,** a long, slitlike serous pocket between the upper part of the testis and the overlying epididymis. **Eternod's s** a loop of vessels connecting the vessels of chorion with those in the under side of th sac. **ethmoidal s., s. ethmoida′lis** one of the paranasal sinuses, located i moid bone and communicating with th infundibulum and bulla and with th highest meatuses of the nasal c *cellulae ethmoidales.*) **falcial s** s. sagittalis inferior. **Forss** space in the wall of the st folds of the mucosa: seen nation. **frontal s.,** s **bony,** s. frontalis oss B N A], one of th located in the frontal bone, and communicating by way of the nasofrontal duct with the middle meatus of the nasal cavity on the same side. Called also *frontal s.* (See also *s. frontalis osseus.*) **s. fronta'lis os'seus** [N A, B N A], an irregular air cavity situated in the frontal bone on either side, deep to the superciliary arch; separated from its fellow of the opposite side by a bony septum, and communicating with the middle meatus of the bony nasal cavity on the same side. Called also *bony frontal s.* **Guerin's s.,** a diverticulum behind Guérin's fold. **Huguier's s.,** a depression in the tympanum between the fenestra ovalis and the fenestra rotunda. **s. interarcua'lis,** fossa tonsillaris. **s. intercaverno'si** [N A], two spaces that connect the two cavernous sinuses, one passing anterior and the other posterior to the infundibulum of the hypophysis. Called also *intercavernous s's.* **s. intercaverno'sus ante'rior** [B N A], the anterior of the two spaces connecting the cavernous sinuses. See *s. intercavernosi.* **s. intercaverno'sus poste'rior** [B N A], the posterior of the two spaces connecting the cavernous sinuses. See *s. intercavernosi.* **intercavernous s's,** s. intercavernosi. **s. of internal jugular vein, inferior,** bulbus venae jugularis inferior. **s. of internal jugular vein, superior,** bulbus venae jugularis superior. **s. of kidney,** s. renalis. **lacteal s's, s. lacteus, s. lactif'eri** [N A, B N A], **lactiferous s's,** enlargements in the lactiferous ducts just before they open onto the mammary papilla. **laryngeal s., s. of larynx,** ventriculus laryngis. **lateral s.,** s. transversus durae matris. **s. lie'nis** [N A], dilated venous sinuses, not lined by ordinary endothelial cells, found in the splenic pulp. Called also *s's of spleen.* **Lieutaud's s.,** a straight sinus running between the inferior longitudinal sinus and the lateral sinus. **longitudinal s., inferior,** s. sagittalis inferior. **longitudinal s., superior,** s. sagittalis superior. **lunate s. of radius,** incisura ulnaris radii. **lunate s. of ulna,** incisura radialis ulnae. **lymphatic s's,** irregular tortuous spaces within lymphatic tissue (nodes) through which a continuous stream of lymph passes, to enter the efferent lymphatic vessels. **s. of Maier,** a slight diverticulum from the upper part of the lacrimal sac, into which the lacrimal canaliculi open, either together or separately. **marginal s.,** a venous channel near the edge of the placenta. **mastoid s.** See *cellulae mastoideae.* **s. maxilla'ris** [N A], **s. maxilla'ris [Highmo'ri]** [B N A], one of the paired paranasal sinuses, located in the body of the maxilla on either side and communicating with the middle meatus of the nasal cavity on the same side. Called also *maxillary s.* (See also *s. maxillaris osseus.*) **s. maxilla'ris os'seus** [N A, B N A], an air cavity of variable size and shape located in the body of each maxilla, communicating with the middle meatus of the bony nasal cavity on the same side. Called also *bony maxillary s.* **maxillary s.,** s. maxillaris. **maxillary s., bony,** s. maxillaris osseus. ... **s. Mey'eri,** a small depression in ... external auditory canal just in ... brana tympani. **middle s. of** ... atlantis. **s. of Morgagni.** ... 2. Sinus aortae. 3. Ventricu- ... **s's of male urethra,** ... **lique s. of pericar-** ... **car'dii** [N A], a blind ... hind the left atrium, ... dial reflections that ... ulmonary veins. ... [N A, B N A], a ... ter that begins ... inal sinuses, ... margin of ... nce of the ... **asal s's,** ... mucosa- ... es which ... uding the ... phenoidal

sinuses. **parasinoidal s.,** any one of several spaces in the dura mater opening into one of the dural sinuses. Called also *lacuna lateralis* or *lacus lateralis.* **s. pericar'dii,** s. transversus pericardii. **s. pericra'nii,** a soft fluctuating vascular tumor of the scalp which communicates directly with an intracranial sinus through a defect in the skull. **peroneal s. of tibia,** incisura fibularis tibiae. **Petit's s.,** s. aortae. **petrosal s., inferior,** s. petrosus inferior. **petrosal s., superior,** s. petrosus superior. **s. petro'sus infe'rior** [N A, B N A], a venous sinus arising from the cavernous sinus and running along the line of the petrooccipital synchondrosis to the internal jugular vein. Called also *inferior petrosal s.* **s. petro'sus supe'rior** [N A, B N A], a sinus arising at the cavernous sinus, passing along the attached margin of the cerebellar tentorium, and draining into the transverse sinus. Called also *superior petrosal s.* **phrenicocostal s., s. phrenicocosta'lis** [B N A], recussus costodiaphragmaticus pleurae. **pilonidal s.,** a suppurating sinus containing a tuft of hair, occurring chiefly in the coccygeal region, but also in other regions of the body. See also *coccygeal s.* **piriform s.,** recessus piriformis. **s. pleu'rae** [B N A], **pleural s.,** recessus pleuralis. **pleuroperitoneal s.,** hiatus pleuroperitonealis. **s. pocula'ris,** utriculus prostaticus. **s. poste'rior ca'vi tym'pani** [N A, B N A], a groove in the posterior wall of the tympanic cavity above the pyramidal eminence. Called also *posterior s. of tympanic cavity.* **s. precervica'lis,** the depression at the side of the neck, produced in the developing embryo by the growth of the branchial arches. **prostatic s., s. prostat'icus** [N A], the posterolateral recess between the seminal colliculus and the wall of the urethra. **s's of pulmonary trunk,** s. trunci pulmonalis. **pyriform s.,** recessus piriformis. **rectal s's, s. recta'les** [B N A], s. anales. **s. rec'tus** [N A, B N A], a venous sinus of the dura mater situated in the line of union of the cerebral falx and the cerebellar tentorium, formed by the junction of the great cerebral vein and the inferior sagittal sinus, and ending in the confluence of the sinuses. Called also *straight s.* **renal s., s. rena'lis** [N A, B N A], a cavity within the substance of the kidney, occupied by the renal pelvis, calices, vessels, nerves, and fat. **s. reu'niens,** the sinus venosus of the embryonic heart. **rhomboid s.** 1. Fossa rhomboidea. 2. Cavum septi pellucidi. **rhomboid s. of Henle,** ventriculus terminalis medullae spinalis. **s. rhomboi'deus cer'ebri,** cavum septi pellucidi. **Ridley's s.,** s. circularis. **Rokitansky-Aschoff s's,** small outpouchings of the mucosa of the gallbladder extending through the lamina propria and the muscular layer. **sacrococcygeal s.,** pilonidal s. **sagittal s., inferior,** s. sagittalis inferior. **sagittal s., superior,** s. sagittalis superior. **s. sagitta'lis infe'rior** [N A, B N A], a small venous sinus of the dura mater, situated in the posterior half of the lower concave border of the cerebral falx and opening into the upper end of the straight sinus. Called also *inferior sagittal s.* **s. sagitta'lis supe'rior** [N A, B N A], a single, long, arched venous sinus of the dura mater that follows the attached margin of the falx cerebri from the foramen cecum back to the internal occipital protuberance, to end in the confluence of the sinuses. Called also *superior sagittal s.* **semilunar s. of tibia,** incisura fibularis tibiae. **sigmoid s., s. sigmoi'deus** [N A], either of two venous sinuses within the dura mater that are continuations of the transverse sinuses; each curves downward from the tentorium cerebelli to become continuous with the superior bulb of the internal jugular vein. **sphenoidal s.,** s. sphenoidalis. **sphenoidal s., bony,** s. sphenoidalis osseus. **s. sphenoida'lis** [N A, B N A], one of the paired paranasal sinuses, located in the anterior part of the body of the sphenoid bone and communicating with the highest meatus of the nasal cavity on the same side. Called also *sphenoidal s.* (See also *s. sphenoidalis osseus.*) **s. sphenoida'lis os'seus** [N A, B N A], an air cavity of variable size and shape situated in the anterior part of the body of the sphenoid bone; separated from its fellow of the opposite side by a septum, and opening into the nasal cavity above the superior nasal concha on the same side. Called also *bony sphenoidal s.* **sphenoparietal s., s. sphenoparieta'lis** [N A, B N A], one of two venous sinuses in the dura mater, one on either side, beginning at one of the meningeal veins next to the apex of the small wing of the sphenoid bone and passing into the anterior part of the cavernous sinus. **s's of spleen,** s. lienis. **straight s.,** s. rectus. **subarachnoidal s's,** cisternae subarachnoideales. **subpetrosal s.,** s. petrosus inferior. **superpetrosal s.,** s. petrosus superior. **tarsal s., s. tar'si** [N A, B N A], the space between the calcaneus and talus, containing the interosseous ligament. **tentorial s.,** s. rectus. **terminal s.,** a vein which encircles the vascular area in the blastoderm. **tonsillar s., s. tonsilla'ris** [B N A], fossa tonsillaris. **transverse s. of dura mater,** s. transversus durae matris. **transverse s. of pericardium,** s. transversus pericardii. **s. transver'sus du'rae ma'tris** [N A, B N A], either of two large venous sinuses of the dura mater that begin in the confluence of the sinuses near the internal occipital protuberance, each then following the attached margin of the cerebellar tentorium around the temporal bone, and there continuing as the sigmoid sinus. At their origin in the confluence, the right and left sinuses communicate with each other, and with the superior sagittal sinus and the straight sinus. Called also *transverse s. of dura mater.* **s. transver'sus pericar'dii** [N A, B N A], a passage within the pericardial sac between the aorta and pulmonary trunk in front and the atria behind. Called also *transverse s. of pericardium.* **traumatic s.,** a sinus due to trauma. **s. trun'ci pulmona'lis** [N A], slight dilatations in the wall of the pulmonary trunk immediately above the pulmonary valve. Called also *s's of pulmonary trunk.* **s. tym'pani** [N A, B N A], **tympanic s.,** a deep fossa on the medial wall of the tympanic cavity. It is bounded behind by the eminentia pyramidalis, below by the subiculum promontorii, and it goes over in front into the fossula fenestrae cochleae. **s. of tympanic cavity, posterior,** s. posterior cavi tympani. **s. un'guis** [N A], the space underlying the advancing free edge of the fingernail or toenail. **urogenital s., s. urogenita'lis** [N A, B N A], an elongated sac formed by division of the cloaca in the early embryo, communicating with the mesonephric ducts and bladder, and forming the vestibule in the female and most of the urethra in the male. **uterine s's,** venous channels in the wall of the uterus in pregnancy. **uteroplacental s's,** blood spaces between the placenta and the uterine sinuses. **s. of Valsalva,** s. aortae. **s. of venae cavae, s. vena'rum cava'rum** [N A, B N A], the posterior portion of the right atrium that is bounded medially by the interatrial septum and laterally by the crista terminalis. It represents part of the sinus venosus of the embryo. **s. veno'sus** [N A, B N A], the common venous receptacle in the embryo, attached to the posterior wall of the primitive atrium; it receives the umbilical and vitelline veins and the ducts of Cuvier. Called also *venous s.* **s. veno'sus scle'rae** [N A, B N A], a circular channel at the junction of the sclera and cornea. Called also *venous s. of sclera* and *Schlemm's canal.* **venous s's of dura mater,** s. durae matris. **venous s. of sclera,** s. venosus sclerae. **s. ventric'uli,** Forssell's s. **s. vertebra'les longitudina'les** [B N A], venous channels within the membranes enclosing the spinal cord. Omitted in N A.

sinusal (si'nus-al). Pertaining to a sinus.

sinusitis (si″nus-i'tis). Inflammation of a sinus. The condition may be purulent or nonpurulent, acute or chronic. Depending on the site of involvement it is known as ethmoid, frontal, maxillary, or sphenoid sinusitis.

sinusoid (si'nus-oid) [*sinus* + Gr. *eidos* form]. 1. Resembling a sinus. 2. A form of terminal blood channel consisting of a large, irregular anastomosing vessel, having a lining of reticuloendothelium but little or no adventitia. Sinusoids are found in the liver, suprarenals, heart, parathyroid, carotid gland, spleen, hemolymph glands, and pancreas. **myocardial s's,** blood sinusoids that lie between the myocardial bundles or fibers.

sinusoidalization (si″nu-soi″dal-i-za'shun). The application of a sinusoidal current.

sinusology (si″nus-ol'o-je). That branch of medicine which has to do with the sinuses.

sinusotomy (si″nu-sot'o-me) [*sinus* + Gr. *tomē* a cutting]. Incision into a sinus.

sinuventricular (si″nu-ven-trik'u-lar). Sinoventricular.

SiO_2. Silicon dioxide.

Si op. sit. Abbreviation for L. *si o'pus sit,* if it is necessary.

siphac (si'fak). An obsolete name for the peritoneum.

siphon (si'fun) [Gr. *siphōn* tube]. A bent tube of two unequal arms: used in the transfer of liquids, also in wound drainage and in lavage of the stomach. **Duguet's s.,** a rubber tube armed with a trocar for performing thoracentesis without aspiration.

siphonage (si'fun-ij). The use of the siphon, as in washing the stomach or in draining wounds.

Siphonaptera (si″fo-nap'ter-ah) [Gr. *siphon* tube + *apteros* wingless]. An order of laterally compressed, highly chitinized and sclerotized small wingless blood-sucking ectoparasites of mammals and birds, commonly known as fleas. More than 800 species have been described, grouped in six or more families.

siphonoma (si″fon-o'mah). Cylindroma.

Siphunculata (si-fun″ku-la'tah). An order of insects including the lice.

Siphunculina (si-fun″ku-li'nah). A genus of insects of the order Diptera. **S. funic'ola,** the common "eye-fly" of India, where it spreads both conjunctivitis and Naga sore; trachoma may also be transmitted by it.

Sippy method, treatment (sip'e) [Bertram Welton *Sippy,* American physician, 1866–1924]. See under *treatment.*

siqua (si'kwah) [coined from L. *sidentis altitudinis quadratio,* the square of the sitting height]. Pirquet's unit for calculating the area of the absorptive surface of the intestine; it is the square of the sitting height (in centimeters).

sirenomelus (si″ren-om'ĕ-lus) [Gr. *seirēn* siren + *melos* limb]. A fetal monster with fused legs and no feet.

siriasis (sir-i'ah-sis) [Gr. *seiriasis* a disease produced by the heat of the sun]. Thermic fever, or sunstroke.

sirikaya (sir″ĭ-ka'yah). The tree *Anona squamosa,* whose leaves are sudorific and bark purgative.

sirup (sir'up). Syrup.

-sis. A termination or ending of words of Greek origin, signifying state or condition. With a com bining vowel it usually appears as *-asis, -e* *-iasis,* or *-osis.*

sismotherapy (sis″mo-ther'ah-pe). Seis apy.

sissorexia (sis″o-rek'se-ah). A tend spleen to accumulate blood corpuscl

sister (sis'ter). The nurse in char ward (Great Britain).

Sisto's sign (sēs'tōz) [Genero trician, died 1923]. See und

sisto-amylase (sis″to-a which paralyzes the act

Sistrurus (sis-troo'r

Sisyrinchium galaxioides (sis″ĭ-rin′ke-um gah-lak″se-oi′dēz). A South American iridaceous plant; its bulbs are purgative and diuretic.

sitfast (sit′fast). An inverted conical area of dry gangrene involving the skin and superficial fasciae of the back in saddle animals, caused by arrest of blood supply from pressure.

sitieirgia (sit″e-īr′je-ah) [Gr. *sition* food + *eirgein* to bar out]. Morbid rejection of food.

sitiology (sit″e-ol′o-je). Sitology.

sitiomania (sit″e-o-ma′ne-ah). Sitomania.

sitiophobia (sit″e-o-fo′be-ah). Sitophobia.

sito- (si′to) [Gr. *sitos* food]. Combining form denoting relationship to food.

sitology (si-tol′o-je). The sum of knowledge regarding food, diet and nutrition.

sitomania (si″to-ma′ne-ah) [*sito-* + Gr. *mania* madness]. 1. Excessive hunger, or insane craving for food. 2. Periodic bulimia.

sitophobia (si″to-fo′be-ah) [*sito-* + Gr. *phobein* to be affrighted by]. A morbid fear of eating.

sitosterol (si-tos′ter-ol). A generic term for a group of closely related natural plant sterols, the individual compounds being designated by Greek letters, and sometimes subscript numerals, as α_1, α_2, α_3, β, and γ, on the basis of differing characteristics. A pharmaceutical preparation, called "sitosterols," and consisting of β-sitosterol and certain saturated sterols, has been used as an antihypercholesterolemic agent.

sitotaxis (si″to-tak′sis). Sitotropism.

sitotherapy (si″to-ther′ah-pe) [*sito-* + Gr. *therapeia* treatment]. Treatment by food; dietotherapy.

sitotoxin (si″to-tok′sin). Any basic poison generated in a cereal food by a plant microorganism.

sitotoxism (si″to-tok′sizm) [*sito-* + Gr. *toxikon* poison]. Poisoning from ingested foods; food poisoning.

sitotropism (si-tot′ro-pizm) [*sito-* + Gr. *tropos* a turning]. Response of living cells to the presence of nutritive elements.

situation (sit″u-a′shun). The combination of factors with which an individual is confronted. In psychology, applied to the stimulus pattern, or the total sum, of all the factors affecting an individual at a given time.

situs (si′tus), pl. *si′tus* [L.]. Site, or position. **s. inver′sus vis′cerum,** lateral transposition of the viscera of the thorax and abdomen. **s. per-ver′sus,** dislocation of any viscus. **s. sol′itus,** the normal position of the viscera. **s. trans-ver′sus,** s. inversus viscerum.

Si vir. perm. Abbreviation for L. *si vi′res permit′tant,* if the strength will permit.

606 (siks-o-siks). Arsphenamine.

Sjögren's disease (sho′grenz) [Henrick *Sjögren,* Swedish ophthalmologist, born 1899]. See under *disease.*

Sjögren's syndrome (sho′grenz) [Tage *Sjögren,* ... ician, 1859–1939]. See under *syn-* ...

... **od** (sho′kwistz) [John August ... ysician, 1863–1934]. See under ...

... *streptokinase.* 2. Abbre- ... *ng.* Used with numbers, ... signate various chemi- ... been used experi- ... f cancer at Sloan- ... Research.

... s dung]. Beta- ... g, crystalline ... human feces.

... of proteins ... amino acid

skatophagy (skah-tof′ah-je). Scatophagy.

skatosin (skah-to′sin). A base, $C_{10}H_{16}N_2O_2$, derived from certain proteins.

skatoxyl (skah-tok′sil). An oxidation product of skatole, $CH_3.C_8H_6NO$, found in the urine in certain cases of disease of the large intestine.

skein (skān). The threadlike figure seen in the earlier stages of mitosis. **Holmgren's s's, test s's.** See *Holmgren's test,* under *tests.*

skelalgia (ske-lal′je-ah) [Gr. *skelos* leg + *algos* pain + *-ia*]. Pain in the leg.

skelasthenia (ske″las-the′ne-ah) [Gr. *skelos* leg + *a* neg. + *sthenos* strength + *-ia*]. Weakness of the legs.

skelatony (ske-lat′o-ne). Circulatory atony of the leg.

skeletal (skel′ĕ-tal). Pertaining to the skeleton.

skeletin (skel′ĕ-tin). Any one of a number of gelatinous substances occurring in invertebrate tissue, and including chitin, sericin, spongin, etc.

skeletization (skel″ĕ-ti-za′shun). 1. Extreme emaciation. 2. The removal of the soft parts from the skeleton.

skeletogenous (skel″ĕ-toj′e-nus). Producing skeletal or bony structures.

skeletogeny (skel″ĕ-toj′e-ne). The formation of the skeleton; the origin and development of the skeleton.

skeletography (skel″ĕ-tog′rah-fe) [*skeleton* + Gr. *graphein* to write]. A description of the skeleton.

skeletology (skel″ĕ-tol′o-je) [*skeleton* + *-logy*]. The sum of what is known regarding the skeleton.

skeleton (skel′ĕ-ton) [Gr. "a dried body, mummy"]. The hard framework of the animal body, especially the bony framework of the body of higher vertebrate animals; the bones of the body collectively. See *dermoskeleton, endoskeleton, exoskeleton, neuroskeleton,* and *splanchnoskeleton.* **appendicular s.,** the bones of the limbs; the *s. membri inferioris liberi* and *s. membri superioris liberi.* **axial s.,** the bones of the cranium and vertebral column. **cardiac s.,** the connective tissue framework of the heart, which supports and gives attachment to the musculature. **s. extremita′tis inferio′ris li′berae** [B N A], s. membri inferioris liberi. **s. extremita′tis superio′ris li′berae** [B N A], s. membri superioris liberi. **s. of heart,** cardiac s. **s. mem′bri inferio′ris li′beri** [N A], the bones of the thigh, leg, and foot. Called also *s. extremitatis inferioris liberae* [B N A]. **s. mem′bri superio′ris li′beri** [N A], the bones of the arm, forearm, and hand. Called also *s. extremitatis superioris liberae* [B N A]. **visceral s.,** that portion of the skeleton which protects the viscera, as the sternum, ribs, and ossa coxae.

skeletopia, skeletopy (skel″ĕ-to′pe-ah, skel′ĕ-to″pe) [*skeleton* + Gr. *topos* place]. The position of an organ in relation to the skeleton.

Skene's catheter, gland (skēnz) [Alexander J. C. *Skene,* American gynecologist, 1838–1900]. See under *catheter* and *gland.*

skenitis (ske-ni′tis). Inflammation of Skene's glands.

skenoscope (ske′no-skōp) [*Skene's* glands + Gr. *skopein* to examine]. An endoscope for examining Skene's glands.

skeocytosis (ske″o-si-to′sis) [Gr. *skaios* left + *kytos* hollow vessel + *-osis*]. Presence of immature forms of white cells in the blood; called also *deviation to the left.*

skeptophylaxis (skep″to-fi-lak′sis) [Gr. *skēptein* to support + *phylaxis* a guarding]. 1. A condition in which a minute dose of a substance poisonous to animals will produce immediate temporary immunity to the action of the poison, although the blood of the animal may be highly toxic during that period of immunity (Lambert, Ancel, and Bouin, 1910). 2. The method of allergic desensitization by the preliminary injection of a small

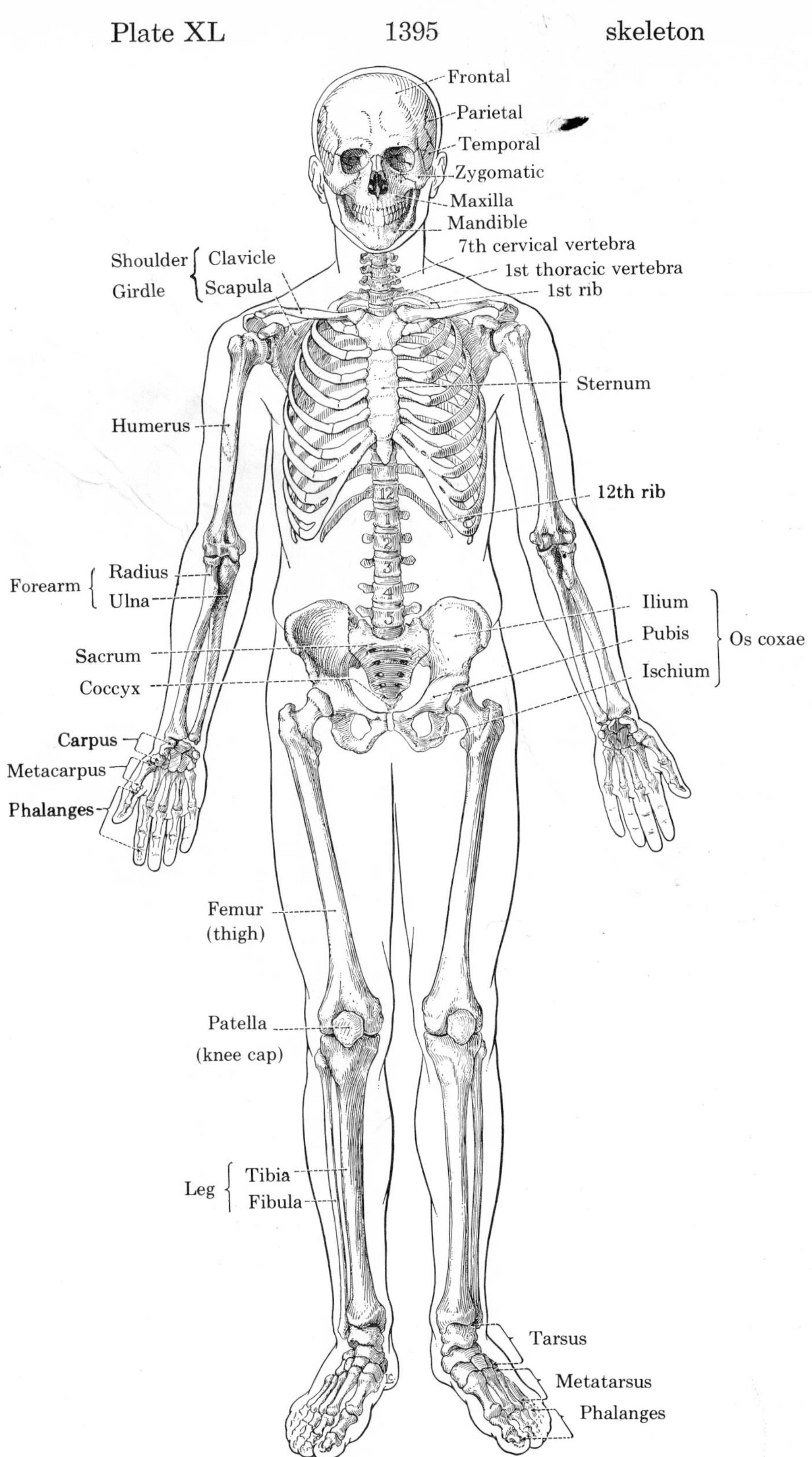

ANTERIOR VIEW OF HUMAN SKELETON

(King and Showers)

amount of the allergen as is commonly done before the injection of an antiserum.

skewfoot (sku′foot). A general term for any deformity of the foot in which its forepart deviates toward the midline. See *metatarsus varus* and *pes varus.*

skia- (ski′ah) [Gr. *skia* shadow]. Combining form denoting reference to shadows, especially of internal structures as produced by roentgen rays.

skiagram (ski′ah-gram) [*skia-* + Gr. *gramma* a writing]. A roentgenogram.

skiagraph (ski′ah-graf). A roentgenogram.

skiagraphy (ski-ag′rah-fe). Roentgenography.

skialytic (ski″ah-lit′ik) [*skia-* + Gr. *lytikos* destroying]. Eliminating or destroying shadows.

skiameter (ski-am′e-ter) [*skia-* + Gr. *metron* measure]. An instrument for measuring the intensity of the roentgen rays, and thus determining how long an exposure is needed.

skiametry (ski-am′e-tre). An objective method for investigating, diagnosing, and evaluating refractive errors of the eye, by projection of a beam of light into the eye and observation of the movement of the illuminated area on the retinal surface and of the refraction by the eye of the emergent rays. Called also *pupilloscopy, retinoscopy, skiascopy,* and *shadow test.*

skiascope (ski′ah-skōp). An instrument for performing skiametry.

skiascopy (ski-as′ko-pe) [*skia-* + Gr. *skopein* to examine]. 1. Skiametry. 2. Examination of the body by the roentgen ray; fluoroscopy.

Skillern's fracture (skil′ernz) [Penn Gaskell *Skillern,* Jr., American surgeon, born 1882]. See under *fracture.*

skin (skin). The outer integument, or covering, of the body, consisting of the corium and epidermis. Called also *cutis.* Beneath the skin is the *subcutaneous connective tissue,* consisting of oblique elastic fibers extending between the corium and fasciae or deeper tissues, and containing lymphatic and blood vessels, nerves, and generally fat. **alligator s.,** ichthyosis sauroderma. **beaters' s.,** goldbeaters' s. **bronzed s.,** melasma suprarenale. **chamois s.,** a soft wash leather of sheep skin: used in surgery. **crocodile s.,** ichthyosis sauroderma. **elastic s.,** cutis hyperelastica. **false s.,** epidermis. **glossy s.,** the shining glazed skin observed in atrophoderma neuriticum. **goldbeaters' s.,** a very thin, tough membrane prepared from ox's cecum and from the intestine of other animals. **India rubber s.,** cutis hyperelastica. **loose s.,** dermatolysis. **paper s.,** parchment s. **parchment s.** 1. The thin, atrophic-looking, stretched skin of cutaneous atrophy; xeroderma. 2. A dry condition of the skin of cattle and sheep, especially such a condition accompanying verminous bronchitis. **piebald s.,** a condition in which the pigment of the skin is not uniformly distributed but is less in some areas, as in leukoderma and vitiligo. **pig s.,** a dimpled condition of the skin due to lymphatic edema. **sailors' s.,** a condition in which the skin is of a bluish-red color, thickened, and covered with warty growths. **scarf s.,** epidermis. **true s.,** corium.

skiodan (ski′o-dan). Trade mark for preparations of methiodal.

sklero-. For words beginning thus, see those beginning *sclero-.*

Sklowsky's symptom (sklow′skēz) [E. L. *Sklowsky,* German physician]. See under *symptom.*

Skoda's rale, sign, etc. (sko′dahz) [Josef *Skoda,* Austrian physician, 1805–1881]. See under the nouns.

skodaic (sko-da′ik). Named for Josef *Skoda.* See under *resonance.*

skole-. For words beginning thus, see those beginning *scole-.*

skopometer (sko-pom′e-ter). An instrument for measuring color, cloudiness, and other optical phenomena of liquids without using standards for comparison.

skoto-. For words beginning thus, see those beginning *scoto-.*

skull (skul). The bony framework of the head, composed of the cranial bones and the bones of the face. It includes the ethmoid, frontal, hyoid, lacrimal, nasal, occipital, palatine, parietal, sphenoid, temporal, and zygomatic bones, and the inferior nasal concha, mandible, maxilla, and vomer. Called also *cranium.* **hot cross bun s.** See *Parrot's sign,* def. 2. **lacuna s.,** craniolacunia. **maplike s.,** a skull marked by irregular tracings resembling outlines on a map: seen in x-ray films of the cranial bones in Schüller-Christian disease. **natiform s.** See *Parrot's sign,* def. 2. **steeple s., tower s.,** oxycephaly. **West's lacuna s., West-Engstler's s.,** a honeycomb appearance of the skull in roentgenograms, associated with spina bifida or meningocele and occasionally with encephalocele.

S.L.A. Abbreviation for L. *sacro-laeva anterior* (left sacro-anterior) position of the fetus.

slant (slant). 1. A sloping surface of agar in a test tube. 2. A slant culture.

sleep (slēp). A period of rest for the body and mind, during which volition and consciousness are in partial or complete abeyance and the bodily functions partially suspended. **crescendo s.,** sleep which is marked by gradually increasing movements on the part of the sleeper. **electric s.,** loss of voluntary movement and presence of general anesthesia induced by the application to the head of a rapidly interrupted electric current. **frozen s.,** treatment of cancer by local exposure of the tissues to a temperature of 40–50°F. and a lowering of the general body temperature to 70–90°F. **paroxysmal s.,** narcolepsy. **prolonged s.,** treatment of neuroses by sustained and continuous sleep for several days under profound drug narcosis. Called also *dauerschlaf* and *dauernarcose.* **temple s.,** incubation, def. 3. **twilight s.,** a condition of analgesia and amnesia, produced by hypodermic administration of morphine and scopolamine. In this state the patient, while responding to pain, does not retain it in her memory. It is employed in the conduct of labor.

slide (slīd). A glass plate on which objects are placed for microscopical examination. **Robinson-Cohen s.,** a modification of the astigmatic dial used in refraction of the eye.

slijmziekte (slim′zēk-te). A bacterial wilt disease of peanuts.

sling (sling). A bandage or suspensory for supporting all or a particular part of the body. **Glisson's s.,** a leather collar applied around the neck and under the chin to which is attached an extension apparatus over a pulley at the head of the patient's bed: for applying extension to the vertebral column. **s. of the lenticular nucleus,** ansa nuclei lenticularis. **Rauchfuss' s.,** an appliance for attaching to a bed for the purpose of supporting the spine in such a way that discharges from the diseased part may escape.

Sling. (Christopher.)

slit (slit′). 1. A long narrow opening or incision. 2. To make a long narrow opening or incision. **gill s.,** a long narrow opening serving as a respiratory passage in fishes and salamanders, and often a similar opening in the developing embryo of higher vertebrates.

slope (slōp). 1. An inclined plane; a surface which is neither horizontal nor vertical. 2. To deviate from the horizontal and from the vertical plane; said of a surface intersecting the horizontal at an angle between 1 and 90 degrees.

slough (sluf). A mass of dead tissue in or cast out from living tissue.

sloughing (sluf'ing). The formation or separation of a slough.

slows (slōz). Trembles.

S.L.P. Abbreviation for L. *sacro-laeva posterior* (left sacroposterior) position of the fetus.

S.L.T. Abbreviation for L. *sacro-laeva transversa* (left sacrotransverse) position of the fetus.

Sluder's method, neuralgia, operation (slu'derz) [Greenfield *Sluder*, American laryngologist, 1865–1928]. See under *operation* and *neuralgia*.

sludge (sluj). A suspension of solid or semisolid particles in a fluid which itself may or may not be a truly viscous fluid. **activated s.,** sludge from well aerated sewage, which, being well supplied with oxidizing bacteria, ensures the presence of sufficient oxidizing organisms to activate the next tankful of sewage. **dewatered s.,** sludge from which the water has been removed by drying or pressing.

sludging (sluj'ing). The settling out of solid particles from solution. **s. of blood.** See *intravascular agglutination*, under *agglutination*.

Sm. Chemical symbol for *samarium*.

smallpox (smawl'poks). Variola; an acute infectious disease caused by a virus, and characterized by vomiting, lumbar pains, an eruption which is first papular, then vesicular, and finally pustular, and by fever which is marked by a distinct remission, beginning with the eruption and continuing until the latter becomes pustular. The period of incubation is about twelve days, and the eruption consists in infiltration of cells into the skin, which cells undergo liquefaction, with the production of suppuration. The eruption appears about the third or fourth day after the prodromal symptoms of chills and fever, with the formation of small red spots on the forehead, face, and wrists. These change into smooth, round papules, which feel like shot under the skin. This eruption spreads over the body, and about the third day the papules become converted into vesicles with a depression or umbilication at the top. The vesicles gradually become converted into pustules, which increase in size and dry up and break, forming soft, yellow crusts, which have a peculiar offensive odor. After a week the scabs fall off, leaving pitted scars or pock-marks. **black s.,** hemorrhagic s. **bovine s.,** vaccinia. **Canadian s.,** horse pox. **coherent s.,** a kind on which the pustules cohere at the edges, but do not become confluent. **confluent s.,** a severe form in which the pustules become more or less confluent. **discrete s.,** a form in which the pustules remain more or less distinct. **equine s.,** horse pox. **hemorrhagic s.,** a form in which hemorrhage occurs into the vesicles or from the mucous surfaces. **inoculation s.,** smallpox resulting from the direct, purposeful transfer of variola virus from a patient to a well person, which was widely practiced before the advent of vaccination. **malignant s.,** a severe and very fatal form of hemorrhagic smallpox. **mild s.,** alastrim. **modified s.,** varioloid. **ovine s.,** ovinia. **Sanaga s.,** alastrim.

smear (smēr). A specimen for microscopic study prepared by spreading the material across the glass slide.

Smee cell (sme) [Alfred *Smee*, English surgeon, 1818–1877]. See under *cell*.

smegma (smeg'mah) [Gr. *smēgma* soap]. A thick, cheesy, ill-smelling secretion, consisting principally of desquamated epithelial cells, and found chiefly about the external genitals. **s. clitor'idis** [B N A], the thick, cheesy secretion found on and around the clitoris. Omitted in N A. **s. embryo'num,** vernix caseosa. **s. praepu'tii** [B N A], the thick, cheesy secretion found under the prepuce (preputium). Omitted in N A.

smegmatic (smeg-mat'ik). Pertaining to or composed of smegma.

smegmolith (smeg'mo-lith) [*smegma* + Gr. *lithos* stone]. A calcareous concretion in the smegma.

smell-brain (smel'brān). The rhinencephalon.

Smellie's method (smel'ēz) [William *Smellie*, British obstetrician, 1697–1763]. See under *method*.

smilacin (smi'lah-sin) [Gr. *smilakinos* pertaining to smilax]. A poisonous glycoside, $C_{18}H_{36}O_6$, from sarsaparilla.

Smilax (smi'laks) [L., Gr. "bindweed"]. A genus of climbing smilaceous plants, which are the source of sarsaparilla.

Smith's disease, sign [Eustace *Smith*, London physician, 1835–1914]. See under *disease* and *sign*.

Smith's dislocation, fracture [Robert William *Smith*, Irish surgeon, 1807–1873]. See under *dislocation* and *fracture*.

Smith's operation [Henry *Smith*, English surgeon in India, 1823–1894]. See under *operation*, def. 2.

Smith's phenomenon [Theobald *Smith*, American pathologist, 1859–1934]. See *Theobald Smith phenomenon*, under *phenomenon*.

Smith's test [Walter George *Smith*, Irish physician, born 1844]. See under *tests*.

Smith-Petersen nail [Marius Nygaard *Smith-Petersen*, American orthopedic surgeon, 1886–1953]. See under *nail*.

S.M.O. Abbreviation for *Senior Medical Officer* (in Navy), and for *Medical Officer of Schools*.

smog (smog). A mixture of smoke and fog; a colloid system in which the disperse phase consists of a mixture of gas and moisture and the dispersion medium is air.

smoke (smōk). A colloid system in which the disperse phase and the dispersion medium are both gas.

smudging (smuj'ing). A defect of speech in which the difficult consonants are omitted.

smut (smut). A disease of cereal grasses (wheat, oats, rye, Indian corn) caused by fungi of the genus *Ustilago* and *Urocystis*. See *Ustilago* and *Urocystis*. **corn s.,** a smut of maize which is caused by *Ustilago maydis* and is used like ergot. **rye s.,** ergot.

Sn. Chemical symbol for *tin* [L. *stannum*].

S.N. Abbreviation for L. *secun'dum natu'ram*, according to nature.

SN 7618. Chloroquine.

SN 13,272. Primaquine.

SN 13,276. Pentaquine.

snail (snāl). A gastropod mollusk with a spiral shell. Certain fresh-water snails in tropical countries are intermediate hosts of parasitic trematodes; the miracidium of the fluke developing into a cercaria in the body of the snail.

snake (snāk). A limbless reptile, many species of which are poisonous. **coral s.,** a venomous snake of the United States belonging to the genus *Elaps*. **poisonous s's,** snakes that secrete substances capable of producing a deleterious effect on the blood (hematoxins) or nervous system (neurotoxins), which are injected into the body of the victim by their bite. See *table*, page 1398.

snap (snap). A short sharp sound. **opening s.,** a short sharp sound occurring just after the beginning of the second heart sound: heard in the fourth left interspace in mitral stenosis.

snare (snār). A wire loop or noose for removing polypi and tumors, being placed around them and tightened so as either to cut them off at the base or to tear them out by the roots. **cold s.,** a snare that has not been heated. **hot s.,** a wire snare heated by a galvanic current, and used to burn off growths. Called also *galvanocaustic s.* **Jarvis's s.,** a wire snare operated by a screw in the handle.

sneeze (snēz). 1. To expel air forcibly and spasmodically through the nose and mouth. 2. An involuntary, sudden, violent, and audible expulsion of air through the mouth and nose.

IMPORTANT POISONOUS SNAKES OF THE WORLD*

FAMILY AND TYPE OF FANGS	COMMON NAMES	TYPE OF VENOM	DISTRIBUTION	REMARKS
COLUBRIDAE; rear, immovable, grooved	Colubrids	Mostly mild	Warm parts of both hemispheres	Over 1000 species, the few poisonous ones not dangerous
Example:	Boomslang	Hemorrhagin	South Africa	Arboreal, timid
ELAPIDAE; front, immovable, grooved	Elapids	Predominantly neurotoxin	Mostly in Old World	Over 150 species, very poisonous
Examples:	Cobras	Mostly neurotoxin	Africa, India, Asia, Philippines, Celebes	Spitting cobra in Africa aims at eyes
	Kraits	Strong neurotoxin	India, S.E. Asia, Indonesia	Sluggish, often buried in dust
	Mambas	Neurotoxin	Tropical W. Africa	Arboreal
	Blacksnake	Neurotoxin	Australia	Large snake, wet terrain
	Copperhead	Neurotoxin	Australia, Tasmania, Solomons	Damp environment
	Brown snake	Neurotoxin	Australia, New Guinea	Slender
	Tiger snake	Strong neurotoxin	Australia	Dry environment; aggressive; very dangerous
	Death adder	Neurotoxin	Australia, New Guinea	Sandy terrain
	Coral snakes	Neurotoxin	United States, tropical America	About 26 species, 2 in southern U. S. A.
HYDROPHIDAE; front, immovable, hollow	Sea snakes	Some mild; others very toxic	Tropical, Indian and Pacific Oceans	Gentle. Rudder-like tail. Over 50 species
VIPERIDAE; front, movable, hollow	True vipers	Predominantly hematoxin	Entirely in Old World	About 50 species
Examples:	European viper	Hematoxin	Europe (rare), N. Africa, Near East	Dry rocky country
	Russell's viper	Hematoxin	S.E. Asia, Java, Sumatra	Mostly open terrain; deadly
	Sand vipers	Hematoxin	N. Sahara	Buried in sand
	Puff adder	Hematoxin	Arabia, Africa	Open terrain; sluggish
	Gaboon viper	Neurotoxin and hematoxin	Tropical W. Africa	Forests; deadly
	Rhinoceros viper	Hematoxin	Tropical Africa	Wet forests
	Habu viper	Neurotoxin	Okinawa	Caves and dry rocky country
CROTALIDAE; front, movable, hollow	Pit vipers	Predominantly hematoxin	Old and New Worlds; none in Africa	Over 80 species; pit between eye and nostril
Examples:	Rattlesnakes†	Predominantly hematoxin	N., Central and S. America	South American form neurotoxic
	Bushmaster	Hematoxin	Central and S. America	Large. In wet forests
	Fer-de-lance	Hematoxin	Central America, N. South America, few West Indies	Common on plantations
	Palm vipers	Hematoxin(?)	S. Mexico, Central and South America	Arboreal; small, greenish. Bite face
	Copperhead	Hematoxin	United States	Dry stony terrain
	Water moccasin	Hematoxin	Southeast U. S. A. to Texas	Swamps
	Asiatic pit vipers	Hematoxin	Southeast Asia, Formosa	Most arboreal

* Manual of Tropical Medicine, Hunter, Frye, and Swartzwelder.
†All rattlesnakes are poisonous.

Snell's law (snelz) [Simeon *Snell*, English ophthalmologist, 1851–1909]. See under *law*.

Snellen's reform eye, test, type (snel′enz) [Hermann *Snellen*, ophthalmologist in Utrecht, 1834–1908]. See under *eye, tests*, and *test type*.

Snider match test (sni′der) [Thomas H. *Snider*, American physician, born 1925]. See under *test*.

snow (sno). A freezing or frozen mixture consisting of discrete particles or crystals. **carbon dioxide s.,** the substance formed by rapid evaporation of liquid carbon dioxide; it gives a temperature of about 110 degrees below zero Fahrenheit (−79°C.), and is used locally in various conditions of the skin.

snuff (snuf). A medicinal or errhine powder to be inhaled into the nose. **catarrh s.,** a powder used by insufflation for coryza. **Ferrier's s.,** a mixture of bismuth and morphine for insufflation. **white s.,** a mixture of menthol and cocaine for insufflation.

snuffles (snuf′f′lz). A catarrhal discharge from the nasal mucous membrane in infants, generally in congenital syphilis.

SO_2. Sulfur dioxide.

soap (sōp) [L. *sapo*]. Any compound of one or more fatty acids, or their equivalents, with an alkali. Soap is detergent and is much employed in liniments, enemas, and in making pills. It is also a mild aperient, antacid and antiseptic. **animal s.,** sapo domesticus. **arsenical s.,** a soap containing arsenic: used in taxidermy to preserve skins. **carbolic s.,** a disinfectant soap containing 10 per cent of phenol. **castile s.,** a hard soap, either white or mottled, prepared from olive oil and soda. **curd s.,** sapo domesticus. **green s.** See *soft s.* **guaiac s.,** a resin of guaiacum saponified with liquor potassae. **hard s.,** soda s. **McClintock's s.,** a disinfectant soap containing an active mercury salt. **medicinal soft s.,** a preparation of vegetable oil, oleic acid, potassium hydroxide, glycerin, and water, used as a skin cleanser. **potash s.,** soft s. **soda s.,** soap made from soda and olive oil. Called also *hard s.* **soft s.,** a liquid soap made from potash and some oil. The official medicinal soft soap is a potassium soap made by the saponification of vegetable oils, excluding coconut oil and palm kernel oil, without the removal of glycerin. It is used as a detergent and stimulant. Called also *sapo mollis medicinalis* and *green s.* **Starkey's s.,** a soap made of potassium carbonate, turpentine oil, and Venice turpentine in equal parts. **superfatted s.,** a soap having an excess of fat over that necessary to neutralize all the alkali. **zinc s.,** a soap containing zinc oxide or zinc sulfate: for use as an ointment or plaster.

socaloin (so-kal′o-in). A variety of aloin, $C_{15}H_{16}O_7$, from Socotrine aloes.

socia (so′she-ah) [L. "a comrade, associate"]. A detached part or exclave of an organ. **s. parot′idis,** a detached part of the parotid gland.

sociologist (so″se-ol′o-jist). An individual skilled in sociology.

sociology (so″se-ol′o-je) [L. *socius* fellow + *-logy*]. The science dealing with social relations and phenomena.

sociometry (so″se-om′e-tre) [L. *socius* fellow + *metrum* a measure]. The branch of sociology concerned with the measurement of human social behavior.

socket (sok′et). A hollow or depression, into which a corresponding part fits. **dry s.,** a condition sometimes occurring after tooth extraction, resulting in exposure of bone with localized osteomyelitis of an alveolar crypt, and symptoms of severe pain. **tooth s's,** the dental alveoli, the cavities in the maxilla and mandible in which the teeth are embedded. Called also *alveoli dentales maxillae* and *alveoli dentales mandibulae.*

soda (so′dah). A term loosely applied to sodium bicarbonate (baking soda), sodium hydroxide (caustic soda), or sodium carbonate (washing soda). **baking s.,** sodium bicarbonate. **caustic s.,** sodium hydroxide. **chlorinated s.,** a mixture of sodium chloride and sodium hypochlorite. **s. cum cal′ce,** an escharotic preparation of equal parts of sodium hydroxide and lime. **washing s.,** sodium carbonate.

sodemia (so-de′me-ah). The presence of sodium in the blood.

sodiarsphenamine (so″di-ars-fen′ah-min). Sodium arsphenamine. See under *arsphenamine.*

sodic (so′dik). Containing soda or sodium.

sodii (so′de-i) [L.]. Genitive of *sodium.*

sodiocitrate (so″de-o-sit′rāt). A compound containing sodium and a salt of citric acid.

sodiotartrate (so″de-o-tar′trāt). A compound containing sodium and a salt of tartaric acid.

sodium (so′de-um), gen. *so′dii* [L. *na′trium,* gen. *na′trii*]. A soft, silver white, alkaline metallic element; symbol, Na; atomic number, 11; atomic weight, 22.990; specific gravity, 0.971. With a valence of 1, it has a strong affinity for oxygen and other nonmetallic elements. Sodium provides the chief cation of the extracellular body fluids. **s. acetate,** a compound, $CH_3.COONa.3H_2O$: used as a systemic and urinary alkalizer. **s. acetrizoate,** sodium 3-acetamido-2,4,6-triiodobenzoate: used as a contrast medium in angiocardiography and in roentgen visualization of the urinary and biliary tracts. **s. acid phosphate,** s. biphosphate. **s. alginate,** a purified carbohydrate product extracted from brown seaweeds with dilute alkali: used for its emulsifying, stabilizing, suspending, thickening, and water-binding qualities in foods, medicines, and cosmetics. **s. aminopterin.** See under *aminopterin.* **s. aminosalicylate,** an antibacterial (tuberculostatic) compound, $C_7H_6NNaO_3.2H_2O$. **s. antimonyltartrate,** antimony sodium tartrate. See under *antimony.* **s. antimonylthioglycollate,** an organic compound of antimony, $CO_2.CH_2.S.Sb.S.CH_2.COONa$: used in the treatment of granuloma inguinale. **s. arsenate,** Na_2HAsO_4, an odorless, amorphous white powder: used when effects of arsenic are desired. **s. ascorbate,** a compound, $C_6H_7NaO_6$, prepared by interaction of ascorbic acid and sodium bicarbonate: used in solution for the parenteral administration of ascorbic acid (vitamin C). **s. aurothiomalate,** gold sodium thiomalate. See under *gold.* **s. aurothiosulfate,** gold sodium thiosulfate. See under *gold.* **s. benzoate,** a white, odorless, granular or crystalline powder, C_6H_5COONa: used chiefly as a test of liver function. **s. benzosulfimide,** saccharin sodium. See under *saccharin.* **s. bicarbonate,** a white, crystalline powder, $NaHCO_3$: used as a gastric antacid, and frequently administered with other medications to produce alkalinity of the urine. **s. biphosphate,** a white, crystalline powder, or colorless crystals, $NaH_2PO_4.2H_2O$: used to render the urine acid. **s. bisulfite,** a white or yellowish white granular powder or crystals, $NaHSO_3$: used as an antiseptic and as an antioxidant in various pharmaceutical preparations. **s. borate,** an odorless compound, $NA_2B_4O_7$, occurring as a white, crystalline powder, or as colorless, transparent crystals: used in various pharmaceutical preparations for external use. **s. bromide,** a substance in white or colorless crystals, NaBr: used in epilepsy, hysteria, and as a hypnotic sedative. **s. cacodylate,** an arsenical remedy, $(CH_3)_2AsO.ONa.3H_2O$, in the form of white crystals, or a white, granular powder, soluble in water: formerly used in tuberculosis, anemia, malaria, psoriasis, etc. **s. caprylate,** the sodium salt of caprylic acid: used in treatment of fungal infections of the skin. **s. carbonate,** a salt in large, colorless crystals, $Na_2CO_3.10H_2O$: sometimes used in solution as a mouth wash or vaginal douche, or as a lotion on the skin. **s. carbonate, monohydrated,** a compound, $Na_2CO_3.H_2O$, occurring in colorless crystals or a white, crystalline powder, with uses similar to those of calcium carbonate. **carboxymethyl cellulose s.,** the sodium salt of a polycarboxymethyl ether of cellulose: used as a bulk laxative. **s. chlorate,** a salt, $NaClO_3$, with properties similar to those of potassium chlorate, and occurring in colorless or white crystals or granules. **s. chloride,** a white, crystalline compound, NaCl, soluble in water, a necessary constituent of the human body and consequently of food. A 0.75–0.90 per cent solution (*isotonic sodium chloride solution*) is used for intravenous and hypodermic injection in many conditions, as a local application in rhinitis, conjunctivitis, etc., and as a preservative for microscopical specimens. **s. citrate,** a white, crystalline salt, $Na_3C_6H_5O_7.2H_2O$: used as an antacid and sometimes as a diuretic, expectorant, and sudorific. It is largely used as an anticoagulant in blood for transfusion. **s. cyanide,** a powder soluble in water, NaCN: used like potassium cyanide. **s. dimethylarsenate,** s. cacodylate. **s. fluoride,** a white, odorless powder, NaF: used in the fluoridation of water, and also applied locally to the teeth, in 2 per cent solution, to reduce the incidence of dental caries. **s. fluosilicate,** s. silicofluoride. **s. folate,** sodium N-[4-{[(2-amino-4-hydroxy-6-pteridyl)methyl]amino}benzoyl]glutamate: used in various anemias and in control of diarrhea in sprue. **glucosulfone s.,** p,p′-diaminodiphenylsulfone-N,N′-di-(dextrose sodium sulfonate): used in treatment of leprosy and tuberculosis. **s. glutamate,** the monosodium salt of L-glutamic acid: used in treatment of encephalopathies associated with diseases of the liver. **s. glycerophosphate,** $C_3H_5(OH)_2PO_4Na_2$: formerly thought useful in various conditions of disordered metabolism. **s. glycocholate,** a yellowish white, bitter salt, $NaC_{26}H_{42}O_6N$, with a pH of 6.6: used as a laboratory reagent. **s. gold thiosulfate,** gold sodium thiosulfate. See under *gold*. **s. hydrate,** s. hydroxide. **s. hydroxide,** a hard, white solid, NaOH, soluble in water; strongly alkaline and caustic, and used chiefly in various chemical and pharmaceutical manipulations. **s. hypochlorite,** a compound, NaClO: used in solution as a germicide, deodorant, and bleach. **s. hypophosphite,** a salt, $NaPH_2O_2.H_2O$, occurring in colorless, rectangular plates, or as a white, granular powder. **s. hyposulfite,** s. thiosulfate. **s. indigotindisulfonate,** the sodium salt of indigotindisulfonic acid, $C_{16}H_8N_2O_8S_2Na_2$, a blue powder or purple mass: used as a stain in histology and as a test for renal permeability and for sugar in the urine. Called also *indigo carmine*. **s. iodate,** $NaIO_3$, a salt used as an alterative, especially in diseases of the mucous surfaces. **s. iodide,** a binary haloid, NaI, occurring in colorless crystals: used in various conditions as a source of iodine. **s. iodipamide,** sodium N,N′-adipyl-bis(3-amino-2,3,6-triiodobenzoate) water-soluble organic iodine compound: used in roentgenography of the biliary tract. **s. iodohippurate,** a compound which may be administered orally, intravenously, or by retrograde injection, as a contrast medium in roentgenography of the urinary tract. **s. iodomethamate,** a white, odorless powder, $C_8H_3I_2NNa_2O_5$: used as a contrast medium in excretory urography, aortography, angiocardiography, and cerebral arteriography. **s. lactate,** $C_3H_5NaO_3$, the sodium salt of racemic or inactive lactic acid: used parenterally in one-sixth to one-fourth molar solution to combat acidosis. **s. lauryl sulfate,** a surface-active agent, $CH_3(CH_2)_{10}CH_2OSO_3Na$, occurring in white or light yellow crystals: used as an ingredient in toothpastes. **s. levothyroxine,** the sodium salt of the levo isomer of thyroxine: used in replacement therapy. **s. liothyronine,** the sodium salt of L-3,3′,5-triiodothyronine: used in the treatment of hypothyroidism, metabolic insufficiency, and such gynecologic disorders as premenstrual tension, dysmenorrhea, or amenorrhea. **s. methicillin,** sodium 6(2′,6′-dimethoxybenzamido)penicillinate monohydrate, a semisynthetic penicillin salt for parenteral administration. **s. methylarsonate,** a crystalline powder, $CH_3AsO(ONa)_2.5H_2O$, easily soluble in water and less soluble in alcohol, sometimes employed for its arsenical effects. **s. morrhuate,** sodium salts of the fatty acids of cod liver oil: used as a sclerosing agent for varicose veins and hemorrhoids. **s. nitrate,** a compound, $NaNO_3$, occurring as colorless crystals or in white granules or powder; formerly used as a diuretic and in treatment of dysentery, but now used as a reagent and in certain industrial processes. **s. nitrite,** a white crystalline salt, $NaNO_2$: used as an antispasmodic in angina pectoris, Raynaud's disease, asthma, and such conditions as lead colic and spastic colitis; also used as an antidote in cyanide poisoning. **s. oleate,** the sodium salt of oleic acid; formerly considered useful in treatment of gallstones. **s. oxacillin,** a semisynthetic penicillin salt for oral administration. **s. para-aminohippurate,** a compound, $C_9H_9N_2NaO_3$, which is injected intravenously in studies for the measurement of effective renal plasma flow and determination of the functional capacity of the tubular excretory mechanism. **s. para-aminosalicylate,** s. aminosalicylate. **s. perborate,** a compound, $NaBO_3.4H_2O$, prepared by interaction of boric acid or sodium borate with sodium or hydrogen peroxide: used as an oxidant and local anti-infective. **s. peroxide,** a white powder, Na_2O_2, soluble in water in which it liberates oxygen: used as a dental bleach and in ointment form in acne and rosacea pustulosa. **s. phenolsulfonate,** an odorless, saline compound, $NaC_6H_5OSO_3.2H_2O$, in colorless transparent prisms or crystalline granules: sometimes employed as an intestinal antiseptic. **s. phosphate,** a salt, $Na_2HPO_4.7H_2O$: used as a mild saline purgative and cholagogue. **s. phosphate, effervescent,** a dry granular mixture of citric acid, exsiccated sodium phosphate, tartaric acid, and sodium bicarbonate. **s. phosphate, exsiccated,** the anhydrous salt, Na_2HPO_4: used in preparing effervescent sodium phosphate. **potassium s. tartrate.** See under *potassium*. **s. propionate,** a granular, crystalline powder, $CH_3CH_2.COONa.xH_2O$: used in superficial fungus infections. **s. psylliate,** the sodium salt of the liquid fatty acids obtained by hydrolysis of the fixed oil of the seeds of *Plantago ovata:* used as a sclerosing agent. **s. pyroborate,** s. borate **s. pyrophosphate,** a compound, $Na_4P_2O_7$ produced by heating sodium phosphate at a red heat. **s. rhodanate,** s. thiocyanate. **s. salicylate,** a white, crystalline salt, $OH.C_6H_4.COONa$: used as an analgesic. **s. santoninate,** a colorless crystalline compound, $C_{15}H_{19}NAO_4.3\frac{1}{2}H_2O$, once used as a vermifuge. **s. silicate,** a compound of sodium, silicon, and oxygen in various ratios, which has been used as an antiseptic and for other purposes in medicine. **s. silicofluoride,** a white, granular powder, Na_2SiF_6: sometimes added to water to produce 0.7 to 1 part per million of fluorine, to prevent dental caries. **s. stearate,** a compound, $C_{18}H_{35}NaO_2$, produced by interaction of sodium carbonate and commercial stearic acid. The official preparation consists of a mixture of sodium stearate with varying proportions of sodium palmitate ($C_{16}H_{31}NaO_2$). **s. succinate,** a compound, $(CH_2.CO.ONa)_2$: formerly used in catarrhal jaundice. **s. sulfanilate,** a salt in white plates, $C_6H_4(NH_2)SO_2NaO$: used in acute nasal catarrh. **s. sulfate,** a white, efflorescent salt, $Na_2SO_4.10H_2O$: hydragogue cathartic. **s. sulfite,** a compound, $Na_2SO_3.7H_2O$, occurring as colorless, efflorescent crystals: formerly used in treatment of dyspepsia, and externally in parasitic infections. **s. sulfite, anhydrous,** a fairly stable compound, Na_2SO_3, occurring as white small crystals or powder: used as a reagent. **s. sulfite, exsiccated,** s. sulfite, anhydrous. **s. sulfocarbolate,** s. phenolsulfonate. **s. sulfocyanate,** s. thiocyanate. **s. sulfoxone,** disodium sulfonylbis(p-phenyleneimino)di(methanesulfinate), $C_{14}H_{14}N_2Na_2O_6S_3$: used in treatment of leprosy. **s. tetraborate,** s. borate. **s. tetradecyl sulfate,** sodium 7-ethyl-2-methyl-4-hendecanol sulfate, a white, waxy, odorless solid: used in solution as a sclerosing agent. **s. thiocyanate,** white or colorless, odorless crystals, NaSCN, with a cooling, salty taste: used for the same purposes as potassium thiocyanate. **s. thiosulfate,** a coarse, crystalline powder, $Na_2S_2O_3.5H_2O$: formerly recommended in treatment of cyanide poisoning and poisoning with heavy metals, in arsphenamine reactions involving the skin, and in argyria; used also in measuring the volume of extracellular body fluid and the renal glomerular filtration rate.

sodokosis (so″do-ko′sis). Rat-bite fever.

sodoku (so′do-koo) [Japanese *so* rat + *doku* poison]. A relapsing type of infection caused by *Spirillum minus*, transmitted by the bite of an infected rat, and characterized by a delayed local inflammatory reaction at the site of the bite, with lymphangitis, regional lymphadenitis, rigors, and fever of sudden onset; first described in Japan.

sodomist (sod′o-mist). One who practices sodomy.

sodomite (sod′o-mīt). Sodomist.

sodomy (sod′o-me) [after the city of *Sodom*]. A form of paraphilia, variously defined by law to include sexual contact between humans and animals of other species, and mouth-genital or anal contact between humans.

sodophthalyl (so″do-thal′il). Disodoquinone phenolphthalein: used as a laxative.

Soemmering's foramen, ganglion, spot (sem′er-ingz) [Samuel Thomas *Soemmering*, German anatomist, 1755–1830]. See under the nouns.

softening (sof′en-ing) [Gr. *malakia*]. The process of becoming soft; any morbid process of becoming soft, as of the brain or spinal cord, or of the vascular coats. **anemic s.,** disintegration of brain matter from deficient blood supply. **s. of the brain.** 1. A popular designation for paralytic dementia. 2. True softening of the brain substance; encephalomalacia. **colliquative s.,** softening in which the tissues become liquefied. **gray s.,** a stage in which the fat produced by degeneration has been more or less absorbed. **green s.,** a stage in which there is green pus present in the degenerated spot. **hemorrhagic s.,** softening of a part due to hemorrhage into it. **inflammatory s.,** a form of red softening due to inflammation. **mucoid s.,** myxomatous degeneration. **pyriform s.,** yellow s. **red s.,** softening of a patch or of patches of brain substance, with local redness due to congestion. **s. of the stomach,** gastromalacia; softening of the stomach walls due to an extremely acid condition of its contents: the condition is usually seen after death. **white s.,** the stage next following yellow softening, in which the spot has become white from the presence of fatty deposit. **yellow s.,** the second of the three stages of the myelic process, characterized by fatty degeneration; the stage following red softening, in which the patch has become yellow as a result of degenerative changes in the brain substance.

soja bean (so′yah). Soy bean.

sokosha (so-ko′shah). Rat-bite fever.

Sol. Abbreviation for *solution.*

sol (sol). 1. A colloid system in which the dispersion medium is liquid. 2. A contraction of *solution.* **metal s.,** a colloidal solution of a metal. Such solutions have properties similar to those of enzymes, and are therefore sometimes called inorganic enzymes.

solandrine (so-lan′drin). An alkaloid from the plant *Solandra laevis*, having properties like those of hyoscine.

solangustine (so″lan-gus′tin). A crystalline alkaloid, $C_{33}H_{53}NO_7.H_2O$, from *Solanum angustifolium.*

solanoid (so′lah-noid) [L. *solanum* potato + Gr. *eidos* form]. Resembling a raw potato in texture.

solanoma (so″lah-no′mah). A solanoid cancer.

Solanum (so-la′num) [L. "nightshade"]. A genus of herbs and shrubs, including the potato, several of the nightshades, and many poisonous and medicinal species. **S. carolinen′se,** a plant of the United States. The fluidextracts of the root and berries have been used in epilepsy. **S. mammo′sum,** the so-called apple of Sodom, a plant of North America, and its homeopathic preparation. **S. olea′ceum,** the jaquerioba, an herb of tropical America, and a homeopathic preparation of its blossoms. **S. tubero′sum,** the common potato.

solar (so′lar) [L. *solaris*]. 1. Pertaining to the sun. 2. Noting the great sympathetic plexus and its principal ganglia: so called from their radiating nerves.

solargentum (sol″ar-jen′tum). A brand of mild silver protein.

solarium (so-la′re-um) [L.]. A room especially designed to allow exposure to light of the sun or to artificial light.

solarization (so″lar-i-za′shun). Exposure to sunlight and the effects produced thereby; especially the decreased transparency that takes place in glass after long exposure to ultraviolet radiation.

solarize (so′lar-iz) [L. *sol* sun]. To expose to the rays of the sun.

solation (sol-a′shun). The conversion of a gel into a sol.

Soldaini's reagent, test (sol″dah-e′nēz) [Arturo *Soldaini*, Italian chemist]. See under *tests.*

solder (sod′er). 1. A fusible alloy of metals used to unite the edges or surfaces of two pieces of metal. 2. To produce a union between two pieces of metal by use of a fusible alloy.

sole (sōl) [L. *solea; planta*]. The bottom of the foot. **convex s., dropped s.,** pumiced foot.

soleno- (so′lĕ-no) [Gr. *sōlēn* a channel, gutter, pipe]. Combining form denoting relationship to a pipe or gutter; tubular or grooved.

Solenoglypha (so″lĕ-nog′lĭ-fah) [*soleno-* + Gr. *glyphein* to cut out with a knife]. A group of poisonous snakes with fangs that are hollow like a hypodermic needle and that normally fold back against the roof of the mouth but can be erected for striking and piercing. Examples are the massausauga and the rattlesnakes.

solenoid (so′lĕ-noid) [Gr. *sōleno-eides* pipe-shaped, grooved]. A coil of wire spaced equally between turns, which acts like a magnet when an electric current is passed through it.

solenoma (so″lĕ-no′mah). Endometrioma.

solenonychia (so″lĕ-no-nik′e-ah) [*soleno-* + Gr. *onyx, onychos* nail + *-ia*]. A longitudinal tubular deformation of the nail plate, sometimes occurring as the result of formation of an excrescence of the proximal nail bed, the nail forming around it as it grows distally.

Solenopotes (so″lĕ-no-po′tēz) [*soleno-* + Gr. *pōtēs* a drinker]. A genus of lice of the order Anoplura. **S. capilla′tus,** a species of sucking lice occasionally found parasitic on cattle.

solferino (sol″fer-e′no). Fuchsin.

solganal (sol′gah-nal). Trade mark for a preparation of aurothioglucose.

solid (sol′id) [L. *solidus*]. 1. Not fluid or gaseous; not hollow. 2. A substance or tissue not fluid or gaseous. **color s.,** a three-dimensional geometrical body, devised to show the relation of all hues and brightnesses, including black, white, and grays, in their various modes.

Solidago (sol″ĭ-da′go) [L.]. A genus of composite-flowered plants: the golden-rods. *S. virgau′rea*, of Europe and North America, is aromatic and diuretic.

solidism (sol′ĭ-dizm) [L. *solidus* solid]. The obsolete doctrine that changes in the solids of the body, such as expansion or contraction, are the causes of every disease.

solidist (sol′ĭ-dist). One who accepts the doctrine of solidism.

solidistic (sol″ĭ-dis′tik). Pertaining to solidism or to the solidists.

solipsism (sōl′ip-sizm) [L. *solus* alone + *ipse* one's self]. The belief that the world exists only in the mind of the individual, or that it consists solely of the individual himself and his own experiences.

solipsistic (sōl″ip-sis′tik). Pertaining to or characterized by solipsism.

solitary (sol′ĭ-ter″e) [L. *solitarius*]. Placed alone; not grouped with others.

sol-lunar (sol-lu′nar) [L. *sol* sun + *luna* moon]. Pertaining to or caused by the sun and moon.

solubility (sol″u-bil′ĭ-te). The quality or fact of being soluble; susceptibility of being dissolved.

soluble (sol′u-b'l) [L. *solubilis*]. Susceptible of being dissolved.

solum (so′lum), pl. *so′la* [L.]. [N A] The bottom or lowest part. **s. tym′pani,** paries jugularis cavi tympani. **s. un′guis,** matrix unguis.

solute (so′lūt). A substance dissolved in a solution. A solution consists of a solute and a solvent.

solutio (so-lu′she-o) [L., from *solvere* to dissolve]. Solution.

solution (so-lu′shun) [L. *solutio*]. 1. A liquid consisting of a mixture of two or more substances which are molecularly dispersed through one another in a homogeneous manner; defined in pharmacology as a liquid preparation containing one or several soluble chemical substances usually dissolved in water and not, for various reasons, falling into another category. 2. The process of dissolving. 3. A loosening or separation. **A.C.D. s., acid citrate dextrose s.** See *anticoagulant acid citrate dextrose s.* **alcoholic s.,** a solution in which alcohol is used as the solvent. **Alsever's s.,** a solution for preserving sheep's red blood cells for use in complement fixation tests. **aluminum acetate s.,** a preparation of aluminum subacetate and glacial acetic acid: used for its antiseptic and astringent action on the skin. **aluminum subacetate s.,** a solution yielding 2.3–2.6 per cent of aluminum oxide and 2.5–6.1 per cent of acetic acid: used topically on the skin as an antiseptic and astringent. **amaranth s.,** a clear, vivid red fluid, produced by dissolving amaranth in purified water, each 100 ml. containing 0.9–1.1 Gm. of $C_{20}H_{11}N_2Na_3O_{10}S_3$. **amaranth s., compound,** a solution composed of amaranth solution, caramel, alcohol, and purified water: used as a coloring agent. **ammonia s., diluted,** a colorless, transparent liquid of alkaline reaction, containing in each 100 ml. 9–10 Gm. of NH_3. Called also *ammonia water*, or *diluted ammonium hydroxide solution.* **ammonia s., strong,** a colorless, transparent liquid, strongly alkaline in reaction, containing 27–30 per cent of NH_3. Called also *stronger ammonia water* or *stronger ammomium hydroxide solution.* **ammonium acetate s.,** a clear, colorless liquid, containing ammonium acetate. **ammonium citrate s., alkaline,** a preparation of dibasic ammonium citrate and strong ammonia solution: used in tests for zinc. **ammonium hydroxide s., diluted,** ammonia s., diluted. **ammonium hydroxide s., stronger,** ammonia s., strong. **anisotonic s.,** a solution having an osmotic pressure differing from that of the standard of reference. **anticoagulant acid citrate dextrose s.,** a sterile solution generally used as an anticoagulant for blood obtained for transfusion purposes, and commonly consisting of dihydrous trisodium citrate, monohydrous citric acid, and dextrose. **antiseptic s.,** a clear, colorless liquid, containing boric acid, thymol, chlorothymol, menthol, eucalyptol, methyl salicylate, thyme oil, alcohol, and purified water: a weak antibacterial solution for external use. **aqueous s.,** a solution in which water is used as the solvent. **aromatic s., alkaline,** a preparation of glycerin, potassium bicarbonate, sodium borate, and other ingredients: used as a mouth wash. **arsenic chloride s.,** arsenious acid s. **arsenic and mercuric iodides s.,** a clear, colorless to faint yellow solution, compounded of arsenic triiodide, red mercuric iodide, and distilled water. **arsenical s.,** potassium arsenite s. **arsenious acid s.,** a clear, colorless, odorless liquid, with an acid reaction, containing arsenic trioxide. **benzalkonium chloride s.,** a clear, colorless, aqueous solution, with an aromatic odor and a slightly bitter taste, which contains 93–107 per cent of the labeled amount of benzalkonium chloride. **benzethonium chloride s.,** a clear colorless liquid, without odor and with a slightly bitter taste, which contains 93–109 per cent of the labeled amount of benzethonium chloride. **boric acid s.,** a clear, colorless, odorless liquid, each 100 ml. of which contains at least 4.25 Gm. of boric acid. Called also *saturated boric acid solution.* **Bouin's s.** See under *fluid.* **buffer s.,** a solution which resists appreciable change in its hydrogen ion concentration when acid or alkali is added to it. **Burnett's s.** See under *fluid.* **Burow's s.,** aluminum acetate s. **calciferol s.,** a solution of calciferol in an edible vegetable oil or other vehicle, each gram containing not less than 0.25 mg. of calciferol. **calcium hydroxide s.,** clear, colorless liquid with an alkaline reaction, each 100 ml., at 25° C., containing not less than 140 mg. of calcium hydroxide. **carmine s.,** a deep red, rather viscous liquid, compounded of carmine, diluted ammonia solution, glycerin, and water. **centinormal s.,** hundredth-normal s. **coal tar s.,** a solution of coal tar and polysorbate 80 in alcohol. **coal tar s., chloroformic,** a yellowish brown liquid, compounded by dissolving coal tar in chloroform. **cochineal s.,** a dark, purplish red fluid with a slightly aromatic odor, compounded of cochineal, potassium carbonate, alum, potassium bitartrate, glycerin, and water. **Cohn's s.,** a synthetic medium for growing yeast and molds, containing monopotassium acid phosphate, calcium phosphate, magnesium sulfate, and ammonium tartrate, in water. **colloid s., colloidal s.,** a preparation consisting of minute particles of matter suspended in a solvent, the solvent being called the continuous phase, and the suspended matter, the disperse phase. Called also *disperse system.* See *dispersoid* and *emulsoid.* **contrast s.,** a solution of a substance opaque to the roentgen ray, used to facilitate roentgen visualization of some organ or structure in the body. **cresol s., compound,** cresol s., saponated. **cresol s., saponated,** a mixture of cresol, vegetable oil, potassium hydroxide, alcohol, and water: used as a disinfectant. **crystal violet s.,** methylrosaniline chloride s. **Czapek-Dox s.,** a solution used for growing molds, containing glucose, sodium nitrate, monopotassium phosphate, potassium chloride, magnesium sulfate, iron sulfate, and water. **Dakin's s.,** a buffered aqueous solution of sodium hypochlorite: used as a bactericide. See *Carrel-Dakin treatment,* under *treatment.* **Dakin's s., modified,** sodium hypochlorite s., diluted. **decimolar s.,** a solution having one-tenth the strength of a molar solution. **decinormal s.,** tenth-normal s. **disclosing s.,** a solution which is used for the purpose of making something apparent, such as one to be painted on the surface of a tooth in order to stain, and thus render visible, foreign matter or bacterial plaques. **Dobell's s.,** sodium borate s., compound. **Donovan's s.,** arsenic and mercuric iodides s. **double-normal s.,** a solution having double the strength of a normal solution: designated 2 N. **Dunham's s.,** a solution of peptone and sodium chloride in water. **dl-ephedrine hydrochloride s.,** racephedrine hydrochloride s. **ephedrine sulfate s.,** a clear, colorless solution with a slightly camphoraceous odor and taste, and a neutral or acid reaction, compounded of ephedrine sulfate, chlorobutanol, sodium chloride, and purified water. **epinephrine s.,** a nearly colorless, slightly acid solution of epinephrine in purified water, prepared with the aid of hydrochloric acid, each 100 ml. containing 90–115 mg. of epinephrine. **epinephrine bitartrate ophthalmic s.,** a solution of epinephrine bitartrate and boric acid in purified water: used as a mydriatic. **ethereal s.,** a solution in which ether is used as the solvent. **ethylenediamine s.,** a clear, colorless or slightly yellow solution, containing not less than 67 per cent of ethylenediamine. **Farrant's s.,** a mounting preparation used in bacteriological work, containing glycerin, water, arsenious acid solution, and gum arabic. **Fehling's s.,** dissolve 34.66 Gm. of copper sulfate in water to make 500 ml., dissolve 173 Gm. of crystallized potassium sodium tartrate and 50 Gm. of sodium hydroxide in water to make 500 ml. Keep the two solutions in small well-stoppered bottles; for use, mix equal parts of the two solutions. **ferric chloride s.,** a yellowish orange liquid with a faint odor of hydrochloric acid and an acid reaction, containing 37.2–42.7 Gm. of ferric chloride and 3.85–6.6 Gm. of hydrochloric acid in each 100 ml. **ferric subsulfate s.,** an aqueous solution of basic ferric sulfate: used as an astringent. **fiftieth-normal s.,** a solution having one-fiftieth the strength of a normal solution: designated N/50 or 0.02 N. **fixative s.** See *fixative.* **Flemming's s.,** a solution for hardening histological specimens, consisting of chromium trioxide, osmium tetroxide, glacial acetic acid, and water. **Fonio's s.,** a solution of magnesium sulfate in water: used as a diluent for blood platelets. **formaldehyde s.,** a solution of 37 per cent formaldehyde: used as a disinfectant. **formol-Zenker s.,** a fixing solution consisting of Zenker's solution and formaldehyde solution. **Fowler's s.,** potassium arsenite s. **gelatine s., special intravenous,** a 5 or 6 per cent sterile, pyrogen-free solution of gelatin in isotonic sodium chloride solution: used as a plasma volume expander. **gentian violet s.,** methylrosaniline chloride s. **Gilson's s.,** a fixative solution consisting of mercuric chloride, nitric acid, glacial acetic acid, 70 per cent alcohol, and water. **Gower's s.,** a solution of sodium sulfate, glacial acetic acid, and water, which is used for the dilution of blood for examination under the microscope. **Gram's s.** See *gram stain,* in *Table of Stains and Staining Methods.* **gram molecular s.,** molar s. **half-normal s.,** a solution having half the strength of a normal solution: designated N/2. **Hamdi's s.,** a solution for preserving histological specimens, consisting of sodium sulfate, salt, glycerin, and water. **Harrington's s.,** a solution for hand disinfection, consisting of alcohol, hydrochloric acid, water, and corrosive mercuric chloride. **Hartman's s.,** a solution once used for dentin desensitization, consisting of thymol, 95 per cent ethyl alcohol, and sulfuric ether. **Hartmann's s.,** a solution containing sodium chloride, sodium lactate, and phosphates of calcium and potassium: used parenterally in acidosis and alkalosis. **Hayem's s.,** one used in diluting blood for microscopical examination, consisting of mercury bichloride, sodium chloride, sodium sulfate, and water. **hundredth-normal s.,** a solution having one-hundredth the strength of a normal solution: designated N/100 or 0.01 N. **hydrogen dioxide s.,** hydrogen peroxide s. **hydrogen peroxide s.,** a solution containing 2.5–3.5 Gm. of hydrogen peroxide per 100 ml.: used as a local anti-infective to the skin and mucous membrane. **hyperbaric s.,** a solution having a greater specific gravity than a standard of reference, such as one used for spinal anesthesia having a specific gravity greater than that of the spinal fluid, causing it to migrate downward and produce anesthesia below the level of injection. **hyperosmotic s., hypertonic s.,** a solution having an osmotic pressure greater than that of a standard of reference, such as the blood serum. **hypobaric s.,** a solution having a specific gravity less than that of a standard of reference, such as one used for spinal anesthesia having a specific gravity less than that of the spinal fluid, causing it to migrate upward and produce anesthesia above the level of injection. **hyposmotic s., hypotonic s.,** a solution having an osmotic pressure less than that of a standard of reference, such as the blood serum. **iodine s.,** a transparent, reddish brown liquid, with the odor of iodine, each 100 ml. of which contains 1.8–2.2 Gm. of iodine and 2.1–2.6 Gm. of sodium iodide. **iodine s., compound,** iodine s. strong., **iodine s., strong,** a solution consisting of 5 per cent iodine and 10 per cent potassium iodide in water: used in treatment of goiter. **iron and ammonium acetate s.,** a clear, reddish brown liquid, with an aromatic odor, compounded of ferric chloride tincture, diluted acetic acid, ammonium acetate solution, aromatic elixir, glycerin, and distilled water. **isobaric s.,** a solution having the same specific gravity as a standard of reference, such as one used for spinal anesthesia having a specific gravity the same as that of the spinal fluid, causing it to remain and produce anesthesia at the level of injection. **isosmotic s., isotonic s.,** a solution having an osmotic pressure the same as that of some other solution with which it is compared, such as physiological salt solution, which has the same osmotic pressure as blood serum. **Javelle s.,** a solution of sodium or potassium hypochlorite used as a wound antiseptic and in the purification of water. **Kaiserling s.** 1. *For fixation:* formalin 400 ml., water 2,000 ml., potassium nitrate 30 Gm., potassium acetate 60 Gm. 2. *For restoring color:* alcohol 80 per cent. 3. *For preservation:* potassium acetate 200 Gm., glycerol 400 ml., sodium arsenate 100 Gm., water 2,000 ml. **Koppeschaar's s.,** a tenth-normal solution of bromine: used as a test. **Labarraque's s.,** sodium hypochlorite solution, diluted with an equal volume of water. **Lang's s.** See under *fluid.* **Lange's s.,** a solution of colloidal gold. **lead subacetate s.,** an aqueous solution of lead acetate and lead monoxide: used as an astringent. **lead subacetate s., diluted,** a colorless, slightly turbid liquid, with a sweet, astringent taste, prepared by diluting lead subacetate solution with water. **lime s., sulfurated,** a solution of lime and sublimed sulfur in water: used as a scabicide. **liver s.,** a brownish liquid prepared from mammalian livers and containing the soluble thermostable fraction which stimulates hematopoiesis in patients with pernicious anemia. **Locke's s.,** a solution of sodium chloride, calcium chloride, potassium chloride, sodium bicarbonate, and dextrose: used in physiological experiments to keep the mammalian heart beating. **Locke's s., citrated,** a solution of sodium chloride, potassium chloride, calcium chloride, sodium citrate, and water, with pH adjusted to 7.4. **Locke-Ringer's s.,** a test solution containing sodium chloride, potassium chloride, calcium chloride, magnesium chloride, sodium bicarbonate, dextrose, and water. **Lugol's s.,** iodine s., strong. **Magendies's s.,** a solution containing morphine sulfate. **magnesium citrate s.,** a solution of magnesium carbonate, with citric acid and other flavoring agents: used as a cathartic. **malt extract s.,** a solution of malt extract in water: used as a bacteriological culture medium. **Manson's s.,** a solution of methylene blue, borax, and water, used for staining blood parasities. **Mayer's s.,** a solution of potassium phosphate, magnesium sulfate, and calcium phosphate in water: used as a culture medium. **Mencière's s.** See under *mixture.* **merbromin s.,** a clear, red liquid with a yellow-green fluorescence, compounded of merbromin and water, each 100 ml. of which contains 1.8–2.2 Gm. of merbromin. **merbromin s., surgical,** a clear, red liquid with a yellow-green fluorescence, compounded of merbromin, water, acetone, and neutralized alcohol, the merbromin containing 24–26.7 per cent of mercury, and 18–21.3 per cent of bromine. **methylrosaniline chloride s.,** a purple liquid with a slight odor of alcohol, containing methylrosaniline chloride, alcohol, and purified water, each 100 ml. containing 0.95–1.05 Gm. of methylrosaniline chloride. **molal s.,** a solution containing 1 mole of solute dissolved in 1,000 Gm. of solvent. **molar s.,** a solution each liter of which contains 1 gram-molecule of the active substance: designated M/1 or 1 M. The concentration of other solutions may be expressed in relation to that of molar solutions as tenth-molar (M/10 or 0.1 M), etc. **molecular disperse s.,** a solution in which the dispersed particles have a diameter of about 0.1 micromicron. **Monsel's s.,** ferric subsulfate s. **Naegeli's s.,** a synthetic culture medium containing dibasic potassium phosphate, magnesium sulfate, calcium chloride, and ammonium tartrate, in water: used for growing yeasts and molds. **naphazoline hydrochloride s.,** a solution of naphazoline hydrochloride in water, adjusted with suitable buffers, each 100 ml. containing 45–55 mg. of the compound. **Nessler's s.** See under *reagent.* **nitrate s.,** a solution of peptone, potassium nitrate, and water: used as a bacteriological culture medium. **nitrofurazone s.,** a clear, light yellow, somewhat viscous liquid, with a faint, characteristic odor, each 100 Gm. of which contains 190–210 mg. of nitrofurazone. **nitromersol s.,** a clear, reddish orange liquid, compounded of nitromersol, sodium hydroxide, monohydrated sodium carbonate, and purified water, each 100 ml. of which yields 180–220 mg. of nitromersol.

normal s., a solution each liter of which contains 1 gram equivalent weight of the active substance: designated N/1 or 1 N. **normal saline s., normal salt s.,** physiological salt s. **normobaric s.,** isobaric s. **Orth's s.,** a solution for fixing histological specimens, consisting of Müller's fluid and formaldehyde solution. **parathyroid s.,** parathyroid injection. **Pasteur's s.,** a solution of ammonium tartrate, cane sugar, and ash from yeast, in water: used as a medium for growing yeasts and molds. **Perenyi's s.,** an embryological fixing solution, consisting of 10 per cent solution of nitric acid, alcohol, and 0.5 per cent solution of chromic acid. **phenylephrine hydrochloride s.,** a clear, colorless, or slightly yellow liquid, which contains 95–105 per cent of the labeled amount of phenylephrine hydrochloride. **physiological salt s., physiological sodium chloride s.,** an aqueous solution of sodium chloride and other components, having an isosmotic pressure identical to that of blood serum. **Pickrell's s.,** a solution of sulfadiazine in ethanolamine, with sodium benzoate as preservative. **Pitkin's s.,** a solution of procaine in a solvent having a specific gravity lower than that of the spinal fluid: used as a spinal anesthetic. **pituitary s., pituitary s., posterior,** posterior pituitary injection. **potassium arsenite s.,** a solution of arsenic trioxide, potassium bicarbonate, and alcohol in water, used as an antileukemic agent. **potassium iodide s.,** a clear, colorless, odorless liquid with a strongly salty taste and neutral or alkaline reaction, each 100 ml. of which contains 97–103 Gm. of potassium iodide. **racephedrine hydrochloride s.,** a clear, colorless solution with a camphoraceous odor and taste, compounded of racephedrine hydrochloride, chlorobutanol, and Ringer's solution. **radiocyanocobalamine s.,** a solution suitable for oral administration, containing cyanocobalamin labeled with cobalt-60: used as an aid in diagnosing pernicious anemia. **radiogold s.,** a colloidal solution of radioactive gold (Au^{198}): used as a neoplastic suppressant. **Rees-Ecker s.,** a solution consisting of sodium citrate, neutral formaldehyde, and brilliant cresyl blue: used as a diluting fluid for direct platelet counts. **Ringer's s.,** a clear, colorless liquid, with a mild saline taste, containing, in each 100 ml., 820–900 mg. of sodium chloride, 25–35 mg. of potassium chloride, and 30–36 mg. of calcium chloride, prepared with recently boiled purified water: for topical use. **Ruge's s.,** a solution of glacial acetic acid, 40 per cent formalin, and water: used as a stain. **saline s., salt s.,** a solution of sodium chloride, or common salt, in purified water. **saponated cresol s.** See *cresol s., saponated.* **saturated s.,** a solution in which the solvent has taken up all of the dissolved substance that it can hold in solution. **Schällibaum's s.,** a solution of celloidin and oil of cloves: used in histological work to attach paraffin sections to slides. **sclerosing s.,** a solution of an irritant substance for injection into a vein to produce obliteration of the vein, or into a hernia to induce fibrous formation and obliteration of the sac. **seminormal s.,** half normal s. **Seyderhelm's s.,** a colloidal mixture of Congo red and trypan blue, for staining urinary sediment. **silver nitrate s., ammoniacal,** a clear, colorless, almost odorless liquid, compounded of silver nitrate, water, and strong ammonia solution: used as a dental protective. **silver nitrate ophthalmic s.,** a solution of silver nitrate in a buffered water medium, containing 0.95–1.05 per cent of $AgNO_3$: used as a local anti-infective applied topically to the conjunctiva. **sodium borate s., compound,** a solution containing sodium borate, sodium bicarbonate, liquefied phenol, glycerin, and purified water: used as a gargle or mouth wash. **sodium chloride s.,** a sterile solution of sodium chloride in purified water, containing 0.85–0.95 per cent of NaCl: topical use only. **sodium citrate anticoagulant s.,** a sterile solution of sodium citrate in water: used to prevent coagulation of blood plasma and of whole blood. **sodium hypochlorite s.,** a clear, pale, greenish yellow liquid with the odor of chlorine, containing 4–6 per cent of sodium hypochlorite. **sodium hypochlorite s., diluted,** a colorless to light yellow liquid with a faint odor of chlorine, compounded of sodium hypochlorite solution, sodium bicarbonate, and water, each 100 ml. containing 450–500 mg. of NaClO. **sodium phosphate s.,** a clear colorless liquid without odor and with a salty taste, the consistency of thick syrup, each 100 ml. of which contains the equivalent of 71–79 Gm. of sodium phosphate. **sodium radio-iodide s.,** a solution containing radioactive iodine (I^{131}), used in diagnostic studies of thyroid disease and in detection and treatment of thyroid carcinoma. **sodium radio-phosphate s.,** a solution containing radioactive phosphorus (P^{32}): used as a suppressant of certain neoplasms and polycythemia. **sorbitol s.,** a clear, colorless, syrupy liquid with a sweet taste and without odor, recommended as a sweetening agent for diabetics and as a diuretic, and used in various pharmaceutical preparations. **standard s.,** one which contains in each liter a definitely stated amount of reagent; usually expressed in terms of normality (equivalent weight of active substance per liter of solution). **sulfurated lime s.** See *lime s., sulfurated.* **supersaturated s.,** a solution that contains in solution more of the solute than it can permanently hold. **surgical s. of chlorinated soda.** See *sodium hypochlorite s., diluted.* **susa s.,** a decalcifying solution composed of corrosive sublimate, sodium chloride, trichloracetic acid, glacial acetic acid, formalin, and water. **tenth-normal s.,** one having one-tenth the strength of a normal solution: designated N/10 or 0.1 N. **test s's,** standard solutions of specified chemical substances used in performing certain test procedures. **thousandth-normal s.,** a solution having one-thousandth the strength of a normal solution: designated N/1,000 or 0.001 N. **Toison's s.,** a fluid used in diluting blood for the counting of the erythrocytes, consisting of crystal violet, sodium chloride, sodium sulfate, glycerin, and water. **tribromoethanol s.,** a clear colorless liquid, a solution of tribromoethanol in amylene hydrate, each 100 ml. of which contains 99–101 Gm. of tribromoethanol. **tribromoethyl alcohol s.,** tribromoethanol s. **Tyrode's s.,** a modified Locke's solution containing magnesium, used especially for perfusing the intestine of the rabbit. **tyrothricin s.,** a solution of tyrothricin in alcohol. **Uschinsky's s.,** a solution in water of asparagin, ammonium lactate, neutral sodium phosphate, and sodium chloride: used as a culture medium for bacteria. **Vleminckx' s.,** lime s., sulfurated. **volumetric s.,** one which contains a specific quantity of solvent per stated unit of volume. See also *standard s.* **Winogradsky's s.** 1. *For growing nitrifying organisms:* Potassium phosphate, magnesium sulfate, calcium chloride, sodium chloride, and ammonium sulfate, in water. 2. *For growing nitrosifying organisms:* Ammonium sulfate, potassium sulfate, and basic magnesium carbonate, in water. **Zenker's s.,** a fixative solution consisting of mercury bichloride, potassium dichromate, glacial acetic acid, and water. **Ziehl's s.,** See *Table of Stains and Staining Methods.*

solv. Abbreviation for L. *sol've,* dissolve.

solvable (sol′vah-b'l). Soluble.

solvate (sol′vāt). A compound of one or more molecules of a solvent with the ions or with the molecules of a dissolved substance.

solvation (sol-va′shun). Chemical combination of a solvent with the solute.

solvent (sol′vent) [L. *solvens*]. 1. Dissolving; effecting a solution. 2. A liquid that dissolves or that is capable of dissolving.

solvolysis (sol-vol′ĭ-sis). A general term for double decomposition reactions of the type of hydrolysis, ammonolysis, and sulfolysis.

soma (so′mah) [Gr. *sōma* body]. 1. The body as distinguished from the mind. 2. The body tissue as distinguished from the germ cells. 3. Trade mark for preparations of carisoprodol.

somacule (so′mah-kūl). The smallest possible particle of protoplasm.

somal (so′mal). Pertaining to the body.

somaplasm (so′mah-plazm). Somatoplasm.

somasthenia (sōm″as-the′ne-ah) [*soma* + *a* neg. + Gr. *sthenos* strength + *-ia*]. A condition of bodily weakness, poor appetite and sleep, and inability to maintain a normal active life without easy exhaustion.

somatalgia (so″mah-tal′je-ah) [*somato-* + Gr. *algos* pain + *-ia*]. Bodily pain.

somatasthenia (so″mat-as-the′ne-ah). Somasthenia.

somatesthesia (so″mat-es-the′ze-ah) [*somato-* + Gr. *aisthēsis* perception + *-ia*]. The consciousness of having a body.

somatesthetic (so″mat-es-thet′ik). Pertaining to somatesthesia.

somatic (so-mat′ik) [Gr. *sōmatikos*]. Pertaining to or characteristic of the body (soma).

somaticosplanchnic (so-mat″ĭ-ko-splank′nik). Somaticovisceral.

somaticovisceral (so-mat″ĭ-ko-vis′er-al). Pertaining to the body and viscera.

somatist (so′mah-tist). A scientist who believes that neuroses and psychoses are of physical origin and are based on bodily lesions.

somatization (so″mah-ti-za′shun). In psychiatry, the conversion of mental experiences or states into bodily symptoms.

somato- (so′mah-to) [Gr. *sōma, sōmatos* body]. Combining form denoting relationship to the body.

somatoceptor (so-mat′o-sep″tor). A receptor concerned in receiving stimuli of the skeletal and somatic musculature.

somatochrome (so-mat′o-krōm) [*somato-* + Gr. *chrōma* color]. Any nerve cell which has a well-marked cell body completely surrounding the nucleus, its colorable protoplasm having a distinct contour: used also adjectively.

somatoderm (so-mat′o-derm) [*somato-* + Gr. *derma* skin]. The somatic layer of mesoderm.

somatodidymus (so″mah-to-did′ĭ-mus). A fetal monster exhibiting somatodymia.

somatodymia (so″mah-to-dim′e-ah) [*somato-* + Gr. *didymos* twin + *-ia*]. A developmental anomaly resulting in the production of conjoined twins whose trunks are fused into one.

somatogenesis (so″mah-to-jen′e-sis) [*somato-* + Gr. *genesis* production]. The formation or emergence of bodily structure out of hereditary sources; the formation of somatoplasm out of germ plasm.

somatogenetic (so-mat″o-je-net′ik). 1. Pertaining to somatogenesis. 2. Somatogenic.

somatogenic (so″mah-to-jen′ik) [*somato-* + Gr. *gennan* to produce]. Originating in the cells of the body.

somatogram (so-mat′o-gram) [*somato-* + Gr. *gramma* a writing]. A roentgenogram of the body.

somatology (so″mah-tol′o-je) [*somato-* + *-logy*]. The sum of what is known regarding the body; the study of the anatomy and physiology of the body.

somatome (so′mah-tōm) [*soma* + Gr. *temnein* to cut]. 1. An appliance for cutting the body of the fetus. 2. A somite.

somatomegaly (so″mah-to-meg′ah-le) [*somato-* + Gr. *megaleios* stately + *-ia*]. Abnormal size of body; gigantism.

somatometry (so-mah-tom′e-tre) [*somato-* + Gr. *metron* measure]. Measurement of the body.

somatomic (so″mah-tom′ik). Pertaining to a somatome.

somatopagus (so″mah-top′ah-gus) [*somato-* + Gr. *pagos* thing fixed]. A double fetal monster with trunks more or less merged.

somatopathic (so″mah-to-path′ik) [*somato-* + Gr. *pathos* disease]. Pertaining to or characterized by somatopathy.

somatopathy (so″mah-top′ah-the). A bodily disorder as distinguished from a mental one.

somatophrenia (so″mah-to-fre′ne-ah) [*somato-* + Gr. *phrēn* mind + *-ia*]. A mental condition which exaggerates or imagines body ills.

somatoplasm (so-mat′o-plasm) [*somato-* + Gr. *plasma* anything formed or molded] The protoplasm of the body cells as distinguished from that of the germ cells. Cf. *germ plasm.*

somatopleural (so″mah-to-ploor′al). Pertaining to the somatopleure.

somatopleure (so-mat′o-ploor) [*somato-* + Gr. *pleura* side]. The embryonic body wall, formed by ectoderm and somatic mesoderm.

somatopsychic (so″mah-to-si′kik) [*somato-* + Gr. *psychē* soul]. Pertaining to both body and mind.

somatopsychosis (so″mah-to-si-ko′sis) [*somato-* + *psychosis*]. Southard's name for a mental disease symptomatic of bodily disease.

somatoschisis (so″mah-tos′kĭ-sis) [*somato-* + Gr. *schisis* fissure]. A developmental anomaly characterized by a fissure of the trunk.

somatoscopy (so″mah-tos′ko-pe) [*somato-* + Gr. *skopein* to examine]. Viewing or examination of the body.

somatosexual (so″mah-to-seks′u-al) [*somato-* + L. *sexus* sex]. Pertaining to both physical and sex characteristics; pertaining to the physical manifestations of sexual development.

somatosplanchnopleuric (so″mah-to-splank″no-ploor′ik). Pertaining to the somatopleure and the splanchnopleure.

somatotherapy (so″mah-to-ther′ah-pe) [*somato-* + Gr. *therapeia* treatment]. Treatment aimed at curing the ills of the body.

somatotomy (so″mah-tot′o-me) [*somato-* + Gr. *tomē* a cutting]. The anatomy or dissection of the body.

somatotonia (so″mah-to-to′ne-ah) [*somato-* + Gr. *tonos* tension + *-ia*]. A group of traits dominated by muscular activity and vigorous body assertiveness (Sheldon).

somatotridymus (so″mah-to-trid′ĭ-mus) [*somato-* + Gr. *tri-* three + *didymos* twin]. A fetal monster with three trunks.

somatotrophic (so″mah-to-trōf′ik) [*somato-* + Gr. *trophē* nourishment]. Having a stimulating effect on body nutrition and growth.

somatotrophin (so″mah-to-tro′fin). Growth hormone. See under *hormone.*

somatotropic (so″mah-to-trop′ik) [*somato-* + Gr. *tropos* a turning]. 1. Having an affinity for or attacking the body or the body cells; also having an influence on the body. 2. Having the properties of a somatropin.

somatotropin (so″mah-to-tro′pin). Growth hormone. See under *hormone.*

somatotype (so-mat′o-tip) [*somato-* + *type*]. A particular category of body build, determined on the basis of certain physical characteristics. See *ectomorphy*, *endomorphy*, and *mesomorphy.*

somatotyping (so-mat″o-tip′ing). A method of studying objectively the physical types of individuals.

somatotypy (so-mat′o-ti″pe). The determination of the type of body build.

somatropin (so-mat′ro-pin). H. M. Evans' name for the growth-promoting principle of the anterior pituitary.

sombulex (som′bu-leks). Trade mark for a preparation of hexobarbital.

somesthesia (so″mes-the′ze-ah). Somatesthesia.

somesthetic (so″mes-thet′ik). Somatesthetic.

somite (so′mīt). One of the paired, blocklike masses of mesoderm, arranged alongside the neural tube of the embryo, forming the vertebral column. Called also *mesoblastic* or *mesodermal segment.*

somnambulance (som-nam′bu-lans). Somnambulism.

somnambulation (som-nam″bu-la′shun). Somnambulism.

somnambulism (som-nam′bu-lizm) [L. *somnambulismus; somnus* sleep + *ambulare* to walk]. 1. Habitual walking in the sleep. 2. A hypnotic state in which the subject has the full possession of his senses but no subsequent recollection.

somnambulist (som-nam′bu-list). A person who walks in his sleep.

somnarium (som-na′re-um). An institution for the treatment of functional neuroses by sleep.

somni- (som′ne) [L. *somnus* sleep]. Combining form denoting relationship to sleep.

somnifacient (som″nĭ-fa′shent) [*somni-* + L. *facere* to make]. 1. Causing sleep; hypnotic. 2. An agent that induces sleep.

somniferin (som-nif′er-in) [*somni-* + L. *ferre* to bring]. A derivative of morphine, said to be safer and more effective than morphine.

somniferine (som-nif′er-ĭn). A narcotic alkaloid from *Withania somnifera.*

somniferous (som-nif′er-us) [*somni-* + L. *ferre* to bring]. Inducing or causing sleep.

somnific (som-nif′ik). Somniferous.

somniloquence (som-nil′o-kwens). Somniloquism.

somniloquism (som-nil′o-kwizm) [*somni-* + L. *loqui* to speak]. The habit of talking in one's sleep.

somniloquist (som-nil′o-kwist). One who talks in his sleep.

somniloquy (som-nil′o-kwe). Somniloquism.

somnipathist (som-nip′ah-thist) [*somni-* + Gr. *pathos* disease]. A person in or subject to hypnotic trance.

somnipathy (som-nip′ah-the) [*somni-* + Gr. *pathos* disease]. Any disorder of sleep; a condition of hypnotic trance.

somnocinematograph (som″no-sin″e-mat′o-graf) [*somnus* + *cinematograph*]. An apparatus for recording movements made during sleep.

somnolence (som′no-lens) [L. *somnolentia* sleepiness]. Sleepiness; also unnatural drowsiness.

somnolent (som′no-lent) [L. *somnolentus*]. Affected with somnolence.

somnolentia (som″no-len′she-ah) [L.]. 1. Drowsiness, or somnolence. 2. Sleep drunkenness; a condition of incomplete sleep marked by loss of orientation and by excited or violent behavior.

somnolism (som′no-lizm). A state of mesmeric, or hypnotic, trance.

somnos (som′nos). Trade mark for preparations of chloral hydrate.

somnus (som′nus) [L.]. Sleep.

somopsychosis (so″mo-si-ko′sis) [Gr. *sōma* body + *psychosis*]. A mental disorder in which the symptoms are chiefly bodily, that is, sensory, motor, or visceral, in character.

somosphere (so′mo-sfēr) [Gr. *sōma* body + *sphaira* sphere]. One of the elements of the archiplasm.

sonde (sond) [Fr.]. Sound. **s. coudé** (sond′kooda′) [Fr. "bent sound"], a catheter with an elbow, or sharp, beaklike bend, near the end.

sone (sōn). A unit of loudness, being the loudness of a simple tone of 1,000 cycles per second, 40 decibels above a listener's threshold.

sonifer (son′ĭ-fer) [L. *sonus* sound + *ferre* to bear]. A variety of ear trumpet.

sonitus (son′ĭ-tus) [L. "sound"]. A sounding or tinkling in the ears; tinnitus aurium.

Sonne dysentery (son′e) [Carl *Sonne*, Danish bacteriologist, 1882–1948]. See under *dysentery.*

Sonnenburg's test (son′en-bergz) [Eduard *Sonnenburg*, Berlin surgeon, 1848–1915]. See under *tests.*

sonometer (so-nom′e-ter) [L. *sonus* sound + *metrum* measure]. 1. An apparatus for testing acuteness of hearing. 2. An instrument for measuring the ratios of sound vibrations in various bodies.

sonorous (so-no′rus) [L. *sonorus*]. Resonant; sounding.

soor (sōr) [Ger.]. Thrush.

sophistication (so-fis″tĭ-ka′shun) [Gr. *sophistikos* deceitful]. The adulteration of food or medicine.

sophomania (sof″o-ma′ne-ah) [Gr. *sophos* wise + *mania* madness]. An insane belief in one's own great wisdom.

Sophora (so-fo′ra) [Arabic *sofara*]. A genus of leguminous trees and shrubs. The root and seed of *S. tomentosa* are used in India to arrest choleraic vomiting. For certain poisonous species, see *loco.*

sophoretin (sof″o-re′tin). Quercetin.

sophorin (sof′o-rin). Rutin.

sopor (so′por) [L.]. Sound, deep, or profound sleep.

soporiferous (so″po-rif′er-us) [L. *sopor* deep sleep + *ferre* to bring]. Inducing deep or profound slumber.

soporific (so″po-rif′ik) [L. *soporificus*]. 1. Causing or inducing profound sleep. 2. A drug or other agent which induces sleep.

soporous (so′por-us) [L. *soporus*]. Associated or affected with coma or profound slumber.

S. op. s. Abbreviation for L. *si o′pus sit,* if it is necessary.

Sorangiaceae (so-ran″je-a′se-e). A systematic family of Schizomycetes, order Myxobacterales, made up of saprophytic soil microorganisms, and comprising a single genus, *Sorangium.*

Soranus (so-ra′nus) **of Ephesus** (2nd century A.D.). A celebrated Greek physician of the Methodist school, and the most renowned gynecologist and obstetrician of antiquity. He practiced in Alexandria and, later, in Rome. His surviving writings on obstetrics, gynecology, and pediatrics are outstanding.

sorbefacient (sor″be-fa′shent) [L. *sorbere* to suck + *facere* to make]. 1. Promoting absorption. 2. An agent that promotes absorption.

sorbin (sor′bin). Sorbose.

sorbinose (sor′bĭ-nōs). Sorbose.

sorbite (sor′bit). Sorbitol.

sorbitol (sor′bĭ-tol). A crystalline, hexahydric alcohol, $CH_2OH.(CHOH)_4CH_2OH$, from the tree *Sorbus aucuparia.*

sorbose (sor′bōs). A ketohexose, $CH_2OH-(CHOH)_3CO.CH_2OH$, resembling levulose in its properties.

sordes (sor′dēz) [L. "filth"]. The dark-brown, foul matter which collects on the lips and teeth in low fevers. It consists of a mixture of food, epithelial matter, and microorganisms. **s. gas′tricae,** undigested food, mucus, etc., in the stomach.

sore (sōr). A popular term for almost any lesion of the skin or mucous membranes. **bed s.,** decubitus ulcer. **chrome s.,** chrome ulcer. **Cochin China s.,** cutaneous leishmaniasis. **cold s.,** herpes labialis. **Delhi s.,** cutaneous leishmaniasis. **desert s.,** a form of tropical ulcer resembling varicose ulcer and appearing on the face, back of hands and lower extremities. It occurs in desert areas of Africa, Australia and the Near East. Called also *Gallipoli s., Umballa s., veldt s.* and *Barcoo rot.* **fungating s.,** a soft chancre with granulations. **Gallipoli s.,** desert s. **hard s.,** chancre. **Kandahar s., Lahore s., Madagascar s., Moultan s.,** cutaneous leishmaniasis. **Naga s.,** a form of tropical ulcer occurring among workers in tea gardens in Assam. **Natal s., oriental s., Penjdeh s.,** cutaneous leishmaniasis. **pressure s.,** decubitus ulcer. **soft s.,** chancroid. **summer s's,** sores on the skin of horses caused by penetration of the larva of

Habronema megastomum. **Umballa s.,** desert s. **veldt s.,** desert s. **venereal s.,** any sore that accompanies or manifests a venereal disease, especially a chancroid. **water s.,** ground itch.

Sorensen's reagent (sor′en-senz) [Søreh Peter Lauritz *Sorensen,* Danish chemist, 1868–1939]. See under *reagent.*

sore throat (sōr thrōt). See *laryngitis, pharyngitis,* and *tonsillitis.* **clergyman's s. t.,** dysphonia clericorum. **diphtheria s. t.,** croupous tonsillitis. **epidemic streptococcus s. t.,** septic s. t. **Fothergill's s. t.,** ulcerative angina of severe scarlatina. **hospital s. t.,** septic inflammation of the pharynx and fauces sometimes affecting nurses and interns in hospitals. **putrid s. t.,** gangrenous pharyngitis. **septic s. t.,** a severe type of sore throat occurring in epidemics, marked by intense local hyperemia with or without a grayish exudate and enlargement of the cervical lymph glands. It is caused by a peculiar type of hemolytic streptococcus, the infection being spread by direct contact or by milk. Called also *streptococcus sore throat* and *streptococcus tonsillitis.* **spotted s. t.,** follicular tonsillitis. **streptococcus s. t.,** septic s. t. **ulcerated s. t.,** gangrenous pharyngitis.

Soret band, effect, phenomenon (so-ra′) [C. *Soret,* French physicist, died 1931]. See under *band* and *effect.*

soroche, sorroche (so-ro′cha) [Sp. "antimony"]. Mountain sickness of the Andes, incorrectly ascribed to metallic exhalations.

sororiation (so-ro″re-a′shun) [L. *sororiare* to increase together]. Increase in size of the breasts at puberty.

sorption (sorp′shun) [L. *sorbere* to suck in]. 1. The incorporation of water within a colloid. 2. The processes involved in the net movement of components of adjoining materials across the boundary separating them; applied to the bidirectional movements of substances across the mucosa of the gastrointestinal tract and the net result of such movements, including absorption, enterosorption, exsorption, and insorption.

S.O.S. Abbreviation for L. *si o′pus sit,* if it is necessary.

soteria (so-ter′e-ah) [Gr. *sōtēria* a way or means of safety; a guarantee of safekeeping]. The experiencing of a feeling of security and protection, apparently out of proportion to the stimulus, derived from an external object, which becomes a neurotic object-source of comfort.

soterocyte (so′ter-o-sīt) [Gr. *sōtēr* savior + *kytos* hollow vessel]. A blood platelet.

SOTT. Abbreviation for *synthetic medium old tuberculin trichloracetic acid precipitated.*

Sottas disease (sot′tahz) [Jules *Sottas,* French neurologist, born 1866]. Progressive hypertrophic interstitial neuropathy.

soudan (soo-dan′). Sudan.

soudanite (soo′dan-ēt) [Fr.; from *Sudan* (Arabic *sudan* black), in Africa]. A fever of tropical Africa, often leading to homicidal mania.

souffle (soof′f′l) [Fr. "a puff"; L. *suffare* to blow]. A soft, blowing, auscultatory sound. **cardiac s.,** any cardiac murmur of a blowing quality. **electric s.,** the aura, or slight current of electrified air, which passes from a static electric machine while it is in action. **fetal s.,** a blowing sound sometimes heard in pregnancy: supposed to be due to compression of the umbilical vessels. **funic s., funicular s.,** a hissing souffle synchronous with the fetal heart sounds, and supposed to be produced in the umbilical cord. **mammary s.,** a murmur sometimes observed in the second, third, or fourth intercostal space during pregnancy and the puerperium, attributed to change of dynamics in blood flow through the internal mammary artery. **placental s.,** a souffle supposed to be produced by the blood current in the placenta. **splenic s.,** a sound said to be sometimes audible over a diseased spleen. **umbilical s.,** funic s. **uterine s.,** a sound made by the blood within the arteries of the gravid uterus.

soulal (soo′lal). A severe form of scabies in Arabs.

souma, soumaya (soo′mah, soo-mah′yah). A disease of cattle, horses, goats, and camels in the Sudan; caused by the *Trypanosoma vivax,* which is transmitted by various species of *Glossina.*

sound (sownd) [L. *sonus*]. 1. The effect produced on the organ of hearing by the vibrations of the air or other medium. 2. Mechanical radiant energy, the motion of particles of the material medium through which it travels (air, water, or solids) being along the line of transmission (longitudinal); such energy, of frequency between 20 and 20,000 cycles per second, provides the stimulus for the subjective sensation of hearing. 3. An instrument to be introduced into a cavity, so as to detect a foreign body or to dilate a stricture. 4. A noise, normal or abnormal, heard within the body. For other sounds see under *bruit, fremitus, murmur,* and *rale.* **anasarcous s.,** a bubbling sound of moist quality often heard over edematous skin. **auscultatory s.,** any sound heard on auscultation. **bandbox s.,** a highly resonant sound elicited by percussion over the chest in cases of emphysema of the lung. **Beatty-Bright friction s.,** the friction sound of pleurisy. **bell s.,** bruit d'airain. **Bellocq's s.** See under *cannula.* **bellows s.,** an endocardial murmur resembling the sound made by a bellows. **Béniqué's s.,** a lead or tin sound, having a wide curve, for dilating urethral strictures. **bottle s.,** amphoric rale. **cardiac s's,** heart s's. **coin s.,** bruit d'airain. **cracked-pot s.,** a percussion sound indicative of a pulmonary cavity into which the breath may pass. **cracked-pot s., cranial,** a peculiar sound due to the separation of the cranial sutures from a cerebellar tumor. **entotic s's,** sounds that originate within the ear, such as tinnitus. **esophageal s.,** a long, flexible sound for exploring the esophagus. **first s.** See *heart s's.* **flapping s.,** the peculiar sound made by the closure of the heart valves. **friction s.,** any sound produced by the rubbing of one surface over another. **heart s's,** sounds heard over the cardiac region. The first is dull and prolonged, and occurs along with the systole of the ventricles; the second occurs along with the closure of the semilunar valves, and is short and sharp. A third heart sound, weak, low-pitched, and dull, is sometimes heard following the second heart sound, and is thought to be caused by vibrations of the ventricular walls when they are suddenly distended by the rush of blood from the atria. **hippocratic s.,** the succussion sound heard in pyopneumothorax or seropneumothorax. **Korotkoff s's,** sounds heard during auscultatory blood pressure determination, produced by sudden distention of the artery, the walls of which were previously relaxed because of the surrounding pneumatic cuff. **lacrimal s.,** a sound of small caliber for use in the lacrimal canal. **metallic s.,** a sound having a metallic quality heard especially over cavities in the chest. **mid-diastolic s.,** a sharp sound heard on auscultation just before the first sound of the heart, produced by the auricular systole when the auricular and ventricular systoles are discontinuous. **muscle s.,** the sound heard over a muscle when in a condition of contraction. **peacock s.,** a quality of voice due to various defects and lesions of the air passages. **percussion s.,** any sound obtained by percussion. **physiological s's,** sounds heard when the auditory canals are plugged, caused by the rush of blood through blood vessels in or near the inner ear and by adjacent muscles in continuous low frequency vibration. **pistol-shot s.,** a sharp sound accompanying each pulsation heard by the stethoscope pressed over the femoral artery in aortic insufficiency. **respiratory s.,** any sound heard on auscultation over any portion of the respiratory tract. **second s.** See *heart s's.* **shaking s.,** succussion s. **siphon s.,** a variety of tube or siphon for the stomach. **sizzling s's,** sounds as of fermentation in the stomach. **subjective s.** 1. Phonism. 2. The sound sometimes produced by the blood current in the ears of the auscultator. **succussion s's,** splashing sounds heard on succussion over a distended stomach and in hydropneumothorax. **tick-tack s's,** heart sounds in which there is little or no difference in the quality of the first and second sounds: seen in infants and persons with feeble hearts, characteristic of embryocardia. **to-and-fro s.,** the peculiar friction sound heard in pericarditis and pleuritis. **urethral s.,** a long, slim, slightly conical instrument of steel for exploring and dilating the urethra. **water-wheel s.,** bruit de moulin. **white s.,** that produced by a mixture of all frequencies of mechanical vibration perceptible as sound. **Winternitz's s.,** a double-current catheter. **xiphisternal crunching s.,** a peculiar sound, of unknown origin, frequently heard (20 per cent of healthy men) over the lower sternum and xiphoid process.

Souques's phenomenon, sign (soo′kez) [Alexandre Achille *Souques*, French neurologist, 1860–1944]. See under *phenomenon* and *sign*.

Southey's tubes (south′ēz) [Reginald S. *Southey*, English physician, 1835–1899]. See under *tube*.

Soxhlet's apparatus (soks′lets) [Franz Ritter von *Soxhlet*, German chemist, 1848–1926]. See under *apparatus*.

soya (so′yah). See *soy bean*.

soy bean (soy). The bean of the leguminous plant, *Soja hispida* (*Glycine soja*) or Chinese bean. It contains little starch and is rich in albuminoids, and from it is prepared a meal which is used in making bread for diabetics. It also furnishes an enzyme, urease. See *urease*.

Soyka's plates (soi′kahz) [Isidor *Soyka*, Prague pathologist, 1850–1889]. See under *plate*.

Soymida febrifuga (soi′mĭ-dah feb-rif′u-gah). A tree of southern Asia. The bark is bitter, astringent, and aromatic.

sozalbumin (so″zal-bu′min) [Gr. *sōzein* to save + *albumin*]. Any defensive protein that is not a toxalbumin.

sozin (so′zin) [Gr. *sōzein* to save]. Any defensive protein occurring normally in the body, distinguished as *mycosozins* and *toxosozins*, depending on their action.

sp. Abbreviation for L. *spir′itus*, spirit.

space (spās). 1. A delimited area. 2. An actual or potential cavity of the body. Called also *spatium* [N A]. 3. The areas of the universe beyond the earth and its atmosphere. **apical s.,** the region between the wall of the alveolus and the apex of the root of a tooth. **arachnoid s.** See *cavum subarachnoideale* and *cavum subdurale*. **axillary s.,** axilla. **Blessig's s's,** confluent spaces permeating the periphery of the retina in old people, as a result of cystoid degeneration. **Bogros's s.,** a region bounded by the peritoneum above and the fascia transversalis below, in which the lower part of the external iliac artery can be found without cutting the peritoneum. **bregmatic s.,** the anterior fontanel (fonticulus frontalis). **Broca's s.,** the central part of the anterior olfactory lobe of the brain. **Burns's s.,** fossa jugularis. **cardiac s.,** the space on the surface of the chest which overlies the heart. The *deep cardiac s.* is the portion overlying the lung-covered parts of the heart. The *superficial cardiac s.* is the area overlying the portion of the heart that is not covered by the lung. **cartilage s's,** the spaces in hyaline cartilage which contain the cartilage cells. **cathodal dark s.,** Crookes s. **cell s's,** the spaces in the ground substance of connective tissue enclosing the connective tissue corpuscles. **chyle s's,** the central lymphatic spaces of the villi of the intestine. **circumlental s.,** the space between the ciliary body and the equator of the lens. **Colles' s.,** a space under the perineal fascia containing the transversus perinei, ischiocavernosus, and bulbocavernosus muscles, the posterior scrotal or labial vessels and nerves, and the bulbous portion of the urethra. **complemental s.,** portions of the pleural cavity that are not occupied by lung tissue, such as the triangular spaces below the lower borders of the lungs and irregular spaces about the heart. **corneal s's,** the spaces between the lamellae of the substantia propria of the cornea which contain corneal cells and interstitial lymph. **Cotunnius' s.,** the space within the membranous labyrinth. **Crookes s.,** a dark space at the cathode of a nearly exhausted roentgen-ray tube through which a current is being passed. Called also *cathodal dark s.* **cupola s.,** pars cupularis recessus epitympanici. **Czermak's s's,** spatia interglobularia. **dead s.** 1. Space remaining as a result of failure of proper closure of surgical or other wounds, permitting the accumulation of blood or serum and resultant delay in healing. 2. In the respiratory tract, the mouth, nose, pharynx, larynx, trachea, bronchi, and bronchioles (*anatomic dead space*), or these plus the space in the alveoli occupied by gas which does not participate in oxygen–carbon dioxide exchange (*physiologic dead space*). **s's in dentin,** spatia interglobularia. **Disse's s's,** small spaces which separate the sinusoids of the liver from the liver cells and which carry the lymph of the liver. **Douglas' s.,** excavatio rectouterina. **epicerebral s.,** the potential space between the brain and the pia mater. **epidural s.,** cavum epidurale. **epispinal s.,** the potential space between the substance of the spinal cord and the pia mater. **epitympanic s.,** recessus epitympanicus. **escapement s's,** spaces which permit the escape of material being comminuted between the occlusal surfaces of the teeth, provided by the cusps and ridges, sulci and developmental ridges of the teeth, and the embrasures between the teeth. **Faraday's dark s.,** the dark region separating the negative glow from the positive column in a Crookes tube. **Fontana's s's,** spatia anguli iridocornealis. **free way s.,** interocclusal clearance. **globular s's of Czermak,** spatia interglobularia. **H. s.,** Holzknecht's s. **haversian s.,** haversian canal. **Henke's s.,** a space containing connective tissue between the spinal column and the pharynx and esophagus. **His's perivascular s.,** the space between the adventitia of the blood vessels of the brain and cord and the perivascular limiting membrane of glia tissue. **Holzknecht's s.,** the middle one of the three clear lung fields in the roentgenogram of the chest in oblique projection when the rays pass from the left posteriorly to the right anteriorly: called also *H. s.*, *prevertebral s.*, and *retrocardiac s.* **interarytenoid s.,** pars intercartilaginea rima glottidis. **intercostal s.,** spatium intercostale. **intercrural s.,** a triangular space between the crura cerebri. **interfascial s.,** spatium intervaginale. **interglobular s's,** spatia interglobularia. **interlamellar s's,** the spaces between the lamellae of the cornea. **interocclusal s.,** interocclusal clearance. **interosseous s's of metacarpus,** spatia interossea metacarpi. **interosseous s's of metatarsus,** spatia interossea metatarsi. **interpeduncular s.,** fossa interpeduncularis. **interpleural s.,** mediastinum. **interproximal s., interproximate s.,** the space between the proximal surfaces of adjoining teeth; sometimes used to designate especially the space between the proximal surfaces of adjoining teeth that is gingival to the area of contact (*septal s.*). Cf. *embrasure*. **interradicular s.,** the space between roots; in dentistry applied to the entire extent of the space between the roots of a tooth, from apex to base. **interseptal s.,** a space between the two folds uniting to form the spurious septum in the heart of the early embryo. **intervaginal s.,** spatium intervaginale. **intervaginal s's of optic nerve,** spatia intervaginalia nervi optici. **intervalvular s's,** the intervals (1) between the aortic sinuses, and (2) between the pulmonary sinuses on the outer side, respectively, of the aorta and of the pulmonary artery. **intervillous s.,** the cavernous space of the placenta into which project the chorionic villi and through which maternal blood circulates. **s's of iridocorneal angle,** spatia anguli irido cornealis. **Kiernan's s's,** the dilated triangular spaces in the fissures between the liver lobules, containing the larger interlobular branches of the portal vein, hepatic artery, and hepatic duct. **Kretschmann's s.,** a depressed area in the recessus epitympanicus, below Prussak's space. **Kuhnt's s's,** a succession of radiating spaces in the eye containing aqueous humor. **Larrey's s's,** intervals between those parts of the diaphragm which are attached to the ribs and that which is attached to the sternum. **leeway s.** See *Nance's leeway s.* **Leshaft's s.,** a rhombus which in some persons exists between the external oblique muscle in front, the latissimus dorsi behind, the serratus posticus above, and the internal oblique below: frequently the site of pointing of an abscess, or occurrence of a hernia. **lymph s.,** any space in tissue occupied by lymph. **Magendie's s's,** lymph spaces between the pia and arachnoid, corresponding to the principal sulci of the brain. **Malacarne's s.,** substantia perforata posterior. **Marie's quadrilateral s.** See *quadrilateral s. of Marie.* **Meckel's s.,** cavum trigeminale. **mediastinal s.,** mediastinum. **medullary s.,** the central cavity and the intervals between the trabeculae of bone which contain the marrow. **midpalmar s.,** the palmar space lying between the middle metacarpal bone and the radial side of the hypothenar eminence. **Mohrenheim's s.,** a groove on the deltoid muscle for the cephalic vein and a branch of the acromiothoracic artery. **Nance's leeway s.,** the amount by which the space occupied by the deciduous canine and first and second deciduous molars exceeds that occupied by the canine and premolar teeth of the permanent dentition, usually averaging 1.7 mm. on each side of the dental arch. **Nuel's s.,** spaces between the slender processes of the phalangeal cells of the spiral organ. **palmar s.,** a large fascial space in the hand, divided by a fibrous septum into the midpalmar space and the thenar space. **parapharyngeal s.,** pharyngomaxillary s. **parasinoidal s's,** spaces in the dura mater, along the superior longitudinal sinus, which receive the venous blood. **Parona's s.,** a space between the pronator quadratus muscle and the deep flexor tendons in the forearm, about 2 inches above the wrist, in direct continuity with the tendon sheaths and the midpalmar space. **perforated s., anterior,** substantia perforata anterior. **perforated s., posterior,** substantis perforata posterior. **perichorioidal s., perichoroidal s.,** spatium perichoroideale. **perilymphatic s.,** spatium perilymphaticum. **perineal s., deep,** spatium perinei profundum. **perineal s., superficial,** spatium perinei superficiale. **perineural s's,** spaces within the sheaths of the roots of nerves arising directly from the central nervous system. **peripharyngeal s.,** retropharyngeal s. **perivascular s.,** a lymph space occurring within the walls of an artery. **perivitelline s.,** a space between the ovum and the zona pellucida; in the ovum of some animals, a fluid-filled space separating the fertilization membrane from the surface of the egg. **pharyngomaxillary s.,** the space included between the lateral wall of the pharynx, the internal pterygoid muscle, and the cervical vertebrae. **phrenocostal s.,** the space between the outer edge of the diaphragm and the costal surface. **plantar s's,** three fascial spaces in the foot, divided by septa into *middle, lateral,* and *median plantar spaces.* **pneumatic s.,** a portion of bone occupied by air-containing cells; applied especially to spaces in the bones of the head constituting the paranasal sinuses. **Poiseuille's s.,** that part of the lumen of tube, at its periphery, where no flow of liquid occurs, as next to the wall of a blood vessel, where the red cells are motionless and constitute a layer over which the inner layers of liquid slide. **popliteal s.,** fossa poplitea. **postperforated s.,** substantia perforata posterior. **preperitoneal s.,** spatium retropubicum. **preputial s.,** the space between the prepuce and the glans penis. **prevertebral s.,** Holzknecht's s. **prevesical s.,** spatium retropubicum. **prezonular s.,** portion of the eyeball anterior to the zonula ciliaris, occupied by the aqueous humor. **proximal s., proximate s.,** interproximal s. **Prussak's s.,** recessus membranae tympani superior. **quadrilateral s. of Marie,** a space in the cerebral hemisphere bounded externally by the cortex, medially by the internal capsule, and anteriorly and posteriorly by the insula. **retrobulbar s.,** the space lying behind the fascia of the bulb of the eye, containing the eye muscles and the ocular vessels and nerves. **retrocardiac s.,** Holzknecht's s. **retro-inguinal s.,** Bogros' s. **retro-ocular s.,** retrobulbar s. **retroperitoneal s.,** spatium retroperitoneale. **retropharyngeal s.,** the space behind the pharynx, containing areolar tissue. **retropubic s., Retzius s.,** spatium retropubicum. **Robin's s's,** minute lymph spaces in the external coat of an artery communicating with lymphatic vessels. **Schwalbe's s's,** spatia intervaginalia nervi optici. **semilunar s.** See *Traube's semilunar s.* **septal s.,** that portion of the interproximal space gingival to the contact area of adjacent teeth in a dental arch. **subarachnoid s.,** cavum subarachnoideale. **subdural s.,** cavum subdurale. **subgingival s.,** the space between the gingiva and the tooth surface which it covers. **submaxillary s.,** submaxillary triangle. **subphrenic s.,** the space between the diaphragm and subjacent organs. **subumbilical s.,** the somewhat triangular space within the body cavity just below the umbilicus. **suprasternal s.,** fossa jugularis. **Tarin's s.,** recessus anterior fossae interpeduncularis. **Tenon's s.** spatium intervaginale. **thenar s.,** the palmar space lying between the middle metacarpal bone and the tendon of the flexor pollicis longus. **thiocyanate s.,** a quantitative expression of the space occupied by the extracellular fluid in the body, computed after intravenous injection of sodium thiocyanate. **thyrohyal s.,** the depressed space between the thyroid cartilage and hyoid bone in front. **Traube's semilunar s.,** an area on the left side and front of the lower part of the chest, over which the air in the stomach produces a vesiculotympanitic sound. **Tröltsch's s's.** See *recessus membranae tympani anterior* and *recessus membranae tympani posterior.* **urogenital s.,** rima pudendi. **Virchow-Robin s's,** spaces surrounding the blood vessels as they enter the brain, the inner wall being formed by a prolongation of a membrane like the arachnoid, and the outer wall by a continuation of the pia, the intervening channel communicating with the subarachnoid space. **web s's,** the areas of loose connective tissue and fat between the bases of the fingers. **Westberg's s.,** the space between the pericardium and the beginning of the aorta. **yolk s.,** the space formed by retraction of the vitellus of the ovum from the zona pellucida. **Zang's s.,** fossa supraclaviculares minor. **zonular s's,** spatia zonularia.

spadic (spa′dik). The native name in western South America for the leaves of the coca plant, used for chewing.

spagiric (spah-jir′ik) [Gr. *span* to draw + *ageirein* to bring together]. Pertaining to the obsolete paracelsian system of medicine.

spagirist (spaj′ĭ-rist). A follower of the paracelsian system of medicine.

Spahlinger's treatment (spah′lin-jerz) [Henry *Spahlinger*, a nonmedical research worker of Geneva]. See under *treatment.*

Spallanzani's law (spal″an-zan′ēz) [Lazaro

Spallanzani, eminent Italian anatomist, 1729–1799]. See under *law*.

spallation (spawl-la′shun). Splintering; the process of breaking into small bits. See *spallation products*, under *product*.

span (span). A measurement of reach or extent; applied to the greatest distance from fingertip to fingertip of the widely outstretched arms.

spanemia (spah-ne′me-ah) [*spano-* + Gr. *haima* blood + *-ia*]. Poverty or thinness of the blood; anemia.

spanemic (spah-ne′mik). 1. Pertaining to or affected with spanemia; anemic. 2. A medicine that tends to impoverish the blood.

spano- (span′o) [Gr. *spanos* scarce]. Combining form meaning scanty or scarce.

spanogyny (span′o-jin″e) [*spano-* + Gr. *gynē* woman]. Scarcity of women; decrease in female births.

spanomenorrhea (span″o-men″o-re′ah) [*spano-* + *menorrhea*]. Scanty menstruation.

spanopnea (span″op-ne′ah) [*spano-* + Gr. *pnoia* breath]. A nervous affection, with slow, deep breathing and a subjective feeling of dyspnea.

sparadrap (spar′ah-drap) [L. *sparadrapum*]. A medicated bandage or plaster.

sparer (spar′er). A substance which is destroyed in metabolism, but which, through its destruction, lessens the destruction of other substances.

sparganosis (spar″gah-no′sis). Infection with spargana which invade the subcutaneous tissues, causing inflammation and fibrosis. If the lymphatics are involved elephantiasis results.

sparganum (spar-ga′num), pl. *sparga′na* [Gr. *sparganon* swaddling clothes]. A migrating larva of a tapeworm, especially when the adult stage is not known. **s. bax′teri,** a species found in an abscess of the thigh in Africa. **s. manso′ni,** a species found in China and Japan, perhaps the same as *Diphyllobothrium mansonoides*. **s. prolif′erum,** a species found in the connective tissue of man in Japan and in the United States.

spargosis (spar-go′sis) [Gr. *spargōsis* swelling]. Excessive swelling or distention, particularly distention of the mammae with milk.

sparine (spar′ēn). Trade mark for preparations of promazine.

spark (spark). A flash of light attended with a crackling sound, made by a discharge of electricity. **direct s.,** an electric spark which passes through the body from electrodes without the use of a Leyden jar.

sparteine (spar′te-in) [L. *spartium* broom]. A clear liquid alkaloid, $(CH_2)_2C_5H_8N.CH_2.C_5H_8N(CH_2)_2$, from broom (*Scoparius*): It is poisonous, and acts like digitalis. **s. sulfate,** a white, crystalline compound, $C_{15}H_{26}N_2.H_2SO_4 + 5H_2O$; a cardiac poison: used like digitalis.

spartium (spar′she-um) [Gr. *sparton*]. Scoparius.

spasm (spazm) [L. *spasmus;* Gr. *spasmos*]. 1. A sudden, violent, involuntary contraction of a muscle or a group of muscles, attended by pain and interference with function, producing involuntary movement and distortion. 2. A sudden but transitory constriction of a passage, canal, or orifice. **s. of accommodation,** spasm of the ciliary muscles, producing excess of accommodation for near objects. **athetoid s.,** a spasm in which the affected member makes movements like those of athetosis. **Bell's s.,** convulsive tic. **bronchial s.,** spasmodic contraction of the muscular coat of the bronchial tubes, such as occurs in asthma. **cadaveric s.,** rigor mortis causing movements of the limbs. **canine s.,** risus sardonicus. **carpopedal s.,** spasm of the hand or foot, or of the thumbs and great toes, seen in calcium tetany, rickets and laryngismus stridulus. **cerebral s.,** spasm due to a cerebral lesion. **clonic s.,** a spasm in which rigidity of the muscles is followed immediately by relaxation. **cynic s.,** risus sardonicus. **dancing s.,** palmus. **facial s.,** clonic spasm of the muscles supplied by the facial nerve, either involving the entire side of the face or confined to a limited region around the eye. **fixed s.,** permanent rigidity of a muscle or set of muscles. **functional s.,** occupation neurosis. **glottic s.,** laryngospasm. **habit s.** See *tic*, def. 2. **handicraft s.,** occupation neurosis. **hephestic s.,** hephestic hemiplegia. **histrionic s.,** convulsion of the facial muscles analogous to writers' cramp. **inspiratory s.,** spasmodic contraction of the muscles of inspiration. **intention s.,** muscular spasm occurring on attempting voluntary movement. **lock s.,** a firm tonic spasm that seems to lock the fingers together, as in writers' cramp and in similar affections. **malleatory s.,** malleation. **massive s.,** a seizure characterized by contraction of most of the body musculature. **mimic s.,** involuntary contraction of the facial muscles. **mixed s.,** a spasm in which there are both extensor and flexor movements. **mobile s.,** a tonic spasm with irregular movements of the extremities. It occurs especially after hemiplegia, and is then called *spastic hemiplegia* and *posthemiplegic chorea*. **myopathic s.,** that which accompanies a disease of the muscles. **nictitating s.,** winking s. **nodding s.,** clonic spasm of the sternomastoid muscles, producing bowing motions. Called also *salaam convulsions*. **occupation s.,** occupation neurosis. **perineal s.,** vaginodynia. **phonatory s.,** spasm of the tensors of the vocal bands. **professional s.,** occupation neurosis. **progressive torsion s.,** dystonia musculorum deformans. **respiratory s.,** spasm of the muscles of respiration. **retrocollic s.,** spasmodic retroflexion of the head. **Romberg's s.,** masticatory spasm of the muscles supplied by the fifth nerve. **rotatory s.,** intermittent spasm of the splenius muscle causing rotation of the head. **salaam s.,** nodding s. **saltatory s.,** clonic spasm of the muscles of the legs, producing a peculiar jumping or springing motion in the patient. Called also *palmus*. **Smith's s.,** hephestic hemiplegia. **synclonic s.,** clonic spasm of more than one muscle. **tetanic s.** 1. The muscular spasm occurring in tetanus. 2. Tonic spasm. **tonic s.,** spasm in which rigidity persists for a considerable time. **tonoclonic s.,** a convulsive twitching of the muscles. **tooth s.,** infantile eclampsia. **torsion s.,** spasm marked by a twisting or turning of the body, especially of the pelvis. **toxic s.,** that which is due to a poison. **winking s.,** spasmodic twitching of the orbicularis palpebrarum muscle and of the eyelid. **writers' s.,** writers' cramp.

spasmo- (spaz′mo) [L. *spasmus;* Gr. *spasmos*]. Combining form denoting relationship to a spasm.

spasmodermia (spaz″mo-der′me-ah) [*spasmo-* + Gr. *derma* skin + *-ia*]. A spasmodic affection of the skin.

spasmodic (spaz-mod′ik) [Gr. *spasmōdēs*]. Of the nature of a spasm.

spasmodism (spaz′mo-dizm). A spasmodic condition due to medullary excitation.

spasmogen (spaz′mo-jen) [*spasmo-* + Gr. *gennan* to produce]. A substance that produces or causes spasms.

spasmogenic (spaz″mo-jen′ik). Relating to the production of or causing spasms.

spasmology (spaz-mol′o-je) [*spasmo-* + *-logy*]. The sum of what is known regarding spasms.

spasmolygmus (spaz″mo-lig′mus) [*spasmo-* + Gr. *lygmos* hiccup]. Spasmodic hiccup.

spasmolysant (spaz-mol′ĭ-zant). 1. Relieving or relaxing spasms. 2. An agent that relieves spasm.

spasmolysis (spaz-mol′ĭ-sis). The elimination or checking of spasm.

spasmolytic (spaz″mo-lit′ik). Checking spasms; antispasmodic.

spasmomyxorrhea (spaz″mo-mik″so-re′ah). Myxorrhea intestinalis.

spasmophemia (spaz″mo-fe′me-ah) [*spasmo-* + Gr. *phēmē* speech + *-ia*]. Stuttering; a form of dysphemia in which there are intermittent periods during which sound is blocked.

spasmophile (spaz′mo-fīl). Spasmophilic.

spasmophilia (spaz″mo-fil′e-ah) [*spasmo-* + Gr. *philein* to love]. Spasmophilic diathesis; a condition in which the motor nerves show abnormal sensitiveness to mechanical or electric stimulation, and the patient shows a tendency to spasm, tetany, and convulsions.

spasmophilic (spaz″mo-fil′ik). Marked by a tendency to spasms.

spasmotin (spaz′mo-tin). A poisonous ecbolic and acid principle, $C_{20}H_{21}O_9$, from ergot.

spasmotoxin (spaz″mo-tok′sin) [*spasmo-* + Gr. *toxikon* poison]. Tetanus toxin.

spasmus (spaz′mus) [L.]. Spasm. **s. nu′tans,** nodding spasm.

spastic (spas′tik) [Gr. *spastikos*]. 1. Of the nature of or characterized by spasms. 2. Hypertonic, so that the muscles are stiff and the movements awkward. See *cerebral palsy*, under *palsy*.

spasticity (spas-tis′ĭ-te). A state of increase over the normal tension of a muscle, resulting in continuous increase of resistance to stretching.

spatia (spa′she-ah) [L.]. Plural of *spatium*.

spatial (spa′shal). Pertaining to space.

spatic (spa′tik). Pertaining to a space, especially an interproximal space.

spatium (spa′she-um), pl. *spa′tia* [L.]. A delimited area; used in anatomical nomenclature as a general term to designate an actual or potential open place. Called also *space*. **spa′tia an′guli i′ridis [Fonta′nae]** [B N A], **spa′tia an′guli iridocornea′lis** [N A], the spaces between the fibers of the pectinate ligament through which communication is effected between the anterior chamber and the sinus venosus. Called also *spaces of iridocorneal angle*. **s. intercosta′le** [N A], the space intervening between two adjacent ribs. Called also *intercostal space*. **spa′tia intercosta′lia** [B N A]. See *spatium intercostale*. **s. interfascia′le [Teno′ni]** [B N A], s. intervaginale. **spa′tia interglobula′ria** [N A, B N A], numerous small irregular spaces on the the outer surface of the dentin in the root of the tooth. Called also *interglobular spaces*. **spa′tia interos′sea metacar′pi** [N A, B N A], the four spaces between the metacarpal bones. Called also *interosseous spaces of metacarpus*. **spa′tia interos′sea metatar′si** [N A, B N A], the four spaces between the metatarsal bones. Called also *interosseous spaces of metatarsus*. **s. intervagina′le** [N A], the space between the bulbar fascia and the eyeball. Called also *s. interfasciale* [*Tenoni*] [B N A], and *intervaginal space*. **spa′tia intervagina′lia ner′vi op′tici** [N A, B N A], the subdural and subarachnoid spaces between the internal and external sheaths of the optic nerve. Called also *intervaginal spaces of optic nerve*. **s. perichorioidea′le** [B N A], **s. perichoroidea′le** [N A], any one of the spaces between the laminae of the non-vascular layer of the choroid nearest the sclera. Called also *perichoroidal space*. **s. perilymphat′icum** [N A, B N A], the fluid-filled space separating the membranous from the osseous labyrinth. Called also *perilymphatic space*. **s. perine′i profun′dum** [N A], the area between the superior and inferior fascia of the urogenital diaphragm. Called also *deep perineal space*. **s. perine′i superficia′le** [N A], the region between the inferior fascia of the urogenital diaphragm and the membranous layer of the superficial perineal fascia. It contains the root of the penis and associated muscles. Called also *superficial perineal space*. **s. retroperitonea′le** [N A], the space between the posterior parietal peritoneum and the posterior abdominal wall, containing the kidneys, suprarenal glands, ureters, duodenum, ascending and descending colon, pancreas, and the large vessels and nerves. Called also *retroperitoneal space*. **s. retropu′bicum** [N A], the extraperitoneal space between the inferior aspect of the apex of the bladder, and the transversalis fascia and the posterosuperior aspect of the pubic symphysis, extending along the sides of the bladder to the lateral ligaments and limited below by the puboprostatic ligaments. Called also *retropubic space*. **spa′tia zonula′ria** [N A, B N A], the lymph-filled interstices between the fibers of the zonula ciliaris, communicating with the posterior chamber of the eye. Called also *zonular spaces*.

spatula (spat′u-lah) [L.]. A flat, blunt, usually flexible instrument, used for spreading plasters and for mixing ointments and masses. **s. mal′lei,** the flat end of the handle of the malleus, attached to the membrana tympani. **Roux's s.,** a small steel spatula for transferring infected material to culture tubes.

spatular (spat′u-lar). Spatulate.

spatulate (spat′u-lāt) 1. Having a flat blunt end. 2. To mix or manipulate with a spatula.

spatulation (spat″u-la′shun). The mixing of combined materials to a homogeneous mass by repeatedly scraping them up and smoothing out the mass on a flat surface with a spatula.

spavin (spav′in). In general, an exostosis, usually medial, of the tarsus of equidae, distal to the tibiotarsal articulation and often involving the metatarsals. **blood s.,** a dilatation of either or both of the medial metatarsal or of the saphenous veins, forming a soft enlargement on the dorsomedial surface of the tarsus in equidae. **bog s.,** a distention of the synovial capsule of the tibiotarsal joint in equidae. **bone s.,** osteo-periostitis or arthritis of the inter-tarsal or tarsometatarsal articulations in equidae, commonly followed by exostosis and ankylosis. Classified as visible, occult, anterior, posterior and high. **Jack s.,** a very large exostotic spavin.

spavined (spav′ind). Affected with spavin.

spay (spa). To deprive of the ovaries by surgical removal.

SPCA. Abbreviation for *serum prothrombin conversion accelerator* (blood coagulation factor VII).

spearmint (spēr′mint). The dried leaf and flowering top of *Mentha spicata* or of *Mentha cardiaca:* used as a flavoring agent.

specialism (spesh′al-izm). Devotion to a special department of medicine or surgery.

specialist (spesh′al-ist). A practitioner who devotes himself to a special class of diseases.

specialization (spesh″al-i-za′shun). In medicine, medical practice limited to some special department of medicine or surgery.

species (spe′shēz) [L.]. 1. A taxonomic category subordinate to a genus (or subgenus), and superior to a subspecies or variety, composed of individuals possessing common characters distinguishing them from other categories of individuals of the same taxonomic level. 2. A mixture of dried herbs, seeds, or barks, used chiefly as a decoction; obsolete. **diovulatory s.,** a species of animal, the females of which ordinarily discharge two ova in one ovulatory cycle. **monovulatory s.,** a species of animal, the females of which usually discharge only one ovum in any one ovulatory cycle. **polyovulatory s.,** a species of animal, the females of which normally discharge several (3–16) ova at each ovulatory cycle. **type s.,** the original species from which a description of the genus of organisms is made.

specific (spe-sif′ik) [L. *specificus*]. 1. Pertaining to a species. 2. Produced by a single kind of microorganism. 3. A remedy specially indicated for any particular disease. 4. In immunology, pertaining to the special affinity of antigen for the corresponding antibody.

specificity (spes″ĭ-fis′ĭ-te). The quality or state of being specific. **organ s.** See *organ-specific antigen*, under *antigen*.

specificness (spe-sif′ik-nes). Specificity.

specillum (spe-sil′um) [L. *specere* to look]. A sound or probe.

specimen (spes′ĭ-men). 1. A sample or part of a thing, or of several things, taken to show or to determine the character of the whole, as a specimen of urine. 2. A preparation of tissue for pathological examination or of a normal tissue, organ, or organism for study of its structure. **corrosion s.,** a preparation of an organ, such as the liver, by injection of certain structures, as the arteries and veins, and chemical digestion of surrounding substance.

spectacles (spek′tah-k′lz) [L. *spectacula; spectare* to see]. A pair of lenses in a frame to assist vision. See also *glasses* and *lens.* **compound s.,** spectacles fitted with extra colored glasses, or extra lenses, to be used as occasion requires. **decentered s.,** spectacles with lenses formed from eccentric portions of two convex lenses. **divided s.,** bifocal glasses. **Masselon's s.,** spectacles with an attachment for keeping the upper lid raised in cases of paralytic ptosis. **mica s.,** spectacles of sheet mica: used to protect the eye from foreign bodies. **pantoscopic s.,** bifocal glasses. **periscopic s.,** spectacles with either menisci or concavoconvex lenses, with the concave surfaces toward the eyes: these allow the eyes considerable latitude of motion. **prismatic s.,** spectacles with prismatic lenses for correcting muscular defects. **pulpit s.,** spectacles containing the lenses in the lower segments of the glasses only. **stenopeic s.,** spectacles fitted with metal plates, having each a small central aperture. **tinted s.,** spectacles of a glass so colored as to protect the eyes from the effects of too bright light. **wire frame s.,** a kind of spectacles of wire gauze worn to protect the eye from the entrance of foreign bodies.

spectral (spek′tral). Pertaining to a spectrum; performed by means of a spectrum.

spectrochrome (spek′tro-krōm) [L. *spectrum* + Gr. *chrōma* color]. A term applied to a method of treatment consisting of exposure of the part to be treated to light of various colors.

spectrocolorimeter (spek″tro-kul″or-im′e-ter). An ophthalmospectroscope used in detecting color blindness for one color.

spectrograph (spek′tro-graf). An instrument for photographing spectra on a sensitive photographic plate.

spectrometer (spek-trom′e-ter). 1. An instrument for measuring the index of refraction by measuring the external angle of a prism of the substance. 2. A spectroscope for measuring the wavelengths of rays of a spectrum.

spectrometry (spek-trom′e-tre) [L. *spectrum* image + *metrum* measure]. The determination of the places of the lines in a spectrum.

spectrophobia (spek″tro-fo′be-ah) [L. *spectrum* image + Gr. *phobein* to be affrighted by]. Morbid dread of mirrors or of seeing one's face in a mirror.

spectrophotometer (spek″tro-fo-tom′e-ter) [*spectrum* + *photometer*]. 1. An apparatus for measuring the light sense by means of a spectrum. 2. An apparatus for estimating the quantity of coloring matter in solution by the quantity of light absorbed (as indicated by the spectrum) in passing through the solution.

spectrophotometry (spek″tro-fo-tom′e-tre). The use of the spectrophotometer.

spectropolarimeter (spek″tro-po″lar-im′e-ter). A combined spectroscope and polariscope for determining optical rotation.

spectropyrheliometer (spek″tro-pir-he″le-om′e-ter) [*spectrum* + Gr. *pyr* fire + *hēlios* sun + *metrum* measure]. An instrument for measuring the radiation from the sun.

spectroscope (spek′tro-skōp) [*spectrum* + Gr. *skopein* to examine]. An instrument for developing and analyzing the spectrum of a body.

spectroscopic (spek″tro-skop′ik). Of, pertaining to, or performed by, the spectroscope.

spectrum (spek′trum), pl. *spec′tra* [L. "apparition"]. A charted band of wavelengths of electromagnetic vibrations obtained by refraction and diffraction. See *invisible s.* and *visible s.* By extension, a measurable range of activity, such as the range of bacteria affected by an antibiotic (antibacterial s.) or the complete range of manifestations of a disease. **absorption s.,** one afforded by light which has passed through various gaseous mediums, each gas absorbing those rays of which its own spectrum is composed. **chemical s.,** that part of the spectrum which includes the ultraviolet or actinic rays. **chromatic s.,** that portion of the range of wavelengths of electromagnetic vibrations (from 7700 to 3900 A.U.) which gives rise to the sensation of color (red to violet) to the normally perceptive eye; coincident with the visible spectrum. **color s.,** chromatic s. **continuous s.,** one in which Fraunhofer's lines are not developed. **diffraction s.,** a spectrum formed by the passage of light through a diffraction grating. **fortification s.,** teichopsia. **gaseous s.,** one which is afforded by an incandescent gas. **invisible s.,** that made up of vibrations of wavelengths less than 3900 A.U. (ultraviolet, grenz rays, x-rays, and gamma rays) and between 7700 and 120,000 A.U. (infrared). **ocular s.,** after-image. **prismatic s.,** one produced by the passage of light through a prism. **solar s.,** that portion of the range of wavelengths of electromagnetic vibrations emanating from the sun, including the visible (chromatic, or color) spectrum and small portions of the infrared and ultraviolet radiations at either extreme. **thermal s.,** that portion of the range of wavelengths of electromagnetic vibrations (>7700 A.U.) containing the infrared or heat rays. **toxin s.,** a diagrammatic representation of the neutralizing power of an antitoxin. **visible s.,** that portion of the range of wavelengths of electromagnetic vibrations (from 7700 to 3900 A.U.) which is capable of stimulating specialized sense organs and is perceptible as light. **x-ray s.,** the spectrum of a heterogeneous beam of roentgen rays produced by a suitable grating, generally a crystal.

speculum (spek′u-lum) pl. *spec′ula* [L. "mirror"]. 1. An appliance for opening to view a passage or cavity of the body. 2. The septum pellucidum.

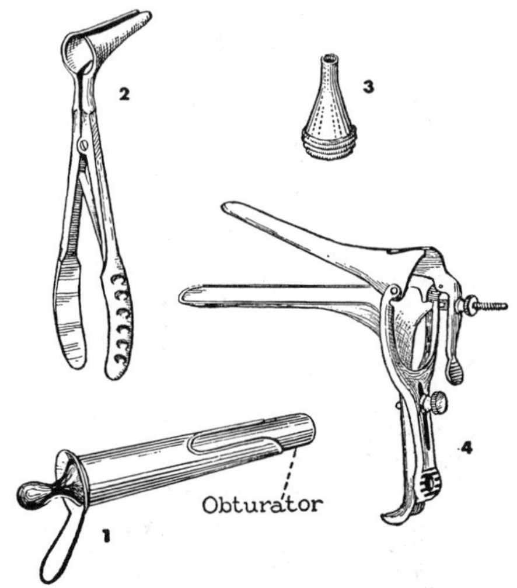

Specula: 1, rectal (David); 2, nasal (Vienna model); 3, ear (Boucheron); 4, vaginal (Pederson).

Bozeman's s., a bivalve speculum the blades of which remain parallel when separated. **Brinkerhoff's s.,** a rectal speculum consisting of a conical tube having a closed extremity, but provided with a sliding bar on the side which provides an opening. **Cook's s.,** a three-pronged rectal speculum. **Cusco's s.,** a form of vaginal speculum, the two blades of which are worked by a screw. **duck-billed s.,** a form of two-valved vaginal speculum. **eye s.,** an appliance for keeping the eyelids apart. **Fergusson's s.,** a cylindrical vaginal speculum made of silvered glass. **Fränkel's s.,** a form of nasal speculum. **Gru-**

ber's s., a form of ear speculum. **Hartmann's s.,** a form of nasal speculum. **s. Helmon'tii,** the central tendon of the diaphragm. **Kelly's s.,** a rectal speculum tubular in shape and fitted with an obturator. **Martin's s.,** a rectal speculum, consisting of a conical cylinder with an obturator. **Mathews' s.,** a four-pronged rectal speculum. **Mayer's s.,** a tubular vaginal glass speculum. **Politzer's s.,** a form of ear speculum. **s. rhomboi'deum,** the lumbodorsal fascia. **Simmond's s.,** a form of vaginal speculum. **Sims's s.,** a double duck-billed vaginal speculum. **stop s.,** an eye speculum with an appliance for controlling the degree to which its branches spread. **wire bivalve s.,** a two-valved vaginal speculum made of heavy wire.

spedalskhed (sped-alsk'hed) [Norwegian]. Leprosy.

Spee's curve (spāz) [Ferdinand Graf von *Spee*, German embryologist, born 1855]. See under *curve*.

speech (spēch). The utterance of vocal sounds conveying ideas. **clipped s.,** utterance in which the words uttered are slurred over and uncompleted: sometimes one of the features of general paresis. **echo s.,** echolalia. **esophageal s.,** speech produced by vibration of the column of air in the esophagus against the contracting cricopharyngeal sphincter, after laryngectomy. **explosive s.,** loud, sudden enunciation, seen in certain brain diseases. **incoherent s.,** speech in which the consecutive ideas expressed are not related: due to disturbance of the train of thought. **jumbled s.,** anarthria. **mirror s.,** a speech abnormality in which the order of syllables in a sentence is reversed. **plateau s.,** speech which is characterized by a level, monotonous, unvaried pitch. **scamping s.,** clipped s. **scanning s.,** speech in which the syllables are separated by prolonged pauses. **slurred s.,** clipped s. **staccato s.,** speech in which each syllable is uttered separately: seen in multiple sclerosis.

Spemann's induction [Hans *Spemann*, German zoologist, 1869–1941; noted for his researches on embryonic development, and winner of the Nobel prize for medicine and physiology in 1935]. See under *induction*.

Spencer-Parker vaccine (spen'ser-par'ker) [Roscoe Roy *Spencer*, American physician, born 1888; Ralph R. *Parker*, American zoologist, 1888–1949]. See under *vaccine*.

Spencer Wells facies. See *Wells' facies*, and under *facies*.

Spengler's fragments, immune body, tuberculin, etc. (speng'lerz) [Carl *Spengler*, Swiss physician, 1860–1937]. See under the nouns.

Spens's syndrome (spenz) [Thomas *Spens*, Scottish physician, 1764–1842]. Adams-Stokes disease.

sperm (sperm) [Gr. *sperma* seed]. 1. The semen or testicular secretion. 2. One of the mature germ cells of a male animal. **muzzled s.,** spermatozoa which are unable to adhere to the ovum.

sperma (sper'mah). [B N A] Semen. Omitted in N A.

spermaceti (sper″mah-set'e) [Gr. *sperma* seed + *kētos* whale]. A waxy substance obtained from the head of the sperm whale, *Physeter macrocephalus:* used as an ingredient in petrolatum rose water ointment.

spermacrasia (sper″mah-kra'zhe-ah) [Gr. *sperma* seed + *akrasia* ill mixture]. Deficiency of spermatozoa in the semen.

spermagglutination (sperm″ah-gloo″tĭ-na'-shun). The agglutination of spermatozoa.

spermalist (sper'mah-list). Spermist.

spermase (sper'mās). An oxidizing enzyme found in barley.

spermateliosis (sper″mah-te″le-o'sis). Spermiogenesis.

spermatemphraxis (sper″mat-em-frak'sis) [Gr. *sperma* seed + *emphraxis* stoppage]. Obstruction to the discharge of semen.

spermatic (sper-mat'ik) [L. *spermaticus;* Gr. *spermatikos*]. Pertaining to the semen; seminal.

spermaticide (sper-mat'ĭ-sīd). Spermicide.

spermatid (sper'mah-tid). A cell derived from a secondary spermatocyte by fission, and developing into a spermatozoon. Called also *spermatoblast*.

spermatin (sper'mah-tin). An albuminoid substance derived from the semen. It is related to mucin and to nucleo-albumin.

spermatism (sper'mah-tizm) [Gr. *spermatismos*]. The production or discharge of semen.

spermatitis (sper″mah-ti'tis). Inflammation of a vas deferens; deferentitis or funiculitis.

spermato-, spermo- (sper'mah-to) [Gr. *sperma, spermatos* seed]. Combining form denoting relationship to seed, specifically to the male generative element.

spermatoblast (sper'mah-to-blast″) [*spermato-* + Gr. *blastos* germ]. A term originally applied to the supporting cells of Sertoli, but now used with the same meaning as *spermatid*.

spermatocele (sper'mah-to-sēl″) [*spermato-* + Gr. *kēlē* tumor]. A cystic distention of the epididymis or the rete testis containing spermatozoa.

spermatocelectomy (sper-mat″o-se-lek'to-me) [*spermatocele* + Gr. *ektomē* excision]. Operative excision of a lesion of the epididymis (spermatocele).

spermatocidal (sper″mah-to-si'dal). Spermicidal.

spermatocyst (sper'mah-to-sist″) [*spermato-* + Gr. *kystis* sac, bladder]. 1. A seminal vesicle. 2. A spermatocele.

spermatocystectomy (sper″mah-to-sis-tek'to-me) [*spermatocyst* + Gr. *ektomē* excision]. Excision of the seminal vesicles.

spermatocystitis (sper″mah-to-sis-ti'tis). Seminal vesiculitis.

spermatocystotomy (sper″mah-to-sis-tot'o-me) [*spermatocyst* + Gr. *tomē* a cutting]. The operation of making an incision into the seminal vesicles for the purpose of drainage.

spermatocytal (sper″mah-to-si'tal). Pertaining to a spermatocyte.

spermatocyte (sper'mah-to-sīt″) [*spermato-* + *-cyte*]. The mother cell of a spermatid. **primary s.,** a cell derived from a spermatogonium and dividing into two secondary spermatocytes. Called also *spermiocyte*. **secondary s.,** one of the two cells into which a primary spermatocyte divides, and which in turn gives origin to spermatids. Called also *prespermatid*.

spermatocytogenesis (sper″mah-to-si″to-jen'e-sis). The first stage of formation of spermatozoa in which the spermatogonia develop into spermatocytes and then into spermatids.

spermatogenesis (sper″mah-to-jen'e-sis) [*spermato-* + Gr. *genesis* production]. The process of formation of spermatozoa, including spermatocytogenesis and spermiogenesis.

spermatogenic (sper″mah-to-jen'ik) [*spermato-* + Gr. *gennan* to produce]. Producing semen or spermatozoa.

spermatogenous (sper″mah-toj'e-nus). Spermatogenic.

spermatogeny (sper″mah-toj'e-ne). Spermatogenesis.

spermatogone (sper'mah-to-gōn″). Spermatogonium.

spermatogonium (sper″mah-to-go'ne-um) [*spermato-* + Gr. *gonē* generation]. An undifferentiated germ cell of a male, originating in a seminal tubule and dividing into two primary spermatocytes. Called also *spermatophore, spermatospore,* and *spermospore*.

spermatoid (sper'mah-toid) [*spermato-* + Gr. *eidos* form]. 1. Resembling semen. 2. A male or flagellated form of the malarial microparasite.

spermatology (sper″mah-tol'o-je) [*spermato-* + *-logy*]. The sum of what is known regarding the semen.

spermatolysin (sper″mah-tol′ĭ-sin). A substance causing spermatolysis.

spermatolysis (sper″mah-tol′ĭ-sis) [*spermato-* + Gr. *lysis* dissolution]. Destruction or solution of spermatozoa.

spermatolytic (sper″mah-to-lit′ik). Pertaining to, characterized by, or causing spermatolysis.

spermatomere (sper′mah-to-mēr″). Spermatomerite.

spermatomerite (sper″mah-to-me′rīt) [*spermato-* + Gr. *meros* part]. One of the chromosomes into which the sperm nucleus resolves during fertilization of the ovum.

spermatomicron (sper″mah-to-mi′kron). A minute particle found in the semen of various animals; seen best with a dark-field microscope, when they show brownian motion.

spermatopathia (sper″mah-to-path′e-ah) [*spermato-* + Gr. *pathos* affection]. A morbid condition of the semen.

spermatopathy (sper″mah-top′ah-the). Spermatopathia.

spermatophobia (sper″mah-to-fo′be-ah) [*spermato-* + *phobia*]. A morbid dread of being affected with spermatorrhea.

spermatophore (sper′mah-to-fōr″) [*spermato-* + Gr. *phorein* to carry]. 1. Spermatogonium. 2. A capsule, containing several spermatozoa, extruded by some of the lower animals.

spermatopoietic (sper″mah-to-poi-et′ik) [*spermato-* + Gr. *poiētikos* creative, productive]. Subserving or promoting the secretion of semen.

spermatorrhea (sper″mah-to-re′ah) [*spermato-* + Gr. *rhoia* flow]. Involuntary, too frequent, and excessive discharge of semen without copulation.

spermatoschesis (sper″mah-tos′kĕ-sis) [*spermato-* + Gr. *schesis* check]. Suppression of the secretion of semen.

spermatosome (sper-mat′o-sōm). Spermatozoon.

spermatospore (sper-mat′o-spōr) [*spermato-* + Gr. *sporos* spore]. A spermatogonium.

spermatotoxin (sper″mah-to-tok′sin). Spermotoxin.

spermatovum (sper″mat-o′vum) [*spermato-* + L. *ovum* egg]. A fecundated ovum.

spermatoxin (sper″mah-tok′sin). Spermotoxin.

spermatozoa (sper″mah-to-zo′ah). Plural of *spermatozoon.*

spermatozoal (sper″mah-to-zo′al). Pertaining to spermatozoa.

spermatozoicide (sper″mah-to-zo′ĭ-sīd). Spermicide.

spermatozoid (sper′mah-to-zoid) [*spermatozoon* + Gr. *eidos* form]. 1. Spermatozoon. 2. The male germ cell in plants.

spermatozoon (sper″mah-to-zo′on), pl. *spermatozo′a* [*spermato-* + Gr. *zōon* animal]. A mature male germ cell, the specific output of the testes. It is the generative element of the semen which serves to impregnate the ovum. It consists of a head, or nucleus, a neck, a middle piece, and a tail with an end piece.

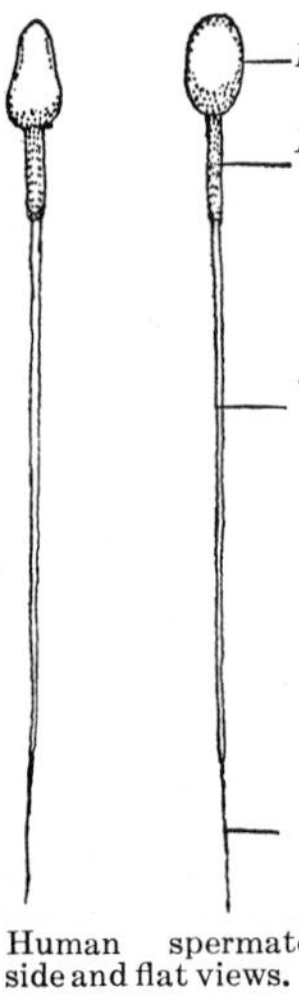

Human spermatozoon, side and flat views. (Hill.)

spermaturia (sper″mah-tu′re-ah) [*spermato-* + Gr. *ouron* urine + *-ia*]. Seminuria.

spermectomy (sper-mek′to-me). Excision of a portion of the spermatic cord.

spermia (sper′me-ah). Plural of *spermium.*

spermiation (sper″me-a′shun). The freeing of mature spermatozoa from the Sertoli cells.

spermicidal (sper″mĭ-si′dal) [*sperm* + L. *caedere* to kill]. Destructive to spermatozoa.

spermicide (sper′mĭ-sīd). An agent that is destructive to spermatozoa.

spermid (sper′mid). Spermatid.

spermidine (sper′mĭ-din). A base, $C_7H_{19}N_3$, isolated from animal tissue.

spermiduct (sper′mĭ-dukt) [*sperm* + L. *ductus* duct]. The ejaculatory duct and vas deferens together.

spermine (sper′min). A base, $NH_2(CH_2)_3NH(CH_2)_4NH(CH_2)_3NH_2$, from semen, sputum, and various other animal substances. **s. phosphate,** the substance, $(C_2H_5N)_4H_4Ca(PO_4)_2$, of which the Charcot-Neumann crystals are composed: found also in various organs and secretions in leukemia, asthma, and emphysema.

spermiocyte (sper′me-o-sīt) [*spermia* + *-cyte*]. A primary spermatocyte.

spermiogenesis (sper″me-o-jen′e-sis). The second stage in the formation of spermatozoa in which the spermatids transform into spermatozoa.

spermiogonium (sper″me-o-go′ne-um). Spermatogonium.

spermiogram (sper′me-o-gram″). A diagram of the various cells formed during the development of the sperm.

spermioteleosis (sper″me-o-te″le-o′sis) [*spermio-* + Gr. *teleiōsis* perfection, completion]. The progressive development of the spermatogonium through the successive changes necessary for becoming a mature spermatozoon.

spermioteleotic (sper″me-o-te″le-ot′ik) [*spermio-* + Gr. *teleiōtikos* perfective]. Pertaining to or characteristic of spermioteleosis.

spermist (sper′mist). A believer in the theory of preformation, holding that the spermatozoon was a complete miniature individual.

spermium (sper′me-um), pl. *sper′mia.* The mature spermatozoon.

spermo-. See *spermato-.*

spermoblast (sper′mo-blast) [*spermo-* + Gr. *blastos* germ]. A spermatid.

spermoculture (sper′mo-kul″tūr). Bacterial examination of cultures of the semen.

spermocytoma (sper″mo-si-to′mah). Seminoma.

spermolith (sper′mo-lith) [*spermo-* + Gr. *lithos* stone]. A calculus in the spermiduct.

spermoloropexis (sper″mo-lo″ro-pek′sis). Spermoloropexy.

spermoloropexy (sper″mo-lo′ro-pek″se) [*spermo-* + Gr. *lōron* thong + *pēxis* fixation]. Fixation of the spermatic cord to the periosteum of the pubes in operation for undescended testicle.

spermolysin (sper-mol′ĭ-sin). Spermatoxin.

spermolysis (sper-mol′ĭ-sis). Spermatolysis.

spermolytic (sper″mo-lit′ik). Spermatolytic.

spermoneuralgia (sper″mo-nu-ral′je-ah) [*spermo-* + Gr. *neuron* nerve + *-algia*]. Neuralgic pain in the spermatic cord.

Spermophilus (sper-mof′ĭ-lus). A genus of marmots of Manchuria, several species of which may harbor rat fleas.

spermophlebectasia (sper″mo-fle″bek-ta′ze-ah) [*spermo-* + Gr. *phleps* vein + *ektasis* distention + *-ia*]. Varicosity of the spermatic veins.

spermoplasm (sper′mo-plazm) [*spermo-* + Gr. *plasma* plasm]. The protoplasm of the spermatids.

spermosphere (sper′mo-sfēr) [*spermo-* + Gr. *sphaira* sphere]. A group or mass of spermatids formed by the segmentation of a secondary spermatocyte.

spermospore (sper′mo-spōr). Spermatogonium.

spermotoxic (sper″mo-tok′sik). Pertaining to a spermotoxin.

spermotoxin (sper″mo-tok′sin). A toxin destructive to spermatozoa; especially an antibody produced by injecting an animal with spermatozoa.

spes (spēs) [L.]. Hope. **s. phthis′ica,** a feeling

of hopefulness of recovery frequently characteristic of patients with tuberculosis.

SPF. Abbreviation for *specific-pathogen free*, a term applied to gnotobiotic animals reared for use in laboratory experiments, and known to be free of specific pathogenic microorganisms.

sp. gr. Abbreviation for *specific gravity*.

sph. Abbreviation for *spherical* or *spherical lens*.

sphacelate (sfas′ĕ-lāt). To become gangrenous.

sphacelation (sfas″ĕ-la′shun). The formation of a sphacelus: mortification.

sphacelism (sfas′ĕ-lizm) [Gr. *sphakelismos*]. Sphacelation or necrosis; sloughing.

sphaceloderma (sfas″ĕ-lo-der′mah) [*sphacelus* + Gr. *derma* skin]. Gangrene of the skin.

sphacelotoxin (sfas″ĕ-lo-tok′sin) [*sphacelus* + Gr. *toxikon* poison]. 1. Spasmotin. 2. A poisonous, yellow resin obtainable from ergot.

sphacelous (sfas′ĕ-lus). Affected with gangrene; sloughing.

sphacelus (sfas′ĕ-lus) [L.; Gr. *sphakelos*]. A slough or mass of gangrenous tissue.

sphaer-. For words beginning thus, see also those beginning *spher-*.

Sphaeranthus (sfe-ran′thus). A genus of plants. **S. in′dicus** furnishes an aphrodisiac oil.

Sphaeria (sfe′re-ah). A genus of fungi. **S. sinen′sis,** a fungus found in China, where it is highly esteemed as a medicine.

sphaero-. For words beginning thus, see also those beginning *sphero-*.

Sphaerophorus (sfe-ro′fo-rus). A genus of minute, gram-negative, non-sporulating obligate anaerobic pleomorphic bacteria found in necrotic tissues as a secondary invader. **S. necroph′orus,** a microorganism which is pathogenic for animals, producing multiple sclerotic abscesses in cattle, and necrotic foci in the liver of cattle and hogs.

Sphaerotilus (sfe-ro′tĭ-lus). A genus of microorganisms of the family Chlamydobacteriaceae, order Chlamydobacteriales, made up of attached or free-floating filaments, frequently showing false branching. It includes three species, *S. dicho′tomus*, *S. flu′itans*, and *S. na′tans*.

sphagiasmus (sfa″je-az′mus) [Gr. *sphagiasmos* a slaying, sacrificing]. 1. Contraction of the neck muscles in an epileptic attack. 2. Petit mal.

sphagitides (sfah-jit′ĭ-dēz) [Gr. *sphagitis* jugular; *sphagē* throat]. An old name for the so-called jugular vessels.

sphagitis (sfa-ji′tis) [Gr. *sphagē* throat + *-itis*]. Any throat inflammation.

sphenethmoid (sfen-eth′moid). Spheno-ethmoid.

sphenion (sfe′ne-on), pl. *sphe′nia* [Gr. *sphēn* wedge + *on* neuter ending]. The cranial point at the sphenoid angle of the parietal bone.

spheno- (sfe′no) [Gr. *sphēn* wedge]. Combining form denoting relationship to the sphenoid bone or to a wedge, or meaning wedge-shaped.

sphenobasilar (sfe″no-bas′ĭ-lar). Pertaining to the sphenoid bone and the basilar part of the occipital bone.

sphenoccipital (sfe″nok-sip′ĭ-tal). Spheno-occipital.

sphenocephalus (sfe″no-sef′ah-lus). A fetal monster exhibiting sphenocephaly.

sphenocephaly (sfe″no-sef′ah-le) [*spheno-* + Gr. *kephalē* head]. A developmental anomaly characterized by a wedge-shaped appearance of the head.

spheno-ethmoid (sfe″no-eth′moid). Noting the curved plate of bone in front of the lesser wing of the sphenoid bone.

sphenofrontal (sfe″no-frun′tal). Pertaining to the sphenoid and frontal bones.

sphenoid (sfe′noid) [*spheno-* + Gr. *eidos* form]. Wedge-shaped; designating especially a very irregular wedge-shaped bone at the base of the skull (os sphenoidale, or sphenoid bone).

sphenoidal (sfe-noi′dal). Pertaining to the sphenoid bone.

sphenoiditis (sfe″noi-di′tis). Inflammation of the sphenoidal sinus.

sphenoidostomy (sfe″noi-dos′to-me) [*sphenoid* + Gr. *stomoun* to provide with an opening, or mouth]. Operative removal of the anterior wall of the sphenoidal sinus.

sphenoidotomy (sfe″noi-dot′o-me). Incision into the sphenoidal sinus.

sphenomalar (sfe″no-ma′lar). Pertaining to the sphenoid and malar bones.

sphenomaxillary (sfe″no-mak′sĭ-ler″e). Pertaining to the sphenoid bone and the maxilla.

sphenometer (sfe-nom′e-ter) [*spheno-* + Gr. *metron* measure]. An instrument for measuring a wedge of bone removed in operations for correcting curvatures.

spheno-occipital (sfe″no-ok-sip′ĭ-tal). Pertaining to the sphenoid and occipital bones.

sphenopalatine (sfe″no-pal′ah-tin). Pertaining to or in relation with the sphenoid and palatine bones.

sphenoparietal (sfe″no-pah-ri′ĕ-tal). Pertaining to the sphenoid and parietal bones.

sphenopetrosal (sfe″no-pe-tro′sal). Pertaining to the sphenoid bone and the petrosa.

sphenorbital (sfe-nor′bĭ-tal). Pertaining to the sphenoid bone and the orbits.

sphenosis (sfe-no′sis) [Gr. *sphēnōsis* a wedging or closing up]. A wedging of the fetus in the pelvis.

sphenosquamosal (sfe″no-skwa-mo′sal). Pertaining to the sphenoid bone and the squamous portion of the temporal bone.

sphenotemporal (sfe″no-tem′po-ral). Pertaining to the sphenoid and temporal bones.

sphenotic (sfe-not′ik) [*spheno-* + Gr. *ous* ear]. Noting a fetal bone which becomes that part of the sphenoid which is adjacent to the carotid groove.

sphenotresia (sfe″no-tre′ze-ah) [*spheno-* + Gr. *trēsis* boring]. Boring of the skull in craniotomy.

sphenotribe (sfe′no-trīb) [*spheno-* + Gr. *tribein* to rub]. An instrument for crushing the basal portion of the fetal skull.

sphenotripsy (sfe′no-trip″se). The crushing of the fetal head with the sphenotribe.

sphenoturbinal (sfe″no-tur′bĭ-nal). Noting a thin, curved bone in front of each of the lesser wings of the sphenoid, with which bone it becomes fused.

sphenovomerine (sfe″no-vo′mer-in). Pertaining to the sphenoid and to the vomer.

sphenozygomatic (sfe″no-zi″go-mat′ik). Pertaining to the sphenoid and zygomatic bones.

sphere (sfēr) [Gr. *sphaira* sphere]. A ball or globe. **attraction s.,** centrosome. **embryotic s.,** the morula. **Morgagni's s's,** Morgagni's globules. **nuclear s's,** rounded droplets seen in pathologic erythrocytes. They are liquid remains of nuclei. **segmentation s.** 1. The morula. 2. A blastomere. **vitelline s., yolk s.,** the morula.

spheresthesia (sfe″res-the′ze-ah) [Gr. *sphaira* sphere + *aisthēsis* perception + *-ia*]. A morbid sensation, as of contact with a ball.

spherical (sfer′ĭ-kal) [Gr. *sphairikos*]. Pertaining to a sphere; sphere-shaped.

sphero- (sfe′ro) [Gr. *sphaira* a ball or globe]. Combining form meaning round, or denoting relationship to a sphere.

spherobacteria (sfe″ro-bak-te′re-ah) [*sphero-* + Gr. *baktērion* bacterium]. A group of bacterial organisms to which the micrococci belong.

spherocylinder (sfe″ro-sil′in-der). A combined spherical and cylindrical lens.

spherocyte (sfe′ro-sīt) [*sphero-* + Gr. *kytos* cell]. A small, globular, completely hemoglobinated erythrocyte without the usual central pallor, found characteristically in hereditary spherocytosis but also observed in acquired hemolytic anemia.

spherocytic (sfe″ro-sit′ik). Characterized by the presence of spherocytes.

spherocytosis (sfe″ro-si-to′sis). The presence of spherocytes in the blood. **hereditary s.,** a familial hemolytic disease characterized by abnormal thickness of the erythrocytes.

spheroid (sfe′roid) [*sphero-* + Gr. *eidos* form]. A globular body, or one resembling a sphere.

spheroidal (sfe-roi′dal). Having the form or shape of a sphere.

spheroidin (sfe-roi′din) [*Sphaeroides* (Gr. *sphaira* sphere) a puffer fish + *-in,* suffix denoting a chemical compound]. A toxic fraction from tetraodontoxin, believed to have the empirical formula $C_{12}H_{17}O_{13}N_3$.

spheroiding (sfe′roid-ing). The formation of globules; in dentistry, the drawing together of amalgam on hardening, so that it recedes from the angles of a tooth cavity.

spherolith (sfe′ro-lith) [*sphero-* + Gr. *lithos* stone]. Any one of the minute spherical deposits found in the kidney tissue of the newborn. They are probably uratic deposits.

spheroma (sfe-ro′mah). A globular tumor.

spherometer (sfe-rom′e-ter) [*sphero-* + Gr. *metron* measure]. An instrument for measuring the curvature of a surface.

Spherophorus (sfer-of′o-rus). Sphaerophorus.

spheroplast (sfer′o-plast). A spherical bacterial or plant cell, produced in hypertonic media under conditions that result in partial or complete absence of the cell wall; identical with *protoplast,* except that spheroplast does not of necessity imply complete absence of the wall.

spherospermia (sfe-ro-sper′me-ah) [*sphero-* + Gr. *sperma* seed]. A round, tailless spermatozoon.

spherule (sfer′ūl). A small sphere. **s's of Fulci,** numerous spherical red bodies seen in the spinal cord in inflammatory conditions of the cord. **paranuclear s.,** the archiplasm.

sphincter (sfingk′ter) [L.; Gr. *sphinktēr* that which binds tight]. A ringlike band of muscle fibers that constricts a passage or closes a natural orifice. Called also *musculus sphincter* [N A]. **s. a′ni.** See *musculus sphincter ani externus* and *musculus sphincter ani internus.* **cardiac s.,** muscle fibers about the opening of the esophagus into the stomach. **cornual s.,** tubal s. **Eisler-Schneider s.,** tubal s. **s. of eye,** musculus orbicularis oculi. **Giordano's s.,** musculus sphincter ductus choledochi. **Henle's s.,** muscle fibers surrounding the prostatic urethra. **hepatic s.,** a thickened portion of the muscular coat of the hepatic veins near their entrance into the inferior vena cava. **s. of hepatopancreatic ampulla,** musculus sphincter ampullae hepatopancreaticae. **Hyrtl's s.,** an incomplete band of muscle fibers in the rectum a few inches above the anus. **inguinal s.,** a ring of muscle fibers around the spermatic cord at the internal opening of the inguinal canal. **s. i′ridis,** musculus sphincter pupillae. **Nélaton's s.,** an occasional and often incomplete band of muscle fibers about the rectum at the level of the prostate. **O'Beirne's s.,** circular muscle fibers in the wall of the large intestine at the junction of the sigmoid colon and rectum. **s. oc′uli,** musculus orbicularis oculi. **Oddi's s.,** the sheath of muscle fibers investing the associated bile and pancreatic passages as they traverse the wall of the duodenum. **s. o′ris,** musculi orbicularis oris. **palatopharyngeal s.,** Passavant's bar. **prepyloric s.,** a band of muscle fibers in the wall of the stomach proximal to the pyloric sphincter. **s. pupil′lae,** musculus sphincter pupillae. **pyloric s.,** a thickening of the middle layer of the muscular wall of the stomach around the opening into the duodenum. Called also *musculus sphincter pylori* [N A]. **rectal s.,** Hyrtl's s. **third s.,** the middle one of the plicae transversales recti, which sometimes blocks the lumen of the rectum. **tubal s.,** an encircling band of muscle fibers at the junction of the uterine tube and the uterus. **s. ure′thrae,** musculus sphincter urethrae. **s. vagi′nae,** the musculus bulbospongiosus in the female. **s. vesi′cae,** musculus sphincter vesicae urinariae.

sphincteral (sfingk′ter-al). Pertaining to a sphincter.

sphincteralgia (sfingk″ter-al′je-ah) [*sphincter* + Gr. *algos* pain + *-ia*]. Pain in a sphincter muscle, as of the anus.

sphincterectomy (sfingk″ter-ek′to-me) [*sphincter* + Gr. *ektomē* excision]. 1. Excision or resection of a sphincter, especially one of the sphincters of the large intestine. 2. Oblique blepharotomy.

sphincteric (sfingk-ter′ik). Pertaining to a sphincter.

sphincterismus (sfingk″ter-iz′mus). Spasm of the sphincter ani.

sphincteritis (sfingk″ter-i′tis). Inflammation of a sphincter, particularly, inflammation of the sphincter of Oddi.

sphincterolysis (sfingk″ter-ol′ĭ-sis) [*sphincter* + Gr. *lysis* dissolution]. The operation of separating the iris from the cornea in anterior synechia.

sphincteroplasty (sfingk′ter-o-plas″te) [*sphincter* + Gr. *plassein* to mold]. The plastic surgical repair of a defective sphincter.

sphincteroscope ((sfingk′ter-o-skōp″) [*sphincter* + Gr. *skopein* to examine]. A speculum for inspecting the anal sphincter.

sphincteroscopy (sfingk″ter-os′ko-pe). Inspection of the anal sphincter.

sphincterotome (sfingk′ter-o-tōm″). 1. An instrument for cutting a sphincter. 2. A special instrument used at operation to relieve postcholecystectomy syndrome.

sphincterotomy (sfingk″ter-ot′o-me) [*sphincter* + Gr. *tomē* a cutting]. The cutting of a sphincter. **internal s.,** incision of the internal sphincter of the anus, used in treatment of anal fissure.

sphingogalactoside (sfing″go-gah-lak′to-sīd). A substance composing part of the material characteristic of the spleen in Gaucher's disease.

sphingoin (sfing′go-in). A leukomaine, $C_{17}H_{35}NO_2$, from the substance of the brain.

sphingol (sfing′gol). An alcohol, $C_9H_{18}O$, obtained from sphingomyelinic acid by hydrolysis.

sphingolipid (sfing″go-lip′id) [Gr. *sphingein* to bind tight + lipid]. A phospholipid containing sphingosine, occurring in particularly high concentrations in brain and nerve tissue; the designation includes cerebrosides, gangliosides, and sphingomyelins.

sphingolipidoses (sfing″go-lip″ĭ-do′sēz). Plural of *sphingolipidosis.*

sphingolipidosis (sfing″go-lip″ĭ-do′sis), pl. *sphingolipidoses.* A general designation applied to a disease characterized by abnormal storage of sphingolipids, such as Gaucher's disease, Niemann-Pick disease, Pfaundler-Hurler disease, and Tay-Sachs disease.

sphingomyelin (sfing″go-mi′ĕ-lin). A general designation of a group of phospholipids which on hydrolysis yield phosphoric acid, choline, sphingosine and a fatty acid.

sphingosine (sfing′go-sin). A basic amino alcohol, present in sphingomyelin.

sphingosinol (sfing-go′sĭ-nol). Sphingosine.

sphygmic (sfig′mik) [Gr. *sphygmikos*]. Pertaining to the pulse. See *sphygmic period,* under *period.*

sphygmo- (sfig′mo) [Gr. *sphygmos* pulse]. Combining form denoting relationship to the pulse.

sphygmobologram (sfig″mo-bo′lo-gram). A tracing made by the sphygmobolometer.

sphygmobolometer (sfig″mo-bo-lom′e-ter) [*sphygmo-* + Gr. *bōlos* mass + *metron* measure].

An instrument for measuring and recording the energy of the pulse wave, and so, indirectly, the strength of the systole.

sphygmobolometry (sfig″mo-bo-lom′e-tre). The use of the sphygmobolometer.

sphygmocardiogram (sfig″mo-kar′de-o-gram). The tracing made by a sphygmocardiograph.

sphygmocardiograph (sfig″mo-kar′de-o-graf) [*sphygmo-* + Gr. *kardia* heart + *graphein* to write]. An instrument for recording the pulse waves and heart beat at the same operation.

sphygmocardioscope (sfig″mo-kar′de-o-skōp) [*sphygmo-* + Gr. *kardia* heart + *skopein* to examine]. An apparatus that records on a disk, the behavior of the pulse, heart action, and sounds.

sphygmochronograph (sfig″mo-kro′no-graf) [*sphygmo-* + Gr. *chronos* time + *graphein* to write]. A form of self-registering sphygmograph.

sphygmodynamometer (sfig″mo-di″nah-mom′-e-ter) [*sphygmo-* + Gr. *dynamis* power + *metron* measure]. An instrument for determining the force of the pulse.

sphygmogenin (sfig-moj′e-nin) [*sphygmo-* + Gr. *gennan* to produce]. Epinephrine.

sphygmogram (sfig′mo-gram) [*sphygmo-* + Gr. *gramma* a writing]. A sphygmographic tracing; the record or tracing made by a sphygmograph. It

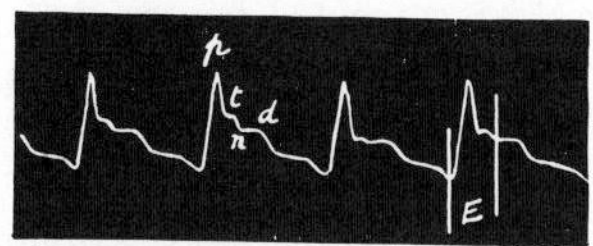

Radial sphygmogram from a healthy individual: *p*, The percussion wave; *t*, tidal or predicrotic wave; *n*, dicrotic or aortic notch; *d*, dicrotic wave; *E*, the sphygmic period during which the semilunar valves are open. (Hay.)

consists of a curve having a sudden rise (*primary elevation*), followed by a sudden fall, after which there is a gradual descent marked by a number of secondary elevations.

sphygmograph (sfig′mo-graf) [*sphygmo-* + Gr. *graphein* to write]. An instrument for registering the movements, form, and force of the arterial pulse. Vierordt's sphygmograph (1835) and Marey's (1860) were the earliest. The latter, variously modified, is the kind principally used.

sphygmographic (sfig″mo-graf′ik). Pertaining to the sphygmograph.

sphygmography (sfig-mog′rah-fe). The production of pulse tracings with the sphygmograph.

sphygmoid (sfig′moid) [*sphygmo-* + Gr. *eidos* form]. Resembling the pulse.

sphygmology (sfig-mol′o-je) [*sphygmo-* + *-logy*]. The sum of what is known regarding the pulse.

sphygmomanometer (sfig″mo-mah-nom′e-ter). An instrument for measuring blood pressure in the arteries. There are many forms of the instrument, each named for the person who devised it, as *Riva-Rocci s., Faught's s., Erlanger's s., Janeway's s., Rogers' s., Staunton's s., Tycos s.*

sphygmomanometroscope (sfig″mo-man″o-met′ro-skōp). An apparatus that combines in one the Riva-Rocci cuff, the tonometer, the two manometers of Busch, and the water manometer used for determining the blood pressure of the upper extremity.

sphygmometer (sfig-mom′e-ter) [*sphygmo-* + Gr. *metron* measure]. An instrument for measuring the force and frequency of the pulse.

sphygmometrograph (sfig″mo-met′ro-graf). An apparatus for recording the maximal and minimal arterial pressures.

sphygmometroscope (sfig″mo-met′ro-skōp). An instrument for taking the blood pressure by the auscultatory method.

sphygmo-oscillometer (sfig″mo-os″ĭ-lom′e-ter). A form of sphygmomanometer in which the disappearance and reappearance of the pulse are indicated by an oscillating needle.

sphygmopalpation (sfig″mo-pal-pa′shun). The act of palpating or feeling the pulse.

sphygmophone (sfig′mo-fōn) [*sphygmo-* + Gr. *phōnē* sound]. An apparatus for rendering audible the vibrations of the pulse.

sphygmoplethysmograph (sfig″mo-ple-thiz′-mo-graf). A plethysmograph which traces a record of the pulse, together with the curve of fluctuation of volume.

sphygmoscope (sfig′mo-skōp) [*sphygmo-* + Gr. *skopein* to examine]. A device for rendering the pulse beat visible. **Bishop's s.,** an apparatus for measuring the blood pressure, especially the diastolic pressure.

sphygmoscopy (sfig-mos′ko-pe). Examination of the pulse.

sphygmosignal (sfig′mo-sig″nal). Vaquez' instrument for making visible the changes in the amplitude of the pulse.

sphygmosystole (sfig″mo-sis′to-le) [*sphygmo-* + *systole*]. That part of the sphygmogram that corresponds to the systole of the heart.

sphygmotonogram (sfig″mo-to′no-gram). The graphic record produced by the sphygmotonograph.

sphygmotonograph (sfig″mo-to′no-graf) [*sphygmo-* + Gr. *tonos* tension + *graphein* to write]. An instrument for recording simultaneously the blood pressure, the carotid or jugular pulse, the brachial pulse, and the time in fifths of a second.

sphygmotonometer (sfig″mo-to-nom′e-ter) [*sphygmo-* + Gr. *tonos* tension + *metron* measure]. An instrument for measuring the elasticity of the arterial walls.

sphygmoviscosimetry (sfig″mo-vis″ko-sim′e-tre) [*sphygmo-* + *viscosity* + Gr. *metron* measure]. Measurement of the blood pressure and the viscosity of the blood.

sphyrectomy (sfi-rek′to-me) [Gr. *sphyra* malleus + *ektomē* excision]. Surgical removal of the malleus.

sphyrotomy (sfi-rot′o-me) [Gr. *sphyra* malleus + *tomē* a cutting]. Surgical removal of a portion of the malleus.

SPI. Abbreviation for *serum precipitable iodine.*

spica (spi′kah) [L. "ear of wheat"]. A figure-of-8 bandage with turns that cross one another. See under *bandage.*

spicular (spik′u-lar). Pertaining to a spicule.

spicule (spik′ūl) [L. *spiculum*]. A sharp, needle-like body.

spiculum (spik′u-lum), pl. *spic′ula* [L.]. Spicule.

spider (spi′der). 1. An arthropod of the class Arachnida, some species of which have poisonous bites. Cf. *arachnidism.* 2. A spider-like nevus. **arterial s.,** nevus araneus. **black widow s.** See *Latrodectus.* **vascular s.,** nevus araneus.

spider burst (spi′der burst). Radiating lines of capillaries on the leg caused by venous dilatation but without distinct varicosity.

spider-lick (spi′der-lik). A troublesome affection of the skin in India due to an insect.

Spiegler's test, tumors (spe′glerz) [Edward *Spiegler*, dermatologist of Vienna, 1860–1908]. See under *tests* and *tumor.*

Spielmeyer-Stock disease (spēl′mi-er stok) [Walter *Spielmeyer*, Munich neurologist, 1879–1935; Wolfgang *Stock*, Jena ophthalmologist, born 1874]. See under *disease.*

Spigelia (spi-je′le-ah) [Adriaan van der *Spieghel*, 1578–1625]. A genus of loganiaceous plants. The rhizome and roots of *S. marilan′dica* have been used as an anthelmintic.

spigelian line, lobe (spi-je′le-an) [Adriaan van der *Spieghel* (L. Spigelius), Flemish anatomist, 1578–1625]. See under *line* and *lobe.*

spigelin (spi-je′lin). A bitter volatile principle from *Spigelia marilandica* and *S. anthelmia*, of tropical America: purgative.

spignet (spig′net). Aralia.

spike (spīk). A sharp upward deflection in a curve, such as the main deflection of the oscillographic tracing of the action potential wave, the following smaller wave being called the *afterpotential.*

spikenard (spīk′nard) [L. *nardus*, or *spica nardi*]. The plant, *Nardostachys jatamansi;* also various fragrant valerianaceous and other plants: now chiefly used in oriental medicine. **American s.,** aralia. **false s.,** *Andropogon nardus*, an aromatic and stimulant East Indian grass; also *Smilacina racemosa*, a North American plant.

Spilanthes (spi-lan′thēz) [Gr. *spilos* spot + Gr. *anthos* flower]. A genus of composite-flowered plants. *S. acmella*, the Para cress of tropical America and Asia, formerly used as a remedy for toothache.

spiloma (spi-lo′mah) [Gr. *spilōma* spot]. Nevus.

spiloplania (spi″lo-pla′ne-ah)[Gr. *spilos* spot + *planos* wandering]. A transient erythema.

spiloplaxia (spi″lo-plak′se-ah) [Gr. *spilos* spot + *plax* plate]. A red spot seen in cases of leprosy or pellagra.

spilus (spi′lus) [Gr. *spilos* spot]. Nevus.

spina (spi′nah), pl. *spi′nae* [L.]. A thornlike process or projection; used in anatomical nomenclature as a general term to denote such a process. **s. angula′ris** [B N A], spina ossis sphenoidalis. **s. bif′ida,** a developmental anomaly characterized by a defect in the bony encasement of the spinal cord. **s. bif′ida ante′rior,** a defect of closure on the anterior surface of the bony spinal canal, often associated with defective development of the abdominal and thoracic viscera. **s. bif′ida cys′tica,** spina bifida in which there is protrusion through the defect of a cystic swelling involving the meninges (meningocele), spinal cord (myelocele), or both (meningomyelocele). **s. bif′ida occul′ta,** spina bifida in which there is a defect of the bony spinal canal without protrusion of the cord or meninges. **s. bif′ida poste′rior,** a defect of closure on the posterior surface of the bony spinal canal. **s. fronta′lis** [B N A], s. nasalis ossis frontalis. **s. hel′icis** [N A, B N A], a small, forward-projecting cartilaginous process on the anterior portion of the helix at about the junction of the helix and its crus, just above the tragus. Called also *spine of helis.* **s. ili′aca ante′rior infe′rior** [N A, B N A], a blunt bony process projecting forward from the lower part of the anterior margin of the ilium, just above the acetabulum. Called also *inferior anterior iliac spine.* **s. ili′aca ante′rior supe′rior** [N A, B N A], a blunt bony projection on the anterior border of the ilium, forming the anterior end of the iliac crest. Called also *superior anterior iliac spine.* **s. ili′aca poste′rior infe′rior** [N A, B N A], a blunt bony projection from the posterior border of the ilium, corresponding to the posterior lower extremity of the facies auricularis and the posterior upper extremity of the incisura ischiadica major. Called also *inferior posterior iliac spine.* **s. ili′aca poste′rior supe′rior** [N A, B N A], a blunt bony projection on the posterior border of the ilium, forming the posterior end of the iliac crest. Called also *superior posterior iliac spine.* **s. intercondyloi′dea,** eminentia intercondylaris. **s. ischiad′ica** [N A, B N A], a strong process of bone projecting backward and medialward from the posterior border of the ischium, on a level with the lower border of the acetabulum and serving to separate the major and minor ischiadic notches. Called also *ischial spine.* **s. mea′tus,** s. supra meatum. **s. menta′lis** [N A, B N A], a small bony projection on the internal surface of the mandible, near the lower end of the midline, serving for attachment of the genioglossal and geniohyoid muscles. Called also *mental spine.* **s. nasa′lis ante′rior maxil′lae** [N A, B N A], the sharp anteriosuperior projection at the anterior extremity of the nasal crest of the maxilla. Called also *anterior nasal spine.* **s. nasa′lis os′sis fronta′lis** [N A], a rough and somewhat irregular process of bone projecting downward and forward from the front part of the inferior surface of the pars nasalis of the frontal bone and fitting between the nasal bones and the ethmoid bone. Called also *spina frontalis* [B N A], and *nasal spine of frontal bone.* **s. nasa′lis os′sis palati′ni** [N A], **s. nasa′lis poste′rior os′sis palati′ni** [B N A], a small, sharp, backward-projecting bony spine forming the medial posterior angle of the horizontal portion of the palatine bone. Called also *nasal spine of palatine bone* and *posterior nasal spine.* **s. os′sis sphenoida′lis** [N A], a small bony process projecting downward from the inferior aspect of the great wing of the sphenoid bone where the wing projects into the angle between the petrous and squamous portions of the temporal bone; it is just posterior to the foramen spinosum and serves for attachemnt of the sphenomandibular and pterygospinous ligaments. Called also *s. angularis* [B N A], and *spine of spenoid bone.* **spi′nae palati′nae** [N A, B N A], ridges which are laterally placed on the inferior surface of the maxillary part of the hard palate, separating the palatine sulci. Called also *palatine spines.* **s. scap′ulae** [N A, B N A], a triangular plate of bone attached by one edge to the back of the scapula, its tip being at the vertebral border of the scapula; it passes laterally toward the shoulder joint and at its base bears the acromion. Called also *spine of scapula.* **s. su′pra mea′tum** [N A, B N A], a pointed process that sometimes projects from the temporal bone, just above and at the back of the external acoustic meatus. Called also *suprameatal spine.* **s. tib′iae,** tuberositas tibiae. **s. trochlea′ris** [N A, B N A], a spicule of bone on the anteromedial part of the orbital surface of the frontal bone for attachment of the trochlea of the superior oblique muscle; when absent, it is represented by the trochlear fovea. Called also *trochlear spine.* **s. tympan′ica ma′jor** [N A, B N A], a spine of the temporal bone forming the anterior edge of the tympanic notch (deficient part of tympanic sulcus). Called also *greater tympanic spine.* **s. tympan′ica mi′nor** [N A, B N A], a spine of the temporal bone forming the posterior edge of the tympanic notch. Called also *lesser tympanic spine.* **s. vento′sa,** a true dactylitis occurring mostly in infants and young children, characterized by enlargement of the fingers or toes, with caseation, sequestration, and sinus formation.

spinacin (spi′nah-sin). A protein obtained from the cytoplasm of the cells of spinach leaves. It is insoluble in water and in salt solutions, but soluble in very slight excess of either acid or alkali.

spinae (spi′ne) [L.]. Plural of *spina.*

spinal (spi′nal) [L. *spinalis*]. Pertaining to a spine or to the vertebral column.

spinalgia (spi-nal′je-ah) [*spine* + Gr. *algos* pain + *-ia*]. Pain in the spinal region. **Petruschky's s.,** tenderness in the interscapular region in tuberculosis of the bronchial lymph nodes.

spinalis (spi-na′lis) [L.]. Spinal.

spinant (spi′nant). Any agent which acts directly upon the spinal cord, increasing its reflex activity.

spinate (spi′nāt) [L. *spinatus*]. Having thorns; shaped like a thorn.

spinawl (spīn′awl). An awl with sharp cutting edges for making a preliminary skin opening for introducing a lumbar puncture needle.

spindle (spin′d′l). 1. The fusiform figure of achromatin in the cell nucleus during mitosis. It consists of fine threads radiating out from the centrosomes and connecting the centrosomes with one another. Called also *achromatic s., nuclear s.* 2. See *brain waves,* under *wave.* **aortic s.,** the dilated part of the aorta just below the isthmus. **Axenfeld-Krukenberg s.,** Krukenberg's s. **central s.,** the bundle of fibers in the axial part of the spindle of an amphiaster. **cleavage s.,** any spindle formed during cleavage of the ovum. **enamel s's,** spindle-shaped extensions of the dentinal tubules passing across the dentinoenamel junction into the enamel. **His' s.,** aortic s.

Krukenberg's s., a vertical spindle-shaped, brownish-red opacity on the posterior surface of the cornea. **Kuhne's s.**, muscle s. **muscle s.**, a mechanoreceptor found between the skeletal muscle fibers; the muscle spindles are arranged in parallel with muscle fibers, and respond to passive stretch of the muscle but cease to discharge if the muscle contracts isotonically, thus signaling muscle length. The muscle spindle is the receptor responsible for the stretch or myotatic reflex. **neuromuscular s.**, muscle s. **nuclear s.** See *spindle*, def. 1. **tendon s.**, Golgi tendon organ. **tigroid s's**, Nissl bodies.

spine (spin). 1. A thornlike process or projection. Called also *spina* [N A]. 2. The spinal column (columna vertebralis [N A]). 3. The central ridge on the internal surface of a horse's hoof, between the branches of the frog. Called also *frog-stay*. **alar s., angular s.**, spina ossis sphenoidalis. **bamboo s.**, the ankylosed spine produced by rheumatoid spondylitis; so called because of the roentgenographic appearance caused by lipping of the vertebral margins. **basilar s.**, tuberculum pharyngeum. **Civinini's s.**, processus pterygospinosus. **cleft s.** See *spina bifida*. **dorsal s.**, columna vertebralis. **Erichsen's s.**, an obscure condition occurring as the result of alleged accidental injury to the vertebral column. **ethmoidal s. of Macalister**, crista sphenoidalis. **frontal s., external**, spina nasalis ossis frontalis. **s. of greater tubercle of humerus**, crista tuberculi majoris. **s. of helix**, spina helicis. **hemal s.**, a dependent projection from the hemal arch in lower vertibrates; considered to be represented in man by the sternum. **s. of Henle**, spina supra meatum. **hysterical s.**, simulated vertebral disease in neurotic patients. **iliac s., anterior, inferior**, spina iliaca anterior inferior. **iliac s., anterior, superior**, spina iliaca anterior superior. **iliac s., posterior, inferior**, spina iliaca posterior inferior. **iliac s., posterior, superior**, spina iliaca posterior superior. **iliopectineal s.**, eminentia iliopubica. **intercondyloid s.**, eminentia intercondylaris. **ischial s., s. of ischium**, spina ischiadica. **jugular s.**, processus jugularis ossis occipitalis. **kissing s's**, a condition in which the spinous processes of adjacent vertebra are in contact. **s. of lesser tubercle of humerus**, crista tuberculi minoris. **s. of maxilla**, spina nasalis anterior maxillae. **meatal s.**, spina supra meatum. **mental s.**, spina mentalis. **mental s., external**, protuberantia mentalis. **nasal s., anterior**, spina nasalis anterior maxillae. **nasal s., posterior**, spina nasalis ossis palatini. **nasal s. of frontal bone**, spina nasalis ossis frontalis. **nasal s. of maxilla, anterior**, spina nasalis anterior maxillae. **nasal s. of palatine bone**, spina nasalis ossis palatini. **neural s.**, processus spinosus vertebrarum. **obturator s.**, crista obturatoria. **occipital s., external**, protuberantia occipitalis externa. **occipital s., internal**, protuberantia occipitalis interna. **palatine s's**, spinae palatinae. **peroneal s. of os calcis**, trochlea peronealis calcanei. **pharyngeal s.**, tuberculum pharyngeum. **poker s.**, the ankylosed spine produced by rheumatoid spondylitis; so called because of its rigidity. **s. of pubic bone, s. of pubis**, tuberculum pubicum ossis pubis. **rigid s.**, poker s. **s. of scapula**, spina scapulae. **sciatic s.**, spina ischiadica. **s. of sphenoid bone, sphenoidal s.**, spina ossis sphenoidalis. **suprameatal s.**, spina supra meatum. **s. of tibia, tibial s.**, tuberositas tibiae. **trochanteric s., greater**, labium laterale lineae asperae femoris. **trochanteric s., lesser**, labium mediale lineae asperae femoris. **trochlear s.**, spina trochlearis. **tympanic s., anterior, tympanic s., greater**, spina tympanica major. **tympanic s., lesser, tympanic s., posterior**, spina tympanica minor. **typhoid s.**, a painful condition of the spine due to osteomyelitis of the vertebrae following typhoid fever. **s. of vertebra**, processus spinosus vertebrarum.

spinel (spi-nel′). A colored mineral sometimes used to produce markings or defects in porcelain restorations to simulate more closely the appearance of natural teeth.

Spinelli's operation (spe-nel′ēz) [Pier Giuseppe *Spinelli*, Italian gynecologist, 1862–1929]. See under *operation*.

spinibular (spi-nib′u-lar). Spinobulbar.

spinicerebellar (spi″ne-ser″e-bel′ar). Spinocerebellar.

spinifugal (spi-nif′u-gal) [L. *spina* spine + *fugere* to flee]. Going, conducting, or moving away from the spinal cord.

spiniperipheral (spi″ne-pe-rif′er-al). Spinoperipheral.

spinipetal (spi-nip′e-tal) [L. *spina* spine + *petere* to seek]. Tending, conducting, or moving toward the spinal cord.

Spinitectus gracilis (spi″ne-tek′tus gras′ĭ-lis). A parasitic nematode in the intestines of fishes in the United States.

spinitis (spi-ni′tis). Myelitis.

spinnbarkeit (spin′bahr-kit) [Ger.]. The formation of a thread by cervical mucus when blown onto a glass slide and drawn out by a coverglass; the time at which it can be drawn to the maximum length usually precedes or coincides with the time of ovulation.

spinobulbar (spi″no-bul′bar). Pertaining to the spinal cord and the medulla oblongata.

spinocellular (spi″no-sel′u-lar). Containing, made up of, or marked by, prickle cells.

spinocerebellar (spi″no-ser″e-bel′ar). Pertaining to the spinal cord and the cerebellum.

spinocortical (spi″no-kor′tĭ-kal). Corticospinal.

spinocostalis (spi″no-kos-ta′lis). The superior and inferior serratus posterior muscles together.

spinogalvanization (spi″no-gal″vah-ni-za′-shun). Galvanization of the spinal cord, performed by moving the anode slowly up and down the spine.

spinoglenoid (spi″no-gle′noid). Pertaining to the spine of the scapula and the glenoid cavity.

spinogram (spi′no-gram). A roentgenogram of the spine or of the spinal cord.

spinomuscular (spi″no-mus′ku-lar). Pertaining to the spinal cord and to the muscles.

spinoneural (spi″no-nu′ral). Pertaining to the spinal cord and to the nerves.

spinoperipheral (spi″no-pe-rif′er-al). Pertaining to the spinal cord and the periphery.

spinopetal (spi-nop′e-tal). Spinipetal.

spinose (spi′nōs). Spinous.

spinotectal (spi″no-tek′tal). Tectospinal.

spinous (spi′nus) [L. *spinosus*]. 1. Like a spine. 2. Pertaining to a spine or to a spinelike process.

spinthariscope (spin-thar′ĭ-skōp) [Gr. *spintharis* spark + *skopein* to examine]. An instrument for viewing the emanations of radium.

spintherism (spin′ther-izm) [Gr. *spinthērizein* to emit sparks]. The appearance as of sparks before the eyes.

spintherometer (spin″ther-om′e-ter) [Gr. *spinthēr* spark + *metron* measure]. An apparatus for measuring the changes which occur in the vacuum of the roentgen-ray tube, and hence the penetrating power of the rays.

spintheropia (spin″ther-o′pe-ah) [Gr. *spinthēr* spark + *ōpē* sight + *-ia*]. Spintherism.

spintometer (spin-tom′e-ter). Spintherometer.

spir. Abbreviation for L. *spir′itus*, spirit.

spiracle (spir′ah-k'l) [L. *spirare* to breathe]. A breathing orifice of arthropods and of some vertebrates.

spiradenitis (spi″rad-e-ni′tis) [Gr. *speira* coil + *adēn* gland + *-itis*]. Hidradenitis suppurativa.

spiradenoma (spi″rad-e-no′mah). Adenoma of the sweat glands.

spiral (spi′ral) [L. *spiralis*]. Winding about a center like a coil or the thread of a screw. **Curschmann's s's,** coiled mucinous fibrils sometimes found in the sputum of bronchial asthma. **Golgi-Rezzonico s.** See under *thread.* **Herxheimer's s's.** See under *fiber.* **Perroncito's s's.** See under *apparatus.* **tendon s.,** a spiral receptor connected with a tendon.

Spiranthes (spi-ran′thēz) [Gr. *speira* coil + *anthos* flower]. A genus of orchidaceous plants. **S. autumna′lis,** a species reputed to be aphrodisiac. **S. diuret′ica,** a species of Chile: said to be a valuable diuretic.

spirem (spi′rem). Spireme.

spireme (spi′rēm) [Gr. *speirēma* coil]. Skein. See *mitosis.*

spirilla (spi-ril′ah) [L.]. Plural of *spirillum.*

Spirillaceae (spi″ril-la′se-e). A family of Schizomycetes (order Pseudomonadales, suborder Pseudomonadineae), made up of gram-negative, simple curved or spirally twisted rods, frequently forming chains of spirally twisted cells. It includes 10 genera, *Cellfalcicula, Cellvibrio, Desulfovibrio, Methanobacterium, Microcyclus, Myconostoc, Paraspirillum, Selenomonas, Spirillum,* and *Vibrio.*

spirillemia (spi″ril-e′me-ah) [*spirilla* + Gr. *haima* blood + *-ia*]. The presence of spirilla in the blood.

spirillicidal (spi-ril″ĭ-si′dal). Destroying spirilla.

spirillicide (spi-ril′ĭ-sīd) [*spirilla* + L. *caedere* to kill]. 1. Destroying spirilla. 2. An agent which destroys spirilla.

spirillicidin (spi-ril″ĭ-si′din). A substance formed in the blood of patients immunized against spirilla and capable of destroying spirilla.

spirillolysis (spi″rĭ-lol′ĭ-sis) [*spirilla* + Gr. *lysis* dissolution]. The breaking up of or destruction of spirilla.

spirillosis (spi″rĭ-lo′sis). 1. Any disease condition attended or marked by the presence of spirilla in the body. 2. A disease of fowls marked by diarrhea, fever, malaise, and death in a few days. It is caused by *Spironema gallinarum* transmitted by ticks of the species *Argas miniatus.*

spirillotropic (spi″rĭ-lo-trop′ik). Having an affinity for spirilla.

spirillotropism (spi″rĭ-lot′ro-pizm) [*spirilla* + Gr. *tropos* a turning]. The property of having an affinity for spirilla.

Spirillum (spi-ril′lum). A genus of microorganisms of the family Spirillaceae, suborder Pseudomonadineae, order Pseudomonadales, made up of cells which form long spirals, or portions of a turn. It includes nine species, *S. iterso′nii, S. kutsch′eri, S. lipo′ferum, S. mi′nus, S. ser′pens, S. ten′ui, S. un′dula, S. virginia′num,* and *S. vol′utans.* One species, *Spirillum minus,* is pathogenic for guinea pigs, mice, rats, and monkeys, and is the cause of rat-bite fever (sodoku) in man. Many of the organisms placed in this genus in earlier taxonomic nomenclature have been reclassified in other genera.

spirillum (spi-ril′um), pl. *spiril′la* [L.]. 1. A relatively rigid, spiral-shaped bacterium. 2. An organism of the genus *Spirillum.* **Deneke's s.,** *Vibrio tyrogenus.* **s. of Finkler and Prior,** *Vibrio proteus.* **Gamaleia's s.,** *Vibrio metchnikovii.* **s. of Vincent,** *Borrelia vincentii.* **s. of Wernicke,** a pathogenic species from water.

spirit (spir′it) [L. *spiritus*]. 1. Any volatile or distilled liquid. 2. A solution of a volatile material in alcohol. **ammonia s., ammonia s., aromatic,** a preparation containing 1.7–2.1 per cent of ammonia, and 3.5–4.5 per cent of ammonium carbonate and miscellaneous oils: used as an inhalant to revive a person who has fainted. **anise s.,** a mixture of anise oil and alcohol. **benzaldehyde s.,** a mixture of benzaldehyde, alcohol, and distilled water. **camphor s.,** a solution of camphor in alcohol: used as a local irritant. **cardamom s., compound,** a preparation of cardamom oil with other volatile oils and alcohol: used as a flavored vehicle. **cinnamon s.,** an alcoholic solution of cinnamon oil, each 100 ml. of which contains 9–11 ml. of the oil. **ether s.,** a transparent, colorless liquid with a burning sweetish taste and an ether odor, consisting of ethyl oxide and alcohol. **ether s., compound,** a mixture of ethyl oxide, alcohol, and ethereal oil. **ethyl nitrite s.,** an alcoholic solution containing 3.5–4.5 per cent of ethyl nitrite. **glyceryl trinitrate s.,** a clear, colorless liquid with the odor of alcohol, compounded of glyceryl trinitrate 1–1.1 per cent in alcohol. **lavender s.,** an alcoholic solution of lavender oil, each 100 ml. of which contains 4–6 ml. of lavender oil. **lavender s., compound,** compound lavender tincture. **s. of Mindererus,** ammonium acetate solution. **myrcia s., compound,** a preparation of myrcia oil,, orange oil, pimenta oil, alcohol, and water. **nitroglycerin s.,** glyceryl trinitrate s. **s. of nitrous ether,** ethyl nitrite s. **orange s., compound,** an alcoholic preparation containing orange, lemon, coriander, and anise oils: used as a flavoring agent. **peppermint s.,** a preparation of peppermint, peppermint oil, and alcohol. **perfumed s.,** an aqueous solution of various fragrant oils, such as bergamot, lavender, lemon, orange flower, and rosemary, with alcohol, to which ethyl acetate has been added. **spearmint s.,** an alcoholic solution of spearmint oil and powdered spearmint, each 100 ml. of which contains 9–11 ml. of spearmint oil. **sweet s. of nitre,** ethyl nitrite s. **s. of turpentine,** turpentine oil. **vanillin s., compound,** a preparation of vanillin and cardamom, cinnamon, and orange oils in alcohol. **s. of wine,** alcohol.

spirituous (spir′it-u-us) [L. *spirituosus*]. Alcoholic; containing a considerable proportion of alcohol.

Spiro's test (spe′ro) [Karl *Spiro,* German chemist, 1867–1932]. See under *tests.*

Spirocerca sanguinolenta (spi″ro-ser′kah sang″gwĭ-no-len′tah). A nematode of the family Spiruridae, found in the walls of the aorta, esophagus, and stomach of dogs.

Spirochaeta (spi″ro-ke′tah) [Gr. *speira* coil + *chaitē* hair]. A genus of microorganisms of the family Spirochaetaceae, order Spirochaetales, made up of flexible, undulating, spiral-shaped rods, found in fresh- or sea-water slime, especially when hydrogen sulfide is present. It includes five species, *S. daxen′sis, S. eurystrep′ta, S. mari′na, S. plica′tilis,* and *S. stenostrep′ta.* Most of the organisms placed in this genus in earlier taxonomic nomenclature have been reclassified in other genera.

Spirochaetaceae (spi″ro-ke-ta′se-e). A family of Schizomycetes (order Spirochaetales), made up of coarse spiral organisms, 30 to 5000 μ long, with definite protoplasmic structures, found in the intestinal tracts of bivalve mollusks and in stagnant fresh or salt water. It includes three genera, *Cristaspira, Saprospira,* and *Spirochaeta.*

Spirochaetales (spi″ro-ke-ta′lēz). An order of class Schizomycetes, made up of slender, flexuous, motile organisms, 6 to 500 μ long, in the form of spirals with at least one complete turn. It includes two families, *Spirochaetaceae* and *Treponemataceae.*

spirochetal (spi″ro-ke′tal). Pertaining to or caused by spirochetes.

spirochete (spi′ro-kēt). 1. A spiral-shaped bacterium; a general term for any microorganism of the order Spirochaetales. 2. An organism of the genus *Spirochaeta.*

spirochetemia (spi″ro-ke-te′me-ah) [*spirochete* + Gr. *haima* blood + *-ia*]. The presence of spirochetes in the blood.

spirocheticidal (spi″ro-ke″tĭ-si′dal) [*spirochete* + L. *caedere* to kill]. Destructive to spirochetes.

spirocheticide (spi″ro-ke′tĭ-sīd). An agent that causes the destruction of spirochetes.

spirochetogenous (spi″ro-ke-toj′e-nus). Caused by spirochetes.

spirochetolysin (spi″ro-ke-tol′ĭ-sin). A substance which causes lysis of spirochetes.

spirochetolysis (spi″ro-ke-tol′ĭ-sis) [*spirochete* + Gr. *lysis* dissolution]. The destruction of spirochetes by lysis.

spirochetolytic (spi″ro-ke″to-lit′ik). Pertaining to, characterized by, or causing spirochetolysis.

spirochetosis (spi″ro-ke-to′sis). Infection caused by the presence of spirochetes. **s. arthrit′ica,** a rheumatoid affection of the joints caused by *Spirochaeta forans* (H. Reiter, 1916). **broncho-pulmonary s.,** bronchospirochetosis. **fowl s.,** a disease of fowls caused by *Borrelia gallinarum* and spread by the fowl tick *Argas persicus.* **gastric s.,** grass sickness. **icterogenic s., s. icterohaemorrhag′ica,** spirochetal jaundice. **s. riveren′sis,** a spirochetal chronic meningitis occurring in the department of Rivera in Brazil.

spirochetotic (spi″ro-ke-tot′ik). Pertaining to or characterized by spirochetosis.

spirocheturia (spi″ro-ke-tu′re-ah) [*spirochete* + Gr. *ouron* urine + *-ia*]. The presence of spirochetes in the urine.

spirofibrilla (spi″ro-fi-bril′lah), pl. *spirofibrillae.* Fayod's name for one of the hypothetical hollow, twisted fibrils forming the spirospartae, which constitute the protoplasm and nuclei of vegetable cells.

spirogram (spi′ro-gram) [L. *spirare* to breathe + Gr. *gramma* a writing]. A tracing or graph of respiratory movements.

spirograph (spi′ro-graf) [L. *spirare* to breathe + Gr. *graphein* to write]. An instrument for registering the respiratory movements.

spirographidin (spi″ro-graf′ĭ-din). A hyalin derived from spirographin.

spirographin (spi-rog′rah-fin). A hyalogen derivable from the skeletal structures of *Spirographis,* a wormlike animal.

spirography (spi-rog′rah-fe). The graphic measurement of breathing, including breathing movements and breathing capacity.

spiroid (spi′roid). Resembling a spiral.

spiro-index (spi″ro-in′deks) [L. *spirare* to breathe + *index*]. The value obtained by dividing the vital capacity by the height of the individual.

spirolactone (spi″ro-lak′tōn). A compound bearing 17α-propionic acid as gamma-lactone with 17β-hydroxyl, capable of opposing the action of sodium-retaining steroids on renal transport of sodium and potassium. Three such compounds have been studied. The first contained angular methyl at C_{13} and C_{10}, and is 3-(3-keto-17β-hydroxy-4-androsten-17α-yl)-propionic acid-γ-lactone; the second, without angular methyl at C_{10}, is more potent, and the third, with a thioacetyl group at C_7, is highly active orally.

spiroma (spi-ro′mah). Spiradenoma.

spirometer (spi-rom′e-ter) [L. *spirare* to breathe + *metrum* measure]. An instrument for measuring the air taken into and exhaled from the lungs.

spirometric (spi″ro-met′rik). Pertaining to spirometry or the spirometer.

spirometry (spi-rom′e-tre). The measurement of the breathing capacity of the lungs. **bronchoscopic s.,** bronchospirometry.

Spironema (spi″ro-ne′mah) [Gr. *speira* coil + *nēma* thread]. A name in Pribram's classification for a genus of spiral-shaped organisms, most of which are now included in the genus Borrelia.

spirophore (spi′ro-fōr) [L. *spirare* to breathe + Gr. *phorein* to bear]. An apparatus to effect artificial respiration.

Spiroschaudinnia (spi″ro-shaw-din′e-ah). A genus name proposed by Sambon (1907) for a group of spiral-shaped microorganisms found in the blood, most of which are now included in the genus Borrelia.

spiroscope (spi′ro-skōp) [L. *spirare* to breathe + Gr. *skopein* to examine]. An apparatus for respiration exercises by which the patient can see the amount of water displaced in a given time and thus gauge his respiratory capacity.

spiroscopy (spi-ros′ko-pe). The use of the spiroscope.

spirosparta (spi″ro-spar′tah) [Gr. *speira* coil + *spartē* a rope], pl. *spirospar′tae.* Fayod's name for one of the ropelike structures, formed by spirofibrillae, which constitute the protoplasm and nuclei of vegetable cells.

spissated (spis′āt-ed) [L. *spissatus*]. Inspissated: thickened by evaporation.

spissitude (spis′ĭ-tūd) [L. *spissitudo*]. The state or quality of being inspissated.

Spitzka's nucleus, tract (spits′kahz) [Edward Charles *Spitzka,* New York neurologist, 1852–1914]. See under the nouns.

Spitzka-Lissauer tract (spits′kah lis′ow-er) [E. C. *Spitzka;* Heinrich *Lissauer,* German neurologist, 1861–1891]. Lissauer's tract.

Spivack's operation, rule (spiv′aks) [Julius L. *Spivack,* American surgeon, 1889–1956]. See under *operation* and *rule.*

Spix's spine (spik′sez) [Johann Baptist *Spix,* German naturalist, 1781–1826]. See under *spine.*

splanchnapophyseal (splank″nap-o-fiz′e-al). Pertaining to a splanchnapophysis.

splanchnapophysis (splank″nah-pof′ĭ-sis) [*splanchno-* + *apophysis*]. A skeletal element, like the lower jaw, connected with the alimentary canal.

splanchnectopia (splank″nek-to′pe-ah) [*splanchno-* + Gr. *ektopos* out of place + *-ia*]. Displacement of a viscus.

splanchnemphraxis (splank″nem-frak′sis) [*splanchno-* + Gr. *emphraxis* stoppage]. Obstruction of a viscus, particularly the intestine.

splanchnesthesia (splank″nes-the′ze-ah) [*splanchno-* + Gr. *aisthēsis* perception + *-ia*]. Visceral sensation.

splanchnesthetic (splank″nes-thet′ik). Pertaining to splanchnesthesia.

splanchnic (splank′nik) [Gr. *splanchnikos;* L. *splanchnicus*]. Pertaining to the viscera.

splanchnicectomy (splank″ne-sek′to-me) [*splanchnic* + Gr. *ektomē* excision]. Excision of a section (resection) of the greater splanchnic nerve; splanchnic neurectomy. This operation is combined with sympathectomy for the relief of essential hypertension.

splanchnicotomy (splank″ne-kot′o-me) [*splanchnic* + Gr. *tomē* a cutting]. Division of a splanchnic nerve.

splanchno- (splank′no) [Gr. *splanchnos* viscus]. Combining form denoting relationship to a viscus, or to the splanchnic nerve.

splanchnoblast (splank′no-blast) [*splanchno-* + Gr. *blastos* germ]. The rudiment or anlage of any viscus.

splanchnocele (splank′no-sēl) [*splanchno-* + Gr. *kēlē* hernia]. Hernial protrusion of a viscus.

splanchnocoele (splank′no-sēl) [*splanchno-* + Gr. *koilos* hollow]. That portion of the body cavity, or coelom, from which are developed the abdominal, pericardial, and pleural cavities. Called also *pleuroperitoneal cavity* and *ventral coelom.*

splanchnocranium (splank″no-kra′ne-um) [*splanchno-* + *cranium*]. Those parts of the skull that are of branchial arch origin.

splanchnoderm (splank′no-derm). Splanchnopleure.

splanchnodiastasis (splank″no-di-as′tah-sis) [*splanchno-* + Gr. *diastasis* separation]. Separation of a viscus; displacement of a viscus.

splanchnodynia (splank″no-din′e-ah) [*splanch-*

no- + Gr. *odynē* pain + *-ia*]. Pain in an abdominal organ.

splanchnography (splank-nog′rah-fe) [*splanchno-* + Gr. *graphein* to write]. The descriptive anatomy of the viscera.

splanchnolith (splank′no-lith) [*splanchno-* + Gr. *lithos* stone]. An intestinal calculus or concretion.

splanchnologia (splank″no-lo′je-ah). Splanchnology; in N A terminology *splanchnologia* encompasses the nomenclature relating to the digestive, respiratory, and urogenital organs, and the peritoneum, ductless glands, and paraganglia.

splanchnology (splank-nol′o-je) [*splanchno-* + Gr. *logos* treatise]. The scientific study of the viscera of the body; applied also to the body of knowledge relating thereto.

splanchnomegalia (splank″no-mĕ-ga′le-ah). Splanchnomegaly.

splanchnomegaly (splank″no-meg′ah-le) [*splanchno-* + Gr. *megas* large]. Enlargement of the viscera.

splanchnomicria (splank″no-mik′re-ah) [*splanchno-* + Gr. *mikros* small]. Abnormal smallness of the viscera.

splanchnopathy (splank-nop′ah-the) [*splanchno-* + Gr. *pathos* disease]. Disease of the viscera.

splanchnopleural (splank″no-ploor′al). Pertaining to the splanchnopleure.

splanchnopleure (splank′no-ploor) [*splanchno-* + Gr. *pleura* side]. The layer formed by the union of the splanchnic mesoderm with entoderm. From it are developed the muscles and the connective tissue of the digestive tube.

splanchnoptosia (splank″no-to′se-ah). Splanchnoptosis.

splanchnoptosis (splank″no-to′sis) [*splanchno-* + Gr. *ptōsis* falling]. The prolapse, or falling down, of the viscera. Called also *abdominal ptosis, visceroptosis* and *Glénard's disease.*

splanchnosclerosis (splank″no-skle-ro′sis) [*splanchno-* + Gr. *sklērōsis* hardening]. Induration of the viscera.

splanchnoscopy (splank-nos′ko-pe) [*splanchno-* + Gr. *skopein* to examine]. The inspection of the viscera by transillumination.

splanchnoskeleton (splank″no-skel′e-ton) [*splanchno-* + Gr. *skeleton* a dried body, mummy]. The totality of the skeletal structures connected with the viscera, especially the bony structure that forms within certain organs of animals, as in the tongue, eye, penis, etc.

splanchnosomatic (splank″no-so-mat′ik) [*splanchno-* + Gr. *sōmatikos* of or for the body]. Pertaining to the viscera and the body.

splanchnostaxis (splank″no-stak′sis) [*splanchno-* + Gr. *staxis* dripping]. The dripping or leaking of blood from minute splanchnic vessels; spontaneous abdominal bleeding.

splanchnotomy (splank-not′o-me) [*splanchno-* + Gr. *tomē* a cutting]. The anatomy or dissection of the viscera.

splanchnotribe (splank′no-trīb) [*splanchno-* + Gr. *tribein* to crush]. An instrument for crushing the intestine and so closing its lumen.

splayfoot (spla′foot). Flatfoot; talipes valgus.

spleen (splēn) [Gr. *splēn;* L. *splen*]. A large glandlike but ductless organ situated in the upper part of the abdominal cavity on the left side and lateral to the cardiac end of the stomach. Called also *lien* [N A]. It is of a flattened oblong shape and about 125 mm. long; it has a purple color and a pliable consistency. It disintegrates the red blood corpuscles and sets free the hemoglobin, which the liver converts into bilirubin, and has other important functions, the full scope of which is not entirely determined. **accessory s.,** a connected or detached outlying portion, or exclave, of the spleen. Called also *lien accessorius.* **bacon s.,** a spleen with areas of amyloid degeneration, giving its cut surfaces the appearance of fried bacon. **cyanotic s.,** a contracted form of spleen due to passive congestion. **diffuse waxy s.,** amyloid degeneration of the spleen involving especially the coats of the venous sinuses and the reticulum of the organ. **enlarged s.,** hypertrophy of the spleen due to chronic malarial poisoning. Called also *splenomegaly* and *ague cake.* **flecked s. of Feitis,** multiple necroses of the spleen, characterized by nonembolic multiple areas of anemic necrosis. **floating s.,** a spleen displaced and preternaturally movable. Called also *wandering s.* **Gandy-Gamna s.,** siderotic splenomegaly. **hard-baked s.,** a condition of the spleen in Hodgkin's disease, marked by the presence of grayish areas resembling the diseased lymph nodes in structure. **lardaceous s.,** waxy s. **movable s.,** floating s. **porphyry s.,** a spleen which is the seat of nodular infiltration. **sago s.,** a spleen having on its cut surface the appearance of grains of sago: due to amyloid infiltration. **speckled s.,** flecked s. **wandering s.,** floating s. **waxy s.,** a spleen affected with amyloid degeneration. Called also *lardaceous s.*

splen (splen) [Gr. *splēn*]. Spleen.

splen-. See *spleno-*.

splenadenoma (splēn″ad-e-no′mah) [*splen-* + Gr. *adēn* gland + *-oma*]. Hyperplasia of the spleen pulp.

splenalgia (sple-nal′je-ah) [*splen-* + Gr. *algos* pain + *-ia*]. Neuralgic pain in the spleen.

splenatrophy (splen-at′ro-fe). Atrophy of the spleen.

splenauxe (sple-nawk′se) [*splen-* + Gr. *auxē* increase]. Enlargement of the spleen.

splenceratosis (splen″ser-ah-to′sis). Splenokeratosis.

splenculus (spleng′ku-lus) [L. "little spleen"]. An accessory spleen, or splenic exclave.

splenectasis (sple-nek′tah-sis) [*splen-* + Gr. *ektasis* enlargement]. Enlargement of the spleen.

splenectomize (sple-nek′to-mīz). To deprive of the spleen by surgical removal.

splenectomy (sple-nek′to-me) [*splen-* + Gr. *ektomē* excision]. Excision or extirpation of the spleen. **subcapsular s.,** splenectomy in which the capsule of the organ is incised and the spleen decapsulated and removed.

splenectopia (sple-nek-to′pe-ah) [*splen-* + Gr. *ek* out + *topos* place + *-ia*]. Displacement of the spleen; wandering or floating spleen.

splenectopy (sple-nek′to-pe). Splenectopia.

splenelcosis (sple″nel-ko′sis) [*splen-* + Gr. *helkōsis* ulceration]. Ulceration of the spleen.

splenemia (sple-ne′me-ah) [*splen-* + Gr. *haima* blood + *-ia*]. Congestion of the spleen with blood.

splenemphraxis (sple″nem-frak′sis) [*splen-* + Gr. *emphraxis* stoppage]. Congestion of the spleen.

spleneolus (sple-ne′o-lus). Accessory spleen.

splenepatitis (sple″nep-ah-ti′tis) [*splen-* + Gr. *hēpar* liver + *-itis*]. Inflammation of the spleen and liver.

splenetic (sple-net′ik). Affected with splenic disorder; ill humored.

splenial (sple′ne-al). Pertaining to the splenium or to the splenius muscle.

splenic (splen′ik) [Gr. *splēnikos;* L. *splenicus*]. Pertaining to the spleen.

splenicterus (splen-ik′ter-us) [*splen-* + Gr. *ikteros* jaundice]. Inflammation of the spleen associated with jaundice.

splenification (splen″ĭ-fi-ka′shun). Splenization.

spleniform (splen′ĭ-form). Resembling the spleen.

spleniserrate (splen″ĭ-ser′āt). Pertaining to the splenius and the serratus muscles.

splenitis (sple-ni′tis) [*splen-* + *-itis*]. Inflammation of the spleen: a condition that is usually produced by pyemia. It is attended by enlargement of the organ with pus, and is marked by much local pain. **spodogenous s.,** that due to accumulation of foreign particles in the spleen.

splenium (sple′ne-um) [L.; Gr. *splēnion*]. A band-like structure; a bandage or compress. **s. cor′poris callo′si** [N A, B N A], the posterior rounded end of the callosum.

splenization (splen″ĭ-za′shun). That condition of a part, especially the lung, in which it has the appearance of the tissue of the spleen, due to engorgement and condensation. **hypostatic s.**, that produced by hypostatic pneumonia.

spleno-, splen- [Gr. *splēn* spleen]. Combining form denoting relationship to the spleen.

splenocele (sple′no-sēl) [*spleno-* + Gr. *kēlē* hernia]. Hernia of the spleen.

splenoceratosis (sple″no-ser″ah-to′sis). Splenokeratosis.

splenocleisis (sple″no-kli′sis) [*spleno-* + Gr. *kleisis* closure]. 1. Irritation of the surface of the spleen to induce the development of new fibrous tissue. 2. Extraperitoneal transplantation of a portion of the spleen beneath the rectus muscle.

splenocolic (sple″no-kol′ik) [*spleno-* + Gr. *kolon* colon]. Pertaining to the spleen and colon.

splenocyte (splen′o-sīt). The monocyte characteristic of the spleen.

splenodiagnosis (sple″no-di″ag-no′sis). Diagnosis of typhoid fever by noting the effect on the spleen of injections of extracts of typhoid bacilli.

splenodynia (sple″no-din′e-ah) [*spleno-* + Gr. *odynē* pain + *-ia*]. Pain in the spleen.

splenogenous (sple-noj′e-nus). Arising in or formed by the spleen.

splenogram (sple′no-gram). 1. A roentgenogram of the spleen. 2. A differential count of the cells found in a stained preparation of material obtained by splenic puncture.

splenogranulomatosis (splen″o-gran″u-lo″mah-to′sis). A granulomatous condition of the spleen. **s. siderot′ica,** Gamna's disease.

splenography (sple-nog′rah-fe) [*spleno-* + Gr. *graphein* to write]. 1. Roentgenography of the spleen. 2. A description of the spleen.

splenohepatomegalia (sple″no-hep″ah-to-me-ga′le-ah). Splenohepatomegaly.

splenohepatomegaly (sple″no-hep″ah-to-meg′ah-le) [*spleno-* + Gr. *hēpar* liver + *megas* large]. Enlargement of the spleen and liver.

splenoid (sple′noid) [*spleno-* + Gr. *eidos* form]. Resembling the spleen.

splenokeratosis (sple″no-ker″ah-to′sis) [*spleno-* + Gr. *keras* horn + *-osis*]. Hardening of the spleen.

splenolaparotomy (sple″no-lap″ah-rot′o-me). Laparosplenotomy.

splenology (sple-nol′o-je) [*spleno-* + *-logy*]. The sum of knowledge regarding the spleen, its functions and diseases.

splenolymphatic (sple″no-lim-fat′ik). Pertaining to the spleen and lymph glands.

splenolysin (sple-nol′ĭ-sin) [*spleno-* + Gr. *lyein* to dissolve]. A lysin destructive to splenic tissue.

splenolysis (sple-nol′ĭ-sis). Destruction of spleen tissue.

splenoma (sple-no′mah), pl. *splenomas* or *spleno′mata* [*spleno-* + *-oma*]. A tumor of the spleen.

splenomalacia (sple″no-mah-la′she-ah) [*spleno-* + Gr. *malakia* softness]. Abnormal softness of the spleen; softening of the spleen.

splenomedullary (sple″no-med′u-ler″e). Of or pertaining to the spleen and bone marrow.

splenomegalia (sple″no-me-ga′le-ah). Splenomegaly.

splenomegaly (sple″no-meg′ah-le) [*spleno-* + Gr. *megas* large]. Enlargement of the spleen. The term is principally applied to a disease marked by hypertrophy of the spleen, with progressive anemia and with no leukemia or disease of the lymph glands. **congestive s.** See *Banti's disease.* **Egyptian s.** is caused by *Schistosoma mansoni.* **Gaucher's s.** See under *disease.* **hemolytic s.,** hemolytic jaundice. **hypercholesterolemic s.,** a form of splenomegaly in which there is an unusual accumulation of cholesterol in the blood. **infantile s.,** anaemia infantum pseudoleukaemica. **infective s., infectious s.,** splenomegaly which is associated with an infection. **myelophthisic s.,** enlargement of the spleen marked by decrease in myeloid tissue and by fibrosis. **Niemann's s.** See under *disease.* **siderotic s.,** splenomegaly characterized by marked fibrosis with deposit of iron and calcium (Gandy-Gamna nodules). Called also *Gandy-Nanta's disease.* **spodogenous s.,** enlargement of the spleen attributed to accumulation of erythrocytes in the organ. **tropical s., febrile,** kala-azar.

splenometry (sple-nom′e-tre). Determination of the size of the spleen.

splenomyelogenous (sple″no-mi″ĕ-loj′e-nus). Formed in the spleen and bone marrow; splenomedullary.

splenomyelomalacia (sple″no-mi″ĕ-lo-mah-la′she-ah) [*spleno-* + Gr. *myelos* marrow + *malakia* softening]. Softening of the spleen and bone marrow.

splenoncus (sple-nong′kus) [*spleno-* + Gr. *onkos* bulk, mass]. Tumor of the spleen.

splenonephric (sple″no-nef′rik). Pertaining to the spleen and the kidney.

splenonephroptosis (sple″no-nef″rop-to′sis) [*spleno-* + Gr. *nephros* kidney + *ptōsis* falling]. Downward displacement of the spleen and kidney on the same side.

splenopancreatic (sple″no-pan″kre-at′ik). Pertaining to the spleen and the pancreas.

splenoparectasis (sple″no-par-ek′tah-sis) [*spleno-* + Gr. *parektasis* extension]. Excessive enlargement of the spleen.

splenopathy (sple-nop′ah-the) [*spleno-* + Gr. *pathos* disease]. Any disease of the spleen.

splenopexia (sple″no-pek′se-ah). Splenopexy.

splenopexis (sple′no-pek″sis). Splenopexy.

splenopexy (sple′no-pek″se) [*spleno-* + Gr. *pexis* fixation]. Surgical fixation of a wandering spleen to the abdominal wall by sutures.

splenophrenic (splen-o-fren′ik) [*spleno-* + Gr. *phrēn* diaphragm]. Pertaining to the spleen and diaphragm.

splenopneumonia (splen″o-nu-mo′ne-ah). Pneumonia attended with splenization of the lung.

splenoportography (sple″no-por-tog′rah-fe). Splenic portography.

splenoptosia (sple″nop-to′se-ah). Splenoptosis.

splenoptosis (sple″nop-to′sis) [*spleno-* + Gr. *ptōsis* falling]. Prolapse or downward displacement of the spleen.

splenorenopexy (sple″no-re′no-pek″se). Nephrosplenopexy.

splenorrhagia (sple″no-ra′je-ah) [*spleno-* + Gr. *rhēgnynai* to burst forth]. Hemorrhage from the spleen.

splenorrhaphy (sple-nor′ah-fe) [*spleno-* + Gr. *rhaphē* suture]. Suture of wounds of the spleen.

splenosis (sple-no′sis). A condition in which multiple implants of splenic tissue are present throughout the peritoneal cavity. **pericardial s.,** development between the heart and pericardium of splenic tissue deliberately introduced into the pericardial cavity as a means of increasing the blood supply to the heart muscle.

splenotherapy (sple″no-ther′ah-pe). Treatment by administering splenic tissue.

splenotomy (sple-not′o-me) [*spleno-* + Gr. *tomē* a cutting]. Surgical incision of the spleen.

splenotoxin (sple″no-tok′sin). A toxin produced by or acting on the spleen.

splenotyphoid (sple″no-ti′foid). Typhoid fever with marked splenic involvement.

splenulus (splen′u-lus). A little spleen; an accessory spleen.

splenunculus (sple-nung′ku-lus). Lienunculus.

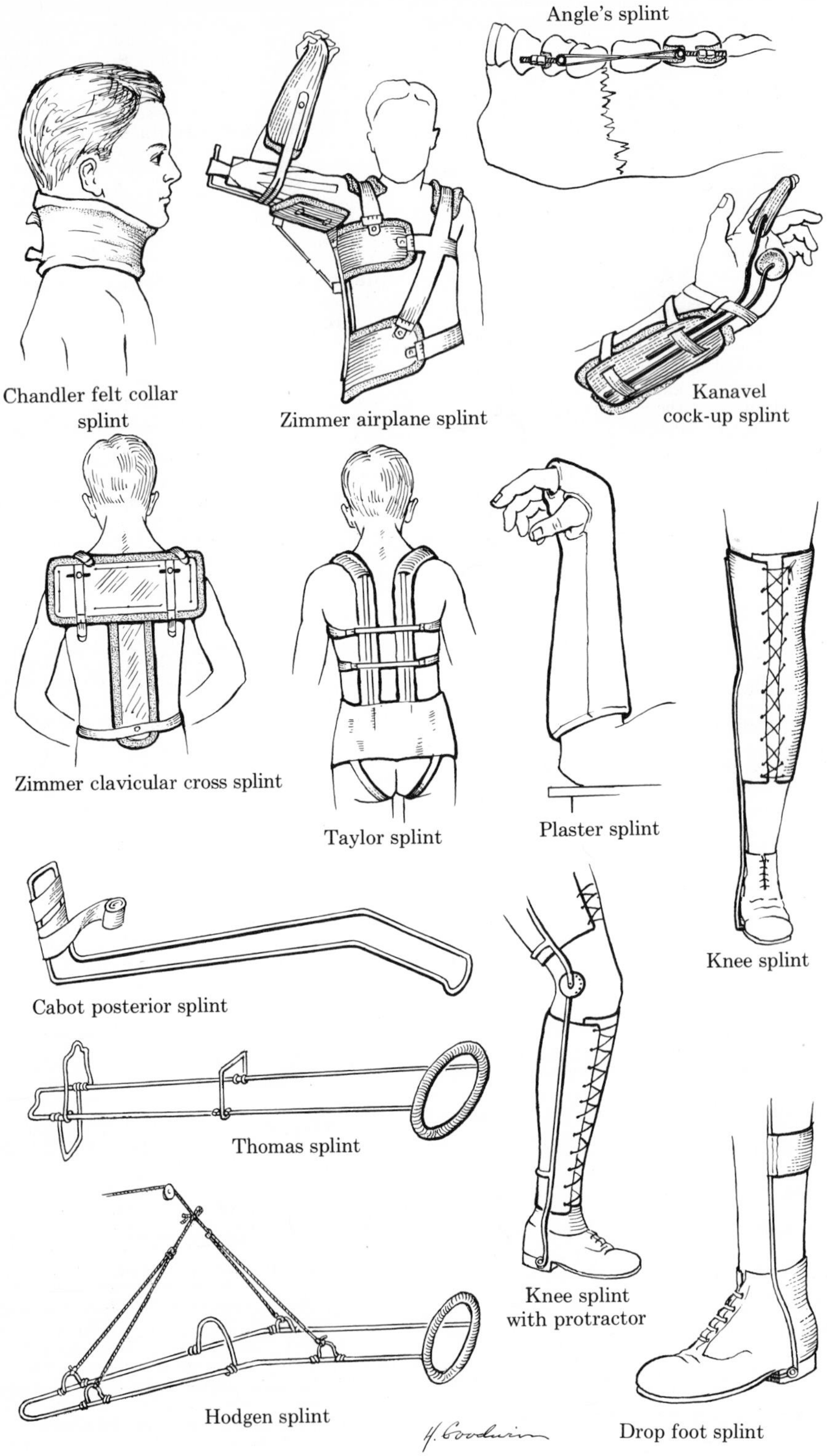

Angle's splint

Chandler felt collar splint

Zimmer airplane splint

Kanavel cock-up splint

Zimmer clavicular cross splint

Taylor splint

Plaster splint

Knee splint

Cabot posterior splint

Thomas splint

Knee splint with protractor

Hodgen splint

Drop foot splint

H. Goodwin

VARIOUS TYPES OF SPLINT

splint (splint). 1. A rigid or flexible appliance for the fixation of displaced or movable parts. 2. [pl.]. A condition characterized by development of exostoses on the rudimentary second or fourth metacarpal or metatarsal bone in the horse. **Agnew's s.** 1. One for fracture of the patella. 2. One used in fracture of the metacarpus. **anchor s.**, a splint for fracture of the jaw, with metal loops fitting over the teeth and held together by a rod. **Anderson s.**, a splint for external internal fixation of fractures: two or more long screws, Kirschner wire, or nails are inserted through the tissues into the bone above and below the fracture; each group of screws, wires or nails is attached to an external plate and the plates are joined by an adjustable screw. **Angle's s.** See illustration. **Asch's s.**, a tube splint for fracture of the nose. **Ashhurst's s.**, a bracketed splint of wire with a foot piece: made to cover the thigh and leg, and used after excision of the knee joint. **Balkan s.**, an apparatus for continuous extension in treatment of fractures of the femur. It consists of an overhead bar, supported from the floor with pulleys attached, which supports the leg in a metal sling. **banjo traction s.**, a splint for the fingers constructed from a steel rod shaped like a banjo. **Bavarian s.**, a dressing formed by two pieces of flannel, folded once and sutured along the margin of the fold; between the layers of each fold, plaster cream is introduced, the seam serving as a hinge in the removal of the splint. **Böhler s.**, a piece of wood measuring 12 × 6 × 2 inches, rounded at the upper end to fit the axilla. **Bond's s.**, a form of splint for fracture of the lower end of the radius. **Bowlby's s.**, a splint for fracture of the shaft of the humerus. **bracketed s.**, a splint composed of two pieces of metal or wood joined by brackets. **Cabot's s.**, a posterior wire splint (see illustration). **Carter's intranasal s.**, a fenestrated steel bridge, the wings of which are connected by a hinge: used in the bridge splint operation for depressed bridge of the nose. **Chandler felt collar s.** See illustration. **Chatfield-Girdleston s.**, an apparatus for enabling a paralyzed poliomyelitis patient with bilateral deltoid paralysis to walk with crutches. **coaptation s's**, small splints adjusted about a fractured limb for the purpose of producing coaptation of fragments. **Cramer's s.**, a flexible wire splint consisting of parallel stout wires between which smaller wires are stretched like the rounds of a ladder. **Denis Browne s.**, a splint for the correction of talipes equinovarus. **DePuy s.**, an adjustable clavicular brace for fracture of the clavicle. **drop foot s.** See illustration. **Dupuytren's s.**, a splint to prevent eversion in Pott's fracture. **dynamic s.**, a support or protective apparatus for the hand or any other part of the body which also aids in initiating and performing motion of that part or adjacent parts and assists in dealing with the forces resulting from the action, thus assisting in those motions necessary to perform the activities of daily living. **Engelmann s.**, a big splint consisting of two strips of metal connecting at the top with a ring which fits over the thigh as high as it can be pushed up against the crotch. It is fastened at the lower end with a spike in each side which is driven into the shoe between the sole and upper, close to the heel. **Fox's s.**, an apparatus for fractured clavicle. **functional s.**, dynamic s. **Gibson's s.**, a form of Thomas splint. **Gilmer's s.**, a silver wire fastening for holding the lower teeth to the upper ones in fracture of the mandible. **Gooch s.**, a flexible coaptation splint consisting of strips of wood arranged edge to edge and glued to cloth or leather. **Gordon's s.**, a side splint for the arm and hand in Colles' fracture. **Gunning's s.**, an interdental splint used in treating fractured mandible. **Hammond's s.**, a wire splint used for repositioning the teeth in orthodontics. **Hodgen s.**, a wire splint for fracture of the femur below the upper third. See illustration. **interdental s.**, a splint for fracture of the jaw, held in place by wires passed around the teeth. **Jones' nasal s.**, a splint for fracture of the nasal bones. **Kanavel's cock-up s.**, a splint for application to stiffened hands. See illustration. **Keller-Blake s.**, a hinged half-ring modification of the Thomas traction splint for fracture of the femur. **knee s.** See illustration. **Levis' s.**, a splint of perforated metal extending from below the elbow to the end of the palm. **Liston's s.**, a simple straight splint adapted to the side of the leg and body. **live s.**, dynamic s. **McGee's s.**, a splint for fracture of both rami of the mandible. **McIntire's s.**, a posterior splint for the leg and thigh, in the form of a double inclined plane. **Mason's s.**, a splint for the after-treatment of amputation at the elbow. **plaster s.**, a splint composed of gauze impregnated with plaster of paris. **poroplastic s.**, a splint which can be softened with water and molded upon the limb. **Porzett s.**, a splint for controlling movement of the arms and of the head of the child after harelip operations. **Sayre's s.**, one of three varieties of splint: one for the ankle, one for the knee, and one for use in hip joint disease. **shin s's**, strain of the flexor digitorum longus muscle occurring in athletes, marked by pain along the shin bone. **Simpson's s.**, a shaped tampon of cotton for inserting into the nasal fossa. **Stader s.**, a splint for external internal fixation of fractures, consisting of a metal bar having a steel pin at each end for insertion into the bone on either side of the fracture so that the bar bridges the fracture: the ends of the fractured bone are drawn together by adjusting screws. **Stromeyer's s.**, a splint consisting of two hinged portions which can be fixed at any angle. **T s.**, a T-shaped splint made by tacking a transverse piece of splint board across the end of a vertical piece. **Taylor s.** See illustration. **therapeutic s.**, dynamic s. **Thomas' knee s.**, a splint for removing the pressure of the weight of the body from the knee joint by transferring it to the ischium and perineum. See illustration. **Thomas' posterior s.**, a form of splint used in hip joint disease. **Tobruk s.**, an immobilizing split plaster cast applied from the foot to the groin; with skin traction tapes through openings in the plaster and connected with a Thomas splint. It was used in the North African campaign of World War II. **Toronto s.** 1. A splint for poliomyelitis cases in which adjustable splints for the arms and legs are used with and attached to a Bradford frame. 2. A splinting catheter for use in the ureter after plastic operation. **Valentine's s.**, a splint for fracture of the clavicle. **Volkmann's s.**, a guttered splint with a foot piece and two lateral supports: for fracture of the lower extremity. **Wertheim s.**, a splint for fracture of a metacarpal bone. **Zimmer s.**, one used in ambulatory patients to immobilize the head and neck after injury to the cervical vertebrae. **Zimmer airplane s.** See illustration.

splinter (splin′ter). 1. A small fragment, as a piece of fractured bone. 2. To break into small fragments.

splinting (splint′ing). 1. Application of a splint, or treatment by use of a splint. 2. In dentistry, the application of a fixed restoration to join two or more teeth into a single rigid unit. 3. Rigidity of muscles occurring as a means of avoiding pain caused by movement of the part.

splints (splintz). See *splint*, def. 2.

splitting (split′ing). Division into fragments. In chemistry, the separation of a complex substance into two or more simpler substances. **s. of heart sounds**, a reduplication or doubling of the first or second heart sound, due to failure of the valves on the two sides of the heart to close at precisely the same instant.

spodiomyelitis (spo″de-o-mi″ĕ-li′tis) [Gr. *spodios* ash colored + *myelos* marrow + *-itis*]. Acute anterior poliomyelitis.

spodo- (spod′o) [Gr. *spodos* ashes]. Combining form denoting relation to waste materials.

spodogenous (spo-doj′e-nus) [*spodo-* + Gr. *gennan* to produce]. Pertaining to or caused by waste materials in an organ.

spodogram (spod′o-gram) [*spodo-* + Gr. *gramma* a mark]. The pattern created by the ash after incineration of a minute amount of tissue or other material. Called also *ash picture*.

spodography (spo-dog′rah-fe) [*spodo-* + Gr. *graphein* to write]. The incineration of a minute quantity of tissue and observation of the ashes (spodogram) under a dark-field microscope, as a means of studying the mineral constitutents of the cells.

spodophagous (spo-dof′ah-gus) [*spodo-* + Gr. *phagein* to devour]. Eating up or destroying the waste materials of the body.

spodophorous (spo-dof′o-rus) [*spodo-* + Gr. *phorein* to bear]. Removing waste materials.

spondyl- (spon′dil). See *spondylo-*.

spondylalgia (spon″dĭ-lal′je-ah). Pain in a vertebra.

spondylarthritis (spon″dil-ar-thri′tis) [*spondyl-* + Gr. *arthron* joint + *-itis*]. Arthritis of the spine. **s. ankylopoiet′ica,** rheumatoid spondylitis.

spondylarthrocace (spon″dil-ar-throk′ah-se) [*spondyl-* + Gr. *arthron* joint + *kakē* badness]. Tuberculosis of the vertebrae.

spondylexarthrosis (spon″dil-eks″ar-thro′sis) [*spondyl-* + Gr. *exarthrōsis* dislocation]. Dislocation of a vertebra.

spondylitic (spon″dĭ-lit′ik). Pertaining to or characterized by spondylitis.

spondylitis (spon″dĭ-li′tis). Inflammation of the vertebrae. **s. ankylopoiet′ica, s. ankylo′sans, ankylosing s.,** rheumatoid s. **Bechterew's s.,** rheumatoid s. **s. defor′mans,** rheumatoid s. **hypertrophic s.,** spondylitis with evidences of hypertrophic changes in the vertebrae. **s. infectio′sa,** inflammation of the vertebrae caused by a specific pathogen. **Kümmell's s.** See under *disease*. **Marie-Strümpell s.,** rheumatoid s. **muscular s.,** a morbid condition of the spine resulting from muscular weakness and not a true inflammation. **posttraumatic s.,** Kümmell's disease. **rheumatoid s.,** a systemic illness of unknown etiology, affecting young males predominantly, and producing pain and stiffness as a result of inflammation of the sacroiliac, intervertebral, and costovertebral joints; paraspinal calcification, with ossification and ankylosis of the spinal joints, may cause complete rigidity of the spine and thorax. **rhizomelic s., s. rhizome′lica, s. rhizomélique′,** rheumatoid s. **traumatic s.,** spondylitis occurring as a result of injury to the vertebrae. **s. tuberculo′sa,** spondylitis caused by infection with the tubercle bacillus. **s. typho′sa,** inflammation of the vertebrae following typhoid fever.

spondylizema (spon″dĭ-li-ze′mah) [*spondyl-* + Gr. *izēmia* depression]. Downward displacement of a vertebra in consequence of the destruction or softening of the one below it.

spondylo-, spondyl- (spon′dĭ-lo, spon′dil) [Gr. *spondylos* vertebra]. Combining form denoting relationship to a vertebra, or to the spinal column.

spondylocace (spon″dĭ-lok′ah-se) [*spondylo-* + Gr. *kakē* badness]. Tuberculosis of the vertebrae.

spondylodesis (spon″dĭ-lod′ĕ-sis) [*spondylo-* + Gr. *desis* binding]. The operation of fusing the vertebrae by a short bone graft in cases of tuberculous spine.

spondylodiagnosis (spon″dĭ-lo-di″ag-no′sis) [*spondylo-* + *diagnosis*]. Diagnosis by the reflexes obtained by stimulating the vertebrae.

spondylodidymia (spon″dĭ-lo-di-dim′e-ah) [*spondylo-* + Gr. *didymos* twin + *-ia*]. Teratic union of twins by the vertebrae.

spondylodymus (spon″dĭ-lod′ĭ-mus). A twin monster united by the vertebrae.

spondylodynia (spon″dĭ-lo-din′e-ah) [*spondyl-* + Gr. *odynē* pain + *-ia*]. Pain in a vertebra.

spondylolisthesis (spon″dĭ-lo-lis′the-sis) [*spondyl-* + Gr. *olisthanein* to slip]. Forward displacement of one vertebra over another, usually of the fifth lumbar over the body of the sacrum, or of the fourth lumbar over the fifth.

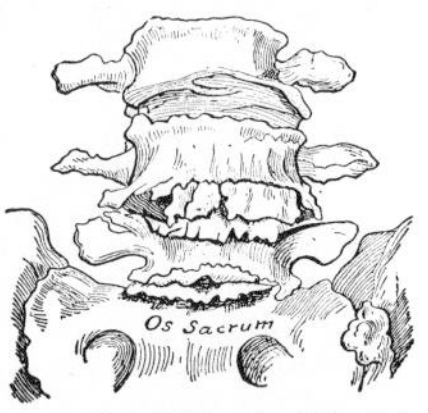

Os Sacrum

Spondylolisthesis (Davis).

spondylolisthetic (spon″dĭ-lo-lis-thet′ik). Pertaining to or caused by spondylolisthesis.

spondylolysis (spon″dĭ-lol′ĭ-sis [*spondylo-* + Gr. *lysis* dissolution]. Dissolution of a vertebra; a condition marked by platyspondylia, aplasia of the vertebral arch, and separation of the pedicle.

spondylomalacia (spon″dĭ-lo-mah-la′she-ah). Softening of vertebrae. **s. traumat′ica,** Kümmell's disease.

spondylopathy (spon″dĭ-lop′ah-the) [*spondylo-* + Gr. *pathos* disease]. Any disorder of the vertebrae. **traumatic s.,** Kümmell's disease.

spondyloptosis (spon″dĭ-lo-to′sis). Spondylolisthesis.

spondylopyosis (spon″dĭ-lo-pi-o′sis) [*spondylo-* + Gr. *pyōsis* suppuration]. Suppuration of a vertebra or of vertebrae.

spondyloschisis (spon″dĭ-los′kĭ-sis) [*spondylo-* + Gr. *schisis* fissure]. Congenital fissure of a vertebral arch.

spondylosis (spon″dĭ-lo′sis). Ankylosis of a vertebral joint. **s. chron′ica ankylopoiet′ica, rhizomelic s.,** spondylitis ankylopoietica.

spondylosyndesis (spon″dĭ-lo-sin′de-sis) [*spondylo-* + Gr. *syndesis* a binding together]. Operative immobilization or ankylosis of the spine; spinal fusion.

spondylotherapy (spon″dĭ-lo-ther′ah-pe) [*spondylo-* + Gr. *therapeia* treatment]. Treatment by physical methods applied to the spinal region; spinal therapeutics.

spondylotomy (spon″dĭ-lot′o-me) [*spondylo-* + Gr. *temnein* to cut]. Rachitomy.

spondylous (spon′dĭ-lus). Pertaining to a vertebra.

spongarion (spon-ga′re-on) [Gr.]. An ancient eye salve.

sponge (spunj) [L., Gr. *spongia*]. 1. The elastic fibrous skeleton of *Euspongia officinalis*, a marine animal organism: used mainly as an absorbent. 2. An absorbent pad of folded gauze or cotton. **Bernay's s.,** compressed disks of cotton which expand under moisture: used in checking epistaxis. **burnt s.,** spongia usta. **ear s.,** a small piece of sponge attached to a handle and used for washing the ear. **fibrin s.,** a spongy form of fibrin, used as a hemostatic. **gelatin s.,** a spongy form of denatured gelatin used as a hemostatic, especially when wet with thrombin. **gelatin s., absorbable,** a sterile, absorbable, water-insoluble gelatin-base sponge: used in the control of capillary bleeding.

spongeitis (spon″je-i′tis). Spongiitis.

spongia (spon′je-ah) [L.; Gr.]. Sponge. **s. compres′sa,** a sponge tent. **s. gelati′na absorben′da,** absorbable gelatin sponge. **s. us′ta** [L. "burnt sponge"], an alterative; its qualities are due to the contained iodine.

spongiform (spon′jĭ-form) [L. *spongia* sponge + *forma* shape]. Resembling a sponge.

spongiitis (spon″je-i′tis). Inflammation of the corpus spongiosum of the penis; periurethritis.

spongin (spon′jin). A horny, albuminoid material forming the basis of sponge.

spongio- (spon′je-o) [L., Gr. *spongia* sponge].

Combining form meaning like a sponge, or denoting relationship to a sponge.

spongioblast (spon′je-o-blast) [*spongio-* + Gr. *blastos* germ]. 1. Any one of the embryonic epithelial cells, developed about the neural canal, which becomes transformed, some into neuroglia and some into ependyma cells. 2. Amacrine.

spongioblastoma (spon″je-o-blas-to′mah). A tumor containing spongioblasts; gliosarcoma or glioblastoma. In *s. multifor′me* the cells are of various forms of arrangements; in *s. unipola′re* the spongioblasts are mostly unipolar.

spongiocyte (spon′je-o-sīt). 1. A neuroglia cell. 2. One of the cells with spongy vacuolated protoplasm in the cortex of the suprarenal gland.

spongiocytoma (spon″je-o-si-to′mah). Spongioblastoma.

spongioid (spon′je-oid) [*spongio-* + Gr. *eidos* form]. Resembling a sponge in structure or appearance.

spongiopilin (spon″je-o-pi′lin) [*spongio-* + Gr. *pilos* felt]. A fabric formed of sponge and wool felted together with a layer of caoutchouc applied to one surface: used like a poultice.

spongioplasm (spon′je-o-plazm) [*spongio-* + Gr. *plasma* anything formed or molded]. 1. A substance which forms the network of fibrils pervading the cell substance and forming the reticulum of the fixed cell. 2. The granular material of an axon.

spongiosis (spon″je-o′sis). Intercellular edema of the spongy layer (malpighian layer) of the skin.

spongiositis (spon″je-o-si′tis). Inflammation of the corpus spongiosum.

spongosterol (spon-gos′ter-ol). An isomer of cholesterol found in sponges.

spongy (spun′je). Of a spongelike appearance or texture.

spontaneous (spon-ta′ne-us) [L. *spontaneus*]. 1. Voluntary; instinctive. 2. Occurring without external influence.

spontin (spon′tin). Trade mark for a lyophilized preparation of ristocetins A and B.

spoon (spo͞on). A metallic instrument with an oval bowl placed on a handle. **Daviel's s.,** an instrument used in removing the eye lens. **excavator s.,** a spoon-shaped dental excavator. **marrow s.,** a gouge for removing marrow from bones. **sharp s.,** a spoon with a sharp-edged bowl: used for scraping away granulations, etc. **test s.,** a small spoon with a spatula-like handle for taking up small quantities of a powder, etc. in chemical experiments. **Volkmann's s.,** sharp s.

sporadic (spo-rad′ik) [Gr. *sporadikos* scattered; L. *sporadicus*]. Not widely diffused or epidemic; occurring only occasionally.

sporadoneure (spo-rad′o-nūr) [Gr. *sporadikos* sporadic + *neuron* nerve]. An isolated nerve cell occurring in any of the tissues.

sporangia (spo-ran′je-ah). Plural of *sporangium.*

sporangial (spo-ran′je-al). Pertaining to a sporangium.

sporangiophore (spo-ran′je-o-fōr). The threadlike stalk which bears at its tip the sporangium of molds.

sporangium (spo-ran′je-um), pl. *sporan′gia* [*spore* + Gr. *angeion* vessel]. Any encystment containing spores or sporelike bodies as in the larval state of trematode parasites or in certain of the mold fungi.

sporation (spo-ra′shun). Sporulation.

spore (spōr) [L. *spora;* Gr. *sporos* seed]. The reproductive element of one of the lower organisms, such as a protozoan or a cryptogamic plant. *Exospores* or *conidiospores* are nonsexual spores arising from the end of the hyphae by budding. Large ones are called *macroconidia;* small ones, *microconidia. Endospores* or *gonidospores* are formed in the interior of special spore cases called *sporangia.* Endospores that are free and provided with locomotive flagella are *zoospores,* their cases being termed *zoosporangia.* An *ascospore* is a variety of endospore contained in a special spore case called an ascus. *Basidiospores* are spores formed at the ends of club-shaped structures called *basidia. Zygospores* are spores formed by a conjugation between two special hyphae. *Chlamydospores* are asexual resting spores, with thick walls, produced by enlargement of special cells. *Oospores* are spores formed by fertilization in a manner similar to true seeds. **asexual s.,** a spore produced by division within the walls of a mother cell. **bacterial s's,** inactive resting or resistant forms produced within the body of a bacterium. **black s's of Ross,** degenerated and pigmented malarial oocysts in the body of a mosquito. **swarm s's,** spores made up of numerous active motile individuals. **washed s's,** spores of bacteria which have been freed from their toxin by washing.

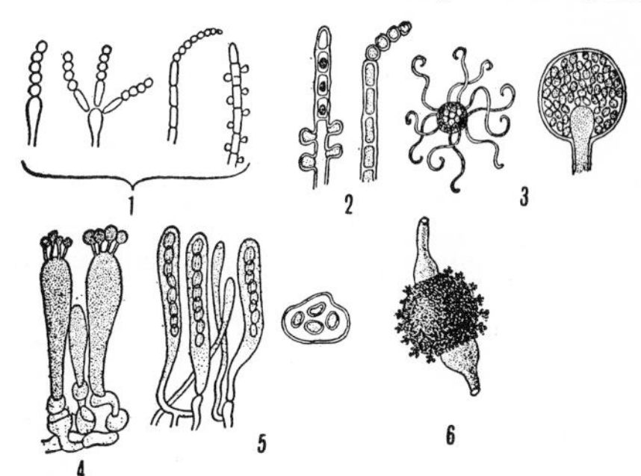

Various types of spores in fungi: 1, Conidiospores. 2, Chlamydospores. 3, Gonidiospores. 4, Basidiospores. 5, Ascospores. 6, Zygospores. (de Rivas.)

sporenrest (spo′ren-rest) [Ger.]. The mass of protoplasm left after the completion of sporulation of two congregating protozoan cells. Called also *sporal residuum.*

sporetia (spo-re′she-ah). That part of the extranuclear chromatin of a cell that is concerned in the reproductive function of the cell.

sporicidal (spo″rĭ-si′dal) [*spore* + L. *caedere* to kill]. Destroying spores.

sporicide (spo′rĭ-sīd). An agent that destroys spores.

sporidia (spo-rid′e-ah). Plural of *sporidium.*

sporidiosis (spo-rid″e-o′sis). Infection with sporidia.

sporidium (spo-rid′e-um), pl. *sporid′ia.* A protozoan organism in one of the spore stages of its growth: frequently seen in the vertebrate organism as a parasite.

sporiferous (spo-rif′er-us) [*spore* + L. *ferre* to bear]. Producing or bearing spores.

sporiparous (spo-rip′ah-rus) [*spore* + L. *parere* to produce]. Producing spores.

sporo- (spo′ro) [Gr. *sporos* seed]. Combining form denoting relationship to a spore.

sporoagglutination (spo″ro-ah-gloo″tĭ-na′shun). Agglutination of spores in the diagnosis of sporotrichosis.

sporoblast (spo′ro-blast) [*sporo-* + Gr. *blastos* germ]. One of the bodies developed within the oocyst of the malarial parasite in the mosquito from which the sporozoite later develops.

sporocyst (spo′ro-sist) [*sporo-* + Gr. *kystis* sac, bladder]. 1. Any cyst or sac containing spores or reproductive cells, especially in a vegetal or animal organism of a low type; a saclike organism which develops from a miracidium in the body of a snail host and contains germ cells which give rise to other sporocysts or to rediae. 2. The envelope formed about a sporoblast in the course of its development into a spore. Called also *spore membrane.*

sporoduct (spo′ro-dukt). A tubelike structure in the walls of certain sporocysts through which the spores are given off.

sporogenesis (spo″ro-jen′e-sis) [*sporo-* + Gr. *genesis* production]. The formation of spores; reproduction by spores.

sporogenic (spo″ro-jen′ik). Capable of developing into or producing spores.

sporogenous (spo-roj′e-nus) [*sporo-* + Gr. *gennan* to produce]. Reproduced by spores.

sporogeny (spo-roj′e-ne) [*sporo-* + Gr. *gennan* to produce]. The development of spores.

sporogony (spo-rog′o-ne) [*sporo-* + Gr. *goneia* generation]. The sexual cycle of sporozoa: especially the life-cycle of the malarial parasite (Plasmodium) in the stomach and body of the mosquito. Cf. *schizogony*.

sporomycosis (spo″ro-mi-ko′sis) [*sporo-* + Gr. *mykēs* fungus]. A condition caused by infection with the spores of a fungus.

sporont (spo′ront) [*sporo-* + Gr. *ōn, ontos* being]. A mature protozoan in its sexual cycle. Cf. *schizont*.

sporophore (spo′ro-fōr) [*sporo-* + Gr. *phorein* to bear]. That part of an organism that supports the spores.

sporophyte (spo′ro-fit) [*sporo-* + Gr. *phyton* plant]. The diploid or asexual stage in the antithetic alternation of generation.

sporoplasm (spo′ro-plazm) [*sporo-* + Gr. *plasma* anything formed or molded]. The protoplasm of reproductive cells.

sporoplasmic (spo″ro-plaz′mik). Pertaining to or of the nature of sporoplasm.

sporotheka (spo″ro-the′kah) [*sporo-* + Gr. *thēkē* case]. The envelope enclosing a number of exotospores of the malarial parasite before they leave the body of the mosquito host.

Sporothrix (spo′ro-thriks). Sporotrichum.

sporotrichin (spo-rot′rĭ-kin). A derivative of *Sporotrichum schenkii* used as a skin test in the diagnosis of sporotrichosis.

sporotrichosis (spo″ro-tri-ko′sis). A chronic infection caused by *Sporotrichum schenckii* and marked by the formation in the lymph nodes, skin or subcutaneous tissues of nodular lesions which tend to break down and form indolent ulcers. It may also occur as a generalized systemic disease (*extracutaneous s.*) affecting the muscles, bones, joints, and mucous membranes.

Sporotrichum (spo-rot′rĭ-kum) [*sporo-* + Gr. *thrix* hair]. A genus of fungi of which the species **S. schenck′ii** is the cause of sporotrichosis; also called *S. beurman′ni, S. councilman′i, S. jeansel′mei, S. e′qui*.

Sporotrichum (de Rivas).

Sporozoa (spo″ro-zo′ah) [*sporo-* + Gr. *zōon* animal]. A class of endoparasitic protozoans. They reproduce by sporulation and have no organs of locomotion. It includes the *Gregarinae*, the *Coccidia*, the *Haemosporidia*, the *Sarcosporidia*, the *Microsporidia*, and the *Myxosporidia*.

sporozoa (spo″ro-zo′ah). Plural of *sporozoon*.

sporozoan (spo″ro-zo′an). 1. Pertaining to sporozoa. 2. A sporozoon.

sporozoite (spo″ro-zo′it) [*sporo-* + Gr. *zōon* animal]. A spore formed after fertilization; any one of the sickle-shaped nucleated germs formed by division of the protoplasm of a spore of a sporozoan organism. In malaria, the sporozoites are the forms of the plasmodium which are liberated from the oocysts in the mosquito, which accumulate in the salivary glands and which are transferred to man in the act of feeding. Called also *falciform body*. See illustration on Plasmodium.

sporozooid (spo″ro-zo′oid). 1. Resembling a sporozoon. 2. A falciform body resembling a sporozoon.

sporozoon (spo″ro-zo′on), pl. *sporozo′a*. 1. Any organism or species belonging to the class Sporozoa. 2. The female malarial parasite in the stage formed by the capsulation of a macrogamete; by division it is transformed into a crop of sporozoites.

sporozoosis (spo″ro-zo-o′sis). Infection with sporozoa.

sport (spōrt). A freak of nature; lusus naturae.

sporular (spōr′u-lar). Pertaining to a spore.

sporulation (spōr″u-la′shun). The formation of spores. A form of reproduction consisting of spontaneous division of the cell into four or more daughter elements, each with a part of the original cell nucleus. Called also *spore formation*. **arthrogenous s.**, the change of bacteria into resistant forms which, in favorable conditions, will reproduce themselves. **endogenous s.**, sporulation of a protozoon within its host. **exogenous s.**, sporulation of a protozoon to produce the infection of fresh hosts.

sporule (spor′ūl). A small spore.

spot (spot). A circumscribed area or place; a loculus or macula. **acoustic s's**, maculae [N A]. **Bier's s's**, pallid patches on a congested and engorged skin which has been deprived of its normal circulation: these patches spread and coalesce. **Bitot's s's**, shiny, gray, triangular spots on the conjunctiva, associated with vitamin A deficiency. Called also *xerosis corneae*. **blind s.**, the area marking the site of entrance of the optic nerve on the retina (optic disk); so called because there are no sensory receptors in this region and hence no response to stimuli restricted to it. **blue s.** 1. Macula caerulea. 2. Mongolian spot. **café au lait s's** (kah-fa′o-la′) [Fr.], pigmented areas of the skin in von Recklinghausen's disease. **Carleton's s's**, sclerosed spots in the bones in gonorrheal disease. **Cayenne pepper s.**, a papillary varix. **cherry-red s.**, a red spot seen on the retina of each eye in the region of the macula lutea in amaurotic family idiocy. Called also *Tay's sign*. **Christopher's s's**, Maurer's dots. **cold s.**, any one of the temperature spots where cold is normally perceived, but not heat. **cotton-wool s's**, irregular white spots on the retina, made up of cells filled with fat or cholesterol: seen in arteriosclerotic Bright's disease. **cribriform s.**, macula cribrosa. **deaf s.**, deaf point. **de Morgan's s's**, red spots, like nevi, sometimes seen on the skin of old people. **embryonic s.**, area germinativa. **epigastric s.**, a point of tenderness exactly over the xiphoid process. **eye s.**, the rudiment of an eye in the embryo. **Filatow's s's**, Koplik's s's. **flame s's**, large hemorrhagic spots in the eyeground. **Flindt's s's**, Koplik's s's. **focal s.**, the spot or area of the target of an x-ray tube from which the roentgen rays are emitted. **Fordyce's s's**, isolated sebaceous glands in the oral mucosa, presenting as yellowish, milium-like bodies. **germinal s.**, the nucleolus of an ovum. **Graefe's s's**, spots over the vertebrae, pressure on which produces relaxation of blepharofacial spasm. **hot s.** 1. Any one of the temperature spots where heat is normally perceived, but not cold. 2. The sensitive area of a neuroma. **hypnogenetic s.**, any superficial area stimulation of which will bring on sleep. **Jacquemier's s.** See under *sign*. **Janeway's s's**, small nodular hemorrhagic spots on the palms and soles in cases of subacute bacterial endocarditis. **Koplik's s's**, small, irregular, bright red spots on the buccal and lingual mucosa, with a minute bluish white speck in the center of each, that are pathognomonic of beginning measles. **light s.**, cone of light. **liver s.**, a lay term for brownish spots on the skin. See *chloasma, Fasciola hepatica, morphea,* and *tinea versicolor.* **Mariotte's s.,** blind s. **Maurer's s's.** See under *dot.* **Maxwell's s.,** macula retinae. **milk s's.** 1. Whitish spots of fibrous thickening seen on the visceral layer of the pericardium in postmortem examination. 2. Dense masses of macrophages in the omentum. **Mongolian s.,** a brownish or bluish plaque of varying size, usually in the sacral area, present at birth and involuting in early life. **pain s's,** spots on the skin where alone the sense of pain can be produced by a stimulus. **pelvic s's,** round or oval shadows often seen on fluoroscopic examination in the region of the inferior spine of the ilium and the horizontal ramus of the pubic bone. **plague s's,** ecchymotic spots seen in some cases of bubonic plague, probably due to the bites of vermin. **rose s's,** a scattered eruption of rose-colored spots, appearing on the abdomen and loins during the first seven days of typhoid fever. Called also *typhoid spots* and *typhoid roseola.* **Roth's s's,** round or oval white spots sometimes seen in the retina early in the course of subacute bacterial endocarditis. **ruby s's,** de Morgan s's. **sacral s.,** Mongolian s. **silver s.,** a mycetoma of lice occupied by symbionts and essential to the life of the louse. **snow bank s's,** cotton-wool s's. **Soemmering's s.,** macula retinae. **soldier s's,** milk s's. **spongy s.,** the vascular zone. **Stephen's s's,** Maurer's dots. **Tardieu's s's,** spots of ecchymosis under the pleura following death by suffocation. **Tay's s.,** a red spot (the choroid) surrounded by a white circle, seen through the fovea centralis in amaurotic idiocy. **temperature s's,** hot and cold spots; spots on the skin normally anesthetic to pain and pressure and sensitive respectively to heat and cold; they are arranged in lines, often somewhat curved: they show the peculiar arrangement of the end-apparatus with respect to the temperature sense. **tendinous s.,** macula albida. **Trousseau's s.,** tache cérébrale. **typhoid s's,** rose s's. **vital s.,** a name sometimes given to the respiratory center in the medulla oblongata, because it is indispensable for breathing and therefore for life. **Wagner's s.,** the nucleolus of the human ovum. **warm s's,** minute areas in the skin that are peculiarly sensitive to temperatures above body temperature. **white s's,** grayish, elevated spots, of varying size, sometimes seen on the ventricular surface of the anterior leaflet of the mitral valve. **Willner's s's,** efflorescent spots, soon becoming pustules, on the internal layer of the prepuce; seen in the early stages of variola. **yellow s.,** macula retinae.

sprain (sprān). A joint injury in which some of the fibers of a supporting ligament are ruptured but the continuity of the ligament remains intact. **riders' s.,** sprain of the adductor longus muscle of the thigh, resulting from strain in riding horseback. **Schlatter's s.** See under *disease.*

spray (spra). A liquid minutely divided as by a jet of air or steam. **ether s.,** ether applied in a nebulized form to produce local anesthesia by chilling the part. **needle s.,** a water spray which is administered through a device having needle-sized jets. **Peet-Schultz s.,** a nasal spray for preventive application against poliomyelitis. **Tucker's s.,** a nasal spray for asthma containing 1 per cent cocaine and 5 per cent potassium nitrate.

Sprengel's deformity (spreng'elz) [Otto Gerhard Karl *Sprengel*, German surgeon, 1852–1915]. See under *deformity.*

sprew (sproo). Sprue.

spring-halt (spring'halt). Myoclonus of the hind leg of a horse, causing a gait in which the leg is suddenly raised and then stamped on the ground.

sprue (sproo). 1. A chronic disease marked by sore mouth, with a raw-looking tongue, gastrointestinal catarrh with periodic diarrhea in which the stools are frothy, fatty (steatorrhea) and fetid. There are loss of weight, asthenia, and a blood picture resembling that of pernicious anemia. 2. In dentistry, used to designate both the hole through which metal or other material is poured or forced into a mold and the waste piece of material cast in such a hole. **Belyando s.,** grass sickness.

Spt. Abbreviation for L. *spir'itus,* spirit.

spur (spur). A projecting body, as from a bone. In dentistry, a piece of metal projecting from a plate, band, or other dental appliance. **calcaneal s.,** a bone excrescence on the lower surface of the os calcis which frequently causes pain on walking. **Morand's s.,** hippocampus minor. **occipital s.,** an abnormal process of bone on the occipital bone behind the posterior process of the atlas. **olecranon s.,** an abnormal process of bone at the insertion of the triceps muscle.

spurious (spu're-us) [L. *spurius*]. Simulated; not genuine; false.

sputamentum (spu"tah-men'tum) [L.]. Sputum.

sputum (spu'tum) [L.]. Matter ejected from the lungs, bronchi, and trachea, through the mouth. **s. aerogino'sum,** green expectoration. **albuminoid s.,** a yellowish, frothy sputum of persons from whom large amounts of pleural fluid have been withdrawn: believed to be due to pulmonary edema. **s. coc'tum,** the opaque mucopus of the later stages of bronchitis and laryngitis. **s. cru'dum,** the clear, tenacious mucus of the early stages of laryngitis and bronchitis. **s. cruen'tum,** bloody sputum. **egg yolk s.,** sputum of a bright-yellow color, as in some cases of jaundice. **globular s.,** sputum in yellow, spherical lumps: characteristic of the last stages of tuberculosis. **green s.,** sputum stained with a green pigment, as in certain cases of jaundice. **icteric s.,** sputum stained with a greenish or yellow tint by bile pigments, as in jaundice. **moss-agate s.,** a grayish, opalescent, gelatinous mottled sputum, usually projected from the mouth in a more or less globular form during coughing: characteristic of diseases of the trachea (Chevalier Jackson). **nummular s.,** sputum in rounded disks, shaped somewhat like coins. **prune juice s.,** dark, reddish-brown, bloody sputum of certain forms of pneumonia, cancer of the lung, gangrene, etc. **rusty s.,** sputum stained with blood or blood pigments; seen in pneumonia, etc.

SQ. Abbreviation (symbol) for *subcutaneous.*

squalene (skwal'ēn). An unsaturated hydrocarbon from the liver oil of sharks and certain other elasmobranch fishes. It is $[(CH_3)_2C{:}CH(CH_2)_2C(CH_3){:}CH(CH_2)_2C(CH_3){:}CH.CH_2]_2$.

squama (skwa'mah), pl. *squa'mae* [L.]. A scale or platelike structure. **s. alveola'ris,** a thin plate covering the bare areas of pulmonary alveoli. **frontal s., s. of frontal bone, s. fronta'lis** [N A, B N A], the broad, curved portion of the frontal bone, situated above the supraorbital margin and forming the forehead. **mental s., external,** protuberantia mentalis. **occipital s.,** s. occipitalis. **occipital s., superior,** os interparietale. **s. occipita'lis** [N A, B N A], the largest of the four parts of the occipital bone, extending from the posterior edge of the foramen magnum to the lambdoid suture, its external surface bearing the external occipital protuberance. **perpendicular s.,** s. frontalis. **temporal s., s. of temporal bone, s. tempora'lis** [B N A], pars squamosa ossis temporalis.

squamae (skwa'me) [L.]. Plural of *squama.*

squamate (skwa'māt) [L. *squamatus,* from *squama* scale]. Scaly; having or resembling scales.

squamatization (skwa"mah-ti-za'shun). The transformation of cells of other types into squamous cells; squamous metaplasia.

squame (skwām) [L. *squama*]. A scale or scalelike substance.

squamocellular (skwa"mo-sel'u-lar) [L. *squama* scale + *cellula* cell]. Having squamous cells.

squamofrontal (skwa"mo-fron'tal). Pertaining to the squama frontalis.

squamomastoid (skwa"mo-mas'toid). Pertaining to the squamous and mastoid portions of the temporal bone.

squamo-occipital (skwa″mo-ok-sip′ĭ-tal). Pertaining to the squama occipitalis.

squamoparietal, squamosoparietal (skwa″-mo-pah-ri′ĕ-tal, skwa-mo″so-pah-ri′ĕ-tal). Pertaining to the squamous and parietal bones.

squamopetrosal (skwa″mo-pe-tro′sal). Pertaining to the squamous and petrous portions of the temporal bone.

squamosa (skwa-mo′sah) [L.]. Scaly, or platelike. See *pars squamosa.*

squamosal (skwa-mo′sal). 1. Squamous. 2. The squamosa.

squamosphenoid (skwa″mo-sfe′noid). Pertaining to the squamous portion of the temporal bone and to the sphenoid bone.

squamotemporal (skwa″mo-tem′po-ral). Pertaining to the squamous portion of the temporal bone.

squamous (skwa′mus) [L. *squamosus* scaly]. Scaly, or platelike.

squamozygomatic (skwa″mo-zi″go-mat′ik). Pertaining to the squamous portions of the temporal bone and the zygomatic bone.

squarrose (skwar′ōs) [L. *squarrosus*]. Covered with scurf or dandruff.

squarrous (skwar′us). Squarrose.

squatting (skwot′ting). A position of flexion of the knees and hips, the buttocks being lowered to the level of the heels, sometimes adopted by the parturient at delivery. Children with certain types of cyanotic cardiac defects frequently adopt the position, as it results in an increase in systemic blood flow and, by impeding venous return from the legs, minimizes the tendency of the arterial oxygen saturation to fall with exercise.

squeeze (skwēz). Subjection to pressure; compression. **tussive s.,** the compression of the lung in coughing, which forces material from the alveoli and smaller air passages into the bronchi.

squill (skwil) [L. *scilla;* Gr. *skilla*]. The fleshy inner scales of the bulb of the white variety of *Urginea maritima,* a liliaceous plant. It contains *scillitin, scillin, scillipicrin, scillotoxin,* and several other principles, and is expectorant and diuretic. See *scillaren.*

squillitic (skwil-lit′ik) [L. *scilliticus;* Gr. *skillitikos*]. Pertaining to or containing squill.

squint (skwint). Strabismus. **convergent s.,** esotropia. **divergent s.,** exotropia. **upward and downward s.,** hypertropia.

Squire's catheter (skwīrz) [Trumann Hoffman *Squire,* American surgeon, 1823–1889]. See under *catheter.*

S.R. Abbreviation for *sedimentation rate,* and *sigma reaction.*

Sr. Chemical symbol for *strontium.*

S.R.N. Abbreviation for *State Registered Nurse* (England and Wales).

S romanum (es ro-mah′num). The sigmoid colon.

ss. Abbreviation for L. *se′mis,* one half.

s.s. Abbreviation for *soapsuds.*

Ssabanejew-Frank operation (sab-an′ej-ef frank) [J. *Ssabanejew,* Russian surgeon; Rudolf *Frank,* Vienna surgeon, 1862–1913]. See *Frank's operation,* under *operation.*

SSS. Abbreviation for *specific soluble substance* (polysaccharide haptene).

s.s.s. Abbreviation for L. *stra′tum su′per stra′tum,* layer upon layer.

S.S.V. Abbreviation for L. *sub sig′no vene′ni,* under a poison label.

St. Abbreviation for L. *stet,* let it stand; or *stent,* let them stand.

STA. Abbreviation for *serum thrombotic accelerator.*

S. T. 37 (es″te thir″te sev′en). Trade mark for a solution of hexylresorcinol.

stabilarsan (sta-bil′ar-san). A double glycoside of arsphenamine, $C_6H_{11}O_5.NH(OH)C_6H_3As$.

stabile (stab′il) [L. *stabilis* stable, abiding]. Not moving; stationary; noting an electric current applied by electrodes kept stationary on a part, as opposed to *labile.* **heat s.,** thermostabile.

stability (stah-bil′ĭ-te). The quality of maintaining a constant character in the presence of forces which threaten to disturb it; resistance to change. **dimensional s.,** the resistance of a material to change in its shape or measurements.

stabilization (sta″bil-i-za′shun). The creation of a stable state.

stable (sta′b'l). Not moving, fixed, firm; resistant to change.

staccato (stah-kah′to) [Ital. "detached"]. Noting a manner of utterance in which the speech is delivered in a quick, jerky manner, with an interval between each two syllables.

stachydrine (stah-kid′rin). An alkaloid from *Stachys tubifera* and the fruit of *Citrus grandis.* It is N-methylproline-methylbetaine.

stachyose (stak′e-ōs). An indigestible tetrasaccharide, $C_{24}H_{42}O_{21}$, from the tubers of *Stachys tubifera,* the seeds of various Leguminosae and the roots and rhizomes of Labiatiae.

Stacke's operation (stak′ez) [Ludwig *Stacke,* German otologist, 1859–1918]. See under *operation.*

stactometer (stak-tom′e-ter) [Gr. *staktos* oozing out in drops + *metron* measure]. An instrument for measuring drops.

Stader splint (sta′der) [Otto *Stader,* American veterinary surgeon]. See under *splint.*

Staderini's nucleus (stad″er-e′nēz) [Rutilio *Staderini,* Italian anatomist]. Nucleus intercalatus.

stadium (sta′de-um), pl. *sta′dia* [L.; Gr. *stadion* course]. A stage or period in a disease. **s. ac′mes,** the height of a disease. **s. augmen′ti,** s. incrementi. **s. calo′ris,** the hot stage of a fever or disease. **s. decremen′ti,** the period of decrease of severity in a disease; the defervescence of fever. **s. defervescen′tiae,** s. decrementi. **s. fluorescen′tiae,** the stage of development of the eruption in an exanthematous disease. Called also *eruptive stage.* **s. frig′oris,** the cold stage of an intermittent fever. **s. incremen′ti,** the period of increase in the intensity of a disease; the stage of development of fever. **s. invasio′nis,** the incubative stage. **s. sudo′ris,** the sweating stage of a malarial paroxysm.

Staehelin's test (sta′ĕ-linz) [Rudolf *Staehelin,* Swiss clinician, 1875–1943]. See under *tests.*

staff (staf). 1. A wooden rod or a rodlike structure, especially when used as a symbol. 2. A grooved sound used as a guide for the knife in lithotomy. 3. The professional personnel of a hospital. **s. of Æsculapius,** a rod or staff with a snake entwined around it, which always appeared in the ancient representations of Æsculapius, the god of medicine. It is the symbol of medicine and is the official insignia of the American Medical Association. **attending s.,** the corps of attending physicians and surgeons of a hospital. **consulting s.,** the corps of physicians and surgeons attached to a hospital who do not visit regularly, but may be consulted by members of the attending staff. **house s.,** the resident physicians and surgeons of a hospital. **s. of Wrisberg,** an appearance seen in the normal larynx during examination with the laryngoscope.

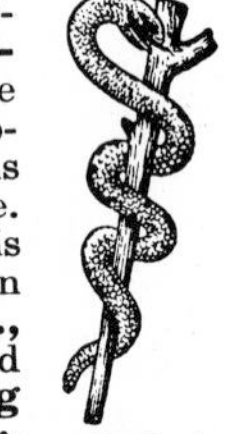

Staff of Æsculapius.

stage (stāj). 1. A period or distinct phase in the course of a disease, the life history of an organism, or any biological process. 2. The platform of a microscope on which a slide is placed for viewing of the specimen. **algid s.,** a condition characterized by a flickering pulse, subnormal temperature and varied nervous symptoms. **amphibolic s.,** the stage which intervenes between the acme and the decline of an attack. **asphyxial s.,** the preliminary stage of an attack of epidemic cholera: marked by cramps, severe pain, and great thirst. **cold s.,** the chill or rigor of a malarial attack. **defervescent s.,** stadium decrementi. **eruptive s.,** stadium fluorescentiae. **expulsive s.,** the stage of labor during which the child is being expelled from the uterus; the second stage of labor. **s. of fervescence,** pyrogenetic stage. **first s.** (of labor), the earliest stage of labor, ending with dilatation of the os uteri. **flexion s.,** the stage in labor in which the arm of the fetus presses against its breast. **fourth s.** (of labor), the period intervening between the end of the third stage of labor and occurrence of a satisfactory reaction of the mother to delivery. **hot s.,** the period of pyrexia in a malarial paroxysm. **incubative s.,** the early stage of an infectious disease, marked by the formation of toxins and the appearance of prodromal symptoms. **s. of invasion,** the time during which the system is coming under a morbific influence. **knäuel s.,** skein. **s. of latency,** the incubation period of any infectious disorder. **mechanical s.,** a platform of a microscope by which the specimen being viewed can be moved in either of two mutually perpendicular directions. **placental s.,** third s. **precystic s.,** the stage in the life cycle of an ameba in which it becomes nonmotile and secretes a wall about itself to become a cyst. **pre-eruptive s.,** the stage after infection and before eruption. **premenstrual s.,** the condition of the uterine mucosa after ovulation and the formation of a corpus luteum. **prodromal s.,** incubative stage. **progestational s.,** the secretory stage of the endometrial cycle immediately preceding menstruation or implantation of the embryo. **proliferative s.,** the phase of the uterine mucosa following the first stage of rest: the mucosa shows hypertrophy of the glands and increase of the lining epithelium. **pyretogenic s., pyrogenetic s.,** the stage of invasion of a febrile attack. **Ranke's s's,** in tuberculosis, (1) primary infection, usually in early growth; (2) generalized infection of the glands, joints, skin, also miliary tuberculosis; (3) chronic tuberculosis, chiefly of the lungs. **rest s.,** the stage of the uterine mucosa immediately following the completion of menstruation. **resting s.,** the stage of a cell or its nucleus when no mitotic changes are going on. **ring s.** See *signet ring,* under *ring.* **sauroid s.** See *sauroid cell,* under *cell.* **second s.** (of labor), period during which the infant is expelled from the uterus. **senile leukocyte s.,** the stage at which neutrophils have reached their maximum lobation. **stepladder s.,** an early stage of enteric fever: so called from the peculiar form of the temperature curve. **sweating s.,** the final stage of a malarial paroxysm, marked by sweating. **third s.** (of labor), the period following expulsion of the infant and ending with expulsion of the placenta and membranes from the uterus. **vegetative s.,** resting s. **zooglea s.,** the stage in the life history of a microorganism in which it forms zooglea.

staggers (stag′erz). 1. A functional and organic disease of the brain and cord of domestic animals, especially a disease of sheep caused by presence in the brain of *Coenurus cerebralis,* and marked by unsteadiness of gait. Called also *blind staggers, gid, sturdy, turnsick, turnsickness, leaping ill, thorter ill,* and *coenurosis.* 2. A form of vertigo occurring in decompression sickness. **blind s.** 1. See *staggers,* def. 1. 2. An acute form of selenium poisoning. **grass s.,** loco poisoning. **mad s.** See *staggers,* def. 1. **sleepy s., stomach s.,** a disease of horses, of unknown causation, but usually associated with the eating of moldy hay and grain. Called also *forage poisoning.*

stagnin (stag′nin). An extract derived from the spleen of horses by autolysis. It is a powerful styptic and hemostatic.

Stahl's ear (stahlz) [Friedrich Karl *Stahl,* German physician, 1811–1873]. See under *ear.*

Stahr's gland (stahrz) [Hermann *Stahr,* German anatomist and pathologist, born 1868]. A lymph gland situated on the facial artery.

stain (stān). 1. Any dye, reagent, or other material used in producing coloration, such as a substance used in coloring tissues or microorganisms for microscopical study. See *Table of Stains and Staining Methods* and names of specific compounds. 2. A superficial discoloration, or a colored spot on the skin. **acid s.,** a stain which is acid in reaction and more readily colors the protoplasm of cells. **after s.** See *after-stain.* **basic s.,** a stain which is basic in reaction and shows an affinity for the nuclei of cells. **contrast s.,** material used to color an unstained portion of a tissue after another portion has been stained with another dye. **counter s.** See *counter-stain.* **metachromatic s.,** a stain that colors certain cell constituents a color different from that of the stain itself. **neutral s.,** a combination of an acid and a basic stain for staining neutrophil tissues. **nuclear s.,** a stain which has a special affinity for the nuclei of cells. **plasmatic s., plasmic s.,** a stain which colors the tissue uniformly throughout. **port-wine s.,** nevus flammeus. **protoplasmic s.,** a stain which has a special affinity for the protoplasm of cells. **selective s.,** a stain which has a special affinity for a certain tissue element, staining it more vividly than, or to the exclusion of, other elements of the same specimen.

staining (stān′ing). The artificial coloration of a substance, such as the introduction or application of material to facilitate examination of tissues, microorganisms, or other cells under the microscope. For various methods, see *Table of Stains and Staining Methods.* **bipolar s.,** staining at the two poles only, or staining differently at the two poles. **differential s.,** staining with a substance for which different bacteria or different elements of the bacteria or specimen being stained show varying affinities, resulting in their differentiation. **double s.,** staining with two different dyes which have an affinity for different tissue elements. **fluorescent s.,** the coloration of tissues with a fluorescent dye. **intravital s.,** vital s. **multiple s.,** staining with several different dyes to facilitate identification of different tissue elements. **negative s.,** staining of the background and not the organism, to facilitate the microscopical study of bacteria. **polar s.,** staining in which the ends of the rod stain deeply while the central portion is nearly or quite unstained, as in the pasteurellas. **postvital s.,** staining that occurs after death of a tissue which has been previously stained by vital methods. **preagonal s.,** vital s. **simple s.,** staining with a single substance, such as the staining of microorganisms with a single dye. **substantive s.,** the coloration of tissues by direct absorption of dyes in which they are immersed. **supravital s.,** staining of living tissue removed from the body. **triple s.,** staining with three different dyes to facilitate identification of the different elements. **vital s.,** staining of a tissue by a dye which is introduced into a living organism and which, by virtue of elective attraction to certain tissues, will stain those tissues. Called also *intravital staining.*

TABLE OF STAINS AND STAINING METHODS

Listing some of the preparations and methods most commonly employed in histologic and pathologic technique (*arranged alphabetically*).

Achucárro's s.: A silver-tannin stain for impregnating connective tissue. **acid-fast s.:** A staining procedure for demonstrating acid-fast microorganisms. After being stained with carbolfuchsin, either hot or by prolonged (16–24 hour) exposure, the microorganisms resist decolorization with dilute acid and do not show the counterstain (usually methylene blue) that is taken up by the decolorized, non-acid-fast microorganisms and tissue elements. **acid fuchsin s.:** A diffuse stain containing acid fuchsin and diluted hydrochloric acid in purified water, for demonstrating axons. **Albert's diphtheria s.:** A stain containing toluidine blue and methyl (or malachite) green. Following treatment with iodine solution, the metachromatic granules appear black, the bars dark green to black, and the remainder of the diphtheria bacillus a light green. **alum-carmine s.:** A preparation of ordinary alum and carmine. **Alzheimer s.:** A methylene blue and eosin polychrome stain for demonstrating Negri bodies. **Anthony's capsule s.:** A method of staining the capsules of bacteria in which the microorganisms are heavily stained with acetic acid–crystal violet, followed by treatment with copper sulfate solution. The bacterial cells appear dark blue, and the capsules bluish violet. **azan s.:** Heidenhain's modification of Mallory's triple stain. **basic fuchsin s.:** A stain containing basic fuchsin in distilled water. **Benda's s.:** A method for demonstrating nerve tissue. **Bensley's neutral gentian orange G s.:** A preparation used for demonstrating secretion granules. **Best's carmine s.:** A stain for demonstrating glycogen. **Bethe's method:** A method of fixing methylene blue stains of nerve fibers. **Bielschowsky's s.:** An ammoniacal silver stain for demonstrating axons and neurofibrils. **Bodian method:** A method of staining nerve fibers and nerve endings with colloidal silver. **Cajal method:** A method of staining astrocytes by a gold chloride–mercuric chloride compound. **Cajal's double method:** A method of demonstrating ganglion cells. **carbolfuchsin s.:** A stain for microorganisms containing basic fuchsin and dilute phenol as a mordant. **carbol-gentian violet s.:** A solution containing gentian violet and carbolic acid. **Castaneda's s.:** A method of demonstrating rickettsiae. **Ciaccio's s.:** A stain for demonstrating lipoids. **Cox's modification of Golgi's corrosive sublimate method:** A method for staining ganglion cells. **Davenport's s.:** A stain for demonstrating various elements of nerve tissue, dependent upon the special affinity of nerve cells and their processes for silver. **Delafield's hematoxylin:** A preparation of hematoxylin, used as a nuclear stain. **Ehrlich's acid hematoxylin:** A preparation of hematoxylin, used as a nuclear stain. **Ehrlich's neutral s.:** A mixture of methylene blue and acid fuchsin, used to stain blood corpuscles. **Ehrlich's triacid s.:** A stain containing acid fuchsin, orange G, and methyl green; used for demonstrating various formed elements in the blood. **Feulgen method:** A method of demonstrating chromatin and deoxyribose nucleic acid. **Fontana's s.:** A method of staining spirochetes by silver impregnation, using ammoniacal silver nitrate solution. **Giemsa s.:** A solution containing azure II-eosin, azure II, glycerin, and methanol: used for staining protozoan parasites such as trypanosomes, Leishmania, etc., Leptospira, Borrelia, viral inclusion bodies, and Rickettsia. **Golgi's mixed method:** A method of staining nerve cells and all of their processes; historically of very great importance. **Gomori's s's:** Stains used for histological demonstration of enzymes, especially phosphatases and lipases in sections; also methods for demonstration of connective tissue fibers and secretion granules. **Goodpasture's s.:** A method for demonstrating the peroxidase reaction. **Gram's method,** or **gram s.:** An empirical staining procedure devised by Gram in which microorganisms are stained with crystal violet, treated with 1:15 dilution of Lugol's iodine, decolorized with ethanol or ethanol-acetone, and counterstained with a contrasting dye, usually safranin, Those microorganisms that retain the crystal violet stain are said to be gram-positive, and those that lose the crystal violet stain by decolorization but stain with the counterstain are said to be gram-negative. **Harris' hematoxylin:** A nuclear stain. **Harris' method:** A method for demonstrating Negri bodies. **Heidenhain's iron hematoxylin s.:** An important cytological method for the demonstration of most cellular structures: nuclei, chromosomes, centrioles, fibrils, mitochondria, cilia, etc. **hemalum s.:** A nuclear stain containing hematoxylin and alum, widely used, especially in combination with eosin. **hematoxylin-eosin s.:** A mixture of hematoxylin in distilled water and aqueous eosin solution, employed almost universally for routine examination of tissues. Numerous variations are employed in execution of the stain. **hematoxylin-eosin-azure II:** Maximow's method for the staining of blood-forming organs. **Hiss capsule s.:** A method of demonstrating bacterial capsules by mixing the bacterial suspension with India ink, drying and fixing, and staining with crystal violet or basic fuchsin. The bacterial cells are stained violet or red, and the capsules appear as unstained halos against the black background. **Hortega method:** A method of demonstrating microglia, employing ammoniacal silver carbonate. **iron hematoxylin method:** A staining procedure in which the sections are treated with an iron salt, stained with hematoxylin, and differentiated with the same iron salt. **Janus green B:** A stain used supravitally for the demonstration of mitochondria. **Jenner's method:** A method for demonstrating blood corpuscles. **Leishman's s.:** A mixture of methylene blue and eosin for staining blood cells and certain parasites. **Levaditi's method:** A method for demonstrating *Treponema pallidum* in sections, employing reduced silver. **lithium-carmine s.:** A diffuse stain used intravitally for the demonstration of macrophages. **Löffler's alkaline methylene blue:** Methylene blue solution made slightly alkaline with potassium hydroxide. **Löffler's flagella s.:** A staining procedure for the demonstration of bacterial flagella. The smear is fixed in ferric chloride–tannic acid solution, and stained with methylene blue–aniline (or carbol-) fuchsin. **Lorrain Smith s.:** Nile blue sulfate staining fatty acids blue and neutral fat pink. **Macchiavello's s.:** A rickettsial stain in which the heat-fixed smear is stained with basic fuchsin, decolorized in citric acid, and counterstained with methylene blue. Rickettsiae are stained red, and tissue components blue. The stain may also be used for the elementary bodies of viruses of the psittacosis-lymphogranuloma venereum group. **Mallory's acid fuchsin, orange G, and aniline blue s.:** A stain for demonstrating connective tissue and secretion granules. **Mallory's phosphotungstic acid–hematoxylin s.:** A stain used for demonstrating nuclear and cytoplasmic detail and connective tissue fibers. **Mallory's triple s.:** Mallory's acid fuchsin, orange G, and aniline blue s. **Marchi's method:** A method of demonstrating degenerated nerve fibers, the tissue first being fixed in a solution containing potassium bichromate, which prevents the normal myelinated fibers from staining with osmic acid. **Masson s.:** A trichrome stain for connective tissue. **Maximow's method:** Hematoxylin-eosin-azure II. **May's spore s.:** A method of staining the spores of bacteria in which they are treated with 5 per cent chromic acid, then with ammonia, stained with hot carbol-fuchsin, decolorized with dilute sulfuric acid, and counterstained with methylene blue. The spores appear red, and the vegetative cells blue. **May-Grünwald s.:** An alcoholic neutral mixture of methylene blue and eosin. **Mayer's hemalum:** An aqueous solution of hematein, alum, thymol, and 90 per cent alcohol. **Mayer's mucihematein:** A specific stain for mucus. **methyl green-pyronine s.:** Unna-Pappenheim s. **methyl violet s.:** An aniline dye used as a bacteriological stain. **methylene blue:** An aniline dye much used as a staining agent; prepared in a saturated solution (7 per cent) in absolute alcohol, which is diluted for use. **Michaelis' s.:** A mixture of alcoholic solution of methylene blue and a solution of eosin in acetone: used for demonstrating blood corpuscles. **Milligan's trichrome s.:** A differential stain for connective tissue and smooth muscle. Nuclei and muscle appear magenta; collagen appears green or blue, depending on whether fast green or aniline blue is used as a counter stain; and red blood cells appear orange to orange red. **neutral red:** An important supravital stain for the demonstration of vacuoles in cells, and especially of the vacuome. **Nissl's method:** A method employed in the study of nerve cell bodies. **Pal's modification of Weigert's myelin sheath s.:** A method for the study of myelinated nerves, the specimen being treated for several weeks in a solution containing potassium bichromate. **Papanicolaou's s.:** A method of staining smears of various body secretions, from the respiratory, digestive or genitourinary tract, for the examination of exfoliated cells, to detect the presence of a malignant process. **Pappenheim's s.:** A method for differentiating basophilic granules of erythrocytes and nuclear fragments. **Perdrau's method:** A modification of Bielschowsky's method for staining collagen and reticulin. **Perls' s.** See under *tests*. **peroxidase s.:** See Goodpasture's s. **phosphotungstic acid-hematoxylin s.** See *Mallory's phosphotungstic acid-hematoxylin s.* **polychrome methylene blue:** A stain for demonstrating plasma cells and mast cells, employing potassium carbonate and methylene blue. **Ranson's pyridine silver s.:** A stain used for demonstrating nerve cells and their processes. **Romanowsky's s.:** The prototype of the many eosin-methylene blue stains for blood smears and malarial parasites. **Shaeffer's spore s.:** A method of staining spores with hot malachite green, rinsing the stain out of the vegetative cells with water, and counterstaining with safranin. The spores appear bright green, and the vegetative cells pink. **spore s.:** A method of staining the spores of bacteria, usually with carbol-fuchsin or malachite green, heat being used to drive the stain into the spores, which later resist decolorization with ethanol or dilute acid. The preparation is usually counterstained with a dye of a contrasting color. **tetrachrome s.:** A stain combining eosin Y, methylene blue, azur A, and methylene violet, in methyl alcohol. **Unna's alkaline methylene blue:** A strongly alkaline solution of methylene blue which is valuable for staining plasma cells. **Unna-Pappenheim s.** A stain for plasma cells, employing methyl green and pyronine; also widely used for demonstrating nucleoproteins. **van Gieson's solution of trinitrophenol and acid fuchsin:** A stain for connective tissue, consisting of acid fuchsin and aqueous solution of trinitrophenol. **Verhoeff's s.:** A stain for demonstrating elastic tissue. **von Kossa's s.:** A silver nitrate stain for bone mineral. **Weigert's fibrin s.:** A method, many variations of which have been used in both fixation and staining; stains gram-positive bacteria as well as fibrin. **Weigert's iron hematoxylin s.:** A simple method for staining most nuclear and cytoplasmic constituents. **Weigert's myelin sheath m.:** A method of demonstrating the myelin sheath of nerve cell processes. **Weigert's neuroglia fiber s.:** A complicated method for demonstrating fibrous glia, which works best on human material. **Weigert's resorcin-fuchsin s.:** A method for the demonstration of elastic fibers. **Weil's s.:** A method for staining myelin sheaths. **Wright's s.:** A mixture of eosin and methylene blue, used for demonstrating blood corpuscles and malarial parasites. **Ziehl's carbol-fuchsin s.** See *carbol-fuchsin s.* **Ziehl-Neelsen s.** See *acid-fast s.* **Ziehl-Neelsen carbol-fuchsin:** A mixture of basic fuchsin, alcohol, liquefied phenol and purified water.

---

staitinodermia (sti″tĭ-no-der′me-ah) [Gr. *staitinos* doughy + *derma* skin + *-ia*]. A doughy or rubbery condition of the skin.

stalactite (stah-lak′tīt). A long filamentous formation which hangs down from the surface of a broth culture of *Pasteurella pestis* into the liquid below.

stalagmometer (stal″ag-mom′e-ter) [Gr. *stalagmos* dropping + *metron* measure]. An instrument for measuring surface tension by determining the exact number of drops in a given quantity of a liquid. See *miostagmin reaction,* under *reaction.*

stalagmon (stah-lag′mon). A colloidal substance which changes the surface tension of a liquid containing it.

staling (stāl′ing). Urination in cattle and horses.

stalk (stawk). An elongated, more or less slender anatomical structure resembling the stalk of a plant. **abdominal s.,** the umbilical cord. **allantoic s.,** the more slender tube, interposed in most mammals between the urogenital sinus and the allantoic sac. **belly s.,** the umbilical cord. **body s.,** a bridge of mesoderm connecting the caudal end of the young embryo with the chorion and eventually giving passage to the allantois with its important accompanying blood vessels. **cerebellar s.,** any one of the cerebellar peduncles. **hypophyseal s.,** the structure through which the hypophysis cerebri receives nerve fibers from the hypothalamus. **optic s.,** a slender structure attaching the optic vesicle to the brain wall in the early embryo. **yolk s.,** the vitelline duct.

stamen (sta′men). The structure of a flower which bears the male gamete, or pollen.

stamina (stam′ĭ-nah) [L.]. Vigor or endurance.

stammering (stam′er-ing). Stuttering.

Stamnosoma (stam″no-so′mah) [Gr. *stamnos* jar + *sōma* body]. A genus of flukes. *S. arma′tum* and *S. formosa′num* have been found in man.

standard (stan′dard). Something established as a measure or model to which other similar things should conform. **Pignet's s.** See *Pignet's formula,* under *formula.*

standardization (stan″dard-i-za′shun). 1. The bringing of any preparation to a specified standard as to quality or ingredients. 2. The formulation of standards for a substance or for a procedure.

standardize (stan′dard-īz). To compare with or conform to a standard; to establish standards.

standstill (stand′stil). A quiet state resulting from the suspension of activity or movement. **atrial s.,** cessation of contraction of the atria of the heart. **auricular s.,** atrial s. **cardiac s.,** cessation of contraction of the myocardium. See also *cardioplegia.* **respiratory s.,** suspension of the movements of respiration; termed *expiratory s.* when it occurs at the end of an expiration, and *inspiratory s.* when it occurs at the end of an inspiration. **ventricular s.,** cessation of contraction of the ventricles of the heart.

Stanley bacillus (stan′le) [*Stanley,* England]. A type of Salmonella isolated from cases of food poisoning occurring there.

stannate (stan′āt). Any salt of stannic acid.

stannic (stan′ik). Containing tin as a quadrivalent element. **s. chloride,** an irritant war smoke, $SnCl_4$.

stanniferous (stan-nif′er-us) [L. *stannum* tin + *ferre* to bear]. Containing tin.

Stannius' ligature (stan′e-us) [Herman Friedrich *Stannius*, German biologist, 1808–1883]. See under *ligature.*

stannous (stan′us). Containing tin as a bivalent element.

stanolone (stan′o-lōn). Chemical name: 17β-hydroxy-3-androstanone: used as an androgenic substance.

stanozolol (stan′o-zo-lol). A steroid compound with marked anabolic but weak androgenic activity, 17β-hydroxy-17α-methylandrostano[3,2-c]pyrazole: used to improve appetite and promote gain in weight.

stapedectomy (sta″pe-dek′to-me) [L. *stapes* stirrup + Gr. *ektomē* excision]. Excision of the stapes.

stapedial (stah-pe′de-al). Pertaining to the stapes.

stapediolysis (stah-pe″de-ol′ĭ-sis). Mobilization of the stapes in the surgical treatment of otosclerosis.

stapedioplasty (stah-pe″de-o-plas′te). Replacement of the stapes with other material (wire, bone, or plastic) in correction of defective hearing resulting from otosclerosis, the prosthesis serving to conduct the sound waves from the incus to the oval window (fenestra vestibuli).

stapediotenotomy (stah-pe″de-o-te-not′o-me). The cutting of the tendon of the stapedius muscle.

stapediovestibular (stah-pe″de-o-ves-tib′u-lar). Pertaining to the stapes and vestibule.

stapes (sta′pēz) [L. "stirrup"]. [N A, B N A] The innermost of the auditory ossicles, shaped somewhat like a stirrup. It articulates by its head with the incus, and its base is inserted into the fenestra vestibuli. Called also *stirrup.*

Staph (staf). Abbreviation for *Staphylococcus.*

staphcillin (staf-sil′lin). Trade mark for a preparation of dimethoxyphenyl penicillin sodium.

staphisagria (staf″ĭ-sa′gre-ah) [Gr. *staphis* raisin + *agrios* wild]. The poisonous seeds of *Delphinium staphisagria*, stavesacre, or lousewort. The plant and its seeds are poisonous and narcotic. The seed is sometimes employed as a vermifuge, but mainly for destroying lice.

staphisagrine (staf″ĭ-sa′grin). A poisonous alkaloid, $C_{22}H_{33}NO_5$, from staphisagria.

staphyl-. See *staphylo-.*

staphylagra (staf″ĭ-la′grah) [*staphyl-* + Gr. *agra* a way of catching]. A forceps for holding the uvula.

staphylectomy (staf″ĭ-lek′to-me) [*staphyl-* + Gr. *ektomē* excision]. Uvulectomy; excision of the uvula.

staphyledema (staf″il-e-de′mah) [*staphyl* + Gr. *oidēma* swelling]. An enlargement or swollen state of the uvula.

staphylematoma (staf″il-em″ah-to′mah). Hemorrhage from the uvula (Pauli).

staphylin (staf′ĭ-lin). A lysogenic substance produced by active strains of staphylococci which prevents the growth of *Corynebacterium diphtheriae.*

staphyline (staf′ĭ-līn). 1. Shaped like a bunch of grapes. 2. Pertaining to the uvula.

staphylinus (staf″ĭ-li′nus) [L.]. Pertaining to the uvula.

staphylion (stah-fil′e-on) [Gr. "little grape"]. 1. An encephalometric landmark on the posterior edge of the hard palate at the median line. 2. The uvula. 3. A nipple or teat.

staphylitis (staf″ĭ-li′tis). Inflammation of the uvula.

staphylo-, staphyl- (staf′ĭ-lo, staf′il) [Gr. *staphylē* a bunch of grapes]. Combining form denoting resemblance to a bunch of grapes, used especially to denote relationship to the uvula.

staphyloangina (staf″ĭ-lo-an′jĭ-nah). A mild form of sore throat, marked by a pseudomembranous deposit in the throat due to a staphylococcus.

staphylobacterin (staf″ĭ-lo-bak′ter-in). A bacterial vaccine prepared from staphylococci.

staphylocide (staf″ĭ-lo-sīd). Staphylococcide.

staphylocoagulase (staf″ĭ-lo-ko-ag′u-lās). A coagulase produced by staphylococci which is important in the initiation of staphylococcic infections.

staphylococcal (staf″ĭ-lo-kok′al). Pertaining to or caused by staphylococci.

staphylococcemia (staf″ĭ-lo-kok-se′me-ah) [*staphylococcus* + Gr. *haima* blood + *-ia*]. A condition characterized by the presence of staphylococci in the blood.

staphylococci (staf″ĭ-lo-kok′si). Plural of *staphylococcus.*

staphylococcia (staf″ĭ-lo-kok′se-ah). 1. Skin suppuration due to a staphylococcus. 2. A secondary infection with a staphylococcus.

staphylococcic (staf″ĭ-lo-kok′sik). Pertaining to or caused by staphylococci.

staphylococcide (staf″ĭ-lo-kok′sīd). An agent that is destructive to staphylococci.

Staphylococcus (staf″ĭ-lo-kok′kus) [Gr. *staphylē* bunch of grapes + *kokkus* berry]. A genus of microorganisms of the family Micrococcaceae, order Eubacteriales. **S. au′reus,** a species comprising the pigmented, coagulase-positive, mannitol-fermenting pathogenic form. **S. epider′midis,** a species made up of non-pigmented, coagulase-negative, mannitol-negative non-pathogenic microorganisms commonly found on the skin.

staphylococcus (staf″ĭ-lo-kok′us), pl. *staphylococ′ci.* 1. A spherical bacterium occurring predominantly in irregular masses of cells as a consequence of failure of the daughter cells to separate following cell division in more than one plane. 2. An organism of the genus *Staphylococcus.*

staphyloderma (staf″ĭ-lo-der′ma). Cutaneous pyogenic infection by staphylococci.

staphylodermatitis (staf″ĭ-lo-der″mah-ti′tis). Inflammation of the skin due to staphylococci.

staphylodialysis (staf″ĭ-lo-di-al′ĭ-sis) [*staphylo-* + Gr. *dialysis* loosing]. Relaxation of the uvula.

staphyloedema (staf″ĭ-lo-e-de′mah). Staphyledema.

staphylohemia (staf″ĭ-lo-he′me-ah) [*staphylo-* + Gr. *haima* blood + *-ia*]. The presence of staphylococci in the blood.

staphylokinase (staf″ĭ-lo-ki′nās). A bacterial kinase produced by certain strains of staphylococci, which is capable of activating plasminogen in the blood of various species of animals.

staphyloleukocidin (staf″ĭ-lo-lu″ko-si′din). A toxin from staphylococcus cultures that is destructive to leukocytes.

staphylolysin (staf″ĭ-lol′ĭ-sin). A principle with hemolytic activity produced by staphylococci. **α s., alpha s.,** a hemolysin produced by pathogenic staphylococci which lyses both sheep and rabbit erythrocytes at 37°C. and has leukocidin activity. **β s., beta s.,** a hot-cold hemolysin produced by staphylococci which lyses sheep but not rabbit erythrocytes in the cold following preliminary incubation at 37°C. **δ s., delta s.,** a hemolysin produced by pyogenic staphylococci which lyses red cells from man, monkey, horse, rat, mouse, and guinea pig, as well as from sheep and rabbit; it differs immunologically from the α and β staphylolysins, and in purified preparation is both dermonecrotic and lethal. **ε s., epsilon s.,** a hemolysin formed almost exclusively by nonpathogenic, coagulase-negative strains of staphylococci. **γ s., gamma s.,** a hemolysin produced by staphylococci which is similar to the α staphylolysin but is serologically distinguishable from it.

staphyloma (staf″ĭ-lo′mah) [Gr. *staphylōma* a defect in the eye inside the cornea]. Protrusion of the cornea or sclera, resulting from inflammation. **annular s.** 1. A staphyloma surrounded by an atrophic choroid coat. 2. Staphyloma of the sclera in the ciliary region, extending around the margin of the cornea. **anterior s.,** scleral staphyloma in the anterior part of the eye; keratoglobus. **ciliary s.,** scleral staphyloma in the part covered by the ciliary body. **s. cor′neae.** 1. Protrusion of the cornea, caused by the cornea losing its transparency and projecting beyond the eyelid. Called also *conical cornea, prolapsus corneae,* and *projecting staphyloma.* 2. Staphyloma formed by an iris which has protruded through a wound in the cornea. **s. cor′neae racemo′sum,** staphyloma corneae (2) in which there are a number of perforations from which small portions of iris protrude. **equatorial s.,** scleral staphyloma occurring in the equatorial region of the eye. **intercalary s.,** that which occurs in the rim of sclera anterior to the insertion of the ciliary body. **posterior s., s. posti′cum,** the backward bulging of the sclera at the posterior pole of the eye. **projecting s.,** s. corneae. **retinal s.,** a forward bulging of the retina. **Scarpa's s.,** posterior staphyloma. **scleral s.,** protrusion of the contents of the eyeball at a point where the sclera has become too thin. **uveal s.,** protrusion of the uvea through a ruptured sclera.

staphylomatous (staf″ĭ-lom′ah-tus). Pertaining to or resembling staphyloma.

staphylomycosis (staf″ĭ-lo-mi-ko′sis) [*staphylo-* + Gr. *mykēs* fungus + *-osis*]. Any systemic disorder due to staphylococci; staphylococcus infection.

staphyloncus (staf″ĭ-long′kus) [*staphylo-* + Gr. *onkos* mass]. A tumor or swelling of the uvula.

staphylopharyngorrhaphy (staf″ĭ-lo-far″in-gor′ah-fe) [*staphylo-* + Gr. *pharynx* pharynx + *rhaphē* suture]. The stitiching of the halves of the velum palatini to the posterior wall of the pharynx.

staphyloplasmin (staf″ĭ-lo-plaz′min). A poison produced in the organism of a staphylococcus, producing suppuration.

staphyloplasty (staf′ĭ-lo-plas″te) [*staphylo-* + Gr. *plassein* to mold]. Plastic surgery of the uvula.

staphyloptosia (staf″ĭ-lop-to′se-ah) [*staphylo-* + Gr. *ptōsis* falling + *-ia*]. Elongation of the uvula.

staphyloptosis (staf″ĭ-lop-to′sis). Staphyloptosia.

staphylorrhaphy (staf″ĭ-lor′ah-fe) [*staphylo-* + Gr. *rhaphē* suture]. Suturation of a fissure of the soft palate and uvula.

staphyloschisis (staf″ĭ-los′kĭ-sis) [*staphylo-* + Gr. *schisis* splitting]. Fissure of the uvula and soft palate.

staphylostreptococcia (staf″ĭ-lo-strep″to-kok′-se-ah). A secondary pyogenic infection with a staphyloloccus and a streptococcus.

staphylotome (staf′ĭ-lo-tōm) [Gr. *staphylotomon*]. A knife for cutting the uvula.

staphylotomy (staf″ĭ-lot′o-me) [*staphylo-* + Gr. *tomē* a cutting]. 1. Incision of the uvula. 2. The removal of a staphyloma by cutting.

staphylotoxin (staf″ĭ-lo-tok′sin). A toxin occurring in cultures of staphylococci.

staphylotropic (staf″ĭ-lo-trop′ik). Having a selective affinity for staphylococci.

star (star). Any structure with an appearance like that of a star. **daughter s.** See *diaster.* **dental s.,** a marking on the incisor teeth of horses, first appearing in the lower central incisors at about the age of eight years: used in judging a horse's age. **lens s's,** starlike lines formed within the lens of the eye by fibers which pass from the anterior to the posterior surface. **mother s.,** monaster. **polar s's,** the starlike figures of the diaster. **s's of Verheyen,** venae stellatae renis. **Winslow's s's,** whorls of capillary vessels from which arise the vorticose veins of the choroid coat of the eye.

starch (starch) [L. *amylum*]. A polysaccharide from various plant tissues, having the formula $(C_6H_{10}O_5)_n$. A pharmaceutical preparation consisting of granules separated from the mature grain of *Zea mays* is used as a dusting powder. **animal s.,** glycogen. **cassava s.,** the starch from *Manihot utilissima* and *M. aipi.* **corn s.,** a starch from maize. **iodized s.,** starch that has been treated with iodine, of which it contains 5 per cent: alterative and antidotal. **lichen s., moss s.,** lichenin. **sago s.,** starch from the sago palm. **soluble s.,** the first stage in the hydrolysis of starch.

stare (stār). A fixed, unblinking gaze. **postbasic s.,** a peculiar expression of the eyes in posterior basic meningitis due to downward rolling of the eyeball and retraction of the upper lid.

Starling's hypothesis, law (star′lingz) [Ernest Henry *Starling,* English physiologist, 1866–1927]. See under *hypothesis* and *law.*

starter (star′ter). A culture of microorganisms used to initiate fermentation, as in dairy products.

Startin's bandage, mixture (star′tinz) [James *Startin,* London dermatologist, 1851–1910]. See under *bandage* and *mixture.*

starvation (star-va′shun). Long-continued deprival of food.

stasibasiphobia (stas″ĭ-bas″ĭ-fo′be-ah) [Gr. *stasis* standing + *basis* step + *phobein* to be affrighted by]. Morbid distrust of one's ability to stand or walk.

stasidynic (stas″ĭ-din′ik) [Gr. *stasis* standing + *dynasthai* to be able]. Unaffected by either oxidation or reduction.

stasimetry (stas-im′e-tre). The measurement of the consistency of soft bodies.

stasimorphia (stas″ĭ-mor′fe-ah). Stasimorphy.

stasimorphy (stas″ĭ-mor′fe) [Gr. *stasis* standing + *morphē* form]. Deformity or abnormality of shape in any organ, due to arrest of development.

stasiphobia (stas″ĭ-fo′be-ah) [Gr. *stasis* standing + *phobein* to be affrighted by]. Morbid dread of standing erect.

stasis (sta′sis) [Gr. *stasis* a standing still]. A stoppage of the flow of blood or other body fluid in any part. **diffusion s.,** stasis in which there is diffusion of lymph or serum. **foot s.,** trench foot. **ileal s.,** abnormal delay in the passage of the intestinal contents through the ileum; it is usually due to dilatation of the ileum. **intestinal s.,** a condition of intestinal atony, frequently with visceral ptosis, intestinal kinks, bands, or adhesions, resulting in constipation, auto-intoxication, neurasthenia, etc. **papillary s.,** choked disk. **pressure s.,** stoppage of the circulation caused by undue pressure on a part. **urinary s.,** stoppage of the flow or discharge of urine, which may occur at any level of the urinary tract. **venous s.,** venous insufficiency.

stasobasiphobia (stas″o-bas″ĭ-fo′be-ah). Stasibasiphobia.

stasophobia (stas″o-fo′be-ah). Stasiphobia.

Stas-Otto method (stahs-ot′o) [Jean Servais *Stas,* a Belgian chemist, 1813–1891]. A method of separating alkaloids and similar amino compounds.

Stat. Abbreviation for L. *sta′tim,* immediately.

stat. The German unit for measuring the amount of radium emanation: it is equivalent to 0.364 microcurie.

state (stāt) [L. *status*]. 1. Condition or situation; status. 2. The crisis, or the turning point of an attack of disease. **anelectrotonic s.,** the condition which obtains in a nerve near the anode during the passage of a continuous current. **anxiety tension s.,** neuromuscular hypertension. **anxious s.,** a state of fear with no particular object as in panophobia. **catelectrotonic s.,** the condition of a nerve near the cathode during the passage of an electric current. **central excitatory s.,** a condition in which there is stored up in a reflex center of the cord a number of stimuli which do not reveal themselves in reflex response.

constitutional psychopathic s., inability to adjust to ordinary social and environmental conditions, as indicated by disorders of conduct, in the absence of any other recognized mental disease. **correlated s.,** dynamic equilibrium. **dream s.,** a state of defective consciousness in which the environment is imperfectly perceived. **epileptic s.,** status epilepticus. **hypnagogic s.,** that state of semiconsciousness which immediately precedes falling asleep. **hypnoidal s.,** a condition in which portions of unrecognized past experience come up into consciousness from the subconscious life. **hypnoidic s.,** a state in which more or less connected experiences of the past come up into consciousness from the subconscious state. **hypnoleptic s.,** a state occurring between two experiences of double personality. **hypnopompic s.,** that state of semiconsciousness which immediately precedes complete awakening from sleep. **local excitatory s.,** the condition of a nerve produced by an ineffectual stimulus. **marble s.,** a change in the corpus striatum consisting in the appearance of myelin fibers where normally ganglion cells are found. **plastic s., pluripotent s.,** the state of parts of the zygote or early embryo in which they may develop into any adult tissue or part. **refractory s.,** a condition of subnormal excitability of muscle and nerve following excitation. **resting s.,** the physiological condition achieved by complete bed rest for a period of at least one hour, a condition required in a number of different tests of various body functions. **steady s.,** dynamic equilibrium. **twilight s.,** a temporary absence of consciousness in which the patient may perform certain acts involuntarily and without remembrance of them afterward. **typhoid s.,** a condition of great muscular weakness and stupor, with dry, brown tongue, sordes on the teeth, muttering delirium, feeble pulse, involuntary discharge of feces and urine: seen in certain wasting diseases, as typhoid and other fevers.

static (stat′ik) [L. *staticus;* Gr. *statikos*]. 1. At rest; in equilibrium; not in motion. 2. Not dynamic.

statics (stat′iks). That phase of mechanics which deals with the action of forces and systems of forces on bodies at rest.

statim (sta′tim) [L.]. Immediately, at once. Abbreviated *stat.*

station (sta′shun) [L. *statio,* from *stare* to stand still]. 1. The position assumed in standing; the manner of standing; in ataxic conditions it is sometimes pathognomonic. See *attitude.* 2. A specified site to which wounded soldiers are brought. **aid s.,** a place for assembling and collecting the wounded in battle for their evacuation to the rear. **dressing s.,** a sheltered temporary retreat for soldiers wounded in battle who have been collected on the field by the litter bearers and brought in from the aid station. **hospital s.,** a station attached to an army division to which patients are brought from aid stations. **rest s.,** a place for temporary relief of sick and wounded transported by hospital trains or ambulances located at definite points on a military road or railway. **Romberg s.,** the position assumed by the patient when the Romberg sign is being sought, i.e., standing upright with the feet close together.

stationary (sta′shun-er″e) [L. *stationarius*]. Not subject to variations or to changes of place.

statistics (stah-tis′tiks). Numerical facts pertaining to a body of things; also the science which deals with the collection and tabulation of such facts. **vital s.,** that branch of biometry which deals with the data and laws of human mortality, morbidity, natality, and demography; called also *biostatistics.*

statoconia (stat″o-ko′ne-ah) [Gr. *statos* standing + *konos* dust] (pl.). [N A] Minute calciferous granules within the gelatinous statoconic membrane surmounting the maculae. Called also *otoconia* [B N A].

statocyst (stat′o-sist) [Gr. *statos* standing + *kystis* sac, bladder]. One of the sacs of the labyrinth to which is attributed an influence in the maintenance of static equilibrium.

statolith (stat′o-lith). One of the granules constituting the otoconia.

statometer (stah-tom′e-ter) [Gr. *statos* standing + *metron* measure]. An apparatus for measuring the degree of exophthalmos.

statosphere (stat′o-sfēr). Centrosphere.

statural (stat′u-ral). Pertaining to stature.

stature (stat′ūr) [L. *statura*]. The height or tallness of a person standing.

status (sta′tus) [L.]. State or condition. **s. angino′sus,** a condition resembling angina due to paroxysmal tachycardia but without coronary thrombosis. **s. arthrit′icus,** the gouty diathesis; predisposition to gout. **s. asthmat′icus,** asthmatic crisis; asthmatic shock; a sudden intense and continuous aggravation of a state of asthma, marked by dyspnea to the point of exhaustion and collapse. **s. calcif′ames,** calcium hunger. **s. cholera′icus,** a state occurring in the algid stage of cholera, characterized by a dull countenance, weak pulse and cold skin. **s. chore′icus,** a severe and persistent form of chorea. **s. convul′sivus,** a condition marked by a series of convulsions following one after the other. **s. criba′lis, s. cribro′sus,** a sievelike condition of the brain due to dilatation of the perivascular lymph spaces. **s. crit′icus,** a severe and persistent form of tabetic crises. **s. degenerati′vus,** a condition characterized by the presence of an unusual number of degenerative stigmata in a single individual. **s. dysgraph′icus,** dysgraphia. **s. dysmyelina′tus, s. dysmyelinisa′tus,** a condition marked by reduction in number of the myelin sheaths of the globus pallidus and substantia nigra with accumulations of iron pigment. Seen in children, the condition is marked by rigidity of the lower extremities and increasing mental deficiency. Called also *Hallervorden-Spatz syndrome.* **s. dysraph′icus,** faulty closure of the neural tube resulting in faulty formation of midline adult structures, such as the spine, sternum, breasts and palate. **s. epilep′ticus,** a series of rapidly repeated epileptic convulsions without any periods of consciousness between them. **s. gas′tricus,** a disordered state of the stomach: gastric indigestion. **s. hemicra′nicus,** a state marked by constantly recurring attacks of migraine. **s. lacuna′ris, s. lacuno′sus,** a condition of the brain marked by numerous small infarcts or losses of substance. **s. lymphat′icus,** lymphatism. **s. marmora′tus,** a condition marked by excessive myelinization of the nerve fibers of the corpus striatum, with spasticity, hyperkinesis, and choreatic movements. Called also *Little's disease, Vogt's disease* and *état marbré.* **s. nervo′sus,** the typhoid state. **s. parathyreopri′vus,** a condition due to absence of parathyroid. **petit mal s.,** a state of mental confusion lasting for minutes or hours, and distinguished by nearly continuous dart-dome discharges of the electroencephalogram. **s. prae′sens,** the condition of a patient at the time of observation. **s. rap′tus,** a condition of ecstasy. **s. spongio′sus,** extensive vacuolization of the cerebral cortex. **s. thymicolymphat′icus,** a condition resembling lymphatism, with enlargement of the lymphadenoid tissue generally and with enlargement of the thymus as the special influencing factor. **s. thy′micus,** lymphatism. **s. typho′sus,** the typhoid state. **s. verruco′sus,** a wartlike appearance of the cerebral cortex. **s. vertigino′sus,** a prolonged condition of vertigo.

statuvolence (stat-u′vo-lens) [L. *status* state + *volens* willing]. A voluntary, self-induced state of hypnotism.

statuvolent (stat-u′vo-lent). Affected with or able to enter a condition of statuvolence.

statuvolic (stat″u-vol′ik). Statuvolent.

statuvolism (stat-u′vo-lizm). Statuvolence.

Staub-Traugott effect, test (stawb-traw′got) [Hans *Staub*, Swiss (Basel) internist, born 1890; Carl *Traugott*, Frankfort internist, born 1885]. See under *effect.*

staurion (staw′re-on) [Gr., dim. of *stauros* cross]. A point at the crossing of the median and transverse palatine sutures.

stauroplegia (staw″ro-ple′je-ah) [Gr. *stauros* cross + *plēgē* stroke]. Crossed hemiplegia.

stavesacre (stāvz′a-ker). Staphisagria.

staxis (stak′sis) [Gr. "a dripping"]. Hemorrhage.

stay (sta). A narrow structure that gives support, such as the bar of a horse's hoof. **s. of white line,** adminiculum lineae albae.

STD. Abbreviation for *skin test dose.*

steapsin (ste-ap′sin) [Gr. *stear* fat + *pepsis* digestion]. The lipase of the pancreatic juice.

steapsinogen (ste″ap-sin′o-jen). A proenzyme of steapsin.

stearate (ste′ah-rāt). Any compound of stearic acid.

stearentin (ste′ah-ren″tin) [Gr. *stear* fat + *enteron* intestine]. Greenish sebaceous matter occurring in feces of suckling infants.

steariform (ste-ar′ĭ-form). Fatlike.

stearin (ste′ah-rin). A white, crystalline fat, glyceryl tristearate, $C_3H_5(C_{18}H_{35}O_2)_3$, found in the harder fats, such as tallow.

Stearns's alcoholic amentia (sternz) [A. Warren *Stearns*, American physician, 1885–1959]. See under *amentia.*

stearo-, steato- (ste′ah-ro, ste′ah-to) [Gr. *stear*, *steatos* fat]. Combining forms denoting relationship to fat.

stearoconotum (ste″ah-ro-ko-no′tum) [*stearo-* + Gr. *konis* dust or powder]. A yellow, pulverulent fat found in the brain mass.

stearodermia (ste″ah-ro-der′me-ah) [*stearo-* + Gr. *derma* skin + *-ia*]. A disease of the skin involving the sebaceous glands.

stearopten (ste″ah-rop′ten) [*stearo-* + Gr. *ptēnos* volatile]. A camphor; the more solid substance which, combined with an eleopten, constitutes a typical volatile oil.

stearrhea (ste″ah-re′ah) [*stearo-* + Gr. *rhoia* flow]. Steatorrhea.

steatadenoma (ste-at″ad-e-no′mah). Adenoma of the sebaceous glands.

steatite (ste′ah-tit). Talcum.

steatitis (ste″ah-ti′tis) [*steato-* + *-itis*]. Inflammation of adipose tissue.

steato- (ste′ah-to). See *stearo-.*

steatocele (ste-at′o-sēl) [*steato-* + Gr. *kēlē* tumor]. A fatty mass formed within the scrotum.

steatocryptosis (ste″ah-to-krip-to′sis) [*steato-* + Gr. *kryptos* concealed]. Disorder of the function of the sebaceous glands.

steatocystoma (ste″ah-to-sis-to′mah). A sebaceous cyst. **s. mul′tiplex,** steatomatosis.

steatogenous (ste″ah-toj′e-nus) [*steato-* + Gr. *gennan* to produce]. Producing fat.

steatolysis (ste″ah-tol′ĭ-sis) [*steato-* + Gr. *lysis* dissolution]. The emulsifying process fats undergo preparatory to absorption.

steatolytic (ste″ah-to-lit′ik). Pertaining to, characterized by, or promoting steatolysis.

steatoma (ste″ah-to′mah), pl. *steato′mata* or *steatomas.* 1. A sebaceous cyst. 2. Lipoma.

steatomatosis (ste″ah-to-mah-to′sis). The presence of numerous sebaceous cysts.

steatomery (ste″ah-tom′er-e) [*steato-* + Gr. *meros* part]. A deposit of fat on the outer aspect of the thighs and buttocks.

steatomosis (ste″ah-to-mo′sis). Steatomatosis.

steatonecrosis (ste″ah-to-ne-kro′sis). Fatty necrosis.

steatopathy (ste″ah-top′ah-the) [*steato-* + Gr. *pathos* disease]. Disease of the sebaceous glands.

steatopygia (ste″ah-to-pij′e-ah) [*steato-* + Gr. *pygē* buttock + *-ia*]. Excessive fatness of the buttocks; Hottentot bustle.

steatopygous (ste″ah-top′ĭ-gus). Pertaining to or characterized by steatopygia.

steatorrhea (ste″ah-to-re′ah) [*steato-* + Gr. *rhoia* a flow]. The excessive loss of fats in the feces. **idiopathic s.,** Thaysen's name for a condition probably identical with sprue.

steatosis (ste″ah-to′sis). 1. Fatty degeneration. 2. Disease of the sebaceous glands. **s. cardi′aca,** cardiomyoliposis. **cholesterin s.,** a form of xanthoma in which the lipid in the foam cells is cholesterol.

steatotrochanteria (ste″ah-to-tro″kan-te′re-ah). Steatomery.

steatozoon (ste″ah-to-zo′on) [*steato-* + Gr. *zōon* animal]. *Demodex folliculorum.*

stechiology (stek″e-ol′o-je). Stoichiology.

stechiometry (stek″e-om′e-tre). Stoichiometry.

steclin (stek′lin). Trade mark for preparations of tetracycline hydrochloride.

Steell's murmur (stēlz) [Graham *Steell*, English physician, 1851–1942]. See under *murmur.*

Steenbock unit (stēn′bok) [Harry *Steenbock*, American biochemist, born 1886]. See under *unit.*

stege (ste′je) [Gr. *stegos* roof]. The internal layer of the rods of Corti.

stegnosis (steg-no′sis) [Gr. *stegnōsis* obstruction]. Constriction; stenosis.

stegnotic (steg-not′ik). Pertaining to, characterized by, or promoting stegnosis; astringent.

Stegomyia (steg″o-mi′yah) [Gr. *stegos* roof + *myia* fly]. A subgenus of mosquitoes. *S. argen′teus, S. cal′opus* and *S. fascia′tus* are old names for *Aedes aegypti.*

Stein's test (stīnz) [Stanislav Aleksandr Fyodorovich von *Stein*, Russian otologist, born 1855]. See under *tests.*

Stein-Leventhal syndrome (stīn-lev′en-thal) [Irving F. *Stein*, Sr., American gynecologist, born 1887; Michael L. *Leventhal*, American obstetrician and gynecologist, born 1901]. See under *syndrome.*

Steinach's method, operation (sti′nahks) [Eugen *Steinach*, Austrian physician, 1861–1944]. See under *operation.*

Steiner's tumors (sti′nerz) [Gabriel *Steiner*, German neurologist, born 1883]. Jeanselme's nodules.

Steinmann's extension, pin (stīn′manz) [Fritz *Steinmann*, Bern surgeon, 1872–1932]. See *nail extension,* under *extension.*

stelazine (stel′ah-zēn). Trade mark for preparations of trifluoperazine.

stella (stel′ah), pl. *stel′lae* [L.]. Star. **s. len′tis hyaloi′dea,** the posterior pole of the crystalline lens. **s. len′tis irid′ica,** the anterior pole of the crystalline lens.

Stellaria (stel-la′re-ah). A genus of caryophyllaceous plants: the chickweeds. *S. holos′tea* and *S. me′dia* were formerly used as demulcent medicines.

stellate (stel′āt) [L. *stellatus*]. Shaped like a star; arranged in a roset, or in rosets.

stellectomy (stel-lek′to-me). The operation of dividing the cervical sympathetic cord above the stellate ganglion: done for the relief of angina pectoris.

stellite (stel′it). A very hard, noncorrosive alloy of cobalt, chromium, and tungsten used for surgical instruments.

stellreflexe (stel″re-flek′sě) [Ger.]. A postural reflex.

stellula (stel′u-lah), pl. *stel′lulae* [L., dim. of *stella*]. Little star. **stel′lulae vasculo′sae winslow′ii,** Winslow's stars. **stel′lulae verhey′enii,** venae stellatae renis.

stellulae (stel′u-le) [L.]. Plural of *stellula.*

Stellwag's sign (stel′vagz) [Carl *Stellwag* von Carion, Austrian oculist, 1823–1904]. See under *sign.*

stem (stem). A supporting structure comparable to the stalk or stem of a plant. **brain s.,** all of the brain except the cerebellum, the cerebrum, and the white matter connected with them: it includes the motor and sensory tracts and the cranial nerve nuclei. Called also *segmental apparatus* and *brain axis.*

Stender dish (sten′der) [Wilhelm P. *Stender,* manufacturer in Leipzig]. See under *dish.*

stenediol (sten′di-ol). Trade mark for preparations of methandriol.

stenion (sten′e-on), pl. *sten′ia* [Gr. *stenos* narrow + *-on* neuter ending]. An encephalometric landmark, the craniometrical point situated at each end of the smallest transverse diameter of the head in the temporal region.

Steno (ste′no). See *Stensen.*

steno- (sten′o) [Gr. *stenos* narrow]. Combining form meaning contracted or narrow.

stenobregmatic (sten″o-breg-mat′ik) [*steno-* + Gr. *bregma* the front part of the head]. Having the upper and anterior portion of the head narrowed.

stenocardia (sten″o-kar′de-ah). Angina pectoris.

stenocephalia (sten″o-se-fa′le-ah) [*steno-* + Gr. *kephalē* head + *-ia*]. Excessive narrowness of the head.

stenocephalous (sten″o-sef′ah-lus). Having a narrow head.

stenocephaly (sten″o-sef′ah-le). Stenocephalia.

stenochoria (sten″o-ko′re-ah) [*steno-* + Gr. *chōros* space]. Stenosis, or narrowing.

stenocompressor (sten″o-kom-pres′or). An instrument for closing the opening of Stensen's duct during dental operations.

stenocoriasis (sten″o-ko-ri′ah-sis) [*steno-* + Gr. *korē* pupil]. Contraction of the pupil of the eye.

stenocrotaphia (sten″o-kro-ta′fe-ah) [*steno-* + Gr. *krotaphos* temple + *-ia*]. Narrowness of the temporal region.

stenocrotaphy (sten″o-krot′ah-fe). Stenocrotaphia.

stenopeic (sten″o-pe′ik) [*steno-* + Gr. *opē* opening]. Having a narrow slit or opening.

stenophotic (sten″o-fo′tik) [*steno-* + Gr. *phōs* light]. Able to see in a weak light.

stenosal (ste-no′sal). Stenotic.

stenosed (ste-nōst′). Narrowed or constricted.

stenosis (ste-no′sis) [Gr. *stenōsis*]. Narrowing or stricture of a duct or canal. **aortic s.,** a narrowing of the aortic orifice of the heart or of the aorta itself. **cardiac s.,** a narrowing or diminution of any heart passage or cavity. **cicatricial s.,** stenosis caused by the contraction or shriveling of a cicatrix. **Dittrich's s.,** stenosis of the conus arteriosus. **granulation s.,** stenosis or narrowing caused by the deposit of granulations or by their contraction. **mitral s.,** a narrowing of the left atrioventricular orifice. **postdiphtheritic s.,** stenosis of the larynx or trachea following diphtheria. **preventricular s.,** preventriculosis. **pulmonary s.,** narrowing of the opening between the pulmonary artery and the right ventricle. **pyloric s.,** hypertrophic obstruction of the pyloric orifice of the stomach, usually congenital (H. Beardsley, 1788). **tricuspid s.,** narrowing or stricture of the tricuspid orifice of the heart.

stenostegnosis (sten″o-steg-no′sis). Stenostenosis.

stenostenosis (sten″o-ste-no′sis) [*Stensen's duct* + Gr. *stenōsis* narrowing]. Stenosis or constriction of Stensen's duct.

stenostomia (sten″o-sto′me-ah) [*steno-* + Gr. *stoma* mouth + *-ia*]. Narrowing of the mouth.

stenothermal (sten″o-ther′mal). Stenothermic.

stenothermic (sten″o-ther′mik) [*steno-* + Gr. *thermē* heat]. Able to withstand only a small range of temperature: a term applied to bacteria which can develop only at a certain temperature or within a narrow range of temperature.

stenothorax (sten″o-tho′raks) [*steno-* + Gr. *thōrax* chest]. Abnormal narrowness of the chest.

stenotic (ste-not′ik) [Gr. *stenotēs* narrowness]. Pertaining to or characterized by stenosis; abnormally narrowed.

Stensen's duct, experiment, foramen (sten′senz) [Niels *Stensen,* Danish priest-physician, anatomist, physiologist and theologian, 1638–1686]. See under the nouns.

stent (stent). 1. An impression of the mouth and oral structures made of Stent's mass. 2. A mold for keeping a graft in place, made of Stent's mass. By extension used to designate a device or mold of any suitable material, used to hold a graft in place or to provide support for tubular structures that are being anastomosed.

Stent's composition, mass (stentz) [C. *Stent,* English dentist of the 19th century]. See under *mass.*

stentorin (sten′to-rin). A blue pigment derived from certain protozoa.

step (step). One of a series of footrests on different levels, or a structure resembling it. **Krönig's s's,** extension of the lower part of the right edge of cardiac dulness in a steplike form: seen in hypertrophy of the right heart.

stephanial (ste-fa′ne-al). Pertaining to the stephanion.

stephanion (ste-fa′ne-on) [Gr. *stephanos* crown + *-on* neuter ending]. The point on the side of the cranium at which the coronal suture meets the temporal line of the frontal bone.

Stephanofilaria (stef″ah-no-fi-la′re-ah). A genus of filarial nematodes. **S. stile′si,** a species causing skin infection in domestic animals.

Stephanurus (stef″ah-nu′rus). A genus of nematode parasites. **S. denta′tus,** a species parasitic in the urinary tract of swine.

Stephenson's wave (ste′ven-sonz) [William *Stephenson,* Scottish obstetrician, 1837–1908]. See under *wave.*

steradian (ste-ra′de-an) [Gr. *ster-* solid + *radian*]. The unit of measurement of solid angles, equivalent to the angle subtended at the center of a sphere by an area on its surface equal to the square of its radius.

sterane (ster′ān). Trade mark for preparations of prednisolone.

sterco- (ster′ko) [L. *stercus* dung]. Combining form denoting relation to feces.

stercobilin (ster″ko-bi′lin) [*sterco-* + *bilin*]. A reduction product, $C_{33}H_{46}N_4O_6$, of bilirubin, excreted in the feces and giving them their brown color.

stercobilinogen (ster″ko-bi-lin′o-jen). Urobilinogen.

stercolith (ster′ko-lith) [*sterco-* + Gr. *lithos* stone]. A fecal concretion.

stercoporphyrin (ster″ko-por′fĭ-rin). Coproporphyrin.

stercoraceous (ster″ko-ra′shus) [L. *stercoraceus*]. Consisting of or containing feces; fecal.

stercoral (ster′ko-ral). Stercoraceous.

stercoremia (ster″ko-re′me-ah) [*sterco-* + Gr *haima* blood + *-ia*]. A toxic state occasioned by poisons absorbed from unexpelled feces.

stercorin (ster′ko-rin). Coprosterol.

stercorolith (ster′ko-ro-lith). Stercolith.

stercoroma (ster″ko-ro′mah). A large accumulation of fecal matter forming a tumor-like mass in the rectum.

stercorous (ster′ko-rus) [L. *stercorosus*]. Of the nature of excrement.

Sterculia (ster-ku′le-ah). A genus of trees and shrubs, including many species, mostly tropical: some have edible seeds and others are medicinal, while still others afford a gum resembling tragacanth. The hairs of *S. apetala* of Panama may be very irritating.

stercus (ster′kus), pl. *ster′cora* [L.]. Dung, or feces.

stere (stēr) [Gr. *stereos* solid]. A cubic meter.

stereo- (ste′re-o) [Gr. *stereos* solid]. Combining form meaning solid, having three dimensions, or firmly established.

stereoagnosis (ste″re-o-ag-no′sis). Astereognosis.

stereoarthrolysis (ste″re-o-ar-throl′ĭ-sis) [*stereo-* + Gr. *arthron* joint + *lysis* dissolution]. Operative formation of a movable new joint in cases of bony ankylosis.

stereoauscultation (ste″re-o-aws″kul-ta′shun). Auscultation by means of two phonendoscopes each on different parts of the chest. One tube of each instrument is placed in the ears, the other tube of each being closed with the fingers.

stereoblastula (ste″re-o-blas′tu-lah). A solid blastula, all of whose cells reach the external surface.

stereocampimeter (ste″re-o-kam-pim′e-ter) [*stereo-* + L. *campus* field + *metrum* measure]. An instrument for studying unilateral central scotomas and defects in the central retinal area.

stereocardiography (ster″e-o-kar″de-og′rah-fe). Spatial vectorcardiography.

stereochemical (ste″re-o-kem′e-kal). Pertaining to stereochemistry, or to the space relations of the atoms of a molecule.

stereochemistry (ste″re-o-kem′is-tre). That chemical theory which supposes an arrangement of the atoms of certain molecules in three dimensional spaces; that branch of chemistry which treats of the space relations between atoms.

stereocilia (ste″re-o-sil′e-ah). Plural of *stereocilium.*

stereocilium (ste″re-o-sil′e-um), pl. *stereocilia.* A non-motile protoplasmic filament on the free surface of a cell. Cf. *kinocilium.*

stereo-cinefluorography (ste″re-o-sin″e-floo″-or-og′rah-fe). Photographic recording by motion picture camera of x-ray images produced by stereofluoroscopy, affording three-dimensional visualization.

stereocognosy (ste″re-o-kog′no-se). Stereognosis.

stereoencephalotome (ster″e-o-en-sef′ah-lo-tōm). A guiding instrument used in stereoencephalotomy.

stereoencephalotomy (ster″e-o-en-sef″ah-lot′-o-me) [*stereo-* + Gr. *enkephalos* brain + *tomē* a cutting]. Production of sharply circumscribed lesions in subcortical ganglia or pathways by means of electrodes whose direction and position in space are exactly determined by mechanical guides, thereby avoiding, as far as possible, unintended lesions in other areas. See *mesencephalotomy, pallidotomy,* and *thalamotomy.*

stereofluoroscopy (ste″re-o-floo″o-ros′ko-pe). Stereoscopic fluoroscopy.

stereognosis (ste″re-og-no′sis) [*stereo-* + Gr. *gnōsis* knowledge]. 1. The faculty of perceiving and understanding the form and nature of objects by the sense of touch. 2. Perception by the senses of the solidity of objects.

stereognostic (ste″re-og-nos′tik). Pertaining to stereognosis.

stereogram (ste′re-o-gram). 1. A stereoscopic roentgenogram. 2. A stereoscopic drawing.

stereograph (ste″re-o-graf). A stereoscopic roentgenogram.

stereoisomer (ste″re-o-i′so-mer). A compound exhibiting, or capable of exhibiting, stereoisomerism.

stereoisomeric (ster″e-o-i″so-mer′ik). Pertaining to or exhibiting stereoisomerism.

stereoisomerism (ster″e-o-i-som′er-izm) [*stereo-* + *isomerism*]. A type of isomerism in which two or more compounds possess the same molecular and structural formulas but different spatial or configurational formulas, the spatial relationships of the atoms being different, but not the linkages. Stereoisomerism is divided into two branches, *optical isomerism* (which includes enantiomorphism and diastereoisomerism), and *geometric isomerism.* See also *mutarotation* and *racemization.*

stereometer (ste″re-om′e-ter) [*stereo-* + Gr. *metron* measure]. An instrument for performing stereometry.

stereometry (ste″re-om′e-tre). The measurement of the cubic or solid contents of a solid body, or of the capacity of a hollow space.

stereo-ophthalmoscope (ste″re-o-of-thal′mo-skōp). An ophthalmoscope by which the fundus of the eye is viewed with both eyes through two eyepieces.

stereophantoscope (ste″re-o-fan′to-skōp) [*stereo-* + Gr. *phantos* visible + *skopein* to examine]. A large stereoscopic machine with rotating disks in the place of pictures.

stereophorometer (ste″re-o-fo-rom′e-ter). A prism-refracting instrument for use in orthoptic training.

stereophoroscope (ste″re-o-for′o-skōp) [*stereo-* + Gr. *phoros* bearing + *skopein* to examine]. A form of zoetrope, employed in the study of visual perception.

stereophotography (ste″re-o-fo-tog′rah-fe). Stereoscopic photography.

stereophotomicrograph (ste″re-o-fo-to-mi′-kro-graf). A stereoscopic photograph of a microscopical subject.

stereoplasm (ste′re-o-plazm) [*stereo-* + Gr. *plasma* anything formed or molded]. The more solid portions of protoplasm.

stereopsis (ste″re-op′sis) [*stereo-* + Gr. *opsis* vision]. Stereoscopic vision.

stereoradiography (ste″re-o-ra″de-og′rah-fe). Stereoroentgenography.

stereoroentgenography (ste″re-o-rent″gen-og′-rah-fe). The making of a roentgenogram giving an impression of depth as well as of width and height.

stereoroentgenometry (ste″re-o-rent″gen-om′-e-tre). Measurement of the solid dimensions of a radiopaque object from its stereoscopic roentgenograms.

stereoscope (ste′re-o-skōp″) [*stereo-* + Gr. *skopein* to examine]. An instrument for producing the appearance of solidity and relief by combining the images of two similar pictures of an object.

stereoscopic (ste″re-o-skop′ik). Having the effect of a stereoscope: giving to objects seen a solid appearance.

stereoskiagraphy (ste″re-o-ski-ag′rah-fe). Stereoroentgenography.

stereospecific (ster″e-o-spe-sif′ik). Exhibiting marked structural specificity in interacting with a substrate or a limited class of substrates: used of enzymes, permeases.

stereotaxic (ste″re-o-tak′sik). Pertaining to or characterized by precise positioning in space.

stereotaxis (ste″re-o-tak′sis). Stereotropism.

stereotropic (ste″re-o-trop′ik). Pertaining to or characterized by stereotropism.

stereotropism (ste″re-ot′ro-pizm) [*stereo-* + Gr. *tropos* a turning]. The movement of an organism in response to contact with a solid or with a rigid surface.

stereotypy (ste′re-o-ti″pe) [*stereo-* + Gr. *typos* type]. The persistent repetition of senseless acts or words. It may be a persistent maintaining of a bodily attitude (*s. of attitude*), repetition of senseless movements (*s. of movement,* echopraxia), or constant repetition of certain words or phrases (*s. of speech,* echolalia, verbigeration).

steric (ste′rik). Pertaining to the arrangement of atoms in space; pertaining to stereochemistry.

sterid (ster′id). Steroid.

sterigma (ste-rig′mah), pl. *sterig′mata* [Gr. *stērigma* support]. Any one of the radially arranged outgrowths crowded together on the upper half of the sphere into which the conidia bearers of an aspergillus expand.

Sterigmatocystis (ste-rig″mah-to-sis′tis). Sterigmocystis.

Sterigmocystis (ste-rig″mo-sis′tis). A genus of mold resembling Aspergillus except that secondary phialides project from each primary phialide. *S. nid′ulans* has been found in otomycosis and in the white granules of mycetoma.

sterile (ster′il) [L. *sterilis*]. 1. Not fertile; infertile; barren; not producing young. 2. Aseptic; not producing microorganisms; free from microorganisms.

sterility (ste-ril′ĭ-te) [L. *sterilitas*]. 1. The state of being free from microorganisms. 2. The inability to produce offspring, that is, the inability to conceive or to induce conception. **absolute s.,** complete and irremediable inability to produce offspring. **one-child s.,** inability to produce further offspring after having produced one. **primary s.** 1. Inability to produce offspring because of the congenital absence of some factor essential for reproduction. 2. Sterility in which no offspring has ever been produced. **relative s.,** inability to produce offspring only because of certain non-sterilizing conditions, such as oligo-ovulation or oligospermia, conception, or induction of conception, still being a possibility. **secondary s.** 1. Inability to produce further offspring after having conceived or induced conception. See *one-child s.* and *two-child s.* 2. Inability to produce offspring resulting from a non-congenital defect. **two-child s.,** inability to produce further offspring after having produced two.

sterilization (ster″ĭ-li-za′shun). 1. The complete destruction of microorganisms by heat (wet steam under pressure at 120°C. for 15 minutes, or dry heat at 360–380°C. for 3 hours), or by bactericidal chemical compounds. 2. Any procedure by which an individual is made incapable of reproduction, such as castration, vasectomy, or salpingectomy. **chemical s.,** sterilization accomplished by means of a chemical substance. **eugenic s.,** the process of rendering a person incapable of reproduction because the offspring would probably be undesirable types. **fractional s., intermittent s.,** destruction of microorganisms by successive application of the procedure at intervals, to allow spores to develop into adult forms, which are more easily destroyed. **mechanical s.,** the eradication of microorganisms by passing the fluid through a bacteria-proof filter.

sterilize (ster′ĭ-līz). 1. To render sterile; to free from microorganisms. 2. To render incapable of reproduction.

sterilizer (ster′ĭ-līz″er). A mechanism used in sterilizing substances. **Arnold s.,** an apparatus for sterilizing objects by means of live steam at atmospheric pressure.

sterisil (ster′ĭ-sil). Trade mark for a preparation of hexetidine.

Stern's position (sternz) [Heinrich *Stern*, American physician, 1862–1918]. See under *position*.

sternad (ster′nad). Toward the sternum, or sternal aspect.

sternal (ster′nal) [L. *sternalis*]. Pertaining to the sternum.

sternalgia (ster-nal′je-ah) [Gr. *sternon* sternum + *algos* pain + *-ia*]. 1. Pain in the sternum. 2. Angina pectoris.

Sternberg's disease (stern′bergz) [Karl *Sternberg*, German pathologist, 1872–1935]. Lymphogranulomatosis.

sternebra (ster′ne-brah), pl. *ster′nebrae* [*sternum* + *vertebrae*]. Any one of the segments of the sternum in early life.

sternen (ster′nen). Pertaining to the sternum alone.

sterno- (ster′no). Combining form denoting relationship to the sternum.

sternoclavicular (ster″no-klah-vik′u-lar). Pertaining to the sternum and clavicle.

sternoclavicularis (ster″no-klah-vik″u-la′ris) [L.]. Sternoclavicular.

sternocleidal (ster″no-kli′dal) [*sterno-* + Gr. *kleis* key]. Sternoclavicular.

sternocostal (ster″no-kos′tal) [*sterno-* + L. *costa* rib]. Pertaining to the sternum and ribs.

sternodymia (ster″no-dim′e-ah). The union of two monster fetuses by the anterior wall of the chest.

sternodymus (ster-nod′ĭ-mus) [*sterno-* + Gr. *didymos* twin]. A pair of twin monsters united by the anterior wall of the chest.

sternodynia (ster″no-din′e-ah). Sternalgia.

sternoglossal (ster″no-glos′al). Pertaining to the sternum and the tongue.

sternogoniometer (ster″no-go″ne-om′e-ter). An instrument for measuring the sternal angle.

sternohyoid (ster″no-hi′oid). Pertaining to the sternum and to the hyoid bone.

sternoid (ster′noid). Resembling the sternum.

sternomastoid (ster″no-mas′toid). Pertaining to the sternum and the mastoid process of the temporal bone.

sternopagia (ster″no-pa′je-ah). Sternodymia.

sternopagus (ster-nop′ah-gus) [Gr. *sternon* sternum + *pagos* thing fixed]. Sternodymus.

sternopericardial (ster″no-per″ĭ-kar′de-al). Pertaining to the sternum and the pericardium.

sternoscapular (ster″no-skap′u-lar). Pertaining to the sternum and the scapula.

sternoschisis (ster-nos′kĭ-sis) [*sterno-* + Gr. *schisis* cleft]. A developmental anomaly characterized by a fissure of the sternum.

sternothyreoideus (ster″no-thi″re-oi′de-us) [L.]. Sternothyroid.

sternothyroid (ster″no-thi′roid). Pertaining to the sternum and to the thyroid cartilage or gland.

sternotomy (ster-not′o-me) [*sterno-* + Gr. *tomē* a cutting]. The operation of cutting through the sternum.

sternotracheal (ster″no-tra′ke-al) [*sterno-* + *trachea*]. Pertaining to the sternum and to the trachea.

sternotrypesis (ster″no-tri-pe′sis) [*sterno-* + Gr. *trypēsis* trephination]. Surgical perforation of the sternum.

sternovertebral (ster″no-ver′te-bral). Pertaining to the sternum and vertebrae.

sternoxiphopagus (ster″no-zi-fop′ah-gus) [*sterno-* + *xiphoid* process + Gr. *pagus* thing fixed]. A double monster consisting of two similar components united in the frontal plane, in the region of the sternum and xiphoid process.

sternum (ster′num) [L.; Gr. *sternon*]. [N A, B N A] A longitudinal unpaired plate of bone forming the middle of the anterior wall of the thorax, and articulating above with the clavicles and along the sides with the cartilages of the first seven ribs. It consists of three portions, the manubrium, the body, and the xiphoid process. **cleft s.,** a sternum which is longitudinally fissured.

sternutatio (ster″nu-ta′she-o) [L.]. Sternutation. **s. convulsi′va,** paroxysmal and convulsive sneezing.

sternutation (ster″nu-ta′shun) [L. *sternutatio*]. The act of sneezing; a sneeze.

sternutator (ster′nu-ta″tor). A gas or other substance that causes sneezing.

sternutatory (ster-nu′tah-tor″e). [L. *sternutatorius*]. 1. Producing or causing sneezing. 2. An agent that causes sneezing.

sternzellen (stern′tsel-en) [Ger. "star cells"]. Kupffer's cells.

steroid (ste′roid). A group name for compounds that resemble cholesterol chemically and that contain also a hydrogenated cyclopentophenanthrene-ring system. Some of the substances included in this group are the sex hormones, cardiac aglycones, bile acids, sterols proper, toad poisons, saponins, and some of the cancerigenic hydrocarbons.

steroidogenesis (ste-roi″do-jen′e-sis). The production of steroids, as by the adrenal glands.

sterol (ste′rol) [Gr. *stereos* solid + *-ol* (L. *oleum* oil)]. A monohydroxy alcohol of high molecular weight; one of a class of compounds widely distributed in nature, which, because their solubilities are similar to those of fats, have been classified with the lipids. Cholesterol is the best known member of the group.

steroline (ste′rol-in). A general term for glycosidal derivatives of terpenes and sterols.

sterolytic (ste″ro-lit′ik). Capable of dissolving sterols.

sterosan (ster′o-san). Trade mark for preparations of chlorquinaldol.

stertor (ster′tor) [L.]. An act of snoring; stertorous or sonorous breathing. **hen-cluck s.,** a respiration sound like a hen's cluck in cases of postpharyngeal abscess.

stertorous (ster′to-rus). Characterized by stertor.

steth- (steth). See *stetho-*.

stethacoustic (steth″ah-koo′stik). Heard with the stethoscope.

stethalgia (steth-al′je-ah). Pain in the chest or chest wall.

stetharteritis (steth″ar-te-ri′tis). Inflammation of the arteries of the chest.

stethemia (steth-e′me-ah) [*steth-* + Gr. *haima* blood + *-ia*]. Congestion of the lungs.

stethendoscope (steth-en′do-skōp) [*steth-* + Gr. *endon* within + *skopein* to examine]. A fluoroscope used in examination of the chest.

stetho-, steth- (steth′o, steth) [Gr. *stēthos* chest]. Combining form denoting relationship to the chest.

stethocyrtograph (steth″o-ser′to-graf). Stethokyrtograph.

stethogoniometer (steth″o-go″ne-om′e-ter) [*stetho-* + Gr. *gōnia* angle + *metron* measure]. An apparatus for measuring the curvature of the chest.

stethograph (steth′o-graf) [*stetho-* + Gr. *graphein* to write]. An instrument for recording movements of the chest.

stethography (steth-og′rah-fe). 1. Use of the stethograph to record movements of the chest. 2. Phonocardiography.

stethokyrtograph (steth″o-kir′to-graf) [*stetho-* + Gr. *kyrtos* bent + *graphein* to write]. An instrument for recording and measuring the curves of the chest.

stethometer (steth-om′e-ter) [*stetho-* + Gr. *metron* measure]. An instrument for measuring the circular dimension or expansion of the chest.

Stethomyia (steth″o-mi′yah). A subgenus of anopheline mosquitoes.

stethomyitis (steth″o-mi-i′tis) [*stetho-* + Gr. *mys* muscle + *-itis*]. Inflammation of the muscles of the chest.

stethomyositis (steth″o-mi″o-si′tis). Stethomyitis.

stethoparalysis (steth″o-pah-ral′ĭ-sis). Paralysis of the chest muscles.

stethophone (steth′o-fōn) [*stetho-* + Gr. *phōnē* voice]. 1. An instrument designed to transmit stethoscopic sounds so that many persons can hear them simultaneously. 2. A term proposed as a more accurate name for stethoscope.

stethophonometer (steth″o-fo-nom′e-ter) [*stetho-* + Gr. *phōnē* voice + *metron* measure]. An instrument for measuring the intensity of auscultatory sounds.

stethopolyscope (steth″o-pol′ĭ-skōp) [*stetho-* + Gr. *polys* many + *skopein* to examine]. A stethoscope for the simultaneous use of several persons.

stethoscope (steth′o-skōp) [*stetho-* + Gr. *skopein* to examine]. An instrument of various form, size, and material for performing mediate auscultation. By means of this instrument the respiratory, cardiac, pleural, arterial, venous, uterine, fetal, intestinal, and other sounds are conveyed to the ear of the observer. **binaural s.,** one with two adjustable branches, designed for use with both ears. **Cammann's s.,** a binaural stethoscope. **differential s.,** one by means of which sounds at two different portions of the body may be compared.

stethoscopic (steth″o-skop′ik). Pertaining to or performed by means of the stethoscope.

stethoscopy (steth-os′ko-pe). Examination by means of the stethoscope.

stethospasm (steth′o-spazm). Spasm of the chest muscles.

Stevens-Johnson syndrome [Albert Mason *Stevens*, 1884–1945, and Frank Chambliss *Johnson*, 1894–1934, American pediatricians]. Ectodermosis erosiva pluriorificialis.

Stewart's purple (stu′arts) [Douglas Hunt *Stewart*, New York surgeon, 1860–1933]. See under *purple*.

STH. Abbreviation for *somatotropic* (growth) *hormone*.

sthenia (sthe′ne-ah) [Gr. *sthenos* + *-ia*]. A condition of strength and activity.

sthenic (sthen′ik). Active; strong.

stheno- (sthen′o) [Gr. *sthenos* strength]. Combining form denoting relationship to strength.

sthenometer (sthen-om′e-ter). An instrument for measuring the muscular strength of a part.

sthenometry (sthen-om′e-tre) [*stheno-* + Gr. *metron* measure]. The measurement of bodily strength.

sthenophotic (sthen″o-fo′tik) [*stheno-* + Gr. *phōs* light]. Able to see in a strong light.

sthenoplastic (sthen″o-plas′tik) [*stheno-* + Gr. *plastikos* formed]. A term applied to the body form which resembles the long or dolichomorphic form.

sthenopyra (sthen″o-pi′rah) [*stheno-* + Gr. *pyr* fire]. Sthenic fever.

stibamine (stib′ah-min). Sodium amino-phenylstibinate: used in the treatment of kala-azar. **s. glucoside,** a pentavalent antimony compound: used in the treatment of kala-azar, schistosomiasis, and filariasis. **urea s.,** the carbamide salt of para-amino-phenyl-stibinic acid, $NH_2.CO.NH_2.C_6H_4SbO(OH)_2$: used in the treatment of kala-azar.

stibialism (stib′e-al-izm) [L. *stibium* antimony]. Poisoning with antimony.

stibiated (stib′e-āt″ed). Containing antimony.

stibiation (stib″e-a′shun) [L. *stibium* antimony]. Administration of antimonials in large quantities; treatment by bringing the patient under the full influence of antimony.

stibium (stib′e-um) [L.]. Antimony.

stibonium (stĭ-bo′ne-um). The radical SbH_4.

stibophen (stib′o-fen). Chemical name: [3,5-di(sodium sulfonate)-6-sodoxyphenyl][3,5-di(sodium sulfonate)-o-phenylene]: used as an antischistosomal and antileishmanial agent.

stichochrome (stik′o-krōm) [Gr. *stichos* row + *chrōma* color]. Any nerve cell having the stainable substance (chromophilic bodies) arranged in more or less regular striae or layers.

Sticker's disease (stik′erz) [Georg *Sticker*, German physician, born 1860]. Erythema infectiosum.

Sticta (stik′tah) [Gr. *stiktos* punctured]. A genus of lichens; lungwort.

stictacne (stik-tak′ne) [Gr. *stiktos* punctured + *acne*]. Acne punctata.

Stieda's disease, fracture (ste′dahz) [Alfred *Stieda*, German surgeon, born 1869]. See *Pellegrini-Stieda disease*, and under *fracture*.

Stieglitz test (ste′glitz) [Edward J. *Stieglitz,* American physician, 1899–1958]. See under *tests.*

Stierlin's sign, symptom (stēr′linz) [Eduard *Stierlin,* Munich surgeon, 1878–1919]. See under *symptom.*

stigma (stig′mah), pl. *stigmas* or *stig′mata* [Gr. "mark"]. 1. A spot, dot, or impression upon the skin. 2. Follicular stigma. 3. Any mental or physical mark or peculiarity which aids in the identification or in the diagnosis of a condition. **baker's s.,** lumps on the backs of the fingers of bakers, produced by kneading dough. **stigmata of Benecki,** stigmata ventriculi. **costal s.,** Stiller's sign. **s. of degeneracy,** any of the bodily abnormalities which are found in considerable number in degenerate persons. **follicular s.,** a spot on the surface of an ovary where the graafian follicle will rupture. **Giuffrida-Ruggieri s.,** abnormal shallowness of the glenoid fossa. **hysteric s.,** a bodily mark or sign characteristic of hysteria. **malpighian s's,** the points where the smaller veins enter into the larger veins of the spleen. **stig′mata ma′ydis,** the silk or stigmata of maize; corn silk: a diuretic. See *Zea.* **psychic s.,** mental conditions marked by susceptibility to suggestion. **somatic s.,** the bodily signs of certain nervous diseases. **stig′mata ventric′uli,** porelike erosions and petechiae on the gastric mucosa associated with a form of acute gastric ulcer.

stigmal (stig′mal). Pertaining to a stigma.

stigmasterol (stig-mas′ter-ol). A plant sterol, $C_{29}H_{48}O$, occurring in physostigma, cacao butter, rape oil, and elsewhere.

stigmata (stig′mah-tah) [Gr.]. Plural of *stigma.*

stigmatic (stig-mat′ik). Pertaining to a stigma.

stigmatism (stig′mah-tizm). 1. The condition due to or marked by stigmas. 2. The accurate rendition of points by a lens system.

stigmatization (stig″mah-ti-za′shun). 1. The formation of impressions on the skin. 2. The formation of bleeding points or of red lines upon the skin by hypnotic suggestion.

stigmatometer (stig″mah-tom′e-ter). An instrument for testing the refraction of the eye by the objective method and for direct ophthalmoscopy.

stigmatosis (stig″mah-to′sis). A skin disease marked by ulcerated spots.

stijfziekte (stēf-zēk′te) [Dutch]. A phosphorus-deficiency disease of the joints of young cattle in South Africa: marked by retardation of growth, skeletal abnormalities, stiffness, and lameness.

stilalgin (stil-al′jin). Mephenesin.

stilbene (stil′bēn). Toluylene.

stilbestrol (stil-bes′trol). Diethylstilbestrol.

stilbetin (stil-be′tin). Trade mark for a preparation of diethylstilbestrol.

stilet (sti-let′) [Fr. *stilette*]. Stylet.

stilette (sti-let′) [Fr.]. Stylet.

stili (sti′li) [L.]. Plural of *stilus.*

Still's disease (stilz) [Sir George Frederick *Still,* English physician, 1868–1941]. See under *disease.*

stillbirth (stil′berth). The birth of a dead child. See *fetal death.*

stillborn (stil′born). Born dead.

Stiller's sign, theory (stil′erz) [Berthold *Stiller,* physician in Budapest, 1837–1922]. See under *sign* and *theory.*

stillicidium (stil″ĭ-sid′e-um) [L. *stilla* drop + *cadere* to fall]. 1. A dribbling or flowing by drops. 2. Epiphora. **s. lacrima′rum,** epiphora. **s. na′rium,** coryza. **s. uri′nae,** strangury.

Stilling's canal, cells, nucleus, raphe, etc., (stil′ingz) [Benedict *Stilling,* German anatomist 1810–1879]. See under the nouns.

Stillingia (stil-lin′je-ah) [Benjamin *Stillingfleet,* English botanist, 1702–1771]. A genus of euphorbiaceous trees, shrubs, and herbs. The root of *S. sylvat′ica,* a plant of North America, is sialagogue and diuretic.

stilus (sti′lus), pl. *sti′li* [L.]. Stylus.

stimulant (stim′u-lant) [L. *stimulans*]. 1. Producing stimulation; especially producing stimulation by causing tension on muscle fiber through the nervous tissue. 2. An agent or remedy that produces stimulation. **alcoholic s.,** one of which ethylic alcohol is the basis, such as wine, brandy, whisky, and malt liquors. **bronchial s.,** an agent which stimulates ejection of material from the bronchial tubes. **cardiac s.,** one which increases the heart's action. **cerebral s.,** one which exalts the functional activities of the brain. **cutaneous s.,** a diaphoretic agent which acts by stimulating the skin. **diffusible s.,** one which acts promptly and strongly, but transiently. **gastric s.,** one which promotes the digestion of food in the stomach. **general s.,** one which acts upon the whole body. **genital s.,** an aphrodisiac. **hepatic s.,** one which stimulates the functions of the liver. **intestinal s.,** a cathartic agent. **local s.,** one which affects only, or mainly, that part to which it is applied. **nervous s.,** one which acts mainly upon the nerve centers: a cerebral or a spinal stimulant. **renal s.,** a stimulating diuretic. **respiratory s.,** one which increases the respiratory movements. **spinal s.,** one which acts upon and through the spinal cord. **stomachic s.,** gastric s. **topical s.,** local s. **uterine s.,** an agent which stimulates uterine contraction or the menstruation. **vascular s., vasomotor s.,** one which affects the vasomotor centers.

stimulate (stim′u-lāt). To excite to functional activity.

stimulation (stim″u-la′shun) [L. *stimulatio,* from *stimulare* to goad]. The act or process of stimulating; the condition of being stimulated. **areal s.,** stimulation of an extended portion of a sense organ. **audio-visual-tactile s.,** the simultaneous rhythmic excitation of the receptors for the senses of hearing, sight, and touch. **non-specific s.,** stimulation of a sense organ by other than the specific exciting agent. **paradoxical s.,** application of a warm object to one of the cold spots of the body produces a sensation of cold. **paraspecific s.,** non-specific s. **punctual s.,** excitation of a sense organ by stimulation at a single point.

stimulin (stim′u-lin). A name given by Metchnikoff to an element in the blood serum that stimulates the action of phagocytes.

stimulus (stim′u-lus), pl. *stim′uli* [L. "goad"]. Any agent, act, or influence that produces functional or trophic reaction in a receptor or in an irritable tissue. **adequate s.,** a stimulus of the specific form of energy to which the receptor is most sensitive. Called also *homologous s.* **chemical s.,** a chemical substance capable of exciting a response in an organism mediated through specialized nerve endings. **electric s.,** a galvanic, induced, or other electric current or shock as applied to a responsive tissue. **heterologous s.,** one which produces an effect or sensation when applied to any part whatever of a nerve tract. **heterotopic s.,** a stimulus to heart contraction arising elsewhere than in the sino-atrial node, the normal pacemaker of the heart. **homologous s.,** adequate s. **liminal s.,** one near the threshold. **mechanical s.,** a stimulant application of mechanical force, as in friction or pinching. **nomotopic s.,** a stimulus to heart contraction arising in the sino-atrial node. **subliminal s.,** one well below the threshold. **supraliminal s.,** one well above the threshold. **thermal s.,** application of heat. **threshold s.,** a stimulus of such strength that it may or may not be effective.

sting (sting). An injury caused by the venom of a plant or animal (biotoxin) introduced into the individual or with which he has come in contact, together with the mechanical trauma caused by the organ responsible for its introduction. **Irukandji s.,** a clinical syndrome observed in the vicinity of Cairns, Queensland, Australia, attributed to stinging by an unknown agent, supposedly a small transparent jellyfish.

Stintzing's tables (stint′zingz) [Roderich *Stintzing*, Jena internist, 1854–1933]. Tables showing the average value of the normal electric excitability of the muscles and nerves.

Stipa viridula (sti′pah vi-rid′u-lah). A grass of the southwestern United States, called *sleepygrass*: poisonous to cattle and horses; said to be a powerful narcotic, diuretic, sudorific, and cardiac poison.

stippling (stip′pling). A spotted condition or appearance, such as an appearance of the retina as if dotted with light and dark points, or the spotted appearance of red blood corpuscles in basophilia. See *basophilia*. It may also be the result of irregular indentations or undulations in a surface, such as the adaptive specialization of normal gingivae which sometimes disappears in disease. **malarial s.,** the finely granular appearance often seen in stained red blood corpuscles which harbor tertian malarial parasites. The granules are called *Schüffner's granules*. **Maurer's s.,** Maurer's dots. **Schüffner's s.,** malarial s.

stirpicultural (ster″pĭ-kul′tu-ral). Pertaining to stirpiculture.

stirpiculture (ster′pĭ-kul″tūr) [L. *stirps* stock + *cultura* culture]. The systematic attempt at improving a stock or race by attention to the laws of breeding.

stirrup (stir′up). 1. A structure or device resembling the stirrup of a saddle, or the portion of an apparatus on which to rest the feet. 2. The stapes. **Finochietto's s.,** an apparatus for exerting skeletal traction in leg fractures, with a U-shaped steel band, passed over the posterior process of the calcaneous and fixed by a cross bar, from which traction is applied.

stitch (stich). 1. To pass through tissue, by means of a needle, lengths of thread, catgut, wire, or other material, usually for the purpose of approximating wound edges but also for the purpose of fixing or mobilizing an organ or other body part. 2. A single passage of suture material through tissues, for their approximation or mobilization. See under *suture*. 3. A severe pain, generally at the costal margin on one side.

stithe (stīth). Incus.

stizolobin (sti″zo-lo′bin). The globulin of the Chinese velvet bean.

stochastic (sto-kas′tik) [Gr. *stokastikos* skillful in aiming at, able to guess]. Able to conjecture skillfully; arrived at by skillful conjecturing.

stoechiology (stek″e-ol′o-je). Stoichiology.

stoechiometry (stek″e-om′e-tre). Stoichiometry.

Stoerk's blennorrhea (sterks) [Carl *Stoerk*, Austrian laryngologist, 1832–1899]. See under *blennorrhea*.

Stoffel operation (stof′el) [Adolf *Stoffel*, German orthopedist, born 1880]. See under *operation*.

stoichiology (stoi″ke-ol′o-je) [Gr. *stoicheion* element + *-logy*]. The science of elements, especially the physiology of the cellular elements of tissues.

stoichiometry (stoi″ke-om′e-tre) [Gr. *stoicheion* element + *metron* measure]. The study of the numerical relationships of chemical elements and compounds and the mathematical laws of chemical changes; the mathematics of chemistry.

Stokes's amputation, operation [Sir William *Stokes*, Irish surgeon, 1839–1900]. Gritti-Stokes amputation.

Stokes's disease, expectorant, law, liniment, sign, etc. (stōks) [William *Stokes*, Irish physician, 1804–1878]. See under the nouns.

Stokes's lens [George Gabriel *Stokes*, English physicist, 1819–1903]. See under *lens*.

Stokes's reagent (stōks) [William Royal *Stokes*, American pathologist, born 1870]. See under *reagent*.

Stokes-Adams disease, syncope, syndrome [William *Stokes*, Irish physician, 1804–1878; Robert *Adams*, Irish physician, 1791–1875]. See *Adams-Stokes disease*, under *disease*.

Stokvis' disease, test (stok′vis) [Barend J. E. *Stokvis*, Dutch physician, 1834–1902]. See under *disease* and *tests*.

stoma (sto′mah), pl. *sto′mas* or *sto′mata* [Gr. "mouth"]. 1. Any minute pore, orifice, or opening on a free surface; specifically, one of the openings (stigma, or pseudostoma) between epithelial cells of a lymph space, forming a means of communication between adjacent lymph channels. 2. The opening established in the abdominal wall by colostomy, cecostomy, ileostomy, etc.; also the opening between two portions of the intestine in an anastomosis.

stomacace (sto-mak′ah-se) [Gr. *stoma* mouth + *kakē* badness]. Ulcerative stomatitis.

stomach (stum′ak) [L. *stomachus;* Gr. *stomachos*]. The musculomembranous expansion of the alimentary canal between the esophagus and the duodenum. Called also *ventriculus* [N A]. The proximal portion is the cardiac part; the distal portion, the pyloric part. The upper concave surface or edge is the *lesser curvature;* the lower convex edge is the *greater curvature*. The coats of the stomach are four: An outer, peritoneal, or *serous* coat; a *muscular coat*, made up of longitudinal, oblique, and circular fibers; a *submucous* coat; and the *mucous* coat or membrane forming the inner lining. The secretion of the stomach, the *gastric* juice, contains hydrochloric acid and various digestive enzymes. **aviator's s.,** aeroneurosis. **bilocular s.,** hour-glass s. **cardiac s.,** the portion of the stomach close to the esophagus. **cascade s.,** an atypical form of hour-glass stomach, characterized roentgenologically by a drawing up of the posterior wall. An opaque medium first fills the upper sac and then cascades into the lower sac. **cup-and-spill s.,** a roentgenographic finding in which the barium remains for a time in the gastric fundus, before spilling over into the main cavity of the stomach, as a result of pressure by a distended colon. **dumping s.,** a complication that sometimes follows gastro-enterostomy, in which food is emptied rapidly through the new opening, producing intestinal distention and discomfort. See *dumping syndrome*, under *syndrome*. **Holzknecht s.,** a stomach the roentgen picture of which shows it placed diagonally with the pylorus at the lower end of the diagonal. **hour-glass s.,** a stomach more or less completely and permanently divided into two parts, so that it resembles an hour-glass in shape. **leather bottle s.,** linitis plastica. **miniature s.,** Pavlov's s. **Pavlov's s.,** a portion of the stomach of a dog isolated from communication with the rest of the stomach and opening on to the abdominal wall through a fistula: used in studying gastric secretion. **powdered s.,** the dried and powdered defatted wall of the stomach of the hog, *Sus scrofa:* used in anemia. **red s.,** a condition in which the pyloric end of the stomach is dark red. **sclerotic s.,** linitis plastica. **thoracic s.,** a stomach which is situated or drawn up above the level of the diaphragm. **trifid s.,** a stomach with two constrictions, producing three pouches. **upside-down s.,** thoracic s. **wallet s.,** baglike distention of the stomach. **waterfall s.,** cascade s. **water-trap s.,** a stomach with an extremely high pylorus, so that it does not readily empty itself.

stomachal (stum′ah-kal). Pertaining to the stomach.

stomachalgia (stum″ah-kal′je-ah). Pain in the stomach.

stomachic (sto-mak′ik) [L. *stomachicus;* Gr. *stomachikos*]. 1. Pertaining to the stomach. 2. A medicine which promotes the functional activity of the stomach; a stomachic tonic.

stomachodynia (stum″ah-ko-din′e-ah) [*stomach* + Gr. *odynē* pain + *-ia*]. Pain in the stomach.

stomachoscopy (sto″mah-kos′ko-pe) [*stomach* +

Gr. *skopein* to examine]. Examination of the stomach.

stomadeum (sto″mah-de′um). Stomodeum.

stomal (sto′mal). Pertaining to a stoma or stomata.

stomalgia (sto-mal′je-ah). Stomatalgia.

stomata (sto′mah-tah) [L.]. Plural of *stoma*.

stomatal (sto′mah-tal). Pertaining to stomata.

stomatalgia (sto″mah-tal′je-ah). Pain in the mouth.

stomatic (sto-mat′ik). Pertaining to the mouth.

stomatitides (sto″mah-tit′ĭ-dēz). Plural of *stomatitis*. A general term applied collectively to inflammatory conditions of the oral mucosa.

stomatitis (sto-mah-ti′tis), pl. *stomatit′ides* [*stomato-* + *-itis*]. Inflammation of the oral mucosa, due to local or systemic factors, which may involve the buccal and labial mucosa, palate, tongue, floor of the mouth, and the gingivae. **angular s.,** superficial erosions and fissuring at the angles of the mouth; it may occur in riboflavin deficiency and in pellagra or result from sensitivity to denture material. **aphthobullous s.,** foot-and-mouth disease. **s. aphtho′sa, aphthous s.,** herpetic s. **s. arsenica′lis,** stomatitis due to arsenical poisoning. **epidemic s., epizootic s.,** foot-and-mouth disease. **erythematopultaceous s.,** stomatitis characterized by a reddened mucous membrane, covered with a layer of thick, sticky matter: seen in uremia. **s. exanthemat′ica,** stomatitis secondary to an exanthematous disease. **fusospirochetal s.,** necrotizing ulcerative s. **s. gangreno′sa, gangrenous s.,** a severe fusospirochetal infection of grave prognosis, occurring in debilitated patients, with gangrene of the oral and facial tissues. Called also *cancrum oris* and *noma*. **gonococcal s.,** a rare infection of the oral mucosa caused by *Neisseriae gonorrheae*, occurring in newborn infants (infected from the birth canal) and in adults. **herpetic s., s. herpet′ica,** an acute infection of the oral mucosa, caused by the virus of herpes simplex, with vesicle formation. Called also *canker sore*. **s. hyphomycet′ica,** thrush. **infectious s.,** a general term for a usually mild infection of the oral mucosa, beginning with a circumscribed red, itchy area. **infectious pustular s.,** a filtrable-virus disease of horses, marked by pustular eruption on the mucous membrane of the mouth; transmissible to cattle, sheep, hogs, and fowls. **s. intertrop′ica,** sprue. **s. medicamento′sa,** eruptive involvement of the oral mucosa resulting from an allergic reaction to some medication, such as antibiotics, arsenic, barbiturates, or salicylates. **membranous s.,** infection of the oral mucosa, accompanied by the formation of false membrane. **mercurial s.,** stomatitis due to mercurial poisoning. **s. myceto-genet′ica,** stomatitis resulting from a fungus infection. **mycotic s.,** thrush. **necrotizing ulcerative s.,** stomatitis caused by extension to the oral mucosa of necrotizing ulcerative gingivitis, characterized by ulceration, pseudomembrane, and odor, with lesions involving the palate or pharynx, as well as the oral mucosa. **s. nicoti′na,** irritation of the palate resulting from the coal tar products of tobacco, sometimes contributing to neoplasia. **non-specific s.,** inflammation of the oral mucosa occurring in association with other conditions, such as menstruation, diabetes, or uremia. **s. scorbu′tica,** stomatitis associated with vitamin C deficiency. **syphilitic s.,** stomatitis due to systemic syphilis. **s. traumat′ica,** stomatitis produced by some mechanical, thermal, or chemical cause. **tropical s.,** sprue. **ulcerative s.,** stomatitis characterized by the appearance of shallow ulcers on the cheeks, tongue, and lips. **ulcerative s. of sheep,** orf. **s. venena′ta,** lesions of the oral mucosa resulting from contact with ordinarily innocuous substances such as denture bases, dentifrices, lipstick, food items, or flavoring in gum and candy. **vesicular s.,** herpetic s. **vesicular s. of horses,** an acute febrile infectious disease of horses marked by a vesicular eruption on the tongue and mucous membrane of the mouth and lips. **Vincent's s.,** necrotizing ulcerative s. **vulcanite s.,** stomatitis due to contact with a vulcanite dental plate.

stomato- (sto′mah-to) [Gr. *stoma, stomatos* mouth]. Combining form denoting relationship to the mouth.

stomatocace (sto″mah-tok′ah-se) [*stomato-* + Gr. *kakē* badness]. Ulcerative stomatitis.

stomatodynia (sto″mah-to-din′e-ah) [*stomato-* + Gr. *odynē* pain + *-ia*]. Pain in the mouth.

stomatodysodia (sto″mah-to-dis-o′de-ah) [*stomato-* + Gr. *dysōdia* stench]. A bad odor coming from the mouth.

stomatogastric (sto″mah-to-gas′trik). Pertaining to the stomach and the mouth.

stomatography (sto″mah-tog′rah-fe) [*stomato-* + Gr. *graphein* to write]. A description of the mouth.

stomatolalia (sto″mah-to-lal′e-ah). Speaking through the mouth with the nares closed.

stomatological (sto″mah-to-loj′e-kal). Pertaining to stomatology.

stomatologist (sto″mah-tol′o-jist). An expert in stomatology.

stomatology (sto″mah-tol′o-je). That branch of medicine which treats of the mouth and its diseases.

stomatomalacia (sto″mah-to-mah-la′she-ah) [*stomato-* + Gr. *malakia* softness]. Softening of the structures of the mouth.

stomatomenia (sto″mah-to-me′ne-ah) [*stomato-* + Gr. *mēniaia* menses]. Bleeding from the mucous membrane of the mouth at the time of menstruation.

stomatomy (sto-mat′o-me) [*stoma-* + Gr. *tomē* a cutting]. The surgical incision of the os uteri.

stomatomycosis (sto″mah-to-mi-ko′sis) [*stomato-* + Gr. *mykēs* fungus]. Any mouth disease due to a fungus.

stomatonecrosis (sto″mah-to-ne-kro′sis). Stomatitis gangrenosa.

stomatonoma (sto″mah-to-no′mah). Stomatitis gangrenosa.

stomatopathy (sto″mah-top′ah-the) [*stomato-* + Gr. *pathos* suffering]. Any disorder of the mouth.

stomatophylaxis (sto″mah-to-fi-lak′sis). Oral prophylaxis.

stomatoplastic (sto″mah-to-plas′tik). Pertaining to stomatoplasty.

stomatoplasty (sto′mah-to-plas″te) [*stomato-* + Gr. *plassein* to mold]. Plastic surgery of, or operative repair of, defects of the mouth or of the os uteri.

stomatorrhagia (sto″mah-to-ra′je-ah) [*stomato-* + Gr. *rhēgnynai* to burst forth]. Hemorrhage from the mouth. **s. gingiva′rum,** hemorrhage from the gingivae.

stomatoschisis (sto″mah-tos′kĭ-sis) [*stomato-* + Gr. *schisis* split]. Harelip.

stomatoscope (sto-mat′o-skōp) [*stomato-* + Gr. *skopein* to examine]. An instrument used in inspecting the mouth.

stomatosis (sto″mah-to′sis). Stomatopathy.

stomatotomy (sto″mah-tot′o-me). Stomatomy.

stomatotyphus (sto″mah-to-ti′fus). Typhus fever with severe lesions of the mouth.

stomencephalus (sto″men-sef′ah-lus). Stomocephalus.

stomion (sto′me-on) [Gr. *stomion*, dim. of *stoma* mouth]. An anthropometric landmark, being the central point in the oral fissure when the lips are closed.

stomocephalus (sto″mo-sef′ah-lus) [*stomo-* + Gr. *kephalē* head]. A monster fetus with a rudimentary head and jaws, so that the skin hangs in folds about the mouth.

stomodeal (sto″mo-de′al). Pertaining to the stomodeum.

stomodeum (sto″mo-de′um) [*stomo-* + Gr. *hodaios* pertaining to a way]. An invagination of the ectoderm of the embryo at the point where later the mouth is formed.

stomoschisis (sto-mos′kĭ-sis) [*stomo-* + Gr. *schisis* a splitting]. Fissure of the mouth.

Stomoxys (sto-mok′sis). A genus of flies. **S. cal′citrans,** the common stable fly; it is annoying to man and beast, and is capable of transmitting anthrax, tetanus, and infectious anemia of horses. Called also *stable fly* and *legsticker.*

Stomoxys calcitrans.

-stomy (sto′me) [Gr. *stomoun* to provide with an opening, or mouth]. Word termination denoting the surgical creation of an artificial opening into a hollow organ (colostomy, tracheostomy) or a new opening between two such structures (gastroenterostomy, pyeloureterostomy).

stone (stōn). 1. A mass of extremely hard and unyielding material; a calculus. 2. A unit of weight recognized in Great Britain, being the equivalent of 14 pounds (avoirdupois), or about 6.34 kg. (metric). **artificial s.,** a specially calcined gypsum derivative used for making impressions of oral structures; similar to plaster of paris but with non-porous grains, so that the product is stronger than one made of plaster of paris. **bladder s.,** vesical calculus. **blue s.,** copper sulfate. **chalk s.,** a gouty concretion, usually of the hands or feet, which consists mainly of sodium urate, sometimes combined with various lime salts. **dental s.** 1. Denticle. 2. Artificial stone. **eye s.,** the operculum of a small shell or other small calcareous object: used for removing foreign bodies from the eye. **lung s.,** lung calculus. **metabolic s.,** cholesterol calculus. **pulp s.,** denticle. **rotten s.,** a siliceous mineral much used as a polishing material. **s.-searcher,** a sound for exploring the bladder wherein a calculus is suspected. **skin s's,** calcareous nodules sometimes seen in the subcutaneous tissues. **staghorn s.** See under *calculus.* **struvit s.** See under *calculus.* **tear s.,** dacryolith. **vein s.,** phlebolith. **womb s.,** a calcified fibroid tumor of the uterus.

Stookey's reflex (stook′ēz) [Byron *Stookey,* New York neurologic surgeon, born 1887]. See under *reflex.*

stool (stōōl). The fecal discharge from the bowels. **bilious s.,** the yellowish or brownish stools, turning darker on exposure, that are characteristic of bilious diarrhea. Bilious stools are green if the bowel contents are very acid. **caddy s.,** the stools seen in yellow fever; they look like dark, sandy mud. **fatty s.,** stools containing fat: seen in diseases of the pancreas. **lienteric s.,** a stool that contains much undigested food. **mucous s.,** a stool containing a large amount of mucus: seen in intestinal inflammation. **pea soup s.,** the characteristic liquid evacuation of typhoid fever. **pipe-stem s.,** a stool resembling the shape of a pipe stem, seen in stricture of the lower rectum. **ribbon s.,** a long flattened stool seen in lower rectal stricture. **rice water s.,** the characteristic watery evacuations of cholera. **sago-grain s.,** stools of amebiasis in which the liquid feces contain small flecks of blood-stained mucus. **spinach s.,** dark-green stool resembling cooked spinach, resulting from the use of calomel in infants.

storax (sto′raks) [L. *storax, styrax;* Gr. *styrax*]. A balsam from the trunk of *Liquidambar orientalis,* a tree of western Asia, or of *L. styraciflua* of North America. It is used locally in scabies. Also called *styrax.*

storm (storm). An outburst; a temporary and sudden increase in symptoms. **brain s.,** a succession of sudden and severe paroxysms of cerebral disturbance. **nerve s.,** a sudden outburst of nervous disorder.

Storm van Leeuwen's chamber [William *Storm van Leeuwen,* a pharmacist in Leyden, 1882–1933]. See under *chamber.*

stoss (stos) [Ger.]. See *stosstherapy.*

stosstherapy (stos′ther-ah-pe) [Ger. *stoss* shock, stroke + *therapy*]. Treatment of a disease by a single massive dose of a therapeutic agent, or by short-term administration of unphysiologically large doses.

Str. Abbreviation for *Streptococcus.*

strabismic (strah-biz′mik). Pertaining to or of the nature of strabismus.

strabismometer (strah-biz-mom′e-ter) [*strabismus* + Gr. *metron* measure]. An apparatus for measuring strabismus.

strabismus (strah-biz′mus) [Gr. *strabismos*]. Deviation of the eye which the patient cannot overcome. The visual axes assume a position relative to each other different from that required by the physiological conditions (Parsons). The various forms of strabismus are spoken of as tropias, their direction being indicated by the appropriate prefix, as *eso*tropia, *exo*tropia, etc. Called also *manifest deviation* and *squint.* **absolute s.,** that which occurs at all distances of the fixation point. **accommodative s.,** that which is due to excessive or deficient accommodative effort. **alternating s., bilateral s., binocular s.,** that which affects each eye alternately. **Braid's s.,** the turning of the eyes simultaneously upward and inward; a means sometimes adopted of inducing the hypnotic state. **concomitant s.,** that which is due to a faulty insertion of the eye muscles, resulting in the same amount of deviation in whatever direction the eyes are looking, because the squinting eye follows the movements of the other eye. **constant s.,** strabismus that is constantly present. **convergent s.,** that in which the visual axes converge; cross-eye or esotropia. **cyclic s.,** intermittent strabismus that recurs at regular intervals. **s. deor′sum ver′gens,** that in which the visual axis of the squinting eye falls below the fixation point. **divergent s.,** that in which the visual axes diverge; exotropia. **dynamic s.,** the tendency to strabismus due to insufficiency of the ocular muscles, but which may be overcome by the effort of binocular vision. **external s.,** divergent s. **horizontal s.,** strabismus in which the deviation of the visual axis is in the horizontal plane. See *esotropia* and *exotropia.* **intermittent s.,** that which occurs only at intervals. **internal s.,** convergent s. **kinetic s.,** strabismus due to overactivity of the muscles controlling ocular movements. **latent s.,** that which occurs only when one eye is occluded. **manifest s.,** strabismus which occurs when vision by both eyes is possible. **mechanical s.,** that due to pressure or traction on the eye, as by a tumor, producing deflection. **monocular s., monolateral s.,** unilateral s. **muscular s.,** concomitant s. **nonconcomitant s.,** that in which the amount of deviation of the squinting eye varies according to the direction in whch the eyes are turned. **paralytic s.,** that which is due to paralysis of an eye muscle. **paralytic s., acute,** strabismus attended by dizziness and double vision. **periodic s.,** that which is seen only during efforts at accommodation. **relative s.,** that which occurs for some and not for other distances of the fixation point. **spasmodic s.,** that which is due to spasm of the muscles of the eye. **suppressed s.,** heterophoria. **s. sur′sum ver′gens,** that in which the visual axis of the squinting eye falls above the fixation point. **unilateral s., uniocular s.,** strabismus affecting only one eye. **vertical s.,** strabismus in which the deviation of the visual axis is in the vertical plane. See *hypertropia* and *hypotropia.*

strabometer (strah-bom′e-ter). Strabismometer.

strabometry (strah-bom′e-tre). Measurement of the amount of strabismus.

strabotome (strab′o-tōm). A knife for performing strabotomy.

strabotomy (strah-bot′o-me) [Gr. *strabos* squinting + *tomē* a cutting]. The cutting of the tendon of a muscle of the eye in treatment of strabismus.

Strachan's disease (strawnz) [William Henry Williams *Strachan*, English physician of the 19th century]. Pellagra.

strain (strān). 1. To overexercise; to use to an extreme and harmful degree. 2. To filter or subject to colation. 3. An overstretching or overexertion of some part of the musculature. 4. Excessive effort or undue exercise. 5. A group of organisms within a species or variety, characterized by some particular quality, as rough or smooth strains of bacteria. **heterologous s.,** a strain of microorganisms sufficiently different from the original strain so that on inoculation they produce a superinfection. **high-jumper's s.,** strain of the rotator muscles of the thigh occurring in high jumpers. **homologous s.,** a strain of microorganisms so similar to the original strain that on inoculation they are unable to produce superinfection. **R s., rough s.,** the rough strain that results from microbic dissociation; R colonies have a dull, uneven surface and irregular border, the growth in fluid media tends to flake out, no capsules are seen and the culture tends to be less virulent. **S s., smooth s.,** the smooth strain that results from microbic dissociation. The S colonies have a smooth surface and an unbroken border, growth in fluid media tends to be diffuse, capsules, if present at all, are found in this strain, and the culture tends to be more virulent. **Vi s.,** a strain of *Eberthella typhi* which is encapsulated and virulent.

strainer (strān′er). An apparatus for straining.

strait (strāt). A narrow passageway. **pelvic s., inferior,** the pelvic outlet. **pelvic s., superior,** the pelvic inlet.

stramonium (strah-mo′ne-um). The dried leaf and flowering or fruiting tops of *Datura stramonium:* used in parasympathetic blockade.

strand (strand). A thread or fiber. **Billroth's s.,** trabecula lienis. **lateral enamel s.,** a structure in a developing tooth connecting the enamel organ with the dental lamina.

strangalesthesia (strang″g'l-es-the′ze-ah) [Gr. *strangalizein* to choke + *aisthēsis* perception + *-ia*]. Zonesthesia.

strangle (strang′g'l) [L. *strangulare*]. To choke, or to be choked by compression or other obstruction of the windpipe.

strangles (strang′g'lz). 1. An infectious disease of horses, characterized by a mucopurulent inflammation of the respiratory mucous membrane, and caused by the *Streptococcus equi.* 2. A condition in swine, characterized by infection of the lymph nodes, producing heavily encapsulated abscesses in the region of the pharynx.

strangulated (strang′gu-lāt″ed) [L. *strangulatus*]. Congested by reason of constriction or hernial stricture. See *hernia.*

strangulation (strang″gu-la′shun) [L. *strangulatio*]. 1. Choking or throttling arrest of respiration, due to occlusion of the air passage. 2. Arrest of the circulation in a part, due to compression.

stranguria (strang-gu′re-ah). Strangury.

strangury (strang′gu-re) [Gr. *stranx* drop + *ouron* urine]. Slow and painful discharge of the urine: due to spasm of the urethra and bladder.

strap (strap). 1. A band or slip, as of adhesive plaster, used in attaching parts to each other. 2. To bind down tightly. **crib s.,** a strap to be placed around the neck of a horse to prevent cribbing by compressing the windpipe. **Wyman's s's,** a set of straps for keeping a violently disturbed person in bed.

strapping (strap′ing). The application of strips of adhesive plaster, one overlapping the other, so as to cover a part and exert pressure upon it. See Plate XLII.

Strasburger's cell-plate (strahs-burg′erz) [Edward *Strasburger*, German histologist, 1844–1912]. Midbody.

Strassburg's test (strahs′boorgz) [Gustav Adolf *Strassburg*, German physiologist, born 1848]. See under *tests.*

Strassmann's phenomenon (strahs′manz) [Paul Ferdinand *Strassmann*, Berlin gynecologist, 1866–1938]. See under *phenomenon.*

strata (stra′tah) [L.]. Plural of *stratum.*

stratification (strat″ĭ-fi-ka′shun) [L. *stratum* layer + *facere* to make]. Disposal in layers.

stratified (strat′ĭ-fīd). Disposed in layers.

stratiform (strat′ĭ-form) [L. *stratum* layer + *forma* form]. Having the form of strata.

stratigram (strat′ĭ-gram). A roentgenogram of a selected layer of the body made by stratigraphy.

stratigraphy (strah-tig′rah-fe) [L. *stratum* layer + Gr. *graphein* to write]. See *body section roentgenography,* under *roentgenography.*

stratum (stra′tum), pl. *stra′ta* [L.]. A sheetlike mass of substance of nearly uniform thickness. Called also *layer.* **s. adamanti′num,** the enamel of a tooth (enamelum [N A]). **s. al′bum profun′dum cor′poris quadrigem′ini** [B N A], a layer of white matter between the corpora quadrigemina and the central gray layer of the cerebral aqueduct. Omitted in N A. **Arlt's s.,** s. zonale thalami. **ashy s. of cerebellum,** s. moleculare cerebelli. **s. bacillo′rum,** s. neuroepitheliale retinae. **s. basa′le,** the deepest layer of the mucosa of the uterus, the cells of which undergo minimal change during the sexual cycle. **s. basa′le epider′midis** [N A], the deepest stratum of the epidermis, composed of a single layer of deeply basophilic cells. Called also *basal layer of epidermis.* **cerebral s. of retina, s. cerebra′le ret′inae** [N A], the internal, transparent, light-sensitive layer of the optic part of the retina. **s. cine′reum cerebel′li** [B N A], s. moleculare cerebelli. **s. cine′reum collic′uli superio′ris,** s. griseum colliculi superioris. **circular s. of muscular tunic of colon,** s. circulare tunicae muscularis coli. **circular s. of muscular tunic of rectum,** s. circulare tunicae muscularis recti. **circular s. of muscular tunic of small intestine,** s. circulare tunicae muscularis intestini tenuis. **circular s. of muscular tunic of stomach,** s. circulare tunicae muscularis ventriculi. **s. circula′re membra′nae tym′pani** [N A, B N A], the layer of circularly coursing fibers deep to the mucous layer of the tympanic membrane; it is best developed near the periphery. Called also *circular layer of tympanic membrane.* **s. circula′re tu′nicae muscula′ris co′li** [N A], the inner layer of circularly coursing fibers in the muscular coat of the colon. Called also *circular layer of muscular tunic of colon.* **s. circula′re tu′nicae muscula′ris intesti′ni ten′uis** [N A, B N A], the inner layer of circularly coursing fibers in the muscular coat of the small intestine. Called also *circular layer of muscular tunic of small intestine.* **s. circula′re tu′nicae muscula′ris rec′ti** [N A], the inner layer of circularly coursing fibers in the muscular coat of the rectum. Called also *circular layer of muscular tunic of rectum.* **s. circula′re tu′nicae muscula′ris tu′bae uteri′nae** [B N A], the layer of circularly coursing fibers in the muscular coat of the uterine tube. Omitted in N A. **s. circula′re tu′nicae muscula′ris ure′thrae mulie′bris** [B N A], the layer of circularly coursing fibers in the muscular coat of the female urethra. Omitted in N A. **s. circula′re tu′nicae muscula′ris ventric′uli** [N A, B N A], the layer of circularly coursing fibers in the muscular coat of the stomach. Called also *circular layer of muscular tunic of stomach.* **s. compac′tum,** the superficial layer of the endometrium, and especially of the decidua basalis. Called also *compact layer.* **connective tissue s. of mesentery,** lamina mesenterii propria. **s. cor′neum epider′-**

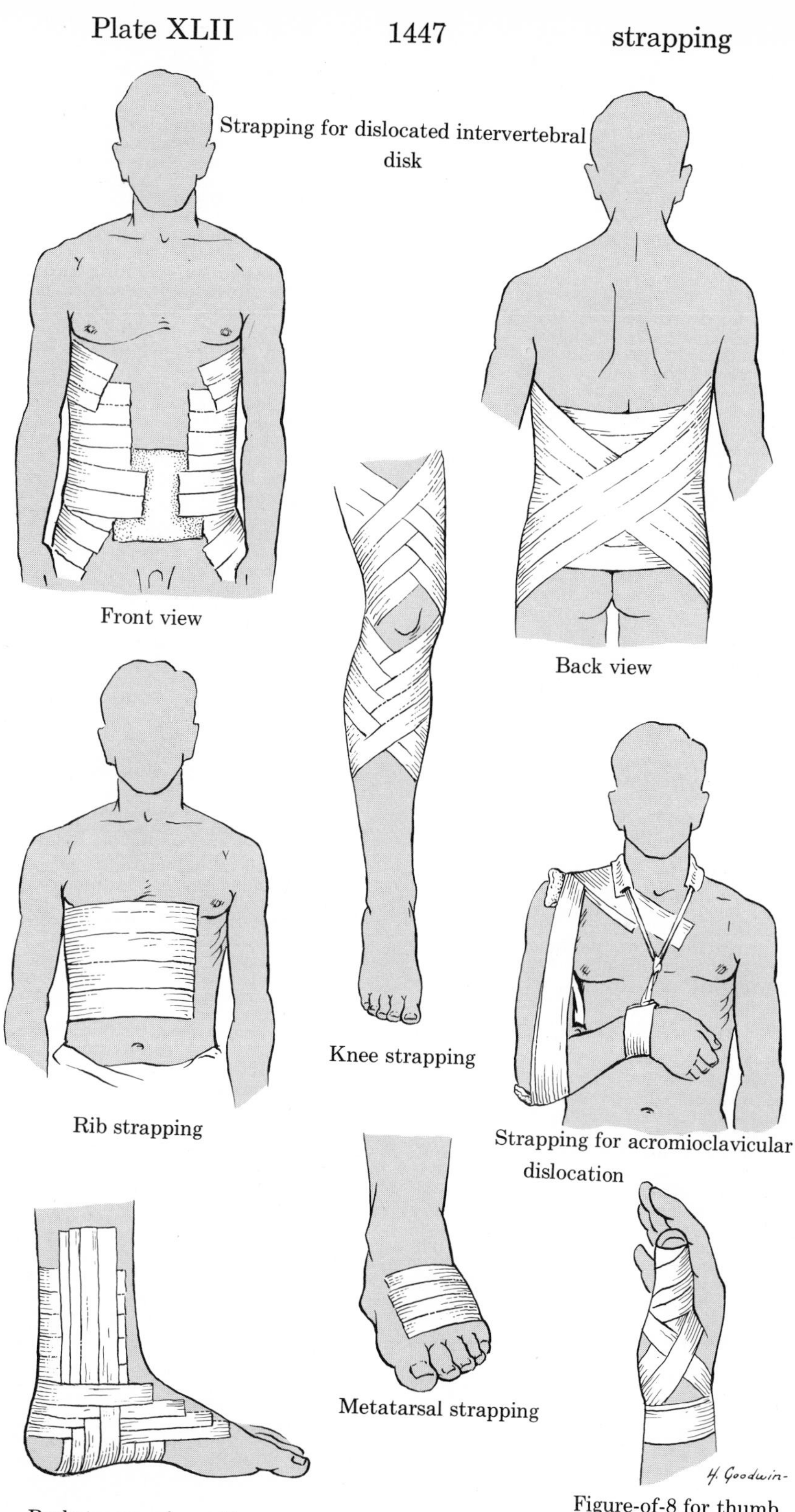

VARIOUS TYPES OF STRAPPING

midis [N A], the outermost layer of the epidermis, consisting of cells that are dead and desquamating; the B N A term embraced also the layers now called *s. lucidum epidermidis* and *s. granulosum epidermidis.* Called also *horny layer of epidermis.* **s. cor'neum un'guis** [N A, B N A], the outer, compact layer of the nail. Called also *nail plate* and *horny layer of nail.* **s. cuta'neum mem-bra'nae tym'pani** [N A, B N A], a very thin form of skin that constitutes the lateral layer of the tympanic membrane. Called also *cutaneous layer of tympanic membrane.* **s. cylin'dricum epider'midis,** N A alternative for *s. basale epidermidis.* **s. denta'tum epider'midis,** s. germinativum epidermidis (Malpighii). **s. dis-junc'tum,** a layer of partially detached cells on the free surface of the epidermis. **s. ebo'ris,** the dentin of a tooth (dentinum [N A]). **s. exter'num tu'nicae muscula'ris duc'tus deferen'tis** [B N A], the outer layer of fibers in the muscular coat of the ductus deferens. Omitted in N A. **s. exter'num tu'nicae muscula'ris ure'teris** [B N A], the outer layer of fibers in the muscular coat of the ureter. Omitted in N A. **s. exter'num tu'nicae muscula'ris ves'-icae urina'riae** [B N A], the outer layer of fibers in the muscular coat of the urinary bladder. Omitted in N A. **s. fibro'sum cap'sulae articula'ris** [B N A], membrana fibrosa capsulae articularis. **s. filamento'sum,** s. germinativum epidermidis [Malpighii]. **s. func-tiona'le,** the surface layer of the mucosa of the uterus, the cells of which participate in the changes occurring during the sexual cycle. **s. gangli-ona're ner'vi op'tici** [N A], the layer of the cerebral stratum of the retina that contains the multipolar neurons, the axons of which form the fibers of the optic nerve. Called also *ganglionic layer of optic nerve.* **s. gangliona're ret'inae** [N A], the layer of the cerebral stratum of the retina that contains the bipolar cells. Called also *ganglionic layer of retina.* **ganglionic s. of optic nerve,** s. ganglionare nervi optici. **gan-glionic s. of retina,** s. ganglionare retinae. **s. ganglio'sum cerebel'li** [B N A], the thin middle gray layer of the cortex cerebelli, consisting of a single layer of Purkinje cells. Omitted in N A. **s. gelatino'sum,** the innermost of the four layers of the olfactory lobe. **s. germinati'-vum epider'midis [Malpig'hii]** [B N A], the innermost layer of the epidermis, embracing the layers now called *s. basale epidermidis* and *s. spinosum epidermidis.* **s. germinati'vum un'guis** [N A, B N A], the lower layer of the nail, from which the nail grows; it is continuous with the stratum basale and stratum spinosum of the epidermis. Called also *germinative layer of nail.* **s. granulo'sum cerebel'li** [N A, B N A], the deep layer of the cortex of the cerebellum. It contains may small neurons (granule cells) and is separated from the molecular layer by the Purkinje cells. Called also *granular layer of cerebellum.* **s. granulo'sum epider'midis** [N A], the layer of the skin between the stratum lucidum and the stratum spinosum. Called also *granular layer of epidermis.* **s. granulo'sum follic'uli ooph'ori vesiculo'si** [B N A], **s. granulo'-sum follic'uli ova'rici vesiculo'si** [N A], **s. granulo'sum ova'rii,** the layer of follicle cells lining the theca of a vesicular ovarian follicle. **gray s. of cerebellum,** s. moleculare cerebelli. **s. gris'eum centra'le cer'ebri** [B N A], substantia grisea centralis cerebri. **s. gris'eum collic'uli superio'ris** [N A, B N A], a thick layer, containing few myelinated fibers, near the outer surface of the superior colliculus. Called also *gray layer of superior colliculus.* **s. interme'-dium,** the layer of cells of the enamel organ of a tooth just peripheral to the ameloblastic layer. **s. inter'num tu'nicae muscula'ris duc'tus deferen'tis** [B N A], the inner layer of fibers in the muscular coat of the ductus deferens. Omitted in N A. **s. inter'num tu'nicae muscula'ris ure'teris** [B N A], the inner layer of fibers in the muscular coat of the ureter. Omitted in N A. **s. inter'num tu'nicae muscula'ris ves'icae urina'riae** [B N A], the inner layer of fibers in the muscular coat of the urinary bladder. Omitted in N A. **s. interoliva're lemnis'ci** [B N A], fibers from the posterior columns of the spinal cord that pass upward between the olives to the ventrolateral nucleus of the thalamus. Omitted in N A. **s. lacuno'sum,** one of the constituent layers of the hippocampus. **s. lemnis'ci,** s. interolivare lemnisci. **longitudinal s. of muscular tunic of colon,** s. longitudinale tunicae muscularis coli. **longitudinal s. of muscular tunic of rectum,** s. longitudinale tunicae muscularis recti. **longitudinal s. of muscular tunic of small intestine,** s. longitudinale tunicae muscularis intestini tenuis. **longitudinal s. of muscular tunic of stomach,** s. longitudinale tunicae muscularis ventriculi. **s. longitudina'le tu'nicae mus-cula'ris co'li** [N A], the outer layer of the muscular coat of the colon, consisting of longitudinally coursing fibers; it is thick in the regions of the three teniae coli and very thin between them. Called also *longitudinal layer of muscular tunic of colon.* **s. longitudina'le tu'nicae mus-cula'ris intesti'ni ten'uis** [N A, B N A], the outer layer of the muscular coat of the small intestine, consisting of longitudinally coursing fibers. Called also *longitudinal layer of muscular tunic of small intestine.* **s. longitudina'le tu'nicae muscula'ris rec'ti** [N A], the outer layer of the muscular coat of the rectum, consisting of longitudinally coursing fibers. Called also *longitudinal layer of muscular tunic of rectum.* **s. longitudina'le tu'nicae muscula'ris tu'bae uteri'nae** [B N A], the layer of longitudinally coursing fibers in the muscular coat of the uterine tube. Omitted in N A. **s. longi-tudina'le tu'nicae muscula'ris ure'thrae mulie'bris** [B N A], the layer of longitudinally coursing fibers in the muscular coat of the female urethra. Omitted in N A. **s. longitudina'le tu'nicae muscula'ris ventric'uli** [N A, B N A], the layer of longitudinally coursing fibers in the muscular coat of the stomach. Called also *longitudinal layer of muscular tunic of stomach.* **s. lu'cidum epider'midis** [N A], the clear translucent layer of the skin, just beneath the stratum corneum. Called also *clear layer of skin.* **s. malpig'hii,** s. germinativum epidermidis (Malpighii). **s. me'dium tu'nicae muscula'ris duc'tus deferen'tis** [B N A], the middle layer of the muscular coat of the ductus deferens. Omitted in N A. **s. me'dium tu'nicae mus-cula'ris ure'teris** [B N A], the middle layer of the muscular coat of the ureter. Omitted in N A. **s. me'dium tu'nicae muscula'ris ves'icae urina'riae** [B N A], the middle layer of the muscular coat of the urinary bladder. Omitted in N A. **s. molecula're cerebel'li** [N A], the superficial layer of the cortex of the cerebellum, containing a relatively small number of stellate neurons. Called also *s. cinereum cerebelli* [B N A], and *molecular layer of cerebellum.* **s. muco'sum membra'nae tym'pani** [N A, B N A], the inner layer of the tympanic membrane, continuous with the mucosa lining the tympanic cavity. Called also *mucous layer of tympanic membrane.* **s. neuroepithelia'le ret'inae** [N A], the outer layer of the cerebral stratum of the retina, which contains the rods and cones. Called also *neuroepithelial layer of retina.* **s. nuclea're medul'lae oblonga'tae** [B N A], a tract of gray substance in the medulla oblongata, containing the nuclei of the lower cranial nerves. Omitted in N A. **Oehl's s.,** s. lucidum epidermidis. **s. olfacto'rium,** one of the four layers of the olfactory lobe. **s. op'ticum,** a layer of white fibers in the superior colliculus, just below the stratum griseum. **s. o'riens,** the layer of polymorphic cells of the hippocampus. **s. papilla're cor'ii** [N A], **s. papilla're cu'tis,** the outer layer of the corium, characterized by ridges and papillae which protrude into the epidermis. Called also *corpus papillare corii*

[B N A], and *papillary layer of corium.* **s. perichorioi'deum,** lamina suprachoroidea. **s. pigmen'ti bul'bi oc'uli** [N A, B N A], a layer of pigmented epithelium, the outer of the two parts of the retina, extending from the entrance of the optic nerve to the pupillary margin of the iris, and comprising the stratum pigmenti retinae, stratum pigmenti corporis ciliaris, and stratum pigmenti iridis. Called also *pigmented layer of eyeball.* **s. pigmen'ti cor'poris cilia'ris** [N A, B N A], the part of the pigmented layer of the eyeball that rests on the ciliary body. Called also *pigmented layer of ciliary body.* **s. pigmen'ti i'ridis** [N A, B N A], the part of the pigmented layer of the eyeball that rests on the posterior surface of the iris. Called also *pigmented layer of iris.* **s. pigmen'ti ret'inae** [N A, B N A], the part of the pigmented layer of the eyeball that forms the outer layer of the pars optica of the retina. Called also *pigmented layer of retina.* **s. Purkin'je,** s. gangliosum cerebelli. **s. pyramida'le,** the innermost layer but one of the strata of the human brain cortex. **s. radia'tum,** a layer of the hippocampus, crossed at right angles to its surfaces by the processes of large pyramidal cells which lie along its border. **s. radia'tum membra'nae tym'pani** [N A, B N A], the layer of fibers beneath the cutaneous layer of the tympanic membrane, radiating outward from the manubrium of the malleus to pass into the fibrocartilaginous ring. Called also *radiate layer of tympanic membrane.* **s. reticula're co'rii** [N A], **s. reticula're cu'tis,** the inner layer of the corium, consisting chiefly of dense fibrous tissue. Called also *tunica propria corii* [B N A], and *reticular layer of corium.* **s. reticula'tum,** s. zonale thalami. **s. spino'sum epider'midis** [N A], the layer of the skin between the stratum granulosum and the stratum basale, characterized by the presence of prickle cells. Called also *spinous layer of epidermis.* **s. spongio'sum.** 1. The middle layer of the endometrium. 2. Corpus spongiosum urethrae muliebris. **s. subcuta'neum,** tela subcutanea. **s. submuco'sum,** the inner layer of the myometrium, which is in contact with the endometrium. Called also *s. subvasculare.* **submucous s. of bladder,** tela submucosa vesicae urinariae. **submucous s. of colon,** tela submucosa coli. **submucous s. of rectum,** tela submucosa recti. **submucous s. of small intestine,** tela submucosa intestini tenuis. **submucous s. of stomach,** tela submucosa ventriculi. **s. subsero'sum,** the outer layer of the myometrium, which is in contact with the serous coat of the uterus. **s. subvascula're,** s. submucosum. **s. supravascula're,** the layer of the myometrium that lies between the stratum vasculare and the stratum subserosum. **s. synovia'le cap'sulae articula'ris** [B N A], membrana synovialis capsulae articularis. **s. vascula're,** the middle layer of the myometrium, forming most of its bulk, and composed of circular and spiral fibers. **white s. of quadrigeminal body, deep,** s. album profundum corporis quadrigemini. **s. zona'le cor'poris quadrigem'ini** [B N A], a superficial layer of white fibers of the corpora quadrigemina. Omitted in N A. **s. zona'le thal'ami** [N A, B N A], a layer of white nerve fibers covering the dorsal surface of the thalamus. Called also *zonal layer of thalamus.*

Straus's phenomenon, reaction, sign (strows'ez) [Isador *Straus*, French physician, 1854–1896]. See under *reaction* and *sign.*

Strauss's cannula, needle, sign (strows'ez) [Hermann *Strauss*, physician in Berlin, 1868–1944]. See under *needle* and *sign.*

streak (strēk). A line, stripe, or trace. **angioid s's,** pigment striae appearing in the retina after hemorrhage. **germinal s.,** primitive s. **Knapp's s's,** lines resembling blood vessels seen occasionally in the retina after hemorrhage. **medullary s.,** the neural, or medullary, groove. **meningeal s.,** tache cérébrale. **primitive s.,** a faint white trace at the aftermost end of the germinal area, formed by the movement of cells, and constituting the first indication of the development of the separate germ layers.

stream (strēm). A current or flow of water or other fluid. **axial s.,** the core of rapid flow in the center of a channel, as in the lumen of a blood vessel, bordered or surrounded by a zone in which the elements move less rapidly, or are motionless.

streblomicrodactyly (streb″lo-mi″kro-dak'tĭ-le) [Gr. *streblos* twisted + *mikros* small + *daktylos* finger]. Streptomicrodactyly.

stremma (strem'ah) [Gr. "a twist"]. A sprain.

streph-. See *strepho-.*

strephenopodia (stref″ĕ-no-po'de-ah) [*streph-* + Gr. *en* in + *pous* foot]. Talipes varus.

strephexopodia (stref″ek-so-po'de-ah) [*streph-* + Gr. *exō* out + *pous* foot]. Talipes valgus.

strepho-, streph- (stref'o, stref) [Gr. *strephein* to twist]. Combining form meaning twisted.

strephopodia (stref″o-po'de-ah). Talipes equinus.

strephosymbolia (stref″o-sim-bo'le-ah) [*strepho-* + Gr. *symbolon* symbol + *-ia*]. 1. A disorder of perception in which objects seem reversed as in a mirror. 2. A reading difficulty inconsistent with a child's general intelligence, beginning with confusion between similar but oppositely oriented letters (b–d, q–p) and a tendency to reverse direction in reading.

strephotome (stref'o-tōm). An instrument like a corkscrew for invaginating the hernial sac.

strepitus (strep'ĭ-tus) [L.]. A noise; a sound heard on auscultation. **s. uteri'nus,** the sound of flowing blood in the pregnant uterus heard after the first trimester of pregnancy.

strepogenin (strep″o-gen'in). A factor present in casein and certain other proteins which is essential to optimal growth of animals.

strepsinema (strep″sĭ-ne'mah) [Gr. *strepsis* a twist + *nēma* thread]. The threads of chromatin in the strepsitene stage.

strepsitene (strep'sĭ-tēn). A stage of meiosis, after the diplotene stage, in which the threads become twisted about each other.

streptamine (strep-tam'in). One of the fractions derived from the degradation of streptomycin, the other fraction being streptidine. It is 1,3-diamino-2,4,5,6-tetrahydroxycyclohexane.

strepticemia (strep″tĭ-se'me-ah). Streptococcemia.

streptidine (strep'tĭ-dīn). One of the fractions derived from streptomycin. It is 1,3-diguanido-2,4,5,6-tetrahydroxycyclohexane. See *streptamine.*

strepto- (strep'to) [Gr. *streptos* twisted]. Combining form meaning twisted.

strepto-angina (strep″to-an'jĭ-nah). A pseudomembranous deposit in the throat due to a streptococcus.

streptobacilli (strep″to-bah-sil'i). Plural of *streptobacillus.*

Streptobacillus (strep″to-bah-sil'lus). A name given a genus of microorganisms of family Bacteroidaceae, order Eubacteriales, said to be made up of pleomorphic bacteria which vary from short rods to long, interwoven filaments. *S. monilifor'mis,* an etiological agent of rat-bite fever and Haverhill fever.

streptobacillus (strep″to-bah-sil'us), pl. *streptobacil'li.* 1. A rod-shaped bacterium remaining loosely attached end-to-end in long chains as a consequence of failure of daughter cells to separate following cell division. 2. An organism of the genus *Streptobacillus.*

streptobacteria (strep″to-bak-te're-ah) (pl.). A group including those bacteria (*Streptothrix,* etc.) which are linked together into twisted chains.

streptobacterin (strep″to-bak'ter-in). The vaccine prepared from streptococci.

streptococcal (strep″to-kok'al). Pertaining to or due to a streptococcus.

Streptococceae (strep″to-kok′se-e). A tribe of microorganisms of the family Lactobacillaceae, order Eubacteriales, made up of spherical or elongated cells which divide in one plane only, and usually occur in pairs or chains. It includes five genera, *Diplococcus*, *Leuconostoc*, *Pediococcus*, *Peptostreptococcus*, and *Streptococcus*.

streptococcemia (strep″to-kok-se′me-ah) [*streptococcus* + Gr. *haima* blood + *-ia*]. The presence of streptococci in the blood; streptococcus infection.

streptococci (strep″to-kok′si). Plural of *streptococcus*.

streptococcic (strep″to-kok′sik). Streptococcal.

streptococcicide (strep″to-kok′sĭ-sīd). An agent that is destructive to streptococci.

streptococcicosis (strep″to-kok″sĭ-ko′sis). A general term for all streptococcal infections.

streptococcolysin (strep″to-kok-kol′ĭ-sin). Streptolysin.

Streptococcus (strep″to-kok′us) [*strepto-* + Gr. *kokkos* berry]. A genus of microorganisms of the tribe Streptococceae, family Lactobacillaceae, order Eubacteriales. The genus is separable into the pyogenic group, the viridans group, the enterococcus group, and the lactic group. The first group includes the β-hemolytic human and animal pathogens, the second and third include α-hemolytic parasitic forms occurring as normal flora in the upper respiratory tract and the intestinal tract, respectively, and the fourth is made up of saprophytic forms associated with the souring of milk. **S. agalac′tiae,** β-hemolytic streptococci of group B, causing mastitis in cattle and seldom infecting man. **S. bo′vis,** a serologically heterogeneous species found in the bovine alimentary tract and sometimes in human feces; also sometimes associated with subacute endocarditis. **S. e′qui,** β-hemolytic streptococci of group C, the specific etiologic agent of strangles in horses; it is non-pathogenic for man. **S. equisim′ilis,** β-hemolytic streptococci of group C, producing about 5 per cent of human streptococcal disease, and known as "human C." **S. faeca′lis,** α-hemolytic streptococci of the entercoccus group, found as a normal inhabitant of the intestinal tract and a cause of subacute bacterial endocarditis; three varieties are sometimes recognized. **S. mi′tis,** α-hemolytic streptococci of the viridans group, found in the normal upper respiratory tract and etiologically related to regional focal abscesses and subacute bacterial endocarditis. **S. pyog′enes,** β-hemolytic, toxigenic pyogenic streptococci of group A, causing septic sore throat, scarlet fever, rheumatic fever, puerperal sepsis, acute glomerulonephritis, and other conditions in man. **S. saliva′rius,** α-hemolytic streptococci of the viridans group, making up a part of the normal flora of the upper respiratory tract, and occasionally associated with apical abscesses of the teeth and subacute bacterial endocarditis. **S. zooepidem′icus,** β-hemolytic streptococci of group C, commonly causing pyogenic disease in lower animals and known as "animal pyogenes"; it is rarely found in man.

streptococcus (strep-to-kok′us), pl. *streptococ′ci*. 1. A spherical bacterium occurring predominantly in chains of cells often surrounded by continuous capsular material as a consequence of failure of daughter cells to separate following cell division in one plane. 2. An organism of the genus *Streptococcus*. **alpha s.** See under *hemolytic s.* **anhemolytic s.,** a streptococcus which does not cause any change in the medium when cultured on blood-agar. **Bargen's s.,** *Streptococcus bovis*. **beta s.** See under *hemolytic s.* **Fehleisen's s.,** *Streptococcus pyogenes*. **gamma s.,** anhemolytic s. **hemolytic s.,** any streptococcus that is capable of hemolyzing red blood corpuscles, or of producing a zone of hemolysis about the colonies on blood-agar. The great majority of streptococci found in pathologic processes belong to this type. The hemolytic streptococci have been classified as the *alpha* (α-hemolytic) or *viridans type*, which produces about the colony on blood-agar a zone of greenish discoloration considerably smaller than the clear zone produced by the beta type; and the *beta* (β-hemolytic) *type*, which produces a clear zone of hemolysis immediately surrounding the colony on blood-agar. **s. of Ostertag,** a species causing vaginitis verrucosa in cattle.

streptocyte (strep′to-sīt). An amebiform body occurring in beadlike strings from the vesicles of foot-and-mouth disease.

streptoderma (strep″to-der′mah). Cutaneous pyogenic infection by streptococci.

streptodermatitis (strep″to-der″mah-ti′tis). Dermatitis produced by streptococci.

streptodornase (strep″to-dor′nās) [*strepto*cocci + *de*oxy*r*ibo*n*ucle*ase*]. A substance produced by hemolytic streptococci that catalyzes the depolymerization of deoxyribonucleic acid. **streptokinase-s.** See under *streptokinase*.

streptoduocin (strep″to-du′o-sin). An antibiotic compound consisting of approximately equal parts of dihydrostreptomycin sulfate and streptomycin sulfate.

streptogenin (strep″to-jen′in). A hypothetical substance in the proteins of milk and other foods, the lack of which causes sub-optimal growth in bacteria and laboratory animals.

streptokinase (strep″to-ki′nās) [*strepto*coccus + *kinase*]. An enzyme produced by streptococci that catalyzes the conversion of plasminogen to plasmin. **s.-streptodornase,** a mixture of enzymes elaborated by hemolytic streptococci, used as a proteolytic and fibrinolytic agent.

streptoleukocidin (strep″to-lu″ko-si′din). A toxin from streptococcus cultures which is destructive to leukocytes.

streptolysin (strep-tol′ĭ-sin) [*strepto*coccus + hemo*lysin*]. A filterable hemolysin produced by various streptococci. **s. O,** a hemolysin which is inactive in the oxidized state but is readily activated by treatment with mild reducing agents, such as sulfite. **s. S,** a hemolysin which is sensitive to treatment with heat or acid, but is not inactivated by oxygen.

streptomicrodactyly (strep″to-mi″kro-dak′tĭ-le) [*strepto* + Gr. *mikros* small + *daktylos* finger] Camptodactyly in which the little fingers only are involved.

Streptomyces (strep″to-mi′sēz) [*strepto-* + Gr. *mykēs* fungus]. A genus of microorganisms of the family Streptomycetaceae, order Actinomycetales, separable into 150 different species, usually soil forms but occasionally parasitic on plants and animals, and notable as the source of various antibiotics, such as the tetracyclines.

Streptomycetaceae (strep″to-mi″se-ta′se-e). A family of Schizomycetes, order Actinomycetales, made up of primarily soil forms, sometimes thermophilic in rotting manure, and some parasitic species. It includes three genera: *Micromonospora*, *Streptomyces*, and *Thermoactinomyces*.

streptomycin (strep′to-mi″sin). An antibiotic substance produced by the soil actinomycete, *Streptomyces griseus*.

streptomycosis (strep″to-mi-ko′sis). Infection with fungi of the genus Streptomyces.

streptonivicin (strep″to-ni′vĭ-sin). Novobiocin.

streptosepticemia (strep″to-sep″tĭ-se′me-ah). Septicemia due to a streptococcus.

Streptosporangium (strep″to-spo-ran′je-um) [*strepto-* + Gr. *sporos* seed + *angeion* vessel]. A genus of microorganisms of the family Actinoplanaceae, order Actinomycetales, made up of mycelium-forming saprophytic microorganisms found in soil and water.

streptothricin (strep″to-thri′sin). An antibiotic substance which is active against both gram-negative and gram-positive bacteria.

streptothricosis (strep″to-thri-ko′sis). Streptotrichosis.

Streptothrix (strep′to-thriks) [*strepto-* + Gr. *thrix* hair]. A name formerly given a genus of microorganisms, species of which are now classified under *Actinomyces, Streptomyces, Nocardia,* and other genera.

streptotrichal (strep-tot′rĭ-kal). Pertaining to or caused by streptothrix.

streptotrichosis (strep″to-tri-ko′sis). Infection with organisms of the former genus Streptothrix. See *actinomycosis* and *nocardiosis.*

stress (stres). 1. Forcibly exerted influence; pressure. In dentistry the pressure of the upper teeth against the lower in mastication. 2. The sum of all non-specific biological phenomena elicited by adverse external influences, including damage and defense. It may be localized, as in the local adaptation syndrome (L.A.S.), or systemic, as in the general adaptation syndrome (G.A.S.).

stress-breaker (stres′brāk-er). A device which abolishes or lessens the occlusal forces acting on abutment teeth.

stretcher (strech′er). A litter for carrying the sick or injured.

stria (stri′ah), pl. *stri′ae* [L. "a furrow, groove"]. 1. A streak, or line. 2. A narrow bandlike structure; used in anatomical nomenclature as a general term to designate such longitudinal collections of nerve fibers in the brain. **acoustic striae,** striae medullares ventriculi quarti. **stri′ae albican′tes,** striae atrophicae. **striae of Amici,** lines which mark or separate the alleged disks of sarcous matter from each other. **stri′ae atro′phicae,** white or colorless striae on the abdomen, breasts, or thighs, caused by mechanical stretching of the skin, such as occurs in pregnancy or excessive obesity, with weakening of the elastic tissue; such striae may also be colored, and are often associated with increased urinary corticoid excretion. **auditory striae,** striae medullares ventriculi quarti. **striae of Baillarger,** Baillarger's lines. **stri′ae cilia′res,** slight dark ridges running parallel with each other from the teeth of the ora serrata to the valleys between the ciliary processes. **stri′ae cu′tis disten′sae, stri′ae disten′sa,** striae atrophicae. **s. for′nicis,** s. medullaris thalami. **Francke's striae,** small cutaneous venous ectasias of red wine color appearing near the seventh cervical vertebra. **striae of Gennari,** Baillarger's lines. **stri′ae gravida′rum,** striae atrophicae following pregnancy. **habenular s.,** s. medullaris thalami. **s. interme′dia trigo′ni olfacto′rii** [B N A], **intermediate stria of olfactory trigone,** a more or less distinct branch of the posterior end of the olfactory tract, which spreads out in the olfactory trigone and the anterior perforated substance. Omitted in N A. **s. kaesbechtere′wi,** Bechterew's layer. **Knapp's striae,** streaks sometimes seen in the retina after hemorrhage. **s. lancis′ii,** s. longitudinalis medialis corporis callosi. **Langhans' s.,** a layer of canalized fibrin in the developing placenta on the external surface of the chorion adjacent to the intervillous space. **longitudinal s. of corpus callosum, lateral,** s. longitudinalis lateralis corporis callosi. **longitudinal s. of corpus callosum, medial,** s. longitudinalis medialis corporis callosi. **s. longitudina′lis latera′lis cor′poris callo′si** [N A, B N A], a white, longitudinal band along the lateral part of the upper surface of the corpus callosum, covered by the gyrus cinguli and passing back to the hippocampus. Called also *lateral longitudinal s. of corpus callosum.* **s. longitudina′lis media′lis cor′poris callo′si** [N A, B N A], a white, longitudinal line near the middle of the upper surface of the corpus callosum, which passes back to the hippocampus. Called also *medial longitudinal s. of corpus callosum.* **mallear s. of tympanic membrane, s. mallea′ris membra′nae tym′pani** [N A], **s. malleola′ris membra′nae tym′pani** [B N A], a nearly vertical radial band seen on the outer surface of the tympanic membrane; it extends from the umbo upward to the prominentia mallearis and is caused by the manubrium mallei. **s. media′lis trigo′ni olfacto′rii** [B N A], the portion of the posterior end of the olfactory tract that turns medialward to the area parolfactoria. Omitted in N A. **stri′ae medulla′res acus′ticae, stri′ae medulla′res fos′sae rhomboi′deae** [B N A], striae medullares ventriculi quarti. **s. medulla′ris thal′ami** [N A, B N A], a fiber bundle that arises from the medial olfactory area, subcallosal gyrus, preoptic area, and amygdaloid nuclei, and runs backward along the dorsomedial border of the thalamus to reach the habenular nucleus. **stri′ae medulla′res ventric′uli quar′ti** [N A], bundles of white fibers coursing transversely across the floor of the fourth ventricle. They arise from the arcuate nuclei, pass dorsally close to the midline, and after having reached the fourth ventricle finally enter the inferior cerebellar peduncle. Called also *striae medullares fossae rhomboideae* [B N A], and *medullary striae of fourth ventricle.* **medullary striae of fourth ventricle, medullary striae of rhomboid fossa,** striae medullaris ventriculi quarti. **medullary s. of thalamus.** 1. Stria medullaris thalami. 2. See *laminae medullares thalami.* **meningitic s.,** tache cérébrale. **Nitabuch's s.,** a layer of canalized fibrin in the developing placenta, along the decidual surface, where the trophoblast and decidua merge. **s. olfacto′ria** [N A], **s. olfacto′ria latera′lis** [B N A], **olfactory s.,** a band of fibers running from the olfactory region toward the insula. **s. patella′ris,** a transverse stria above the upper border of the patella, seen after an attack of some infectious disease, such as typhoid fever. **s. pinea′lis,** s. medullaris thalami. **Retzius' parallel striae,** brown lines crossing the enamel prisms, seen on cutting the tooth enamel. **Rohr's s.,** a layer of canalized fibrin in the developing placenta, within the intervillous space at the fetal-maternal junction. **Schreger's striae,** darkish, irregular lines crossing the enamel rods and striae of Retzius of the tooth enamel. **s. semicircula′ris,** s. terminalis. **s. termina′lis** [N A, B N A], a band of fibers along the lateral margin of the ventricular surface of the thalamus, covering the thalamostriate vein and, following the course of the vein, marking the line of separation between the thalamus and the caudate nucleus; it extends from the region of the interventricular foramen to the inferior horn of the lateral ventricle, carrying fibers from the amygdaloid nuclei to the septal, hypothalamic, and thalamic areas. **stri′ae transver′sae cor′poris callo′si** [B N A], transverse bands on the upper surface of the corpus callosum, constituted by bundles of fibers. **s. vascula′ris duc′tus cochlea′ris** [N A, B N A], a layer of fibrous vascular tissue covering the outer wall of the cochlear duct, which is thought to secrete the endolymph. **s. ventric′uli ter′tii,** s. medullaris thalami. **Wickham's striae,** grayish lines forming a network on the surface of the papules characteristic of lichen planus.

striae (stri′e) [L.]. Plural of *stria.*

striascope (stri′ah-skōp). An instrument for use in ophthalmologic refraction.

striatal (stri-a′tal). Pertaining to the corpus striatum.

striated (stri′āt-ed) [L. *striatus*]. Striped; marked by striae.

striation (stri-a′shun). 1. The quality of being marked by stripes or striae. 2. A streak or scratch. **Baillarger's s's.** See under *line.* **tabby cat s., tigroid s.,** a striation or marking on muscle tissue that has undergone marked fatty degeneration; seen especially in degenerated heart muscle.

striatran (stri′ah-tran). Trade mark for a preparation of emylcamate.

striatum (stri-a′tum) [L.]. Striped, or grooved.

Strickler's solution (strik′lerz) [Albert *Strickler,* American dermatologist, born 1886]. See under *solution.*

stricture (strik'tūr) [L. *strictura*]. The abnormal narrowing of a canal, duct, or passage, either from cicatricial contraction or the deposit of abnormal tissue. **annular s.,** a ringlike obstruction around the walls of an organ. **bridle s.,** a fold of membrane stretched across a canal, and partially closing it. **cicatricial s.,** one which follows a wound or sore, producing cicatricial contraction. **contractile s.,** one which may be mechanically dilated, but which soon returns to its contracted condition. Called also *recurrent s.* **false s., functional s.,** spasmodic s. **Hunner's s.,** stricture of the ureter due to local inflammation of the wall of the ureter. **hysterical s.,** spasmodic stricture of the esophagus seen in hysterical subjects. **impermeable s.,** one that does not permit the passage of an instrument. **irritable s.,** one in which the passage of an instrument produces severe pain. **organic s.,** a stricture due to a structural change in or about a canal, as the deposit of adventitious tissue, plastic inflammation, or neoplasmic growths. **permanent s.,** organic s. **recurrent s.,** contractile s. **spasmodic s., spastic s.,** one that is due to muscular spasm. Called also *false s., functional s.,* and *temporary s.* **temporary s.,** spasmodic s.

stricturoscope (strik'tu-ro-skōp). An instrument for examining strictures of the rectum.

stricturotome (strik'tu-ro-tōm). A knife for cutting strictures.

stricturotomy (strik"tu-rot'o-me). The cutting of a stricture.

strident (stri'dent). Stridulous.

stridor (stri'dor) [L.]. A harsh, high-pitched respiratory sound such as the inspiratory sound often heard in acute laryngeal obstruction. Cf. *laryngismus stridulus.* **s. den'tium,** bruxism. **s. serrat'icus,** a sound like that made by filing a saw, caused by respiration through a tracheostomy tube.

stridulous (strid'u-lus) [L. *stridulus*]. Attended with stridor; shrill and harsh in sound.

stringhalt (string'hawlt). Sudden and extreme flexion of the hind leg of a horse, producing a jerking motion in walking.

striocellular (stri"o-sel'u-lar) [L. *stria* streak + *cellular*]. Composed of striated muscle fibers and cells.

striocerebellar (stri"o-ser"e-bel'ar). Pertaining to the cerebellum and the corpus striatum.

striomuscular (stri"o-mus'ku-lar). Pertaining to or composed of striated muscle.

striospinoneural (stri"o-spi"no-nu'ral). Pertaining to the corpus striatum, the spinal cord, and the nerves: a term applied to a system of nerve fibers.

strip (strip). To press the contents from a canal, such as the urethra, by running the finger along it.

stripe (strīp). A streak or stria. **Baillarger's s's, Gennari's s's.** See *Baillarger's lines.* **Hensen's s.** 1. A band near the middle of the under surface of the membrana tectoria of the ear. 2. A slightly stainable central section in certain insect muscles. **Mees's s's,** diagonal white stripes on the fingernails in arsenic poisoning. **Vicq d'Azyr's s's,** the third and fifth stripes from within outward of the cortex of the cerebellum parallel to the surface.

strobila (stro-bi'lah), pl. *strobi'lae* [L.; Gr. *strobilos* anything twisted up]. The entire adult tapeworm including the scolex, neck, and proglottides.

strobile (stro'bīl). Strobila.

strobiloid (stro'bĭ-loid). Resembling a row of tapeworm segments.

strobilus (stro-bi'lus) [L.; Gr. *strobilos* anything twisted up]. Strobila.

stroboscope (stro'bo-skōp) [Gr. *strobos* whirl + *skopein* to examine]. An instrument by which the successive phases of animal movements may be studied; motion may appear to come to rest.

stroboscopic (stro"bo-skop'ik). Pertaining to the stroboscope.

Stroganoff's (Stroganov's) treatment (stro-gan'ofs) [Vasilii Vasilovich *Stroganov,* Russian obstetrician, born 1857]. See under *treatment.*

stroke (strōk). A sudden and severe attack, as of apoplexy or paralysis. **apoplectic s.,** an attack of apoplexy. **back s.** 1. The recoil of the ventricles at the time the blood is forced into the aorta. 2. The influence which a peripheral organ of response exerts back upon the nerve center from which the response was generated. **cold s.,** a condition analogous to heat stroke due to exposure to excessive cold. **heat s.,** a condition caused by exposure to excessive heat, natural or artificial, and marked by dry skin, vertigo, headache, thirst, nausea and muscular cramps. It may occur in one of three forms: (1) *thermic fever* or *sunstroke;* (2) *heat exhaustion;* or, more rarely, (3) *heat cramps.* **light s.,** a fatal narcosis produced in sensitized mice by exposure to light. **lightning s.,** loss of consciousness and shock with burns, frequently fatal, caused by lightning. **paralytic s.,** a sudden attack of paralysis from injury to the brain or cord. **sun s.** See *sunstroke.*

stroma (stro'mah), pl. *stro'mata* [Gr. *strōma* anything laid out for lying or sitting upon]. The structural elements of an organ; used in anatomical nomenclature as a general term to designate the tissue that forms the ground substance, framework, or matrix of an organ, as distinguished from that constituting its functional element, or parenchyma. **s. of cornea,** substantia propria corneae. **s. glan'dulae thyreoi'deae** [B N A], **s. glan'dulae thyroi'deae** [N A], the tissue that forms the framework of the thyroid gland. Called also *s. of thyroid gland.* **s. i'ridis** [N A, B N A], **s. of iris,** the soft mass of connective tissue fibers that make up the major portion of the iris. **s. ova'rii** [N A, B N A], **s. of ovary,** the fibrous tissue and smooth muscle composing the framework of the ovary. **Rollet's s.,** that part of a red blood corpuscle which remains after the hemoglobin has been removed. **s. of thyroid gland,** s. glandulae thyroideae. **vitreous s., s. vit'reum** [N A, B N A], the framework of firmer material making up the vitreous body of the eye, and enclosing within its meshes the more fluid portion (humor vitreus).

stromal (stro'mal). Stromatic.

stromatic (stro-mat'ik). Pertaining to or resembling stroma.

stromatin (stro'mah-tin). The protein constituent of the stroma of erythrocytes.

stromatogenous (stro"mah-toj'e-nus) [*stroma* + Gr. *gennan* to produce]. Originating in the stroma or connective tissue of an organ.

stromatolysis (stro"mah-tol'ĭ-sis) [*stroma* + Gr. *lysis* dissolution]. Destruction of the stroma of a cell, especially that of a red blood corpuscle.

stromatosis (stro"mah-to'sis). Adenomyosis in which the invading endometrial substance is stromal and not glandular.

Stromeyer's cephalhematocele, splint (stro'mi-erz) [Georg Friedrich Louis *Stromeyer,* German surgeon, 1804–1876]. See under the nouns.

stromuhr (strōm'oor) [Ger. "stream clock"]. Ludwig's instrument for measuring the velocity of the blood flow (1867); a rheometer.

Strong's bacillus (strongz) [Richard Pearson *Strong,* American physician, 1872–1948]. A variety of paradysentery bacillus (*Shigella*).

strongyliasis (stron"jĭ-li'ah-sis). Strongylosis.

Strongyloides (stron"jĭ-loi'dēz). A genus of nematodes (roundworms) widely distributed in the intestinal contents of mammals. **S. ca'nis,** a species found in dogs. **S. intestina'lis,** *S. stercoralis.* **S. papillo'sus,** a species found in sheep, goats, rabbits, and rats. **S. rat'ti,** a species found in rats. **S. stercora'lis,** a roundworm occurring widely in tropical and subtropical countries. The female worm and her larvae inhabit the mucosa and submucosa of the small intestine where they cause diarrhea and ulceration (intestinal strongyloidiasis). The larvae expelled from an infected person with his feces develop in the soil and penetrate the human skin on contact. They eventually reach the lungs where they cause hemorrhage (pulmonary strongyloidiasis).

strongyloidiasis (stron″jĭ-loi-di′ah-sis). Infection with *Strongyloides stercoralis.*

strongyloidosis (stron″jĭ-loi-do′sis). Strongyloidiasis.

strongylosis (stron″jĭ-lo′sis). Infection with worms of the genus Strongylus.

Strongylus (stron′jĭ-lus) [Gr. *strongylos* round]. A genus of parasitic nematode worms. **S. equi′nus,** a worm parasitic in the intestines of horses; called also *palisade worm.* **S. fila′ria** causes hoose of sheep. **S. gibso′ni,** a species found in cattle and swine, and occasionally in man. **S. gi′gas,** *Dioctophyma renale.* **S. longivagina′tus,** a species found in the lungs of sheep, swine, and rabbits. **S. micru′rus** causes the disease hoose in calves. **S. paradox′us,** *Metastrongylus apri.* **S. rena′lis,** *Dioctophyma renale.* **S. sub′tilis,** *Trichostrongylus instabilis.* **S. vulga′ris,** a species found in horses.

strongylus (stron′jĭ-lus), pl. *stron′gyli.* An individual organism of the genus Strongylus.

strontia (stron′she-ah). An earthy substance, strontium oxide, SrO.

strontium (stron′she-um) [*Strontian* in Scotland]. A dark yellowish metal: symbol, Sr; atomic number, 38; atomic weight, 87.62. **s. bromide,** a clear, colorless, crystalline substance, $SrBr_2 + 6H_2O$: used like other bromides. **s. salicylate,** a salt, $(OH.C_6H_4.CO.O)_2Sr$, in white crystals, soluble in 40 parts of water and freely in alcohol.

strontiuresis (stron″she-u-re′sis). The elimination of strontium from the body through the kidneys.

strontiuretic (stron″she-u-ret′ik). Pertaining to, characterized by, or promoting strontiuresis.

strophocephalus (strof″o-sef′ah-lus). A fetal monster exhibiting strophocephaly.

strophocephaly (strof″o-sef′ah-le) [Gr. *strophos* a twisted band + *kephalē* head]. A developmental anomaly characterized by distortion of the head and face.

strophosomus (strof″o-so′mus) [Gr. *strophos* a twisted band + *sōma* body]. A celosomus, especially in chicks, in which the extremities are reflexed onto the back with the distal ends resting on the head.

strophulus (strof′u-lus) [L.]. A papular eruption of infants, called tooth rash or gum rash, of several varieties. See *miliaria.* **s. al′bus,** a variety known as white gum, or milium. **s. can′didus,** a variety of strophulus in which the papules are larger, are not inflamed, but have a smooth, shining surface, which gives them a lighter color than the cuticle near them. **s. confer′tus,** a variety with crowded papillae. **s. infan′tum.** See *strophulus* and *miliaria.* **s. intertinc′tus,** spotted strophulus, or red gum: a form in which the child's skin appears like cotton printed with red. **s. prurigino′sus,** a form characterized by intensely itching papules: seen chiefly in children. **s. volat′icus,** a form characterized by a fugitive eruption.

struck (struk). A gastrointestinal disease of sheep in Kent, England, caused by *Clostridium perfringens* type C.

structural (struk′tūr-al). Pertaining to or affecting the structure.

structural-functional (struk″tūr-al-funk′shun-al). Pertaining to both the structure and the function of a part, as of the brain.

structure (struk′tūr) [L. *struere* to build]. The components and their manner of arrangement in constituting a whole. **antigenic s.** (of microorganisms), the mosaic of individual antigens present in cells of microorganisms.

struma (stroo′mah) [L.]. 1. Scrofula. 2. Goiter. **s. aberran′ta,** goiter affecting an accessory thyroid gland. **adrenal s.,** suprarenal hyperplasia. **s. aneurysmat′ica,** vascular goiter in which the vessels are dilated. **s. basedowifica′ta,** toxic goiter. **s. ba′seos lin′guae,** an accessory and ectopic portion of thyroid tissue at the base of the tongue. **s. calculo′sa,** a goiter that has undergone calcification. **cast iron s.,** Riedel's s. **s. colloi′des,** distention of the follicles of the thyroid gland with colloid secretion. **s. colloi′des cys′tica,** a colloid goiter in which the walls of the follicles have broken down, forming cysts or cystlike cavities. **s. cys′tica os′sea,** a goiter in which bone has formed. **s. endothora′cia,** mediastinal goiter. **s. fibro′sa,** thyroid enlargement caused by hyperplasia of the connective tissue. **s. follicula′ris,** parenchymatous goiter. **s. gelatino′sa,** colloid goiter. **Hashimoto's s.,** s. lymphomatosa. **s. hyperplas′tica,** s. fibrosa. **ligneous s.,** Riedel's s. **s. lipomato′des aberra′ta re′nis,** hypernephroma. **s. lymphat′ica,** status lymphaticus. **s. lymphomato′sa,** a progressive disease of the thyroid gland, with extensive acidophilic degeneration of its epithelial elements and replacement by lymphoid and fibrous tissue. Called also *Hashimoto's disease* and *Hashimoto's thyroiditis.* **s. malig′na,** cancer of the thyroid body. **s. mol′lis,** thyroid enlargement due to hyperplasia of the cellular and colloid elements. **s. nodo′sa,** adenoma of the thyroid gland. **s. ova′rii,** a rare teratoid tumor of the ovary which contains iodine and histologically resembles colloid goiter. **s. parenchymato′sa,** enlargement of the thyroid gland due to follicular hyperplasia. **s. pituita′ria,** permanent enlargement of the pituitary body. **s. postbranchia′lis,** Getsowa's name for adenocarcinoma of the thyroid originating in a lateral anlage of the thyroid. **retrosternal s.,** substernal s. **Riedel's s.,** a chronic proliferating, fibrosing, inflammatory process involving usually one but sometimes both lobes of the thyroid gland, as well as the trachea and the muscles, fascia, nerves, and vessels in the vicinity of the gland. Called also *Riedel's disease* and *ligneous thyroiditis.* **substernal s.,** a goiter that extends down back of the sternum. **s. suprarena′lis,** a peculiar tumor of the suprarenal gland, consisting mainly of fatty tissue. **thymus s.,** persistence of the thymus gland beyond the time when it usually atrophies. **s. vasculo′sa,** vascular goiter.

strumectomy (stroo-mek′to-me) [L. *struma* goiter + Gr. *ektomē* excision]. Surgical removal of a goiter. **median s.,** excision of a median goiter or an enlarged isthmus of the thyroid.

strumiform (stroo′mĭ-form) [L. *struma* scrofula + *forma* shape]. Resembling scrofula.

strumiprival (stroo-mip′rĭ-val). Strumiprivous.

strumiprivic (stroo″mĭ-priv′ik). Strumiprivous.

strumiprivous (stroo″mĭ-pri′vus) [L. *strumiprivus; struma* goiter + *privus* deprived]. Caused by the removal of the thyroid gland.

strumitis (stroo-mi′tis). Inflammation of the thyroid gland. **eberthian s.,** strumitis due to infection with the typhoid bacillus.

strumoderma (stroo″mo-der′mah). Scrofuloderma.

strumosis (stroo-mo′sis). The state of being strumous.

strumous (stroo′mus) [L. *strumosus*]. Scrofulous; affected with or of the nature of scrofula.

Strümpell's disease, sign, etc. (strim′pelz) [Adolf von *Strümpell,* physician in Leipzig, 1853–1925]. See under the nouns.

Strümpell-Leichtenstern disease (strim′pel-lik′ten-stern) [A. von *Strümpell;* Otto *Leichtenstern,* German physician, 1845–1900]. Hemorrhagic encephalitis.

Strümpell-Marie disease (strim′pel-mah-re′) [A. von *Strümpell;* Pierre *Marie,* French physician, 1853–1940]. Rheumatoid spondylitis.

Strümpell-Westphal pseudosclerosis (strim'pel-vest'fawl) [A. von *Strümpell;* C. F. O. *Westphal,* German neurologist, 1833–1890]. See *pseudosclerosis.*

Strunsky's sign (strun'skēz) [Max *Strunsky,* New York orthopedic surgeon, born 1873]. See under *sign.*

Struve's test (stroo'vez) [Heinrich *Struve,* physician in Petrograd]. See under *tests.*

strychnine (strik'nin). The alkaloid from seeds of *Strychnos nux-vomica:* used as a central nervous system stimulant. **s. hydrochloride,** a crystalline salt, $C_{21}H_{22}N_2O_2.HCl + 2H_2O$. **s. nitrate,** a salt, $C_{21}H_{22}N_2O_2.HNO_3$: used for dipsomania. **s. phosphate,** a salt, $C_{21}H_{22}N_2O_2.H_3PO_4.2H_2O$, used in compounding iron, quinine, and strychnine phosphates elixir. **s. sulfate,** a white, crystalline salt, $(C_{21}H_{22}N_2O_2)_2.H_2SO_4.5H_2O$: it is employed more than any other of the strychnine salts.

strychninism (strik'nin-izm). A toxic condition due to the misuse of strychnine; chronic strychnine poisoning.

strychninization (strik"nin-i-za'shun). The act of bringing under the influence of strychnine.

strychninomania (strik"nin-o-ma'ne-ah) [*strychnine* + Gr. *mania* madness]. Mental aberration due to strychnine poisoning.

strychnism (strik'nizm). Poisoning by strychnine.

strychnize (strik'nīz). To put under the influence of strychnine.

Strychnos (strik'nos) [Gr. "nightshade"]. A genus of loganiaceous tropical trees. See *curare, nux vomica,* and *strychnine.*

S.T.S. Abbreviation for *serologic test for syphilis.*

S.T.U. Abbreviation for *skin test unit.*

stump (stump). The distal end of the part of the limb left in amputation. **conical s.,** a cone-shaped amputation stump produced as a result of undue retraction of the muscles.

stun (stun). To knock senseless; to render unconscious by a blow or other force; to daze.

stupe (stūp) [L. *stupa* tow]. A cloth, sponge, or the like, for external application, charged with hot water, wrung out nearly dry, and then made irritant or otherwise medicated.

stupefacient (stu"pĕ-fa'shent) [L. *stupefacere* to make senseless]. 1. Inducing stupor. 2. An agent that induces stupor.

stupefactive (stu"pĕ-fak'tiv). Producing narcosis or stupor.

stupor (stu'por) [L.]. Partial or nearly complete unconsciousness; also, in psychiatry, a disorder marked by reduced responsiveness. **anergic s.,** a form of dementia in which the patient is quiet, listless, and nonresistant. **benign s.,** a condition of stupor sometimes observed in the depressive phase of manic-depressive psychosis. **delusion s.,** stuporous insanity or acute dementia. **epileptic s.,** stupor following an epileptic convulsion; called also *postconvulsive s.* **lethargic s.,** trance. **postconvulsive s.,** epileptic s.

stuporose (stu'por-ōs). Stuporous.

stuporous (stu'por-us). Affected with or characterized by stupor.

stupp (stup). A poisonous kind of soot which accumulates in the condensers of mercury smelters. It contains metallic mercury in a finely divided condition.

sturdy (stur'de). Staggers in sheep.

Sturge's disease (ster'jez) [W. A. *Sturge,* British physician of 19th century]. Nevoid amentia.

Sturm's conoid, interval (sturmz) [Johann Christoph *Sturm,* 1635–1703]. See under *conoid,* and *focal interval,* under *interval.*

stuttering (stut'er-ing). A problem of speech behavior involving three definitive factors: (1) speech disfluency, most significantly repetitions of parts of words and whole words, prolongations of sounds, interjections of sounds or words, and unduly prolonged pauses; (2) reactions of the listeners to the speaker's disfluency as evaluated by them as undesirable, abnormal, or unacceptable; and (3) the reactions of the speaker to the listeners' reactions, as well as to his own speech disfluency and to his conception of himself as a stutterer. Stammering is the term generally applied to the condition in England and throughout the British Commonwealth. **labiochoreic s.,** labiochorea. **urinary s.,** interruption of the flow during urination.

sty (sti) [L. *hordeolum*]. Inflammation of one or more of the sebaceous glands of the eyelids. **meibomian s.,** inflammation of a meibomian gland at the posterior surface of the lid. **zeisian s.,** inflammation of a zeisian gland, occurring at the edge of the lids.

stycosis (sti-ko'sis). The presence of calcium sulfate in the organs of the body, especially the lymph glands.

stye (sti). Sty.

style (stīl). Stylet.

stylet (sti'let) [L. *stilus;* Gr. *stylos* pillar]. 1. A wire run through a catheter or cannula to render it stiff or to clear it. 2. A slender probe.

styliform (sti'lĭ-form) [L. *stilus* stake, pole + *forma* shape]. Resembling or shaped like a bodkin; styloid.

styliscus (sti-lis'kus) [L.; Gr. *styliskos* pillar]. A slender cylindrical tent.

stylo- (sti'lo) [L. *stilus* a stake, pole; Gr. *stylos* pillar]. Combining form denoting resemblance to a stake or pole, used especially to denote relationship to the styloid process of the temporal bone.

stylohyal (sti"lo-hi'al). Pertaining to the styloid process and the hyoid bone.

stylohyoid (sti"lo-hi'oid). Pertaining to the styloid process and to the hyoid bone.

styloid (sti'loid) [Gr. *stylos* pillar + *eidos* form]. Resembling a pillar; long and pointed.

styloiditis (sti"loid-i'tis). Inflammation of tissues about the styloid process; especially an irritation of the nerve due to rubbing against the styloid process.

stylomandibular (sti"lo-man-dib'u-lar). Pertaining to the styloid process and the inferior maxillary bone.

stylomastoid (sti"lo-mas'toid). Pertaining to the styloid and mastoid processes.

stylomaxillary (sti"lo-mak'sĭ-ler"e). Pertaining to the styloid process and to the maxilla.

stylomyloid (sti"lo-mi'loid) [*stylo-* + Gr. *mylē* mill + *eidos* form]. Pertaining to the styloid process and to the region of the molar teeth.

Stylosanthes (sti"lo-san'thēz) [*stylo-* + Gr. *anthos* flower]. A genus of leguminous herbs, chiefly South American. *S. ela'tior,* the pencil-flower of North America, is a uterine sedative.

stylostaphyline (sti"lo-staf'ĭ-līn). Pertaining to the styloid process of the temporal bone and the velum palati.

stylosteophyte (sti-los'te-o-fīt). A pillar-shaped exostosis.

stylostixis (sti"lo-stik'sis) [*stylo-* + Gr. *stixis* pricking]. Acupuncture.

stylus (sti'lus) [L. *stilus*]. 1. A stilet. 2. A pencil-shaped medicinal preparation, as a stick of caustic.

stymatosis (sti"mah-to'sis) [Gr. *styma* priapism]. Priapism with a bloody discharge.

stypage (sti'pij, ste-pahzh') [Fr.]. The application of a stype to produce local anesthesia.

stype (stīp) [Gr. *styppeion* tow]. A tampon or pledget.

stypsis (stip'sis) [Gr. *stypsis* contraction]. 1. Astringency; astringent action. 2. Treatment by astringents.

styptic (stip'tik) [Gr. *styptikos*]. 1. Astringent; arresting hemorrhage by means of an astringent quality. 2. An astringent and hemostatic remedy. **Binelli's s.,** a solution of creosote, used for arresting hemorrhage. **chemical s.,** one which arrests hemorrhage by causing coagulation through chemical action. **mechanical s.,** one which acts by causing coagulation mechanically, as a pledget of cotton. **vascular s.,** one which acts by producing contraction of the wounded vessels.

stypven (stip′ven). Trade mark for a preparation of Russell's viper venom: used as a hemostatic agent.

styramate (stir′ah-māt). Chemical name: 2-hydroxy-2-phenylethyl carbamate: used as a skeletal muscle relaxant.

styrol (sti′rol). A fragrant liquid or oily hydrocarbon, vinyl benzene, $C_6H_5.CH{:}CH_2$, from storax. Called also *cinnamene, cinnamol,* and *phenylethene.*

styrolene (sti′ro-lēn). Styrol.

styrone (sti′ron). Cinnamyl alcohol, phenyl allyl alcohol, $C_6H_5CH{:}CH.CH_2OH$: used as an antiseptic, and in microscopy and histology as a bleach.

su. Abbreviation for L. *su′mat,* let him take.

suavitil (swav′ĭ-til). Trade mark for a preparation of benactyzine.

sub- [L. *sub* under]. Prefix signifying *under, near, almost,* or *moderately.*

subabdominal (sub″ab-dom′ĭ-nal). Situated near or below the abdomen.

subabdominoperitoneal (sub″ab-dom″ĭ-no-per″ĭ-to-ne′al). Situated below the abdominal peritoneum.

subacetabular (sub″as-e-tab′u-lar). Situated below the acetabulum.

subacetate (sub-as′e-tāt). Any basic acetate.

subacid (sub-as′id). Somewhat acid.

subacidity (sub″ah-sid′ĭ-te). Deficient acidity.

subacromial (sub″ah-kro′me-al). Situated below or beneath the acromion.

subacute (sub″ah-kūt′). Somewhat acute; between acute and chronic.

subalimentation (sub″al-ĭ-men-ta′shun). Insufficient nourishment.

subanal (sub-a′nal). Situated below the anus.

subapical (sub-ap′e-kal). Situated below an apex.

subaponeurotic (sub″ap-o-nu-rot′ik). Situated beneath an aponeurosis.

subarachnoid (sub″ah-rak′noid). Situated or occurring beneath the arachnoid.

subarachnoiditis (sub″ah-rak″noid-i′tis). Inflammation occurring on the lower surface of the arachnoid.

subarcuate (sub-ar′ku-āt) [*sub-* + L. *arcuatus* arched]. Somewhat arched or bent.

subareolar (sub″ah-re′o-lar). Beneath the areola.

subastragalar (sub″as-trag′ah-lar). Situated or occurring under the astragalus (talus).

subastringent (sub″as-trin′jent). Moderately astringent.

subatloidean (sub″at-loi′de-an). Situated beneath the atlas.

subaural (sub-aw′ral). Situated beneath the ear.

subaurale (sub″aw-ra′le). An anthropometric landmark, the lowest point on the inferior border of the ear lobule when the subject is looking straight ahead.

subauricular (sub″aw-rik′u-lar). Below the pinna (auricle) of the ear.

subaxial (sub-ak′se-al). Below an axis.

subaxillary (sub-ak′sĭ-ler″e). Below the axilla, or armpit.

subbasal (sub-ba′sal). Below a base.

subbrachial (sub-bra′ke-al). Beneath the brachium (in cerebral anatomy).

subbrachycephalic (sub″bra-ke-se-fal′ik). Somewhat brachycephalic; having a cephalic index of 78 to 79.

subcalcareous (sub″kal-ka′re-us). Slightly calcareous.

subcalcarine (sub-kal′kar-īn). Beneath the calcarine fissure.

subcalorism (sub-ka′lor-izm). Frigorism.

subcapsular (sub-kap′su-lar). Situated below a capsule.

subcapsuloperiosteal (sub-kap″su-lo-per″e-os′te-al). Beneath the capsule and the periosteum of a joint.

subcarbonate (sub-kar′bo-nāt). Any basic carbonate.

subcartilaginous (sub″kar-tĭ-laj′ĭ-nus). 1. Situated beneath a cartilage. 2. Partly cartilaginous.

subcentral (sub-sen′tral). Located near the center; situated ventrad of the central fissure of the cerebrum.

subcerebellar (sub″ser-e-bel′ar). Beneath the cerebellum.

subcerebral (sub-ser′e-bral). Beneath the cerebrum.

subchloride (sub-klo′rīd). That chloride of any series which contains the smallest proportion of chlorine.

subchondral (sub-kon′dral). Beneath a cartilage.

subchordal (sub-kor′dal). Situated below the notochord or below the vocal cords.

subchorionic (sub″ko-re-on′ik). Situated beneath the chorion.

subchoroidal (sub″ko-roi′dal). Beneath the choroid.

subchronic (sub-kron′ik). Between chronic and subacute.

subclavian (sub-kla′ve-an). Situated under the clavicle.

subclavicular (sub″klah-vik′u-lar). Situated under the clavicle.

subclinical (sub-klin′ĭ-kal). Without clinical manifestations: said of the early stages, or a slight degree, of a disease.

subconjunctival (sub″kon-junk-ti′val). Situated or occurring beneath the conjunctiva.

subconscious (sub-kon′shus). 1. Imperfectly or partially conscious. 2. Preconscious.

subconsciousness (sub-kon′shus-nes). The state of being partially conscious.

subcontinuous (sub″kon-tin′u-us). Nearly continuous; remittent.

subcoracoid (sub-kor′ah-koid). Situated beneath the coracoid process.

subcortex (sub-kor′teks). That part of the brain substance which underlies the cortex.

subcortical (sub-kor′tĭ-kal). Situated beneath the cortex.

subcostal (sub-kos′tal). Situated beneath a rib.

subcostalgia (sub″kos-tal′je-ah). Pain over the subcostal nerve, i.e., in the region of the appendix, epigastrium, and kidney.

subcranial (sub-kra′ne-al). Beneath the cranium.

subcrepitant (sub-krep′ĭ-tant). Nearly or indistinctly crepitant.

subcrepitation (sub″krep-ĭ-ta′shun). An indistinctly crepitant sound.

subculture (sub′kul-tūr). A culture of bacteria derived from another culture.

subcuneus (sub-ku′ne-us). A group of convolutions under the cuneus, and continuous with the gyrus fornicatus.

subcutaneous (sub″ku-ta′ne-us). Situated or occurring beneath the skin.

subcuticular (sub″ku-tik′u-lar). Situated beneath the epidermis.

subcutis (sub-ku′tis) [*sub-* + L. *cutis* skin]. The subcutaneous tissue.

subdelirium (sub″de-lir′e-um). Partial or mild delirium.

subdeltoid (sub-del′toid). Beneath the deltoid muscle.

subdental (sub-den′tal) [*sub-* + L. *dens* tooth]. Beneath the teeth.

subdermal (sub-der′mal). Situated or occurring beneath the skin.

subdermic (sub-der′mik). Subdermal.

subdiaphragmatic (sub″di-ah-frag-mat′ik). Situated under the diaphragm; subphrenic.

subdorsal (sub-dor′sal). Situated below the dorsal region.

subduct (sub-dukt′). To depress or draw down.

subduction (sub-duk′shun). A drawing downward; specifically the duction of the eyeball exerted by the inferior rectus muscle.

subdural (sub-du′ral). Situated beneath the dura.

subencephalon (sub″en-sef′ah-lon). Medulla oblongata.

subendocardial (sub″en-do-kar′de-al). Situated beneath the endocardium.

subendothelial (sub″en-do-the′le-al). Situated beneath an endothelial membrane.

subendothelium (sub″en-do-the′le-um). Debove's membrane.

subendymal (sub-en′dĭ-mal). Situated beneath the endyma.

subepidermal, subepidermic (sub″ep-ĭ-der′-mal, sub″ep-ĭ-der′mik). Situated or occurring beneath the epidermis.

subepiglottic (sub″ep-ĭ-glot′ik). Below the epiglottis.

subepithelial (sub″ep-ĭ-the′le-al). Situated beneath the epithelium.

suberin (soo′ber-in). An insoluble variety of cellulose derived from cork.

suberitin (soo-ber′ĭ-tin) [*Suberites*, a marine sponge (from L. *suber* cork) + chemical suffix *-in*]. A toxic substance derived from the marine sponge, *Suberites domunculus*, which, when injected into dogs, produces intestinal hemorrhages and respiratory distress.

subexcite (sub″ek-sīt′). To excite in a partial manner.

subextensibility (sub″eks-ten″sĭ-bil′ĭ-te). Decreased extensibility.

subfalcial (sub-fal′se-al). Beneath the falx cerebri.

subfamily (sub-fam′ĭ-le). A taxonomic order sometimes established, subordinate to a family and superior to a tribe.

subfascial (sub-fash′al). Situated beneath a fascia.

subfebrile (sub-feb′ril). Somewhat febrile.

subfertile (sub-fer′til). Characterized by less than normal fertility.

subfertility (sub″fer-til′ĭ-te). The state of being less than normally fertile; relative sterility.

Sub fin. coct. Abbreviation for L. *sub fi′nem coctio′nis*, toward the end of boiling.

subfissure (sub-fish′ur). A fissure of the brain concealed by two overlapping convolutions.

subflavous (sub-fla′vus) [*sub-* + L. *flavus* yellow]. Yellowish.

subfoliar (sub-fo′le-ar). Pertaining to a subfolium.

subfolium (sub-fo′le-um) [*sub-* + L. *folium* leaf]. Any one of the elementary divisions of a cerebellar folium.

subfrontal (sub-frun′tal). Situated beneath a frontal lobe or convolution.

subgaleal (sub-ga′le-al). Situated beneath the galea aponeurotica.

subgallate (sub-gal′āt). A basic gallate.

subgemmal (sub-jem′al) [*sub-* + L. *gemma* bud]. Situated under a taste bud or other bud.

subgerminal (sub-jer′mĭ-nal). Below or under the germ.

subgingival (sub-jin′jĭ-val). Beneath the gingiva.

subglenoid (sub-gle′noid). Situated under the glenoid fossa.

subglossal (sub-glos′al). Sublingual.

subglossitis (sub″glos-si′tis) [*sub-* + L. *glossa* tongue + *-itis*]. Inflammation of the lower surface of the tongue.

subglottic (sub-glot′ik). Beneath the glottis.

subgranular (sub-gran′u-lar). Somewhat granular.

subgrondation (sub″gron-da′shun) [Fr.]. The depression of one fragment of bone beneath another.

subgyre (sub′jir). Subgyrus.

subgyrus (sub-ji′rus). Any gyrus that is partly concealed or covered by another or by others.

subhepatic (sub″he-pat′ik). Situated beneath the liver.

subhumeral (sub-hu′mer-al). Below or beneath the humerus.

subhyaloid (sub-hi′ah-loid). Situated or occurring beneath the hyaloid membrane.

subhyoid (sub-hi′oid). Subhyoidean.

subhyoidean (sub″hi-oi′de-an). Situated or occurring under the hyoid.

subicteric (sub″ik-ter′ik). Somewhat jaundiced.

subicular (sŭ-bik′u-lar). Of or pertaining to the uncinate gyrus.

subiculum (sŭ-bik′u-lum) [L., from *subicere* to raise, lift]. An underlying or supporting structure. **s. cor′nu ammo′nis, s. hippocam′pi,** gyrus parahippocampalis. **s. promonto′rii ca′vi tym′pani** [N A, B N A], **s. of promontory of tympanic cavity,** a ridge of bone bounding the tympanic sinus posteriorly.

subiliac (sub-il′e-ak). Below the ilium.

subilium (sub-il′e-um). The lowest portion of the ilium.

subimbibitional (sub″im-bĭ-bish′on-al). Due to deficient intake of liquid.

subinfection (sub″in-fek′shun). 1. Auto-infection due to weakening of the resisting cells of the organism from constant effort in overcoming toxic cells. 2. A condition in which bacteria that have gained entrance to the system become destroyed, and with their destruction liberate toxins which poison the cells around them.

subinflammation (sub″in-flah-ma′shun). A slight or mild inflammation.

subinflammatory (sub″in-flam′ah-tor″e). Pertaining to or causing only mild inflammation.

subintegumental (sub″in-teg″u-men′tal). Beneath the skin.

subintimal (sub-in′tĭ-mal). Beneath the intima.

subintrance (sub-in′trans). Recurrence of a paroxysm after a shorter period than usual.

subintrant (sub-in′trant) [L. *subintrans* entering by stealth]. 1. Beginning before the completion of a previous cycle or paroxysm; anticipating. 2. Characterized by recurrence at lessening intervals.

subinvolution (sub″in-vo-lu′shun). Incomplete involution; failure of a part to return to its normal size and condition after enlargement from functional activity.

subiodide (sub-i′o-dīd). That iodide of any series which contains the smallest proportion of iodine.

subjacent (sub-ja′sent) [*sub-* + L. *jacere* to lie]. Lying beneath or underneath.

subject[1] (sub-jekt′) [L. *subjectare* to throw under]. To cause to undergo, or submit to; to render subservient.

subject[2] (sub′jekt) [L. *subjectus* cast under]. 1. A person or animal which has been the object of treatment, observation, or experiment. 2. A body for dissection.

subjective (sub-jek′tiv) [L. *subjectivus*]. Pertaining to or perceived only by the affected individual; not perceptible to the senses of another person.

subjectoscope (sub-jek′to-skōp) [*subjective sensation* + Gr. *skopein* to examine]. An instrument used in the study of subjective visual sensations.

subjee (sub′je) [Hind. *sabzī*, literally, "greenness"]. The capsules and larger leaves of *Cannabis indica*.

subjugal (sub-ju′gal). Situated below the zygomatic bone.

sublatio (sub-la′she-o) [L.]. Sublation. **s. retinae,** detachment of the retina.

sublation (sub-la′shun) [L. *sublatio*]. A lifting up, or elevation.

sublesional (sub-le′shun-al). Performed or occurring beneath a lesion.

sublethal (sub-le′thal). Not quite fatal; insufficient to cause death.

sublimate (sub′lĭ-māt) [L. *sublimatum*]. 1. A substance obtained or prepared by sublimation. 2. To divert consciously unacceptable instinctual drives into personally and socially acceptable channels through a mechanism operating outside of and beyond conscious awareness. **corrosive s.,** mercury bichloride.

sublimation (sub″lĭ-ma′shun) [L. *sublimatio*]. 1. The direct change of state from solid to vapor. 2. Freud's term for the process of deviating sexual motive powers from sexual aims or objects to new aims or objects other than sexual.

sublime (sub-līm′) [L. *sublimare*]. To volatilize a solid body by heat and then to collect it in a purified form as a solid or powder.

subliminal (sub-lim′ĭ-nal) [*sub-* + L. *limen* threshold]. Below the limen, or threshold, of sensation.

sublimis (sub-li′mis) [L.]. Superficial; B N A alternative for *superficialis*.

sublingual (sub-ling′gwal). Located beneath the tongue.

sublinguitis (sub″ling-gwi′tis). Inflammation of the sublingual gland.

sublobe (sub′lōb). A division of a lobule.

sublobular (sub-lob′u-lar). Situated beneath a lobule.

sublumbar (sub-lum′bar). Situated beneath the lumbar region.

subluxation (sub″luk-sa′shun) [*sub-* + L. *luxatio* dislocation]. An incomplete or partial dislocation. **Volkmann's s.,** a type of tuberculous arthritis marked by flexion contracture of the knee, external rotation of the leg, valgus position of the knee, and bending of the upper third of the tibia.

sublymphemia (sub″lim-fe′me-ah). Hypolymphemia.

submammary (sub-mam′ar-e). Situated or occurring beneath a mammary gland.

submandibular (sub″man-dib′u-lar). Below the mandible.

submania (sub-ma′ne-ah). Hypomania.

submarginal (sub-mar′jĭ-nal). Situated beneath or near a margin.

submaxilla (sub″mak-sil′ah) [*sub-* + L. *maxilla* jaw]. The mandible.

submaxillaritis (sub-mak″sĭ-ler-i′tis). Inflammation of the submaxillary gland.

submaxillary (sub-mak′sĭ-ler″e). Situated beneath the maxilla.

submedial, submedian (sub-me′de-al, sub-me′de-an). Beneath or near the middle.

submembranous (sub-mem′brah-nus). Partly membranous.

submeningeal (sub″me-nin′je-al). Under or beneath the meninges.

submental (sub-men′tal) [*sub-* + L. *mentum* chin]. Situated below the chin.

submersion (sub-mer′shun) [*sub-* + L. *mergere* to dip]. The act of placing or the condition of being under the surface of a liquid.

submicron (sub-mi′kron). A particle varying in size from 10^{-5} cm. to 5×10^{-7} cm.

submicroscopical (sub″mi-kro-skop′ĭ-kal). Too small to be visible with the light microscope.

submorphous (sub-mor′fus). Neither amorphous nor perfectly crystalline.

submucosa (sub″mu-ko′sah). The layer of areolar tissue situated beneath the mucous membrane. See under *tela* terms beginning *t. submucosa.*

submucosal (sub″mu-ko′sal). Pertaining to the submucosa, or situated beneath the mucous membrane.

submucous (sub-mu′kus). Situated or performed beneath the mucous membrane.

subnarcotic (sub″nar-kot′ik). Moderately narcotic.

subnasal (sub-na′zal). Situated below the nose.

subnasale (sub″na-sa′le). An anthropometric landmark, the point at which the nasal septum merges, in the midsagittal plane, with the upper lip.

subnatant (sub-na′tant). 1. Situated below or at the bottom of something. 2. The underlying liquid after precipitation of a solid component of a system.

subneural (sub-nu′ral). Situated beneath a nerve or the neural axis.

subnitrate (sub-ni′trāt). A basic nitrate.

subnormal (sub-nor′mal). Below or less than normal; characterized by qualities, such as intelligence, lower than the level usually observed.

subnotochordal (sub″no-to-kor′dal). Situated beneath the notochord.

subnucleus (sub-nu′kle-us). A partial or secondary nucleus into which a large nerve nucleus may be split up.

subnutrition (sub″nu-trish′un). Defective nutrition.

suboccipital (sub″ok-sip′ĭ-tal). Situated below the occiput.

suboperculum (sub″o-per′ku-lum). The portion of the occipital gyrus that overlies the insula.

suboptimal (sub-op′tĭ-mal). Less than the optimum.

suboptimum (sub-op′tĭ-mum). A condition lower than that which is optimal or best.

suborbital (sub-or′bĭ-tal). Situated beneath the orbit.

suborder (sub-or′der). A taxonomic category sometimes established, subordinate to an order and superior to a family.

suboxidation (sub″ok-sĭ-da′shun). Deficient oxidation.

suboxide (sub-ok′sīd). That oxide in any series which contains the smallest proportion of oxygen.

subpapular (sub-pap′u-lar). Indistinctly papular.

subparalytic (sub″par-ah-lit′ik). Partially paralytic.

subparietal (sub″pah-ri′ĕ-tal). Situated below a parietal bone, convolution, or fissure.

subpatellar (sub″pah-tel′ar). Situated below the patella.

subpectoral (sub-pek′tor-al). Situated beneath the pectoral muscles.

subpeduncular (sub″pe-dung′ku-lar). Situated beneath a peduncle.

subpelviperitoneal (sub-pel″ve-per″ĭ-to-ne′al). Situated beneath the pelvic peritoneum.

subpericardial (sub″per-ĭ-kar′de-al). Situated beneath the pericardium.

subperiosteal (sub″per-e-os′te-al). Situated beneath the periosteum.

subperiosteocapsular (sub″per-e-os″te-o-kap′su-lar). Subcapsuloperiosteal.

subperitoneal (sub″per-ĭ-to-ne′al). Situated or occurring beneath the peritoneum.

subperitoneo-abdominal (sub″per-ĭ-to-ne″o-ab-dom′ĭ-nal). Occurring beneath the abdominal peritoneum.

subperitoneopelvic (sub″per-ĭ-to-ne-o-pel′vik). Occurring beneath the peritoneum of the pelvis.

subpharyngeal (sub″fah-rin′je-al). Situated below the pharynx.

subphrenic (sub-fren′ik). Situated under the diaphragm; subdiaphragmatic.

subphylum (sub-fi′lum), pl. *subphy′la.* A taxonomic category sometimes established, subordinate to a phylum and superior to a class.

subpial (sub-pi′al). Situated beneath the pia mater.

subpituitarism (sub″pĭ-tu′ĭ-tar-izm). Hypopituitarism.

subplacenta (sub″plah-sen′tah). The decidua basalis.

subpleural (sub-ploor′al). Situated beneath the pleura.

subplexal (sub-plek′sal). Situated beneath a plexus.

subpontine (sub-pon′tin). Situated below the pons.

subpreputial (sub″pre-pu′shal). Situated below the prepuce.

subpubic (sub-pu′bik). Situated or performed below the pubic arch.

subpulmonary (sub-pul′mo-ner″e). Situated or occurring below the lung.

subpulpal (sub-pul′pal). Below the dental pulp.

subpyramidal (sub″pi-ram′ĭ-dal). Below a pyramid.

subrectal (sub-rek′tal). Below the rectum.

subretinal (sub-ret′ĭ-nal). Below the retina.

subrostral (sub-ros′tral). Beneath the rostrum.

subsalt (sub′sawlt). Any basic salt.

subscaphocephaly (sub″skaf-o-sef′ah-le). The condition of being moderately scaphocephalic.

subscapular (sub-skap′u-lar). Situated below or under the scapula.

subscleral (sub-skle′ral). Located or occurring beneath the sclera.

subsclerotic (sub-skle′rot-ik). 1. Subscleral. 2. Partly sclerosed.

subscription (sub-skrip′shun). That part of a prescription which gives the directions for compounding the ingredients. See *prescription.*

subserosa (sub″se-ro′sah). A layer of tissue situated beneath a serous membrane.

subserous (sub-se′rus). Situated beneath a serous membrane.

subsibilant (sub-sib′ĭ-lant). Having a muffled, whistling sound.

subsonic (sub-son′ik). Infrasonic.

subspinale (sub″spi-na′le). A cephalometric landmark, being the deepest midline point on the premaxilla between the anterior nasal spine and the prosthion.

subspinous (sub-spi′nus). Situated below a spinous process.

subsplenial (sub-sple′ne-al). Beneath the splenium of the corpus callosum.

substage (sub′stāj). That part of the microscope which is situated beneath the stage.

substance (sub′stans) [L. *substantia*]. The material constituting an organ or body. Called also *substantia* [N A]. **accessory food s.,** vitamin. **ad s.,** a name given to the substance which effects transmission of a nerve impulse across a synapse. **adamantine s. of tooth,** enamelum. **agglutinable s.,** a substance existing in erythrocytes and bacteria, with which an agglutinin unites to produce specific agglutination. **agglutinating s.,** agglutinin. **α-s., alpha s.,** reticular s. **anti-immune s.,** antiamboceptor. **arborescent white s. of cerebellum,** arbor vitae cerebelli. **autacoid s.,** autacoid. **bactericidal s.,** complement. **β-s., beta s.** See *Heinz-Ehrlich bodies.* **black s.,** substantia nigra. **Blum s.,** katechin. **bony s. of tooth,** cementum. **cement s., cementing s.,** material which serves to hold together the different components of a tissue, as the intercellular substance in endothelium or the interprismatic substance in tooth enamel. **central intermediate s. of spinal cord,** substantia intermedia centralis medullae spinalis. **chromophil s.** See *Nissl bodies.* **colloid s.,** a jelly-like material formed in colloid degeneration. **compact s. of bones,** substantia compacta ossium. **contact s.,** catalyst. **cortical s. of bone,** substantia corticalis ossium. **cortical s. of cerebellum,** cortex cerebelli. **cortical s. of cerebrum,** cortex cerebri. **cortical s. of kidney,** cortex renis. **cortical s. of lens,** cortex lentis. **cortical s. of lymph nodes,** cortex nodi lymphatici. **cortical s. of suprarenal gland,** cortex glandulae suprarenalis. **cytotoxin s.,** cytolysin. **depressor s.,** a substance that tends to decrease activity or blood pressure. **dotted s.,** a granular material which makes up a large part of the central nervous system of invertebrates. **exophthalmos-producing s.,** a substance isolated from crude anterior pituitary extracts which produces exophthalmos in experimental animals. **external s. of suprarenal gland,** cortex glandulae suprarenalis. **fundamental s. of tooth,** dentinum. **gelatinous s. of gray substance,** substantia gelatinosa substantiae griseae. **gelatinous s. of spinal cord,** substantia gelatinosa medullae spinalis. **glandular s. of prostate,** substantia glandularis prostatae. **gray s.,** substantia grisea. **gray s. of cerebrum, central,** substantia grisea centrale cerebri. **gray s. of spinal cord,** substantia grisea medullae spinalis. **ground s.,** the homogeneous material of supporting tissues in which connective tissue cells and fibers are embedded. **H s.,** released s. **hemolytic s.,** a material in serum which destroys erythrocytes of blood added to it: a cytase or alexin. **interfibrillar s. of Flemming, interfilar s.,** hyaloplasm, def. 1. **intermediate s. of spinal cord, lateral,** substantia intermedia lateralis medullae spinalis. **intermediate s. of suprarenal gland, internal s. of suprarenal gland,** medulla glandulae suprarenalis. **interosseos s. of Reinke,** cementum. **interprismatic s.,** the ground substance in which the enamel rods are embedded. **interspongioplastic s.,** cytochylema. **interstitial s.,** ground s. **intertubular s. of tooth, ivory s. of tooth,** dentinum. **s. of lens,** substantia lentis. **medullary s.** 1. The white matter of the central nervous system, consisting of axons and their myelin sheaths. 2. The soft, marrow-like substance of the interior of an organ. See under *medulla.* **medullary s. of bones,** medulla ossium. **medullary s. of bones, red,** medulla ossium rubra. **medullary s. of bones, yellow,** medulla ossium flava. **medullary s. of kidney,** medulla renis. **medullary s. of suprarenal gland,** medulla glandulae suprarenalis. **metachromatic s.,** fine particles seen in erythrocytes, especially after supravital staining. **metaplastic s's,** cytoplasmic inclusions. **molecular s.,** neuropil. **muscular s. of prostate,** substantia muscularis prostatae. **s. of Nissl.** See *Nissl bodies.* **no-threshold s's,** those substances in the blood which are excreted into the urine in proportion to their absolute amount in the blood. Cf. *threshold s's.* **onychogenic s.,** the nail-forming substance which occurs in parallel fibrils in the nail matrix. **organ-forming s's,** specialized materials that become segregated in definite blastomeres, thus bringing about a mosaic type of development. **P.-P. s., pellagra-preventing s.,** a substance which, used in the diet, will prevent or abolish pellagra. **perforated s., anterior,** substantia perforata anterior. **perforated s., posterior,** substantia perforata posterior. **periventricular gray s.,** diffuse collections of small cells immediately surrounding the ependymal lining of the third ventricle. **petrous s. of tooth,** cementum. **prelipid s.,** degenerated nerve tissue which has not yet been converted into fat. **pressor s.,** any substance that tends to increase blood pressure. **preventive s.,** amboceptor. **proper s. of cornea,** substantia propia corneae. **proper s. of sclera,** substantia propria sclerae. **proper s. of tooth,**

dentinum. **reaction s.,** a substance formed in the body of an animal on immunization with cellular products from an animal of another species. Called also *adaptation product.* **receptive s.,** a hypothetical substance supposed to exist in muscle tissue, especially near the motor end-plates of the nerves, and to conduct excitation. **red s. of spleen,** pulpa lienis. **Reichert's s.,** the posterior portion of the anterior perforated substance. **Reichstein's s. Fa,** cortisone. **Reichstein's s. M,** hydrocortisone, or cortisol. **released s.,** a histamine-like substance liberated at the site of inflammation and responsible for increased vascular permeability; called also *H s.* **reticular s.,** the netlike mass of threads seen in erythrocytes after vital staining; called also *alpha s.* and *filar mass.* **reticular s., white, of Arnold,** formatio reticularis pontis. **Rolando's gelatinous s.,** substantia gelatinosa medullae spinalis. **Rollett's secondary s.,** the transparent material lying in narrow zones on each side of Krause's disks. **sarcous s.,** the substance composing the sarcous element of muscle. **s. sensibilis'atrice, sensibilizing s., sensitizing s.,** amboceptor. **Soemmering's gray s.,** substantia nigra. **specific capsular s., specific soluble s.,** bacterial haptene. **spongy s. of bones,** substantia spongiosa ossium. **threshold s's,** those substances in the blood, such as sodium chloride and sugar, which are excreted into the urine only as far as they exceed a certain threshold value. Cf. *no-threshold s's.* **thromboplastic s.,** zymoplastic s. **tigroid s.** See *Nissl bodies.* **transmitter s.,** a chemical substance (mediator) which induces activity in an excitable tissue, such as nerve or muscle. **vitreous s. of tooth,** enamelum. **white s.,** substantia alba. **white s. of Schwann,** material composing the medullary sheath of a nerve fiber; myelin. **white s. of spinal cord,** substantia alba medullae spinalis. **zymoplastic s.,** a substance in the tissues which hastens the coagulation of the blood (A. Schmidt). Called also *thromboplastic s., thromboplastin, thrombokinase, coagulin,* and *cytogen.*

substandard (sub-stan'dard). Falling short of the accepted or usual standard.

substantia (sub-stan'she-ah), pl. *substan'tiae* [L.]. Material of which a tissue, organ, or body is made up; used as a general term in anatomical nomenclature. Called also *substance.* **s. adamanti'na den'tis** [B N A], enamelum. **s. al'ba** [N A, B N A], the white nervous tissue, constituting the conducting portion of the brain and spinal cord, and composed mostly of myelinated nerve fibers. Called also *white substance.* **s. al'ba medul'lae spina'lis** [N A], the white substance of the spinal cord, consisting of long myelinated nerve fibers arranged in parallel longitudinal bundles. **s. cine'rea,** s. grisea. **s. cine'rea interme'dia, s. cine'rea me'dia of Stieda,** nucleus interpeduncularis. **s. compac'ta os'sium** [N A, B N A], bone substance which is dense and hard. Called also *compact bone.* **s. cortica'lis cerebel'li** [B N A], cortex cerebelli. **s. cortica'lis cer'ebri** [B N A], cortex cerebri. **s. cortica'lis glan'dulae suprarena'lis** [B N A], cortex glandulae suprarenalis. **s. cortica'lis len'tis** [B N A], cortex lentis. **s. cortica'lis lymphoglan'dulae** [B N A], cortex nodi lymphatici. **s. cortica'lis os'sium** [N A, B N A], the substance comprising the hard outer layer of a bone. **s. cortica'lis re'nis** [B N A], cortex renis. **s. denta'lis pro'pria,** dentinum. **s. ebur'nea den'tis** [B N A], dentinum. **s. ferrugin'ea,** locus ceruleus. **s. ferrugin'ea supe'rior,** nucleus fastigii. **s. fundamenta'lis den'tis,** dentinum. **s. gelatino'sa centra'lis** [N B A], s. gelatinosa substantia griseae. **s. gelatino'sa colum'nae posterio'ris,** s. gelatinosa medullae spinalis. **s. gelatino'sa medul'lae spina'lis** [N A], **s. gelatino'sa [Rolan'di]** [B N A], the gelatinous-appearing cap that forms the dorsal part of the posterior horn of the spinal cord. Called also *gelatinous substance of spinal cord.* **s. gelatino'sa substan'tiae gris'eae** [N A], the neuroglia and the processes of the ependymal cells surrounding the ependyma of the central canal. Called also *s. gelatinosa centralis* [B N A], and *gelatinous substance of gray substance.* **s. glandula'ris prosta'tae** [N A], tissue composed of branched tubuloalveolar glands, outgrowths of the tunica mucosa of the urethra, which terminate in excretory ducts opening into the urethra; it is enclosed in muscular substance and permeated by muscular strands. Called also *corpus glandulare prostatae* [B N A], and *glandular substance of prostate.* **s. gris'ea** [N A, B N A], the gray nervous tissue composed of nerve cell bodies, unmyelinated nerve fibers, and supportive tissue. Called also *gray substance.* **s. gris'ea centra'lis cer'ebri** [N A], the gray substance in the brain surrounding the cerebral aqueduct. Called also *stratum griseum centrale cerebri* [B N A], and *central gray substance of cerebrum.* **s. gris'ea centra'lis medul'lae spina'lis** [B N A]. See *s. intermedia centralis medullae spinalis* and *s. intermedia lateralis medullae spinalis.* **s. gris'ea medul'lae spina'lis** [N A], the gray substance of the spinal cord, containing fewer myelinated fibers but more nerve cell bodies, unmyelinated nerve fibers, and blood vessels than the white substance. **s. hyali'na,** the more fluid interstitial part of the protoplasm of a cell. Cf. *s. opaca.* **s. innomina'ta,** nerve tissue immediately caudad to the anterior perforated substance. **s. innomina'ta of Reil,** ansa peduncularis. **s. interme'dia centra'lis medul'lae spina'lis** [N A], the gray substance surrounding the central canal of the spinal cord. Called also *central intermediate substance of spinal cord.* **s. interme'dia latera'lis medul'lae spina'lis** [N A], the gray substance of the spinal cord that intervenes between the central intermediate substance, the lateral column, and the anterior and posterior columns. Called also *lateral intermediate substance of spinal cord.* **s. intertubula'ris den'tis,** dentinum. **s. len'tis** [N A, B N A], the fibrous material making up the bulk of the lens of the eye. **s. medulla'ris glan'dulae** [B N A], medulla glandulae suprarenalis. **s. medulla'ris lymphoglan'dulae** [B N A], medulla nodi lymphatici. **s. medulla'ris re'nis** [B N A], medulla renis. **s. metachromaticogranula'ris.** See *Heinz-Ehrlich bodies.* **s. muscula'ris prosta'tae** [N A], the muscular stroma of the prostate, which is intimately blended with the fibrous capsule and permeates the glandular substance. Called also *musculus prostaticus* [B N A], and *muscular substance of prostate.* **s. ni'gra** [N A, B N A], a layer of pigmented gray substance that separates the tegmentum from the basis pedunculi cerebri. Called also *body of Vicq d'Azyr, ganglion of Soemmering, locus niger,* and *black substance.* **s. opa'ca,** the reticulum of the protoplasm of a cell. Cf. *s. hyalina.* **s. os'sea den'tis** [B N A], cementum. **s. perfora'ta ante'rior** [N A, B N A], an area on the ventral surface of the brain just lateral to the optic chiasm which is pierced by numerous small arteries. Called also *anterior perforated substance.* **s. perfora'ta poste'rior** [N A, B N A], an area on the ventral surface of the brain between the cerebral peduncles which is pierced by numerous branches of the posterior cerebral artery. Called also *posterior perforated substance.* **s. pro'pria cor'neae** [N A, B N A], the fibrous, tough, and transparent main part of the cornea, between the anterior and the posterior limiting lamina. **s. pro'pria den'tis,** dentinum, **s. pro'pria scle'rae** [N A], the chief part of the sclera, lying between the lamina fusca and the episcleral lamina, composed of dense bands of fibrous tissue, mostly parallel with the surface, and crossing each other in all directions. It is structurally continuous with the substantia propria corneae. **s. reticula'ris**

al′ba of Arnold, formatio reticularis pontis. **s. reticula′ris al′ba gy′ri fornica′ti [Arnol′di]** [B N A], a name given to a reticular mixture of gray and white substance on the portion of the surface of the gyrus parahippocampalis that adjoins the gyrus dentatus. Omitted in N A. **s. reticula′ris al′ba medul′lae oblonga′tae,** B N A term for the white substance forming part of the formatio reticularis medullae oblongatae [N A]. **s. reticula′ris gris′ea medul′lae oblonga′tae,** B N A term for the gray substance forming part of the formatio reticularis medullae oblongatae [N A]. **s. reticulo-filamento′sa,** reticular substance. **s. Rolan′di,** s. gelatinosa medullae spinalis. **s. spongio′sa medul′lae spina′lis.** See *s. intermedia centralis medullae spinalis, s. intermedia lateralis medullae spinalis,* and *columnae griseae.* **s. spongio′sa os′sium** [N A, B N A], bone substance made up of thin intersecting lamellae, usually found internal to compact bone. Called also *spongy bone.* **s. vit′rea den′tis,** enamelum.

substernal (sub-ster′nal). Situated beneath the sternum.

substernomastoid (sub″ster-no-mas′toid). Beneath the sternomastoid muscle.

substitute (sub′stĭ-tūt). A material which may be used in place of another. **blood s., plasma s.,** a fluid which may be used instead of whole blood or plasma for replacement of circulating fluid in the body.

substitution (sub″stĭ-tu′shun) [L. *substitutio,* from *sub* under + *statuere* to place]. The act of putting one thing in the place of another; especially the chemical replacement of one substance by some other. **cell s.,** in hematology, the physiological regeneration of the blood cells.

substitutive (sub′stĭ-tu″tive). Effecting a change or substitution.

substrate (sub′strāt) [L. *sub* under + *stratum* layer]. A substance upon which an enzyme acts, known also as *zymolyte.*

substratum (sub-stra′tum) [L.]. 1. A substrate. 2. A lower layer or stratum.

substructure (sub′struk-tūr). The underlying or supporting portion of an organ or appliance. In dentistry, that portion of an implant denture which is embedded in the tissues of the jaw.

subsulcus (sub-sul′kus). A sulcus concealed by another.

subsulfate (sub-sul′fāt). A basic sulfate.

subsultus (sub-sul′tus) [L. *subsilire* to spring up]. A spasmodic movement. **s. ten′dinum,** a twisting movement of the muscles and tendons such as is observed in a typhoid state.

subsylvian (sub-sil′ve-an). Situated beneath the fissure of Sylvius.

subtarsal (sub-tar′sal). Situated below the tarsus.

subtegumental (sub″teg-u-men′tal). Subcutaneous.

subtemporal (sub-tem′por-al). Beneath the temple or any temporal structure or part.

subtenial (sub-te′ne-al). Situated beneath the tenia.

subtentorial (sub-ten′to-re-al). Situated beneath the tentorium.

subterminal (sub-ter′mĭ-nal). Situated near the end or extremity.

subtetanic (sub″te-tan′ik). Mildly tetanic: said of convulsions less severe than those of tetanus.

subthalamic (sub″thah-lam′ik). Situated below the thalamus.

subthalamus (sub-thal′ah-mus). The ventral thalamus or subthalamic tegmental region; the portion of the diencephalon which lies between the thalamus and the tegmentum of the mesencephalon.

subthyroidism (sub-thi′roid-izm). Hypothyroidism.

subtile (sub′til) [L. *subtilis*]. Keen and acute.

subtle (sut″l) [L. *subtilis*]. 1. Very fine. 2. Subtile.

subtotal (sub-to′tal). Nearly but not quite total.

subtrapezial (sub″trah-pe′ze-al). Situated beneath the trapezius muscle.

subtribe (sub′trīb). A taxonomic category sometimes established, subordinate to a tribe and superior to a genus.

subtrochanteric (sub″tro-kan-ter′ik). Situated below a trochanter.

subtrochlear (sub-trok′le-ar). Situated beneath the trochlea.

subtuberal (sub-tu′ber-al). Situated under a tuber.

subtympanic (sub″tim-pan′ik). 1. Below the tympanum. 2. Having a somewhat tympanic quality.

subtypical (sub-tip′ĭ-kal). Falling short of being typical.

sububeres (sub-u′ber-ēz) [L., pl.]. Unweaned or suckling children.

subumbilical (sub″um-bil′e-kal). Situated beneath the umbilicus.

subungual (sub-ung′gwal) [*sub-* + L. *unguis* nail]. Situated beneath a nail.

suburethral (sub″u-re′thral). Situated or occurring beneath the urethra.

subvaginal (sub-vaj′ĭ-nal). Situated under a sheath, or below the vagina.

subvertebral (sub-ver′te-bral). Situated on the ventral side of the vertebral column.

subvirile (sub-vir′il). Characterized by deficient virility.

subvitaminosis (sub-vi″tah-min-o′sis). A condition due to vitamin deficiency.

subvitrinal (sub-vit′rĭ-nal). Situated beneath the vitreous.

subvolution (sub″vo-lu′shun) [*sub-* + L. *volvere* to turn]. The operation of turning over of a flap; especially the operation of dissecting and turning up a pterygium, so that the outer or cutaneous surface comes in contact with the raw surface of the dissection. It is done to prevent readhesion.

subwaking (sub-wāk′ing). Intermediate between waking and sleeping.

subzonal (sub-zo′nal). Situated beneath a zone, as below the zona pellucida.

subzygomatic (sub″zi-go-mat′ik). Situated below the zygoma.

sucaryl (su′kah-ril). Trade mark for a non-caloric sweetening agent (cyclamate calcium or cyclamate sodium) for use in restricted diets.

succagogue (suk′ah-gog). [L. *succus* juice + Gr. *agōgos* leading]. 1. Inducing glandular secretion. 2. An agent that stimulates glandular secretion.

succedaneous (suk″se-da′ne-us). Ensuing; in place of; of the nature of a succedaneum.

succedaneum (suk″se-da′ne-um) [L. *succedaneus* taking another's place]. A medicine or material that may be substituted for another of like properties.

succenturiate (suk″sen-tu′re-āt) [L. *succenturiare* to substitute]. Accessory; serving as a substitute.

succinate (suk′sĭ-nāt). Any salt of succinic acid.

succino-dehydrogenase (suk″sĭ-no-de-hi-dro′je-nās). An enzyme which splits off hydrogen from succinic acid: it occurs in muscle.

succinoresinol (suk″sĭ-no-rez′ĭ-nol). A resinol from amber, $C_{12}H_{20}O$.

succinous (suk′sĭ-nus). Pertaining to amber.

succinum (suk′sĭ-num) [L.]. Amber.

succinylcholine (suk″sĭ-nil-ko′lēn). Chemical name: bis [2-dimethylaminoethyl] succinate: used as a skeletal muscle relaxant.

succinylsulfathiazole (suk″sĭ-nil-sul″fah-thi′ah-zōl). Chemical name: 4′-(2-thiazolylsulfamoyl)-succinanilic acid: used as an antibacterial agent.

succorrhea (suk″o-re′ah) [L. *succus* juice + Gr. *rhoia* flow]. An excessive flow of a juice or secretion, as in ptyalism.

succuba (suk′u-bah) [L.; from *succumbere* to lie under]. An imaginary female monster, or demon.

succubus (suk′u-bus) [L.; from *succumbere* to lie under]. An imaginary monster, or demon, formerly regarded as a cause of nightmare.

succus (suk′kus), pl. *suc′ci* [L.]. Any fluid derived from living tissue; used in anatomical nomenclature [B N A] as a general term for a bodily secretion or a fluid derived from body tissue. Called also *juice.* **s. cera′si,** cherry juice. **s. enter′icus** [B N A], the liquid secreted by the glands in the wall of the small intestine. Omitted in N A. **s. gas′tricus** [B N A], the liquid secretion of the glands of the stomach. Omitted in N A. **s. pancreat′icus** [B N A], the liquid secretion of the pancreas, which is discharged into the duodenum. Omitted in N A. **s. prostat′icus** [B N A], the secretion of the prostate gland, which contributes to formation of the semen. Omitted in N A. **s. ru′bi idae′i,** raspberry juice.

succussion (sŭ-kush′un) [L. *succussio* a shaking from beneath, earthquake]. A splashing sound heard when a patient is shaken, indicative of the presence of fluid and air in a body cavity. **hippocratic s.,** a splashing sound heard in the chest when the patient is shaken, usually pathognomonic of pneumohydrothorax.

sucholo-albumin (su″ko-lo-al-bu′min) [L. *sus* pig + Gr. *cholē* bile + *albumin*]. A poisonous protein characteristic of hog cholera, and obtained from cultures of the bacillus. It is injected for the purpose of giving immunity to the disease.

sucholotoxin (su″ko-lo-tok′sin) [L. *sus* pig + Gr. *cholē* bile + *toxin*]. A toxin from cultures of the bacillus of hog cholera.

suckle (suk″l). To derive or to provide nourishment by feeding at the breast.

sucostrin (su-kos′trin). Trade mark for a preparation of succinylcholine.

Sucquet-Hoyer anastomosis (sik-a′oy-ār) [*Sucquet;* Henryk *Hoyer,* Polish anatomist, 1864–1947]. See under *anastomosis.*

sucramin (su′krah-min). The ammonium salt of gluside.

sucrase (su′krās). Invertin.

sucrate (su′krāt). A compound of a substance with sucrose.

sucre (su′k′r) [Fr.]. Sugar. **s. actuelle′,** actual sugar. **s. virtuelle′,** virtual sugar.

sucroclastic (su″kro-klas′tik). [Fr. *sucre* sugar + Gr. *klastos* broken]. Splitting up sugar.

sucrol (su′krol). Dulcin.

sucrose (su′krōs) [L. *sucrosum*]. A disaccharide, $C_{12}H_{22}O_{11}$, crystallizing in prisms, soluble in water, and turning the plane of polarization to the right. By boiling with acids and by the action of certain enzymes it is hydrolyzed and converted into dextrose and levulose. It is extensively used as a food and as a sweetening agent, and is much employed in pharmacy, forming the basis of many pharmaceutical preparations.

sucrosemia (su″kro-se′me-ah) [*sucrose* + Gr. *haima* blood + *-ia*]. The presence of sucrose in the blood.

sucrosum (su-kro′sum) [L.]. Sucrose.

sucrosuria (su″kro-su′re-ah) [*sucrose* + Gr. *ouron* urine + *-ia*]. The presence of sucrose in the urine.

suction (suk′shun) [L. *sugere* to suck]. The act or process of sucking or of aspirating, as in the production of adhesion between two surfaces by exhaustion of the air between them. **posttussive s.,** a sucking sound heard over a lung cavity just after a cough.

suctorial (suk-to′re-al). Fitted for performing suction.

sucuuba (soo″koo-oo′bah). The *Plumeria phagedenica,* a medicinal plant of South America.

sudafed (soo′dah-fed). Trade mark for preparations of pseudoephedrine hydrochloride.

sudamen (su-da′men), pl. *sudam′ina* [L., from *sudare* to sweat]. A whitish vesicle caused by the retention of sweat in the sudorific ducts or the layers of the epidermis. The vesicles are about the size of millet seeds, and the eruption occurs after profuse sweating, or in certain febrile diseases.

sudamina (su-dam′ĭ-nah) [L.]. Plural of *sudamen.*

sudaminal (su-dam′ĭ-nal). Pertaining to or resembling sudamina.

Sudan (su-dan′). A diazo-compound, $C_{20}H_{14}N_{12}O$, in the form of a brown powder, used as a stain for fat: called also *pigment brown.* **S. I,** $C_6H_5.N{:}N.C_{10}H_6.OH$. **S. II,** $(CH_3)_2C_6H_3.N{:}N.C_{10}H_6.OH$. **S. G, S. III,** a red fat-soluble azo dye, $C_6H_5.N.N.C_6H_4.N{:}N.C_{10}H_6.OH$: an important stain for the demonstration of neutral fats. **S. IV,** scarlet red. **S. yellow G,** a brown powder, $C_{12}H_{10}N_2O_2$: used as a stain for fats.

sudanophil (su-dan′o-fil). An element that stains readily with Sudan.

sudanophilia (su-dan″o-fil′e-ah) [*sudan* + Gr. *philein* to love]. 1. Affinity for Sudan stain. 2. A condition in which the leukocytes contain particles that stain readily with Sudan red. The condition is thought to be indicative of suppuration.

sudanophilic (su-dan″o-fil′ik). Staining readily with Sudan.

sudanophilous (su″dan-of′ĭ-lus). Sudanophilic.

sudarium (su-da′re-um) [L.]. A sweat bath.

sudarshan shurna (soo-dar′shan shoor′nah). A Hindu febrifuge containing fifty kinds of drugs.

sudation (su-da′shun) [L. *sudatio*]. 1. The excretion of sweat. 2. Excessive sweating.

sudatoria (su″dah-to′re-ah). 1. Hyperhidrosis. 2. Plural of *sudatorium.*

sudatorium (su-dah-to′re-um), pl. *sudato′ria* [L.]. 1. A hot air bath. 2. A room for the administration of hot air baths.

Sudeck's atrophy, disease, point (soo′deks) [Paul Hermann Martin *Sudeck,* Hamburg surgeon, 1866–1938]. See *post-traumatic osteoporosis,* and under *point.*

sudogram (su′do-gram) [L. *sudor* sweat + Gr. *gramma* a writing]. A graphic representation of the areas of the body on which sweating is present, after injection of a dye which is excreted by the sweat glands.

sudokeratosis (su″do-ker″ah-to′sis). Keratosis of the sweat ducts.

sudomotor (su″do-mo′tor) [L. *sudor* sweat + *motor* move]. Exerting an influence on the sweat glands.

sudor (su′dor) [L.]. Sweat, or perspiration; an official term in B N A, but omitted in N A. **s. an′glicus** ["English sweat"], miliary fever. **s. cruen′tus, s. sanguin′eus,** the secretion of red (blood-tinged) sweat; hematidrosis. **s. urino′sus,** the secretion of urinous sweat; uridrosis.

sudoral (su′dor-al) [L. *sudor* sweat]. Pertaining to sweat; characterized by sweating.

sudoresis (su″do-re′sis). Profuse sweating.

sudoriceratosis (su-dor″ĭ-ker″ah-to′sis). Sudokeratosis.

sudoriferous (su″dor-if′er-us) [L. *sudor* sweat + *ferre* to bear]. 1. Conveying sweat. 2. Sudoriparous.

sudorific (su″dor-if′ik) [L. *sudorificus*]. 1. Promoting the flow of sweat; diaphoretic. 2. An agent that causes sweating.

sudorikeratosis (su-dor″ĭ-ker″ah-to′sis). Sudokeratosis.

sudoriparous (su″dor-ip′ah-rus) [L. *sudor* sweat + *parere* to produce]. Secreting or producing sweat.

sudorrhea (su″do-re′ah). [L. *sudor* sweat + Gr. *rhoia* flow]. Excessive sweating; hyperhidrosis.

suet (su′et) [L. *sevum*]. The fat from the abdominal cavity of a ruminant animal, especially the sheep or ox: used in the preparation of cerates and ointments and as an emollient. The preparation employed in pharmacy is the internal fat of the abdomen of the sheep. **benzoinated s.,** prepared suet 1000, benzoin 30. **prepared s.,** the internal fat of the abdomen of the sheep purified by melting and straining.

suffocant (suf′o-kant). An agent that causes suffocation.

suffocation (suf″o-ka′shun) [L. *suffocatio*]. The stoppage of respiration, or the asphyxia that results from it.

suffraginis (suf-fraj′ĭ-nis) [L.]. The large pastern bone or first phalanx of the horse.

suffumigation (suf″fu-mĭ-ga′shun) [L. *sub* under + *fumigatio* smoking]. 1. A fumigation from below. 2. A substance to be burned in fumigation.

suffusion (sŭ-fu′zhun) [L. *suffusio*]. 1. The process of overspreading, or diffusion. 2. The condition of being moistened or of being permeated through, as by blood.

sugar (shoog′ar) [L. *saccharum;* Gr. *sakcharon*]. A sweet carbohydrate of various kinds, and of both animal and vegetable origin. It is an aldehyde or ketone derivative of polyhydric alcohols. The two principal groups of sugars are the disaccharides, having the formula $C_{12}H_{22}O_{11}$, and the monosaccharides, $C_6H_{12}O_6$; all are white, crystallizable solids, soluble in water and dilute alcohol. The disaccharides are sucrose or saccharose, *beet s., cane s., maple s., palm s., malt s.* (maltose), *milk s.* (lactose), *larch s.* (melizitose), and others. The monosaccharides include ordinary dextrose (δ-glucose) (*diabetic s., grape s., liver s., potato s., starch s.*), levulose (*fruit s.*), invert inosite (*heart s., muscle s.*). Besides these, a very considerable number of artificial and other sugars are known to chemistry. **actual s.** (sucre actuelle of Lépine), the free glucose in the blood. **anhydrous s.,** anhydrosugar. **barley s.,** a clear hard form of sugar formed by heating ordinary granulated sugar (sucrose) to 160° F. **beechwood s.,** xylose. **beet s.,** sucrose derived from the root of the beet. **blood s.,** glucose, the form in which carbohydrate is carried in the blood, usually in a concentration of 70–120 mg. per 100 ml. **brain s.,** cerebrose. **burnt s.,** caramel. **cane s.,** sucrose. **collagen s.,** glycocoll. **diabetic s.,** the dextrose which is found in the urine in diabetes mellitus. **fruit s.,** levulose. **gelatin s.,** amino-acetic acid. **grape s.,** dextrose. **heart s.,** inosite. **invert s.,** the mixture of dextrose and levulose obtained by hydrolysing sucrose. A solution of invert sugar is used in the injection treatment of varicose veins. **s. of lead,** lead acetate. **Leo's s.,** laiose. **liver s.,** dextrose from the liver. **malt s.,** maltose. **maple s.,** saccharose from maple sap. **milk s.,** lactose. **muscle s.,** inositol. **oil s.,** eleosaccharum. **reducing s.,** a sugar which will reduce an alkaline copper tartrate solution. **simple s.,** a monosaccharide. **starch s.,** dextrin. **sulfur s.,** thioglucose. **threshold s.,** the lower limit of hyperglycemia at which dextrose appears in the urine. **virtual s.** (sucre virtuelle of Lépine), sugar in the blood in a colloidal state. **wood s.,** xylose.

sugarin (shoog′ar-in). Methylbenzoylsulfimide; a crystalline substance said to be 500 times as sweet as sugar.

suggestibility (sug-jes″tĭ-bil′ĭ-te). A condition of abnormal susceptibility to suggestion.

suggestible (sug-jes′tĭ-b′l). Abnormally susceptible to suggestion.

suggestion (sug-jes′chun) [L. *suggestio*]. 1. The impartation of an idea to a subject from without. 2. An idea introduced from without. **hypnotic s.,** a suggestion imparted to a person in the hypnotic state, by which he is led to believe certain things contrary to fact or induced to perform certain actions. **post-hypnotic s.,** implantation in the mind of a subject during hypnosis of a suggestion to be acted upon after recovery from the hypnotic state. **traumatic s.** See *autosuggestion.*

suggillation (sug″jĭ-la′shun) [L. *suggillatio*]. 1. A bruise or ecchymosis. 2. A mark of postmortem lividity.

suicide (soo′ĭ-sīd) [L. *sui* of himself + *caedere* to kill]. The taking of one's own life. **psychic s.,** the termination of one's own life without employment of physical agents.

suint (swint). The fatty natural potash soap derivable from sheep's wool; lanolin is prepared from it.

suit (sūt). An outer garment covering the entire body. **anti-blackout s., anti-g s., g s.,** a garment worn by aviators, designed to increase their ability to withstand without ill effects the acceleratory forces experienced in certain aerial maneuvers.

sukkla pakla (sook′lah pak′lah) [Hind. "dry suppuration"]. Ainhum.

sulamyd (sul′am-id). Trade mark for a preparation of sulfacetamide.

sulcate (sul′kāt) [L. *sulcatus*]. Furrowed or marked with sulci.

sulci (sul′si) [L.]. Plural of *sulcus.*

sulciform (sul′sĭ-form). Formed like a groove.

sulculus (sul′ku-lus), pl. *sul′culi* [L.]. A small or minute sulcus.

sulcus (sul′kus), pl. *sul′ci* [L.]. 1. A groove, trench, or furrow; used in anatomical nomenclature as a general term to designate such a depression, especially one of those on the surface of the brain, separating the gyri. 2. A linear depression in the surface of a tooth, the sloping sides of which meet at an angle. **alveolabial s.,** the furrow between the dental arch and the lips. **alveolingual s.,** the depression between the dental arch and the tongue. **s. ampulla′ris** [N A, B N A], **ampullary s.,** a transverse groove on the membranous ampulla of each semicircular duct, for the ampullary branch of the pars vestibularis nervi octavi. **angular s.,** incisura angularis ventriculi. **s. anthel′icis transver′sus** [N A, B N A], the depression on the medial surface of the pinna corresponding to the lower crus of the anthelix. Called also *transverse s. of anthelix.* **aortic s., s. aor′ticus,** a longitudinal groove on the median surface of the left lung corresponding to the thoracic aorta. **s. arte′riae occipita′lis** [N A, B N A], the groove just medial to the mastoid notch on the temporal bone, lodging the occipital artery. Called also *s. of occipital artery.* **s. arte′riae subcla′viae** [N A], a transverse groove on the cranial surface of the first rib, just posterior to the anterior scalene tubercle; it lodges the subclavian artery. Called also *s. subclavius* [B N A], and *s. of subclavian artery.* **s. arte′riae tempora′lis me′diae** [N A, B N A], a nearly vertical groove running just superior to the external acoustic meatus on the external surface of the squamous part of the temporal bone; it lodges the middle temporal artery. Called also *s. of middle temporal artery.* **s. arte′riae vertebra′lis atlan′tis** [N A, B N A], the groove on the cranial surface of the posterior arch of the atlas; it lodges the vertebral artery and the first spinal nerve. Called also *s. of vertebral artery of atlas.* **arterial sulci, sul′ci arterio′si** [N A, B N A], grooves on the internal surfaces of the cranial bones for the meningeal arteries. Called also *arterial grooves.* **atrioventricular s.,** s. coronarius cordis. **s. of auditory tube,** s. tubae auditivae. **s. of auricle, posterior, s. auric′ulae poste′rior** [N A, B N A], the slight depression on the pinna that separates the anthelix from the antitragus. **s. of auricular branch of vagus nerve,** s. canaliculi mastoidei. **basilar s. of occipital bone,** s. sinus petrosi inferioris ossis occipitalis. **basilar s. of pons, s. basila′ris pon′tis**

[N A, B N A], the anteromedian groove in the pons, lodging the basilar artery. **bicipital s., lateral,** s. bicipitalis lateralis. **bicipital s., medial,** s. bicipitalis medialis. **s. bicipita'lis latera'lis** [N A, B N A], a longitudinal groove on the lateral side of the arm which marks the limit between the lateral border of the biceps muscle and the brachialis. Called also *lateral bicipital groove.* **s. bicipita'lis media'lis** [N A, B N A], a longitudinal groove on the medial side of the arm which marks the limit between the medial border of the biceps muscle and the brachialis. Called also *medial bicipital groove.* **calcaneal s., s. calca'nei** [N A, B N A], a rough, deep groove on the upper surface of the calcaneus, between the medial and the posterior articular surfaces and giving attachment to the interosseous talocalcaneal ligament. **calcarine s., s. calcari'nus** [N A], a sulcus on the medial surface of the occipital lobe, separating the cuneus from the lingual gyrus. Called also *fissura calcarina* [B N A]. **callosal s.,** s. corporis callosi. **callosomarginal s.,** s. cinguli. **s. callo'sus,** s. corporis callosi. **s. canalic'uli mastoi'dei** [B N A], a groove in the petrous portion of the temporal bone for the mastoid canaliculus. Omitted in N A. **s. cana'lis innomina'tus,** s. nervi petrosi minoris. **s. carot'icus os'sis sphenoida'lis** [N A, B N A], **carotid s.,** the groove on the side of the body of the sphenoid bone that lodges the internal carotid artery and the cavernous sinus. **carpal s., s. car'pi** [N A, B N A], a broad deep groove on the volar surface of the carpal bones, which transmits the flexor tendons and the median nerve into the palm of the hand. **central s. of cerebrum,** s. centralis cerebri. **s. centra'lis cer'ebri** [N A], **s. centra'lis cere'bri [Rolandi]** [B N A], a groove that runs obliquely across the superolateral surface of the cerebral hemisphere, separating the frontal from the parietal lobe. Called also *central s. of cerebrum.* **sul'ci cerebel'li** [B N A], **sulci of cerebellum,** fissurae cerebelli. **cerebral s., lateral,** s. lateralis cerebri. **sul'ci cer'ebri** [N A, B N A], **sulci of cerebrum,** the furrows between the gyri of the cerebrum. **s. of chiasm, s. chias'matis** [N A, B N A], a furrow on the superior surface of the sphenoid bone located just anterior to the tuberculum sellae, and lodging the optic chiasm. **cingulate s., s. cin'guli** [N A, B N A], **s. of cingulum,** a long, irregularly shaped sulcus on the medial surface of a hemisphere, which separates the cingulate gyrus below from the superior frontal gyrus and the paracentral lobule above. It may be divided into frontal and marginal portions. **circular s. of insula, s. circula'ris in'sulae** [N A], **s. circula'ris [Rei'li]** [B N A], a groove that separates the floor of the insula from the opercula. **collateral s., s. collatera'lis** [N A], a longitudinal sulcus on the inferior surface of the cerebral hemisphere between the fusiform gyrus and the parahippocampal gyrus. Called also *fissura collateralis* [B N A]. **s. col'li mandib'ulae,** the shallow groove between the ridge of the mandibular neck and the line of attachment of the sphenomandibular ligament. **s. corona'rius cor'dis** [N A, B N A], **coronary s. of heart,** a groove on the external surface of the heart, separating the atria from the ventricles; portions of it are occupied by the major arteries and veins of the heart. **s. cor'poris callo'si** [N A, B N A], **s. of corpus callosum,** a sulcus encircling the convex aspect of the corpus callosum at the bottom of the longitudinal cerebral fissure. **s. cos'tae** [N A, B N A], **costal s.,** a sulcus that follows the inferior and internal surface of a rib anteriorly from the tubercle, gradually becoming less distinct; it lodges the intercostal vessels and nerves. **costal s., inferior,** s. costae. **s. cru'ris hel'icis** [N A, B N A], **s. of crus of helix,** a transverse sulcus on the medial surface of the pinna, corresponding to the crus helicis on the lateral surface. **cuboid, s.,** s. tendinum musculorum peroneorum calcanei. **sul'ci cu'tis** [N A, B N A], the fine depressions on the surface of the skin between the ridges of the skin. Called also *sulci of skin.* **ethmoidal s. of Gegenbaur,** foramen ethmoidale anterius. **ethmoidal s. of nasal bone, s. ethmoida'lis os'sis nasa'lis** [N A, B N A], a groove that extends the entire length of the posteromedial surface of the nasal bone and lodges the anterior ethmoid nerve. **s. of Eustachian tube,** s. tubae auditivae. **frontal s.** 1. See *s. frontalis inferior* and *s. frontalis superior.* 2. Sulcus sinus sagittalis superioris ossis frontalis. **frontal s., inferior,** s. frontalis inferior. **frontal s., superior,** s. frontalis superior. **s. fronta'lis infe'rior** [N A, B N A], a short longitudinal sulcus that separates the inferior and middle frontal gyri. Called also *inferior frontal s.* **s. fronta'lis supe'rior** [N A, B N A], a longitudinal sulcus that separates the middle and superior frontal gyri. Called also *superior frontal s.* **gingival s.,** a furrow surrounding a tooth, bounded internally by the surface of the tooth and externally by the epithelium lining the free gingiva. **gluteal s., s. glu'teus** [N A], a curved transverse groove or fold on the back of the lower member, separating the upper part of the thigh from the nates. **greater palatine s. of maxilla,** s. palatinus major maxillae. **greater palatine s. of palatine bone,** s. palatinus major ossis palatini. **s. of greater petrosal nerve,** s. nervi petrosi majoris. **s. ham'uli pterygoi'dei** [N A, B N A], a smooth groove on the lateral surface of the medial pterygoid plate of the sphenoid bone, in the angle at the base of the pterygoid hamulus; it lodges the tendon of the tensor veli palatini muscle. Called also *s. of pterygoid hamulus.* **Harrison's s.,** Harrison's groove. **hippocampal s., s. hippocam'pi** [N A], the sulcus that extends from the splenium of the corpus callosum almost to the tip of the temporal lobe, and forms the medial boundary of the parahippocampal lobe. Called also *fissura hippocampi* [B N A]. **s. horizonta'lis cerebel'li** [B N A], fissura horizontalis cerebelli. **hypothalamic s., s. hypothalam'icus** [N A], **s. hypothalam'icus [Monro'i]** [B N A], a shallow curved sulcus on the wall of the third ventricle, extending from the interventricular foramen to the cerebral aqueduct. **s. of inferior petrosal sinus of occipital bone,** s. sinus petrosi inferioris ossis occipitalis. **s. of inferior petrosal sinus of temporal bone,** s. sinus petrosi inferioris ossis temporalis. **infraorbital s. of maxilla, s. infraorbita'lis maxil'lae** [N A, B N A], a groove in the orbital surface of the maxilla, commencing near the middle of the posterior edge of the surface and running anteriorly for a short distance to become continuous with the infraorbital canal. **infrapalpebral s., s. infrapalpebra'lis** [N A, B N A], the furrow below the lower eyelid. **s. of innominate canal,** s. nervi petrosi minoris. **interarticular s. of calcaneus,** s. calcanei. **interarticular s. of talus,** s. tali. **intercalary s.,** a sulcus above and parallel to the corpus callosum. **intermediate s. of spinal cord, anterior,** s. intermedius anterior medullae spinalis. **intermediate s. of spinal cord, posterior,** s. intermedius posterior medullae spinalis. **s. interme'dius,** a slight groove about 2.5 cm. from the duodenopyloric constriction of the stomach. **s. interme'dius ante'rior medul'lae spina'lis** [B N A], an occasional furrow between the anterior median fissure and the anterior lateral sulcus of the spinal cord. Omitted in N A. **s. interme'dius poste'rior medul'lae spina'lis** [N A, B N A], a furrow in the cervical part of the spinal cord between the fasciculus gracilis and the fasciculus cuneatus. Called also *posterior intermediate s. of spinal cord.* **interpapillary sulci of Rauber,** sulci cutis. **interparietal s., s. interparieta'lis** [B N A], s. intraparietalis. **intertubercular s. of humerus, s. intertubercula'ris**

hu′meri [N A, B N A], a longitudinal groove on the anterior surface of the humerus, lying between the tubercula above and between the cristae tuberculi farther down, and lodging the tendon of the long head of the biceps muscle. **interventricular s., anterior,** s. interventricularis anterior. **interventricular s., posterior,** s. interventricularis posterior. **interventricular s. of heart,** s. coronarius cordis. **s. interventricula′ris ante′rior** [N A], a groove on the sternocostal surface of the heart marking the position of the interventricular septum and the line of separation between the ventricles. Called also *s. longitudinalis anterior cordis* [B N A], and *anterior interventricular s.* **s. interventricula′ris poste′rior** [N A], a groove on the diaphragmatic surface of the heart marking the position of the interventricular septum and the line of separation between the ventricles. Called also *s. longitudinalis posterior cordis* [B N A], and *posterior interventricular s.* **intraparietal s., s. intraparieta′lis** [N A], an irregular suclus on the convex surface of the parietal lobe of the cerebrum and between the inferior and superior parietal lobuli. Called also *s. interparietalis* [B N A]. **Jacobson's s.** 1. Sulcus promontorii cavi tympani. 2. Sulcus tympanicus ossis temporalis. **labiodental s.,** the arched groove in the embryo which separates off the anterior part of the mandibular process, thus helping to form the lower lip. **lacrimal s. of lacrimal bone,** s. lacrimalis ossis lacrimalis. **lacrimal s. of maxilla,** s. lacrimalis maxillae. **s. lacrima′lis maxil′lae** [N A, B N A], a groove directed inferiorly and somewhat posteriorly on the nasal surface of the body of the maxilla, just anterior to the large opening into the maxillary sinus; it is converted into the nasolacrimal canal by the lacrimal bone and inferior nasal concha. Called also *lacrimal s. of maxilla.* **s. lacrima′lis os′sis lacrima′lis** [N A, B N A], a deep vertical groove on the anterior part of the lateral surface of the lacrimal bone, which with the maxilla forms the fossa for the lacrimal sac. Called also *lacrimal s. of lacrimal bone.* **lateral s. for lateral sinus of occipital bone,** s. sinus transversi. **lateral s. for lateral sinus of parietal bone,** s. sinus sigmoidei ossis parietalis. **lateral s. of medulla oblongata, anterior,** s. lateralis anterior medullae oblongatae. **lateral s. of medulla oblongata, posterior,** s. lateralis posterior medullae oblongatae. **lateral s. for sigmoidal part of lateral sinus,** s. sinus sigmoidei ossis temporalis. **lateral s. of spinal cord, posterior,** s. lateralis posterior medullae spinalis. **s. latera′lis ante′rior medul′lae oblonga′tae** [N A, B N A], a longitudinal sulcus on the surface of the medulla oblongata, lateral to the pyramid and medial to the funiculus lateralis below and the olive above; through it emerge the fibers of the hypoglossal nerve. Called also *anterior lateral s. of medulla oblongata.* **s. latera′lis ante′rior medul′lae spina′lis** [B N A], the longitudinal band on the anterolateral surface of the spinal cord through which the ventral nerve roots appear. Omitted in N A. **s. latera′lis cer′ebri** [N A], a deep cleft beginning at the anterior perforated substance, extending laterally between the temporal and frontal lobes, and turning posteriorly between the temporal and parietal lobes. It divides into posterior, ascending, and anterior branches. Called also *fissura cerebri lateralis* [*Sylvii*] [B N A], and *lateral cerebral s.* **s. latera′lis mesenceph′ali** [B N A], a longitudinal groove on the side of the mesencephalon, separating the crus cerebri from the tegmentum. Omitted in N A. **s. latera′lis pedun′culi cer′ebri,** s. lateralis mesencephali. **s. latera′lis poste′rior medul′lae oblonga′tae** [N A, B N A], an upward extension of the posterolateral sulcus of the spinal cord; through it emerge the fibers of the glossopharyngeal, vagus, and accessory nerves. Called also *posterior lateral s. of medulla oblongata.* **s. latera′lis poste′rior medul′lae spina′lis** [N A, B N A], a longitudinal sulcus on the posterolateral surface of the spinal cord. It gives entrance to the dorsal nerve roots and separates the lateral and posterior funiculi. Called also *posterior lateral s. of spinal cord.* **s. of lesser petrosal nerve,** s. nervi petrosi minoris. **s. lim′itans** [N A], a groove midway on the inner surface of each lateral wall of the neural tube, which separates it into a dorsal, alar plate and a ventral, basal plate. Called also *s. limitans ventriculorum cerebri* [B N A]. **s. lim′itans fos′sae rhomboi′deae** [N A, B N A], a longitudinal groove on the lateral side of the medial eminence, extending the entire length of the floor of the fourth ventricle. **s. lim′itans in′sulae,** s. circularis insulae. **s. lim′itans ventriculo′rum cer′ebri** [B N A], s. limitans. **longitudinal s. of frontal bone,** s. sinus sagittalis superioris ossis frontalis. **longitudinal s. of heart, anterior,** s. interventricularis anterior. **longitudinal s. of heart, posterior,** s. interventricularis posterior. **longitudinal s. of occipital bone,** s. sinus sagittalis superioris. **longitudinal s. of parietal bone,** s. sagittalis ossis parietalis. **s. longitudina′lis ante′rior cor′dis** [B N A], s. interventricularis anterior. **s. longitudina′lis os′sis occipitis,** s. sinus sagittalis superioris. **s. longitudina′lis poste′rior cor′dis** [B N A], s. interventricularis posterior. **lunate s., s. luna′tus** [N A], a small semilunar furrow sometimes seen on the lateral surface of the occipital lobe of the cerebrum; this sulcus is conspicuous in the brain of certain apes and was called by Reidinger *Affenspalte* [Ger. "ape fissure"]. **malleolar s., s. malleola′ris tib′iae** [N A, B N A], a short longitudinal groove on the posterior surface of the medial malleolus of the tibia, which lodges the tendons of the posterior tibial muscle and the long flexor muscle of the toes. **mandibular s.,** s. colli mandibulae. **s. of mastoid canaliculus,** s. canaliculi mastoidei. **s. ma′tricis un′guis** [N A, B N A], **s. of matrix of nail,** the cutaneous fold in which the proximal part of the nail is embedded. **medial s. of crus cerebri, s. media′lis cru′ris cer′ebri** [N A], a longitudinal furrow on the medial surface of a cerebral peduncle, marking the separation of the crus cerebri from the tegmentum and lodging the root of the oculomotor nerve. Called also *s. nervi oculomotorii* [B N A]. **s. media′lis mesenceph′ali,** s. medialis cruris cerebri. **median s. of fourth ventricle,** s. medianus ventriculi quarti. **median s. of medulla oblongata, posterior,** s. medianus posterior medullae oblongatae. **median s. of spinal cord, posterior,** s. medianus posterior medullae spinalis. **median s. of tongue,** s. medianus linguae. **s. media′nus lin′guae** [N A, B N A], a shallow groove on the dorsal surface of the tongue in the midline. Called also *median s. of tongue.* **s. media′nus poste′rior medul′lae oblonga′tae** [N A], a narrow groove, existing only in the closed part of the medulla oblongata, which is the continuation of the posterior median sulcus of the spinal cord. Called also *fissura mediana posterior medullae oblongatae* [B N A], and *posterior median s. of medulla oblongata.* **s. media′nus poste′rior medul′lae spina′lis** [N A, B N A], a shallow vertical groove on the posterior surface of the spinal cord in the median plane. Called also *posterior median s. of spinal cord.* **s. media′nus ventric′uli quar′ti** [N A], a groove in the floor of the fourth ventricle along the midline. Called also *median s. of fourth ventricle.* **meningeal sulci,** sulci arteriosi. **mentolabial s., s. mentolabia′lis** [N A, B N A], the depression between the lower lip and the chin. **s. mesenceph′ali media′lis,** s. medialis cruris cerebri. **s. of middle temporal artery,** s. arteriae temporalis mediae. **s. of Monro,** s. hypothalamicus. **muscular s. of tympanic cavity,** semicanalis musculi tensoris tympani. **s. mus′culi flexo′ris hal′lucis lon′gi calca′nei** [B N A], s. tendinis musculi flexoris hallucis longi calcanei. **s. mus′culi flexo′ris hal′lucis lon′gi ta′li** [B N A], s. tendinis musculi flexoris hallucis longi tali. **s. mus′culi peronae′i calca′nei** [B N A], s. tendinum musculorum peroneorum calcanei. **s. mus′culi peronae′i os′sis cuboi′dei** [B N A], s. tendinis musculi peronei longi. **mylohyoid s. of mandible, s. mylohyoi′deus mandib′ulae** [N A, B N A], a groove on the medial surface of the ramus of the mandible, passing downward and forward from the foramen mandibulare and lodging the mylohyoid artery and nerve. **nasal s., posterior,** meatus nasopharyngeus. **s. of nasal process of maxilla,** s. lacrimalis maxillae. **nasolabial s., s. nasolabia′lis** [N A, B N A], the depression between the nose and the upper lip. **s. ner′vi oculomoto′rii** [B N A], s. medialis cruris cerebri. **s. ner′vi petro′si majo′ris** [N A], a small groove in the floor of the middle cranial fossa, running anteromedially from the hiatus of the facial canal to the foramen lacerum, and lodging the greater petrosal nerve. Called also *s. nervi petrosi superficialis majoris* [B N A], and *s. of greater petrosal nerve.* **s. ner′vi petro′si mino′ris** [N A], a small groove in the floor of the middle cranial fossa, running anteromedially just lateral to the sulcus of the greater petrosal nerve, and lodging the lesser petrosal nerve. Called also *s. nervi petrosi superficialis minoris* [B N A], and *s. of lesser petrosal nerve.* **s. ner′vi petro′si superficia′lis majo′ris** [B N A], s. nervi petrosi majoris. **s. ner′vi petro′si superficia′lis mino′ris** [B N A], s. nervi petrosi minoris. **s. ner′vi radia′lis** [N A, B N A], a broad oblique groove on the posterior surface of the humerus for the radial nerve and the deep brachial artery. Called also *radial groove* and *s. of radial nerve.* **s. ner′vi spina′lis** [N A, B N A], the groove on the upper surface of each transverse process of a cervical vertebra, extending from the foramen transversarium lateralward and separating the anterior and posterior tubercles. It lodges the ventral branch of a cervical nerve. Called also *s. of spinal nerve.* **s. ner′vi ulna′ris** [N A, B N A], a shallow vertical groove on the posterior surface of the medial epicondyle of the humerus for the ulnar nerve. Called also *groove of ulnar nerve.* **nymphocaruncular s., nymphohymeneal s.,** a groove between either labium minus and the carunculae hymenales. **obturator s. of pubis, s. obturato′rius os′sis pu′bis** [N A, B N A], a groove that obliquely crosses the inferior surface of the superior ramus of the pubis, giving passage to the obturator vessels and nerve. **occipital sulci, lateral,** sulci occipitales laterales. **occipital sulci, superior,** sulci occipitales superiores. **occipital s., transverse,** s. occipitalis transversus. **s. of occipital artery,** s. arteriae occipitalis. **s. occipita′lis ante′rior,** a variable, vertically disposed furrow on the convex surface of the cerebrum, which by some is taken as the line of division between the parietal and the occipital lobes. **sul′ci occipita′les latera′les** [B N A], horizontal furrows that divide the lateral occipital gyri into upper and lower portions. Omitted in N A. **sul′ci occipita′les superio′res** [B N A], irregular sulci associated with the superior occipital gyri. Omitted in N A. **s. occipita′lis transver′sus** [N A, B N A], a vertical sulcus back of the gyrus angularis, which may help to form the anterior boundary of the occipital lobe or may lie within it. Called also *transverse occipital s.* **s. occip′itis,** s. sinus sagittalis superioris. **occipitotemporal s., s. occipitotempora′lis** [N A], a longitudinal sulcus on the inferior surface of the temporal lobe that separates the inferior temporal gyrus from the lateral occipitotemporal gyrus. Called also *s. temporalis inferior* [B N A]. **s. oculomoto′rius,** s. medialis cruris cerebri. **s. olfacto′rius lo′bi fronta′lis** [N A, B N A], a straight parasagittal sulcus on the inferior surface of the frontal lobe, lodging the olfactory bulb and tract, and separating the gyrus rectus from the gyri orbitales. Called also *olfactory s. of frontal lobe.* **s. olfacto′rius na′si** [N A, B N A], a shallow sulcus on the wall of the nasal cavity, passing upward from the level of the anterior end of the middle concha just above the agger nasi to the lamina cribrosa. Called also *olfactory s. of nose.* **olfactory s. of frontal lobe,** s. olfactorius lobi frontalis. **olfactory s. of nose,** s. olfactorius nasi. **optic s.,** s. chiasmatis. **orbital sulci of frontal lobe, sul′ci orbita′les lo′bi fronta′lis** [N A, B N A], irregular sulci between the orbital gyri of the frontal lobe. **palatine sulci of maxilla, sul′ci palati′ni maxil′lae** [N A, B N A], the laterally placed furrows, between the palatine spines on the inferior surface of the hard palate, that lodge the palatine vessels and nerves. **palatinovaginal s., s. palatinovagina′lis** [N A], the groove on the vaginal process of the pterygoid process of the sphenoid bone that participates in formation of the palatinovaginal canal. **s. palati′nus ma′jor maxil′lae** [N A], the sulcus on the nasal surface of the maxilla which, along with the corresponding one on the perpendicular plate of the palatine bone, forms the canal for the greater palatine nerve. Called also *greater palatine s. of maxilla.* **s. palati′nus ma′jor os′sis palati′ni** [N A], a vertical groove on the maxillary surface of the perpendicular plate of the palatine bone; it articulates with the maxilla to form the canal for the greater palatine nerve. Called also *s. pterygopalatinus ossis palatini* [B N A], and *greater palatine s. of palatine bone.* **paracolic sulci, sul′ci paracol′ici** [N A], small shallow and variable peritoneal pockets situated lateral to the descending colon. Called also *recessus paracolici* [B N A]. **paraglenoid sulci of hip bone, sul′ci paraglenoida′les os′sis cox′ae** [B N A], slight grooves, anterior and inferior to the auricular surface of the ilium, that serve for attachment of the ventral and interosseous sacroiliac ligaments. Omitted in N A. **parietooccipital s.** 1. Sulcus parietooccipitalis. 2. Sulcus intraparietalis. **s. parietooccipita′lis** [N A], a sulcus in the medial surface of each cerebral hemisphere, running upward from the calcarine sulcus and marking the boundary between the cuneus and precuneus, and also between the parietal and occipital lobes. Called also *fissura parietooccipitalis* [B N A], and *parietooccipital s.* **s. parolfacto′rius ante′rior** [B N A], a sulcus on the medial surface of the cerebral hemisphere, between the area parolfactoria behind and the inferior frontal gyrus in front. Omitted in N A. **s. parolfacto′rius poste′rior** [B N A], a curved sulcus on the medial surface of the cerebral hemisphere, below the splenium of the corpus callosum and between the gyrus paraterminalis and the area parolfactoria. Omitted in N A. **petrobasilar s.,** s. sinus petrosi inferioris ossis temporalis. **petrosal s. of occipital bone, inferior,** s. sinus petrosi inferioris ossis occipitalis. **petrosal s. of temporal bone, inferior,** s. sinus petrosi inferioris ossis temporalis. **petrosal s. of temporal bone, posterior,** s. sinus petrosi inferioris ossis temporalis. **petrosal s. of temporal bone, superior,** s. sinus petrosi superioris. **s. petro′sus infe′rior os′sis occipita′lis** [B N A], s. sinus petrosi inferioris ossis occipitalis. **s. petro′sus infe′rior os′sis tempora′lis** [B N A], s. sinus petrosi inferioris ossis temporalis. **s. petro′sus supe′rior os′sis tempora′lis** [B N A], s. sinus petrosi superioris. **polar s.,** any one of the small fissures which surround the posterior end of the calcarine sulcus. **postcentral s., s. postcentra′lis** [N A], a sulcus on the superolateral surface of the cerebrum, separating the postcentral gyrus from the remainder of the parietal lobe. **postclival s.,** a fissure of the cerebellum between the declive and the folium vermis. **postnodular s.,** a sulcus on the under side of the cerebellum between the nodule and the uvula. **postpyramidal s.,** a sulcus on the under side of the cerebellum between the pyramid and the tuber vermis. **s. praecentra'lis** [B N A], s. precentralis. **precentral s., s. precentra'lis** [N A], a vertical sulcus on the convex surface of a cerebral hemisphere, separating the precentral gyrus from the remainder of the frontal lobe. **preclival s.,** a fissure of the cerebellum between the culmen and the declive. **prepyramidal s.,** a sulcus on the inferior surface of the cerebellum between the uvula and the pyramid. **prerolandic s.,** s. precentralis. **s. promonto'rii ca'vi tym'pani** [N A, B N A], a groove in the surface of the promontory of the tympanic cavity, lodging the tympanic nerve. **s. of pterygoid hamulus,** s. hamuli pterygoidei. **pterygoid s. of pterygoid process,** s. pterygopalatinus processus pterygoidei. **pterygopalatine s. of palatine bone,** s. palatinus major ossis palatini. **pterygopalatine s. of pterygoid process,** s. pterygopalatinus processus pterygoidei. **s. pterygopalati'nus os'sis palati'ni** [B N A], s. palatinus major ossis palatini. **s. pterygopalati'nus proces'sus pterygoi'dei** [N A, B N A], a small groove on the inferior surface of the vaginal process of the medial pterygoid plate of the sphenoid bone, forming part of the wall of the vomerovaginal canal. Called also *pterygopalatine s. of pterygoid process.* **s. pulmona'lis thora'cis** [N A, B N A], **pulmonary s. of thorax,** a large vertical groove in the posterior part of the chest cavity, one on either side of the bodies of the vertebrae posterior to the level of their ventral surface, lodging the posterior, bulky portion of the lung. **radial s. of humerus, s. of radial nerve,** s. nervi radialis. **Reil's s.,** s. circularis insulae. **retrocentral s.,** s. postcentralis. **rhinal s., s. rhina'lis** [N A], a fissure on the inferior surface of the hemisphere, separating the anterior part of the parahippocampal gyrus from the rest of the temporal lobe. **sagittal s. of frontal bone,** s. sinus sagittalis superioris ossis frontalis. **sagittal s. of occipital bone,** s. sinus sagittalis superioris ossis occipitalis. **sagittal s. of parietal bone,** s. sagittalis ossis parietalis. **s. sagitta'lis os'sis fronta'lis** [B N A], s. sinus sagittalis superioris ossis frontalis. **s. sagitta'lis os'sis occipita'lis** [B N A], s. sinus sagittalis superioris ossis occipitalis. **s. sagitta'lis os'sis parieta'lis** [N A, B N A], a shallow sulcus along the sagittal margin on the internal surface of the parietal bone; with its fellow of the opposite side it forms a groove for the middle portion of the superior sagittal sinus. Called also *sagittal s. of parietal bone.* **s. scle'rae** [N A, B N A], **scleral s., sclerocorneal s.,** the groove at the junction of the sclera and cornea. **s. of semicanal of humerus,** s. intertubercularis humeri. **s. of semicanal of vidian nerve,** s. nervi petrosi majoris. **semilunar s. of radius,** incisura ulnaris radii. **sigmoid s., s. of sigmoid sinus,** s. sinus sigmoidei. **s. of sigmoid sinus of occipital bone,** s. sinus sigmoidei ossis occipitalis. **s. of sigmoid sinus of parietal bone,** s. sinus sigmoidei ossis parietalis. **s. of sigmoid sinus of temporal bone,** s. sinus sigmoidei ossis temporalis. **s. sigmoi'deus os'sis tempora'lis** [B N A], s. sinus sigmoidei ossis temporalis. **s. si'nus petro'si inferio'ris os'sis occipita'lis** [N A], the groove in the floor of the posterior cranial fossa at the line of junction between the basilar part of the occipital and the petrous portion of the temporal bone; it lodges the inferior petrosal sinus. Called also *s. petrosus inferior ossis occipitalis* [B N A], and *s. of inferior petrosal sinus of occipital bone.* **s. si'nus petro'si inferio'ris os'sis tempora'lis** [N A], a groove on the posteromedial edge of the internal surface of the petrous portion of the temporal bone, which, with a corresponding groove on the adjacent basilar part of the occipital bone, lodges the inferior petrosal sinus. Called also *s. petrosus inferior ossis temporalis* [B N A], and *s. of inferior petrosal sinus of temporal bone.* **s. si'nus petro'si superio'ris** [N A], a small posterolaterally directed sulcus that runs along the internal surface of the petrous part of the temporal bone on the angle separating the posterior and middle cranial fossae; it lodges the superior petrosal sinus. Called also *s. petrosus superior ossis temporalis* [B N A], and *s. of superior petrosal sinus.* **s. si'nus sagitta'lis superio'ris os'sis fronta'lis** [N A], a median groove on the cerebral surface of the squama of the frontal bone; in the upper part only, it is continuous with the sagittal sulcus of the parietal bone and lodges the anterior portion of the superior sagittal sinus. Called also *s. sagittalis ossis frontalis* [B N A], and *s. of superior sagittal sinus of frontal bone.* **s. si'nus sagitta'lis superio'ris os'sis occipita'lis** [N A], a broad sulcus on the internal surface of the squama of the occipital bone, generally to the right of the superior division of the cruciform eminence; it lodges the posterior part of the superior sagittal sinus. Called also *s. sagittalis ossis occipitalis* [B N A], and *s. of superior sagittal sinus of occipital bone.* **s. si'nus sigmoi'dei** [N A], an S-shaped sulcus beginning on the internal surface of the posteroinferior edge of the parietal bone and continuous with the lateral end of the sulcus of the transverse sinus; it passes onto the internal surface of the mastoid part of the temporal bone, where it bends inferiorly and medially to continue onto the lateral portion of the occipital bone, ending at the jugular foramen. It lodges the sigmoid sinus. Called also *s. of sigmoid sinus.* **s. si'nus sigmoi'dei os'sis occipita'lis** [N A], the portion of the sulcus of the sigmoid sinus found on the occipital bone. **s. si'nus sigmoi'dei os'sis parieta'lis** [N A], a short groove on the internal surface of the posteroinferior angle of the parietal bone, continuous with both the sulcus for the sigmoid sinus on the temporal bone and the sulcus for the transverse sinus on the occipital bone; it lodges the superior part of the sigmoid sinus. Called also *s. transversus ossis parietalis* [B N A], and *s. of sigmoid sinus of parietal bone.* **s. si'nus sigmoi'dei os'sis tempora'lis** [N A], the portion of the sulcus of the sigmoid sinus found on the temporal bone. Called also *s. sigmoideus ossis temporalis* [B N A]. **s. si'nus transver'si** [N A], a wide groove that passes horizontally, lateralward and forward from the internal occipital protuberance to the parietal bone, where it becomes continuous with the sulcus of the sigmoid sinus; it lodges the transverse sinus. Called also *s. transversus ossis occipitalis* [B N A], and *s. of transverse sinus.* **sulci of skin,** sulci cutis. **s. of spinal nerve,** s. nervi spinalis. **spiral s., external,** s. spiralis externus. **spiral s., internal,** s. spiralis internus. **spiral s. of humerus,** s. nervi radialis. **s. spira'lis** [B N A]. See *s. spiralis externus* and *s. spiralis internus.* **s. spira'lis exter'nus** [N A], a concavity within the cochlear duct immediately above the basilar crest. Called also *external spiral s.* **s. spira'lis inter'nus** [N A], the C-shaped concavity within the cochlear duct formed by the limbus laminae spiralis and its tympanic and vestibular labia along the edge of the osseous spiral lamina. Called also *internal spiral s.* **s. subcla'viae** [B N A], s. arteriae subclaviae. **subclavian s.,** s. arteriae subclaviae. **subclavian s. of lung,** s. subclavius pulmonis. **s. of subclavian artery,** s. arteriae subclaviae. **s. of subclavian vein,** s. venae subclaviae. **s. subcla'vius,** s. arteriae subclaviae. **s. subcla'vius pulmo'nis** [B N A], a broad, shallow, transverse groove across the top of the lung, lodging the subclavian artery. Omitted in N A. **subparietal s., s. subparieta'lis** [N A, B N A], a sulcus on the medial surface of a cerebral hemisphere, above the splenium of the corpus callosum, separating the precuneus from the cingulate gyrus. **s. of superior petrosal sinus,** s. sinus petrosi superioris. **s. of superior sagittal sinus of frontal bone,** s. sinus sagittalis superioris ossis frontalis.

s. of superior sagittal sinus of occipital bone, s. sinus sagittalis superioris ossis occipitalis. **supraorbital s.,** foramen supraorbitalis. **suprasplenial s.,** s. subparietalis. **s. Syl′vii,** fossa lateralis cerebri. **s. ta′li** [N A, B N A], **s. of talus,** a transverse groove on the inferior surface of the talus, between the medial and the posterior articular surface, which helps to form the sinus tarsi. **temporal s., inferior, temporal s., middle,** s. temporalis inferior [N A]. **temporal s., superior,** s. temporalis superior. **temporal sulci, transverse,** sulci temporales transversi. **temporal s. of temporal bone,** s. arteriae temporalis mediae. **s. tempora′lis infe′rior.** 1. [N A] A longitudinal sulcus on the lateral surface of the temporal lobe, separating the middle and the inferior temporal gyri. Formerly called *s. temporalis medius* [B N A]. 2. [B N A] Sulcus occipitotemporalis. **s. tempora′lis me′dius** [B N A], s. temporalis inferior [N A]. **s. tempora′lis supe′rior** [N A, B N A], a longitudinal sulcus on the lateral surface of a cerebral hemisphere, passing downward and forward from the gyrus angularis to the temporal pole and separating the superior and the middle temporal gyri. Called also *superior temporal s.* **sul′ci tempora′les transver′si** [N A, B N A], irregularly vertical sulci in the part of the temporal lobe that lies within the insula. Called also *transverse temporal sulci.* **s. ten′dinum musculo′rum fibula′rium calca′nei,** N A alternative for *s. tendinum musculorum peroneorum calcanei.* **s. ten′dinis mus′culi flexo′ris hal′lucis lon′gi calca′nei** [N A], an inferior groove on the medial surface of the calcaneus, lodging the tendon of the flexoris hallucis longus muscle. Called also *s. musculi flexoris hallucis longi calcanei* [B N A]. **s. ten′dinis mus′culi flexo′ris hal′lucis lon′gi ta′li** [N A], the sagittal groove on the posterior surface of the body of the talus that transmits the tendon of the flexor hallucis longus muscle. Called also *s. musculi flexoris hallucis longi tali* [B N A]. **s. ten′dinum musculo′rum peroneo′rum calca′nei** [N A], a slight groove on the inferior part of the lateral surface of the calcaneus, lodging the tendons of the peroneus longus and brevis muscles. Called also *s. musculi peronaei calcanei* [B N A], and *s. of tendons of peroneus muscles.* **s. ten′dinis mus′culi perone′i lon′gi** [N A], a deep groove on the inferior surface of the cuboid bone, which in certain foot positions lodges the tendon of the peroneus longus muscle. Called also *s. musculi peronaei ossis cuboidei* [B N A], and *s. of tendon of peroneus longus muscle.* **s. of tendon of flexor hallucis longus muscle of calcaneus,** s. tendinis musculi flexoris hallucis longi calcanei. **s. of tendon of flexor hallucis longus muscle of talus,** s. tendinis musculi flexoris hallucis longi tali. **s. of tendons of peroneus muscles,** s. tendinum musculorum peroneorum calcanei. **s. of tendon of peroneus longus muscle,** s. tendinis musculi peronei longi. **terminal s. of right atrium,** s. terminalis atrii dextri. **terminal s. of tongue,** s. terminalis linguae. **s. termina′lis a′trii dex′tri** [N A, B N A], a shallow groove on the posterior external surface of the right atrium of the heart that connects the right sides of the superior and inferior venae cavae; it represents the junction of the sinus venosus with the primitive atrium in the embryo, and corresponds to a ridge on the internal surface, the crista terminalis. Called also *terminal s. of right atrium.* **s. termina′lis lin′guae** [N A, B N A], a more or less distinct groove on the tongue, extending from the foramen cecum forward and lateralward to the margin of the tongue on either side, and dividing the dorsum of the tongue from the root. It is marked by a row of vallate papillae. Called also *terminal s. of tongue.* **s. of tongue.** See *s. medianus linguae* and *s. terminalis linguae.* **transverse s. of anthelix,** s. anthelicis transversus. **transverse s. of heart,** s. coronarius cordis. **transverse s. of occipital bone,** s. sinus transversi. **transverse s. of parietal bone,** s. sinus sigmoidei ossis parietalis. **s. of transverse sinus,** s. sinus transversi. **transverse s. of temporal bone,** s. sinus sigmoidei ossis temporalis. **s. transver′sus os′sis occipita′lis** [B N A], s. sinus transversi. **s. transver′sus os′sis parieta′lis** [B N A], s. sinus sigmoidei ossis parietalis. **s. tu′bae auditi′vae** [N A, B N A], **s. tu′bae eusta′chii,** a groove on the medial part of the base of the spine of the sphenoid bone; it lodges a portion of the cartilaginous part of the auditory tube. Called also *s. of auditory tube.* **Turner's s.,** s. intraparietalis. **tympanic s. of temporal bone, s. tympan′icus os′sis tempora′lis** [N A, B N A], a narrow groove in the medial part of the external acoustic meatus of the temporal bone, into which the tympanic membrane fits. It is deficient above. Called also *tympanic s. of temporal bone.* **s. of ulnar nerve,** s. nervi ulnaris. **s. of umbilical vein,** s. venae umbilicalis. **sulci for veins,** sulci venosi. **s. of vena cava, s. ve′nae ca′vae** [N A], a groove on the upper part of the posteroinferior surface of the liver, separating the right lobe from the caudate lobe and lodging the inferior vena cava. Called also *fossa venae cavae* [B N A]. **s. ve′nae subcla′viae** [N A], a transverse groove on the cranial surface of the first rib, just anterior to the anterior scalene tubercle; it lodges the subclavian vein. Called also *s. of subclavian vein.* **s. ve′nae umbilica′lis** [N A], the impression on the visceral surface of the liver in the fetus, which lodges the umbilical vein. Called also *s. of umbilical vein.* **sul′ci veno′si** [N A, B N A], **venous sulci,** grooves on the internal surfaces of the cranial bones for the meningeal veins. Called also *venous grooves.* **s. ventra′lis medul′lae spina′lis,** fissura mediana anterior medullae spinalis. **vermicular s.,** a fissure between the vermis and the hemisphere of the cerebellum. **s. of vertebral artery of atlas,** s. arteriae vertebralis atlantis. **vertical s.,** s. precentralis. **vomerovaginal s., s. vomerovagina′lis** [N A], the groove on the vaginal process of the pterygoid process of the sphenoid bone that helps form the vomerovaginal canal. **Waldeyer's s.** See *s. spiralis externus* and *s. spiralis internus.* **s. of wrist,** s. carpi.

sulfacetamide (sul″fah-set′ah-mīd). Chemical name: N-sulfanilylacetamide: used as an antibacterial agent.

sulfacid (sulf-as′id). Sulfonic acid.

sulfadiazine (sul″fah-di′ah-zēn). Chemical name: N^1-2-pyrimidinylsulfanilamide: used as an antibacterial agent.

sulfadimetine (sul″fah-di′mĕ-tēn). Sulfisomidine.

sulfadimidine (sul″fah-di′mĭ-dēn). Sulfamethazine.

sulfaethidole (sul″fah-eth′ĭ-dōl). Chemical name: N^1-(5-ethyl-1,3,4-thiadiazol-2-yl) sulfanilamide: used as an antibacterial agent.

sulfafurazole (sul″fah-fu′rah-zōl). Sulfisoxazole.

sulfaguanidine (sul″fah-gwan′ĭ-dēn). Chemical name: N^1-amidinosulfanilamide: used as an antibacterial agent.

sulfamerazine (sul″fah-mer′ah-zēn). Chemical name: N^1-(4-methyl-2-pyrimidinyl)sulfanilamide: used as an antibacterial agent.

sulfamethazine (sul″fah-meth′ah-zēn). Chemical name: N^1-(4,6-dimethyl-2-pyrimidinyl)sulfanilamide: used as an antibacterial agent.

sulfamethizole (sul″fah-meth′ĭ-zōl). Chemical name: N^1-(5-methyl-1,3,4-thiadiazol-2-yl)sulfanilamide: used as an antibacterial agent.

sulfamethoxypyridazine (sul″fah-meth-ok′se-pi-rid′ah-zēn). Chemical name: N^1-(6-methoxy-3-pyridazinyl)sulfanilamide: used as an antibacterial agent.

sulfamethyldiazine (sul″fah-meth″il-di′ah-zēn). Sulfamerazine.

sulfamethylthiadiazole (sul″fah-meth″il-thi″-ah-di′ah-zōl). Sulfamethizole.

sulfamezathine (sul″fah-mez′ah-thēn). Trade mark for a preparation of sulfamethazine.

sulfamido (sul-fam′ĭ-do). One of a group of compounds containing an amino-sulfone group $SO_2.NH_2$.

sulfamine (sul-fam′in). The univalent radical, $—SO_2NH_2$.

sulfamylon (sul″fah-mi′lon). Trade mark for preparations of mafenide.

sulfanemia (sulf″ah-ne′me-ah). Anemia due to the use of sulfonamide drugs.

sulfanilamide (sul″fah-nil′ah-mīd). Chemical name: p-aminobenzenesulfonamide: used as an antibacterial agent.

sulfanilate (sulf-an′ĭ-lāt). A salt of sulfanilic acid.

sulfanuria (sulf″ah-nu′re-ah). Anuria resulting from the use of sulfonamide drugs.

sulfapyridine (sul″fah-pir′ĭ-dēn). Chemical name: N^1-2-pyridylsulfanilamide: used as an antibacterial agent.

sulfarsphenamine (sulf″ar-sfen′ah-min). The disodium salt of dihydroxy-diaminoarsenobenzene-monomethylene sulfonate, $NH_2(OH)C_6H_3.As:As-C_6H_3(OH)NH.CH_2.SO_2.ONa$. It contains 18–20 per cent of arsenic and is used in the treatment of syphilis. It differs from neoarsphenamine in having two side chains instead of one and in that the sulfur has a valence of four instead of two.

sulfasuxidine (sul″fah-suk′sĭ-dēn). Trade mark for preparations of succinylsulfathiazole.

sulfatase (sul′fah-tās). An enzyme that catalyzes the hydrolysis of various sulfuric acid esters into sulfuric acid and alcohol.

sulfate (sul′fāt) [L. *sulphas*]. Any salt of sulfuric acid. **acid s.,** one in which only one half of the hydrogen of the sulfuric acid is replaced: a bisulfate. **basic s.,** one in which the normal sulfate of the base is combined with a hydroxide of the same base; a subsulfate. **conjugated s's,** aromatic substances, such as phenol, scatoxyl, and indoxyl, which occur in the urine along with mineral sulfates. **cupric s.,** a compound, $CuSO_4.5H_2O$, occurring as deep blue, triclinic crystals or blue crystalline granules or powder: used as a fungicide, and as an emetic. **ethereal s's,** conjugated s's. **ferrous s.,** pale bluish-green odorless crystals or granules, $FeSO_4.7H_2O$: used in treatment of iron deficiency anemia. **mineral s's,** sulfates in the urine which are combinations of sulfuric acid with mineral substances such as sodium, potassium, calcium, and magnesium. **neutral s., normal s.,** one in which all the hydrogen of the sulfuric acid is replaced. **preformed s's,** mineral s's.

sulfatemia (sul″fāt-e′me-ah). The presence of sulfates in the blood.

sulfathalidine (sul″fah-thal′ĭ-dēn). Trade mark for phthalylsulfathiazole.

sulfathiazole (sul″fah-thi′ah-zōl). Chemical name: N^1-2-thiazolylsulfanilamide: used as an antibacterial agent.

sulfatide (sul′fah-tīd). One of a class of lipoid substances which are esters of sulfuric acid. They are found largely in the medullated nerve fibers.

sulfhemoglobin (sulf″he-mo-glo′bin). Sulfmethemoglobin.

sulfhemoglobinemia (sulf″he-mo-glo″bin-e′me-ah). The presence of sulfmethemoglobin in the blood.

sulfhydrate (sulf-hi′drāt). Any compound of a base with sulfhydric acid or, more correctly, with the radical sulfhydryl, SH, or hydrogen sulfide.

sulfhydryl (sulf-hi′dril). The univalent radical, —SH.

sulfide (sul′fīd). Any binary compound of divalent sulfur; a compound of sulfur with another element or base.

sulfindigotate (sul-fin′dĭ-go-tāt). Any salt of sulfindigotic acid.

sulfinpyrazone (sul″fin-pi′rah-zōn). Chemical name: 1,2-diphenyl-4-(2′-phenylsulfinethyl)-3,5-pyrazolidinedione: used as a uricosuric agent in treatment of gout.

sulfinyl (sul′fĭ-nil). The bivalent radical, —SO—.

sulfisomidine (sul-fi-som′ĭ-dēn). Chemical name: N^1-(2,6-dimethyl-4-pyrimidinyl) sulfanilamide: employed as an antibacterial agent.

sulfisoxazole (sul″fi-sok′sah-zōl). Chemical name: N^1-(3,4-dimethyl-5-isoxazolyl)sulfanilamide: used as an antibacterial agent.

sulfite (sul′fīt) [L. *sulfis*]. Any salt of sulfurous acid.

sulfmethemoglobin (sulf″met-he″mo-glo′bin). A greenish substance formed by treating blood with hydrogen sulfide or by the absorption of this gas from the intestinal tract. It is the cause of the greenish color seen in the abdominal walls and along the vessels of cadavers. Called also *sulfhemoglobin.*

sulfo-. A prefix used in naming chemical compounds, indicating presence of divalent sulfur or of the group SO_2OH.

sulfo-acid (sul″fo-as′id). Sulfonic acid.

sulfobromophthalein (sul″fo-bro″mo-thal′e-in). Chemical name: phenoltetrabromphthalein disodium sulfonate: used in tests of liver function.

sulfocarbamide (sul″fo-kar′bah-mīd). Thiourea.

sulfoconjugation (sul″fo-kon″ju-ga′shun). The formation of conjugated sulfates.

sulfocyanate (sul″fo-si′ah-nāt). Thiocyanate.

sulfogel (sul′fo-jel). A gel in which sulfuric acid is the medium instead of water.

sulfohydrate (sul″fo-hi′drāt). Sulfhydrate.

sulfoichthyolate (sul″fo-ik′the-o-lāt). A salt of sulfoichthyolic acid. See *ichthammol.*

sulfolipid (sul″fo-lip′id). A lipid which on hydrolysis yields sulfuric acid.

sulfolysis (sul-fol′ĭ-sis) [*sulfo-* + Gr. *lysis* dissolution]. A double decomposition, similar to hydrolysis, but in which sulfuric acid takes the place of water.

sulfomucin (sul″fo-mu′sin). A glucoprotein found in cartilage, cornea, and gastrointestinal mucosa, which contains sulfuric acid, uronic acid, and chondrosamine or glucosamine.

sulfonamide (sul-fon′ah-mīd). The chemical group SO_2NH_2. The sulfonamide compounds are a group of compounds with one or more benzene rings, amino groups, and a sulfonamide group.

sulfonamidemia (sul″fōn-am″ĭ-de′me-ah). The presence of a sulfonamide compound in the blood.

sulfonamidocholia (sul″fōn-am″ĭ-do-ko′le-ah). The presence of a sulfonamide compound in the bile.

sulfonamidotherapy (sul″fōn-am″ĭ-do-ther′ah-pe). Treatment with sulfonamide compounds.

sulfonamiduria (sul″fōn-am″ĭ-du′re-ah). The presence of a sulfonamide compound in the urine.

sulfone (sul′fōn). 1. The radical SO_2. 2. Any sulfur alcohol or ether; any compound of SO_2 with one or two hydrocarbons. It is analogous to ketone. **Angeli's s.,** glucosulfone sodium.

sulfonethylmethane (sul″fōn-eth″il-meth′ān). A crystalline powder, $(C_2H_5)(CH_3)C(SO_2C_2H_5)_2$, a hypnotic resembling sulfonmethane.

sulfonic (sul-fon′ik). Indicating chemical compounds containing the monovalent $—SO_2OH$ or $—SO_3H$ radical.

sulfonmethane (sul″fōn-meth′ān). A white, crystalline compound, $(CH_3)_2C(SO_2C_2H_5)_2$, diethylsulfonedimethylmethane, readily soluble in alcohol and slowly in 100 parts of water. It has moderate hypnotic properties, and is used in insomnia of functional origin.

sulfonsol (sul-fon′sol). Trade mark for oral trisulfapyrimidines suspension.

sulfonyl (sul′fo-nil). The bivalent radical, $—SO_2—$.

sulfoparaldehyde (sul″fo-pah-ral′de-hīd). A crystalline substance, $(CH_3.CHS)_3$, or trithioacetaldehyde; insoluble in water, but soluble in alcohol, and used as a hypnotic.

sulfoprotein (sul″fo-pro′te-in). Any one of a series of albumins containing loosely combined sulfur.

sulfopyretotherapy (sul″fo-pi-ret″o-ther′ah-pe). Artificial fever therapy produced by the intramuscular injection of sulfur solution.

sulfosalt (sul′fo-sawlt). A salt of sulfonic acid.

sulfosol (sul′fo-sol). A sol in which sulfuric acid is the dispersion medium.

sulfoxide (sul-fok′sīd). 1. The bivalent radical, $=SO$. 2. Any member of a group of compounds intermediate between the sulfides and the sulfones.

sulfoxism (sul-fok′sizm). Sulfuric acid poisoning.

sulfur (sul′fur), gen. *sul′furis* [L.]. A nonmetallic element existing in many allotropic forms; symbol, S; atomic number, 16; atomic weight, 32.064. Sulfur is a laxative and diaphoretic and is used in diseases of the skin and respiratory organs, and in hemorrhoids, habitual constipation, etc. **colloidal s.,** sulfur in a state of extremely fine division. **s. dioxide,** a corrosive gas, SO_2: used as an antioxidant. **flower of s.,** sublimed s. **hepar-s.,** sulfurated potash. **s. hydride,** H_2S, a gas having the smell of rotten eggs. **s. iodide,** a binary compound, S_2I_2: used in ointments. **lac s.,** precipitated s. **liver of s.,** sulfurated potash. **s. lo′tum,** washed s. **milk of s.,** precipitated s. **s. monochloride,** a lacrimating war gas, S_2Cl_2. **precipitated s.,** milk of sulfur; sulfur precipitated from a solution of calcium pentasulfide and thiosulfate: it contains more or less calcium sulfide, etc. **roll s.,** sulfur melted and cast in the form of rolls. **sublimed s.,** sulfur in fine, yellow powder, obtained by cooling the heated vapor of ordinary sulfur. **s. trioxide,** sulfuric acid anhydride, SO_3. **s. vasogen,** an ointment containing sulfur and vasogen, either semisolid or fluid: useful in seborrhea. **vegetable s.,** lycopodium. **washed s.,** sublimed sulfur purified by washing with water.

sulfuraria (sul″fu-ra′re-ah). A yellow powder, the sediment from certain springs in Italy, said to contain sulfur, calcium sulfide, strontium sulfate, silica, etc.: used in skin diseases.

sulfurated, sulfureted (sul′fu-rāt″ed, sul′fu-ret″ed). Combined or charged with sulfur.

sulfurator (sul′fu-ra″tor). An apparatus for applying sulfur fumes, as in disinfecting.

sulfuret (sul′fu-ret). Sulfide.

sulfurize (sul′fu-rīz). To cause to combine with sulfur.

sulfuryl (sul′fu-ril). The radical SO_2.

sulfydryl (sul-fi′dril). Sulfhydryl.

Sulkowitch's test (sul′ko-wich″ez) [Hirsh Wolf *Sulkowitch*, American physician, born 1906]. See under *tests.*

sullage (sul′ij). Sewage.

sulph-. For words beginning thus, see those beginning *sulf-*.

sul-spansion (sul-span′shun). Trade mark for a suspension of sulfaethidole.

sum. Abbreviation for L. *su′mat,* let him take; or *sumen′dum,* to be taken.

sumac (su′mak). A name of various species of *Rhus,* applied principally to the nonpoisonous species: astringent. **swamp s.,** *Rhus venenata.*

summation (sum-ma′shun) [L. *summa* total]. The accumulative effects of a number of stimuli applied to a muscle, a nerve or a reflex arc. **central s.,** the condition in which successive subliminal stimuli accumulate in a reflex center until they finally produce a reflex discharge.

summit (sum′it) [L. *summus,* superlative of *superus*]. The highest point. **s. of bladder,** apex vesicae urinariae. **s. of nose,** radix nasi.

Sumner's sign (sum′nerz) [F. W. *Sumner,* British surgeon]. See under *sign.*

sunburn (sun′bern). Injury to the skin, with erythema, tenderness, and vesiculobullous changes, following excessive exposure to sunlight, and produced by ultraviolet rays, which are not filtered out by clouds.

sunstroke (sun′strōk). Insolation, or thermic fever; a condition produced by exposure to the sun, and marked by convulsions, coma, and a high temperature of the skin.

super- [L. *super* above]. A prefix signifying above, or implying excess.

superabduction (su″per-ab-duk′shun). Extreme or excessive abduction.

superacid (su″per-as′id). Excessively acid.

superacidity (su″per-ah-sid′ĭ-te). Excessive acidity.

superacromial (su″per-ah-kro′me-al). Above or upon the acromion.

superactivity (su″per-ak-tiv′ĭ-te). Activity greater than normal.

superacute (su″per-ah-kūt′). Extremely acute.

superalbal (su″per-al′bal) [*super-* + L. *alba* white]. Situated in the upper part of the white substance of the brain.

superalbuminosis (su″per-al-bu″mĭ-no′sis). Excessive formation of albumin.

superalimentation (su″per-al″ĭ-men-ta′shun). Therapeutic treatment by excessive feeding beyond the requirements of the appetite: employed in wasting diseases. Called also *gavage.*

superalkalinity (su″per-al″kah-lin′ĭ-te). Excessive alkalinity.

superaurale (su″per-aw-ra′le). An anthropometric landmark, the highest point on the superior border of the helix of the ear.

supercallosal (su″per-kah-lo′sal). Situated above the corpus callosum.

supercarbonate (su″per-kar′bon-āt). Bicarbonate.

supercentral (su″per-sen′tral). 1. Above a center. 2. Above the central sulcus of the brain.

supercerebellar (su″per-ser″e-bel′ar). In the upper part of the cerebellum.

supercerebral (su″per-ser′e-bral). In the upper part of the cerebrum.

supercilia (su″per-sil′e-ah) [L., pl. of *supercilium*]. [N A, B N A] The hairs growing on the transverse elevation at the junction of the forehead and the upper lid of either eye. Called also *eyebrow.*

superciliary (su″per-sil′e-a-re) [L. *superciliaris*]. Pertaining to the eyebrow.

supercilium (su″per-sil′e-um), pl. *supercil′ia* [L.]. [N A, B N A] The transverse elevation at the junction of the forehead and the upper eyelid. See *eyebrow* (def. 1), and see also *supercilia.*

superclass (su′per-klas). A taxonomic category sometimes established, subordinate to a phylum and superior to a class.

superdicrotic (su″per-di-krot′ik). Hyperdicrotic.

superdistention (su″per-dis-ten′shun). Excessive distention.

superduct (su″per-dukt′) [*super-* + L. *ducere* to draw]. To carry up or elevate.

superdural (su″per-du′ral). Situated above or external to the dura mater.

super-ego (su″per-e′go). A part of the psyche with components derived from both the id and the ego, functioning largely in the unconscious zone, and acting as a monitor over the ego.

superexcitation (su″per-ek″si-ta′shun) [*super-*

+ L. *excitatio* excitement]. Extreme or excessive excitement.

superextended (su″per-eks-tend′ed). Extended beyond the normal.

superextension (su″per-eks-ten′shun). Excessive extension.

superfamily (su″per-fam′ĭ-le). A taxonomic category sometimes established, subordinate to an order and superior to a family.

superfatted (su″per-fat′ed). Containing more fat than can be combined with the quantity of alkali present.

superfecundation (su″per-fe″kun-da′shun) [*super-* + L. *fecundare* to fertilize]. Fertilization of an ovum taking place after one ovum has already been fertilized, or the more or less simultaneous fertilization of two ova by spermatozoa of different males.

superfemale (su″per-fe′māl). A female organism whose cells contain more than the ordinary number of sex-determining (X) chromosomes.

superfetation (su″per-fe-ta′shun) [*super-* + *fetus*]. The fertilization and subsequent development of an ovum when a fetus is already present in the uterus.

superfibrination (su″per-fib″rĭ-na′shun). The formation of an excessive amount of fibrin in the blood.

superficial (su″per-fish′al) [L. *superficialis*]. Pertaining to or situated near the surface.

superficialis (su″per-fish″e-a′lis). Superficial; in official anatomical nomenclature, used to designate a structure situated closer than another to the surface of the body.

superficies (su″per-fish′e-ēz) [L.]. An outer surface.

superfissure (su″per-fish′er). A fissure formed by the overlapping of two cerebral convolutions.

superflexion (su″per-flek′shun). Extreme or excessive flexion.

superfrontal (su″per-frun′tal). Situated at the upper or frontal part of a structure.

superfunction (su″per-funk′shun). Excessive activity of an organ or structure.

supergenual (su″per-jen′u-al). Above the knee.

supergyre (su′per-jir). A cerebral convolution which overlaps another.

superimpregnation (su″per-im″preg-na′shun) [*super-* + *impregnation*]. Fertilization of a second ovum occurring after one has already been fertilized.

superinduce (su″per-in-dūs′). To induce or bring on in addition to some already existing condition.

superinfection (su″per-in-fek′shun). A condition produced by sudden growth of a type of bacteria different from the original offenders in a wound or lesion under treatment.

superinvolution (su″per-in″vo-lu′shun). Hyperinvolution.

superior (su-pe′re-or) [L. "upper"; neut. *superius*]. Situated above, of directed upward; in official anatomical nomenclature, used in reference to the upper surface of an organ or other structure, or to a structure occupying a higher position.

superlactation (su″per-lak-ta′shun). Hyperlactation.

superlethal (su″per-le′thal). More than sufficient to cause death.

superligamen (su″per-li-ga′men) [*super-* + L. *ligamen* bandage]. A bandage applied over a surgical dressing to keep it in place.

supermaxilla (su″per-mak-sil′ah). The maxilla.

supermedial (su″per-me′de-al). Situated above the middle.

supermicroscope (su″per-mi′kro-skōp). An electron microscope giving extremely high magnification.

supermoron (su″per-mo′ron). A person who is above the grade of a moron, being only slightly deficient mentally.

supermotility (su″per-mo-til′ĭ-te). Excessive motility.

supernatant (su″per-na′tant) [*super-* + L. *natare* to swim]. 1. Situated above or on top of something. 2. The overlying liquid after precipitation of a solid component of a system.

supernate (su′per-nāt). Supernatant, def. 2.

supernormal (su″per-nor′mal). More than normal.

supernumerary (su″per-nu′mer-ar″e) [L. *supernumerarius*]. In excess of the regular or normal number.

supernutrition (su″per-nu-trish′un). Excessive nutrition.

superoccipital (su″per-ok-sip′ĭ-tal). At the upper part of the occiput.

superofrontal (su″per-o-fron′tal). Superfrontal.

superolateral (su″per-o-lat′er-al). Above and at the side.

superovulation (su″per-ov″u-la′shun). Extraordinary acceleration of ovulation.

superparasite (su″per-par′ah-sīt). Hyperparasite.

superparasitism (su″per-par′ah-si″tizm). Infestation with more parasites of one species than the host can support or bring to maturity.

superphosphate (su″per-fos′fāt). Any acid phosphate.

superpigmentation (su″per-pig″men-ta′shun). Excessive pigmentation.

super-regeneration (su″per-re-jen″er-a′shun). The development of superfluous tissue, organs, or parts as a result of regeneration.

supersalt (su′per-sawlt). Any salt with an excess of acid; a persalt or acid salt.

supersaturate (su″per-sat′u-rāt). To add more of an ingredient than can be held in solution permanently.

superscription (su″per-skrip′shun) [L. *superscriptio*]. The sign ℞ before a prescription. See *prescription*.

supersecretion (su″per-se-kre′shun). Excessive secretion.

supersedent (su″per-se′dent). A remedy which cures or prevents a disease in a part.

supersensitization (su″per-sen″sĭ-ti-za′shun). Hypersensitization.

supersoft (su″per-soft′). Extremely soft; applied to roentgen rays of extremely long wavelengths, large absorption coefficients, and low penetrating power.

supersonic (su″per-son′ik) [*super-* + L. *sonus* sound]. Having a speed greater than the velocity of sound, that is, faster than approximately one-fifth mile per second (or 720 miles an hour) in air.

supersonics (su″per-son′iks). The general science relating to phenomena associated with speed greater than the velocity of sound (as in case of aircraft and projectiles traveling faster than sound).

supersphenoid (su″per-sfe′noid). Above the sphenoid bone.

superstructure (su″per-struk′tūr). The overlying or visible portion of an appliance. In dentistry, that portion of an implant denture which is outside the tissues of the mouth.

supersulcus (su″per-sul′kus). Superfissure.

supertension (su″per-ten′shun). Extreme or excessive tension.

supervenosity (su″per-ve-nos′ĭ-te). An abnormally diminished level of oxygen in venous blood.

supervention (su″per-ven′shun). The development of some condition in addition to an already existing one.

supervirulent (su″per-vir′u-lent). Excessively virulent.

supervisor (su′per-vīz″er). An individual who oversees the activities of others, such as a nurse who oversees the nursing activities in a specific ward or department of a hospital.

supervitaminosis (su″per-vi″tah-min-o′sis). Hypervitaminosis.

supervoltage (su′per-vol″tij). Very high voltage: said of high voltage roentgen ray therapy.

supinate (su′pĭ-nāt). To assume or place in a supine position.

supination (su″pĭ-na′shun) [L. *supinatio*]. The act of assuming the supine position, or the state of being supine. Applied to the hand, the act of turning the palm forward (anteriorly) or upward, performed by lateral rotation of the forearm. Applied to the foot, it generally implies movements resulting in raising of the medial margin of the foot, hence of the longitudinal arch. Cf.

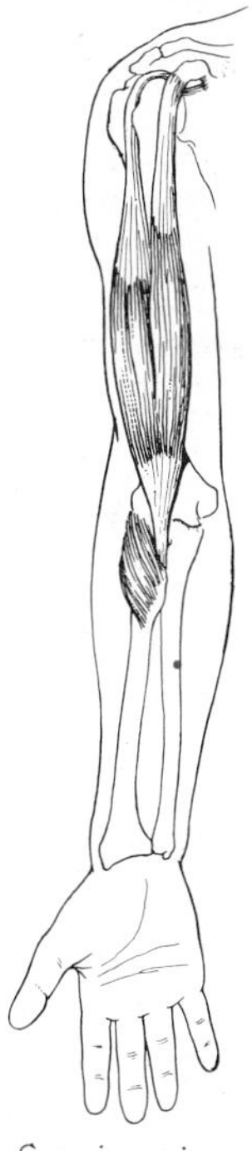

Supination

Supinators contracted; forearm, hand supinated. (King and Showers.)

supine (su′pīn) [L. *supinus* lying on the back, face upward]. Lying with the face upward. See also *supination*.

suplago-albumin, suplagalbumin (su-pla″go-al-bu′min, su-pla″gal-bu′min) [L. *sus* swine + *plaga* plague + *albumin*]. An albumose of swine plague.

suplagotoxin (su-pla″go-tok′sin) [L. *sus* swine + *plaga* plague + *toxin*]. One of the ptomaines of swine plague.

suppedania (sup″e-da′ne-ah) [L. *sub* under + *pes* foot]. Local applications to the soles of the feet.

supplemental (sup″lĕ-men′tal). Serving as a supplement or addition.

support (su-port′). An appliance which helps maintain a part in position. **Abée's s.,** an appliance for producing compression over the breast region to quiet an overacting heart.

suppositoria (su-poz′ĭ-to″re-ah) [L.]. Plural of *suppositorium*.

suppositorium (su-poz′ĭ-to″re-um), pl. *suppos′itoria* [L.]. Suppository.

suppository (sŭ-poz′ĭ-to-re) [L. *suppositorium*]. An easily fusible medicated mass to be introduced into an orifice of the body. **glycerin s.,** a suppository made up of a mixture of glycerin and sodium stearate: used as a rectal evacuant.

suppression (sŭ-presh′un) [L. *suppressio*]. 1. The sudden stoppage of a secretion, excretion, or normal discharge. 2. In psychoanalysis, conscious inhibition as contrasted with repression which is unconscious.

suppurant (sup′u-rant) [L. *suppurans*]. 1. Characterized by suppuration. 2. An agent that causes suppuration.

suppurantia (sup″u-ran′she-ah). Substances that cause suppuration.

suppuration (sup″u-ra′shun) [L. *sub* under + *puris* pus]. The formation of pus; the act of becoming converted into and discharging pus. **alveodental s.,** periodontitis with the formation of pus.

suppurative (sup′u-ra″tiv). Producing pus, or associated with suppuration.

supra- [L. "above"]. Prefix signifying above or over.

supra-acromial (su″prah-ah-kro′me-al). Situated above or over the acromion.

supra-anal (su-prah-a′nal). Situated above the anus.

supra-auricular (su″prah-aw-rik′u-lar). Situated above the ear.

supra-axillary (su″prah-ak′sĭ-ler″e). Situated above the axilla.

suprabuccal (su″prah-buk′al). Above the buccal region.

suprabulge (su′prah-bulj). The surfaces of a tooth occlusal to the height of contour, or sloping occlusally. Cf. *infrabulge*.

supracerebellar (su″prah-ser″e-bel′ar). On the upper surface of the cerebellum.

supracerebral (su″prah-ser′e-bral). Over or on the surface of the cerebrum.

suprachoroid (su″prah-ko′roid). Situated above or upon the choroid.

suprachoroidea (su″prah-ko-roi′de-ah). The outermost layer of the choroid coat; the loose tissue between the sclerotic and the choroid coat of the eye. Called also *ectochoroidea* and *suprachoroid lamina*.

supraciliary (su″prah-sil′e-er″e). Superciliary.

supraclavicular (su″prah-klah-vik′u-lar). Situated above the clavicle.

supraclavicularis (su″prah-klah-vik″u-la′ris) [L.]. Supraclavicular.

supraclusion (su″prah-kloo′zhun). The condition in which the occluding surface of a tooth extends beyond the normal occlusal plane.

supracommissure (su″prah-kom′ĭ-sūr). A cerebral commissure situated in front of the stalk of the pineal body.

supracondylar (su″prah-kon′dĭ-lar). Situated above a condyle or condyles.

supracondyloid (su″prah-kon′dĭ-loid). Supracondylar.

supracostal (su″prah-kos′tal). Situated above or upon a rib or ribs.

supracotyloid (su″prah-kot′ĭ-loid). Situated above the acetabulum.

supracranial (su″prah-kra′ne-al). On the upper surface of the cranium.

supradiaphragmatic (su″prah-di″ah-frag-mat′ik). Situated above the diaphragm.

supradural (su″prah-du′ral). Situated above the dura mater.

supra-epicondylar (su″prah-ep″ĭ-kon′dĭ-lar). Situated above an epicondyle.

supra-epitrochlear (su″prah-ep″ĭ-trok′le-ar). Situated above the medial epicondyle of the humerus.

supraglenoid (su″prah-gle′noid). Situated above the glenoid cavity.

supraglottic (su″prah-glot′ik). Situated above the glottis.

suprahepatic (su″prah-he-pat′ik). Situated above the liver.

suprahyoid (su″prah-hi′oid). Situated above the hyoid bone.

supra-inguinal (su″prah-in′gwĭ-nal). Situated above the groin.

supra-intestinal (su″prah-in-tes′tĭ-nal). Situated above the intestine.

supraliminal (su″prah-lim′ĭ-nal). Above the limen of sensation; more than just perceptible.

supralumbar (su″prah-lum′bar). Situated above the loin.

supramalleolar (su″prah-mah-le′o-lar). Situated above a malleolus.

supramammary (su″prah-mam′ah-re). Situated above a mammary gland.

supramandibular (su″prah-man-dib′u-lar). Situated above the mandible.

supramarginal (su″prah-mar′jĭ-nal). Situated above a margin.

supramastoid (su″prah-mas′toid). Situated above the mastoid portion of the temporal bone.

supramaxilla (su″prah-mak-sil′ah). The maxilla.

supramaxillary (su″prah-mak′sĭ-ler″e). 1. Pertaining to the upper jaw. 2. Situated above the maxilla.

supramaximal (su″prah-mak′sĭ-mal). Above the maximum.

suprameatal (su″prah-me-a′tal). Situated above a meatus.

supramental (su″prah-men′tal) [*supra-* + L. *mentum* chin]. Situated above the chin.

supramentale (su″prah-men-ta′le). A cephalometric landmark, being the most posterior midline point in the concavity between the infradentale and pogonium.

supranasal (su″prah-na′zal). Above the nose.

supraneural (su″prah-nu′ral) [*supra-* + Gr. *neuron* nerve]. Above a nerve, or above a neural axis.

supranormal (su″prah-nor′mal). Greater than normal; present or occurring in excess of normal amounts or values.

supranuclear (su″prah-nu′kle-ar). Situated or occurring above or on the cortical side or surface of a nucleus.

supraoccipital (su″prah-ok-sip′ĭ-tal). Situated above or in the upper portion of the occiput.

supraocclusion (su″prah-ŏ-kloo′zhun). Supraclusion.

supraocular (su″prah-ok′u-lar). Above the eye.

supraoptimal (su″prah-op′tĭ-mal). Greater than optimal.

supraoptimum (su″prah-op′tĭ-mum). A condition or quantity exceeding the optimum.

supraorbital (su″prah-or′bĭ-tal). Situated above the orbit.

suprapatellar (su″prah-pah-tel′ar). Situated above the patella.

suprapelvic (su″prah-pel′vik). Situated above the pelvis.

suprapineal (su″prah-pi′ne-al). Situated above the pineal gland.

suprapontine (su″prah-pon′tĭn). Situated above or in the upper part of the pons.

suprapubic (su″prah-pu′bik). Situated or performed above the pubic arch.

suprarenal (su″prah-re′nal) [*supra-* + L. *ren* kidney]. Situated above a kidney; pertaining to the suprarenal gland.

suprarenalectomy (su″prah-re″nal-ek′to-me) [*suprarenal* + Gr. *ektomē* excision]. Adrenalectomy; excision of the adrenal gland.

suprarenalemia (su″prah-re″nal-e′me-ah) [*suprarenal* + Gr. *haima* blood + *-ia*]. Increase of adrenal secretion (epineprhine) in the blood.

suprarenalism (su″prah-re′nal-izm). The condition produced by abnormal adrenal activity.

suprarenalopathy (su″prah-re″nal-op′ah-the) [*suprarenal* + Gr. *pathos* disease]. A disorder due to derangement of the adrenal gland.

suprarene (su″prah-rēn′) [*supra* + L. *ren* kidney]. An adrenal gland.

suprarenin (su″prah-ren′in). Trade mark for a preparation of epinephrine bitartrate.

suprarenogenic (su″prah-re″no-jen′ik). Originating in the adrenal gland; due to abnormal adrenal activity.

suprarenoma (su″prah-re-no′mah). A tumor derived from the adrenal tissue.

suprarenopathy (su″prah-re-nop′ah-the). Suprarenalopathy.

suprarenotropic (su″prah-re″no-trop′ik). Having an influence on the adrenal gland; adrenotropic.

suprarenotropism (su″prah-re-not′ro-pizm). An endocrine make-up in which the adrenal hormone is dominant.

suprascapular (su″prah-skap′u-lar). Situated on the upper part of the scapula.

suprascleral (su″prah-skle′ral). On the outer surface of the sclera.

suprasellar (su″prah-sel′ar). Above the sella turcica.

supraseptal (su″prah-sep′tal). Situated above a septum.

suprasonics (su″prah-son′iks). Ultrasonics.

supraspinal (su″prah-spi′nal). Situated upon or above a spine.

supraspinous (su″prah-spi′nus). Situated above a spine or a spinous process.

suprastapedial (su″prah-stah-pe′de-al). Situated above the stapes.

suprasternal (su″prah-ster′nal). Situated above the sternum.

suprasterol (su″prah-ster′ol). An isomer of ergosterol.

suprasylvian (su″prah-sil′ve-an). Situated above the sylvian fissure.

supratemporal (su″prah-tem′po-ral). Situated above the temporal bone, fossa, or region.

suprathoracic (su″prah-tho-ras′ik). Situated above or cephalad of the thorax.

supratonsillar (su″prah-ton′sĭ-lar). Situated above a tonsil.

supratrochlear (su″prah-trok′le-ar). Situated above the trochlea.

supraturbinal (su″prah-ter′bĭ-nal). The superior turbinal bone.

supratympanic (su″prah-tim-pan′ik). Above the tympanum.

supra-umbilical (su″prah-um-bil′ĭ-kal). Situated above the umbilicus.

supravaginal (su″prah-vaj′ĭ-nal). Situated above or outside of a sheath, specifically above the vagina.

supravergence (su″prah-ver′jens). The movement of one eye upward vertically as compared with movement of the other eye.

supraversion (su″prah-ver′zhun). The condition of a tooth when it is abnormally elongated from its socket.

supraxiphoid (su″prah-zi′foid). Above the xiphoid process.

sura (su′rah) [L.] [N A, B N A]. The muscular posterior portion of the leg. Called also *calf*.

sural (su′ral). Pertaining to the calf of the leg.

suralimentation (sur″al-ĭ-men-ta′shun). Superalimentation.

suramin sodium (su′rah-min so′de-um). Chemical name: hexasodium sym.-bis (m-aminobenzoyl-m-amino-p-methyl-benzoyl-l-naphthylamino-4, 6,8-trisulfonate) carbamide: used as an antitrypanosomal and antifilarial agent.

surcingle (sur′sing-g'l) [L. *super* over + *cingulum* belt]. Cauda nuclei caudati.

surdimute (sur′dĭ-mūt) [L. *surdus* deaf + *mutus* mute]. 1. Both deaf and dumb. 2. An individual who can neither hear nor speak.

surdimutism (sur″dĭ-mu′tizm). Deaf-mutism.

surdimutitas (sur″dĭ-mu′tĭ-tas) [L. *surdus* deaf + *mutus* unable to speak + *-tas* state]. Deaf-mutism.

surditas (sur′dĭ-tas) [L.]. Deafness. **s. congen′ita,** congenital deafness.

surdity (sur′dĭ-te) [L. *surditas*]. Deafness.

surexcitation (sur″ek-si-ta′shun) [L. *super* over + *excitation*]. Excessive excitation.

surfacaine (sur′fah-kān). Trade mark for preparations of cyclomethycaine.

surface (sur′fis). The outer part or an external aspect of a solid body. For names included in official anatomical nomenclature, see under *facies*. **alveolar s. of maxilla,** arcus alveolaris maxillae. **anterior s.,** that surface which is toward the front of the body (on or nearest the ventral aspect) in man (*facies anterior* [N A]), or directed toward the head (away from the tail) in quadrupeds; in dentistry, the proximal surface of a premolar or molar tooth that is closest to the midline of the dental arch. **anterior s. of**

manubrium and gladiolus, planum sternale. **anterior s. of sacrum,** facies pelvina ossis sacri. **anterior s. of scapula,** facies costalis scapulae. **anterior s. of stomach,** paries anterior ventriculi. **approximal s.,** proximal s. **articular s.,** that surface of a bone or cartilage which forms a joint with another (*facies articularis* [N A]). **articular s. of acetabulum,** facies lunata acetabuli. **articular s. of sacral bone, lateral,** facies auricularis ossis sacri. **axial s.,** any surface parallel with an axis; in dentistry, any surface of a tooth which is parallel with its long axis, including the buccal, distal, labial, lingual, and medial surfaces. **basal s.,** that surface of a denture the detail of which is determined by the impression and which rests upon the supporting tissues of the mouth. **buccal s.,** the surface of a posterior tooth (or of a denture) which faces the cheek (*facies buccalis dentis* [N A]). **condyloid s. of tibia,** facies articularis superior tibiae. **contact s.,** the portion of the surface of a tooth which lies in contact with the next tooth in the same row. See also *proximal s.* **diaphragmatic s.,** the surface of an organ of the thoracic or abdominal cavity that is directed toward the diaphragm (*facies diaphragmatica* [N A]). **distal s.,** that surface of a structure which is farther from a point of reference; in dentistry, the proximal surface of a tooth farthest from the midline of the dental arch (*lateral s.* or *posterior s.*). **dorsal s.** 1. The aspect of a structure that is directed toward the back of the body, or posteriorly, in man (*facies dorsalis, facies posterior* [N A]). 2. That surface which is upper or higher, or toward or nearest the back, in quadrupeds. **extensor s.,** the aspect of a joint of a limb (such as the knee or the elbow) on the side toward which the movement of extension is directed. **facial s.,** the surface of a tooth or denture which faces toward the lip or cheek; a labial or buccal surface. **flexor s.,** the aspect of a joint of a limb (such as the knee or the elbow) on the side toward which the movement of flexion is directed. **foundation s.,** basal s. **impression s.,** the surface of a denture that is determined by the impression made of the structures in the mouth. **incisal s.,** the surface of an anterior tooth that comes in contact with a tooth of the opposite jaw when the jaws are closed. **inferior s.,** that surface which is lower (directed away from the head, in man) (*facies inferior* [N A]). **labial s.,** the surface of an anterior tooth (or of a denture) which faces the lip (*facies labialis dentis* [N A]). **lateral s.,** a surface nearer to or directed toward the side of the body (*facies lateralis* [N A]); in dentistry, the proximal surface of an incisor or canine tooth that is farthest from the midline of the dental arch. **lingual s.,** the surface of a tooth (or of a denture) which faces the tongue (*facies lingualis dentis* [N A]). **masticatory s.,** occlusal s.; often thought of as restricted to the tooth surfaces actually participating in mastication (*occlusal s., working*). **medial s.,** a surface nearer to or directed toward the midline of the body (*facies medialis* [N A]); in dentistry, the proximal surface of an incisor or canine tooth that is closest to the midline of the dental arch. **mesial s.,** medial s. **morsal s's,** the occlusal surfaces of the mandibular and maxillary teeth which make contact in centric occlusion. **occlusal s.,** the surface of a posterior tooth (or of a denture) which comes in contact with structures of the opposite jaw when the jaws are closed; sometimes, by extension, used to designate the incisal surface of the anterior teeth as well (*facies masticatoria* [N A]). **occlusal s., working,** the occlusal surface of a tooth upon which mastication can occur. **polished s.,** one that is smoothed to a fine finish; in dentistry, that portion of the surface of a denture that is usually polished, including the palatal surface, and the buccal and lingual surfaces of the teeth. **posterior s.,** that surface which is toward the back of the body (on or nearest the dorsal aspect) in man (*facies posterior, facies dorsalis* [N A]), or directed toward the tail in quadrupeds; in dentistry, the proximal surface of a premolar or molar tooth that is farthest from the midline of the dental arch. **posterior s. of sacrum,** facies dorsalis ossis sacri. **posterior s. of scapula,** facies dorsalis scapulae. **posterior s. of stomach,** paries posterior ventriculi. **proximal s.,** a surface that is nearer to a point of reference; used in dentistry to designate that surface of a tooth which faces an adjoining tooth in the same dental arch (*facies contactus dentis* [N A]). **proximate s.,** proximal s. **subocclusal s.,** a portion of the surface of a tooth which is directed toward but does not make contact with the occlusal surface of its opposite number in the other jaw. **superior s.,** that surface which is upper or higher (directed toward the head, in man) (*facies superior* [N A]). **tentorial s.,** the portion of the cerebral surface that is in contact with the tentorium cerebelli. **ventral s.** 1. The anterior surface, in man. 2. That surface which is lower, or on or nearest the abdominal aspect in quadrupeds.

surfactant (surf-ak′tant). A surface-active agent.

surgeon (sur′jun) [L. *chirurgio;* Fr. *chirurgien*]. A practitioner of surgery. **barber s.,** formerly a barber who was authorized to practice surgery. **contract s.,** in the U. S. Army a physician or dentist engaged for temporary service in the medical department; called also *acting assistant surgeon.* **s. general,** the chief surgeon of an army or navy. **house s.,** the chief surgical intern of a hospital. **post s.,** the surgeon of an established army post.

surgery (sur′jer-e) [L. *chirurgia,* from Gr. *cheir* hand + *ergon* work]. 1. That branch of medicine which treats diseases, wholly or in part, by manual and operative procedures. 2. A place for the performance of surgical operations. **abdominal s.,** the surgery of the abdominal viscera. **antiseptic s.,** surgery conducted in accordance with antiseptic principles. **arthrosteopedic s.,** surgery of the extremities and skeleton. **aseptic s.,** surgery that is carried out so nearly free of bacteria that infection or suppuration does not result. **aural s.,** the surgical treatment of diseases of the ear. **cerebral s.,** that which deals with operations upon the brain. **cineplastic s.,** creation of a skin-lined tunnel through a muscle adjacent to the stump of an amputated limb, to permit use of the muscle in operating a prosthesis. **clinical s.,** surgery as practiced in the teaching clinic. **conservative s.,** surgery which looks to the preservation or the restoration of disabled parts, rather than their removal. **cosmetic s.,** that department of surgery which deals with procedures designed to improve the patient's appearance by plastic restorations, removal of blemishes, etc. **decorative s.,** cosmetic s. **dental s.,** that branch of the healing arts which deals with the surgical and adjunctive treatment of diseases, injuries, and defects of the teeth. **dentofacial s.,** that branch of the healing arts which deals with the surgical and adjunctive treatment of diseases, injuries, and defects involving the face and structures of the mouth. **featural s.,** plastic surgery of the face. **general s.,** that which deals with surgical cases of all kinds. **ionic s.,** surgical ionization and electrolysis. **major s.,** surgery which is concerned with the more important and dangerous operations. **minor s.,** the surgery which has low mortality, requires few assistants, and is usually performed outside of the hospital. **operative s.,** the operative or more mechanical part of surgery; that which deals with methods or with operative procedures. **oral s.,** that branch of the healing arts which deals with the diagnosis and the surgical and adjunctive treatment of diseases, injuries, and defects of the mouth, the jaws, and associated structures. **orificial s.,** the surgery of the orifices of the body, as the mouth, anus, vulva, etc. **orthopedic s.,** that branch of surgery which deals with the correction of deformities; orthopedics. **pelvic s.,** the surgery of the pelvis; chiefly in gynecological and obstetrical cases. **plastic s.,** surgery concerned with the restoration or reconstruction of body structures that are defective or damaged by injury or disease. **rectal s.,** the surgical treatment of diseases of the rectum. **stereotaxic brain s.,** stereoencephalotomy. **structive s., structural s.,** surgery that concerns itself with morphologic changes and functional amelioration both in the internal cavities of the body and in the body periphery. **subcutaneous s.,** the performance of surgical operations through a very small opening in the skin. **veterinary s.,** the surgery of domestic animals.

surgical (sur′je-kal). Of, or pertaining to, surgery.

surgiology (sur″je-ol′o-je). A term proposed to include research in physiology as connected with surgery, experimental surgery, etc.

surinamine (su-rin′ah-min). A methyl tyrosine, paraoxyphenyl-alphamethylamino-propionic acid, $OH.C_6H_4.CH_2.CH(COOH).NH.CH_3$, found in many plants.

surital (sur′ĭ-tal). Trade mark for preparations of thiamylal.

surra (soor′ah). A disease of horses, camels, and other domestic animals in India, China, Africa, and the Philippine Islands, said to be caused by an animal microparasite, the *Trypanosoma evansi.* It is marked by fever, petechia of mucous surfaces, edema, progressive anemia, and emaciation, ending in death. It is transmitted by the bite of gadflies or horseflies (Tabanidae) and probably also by fleas.

surrogate (sur′o-gāt) [L. *surrogatus* substituted]. Something used as a substitute for another. In psychoanalysis, an imagined person who conceals from conscious recognition the identity of that person, e.g., in dreams a king may represent the dreamer's father (**father s.**).

sursanure (sur-săn′ūr). An old name for a sore healed outwardly, but not inwardly.

sursumduction (sur″sum-duk′shun) [L. *sursum* upward + *ducere* to lead]. The turning upward of a part, as of the eyes.

sursumvergence (sur″sum-ver′jens) [L. *sursum* upward + *vergere* to turn]. An upward movement, especially of the eyes.

sursumversion (sur″sum-ver′zhun) [L. *sursum* upward + *vertere* to turn]. An act of turning or directing upward; especially the simultaneous and equal upward turning of both eyes.

suruçucu (soo″roo-soo′koo). The *Lachesis mutus,* a venomous snake of South America.

susceptibility (sus-sep″tĭ-bil′ĭ-te). The state of being readily affected or acted upon. In immunology, the condition may be acquired, familial, individual, inherited, racial, specific, etc., the same as is immunity. **differential s.,** nonhomogeneity in response by the various regions of an embryo when subjected to a diffusely applied injurious agent.

susceptible (sus-sep′tĭ-b'l). 1. Capable of impression; readily acted on. 2. An individual who is not known to have become immune to an infectious disease by either natural or artificial means.

suscitate (sus′ĭ-tāt). To arouse to greater activity.

suscitation (sus″ĭ-ta′shun) [L. *suscitatio*]. An arousal or excitation.

susotoxin (su″so-tok′sin) [L. *sus* hog + *toxin*]. A ptomaine or toxin, $C_{10}H_{26}N_2$, from cultures of the hog cholera bacillus. It causes convulsions and death when injected into animals.

suspenopsia (sus″pen-op′se-ah) [L. *suspendere* to cause to waver + Gr. *opsis* vision + *-ia*]. A condition of frequently occurring momentary suppression of attention in the visual cortex to impulses arising in the central retinal areas.

suspensiometer (sus-pen″se-om′e-ter). An instrument for standardizing bacterial and other suspensions.

suspension (sus-pen′shun) [L. *suspensio*]. 1. A condition of temporary cessation, as of animation, of pain, or of any vital process. 2. Treatment, chiefly of spinal disorders, by suspending the patient by the chin and the shoulders. 3. A preparation of a finely divided drug intended to be incorporated (suspended) in some suitable liquid vehicle before it is used, or already incorporated in such a vehicle. **cephalic s.,** suspension of a patient by the head in order to make extension of the vertebral column. **colloid s.,** a suspension in which the suspended particles are very small. **insulin isophane s.,** a sterile suspension made from zinc-insulin crystals modified by the addition of protamine, having an intermediate action. **insulin protamine zinc s.,** a sterile suspension of insulin modified by the addition of zinc chloride and protamine, having a prolonged action. **insulin zinc s.,** a sterile suspension of insulin modified by the addition of zinc chloride, having an intermediate action. **selenium sulfide s.,** a preparation containing 2.5 per cent of selenium sulfide: used externally in treatment of non-inflammatory, non-exudative seborrhea. **trisulfapyrimidines oral s.,** a suspension of sulfadiazine, sulfamerazine, and sulfamethazine: used as an antibacterial agent.

suspensoid (sus-pen′soid). Suspension colloid.

suspensorius (sus″pen-so′re-us) [L.]. Suspensory.

suspensory (sus-pen′so-re) [L. *suspensorius*]. 1. Serving to hold up a part. 2. A ligament, bone, muscle, sling, or bandage which serves to hold up a part.

suspirious (sus-pi′re-us). Breathing heavily; sighing.

sustentacular (sus′ten-tak′u-lar) [L. *sustentare* to support]. Sustaining or supporting. See under *cell.*

sustentaculum (sus″ten-tak′u-lum), pl. *sustentac′ula* [L.]. A support. **s. li′enis,** ligamentum phrenicolienale. **s. ta′li** [N A, B N A], **s. of talus,** a process of the calcaneus which supports the astragalus.

susurrus (su-sur′us) [L.]. Murmur.

sutho (su′tho). A kind of leprosy occurring in Korea.

sutika (su′tik-ah). A disease of pregnant women of Bengal, marked by digestive troubles and fever during pregnancy, with progressive pernicious anemia occurring after delivery.

Sutton's disease (sut′onz). 1. [Richard Lightburn *Sutton,* American dermatologist, 1878–1952]. Leukoderma acquisitum centrifugum. 2. [Richard L. *Sutton,* Jr., American dermatologist, born 1908]. Granuloma fissuratum.

sutura (su-tu′rah), pl. *sutu′rae* [L. "a seam"]. [N A, B N A] A type of fibrous joint in which the apposed bony surfaces are so closely united by a very thin layer of fibrous connective tissue that no movement can occur; found only in the skull. Called also *suture, sutura vera,* and *true suture.* **s. corona′lis** [N A, B N A], the line of junction of the frontal bone with the two parietal bones. Called also *coronal suture.* **sutu′rae cra′nii** [N A, B N A], the sutures between the various bones of the skull, named generally for the specific components participating in their formation. Called also *cranial sutures.* **s. denta′ta,** s. serrata. **s. ethmoideomaxilla′ris** [N A, B N A], the line of junction between the orbital lamina of the ethmoid bone and the orbital surface of the maxilla. Called also *ethmoideomaxillary suture.* **s. fronta′lis** [N A, B N A], the usually transient line of junction between the right and left halves of the frontal bone. The inferior part often persists in the adult; if the entire suture persists, it is called the metopic suture. Called also *frontal suture.* **s. frontoethmoida′lis** [N A, B N A], the line of junction in the anterior cranial fossa between the frontal bone and the cribriform plate of the ethmoid bone. Called also *frontoethmoidal suture.* **s. frontolacrima′lis** [N A, B N A], the line of junction between the upper edge of the lacrimal bone and the orbital part of the frontal bone. Called also *frontolacrimal suture.* **s. frontomaxilla′ris** [N A, B N A], the line of junction between the frontal bone and the frontal process of the maxilla. Called also *frontomaxillary suture.* **s. frontonasa'lis** [N A], the line of junction between the frontal and the two nasal bones. Called also *s. nasofrontalis* [B N A], and *frontonasal suture.* **s. frontozygomat'ica** [N A], the line of junction between the zygomatic bone and the zygomatic process of the frontal bone. Called also *s. zygomaticofrontalis* [B N A], and *frontozygomatic suture.* **s. harmo'nia,** s. plana. **s. incisi'va** [N A, B N A] an indistinct suture sometimes seen extending laterally from the incisive fossa to the space between the canine tooth and the lateral incisor, indicating the line of fusion between the premaxilla and the maxilla. Called also *incisive suture.* **s. infraorbita'lis** [N A, B N A], a suture sometimes seen extending from the infraorbital foramen to the infraorbital groove. Called also *infraorbital suture.* **s. intermaxilla'ris** [N A, B N A], the line of junction between the maxillary bones of either side, just below the anterior nasal spine. Called also *intermaxillary suture.* **s. internasa'lis** [N A, B N A], the line of junction between the two nasal bones. Called also *internasal suture.* **s. lacrimoconcha'lis** [N A, B N A], the line of junction between the lacrimal bone and the inferior nasal concha. Called also *lacrimoconchal suture.* **s. lacrimomaxilla'ris** [N A, B N A], a suture on the inner wall of the orbit, between the lacrimal bone and the maxilla. Called also *lacrimomaxillary suture.* **s. lambdoi'dea** [N A, B N A], the line of junction between the occipital and parietal bones, shaped like the Greek letter lambda. Called also *lambdoid suture.* **s. limbo'sa,** a type of suture in which there is interlocking of the beveled surfaces of the bones. **s. nasofronta'lis** [B N A], s. frontonasalis. **s. nasomaxilla'ris** [N A, B N A], the line of junction between the lateral edge of the nasal bone and the frontal process of the maxilla. Called also *nasomaxillary suture.* **s. no'tha,** a type of suture formed by apposition of the roughened surfaces of the two participating bones. **s. occipitomastoi'dea** [N A, B N A], an extension of the lambdoid suture between the occipital bone and the posterior edge of the mastoid portion of the temporal bone. Called also *occipitomastoid suture.* **s. palati'na media'na** [N A, B N A], the line of junction between the horizontal part of the palatine bones of either side. Called also *median palatine suture.* **s. palati'na transver'sa** [N A, B N A], the line of junction between the palatine processes of the maxillae and the horizontal parts of the palatine bones. Called also *transverse palatine suture.* **s. palatoethmoida'lis** [N A, B N A], the line of junction between the orbital process of the palatine bone and the orbital lamina of the ethmoid bone. Called also *palatoethmoidal suture.* **s. palatomaxilla'ris** [N A, B N A], the suture in the floor of the orbit, between the orbital processes of the palatine bone and the orbital portion of the maxilla. Called also *palatomaxillary suture.* **s. parietomastoi'dea** [N A, B N A], the line of junction between the posterior inferior angle of the parietal bone and the mastoid process of the temporal bone. Called also *parietomastoid suture.* **s. pla'na** [N A], a type of suture in which there is simple apposition of the contiguous surfaces, with no interlocking of the edges of the participating bones. Called also *flat suture.* **s. sag'ittalis** [N A, B N A], the line of junction between the two parietal bones. Called also *sagittal suture.* **s. serra'ta** [N A, B N A], a type of suture in which the participating bones are united by interlocking processes resembling the teeth of a saw. Called also *serrated suture.* **s. sphenoethmoida'lis** [N A, B N A], the line of junction between the body of the sphenoid bone and the orbital lamina of the ethmoid bone. Called also *sphenoethmoidal suture.* **s. sphenofronta'lis** [N A, B N A], a long suture joining the orbital part of the frontal bone to the greater and lesser wings of the sphenoid bone on either side of the skull. Called also *sphenofrontal suture.* **s. sphenomaxilla'ris** [N A, B N A], a suture occasionally seen between the pterygoid process of the sphenoid bone and the maxilla. Called also *sphenomaxillary suture.* **s. sphenoorbi'talis** [B N A], the line or junction between the orbital process of the palatine bone and the body of the sphenoid bone. Omitted in N A. **s. sphenoparieta'lis** [N A, B N A], the line of junction between the great wing of the sphenoid bone and the parietal bone. Called also *sphenoparietal suture.* **s. sphenosquamo'sa** [N A, B N A], the line of junction between the great wing of the sphenoid bone and the squamous part of the temporal bone. Called also *sphenosquamous suture.* **s. sphenozygomat'ica** [N A, B N A], the line of junction between the great wing of the sphenoid bone and the zygomatic bone. Called also *sphenozygomatic suture.* **s. squamo'sa** [N A, B N A], a type of suture formed by overlapping of the broad beveled edges of the participating bones. Called also *squamous suture.* **s. squamo'sa cra'nii** [N A, B N A], the suture between the squamous part of the temporal bone and the parietal bone. Called also *squamous suture of cranium.* **s. squamosomastoi'dea** [N A, B N A], a suture existing early in life between the squamous and mastoid portions of the temporal bone. Called also *squamosomastoid suture.* **s. temporozygomat'ica** [N A], the line of junction between the zygomatic process of the temporal bone and the temporal process of the zygomatic bone. Called also *s. zygomaticotemporalis* [B N A], and *temporozygomatic suture.* **s. ve'ra,** a true suture, in which no movement of the participating bones can occur. **s. zygomaticofronta'lis** [B N A], s. frontozygomatica. **s. zygomaticomaxilla'ris** [N A, B N A], the line of junction between the zygomatic bone and the zygomatic process of the maxilla. Called also *zygomaticomaxillary suture.* **s. zygomaticotemporalis** [B N A], s. temporozygomatica.

sutural (su'tu-ral). Of or pertaining to a suture.

suturation (su″tu-ra'shun). The act or process of suturing, sewing, or stitching.

suture (su'tūr) [L. *sutura* a seam]. 1. A type of fibrous joint in which the opposed surfaces are closely united. See *sutura.* 2. A stitch or series of stitches made to secure apposition of the edges of a surgical or accidental wound; used also as a verb to indicate the application of such stitches. 3. Material used in closing a surgical or accidental wound with stitches. **absorbable s.,** a strand of material used for closing wounds, which becomes dissolved in the body fluids and disappears, such as catgut and tendon. **Albert's s.,** a form of Czerny suture in which the first row of stitches is passed through the entire thickness of the intestine. **Appolito's s.,** Gely's s. **apposition s.,** a superficial suture used for the exact approximation of the cutaneous edges of a wound. **approximation s.,** a deep suture for securing apposition of the deep tissues of a wound. **arcuate s.,** sutura coronalis. **basilar s.,** fissura sphenooccipitalis. **bastard s.,** false s. **Béclard's s.,** a continuous through-and-through suture in which the needle is threaded with a white and a colored thread; when the suture is withdrawn, the white thread is pulled from one end and the colored one from the other. **Bell's s.,** a form of glovers' suture in which the needle is passed from within outward alternately on the two edges of the wound. **biparietal s.,** sutura sagittalis. **bolster s.,** a suture the ends of which are tied over a roll of gauze or a piece of rubber tubing, in order to lessen the tension on the skin. **Bozeman's s.,** a form of button suture. **bregmatomastoid s.,** sutura parietomastoidea. **buried s.,** one that is placed deep in the tissues and concealed by the skin. **button s.,** one in which the suture material is passed through a button-like disk to prevent the knot from cutting through the skin. **catgut s.,** material for wound closure, prepared from strands of submucosa of the proximal portion of the small intestine of

Over-and-over suture

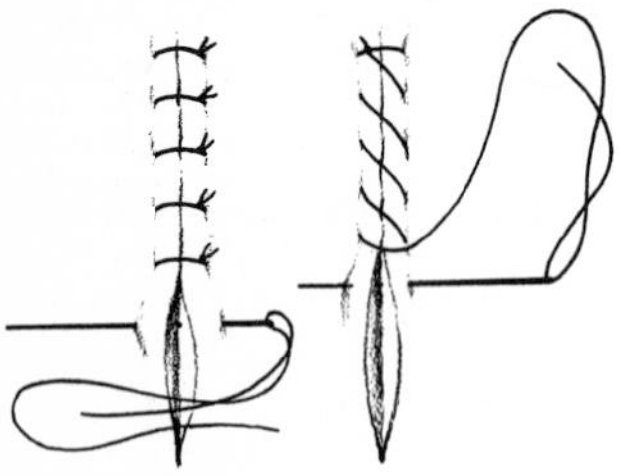

Vertical mattress suture

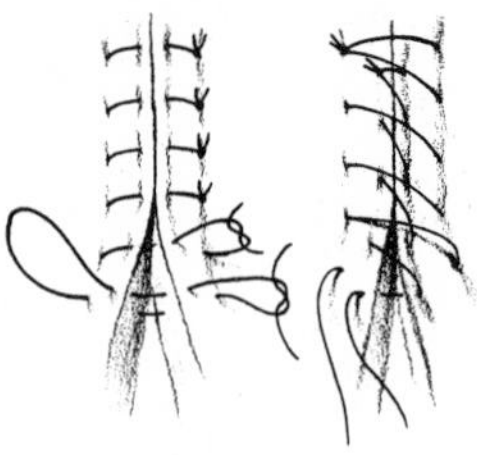

Horizontal mattress suture

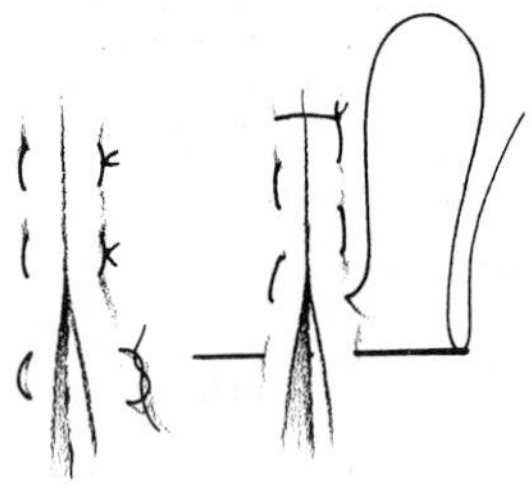

Lembert suture

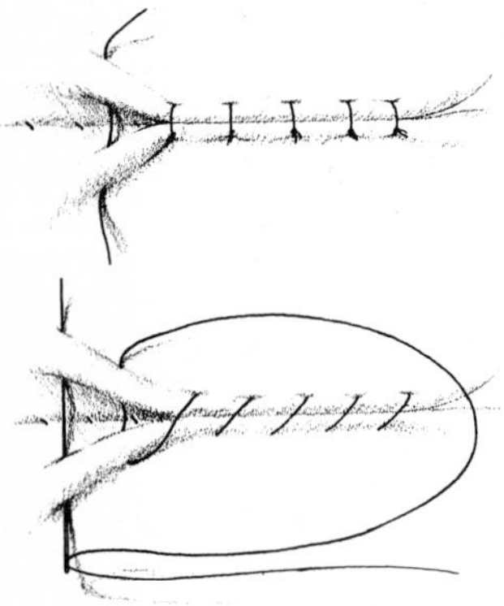

Lock-stitch suture

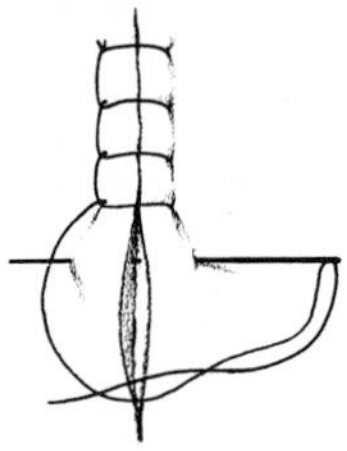

Connell suture

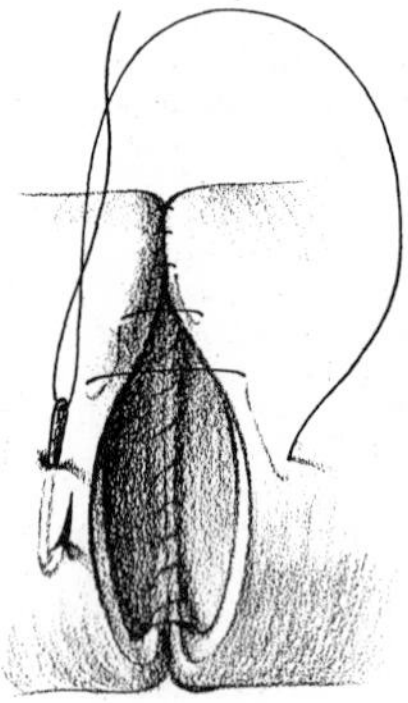

Purse-string suture

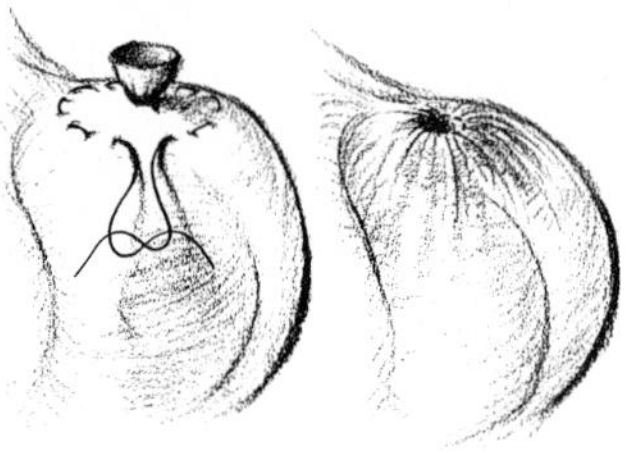

Halsted suture

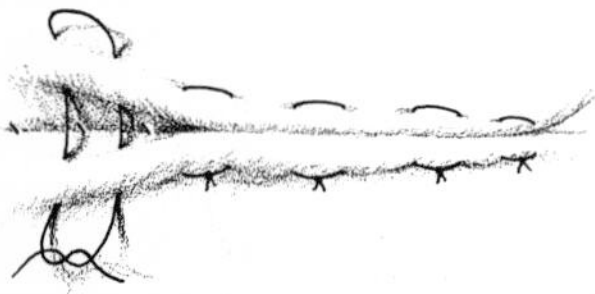

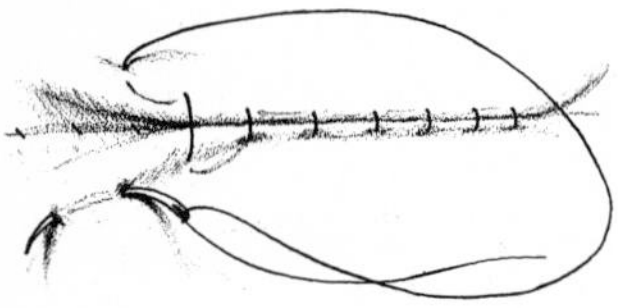

Everting sutures

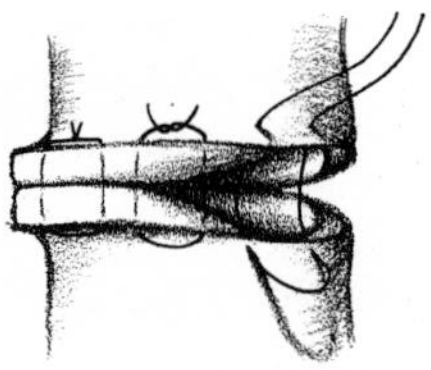

Subcuticular suture

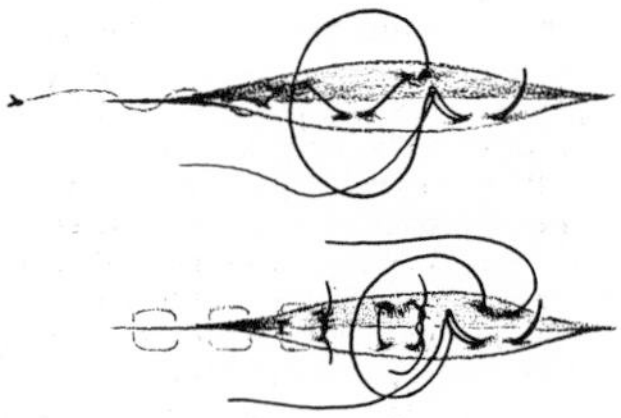

Cushing suture

VARIOUS TYPES OF SUTURES AND KNOTS

(Nealon)

sheep. **chain s.,** a continuous suture in which each loop of thread is caught by the next adjacent loop. **circular s.,** one that is applied to the entire circumference of an organ. **clavate s.,** quilled s. **coaptation s.,** apposition s. **cobblers' s.,** one made with suture material threaded through a needle at each end. **compound s.,** quilled s. **Connell s.,** a U-shaped continuous suture used in intestinal anastomosis, the stitches being placed parallel to and about 4 mm. from the edge of the wound, and passing through all the layers of the bowel. See illustration. **continuous s.,** one in which a continuous, uninterrupted length of material is used for a series of stitches. **coronal s.,** sutura coronalis. **cranial s's,** the lines of junction between the bones of the skull. See *suturae cranii* [N A]. **Cushing s.,** a continuous inverting suture used for closing the outer layers of tissue in surgery of the gastrointestinal tract. See illustration. **cutaneous s. of palate,** raphe palati. **Czerny's s.** 1. An intestinal suture in which the thread is passed through the mucous membrane alone. 2. A method of uniting a ruptured tendon by splitting one of the ends and suturing the other end into the slit. **Czerny-Lembert s.,** a combination of Czerny and Lembert sutures in circular enterorrhaphy. **dentate s.,** sutura serrata. **double-button s.,** a form of suture in which the suture material is passed deep to the surface across the edges of the wound, between two buttons placed one on either side of the suture line. **dry s.,** one in which the stitches are placed through two strips of adhesive plaster applied along either edge of a wound. **Dupuytren's s.,** a continuous Lembert suture. **Duvergier's s.,** the suturation of an intestine over a section of a calf's trachea. **Emmet's s.,** a series of double Lembert sutures used in closing intestinal wounds. **ethmoideomaxillary s.,** sutura ethmoideomaxillaris. **everting s.,** a method by which the approximated edges of a wound are everted; used in early blood vessel surgery to bring about apposition of the tunica intima of the divided segments. See illustration. **false s.,** a line of junction between apposed surfaces, without fibrous union of the bones. **figure-of-eight s.,** one in which the thread follows the contours of the figure 8; it may be almost entirely within or entirely outside the tissues. **flat s.,** sutura plana. **frontal s.,** sutura frontalis. **frontoethmoidal s.,** sutura frontoethmoidalis. **frontolacrimal s.,** sutura frontolacrimalis. **frontomalar s.,** sutura frontozygomatica. **frontomaxillary s.,** sutura frontomaxillaris. **frontonasal s.,** sutura frontonasalis. **frontoparietal s.,** sutura coronalis. **frontosphenoid s.,** sutura sphenofrontalis. **frontozygomatic s.,** sutura frontozygomatica. **furrier's s.,** a method of stitching intestinal wounds by piercing first one margin of the incision and then the other from within outward; overlying sutures are placed through the seromuscular layers to reinforce the closure and prevent leakage. **Gaillard-Arlt s.,** a suture used in correction of entropion. **Gély's s.,** a continuous suture for repair of intestinal wounds, made by a thread with a needle at each end, and consisting of a series of cross-stitches closing the wound. **glovers' s.,** lock-stitch s. **s. of Goethe,** sutura incisiva. **Gould's s.,** a reversed type of mattress suture, with the stitch closer to the line of incision than the site of emergence of the ends of the material; used in closing intestinal wounds. **Gussenbauer's s.,** a figure-of-eight suture used in repairing a rent of the intestine. **Halsted s.,** a modification of the Lembert suture, consisting of a stitch parallel to the wound on one side, with the two free ends of the material emerging on the other side, where they are tied. See illustration. **harelip s.,** a figure-of-eight suture used in the correction of harelip. **Harris' s.,** a method used in intestinal anastomosis. **hemostatic s's,** sutures used to control oozing of blood from raw areas, consisting of two loops of an over-and-over suture, placed at right angles to each other. **incisive s.,** sutura incisiva. **India rubber s.,** rubber s. **infraorbital s.,** sutura infraorbitalis. **interendognathic s.,** sutura palatina mediana. **intermaxillary s.,** sutura intermaxillaris. **internasal s.,** sutura internasalis. **interparietal s.,** sutura sagittalis. **interrupted s.,** a form of suture in which each stitch is made with a separate piece of suture material, threaded on a different needle. **intradermic s.,** a suture applied parallel with the edges of the wound, but below the surface of the skin, the needle being inserted at opposite points in the deep layers of the skin. **inverting s.,** a method by which the approximated edges are inverted; used in intestinal anastomosis to appose the serosal surfaces of the two segments, as in the Cushing or Lembert suture. **Jobert's s.,** an interrupted suture of various kinds for suturing a divided intestine, the end of the proximal segment being invaginated into the proximal end of the distal segment. **jugal s.,** sutura sagittalis. **lace s.,** a series of fine stitches closing a wound or fistula. **lacrimoconchal s.,** sutura lacrimoconchalis. **lacrimoethmoidal s.,** the vertical line of junction, on the medial wall of the orbit, between the lacrimal bone and the orbital plate of the ethmoid bone. **lacrimomaxillary s.,** sutura lacrimomaxillaris. **lacrimoturbinal s.,** sutura lacrimoconchalis. **lambdoid s.,** sutura lambdoidea. **Le Dentu's s.,** for a divided tendon: Two stitches are passed on each side, right and left, and are tied in front; a third is taken from right to left above and below the cut, and is tied on one side. **Le Dran's s.,** an intestinal suture in which single threaded stitches about one inch apart are tied on each side of the wound separately, and the two bundles are then tied together. **Le Fort's s.,** for a divided tendon: A single loop is passed above the cut, entering at one side, coming out and going in in front; it is then passed below the cut at each side, coming out in front, and is there tied. **Lembert s.,** an inverting suture commonly used in gastrointestinal surgery, the needle being inserted about 2.5 mm. lateral to the edge of the incision, through the serous and muscular tunics but not the submucosa and brought out near the edge of the incision, then being inserted near the edge of the incision on the other side and brought out at the more distant point, without having entered the lumen of the organ. It may be either interrupted or continuous. See illustration. **Littre's s.,** a form used in operations for intestinal gangrene: The lower end of the bowel is ligated, and the upper end is joined to the inguinal ring to form an artificial anus. **living s.,** material for stitching wounds, prepared from freshly removed fascia of the patient. **lock-stitch s.,** a continuous hemostatic suture used in intestinal surgery, the needle being passed through all layers of the bowel and the loop of suture material being made to fall over the point of emergence of the needle, which comes up through the loop, forming a self-locking stitch when the strand is pulled taut. See illustration. **Löffler's s.,** a method, used mainly for intestinal wounds, in which interrupted wire loops are crossed and attached to the wound. **longitudinal s.,** sutura sagittalis. **longitudinal s. of palate,** sutura palatina mediana. **loop s.,** interrupted s. **malomaxillary s.,** sutura zygomaticomaxillaris. **mamillary s., mastoid s.,** sutura occipitomastoidea. **mattress s., horizontal,** a method in which the stitches are made parallel with the edges of the wound, the suture material crossing under the wound edges from one side to the other. It may be either continuous or interrupted. See illustration. **mattress s., right-angle,** mattress s., vertical. **mattress s., vertical,** a method in which the stitches are made at right angles to the edges of the wound, taking both deep and superficial bites, the superficial bite making for more exact apposition of the skin margins. See illustration. **Maunsell s.,** a method of approximating the mesenteric border of the divided intestine. **metopic s.,** a name given the frontal suture when it persists in the adult skull. **nasal s.,** sutura internasalis. **nasofrontal s.,** sutura frontonasalis. **nasomaxillary s.,** sutura nasomaxillaris. **nerve s.,** material for uniting the ends of a divided nerve. **nonabsorbable s.,** material for closing wounds which is not absorbed in the body, such as silk, cotton, and stainless steel, or synthetic material such as nylon. **noose s.,** interrupted s. **occipital s.,** sutura lambdoidea. **occipitomastoid s.,** sutura occipitomastoidea. **occipitoparietal s.,** sutura lambdoidea. **occipitosphenoidal s.,** fissura sphenooccipitalis. **over-and-over s.,** a method in which equal bites of tissue are taken on each side of the wound and the edges approximated; it may be either interrupted or continuous. See illustration. **overlapping s.,** a squamous suture (sutura squamosa), such as the sutura squamosa cranii. **palatine s., anterior,** sutura incisiva. **palatine s., median, palatine s., middle,** sutura palatina mediana. **palatine s., posterior, palatine s., transverse,** sutura palatina transversa. **palatoethmoidal s.,** sutura palatoethmoidalis. **palatomaxillary s.,** sutura palatomaxillaris. **Palfyn's s.,** a method of repairing intestinal wounds, loops of thread being passed through the intestinal wall, and the ends secured to the skin. **Pancoast's s.,** a form of plastic suture. **Paré's s.,** the use of strips of cloth applied along the edges of a wound, and then stitched together so as to bring the margins of the wound into apposition. **parietal s.,** sutura sagittalis. **parietomastoid s.,** sutura parietomastoidea. **parietooccipital s.,** sutura lambdoidea. **Petit's s.,** a suture for intestinal wounds, in which stitches are placed three lines apart, the ends on each side tied together, and then twisted into two bundles. **petrobasilar s., petrosphenobasilar s.,** synchondrosis petrooccipitalis. **petrosphenooccipital s. of Gruber,** fissura petrooccipitalis. **petrosquamous s.,** fissura petrosquamosa. **pin s.,** a figure-of-eight suture in which the suture material is passed around pins inserted in the tissues at the side of the wound. **plastic s.,** a method in which a tongue is cut in one lip of the wound and a groove in the other, the tongue and groove then being stitched together, and the ends of the thread tied over a roll of adhesive plaster. **plate s.,** lead plate s. **premaxillary s.,** sutura incisiva. **presection s.,** a stitch or series of stitches placed in the tissues before an incision is made. **primary s.,** one that is placed in a wound immediately after it has been received. **purse-string s.,** a type of inverting suture commonly used to bury the stump of the appendix, a continuous running suture being placed about the opening, and then drawn tight. See illustration. **quilled s.,** one in which a double thread is employed and tied over quills or a soft catheter, in order that the stitches may be relaxed when the tension becomes too great. **quilt s., quilted s.,** a continuous mattress suture in which each stitch is tied as soon as formed, and the successive stitches are passed in opposite directions. **Ramdohr's s.,** a method of stitching the divided intestine after the distal end of the proximal segment has been invaginated into the proximal end of the distal segment. **relaxation s., relief s.,** any suture which closes a wound temporarily, but is so formed that it may be loosened in order to relieve the tension should it become too great. **retention s.,** a reinforcing suture for abdominal wounds, utilizing exceptionally strong material like braided silk or stainless steel, and including a large amount of tissue in each stitch: intended to relieve pressure on the primary suture line. **rhabdoid s.,** sutura sagittalis. **Richter's s.,** a method of closing intestinal wounds in which interrupted metallic loops are used, their ends being brought out of the external wound. **Rigal's s.,** rubber s. **Ritisch's s.,** a method of enterorrhaphy, a stitch being taken through the bowel wall from side to side, the ends twisted and then brought out through the external wound. **rubber s.,** a figure-of-eight suture in which rubber bands are used instead of thread. **Saenger's s.,** closure of the uterine wound in cesarean section by eight or ten deep silver wire sutures, with twenty or more superficial stitches taken through the peritoneum. **sagittal s.,** sutura sagittalis. **scaly s.,** sutura squamosa. **secondary s.,** suturation of a wound at a considerable period (more than a week) after operation, especially when the wound has been primarily sutured and tamponed. **seroserous s.,** a method of suturation in which two serous surfaces are apposed. **serrated s.,** sutura serrata. **shotted s.,** one in which the two ends of the wire are passed through a perforated shot, which is then compressed. **silkworm gut s.,** material prepared from the entrails of the silkworm, for use in wound closure. **Simon's s.,** a method of closing the lacerated perineum and ruptured sphincter ani, in which the rectal mucosa, the vaginal mucosa, and the skin are separately sutured. **Sims's s.,** a shotted suture. **s's of skull,** suturae cranii. **sphenoethmoidal s.,** sutura sphenoethmoidalis. **sphenofrontal s.,** sutura sphenofrontalis. **sphenomalar s.,** sutura sphenosquamosa. **sphenomaxillary s.,** sutura sphenomaxillaris. **sphenooccipital s.,** fissura sphenooccipitalis. **sphenoorbital s.,** sutura sphenoorbitalis. **sphenoparietal s.,** sutura sphenoparietalis. **sphenopetrosal s.,** synchondrosis petrooccipitalis. **sphenosquamous s., sphenotemporal s.,** sutura sphenosquamosa. **sphenozygomatic s.,** sutura sphenozygomatica. **squamosomastoid s.,** sutura squamosomastoidea. **squamosoparietal s.,** sutura squamosa cranii. **squamososphenoid s.,** sutura sphenosquamosa. **squamous s.,** sutura squamosa. **squamous s. of cranium,** sutura squamosa cranii. **staple s.,** closure of a wound by U-shaped wires passed through the edges. **subcuticular s.,** a method of skin closure involving placement of stitches in the subcuticular tissues parallel with the line of the wound, the suture material being first anchored at one end of the wound; after all the stitches have been placed, it is drawn tight and anchored at the other end. See illustration. **superficial s.,** one that is placed through the skin only, or which does not include any deep tissue. **Taylor's s.,** a method of approximation of the flaps by cobblers' sutures after amputation of the cervix uteri. **temporal s.,** sutura squamosa cranii. **temporomalar s., temporozygomatic s.,** sutura temporozygomatica. **tension s.,** relaxation s. **tongue-and-groove s.,** plastic s. **transverse s. of Krause,** sutura infraorbitalis. **triangular s.,** Simon's s. **true s.,** sutura vera. **twisted s.,** figure-of-eight s. **uninterrupted s.,** continuous s. **uteroparietal s.,** stitching of the uterus to the inner surface of the abdominal wall at the incision line after cesarean section. **visceroparietal s.,** the stitching of a viscus to the abdominal wall. **Wölfler's s.** 1. For a divided intestine: The mucosa is united by a continuous suture, tied for a part of the circumference on the inside, and for a part on the outside, of the gut, the serous surfaces being united by Lembert sutures. 2. For a divided tendon: The stitch enters the tendon from one side above the cut, comes out twice in front, both above and below, and is tied on the side where it first entered. **Wysler s.,** a seromuscular-seromuscular suture for approximating the peritoneal layers of the intestine. **zygomaticofrontal s.,** sutura frontozygomatica. **zygomaticomaxillary s.,** sutura zygomaticomaxillaris. **zygomaticotemporal s.,** sutura temporozygomatica.

suvren (suv′ren). Trade mark for a preparation of captodiamine.

suxamethonium (suk″sah-mĕ-tho′ne-um). Succinylcholine.

Suzanne's gland (soo-zanz′) [Jean Georges *Su-*

zanne, French physician, born 1859]. See under *gland.*

SV. Abbreviation for *simian virus.*

s.v. Abbreviation for L. *spir'itus vi'ni,* alcoholic spirit.

s.v.r. Abbreviation for L. *spir'itus vi'ni rectifica'tus,* rectified spirit of wine.

s.v.t. Abbreviation for L. *spir'itus vi'ni ten'uis,* proof spirit.

swab (swahb). 1. A device for moistening the lips of a helpless patient. 2. A wire with a tuft of sterilized cotton at the end: used in collecting material for bacteriological study. **Graham s.,** a swab similar to the NIH swab but using Scotch tape held by forceps. **NIH s.,** a glass rod with a square of cellophane attached: used for collecting suspected material from a mucous surface. The cellophane square is transferred to a microscope slide for examination. **West s.** See *West tube method,* under *method.*

swage (swāj). 1. To shape metal by hammering or by adapting it to a die. 2. A tool or form, often one of a pair, for shaping metal by pressure.

swager (swāj'er). An apparatus fitted with dies and counterdies for shaping crowns, inlays, etc., in dental work.

swallowing (swahl'o-ing). The taking in of a substance through the mouth and pharynx, past the cricopharyngeal constriction into the esophagus.

swarming (sworm'ing). Spreading in a swarm: a term applied to bacteria which spread over the surface of the colony.

swayback (swa'bak). 1. Abnormal downward curvature of the spinal column in the dorsal region in horses. 2. Enzootic ataxia; a congenital demyelinizing disease of lambs, characterized by incoordination, tremor, blindness, and spastic paralysis.

sweat (swet). The perspiration; the clear liquid exuded from or excreted by the sudoriparous glands. It possesses a characteristic odor, and a salty taste; its reaction is normally alkaline, but when mixed with sebum, it is acid. It contains sodium chloride, cholesterin, fats and fatty acids, and traces of albumin, urea, and other compounds. **bloody s.,** hemathidrosis. **blue s.,** chromhidrosis in which the sweat has a blue color. **fetid s.,** bronchidrosis. **green s.,** a greenish sweating seen among workers in copper. **intestinal s.,** colliquative diarrhea. **night s.,** sweating during sleep: a symptom frequently occurring in phthisis. **phosphorescent s.,** phosphorescent perspiration, sometimes observed in miliaria and after the eating of phosphorescent fish. **urinary s.,** urhidrosis.

sweating (swet'ing). The act of perspiring. **colliquative s.,** a copious clammy perspiration.

Swediaur's disease (swa″de-aw'erz) [François Xavier *Swediaur,* Austrian physician, 1748–1824]. See under *disease.*

sweeny (swe'ne). Atrophy of the muscles in the shoulder of a horse.

swellhead (swel'hed). Lechuguilla fever.

swelling (swel'ing). 1. A transient abnormal enlargement or increase in volume of a body part or area not caused by proliferation of cells. 2. An eminence, or elevation. **albuminous s.,** cloudy s. **arytenoid s.,** an eminence on each side of the primitive laryngeal orifice that presages the future larynx. **blennorrhagic s.,** swelling of the knee in gonorrheal synovitis. **Calabar s's,** elevations about one half the size of an egg, appearing on various portions of the body, and due to infection with *Loa loa.* **cloudy s.,** an early stage of toxic degenerative changes, especially in the protein constituents of organs in infectious diseases. The tissues appear swollen, parboiled and opaque but revert to normal when the cause is removed. Called also *albuminous degeneration.* **fugitive s.,** an extremely short-lived swelling. **genital s.,** an elevation on each side of the primitive phallus that becomes either a labial or a scrotal swelling. **giant s.,** angioneurotic edema. **glassy s.,** amyloid degeneration. **hunger s.,** edematous swellings in wet beriberi. **Kamerun s's,** Calabar s's. **labial s.,** the primordium of a labium majus. **labioscrotal s.,** genital s. **scrotal s.,** the primordium of a lateral half of the scrotum. **Soemmerring's crystalline s.,** annular edema of the lower portion of the lens capsule after the removal of a cataractous lens. **tropical s's,** Calabar s's. **tympanic s.,** intumescentia tympanica. **white s.,** the swelling produced by tuberculous arthritis.

Swieten (sve'ten). See *van Swieten.*

Swift's disease (swifts) [W. *Swift,* Australian physician]. Erythredema.

Swift-Ellis treatment (swift-el'is) [Homer F. *Swift,* American physician, 1881–1953; Arthur W. M. *Ellis,* English physician, born 1883]. See under *treatment.*

swing (swing). A kind of suspensory cradle or sling.

swinny (swin'e). Sweeny.

swoon (swo͞on). Syncope.

sycephalus (si-sef'ah-lus). Syncephalus.

sychnosphygmia (sik″no-sfig'me-ah) [Gr. *sychnos* frequent + *sphygmos* pulse + *-ia*]. Tachycardia.

sychnuria (sik-nu're-ah) [Gr. *sychnos* frequent + *ouron* urine + *-ia*]. Pollakiuria.

sycoma (si-ko'mah) [Gr. *sykōma,* from *sykon* fig]. A wart or condyloma.

sycosiform (si-ko'sĭ-form). Resembling sycosis.

sycosis (si-ko'sis) [Gr. *sykōsis,* from *sykon* fig]. 1. A disease marked by inflammation of the hair follicles, especially of the beard, forming papules or pustules that are perforated by the hairs and are surrounded by infiltrated skin. It is a chronic pustular staphylococcus infection and often occurs in general debility and constitutional disturbances. 2. A kind of ulcer on the eyelids. **bacillogenic s.,** sycosis said to be caused by the *Bacillus sycosiferus foetidus.* **s. bar'bae,** sycosis of the beard. **coccogenic s.,** sycosis of the hair follicles of the beard from infection of the follicles by staphylococci. **s. contagio'sa,** tinea barbae. **s. frambоe'sia, s. framboesiaefor'mis,** folliculitis keloidalis. **hyphomycotic s.,** tinea barbae. **lupoid s.,** a chronic, scarring form of deep sycosis barbae, characterized by a persistent, slowly enlarging circinate patch with follicular papulopustules in the active, advancing border, and healing with scarring occurring in the central area. **nonparasitic s.,** coccogenic s. **s. nu'chae necro'tisans,** keloidal folliculitis. **parasitic s.,** tinea barbae. **s. staphylog'enes,** s. vulgaris. **s. tarsi,** blepharitis. **s. vulga'ris,** a form due to infection with pus cocci.

sycotrol (si'ko-trol). Trade mark for a preparation of pipethanate hydrochloride.

Sydenham's chorea, cough (sid'en-hams) [Thomas *Sydenham,* a celebrated English physician, sometimes called the "English Hippocrates," 1624–1689]. See under the nouns.

syllabize (sil'ah-bīz). To divide speech sounds into syllables.

syllabus (sil'ah-bus) [L., a collection]. An outline of a course of lectures.

syllepsiology (sil″ep-se-ol'o-je) [Gr. *syllēpsis* conception + *-logy*]. The sum of knowledge regarding conception or pregnancy.

syllepsis (sil-lep'sis). Conception, or pregnancy.

sylvan (sil'van). A liquid obtained along with tetrol from distillation of pine wood.

sylvatic (sil-vat'ik). Sylvan; pertaining to, located in, or living in the woods.

sylvian (sil've-an). Described by or named for François de la Boe (Latinized Sylvius), 1614–1672, a French anatomist (*sylvian fissure*); the name has also been ascribed to Jacobus *Sylvius* (Jacques Dubois), 1478–1555, a French anatomist who was a teacher of Vesalius (*sylvian aqueduct*).

sym. Abbreviation for *symmetrical.*

symballophone (sim-bal′o-fōn) [Gr. *syn* together + *ballein* to throw + *phōnē* sound]. A special type of double stethoscope making possible the comparison of sounds and detection of their direction.

symbion (sim′bi-on). Symbiont.

symbionic (sim-bi-on′ik). Pertaining to or characterized by symbiosis.

symbiont (sim′bi-ont) [Gr. *syn* together + *bioun* to live]. An organism which lives in a state of symbiosis.

symbiosis (sim″bi-o′sis) [Gr. *symbiōsis*]. 1. The living together or close association of two dissimilar organisms, each of the organisms being known as a *symbiont*. The association may be beneficial to both (mutualism), beneficial to one without effect on the other (commensalism), beneficial to one and detrimental to the other (parasitism), detrimental to one without effect on the other (amensalism), or detrimental to both (synnecrosis). 2. A condition in which a characteristic or a symptom becomes a part of the patient's personality. **antagonistic s., antipathetic s.,** an association between two organisms which is to the disadvantage of one of them; parasitism. **conjunctive s.,** association between two different organisms, with bodily union between them. **constructive s.,** an association between two organisms which is of benefit to the physiologic processes of one of them. **disjunctive s.,** symbiosis without actual union of the organisms.

symbiote (sim′bi-ōt). Symbiont.

Symbiotes (sim″be-o′tēs) [Gr. *symbiōtēs* one who lives with]. A genus of the tribe Wolbachieae, family Rickettsiaceae, order Rickettsiales, occurring as a single species, *S. lectula′rius*, which is parasitic on the bedbug.

symbiotic (sim″bi-ot′ik). Associated in symbiosis; living together.

symblepharon (sim-blef′ah-ron) [Gr. *syn* together + *blepharon* eyelid]. An adhesion between the tarsal conjunctiva and the bulbar conjunctiva. **anterior s.,** attachment of the lid to the eyeball by fibrous bands. **posterior s.,** adhesion between the lid and the eyeball extending into the fornix. **total s.,** adhesion of the entire conjunctival surfaces between the lid and the eyeball.

symblepharopterygium (sim-blef″ah-ro-ter-ij′e-um). A combination of symblepharon and pterygium; a form of symblepharon in which the lid is joined to the eyeball by a cicatricial band resembling a pterygium.

symbol (sim′bul) [Gr. *symbolon*, from *symballein* to interpret]. A mark or character representing some quality or relation. In chemistry, a symbol is a letter or combination of letters representing an atom or a group of atoms. In psychiatry, an unconscious substitute which allows the libido to turn to an object not consciously concerned with sexuality. **phallic s.,** in psychoanalysis, any pointed or upright object which may represent the phallus or penis.

symbolia (sim-bo′le-ah). Ability to recognize the nature of objects by the sense of touch.

symbolism (sim′bol-izm). 1. An abnormal mental condition in which every occurrence is conceived of as a symbol of the patient's own thoughts. 2. In psychoanalysis, a mechanism of unconscious thinking, usually of a sexual nature, whereby the real meaning becomes transformed so as not to be recognized as sexual by the super-ego.

symbolization (sim″bol-i-za′shun). A mental mechanism of the subconscous which consists in the representation of one object, idea or quality by another.

symbolophobia (sim″bol-o-fo′be-ah) [Gr. *symbolon* symbol + *phobein* to be affrighted by]. A morbid fear that one's acts may contain some symbolic meaning.

symbrachydactylia (sim-brak″e-dak-til′e-ah) [Gr. *syn* together + *brachys* short + *daktylos* finger + *-ia*]. A condition in which the fingers or toes are short and adherent; webbed fingers or toes.

symbrachydactylism (sim-brak″e-dak′til-izm). Symbrachydactylia.

Syme's operation (sīmz) [James *Syme*, Scottish surgeon, 1799–1870]. See under *operation*.

symelus (sim′e-lus). Symmelus.

Symington's body (si′ming-tonz) [Johnson *Symington*, Scottish anatomist, 1851–1924]. The anococcygeal body. See under *body*.

symmelia (sim-me′le-ah) [Gr. *syn* together + *melos* limb + *-ia*]. A developmental anomaly characterized by an apparent fusion of the lower limbs. There may be three feet (*tripodial s.*), two feet (*dipodial s.*), one foot (*monopodial s.*), or no feet (*apodial s.*).

symmelus (sim′e-lus). A fetal monster exhibiting symmelia.

symmetrical (sĭ-met′re-kal) [Gr. *symmetrikos*]. Pertaining to or exhibiting symmetry. In chemistry, denoting compounds which contain atoms or groups at equal intervals in the molecule.

symmetromania (sim″e-tro-ma′ne-ah) [*symmetry* + Gr. *mania* madness]. An insane tendency to make symmetrical motions, as of both arms instead of one.

symmetry (sim′ĕ-tre) [Gr. *symmetria; syn* with + *metron* measure]. The regular or reversed disposition of parts around a common axis, or on each side of any plane of the body. **inverse s.,** correspondence as between an object and its mirror image, in which one side of one object corresponds with the opposite side of another.

sympathectomize (sim″pah-thek′to-mīz). To deprive of sympathetic innervation.

sympathectomy (sim″pah-thek′to-me) [*sympathetic* + Gr. *ektomē* excision]. The transection, resection, or other interruption of some portion of the sympathetic nervous pathways. Operations may be named according to the topographic location of the nerve, ganglion or plexus operated on, as *cervical, dorsal, lumbar*, or *thoracolumbar s.*, or in reference to the diaphragm, as *subdiaphragmatic, supradiaphragmatic*, or *transdiaphragmatic s.* **chemical s.,** interruption by chemical means of a sympathetic nervous pathway. **periarterial s.,** surgical removal of the sheath of an artery containing the sympathetic nerve fibers. The operation produces temporary vasodilatation leading to improved nutrition of the part supplied by the vessel. It is indicated for trophic disorders (Leriche). Called also *arterial decortication*.

sympatheoneuritis (sim-path″e-o-nu-ri′tis). Inflammation of the sympathetic nerve.

sympathesis (sim-path′e-sis). The morbid sympathies and synergies of the organism.

sympathetectomy (sim″pah-the-tek′to-me). Sympathectomy.

sympathetic (sim″pah-thet′ik) [Gr. *sympathētikos*]. 1. Pertaining to, caused by, or exhibiting, sympathy. 2. The sympathetic nerve or system of nerves.

sympatheticalgia (sim″pah-thet″ĭ-kal′je-ah). Pain in the cervical sympathetic ganglion.

sympatheticoma (sim″pah-thet″ĭ-ko′mah). Sympathoma.

sympatheticomimetic (sim″pah-thet″ĭ-ko-mi-met′ik) [*sympathetic* + Gr. *mimētikos* imitative]. Sympathomimetic.

sympatheticoparalytic (sim″pah-thet″ĭ-ko-par″ah-lit′ik). Due to or affected with paralysis of the sympathetic nervous system.

sympatheticotonia (sim″pah-thet″ĭ-ko-to′ne-ah). A condition in which the sympathetic nervous system dominates the general functioning of the body organs, characterized by vascular spasm, heightened blood pressure, dermographic formation of goose flesh, and activity of the ciliospinal reflex.

sympatheticotonic (sim″pah-thet″ĭ-ko-ton′ik) [*sympathetic* + Gr. *tonos* tension]. Pertaining to or characterized by sympatheticotonia.

sympathetoblast (sim″pah-thet′o-blast). One of

the embryonic nerve cells from the sympathetic system which develops into a sympathetic cell.

sympathic (sim-path′ik). Sympathetic.

sympathicectomy (sim-path″ĭ-sek′to-me). Sympathectomy.

sympathicoblast (sim-path′ĭ-ko-blast″). The primitive pluripotential undifferentiated cell which develops into a sympathetic nerve cell.

sympathicoblastoma (sim-path″ĭ-ko-blas-to′-mah). A malignant tumor containing sympathicoblasts.

sympathicodiaphtheresis (sim-path″ĭ-ko-di″-af-the-re′sis). Doppler's operation.

sympathicogonioma (sim-path″ĭ-ko-go″ne-o′-mah). A tumor composed of sympathogonia, being a malignant growth of intra-uterine life or early infancy.

sympathicolytic (sim-path″ĭ-ko-lit′ik). Sympatholytic.

sympathicomimetic (sim-path″ĭ-ko-mi-met′ik). Sympathomimetic.

sympathiconeuritis (sim-path″ĭ-ko-nu-ri′tis). Inflammation of the sympathetic nerve.

sympathicopathy (sim-path″ĭ-kop′ah-the). Any disease due to disorder of the sympathetic nervous system.

sympathicotherapy (sim-path″ĭ-ko-ther′ah-pe). Treatment of certain diseases by stimulation or irritation of the turbinals and nasal septum, on the theory that such stimulation influences the sympathetic nerve.

sympathicotonia (sim-path″ĭ-ko-to′ne-ah). Sympatheticotonia.

sympathicotonic (sim-path″ĭ-ko-ton′ik). Sympatheticotonic.

sympathicotripsy (sim-path″ĭ-ko-trip′se) [*sympathetic ganglion* + Gr. *tribein* to crush]. The surgical crushing of a nerve, ganglion or plexus of the sympathetic (vegetative) nervous system.

sympathicotrope (sim-path′ĭ-ko-trōp). Sympathicotropic.

sympathicotropic (sim-path″ĭ-ko-trop′ik) [*sympathetic* + Gr. *tropikos* turning]. **1.** Having an affinity for the sympathetic nervous system. 2. An agent that has an affinity for or exerts its principal effect upon the sympathetic nervous system.

sympathicus (sim-path′ĭ-kus). The sympathetic nervous system.

sympathin (sim′pah-thin). A substance secreted by the sympathetic nerve endings and appearing in the blood stream after sympathetic excitation and serving to increase the action of sympathetic nerve fibers. *Sympathin E* (excitatory) acts as a vasoconstrictor; *sympathin I* (inhibitory) is a vasodilator.

sympathism (sim′pah-thizm). Susceptibility to hypnotic influence; suggestibility; the alleged transfer of feelings from one person to another.

sympathist (sim′pah-thist). One susceptible to sympathism.

sympathoblast (sim-path′o-blast) [*sympathetic* + Gr. *blastos* germ]. Sympathicoblast.

sympathoblastoma (sim″pah-tho-blas-to′mah). Sympathicoblastoma.

sympathoglioblastoma (sim″pah-tho-gli″o-blas-to′mah). A tumor composed of sympathicoblasts with a few neuroblasts and spongioblasts.

sympathogonia (sim″pah-tho-go′ne-ah) [pl., *sympathetic* + Gr. *gonē* seed]. Embryonic cells which develop into sympathetic cells.

sympathogonioma (sim″pah-tho-go″ne-o′mah). A tumor composed of sympathogonia.

sympatholytic (sim″pah-tho-lit′ik) [*sympathetic* + Gr. *lytikos* dissolving]. 1. Opposing the effects of impulses conveyed by adrenergic postganglionic fibers of the sympathetic nervous system. 2. An agent that opposes the effects of impulses conveyed by adrenergic postganglionic fibers of the sympathetic nervous system.

sympathoma (sim″pah-tho′mah). A tumor containing tissue resembling that of the sympathetic nervous system.

sympathomimetic (sim″pah-tho-mi-met′ik) [*sympathetic* + Gr. *mimētikos* imitative]. **1.** Mimicking the effects of impulses conveyed by adrenergic postganglionic fibers of the sympathetic nervous system. 2. An agent that produces effects similar to those of impulses conveyed by adrenergic postganglionic fibers of the sympathetic nervous system.

sympathy (sim′pah-the) [Gr. *sympatheia*]. **1.** An influence produced in any organ by disease or disorder in another part. 2. A relation which exists between the mind and the body, causing the one to be affected by the other. 3. The influence exerted by one individual upon another, or received by one from another, and the effects thus produced, as seen in hypnotism, in yawning, and in the transfer of hysterical symptoms.

sympectothiene (sim-pek″to-thi′ēn). Ergothioneine.

sympectothion (sim-pek″to-thi′on) [Gr. *syn* together + *pexis* fixation + *theion* sulfur]. Ergothioneine.

symperitoneal (sim″per-ĭ-to-ne′al). Uniting two or more parts of the peritoneum artificially.

sympexion (sim-pek′se-on), pl. *sympex′ia* [Gr. *sympēxis* condensation, coagulation + *on* neuter ending]. A concretion.

sympexis (sim-pek′sis). Arrangement of erythrocytes according to the laws of surface tension.

symphalangia (sim″fah-lan′je-ah) [Gr. *syn* together + *phalanges* + *-ia*]. End-to-end fusion of contiguous phalanges of a digit, usually associated with other deformity of the hand or foot.

symphalangism (sim-fal′an-jizm). Symphalangia.

symphoricarpus (sim″fōr-ĭ-kar′pus) [Gr. *symphorein* to bear together + *karpos* fruit]. A homeopathic preparation of the fruit of *Symphoricarpos racemosus*, or snowberry, a shrub of North America.

Symphoromyia (sim″fo-ro-mi′yah). A genus of biting flies of western North America.

symphyocephalus (sim″fe-o-sef′ah-lus) [Gr. *syn* together + *phyein* to grow + *kephalē* head]. A double monstrosity joined at the head.

symphyogenetic (sim″fe-o-je-net′ik) [Gr. *syn* together + *phyein* to grow + *gennan* to produce]. Concerning the combined effects of hereditary determiners and environmental factors in producing the organism's structure and behavior.

symphyseal (sim-fiz′e-al). Pertaining to a symphysis.

symphyseorrhaphy (sim-fiz″e-or′ah-fe). Symphysiorrhaphy.

symphyses (sim′fĭ-sēz). Plural of *symphysis*.

symphysial (sim-fiz′e-al). Symphyseal.

symphysic (sim-fiz′ik). Characterized by abnormal fusion of adjacent parts.

symphysiectomy (sim-fiz″e-ek′to-me) [*symphysis* + Gr. *ektomē* excision]. Resection of the symphysis pubis in order to facilitate impending and possible future deliveries.

symphysiolysis (sim-fiz″e-ol′ĭ-sis) [*symphysis* + Gr. *lysis* dissolution]. Separation or slipping of symphyses, especially the symphysis pubis.

symphysion (sim-fiz′e-on) [*symphysis* + Gr. *on* neuter ending]. The middle point of the outer border of the alveolar process of the lower jaw.

symphysiorrhaphy (sim-fiz″e-or′ah-fe) [*symphysis* + Gr. *rhaphē* suture]. Suture of a divided symphysis.

symphysiotome (sim-fiz′e-o-tōm). A knife used in performing symphysiotomy.

symphysiotomy (sim-fiz″e-ot′o-me) [*symphysis* + Gr. *tomē* a cutting]. The division of the fibrocartilage of the symphysis pubis, in order to facilitate delivery, by increasing the diameter of the pelvis.

symphysis (sim′fĭ-sis), pl. *sym′physes* [Gr. "a growing together, natural junction"]. A site or line of union; used in official anatomical nomenclature to designate a type of cartilaginous joint in which the apposed bony surfaces are firmly united by a plate of fibrocartilage. **cardiac s.,** adhesion of the parietal and visceral layers of the pericardium. **s. mandib′ulae, s. men′ti,** the line of union, in the median plane, of the two halves of the fetal lower jaw. **s. os′sium pu′bis** [B N A], **pubic s.,** s. pubica. **s. pu′bica** [N A], **s. pu′bis,** the joint formed by union of the bodies of the pubic bones in the median plane by a thick mass of fibrocartilage. Called also *s. ossium pubis* [B N A], and *pubic s.* **s. sacrococcyg′ea** [B N A], **sacrococcygeal s.,** junctura sacrococcygea. **sacroiliac s.,** articulatio sacroiliaca.

symphysodactylia (sim″fĭ-so-dak-til′e-ah) [Gr. *symphysis* a growing together + *daktylos* finger + *-ia*]. Union of the fingers or toes.

Symphytum (sim′fĭ-tum) [L.; Gr. *symphyton*]. A genus of boraginaceous plants; *S. officinale* is the comfrey of Europe and North America.

symphytum (sim′fĭ-tum). A homeopathic preparation of *Symphytum officinale.*

symplasm (sim′plazm). A tissue in which there is no cellular structure.

symplasmatic (sim″plaz-mat′ik). Marked by union of protoplasm.

symplast (sim′plast). Symplasm.

symplex (sim′pleks). A chemical compound in which a high molecular substance is bound by residual valencies: such are activators, adsorbents, hemoglobin, and toxin-antitoxin.

Symplocarpus foetidus (sim″plo-kar″pus fet′ĭ-dus). *Dracontium foetidum.*

sympodia (sim-po′de-ah) [Gr. *syn* together + *pous* foot + *-ia*]. Sirenomelia.

symptom (simp′tum) [L. *symptoma;* Gr. *symptōma* anything that has befallen one]. Any functional evidence of disease or of a patient's condition; a change in a patient's condition indicative of some bodily or mental state. See also *sign.* **abstinence s's,** withdrawal s's. **accessory s.,** any symptom not pathognomonic. **Anton's s.,** failure to recognize one's own blindness. **assident s.,** accessory s. **Bárány's s.** 1. In disturbances of equilibrium of the vestibular apparatus the direction of the fall is influenced by changing the position of the patient's head. 2. If the normal ear is irrigated with hot water (110–120°F.), a rotatory nystagmus is developed toward the side of the irrigated ear; if the ear is irrigated with cold water, a rotatory nystagmus is developed away from the irrigated side. There is no nystagmus if the labyrinth is diseased. Called also *caloric test.* **Bechterew's s.,** paralysis of the facial muscles for automatic movements. **Béhier-Hardy s.** See under *sign.* **Bernhardt's s.** See under *sign.* **Biernacki's s.** See under *sign.* **Bogue's s.,** if, in a child from 4 to 7 years old, the maxillary arch between the second deciduous molars is less than 28 mm. broad, orthodontic treatment is indicated. **Bolognini's s.** See under *sign.* **Bonhoeffer's s.,** loss of normal muscle tonus in chorea. **Brauch-Romberg s.** See *Romberg's sign,* under *sign.* **Buerger's s.,** in thrombo-angiitis obliterans, the pain in the affected leg when the patient is lying down is relieved only by lying with the leg hung over the side of the bed. **Burghart's s.,** fine râles over the anterior inferior edge of the lung; an early sign of pulmonary tuberculosis. **Capgras s.,** the mental impression, but not an actual hallucination, of a person that he is not alone. **cardinal s.** 1. A symptom of greatest significance to the physician, establishing the identity of the illness. 2. [Pl.]. The symptoms shown in the pulse, temperature, and respiration. **Castellani-Low s.,** a fine tremor of the tongue seen in sleeping sickness. **characteristic s.,** a symptom that is almost universally associated with a particular disease or condition. **Colliver's s.,** a peculiar twitching, tremulous, or convulsive movement of the limbs, face, jaw, and sometimes of the entire body, seen in the preparalytic stage of poliomyelitis. **concomitant s.,** a symptom not essential to a disease, but which may have an accessory value in its diagnosis. **consecutive s.,** a symptom appearing during convalescence from a disease, but having no connection with the disease. **constitutional s.,** a symptom which is indicative of or due to disorder of the whole body. **crossbar s. of Fraenkel,** blocking of the peristaltic wave on the lesser curvature of the stomach at the site of an ulcer, on fluoroscopy of the stomach. **deficiency s.,** a symptom which is due to a deficiency of the secretion of some endocrine gland. **delayed s.,** one which does not appear for some time after the occurrence of the causes which produce it. **direct s.,** one which is directly caused by the disease. **dissociation s.,** anesthesia to pain and to heat and cold without loss of tactile sensibility; seen in syringomyelia. **drug s.,** a homeopathic term for any symptom shown by a person who is proving a drug. **endothelial s.** See *Rumpel-Leede phenomenon,* under *phenomenon.* **Epstein's s.,** a symptom seen in neurotic infants, consisting of failure of the upper lid to move downward, giving the child a frightened expression. **equivocal s.,** a symptom which may be produced by several different diseases. **esophagosalivary s.,** excessive flow of saliva in patients with cancer of the esophagus. **Francke's s.,** red streaks near the border of the gums in influenza. **Fröschel's s.,** if a child does not react to tickling at the opening of the auditory canal, yet is ticklish throughout the rest of his body, disease of the auditory apparatus is indicated. **Ganser's s.,** the giving of wrong or absurd answers to questions: seen in certain psychotic conditions. **general s.,** constitutional s. **Gersuny's s.,** in fecal tumors, if the finger be pressed slowly into the mass so that the intestinal mucous membrane sticks to the mass and then the finger is withdrawn gradually, it is possible to perceive the loosening of the mucous membrane from the fecal mass. **Goldthwait's s.** See under *sign.* **guiding s.,** characteristic s. **Haenel s.,** in tabes there is a lack of sensation on pressure over the eyeballs. **halo s.,** the seeing of colored rings around an individual light source: indicative of glaucoma. **Hochenegg's s.,** enormous distention of the rectal ampulla with gas in intestinal stenosis and appendicitis. **Howship's s.,** Romberg-Howship sign. **Huchard's s.** See under *sign.* **incarceration s.,** periodically recurring symptoms of displaced kidney, such as nephralgia, gastralgia, and severe collapse. Called also *Dietl's crisis.* **indirect s.,** a symptom which points to a condition that may or may not be due to a particular disease or lesion. **induced s.,** one produced intentionally. **Jonas' s.,** spasm of the pylorus in rabies. **Kerandel's s.** See under *sign.* **Kocher's s.,** a symptom of exophthalmic goiter: the examiner places his hand on a level with the patient's eyes and then lifts it higher; the patient's upper lid springs up more quickly than does his eyeball. **Kussmaul's s.** See under *sign.* **labyrinthine s's,** a group of symptoms indicating disease of the internal ear. **Lade s.,** a peculiar diarrhea or very soft stool occurring fourteen days prior to the eruption of varicella. **Leser-Trélat s.,** de Morgan spots. See under *spot.* **Liebermeister's s.,** an anemic area on the tongue: an early symptom of air embolism. **Liebreich's s.,** a symptom of red-green color blindness in which light effects appear red and shadows green. **local s.,** one due to local disease or to a particular lesion. **localizing s's,** symptoms that indicate the location of a lesion. **Loewi's s.** See under *tests.* **Magendie's s.** See under *sign.* **Magnan's s.,** a sensation as of a round body beneath the skin:

sometimes experienced in chronic cocainism. **Mannaberg's s.** See under *sign.* **Mannkopf's s.** See under *sign.* **neighborhood s.,** a symptom produced in an organ by disease in a neighboring organ, as by pressure of a tumor in one organ on an organ adjacent to it. **nostril s.,** dilatation of the nostrils during expiration and dropping during inspiration. **objective s.,** one that is obvious to the senses of the observer. **Oehler's s.,** coldness and pallor of the feet in intermittent claudication. **passive s.,** static s. **pathognomonic s.,** one that establishes with certainty the diagnosis of the disease. **Pel-Ebstein s.,** the chronic relapsing pyrexia of Hodgkin's disease; called also *Pel-Ebstein pyrexia.* **Pratt's s.** See under *sign.* **precursory s., premonitory s.,** signal s. **presenting s.,** the symptom or group of symptoms of which the patient complains the most or from which he seeks relief. **pressure s.,** a nervous symptom due to pressure upon the brain or spinal cord. Pressure symptoms consist of spasms, increased muscular tonicity, pain, hyperesthesia, and, in severe cases, paralysis. **rainbow s.,** halo s. **rational s.,** subjective s. **reflex s.,** a symptom occurring in a part remote from that which is affected by the disease. **Remak's s.,** polyesthesia; also a prolongation of the lapse of time before a painful impression is perceived; both are noted in tabes dorsalis. **Roger's s.,** a temperature below the normal in the third stage of tuberculous meningitis. **Rumpf's s.** See under *sign.* **Seguin's signal s.,** the involuntary contraction of the muscles just before an epileptic attack. **signal s.,** a sensation, aura, or other subjective experience that gives warning of the approach of an epileptic or other seizure. **Simon's s.,** polyuria seen in cancer of the breast caused by metastasis of cancer to the pituitary body. **Skeer's s.** See under *sign.* **Sklowsky's s.,** when light pressure with the index finger is made upon the healthy skin near, and then over, a vesicle in varicella, the wall of the vesicle easily collapses and the contents are discharged. **Snow's s.,** bulging of the sternum in cancerous involvement of the thymus secondary to cancer of the breast. **static s.,** a condition indicative of the state of some particular organ independent of the rest of the body. Called also *passive s.* **Stellwag's s.** See under *sign.* **sticky s.,** Gersuny's s. **Stierlin's s.,** indurating and ulcerative processes, especially tuberculosis of the cecum and ascending colon, are shown in the roentgen plate by absence of the normal shadow following a contrast meal. **subjective s.,** one that is perceptible to the patient only. **sympathetic s.,** one due to sympathy, as when pain or other disorder affects a part when some other part is the seat of the disease proper. **Tar's s.,** in health the lower borders of the lungs are situated as deeply in the lying down position with moderate exhalation as in the upright position with deep inhalation: in infiltrating process of the lungs this is not the case. **Trendelenburg's s.,** a waddling gait due to paralysis of the gluteal muscles. See also *Trendelenburg's test,* def. 2, under *tests.* **Trunecek's s.,** a perceptible pulsation of the subclavian artery at the point of insertion of the sternocleidomastoid muscle in sclerosis of the aorta. **Wanner's s.,** decrease of sound conduction through the bones of the head, without pain in the labyrinth, points to organic change in the skull. **Wartenberg's s.** 1. Itching of the nostrils and tip of the nose indicative of cerebral tumor. 2. Flexion of the thumb occurring on flexion of the other fingers against resistance: seen in pyramidal lesions. **Weber's s.** See under *sign.* **Wernicke's s.** See under *sign.* **Westphal's s.** See under *sign.* **Winterbottom's s.** See under *sign.* **withdrawal s's,** symptoms which follow the sudden withholding of a drug to which a person has become addicted.

symptomatic (simp″to-mat′ik) [Gr. *symptōmatikos*]. Pertaining to or of the nature of a symptom.

symptomatology (simp″tom-ah-tol′o-je). 1. That branch of medicine which treats of symptoms; the systematic discussion of symptoms. 2. The combined symptoms of a disease.

symptomatolytic (simp″to-mah-to-lit′ik) [*symptom* + Gr. *lytikos* dissolving]. Causing the disappearance of symptoms.

symptome (samp-tōm′) [Fr.]. Symptom. **s's complice′** [Fr. "symptom complex"], a group of symptoms characteristic of a certain condition.

symptomolytic (simp″to-mo-lit′ik). Symptomatolytic.

symptosis (simp-to′sis) [Gr. *syn* together + *ptōsis* fall]. The gradual wasting of the whole body or of any organ.

sympus (sim′pus) [Gr. *syn* together + *pous* foot]. A monster fetus exhibiting fusion of the lower limbs. Called also *sirenomelus.* **s. a′pus,** a variety in which the feet are wanting. **s. di′pus,** a form in which both feet are present. **s. mo′nopus,** a form in which one foot is present.

Syms's tractor (simz′ez). [Parker *Syms,* American surgeon, 1860–1933]. See under *tractor.*

syn- [Gr. *syn* with, together]. Prefix signifying union or association.

synadelphus (sin″ah-del′fus) [*syn-* + Gr. *adelphos* brother]. A monster with a single body and eight limbs.

synaetion (sin-e′te-on) [Gr. *synaitios* being a joint cause]. The secondary or cooperative cause of a disease.

synalar (sin′ah-lar). Trade mark for a preparation of fluocinolone acetonide.

synalgia (sin-al′je-ah). Pain experienced in one place as the result of a lesion in another.

synalgic (sin-al′jik). Affected with or of the nature of synalgia.

synanastomosis (sin″ah-nas″to-mo′sis). The anastomosis of several vessels.

synanche (sin-an′ke). Cynanche.

synanthema (sin″an-the′mah) [*syn-* + Gr. *anthein* to bloom]. A local eruption consisting of a group of papules.

synanthrin (sin-an′thrin). Inulin.

synanthrose (sin-an′thrōs). Levulin.

synaphymenitis (sin-af″ĭ-men-i′tis). Conjunctivitis.

synapse (sin′aps) [Gr. *synapsis* a conjunction, connection]. The anatomical relation of one nerve cell to another; the region of contact between proc-

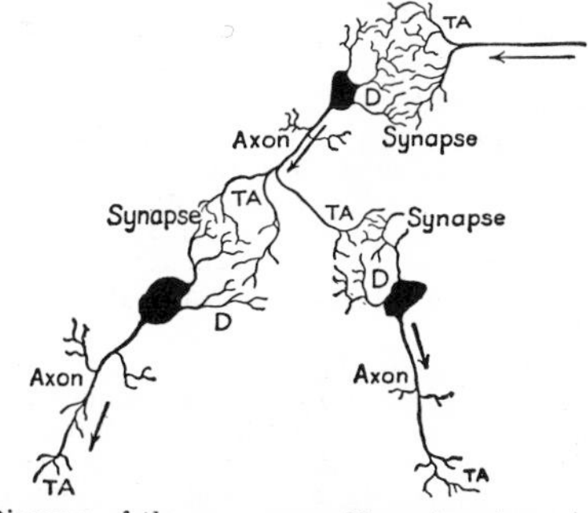

Diagram of three synapses. Nerve impulse is indicated by arrows, showing that the direction of passage is from terminal arborization (TA) of axon of one neuron to dendrites (D) of another neuron. (Williams.)

esses of two adjacent neurons, forming the place where a nervous impulse is transmitted from one neuron to another (Foster). Called also *synaptic junction.*

synapsis (sĭ-nap′sis) [Gr. "conjunction"]. The pairing off and union of homologous chromosomes from the male and female pronuclei at the start of meiosis. Called also *syndesis.*

synaptase (sĭ-nap′tās) [Gr. *synaptos* joined]. Emulsin.

synaptene (sĭ-nap′tēn). Amphitene.

synaptic (sĭ-nap′tik). Pertaining to or affecting a synapse.

synaptology (sin″ap-tol′o-je). That branch of neurology which deals with the synaptic correlations of the nervous system.

synarthrodia (sin″ar-thro′de-ah) [*syn-* + Gr. *arthrōdia* joint]. Synarthrosis.

synarthrodial (sin″ar-thro′de-al). Pertaining to synarthrodia.

synarthrophysis (sin″ar-thro-fi′sis) [*syn-* + Gr. *arthron* joint + *physis* growth]. Any ankylosing process; progressive ankylosis of joints.

synarthroses (sin″ar-thro′sēz). Plural of *synarthrosis.*

synarthrosis (sin″ar-thro′sis), pl. *synarthro′ses* [*syn-* + Gr. *arthrōsis* joint]. A form of articulation in which the bony elements are united by continuous intervening fibrous tissue. See *junctura fibrosa.*

synase (sin′ās). An enzyme which catalyzes a synthetic process.

synathresis (sin″ath-re′sis). Synathroisis.

synathroisis (sin″ath-roi′sis) [*syn-* + Gr. *athroisis* collection]. Local hyperemia or congestion.

syncaine (sin-ka′in). Procaine hydrochloride.

syncanthus (sin-kan′thus) [*syn-* + Gr. *kanthos* canthus]. Adhesion of the eyeball to the orbital structures.

syncaryon (sin-kar′e-on) [*syn-* + Gr. *karyon* nucleus]. The nucleus formed by fusion of two pronuclei.

syncelom (sin-se′lom). The perivisceral cavities of the body considered as one structure, including the pleural, cardiac, and peritoneal cavities, and tunica vaginalis.

syncephalus (sin-sef′ah-lus) [*syn-* + Gr. *kephalē* head]. A double fetal monster with one head, there being a single face with four ears, two on the back of the head.

synchesis (sin′ke-sis). Synchysis.

synchilia (sin-ki′le-ah) [*syn-* + Gr. *cheilos* lip + *-ia*]. Congenital adhesion of the lips.

synchiria (sin-ki′re-ah) [*syn-* + Gr. *cheir* hand + *-ia*]. A condition in which the sensation produced by a stimulus applied to one side of the body is referred to both sides.

syncholia (sin-ko′le-ah) [*syn-* + Gr. *cholē* bile + *-ia*]. The secretion of substances of exogenous origin in the bile.

synchondrectomy (sin″kon-drek′to-me) [*synchondrosis* + Gr. *ektomē* excision]. Surgical excision of a synchondrosis, especially of the symphysis of the pubic bone.

synchondroseotomy (sin″kon-dro″se-ot′o-me) [*synchondrosis* + Gr. *tomē* a cutting]. An operation for exstrophy of the bladder done by cutting through the sacroiliac liagments and forcibly drawing together the pelvic bones.

synchondroses (sin″kon-dro′sēz). Plural of *synchondrosis.*

synchondrosis (sin″kon-dro′sis), pl. *synchondro′ses* [Gr. *synchondrōsis* a growing into one cartilage]. A type of cartilaginous joint that is usually temporary, the intervening hyaline cartilage ordinarily being converted into bone before adult life. **s. arycornicula′ta** [B N A], the cartilaginous union between the upper end of the arytenoid cartilage and the base of the corniculate cartilage. Omitted in N A. **costoclavicular s.,** ligamentum costoclaviculare. **synchondro′ses cra′nii** [N A, B N A], **synchondroses of cranium,** the cartilaginous junctions between certain bones of the cranium. **epiphyseal s., s. epiphy′seos** [B N A], cartilago epiphysialis. **intersphenoidal s., s. intersphenoida′lis** [B N A], the cartilaginous union of the two halves of the body of the sphenoid bone in the fetus. Omitted in N A. **intraoccipital s., anterior,** s. intraoccipitalis anterior. **intraoccipital s., posterior,** s. intraoccipitalis posterior. **s. intraoccipita′lis ante′rior** [N A, B N A], the cartilaginous union of the pars basilaris with the partes laterales of the occipital bone in the newborn. Called also *anterior intraoccipital s.* **s. intraoccipita′lis poste′rior** [N A, B N A], the cartilaginous union of the squama with the partes laterales of the occipital bone in the newborn. Called also *posterior intraoccipital s.* **petro-occipital s., s. petrooccipita′lis** [N A, B N A], the plate of cartilage in the petrooccipital fissure which helps to unite the basilar portion of the occipital bone and the petrous portion of the temporal bone. **pubic s., s. pu′bis,** symphysis pubica. **sacrococcygeal s.,** junctura sacrococcygea. **synchondroses of skull,** synchondroses cranii. **sphenobasilar s., spheno-occipital s.,** s. sphenooccipitalis. **s. sphenooccipita′lis** [N A, B N A], the cartilaginous union of the anterior end of the basilar portion of the occipital bone with the posterior surface of the body of the sphenoid bone. **s. sphenopetro′sa** [N A, B N A], **sphenopetrosal s.,** the cartilaginous union of the lower border of the great wing of the sphenoid bone with the petrous portion of the temporal bone in the sphenopetrosal fissure. **sternal s., s. sterna′lis** [N A, B N A], the cartilaginous union between the manubrium and the body of the sternum.

synchondrotomy (sin″kon-drot′o-me) [*synchondrosis* + Gr. *tomē* a cutting]. The division of the symphysis pubis or of any other synchondrosis.

synchopexia (sin″ko-pek′se-ah). Tachycardia.

synchronia (sin-kro′ne-ah). 1. Synchronism. 2. The formation of parts or tissues at the usual time. Cf. *heterochronia.*

synchronism (sin′kro-nizm). Occurrence at the same time; the quality of being synchronous.

synchronous (sin′kro-nus) [*syn-* + Gr. *chronos* time]. Occurring at the same time.

synchrotone (sin′kro-tōn). Hallberg's tunable ultrashort-wave generator.

synchrotron (sin′kro-tron). A machine for generating high-speed electrons or protons. It combines features of the cyclotron and betatron and will produce 70 million volts.

synchysis (sin′kĭ-sis) [Gr. "a mixing together"]. A softening or fluid condition of the vitreous body of the eye; synchysis corporis vitrei. **s. scintil′lans,** spintherism; flashes of reflected light from crystals of cholesterol or fatty acids floating in the vitreous humor.

syncinesis (sin″si-ne′sis). Synkinesis.

synciput (sin′si-put). Sinciput.

synclinal (sin-kli′nal) [Gr. *synklinein* to lean together]. Bent or inclined together.

synclitic (sin-klit′ik). Pertaining to or marked by synclitism.

synclitism, syncliticism (sin′klit-izm, sin-klit′ĭ-sizm) [Gr. *synklinein* to lean together]. Parallelism between the planes of the fetal head and those of the pelvis.

synclonus (sin′klo-nus) [*syn-* + Gr. *klonos* turmoil]. 1. Muscular tremor, or the successive clonic contraction of various muscles together. 2. Any disease characterized by muscular tremors. **s. beriber′ica,** muscular tremors associated with beriberi.

syncopal (sin′ko-pal). Pertaining to or characterized by syncope.

syncope (sin′ko-pe) [Gr. *synkopē*]. 1. A sudden loss of strength. 2. A temporary suspension of consciousness due to cerebral anemia; a faint. **Adams-Stokes s.,** Adams-Stokes disease. **s. angino′sa,** cardiac spasm caused by closure of the coronary arteries. **carotid s.,** carotid sinus syndrome. **digital s.,** a sudden temporary loss of strength in the fingers. **laryngeal s.,** laryngeal vertigo. **local s.,** Raynaud's disease. **tussive s.,** fainting associated with paroxysms of coughing. **vasovagal s.,** carotid sinus syndrome.

syncopic (sin-kop′ik). Syncopal.

syncretio (sin-kre′she-o) [L.]. A growing together

or adhesion, as between inflamed serous surfaces in contact.

syncurine (sin′ku-rēn). Trade mark for a preparation of decamethonium bromide.

syncyanin (sin-si′ah-nin). A blue pigment produced by *Pseudomonas syncyanea.*

syncytial (sin-sish′al). Of, pertaining to, or producing, a syncytium.

syncytiolysin (sin″sit-e-ol′ĭ-sin). A lysin destructive to the syncytium; formed in the blood of an animal into which matter from the placenta of another animal has been injected.

syncytioma (sin-sit″e-o′mah). A tumor in which the uterine wall is infiltrated with large syncytial wandering cells. **s. malig′num,** a form of tumor, epithelial in nature, originating at the placental site during pregnancy or the puerperium. It is composed of large cells derived from the syncytium and smaller ones from the epithelium of the chorionic villi (Langhans' cells). Called also *deciduoma malignum, sarcoma deciduocellulare,* and *chorioepithelioma.*

syncytiotoxin (sin-sit″e-o-tok′sin). A toxin that has a specific action on the placenta.

syncytiotrophoblast (sin-sit″e-o-trof′o-blast). Syntrophoblast.

syncytium (sin-sit′e-um). A multinucleate mass of protoplasm produced by the merging of cells.

syncytoid (sin′sĭ-toid). Resembling a syncytium.

syncytotoxin (sin″sĭ-to-tok′sin). A cytolytic serum produced by immunizing animals with placental cells.

syndactylia (sin″dak-til′e-ah). Syndactyly.

syndactylism (sin-dak′tĭ-lizm). Syndactyly.

syndactylous (sin-dak′tĭ-lus). Pertaining to or characterized by syndactyly.

syndactylus (sin-dak′tĭ-lus). An individual exhibiting syndactyly.

syndactyly (sin-dak′tĭ-le) [Gr. *syn* with + *daktylos* finger]. The most common congenital anomaly of the hand, marked by persistence of the webbing between adjacent digits, so they are more or less completely attached; generally considered an inherited condition, the anomaly may also occur in the foot. **complete s.,** syndactyly in which the connection extends from the base of the involved digits to the tip. **complicated s.,** syndactyly in which the bones or nails of the involved digits are fused. **double s.,** syndactyly involving three digits (two webs). **partial s.,** syndactyly in which the connecting web extends only part way up from the base of the involved digits. **simple s.,** syndactyly in which the connecting web consists only of skin. **single s.,** syndactyly involving two digits (a single web). **triple s.,** syndactyly involving four digits (three webs).

syndectomy (sin-dek′to-me) [Gr. *syndesmos* band + *ektomē* excision]. Excision of a circular strip of the conjunctiva for the cure of pannus. Called also *circumcision of the cornea* and *peritomy.*

syndelphus (sin-del′fus). Synadelphus.

syndesis (sin′de-sis) [*syn-* + Gr. *desis* binding]. 1. Artificial ankylosis; arthrodesis. 2. Synapsis.

syndesmectomy (sin″des-mek′to-me) [*syndesmo-* + Gr. *ektomē* excision]. Excision of a ligament or a portion of a ligament.

syndesmectopia (sin″des-mek-to′pe-ah) [*syndesmo-* + Gr. *ektopos* out of place + *-ia*]. Unusual situation of a ligament.

syndesmitis (sin″des-mi′tis) [*syndesmo-* + *-itis*]. 1. Inflammation of a ligament or ligaments. 2. Conjunctivitis. **s. metatar′sea,** inflammation of the metatarsal ligaments occurring in foot soldiers during strenuous marches: called also *march tumor.*

syndesmo- (sin-des′mo) [Gr. *syndesmos* band or ligament]. Combining form denoting relationship to connective tissue or particularly the ligaments.

syndesmochorial (sin″des-mo-ko′re-al). A type of placentation, occurring in ruminants, characterized by limited destruction of the endometrial epithelium.

syndesmography (sin″des-mog′rah-fe) [*syndesmo-* + Gr. *graphein* to write]. A description of the ligaments.

syndesmologia (sin″des-mo-lo′je-ah). Syndesmology; in N A terminology *syndesmologia* encompasses the nomenclature relating to the articulations (joints) and ligaments.

syndesmology (sin″des-mol′o-je) [*syndesmo-* + Gr. *logos* treatise]. The scientific study of ligaments, by extension including also study of the articulations and joints; applied also to the body of knowledge relating thereto.

syndesmoma (sin″des-mo′mah). A neoplasm or tumor composed of connective tissue.

syndesmo-odontoid (sin-des″mo-o-don′toid). The posterior of the two atlo-axoid articulations formed between the anterior surface of the transverse ligaments and the back of the odontoid process.

syndesmopexy (sin-des′mo-pek″se) [*syndesmo-* + Gr. *pēxis* fixation]. The operative fixation of a dislocation by using the ligaments of the joint.

syndesmophyte (sin-des′mo-fīt) [*syndesmo-* + Gr. *phyton* plant]. An osseous excrescence, or bony outgrowth, from a ligament.

syndesmoplasty (sin-des′mo-plas″te) [*syndesmo-* + Gr. *plassein* to form]. Plastic operation on a ligament.

syndesmorrhaphy (sin″des-mor′ah-fe) [*syndesmo-* + Gr. *rhaphē* suture]. Suture or repair of ligaments.

syndesmosis (sin″des-mo′sis), pl. *syndesmo′ses* [Gr. *syndesmos* band]. [N A, B N A] A type of fibrous joint in which the intervening fibrous connective tissue forms an interosseous membrane or ligament. **tibiofibular s., s. tibiofibula′ris** [N A], a firm fibrous union formed at the distal end of the tibia and fibula between the fibular notch of the tibia and a roughened triangular surface on the fibula. **s. tympanostape′dia** [N A, B N A], **tympanostapedial s.,** the connection of the base of the stapes with the secondary membrane in the fenestra vestibuli.

syndesmotomy (sin″des-mot′o-me) [*syndesmo-* + Gr. *tomē* a cutting]. The dissection or cutting of a ligament.

syndrome (sin′drōm) [Gr. *syndromē* concurrence]. A set of symptoms which occur together; the sum of signs of any morbid state; a symptom complex. **abdominal s.,** recurrent attacks of abdominal cramp continuing over a long period: seen in childhood rheumatic diseases. **Abercrombie's s.,** amyloid degeneration. **abstinence s.** See under *symptom.* **Achard-Thiers s.,** diabetes in bearded women. **Adair-Dighton s.,** a familial syndrome of blue scleras, fragilitas ossium, and deafness. **Adams-Stokes s.** See under *disease.* **addisonian s.,** the complex of symptoms resulting from adrenal insufficiency. See *Addison's disease,* under *disease.* **Adie's s.,** a syndrome consisting of a pathological pupil reaction (pupillotonia), the most important element of which is a myotonic condition on accommodation; the pupil on the affected side contracts on near vision more slowly than does the pupil on the opposite side, and it also dilates more slowly. The affected pupil does not usually react to direct or indirect light, but it may do so in an abnormal fashion. Certain tendon reflexes are absent or diminished, but there are no motor or sensory disturbances, nor demonstrable changes indicative of disease of the nervous system. **adiposogenital s.,** adiposogenital dystrophy. **adrenogenital s.,** hyperfunction of the adrenal cortex, with pseudohermaphroditism and virilism in the female, usually evident at birth, and precocious sexual development (macrogenitosomia precox) in the male, usually not appearing until three or four years after birth. **Albright's s., Albright-McCune-Stern-**

berg s., asymmetric disease of the bones (osteitis fibrosa cystica), melanotic pigmentation of the skin and sexual precocity in the female. **Aldrich's s.,** a condition characterized by chronic eczema, chronic suppurative otitis media, anemia, and thrombocytopenic purpura; transmitted as a sex-linked recessive by the unaffected female to the male. **amnestic s.,** Korsakoff's psychosis. **amyostatic s.,** hepatolenticular degeneration. **Andersen's s.,** bronchiectasis, cystic fibrosis of the pancreas, and vitamin A deficiency. **Angelucci's s.,** excitable temperament, palpitation, and vasomotor disturbance in patients with spring conjunctivitis. **anginal s., anginose s.,** the pain and other symptoms of chronic myocardial disease. **anterior cornual s.,** muscular atrophy due to lesions of the anterior cornua of the spinal column. **anxiety s.,** the physical symptoms accompanying anxiety, such as palpitation of the heart, rapid and shallow respiration, sweating, pallor and a feeling of panic. **Apert's s.,** acrocephalosyndactylia. **Arnold's nerve reflex cough s.,** a reflex cough due to irritation of the area supplied by Arnold's nerve (the auricular branch of the vagus nerve). This area is the posterior and inferior portion of the external auditory canal and the posterior half of the tympanic membrane. **Arnold-Chiari s.** See under *deformity.* **arterial-pulmonary s.,** the train of symptoms caused by extravascular stenosis of the pulmonary artery, consisting of atrophy of the pericardial muscle with arterial pulsation, systolic thrill and exaggerated diastolic impulse in the second or third interspace. **Ascher's s.,** blepharochalasis occurring in association with goiter (adenoma of the thyroid) and redundancy of the mucous membrane and submucous tissue of the upper lip. **asphyctic s.,** polypnea, bradycardia, cyanosis, and anxiety. **auriculotemporal s.,** the appearance of a red area and of sweating on the cheek in connection with eating: seen in lesions of the parotid gland and due to some involvement of the auriculotemporal nerve. **Avellis's s.,** ipsilateral paralysis of vocal cord and soft palate, loss of pain and temperature sensibility in contralateral leg, trunk, arm, neck and in the skin over the scalp. Called also *ambiguospinothalamic paralysis* and *s. of nucleus ambiguus* and *spinal fillet.* **Ayerza's s.** 1. Syphilis of the pulmonary artery. 2. Dilatation of the pulmonary artery due to mitral stenosis. 3. Hypertension of lesser circulation due to disease of the lung. 4. Arteriosclerosis of the lesser circulation. See also *Ayerza's disease.* **Babinski's s.,** the association of cardiac and arterial disorders with chronic syphilitic meningitis, tabes dorsalis, paralytic dementia, and other late syphilitic manifestations. **Babinski-Fröhlich s.,** Fröhlich's s. **s. of Babinski-Nageotte,** contralateral hemiplegia; contralateral hemianesthesia of discriminative sensibility of arm, leg, trunk, neck, and scalp; ipsilateral lateropulsion, hemiasynergia, and hemiataxia; myosis, enophthalmos, and ptosis; due to multiple lesions affecting the pyramid and fillet, the cerebellar peduncle and the reticular formation. **Babinski-Vacquez s.,** Babinski's s. **Banti's s.** See under *disease.* **Bard-Pic s.,** chronic progressive icterus, marked enlargement of the gallbladder, rapid cachexia in carcinoma of the head of the pancreas. **Bardet-Biedl s.,** Laurence-Biedl s. **Barré-Guillain s.,** Guillain-Barré s. **Bassen-Kornzweig s.,** progressive ataxic neuropathy associated with atypical retinitis pigmentosa with involvement of the macula and presence in the blood of erythrocytes having pseudopodia of irregular length and number, giving them a crenated appearance (acanthocytes). **Beau's s.,** asystolia. **Behçet's s.,** recurrent ulceration of the genitals, aphthous lesions of the mouth, uveitis or iridocyclitis followed by hypopyon. **s. of Benedikt,** paralysis of the parts supplied by the oculomotor nerve of one side, with paresis and tremor of the upper extremity on the other. **Bernard's s., Bernard-Horner s.,** Horner's s. **Bernard-Sergent s.,** diarrhea, vomiting, and collapse characteristic of Addison's disease. **Bernhardt-Roth s.,** meralgia paraesthetica. **Bernheim's s.,** a syndrome due to enlargement of the left ventricle and stenosis of the right ventricle caused by a hypertrophied interventricular septum; characterized by enlargement of the liver, distention of the veins of the neck, edema, and absence of pulmonary congestion or dyspnea. **Bertolotti's s.,** sacralization of the fifth lumbar vertebra together with sciatica and scoliosis. **Bianchi's s.,** a sensory aphasic syndrome with apraxia and alexia, seen in lesions of the left parietal lobe. **Biedl's s., Biemond's s.,** Laurence-Biedl s. **Blatin's s.,** hydatid thrill. **Blum's s.,** chloropenic azotemia. **body of Luys s.,** choreiform contractions of one side of the body, especially the shoulder and hip, speech defects, and hypotonia in lesions of the body of Luys. **Bonnevie-Ullrich s.,** a condition characterized by pterygium colli, lymphangiectatic edema of hands and feet, ocular hypertelorism, short stature, and other developmental anomalies. **Bonnier's s.,** a series of symptoms due to lesion of Deiters' nucleus or of the vestibular tracts related thereto; it consists of vertigo, pallor, and various aural and ocular disturbances. **Bouillaud's s.,** the coincidence of pericarditis and endocarditis in acute articular rheumatism. **Bouveret's s.,** auricular paroxysmal tachycardia. **brachial s.,** a morbid condition resulting from compression or irritation of nerves of the brachial plexus. **Brennemann's s.,** mesenteric and retroperitoneal lymphadenitis as a sequel of throat infections. **Briquet's s.,** shortness of breath and aphonia dependent on hysterical paralysis of the diaphragm. **Brissaud-Marie s.,** hysterical glossolabial hemispasm. **Brissaud-Sicard s.,** spasmodic hemiplegia caused by lesions of the pons. **Bristowe's s.,** a series of ingravescent symptoms characteristic of tumor of the corpus callosum: (1) gradual onset of hemiplegia; (2) association of hemiplegia on one side, vague hemiplegic symptoms on the other; (2) stuporousness and drowsiness, difficulty of swallowing, and speechlessness; (4) absence of direct implication of the cranial nerves; (5) death from coma. **Brock s.,** middle lobe s. **Brown-Séquard s.,** paralysis of motion on one side of the body and of sensation on the other, due to a lesion involving one side of the spinal cord. **Brugsch's s.,** acropachyderma. **Bruns' s.,** association of vertigo with sudden movements of the head, assumed to be characteristic of cysticercus infection of the fourth ventricle. **bulbar s.,** Dejerine's syndrome, def. 2. **bundle of Kent s.,** Wolff-Parkinson-White s. **Burnett's s.,** milk-alkali s. **Bywater's s.,** ischemic muscular necrosis. **callosal s.,** an association of symptoms thought to result from a lesion of the corpus callosum. **Capgras's s.,** a mental condition in which the patient cannot identify the person appearing before him. **capsular thrombosis s.,** complete hemiplegia involving the face, arm and leg, with rigidity and contractions due to occlusion of the perforating branches of the middle archal artery. **capsulothalamic s.,** a syndrome of lesions of the thalamus and internal capsule consisting of elevation of the affective tone and instability of the emotions, hemianesthesia, and hemiplegia of the affected side. **cardiac asthma s.,** Ridley's s. **carotid sinus s.,** dizziness, fainting and sometimes convulsive seizures that result from overactivity of the carotid sinus reflex. **carpal tunnel s.,** a complex of symptoms resulting from compression of the median nerve in the carpal tunnel, with pain and burning or tingling paresthesias in the fingers and hand, sometimes extending to the elbow. **cavernous sinus s.,** edema of the conjunctiva, proptosis, edema of upper lid and root of the nose, together with paralysis of the third, fourth, and sixth nerves, due to thrombosis of the cavernous sinus. **centroposterior s.,** syringomyelic dissociation of sensibility and vasomotor disorders, due to lesions of the centroposterior portion of the gray matter of the spinal cord. **cerebellar s.,** Nonne's s. **cervical s.,** a condition caused by irritation of the cervical nerve roots. **cervical rib s., cervicobrachial s.,** scalenus s. **Cestan's s., s. of Cestan-Chenais,** contralateral hemiplegia; contralateral hemianesthesia of the leg, trunk, arm, neck, and scalp; ipsilateral lateropulsion and hemiasynergia; miosis, enophthalmos, and ptosis; ipsilateral palatoplegia and laryngoplegia: due to scattered lesions of the pyramid, fillet, inferior cerebellar peduncle, nucleus ambiguus, and oculopupillary center. **Cestan-Raymond s.,** Raymond-Cestan s. **Charcot's s.** 1. Intermittent claudication. 2. Intermittent hepatic fever. **Charcot-Weiss-Barber s.,** carotid sinus s. **Charlin's s.,** pain, iritis, corneitis, rhinorrhea and tenderness along the nose in eye disturbance of nasal origin. **Chauffard's s., Chauffard-Still s.,** polyarthritis with fever and enlargement of the spleen and lymph nodes in persons infected with nonhuman tuberculosis. **Chiari's s.,** a symptom complex due to primary obliterating endophlebitis of the hepatic veins. **Chiari-Arnold s.** See under *deformity.* **Chiari-Frommel s.,** Frommel's disease. **chiasma s., chiasmatic s.,** a syndrome indicative of lesion affecting the optic chiasma: impairment of vision, limitations of the field of vision, central scotoma, headache, vertigo and syncope. **chorea s.,** Hunt's striatal s., def. 2. **Christian's s.** See *Schüller-Christian disease*, under *disease.* **Citelli's s.,** mental backwardness, loss of power of concentration, drowsiness or insomnia: seen in persons with adenoids or sinus infection. **Clarke-Hadfield s.,** congenital pancreatic disease with infantilism; with enlarged liver, bulky fatty stools and extensive atrophy of pancreas in undersized and underweight child. **Claude's s.,** rubrospinal cerebellar peduncle s.; inferior s. of red nucleus; paralysis of the third nerve on one side and asynergia on the other side together with dysarthria. **Claude-Bernard-Horner s.,** Horner's s. **closed head s.,** the complex of symptoms characteristic of cerebral injury without cranial penetration. **Clough and Richter's s.,** anemia in which the red corpuscles exhibit a severe degree of auto-agglutination. **Collet's s., Collet-Sicard s.,** glossolaryngoscapulopharyngeal hemiplegia due to complete lesion of the ninth, tenth, eleventh and twelfth cranial nerves. **compression s.,** shock with hematuria and oliguria following long continued pressure on a limb, as in bombed buildings. **concussion s.,** encephalopathy due to trauma. **cor pulmonale s.,** dilatation of the right ventricle and pulmonary artery, increase in the pulmonary second sound, gallop rhythm, pain, cough, cyanosis: in pulmonary embolism. **s. of corpus striatum,** Vogt's s. **Costen's s.,** temporomandibular joint s. **costoclavicular s.,** pain or other difficulties in the arm and/or hand, apparently due to pressure, stretching, or friction on the nerves or vessels at the cervicobrachial outlet. **Cotard's s.,** paranoia with delusions of negation, a suicidal tendency, and sensory disturbances. **Courvoisier-Terrier s.,** dilatation of the gallbladder, retention jaundice, and discoloration of the feces, indicating obstruction due to a tumor of the ampulla of Vater. **Crigler-Najjar s.,** a form of congenital familial nonhemolytic jaundice, occurring in infants and characterized by presence in the blood of excessive amounts of unconjugated bilirubin, and by kernicterus. **s. of crocodile tears,** spontaneous lacrimation occurring parallel with the normal salivation of eating. It follows facial paralysis and seems to be due to straying of the regenerating nerve fibers, some of those destined for the salivary glands going to the lacrimal glands. **crush s.,** the edema, oliguria, and other symptoms of renal failure which follow the crushing of a part, especially a large muscle mass. See *lower nephron nephrosis*, under *nephrosis.* **Cruveilhier-Baumgarten s.,** splenomegaly, portal hypertension and patent umbilical vein. **cubital tunnel s.,** a complex of symptoms resulting from injury or compression of the ulnar nerve at the elbow, with pain along the ulnar aspect of the hand and forearm, and disability of the hand. **Cushing's s.** 1. Pituitary basophilism. 2. In tumors of the cerebellopontine angle and acoustic tumors: subjective noises, impairment of hearing, ipsilateral paralysis of the sixth and seventh nerves. **Cyriax' s.,** slipping rib cartilage. **Da Costa's s.,** neurocirculatory asthenia. **Danlos' s.,** a tetrad of symptoms consisting of overextensibility of joints, hyperelasticity of the skin, fragility of the skin and pseudotumors following trauma. **defibrination s.,** a condition in which the blood is rendered incoagulable owing to severe hypofibrinogenemia occurring as a result of massive release of thromboplastic material and the consumption of fibrinogen or destruction of formed fibrin by fibrinolysins; this may occur in a number of situations, particularly following shock and obstetrical complications such as amniotic fluid embolism, premature separation of the placenta, and prolonged retention of a dead fetus. **Dejerine's s.** 1. A syndrome in cortical sensory disturbances characterized by impairment of sensory discrimination (astereognosis), judgment of intensity and recognition of differences. 2. Of bulbar lesions, those in the upper part of the bulb produce paralysis of the twelfth nerve of the side of the lesion and hemiplegia on the opposite side; lesions in the lower part of the bulb cause paralysis of the larynx and soft palate. 3. Symptoms of radiculitis; namely, distribution of the pain, motor and sensory defects in the region of the radicular or segmental disturbance of the nerve roots rather than along the course of the peripheral nerve. 4. A syndrome resembling tabes dorsalis, with deep sensibility depressed but tactile sense normal. It is due to lesion of the long root fibers of the posterior column. **s. of Dejerine-Roussy,** thalamic s. **de Toni-Fanconi s.,** Fanconi's s. **Dighton-Adair s.,** Adair-Dighton s. **Di Guglielmo s.,** erythremic myelosis. **Doan and Wiesman's s.,** neutropenia, splenomegaly, and functional overactivity of the bone marrow. **Down's s.,** mongolism. **Dresbach's s.,** sickle cell anemia. **Duane's s.,** narrowing of the palpebral opening on the side on which the external rectus muscle is paralyzed when the patient looks toward the opposite side. **Dubin-Johnson s.,** chronic idiopathic jaundice characterized by clinical exacerbations and remissions, and by the presence of a brown, coarsely granular pigment in the hepatic cells, which is pathognomonic of the condition. **Dubin-Sprinz s.,** Dubin-Johnson s. **Dubreuil-Chambardel s.,** caries of the upper incisor teeth in persons between the ages of fourteen and seventeen followed after an interval by caries in the other teeth. **Duchenne's s.,** the collective signs of labioglossopharyngeal paralysis. **Duchenne-Erb s.** See under *paralysis.* **dumping s.,** nausea, weakness, sweating, palpitation, varying degrees of syncope, often a sensation of warmth, and sometimes diarrhea, occurring after ingestion of food by patients who have had partial gastrectomy. **Duplay's s.,** frozen shoulder. **Dupré's s.,** meningism, def. 1. **dysglandular s.,** the series of symptoms caused by an abnormality of the internal secretions. **dystrophia-dystocia s.,** difficult labor in a woman characterized by short, stocky build, obesity, a relatively long torso with short thighs, and a masculine escutcheon. **Eddowes' s.,** blue scleras, otosclerosis, and fragility of the bones occurring as a familial syndrome. **effort s.,** neurocirculatory asthenia. **egg-white s.** See under *injury.* **Ehlers-Danlos s.,** Danlos' s. **Eisenmenger's s.,** displacement of the aorta to the right, defect of the septum, hypertrophy of the right ventricle, enlargement of the infundibulum and of the pulmonary artery and pulmonary valve. **Ellis-van Creveld s.,** chondroectodermal dysplasia. **encephalotrigeminal vascular s.,** the combination of multiple angiomas of the brain and vascular nevi in the trigeminal region. **epiphys-**

ial s., precocious development of external genitalia and sexual function, precocious abnormal growth of long bones, appearance of signs of internal hydrocephalus, absence of all other motor and sensory symptoms indicating lesion of the pineal body. Called also *Pellazzi's s.*, *pineal s.*, and *s. of macrogenitosomia precox.* **Epstein's s.**, nephrotic s. **Erb's s.**, the totality of signs of asthenic bulbar paralysis. **Faber's s.**, hypochromic anemia. **Fabry's s.**, angiokeratoma corporis diffusion. **Fallot's s.**, tetralogy of Fallot. **Fanconi s.**, congenital hypoplastic anemia, def. 2. **Felty's s.**, a combination of chronic arthritis, splenomegaly, leukopenia, and the appearance of pigmented spots on the skin of the lower extremities. **Fitz's s.**, a series of symptoms indicative of acute pancreatitis, consisting of epigastric pain, vomiting, collapse, followed within twenty-four hours by a circumscribed swelling in the epigastrium or by tympanites. **Forssman's carotid s.**, neurologic disturbances following injection of a small dose of serum containing Forssman's antibodies into the carotid artery of a guinea pig, including disequilibrium, rotatory movement along the vertical and the longitudinal axis, forced deviation of the eyeballs, and nystagmus. **Foster Kennedy s.**, Kennedy's s. **four-day s.**, idiopathic respiratory distress of newborn; so called because the infant usually recovers or dies within four days. **Foville's s.**, crossed paralysis of the limbs on one side of the body and of the face on the opposite side, together with loss of power to rotate the eyes to that side. **Frey's s.**, auriculotemporal s. **Friderichsen-Waterhouse s.**, Waterhouse-Friderichsen s. **Friedmann's vasomotor s.**, a train or cycle of symptoms due to a progressive subacute encephalitis of traumatic origin, including a sense of fulness in the head, headache, vertigo, irritability, insomnia, easy fatigability, and defect of memory. **Fröhlich's s.**, adiposogenital dystrophy. **Froin's s.**, a condition of the lumbar spinal fluid consisting of a transparent clear yellow color (xanthochromia), with the finding of large amounts of globulin, rapid coagulation, and the absence of an increased number of cells. It is seen in certain organic nervous diseases in which the lumbar fluid is cut off from communication with the fluid in the ventricles. Called also *loculation s.* **Fuchs's s.**, unilateral heterochromia, precipitates in the cornea, and secondary cataract. **Gailliard's s.**, dextrocardia from retraction of lungs and pleura to the right. **Gaisböck's s.**, polycythemia hypertonica. **Ganser's s.**, amnesia, disturbance of consciousness, hallucinations, generally of hysterical origin: the condition is marked by senseless answers to questions and by absurd acts. Called also *acute hallucinatory mania.* **gastrocardiac s.**, disturbances of the circulatory system, particularly of the heart, produced by faulty function of the stomach. **Gee-Herter-Heubner s.**, celiac disease. **Gélineau's s.**, narcolepsy. **general adaptation s.**, the total of all nonspecific systemic reactions of the body to long-continued exposure to systemic stress. **Gerhardt's s.**, bilateral abductor paralysis of the vocal cords causing inspiratory dyspnea. **Gerlier's s.** 1. Gerlier's disease. 2. Hunt's syndrome. **Gerstmann's s.**, a combination of finger agnosia, right-left disorientation, agraphia, acalculia, right homonymous diplopia and, in addition, right homonymous hemianopsia, due to left-sided lesion in the angular gyrus. **s. of globus pallidus**, paralysis agitans, juvenile. **Gopalan's s.**, a symptom complex resulting from malnutrition, with signs suggestive of riboflavin deficiency, a burning sensation in the extremities, a feeling of "pins and needles" in their distal parts, and hyperhidrosis. **Gougerot's s.**, a skin reaction characterized by crops of papules, macules and small nodules. **Gouley's s.**, constriction of the pulmonary artery by adhesive pericarditis in severe rheumatic heart disease. **Gowers' s.**, paroxysmal vasovagal attacks. **Gradenigo's s.**, palsy of the sixth nerve and severe unilateral headache in suppurative disease of the middle ear, caused by involvement of the abducens and trigeminal nerves by direct spread of the infection. **Graham-Little s.**, lichen planus associated with acuminate follicular papules and alopecia. **gray spinal s.**, muscular atrophy, syringomyelic disturbances of sensation, and vasomotor troubles, due to lesions of the gray matter of the spinal cord. **Grönblad-Strandberg s.**, angioid streaks in the retina together with pseudoxanthoma elasticum of the skin. **Guillain-Barré s.**, a syndrome described in encephalitis of virus origin consisting of absence of fever, pain or tenderness in the muscles, motor weakness, abolition of tendon reflexes, great increase in the protein in the cerebrospinal fluid without corresponding increase in cells. Called also *radiculoneuritis*, *encephalomyeloradiculoneuritis*, and *acute infective polyneuritis.* **Gunn's s.**, the association of movements of the upper eyelid with those of the jaw. **Hadfield-Clark s.**, Clark-Hadfield s. **Hallervorden-Spatz s.**, beginning in childhood there are progressive rigidities beginning on the legs, athetoses, mental deterioration and retardation of speech and of emotion: due to gradual degeneration of the pallidum and pars reticularis of the substantia nigra. **Hamman's s.** See under *disease.* **Hamman-Rich s.**, diffuse interstitial pulmonary fibrosis. **Hand's s.**, **Hand-Schüller-Christian s.**, Schüller-Christian disease. **hand-shoulder s.**, reflex sympathetic dystrophy of the upper extremity. **Hanot's s.**, Hanot's disease. **Hanot-Chauffard s.**, hypertrophic cirrhosis with pigmentation and diabetes mellitus. **Hare's s.**, Pancoast's s., def. 1. **Harris' s.**, spontaneous hyperinsulism. **Hassin's s.**, protrusion of the ear on the side of the lesion combined with Horner's syndrome, in disease of the sympathetic nerve in the cervical region. **Hayem-Widal s.**, hemolytic jaundice. **hemiparaplegic s.**, Brown-Séquard s. **hemohistioblastic s.**, reticuloendotheliosis. **hemopleuropneumonic s.**, dyspnea, hemoptysis, tachycardia, and fever, with dullness at the base of the chest and tubular respiration over the middle zone of the chest: indicative of pneumonia and hydrothorax in puncture wounds of the chest. **hemorrhagic fever s.**, a highly fatal type of dengue observed in the Philippines and Thailand. **Hench-Rosenberg s.**, palindromic rheumatism. **hepatorenal s.**, **Heyd's s.**, renal changes and symptoms produced by traumatism of the liver: abdominal distention, nausea, vomiting, fever, rapid pulse, albuminuria, delirium, and coma, occurring as a syndrome in inflammation of the liver and gallbladder. **Hines-Bannick s.**, intermittent attacks of low temperature and disabling sweating. **Hoffmann-Werdnig s.**, precocious hereditary spinal muscular atrophy, marked by hypotonia, and muscular paralysis, contracture, and atrophy. **Holmes-Adie s.**, Adie's s. **Homén's s.**, giddiness, a drunken gait, indistinct speech, impairment of memory, and gradually increasing dementia, with rigidity of the body, especially the legs: due to lesion of the lenticular nucleus. **Horner's s.**, **Horner-Bernard s.**, sinking in of the eyeball, ptosis of the upper eyelid, slight elevation of the lower lid, constriction of the pupil, narrowing of the palpebral fissure, and anhidrosis caused by paralysis of the cervical sympathetic. **Horton's s.**, histamine cephalalgia. **humoral s.**, change in the chemistry of the body fluids (chloride deficiency in the blood and dehydration of the tissues) associated with intestinal obstruction. **Hunt's s.** 1. Herpetic inflammation of the geniculate ganglion, marked by herpes zoster of the auricular region, with or without facial palsy. 2. Juvenile paralysis agitans. **Hunt's striatal s's.** 1. Paleostriatal or pallidal syndrome characterized by paralysis of automatic associated movements, muscular rigidity, and rhythmic tremor of the paralysis agitans type, produced by atrophy or degeneration of the pallidal system of the corpus striatum. Called also *paralysis agitans syn-*

drome. 2. Neostriatal syndrome characterized by spontaneous choreiform movements of automatic associated type, produced by atrophy or degeneration of the neostriatal or striopallidal system of the corpus striatum. Called also *chorea syndrome.* 3. Mixed striatal syndromes from involvement of both systems; characterized by symptoms of chorea and paralysis agitans in various combinations. Athetosis, dystonia musculorum, and progressive lenticular degeneration. **Hunterian glossitis s.**, idiopathic pernicious anemia with combined sclerosis of the spinal cord and constitutional achylia gastrica. **Hurler's s.**, lipochondrodystrophy. **Hutchinson's s.** 1. Adrenal sarcoma of infants with metastases to the orbit. 2. Hutchinson's triad. **Hutchinson-Gilford s.**, progeria. **hyaline membrane s.**, idiopathic respiratory distress of newborn; so called because of the autopsy finding of a hyaline membrane lining the bronchioles, alveolar ducts, and alveoli. **hypercalcemia s.**, milk-alkali s. **hyperophthalmopathic s.**, proptosis, paresis of the external ocular muscles, swelling of the lids, edema of the conjunctiva and retrobulbar pain. **hypophyseal s.**, adiposogenital dystrophy. **Jackson's s.**, paralysis of the soft palate, larynx, and one half of the tongue, joined to that of the sternomastoid and trapezius muscles. Called also *syndrome of vago-accessory-hypoglossal paralysis.* **Jacquet's s.** See under *disease.* **jejunal s.**, dumping syndrome. **jugular foramen s.**, Vernet's s. **Karroo s.**, a condition observed in youth among South African Boers in the Karroo region, consisting of high fever, alimentary tract disturbance and tenderness in the lymph glands of the neck. **Kartagener's s.**, associated bronchiectasis, sinusitis, and situs inversus. **Kast's s.**, multiple hemangiomata associated with chondromata. **Kennedy's s.**, retrobulbar optic neuritis, central scotoma, optic atrophy on the side of the lesion and papilledema on the opposite side: occurring in tumors of the frontal lobe of the brain which press downward. **Kimmelstiel-Wilson s.**, intercapillary glomerulosclerosis, with diabetes, nephrosis, and gross albuminuria. **Kleine-Levin s.**, the syndrome of periodic somnolence, morbid hunger, and motor unrest. **Klinefelter's s.**, a condition characterized by the presence of small testes, with fibrosis and hyalinization of seminiferous tubules, without involvement of Leydig cells, and by increase in urinary gonadotropins; associated with an abnormality of the sex chromosomes. **Klippel-Feil s.**, a condition characterized by shortness of the neck resulting from reduction in the number of cervical vertebrae or the fusion of multiple hemivertebrae into one osseous mass; the hairline is low and motion of the neck is limited. **Klumpke-Dejerine s.**, Klumpke's paralysis. **Kocher's s.**, the leukopenia due to granulocytopenia with relative and absolute lymphocytosis and moderate eosinophilia occasionally accompanying thyrotoxicosis. **König's s.**, constipation alternating with diarrhea and attended with abdominal pain, meteorism, and gurgling sounds the right iliac fossa. **Korsakoff's s.** See under *psychosis.* **Landry's s.**, acute ascending paralysis. **Lasègue's s.** See *Lasègue's sign*, def. 2. **lateral cord and associated anterior cornual s.**, spastic muscular atrophy due to lesion of the lateral elements of the spinal cord and of its anterior cornua. **Laubry-Soule s.**, elevation of the left side of the diaphragm with aerogastrocolia in coronary artery disease. **Launois' s.**, gigantism due to excessive pituitary secretion. **Laurence-Biedl s., Laurence-Moon-Biedl s.**, a syndrome composed of obesity, hypogenitalism, retinitis pigmentosa, mental deficiency, skull defects, and sometimes syndactylism. **Läwen-Roth s.**, dwarfism with stippled epiphyses and thyroid deficiency. **Leredde's s.**, severe dyspnea on exertion dating from early life, combined with advanced emphysema, recurrent attacks of acute febrile bronchitis; a remote sequel of syphilis, usually congenital. **Leriche s.**, idiopathic thrombosis of the terminal aorta. **Lermoyez's s.**, tinnitus and deafness preceding an attack of vertigo and then subsiding after the vertigo has become established. **Leschke s.**, general weakness, development of numerous brownish pigmented spots on the skin, hyperglycemia. **Lévi's s.**, paroxysmal hyperthyroidism. **Lévy-Roussy s.**, Roussy-Lévy s. **Lhermitte and McAlpine s.**, combined pyramidal and extrapyramidal system disease. **Libman-Sacks s.** See under *disease.* **Lichtheim's s.** 1. Dorsolateral degeneration of the spinal cord. 2. Splenomegalic pernicious anemia with funicular myelosis. **Lightwood's s.**, renal tubular acidosis. **liver-kidney s.**, hepatorenal s. **loculation s.**, Froin's s. **Löffler's s.**, a condition characterized by transient infiltrations of the lungs associated with an increase of the eosinophilic leukocytes in the blood and with only slight systemic manifestations: called also *Löffler's eosinophilia.* **Lowe's s.**, oculocerebrorenal s. **Lutembacher's s.**, acquired rheumatic mitral stenosis associated with an atrial septal defect. **lymphoproliferative s.**, a general term applied to a group of diseases which are characterized by proliferation of lymphoid tissue, such as lymphocytic leukemia and malignant lymphoma. **McArdle s.**, myopathy due to inability of skeletal muscles to properly utilize muscle glycogen. **Mackenzie's s.**, associated paralysis of the tongue, soft palate, and vocal cord on the same side. **Maffucci's s.**, dyschondroplasia with hemangiomata. **malabsorption s.**, a condition characterized by weight loss, increased excretion of fat and protein in the stools, and varying degrees of anemia and electrolyte depletion. **Malin's s.**, anemia in which the red corpuscles are ingested by the leukocytes: called also *phagocytic anemia* and *autoerythrophagocytosis.* **Marañón's s.**, a syndrome consisting of scoliosis and flatfoot, with ovarian insufficiency. **Marchiafava-Micheli s.**, hemoglobinuria usually only at night, associated with one or more of the following: hemosiderinuria, albuminuria, normochromic anemia, leukopenia, thrombocytopenia, reticulocytosis, elevation of the icterus index, periods of jaundice, and often palpable spleen. **Marcus Gunn s.**, Gunn's s. **Marfan's s.**, congenital anomalies of the heart occurring in association with multiple somatic deformities. **Marie's s.** 1. Acromegaly caused by disorder of the pituitary secretion. 2. Hypertrophic osteoarthropathy. **Marie-Robinson s.**, melancholia, insomnia, and impotence in a form of levulosuria. **Meigs' s.**, ascites and hydrothorax associated with ovarian fibroma or other pelvic tumor. **Meniere's s.**, deafness, tinnitus, and dizziness, occurring in association with nonsuppurative disease of the labyrinth. Called also *endolymphatic* or *labyrinthine hydrops.* **mesodermal s.**, an abnormal condition in which many mesodermal tissues are involved. **metameric s.**, segmentary s. **middle lobe s.**, atelectasis of the right middle lobe, with chronic pneumonitis, resulting from compression of the bronchus by tuberculotic hilar lymph nodes. **middle radicular s.**, paralysis of the triceps muscle and the dorsal extensors of the hand due to paralysis of the root of the seventh cervical nerve. **Mikulicz's s.**, chronic lymphocytic infiltration and enlargement of the lacrimal and salivary glands, associated with other specific disease, such as sarcoidosis, malignant lymphoma, or collagen disease. **Milian's s.**, Milian's erythema. **milk-alkali s.**, a syndrome characterized by hypercalcemia without hypercalciuria or hypophosphatemia, with only mild alkalosis, normal serum phosphatase, severe renal insufficiency with hyperazotemia and calcinosis, attributed to ingestion of milk and absorbable alkali for long periods of time. **Milkman's s.**, a generalized bone disease marked by multiple transparent stripes of absorption in the long and flat bones. **Millard-Gubler s.**, alternating abducens facial hemiplegic paralysis. **Minkowski-Chauffard s.**, hemolytic jaundice. **Möbius s.**, akinesia algera. **Monakow's**

s., hemiplegia on the side opposite the lesion in occlusion of the anterior choroidal artery: sometimes with hemianesthesia and hemianopia. **Moore's s.,** abdominal epilepsy. **Morel's s.,** hyperostosis of the frontal bone, obesity, headache, nervous disturbance, and a tendency to mental disorder. **Morgagni's s.,** internal frontal hyperostosis, virilism, and obesity. **Morgagni-Stewart-Morel s.,** a syndrome which is a combination of the syndromes described by Morel and Morgagni. **Morquio's s.,** a form of eccentro-osteochondrodysplasia in which the skeletal changes are chiefly in the vertebral column and which is inherited recessively. **Morton's s.,** a congenital insufficiency of the first metatarsal segment of the foot, characterized by metatarsalgia due to shortening or relaxation of the part. **Morvan's s.,** recurring painless whitlows, usually symmetrically placed on the hands, though sometimes on the lower extremities, seen in cases of syringomyelia and occasionally in leprosy. **Mosse's s.,** erythremia with cirrhosis of the liver. **Munchausen's s.,** a condition characterized by habitual presentation for hospital treatment of an apparent acute illness, the patient giving a plausible and dramatic history, all of which is false. **Murchison-Sanderson s.,** Pel-Ebstein disease. **myasthenia gravis s.,** Erb's s., def. 2. **myeloproliferative s.,** a general term applied to a group of diseases which may be related histogenetically and are characterized, at varying times and in varying degrees, by medullary and extramedullary proliferation of one or more lines of bone marrow constituents, including the myelocytic, erythroblastic, and megakaryocytic forms, in addition to the various cells derived from the reticulum and mesenchymal elements; the group includes acute and chronic myelocytic leukemia, erythremia, myelofibrosis with myeloid metaplasia, hemorrhagic thrombocythemia, erythremic myelosis, and erythroleukemia. **Naffziger's s.,** scalenus s. **nephrotic s.,** a condition characterized by massive edema, heavy proteinuria, hypoalbuminemia, and peculiar susceptibility to intercurrent infections. **neurocutaneous s.,** the formation of nevi and deformities of the skeleton with symtoms of degeneration in the central nervous system. **nitritoid s.,** nitritoid crisis. **Nonne's s.,** a syndrome consisting of the various disturbances of synergic motor control, asynergia, dysmetria, speech disturbances, incoordination, etc., pointing to disease of the cerebellum. Called also *cerebellar s.* and *s. of cerebellar agenesis.* **Nonne-Milroy-Meige s.,** Milroy's disease. **nonsence s.,** Ganser's s. **Nothnagel's s.,** unilateral oculomotor paralysis combined with cerebellar ataxia, in lesions of the cerebral peduncles. **oculocerebrorenal s.,** a type of vitamin D–refractory rickets associated with glaucoma, mental retardation, and tubule reabsorption dysfunction as evidenced by hypophosphatemia, acidosis, and aminoaciduria. **Ogilvie's s.,** a condition simulating colonic obstruction, with persistent contraction of intestinal musculature. Also called *false colonic obstruction.* **orodigitofacial s.,** orofacial-digital syndrome. **orofacial-digital s.,** a condition characterized by hypertrophy of the frenula, oligophrenia, trembling, and anomalies of the hands. **Ostrum-Furst s.,** congenital synostosis of the neck, platybasia and Sprengel's deformity. **outlet s.,** brachial s. **paleostriatal s.** 1. Hunt's striatal syndrome, def. 1. 2. Paralysis agitans. **pallidal s.,** Hunt's striatal s., def. 1. **pallidomesencephalic s.,** a syndrome made up of rigidity, poverty of movement, and bradykinesia, amounting to a parkinsonian state. **Pancoast's s.** 1. Roentgenographic shadow at apex of lung, neuritic pain in the arm, atrophy of the muscles of the arm and hand, and Horner's syndrome, observed in tumor near the apex of the lung. 2. Osteolysis in the posterior part of one or more ribs and sometimes also involving the corresponding vertebra. **pancreaticohepatic s.,** extensive destruction of pancreatic tissue and fatty metamorphosis of the liver. **paralysis agitans s.,** Hunt's striatal s., def. 1. **paratrigeminal s.,** association of the syndrome of the sympathetic with trigeminal paralysis. **Parinaud's s.,** paralysis of conjugate, upward movement of the eyes without paralysis of convergence: seen in lesion of the midbrain. **Parke's s.,** infantile epidemic acidosis with acetonemic vomiting. **Parkinson's s., parkinsonian s.,** muscular rigidity, immobile facies, tremor, which tends to disappear on volitional movement, abolition of associated and automatic movements, and salivation, due to lesion of the globus pallidus. This syndrome is characteristic of paralysis agitans (Parkinson's disease), and is a frequent sequel of lethargic encephalitis. Called also *parkinsonism.* **Paterson's s.,** Plummer-Vinson s. **Patton's s.,** Graves's s., def. 1. **Pellazzi's s.,** epiphysial s. **Pepper s.,** when the right adrenal is affected with neuroblastoma, the metastases are largely limited to the liver. **pericolic-membrane s.,** symptoms resembling those of chronic appendicitis due to the pressure of pericolic membranes. **Peutz s.,** hereditary intestinal polyposis. **Peutz-Jeghers s.,** gastrointestinal polyposis associated with excessive melanin pigmentation of the skin and mucous membranes, commonly a familial condition. **phrenogastric s.,** elevation of the left diaphragm with excess gas in the stomach occurring in coronary disease. **physiopathic s.,** a combination of glossy skin on the fingers, decalcification of the phalanges, and paresis. **Picchini's s.,** inflammation of the three serous membranes connected with the diaphragm, sometimes involving the meninges, synovial sheaths, and tunica vaginalis of the testicle; caused by a trypanosome. **Pick's s.** 1. Pick's disease. 2. Palpitation of the heart: a feeling of oppression on the chest, dyspnea, cyanosis, and dropsical phenomena: seen in certain heart diseases. **Pickwickian s.,** the complex of exogenous obesity, somnolence, hypoventilation, and erythrocytosis. **Pierre Robin s.,** micrognathia occurring in association with cleft palate and glossoptosis. **pineal s.,** epiphysial s. **Pins' s.** See under *sign.* **pituitary s.,** Marie's s., def. 1. **Plummer-Vinson s.,** dysphagia with glossitis, hypochromic anemia, splenomegaly, and atrophy in the mouth, pharynx and upper end of the esophagus. Called also *sideropenic dysphagia.* **pluriglandular s.,** polyglandular s. **polyglandular s.,** a series of symptoms believed to be due to pathologic action of several ductless glands. **pontine s.,** Raymond-Cestan s. **postcommissurotomy s.,** fever, chest pain, pneumonitis, and cardiomegaly, occurring frequently in patients who have undergone mitral commissurotomy, and attributed by some to reactivation of rheumatic fever. **posterior cord s.,** sensory and ataxic phenomena derived from a lesion of the posterior columns, as in locomotor ataxia. **posterolateral s.,** an ataxic and spasmodic condition due to lesion of the posterolateral elements of the spinal cord. **postgastrectomy s.,** dumping s. **postirradiation s.,** a symptom complex caused by massive irradiation, with hemorrhage, anemia, and malnutrition. **postpericardiotomy s.,** delayed pericardial or pleural reaction following opening of the pericardium, characterized by fever, chest pain, and signs of pleural and/or pericardial inflammation. **Potain's s.,** dyspepsia with dilatation of the right ventricle and increase of the pulmonary sound: observed in gastrectasis. **Pozzi's s.,** leukorrhea and backache without enlargement of the uterus: characteristic of endometritis. **premotor s.,** the association of spastic hemiplegia with increased reflexes, disturbances of skilled movements, forced grasping and transient vasomotor disturbance: occurs in lesions of the premotor cortex. **Profichet's s.,** a gradual growth of calcareous nodules in the subcutaneous tissues (skin stones) especially about the larger joints, with a tendency to ulceration or cicatrization and attended by atrophic and nervous symptoms. **Putnam-Dana s.,** a sclerosis of the lateral and dorsal columns of the spinal cord. **radicular s.,** a syndrome due to lesion of the roots of the spinal nerves, consisting of restricted mobility of the spine and root pain. **Raymond-Cestan s.,** a syndrome due to obstruction of twigs of the basilar artery causing lesions of the pontine region: it is characterized by quadriplegia, anesthesia and nystagmus. **Refsum's s.,** hemeralopia, atypical retinitis pigmentosa, and chronic polyneuritis. **Reichmann's s.,** gastrosuccorrhea. **Reiter's s.,** a combination of arthritis, conjunctivitis, and urethritis, all nongonorrheal. **Rénon-Delille s.,** lowered blood pressure, tachycardia, oliguria, insomnia, hyperhidrosis, intolerance of heat, as signs of dyspituitarism. **respiratory distress s.,** idiopathic respiratory distress of newborn. **s. of retroparotid space,** Villaret's s. **Ridley's s.,** sudden dyspnea with edema of the lungs in cardiac asthma. **Riley-Day s.,** dysautonomia. **Roger's s.,** a continuous excessive secretion of saliva as the result of cancer in the esophagus, or other esophageal irritation. **rolandic vein s.,** hemiplegia resulting from interference with the cerebral venous circulation. **Romberg-Paessler s.,** low blood pressure, rapid heart action, tympanites, and shock: symptoms caused by dilatation of the blood vessels in the splanchnic area. **Rosenbach's s.,** paroxysmal tachycardia with gastric and respiratory complications. **Roth's s.,** meralgia paraesthetica. **Rothmund's s.,** heredofamilial atrophic dermatoses with wasting of the muscles, juvenile cataracts, and endocrine features. **Roussy-Lévy s.,** progressive neuropathic (peroneal) muscular atrophy with scoliosis and cerebellar ataxia. **Rust's s.,** stiff neck, stiff carriage of the head, with the necessity of grasping the head with both hands in lying down or rising up from a horizontal posture, occurring in phthisis, cancer, fracture of the spine, rheumatic or arthritic processes, or syphilitic periostitis. **Sawii s.,** an exfoliative dermatitis of unknown etiology. **scalenus s., scalenus anticus s.,** pain over the shoulder, often extending down the arm or radiating up the back of the neck due to compression of the nerves and vessels between a cervical rib and the scalenus anticus muscle: called also *Naffziger's s.* and *cervical rib s.* **scapulocostal s.,** pain in the superior or posterior aspect of the shoulder girdle, radiating to contiguous regions, as a result of long-standing alteration of the relationship of the scapula and the posterior thoracic wall. **Schanz's s.,** a series of symptoms indicating spinal weakness, consisting of a sense of fatigue, pain on pressure over the spinous processes, pain on lying prone, and indications of spinal curvature. **Schaumann's s.,** a combination of Boeck's sarcoid, hilus adenitis, iridocyclitis, osteitis multiplex cystoides and other symptoms; generalized sarcoidosis. **Schmidt's s.,** paralysis on one side, affecting the vocal cord, the velum palati, the trapezius muscle, and the sternocleidomastoid muscle, due to a lesion of the nucleus ambiguus and nucleus accessorius. **Schönlein-Henoch s.** See under *purpura.* **Schroeder's s.,** high blood pressure with abnormal diminution of the salt content of the sweat, due to overactivity of the adrenal glands, and with notable gain in weight. **Schüller's s., Schüller-Christian s.,** Schüller-Christian disease. **Schultz s.,** agranulocytosis. **scimitar s.,** anomalous drainage of the right lung into the inferior vena cava. **segmentary s.,** a syndrome which is produced by a lesion of the gray matter of the spinal cord. Called also *metameric s.* **Selye s.,** general adaptation s. **Senear-Usher s.,** pemphigus erythematosus. **Sézary s., Sézary reticulosis s.,** an exfoliative erythroderma produced by cutaneous infiltration of reticular lymphocytes and associated with alopecia, edema, hyperkeratosis, and pigment and nail changes; although bone marrow and lymph nodes are normal, reticulemia may occur. **Sheehan's s.,** hypopituitarism occurring in a woman after severe hemorrhage or shock at delivery, commonly characterized by failure of lactation, loss of body hair, and amenorrhea. **shoulder-hand s.,** a clinical disorder of the upper extremity, characterized by pain and stiffness in the shoulder, with puffy swelling and pain in the ipsilateral hand, sometimes occurring after myocardial infarction but also produced by other known or unknown causes. **Sicard's s.,** Collet-Sicard s. **Siemens' s.,** hereditary ectodermal dysplasia. **Silverskiöld's s.,** a form of eccentro-osteochondrodysplasia in which the skeletal changes are chiefly in the extremities and which is inherited as a dominant character. **Silvestrini-Corda s.,** eunuchoid body type, absence of body hair, defective libido, atrophy of the testes, sterility, and gynecomastia: a syndrome indicative of abnormally high estrogenic activity, due to failure of the liver to inactivate the estrogens. **Simmonds' s.** See under *disease.* **Simon's s.,** primary cancer of the female breast with metastasis to the hypophysis and consequent polyuria. **Sjögren's s.,** a symptom complex in which keratoconjunctivitis sicca is associated with pharyngitis sicca, enlargement of the parotid glands, and chronic polyarthritis. **Sluder's s.** See under *neuralgia.* **Spens's s.,** Adams-Stokes disease. **split-brain s.,** an association of symptoms produced by disruption of or interference with the connection between the hemispheres of the brain. **Spurway s.,** osteogenesis imperfecta associated with blue sclerae. **Stein-Leventhal s.,** a clinical symptom complex characterized by secondary amenorrhea and anovulation (hence sterility), and regularly associated with bilateral polycystic ovaries; excretion of follicle-stimulating hormone and 17-ketosteroids is essentially normal. **Stevens-Johnson s.,** ectodermosis erosiva pluriorificialis. **Stewart-Morel s.,** Morel's s. **stiff-man s.,** a condition characterized by progressive fluctuating muscular rigidity and spasm. **Still-Chauffard s.,** Chauffard's s. **Stokes's s., Stokes-Adams s.,** Adams-Stokes disease. **striatal s.,** Hunt's striatal s. **Stryker-Halbeisen s.,** scaly itching erythroderma on the face, neck and upper chest with macrocytic anemia; probably a syndrome of vitamin deficiency. **Sturge's s., Sturge-Kalischer-Weber s.,** nevoid amentia. **Sturge-Weber s.,** vascular nevi along the course of the superior and middle branches of the trigeminal nerve, glaucoma on the same side, and nevi of the pia. **subclavian steal s.,** deficiency of cerebral circulation caused by the vertebral artery functioning as a source of collateral arterial supply to the upper extremity, as a result of atherosclerotic obstruction of the proximal portion of the subclavian artery. **Sudeck-Leriche s.,** posttraumatic osteoporosis associated with vasospasm. **suprarenogenic s.,** adrenal disorder characterized by adiposity, pigmentation, and hairiness. **supraspinatus s.,** tenderness over the supraspinatus tendon, a painful arc on movement of the arm, and a reversal of scapulohumeral rhythm. **Tapia's s.,** unilateral paralysis of the tongue and larynx, the velum palati being unaffected. **Taussig-Bing s.,** pulmonic stenosis and nonfunctioning right ventricle, with both mitral and aortic insufficiency. **tegmental s.,** hemiplegia, alternating with disordered eye movements, indicative of lesions of the tegmentum. **temporomandibular joint s.,** dysfunction of the temporomandibular joint caused by deforming arthritis resulting from mandibular overclosure or displacement. **Terry's s.,** retrolental fibroplasia. **testicular feminization s.,** an extreme form of male pseudohermaphroditism, with female external development, including secondary sex characteristics, but with presence of testes and absence of uterus and tubes. **thalamic s.,** a combination of the following symptoms: (1) Superficial persistent hemianesthesia; (2) mild hemiplegia; (3) mild hemiataxia and more or less complete asterognosis; (4) severe and persistent pains in the hemiplegic side; (5) choreo-athetoid movements in the members of the paralyzed side.

Called also *Dejerine-Roussy s.* and *thalamic hyperesthetic anesthesia.* **Thibierge-Weissenbach s.,** calcinosis. **Thiele s.,** tenderness and pain in the region of the lower portion of the sacrum and coccyx, or in contiguous soft tissues and muscles. **thromboembolic s.,** the association between the formation of thrombi in the deep veins of the leg and pulmonary embolism. **Tietze's s.,** painful nonsuppurative swellings of costal cartilages. **Timme's s.,** ovarian and adrenal insufficiency with compensatory hypopituitarism. **Tommaselli's s.** See under *disease.* **Treacher-Collins s.,** mandibular facial dysostosis. **Troisier's s.,** bronzed cachexia occurring in diabetes. **Turner's s.,** retarded growth and sexual development, webbing of neck, low posterior hair line margin, increased carrying angle of elbow, cubitus valgus; associated with an abnormality of the sex chromosomes. **vago-accessory s.,** Schmidt's s. **van der Hoeve's s.,** a combination of blue scleras, osteogenesis imperfecta, and otosclerosis. **vascular s.,** any syndrome due to occlusion of vessels supplying the nervous system. **Vernet's s.,** paralysis of the ninth, tenth, and eleventh cranial nerves, marked by paralysis of the superior constriction of the pharynx and difficulty in swallowing solids; paralysis of the soft palate and fauces with anesthesia of these parts and of the pharynx, and loss of taste in the posterior third of the tongue; paralysis of the vocal cords and anesthesia of the larynx; paralysis of the sternocleidomastoid and trapezius muscles. **Villaret's s.,** paralysis of the superior constriction of the pharynx and difficulty in swallowing solids; paralysis of soft palate and fauces with anesthesia of these parts and of the pharynx; loss of taste in the posterior third of the tongue; paralysis of the vocal cords and anesthesia of the larynx; paralysis of the sternocleidomastoid and trapezius. **Vogt's s.,** athetosis, rhythmic oscillation of the limbs, spasmodic outbursts of laughing and crying, absence of paralysis, no disturbance of sensation, no mental disturbance; a syndrome due to lesion of the corpus striatum. Called also *syndrome of double athetosis* and *syndrome of corpus striatum.* **Vogt-Koyanagi s.,** exudative iridocyclitis and choroiditis associated with patchy depigmentation of the skin and hair; the lashes and eyebrows also become whitened, and there may also be retinal detachment and associated deafness and tinnitus. **Volkmann's s.,** post-traumatic muscular hypertonia and degenerative neuritis; Volkmann's contracture. **Wallenberg's s.,** Babinski-Nageotte s. **Waterhouse-Friderichsen s.,** the malignant or fulminating form of meningococcus meningitis, which is marked by sudden onset and short course, fever, coma, and collapse, cyanosis, hemorrhages from the skin and mucous membranes and bilateral adrenal hemorrhage. **s. of Weber,** paralysis of the oculomotor nerve on the same side as the lesion, producing ptosis, strabismus, loss of light reflex and of accommodation; also spastic hemiplegia on the side opposite the lesion with increased reflexes and loss of superficial reflexes. Called also *syndrome of cerebral peduncle* and *alternating oculomotor hemiplegia.* **Weber-Dubler s.,** complete hemiplegia on the side opposite the lesion with oculomotor paralysis on the side of the lesion in disease of the cerebral peduncles. **Weingarten's s.,** tropical eosinophilia. **Werdnig-Hoffmann s.** See under *paralysis.* **Werner's s.,** premature senility of an adult, characterized by early graying and some loss of the hair, cataracts, hyperkeratinization, and scleroderma-like changes in the skin of the lower extremities, followed by chronic ulceration. **Wernicke's s.,** presbyophrenia. **Widal s.,** ictero-anemia. **Wilson's s.,** progressive lenticular degeneration. **Wolff-Parkinson-White s.,** a defect in the functioning of the heart, recognized in the electrocardiogram by occurrence of a short P-R interval and prolonged QRS time: seen in patients with paroxysmal tachycardia. **Wright's s.** 1. (Irving S. Wright). A neurovascular syndrome caused by hyperabduction of the arm. Such hyperabduction may cause occlusion of the subclavian artery, leading to gangrene, or may produce sensory symptoms due to stretching of the brachial plexus. 2. A condition marked by multifocal areas of osteitis fibrosa, patchy cutaneous pigmentation and precocious puberty. **Young's s.,** amyotrophic lateral sclerosis of bulbar type associated with platybasia. **Zollinger-Ellison s.,** a triad comprising (1) intractable, sometimes fulminating, and in many ways atypical peptic ulcers; (2) extreme gastric hyperacidity; and (3) non–beta cell, non–insulin-secreting islet cell tumors, which might be single or multiple, small or large, innocent or malignant.

syndromic (sin-dro′mik). Occurring as a syndrome.

syndrox (sin′droks). Trade mark for preparations of methamphetamine.

synechia (sĭ-nek′e-ah), pl. *synech′iae* [Gr. *synecheia* continuity]. Adhesion of parts; especially, adhesion of the iris to the cornea or to the lens. **anterior s.,** adhesion of the iris to the posterior surface of the cornea after perforation resulting from keratitis. **s. pericar′dii,** concretio cordis. **posterior s.,** adhesion of the iris to the capsule of the lens. **total s.,** adhesion of the whole surface of the iris to the lens. **s. vul′vae,** a congenital condition in which the labia minora are sealed together.

synechotome (sin-ek′o-tōm). A cutting instrument for use in synechotomy.

synechotomy (sin″e-kot′o-me) [*synechia* + Gr. *tomē* a cutting]. The operation of cutting a synechia.

synechtenterotomy (sin″ek-ten″ter-ot′o-me) [Gr. *synechēs* joined together + *enteron* bowel + *tomē* a cutting]. The division of an intestinal adhesion.

synecology (sin″e-kol′o-je). The study of the environment of organisms in the mass, as distinguished from *auto-ecology.*

synencephalia (sin″en-se-fa′le-ah) [*syn-* + Gr. *enkephalos* brain + *-ia*]. A developmental anomaly in which there are two bodies and one head.

synencephalocele (sin″en-sef′ah-lo-sēl″) [*syn-* + Gr. *enkephalos* brain + *kēlē* tumor]. Encephalocele with adhesions to the adjoining parts.

synencephalus (sin″en-sef′ah-lus). A fetal monster exhibiting synencephalia.

syneresis (sĭ-ner′ĕ-sis) [Gr. *synairesis* a taking or drawing together]. A drawing together of the particles of the dispersed phase of a gel, with separation of some of the disperse medium and shrinkage of the gel, such as occurs in the clotting of blood.

synergenesis (sin″er-jen′e-sis). The doctrine that every cell transmits its protoplasm to every generation of cells derived from it.

synergetic (sin″er-jet′ik). Working together: said of muscles which cooperate in performing an action.

synergia (sin-er′je-ah). Synergy.

synergic (sin-er′jik). Acting together or in harmony.

synergism (sin′er-jizm). The joint action of agents so that their combined effect is greater than the algebraic sum of their individual effects.

synergist (sin′er-jist). 1. A medicine that aids or cooperates with another; an adjuvant. 2. An organ that acts in concert with another. **pituitary s.,** a substance occurring in extracts of the anterior pituitary which enhances the action of gonadotropic extracts of the urine of pregnant women or placenta.

synergistic (sin″er-jis′tik). Acting together; enhancing the effect of another force or agent.

synergy (sin′er-je) [L. *synergia;* Gr. *syn* together + *ergon* work]. Correlated action or cooperation on the part of two or more structures or drugs. In neurology, the faculty by which movements are properly grouped for the performance of acts requiring special adjustments.

synesthesia (sin″es-the′ze-ah) [*syn-* + Gr. *aisthēsis* perception + *-ia*]. A secondary sensation accompanying an actual perception; the experiencing of a sensation in one place, due to stimulation applied to another place; also the condition in which a stimulus of one sense is perceived as sensation of a different sense, as when a sound produces a sensation of color. **s. al′gica,** a painful synesthesia.

synesthesialgia (sin″es-the″ze-al′je-ah). A condition in which a stimulus produces pain on the affected side but no sensation or even a pleasant one on the normal side of the body.

synezesis (sin″e-ze′sis). Synizesis.

syngamous (sin′gah-mus) [*syn-* + Gr. *gamos* marriage]. 1. Pertaining to or characterized by syngamy. 2. Having the sex of the individual determined at the time when the ovum is fertilized.

Syngamus (sin′gah-mus). A genus of worms that are parasitic in fowl and other birds. **S. tra′chea,** a species of worms which are parasitic in chickens, pheasants, turkeys, and various wild birds, inhabiting the trachea and interfering with respiration when present in large numbers.

syngamy (sin′gah-me) [*syn-* + Gr. *gamos* marriage]. 1. Sexual reproduction. 2. The union of the gametes in fertilization.

syngenesioplastic (sin″je-ne″se-o-plas′tik) [*syn-* + Gr. *genesis* origin + *plassein* to form]. Denoting transplantation of tissue from one individual to a related individual of the same species, as from a mother to her child, or from a brother to a sister.

syngenesiotransplantation (sin″je-ne″se-o-trans″plan-ta′shun). Syngenesioplastic transplantation.

syngenic (sin-jen′ik) [*syn-* + Gr. *gennan* to produce]. Congenital.

syngignoscism (sin-jig′no-sizm) [*syn-* + Gr. *gignōskein* to know]. Hypnotism or hypnotic influence.

syngonic (sin-gon′ik) [*syn-* + Gr. *gonē* seed]. Having the sex of the individual determined at the time when the ovum is fertilized.

synidrosis (sin″ĭ-dro′sis) [*syn-* + Gr. *hidrōsis* a sweating]. Sweating associated with some other condition.

synizesis (sin″ĭ-ze′sis) [Gr. *synizēsis*]. 1. Occlusion. 2. A stage in mitosis in which the nuclear chromatin is massed. **s. pupil′lae,** occlusion of the pupil.

synkainogenesis (sin″ki-no-jen′e-sis) [*syn-* + Gr. *kainos* new + *genesis* production]. The process of developing a new formation simultaneously with another formation.

synkaryon (sin-kar′e-on) [*syn-* + Gr. *karyon* nucleus]. The nucleus produced by the fusion of two pronuclei; the fertilization nucleus.

synkavite (sin′ka-vit). Trade mark for preparations of menadiol sodium diphosphate.

synkinesia (sin″ki-ne′ze-ah). Synkinesis.

synkinesis (sin″ki-ne′sis) [*syn-* + Gr. *kinēsis* movement]. An associated movement; an unintentional movement accompanying a volitional movement. **imitative s.,** an involuntary movement on the healthy side accompanying an attempt at movement on the paralyzed side. **mouth-and-hand s.** See *Saunders' sign*, under *sign*. **spasmodic s.,** a movement on the paralyzed side attending a voluntary movement on the healthy side.

synkinetic (sin″ki-net′ik). Pertaining to or of the nature of synkinesis.

synnecrosis (sin″ne-kro′sis) [*syn-* + Gr. *nekrōsis* a state of death]. A relationship between populations (or individuals) resulting in mutual depression or death.

synneurosis (sin″nu-ro′sis) [*syn-* + Gr. *neuron* nerve]. Syndesmosis.

synocha (sin′o-kah) [L.; Gr. *synochos* jointed together]. A continued fever.

synochal (sin′o-kal). Of or pertaining to synocha.

synochus (sin′o-kus). Synocha.

synocytotoxin (sin″o-si″to-tok′sin). Syncytotoxin.

synonychia (sin″o-nik′e-ah) [*syn-* + Gr. *onyx* nail + -ia]. Fusion of the nails of two or more digits in complicated syndactyly.

synophridia (sin″of-rid′e-ah). Synophrys.

synophrys (sin-of′ris) [Gr. "with meeting eyebrows"]. The condition in which the eyebrows grow together.

synophthalmia (sin″of-thal′me-ah) [*syn-* + Gr. *ophthalmos* eye + *-ia*]. The usual form of cyclopia, in which the two eyes are more or less completely fused into one.

synophthalmus (sin″of-thal′mus). Cyclops.

synophylate (sin″o-fi′lāt). Trade mark for preparations of theophylline sodium glycinate.

synopsy (sin′op-se) [Gr. *syn* together + *opsis* vision]. 1. A form of synesthesia in which certain colors are associated with certain tones. 2. The abnormal suggestion of types of the human face or figure by the various numerals.

synoptophore (sin-op′to-fōr). An instrument for diagnosing strabismus and for treating it by orthoptic methods.

synoptoscope (sin-op′to-skōp) [*syn-* + Gr. *optos* seen + *skopein* to examine]. An instrument for examining the eye in strabismus.

synorchidism (sin-or′kĭ-dizm). Synorchism.

synorchism (sin′or-kizm) [*syn-* + Gr. *orchis* testicle]. Fusion of the two testes into one mass, which may be located in the scrotum or in the abdomen.

synoscheos (sin-os′ke-os) [*syn-* + Gr. *oscheon* scrotum]. Adhesion between the penis and scrotum.

synosteology (sin″os-te-ol′o-je) [*syn-* + Gr. *osteon* bone + *-logy*]. The sum of knowledge regarding the joints and articulations.

synosteosis (sin″os-te-o′sis). Synostosis.

synosteotic (sin″os-te-ot′ik). Pertaining to or marked by synosteosis.

synosteotomy (sin″os-te-ot′o-me) [*syn-* + Gr. *osteon* bone + *tomē* a cutting]. The dissection of the joints.

synostosis (sin″os-to′sis), pl. *synosto′ses* [*syn-* + Gr. *osteon* bone]. 1. [N A] A union between adjacent bones or parts of a single bone formed by osseous material, such as ossified connecting cartilage or fibrous tissue. 2. The osseous union of bones that are normally distinct. **radio-ulnar s.,** bony fusion of the proximal ends of the radius and ulna. **tribasilar s.,** fusion in infancy of the three bones at the base of the skull, producing mental retardation.

synostotic (sin″os-tot′ik). Synosteotic.

synotia (si-no′she-ah) [*syn-* + Gr. *ous* ear]. A developmental anomaly characterized by persistence of the ears in their horizontal position beneath the mandible.

synotus (si-no′tus) [*syn-* + Gr. *ous* ear]. A monster fetus exhibiting synotia.

synousiology (si-noo″se-ol′o-je) [Gr. *synousia* sexual intercourse + *logos* treatise]. The science and art of sexual intercourse.

synovectomy (sin″o-vek′to-me) [*synovia* + Gr. *ektomē* excision]. Excision of a synovial membrane, as of that lining the capsule of the knee joint, performed in treatment of rheumatoid arthritis of the knee.

synovia (si-no′ve-ah) [L.; Gr. *syn* with + *ōon* egg]. [N A, B N A] A transparent alkaline, viscid fluid, resembling the white of an egg, secreted by the synovial membrane, and contained in joint cavities, bursae, and tendon sheaths. Also called *synovial fluid.*

synovial (sĭ-no′ve-al) [L. *synovialis*]. Of, or pertaining to, or secreting, synovia.

synovialis (sĭ-no″ve-a′lis) [L.]. Synovial.

synovialoma (sĭ-no″ve-ah-lo′mah). Synovioma.

synovianalysis (sĭ-no″ve-ah-nal′ĭ-sis). The laboratory examination of joint fluid (synovia).

synovin (sin′o-vin). The mucin found in synovia.

synovioblast (sĭ-no′ve-o-blast). A fibroblast of synovial membrane.

synovioma (sĭ-no″ve-o′mah). A tumor of synovial membrane origin.

synoviparous (sin″o-vip′ah-rus) [*synovia* + L. *parere* to produce]. Producing synovia.

synovitis (sin″o-vi′tis). Inflammation of a synovial membrane. It is usually painful, particularly on motion, and is characterized by a fluctuating swelling, due to effusion within a synovial sac. Synovitis is qualified as *fibrinous, gonorrheal, hyperplastic, lipomatous, metritic, puerperal, rheumatic, scarlatinal, syphilitic, tuberculous, urethral,* etc. **bursal s.,** bursitis. **dendritic s.,** that in which villous growths are developed within the sac. **dry s.,** synovitis with but little effusion. **fungous s.,** fungous arthritis. **purulent s.,** that in which there is an effusion of pus in a synovial sac. **serous s.,** synovitis with copious nonpurulent effusion. **s. sic′ca,** dry synovitis. **simple s.,** that in which the effusion is clear or but slightly turbid. **tendinous s.,** inflammation of a tendon sheath. **vaginal s.,** tendinous synovitis. **vibration s.,** synovitis produced by the passage of a missile through the tissues near a joint, but without actually wounding the joint.

synovium (sĭ-no′ve-um). A synovial membrane.

synphalangism (sin-fal′an-jizm). Symphalangia.

synpneumonic (sin″nu-mon′ik). Occurring in association with pneumonia.

synprolan (sin′pro-lan). The name applied by Zondek to the synergistic principle in the anterior pituitary which enhances the action of the gonadotropic substance ("prolan") in the urine of pregnant women. See *pituitary synergist.*

synreflexia (sin″re-flek′se-ah). The association existing between various reflexes.

syntactic (sin-tak′tik). Pertaining to or affecting syntax, or the proper arrangement of words in speech.

syntaxis (sin-tak′sis) [Gr. "a putting together in order"]. Articulation.

syntectic (sin-tek′tik). Pertaining to or characterized by syntexis.

syntenosis (sin″te-no′sis) [*syn-* + Gr. *tenōn* tendon]. A hinge joint surrounded by tendons.

synteresis (sin″ter-e′sis) [*syn-* + Gr. *tērein* to watch over]. Preventive treatment; prophylaxis.

synteretic (sin″ter-et′ik). Prophylactic.

syntexis (sin-tek′sis) [Gr. *syntēxis* colliquation]. Wasting or emaciation.

synthermal (sin-ther′mal) [*syn-* + Gr. *thermē* heat]. Having the same temperature.

synthescope (sin′thĕ-skōp) [Gr. *synthesis* placing together + *skopein* to examine]. An instrument for observing the visible effect of placing two liquids in contact.

synthesis (sin′thĕ-sis) [Gr. "a putting together, composition"]. 1. The artificial building up of a chemical compound by the union of its elements. 2. The process of bringing back into consciousness activities or experiences that have become split off or disassociated. Cf. *dissociation* (3), and *subconscious.* **s. of continuity,** union of the lips of a wound or the ends of a fractured bone. **morphologic s.,** histogenesis.

synthesize (sin″thĕ-sīz′). To produce by means of synthesis.

synthetic (sin-thet′ik) [L. *syntheticus;* Gr. *synthetikos*]. 1. Pertaining to, of the nature of, or participating in synthesis. 2. Produced by synthesis; artificial.

synthetism (sin′thĕ-tizm) [Gr. *synthetos* put together]. The complete treatment of a fracture.

synthorax (sin-tho′raks). Thoracopagus.

synthroid (sin′throid). Trade mark for a preparation of sodium levothyroxine.

syntocinon (sin-to′sĭ-non). Trade mark for a solution of synthetic oxytocin.

syntone (sin′tōn). A person of syntonic type.

syntonic (sin-ton′ik) [*syn-* + Gr. *tonos* tension]. A term applied by Bleuler to the stable integrated type of personality which responds normally to the environment, as contrasted with the schizoid type.

syntonin (sin′to-nin). An acid metaprotein which precipitates from a gastric digestion mixture at or near the neutral point.

syntopie, syntopy (sin′to-pe) [*syn-* + Gr. *topos* place]. The position of an organ in relation to neighboring organs.

syntoxoid (sin-tok′soid). Any toxoid having exactly the same affinity for an antitoxin as that possessed by the associated toxin. See *toxoid.*

syntripsis (sin-trip′sis) [*syn-* + Gr. *tribein* to rub]. The comminution or crushing of a bone; comminuted fracture.

syntropan (sin′tro-pan). Trade mark for a preparation of amprotropine phosphate.

syntrophism (sin′trōf-izm) [*syn-* + Gr. *trophē* nourishment]. Stimulation of the growth of a microorganism resulting from admixture with or nearness of another strain.

syntrophoblast (sin-trof′o-blast). The outer syncytial layer of the trophoblast.

syntrophus (sin′tro-fus) [Gr. *syntrophos* congenital]. Any congenital or inherited disease.

syntropic (sin-trop′ik) [*syn-* + Gr. *trepein* to turn]. 1. Turning or pointing in the same direction, as the ribs of the vertebral spines. 2. Pertaining to syntropy. 3. Meyer's term for a well-balanced personality with a normal social outlook: called also *koinotropic.*

syntropy (sin′tro-pe) [*syn-* + Gr. *tropos* a turning]. The correlation of several factors, as the relation of certain physical characteristics or diseases to the development or incidence of other diseases.

synulosis (sin″u-lo′sis) [Gr. *synoulōsis*]. Complete cicatrization.

synulotic (sin″u-lot′ik) [Gr. *synoulōtikos*]. 1. Favoring cicatrization. 2. An agent that favors cicatrization.

Synura (sin-u′rah). A genus of flagellates which sometimes impart an unpleasant taste to drinking water.

synxenic (sin-zen′ik) [*syn-* + Gr. *xenos* a guest-friend, stranger]. Associated with a known number of microbic species; applied to laboratory animals whose microfauna and microflora are known (gnotobiotes).

Syphacia (si-fa′se-ah). A nematode parasite found in the intestines of rodents. **S. obvela′ta,** a common cecal parasite of laboratory rats that has been reported occasionally in man.

syphilid (sif′ĭ-lid). A general term for the cutaneous eruptions of syphilis. **acneiform s.,** pustular s. **acuminate papular s.,** follicular s. **annular s.,** a syphilitic eruption in ring-shaped patches. **bullous s.,** a syphilitic eruption in the form of enlarged pustules. **corymbose s.,** a form of syphilid consisting of large papules, each surrounded by a circle of small papules. **ecthymatous s.,** pustular s. **erythematous s.,** syphilitic roseola; an eruption of reddish macules in the secondary stage. Called also *macular s.* **flat papular s.,** lenticular s. **follicular s.,** a papular syphilid of the hair follicles. Called also *miliary syphilid* and *syphilitic lichen.* **frambesioid s.,** vegetating s. **gummatous s.,** a gumma. **herpetiform s.,** vesicular syphilid in which the lesions are massed in irregular serpiginous forms. **impetiginous s.,** a syphilid consisting of small pustules covered by yellowish or brownish crusts on the scalp. Called also *syphilitic impetigo.* **lenticular s.,** a secondary eruption with condylomas, or moist, flat papules. **miliary s.,** follicular s. **nodular s.,** tuberculous syphiloderm. **nummular s.,** papulosquamous

s. **palmar s.**, a syphilid on the hands. **papular s.**, lichen syphiliticus. **papulosquamous s.**, a cutaneous manifestation of tertiary syphilis consisting of scaly papules. **pemphigoid s.**, syphilitic pemphigus. **pigmentary s.**, syphilitic leukoderma. **plantar s.**, a syphilid on the sole of the foot. **pustular s.**, an ulcerating syphilid, usually resulting in a pigmented scar or depression. **rupial s.**, syphilitic rupia. **secondary s.**, any syphilid peculiar to the secondary stage of syphilis. **serpiginous s.**, a syphilid which spreads on one side while healing on the other. **tertiary s.**, a syphilid occurring in the tertiary stage of syphilis. **varicelliform s.**, a variety of vesicular syphilid in which the vesicles are situated on a raised surface, of a dull-red color, contain a cloudy fluid, and dry into thick greenish crusts. **varioliform s.**, pustular syphilid. **vegetating s.**, a syphilid in the form of warty growths. **vesicular s.**, a cutaneous manifestation of secondary syphilid consisting of vesicles.

syphilide (sif'ĭ-lid), pl. *syphil'ides* [Fr.]. Syphilid.

syphilidography (sif″ĭ-lĭ-dog'rah-fe). Syphilography.

syphilidologist (sif″ĭ-lĭ-dol'o-jist). Syphilologist.

syphilimetry (sif″ĭ-lim'e-tre) [*syphilis* + Gr. *metron* measure]. 1. The measurement of the intensity of the syphilitic infection at a given time. 2. See *Vernes' test*, def. 1, under *tests*.

syphilin (sif'ĭ-lin). 1. The contagious principle of syphilis. 2. Syphiline.

syphiline (sif'ĭ-lin). A concentrated glycerinated extract of the liver of a syphilitic fetus, used in testing for syphilis.

syphilionthus (sif″ĭ-le-on'thus) [*syphilis* + Gr. *ionthos* eruption]. Any copper-colored, scaly syphilid.

syphiliphobia (sif″ĭ-lĭ-fo'be-ah). Syphilophobia.

syphilis (sif'ĭ-lis) [*Syphilus*, the name of a shepherd infected with the disease in the poem of Fracastorius (1530), in which the term first appears. Derived perhaps from Gr. *syn* together + *philein* to love, or from Gr. *siphlos* crippled, maimed]. A contagious venereal disease leading to many structural and cutaneous lesions, due to a microorganism, the *Treponema pallidum* and transmitted usually by direct contact. Its primary local seat is a hard or true chancre, whence it extends by means of the lymphatics to the skin, mucosa, and to nearly all the tissues of the body, even to the bones and periosteum. **acquired s.**, syphilis resulting from contact, usually coitus. **congenital s.**, syphilis existing at birth; characterized by coryza, cutaneous eruptions, wasting of the tissues, parenchymatous keratitis, malformed teeth, and craniotabes. **constitutional s.**, syphilis after it has ceased to be a mere local manifestation, and has more or less completely affected the whole organism. **s. d'emblée** (dah-bla'), syphilis which develops without the formation of an initial sore. **equine s.**, dourine. **s. heredita'ria tar'da**, congenital syphilis that manifests itself some time after birth. **horse s.**, dourine. **s. innocen'tum, s. inson'tium**, syphilis not acquired by coitus. **late s.**, the last stage of untreated syphilis. **latent s.**, syphilis in the stage following primary and secondary stages, when no signs or symptoms are present. **primary s.**, syphilis in its first stage; the primary lesion (*chancre*) usually appears between ten and forty days after infection, and is painless; the nearby lymph nodes become hard and swollen, are painless, do not ulcerate, and slowly return to their normal condition. **quaternary s.**, parasyphilis. **rabbit s.**, a naturally occurring disease in rabbits caused by *Treponema cuniculi*. **secondary s.**, syphilis in the second of its three stages: it begins after six weeks and usually within three months. It is attended with fever, copper-hued and multiform skin eruptions, with no itching, iritis, alopecia, mucous patches, and severe pains in the head, joints, and periosteum. **tertiary s.**, the stage characterized by a set of peculiar skin affections, including rupia, gumma, syphilitic pemphigus and ecthyma. Bone lesions are often present, and the internal viscera may become extensively diseased.

syphilitic (sif″ĭ-lit'ik) [L. *syphiliticus*]. Affected with, caused by, or pertaining to syphilis.

syphiloderm (sif'ĭ-lo-derm″) [*syphilis* + Gr. *derma* skin]. Any syphilitic affection of the skin.

syphiloderma (sif″ĭ-lo-der'mah). Syphiloderm.

syphilodermatous (sif″ĭ-lo-der'mah-tus). Of or relating to a syphilid.

syphilogenesis (sif″ĭ-lo-jen'e-sis). The development of syphilis.

syphilogenous (sif″ĭ-loj'e-nus). Causing or producing syphilis.

syphilographer (sif″ĭ-log'rah-fer). A writer on the subject of syphilis.

syphilography (sif″ĭ-log'rah-fe) [*syphilis* + Gr. *graphein* to write]. 1. A treatise upon or description of syphilis. 2. The bibliography of syphilis.

syphiloid (sif'ĭ-loid). 1. Resembling syphilis. 2. Any disease resembling syphilis occurring as an epidemic at various times in certain countries.

syphilologist (sif″ĭ-lol'o-jist). An expert in the theory or treatment of syphilis.

syphilology (sif″ĭ-lol'o-je). The sum of what is known regarding syphilis.

syphiloma (sif″ĭ-lo'mah). A tumor of syphilitic origin; a gumma.

syphilomania (sif″ĭ-lo-ma'ne-ah) [*syphilis* + Gr. *mania* madness]. Syphilophobia.

syphilopathy (sif″ĭ-lop'ah-the) [*syphilis* + Gr. *pathos* disease]. Any syphilitic manifestation.

syphilophobia (sif″ĭ-lo-fo'be-ah) [*syphilis* + Gr. *phobein* to be affrighted by]. 1. Morbid fear of syphilis. 2. The delusion of being infected with syphilis.

syphilophobic (sif″i-lo-fo'bik). Pertaining to or characterized by syphilophobia.

syphilophyma (sif″ĭ-lo-fi'mah) [*syphilis* + Gr. *phyma* growth]. Any syphilitic growth or excrescence.

syphilopsychosis (sif″ĭ-lo-si-ko'sis). Any syphilitic mental disease.

syphilosis (sif″ĭ-lo'sis). Generalized syphilitic disease.

syphilotherapy (sif″ĭ-lo-ther'ah-pe). The treatment of syphilis.

syphilous (sif'ĭ-lus). Syphilitic.

syphionthus (sif″e-on'thus). Syphilionthus.

syphitoxin (sif″ĭ-tok'sin) [*syphilitis* + *toxin*]. An antisyphilitic serum.

syphonoma (si″fo-no'mah). Cylindroma.

Syr. Abbreviation for L. *syrupus*, syrup.

syrigmophonia (sir″ig-mo-fo'ne-ah) [Gr. *syrigmos* a shrill piping sound + *phōnē* voice + *-ia*]. A high, whistling sound of the voice.

syrigmus (sĭ-rig'mus) [Gr. *syrigmos* a shrill piping sound]. A ringing in the ears.

syringadenoma (sĭ-ring″ad-e-no'mah). Adenoma of the ducts of the sweat glands.

syringadenous (sĭ-ring-ad'e-nus) [Gr. *syrinx* pipe or tube + *adēn* gland]. Pertaining to the sweat glands.

syringe (sir'inj) [L. *syrinxe;* Gr. *syrinx*]. An instrument for injecting liquids into any vessel or cavity. **Anel's s.**, a delicate syringe for the treatment of the lacrimal passages. **chip s.**, a small, fine-nozzled syringe used to direct a current of air into a tooth cavity being excavated, to remove the small fragments detached from the tooth. **dental s.**, a small syringe for use in operative dentistry. **fountain s.**, an apparatus which injects a liquid by the action of gravity. **Higginson's s.**, a form of rectal enema syringe. **hypodermic s.**, one by means of which liquids are injected through a hollow needle into the subcutaneous tissues. **Luer's s., Luer-Lok s.**, a glass syringe for intravenous and hypodermic use. **Neisser's s.**, a urethral syringe for use in gonorrhea. **Pravaz's**

s., a hypodermic needle fitted to a long, slender cannula and trocar. **probe s.**, a syringe whose point may be used also as a probe: used mostly in treating the lacrimal passages. **tooth s.**, dental s.

syringectomy (sir″in-jek′to-me) [*syringo-* + Gr. *ektomē* excision]. The excision of the walls of a fistula.

syringin (si-rin′jin). A white, crystalline glycoside, $C_{17}H_{24}O_9$, soluble in hot water and in hot alcohol, from the bark of lilac, *Syringa vulgaris:* antiperiodic.

syringitis (sir″in-ji′tis). Inflammation of the eustachian tube.

syringo- (si-ring′go) [Gr. *syrinx* pipe, tube, fistula]. Combining form denoting relationship to a tube or a fistula.

syringobulbia (si-ring″go-bul′be-ah) [*syringo-* + Gr. *bolbos* bulb + *-ia*]. The presence of cavities in the medulla oblongata.

syringocele (si-ring′go-sēl). A cavity-containing herniation of the spinal cord through the bony defect in spina bifida.

syringocoele (si-ring′go-sēl) [*syringo-* + Gr. *koilia* hollow]. The central canal of the spinal cord (canalis centralis medullae spinalis [N A]).

syringocystadenoma (si-ring″go-sis″tad-e-no′-mah) [*syringo-* + *cystadenoma*]. Adenoma of the sweat glands; a skin disease marked by an eruption of small, hard papules: called also *hidradenoma* and *adenoma hidradenoides.*

syringocystoma (si-ring″go-sis-to′mah) [*syringo-* + Gr. *kystis* cyst + *-oma*]. A cystic tumor of the sweat glands.

syringo-encephalia (si-ring″go-en″se-fa′le-ah) [*syringo-* + Gr. *enkephalos* brain + *-ia*]. The formation of abnormal cavities in the brain substance.

syringo-encephalomyelia (si-ring″go-en-sef″-ah-lo-mi-e′le-ah) [*syringo-* + Gr. *enkephalos* brain + *myelos* marrow + *-ia*]. The existence of cavities in the substance of the brain and spinal cord.

syringoid (si-ring′goid) [L. *syringoides,* from Gr. *syrinx* pipe + *eidos* form]. Resembling a pipe or tube; fistulous.

syringoma (sir″ing-go′mah). Adenoma of sweat glands.

syringomeningocele (si-ring″go-me-nin′go-sēl) [*syringo-* + Gr. *mēninx* membrane + *kēlē* tumor]. A meningocele resembling a syringomyelocele.

syringomyelia (si-ring″go-mi-e′le-ah) [*syringo-* + Gr. *myelos* marrow + *-ia*]. A condition marked by abnormal cavities filled with liquid in the substance of the spinal cord. **s. atroph′ica,** cavitary myelitis.

syringomyelitis (si-ring″go-mi″ĕ-li′tis). Inflammation of the spinal cord, with the formation of cavities in its substance.

syringomyelocele (si-ring″go-mi′ĕ-lo-sēl) [*syringo-* + Gr. *myelos* marrow + *kēlē* tumor]. Hernial protrusion of the spinal cord through the bony defect in spina bifida, the mass containing a cavity connected with the central canal of the spinal cord.

syringomyelus (si-ring″go-mi′ĕ-lus). Dilatation of the central canal of the spinal cord, the gray matter being converted into connective tissue.

syringopontia (si-ring″go-pon′she-ah). A condition in which cavities exist in the pons.

Syringospora (si″ring-gos′po-rah). Former name of a genus of fungi now called *Candida.*

syringosystrophy (si-ring″go-sis′tro-fe) [*syringo-* + Gr. *systrophē* a twist]. Torsion of the oviduct.

syringotome (si-ring′go-tōm). A knife for cutting a fistula.

syringotomy (sir″in-got′o-me) [*syringo-* + Gr. *tomē* a cutting]. The operation of incising a fistula, particularly an anal fistula.

syrinx (sir′inks) [Gr. "a pipe"]. 1. A tube or pipe; also a fistula. 2. The lower or posterior larynx of birds, being that one of the two larynges of birds in which the voice is produced.

syrosingopine (si″ro-sing′go-pīn). Chemical name: carbethoxysyringoyl methylreserpate: used as an antihypertensive agent.

syrup (sir′up) [L. *syrupus;* Arabic *sharāb*]. A concentrated solution of a sugar, such as sucrose, in water or other aqueous liquid, sometimes with some medicinal substance added. Such preparations are usually used as flavored vehicles for other drugs. **acacia s.**, a preparation of powdered acacia, sodium benzoate, vanilla tincture, sucrose, and water: used as a flavored vehicle for drugs. **bromides s.**, a preparation containing potassium, sodium, ammonium, calcium, and lithium bromides: used as a central nervous system depressant. **cacao s.**, a preparation of cacao, sucrose, liquid glucose, glycerin, and other ingredients: used as a flavored vehicle in compounding prescriptions. **cherry s.**, a mixture of cherry juice, sucrose, alcohol, and purified water: used as a flavored vehicle for drugs. **chlorpheniramine maleate s.**, a liquid preparation containing between 45 and 55 mg. of chlorpheniramine maleate per 100 ml., and 6 to 8 per cent of alcohol: used as an antihistaminic. **chlorpromazine hydrochloride s.**, a liquid preparation containing between 190 and 210 mg. of chlorpromazine hydrochloride per 100 ml.: used as a tranquilizer. **citric acid s.**, a preparation of lemon tincture, hydrous citric acid, and purified water, in syrup: used as a flavored vehicle for drugs. **cocoa s.**, cacao s. **dextromethorphan hydrobromide s.**, a liquid preparation of dextromethorphan hydrobromide: used as an antitussive. **diethylcarbamazine citrate s.**, a syrup containing between 2.28 and 2.52 Gm. of diethylcarbamazine citrate per 100 ml.: used as an antifilarial. **dihydrocodeinone bitartrate s.**, a solution of dihydrocodeinone bitartrate in purified water and cherry syrup: used as an antitussive. **dimenhydrinate s.**, a liquid preparation of dimenhydrinate, containing between 295 and 330 mg. of dimenhydrinate in each 100 ml.: used as an antihistaminic and antinauseant. **ephedrine sulfate s.**, a solution of ephedrine sulfate, citric acid, amaranth solution, caramel, lemon oil, orange oil, benzaldehyde, vanillin, alcohol, and sucrose, in purified water: used as a sympathomimetic. **eriodictyon s., aromatic,** a solution of eriodictyon fluidextract, potassium hydroxide solution, compound cardamom tincture, sassafras oil, lemon oil, clove oil, alcohol, sucrose, and magnesium carbonate, in purified water: used as a vehicle for drugs. **ferrous iodide s.**, a solution of iron, iodine, hypophosphorous acid, and sucrose, in purified water: used as a hematinic. **ferrous sulfate s.**, a mixture of ferrous sulfate, hydrous citric acid, peppermint spirit, sucrose, and purified water, each 100 ml. of which contains 3.75–4.25 Gm. of ferrous sulfate. **glycyrrhiza s.**, a mixture of glycyrrhiza fluidextract, fennel and anise oil, and syrup: used as a flavored vehicle in compounding prescriptions. **hydriodic acid s.**, a solution of diluted hydriodic acid and sucrose in purified water, each 100 ml. of which contains 1.3–1.5 Gm. of HI: used as an expectorant. **ipecac s.**, a mixture of ipecac fluidextract, glycerin, and syrup: used as an expectorant and emetic. **licorice s.**, glycyrrhiza s. **medicated s.**, one to which a medicinal substance has been added. **orange s.**, a preparation of sweet orange peel tincture, citric acid, talc, and sucrose, in purified water: used as a flavored vehicle for pharmaceuticals. **phenindamine tartrate s.**, a syrup containing between 190 and 220 mg. of phenindamine tartrate in each 100 ml.: used as an antihistaminic. **piperazine citrate s.**, a syrup containing between 10 and 12 Gm. of anhydrous piperazine citrate in each 100 ml.: used as an anthelmintic. **prochlorperazine ethanedisulfanate s.**, a syrup containing, in each 100 ml., an amount of prochlorperazine ethanedisulfanate equivalent to 95–105 mg. of prochlorperazine: used as an antiemetic and tranquilizer. **promethazine hydrochloride s.**, a syrup containing, in each 100 ml., between 112 and 138 mg. of promethazine hydrochloride: used as an antihistaminic. **raspberry s.**, a syrup consisting of raspberry juice, sucrose, and alcohol, in purified water: used as a flavored vehicle for drugs. **sarsaparilla s., compound**, a solution of sarsaparilla and glycyrrhiza fluidextracts, sassafras and anise oils, methyl salicylate, alcohol, and syrup: used as a vehicle for drugs. **senna s.**, a solution of senna fluidextract, coriander oil, sucrose, and purified water: used as a cathartic. **simple s.**, one compounded from purified water and sucrose. **s. of tolu**, tolu balsam s. **tolu balsam s.**, a mixture of tolu balsam tincture, magnesium carbonate, sucrose, and purified water: used as a flavored vehicle for drugs. **white pine s., compound**, a solution containing coarsely powdered white pine, wild cherry, aralia, poplar bud, sanguinaria, and sassafras, combined with amaranth solution, chloroform, sucrose, glycerin, alcohol, and water: used as an antitussive and as a vehicle for other drugs. **white pine s., compound, with codeine**, compound white pine syrup combined with codeine phosphate dissolved in purified water: used as an antitussive. **wild cherry s.**, a mixture of a percolate of wild cherry, glycerin, sucrose, alcohol, and water: used as a flavored vehicle. **Yerba santa s., aromatic**, aromatic eriodictyon s.

syrupus (sĭ-ru′pus) [L.]. Syrup. **s. auran′tii**, orange syrup. **s. cera′si**, cherry syrup. **s. cor′rigens**, aromatic eriodictyon syrup. **s. pi′ni al′bae compos′itus**, compound white pine syrup. **s. pi′ni al′bae compos′itus cum co′deina**, compound white pine syrup with codeine. **s. pru′ni virginia′nae**, wild cherry syrup. **s. ru′bi i′daei**, raspberry syrup. **s. sarsaparil′lae compos′itus**, compound sarsaparilla syrup.

syssarcosic (sis″sar-ko′sik). Syssarcotic.

syssarcosis (sis″sar-ko′sis) [Gr. *syn* together + *sarkōsis* fleshy growth]. The union or connection of bones by means of muscle. An example is the connection between the hyoid bone and the lower jaw, the scapula, and the breast bone.

syssarcotic (sis″sar-kot′ik). Pertaining to or of the nature of a syssarcosis.

syssomus (sis-so′mus) [Gr. *syn* with + *sōma* body]. A double fetal monster with two heads and with the bodies united.

systaltic (sis-tal′tik) [Gr. *systaltikos* drawing together]. Alternately contracting and expanding.

systatic (sis-tat′ik). Affecting several of the sensory faculties at the same time.

system (sis′tem) [Gr. *systēma* a complex or organized whole]. 1. A set or series of interconnected or interdependent parts or entities (objects, organs, or organisms) which function together in a common purpose or produce results impossible of achievement by one of them acting or operating alone. 2. A school or method of practice based on a specific set of principles, as the eclectic or galenic school. **absorbent s.**, systema lymphaticum. **accessory portal s. of Sappey**, small compensatory blood vessels formed around the liver and gallbladder in cases of cirrhosis of the liver. **adipose s.**, the fatty tissue of the body, considered collectively. **alimentary s.**, the organs concerned with the conversion and absorption of nutritional elements in the body. See *apparatus digestorius.* **association s.**, the tracts of fibers in the brain by means of which perceptions are associated and thought rendered possible. **autonomic nervous s.**, the portion of the nervous system concerned with regulation of the activity of cardiac muscle, smooth muscle, and glands. See *systema nervosum autonomicum* [N A]. **Bertillon s.**, a system of identification of individuals, based on description of physical characteristics, including such data as eye and hair color, blemishes or scars, and various measurements of the body. **biological s.**, a system composed of living material; such systems range from a collection of separate molecules to an assemblage of separate organisms. **blood-vascular s.**, the blood vessels of the body. **Borstal s.**, a system of treating criminals, especially juvenile ones, by removing them from evil environment and placing them under wholesome influences. **brunonian s.**, brunonianism. **bulbospiral s.**, muscle bundles in the heart which arise in and are attached to the conus arteriosus and the root of the aorta. **case s.**, a method of teaching based on the logical analysis of, and deductions formed from, reported cases of disease. **centimeter-gram-second s.** See *C.G.S.* **central nervous s.**, that portion of the nervous system consisting of the brain and spinal cord (systema nervosum centrale [N A]). **centrencephalic s.**, the system of neurons located in the central core of the upper brain stem from the thalamus down to the medulla oblongata, and connecting the two hemispheres of the brain. **cerebellorubral s.**, motor fibers joining the dentate nucleus of the cerebellum with the red nucleus of the opposite side. **cerebellorubrospinal s.**, the cerebellorubral and rubrospinal systems considered together. **cerebrospinal s.**, the brain and spinal cord (systema nervosum centrale [N A]). **chromaffin s.**, the cells of the body which characteristically stain strongly with chromium salts, considered collectively; they occur along the sympathetic nerves, in the adrenal, carotid, and coccygeal glands, and in various other organs. **circulatory s.**, the channels through which the nutrient fluids of the body circulate; often restricted to the vessels conveying blood. **dentinal s.**, all the tubules radiating from a single pulp cavity. **dermal s., dermoid s.**, the skin and its appendages, including both the hair and the nails (integumentum commune [N A]). **digestive s.**, the organs associated with the ingestion and digestion of food. See *apparatus digestorius* [N A]. **dioptric s.**, a system of lenses or of different media for refracting light. **disperse s., dispersion s.**, a colloid solution. **dosimetric s.**, a regular and determinate system of administration of a therapeutic agent. **ecological s.** See *ecosystem.* **endocrine s.**, the system of glands which elaborate internal secretions, including the pituitary, parathyroid, thyroid, and suprarenal glands (glandulae sine ductibus [N A]). **endothelial s.** See *reticuloendothelial s.* **esthesiodic s.**, the afferent elements of the spinal cord, concerned in the transmission of sensory impulses. **exteroceptive nervous s.**, that portion of the afferent elements of the somatic nervous system which is sensitive to stimuli originating outside the body. **exterofective s.**, the central nervous system as helping to maintain homeostasis from without. **genitourinary s.**, the organs of reproduction, together with the organs concerned in the production and excretion of urine (apparatus urogenitalis or systema urogenitale [N A]). **glandular s.**, the glandular tissue of the body considered collectively. **Grancher s.**, the early removal of young children from contact with patients with tuberculosis, to save them from infection. **haversian s.**, a haversian canal and its concentrically arranged lamellae, constituting the basic unit of structure of compact bone. See *osteon.* **hematopoietic s.**, the tissues concerned in production of the blood, including bone marrow and lymphatic tissue. **heterogeneous s.**, a system or structure made up of mechanically separable parts, as an emulsion. **homogeneous s.**, a system or structure made up of parts which cannot be mechanically separated, as a solution. **hormonopoietic s.**, the tissues concerned in the production of hormones, considered collectively (endocrine s.). **interoceptive nervous s.**, the afferent portion of the visceral nervous system, transmitting impulses arising in the various viscera. **interofective s.**, the autonomic nervous system as the guardian and keeper of homeostasis from within. **interrenal s.**, cortex glandulae suprarenalis. **involuntary nervous s.**, Gas-

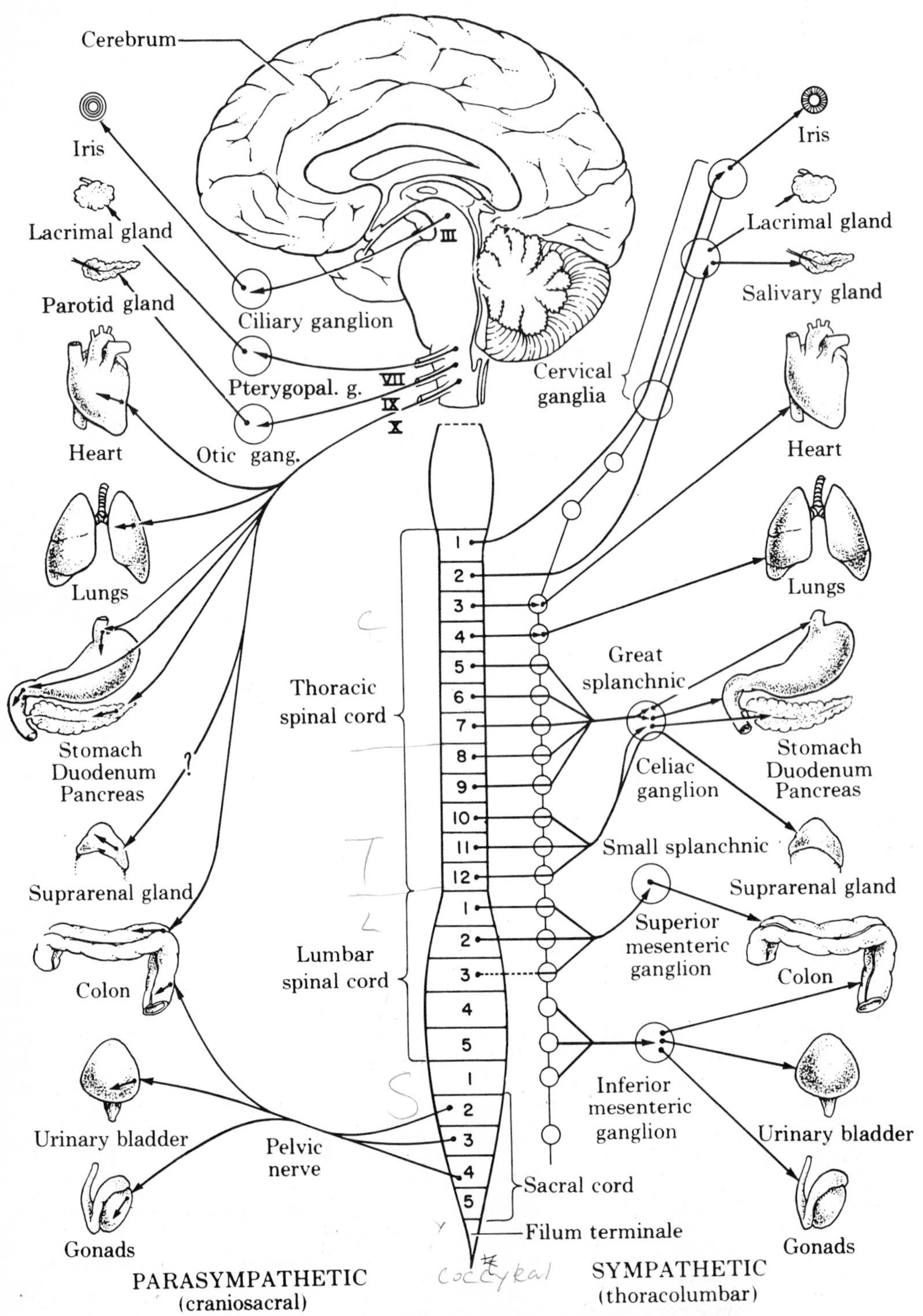

THE AUTONOMIC NERVOUS SYSTEM

(Villee)

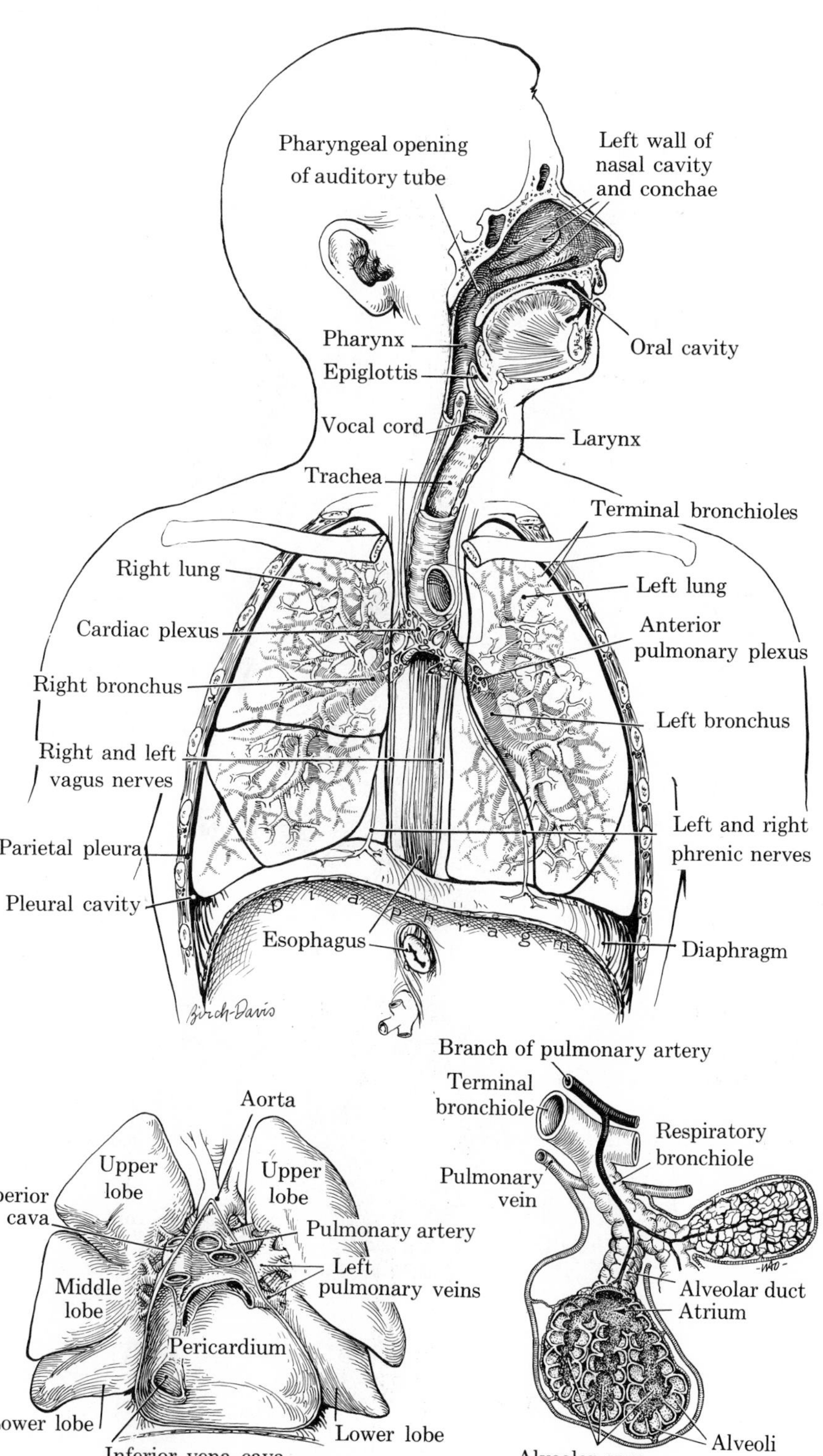

ORGANS OF THE RESPIRATORY SYSTEM

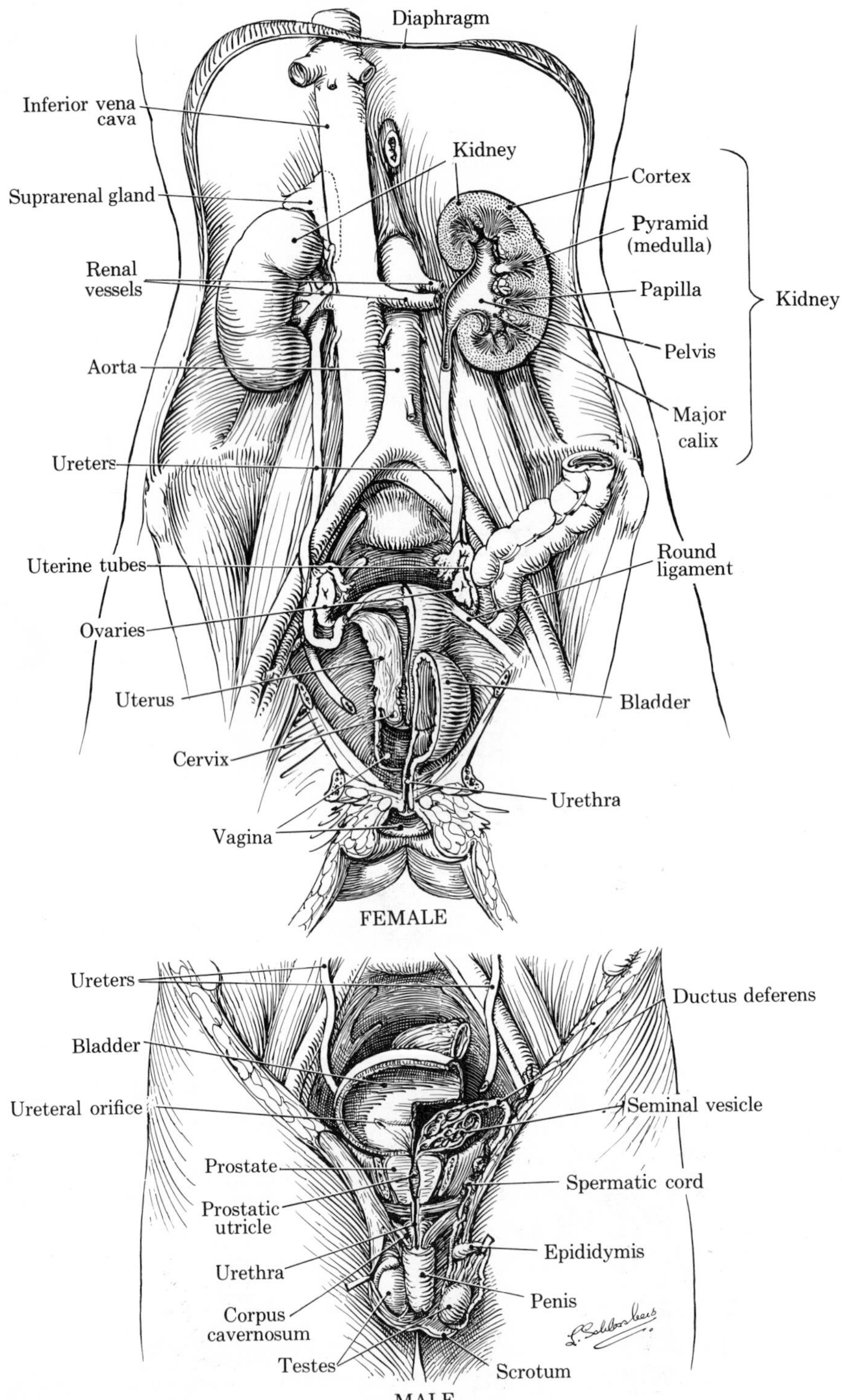

ORGANS OF THE UROGENITAL SYSTEM

kill's name for the autonomic nervous system (systema nervosum autonomicum [N A]). **kinesiodic s.,** the efferent elements of the spinal cord, concerned in the transmission of motor impulses. **kinetic s.** 1. Crile's term for the system of organs through which latent energy is converted into heat and motion, including the brain, thyroid, liver, adrenals, pancreas, and muscles. 2. Hunt's term for the motion systems of the efferent nervous system, which subserve the various reflex, automatic-associated, and isolated synergetic types of movement. Cf. *static s.* **labyrinthine s.,** those parts of the vestibulocochlear organ concerned with the maintenance of equilibrium. **lymphatic s.,** the lymphatic vessels and the lymphatic or lymphoid tissue, considered collectively (systema lymphaticum [N A]). **macrophage s.,** reticuloendothelial s. **masticatory s.,** the organs and structures which function primarily in mastication, including the jaws, the teeth with their supporting structures, the temporomandibular articulation, mandibular musculature, tongue, lips, cheeks, and oral mucosa. **meter-kilogram-second s.** See *M.K.S.* **metric s.,** a decimal system of weights and measures based on the meter. **muscular s.,** all the muscles of the body considered collectively. **neokinetic s.,** that part of the nervous motor mechanism that is concerned with voluntary muscular movements. See *neokinetic.* **nervous s.,** the chief organ system which correlates the adjustments and reactions of an organism to internal and environmental conditions. Called also *systema nervosum* [N A]. It comprises the central and peripheral nervous systems: the former is composed of the brain and spinal cord, and the latter includes all the other neural elements. See also *autonomic nervous s., parasympathetic nervous s.,* and *sympathetic nervous s.* **paleokinetic s.,** that part of the nervous motor mechanism that is concerned with automatic associated movements. See *paleokinetic.* **pallidal s.,** an efferent motor system of the corpus striatum, originating in the globus pallidus cells of the caudate and lenticular nuclei, the axons of which traverse the ansa lenticularis to the hypothalamic region. **parasympathetic nervous s.,** the craniosacral portion of the autonomic nervous system (pars parasympathica systematis nervosi autonomici [N A]). **pedal s.,** the pyramidal tract, or caudate nucleus, and the anterior and posterior caudate fibers. **peripheral nervous s.,** that portion of the nervous system consisting of the nerves and ganglia outside the brain and spinal cord (systema nervosum periphericum [N A]). **Pinel's s.,** a method of management of the emotionally and mentally disturbed without the use of forcible restraint. **plenum s.,** a system of ventilation based on the mechanical propulsion of air into the room. **portal s.,** an arrangement of vessels whereby blood collected from one set of capillaries passes through a large vessel or vessels and then through a second set of capillaries before it returns to the systemic circulation; such an arrangement occurs in the hypophysis and the liver. **posture s.,** static s. **pressoreceptor s.,** the portion of the autonomic nervous system sensitive to stimulation by changes in pressure. **projection s.,** tracts of nerve fibers in the brain by means of which external objects are brought into consciousness. **proprioceptive nervous s.,** that portion of the afferent elements of the somatic nervous system which is sensitive to stimuli originating inside the body (from muscles, bones, joints, and ligaments). **respiratory s.,** the tubular and cavernous organs that allow the atmospheric air to reach the circulatory system. See *apparatus respiratorius* [N A]. **reticuloendothelial s.,** the cells of the body having both endothelial and reticular attributes and showing a common phagocytic behavior toward dyestuffs, including cells of the spleen and lymph nodes, Kupffer cells of the liver, the reticuloendothelium of bone marrow, and the clasmatocytes; this system is concerned in blood cell formation and destruction, storage of fatty materials, and the metabolism of iron and pigment, and plays a defensive role in inflammation and immunity. **rubrospinal s.,** the red nucleus and fibers connecting it with the opposite side of the spinal cord. **sinospiral s.,** muscle bundles in the heart which arise from and are inserted into the region of the primitive venous sinus. **somatic nervous s.,** the elements of the nervous system concerned with the transmission of impulses to and from the nonvisceral components of the body, such as the skeletal muscles, bones, joints, ligaments, skin, and eye and ear. **static s.,** Hunt's term for the motion systems of the efferent nervous system which subserve static or postural functions, viz., tonus, posture, attitude, and equilibrium. Cf. *kinetic s.,* def. 2. Called also *posture s.* **stomatognathic s.,** the structures of the mouth and jaws, considered collectively, as they subserve the functions of mastication, deglutition, respiration, and speech. **sympathetic nervous s.** 1. The thoracolumbar portion of the autonomic nervous system (pars sympathica systematis nervosi autonomici [N A]). 2. The autonomic nervous system (formerly called *systema nervorum sympathica* in B N A). **urogenital s.,** the organs concerned in the production and excretion of urine, together with the organs of reproduction (apparatus urogenitalis or systema urogenitale [N A]). **uropoietic s.,** the organs concerned in secretion of urine (organa uropoietica). **vascular s.,** the vessels of the body, especially the blood vessels. **vasomotor s.,** the part of the nervous system that controls the caliber of the blood vessels. **vegetative nervous s.,** Meyer and Gottlieb's name for the autonomic nervous system (systema nervosum autonomicum [N A]). **vestibular s.,** labyrinthine s. **visceral nervous s.,** the elements of the nervous system concerned with the transmission of impulses from the viscera and to involuntary muscle and glands.

systema (sis-te′mah) [Gr. *systēma* a complex or organized whole]. A series of interconnected or interdependent organs which together accomplish a specific function. Called also *system.* **s. digesto′rium,** N A alternative for *apparatus digestorius.* **s. lymphat′icum** [N A, B N A], the lymphatic vessels and the lymphatic or lymphoid tissue, considered collectively. Called also *lymphatic system.* **s. nervo′rum centra′le** [B N A], s. nervosum centrale. **s. nervo′rum peripher′icum** [B N A], s. nervosum periphericum. **s. nervo′rum sympath′icum** [B N A], s. nervosum autonomicum. **s. nervo′sum** [N A], the chief organ system that correlates the adjustments and reactions of the organism to internal and environmental conditions, composed of the central and the peripheral nervous system; the former comprises the brain and spinal cord, and the latter includes all other neural elements. Called also *nervous system.* **s. nervo′sum autonom′icum** [N A], the portion of the nervous system concerned with regulation of activity of cardiac muscle, smooth muscle, and glands; usually restricted to the two visceral efferent systems, the pars sympathica systematis nervosi autonomici (thoracolumbar part) and the pars parasympathica systematis nervosi autonomici (craniosacral part). Called also *s. nervorum sympathicum* [B N A], and *autonomic nervous system.* **s. nervo′sum centra′le** [N A], that portion of the nervous system consisting of the brain and spinal cord. Called also *s. nervorum centrale* [B N A], and *central nervous system.* **s. nervo′sum peripher′icum** [N A], that portion of the nervous system consisting of the nerves and ganglia outside the brain and spinal cord. Called also *s. nervorum periphericum* [B N A], and *peripheral nervous system.* **s. respirato′rium,** N A alternative for *apparatus respiratorius.* **s. urogenita′le,** N A alternative for *apparatus urogenitalis.* **s. vaso′rum,** the blood and lymph vessels of the body and all their ramifications, considered collectively.

systematic (sis″te-mat′ik) [Gr. *systēmatikos*]. Pertaining or according to a system.

systematization (sis-tem″ah-ti-za′shun). Arrangement according to a system. In psychiatry, the arrangement of ideas into a logical sequence, or of delusions into a superficially coherent system.

systematized (sis′te-mah-tizd). Made systematic or arranged according to a system.

systematology (sis″tĕ-mah-tol′o-je) [Gr. *systēma* system + *-logy*]. The doctrine or bibliography of systematic arrangements.

systemic (sis-tem′ik). 1. Pertaining to or affecting the body as a whole. 2. Systematic.

systemoid (sis′tĕ-moid) [Gr. *systēma* system + *eidos* form]. 1. Resembling a system. 2. Noting tumors made up of various kinds of tissue.

systogene (sis′to-jēn). Tyramine.

systole (sis′to-le) [Gr. *systolē* a drawing together, contraction]. The contraction, or period of contraction, of the heart, especially that of the ventricles. It coincides with the interval between the first and the second heart sound, during which the blood is forced into the aorta and the pulmonary trunk. **aborted s.,** a systole not reflected by pulsation of a peripheral artery on account of mitral regurgitation. **anticipated s.,** a ventricular systole which occurs before the ventricle is filled. **arterial s.,** the rhythmic contraction of an artery. **atrial s., auricular s.,** the contraction of the atria by which the blood is forced from them into the ventricles: it precedes the true or ventricular systole. **catalectic s.,** an aborted or imperfect systole. **extra s.,** a premature contraction of an atrium or ventricle, or of both, while the fundamental rhythm is maintained at the sinus. **hemic s.,** an independently occurring systole of a ventricle. **ventricular s.,** the contraction of the ventricles of the heart by which the blood is forced into the aorta and the pulmonary trunk.

systolic (sis-tol′ik). Pertaining to or produced by the systole; occurring along with the ventricular systole.

systolometer (sis″to-lom′e-ter) [Gr. *systolē* systole + *metron* measure]. An instrument for determining the quality of the heart sounds.

systremma (sis-trem′ah) [Gr. "anything twisted up together"]. A cramp in the muscles of the calf of the leg.

sytobex (si′to-beks). Trade mark for a parenteral preparation of crystalline vitamin B_{12}. See *cyanocobalamin.*

syzygial (sĭ-zij′e-al). Pertaining to syzygy.

syzygiology (sĭ-zij″e-ol′o-je). The study of the relationship of the whole as contrasted to that of isolated parts and functions.

Syzygium (sĭ-zij′e-um). A genus of tropical myrtaceous trees. *S. jambolanum,* the jambul tree of India, is astringent.

syzygium (sĭ-zij′e-um). Syzygy.

syzygy (siz′ĭ-je) [Gr. *syzygia* a union of branches with the trunk]. 1. The conjunction and fusion of organs without loss of identity. 2. An animal microorganism supposed to be formed by the fusion of several larval parasites.

Szabo's test (sah′bōz) [Dionys *Szabo,* Budapest physician, 1856–1918]. See under *tests.*

sze-giao-han (Chinese "four legs cold"]. Chinese name for a virus encephalitis of water buffaloes.

Szent-Györgyi reaction (sent-jor′jĭ) [Albert *Szent-Györgyi,* Hungarian biochemist in America, born 1893, noted for his isolation of ascorbic acid and research in muscle contraction; winner of the Nobel prize for medicine and physiology in 1937]. See under *reaction.*

T

T. Abbreviation for *temperature, thoracic* (in vertebral formulas), and intra-ocular *tension.* Normal intra-ocular tension is indicated by the symbol Tn, while T + 1, T + 2, etc., indicate stages of increased tension, and T − 1, T − 2, etc., indicate stages of decreased tension.

t. Abbreviation for *temporal.*

τ. Symbol for *life* (time).

$\tau_{\frac{1}{2}}$. Symbol for *half-life* (time).

T-1824. Evans blue.

TA. Abbreviation for *alkaline tuberculin.*

T. A. Abbreviation for *toxin-antitoxin.*

Ta. Chemical symbol for *tantalum.*

tabacin (tab′ah-sin). A glycoside occurring in tobacco.

tabacism (tab′ah-sizm). Tabacosis.

tabacosis (tab″ah-ko′sis). Poisoning by tobacco, and chiefly by the inhalation of tobacco dust; also a form of pneumoconiosis caused by tobacco dust **(t. pulmo′num).**

tabacum (tab′ah-kum) [L.]. Tobacco.

tabagism (tab′ah-jizm). The condition produced by excessive use of tobacco; nicotinism.

tabanid (tab′ah-nid). Any gadfly of the family Tabanidae, of which the genus *Tabanus* is the type. Other genera are *Chrysops, Goniops, Silvius, Haematopoda,* and *Diachlorus.* Many of the species inflict painful bites upon men and animals, and some species are mechanical vectors of diseases.

Tabanus (tah-ba′nus) [L. "gadfly"]. A genus of biting flies; the horse flies. They transmit trypanosomes and anthrax to the lower animals. **T. atra′tus,** the common black horse fly of North America. **T. bovi′nus,** the gadfly of cattle in Asia, Africa, and South America. **T. ditaenia′tus, T. fascia′tus, T. gra′tus,** the Seroot flies of the Sudan, which are very troublesome to man and beast.

Tabanus bovinus.

tabardillo (tab″ar-dēl′yo) [Sp.]. Murine typhus.

tabatière anatomique (tah-bah″te-ār′ ah-nah-to-mēk′) [Fr. "anatomical snuffbox"]. The hollow on the back of the hand and at the base of the thumb, between the tendons of the extensor pollicis longus and extensor pollicis brevis muscles.

tabefaction (tab″e-fak′shun). The wasting of the body; tabes.

tabella (tah-bel′ah), pl. *tabel′lae* [L.]. A medicated tablet or troche.

tabes (ta′bēz) [L. "wasting away, decay, melting"]. 1. Any wasting of the body; progressive atrophy of the body or a part of it. 2. Tabes dorsalis. **abortive t.,** rudimentary t. **cerebral t.,** dementia paralytica. **cervical t.,** tabes dorsalis in which the upper extremities are first affected. **diabetic t.,** a peripheral neuritis occurring in diabetic patients with symptoms of locomotor ataxia; called also *diabetic neurotabes.* **t. dorsa′lis,** a degeneration of the dorsal columns of the spinal cord and of the sensory nerve trunks, with wasting. The disease is marked by paroxysms or crises of intense pain, incoordination, disturbances of sensation, loss of reflexes, paroxysms of functional disturbance of various organs, as the stomach, larynx, etc.; also by various trophic disturbances, especially of the bones and joints, incontinence or retention of urine, failure of sexual power, etc. The course of the disease is usually slow but progressive, and, although it may often be temporarily arrested, complete cure is very rare. The disease occurs after middle life, and is more frequent in the male sex. It is also known as *syphilitic posterior spinal sclerosis*. **t. ergot′ica,** a condition resembling tabes dorsalis, due to ergotism. **Friedreich's t.,** Friedreich's ataxia. **hereditary t.,** hereditary ataxia. **t. infan′tum,** tabes as seen in infants with congenital syphilis. **t. infe′rior,** tabes dorsalis affecting the lower extremities. **interstitial t.,** tabes marked by a primary proliferation of the neuroglia, due to chronic thickening of the blood vessels of the posterior columns. **marantic t.,** tabes dorsalis marked by extreme emaciation. **t. mesenter′ica, t. mesara′ica,** tuberculosis of the mesenteric glands in children, resulting in digestive derangement and wasting of the body. **monosymptomatic t.,** tabes dorsalis exhibiting a single symptom. **nerve t.,** tabes resulting from parenchymatous degeneration of the posterior columns of the spinal cord. **peripheral t.,** pseudotabes. **rudimentary t.,** tabes dorsalis which shows only a few symptoms, the condition remaining stationary for a long time; called also *abortive t.* **spasmodic t.,** lateral sclerosis of the spinal cord. **t. spina′lis,** locomotor ataxia. **t. supe′rior,** cervical tabes. **vessel t.,** tabes due to an obliterative endarteritis occurring within a principal vessel supplying the posterior column of the spinal cord.

tabescent (tah-bes′ent) [L. *tabescere* to waste away]. Wasting away; shriveling.

tabetic (tah-bet′ik). Pertaining to or affected with tabes.

tabetiform (tah-bet′ĭ-form). Resembling tabes.

tabic (tab′ik). Tabetic.

tabid (tab′id) [L. *tabidus* melting, dissolving]. Tabetic; wasting away.

tabification (tab″ĭ-fi-ka′shun) [L. *tabes* wasting away + *facere* to make]. The process of wasting away.

tablature (tab′lah-tūr). The separation of the chief cranial bones into inner and outer tables, which are separated by a diploe.

table (ta′b′l) [L. *tabula*]. A flat layer or surface. **inner t. of bones of skull,** lamina interna ossium cranii. **inner t. of frontal bone,** facies interna ossis frontalis. **outer t. of bones of skull,** lamina externa ossium cranii. **outer t. of frontal bone,** facies externa ossis frontalis. **vitreous t.,** lamina interna ossium cranii. **water t.,** the upper surface of the impervious strata on which the ground water lies deep to the surface of the earth.

tablespoon (ta′b′l-spo͞on). A household unit of capacity, approximately equivalent to 4 fluid drams, or 15 milliliters.

tablet (tab′let). A solid dosage form of varying weight, size, and shape, which may be molded or compressed, and which contains a medicinal substance in pure or diluted form. **buccal t.,** a small flat, oval tablet to be held between the cheek and gum, permitting direct absorption through the oral mucosa of the medicinal substance contained therein. **dispensing t.,** a compressed or molded tablet containing a large quantity of a drug, used by dispensing pharmacists in compounding prescriptions. **hypodermic t.,** one to be dissolved in water, containing a medicinal substance for hypodermic injection. **sublingual t.,** a small flat, oval tablet to be held beneath the tongue, permitting direct absorption of the medicinal substance contained therein. **t. triturate,** a small, usually cylindrical molded disk containing a medicinal substance diluted with a mixture of lactose and powdered sucrose, in varying proportions, with a moistening agent.

taboparalysis (ta″bo-pah-ral′ĭ-sis). Taboparesis.

taboparesis (ta″bo-pah-re′sis, ta″bo-par′e-sis). A form of dementia paralytica occurring concomitantly with tabes dorsalis.

tabophobia (ta″bo-fo′be-ah) [L. *tabes* + Gr. *phobein* to be affrighted by]. A morbid fear of tabes.

tabula (tab′u-lah), pl. *tab′ulae* [L.]. Table. **t. exter′na os′sis cra′nii,** lamina externa ossis cranii. **t. inter′na os′sis cra′nii, t. vit′rea,** lamina interna ossis cranii.

tabular (tab′u-lar) [L. *tabula* a board or table]. Resembling or shaped like a table.

tacahout (tak″ah-ho͞ot′) [Arabic]. A kind of gall from tamarisk trees: a source of gallic acid.

tacamahac (tak′ah-ma-hak″). A resin derived from various trees.

tacaryl (tak′ah-ril). Trade mark for preparations of methdilazine.

tache (tahsh) [Fr.]. A spot, or blemish. **t. blanche** (blahnsh) [Fr. "white spot"], a white spot on the liver in certain infectious diseases. **t. bleuâtre** (bleu-ahtr′) [Fr. "bluish spot"], a kind of bluish spot on the skin: said to occur in certain cases of typhoid fever, and sometimes caused by lice. **t. cérébrale** (sa-ra-brahl′) [Fr. "cerebral spot"], a congested streak produced by drawing the nail across the skin: a concomitant of various nervous or cerebral diseases. Called also *t. méningéale.* **t's laiteuses** (la-tēz′) [Fr. "milky spots"], small spots, of a milky appearance in the omentum, made up of lymphoid cells and macrophages and especially prominent in the rabbit. 2. Lymphangeal nodules. **t. méningéale** (ma-nin-zha-al′) [Fr. "meningeal spot"], t. cérébrale. **t. motrice** (mo-trēs′) [Fr. "motor spot"], a kind of motor nerve ending in which the nerve fibril passes to a muscle cell, where it ends in a slight enlargement. **t. noir** (nwahr) [Fr. "black spot"], an ulcer covered with a black adherent crust, a characteristic local reaction occurring at the presumed site of the infective bite in certain tick-borne rickettsioses, such as scrub typhus or boutonneuse fever. **t. spinale** (spe-nahl′) [Fr. "spinal spot"], a bulla resembling a burn, and due to spinal cord disease. **t. vierge** (ve-ārzh′) [Fr. "virginal spot"], a small area on a bacterial culture on which there is no growth.

tacheometer (tak″e-om′e-ter). Tachometer.

tachetée (tahsh″ĕ-ta′) [Fr.]. Tachetic.

tachetic (tah-ket′ik). Marked by spots or blotches.

tachistoscope (tah-kis′to-skōp) [Gr. *tachistos* swiftest + *skopein* to examine]. A kind of stereoscope in which vision is interrupted by a movable diaphragm.

tacho- (tak′o) [Gr. *tachos* speed]. Combining form denoting relationship to speed.

tachogram (tak′o-gram) [*tacho-* + Gr. *gramma* mark]. A graphic record of the movement and velocity of the blood current.

tachography (tah-kog′rah-fe) [*tacho-* + Gr. *graphein* to write]. The recording of the speed of the blood current.

tachometer (tah-kom′e-ter) [*tacho-* + Gr. *metron* measure]. Hemotachometer.

tachy- (tak′e) [Gr. *tachys* swift]. Combining form meaning swift or rapid.

tachyauxesis (tak″e-awk-ze′sis) [*tachy-* + Gr. *auxēsis* growth]. Heterauxesis in which the part grows more rapidly than the whole.

tachycardia (tak″e-kar′de-ah) [*tachy-* + Gr. *kardia* heart]. Excessive rapidity in the action of the heart. The term is usually applied to a pulse rate above 100 per minute. **auricular t.,** auricular flutter. **constant t.,** a continuous tachycardia observed in certain diseases. **essential t.,** that which is paroxysmal and is due to a cardiac neurosis. **orthostatic t.,** disproportionate rapidity of the pulse on rising from a reclining to a standing position. **paroxysmal t.,** a condition marked by attacks of excessively rapid heart action which come on abruptly and terminate just as abruptly. **reflex t.,** rapid action of the heart caused by disturbances somewhere else than in the circulatory apparatus. **sinus t.,** simple tachycardia. **t. strumo′sa exophthal′mica,** exophthalmic goiter.

tachycardiac (tak″e-kar′de-ak). 1. Pertaining to, characterized by, or causing tachycardia. 2. An agent that acts to accelerate the pulse.

tachycardic (tak″e-kar′dik). Tachycardiac.

tachygenesis (tak″e-jen′e-sis) [*tachy-* + Gr. *genesis* production]. The acceleration and compression of ancestral stages in embryonic development.

tachylalia (tak″e-la′le-ah) [*tachy-* + Gr. *lalein* to speak + *-ia*]. Rapidity of speech.

tachymeter (tah-kim′e-ter) [*tachy-* + Gr. *metron* measure]. Any instrument for measuring rapidity of motion of any body.

tachyphagia (tak″e-fa′je-ah) [*tachy-* + Gr. *phagein* to eat + *-ia*]. Rapid or hasty eating.

tachyphasia (tak″e-fa′ze-ah) [*tachy-* + Gr. *phasis* speech + *-ia*]. Tachyphrasia.

tachyphemia (tak″e-fe′me-ah) [*tachy-* + Gr. *phēmē* speech + *-ia*]. Tachyphrasia.

tachyphrasia (tak″e-fra′ze-ah) [*tachy-* + Gr. *phrasis* speech + *-ia*]. Extreme volubility of speech: sometimes a sign of mental disorder.

tachyphrenia (tak″e-fre′ne-ah) [*tachy-* + Gr. *phrēn* mind + *-ia*]. Mental hyperactivity.

tachyphylaxis (tak″e-fi-lak′sis) [*tachy-* + Gr. *phylaxis* protection]. 1. Rapid immunization against the effect of toxic doses of an extract by previous injection of small doses of the same (Gley, 1911). 2. The decreasing responses which follow consecutive injections made at short intervals.

tachypnea (tak″ip-ne′ah) [*tachy-* + Gr. *pnoia* breath]. Excessive rapidity of respiration; a respiratory neurosis marked by quick, shallow breathing.

tachypragia (tak″e-prag′e-ah) [*tachy-* + Gr. *prassein* to act]. Rapidity of action.

tachypsychia (tak″e-si′ke-ah) [*tachy-* + Gr. *psychē* soul + *-ia*]. Rapidity of psychic processes.

tachyrhythmia (tak″e-rith′me-ah) [*tachy-* + Gr. *rhythmos* rhythm + *-ia*]. Tachycardia.

tachysterol (tak-is′te-rol). An isomer of ergosterol produced by irradiation.

tachysynthesis (tak″e-sin′thĕ-sis). Tachyphylaxis.

tachysystole (tak″e-sis′to-le). Abnormally rapid systole; extrasystole. **atrial t., auricular t.,** atrial flutter.

tachytrophism (tak″e-tro′fizm) [*tachy-* + Gr. *trophē* nutrition]. Rapid metabolism.

tacosal (tak′o-sal). Trade mark for a preparation of diphenylhydantoin.

tacosis (tah-ko′sis). Takosis.

tactile (tak′til) [L. *tactilis*]. Pertaining to the touch.

tactilogical (tak″tĭ-loj′e-kal). Pertaining to touch: tactual.

taction (tak′shun) [L. *tactio*]. 1. A touch; an act of touching. 2. The sense of touch; perception by the touch.

tactometer (tak-tom′e-ter) [L. *tactus* touch + *metrum* measure]. An instrument for measuring the acuteness of the sense of touch; an esthesiometer.

tactor (tak′tor). A tactile end-organ.

tactual (tak′tu-al) [L. *tactus* touch]. Pertaining to or accomplished by the touch.

tactus (tak′tus) [L.]. Touch. **t. erudi′tus** [L. "trained touch"], delicacy of touch acquired by practice. **t. ex′pertus** [L. "experienced touch"], t. eruditus.

taedium (te′de-um) [L.]. Weariness; boredom. **t. vi′tae** [L. "weariness of life"], morbid disgust with life.

Taenia (te′ne-ah) [L. "a flat band," "bandage," "tape"]. A genus of common tapeworms. **T. africa′na,** a tapeworm resembling *T. saginata*, found in Negroes of German East Africa. **T. antarc′tica,** a species from dogs in Antarctic regions. **T. balan′iceps,** a species from dogs and bobcats in Nevada and New Mexico. **T. brachyso′ma,** a species infesting dogs in Italy. **T. bru′nerri,** a species found in Algeria. **T. cer′vi,** a species from dogs in Denmark. **T. confu′sa,** a species found in the Mississippi valley. **T. cras′siceps,** a cestode parasite of foxes in Alaska and Canada, found in rodents as an intermediate host. **T. crassicol′lis,** a species found in cats which passes its encysted stage in the liver of rats, where it produces sarcomas. **T. cucur′bitum,** *T. saginata.* **T. demerarien′sis,** a South American tapeworm, rarely observed in man. **T. echinococ′cus,** *Echinococcus granulosus.* **T. ellip′tica,** a species measuring from 6 to 12 inches, occurring in the intestines of dogs and cats. **T. fenestra′ta,** a tapeworm the segments of which have burst and have discharged their eggs, leaving a ring of tissue only. **T. fus′a,** a tapeworm of which the segments are more or less fused or consolidated. **T. hydatige′na,** a tapeworm that is parasitic in dogs and wild carnivora, found in the liver and abdominal cavity of cloven-hoofed animals as intermediate hosts. **T. krab′bei,** a cestode parasite found in bobcat, dog, and wolf in the northern United States, Canada, and Alaska. **T. madagascarien′sis,** *Raillietina madagascariensis.* **T. margina′ta,** a small cestode, 1.5–4 meters in length, found in dogs. **T. mediocanella′ta,** *T. saginata.* **T. na′na,** *Hymenolepis nana.* **T. o′vis,** a species parasitic in dogs; found in the musculature of sheep and goats as intermediate hosts. **T. philippi′na,** a species found in the Philippines. **T. pisifor′mis,** a tapeworm commonly found in dogs; also parasitic in cats, foxes, wolves, and other animals. **T. sagina′ta,** the common tapeworm of man, a species 12 to 25 feet long, found in the adult form in the human intestine, and in the larval state (*Cysticercus bovis*) in the muscles and other organs of the ox. Man acquires the disease by eating infected meat. It is known as the *beef tapeworm* and *fat tapeworm*, and is also called *T. mediocanellata.* **T. so′lium,** the pork tapeworm, or armed tapeworm, a species 3 to 6 feet long, found in the intestine of man, and in the larval state (*Cysticerus cellulosae*) in the muscles of the hog. Its head is armed with a double row of hooklets. It gains access to the human intestine through ingestion of inadequately cooked or measly pork. It is rare in America, but common in certain parts of Europe. **T. taeniaefor′mis,** a cestode parasite commonly found in cats, and more rarely in dogs, foxes, and other animals, having rats, mice, and other rodents as intermediate host.

taenia (te′ne-ah), pl. *tae′niae* [L.]. 1. [B N A] A flat strip of soft tissue (tenia [N A]). 2. An individual organism of the genus Taenia. Called also *tenia.* **tae′niae acus′ticae,** striae medullares ventriculi quarti. **t. chorioi′dea** [B N A], tenia choroidea. **t. cine′rea,** a band of gray substance on the floor of the fourth ventricle outside the striae medullares ventriculi quarti. **tae′niae co′li** [B N A], teniae coli. **t. fim′briae** [B N A], the line of attachment of the choroid plexus of the lateral ventricle to the fimbria of the hippocampus; included as an unnamed portion of the tenia fornicis [N A]. **t. for′nicis** [B N A], the line of attachment of the choroid plexus of the lateral ventricle to the fornix. See *tenia fornicis* [N A]. **t. hippocam′pi,** fimbria hippocampi. **t. li′bera** [B N A], tenia libera. **t. medulla′ris thal′ami op′tici, medullary t. of thal-**

amus, tenia thalami. **t. mesocol'ica** [B N A], tenia mesocolica. **t. omenta'lis** [B N A], tenia omentalis. **t. pon'tis,** a bundle of fibers sometimes found along the rostral border of the pons and the pedunculus cerebellaris medius, running an isolated course to the cerebellum. **tae'niae pylo'ri,** ligamenta pylori. **t. semicircula'ris cor'poris stria'ti,** stria terminalis corporis striati. **t. tec'tae,** stria longitudinalis lateralis corporis callosi. **tae'niae tela'rum** [B N A]. See *tenia telae* [N A]. **t. termina'lis.** 1. Taenia fimbriae. 2. A slight ridge on the inner surface of the right atrium that marks the position of the sinoatrial node. **t. thal'ami** [B N A], tenia thalami. **t. tu'bae,** a thickened band of peritoneum along the upper border of the uterine tube. **taeniae of Valsalva,** teniae coli. **t. ventric'uli quar'ti** [B N A], tenia ventriculi quarti. **t. ventric'uli ter'tii,** tenia thalami. **t. viola'cea,** a bluish stripe running longitudinally in the floor of the fourth ventricle.

taenia-. For other words beginning thus, see also those beginning *tenia-*.

taeniae (te'ne-e). Plural of *taenia.*

Taeniarhynchus (te″ne-ah-ring'kus). A genus name formerly given to beef tapeworms. See *Taenia confusa* and *Taenia saginata.*

taeniasis (te-ni'ah-sis). Teniasis.

taeniola (te-ni'o-lah) [L., dim. of *taenia*]. A slender bandlike structure. **t. cine'rea,** taenia cinerea. **t. cor'poris callo'si of Reil,** lamina rostralis.

Taeniorhynchus (te″ne-o-ring'kus). A genus of mosquitoes now called *Mansonia.*

Taenzer's disease (ten'zerz) [Paul *Taenzer,* Bremen dermatologist, 1858–1919]. Ulerythema ophryogenes.

T.A.F. Abbreviation for German *Tuberculin Albumose Frei,* or albumose-free tuberculin; also for *toxoid-antitoxin floccules.*

tagathen (tag'ah-then). Trade mark for a preparation of chlorothen citrate.

tagatose (tag'ah-tōs). A ketohexose, CH_2OH-$(CHOH)_3$.CO.CH_2OH, isomeric with levulose.

tagesrest (tah'gez-rest) [Ger.]. Day residue.

tagliacotian operation (tah″le-ah-ko'she-an) [Gasparo *Tagliacozzi* (1546–1599) of Bologna, who was a pioneer of plastic surgery and especially renowned for his interest in rhinoplasty]. See *Italian operation,* under *operation.*

tagma (tag'mah), pl. *tagmas* or *tag'mata* [Gr. "a thing arranged"]. An aggregate of molecules; the ultimate molecular mass of protoplasm. See *micelle.*

tahaga (tah-hah'gah). A disease of camels in Algeria, similar to surra, caused by *Trypanosoma evansi.*

tail (tāl) [L. *cauda;* Gr. *oura*]. A slender appendage. Called also *cauda* [N A]. **t. of caudate nucleus,** cauda nuclei caudati. **t. of epididymis,** cauda epididymidis. **occult t.,** supernumerary segments of the coccyx, present in the buttock. **t. of pancreas,** cauda pancreatis. **t. of Spence,** the projection of mammary glandular tissue extending into the axillary region, sometimes forming a visible mass which may enlarge premenstrually or during lactation. **t. of spleen,** extremitas anterior lienis.

tailgut (tāl'gut). A prolongation of the hindgut into the tail of the early embryo.

Tait's knot, law, operation (tāts) [Lawson *Tait,* English surgeon, 1845–1899]. See under the nouns.

taka-diastase (tah'kah di'as-tās) [Jokichi *Takamine,* Japanese chemist in New York, 1854–1922]. The trade name for a digestive substance formed by the action of the spores of the fungus *Aspergillus oryzae* on the bran of wheat: used as a digestant.

Takata's reagent (tak-ah'tahz) [Maki *Takata,* Japanese pathologist, born 1892]. See under *reagent.*

Takata-Ara test (tak-ah'tah ah'rah) [Maki *Takata;* Kiyoshi *Ara,* Japanese pathologist]. See under *tests.*

Takayama's reagent, solution (tah″kah-yah'mahz) [Masao *Takayama,* Japanese physician, born 1871]. See under *solution.*

takosis (tah-ko'sis) [Gr. *tēkein* to cause wasting]. A contagious disease of goats caused by the *Micrococcus caprinus.*

Tal. Abbreviation for L. *tal'is,* such a one.

talalgia (tal-al'je-ah). Pain in the heel or ankle.

talantropia (tal″an-tro'pe-ah) [Gr. *talanton* balance + *tropos* a turning + *-ia*]. Nystagmus.

Talauma elegans (tal-aw'mah el'e-gans). A plant of Java, valued as a stomachic, antispasmodic, and antihysteric remedy.

talbutal (tal'bu-tal). Chemical name: 5-allyl-5-sec-butylbarbituric acid: used as a hypnotic and sedative.

talc (talk). A native, hydrous magnesium silicate, sometimes containing a small proportion of aluminum silicate: used as a dusting powder. Called also *purified talc.*

talcosis (tal-ko'sis). A morbid condition resulting from the inhalation or implantation in the body of talc. **pulmonary t.,** a morbid condition of the lungs resulting from inhalation of particles of talc.

talcum (tal'kum) [L.]. Talc.

taliacotian (tal″e-ah-ko'shan). Tagliacotian.

taliped (tal'ĭ-ped). 1. Clubfooted. 2. A clubfooted person.

talipedic (tal″ĭ-pe'dik). Clubfooted.

talipes (tal'ĭ-pēz) [L. "clubfoot"]. A congenital deformity of the foot, which is twisted out of shape or position. See also under *pes.* **t. calcaneoval'gus,** a deformity of the foot in which the heel is turned outward from the midline of

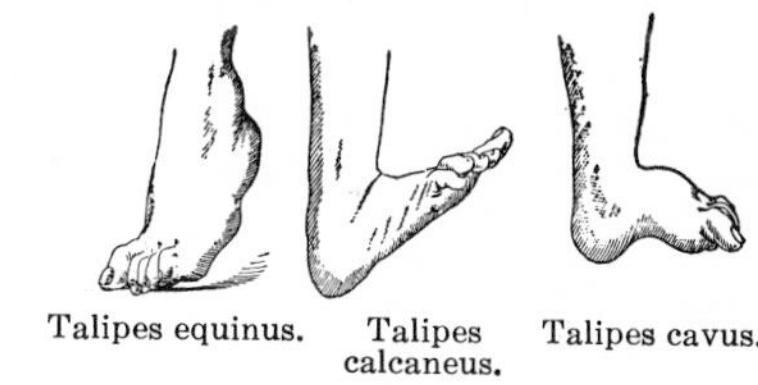

Talipes equinus. Talipes calcaneus. Talipes cavus.

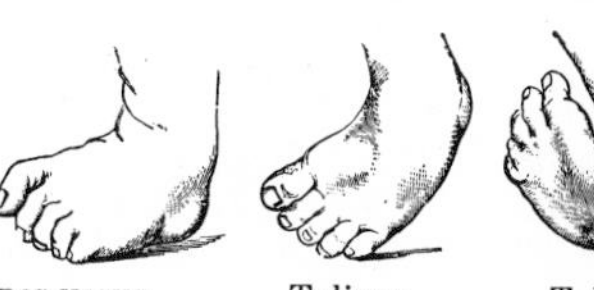

Talipes varus. Talipes equinovarus. Talipes calcaneovarus.

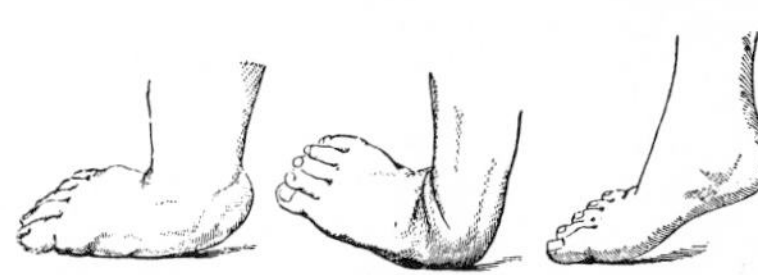

Talipes valgus. Talipes calcaneovalgus. Talipes equinovalgus.

the body and the anterior part of the foot is elevated. **t. calcaneova'rus,** a deformity of the foot in which the heel is turned toward the midline of the body and the anterior part is elevated. **t. calca'neus,** a deformity in which the foot is dorsiflexed. **t. cavoval'gus,** a deformity in which the longitudinal arch of the foot is abnormally high, and the heel is turned outward from the midline of the body. **t. ca'vus,** a deformity in which the longitudinal arch of the foot is abnormally high. **t. equinoval'gus,** a deformity of the foot in which the heel is elevated and turned outward from the midline of the body. **t. equinova'rus,** a deformity of the foot in which the heel is turned inward from the midline of the leg and the foot is plantar flexed. This is associated with the raising of the inner border of the foot (supination) and displacement of the anterior part of the foot so that it lies medially to the vertical axis of the leg (adduction). With this type of foot the arch is higher (cavus) and the foot is in equinus (plantar flexion). This is a typical clubfoot. **t. equi'nus,** a deformity in which the foot is plantar flexed, causing the person to walk on the toes without touching the heel. **t. planoval'gus,** a deformity of the foot in which the heel is turned outward from the midline of the leg and the outer border of the anterior part of the foot is higher than the inner border. This results in a lowering of the longitudinal arch. The condition may be congenital and permanent, or it may be spasmodic as a result of reflex spasm of the muscles controlling the foot. **t. val'gus,** a deformity of the foot in which the heel is turned outward from the midline of the leg. **t. va'rus,** a deformity of the foot in which the heel is turned inward from the midline of the leg.

talipomanus (tal″ĭ-pom'ah-nus) [L. *talipes* clubfoot + *manus* hand]. Clubhand; a deformity of the hand in which it is twisted out of shape or position. It usually consists of strong flexion and adduction of the hand.

Tallerman's apparatus (tal'er-manz) [Lewis A. *Tallerman*, English inventor]. See under *apparatus.*

tallow (tal'o). Suet. **bayberry t.,** a fat obtained from the berries of the wax myrtle (*Myrica cerifera*).

Tallqvist's scale (tahl'kvists) [Theodor Waldemar *Tallqvist*, Finnish physician, 1871–1927]. See under *scale.*

Talma's disease, operation (tal'mahz) [Sape *Talma*, physician in Utrecht, 1847–1918]. See under *disease* and *operation.*

talocalcaneal (ta″lo-kal-ka'ne-al). Pertaining to the talus and calcaneus.

talocrural (ta″lo-kroo'ral) [L. *talus* ankle + *crus* leg]. Pertaining to the talus and the bones of the leg.

talofibular (ta″lo-fib'u-lar). Pertaining to the talus and the fibula.

talon (tal'on) [L. "bird's claw"]. A low cusp or posterior prolongation of a molar tooth.

talonavicular (ta″lo-nah-vik'u-lar). Pertaining to the talus and the navicular bone.

talonid (tal'o-nid). The posterior part of a lower molar tooth.

taloscaphoid (ta″lo-skaf'oid). Talonavicular.

talose (ta'lōs). An aldehyde hexose, CH_2OH-$(CHOH)_4CHO$, isomeric with dextrose.

talotibial (ta″lo-tib'e-al). Pertaining to the talus and the tibia.

talus (ta'lus), pl. *ta'li* [L. "ankle"]. 1. [NA, B N A] The highest of the tarsal bones and the one which articulates with the tibia and fibula to form the ankle joint. Called also *ankle bone.* 2. The ankle.

T.A.M. Abbreviation for *toxoid-antitoxin mixture.*

tama (ta'mah). Swelling of the feet and legs.

tambour (tam-boor') [Fr. "drum"]. A drum-shaped appliance used in transmitting movements in a recording instrument. It consists of a cylinder having an elastic membrane stretched over it, and to which passes a tube that transmits the air. It is connected with a recording apparatus.

tamisage (tam-ĭ-sahzh') [Fr.]. Thorough washing, sieving and inspection of a patient's stools, as in the search for parasites.

tampan (tam'pan). See *Argus persicus* and *Ornithodorus moubata.*

tampicin (tam'pĭ-sin). A glycoside, $C_{34}H_{54}O_{14}$, from Tampico jalap, *Ipomoea simulans.*

tampon (tam'pon) [Fr. "stopper, plug"]. A pack; a plug made of cotton, sponge, or oakum: variously used in surgery to plug the nose, vagina, etc., for the control of hemorrhage or the absorption of secretions. **Corner's t.,** a tampon composed of omentum for insertion into a gastric or intestinal wound. **Dührssen's t.,** tamponade of the vagina with iodoform gauze in uterine hemorrhage. **kite tail t.,** a tampon made up of several pledgets tied to a string at intervals. **tracheal t.,** an inflatable rubber bag surrounding a tracheotomy tube: used to prevent the entrance of blood into the trachea in operations on the mouth and nose. **Trendelenburg's t.,** an inflatable bag of rubber surrounding a tracheotomy tube: used for preventing the escape of blood down the sides of the tube.

tamponade (tam″pon-ād') [Fr. *tamponner* to stop up]. The surgical use of the tampon. **cardiac t., heart t.,** acute compression of the heart which is due to effusion of the fluid into the pericardium or to the collection of blood in the pericardium from rupture of the heart or a coronary vessel. **chronic t.,** chronic compression of the heart caused by calcification of the pericardium. **Rose's t.,** cardiac tamponade.

tamponage (tam-po-nahzh'). Tamponade.

tamponing (tam'pon-ing). Tamponade.

tamponment (tam-pon'ment). The act of plugging with a tampon.

Tamus (ta'mus) [L.]. A genus of dioscoreaceous plants. *T. communis* is an old-world plant called black bryony: used homeopathically.

tan (tan). 1. To color or become of a brownish color from exposure to sun and wind. 2. The brownish color of the skin and hands acquired by exposure to the sun and air.

tandearil (tan-de'ah-ril). Trade mark for a preparation of oxyphenbutazone.

tang (tang). A projecting shank on a dental appliance; a minor connector.

tanghin (tan'gēn). The apocynaceous tree, *Cerbera tanghin*, of Madagascar, and its exceedingly poisonous seed: also an extract prepared from it.

Tangier disease (tan-jēr') [*Tangier* Island, in Chesapeake Bay, where the disease was first discovered]. See under *disease.*

tangoreceptor (tang″go-re-sep'tor) [L. *tangere* to touch + *receptor*]. A sense organ that responds only to physical contact, such as touch.

tank (tank). An artificial receptacle for liquids. **activated sludge t.,** a tank through which sewage flows slowly or intermittently while compressed air is allowed to bubble up through it. **anaerobic t.,** septic t. **biological t.,** a modified septic tank. **digestion t.,** a deep septic tank in which sludge is separated and submitted to septic action without making the rest of the sewage offensive. Called also *Emsher* or *Imhoff t.* **Dortmund t.,** a deep vertical flow settling tank for removing sludge from sewage. **Emsher t.,** digestion t. **Hubbard t.,** a tank in which a patient may be immersed for the purpose of permitting him to take underwater exercise. **hydrolytic t.,** septic t. **Imhoff t.,** digestion t. **septic t.,** a tank for the receipt of sewage, there to remain for a time in order that the solid matter may settle out and a certain amount of putrefaction occur from the action of the anaerobic bacteria present in the sewage. Called also *anaerobic t.* and *hydrolytic t.* **settling t.,** a basin in which the rate of flow of the sewage is reduced and the sludge allowed to settle out.

tannal (tan'al). Aluminum tannate. **insoluble t.,** basic aluminum tannate; a brown-yellow powder, $Al_2(OH)_4(C_{14}H_9O_9)_2 + 10H_2O$: astringent. **soluble t.,** aluminum tannotartrate; a yellowish-brown powder, $Al_2(C_4H_6O_6)_2(C_{14}H_9O_9)_2 + 6H_2O$: astringent.

tannalin (tan'al-in). A formaldehyde solution.

tannase (tan'ās). An esterase found in various tannin-bearing plants and produced in cultures by *Aspergillus niger* and *Penicillium glaucum*, which catalyzes the hydrolysis of various ester linkages in gallic acid compounds.

tannate (tan′āt) [L. *tannas*]. Any salt of tannic acid: all the tannates are astringent.

tannin (tan′in). Tannic acid. **t. albuminate exsiccata,** albutannin. **diacetyl t., t. diacetylate,** acetyltannic acid. **pathologic t.,** any tannin derived from galls, or vegetable excrescences due to a local disease of the plant. **physiologic t.,** any tannin normally produced by a healthy plant.

tanning (tan′ing). The treatment of burns with tannin.

Tanret's reaction, test (tahn-rāz′) [Charles *Tanret*, French physician, 19th century]. See under *tests*.

Tansini's operation, sign (tan-se′nēz) [Iginio *Tansini*, Italian surgeon, 1855–1943]. See under *operation* and *sign*.

tantalum (tan′tah-lum). A rare metallic element; symbol, Ta; atomic number, 73; atomic weight, 180.948. It is a noncorrosive and malleable metal and has been used for plates or disks to replace cranial defects due to wounds, for wire sutures, and for making prosthetic appliances.

tantrum (tan′trum). A violent display of bad temper.

taon (tah-on′). Infantile beriberi occurring in the Philippine Islands.

tap (tap). 1. A quick, light blow. 2. To drain off fluid by paracentesis. 3. A variety of East Indian jungle fever. **bloody t.,** a lumbar puncture in which the fluid obtained is bloody or pinkish. **front t.,** a tap on the muscles of the front of the leg, producing contraction of the muscles of the calf in spinal irritability. **heel t.,** reflex movement of the toes on tapping the heel: occurring in pyramidal tract diseases such as multiple sclerosis.

tapazole (tap′ah-zol). Trade mark for a preparation of methimazole.

tapeinocephalic (tap″ĭ-no-se-fal′ik). Characterized by tapeinocephaly.

tapeinocephaly (tap″ĭ-no-sef′ah-le) [Gr. *tapeinos* low-lying + *kephalē* head]. A low form of the skull, which is also flattened at front, having a vertical index below 72.

tapetal (tah-pe′tal). Pertaining to a tapetum, especially to the tapetum lucidum.

tapetum (tah-pe′tum), pl. *tape′ta* [L.; Gr. *tapētion*, dim. of *tapēs* a carpet, rug]. 1. A covering structure, or layer of cells. 2. [B N A] A stratum in the human brain constituted by the fibers from the body and splenium of the corpus callosum sweeping outward over the lateral ventricle and forming the roof and lateral wall of its posterior horn, and the lateral wall of its inferior horn. Omitted in N A. **t. alve′oli,** periodontium. **t. cellulo′sum,** a type of tapetum lucidum, being the more complex, more cellular type found in all but two species of the order Carnivora and in the seals. **t. choroi′deae,** t. lucidum. **t. cor′poris callo′si,** tapetum, def. 2. **t. fibro′sum,** a type of tapetum lucidum, being the simpler, fibrous type found almost exclusively in hoofed animals, in a few fish, and in marsupials, elephants, and whales. **t. lu′cidum,** the iridescent pigment epithelium of the choroid of animals which gives their eyes the properties of shining in the dark. Called also *t. choroideae*. **t. ni′grum,** stratum pigmenti bulbi oculi. **t. oc′uli,** stratum pigmenti retinae. **t. ventric′uli,** fasciculus longitudinalis superior cerebri.

tapeworm (tāp′werm). A parasitic intestinal cestode worm, or species of a flattened, tapelike form, and composed of separate joints. Those infesting man are principally of the genera *Taenia, Diphyllobothrium, Hymenolepis, Sparganum, Echinococcus,* and *Dipylidium*. The ova of tapeworms are taken into the alimentary canal of the intermediate host, whence they make their way into the tissues, where they form small, cystlike masses, called *scolices* or *cysticerci*. See *hydatid*. When the flesh of the original host is eaten, the scolices develop within the alimentary canal of the new host into a *strobilus*, or adult tapeworm, which consists of a head, neck, and a various (often very great) number of oblong joints, or segments, called *proglottides*, each of which is hermaphroditic and produces ova. **African t.,** *Taenia africana*. **armed t.,** *Taenia solium*, the commonest species of tapeworm. **beef t.,** *Taenia saginata*. **broad t.,** *Diphyllobothrium latum*. **dog t.,** *Echinococcus granulosus*. **double-pored dog t.,** *Dipylidium caninum*. **dwarf t.,** *Hymenolepis nana*. **fat t.,** *Taenia saginata*. **fish t.,** *Diphyllobothrium*. **fringed t.,** *Thysanosoma*. **heart-headed t.,** *Diphyllobothrium cordatus*. **hydatid t.,** *Echinococcus granulosus*. **Japanese double cord t.,** *Diplogonoporus grandis*. **Madagascar t.,** *Raillietina madagascariensis*. **Manson's larval t.,** *Diphyllobothrium mansonoides*. **measly t.** 1. *Taenia saginata*. 2. *Taenia solium*. **pork t.,** *Taenia solium*. **rat t.,** *Hymenolepis diminuta*. **Swiss t.,** *Diphyllobothrium latus*. **unarmed t.,** *Taenia saginata*. **Ward's Nebraskan t.,** *Taenia confusa*.

taphophilia (taf″o-fil′e-ah) [Gr. *taphos* grave + *philein* to love]. Morbid interest in graves and cemeteries.

taphophobia (taf″o-fo′be-ah) [Gr. *taphos* grave + *phobein* to be affrighted by]. Obsessive fear of being buried alive.

Tapia's syndrome (tap′e-ahz) [Antonia García *Tapia*, Spanish otolaryngologist, 1875–1950]. See under *syndrome*.

tapinocephalic (tap″ĭ-no-se-fal′ik). Tapeinocephalic.

tapinocephaly (tap″ĭ-no-sef′ah-le). Tapeinocephaly.

tapioca (tap″e-o′kah). A fecula, or starch, derived from the root of *Jatropha manihot*, or manioc: used as a food.

tapiroid (ta′pĭ-roid). Resembling the snout of a tapir.

tapotage (tah-po-tahzh′). Coughing and expectoration following percussion in the supraclavicular region: a sign sometimes obtained in pulmonary tuberculosis.

tapotement (tah-pōt-maw′) [Fr.]. A tapping or percussing movement in massage. It includes clapping, beating, and punctation.

tar (tahr). A dark-brown or black, viscid liquid, obtained by roasting the wood of various species of pine, or as a by-product of the destructive distillation of bituminous coal. It is a mixture of complex composition, and is the source of a number of substances, as cresol, creosol, guaiacol, naphthalene, paraffin, phenol, toluene, xylene, etc. It is used in chronic bronchitis, diarrhea, and diseases of the urinary organs, and externally in certain skin diseases. **coal t.,** tar obtained as a by-product of the destructive distillation of bituminous coal: applied locally as ointment or solution to skin lesions. **gas t.,** a coal tar derived from the coal, rosin, petroleum, and other material used in gas works. **juniper t.,** the volatile oil obtained from the woody portions of *Juniperus oxycedrus:* used as a local anti-eczematic. **pine t.,** a viscid, blackish brown liquid obtained by destructive distillation of the wood of various pine trees: used externally as a stimulant and antiseptic in various skin diseases.

Tar's symptom (tahrz) [Aloys *Tar*, Budapest physician, born 1886]. See under *symptom*.

Taraktogenos kurzii (tar″ak-toj′e-nos kur′ze-e). The tropical tree from the seeds of which chaulmoogra oil is obtained.

tarantism (tar′an-tizm). A variety of dancing mania, popularly believed to be caused by the bite of a tarantula, and to be cured by dancing.

tarantula (tah-ran′tu-lah). A venomous spider. **American t.,** a large, dark, ferocious looking spider, *Eurypelma hentzii*, having a poisonous bite. **black t.,** a venomous spider of Panama, *Sericopelma communis*. **European t.,** the true tarantula, the large European wolf spider, *Lycosa tarentula,* the bite of which was believed to cause death.

tarassis (tah-ras′is) [Gr. *taraxis* confusion]. A term proposed by Sanoaville de Lachèse (1886) for hysteria in the male.

taraxacin (tah-raks′ah-sin). A bitter principle from the root of the common dandelion.

Taraxacum (tah-rak′sah-kum) [L]. A genus of composite-flowered plants. The dried root of *T. officinale,* the common dandelion, contains the principle taraxacin and is a simple bitter.

taraxacum (tah-rak′sah-kum). The dried rhizome and root of *Taraxacum officinale* or of *Taraxacum laevigatum:* used as a constituent of glycerinated gentian elixir.

taraxigen (tah-rak′sĭ-jen). See *taraxy.*

taraxin (tah-rak′sin). See *taraxy.*

taraxis (tah-rak′sis). An obsolete name for conjunctivitis.

taraxy (tah-rak′se) [Gr. *taraxis* disturbance]. Novy's name for anaphylaxis, on the theory that the condition is due to a poisonous substance (*taraxin*) which is formed in the blood on the injection of an alien substance, as the result of a reaction with a substance which already exists in the blood serum (*taraxigen*).

tarbadillo (tahr″bah-dēl′yo) [Sp.]. Tabardillo.

Tardieu's spots (tar-dyuz′) [Auguste Ambroise *Tardieu,* French physician, 1818–1879]. See under *spot.*

tardive (tahr′div) [Fr. "tardy, late"]. Marked by lateness, late; applied to a disease in which the characteristic lesion is late in appearing.

tare (tār). 1. The weight of the vessel in which a substance is weighed. 2. To take the weight of a vessel which is to contain a substance, in order to allow for it when the vessel and the substance are weighed together.

tarentism (tar′en-tizm). Tarantism.

tarentula (tah-ren′tu-lah). Tarantula.

target (tahr′get). An object or area toward which something is directed, such as the metal or plate of a roentgen ray tube on which the electrons impinge and from which the roentgen rays are sent out.

Tarin, Tarinus, band of, valve of, etc. (tah-ră′, tah-ri′nus) [Pierre *Tarin,* French anatomist, 1700–1761]. See under the nouns.

Tarnier's forceps, sign (tar-ne-āz′) [Etienne Stéphene *Tarnier,* French obstetrician, 1828–1897]. See under *forceps* and *sign.*

tarsadenitis (tahr″sad-e-ni′tis). An inflammation of the tarsus of the eyelid and of the meibomian glands.

tarsal (tahr′sal) [L. *tarsalis*]. 1. Pertaining to the tarsus of an eyelid or to the instep. 2. Any one of the bones of the tarsus.

tarsalgia (tahr-sal′je-ah). Pain in the ankle or foot.

tarsalis (tahr-sa′lis) [L.]. Tarsal.

tarsectomy (tahr-sek′to-me) [*tarso-* + Gr. *ektomē* excision]. 1. Excision of the tarsus, or a part of it. 2. Excision of a tarsal cartilage.

tarsectopia (tahr″sek-to′pe-ah) [*tarso-* + Gr. *ektopos* out of place + *-ia*]. Dislocation of the tarsus.

tarsitis (tahr-si′tis). Inflammation of the tarsus, or margin of an eyelid; blepharitis.

tarso- (tahr′so) [Gr. *tarsos* a broad flat surface]. Combining form denoting relationship to the edge of the eyelid, or to the instep of the foot.

tarsocheiloplasty (tahr″so-ki′lo-plas″te) [*tarso-* + Gr. *cheilos* lip + *plassein* to mold]. A plastic operation upon the edge of the eyelid, as in treatment of trichiasis.

tarsoclasis (tahr-sok′lah-sis) [*tarso-* + Gr. *klasis* breaking]. The operation of fracturing the tarsus of the foot.

tarsomalacia (tahr″so-mah-la′she-ah) [*tarso-* + Gr. *malakia* softening]. Softening of the tarsus of an eyelid.

tarsomegaly (tahr″so-meg′ah-le). Enlargement of the os calcis.

tarsometatarsal (tahr″so-met″ah-tahr′sal). Pertaining to the tarsus and the metatarsus.

tarso-orbital (tahr″so-or′bĭ-tal). Pertaining to the tarsus and the orbit.

tarsophalangeal (tahr″so-fah-lan′je-al). Pertaining to the tarsus and the phalanges of the toes.

tarsophyma (tahr″so-fi′mah) [*tarso-* + Gr. *phyma* growth]. Any tarsal tumor.

tarsoplasia (tahr″so-pla′se-ah). Tarsoplasty.

tarsoplasty (tahr′so-plas″te) [*tarso-* + Gr. *plassein* to form]. Plastic surgery of the tarsus of an eyelid.

tarsoptosis (tahr″sop-to′sis) [*tarso-* + Gr. *ptōsis* falling]. Falling of the tarsus; flatfoot.

tarsorrhaphy (tahr-sor′ah-fe) [*tarso-* + Gr. *rhaphē* suture]. The operation of suturing together a portion of (*partial t.*) or the entire (*total t.*) upper and lower eyelids for the purpose of shortening or closing entirely the palpebral fissure. The terms *external t., median t.,* and *internal t.* are used to indicate the portion of the lids brought together in partial tarsorrhaphy. Called also *blepharorrhaphy.*

tarsotarsal (tahr″so-tahr′sal). Pertaining to the articulation between the two rows of tarsal bones.

tarsotibial (tahr″so-tib′e-al). Pertaining to the tarsus and the tibia.

tarsotomy (tahr-sot′o-me) [*tarso-* + Gr. *tomē* a cutting]. The operation of incising the tarsus, or an eyelid; blepharotomy.

tarsus (tahr′sus) [L.; Gr. *tarsos* a frame of wickerwork; any broad flat surface]. 1. [N A, B N A] The region of the articulation between the foot and the leg. See also *tarsus osseus.* 2. One of the plates of connective tissue forming the framework of an eyelid. See *t. inferior palpebrae* and *t. superior palpebrae.* **bony t.,** t. osseus. **t. infe′rior palpe′brae** [N A, B N A], the firm framework of connective tissue that gives shape to the inferior eyelid. **t. os′seus** [N A, B N A], the seven bones constituting the articulation between the foot and the leg: the talus, calcaneus, and navicular, in the proximal row; and the cuboid and the lateral, intermediate, and medial cuneiform bones, in the distal row. Called also *bony t.* **t. supe′rior palpe′brae** [N A, B N A], the firm framework of connective tissue that gives shape to the upper eyelid.

tartar (tahr′tahr) [L. *tartarum;* Gr. *tartaron*]. 1. The lees, or sediment, of a wine cask; crude potassium bitartrate. 2. Dental calculus. **borated t.,** a white powder prepared by evaporating a solution of 2 parts of sodium borate and 5 parts of potassium bitartrate. **cream of t.,** potassium bitartrate. **t. emetic,** antimony potassium tartrate. See under *antimony.* **serumal t.,** subgingival calculus. Called also *hematogenic calculus.* **vitriolated t.,** potassium tartrate.

tartarated (tahr′tahr-āt″ed). Charged with tartaric acid.

tartarized (tahr′tahr-īzd). Tartarated.

tartrate (tahr′trāt) [L. *tartras*]. Any salt of tartaric acid. **acid t.,** a bitartrate; any salt of tartaric acid in which one atom only of hydrogen is replaced by a base. **normal t.,** one in which two hydrogen atoms are replaced; various tartrates are employed as remedial agents.

tartrated (tahr′trāt-ed) [L. *tartratus*]. Containing tartar or tartaric acid.

tartro-bismuthate (tahr″tro-biz′mu-thāt). Bismuthotartrate.

tasikinesia (tas″ĭ-ki-ne′ze-ah) [Gr. *tasis* straining + *kinēsis* motion + *-ia*]. A morbid inclination to get up and walk; inability to remain seated.

taste (tāst) [L. *gustus*]. The peculiar sensation caused by the contact of soluble substances with the tongue; the sense effected by the tongue, the gustatory and other nerves, and the gustation center. **color t.,** pseudogeusesthesia. **franklinic t.,** a sour taste produced by stimulating the tongue with static electricity.

taste-blindness (tāst-blīnd′nes). Inability to taste certain substances, such as phenylthiocarbamide.

taster (tās′ter). An individual capable of tasting a particular test substance, such as phenylthiocarbamide, used in certain genetic studies.

T.A.T. Abbreviation for *toxin-antitoxin.*

tätte melk (tet′ĕ melk). A food article in Sweden, prepared by inoculating milk with leaves of *Pinguicula vulgaris.*

tattooing (tat-too′ing). The insertion of permanent colors in the skin by introducing them through punctures. **t. of the cornea,** the permanent coloring of the cornea chiefly to conceal leukomatous spots.

Tatum (ta′tum), Edward Lawrie. United States biochemist, born 1909; co-winner, with George Wells Beadle and Joshua Lederberg, of the Nobel prize in medicine and physiology for 1958, for work in genetics and heredity.

Tatusia novemcincta (tah-tu′se-a no″vem-sink′ta). A trypanosome found in the armadillo, transmitted by the insect *Triatoma geniculata* (Chagas, 1912).

tauranga (taw-ran′gah). Bush disease.

taurine (taw′rin). 1. A crystallizable acid, aminoethyl-sulfonic acid, $NH_2(CH_2)_2SO_2OH$, from the bile, produced from the decomposition of taurocholic acid. It is found also in small quantities in the tissues of the lungs and muscles. Its crystals are colorless and are readily soluble in water. 2. A nutrient jelly from beef.

taurocholaneresis (taw″ro-ko″lan-er′e-sis) [*taurocholic* acid + Gr. *hairesis* a taking]. Increase in the output or elimination of taurocholic acid in the bile. Cf. *cholaneresis.*

taurocholanopoiesis (taw″ro-ko-lan″o-poi-e′-sis). Synthesis of taurocholic acid by the liver.

taurocholate (taw″ro-ko′lāt). Any salt of taurocholic acid.

taurocholemia (taw″ro-ko-le′me-ah). The presence of taurocholic acid in the blood.

taurophobia (taw″ro-fo′be-ah) [L. *taurus* bull + *phobia*]. Morbid fear of bulls.

Taussig-Bing syndrome (taw′sig-bing) [Helen B. *Taussig,* American pediatrician, born 1898; Richard J. *Bing,* American surgeon, born 1909]. See under *syndrome.*

tauto- (taw′to) [Gr. *tauto* the same]. Combining form meaning the same.

tautomenial (taw″to-me′ne-al) [*tauto-* + Gr. *mēniaia* menses]. Pertaining to the same menstrual period.

tautomer (taw′to-mer). A chemical compound exhibiting, or capable of exhibiting, tautomerism.

tautomeral (taw-tom′er-al) [*tauto-* + Gr. *meros* part]. Pertaining to the same part; especially sending processes to help in the formation of the white matter in the same side of the spinal cord: used of certain neurons and neuroblasts. See *tautomeral cells,* under *cell.*

tautomeric (taw″to-mer′ik). Exhibiting, or capable of exhibiting, tautomerism.

tautomerism (taw-tom′er-izm) [*tauto-* + Gr. *meros* part]. A form of stereoisomerism in which the compounds are mutually interconvertible, under normal conditions, forming a mixture which is in dynamic equilibrium. See *prototropy* and *anionotropy.*

Tawara's node (tah-wah′rah) [K. Sunao *Tawara,* Japanese pathologist, born 1873]. See under *node.*

taxa (tak′sah). Plural of *taxon.*

taxis (tak′sis) [Gr. "a drawing up in rank and file"]. 1. An orientation movement of a motile organism in response to an external stimulus. Such a response may be either positive (toward) or negative (away from the stimulus). Used also as a word termination, affixed to a stem denoting the nature of the stimulus (stereotaxis). 2. Exertion of force in the manual replacement of a displaced organ or part, as of the protruded intestine in hernia. **bipolar t.,** the repositioning of a retroverted uterus by upward pressure through the rectum, the cervix being pulled down in the vagina.

Taxodium distichum (taks-o′de-um dis-tik′-um). The cypress, a timber tree of North America. The resin was formerly used in rheumatism.

taxology (taks-ol′o-je). Taxonomy.

taxon (tak′son), pl. *tax′a* [Gr. *taxis* a drawing up in rank and file + *on* neuter ending]. A particular group (category) into which related organisms are classified, such as a species, genus, family, order, or class.

taxonomic (tak″so-nom′ik). Pertaining to taxonomy.

taxonomy (taks-on′o-me) [L. *taxinomia;* Gr. *taxis* a drawing up in rank and file + *nomos* law]. The orderly classification of organisms into appropriate categories (taxa) on the basis of relationships among them, with the application of suitable and correct names.

Tay's disease, choroiditis, spot (tāz) [Warren *Tay,* English physician, 1843–1927]. See under *choroiditis* and *spot.*

Tay-Sachs disease (ta saks′) [Warren *Tay;* Bernard *Sachs,* New York neurologist, 1858–1944]. Amaurotic family idiocy.

Taylor's apparatus (ta′lerz) [Charles Fayette *Taylor,* surgeon in New York, 1827–1899]. See under *apparatus.*

Taylor's disease (ta′lerz) [Robert William *Taylor,* American dermatologist, 1842–1908]. Idiopathic localized atrophy of the skin.

tazettine (tāz′ĕ-tin). A crystalline alkaloid, $C_{18}H_{21}O_5N$, from the bulbs of *Narcissus tazetta.*

TB. See under *tuberculin.*

Tb. Chemical symbol for *terbium.*

T.b. Abbreviation for *tubercle bacillus,* and, in speaking, for *tuberculosis.*

TBB 1-698. Tibione.

TBN. Abbreviation for *bacillus emulsion.* See under *tuberculin.*

TBP. Bithionol.

TC. See under *tuberculin.*

Tc. Chemical symbol for *technetium.*

TCD$_{50}$. Abbreviation for *median tissue culture dose.* See *TCID$_{50}$*.

TCID$_{50}$. Abbreviation for *median tissue culture infective dose;* that quantity of a cytopathogenic agent (virus) that will produce a cytopathic effect in 50 per cent of the cultures inoculated.

t.d.s. Abbreviation for L. *ter di′e sumen′dum,* to be taken three times a day.

Te. 1. Chemical symbol for *tellurium.* 2. Abbreviation for *tetanus.*

TEA. Tetraethylammonium.

tea (te) [L. *thea*]. 1. The dried leaves of *Thea chinensis,* containing caffeine and tannic acid, or a decoction thereof. 2. Any decoction or infusion. **beef t.,** an infusion of lean beef.

TEAC. Acronym for tetraethylammonium chloride.

Teale's amputation (tēlz) [Thomas Pridgin *Teale,* English surgeon, 1801–1868]. See under *amputation.*

tears (tērz) [L. *lacrimae;* Gr. *dakrya*]. 1. The watery secretion of the lacrimal glands which serves to moisten the conjunctiva. The secretion is slightly alkaline and saline. 2. Small, naturally formed, droplike masses of a gum or resin. **crocodile t.,** lacrimation on chewing and eating, a syndrome occurring in facial paralysis.

teart (tert). Molybdenosis of farm animals caused

by feeding on vegetation grown on soil that contains unusual amounts of molybdenum.

tease (tēz). To pull a tissue apart with needles for microscopical examination.

teaspoon (te′spo͞on). A spoon of small size, containing about 1 fluid dram or 4 milliliters.

teat (tēt). The nipple of the mammary gland.

teatulation (tet-u-la′shun). The formation of a nipple-like elevation.

technetium (tek-ne′she-um). The metallic chemical element of atomic number 43; atomic weight, 99; symbol, Tc.

technic (tek′nik). Technique.

technical (tek′nĭ-kal). Pertaining to technique.

technician (tek-nish′an). A person trained in and expert in the performance of technical procedures.

technique (tek-nēk′) [Fr.]. The method of procedure and the details of any mechanical process or surgical operation. **Kristeller t.** See under *method*. **squash t.,** a method of preparing cells for chromosome study, suspending them in hypotonic solution, then incubating them and exposing them to colchicine for one hour; after fixing and staining, a drop of the stained material is placed on a glass slide and covered with a glass slip, which is then pressed against the slide with one thumb. **time diffusion t.,** a form of spinal anesthesia in which the anesthetic, of low specific gravity, is injected by lumbar puncture, with the patient in the sitting position. The anesthetic is allowed to flow upward for a measured number of seconds and then the patient is placed in the horizontal position.

technocausis (tek″no-kaw′sis) [Gr. *technē* art + *kausis* burning]. The use of the actual cautery.

technologist (tek-nol′o-jist). Technician.

technology (tek-nol′o-je) [Gr. *technē* art + *logos* treatise]. Scientific knowledge; the sum of the study of a technique. **splint t.,** the scientific study of splints for surgeon's use.

technometer (tek-nom′e-ter). An instrument which measures and indicates an x-ray exposure.

technopsychology (tek″no-si-kol′o-je) [Gr. *technē* art + *psychology*]. The psychology of the workman and his adaptation to his work.

tecosis (te-ko′sis). Takosis.

tectocephalic (tek″to-se-fal′ik). Characterized by tectocephaly.

tectocephaly (tek″to-sef′ah-le) [L. *tectum* roof + Gr. *kephalē* head]. Scaphocephalism.

tectology (tek-tol′o-je) [Gr. *tektōn* builder + *-logy*]. The science which treats of the building up of organisms from organic elements; the doctrine of structure.

tectonic (tek-ton′ik). Pertaining to plastic surgery or to surgery for the restoration of lost parts.

tectorial (tek-to′re-al) [L. *tectum* roof]. Of the nature of a roof or covering.

tectorium (tek-to′re-um), pl. *tecto′ria* [L. "roof"]. Membrana tectoria ductus cochlearis.

tectospinal (tek″to-spi′nal). Pertaining to the tectum mesencephali and the spinal cord.

tectum (tek′tum). Any rooflike structure. **t. mesenceph′ali** [N A], **t. of mesencephalon,** the dorsal part of the mesencephalon, comprising the superior and inferior colliculi and the tectal lamina.

teeth (tēth). Plural of *tooth*.

teething (tēth′ing). The eruption of the teeth.

tegmen (teg′men), pl. *teg′mina* [L. "cover"]. Any covering, or shelter; used in anatomical nomenclature as a general term to designate a covering structure or roof. **t. an′tri,** t. tympani. **t. cel′lulae,** t. mastoideum. **t. cra′nii,** calvaria. **t. cru′ris,** tegmentum, def. 2. **t. mastoideotympan′icum,** the tegmen mastoideum and tegmen tympani, which together roof over the mastoid cells. **t. mastoid′eum,** the bony roof of the mastoid cells. **t. tym′pani.** 1. [N A, B N A] the thin layer of translucent bone, on the petrous part of the temporal bone in the floor of the middle cranial fossa, separating the tympanic antrum from the cranial cavity. Called also *roof of tympanum*. 2. Paries tegmentalis cavi tympani. **t. ventric′uli quar′ti** [N A, B N A], the roof of the fourth ventricle, formed by the superior and inferior medullary vela.

tegmental (teg-men′tal). Pertaining to or of the nature of a tegmen or tegmentum.

tegmentum (teg-men′tum), pl. *tegmen′ta* [L.]. 1. A covering. 2. [N A, B N A] The part of the cerebral peduncle dorsal to the substantia nigra, comprising various nuclei, fiber tracts, and reticular formations. **t. au′ris,** membrana tympani. **hypothalamic t.,** subthalamic t. **t. of pons, t. rhombenceph′ali** [N A], the dorsal half of the pons. **subthalamic t.,** the portion of the tegmentum of the cerebral peduncle extending beneath the thalamus.

tegument (teg′u-ment) [L. *tegumentum*]. The integument or skin.

tegumental (teg″u-men′tal). Of the nature of a tegument.

tegumentary (teg″u-men′ter-e). Pertaining to the skin or tegument.

Teichmann's crystals, test (tīk′mahnz) [Ludwig Carl *Teichmann*-Stawiarski, German histologist, 1825–1895]. See under *crystal* and *tests*.

teichopsia (ti-kop′se-ah) [Gr. *teichos* wall + *opsis* vision + *-ia*]. The sensation of a luminous appearance before the eyes, with a zigzag, wall-like outline. Called also *fortification spectrum, flittering scotoma, scintillating scotoma,* and *scotoma scintilans*.

T-1824. Evans blue.

teinodynia (ti″no-din′e-ah). Tenodynia.

teinte B (tant ba) [Fr.]. Tint B.

teknocyte (tek′no-sīt) [Gr. *teknon* that which is born + *kytos* cell]. A young neutrophil leukocyte.

tela (te′lah), pl. *te′lae* [L. "something woven," "web"]. Any weblike tissue; used as a general term in anatomical nomenclature to designate a thin membrane resembling a web. **t. ara′nea,** a spider web. **t. cellulo′sa,** t. conjunctiva. **t. chorioi′dea ventric′uli quar′ti** [B N A], t. choroidea ventriculi quarti. **t. chorioi′dea ventric′uli ter′tii** [B N A], t. choroidea ventriculi tertii. **t. choroidea of fourth ventricle,** t. choroidea ventriculi quarti. **t. choroidea of third ventricle,** t. choroidea ventriculi tertii. **t. choroi′dea ventric′uli quar′ti** [N A], the fold of pia mater forming the roof of the fourth ventricle. **t. choroi′dea ventric′uli ter′tii** [N A], the fold of pia mater forming the roof of the third ventricle. **t. conjuncti′va** [N A, B N A], a general term used to designate connective tissue. **t. elas′tica** [N A, B N A], a general term used to designate elastic tissue. **t. subcuta′nea** [N A, B N A], the subcutaneous connective tissue or superficial fascia. **t. submuco′sa** [N A, B N A], the layer of loose connective tissue between the lamina muscularis mucosae and the tunica muscularis in most parts of the digestive, respiratory, urinary, and genital tracts. **t. submuco′sa bronchio′rum** [N A, B N A], the layer of tissue underlying the tunica mucosa of the bronchi. **t. submuco′sa co′li** [N A, B N A], the layer of tissue underlying the tunica mucosa of the colon. **t. submuco′sa esoph′agi** [N A], the layer of tissue underlying the tunica mucosa of the esophagus. **t. submuco′sa intesti′ni ten′uis** [N A, B N A], the submucous layer of the wall of the small intestine. **t. submuco′sa pharyn′gis** [N A, B N A], the tissue underlying the tunica mucosa of the pharynx. **t. submuco′sa rec′ti** [N A, B N A], the submucous layer of the wall of the rectum. **t. submuco′sa tra′cheae** [N A, B N A], the tissue underlying the tunica mucosa of the trachea. **t. submuco′sa tu′bae uteri′nae** [B N A], the submucous layer of the wall of the uterine tube. Omitted in N A. **t. submuco′sa ventric′uli** [N A, B N A], the tissue underlying the tunica mucosa of the stomach. **t. submuco′sa ves′icae urina′riae** [N A, B N A], the submucous layer of the wall of the urinary bladder. **t. subsero′sa** [N A, B N A], a layer of loose areolar tissue underlying the tunica serosa of various organs. **t. subsero′sa co′li** [N A], loose areolar tissue underlying the tunica serosa of the colon. **t. subsero′sa hep′atis** [N A], loose areolar tissue underlying the tunica serosa of the liver. **t. subsero′sa intesti′ni ten′uis** [N A], the subserous layer of the wall of the small intestine. **t. subsero′sa peritone′i** [N A], a web of loose areolar tissue underlying the tunica serosa of the peritoneum. **t. subsero′sa tu′bae uteri′nae** [N A], the subserous layer of the wall of the uterine tube. Called also *tunica adventitia tubae uterinae* [B N A]. **t. subsero′sa u′teri** [N A], the areolar tissue underlying the tunica serosa of the uterus. **t. subsero′sa ventric′uli** [N A], the tissue underlying the tunica serosa of the stomach. **t. subsero′sa ves′icae fel′leae** [N A], the tissue underlying the tunica serosa of the gallbladder. **t. subsero′sa ves′icae urina′riae** [N A], the subserous layer of the wall of the urinary bladder.

telae (te′le) [L.]. Plural of *tela.*

telalgia (tel-al′je-ah). Pain occurring in a part distant from the lesion; referred pain.

telangiectasia (tel-an″je-ek-ta′ze-ah) [*tele-*(1) + Gr. *angeion* vessel + *ektasis* dilatation + *-ia*]. A condition characterized by dilatation of the capillary vessels and minute arteries, forming a variety of angioma. **essential t.,** capillary dilatation due to static mechanical abnormality. **hereditary hemorrhagic t.,** a hereditary disorder marked by a tendency to bleeding due to local lesions of the capillaries. Called also *Osler's disease.* **t. lymphat′ica,** lymphangioma formed by dilatation of the lymph vessels. **t. macula′ris erupti′va per′stans,** urticarial eruption marked by persistent red macules with very little pigmentation. **spider t.,** nevus araneus. **t. verruco′sa,** angiokeratoma.

telangiectasis (tel-an″je-ek′tah-sis), pl. *telangiec′tases.* The spot formed on the skin by a dilated capillary or terminal artery.

telangiectatic (tel-an″je-ek-tat′ik). Pertaining to or characterized by telangiectasia.

telangiectodes (tel-an″je-ek-to′dēz). Marked by telangiectasia.

telangiectoma (tel-an″je-ek-to′mah). Telangioma.

telangiitis (tel-an″je-i′tis) [*tele-*(1) + Gr. *angeion* vessel + *-itis*]. Inflammation of the capillaries.

telangioma (tel-an″je-o′mah) [*tele-*(1) + Gr. *angeion* vessel + *-oma*]. A tumor made up of dilated capillaries.

telangion (tel-an′je-on) [*tele-*(1) + Gr. *angeion* vessel]. A terminal artery.

telangiosis (tel″an-je-o′sis) [*tele-*(1) + Gr. *angeion* vessel + *-osis*]. Any disease of the capillary vessels.

telar (te′lar). Pertaining to, affecting or resembling tela.

tele- (tel′e). 1. [Gr. *telos* end]. Combining form denoting relation to the end. 2. [Gr. *tēle* far off, at a distance]. Combining form meaning operating at a distance, or far away.

telebinocular (tel″e-bi-nok′u-lar). A prism-refracting instrument for use in orthoptic training.

telecardiogram (tel″e-kar′de-o-gram). The tracing obtained by telecardiography.

telecardiography (tel″e-kar″de-og′rah-fe) [*tele-*(2) + Gr. *kardia* heart + *graphein* to write]. The recording of alterations in the electric potential of the heart, the impulses being transmitted by telephone wires from the subject to the receiving apparatus, permitting the record to be read by one at a distance from the patient.

telecardiophone (tel″e-kar′de-o-fōn) [*tele-*(2) + Gr. *kardia* heart + *phōnē* voice]. An apparatus for rendering heart sounds audible to listeners at a distance from the patient.

teleceptive (tel′e-sep″tiv). Pertaining to a teleceptor.

teleceptor (tel′e-sep″tor) [*tele-*(2) + *receptor*]. A sensory nerve terminal which is sensitive to stimuli originating at a distance. Such nerve endings exist in the eyes, ears, and nose.

telecinesia (tel″e-si-ne′ze-ah). Telekinesis.

telecinesis (tel″e-si-ne′sis). Telekinesis.

telecord (tel′e-kord). An apparatus for attachment to an x-ray machine; by means of it each cardiac phase can be photographed in series.

telecurietherapy (tel″e-ku″re-ther′ah-pe) [*tele-*(2) + *curietherapy*]. Treatment with radium or radon by using the radium element at a distance from the body.

teledactyl (tel″e-dak′til) [*tele-*(2) + Gr. *daktylos* finger]. An appliance for picking up objects from the ground without stooping: used in spinal diseases.

teledendrite, teledendron (tel″e-den′drīt, tel″e-den′dron). Telodendron.

telediastolic (tel″e-di″ah-stol′ik) [*tele-*(1) + *diastole*]. Pertaining to the last phase of the diastole.

telegony (tel-eg′o-ne) [*tele-*(2) + Gr. *gonē* offspring]. The alleged appearance in the offspring of one sire of characteristics derived from a previous sire to whom the dam has borne offspring.

telekinesis (tel″e-ki-ne′sis) [*tele-*(2) + Gr. *kinēsis* movement]. The power claimed by certain persons of moving objects without contact with the object moved; also motion produced without contact with a moving body.

telekinetic (tel″e-ki-net′ik). Pertaining to telekinesis.

telelectrocardiogram (tel″e-lek″tro-kar′de-o-gram). Telecardiogram.

telemetry (tel-em′e-tre) [*tele-*(2) + Gr. *metron* measure]. The making of measurements at a distance from the subject, the measurable evidence of the phenomena under investigation being transmitted by radio signals. See *radioelectrocardiography* and *radioencephalography.*

telemnemonike (tel″e-ne-mon′ĭ-ke) [*tele-*(2) + Gr. *mnēmonikos* pertaining to memory]. The gaining of consciousness of things in the memory of another person.

telencephal (tel-en′se-fal). Telencephalon.

telencephalic (tel″en-se-fal′ik). Pertaining to the telencephalon.

telencephalization (tel″en-sef″al-i-za′shun). The transfer to the telencephalon, during the process of evolution, of the direction of the more complex nerve reactions.

telencephalon (tel″en-sef′ah-lon) [*tele-*(1) + Gr. *enkephalos* brain]. 1. [N A, B N A] The anterior portion of the brain, including the lamina terminalis and the cerebral hemispheres, which comprise the cerebral cortex, the corpus striatum, and the rhinencephalon. Called also *endbrain.* 2. The anterior of the two vesicles formed by specialization of the prosencephalon in the developing embyro.

teleneurite (tel″e-nu′rīt). The end expansion of an axis-cylinder.

teleneuron (tel″e-nu′ron) [*tele-*(1) + Gr. *neuron* nerve]. A nerve ending.

teleological (te″le-o-loj′ĭ-kal). 1. Pertaining to teleology. 2. Serving an ultimate purpose in development.

teleology (tel″e-ol′o-je) [*tele-*(1) + Gr. *logos* treatise]. The doctrine of final causes, or of adaptation to a definite purpose.

teleomitosis (tel″e-o-mi-to′sis) [*tele-*(1) + *mitosis*]. Completed mitosis.

teleonomic (tel″e-o-nom′ik). Pertaining to or having evolutionary survival value.

teleonomy (tel″e-on′o-me) [*teleo-* + Gr. *nomos*, law]. The doctrine that the existence of a structure or a function in an organism implies that it has had evolutionary survival value.

teleorganic (tel″e-or-gan′ik). Necessary to life.

teleoroentgenogram (tel″e-o-rent-gen′o-gram). Teleroentgenogram.

teleoroentgenography (tel″e-o-rent″gen-og′-rah-fe). Teleroentgenography.

teleost (tel′e-ost). One of an order of fish known as the bony fish.

teleotherapeutics (tel″e-o-ther″ah-pu′tiks) [*tele*-(2) + *therapeutics*]. Suggestive therapeutics.

telepaque (tel′e-pāk). Trade mark for a preparation of iopanoic acid.

telepathist (te-lep′ah-thist). A professed mind-reader.

telepathize (te-lep′ah-thīz). To affect by sympathetic or other subtle means.

telepathy (te-lep′ah-the) [*tele*-(2) + Gr. *pathos* feeling]. Extrasensory perception of the mental activity of another person. Cf. *clairvoyant*.

telephium (te-lef′e-um). An intractable ulcer.

telephonophobia (tel″e-fo″no-fo′be-ah). Pathologic fear of telephones.

teleradiography (tel″e-ra″de-og′rah-fe). Teleroentgenography.

teleradium (tel″e-ra′de-um) [*tele*-(2) + *radium*]. A massive dose of radium applied at some distance from the body.

telergic (tel-er′jik). Acting at a distance.

telergy (tel′er-je) [*tele*-(2) + Gr. *ergon* work]. 1. Automatism. 2. A hypothetical action of one brain on another at a distance.

teleroentgenogram (tel″e-rent-gen′o-gram). The picture or film obtained by teleroentgenography.

teleroentgenography (tel″e-rent″gen-og′rah-fe). Roentgenography with the x-ray tube 6½ to 7 feet away from the plate in order more nearly to secure parallelism of the rays.

teleroentgentherapy (tel″e-rent″gen-ther′ah-pe). Roentgen-ray therapy with the x-ray tube at a distance (6–7 feet) away from the body.

Telesphorus (tel-es′fo-rus) [Gr. *telesphoros* bringing to an end]. The god of convalescence, a deity worshipped in company with Æsculapius, the god of healing, and Hygeia, the goddess of health.

telesthesia (tel″es-the′ze-ah) [*tele*-(2) + Gr. *aisthēsis* perception + *-ia*]. Telepathy; perception at a distance.

telesthetoscope (tel″es-thet′o-skōp) [*tele*-(2) + Gr. *aisthēsis* perception + *skopein* to examine]. A combination of stethoscope and electrical amplification by which persons at a distance from the patient can hear the heart and lung sounds, as in demonstrating to a class or to a medical audience.

telesyphilis (tel″e-sif′ĭ-lis). Metasyphilis.

telesystolic (tel″e-sis-tol′ik) [*tele*-(1) + *systole*]. Pertaining to the last phase of the systole.

teletactor (tel″e-tak′tor) [*tele*-(2) + L. *tangere* to touch]. An instrument for communicating with the deaf by means of touch on a vibrating plate.

teletherapy (tel″e-ther′ah-pe) [*tele*-(2) + Gr. *therapeia* treatment]. 1. Radiation treatment with massive doses administered at a distance from the body. 2. Suggestive therapeutics.

telethermometer (tel″e-ther-mom′e-ter). An apparatus for determining temperature on which the reading is made at a distance from the object or subject which is being studied.

tellurate (tel′u-rāt). Any salt of telluric acid.

telluric (tel-lu′rik). 1. Pertaining to or originating from the earth. 2. Pertaining to the element tellurium.

tellurism (tel′u-rizm) [L. *tellus* earth]. The alleged production of disease by emanations from the earth or soil (telluric effluvium, or miasma).

tellurite (tel′u-rīt). Any salt of tellurous acid.

tellurium (tel-lu′re-um) [L. *tellus* earth]. A nonmetallic or metalloid element; symbol, Te; specific gravity, 6.24; atomic weight, 127.60; atomic number, 52.

Tellyesniczky's fluid (tel″yets-nits′kēz) [Kálmár *Tellyesniczky*, Budapest anatomist, 1868–1932]. See under *fluid*.

telo- (tel′o) [Gr. *telos* end]. Combining form denoting relationship to an end.

telobiosis (tel″o-bi-o′sis) [*telo*- + Gr. *biōsis* way of life]. The end-to-end union of embryos through operative procedures.

telocinesia, telocinesis (tel″o-si-ne′se-ah, tel″-o-si-ne′sis). Telophase.

telocoele (tel′o-sēl) [*telo*- + Gr. *koilia* cavity]. The cavity of the telencephalon.

telodendria (tel″o-den′dre-ah). Plural of *telodendrion.*

telodendrion (tel″o-den′dre-on), pl. *teloden′dria.* Telodendron.

telodendron (tel″o-den′dron) [*telo*- + Gr. *dendron* tree]. One of the many fine terminal branches of an axon.

telogen (tel′o-jen). The quiescent, or resting, phase of the hair cycle, following catagen, the hair having become a club hair and not growing further.

telognosis (tel″og-no′sis) [*tele*otelephonic diag*nosis*]. Diagnosis based on interpretation of roentgenograms transmitted by telephonic or radio communication.

telokinesis (tel″o-ki-ne′sis) [*telo*- + Gr. *kinēsis* motion]. Telophase.

telolecithal (tel″o-les′ĭ-thal) [*telo*- + Gr. *lekithos* yolk]. Having the yolk concentrated toward one pole which, because of that concentration, is designated the vegetal pole.

telolemma (tel″o-lem′ah) [*telo*- + Gr. *lemma* rind]. The twofold covering of a motorial end-plate, made up of sarcolemma and an extension of Henle's sheath.

telomere (tel′o-mēr) [*telo*- + Gr. *meros* part]. A term applied to each of the extremities of a chromosome, which possess special properties, among them a polarity which prevents their reunion with any fragment after a chromosome has been broken.

telophase (tel′o-fāz) [*telo*- + Gr. *phasis* phase]. The last of the four stages of mitosis. See *mitosis.*

telophragma (tel″o-frag′mah) [*telo*- + Gr. *phragmos* a fencing in]. Krause's membrane. See *inophragma* and *mesophragma.*

teloreceptor (te′lo-re-sep″tor). Teleceptor.

telorism (tel′o-rizm). See *hypertelorism.*

telosynapsis (tel″o-sĭ-nap′sis) [*telo*- + Gr. *synapsis* conjunction]. The union of chromosomes end to end during meiosis. Cf. *parasynapsis.*

telotism (tel′o-tizm). 1. The complete performance of a function. 2. A complete erection of the penis.

telson (tel′son). A scorpion's sting.

TEM. Triethylene melamine, a compound used orally in the experimental treatment of leukemia.

temaril (tem′ah-ril). Trade mark for preparations of trimeprazine tartrate.

temp. dext. Abbreviation for L. *tem′pori dex′tro,* to the right temple.

temperament (tem′per-ah-ment) [L. *temperamentum* mixture]. The peculiar physical character and mental cast of an individual. **atrabilious t.** Same as *melancholic t.* **bilious t.,** that characterized by a dark or sallow complexion, black hair, and a slow or moderate circulation of the blood. **choleric t.** Same as *bilious t.* **lymphatic t.,** one characterized by a fair but not ruddy complexion, light hair, and a general softness or laxity of the tissues. It results, according to the old physiologists, from the predominance of lymph or phlegm in the system. **melancholic t.,** one characterized by a predominance of *black bile* (which was supposed to be secreted by the spleen), rendering the disposition melancholic and morose, and, when in great excess, producing hypochondriasis. **nervous t.,** one characterized by the predominance of the nervous element, and by great activity or susceptibility of the great nervous center, the brain. **phlegmatic t.,** lymphatic t. **sanguine t., sanguineous t.,** one characterized by fair and ruddy complexion, yellow, red, or light auburn hair, a full, muscular development, large, full veins, and an active pulse, all indicating an abundant supply of blood.

temperantia (tem″per-an′she-ah). Sedatives.

temperature (tem′per-ah-tūr) [L. *temperatura*]. The degree of sensible heat or cold. **absolute t.,** temperature reckoned from absolute zero (−273.15°C. or −459.67°F.), expressed on an absolute scale (Kelvin or Rankine). **body t.,** the temperature of the body. **body t., basal,** the temperature of the body under conditions of absolute rest. **critical t.,** a temperature below which a gas may be reduced to liquid form by pressure. **maximum t.,** in bacteriology, the temperature above which growth does not take place. **mean t.,** the average temperature in a locality for a given period of time. **minimum t.,** in bacteriology, temperature below which growth does not take place. **normal t.,** that of the human body in health, 98.6°F. or 37°C. This is maintained by the thermotaxic nerve mechanism, which maintains a balance between the thermogenetic, or heat-producing, and the thermolytic, or heat-dispelling, processes. **optimum t.,** the temperature most favorable to the development of cultures of a given species of microorganism. **room t.,** the ordinary temperature of a room, 65–80°F. **subnormal t.,** temperature below the normal.

template (tem′plāt). A pattern or mold. In dentistry, a curved or flat plate used as an aid in setting teeth for a denture. In immunology, the term *templating* has been applied to the concept that the action of antigen on specific precipitins is influenced by the protein reserve of the body (antibody matrix) which sets the pattern of action of protective antibodies. **surgical t.,** a thin plate of transparent resin shaped to duplicate the surface of an impression for an immediate denture and used as a guide in surgically shaping the alveolar process of the jaw to fit the prosthesis.

temple (tem′p'l) [L. *tempula*, dim. of *tempora*, pl. of *tempus*]. The lateral region of the upper part of the head. See *tempora.*

tempolabile (tem″po-la′bil) [L. *tempus* time + *labilis* unstable]. Subject to change with the passage of time.

tempora (tem′po-rah) [L., pl. of *tempus*]. [N A, B N A] The region on either side of the head, above the zygomatic arch.

temporal (tem′po-ral) [L. *temporalis*]. 1. Pertaining to the lateral region of the head, above the zygomatic arch. 2. Pertaining to time; limited as to time; temporary.

temporalis (tem-po-ra′lis) [L.]. Pertaining to the lateral region of the head, above the zygomatic arch.

temporo-auricular (tem″po-ro-aw-rik′u-lar). Pertaining to the temporal and auricular regions.

temporofacial (tem″po-ro-fa′shal). Pertaining to a temple and the face.

temporofrontal (tem″po-ro-fron′tal). Pertaining to the temporal and frontal bones or regions.

temporohyoid (tem″po-ro-hi′oid). Pertaining to the temporal and hyoid bones.

temporomalar (tem″po-ro-ma′lar). Temporozygomatic.

temporomandibular (tem″po-ro-man-dib′u-lar). Pertaining to the temporal bone and the mandible.

temporomaxillary (tem″po-ro-mak′sĭ-ler″e). Pertaining to the temporal bone, or region, and the maxilla.

temporo-occipital (tem″po-ro-oks-ip′ĭ-tal). Pertaining to the temporal and occipital bones or regions.

temporoparietal (tem″po-ro-pah-ri′ĕ-tal). Pertaining to the temporal and parietal bones or regions.

temporopontile (tem″po-ro-pon′til). Pertaining to the temporal lobe and the pons.

temporospatial (tem″po-ro-spa′shal) [L. *tempus* time + *spatium* space]. Pertaining to both time and space.

temporosphenoid (tem″po-ro-sfe′noid). Pertaining to the temporal and sphenoid bones.

temporozygomatic (tem″po-ro-zi″go-mat′ik). Pertaining to the temporal and zygomatic bones, or to the region of the zygomatic arch.

tempostabile (tem″po-sta′bil) [L. *tempus* time + *stabilis* stable]. Not subject to change with the passage of time.

tempra (tem′prah). Trade mark for preparations of acetaminophen.

temp. sinist. Abbreviation for L. *tem′pori sinis′tro*, to the left temple.

temulence (tem′u-lens) [L. *temulentia*]. Drunkenness; intoxication.

tenacious (te-na′shus) [L. *tenax*]. Holding fast; adhesive.

tenacity (te-nas′ĭ-te). Toughness; the condition of being tough. **cellular t.,** the inherent tendency of all cells to persist in a given form or direction of activity.

tenaculum (te-nak′u-lum) [L.]. 1. A hooklike instrument for seizing and holding parts. 2. Any

Tenaculum (Da Costa).

fibrous band for holding parts in their places. **t. ten′dinum,** retinaculum tendinum.

tenalgia (te-nal′je-ah) [Gr. *tenōn* tendon + *algos* pain + *-ia*]. Pain in a tendon.

tenderness (ten′der-nes). Abnormal sensitiveness to touch or pressure. **pencil t.,** local tenderness on pressure with the rubber tip of a pencil. **rebound t.,** a sensation of pain felt on the release of pressure.

tendinitis (ten″dĭ-ni′tis). Inflammation of tendons and of tendon-muscle attachments. **t. of horse,** inflammation of the flexor tendons, due to strain of wrenching, and causing great tenderness and lameness. **t. ossif′icans traumat′ica,** a condition in which areas of ossification develop in tendons as a result of trauma. **t. sten′osans, stenosing t.,** stenosing tendovaginitis of the flexor tendons of the finger.

tendinoplasty (ten′dĭ-no-plas″te) [L. *tendo* tendon + Gr. *plassein* to mold]. The plastic surgery of the tendons.

tendinosuture (ten″dĭ-no-su′tūr) [L. *tendo* tendon + *sutura* sewing]. The suturing of a tendon.

tendinous (ten′dĭ-nus) [L. *tendinosus*]. Pertaining to, resembling, or of the nature of a tendon.

tendo (ten′do), pl. *ten′dines* [L.]. [N A, B N A] A fibrous cord of connective tissue in which the fibers of a muscle end and by which the muscle is attached to a bone or other structure. Called also *tendon.* **t. Achil′lis,** official alternative for *t. calcaneus.* **t. calca′neus** [N A, B N A], a powerful tendon at the back of the heel which attaches the triceps surae muscle to the tuberosity of the calcaneus. Called also *tendo Achillis, Achilles tendon,* and *calcaneal tendon.* **t. conjuncti′vus,** N A alternative for *falx inguinalis.* **t. cordifor′mis,** centrum tendineum. **t. crico-esophage′us** [N A], the tendon giving origin to the longitudinal fibers of the esophagus that come from the upper part of the lamina of the cricoid cartilage. Called also *cricoesophageal tendon.* **t. oc′uli, t. palpebra′rum,** ligamentum palpebrale mediale.

tendolysis (ten-dol′ĭ-sis) [L. *tendo* tendon + Gr. *lysis* dissolution]. The operation of freeing a tendon from adhesions.

tendomucin (ten″do-mu′sin). A mucin derivable from tendons and closely related to submaxillary mucin and to the colloid of cancers.

tendomucoid (ten″do-mu′koid). Tendomucin.

tendon (ten′dun) [L. *tendo;* Gr. *tenōn*]. A fibrous cord by which a muscle is attached. See *tendo.* **Achilles t.,** tendo calcaneus. **calcaneal t.,** tendo calcaneus. **central t. of diaphragm,** centrum tendineum. **central t. of perineum,** centrum tendineum perinei. **common t.,** a tendon that serves more than one muscle. **conjoined t.,** falx inguinalis. **cordiform t. of diaphragm,** centrum tendineum. **coronary t's,** the fibrous rings surrounding the orifices of the ventricles leading to the aorta and the pulmonary trunk. See *anuli fibrosi cordis.* **cricoesophageal t.,** tendo cricoesophageus. **hamstring t.** See *hamstring.* **t. of Hector, heel t.,** tendo calcaneus. **intermediate t. of diaphragm,** centrum tendineum. **kangaroo t.,** the prepared tendon from the tail of certain species of kangaroo: used as a material for sutures or ligatures. **membranaceous t.,** aponeurosis. **patellar t., anterior, patellar t., inferior,** ligamentum patellae. **pulled t.,** disruption of the fibers attaching a muscle to its point of origin, occurring as the result of unusual muscular effort. **riders' t.,** injury to the adductor tendons of the thigh incurred in horseback riding. **slipped t.,** perosis. **trefoil t.,** centrum tendineum. **t. of Zinn,** zonula ciliaris.

tendoplasty (ten′do-plas″te) [L. *tendo* tendon + Gr. *plassein* to mold]. Plastic surgery of the tendons.

tendosynovitis (ten″do-sin″o-vi′tis). Tenosynovitis.

tendotome (ten′do-tōm). Tenotome.

tendotomy (ten-dot′o-me). Tenotomy.

tendovaginal (ten″do-vaj′ĭ-nal) [L. *tendo* tendon + *vagina* sheath]. Pertaining to a tendon and its sheath.

tendovaginitis (ten″do-vaj″ĭ-ni′tis). 1. Inflammation of a tendon and its sheath. 2. Tenosynovitis.

tenectomy (te-nek′to-me) [Gr. *tenōn* tendon + *ektomē* excision]. Excision of a lesion of a tendon or of a tendon sheath.

tenesmic (te-nez′mik). Pertaining to or of the nature of tenesmus.

tenesmus (te-nez′mus) [L.; Gr. *teinesmos*]. Straining; especially ineffectual and painful straining at stool or in urination. **rectal t.,** painful, long-continued, and ineffective straining at stool. **vesical t.,** that which sometimes accompanies urination.

tenia (te′ne-ah), pl. *te′niae* [L. "a flat band," "bandage," "tape"]. 1. [N A] A flat band or strip of soft tissue. Called also *taenia* [B N A]. 2. An individual organism of the genus Taenia. **te′niae acus′ticae,** striae medullares ventriculi quarti. **t. choroi′dea** [N A], the line of attachment of the lateral choroid plexus to the medial wall of the cerebral hemisphere. **te′niae co′li** [N A], three thickened bands, about ¼ inch wide and one-sixth shorter than the colon, formed by the longitudinal fibers in the muscular tunic of the large intestine and extending from the root of the vermiform appendix to the rectum, where the fibers spread out and form a continuous layer encircling the tube: they include the *t. libera, t. mesocolica,* and *t. omentalis.* **t. for′nicis** [N A], **t. of fornix,** the line of attachment of the choroid plexus of the lateral ventricle to the fornix, including the line of its attachment to the fimbria of the hippocampus (taenia fimbriae [B N A]). **t. of fourth ventricle,** t. ventriculi quarti. **t. li′bera** [N A], the thickened band formed by longitudinal muscle fibers of the large intestine, almost equidistant from the tenia mesocolica and the tenia omentalis. **t. mesocol′ica** [N A], the thickened band of longitudinal muscle fibers of the large intestine along the site of attachment of the mesocolon. **t. omenta′lis** [N A], the band of longitudinal muscle fibers of the large intestine along the site of attachment of the greater omentum. **t. plex′us choroi′dei ventric′uli quar′ti, t. si′nus rhomboi′deae,** t. ventriculi quarti. **t. te′lae** [N A], the line of attachment of the ependymal cells of the choroid plexus to various portions of the brain. Called *taenia telarum* [B N A]. **t. thal′ami** [N A], **t. of thalamus,** the line of attachment of the ependymal cells of the roof of the third ventricle to the dorsal margin of the thalamus. **t. of third ventricle,** t. thalami. **t. ventric′uli quar′ti** [N A], the line of attachment of the ependymal cells of the choroid plexus to the caudal part of the fourth ventricle. Called also *t. of fourth ventricle.* **t. ventric′uli ter′tii,** t. thalami.

teniacide (te′ne-ah-sīd) [L. *taenia* tapeworm + *caedere* to kill]. 1. Destructive to tapeworms. 2. An agent that destroys tapeworms.

teniafuge (te′ne-ah-fūj) [L. *taenia* tapeworm + *fugare* to put to flight]. 1. Expelling tapeworms. 2. An agent that expels tapeworms.

tenial (te′ne-al). Pertaining to a taenia.

tenicide (ten′ĭ-sīd). Teniacide.

teniform (ten′ĭ-form). Resembling a taenia, or a tapeworm.

tenifugal (te-nif′u-gal). Expelling tapeworms.

tenifuge (ten′ĭ-fūj). Teniafuge.

tenioid (te′ne-oid). Teniform.

teniola (te-ne′o-lah) [L. *taeniola*]. A thin, grayish ridge which separates the striae of the floor of the fourth ventricle from the cochlear part of the acoustic nerve. Called also *taeni′ola cine′rea.*

teniotoxin (te″ne-o-tok′sin). A poisonous principle occurring in tapeworms.

tennysine (ten′ĭ-sin). An alkaloid or leukomaine derivable from the brain substance.

teno-, tenonto- (ten′o, ten-on′to) [Gr. *tenōn, tenontos* tendon]. Combining form denoting relationship to a tendon.

tenodesis (ten-od′e-sis) [*teno-* + Gr. *desis* a binding together]. Tendon fixation; suturing of the proximal end of a tendon to the bone.

tenodynia (ten″o-din′e-ah) [*teno-* + Gr. *odynē* pain]. Pain in a tendon.

tenofibril (ten′o-fi″bril). Tonofibril.

tenomyoplasty (ten″o-mi′o-plas″te) [*teno-* + Gr. *mys* muscle + *plassein* to form]. A plastic operation involving tendon and muscle: applied especially to an operation for inguinal hernia.

tenomyotomy (ten″o-mi-ot′o-me) [*teno-* + Gr. *mys* muscle + *tomē* a cutting]. Excision of a portion of tendon and muscle.

Tenon's capsule, space, etc. (te′nonz) [Jacques René *Tenon,* French surgeon, 1724–1816]. See under the nouns.

tenonectomy (ten″o-nek′to-me) [*teno-* + Gr. *ektomē* excision]. Excision of a part of a tendon for the purpose of shortening it.

tenonitis (ten″o-ni′tis). 1. Tenontitis. 2. Inflammation of Tenon's capsule.

tenonometer (ten″o-nom′e-ter) [Gr. *teinein* to stretch + *metron* measure]. An apparatus for measuring intra-ocular tension.

tenonostosis (ten″on-os-to′sis). Tenostosis.

tenontagra (ten″on-ta′grah, ten-on′tag-rah) [*tenonto-* + Gr. *agra* seizure]. A gouty affection of the tendons.

tenontitis (ten″on-ti′tis). Inflammation of a tendon. **t. prolif′era calca′rea,** inflammation of a tendon, with degeneration and the formation of calcareous matter.

tenonto-. See *teno-.*

tenontodynia (ten″on-to-din′e-ah) [*tenonto-* + Gr. *odynē* pain + *-ia*]. Pain in the tendons.

tenontography (ten″on-tog′rah-fe) [*tenonto-* + Gr. *graphein* to write]. A written description or delineation of the tendons.

tenontolemmitis (ten-on″to-lem-mi′tis) [*tenonto-* + Gr. *lemma* rind + *-itis*]. Tenosynovitis.

tenontology (ten″on-tol′o-je). The sum of what is known regarding the tendons.

tenontomyoplasty (ten-on″to-mi′o-plas″te). Tenomyoplasty.

tenontomyotomy (ten-on″to-mi-ot′o-me). Tenomyotomy.

tenontophyma (ten-on″to-fi′mah) [*tenonto-* + Gr. *phyma* growth]. A tumorous growth in a tendon.

tenontoplasty (ten-on′to-plas″te). Tenoplasty.

tenontothecitis (ten-on″to-the-si′tis) [*tenonto-* + Gr. *thēkē* sheath + *-itis*]. Inflammation of a tendon sheath.

tenontotomy (ten″on-tot′o-me). Tenotomy.

tenophony (te-nof′o-ne) [*teno-* + Gr. *phōnē* sound]. An auscultatory sound supposed to be produced by the chordae tendineae.

tenophyte (ten′o-fit) [*teno-* + Gr. *phyton* growth]. A growth or concretion in a tendon.

tenoplastic (ten″o-plas′tik). Of or relating to tenoplasty.

tenoplasty (ten′o-plas″te) [*teno-* + Gr. *plassein* to shape]. Plastic surgery of the tendons; operative repair of a defect in a tendon.

tenoreceptor (ten″o-re-sep′tor) [*teno-* + *receptor*]. A proprioceptor situated in tendon: such receptors are stimulated by contraction.

tenorrhaphy (ten-or′ah-fe) [*teno-* + Gr. *rhaphē* suture]. The union of a divided tendon by a suture.

tenositis (ten″o-si′tis). Inflammation of a tendon.

tenostosis (ten″os-to′sis) [*teno-* + Gr. *osteon* bone + *-osis*]. Ossification of a tendon.

tenosuspension (ten″o-sus-pen′shun). An operation for habitual dislocation of the shoulder by passing a strip of peroneus longus tendon through the head of the humerus and through the acromion process.

tenosuture (ten″o-su′tūr) [*teno-* + L. *sutura* suture]. Tenorrhaphy.

tenosynitis (ten″o-si-ni′tis). Tendovaginitis.

tenosynovectomy (ten″o-sin″o-vek′to-me). Excision or resection of a tendon sheath.

tenosynovitis (ten″o-sin″o-vi′tis). Inflammation of a tendon sheath. **t. acu′ta purulen′ta,** tenosynovitis with pus formation. **adhesive t.,** tenosynovitis in which the tendons become bound in an inflammatory mass. **t. crep′itans,** a form accompanied by a crackling sound in the soft tissues on movement. **gonococcic t., gonorrheal t.,** tenosynovitis due to metastatic gonococcal infection. **t. granulo′sa,** tuberculosis of tendon sheaths, which become filled with granulation tissue. **t. hypertroph′ica,** a condition marked by swellings along the tendons and their sheaths. **t. sero′sa chron′ica,** tenosynovitis with serous effusion. **t. sten′osans,** a painful condition of the wrist, marked by thickening and narrowing of the tendon sheath of the extensor brevis and abductor longus pollicis (De Quervain). **tuberculous t.,** chronic tuberculous infection of tendon sheaths and bursae. **villonodular t.,** a condition characterized by exaggerated proliferation of synovial membrane cells, producing a solid tumor-like mass, commonly occurring in periarticular soft tissues and less frequently in joints. **villous t.,** chronic infection of tendon sheaths and bursa, with proliferation of villous projections from the surface of the membranes.

tenotome (ten′o-tōm). A cutting instrument used in tenotomy.

tenotomist (ten-ot′o-mist). An expert in performing tenotomy.

tenotomize (ten-ot′o-mīz). To perform tenotomy.

tenotomy (ten-ot′o-me) [*teno-* + Gr. *tomē* a cutting]. The cutting of a tendon as for strabismus or clubfoot. **curb t.,** the operation of cutting an eye muscle in squint and inserting it farther back on the globe of the eye. **graduated t.,** the incomplete division of a tendon.

tenovaginitis (ten″o-vaj″ĭ-ni′tis). Inflammation of a tendon sheath.

tense (tens). Drawn tight; rigid.

tensilon (ten′sĭ-lon). Trade mark for a solution of edrophonium chloride.

tensio-active (ten″se-o-ak′tiv). Having an effect on surface tension.

tensiometer (ten″se-om′e-ter) [*tension* + Gr. *metron* measure]. An apparatus for measuring the surface tension of liquids.

tension (ten′shun) [L. *tensio;* Gr. *tonos*]. 1. The act of stretching. 2. The condition of being stretched or strained; the amount to which anything is stretched or strained. 3. Voltage. **arterial t.,** the strain on an artery produced by the blood current at full pulse. **electric t.,** electromotive force. **gaseous t.,** the elasticity of a gas, or its tendency to expand. **intraocular t.** See under *pressure.* **intravenous t.,** the strain produced by the blood current upon the coats of a vein. **muscular t.,** the condition of moderate contraction produced by stretching a muscle. **premenstrual t.,** a syndrome sometimes occurring during the ten days preceding menstruation, marked by emotional instability, irritability, insomnia, and headache. There may also be pain in the breasts, abdominal distention, bearing-down pelvic discomfort, nausea, anorexia, constipation, urinary frequency, and general weakness. **surface t.,** the tension or resistance which acts to preserve the integrity of a surface, such as the tension or resistance to rupture possessed by the surface film of a liquid, or the tension or strain upon the surface of a liquid in contact with another substance with which it does not mix. **tissue t.,** a state of equilibrium between tissues and cells which prevents overaction of any part.

tensiophone (ten′se-o-fōn) [L. *tensio* tension + Gr. *phōnē* sound]. An instrument for obtaining auscultatory and palpatory readings of the blood pressure.

tensometer (tens-om′e-ter). An apparatus by which the tensile strength of materials can be determined.

tensor (ten′sor) [L., "stretcher," "puller"]. Any muscle that stretches or makes tense.

tent (tent) [L. *tenta,* from *tendere* to stretch]. 1. A covering of fabric arranged to enclose an open space, especially such an arrangement over a patient's bed for the purpose of administering oxygen or medications active by inhalation. 2. A conical and expansible plug of soft material, as lint, gauze, etc., for dilating an orifice or for keeping a wound open, so as to prevent its healing except at the bottom. **laminaria t.,** a tent made of sea tangle, or laminaria. **oxygen t.,** a tent erected over a bed into which a constant flow of oxygen can be maintained. **sponge t.,** a slender, cone-shaped piece of compressed sponge: used for dilating the os uteri. **steam t.,** a tent erected over a bed into which steam is passed: used in certain respiratory conditions. **tupelo t.,** one made of the wood of the root of the water-tupelo, a tree (*Nyssa uniflora*) of North America.

tentacle (ten′tah-k′l). A slender whiplike organ in invertebrates for feeling or motion.

tentative (ten′tah-tiv). Experimental and subject to change.

tenthmeter (tenth-me′ter). One ten-millionth of a meter.

tentiginous (ten-tij′ĭ-nus). Characterized by maniacal lust.

tentigo (ten-ti′go) [L. "lecherousness"]. Psychopathic lasciviousness.

tentorial (ten-to′re-al). Pertaining to the tentorium.

tentorium (ten-to′re-um), pl. *tento′ria* [L. "tent"].

An anatomical part resembling a tent or a covering. **t. cerebel'li** [N A, B N A], **t. of cerebellum,** the extension of dura mater that forms a partition between the cerebrum and cerebellum and covers the upper surface of the cerebellum. **t. of hypophysis,** diaphragma sellae.

tentum (ten'tum). The penis.

tenulin (ten'u-lin). A crystalline principle, $C_{17}H_{22}O_5$, from *Helenium tenuifolium* and other species that is mildly sternutatory and poisonous to fish.

tephromalacia (tef"ro-mah-la'she-ah) [Gr. *tephros* ash-colored + *malakia* softening]. Softening of the gray matter of the brain or cord.

tephromyelitis (tef"ro-mi"ĕ-li'tis) [Gr. *tephros* ash-colored + *myelos* marrow + *-itis*]. Inflammation of the gray substance of the spinal cord.

tephrosis (tef-ro'sis) [Gr. *tephrōsis*]. Incineration or cremation.

tephrylometer (tef"ril-om'e-ter) [Gr. *tephros* ash-colored + *hylē* matter + *metron* measure]. A graduated glass tube for measuring the thickness of the gray matter of the brain.

tepidarium (tep"ĭ-da're-um) [L., from *tepidus* lukewarm]. A warm bath: more correctly, a place for a warm bath.

tepor (te'por) [L. "lukewarmness"]. Gentle heat.

TEPP. Acronym for *tetraethylpyrophosphate*.

ter- [L. *ter* thrice]. Prefix meaning three, three-fold.

tera- (ter'ah) [Gr. *teras* monster]. Combining form used in naming units of measurement to indicate a quantity one trillion (10^{12}) times the unit specified by the root with which it is combined.

terabdella (ter"ab-del'ah) [Gr. *teirein* to bore + *bdella* leech]. A form of mechanical leech.

teracurie (ter"ah-ku're). A unit of radioactivity, being one trillion (10^{12}) curies.

teras (ter'as), pl. *ter'ata* [L.; Gr.]. A fetal monster. **ter'ata anadid'yma,** anadidymus; sometimes applied to a double monster with duplication of the cephalic pole and single toward the podalic pole. **ter'ata kata-anadid'yma,** anakatadidymus. **ter'ata katadid'yma,** katadidymus; sometimes applied to a double monster with duplication of the podalic pole and single toward the cephalic pole.

terata (ter'ah-tah). Plural of *teras*.

teratic (ter-at'ik) [Gr. *teratikos*]. Monstrous; having the characters of a monster.

teratism (ter'ah-tizm) [Gr. *teratisma*]. An anomaly of formation or development; the condition of a fetal monster. See under *teras, monster,* and *monstrum,* and names of specific fetal monsters.

terato- (ter'ah-to) [Gr. *teras, teratos* monster]. Combining form denoting relationship to a monster.

teratoblastoma (ter"ah-to-blas-to'mah). A neoplasm containing embryonic elements and differing from a teratoma in that its tissue does not represent all the germinal layers.

teratocarcinogenesis (ter"ah-to-kar"sĭ-no-jen'e-sis). The production of teratomas.

teratogen (ter'ah-to-jen). An agent or factor that causes the production of physical defects in the developing embryo.

teratogenesis (ter"ah-to-jen'e-sis) [*terato-* + Gr. *genesis* production]. The production of physical defects in offspring in utero.

teratogenetic (ter"ah-to-je-net'ik). Pertaining to teratogenesis.

teratogenic (ter"ah-to-jen'ik). Tending to produce anomalies of formation, or teratism.

teratogenous (ter"ah-toj'e-nus). Developed from fetal remains.

teratogeny (ter"ah-toj'e-ne). Teratogenesis.

teratoid (ter'ah-toid) [*terato-* + Gr. *eidos* form]. Resembling a monster.

teratologic, teratological (ter"ah-to-loj'ik, ter"ah-to-loj'ĭ-kal). Pertaining to teratology.

teratology (ter"ah-tol'o-je). That division of embryology and pathology which deals with abnormal development and congenital malformations.

teratoma (ter"ah-to'mah), pl. *teratomas* or *terato'mata*. A true neoplasm made up of a number of different types of tissue, none of which is native to the area in which it occurs.

teratomatous (ter"ah-to'mah-tus). Pertaining to, or of the nature of, teratoma.

teratophobia (ter"ah-to-fo'be-ah) [Gr. *teras* monster + *phobein* to be affrighted by]. 1. Morbid fear or aversion to monsters. 2. Morbid dread of giving birth to a teratism.

teratosis (ter"ah-to'sis) [Gr. *teras* monster + *-osis*]. Teratism.

teratospermia (ter"ah-to-sper'me-ah). The presence of malformed spermatozoa in the semen.

terbium (ter'be-um). A rare metallic element; symbol, Tb; atomic number, 65; atomic weight, 158.924.

terchloride (ter-klo'rīd). Trichloride.

tere (te're) [L.]. Rub.

terebene (ter'e-bēn) [L. *terebenum*, from *terebinthus* turpentine]. A thin, yellowish, fragrant mixture of terpene hydrocarbons, $C_{10}H_{16}$, obtained from oil of turpentine by the action of sulfuric acid. It is antiseptic and expectorant, and has been used in catarrh, bronchitis, cystitis, fermentative dyspepsia, genito-urinary disease, and as an application to gangrenous wounds, etc.

terebenthene (ter"e-ben'thēn). Oil of turpentine.

terebinth (ter'e-binth) [L. *terebinthus*]. 1. The tree *Pistacia terebinthus*, which affords Chian turpentine. 2. Turpentine.

terebinthina (ter"e-bin'thĭ-nah) [L.]. Turpentine.

terebinthinate (ter"e-bin'thĭ-nāt). Resembling or containing turpentine.

terebinthinism (ter"e-bin'thĭ-nizm). Poisoning with oil of turpentine.

terebrachesis (ter"e-bra-ke'sis). The operation of shortening the round ligament.

terebrant, terebrating (ter'e-brant, ter'e-brāt"ing) [L. *terebrans* boring]. Of a boring or piercing quality.

terebration (ter"e-bra'shun) [L. *terebratio*]. An act of boring or trephining; also a boring pain.

teres (te'rēz) [L.]. Long and round.

terfonyl (ter'fo-nil). Trade mark for preparations of sulfamethazine, sulfadiazine, and sulfamerazine (trisulfapyrimidines).

tergal (ter'gal) [L. *tergum* back]. Pertaining to the back or the dorsal surface.

tergolateral (ter"go-lat'er-al) [L. *tergum* back + *latus* side]. Dorsolateral.

ter in die (ter in de'a) [L.]. Three times a day.

term (term) [L. *terminus*, from Gr. *terma*]. 1. A word or combination of words commonly used to designate a specific entity. 2. A limit or boundary. 3. A definite period or specified time of duration, such as the culmination of pregnancy at the end of nine months. **ontogenetic t's,** termini ontogenetici.

termatic (ter-mat'ik). Pertaining to the terma.

terminad (ter'mĭ-nad) [L. *terminus* limit + *ad* to]. Toward the end or terminus.

terminal (ter'mĭ-nal) [L. *terminalis*]. 1. Forming or pertaining to an end; placed at the end. 2. A termination, end or extremity. See *ending*.

terminatio (ter"mĭ-na'she-o), pl. *terminatio'nes* [L. "a limiting, bounding]. An ending; the site of discontinuation of a structure. **terminatio'nes nervo'rum li'berae** [N A], those neural receptors having the simplest form, in which the peripheral nerve fiber divides into fine branches that terminate freely in connective tissue or epithelium. Called also *free nerve endings*.

termination (ter"mĭ-na'shun) [L. *terminatio*]. A distal end; a cessation.

terminationes (ter″mĭ-na″she-o′nēz) [L.]. Plural of *terminatio.*

termini (ter′mĭ-ni) [ML.]. Plural of *terminus.*

terminology (ter″mĭ-nol′o-je) [L. *terminus* term + *-logy*]. Nomenclature; a system of scientific or technical appellations; the science which deals with the investigation, arrangement, and construction of terms.

terminus (ter′mĭ-nus), pl. *ter′mini* [ML.]. 1. A term; expression. 2. An ending. **ter′mini ad extremita′tes spectan′tes** [B N A], termini ad membra spectantes. **ter′mini ad mem′bra spectan′tes,** the NA category embracing terms relating to the upper and lower limbs. Called also *termini ad extremitates spectantes* [B N A]. **ter′mini genera′les,** a category in official anatomical nomenclature including general terms (that is, terms not applied exclusively to one specific structure but to all structures belonging to the particular category or to which the term is applicable). **ter′mini ontogenet′ici** [N A, B N A], terms relating to development, including those pertaining to the placenta and other fetal membranes or other structures. Called also *ontogenetic terms.* **ter′mini si′tum et directio′nem par′tium cor′poris indican′tes,** a category in official anatomical nomenclature embracing terms indicating position and direction of parts of the body.

termone (ter′mōn). A hormone allegedly given off by male and by female gametes, which tends to influence the sex of the resulting zygote.

ternary (ter′nah-re) [L. *ternarius*]. 1. Third in order. 2. Made up of three distinct elements or radicals.

ternitrate (ter-ni′trāt). A trinitrate.

teroxide (ter-ok′sīd) [L. *ter* three + *oxide*]. Trioxide.

terpane (ter′pān). Methane.

terpene (ter′pēn). Any hydrocarbon of the formula $C_{10}H_{16}$, derivable chiefly from essential oils, resins, and other vegetable aromatic products. They may be acyclic, bicyclic, or monocyclic, and differ somewhat in physical properties.

terpenism (ter′pen-izm). Poisoning with terpene.

terpin (ter′pin) [L. *terpinum*]. A product, $(CH_3)_2$-$C(OH).C_6H_9(OH).CH_3$, obtained by the action of nitric acid on oil of turpentine and alcohol. **t. hydrate,** a bitter, colorless, crystalline compound, $C_{10}H_{20}O_2 + H_2O$: used as an expectorant.

terpineol (ter-pin′e-ol). An alcohol, $(CH_3)_2$.-$C(OH).C_6H_8.CH_3$, consisting of a mixture of several isomers occurring in many essential oils; formerly used as an antiseptic, but now used as a perfuming agent.

terpinol (ter′pĭ-nol). An oily, fragrant liquid, $(C_{10}H_{16})_2H_2O$, prepared by distilling terpin hydrate with dilute hydrochloric or sulfuric acid. It is soluble in ether and alcohol, but almost insoluble in water. Formerly used in bronchial affections and as a perfume. **t. hydrate,** terpin hydrate.

terra (ter′ah) [L.]. Earth. **t. al′ba,** white clay: used as an adsorbent. **t. japon′ica** [L. for "Japanese earth"], pale catechu, or gambir. **t. lem′nia,** a yellowish, ferruginous clay. **t. mer′ita,** turmeric. **t. pondero′sa,** barium sulfate, or baryta. **t. sigilla′ta** [L. "sealed earth" of ancient Lemnos], Armenian bole, sold in masses stamped with a seal. **t. silic′ea purifica′ta,** purified silicious or infusorial earth; silicious earth, boiled, washed, and calcined. It is a fine gray powder and is used in certain pharmaceutical operations.

terramycin (ter′ah-mi″sin). Trade mark for preparations of oxytetracycline.

terrein (ter′e-in). A compound, $C_8H_{10}O_2$, formed by the action of *Aspergillus terreus.*

Terrillon's operation (ter″e-yawz′) [Octave Roch *Terrillon,* French surgeon, 1844–1895]. See under *operation.*

terror (ter′er). Intense fright. **day t's,** pavor diurnus. **night t's,** pavor nocturnus.

tersulfide (ter-sul′fīd). Trisulfide.

tertian (ter′shun) [L. *tertianus*]. Recurring every third day, counting the day of occurrence as the first day; applied to the type of fever caused by certain forms of malarial parasites. **double t.,** an intermittent fever in which there are two sets of recurrences, each tertian, but differing somewhat in character.

tertiarism (ter′she-ah-rizm). The combined symptoms of tertiary syphilis.

tertiary (ter′she-er-e) [L. *tertiarius*]. Third in order.

tertigravida (ter″she-grav′ĭ-dah) [L. *tertius* third + *gravida* pregnant]. A woman pregnant for the third time. Also written gravida III.

tertipara (ter-ship′ah-rah) [L. *tertius* third + *parere* to bring forth, produce]. A woman who has had three pregnancies which resulted in viable offspring. Also written Para III.

teslaization (tes″la-i-za′shun) [Nikola *Tesla,* a Serbian electrician in New York, 1856–1943]. Treatment by Tesla's currents: arsonvalization.

tessalon (tes′sah-lon). Trade mark for a preparation of benzonatate.

tessellated (tes′el-lāt″ed) [L. *tessellatus; tessella* a square]. Divided into squares, like a checker board.

test (test) [L. *testum* crucible]. 1. An examination or trial. 2. A significant chemical reaction. 3. A reagent. For specific tests, see *Table of Tests.* See also under *method, phenomenon, reaction, reagent, sign,* and *symptom.*

test card (test kard). A card printed with various letters or symbols, used in testing vision. **stigmometric t. c.,** a card with dots and squares arranged in groups, for testing vision (Fridenberg).

test letter (test let′er). See *test type.*

A TABLE OF TESTS

(See also under *method*, *phenomenon*, *reaction*, *sign*, and *symptom*.)

Abderhalden's t. See under *reaction*.

Abelin's t. (*for arsphenamine*). See under *reaction*.

Abrams' t. (*for lead in the urine*): Add ammonium oxalate to urine (1:150) and introduce metallic magnesium (wire or rod). Lead is precipitated on the magnesium, and can be identified by warming with a fragment of iodine (yellow lead iodide), or dissolving in nitric acid and applying other reagents.

acetanilid t. See *Yvon's t.*

acetic acid t. (*for albumin in urine*): A few drops of acetic acid are added to the boiled urine, when a white precipitate is formed.

acetic acid and potassium ferrocyanide t. (*for proteins*): Acidify the unknown with acetic acid and add a few drops of potassium ferrocyanide. Protein produces a white flocculent precipitate.

aceto-acetic acid t. See *Arnold's t.*, *Harding and Ruttan's t.*, *Hurtley's t.*, *Lindemann's t.*, and *Nobel's t.*

acetone t.: A test for the presence of acetone in the urine made by adding a few drops of sodium nitroprusside, shaking, and pouring over the mixture stronger ammonia water: a magenta-colored line is formed over the area of contact if acetone is present. See also *Bayer's t.*, *Behre and Benedict's t.*, *Braun's t.*, *Chautard's t.*, *Denigès' t.* (2), *Frommer's t.*, *Gerhardt's t.*, *Gunning's t.*, *Lange's t.* (2), *Legal's t.* (1), *Lieben's t.*, *Lieben-Ralfe t.*, *Malerba's t.*, *Nobel's t.* (1), *Penzoldt's t.* (1), *Ralfe's t.* (1), *Rantzman's t.*, *Reynold's t.*, *Rothera's t.*, *Stock t.*

acetonitril t. (*for hyperthyroidism*): The blood of such patients increases the resistance of mice to poisoning by acetonitril and morphine.

Achard and Castaigne's t. See *methylene blue t.*

acidity reduction t.: 250 cc. of 0.4 per cent hydrochloric acid is introduced into an empty stomach through a tube. Samples are withdrawn at intervals of fifteen minutes and titrated for free acid.

acidosis t. See *Sellard's t.*

Acree-Rosenheim t. (*for proteins*): A few drops of formaldehyde solution (1:5000) are placed in a solution of the suspected matter. A little concentrated sulfuric acid is slowly placed in the test tube so that the solutions do not mix. At the line of contact a violet color appears if proteins are present.

acrolein t. (*for glycerol and fats*): Heat the substance with an equal quantity of potassium acid sulfate and note the peculiar penetrating odor of acrolein.

Adamkiewicz's t. (*for proteins*): Add the substance to a mixture of 1 volume of strong sulfuric acid and 2 volumes of glacial acetic acid and heat it. A reddish-violet color shows the presence of proteins.

Adams' t. (*for fat in milk*): Dry a known quantity of milk on filter paper, extract in Soxhlet's apparatus, dry to constant weight, and weigh.

Addis' t. See under *count*.

Adler's t. See *benzidine t.*

Admiralty t.: A test for the efficiency of excremental disinfectants in which gelatin and starch are used as the organic test substances.

adrenalin t. See *epinephrine t.*

agglutination t.: One of various specific and nonspecific tests the results of which depend on agglutination of bacteria or of other cells: used as an aid in diagnosis of certain bacterial or of viral and rickettsial diseases, and of rheumatoid arthritis.

Agostini's t. (*for dextrose*): Mix 5 drops of the urine with 5 drops of a 0.5 per cent solution of gold chloride and 3 drops of a 20 per cent solution of potassium hydroxide, and warm the mixture; dextrose will give a red tint.

Aiello's t.: Add 0.5–0.8 cc. of concentrated hydrochloric acid and 2–3 drops of a 2 per cent solution of formaldehyde to 2–3 cc. of spinal fluid. Overlay with a 0.06 per cent solution of sodium nitrite. A violet ring indicates tryptophan.

air t. See *Franken's t.*

Albarran's t. (*for renal inadequacy*): A test for the renal function based upon the principle that the greater the destruction of epithelium in the kidney, the less likely is that organ to respond by an increase in secretion after the administration of quantities of water. Called also *polyuria t.*

albumin t. See *acetic acid t.*, *Almén's t.* (1), *Alper's t.*, *ammonium sulfate t.* (2), *Axenfeld's t.*, *Barral's t.*, *Berzelius' t.*, *Blum's t.*, *Boedeker's t.*, *Boston's t.*, *Bychowski's t.*, *Carrez's t.*, *Castellani's t.*, *Cohen's t.*, *Esbach's t.*, *Exton's t.*, *Fürbringer's t.*, *Geissler's t.*, *Heller's t.* (1), *Heynsius' t.*, *Hindenlang's t.*, *Ilimow's t.*, *Johnson's t.*, *Lessilur-Prirey t.*, *MacWilliams' t.*, *magnesionitric t.*, *Méhu's t.*, *Millard's t.*, *Oliver's t.* (1), *Osgood-Haskin's t.*, *oxyphenyl sulfonic acid t.*, *Parnum's t.*, *Pollacci's t.*, *Posner's t.* (1), *Purdy's t.* (2), *Raabe's t.*, *Rees' t.*, *Riegler's t.* (1), *Roberts' t.* (1), *Spiegler's t.*, *Tanret's t.*, *Tidy's t.* (1), (2), *Tretop's t.*, *Tsuchiya's t.*, *Ulrich's t.*, *Zouchlos' t.* See also the tests listed under *protein t.*

albumin A t. See *Zahn t.*, 2d def.

alcadd t. (*al*coholic *add*iction): A test devised for the rapid identification of alcoholic addicts or for those with a tendency toward alcoholism.

alcohol t. See *Anstie's t.*, *Berthelot's t.*, (2), *chromic acid t.*, *ethyl acetate t.*, *iodoform t.* (2), *Woodbury's t.*

aldehyde t. See *formol-gel t.*, *Napier's serum t.*, and *Tollen's t.* (1).

Aldrich-McClure t. See *McClure-Aldrich t.*

Alfraise's t. (*for iodine*): A reagent consisting of 1 drop of hydrochloric acid in 100 parts of water, 1 of starch, and 1 of potassium nitrate. This is boiled, and 1 drop of the reagent is added to the liquid that is being tested, when a blue color will be produced if iodine is present.

alizarin t. (*for gastric secretion*): After a test drink containing alizarin the intensity of coloration of the urine gives an indication as to the degree of acidity of the urine.

alkali t. See *Bachmeier's t.*, *Degener's t.*

alkali denaturation t.: A moderately sensitive spectrophotometric method for determining the concentration of fetal (F) hemoglobin, which depends on the resistance of the hemoglobin molecule to denaturation of its globin moiety when exposed to alkali.

alkali tolerance t.: 20 Gm. of sodium bicarbonate given while fasting should raise the pH of the urine to 8 within two hours.

alkaloid t. See *Arnold's t.* (2), *Bouchardat's t.*, *Erdman's t.*, *Fröhde's t.*, *Frohn's t.*, *Mayer's t.*, *Vitali's t.* (1) and (2), *Winckler's t.* (1), *Wormley's t.*, *Yvon's t.* (2).

Allen's t.: 1. (*For glucose in the urine.*) Made by adding urine to boiling Fehling's solution, and allowing it to cool, when turbidity will be seen if dextrose is present. 2. (*For phenol.*) To 2 drops of the suspected liquid add 5 drops of hydrochloric acid and 1 of nitric acid. Phenol, if present, will produce a cherry-red color. 3. (*For strychnine.*) Extract with ether, concentrate by letting fall drops into a warmed porcelain capsule, cool the residue, and treat with sulfuric acid and manganese dioxide. Strychnine gives a violet color. 4. (*For tinea versicolor.*) Compound solution of iodine is applied to the suspected eruption: a dark mahogany stain will be produced if the eruption is tinea. (Charles Warren Allen.) 5. (*For occlusion of* *ulnar or radial arteries.*) The patient makes a tight fist so as to express the blood from the skin of the palm and fingers: the examiner makes digital compression on either the radial or the ulnar artery. If on opening the hand blood fails to return to the palm and fingers, there is indicated obstruction to the blood flow in the artery that has not been compressed. (Edgar V. Allen.)

Allen-Doisy t. (*for estrogenic substance in laboratory animals*): A positive test is the presence in the vaginal secretion of cornified epithelial cells: a negative test shows only leukocytes in the secretion.

Allesandri-Guaceni t. (*for nitric acid; nitrates*): Dissolve a few drops of phenol in hydrochloric acid by heating twelve hours on a water bath. Heat 10 drops of the reagent with the dry residue of suspected liquid on the water bath. Nitric acid or nitrates give an intense violet color, changed by ammonia to green.

Almén's t.: 1. (*For albumin in urine.*) One part of Almén's reagent is added to 6 parts of the urine: a cloudiness is produced when albumin is present. 2. (*For blood or blood pigment.*) Shake the suspected liquid with a mixture of equal parts of tincture of guaiacum and oil of turpentine: blood pigment, if present, will turn the mixture blue. 3. (*For dextrose.*) Heat the liquid with bismuth subnitrate dissolved in sodium hydroxide solution and sodium potassium tartrate; dextrose will cause the mixture to become dark brown or nearly black, and to deposit a black precipitate.

aloin t. See *Rossel's aloin t.*

Alper's t. (*for albumin in the urine*): Acidulate the urine with hydrochloric acid and add equal volumes of a 1 per cent mercury succinimide solution: a white cloudiness forms.

alpha t.: A psychological test designed to determine the mental capacity of persons able to read English.

alphanaphthol t. See *Molisch's t.* (2).

Althausen t.: A test for the velocity of intestinal absorption by determining at intervals the concentration of galactose in the blood after the oral administration of sugar.

Amann's t. (*for indican in urine*): To 20 cc. of urine are added a few drops of pure sulfuric acid, 5 cc. of chloroform, and then 5 cc. of a 10 per cent solution of sodium pyrosulfate. They are mixed gently for several minutes. The chloroform is then allowed to settle and will be colored blue by the indigo.

amidopyrine t. See *aminopyrine t.*

amino-acid nitrogen t. See *ninhydrin t., triketohydrindene hydrate t.*

aminopyrine t. (*for occult blood in feces*): A small portion of the feces is stirred up in 3 to 4 cc. of distilled water and filtered. To the filtrate add 3 or 4 cc. of a 90 per cent alcoholic solution of aminopyrine and several drops of a 30 per cent acetic acid with hydrogen peroxide. A violet-blue color indicates occult blood.

ammonia t. See *Brown's t.* (2), *Nessler's t., Ronchese's t.*

ammonium sulfate t. (*for spinal fluid*): 1. *For globulin:* In a test tube place 2 cc. of a solution of 85 Gm. of ammonium sulfate in 100 cc. of water. Overlay with spinal fluid. A clean-cut, grayish-white ring appearing within five minutes indicates excess of globulin. 2. *For albumin:* Mix contents of tube, filter, add acetic acid and boil. A gray cloud indicates increase of albumin. A faint opalescence is normal.

amylase t.: 1. (*For kidney function.*) The urine is tested for starch: a diminution below the normal starch content indicates a diminution of kidney function. 2. See *Hawk's t.*

amyl nitrite t. (*for spinal block*): Note whether or not the rise in intracranial pressure following amyl nitrite injections is transmitted to the spinal intrathecal cavity.

amylopsin t.: Add 0.5 cc. of duodenal contents to 50 cc. of a 3 per cent solution of soluble starch. Incubate for one-half hour and test for reducing sugars.

Andersch and Gibson t.: A test for the amount of fibrinogen in the blood plasma.

Anderson's t. (*to distinguish pyridine chloroplatinate from quinoline chloroplatinate*): Boil the salt in water; the pyridine salt becomes an insoluble double salt, and gives off hydrogen chloride, but the quinoline salt remains in solution.

Anderson and Goldberger's t. (*for typhus fever*): The patient's blood is injected into the peritoneal cavity of guinea-pigs, when, if the disease is typhus, a typical temperature curve will be obtained.

André's t. (*for quinine*): Chlorine and ammonia produce a green color changing to blue on saturation with acid. Excess of acid changes the color to violet or bright red, but ammonia again turns it green.

Andreasch's t. (*for cysteine*): Dissolve the substance in hydrochloric acid, and add a few drops of a dilute solution of ferric chloride and a little ammonia water. Cysteine causes the liquid to assume a dark purplish tint.

Andrewes' t. (*for uremia*): To one volume of serum two volumes of alcohol are added. The mixture is centrifuged and the alcoholic supernatant layer removed. To four volumes of this alcoholic extract are added two volumes of alcohol and one volume of freshly prepared diazo reagent, as in van den Bergh's test. In uremia the mixture slowly develops a brown-buff color.

Anstie's t. (*for alcohol in the urine*): A reagent consisting of a solution of potassium dichromate, 1, in concentrated sulfuric acid, 300, is added by drops. An emerald-green color signifies the presence of alcohol in toxic quantity.

antiformin t. See *antiformin.*

antimony t. See *Marsh's t.*

antipyrine t. See *Fieux's t.*

antithrombin t.: A test for typhoid based on the action of thrombin on the patient's serum.

antitrypsin t.: A test based on the power of the blood serum to inhibit the action of trypsin. The antitryptic power of the blood serum is increased in carcinoma, nephritis, pregnancy, etc. Called also *Bergmann-Meyer t., Fuld-Goss t.,* and *Müller-Jochmann t.*

Antonucci t.: A method for rapid cholecystography with tetraiodophenolphthalein.

anvil t.: The striking of a part with the closed fist used like a hammer: a blow so given on the sole of the foot with the leg extended produces pain in the hip in early hip-joint disease; such a blow given over the top of the head elicits pain in a diseased vertebra.

apomorphine t. See *Bedson's t.*

aptitude t's. Tests given to determine aptitude or ability to undertake the study of medicine or other professions.

Arakawa's t. (*for peroxidase in milk*). See under *reagent.*

Archetti's t. (*for caffeine*): Heat a solution of potassium ferricyanide with half its volume of nitric acid to boiling, then dilute with water. The reagent gives a precipitate of Prussian blue with caffeine (uric acid does also).

Arloing-Courmont t.: The Widal reaction in tuberculosis.

Arnold's t.: 1. (*For aceto-acetic acid in urine.*) *a.* Dissolve 1 Gm. of para-amido-acetophenone in 80 to 100 cc. water by shaking and adding hydrochloric acid by drops, then add more concentrated acid until the solution is colorless. *b.* Dissolve 1 Gm. sodium nitrite in 100 cc. distilled water. Just before using mix 2 parts *a* with 1 part *b*, add an equal volume of urine, and 2 or 3 drops concentrated ammonia water: an intense brownish-red color develops. Now add 1 volume of this colored urine to 10 or 12 volumes of concentrated hydrochloric acid, 2 to 4 drops of ferric chloride, and 3 cc. of chloroform; a beautiful purplish-violet color develops in the chloroform if aceto-acetic acid is present. Strongly colored urine should first be decolorized with animal charcoal. 2. (*Alkaloidal tests.*) *a.* Some alkaloids heated on the water bath with syrupy phosphoric acid obtained by dissolving metaphosphoric acid or phosphoric acid anhydride in phosphoric acid yield characteristic color reactions: aconitine, violet; nicotine, yellow; coniine, green. *b.* Triturated with concentrated sulfuric acid, many alkaloids yield characteristic color reactions upon adding 30 to 40 per cent alcoholic (in some instances aqueous) potassium hydroxide solution.

Aron's t. (*for cancer*): A biopsy specimen of the adrenal cortex of a rabbit is taken. The animal is then injected with urinary extract from the patient. After two days the rabbit is killed and its adrenal cortex compared with the biopsy specimen.

arsenic t. See *Bettendorff's t., Fleitmann's t., Gutzeit's t., Marsh's t., Reinsch's t.* (1).

arsphenamine t. See *Abelin reaction*, under *reaction.*

Aschheim-Zondek t. (*for pregnancy*): The subcutaneous injection of the urine of pregnant women into immature female mice is followed by swelling, congestion, and hemorrhages of the ovaries and premature maturation of the ovarian follicles.

Aschner's t., Aschner-Danini t. See *Aschner's phenomenon*, under *phenomenon.*

Ascoli's t. 1. [Alberto *Ascoli*]. The formation of a ring of precipitate at the junction of the two fluids when the extract of the infected tissue of an anthrax animal, after boiling with saline solution, is added to anthrax immune serum. 2. [Maurizio *Ascoli*]. See *miostagmin reaction*, under *reaction.*

association t.: A test based on associative reaction. It is usually performed by mentioning words to a patient and noting what other words the patient will give as the ones called up in his mind. The reaction time is also noted.

Atkinson and Kendall's t. (*for blood*): A modified form of Teichmann's test.

atropine t.: 1. See *Dehio's t.* and *Reuss's t.* 2. (*For typhoid infections.*) The patient is given atropine $\frac{1}{30}$ grain (0.002 Gm.) hypodermically at least one hour after eating and while in the prone position. The pulse is counted minute by minute one-half hour after the injection. Normally there should be a rise of at least 15 beats per minute over the rate preceding administration of the drug. This increased rate is absent in typhoid infection. Called also *Norris' t.*

attention-alertness t. See *Bourdon's t.*

Auricchio and Chieffi's t.: A test for leishmaniasis based on the fact that the serum of patients flocculates rapidly on the addition of a solution of iron peptonate.

autohemolysis t.: One performed in investigation of certain hemolytic states, particularly the congenital, non-spherocytic hemolytic anemias. Defibrinated blood is incubated at 37 C., under sterile conditions, for 24 and 48 hours, and the amount of spontaneous hemolysis is quantitated.

auto-urine t. (*for tuberculosis*): Into the superficial layers of the patient's skin is injected 0.05 cc. of the patient's own urine. If the patient is actively tuberculous a local reaction develops which consists of a palpable lump of infiltration. Called also *Wildbolz's t.*

Axenfeld's t. (*for albumin in urine*): Acidulate the urine with formic acid, and drop by drop add a 0.1 per cent solution of gold chloride. On warming, albumin, if present, will produce a red tint, which more of the gold chloride will turn to a blue. Many other substances will produce the blue tint, but not the red.

Ayer's t. (*for spinal block*): With a spinal manometer, the pressure in lumbar puncture and that in a cisterna magna puncture should be identical in the normal subject.

Ayer-Tobey t. See *Tobey-Ayer t.*

A-Z t. Aschheim-Zondek test.

azorubin t. (*for liver function*): 4 cc. of a 1 per cent solution of azorubin S are injected intravenously. In healthy subjects 95 per cent of the dye is excreted by the liver and 5 per cent in the urine. In liver disturbance the dye increases in the urine.

Babcock's t. (*for fat in milk*): To 17.6 cc. of milk add 17.5 cc. sulfuric acid, specific gravity 1.82–1.83; centrifuge five minutes; bring level of liquid up to base of neck by adding hot water, at about 140 F.; centrifuge three minutes; add hot water to bring fat column well up into neck; centrifuge two minutes; read directly from scale on neck.

Babinski's t. See under *sign.*

Babinski-Weil t.: The patient, with his eyes shut, is made to walk forward and backward ten times in a clear space. A person with labyrinthine disease deviates from the straight path, bends to one side when walking forward and to the other side when walking backward.

Bachman t. (*for trichinosis*): A 1 per cent solution of powdered trichina larvae is injected intradermally. Within a week a well-defined area of edema develops if the patient has trichinosis.

Bachmeier's t. (*for alkalis*): Tannin solution produces a red to reddish-brown color, changing to dirty green.

bactericidal t. See *Neisser and Wechsberg's t.*, and *Wright's method*, def. 2, under *method.*

bacteriolytic t. See *Pfeiffer's phenomenon*, under *phenomenon.*

Baeyer's t.: 1. (*For dextrose.*) Boil the liquid with orthonitrophenylpropiolic acid and sodium carbonate: if dextrose is present, indigo is formed; but an excess of dextrose will destroy the blue tint by forming white indigo. 2. (*For indol.*) The suspected substance is dissolved in water, acidulated with 2 or 3 drops of fuming nitric acid; a 2 per cent solution added drop by drop produces a red color and then a red deposit of nitrosoindole nitrate.

balance t.: A functional test made by comparing the intake and output of a normal constituent, as of the urine.

Baldwin's t. (*for retrocecal appendicitis*): The colon is inflated with air: the band of colonic resistance formerly impossible to demonstrate becomes evident.

Balfour's t.: The ascertainment of whether the heart is still active in cases of apparent death by inserting pins bearing paper streamers into the skin over the heart. Movement of the heart muscles will be shown by movement of the papers.

ball t. See *Müller's test* (3).

Bang t.: An agglutination test for the detection of brucellosis in cattle.

Bárány's t. See under *symptom.*

Bárány's pointing t.: Have the patient point at a fixed object alternately with the eyes open and closed. A constant error with the eyes closed indicates a brain lesion.

Barberio's t. (*for semen*): To a drop of seminal fluid on a glass slide $\frac{1}{2}$ drop of saturated aqueous solution of trinitrophenol (picric acid) is added, when a precipitate of yellow, strongly refractive, needle-shaped crystals is formed.

Bardach's t. (*for protein*): A test dependent on the fact that, in the presence of protein, acetone and potassium mercuric iodide and alkali react to yield canary-yellow needles instead of the usual hexagonal crystals of iodoform.

Bareggi's t. (*for typhoid fever*): The clot formed in the blood of typhoid patients after twenty-four hours is watery and soft, with only a small amount of separated serum.

Barfoed's t. (*for monosaccharides*): Boil 5 cc. of Barfoed's solution (dissolve 4.5 Gm. of neutral crystallized copper acetate and 1.2 cc. of 50 per cent acetic acid in 100 cc. of water) and add the unknown slowly and with boiling. Monosaccharides reduce this mixture (formation of a red precipitate), while disaccharides do so only very slowly if at all, and so can be distinguished from the former.

Bargehr t.: A test for leprosy based on the fact that persons associated with lepers develop specific antibodies which confer immunity on them.

Barral's t. (*for albumin and biliary pigments*): Overlay the urine with a 20 per cent solution of sozolic acid: a white ring develops at the contact point if albumin is present; a green ring if biliary pigments are present.

bar-reading t. A test for binocular and stereoscopic vision, which consists of holding a ruler midway between the eyes and the printed page.

Basham's t. (*for bile pigment*): The liquid is shaken with chloroform, evaporated, and a drop of nitric acid added, when a play of bright colors is produced, finally becoming a fine red.

basophil t. (*for sensitivity*): A drop of the subject's blood is mixed with a small amount of solution of the substance being tested; disintegration of the basophils accompanies the release of histamine and is evidence of hypersensitivity to the substance.

Bass-Watkin t. (*for agglutination*): A form of the Widal test so modified that it can be performed at the bedside in about five minutes. Place ¼ drop of the patient's blood on a glass slide, dissolve in 1 drop of water, add 1 drop of a rather heavy killed suspension of typhoid bacilli, and mix by tilting the slide from side to side. In a positive case small grayish clumps and a fine granular sediment form within two minutes.

Bauer's t.: 1. A modification of the Wassermann test by relying entirely on the antisheep amboceptor present in the patient's serum. 2. Galactose tolerance test; test of carbohydrate tolerance of the liver, performed by administering 30 Gm. of galactose, the urine being tested later for galactose by means of Fehling's solution: the elimination of more than 3 Gm. indicates hepatic functional impairment. 3. (*For milk.*) To 2 cc. of milk add 1 drop of 0.25 per cent aqueous solution of Nile-blue sulfate. The blue color can be extracted from human milk, but not from cow's milk by means of ether.

Baumann's t. (*for dextrose*): To a watery solution of the substance add benzoyl chloride and an excess of sodium hydroxide, and shake until the odor of benzoyl chloride disappears and a precipitate of the benzoic acid ester of dextrose is formed.

Baumann and Goldmann's t. (*for cystine*): A solution containing the cystine is shaken with sodium hydroxide and benzoyl chloride: a voluminous precipitate is formed, composed of benzoyl cystine.

Bayer's t. (*for acetone in the urine*): Equal volumes of urine and nitrobenzenaldehyde are mixed with alkaline water: acetone turns it to an indigo-blue tint.

Bayrac's t. (*for uric acid in urine*): Evaporate 50 cc. of urine to dryness on the water bath, treat residue with hydrochloric acid (1:5), wash with alcohol, dissolve in 20 drops of sodium hydroxide solution heated to 90 or 100 C. on water bath, and decompose with sodium hypobromite in the apparatus for determining urea. Each 1 cc. of nitrogen at ordinary temperature equals 0.00357 Gm. uric acid.

B. C. G. t. See *bicolor guaiac t.*

bead t. (*for digestive function*). See *Einhorn's bead t.*

Bechterew's t.: The patient seated in bed is directed to stretch out both legs. In sciatica he cannot do this, but can stretch out each leg in turn.

Becker's t.: 1. (*For picrotoxin.*) Fehling's solution is added and the mixture is warmed: if the alkaloid is present, the solution is reduced. 2. (*For astigmatism.*) The patient looks at a test card containing lines radiating in sets of three and points out which seem blurred.

Bedson's t. (*for apomorphine*): On boiling morphine solution containing apomorphine with potassium hydroxide a brown color develops.

Behre and Benedict's t. (*for acetone bodies*): Distill out the acetone bodies from acid solution. and determine colorimetrically with salicylic aldehyde and alkali. A red color is dihydroxy benzalacetone.

Bell's t.: 1. (*For percentage of free hydrochloric acid in stomach contents.*) Filter the contents, and to 4 cc. add drop by drop a solution of dimethyl-amido-azobenzol until the pink color ceases to grow darker. Compare with Bell's color scale for percentage. 2. (*For alum in flour or bread.*) Fresh 5 per cent logwood tincture in methylated spirit. Moisten 10 Gm. flour with water, then add 1 cc. tincture and an equal quantity saturated ammonium carbonate solution. Sample, if pure, gives pinkish color, gradually fading to buff or brown. If alum is present, a lavender or bluish tint is formed, becoming more marked on drying.

Bellerby's t. See *Xenopus t.*

belt t. (*for enteroptosis*): The lower abdomen of the patient is encircled by both hands and lifted up. The patient will experience a sensation of relief if enteroptosis is present.

Bendien's t.: 1. A vanadic acid flocculation and spectrophotometric test for cancer. 2. A serum test for prognosis in tuberculosis.

Benedict's t.: 1. (*For dextrose.*) 200 Gm. of sodium or potassium citrate and 200 Gm. crystallized sodium carbonate and 125 Gm. of potassium sulfocyanate are dissolved in 800 cc. of boiling water. This is cooled and filtered and 18 Gm. copper sulfate dissolved in 100 cc. of water are added and the whole diluted to make 1 liter. To 5 cc. of this reagent, in a test tube, 8 or 10 drops of the solution to be tested are added. Boil for one or two minutes and allow to cool slowly. If dextrose is present the solution will be filled with a precipitate red, yellow, or green in color. 2. (*For urea.*) The urea is hydrolyzed to ammonium carbonate by $KHSO_4$ and $ZNSO_4$, made alkaline, and distilled as usual.

Benedict and Denis' t. (*for total sulfur in urine*). See under *method.*

Benedict and Murlin's t. (*for amino-acid nitrogen in urine*). See under *method.*

bentonite t.: A flocculation test for rheumatoid arthritis in which sensitized bentonite particles are added to inactivated serum; results are considered positive when half of the particles are clumped and half still remain in suspension.

benzidine t. (*for blood*): To a saturated solution of benzidine in glacial acetic acid add an equal volume of 3 per cent hydrogen peroxide and 1 cc. of the unknown. A blue color indicates blood.

benzidine peroxidase t. (*for raw milk*): To 10 cc. of the milk add 2 cc. of a 4 per cent alcoholic solution of benzidine and sufficient acetic acid to coagulate the milk. Mix and allow 2 cc. of a 3 per cent solution of hydrogen peroxide to flow slowly down the wall of the tube. An immediate blue color indicates raw milk (not heated to 78 C.).

benzoin t. (*for cerebrospinal syphilis*): When a colloidal solution of benzoin resin is added to syphilitic cerebrospinal fluid, flocculation or precipitation occurs.

Bercovitz t. (*for pregnancy*): Into the patient's eye is instilled 5 or 6 drops of the patient's blood diluted with 1 drop of normal saline: dilatation or contraction of the pupil constitutes a positive reaction.

Berenreuther t.: A test of interests and attitudes, consisting of 125 questions to be answered by yes or no.

Bergmann-Meyer t. See *antitrypsin t.*

Berthelot's t. 1. (*For phenol.*) An ammoniacal solution of phenol treated with solution of chlorinated soda takes on a fine blue color. 2. (*For* *alcohol.*) Shake with a few drops of benzyl chloride and an excess of sodium hydroxide until the irritating odor of benzyl chloride disappears. The aromatic odor of ethyl benzoate indicates alcohol.

Bertoni-Raymondi t. (*for nitrous acid in blood*): Dialyze, evaporate the dialysate to dryness, take up with hot alcohol, and add starch paste and potassium iodide: a blue color develops.

Bertrand's t. (*for dextrose*): Boil the unknown with an excess of Fehling's solution, filter out the cuprous oxide, dissolve in an acid solution of ferric sulfate, and titrate with potassium permanganate.

Berzelius's t. (*for albumin*): Albumin is precipitated from solution by a fresh concentrated solution of metaphosphoric acid.

beta t.: A psychological test for intelligence to be used instead of the alpha test on persons unacquainted with English.

beta-oxybutyric acid t. See *Black's t., Hart's t., Kultz's t., Osterberg's t.*

Bettendorff's t. (*for arsenic*): The liquid to be tested is mixed with hydrochloric acid; a freshly prepared solution of stannous chloride is added, and a bit of tinfoil is put into it, when a brown color or precipitate is formed.

Bettmann's t. See *Bettendorff's t.*

Bial's t. (*for pentose in urine*): Make a reagent consisting of 500 cc. of 30 per cent hydrochloric acid, 1 Gm. of orcin, and 25 drops liquor ferri sesquichloratis (G. Ph.). Five cc. of this reagent are boiled in a test tube, and after removal from the flame, several drops of urine are added. A green color appearing at once indicates pentose.

bicarbonate tolerance t. See *Sellards' t.*

bicolor guaiac t.: A colloidal reaction in the cerebrospinal fluid: the reagents are a suspension of guaiac resin with two colored solutions, naphthol green and brilliant basic fuchsin. Called also *B. C. G. t.*

bile acid t. See *Bischoff's t., Drechsel's t., Francis' t.* (1), *Hay's t., Mylius' t., Neukomm's t., Oliver's t.* (4), *Pettenkoffer's t., Strassburg's t., Tyson's t., Udránsky's t.* (1).

bile pigment t. See *Barral's t., Basham's t., Bonanno's t., Brucke's t.* (1), *Capranica's t.* (1), *Cunisset's t., Dragendorff's t., Dumontpallier's t., Fleischl's t., foam t., Gerhardt's t.* (3), *Gluzinski's t.* (1), *Gmelin's t., Hammarsten's t.* (2), *Huppert's t., Huppert-Cole t., Jolles' t.* (1), *Kapsinow's t., Krokiewicz's t., Maréchal's t., Masset's t., Nakayami t., Nobel's t.* (2), *Quinlan's t., Rosenbach-Gmelin t., Salkowski and Schipper's t., sand t., Schmidt's t.* (1), *Smith's t.* (1), *Stokvis' t., Torquay's t., Trousseau's t., Ultzmann's t., Vitali's t.* (3) and (4).

bile solubility t. (*for differentiation between pneumococci and streptococci*): The broth culture to be tested is divided into two parts in separate test tubes. Add 0.5 cc. of sterile ox bile to one tube and 0.5 cc. of salt solution to the other (control) tube. Pneumococci generally dissolve and the cultures become clear; cultures of streptococci remain cloudy.

bilirubin t. See *Fouchet's t., Harrison spot t., Schmidt's t.* (1), *Van den Bergh's t.* (1), (2).

Binet's t.: A method of testing the mental capacity of children and youth by asking a series of questions adapted to, and standardized on, the capacity of normal children at various ages. According to the answers given the mental age of the subject is ascertained.

Binet-Simon t. See *Binet's t.*

Bing's entotic t.: When words are not audible through an ear trumpet as ordinarily applied, but may be heard when spoken into a trumpet joined to a catheter in the eustachian tube, it is probable that there is a lesion of the incus or malleus.

Binz's t. (*for quinine in urine*): The reagent consists of 2 parts iodine, 1 part potassium iodide, and 40 parts water.

Bio Lab t.: A modification of the Ide test for syphilis.

biological t. See *serum t.*

Birkhaug t.: A skin test for rheumatism: intracutaneous injection of 0.1 cc. of a 1 to 100 dilution of the toxin of a streptococcus derived from a case of rheumatic fever.

Bischoff's t. (*for biliary acids*): Heated with diluted sulfuric acid and cane sugar these yield a red color.

bismuth t. See *Nylander's t.*

bitterling t. (*for pregnancy*): A small carplike fish of Japan (the bitterling) is placed in a quart of fresh water containing 2 teaspoonfuls of the woman's urine; if the woman is pregnant, there grows out from the belly of the bitterling its long tubular oviduct.

biuret t.: 1. (*For proteins.*) To the unknown solution add strong potassium hydroxide solution and then a few drops of very dilute copper sulfate solution. A pinkish-violet color indicates the presence of biuret or of a similar double —CO.OH— grouping. 2. (*For urea.*) Melt the substance in a dry test tube and heat it, then cool, and dissolve in water; add caustic soda, and mix drop by drop a dilute solution of copper sulfate: a pink and finally a bluish color is produced.

Black's t. (*for beta-oxybutyric acid*): Evaporate 50 cc. of urine in a small dish to about one-fourth; acidify with a few drops of hydrochloric acid and add plaster of paris to a thick paste. When the mass begins to harden, break it up into a meal; add 30 cc. of ether and mix. Draw the clear ether into an evaporating dish; evaporate over a water bath and dissolve the residue in 10 cc. of water. Neutralize with an excess of dry barium carbonate; pour into a test tube, add a few drops of hydrogen peroxide and 5 drops of 10 per cent ferric chloride. A red color indicates beta-oxybutyric acid.

Blackberg and Wanger's t. (*for melanin*): Concentrate the urine to one-third, add 1 per cent of potassium persulfate, and let it stand two hours. Precipitate the melanin with an equal volume of methyl alcohol. Filter, wash and dry.

blanche t.: Blanching of the tissues just lingual to the maxillary medial incisors after a tug on the upper lip indicates persistence of attachment of a heavy fibrous frenum which may well interfere with normal developmental closure of the spacing between the teeth.

Blaxland's t. (*for differentiating between a large ovarian cyst and ascites*): A flat ruler is laid upon the abdomen just above the level of the anterior superior iliac spines: with the fingers of both hands this is pressed firmly and steadily backward toward the lumbar spine. In ovarian cyst the pulsations of the abdominal aorta can be felt.

blister t. (*for infectious disease*): A blister is raised on the skin and its contents examined. If the proportion of eosinophils present is less than 25 per cent infectious disease is probable. Called also *Roger-Josué t.*

Block-Steiger t.: A test for simulated deafness based on the fact that if two tuning-forks, vibrating in unison, but one struck stronger than the other, be held before the two ears of a person with normal hearing, the louder fork only will be heard.

blood t. A popular term for a serologic test for diagnosing syphilis.

blood, tests for. See *Almén's t.* (2), *aloin-turpentine t., aminopyrine t., benzidine t., Cowie's guaiac t., Day's t., Deen's t., Donogany's t., Einhorn's t., Fleig's t., Gannther's t., Gregorson and Boas' t., guaiac t., Heller's t.* (2), *hematein t., hydrogen peroxide t., Klimow's t., Kobert's t., Ladendorff's t., Lechini's t., Lyle and Curtman's t., Meyer's t.* (3), *phenolphthalein t., Rose's t., Rosenthal's t.* (1), *Rossel's aloin t., Ruttan and Hardisty's t., sand t., Saundby's t., Schalfijew's t., Schönbein's t., serum t., Stokes' t., Struve's t., Taylor's t., Teichmann's t., von Zeynek and Nencki's t., Weber's t.* (3), *Williamson's t.*

blood cholesterol t.: Increase of the cholesterol

content of the blood indicates deficiency of the cholaligenic power of the liver.

blood-urea clearance t.: A test for renal function based on the volume of blood which is cleared of its urea per minute.

Bloor's t. 1. (*For fat.*) The protein is precipitated, the fat is saponified, and the amount determined nephelometrically. 2. (*For cholesterol in blood.*) Extract the blood with a mixture of alcohol and ether and evaporate to dryness. Extract residue with chloroform and add acetic anhydride and sulfuric acid.

Bloxam's t. (*for urea*): If a nitrate is present, add a few drops of an ammonium chloride solution; if absent, acidulate with hydrochloric acid. Evaporate to dryness in a watch glass, and heat cautiously as long as thick, white fumes evolve. Dissolve the residue in a drop or two of ammonia, add a drop of barium chloride solution, and stir. If urea is present, a crystalline streak of barium cyanurate will form in the track of the rod.

Blum's t. (*for albumin*): Dissolve 0.03 to 0.05 Gm. manganous chloride in a little water; acidulate with hydrochloric acid, and treat with 100 cc. 10 per cent solution sodium metaphosphate. Then add lead oxide a little at a time; let the liquid settle, and filter. Resulting pink solution of manganic metaphosphate detects albumin in urine. Place reagent in a test tube and filter urine into it.

Blumenau's t. (*for tuberculosis*): A drop of tuberculin is applied to the forearm and covered with adhesive plaster: an eruption develops if the patient has tuberculosis.

Blyth's t. (*for lead in drinking water*): A little alcoholic tincture of cochineal makes a precipitate with it.

Boas' t.: 1. (*For atony of the bowels.*) The colon is unloaded and injected with water; the quantity of water necessary to elicit a splashing sound on succussion is noted as a measure of the degree of atony. 2. (*For hydrochloric acid in the stomach contents.*) Dissolve 5 Gm. of resorcinol and 5 Gm. of sugar in 100 cc. of dilute alcohol. A thin layer of this reagent is warmed upon a porcelain dish. If a glass rod is dipped in this layer and touched to a drop of the filtered stomach liquid, a scarlet streak is formed. Called also *resorcinol t.* 3. (*For free hydrochloric acid in the stomach contents.*) Resublimed resorcinol, 5 parts; cane sugar, 3 parts; 94 per cent alcohol, to make 100 parts; boil the fluid with the reagent: free hydrochloric acid will give a transient rose-red mirror. 4. (*For lactic acid.*) Test for lactic acid in gastric juice depends on oxidation of the acid to aldehyde and formic acid by action of sulfuric acid and manganese. The aldehyde is detected by addition of Nessler's reagent or by formation of iodoform when iodine solution is added. 5. Same as *chlorophyll t.*

Bodal's t.: Test of color perception by the use of colored blocks.

Boedeker's t. (*for albumin*): The liquid is treated with acetic acid, and potassium ferrocyanide in solution is added drop by drop: albumin will form a white precipitate.

Boerner-Luckens t.: A flocculation test for syphilis.

Bohmansson's t. (*for dextrose*): To 10 cc. of the urine add 2 cc. of 25 per cent hydrochloric acid and 5 cc. of bone black. Shake well, filter, and make Nylander's test on the filtrate.

Bolen t. (*for cancer*): A diagnostic test based on differences in clot retraction in cancerous and noncancerous persons.

Boltz's t. (*for diagnosis of dementia paralytica*): Place 1 cc. of fresh cerebrospinal fluid in a small glass test tube and to it add 0.3 cc. of acetic anhydride. Shake the mixture well and then add, drop by drop, 0.8 cc. of concentrated sulfuric acid. Shake the mixture gently once more. Then hold the test tube against a white background. The presence of a lilac tint indicates a positive reaction; a brownish-yellow, reddish-yellow, or clear fluid is noted if the reaction is a negative one.

Bonanno's t. (*for bile pigments*): To 5 cc. of the unknown add a few drops of concentrated hydrochloric acid containing 2 per cent of sodium nitrite. An emerald green color indicates bile pigments.

bone conduction t.: If a vibrating tuning-fork, when the handle is placed against the skull, is heard more distinctly than when held near the ear, it indicates loss in conduction through the middle ear.

borates and boric acid t.: Dry the milk and ash the residue. Add 1 cc. of water and 2 drops of hydrochloric acid. Soak a strip of turmeric paper in the solution one minute and allow it to dry in the air. A deep red color which changes to green or blue on treatment with dilute alkali indicates boric acid.

Borchardt's t. (*for levulose in urine*): A few cubic centimeters of a mixture of equal parts of water and concentrated hydrochloric acid are heated for one and one half minutes with an equal amount of urine and a few crystals of resorcin. The mixture is allowed to cool and is made alkaline with sodium carbonate; then poured into a test tube and shaken with acetic ether: a yellow color in the ether indicates the presence of levulose.

Borden's t. (*for typhoid fever*): A modification of the Widal test. The patient's blood serum is mixed with salt solution and then with a suspension of killed typhoid bacilli, so as to bring the dilution up to 1 to 50. The positive reaction consists in the sinking of the clump of bacteria to the bottom of the test tube, leaving a clear fluid above a small white mass of agglutinated bacilli.

Bordet's t. See *serum t.*

Boston's t.: A method of performing the ring tests for albumin in which the fluids are brought into contact in a glass pipet.

Botelho's t. (*for cancer*): To centrifugated suspect blood serum dilute nitric acid and an iodine reagent are added in several small amounts at short intervals, the test tube being shaken after each addition. Normal serum remains clear, that of cancer patients continues clouded.

Böttger's t.: 1. [R. *Böttger*] (*for carbon monoxide*): Paper moistened with palladium chloride solution (0.0002 Gm. in 100 cc.) becomes darkened in the presence of carbon monoxide. 2. [W. C. *Böttger*] (*for dextrose in the urine*): The urine is treated with sodium hydroxide and then boiled with a very small amount of bismuth subnitrate; if dextrose is present the precipitate is black.

Bottu's t. (*for dextrose*): To 8 cc. of Bottu's reagent (3.5 Gm. of orthonitro-phenyl-propiolic acid and 5 cc. of freshly prepared 10 per cent solution of sodium hydroxide per liter) in a test tube add 1 cc. of the urine and mix. Boil the upper portion, add one more cc. of the mixture, and heat again. A blue color accompanied by the precipitation of small particles of indigo indicates dextrose.

Bouchardat's t. (*for alkaloids*): Potassium triiodide as a test for alkaloids gives a brown precipitate, soluble in alcohol.

Bouin and Ancel t.: A test for the presence of progestin.

Bourdon's t. (*for mental alertness*): A test based on the accuracy and time required for a patient to strike out certain letters, numbers or words as required.

Bourget's t. (*for iodides in urine and saliva*): Impregnate a filter paper with a 5 per cent starch solution, dry, and cut into squares 5 cm. each. Then drop 2 or 3 drops of a 5 per cent ammonium persulfate solution in the center of each square, and dry the pieces in the dark. Even with traces of iodine the prepared paper gives an intensely blue color.

Boveri's t. (*for excess of globulin in cerebrospinal fluid*): Over 1 cc. of cerebrospinal fluid in a test tube is poured an equal quantity of a 1:1000 solution of potassium permanganate. If there is excess of globulin a yellow ring will form at the line of junction, and on shaking, the entire contents of the tube will become bright yellow.

Boyksen's t. (*for cancer*): Serum from animals immunized with cancer material is injected intracutaneously. The resulting reaction is said to be more frequently positive in cancer patients than in controls.

Bozicevich's t.: A test for the detection of trichinosis.

bracelet t.: The production of pain on moderate lateral compression of the lower ends of the radius and ulna: observed in rheumatoid arthritis.

Brahmachari's t.: A test for leishmaniasis based on the degree of opacity produced on diluting the serum with water, on the theory that the serum is characterized by an excess of globulin.

Bram's t.: Persons with exophthalmic goiter are more tolerant of quinine hydrobromide than normal persons.

Brande's t. (*for quinine*): When a solution of quinine is treated with chlorine water and ammonia, a green color is produced.

Braun's t. (*for dextrose in urine*): The urine is alkalinized with sodium hydroxide and boiled with a solution of trinitrophenol: if dextrose is present, a deep-red color is produced. Acetone gives the same reaction, though less decidedly; while creatine will give it even in a cold solution.

Braun-Husler t.: To 1 cc. of cerebrospinal fluid add 5 cc. of 1:300 aqueous solution of hydrochloric acid: the mixture becomes cloudy if there is an excess of globulin in the cerebrospinal fluid.

Bremer's t. (*for diabetic blood*): The blood is prepared for staining, dried in a hot-air sterilizer, and stained with methylene blue and eosin. The red corpuscles of normal blood become brownish; but those of diabetic blood take on a greenish-yellow tint.

Brieger's t.: 1. (*For pyrocatechin.*) Add 1 drop of urine to 1 drop of very dilute ferric chloride solution on a watch glass—pyrocatechin causes an emerald-green color; on adding now a dilute solution of sodium bicarbonate or ammonium carbonate, the fluid becomes violet, changing back to green with acetic acid. 2. (*For strychnine.*) Pure chromic acid is added, and a violet color is produced. 3. See *cachexia reaction*, under *reaction*.

bromine t.: 1. (*For melanin.*) See *Zeller's t.* 2. (*For tryptophan.*) See *tryptophan t.* 3. (*For pregnancy.*) A chemical test for the histamine found in the pituitary hormone excreted in the urine; in a test tube 2.5 cc. of urine are mixed with 1 cc. of bromine water, heating the solution to boiling. A positive reaction is indicated by a pink coloration.

bromsulphalein t. See *bromsulphalein*.

Brouha t. (*for pregnancy*): Immature male mice are injected subcutaneously with the morning urine of the patient daily for from eight to ten days: the mice are then killed and if their seminal vesicles are abnormally enlarged, swollen or distended with fluid the test is positive.

Brown's t. (*T. K.*): A modification of the Friedman test in which the patient's blood serum is used instead of urine.

Brown's t. (*for quantitative estimation of ammonia in urine*): Heat 60 cc. of urine with 3 Gm. of basic lead acetate, stir well, let stand for a few minutes, and filter. This removes nitrogenous substances. Heat the filtrate with 2 Gm. neutral potassium oxalate, stir well, and filter. Take 10 cc. of the filtrate, add 50 cc. of water and 15 Gm. of neutral potassium oxalate, and estimate the ammonia.

Brown fever t. (*for lesions of the sympathetic nervous system*): Fever is induced with intravenous typhoid vaccine and the increase of surface temperature is measured at half-hour intervals with a galvanometer.

brucellin t., An allergic skin test made by the intradermal injection of melitin for the diagnosis of undulant fever.

Bruck's serochemical t. (*for syphilis*): Nitric acid when added to syphilitic blood serum causes a precipitate to form. Bruck's technic is based on an acid containing, per hundred Gm., 24.77 Gm. of nitric acid, or, per hundred cc., 28.48 cc. of nitric acid with a specific gravity of 1.149. He uses 0.3 cc. To 0.5 cc. of clear serum 2 cc. of distilled water are added. This is shaken, and then 0.3 cc. of nitric acid is added with a standardized pipet. This is shaken and permitted to stand at room temperature for ten minutes. Then 16 cc. of distilled water at 15 C. is added and shaken slowly three or four times so as not to foam. This shaking is repeated ten minutes later, and then the tube is set aside for one-half hour. If the serum is syphilitic, it shows a distinct flocculent turbidity. In twelve hours a precipitate is piled up on the floor of the test tube. If the serum is nonsyphilitic, there is no precipitate at any time.

Brücke's t.: 1. (*For bile pigments in urine.*) It is made by shaking with nitric acid, and then slowly adding sulfuric acid, when color reactions follow. 2. (*For proteins.*) The suspected liquid is acidulated with hydrochloric acid and treated with potassic iodide, when the proteins will be precipitated. 3. (*For urea.*) The suspected liquid is heated with an alcoholic solution of fusel oil, filtered, and treated with a solution of oxalic acid in fusel oil, when a crystalline deposit is formed.

Brugsch's t.: Potassium ferrocyanide is injected intradermally as a test for iron in the skin.

Bryce's t.: The determination of a degree of immunity against smallpox conferred by vaccination by repeating the inoculation after the lapse of several days; if the first is successful, the second will rapidly overtake it.

Bufano t. (*for liver function*): Intravenous injection of 10 cc. of a 12 per cent solution of glycocoll is preceded and followed by measurement of the blood amino nitrogen. Normally there is a decrease in the amino acid after the injection.

Burchard-Liebermann t. See *Liebermann's t.*

Bürger's t.: In persons without metabolic disturbance there develops a hypercholesterolemia after the ingestion of cholesterol.

Burnam's t. (*for formaldehyde in urine*): To 10 cc. of urine in a test tube is added 3 drops of a 5 per cent solution of phenylhydrazine hydrochloride, 3 drops of a 5 per cent solution of sodium nitroprusside, and then a few drops of sodium hydroxide solution are poured down the side of the test tube. If formaldehyde is present, a deep purplish color is seen, changing to dark green, and then to pale yellow.

Busacca's t.: 1. One cc. of sterilized gelatin is rendered fluid by heating and is then injected intracutaneously. In syphilitic subjects this injection is followed within six hours by a reddened infiltrated area. 2. From 0.2 to 0.3 cc. of horse serum injected into the forearm produces a cutaneous skin reaction in tuberculosis in infants.

Buscaino's t.: Three cc. of urine are mixed with 1.5 cc. of a 5 per cent solution of silver nitrate and the whole boiled for thirty minutes. The color of the precipitate indicates the reaction; a white precipitate is negative; a brown or black precipitate indicates disease of the brain.

butter t.: A test for pancreatic insufficiency based on the fact that in deficiency of the external secretion of the pancreas so much fat may be present in the stool after the ingestion of butter that the stool looks like butter.

butyric acid t. See *pineapple t.*, and *Noguchi reaction*, under *reaction*.

Bychowski's t. (*for albumin in urine*): Two drops of urine are placed in a test tube of hot water and shaken: the water becomes cloudy if albumin is present.

caffeine t. See *Archetti's t.*, *Delff's t.*

Caillan's t. (*for dextrose in urine*): Shake 2 parts of urine with 1 part of chloroform: on settling, dextrose will be present in the upper layer.

calcium t.: See *Clark's t.*

Callaway's t.: A test for dislocation of the humerus, consisting in the fact that the circumference of the affected shoulder, measured over the acromion and through the axilla, is greater than that on the unaffected side.

Calmette's t. See *ophthalmic reaction* under *reaction.*

caloric t. See *Barany's symptom,* under *symptom.*

Calvert's t.: The patient takes his usual food, but no fluids from 12 noon. At 9 P. M. the bladder is emptied and 15 Gm. of urea are drunk in 4 oz. of water; at 10 P. M. the bladder is again emptied and the urine discarded. The patient then goes to bed and all the night urine, together with that passed on rising—say 7 A. M.—is kept. A sample (*a*) of these mixed portions is analyzed for its urea content. The patient then drinks 30 oz. of weak tea or water and the urine passed up to the end of two hours—9 A. M.—is kept and a sample (*b*) again analyzed for its urea percentage. The two specimens *a* and *b* represent the maximum and minimum concentrations of urea in the urine and the difference between them represents the urea range.

Cammidge's t. See under *reaction.*

Campani's t. (*for dextrose*): A mixture of a concentrated solution of lead subacetate and a dilute solution of copper acetate is productive of a yellow or red color.

Campbell's t.: The erythrocytes of pellagrous blood cause more rapid discoloration of iodine solutions than do other red corpuscles.

camphor t.: If $7\frac{1}{2}$ grains of camphor are given by mouth it should cause glycuronic acid to appear in the urine. This will not occur in liver disease.

cane sugar t. See *Niclés' t.*

Cantani t. (*in syphilis*): Reagent A, 56 Gm. of powdered ox heart, 300 cc. of 95 per cent ethyl alcohol, 150 cc. of 99.2 per cent ethyl alcohol and 2.5 Gm. of cholesterol; reagent B, 20 Gm. of egg lecithin, 370 cc. of 95 per cent ethyl alcohol and 3.75 cc. of pure phenol; reagent C, 225 cc. of 95 per cent ethyl alcohol, 25 cc. of pure phenol and 0.1 cc. of a 5 per cent solution of petrolatum in benzine. One part of reagent A, one part of reagent B and 0.5 part of reagent C are placed in a tube with two parts of a 3 per cent solution of sodium chloride. It is shaken for seven minutes before using. Eight times the original amount of sodium chloride solution is put in another tube and after seven minutes the contents of the second tube are poured into the first tube and thoroughly mixed. Twenty-five hundredths cubic centimeters of the mixture is poured into the tubes (generally five) containing the serum to be examined; the tubes are shaken at the rate of from 150 to 200 times per minute for four minutes, then left at rest for two minutes, and 2 cc. of an 0.85 per cent solution of sodium chloride is added to each tube. Negative serums show opalescence without flocculation; positive serums, clear flocculation; strongly positive serums, heavy flocculation with clarification of the liquid.

capillary resistance t.: Apply blood pressure cuff for five minutes tightly enough to obstruct venous return only and note the number of petechiae thus produced.

capon comb growth t.: A test for the presence of testis hormone based on the growth response of the comb of a capon following subcutaneous injection of the test material.

Cappagnoli's t. (*for dextrose*): A solution of cupric hydroxide and potassium hydroxide is added, when a blue color is produced.

Capranica's t.: 1. (*For bile pigments.*) Shake the liquid with chloroform containing bromine: it turns green, blue, violet, yellowish red, and then becomes nearly colorless. 2. (*For guanine.*) A warm solution of guanine hydrochloride gives a yellow precipitate in silky needles with a cold saturated solution of trinitrophenol. 3. (*For guanine.*) Mix the solution with a concentrated solution of potassium ferrocyanide: a yellowish-brown precipitate in prisms appears. 4. (*For guanine.*) Add to the suspected solution a concentrated solution of potassium dichromate: guanine will cause an orange-red precipitate in crystals.

carbohydrate t. See *Moore's t., Schiff's t.*

carbohydrate tolerance t. See *Killian's t.*

carbon monoxide t. See *Böttger's t.* (1), *Dejust's t., Hoppe-Seyler t.* (1), *Katayama's t., Preyer's t., Rubner's t.* (1), *Salkowski's t.* (1), *tannin t., Wetzel's t., Zaleski's t.*

carbon monoxide hemoglobin t. See *tannin t.*

Carnot's t. (*for atonic dilatation of the stomach*): The patient's stomach is emptied by the stomach pump and 500 cc. of water introduced. The patient remains in an erect posture for an hour, after which the water is withdrawn and measured. Then 500 cc. of water are introduced and the patient placed on his right side for an hour. In this position the stomach should be nearly empty in an hour.

carotinemia t.: To 2 cc. of serum add 2 cc. of 95 per cent alcohol and 2 cc. of petroleum ether. Compare the color of the ether layer with a standard.

Carr-Price t.: A quantitative color test for vitamin A in oils.

Carrez's t. (*for albumin*): One gram of resorcinol is dissolved in 2 cc. of distilled water in a test tube and the urine is poured upon the surface. A white ring shows albumin.

Casamajor's t. (*for glucose*): The suspected liquid is shaken with methyl alcohol; glucose makes the mixture cloudy.

casein t. See *Leiner's t.*

Casilli's t.: An adaptation of the Kahn antigen for slide agglutination.

Casoni's intradermal t. (*for hydatid disease*): Injection into the skin of hydatid fluid; subsequent increase in size of the white papule so produced indicates hydatid disease.

Castellani's t.: 1. (*For albuminuria.*) The filtered urine 5 cc., is placed in a test tube and 1.5 cc. of liquefied phenol is added by pouring it slowly down the sides of the tube by means of a pipet. The liquefied phenol will collect at the bottom of the tube. If within two minutes a definite white ring forms where the two liquids come in contact the test is considered positive; namely, the urine contains albumin. 2. An agglutination test for ascertaining the existence of a mixed infection with allied species of organisms.

catoptric t.: A test for cataract made by observing the reflections from the cornea and from the surfaces of the crystalline lens.

cellulose t. See *Cutola t., Schultze's t.* (1).

cephalin-cholesterol flocculation t. See *Hanger's t.*

Chapman's t. (*for acute abdominal conditions*): The patient is told to assume a supine position with his arms at his sides and then to raise himself by the abdominal muscles alone: when he fails to rise or feels great pain in doing so the test is positive.

Chautard's t. (*for acetone in the urine*): A drop of aqueous solution of magenta is dissolved with sulfurous acid and added to the urine, when a violet color is produced.

Chediak's t. (*for syphilis*): A drop of blood is put on a slide, stirred for one minute and thus defibrinated, then exposed to the air and dried. To the dried drop 0.015 cc. of a solution containing 3.5 per cent of sodium chloride and 0.3 per cent of sodium carbonate is added. The blood is diluted with this solution and is placed in a paraffin ring (1.5 cm. in diameter) on another slide. Then 0.03 cc. of a dilution of the Meinicke clarification extract made with the aforementioned freshly prepared salt solution in a ratio of 1:10 is added. Before use, the extract and diluting fluid are heated separately for eight minutes in the water bath at 56 C. (132.8 F.), and, after being mixed, the solution remains two minutes longer in the water bath. The slide is shaken for three minutes and kept for thirty minutes in the moist chamber at room temperature. In negative tests the microscope reveals brown granules, but the positive reaction is indicated by black floccules and clots in the reddish-brown fluid.

Chick-Martin t.: A test for the efficiency of excremental disinfectants in which dried human feces are used as the test material. See under *method.*

Chiene's t.: Two strips of lead or tape are carried across the front of the body, the upper over the anterior superior spines, the lower over the great trochanters; convergence of these lines points to the side of upward displacement of the trochanter in fracture of the neck of the femur.

Chimani-Moos t.: A test for detecting simulated deafness.

chloride balance t. See *balance t.*

chlorophyll t. (*for gastric motility*): On a fasting stomach the patient drinks 400 cc. of water which has been colored green by the addition of 20 drops of chlorophyll solution. After half an hour the residue is aspirated from the stomach, and the amount that has passed out of the stomach in one-half hour is ascertained.

cholera red t. (*for indole*): To the unknown add one tenth its volume of a 0.02 per cent solution of potassium nitrite and mix. Underlay with sulfuric acid. The purple color will change to bluish green on neutralization with potassium hydroxide.

cholesterol t. See *Bloor's t.* (2), *Bürger's t., Liebermann-Burchardt's t., Obermüller's t., Salkowski's t.* (2), *Schiff's t.* (2), (3), *Schultze's t.* (2), and *Zwenger's t.*

choline t. See *Rosenheim's t.*

Chopra's antimony t. (*for kala-azar*): Patient's diluted serum is treated with 4 per cent solution of urea stibamine: a flocculent precipitate constitutes a positive reaction.

Chorine's t. (*for malaria*): Dilute the serum with 10 parts of distilled water. Determine the optical density at once with the photometer of Vernes, Bricq, and Yvonne. Incubate three hours, allow to stand thirty minutes and take a second reading. The difference in the two readings in degrees represents the index of the serum.

Chrobak t.: If irritation of an eroded cervix by a sound causes bleeding and crumbling of the tissue, cancer is indicated.

chromatin t. (*for determination of genetic sex*): Examination of body cells for presence of the sex chromatin situated at the periphery of the nucleus in normal females but not in normal males.

chromic acid t. (*for alcohol*): Warm with dilute sulfuric acid or hydrochloric acid and add 1 to 2 drops of very dilute potassium dichromate solution. The color will change from red to green and the odor of acetaldehyde will appear.

Ciamician and Magnanini's t. (*for skatole*): Warm the solution with sulfuric acid: skatole produces a purplish-red tint.

Cipollina's t. (*for dextrose or levulose in urine*): Four cc. of urine, 5 drops of pure phenylhydrazine, and 0.5 cc. of glacial acetic acid are boiled for one minute. Four or 5 drops of potassium hydroxide solution are added and the mixture boiled again for a few seconds. Cool and examine for crystals of phenyl-levulosazone or phenyl-dextrosazone.

citochol t. See *Sachs-Witebsky t.*

Clark t. (*John S.*): Bleeding upon palpation of the interior of the uterus with a sound: indicative of cancer.

Clark's t. (*for calcium in blood*): Precipitate the calcium with ammonium oxalate, remove excess of oxalate, dissolve precipitate in sulfuric acid and titrate against potassium permanganate.

Clauberg t.: A biological assay method for the standardization of corpus luteum preparations or progesterone. Immature rabbits are primed with estrogen before the material to be tested is administered. The degree of endometrial development is observed.

Clive's t.: An acetic anhydride method of testing the blood serum for syphilis.

coagulation t. (*for proteins in urine*): Acidify the urine with acetic acid and boil. A white coagulum or a white precipitate or a cloudiness indicates protein.

cobra venom t. See *Weil's t.*

coccidioidin t.: An intracutaneous test for coccidioidal granuloma.

cockscomb t.: A test for the activity of the ergot preparations, based on the fact that ergot, when administered to a cock, produces a blue coloration of its comb.

coffee t. (*for glaucoma*): The patient drinks 1 or 2 cups of strong black coffee: if the intra-ocular tension rises 15–20 mg. Hg in from twenty to forty minutes, glaucoma is indicated.

Cohen's t. (*for albumin*): To the acidulated solution add a solution of potassium bismuthic iodide and potassium iodide: albumin is precipitated.

Cohn's t.: A test for color perception by the use of variously colored embroidery patterns.

coin t.: A test for pneumothorax made by auscultating the chest while a silver coin laid against the chest is struck with another coin. A metallic, ringing sound is produced over a cavity containing air.

colchicin t. See *Zeisel's t.*

cold pressor t. See *Hines and Brown t.*

Cole's t.: 1. (*For dextrose.*) Add acetic acid to the urine and filter through blood charcoal to remove other reducing substances. Then make a modified Fehling's test. 2. (*For lactose.*) Absorb the lactose on to blood charcoal, extract it again with hot dilute acetic acid and make an osazone test. 3. (*For uric acid.*) Add 2 drops of ammonium hydroxide to 5 cc. of urine and then saturate with ammonium chloride. Pour off the supernatant fluid, filter, evaporate residue, and make murexid test.

colloidal benzoin t. See *benzoin t.*

colloidal gold t. See *Lange's t.*

Comessatti's t. (*for epinephrine*): To 5 cc. of the unknown solution add an equal volume of 1 per cent sodium acetate solution and 1 cc. of 0.1 per cent mercuric chloride solution. A rose color indicates epinephrine.

concentration t.: A test for renal function: the patient is placed under conditions which cause the normal person to elaborate urine containing one or more constituents in high concentration and the results observed to see whether the patient is able to attain this concentration. See *urea concentration t., xylose concentration t.*

Congo red t. (*for amyloidosis*): Congo red is injected intravenously; if more than 60 per cent of the dye disappears after one hour, amyloidosis is indicated.

conjugate glycuronates t. See *Tollen's t.*

conjunctival t. 1. See *ophthalmic reaction* under *reaction.* 2. The local reaction which occurs when a pollen or an extract of the pollen is instilled into the conjunctival sac of a person sensitive to that pollen.

connective tissue t. See *Schmidt's t.* (5).

contact t. See *patch t.*

Contejean t.: Dissolve freshly precipitated cobalt carbonate in specimen, a red color changing to blue on evaporation indicates free HCl.

Cooke's t. (*for purine bodies in urine*): In a centrifuge tube take 10 cc. urine and add 1 Gm. sodium carbonate and 1 or 2 cc. strong ammonia. Shake until the sodium carbonate is dissolved. The earthy phosphates will be precipitated. Centrifuge and pour off clear fluid. Add 2 cc. ammonia and 2 cc. silver ammonionitrate solution. Centrifuge again.

Each 0.1 cc. of sediment represents 0.001176 Gm. of purine bodies.

Coombs' t. (*for antibodies in blood*): Two drops of a 2 per cent suspension of the red cells to be tested is mixed with two drops of rabbit antihuman globulin serum in a small serologic test tube, incubated for 30 minutes at 37 C. and centrifuged at 1000 r.p.m. for two minutes, then checked for agglutination, which indicates the presence of globulin antibodies on the surface of the red cells. Used to detect sensitized red cells in erythroblastosis fetalis and to diagnose other hemolytic syndromes.

Cope's t.: With patient on his back, the examiner flexes the right thigh and rotates the hip joint internally: an inflamed appendix will be irritated by this movement and pain will be felt in the hypogastrium.

copper soap t. (*for lipase*): Make up a hydrogel with 1 per cent of agar-agar, 2½ per cent of starch, and 2½ per cent of a neutral fat; pour into Petri dishes, cool, and place drops of the unknown on its surface. Incubate at 38 C. one hour and pour over the surface a saturated solution of cupric sulfate. Bluish-green spots of copper soap where the drops were indicate lipase action.

Corner-Allen t.: A biological method of assay for progesterone or corpus luteum preparations containing it. The rabbits are mated, the ovaries removed eighteen hours later and the material to be assayed injected. The results are read according to the intensity of the endometrial changes.

Costa t. (*for the activity of infections*): A test based on observing the rapidity with which precipitation is produced in blood serum by a procaine formaldehyde reagent.

cover t.: A test for imbalance of ocular muscles, made by covering one eye and noting its movement while uncovering it again.

Cowie's guaiac t. (*for blood in feces*): Add glacial acetic acid to the feces and extract with ether. To the filtrate add an equal volume of water, some powdered guaiac resin, and old turpentine or hydrogen peroxide. A blue color indicates blood.

Craft's t.: In organic disease of the pyramidal tract, stroking with a blunt point upward over the dorsal surface of the ankle, the leg being extended and the muscles relaxed, produces dorsal extension of the great toe.

Craig's t.: 1. (*For tuberculosis.*) A complement-fixation test for tuberculosis in which the antigen is made by growing several strains of bacilli on an alkaline bouillon containing a teaspoonful of aseptically removed egg white and egg yolk for each 250 cc. of bouillon. 2. A modification of the Wassermann test using a human hemolytic serum instead of a sheep hemolytic serum.

Cramer's t. (*for dextrose*): Place 3 cc. of Cramer's "2.5 reagent" (0.4 Gm. of mercuric oxide and 6 Gm. of potassium iodide dissolved in 100 cc. of water and the reaction so adjusted that 10 cc. will be neutralized to phenolphthalein by 2.5 cc. of N/10 acid) in a test tube and boil. Add 3 cc. of the urine and again boil. If positive the mixture becomes turbid, darkens, and a precipitate of finely divided mercury settles out.

Crampton's t.: A test for physical resistance and condition based on the difference between the pulse and blood pressure in the recumbent position and in the standing position. A difference of 75 or more indicates good condition; one of 65 or less shows a poor condition.

creatinine t. See *balance t., Braun's t., Jaffé's t.* (1), *Kerner's t., Salkowski's t.* (5), *Thudichum's t., von Maschke's t., Weyl's t.*

creatinine clearance t.: A test for renal function based on the rate at which ingested creatinine is filtered through the renal glomeruli.

Crismer's t. (*for dextrose*): The solution is made alkaline, and is boiled with 1 part of safranine in 1000 parts of water: if dextrose is present, the mixture is decolorized or turned to a pale yellow.

Cronin Lowe t.: A precipitation test for malignancy.

Cuboni's t. (*for pregnancy*): The urine of mares is filtered, 1 cc. of concentrated hydrochloric acid is added to every 5 cc. of urine; the mixture is left in a test tube in a boiling-water bath for ten minutes. After cooling, 6 cc. of benzol are added to the same quantity of urine and the mixture shaken. The urine is poured off and the benzol collected, allowed to settle, and passed through a paper filter. Of this benzol extract 3 cc. is dried by heating to 60 to 80 C., 0.8 cc. concentrated sulfuric acid is poured over it in the test tube, the whole heated for a few minutes in a water-bath of 78 to 80 C., and finally the results are observed. The reaction is negative (the subject is not pregnant) if the fluid obtained is of a reddish-brown, or brown color, and not fluorescent; if the reaction is positive, the fluid shows a green fluorescence with transmitted light.

cuff t.: A test for angina pectoris by producing ischemia in the left arm for five minutes by raising the pressure in a blood-pressure cuff on the arm to 50 mm. above the usual systolic pressure. This produces an anginal attack in angina.

Cuignet's t.: A test for simulated unilateral blindness. With the patient reading a book, the examiner inserts a pencil vertically between the eyes and the book. If patient continues to read uninterruptedly, he is seeing with both eyes.

Cunisset's t. (*for bile in the urine*): The urine is shaken with chloroform: if biliary matter is present, a yellow color is produced.

currant t.: If, after a meal of currants, the seeds do not appear in the stools in twenty-four hours, there is defective motility.

Curschmann t.: In patients who have an attack of appendicitis, if the leukocyte count does not exceed 6000, the disease has reached a period of sufficient quiescence to justify operation.

Cutler-Power-Wilder t. (*for Addison's disease*): The sodium chloride in the diet is restricted for a few days, and potassium citrate is administered. A marked rise in urinary chloride concentraction on the third day indicates adrenal insufficiency.

Cutola t.: A 50 per cent hydriodic acid solution containing iodine colors cellulose blue.

Cutting's t. (*for spinal fluid*): Add a colloidal suspension of gum mastic to a series of dilutions of the spinal fluid. A heavy white precipitate is positive.

cysteine t. See *Andreasch's t., nitroprusside t.* (1), *Sullivan's t.*

cystine t. See *Baumann and Goldmann's t., Liebig's t., Müller's t.* (1).

cytosin t. See *Wheeler and Johnson's t.*

Daclin t.: Shake 10 cc. of urine with 5 cc. of chloroform; allow this mixture to separate; decant the chloroform layer; evaporate this at a gentle heat; treat the residue with 2 drops of pure H_2SO_4. A violet color indicates santonine.

Dalldorf's t. (*for fragility of the skin capillaries*): Observation of the development of petechiae following the application of a suction cup to the outer surface of the arm.

D'Amato's t.: In person sensitized to the causative organism of a disease such as typhoid, paratyphoid, undulant fever, syphilis, the injection of the corresponding vaccine produces a hemoclastic reaction. In bearers of malignant tumors the injection of neoplastic extracts produces a specific hemoclastic reaction.

Darányi t. (*for pulmonary tuberculosis*): To 0.2 cc. of serum add 1.1 cc. of diluted alcohol (1 cc. of 96 per cent alcohol to which has been added 4 cc. of 2 per cent NaCl solution). Mix and place in a water bath at 60 C. for twenty minutes. Readings of the degree of flocculation are made at one-half, one, two, three, and twenty-four hours. Flocculation in one-half to one hour is termed plus-four; after two hours, plus-three; after three hours, plus-two; and after twenty-four hours, plus-one.

dark-adaptation t. (*for vitamin A deficiency*): A test based on the fact that with a deficient intake of vitamin A the ability to see a dimly illuminated object in a dark room is diminished.

Davy's t. (*for phenol*): To a drop or two of the suspected solution add 3 or 4 drops of a solution of 1 part of molybdic acid in 10 or 15 parts of concentrated sulfuric acid: if phenol is present, a pale yellow-brown tint is produced, changing to a reddish brown and then to a fine purple.

Day's t. (*for blood*): The suspected substance is treated with fresh guaiacum tincture and then with hydrogen dioxide: if blood is present, a blue tint is produced.

Dedichen's t. (*for liver function*): A test based on the assumption that urobilinuria is a sign of absolute liver insufficiency. Tincture of iodine is added to the urine, drop by drop, and then an equal amount of Schlesinger's reagent. The mixture is filtered. If urobilin is present, fluorescence takes place.

Deen's t. (*for blood in gastric juice*): To the gastric juice is added 1 cc. of a fresh tincture of guaiac and 1 cc. of Hühnerfeld's solution (2 cc. of glacial acetic acid, 1 cc. of distilled water, and 100 cc. each of oil of turpentine and alcohol). On shaking, the fluid turns blue if blood is present. Iron compounds give the same reaction as blood.

Degener's t. (*for alkalis*): Phenacetolin is turned red by alkalis.

Dehio's t.: If bradycardia is relieved by injections of atropine, the condition is caused by irritation of the vagus; but if the bradycardia is not relieved, the cause is some affection of the heart muscle.

dehydrocholate t. (*for the speed of blood circulation*): Sodium dehydrocholate solution is injected intravenously. The usual time elapsing until a bitter taste in the mouth occurs is thirteen seconds.

Dejust's t. (*for carbon monoxide*): If air containing carbon monoxide is passed through an ammoniacal silver solution, metallic silver will be deposited and the solution will take on a brown or black color.

Delff's t. (*for caffeine*): A solution of red mercuric oxide and potassium iodide: used as a test for caffeine, which it throws down as a crystalline precipitate.

Denigès' t.: 1. (*For uric acid.*) Add nitric acid, which changes uric acid into alloxan, heat gently so as to drive off free nitric acid; add a few drops of sulfuric acid and of commercial benzol, which contains thiophen. This gives a blue color if alloxan has been formed. 2. (*For acetone in urine.*) About 1 inch of the distillate in a test tube is mixed with an equal amount of a solution of the subsulfate of mercury (mercuric oxide 50, sulfuric acid 200, water up to 1000) and the mixture allowed to simmer in a stoppered flask for about five minutes. A white crystalline precipitate occurs on cooling, which is very distinctive in appearance. If acetone is present in excess, the test is less distinct. If but a trace is present, a trace of sodium chloride will aid the precipitation. The precipitate is not soluble in dilute hydrochloric acid. 3. (*For morphine.*) To 10 cc. of the unknown add 1 cc. of hydrogen peroxide, 1 cc. of ammonium hydroxide and 1 drop of 4 per cent solution of copper sulfate. A red color indicates morphine.

Dennis and Silverman's t. (*for the pH of stomach contents*): A few drops of stomach contents are placed on test papers impregnated with Töpfer's reagent and with thymol blue. These are then matched up with similar test papers to which buffered solutions of known pH are applied.

Derrien's t. (*for alphadinitrophenol in the urine*): To 10 cc. of urine add 1 cc. of 10 per cent H_2SO_4 and 1 cc. of 0.5 per cent $NaNO_2$. Shake and keep in the dark five minutes. Place 2 cc. of a fresh 0.5 per cent betanaphthol solution in ammonia water (22 B) in a 25 cc. capacity tube and add the treated urine. Shake and after one minute add 10 cc. of sulfuric ether. Shake and cork. If the ether is violet, wine color or orange-red the reaction is positive; if colorless or yellow, negative.

desmoid t. See under *reaction.*

dextrose t. See *Agostini's t., Allen's t.* (1), *Almén's t.* (3), *Baeyer's t.* (1), *Barfoed's t., Baumann's t., Benedict's t.* (1), *Bertrand's t., Bohmansson's t., Böttger's t., Bottu's t., Braun's t., Caillan's t., Campani's t., Cappagnoli's t., Casamajor's t., Cipollina's t., Cole's t.* (1), *Cramer's t., Crismer's t., Donaldson's t.* (1), *Edelfsen's t., Fehling's t., fermentation t., Fischer's t., Folin's t.* (4), *Folin-McEllroy t., Gawalowski's t., Gentele's t., Gerrard's t., Hager's t., Haines' t., Hassall's t., Heller's t.* (3), *Horsley's t., hydroxylamine t., Jaffé's t.* (1), *Knapp's t.* (1), *Kowarsky's t.* (1), *Loewe's t., Löwenthal's t., Mathew's t., Maumené's t., Molisch's t.* (1), (2), *Moore's t., Mulder's t.* (1), *mycologic t., Nicklés' t., nitropropiol t., Nylander's t., Oliver's t.* (2), *Pavy's t. Pélouse-Moore t., Penzoldt's t.* (2), *Purdy's t.* (1), *Riegler's t.* (3), *Robert's t.* (2), *Rubner's t.* (2), *saccharimeter t., Sachsse's t., safranine t., Salkowski's t.* (4), *Schmidt's t.* (2), *silver t., Soldaini's t., Tollen's t., Trommer's t., von Jaksch's t.* (2), *Wender's t., Worm-Müller t.*

diacetic acid t. See *aceto-acetic acid t.*

diacetyl t. (*for urea*): The solution to be tested is mixed with concentrated hydrochloric acid and diacetyl monoxime. A yellow color develops on boiling if urea is present.

dialysis t. See *Abderhalden's reaction,* under *reaction.*

Diamond slide t.: A serologic test for Rh typing performed on open microscope slides.

diastase t. See *Wohlgemuth's t.*

diazo t. See *Ehrlich's diazo reaction,* under *reaction.*

Dick t. (*for susceptibility to scarlet fever*): A small amount of scarlet fever toxin is injected intracutaneously; appearance within 24 to 48 hours of a small area of reddening of the skin indicates susceptibility of the subject.

Dicken's t. (*for salvarsan*): To 10 cc. of urine add 3 drops of hydrochloric acid and 10 drops of a 0.5 per cent solution of sodium nitrite. Mix 5 cc. of 10 per cent resorcinol and 3 cc. of a 20 per cent solution of sodium carbonate. Stratify the two solutions, a rose-red ring indicates salvarsan; a yellow ring, atoxyl.

Dienst t. (*for pregnancy*): A test based upon the increase of antithrombin in the serum and in the urine of pregnant women.

digestive function t. See *Einhorn's bead t.*

digitalin t. See *Grandeau's t.*

dilution t. See *Strauss' t.* (2), *Volhard t.,* and *water t.*

dimethylamino-azobenzene t. (*for free hydrochloric acid*): To a little of the filtered gastric juice in a test tube add a drop of 0.5 per cent alcoholic solution of dimethylamino-azobenzene; in the presence of free hydrochloric acid there will at once appear a cherry-red color.

dirt t. (*for milk*): Filter a pint of milk through a little disk of absorbent cotton and note the stain produced.

Dold's t.: A flocculation test for syphilis.

Dolman's t. (*for ocular dominance*): The patient holds in both hands a card with a hole in it through which to sight at a light.

Donaldson's t. 1. (*For sugar.*) Add to a suspected fluid a few drops of a solution of 5 parts of sodium carbonate, 5 of potassium hydroxide, 6 of potassium bitartrate, 4 of cupric sulfate, and 32 of water; heat it, and if sugar is present, a yellow-green color will be produced. 2. (*For amebic cysts.*) Add Donaldson's stain to a small amount of the feces; amebic cysts are stained yellow or brown.

Donath's t. (*for paroxysmal hemoglobinuria*). See under *phenomenon.*

Donath-Landsteiner t. (*for paroxysmal hemoglobinuria*): A test based on the fact that the blood of patients with this disease contains iso- and auto-hemolysin which unites with red cells only at low temperatures (2 to 10 C.), hemolysis occurring only after warming with the complement to 37 C.

Donders' t.: A color vision test performed by lanterns with sides of colored glass.

Donné's t. (*for pus in urine*): Separate sediment from the urine, add to it a piece of solid potassium hydroxide, and stir. If pus is present the sediment will become slimy and tough, while mucus will pass into solution.

Donogany's t. (*for blood in urine*): One cc. of ammonium sulfide solution and 1 cc. of pyridine solution are added to 10 cc. of urine: an orange color appears if blood is present.

Dorn-Sugarman t.: A test for sex determination by observing the effect on the testicles of rabbits who have been injected with the urine of the pregnant woman.

double-blind t., a study of the effects of a specific agent in which neither the administrator nor the recipient, at the time of administration, knows whether the active or an inert substance is being given.

Dowell t. (*for pregnancy*): Extract of anterior pituitary is injected intradermally into the flexor surface of the arm: in pregnant women, erythema develops about the injected site.

Dragendorff's t. (*for bile pigments*): Wet an unglazed porcelain plate with the suspected urine, which is soon absorbed; add a drop or more of nitric acid: if bile pigments are present, colored rings are formed.

Drechsel's t.: 1. (*For bile.*) On heating the liquid on a water bath with phosphoric acid and cane sugar, a reddish-brown color will be produced if bile is present. 2. (*For xanthine.*) Made by adding cupric chloride to an ammoniacal solution of the substance: xanthine, if present, causes a muddy precipitate.

Dreyer's t.: An agglutination test for the differentiation of typhoid and paratyphoid infections from other infections in persons vaccinated against typhoid-paratyphoid infection.

drinking t. (*for glaucoma*): One quart of water is ingested as rapidly as possible before breakfast. The intraocular pressure is measured every fifteen minutes. A rise of from 8 to 15 mg. Hg in less than one-half hour indicates glaucoma.

Duane's t.: The employment of a candle blaze and prisms to measure the degree of ocular heterophoria.

Dugas' t.: A test for the existence of dislocation of the shoulder, made by placing the hand of the affected side on the opposite shoulder and bringing the elbow to the side of the chest. If this cannot be accomplished, dislocation exists.

Duke's t. (*for bleeding time*): Clean finger, make light puncture, remove blood drop at intervals until bleeding stops. Note elapsed time.

Dumontpallier's t. (*for bile pigments*): Over the liquid to be tested pour carefully iodine tincture: if bile pigment is present, a green ring is seen between the two liquids.

Dungern's t. See *von Dungern's t.*

Dupont's t. (*for death*): The action of a drop of atropine in the pupil is observed.

Dwight-Frost t.: Strain applied to the heart muscle by marked variation in intrathoracic pressure will cause the tonicity of the heart muscle to vary as recorded by the systolic pressure.

Eagle t. (*for syphilis*): An alcoholic beef heart antigen is prepared and is fortified by a combination of cholesterol and sitosterol to the point of oversaturation. One cc. of the fortified antigen is mixed with 1.3 cc. of a 4 per cent sodium chloride solution. This antigen-saline mixture is left at rest for thirty minutes, and 0.04 cc. is then placed into test tubes, followed by 0.4 cc. of the serum. The set is shaken in the Kahn shaker for two minutes, and the racks are incubated at 37 C. for four hours or longer. The tubes are then centrifugated for ten minutes. Physiologic solution of sodium chloride, 1.2 cc., is then run into each tube and the results are read.

Ebbighaus' t. (*for mental disease*): The examiner gives the patient sentences from which several words have been omitted, and asks him to complete them.

Eberson's t. (*for pregnancy*): A modification of the Aschheim-Zondek test by concentrating the pituitary hormone produced in the patient's urine and injecting it into an immature female rat.

edestin t. (*for gastric cancer based on the presence of peptid-splitting ferment*): The gastric juice is filtered, neutralized with normal Na_2CO_3 solution, using phenolphthalein as indicator, and then brought to an alkalinity equal to N/100 Na_2CO_3, in order to inactivate pepsin. Place 2 cc. of a 0.1 per cent solution of edestin in 0.1 per cent Na_2CO_3 in each of four test tubes. To three tubes add 2 cc., 1 cc., and 0.5 cc. of the faintly alkalinized gastric fluid, reserving the fourth tube as a control and adding to it only a drop of phenolphthalein solution. Place the four tubes in an incubator at 37 C. At the end of four hours exactly neutralize the contents of each of the tubes with 5 per cent acetic acid. When the neutral point is reached all the undigested edestin will be precipitated. The degree of digestion is indicated by the amount of turbidity compared with that in the control tube. Absence of turbidity indicates complete digestion.

Edlefsen's t. (*for dextrose*). See under *reagent.*

Ehrard's t.: A test for detecting simulated deafness.

Ehrlich's t. 1. See *Ehrlich's diazo reaction*, under *reaction.* 2. The benzaldehyde test for urobilinogen. See *para-dimethyl-amino-benzaldehyde t.*

Ehrmann's t. (*for mydriatic substances*): The suspected substance is applied to an enucleated frog's eye, dilatation indicating the presence of a mydriatic substance.

Ehrmann's pancreatic t. (*for pancreatic efficiency*): After a test meal of hydrated fats and of chopped meat the gastric contents and feces are examined for the fat-splitting of pancreatic lipase and for the presence of undigested muscle fibers which are characteristic for decrease of trypsin.

Eijkman's t. 1. (*For phenol.*) Add to the suspected solution a few drops of an alcoholic solution of ethylic ether and nitrous acid, each, 1 part, and concentrated sulfuric acid, 2 parts: a red color is produced. 2. B. coli will form gas in a glucose broth medium that is held at 43–45 C.; aerogenes will not.

Einhorn's t. (*for blood in stomach, feces, and urine*): The fluid is tested by paper sensitized with benzidine. The benzidine paper is immersed in the fluid to be examined, and a few drops of hydrogen dioxide are added, when a blue color is formed if blood is present: the color should appear in a few seconds.

Einhorn's bead t. (*for digestive function*): A sample of the food to be examined is wrapped in gauze to which a colored glass bead is attached, and the whole is placed in a gelatin capsule, which is swallowed. The bead serves to help find and identify the gauze in the feces, and the digestive function is judged by the time the bead is passed and by the digestion of the food sample.

Einhorn's digestion t's. 1. *Protein:* Place a capillary tube filled with 1 per cent hemoglobin agar in duodenal contents and incubate for twenty-four hours. The average length of clear digested end-portions is the index of tryptic digestion. 2. *Starch:* Place a capillary tube filled with a 5 per cent starch agar in duodenal contents and incubate for twenty-four hours. Push contents out onto a slide and cover with Lugol's solution. The average length of the uncolored end-portions is the index of amylolytic digestion. 3. *Olive oil:* Place a capillary tube filled with 25 per cent olive oil, Nile-blue agar in duodenal contents and incubate for twenty-four hours. The average length of the undigested (violet colored) end-portions is the index of steatolytic digestion.

Eiselt's t. (*for melanin in the urine*): Oxidizing agents like nitric and sulfuric acids or potassium dichromate render the urine dark colored if melanin is present.

Eitelberg's t.: A large tuning-fork is held near the ear, at intervals, for from twenty to thirty minutes. If the ear is normal the perception of the vibrations increases after each interval; but if there is a lesion of the conducting apparatus, the perception decreases.

Ellermann and Erlandsen's t. See *tuberculin titer t.*

Elsberg's t.: A method of testing the sense of smell for determining the existence of brain tumor.

Elton's ring t.: A test for the presence of bilirubinate in the blood serum.

Ely's t.: With the patient prone, if flexion of the leg on the thigh causes the buttocks to arch away from the table and the leg to abduct at the hip joint, there is contracture of the lateral fascia of the thigh.

Emanuel-Cutting t. See *mastic t.*

emulsoid-gelatin t. See *gel t.*

epinephrine t.: 1. In persons with exophthalmic goiter the injection of 1 mg. of epinephrine produces a lowering of blood pressure in vagotonic patients and an exaggerated rise of temperature in patients with sympathicotonia. 2. See *Goetsch's skin reaction*, under *reaction*. 3. See *Comessatti's t.*, *Meyer's t.* (1), *Vulpian t.*

epiphanin t. See under *reaction.*

Erdmann's t. (*for alkaloids*). See under *reagent.*

Erichsen t. See under *sign.*

erythrocyte sedimentation t. See *Fahraeus t.*, and under *rate.*

Esbach's t. (*for albumin*). See under *reagent.*

Escherich's t.: A modification of the von Pirquet reaction in which the tuberculin is injected subcutaneously.

Escudero's t. (*for gout*): After a meal containing a given quantity of purines, the quantity eliminated after a period of twenty-four to forty-eight hours is measured: if more than 50 per cent is eliminated gout is excluded.

ether t.: A small amount of a 25 per cent solution of sulfuric acid is added to urine in a test tube and a thin layer of ether is floated over it: the contents of the tube are shaken and allowed to stand. If the froth becomes sticky allergic asthma is indicated.

ethyl acetate t. (*for alcohol*): Add an equal volume of concentrated sulfuric acid and a little sodium acetate and heat. The ethereal odor of ethyl acetate indicates alcohol.

ethyl butyrate t. (*for pancreatic lipase*): A neutral mixture of water, ethyl butyrate, and litmus turns red when acted on by lipase due to the liberation of butyric acid.

euglobulin lysis t., a test which measures blood fibrinolytic activity by determining the time required to dissolve an incubated clot composed of precipitated plasma euglobulin and exogenous thrombin.

Eustis's t.: A test for heart efficiency which depends on the rise in the systolic blood pressure following an increase in pressure within the chest caused by forcible expiration of the full breath.

Ewald's t.: 1. (*For hydrochloric acid in stomach contents.*) Mix 2 cc. of a 10 per cent solution of potassium thiocyanate, 0.5 cc. of a neutral solution of iron acetate, and 7.5 cc. of water. This makes a ruby-red solution. A few drops are put into a porcelain dish and a drop or two of the suspected liquid are added. If HCl is present, a slight violet is seen; but on mixing the color becomes brown. 2. (*For motility of the stomach.*) The injection of phenyl salicylate after a light meal. The phenyl salicylate passes into the intestine, where it is decomposed and salicyluric acid secreted in the urine. Normally the salicyluric acid should appear in from one to two hours, and may be detected by adding to the urine a weak solution of ferric chloride, when a purple color will appear. Called also *salol t.*

extinction t.: Schultz-Charlton phenomenon.

Exton's t. (*for albumin in urine*): Heat together equal volumes of Exton's reagent and urine. A precipitate indicates the presence of albumin.

Exton and Rose's glucose tolerance t.: 50 Gm. of glucose are given and thirty minutes later another 50 Gm. The blood sugar level at sixty minutes should not be greater than at thirty minutes.

Fabre's t.: A test for barbital based on the formation of crystalline dicanthyl compounds developed in the presence of acetic acid.

Fahraeus' t.: A quantitative measure of the speed with which red blood corpuscles settle. The results are important in the diagnosis of pregnancy and of some pathologic conditions.

Falk and Tedesco's t.: A test for bronchial disease based on the fact that if salicylates are given to a patient in whom the bronchial mucosa is injured, salicylic acid will appear in the sputum.

Falls' t. (*for pregnancy*): A dilute suspension of colostrum is injected intradermally into the forearm of the patient: in the presence of pregnancy the wheal that is produced will have a pearly appearance without any pink areola.

Farber's t.: Presence of swallowed vernix cells in the meconium of a newborn baby indicates partial intestinal stenosis; their absence indicates intestinal atresia.

fat t. See *acrolein t.*, *Adams' t.*, *Babcock's t.*, *Bloor's t.* (1), *Meigs's t.*, *Saathoff's t.*

fatigue t. See under *reaction.*

Faust's t. (*for amebic cysts*): Fix a smear of the feces in Schaudinn's fluid then stain successively with alcoholic iodine, 2 per cent iron-alum and 0.5 per cent hematoxylin.

Fearon's t. (*for vitamin A*): Add 1 Gm. of phosphorus pentoxide to 5 cc. of oil. A purple color indicates vitamin A.

feather-germ t.: Into a brown Leghorn capon from which some feathers in the saddle area are removed thyroid extract is injected. Several days later the new feathers that have formed are plucked and will show a black line at the bases of the feather germs.

Fehling's t. (*for dextrose in the urine*): Mix the suspected liquid with freshly prepared Fehling's solution (q.v. under *solution*) and boil. A red precipitate of cuprous oxide shows the presence of dextrose.

fermentation t. (*for dextrose*): Fill a graduated fermentation tube with the urine or unknown solution, add a small portion of compressed yeast, and incubate for twelve hours. The amount of gas that accumulates in the closed arm indicates the amount of dextrose present.

ferric chloride t.: 1. (*For thiocyanates in saliva.*) Add a few drops of dilute ferric chloride to saliva and acidify with hydrochloric acid. Red ferric thiocyanate forms, which is decolorized by adding mercury bichloride. 2. (*For salicylic acid.*) See *Remont's t.*

Feulgen's t. (*for animal nucleic acid*): Hydrolyze with HCl solution and treat with 1 per cent solution of decolorized rosaniline; a red color develops.

fibrinogen t. (*for liver function*): Decrease in the amount of fibrinogen in the blood plasma below the normal amount points to liver injury. Whipple adds 1 cc. of a 2.5 per cent solution of calcium chloride to 1 cc. of plasma and judges the amount of fibrinogen by the toughness of the resulting clot. Rowntree heats the plasma on a water bath at 59 C. for twenty to thirty minutes, then washes, dries and weighs the clot.

fibroderm bismuth capsule t. See *Schwarz's t.* (2).

Fieux's t. (*for antipyrine*): To the suspected liquid add 12 drops of sulfuric acid and 2.5 Gm. of sodium metaphosphate; filter, and to the filtrate add a few drops of a solution of sodium nitrate. If antipyrine is present, a green color will be produced.

film t. See *Ross' t.*

filter paper microscopic t. (*for syphilis*): A flocculation test utilizing different quantities of whole blood, obtainable by puncture of ear lobe, finger, heel or toe, collected on filter paper and dried, then tested with standard VDRL antigen.

Finckh's t. (*for mental disease*): The patient is directed to explain the meaning of proverbs, such as "when the cat's away the mice will play," etc.

finger-to-finger t.: Similar to finger-nose test, for testing coordinated movements of the extremities.

finger-nose t. (*for coordinated movements of the extremities*): The patient is directed to close his eyes, and, with arm extended to one side, slowly to endeavor to touch the end of his nose with the point of his index finger.

Fischer's t. (*for dextrose*): The urine is boiled with phenylhydrazine and sodium acetate. If dextrose is present yellow crystals of phenylglucosazone will be formed.

fish t. See *erythrophore reaction*, under *reaction.*

Fishberg concentration t. (*for renal function*): Patient is given supper with not more than 200 cc. of fluid and nothing thereafter. Urine voided during the night is discarded. The morning urine is saved, the patient kept in bed, and the urine of one hour later and of two hours later is saved. If the specific gravity of any of these three specimens is less than 1.024 there is impairment of renal function.

Fishberg and Friedfeld t. See *xylose concentration t.*

fistula t.: The air in the external auditory canal is compressed or rarefied: if there is erosion of the inner osseous wall of the tympanum, nystagmus will be produced, provided the labyrinth still functionates.

fixation t. See *fixation of the complement*, under *fixation.*

Flack t.: A test of physical efficiency: after a full inspiration the subject blows as long as he can into a mercury manometer with a force of 40 mm. mercury.

Fleig's t. (*for blood in the urine*): A test based on the fact that fluorescein is easily reduced to fluorescin in the presence of oxygenated water and a catalytic agent, such as hemoglobin and its derivatives.

Fleischl's t. (*for bile pigments in urine*): Heat the urine with a strong solution of sodium nitrate and add sulfuric acid with a pipet. The acid sinks to the bottom of the tube and forms colored layers.

Fleitmann's t. (*for arsenic compound*): In a tube containing the suspected fluid hydrogen is generated from zinc and solution of potassium hydroxide. The mouth of the tube is closed by a piece of filter paper moistened with a solution of silver nitrate. On heating, if an inorganic arsenic compound is present, the filter paper will turn black.

flicker t.: Determination of the flicker fusion threshold of an individual as a means of diagnosing existent or incipient high blood pressure and certain forms of heart disease, or to determine the effect of a drug on blood vessel spasm.

flicking t. (*for purpura*): The veins are distended by applying a tourniquet over the elbow: the distended vein is flicked with the operator's finger and if petechiae appear purpura is indicated.

flocculation t.: One in which a positive result depends on the degree of flocculent precipitation produced in the material being tested, as in the *Sachs-Georgi t., Sachs-Witebsky t.*, or *Vernes' t.*

Florence t. (*for spermatic fluid*): To the suspected substance add a strong aqueous solution of iodine and potassium iodide. If spermatic fluid is present, brown plates or needles will be formed.

Fluhmann's t.: A modification of the Allen-Doisy test for estrogenic substance in the body, using mice in which a positive reaction is the mucinification of the vaginal mucosa.

foam t. (*for bile pigments*): Shake the specimen of urine in a test tube: a brownish-yellow foam indicates bile pigments.

Focker's t.: To urine rendered alkaline with sodium hydroxide add a solution of ammonium chloride: a precipitate of acid ammonium urate is formed.

Folin's t.: 1. (*For quantity of urea.*) See *Folin's microchemical method (for urea)*, under *method.* 2. (*For quantity of uric acid.*) See *Folin-Shaffer method (for uric acid)*, under *method.* 3. (*For uric acid.*) To the unknown add a saturated solution of oxalic acid and evaporate to dryness. Cool and extract phenols with 95 per cent alcohol. Dissolve residue in water, add sodium carbonate, and Folin's sodium phosphotungstate reagent. A blue color indicates uric acid. 4. (*For sugar in normal urine.*) Shake the urine with trinitrophenol and bone black to remove creatinin. Filter, add a small amount to Folin's sugar reagent, shake while boiling for one and a half minutes, and centrifugalize. A red layer of cuprous oxide in bottom of tube indicates sugar. 5. (*For amino acids.*) Amino acids develop a pink color in the presence of betanaphthaquinone sulfonic acid and alkali.

Folin and Denis' t. (*for tyrosine*): To 1 to 2 cc. of the unknown add an equal volume of the reagent (containing 10 per cent of sodium tungstate, 2 per cent of phosphomolybdic acid), and 3 to 10 cc. of a saturated solution of sodium carbonate. A blue color indicates tyrosine.

Folin and McEllroy's t. (*for dextrose*): (Reagent: 100 Gm. of sodium pyrophosphate, 30 Gm. of disodium phosphate, and 50 Gm. of dry sodium carbonate in 1 liter of water. Dissolve with heat and add 13 Gm. of copper sulfate dissolved in 200 cc. of water.) To 5 cc. of the reagent add 5 to 8 drops of the urine and boil. In the presence of sugar the hot solution is filled with a colloidal greenish-yellow or reddish precipitate.

Folin and Wu's t. See under *method.*

formaldehyde t. See *Burnam's t., Jorissen's t., Kentmann's t., Leach's t., Lebbin's t., Luebert's t., Schiff's t.* (6).

formalin t., formaldehyde t.: A test for syphilis based on the fact that the addition of a small quantity of solution of formaldehyde to syphilitic serum produces gelatinization.

formol-gel t.: A test for kala-azar: a drop of the patient's serum is placed on a slide, which is then inverted over a watch glass containing a few drops of liquor formaldehyde. The serum from cases of kala-azar will solidify into a stiff opaque jelly.

Fornet's ring t. See *Fornet's reaction*, under *reaction.*

Foshay's t. (*for tularemia*): A suspension of *Pasteurella tularensis* is injected into the skin: a positive reaction resembles that in a positive tuberculin test.

Foubert's t. (*of death*): Testing the heart for movement by inserting the finger through an incision in an intercostal space.

Fouchet's t. (*for bilirubin in blood*): To a sample of the blood serum there is added an equal part of a reagent consisting of 5 Gm. trichloracetic acid, 20 cc. water, and 2 cc. ferric chloride; a green color is produced if bilirubin is present.

Fournier t.: The patient is asked to rise on command from a sitting position: he is asked to rise and walk, then stop quickly on command: he is asked to walk and turn around quickly on command. The ataxic gait is thus brought out.

FPM t. See *filter paper microscopic t.*

fragility t.: Add 1 drop of blood to 25-cc. portions of salt solutions varying in concentration from 0.28 to 0.50 per cent. Shake and allow to stand two hours. Note concentration at which hemolysis begins to show a tinge of pink. Normal bloods begin at 0.42 to 0.44 and are complete at 0.36 to 0.32.

Francis' t. 1. (*For bile acids in urine.*) In a test tube is placed 2 Gm. of dextrose in 15 Gm. of sulfuric acid: the urine is placed on top of this, when a purple color forms if bile acids are present. 2. An intracutaneous test in pneumonia for ascertaining the body response to the infection and whether the specific antibodies are present after treatment with antipneumococcus serum. The homologous pneumococcus polysaccharide is used in the skin test.

Frank and Goldberger t. (*for pregnancy*): The female sex hormone from 40 cc. of the patient's blood is injected into a castrated mouse and the results are interpreted from vaginal spreads.

Frank and Nothmann's t.: The occurrence of glycosuria with a blood sugar content below 1.9 after administration of 100 Gm. of dextrose indicates pregnancy which is of longer duration than three weeks and less than three months.

Fränkel's t.: Examination of the nasal cavity with the patient's head bent down between his knees and rotated so that the side to be examined is turned upward. If pus is seen in the middle meatus, suppuration in some of the anterior accessory sinuses is indicated.

Franken's t. (*for completeness of placenta*): The placenta held by the umbilical cord is put in a wash basin containing warm water; air is introduced through the umbilical vein. In this way defects in the placenta can be recognized.

Frei t.: Sterile pus from the lesion is injected intracutaneously: the development of a raised red papule indicates venereal lymphogranuloma.

Friderichsen's t. (*for vitamin A deficiency*): Determination of the weakest light stimulus which will give rise to an oculomotor reflex. A variation from normal indicates vitamin A deficiency.

Friedman's t., Friedman-Lapham t. (*for pregnancy*): The injection of the urine of a pregnant woman into female rabbits will cause the formation of corpora lutea and corpora haemorrhagica in the rabbits.

Friedman-Hamburger t. See *edestin t.*

Fröhde's t.: A 1 per cent solution of sodium molybdate in sulfuric acid: a test for alkaloids.

Frohn's t.: The use of the double iodide of bismuth and potassium as a test for alkaloids.

Frommer's t. (*for acetone in urine*): Alkalinize about 10 cc. of the urine with 2 or 3 cc. of 40 per cent sodium hydroxide solution, add 10 or 12 drops of 10 per cent alcoholic solution of salicylous acid (salicyl aldehyde), heat the upper portion to about 70 C. (it should not reach the boiling point), and keep at this temperature five minutes or longer. In the presence of acetone an orange color, changing to deep red, appears in the heated portion.

fructose t. See *levulose t.*

Fuchs's t.: A test for cancer based on the observation that the serum of normal persons digests all fibrin except that of normal persons while the serum of cancer subjects digests all fibrin except that of cancer subjects.

Fuelgen t. (*for deoxyribonucleic acid*): A microchemical test for the specific type of nucleic acid found in chromatin.

Fuld's t. (*for antitryptic power of blood serum*): Three solutions are used: a 0.1 per cent solution of Grübler's dry trypsin in slightly alkaline normal saline, a 0.2 per cent neutral solution of casein, and an alcoholic solution of acetic acid. A series of test tubes are prepared containing definite amounts of casein solution and of diluted blood serum and increasing amounts of trypsin solution. After incubating, 1 or 2 drops of the acetic acid solution are added to each test tube. If any turbidity appears it indicates the presence of undigested casein. The amount of trypsin necessary to digest the casein completely in one-half hour can then be determined.

Fuld-Goss t. See *antitrypsin t.*

fundus reflex t. Skiascopy.

Fürbringer's t. (*for albumin*): In the urine are placed gelatin capsules opened at each end and containing mercuric chloride, sodium chloride, and citric acid. If albumin is present cloudiness or a flocculent precipitate is produced.

furfurol t. (*for proteins*): Heat the suspected substance with sulfuric acid. If proteins are present, furfurol is formed.

Gairdner's coin t. See *coin t.*

galactose t. See *mucic acid t., phloroglucin t.*

galactose tolerance t. See *Bauer's t.* (2).

Galli Mainini t. (*for pregnancy*): 10 cc. of urine from the patient is injected into a normal male batrachian (frog or toad). The presence of spermatozoa in a drop of the batrachian's urine indicates the existence of pregnancy.

Gallois' t. (*for inosite*, proteins, tyrosine, and other sugars being present): Evaporate a solution of the suspected substance to partial dryness, and moisten the residue with a solution of mercuric nitrate. On drying, it assumes a yellow color, which heating turns to a bright red, which disappears when the liquid cools.

Ganassini's t. (*for uric acid*): Precipitate the alkaline urate with $ZnCl_2$. In contact with the air the precipitate turns blue.

Gannther's t.: Hydrogen dioxide, H_2O_2, liberates oxygen when brought into contact with blood.

Gardiner-Brown t.: A vibrating tuning-fork is placed on the mastoid process of the patient: if the vibrations are heard longer than they can be felt by the examiner, or if they cease to be heard while they can still be felt by the examiner, there is disease of the middle ear.

Garriga's t.: A flocculation test for syphilis.

Garrod's t.: 1. (*For hematoporphyrin in urine.*) To 100 cc. of urine, 20 cc. of a 10 per cent solution of sodium hydroxide is added, and the whole is filtered. The filtrate is washed in water-free alcohol and the precipitate dissolved in hydrochloric acid. The test is completed with the spectroscope, which gives two absorption bands indicative of hematoporphyrin. 2. (*For uric acid in the blood.*) 30 cc. of blood serum are treated with 0.5 cc. of acetic acid. A fine thread is immersed in it, on which are formed crystals of uric acid.

gastric function t. See *Einhorn bead t., Ewald's t.* (2), *iodipin t., Klemperer's t., Penzoldt's t.* (3), *Rehfuss t., Sahli's t., Sahli's glutoid t., Schmidt's t.* (5), *Schwarz's t.* (2).

Gate and Papacostas' t. See *formalin t.*

Gault t.: A test for simulated deafness by closing the good ear and then making a sound near the supposed bad ear: a winking motion of the lid on the tested side indicates hearing.

Gauran t.: A complement fixation test for the diagnosis of gonorrheal infection.

Gawalowski's t. (*for glycosuria*): Ammonium molybdate is added to suspected urine and heated to 100 C. If dextrose is present, the solution becomes blue.

Gay-Force t. See *typhoidin t.*

Gayer t. (*for Cannabis indica*): The amount of the extract or pure drug which injected intravenously produces full anesthesia of the cornea in rabbits.

Geissler's t. (*for albumin in the urine*): A test paper is dipped in citric acid and dried; another is dipped in a solution containing 3 per cent of mercuric chloride and 14 per cent of potassium iodide, and dried; the two papers are placed in the urine. If there is albumin present, a precipitate will be formed.

gel t. Differentiation of syphilitic serum by the opacity and rapid precipitation produced by addition of glacial acetic acid to small quantities of the serum (J. E. R. MacDonagh, 1916).

Gellé's t.: A rubber tube is inserted in the ear and a tuning-fork is brought in contact with it. By means of a bulb on the tube pressure or suction is made. If the ear is normal, the vibrations of the fork are distinctly perceived; but they are not perceived if there is any lesion of the ossicular chain.

Gentele's t. (*for dextrose or uric acid*): Add to the suspected liquid a solution of potassium ferrocyanide made alkaline with sodium hydroxide. On heating it becomes decolorized.

Geraghty's t.: The phenolsulfonphthalein test.

Gerhardt's t.: 1. (*For acetone in the urine.*) Add a solution of ferric chloride and a red color is produced. This test is not reliable (Carl J. Gerhardt). 2. (*For aceto-acetic acid in the urine.*) Filter, in order to remove the phosphates, and add a few drops of a solution of ferric chloride, which produces a deep-red color, which disappears when sulfuric acid is added. 3. (*For bile pigments in the urine.*) It is made by shaking with an equal measure of chloroform and soon after adding tincture of iodine and potassium hydroxide to the separated chloroform, when a yellow or yellowish-brown color is produced. (Charles Frederic Gerhardt.)

Gerrard's t. (*for dextrose in the urine*): Fehling's solution is treated with a 5 per cent solution of potassium cyanide until the blue color begins to disappear. The suspected liquid is heated with this mixture, and if there is dextrose present, more or less discoloration takes place.

Ghedini-Weinberg t.: A biological test for the diagnosis of echinococcus cyst, using human cystic fluid as the antigen.

Gibbon and Landis t. (*for peripheral circulation*): A pair of extremities (the hands, if the feet are to be tested; the feet, if the hands are to be tested) are immersed in a bath of 43–45 C. If the temperature in the unimmersed extremities rises, the circulation is normal.

Gies' biuret t. (*for proteins*): Gies uses the following reagent in making the test: mix 25 cc. of a 3 per cent solution of cupric sulfate and 975 cc. of a 10 per cent solution of potassium hydroxide.

girdle t. (*for splanchnoptosis*): The examiner, standing behind the patient, places his arms around the patient, so that his hands meet in front of the patient's abdomen; he squeezes and raises the viscera and then allows them to fall suddenly. If the patient feels relieved by the raising pressure and experiences distress on the release, the condition is probably one of splanchnoptosis.

Glénard's t. See *girdle t.*

globulin t. See *ammonium sulfate t.* (1), *Boveri's t.*, *Braun-Husler t.*, *Gordon's t.*, *Hammarsten's t.* (1), *Kaplan's t.*, *Lange's t.* (1), *Mayerhofer's t.*, *Noguchi's t.* (2), *Nonne-Apelt t.*, *Pandy's t.*, *Pohl's t.*, *Ross-Jones t.*, *Weichbrodt's t.*

glucose t. See *dextrose t.*

glucose tolerance t.: A test of hepatic function based on the power of the normal liver to absorb and store large quantities of glucose. Blood sugar should return to normal in two to two and one-half hours after taking 100 Gm. of glucose into a fasting stomach. See also *Exton and Rose's glucose tolerance t.*

glutoid t. See *Sahli's glutoid t.*

Gluzinski's t.: 1. (*For bile pigments.*) Boil the solution with solution of formaldehyde until it becomes green; adding a little hydrochloric acid changes the tint to an amethyst violet. 2. (*For differentiation between ulcer and cancer of stomach.*) Examination of the gastric contents recovered from a fasting patient: (1) After a test breakfast consisting of the white of a boiled egg and 200 cc. of water, which is recovered after three quarters of an hour. (2) After a test dinner consisting of a beefsteak and 250 cc. of water, which is recovered after three and three-quarters hours. In ulcer, both the breakfast and the dinner give the reaction of free HCl. In beginning cancer the first meal will give reaction of free HCl, while the second meal will show only a slight trace or none at all.

glycerol t. See *acrolein t.*, *hypochlorite-orcinol t.*

glycerol-cholesterol t. See *Hinton's t.*

glycerophosphate t. (*for renal function*): 500 mg. of sodium glycerophosphate are injected intravenously, and then the free and total phosphorus in the urine collected during the following hour is determined.

glycuronates t. See *phloroglucin t.*, *Tollens' t.* (4), *Tollens, Neuberg and Schwket's t.*

glycyltryptophan t. (*for carcinoma of stomach*): Filtered gastric contents and glycyltryptophan are placed in a test tube and kept at body temperature for twenty-four hours: if, on the addition of a few drops of bromine, a reddish-violet color is formed, carcinoma is indicated.

glyoxylic acid t. See *Hopkins-Cole test.*

Gmelin's t. (*for bile pigments*): Fuming nitric acid is so added to the suspected urine that it forms a layer under it. Near the junction of the two liquids rings are formed—a green ring above, and under it a blue, violet red, and reddish yellow. If the green and violet-red rings are absent, the reaction shows the probable presence of lutein.

Goetsch's t. See *Goetsch's skin reaction*, under *reaction.*

gold number t. See *Lange's t.* (1).

Goldscheider's t. (*for cutaneous thermal sensibility*): Consists in touching the skin with the slightly pointed end of a metallic cylinder varyingly heated.

gold-sol t. See *Lange's t.* (1).

Gordon's t.: A test for the presence of globulin-albumin in the spinal fluid. One cc. of spinal fluid is placed in a small test tube and 0.1 cc. of 1 per cent solution of corrosive mercuric chloride in distilled water. The formation of a cloud or precipitate after standing an hour indicates a positive reaction.

Gordon's biological t. (*for Hodgkin's disease*): Lymphadenomatous tissue injected intracerebrally into rabbits causes the development of a characteristic lesion in the rabbits' nervous tissues, accompanied by ataxia, spasm, and paralysis.

Göthlin's t.: A test for the adequacy of vitamin C in the blood (capillary fragility), done by testing the capillary resistance in the arm.

Graefe's t. (*for heterophoria*): On holding a prism of 10 degrees before one eye, base up or down, two images are formed. One of these images is displaced laterally in heterophoria.

Graham's t.: The intravenous or oral administration of tetraiodophthalein sodium prior to roentgenologic examination of the gallbladder.

Grandeau's t. (*for digitalin*): The substance is dissolved in concentrated sulfuric acid, to which bromine is added: a rose color is formed if digitalin is present.

Gräupner's t. (*for cardiac efficiency*): A test based on the fact that the blood pressure of strong hearts rises during exercise, while that of weak hearts falls. The exercise is furnished by turning a wheel provided with a brake and permitting the measurement of the work done.

Gregerson and Boas' t. (*for blood*): A modification of the benzidine test to make it less sensitive for use in testing feces. Use a 0.5 per cent solution of benzidine instead of a saturated solution and barium peroxide instead of hydrogen peroxide.

Greig t. (*for the identification of Vibrio cholerae*): A mixture of a broth culture of vibrios is mixed with a suspension of sheep or goat erythrocytes, and incubated. By this test the true cholera vibrio is non-hemolytic.

Greppi-Villa t.: Splenic contraction after injection of epinephrine, for the diagnosis of thrombophlebitic solenic tumors.

Griess's t. (*for nitrites in the saliva*): Mix it with 5 parts of water; add a few drops of dilute solution of sulfuric acid and a few drops of metadiamidobenzene: this produces a strong yellow color if nitrites are present.

Grigg's t. (*for proteins*): Metaphosphoric acid precipitates them all except the peptones.

Gröbly's t. (*for malignancy*): The total phosphorus content of the blood is determined by Neumann's method and the amount of phosphorus in mg. per 100 cc. is divided by the first two figures of the erythrocyte count. If the quotient thus obtained does not exceed 3.17, malignancy may be excluded.

Grocco's t.: In slight cases of purpura and peliosis rheumatica, if an elastic ligature is placed around the forearm, punctiform hemorrhages will appear in the bend of the elbow.

Gross' t.: 1. (*For trypsin in feces.*) In a mortar thoroughly rub up a portion of the fecal mass with three times its bulk of 0.1 per cent sodium carbonate solution. Filter. Mix 10 cc. of the filtrate with 100 cc. of a fresh solution consisting of 0.5 Gm. Grübler's pure casein, 1 Gm. sodium carbonate, and 1000 cc. distilled water. Add a little toluol to prevent bacterial activity and place in an incubator at about 38 C. At intervals remove a few cubic centimeters and test for casein by adding a few drops of acetic acid of about 1 per cent strength. A white cloud appears as long as any casein remains undigested. With the patient upon a protein diet, there is normally a sufficient amount of trypsin to digest all the casein in from ten to fifteen hours. Delay or complete failure of digestion shows diminution or absence of trypsin. 2. A color reaction for the diagnosis of carcinoma.

group t.: A test of intelligence or aptitude given to a number of persons at one time.

Gruber's t. (*for the sensitiveness of the ear to sounds*): The end of the finger is inserted in the ear after the sound of a tuning-fork has ceased to be heard. The tuning-fork is then held against the finger, when the sound again becomes audible.

Gruber-Widal t. See under *reaction.*

Grünbaum's t.: In Addison's disease adrenal extract does not raise the arterial tension.

Grünbaum-Widal t. See *Widal t.*

Gruskin t.: 1. (*For malignancy.*) Inject intradermally a serum containing an alcoholic extract of embryonic tissue cells: a slight area of infiltration, with pseudopod formation, occurs in positive cases. 2. (*For pregnancy.*) An antigen prepared from the fetal layer of the human placenta (pregnacol) is injected intradermally. If pseudopods arise from the wheal at the site of injection, the test is positive. 3. (*For tuberculosis.*) A preparation of the fibrin from tuberculous guinea pigs is injected intracutaneously. The appearance of pseudopodia extending outward from the wheal within six minutes is positive.

guaiac t. (*for blood*): A blood stain treated with tincture of guaiacum, and then with hydrogen dioxide, assumes a blue tint.

Gunning's t. (*for acetone in urine*): To a few cubic centimeters of urine or distillate in a test tube add a few drops of tincture of iodine and of ammonia alternately until a heavy black cloud appears. This cloud will gradually clear up and, if acetone is present, iodoform, usually crystalline, will separate out. The iodoform can be recognized by its odor or by detection of the crystals microscopically. Iodoform crystals are yellowish six-pointed stars or six-sided plates.

Gunning-Lieben t. See *Gunning's t.*

Günzburg's t. (*for hydrochloric acid in the stomach contents*): Dissolve 2 Gm. of phloroglucin and 1 Gm. of vanillin in 30 cc. of alcohol; of this mix 2 drops with 2 drops of filtered gastric juice; heat it slowly in a porcelain cell. Free HCl produces a bright-red color; it is not present if the color is brownish red or brown.

Guterman t. (*for pregnancy*): A test which is based on the color developed when pregnanediol from the urine of the woman is treated with sulfuric acid.

Gutzeit's t. (*for arsenic*): A paper is moistened with an acidulated silver nitrate solution and exposed to the fumes from the suspected liquid, which is mixed with zinc and dilute sulfuric acid. The formation of a yellow spot on the paper indicates the presence of inorganic arsenic compounds.

Hager's t. (*for dextrose*): See under *reagent.*

Haines' t. (*for dextrose*): Copper sulfate, 30 grains; glycerin, ½ fl.oz.; liquor potassae, 5 fl.oz.; water, sufficient to make 6 fl.oz. When boiled and a little urine added, and again boiled, a yellow or reddish-yellow precipitate is produced.

Hallion's t. See *Tuffier's t.*

Ham t.: A test performed by incubating red cells in an acid environment. Frank hemolysis, originally described as specific for paroxysmal hemoglobinuria, is also observed when spherocytic cells are present in sufficient numbers in other congenital or acquired hemolytic anemias.

Hamburger's t.: A test made by injecting 0.1 cc. of a 1:10,000 dilution of tuberculin just below the skin; subcutaneous infiltration follows in twenty-four hours if the patient is tubercular.

Hamel's t. (*for slight jaundice*): A little blood is drawn by puncture from the lobe of the ear into a capillary tube and the tube is allowed to stand for a few hours. The serum which collects in the upper part of the tube will be yellow if jaundice is present.

Hamilton's t.: When the shoulder joint is luxated, a rule or straight rod applied to the humerus can be made to touch the outer condyle and the acromion at the same time.

Hammarsten's t.: 1. (*For globulin.*) In a neutral solution suspected to contain globulin dissolve magnesium sulfate to saturation; the globulin will be precipitated and may be filtered out. 2. (*For bile pigment.*) To one volume of acid mixture (1 part HNO_3 and 19 parts HCl, each 25 per cent) add four volumes of alcohol. Then add a few drops of the unknown. A green color indicates biliverdin.

Hammer's t.: A complement fixation test for tuberculosis, in which the antigen is a mixture of Koch's old tuberculin and an extract of tuberculous granulation tissue.

Hammerschlag's t.: Determination of the specific gravity of the blood by allowing drops of the blood to fall into benzene-chloroform mixtures of known densities.

Hanganatziu-Deicher t. (*for glandular fever*): The serum of the patient is inactivated by a temperature of 58 C. Then a series of dilutions of serum with physiologic solution of sodium chloride is set up (1:4, 1:8, 1:16 and so on up to 1:4096). To each 0.5 cc. of serum dilution, 0.5 cc. of a 2 per cent suspension of washed corpuscles of sheep's blood and then 1 cc. of sodium chloride solution are added. The tubes are put in the incubator for two hours and then in the ice-box over night. In infectious mononucleosis there is a thick clotted conglobation of the corpuscles of the sheep's blood up into the high dilutions; otherwise agglutination is either entirely absent or extremely weak in the 1:4, 1:8 and, in exceptional cases, the 1:16 tubes.

Hanger's t.: A test for the presence of liver cell disease, based on the flocculation of a cephalin-cholesterol emulsion by the patient's serum.

Hanke and Koessler's t. (*for phenols, hydroxy-aromatic acids, and imidazoles*): To 5 cc. of 1.1 per cent sodium carbonate solution add 2 cc. of para-diazobenzene sulfonic acid reagent. Then add 1 cc. of solution to be tested.

Harding and Ruttan's t. (for *aceto-acetic acid*): Acidify the urine with acetic acid, add ½ cc. of N/10 sodium nitroprusside, and then overlay the solution with concentrated aqueous NH_4OH. A violet ring is produced.

Harris and Ray t.: A microtitration for vitamin C in the urine.

Harrison spot t. (*for bilirubin in urine*): Add to 10 cc. of urine 5 cc. of a 10 per cent solution of barium chloride, mix and filter. Spread filter paper on dry filter paper. Add one to two drops of Fouchet's reagent (trichloroacetic acid 25 Gm., water 100 cc. and 10 per cent solution of ferric chloride 10 cc.); a positive reaction gives a blue to green color (Godfried).

Harrower's t. (*for hypothyroidism*): Four ½-grain doses of thyroid extract are given the first day, four 1-grain doses the second day, and four 2-grain doses the third day. A record of the pulse rate is kept during these days as an indication of the amount of hypothyroidism.

Hart's t. (*for oxybutyric acid in urine*): Remove acetone and diacetic acid by diluting 20 cc. urine with 20 cc. of water, adding a few drops of acetic acid, and boiling down to 10 cc. To this add 10 cc. of water, mix, and divide between two test tubes. To one tube add 1 cc. of hydrogen peroxide, warm gently, and cool. This transforms β-hydroxybutyric acid to acetone. Now apply Lange's test for acetone to each tube. A positive reaction in the tube to which hydrogen peroxide has been added shows the presence of β-oxybutyric acid in the original sample of urine.

Hassall's t. (*for dextrose*): The microscopical observation of growth of the *Saccharomyces cerevisiae* in urine: a sign of the presence of sugar.

Hawk's t. (*for fecal amylase*): Rub up and dilute the feces with seven volumes of a neutral mixture of Na_2HPO_4, NaH_2PO_4, and NaCl. Add varying amounts of this to tubes containing soluble starch and toluene and incubate for twenty-four hours. Test for digestion with iodine.

Hay's t. (*for bile salts*): A pinch of sublimated sulfur is dropped in the urine: the sulfur sinks if bile is present, but floats if it is absent.

Hecht's t. (*for syphilis*): A modification of Wassermann's reaction, based on the fact that normal human serum is capable of dissolving ten times its volume of a 2 per cent solution of sheep's blood.

Hecht-Weinberg t. See *Hecht's t.*

Hecht-Weinberg-Gradwohl t. (*for syphilis*): A modification of the Wassermann test using not only the natural antisheep amboceptor in human serum, but also the native hemolytic complement, the hemolytic index of the human serum being determined before the sheep corpuscles are added to the tube.

heel-knee t.: The patient, lying on his back, is asked to close his eyes and touch the knee of one leg with the heel of the other and then to pass the heel slowly down the front of the shin to the ankle.

heel-tap t. See *heel tap*, under *tap*.

Heichelheim's t. See *iodipin t.*

Heller's t.: 1. (*For albumin in urine.*) Stratify cold nitric acid below the urine in a test tube; albumin will form a white coagulum between the urine and the acid. 2. (*For blood in the urine.*) Add potassium hydroxide solution and heat; the earthy phosphates are precipitated, and if blood is present, they are stained red by hematin. 3. (*For dextrose in urine.*) Add a solution of potassium hydroxide: sugar will cause a brownish or reddish precipitate.

hematein t. (*for blood*): To 5 cc. of the unknown add 5 cc. of sodium hydroxide, 2 drops of hematein solution, and 10 drops of hydrogen peroxide. If blood is present the contents will turn rapidly to violet red, then to clear brown, and then to pale yellow. Without blood these changes occur more slowly.

hematoporphyrin t. See *Garrod's t.* (1).

hemin t. (*for blood*). See *Teichmann's t.*

hemoglobin t. See *Almén's t., Heller's t., Kobert's t., Newcomer's t., sand t., Stokes's t., Tallqvist's t.*

hemosiderin t. See *Perl's t., Rous's t.*

Hench-Aldrich t. (*for the mercury-combining power of saliva*): Titrate 5 cc. of saliva with a 5 per cent solution of bichloride of mercury until a drop gives a reddish-brown color with a saturated solution of sodium carbonate.

Henderson's t.: The patient takes a deep breath and holds it as long as he can. If he cannot hold it for more than twenty seconds, he is not a good anesthetic risk, because of the presence of acidosis.

Henle-Coenen t.: The amount of retrograde flow of blood which is obtained from the open end of the distal stump of a divided artery, while the proximal portion is being compressed with a clamp, is a measure (or index) of the adequacy of the collateral circulation.

Hennebert's t. See under *sign.*

Henry's t. (*for malaria*): A serum-flocculation test in which a nonspecific melanic antigen (melanoflocculation) and fine-grained iron antigen (ferroflocculation) are employed.

Henshaw t.: A test to aid in the selection of the appropriate homeopathic remedy in a given case of disease. A visible flocculation zone develops in the patient's blood serum when brought into contact with a potentized remedy homeopathically indicated in the case.

hepatic function t. See *liver function t.*

Hering's t.: On looking with both eyes through a tube blackened within and having a thread running vertically across the farther end, a small round body being placed either before or behind the thread—if vision is binocular, the subject is able at once to tell whether the ball is nearer to him than the thread or farther off; but if vision is monocular, he cannot tell whether it is nearer or farther than the thread.

Herman-Perutz t. See *Perutz reaction*, under *reaction.*

Herring's t., Herring-Binet t.: A modification of the Binet-Simon test for intelligence.

Herter's t.: 1. (*For indole.*) To the unknown add 1 drop of a 2 per cent solution of beta-naphthaquinone-sodium-mono-sulfonate. Now add a drop of a 10 per cent solution of potassium hydroxide and a blue or bluish-green color indicates indole. 2. (*For skatole.*) To the unknown add 1 cc. of an acid solution of para-dimethyl-amino-benzaldehyde and heat to boiling. The purplish-blue color is intensified by the addition of hydrochloric acid.

Herz's t. (*for efficiency of the myocardium*): After slowly flexing and extending the forearm, the pulse rate increases when the myocardium is strong and decreases when it is weak.

Herzberg's t. (*for free hydrochloric acid in the gastric juice*): Moisten a paper with a solution of Congo red and dry it: free HCl colors it blue or bluish black.

Hess capillary t. (*for condition of the capillary walls*): See *tourniquet t.*, def. 1.

Heynsius' t. (*for albumin*): To a suspected liquid add enough acetic acid to render acidulous, and then boil with a saturated solution of sodium chloride; albumin will form a flocculent precipitate.

Hildebrandt's t. (*for urobilin in urine*): The reagent consists of an unfiltered solution of 10 parts of zinc acetate and 90 parts of absolute alcohol. The reagent is shaken before using and equal parts of reagent and urine are mixed, the precipitate which forms being filtered off. With increase of urobilin the filtrate shows a distinct green fluorescence, either directly or after the addition of ammonia.

Hindenlang's t. (*for albumin*): To the liquid to be tested add solid metaphosphoric acid; albumin, if present, forms a precipitate.

Hines and Brown t.: Cold pressor test; a test which measures the response of the blood pressure to the immersion of one hand in ice water: indicative of susceptibility to hypertension.

Hinton t. (*for syphilis*): (1) Pipet into the first tube 0.1 cc. of serum, into the second, 0.2 cc., and into the third, 0.3 cc. with a 1 cc. pipet graduated in one tenths. (2) Add 0.5 cc. of the glycerinated indicator to each tube with a 10 cc. pipet. (3) Shake thoroughly the rack containing the tests by first inclining it at an angle of about 60 degrees to the body and then thrusting it quickly forward and backward. By repeating this ten times one obtains a quick but thorough mixture of the serum with the glycerinated indicator. The presence of distinct foam in each tube is the only safe criterion of adequate mixing. (4) Place the rack containing the tubes in the Wassermann bath or incubator which registers a temperature continuously between 25 and 28 C. for from twelve to eighteen hours (overnight). At the end of six hours the difference between the positive and negative reactions is marked, but the final decision should not be made in less than twelve hours, and preferably only after eighteen hours.

hippuric acid t. See *Lücke's t.*, *Quick's t.* (1), *Spiro's t.* (2).

Hirschfeldt's t. (*for cancer*): A complement fixation test for detecting in cancer patients antibodies for cancer lipoids.

Hirst t., Hirst and Hare t. (*for influenza*): Heterophile antibodies, if present in the blood, agglutinate chicken erythrocytes.

histamine t.: 1. One cc. of a 0.1 per cent solution of histamine is injected subcutaneously as a stimulant of gastric secretion. 2. (*For lesions of the sympathetic nervous system.*) A small area of skin on the wrist, ankle or knee is cleansed with alcohol, which is allowed to dry. A drop of 1:1000 solution of histamine phosphate is placed on it and introduced into the epidermis by multiple needle punctures in a manner similar to that used for cowpox vaccination. The excess histamine is gently removed. (*a*) A reddish purple spot appears as the result of local capillary dilatation. (*b*) A local wheal succeeds, because of transudation of serum from increased permeability of the capillaries. (*c*) A flare results as the effect of dilatation of the arteries by the reflex of a local axon.

histidine t. (*for pregnancy*): A test based on the presence of histidine in pregnancy urine. To 5 cc. of the filtered urine a bromine reagent is added (1 cc. of bromine with 100 cc. of glacial acetic acid); then an alkaline reagent. A violet or purple color indicates the presence of histidine.

histidine loading t. (*for folic acid deficiencies*): A loading dose of histidine is given, and the resultant urinary excretion of excess formiminoglutamic acid, secondary to decreased amounts of tetrahydrofolic acid, is measured.

Hitzig t. (*for vestibular apparatus*): The positive electrode of a galvanic current is applied just in front of the ear being examined, while the negative electrode is held in the patient's hand, the patient standing with feet together and eyes closed. A current of 5 milliamperes causes a leaning toward the positive pole in normal persons.

hock t.: A test for spavin in horses made by holding up the limb with a hock bent sharply. The horse is then started suddenly, and in cases of spavin the first steps are very lame.

Hoffmann's t. (*for tyrosine*): Add mercuric nitrate to the suspected liquid and boil it; then add nitric acid with a little nitrous acid. A red color is produced if tyrosine is present, and a red precipitate is seen.

Hofmann's t.: A modification of the Aschheim-Zondek test in which 13 cc. of the patient's blood serum is used instead of urine.

Hofmeister's t.: 1. (*For leucine.*) Warm the suspected liquid with mercurous nitrate; if leucine is present, metallic mercury is deposited. 2. (*For peptones.*) Mix phosphotungstic and hydrochloric acids; let the mixture stand twenty-four hours, and filter. With this reagent a solution containing peptones with no albumin will afford a precipitate.

Hogben t. See *Xenopus t.*

Holmgren's t.: The use of skeins of colored worsted as a test of the perception of colors. A skein is given to the subject of the test, and he is asked to match it out of a set of variously colored skeins.

Holten's t.: A creatinine clearance test for renal efficiency.

Hopkins' thiophene t. (*for lactic acid*): Add a few drops of stomach contents to 5 cc. of concentrated sulfuric acid containing a little cupric sulfate and heat two minutes. Cool and add a very little thiophene. A cherry-red color indicates lactic acid.

Hopkins-Cole t. (*for protein*): Glyoxylic acid is prepared by the action of sodium amalgam on a solution of oxalic acid. A few drops of this solution are added to the protein solution and strong sulfuric acid is poured down the side of the tube. A bluish-violet color is produced at the junction of the two fluids due to the presence of tryptophan.

Hoppe-Seyler t.: 1. (*For carbon monoxide in the blood.*) Add to blood twice its volume of a solution of sodium hydroxide of 1.3 specific gravity: normal blood will form a dingy brown mass with a green shade if spread thin on a white surface; but if carbon monoxide is present, the mass is red, and so is the thin layer. 2. (*For xanthine.*) Add the substance to be tested to a mixture of chlorinated lime in a porcelain dish; a dark-green ring is formed at first.

hormone t. See *Aschheim-Zondek t.*, *Siddall t.*

Horsley's t. (*for dextrose*): The solution is boiled with potassium hydroxide and potassium chromate; if dextrose is present a green color is produced.

Hotis t. (*for garget or mastitis in cows*): Fresh milk containing bromcresol purple is incubated for twenty-four hours. A positive reaction is the formation of yellow flakes on the sides of the test tube.

Houghton's t.: Ergot is given to a white leghorn cock; if the comb becomes darkened, the drug is of standard strength.

Howell's t. (*for prothrombin*): A test for the amount of prothrombin in the blood depending on the clotting time of the oxalated plasma treated with calcium chloride and thromboplastin.

Huddleson's t.: An agglutination test for brucellosis in man.

Huggins t. (*for cancer*): A sample of patient's blood is treated with iodoacetate and is heated. The serum albumin clots more readily in healthy subjects than in subjects who have cancer.

Huhner t.: Examination of the secretions aspirated from the vaginal fornix and the endocervical canal after coitus, to determine the number and condition of spermatozoa present and the extent to which they have penetrated the cervical mucus.

human erythrocyte agglutination t.: An adaptation of the sheep cell agglutination test, human Rh-positive cells coated with incomplete anti-Rh antibody being used instead of the sheep red blood cells sensitized with rabbit gamma globulin. The sera of some patients with rheumatoid arthritis will agglutinate these cells. The agglutination may be inhibited by some normal sera, and not others, and this test is the basis for the determination of the inherited gamma globulin groups (Gm system).

Hunt's t. See *acetonitril t.*

Huppert's t. (*for bile pigments*): The suspected solution is treated with lime water or calcium chloride solution and then with a solution of ammonium or sodium carbonate. The precipitate of bile pigments may be removed by shaking with chloroform, after washing with water and acidulating with acetic acid. Bilirubin colors the chloroform yellow and the acetic acid solution green.

Huppert-Cole t. (*for bile pigments*): To 50 cc. of the unknown add an excess of baryta water or lime water. To the precipitate add 5 cc. of 95 per cent alcohol, 2 drops of strong sulfuric acid, and 2 drops of a 5 per cent solution of potassium chlorate. Boil, and the supernatant liquid will be emerald or bluish-green if bile is present.

Hurtley's t. (*for aceto-acetic acid*): To 10 cc. of the unknown add 2 cc. of strong hydrochloric acid and 1 cc. of fresh 1 per cent sodium nitrite solution. Shake and add 15 cc. of concentrated ammonium hydroxide and 5 cc. of 10 per cent ferrous sulfate. A violet or purple color develops slowly if aceto-acetic acid is present.

hydrobilirubin t. See *Schmidt's t.*

hydrochloric acid t. See *Bell's t.* (1), *Boas' t.* (2), (3), *Contejean t., Dennis and Silverman's t., dimethylamino-azobenzene t., Ewald's t.* (1), *Günzburg's t., Herzberg's t., Leo's t., Lüttke's t., Maly's t.* (1), (2), *Mohr's t., Rabuteau's t.* (1), (2), *Riegler's t.* (2), *Scivoletto's t., Szabo's t., Töpfer's t., Uffelmann's t., von Jaksch's t.* (1), *Winckler's t.* (2), *Witz's t.*

hydrogen peroxide t. (*for blood*): A 20 per cent solution of hydrogen peroxide is added to the suspected fluid, when, if blood is present even in minute proportion, bubbles will rise, forming foam on the surface of the fluid.

hydrophilia skin t.: Two tenths cc. of an 0.85 per cent salt solution is injected intradermally. While the resulting swelling of the cuticle normally disappears in an hour or an hour and a half, in edema and ascites it disappears in from five to thirty-five minutes.

hydrostatic t.: Floating of the lungs of a dead infant when placed in water indicates that the child was born alive. Called also *Raygat's t.*

hydroxylamine t. (*for dextrose*). See *Bang's method*, under *method.*

hyperemia t. See *Moschcowitz's t.*

hyperpnea t. See *Rosett's t.*

hypochlorite-orcinol t. (*for glycerin*): To 3 cc. of the unknown add 3 drops of N/1 sodium hypochlorite solution and boil one minute to drive off chlorine. Then add an equal volume of strong hydrochloric acid and a little orcinol. Boil, and a violet or greenish-blue color indicates glycerine or a sugar, or some substance that can be oxidized to a sugar.

hypoxanthine t. See *Kossel's t.*

icterus index t.: The comparison by dilution colorimetry of the blood serum with a standard solution of potassium bichromate.

Ide t. (*for syphilis*): One drop of blood, or serum, or cerebrospinal fluid, is mixed with saline on a hollow glass slide and the antigen is added. The slide is then shaken for four to five minutes and the result read under the low-power objective of a microscope or with a powerful lens. Positive reactions show purplish-blue colored clumps, while in a negative reaction there is no sign of clumping. The preparation of the antigen: oxheart is extracted with alcohol, and then to the extract are added measured amounts of cholesterin, gum benzoin, and dyes (crystal violet and azure II).

Iefimov t. (*for animal parasites in intestine*): 5 to 10 cc. of freshly voided urine is brought to the boiling point and a few drops of Mellon's reagent are added. The formation of a gray color indicates a positive reaction.

Ilimow's t. (*for albumin*): Acidulate with acid sodium phosphate, filter, and add a solution of phenol (1:20). A cloudy precipitate indicates albumin.

Ilosvay's t. (*for nitrites*). See under *reagent.*

Imhof's t.: An autoserum test for tuberculosis.

imidazole t. See *Hanke and Koessler's t.*

indican t. See *Amann's t., Jaffé's t.* (2), *Jolles' t.* (2), *MacMunn's t., Obermeyer's t., Porter's t.* (2), *Wang's t., Weber's t.* (2).

indigo carmine t. (*for renal permeability*): A solution of indigo carmine is injected intramuscularly and the time of its appearance in the urine is noted. Normally, it begins to appear in about five minutes. Delay beyond this points to defective renal adequacy.

indigo red t. See *Rosenbach's t., Rosin's t.*

indole t. See *Baeyer's t.* (2), *cholera red t., Herter's t.* (1), *Kondo's t., Legal's t.* (2), *Nencki's t., nitroso-indole-nitrate t., pine wood t., Salkowski's t.* (3), *vanillin t.*

indophenol t. (*for the presence of oxidizing enzymes in cells and for detecting the presence of myeloblasts, etc.*): Cover glass films of the cells are fixed in alcohol. Float for ten to twenty minutes, face down, upon a freshly prepared solution of equal parts of 1 per cent aqueous solutions of dimethyl-para-phenylendiamine and of alpha-naphthol. Rinse and mount in glycerin. The cytoplasm of cells containing oxidase (myeloblasts, myelocytes, polymorphonuclears, and large mononuclears) will be colored blue by indophenol.

inkblot t. See *Rorschach t.*

inoculation t. (*for acute anterior poliomyelitis*): The cerebrospinal fluid of the suspected patient (i.e., before the appearance of paralytic symptoms) is injected into a monkey. Paralysis will appear in the monkey within seven days if the patient is affected.

inosite t. See *Gallois' t., Scherer's t.* (1), *Seidel's t.*

intelligence t. See *alpha t., beta t., Binet t., Kuhlmann t., performance t., Pintner-Patterson t., Rorschach t., Stanford t., Terman t., vocabulary t., Yerkes-Bridges t.*

intracutaneous tuberculin t. See *Mantoux t.*

intradermal salt solution t. See *McClure-Aldrich t.*

inulin clearance t. See under *inulin.*

iodine t.: 1. (*For starch.*) When a compound solution of iodine is added to starch, and especially to an acid or neutral solution of cooked starch paste, a deep-blue color is produced which disappears on heating and reappears on cooling. Erythrodextrin and glycogen give a red color with iodine. 2. See *Alfraise's t., Bourget's t., Lesser's t., Winckler's t.* (3).

iodipin t. (*for motility of the stomach*): Iodipin is given in a gelatin capsule. The saliva is then examined every fifteen minutes for iodine. The presence of iodine in the saliva indicates that the iodipin has reached the intestine, as it is not decomposed in the stomach. Called also *Heichelheim's t.*

iodoform t.: 1. (*For acetone.*) See *Gunning's t.* 2. (*For alcohol.*) Make the unknown alkaline and add a few drops of iodine solution. Heat gently, and yellow iodoform crystals indicate alcohol or some similar body.

iron t. See *Brugsch's t., Tizzoni's t.*

irrigation t.: The patient is examined with the bladder full. The anterior urethra is washed out with a warm solution of boric acid (3 per cent), the perineum being compressed to prevent the entrance of the fluid into the posterior urethra. When the washings are perfectly clear the patient voids his urine and any turbidity must come from the posterior urethra.

Ishihara's t.: 1. A test for color vision made by the use of a series of plates composed of round dots of various sizes and colors. 2. A flocculation test for syphilis, using as antigen an alcoholic extract of the kidney of a pregnant rabbit.

Israelson's t.: The reagent consists of 1 part of alcoholic extract of dried brain of rabbit, guinea pig or beef, 9 parts of physiologic solution of sodium chloride and one or two drops of a 0.2 per cent solution of fuchsin for each cubic centimeter of the reagent. To one drop of the suspected serum, placed on a microscopic slide, one drop of reagent is added and mixed with the aid of a glass rod. In positive reactions there are rosy, flaky shreds in transparent fluid. In negative reactions the appearance is uniformly rosy. In weakly positive reactions, the flocculent particles are very small but are plainly visible under the magnifying lens.

Ito-Reenstierna t.: Intracutaneous injection of a vaccine of killed Ducrey bacilli elicits a positive skin reaction in persons who have been infected with chancroid.

Jacobsthal's t. (*for serodiagnosis of syphilis*): 1.

The patient's serum is mixed with alcoholic extract of syphilitic liver in the proportion of 1 to 10, and the resulting precipitate is examined with the dark field illuminator. A strong positive reaction appears as a clumpy precipitate, a weak positive reaction as a small conglomeration of little fat particles, while a negative reaction is shown as a thick emulsion of fine dancing particles: called also *optic serodiagnosis of syphilis.* 2. A modification of the Wassermann test in which complement fixation is done at a low temperature.

Jacoby's t. (*for pepsin*): The greatest dilution of gastric juice which will clarify an acid solution of ricin in three hours at 38 C. gives the number of peptic units in the juice.

Jacquemin's t. (*for phenol*): Add to the suspected liquid an equal quantity of aniline and some sodium hypochlorite in solution: a blue color is produced.

Jadassohn's t. See *irrigation t.*

Jadassohn-Bloch t.: A skin test for allergic conditions made by holding the suspected substance in contact with the skin for a considerable time by binding it on.

Jaffé's t.: 1. (*For creatinine and dextrose.*) To the liquid add trinitrophenol and then make alkaline with sodium hydroxide. A red color without heating indicates creatinine; a red color after heating indicates dextrose. 2. (*For indican.*) To the suspected liquid are added an equal amount of concentrated hydrochloric acid, 1 cc. of chloroform, and a few drops of a strong solution of chlorinated soda. The chloroform is colored blue if indican is present.

Jaksch's t. See *von Jaksch's t.*

Janet's t.: A test for differentiating between functional and organic anesthesia. The patient is instructed to say "yes" or "no," according as he does or does not feel the examiner's touch. He may say "no" in functional anesthesia, but he will say nothing in cases of organic anesthesia.

Jansen's t. (*for osteo-arthritis deformans of the hip*): The patient is told to cross his legs with a point just above the ankle resting on the opposite knee. This motion is impossible when the disease exists.

Javorski's t., Jaworski's t.: In hourglass stomach a splashing sound will be heard on succussion of the pyloric portion after siphonage.

jelly-film t. See *Ross' t.*

Jendrasic's t. (*for water-soluble vitamin B*): Prepare the reagent by mixing equal volumes of N/10 ferric chloride and N/10 potassium ferricyanide and use at once. To a concentrated aqueous solution of the substance add about 2 per cent of acetic acid, then add the reagent as long as the depth of the blue color increases. Stopper, let stand ten minutes, and read. One to five volumes of distilled water may be added to reduce the color. A distinct blue color or a bright blue precipitate is positive. A green color is negative.

Jenner-Kay t.: A test for serum phosphatase.

Jenning's t.: A modification of Holmgren's test for color perception. Small patches of colored worsted are placed so as to be protected from light and dust. The person to be examined indicates his color selection by pricking the record sheet with a pointed pencil.

Johnson's t. (*for albumin*): Put the urine in a test tube and carefully pour upon it a strong solution of trinitrophenol: a white coagulum of albumin appears at the junction of the liquids which heating augments.

Jolles' t.: 1. (*For bile pigments in urine.*) The urine is shaken with barium chloride solution, chloroform, and a few drops of hydrochloric acid. The precipitate is removed and partially dried. Treatment with 2 drops of strong sulfuric acid will bring out the characteristic colors of the bile pigments. 2. (*For indican.*) To the urine add a little alcoholic solution of thymol and fuming hydrochloric acid containing 0.5 per cent of ferric chloride. Chloroform shaken with this mixture becomes violet in color.

Jones and Cantarow t. See *urea concentration t.*

Jorissen's t. (*for formaldehyde*): Add 0.5 cc. of a 1 per cent solution of phloroglucinol in 10 per cent sodium hydroxide to 1 cc. of the urine. A bright red color indicates free formaldehyde.

Justus' t. (*for syphilis*): Administration of mercury by inunction or subcutaneously, when, if syphilis is present, there will be a fall of hemoglobin of from 10 to 20 per cent.

Kabatschnik's t. (*for hearing*): A tuning-fork is held near the open ear and removed the moment the sound ceases; it is then applied to the nail of the examiner's finger and this finger is placed so as to close the patient's external auditory meatus. In a normal ear the sound will be heard again, although the fork has not been struck a second time.

Kafka's t. (*for cerebrospinal syphilis*): A modification of the mastic test, made with a solution of sodium bicarbonate, sodium chloride, mastic resin, and a stain; called also the *stained normomastic t.*

Kahn t.: 1. [R. L. Kahn]. A precipitation test for syphilis. The serum is inactivated as in the Wassermann test. To 0.3 cc. of serum in a test tube is added 0.05 cc. of diluted antigen. After shaking for three minutes the tube is incubated at 37 C. overnight. A positive reaction is shown by the presence of one or more lumps of precipitate. In the "presumptive" Kahn test a sensitized antigen is employed. 2. [Herbert Kahn]. A test for the presence of cancer based on quantitative determination of a certain constituent of the patient's blood called albumin A.

kairin t. See *Petri's t.*

Kamnitzer's t. (*for pregnancy*): The administration of 2.5 mg. of phloridzin causes glycosuria.

Kantor and Gies' t. (*for proteins*): Test papers, made by dipping them in Gies' reagent (see under *Gies' t.*), drying and cutting into strips, are used in making their biuret test.

Kapeller-Adler t.: A test for histidine in the urine of pregnant women: suggested as a test for pregnancy.

Kaplan's t. (*for globulin-albumin in spinal fluid*): To 0.2 cc. of the fluid in a test tube is added 0.3 cc. of distilled water. This is boiled up twice. Three drops of a 5 per cent solution of butyric acid in physiologic salt solution are added and the mixture carefully underlaid with 0.5 cc. of a saturated aqueous solution of ammonium sulfate. After twenty minutes a definite ring will form at the point of contact if globulin-albumin is present.

Kapsinow's t. (*for bile pigments*): Add Obermayer's reagent to the urine and heat. A green color indicates bile pigments.

Kashiwado's t. (*for pancreatic disease*): The patient swallows stained nuclei from a calf's thymus mixed with lycopodium grains. These later serve to indicate the portion of the feces which is to be examined.

Kastle's t. (*for raw milk*): To 5 cc. of the milk add 0.3 cc. of N/10 hydrogen peroxide solution and 1 cc. of a 1 per cent solution of tricresol. Raw milk will give a slight yellow color, boiled milk will not.

Kastle-Meyer t. See *phenolphthalein t.*

Katayama's t. (*for carbonyl-hemoglobin*): To 5 drops of blood add 10 cc. of water, 5 drops of orange-colored ammonium sulfide, and enough acetic acid to make the mixture acid. CO causes a rose-red color; normal blood, a dirty greenish gray.

Kathrein's t. See *Maréchal's t.*

Katzenstein's t. (*for efficiency of the myocardium*): On constriction of the femoral arteries the systolic blood pressure is increased in cases where the myocardium is efficient.

Kauffmann's t. (*for circulation*): The subject drinks 150 cc. of water, four times, at hour intervals. The foot of the bed is then raised about 25 cm. If there is insufficiency of the circulation, the diuresis increases during the following two hours.

Keller's ultraviolet t.: The use of photosensitive test papers for determining the presence of erythema-producing waves in compound radiations.

Kelling's t.: 1. (*For lactic acid in the stomach.*) The stomach contents are diluted with water, and to them are added one or two drops of a 5 per cent watery solution of ferric chloride. A greenish-yellow color is formed when lactic acid is present. 2. A test for the presence and location of an esophageal diverticulum by the sound of swallowing. 3. (*For gastric carcinoma.*) A test based on the fact that the serum of cancer patients will dissolve the red corpuscles of the hen.

Kelly's t. (*for differentiating between saphenous varix and femoral hernia*): Compress the veins below the knee with the left hand applied to the calf: with the right hand squeeze sharply the inner side of the thigh just above the knee. The blood will be sent back through the internal saphenous vein and will make the swelling in the groin quiver.

Kentmann's t. (*for formaldehyde*): Dissolve in a test tube 0.1 Gm. of morphine in 1 cc. of sulfuric acid; add, without mixing, an equal volume of the liquid to be tested: in a short time the latter will take on a reddish-violet color if any formaldehyde is present.

Kerner's t. (*for creatinine*): Acidify the suspected solution and add phosphomolybdic or phosphotungstic acid in solution: if creatinine is present, it will form a crystalline precipitate.

kidney function t. See *amylase t.* (1), *blood-urea clearance t., concentration t., creatinine clearance t., Fishberg concentration t., glycerophosphate t., indigo carmine t., lactose t.* (1), *methylene blue t.* (1), *Mosenthal's t., Nyiri's t., phenolsulfonphthalein t., phlorizin t., potassium iodide t., Pregl's t., Rehberg's t., Simonelli's t., Strauss's t.* (2), (4), *urea balance t., urea concentration t., urine concentration t., Volhard's t.* (2), *Wohlgemuth's t., xylose clearance or tolerance t., xylose concentration t.*

Killian's t. (*for carbohydrate tolerance*): Two hours after a standard breakfast give patient 200 cc. of water. One hour later give 1.75 Gm. of dextrose per kilogram of body weight. Determine amount of dextrose in blood specimens taken at hourly intervals. Also in the twenty-four-hour specimen of urine.

Kinberg's t. (*for liver function*): After a low nitrogen content diet for several days, 50 Gm. of gelatin dissolved in hot chocolate is taken fasting. In liver disease there is an increase in the output of amino-acids, except in congestion of the liver and catarrhal jaundice.

Kitzmiller t. See *antithrombin t.*

Kiutsi-Malone t. (*for pregnancy*): A modification of the Abderhalden test based on the presence of specific enzymes in the urine.

Kjeldahl's t. (*for nitrogen*). See under *method.*

Klausner's t. (*for syphilis*): The patient's serum is placed in a test tube and covered with distilled water. A turbidity at the plane of contact indicates syphilis.

Klein t. See under *reaction.*

Klemperer's t. (*for motor power of stomach*): Wash out the stomach and introduce by the stomach tube 100 cc. of olive oil. After two hours withdraw the oil. As the stomach cannot absorb the oil, the amount withdrawn subtracted from the amount introduced indicates the amount passed out of the stomach. In the normal stomach not more than 20 to 40 cc. should remain after two hours.

Klimow's t. (*blood in urine*): To a specimen of urine is added an equal quantity of H_2O_2 and a little powdered aloin: formation of a purple color indicates the presence of blood.

Kline t., Kline-Young t.: A microscope slide precipitation test for syphilis.

Knapp's t.: 1. (*For sugar in the urine.*) Ten Gm. of mercuric cyanide are dissolved in 100 cc. of a solution of caustic soda and diluted: heated with diabetic urine, metallic mercury is precipitated. 2. (*For organic acids in stomach.*) Stomach contents are filtered and 1 cc. treated with 5 cc. of ether. The extract is floated on dilute iron solution in test tubes, and the various colored rings formed will indicate the presence of the various acids.

Kober t.: 1. (*For estrogens.*) When estrogens are treated with a mixture of sulfuric acid and phenolsulfonic acid and then diluted with water a clear, pink color is formed. 2. (*For proteins in milk.*) The proteins are precipitated with sulfosalicylic acid and the precipitate estimated nephelometrically.

Kobert's t. (*for hemoglobin*): The suspected liquid is treated with zinc powder or a solution of zinc sulfate; the resulting precipitate is stained red by alkalis.

Koch's t. (*for hemorrhagic diathesis*): With a needle pricks are made into the subcutaneous tissue. In hemorrhagic diathesis a bloody effusion develops around the pricks.

Koenecke's t. (*for estimating the functional activity of the bone marrow*): A dose of 10 cc. of a 5 per cent solution of sodium nucleinate is injected into the buttocks, the leukocytes being counted before and after the injection. Reduction or only slight increase (by 20 or 40 per cent) in the number of leukocytes after the injection indicates hypofunction of the bone marrow. A positive reaction (increase of leukocytes by from 40 to 200 per cent) testifies to normal functioning.

Koh's t.: A test for determining the existence of emotional disorders in children.

Kolmer's t.: 1. A modification of the Wassermann test for syphilis. 2. A specific complement-fixation test for various bacterial diseases.

Kondo's t. (*for indole or skatole*): To 1 cc. of the unknown add 3 drops of solution of formaldehyde and 1 cc. of concentrated sulfuric acid. A violet-red color indicates indole; a yellow or brown color, skatole.

Konew's t. (*for glanders*): A test tube is filled to the depth of 3 cm. with mallease, and blood serum from the suspected subject is introduced by means of a pipet at the bottom of the tube beneath the mallease. If the patient is affected with glanders a white cloudiness will appear along the line separating the two liquids. Called also *ring t.*

Konsuloff's t. (*for pregnancy*): A test based on the fact that the melanophores are increased in pregnancy and are excreted in the urine.

Korotkoff's t.: In aneurysm, if the blood pressure in the peripheral circulation remains fairly high while the artery above the aneurysm is compressed, the collateral circulation is good.

Kossel's t. (*for hypoxanthine*): The liquid to be tested is treated with zinc and hydrochloric acid and with sodium hydroxide in excess: if hypoxanthine is present, a ruby-red color is produced.

Kottmann's t. (*for thyroid function*): To 1 cc. of clear blood serum add 0.25 cc. of 0.5 per cent solution of KI and 0.3 cc. of 0.5 per cent solution of $AgNO_3$. Expose serum for five minutes to light of 500-watt Mazda lamp at 25 cm. distance. Then add 0.5 cc. of 0.25 per cent solution of hydrochinone. Normal serum turns brown in a short time; that of patients with hypothyroidism in a shorter time; that of patients with hyperthyroidism only after considerable delay.

Kowarsky's t.: 1. (*For dextrose in urine.*) In a test tube place 5 drops of pure phenylhydrazine, 10 drops of glacial acetic acid, and 1 cc. of saturated solution of sodium chloride. To the mass which results add 2 or 3 cc. of urine; boil two minutes, and cool. If dextrose is present, crystals of phenylglucosazone will be seen with the microscope. 2. (*Blood test for diabetes.*) Test of the patient's blood based on the reduction of a copper solution by the sugar in the blood to cuprous oxide, and the dissolving of the latter in an acid solution of ferrous sulphate, which causes the separation of an equal amount of ferrous oxide, which is measured by titration with potassium permanganate.

Krauss' t. See under *reaction.*

Krokiewicz's t. (*for bile pigment in urine*): 1 cc. of a 1 per cent solution of sodium nitrate and 1 cc. of a 1 per cent solution of sulfanilic acid are mixed and added drop by drop to 0.5 cc. of urine. The amount added must not exceed 10 drops. The mixture becomes bright red, changing to amethyst on the addition of 1 or 2 drops of concentrated hydrochloric acid and a large amount of water.

Kuhlmann t.: A modification of the Binet-Simon test for intelligence so changed as to adapt it for use on infants.

Külz's t. (*for β-hydroxybutyric acid*): 1. The fermented urine is evaporated to a syrupy consistence, strong sulfuric acid in equal volume is added, and the mixture is distilled. If hydroxybutyric acid is present, α-crotonic acid will be formed, which will crystallize. 2. If, after fermentation, the urine shows dextrorotatory properties, β-hydroxybutyric acid is present.

Kurzrok-Miller t.: An in vitro test of compatibility of cervical mucus and spermatozoa, involving observation, under the microscope, of the behavior of sperm placed beside a sample of mucus taken from the cervical canal at the time of ovulation.

Kustallow's t. (*for pregnancy*): The addition of a drop of urine of a pregnant woman to a drop of hay solution on a slide causes arrest of movement and agglutination of the infusoria.

Kveim t. (*for sarcoidosis*): Intracutaneous injection of an antigen prepared from human sarcoid tissue, usually lymph nodes or spleen; appearance in about a week of a red-purple papule which increases in size and on biopsy resembles the tuberculoid granulomas of sarcoidosis is considered positive for sarcoidosis.

Laborde's t. (*for death*): Oxidation of a needle plunged into the muscle of a limb after twenty to sixty minutes if life is present.

lactic acid t. See *Boas' t.* (4), *Hopkins' thiophene t., Kelling's t.* (1), *MacLean t., Strauss's t.* (1), *Uffelmann's t.*

lactose t.: 1. (*For renal function.*) Twenty Gm. of lactose dissolved in 20 cc. of distilled water are injected under aseptic precautions into a vein at the bend of the elbow. The urine is collected hourly and tested (Nylander's test) until the sugar reaction ceases to be positive. If lactose secretion continues for more than five hours renal disease is indicated. 2. See *Cole's t.* (2), *Mathews' t., Meyer's t.* (2), *Moore's t., mucic acid t., Rubner's t.* (2).

Ladendorff's t. (*for blood*): Treat the suspected liquid with tincture of guaiacum, and afterward with eucalyptus oil: the upper stratum of the mixture is turned violet and the lower blue if blood is present.

Landau color t. (*for syphilis*): To 0.2 cc. of clear serum from the patient add 0.01 cc. of a reagent consisting of a 1 per cent solution of iodine in carbon tetrachloride. Shake thoroughly until the iodine color has disappeared. Let stand for four or five hours. A positive reaction is shown by a clear, transparent, yellow color; a negative one by an opaque grayish color.

Lang's t. (*for taurine*): The solution to be tested is boiled with freshly prepared mercuric oxide: taurine will cause a white precipitate to appear.

Lange's t.: 1. (*For the presence of protein—globulin—in the cerebrospinal fluid, and thus for the diagnosis of cerebrospinal syphilis.*) It is performed by the addition of a preparation of colloidal gold to ten dilutions of spinal fluid, ranging from 1:10 to 1:5120. The results are interpreted according to the changes in color which result. When no change occurs the reaction is negative and is recorded as 0. The color changes depend upon the amount of gold precipitated and are recorded as 1, 2, 3, 4, 5, the last being clear, owing to complete precipitation of the gold. Syphilis of the nervous system gives a reaction in the first five dilutions: tuberculous meningitis reacts in the middle dilutions, pyogenic meningitis reacts in the high dilutions, while general paresis gives a reaction different from that given by cerebrospinal syphilis or tabes. Called also *gold-sol test, gold number method,* and *colloidal gold chloride test.* 2. (*For acetone in urine.*) 15 cc. of urine are mixed with 0.5 to 1 cc. of acetic acid, and a few drops of a freshly prepared concentrated solution of sodium nitroprusside added. The mixture is overlaid with ammonia. At the point of junction a characteristic violet ring is formed.

lantern t.: A test for color blindness made with a set of specially devised lanterns.

latex fixation t.: A serological test for rheumatoid factor, helpful in the diagnosis of rheumatoid arthritis.

Laughlen t.: A precipitation test for the serologic diagnosis of syphilis. Blood is taken from a finger or an ear lobe. The serum is mixed with several drops of the antigen, benzoin, cholesterol, scarlet red, salt water, and alcoholic beef-heart extract. If syphilis is present, coarse particles develop in the colorless fluid, and clumps of red granules appear.

Lautier's t. (*for tuberculosis*): A few drops of a 1 per cent solution of Old Tuberculin are placed on the arm, covered with cotton, and left for forty-eight hours: if tuberculosis is present there will develop a patch of vesicles on an elevated reddened base.

Leach's t. (*for formaldehyde*): To 10 cc. of milk add 10 cc. of concentrated hydrochloric acid containing 0.02 per cent of ferric chloride. Heat, and if formaldehyde is present a violet color will be produced.

lead t. See *Abrams' t., Blyth's t.*

Lebbin's t. (*for formaldehyde in milk*): A small amount of milk is boiled with a mixture of 0.05 Gm. of resorcinol and the same quantity of a 5 per cent solution of sodium hydroxide. Change from a yellow to a red color indicates the presence of formaldehyde.

Lechini's t. (*for blood in urine*): Ten cc. of urine are treated with 1 drop of acetic acid and 3 cc. of chloroform: with blood the chloroform layer becomes red.

Lee's t. (*for rennin*): Add 5 drops of gastric juice to 5 cc. of milk. Coagulation should take place in twenty minutes in the incubator.

Lee-Vincent t.: A test for calcium deficiency as a cause of delayed coagulation time.

Legal's t.: 1. (*For acetone.*) Render the urine acid with HCl and distil it. Solution of sodium hydroxide and sodium nitroprusside added to the distillate produce a ruby-red tint, which acetic acid changes to purple. Creatinine will also produce a red color, but this color disappears when acetic acid is put in. 2. (*For indole.*) To the unknown add a few drops of sodium nitroprusside. Make alkaline with potassium hydroxide. The violet color changes to blue on the addition of acetic acid.

Leiner's t. (*for casein or paracasein*): A piece of feces is fixed by heat on a slide and stained with a solution of acid fuchsin and methyl green. A pale blue or violet color is formed.

Le Nobel's t. See *Nobel's t.*

lentochol t. See *Sachs-Georgi t.*

Leo's t. (*for free hydrochloric acid*): Calcium carbonate is added to the solution, which is neutralized if the acidity is due to free acid, but not if due to acid salts.

lepromin t. (*for leprosy*). See *lepromin.*

Lesser's t.: Any iodine-containing secretion turns yellow when treated with calomel.

Lesieur-Privey t.: A test for albumin in the

sputum, the presence of which is believed to indicate the existence of pulmonary tuberculosis.

leucine t. See *Hofmeister's t.* (1), *Scherer's t.* (2).

Levinson t. (*for tuberculous meningitis and other intracranial conditions*): One cc. of spinal fluid is placed in each of the two test tubes 8 mm. in diameter. To one is added 1 cc. of a 1 per cent solution of mercuric chloride and, to the other, 1 cc. of a 3 per cent solution of sulfosalicylic acid. The tubes are well shaken, stoppered and allowed to stand at room temperature for forty-eight hours. At the end of twenty-four and forty-eight hours the column of precipitate in each tube is measured in millimeters. When the height of the precipitate in the first test tube is seen to be twice that of the precipitate in the second tube, the result of the test is positive.

levulose t. See *Borchardt's t., Cipollina's t., methylphenyl-hydrazine t., Rubner's t.* (2), *Selivanoff's t.*

levulose tolerance t.: A test of hepatic function based on the power of the liver to absorb and store large quantities of levulose.

Lewis and Pickering t.: The employment of a rapid rise of temperature to produce vasodilatation in the part to be tested for the state of the peripheral circulation.

Lichtheim t.: If a patient is able to indicate the number of syllables in a word which he cannot utter, it indicates that the cortex is less involved than the association fibers.

Lieben's t. (*for acetone in urine*): Acidulate and distill it, and treat with ammonia and tincture of iodine: if acetone is present, a yellow precipitate of iodoform is produced.

Lieben-Ralfe t. (*for acetone*): Boil 1.3 Gm. of potassium iodide in 3.75 cc. of solution of potassium hydroxide; float the urine on the surface of the reagent in a test tube: a precipitate of phosphate is formed at the upper surface of the reagent, which, if acetone is present, will be rendered yellow by iodoform.

Liebermann's t. (*for proteins*): A precipitate is made from the urine with alcohol; wash this with ether and heat with strong hydrochloric acid: this produces a fine violet-blue color if proteins are present.

Liebermann-Burchardt t. (*for cholesterol*): Dissolve the suspected substance in chloroform, add acetic anhydride, and treat with strong sulfuric acid; if cholesterol is present, a violet color is produced, which soon changes to green.

Liebig's t. (*for cystine*): Boil the suspected substance with a sodium hydroxide solution and a little lead sulfide: if cystine is present, the lead sulfide will form a black precipitate.

Ligat's t. (*for cutaneous hyperesthesia in abdominal disease*): The skin is pinched between the thumb and forefinger and lifted up from the parts below.

Lignières' t.: A modification of the cuti-reaction consisting in shaving the skin and rubbing in a few drops of raw tuberculin. In tuberculous persons there appear papules whose color varies from pale pink to deep red.

Lindemann's t. (*for aceto-acetic acid in urine*): To about 10 cc. of urine add 5 drops of 30 per cent acetic acid, 5 drops Lugol's solution, and 2 or 3 cc. chloroform, and shake. The chloroform does not change color if diacetic acid is present, but becomes reddish violet in its absence. Uric acid also decolorizes iodine, and if much is present double the amount of Lugol's solution should be used.

Lindner's t. See under *sign*.

Links' t. (*for carcinoma*): A serum test for early carcinoma based on the relationship of the potassium and magnesium content of the serum to the erythrocyte count of the blood.

Linzenmeier's t.: An application of a blood sedimentation test to the diagnosis of pregnancy: a definite increase in the sedimentation rate of red corpuscles indicates the presence of pregnancy.

lipase t.: 1. (*For liver function.*) A test based on the fact that lipase is present in the blood plasma of normal persons in a constant amount. Liver injury will cause a rise in the lipase of the blood plasma as measured by the power of the blood to split ethyl butyrate. 2. See *copper soap t., litmus milk t., ethyl bityrate t.*

Lipps's t. See *sand t.*

Lipschuetz's t.: To a solution of sterol in glacial acetic acid add a granule of benzoyl peroxide: a green color appears at once.

litmus milk t. (*for pancreatic lipase*): Add pancreatic lipase to litmus milk, incubate, and note change of color.

liver function t. See *azorubin t., Bauer's t.* (2), *Bufano t., camphor t., Dedichen's t., fibrinogen t., Hanger's t., Kinberg's t., levulose tolerance t., lipase t., Macdonald's t., phenoltetrachlorphthalein t., Quick's t., rose bengal t., Rosenthal's t.* (2), *santonin t., Strauss's t.* (3), *Weltmann's serum t.* (1), *Zappacosta's t.*

Livierato's t. (*for hypotonia of the myocardium*): 1. Right enlargement of the area of dullness over the heart on mechanical stimulation of the abdominal aortic plexus; called also *abdominocardiac sign.* 2. Spontaneous enlargement of the right heart, occurring on change from the reclining to the erect posture, and spontaneous return to the previous condition when the subject lies down again; called also *orthocardiac reflex.*

Loewe's t. (*for dextrose in urine*): Treat the urine with a solution of sodium carbonate containing bismuth subnitrate and glycerine: sugar gives a dark precipitate.

Loewi's t.: Three drops of epinephrine chloride solution 1:1000 are instilled into the conjunctival sac, followed in five minutes by 3 more drops. This produces dilatation of the pupil in pancreatic insufficiency, diabetes, and hyperthyroidism.

Lombard's t.: A test for simulated deafness using a noise apparatus.

Löwenthal's t. (*for dextrose not in urine*): Boil the suspected substance with a solution of ferric chloride, tartaric acid, and sodium carbonate; if dextrose is present, the liquid becomes dark, and iron oxide is freely precipitated.

Lowy's t.: A modified Abderhalden test for the diagnosis of cancer.

Lücke's t. (*for hippuric acid*): Add boiling hot nitric acid and then evaporate; heat the dry residue: a strong odor of nitrobenzene proves the presence of hippuric acid.

Luebert's t. (*for formaldehyde in milk*): Five Gm. of coarsely powdered potassium sulfate are placed in a 100 cc. flask; 5 cc. of suspected milk are put over it by a pipet, and 10 cc. of sulfuric acid (specific gravity, 1.84) are run down the side of the flask. If formaldehyde is present, a violet coloration soon occurs: if none is present, the fluid becomes brown or black.

Luenbach-Koeppe t.: A modification of the Visscher-Bowman test.

luetin t. See *Noguchi's luetin reaction,* under *reaction.*

lupus induction t.: Serum from a patient suspected of having lupus erythematosis is mixed with normal blood and rotated in a vial with glass beads to induce the formation of the LE cell.

Lüttge-Mertz t.: A modification of the Abderhalden test for pregnancy.

Lüttke's t. (*for free hydrochloric acid in the gastric juice*): A quantitative determination in succession of the total chlorides, the chlorine in the fixed chlorides, and then the combined and free HCl.

Lyle and Curtman's t. (*for blood*): Boil the stool with acetic acid, extract it with ether, and to the ethereal extract add a little guaiaconic acid in 95 per cent alcohol. A decided green or light-blue or purple color indicates the presence of blood.

lysis time t.: A test to measure blood fibrinolytic activity, performed by clotting precipitated euglobulin with thrombin and making serial observations of the lysis of the clot.

McClure-Aldrich t.: An 0.8 per cent solution of sodium chloride is injected intradermally; the rate with which it is absorbed (disappearance of wheal or Q. R. Z.) is decreased from the normal time in intoxications.

MacDonagh's t. See *gel t.*

Macdonald's t.: A test for liver function by the injection of 2 mg. per kilogram of bromsulphalein and the taking of blood specimens every five minutes for thirty minutes after the injection.

Macht t.: The effect of blood serums on the growth of seedlings of *Lupinus albus*: the serum of pernicious anemia and other abnormal blood conditions delays the growth of the seedlings.

McKendrick t.: A skin reaction for the diagnosis of enteric infection: cultures of *Bacillus typhosus*, paratyphosus A and B are injected intracutaneously.

McKinnon's t. (*for smallpox*): Material from the patient's lesion is inoculated intradermically into a normal rabbit and into a vaccinated rabbit. If the material contains smallpox virus the normal rabbit, but not the immunized one, will develop a local lesion.

Maclagan's t. See *thymol turbidity t.*

MacLean t. (*for lactic acid in gastric juice*): To 5 cc. of gastric juice add 5 drops of the following reagent: ferric chloride, 5 Gm.; concentrated hydrochloric acid, 1.5 cc.; saturated solution of bichloride of mercury, 100 cc.

MacLean-de Wesselow t. See *urea concentration t.*

MacMunn's t. (*for indican*): Boil the urine in an equal quantity of hydrochloric acid and a little nitric acid; cool, and shake with chloroform, which becomes violet, and shows one absorption band due to indigo blue and one due to indigo red.

MacQuarrie t.: A pencil and paper test for estimating general mechanical ability.

MacWilliams' t. (*for albumin*): Take 20 cc. of urine and add 2 drops of a saturated solution of salicylsulfonic acid: if albumin is present, a cloudiness or precipitate will be seen: if albumoses or peptones are present, this precipitate will disappear on boiling, but appears again on cooling.

magnesionitric t.: A test for albumin in the urine made with 1 part each of nitric acid and magnesium sulfate.

Magpie's t. (*for salts of mercury*): Stannous chloride is added to the suspected solution, when a white and gray precipitate is formed, consisting of metallic mercury and mild mercurous chloride.

Malerba's t. (*for acetone*): Add a solution of dimethyl-paraphenylendiamine: a fine red or reddish color is seen.

Malmejde's t.: If the urine of a tuberculous person is collected in sterile bottles and kept in free contact with air, but protected from dust, it preserves its acid reaction for from twelve days to three months, whereas the urine of healthy persons becomes alkaline in from three to ten days. Called also *uro-reaction.*

Malot's t. A test for the quantitative determination of phosphoric acid in urine by the reaction with cochineal and a uranium salt.

maltose t. See *Rubner's t.* (2).

Maly's t.: 1. (*For free hydrochloric acid in the gastric juice.*) A solution of methylene blue is added: the free acid will turn it from a violet to a green or blue tint. 2. (*For free hydrochloric acid in stomach contents.*) Filter into a glass dish and stain blue with ultramarine; place a piece of lead paper over it and cover; warm the mixture. The free acid will turn the blue to brown and darken the lead paper.

Mandel's t. (*for proteins*): Add to the suspected liquid a 5 per cent solution of chromic acid: proteins will cause a precipitation.

Manoiloff's t. (*for pregnancy*): To 5 drops of serum in a test tube add 1 cc. of a 2 per cent solution of diuretin in water and a 0.2 per cent alcoholic solution of Nile blue. Shake. A yellow or rose color means pregnancy: a blue or bluish color not pregnant.

Manson evaluation t.: A test for the psychometric differentiation of alcoholics and non-alcoholics.

Mantoux t. (*for tuberculosis*): Intracutaneous injection of increasing amounts of Old Tuberculin in the absence of local reaction.

Manzullo's t. See *tellurite t.*

Maréchal's t. (*for bile pigments in urine*): Drop tincture of iodine carefully into the tube: when the drops touch the urine, a green color is seen.

Maréchal-Rosin t. See *Maréchal's t.*

Marie's three-paper t.: A test for attention and recall: three pieces of paper are given to the subject who is told to cross the room, drop one piece into the waste basket, place another on the table, and return the third to the examiner.

Markee t. (*for pregnancy*): Either of two tests based on the effect produced on endometrial transplants inserted into the anterior chamber of the eye of rabbits by the injection of the follicular hormone of the woman's urine.

Marlow's t. (*for heterophoria*): One eye is occluded by a bandage for some time: after the bandage is removed, measurements for heterophoria are made.

Marquardt's t. (*for fusel oil*): Add a few drops of dilute potassium permanganate until the light pink color persists. Cork for twenty-four hours. Add more permanganate if necessary to keep the pink color. Note the sickening odor of valeric acid.

Marquis's t. (*for morphine*): Evaporate the unknown to dryness on a white porcelain plate and touch with a mixture of 3 cc. of concentrated sulfuric acid and 2 drops of formalin. A purple-red color changing to violet and then to blue indicates morphine.

Marris' atropine t. (*for typhoid and paratyphoid A and B infections*): The patient lies horizontally and completely quiet throughout the test, which is not employed till at least one hour after the last meal. The pulse rate is counted minute by minute until it is found to be steady—usually a matter of ten minutes. Atropine sulfate is then injected hypodermically, the dose being $\frac{1}{33}$ grain, preferably over the triceps region, to ensure rapid absorption. Twenty-five minutes later the pulse is again counted minute by minute, until it is clear that any rise which may have followed the injection has begun to pass off. The difference between the average pulse rate before the injection and the maximum reached after it gives the "escape," or acceleration of the pulse rate, brought about by the dose of atropine. If the escape is 14 or less the case may be regarded as one of typhoid or paratyphoid fever. If it is 15 or more, the reaction is said to be negative.

Marsh's t. (*for arsenic or antimony*): Hydrogen obtained from zinc and dilute sulfuric acid is allowed to act on the suspected substance; if arsenic is present, hydrogen arsenide (AsH_3) is formed. Ignite this gas and hold a piece of porcelain in the jet of flame: metallic arsenic is deposited. For antimony the same test is serviceable, but the arsenical mirror is dissolved by sodium hypochlorite solution, while the antimonial mirror is not affected by it.

Marshall's t. (*for urea*): Treat the specimen with urease and titrate the ammonia so formed. See under *method.*

Maschke's t. See *von Maschke's t.*

Masselon t.: Requiring the patient to compose a complete sentence in which several given words are to be included.

Masset's t. (*for bile pigments in urine*): Add 2 or 3 drops of sulfuric acid and a crystal of potassium nitrite: a grass-green color shows the presence of bile pigments.

Master "2-step" exercise t. (*of coronary circulation*): An electrocardiographic test, the tracings being recorded while the subject repeatedly ascends and descends two steps, each 9 inches high, as well as immediately and 2 and 6 minutes after cessation of the climbs. The amount of work (number of trips) is standardized for age, weight, and sex.

mastic t. (*for cerebrospinal syphilis*): A test depending on the precipitation of a solution containing mastic in cases of syphilis, and no change in the solution in negative cases. Called also *Emanuel-Cutting test.*

Matas' t. See *tourniquet t.*, def. 2.

Mátéfy t.: A serum test for the early diagnosis of pulmonary tuberculosis.

Mathews' t. (*for lactose and dextrose*): If both dextrose and lactose are suspected, make a total quantitative test by Benedict's method. Add yeast to the urine and ferment out the dextrose, then make a second quantitative determination. The second determination is or may be lactose; confirm with the osazone test. The difference between the two determinations is dextrose.

Maumené t. (*for dextrose*): Heat the urine with a little stannous chloride; if sugar is present, a dark-brown precipitate will be formed.

Mauthner's t.: A method of testing color blindness by the use of small bottles filled with different pigments, some with one only and some with two, the latter containing either pseudoisochromatic or isochromatic solutions.

Mayer's t. (*for alkaloids*): Mercuric chloride, 13½ Gm., and potassium iodide, 50 Gm., are dissolved in 1000 cc. of water: this is used as a test for alkaloid, with which it gives a white precipitate.

Mayerhofer's t.: The reduction of a decinormal solution of potassium permanganate solution by 1 cc. of spinal fluid in an acid medium as an index of the amount of protein substance present in the fluid: used as an indication of the existence of tuberculous meningitis.

Mazer-Hoffman t.: A test for pregnancy based on the presence of female sex hormone in the urine as detected by examining the vaginal smears of mice which have been injected with the patient's urine.

Mazzini t.: A flocculation test for the diagnosis of syphilis.

Méhu's t. (*for albumin in urine*): Add a little nitric acid, and mix with 10 volumes of a solution of 2 parts of alcohol, 1 part of phenol, and 1 part of acetic acid; shake it and a white precipitate appears. This test is said not to be entirely trustworthy.

Meigs's t. (*for fat in milk*): To 10 cc. of milk in a special apparatus add 20 cc. of water, 20 cc. of ethyl ether, and shake. Then add 20 cc. of 95 per cent alcohol. Remove the ethereal layer, evaporate, and weigh.

Meinicke t. (*for syphilis*): 1. Flocculation test: alcoholic extract of horse's heart diluted with water and a 2 per cent sodium chloride solution is added to the blood serum. After incubation for twenty-four hours flocculation is produced in syphilis. 2. Turbidity test: the same solution, greatly diluted and containing balsam of tolu, gives a turbid mixture in syphilis. 3. Clearing or clarification test: a milky dilution of alcoholic beef heart containing balsam of tolu will be cleared by the addition of syphilitic blood serum.

melanin t. See *Blackberg and Wagner's t., Eiselt's t., Thormählen's t., von Jaksch's t.* (3), *Zeller's t.* (1).

melitin t. See *brucellin t.*

Meltzer-Lyon t. (*for biliary disease*): A strong solution of magnesium sulfate is instilled into the duodenum by means of a tube, with the hope that this will paralyze the sphincter of Oddi, and that this paralysis will be followed by reflex contraction of the gallbladder, thus permitting the collection of separate specimens of bile from the common duct, the gallbladder, and the liver.

Mendel's t. See *Mantoux t.*

Mendeléeff's t.: A test for cancer based on the theory that there is a specific difference between the coagulating powers of leukocytic and erythrocytic extracts in cancerous and noncancerous subjects.

Mendelsohn's t.: A test for efficiency of the heart muscle based on the rapidity of the recovery of the pulse from its acceleration produced by exertion.

mercury t. See *Magpie's t., Reinsch's t.* (2), *Vogel and Lee's t.*

Mérieux-Baillion t.: The serum from a tuberculous person is injected into the person to be tested; if the latter is tuberculous a reaction will be produced.

Mester's t. (*for rheumatic disease*): Blood is withdrawn from the middle finger of the right hand of a fasting patient before and again thirty and sixty minutes after administration of two or three intracutaneous injections of 0.2 cc. each of a sterile 0.1 per cent aqueous solution of salicylic acid, and the number of leukocytes is determined after each withdrawal. The injections are made at the flexor aspect of the right forearm at a distance of about 5 cm. from each other. They are followed by severe pain and burning sensation of short duration and by the formation, at the points of the injections, of wheals which disappear in a few hours. Positive results are shown by transient leukopenia within the first thirty minutes after administration of the injections.

methylene blue t.: 1. (*For renal permeability.*) A solution of methylene blue is injected intramuscularly and the time of its appearance in the urine is noted. Normally, it appears in about thirty minutes. When delayed beyond this, renal permeability is reduced. Called also *Achard and Castaigne's t.* 2. (*For milk.*) To 10 cc. of milk add 1 cc. of standard methylene blue solution, stopper, mix and incubate at 37 C. in the dark. Mix each half hour. Good quality milk should not decolorize the mixture in less than six to eight hours.

methyl-phenyl-hydrazine t. (*for levulose*): Add 4 Gm. of methyl-phenyl-hydrazine to 10 cc. of unknown (containing about 2 Gm. of levulose) and enough alcohol to clarify the solution. Add 4 cc. of 50 per cent acetic acid and heat from five to ten minutes. Reddish-yellow needles of methyl-phenyl-levulosazone indicate levulose.

Mett's t. (*for estimating pepsin*): Tubes of coagulated albumin are introduced into the unknown and into a standard pepsin HCl mixture and the amount of digestion occurring in a given time is noted.

Meyer's t.: 1. The blood vessel of a freshly killed ox is placed in the solution to be tested; if it contracts, epinephrine is assumed to be present. 2. (*For lactose.*) Precipitate the proteins of the milk with phosphotungstic acid and titrate the filtrate with Benedict's solution. 3. (*For blood.*) See *Meyer's reagent*, under *reagent.*

Michaelides' t.: A seroreaction for syphilis in which ox bile is used as the antigen.

Michailow's t. (*for proteins*): Add ferrous sulfate to the solution, underlay it with strong sulfuric acid and a drop or so of nitric acid: a brown ring and red coloration indicate the presence of proteins.

microprecipitation t.: A precipitation test in which a minute quantity of the serum is employed.

Middlebrook-Dubos hemagglutination t.: A test for the detection of serum antibodies to certain components of *Mycobacterium tuberculosis.*

milk t. See *Babcock's t., Bauer's t.* (3), *benzidine peroxidase t., Kastle's t., Kober t.* (2), *methylene blue t.* (2), *phosphatase t., Storck's t., Wilkinson and Peter's t.*

Millard's t. (*for albumin*): Make a reagent of 2 parts of liquefied carbolic acid, 6 parts of glacial acetic acid, and 22 parts of a solution of potassium hydroxide: this precipitates albumin.

Miller-Kurzrok t.: A laboratory procedure to

test the ability of the sperm to penetrate the mucus plug in the woman's cervix.

40 millimeter t. (*for athletic efficiency*): The subject sits with nasal respiration occluded with a clamp, and by expiring through a mouthpiece, sustains a column of mercury at the height of 40 mm. as long as he can. The pulse rate is taken meanwhile, every five seconds. In a satisfactory test the pulse rate is unaltered for a minute or more.

Millon's t. (*for proteins and nitrogenous compounds*): A solution is made of 10 Gm. of mercury and 20 Gm. of nitric acid; this is diluted with an equal volume of water and decanted after standing twenty-four hours. This reagent gives a red color with proteins and other substances, such as tyrosine, phenol, and thymol, which contain the hydroxy-phenyl group.

Mills's t. (*for tennis elbow*): With the wrist and fingers fully flexed and the forearm pronated complete extension of the elbow is painful.

miostagmin t. See under *reaction.*

mirror t.: A mirror is held horizontally above the larynx and the patient instructed to cough. The mirror is thus sprayed with bronchial secretion. Small flecks of yellowish secretion on the mirror indicate tuberculous expectoration.

Mitscherlich's t. (*for phosphorus in the stomach*): The contents of the stomach are made acid and distilled in the dark. The condenser will contain a luminous ring. Small amounts of alcohol, ether, or turpentine will prevent the reaction.

Mitsuda-Rost t. See *lepromin.*

Mittelmeyer's t.: The patient is directed to take marching steps on one spot without progressing: in vestibular disorder he will turn to the side homolateral to vestibular loss, or contralateral to vestibular excitation.

Mohr's t. (*for hydrochloric acid in the stomach contents*): Dilute to a light-yellow color a solution of iron acetate, free from alkaline acetates; add a few drops of a solution of potassium thiocyanate, and then the filtered contents of the stomach: if they contain the acid, a red coloring ensues, which is destroyed by sodium acetate.

Molisch's t.: 1. (*For dextrose in urine.*) Add 2 cc. of urine, 2 drops of a 15 per cent solution of thymol, and an equal volume of strong sulfuric acid, and a deep-red color results. 2. (*For dextrose in urine.*) To 1 cc. of urine add 2 or 3 drops of a 5 per cent solution of alpha-naphthol in alcohol, then add 2 cc. of strong sulfuric acid; a deep-violet color is produced, and a violet precipitate follows if water is added. 3. (*For proteins.*) The substance is treated with a 15 per cent alcoholic solution of alphanaphthol and then with concentrated sulfuric acid; a violet color is formed if proteins are present.

Moloney t. (*for delayed sensitivity to diphtheria toxoid*): The intradermal injection of 0.02 Lf diphtheria toxoid in 0.1 ml.; appearance in 24 hours of an area of redness with induration greater than 1 cm. in diameter is indicative of a positive reaction.

monosaccharide t. See *Barfoed's t.*

Montigne's t.: Heat an alcoholic solution of a sterol with silicotungstic acid: a red-brown color appears.

Moore's t. (*for dextrose or any carbohydrate*): Boil the suspected solution with sodium or potassium hydroxide; if dextrose or lactose is present, a yellow or brown color is produced.

Morelli's t. (*to differentiate between an exudate and a transudate*): Add a few drops of the suspected fluid to a saturated solution of mercuric chloride in a test tube; a flaky precipitate indicates a transudate, a clot indicates an exudate.

Moretti's t. (*for typhoid fever*): Twenty-five cc. of urine are saturated with 20 Gm. of crystallized ammonium sulfate. After a quarter of an hour the urine is filtered and diluted to about one third. To 10 cc. of the filtrate one fifth of its volume of a 10 per cent solution of sodium hydroxide is added, and then a drop of 5 per cent tincture of iodine. The solution is shaken, and if the reaction is positive a persistent golden-yellow color is produced.

Moritz t.: See *Rivalta's reaction,* under *reaction.*

Mörner's t.: 1. (*For tyrosine.*) To a small quantity of the crystals in a test tube add a few cubic centimeters of Mörner's reagent (solution of formaldehyde, 1 cc.; distilled water, 45 cc.; concentrated sulfuric acid, 55 cc.). Heat gently to the boiling point. A green color shows the presence of tyrosine. 2. See *nitroprusside t.* (1).

Moro's t. See under *reaction.*

morphine t. See *Denigès' t.* (3), *Marquis's t., Oliver's t.* (3), *Weppen's t.* (1).

Morton's t.: In metatarsalgia, transverse pressure across the heads of the metatarsals causes a sharp pain, especially between the second and third metatarsals.

Moschcowitz t.: A test for arteriosclerosis made by rendering the lower limb bloodless by means of an Esmarch bandage. This is removed after five minutes have elapsed, when, in a normal limb, the color will return in a few seconds, but in one affected by arteriosclerosis the return of color takes place much more slowly. Called also *hyperemia t.*

Mosenthal's t. (*for kidney function*): With the patient on a prescribed general diet take samples of urine in two-hour periods during the day and once at night. Examine them for volume, specific gravity, total nitrogen and chlorides, and compare with normal.

Moynihan's t. (*for hourglass stomach*): The two parts of a Seidlitz powder are given separately: in hourglass stomach two separated protrusions on the abdominal wall can be observed.

mucic acid t. (*for galactose, lactose,* etc.): To the unknown add 20 per cent of its volume of nitric acid and evaporate on water bath to about 20 per cent of its original volume. A fine white precipitate of mucic acid indicates galactose or a carbohydrate containing galactose.

mucification t.: The vagina of a mouse is injected with blood serum: the extent of mucification of the mucosa developing in four days is noted.

Muck's t. (*for pregnancy, albuminuria, and eclampsia*): Application of adrenalin chloride (1 to 1000) to the anterior part of the inferior meatus of the nose: a silvery gray blanching of the area touched indicates a positive reaction.

Mulder's t.: 1. (*For dextrose.*) Alkalinize the solution with sodium carbonate: on adding a solution of indigo-carmine and heating the mixture is decolorized, but becomes blue again when shaken with air. 2. (*For proteins.*) Treat the suspected substance with nitric acid: proteins are turned yellow by it; alkalinize the substance and it becomes an orange yellow, due to the presence of the phenyl group. Called also *xanthoproteic reaction.*

Müller's t.: 1. (*For cystine.*) Boil the substance with potassium hydroxide until dissolved; when cold, dilute it with water: a solution of sodium nitroprusside produces a violet coloration, which soon changes to a yellow. (Edward Müller.) 2. A drop of pus is allowed to fall into a small vessel containing some Millon's reagent. Ordinary pus forms a little lump that soon disintegrates and colors the liquid bright red. Tuberculous pus forms a tough skin on the surface of the fluid, which, if pushed down, takes on a globular shape. 3. (*For syphilis.*) A conglobation or clotting reaction for the diagnosis of syphilis, employing cholesterinized ox heart extract and an inactivated serum. (Rudolf Müller.)

Müller-Jochmann t.: 1. When a trace of pus is placed on some sterile coagulated blood serum, and the latter put in an incubator, no change takes place if the pus is tuberculous. Ordinary pus, on the other hand, will form a cup-shaped depression in the culture medium. 2. See *antitrypsin t.*

Murata t.: A ring modification of the Sachs-Georgi test for syphilis.

murexide t. See *Weidel's t.* (1).

Murphy's t.: The patient sits with his arms folded in front of him: the examiner's thumb is placed under the twelfth rib and short jabbing movements are made. Thus deep-seated tenderness and muscular rigidity are determined. Called also *Murphy's kidney punch.*

mycobiologic t.: Mycologic test.

mycologic t. (*for sugar in urine*): To the specimen of urine an equal quantity of 1 per cent peptone solution is added. This mixture is sown with some species of *Monilia.* If sugar is present, gas is developed.

Myers and Fine t. (*for amylolytic activity*): Add decreasing amounts of stomach contents to constant amounts of starch solution and note by means of iodine the amount required to completely hydrolyze the starch.

Mylius' t. (*for bile acids*): To each cubic centimeter of the solution of bile acids add 1 cc. of strong sulfuric and 1 drop of furfurol solution; if bile acids are present, a red color is produced, which turns to a bluish violet in the course of a day or so.

Nagel's t.: A test for color vision performed by means of cards with the colors printed in concentric circles.

Nagle's t. (*for tolerance to alcohol*): 0.03 cc. of 60 per cent ethyl alcohol is injected intracutaneously in the deltoid region. The size and intensity of the zone of erythema which develops around the wheal indicates the relative susceptibility of the patient.

Nakayama's t. (*for bile pigments*): Add 5 cc. of acid urine to the same amount of 10 per cent barium chloride solution and centrifugalize. To the precipitate is added 2 cc. of a reagent consisting of 99 parts of 95 per cent alcohol, 1 part of fuming hydrochloric acid to a liter of which 4 Gm. of ferric chloride has been added. The fluid is boiled, when a green color is obtained, which, on the addition of yellow nitric acid, becomes violet or red.

Napier's serum t. (*for kala-azar*): Add one drop of 40 per cent formaldehyde to 1 cc. of blood serum. If the serum becomes white and opalescent it indicates kala-azar.

Nasso's t.: An autoliquor test for tuberculosis.

Nathan's t. (*for tuberculosis*): A piece of gauze 1 cm. in diameter is moistened in Old Tuberculin and applied to healthy skin on the flexor surface of the forearm. The edges are secured to the skin by adhesive substance. The dressing is removed twenty-four hours later and the reaction is observed for the next five or six days. When positive, the reaction is characterized by the appearance of small vesicopapular lesions on a normal or somewhat hyperemic base.

Neisser and Wechsberg's t. (*for bactericidal power of blood*): Patient's serum is inactivated, mixed with fresh guinea-pig complement, and the bacteria incubated and then plated on agar.

Nencki's t. (*for indole*): Treat the suspected material with nitric acid and a little nitrous acid: a red color follows, and in concentrated solution a red precipitate may appear.

neosalvarsan t. See *Abelin's reaction,* under *reaction.*

Nessler's t. (*for free ammonia*). See under *reagent.*

Neubauer and Fischer's t.: The glycyltryptophan test.

Neufeld's t. (*for pneumococci*): Application of a specific antipneumococcus serum to sputum causes swelling of the capsules of the homologous pneumococci.

Neukomm's t. (*for bile acids*): A drop of the suspected substance is placed on a small white porcelain cover with a drop of dilute cane sugar solution and one of dilute sulfuric acid. The mixture is carefully evaporated over a flame, a violet stain being left if bile acids are present.

neutralization t.: A test for the bacterial neutralization power of a substance by testing its action on the pathogenic properties of the organism concerned.

Newcomer's t. (*for hemoglobin*): Hemolyze blood with hydrochloric acid and match color with standard disk.

Nickerson-Kveim t. See *Kveim t.*

Niclés' t. (*for distinguishing cane sugar from dextrose*): Heat the sugar with carbon tetrachloride to 100 C. This blackens cane sugar, but not dextrose.

ninhydrin t. (*for amino-acid nitrogen*). See under *reaction.*

Nippe's t. (*for blood*): A modified form of Teichmann's test.

nitrate reduction t. See *Ilosvay's reagent,* under *reagent.*

nitrates t. See *Allesandri-Guaceni t.*

nitric acid t.: 1. (*For albumin.*) See *Heller's t.* (1). 2. See *Allesandri-Guaceni t., Weyl's t.* (2).

nitric acid-magnesium sulfate t. (*for albumin*). See *Roberts' t.* (1).

nitrites t. (*in saliva*): To the saliva add 1 or 2 drops of H_2SO_4, a few drops of KI solution, and some starch paste. A blue color indicates nitrites. See also *Griess's t., Ilosvay's t., Schaffer's t.*

nitrogen partition t.: A test of hepatic function based on alterations in the distribution of nitrogen in the various nitrogenous bodies of the blood and urine.

nitropropiol t. (*for sugar in urine*): The urine is mixed with an alkali and heated with orthonitrophenylpropiolic acid, when the color reaction will be seen.

nitroprusside t.: 1. (*For cysteine.*) If a protein containing cysteine is dissolved in water and 2 to 4 drops of a 4 or 5 per cent solution of sodium nitroprusside and then a few drops of ammonia are added, a deep purple-red color appears; called also *Morner's t.* 2. (*For acetone.*) See *Legal's t.* (1). 3. (*For indole.*) See *Legal's t.* (2). 4. (*For creatinine.*) See *Weyl's t.* (1).

nitroso-indole-nitrate t. (*for indole and skatole*): Acidify the unknown with nitric acid and add a few drops of potassium nitrite. A red color or a red precipitate indicates indole; a white turbidity, skatole.

Nobel's t.: 1. (*For aceto-acetic acid and acetone.*) Stratify ammonium hydroxide on urine acidified with acetic acid and to which a little sodium nitroprusside has been added. A violet ring at the junction indicates aceto-acetic acid or acetone. 2. (*For bile pigments.*) Add zinc chloride and a little of the tincture of iodine; a dichroic coloration follows.

Noguchi's t.: 1. See *Noguchi's reaction,* under *reaction.* 2. (*For globulin.*) To 0.5 cc. of Noguchi's reagent add 0.1 cc. of spinal fluid. Boil and add 0.1 cc. of N/1 sodium hydroxide. A flocculent precipitate indicates globulin.

Nonne's t. (*for excess of globulin in the spinal fluid*). See *Ross-Jones t.*

Nonne-Apelt t. See under *reaction.*

nonverbal t.: A mental test in which language is not used.

Norris' atropine t. See *atropine t.* (2).

Nothnagel's t.: A crystal of a sodium salt placed upon the serous surface of the bowel in operations on the intestine causes an ascending peristalsis, and thus shows the direction of the exposed gut.

nuclear t., nucleus t. (*for proteolytic pancreatic function*): A test based on the fact that cell nuclei are digested by the pancreatic juice, and not by the stomach.

nucleo-albumin t. See *Ott's t.*

Nyiri's t.: A concentration test for kidney function by the use of thiosulfate.

Nylander's t. (*for dextrose in urine*): Dissolve 2 parts of bismuth subnitrate and 4 of sodium and potassium tartrate in 100 cc. of a 10 per cent solution of sodium hydroxide; of this add 1 part to 10 of the suspected urine and boil five minutes; a black coloration or black precipitate indicates a reducing sugar.

nystagmus t. See *Bárány's symptom,* under *symptom.*

Ober's t.: With the patient on his left side with his left leg and thigh flexed, the examiner holds the patient's right leg abducted and extended. If on the sudden withdrawal of the examiner's support the right leg holds up instead of dropping, there is contraction of the tensor fasciae femoris.

Obermeyer's t. (*for indican in urine*): Precipitate the urine with a 1:5 lead acetate solution with care, lest an excess of the reagent be taken; filter and agitate the filtrate with an equal amount of fuming hydrochloric acid containing a little of the solution of ferric chloride; to this add chloroform which is turned blue by indigo.

Obermüller's t. (*for cholesterin*): Put the substance to be tested in a test tube and melt it with a drop or two of propionic anhydride over a small flame: on cooling, the mass becomes successively blue, green, orange, carmine, and copper colored.

obturator t. See *Cope's t.*

occult blood t. See tests listed under *blood t.*

Oliver's t.: 1. (*For albumin.*) Underlay the urine with a 1:4 solution of sodium tungstate and a 10:6 solution of citric acid: a white coagulum at the junction of the two layers shows the presence of albumin. 2. (*For sugar.*) Boil the suspected liquid with indigo carmine: sugar will change the blue to a red or yellow. 3. (*For morphine.*) If, to a solution of morphine, a few cubic centimeters of hydrogen peroxide is added and the mixture is stirred with a piece of copper wire, the solution takes on a deep port wine color, with the evolution of gas. 4. (*For bile acids.*) To 5 cc. of the unknown add 2 to 3 drops of acetic acid and filter. An equal volume of 1 per cent solution of peptone will produce a precipitate insoluble in excess of acetic acid if bile acids are present.

one-stage prothrombin time t. See *Quick's t.,* def. 2.

orcinol t. (*for pentose in urine*). See *Bial's t.*

organoleptic t.: A test by the senses.

orientation t.: See if patient can give correctly the time of day, the day of the week and of the month, the year and place.

orthotoluidine t. (*for blood*). See *Ruttan and Hardisty's t.*

osazone t. (*for sugars*). See *Kowarsky's t.* (1) and *von Jaksch's t.* (2).

Osgood-Haskins t. (*for albumin*): To 5 cc. of urine add 1 cc. of 50 per cent acetic acid. A precipitate at room temperature indicates bile salts, urates, or resin acids. Add 3 cc. of a saturated solution of sodium chloride. A precipitate suggests Bence Jones protein or globulin. The Bence Jones protein will redissolve on heating.

osmotic resistance t.: A test to determine the liberation of platelet factor 3, necessary for the formation of intrinsic thromboplastin; performed by comparing the clot-promoting abilities of platelets suspended in distilled water with the abilities of those suspended in saline solution.

Osterberg's t. (*for beta-oxybutyric acid*): To 800 mg. of ammonium sulfate add 0.15 cc. of concentrated ammonium hydroxide solution, 2 drops of a 5 per cent solution of nitroprusside and 1 cc. of the urine. Dilute to 50 cc. and compare with a standard.

Otani's t. (*for typhoid, paratyphoid, and dysentery*): A small amount of the citrated blood of the patient is taken up in a capillary pipet, and to this is added an equal amount of a fine emulsion of the bacilli of the disease in question. After autoclaving, a drop of the contents is placed on a slide, stained, and the phagocytes counted. If 30 per cent or more of the phagocytes have taken up bacilli the test is positive.

Ott's t. (*for nucleo-albumin in urine*): To the urine is added an equal volume of saturated solution of sodium chloride, and then Almén's reagent (dissolve 5 Gm. of tannic acid in 240 cc. of 50 per cent alcohol and add 10 cc. of 25 per cent acetic acid); a precipitate forms when nucleo-albumin is present.

oxyphenylsulfonic acid t. (*for albumin in urine*): Dissolve in 20 parts of water 3 parts of oxyphenylsulfonic acid and 1 part of salicylsulfonic acid; add to 1 cc. of urine a drop of the reagent: if albumin is present, a clear white precipitate appears.

Pachon's t.: Measuring of the blood pressure for the purpose of determining the state of the collateral circulation in aneurysm.

Page and van Slyke's t. (*for plasma protein contents below the edema-producing level*): Place a drop of the plasma in fluorobenzene; if it rises it has a specific gravity less than 1.0235.

Paget's t.: A solid tumor is most hard in its center, whereas a cyst is least hard in its center.

palmin t., palmitin t. (*for pancreatic efficiency*): After a test meal containing palmitin, the contents of the stomach are examined for the presence of fatty acids. They will be found in cases in which the pancreas is normal, for the presence of fat in the stomach causes the pylorus to open and admit the pancreatic juice, which splits palmitin into fatty acids.

pancreatic function t. See *Kashiwado's t., litmus milk t., nuclear t., palmin t., Sahli-Nencki t., secretin t.*

Pandy's t.: A test for globulin in the cerebrospinal fluid. Mix 80 to 100 cc. pure phenol with distilled water, shake, and place in incubator several hours. After several days at room temperature pour off top watery part which serves as the reagent. With a Pasteur pipet a drop (0.01 cc.) of the fluid to be tested is deposited on the bottom of a watch crystal filled with the reagent. If no cloudy precipitate forms within five seconds the reaction is negative.

para-dimethyl-amino-benzaldehyde t. (*for urobilinogen*): To the unknown add an equal volume of hydrochloric acid and boil. Then add 2 drops of a 5 per cent solution of para-dimethyl-amino-benzaldehyde in 10 per cent sulfuric acid. A red to violet color indicates urobilinogen. Called also *Ehrlich's t.*

Parnum's t. (*for albumin*): Filter the urine, and add one sixth of its volume of a saturated solution of magnesium or sodium sulfate; acidulate with acetic acid and boil: if albumin is present, a white precipitate is formed.

partial thromboplastin time t.: A one-stage clotting test to detect deficiencies of the components of the intrinsic thromboplastin system, performed by measuring the clotting time of recalcified plasma after addition of crude cephalin brain extract.

patch t.: A test for hypersensitiveness made by applying to the skin the substances in question by means of small pieces of linen or blotting paper impregnated with the substances: on removal of the patches the reactions of the skin are noted. The same method is used for applying tuberculin test for tuberculosis (*Vollmer's t.*).

paternity t.: A test to determine the blood groups of mother, child, and alleged father for the purpose of excluding the possibility of paternity.

Patrick's t.: With the patient supine the thigh and knee are flexed and the external malleolus is placed over the patella of the opposite leg; the knee is depressed, and if pain is produced thereby arthritis of the hip is indicated. Patrick calls this test *fabere sign*, from the initial letters of movements that are necessary to elicit it, namely, flexion, abduction, external rotation, extension.

Patterson's t.: A chemical spot test for the diagnosis of uremia. A drop of Ehrlich's reagent is applied to a drop of blood placed on a white filter paper: if there is greatly increased blood urea, the spot on the filter paper turns a greenish color.

Paul's t.: Pus from a suspected pustule is rubbed into the scarified eye of a rabbit; if the pus is variolous or vaccinal, a condition of epitheliosis develops in the rabbit in from thirty-six to forty-eight hours.

Paul-Bunnell t.: A method of testing for the presence of heterophil antibodies in the blood: the blood of patients with infectious mononucleosis contains antibodies for the red blood cells of sheep.

Paunz' t. (*for amyloidosis*): Inject intravenously 10 cc. per kg. of a 0.6 per cent solution of Congo red. After one hour withdraw some blood and to the serum add a little hydrochloric acid. No blue color in the coagulated proteins indicates amyloidosis.

Pavy's t. (*for dextrose in urine*): Prepare a reagent by mixing 120 cc. of Fehling's solution with 200 cc. of ammonia (specific gravity 0.88), 400 cc. of a solution of sodium hydroxide (specific gravity 1.14), and 1000 cc. of water; boil the suspected liquid with this solution: if dextrose is present, the reagent is decolorized.

Peck t. (*for purpura haemorrhagica*): 0.1 to 0.2 cc. of titrated moccasin venom is injected intradermally. At a different site physiologic salt solution is injected. The appearance, after one hour, of a purpuric lesion at the site of the first injection and no reaction to the control injection indicates purpura.

Pélouse-Moore t. (*for sugar in urine*): Boil with a solution of potassa, cool, and add 1 drop of concentrated sulfuric acid, when the odor of burnt sugar will be given off.

Pels and Macht t.: The blood of patients affected with certain diseases (pernicious anemia, pemphigus) has a more poisonous effect on living plant protoplasm than does normal blood.

pentose t. See *Bial's t., phloroglucin t.*

Penzoldt's t.: 1. (*For acetone.*) To the suspected liquid add a warm saturated solution of orthonitrobenzaldehyde, and render it alkaline with sodium hydroxide: if acetone is present, the mixture becomes yellow and then green; thereafter a precipitate forms which, on shaking with chloroform, gives a blue color. 2. (*For dextrose in urine.*) Add sodium hydroxide solution and a slightly alkaline solution of sodium diazobenzosulfonate; shake the mixture until it foams: a red or yellow-red color is produced, the foam also being red. 3. (*For stomach absorption.*) A capsule containing 3 grains of potassium iodide is given and a glass of water taken. Dried starch paper is moistened with the patient's saliva, and then a drop of fuming nitric acid placed on the paper. A blue or violet color will form.

Penzoldt-Fischer t. (*for phenol*): Alkalinize strongly the substance to be tested and dissolve in a solution of diazobenzolsulfonic acid: phenol, if present, produces a deep-red color.

peppermint t. (*for pulmonary perforation*): The pneumothorax cavity is filled with the vapor of essence of peppermint. If there is a pulmonary perforation the patient will recognize the characteristic smell.

pepsin t. See *Jacoby's t., Mett's t.*

peptone t. See *Hofmeister's t.* (2), *Ralfe's t.* (2), *Randolph's t.*

perchloride t.: A port wine colored reaction obtained by treating the urine of pregnant women affected with hyperemesis with solution of ferric chloride. The intensity of the reaction indicates the gravity of the case.

percutaneous tuberculin t. See *Moro's t.*

Peret's t. (*for tumors*): From 3 to 5 cc. of blood is withdrawn from the patient's ulnar vein; after removal of the clot, 0.1 cc. of the serum is placed in a test tube; a physiologic solution is added to make 1 cc. Then a 0.25 per cent solution of saponin is added and 1 cc. of a 2 per cent suspension of sheep's erythrocytes is poured in. In 44 cases of a supposed cancer of the internal organs, the lipoid index of the reaction was low (from 0.49 to 0.53), which is characteristic for the serums of patients who have cancer.

performance t.: An intelligence test in which the subject is required to do certain things rather than to answer questions.

Peria's t. (*for tyrosine*). See *Piria's t.*

Perls' t.: A test for hemosiderin made by treating the substance with hydrochloric acid and potassium ferrocyanide: the Prussian blue reaction is produced if hemosiderin is present.

permanganate t. See *Weiss permanganate t.*

peroxidase t. See *Arakawa's reagent,* under *reagent,* and *Goodpasture's stain,* under *stain.*

Perthes' t. (*for collateral circulation in varicose veins*). See *tourniquet t.,* def. 3.

Peterman's t. (*for syphilis*): 0.05 cc. of inactivated serum of the patient is stirred with 0.01 cc. of diluted beef heart antigen; this is inactivated between microscope slides at 37 C. for ten minutes and examined microscopically.

Petri's t.: 1. (*For kairin in urine.*) Add acetic acid and calcium chloride in solution, when a fuchsin-red color is produced. 2. (*For proteins.*) Add diazobenzolsulfonic acid and sodium hydroxide: an orange or brownish color is formed, and on shaking a red froth is produced.

Pettenkofer's t. (*for bile acids in urine*): Drop a solution of the suspected material into a mixture of sugar and sulfuric acid: a purplish-crimson color is produced. This test is also given by amino-myelin, cephalin, lecithin, and myelin.

Petzetaki's t. (*for typhoid fever*): Fifteen cc. of urine are placed in a test tube and to this is added a little 5 per cent alcoholic solution of iodine; if the upper part of the urine takes on a golden-yellow color, the test is positive.

phenacetin t. (*in urine*): To the urine add a little concentrated hydrochloric acid, a little 1 per cent solution of sodium nitrite and a little alkaline alpha-naphthol solution. Make alkaline and a red color indicates phenacetin.

phenol t. See *Allen's t.* (2), *Berthelot's t.* (1), *Davy's t., Eijkman's t.* (1), *Hanke and Koessler's t., Jacquemin's t., Penzoldt-Fischer t., Plugge's t.*

phenolphthalein t.: 1. (*For blood.*) Boil a thin fecal suspension, cool, and add it to half as much reagent (made by dissolving 1 to 2 Gm. of phenolphthalein and 25 Gm. of potassium hydroxide in water. Add 10 Gm. of metallic zinc and heat until decolorized). A pink color indicates the presence of blood. 2. (*In urine.*) Make the urine alkaline and a red color indicates phenolphthalein.

phenolsulfonphthalein t. (*for kidney function*): Inject 1 cc. of 0.6 per cent solution of the monosodium salt of phenolsulfonphthalein intravenously or intramuscularly and collect the urine at hourly intervals. Make specimens alkaline with sodium hydroxide and match color in colorimeter with standard solution. Usually 60 to 75 per cent of the dye is excreted in two hours; 40 per cent or less indicates impaired function.

phenoltetrachlorophthalein t. (*for liver function*): Phenoltetrachlorophthalein is injected intravenously, and normally it appears in the feces, being excreted by the liver with the bile, and giving a bright color to the feces. A drop in the normal excretion of this substance points to liver injury.

phenylhydrazine t. See *Kowarsky's t.* (1), *von Jaksch's t.* (2).

phlorizin t. (*for renal insufficiency*): The bladder is emptied and a hypodermic injection given of a mixture of 5 to 10 Gm. each of sodium carbonate and phlorizin. Sugar will appear in the urine within half an hour if the kidney is healthy. If only a small quantity of sugar appears, there is probably renal insufficiency; if none at all, then serious kidney disease probably exists.

phloroglucin t. (*for galactose, pentose, and glycuronates in urine*). A solution of phloroglucin in hydrochloric acid is added to the urine and warmed, a red color forming if suspected substances are present.

phosphatase t. (*for adequate pasteurization of milk*): *Mycobacterium tuberculosis* is killed more easily than milk phosphatase is destroyed by heat, so if there is no phosphatase in the milk, the pasteurization has been adequate. Add 2,6-dibromoquinonechloroimide and disodium phenyl phosphate to the sample of borax buffered milk. If phosphatase is present, the phenol will be set free and will undergo an indophenol reaction with the production of a blue color.

phosphoric acid t. See *Malot's t., Mitscherlich's t.*

phrenic-pressure t.: Pressure is applied to the phrenic nerve on both sides over the clavicles. If the patient feels pain, the lesion is in the pleural space; if he does not feel pain, the lesion is in the abdomen.

phthalein t. See *phenolsulfonphthalein t.*

phytotoxin t. See *Macht t.*

Piazza's t. (*for tuberculosis*): The patient's urine is mixed with the serum of a guinea pig or rabbit which has received an injection of Koch's Old Tuberculin: the formation of a precipitate is positive.

picrotoxin t. See *Becker's t.*

Pincus t.: Typical colors are produced on heating 17-ketosteroids with concentrated antimony trichloride in glacial acetic acid.

pineapple t. (*for butyric acid in stomach*): A few drops of sulfuric acid and alcohol are added to a dried ethereal extract of the gastric juice. If butyric acid is present, an odor of pineapple will be given off, caused by the formation of ethylbutyrate.

pine wood t. (*for indole*): A pine splinter moistened with concentrated hydrochloric acid is turned cherry red by a solution of indole.

Pintner-Patterson t.: A series of performance tests designed to estimate the ability to manage concrete objects.

Piorkowski's t. (*for typhoid bacilli*): Alkaline urine is boiled with a small amount of peptone and gelatin. The filtered product is sterilized and inoculated with the suspected substances. Plate cultures are made. Typhoid colonies will develop in twenty-four hours.

Piotrowski's t. See *biuret t.* (1).

Piria's t. (*for tyrosine*): Moisten the suspected material with strong sulfuric acid and warm it; then dilute and warm it again; neutralize it with barium carbonate, filter, and add ferric chloride in dilute solution: if tyrosine is present, a violet color is seen, which is destroyed by an excess of ferric chloride.

Pirquet's t. See under *reaction.*

plasmacrit t., a rapid but reasonably sensitive and specific screening test for syphilis, using plasma from microhematocrit tubes.

Plesch's t. (*for persistent ductus arteriosus*): Determination of the amount of oxygen and of carbonic acid in the blood that traverses the lungs.

Plugge's t. (*for phenol*): A dilute solution containing phenol becomes red on mixture with a mercuric nitrate solution containing a trace of nitrous acid; mercury is also precipitated and the odor of salicylol is given off.

Poehl's t. (*for determining the presence of the cholera bacillus*): Add 10 drops of concentrated sulfuric acid to 7 cc. of the pure culture, when a rose color will be formed, deepening to a purple.

Pohl's t. (*for globulins*): These substances are precipitated from solution by ammonium sulfate.

pointing t. See *Bárány's pointing t.*

Politzer's t. (*for deafness in one ear*): When a tuning-fork is placed in front of the nares it is heard only by an unaffected ear during deglutition.

Pollacci's t. (*for albumin in urine*): Dissolve in 100 cc. of water 1 Gm. of tartaric acid, 5 Gm. of mercuric chloride, and 10 Gm. of sodium chloride, and add 5 cc. of solution of formaldehyde. This solution added to urine will cause coagulation of albumin in a white zone.

Pollatschek-Porges t. See *Porges-Pollatschek t.*

polyuria t. See *Albarran's t.*

Porges-Meier t. (*for syphilis*): A 1 per cent emulsion of lecithin in physiologic salt solution is mixed with an equal volume of blood serum and allowed to stand for five hours. Blood serum from the patient to be tested is added, when the lecithin will be precipitated if the patient has syphilis.

Porges-Pollatschek t. (*for pregnancy*): One-fifth cc. of the hormone of the hypophysis is injected intracutaneously into the skin. If the woman is not pregnant, a distinct red circle, about an inch in diameter, is formed, after a few hours, at the site of the injection, and remains visible for from twenty-four to thirty-six hours. In pregnancy there is no reaction.

Porges-Salomon t. (*for syphilis*): A 1 per cent sodium glycocholate solution is mixed with an equal volume of clear activated serum from the patient. If the serum is syphilitic, distinct flocculi will appear at the top of the fluid.

porphobilinogen t. See *Watson-Schwartz t.*

Porter's t.: 1. (*For excess of uric acid.*) The upper portion of the urine is boiled in a test tube and a few drops of 4 per cent acetic acid added; in a few hours crystals of uric acid will form just below the surface. 2. (*For indican.*) Ten cc. of urine is shaken with an equal amount of hydrochloric acid and 5 drops of a 0.5 per cent solution of potassium permanganate; add 5 cc. of chloroform and shake. A purple color with a deposit of blue matter indicates indican.

Porteus maze t.: A performance test in which the subject is required to trace with a pencil through printed mazes of increasing difficulty.

Posner's t.: 1. (*For the source of albumin in urine.*) A twenty-four-hour sample of urine is preserved with solution of formaldehyde, shaken, and the leukocytes counted in the blood-counting chamber—100,000 leukocytes per 2 cc. of urine indicate 0.1 per cent of albumin. In this case the albumin is probably due solely to the pus. If albumin is present in greater proportion than this, it is probably due to Bright's disease. 2. (*For proteins.*) Posner makes a ring biuret test by mixing the potassium hydroxide solution and the unknown and then stratifying very dilute copper sulfate solution on top of the mixture.

potassium iodide t. (*for renal function*): The patient receives 0.5 Gm. of potassium iodide in solution by mouth, and the urine is tested every two hours for iodine. If iodine secretion is prolonged beyond sixty hours, excretion through the renal tubules is indicated.

Pratt's t.: A modification of Volhard's test combining the dilution and concentration test.

precipitin t., precipitation t.: A test in which the positive reaction consists in the formation and deposit of a precipitate in the fluid being tested.

Pregl's t. (*for kidney function*): Determine specific gravity of the urine obtained by catheterization of the ureters. Using Haeser's coefficient estimate the amount of solid substances excreted, and compare it with the weight of ash. The diseased kidney may excrete the same volume of water, but less solid material. A predominance of mineral substances (ash) over the organic also speaks for a lower function of the kidney.

pregnancy t. See *Aschheim-Zondek t., Bercovitz t., bitterling t., bromine t.* (3), *Brouha t., Brown's t., Cuboni's t., Dienst t., Dowell t., Eberson's t., Falls' t., Frank and Goldberger t., Frank and Nothmann's t., Friedman's t., Galli Mainini t., Gruskin t.* (2), *Guterman t., histidine t., Kamnitzer's t., Kapeller-Adler t., Kiutsi-Malone t., Konsuloff's t., Kustallow's t., Linzenmeier's t., Manoiloff's t., Markee t., Mazer-Hoffman t., Muck's t., Porges-Pollatschek t.,* *prostigmine t., Renton's t., Schneider t., Siddall t., Venning Browne t., Visscher-Bowman t., Voge's t., von Pall's t., Weisman's t., Wilson's t.,* and *Xenopus t.*

Prendergast's t. (*for typhoid fever*): Intradermal injection of 5 mg. of typhoid vaccine. In the non-typhoid patients there develops within twenty-four hours an area of redness about the site of the injection, while in the typhoid patient there is no reaction.

presumptive t. (*for B. coli in drinking water*): The fermentation of lactose with the production of acid and gas in suitable culture media.

Preyer's t.: A spectroscopic test for carbon monoxide in the blood.

Proetz t. (*for acuity of sense of smell*): Use of a series of substances each in 10 different concentrations in a liter of petrolatum of specific gravity 0.880, to determine the least concentration at which the substance can be recognized: termed *olfactory coefficient* or *minimal identifiable odor.*

prostigmine t. (*for pregnancy*): Administration of prostigmine to a woman who has missed her regular menstruation will bring on menstruation if she is not pregnant.

protein t. See *acetic acid and potassium ferrocyanide t., Acree-Rosenheim t., Adamkiewicz's t., Bardach's t., biuret t.* (1), *Brücke's t.* (2), *coagulation t., Ehrlich's t., furfurol t., Gies' biuret t., Grigg's t., Hopkins-Cole t., Kantor and Gies' t., Kober t.* (2), *Liebermann's t., Mandel's t., Michailow's t., Millon's t., Molisch's t.* (3), *Mulder's t.* (2), *Petri's t.* (2), *Posner's t.* (2), *Reichl's t., Schulte's t., Schultze's t.* (3), *Sicard-Cantelouble t., sulfur t., triketohydrindene-hydrate t., von Aldor's t.* See also tests listed under *albumin t.*

protein tyrosin t. (*for malaria*): To 0.1 cc. of serum add 3 cc. of a 14 per cent solution of sodium sulfate, mix and incubate for three hours. Centrifuge and wash the precipitate with fresh solution of sodium sulfate. Dissolve the precipitate in 1.75 cc. of water and add 0.1 cc. of a 5N solution of sodium hydroxide. Heat on water bath for ten minutes, add 0.15 cc. of Folin and Ciocalteu's phenol reagent and compare with a standard.

proteose t.: Proteose does not coagulate on boiling, but gives a ring test with trichloracetic acid.

prothrombin t. See *Howell's t., Quick's t.* (2), *Smith's t.* (2).

prothrombin consumption t.: A test used, for the most part, to measure the formation of intrinsic thromboplastin by determining the residual serum prothrombin after blood coagulation is complete. Because the test is made on whole blood, it also measures, indirectly, the thromboplastic function of platelets.

prothrombin-proconvertin t.: A test used in the control of coumarin-type anticoagulants similar to the Quick method, except that it employs a saline extract of brain as a thromboplastin and requires the presence of excess blood coagulation factor V, usually derived from deprothrombinized ox plasma.

protozoan t.: The use of protozoan protoplasm as a test for pathologic tissue change, by observing the rate of reproduction of cultures of paramecium bred on normal and pathologic tissue.

psychometric t's. See *intelligence t.*

Purdy's t.: 1. (*For dextrose.*) See *Purdy's fluid,* under *fluid.* 2. (*For albumin.*) Fill a test tube two thirds full of the clear urine, add one sixth of its volume of a saturated solution of sodium chloride and 5 to 10 drops of 50 per cent acetic acid. Gently heat the upper part of the tube and look for a cloud.

purine bodies t. See *Cook's t.*

pus t. See *Donné's t., Vitali's t.* (6), *Waterhouse pus t.*

pyramidon t. 1. (*For occult blood in feces.*) See *aminopyrine t.* 2. (*In urine.*) To the urine add tincture of iodine. A yellow ring indicates pyramidon.

pyridine t. See *Anderson's t.*

pyrocatechin t. See *Brieger's t.* (1).

quadriceps t. (*for hyperthyroidism*): The patient sits well forward on the edge of a straight chair and holds the leg out at right angles to the body. Normal persons can hold this position for at least a minute; those with thyroidism can maintain it for only a few seconds.

Queckenstedt's t. See under *sign.*

quellung t. See *Neufeld's t.*

Quick's t.: 1. (*For liver function.*) A test based on excretion of hippuric acid following the administration of sodium benzoate. 2. (*One-stage prothrombin time.*) By adding an extrinsic thromboplastin such as dried rabbit brain and calcium to oxalated blood the integrity of the prothrombin complex, composed of factors II, V, VII, X, may be defined; used widely to control administration of coumarin-type anticoagulants.

quinine t. See *André's t., Binz's t., Brande's t., thalleioquin t.*

Quinlan's t. (*for bile*): A 3-mm. layer of the suspected liquid is examined by the spectroscope: if bile is present, some of the violet color of the spectrum will be absorbed.

Raabe's t. (*for albumin*): Filter the urine into a test tube and drop a crystal of trichloracetic acid into it: albumin will form a white ring about the crystal; uric acid may form a similar ring, but it is not so well defined.

Rabuteau's t.: 1. (*For hydrochloric acid in urine.*) Add a little indigosulfonic acid to color the urine, and sulfurous acid to decompose what hydrochloric acid may be present: the urine will be decolorized. 2. (*For hydrochloric acid in stomach contents.*) One Gm. of potassium iodate and 0.5 Gm. of potassium iodide are added to 50 cc. of starch mucilage; filtered stomach liquids are added to it: free hydrochloric acid will render the mixture blue.

Ralfe's t.: 1. (*For acetone in urine.*) Boil 4 cc. of solution of potassium hydroxide with 1.5 Gm. of potassium iodide; overlay it with 4 cc. of urine: a yellow ring with specks of iodoform appears at the plane of contact. 2. (*For peptones in urine.*) Put 4 cc. of Fehling's solution in a test tube and overlay it with urine: a rose-colored ring shows the presence of peptones.

Ramon's flocculation t.: To a series of tubes containing a constant amount of diphtheria toxin, antitoxin is added in increasing amounts: when a zone of flocculation appears, the tube showing it contains a completely neutralized mixture of toxin and antitoxin.

Randolph's t. (*for peptones in urine*): Add 2 drops of a saturated solution of potassium iodide and 3 drops of Millon's reagent to 5 cc. of cold and slightly acid urine: a yellow precipitate shows the presence of peptones.

Rantzman's t.: A modification of Lang's (sodium nitroprusside) test for acetone in which ammonium nitrate is used as a preservative.

rash-extinction t. See *Schultz-Charlton phenomenon,* under *phenomenon.*

Raygat's t. See *hydrostatic t.*

reckoning t.: A mental test, consisting in requiring the patient to add in pairs a series of numbers. The total number of sums accomplished per minute indicates the patient's capacity for mental work, while their accuracy indicates the patient's fixed associations and power of attention.

red t. See *phenolsulfonphthalein t.*

Rees's t. (*for albumin*): Small amounts of albumin are precipitated from solution by tannic acid in alcoholic solution.

Reh's t.: A modification of the Schick test in which the diphtheria toxin is applied by punctate scarification.

Rehberg's t.: A test for kidney function based on the excretion of creatinine administered 2 Gm. in 500 cc. of water.

Rehfuss' t.: A test for studying gastric secretion. By means of a specially devised tube (*Rehfuss tube*) inserted into the stomach immediately after an Ewald test meal a specimen of the contents is drawn off at fifteen-minute intervals until the close of digestion. Each specimen is examined and the results are plotted in a graphic curve, the abscissa of which is the number of minutes at which the gastric contents were removed, and the ordinate the number of cubic centimeters of decinormal sodium hydroxide solution necessary to titrate the free acidity and the total acidity of the gastric contents.

Reichl's t. (*for proteins*): Add 2 or 3 drops of an alcoholic solution of benzaldehyde and a quantity of sulfuric acid previously diluted to twice its volume with water; then add a few drops of ferric sulfate solution. The mixture will sooner or later take on a deep-blue color.

Reid Hunt's t. See *acetonitril test.*

Reinsch's t.: 1. (*For arsenic.*) Acidulate the liquid with HCl, insert a strip of clean copper, and boil; if arsenic is present, a gray or bluish film of copper is deposited. Remove the copper, wash, dry, insert in a long glass tube, and heat. The arsenic sublimes to the cooler parts of the tube as octahedral crystals. 2. (*For mercury in urine.*) Acidify the urine with HCl and place in it a piece of clean copper foil. After twelve to twenty-four hours remove foil, wash, and dry, introduce into a tube, and distill off the mercury as in the arsenic test.

Remont's t. (*for salicylic acid*): Make the milk acid with sulfuric acid, extract the salicylic acid with ether, and identify it by the purple or violet color produced on the addition of ferric chloride.

renal function t. See *kidney function t.*

rennin t. See *Lee's t., Riegel's t.*

Renton's t.: A test for pregnancy dependent on the presence of histidine in the urine of pregnant women.

resorcinol t. (*for hydrochloric acid*). See *Boas's t.* (2).

resorcinol-hydrochloric acid t. (*for levulose*). See *Selivanoff's t.*

resorption skin t. See *hydrophilia skin t.*

Reuss's t. (*for atropine*): The substance examined is treated with sulfuric acid and oxidizing agents: if atropine is present, an odor of roses and orange-flowers is given off.

Reynold's t. (*for acetone*): To the liquid to be examined add freshly prepared mercuric oxide; shake and filter, overlay the filtrate with ammonium sulfide, when it is turned black.

rhubarb t. (*in urine*): Make the urine alkaline and a red color indicates rhubarb.

Rieckenberg's t. See under *phenomenon.*

Riegel's t. (*for rennin*): To 10 cc. of milk there is added 5 cc. of neutral gastric juice; this is incubated fifteen minutes, when coagulation will occur if rennin is present.

Riegler's t.: 1. (*For albumin.*) Ten Gm. of beta-naphtholsulfonic acid are dissolved in 200 cc. of distilled water and filtered; 5 cc. of urine are treated with 20 to 30 drops of solution. Turbidity shows the presence of albumin. 2. (*For hydrochloric acid in the gastric juice.*) Congo red is changed to blue if hydrochloric acid is present. 3. (*For dextrose.*) Place in a test tube 0.1 Gm. of phenyl-hydrazine-hydrochloride, 0.25 Gm. of sodium acetate, and 20 drops of the urine. Heat to boiling. Add 10 cc. of a 3 per cent solution of potassium hydroxide and gently shake the tube. A red color indicates sugar.

Rimini's t. See *Burnam's t.*

ring t.: 1. (*For antibiotic activity.*) The solution is placed in a ring resting on the surface of seeded agar and the size of the surrounding clear area of inhibition indicates the activity. 2. (*For glanders.*) See *Konew's t.* 3. (*For protein.*) See *Heller's t., Posner's t., Roberts' t.*

Ringold t. (*for cancer*): A test based on the principle that in the blood smear of a cancer patient, in contrast with that of a healthy person, the nuclei of the large lymphocytes and monocytes appear divided, and are often crushed together or overlap one another.

Rinne t.: A hearing test made, with the opposite ear masked, with tuning forks of 256, 512, and 1024 cycles, by alternately placing the stem of the vibrating fork on the mastoid process of the temporal bone of the patient and holding it ½ inch from the external auditory meatus until it is no longer heard at one of these positions. The result is expressed as "Rinne positive" when it is heard longer by air, as "Rinne equal" when it is heard the same by air and bone, and "Rinne negative" when heard longer by bone.

Rivalta's t. See under *reaction.*

Roberts' t.: 1. (*For albumin.*) Underlay the urine with a mixture containing 5 parts of saturated solution of magnesium sulfate and 1 part of nitric acid; a white ring or layer forms at the plane of junction. 2. (*For dextrose.*) Determine the specific gravity of the urine at a certain temperature; add a little tartaric acid and some yeast; after twenty-four hours filter and again find the specific gravity. Each degree of density lost represents a grain of dextrose in a fluidounce of the urine.

Roffo's t.: To 2 cc. of fresh centrifugalized blood serum are added 5 drops of a 5 per cent solution of neutral red. The normal yellow of the serum changes to red if the subject has cancer.

Roger's t. See *camphor t.*

Roger-Josué t. See *blister t.*

Römer's t.: Intracutaneous injection of tuberculin into a tuberculous guinea-pig produces a papule with a hemorrhagic center: this is called cockade reaction.

Ronchese t. (*for quantitative determination of ammonia in urine*): One based on the action of solution of formaldehyde on the ammonia salts. A 10 per cent solution of sodium carbonate is added, a drop at a time, to the urine until the reaction becomes neutral. The solution of formaldehyde (40 per cent) is neutralized with a one-fourth normal soda solution against phenolphthalein until a slight pink tint develops. Then 25 cc. of the neutral urine and 10 cc. of the neutral solution of formaldehyde are mixed and titrated against decinormal sodium carbonate solution until a deep pink develops. The calculation is simple: 1 cc. of the decinormal sodium carbonate solution for 100 cc. of urine corresponds to 0.017 Gm. ammonia in 1000 cc. of urine.

Rorschach t.: A test for intelligence which measures also the emotional elements of the personality. It consists of a series of 10 ink blot designs, some black and some in colors. The patient is directed to look at the cards and simply tell what he sees.

Rose's t. (*for blood*): The scrapings from a blood stain are boiled in dilute caustic potash: when examined the liquid will show a greenish color in a thin layer and a red color in a thicker layer.

rose bengal t. (*for liver function*): Rose bengal (1 per cent in sodium chloride solution) is injected into the blood stream. Normally it disappears from the blood rapidly: delay in the normal disappearance time points to diminished activity of the liver.

Rose-Waaler t. (*for rheumatoid factors*). See *sheep cell agglutination t.*

Rosenbach's t. 1. (*For indigo red.*) Boil with nitric acid, and a blue color will be formed. 2. (*For circulating cold hemolysins.*) Immersion of the hands or feet in ice water will be followed by symptoms of paroxysmal cold hemoglobinuria if cold hemolysins are present.

Rosenbach-Gmelin t. (*for bile pigment*): Filter the urine through a very small filter; put a drop of nitric acid with a trace of nitrous acid on the inside of the filter, when a pale-yellow spot will appear, surrounded with yellowish-red, violet, blue, and green rings.

Rosenheim's t. (*for cholera*): Add iodine potassium iodide solution (2 Gm. of iodine and 6 Gm. of potassium iodide in 100 cc. of water) to an alcoholic extract of the material. Dark-brown plates and prisms may be seen with a microscope if cholera is present.

Rosenheim-Drummond t. (*for vitamin A*): Dissolve 1 or 2 drops of cod liver oil in about 5 cc. of an anhydrous fat solvent. Add 1 drop of concentrated sulfuric acid. A temporary deep-violet color indicates vitamin A.

Rosenthal's t.: 1. (*For blood in urine.*) Add potassium hydroxide solution to the urine, remove the precipitate and dry it; a small amount is placed on a slide with a crystal of sodium chloride; apply a cover glass and cause a few drops of glacial acetic acid to flow under it; warm the plate, and when it is cool hemin crystals will appear if blood is present. 2. (*For liver function.*) A modification of the phenoltetrachlorophthalein test based on the amount of the dye which remains in the blood at definite periods after injection of 5 mg. per kilogram of body weight. The normal liver will remove most of the dye from the blood in fifteen minutes and all of it within an hour.

Rosett's t.: Internal aeration of the blood may produce a convulsion in epileptic subjects.

Rosin's t. (*for indigo red*): Render the liquid alkaline with sodium carbonate and extract with ether: this is colored red.

Ross's t. (*for syphilis*): To a 2 per cent agar solution (5 cc.) add 0.4 cc. of Unna's polychrome blue, 0.4 cc. of a 5 per cent aqueous solution of sodium bicarbonate, and 4.2 cc. of sterile water. This is poured in a thin layer on a slide, and when it has solidified the material to be examined is placed on a cover glass and dropped on the slide; if spirochetes are present they are stained. Called also *film test* and *thick-film t.*

Ross-Jones t. (*for excess of globulin in cerebrospinal fluid*): One cc. of cerebrospinal fluid is floated over 2 cc. of concentrated ammonium sulfate solution; excess of globulin produces a fine white ring at the line of junction.

Rossel's aloin t. (*for blood in stools*): About 1 drachm of the feces is put in a test tube and extracted with 5 to 10 cc. of ether to remove the fat. After pouring off the ether the feces are thoroughly shaken up with 5 cc. of glacial acetic acid. The acid is then poured into another test tube and extracted with 5 to 10 cc. of ether. The test is then made with this ether. To that ether are added 20 to 30 drops of old oil of turpentine and 10 to 15 drops of a 1 to 4 per cent solution of Barbados aloin in 60 to 70 per cent alcohol. In the presence of blood the mixture takes on a light red color, turning to bright cherry red in about ten minutes.

Rothera's t. (*for acetone*): To 5 cc. of urine add a little solid ammonium sulfate and add 2 to 3 drops of a fresh 5 per cent solution of sodium nitroprusside and 1 to 2 cc. of stronger ammonia water. A permanganate color forms if acetone is present.

Rotter's t. (*for vitamin C in the body*): Cutaneous injection of 2,6-dichlorphenolindophenol produces colorization of the tissues: decolorization occurring in ten minutes indicates adequate vitamin C.

Rous's t. (*for hemosiderin*): Centrifuge the urine. To the sediment add 5 cc. of a 2 per cent solution of potassium ferrocyanide and 5 cc. of a 1 per cent solution of hydrochloric acid. Hemosiderin granules stain blue.

Roussin's t.: Microscopic examination of suspected blood stains.

Rowntree and Geraghty's t. See *phenolsulfonphthalein t.*

Rubin's t.: A test for patency of the fallopian tubes made by transuterine insufflation with carbon dioxide. If the tubes are patent the gas enters the peritoneal cavity and may be demonstrated by the fluoroscope or roentgenogram. This subphrenic pneumoperitoneum causes pain in both shoulders of the patient. If the manometer registers not over 100 mm. Hg the tubes are patent; if between 120 and 130, there is stenosis or stricture, but not complete occlusion; if it rises to 200, the tubes are completely occluded.

Rubino's t. See under *reaction.*

Rubner's t.: 1. (*For carbon monoxide in blood.*) Shake the blood with 4 or 5 volumes of lead acetate in solution: if the blood contains CO, it will retain its bright color; if not, it becomes a chocolate brown. 2. (*For lactose, dextrose, maltose,* and *levulose in urine.*) Add lead acetate to the urine, boil, and then add an excess of ammonium hydroxide. Lactose gives a brick-red color; dextrose gives a coffee-brown color; maltose gives a light-yellow color; and levulose gives no color at all.

Ruge and Phillipp's t.: A test for the virulence of microorganisms based on their ability to survive and multiply in the patient's blood in vitro.

Ruhemann's t. (*for uric acid in urine*). See under *method.*

ruler t. See *Hamilton's test.*

Rumpel-Leede t. See under *phenomenon.*

Russo's t. See under *reaction.*

Ruttan and Hardisty's t. (*for blood*): Blood in the presence of a 4 per cent glacial acetic acid solution of orthotolidine and hydrogen peroxide gives a bluish color.

Ryan's skin t.: A test for fatigue by making, with a blunt instrument, a stroke on the skin of the forearm and noting by means of a stop watch the time that elapses between the moment of stimulation and the moment at which the white streak thus produced begins to fade. The time is shorter in fatigued persons.

Rytz t. (*for syphilis*): The test requires only one tube for each serum. In a tube 75 mm. by 10 mm., 0.15 cc. of serum is placed and heated in a water bath at 60 C. for three minutes; 0.05 cc. of half saturated ammonium sulfate is added and mixed by shaking. The antigen emulsion, 0.05 cc., is added, mixed by shaking, and 1 cc. of a 0.9 per cent solution of sodium chloride is added and rotated in such a manner that the antigen particles become evenly distributed. This is shaken in the Kahn shaker for three minutes, and then 2 cc. of a 0.9 per cent solution of sodium chloride is added and the tube is inverted slowly two or three times just before the reading is taken. A 1 plus reaction consists of tiny, densely scattered flocculation particles in a slightly opalescent fluid. Plus 2, 3 and 4 reactions show clumps of flocculation in a clear fluid, the clumps varying in size according to the positiveness of the serum. A negative test shows only minute antigen particles in a slightly hazy fluid without clumping.

Saathoff's t. (*for fat in stools*): Rub up the feces with sudan and warm. Fat droplets stain yellow to red.

Sabrazès t.: With the patient in a reclining position, at the end of a normal inspiration the nose is pinched and the patient is instructed to hold the breath for as long a time as possible: a period of twenty to thirty seconds is normal; fifteen seconds indicates mild acidosis; five to ten seconds, severe acidosis.

saccharimeter t.: Dextrose in solution rotates the plane of polarized light to the right, while levulose turns it to the left.

Sachs's t.: The placenta is floated in water: if it takes up a horizontal position it is intact; if its position is vertical or oblique, the placenta is incomplete.

Sachs-Georgi t. (*for syphilis*): 1 cc. of a solution of cholesterinized alcoholic extract of human or beef heart (1 part) and 0.9 per cent sodium chloride solution (9 parts), when added to 0.3 cc. of syphilitic serum, will cause a flocculent precipitation; called also *lentochol reaction.*

Sachs-Witebsky t. (*for syphilis*): A quickly performed seroreaction for syphilis using a more concentrated cholesterinized extract of beef heart than that used in the Sachs-Georgi test; called also *citochol reaction*.

Sachsse's t. (*for sugar in the urine*): A solution of 18 Gm. of red mercuric iodide, 25 Gm. of potassium iodide, 80 Gm. of potassium hydroxide, in water enough to make a liter: sugar, if present, causes a black precipitate.

safranine t. (*for sugar in the urine*): Add normal sodium hydroxide solution to an equal quantity of urine, add safranine, and heat to 180 F., when the safranine will be dissolved if sugar is present.

Sahli's t. (*for motive and digestive power of stomach*): The patient is fed a soup made of definite amounts of water, flour, butter, and salt, and in an hour the stomach contents are removed. The amount of fat present shows how much of the meal has been digested, and the acidity indicates how much the stomach has secreted.

Sahli's desmoid t. See *desmoid reaction*, under *reaction*.

Sahli's glutoid t. (*for digestive function*): A glutoid capsule containing 0.15 Gm. of iodoform is taken with an Ewald breakfast. The capsule is not digested by the stomach fluid, but is readily digested by pancreatic juice. Appearance of iodine in the saliva and urine within four to six hours indicates normal gastric motility, normal intestinal digestion, and normal absorption. Glutoid capsules are prepared by soaking gelatin capsules in solution of formaldehyde.

Sahli-Nencki t. (*for lipolytic activity of the pancreas*): The administration of salol, which is to be excreted as salicylic acid.

salicylaldehyde t. (*for acetone*). See *Frommer's t.*

salicylic acid t. See *Remont's t., Siebold and Bradbury's t.*

saline wheal t. See *McClure-Aldrich t.*

Salkowski's t.: 1. (*For CO in the blood.*) Add to the blood 20 volumes of water and sodium hydroxide in solution (specific gravity, 1.34). If CO is present, it becomes cloudy and then red; flakes of red afterward float on the surface. 2. (*For cholesterol.*) Dissolve in chloroform and add an equal volume of strong sulfuric acid: if cholesterol is present, the solution becomes bluish red, and slowly changes to a violet red, the sulfuric acid becomes red, with a green fluorescence. 3. (*For indole.*) To the solution to be tested add a little nitric acid, and drop in slowly a solution of potassium nitrite (2 per cent): a red color shows that indole is present, and a red precipitate is afterward formed. 4. (*For dextrose.*) A modified form of Trommer's test. 5. (*For creatinine.*) To the yellow solution obtained in Weyl's test add an excess of acetic acid and heat. A green color results, which turns to blue.

Salkowski-Ludwig t. (*for uric acid*): A solution of silver ammonionitrate and ammonium and magnesium chlorides precipitates uric acid.

Salkowski and Schipper's t. (*for bile pigments*): To 10 cc. of the unknown add 5 drops of a 20 per cent solution of sodium carbonate and 10 drops of a 20 per cent solution of calcium chloride. To the precipitate add 3 cc. of alcohol containing 5 per cent of strong hydrochloric acid and a few drops of sodium nitrite. Heat. A green color indicated bile pigments.

salol t. See *Ewald's t.* (2).

Salomon's t.: Testing of the stomach washing by means of Esbach's reagent, after twenty-four hours without protein food. The presence of albumin indicates ulcerative cancer.

salvarsan t. See *Dicken's t.*

sand t. (*for bile and hemoglobin in urine*): A layer of white sand is spread on a plate and on this is poured some of the urine. If the urine contains pigments, a spot is left on the sand, which is brown with hemoglobin and greenish with bile pigment. Called also *Lipp's t.*

Sandrock t. (*for thrombosis*): Vigorous friction is applied to the part; the degree of hyperemia which follows is an indication of the condition of the circulation.

Sanford's t.: Prepare a series of dilutions of salt from 0.28 to 0.5 per cent. Add 1 drop of blood to each dilution, mix, allow to settle and note the tubes which show hemolysis.

santonin t.: 1. (*For the antitoxic efficiency of the liver.*) The patient is given 0.02 Gm. of santonin on a fasting stomach. The urine is examined hourly for oxysantonin by treating it with a dilute sodium hydroxide solution which will produce a red color with oxysantonin. 2. See *Daclin t.*

Saundby's t. (*for blood in feces*): To a small quantity of feces in a test tube 10 drops of a saturated benzidine solution is added. To this is added 30 drops of hydrogen peroxide solution, when a dark blue color will develop if blood is present.

scarification t. See *Pirquet reaction*, under *reaction*.

Schaffer's t. (*for nitrites in urine*): Decolorize 4 cc. of urine with animal charcoal and add to it 4 cc. of 10 per cent acetic acid and 3 drops of 5 per cent solution of potassium ferrocyanide: an intense yellow color indicates nitrites.

Schalfijew's t. (*for blood*): Treat defibrinated blood with excess of glacial acetic acid, heat to 80 C., cool, and examine for hemin crystals.

Scherer's t.: 1. (*For inosite.*) Evaporate on platinum foil with nitric acid; add ammonia water and a single drop of calcium chloride in solution, reevaporate to dryness: a rose-red coloration indicates the presence of inosite. 2. (*For pure leucine.*) A small portion of leucine with a few drops of nitric acid are evaporated on platinum foil. The transparent residue turns a brownish color on the addition of a sodium hydroxide solution. When the mixture is concentrated an oil-like drop is obtained. 3. (*For tyrosine.*) Treat with nitric acid and dry with care on platinum foil; the formation of nitrotyrosine nitrate renders it yellow, and sodium hydroxide solution changes the color to reddish yellow.

Schick t.: Intracutaneous injection of a quantity of diphtheria toxin equal to one fiftieth of the minimal lethal dose diluted in salt solution. Since one thirtieth of a unit of antitoxin per cubic centimeter of blood is sufficient to neutralize this amount of toxin; if the patient has less than this amount the toxin is not neutralized, and an area of inflammation is produced on the skin at the site of the injection. The test is a measure of immunity to diphtheria.

Schiff's t.: 1. (*For carbohydrates in urine.*) Warm and add sulfuric acid; expose to the fumes of the urine a paper dipped in a mixture of equal volumes of xylidine and glacial acetic acid with alcohol and dried: the paper becomes red if carbohydrates are present. 2. (*For cholesterol.*) Add a reagent composed of 2 parts of sulfuric acid with 1 part of a dilute solution of ferric chloride; evaporate to dryness and a violet color is produced. 3. (*For cholesterol.*) Evaporate with nitric acid and add ammonia water; a red color not changed by alkalis is produced. 4. (*For allantoin and urea.*) Add a solution of furfurol in hydrochloric acid; a yellow color appears, turning to purple and then to a brownish black. 5. (*For uric acid.*) Treat silver nitrate paper with an alkaline solution of the suspected substance; a brown stain shows the presence of uric acid. 6. (*For formaldehyde in milk.*) The solution consists of an aqueous solution of magenta, 40 cc.; distilled water, 250 cc.; aqueous solution of sodium bisulfite, 10 cc.; pure concentrated sulfuric acid, 10 cc., which is allowed to stand until it is colorless; 2 cc. of this solution is added to a test tube two thirds full of milk. If formaldehyde is present, a pink or lilac color will appear in from thirty to sixty seconds.

Schiller's t. (*for cancer of cervix*): A test for early squamous-cell cancer by treating the tissue with a solution of 1 Gm. of pure iodine and 2 Gm. of potassium iodide in 300 cc. of water: if the cervix is healthy, the surface turns brown; if there is cancer, the treated area turns white or yellow, because cancer cells do not contain glycogen and therefore do not stain with iodine.

Schilling t. (*for gastrointestinal absorption of vitamin B_{12}*): A measured amount of radioactive vitamin B_{12} is given orally, followed by a parenteral flushing dose of the non-radioactive vitamin, and the percentage of radioactivity is determined in the urine excreted over a 24-hour period. A low urinary excretion which becomes normal after the test is repeated with intrinsic factor is diagnostic of primary pernicious anemia.

Schirmer's t. (*for keratoconjunctivitis sicca*): A piece of filter paper is inserted into the conjunctival sac over the lower lid with the end of the paper hanging down on the outside. If the projecting paper remains dry after 15 minutes, deficient tear formation is indicated.

Schlesinger's t. (*for urobilin*): To about 5 cc. of the urine in a test tube add a few drops of Lugol's solution to transform the chromogen into the pigment. Now add 4 or 5 cc. of a saturated solution of zinc chloride in absolute alcohol and filter. A greenish fluorescence, best seen when the tube is viewed against a black background and the light is concentrated upon it with a lens, shows the presence of urobilin. Bile pigment, if present, should be removed by adding about one fifth volume of 10 per cent calcium chloride solution and filtering.

Schmidt's t. 1. (*For bile.*) Particles of fresh feces are rubbed up with concentrated aqueous solution of corrosive mercuric chloride in a glass dish. After standing covered for twenty-four hours the matter is examined, bilirubin appearing as green particles, hydrobilirubin as red ones. 2. (*For sugar.*) Lead acetate is added and precipitated with ammonia water; on heating, the white precipitate remains unchanged if saccharose or milk sugar is present, but if dextrose is present, an orange tint is seen. 3. (*For proteolytic pancreatic function.*) See *nucleus t.* 4. (*For intestinal indigestion.*) The patient is placed upon a definite diet. After a few days the feces are examined for fermentation. If this occurs within forty-eight hours it points to the imperfect intestinal digestion of starch. 5. (*For digestive function of the stomach.*) A test based upon the fact that when the gastric secretion is absent or greatly diminished, connective tissue masses appear in the stool after eating raw chopped meats.

Schneider t.: A test for pregnancy in which female rabbits are employed.

Schneider's t. (*for urobilinogen and urobilin*): Add Ehrlich's reagent to the duodenal contents and note rapidity and intensity of development of red color.

Schönbein's t.: 1. (*For blood.*) Blue coloration obtained by adding solution of hydrogen peroxide to tincture of guaiac mixed with suspected blood. 2. (*For copper.*) A solution containing a copper salt becomes blue if potassium cyanide and tincture of guaiac are added.

Schopfer's t.: Minute amounts of vitamin B in the blood catalyze the mold *Phycomyces blakesleeanus.*

Schroeder's t. (*for urea*): Add a crystal of the substance to a solution of bromine in chloroform: the urea will decompose and gas will be formed.

Schubert-Dannmeyer t.: A test for cancer based on the difference of certain electrical properties between a lipin extract of cancer serum and that from normal serum.

Schulte's t. (*for proteins*): Remove all coagulable protein, precipitate with six volumes of absolute alcohol, dissolve the precipitate in water, and apply the biuret test.

Schultz's t. (*for coagulation time of blood*): Fill capillary tube with blood and note time of coagulation by breaking off pieces of the tube from time to time and shaking out the contents.

Schultz-Charlton t. See under *phenomenon.*

Schultze's t.: 1. (*For cellulose.*) Iodine is dissolved to saturation in a zinc chloride solution (specific gravity, 1.8), and 6 parts of potassium iodide are added: this reagent colors cellulose blue. 2. (*For cholesterol.*) Evaporate with nitric acid, using a porcelain dish and water bath. If cholesterol is present, a yellow deposit is formed, which changes to yellowish red when ammonia is added. 3. (*For proteins.*) To a suspected solution add a very little of a dilute solution of cane sugar and concentrated sulfuric acid; keep it at 60 C., and a bluish-red coloration is produced.

Schultze's indophenol oxydase t. See *indophenol t.*

Schumm's t.: 1. See *benzidine t.* 2. (*For hematin in plasma.*) A given volume of plasma is covered with a layer of ether; one-tenth the volume of concentrated ammonium sulfide (analar) is then run in with a pipette and subsequently mixed by shaking. A positive reaction is indicated by the appearance of a hemochromogen with a sharply defined α band at 558 mμ in a depth up to 4 cm. of plasma.

Schürmann's t. (*for syphilis*): A color reaction proposed for the recognition of syphilitic blood serum.

Schwabach t.: A hearing test made, with the opposite ear masked, with tuning forks of 256, 512, 1024, and 2048 cycles, alternately placing the stem of the vibrating fork on the mastoid process of the temporal bone of the patient and that of the examiner (whose hearing should be normal) until it is no longer heard by one of them. The result is expressed as "Schwabach prolonged" if heard longer by the patient, as "Schwabach shortened" if heard longer by the examiner, and as "Schwabach normal" if heard for the same time by both.

Schwartz's t. (*for varicose veins*): The flats of the fingers are placed along the course of the supposed varicose saphenous vein in the thigh and some prominent part of the vessel below is tapped: a shock is transmitted to the fingers above if the vein is varicose.

Schwartz-McNeil t.: A complement fixation test for gonorrhea in which the antigen is an autolysate of a large number of strains of gonococci.

Schwarz's t.: 1. Heat the substance with charcoal: the odor of mercaptan indicates the presence of sulfonal. (K. L. H. Schwarz.) 2. (*For digestive function of stomach.*) With a test breakfast there is administered a capsule of goldbeaters' skin containing 4 Gm. of bismuth carbonate and 0.25 Gm. of neutral pepsin. The patient is then examined fluoroscopically. At first the capsule appears as a circular, sharply defined area, but if it is dissolved by the stomach juice the area becomes a broad band. If the shadow of the capsule remains unchanged after five hours, anacidity of the stomach is indicated. Called also *fibroderm bismuth capsule t.* (G. Schwarz.)

Scivoletto's t. (*for hydrochloric acid in urine*): Dip filter paper in starch paste and dry; sprinkle it with urine and dry; hang it in a flask containing strontium acetate in solution: a blue color indicates the presence of the acid.

scratch t.: Cutireaction.

screen t. See *cover t.*

secretin t.: A test for pancreatic function done by examining the pancreatic secretion produced by the intravenous injection of secretin.

sedimentation t.: 1. See *agglutination t.* 2. See *erythrocyte sedimentation reaction,* under *reaction.*

Seidel's t. (*for inosite*): Evaporate in a platinum crucible with nitric acid, and treat with ammonia and strontium acetate in solution: inosite, if present, causes a green coloration and a violet precipitate.

Seidlitz powder t. (*for diaphragmatic hernia*): The stomach is distended by the administration of a Seidlitz powder which will cause roentgen visualization of the herniated stomach loop.

Selivanoff's t. (*for fructose in urine*): To the urine is added an equal volume of hydrochloric acid containing resorcinol in the following proportion: 0.5 resorcinol, 30 cc. water, and 30 cc. concentrated hydrochloric acid. Formation of a burgundy-red color after heating indicates fructose.

Sellards' t. (*for acidosis*): The patient is given 5 Gm. of sodium bicarbonate, dissolved in water, by mouth, every two or three hours until the urine, passed before each dose, becomes neutral or faintly alkaline. Tolerance of 20 to 30 Gm. shows moderate acidosis; tolerance of from 75 to 100 Gm. indicates distinct acidosis. Called also *bicarbonate tolerance t.*

semen t. See *Barberio's t.*, *Florence t.*, *Huhner t.*

Senn's t.: The introduction of hydrogen into the intestines by the rectum as an aid in the diagnosis of intestinal perforations.

senna t. (*in urine*): Make the urine alkaline and a red color indicates senna.

sensitized sheep cell t. See *sheep cell agglutination t.*

sero-enzyme t. See *Abderhalden's t.*

serologic t.: Any laboratory test on the blood serum of a patient.

serum t. (*for blood, meat, sperm, etc.*): The antigen, human blood serum, is injected several times, at intervals, into a rabbit. The suspected specimen is dissolved in physiologic salt solution and added to the serum of a rabbit treated in the way mentioned. The serum will become clouded if the suspected specimen is of the same species as the antigen used for immunizing the rabbit. Called also *biological t.*, *Bordet's t.*, and *Uhlenhuth's t.*

serum neutralization t.: A test for the previous existence of yellow fever, using a mouse-adapted virus.

Sgambati's t. See under *reaction.*

shadow t.: Testing the refraction of the eye by means of a retinoscope or a skiascope.

Shaw-Mackenzie t.: A test for cancer based on the action of carcinoma extract on the blood serum of the patient.

Shear's t. (*for vitamin D*): To the oil add an equal volume of acid aniline (1 part concentrated HCl and 15 parts aniline). Mix and boil. A green color changing to red indicates vitamin D.

sheep cell agglutination t.: A method for detecting the presence of rheumatoid factors (R.F.) in serum by the agglutination of sheep red blood cells sensitized with rabbit gamma globulin.

Sicard-Cantelouble t.: Place 4 cc. of spinal fluid in a specially graduated tube, add 12 drops of a 33 per cent trichloracetic acid, mix and read the amount of protein precipitated after twenty-four hours' sedimentation.

sickling t.: A method to demonstrate hemoglobin S and the sickling phenomenon in erythrocytes, particularly in the heterozygous state, performed by reducing the environmental oxygen to which the red cells are exposed. This may be done by simply sealing a drop of blood under a coverslip or, to hasten the morphologic change, by adding 2 per cent sodium metabisulfite or sodium dithionite to the preparation.

Siddall t. (*for pregnancy*): Injection of the blood serum of a pregnant woman into a mouse causes enlargement of the animal's uterus.

Siebold and Bradbury's t. (*for salicylic acid in urine*): Alkalinize with potassium carbonate; add a solution of lead nitrate in excess; filter, and add a dilute solution of ferric chloride, when a violet color will be produced.

sigma t. See under *reaction.*

silver t. (*for dextrose in the urine*): Boil it with silver nitrate solution and an excess of ammonia: metallic silver will be deposited. Tartaric acid and aldehyde also produce this reaction.

Simonelli's t. (*for renal inadequacy*): Iodine is administered and the urine and saliva tested for iodine. If iodine does not appear in the urine at the same time as in the saliva, the kidneys are diseased.

Sims' t.: A post-coital test for the ability of the spermatozoa to penetrate the cervical mucus.

single-blind t., a study of the effects of a specific agent in which the administrator, but not the recipient, knows the nature of the agent being given.

Sivori and Rebaudi t.: A test for tuberculosis based on change in the ferments affecting the protein similar to the Abderhalden test.

skatole t. See *Ciamician and Magnanini's t.*, *Herter's t.* (2), *Kondo's t.*, *nitroso-indole-nitrate t.*

skin t. See *cutaneous reaction*, under *reaction.*

slide t. See *Kline t.*

smear t. See *Papanicolaou's stain*, under *stains and staining.*

Smith's t.: 1. (*For bile pigments.*) Overlay the suspected liquid with tincture of iodine diluted 1:10; a green ring or plane appears at the junction of the two liquids in the tube. 2. (*For prothrombin time.*) A test using a thromboplastin extract added to freshly drawn blood.

Snellen's t.: 1. (*For pretended blindness in one eye.*) The patient is requested to look at alternate red and green letters; the admittedly sound eye is covered with a red glass and if the green letters are read, evidence of fraud is present. 2. Determination of visual acuity by means of Snellen test types.

Snider match t. (*a screening test for pulmonary ventilation*): An ordinary book match which is burned nearly half way is held 6 inches from the mouth of the patient, who attempts to extinguish it by exhaling, after taking as deep a breath as possible, and without bringing the lips together.

sniff t.: When a patient sniffs, the paralyzed half of the diaphragm is seen to rise and the intact half to descend, as observed by fluoroscopy.

sodium chloride balance t. See *balance t.*

Soldaini's t. (*for glucose in the urine*): Dissolve 15 Gm. of copper carbonate and 416 Gm. of potassium bicarbonate in 1400 cc. of water for a reagent; 2 parts of urine are boiled with 1 part of the reagent. A yellow precipitate of cupric oxide shows the presence of dextrose.

Solera's t. (*for thiocyanates*): Saturate filter paper with ½ per cent starch paste containing 1 per cent of iodic acid. Dry and preserve as test paper. A piece of this paper moistened with saliva will turn blue if thiocyanate is present.

solubility t. (*for pneumococcus*): Reagent: sodium desoxycholate 10 Gm., alcohol 10 cc., water 90 cc. Add 2 drops of the reagent to 1 cc. of a broth culture. Pneumococci dissolve within five minutes.

Sonnenschein's t. (*for strychnine*): The substance is dissolved in a drop of sulfuric acid, some cerosoceric oxide is added, and stirred with a glass rod. A deep-blue color is formed, changing to violet, and finally to cherry red.

soy bean t. See *urease t.*

specific gravity t. See *Fishberg concentration t.*, *Volhard's t.* (2).

sphenopalatine t.: The sphenopalatine ganglion is anesthetized with butyn in order to determine whether the efferent current which is motivating a symptom is routed through either sphenopalatine ganglion, and if so, whether the left one or the right one.

Spiegler's t. (*for albumin*): Acidulate with acetic acid and filter; prepare a reagent with 8 Gm. of mercuric chloride, 10 Gm. of sodium chloride, and 4 Gm. of tartaric acid in 200 cc. of water and 20 cc. of glycerin; overlay the reagent with the filtrate. If albumin is present, a white ring appears at the junction of the liquids.

spinal t.: Any laboratory serologic test of the spinal fluid.

Spiro's t.: 1. A test for the determination of ammonia and urea, embracing a combination of Folin's method for urea and the Moerner-Sjöqvist method for urea. 2. (*For hippuric acid.*) Warm the unknown with acetic anhydride, anhydrous sodium acetate and benzaldehyde. Cool, and crystals of phenyl-amino-cinnamic acid-lactimide form.

sponge t.: A test performed by passing a hot sponge up and down the spine; if any lesion of the spine is present, pain is felt as the sponge passes over its locality.

Staehlin's t. (*for functional efficiency of myocardium*): The pulse rate after walking is more accelerated in impending heart failure than in health.

Stanford t.: A modified Binet test.

Stange's t.: After a few preliminary deep inspirations, the patient takes a deep breath and holds it as long as possible; unless he can hold it for at least thirty seconds he is not a good anesthetic risk.

starch t. See *iodine t.* (1).

station t.: A test for disturbances of coordination, made by placing the patient in an erect posture, with the heels and toes of the two feet together: if the swaying of the body is beyond normal, coordination is defective.

steapsin t.: See *ethyl butyrate t.*

Stein's t.: Inability to stand on one foot with the eyes shut: seen in disease of the labyrinth.

Steinle-Kahlenberg t.: Heat a chloroform solution of a sterol with antimony pentachloride. The purple color changes to cobalt blue in the light.

Stenger t.: A test for detecting simulation of unilateral deafness.

Stern's t.: A modification of the Wassermann test by using fresh active serum and the patient's complement, and overcoming nonspecific reactions by two fifths to one fifth of the usual dose of extract and three or four times the amboceptor unit.

Stern's fermentation t.: Grow the organisms in a fuchsin-sulfite glycerol meat extract culture medium. A Stern positive organism produces a deep lilac color.

Stewart's t.: Estimation of the amount of collateral circulation, in aneurysm of the chief artery of a limb, with a calorimeter.

Stieglitz t.: A marked fall in diastolic blood pressure following the inhalation of amyl nitrite indicates absence of hardening of the cerebral vessels.

Stock t. (*for acetone in urine*): The distillate of the urine is used. From 50 to 100 cc. of urine is made acid by the addition of either acetic, hydrochloric, or sulfuric acid. The first 10 cc. of distillate will contain all the possible acetone. About 1 inch of the distillate is placed in a test tube; a drop or two of a 10 per cent solution of hydroxylamine hydrochloride is added, and sufficient sodium hydroxide or carbonate solution to render the solution alkaline to liberate hydroxylamine; the mixture is shaken and a couple of drops of pyridine is added and the mixture shaken; then 1 inch of ether is added and the mixture shaken. Bromine water is then added drop by drop, with mixing, until the ether layer becomes yellow; then a few drops of strong hydrogen peroxide is added; if acetone is present the ether will turn a distinctive green blue.

Stokes's t. (*for oxyhemoglobin*): Prepare a reagent by dissolving ferrous sulfate, adding tartaric or citric acid, and alkalinizing with ammonia. This reagent reduces hemoglobin.

Stokvis' t. (*for bile pigment*): With 25 cc. of urine mix 8 cc. of a 1:5 zinc acetate solution; wash the precipitate in water on a filter, and dissolve in ammonia water. Filter again, and in a short time the filtrate shows a bluish-green tint.

Storck's t. (*for human milk*): The ferment of human milk will decompose hydrogen dioxide.

Strange's t. See *Henderson's t.*

Strassburg's t. (*for bile acids in albumin-free urine*): Add cane sugar to the urine; dip filter paper into it and dry. A drop of sulfuric acid on the paper will cause a red or violet spot if bile acids are present.

Straus's biological t. (*for glanders*): See *Straus' reaction*, under *reaction.*

Strauss's t.: 1. (*For lactic acid in stomach.*) Extract the lactic acid from the stomach contents by means of ether. To the ether add distilled water and a little ferric chloride solution; a green color indicates lactic acid. 2. A concentration test for kidney function by the ingestion of water. 3. A levulose tolerance test for hepatic function. 4. A urea balance test for renal function.

Struve's t. (*for blood in the urine*): Alkalinize the urine and add tannic and acetic acids until the reaction becomes acid and a dark precipitate is formed. When this is dried, crystals of hemin may be obtained from it by adding ammonium chloride and glacial acetic acid.

strychnine t. See *Allen's t.* (3), *Brieger's t.* (2), *Sonnenschein's t.*, *Wenzell's t.*

Stypven time t.: A test similar to the Quick one-stage prothrombin time test, but performed with Russell's viper venom as the thromboplastic agent; useful in defining deficiencies of blood coagulation factor X.

sugar t. See tests listed under *dextrose t.*, *galactose t.*, *levulose t.*, and *maltose t.*

sulfonal t. See *Schwarz's t.* (1).

sulfosalicylic acid t. Same as *Exton's t.*

sulfur t. (*for protein*): The suspected liquid is heated with an excess of sodium hydroxide and a small quantity of acetate of lead. If proteins are present, a black precipitate of lead sulfide is formed.

Sulkowitch's t. (*for calcium in urine*): The precipitation of calcium in urine as an oxalate with use of a reagent consisting of 2.5 Gm. of oxalic acid, 2.5 Gm. of ammonium oxalate, and 5 cc. of glacial acetic acid dissolved in 150 cc. of distilled water.

Sullivan's t. (*for cysteine*): To 1 or 2 cc. of the unknown solution add 1 to 2 drops of a 0.5 per cent solution of 1,2-naphthoquinone-4-sodium sulfonate and then 5 cc. of a 20 per cent sodium thiosulfate made up in 0.25 normal sodium hydroxide. A brilliant red color indicates a free SH group, cysteine rather than cystine.

Suranyi's t.: An albumin reaction for the diagnosis of carcinoma.

syphilis t. See *Bauer's t.* (1), *benzoin t.*, *Boerner-Lucken's t.*, *Bruck's serochemical t.*, *Busacca's t.* (1), *Cantani t.*, *Casilli's t.*, *Chediak's t.*, *Clive's t.*, *Craig's t.* (2), *Cutting's t.*, *Eagle t.*, *filter paper microscopic t.*, *Garriga's t.*, *gel t.*, *Hecht's t.*, *Hecht-Weinberg-Gradwohl t.*, *Hennebert's t.*, *Hinton t.*, *Ide t.*, *Ishihara's t.* (2), *Jacobsthal's t.* (1), (2), *Justus' t.*, *Kafka's t.*, *Kahn t.* (1), *Klausner's t.*, *Kline t.*, *Kolmer's t.* (1), *Landau color t.*, *Lange's t.* (1), *Laughlen t.*, *mastic t.*, *Mazzini t.*, *Meinicke t.* (1), (2), (3), *Michaelides' t.*, *Müller's t.* (3), *Murata t.*, *Peterman's t.*, *Porges-Meier t.*, *Porges-Salomon t.*, *Ross's t.*, *Rytz t.*, *Sachs-Georgi t.*, *Sachs-Witebsky t.*, *Schürmann's t.*, *Stern's t.*, *Takata-Ara t.*, *Tschernogowbou's t.*, *Ucko's t.*, *Vernes' t.* (1), *von Dungern's t.* (2), *Weil's t.* See also the following under *reaction: Fornet's r.*, *Jarisch-Herxheimer r.*, *Klausner's r.*, *Noguchi's r.*, *Noguchi's luetin r.*, *pallidin r.*, *Perutz's r.*, *Targowla r.*, *Wassermann r.*, *Wassermann r., provocative.*

Szabo's t. (*for HCl in the stomach contents*): Add to the suspected liquid a reagent containing equal parts of a 0.5 per cent solution of sodioferric tartrate and ammonium thiocyanate. If HCl is present, the reagent is changed from a pale yellow to a brownish red.

Takata-Ara t.: By mixing a mercuric chloride solution with sodium carbonate in the presence of the normal spinal fluid a colloidal solution of mercuric oxide is formed which turns a deep bluish violet by adding a solution of diamond-fuchsin. With pathologic spinal fluids the reaction is different. The abnormal protein content of the latter causes either a flocculation of the mercuric oxide with a discoloration of the fluid or color changes from bluish violet to pink with practically no precipitation. The first type of reaction, according to Takata and Ara, is typical of syphilis of the central nervous system while the change of the color occurs in bacterial meningitis.

Tallqvist's t. (*for hemoglobin*): Place a drop of blood on the paper provided and compare color while fresh with the color scale.

tannic acid t. (*for nucleo-albumin*). See *Ott's t.*

tannin t. (*for carbon monoxide hemoglobin*): Dilute the blood with 4 volumes of distilled water and add a little potassium ferricyanide to change the oxyhemoglobin into methemoglobin. Divide into two parts and thoroughly oxygenate one by shaking to decompose the carbon monoxide hemoglobin in it. Add to each part a little yellow ammonium sulfide and a little tannin solution. A bright red precipitate in the part not shaken indicates carbon monoxide hemoglobin. The methemoglobin in the other part gives a dirty, olive-green precipitate.

Tanret's t. (*for albumin*): Tanret's reagent gives a white precipitate with albumin.

tape t. of Wolff: Consists of cleansing the skin in the paravertebral region between the eighth and eleventh thoracic vertebrae with green soap and water. When dried, the area is bathed with benzene. After drying again, a drop of tuberculin ointment the size of a pea is applied over the right side of the cleansed area and on the left side a drop of control ointment is used. Both drops are then covered with pieces of adhesive tape 2 inches square. This is tightly applied. In forty-eight hours the tape is soaked with benzene and removed. Ten minutes later the reaction is observed. When positive, the area over which the tuberculin ointment was applied shows papules, erythema, induration and pigmentation.

Tardieu's t. (*for infanticide*): Presence of air-bubbles in gastric mucosa after establishment of fetal respiration.

Targowla's t. See under *reaction.*

taurine t. See *Lang's t.*

Taylor's t.: A modification of Schönbein's test for blood, the blue precipitate forming a deep sapphire blue solution when taken up by alcohol or ether.

Teichmann's t. (*for blood*): The suspected liquid is put under a cover glass with a crystal of sodium chloride and a little glacial acetic acid; heat carefully without boiling and then cool. If blood is present, rhombic crystals of hemin will appear.

tellurite t. (*for diphtheria*): A 2 per cent solution of potassium tellurite is applied to the membrane or exudate in the throat: any area affected with diphtheria will become blackened in from five to ten minutes (Manzullo, 1938).

Terman t.: The Stanford modification of the Binet-Simon test.

thalleioquin t. (*for quinine*): A neutralized solution of the suspected liquid is treated with chlorine, or bromine water, and then with an excess of ammonia, when the green substance, thalleioquin, will be formed.

thermoprecipitin t.: The finely divided organ or part is mixed with 5 to 10 parts of water, boiled, filtered, and stratified with a specific serum. A precipitate forming in five minutes is positive.

thick film t. See *Ross's t.*

thiochrome t. (*for thiamine*): Oxidize the thiamine to thiochrome and then recognize the latter by its blue-violet fluorescence in ultraviolet radiation.

thiocyanate t. See *ferric chloride t.* (1), *Solera's t.*

Thomas-Binetti t: Rapid decoloration of methylene blue by cancer serum in the presence of cancer extracts.

Thompson's t. (*for gonorrhea*). See *two-glass t.*

Thormählen's t. (*for melanin in urine*): Treat with a solution of sodium nitroprusside, potassium hydroxide, and acetic acid. If melanin is present, a deep-blue color will form.

Thorn t.: A test of adrenal cortical response after injection of ACTH or of epinephrine.

thread t. See *Garrod's t.* (2).

three-glass t.: On arising in the morning the patient urinates successively into three glass receptacles labeled I, II, and III. In acute anterior urethritis the urine in I will be turbid from pus, while II and III will be clear; but in posterior urethritis the urine in all three glasses will be turbid. Blood in I comes only from the anterior urethra, but if it comes from the posterior urethra all three will contain blood. Shreds in glass III point to chronic prostatitis.

three-paper t. See *Marie's three-paper t.*

thromboplastin generation t.: A sensitive test for delineation of defects in formation of intrinsic thromboplastin and hence deficiencies of the factors involved. Patient plasma, serum, calcium chloride, and autologous platelets or platelet lipid substitute are incubated concurrently, and, at appropriate intervals, the clotting times of normal citrated plasma substrate, to which aliquots of the incubation mixture are added in sequential fashion, are determined.

Thudichum's t. (*for creatinine*): Add to the suspected substance a dilute solution of ferric chloride. A dark-red color indicates the presence of creatinine.

thumb-nail t. (*for fractured patella*): The thumb nail is passed over the subcutaneous surface of the patella: a fracture will be felt as a sharp crevice.

thymol turbidity t. (*for disordered liver metabolism*): Direct precipitation of a protein from the serum of a patient with hepatic insufficiency by means of a solution of thymol.

thyroid t. See under *sign.*

Tidy's t.: 1. (*For albumin in urine.*) Add equal volumes of phenol and glacial acetic acids. Albumin will form a white precipitate. 2. (*For albumin in urine.*) Add 15 drops of alcohol and 15 drops of phenol. Albumin will form a white precipitate.

Tizzoni's t. (*for iron in tissues*): Treat a section of tissue with a 2 per cent solution of potassium ferrocyanide, and then with a 0.5 per cent solution of HCl. The tissue will be stained a blue color if iron is present.

TNT t. See *Webster's t.*

Tobey-Ayer t. (*in the diagnosis of lateral sinus thrombosis*): After spinal puncture a manometer is attached to the puncture needle: compression on both jugular veins causes the fluid to rise in the manometer; pressure on one jugular vein alone, causes a rise in spinal fluid pressure if the lateral sinus is normal, but little or no rise if there is thrombosis of the sinus on the same side as compression of the vein. The significance of the test is greater on the right side than on the left.

Tollens' t.: 1. (*For aldehyde.*) Treat the suspected solution with an ammoniacal solution of silver nitrate and potassium hydroxide. If aldehyde is present, a mirror of metallic silver appears. 2. (*For dextrose.*) Prepare a reagent by precipitating a silver nitrate solution with potassium hydroxide and dissolving with ammonia. This is reduced by dextrose. 3. (*For pentose.*) See *phloroglucin t.* 4. (*For conjugate glycuronates.*) To 5 cc. of the urine add 1 cc. of a 1 per cent solution of naphthoresorcinol in 95 per cent alcohol and 5 cc. of strong hydrochloric acid. Boil and cool. An ether extract of this mixture is violet red if glycuronates are present.

Tollens, Neuberg, and Schwket's t. (*for glycuronic acid*): Extract the glycuronic acid from acidified urine with ether, add water, evaporate the ether, and make orcinol test.

tongue t. See under *phenomenon.*

Töpfer's t's: Quantitative tests for hydrochloric acid in gastric contents. 1. (*For total acidity.*) One per cent solution of phenolphthalein is used as the indicator. 2. (*For free HCl.*) Five-tenths per cent alcoholic solution of dimethyl-amino-azobenzene is used as the indicator. 3. (*For combined HCl.*) One per cent aqueous solution of sodium alizarin sulfonate is used as the indicator.

Torquay's t. (*for bile*): A small amount of the suspected liquid is added to a test tube containing an aqueous solution of methyl violet, 1:2000. Bile will change the blue color to red.

tourniquet t.: 1. (*For capillary fragility.*) After application of pressure midway between diastolic and systolic for 5–10 minutes by a manometer cuff, the petechiae are counted in a previously marked area, 2.5 cm. in diameter, on the inner aspect of the forearm, about 4 cm. below the crease of the elbow. A number between 10 and 20 is marginal, above 20, abnormal. Called also *Hess capillary t.* 2. (*For collateral circulation.*) After hyperemia of the limb has been artificially produced by application of the tourniquet, the tourniquet is removed and the extent of collateral circulation is determined by compressing the main artery. Called also *Matas' t.* 3. (*For collateral circulation in patients with varicose veins.*) A bandage is applied to the upper part of the leg below the knee and the patient walks around with it on; the varicose veins of the leg will become evacuated from continuous compression if there is sufficient collateral circulation in the deep veins. Called also *Perthes' t.*

Trambusti t. (*for tuberculosis*). See under *reaction.*

trapeze t.: When the patient hangs from a trapeze, a spinal deformity will disappear if the deformity is postural but will remain if it is structural.

Trendelenburg's t.: 1. Raise the leg above the level of the heart until the veins are empty; then lower it quickly. If the veins become distended at once varicosity and incompetence of the valves are indicated. 2. The patient, stripped and with back to the examiner, is told to lift first one foot and then the other. The position and movements of the gluteal fold are watched: when standing on the affected limb the gluteal fold on the sound side falls instead of rising: seen in poliomyelitis, ununited fracture of the femoral neck, coxa vara, and congenital dislocations.

Tretop's t.: To fresh urine in a test tube a few drops of 40 per cent formalin are added: albumin in the urine is coagulated.

Triboulet's t. (*for tuberculous ulceration of the intestines*): A lump of feces as large as a walnut is dissolved in 20 cc. of distilled water and filtered; 3 cc. of the filtrate is diluted with 12 cc. of distilled water; 20 minims of Triboulet's reagent (sublimate 3.5, acetic acid 1, aqua dest. ad 100) are added. As a control the same solution is prepared without Triboulet's reagent. The test tubes containing the two solutions are well shaken, and are compared after five and twenty-four hours. A positive reaction is indicated by a cloudy gray or brown deposit.

trichophytin t. (*for trichophyton infection*): When filtrates of the ringworm microorganism are injected into persons who have been infected with the disease, a reaction is produced somewhat resembling the tuberculin reaction.

tricresol peroxidase t. (*for raw milk*). See *Kastle's t.*

triketohydrindene hydrate t.: Add a small amount of 1 per cent solution of ninhydrine and boil. A blue color indicates a free carboxyl and alpha-amino group in proteins, peptones, peptides, or amino acids.

Trommer's t. (*for dextrose in the urine*): To 2 parts of urine 1 part of potassium or sodium hydroxide is added; a very dilute solution of copper sulfate is then added drop by drop, and then the whole is boiled. Sugar, if present, causes precipitation of an orange-red deposit.

Trousseau's t. (*for bile in urine*): Tincture of iodine diluted with 10 parts of alcohol is added to urine in a test tube. A green ring is formed where the liquids touch if bilirubin is present.

trypsin t. See *antitrypsin t., Gross' t.* (1).

tryptophan t.: 1. Testing of the stomach contents for the presence of tryptophan, which indicates the presence of carcinoma of the stomach. The test is performed by adding to the suspected liquid a few drops of 3 per cent acetic acid, and then adding to this carefully, drop by drop, a few drops of bromine water. A reddish-violet color is formed if tryptophan is present. 2. (*For tuberculous meningitis.*) Add hydrochloric acid and formalin and then overlay with sodium nitrate solution. A violet ring is positive.

Tschernogowbou's t.: A modification of the Wassermann test by using the natural amboceptor and complement in the patient's serum against guinea-pig erythrocytes.

Tsuchiya's t. (*for albumin*): A modified Esbach test in which Tsuchiya's reagent is used instead of Esbach's reagent.

tuberculin t.: A test for the existence of tuberculosis, consisting in the subcutaneous injection of 5 mg. of tuberculin. In healthy persons it produces no appreciable effect, but in tuberculous patients it produces a moderate fever, which lasts for several hours, and also a swelling and redness in tuberculous lesions of the patient. See also *ophthalmic reaction, cutireaction of von Pirquet, Calmette's reaction, Moro's reaction,* under *reaction,* and *Mantoux t.*

tuberculin patch t.: A test made by applying to the skin a piece of surgical adhesive on which some Old Tuberculin has been placed.

tuberculin titer t.: A test for the hypersensitivity of the organism to tuberculin by a graduated cutaneous tuberculin test with varying concentrations of the tuberculin. Called also *Ellerman and Erlandsen's t.*

tuberculous albumin reaction t. See *Lessilur-Prirey t.*

Tuffier's t.: In aneurysm, when the main artery and vein of a limb are compressed, swelling of the veins of the hand or foot will occur only if the collateral circulation is free.

two-glass t. (*for urethritis*): The patient collects his urine on rising, the first part in one glass and the second part in a separate glass. If he has anterior urethritis the first portion will be turbid and the second portion clear; if he has both anterior and posterior urethritis both portions will be turbid.

two-stage prothrombin t.: A method of quantitating prothrombin after tissue thromboplastin and excess factor V have converted it to thrombin, by determining the clotting time of a standard fibrinogen solution to which the previously generated thrombin has been added.

Twort t. (*for carcinogenic oil*): A few drops of the oil are injected into an animal and subsequently recovered for examination. If the oil is toxic its physical characters will be altered.

typhoidin t.: A cutaneous test for typhoid fever made by inoculating typhoidin into the skin of the forearm. A positive reaction consisting in the formation of an indurated and reddened area at the site of inoculation.

tyrosine t. See *Folin and Denis' t., Hoffmann's t., Mörner's t.* (1), *Piria's t., Scherer's t.* (3), *Udránszky's t.* (2), *Wurster's t.* (2).

Tyson's t. (*for bile acids in urine*): 180 to 240 cc. of urine are evaporated to dryness on the water bath. The residue is extracted with absolute alcohol, and to the extract 12 to 14 volumes of ether are added. The bile acids are precipitated, then are filtered off, dissolved in water, and the aqueous solution decolorized with animal charcoal.

Tzanck t.: Examination of tissue from the floor of a lesion, in vesicular or bullous diseases, to discover the type of cell present as a means of diagnosing the disease. Certain cells are pathognomonic of varicella, herpes simplex, herpes zoster, or pemphigus.

Ucko's t.: A modified method for performing the Takata-Ara test: it is a precipitation reaction produced by mercury in serum of hepatic patients.

Udránszky's t.: 1. (*For bile acids.*) Take 1 cc. of a solution of the suspected substance, add a drop of 0.1 per cent solution of furfurol in water, underlay with strong sulfuric acid, and cool. If bile is present, a bluish-red color is formed. 2. (*For tyrosine.*) Take 1 cc. of the suspected substance in solution, add a drop of 0.5 per cent aqueous solution of furfurol, underlay with 1 cc. of concentrated sulfuric acid. A pink color shows the presence of tyrosine.

Uffelmann's t. (*for lactic acid in the gastric contents*): To a quantity of material taken from the stomach there is added a few drops of a reagent containing 3 drops of a solution of ferric chloride, 3 drops of a concentrated solution of phenol, and 20 cc. of water. Hydrochloric acid, if present, decolorizes this solution, while lactic acid turns it yellow.

Uhlenhuth's t. See *serum t.*

Ulrich's t. (*for albumin*): The reagent consists of saturated solution of common salt, 98 cc.; glacial acetic acid, 2 cc. It must be perfectly clear. Boil a few cubic centimeters of this fluid in a test tube, and immediately overlay with the urine. Albumin and globulin give a white ring at the zone of contact.

Ultzmann's t. (*for bile pigments*): To 10 cc. of the urine to be tested add 3 or 4 cc. of a 1:3 solution of potassium hydroxide and an excess of HCl. Bile pigments will cause an emerald-green coloration.

Umber's t. (*for scarlet fever*): To a small quantity of urine there are added 2 drops of a solution made with 30 cc. concentrated hydrochloric acid, 2 Gm. of para-dimethyl-amino-benzaldehyde and 70 cc. of water. A red reaction indicates scarlet fever.

uracil t. See *Wheeler and Johnson's t.*

urea t. See *Benedict's t.* (2), *biuret t.* (2), *Bloxam's t.*, *Brücke's t.* (3), *diacetyl t.*, *Folin's t.* (1), *Marshall's t.*, *Schiff's t.* (4), *Schroeder's t.*, *Spiro's t.* (1), *urease t.*, *Van Slyke t.* (2).

urea clearance t. See *blood-urea clearance t.*

urea concentration t. (*for renal efficiency*): A test based on the fact that urea is absorbed rapidly from the stomach into the blood, and is excreted unaltered by the kidneys: 15 Gm. of urea is given with 100 cc. of fluid, and the urine which is collected at the end of two hours is tested for urea concentration. Called also *Maclean-de Wesselow t.* and *Jones and Cantarow t.*

urease t.: A test for urea based on the conversion of urea into ammonium carbonate by the urease of soy bean. See *Marshall's method*, under *method.*

uric acid t. See *Bayrac's t.*, *Cole's t.* (3), *Denigès' t.* (1), *Folin's t.* (2), (3), *Ganassini's t.*, *Garrod's t.* (2), *Gentele's t.*, *Porter's t.* (1), *Salkowski-Ludwig t.*, *Schiff's t.* (5), *von Jaksch's t.* (4), *Weidel's t.* (1).

urine concentration t.: Under a controlled diet the specific gravity of the urine should reach 1.18 or more at certain times.

urobilin t. See *Hildebrandt's t.*, *para-dimethyl-amino-benzaldehyde t.*, *Schlesinger's t.*, *Schneider's t.*

urochromogen t. See *Weiss's t.*

urorosein t.: Add to the urine half as much concentrated hydrochloric acid and a few drops of a 1 per cent solution of potassium nitrate. A red color indicates urorosein.

Urriolla's t.: The discovery of blood pigment in the urine is indicative of the existence of malaria.

Valenta's t. (*for foreign fats in butter*): The butter is heated with an equal amount of glacial acetic acid and then cooled. If opacity begins to show at 96 F., there is adulteration; if opacity is not observed until about 62 F., the butter is pure.

Valsalva's t. (*for pneumothorax*): After a deep inspiration the mouth and nose are held tightly closed, and a strong attempt at expiration is made. This determines the possibility of the inflation of lung tissue compressed by pneumothorax.

valve t.: Auscultation of the heart while the patient lies with the legs raised obliquely and the arms lifted perpendicularly.

van Deen's t. See *Deen's t.*

van den Bergh's t.: 1. (*The direct test.*) Dilute 1 cc. of the serum with 2 cc. of distilled water and add 0.25 to 50 cc. of freshly prepared diazo reagent (q.v. under *reagent*). A bluish-violet color beginning immediately and becoming maximal in from ten to thirty seconds is called a *prompt* or *immediate direct reaction*, indicating the presence of uncombined bilirubin and therefore the existence of obstructive jaundice. A reddish coloration beginning after from one to fifteen minutes and gradually deepening to a violet is called a *delayed direct reaction*, which indicates impaired liver function. A reddish color which appears at once and deepens to a violet is called a *biphasic direct reaction.* 2. (*The indirect test.*) To 0.5 cc. of serum add 1 cc. of 96 per cent alcohol and centrifugalize. To 1 cc. of the clear supernatant fluid add 0.25 cc. of the diazo reagent. A violet-red color appears at once if positive and is due to bilirubin fixed to the blood protein, pointing to hemolytic jaundice. This test can be made in a quantitative manner by determining the dilution of the serum which gives a color corresponding to a dilution of azobilirubin of 1:200,000.

van der Velden's t. See *Maly's t.*

vanillin t. (*for indole*): To 5 cc. of the culture add 5 drops of 5 per cent vanillin solution in 95 per cent alcohol and 2 cc. of hydrochloric acid. Indole gives an orange color; tryptophan, a reddish-violet color.

Van Slyke t.: 1. (*For amino-nitrogen.*) Nitrous acid acting on amino-nitrogen sets free nitrogen gas, which is collected and its volume determined. 2. (*For urea.*) Treat the sample with urease, pass the ammonia so formed into fiftieth normal acid, and titrate the excess of acid.

Van Slyke and Cullen's t. See under *method.*

Vaughn and Novy's t. (*for tyrotoxicon*): Adding 2 or 3 drops each of sulfuric and carbolic acids and a few drops of an aqueous solution of the suspected substance to tyrotoxicon gives a yellow or orange-red color.

Venning Browne t.: The presence of pregnanediol in the urine indicates the presence of corpus luteum hormone in the body.

ventilation t.: Measurement of the quantity of air expired by a person during a period of exercise.

Vernes' t.: 1. (*For syphilis.*) Direct method: A test based on the degree of flocculation produced by various blood serums on a specially prepared extract of dried horse heart muscle, called perethynol. Indirect method: A test based on measuring the amount of flocculation produced in perethynol according to the degree of inhibition of hemolysis of sheep corpuscles by swine serum. The degree of flocculation by normal serum and that by syphilitic serum is noted during a course of time, and the various readings are plotted into curves (syphilimetry). Normal serums give a horizontal line, but with syphilitic serums the curve of flocculation oscillates up and down. 2. (*For tuberculosis.*) The patient's blood is mixed with an equal amount of 1.25 per cent aqueous solution of resorcin. If the optic density of the mixture is below 15, the subject is free from tuberculosis; if it is above 30 the subject has tuberculosis.

virulence t. (*for diphtheria*): Inject 4 cc. of a broth culture subcutaneously into each of two guinea pigs. Into the control inject also 1 cc. of antitoxin. The control should survive, the other should die.

Visscher-Bowman t. (*for pregnancy*): A chemical test for pregnancy, depending on the presence of anterior pituitary hormones in the urine.

Vitali's t.: 1. (*For alkaloids.*) Evaporate with

fuming nitric acid and add a drop of potassium hydroxide, when color reactions will occur. For atropine the color is violet, turning to red. 2. (*For alkaloids.*) Add sulfuric acid, potassium chlorate, and an alkaline sulfide. Various color reactions will follow. 3. (*For bile pigments.*) Add a few drops of potassium nitrate in solution and dilute sulfuric acid. The color reactions are green, followed by blue or red and yellow. 4. (*For bile pigments.*) Add quinine bisulfate in solution and follow with ammonia water, sulfuric acid, a crystal of sugar, and alcohol. A violet color results. 5. (*For thymol.*) Distil, and pass the vapor through a mixture of chloroform and potassium hydroxide solution. A red color results. 6. (*For pus in the urine.*) The urine is acidified with acetic acid and filtered. On the filter paper thus obtained a small quantity of guaiacum is dropped. The paper will turn a dark blue if pus is present.

vitamin t. See *Carr-Price t., Fearon's t., Rosenheim-Drummond t., Schopfer's t., Shear's t.*

vocabulary t.: A form of intelligence test based on the subject's knowledge of a selected list of words.

Voelcker and Joseph's t. See *indigo carmine t.*

Voge's t. (*for pregnancy*): Treatment of the urine with bromine water, which produces a pink coloration if histidine is present, indicating pregnancy.

Vogel and Lee's t. (*for mercury*): Add 3 per cent of hydrochloric acid and concentrate the urine to one fifth its original volume. Add a piece of clean copper wire. A silvery film indicates mercury. To confirm, place the wire in a tube with a plug of gold foil and distill the mercury over onto the gold. Sublime a crystal of iodine onto the mercury and form the red iodide of mercury.

Voges-Proskauer t. See under *reaction.*

Volhard's t.: 1. (*For chlorides.*) The chlorides are precipitated by a known amount of $AgNO_3$. The excess of $AgNO_3$ is then titrated with KCNS. See under *method.* 2. (*Specific gravity test for renal function.*) The patient is given 1500 cc. of water to drink within three quarters of an hour in the early morning, and then nothing but a dry diet for the rest of the day. Following the ingestion of water, the specific gravity of the urine drops below 1.002 and the water taken is eliminated in about four hours. Later in the day, the specific gravity rises, passing 1.025 late in the afternoon.

Vollmer's t.: A proprietary tuberculin patch test done with an adhesive strip on which are two test squares and one control square of filter paper, the test squares saturated with concentrated Old Tuberculin and the control square with uninoculated broth.

von Aldor's t. (*for proteoses*): Precipitate the urine with phosphotungstic acid, wash the precipitate with alcohol, bring into solution with potassium hydroxide, and apply the biuret test.

von Dungern's t.: 1. A complement fixation test for the diagnosis of malignant disease. 2. A chemical serum test for syphilis, made with an alkaline indigo solution.

von Frisch t. (*for collateral circulation*): A normal coloration of the peripheral parts on pressure over the artery on the side proximal to the injury and appearance of venostasis on the peripheral side of the temporarily occluded vein.

von Jaksch's t.: 1. (*For free HCl in gastric juice.*) A test paper prepared with benzopurpurine B takes on a fine violet color if HCl is present. If present in considerable amount, it becomes dark blue. 2. (*For dextrose in urine.*) A mixture of 3 parts of sodium acetate and 2 parts of phenylhydrazine hydrochloride is added to the urine; warm it, and put the test tube in hot water for half an hour. On cooling, yellow needles of phenylglucosazone are seen as a precipitate. 3. (*For melanin.*) Add to the suspected liquid a few drops of a solution of ferric chloride. If melanin is present, a gray appearance is produced. After precipitation add more ferric chloride, and the precipitate will be redissolved. 4. (*For uric acid.*) Heat the powder slowly on a glass dish with a few drops of bromine water or chlorine water: the substance becomes red. After cooling, add ammonia, and it becomes purplish red.

von Maschke's t. (*for creatinine*): To the suspected solution add a few drops of Fehling's solution, after mixing with a cold solution of sodium carbonate: an amorphous, flocculent precipitate proves the presence of creatinine.

von Pall's t. (*for pregnancy*): The diastase content of the urine gives indications for an existing pregnancy.

von Pirquet's t. See *Pirquet's reaction,* under *reaction.*

von Recklinghausen's t. (*of heart function*): A test based on the proposition that the product of the frequency of the pulse by the amplitude of the blood pressure is equal to the amount of blood expelled by the heart in a second, divided by the distensibility of the circulatory system.

von Zeynek and Mencki's t. (*for blood*): Precipitate the urine with acetone, extract the precipitate with acidified acetone, and examine the colored extract under the microscope for small hemin crystals.

Vulpian t. (*for epinephrine*): Add a few drops of ferric chloride solution, and a green color indicates epinephrine.

Waaler-Rose t. (*for rheumatoid factors*). See *sheep cell agglutination t.*

Wagner's t. (*for occult blood*). See *benzidine t.*

Walter's bromide t.: A test based on the fact that in normal persons the ratio of the amount of bromide in the blood and cerebrospinal fluid is constant: in persons with mental disorder the ratio may vary.

Wang's t. (*quantitative test for indican*): The indican is converted into indigosulfuric acid and titrated by means of a potassium permanganate solution.

Warren's t. See *Trommer's t.*

Wassermann t. See under *reaction.*

water t. (*for Addison's disease*): The volume of urine excreted from 10:30 p.m. to 8:30 a.m. is measured. Twenty cc. of water per kilogram of body weight (9 cc. per pound) is administered without breakfast. The urine is collected at 9:30, 10:30, 11:30 a.m., and at 12:30 p.m. If the volume of any single specimen exceeds the volume of urine excreted during the night, Addison's disease is ruled out.

water-gurgle t. (*for stricture of the esophagus*): The swallowing of water causes a peculiar gurgle heard on auscultation.

Waterhouse pus t.: If pain in a local inflammation is increased by the application of a constricting bandage, pus is present.

Watson-Schwartz t.: A simple qualitative procedure, depending upon the chloroform- and butanol-insolubility of porphobilinogen aldehyde, for differentiating porphobilinogen from urobilinogen and other Ehrlich reactors: of value in the diagnosis of acute porphyria.

Weber's t.: 1. A hearing test made by placing the stem of a vibrating 256 tuning fork on the vertex or on the midline of the forehead just above the glabella. The result is expressed as "Weber negative" if it is heard as in the midline, and as "Weber right" or "Weber left," respectively, if it is referred to the right or the left ear. 2. (*For indican.*) Boil 30 cc. of suspected urine with an equal volume of hydrochloric acid containing a little nitric acid; cool it, and shake with ether: if indican is present, the ether will become red or violet and the froth will be blue. 3. (*For blood.*) Mix the blood with 30 per cent acetic acid and extract with ether. To the ethereal extract add an alcoholic solution of guaiac and hydrogen peroxide. A blue color indicates blood.

Webster's t. (*for TNT in urine*): The urine is extracted with ether, then acidified with a mineral acid, and again extracted with ether. In the latter extract the presence of the azoxy-compound formed from TNT is shown by the development of a violet tint on the addition of alcoholic potash.

Weichbrodt's t. (*for globulin*): To 0.7 cc. of spinal fluid add 0.3 cc. of a 1 per cent solution of mercuric bichloride. A cloudiness or opalescence indicates globulin.

Weidel's t.: 1. (*For uric acid.*) The substance tested is treated with nitric acid, evaporated, and moistened with ammonia water: if uric acid is present, murexide will be formed, and a purple color is produced. Called also *murexide t.* 2. (*For xanthine.*) Warm with freshly prepared chlorine water containing a trace of nitric acid until gas ceases to be produced: contact with gaseous ammonia develops a pink or purple color. 3. (*For xanthine bodies.*) Dissolve in warm chlorine water, evaporate, and treat with ammonia water, a pink or purple color will form, changing to violet on the addition of sodium or potassium hydroxide solution.

Weil's t. (*for syphilis*): A test for syphilis based on the fact that the erythrocytes of syphilitics are especially resistant to the hemolyzing power of cobra venom.

Weil-Felix t. See under *reaction.*

Weinberg's t.: A complement-fixation test for hydatid disease.

Weinstein's t. See *tryptophan t.*

Weisman's t.: A modification of the Aschheim-Zondek test, using female mice as the test animals.

Weiss permanganate t. See *Weiss's t.*

Weiss's t. (*for urochromogen*): To 2 cc. of the urine add 4 cc. of distilled water and 3 drops of a 1:1000 solution of potassium permanganate. A canary yellow color indicates urochromogen.

Welland's t.: A vertical bar placed between the eyes and letters to be read shows the degree of binocular fixation.

Weltmann's serum t.: 1. (*For hepatic diseases, diseases of the biliary tract and hemolytic icterus.*) To an equal amount of serum (0.1 cc.) add 5 cc. of a solution of calcium chloride in distilled water diluted in arithmetical progression from 0.1 per hundred to 0.1 per thousand and boil the whole batch on a water bath for fifteen minutes, during which time the tubes must be shaken continually. In advanced cirrhosis the reaction shows a marked and constant increase of the coagulation column. Inflammatory processes of the biliary tract and tumors of the liver and of the biliary system show either shortening of the coagulation column or normal values. 2. A serum coagulation test for the prognosis in pulmonary tuberculosis, indicating whether the process is exudative or fibrous in type. 3. Coagulation of blood serum by solutions of calcium chloride: a prognostic test in rheumatic fever.

Wender's t. (*for dextrose*): Make a reagent by dissolving 1 part of methylene blue in 300 parts of distilled water; alkalinize this with potassium hydroxide and heat with a suspected solution: dextrose, if present, will decolorize it.

Wenzell's t. (*for strychnine*): Treat the suspected material with a solution of 1 part of potassium permanganate in 2000 parts of sulfuric acid: strychnine, even in very small proportion, will cause color reactions.

Weppen's t.: 1. (*For morphine.*) Treatment with sugar, bromine, and sulfuric acid: a red color shows the presence of morphine. 2. (*For veratrin.*) Add sugar and sulfuric acid: a yellow, green, or blue color is formed.

Wernicke's t. See *hemiopic pupillary reaction,* under *reaction.*

Wetzel's t. (*for carbon monoxide in blood*): To the blood to be examined add 4 volumes of water and treat with 3 volumes of a 1 per cent tannin solution. If CO is present, the blood becomes carmine red; normal blood slowly assumes a grayish hue.

Weyl's t.: 1. (*For creatinine.*) To the suspected solution add a little of a dilute solution of sodium nitroprusside, and then carefully put in a few drops of a weak solution of sodium hydroxide: a ruby-red color results, changing to blue on warming with acetic acid. 2. (*For nitric acid in the urine.*) Distill 200 cc. of urine with 0.2 part of sulfuric or hydrochloric acid, receiving the distillate in a potassium hydroxide solution. If metaphenyldiamine is added, a yellow color will form; if there is added pyrogallic acid in aqueous solution with a little sulfuric acid, the color will be brown; but sulfanilic acid in solution, followed in ten minutes by naphthylamine hydrochlorate, produces a red tint.

Wheeler and Johnson's t. (*for uracil and cytosine*): To the unknown solution add bromine water until the color is permanent, but avoid excess. Now add an excess of barium hydroxide. A purple color indicates one of these substances.

Whipple's t's. See *fibrinogen t., lipase t., phenoltetrachlorophthalein t.*

whisper t.: A test for hearing in which the patient stands at one end of the room with the ear opposite to that being tested closed with the finger and with the eyes closed. The examiner, whispering as he goes, approaches the patient and notes at what point the whisper is perceived by the patient.

Widal's t., Widal's serum t. (1896). See *Gruber-Widal reaction,* under *reaction.*

Widal's hemoclastic crisis t. See *hemoclastic crisis,* under *crisis.*

Wideroe's t.: A test for the character of puncture fluids. A few drops of Millon's reagent is placed in a water glass, and 1 drop of the fluid to be tested is placed on the surface. A film of coagulated protein at once forms. If this film is coherent and can be lifted readily, the exudate is tuberculous; if less readily, it is inflammatory; if it breaks up so that it cannot be lifted at all, it is a transudate.

Widmark's t.: A blood test for the diagnosis of alcoholic intoxication.

Wilbrand's prism t.: A small circle of white paper is placed upon a black surface, and the patient is seated before it with one eye bandaged. He is directed to look at the spot, and a strong prism is placed before the eye in such a way that the image of the spot is thrown upon the blind half of the retina. It is noticed if the eye at once moves to find the object again, and whether the movement is reversed when the prism is withdrawn. The presence of this reaction places the lesion in the cerebrum; the absence of the reaction locates it in the tract.

Wilbur and Addis' t. (*for urobilinogen and urobilin*). See *Schneider's t.*

Wildbolz's t. See *auto-urine t.*

Wilkinson and Peter's t. (*for raw milk*): Benzidine and hydrogen peroxide give a blue color in raw milk, but not in heated milk.

Williamson's blood t.: In a narrow test tube 40 c.mm. of water and 20 c.mm. of blood are placed; to this are added 1 cc. of methylene blue (1:6000) and 40 c.mm. of solution of potassium hydroxide. The tube is placed in a pot of boiling water. If the blood is from a diabetic patient, the blue soon disappears, but not otherwise.

Wilson's t. (*for pregnancy*): A modification of the Friedman test for pregnancy.

Winckler t.: 1. (*For alkaloids.*) A solution of mercuric chloride with an excess of potassium iodide is added: alkaloids will cause a white precipitate. 2. (*For free HCl in the gastric juice.*) Filter the juice into a porcelain cell with a few drops of the 5 per cent alcoholic solution of alpha-naphthol containing 1 per cent or less of dextrose. Heat carefully, and a bluish-violet zone will appear, which rapidly grows darker. 3. (*For iodine.*) Sodium nitrate is mixed with a starch paste: iodine gives a blue color with it.

Winslow's t.: Test for respiration in doubtful

death by observing a vessel of water placed at the bottom of the chest.

Winternitz's t. See *iodipin t.*

Wishart t. (*for acetonemia*): A few drops of plasma are placed in a small test tube. Enough dry powdered ammonium sulfate is added to supersaturate, so that at the end of the test there will still be some of the solid sulfate in the bottom of the tube. A couple of drops of a fresh solution of sodium nitroprusside are next added and shaken, and finally 1 or 2 drops of ordinary ammonia water. On shaking, a purple color develops, a little more slowly than in the case of urine. The intensity of the color indicates the degree of acetonemia.

Witz's t. (*for hydrochloric acid in the gastric juice*): A 1:48 aqueous solution of methyl violet causes a violet color, changing to blue and then green.

Wohlgemuth's t. (*for renal inadequacy*): The urine is mixed with a solution of soluble starch, 1:1000, and is incubated to permit digestive reaction. The fluid is then tested with iodine to determine the amount of starch hydrolysis. The test is based on the fact that the normal kidney tissue secretes a diastatic enzyme which is diminished in proportion as the kidney parenchyma is diseased.

Woldman's t.: A test for gastrointestinal lesion based on the principle that free phenolphthalein may pass through a lesion in the gastrointestinal mucosa and appear in the urine.

Wolff-Eisner t. See *Calmette reaction*, under *reaction.*

Wolff-Junghans t. (*for gastric cancer*): Quantitative estimation of the soluble albumin in the gastric extracts after giving a test meal; marked increase of dissolved albumin indicating malignant disease.

Woodbury's t. (*for alcohol in the urine*): To 2 cc. of urine 1 cc. of sulfuric acid is added, and a crystal of potassium dichromate: a green color will soon form.

Woods's t. (*A. C. Woods*): Complement fixation with uveal pigment for sympathetic ophthalmitis.

Worm-Müller t. (*for dextrose in the urine*): A test made by boiling in a test tube $\frac{1}{3}$ cc. of a 2.5 per cent solution of copper sulfate and 2.5 cc. of a solution of potassium hydroxide. Boil each and mix, and a yellowish or red precipitate will be formed.

Wormley's t. (*for alkaloids*): 1. Made by treating with an alcoholic solution of picric acid, when a yellow precipitate will be formed. 2. Made by treating with a solution of 1 part of iodine and 2 parts of potassium iodide in 60 parts of water: a colored precipitate will be formed.

worsted t. See *Holmgren's t.*

Wreden's t.: Test for death of the fetus by the presence of gelatinous substance in the middle ear, which can only be expelled on establishment of full respiration; never found in a child which has lived for twenty-four hours.

Wurster's t.: 1. (*For hydrogen peroxide.*) Test paper is saturated with the solution of tetramethylparaphenylendiamine: hydrogen peroxide turns it to a blue-violet color. 2. (*For tyrosine.*) The suspected material is dissolved in boiling water and a little quinone: a ruby-red color will form, changing slowly to brown.

Wys's t. See *iodine number*, under *number.*

xanthemia t. See *carotinemia t.*

xanthine t. See *Drechsel's t.* (2), *Hoppe-Seyler t.* (2), *Weidel's t.* (2), (3).

xanthroproteic t. See *Mulder's t.* (2).

Xenopus t. (*for pregnancy*): A female African toad (*Xenopus laevis*) is injected with 2 cc. of urine, or 1 cc. of an extract, into the dorsal lymph sac. A deposit of 5–6 or more eggs within four to twelve hours indicates pregnancy.

xylidine t. See *Schiff's t.* (1).

xylose clearance or tolerance t. (*for renal efficiency*): After the administration of 50 Gm. of xylose, the normal kidney is able to concentrate it to 2.5 per cent within two hours and to excrete 25 per cent within twenty-four hours. In renal insufficiency the percentage is greatly lowered.

xylose concentration t.: Under uniform controlled conditions the ingestion of 50 Gm. of xylose should result in a concentration of 2.5 per cent in the urine within two hours.

Yakinoff's t.: Atoxyl is warmed in a test tube; the slightest yellowish discoloration indicates the presence of dangerous impurities.

Yefimov's t. (*for worms in urine*): 1. From 5 to 10 cc. of urine is treated with 5 or 10 drops of a solution of mercuric nitrate. If the precipitate formed is grayish or dirty, the patient has intestinal worms. 2. The crystals formed by evaporating a drop of urine are examined under the microscope. Granular crystals indicate the presence of cestodes; waxlike ones show the presence of nematodes.

Yerkes-Bridges t.: A modified and improved form of the Binet-Simon test for intelligence.

Young's test (*for cataract*): On a disk with a varied number of pinholes in different portions, the patient's ability to recognize the number of holes is a test of the integrity of macular function.

Yvon's t.: 1. (*For acetanilid in urine.*) Extract it with chloroform and heat the residue with mercurous nitrate, when a green color will form. 2. (*For alkaloids.*) Add a solution of 3 Gm. of bismuth subnitrate, made by boiling in 40 cc. of water, to which are added 14 Gm. of potassium iodide and 40 drops of hydrochloric acid: a red color will show the presence of an alkaloid.

Zaleski's t. (*for carbon monoxide in blood*): To 2 cc. of blood add an equal volume of water and 3 drops of a one-third saturated solution of copper sulfate: if carbon monoxide is present, a brick-red deposit is thrown down; otherwise the precipitate is greenish brown.

Zambrini's t. See under *ptyaloreaction.*

Zangemeister t. (*for paternity*): A decrease in the light permeability (detected by the photometer) when the serum of the child is mixed with that of the father; when the serum of a man other than the father is added to a child's serum this decrease does not occur.

Zappacosta's t. (*for liver function*): Glycocyamine is injected intravenously: if in one quarter of an hour after the injection the substance is still present in the blood, liver function is impaired.

Zeisel's t. (*for colchicine*): Dissolve in hydrochloric acid, boil with ferric chloride, and shake with chloroform: a brown or dark-red layer will form at the bottom.

Zeller's t.: 1. (*For melanin in urine.*) Add bromine water: a yellow precipitate will form, changing slowly to black. 2. See *Moloney's t.*

Zenoni's t.: Sputum is mixed with alcohol and stained with aqueous solution of safranine, when the mucin is colored yellow and the albumin red.

Ziehen's t. (*for mental disease*): The patient is requested to explain the difference between such contrasted objects as ice and water, cat and dog, etc.

Ziffern's t. (*for clotting activity*). See *Smith's t.*

zinc fluorescence t. (*for urobilin*). See *Schlesinger's t.*

Zitovitch's t. (*for cancer*): After inhaling dilute chlorine gas for one-half hour, such as is used for therapeutic purposes, the citrated plasma of the patient shows some hemolysis normally. No hemolysis indicates cancer.

Zondek-Aschheim t. See *Aschheim-Zondek t.*

Zouchlos' t. (*for albumin in the urine*): 1. Precipitate it with a mixture of 1 part of acetic acid and 6 parts of a 10 per cent solution of mercuric chloride. 2. Prepare a reagent with 100 parts of a 10 per cent solution of potassium thiocyanate

A TABLE OF TESTS (*Concluded*)

and 20 parts of acetic acid: drop it slowly into the urine until the albumin appears as a white cloudiness. 3. Add equal parts of succinic acid and potassium thiocyanate: albumin, if present, will be precipitated.

Zsigmondy's gold number t. See *Lange's t.* (1).

Zwenger's t.: 1. (*For cholesterol.*) A crystal of cholesterol with 5 parts of sulfuric acid and 1 part water gives a red ring changing to violet. 2. See *Liebermann's t.*

---

test meal (test mēl). A meal containing material given for the specific purpose for aiding diagnostic examination of the stomach, as by roentgenoscopy or by chemical analysis later of the stomach contents. **Boas' t. m.,** a tablespoonful of oatmeal in a quart of water boiled down to a pint. **Boyden t. m.,** a motor meal for testing the evacuation of the gallbladder, containing three or four egg yolks combined with milk and seasoned with sugar, port wine, etc. **Dock's t. m.,** the same as Ewald's except that one shredded wheat biscuit is substituted for the rolls or bread. **Ehrmann's alcohol t. m.,** 50 cc. of 7 per cent alcohol. **Ewald's t. m.,** two rolls or slices of dry bread and 9 to 12 ounces of water. **Fischer's t. m.,** Ewald's test meal to which is added ¼ pound of finely chopped lean ground steak, broiled and slightly seasoned. **Leube's t. m.,** 12 ounces of soup, 3 to 6 ounces of minced steak, 2 ounces of white bread, and 6 ounces of water. **motor t. m.,** a meal or drink containing a radiopaque substance, permitting roentgenoscopic observation of its progress through the stomach, pylorus, and other portions of the gastrointestinal tract. **Riegel's t. m.,** a plate of soup, 200 Gm. of beefsteak, 50 Gm. of mashed potatoes, and one roll. **Salzer's t. m's,** two meals given four hours apart, the stomach contents being removed one hour after the last meal, when, if the stomach is normal, no remains of the first meal should be found. The first meal consists of soft-boiled eggs, cold roast beef, rice, and milk; the second, of stale bread and water.

test type (test tīp). Printed letters of varying size, used in the testing of visual acuity. See also under *chart.* **Jaeger's t. t.,** ordinary printer's type of seven different sizes imprinted on a card; used in testing near vision. **Snellen's t. t.,** block letters used in testing visual acuity so designed that the whole letter subtends, at the appropriate distance, a visual angle usually of 5 minutes, and each component part subtends an angle of 1 minute. See also *Snellen's chart.*

Two of Snellen's test types.

testa (tes'tah) [L.]. A shell; oyster shell. **t. o'vi,** egg shell. **t. praepara'ta,** oyster shell powdered and washed.

testaceous (tes-ta'she-us) [L. *testa* shell]. Of the nature of shell; having a shell.

testalgia (tes-tal'je-ah) [*testis* + *-algia*]. Pain in the testicle.

testectomy (tes-tek'to-me) [*testis* + Gr. *ektomē* excision]. Removal of a testis; castration.

testes (tes'tēz) [L.]. Plural of *testis.*

testibrachial (tes"tĭ-bra'ke-al). Pertaining to the testibrachium.

testibrachium (tes"tĭ-bra'ke-um) [*testis* + L. *brachium* arm]. Pedunculus cerebellaris superior.

testicle (tes'tĭ-k'l) [L. *testiculus*]. The testis.

testicond (tes'tĭ-kond) [*testis* + L. *condere* to hide]. Having the testes retained within the abdominal cavity, as occurs normally in many mammals, such as the elephant and armadillo.

testicular (tes-tik'u-lar). Pertaining to a testis.

testiculoma (tes-tik"u-lo'mah). A tumor containing testicular tissue. **t. ova'rii,** arrhenoblastoma.

testiculus (tes-tik'u-lus) [L.]. Testis.

testis (tes'tis), pl. *tes'tes* [L.]. [N A, B N A] The male gonad; an egg-shaped gland normally situated in the scrotum, which produces spermatozoa. **Cooper's irritable t.,** a testis affected with neuralgia. **ectopic t.,** a testis which has become lodged in some abnormal location. **inverted t.,** a testis whose position in the scrotum is reversed, the epididymis being attached to the anterior instead of the posterior surface. **t. mulie'bris,** an ovary. **obstructed t.,** a testis whose descent has been prevented by a fascial sheet at the entrance to the scrotum. **pulpy t.,** a testis affected with medullary sarcoma. **t. re'dux,** a testis which tends to be drawn to the upper part of the scrotum. **retained t.,** undescended t. **undescended t.,** a testis which has failed to descend into the scrotum, but remains in the inguinal canal, and the condition so produced. Called also *cryptorchism* or *cryptorchidism.*

testitis (tes-ti'tis). Orchitis.

testitoxicosis (tes"tĭ-tok"sĭ-ko'sis) [*testis* + Gr. *toxikon* poison]. A condition of intoxication which sometimes follows double ligation of the vas deferens.

testoid (tes'toid). 1. A term applied to testicular hormones and other natural or synthetic compounds having a similar effect. 2. A rudimentary testis, especially such a structure occurring in a hermaphrodite.

testopathy (tes-top'ah-the) [*testes* + Gr. *pathos* disease]. Any disease of the testes.

testosterone (tes-tos'ter-ōn). The hormone produced by the testes in the male, which functions in the induction and maintenance of male secondary sex characters. A pharmaceutical compound, 17β-hydroxy-4-androsten-3-one, prepared synthetically from cholesterol or isolated from bull testes, is used as replacement therapy of testicular deficiency, and has been used in palliation of advanced metastatic carcinoma of the female breast. **t. cyclopentylpropionate,** 17β-hydroxy-4-androsten-3-one-3-(cyclopentyl)propionate, a compound that has an effect more protracted than that of testosterone. **t. cypionate,** t. cyclopentylpropionate. **t. enanthate,** $\triangle^4$-androstene-17β-hepatanoate-3-one, a compound which, administered in oil, exerts a prolonged action. **ethinyl t.,** pregneninolone. **t. heptanoate,** t. enanthate. **methyl t.** See *methyltestosterone.* **t. propionate,** a crystalline androgenic steroid, $\triangle^4$-androstene-17β-propionate-3-one, $C_{22}H_{32}O_3$: used to supply testicular hormone in eunuchism and eunuchoidism (hypogonadism); also used in crpytorchism, dysmenorrhea and certain other gynecological conditions, and in palliation of advanced metastatic carcinoma in the female breast.

testryl (tes'tril). Trade mark for a suspension of pure crystalline testosterone.

tetanal (tet'ah-nal). Pertaining to or derived from tetanus.

tetania (te-ta'ne-ah) [L.]. Tetany. **t. gravida'rum,** tetany in pregnant women. **t. parathyreopri'va,** tetany caused by removal of the parathyroids.

tetanic (te-tan'ik) [Gr. *tetanikos*]. 1. Pertaining to or of the nature of tetanus. 2. Producing tetanus.

tetaniform (te-tan'ĭ-form) [*tetanus* + L. *forma* shape]. Like or resembling tetanus.

tetanigenous (tet"ah-nij'e-nus) [*tetanus* + Gr. *gennan* to produce]. Producing tetanus or tetanic spasms.

tetanilla (tet"ah-nil'ah). 1. A form of tetany without rigidity, but attended by mental changes. 2. Paramyoclonus multiplex.

tetanine (tet'ah-nin). A poisonous ptomaine, $C_{13}H_{30}N_2O_4$, from cultures of the bacillus of tetanus, and from the tissues of tetanus patients. It produces paralysis, tetanic convulsions, and death.

tetanism (tet'ah-nizm). A form of more or less

continuous muscular hypertonicity sometimes seen in young infants; a series of clinical conditions resembling those of tetanus, but dependent on infection with an organism other than the *Clostridium tetani*.

tetanization (tet″ah-ni-za′shun). The induction of tetanic convulsions or symptoms.

tetanize (tet′ah-nīz). To throw into a state or condition of tetanus or continuous spasm; to induce tetanoid movements in an organism or a muscle.

tetanocannabin (tet″ah-no-kan′ah-bin). A poisonous principle sometimes found in hemp: it resembles strychnine in its action.

tetanode (tet′ah-nōd). The unexcited stage of tetany.

tetanoid (tet′ah-noid) [*tetanus* + Gr. *eidos* form]. Like or resembling tetanus.

tetanolysin (tet″ah-nol′ĭ-sin) [*tetanus* + *lysin*]. The hemolytic fraction of the exotoxin formed by *Clostridium tetani*, the organism causing tetanus in man and domestic animals.

tetanometer (tet″ah-nom′e-ter) [*tetanus* + Gr. *metron* measure]. An apparatus for measurement and analysis of tetanus.

tetanomotor (tet″ah-no-mo′tor) [*tetanus* + L. *motor* mover]. A device for the mechanical production of tetanic motor spasm.

tetanophilic (tet″ah-no-fil′ik) [*tetanus* + Gr. *philein* to love]. Having an affinity for the toxin of tetanus.

tetanospasmin (tet″ah-no-spaz′min) [*tetano-* + L. *spasmus* spasm + *-in* chemical suffix]. The neurotoxic fraction of the exotoxin formed by *Clostridium tetani*, the organism causing tetanus in man and domestic animals.

tetanotoxin (tet″ah-no-tok′sin) [*tetanus* + *toxin*]. A poisonous ptomaine, $C_5H_{11}N$, from cultures of *Clostridium tetani*.

tetanus (tet′ah-nus) [Gr. *tetanos*, from *teinein* to stretch]. 1. An acute infectious disease caused by a toxin produced in the body by the *Clostridium tetani*, with tonic spasm of the masseter muscles, causing trismus ("lockjaw"), followed by spasms of the back muscles, producing the characteristic opisthotonos. Rarely, the body may be bowed forward or to the side. 2. Continuous tonic spasm of a muscle, steady contraction of a muscle without distinct twitching. **acoustic t.,** a series of induction shocks in a frog's nerve and muscle preparation: the speed is measured by the pitch of a vibrant rod. **anodal closure t.,** tetanic muscular contraction occurring at the anode when the electric circuit is closed. **anodal opening t.,** tetanic muscular contraction occurring at the anode when the electric circuit is opened or broken. **t. anti′cus,** tetanus in which the body is bowed forward. **apyretic t.,** tetany. **artificial t.,** that which is produced as a result of the administration of drugs. **cathodal closure t.,** tetanic muscular contraction occurring at the cathode when the electric circuit is closed. **cathodal opening t.,** tetanic muscular contraction occurring at the cathode when the electric circuit is opened or broken. **cephalic t.,** a rare disease developing after injuries to the scalp, face, or neck, associated with palsies of cranial nerves 3, 4, 6, 7, 9, 10, 12, and invariably associated with some degree of trismus. **cerebral t.,** a form of tetanus produced by inoculating the brain of animals with tetanus antitoxin. It is attended by epileptiform convulsions and excitement. **chronic t.,** a form seen in man in which the onset is later, the progress of the disease is slower, and the prognosis more favorable than in the acute form. **cryptogenic t.,** tetanus which occurs without any wound or other ascertainable cause. **t. dorsa′lis,** t. posticus. **drug t.,** toxic spasm produced by some tetanic drug. **extensor t.,** that which affects especially the extensors. **flexor t.,** tonic spasm of flexor muscles. **head t., hydrophobic t.** See *kopf-tetanus*. **idiopathic t.,** that which does not follow a lesion. **imitative t.,** hysteria which simulates tetanus. **t. infan′tum,** t. neonatorum. **inoculation t.,** experimental tetanus produced by inoculation with a culture of *Clostridium tetani*. **intermittent t.,** tetany. **Janin's t., Klemm's t., kopf t.,** kopf-tetanus. **t. latera′lis,** tetanus in which the body is bent sideways. **localized t.,** tetanic spasm of a single part. **modified t.,** localized tetany. **t. neonato′rum,** tetanus of very young infants, usually due to the infection of the umbilicus. **t. paradox′us,** cephalic tetanus in which trismus is combined with paralysis of the facial or other cranial nerve. **paralytic t.,** kopf-tetanus. **partial t.,** tetany. **t. posti′cus,** tetanus in which the body is bowed backward. **postserum t.,** tetanus which develops even after the administration of tetanus serum. **puerperal t.,** that which occurs in women after childbirth. **Ritter's t.,** tetanic contractions taking place at the opening of a constant current which has been passing for some time along a nerve: seen in tetany. **Rose's t.,** kopf-tetanus. **splanchnic t.,** a form in which the muscles of deglutition and of respiration are severely involved and in which there is severe dysphagia. **toxic t.,** that produced by an overdose of nux vomica or strychnine. **traumatic t.,** that which follows wound poisoning. **uterine t.,** puerperal t. **Wundt's t.,** tetanic contraction in a frog's muscle produced by electric current or injury.

tetany (tet′ah-ne). 1. A syndrome manifested by sharp flexion of the wrist and ankle joints (carpopedal spasm), muscle twitchings, cramps, and convulsions, sometimes with attacks of stridor. It is due to abnormal calcium metabolism and occurs in parathyroid hypofunction, vitamin D deficiency, alkalosis, and as a result of the ingestion of alkaline salts. 2. Tetanus, def. 2. **duration t.,** a continuous tetanic contraction in response to a very strong continuous current: it occurs especially in degenerated muscles; symbol, DT. **epidemic t.,** rheumatic t. **gastric t.,** a severe form due to disease of the stomach, attended by difficult respiration and painful tonic spasms of the extremities. **grass t.,** an often fatal condition that may be produced in "fresh" cows that are turned out into lush pastures. It is apparently due to a deficiency of magnesium in the diet. **hyperventilation t.,** tetany produced by forced inspiration and expiration continued for a considerable time. **lactation t.,** grass tetany. **latent t.,** tetany elicited by the application of electrical and mechanical stimulation. **parathyroid t., parathyroprival t.,** tetany due to removal of the parathyroids. **rheumatic t.,** an acute epidemic disease, not uncommon in Europe, lasting two or three weeks, and seldom fatal. Called also *epidemic t.* **thyroprival t.,** a form due to suspension of the function of the thyroid gland.

tetarcone (tet′ar-kōn). Tetartocone.

tetartanope (tet-ar′tah-nōp). An individual exhibiting tetartanopia.

tetartanopia (tet″ar-tah-no′pe-ah) [Gr. *tetartos* fourth + *an-* neg. + *ōpē* sight + *-ia*]. 1. Quadrantanopia. 2. A rare problematic type of defective color vision, characterized by retention of the sensory mechanism for two hues only (red and green), and lacking that for blue and yellow, which are replaced in the spectrum by an achromatic (gray) band. Coined by G. E. Miller (1924), who conceded yellow as a fourth, "inner" primary. Cf. the correlative terms *protanopia*, *deuteranopia*, and *tritanopia*, in which the color vision deficiency is in the first, second, and third primary, respectively.

tetartanopic (tet″ar-tah-nop′ik). Pertaining to or characterized by tetartanopia.

tetartanopsia (tet″ar-tah-nop′se-ah). Tetartanopia.

tetartocone (tet-ar′to-kōn) [Gr. *tetartos* fourth + *cone*]. The posterior internal cusp of an upper premolar tooth.

tetartoconoid (tet″ar-to-ko′noid). The posterior internal cusp of a lower premolar tooth.

tethelin (teth′e-lin) [Gr. *tethēlōs* flourishing]. A water-soluble phospholipin obtained from the anterior lobe of the pituitary body, which on hydrolysis yields inosite, which accelerates the growth process, and which prolongs the life span (T. Brailsford Robertson).

tetiothalein sodium (te″she-o-thal′e-in so′de-um). Tetraiodophthalein sodium.

tetmil (tet′mil). Ten millimeters taken as a unit of measurement.

tetra- (tet′rah) [Gr. *tetra-* four]. Combining form meaning *four.*

tetra-amylose (tet″rah-am′ĭ-lōs). An anhydride compound obtained from dextrin. It is a polymerized from of diamylose, $[(C_6H_{10}O_5)_2]_2$.

tetrabasic (tet″rah-ba′sik) [*tetra-* + Gr. *basis* base]. Containing four atoms of replaceable hydrogen.

tetrablastic (tet″rah-blas′tik). Having four germ layers.

tetrabrachius (tet″rah-bra′ke-us) [*tetra-* + Gr. *brachiōn* arm]. A double fetal monster having four arms.

tetrabromofluorescein (tet″rah-bro″mo-floo″o-res′e-in). Eosin.

tetrabromophenolphthalein (tet″rah-bro″mo-fe″nol-thal′e-in). An indicator, $C_6H_4.CO.O.C$-$(C_6H_2Br_2OH)_2$, which is colorless with acids and violet with alkalis.

tetrabromophthalein sodium (tet″rah-bro-mo-thal′e-in so′de-um). The sodium salt of tetrabromophenolphthalein, $NaOOC.C_6H_4.C:C_6H_2$-$Br_2O.C_6H_2Br_2ONa$, used for roentgenological examination of the gallbladder, in which organ it appears after intravenous injection.

tetracaine (tet′rah-kān). Chemical name: 2-dimethylaminoethyl-p-butylaminobenzoate: used as a local anesthetic.

tetracetate (tet-ras′e-tāt) [*tetra-* + *acetate*]. A compound of a base with four acetic acid molecules.

Tetrachilomastix (tet″rah-ki″lo-mas′tiks). A flagellate protozoan sometimes found in the intestinal tract of man. **T. bengalen′sis,** a form found commonly in India associated with chronic intestinal complaints. **T. intestina′lis,** a coprozoic, flagellate organism sometimes found in human feces. It is pyriform in shape, has four anterior flagella, and can be cultivated.

tetrachirus (tet″rah-ki′rus) [*tetra-* + Gr. *cheir* hand]. A fetal monster having four hands.

tetrachlorethane (tet″rah-klōr-eth′ān). Acetylene tetrachloride, $CHCl_2.CHCl_2$, formed by the action of chlorine on acetylene.

tetrachloride (tet″rah-klo′rīd). A compound of a radical with four atoms of chlorine.

tetrachlormethane (tet″rah-klōr-meth′ān). Carbon tetrachloride, CCl_4.

tetrachloroethylene (tet″rah-klo″ro-eth′ĭ-lēn). Chemical name: perchloroethylene: used as an anthelmintic.

tetrachlorphenoxide (tet″rah-klōr″fen-ok′sīd). A fungicide used for the preservation of lumber: it may cause a dermatitis in workmen.

tetrachromic (tet″rah-kro′mik) [*tetra-* + Gr. *chrōma* color]. 1. Pertaining to or exhibiting four colors. 2. Able to distinguish only four of the seven colors of the spectrum.

tetracid (tet′ras-id). Capable of replacing four atoms of hydrogen in an acid, or having four atoms of hydrogen replaceable by acid radicals.

tetracrotic (tet″rah-krot′ik) [*tetra-* + Gr. *krotos* beat]. Showing four elevations in the sphygmographic tracing of the pulse.

tetracycline (tet″rah-si′klēn). An antibiotic substance isolated from the elaboration products of certain species of Streptomyces on suitable media. Chemical name: 4-dimethylamino-1,4,4α,5,5α,6,-11,12α-octahydro-3,6,10,12,12α-pentahydroxy-6-methyl-1,11-dioxo-2-naphthacenecarboxamide.

tetracyn (tet′rah-sin). Trade mark for preparations of tetracycline.

tetrad (tet′rad) [Gr. *tetra-* four]. 1. Any element or radicle having a valence, or combining power, of four. 2. A group of four similar or related entities. 3. A group of four chromosomal elements formed in miosis. 4. A square of cells produced by the division into two planes of certain cocci: if of four cells, it is a tetrad of the first power; if of sixteen cells, it is of the second power.

tetradactylous (tet″rah-dak′tĭ-lus). Pertaining to or characterized by tetradactyly.

tetradactyly (tet″rah-dak′tĭ-le) [*tetra-* + Gr. *daktylos* finger]. The condition of having four digits on the hand or foot.

tetra-erythrin (tet″rah-er′ĭ-thrin). Crustaceorubin.

tetraethylammonium (tet″rah-eth″il-ah-mo′-ne-um). The radical $(C_2H_5)_4N$, which, in various compounds (quaternary ammonium compounds—*t. bromide, t. chloride*), has been used as a ganglionic blocking agent.

tetraethylthiuram disulfide (tet″rah-eth″il-thi′u-ram″ di-sul′fīd). A compound $[(C_2H_5)_2N.$-$CS.S]_2$, occurring in slightly yellowish crystals with a bitter taste and a faint odor of violets, which produces hypersensitivity to alcohol. Marketed under various trade names, as abstinyl, antabuse, aversan, and teca.

tetragenic (tet″rah-jen′ik). Produced by the *Micrococcus tetragenus.*

tetragenous (tet-raj′e-nus) [*tetra-* + Gr. *gennan* to produce]. Splitting into groups of four: said of bacteria.

tetragonum (tet″rah-go′num) [L.; Gr. *tetragōnon*]. A square or quadrant; a quadrangular area or space. **t. lumba′le,** the quadrangular space bounded by the four lumbar muscles—by the serratus posterior inferior above, the internal oblique below, the erector spinae internally, and the external oblique externally.

tetragonus (tet″rah-go′nus). The platysma muscle.

tetrahydric (tet″rah-hi′drik). Containing four atoms of replaceable hydrogen: said of an acid or alcohol.

tetrahydropalmatine (tet″rah-hi″dro-pal′mah-tin). A crystalline alkaloid, $C_{21}H_{25}NO_4$, from the roots of *Corydalis tuberosa.*

tetrahydrozoline (tet″rah-hi-dro′zo-lēn). Chemical name: 2-(1,2,3,4-tetrahydro-1-naphthyl)-2-imidazoline, a sympathomimetic agent employed typically as a nasal decongestant.

tetraiodoethylene (tet″rah-i″o-do-eth′ĭ-lēn). Diiodoform.

tetraiodophenolphthalein (tet″rah-i″o-do-fe″-nol-thal′e-in). A dye, $C_6H_4.CO.O.C(C_6H_2I_2OH)_2$, which after intravenous injection is excreted in the bile in sufficient amount to make possible roentgenography of the gallbladder. It has been used in treating typhoid fever carriers.

tetraiodophthalein (tet″rah-i″o-do-thal′e-in). Iodophthalein.

tetraiodothyronine (tet″rah-i″o-do-thi′ro-nēn). Thyroxine; so called because it is formed by the conjugation of two molecules of diiodotyrosine.

tetralogy (tet-ral′o-je). A combination of four elements or factors, such as four concurrent symptoms or defects. **t. of Fallot,** a combination of congenital cardiac defects commonly found in adults, namely, pulmonary stenosis in the conus region, interventricular septal defect, dextroposition of the aorta so that it overrides the interventricular septum and receives venous as well as arterial blood, and right ventricular hypertrophy.

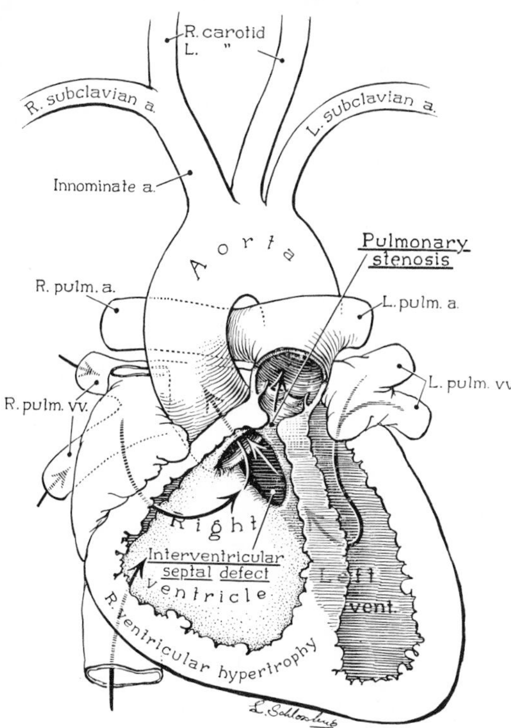

Tetralogy of Fallot. (Blalock and Taussig.)

tetramastigote (tet″rah-mas′tĭ-gōt) [*tetra-* + Gr. *mastix* lash]. 1. Having four flagella. 2. An organism having four flagella.

tetramazia (tet″rah-ma′ze-ah) [*tetra-* + Gr. *mazos* breast + *-ia*]. The condition of having four mammary glands.

Tetrameres (tet-ram′er-ēz). A genus of worms parasitic in the alimentary tract of chickens and other fowl. **T. american′a,** a filaroid parasite of the proventriculus of chickens and other birds.

tetrameric (tet″rah-mer′ik) Having four parts.

tetramethyl (tet″rah-meth′il). A chemical compound each molecule of which contains four methyl groups.

tetramethylammonium hydroxide (tet″rah-meth″il-ah-mo′ne-um hi-drok′sīd). A toxic fraction, $N(CH_3)_4OH$, isolated from the sea anemone, *Actinia equina.*

tetramethylenediamine (tet″rah-meth″il-ēn-di′am-in). Putrescine.

tetramethylputrescine (tet″rah-meth″il-pu-tres′in). An extremely poisonous crystalline base, $N(CH_3)_2(CH_2)_4N(CH_3)_2$, derivable from putrescine. It produces symptoms like those of muscarine poisoning.

tetramine (tet′rah-mēn). Tetramethylammonium hydroxide.

tetramitiasis (tet″rah-mi-ti′ah-sis). Infestation with *Tetramitus.*

Tetramitus mesnili (tet-ram′ĭ-tus mes-ni′le). *Chilomastix mesnili.*

tetramylose (tet-ram′ĭ-lōs). A crystalline amylose, $(C_6H_{10}O_5)_4$.

tetranitrol (tet″rah-ni′trol). Nitro-erythrol.

tetranophthalmos (tet″ran-of-thal′mos) [*tetra-* + Gr. *ophthalmos* eye]. A fetal monster having four eyes.

tetranopsia (tet″ran-op′se-ah). Quadrantanopia.

tetranucleotidase (tet″rah-nu″kle-ot′ĭ-dās). An enzyme that splits nucleic acid into nucleotides.

tetranucleotide (tet″rah-nu′kle-o-tīd). Nucleic acid.

Tetranychus (tet-ran′ĭ-kus) [*tetra-* + Gr. *onyx* nail]. A genus of mites. **T. autumna′lis,** *Trombicula autumnalis.* **T. molestis′simus,** an acarid attacking man and causing severe itching. **T. tela′rius,** the spider mite, which sometimes infests man.

tetraodontoxin (tet-ra″o-don-tok′sin) [*Tetraodon,* from Gr. *tetra* four + *odous* tooth, a puffer fish + *toxikon* poison]. A pure crystalline toxic substance derived from puffer (tetraodontoid) fishes.

tetraodontoxism (tet-ra″o-don-tok′sizm). The most severe form of ichthyosarcotoxism, produced by ingestion of certain fishes of the sub-order Tetraodontoidea.

tetraotus (tet″rah-o′tus) [Gr. *tetraōtos* four eared]. A fetal monster with two nearly separate heads, two faces, four eyes, and four ears.

tetraparesis (tet″rah-par′e-sis). Muscular weakness affecting all four extremities.

tetrapeptide (tet″rah-pep′tid). A peptide which on hydrolysis yields four amino acids.

tetraplegia (tet″rah-ple′je-ah) [*tetra-* + Gr. *plēgē* stroke + *-ia*]. Paralysis of all four extremities.

tetraploid (tet″rah-ploid). 1. Pertaining to or characterized by tetraploidy. 2. An individual or cell having four sets of chromosomes.

tetraploidy (tet′rah-ploi″de). The state of having four sets of chromosomes (4n).

tetrapodisis (tet″rah-po-di′sis). Locomotion on four feet; quadruped locomotion, as in young children.

tetrapus (tet′rah-pus) [*tetra-* + Gr. *pous* foot]. A fetal monster having four feet.

tetrasaccharide (tet″rah-sak′ah-rid). A carbohydrate containing four (hypothetical) saccharide groups, $C_{24}H_{42}O_{21}$.

tetrascelus (tet-ras′e-lus) [*tetra-* + Gr. *skelos* leg]. A fetal monster having four legs.

tetraschistic (tet″rah-skis′tik) [*tetra-* + Gr. *schisis* division]. Divided into four elements by fission.

tetrasomic (tet″rah-so′mik). Pertaining to or characterized by tetrasomy.

tetrasomy (tet′rah-so″me) [*tetra-* + Gr. *sōma* body]. The presence of two additional chromosomes of one type in an otherwise diploid cell (2n + 2).

tetraster (tet-ras′ter) [*tetra-* + Gr. *astēr* star]. A figure in abnormal mitosis characterized by four centrosomal centers or asters.

tetrastichiasis (tet″rah-stĭ-ki′ah-sis) [*tetra-* + Gr. *stichos* row + *-iasis*]. A condition in which there are four rows of eyelashes.

Tetrastoma (tet-ras′to-mah) [*tetra-* + Gr. *stoma* mouth]. A genus of trematodes sometimes found in the urine.

tetratomic (tet″rah-tom′ik). 1. Consisting of four atoms. 2. Having four replaceable atoms.

Tetratrichomonas buccalis (tet″rah-trik-om′-o-nas buk-ka′lis). *Trichomonas buccalis.*

tetravaccine (tet″rah-vak′sēn). A vaccine containing dead cultures of the bacteria of typhoid, paratyphoid A, paratyphoid B, and cholera.

tetravalent (tet-rav′ah-lent). Having a chemical valence or combining power of four.

tetronal (tet′ro-nal). Diethylsulfondiethylmethane, $(C_2H_5)_2.C.(SO_2C_2H_5)_2$, occurring in the form of colorless scales. It is hypnotic.

tetroneurythrin (tet″ron-er′ĭ-thrin). A pigment from certain birds' feathers, mullets, and many invertebrates.

tetrophthalmos (tet″rof-thal′mos) [*tetra-* + Gr. *ophthalmos* eye]. A double-faced fetal monster with two ears and four eyes.

tetrose (tet′rōs). A monosaccharide containing four carbon atoms in a molecule.

tetrotus (tet-ro′tus). Tetraotus.

tetroxide (tet-rok′sīd). A compound of a radical with four oxygen atoms.

tetryl (tet′ril). An organic explosive and expellant, tetra-nitro-methyl-aniline, $(NO_2)_3C_6H_2N(NO)_2\text{-}CH_3$, which may cause an industrial dermatitis.

tetter (tet′er). 1. A popular name for various skin diseases. 2. A skin disease of animals communicable to man, and characterized by intense itching. **blister t.,** pemphigus. **brawny t.,** seborrhoea capitis. **Cantlie's foot t.,** epidermophytosis of the foot. **crusted t.,** impetigo. **dry t.,** squamous or dry eczema. **eating t.,** lupus. **honeycomb t.,** favus. **humid t., moist t.,** eczema. **milky t.,** crusta lactea. **scaly t.,** psoriasis and squamous eczema.

tetterwort (tet′ter-wort). Sanguinaria.

tetum (tet′um). Ancylostomiasis.

tety (te′te). A disease of Madagascar marked by a pustular or scaly eruption about the nose and mouth.

teucrin (tu′krin). A crystalline glycoside, $C_{21}H_{24}O_{11}$, from *Teucrium fruticans.*

Teucrium (tu′kre-um) [Gr. *teukrion* an herb of the germander kind]. A genus of labiate plants called germander. Several old-world species are medicinal.

teutlose (tūt′lōs) [Gr. *teutlon* beet]. A kind of sugar found in beet root.

tewfikose (tu′fĭ-kōs). A sugar occurring in the milk of the Egyptian buffalo, *Bos bubalus.*

texis (tek′sis) [L.; Gr.]. Child-bearing.

textiform (teks′tĭ-form) [L. *textum* any material put together + *forma* form]. Formed like a tissue, network, or web.

textoblastic (teks″to-blas′tik) [L. *textum* any material put together + Gr. *blastos* germ]. Forming adult tissue; regenerative: said of cells.

textoma (teks-to′mah) [L. *textum* any material put together + *-oma*]. A tumor composed of completely differentiated tissue cells.

textometer (teks″to-me′ter) [L. *textum* any material put together + Gr. *mētēr* mother]. Protoplasm regarded as the mother of tissues.

textural (teks′tu-ral). Pertaining to the texture, or constitution, of the tissues.

texture (teks′tūr) [L. *textura*]. 1. Any of the organized tissues or substances of the body. 2. The arrangement of the elementary parts of the body.

textus (teks′tus) [L.]. A tissue.

T.F. Abbreviation for *tuberculin filtrate.*

TGT. Abbreviation for *thromboplastin generation test.*

Th. Chemical symbol for *thorium.*

thalamencephalic (thal″am-en″se-fal′ik). Pertaining to the thalamencephalon.

thalamencephalon (thal″am-en-sef′ah-lon). [N A, B N A] The part of the diencephalon that comprises the thalamus, metathalamus, and epithalamus.

thalami (thal′ah-mi) [L.]. Genitive singular and nominative plural of *thalamus.*

thalamic (thah-lam′ik). Pertaining to the thalamus.

thalamocoele (thal′ah-mo-sēl″) [Gr. *thalamos* inner chamber + *koilia* hollow]. The third ventricle of the brain (ventriculus tertius cerebri [N A]).

thalamocortical (thal″ah-mo-kor′tĭ-kal). Pertaining to the thalamus and cortex.

thalamocrural (thal″ah-mo-kroo′ral). Pertaining to the thalamus and a crus cerebri.

thalamolenticular (thal″ah-mo-len-tik′u-lar). Pertaining to the thalamus and the lenticular nucleus.

thalamomamillary (thal″ah-mo-mam′ĭ-ler″e). Pertaining to the thalamus and mamillary bodies.

thalamopeduncular (thal″ah-mo-pe-dung′ku-lar). Pertaining to the thalamus and a cerebral peduncle.

thalamotegmental (thal″ah-mo-teg-men′tal). Pertaining to the thalamus and tegmentum.

thalamotomy (thal″ah-mot′o-me) [*thalamus* + Gr. *tomē* a cutting]. The production of circumscribed lesions in the thalamus, particularly in treatment of psychotic disorders with a strong emotional component. **anterior t.,** production of lesions in the anterior nucleus of the thalamus. **dorso-medial t.,** production of lesions in the dorso-medial nucleus of the thalamus.

thalamus (thal′ah-mus), pl. *thal′ami* [L.; Gr. *thalamos* inner chamber]. [N A, B N A] The middle and larger portion of the diencephalon, which forms part of the lateral wall of the third ventricle and lies between the hypothalamus and the epithalamus. It comprises medullary laminae and variously named nuclear groups, and is the main relay center for sensory impulses to the cerebral cortex.

thalassanemia (thah-las″sah-ne′me-ah). Thalassemia.

thalassemia (thal″ah-se′me-ah) [Gr. *thalassa* sea (because it was observed originally in persons of Mediterranean stock) + *haima* blood + *-ia*]. A hereditary, genetically determined hemolytic anemia with familial and racial incidence, divided into a number of categories based upon clinical severity and the type(s) of hemoglobin contained in the erythrocytes. In *thalassemia major,* for example, the most severe form of the disease, there is a marked increase in F hemoglobin; in *thalassemia minor,* or trait form, A_2 hemoglobin is elevated above normal. Increasing knowledge indicates that there may be several different thalassemias, depending on the determinants controlling the synthesis of the hemoglobin polypeptide chains. Called also *Cooley's anemia, Mediterranean anemia, erythroblastotic anemia of childhood,* and *familial erythroblastic anemia.*

thalassin (thah-las′sin). A toxic substance derived from tentacles of the sea anemone, *Anemonia sulcata,* which, when injected into dogs, produces allergic symptoms.

thalassophobia (thah-las″so-fo′be-ah) [Gr. *thalassa* sea + *phobein* to be affrighted by]. Morbid dread of the sea.

thalassoposia (thah-las″so-po′ze-ah) [Gr. *thalassa* sea + *posis* drinking + *-ia*]. The ingestion of sea water.

thalassotherapy (thah-las″so-ther′ah-pe) [Gr. *thalassa* sea + *therapeia* treatment]. The treatment of disease by sea bathing, sea voyages, and sea air.

thalgrain (thal′grān). Grain mixed with thallium sulfate: used as a poison for rodents.

thalidomide (thah-lid′o-mīd). Chemical name: α(N-phthalimido)glutarimide, $C_{13}H_{10}N_2O_4$. Used commonly in Europe as a sedative and hypnotic in the early 1960's, it was discovered to be the cause of serious congenital anomalies in the fetus, notably dysmelia, when taken by a woman during early pregnancy.

thalleioquin (thal-i′o-kwin). A greenish, resinous substance, produced in a test for quinine.

thallitoxicosis (thal″ĭ-tok″sĭ-ko′sis). Poisoning by thallium or thallium-containing substances.

thallium (thal′e-um) [Gr. *thallos* green shoot]. A soft, bluish-white metal; symbol, Tl; atomic number, 81; atomic weight, 204.37; specific gravity, 11.85; its salts are active poisons.

thallophyte (thal′o-fīt) [Gr. *thallos* green shoot + *phyton* plant]. One of a group of cryptogamous plants of low structure, including algae, fungi, and lichens. Myxomycetes and bacteria are also sometimes included in this category.

thallospore (thal′o-spōr). A thallus modified to serve as an organ of reproduction.

thallus (thal′us). 1. A simple plant body not differentiated into root, stem, and leaf, which is characteristic of thallophytes. 2. The actively growing vegetative organism as distinguished from reproductive or resting portions, as in fungi.

thalposis (thal-po′sis) [Gr. *thalpos* warmth]. Warmth sense; the sense which perceives warmth.

thalpotic (thal-pot′ik). Pertaining to thalposis.

Thamnidium (tham-nid′e-um) [Gr. *thamnos* bush]. A genus of molds which resembles Mucor and which is often found growing on meat in cold storage. It can grow at 28°F. and forms a profuse hairy growth. The species most frequently found are *T. elegans* and *T. chaetocladioides*.

thamuria (tham-u′re-ah) [Gr. *thamys* often + *ouron* urine + *-ia*]. Frequency of urination.

thanato- (than′ah-to) [Gr. *thanatos* death]. Combining form denoting relationship to death.

thanatobiologic (than″ah-to-bi″o-loj′ik) [*thanato-* + Gr. *bios* life + *-logy*]. Pertaining to death and life.

thanatognomonic (than″ah-to-no-mon′ik) [*thanato-* + Gr. *gnōmonikos* decisive]. Indicating the approach of death.

thanatoid (than′ah-toid) [*thanato-* + Gr. *eidos* form]. Resembling death.

thanatology (than″ah-tol′o-je). The medicolegal study of death and conditions affecting dead bodies.

thanatomania (than″ah-to-ma′ne-ah) [*thanato-* + Gr. *mania* madness]. Suicidal or homocidal mania.

thanatometer (than″ah-tom′e-ter) [*thanato-* + Gr. *metron* measure]. A thermometer used to prove the occurrence of death by registering the reduction of the bodily temperature.

thanatophidia (than″ah-to-fid′e-ah) [*thanato-* + Gr. *ophis* snake]. The deadly serpents collectively; toxicophidia.

thanatophidial (than″ah-to-fid′e-al). Pertaining to venomous snakes.

thanatophobia (than″ah-to-fo′be-ah) [*thanato-* Gr. *phobein* to be affrighted by]. The unwarranted apprehension of imminent death; morbid dread of death.

thanatopsia, thanatopsy (than″ah-top′se-ah, than′ah-top″se) [*thanato-* + Gr. *opsis* view]. Necropsy.

thanatosis (than″ah-to′sis). Gangrene or necrosis.

Thane's method (thānz) [George Dancer *Thane*, British anatomist, 1850–1930]. A method of locating the fissure of Rolando. Its upper end is about one-half inch behind the middle of a line uniting the inion and the glabella, and its lower end about one-quarter inch above and one and one-quarter inches behind the external angular process of the frontal bone.

Thapsia (thap′se-ah) [L.; Gr. *thapsia;* named from the isle of *Thapsus*]. A genus of umbelliferous plants. *T. garganica*, of Northern Africa, affords an irritant resin somewhat used in plasters; the plant is locally employed as a polychrest remedy.

thassophobia (thas″so-fo′be-ah) [Gr. *thassein* to sit idle + *phobein* to be affrighted by]. Morbid dread of sitting idle.

thaumatropy (thaw-mat′ro-pe) [Gr. *thauma* wonder + *tropos* a turning]. The transformation of an organ or structure into another organ or structure.

thaumaturgic (thaw″mah-ter′jik) [Gr. *thauma* wonder + *ergon* work]. Working wonders; magical; miraculous.

Thaysen's disease (thi′senz) [T. E. H. *Thaysen*, Copenhagen physician, 1883–1936]. Idiopathic steatorrhea.

thea (the′ah) [L.]. Tea.

theaism (the′ah-izm). A morbid condition resulting from ingestion of excessive quantities of tea.

thebaic (the-ba′ik) [L. *Thebaicus* Theban, named for Thebes, where opium was once prepared]. Pertaining to or derived from opium.

thebaica (the-ba′ĭ-kah). Opium.

thebaine (the-ba′in). A crystalline, poisonous, and anodyne alkaloid from opium, $C_{19}H_{21}NO_3$, having properties similar to those of strychnine. Also called *dimethyl morphine* and *paramorphine*.

thebaism (the′bah-izm). Opiumism.

thebesian (the-be′ze-an) [named for or described by Adam Christian *Thebesius*, German physician, 1686–1732]. See under *foramen*, *valve*, and *vein*.

theca (the′kah), pl. *the′cae* [L.; Gr. *thēkē*]. An enclosing case or sheath, as of a tendon. **t. cor′dis**, pericardium. **t. exter′na**, tunica externa thecae folliculi. **t. of follicle**, t. folliculi. **t. of follicle of von Baer**, tunica externa thecae folliculi. **t. follic′uli** [N A, B N A], an envelope of condensed connective tissue surrounding a vesicular ovarian follicle, comprising an internal vascular layer and an external fibrous layer. **t. inter′na**, tunica interna thecae folliculi. **t. medul′lae spina′lis, t. of spinal cord, t. vertebra′lis**, dura mater spinalis.

thecae (the′se) [L.]. Plural of *theca*.

thecal (the′kal). Pertaining to a theca.

thecitis (the-si′tis). Inflammation of the sheath of a tendon.

thecodont (the′ko-dont) [Gr. *thēkē* sheath + *odous* tooth]. Having the teeth inserted in sockets or alveoli.

thecoma (the-ko′mah). A theca-cell tumor.

thecostegnosis (the″ko-steg-no′sis) [Gr. *thēkē* sheath + *stegnōsis* narrowing]. Contraction of a tendon sheath.

Theden's bandage (ta′denz) [Johann Christian Anton *Theden*, German surgeon, 1714–1797]. See under *bandage*.

Theile's canal, glands (ti′lez) [Friedrich Wilhelm *Theile*, German anatomist, 1801–1879]. See under *canal* and *gland*.

Theiler's disease [Max *Theiler*, microbiologist, born 1899; winner of the Nobel prize for medicine and physiology in 1951]. See under *disease*.

Theileria (thi-le′re-ah) [Sir Arnold *Theiler*, Swiss microbiologist, 1867–1936]. A genus of minute intraglobular protozoan parasites. **T. annula′ta**, a species pathogenic for cattle. **T. dis′par**, a species which causes heavy mortality of cattle in northern Africa: it is transmitted by the tick *Hyalomma mauritanicum*. **T. hir′ci** causes a fatal disease in sheep and goats. **T. par′va**, a species causing a disease of cattle in South Africa which is similar to Texas cattle fever. See *Rhodesian fever*, under *fever*. **T. tsutsugamu′shi**, *Rickettsia tsutsugamushi*.

theileriasis (thi″lĕ-ri′ah-sis). Infection with *Theileria*.

theinism (the′in-izm). Theaism.

thelalgia (the-lal′je-ah) [Gr. *thēlē* nipple + *algos* pain + *-ia*]. Pain in the nipple.

thelarche (the-lar′ke) [Gr. *thēlē* nipple + *archē* beginning]. The beginning of development of the breasts at puberty.

Thelazia (the-la′ze-ah). A genus of worms allied to Filaria. Several species (*T. callipaeda*, *T. californiensis*) are parasitic in the eyes of animals.

thelaziasis (the″la-zi′ah-sis). Infestation of the eye with *Thelazia*.

theleplasty (the′le-plas″te) [Gr. *thēlē* nipple + *plassein* to form]. A plastic operation upon the nipple.

thelerethism (thel-er′ĕ-thizm) [Gr. *thēlē* nipple + *erethisma* a stirring up]. Erection or protrusion of the nipple.

thelitis (the-li′tis) [Gr. *thēlē* nipple + *-itis*]. Inflammation of a nipple.

thelium (the′le-um), pl. *the′lia* [L.]. 1. A papilla. 2. A nipple.

Thelohania magna (the″lo-ha′ne-ah mag′nah). A microsporidium parasitic in the larvae of the mosquito, *Culex pipiens*.

thelorrhagia (the″lo-ra′je-ah). Hemorrhage from the nipple.

thelothism, thelotism (the′lo-thizm, the′lotizm). Thelerethism.

thelyblast (thel′e-blast) [Gr. *thēlys* female + *blastos* germ]. Feminonucleus.

thelyblastic (thel″e-blas′tik). Pertaining to or of the nature of a thelyblast.

thelygenic (the″le-jen′ik) [Gr. *thēlys* female + *gennan* to produce]. Producing only female offspring.

thelykinin (the″le-ki′nin). Estrone.

thelytocia (thel″e-to′she-ah) [Gr. *thēlys* female + *tokos* birth]. Normal parthenogenesis producing females only.

thelytocous (the-lit′o-kus). Pertaining to or characterized by thelytocia.

thelytoky (the-lit′o-ke). Thelytocia.

Themison (them′ĭ-son) **of Laodicea** (1st century B.C.). A Greek physician who founded the Methodist school of medicine.

thenad (the′nad). Toward the thenar eminence or toward the palm.

thenal (the′nal). Pertaining to the palm or thenar.

thenar (the′nar) [Gr.]. 1. [N A, B N A] The mound on the palm at the base of the thumb. Called also *thenar eminence*. 2. Pertaining to the palm.

thenyldiamine (then″il-di′ah-mēn). Chemical name: 2-[(2-dimethylaminoethyl)-3-thenylamino]-pyridine: used as an antihistaminic.

thenylene (then′ĭ-lĕn). Trade mark for a preparation of methapyrilene hydrochloride.

thenylpyramine (then″il-pir′ah-mēn). Methapyrilene.

Theobaldia (the″o-bal′de-ah) [Frederic Vincent *Theobald*, British zoologist, 1868–1930]. A genus of mosquitoes of the temperate regions of the Old and New Worlds.

Theobroma (the″o-bro′mah) [Gr. *theos* god + *brōma* food]. A genus of sterculiaceous plants. The seeds of *T. cacao* (called theobroma and cacao) contain the alkaloid theobromine, and are used in the preparation of cacao and chocolate.

theobromine (the″o-bro′min). An alkaloid, 3,7-dimethylxanthine, prepared from the dried ripe seed of *Theobroma cacao:* used as a diuretic and as a smooth muscle relaxant.

theobromose (the″o-bro′mōs). Theobromine lithium, $C_7H_7O_2N_4.Li$: used as a diuretic.

theoglycinate (the″o-gli′sĭ-nāt). Trade mark for a preparation of theophylline sodium glycinate.

theolin (the′o-lin). A colorless, volatile liquid hydrocarbon, heptane, C_7H_{16}; obtainable from petroleum, etc. It resembles benzine and has similar uses.

theomania (the″o-ma′ne-ah) [Gr. *theos* god + *mania* madness]. Religious insanity; especially mental disorder in which the patient believes himself inspired by or possessed of divinity.

theomaniac (the″o-ma′ne-ak). Pertaining to or characterized by theomania. By extension sometimes used to designate an individual exhibiting theomania.

theophobia (the″o-fo′be-ah) [Gr. *theos* god + *phobein* to be affrighted by]. Morbid fear of the wrath of God.

theophylline (the″o-fil′in) [L. *thea* tea + Gr. *phyllon* leaf]. A white, odorless, crystalline alkaloid, 1,3-dimethylxanthine, $C_7H_8N_4O_2.H_2O$, derived from tea or produced synthetically: used as a smooth muscle relaxant and as a diuretic. **anhydrous t.,** theophylline which does not contain the molecule of water, $C_7H_8N_4O_2$. **t. cholinate,** oxtriphylline. **t. ethanolamine,** a preparation consisting of 75 per cent of anhydrous theophylline and 25 per cent of ethanolamine, used as a diuretic and bronchodilator. **t. ethylenediamine,** aminophylline. **t. methylglucamine,** a preparation consisting of an equimolecular mixture of theophylline and N-methylglucamine: used as a smooth muscle relaxant. **t. sodium,** a compound of theophylline and sodium, $C_7H_7N_4NaO_2$: used in combination with sodium acetate or glycine. **t. sodium acetate,** a hydrated mixture containing theophylline sodium and sodium acetate in approximately equimolecular proportions, and yielding 55 to 65 per cent of anhydrous theophylline: used as a smooth muscle relaxant. **t. sodium glycinate,** an equilibrium mixture containing theophylline sodium and glycine in approximately equimolecular proportions: used as a smooth muscle relaxant.

Theorell (the″o-rel′), Axel Hugo Teodor. Swedish biochemist, born 1903; winner of the Nobel prize in medicine and physiology for 1955, for his discoveries concerning the nature and mode of action of oxidation enzymes.

theorem (the′o-rem) [Gr. *theorēma* a principle arrived at by speculation]. A proposition capable of demonstration. **Gibbs's t.,** substances which lower the surface tension of the pure dispersion medium tend to collect on its surface. **Hazen's t.,** the proposition that for every death from typhoid fever avoided by the purification of public water supplies two or three deaths are avoided from other causes.

theory (the′o-re) [Gr. *theōria* speculation as opposed to practice]. 1. The doctrine or the principles underlying an art as distinguished from the practice of that particular art. 2. A formulated hypothesis, or, loosely speaking, any hypothesis or opinion not based upon actual knowledge. **Adami's t.,** a hypothesis for the explanation of heredity, resembling Ehrlich's side-chain theory of immunity. **Adler's t.,** the theory that neuroses are developed as compensations for a social or physical inferiority. **Altmann's t.,** a theory that protoplasm is made up of granular particles (bioblasts) grouped in masses and enclosed in indifferent matter. **apposition t.,** the theory that tissues grow by the deposit of cells from without. **Arrhenius' t.,** the theory of electrolytic dissociation. **atomic t.,** the theory that the molecules of a substance are made up of one or more atoms, each representing a definite amount of the element, which amount does not vary in the molecule, whatever combinations the molecule may enter. **avalanche t.,** the theory that nervous influence increases in force as it descends along an efferent nerve. **biochemical t.** See *Ehrlich's biochemical t.* **Bolk's retardation t.,** the theory that man, in his development, has stopped at a stage which, in the higher primates, is still a fetal stage. **Bowman's t.** (*of urinary secretion*), the theory that water and inorganic salts are excreted in the glomeruli, whereas the urea and related bodies are eliminated by the epithelial cells in the convoluted tubes. Cf. *Ludwig's t.* **brunonian t.,** the obsolete opinion of John Brown (1735–1788) that all diseases are due to an excess or lack of stimulus. **Buchner's t.,** a theory of immunity which supposes that the cells of a body which has recovered from an infection undergo a reactive change which protects against similar infections. **Buergi's t.,** two different substances causing identical therapeutic manifestations when combined are increased in their effects if they possess identical pharmacologic points of attack. **cell t.,** the doctrine that all living matter is composed of cells and that cell activity is the essential process of life. **cell-chain t.,** the theory that the nerve fiber consists of a chain of special cells which have only secondarily been brought into relation with the central cell. **chemicoparasitic t.,** the theory that dental caries is caused by combined chemical and parasitic action. **cloaca t.,** the theory assumed by children and some neurotics that a child is born like a passage of the bowels. **clonal-selection t. of immunity,** the theory that immunological specificity is preformed during embryonic life and is mediated through cell clones. **Cohnheim's t.** 1. The theory that the emigration of leukocytes is the essential feature of inflammation. 2. The theory that tumors develop from embryonic rests which do not participate in the formation of normal surrounding tissue. **darwinian t.** See *darwin-*

ism. **De Vries' t.**, t. of mutations. **Dieulafoy's t.**, the theory that appendicitis is always due to the appendix becoming a closed cavity. **dimer t.**, the theory that the tooth organ of primates is composed of two halves, each of which is a representative of an independent tooth in the lower orders of animals. **dualistic t.**, the theory that the blood cells arise from two distinct types of primitive cells, the myeloblasts and lymphoblasts. Cf. *monophyletic t.* **Ehrlich's biochemical t.**, the theory that specific chemical affinity exists between the substance of specific living cells and specific chemical substances. **Ehrlich's side-chain t.**, a theory advanced regarding the phenomena concerned in immunity and cytolysis. According to this theory, the protoplasm of the body cells contains highly complex organic molecules, consisting of a tolerably stable central group, to which are attached less stable lateral chains (or side chains) of atoms or atomic groups. The ordinary chemical transformations in the protoplasm are carried on by means of these lateral chains (or *receptors*), the stable center of the molecule remaining unaffected. The lateral chains contain a group of atoms (*haptophore group*), which is capable of uniting with similar groups in toxins, bacterial cells, and foreign cells. See also *amboceptor* and *complement.* **electron t.**, all bodies are complex structures composed of small particles called atoms together with still smaller particles called electrons. **emergency t.**, Cannon's theory that the adrenal medulla is stimulated to secrete by activity on the part of the sympathetic nervous system in conditions of emotional excitement, pain, etc.; or, in other words, to meet bodily emergencies. **emigration t.**, Cohnheim's t. **enzyme-trace-substance t.**, any substance (not alive) which in trace amounts induces profound biological effects, does so through some enzyme system. **Flourens' t.**, the opinion that the entire cerebrum is concerned in each and every psychic operation or process. **Frerichs' t.**, the theory that uremia is really a poisoning by ammonium carbonate formed by the action on urea of a ferment contained in the blood. **Freud's t.**, hysteria is due to a psychic trauma which was not adequately reacted to when it was received, and remains as an affect memory. **germ t.**, the doctrine that infectious diseases are of microbic origin. **germ layer t.**, the teaching that the embryo develops three primary germ layers, each of which gives rise to definite organ derivatives. **Gestalt t.** See *gestaltism.* **Golgi's t.**, the theory that the neurons communicate by the neuraxons of Golgi's cells and the collaterals of the neuraxons of Deiters' cells. **Goltz's t.**, the theory that the function of the semicircular canals is to transmit sensations of position, and thus materially aid in the sense of equilibrium. **ground water t.**, Pettenkofer's t. **Hammarsten's t.**, that the coagulation of the blood is due to the decomposition of fibrinogen and the production of fibrin by the agency of the fibrinogen. **Helmholtz t.**, a theory of sound perception: each basilar fiber responds sympathetically to a definite tone and stimulates the hair cells of Corti's organ, which rest upon the fiber. The nerve impulse from this stimulation of the hair cells is carried to the brain. **Hering's t.**, the doctrine that color sensation depends on decomposition and restitution of the visual substance: disassimilation producing red, yellow, and white, and restitution producing blue, green, and black. **humoral t.**, the ancient theory that the body contains four humors—blood, phlegm, yellow bile, and black bile, health being the result of their proper adjustment, and disease resulting from their imbalance or irregular distribution. **incasement t.**, the formerly advocated theory that all animals and plants develop from preexisting germs, and that they incase the germs of all future generations, one within another. **ionic t.**, a theory that, on going into solution, the molecules of an electrolyte break up or dissociate into two or more portions, these portions being positively and negatively charged electrically, the positively charged portions being different chemically from those negatively charged. When an electric current is passed through the solution of an electrolyte the positively charged portions are attracted by the negative pole or electrode, and move toward it; the negatively charged portions are attracted by and migrate toward the positive electrode. From this property of moving toward one of the electrodes, these charged molecular fractions of electrolytes are called ions, from the Greek verb meaning "to move." **James-Lange t.**, the theory that emotion is the sensory awareness of response to the emotion-provoking stimulus, particularly autonomic response. **Kern plasma relation t.**, the theory that for each cell there exists a definite size relation of nuclear mass to cell mass. **Ladd-Franklin t.** (*of color vision*) that red, green, and blue stimulating substances are liberated in the nerve endings by suitable light waves from a complex photosensitive molecule. **Lamarck's t.**, the theory that acquired characteristics may be transmitted. **lateral-chain t.**, Ehrlich's side-chain t. **Liebig's t.**, the hydrocarbons which oxidize easily are the foods which produce animal heat. **Ludwig's t.** (*of urinary secretion*), the theory that urine is formed by the simple process of filtration in the glomeruli and diffusion along the urinary tubules. **MacDougal's t.**, the hypothesis that many, if not all variations in nature are formed by chemical modifications of the germ cells. **Maly's t.**, that the hydrochloric acid of the gastric juice is formed by the interaction of the phosphates and the chlorides of the blood. **t. of medicine**, the body of principles of the science and art of medicine as distinguished from the *practice of medicine*, or the application of those principles in actual practice. **mendelian t.** See *Mendel's law*, under *law.* **Metchnikoff's t.**, the theory that bacteria and other harmful elements in the body are attacked and destroyed by cells called phagocytes, and that the contest between such harmful elements and the phagocytes produces inflammation. **Meyer's t.**, the theory that dementia praecox is functional and not organic. **migration t.**, the theory that sympathetic ophthalmia is produced by migration of the pathogenic agent through the lymph channels of the optic nerve. **mnemic t.**, the theory that the cell has an inherited "memory" of the influences that are brought to bear upon it, and that consequently it tends to inherit acquired characteristics. Called also *Semon-Hering hypothesis.* **Monakow's t.**, the theory of diaschisis. See *diaschisis.* **monophyletic t.**, the theory that all forms of blood corpuscles, both red and white, have their origin in one and the same form of primordial blood cell (hemoblast, hemogonium), the several types of corpuscles arising by a process of differentiation. Called also *unitarian t.* Cf. *polyphyletic t.* **t. of mutations**, the theory of heredity, according to which the variability in the germ plasm is such that it may at times give rise not to fluctuating variations, but to marked and permanent variations, and these latter, if advantageous to the animal, are preserved by natural selection. Such permanent variations are called mutations or sports. Called also *De Vries' t.* **myogenic t.**, the theory that the muscle fibers of the heart possess in themselves the power of originating and maintaining the contraction of the heart. **Nernst's t.**, the theory that electric stimulus to the tissues is due to dissociation of the ions which produces a concentration of the salts in the solution which envelops the cell membranes. **neuron t.** (Waldeyer, 1801), the theory that the nervous system consists of innumerable neurons in contiguity, but not in continuity. See *neuron.* **onion t.**, the obsolete opinion that the vitreous is made up of layers arranged like those of an onion. **orange t.**, the obsolete opinion that the vitreous body is composed of radial sectors like those of an orange. **overproduction t.** See *Weigert's law*, under *law.* **paralytic t.**, the doctrine that hyperemia is the most essential fact of inflammation, and is caused by paralysis of the vasomotor nerves. **Pasteur's t.,** the theory that the immunity secured by an attack of a disease is caused by the exhaustion of material needed for the growth of the organism of the disease. **Pekelharing's t.,** a theory of blood coagulation, namely that calcium is loosened from thrombin and unites with fibrinogen to form fibrin. **Pettenkofer's t.,** the theory that epidemics, as of typhoid fever, occur at the time when the ground water is at a low level; and that bacteria of the disease do not pass directly from the sick to the healthy, but pass into the soil, where they ripen when the soil is dry. **phlogiston t.** See *phlogiston.* **pithecoid t.,** the theory that man is descended from apelike ancestors. **Planck's t.,** quantum t. **point de repère t.,** the theory that there is always an external object, however small, to serve as a starting point for hallucination or for illusion (Binet). **polyphyletic t.,** the theory that the various corpuscles and cells of the blood have their origin from two or more distinct varieties of primordial (mother) cells. Cf. *monophyletic t.* **P. O. U. t.,** Ishihara's theory of the placenta-ovary-uterus production of internal secretion. **proteomorphic t.,** the theory that immunity against bacterial infection is handled by the hematopoietic system primarily, and secondarily by all the cells of the body, the waste products of the process being excreted by the liver. **quantum t.,** the theory that the radiation and absorption of energy take place in definite quantities called quanta (E) which vary in size and are defined by the equation E = hv, in which h is Planck's constant and v is the frequency of the radiation. **recapitulation t.** See *recapitulation.* **resonance t.** 1. Helmholtz theory. 2. The theory of specificity which assumes that the surface forces of reacting substances must harmonize. **Ribbert's t.,** that a tumor is formed from the development of cell rests owing to reduced tension in the surrounding tissues. **Schiefferdecker's symbiosis t.,** the theory that among the tissues of the body there is a sort of symbiosis, so that the products of metabolism in one tissue serve as a stimulus to the activities of other tissues. **Schön's t.,** the theory of ocular accommodation that the ciliary muscle exerts on the lens the same effect as is produced on a rubber ball held in both hands and compressed by the fingers. **Semon-Hering t.,** mnemic t. **side-chain t.,** Ehrlich's side-chain t. **Spitzer's t.,** the formation of the septums in the heart are teleologically conditioned, phylogenetically brought about, and mechanically achieved by the appearance and development of the lungs through phylogeny. **Traube's resonance t.** See *resonance t.* **trialistic t.,** the theory that the blood cells arise from three distinct types of primitive cells, the myeloblasts, lymphoblasts, and monocytes. Cf. *monophyletic t.* **undulatory t.,** wave t. **unitarian t.,** monophyletic t. **unitary t.,** the theory that disease is single in its nature and is not made up of separate and distinct morbid entities. **Villemin's t.,** the theory of the infectiousness and specificity of tuberculosis held before the discovery of the bacillus. **Wagner's t.,** migration theory. **wave t.,** the theory that light, heat, and electricity are transmitted through space in the form of waves. **Weismann's t.** See *weismannism.* **Woods-Fildes t.,** the theory that the antibacterial activity of at least some chemotherapeutic drugs (especially the sulfonamides) is a consequence of a competitive inhibition of essential metabolic reactions of the microorganism. **Young-Helmholtz t.,** the doctrine that color vision depends on three sets of retinal fibers, corresponding to the colors red, green, and violet. **Zuntz's t.,** a theory of muscle contraction.

theotherapy (the″o-ther′ah-pe) [Gr. *theos* god + *therapeia* treatment]. The treatment of disease by prayer and religious exercises.

thephorin (thef′o-rin). Trade mark for preparations of phenindamine tartrate.

therapeusis (ther″ah-pu′sis). Therapeutics.

therapeutic (ther″ah-pu′tik) [Gr. *therapeutikos* inclined to serve]. 1. Pertaining to therapeutics, or to the art of healing. 2. Curative.

therapeutics (ther″ah-pu′tiks). 1. The science and art of healing. 2. A scientific account of the treatment of disease. **alimentary t.,** treatment by careful regulation of the diet. **cellular t.,** organotherapy. **dental t.,** that branch of dentistry which deals with the treatment of diseases of the teeth. **dynamic t.,** treatment based on the careful selection of each separate drug for a distinctive purpose. **empiric t.,** treatment by remedies that experience has proved to be useful. **massive sterilizing t.,** therapia sterilisans magna. **mediate t.,** medication of a nursing child through its mother's milk, the remedy being administered to the mother. **mental t.,** treatment directed to influencing the mind, including hypnotic suggestion, etc. **rational t.,** treatment based upon a knowledge of the disease and of the action of the remedies employed. **ray t.,** radiotherapy. **specific t.,** treatment of a disease by a drug that is regarded as specific, as of syphilis by mercury. **stomatologic t.,** the treatment of diseases of the mouth. **suggestive t.,** treatment of disease by hypnotic suggestion. **testicular t.,** treatment by the hypodermic injection of testicular extract. **vibratory t.,** treatment by vibrations of various kinds, as by vibratory motions in massage.

therapeutist (ther″ah-pu′tist). Therapist.

therapia (ther″ah-pi′ah). Therapy. **t. sterili′sans mag′na,** Ehrlich's procedure of treatment by the use of some chemical agent which will destroy the parasites in the body of a patient without being seriously toxic for the patient.

therapist (ther′ah-pist) [Gr. *therapeutēs* one who attends to the sick]. A person skilled in the treatment of disease; often combined with a term indicating the specific type of disorder treated (as *speech therapist*) or a particular type of treatment rendered (as *physical therapist*).

therapy (ther′ah-pe) [Gr. *therapeia* service done to the sick]. The treatment of disease; therapeutics. See also under *treatment.* **anticoagulant t.,** the use of drugs to render the blood sufficiently incoagulable to discourage thrombosis without incurring the risk of hemorrhage. **aseptic pus t.,** the subcutaneous injection of aseptic pus to stimulate the defensive processes of the body. **autoserum t.,** treatment of disease by the injection of the patient's own blood serum. **bacterial t.,** opsonic t. **beam t.** 1. Treatment by the application of light from one of the colors of the spectrum. 2. The treatment of cancer by rays from a large mass of radium situated at a distance from the patient. **biological t.,** treatment of disease by the injection of the substances which produce a biological reaction in the organism. The term includes the use of serums, antitoxins, vaccines, and nonspecific proteins. **buffer t.,** intravenous injection of buffer substances, such as sodium bicarbonate, with the object of raising the hydrogen ion concentration. **carbonic t.,** the administration of carbon dioxide for starting respiration in newborn infants and for resuscitating persons overcome by asphyxiating gases. **Chaoul t.,** short distance, low voltage roentgen therapy. See *Chaoul tube,* under *tube.* **cisternomalarial t.,** the injection into the cisterna magna of a patient of the blood of a person in malarial paroxysm: employed in tabes, dementia paralytica and other syphilitic states. **collapse t.,** treatment of pulmonary tuberculosis by operative immobilization of the diseased lung. **convulsive shock t.** See *shock t.* **corrective t.,** the planning and administration of progressive physical exercise and activities most effective in improving or maintaining general physical and emotional health, through individual or group participation. **Curie t.,** treatment with radium. **deleading t.,** a process of therapy by which bone metabolism is increased and the elimination of lead, radium, etc., is accelerated. A period of high calcium intake alternates with one of low calcium intake together with parathyroid extract, thyroid extract and ammonium chloride. **deep roentgen-ray t.**, roentgen-ray treatment in which the voltages employed are from 150 to 200 kilovolts. **diathermic t.**, treatment by thermo-penetration. **duplex t.**, treatment by diathermic and galvanic currents in combination, both currents being passed through the body at the same time by way of the same two electrodes. **electric convulsive t., electroshock t.** See *shock t.* **emanation t.**, treatment of disease by the emanations from radioactive substances. **fever t.**, treatment of disease by induction of high body temperature, accomplished by physical means or by injection of fever-producing vaccines. **gametocyte t.**, treatment aimed at destruction of the infective forms of the malarial parasites. **grid t.**, therapeutic application of roentgen rays through a metal grid with a series of small, evenly spaced perforations. **heterovaccine t.**, bacterial vaccine therapy by the use of some germ other than the specific cause of the disease. **high-voltage roentgen t.**, deep roentgen-ray t. **hunger t.**, limotherapy. **hyperglycemic t.** See *insulin shock*, under *shock*. **immunization t.**, treatment with antiserum and with actively antigenic substances, e.g., vaccines. **intra-osseous t.**, the infusion of blood or other solutions into the circulation by injection through the bone marrow. **intravenous t.**, treatment by agents introduced directly into a vein, including injection of drugs in solution, blood transfusion, saline infusion, etc. **irritation t.**, stimulation t. **light t.**, the therapeutic application of radiation in the visible spectrum. **liquid air t.** See *refrigeration*. **malarial t., malarization t.** See *malariotherapy*. **massive drip intravenous t.**, the treatment of early syphilis by massive doses of arsenicals (neoarsphenamine, mapharsen) by slow continuous intravenous drip injection. **metatrophic t.**, administering a diet that acts as an adjunct to the drug taken. **milieu t.**, daily participation of patients living at home in group psychiatric therapy at a hospital, providing for observation and utilization of the patient's interpersonal relationships in a social setting, as well as occupational, physical, and individual psychotherapy. **nonspecific t.**, treatment of infections by the injection of nonspecific substances, such as proteins, proteoses, bacterial vaccines, etc., which produce a general and nonspecific effect on cellular activity. **nuclein t.**, the treatment of disease by nucleins from blood serum and from various organs. **occupational t.**, the use of any occupation for remedial purposes. **opsonic t.**, the treatment with bacterial vaccines to increase the opsonic index of the blood; called also *vaccine t.* **organic t.**, organotherapy. **oxygen t.**, the treatment of bronchitis, bronchopneumonia and of other diseases by means of oxygen inhalation. **paraspecific t.**, nonspecific therapy. **phlogetan t.**, the treatment of various conditions by the subcutaneous or intramuscular injection of some derivative of albuminoid bodies containing nucleoprotein. **physical t.**, the treatment of disease by means of physical agents, such as light, heat, cold, water, and electricity, or by use of mechanical apparatus. **protective t.**, sparing t. **protein t.**, injection of foreign proteins by the parenteral route in inflammatory and venereal diseases; nonspecific therapy. **protein shock t.**, protein t. **pulp canal t.**, root canal t. **radium t.**, the treatment of disease by means of radium. **radium beam t.** See *beam t.*, def. 2. **recurrence t.**, inoculation with Treponema. **reflex t.**, treatment by producing a reflex action. **replacement t.**, treatment to replace deficient formation of body products by securing the slow, steady liberation of the therapeutic material within the body as by the implantation of tablets or the injection of oily solutions. **root canal t.**, the treatment of diseases and injuries that affect the roots of the teeth and the pulp canals. **rotation t.**, rotation of the patient during irradiation so that all rays are focused on the spot treated but the skin dose is distributed over the circumference of the body. **serum t.** See *serotherapy*. **shock t.**, the treatment of psychotic patients by induction of coma or convulsions by injecting insulin (*insulin shock*) or metrazol, or by passing an electric current through the brain (electroshock, or electroconvulsive therapy). **short wave t.**, short wave diathermy. **solar t.**, heliotherapy. **sparing t.**, treatment directed to the protecting and sparing of an organ by allowing it to rest as much as possible. Called also *protective t.* **specific t.**, treatment by a remedy which acts directly against the cause of the disease, as of malaria by quinine. **stimulation t.**, treatment by the parenteral injection of certain substances with the result that the nervous vascular systems of the body function more vigorously and the metabolism is increased: called also *irritation t.* **substitution t.**, the administration of a gland of internal secretion to supply the deficiency of that gland. **substitutive t.** See *substitutive medication*, under *medication*. **suggestion t.**, the treatment of disease by hypnotic suggestion. **thyroid t.**, treatment of various diseases by thyroid or by derivatives from it. It is employed in myxedema, cretinism, goiter, obesity, scrofuloderma, psoriasis, pityriasis, lupus, etc. **vaccine t.**, active immunization against a disease by the injection of the bacteria of the disease or their products directly into a patient. **Weiss' fever t.** See *Weiss' treatment*, under *treatment*. **zomo t.**, treatment by the administration of meat juice. **zone t.**, treatment of disorder by mechanical stimulation of a body area located in the same longitudinal zone as the disorder.

theriac (ther′e-ak). Theriaca.

theriaca (the-ri′ah-kah) [Gr. *thēriaka* antidotes to the poison of wild animals, from *thērion* wild animal]. A mixture regarded as effective against bites by poisonous animals; it contained at one time 60 to 70 substances which were pulverized and made into an electuary with honey. **t. androm′achi**, a celebrated mixture of sixty-one drugs, formerly prescribed as an antidote for poisons, supposedly originated by Andromachus (the elder) of Crete.

theriatrics (the″re-at′riks) [Gr. *thērion* beast + *iatrikē* surgery, medicine]. Veterinary medicine.

theriomimicry (the″re-o-mim′ĭ-kre). Imitation of an animal.

Therioplectes (the″re-o-plek′tēz). A genus of tabanid flies.

theriotherapy (the″re-o-ther′ah-pe) [Gr. *thērion* beast + *therapeia* treatment]. Treatment of the diseases of lower animals.

theriotomy (the″re-ot′o-me) [Gr. *thērion* beast + *tomē* a cutting]. The dissection or anatomy of animals.

therm (therm) [Gr. *thermē* heat]. A unit of heat. The word has been used as equivalent to (*a*) large calorie; (*b*) small calorie; (*c*) 1,000 large calories; (*d*) 100,000 British thermal units.

therm-. See *thermo-*.

thermacogenesis (ther″mah-ko-jen′e-sis) [Gr. *thermē* heat + *genesis* production]. The action of a drug in elevating the body temperature.

thermae (ther′me) [L., pl.; Gr. *thermē* heat]. 1. Warm springs or warm baths. 2. Establishments for the therapeutic use of warm medicinal springs.

thermaerotherapy (therm-a″er-o-ther′ah-pe) [*therm-* + Gr. *aēr* air + *therapeia* treatment]. Treatment by the application of hot air.

thermal (ther′mal). Pertaining to or characterized by heat.

thermalgesia (ther″mal-je′ze-ah) [*therm-* + Gr. *algēsis* sense of pain + *-ia*]. A condition in which the application of heat produces pain.

thermalgia (ther-mal′je-ah) [*therm-* + Gr. *algos* pain + *-ia*]. A condition marked by sensations of intense burning pain; causalgia.

thermanalgesia (therm″an-al-je′se-ah). Absence of pain on application of heat.

thermanesthesia (therm″an-es-the′ze-ah) [*therm-* + *an-* neg. + Gr. *aisthēsis* perception + *-ia*]. Lack of ability to recognize sensations of heat and cold; absence of the heat sense.

thermatology (ther″mah-tol′o-je). The scientific study of heat as a therapeutic agent.

thermelometer (ther″mel-om′e-ter). An electric thermometer.

thermesthesia (therm″es-the′ze-ah) [*therm-* + Gr. *aisthēsis* perception + *-ia*]. Ability to recognize heat and cold; the temperature sense.

thermesthesiometer (therm″es-the″ze-om′e-ter) [*thermesthesia* + *metron* measure]. An instrument for measuring sensibility to heat.

thermhyperesthesia (therm″hi-per-es-the′ze-ah). Excessive sensitiveness to high temperatures.

thermhypesthesia (therm″hi-pes-the′ze-ah) [*therm-* + Gr. *hypo* under + *aisthēsis* perception + *-ia*]. Decrease in the normal sensitiveness to heat.

thermic (ther′mik). Of or pertaining to heat.

thermion (ther′me-on). A particle containing an electric charge emitted by an incandescent substance; such as the electrons emitted from the cathode in a Coolidge tube.

thermionics (ther″me-on′iks). The science of the phenomena exhibited by thermions.

thermistor (ther-mis′tor). A special type of resistance thermometer which measures extremely small changes in temperature.

thermo-, therm- (Gr. *thermē* heat]. Combining form denoting relationship to heat.

Thermoactinomyces (ther″mo-ak″tĭ-no-mi′sēz) [*thermo-* + Gr. *aktis, aktinos* a ray + *mykēs* fungus]. A genus of microorganisms of the family Streptomycetaceae, order Actinomycetales, made up of saprophytic soil and water microorganisms distinguished by their ability to grow at high (50–65°C.) temperatures.

thermo-aesthesia (ther″mo-es-the′ze-ah). Thermesthesia.

thermo-algesia (ther″mo-al-je′ze-ah). Thermalgesia.

thermo-analgesia (ther″mo-an″al-je′ze-ah). Thermanalgesia.

thermo-anesthesia (ther″mo-an″es-the′ze-ah). Thermanesthesia.

thermobiosis (ther″mo-bi-o′sis) [*thermo-* + Gr. *biōsis* way of life]. Ability to live in a high temperature.

thermobiotic (ther″mo-bi-ot′ik). Pertaining to or characterized by thermobiosis.

thermocauterectomy (ther″mo-kaw″ter-ek′to-me) [*thermocautery* + Gr. *ektomē* excision]. Excision of an organ (as the uterus) by the thermocautery.

thermocautery (ther″mo-kaw′ter-e). Cauterization by means of a heated wire or point.

thermochemistry (ther″mo-kem′is-tre). The aspect of physical chemistry dealing with heat changes that accompany chemical reactions.

thermochroic (ther″mo-kro′ik) [*thermo-* + Gr. *chroa* color]. Reflecting some of the heat rays and absorbing or transmitting others.

thermochroism, thermochrosis (ther-mok′ro-izm, ther″mo-kro′sis). The state or condition of being thermochroic.

thermocoagulation (ther″mo-ko-ag-u-la′shun). Coagulation of tissue by the action of high-frequency currents: used in removal of growths and also used to produce precisely located lesions in the globus pallidus.

thermocouple (ther′mo-kup″'l). A pair of dissimilar electrical conductors (such as platinum and platinum-rhodium, or copper and constantan), so joined that an electromotive force is developed by the thermoelectric effects when the junctions are at different temperatures: used for measuring temperature differences.

thermocurrent (ther″mo-kur′ent). A thermoelectric current.

thermodiffusion (ther″mo-dĭ-fu′zhun). Diffusion under the influence of elevated temperature.

thermoduric (ther″mo-du′rik) [*thermo-* + L. *durus* enduring]. Capable of withstanding high temperature.

thermodynamics (ther″mo-di-nam′iks) [*thermo-* + Gr. *dynamis* power]. The branch of science which deals with heat, energy, and the interconversion of these, and with related problems.

thermo-electric (ther″mo-e-lek′trik). Pertaining to electricity generated by heat.

thermo-electricity (ther″mo-e″lek-tris′ĭ-te). Electricity generated by heat.

thermo-esthesia (ther″mo-es-the′ze-ah). Thermesthesia.

thermo-esthesiometer (ther″mo-es-the″ze-om′e-ter). Thermesthesiometer.

thermo-excitory (ther″mo-ek-si′tor-e). Exciting or stimulating the production of heat in the body.

thermogenesis (ther″mo-jen′e-sis) [*thermo-* + Gr. *genesis* production]. The production of heat, especially within the animal body.

thermogenetic (ther″mo-je-net′ik). Pertaining to the production of heat.

thermogenic (ther″mo-jen′ik). Producing heat.

thermogenics (ther″mo-jen′iks). The science relating to heat production.

thermogenous (ther-moj′e-nus). Caused by elevation of temperature, or by heat.

thermogram (ther′mo-gram). 1. A graphic record of variations in temperature (heat). 2. The visual record obtained by thermography.

thermograph (ther′mo-graf). 1. An instrument for recording variations in temperature (heat). 2. A thermogram (def. 2). 3. The apparatus or device employed in thermography.

thermographic (ther″mo-graf′ik). Pertaining to a thermogram or to thermography.

thermography (ther-mog′rah-fe) [*thermo-* + Gr. *graphein* to write]. A technique of photographically portraying the surface temperatures of the body, based on the self-emanating infrared radiation; sometimes employed as a means of diagnosing underlying pathologic processes.

thermohyperalgesia (ther″mo-hi″per-al-je′ze-ah). A condition in which the application of moderate heat causes extreme pain.

thermohyperesthesia (ther″mo-hi″per-es-the′-ze-ah). Extreme sensitiveness to high temperatures.

thermohypesthesia (ther″mo-hi″pes-the′ze-ah). A state of diminished sensitiveness to high temperatures.

thermohypo-esthesia (ther″mo-hi″po-es-the′-ze-ah). Thermohypesthesia.

thermo-inactivation (ther″mo-in-ak″tĭ-va′-shun). Destruction of the power to act by exposure to heat.

thermo-inhibitory (ther″mo-in-hib′ĭ-tor″e). Inhibiting or retarding the production of bodily heat.

thermo-integrator (ther″mo-in′te-gra″tor). An apparatus for recording environmental warmth.

thermolabile (ther″mo-la′bil). Easily altered or decomposed by heat.

thermolamp (ther′mo-lamp) [*thermo-* + Gr. *lampē* torch]. A lamp for heating.

thermolaryngoscope (ther″mo-lah-ring′go-skōp). A laryngoscope heated by electricity so that the mirror does not become obscured by condensing moisture.

thermology (ther-mol′o-je) [*thermo-* + *-logy*]. The science of heat.

thermolysis (ther-mol′ĭ-sis) [*thermo-* + Gr. *lysis* dissolution]. 1. Chemical dissociation by means of heat. 2. The dissipation of bodily heat by means of radiation, evaporation, etc.

thermolytic (ther″mo-lit′ik) [*thermo-* + Gr. *lytikos*

dissolving]. Pertaining to, characterized by, or promoting thermolysis.

thermomassage (ther″mo-mah-sahzh′). Massage with heat.

thermomastography (ther″mo-mas-tog′rah-fe). The use of thermography in the diagnosis of lesions of the breast.

thermometer (ther-mom′e-ter) [*thermo-* + Gr. *metron* measure]. An instrument for determining temperatures. In principle, it makes use of some substance with a physical property that varies in magnitude with temperature, to determine a value of temperature on some defined scale. See also under *scale*. **air t.**, one in which the expansible material is air. **alcohol t.**, a liquid-in-glass thermometer in which alcohol is the liquid used. **axilla t.**, a surface thermometer to be used in the axilla. **Celsius t.**, a thermometer employing the Celsius scale (q.v.). **centigrade t.**, one employing the Celsius scale, that is, having the interval between the two established reference points divided into 100 units. **clinical t.**, one for use in determining temperature of the human body. **depth t.**, a thermometer whose sensitive element may be introduced into the tissues, for registering the actual temperature of a tissue. **differential t.**, one for measuring small differences in temperature. **Fahrenheit t.**, a thermometer employing the Fahrenheit scale (q.v.). **fever t.**, clinical t. **gas t.**, one in which the expansible material is a gas, such as air, carbon dioxide, helium, neon, nitrogen, or oxygen. **half-minute t.**, a clinical thermometer with a short time lag. **kata t.** See *katathermometer*. **Kelvin t.**, a thermometer employing the Kelvin scale (q.v.). **liquid-in-glass t.**, the common type of thermometer, containing a liquid which expands with increase in temperature; most of the liquid is in a bulb, but its free surface is in a capillary tube graduated to indicate the degree of temperature causing expansion to each particular point. **maximum t.**, one which registers the highest temperature to which it has been exposed. **mercurial t.**, a liquid-in-glass thermometer in which mercury is the liquid used. **metallic t.**, one in which some solid metal is used as the expansible element. **metastatic t.**, one which indicates minute changes of temperature. **minimum t.**, one which registers the lowest temperature to which it has been exposed. **oral t.**, a clinical thermometer which is placed under the tongue, to record the temperature in the mouth; characteristically the bulb containing the mercury is elongated. **Rankine t.**, a thermometer employing the Rankine scale (q.v.). **Réaumur t.**, a thermometer employing the Réaumur scale (q.v.). **recording t.**, a temperature-sensitive instrument by which the temperature to which it has been exposed is continuously recorded on a specially designed chart. **rectal t.**, a clinical thermometer which is inserted in the rectum, for determining body temperature; characteristically the bulb containing the mercury is pear shaped. **resistance t.**, a thermometer which uses the electric resistance of metals for determining temperature; it consists of a resistance bulb of platinum or other metal wire, and uses a Wheatstone bridge. **self-registering t.**, recording t. **surface t.**, a clinical thermometer for determining the temperature on the surface of the body. **thermocouple t.**, a combination of a thermocouple with some device for measuring its electromotive force, such as a potentiometer; in use the thermocouple's reference junction is kept at a reference temperature (such as the ice point) and its measuring junction at the temperature being measured. **veterinary t.**, a clinical thermometer for taking the body temperature of animals.

thermometric (ther″mo-met′rik). Pertaining to a thermometer or to the measurement of degrees of temperature.

thermometry (ther-mom′e-tre). The measurement of temperatures.

thermoneurosis (ther″mo-nu-ro′sis). Pyrexia of vasomotor origin.

thermopalpation (ther″mo-pal-pa′shun). Palpation for the purpose of determining differences of temperature at different portions of the body.

thermopenetration (ther″mo-pen″e-tra′shun). Application of currents of low tension and high amperage, which produce warmth in the deeper parts of the body; medical diathermy.

thermophagy (ther-mof′ah-je) [*thermo-* + Gr. *phagein* to eat]. The eating of very hot food.

thermophile (ther′mo-fīl). An organism which grows best at temperatures between 55 and 65°C.

thermophilic (ther″mo-fil′ik) [*thermo-* + Gr. *philein* to love]. Growing best at or having a fondness for high temperatures.

thermophobia (ther″mo-fo′be-ah) [*thermo-* + Gr. *phobein* to be affrighted by]. Morbid dread of high temperatures.

thermophore (ther′mo-fōr) [*thermo-* + Gr. *pherein* to bear]. 1. A device or apparatus for retaining heat. 2. An instrument for estimating heat sensibility.

thermophylic (ther″mo-fi′lik) [*thermo-* + Gr. *phylakē* guard]. Resisting the destructive effects of heat (said of certain bacilli).

thermopile (ther′mo-pīl) [*thermo* + L. *pila* pillar, pile]. A number of thermocouples in series; used to increase the sensitivity for a temperature-measuring device, or for the direct conversion of heat into electric energy.

thermoplastic (ther″mo-plas′tik). Softening under heat and capable of being molded into shape with pressure, then hardening on cooling without undergoing chemical change.

thermoplegia (ther″mo-ple′je-ah) [*thermo-* + Gr. *plēgē* stroke + *-ia*]. Heatstroke or sunstroke; thermic fever.

thermopolypnea (ther″mo-pol″ip-ne′ah) [*thermo-* + Gr. *polys* many + *pnoia* breath]. A quickening of the respiration due to great heat or high temperature.

thermopolypneic (ther″mo-pol″ip-ne′ik). Pertaining to or characterized by thermopolypnea.

thermoprecipitation (ther″mo-pre-sip″ĭ-ta′shun). Precipitation by heat.

thermoprecipitin (ther″mo-pre-sip′ĭ-tin). A heated extract of a bacterium used for precipitin tests.

thermoprecipitinogen (ther″mo-pre-sip″ĭ-tin′o-jen). A heated precipitinogen; when injected into animals coctoprecipitins are produced.

thermoradiotherapy (ther″mo-ra″de-o-ther′ah-pe). A method of applying roentgen rays in combination with a heating of the tissues by thermopenetration on the theory that the radiosensitiveness of tissues is increased by heating them.

thermoreceptor (ther″mo-re-sep′tor). A nerve ending that is sensitive to stimulation by heat.

thermoregulation (ther″mo-reg″u-la′shun). Heat regulation.

thermoregulator (ther″mo-reg′u-la″tor). 1. Controlling or regulating heat. 2. Thermostat.

thermoresistance (ther″mo-re-sis′tans). The quality of being neither readily nor greatly affected by heat.

thermoresistant (ther″mo-re-zis′tant). Neither readily nor greatly affected by heat.

thermoscope (ther′mo-skōp) [*thermo-* + Gr. *skopein* to examine]. A differential thermometer.

thermostabile (ther″mo-sta′bil). Not affected by heat; able to withstand the effects of heat without undergoing change.

thermostability (ther″mo-stah-bil′ĭ-te). The quality of withstanding the effects of heat without undergoing change.

thermostasis (ther″mo-sta′sis) [*thermo-* + Gr. *stasis* a placing, setting]. The maintenance of body temperature in warm-blooded animals.

thermostat (ther′mo-stat) [*thermo-* + Gr. *histanai* to halt]. A device interposed in a heating system by which the temperature can be automatically maintained between certain levels.

thermosteresis (ther″mo-ste-re′sis) [*thermo-* + Gr. *sterēsis* deprivation]. The deprivation of heat.

thermostromuhr (ther″mo-strōm′oor). An instrument for measuring the amount of blood flowing in a blood vessel.

thermosystaltic (ther″mo-sis-tal′tik) [*thermo-* + Gr. *systellein* to contract]. Contracting under the influence or stimulus of heat.

thermosystaltism (ther″mo-sis′tal-tizm) [*thermo-* + Gr. *systellein* to contract]. Muscular contraction in response to temperature changes.

thermotactic (ther″mo-tak′tik). Pertaining to thermotaxis.

thermotaxic (ther″mo-tak′sik). Thermotactic.

thermotaxis (ther″mo-tak′sis) [*thermo-* + Gr. *taxis* arrangement]. 1. The normal adjustment of the bodily temperature. 2. The movement of an organism in response to an increase in temperature.

thermotherapy (ther″mo-ther′ah-pe) [*thermo-* + Gr. *therapeia* treatment]. Treatment of disease by the application of heat.

thermotics (ther-mot′iks). The science of heat.

thermotolerant (ther″mo-tol′er-ant). Enduring heat; said of bacteria whose activity is not checked by high temperature.

thermotonometer (ther″mo-to-nom′e-ter) [*thermo-* + Gr. *tonos* tension + *metron* measure]. An instrument for measuring the amount of muscular contraction caused by heat.

thermotoxin (ther″mo-tok′sin). [*thermo-* + *toxin*]. Any toxic substance formed in the living organism by heat.

thermotracheotomy (ther″mo-tra″ke-ot′o-me). Incision of the trachea by actual cautery.

thermotropism (ther-mot′ro-pizm) [*thermo-* + Gr. *tropē* turn]. The orientation of a living cell in response to the stimulus of heat.

theroid (the′roid) [Gr. *thēriōdēs* beast-like). Resembling an animal of a lower order.

theromorph (the′ro-morf) [Gr. *thēr* wild beast + *morphē* form]. A morphologic part of an organism or individual with supernumerary, teratic, or absent parts, giving it a resemblance to a lower animal.

theromorphism (the″ro-mor′fizm). The abnormal resemblance of some part of the organism to the normal structure of the corresponding part of an animal of lower type.

theruhistin (ther″u-his′tin). Trade mark for preparations of isothipendyl.

thesaurismosis (the-saw″riz-mo′sis) [Gr. *thēsauros* treasure]. A metabolic disorder in which some substance accumulates or is stored in certain cells in unusually large amounts. The stored substances may be lipoids, proteins, carbohydrates and other substances. **amyloid t.,** amyloidosis. **bilirubin t.,** jaundice. **calcium t.,** calcinosis. **collagen t.,** scleroderma. **cholesterol t.,** Schüller-Christian disease. **glycogen t.,** glycogenosis. **kerasin t.,** Gaucher's disease. **lipoid t.,** lipoidosis. **melanin t.,** Addison's disease. **phosphatide t.,** Niemann-Pick disease. **urate t.,** gout. **water t.,** edema.

thesaurosis (the″saw-ro′sis) [Gr. *thēsauros* treasure + *-osis*]. A condition resulting from the storing up in the body of unusual amounts of normal or foreign substance. See *thesaurismosis.*

Thessalus (thes′sah-lus) **of Cos** (4th century B.C.). A Greek physician; the son of Hippocrates, he followed his father's teachings closely.

Thessalus (thes′sah-lus) **of Tralles** (1st century A.D.). A Greek physician of the Methodist school and a pupil of Themison.

thiabendazole (thi″ah-ben′dah-zol). A broad-spectrum anthelmintic with a wide range of activity: found useful in ancylostomiasis and strongyloidiasis.

thiamazole (thi-am′ah-zōl). Methimazole.

thiamine (thi′ah-min). A component of the B complex of vitamins, first isolated in 1926; present in beans, green vegetables, sweet corn, egg yolk, liver, corn meal, and brown rice, and found in blood plasma and cerebrospinal fluid in the free state. **t. hydrochloride,** 3-(4-amino-2-methylpyrimidyl-5-methyl)-4-methyl-5β-hydroxyethylthiazolium chloride hydrochloride, used as a vitamin supplement. **t. mononitrate,** a compound prepared by removing the chloride ions from thiamine hydrochloride and reconstituting the salt by treatment with nitric acid: used like thiamine hydrochloride. **phosphorylated t., t. pyrophosphate,** the active form of thiamine, which serves as the cofactor in reactions involving oxidative decarboxylation of certain important intermediates in carbohydrate metabolism. Called also *cocarboxylase.*

thiamylal (thi-am′ĭ-lal). Chemical name: 5-allyl-5-(1-methylbutyl)-2-thiobarbituric acid. **t. sodium,** the sodium salt of thiamylal, sodium 5-allyl-5-(1-methylbutyl)-2-thiobarbiturate, an ultrashort-acting barbiturate used intravenously to induce general anesthesia for procedures of short duration.

thiasine (thi′ah-sin). A sulfur-containing compound isolated from blood.

thiazole (thi′ah-zōl). The chemical ring

S 1
5 2
4 3
N

Thiele's syndrome (thēlz) [George H. *Thiele,* American proctologist, born 1896]. See under *syndrome.*

Thielmann's diarrhea drops, diarrhea mixture (tēl-manz) [Karl Heinrich *Thielmann,* German internist, 1802–1872]. See under *mixture.*

thiemia (thi-e′me-ah) [Gr. *theion* sulfur + *haima* blood + *-ia*]. The presence of sulfur in the blood.

Thiersch's graft, method (tērsh′ez) [Karl *Thiersch,* German surgeon, 1822–1895]. See under *graft.*

thigh (thi). The portion of the lower extremity situated between the hip above and the knee below. **cricket t.,** rupture of some of the fibers of the rectus femoris, which may occur in playing cricket or football; sometimes the tendon of the quadriceps or that of the patella is also ruptured. **drivers' t.,** sciatic neuralgia caused by pressure from the use of the accelerator in driving an automobile. **Heilbronner's t.,** broadening and flattening of the thigh; seen in cases of organic paralysis when the patient lies on his back on a hard mattress. It does not appear in hysterical paralysis.

thigmesthesia (thig″mes-the′ze-ah) [Gr. *thigma* touch + *aisthēsis* perception + *-ia*]. Tactile sensibility.

thigmocyte (thig′mo-sīt). A blood platelet; so called on the theory that the platelet's function is to adhere to nongreasy matter.

thigmotactic (thig″mo-tak′tik). Pertaining to, characterized by, or causing thigmotaxis.

thigmotaxis (thig″mo-tak′sis). Movement occurring in response to the stimulus of contact or touch, which may be toward (*positive t.*) or away from the stimulating object (*negative t.*).

thigmotropic (thig″mo-trop′ik). Pertaining to or exhibiting thigmotropism; responding to the stimulus of contact or touch.

thigmotropism (thig-mot′ro-pizm) [Gr. *thigma* touch + *tropē* turn]. The orientation of an organism in response to the stimulus of contact or touch.

thimerosal (thi-mer′o-sal). Chemical name: sodium ethylmercurithiosalicylate: used as a local antibacterial.

thimethaphan (thi-meth′ah-fan). Trimethaphan.

thio- (thi′o) [Gr. *theion* sulfur]. A prefix signifying the presence of sulfur.

thio-acid (thi″o-as′id). An organic compound produced by replacement of some of the oxygen of the carboxyl group by divalent sulfur.

thio-albumose (thi″o-al′bu-mōs). A deutero-albumose having a large sulfur content.

thio-alcohol (thi″o-al′ko-hol). Mercaptan.

thio-arsenite (thi″o-ar′se-nīt). Any compound of sulfur and arsenic of the type K_3AsS_3.

Thiobacillus (thi″o-bah-sil′lus). A genus of microorganisms of the family Thiobacteriaceae, suborder Pseudomonadineae, order Pseudomonadales, occurring as small, gram-negative, rod-shaped cells. It includes nine species, *T. concreti′vorus*, *T. coprolit′icus*, *T. denitri′ficans*, *T. ferroox′idans*, *T. neopolita′nus*, *T. novel′lus*, *T. thioox′idans*, *T. thio′parus*, and *T. trautwei′nii.*

Thiobacteriaceae (thi″o-bak-te″re-a′se-e). A family of chemosynthetic microorganisms (order Pseudomonadales, suborder Pseudomonadineae) occurring as coccoid or straight or curved rod-shaped cells which oxidize sulfur compounds, usually depositing free sulfur granules inside or outside the cells. It includes five genera, *Macromonas, Thiobacillus, Thiobacterium, Thiospira,* and *Thiovulum.*

Thiobacterium (thi″o-bak-te′re-um). A genus of microorganisms of the family Thiobacteriaceae, suborder Pseudomonadineae, order Pseudomonadales, occurring as rod-shaped sulfur bacteria in fresh or salt water or in the soil. It includes three species, *T. bovis′ta*, *T. crystallif′erum*, and *T. retifor′mans.*

Thiocapsa (thi″o-kap′sah) [*thio-* + Gr. *kapsa* a case, casket]. A genus of microorganisms of the family Thiorhodaceae, suborder Rhodobacteriineae, order Pseudomonadales, occurring as spherical cells within a slime capsule. It includes two species, *T. florida′na* and *T. roseopersici′na.*

thiocarbamide (thi″o-kar′bah-mīd). Thiourea.

thiochrome (thi″o-krōm). The yellow coloring matter of yeast, $C_{12}H_{14}ON_4S$.

thiocyanate (thi″o-si′ah-nat). A salt analogous in composition to a cyanate, but containing sulfur instead of oxygen. Also called *sulfocyanate.*

Thiocystis (thi″o-sis′tis) [*thio-* + Gr. *kystis* sac, bladder]. A genus of microorganisms of the family Thiorhodaceae, suborder Rhodobacteriineae, order Pseudomonadales, occurring as spherical to ovoid cells embedded in a common gelatinous capsule. It includes two species, *T. ru′fa* and *T. viola′cea.*

Thioderma (thi″o-der′mah) [*thio-* + Gr. *derma* skin]. A name formerly given a genus of sulfur bacteria.

Thiodictyon (thi″o-dik′te-on) [*thio-* + Gr. *diktyon* net]. A genus of microorganisms of the family Thiorhodaceae, suborder Rhodobacteriineae, order Pseudomonadales, occurring as rod-shaped cells arranged end to end in a netlike structure. The type species is *T. el′egans.*

thiodiphenylamine (thi″o-di-fen″il-am′in). Phenothiazine.

thiodotherapy (thi′o-do-ther′ah-pe) [*thio-* + *iodine* + *therapy*]. Combined sulfur and iodine therapy.

thio-ether (thi″o-e′ther). A sulfur ether; an ether in which sulfur replaces oxygen.

thioethylamine (thi″o-eth″il-am′in). An amine, $SH(CH_2)_2NH_2$, formed from cysteine by the loss of CO_2.

thioflavine (thi″o-fla′vin) [*thio-* + *flavine*]. A yellow dye, methyl dehydrothio-p-toluidine sulfonate.

thiogenic (thi″o-jen′ik) [*thio-* + Gr. *gennan* to produce]. Able to convert hydrogen sulfide into higher sulfur compounds.

thioglucose (thi″o-glu′kōs). A glucose that contains a sulfhydryl group.

thiol (thi′ol). Sulfhydryl.

thiolhistidine (thi″ol-his′tĭ-din). One of the amino acids.

thiolin (thi′o-lin). A dark-green substance prepared by boiling 1 part of sulfur in 6 parts of linseed oil, and treating the product with sulfuric acid: used like ichthyol in skin diseases. Called also *thiolinic acid*

thiomerin (thi-o′mer-in). Trade mark for preparations of mercaptomerin.

thiomersalate (thi″o-mer′sah-lāt). Thimerosal.

thioneine (thi″o-ne′in) [Gr. *theion* sulfur + *neos* new]. Ergothioneine.

thionic (thi-on′ik). Pertaining to sulfur.

thionine (thi′o-nin). A dark-green dye or stain, aminophenthiazin, $NH_2.C_6H_3(NS).C_6H_3.NH_5$, giving a purple color in solution, and used as a stain in microscopy. **t. hydrochloride,** a purple stain. Called also *Lauth's violet.*

thionyl (thi′o-nil). The radical SO.

thiopectic (thi″o-pek′tik). Fixing sulfur.

Thiopedia (thi″o-pe′de-ah) [*thio-* + Gr. *pedion* a plain]. A genus of microorganisms of the family Thiorhodaceae, suborder Rhodobacteriineae, order Pseudomonadales, occurring as spherical to short rod-shaped cells. The type species is *T. ro′sea.*

thiopental (thi″o-pen′tal). Chemical name: 5-ethyl-5-(1-methylbutyl)-2-thiobarbituric acid. **t. sodium,** the sodium salt of thiopental, sodium 5-ethyl-5-(1-methylbutyl)-2-thiobarbiturate, used intravenously or rectally to induce general anesthesia.

thiopentone (thi″o-pen′tōn). Thiopental.

thiopexic (thi″o-pek′sik). Thiopectic.

thiopexy (thi″o-pek′se) [*thio-* + Gr. *pēxis* fixation]. The fixation of sulfur.

thiophil (thi′o-fil). 1. A thiophilic organism. 2. Thiophilic.

thiophilic (thi″o-fil′ik) [Gr. *theion* sulfur + *philein* to love]. Growing successfully in the presence of sulfur or sulfur compounds.

Thiopolycoccus (thi″o-pol″e-kok′kus). A genus of microorganisms of the family Thiorhodaceae, suborder Rhodobacteriineae, order Pseudomonadales, occurring as spherical cells in irregularly shaped dense aggregates, held together by mucus. The type species *T. ru′ber.*

thiopropazate (thi″o-pro′pah-zāt). Chemical name: 2-chloro-10-{3-[4-(2-acetoxyethyl)piperazinyl]propyl} phenothiazine: used as a tranquilizer.

Thiorhodaceae (thi″o-ro-da′se-e). A family of Schizomycetes (order Pseudomonadales, suborder Rhodobacteriineae), occurring in environments containing sulfides, requiring light but little or no oxygen, and producing a pigment system composed of green bacteriochlorophyll and yellow and red carotenoids. It includes 13 genera: *Amoebobacter, Chromatium, Lamprocystis, Rhabdomonas, Rhodothece, Thiocapsa, Thiocystis, Thiodictyon, Thiopedia, Thiopolycoccus, Thiosarcina, Thiospirillum,* and *Thiothece.*

thioridazine (thi″o-rid′ah-zēn). Chemical name: 2-methylmercapto-10-[2-(N-methyl-2-piperidyl)-ethyl]phenothiazine: used as a tranquilizer.

Thiosarcina (thi″o-sar-si′nah). A genus of microorganisms of the family Thiorhodaceae, suborder Rhodobacteriineae, order Pseudomonadales, occurring as sperical cells in cubical packets. The type species is *T. ro′sea.*

thiosinamine (thi″o-sin′ah-min). A bitter, crystalline substance, $(NH_2)CS.NHCH_2CH{:}CH_2$, allyl sulfocarbamide or allyl thiourea, from oil of mustard and ammonia; used as a resolvent for scar structures, etc., and in lupus, tuberculosis, and arsphenamine dermatitis.

Thiospira (thi″o-spi′rah). A genus of microorganisms of the family Thiobacteriaceae, suborder Pseudomonadineae, order Pseudomonadales, occurring as colorless, slightly bent, large rods with a small number of polar flagella and containing sulfur granules within the cells. It includes two species, *T. bipuncta′ta* and *T. winograd′skyi.*

Thiospirillum (thi″o-spi-ril′lum). A genus of microorganisms of the family Thiorhodaceae, suborder Rhodobacteriineae, order Pseudomonadales, occurring singly as spirally wound cells. It includes five species, *T. jenen'se, T. rosenber'gii, T. ru'fum, T. sangui'neum*, and *T. viola'ceum.*

thiosulfate (thi″o-sul′fāt). Any salt of thiosulfuric acid.

thio-tepa (thi″o-te′pah). Chemical name: tris(1-aziridinyl)phosphine sulfide: used as a neoplastic suppressant.

Thiothece (thi″o-the′se). A genus of microorganisms of the family Thiorhodaceae, suborder Rhodobacteriineae, order Pseudomonadales, occurring as spherical to elongated cells embedded in a gelatinous capsule. The type species is *T. gelatino'sa.*

thiouracil (thi″o-u′rah-sil). A thiourea derivative, 2-mercapto-4-pyrimidone, which affects adversely the synthesis of the thyroid hormone.

Thiovulum (thi-o′vu-lum). A genus of microorganisms of the family Thiobacteriaceae, suborder Pseudomonadineae, order Pseudomonadales, occurring as round to ovoid unicellular organisms, normally containing sulfur in the cytoplasm. The type species is *T. ma'jus.*

thiozine (thi′o-zin). Ergothioneine.

third intention. See under *healing.*

thirst (therst) [L. *sitis*, Gr. *dipsa*]. A sensation, often referred to the mouth and throat, associated with a craving for drink; ordinarily interpreted as a desire for water. **false t.,** thirst which is not associated with a bodily need for water and is not satisfied by the intake of water. **insensible t.,** subliminal t. **real t.,** true t. **subliminal t.,** a sensation of need for water which is insufficient to prompt the ingestion of water but is at times sufficient to maintain drinking once it is initiated. **true t.,** thirst which is associated with a bodily need for water and is satisfied by the ingestion of water. **twilight t.,** subliminal t.

Thiry's fistula (thi′rēz) [Ludwig *Thiry*, Austrian physiologist, 1817–1897]. See under *fistula.*

thixokon (thik′so-kon). Trade mark for a preparation of acetrozoate sodium.

thixolabile (thik″so-la′bil). Easily affected by shaking.

thixotropic (thik″so-trop′ik). Pertaining to or characterized by thixotropy.

thixotropism (thik-sot′ro-pizm). Thixotropy.

thixotropy (thik-sot′ro-pe) [Gr. *thixis* a touch + *tropos* a turning]. The property, exhibited by certain gels, of becoming fluid when shaken and then becoming solid again.

thlipsencephalus (thlip″sen-sef′ah-lus) [Gr. *thlipsis* pressure + *enkephalos* brain]. A monster with a deficient skull, or with the upper part of the skull lacking.

thoko (tho′ko). A skin disease endemic in Fiji; probably yaws.

Thoma's ampulla, fluid (to′mahz) [Richard *Thoma*, German histologist, 1847 1923]. See under *ampulla* and *fluid.*

Thoma-Zeiss counting cell, chamber (to′-mah-zīs) [Richard *Thoma;* Carl *Zeiss*, German optician, 1816–1888]. See under *chamber.*

Thomas' pessary (tom′as) [Theodore Gaillard *Thomas*, New York gynecologist, 1831–1903]. See under *pessary.*

Thomas' splint (tom′as) [Hugh Owen *Thomas*, surgeon in Liverpool, 1834–1891]. See under *splint.*

Thomayer's sign (to′mi-erz) [Josef *Thomayer*, Czech internist in Prague, 1853–1925]. See under *sign.*

Thompson's solution (tom′sonz) [Ashburton *Thompson*, English physician of the 19th century]. See under *solution.*

Thompson's test (tom′sonz) [Sir Henry *Thompson*, English surgeon, 1820–1904]. See under *tests.*

Thomsen's disease (tom′senz) [Asmus Julius *Thomsen*, Danish physician, 1815–1896]. Myotonia congenita.

Thomsen's phenomenon (tom′senz) [Oluf *Thomsen*, Danish physician, 1878–1940]. See under *phenomenon.*

Thomson's fascia (tom′sunz) [Allen *Thomson*, Scottish anatomist, 1809–1884]. See under *fascia.*

Thomson's sign (tom′sunz) [Frederick Holland *Thomson*, British physician, 1867–1938]. Pastia's sign. See under *sign.*

thomsonianism (tom-so′ne-an-izm) [Samuel *Thomson*, a New Hampshire farmer, 1769–1843]. An empiric system of medical practice, chiefly based on use of plants as remedies.

thonzylamine (thon-zil′ah-mīn). Chemical name: 2-[(2-dimethylaminoethyl)(p-methoxybenzyl)amino]pyrimidine: used as an antihistaminic.

thoracal (tho′rah-kal). Thoracic.

thoracalgia (tho″rah-kal′je-ah). Pain in the chest wall.

thoracectomy (tho″rah-sek′to-me) [*thoraco-* + Gr. *ektomē* excision]. Thoracotomy with resection of a portion of a rib.

thoracentesis (tho″rah-sen-te′sis). Thoracocentesis.

thoracic (tho-ras′ik) [L. *thoracicus;* Gr. *thōrakikos*]. Pertaining to the chest.

thoracico-abdominal (tho-ras″ĭ-ko-ab-dom′ĭ-nal). Pertaining to the thorax and abdomen.

thoracicohumeral (tho-ras″ĭ-ko-hu′mer-al). Pertaining to the thorax and the humerus.

thoracispinal (tho-ras″ĭ-spi′nal). Pertaining to the thoracic portion of the spinal column.

thoraco- (tho′rah-ko) [Gr. *thōrax, thōrakos* chest]. Combining form denoting relationship to the chest.

thoracobronchotomy (tho″rah-ko-brong-kot′o-me). Incision into the bronchus through the thoracic wall.

thoracocautery (tho″rah-ko-kaw′ter-e). The division by cautery of adhesion to complete the collapse of the lung in pneumothorax therapy.

thoracoceloschisis (tho″rah-ko-se-los′kĭ-sis) [*thoraco-* + Gr. *koilia* belly + *schisis* fissure]. Fissure of the thorax and abdomen.

thoracocentesis (tho″rah-ko-sen-te′sis) [*thoraco-* + Gr. *kentēsis* puncture]. Surgical puncture of the chest wall for drainage of fluid. Called also *paracentesis thoracis* and *pleuracentesis.*

thoracocyllosis (tho″rah-ko-si-lo′sis) [*thoraco-* + Gr. *kyllōsis* crippling]. Deformity of the chest.

thoracocyrtosis (tho″rah-ko-sir-to′sis) [*thoraco-* + Gr. *kyrtōsis* a being humpbacked]. Abnormal curvature of the thorax, or unusual prominence of the chest.

thoracodelphus (tho″rah-ko-del′fus) [*thoraco-* + Gr. *adelphos* brother]. A double monster with one head, two arms, and four legs, the bodies being joined above the navel.

thoracodidymus (tho″rah-ko-did′ĭ-mus) [*thoraco-* + Gr. *didymos* twin]. Conjoined twins united at the thorax.

thoracodynia (tho″rah-ko-din′e-ah) [*thoraco-* + Gr. *odynē* pain]. Pain in the chest.

thoracogastrodidymus (tho″rah-ko-gas″tro-did′ĭ-mus) [*thoraco-* + Gr. *gastēr* belly + *didymos* twin]. Conjoined twins united at the belly and chest.

thoracogastroschisis (tho″rah-ko-gas-tros′kĭ-sis) [*thoraco-* + Gr. *gastēr* belly + *schisis* fissure]. Fissure of the thorax and abdomen.

thoracograph (tho-rak′o-graf) [*thoraco-* + Gr. *graphein* to write]. An apparatus for obtaining diagrams showing the movements of the chest during respiration.

thoracolaparotomy (tho″rah-ko-lap″ah-rot′o-me) [*thoraco-* + Gr. *lapara* loin + *tomē* a cutting]. Incision through both the thorax and abdomen to gain access to the subphrenic space and adjoining regions.

thoracolumbar (tho″rah-ko-lum′bar). Pertaining to the thoracic and lumbar parts of the spine.

thoracolysis (tho″rah-kol′ĭ-sis) [*thoraco-* + Gr. *lysis* dissolution]. The freeing of the chest wall from adhesions by removal of the precordial ribs. **t. praecordi′aca,** cardiolysis.

thoracomelus (tho″rah-kom′e-lus) [*thoraco-* + Gr. *melos* limb]. A fetal monster with a supernumerary arm or leg attached to the thorax.

thoracometer (tho″rah-kom′e-ter) [*thoraco-* + Gr. *metron* measure]. Stethometer.

thoracometry (tho″rah-kom′e-tre). Measurement of the thorax.

thoracomyodynia (tho″rah-ko-mi″o-din′e-ah) [*thoraco-* + Gr. *mys* muscle + *odynē* pain]. Pain in the muscles of the chest.

thoracopagus (tho″rah-kop′ah-gus) [*thoraco-* + Gr. *pagos* thing fixed]. A double fetal monster consisting of two nearly complete individuals joined in or near the sternal region, so the two components are face to face. **t. epigas′tricus,** an asymmetrical double monster in which the parasitic component is attached to the epigastric region of the autosite. **t. parasit′icus,** an asymmetrical double monster in which the parasitic component is attached to the thorax of the autosite.

thoracoparacephalus (tho″rah-ko-par″ah-sef′ah-lus) [*thoraco-* + Gr. *para* beside + *kephalē* head]. Asymmetrical conjoined twins, a parasite with rudimentary head being attached to the thorax of the autosite.

thoracopathy (tho″rah-kop′ah-the) [*thoraco-* + Gr. *pathos* disease]. Any disease of the thorax or of the thoracic organs.

thoracoplasty (tho″rah-ko-plas′te) [*thoraco-* + Gr. *plassein* to mold]. Plastic surgery of the thorax; operative repair of defects of the chest. **costoversion t.,** removal of several ribs and their replacement "inside out," with one rib placed vertically as a strut, providing a concave bony framework, to keep the underlying lung permanently collapsed.

thoracopneumograph (tho″rah-ko-nu′mo-graf) [*thoraco-* + Gr. *pneuma* breath + *graphein* to write]. An instrument for recording the respiratory movements of the chest.

thoracopneumoplasty (tho″rah-ko-nu′mo-plas″te) [*thoraco-* + Gr. *pneumōn* lung + *plassein* to form]. Plastic surgical operation involving the chest and lung.

thoracoschisis (tho″rah-kos′kĭ-sis) [*thoraco-* + Gr. *schisis* fissure]. Congenital fissure of the chest.

thoracoscope (tho-ra′ko-skōp). 1. An endoscope for examining the pleural cavity; it is pushed into the cavity through an intercostal space. 2. A stethoscope.

thoracoscopy (tho″rah-kos′ko-pe) [*thoraco-* + Gr. *skopein* to examine]. The diagnostic examination of the chest; specifically, the direct examination of the pleural cavity by means of the endoscope; pleural endoscopy.

thoracostenosis (tho″rah-ko-ste-no′sis) [*thoraco-* + Gr. *stenōsis* contraction]. Abnormal contraction of the chest wall.

thoracostomy (tho″rah-kos′to-me) [*thoraco-* + Gr. *stomoun* to provide with an opening, or mouth]. Surgical creation of an opening in the wall of the chest for the purpose of drainage.

thoracotomy (tho″rah-kot′o-me) [*thoraco-* + Gr. *tomē* a cutting]. Surgical incision of the wall of the chest.

thoradelphus (tho″rah-del′fus). Thoracodelphus.

thorax (tho′raks), pl. *tho′races* [Gr. *thōrax*]. [N A, B N A] The part of the body between the neck and the respiratory diaphragm, encased by the ribs; the chest. **amazon t.,** a chest with only one mammary gland, or breast. **t. asthen′icus,** t. paralyticus. **barrel-shaped t.,** a malformed chest which is rounded like a barrel; seen in pulmonary emphysema. **cholesterol t.,** accumulation in the pleural cavities of fluid with a high cholesterol content. **t. paralyt′icus,** the long flat thorax of patients with constitutional visceroptosis. **Peyrot's t.,** a chest that is obliquely oval: seen in large pleural effusions. **pyriform t.,** a pear-shaped thorax, large above, small below.

thorazine (thor′ah-zēn). Trade mark for preparations of chlorpromazine hydrochloride.

Thorel's bundle (to′relz) [Ch. *Thorel,* German physician, 1868–1935]. See under *bundle.*

thoriagram (tho′re-ah-gram) [*thorium* + Gr. *gramma* mark]. A photograph made with thorium.

thorium (tho′re-um) [*Thor,* a Norse deity]. A rare, heavy gray metal, atomic number, 90; atomic weight, 232.038; symbol, Th. A radioactive metal with a half-life of the order of 10^{10} years, thorium is the parent element of a radioactive disintegration series. Because of its radiopacity, various compounds of thorium have been used to facilitate visualization in roentgenography. **t. D,** the last element of the disintegration series derived from thorium, a stable isotope of lead with an atomic weight of 208. **t. dioxide,** ThO_2, used in roentgenography of the alimentary tract. **t. nitrate,** $Th(NO_3)_4.4H_2O$, used externally in parasitic skin diseases and internally in rheumatism. **sodium t. tartrate,** used in roentgenography, especially of the gastrointestinal tract. **t. X,** a radioactive element produced by disintegration of thorium, and an isotope of radium with a half-life of about $3\frac{2}{3}$ days: used in treatment of superficial skin conditions.

Thormählen's test (tor′ma-lenz) [Johann *Thormählen,* German physician]. See under *tests.*

Thornton's sign (thorn′tonz) [Knowsley *Thornton,* British physician, 1845–1904]. See under *sign.*

thoron (tho′ron). Thorium emanation.

thoroughpin (thur′o-pin). A distention of the synovial sheath of the flexor perforans tendon of the horse at the hock joint; also a similar distention on the carpal joint of the foreleg.

thread (thred). A long slender structure, such as a continuous filament of some substance used as suture material. **celluloid t.,** sterilized linen thread impregnated with celluloid solution, used for ligatures and sutures. **t's of Golgi-Rezzonico,** threads of nerve tissue in the incisure of Lanterman surrounding the axis-cylinder in a spiral arrangement: called also *apparatus of Rezzonico.* **Pagenstecher's linen t.,** ordinary linen thread which has been immersed in a solution of celluloid: used as a suture material. **Simonart's t.,** a band formed by the stretching of adhesions between the amnion and fetus when the amniotic cavity is distended with its proper fluid.

threadworm (thred′wurm). Any nematode worm, especially *Enterobius vermicularis.*

thremmatology (threm″ah-tol′o-je) [Gr. *thremma* nursling + *logos* treatise]. The science of the laws of heredity and variation.

threonine (thre′o-nin). An alpha-amino acid, an isomeric form of alpha-amino beta-hydroxy normal butyric acid, $CH_3.CH(OH).CH(NH_2).COOH$: essential for optimal growth in infants and for nitrogen equilibrium in adults.

threose (thre′ōs). A sugar, $C_4H_8O_4$, isomeric with erythrose.

threpsis (threp′sis) [Gr.]. Nutrition.

threpsology (threp-sol′o-je) [Gr. *threpsis* nutrition + *-logy*]. The sum of what is known concerning nutrition; the science of nutrition.

threptic (threp′tik). Pertaining to nutrition; pertaining to the nurturing of offspring by the parents, especially in certain insect species.

threshold (thresh′old). 1. That value at which a stimulus just produces a sensation, is just appreciable, or comes just within the limits of perception. Called also *schwelle.* 2. That degree of concentration of a substance in the blood plasm above which the substance is excreted by the kidneys and below which it is not excreted; such a substance is called a *threshold body.* **absolute t.,**

the lowest possible limit of stimulation that is capable of producing sensation. Called also *stimulus t.* **achromatic t.,** the least intensity of the spectrum that produces a sensation of color. Reduction of intensity below this point produces a sensation of brightness only, without any color distinction. **auditory t.,** the *mini'mum audib'ile*, or slightest perceptible sound. **t. of consciousness,** the *mini'mum sensib'ile*, or lowest limit of sensibility; the point of consciousness at which a stimulus is barely perceived. **convulsant t.,** the minimum amount of electric current or drug required to produce a convulsion in shock treatment. **differential t.,** the lowest limit of discriminative sensibility; the ratio which the difference of two stimuli must bear to half their sum in order that their difference may be just perceptible. **displacement t.,** the threshold of perception of a break in the continuity of a contour or of a border. **double point t.,** the smallest distance apart at which two stimuli of touch are felt as distinct. **erythema t.,** the radioactive dose which just begins to cause erythema of the skin. **flicker fusion t.,** the frequency at which a flickering light just appears to be continuous. See *flicker test*, under *test*. **galvanic t.,** rheobasis. **neuron t.,** that degree of stimulation of a neuron which just suffices to call forth a fruitful excitation (sensation, movement, or the like) in a neuron. **t. of nose,** limen nasi. **parasite t.,** pyrogenic t. **pyrogenic t.,** the number of malarial parasites required to be in the blood to produce fever. **relational t.,** the ratio which two stimuli must have to each other in order that the difference between them may be just perceptible. **renal t.,** that concentration of a substance that is necessary in the blood before more than a normal quantity of it is eliminated in the urine. **resolution t.,** minimum separabile. **sensitivity t., stimulus t.,** absolute t. **swallowing t.,** the minimal stimulation necessary to elicit the reflex action that leads to swallowing. **t. of visual sensation,** the least possible amount of stimulus that gives rise to the sensation of sight.

thrill (thril). A tremor or vibration felt on applying the hand or finger-tips to the body and due to a fremitus. **aneurysmal t.,** the vibratory sensation felt on the palpation of an aneurysm. **aortic t.,** a thrill perceptible over the aortic orifice in disease of its valves. **diastolic t.,** the vibratory sensation felt over the precordium in advanced aortic insufficiency. **fat t.,** a peculiar thrill sometimes felt in abdominal examinations due to excessive fatness of the parietes. **hydatid t.,** a vibration felt on percussing over a hydatid cyst. **presystolic t.,** a thrill occasionally felt just before the systole by the hand placed over the apex of the heart. **purring t.,** a thrill of a quality suggesting the purring of a cat. **systolic t.,** a thrill felt on systole over the precordium in aortic stenosis, pulmonary stenosis and aneurysm of the ascending aorta.

thrix (thriks) [Gr.]. Hair; used as a word termination denoting a resemblance or a relationship to hair. **t. annula'ta,** ringed hair.

throat (thrōt). 1. The pharynx. 2. The fauces. 3. The anterior part of the neck. **sore t.** See *sore throat*, under S. **trench t.,** Vincent's angina.

throb (throb). A pulsating movement or sensation.

throbbing (throb'ing). Beating; attended with a beating sensation.

Throckmorton's reflex [Thomas Bentley *Throckmorton*, American neurologist, born 1885]. See under *reflex*.

throe (thro). A severe pain or paroxysm.

thromballosis (throm″bah-lo'sis). The condition of the venous blood produced by coagulation.

thrombase (throm'bās). Thrombin.

thrombasthenia (throm″bas-the'ne-ah) [*thrombocyte* + Gr. *astheneia* weakness]. A functional defect of blood platelets, especially a deficiency of platelet clot retracting factor. **Glanzmann's t.,** a condition resulting from a qualitative disorder of blood platelets, characterized by prolonged bleeding time, abnormal clot retraction, and decreased spreading and adhesiveness of platelets, probably due to deficiency of certain enzymes and adenosine triphosphate in the platelets. It is inherited, and is manifested clinically by ease of bruising, purpura, and bleeding from mucous membranes. Called also *constitutional thrombocytopathy*.

thrombectomy (throm-bek'to-me) [Gr. *thrombos* clot + *ektomē* excision]. Removal of a thrombus from a blood vessel; properly indicative of such removal by excision. **medical t.,** enzymatic dissolution of a blood clot in situ.

thrombembolia (throm″bem-bo'le-ah). Thromboembolism.

thrombin (throm'bin). The enzyme derived from prothrombin which converts fibrinogen to fibrin. Called also *thrombase* and *fibrin ferment*. A pharmaceutical preparation (*topical t.*), a sterile protein substance prepared from prothrombin of bovine origin through interaction with added thromboplastin in the presence of calcium, is used therapeutically as a local hemostatic.

thrombinogen (throm-bin'o-jen). Prothrombin.

thrombo- (throm'bo) [Gr. *thrombos* clot]. Combining form denoting relationship to a clot, or thrombus.

thromboangiitis (throm″bo-an″je-i'tis) [*thrombo-* + Gr. *angeion* vessel + *-itis*]. Inflammation of the intima of a blood vessel with clot formation. **t. oblit'erans,** an inflammatory and obliterative disease of the blood vessels of the extremities, more frequently the lower extremities, occurring chiefly in young men and leading to ischemia of the tissues and gangrene. Called also *Buerger's disease* and *presenile spontaneous gangrene*.

thromboarteritis (throm″bo-ar″ter-i'tis). Thrombosis occurring in association with inflammation of an artery. **t. purulen'ta,** purulent softening of an arterial thrombosis, with infiltration of the artery walls.

thrombocinase (throm″bo-ki'nās). Thrombokinase.

thromboclasis (throm-bok'lah-sis) [*thrombo-* + Gr. *klasis* a breaking]. The breaking up or dissolution of a thrombus.

thromboclastic (throm″bo-klas'tik). Breaking up thrombi.

thrombocyst (throm'bo-sist) [*thrombo-* + Gr. *kystis* cyst]. The sac which forms around a clot or thrombus.

thrombocystis (throm″bo-sis'tis). Thrombocyst.

thrombocyte (throm'bo-sīt) [*thrombo-* + Gr. *kytos* hollow vessel]. A blood platelet.

thrombocythemia (throm″bo-sĭ-the'me-ah) [*thrombocyte* + Gr. *haima* blood + *-ia*]. A fixed increase in the number of circulating blood platelets. Called also *piastrinemia*. **essential t.,** hemorrhagic t. **hemorrhagic t.,** a clinical syndrome characterized by repeated spontaneous hemorrhages, either external or into the tissues, and a remarkable increase in the number of circulating platelets; regarded as one of the myeloproliferative syndromes. Called also *essential, idiopathic*, or *primary thrombocythemia*, and *megakaryocytic leukemia*. **idiopathic t., primary t.,** hemorrhagic t.

thrombocytin (throm″bo-si'tin). Serotonin.

thrombocytocrit (throm″bo-si'to-krit) [*thrombocyte* + Gr. *krinein* to separate]. An instrument used to measure the volume of packed blood platelets in a given quantity of blood.

thrombocytolysin (throm″bo-si-tol'ĭ-sin). Factor VIII. See under *coagulation factors*.

thrombocytolysis (throm″bo-si-tol'ĭ-sis). Destruction of blood platelets (thrombocytes).

thrombocytopathic (throm″bo-si″to-path'ik). Pertaining to or characterized by thrombocytopathy.

thrombocytopathy (throm″bo-si-top'ah-the). A

general term applied to a qualitative disorder of the blood platelets; sometimes used to designate specifically a qualitative abnormality due mainly to deficiency of platelet factor 3, causing defective generation of intrinsic thromboplastin. **constitutional t.,** Glanzmann's thrombasthenia.

thrombocytopen (throm″bo-si′to-pen). A substance obtained from the spleen of patients with purpura hemorrhagica, originally thought to be specific in its induction of thrombocytopenia in rabbits but no longer so considered, since similar effects may be obtained with other organ extracts.

thrombocytopenia (throm″bo-si″to-pe′ne-ah). [*thrombocyte* + Gr. *penia* poverty]. Decrease in the number of blood platelets. **essential t.,** idiopathic thrombocytopenic purpura. **malignant t.,** aleukia haemorrhagica.

thrombocytopoiesis (throm″bo-si″to-poi-e′sis) [*thrombocyte* + Gr. *poiēsis* a making, creation]. The production of blood platelets.

thrombocytopoietic (throm″bo-si″to-poi-et′ik). Concerned in the formation of thrombocytes.

thrombocytosis (throm″bo-si-to′sis). An unusually large number of thrombocytes in the blood.

thrombocytozyme (throm″bo-si′to-zīm). Cytozyme from thrombocytes.

thromboelastogram (throm″bo-e-las′to-gram). The graphic record of the values determined by thromboelastography.

thromboelastograph (throm″bo-e-las′to-graf). An apparatus used in study of the rigidity of blood or plasma during coagulation.

thromboelastography (throm″bo-e″las-tog′rah-fe). Determination of the rigidity of the blood or plasma during coagulation, by use of the thromboelastograph.

thromboembolia (throm″bo-em-bo′le-ah). Thromboembolism.

thromboembolism (throm″bo-em′bo-lizm). Obstruction of a blood vessel with a thrombus which has broken loose from its site of formation.

thromboendarterectomy (throm″bo-end″ar-ter-ek′to-me) [*thrombo-* + Gr. *endon* within + *artēria* artery + *ektomē* excision]. Removal of an obstructing thrombus together with the inner lining of an obstructed artery. **coronary t.,** excision of blood clot and the intima from an occluded coronary artery.

thromboendarteritis (throm″bo-end-ar″ter-i′tis). Inflammation of the innermost coat of an artery, with thrombus formation.

thromboendocarditis (throm″bo-en″do-kar-di′tis). 1. Deposition of a blood clot on a heart valve which has previously been eroded. 2. An infectious disease of rabbits.

thrombogen (throm′bo-jen) [*thrombo-* + Gr. *gennan* to produce]. Prothrombin.

thrombogenesis (throm″bo-jen′e-sis). The formation of blood clots.

thrombogenic (throm″bo-jen′ik) [*thrombo-* + Gr. *gennan* to produce]. Producing a clot, curd, or coagulum.

thromboid (throm′boid) [Gr. *thromboeidēs*]. Resembling a thrombus.

thrombokinase (throm″bo-kin′ās). Thromboplastin.

thrombokinesis (throm″bo-ki-ne′sis) [*thrombo-* + Gr. *kinēsis* motion]. The formation of a blood clot; clotting of blood.

thrombolymphangitis (throm″bo-lim″fan-ji′tis). Inflammation of a lymph vessel due to a thrombus.

thrombolysis (throm-bol′ĭ-sis) [*thrombo-* + Gr. *lysis* dissolution]. The phenomenon by which preformed thrombi are lysed by a complex series of events, the most important of which involves the local action of plasmin confined within the substance of the thrombus.

thrombolytic (throm″bo-lit′ik). Dissolving or splitting up a thrombus.

thrombometer (throm-bom′e-ter) [*thrombo-* + Gr. *metron* measure]. An apparatus for determining whether a given blood has a tendency to form thrombi.

thrombon (throm′bon) [*thrombo-* + Gr. *on* neuter ending]. The element of the blood consisting of the platelets and their precursors.

thrombopathia (throm″bo-path′e-ah). Thrombocytopathy.

thrombopathy (throm-bop′ah-the). Thrombocytopathy. **constitutional t.,** Glanzmann's thrombasthenia.

thrombopenia (throm″bo-pe′ne-ah). Thrombocytopenia. **essential t.,** idiopathic thrombocytopenic purpura.

thrombopeny (throm′bo-pe″ne). Thrombocytopenia.

thrombophilia (throm″bo-fil′e-ah) [*thrombo-* + Gr. *philein* to love]. A tendency to the occurrence of thrombosis.

thrombophlebitis (throm″bo-fle-bi′tis) [*thrombo-* + Gr. *phleps* vein + *-itis*]. A condition in which inflammation of the vein wall has preceded the formation of the thrombus. Cf. *phlebothrombosis*. **iliofemoral t., postpartum,** thrombophlebitis of the iliofemoral vein following childbirth. Called also *phlegmasia alba dolens puerperarum*. **t. mi′grans,** a recurring migratory phlebitis usually affecting segments of superficial peripheral veins, and sometimes involving major and visceral veins; it may occur in multiple sites simultaneously or at intervals. **t. purulen′ta,** thrombophlebitis with purulent softening of the thrombus, and infiltration of the wall of the vessel. **t. sal′tans,** thrombophlebitis appearing in different isolated sites.

thrombophthisis (throm″bo-thi′sis) [*thrombocyte* + Gr. *phthisis* wasting]. Destruction of thrombocytes (blood platelets) due to disturbance of bone marrow function.

thromboplastic (throm″bo-plas′tik) [*thrombo-* + Gr. *plassein* to form]. Causing or accelerating clot formation in the blood.

thromboplastid (throm″bo-plas′tid). A blood platelet.

thromboplastin (throm″bo-plas′tin). A factor essential to the production of thrombin and proper hemostasis. Called also *prothrombinase*. **extrinsic t.,** the prothrombin activator formed as the result of interaction of coagulation factors III, V, VII, and X which, with factor IV, aids in the formation of thrombin in the second stage of coagulation: called *extrinsic* because not all of the components required for its production (e.g., factor III, or tissue thromboplastin) are derived from intravascular sources. **intrinsic t.,** the prothrombin activator formed as the result of interaction of coagulation factors V, VIII, IX, X, XI, and XII and platelet factor 3 which, with factor IV, aids in the conversion of prothrombin to thrombin in the second stage of coagulation: called *intrinsic* because the components required for its production are derived from intravascular sources. **tissue t.,** coagulation factor III. See under *factor*. So called because it is released by or derived from extravascular tissues.

thromboplastinogen (throm″bo-plas-tin′o-jen). Factor VIII. See under *coagulation factors*.

thrombopoiesis (throm″bo-poi-e′sis). 1. The formation of thrombi. 2. Thrombocytopoiesis.

thrombopoietic (throm″bo-poi-et′ik). Pertaining to or characterized by thrombopoiesis.

thrombosed (throm′bōsd). Affected with thrombosis.

thrombosin (throm-bo′sin). Thrombin.

thrombosinusitis (throm″bo-si″nus-i′tis). Thrombosis of a dural sinus.

thrombosis (throm-bo′sis) [Gr. *thrombōsis*]. The formation, development or presence of a thrombus. **agonal t.,** lardaceous coagula of intravital blood formed in the heart and great vessels before death (Ribbert, 1916). **atrophic t.,** marasmic t. **cardiac t.,** thrombosis of the heart. **cavernous sinus t.,** thrombosis affecting the cavernous sinus. **coagulation t.,** that produced by coagulation of fibrin in a vessel. **compression t.,** that which is due to the compression of a vein between the heart and the thrombus. **coronary t.,** the formation of a clot in a coronary artery, obstructing the flow of blood and causing ischemia and infarction of the myocardium supplied by the vessel. **creeping t.,** thrombosis gradually involving one portion of a vein after another. **dilatation t.,** thrombosis due to the slowing of circulation on account of dilatation of a vein. **embolic t.,** thrombosis following obstruction of a vessel by an embolus. **foam t.** See under *embolism.* **infective t.,** that which is due to a bacterial invasion. **jumping t.,** thrombosis affecting a vein in a part shortly after affecting one in another part. **marantic t., marasmic t.,** thrombosis, chiefly of the longitudinal sinus, occurring in the wasting diseases of infancy and of old age. Called also *atrophic t.* **mesenteric t.,** formation of a clot in an artery or arteriole of the mesentery. **placental t.** 1. A normal formation of thrombi in the placenta. 2. An abnormal extension of the placental thrombus formation to the veins of the uterus. **plate t., platelet t.,** an abnormal accumulation of blood platelets, forming a thrombus. **puerperal t.,** coagulation of blood in the veins occurring after childbirth. **Ribbert's t.,** agonal t. **sinus t.,** thrombosis of a venous sinus. **traumatic t.,** thrombosis due to injury to a part. **venous t.,** phlebitis in which a thrombus is present; thrombophlebitis.

thrombostasis (throm-bos′tah-sis). Stasis of blood in a part, attended with the formation of a thrombus.

thrombosthenin (throm″bo-sthe′nin) [*thrombo-* + Gr. *sthenos* strength + *-in* chemical suffix]. A substance liberated by blood platelets during viscous metamorphosis, important for complete clot retraction and firmness of the clot.

thrombotest (throm′bo-test). A test similar to the one-stage prothrombin test except that it is supposedly sensitive to depression of blood coagulation factor IX and hence has an advantage over the one-stage test in controlling anticoagulant therapy; such superiority, however, has not been demonstrated consistently.

thrombotic (throm-bot′ik). Pertaining to or affected with thrombosis.

thrombotonin (throm″bo-to′nin). Serotonin.

thrombus (throm′bus) [Gr. *thrombos*]. A plug or clot in a blood vessel or in one of the cavities of the heart, formed by coagulation of the blood, and remaining at the point of its formation. Cf. *embolus.* **agglutinative t.,** hyaline t. **agonal t., agony t.,** a clot formed in the heart during the process of dying. **annular t.,** one which has an opening through its center, while the circumference is attached to the wall of the vessel. **antemortem t.,** a white thrombus formed in the heart or in a large vessel before death. **ball t.,** a rounded heart clot. **bile t.,** a plug in one of the intrahepatic bile ducts: seen in inflammatory conditions. **blood plate t.,** one formed by an abnormal accumulation of blood platelets. **calcified t.,** a phlebolith. **coral t.,** a red clot formed by coagulated fibrin enclosing red corpuscles. **currant jelly t.,** a soft, reddish, jelly-like clot. **ferment t.,** a thrombus formed on account of the development of fibrin ferment in the blood. **fibrinous t.,** a thrombus composed mainly of fibrin, and attached to the walls of a blood vessel. **globulin t., hematoblastic t.,** a thrombus composed largely of globulin. **hematostatic t.,** a form due to stagnation of the blood, and made up principally of red corpuscles. **hyaline t.,** a thrombus composed of erythrocytes which have lost their hemoglobin, forming a colorless translucent mass. **infective t.,** a thrombus occurring as a result of septic or bacterial poisoning. **Laennec's t.,** a globular thrombus in the heart, chiefly in cases of fatty degeneration. **laminated t.,** a thrombus whose substance is disposed in layers which sometimes differ in their material. **lateral t.,** a clot attached to the side of a vessel, incompletely obstructing the blood current. **marantic t., marasmic t.,** a form due to wasting disease and deprivation of the blood. See also under *thrombosis.* **mechanical t.,** a form due to mechanical obstruction of the blood current. **milk t.,** an accumulation of curdled milk in a lactiferous duct. **mixed t.,** laminated t. **mural t.,** a thrombus attached to a diseased area of endocardium. **obstructive t.,** one which completely obliterates the lumen of the vessel at its site. **organized t.,** one which is traversed by loops from the vasa vasorum. **pale t.,** a dull-white thrombus. **parasitic t.,** an accumulation of the pigmented bodies of free malarial parasites and their spores in the capillaries of the brain. **parietal t.,** one which is so attached to the wall of a vessel as to form a kind of valve. Called also *valvular t.* **phagocytic t.,** an accumulation of melaniferous leukocytes in the capillaries of the brain. **pigmentary t.,** an accumulation of free pigment in the capillaries of the brain. **plate t.,** a thrombus composed of blood platelets. **postmortem t.,** a thrombus or clot of blood formed in the heart or in a large vessel after death. **primary t.,** one which remains at the place of its origin. **propagated t.,** one which has been carried to a point more or less remote from the place of its origin, or which has grown beyond its original limits. **red t.,** a thrombus of a dark-red color formed by the coagulation of blood which is at rest. **stratified t.,** one made up of layers of different colors. **traumatic t.,** one which results from an injury. **valvular t.,** parietal t. **white t.** 1. One which contains no pigment. 2. One composed chiefly of leukocytes.

thrush (thrush). 1. A disease of infants (sometimes of adults) attended with the formation of aphthae, or whitish spots in the mouth. It is due to infection by the fungus *Candida albicans.* The aphthae are followed by shallow ulcers. The disease is often attended with fever and gastrointestinal irritation. Such infection may spread to the groin, buttocks and other parts of the body. 2. A disease of the horse's foot attended with a fetid discharge. 3. Same as *sprue.* **sheep t.,** orf.

thrypsis (thrip′sis) [Gr. "a breaking in small pieces"]. A comminuted fracture.

Thudichum's test (too′de-koomz) [John Lewis William *Thudichum,* London physician of German birth, 1828–1901]. See under *tests.*

Thuja (thu′jah) [L.; Gr. *thyia*]. A genus of coniferous trees called *arbor vitae.*

thuja (thu′jah). Fresh tops of *Thuja occidentalis,* white cedar: diuretic, antipyretic, sudorific, and emmenagogue.

thujone (thu′jōn). An aromatic terpene ketone present in many essential oils. It is $CH_3.C_6H_6O.CH(CH_3)_2$.

thulium (thu′le-um) [*Thule,* ancient name of Shetland]. A very rare metallic element; symbol, Tm; atomic number, 69; atomic weight, 168.934.

thumb (thum) [L. *pollex, pollux*]. The first digit of the hand, being the most preaxial of the five fingers, having only two phalanges, and being apposable to the four other fingers of the hand. **bifid t.,** a deformed thumb in which the distal phalanx is divided or bifurcated. **tennis t.,** tendinitis with calcification in the flexor pollicis longus, resulting from repeated friction experienced in playing tennis.

thumbprint (thum′print). An imprint of the cutaneous ridges of the fleshy distal portion of the thumb.

thumps (thumps). 1. A disease of swine caused by Ascaris larvae in the lungs. 2. A kind of singultus, or hiccup, of horses, due to spasm of the diaphragm.

thus (thus), gen. *thu'ris* [L.]. Olibanum or frankincense. **American t.,** the turpentine of various American pine trees. See *olibanum.* **gum t.,** turpentine.

thylacitis (thi″lah-si'tis) [Gr. *thylax* pouch + *-itis*]. Inflammation of the oil glands of the skin.

thymasma (thi-mas'mah). Thymic asthma.

thyme (tīm) [L. *thymus;* Gr. *thymos*]. A plant of the genus *Thymus.* The *Thymus vulgaris,* or garden thyme, contains a volatile oil, which is aromatic and carminative. It also contains *thymol, thymene,* and *cumene.* **wild t.,** *Thymus serpyllum,* which contains a volatile oil similar to that of *Thymus vulgaris.*

thymectomize (thi-mek'to-mīz). To deprive of the thymus gland by surgical removal.

thymectomy (thi-mek'to-me) [Gr. *thymos* thymus + *ektomē* excision]. Removal of the thymus.

thymelcosis (thi″mel-ko'sis) [Gr. *thymos* thymus + *helkōsis* ulceration]. Ulceration of the thymus.

thymene (thi'mēn). A clear, oily hydrocarbon, $C_{10}H_{16}$, from the oil of thyme.

thymergasia (thi″mer-ga'se-ah). See *thymergastic.*

thymergastic (thi″mer-gas'tik) [Gr. *thymos* mind + *ergon* work]. Meyer's term for pure affect psychic disorders, characterized by thinking difficulty (the manic-depressive group).

-thymia [Gr. *thymos* mind + *-ia*]. Word termination denoting a condition of mind.

thymian (thim'e-an, tim'e-an) [Ger.]. Thyme.

thymiasis (thi-mi'ah-sis). Thymiosis.

thymic (thi'mik) [L. *thymicus*]. 1. Pertaining to the thymus. 2. Contained in or derived from thyme.

thymicolymphatic (thi″mĭ-ko-lim-fat'ik). Pertaining to the thymus and the lymphatic glands.

thymidine (thi'mĭ-dēn). A compound, thymine desoxyriboside, isolated from liver.

thymin (thi'min). The hypothetical hormone of the thymus.

thymine (thi'min). A pyrimidine base, 5-methyl uracil, $C_5H_6N_2O$, obtained from nucleinic acid: used in treating pernicious anemia and sprue.

thymion (thim'e-on) [Gr.]. A cutaneous wart.

thymiosis (thim″e-o'sis). Yaws.

thymitis (thi-mi'tis). Inflammation of the thymus.

thymo- (thi'mo). 1. [Gr. *thymos* thymus]. Combining form denoting relationship to the thymus gland. 2. [Gr. *thymos* mind, spirit.] Combining form denoting relationship to the soul or emotions.

thymocrescin (thi″mo-kres'in). A hypothetical growth-promoting substance in extracts of the thymus gland.

thymocyte (thi'mo-sīt) [*thymo-*(1) + Gr. *kytos* hollow vessel]. A lymphocyte-like cell occurring in the thymus gland.

thymoform (thi'mo-form). A yellowish, antiseptic powder, thymoloform, $CH_2[C_6H_3(CH)_3(C_3H_7)O]_2$, prepared from formaldehyde and thymol.

thymogenic (thi″mo-jen'ik) [*thymo-*(2) + Gr. *gennan* to produce]. Of affective or hysterical origin.

thymohydroquinone (thi″mo-hi″dro-kwin-ōn'). A compound occurring in the urine after the administration of thymol. It is 2,5-dihydroxy-p-cymene, $CH_3.C_6H_2(OH)_2CH(CH_3)_2$, and is found in various essential oils.

thymokesis (thi″mo-ke'sis). Enlargement of the remnant of the thymus gland that is found in the adult.

thymokinetic (thi″mo-ki-net'ik). Tending to stimulate the thymus gland.

thymol (thi'mol). Chemical name: 5-methyl-2-isopropyl-1-phenol: used as an antibacterial and antifungal agent. **t. iodide,** a mixture of iodine derivatives of thymol, principally dithymol-diiodide, $(C_6H_2.CH_3.C_3H_7.OI)_2$, a reddish-brown powder: used as a deodorant antiseptic dressing like iodoform; also in the treatment of epidermophytosis (athlete's foot). It is used either in the form of the powder or in an ointment made with hydrous wool fat or petrolatum. **t. phthalein.** See *thymol-phthalein.*

thymolize (thi'mo-līz). To treat with thymol.

thymol-phthalein (thi″mol-thal'e-in). An indicator, $C_6H_4.CO.O.C(C_6H_2.CH_3.C_3H_7.OH)_2$, with a pH range of 9.3 to 10.5, being colorless at 9.3 and blue at 10.5.

thymolysin (thi-mol'ĭ-sin). An antibody that damages or kills thymus cells.

thymolysis (thi-mol'ĭ-sis) [*thymo-*(1) + Gr. *lysis* dissolution]. Involution or dissolution of the thymus gland.

thymolytic (thi″mo-lit'ik). Pertaining to, characterized by, or promoting thymolysis.

thymoma (thi-mo'mah) [*thymo-*(1) + *-oma*]. A tumor derived from the epithelial elements of the thymus.

thymometastasis (thi″mo-mĕ-tas'tah-sis). A metastasis from the thymus gland.

thymonucleodepolymerase (thi″mo-nu″kle-o-de-pol'ĭ-mer-ās). An enzyme which catalyzes the depolymerization of thymonucleic acid, thus forming mononucleotides.

thymopathic (thi″mo-path'ik). Pertaining to, characterized by, or causing thymopathy.

thymopathy (thi-mop'ah-the). 1. Any disease of the thymus. 2. Any mental affection or disease; any disturbance of affectivity; a psychopathy.

thymoprivic (thi″mo-priv'ik). Thymoprivous.

thymoprivous (thi-mop'rĭ-vus) [*thymo-*(1) + L. *privus* without]. Pertaining to or caused by removal or atrophy of the thymus.

thymopsyche (thi″mo-si'ke) [*thymo-*(2) + Gr. *psychē* soul]. The affective processes of the mind. Cf. *noopsyche.*

thymotoxic (thi″mo-tok'sik). Toxic for thymus tissue.

thymotoxin (thi″mo-tok'sin). An element that exerts a deleterious effect on the thymus gland.

thymotrope (thi'mo-trōp). A person who exhibits thymotropism.

thymotropic (thi″mo-trop'ik). Pertaining to or marked by thymotropism.

thymotropism (thi-mot'ro-pizm) [*thymus* + Gr. *tropē* a turning]. That type of endocrine constitution in which the influence of the thymus prevails.

thymovidin (thi-mo'vĭ-din). A hormone which originates in the thymus of birds and stimulates the oviduct to the production of normal egg envelopes.

Thymus (thi'mus). A genus of herbs native to south central Europe and grown extensively in other countries. See *thyme.*

thymus (thi'mus) [L.; Gr. *thymos*]. [N A, B N A] A ductless gland-like body situated in the anterior mediastinal cavity which reaches its maximum development during the early years of childhood. It is of a grayish-red color and it usually has two longitudinal lobes joined across a median plane. **accessory t.,** a separated portion of the thymus gland which may be found occasionally. **internal t.,** a body in either lobe of the thyroid of the cat. **persistent t., t. persis'tens hyperplas'tica,** a thymus which persists into adult life, sometimes even becoming hypertrophied.

thymusectomy (thi″mus-ek'to-me) [*thymus* + Gr. *ektomē* excision]. Excision of the thymus.

thynnin (thin'in). A protamine from the sperm of the tunny fish, *Thunnus thynnus.*

thypar (thi'pahr). Deprived of the thyroid and parathyroid glands; lacking thyroid and parathyroid secretions.

thyrasthenia (thi″ras-the'ne-ah) [*thyroid* + Gr. *astheneia* weakness]. Neurasthenia due to deficient thyroid secretion.

thyratron (thi'rah-tron). A form of discharge tube

containing mercury vapor and a multiplicity of electrodes, used as an electric valve to rectify alternating current.

thyremphraxis (thi″rem-frak′sis) [Gr. *thyreos* shield + *empharaxis* stoppage]. Obstruction of the thyroid gland.

thyreo- (thi′re-o). For other words beginning thus, see also those beginning *thyro-*.

thyreoitis (thi″re-o-i′tis). Thyroiditis.

thyro- (thi′ro). Combining form denoting relationship to the thyroid gland.

thyroactive (thi″ro-ak′tiv). Increasing the activity of the thyroid gland.

thyroadenitis (thi″ro-ad″e-ni′tis) [*thyro-* + Gr. *adēn* gland + *-itis*]. Inflammation of the thyroid gland.

thyroantitoxin (thi″ro-an″te-tok′sin). 1. An antitoxin developed in thyroid poisoning. 2. A thyroid preparation, theoretically $C_6H_{11}N_3O_5$.

thyroaplasia (thi″ro-ah-pla′ze-ah) [*thyro-* + *a* neg. + Gr. *plasis* molding + *-ia*]. Defective development of the thyroid gland with deficient activity of its secretion.

thyroarytenoid (thi″ro-ar″ĭ-te′noid). Pertaining to the thyroid and arytenoid cartilages.

thyrocardiac (thi″ro-kar′de-ak). Pertaining to the thyroid and the heart.

thyrocarditis (thi″ro-kar-di′tis). Any affection of the heart muscle occurring in hyperthyroidism.

thyrocele (thi′ro-sēl) [*thyro-* + Gr. *kēlē* tumor]. A tumor of the thyroid gland; goiter.

thyrochondrotomy (thi″ro-kon-drot′o-me) [*thyro-* + Gr. *chondros* cartilage + *tomē* a cutting]. Surgical incision of the thyroid cartilage.

thyrocolloid (thi″ro-kol′oid). The colloid matter of the thyroid gland.

thyrocricotomy (thi″ro-kri-kot′o-me). Incision of the cricothyroid membrane.

thyrodesmic (thi″ro-dez′mik) [*thyro-* + Gr. *desmos* bond]. Thyrotropic.

thyroepiglottic (thi″ro-ep″ĭ-glot′ik). Pertaining to the thyroid and to the epiglottis.

thyrofissure (thi″ro-fish′ur). The operation of making an opening through the thyroid cartilage for the purpose of gaining access to the interior of the larynx.

thyrogenic (thi″ro-jen′ik). Thyrogenous.

thyrogenous (thi-roj′e-nus) [*thyro-* + Gr. *gennan* to produce]. Originating in the thyroid gland.

thyroglobulin (thi-ro-glob′u-lin). An iodine-containing protein occurring in the colloid of the follicles of the thyroid gland, apparently the form in which the thyroid hormones are stored. It has a molecular weight of about 680,000, and on hydrolysis yields several iodine-containing derivatives of tyrosine.

thyroglossal (thi″ro-glos′al). Pertaining to the thyroid gland and the tongue.

thyrohyal (thi″ro-hi′al). 1. Pertaining to the thyroid cartilage and the hyoid bone. 2. Cornu majus ossis hyoidei.

thyrohyoid (thi″ro-hi′oid). Pertaining to the thyroid gland or cartilage and the hyoid bone.

thyroid (thi′roid) [Gr. *thyreoeidēs; thyreos* shield + *eidos* form]. 1. Resembling a shield; scutiform. 2. The thyroid gland (glandula thyroidea [N A]). 3. A pharmaceutical substance derived from thyroid glands obtained from domesticated animals used for food by man, the glands having been deprived of connective tissue and fat and then cleaned, dried, and powdered: used in replacement therapy. **aberrant t.,** a mass of thyroid tissue situated in an abnormal location. **accessory t.,** an exclave or detached portion of thyroid tissue. **intrathoracic t.,** a mass of thyroid tissue that is located within the thoracic cavity. **lingual t.,** thyroid tissue located at the base of the tongue, between the foramen cecum and the hyoid bone. It may project into the pharynx from the dorsum of the tongue, or be entirely within the tongue or located just beneath it; it may also be accessory to a normally located thyroid gland, or be the only thyroid tissue present. **retrosternal t., substernal t.,** a mass of thyroid tissue situated in the thorax behind the sternum.

thyroidea (thi-roi′de-ah). The thyroid gland. **t. accesso′ria, t. i′ma,** accessory thyroid.

thyroidectomize (thi″roid-ek′to-mīz). To deprive of the thyroid gland by surgical removal.

thyroidectomy (thi″roid-ek′to-me) [*thyroid* + Gr. *ektomē* excision]. Surgical removal of the thyroid.

thyroidism (thi′roid-izm). A morbid condition caused by overactivity of the thyroid gland or excessive doses of thyroid.

thyroiditis (thi″roid-i′tis). Inflammation of the thyroid gland. **acute t.,** inflammation of the thyroid gland caused by staphylococcic, streptococcic, or other infection, with suppuration and abscess formation, and progressing to the subacute stage. **acute nonsuppurative t.,** granulomatous t. **chronic t., chronic fibrous t.,** Riedel's struma. **chronic lymphadenoid t., chronic lymphocytic t.,** struma lymphomatosa. **De Quervains 't.,** granulomatous t. **giant cell t., giant follicular t.,** granulomatous t. **granulomatous t.,** a condition characterized by fever, weakness, sore throat, and painful enlargement of the thyroid gland, with granulomas in the gland consisting of masses of colloid surrounded by giant cells and mononuclear cells, and a moderate amount of fibrosis. **Hashimoto's t.,** struma lymphomatosa. **invasive t., ligneous t.,** Riedel's struma. **lymphoid t.,** struma lymphomatosa. **parasitic t.,** Chagas' disease. **pseudotuberculous t.,** granulomatous t. **Riedel's t.,** Riedel's struma. **subacute t., subacute diffuse t.,** granulomatous t. **woody t.,** Riedel's struma.

thyroidization (thi″roid-i-za′shun). Treatment with a preparation of the thyroid.

thyroidomania (thi″roid-o-ma′ne-ah). Mental disorder associated with hyperthyroidism.

thyroidotherapy (thi″roid-o-ther′ah-pe). Thyrotherapy.

thyroidotomy (thi″roid-ot′o-me) [*thyroid* + Gr. *tomē* a cutting]. Surgical incision of the thyroid.

thyroidotoxin (thi″roid-o-tok′sin). A toxin specific for thyroid tissue.

thyroigenous (thi-roi′je-nus). Due to thyroid disorder.

thyrointoxication (thi″ro-in-tok″sĭ-ka′shun). Thyroid poisoning; thyrotoxicosis.

thyroiodine (thi″ro-i′o-din). A non-specific term for iodine as it exists in the hormones of the thyroid gland.

thyrolysin (thi-rol′ĭ-sin). A thyrolytic serum.

thyrolytic (thi″ro-lit′ik) [*thyroid* + Gr. *lysis* dissolution]. Destructive to thyroid tissue.

thyroma (thi-ro′mah). A tumor which contains iodine and goitrous tissue.

thyromegaly (thi″ro-meg′ah-le) [*thyro-* + Gr. *megaleia* bigness]. Enlargement of the thyroid gland.

thyroncus (thi-rong′kus) [*thyroid* + Gr. *onkos* mass, tumor]. Goiter.

thyronucleo-albumin (thi″ro-nu″kle-o-al-bu′min). A nucleo-albumin present in the thyroid gland.

thyro-oxy-indole (thi″ro-ok″se-in′dol). Thyroxin.

thyroparathyroidectomy (thi″ro-par″ah-thi″roid-ek′to-me) [*thyroid* + *parathyroid* + Gr. *ektomē* excision]. Excision of the thyroid and parathyroids.

thyropathy (thi-rop′ah-the) [*thyroid* + Gr. *pathos* disease]. Any disease of the thyroid.

thyropenia (thi″ro-pe′ne-ah) [*thyroid* + Gr. *penia* poverty]. Deficiency of thyroid secretion.

thyrophyma (thi″ro-fi′mah) [*thyroid* + Gr. *phyma* tumor]. Tumor of the thyroid gland.

thyroprival (thi″ro-pri′val) [*thyroid* + L. *privus* without]. Pertaining to, characterized by, or resulting from deprivation or loss of thyroid function.

thyroprivia (thi″ro-priv′e-ah) [*thyroid* + L. *privus* without]. The condition resulting from lack of thyroid hormone, as a consequence of removal of the thyroid gland or suppression of its functions.

thyroprivic, thyroprivous (thi″ro-priv′ik, thi-rop′rĭ-vus). Thyroprival.

thyroptosis (thi″rop-to′sis) [*thyroid* + Gr. *ptōsis* fall]. Downward displacement of the thyroid gland into the thorax.

thyrosis (thi-ro′sis), pl. *thyro′ses.* Any disease based on disordered thyroid action.

thyrotherapy (thi″ro-ther′ah-pe). Treatment of disease by preparations of the thyroid glands of domestic animals used for food by man.

thyrotome (thi′ro-tōm). An instrument for cutting the thyroid cartilage.

thyrotomy (thi-rot′o-me) [*thyroid* + Gr. *tomē* a cutting]. 1. The surgical division of the thyroid cartilage. 2. The operation of cutting the thyroid gland.

thyrotoxemia (thi″ro-tok-se′me-ah). Thyrotoxicosis.

thyrotoxia (thi″ro-tok′se-ah). Thyrotoxicosis.

thyrotoxic (thi″ro-tok′sik). Marked by toxic activity of the thyroid gland.

thyrotoxicosis (thi″ro-tok″sĭ-ko′sis). A morbid condition resulting from overactivity of the thyroid gland.

thyrotoxin (thi″ro-tok′sin). A toxic substance produced in the thyroid.

thyrotrope (thi′ro-trōp). A person with any disorder of the endocrine function of the thyroid.

thyrotrophic (thi″ro-trōf′ik). Thyrotropic.

thyrotrophin (thi″ro-trōf′in). Thyrotropin.

thyrotropic (thi″ro-trop′ik). 1. Pertaining to or marked by thyrotropism. 2. Having an influence on the thyroid gland.

thyrotropin (thi-rot′ro-pin). A hormone of the anterior pituitary that has affinity for or specifically stimulates the thyroid gland.

thyrotropism (thi-rot′ro-pizm) [*thyroid* + Gr. *tropos* a turning]. Affinity for the thyroid; that type of endocrine constitution in which the influence of the thyroid prevails.

thyroxin (thi-rok′sin). Thyroxine.

thyroxine (thi-rok′sin). A crystalline iodine-containing compound, 3,5,3′,5′-tetraiodothyronine, possessing the physiologic properties of thyroid extract; originally isolated by Kendall from the thyroid gland, and later prepared synthetically: used in treatment of hypothyroidism. **levo t.** See *levothyroxine*, under L.

thyroxinemia (thi-rok″sin-e′me-ah). The presence of thyroxine in the blood.

thyroxinic (thi″rok-sin′ik). Pertaining to thyroxine.

thyroxinsodium (thi-rok″sin-so′de-um). A preparation of thyroxine treated with sodium carbonate.

thyroxinum (thi-rok′sĭ-num). Thyroxine.

thyrsus (thir′sus) [Gr. *thyrsos* Bacchic wand]. The penis.

Thysanosoma (this″ah-no-so′mah). A genus of tapeworms. **T. actinioi′des,** the fringed tapeworm, found in the bile ducts and small intestine of sheep, antelope, and deer, in western and southwestern United States.

thysanotrix (thi-san′o-triks). Trichostasis spinulosa.

Ti. Chemical symbol for *titanium.*

tiacarana (te″ah-kar-an′yah). Dermal leishmaniasis of the ulcerative type.

tibia (tib′e-ah) [L. "a pipe, flute"]. [N A, B N A] The inner and larger bone of the leg below the knee; it articulates with the femur and head of the fibula above and with the talus below. **saber t., saber-shaped t.,** a tibia curved outward as a result of gummatous periostitis. **t. val′ga,** a bowing of the leg in which the angulation is away from the midline of the body. **t. va′ra,** a bowing of the leg in which the angulation is toward the midline of the body; bow-leg.

tibiad (tib′e-ad). Toward the tibial aspect.

tibiaeus (tib-e-e′us). Tibialis.

tibial (tib′e-al) [L. *tibialis*]. Pertaining to the tibia.

tibiale (tib″e-a′le). A bone on the tibial side of the tarsus of the embryo, partly represented in the adult by the astragalus. **t. exter′num, t. posti′cum,** a sesamoid bone found in the tendon of the tibialis posterior muscle.

tibialgia (tib″e-al′je-ah). Painful shin, with lymphocytosis and eosinophilia, probably due to defective nutrition or avitaminosis (von Schrötter, 1916).

tibialis (tib″e-a′lis). Tibial; in official anatomical nomenclature, designating relationship to the tibia.

tibien (tib′e-en). Pertaining to the tibia alone or in itself.

tibiocalcanean (tib″e-o-kal-ka′ne-an). Pertaining to the tibia and the calcaneus.

tibiofemoral (tib″e-o-fem′or-al). Pertaining to the tibia and the femur.

tibiofibular (tib″e-o-fib′u-lar). Pertaining to the tibia and the fibula.

tibionavicular (tib″e-o-nah-vik′u-lar). Pertaining to the tibia and the navicular bone.

tibioperoneal (tib″e-o-per″o-ne′al). Tibiofibular.

tibioscaphoid (tib″e-o-skaf′oid). Tibionavicular.

tibiotarsal (tib″e-o-tar′sal). Pertaining to the tibia and the tarsus.

tic (tik) [Fr.]. 1. Any spasmodic movement or twitching, as of the face. 2. A psychoneurosis marked by quick, sudden spasms that are identical with the movements of volitional intent. Tics occur in persons of neurotic tendency, are often hereditary, and usually develop in youth. Called also *mimic spasm, habit spasm,* and *maladie des tics.* **bowing t.,** salaam convulsions, or repeated bowing movements of the head. **convulsive t.,** spasm of those parts of the face supplied by the seventh nerve. **degenerative t.,** tic occurring in connection with degeneration of the central nervous system. **t. de pensée** (de pahsa′), the habit of involuntarily expressing any thought that happens to come to mind. **diaphragmatic t.,** spasmodic twitching movements of the diaphragm. Called also *respiratory t.* **t. douloureux** (doo-loo-roo′), trigeminal neuralgia. **facial t.,** spasm of the facial muscles. **gesticulatory t.,** that marked by spasmodic movements resembling the gestures of an orator or an actor. **t. de Guinon,** Guinon's disease. **habit t.,** habit spasm. **laryngeal t.,** that marked by a noisy expulsion of air through the glottis. **local t.,** a tic affecting only a limited locality, as the eye. **mimic t.,** facial tic. **motor t.,** a tic which is marked only by the spasmodic movement without mental disturbance. It includes facial spasm, blepharospasm, respiratory, laryngeal, rotatory, and other varieties of tic. **t. nondouloureux,** myoclonus. **occupation t.,** occupation spasm. **progressive choreic t.,** a chronic disease beginning in early life, marked by spasms which at first affect the neck muscles, but, as the disease advances, spread to the rest of the body. The disease ends fatally. **psychomotor t.,** a tic that is accompanied with some mental disorder. It includes the peculiar habit spasms of insanity that are attended with delusions or insane ideas—the peculiar conditions known as mental torticollis, latah, miryachit, palmus, and Gilles de la Tourette's disease, or dancing mania. **respiratory t.,** diaphragmatic t. **rotatory t.,** rotatory spasm. **saltatory t.,**

saltatory spasm; a nervous condition marked by rhythmical dancing or jumping movements whenever the patient stands. **t. de sommeil,** an involuntary movement of the head during sleep. **spasmodic t.,** a condition marked by spasmodic movements of groups of muscles occurring at irregular intervals.

Tichodectes canis (tik″o-dek′tēz kah′nis). The biting dog louse which is an intermediate host of *Dipylidium caninum.*

tick (tik). A blood-sucking arachnid parasite of the superfamily Ixodoidea. The ticks are larger than their relatives, the mites. All ticks are divided into two subfamilies, the Argasidae, or soft ticks, and the Ixodidae, or hard ticks. The former includes the genera *Argas, Otobius, Antricola* and *Ornithodoros,* the latter the genera *Boophilus, Amblyomma, Dermacentor, Haemaphysalis, Hyalomma, Ixodes, Rhipicephalus,* and *Rhipicentor.* **adobe t.,** *Argas persicus.* **American dog t.,** *Dermacentor variabilis.* **bandicoot t.,** *Haemaphysalis humerosa.* **bont t.,** *Amblyomma hebraeum.* **brown dog t.,** *Rhipicephalus sanguineus.* **castor bean t.,** *Ixodes ricinus.* **cattle t.,** *Boophilus.* **dog t.,** *Haemaphysalis leachi, Dermacentor variabilis, Rhipicephalus sanguineus.* **ear t.,** *Ornithodoros megnini.* **Kenya t.,** *Rhipicephalus sanguineus.* **Lone Star t.,** *Amblyomma americanum.* **miana t.,** *Argas persicus.* **Pacific coast t.,** *Dermacentor occidentalis.* **pajarcello t.,** *Ornithodoros coriaceus.* **paralysis t.,** *Ixodes pilosus.* **pigeon t.,** *Argas reflexus.* **Rocky Mountain wood t.,** *Dermacentor andersoni.* **russet t.,** *Ixodes pilosus.* **scrub t.,** *Ixodes holocyclus.* **seed t.,** the young six-legged larva of a tick: after moulting it emerges as an eight-legged nymph. **spinous ear t.,** *Ornithodoros megnini.* **tampan t.,** *Ornithodoros moubata.* **winter t.,** *Dermacentor albipictus.* **wood t.,** *Dermacentor andersoni.*

tickling (tik′ling). Light stimulation of a surface, and its reflex effect, such as involuntary laughter, etc.

ticpolonga (tik″po-long′ah). An extremely venomous serpent of Ceylon and India, *Daboia elegans.* Called also *cobra-monil.*

tictology (tik-tol′o-je) [Gr. *tiktein* to give birth + *logos* treatise]. Obstetrics.

t.i.d. An abbreviation for L. *ter in di′e,* three times a day.

tide (tīd). A physiological variation or increase of a certain constituent in body fluids. **acid t.,** temporary increase in the acidity of the urine which sometimes follows fasting. **alkaline t.,** temporary increase in the alkalinity of the urine during gastric digestion. **fat t.,** the increase of fat in the lymph and blood following a meal.

Tidy's test (ti′dēz) [Charles Meymott *Tidy,* English physician, 1843–1892]. See under *tests.*

Tiedemann's glands, nerve (te′dĕ-manz) [Friedrich *Tiedemann,* German physician, 1781–1861]. See under the nouns.

Tietze's disease, syndrome (tēt′sez) [Alexander *Tietze,* Breslau surgeon, 1864–1927]. Painful nonsuppurative swellings of the costal cartilages.

tigan (ti′gan). Trade mark for preparations of trimethobenzamide hydrochloride.

tiglium (tig′le-um), gen. *tig′lii* [L.]. The croton oil plant, *Croton tiglium.*

tigogenin (tig-oj′e-nin). A complex aglycone, $C_{27}H_{44}O_3$, from tigonin.

tigonin (tig′o-nin). A saponin, $C_{56}H_{92}O_{27}$, from *Digitalis purpurea* and *D. lanata.* On hydrolysis, it yields tigogenin, glucose, galactose and rhamnose.

tigretier (te-gret″e-a′) [Fr.]. A form of hysterical dancing mania peculiar to Tigré, a region in Abyssinia.

tigroid (ti′groid) [Gr. *tigroeidēs* tiger-spotted]. Marked like a tiger. A term applied to Nissl bodies or masses of deeply staining substance in the protoplasm of neurons.

tigrolysis (ti-grol′ĭ-sis). Chromatolysis.

tikitiki (te″ke-te′ke). The Japanese name for rice polishings.

Tillaux's disease (te-yōz′) [Paul Jules *Tillaux,* French physician, 1834–1904]. See under *disease.*

Tilletia (til-le′she-ah). A genus of ustilagineous fungi causing smut on cereals.

tilma (til′mah). Lint.

tilmus (til′mus) [Gr. *tilmos* a plucking]. Carphology.

tiltometer (til-tom′e-ter). An instrument for measuring the degree of tilting of the operating table in spinal anesthesia.

timbre (tim′ber, tam′br) [Fr.]. A musical quality in a tone or sound. **t. métallique,** a high-pitched tympanic second sound heard in dilatation of the aorta. When heard in persons under fifty-five years of age it is suggestive of syphilitic aortitis. Called also *Potain's sign* and *bruit de tabourka.*

time (tīm) [Gr. *chronos;* L. *tempus*]. A measure of duration. **apex t.,** the interval at which the apex of the summated twitches of a muscle succeeds the second stimulus applied to the same muscle. **bleeding t.,** the period of duration of bleeding that follows controlled, standardized puncture of the ear-lobe (Duke method) or forearm (Ivy method): a relatively undependable measure of capillary and platelet function. **bleeding t., secondary,** the time required for the arrest of bleeding when the crust is removed from a traumatized area 24 hours after the original injury; this is generally prolonged in patients with factor VIII deficiency (hemophilia A) and with related hemophilioid states. **chromoscopy t.,** the time elapsing between the intramuscular injection of a dye and its appearance in the gastric secretion. **circulation t.,** the time required for blood to flow between two given points. **clot retraction t.,** the time required for the clot (coagulum) to retract from the wall of the vessel containing it. Normal time 18 to 24 hours. **clotting t.,** coagulation t. **coagulation t.,** the time which it takes a drop of blood to coagulate. Normally it is four and one half minutes. **dextrinizing t.,** the time required for saliva to convert starch into sugar. **generation t.,** the time elapsing from one generation to the next, or in bacteria the time from one scission to the next. **inertia t.,** the time required to overcome the inertia of a muscle after the reception of a stimulus from a nerve. **persistence t.,** the time following the contraction of the ventricle of the heart until the occurrence of relaxation. **prothrombin t.,** the coagulation time of the tube which clots earliest after addition of various amounts of calcium chloride to different portions of oxalate plasma. **reaction t.,** the time elapsing between the application of a stimulus and the resulting reaction. **recalcification t.,** the interval required for clot formation when calcium ion is added to platelet-rich plasma: a measure of hemostatic function of the blood. **sedimentation t.** See *erythrocyte sedimentation reaction,* under *reaction.* **thermal death t.,** the duration of exposure required to kill a bacterium at a stated degree of temperature.

timer (tīm′er). A clock mechanism which may be set to automatically signal the expiration of a given interval of time or to activate or cut off certain other apparatus at the desired time.

Timme's syndrome (tim′ez) [Walter *Timme,* New York neurologist, born 1874]. See under *syndrome.*

timopathy (tim-op′ah-the) [L. *timor* fear + Gr. *pathos* disease]. A state characterized by abnormal dread or apprehension.

timovan (tim′o-van). Trade mark for a preparation of prothipendyl hydrochloride.

tin (tin) [L. *stannum*]. A white, metallic element, atomic number, 50; atomic weight, 118.69; valence of 2 or 4; symbol, Sn. Some of its salts are reagents, others are stains, while some of its compounds, particularly the oxide, have been tried in medicine. **t. chloride,** a compound, $SnCl_2 + 2H_2O$, or stannous chloride: used as a test reagent. **t. oxide,** a pure white powder, obtained from the product of a reaction between tin and concentrated nitric acid at a high temperature: used in dentistry as a polishing agent for teeth and metallic restorations in the mouth.

tinct. Abbreviation for *tincture,* or *tinctura.*

tinctable (tink′tah-b'l). Stainable or tingible.

tinction (tink′shun) [L. *tingere* to dye]. 1. The act of staining. 2. The addition of coloring or flavoring agents to a prescription.

tinctorial (tink-to′re-al). Pertaining to dyeing or staining.

tinctura (tink-tu′rah), gen. and pl. *tinctu′rae* [L.]. Tincture.

tincturation (tink″tu-ra′shun). The preparation of a tincture; the treatment of a drug with a menstruum, such as alcohol or ether, for the purpose of preparing a tincture.

tincture (tink′tūr) [L. *tingere* to wet, to moisten]. An alcoholic or hydroalcoholic solution prepared from animal or vegetable drugs or from chemical substances. **arnica t.,** a preparation of powdered arnica in equal parts of alcohol and water: used as a local irritant. **belladonna t.,** an alcoholic preparation of belladonna leaf: used as a parasympatholytic agent. Called also *belladonna leaf t.* **benzoin t.,** a preparation of benzoin in alcohol: applied topically as a protective. **capsicum t.,** a preparation of powdered capsicum in equal parts of alcohol and water: used as an irritant and carminative. **cardamom t., compound,** a preparation of powdered cardamom seed, cinnamon, caraway, and cochineal in glycerin and diluted alcohol: used as a flavoring agent. **digitalis t.,** an alcoholic extract of digitalis: used as a cardiotonic. **ferric chloride t.,** a hydroalcoholic solution of ferric chloride: used as an astringent and hematinic. **ferric citrochloride t.,** a hydroalcoholic solution of ferric chloride and sodium citrate: used as a hematinic. **gentian t., compound,** a preparation of powdered gentian, bitter orange peel, and cardamom seed in a menstruum of glycerin, alcohol, and water: used as a bitter. **t. of green soap,** medicinal soft soap liniment. **hyoscyamus t.,** a preparation of powdered hyoscyamus in alcohol and water: used as a parasympatholytic agent. **iodine t.,** a preparation of iodine and sodium iodide in diluted alcohol, each 100 ml. of which contains 1.8–2.2 Gm. of iodine and 2.1–2.6 Gm. of sodium iodide: used as a local antiinfective on skin and mucous membrane. **iodine t., strong,** an alcoholic solution of iodine and potassium iodide, each 100 ml. of which contains 6.8–7.5 Gm. of iodine and 4.7–5.5 Gm. of potassium iodide: used as an irritant, antibacterial, and antifungal agent. **lemon t.,** a preparation of lemon peel in alcohol: used as a flavoring agent. Called also *lemon peel t.* **myrrh t.,** a preparation of powdered myrrh in alcohol: used as a protective. **nitromersol t.,** a preparation of nitromersol, sodium hydroxide, and acetone, in alcohol and purified water: used as a local antibacterial. **nux vomica t.,** a preparation of powdered nux vomica in equal parts of alcohol, hydrochloric acid, and water: used as a bitter. **opium t.,** a preparation, obtained by percolation of granulated opium and concentration of the product, each 100 ml. of which yields 0.95–1.05 Gm. of anhydrous morphine: used as an intestinal sedative. **opium t., camphorated,** a preparation of powdered opium, anise oil, benzoic acid, and camphor: used as an intestinal sedative. **opium t., deodorized,** opium t. **rhubarb t., aromatic,** a preparation of powdered rhubarb, cinnamon, clove, and myristica in glycerin, alcohol, and water: used as a cathartic. **stramonium t.,** a hydroalcoholic solution of powdered stramonium: used as a parasympatholytic. **sweet orange peel t.,** a preparation produced by the maceration in alcohol of the outer rind of the non-artificially colored fresh ripe fruit of *Citrus sinensis:* used as a flavoring agent. **thimerosal t.,** a preparation of thimerosal, alcohol, acetone, ethylenediamine solution, and monoethanolamine in water: used as a local antibacterial. **tolu balsam t.,** a preparation of tolu balsam in alcohol: used as an ingredient of tolu balsam syrup. **vanilla t.,** a preparation of vanilla and sucrose in equal parts of diluted alcohol and water: used as an ingredient of acacia syrup.

tindal (tin′dal). Trade mark for a preparation of acetophenazine dimaleate.

tinea (tin′e-ah) [L. "a grub, larva, worm"]. A name applied to many different kinds of fungal infection of the skin, the specific type (depending on characteristic appearance, etiologic agent, or site) usually being designated by a modifying term. **t. amianta′cea,** a non-fungal condition of the scalp, characterized by a dense concentration on its surface of silvery-white or gray scales which extend up on the hair shafts to form an asbestos-like encasement. **asbestos-like t.,** t. amiantacea. **t. axilla′ris,** fungal infection of the skin in the axillary region. See also *trichomycosis axillaris.* **t. bar′bae,** infection of the bearded area of the face and neck, caused by various species of fungi, the type depending on the organism involved: the inflammatory type, caused by *Trichophyton mentagrophytes* or *T. verrucosum* (see *t. kerion*); the ringworm type, caused by various species of fungi, with annular lesions resembling those appearing on non-hairy skin; the sycosiform type, caused by *Trichophyton violaceum* or *T. rubrum* (see *t. sycosis*). **t. cap′itis,** fungal infection of the scalp caused by various species of *Microsporum* and *Trichophyton,* the clinical characteristics depending on the causative organism. **t. cilio′rum,** fungal infection of the scalp, involving the eyelashes. **t. circina′ta,** fungal infection of the glabrous skin, characterized by presence of the annular lesions responsible for the appellation "ringworm." **t. cor′poris,** fungal infection of the glabrous skin, usually caused by various species of *Trichophyton* and *Microsporum,* sometimes acquired from animals or other infected persons and often named for some specific characteristic. See *t. circinata, t. profunda,* and *favus.* **t. cru′ris,** a fungal infection common in males, starting in the crural or perineal folds, and extending onto the upper inner surfaces of the thighs; caused usually by *Epidermophyton floccosum* or species of *Trichophyton.* Called also *eczema marginatum* and *epidermophytosis cruris.* **t. decal′vans,** alopecia areata. **t. favo′sa,** favus. **t. furfura′cea,** a dry, scaly form of seborrhea. **t. gal′li,** a fungal disease of the combs of cocks. Called also *whitecomb.* **t. glabro′sa,** t. corporis. **t. imbrica′ta,** a distinctive type of tinea corporis occurring in tropical countries and caused by *Trichophyton concentricum;* the early lesion is annular, with a circle of scales at the periphery, characteristically attached along one edge. New and larger scaling rings form, sometimes reaching as many as 10 per lesion. **t. inguina′lis,** t. cruris. **t. ke′rion,** a highly inflammatory and suppurative fungal infection, mainly of the scalp or of the bearded area of the face and neck, characterized by presence of nodular, boggy, exudative circumscribed tumefactions which are studded with pustules. **t. ni′gra,** a minor fungal infection, caused by *Cladosporium mansoni* or *C. wernecki,* producing strikingly dark lesions with the appearance of stains of spattered silver nitrate on the skin of the hands or, rarely, on other areas. **t. nodo′sa,** piedra. **t. pe′dis,** a chronic superficial fungal infection of the skin of the foot, especially of that between the toes and on the soles, caused by species of *Trichophyton* or by *Epidermophyton floccosum* or *Candida albicans;* of different types and degrees of severity, it may be marked by maceration, cracking, and scaling of the skin, and by intense itching. **t. profun′da,** a type of tinea corporis characterized by elevated, sharply circumscribed, rather boggy tumors, with a bright red exuding granulating surface, simulating highly anaplastic tumors, and sometimes becoming fluctuant and necrotic. **t. syco′sis,** a rare type of tinea barbae, clinically indistinguishable from chronic bacterial folliculitis, leading to crust formation, and breaking or shedding of the hair, caused by *Trichophyton violaceum* or *T. rubra.* **t. tar′si,** ulcerous blepharitis. **t. ton′surans,** tinea capitis caused by *Trichophyton tonsurans,* characterized by irregular, slowly extending patches of partial baldness, with black dots, similar to those observed in infections by *T. violaceum,* produced by breakage of the hairs at the scalp surface. **t. tropica′lis,** the tinea cruris of tropical countries. **t. un′guium,** onychomycosis. **t. versic′olor,** a common chronic, noninflammatory and usually symptomless disorder, characterized only by occurrence of multiple macular patches, of all sizes and shapes, varying from whitish to fawn-colored or brown; seen most frequently in hot, humid tropical regions, and possibly caused by *Pityrosporon orbiculare.*

Tinel's sign (tin-elz′) [Jules *Tinel,* French neurologist, 1879–1952]. See under *sign.*

tingibility (tin″jĭ-bil′ĭ-te). The quality of being tingible.

tingible (tin′jĭ-b'l) [L. *tingere* to stain]. Susceptible of being tinged or stained.

tingling (ting′gling). A pricklike thrill, caused by cold or by striking a nerve. **distal t. on percussion.** See *Tinel's sign,* under *sign.*

tinkle (ting′k'l). An auscultatory sound like the ringing of a small bell: sometimes heard over large pulmonary cavities and in pneumothorax. **metallic t.,** a ringing sound, as of a metallic object, sometimes heard in connection with other respiratory sounds. **metallic t., Bouillaud's,** a clinking sound sometimes heard on the right side of the apex in hypertrophy of the heart.

tinnitus (tin′ĭ-tus, tĭ-ni′tus) [L. "a ringing"]. A noise in the ears, as ringing, buzzing, roaring, clicking, etc. Such sounds may at times be heard by others than the patient. **t. aurium,** a subjective sensation of noises in the ears. **clicking t.,** a clicking sound occurring in the ear in chronic catarrhal otitis media; it may be heard by others than the patient. **Leudet's t.,** a crackling sound in the ear, audible also to an observer, produced by involuntary contraction of an internal muscle, coinciding with a tic of some of the fibers of the mandibular division of the trigeminal (fifth cranial) nerve. **nervous t.,** that which arises from some disturbance of the otic nerve or its central connection. **nonvibratory t.,** tinnitus which is produced by biochemical changes occurring in the nerve mechanism of hearing. **objective t.,** abnormal or pathological sounds originating within the body of the patient, in the region of the ear, which are audible to others than the patient. **vibratory t.,** tinnitus resulting from transmission to the cochlea of vibrations originating in adjacent tissues of the body.

Tinospora (tin-os′po-rah). A genus of menispermaceous vines. The stalk and root of *T. cordifolia* are used in snake bite, etc.

tint B. A color shown by the pastille in an x-ray–measuring instrument that denotes the amount of radiation which will cause depilation.

tintometer (tin-tom′e-ter) [*tint* + Gr. *metron* measure]. An instrument used in determining the relative proportion of coloring matter in a liquid, as in blood.

tintometric (tin″to-met′rik). Pertaining to tintometry.

tintometry (tin-tom′e-tre). The use of the tintometer.

tiotin (ti′o-tin). The chief avidin-uncombinable biotin vitamer in autoclaved urine and other biological materials. (Dean Burk.) Cf. *miotin.*

tip (tip). A pointed extremity of a body part. Called also *apex.* **t. of nose,** apex nasi. **t. of sacral bone,** apex ossis sacri. **t. of tongue,** apex linguae. **Woolner's t.,** tuberculum auriculae.

tiqueur (te-ker′) [Fr.]. A person subject to a tic.

tirebal (tēr-bahl′) [Fr.]. An instrument resembling a corkscrew, for extracting bullets.

tirefond (tēr-fo′) [Fr.]. An instrument like a corkscrew, for raising depressed portions of a bone.

tires (tīrz). Trembles.

tiring (tīr′ing). The operation of passing a wire around a fractured patella, like a tire around a wheel.

Tiselius apparatus (te-sa′le-us) [Arne *Tiselius,* biochemist in Upsula, Sweden, born 1902; winner of the Nobel prize for chemistry in 1948]. See under *apparatus.*

tisic (tiz′ik). Phthisic.

tisis (tis′is). Phthisis.

tissue (tish′u) [Fr. *tissu*]. An aggregation of similarly specialized cells united in the performance of a particular function. **accidental t.,** a tissue growing in or upon a part to which it is foreign. It is either analogous or heterologous. **adenoid t.,** lymphoid t. **adipose t.,** fatty tissue; connective tissue made up of fat cells in a meshwork of areolar tissue. **adrenogenic t.,** the inner zone of the cortex of an adrenal gland which begins to involute shortly after birth. **analogous t.,** an accidental tissue similar to one found normally in other parts of the body. **areolar t.,** connective tissue made up largely of interlacing fibers. **basement t.,** the substance of a basement membrane. **bony t.,** bone, whether normal or of a soft tissue, which has become ossified. **brown fat t.,** fatty tissue in various regions of the body of some mammals which contains a dark pigment. Called also *moruloid* or *mulberry fat.* The masses have been called interscapular gland, hibernating gland, and Bonnot's gland. **cancellous t.,** the loose spongy tissue of the interior and articular ends of bone. **cartilaginous t.,** the substance of the cartilages. **cavernous t.,** erectile t. **cellular t.,** loose connective tissue with large interspaces, like the subperitoneal structure. **chondroid t.,** an embryonic form of cartilage composed of vesicular cells provided with elastic capsules and having collagenous fibers in its interstitial substance. **chordal t.,** the tissue of the notochord. **chromaffin t.,** a tissue composed largely of chromaffin cells, well supplied with nerves and vessels. It occurs in the adrenal medulla and also forms the paraganglia of the body. **cicatricial t.,** the dense fibrous tissue forming a scar or cicatrix and derived directly from a granulation tissue. Called also *scar t.* **compact t.,** the hard external portion of a bone. **connective t.,** the tissue which binds together and is the support of the various structures of the body. It is made up of fibroblasts, fibroglia, collagen fibrils, and elastic fibrils. It is derived from the mesoderm and in a broad sense includes the collagenous, elastic, mucous, reticular, osseous and cartilaginous tissue. Some also include the blood in this group of tissues. Cf. *fibroblast.* **cribriform t.,** areolar t. **dartoid t.,** that which resembles the dartos in structure. **dental t.,** dentin. **elastic t., elastic t., yellow,** connective tissue made up of yellow, elastic fibers, frequently massed into sheets. **endothelial t.,** endothelium. **episcleral t.,** the loose connective tissue over the sclera, between it and the conjunctiva. **epithelial t.,** epithelium. **epivaginal connective t.,** connective tissue surrounding the sheath of the optic nerve. **erectile t.,** tissue containing large venous spaces with which arteries communicate directly, as in the penis and clitoris. Another type formed of dilated venules occurs in the nasal mucosa. The smooth muscle of the nipples constitutes another erectile organ. **extracellular t.,** the total of tissues and body fluids outside of cells, including the plasma volume and all plasma components, the extracellular fluid volume and its components, plus the intercellular and extracellular tissue solids, most notably the collagen, cartilage, bone, elastin, and other connective tissues of the body framework and viscera. **fatty t.,** adipose t. **fibrohyaline t.,** chondroid t. **fibrous t.,** the ordinary connective tissue of the body, made up largely of yellow or white fibers. **fibrous t., white,** that which is composed almost wholly of collagenous fibers. **Gamgee t.,** a surgical dressing consisting of a thick layer of absorbent cotton between two layers of absorbent gauze. **gelatiginous t.,** that which yields gelatin on boiling with water. **gelatinous t.,** mucoid tissue. **glandular t.,** an aggregation of epithelial cells that elaborate secretions. **granulation t.,** a young vascularized connective tissue formed in the process of healing of ulcers and wounds and ultimately forming the cicatrix. **hematopoietic t.,** tissue that takes part in the production of various elements of the blood. **heterologous t.,** one which is unlike any other that is normal to the organism. **homologous t.,** one identical with another in structural type. **hylic t.,** Adami's term for embryonic tissues constituting the body of an organ, in contrast to lining (lepidic) tissue. See also *hylic.* **hyperplastic t.** 1. Tissue affected by hyperplasia. 2. In dentistry, tissue about the maxilla or mandible that is excessively movable, or more readily displaced than is normal. **indifferent t.,** undifferentiated embryonic tissue. **interstitial t.,** the connective tissue between the cellular elements of a body; the stroma. **intertubular t.,** the dense tissue of dentin in which the dentinal tubes are embedded. **junctional t.,** the bridge between the auricle and ventricle of the heart formed by the auriculoventricular node and the auriculoventricular bundle. **lardaceous t.,** one charged with lardacein as a result of a degenerative process. **lepidic t.,** the lining membrane tissue of the embryo. **leprous t.,** abnormal tissue formed under the influence of *Micobacterium leprae,* and peculiar to leprosy. **lymphatic t.,** lymphoid t. **lymphoid t.,** a lattice work of reticular tissue the interspaces of which contain lymphocytes. **mesenchymal t.,** embryonic connective tissue composed of stellate cells and a ground substance of coagulable fluid. **metanephrogenic t.,** the more caudal nephrogenic tissue that gives rise to the nephrons of the permanent kidney. **mucous t.,** a jelly-like connective tissue, such as occurs in the umbilical cord. **muscular t.,** the substance of a muscle. **myeloid t.,** red bone marrow. **nephrogenic t.,** tissue of the nephrotomes which furnishes the material out of which the three kidney-types arise, **nerve t., nervous t.,** the substance of which the nerves and nerve centers are composed. **nodal t.,** tissue made up of nerve and muscle fibers, such as that composing the sino-auricular node of the heart. **osteogenic t.,** the part of the periosteum or perichondrium next to the bone; it is concerned in the formation of osseous tissue. **osteoid t.,** uncalcified bone tissue. **parenchymatous t.,** parenchyma. **periodontal t.,** periodontium. **podophyllous t.,** the tissue on the inner surface of the hoof of an animal. **primitive pulp t.,** hylic t. **reticular t., reticulated t.,** connective tissue consisting of reticular cells and fibers. **rubber t.,** rubber in sheets for use in surgery. **scar t.,** cicatricial t. **sclerous t's,** the cartilaginous, fibrous, and osseous tissues. **shock t.,** that tissue in the animal body which bears the brunt of the antigen-antibody reaction in anaphylaxis. **splenic t.,** the spleen pulp. **subcutaneous t.,** the layer of loose connective tissue situated directly beneath the skin. Called also *tela subcutanea* [N A]. **subcutaneous fatty t.,** panniculus adiposus. **sustentacular t.,** a non-nervous structure of the retina composed of the müllerian fibers of that organ. **symplastic t.,** symplasm. **vesicular supporting t.,** pseudocartilage.

tissular (tish'u-lar). Pertaining to organic tissue.

titanium (ti-ta'ne-um) [L. *titan* the sun]. A rare, dark-gray, metallic element; atomic number, 22; atomic weight, 47.90; symbol, Ti; specific gravity, 4.5: used in homeopathic practice. **t. dioxide,** a white powder, TiO_2,: used as a solar protective, in an ointment or lotion, and as a pigment in the manufacture of artificial teeth.

titer (ti'ter) [Fr. *titre* standard]. The quantity of a substance required to produce a reaction with a given volume of another substance, or the amount of one substance required to correspond with a given amount of another substance. **agglutination t.,** the highest dilution of a serum which causes clumping of bacteria.

titillation (tit"ĭ-la'shun) [L. *titillatio*]. The act or sensation of tickling.

titillomania (tit"ĭ-lo-ma'ne-ah). A morbid desire to scratch.

titrate (ti'trāt). To determine by titration.

titration (ti-tra'shun) [Fr. *titre* standard]. Volumetric determinations by means of standard solutions of known strength. **colorimetric t.,** a method of determining the hydrogen ion concentration by adding an indicator to the unknown and then comparing the color with a set of tubes containing this same indicator in solutions of known hydrogen ion concentration. **electric t., electrode t., electrolytic t.,** a method of determining the hydrogen ion concentration by placing a hydrogen electrode in the unknown solution and measuring the potential developed as compared with some standard electrode by means of a potentiometer. **formol t.** See *Sörensen's method,* under *method.* **potentiometer t.,** electric t.

titre (ti'ter) [Fr.]. Titer.

titrimetric (tit"rĭ-met'rik). Pertaining to analysis by titration.

titrimetry (ti-trim'e-tre) [*titration* + Gr. *metron* measure]. Analysis by titration.

titubant (tit'u-bant). A person who staggers.

titubation (tit"u-ba'shun) [L. *titubatio*]. The act of staggering or reeling; a staggering or stumbling gait, especially one due to a lesion of the spinal system. **lingual t,.** stuttering or stammering.

Tityus serrulatus (tit'e-us ser"u-la'tus). A scorpion of Brazil which inflicts a severe, sometimes fatal, sting.

Tizzoni's test (tid-zo'nēz) [Guido *Tizzoni,* Italian physician, 1853–1932]. See under *tests.*

tjettek (tyet'ek). A deadly poison prepared by the Javanese from the root of *Strychnos tieute.*

TKD. Abbreviation for *tokodynamometer.*

TKG. Abbreviation for *tokodynagraph.*

Tl. Chemical symbol for *thallium.*

TLC. Abbreviation for *tender loving care* and *total lung capacity.*

Tm. 1. Chemical symbol for *thulium.* 2. Symbol for *maximal tubular excretory capacity* (of the kidneys): used in reporting kidney function studies, with inferior letters representing substance used in test, as Tm_{PAH} (maximum tubular excretory capacity for para-aminohippuric acid).

Tn. Symbol for *normal intraocular tension.*

TNT. Abbreviation for *trinitrotoluene.*

TO. 1. An abbreviation for *original tuberculin.* See *tuberculin.* 2. Abbreviation for *tinctura opii,* tincture of opium.

toadskin (tōd'skin). Phrynoderma.

tobacco (to-bak'o) [L. *tabacum*]. The dried and prepared leaves of *Nicotiana tabacum,* a solanaceous plant. Tobacco contains the alkaloid *nicotine,* and unites the qualities of a sedative narcotic with those of an emetic and diuretic. It is also a heart depressant and antispasmodic. **mountain t.** arnica. **poison t.,** hyoscyamus.

tobaccoism (to-bak'o-izm). A morbid condition due to excessive use of tobacco; nicotinism.

Tobey-Ayer test (to'be a'er) [George L. *Tobey,* Jr., Boston otolaryngologist, 1881–1947; James B.

Ayer, Boston neurologist, born 1882]. See under *tests.*

Tobold's apparatus (to′bōlts) [Adelbert August Oskar *Tobold*, German laryngologist, 1827–1907]. See under *apparatus.*

tochil (to′chil). Paragonimiasis.

toclase (to′klās). Trade mark for preparations of carbetapentane citrate.

toco- (to′ko) [Gr. *tokos* childbirth]. Combining form denoting relationship to childbirth, or labor. See also words beginning *toko-.*

tocodynagraph (to″ko-di′nah-graf). Tokodynagraph.

tocodynamometer (to″ko-di″nah-mom′e-ter). Tokodynamometer.

toco-ergometry (to″ko-er-gom′e-tre) [*toco-* + Gr. *ergon* work + *metron* measure]. The measurement of the force of the uterine contractions in labor.

tocograph (tok′o-graf). A recording tokodynamometer.

tocography (to-kog′rah-fe) [*toco-* + Gr. *graphein* to write]. The graphic recording of uterine contractions.

tocokinin (tok″o-kin′in) [*toco-* + Gr. *kinein* to move]. An extract from yeast and certain vegetables which has the properties of an estral hormone.

tocology (to-kol′o-je). Obstetrics.

tocomania (to″ko-ma′ne-ah) [*toco-* + Gr. *mania* madness]. Puerperal mania.

tocometer (to-kom′e-ter) [*toco-* + Gr. *metron* measure]. Tocodynamometer.

tocopherol (to-kof′er-ol) [*toco-* + Gr. *pherein* to carry]. An alcohol which has the properties of vitamin E; isolated from the oil of the germ of wheat kernel, or produced synthetically. **α t., alpha t.,** 2,5,7,8-tetramethyl-2-(4′8′,12′-trimethyltridecyl)-6-chromanol: used empirically in various disorders.

tocophobia (to″ko-fo′be-ah) [*toco-* + Gr. *phobein* to be affrighted by]. Abnormal dread of childbirth.

tocus (to′kus) [L.; Gr. *tokos*]. Labor; childbirth.

Todd bodies (tod) [John Launcelot *Todd*, Canadian physician, 1876–1949]. See under *body.*

Todd's cirrhosis, paralysis, potion, process (todz) [Robert Bentley *Todd*, English physician, 1809–1860]. See under the nouns.

Toddalia (to-dal′e-ah). A genus of rutaceous shrubs. The root of *T. aculeata*, of the East Indies, is an aromatic stomachic.

toddy (tod′e) [Hind. *tāre, tādi*]. 1. The fermented sap of various palm trees. 2. A drink prepared from gin or whisky, sugar, and water.

toe (to). A digit of the foot. **hammer t.,** a condition in which the proximal phalanx of a toe—oftenest that of the second toe—is extended and the second and distal phalanges are flexed, causing a clawlike appearance. **Hong Kong t.,** epidermophytosis of the toes. **mango t.,** epidermophytosis of the toes. **Morton's t.,** metatarsalgia. **pigeon t.,** pes varus; a permanent toeing-in position of the feet. **seedy t.,** a disease of horses' feet marked by a fungous growth of a horny, honeycombed texture between the coffin bone and the wall of the hoof.

toenail (to′nāl). The nail on one of the digits of the foot.

Toepfer (tep′fer). See *Töpfer.*

tofranil (to-fra′nil). Trade mark for preparations of imipramine hydrochloride.

tofukasu (to-foo-ka′soo). A Japanese food prepared from soy beans.

toilet (toi′let). The cleansing and dressing of a surgical or accidental wound, or of an obstetrical patient.

Toison's solution (twah-zawz′) [J. *Toison*, French histologist, born 1858]. See under *solution.*

toko- [Gr. *tokos* childbirth]. For words beginning thus, see also those beginning *toco-.*

tokodynagraph (to″ko-di′nah-graf) [Gr. *tokos* childbirth + *graphein* to write]. The record obtained with a tokodynamometer.

tokodynamometer (to″ko-di″nah-mom′e-ter) [Gr. *tokos* childbirth + *dynamis* power + *metron* measure]. An instrument for measuring the expulsive force of the uterine contractions in labor.

tolazoline (tol-az′o-lēn). Chemical name: 2-benzyl-2-imidazoline: used as a sympatholytic agent and a vasodilator.

tolbutamide (tol-bu′tah-mīd). Chemical name: 1-butyl-3-p-tolylsulfonylurea: used as an oral hypoglycemic agent.

tolerance (tol′er-ans) [L. *tolerantia*]. The ability to endure without ill effect, such as ability to endure the continued or increasing use of a drug. **acquired t.,** the increasing resistance to the usual effects of a drug as in the case of a drug addict. **alkali t.,** ability of the body to endure the administration of alkalis, measured by the amount of alkali that must be given to cause an alkaline urine. This forms a rough measure of the degree of acidosis. **crossed t.,** the lessened susceptibility which persons who have acquired a tolerance for one drug or poison may thereafter exhibit toward another drug. **drug t.,** progressive diminution of susceptibility to the effects of a drug, resulting from its continued administration. **glucose t.,** ability of the body to metabolize glucose. It is measured by the maximum amount of total glucose in a well-balanced diet, equally divided into three meals, which can be taken without having glucosuria at any time during the twenty-four hours. **immunological t.,** a state of indifference or non-reactivity toward a substance that would normally be expected to excite an immunological response.

tolerant (tol′er-ant). Able to endure, without effect, the action of any particular drug or other agent.

toleration (tol″er-a′shun). Tolerance.

tolerific (tol″er-if′ik). Producing tolerance.

Tollens' test (tol′enz) [Bernhard Christian Gottfried *Tollens*, German chemist, 1841–1918]. See under *tests.*

tolonium (to-lo′ne-um). Chemical name: 3-amino-7-dimethylamino-2-methylphenazothionium: used to reduce bleeding tendency in certain hemorrhagic conditions associated with excess of heparinoid substances in the blood.

tolserol (tol′ser-ol). Trade mark for preparations of mephenesin.

toluene (tol′u-ēn). The hydrocarbon, $C_6H_5.CH_3$, methylbenzene; a colorless liquid obtainable from tolu and other resins and from coal tar. Called also *toluol.*

toluidine (tol-u′ĭ-din). A compound, 2-aminotoluene, $CH_3.C_6H_4.NH_2$, made by reducing nitrotoluene. It is homologous with aniline. **t. blue O,** tolonium.

toluol (tol′u-ol). Toluene.

tolusafranine (tol″u-saf′rah-nin). A dibenzoparadiazine dye, $NH_2(CH_3).C_6H_3.N_2.(C_6H_5)Cl.C_6H_3(CH_3).NH_2$, the chief constituent of safranine.

toluyl (tol′u-il). The univalent acid radical, $CH_3.C_6H_4$.

toluylene (tol-u′ĭ-lēn). The hydrocarbon, diphenyl ethylene, $C_6H_5.CH{:}CH.C_6H_5$. Called also *stilbene.*

tolyl (tol′il). The univalent radical, $CH_3.C_6H_4$, isomeric with benzyl. **t. hydroxide,** cresol.

tomatin (to-ma′tin). An antibiotic substance isolated from tomato plants affected with wilt.

-tome [Gr. *tomē* a cutting]. Word termination signifying (*a*) an instrument for cutting or (*b*) a segment.

tomentum (to-men′tum). A network of minute blood vessels of the pia and the cortex cerebri. Called also *t. cerebri.*

Tomes's fibers, layer, process (tōmz) [Sir John *Tomes*, English dentist, 1836–1895]. See under the nouns.

Tommaselli's disease, syndrome (tom″ah-sel′ēz) [Salvatore *Tommaselli*, Italian physician, 1834–1906]. See under *disease*.

Tommasi's sign, test (tom-mas′e) [L. *Tommasi*, Italian physician]. See under *sign*.

tomo- (to′mo) [Gr. *tomē* a cutting]. Combining form denoting relationship to a cutting, or to a designated layer, as might be achieved by cutting or slicing.

tomogram (to′mo-gram). A roentgenogram of a selected layer of the body made by tomography.

tomograph (to′mo-graf). An x-ray machine which makes a roentgenogram of a layer of tissue at any depth.

tomography (to-mog′rah-fe) [*tomo-* + Gr. *graphein* to write]. See *body section roentgenography*, under *roentgenography*.

tomomania (to″mo-ma′ne-ah) [*tomo-* + Gr. *mania* madness]. 1. Undue eagerness to perform surgical operations. 2. An hysterical desire to be operated upon surgically.

tomotocia (to″mo-to′she-ah) [*tomo-* + Gr. *tokos* birth]. Delivery by abdominal section.

-tomy (to′me) [Gr. *tomē* a cutting] Word termination signifying the operation of cutting, or incision.

tonaphasia (ton″ah-fa′ze-ah). Inability to recall a familiar tune; musical aphasia.

tone (tōn) [Gr. *tonos; L. tonus*]. 1. The normal degree of vigor and tension; in muscle, the resistance to passive elongation or stretch. 2. A healthy state of a part; tonus. 3. A particular quality of sound or of voice. **feeling t.,** the condition or state of mind and feeling which accompanies every thought or act. **finger t.,** the sound heard with the phonendoscope on placing the end of the finger on the diaphragm while the instrument is in use. **heart t's,** the sounds heard in the auscultation of the heart. **jecoral t.,** the sound produced by percussion over the liver. **plastic t.,** the posture-maintaining mechanism of muscle by virtue of which a limb passively placed in any position tends to maintain that position. **Williams' tracheal t.** See under *sign*, def 1.

tonga (tong′gah). A native name for frambesia in New Caledonia.

tongue (tung) [L. *lingua*, Gr. *glōssa*]. 1. The movable, muscular organ on the floor of the mouth, subserving the special sense of taste and aiding in mastication, deglutition, and the articulation of sound. Called also *lingua* [N A]. 2. Any structure or part having a shape similar to that of the oral organ of the same name. Called also *lingula* [N A]. **adherent t.,** a tongue that is abnormally attached by folds of mucous membrane to the sides and floor of the mouth. **baked t.,** the dry, brown tongue of typhoid fever. **bald t.,** a tongue characterized by the absence of papillae. **bifid t.,** a tongue that is divided in its anterior part by a longitudinal fissure. **black t., black hairy t.,** a condition characterized by the presence of a brown or greenish furlike patch on the dorsum of the tongue, composed of hypertrophied filiform papillae with microorganisms and some pigment. Called also *anthracosis linguae, glossophytia, hyperkeratosis linguae, keratomycosis linguae, lingua villosa nigra, melanotrichia linguae,* and *nigrities linguae.* **blue t.,** a disease of sheep and cattle in South Africa, caused by a virus, and characterized by hyperemia and edema of the lips, tongue, and oral mucosa. **burning t.,** glossopyrosis. **cardinal t.,** a tongue whose surface is denuded of epithelium, giving it a bright red appearance. **cerebriform t.,** fissured t. **choreic t.,** abrupt, snakelike protrusion and withdrawal of the tongue occurring in chorea. **cleft t.,** bifid t. **coated t.,** a tongue covered with a whitish or yellowish layer consisting of desquamated epithelium, de-

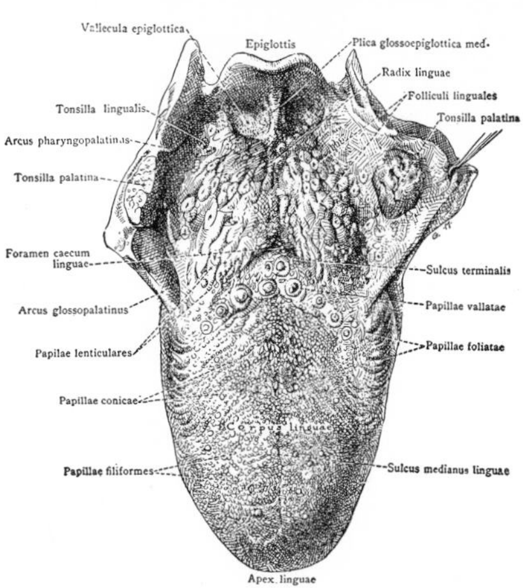

The tongue, showing principal structures. (Eycleshymer and Jones.)

bris, bacteria, fungi, etc. **cobble-stone t.,** a condition characterized by interstitial glossitis, with hypertrophy of the papillae and a verrucous white coating on the tongue. **crocodile t.,** fissured t. **dotted t.,** stippled t. **double t.,** bifid t. **earthy t.,** a tongue that is coated with a deposit of rough, calcareous matter. **encrusted t.,** a heavily coated tongue. **fern leaf t.,** a tongue with a central furrow having lateral branches. **filmy t.,** one marked with symmetrical whitish patches. **fissured t.,** a congenital condition characterized by uniformly arranged fissures radiating forward and outward from the median raphe of the tongue, without evidence of inflammation. **furred t.,** a tongue with papillae so changed as to give the mucous membrane the appearance of whitish fur. **furrowed t.,** fissured t. **geographic t.,** a tongue with denuded patches surrounded by thickened epithelium. Called also *lingua geographica, erythema migrans, pityriasis linguae,* and *glossitis areata exfoliativa.* **glossy t.,** Moeller's glossitis. **grooved t.,** fissured t. **hairy t.,** a tongue the papillae of which have a hairlike appearance. **lobulated t.,** a tongue with a congenital second lobe lying on it. **magenta t.,** the magenta-colored tongue seen in cases of riboflavin deficiency. **mappy t.,** geographic t. **parrot t.,** the dry, horny tongue of low fever, which cannot be protruded. **plicated t.,** fissured t. **raspberry t.,** a red, uncoated tongue, with elevated papillae, such as is seen a few days after appearance of the rash in scarlet fever. **Sandwith's bald t.,** an extremely clean tongue sometimes seen in the late stages of pellagra. **scrotal t.,** fissured t. **smokers' t.,** leukoplakia of the tongue. **t. of sphenoid bone,** lingula sphenoidalis. **split t.,** bifid t. **stippled t.,** a tongue on which each papilla is covered with a separate white patch of epithelium. Called also *dotted t.* **strawberry t.,** a coated tongue with enlarged, red, fungiform papillae, seen in the first 24 hours after appearance of the rash in scarlet fever. **sulcated t.,** fissured t. **white t.,** a condition in which all or part of the papillae and epithelium of the tongue have a dull white color. **wooden t.,** actinomycosis in cattle. **wrinkled t.,** fissured t.

tonguetie (tung′ti). Abnormal shortness of the frenum of the tongue, resulting in limitation of its motion.

tonic (ton′ik) [Gr. *tonikos*]. 1. Producing and restoring the normal tone. 2. Characterized by continuous tension. 3. A term formerly used for a class of medicinal preparations believed to have the power of restoring normal tone to tissue. **bitter t.,** a tonic of bitter taste: used for stimulating the appetite and improving digestion, such as quinine, quassia, and gentian. **cardiac t.,** one which strengthens the heart's action, such as digitalis, strophanthus, or strychnine. **diges-**

tive t., an intestinal or stomachic tonic. **general t.,** one which braces up the whole system: cold baths, electricity, and exercise are general tonics. **hematic t.,** a medicine which improves the quality of the blood: the principal medicines of this class are iron, arsenic, manganese, mercuric chloride, and quinine. **intestinal t.,** one that improves the tone of the intestinal tract. **nervine t.,** one that increases the tone of the nervous system. **stomachic t.,** one which aids the functions of the stomach. Here are classed the alcoholic stimulants, vegetable bitters, hydrochlōric and nitrohydrochloric acids. **vascular t.,** one which increases the tone of the blood vessels. Among them are belladonna, digitalis, ergot, and strychnine.

tonicity (to-nis'ĭ-te). The normal condition of tone or tension; used in colloidal chemistry as the equivalent of effective osmotic pressure.

tonicize (ton'ĭ-sīz). 1. To improve the tone of a part. 2. To induce tonic contraction of a muscle.

tonicoclonic (ton"ĭ-ko-klon'ik). Tonoclonic.

tonitrophobia (ton"ĭ-tro-fo'be-ah) [L. *tonitrus* thunder + Gr. *phobein* to be affrighted by]. Morbid fear of thunder.

tonitruphobia (ton"ĭ-troo-fo'be-ah). Tonitrophobia.

Tonka bean (tong'kah bēn). The seed of *Dipteryx odorata*, a North America tree. It affords coumarin, and is used as a flavoring agent and to disguise odors.

tono- [Gr. *tonos* tension]. Combining form denoting relationship to tone or tension.

tonoclonic (ton"o-klon'ik). Both tonic and clonic; said of a spasm consisting of a convulsive twitching of the muscles.

tonofibril (ton'o-fi"bril). An organoid in the form of a fine fibril seen in cells (and their intercellular bridges), especially epithelial cells: they are supposed by some to give a supporting framework to the cell; others believe they are only tension striae of the protoplasm.

tonogram (to'no-gram). The record produced by tonography.

tonograph (to'no-graf) [*tono-* + Gr. *graphein* to write]. A recording tonometer.

tonography (to-nog'rah-fe). The recording of changes in intraocular pressure produced by the constant application of a known weight on the globe of the eye, reflecting the facility of outflow of the aqueous humor from the anterior chamber.

tonometer (to-nom'e-ter) [*tono-* + Gr. *metron* measure]. An instrument for measuring tension or pressure; usually used specifically in reference to an instrument by which intraocular pressure is measured. **Gärtner's t.,** an instrument for measuring blood pressure by means of a compressing ring applied to the finger. **Goldman's applanation t.,** an instrument for measuring intraocular pressure which eliminates the effects of scleral resistance. **McLean t.,** an instrument which registers intraocular pressure, with a scale from which the pressure can be read directly. **Musken's t.,** an instrument for measuring the tonicity of the Achilles tendon. **Recklinghausen's t.,** an instrument for observing oscillatory blood pressure. **Schiøtz' t.,** an instrument which registers intraocular pressure by direct application to the cornea, the reading on the scale being translated into millimeters of mercury by means of a conversion table.

tonometry (to-nom'e-tre). The measurement of tension or pressure, especially the indirect estimation of the intraocular pressure from determination of the resistance of the eyeball to indentation by an applied force. **digital t.,** estimation of the degree of intraocular pressure by pressure exerted on the eyeball by the finger of the examiner.

tononoscillograph (to"non-os'ĭ-lo-graf). Tonoscillograph.

tonophant (ton'o-fant) [*tono-* + Gr. *phainein* to show]. An instrument for rendering acoustic vibrations visible.

tonoplast (ton'o-plast) [*tono-* + Gr. *plassein* to form]. A small intracellular body which forms powerful osmotic substances within itself and thus swells up to form a small vacuole (De Vries, 1885). The term is now applied to the limiting membrane of an intracellular vacuole, the vacuole membrane.

tonoscillograph (to-nos'ĭ-lo-graf) [*tono-* + L. *oscillare* to swing + Gr. *graphein* to write]. An instrument for recording arterial and capillary pressures and the character of the individual pulse.

tonoscope (ton'o-skop) [*tono-* + Gr. *skopein* to examine]. 1. An apparatus for rendering sound visible by registering the vibrations on a screen. 2. A device for examining the head or brain by means of sound. 3. Tonometer.

tonsil (ton'sil). A small rounded mass of tissue, especially of lymphoid tissue. The term is often used without qualification to designate the palatine tonsil. Called also *tonsilla*. **abdominal t.,** appendix vermiformis. **buried t.,** submerged t. **t. of cerebellum,** tonsilla cerebelli. **eustachian t.** See *noduli lymphatici tubarii tubae auditivae*. **faucial t.** See *palatine t.* **Gerlach's t.** See *noduli lymphatici tubarii tubae auditivae*. **intestinal t.** See *folliculi lymphatici aggregati*. **lingual t.,** tonsilla lingualis. **Luschka's t.,** tonsilla pharyngea. **palatine t.,** a small, almond-shaped mass between the palatoglossal and palatopharyngeal arches on either side, composed mainly of lymphoid tissue, covered with mucous membrane, and containing various crypts and many lymph follicles; believed to act as sources for supply to the mouth and pharynx of phagocytes which destroy bacteria entering the mouth. Called also *tonsilla palatina* [N A]. **pharyngeal t.,** tonsilla pharyngea. **resected t.,** a palatine tonsil part of which has been excised. **submerged t.,** a palatine tonsil that is shrunken and atrophied and is partly or entirely hidden by the palatoglossal arch. **third t.,** tonsilla pharyngea. **t. of torus tubarius,** tonsilla tubaria. **tubal t.** See *noduli lymphatici tubarii tubae auditivae*.

tonsilla (ton-sil'ah), pl. *tonsil'lae* [L.]. A small rounded mass of tissue, especially of lymphoid tissue. Called also *tonsil*. **t. cerebel'li** [N A, B N A], **t. of cerebellum,** a rounded mass forming part of the cerebellum on its inferior surface, between the uvula and the biventral lobule. **t. intestina'lis.** See *folliculi lymphatici aggregati*. **t. lingua'lis** [N A, B N A], an aggregation of lymph follicles on the floor of the oropharyngeal passageway, at the root of the tongue. Called also *lingual tonsil*. **t. palati'na** [N A, B N A], a small, almond-shaped mass between the palatoglossal and palatopharyngeal arches on either side. See *palatine tonsil*. **t. pharyn'gea** [N A, B N A], the diffuse lymphoid tissue and follicles in the roof and posterior wall of the nasopharynx. Called also *pharyngeal tonsil*. **t. tuba'ria** [N A], lymphoid tissue associated with the opening of the auditory tube. Called also *tonsil of torus tubarius*.

tonsillar (ton'sĭ-lar) [L. *tonsillaris*]. Of or pertaining to a tonsil.

tonsillectome (ton"sĭ-lek'tōm). An instrument for performing tonsillectomy.

tonsillectomy (ton"sĭ-lek'to-me) [L. *tonsilla* tonsil + Gr. *ektomē* excision]. Surgical removal of a tonsil or tonsils.

tonsillith (ton'sĭ-lith). Tonsillolith.

tonsillitic (ton"sĭ-lit'ik). Pertaining to or affected with tonsillitis.

tonsillitis (ton"sĭ-li'tis) [L. *tonsilla* tonsil + *-itis*]. Inflammation of a tonsil. **caseous t.,** lacunar t. **catarrhal t., acute,** a form associated with acute catarrhal pharyngitis, in which the tonsils are red and swollen. Called also *erythematous t.* **catarrhal t., chronic,** a form attended by permanent hypertrophy, and usually requiring tonsillectomy. **diphtherial t.** See *diphtheria.* **erythematous t.,** catarrhal t., acute. **follicular t.,** that which especially affects the follicles. **herpetic t.,** a local manifestation of herpes on the tonsil. **lacunar t.,** tonsillitis in which the follicles of the tonsils are filled with plugs of caseous matter. Called also *caseous t.* **t. len'ta,** chronic inflammation of the tonsils producing a prolonged chronic sepsis. **lingual t.,** inflammation of a lymphoid mass at the base of the tongue. **mycotic t.,** a form due to fungi. **parenchymatous t., acute,** quinsy; a form attended with high fever, severe pain, headache, dysphagia, and suppuration. **preglottic t.,** inflammation of the lingual tonsil. **pustular t.,** that which is characterized by the formation of pustules. **streptococcus t.** See *septic sore throat,* under *sore throat.* **superficial t.,** inflammation of the mucous membrane over a tonsil. **suppurative t.,** parenchymatous t., acute. **Vincent's t.,** tonsillitis caused by Vincent's organism.

tonsilloadenoidectomy (ton″sil-o-ad″ĕ-noid-ek′to-me). Excision of palatine tonsils and adenoids.

tonsillohemisporosis (ton″sĭ-lo-hem″ĭ-spo-ro′-sis). Infection of the tonsil with Hemispora.

tonsillolith (ton-sil′o-lith) [*tonsil* + Gr. *lithos* stone]. A concretion or calculus in a tonsil.

tonsillomoniliasis (ton-sil″o-mo″nĭ-li′ah-sis). Infection of the tonsil with Monilia (Candida).

tonsillomycosis (ton-sil″o-mi-ko′sis). Any mycotic infection of the tonsils.

tonsillo-oidiosis (ton-sil″o-o-id″e-o′sis). Infection of the tonsil with Oidium (Candida).

tonsillopathy (ton″sĭ-lop′ah-the) [*tonsil* + Gr. *pathos* disease]. Any disease of the tonsil.

tonsilloprive (ton′sĭ-lo-priv) [*tonsil* + L. *privare* to deprive]. Having the tonsils removed; due to removal or absence of the tonsils.

tonsilloscope (ton-sil′o-skōp) [*tonsil* + Gr. *skopein* to examine]. An instrument for inspecting the tonsils.

tonsilloscopy (ton″sĭ-los′ko-pe). Diagnostic inspection of the tonsils.

tonsillotome (ton-sil′o-tōm). A knife used in tonsillotomy.

tonsillotomy (ton″sĭ-lot′o-me) [L. *tonsilla* tonsil + Gr. *tomē* a cutting]. Incision of a tonsil; the surgical removal of a part of a tonsil.

tonsillotyphoid (ton″sĭ-lo-ti′foid). Pharyngotyphoid.

tonsolith (ton′so-lith). Tonsillolith.

tonus (to′nus) [L.; Gr. *tonos*]. The slight, continuous contraction of muscle, which in skeletal muscles aids in the maintenance of posture and in the return of blood to the heart. See *tone.* **acerebral t.,** tonic contraction of muscles after removal of the cerebrum. **chemical t.,** the state of slight but continuous chemical activity in muscles when at rest. **myogenic t.,** tonic contraction of muscle dependent upon some property of the muscle itself or of its intrinsic nerve cells. **neurogenic t.,** tonic contraction of muscle due to stimulation received through the nervous system.

tooth (tōōth), pl. *teeth.* One of a set of small, bone-like structures of the jaws for masticating the food (dentes [N A]), or a similar structure in various other organisms of the animal or plant kingdom. In man, there are two sets of teeth, the *deciduous teeth,* and the *permanent teeth.* Each tooth has three parts—a *crown,* or *body,* above the gum; a *neck,* between the crown and root; a *root,* or *fang,* embedded within the alveolus. A tooth consists of a solid portion and a pulp cavity. The solid portion includes the *dentin,* or ivory, forming most of the tooth and resembling bone; *enamel,* the hardest of organized bodies, covering the crown; and *cementum,* covering the root. The cementum, or *crusta petrosa,* is true bone. The

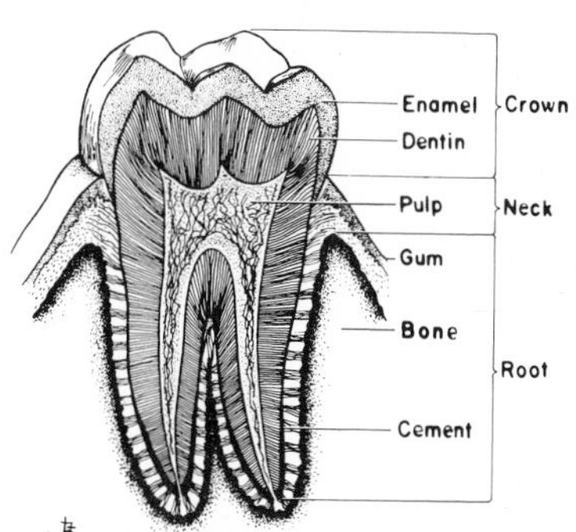

Diagram of a section through a human molar tooth. (Villee.)

pulp cavity within the crown is continuous with a canal in the root which opens at the root apex for the passage of nerves and vessels. This cavity contains the *dental pulp,* a soft, sensitive substance containing many vessels and nerves, and composed of cells and connective tissue. *Eruption,* or "cutting," of the teeth is probably due to growth of the root, the follicle being resorbed by pressure. The order of eruption is: *Deciduous teeth*—Medial incisors, 6 to 8 months; lateral incisors, 7 to 9 months; first molars, 12 to 14 months; canines, 16 to 18 months; second molars, 20 to 24 months. *Permanent teeth*—First molars, 6 or 7 years; medial incisors, 6 to 8 years; lateral incisors, 7 to 9 years; premolars, 10 to 12 years; canines, 9 to 12 years; second molars, 11 to 13 years; third molars, 17 to 21 years. **accessional teeth,** the permanent molars, so called because they do not supplant any deciduous predecessors in the dental arch. Cf. *successional teeth.* **acrylic resin t.,** an artificial tooth made of acrylic resin. **anatomic teeth,** a term applied to artificial teeth in which the cusps and ridges of the natural teeth are reproduced on the occlusal surface. **angular teeth,** canine teeth. **anterior teeth,** the three teeth on either side in each jaw situated closest to the midline of the dental arch, including the incisor and canine (cuspid) teeth. **artificial t.,** a tooth made of porcelain or other synthetic compound in imitation of a natural tooth. See also *denture.* **auditory teeth of Huschke,** dentes acustici. **t. of axis,** dens axis. **azzle teeth,** molar teeth. **barred teeth,** teeth with roots spread out so that their extraction is extremely difficult. **bicuspid teeth,** premolar teeth. **brown opalescent teeth, hereditary.** See *amelogenesis imperfecta.* **buccal teeth,** posterior teeth. **canine teeth,** the four teeth, one on either side in each jaw, immediately lateral to the lateral incisors; the tearing teeth, having a long and conical crown and a single root. Called also *dentes canini* [N A]. **cheek teeth,** posterior teeth. **cheoplastic teeth,** artificial teeth attached to a cheoplastic base without pins. **chiaie teeth,** teeth from which the enamel is eaten away by the action of subterranean gases; seen in those exposed to the emanations of the volcanoes or who drink water impregnated with such gases. **connate t.,** geminate t. **corner t.,** the third incisor on either side of each jaw in the horse. **cross-bite teeth,** posterior teeth designed to permit positioning of the modified buccal cusps of the upper teeth in the fossae of the lower teeth. **cross-pin teeth,** artificial teeth in which the pins are inserted horizontally. **cuspid teeth,** canine teeth. **cuspless teeth,** teeth designed without cusps on the occlusal surface. **deciduous teeth,** the teeth of the first dentition, which are shed and followed, in the dental arch, by the permanent teeth. The 20 deciduous teeth, 10 in each jaw, include 4 incisor, 2 canine, and 4 molar teeth. Called also *dentes decidui* [N A], and *milk* or *temporary teeth.* **diatoric teeth,** artificial teeth with holes in their bases into which the rubber flows and, when processed, attaches the teeth to the base. **t. of**

epistropheus, dens axis. **eye t.,** a canine tooth of the upper jaw, or maxilla. **Fournier teeth,** Moon's teeth. **fused teeth,** a dental structure resulting from the union, early in odontogenesis, of two normally separate tooth germs, the completeness of the fusion depending on the stage at which the union took place. **geminate t.,** a tooth with a single root and root canal, but with two completely or incompletely separated crowns, resulting from invagination of a single tooth germ, causing incomplete formation of two teeth. **Goslee t.,** an interchangeable tooth attached to a metal base. **hag teeth,** upper medial incisors that are widely separated. **hair teeth,** dentes acustici. **Horner's teeth,** incisor teeth horizontally grooved from a deficiency of enamel. **Hutchinson's teeth,** notched and narrow-edged permanent incisors; regarded as a sign of congenital syphilis, but not always of such origin. **impacted t.,** a tooth so placed in the jaw that it is unable to erupt, or unable to attain its normal position in occlusion. **incisor teeth,** the four front teeth in each jaw; the cutting teeth, each with a crown shaped like a wedge, and one long conical root. Called also *dentes incisivi* [N A]. **labial teeth,** anterior teeth. **lion's t.** [Fr. *dent-de-lion* dandelion], Taraxacum. **malacotic teeth,** teeth that are soft in structure and are abnormally susceptible to caries. **malposed t.,** a tooth out of its normal position. **mandibular teeth,** the teeth of the mandible, or lower jaw. **maxillary teeth,** the teeth of the maxilla, or upper jaw. **metal insert teeth,** artificial teeth containing metal in the occlusal surface. **milk teeth,** deciduous teeth. **molar teeth** [L. *molaris* to do with grinding], the most posterior teeth on either side in each jaw, totalling 8 in the deciduous dentition, and usually 12 in the permanent; the grinding teeth, with broad square crowns. The upper molars characteristically have four cusps and three roots; the lower, five cusps and two roots. The third molar, also called *wisdom tooth*, usually has fused roots. Called also *dentes molares* [N A]. **Moon's teeth,** small, domed first molars observed in patients with congenital syphilis. **morsal teeth** [L. *morsus* a seizing], anterior teeth. **mottled teeth,** teeth whose enamel is marked with discoloration. **mulberry t.,** mulberry

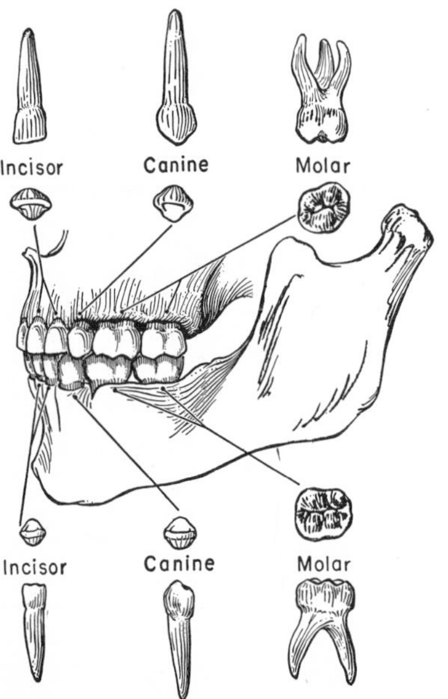

Typical Deciduous Teeth

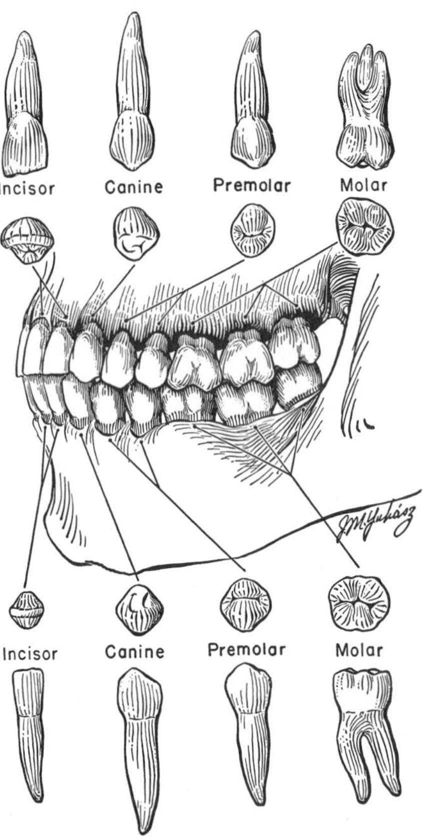

Typical Permanent Teeth

molar. **natal t.,** a prematurely erupted deciduous tooth, visible in the jaw at birth. **nonanatomic teeth,** a term applied to artificial teeth the occlusal surfaces of which are especially designed on the basis of engineering concepts, without regard to the features of natural teeth. **peg t.,** a tooth whose sides converge or taper together incisally, instead of being parallel or diverging mesially and distally; a condition frequently observed in the maxillary medial incisor. **permanent teeth,** the teeth of the second dentition. The 32 permanent teeth, 16 in each jaw, include 4 incisor, 2 canine, 4 premolar, and 6 molar teeth. Called also *dentes permanentes* [N A]. **pink t. of Mummery,** internal resorption of a tooth, so called because of the pink color given the crown by the hyperplastic, vascular pulp filling the area formerly occupied by the resorbed dentin. **pinless teeth,** diatoric teeth. **plastic t.,** an artificial tooth made of synthetic resin. **posterior teeth,** the teeth on either side in each jaw, distal to the canine teeth, including the premolar (bicuspid) and molar teeth. Called also *buccal* or *cheek teeth*. **postpermanent t.,** a tooth that erupts after the permanent teeth have been extracted. **predeciduous t.,** a term applied to a hornified epithelial structure, without roots, occurring on the gingiva over the crest of the ridge of the alveolar process. **premolar teeth,** the four permanent teeth, one on either side in each jaw, distal to the canine teeth, characterized by having a crown with two cusps and a grooved, conical, single root. Called also *dentes premolares* [N A], and *bicuspid teeth*. **primary teeth.** 1. Deciduous teeth. 2. Incisor teeth. **pulpless t.,** a tooth from which the pulp has been extirpated. **rake teeth,** teeth that are widely separated. **sclerotic teeth,** teeth that are hard in structure and are resistant to caries. **screw-driver teeth,** Hutchinson's teeth. **shell t.,** a tooth in which the enamel appears essentially normal, the dentin is extremely thin, and the pulp chamber is enormous. **snaggle t.,** a tooth out of proper line with the others. **stomach t.,** a canine tooth of the lower jaw, or mandible. **straight-pin teeth,** artificial teeth in which the pins are inserted vertically. **"submerged" t.,** a deciduous tooth, most commonly a mandibular second molar, which has undergone a variable degree of root resorption and then become ankylosed to the bone, preventing its exfoliation and subsequent replacement by a permanent tooth. **succedaneous teeth, successional teeth,** the permanent teeth that have deciduous predecessors in the dental arch. **superior teeth,** the teeth of the upper jaw, or maxilla. **supernumerary teeth, supplemental teeth,** natural teeth in excess of the number normally present in the jaw. **temporary teeth,** deciduous teeth. **tube teeth,** artificial teeth having a vertical, cylindrical aperture from the center of the base up into the body of the tooth, into which a pin may be placed or cast for attachment of the tooth to the denture base. **Turner t.,** a permanent tooth with hypoplasia of enamel, resulting from spread to the tooth germ of periapical infection and inflammation involving a primary tooth, usually a mandibular premolar. **virgin t.,** a horse's tooth not yet worn down by use. **vital teeth,** teeth to which the nerve and vascular supply is intact. **wall teeth,** molar teeth. **wandering t.,** a tooth that moves from its normal position in the dental arch. **wang teeth,** molar teeth. **wisdom t.,** one of the third molars, the teeth most distal from the medial line on either side in each jaw, so called because it is the last of the permanent dentition to erupt, usually at the age of 17 to 21 years. Called also *dens serotinus* [N A]. **wolf t.,** a vestigial first premolar tooth sometimes present in the jaw of a horse. **zero degree teeth,** artificial teeth which have no cusp angles in relation to the horizontal on their occlusal surfaces.

Tooth's type (tooths) [Howard Henry *Tooth,* English physician, 1856–1926]. The peroneal form of progressive muscular atrophy.

tooth-borne (tōōth'born). Supported entirely by the teeth: applied to a prosthesis or part of a prosthesis which is entirely supported by the abutment teeth.

topagnosis (top″ag-no'sis) [Gr. *topos* place + *a* neg. + *gnōsis* recognition]. Loss of touch localization.

topalgia (to-pal'je-ah) [Gr. *topos* place + *algos* pain + *-ia*]. Fixed or localized pain: seen in neurasthenia.

topectomy (to-pek'to-me) [*topo-* + Gr. *ektomē* excision]. Ablation of a small and specific area of the frontal cortex in the treatment of mental illness.

topesthesia (top″es-the'ze-ah) [Gr. *topos* place + *aisthēsis* perception + *-ia*]. The power of localizing a tactile sensation.

Töpfer's test (tep'ferz) [Alfred Edouard *Töpfer,* German physician, born 1858]. See under *tests.*

tophaceous (to-fa'shus) [L. *tophaceus: tophus* porous stone]. Hard or gritty.

tophi (to'fi) [L.]. Plural of *tophus.*

topholipoma (tof″o-lĭ-po'mah). A lipoma containing tophi.

tophus (to'fus), pl. *to'phi* [L. "porous stone"]. 1. A chalky deposit of urates found in the tissues about the joints in gout. 2. Dental calculus. **auricular t.,** a tophus on the ear. **dental t.,** dental calculus. **t. syphilit'icus,** a syphilitic node.

tophyperidrosis (tōf″e-per″ĭ-dro'sis) [Gr. *topos* place + *hyper* over + *hidrōs* sweat]. Excessive sweating in certain localized areas.

topical (top'e-kal) [Gr. *topikos*]. Pertaining to a particular spot; local.

Topinard's angle, line (top″e-närz') [Paul *Topinard,* French scientist, 1830–1912]. See under *angle* and *line.*

topitracin (top'ĭ-tra'sin). Trade mark for a preparation of bacitracin.

topo- (top'o) [Gr. *topos* place]. Combining form meaning place.

topoalgia (top″o-al'je-ah). Topalgia.

topo-anesthesia (top″o-an″es-the'ze-ah). Loss of power to localize a tactile sensation.

topodysesthesia (top″o-dis″es-the'ze-ah). Localized dysesthesia.

topognosis (top″og-no'sis) [*topo-* + Gr. *gnōsis* recognition]. Topesthesia.

topographic (top″o-graf'ik). Describing special regions.

topographical (top″o-graf'ĭ-kal). Pertaining to topography.

topography (to-pog'rah-fe) [*topo-* + Gr. *graphein* to write]. The description of an anatomical region or of a special part.

topology (to-pol'o-je) [*topo-* + *-logy*]. 1. Topographical anatomy. 2. The relation between the presenting part of the fetus and the birth canal.

toponarcosis (top″o-nar-ko'sis) [*topo-* + Gr. *narkōsis* benumbing]. Localized anesthesia.

toponeurosis (top″o-nu-ro'sis). A neurosis affecting a limited region.

toponym (top'o-nim). The name of a region as distinguished from an organ.

toponymy (to-pon'ĭ-me) [*topo-* + Gr. *onoma* name]. Terminology pertaining to the position and direction of organs and parts.

topoparesthesia (top″o-par″es-the'ze-ah). Localized paresthesia.

topophobia (top″o-fo'be-ah) [*topo-* + Gr. *phobein* to be affrighted by]. A morbid dread of particular places.

topophylaxis (top″o-fi-lak'sis). The application of a constricting band, intended to confine the phylaxis following arsphenamine injections to the limb in which the injection is made.

topothermesthesiometer (top″o-therm″es-the-ze-om'e-ter) [*topo-* + Gr. *thermē* heat + *aisthēsis* perception + *metron* measure]. An apparatus for measuring the local temperature sense.

topovaccinotherapy (top″o-vak″sĭ-no-ther'ah-pe). Artificial local immunization.

torcular (tor'ku-lar) [L. "wine-press"]. A hollow, or expanded area. **t. Heroph'ili,** confluens sinuum.

Torek operation (to'rek) [Franz J. A. *Torek,* New York surgeon, 1861–1938]. See under *operation.*

torfu (tor'fu). A Japanese food preparation from the soy bean, in white tablets.

tori (to'ri) [L.]. Plural of *torus.*

toric (to'rik). Pertaining to or resembling a torus.

tormina (tor'mĭ-nah) [L.]. The colic.

torminal (tor'mĭ-nal). Pertaining to or characterized by griping pain, or colic.

Tornwaldt's bursitis, disease (torn'vahlts) [Ludwig *Tornwaldt,* 1843–1910]. See under *bursitis.*

tornwaldtitis (torn″vahlt-i'tis). Tornwaldt's bursitis.

torose, torous (to'rōs, to'rus) [L. *torosus* muscular, brawny]. Bulging or knobby.

torpent (tor'pent) [L. *torpere* to be sluggish]. 1. Inactive; in abeyance. 2. An agent that reduces irritation.

torpid (tor'pid) [L. *torpidus* numb, sluggish]. Not acting with normal vigor and facility.

torpidity (tor-pid'ĭ-te). Sluggishness; inactivity, slowness.

torpor (tor'por) [L.]. Lack of response to normal or ordinary stimuli. **t. ret'inae,** a condition in which the retina is excited to action only by stimuli of considerable luminous power.

torque (tork) [L. *torquere* to twist]. A rotary force. In dentistry, the rotation of a tooth on its long axis.

torquing (tork′ing). The twisting of a tooth into position, as in the correction of malposition.

torrefaction (tor″e-fak′shun) [L. *torrefactio*]. The act of roasting or parching.

torrefy (tor′e-fi) [L. *torrefacere*]. To parch, roast, or dry by the aid of heat.

torricellian (to″re-chel′e-an). Named for Evangelista *Torricelli*, Italian physicist, 1608–1647. See under *vacuum*.

torsiometer (tor″se-om′e-ter) [L. *torsio* twist + *metrum* measure]. A form of clinoscope for measuring the amount of rotation of the eyeball on the visual axis.

torsion (tor′shun) [L. *torsio; torquere* to twist]. 1. The act of twisting; the condition of being twisted. In dentistry, the condition of a tooth when it is turned on its long axis. 2. In ophthalmology, any rotation of the vertical corneal meridians. **negative t.,** rotation in a counterclockwise direction. **positive t.,** rotation in a clockwise direction.

torsionometer (tor″shun-om′e-ter) [*torsion* + Gr. *metron* measure]. An apparatus for estimating the degree of rotation of the spinal column.

torsive (tor′siv). Twisted.

torsiversion (tor″sĭ-ver′shun). The turning or rotation of a tooth on its long axis out of its normal position.

torso (tor′so). The trunk without the head or extremities.

torsoclusion (tor″so-kloo′zhun) [L. *torquere* to twist + *cludere* to shut]. 1. Acupressure combined with pressure of the bleeding vessel. 2. Torsiversion.

torso-occlusion (tor″so-ŏ-kloo′zhun). Torsiversion.

torticollar (tor″tĭ-kol′ar). Pertaining to or affected with torticollis.

torticollis (tor″tĭ-kol′is) [L. *tortus* twisted + *collum* neck]. Wryneck; a contracted state of the cervical muscles, producing twisting of the neck and an unnatural position of the head. **congenital t.,** a torticollis due to injury to the sternocleidomastoid muscle on one side at the time of birth and its transformation into a fibrous cord which cannot lengthen with the growing neck. **dermatogenic t.,** torticollis caused by contraction of the skin of the neck. **fixed t.,** an unnatural position of the head due to actual and persistent organic muscular shortening. **hysteric t., hysterical t.,** torticollis due to hysteric contracture. **intermittent t.,** spasmodic t. **labyrinthine t.,** torticollis due to irritation of the semicircular canals on one side. **mental t.,** a form of tic, or habit spasm, in which there is spasmodic contraction of the neck muscles, producing deviation of the head. This deviation usually ceases on the patient lying down, or it may be controlled by slight pressure. **myogenic t.,** a transient condition due to muscular contraction in rheumatism, and to cold. **neurogenic t.,** torticollis due to pressure or irritation of the accessory nerve. **ocular t.,** torticollis due to a high degree of astigmatism. **reflex t.,** torticollis caused by inflammation or suppuration in the neck, enlarged cervical lymph glands or tumor in the tonsil, neck, or pharynx. **rheumatoid t.,** that which is due to rheumatism, chiefly of the sternomastoid and adjacent muscles. **spasmodic t.,** that which is due to spasm of certain muscles, occurring intermittently. **spurious t.,** twisting or stiffness of the neck due to caries of the cervical vertebrae. **symptomatic t.,** stiffness of the neck due to rheumatism.

tortipelvis (tor″tĭ-pel′vis). Dystonia musculorum deformans.

tortua (tor′tu-ah) [L.]. Agony; torture. **t. fa′cies,** Avicenna's name for trigeminal neuralgia.

tortuous (tor′tu-us). Twisted; full of turns and twists.

Torula (tor′u-lah), pl. *toru′lae* [L. "roll"]. A name formerly given a genus of yeastlike fungi. **T. capsula′tus, T. histolyt′ica,** *Cryptococcus neoformans*.

toruli (tor′u-li) [L.]. Plural of *torulus*.

toruliform (tor′u-lĭ-form). Resembling a torula; beaded.

torulin (tor′u-lin). Thiamine.

toruloid (tor′u-loid). Toruliform.

toruloma (tor-u-lo′mah). A tumor or nodule which is one of the lesions of cryptococcosis (torulosis).

Torulopsis histolytica (tor″u-lop′sis his″to-lit′ĭ-kah). *Cryptococcus neoformans*.

torulosis (tor″u-lo′sis). Cryptococcosis.

torulus (tor′u-lus), pl. *tor′uli* [L., dim. of *torus*]. A small elevation; a papilla. **tor′uli tac′tiles** [N A, B N A], the small elevations on the skin of the palm and the sole, richly supplied with sensory nerve endings: called also *tactile elevations*.

torus (to′rus), pl. *to′ri* [L. "a round swelling," "protuberance"]. 1. A bulging projection, a swelling; used in anatomical nomenclature as a general term to designate such a protuberance. 2. A solid developed by the revolution of a circle about any axis other than its diameter. **t. fronta′lis,** a protuberance in the middle line of the root of the nose, on the external surface of the skull. **t. levato′rius** [N A], the mucosal fold covering the levator veli palatini muscle in the lateral wall of the nasal part of the pharynx. **t. mandibula′ris,** an outgrowth of bone found on the lingual surface of the mandible, above the mylohyoid line and usually opposite the premolar tooth; commonly bilateral, and single or multiple in type. **t. occipita′lis** [B N A], a rounded edge occasionally seen on the occipital bone in the region of the superior nuchal line. Omitted in N A. **t. palati′nus** [N A, B N A], a protuberance sometimes found on the hard palate at the junction of the intermaxillary and transverse palatine sutures. **t. tuba′rius** [N A, B N A], the projecting posterior lip of the pharyngeal opening of the auditory tube. **t. ureter′icus,** plica interureterica.

Toti's operation (to′tēz) [Addeo *Toti*, Italian ophthalmologist, born 1861]. See under *operation*.

totipotency (to″te-po′ten-se) [L. *totus* all + *potentia* power]. The ability of a part to develop in any manner, or of a cell to develop into any type of cell.

totipotent (to-tip′o-tent). Totipotential.

totipotential (to″te-po-ten′shal) [L. *totus* all + *potentia* power]. Characterized by ability to develop in any direction: said of cells which can give rise to cells of all orders, i.e., the complete individual. Cf. *unipotential*.

touch (tuch) [L. *tactus*]. 1. The sense by which contact with objects gives evidence as to certain of their qualities. 2. Palpation or exploration with the finger. **abdominal t.,** digital palpation of the abdomen. **double t.,** digital examination of the rectum and vagina at the same time. **rectal t.,** exploration of the rectum with the finger. **royal t.,** the touching or tapping of a person with scrofula; once practiced by the kings of England and France as a supposedly curative measure. Also called *adenochirapsology*. **vaginal t.,** digital exploration of the vagina. **vesical t.,** digital examination of the bladder.

tour (toor) [Fr.]. Turn. **t. de maître** (dĕ mātr) [Fr. "master's turn"], a method of passing the sound or catheter into the male bladder or into the uterus. It is first introduced in a position with its stem parallel to the thighs and between them and its convexity upward, and then, by a sweep, is brought to the ordinary position and carried on into the bladder. The motion is reversed in the uterus.

Tourette's disease (too-retz′). See *Gilles de la Tourette's disease*.

tournesol (tur′nĕ-sol). Litmus.

tourniquet (toor′nĭ-ket) [Fr.]. An instrument for the compression of a blood vessel for the purpose of controlling the circulation and preventing the access of blood to a part. Tourniquets are of various kinds, named chiefly from their inventors. **Dupuytren's t.,** a tourniquet consisting of a semicircular piece of metal with a head at one end, used for compressing the abdominal aorta. **Esmarch's t.,** a tourniquet consisting of a piece of strong, flat rubber tubing, which, after the blood has been driven from the limb by an elastic bandage, is wound about the upper part of the limb so as to arrest the circulation. **field t.,** a padded strap to be buckled on and pressed down by a screw so as to compress an artery. **Fouli's t.,** a rubber cord or tube which is secured by a double grooved block of wood or vulcanite. **garrote t.,** Spanish windlass. **horseshoe t.,** one shaped like a horseshoe to press upon two points. **Momberg's t.** See under *belt.* **Petit's t.** See illustration. **pneumatic t.,** a narrow rubber bag to be bound around a limb, the pressure being raised by pumping in air. **provisional t.,** one applied loosely, to be tightened as occasion may require. **Samway's t.,** formed of strong rubber tubing with an anchor-shaped fastening under which the free end of the tube is caught. **Signorini's t.,** two hinged metal drums with pads at the extremities which are approximated by a screw and pinion. **Spanish t., torcular t.,** Spanish windlass. **Truesdale's t.** See illustration.

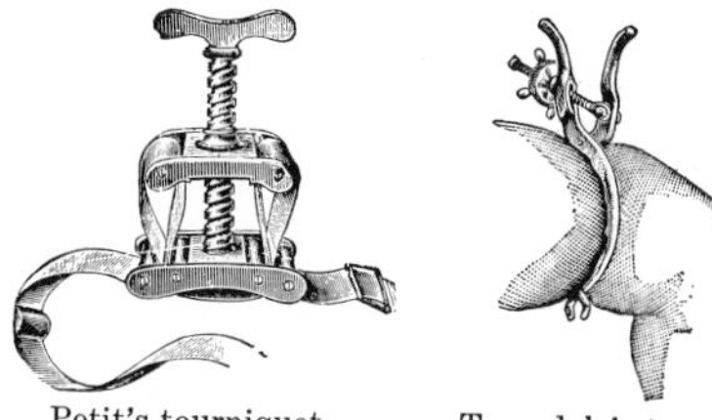

Petit's tourniquet. Truesdale's tourniquet.

tousey (tow′ze) [Sinclair *Tousey,* New York roentgenologist, 1864–1937]. A unit of roentgen-ray power; being the radiance which will produce on a photographic film an effect equal to that produced by a one-candlepower incandescent electric light.

Touton cells (toot′on) [Karl *Touton,* German dermatologist, born 1858]. See under *cell.*

towelette (tow″el-et′). A small towel for the surgeon's or obstetrician's use.

Townsend's mixture (town′sendz) [Joseph *Townsend,* British clergyman, 1739–1816]. See under *mixture.*

toxalbumic (tok″sal-bu′mik). Relating to or caused by toxalbumin.

toxalbumin (tok″sal-bu′min). Any poisonous albumin, whether of bacterial or other origin. Some, like abrin, ricin, and phallin, are found in plant juices; others in serpent venoms, bacterial cultures, etc. See under *toxin.*

toxalbumose (toks-al′bu-mōs). A poisonous albumose.

toxanemia (tok″sah-ne′me-ah). Anemia due to a poison.

Toxascaris (toks-as′kah-ris). A genus of parasitic nematodes of the family Ascaridae. **T. leoni′na,** a species found commonly in lions, tigers, and other large Felidae; found also in dogs and cats, but usually only in older animals. Its larvae differ from those of *Toxocara canis* and *Toxocara cati* by not passing through the lungs of the infected animal.

toxemia (toks-e′me-ah) [*toxin* + Gr. *haima* blood + *-ia*]. A general intoxication due to the absorption of bacterial products (toxins) formed at a local source of infection. **alimentary t.,** toxemia due to absorption from the alimentary canal of chemical poisons. **eclamptic t., eclamptogenic t.,** toxemia of pregnancy. **hydatid t.,** toxemia with urticaria caused by hydatid fluid which has escaped into the peritoneal cavity. **menstrual t.,** that which is due to the absorption of a poison from the altered blood of retained menses. **mucin t.,** toxemia with tetanic symptoms due to excision of the thyroid gland. **preeclamptic t.** See *preeclampsia.* **t. of pregnancy,** a series of pathologic conditions, essentially metabolic disturbances, occurring in pregnant women, and including hyperemesis gravidarum, preeclampsia and fully developed eclampsia.

toxemic (toks-e′mik). Pertaining to or caused by toxemia.

toxenzyme (toks-en′zīm). Any poisonous enzyme.

toxic (tok′sik). Pertaining to, due to, or of the nature of, a poison.

toxicant (toks′ĭ-kant) [L. *toxicans* poisoning]. 1. Poisonous. 2. A poisonous agent.

toxication (tok″sĭ-ka′shun). Poisoning.

toxicemia (toks″ĭ-se′me-ah). Toxemia.

toxicide (tok′sĭ-sīd) [*toxin* + L. *caedere* to kill]. A drug capable of overcoming toxic agents.

toxicity (toks-is′ĭ-te). The quality of being poisonous, especially the degree of virulence of a toxic microbe or of a poison. It is expressed by a fraction indicating the ratio between the smallest amount that will cause an animal's death and the weight of that animal.

toxico- (tok′sĭ-ko) [Gr. *toxikon* poison]. Combining form meaning poisonous or denoting relationship to poison.

toxicodendrol (tok″sĭ-ko-den′drol). A poisonous, nonvolatile oil found in *Rhus toxicodendron.*

toxicodendron (tok″sĭ-ko-den′dron) [*toxico-* + Gr. *dendron* tree]. The poisonous leaves of *Rhus toxicodendron.*

toxicoderma (tok″sĭ-ko-der′mah) [*toxico-* + Gr. *derma* skin]. Any skin disease due to a poison.

toxicodermatitis (tok″sĭ-ko-der″mah-ti′tis). Dermatitis due to a poison.

toxicodermatosis (tok″sĭ-ko-der″mah-to′sis). Toxicoderma.

toxicodermia (tok″sĭ-ko-der′me-ah). Toxicoderma.

toxicodermitis (tok″sĭ-ko-der-mi′tis). Toxicodermatitis.

toxicogenic (tok″sĭ-ko-jen′ik) [*toxico-* + Gr. *gennan* to produce]. Producing or elaborating toxins.

toxicohemia (tok″sĭ-ko-he′me-ah). Toxemia.

toxicoid (tok′sĭ-koid) [*toxico-* + Gr. *eidos* form]. Resembling a poison.

toxicologic (tok″sĭ-ko-loj′ik). Pertaining to toxicology.

toxicologist (tok″sĭ-kol′o-jist). An individual skilled in toxicology.

toxicology (tok″sĭ-kol′o-je). The sum of what is known regarding poisons; the scientific study of poisons, their actions, their detection, and the treatment of the conditions produced by them.

toxicomania (tok″sĭ-ko-ma′ne-ah) [*toxico-* + Gr. *mania* madness]. An intense desire for poisons, narcotic drugs, or intoxicants.

toxicomaniac (tok″sĭ-ko-ma′ne-ak). A person affected with toxicomania.

toxicomucin (tok″sĭ-ko-mu′sin) [*toxico-* + L. *mucus* slime]. A poisonous albuminoid substance derived from cultures of the tubercle bacillus.

toxicopathic (tok″sĭ-ko-path′ik). Pertaining to toxicopathy.

toxicopathy (tok″sĭ-kop′ah-the) [*toxico-* + Gr. *pathos* disease]. Any disease induced by a poison.

toxicopectic (tok″sĭ-ko-pek′tik). Pertaining to, characterized by, or promoting toxicopexis.

toxicopexic (tok″sĭ-ko-pek′sik). Toxicopectic.

toxicopexis (tok″sĭ-ko-pek′sis) [*toxico-* + Gr.

pēxis fixation]. The fixing or neutralizing of a poison in the body.

toxicophidia (tok″sĭ-ko-fid′e-ah) [*toxico-* + Gr. *ophis* snake]. Venomous snakes collectively; thanatophidia.

toxicophobia (tok″sĭ-ko-fo′be-ah) [*toxico-* + Gr. *phobein* to be affrighted by]. Morbid dread of poisons.

toxicophylaxin (tok″sĭ-ko-fi-lak′sin). Any phylaxin which destroys the poisons produced by microorganisms.

toxicosis (tok″sĭ-ko′sis) [Gr. *toxikon* poison + *-osis*]. Any disease condition due to poisoning. **alimentary t.,** sitotoxism. **endogenic t.,** auto-intoxication. **exogenic t.,** poisoning by the ingestion of toxic material, as in the food. **gestational t.,** gestosis. **hemorrhagic capillary t.,** Frank's name for a hemorrhagic condition attributed to capillary weakening from some toxic action. See *Henoch's purpura* under *purpura*. **proteinogenous t.,** an acute and fetal intoxication which appears in white mice which are fed an exclusive diet of various proteins. **retention t.,** that which is due to the nonexcretion of noxious waste products.

toxicosozin (tok″sĭ-ko-so′zin). A defensive protein which counteracts a toxin.

toxidermia (tok″sĭ-der′me-ah). Toxicoderma.

toxidermitis (tok″sĭ-der-mi′tis). Toxicodermitis.

toxiferous (toks-if′er-us) [*toxin* + L. *ferre* to fear]. Conveying or producing a poison.

toxigenic (tok″sĭ-jen′ik). Toxicogenic.

toxigenicity (tok″sĭ-je-nis′ĭ-te). The disease-producing virulence of a parasite which acts by virtue of a soluble toxin.

toxignomic (toks″ig-nom′ik) [*toxin* + Gr. *gnōmē* a means of knowing]. Characteristic of the toxic action of a poison.

toxi-infection (tok″se-in-fek′shun). Toxinfection.

toxi-infectious (tok″se-in-fek′shus). Toxinfectious.

toximucin (tok″sĭ-mu′sin). Toxicomucin.

toxin (tok′sin) [L. *toxicum* poison, from Gr. *toxikos* of or for the bow]. A poison; frequently used to refer specifically to a protein or conjugated protein substance produced by some higher plants, certain animals, and pathogenic bacteria that is highly toxic for other living organisms. Such substances are differentiated from the simple chemical poisons and the vegetable alkaloids by their high molecular weight and antigenicity. **alpha t.,** an antigenic toxin obtained from cultures of *Clostridium perfringens* type A. **amanita t.,** a toxin from *Amanita phalloides*. **animal t.,** one produced by an animal; a zootoxin. **bacterial t's,** toxic substance produced by bacteria, including exotoxins, endotoxins, and toxic enzymes. **Birkhaug's t.,** the toxic filtrate of a streptococcus isolated from a patient with endocarditis and rheumatic fever: used in a skin reaction test for rheumatic fever. **botulinus t.,** one of the five type-specific, immunologically differentiable exotoxins (types A to E, inclusive), produced by *Clostridium botulinum*. **Coley's t.,** an unfiltered mixture of cultures of certain bacteria: once used in treatment of inoperable malignant growths. **dermonecrotic t.,** an exotoxin that produces extensive local necrosis on intradermal inoculation; produced primarily by coagulase-positive staphylococci and regarded as identical with δ staphylolysin. **Dick t.,** erythrogenic t. **diphtheria t.,** exotoxin produced by *Corynebacterium diphtheriae* that is primarily responsible for the pathogenesis of diphtheritic infection; it has been found to be an iron-deficient porphyrin analogue of the iron-porphyrin enzymes. **dysentery t.,** a toxin produced by various species of Shigella. That formed by *Shigella shigae* (*dysenteriae*) (Shiga toxin) resembles diphtheria toxin in nature and activity; all the toxins produced by other dysentery bacilli are endotoxins, immunologically distinct between species but with a closely similar pharmacological action. **erysipelas t.,** a toxin obtained from cultures of the organism causing erysipelas: once used in treatment of malignant growths. **erythrogenic t.,** an exotoxin produced by many, but not all, strains of *Streptococcus pyogenes*, which produces an erythematous reaction on intradermal inoculation in man and to a lesser extent in the rabbit, but not in other animals, and is responsible for the scarlatiniform rash of scarlet fever. **extracellular t.,** a toxin excreted by a bacterial cell; an exotoxin. **fatigue t.,** a toxin formed in the body as a result of muscular effort; a kenotoxin. **fugu t.,** tetraodontotoxin. **gonococcal t.,** an endotoxin present in the gonococcus, which is extractable in dilute alkali. **intracellular t.,** a toxin developed and retained within the bacterial cell; an endotoxin. **meningococcal t.,** an endotoxin present in the meningococcus, which is extractable in dilute alkali. **necrotizing t.,** dermonecrotic t. **normal t.,** a toxin of such strength that 0.01 cc. of the substance will cause death in four days of a guinea pig weighing 250 Gm.: used as a standard of toxin strength. **plant t.,** one produced by a plant; a phytotoxin. **primary t.,** an extracellular toxin immediately after secretion by the bacterial cell and before it has been changed by the albuminoses of the body into a secondary toxin. Cf. *secondary t.* **Salmonella t.,** an endotoxin found in all species of Salmonella and identical with somatic O antigen; it is extractable in trichloracetic acid and glycols. **scarlatinal t.,** erythrogenic t. **secondary t.,** an extracellular toxin secreted by the bacterial cell, after it has been changed by the albuminoses of the body. Cf. *primary t.* **Shiga t.,** the exotoxin formed by *Shigella shigae* (*dysenteriae*), which resembles diphtheria toxin in nature and activity. **soluble t.,** exotoxin. **staphylococcal t.,** a mixture of exotoxins formed by coagulase-positive *Staphylococcus pyogenes* var. *aureus*, including two or more hemotoxins (α, β, and δ hemolysins) having leukocidin activity (α staphylolysin) and dermonecrotic activity (δ staphylolysin), staphylocoagulase, staphylokinase, and enterotoxin. **streptococcal t.,** a mixture of exotoxins formed by *Streptococcus pyogenes*, including the hemotoxins (streptolysin O and streptolysin S), streptokinase, hyaluronidase (invasin), and erythrogenic toxin. **tetanus t.,** the exotoxin of *Clostridium tetani*, consisting of a mixture of a hemotoxin (tetanolysin) and a neurotoxin (tetanospasmin), the latter being of primary importance in the pathogenesis of tetanus. **true t.,** exotoxin.

toxin-antitoxin (tok″sin-an′tĭ-tok″sin). A nearly neutral mixture of diphtheria toxin with its antitoxin. Such a mixture is used for vaccination against diphtheria, the mixture being in such proportion that the diphtheria toxin has 85 per cent of its toxicity neutralized by the antitoxin. Called also *T. A. T.* and *T.-A. mixture*.

toxinemia (tok″sĭ-ne′me-ah) [*toxin* + Gr. *haima* blood + *-ia*]. The poisoning of the blood with toxins.

toxinfection (toks″in-fek′shun). A disease with toxic manifestations but without a recognized infecting microbe.

toxinfectious (toks″in-fek′shus). Pertaining to toxinfection.

toxinic (tok-sin′ik). Pertaining to or caused by a toxin.

toxinicide (tok-sin′ĭ-sīd) [*toxin* + L. *caedere* to kill]. Any agent destructive to toxins.

toxinosis (tok″sĭ-no′sis). Any disease condition due to the presence of a toxin.

toxinotherapy (tok″sĭ-no-ther′ah-pe). Toxitherapy.

toxin-toxoid (tok″sin-tok′soid). A mixture of a toxin and a toxoid.

toxinum (tok-si′num) [L.]. Toxin. **t. diphther′icum detoxica′tum,** diphtheria toxoid.

toxipathic (tok′se-path″ik). Pertaining to or

caused by the pathogenic action of toxins, of whatever origin.

toxipathy (tok-sip′ah-the). Any disease produced by poisoning.

toxipeptone (tok″sĭ-pep′tōn). A poisonous protein or albuminoid substance allied to peptone, especially one produced from peptones by the action of the *Vibrio cholerae.*

toxiphobia (tok″sĭ-fo′be-ah). Toxicophobia.

toxiphoric (tok″sĭ-for′ik) [*toxin* + Gr. *pherein* to bear]. Having an affinity for a toxin.

toxiphrenia (tok″sĭ-fre′ne-ah) [*toxin* + Gr. *phrēn* mind]. Schizophrenia occurring with a toxic, delirious state.

toxiresin (tok″sĭ-rez′in). A poisonous resinous substance obtainable from digitoxin.

toxis (tok′sis) [Gr. *toxikon* poison]. Poisoning; especially, poisoning by toxins.

toxisterol (tok-sis′ter-ol) [*toxin* + *sterol*]. A poisonous isomer of ergosterol, produced by ultraviolet radiation of the latter.

toxitabellae (tok″sĭ-tah-bel′e). Poison tablets.

toxitherapy (tok″sĭ-ther′ah-pe). The therapeutic use of toxins.

toxituberculid (tok″sĭ-tu-ber′ku-lid). A skin lesion attributed to the action of tuberculous toxin.

toxo- (tok′so) [Gr. *toxikon;* L. *toxinum*]. Combining form denoting relationship to a toxin, or poison.

toxo-alexin (tok″so-ah-lek′sin) [*toxo-* + Gr. *alexein* to ward off]. An alexin which tends to produce immunity to bacterial toxins, including toxosozins and toxophylaxins.

Toxocara (tok″so-ka′rah). A genus of nematode worms. **T. ca′nis,** a nematode worm parasitic in the intestine of dogs and sometimes found in man. **T. ca′ti,** a species that is closely related to *T. canis* but is commonly found in cats.

toxocaral (tok″so-kār′al). Pertaining to or caused by Toxocara.

toxocariasis (tok″so-kār-i′ah-sis). Infection by roundworms of the genus Toxocara.

toxoflavin (tok″so-fla′vin). A yellow pigment, isolated from *Bacterium cocovenenans,* which causes food poisoning in Java. It is $C_6H_6N_4O_2$, and probably is isomeric with methyl xanthine.

toxogen (tok′so-jen). Something that produces a poison.

toxogenin (toks-oj′e-nin) [*toxo-* + Gr. *gennan* to produce]. A substance supposed to develop in the blood under the influence of the action of an injected antigen, which, though itself inactive, on the injection of more antigen produces anaphylaxis.

toxoglobulin (tok″so-glob′u-lin). A poisonous globulin.

toxoid (tok′soid) [*toxo-* + Gr. *eidos* form]. A decay product of bacterial exotoxins that has lost toxicity but retains the properties of combining with, or stimulating the formation of, antitoxin. Toxoids of different bacterial species may be administered in combination (e.g., diphtheria and tetanus toxoid), or toxoid may be combined with bacterial vaccine (e.g., diphtheria and tetanus toxoids and pertussis vaccine). **adsorbed t.,** a bacterial toxoid adsorbed on aluminum hydroxide or aluminum hydroxide or aluminum phosphate, slowing its absorption in the body and providing a prolonged antigenic stimulus. **alum t.,** alum-precipitated t. **alum-precipitated t.,** formol toxoid precipitated with potassium alum as an adjuvant and used as an active immunizing agent. **diphtheria t.,** diphtheria toxin rendered nontoxic by treatment with formaldehyde: used in immunizing against diphtheria. **fluid t.,** plain formol toxoid used as an active immunizing agent. **formol t.,** toxoid formed by the prolonged action of formaldehyde on toxins, usually bacterial exotoxins. Called also *anatoxin.* **Glenny t.,** a type of alum-precipitated diphtheria toxoid. **precipitated t.,** a toxoid which has been precipitated, usually by potassium alum, creating an insoluble precipitate which is more slowly absorbed in the body, providing a prolonged antigenic stimulus. **tetanus t.,** a sterile preparation of growth products of *Clostridium tetani,* treated so they no longer cause toxic effects in guinea pigs but are still able to induce active immunity.

toxoid-antitoxoid (tok″soid-an′tĭ-tok″soid). A toxoid mixed with an equivalent amount of antitoxic serum, the precipitate being suspended in saline.

toxo-infection (tok″so-in-fek′shun). Toxinfection.

toxo-infectious (tok″so-in-fek′shus). Toxinfectious.

toxolecithid (tok″so-les′ĭ-thid). Toxolecithin.

toxolecithin (tok″so-les′ĭ-thin). A lecithin compounded with a toxin. as cobra venom.

toxolysin (toks-ol′ĭ-sin). Antitoxin.

toxomucin (tok″so-mu′sin). Toxicomucin.

toxon (tok′son). One of the diphtheritic poisons with less affinity for antitoxin than has toxin and which produces not acute toxic death, but emaciation, paralysis, and a delayed death.

toxone (tok′sōn). Toxon.

toxonoid (tok′so-noid). A toxon which is not toxic, but has the power of binding antitoxin.

toxonosis (tok″so-no′sis). A disease due to poisoning.

toxopeptone (tok″so-pep′tōn). Toxipeptone.

toxopexic (tok″so-peks′ik) [*toxo-* + Gr. *pēxis* fixation]. Fixing a toxin or poison in such a way as to make it harmless to the organism.

toxophilic (tok″so-fil′ik) [*toxo-* + Gr. *philein* to love]. Easily susceptible to a poison; having an affinity for toxins (like certain haptophore groups).

toxophilous (toks-of′ĭ-lus). Toxophilic.

toxophore (tok′so-fōr) [*toxin* + Gr. *phoros* bearing]. The group of atoms in the molecule of a toxin which brings about its specific activity after the molecule has been properly anchored by the haptophore. See *Ehrlich's side-chain theory,* under *theory.*

toxophorous (toks-of′o-rus). Carrying the toxin. See *toxophore.*

toxophylaxin (tok″so-fi-lak′sin). Any phylaxin which destroys or counteracts the poisons produced by bacteria.

Toxoplasma (toks″o-plaz′mah) [*toxo-* + Gr. *plasma* anything formed or molded]. A genus of parasites (sporozoa) found in the endothelial cells of many mammals and birds; has also been reported in man. **T. cunic′uli,** a species causing encephalopathy in the rabbit. **T. gon′dii,** a protozoan parasite causing a chronic infection in a North American rodent, *Ctenodactylus gondi.* **T. pyrog′enes,** a species in the form of oval or crescentic bodies found in the cells of the spleen in tropical splenomegaly (Castellani, 1913).

toxoplasmin (tok″so-plas′min). An antigen prepared from mouse peritoneal fluids rich with *Toxoplasma gondii:* injected intracutaneously as a test for toxoplasmosis.

toxoplasmosis (tok″so-plaz-mo′sis). Infection with, or a condition produced by the presence of, organisms of the genus *Toxoplasma.*

toxoprotein (tok″so-pro′te-in). A toxic protein or a mixture of a toxin and a protein.

toxosozin (tok″so-so′zin). Any sozin which destroys the poisons produced by microorganisms. See *sozin.*

Toxothrix (tok′so-thriks) [Gr. *toxon* a bow + *thrix* hair]. A genus of microorganisms of the family Chlamydobacteriaceae, order Chlamydobacteriales, made up of colorless filamentous, cylindrical cells with a sheath originally thin but later thickened with impregnated iron oxide. It includes two species, *T. gelatino′sa,* and *T. trichog′enes.*

toxuria (toks-u′re-ah). Uremia.

Toynbee's corpuscles, experiment, law, etc. (toin′bēz) [Joseph *Toynbee*, English otologist, 1815–1866]. See under the nouns.

T.P. An abbreviation for *tuberculin precipitation.* See *Calmette's tuberculin*, under *tuberculin.*

TPN. Abbreviation for *triphosphopyridine nucleotide.*

TPNH. Abbreviation for *reduced triphosphopyridine nucleotide.*

T.R. An abbreviation for *tuberculin R*, or new tuberculin. See under *tuberculin.*

tr. Abbreviation for *tincture.*

trabecula (trah-bek′u-lah), pl. *trabec′ulae* [L., dim. of *trabs*]. A little beam; used in anatomical nomenclature as a general term to designate a supporting or anchoring strand of connective tissue, as such a strand extending from a capsule into the substance of the enclosed organ. **trabec′ulae car′neae cor′dis** [N A, B N A], muscular ridges covering a great part of the interior of the walls of the ventricles of the heart: they may stand out in relief only, or be attached as bundles at both ends and free in the middle. **t. cer′ebri,** corpus callosum. **t. cine′rea,** adhesio interthalamica. **trabec′ulae cor′dis,** trabeculae carneae cordis. **trabec′ulae cor′porum cavernoso′rum pe′nis** [N A, B N A], numerous bands and cords of fibromuscular tissue traversing the interior of the corpora cavernosa of the penis, attached to the tunica albuginea and to the septum and creating the cavernous spaces that become filled with blood during erection. Called also *trabeculae of corpora cavernosa of penis.* **trabec′ulae cor′poris spongio′si pe′nis** [N A], numerous bands and cords of fibromuscular tissue traversing the interior of the corpus spongiosum of the penis, creating the cavernous spaces that give the structure its spongy character. Called also *trabeculae of corpus spongiosum of penis.* **trabec′ulae cra′nii,** a pair of longitudinal cranial bars of cartilage in the embryo, bounding the pituitary space that becomes the sella turcica. **fleshy trabeculae of heart,** trabeculae carneae cordis. **trabec′ulae lie′nis** [N A, B N A], fibrous bands that pass into the spleen from the tunica fibrosa and form the supporting framework of the organ. Called also *trabeculae of spleen.* **Rathke's trabeculae,** trabeculae cranii. **septomarginal t., t. septomargina′lis** [N A], a bundle of muscle at the apical end of the right ventricle of the heart, connecting the base of the anterior papillary muscle to the interventricular septum; it usually contains a branch of the atrioventricular bundle. **trabeculae of spleen,** trabeculae lienis.

trabeculae (trah-bek′u-le) [L.]. Plural of *trabecula.*

trabecular (trah-bek′u-lar). Pertaining to a trabecula.

trabecularism (trah-bek′u-lar-izm). The condition of having a trabecular structure.

trabeculate (trah-bek′u-lāt) [L. *trabecula* a small beam or bar]. Marked with cross bars or trabeculae.

trabeculation (trah-bek″u-la′shun). The formation of trabeculae in a part.

trabs (trabs), pl. *tra′bes* [L. "a beam"]. A supporting or anchoring strand or structure. **tra′bes car′neae,** trabeculae carneae cordis. **t. cer′ebri,** corpus callosum.

tracer (trās′er). 1. A dissecting instrument for isolating vessels and nerves. 2. A mechanical device by which the outline of an object or the direction and extent of movement of a part may be graphically recorded. See also *tracing.* 3. A means or agent by which certain substances or structures can be identified or followed. **needlepoint t.,** a mechanical device used in recording jaw movements, in which the tracing is made on a horizontal plate by a weighted or a spring-loaded needle attached to the jaw. **radioactive t.,** a radioactive isotope replacing a stable chemical element in a compound introduced into the body, enabling the course of its metabolism, distribution, and elimination from the body to be traced by a Geiger-Müller counter or other type of counting instrument. **stylus t.,** a mechanical device used in recording jaw movements in which the element producing the tracing is a pointed instrument or stylus. See *needle-point t.*

trachea (tra′ke-ah) [L.; Gr. *tracheia artēria*]. [N A, B N A] The cartilaginous and membranous tube descending from the larynx to the bronchi. **scabbard t.,** a trachea which is flattened by approximation of its lateral walls.

tracheaectasy (tra″ke-ah-ek′tah-se). Dilatation of the trachea.

tracheal (tra′ke-al) [L. *trachealis*]. Pertaining to the trachea.

trachealgia (tra″ke-al′je-ah) [*trachea* + Gr. *algos* pain + *-ia*]. Pain in the trachea.

tracheitis (tra″ke-i′tis). Inflammation of the trachea.

trachelagra (tra″ke-lag′rah, tra-kel′ah-grah) [Gr. *trachēlos* neck + *agra* seizure]. Gout in the neck.

trachelectomy (tra″ke-lek′to-me) [Gr. *trachēlos* neck + *ektomē* excision]. Excision of the cervix uteri.

trachelematoma (tra″ke-lem″ah-to′mah). A hematoma situated in the sternocleidomastoid muscle.

trachelism, trachelismus (tra′kĕ-lizm, tra″kĕ-liz′mus) [Gr. *trachēlismos*]. Spasm of the neck muscles; spasmodic retraction of the head in epilepsy.

trachelitis (tra″kĕ-li′tis). Cervicitis.

trachelo- (tra′kĕ-lo) [Gr. *trachēlos* neck]. Combining form denoting relationship to the neck or to a necklike structure.

trachelobregmatic (tra″kĕ-lo-breg-mat′ik) [*trachelo-* + Gr. *bregma* the front part of the head]. Pertaining to the neck and the bregma.

trachelocele (trak′ĕ-lo-sēl). Tracheocele.

trachelocyllosis (tra″kĕ-lo-si-lo′sis) [*trachelo-* + Gr. *kyllōsis* crooking]. Torticollis.

trachelocyrtosis (tra″kĕ-lo-sir-to′sis) [*trachelo-* + Gr. *kyrtos* curved + *-osis*]. Trachelokyphosis.

trachelocystitis (tra″kĕ-lo-sis-ti′tis) [*trachelo-* + Gr. *kystis* bladder + *-itis*]. Inflammation of the neck of the bladder.

trachelodynia (tra″kĕ-lo-din′e-ah) [*trachelo-* + Gr. *odynē* pain + *-ia*]. Pain in the neck.

trachelokyphosis (tra″kĕ-lo-ki-fo′sis) [*trachelo-* + Gr. *kyphōsis* a being hump backed]. Abnormal curvature of the cervical portion of the spine.

trachelologist (tra″ke-lol′o-jist). One skilled in trachelology.

trachelology (tra″kĕ-lol′o-je) [*trachelo-* + *-logy*]. The study of the neck and its diseases and injuries.

trachelomyitis (tra″kĕ-lo-mi-i′tis) [*trachelo-* + Gr. *mys* muscle + *-itis*]. Inflammation of the muscles of the neck.

trachelopexia (tra″kĕ-lo-pek′se-ah). Trachelopexy.

trachelopexy (tra′kĕ-lo-pek″se) [*trachelo-* + Gr. *pēxis* fixation]. Surgical fixation of the neck of the uterus to some other part.

tracheloplasty (tra′kĕ-lo-plas″te) [*trachelo-* + Gr. *plassein* to mold]. The plastic surgery of the uterine neck; surgical repair of defects of the neck of the uterus.

trachelorrhaphy (tra″kĕ-lor′ah-fe) [*trachelo-* + Gr. *rhaphē* suture]. Suture of the lacerated cervix uteri.

tracheloschisis (tra″kĕ-los′kĭ-sis) [*trachelo-* + Gr. *schisis* fissure]. Congenital fissure of the neck.

trachelosyringorrhaphy (tra″kĕ-lo-sir″ing-gor′ah-fe) [*trachelo-* + Gr. *syrinx* pipe + *rhaphē* suture]. Trachelorrhaphy for fistula of the vagina.

trachelotomy (tra″kĕ-lot′o-me) [*trachelo-* + Gr. *tomē* a cutting]. The surgical cutting of the uterine neck.

tracheo- (tra′ke-o). Combining form denoting relationship to the trachea.

tracheo-aerocele (tra″ke-o-a′er-o-sēl) [*tracheo-* + Gr. *aēr* air + *kēlē* hernia]. A tracheal hernia containing air.

tracheobronchial (tra″ke-o-brong′ke-al). Pertaining to the trachea and bronchi.

tracheobronchitis (tra″ke-o-brong-ki′tis). Inflammation of the trachea and bronchi.

tracheobronchoscopy (tra″ke-o-brong-kos′ko-pe). Inspection of the interior of the trachea and bronchi.

tracheocele (tra′ke-o-sēl) [*tracheo-* + Gr. *kēlē* hernia]. Hernial protrusion of the tracheal mucous membrane.

tracheo-esophageal (tra″ke-o-e-sof′ah-je-al). Pertaining to or communicating with both the trachea and esophagus.

tracheofissure (tra″ke-o-fish′er). The operation of splitting the trachea.

tracheofistulization (tra″ke-o-fis″tu-li-za′shun). Percutaneous puncture of the trachea for the introduction of medicinal agents.

tracheogenic (tra″ke-o-jen′ik). Originating in the trachea.

tracheolaryngeal (tra″ke-o-lah-rin′je-al). Pertaining to the trachea and larynx.

tracheolaryngotomy (tra″ke-o-lar″in-got′o-me). Incision of the trachea and larynx.

tracheomalacia (tra″ke-o-mah-la′she-ah). Softening of the tracheal cartilages.

tracheopathia (tra″ke-o-path′e-ah) [*tracheo-* + Gr. *pathos* disease]. Disease of the trachea. **t. osteoplas′tica,** a condition marked by the formation of a bony and cartilaginous deposit in the tracheal mucosa.

tracheopathy (tra″ke-op′ah-the). Tracheopathia.

tracheopharyngeal (tra″ke-o-fah-rin′je-al). Pertaining to the trachea and pharynx.

Tracheophilus cymbius (tra″ke-of′ĭ-lus sim′be-us). A trematode parasitic in the trachea and esophagus of ducks in Europe.

tracheophonesis (tra″ke-o-fo-ne′sis) [*tracheo-* + Gr. *phōnēsis* sounding]. Auscultation of the heart at the sternal notch.

tracheophony (tra″ke-of′o-ne) [*tracheo-* + Gr. *phōnē* voice]. A sound heard in auscultation over the trachea.

tracheoplasty (tra′ke-o-plas″te) [*tracheo-* + Gr. *plassein* to mold]. Plastic operations upon the trachea.

tracheopyosis (tra″ke-o-pi-o′sis) [*tracheo-* + Gr. *pyon* pus]. Purulent tracheitis.

tracheorrhagia (tra″ke-o-ra′je-ah) [*tracheo-* + Gr. *rhēgnynai* to burst forth]. Hemorrhage from the trachea.

tracheorrhaphy (tra″ke-or′ah-fe) [*tracheo-* + Gr. *rhaphē* suture]. The operation of suturing the trachea.

tracheoschisis (tra″ke-os′kĭ-sis) [*tracheo-* + Gr. *schisis* fissure]. Fissure of the trachea.

tracheoscopic (tra″ke-o-skop′ik). Pertaining to or of the character of tracheoscopy.

tracheoscopy (tra″ke-os′ko-pe) [*tracheo-* + Gr. *skopein* to examine]. The inspection of the interior of the trachea. **percervical t.,** tracheoscopy through a previously made tracheotomy wound; low tracheoscopy. **peroral t.,** tracheoscopy by means of a tracheoscope passed through the mouth, between the vocal cords, and into the trachea; high tracheoscopy.

tracheostenosis (tra″ke-o-ste-no′sis) [*tracheo-* + Gr. *stenōsis* narrowing]. Contraction or narrowing of the trachea.

tracheostoma (tra″ke-os′to-mah) [*tracheo-* + Gr. *stoma* mouth]. An opening into the trachea through the neck.

tracheostomize (tra″ke-os′to-mīz). To perform tracheostomy upon.

tracheostomy (tra″ke-os′to-me) [*tracheo-* + Gr. *stomoun* to provide with an opening or mouth]. Surgical creation of an opening into the trachea through the neck, for insertion of a tube to facilitate the passage of air to the lungs, or the evacuation of secretions.

tracheotome (tra′ke-o-tōm). An instrument for use in incising the trachea.

tracheotomize (tra″ke-ot′o-mīz). To perform tracheotomy upon.

tracheotomy (tra″ke-ot′o-me) [*tracheo-* + Gr. *tomē* a cutting]. Incision of the trachea through the skin and muscles of the neck, for exploration, removal of a foreign body, or for obtaining a biopsy specimen or removal of a local lesion. **inferior t.,** incision of the trachea through the neck, below the isthmus of the thyroid. **superior t.,** incision of the trachea through the neck, above the isthmus of the thyroid.

trachitis (trah-ki′tis). Tracheitis.

trachoma (trah-ko′mah), pl. *tracho′mata* [Gr. *trachōma* roughness]. 1. A viral disease of the conjunctiva and cornea, producing photophobia, pain, and lacrimation, and characterized by pannus and by redness, inflammation, and follicular and papillary hypertrophy of the conjunctiva. 2. Kraurosis vulvae. **Arlt's t.,** granular conjunctivitis; trachoma. **brawny t.,** general lymphoid infiltration of the conjunctiva without granulation. **t. defor′mans,** vulvitis with cicatricial deformity. **diffuse t.,** a form with large-sized granulations. **follicular t., granular t.,** a form in which there are sago-like elevations on the conjunctiva of the lids. **papillary t.,** that in which there are red, papillary growths on the lids. **Türck's t.,** laryngitis sicca. **t. of vocal bands,** development of nodular swellings on the vocal cords. **t. vul′vae,** kraurosis vulvae.

trachomatous (trah-ko′mah-tus). Pertaining to, affected with, or of the nature of, trachoma.

Trachybdella bistriata (tra″ke-del′ah bis″tre-ah′tah). A leech found in Brazil which attacks man and other animals.

trachychromatic (tra″ke-kro-mat′ik) [Gr. *trachys* rough + *chrōma* color]. Strongly or deeply staining.

trachyphonia (tra″ke-fo′ne-ah) [Gr. *trachys* rough + *phōnē* voice + *-ia*]. Roughness of the voice; hoarseness.

tracing (trās′ing). A graphic record produced by copying another, or scribed by an instrument capable of making a visual record of movements. In dentistry, the record of movements of the mandible produced by a tracer; the shape of the tracing depends on the relative location of the marking point and the tracing plate, and the apex of a properly made tracing is considered to indicate the most retruded unstrained position of the mandible in relation to the maxilla (centric jaw relation). **arrow point t.,** Gothic arch t. **extraoral t.,** one made outside the oral cavity. **Gothic arch t.,** a tracing of the movements of the mandible that resembles the shape of an arrowhead, or a Gothic arch. **intraoral t.,** one made within the oral cavity.

track (trak). The path along which something moves, or the mark left by its movement. **fog t.,** the visible trail or track left when an electron or other particle passes through a supersaturated Wilson chamber. It consists of droplets of condensed moisture which can be photographed. **germ t.,** the lineage or continuity of germ cells which can be traced throughout innumerable generations of individuals.

tract (trakt) [L. *tractus*]. A region, principally one of some length; specifically a collection or bundle of nerve fibers having the same origin, function, and termination (tractus [N A]), or a number of organs, arranged in series, subserving a common function. **alimentary t.,** canalis alimentarius. **ascending t.,** any bundle of nerve fibers that conveys impulses toward the brain. **Bech-**

terew's t., a part of the tegmentum connecting the lemniscus lateralis and the medial aspect of the nucleus dorsalis corporis trapezoidei. **biliary t.**, the organs, ducts, etc., which participate in the secretion and transfer of the bile. **Bruce's t.**, septomarginal t. **bulbar t.**, any of the bundles of nerve fibers of the medulla oblongata. **bulbospinal t.**, olivospinal t. **bulbothalamic t., lateral**, tractus bulbothalamicus lateralis. **bulbothalamic t., medial**, tractus bulbothalamicus medialis. **Burdach's t.**, fasciculus cuneatus medullae spinalis. **callosal t., crossed**, fibers from the thalamus which cross in the corpus callosum to the opposite side and pass on to the cerebral cortex. **central t. of auditory nerve**, fibers that pass from the medullary striae to the lateral lemniscus of the opposite side and then up through the brachium of the inferior colliculus into the medial geniculate body and from there to the cortex of the transverse temporal gyri. **central t. of cranial nerves**, fibers from several cranial nerves which pass upward to the thalamus closely associated with the medial lemniscus. **central t. of thymus**, tractus centralis thymi. **central t. of trigeminal nerve**, a more or less distinct bundle of fibers from the trigeminal nerve which passes upward to the thalamus on the dorsal side of the medial lemniscus. **cerebellar t., direct, of Flechsig**, tractus spinocerebellaris posterior. **cerebellorubrospinal t.**, fibers passing from one dentate nucleus of the cerebellum to the contralateral red nucleus, and thence to the spinal cord. **cerebellospinal t.**, tractus vestibulospinalis. **cerebellotegmental t's of bulb**, fastigiobulbar t's. **cerebrospinal t., lateral**, tractus corticospinalis lateralis. **Collier's t.**, the tegmental part of the medial longitudinal fasciculus. **comma t. of Schultze**, fasciculus interfascicularis. **conariohypophyseal t.**, a portion of the cavity of the embryonic brain connecting the pineal body and the pituitary body. **cornucommissural t.**, fibers in the anterior part of the posterior column of the cord, extending through the sacral and lumbar regions. **corticobulbar t.**, corticonuclear t. **corticocerebellar t's**, corticopontile t's. **corticonuclear t.**, nerve fibers running from the cerebral cortex to the motor nuclei of the cranial nerves. **corticopontile t's, corticopontine t's**, bundles of fibers running from the cerebral cortex to the nuclei of the pons. **corticorubral t.**, fibers passing from the cerebral cortex to the red nucleus. **corticospinal t., anterior**, tractus corticospinalis anterior. **corticospinal t., lateral**, tractus corticospinalis lateralis. **corticothalamic t.**, fibers uniting the cerebral cortex with the thalamus. **Deiters' t.**, tractus vestibulospinalis. **descending t.**, any bundle of nerve fibers that conveys impulses from the brain toward the periphery. **digestive t.**, canalis alimentarius. **direct cerebellar t. of Flechsig**, tractus spinocerebellaris posterior. **direct sensory t.**, a band of fibers passing from near the globose nucleus of the cerebellum to the outer wall of the fourth ventricle. **direct spinocerebellar t.**, tractus spinocerebellaris posterior. **dorsolateral t.**, tractus dorsolateralis. **dorsomedian t.**, fasciculus gracilis medullae spinalis. **epicerebral lymph t's**, lymph spaces between the pia mater and the surface of the brain. **fastigiobulbar t's**, bundles of efferent fibers running from the nucleus fastigii to the medulla oblongata. **fiber t's of spinal cord**, distinct bundles in the white substance of the spinal cord, made up of fibers which have the same origin, termination, and function. **fillet t.**, the continuation of the anterior spinocerebellar tract to the outside of the lateral lemniscus. **fillet t., lateral**, a tract leaving the lateral lemniscus at the level of the motor nucleus of the trigeminal nerve, situated between that nucleus and the dorsal nucleus of the trapezoid body on the medial side of the motor root. **Flechsig's t.**, tractus spinocerebellaris posterior. **foraminous spiral t.**, tractus spiralis foraminosus. **Foville's t.**, tractus spinocerebellaris posterior. **frontopontile t., frontopontine t.**, a tract of fibers arising from the pons and extending anteriorly to form part of the cerebral peduncle. **gastrointestinal t.**, the stomach and intestines in continuity. **genitourinary t.**, apparatus urogenitalis. **Goll's t.**, fasciculus gracilis medullae spinalis. **Gowers' t.**, tractus spinocerebellaris anterior. **habenular t.**, a tract of fibers passing from the habenula to the medial side of the red nucleus. **habenulopeduncular t.**, fasciculus retroflexus. **Helweg's t.**, olivospinal t. **iliopubic t.**, tractus iliopubicus. **iliotibial t.**, tractus iliotibialis. **intermediolateral t.**, columna lateralis medullae spinalis. **internuncial t.**, a fiber tract connecting two nuclei or centers. **intersegmental t., lateral.** See *fasciculi proprii.* **intestinal t.**, the small and large intestines in continuity. **Lissauer's t.**, tractus dorsolateralis. **Löwenthal's t.**, tractus tectospinalis. **lymph t.**, a lymph space or system of lymph spaces, as in the brain. **Maissiat's t.**, tractus iliotibialis. **mamillopeduncular t.**, a fiber tract from the mamillary body to the motor centers in the cerebral peduncle. **mamillotegmental t.**, a branch from the mamillothalamic tract running caudally in the tegmentum of the mesencephalon. **mamillothalamic t.**, fasciculus mamillothalamicus. **Marchi's t.**, tractus tectospinalis. **marginal t., crossed**, tractus dorsolateralis. **medullary t., lateral**, a fillet in the most lateral portion of the reticular formation. **medullary t., sagittal**, a tract of nerve fibers in the brain coming from the posterior third of the posterior limit of the internal capsule. Called also *intracerebral optic t.* **mesencephalic t. of trigeminal nerve**, tractus mesencephalicus nervi trigemini. **mesencephalospinal t.**, tractus rubrospinalis. **t. of Meynert**, fasciculus retroflexus. **Monakow's t.**, tractus rubrospinalis. **motor t.**, any bundle of nerve fibers conveying motor impulses from the central nervous system to a muscle. **olfactomamillary t.**, fibers from the olfactory trigone and the substantia perforata anterior which pass back around the tuber cinereum to the mamillary body. **olfactomesencephalic t.**, fibers which pass from the olfactory trigone back to the gray substance of the mesencephalon. **olfactory t.**, tractus olfactorius. **olfactotegmental t.**, a fiber tract from the secondary olfactory area to the cerebral peduncle. **olivocerebellar t.**, tractus olivocerebellaris. **olivospinal t.**, a crossed tract descending from the olivary nucleus to the lower cervical or upper thoracic segments of the spinal cord. Called also *bulbospinal t., Helweg's t., triangular t.*, and *Helweg's bundle.* **ophthalmic t., optic t.**, tractus opticus. **optic t., intracerebral**, sagittal medullary t. **peduncular t., transverse**, a small band of fibers which passes from the brachium of the inferior colliculus to the sulcus medialis cruris cerebri. **t. of Philippe-Gombault**, Gombault-Philippe triangle. **pontocerebellar t.**, pedunculus cerebellaris medius. **pontospinal t.**, tractus reticulospinalis. **predorsal t.**, tractus tectospinalis. **prepyramidal t.**, tractus rubrospinalis. **projection t.** See under *fiber.* **pyramidal t.**, a term applied to the fibers arising in the anterior central gyrus and passing down through the brain stem to the medulla where some of them cross to the opposite side in the decussation of the pyramids and pass down the cord to the motor cells of the anterior horns as the tractus corticospinalis lateralis; those remaining on the same side form the tractus corticospinalis anterior. **pyramidal t., anterior**, tractus corticospinalis anterior. **pyramidal t., crossed**, tractus corticospinalis lateralis. **pyramidal t., direct**, tractus corticospinalis anterior. **pyramidal t., lateral**, tractus corticospinalis lateralis. **pyramidoanterior t.**, tractus corticospinalis anterior. **pyramidolateral t.**, tractus corticospinalis lateralis.

respiratory t., apparatus respiratorius. **reticulospinal t.,** tractus reticulospinalis. **rubroreticular t.,** fibers from the red nucleus to the reticular formation of the pons. **rubrospinal t.,** tractus rubrospinalis. **sagittal t.** See *medullary t., sagittal.* **Schultze's t., semilunar t.,** fasciculus interfascicularis. **sensory t.,** any bundle of nerve fibers conveying sensory impulses from a peripheral receptor to the central nervous system. **septomarginal t.,** a bundle of fibers along the dorsal periphery of the posterior funiculus in the thoracic region, and along the septum in the lumbar region. **solitary t. of medulla oblongata,** tractus solitarius medullae oblongatae. **speech t.,** nerve fibers connecting the speech center with the nuclei of the nerves which supply the muscles of phonation. **spinal t. of trigeminal nerve,** tractus spinalis nervi trigemini. **spinocerebellar t., anterior,** tractus spinocerebellaris anterior. **spinocerebellar t., direct, spinocerebellar t., dorsal, spinocerebellar t., posterior,** tractus spinocerebellaris posterior. **spinocerebellar t., ventral,** tractus spinocerebellaris anterior. **spinomuscular t.,** the motor cells of the medulla oblongata and spinal cord, and the nerve fibers which originate in them. **spino-olivary t.,** an ascending tract of fibers arising from the posterior gray columns of the cord and running to the olivary nucleus. **spinotectal t.,** tractus spinotectalis. **spinothalamic t., anterior,** tractus spinothalamicus anterior. **spinothalamic t., lateral,** tractus spinothalamicus lateralis. **spinothalamic t., ventral,** tractus spinothalamicus anterior. **spiral t., foraminous,** tractus spiralis foraminosus. **Spitzka's t.,** tractus dorsolateralis. **strionigral t.,** a bundle of fibers from the corpus striatum to the substantia nigra. **sulcomarginal t.,** fasciculus sulcomarginalis. **sylvian t.,** the region of the brain about the lateral cerebral sulcus. **tectobulbar t.,** tractus tectobulbaris. **tectocerebellar t.,** a bundle of fibers from the tectum of the mesencephalon to the cerebellum. **tectospinal t.,** tractus tectospinalis. **tegmental t.,** a tract of fibers in the tegmentum, back of the nucleus posterior corporis trapezoidei, believed to connect the latter with the midbrain. **tegmental t., central,** tractus tegmentalis centralis. **tegmentospinal t.,** tractus reticulospinalis. **temporofrontal t.,** a bundle of fibers connecting the temporal and frontal lobes. **temporopontile t., temporopontine t.,** a tract of fibers connecting the temporal lobe and the pons. **thalamobulbar t.,** a tract of descending fibers from the thalamus to the medulla oblongata. **thalamocortical t.,** fibers passing from the thalamus to the cerebral cortex. **thalamo-occipital t.,** radiatio optica. **thalamo-olivary t.,** a bundle of fibers descending from the thalamus to the olivary nucleus. **thalamospinal t.,** a bundle of fibers descending from the thalamus to the spinal cord. **triangular t.,** olivospinal t. **triangular t. of Philippe-Gombault,** Gombault-Philippe triangle. **trigeminothalamic t.,** fibers from the trigeminal nerve to the thalamus. **urinary t.,** the organs and ducts which participate in the secretion and elimination of the urine. **uveal t.,** the vascular tunic of the eye, comprising the choroid, ciliary body, and iris. **vestibulocerebellar t.,** fibers of the pars vestibularis nervi octavi passing to the cortex of the cerebellum. **vestibulospinal t.,** tractus vestibulospinalis. **vestibulospinal t., anterior,** the fibers of the vestibulospinal tract that descend in the anterior funiculus of the spinal cord. **vestibulospinal t., posterior,** the fibers of the vestibulospinal tract that descend in the lateral funiculus of the spinal cord. **t. of Vicq d'Azyr,** fasciculus mamillothalamicus.

tractate (trak′tāt). To attract or to tend to come together.

tractellum (trak-tel′um), pl. *tractel′la* [L.]. An anterior locomotive flagellum.

traction (trak′shun) [L. *tractio*]. The act of drawing. **axis t.,** traction along an axis, as of the pelvis in obstetrics. **elastic t.,** traction by an elastic force or by means of an elastic appliance. **Russell t.,** traction for the knee joint by means of a cuff applied just below the knee. **skeletal t.,** traction applied directly upon the long bones by means of pins, Kirschner's wire, etc. **tongue t.,** a remedial procedure used as a cardiac stimulant.

tractor (trak′tor) [L. "drawer"]. An instrument for making traction. **Perkins' t.,** a metallic appliance formerly drawn across the skin in the attempted cure of various disorders. **Syms's t.,** a tube with an inflatable rubber bag at the end: used to bring down a prostate into the perineal incision.

tractoration (trak″to-ra′shun). An obsolete form of metallotherapy; the treatment of disease by metallic tractors; perkinism.

tractotomy (trak-tot′o-me). The operation of severing or incising a nerve tract. **mesencephalic t.,** surgical division of nerve tracts in the mesencephalon.

tractus (trak′tus), pl. *tractus* [L. "a track," "trail"]. A region, principally one of some length; used in anatomical nomenclature as a general term, especially to designate a collection or bundle of nerve fibers having the same origin and termination, and serving the same function. Called also *tract.* **t. bulbothalam′icus latera′lis,** the ascending tract of internal arcuate fibers that arises from the nucleus cuneatus, forms the lower part of the decussatio lemniscorum, and passes upward in the outer portion of the medial lemniscus to the lateral nucleus of the thalamus. Called also *lateral bulbothalamic tract.* **t. bulbothalam′icus media′lis,** the ascending tract of internal arcuate fibers that arises from the nucleus gracilis, forms the upper part of the decussatio lemniscorum, and passes upward in the medial portion of the medial lemniscus to the lateral nucleus of the thalamus. Called also *medial bulbothalamic tract.* **t. centra′lis thy′mi** [B N A], the medullary core of the thymus; an irregular fibrous bundle carrying the blood vessels and giving attachment to the lobules of the gland. Omitted in N A. **t. corticospina′lis ante′rior** [N A], a group of nerve fibers in the anterior funiculus of the spinal cord, originating in the cerebral cortex. Called also *fasciculus cerebrospinalis anterior* [*pyramidalis anterior*] [B N A], and *anterior corticospinal tract.* **t. corticospina′lis latera′lis** [N A], a group of nerve fibers in the lateral funiculus of the spinal cord, originating in the cerebral cortex. Called also *fasciculus cerebrospinalis lateralis* [*pyramidalis lateralis*] [B N A], and *lateral corticospinal tract.* **t. dorsolatera′lis** [N A], a group of nerve fibers in the lateral funiculus of the spinal cord dorsal to the posterior column, composed mainly of primary pain and temperature fibers which enter the spinal cord, travel the distance of a few segments in the dorsolateral tract, and then synapse in the posterior column. Called also *dorsolateral tract* or *fasciculus.* **t. iliopu′bicus,** a thickened band of tissue that strengthens the lower part of the deep inguinal ring and forms the base of the internal spermatic fascia. Called also *iliopubic tract.* **t. iliotibia′lis** [N A], **t. iliotibia′lis [Maissia′ti]** [B N A], a thickened longitudinal band of fascia lata extending from the tensor muscle downward along the lateral side of the thigh to the lateral condyle of the tibia. Called also *iliotibial tract.* **t. mesencephal′icus ner′vi trigem′ini** [N A], sensory fibers of the entering trigeminal nerve that continue rostrally along the medial aspect of the superior cerebellar peduncle, their cell bodies being located in the nucleus of the mesencephalic tract, which accompanies it. Called also *radix descendens* [*mesencephalica*] *nervi trigemini* [B N A], and *mesencephalic tract of trigeminal nerve.* **t. olfacto′rius** [N A, B N A], a narrow, white triangular band in the olfactory sulcus on the inferior surface of the frontal lobe, which arises in front from the olfactory bulb and enters the posteroinferior surface of the frontal lobe. Called also *olfactory tract.* **t. olivocerebella'ris** [N A], a fiber tract that arises from the olive, crosses to the opposite side to pierce the other olive, and enters the cerebellum through its inferior peduncle. Called also *fibrae cerebello-olivares* [B N A], and *olivocerebellar tract.* **t. op'ticus** [N A, B N A], the central extension of an optic nerve beyond the optic chiasm. It is a white flat bundle that passes to the side and back around the cerebral peduncle and divides into a lateral root and a medial root. Called also *optic tract.* **t. pyramida'lis ante'rior,** N A alternative for *t. corticospinalis anterior.* **t. pyramida'lis latera'lis,** N A alternative for *t. corticospinalis lateralis.* **t. reticulospina'lis** [N A], a group of nerve fibers in the lateral funiculus of the spinal cord, arising from the reticular formation or reticular nuclei throughout the brain stem tegmentum. Called also *reticulospinal tract.* **t. rubrospina'lis** [N A], a group of nerve fibers in the lateral funiculus of the spinal cord, arising in the large cells of the red nucleus of the mesencephalon. Called also *rubrospinal tract.* **t. solita'rius medul'lae oblonga'tae** [N A, B N A], a descending tract in the medulla oblongata, dorsolateral to the central canal or ventrolateral to the caudal part of the fourth ventricle, near the dorsal nucleus of the vagus and glossopharyngeal nerves, and comprising primary visceral afferent fibers from the facial, glossopharyngeal, and vagus nerves. Called also *solitary tract of medulla oblongata.* **t. spina'lis ner'vi trigem'ini** [N A, B N A], a descending tract of the trigeminal nerve that extends from the upper cervical segments of the spinal cord to a mid-pontine level in the medulla oblongata, lying lateral to the nucleus of the spinal tract of the trigeminal nerve, in which its fibers synapse; this tract carries mainly pain and temperature impulses from the face. Called also *spinal tract of trigeminal nerve.* **t. spinocerebella'ris ante'rior** [N A], a group of nerve fibers in the lateral funiculus of the spinal cord, ascending to the cerebellum through the superior cerebellar peduncle. Called also *fasciculus anterolateralis superficialis* [*Gowersi*] [B N A], and *anterior spinocerebellar tract.* **t. spinocerebella'ris poste'rior** [N A], a group of nerve fibers in the lateral funiculus of the spinal cord, ascending to the cerebellum through the inferior cerebellar peduncle. Called also *fasciculus cerebellospinalis* [B N A], and *posterior spinocerebellar tract.* **t. spinotecta'lis** [N A], a group of nerve fibers in the lateral funiculus of the spinal cord, ascending to the superior and inferior colliculi, and carrying somatic sensory impulses. Called also *spinotectal tract.* **t. spinothalam'icus ante'rior** [N A], a group of nerve fibers in the anterior funiculus of the spinal cord, ascending to the thalamus; it mediates tactile sensibility. Called also *anterior spinothalamic tract.* **t. spinothalam'icus latera'lis** [N A], a group of nerve fibers in the lateral funiculus of the spinal cord, ascending to the thalamus; it transmits sensory impulses of pain and temperature. Called also *lateral spinothalamic tract.* **t. spira'lis foramino'sus** [N A, B N A], a spiral area on the fundus of the internal acoustic meatus, below the crista transversa and in front of the area vestibularis inferior; it corresponds to the base of the cochlea and is perforated with numerous holes for the passage of branches of the vestibulocochlear nerve. Called also *foraminous spiral tract.* **t. subarcua'tus,** an area of small cell structure under the arch of the superior semicircular canal. **t. tectobulba'ris,** fibers arising from the cells of the superior colliculus, passing down to the lower border of the pons and ending in the nuclei of the brain stem and in the reticular formation. Called also *tectobulbar tract.* **t. tectospina'lis** [N A], a group of nerve fibers in the lateral funiculus of the spinal cord, arising from the collicular region of the mesencephalon. Called also *tectospinal tract.* **t. tegmenta'lis centra'lis** [N A], a group of nerve fibers, of diverse origin and destination, just outside the central gray substance of the mesencephalon and dorsal to the red nucleus. Called also *central tegmental tract.* **t. triangula'ris,** olivospinal tract. **t. vestibulospina'lis** [N A], a group of nerve fibers, part in the anterior funiculus (anterior vestibulospinal tract) and part in the lateral funiculus (lateral vestibulospinal tract). Both arise in the medulla from various vestibular nuclei and descend into the spinal cord. Called also *vestibulospinal tract.*

tragacanth (trag'ah-kanth). The dried gummy exudation from *Astragalus gummifer* or other species of Astragulus: used as a suspending agent for drugs.

tragal (tra'gal). Pertaining to the tragus.

tragi (tra'ji) [L., pl. of *tragus*]. [N A, B N A] Hair growing on the pinna of the external ear, especially on the cartilaginous projection anterior to the external opening (tragus).

Tragia (tra'je-ah). A genus of poisonous euphorbiaceous plants. Several species (*T. urens*, etc.) are weeds of the southern United States.

tragomaschalia (trag"o-mas-kal'e-ah) [Gr. *tragos* goat + *maschalē* the armpit]. Odorous perspiration from the axilla.

tragophonia (trag"o-fo'ne-ah). Egophony.

tragophony (trah-gof'o-ne) [Gr. *tragos* goat + *phōne* voice]. Egophony.

tragopodia (trag"o-po'de-ah) [Gr. *tragos* goat + *pous* foot]. Knock knee.

tragus (tra'gus), pl. *tra'gi* [L.; Gr. *tragos* goat]. [N A, B N A] The cartilaginous projection anterior to the external opening of the ear. Called also *hircus*.

train (trān). 1. To prepare by instruction and practice for some definite occupation or pursuit. In bacteriology, to develop bacteria to greater virulence by successive injections into animals. 2. A continuous succession of objects or of events, as of discharges of electric or magnetic energy. **hospital t.,** army medical rolling stock consisting of a train of ten railway cars (eight for patients), with definite personnel and material, for transportation of sick and wounded from the line of communications to the interior. **sanitary t.,** an army medical organization composed of camp infirmaries, ambulance companies, and field hospitals commanded by a division surgeon.

trait (trāt). 1. An inherited bodily or mental character. 2. A distinctive behavior pattern. **sickle cell t.,** a tendency to sickling of erythrocytes without the presence of anemia, encountered when the individual is heterozygous in the gene or genes responsible for the condition.

trajector (trah-jek'tor). An instrument for locating a bullet in a wound.

tral (tral). Trade mark for preparations of hexocyclium methylsulfate.

Trambusti's reaction, test (tram-boos'tēz) [Arnaldo *Trambusti*, Italian pathologist, born 1863]. See under *reaction*.

tramitis (tram-i'tis) [L. *trama* woof + *-itis*]. A condition of the pulmonary tissue in early tuberculosis seen in the roentgenogram as pleural adhesions, deviated mediastinum, sclerosed bands, calcified nodes, and areas of increased density.

trance (trans). A profound or abnormal sleep, from which the patient cannot be aroused easily, and not due to organic disease. Voluntary movement is lost, though sensibility and consciousness may remain. It is usually due to hysteria, and may be induced by hypnotism. **alcoholic t.,** a condition of automatism (dissociation of consciousness with complete forgetfulness) resulting from alcoholic indulgence. **death t.,** that in which the patient appears to be dead. **hypnotic t.,** an artificially induced trance. **hysterical t.,** trance occurring as a symptom of hysteria. **in-**

duced t., that which is mainly due to hysteria, but may be caused by hypnotism.

trancopal (tran′ko-pal). Trade mark for a preparation of chlormezanone.

tranquilizer (tran″kwĭ-liz′er) [L. *tranquillus* quiet, calm + *-ize* verb ending meaning to make + *-er* agent]. An agent which acts on the emotional state, quieting or calming the patient without affecting clarity of consciousness. **major t.**, an agent that reduces psychotic symptoms. **minor t.**, an agent useful in treatment of anxiety and tension or of psychoneurosis.

trans- [L. *trans* through]. Prefix meaning through, across, or beyond. In chemistry, denoting the presence of certain atoms or radicals on opposite sides of the molecule.

transacetylation (trans-as″ĕ-til-a′shun). A chemical reaction involving the transfer of the acetyl radical.

transacylase (trans-as′ĭ-lās). An enzyme that catalyzes transacylation.

transacylation (trans-as″ĭ-la′shun). A chemical reaction involving the transfer of the acyl radical between acetic and higher carboxylic acids.

transaminase (trans-am′ĭ-nās). An enzyme that catalyzes the reversible transfer of an amino group from an α–amino acid to an α–keto acid, usually α–ketoglutaric acid. Most, if not all, transaminases contain pyridoxal-5-phosphate as the prosthetic group. **glutamic-oxalacetic t. (GOT),** an enzyme present normally in serum and in various body tissues, especially in the heart and liver; it is released into the serum as the result of tissue injury, hence the concentration in the serum may be increased in myocardial infarction or acute damage to hepatic cells. **glutamic-pyruvic t. (GPT),** an enzyme present normally in serum and body tissues, especially in the liver; it is released into the serum as a result of tissue injury, hence the concentration in the serum may be increased in patients with acute damage to hepatic cells.

transamination (trans″am-i-na′shun). The reversible transfer of an amino group from an amino acid to what is originally an α–keto acid, forming a new amino acid and keto acid, without the appearance of ammonia in the free state.

transanimation (trans-an″ĭ-ma′shun) [*trans-* + L. *anima* breath]. Resuscitation by mouth-to-mouth breathing.

transaortic (trans″a-or′tik). Performed through the aorta; used especially in reference to surgical procedures on the aortic valve, performed through an incision in the wall of the aorta.

transatrial (trans-a′tre-al). Performed through the atrium: used especially in reference to surgical procedures on a cardiac valve, performed through an incision in the wall of the atrium.

transaudient (trans-aw′de-ent). Permitting passage of the mechanical vibrations perceived as sound.

transcalent (trans-ka′lent) [*trans-* + L. *calere* to be hot]. Permitting the passage of radiant heat.

transcondyloid (trans-kon′dĭ-loid). Through the condyles.

transcortical (trans-kor′tĭ-kal). Connecting two different parts of the cerebral cortex; also dependent on disease of the tracts connecting different parts of the cerebral cortex.

transcutaneous (trans″ku-ta′ne-us). Percutaneous.

transdermic (trans-der′mik) [*trans-* + L. *derma* skin]. Passed through the skin.

transduction (trans-duk′shun) [L. *transducere* to lead across]. The transfer of a genetic fragment from one cell to another. **bacterial t.**, the transfer of a character by bacteriophage from a lysogenic parent culture to another bacterial culture made lysogenic by the bacteriophage.

transduodenal (trans″du-o-de′nal). Through the duodenum.

transection (tran-sek′shun) [*trans-* + L. *sectio* a cut]. A section made across a long axis; a cross section.

transepidermal (trans″ep-ĭ-der′mal). Occurring through or across the epidermis.

transfer (trans′fer) [*trans-* + L. *ferre* to carry]. The conveyance of something from one place to another. **ion t.**, the introduction of ions into body tissue accomplished by the use of electric current.

transferase (trans′fer-ās). An enzyme that catalyzes the transfer, from one molecule to another, of a chemical group that does not exist in free state during the transfer.

transference (trans-fer′ens). 1. The passage or conveyance of a symptom or affection from one part to another, a kind of metastasis. 2. In psychiatry, the shifting of an affect from one person to another or from one idea to another; especially the transfer by the patient to the analyst of emotional tones, either of affection or of hostility, based on unconscious identification. If the transfer is favorable it is *positive t.;* if it is unfavorable it is *negative t.*

transferrin (trans-fer′rin) [*trans-* + L. *ferrum* iron + *-in* chemical suffix]. Serum β-globulin that binds and transports iron. Several types (e.g., C, B, D, with others showing a combination of patterns) have been distinguished and related as the products of corresponding dominant somatic genes, Tf^C, Tf^B, and Tf^D. Called also *siderophilin.*

transfix (trans′fiks) [*trans-* + L. *figere* to fix]. To pierce through and through.

transfixion (trans-fik′shun). A cutting through, as in amputation.

transforation (trans″fo-ra′shun) [*trans-* + L. *forare* to pierce]. The perforation or piercing of the fetal skull.

transforator (trans′fo-ra″tor). An instrument for making a transforation.

transformation (trans″for-ma′shun) [*trans-* + L. *formatio* formation]. Change of form or structure; conversion from one form to another. **asbestos t.**, the deposition of extraneous fibers in hyaline cartilage, which gives it a silky glossy appearance. **bacterial t.**, the artificial conversion of serotypes within a bacterial species by treatment of the R form with deoxyribonucleic acid from a heterologous serotype in the S form; studied largely in *Diplococcus pneumoniae* and *Haemophilus influenzae.* **G-F t., globular-fibrous t.**, the reversible change of actin globules into long filaments, in the process of muscle contraction and relaxation.

transformer (trans-for′mer). An induction apparatus for changing electrical energy at one voltage and current to electrical energy at another voltage and current, through the medium of magnetic energy, without mechanical motion. **closed-core t.**, one having a continuous core of magnetic material (usually iron) without any air gap. **step-down t.**, one for lowering the voltage of the original current. **step-up t.**, one for raising the voltage of the original current.

transfusion (trans-fu′zhun) [L. *transfusio*]. The introduction of whole blood, plasma substitutes, or other injectable solution directly into the blood stream. **direct t.**, immediate t. **exchange t.**, repetitive withdrawal of small amounts of blood and replacement with donor blood, until a large proportion of the blood volume has been exchanged: used in newborn infants with erythroblastosis and in patients with severe uremia. **exsanguination t.**, exchange t. **fetomaternal t.**, transplacental passage of fetal blood into the circulation of the maternal organism. **immediate t.**, the transfer of blood from one person to another without use of an intermediate container or exposing it to the air. **indirect t., mediate t.**, transfer of blood from a donor to a flask or other container, and then to the recipient. **placental t.**, return to the newborn, after birth, and through the umbilical vessels, of the blood contained in the placenta. **replacement t., substitution t.,** exchange t.

transgenation (trans″jen-a′shun). Mutation.

transic (tran′sik). Pertaining to or affected with trance.

transiliac (trans-il′e-ak). Across or between the two ilia.

transilient (tran-sil′e-ent) [*trans-* + L. *salire* to leap]. Leaping or passing across.

transillumination (trans″ĭ-lu″mĭ-na′shun). The passage of light through body tissues for purposes of examination, the object or part under examination being interposed between the examiner and the light source.

transinsular (trans-in′su-lar). Across the insula; crossing the insula.

transischiac (trans-is′ke-ak). Between the two ischia.

transisthmian (trans-is′me-an). Across an isthmus, especially the isthmus of the gyrus fornicatus.

transitional (trans-ish′un-al). 1. Changing from one form to another. 2. A mononuclear leukocyte of the largest size, so called because of the supposition that it becomes transformed into a granular leukocyte.

translation (trans-la′shun) [*trans-* + L. *latus* borne]. A removal or change of place.

translocation (trans″lo-ka′shun) [*trans-* + L. *locus* place]. Removal to another place. In genetics, the shifting of a segment or fragment of one chromosome into another part of a homologous chromosome, or into a non-homologous chromosome. **reciprocal t.,** the mutual exchange of fragments between two broken chromosomes, one part of one uniting with part of the other.

translucent (trans-lu′sent) [*trans-* + L. *lucens* shining]. Transmitting light, but diffusing it so that objects beyond are not clearly distinguished.

transmethylation (trans″meth-ĭ-la′shun). The transfer of a methyl group (CH_3—) from the molecules of one compound to those of another.

transmigration (trans″mi-gra′shun) [*trans-* + L. *migratio* migration]. 1. A wandering; especially a change of place from one side of the body to the other. 2. Diapedesis. **external t.,** the passage of an ovum from one ovary to the tube of the other side without going through its own oviduct. **internal t.,** the passage of an ovum from one oviduct to the other by way of the uterus.

transmissible (trans-mis′ĭ-b′l). Capable of being transmitted from one person to another.

transmission (trans-mish′un) [*trans-* + L. *missio* a sending]. A transfer, as of a disease; the communication of inheritable qualities to offspring. **duplex t.,** the transmission of nervous impulses in two directions along a nerve. **synaptic t.,** the transmission of a nerve impulse across a synapse.

transmutation (trans″mu-ta′shun). 1. Evolutionary change of one species into another. 2. The change of one chemical element into another; nucleonics, the changing of an atomic nucleus to one of a different atomic number by nuclear bombardment, causing rearrangement of the protons and neutrons.

transnormal (trans-nor′mal). More than normal.

transocular (trans-ok′u-lar) [*trans-* + L. *oculus* eye]. Across the eye.

transonance (tran′so-nans) [*trans-* + L. *sonans* sounding]. Transmission of a sound originating in one organ through the substance of another organ.

transorbital (trans-or′bĭ-tal). Performed through the bony socket of the eye.

transpalatal (trans-pal′ah-tal). Performed through the roof of the mouth, or palate.

transparent (trans-par′ent) [*trans-* + L. *parere* to appear]. Permitting the passage of rays of light, so that objects may be seen through the substance.

transparietal (trans″pah-ri′ĕ-tal) [*trans-* + L. *paries* wall]. Through or across a wall, as through the intact body wall.

transperitoneal (trans″per-ĭ-to-ne′al). Through or across the peritoneum.

transphosphorylase (trans″fos-for′ĭ-lās). An enzyme that catalyzes the transfer of a phosphate group. See *kinase* (def. 1).

transphosphorylation (trans-fos″for-ĭ-la′shun). The exchange of phosphate groups between organic phosphates, without their going through the stage of inorganic phosphate.

transpirable (tran-spīr′ah-b′l) [*trans-* + L. *spirare* to exhale]. Permitting the passage of perspiration.

transpiration (tran″spi-ra′shun) [*trans-* + L. *spiratio* exhalation]. The discharge of air, sweat, or vapor through the skin; insensible perspiration. **pulmonary t.,** the exhalation of water vapor from the blood circulating through the lungs.

transplacental (trans″plah-sen′tal). Through the placenta.

transplant[1] (trans-plant′). To transfer tissue from one part to another.

transplant[2] (trans′plant). A piece of tissue taken from the body for grafting into another portion of the body or into another individual. **Gallie t.,** strips of fascia lata from the thigh employed as sutures in hernia operations.

transplantar (trans-plan′tar) [*trans-* + L. *planta* sole]. Across the sole.

transplantation (trans″plan-ta′shun) [*trans-* + L. *plantare* to plant]. The grafting of tissues taken from the same body or from another. See *graft.* In dentistry, the insertion, into a prepared dental alveolus, of an autogenous or homologous tooth; it may be a developing tooth germ from the same mouth, or a frozen homologous transplant. **autoplastic t.,** the transplantation of tissue between different parts of the same individual. **heteroplastic t.,** transplantation of tissue between individuals belonging to different species. **heterotopic t.,** transplantation of tissue typical of one area to a different recipient site. **homoplastic t.,** isoplastic t. **homotopic t.,** transplantation of tissue typical of one area to an identical recipient site. **isoplastic t.,** the transplantation of tissue between individuals of the same species. **orthotopic t.,** homotopic t. **syngenesioplastic t.,** transplantation of tissue from one individual to a related individual of the same species, as from a mother to her child, or from a brother to a sister. **tendon t.,** the operation of inserting a piece from the tendon of a sound muscle into the tendon of a paralyzed muscle. **xenoplastic t.,** transplantation of tissue between individuals belonging to different genera.

transpleural (trans-ploor′al). Through the pleura; by way of the pleural sac.

transport (trans′port) [L. *transportare* to carry across]. The movement of materials in biological systems, particularly into and out of cells and across epithelial layers. **active t.,** the movement of materials across cell membranes and epithelial layers resulting directly from the expenditure of metabolic energy.

transposition (trans″po-zish′un) [*trans-* + L. *positio* placement]. 1. Displacement of a viscus to the opposite side. 2. The operation of carrying a tissue flap from one situation to another without severing its connection entirely until it is united at its new location. 3. The exchange of position of two atoms within a molecule.

transsacral (trans-sa′kral). Through or across the sacrum.

transsection (trans-sek′shun). Transection.

transsegmental (trans″seg-men′tal). Extending across a segment of a limb.

transseptal (trans-sep′tal). Through or across a septum.

transsphenoidal (trans″sfe-noi′dal). Performed through the sphenoid bone.

transsternal (trans-ster′nal). Through the sternum.

transtemporal (trans-tem′por-al). Crossing the temporal lobe.

transthalamic (trans″thah-lam′ik). Crossing the thalamus.

transthermia (trans-ther′me-ah) [*trans-* + Gr. *thermē* heat]. Thermopenetration.

transthoracic (trans″tho-ras′ik). Performed through the wall of the thorax, or through the thoracic cavity.

transthoracotomy (trans″tho-rah-kot′o-me) [*trans-* + *thorax* + Gr. *tomē* a cutting]. The operation of cutting across the thorax.

transtracheal (trans-tra′ke-al). Performed by passage through the wall of the trachea.

transubstantiation (tran″sub-stan″she-a′shun) [*trans-* + L. *substantia* substance]. The substitution of one tissue by another.

transudate (trans′u-dāt) [*trans-* + L. *sudare* to sweat]. A fluid substance which has passed through a membrane or been extruded from a tissue, sometimes as a result of inflammation. A transudate, in contrast to an exudate, is characterized by high fluidity and a low content of protein, cells, or of solid materials derived from cells.

transudation (trans″u-da′shun). The passage of serum or other body fluid through a membrane or tissue surface, which may or may not be the result of inflammation.

transuranium (trans″u-ra′ne-um). Beyond uranium. See *transuranic elements*, under *element*.

transureteroureterostomy (trans″u-re″ter-o-u-re″ter-os′to-me). Anastomosis of the distal and of the proximal portion of one ureter to the ureter of the opposite side.

transurethral (trans″u-re′thral). Performed through the urethra.

transvaginal (trans-vaj′ĭ-nal). Performed through the vagina.

transvaterian (trans″vah-te′re-an). Through the papilla of Vater.

transvector (trans-vek′tor). An organism that conveys or transmits a poison which is not generated in its own body but is obtained from another source, such as the mussel, *Mytilus*, which serves as a transvector of paralytic shellfish poison derived from the dinoflagellate, *Gonyaulax*.

transventricular (trans″ven-trik′u-lar). Performed through the ventricle; used especially in reference to surgical procedures on cardiac valves, performed through an incision in the wall of a ventricle.

transversalis (trans″ver-sa′lis) [*trans-* + L. *vertere, versum* to turn]. Transverse; in official anatomical nomenclature it designates a structure situated at a right angle to the long axis of the body or of an organ.

transversarius (trans″ver-sa′re-us). Relating to another part which is transverse.

transverse (trans-vers′) [L. *transversus*]. Placed crosswise; situated at right angles to the long axis of a part.

transversectomy (trans″ver-sek′to-me) [*transverse* + Gr. *ektomē* excision]. Surgical removal of the transverse process of a vertebra.

transversion (trans-ver′zhun). Displacement of a tooth from its proper numerical position in the jaw.

transversocostal (trans-ver″so-kos′tal). Costotransverse.

transversostomy (trans″ver-sos′to-me) [*transverse* + Gr. *stomoun* to provide with an opening, or mouth]. Colostomy in the transverse colon.

transversotomy (trans″ver-sot′o-me) [*transverse* + Gr. *tomē* a cutting]. The operation of cutting the transverse process of a vertebra.

transverso-urethralis (trans-ver″so-u″re-thra′lis). The transverse fibers of the sphincter urethrae muscle.

transversus (trans-ver′sus). Transverse; in official anatomical nomenclature used to designate a position at right angles to a long axis.

transvesical (trans-ves′ĭ-kal). Through the bladder.

transvestism (trans-ves′tizm) [*trans-* + L. *vestitus* clothed]. A sexual deviation characterized by overwhelming desire to assume the attire, and be accepted as a member, of the opposite sex. Called also *cross dressing* and *eonism*.

transvestite (trans-ves′tīt). An individual exhibiting transvestism.

transvestitism (trans-ves′tĭ-tizm). Transvestism.

Trantas' dots (tran′tas) [Alexios *Trantas*, Greek ophthalmologist, born 1867]. See under *dot*.

tranylcypromine (tran″il-si′pro-mēn). Chemical name: trans-dl-2-phenylcyclopropylamine: used as an inhibitor of monoamine oxidase and as an antidepressant.

trapezial (trah-pe′ze-al). Pertaining to a trapezium.

trapeziform (trah-pez′ĭ-form). Trapezoid.

trapeziometacarpal (trah-pe″ze-o-met″ah-kar′pal). Pertaining to or connecting the trapezium and the metacarpus.

trapezium (trah-pe′ze-um) [L.; Gr. *trapezion*]. An irregular four-sided figure. See *os trapezium*.

trapezoid (trap′e-zoid) [L. *trapezoides;* Gr. *trapezoeidēs* table shaped]. Having the shape of a four-sided solid, with two sides parallel and two diverging.

Trapp's coefficient, formula (traps) [Julius *Trapp*, Russian pharmacist, 1815–1908]. See under *formula*.

trasentine (tras′en-tin). Trade mark for preparations of adiphenine.

Traube's curves, membrane, space (trow′bez) [Ludwig *Traube*, German physician, 1818–1876]. See under the nouns.

trauma (traw′mah), pl. *traumas* or *trau′mata* [L.; Gr.]. A wound or injury. **birth t.,** an injury to the infant received in or due to the process of being born. In psychiatry, the psychic shock produced in an infant by the experience of being born. **potential t.,** in dentistry, an alteration in tissue that may at any time result from an existing dental disharmony. **psychic t.,** an emotional shock that makes a lasting impression on the mind, especially upon the subconscious mind.

traumasthenia (traw″mas-the′ne-ah) [*trauma* + *a* neg. + Gr. *sthenos* strength + *-ia*]. Traumatic neurasthenia.

traumatherapy (traw″mah-ther′ah-pe) [*trauma* + Gr. *therapeia* treatment]. That branch of surgery which deals with the treatment of wounds and injuries.

traumatic (traw-mat′ik) [Gr. *traumatikos*]. Pertaining to, occurring as the result of, or causing trauma.

traumatin (traw′mah-tin). A substance in plant tissues which aids in the repair of injured tissue: called also *wound hormone*.

traumatism (traw′mah-tizm) [Gr. *traumatismos*]. 1. A condition of the system due to an injury or wound. 2. A wound.

traumato- (traw′mah-to) [Gr. *trauma, traumatos* wound]. Combining form denoting relationship to trauma, or to a wound or injury.

traumatogenic (traw″mah-to-jen′ik) [*traumato-* + Gr. *gennan* to produce]. 1. Caused by or due to a wound or wounds. 2. Capable of causing trauma.

traumatologist (traw″mah-tol′o-jist). A surgeon experienced in treating accidental injuries.

traumatology (traw″mah-tol′o-je) [*traumato-* + *-logy*]. The branch of surgery which deals with wounds and disability from injuries.

traumatonesis (traw″mah-ton′e-sis). Suture of a wound.

traumatopathy (traw″mah-top′ah-the) [*trau-*

mato- + Gr. *pathos* disease]. Any disease due to wound or injury.

traumatophilia (traw″mah-to-fil′e-ah) [*trauma-to-* + Gr. *philein* to love]. A condition in which the patient takes a subconscious delight in injuries or surgical operations.

traumatopnea (traw″mah-top-ne′ah) [*traumato-* + Gr. *pnoia* breath]. A condition of partial asphyxia with collapse caused by traumatic opening of the pleura.

traumatopyra (traw″mah-to-pi′rah) [*traumato-* + Gr. *pyr* fever]. Traumatic fever.

traumatosis (traw″mah-to′sis). Traumatism.

traumatotherapy (traw″mah-to-ther′ah-pe). Treatment of wounds and accidents.

traumatropism (traw-mat′ro-pizm) [*trauma* + Gr. *tropos* a turning]. The growth or movement of organisms in relation to injury.

travail (trav′āl). Labor; childbirth.

travois (traw-vwah′). A stretcher for the wounded drawn by a single animal, the rear end of the stretcher dragging upon the ground.

tray (tra). A flat-surfaced utensil for the conveyance of various objects or material. **acrylic resin t.,** an impression tray made of acrylic resin. **impression t.,** in dentistry, a contoured metal container to hold the material with which an impression of the jaw or teeth is being made.

treacle (tre′k'l) [Gr. *thēriaka*]. A syrupy substance or mixture. **Venice t.,** theriaca andromachi.

tread (tred). Injury of the coronet of a horse's hoof, due to striking with the shoe of the opposite side. **nail t.,** an injury to the sole of a horse's hoof from treading on a nail.

treatment (trēt′ment). The management and care of a patient for the purpose of combating disease or disorder. **active t.,** that which is directed immediately to the cure of a disease or injury. **Albertini's t.,** complete rest and abstinence from food in aneurysm of the aorta. **albumose t.,** treatment of typhoid fever by the intravenous injection of deutero-albumose. **Allen's t.,** treatment by certain days of fasting, followed by a restricted diet and attended by a careful determination of the quantity of food which the patient can consume without producing glycosuria and glycemia. Called also *starvation t.* **Alonzo Clark t.,** Pepper t. **antigen t.,** the production of active immunity by the injection of antigens, including bacteriotherapy, and the use of vaccine and tuberculins. **Ascoli t.,** intravenous injections of increasing doses of epinephrine in malaria for the purpose of emptying the spleen of the parasites of the disease. **autoserosalvarsan t.,** Swift-Ellis t. **autoserous t.,** treatment of an infectious disease by inoculating the patient with his own serum. **Babe's t.,** treatment of rabies by injection of spinal cord suspensions attenuated by heating. **Bacelli's t.,** treatment of tetanus by intramuscular injection of carbolic acid, together with enemas of chloral hydrate. **Balfour's t.,** treatment of aneurysm by potassium iodide. **Banting t.,** treatment of obesity by a diet free from carbohydrate, but rich in nitrogenous matters. **Bargen's t.,** treatment of ulcerative colitis with Bargen's serum. **Baunscheidt's t.,** baunscheidtism. **Beard's t.,** treatment of cancer by trypsin. **Beauperthuy's t.,** treatment of leprosy with corrosive mercuric chloride. **Bell t.,** treatment of cancer by injections of a preparation of colloidal lead. **Bergeron's t.,** a method of treating tuberculosis of the lungs by injecting a mixture of hydrogen sulfide and carbon dioxide into the rectum. **Bergonié t.,** the application of general faradization for the reduction of corpulence. **Bier's t.** See under *hyperemia.* **Bier's combined t.,** treatment of surgical tuberculosis by artificial hyperemia, heliotherapy, and iodides. **Bird's t.,** treatment of decubitus ulcer by mild galvanic currents. **Blanchard's t.,** the plugging of tuberculotic bone cavities with a mixture of white wax and petrolatum. **Bluemel's t.,** a method of treating the morphine habit, with complete withdrawal of morphine, a liquid diet, cathartics, intravenous sodium chloride solution, and chloral to insure sleep the first few nights. **Boeck's t.,** the treatment of lupus vulgaris by applying a preparation of pyrogallic acid, resorcinol, salicylic acid, gelatin, and talc. **Bouchardat's t.,** treatment of diabetes by use of a diet that excludes substances rich in carbohydrates. **Brandt t.,** a method of treating fever by immersing the patient in a bath of the temperature of the room (65–70°F.) every three hours when the rectal temperature reaches 102.2°F. **Brandt's t.,** treatment of diseases of the fallopian tubes by pressing out their contents into the uterus by massage. **Brehmer's t.,** treatment of pulmonary tuberculosis by the use of dietetic and physical measures. **Brown-Séquard t.,** organotherapy. **Bülau's t.** See under *method.* **Bulgarian t.,** a method of treating neurologic and psychic sequels of epidemic encephalitis with belladonna in white wine. **Calot t.,** treatment of Pott's disease by plaster jackets having an opening over the kyphos on which pressure is made by means of pads. **Cantani's t.,** treatment of cholera by the repeated injection into the bowel of a large quantity of water containing tannic acid and tincture of opium at a temperature of from 100 to 104°F. **Carrel t., Carrel-Dakin t.,** treatment of wounds, based on thorough opening up of the wound, with removal of all foreign material, dead or lacerated tissue, etc.; careful cleansing, and repeated irrigation of the wound with surgical solution of chlorinated soda which has been modified with sodium bicarbonate. **Castellani's t.,** treatment of elephantiasis by complete rest in bed, bandaging with a flannel or rubber bandage, and daily injections of fibrolysin. **causal t.,** treatment that is directed against the cause of a disease. **choline t.,** treatment of cancer by the intravenous injection of borate of choline in connection with the use of radioactive substances. **Coffey-Humber t.,** treatment of cancer by injection of an extract of adrenal cortex of sheep. **Comby-Filatov t.,** the treatment of chorea with large doses of arsenic. **conservative t.** 1. Treatment designed to conserve the vital powers until clear indications develop. 2. Conservative surgery. **Cordier's t.,** treatment of sciatica by injection of filtered air in the region of the sciatic nerve. **Co-Tui t.,** treatment of peptic ulcer by administration of protein hydrolysate. **Cox's t.,** treatment of cholera by intravenous isotonic saline. **curative t.,** active treatment designed to cure an existing disease. **Dancel's t.,** a treatment of obesity by a diet containing as little water as possible. **Debove's t.,** treatment of tuberculosis by a special form of forced feeding. **Demyanovich's t.,** treatment of scabies by rubbing 40 per cent solution of thiosulfate into the skin, followed by a rub of 5 per cent solution of hydrochloric acid. **dietetic t.,** treatment of disease by regulation of the diet. **drug t.,** treatment with drugs, as distinguished from treatment with physical means, such as diet, exercise, electricity, etc. **Dubois's t.** See under *method.* **Durante's t.,** treatment of surgical tuberculosis by injecting iodine into the lesion. **Ebstein's t.** See under *diet.* **Ehrlich-Hata t.** See *arsphenamine.* **electric shock t.** See *shock therapy,* under *therapy.* **Elliott t.,** treatment of pelvic inflammations by inserting into the vagina a thin rubber bag through which a constant circulation of hot water is maintained. **empiric t.,** treatment by means which experience has proved to be beneficial. **envelope t.** See *Bunyan-Stannard envelope.* **Erlangen t.,** treatment of deep-seated cancer by administering at one sitting a dose of high voltage roentgen ray lethal for the cancer cell, multiple small ports of entry being used. **Etappen t.,** treatment of bowlegs and knock knee by plaster of paris bandage and corrective wedging. **eventration t.,** application of roentgen rays to internal structures after opening the abdomen and bringing the malignant area to the edges of the wound. **expectant t.**, treatment designed only to relieve untoward symptoms, leaving the cure mainly to nature. **Felsen t.**, treatment of dysentery and ulcerative colitis by rectal injection of oxygen. **Ferrier's t.**, treatment of tuberculosis by giving lime salts, calcium carbonate, calcium phosphate, sodium chloride, and calcine magnesia. **fever t.**, pyretotherapy. **Fichera's t.**, treatment of cancer by hypodermic injection of autolyzed human fetal tissue. **Finikoff's t.**, treatment for bone tuberculosis: iodized peanut oil is injected intramuscularly every five to eight days and 10 per cent calcium solution intravenously three times a week. **Finsen t.**, treatment of lupus vulgaris by direct application of rays of sunlight or electric light. **Fischer's t.** See under *solution.* **five day t.** See *massive drip intravenous therapy*, under *therapy.* **Flechsig's t.**, for epilepsy, consists in the use of opium, followed by bromides. **Fliess t.**, anesthetization of the nasal conchae for the relief of pain in dysmenorrhea and in nervous stomach pains. **foam t.**, treatment with the foam produced by blowing a current of air through water containing saponin solution. **forest t.**, dasetherapy. **Forlanini's t.**, artificial pneumothorax for the treatment of pulmonary tuberculosis. **Fournier's t.**, treatment of syphilis by administering mercury for two months, then stopping the mercury for a month or more. This is followed by a period of alternate administration and stopping of the mercury. **Fowler-Murphy t.**, Murphy's t., def. 2. **Fränkel's t.**, the use of strophanthin in cardiac failure. **Frenkel's t.** See under *movement.* **Gennerich's t.**, treatment of neurosyphilis by direct introduction into the spinal canal of a neoarsphenamine solution diluted with spinal fluid. **Girard t.**, treatment of seasickness by hypodermic or oral administration of atropine sulfate and strychnine sulfate. **gland t.**, gonadotherapy. **Guelpa t.**, treatment of gout and rheumatism by fasting and free purging. **Guinard's t.**, application of calcium carbide to ulcerating tumors. **Hare's t.**, treatment of dysentery by rectal injections of hot water through a flexible tube passed above the sigmoid flexure. **Hartel t.**, alcoholic injection for trigeminal neuralgia in which the needle is passed through the mouth into the region of the foramen ovale of the sphenoid bone. **Hassin's t.**, epidural injection of neoarsphenamine for the treatment of tabes. **Heiser's t.**, treatment of leprosy by the injection of a mixture of chaulmoogra oil, camphorated oil, and resorcin. **Heiser-Moro t.** See *apple diet*, under *diet.* **high-frequency t.**, diathermy. **Högyes' t.**, treatment of rabies by the subcutaneous injection of a 1 per cent suspension of rabies virus diluted 1:100 or 1:1000. **Huchard's t.**, treatment of dilatation of the stomach by a diet in which there is a strict limitation of the liquid element. **hygienic t.**, directed to the restoration or maintenance of hygienic conditions. **hypoglycemic shock t.**, insulin-shock t. **Imre's t.**, treatment of retinitis pigmentosa by the inhalation of amyl nitrite every second day for several weeks. **insulin-shock t.** See *shock therapy*, under *therapy.* **Jacquet's biokinetic t.**, active gymnastics of the hand and fingers. **Jarotzky's t.**, treatment of gastric ulcer by a diet of whites of eggs, fresh butter with bread and milk or noodles. **Karell t.**, treatment of heart and kidney disease by keeping the patient in bed and giving only 800 cc. of milk daily for four or five days, the diet then being gradually increased until, on the thirteenth day, the regular diet is resumed. **Kaufmann's t.**, treatment of psychoneurosis by application of powerful electric shocks and the giving of loud military orders to perform certain exercises. **Keating-Hart's t.** See under *fulguration.* **Kenny t.**, treatment of infantile paralysis by wrapping the patient's back and limbs in woolen cloths wrung out of hot water: after pain has subsided passive exercise is given and the patient taught to exercise his muscles by himself. **Killgren t.**, a system of medical gymnastics combined with passive exercise, friction, and vibrations, and laying special emphasis on the mechanical treatment of the nerves. **Kissmeyer t.**, treatment of scabies with a lotion of equal parts of soft soap, isopropyl alcohol, and benzyl benzoate. **Kittel's t.**, massage and manipulation for the dispersion of the uratic deposits in gouty joints. **Klapp's creeping t.**, treatment of scoliosis by having the patient creep about on the floor, with exaggerated movements of the spine. **Knopf's t.**, diaphragmatic respiration practice to avoid inflating the apices of the lungs in tuberculosis and to increase the strength of the heart action in cardiac weakness. **Koga t.**, treatment of thrombo-angiitis obliterans by diluting the blood by hypodermoclysis with normal salt solution. **Korányi's t.**, treatment of leukemia by the use of benzol (benzene). **Kromayer's t.**, treatment of syphilis by the inhalation of very finely divided mercury. **Lambert's t.**, a method of treating the opium habit based on gradual reduction of opium and increasing doses of codeine, which is continued for about a week after the opium is withdrawn. **Lambotte's t.**, a method of extension in fractures of the extremities by means of an extensible steel frame fastened to the bone by steel pegs. **Lancereaux's t.**, treatment of internal aneurysm by injecting glycerin subcutaneously. **Landerer's t.**, injections of cinnamic acid for tuberculosis. **La Porte t.**, treatment of chronic osteomyelitis by application over the infected areas of aluminum potassium nitrate in an oatmeal poultice. **Larat's t.**, treatment of diphtheritic paralysis of the palate by faradism. **Läwe's t.**, treatment of abscesses by injection of the patient's venous blood around the inflammatory focus. **Lenhartz t.**, treatment of gastric ulcer based on absolute bed rest, and feeding an abundant diet, chiefly of proteins, on the principle that the excess of acid is thereby neutralized and the healing of the ulcer facilitated. **Lerich's t.** (*of strains*), infiltration of the periarticular tissues with a 0.5–2 per cent solution of procaine. **Leube t.**, treatment of gastric ulcer by rest in bed, the daily use of lukewarm saline laxatives, the application of hot poultices and Priessnitz compresses to the abdomen, and a diet mainly of milk in increasing quantities, fortified later by the addition of cereals, and finally of meat. **light t.**, phototherapy. **McPheeters' t.**, treatment of varicose ulcer by bandaging a rubber sponge over the ulcerated area and directing the patient to walk as much as possible. Called *venous heart treatment.* **Maisler's t.**, gaseous dilatation in the treatment of gonorrhea. **malarial t.**, malariotherapy. **massive drip intravenous t.** See under *therapy.* **Matas' t.**, treatment of neuralgia by the injection of alcohol under the nerve ganglions at the base of the skull. **medicinal t.**, that in which the treatment is mainly accomplished by the use of remedies. **Meltzer t.**, treatment of tetanus by injection into the spinal canal of a solution of magnesium sulfate. **Minot-Murphy t.**, the treatment of pernicious anemia by the addition to the diet of raw liver or liver extract. **Mitchell t.** See *Weir Mitchell t.* **mixed t.**, treatment of syphilis with both potassium iodide and corrosive sublimate. **Muirhead's t.**, treatment of Addison's disease by epinephrine given to the point of tolerance and the administration of adrenal cortex by mouth. **Murphy's t.** 1. Treatment of pulmonary tuberculosis by injecting nitrogen gas into the pleural cavity in order to cause collapse of the lung and consequent obliteration of cavities in it. 2. Treatment of peritonitis by placing the patient in the Fowler position to favor drainage from the pelvis and abdomen, and then irrigating the lower bowel with physiologic salt solution administered slowly. **Nägeli's t.**, treatment of epistaxis by stretching the cervical sympathetic nerve, which stimulates vasoconstriction. **Nauheim t.**, Schott's t. **Neuber's t.**, treatment of tuberculosis of bones and joints by excising the carious tissue and filling the cavity with an emulsion of iodoform in glycerin. **Neuendorf t.,** treatment of rheumatoid arthritis by the mud baths of Neuendorf, Germany. **Noesske's t.,** treatment of gangrene by incising the part and producing suction by means of a vacuum cup, to draw out the stagnant venous blood. **Noorden t.,** oatmeal t. **Nordach t.,** treatment of pulmonary tuberculosis by fresh air, rest, and an abundance of nourishing food. **oatmeal t.,** treatment of diabetes by restricting the protein of the diet and limiting the carbohydrates to oatmeal. **Ochsner t.,** treatment of appendicitis by securing peristaltic rest so that peritoneal adhesions may form. This is secured by abstention from food by the mouth and the use of gastric lavage and rectal irrigations, but no purgatives. **Oertel's t.,** treatment of heart disease, circulatory diseases, obesity, etc., by regulation of diet, diminution of fluid elements in the food, mountain climbing and other systematic exercises, and by massage and Swedish movements. **Oppenheimer's t.,** a method of treating alcoholism and drug habit. **organ t.,** organotherapy. **Orr t.,** treatment of compound fractures and osteomyelitis by débridement of the wound, alignment of fracture, drainage with petrolatum gauze, and immobilization of limb in a plaster cast which is left on until the wound discharge has softened the plaster. **palliative t.,** treatment which is designed to relieve pain and distress, but which does not attempt a cure. **Paul's t.,** the therapeutic use of lymph for cutaneous therapy of chronic rheumatism. **Pepper t.,** the inhibition of peristalsis in peritonitis with large doses of opium. **Percy t.** See under *cautery*. **Petrén's t.,** treatment of diabetes by a diet containing almost no protein or carbohydrate, by large amounts of fat, until the blood sugar is normal. **Pilcz's t.,** inoculation of paretic patients with the toxin of erysipelas to induce remission of the paresis. **plancha t.,** treatment of leprosy by multiple intradermic injections of antileprosy drugs directly into leprous skin lesions. **Playfair's t.,** treatment by rest and feeding. **Plombières t.** See under *douche*. **Politzer's t.,** treatment of disease of the middle ear by blowing air into the nostril while the patient goes through the movements of swallowing. **Potter t.,** treatment of intestinal fistulas by administration of tenth normal solution of hydrochloric acid to neutralize the alkalinity of the pancreatic juice, thus preventing tryptic activity. **preventive t., prophylactic t.,** that in which the aim is to prevent the occurrence of the disease. **Proetz t.,** the filling of paranasal sinuses with fluid by means of intermittent negative pressure for the treatment of sinus infection. **Q A P t.,** treatment of malaria with quinine sulfate until pyrexia is controlled; then with atabrine for five days; followed by plasmochin for five days. **quinine-calcium t.,** treatment of lobar pneumonia by intravenous or intramuscular injection of a solution of calcium and quinine levulinate. **Quintin t.,** subcutaneous injection of sea water solution in treatment of malnutrition, anemia, chronic indigestion, etc. **rational t.,** treatment which is based upon a knowledge of disease and the action of the remedies employed. **refrigerator t.,** treatment of tuberculosis and sleeping sickness by having the patient spend several hours daily in a room at a temperature of 20°F., to stimulate the metabolic processes. **Retan's t.,** treatment of intussusception by distending the colon with a barium mixture, followed by manipulations. **Ricord's t.,** treatment of syphilis by administration of mercury for six months, followed by administration of potassium iodide for three months. **Roeder's t.,** removal of pus and debris from an inflamed tonsil by suction. **Rogers' t.,** treatment of cholera by transfusion of saline solution and oral administration of permanganates. **Rollier t.,** treatment of surgical tuberculosis by systematic exposure of the part to the rays of the sun. **Rotunda t.,** treatment of eclampsia by free administration of fluids when the convulsions appear. **salicyl t.,** treatment of rheumatism with salicylic acid or its derivatives. **sand t.,** treatment with sand baths. **Sceleth t.,** treatment of drug addiction by the use of saline cathartics and a preparation containing scopolamine hydrobromide, pilocarpine hydrobromide, ethyl morphine hydrochloride, fluidextract of cascara sagrada, alcohol, and water. **Schede's t.,** treatment of necrosis of bone by removing dead bone and granulation tissue, which permits the cavity to fill with blood. The resulting clot is kept moist by an aseptic dressing. **Schlösser's t.,** treatment of facial neuralgia by injections of 80 per cent alcohol into the foramen from which the nerve emerges. **Schöler's t.,** injection of tincture of iodine into the vitreous body in detachment of the retina. **Schott's t.,** treatment of heart disease by use of warm saline baths of Nauheim and systematically conducted exercise. **Schroth's t.,** treatment of obesity by the exclusion of water in any form as far as possible. **Semple's t.,** the prevention of rabies by injection of Semple vaccine. **sewage t.,** the processing of sewage to remove or so alter some of its constituents as to render it less offensive or dangerous and more fit to discharge into a public water course. **shock t.** See under *therapy*. **Sicard t.,** treatment of the gastric crises of tabes by bilateral cordotomy between the first and second, or second and third, thoracic segments of the spinal cord. **Sippy t.,** a regimen of treatment of peptic ulcer based on neutralization of hydrochloric acid by frequent feedings and the use of alkalies in carefully regulated but adequate quantities. **slush t.,** the treatment of acne by the application of a mixture of carbon dioxide snow, acetone, and sulfur. **sodoku t.,** treatment of paresis by inoculation with the spirochete which causes sodoku or rat-bite fever. **solar t.,** heliotherapy. **Spahlinger t.,** treatment of pulmonary tuberculosis based on destruction of tuberculous toxins by injecting various bacteriolytic and antitoxic serums, and then therapeutic vaccination with a series of tuberculins. **Spangler's t.,** treatment of epilepsy by injection of rattlesnake venom. **specific t.,** treatment that is particularly adapted to the special disease being treated. **starvation t.,** Allen t. **Stoker's t.,** treatment in bronchiectasis by continuous inhalation of oxygen. **string method t.,** treatment of esophageal stricture by passing a string through the mouth and through a gastric fistula, and then, by pulling the string up and down, cutting through the stricture so that a bougie may easily be passed. Called also *Abbe's string method*. **Stroganoff's t.,** treatment of puerperal eclampsia by morphine, chloral hydrate, and chloroform, according to a definite scheme. **supporting t.,** that which is mainly directed to sustaining the strength of the patient. **surgical t.,** that in which surgical means are those chiefly employed. **Swift-Ellis t.,** treatment of general paresis by intradural injection of blood serum of the patient taken after the injection of arsphenamine (*autoserosalvarsan*). **symptomatic t.,** expectant t. **Tallerman t.,** the localized application of superheated dry air in rheumatism, gout, sprains, neuritis, eczema, etc. **teleradium t.,** treatment by exposure to a large quantity of radium contained in an apparatus at some distance from the body. **terrain t.,** treatment of weak heart, neurasthenia, corpulence, etc., by regular exercise, mountain climbing, regulation of diet, etc. **three-dye t.,** treatment of burns by application of 6 per cent gentian violet, 1 per cent brilliant green, and 0.1 per cent acriflavin base. **thymus t.,** treatment of progressive muscular atrophy by extracts from the thymus gland. **thyroid t.,** treatment of disease by preparations of the thyroid gland of domestic animals used for food by man. **tonic t.** 1. Treatment with tonics. 2. Treatment of syphilis with small doses of mercury continued for a long period. **Towns-Lambert t.,** treatment of drug addiction by systematic purging, gradually reducing amount of the drug to which the patient is addicted, and the use of a mixture of belladonna tincture and of fluidextracts of hyoscyamus and xanthoxylum. **Trueta t.,** treatment of recently inflicted wounds based on five essential points: (1) prompt surgical treatment; (2) cleansing of the wound; (3) excision (débridement) of the wound; (4) drainage with dry gauze; (5) immobilization in a plaster of paris cast. **Tschmarke's t.,** treatment of burn by thorough washing with soap and water and alcohol under general anesthesia. **Tuffnell's t.,** treatment of aneurysm by absolute rest and starvation diet. **under-water t.,** treatment of poliomyelitis patients by permitting active movements in the water of a bath or pool. **Valsalva's t.,** treatment of aneurysm by absolute rest, starvation diet, and bleeding. **Veit's t.,** treatment of puerperal eclampsia with large doses of morphine. **venous heart t.,** McPheeters' t. **Vidal t.,** treatment of lupus vulgaris by scarification. **Wagner's t.,** treatment of general paresis or other form of neurosyphilis by subcutaneous injection of the blood of an untreated malaria patient. **Wagner-Jauregg t.,** treatment of dementia paralytica by infection of the patient with malaria. **Weir Mitchell t.,** a method of treating neurasthenia, hysteria, etc., by absolute rest in bed, frequent and abundant feeding, and the systematic use of massage and electricity. **Widal t.,** treatment of circulatory disorders by excluding sodium chloride as much as possible from the food. **Willems' t.,** treatment of acute arthritis by early evacuation of the effusion or suppuration followed by immediate active movements of the joint. **Woodbridge t.,** treatment of typhoid fever with small doses of calomel, podophyllin, and intestinal antiseptics. **Yeo's t.,** treatment of obesity by giving large amounts of hot drinks and withholding carbohydrates. **Zeller t.,** subarachnoid insufflation of acetylene for meningitis. **Ziemssen's t.,** treatment of anemia by subcutaneous injections of defibrinated human blood. **Zünd-Burguet t.,** treatment of deafness by the electrophonoide.

tredecaphobia (tred″e-kah-fo′be-ah). Triskaidekaphobia.

tree (tre). 1. A perennial of the plant kingdom characterized by having a main stem or trunk and numerous branches. 2. An anatomical structure with branches resembling a tree. **bronchial t.,** the bronchi and their branching structures.

trehala (tre-ha′lah). A manna-like substance deposited by an insect (*Larinus maculatus*) upon an Asiatic plant of the genus *Echinops*.

trehalose (tre-ha′lōs). A disaccharide, $C_{12}H_{22}O_{11}$, from manna and yeast. It is not digestible, but yields dextrose when hydrolyzed with acids.

Treitz's arch, fossa, hernia, muscle, etc. (trits) [Wenzel *Treitz*, Austrian physician, 1819–1872]. See under the nouns.

Trélat's sign (tra-laz′) [Ulysse *Trélat*, French surgeon, 1828–1890]. See under *sign*.

Trematoda (trem″ah-to′dah) [Gr. *trēmatōdēs* pierced]. A class of the Platyhelminthes which includes the flukes. The trematodes or flukes are parasitic in man and animals, infestation resulting from the ingestion of uncooked or insufficiently cooked fish, crustaceans, and vegetation which are the intermediate hosts of the trematodes. The important trematodes belong to the genera (1) Blood: *Schistosoma*. (2) Intestine: *Echinostoma, Fasciolopsis, Gastrodiscoides, Heterophyes, Metagonimus*. (3) Liver: *Clonorchis, Fasciola, Dicrocoelium, Opisthorchis*. (4) Lung: *Paragonimus*.

trematode (trem′ah-tōd). Any parasitic animal organism belonging to the class Trematoda.

trematodiasis (trem″ah-to-di′ah-sis). Infestation with a trematode.

trembles (trem′b'lz). A disease of cattle and sheep in which the animal becomes weak and may suddenly stumble and fall. Persons made ill by milk or butter from an animal so affected are said to have milk sickness, which is often fatal. The condition seems to be caused by the cattle eating white snakeroot (*Eupatorium urticaefolium*), jimmey weed (*Aploppus heterophyllus*), and *A. fruticosus*. Called also *slows* and *milk sickness*.

tremelloid, tremellose (trem′ĕ-loid, trem′ĕ-lōs). Like jelly.

tremetol (trem′ĕ-tol). A toxin in *Eupatorium urticaefolium* which may be the cause of trembles in cattle and milk sickness in man.

tremogram (tre′mo-gram) [*tremor* + Gr. *gramma* mark]. The tracing or record made by a tremograph; a graphic tracing of a tremor. See *ataxiameter*.

tremograph (tre′mo-graf) [*tremor* + Gr. *graphein* to write]. An instrument for recording tremors.

tremolabile (tre″mo-la′bil) [*tremor* + L. *labilis* unstable]. Susceptible to shaking; easily inactivated by shaking: said of a ferment.

tremophobia (tre″mo-fo′be-ah) [*tremor* + Gr. *phobein* to be affrighted by]. A morbid fear of trembling.

tremor (trem′or, tre′mor) [L., from *tremere* to shake]. An involuntary trembling or quivering. **arsenic t.,** a tremor resulting from arsenic poisoning. **coarse t.,** a tremor in which the vibrations are slow. **continuous t.,** a persistent tremor resembling that of paralysis agitans. **t. cor′dis,** palpitation of the heart. **darkness t.,** involuntary movements of the eyes, resembling nystagmus, which occur in young animals kept in the dark. **epileptoid t.,** intermitting clonic spasm with tremor. **familial hereditary t.,** a condition marked by tremor and having a familial hereditary trend. **fibrillary t.,** a fine rhythmical trembling which is due to alternate contraction of the different fibrils of a muscle; fibrillation. **fine t.,** a tremor in which the vibrations are rapid. **flapping t.,** asterixis. **forced t.,** a movement persisting after voluntary motion, due to intermittent stimulation of the nerve centers. **Hunt's t.,** the tremor attending every voluntary movement which is characteristic of cerebellar lesions. **hysterical t.,** tremor seen in hysteria dependent upon uncertain nervous impulse. **intention t.,** a tremor which arises or which is intensified when a voluntary, coordinated movement is attempted. **intermittent t.,** tremor seen in hemiplegia or when attempts at voluntary movement are made. **kinetic t.,** a tremor occurring in a limb during active movement. **t. lin′guae,** trembling of the tongue, as seen in alcoholism, typhoid fever, and paretic dementia. **t. mercuria′lis,** tremor due to mercurial poisoning. **metallic t.,** a tremor seen in various metallic poisonings. **motofacient t.,** a tremor in muscles which participate in an action. **t. opiophago′rum,** the tremor of opium users. **passive t.,** a tremor occurring only when the patient is at rest. **persistent t.,** a tremor occurring whether the patient is at rest or in motion. **t. potato′rum** ["trembling of drinkers"], delirium tremens. **purring t.,** a thrill, like the purring of a cat, felt by the hand placed over the heart, and due to mitral stenosis. **Rendu's t.,** a hysterical intention tremor. **senile t.,** a tremor resulting from the infirmities of age. **static t.,** a tremor occurring on effort to hold one of the limbs in a definite position. **striocerebellar t.,** a combined form of organic tremor with both striatal and cerebellar components. **t. ten′dinum** ["trembling of the tendons"], subsultus tendinum. **toxic t.,** a tremor seen in states of chronic poisoning. **volitional t.,** a trembling of the entire body during voluntary effort; it is seen in multiple sclerosis.

tremorgram (trem′or-gram). Tremogram.

tremulor (trem′u-lor). A machine for the administration of vibratory treatment.

tremulous (trem′u-lus) [L. *tremulus*]. Shaking, trembling, or quivering.

trend (trend). Inclination in a particular direction or course.

Trendelenburg cannula, operation, position, symptom, test (tren-del′en-berg) [Friedrich *Trendelenburg,* surgeon in Leipzig, 1844–1925]. See under the nouns.

trepan (tre-pan′) [Gr. *trypanon* auger]. 1. An obsolete form of the trephine, resembling a carpenter's bit and brace. 2. To trephine.

trepanation (trep″ah-na′shun) [L. *trepanatio*]. An operation with the trepan; trephination. **corneal t.,** excision of a disk of cornea in treatment of staphyloma.

trepanner (tre-pan′er). One who performs a trepanation.

trephination (tref″ĭ-na′shun). The operation of trephining.

trephine (tre-fīn′) [L. *trephina*]. 1. A crown saw for removing a circular disk of bone, chiefly from the skull, or for removing a disk of tissue from the cornea or sclera. 2. To operate upon with the trephine. **Horsley's t.,** a trephine that may be taken apart and cleaned.

Trephine.

trephinement (tre-fīn′ment). The act or process of trephining.

trephiner (tre-fīn′er). One who performs the operation of trephining.

trephocyte (tref′o-sit) [Gr. *trephein* to feed + *kytos* cell]. A cell which furnishes nutrition to the tissues. See *Sertoli's cell,* under *cell.*

trephone (tref′ōn) [Gr. *trephein* to feed]. A hypothetical substance manufactured by certain cells of the body and used by other cells in the building up of their protoplasm (Carrel).

trepidant (trep′ĭ-dant) [L. *trepidans* trembling]. Characterized by tremor.

trepidatio (trep″ĭ-da′she-o) [L.]. Trepidation. **t. cor′dis,** palpitation of the heart.

trepidation (trep″ĭ-da′shun) [L. *trepidatio*]. 1. A trembling or oscillatory movement. 2. Nervous anxiety and fear.

Treponema (trep″o-ne′mah) [Gr. *trepein* to turn + *nema* thread]. A genus of microorganisms of the family Treponemataceae, order Spirochaetales, made up of cells 3 to 18 μ long, in acute, regular or irregular spirals, some of them being pathogenic and parasitic for man and other animals. Many spirochetes formerly classified as Treponema are now considered to be species of Borrelia. **T. calligy′rum,** a parasitic microorganism found in smegma and in lesions of the pudenda; thought to be non-pathogenic. **T. carate′um,** the causative agent of pinta (carate). **T. cunic′uli,** the causative agent of rabbit syphilis; not pathogenic for man. **T. genita′lis,** a parasitic, non-pathogenic microorganism found on human genitalia. **T. macroden′tium,** an apparently non-pathogenic species which has been found in the mouth. **T. microden′tium,** a parasitic spiral microorganism found in the normal human mouth; non-pathogenic. **T. muco′sum,** a parasitic microorganism found in pyorrhea alveolaris; pathogenicity uncertain. **T. pal′lidum,** the causative agent of syphilis in man. **T. perten′ue,** the causative agent of yaws (framboesia tropica) in man.

treponema (trep″o-ne′mah). An organism of the genus Treponema.

Treponemataceae (trep″o-ne″mah-ta′se-e). A family of schizomycetes (order Spirochaetales), made up of coarse or slender spirals, 4 to 16 μ long, sometimes showing terminal filaments and sometimes visible only with dark-field illumination. They commonly occur as parasites in vertebrates, and some of them cause disease. The family includes three genera, *Borrelia, Leptospira,* and *Treponema.*

treponematosis (trep″o-ne-mah-to′sis). An infection with treponema.

treponemiasis (trep″o-ne-mi′ah-sis). Infection with treponema; syphilis.

treponemicidal (trep″o-ne″mĭ-si′dal). Destroying treponema.

treponemosis (trep″o-ne-mo′sis). Infection with treponema.

trepopnea (tre″pop-ne′ah) [Gr. *trepein* to turn + *pnoia* breath]. A condition in which breathing is most comfortable with the patient turned in a definite recumbent position.

treppe (trep′ĕ) [Ger. "staircase"]. The phenomenon of gradual increase in the extent of muscular contraction following rapidly repeated stimulation (H. P. Bowditch, 1871). Also called *staircase phenomenon.*

Tresilian's sign (tre-sil′e-anz) [Frederick James *Tresilian,* English physician, 1862–1926]. See under *sign.*

tresis (tre′sis) [Gr. *trēsis*]. Perforation.

Treves's fold, operation (trēvs) [Sir Frederick *Treves,* English surgeon, 1853–1923]. See under *fold* and *operation.*

tri- [Gr. *treis;* L. *tres* three]. Prefix meaning *three* or *thrice.*

triacetate (tri-as′ĕ-tāt). An acetate which contains three molecules of the acetic acid radical.

triacetin (tri-as′e-tin). Chemical name: glyceryl triacetate: used as an antimycotic agent.

triacetyloleandomycin (tri-as″ĕ-til-o″le-an″do-mi′sin). The triacetyl ester of a substance produced by the growth of species of Streptomyces: used as an antibiotic.

triacetylpyrogallol (tri-as″ĕ-til-pi″ro-gal′ol). Lenigallol.

triacontanol (tri″ah-kon′tah-nol). A solid, white alcohol, $C_{30}H_{59}OH$, from lucerne.

triacid (tri-as′id). A base capable of neutralizing three equivalents of monobasic acid.

triad (tri′ad) [L. *trias:* Gr. *trias* group of three]. 1. Any trivalent element. 2. A group of three entities or objects. **Basedow's t.,** Merseburg t. **Beck's t.,** three symptoms characteristic of acute cardiac compression: (1) a rising venous pressure, (2) a falling arterial pressure, and (3) a small quiet heart. **Bezold's t.,** prolonged bone conduction, lessened perception of deep tones, and negative Rinne's sign, indicating otosclerosis. **Charcot's t.,** nystagmus, intention tremor, and staccato speech. **Dieulafoy's t.,** hypersensitiveness of the skin, reflex muscular contraction, and tenderness at McBurney's point in appendicitis. **Falta's t.,** the three organs cooperating in production of diabetes mellitus: the pancreas, liver, and thyroid. **Grancher's t.,** lessened vesicular quality of breathing, skodaic resonance, and increased vocal fremitus: in early pulmonary tuberculosis. **hepatic t's,** the association of representatives of the hepatic artery, vein, and bile duct at the angles of the lobules of the liver. **t. of Herz,** phrenocardia. **Hutchinson's t.,** diffuse interstitial keratitis, labyrinthine disease, and Hutchinson teeth, seen in inherited syphilis. **Kartagener's t.** See under *syndrome.* **t. of Luciani,** asthenia, atonia, and astasia, the three major symptoms of cerebellar disease. **Merseburg t., Merseburger t.,** goiter, exophthalmos, and tachycardia, the three cardinal symptoms of Basedow's disease: named after Merseburg, the home of Basedow. **Osler's t.,** telangiectasis, capillary fragility, and hereditary hemorrhagic diathesis. **Saint's t.,** hiatus hernia, colonic diverticula, and cholelithiasis, occurring concomitantly. **t. of Schultz,** jaundice, gangrenous stomatitis, and leukopenia.

triage (tre-ahzh′) [Fr. "sorting"]. The sorting out and classification of casualties of war or other disaster, to determine priority of need and proper place of treatment.

triakaidekaphobia (tri″ah-ki″dek-ah-fo′be-ah). Triskaidekaphobia.

trialism (tri′al-izm). Trialistic theory. See under *theory.*

triallylamine (tri″al-il-am′in). A volatile, oily, liquid amine, $(CH_2{:}CH.CH_2)_3N$.

triamcinolone (tri″am-sin′o-lōn). Chemical name: 9α-fluoro-16α-hydroxyprednisolone: used as an anti-inflammatory steroid. **t. acetonide,** an anti-inflammatory steroid, 9α-fluoro-16α,17α-isopropylidenedioxy-Δ^1-hydrocortisone, applied topically in treatment of various dermatoses, and sometimes administered by intra-articular, intrabursal, or intrasynovial injection in the treatment of painful and inflammatory conditions of joints, bursae, or tendon sheaths.

triamine (tri-am′in). A compound containing three amino (—NH_2) groups.

triamylose (tri-am′ĭ-lōs). A polymerized anhydride of glucose, $(C_6H_{10}O_5)_3$, thought to be a constituent of starch.

triangle (tri′ang-g'l) [L. *triangulum; tres* three + *angulus* angle]. A three-cornered area, figure, or object. See also *trigone* and *trigonum*. **Alsberg's t.,** an equilateral triangle with its apex upward, formed by a line passing through the long axis of the femur, a second line passing through the long axis of the neck of the femur, and a third line on a plane passing through the base of the head of the femur. The angle at the apex is known as *Alsberg's angle*, or *angle of elevation*. **Assézat's t.,** facial t. **auditory t.,** area vestibularis. **auricular t.,** one bounded by lines drawn from the tip of the auricle and the two ends of its base of insertion. **t. of auscultation,** the area limited by the lower edge of the trapezius muscle, the latissimus dorsi, and the medial margin of the scapula. **axillary t.,** the triangular area formed by the inner aspect of the arm, the axilla, and the pectoral region. **Beclard's t.,** the area lying between the posterior edge of the hyoglossus muscle, the posterior belly of the digastric muscle, and the greater cornu of the hyoid bone. **Bonwill t.,** an equilateral triangle said by Bonwill to be formed by a line connecting the centers of the mandibular condyles and lines connecting either center with the mesial contact area of the mandibular medial incisors, each side being approximately 4 inches long. **brachial t.,** axillary t. **Calot's t.,** a triangle bounded by the liver, the cystic duct, and the hepatic duct; it is of particular importance surgically because it contains usually the cystic artery, which most commonly arises in the triangle, the right hepatic artery, and possibly accessory hepatic ducts. Called also *cystohepatic t.* **cardiohepatic t.,** the triangular region in the fifth intercostal space of the right side, separating the heart from the upper edge of the liver. **carotid t., inferior,** the part of the trigonum caroticum medial to the omohyoid muscle. Called also *t. of necessity.* **carotid t., superior,** the part of the trigonum caroticum lateral to the omohyoid muscle. Called also *t. of election.* **cephalic t.,** one on the anteroposterior plane of the skull, between the lines from the occiput to the forehead and to the chin, and a third line extending from the chin to the forehead. **cervical t's.** See *t's of neck.* **Codman's t.** 1. A triangular area visible roentgenographically where the periosteum, elevated by a bone tumor, rejoins the cortex of normal bone. 2. See *Codman's sign*, under *sign.* **color t.,** a plane figure with red, green, and blue located at the three apices, and gray at the center, with lines drawn from side to side, as a guide to the color mixing equation needed to produce any intermediate hue. **crural t.,** the triangular area formed by the inner aspect of the thigh and the lower abdominal, inguinal, and genital regions. **cystohepatic t.,** Calot's t. **digastric t.,** trigonum submandibulare. **Einthoven's t.,** a triangle by which it can be demonstrated that the algebraic sum of the potential differences as recorded in electrocardiographic leads I and III will equal that potential difference recorded in lead II. **t. of elbow,** a triangular area on the front of the elbow, having the brachioradialis muscle on the outside and the pronator teres inside, the base being toward the humerus. **t. of election,** superior carotid t. **extravesical t.,** Pawlik's t. **facial t.,** a triangular area whose points are the basion, the alveolar point, and the nasion. **Farabeuf's t.,** one on the upper part of the neck, its sides being formed by the internal jugular vein and the facial vein, and its base by the hypoglossal nerve. **femoral t.,** trigonum femorale. **frontal t.,** one bounded by the maximum frontal diameter and lines from either end of this diameter to the glabella. **Garland's t.,** a triangular area of relative resonance in the lower back, close to the spine on the diseased side, in pleurisy with effusion. **Gerhardt's t.,** a triangular area of dullness to percussion above the third left rib, observed in patent ductus arteriosus. **Gombault-Philippe t.,** a triangular field formed in the conus medullaris by the fibers of the septomarginal tract. **Grocco's t.** See *Grocco's sign*, under *sign.* **Grynfelt's t.,** a space bounded by the twelfth rib and the lower border of the serratus posterior inferior muscle above, by the anterior border of the quadratus lumborum behind, and by the posterior border of the obliquus internus abdominis in front, in which lumbar hernia may occur. **Henke's t.,** a triangular area between the descending portion of the inguinal fold, the lateral portion of the inguinal fold, and the lateral border of the rectus muscle. **Hesselbach's t.,** trigonum inguinale. **hypoglossohyoid t.,** the triangular space in the subhyoid region, bounded above by the hypoglossal nerve, in front by the posterior border of the mylohyoid muscle, and behind and below by the tendon of the digastric muscle. Called also *Pinaud's t.* and *Pirogoff's t.* **iliofemoral t.,** a triangular area bounded by Nélaton's line, a line through the superior iliac spine, and one extending from this spine to the great trochanter. **infraclavicular t.,** trigonum deltoideopectorale. **inguinal t.** 1. Trigonum inguinale. 2. Trigonum femorale. **Jackson's safety t.,** a triangular space bounded below by the lower end of the thyroid cartilage, its apex in the suprasternal notch, and its sides the inner edges of the sternocleidomastoid muscle; so called because it marks the limits of the area through which the trachea may safely be incised in tracheostomy. **Kanavel's t.,** a triangular area in the middle of the palm beneath which lies the common tendon sheath of the digital flexor tendons. **Korányi-Grocco t.** See *Grocco's sign*, under *sign.* **Labbe's t.,** one included between a horizontal line along the lower border of the cartilage of the ninth rib, the line of the false ribs, and the line of the liver, being the area where the stomach lies in contact with the anterior abdominal wall. **Langenbeck's t.,** one having its apex at the anterior superior spine of the ilium, its base along the anatomical neck of the femur, and its external side by the external face of the great trochanter. **Lesser's t.,** one bounded by the hypoglossal nerve above and the two bellies of the digastricus muscle on the other two sides. **Lesshaft's t.,** Grynfelt's t. **Lieutaud's t.,** trigonum vesicae. **Livingston's t.,** a triangular area bounded by lines from the umbilicus to the crest of the ilium, from the latter to the right pubic spine, and from there to the umbilicus, marking an area which is hypersentive to palpation in appendicitis. **lumbocosto-abdominal t.,** a space between the obliquus externus abdominis muscle, the serratus posterior inferior, the erector spinae, and the obliquus internus abdominis. **lymphoid t.** See *Waldeyer's tonsillar ring*, under *ring.* **Macewen's t.,** suprameatal t. **Malgaigne's t.,** superior carotid triangle. **medullary t.,** capsula interna. **mesenteric t.,** a triangular space between the two layers of the mesentery as they diverge to enclose the intestine. **Middeldorpf's t.,** a padded triangular splint for supporting the upper arm in partial extension in fracture of the humerus. **Minor's t.,** an angular defect posterior to the anus, produced by attachment of the superficial portion of the external sphincter to the coccyx. **t. of necessity,** inferior carotid t.

t's of neck, anterior, the inferior and superior carotid triangles, and the submandibular triangle. **t's of neck, posterior,** the occipital and subclavian triangles. **nodal t.,** an area bounded by two lines of lymphatic dilatations converging at the inner aspect of the knee joint, elicited by digital pressure in cases of glandular fever. **occipital t.,** the area bounded by the sternocleidomastoid muscle anteriorly, the trapezius muscle posteriorly, and the omohyoid muscle inferiorly. **occipital t., inferior,** a triangular area having a line between the two mastoid processes as its base and the inion as its apex. **palatal t.,** one limited by the greatest transverse diameter of the palate and lines from either end of this diameter to the alveolar point. **paravertebral t.** See *Grocco's sign*, under *sign*. **Pawlik's t.,** one within the vagina corresponding exactly with the trigonum vesicae, and bounded laterally by Pawlik's folds. **Petit's t.,** trigonum lumbale. **Pinaud's t., Pirogoff's t.,** hypoglossohyoid t. **popliteal t. of femur,** facies poplitea femoris. **pubo-urethral t.,** one in the perineum bounded externally by the ischiocavernosus muscle, internally by the bulbocavernosus, and posteriorly by the transversus perinei superficialis. **Rauchfuss' t.** See *Grocco's sign*, under *sign*. **Reil's t.,** trigonum lemnisci. **retromandibular t.,** a shallow triangular fossa on the mandibular bone posterior to the third molar. **sacral t.,** a shallow triangular depression overlying the sacrum. **Scarpa's t.,** trigonum femorale. **sternocostal t.,** trigonum sternocostale. **subclavian t.,** trigonum omoclaviculare. **subinguinal t.** 1. Hiatus saphenus. 2. Trigonum femorale. **submandibular t., submaxillary t.,** trigonum submandibulare. **submental t.,** a triangle bounded on either side by the anterior belly of the digastric muscle and below by the hyoid bone. **suboccipital t.,** a triangular area lying between the rectus capitis posterior major and the obliquus capitis superior and obliquus capitis inferior muscles. **suprameatal t.,** a triangular space lying between the lower posterior edge of the root of the zygoma and the superior posterior edge of the opening of the external acoustic meatus. Called also *Macewen's t.* **surgical t.,** any triangular area or region in which certain nerves, vessels, or organs are located; established for reference in surgical operations. **Trautmann's t.,** a space with its anterior angle at the prominence containing the labyrinth, bounded behind by the transverse sinus and above by the inferior temporal line. When the bone is removed, the superior petrosal sinus will be encountered at the upper posterior angle of this triangle. **umbilicomammillary t.,** one having its base formed by the line joining the nipples and its apex at the umbilicus. **urogenital t.** diaphragma urogenitale. **vaginal t.,** Pawlik's t. **vesical t.,** trigonum vesicae. **Ward's t.,** the space formed by the angle of the trabeculae in the neck of the femur: a vulnerable point for fracture. **von Weber's t.,** one on the sole of the foot formed by lines connecting the head of the first metatarsal, the head of the fifth metatarsal, and the center of the under surface of the heel. **Wernicke's t.,** crus posterius capsulae internae.

triangular (tri-ang′gu-lar) [L. *triangularis*]. Having three angles or corners.

triangularis (tri-ang″gu-la′ris) [L.]. Triangular.

triantebrachia (tri″an-te-bra′ke-ah) [*tri-* + *antebrachium* + *-ia*]. A developmental anomaly characterized by tripling of the forearm.

Triatoma (tri-at′o-mah). A genus of bugs of the superfamily Reduviidae: called the cone-nosed bugs, important in medicine as vectors of *Trypanosoma cruzi*. **T. megis′ta,** *Panstrongylus megistus*. **T. sanguisu′ga,** the blood-sucking cone nose or Mexican bedbug of the southern United States. Its bite is painful and causes irritation, swelling, and nausea. Other species which are vectors of *Trypanosoma cruzi* are: *T. dimidia′ta*, of Central America; *T. genicula′ta* (*Panstrongylus geniculatus*), which inhabits the burrows of the armadillo; *T. infes′tans*, the unchuca or great black bug of the Argentine and Paraguay; *T. mexica′na*, found in Mexico; *T. nigrova′rius*, widely distributed in South America; *T. protrac′ta*, of the southern United States; *T.* (*Panstrongylus*) *rubrofascia′ta*, the Malay bug of tropical Asia, Madagascar, and parts of Africa, which has a large proboscis and produces a severe sting; *T.* (*Entriatoma*) *sor′dida* of São Paulo; and *T. vit′ticeps*, of Rio de Janeiro.

triatomic (tri″ah-tom′ik). Made up of three atoms, or having three replaceable hydrogen atoms.

triazol 156 (tri′ah-zol). A compound, 4-cyclohexyl 3-ethyl 1-2-4 triazol, used as a convulsant in the treatment of schizophrenia.

tribade (trib′ād). A woman with a large clitoris who practices tribadism.

tribadism (trib′ah-dizm) [Gr. *tribein* to rub]. Mutual friction of the genitals between women.

tribady (trib′ah-de). Tribadism.

tribasic (tri-ba′sik) [*tri-* + L. *basis* base]. Having three replaceable hydrogen atoms.

tribe (trib). A taxonomic category subordinate to a family (or subfamily) and superior to a genus (or subtribe).

Tribolium (tri-bo′le-um). A genus of small beetles that live in and are very destructive to flour and other cereal products. The two most common species, *T. confu′sum* and *T. casta′neum*, are reddish-brown in color and 3.5 mm. in length.

triboluminescence (tri″bo-lu″mĭ-nes′ens) [Gr. *tribein* to rub + *luminescence*]. Luminescence produced by mechanical energy, as by the grinding of certain crystals.

tribrachia (tri-bra′ke-ah) [*tri-* + Gr. *brachion* arm + *-ia*]. A developmental anomaly characterized by tripling of an arm.

tribrachius (tri-bra′ke-us). 1. A fetal monster exhibiting tribrachia. 2. A fetal monster consisting of conjoined twins having only three arms.

tribromaloin (tri″brōm-al′o-in). A yellow, crystalline compound, $C_{17}H_{15}Br_3O_7$, or bromine and barbaloin.

tribromethanol (tri″brōm-eth′ah-nol). Tribromoethanol.

tribromide (tri-bro′mīd). A bromine compound containing three atoms of bromine to one of the base.

tribromoethanol (tri-bro″mo-eth′ah-nol). Chemical name: 2,2,2-tribromoethanol: used as a general anesthetic.

tribromphenol (tri-brōm-fe′nol). Bromol. **t.-bismuth,** bismuth tribromphenate.

tribromtertiarybutylalcohol (tri-brōm-ter″-she-ar″e-bu″til-al′ko-hol). Brometone.

tribulosis (trib″u-lo′sis). Poisoning in sheep in South Africa, caused by wilted plants of the species *Tribulus terrestris*.

triburon (trib′u-ron). Trade mark for preparations of triclobisonium chloride.

tributyrin (tri-bu′tir-in). A colorless fat, C_3H_5-$(OCOCH_2CH_2CH_3)_3$, contained in cows' butter.

tributyrinase (tri″bu-tir′ĭ-nās). An enzyme in the saliva which acts on tributyrin.

tricalcic (tri-kal′sik). Containing three atoms of calcium.

tricellular (tri-sel′u-lar). Three celled.

tricephalus (tri-sef′ah-lus) [*tri-* + Gr. *kephalē* head]. A monster having three heads.

triceps (tri′seps) [*tri-* + L. *caput* head]. Having three heads. **t. su′rae.** See *Table of Musculi*.

triceptor (tri-sep′tor). An intermediary having three combining groups.

Tricercomonas (tri″ser-kom′o-nas). A parasite of man, probably the same as *Enteromonas*.

trichalgia (trik-al′je-ah). Pain when hair is touched.

trichangiectasis (trik″an-je-ek′tah-sis) [*tricho-* + Gr. *angeion* vessel + *ektasis* dilatation]. Dilatation of the capillary vessels.

trichatrophia (trik″ah-tro′fe-ah) [*tricho-* + Gr. *atrophia* atrophy]. An atrophied condition of the hair bulbs, leading to brittleness of the hair.

trichauxe, trichauxis (trik-awk′se, trik-awk′-sis) [*tricho-* + Gr. *auxē* growth]. Hypertrichosis; excessive growth of the hair, in respect to both quantity and length.

tricheiria (tri-ki′re-ah) [*tri-* + Gr. *cheir* hand + *-ia*]. A developmental anomaly characterized by tripling of a hand.

trichesthesia (trik″es-the′ze-ah). Trichoesthesia.

trichiasis (tri-ki′ah-sis) [Gr.]. 1. A condition of ingrowing hairs about an orifice, or of ingrowing eyelashes. 2. The appearance of hairlike filaments in the urine.

Trichina (trĭ-ki′nah). Trichinella.

trichina (trĭ-ki′nah), pl. *trichi′nae.* An individual organism of the genus Trichinella.

trichinae (trĭ-ki′ne). Plural of *trichina.*

Trichinella (trik″ĭ-nel′ah) [Gr. *trichinos* of hair]. A genus of nematode parasites of the family Trichinellidae. **T. spira′lis,** one of the smallest of the parasitic nematodes, being only about 1.5 mm. in length. It is found coiled in a cyst in the muscles of the rat, pig, and man. When such meat is eaten the cyst dissolves, the parasite matures, deposits its larvae in the deep mucosa, whence they enter the lymphatics, are carried to all parts of the body, and again encyst. An extract of Trichinella larvae is used in an intradermal skin test for trichinosis.

Trichinella spiralis encapsulated in muscle.

trichinelliasis (trik″ĭ-nel-li′ah-sis). Trichinosis.

trichinellosis (trik″ĭ-nel-lo′sis). Trichinosis.

trichiniasis (trik″ĭ-ni′ah-sis). Trichinosis.

trichiniferous (trik″ĭ-nif′er-us) [*trichina* + L. *ferre* to bear]. Containing trichinae.

trichinization (trik″ĭ-ni-za′shun). Infestation with *Trichinella spiralis.*

trichinophobia (trik″ĭ-no-fo′be-ah) [*trichina* + Gr. *phobein* to be affrighted by]. Morbid dread of trichinosis.

trichinoscope (trĭ-ki′no-skōp) [*trichina* + Gr. *skopein* to examine]. An instrument for ascertaining the presence of trichinae.

trichinosis (trik″ĭ-no′sis). A disease condition due to infestation with trichinae. It is produced by eating undercooked pork containing *Trichinella spiralis.* It is attended in the early stages by diarrhea, nausea, colic, and fever, and later by stiffness, pain, swelling of the muscles, fever, sweating, and insomnia.

trichinous (trik′ĭ-nus). Affected with or containing trichinae.

trichion (trik′e-on), pl. *trich′ia* [Gr.]. An anthropometric landmark, the point at which the midsagittal plane of the head intersects the hairline.

trichite (tri′kīt). 1. A. Meyer's name for one of the radially arranged needle-shaped crystals composing a starch grain. 2. One of the needle-shaped plastids placed radially around the periphery of a protozoon.

trichitis (tri-ki′tis). Inflammation of the hair bulbs.

trichloraldehyde (tri″klōr-al′de-hīd). Chloral.

trichloride (tri-klo′rīd). Any combination of three atoms of chlorine with one of another element.

trichlormethane (tri″klōr-meth′ān). Chloroform.

trichlormethiazide (tri-klōr″mĕ-thi′ah-zīd). Chemical name: 3-dichloromethyl-6-chloro-7-sulfamyl-3,4-dihydro-1,2,4-benzothiadiazine-1,1-dioxide: used as a diuretic and hypotensive, and in the treatment of edema.

trichloroethylene (tri″klo-ro-eth′ĭ-lēn). A clear, colorless or blue mobile liquid, C_2HCl_3: used as an inhalation analgesic and anesthetic for short operative procedures.

trichloromethylchloroformate (tri-klo″ro-meth″il-klo″ro-for′māt). A chlorine-containing gas which is irritating to lung tissue.

trichlorotrivinylarsine (tri-klo″ro-tri-vi″nil-ar′sin). A sternutatory war gas $(CHCl.CH)_3As$.

tricho- [Gr. *thrix, trichos,* hair]. A prefix denoting relationship to hair.

tricho-aesthesia (trik″o-es-the′ze-ah). Trichoesthesia.

tricho-anesthesia (trik″o-an″es-the′ze-ah). Loss of hair sensibility.

trichobacteria (trik″o-bak-te′re-ah) [*tricho-* + Gr. *baktērion* rod]. 1. A group of bacteria including those forms which possess flagella. 2. The filamentous or threadlike bacteria.

trichobezoar (trik″o-be′zōr) [*tricho-* + *bezoar*]. A hair-ball; a concretion within the stomach or intestines formed of hairs.

Trichobilharzia (trik″o-bil-har′ze-ah). A genus of flukes. **T. ocella′ta,** a blood fluke parasitic in European ducks.

trichocardia (trik″o-kar′de-ah) [*tricho-* + Gr. *kardia* heart]. Hairy heart; a hairy appearance upon the heart, due to exudative pericarditis.

trichocephaliasis (trik″o-sef″ah-li′ah-sis). Trichuriasis.

trichocephalosis (trik″o-sef″ah-lo′sis). Trichuriasis.

Trichocephalus (trik″o-sef′ah-lus) [*tricho-* + Gr. *kephalē* head]. A former genus of nematodes now called *Trichuris.*

trichochromogenic (trik″o-kro″mo-jen′ik) [*tricho-* + Gr. *chrōma* color + *gennan* to produce]. Giving color to the hair.

trichoclasia (trik″o-kla′se-ah). Trichoclasis.

trichoclasis (trik-ok′lah-sis) [*tricho-* + Gr. *klasis* fracture]. Brittleness of the hair; trichorrhexis nodosa.

trichoclasty (trik′o-klas″te). A nervous habit that has to do with the hair, such as stroking the beard, the eyebrows, etc.

trichocryptosis (trik″o-krip-to′sis) [*tricho-* + Gr. *kryptos* concealed]. Disease of the hair follicles.

trichocyst (trik′o-sist) [*tricho-* + Gr. *kystis* bladder]. A cell structure derived from the cytoplasm.

trichodangiitis (trik″o-dan″je-i′tis) [Gr. *trichōdēs* hairlike + Gr. *angeion* vessel + *-itis*]. Inflammation of the capillaries.

trichodarteriitis (trik″o-dar-ter″e-i′tis) [Gr. *trichōdēs* hairlike + *artēria* artery + *-itis*]. Inflammation of the arterioles.

Trichodectes (trik″o-dek′tēz) [*tricho-* + Gr. *dēktēs* biter]. A genus of parasitic insects. **T. can′is** is found in dogs and cats. **T. cli′max,** a biting louse of goats. **T. e′qui,** one of the biting lice found on horses. **T. herm′si,** a biting louse of goats. **T. la′tus,** the dog louse, found on dogs, especially puppies. **T. pilo′sus,** the horse louse. **T. retu′sis,** a biting louse that infests ranch-raised mink. **T. sphaerocephʹalus,** the red-headed sheep louse, found in the wool of sheep in Europe and America.

Trichodina (trik-od′ĭ-nah) [*tricho-* + Gr. *dinos* whirling]. A genus of the ciliate infusoria species of which live on hydras and the gills of fish and salamanders.

trichodophlebitis (trik″o-do-fle-bi′tis) [Gr. *trichōdēs* hairlike + *phleps* vein + *-itis*]. Inflammation of the venules.

trichodynia (trik″o-din′e-ah) [*tricho-* + Gr. *odynē* pain]. Pain when hair is touched.

trichoepithelioma (trik″o-ep″ĭ-the-le-o′mah). A skin tumor whose cell growth starts in the follicles of the lanugo. **t. papillo′sum mul′tiplex,** an eruption of nodules and papules arising in the hair follicles.

trichoesthesia (trik″o-es-the′ze-ah) [*tricho-* + Gr. *aisthēsis* perception + *-ia*]. The sense by which one perceives when one of the hairs of the skin has been touched; hair sensibility.

trichoesthesiometer (trik″o-es-the″ze-om′e-ter) [*tricho-* + Gr. *aisthēsis* perception + *metron* measure]. An electric apparatus for measuring the hair sensibility, or the sensitiveness of the scalp by means of the hairs.

trichofibroacanthoma (trik″o-fi″bro-ak″an-tho′mah). A tumor of the epithelium of the lanugo follicles and of the prickle-cell layer of the skin.

trichofibroepithelioma (trik″o-fi″bro-ep″ĭ-the″le-o′mah). A fibroma of the epithelium of the lanugo follicles.

trichogen (trik′o-jen). An agent which stimulates the growth of the hair.

trichogenous (trĭ-koj′e-nus) [*tricho-* + Gr. *gennan* to produce]. Promoting the growth of the hair.

trichoglossia (trik″o-glos′e-ah) [*tricho-* + Gr. *glōssa* tongue + *-ia*]. A hairy state of the tongue due to a thickening of the papillae.

trichographism (tri-kog′rah-fizm). Pilomotor reflex.

trichohyalin (trik″o-hi′ah-lin) [*tricho-* + *hyalin*]. The hyalin of the hair; eleidin-like matter in the root sheaths of hair.

trichoid (trik′oid) [*tricho-* + Gr. *eidos* form]. Like or resembling a hair, or the hair.

trichokryptomania (trik″o-krip″to-ma′ne-ah) [*tricho-* + Gr. *kryptos* hidden, secret + *mania* madness]. Trichorrhexomania.

tricholabion (tri-ko-la′be-on) [Gr.]. Tweezers for pulling out hairs.

tricholith (trik′o-lith) [*tricho-* + Gr. *lithos* stone]. A hairy concretion.

trichologia (trik″o-lo′je-ah) [*tricho-* + Gr. *legein* to pick out + *-ia*]. The pulling out of the hair by delirous or insane patients.

trichology (tri-kol′o-je). The sum of what is known regarding the hair.

trichoma (tri-ko′mah). 1. Entropion. 2. Plica polonica.

trichomania (trik″o-ma′ne-ah). Trichotillomania.

trichome (tri′kōm) [Gr. *trichōma* a growth of hair, hair generally]. A filamentous or hairlike structure.

Trichomastix cuniculi (trik″o-mas′tiks ku-nik′u-li). A parasitic organism resembling a trichomonad; found in rabbits.

trichomatose (trĭ-ko′mah-tōs). Pertaining to or affected with trichomatosis.

trichomatosis (trik″o-mah-to′sis). Plica polonica or other disease of the hair produced by fungi.

trichomatous (trĭ-kom′ah-tus). Affected with, of the nature of, or pertaining to, trichoma.

trichomonacidal (trik″o-mo″nah-si′dal). Destructive to trichomonads.

trichomonacide (trik″o-mo′nah-sid). An agent destructive to trichomonads.

trichomonad (trĭ-kom′o-nad). A parasite of the genus Trichomonas.

trichomonadicidal (trik″o-mo-nad″ĭ-si′dal). Trichomonacidal.

trichomonal (trĭ-kom′o-nal). Pertaining to or caused by trichomonads.

Trichomonas (trĭ-kom′o-nas) [*tricho-* + Gr. *monas* unit]. A genus of parasitic flagellate protozoa occurring in the form of pear-shaped cells having three flagella in front, an undulating membrane, and a trailing flagellum. They cause a rather serious disease in animals and birds and may cause diarrhea in man. **T. bucca′lis,** a form found in the mouth and especially about the tartar of the teeth. **T. colum′bae, T. columba′rum,** found in birds affected with diphtheria. **T. elonga′ta,** *T. buccalis.* **T. foe′tus,** a species parasitic in the genital tract of cattle. **T. homi′nis,** a common parasite in the intestine of man, frequently found in diarrheal stools. **T. intestina′lis,** *T. hominis.* **T. mu′ris,** a species found in the cecum of the rat. **T. pulmona′lis,** a form, probably the same as *T. vaginalis*, occurring in the lungs in fetid bronchitis and gangrene of the lungs. **T. vagina′lis,** a species found in the vagina, which produces a refractory vaginal discharge. It has also been found in the bladder and urethra of man.

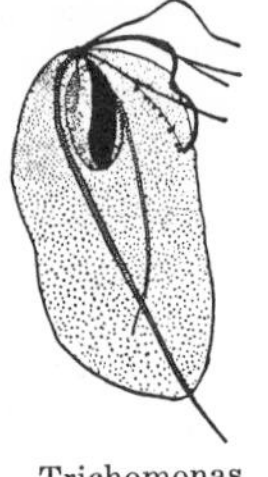

Trichomonas vaginalis (Alfred B. Kupferberg).

trichomoniasis (trik″o-mo-ni′ah-sis). Infection with Trichomonas.

Trichomycetes (trik″o-mi-se′tēs) [*tricho-* + Gr. *mykēs* fungus]. A group of filamentous organisms intermediate between the bacteria and the higher fungi. The group includes Actinomyces, Leptothrix, Cladothrix, and Nocardia.

trichomycetosis (trik″o-mi″se-to′sis). Trichomycosis.

trichomycosis (trik″o-mi-ko′sis) [*tricho-* + Gr. *mykēs* fungus]. Any disease of the hair due to infection by a fungus. **t. axilla′ris, t. chromat′ica,** a minor infection of the axillary and sometimes of the pubic hairs, caused by *Corynebacterium tenuis* and not a fungus, as originally thought, which led to the name; occurring commonly in the tropics, it is characterized by development of dense colonies of bacteria on the hairs, appearing as yellow, or as red or black masses. Called also *t. nodosa, t. palmellina,* and *trichonocardiasis axillaris.* **t. favo′sa,** favus. **t. ni′gra,** t. axillaris in which the bacterial colonies appear as black masses, because of a contaminating chromogenic microorganism. **t. nodo′sa, t. palmelli′na,** t. axillaris. **t. pustulo′sa,** a parasitic hair disease accompanied by the formation of pustules. **t. ru′bra,** t. axillaris in which the bacterial colonies appear as red masses, because of a contaminating chromogenic microorganism.

trichon (trik′on). An autolyzed preparation of the fungi of the genus Trichophyton.

trichonocardiasis, trichonocardiosis (trik″o-no-kar-di′ah-sis, trik″o-no-kar″de-o′sis). A disease of the hair caused by *Nocardia tenuis.* **t. axilla′ris,** trichomycosis axillaris.

trichonodosis (trik″o-no-do′sis). A condition characterized by apparent or actual knotting of the hair, thought to be the result of inability of new hairs to grow freely from their follicles, because of toughness of the surrounding tissues.

trichonosis, trichonosus (trik-o-no′sis, trik-on′o-sus) [*tricho-* + Gr. *nosos* disease]. Any disease of the hair. **t. furfura′cea,** tinea tonsurans. **t. versic′olor,** ringed hair.

trichopathic (trik″o-path′ik). Pertaining to disease of the hair.

trichopathophobia (trik″o-path″o-fo′be-ah) [*tricho-* + Gr. *pathos* disease + *phobein* to be affrighted by]. Morbid anxiety with regard to the hair, its growth, disease, etc.

trichopathy (tri-kop′ah-the) [*tricho-* + Gr. *pathos* disease]. Disease of the hair.

trichophagy (tri-kof′ah-je) [*tricho-* + Gr. *phagein* to eat]. The practice or habit of eating hair.

trichophobia (trik″o-fo′be-ah) [*tricho-* + Gr. *phobein* to be affrighted by]. Morbid dread of hair.

trichophytic (trik″o-fit′ik). 1. Pertaining to trichophytosis. 2. Promoting growth of the hair.

trichophytid (trĭ-kof′ĭ-tid). A generalized eruption which is the expression of an allergic reaction to a trichophyton infection.

trichophytin (trĭ-kof′ĭ-tin). The soluble broth culture products of various species of *Trichophyton:* used in the trichophytin test and for the treatment of trichophyton infections.

trichophytobezoar (trik″o-fi″to-be′zōr) [*tricho-* + Gr. *phyton* plant + *bezoar*]. A bezoar composed of animal hair and vegetable fibers.

Trichophyton (tri-kof′ĭ-ton) [*tricho-* + Gr. *phyton* plant]. A genus of fungi consisting of flat, branched filaments and chains of spores. Species of *Trichophyton* attack the skin, nails and hair. The recognized species are placed in five groups. I. GYPSEUM GROUP: *T. mentagrophy′tes.* II. RUBRUM GROUP: *T. ru′brum.* III. CRATERIFORM GROUP: *T. ton′surans, T. ep′ilans, T. sabourau′di, T. sulfu′reum.* IV. FAVIFORM GROUP: *T. schoenlei′ni, T. concen′tricum, T. ferrugin′eum, T. viola′ceum.* V. ROSACEUM GROUP: *T. rosa′ceum.*

Trichophyton. (de Rivas.)

trichophytosis (trik″o-fi-to′sis). A fungal infection caused by species of *Trichophyton.* **t. bar′bae,** tinea sycosis. **t. cap′itis,** tinea capitis caused by *Trichophyton mentagrophytes, T. tonsurans, T. violaceum, T. schoenleini,* or *T. verrucosum.* **t. cor′poris,** tinea corporis caused by species of *Trichophyton.* **t. cru′ris,** tinea cruris caused by species of *Trichophyton.* **t. un′guium,** fungal infection of the nails caused by species of *Trichophyton.*

trichopoliosis (trik″o-pol″e-o′sis) [*tricho-* + Gr. *poliōsis* grayness]. Grayness of the hair.

Trichoptera (tri-kop′ter-ah) [*tricho-* + Gr. *pteron* wing]. An order of flies, the caddis flies. The hair from the wings produces allergic symptoms in susceptible persons.

trichoptilosis (trik″o-tĭ-lo′sis) [*tricho-* + Gr. *ptilon* feather + *-osis*]. 1. Trichorrhexis nodosa. 2. The condition in which the hairs are covered with feather-like projections.

trichorrhea (trik″o-re′ah) [*tricho-* + Gr. *rhoia* flow]. Rapid loss of the hair.

trichorrhexis (trik″o-rek′sis) [*tricho-* + Gr. *rhēxis* fracture]. A condition in which the hair breaks off. **t. nodo′sa,** a condition which is characterized by what appear to be white nodes on the hairs but are actually sites where the cortex of the shaft has fractured and split into strands, weakening the hairs so they break at these nodes.

trichorrhexomania (trik″o-rek″so-ma′ne-ah) [*tricho-* + Gr. *rhēxis* fracture + *mania* madness]. A morbid tendency to break off the hair by pinching it with the fingernail.

trichoschisis (trik-os′kĭ-sis) [*tricho-* + Gr. *schisis* fissure]. Splitting of the hairs.

trichoscopy (trĭ-kos′ko-pe) [*tricho-* + Gr. *skopein* to examine]. Examination of the hair.

trichosiderin (trik″o-sid′er-in) [*tricho-* + Gr. *sidēros* iron]. An iron-containing brown pigment found in normal human red hair.

trichosis (tri-ko′sis) [Gr. *trichōsis*]. Any disease or abnormal growth of the hair. **t. carun′culae,** abnormal development of the hair on the lacrimal caruncle.

Trichosoma (trik″o-so′mah) [*tricho-* + Gr. *sōma* body]. A genus of roundworms. **T. contor′tum** a roundworm parasitic in domestic fowls.

Trichosomoides (trik″o-so-moi′dēz). A genus of nematode parasites. **T. crassicau′da,** a nematode parasite of rats.

Trichosporon (tri-kos′po-ron) [*tricho-* + Gr. *sporos* seed]. A genus of fungus which may infect the hair. **T. beigel′ii** (*T. gigan′teum*), the cause of white piedra. **T. pedrosia′num,** a species recovered from chromoblastomycosis.

trichosporosis (trik″o-spo-ro′sis). Infestation with Trichosporon. See *trichomycosis* and *piedra.* **t. in′dica, t. nodo′sa, t. trop′ica,** piedra.

trichostachis spinosa (trik″o-stak′is spĭ-no′sah) [*tricho-* + Gr. *stachys* ear of corn]. Trichostasis spinulosa.

trichostasis spinulosa (trĭ-kos′tah-sis spin″u-lo′sa) [*tricho-* + Gr. *stasis* a standing]. A disorder of the hair follicles, which appear to be obstructed with a spinulous dark plug, consisting of numerous lanugo hairs in a horny mass. The skin of the alae nasi and other areas of the face, or of the arms, chest, abdomen, or interscapular area may be affected.

trichostrongylosis (trik″o-stron″jĭ-lo′sis). Infestation with Trichostrongylus.

Trichostrongylus (trik″o-stron′jĭ-lus). A genus of nematode worms of the family Strongylidae, comprising some of the species formerly included in the genus *Strongylus.* **T. insta′bilis,** a species frequently present in sheep and goats and occasionally found in man. **T. orienta′lis,** a species found in Japan. **T. vitri′nus,** a species found in sheep and occasionally in man.

Trichothecium (trik″o-the′se-um) [*tricho-* + Gr. *thēkē* case]. A genus of mold fungi. **T. ro′seum,** a species found in the human ear.

trichotillomania (trik″o-til″o-ma′ne-ah) [*tricho-* + Gr. *tillein* to pull + *mania* madness]. A morbid impulse to pull out one's own hair.

trichotomous (tri-kot′o-mus) [Gr. *tricha* threefold + *tomē* a cutting]. Divided into three parts.

trichotoxin (tri″ko-tok′sin). An antibody which has a toxic action on epithelial cells.

trichotrophy (tri-kot′ro-fe) [*tricho-* + Gr. *trophē* nutrition]. Nutrition of the hair.

trichroic (tri-kro′ik). Pertaining to or characterized by trichroism.

trichroism (tri′kro-izm) [*tri-* + Gr. *chroa* color]. The exhibition of three different colors in three different aspects.

trichromat (tri′kro-mat). A person who has normal color vision.

trichromatic (tri″kro-mat′ik). Trichromic.

trichromatism (tri-kro′mah-tizm). Trichroism.

trichromatopsia (tri″kro-mah-top′se-ah) [*trichroic* + Gr. *opsis* vision + *-ia*]. Ability to see all three primary colors; normal color vision (Hering).

trichromic (tri-kro′mik) [*tri-* + Gr. *chrōma* color]. 1. Pertaining to or exhibiting three colors. 2. Able to distinguish only three of the seven colors of the spectrum.

trichterbrust (trich′ter-broost) [Ger.]. Funnel chest.

trichuriasis (trik″u-ri′ah-sis). The state of being infected with nematodes of the genus Trichuris.

Trichuris (trik-u′ris) [*tricho-* + Gr. *oura* a tail]. A genus of intestinal nematode parasites. **T. trichiu′ra,** the species that principally infests the human subject. It is about 2 inches in length, the front portion of its body, the esophageal zone, being hairlike in slimness. It inhabits the large intestine, and may cause diarrhea, vomiting, and nervous disorders, although it usually produces no symptoms. Also known as *whipworm.*

Trichuris trichiura: A, Females; B, males. The posterior portion of the male is usually coiled as shown in B. Photographs of mounted specimens; natural size. (Todd.)

tricipital (tri-sip′ĭ-tal) [L. *tricipitis* of the triceps]. 1. Pertaining to the triceps. 2. Having three heads.

triclobisonium (tri″klo-bi-so′ne-um). Chemical name: N,N′-bis[1-methyl-3-(2,2,6-trimethylcyclohexyl)propyl]-N,N′-dimethyl-1,6-hexanediamine: used as an antimicrobial agent for skin and wound infections, and as an antitrichomonal agent.

tricofuron (tri″ko-fu′ron). Trade mark for preparations of furazolidone.

tricoloid (tri′ko-loid). Trade mark for preparations of tricyclamol.

tricorn (tri′korn) [*tri-* + L. *cornu* horn]. A lateral ventricle of the brain.

tricornute (tri-kor′nūt) [*tri-* + L. *cornutus* horned]. Having three horns, cornua, or processes.

tricresol (tri-kre′sol). A mixture of three isomeric cresols. See *cresol.*

tricrotic (tri-krot′ik) [Gr. *trikrotos* rowed with a triple stroke; triple beating]. Pertaining to or characterized by tricrotism.

tricrotism (tri′kro-tizm). The quality of having three sphygmographic waves or elevations to one beat of the pulse

tricuspid (tri-kus′pid) [L. *tricuspis*]. 1. Having three points or cusps. 2. Pertaining to the tricuspid valves.

tricyclamol (tri-si′klah-mol). Chemical name: 1-cyclohexyl-1-phenyl-3-pyrrolidino-1-propanol: used in parasympathetic blockade.

Trid. Abbreviation for L. *trid′uum*, three days.

tridactylism (tri-dak′tĭ-lizm) [*tri-* + Gr. *daktylos* finger]. The quality of having only three digits on one hand or foot.

tridactylous (tri-dak′tĭ-lus). Pertaining to or characterized by tridactylism.

trident, tridentate (tri′dent, tri-den′tāt). Three pronged.

tridermic (tri-der′mik) [*tri-* + Gr. *derma* skin]. Derived from the ectoderm, endoderm, and mesoderm.

tridermogenesis (tri″der-mo-jen′e-sis) [*tri-* + Gr. *derma* skin + *genesis* production]. The stage in embryonic development marked by the formation of the three germ layers.

tridermoma (tri″der-mo′mah) [*tri-* + Gr. *derma* skin + *-oma*]. A teratoma containing representatives of all three germ layers.

tridihexethyl (tri″di-heks-eth′il). Chemical name: triethyl(3-hydroxy-3-cyclohexyl-3-phenylpropyl)-ammonium: used in parasympathetic blockade.

tridione (tri-di′ōn). Trade mark for preparations of trimethadione.

tridymite (trid′ĭ-mīt). A mineral consisting, like quartz, of silica.

trielcon (tri-el′kon) [*tri-* + Gr. *helkein* to draw]. A three-branched hook for drawing bullets from wounds and for removing other foreign bodies.

triencephalus (tri″en-sef′ah-lus) [*tri-* + Gr. *enkephalos* brain]. A fetal monster having no organs of sight, hearing, or smell.

-triene (tri′ēn). A chemical suffix indicating the presence of three double bonds.

triethylamine (tri″eth-il-am′in). A somewhat poisonous, oily liquid ptomaine, $N(C_2H_5)_3$, with an ammoniacal smell, derived from decaying fish.

triethylenemelamine (tri-eth″ĭ-lēn-mel′ah-mēn). Chemical name: 2,4,6-tris-(1-aziridinyl)-s-triazine: used as a neoplastic suppressant.

triethylenethiophosphoramide (tri-eth″ĭ-lēn-thi″o-fos-fōr′ah-mīd). Thio-tepa.

trifacial (tri-fa′shal) [L. *trifacialis*]. Designating the fifth cranial nerve (nervus trigeminus [N A]).

trifid (tri′fid) [L. *trifidus*, from *tres* three + *findere* to split]. Split into three parts.

trifluoperazine (tri″floo-o-pār′ah-zēn). Chemical name: 10-[3-(1-methyl-4-piperazinyl)propyl]-2-trifluoromethyl phenothiazine: used as a tranquilizer.

triflupromazine (tri″floo-pro′mah-zēn). Chemical name: 10-(3-dimethylaminopropyl)-2-(trifluoromethyl) phenothiazine: used as a tranquilizer.

trifluromethylthiazide (tri-floor″o-meth″il-thi′ah-zīd). Flumethiazide.

trifoliosis (tri″fo-le-o′sis). A disease of horses marked by irritation of the skin and of the mucous membrane of the mouth and by general disturbance: attributed to the eating of hybrid clover.

trifurcation (tri″fur-ka′shun) [*tri-* + L. *furca* fork]. Division into three branches.

trigastric (tri-gas′trik) [*tri-* + Gr. *gastēr* belly]. Having three bellies: said of a muscle.

trigeminal (tri-jem′ĭ-nal) [*tri-* + L. *geminus* twin]. 1. Triple. 2. Pertaining to the fifth cranial nerve (nervus trigeminus [N A]).

trigeminus (tri-jem′ĭ-nus) [L.]. Triple. See *nervus trigeminus.*

trigeminy (tri-jem′ĭ-ne). The condition of occurring in threes; especially the occurrence of three pulse beats in rapid succession. See *trigeminal pulse*, under *pulse.*

trigenic (tri-jen′ik). Possessing three different alleles at any particular locus on the chromosome.

trigocephalus (tri″go-sef′ah-lus). Trigonocephalus.

trigon (tri′gōn). Trigone.

trigona (tri-go′nah) [L.]. Plural of *trigonum.*

trigonal (tri′go-nal). Triangular; pertaining to a trigone.

trigone (tri′gōn). A triangular area (trigonum [N A]). See also *triangle.* **t. of bladder,** trigonum vesicae. **carotid t.,** trigonum caroticum. **cerebral t.,** fornix cerebri. **collateral t.,** trigonum collaterale. **collateral t. of fourth ventricle,** trigonum nervi vagi. **femoral t.,** trigonum femorale. **fibrous t's of heart,** trigona fibrosa cordis. **t. of habenula, habenular t.,** trigonum habenulae. **Henke's t.,** Henke's triangle. **t. of hypoglossal nerve,** trigonum nervi hypoglossi. **iliopectineal t.,** fossa iliopectinea. **inguinal t.,** trigonum inguinale. **interpeduncular t.,** fossa interpeduncularis. **lumbar t.,** trigonum lumbale. **Müller's t.,** a part of the tuber cinereum that bends over the optic chiasm. **olfactory t.,** trigonum olfactorium. **omoclavicular t.,** trigonum omoclaviculare. **Pawlik's t.,** Pawlik's triangle. **t. of Reil,** trigonum lemnisci. **submandibular t.,** trigonum submandibulare. **urogenital t.,** diaphragma urogenitale. **t. of vagus nerve,** trigonum nervi vagi.

trigonectomy (tri″gōn-ek′to-me) [*trigone* + Gr. *ektomē* excision]. Excision of the base of the bladder (trigonum vesicae).

trigonelline (trig″o-nel′in). An alkaloid found in fenugreek and also in the urine of dogs to which nicotinic acid has been administered. It is a betaine of methyl nicotinic acid.

trigonid (tri-gon′id). The first three cusps of a lower molar tooth.

trigonitis (trig″o-ni′tis) [*trigone* + *-itis*]. Inflammation or localized hyperemia of the trigone of the bladder.

trigonocephalia (trig″o-no-se-fa′le-ah). Trigonocephaly.

trigonocephalic (trig″o-no-se-fal′ik). Pertaining to or characterized by trigonocephaly.

trigonocephalus (trig″o-no-sef′ah-lus). An individual exhibiting trigonocephaly.

trigonocephaly (tri-go″no-sef′ah-le) [Gr. *trigonos* triangular + *kephalē* head]. A deformity of the head characterized by sharp angulation ventrad of the squamous portion of the frontal bones at the site of the suture between them.

trigonotome (tri-go′no-tōm). An instrument for cutting the trigone of the bladder.

trigonum (tri-go′num), pl. *trigo′na* [L.; Gr. *trigōnon*]. A three-cornered area; used as a general term in anatomical nomenclature. Called also triangle and trigone. **t. acus′tici,** area vestibularis. **t. carot′icum** [N A], the triangular region bounded by the posterior belly of the digastric muscle, the sternocleidomastoid muscle, and the anterior midline of the neck. Called also *fossa carotica* [B N A], and *carotid trigone.* **t. cerebra′le,** fornix cerebri. **t. cervica′le.** 1. Trigonum caroticum. 2. Trigonum omoclaviculare. **t. collatera′le** [N A, B N A], the triangular area in the floor of the lateral ventricle between the diverging inferior and posterior horns. Called also *collateral trigone.* **t. collatera′le ventric′uli quar′ti,** t. nervi vagi. **t. col′li latera′le,** regio colli lateralis. **t. coraco-acromia′le,** a triangle bounded by the coracoid process, the apex of the acromion, and the concave border of the clavicle. **t. deltoideopectora′le** [B N A], the deeper part of the infraclavicular region which is exposed by dissection. Omitted in N A. **t. femora′le** [N A, B N A], a triangular area bounded superiorly by the inguinal ligament, laterally by the sartorius muscle, and medially by the adductor longus muscle. Called also *femoral trigone.* **trigo′na fibro′sa cor′dis** [N A, B N A], two thickened and irregularly triangular portions of the fibrous skeleton of the base of the heart, one located between the right and left atrioventricular fibrous rings, posterior to the aortic orifice, and the other between the left atrioventricular fibrous ring and the left posterior margin of the aortic fibrous ring. Called also *fibrous trigones of heart.* **t. haben′ulae** [N A, B N A], the triangular region on the dorsomedial angle of the thalamus, overlying the habenulae and the commissure of the habenulae. Called also *trigone of habenula.* **t. inguina′le** [N A], the area on the inferoanterior abdominal wall bounded by the rectus abdominis muscle, the inguinal ligament, and the inferior epigastric vessels: the site in which a direct inguinal hernia begins. Called also *inguinal trigone.* **t. interpeduncula′re,** fossa interpeduncularis. **t. lemnis′ci** [B N A], a small, more or less distinct triangular area on the side of the isthmus just lateral to the inferior colliculus, bounded below by the superior cerebellar peduncle, dorsomedially by the brachium colliculi inferioris, and anterolaterally by the sulcus lateralis mesencephali. Omitted in N A. **t. lumba′le** [N A], **t. lumba′le [Peti′ti]** [B N A], a small triangular interval between the inferolateral margin of the latissimus dorsi muscle and the external oblique muscle of the abdomen, just above the ilium. Called also *lumbar trigone.* **t. lumbocosta′le,** a triangular opening of variable size between the lateral lumbocostal arch and the pars costalis diaphragmatis. **t. ner′vi hypoglos′si** [N A, B N A], the tapering lower end of the medial eminence of the rhomboid fossa just superficial to the position of the hypoglossal nucleus. Called also *trigone of hypoglossal nerve.* **t. ner′vi va′gi** [N A], an area in the floor of the fourth ventricle superficial to the dorsal nucleus of the vagus nerve. Called also *ala cinerea* [B N A], and *trigone of vagus nerve.* **t. olfacto′rium** [N A, B N A], the triangular enlargement of the olfactory tract as it enters the cerebral hemisphere. Called also *olfactory trigone.* **t. omoclavicula′re** [N A, B N A], a deep region of the neck, corresponding to the fossa supraclavicularis major on the surface, in which the brachial plexus may be palpated, and by downward pressure the subclavian artery can be compressed against the first rib. Called also *omoclavicular trigone* and *subclavian triangle.* **t. sternocosta′le,** a triangular opening between the pars costalis and the pars sternalis diaphragmatis; beyond this point the internal thoracic vessels become the superior epigastric vessels. **t. submandibula′re** [N A], the triangular region of the neck bounded by the mandible, the stylohyoid muscle and posterior belly of the digastric muscle, and the anterior belly of the digastric muscle. Called also *regio submaxillaris* [B N A], and *submandibular trigone.* **t. urogenita′le,** diaphragma urogenitale. **t. va′gi,** t. nervi vagi. **t. ventric′uli latera′lis,** t. collaterale. **t. ves′icae** [N A], **t. ves′icae [Lieutau′di]** [B N A], a smooth triangular portion of the mucous membrane at the base of the bladder. It is bounded behind by the interureteric fold and ends in front in the uvula of the bladder. Called also *trigone of bladder.*

trihexinol (tri-hek′sĭ-nol). Chemical name: α-di-thienyl-(4-dimethylamino-cyclohexyl) carbinol-methylbromide: used in parasympathetic blockade, and in treatment of diarrhea.

trihexyphenidyl (tri-hek″se-fen′ĭ-dil). Chemical name: α-cyclohexyl-α-phenyl-1-piperidine propanol: used in parasympathetic blockade.

trihybrid (tri-hi′brid). A hybrid offspring of parents differing in three mendelian characters.

trihydrate (tri-hi′drāt). Trihydroxide; a compound containing three hydroxyl groups to one base.

trihydric (tri-hi′drik). Containing three hydrogen atoms that are replaceable by bases.

trihydrol (tri-hi′drol). The associated water or ice molecule, $(H_2O)_3$.

trihydroxide (tri″hi-drok′sīd). Trihydrate.

trihydroxyestrin (tri″hi-drok″se-es′trin). Estriol.

tri-iniodymus (tri″in-e-od′ĭ-mus) [*tri-* + Gr. *inion* nape of the neck + *didymos* twin]. A monster with a single body and three heads united posteriorly.

tri-iodide (tri-i′o-dīd). A compound containing three atoms of iodine to one of another element.

tri-iodomethane (tri-i″o-do-meth′ān). Iodoform.

triiodothyronine (tri″i-o″do-thi′ro-nēn). One of the thyroid hormones: an organic iodine-containing compound liberated from thyroglobulin by hydrolysis, and thought to be formed by the conjugation of one molecule each of monoiodotyrosine and diiodotyrosine, or by the partial deiodination of thyroxine. It has several times the biological activity of thyroxine.

triketocholaneresis (tri-ke″to-ko″lan-er′e-sis) [*triketocholic* acid + Gr. *hairesis* a taking]. Increase in the output or elimination of triketocholic acid in the bile. Cf. *cholaneresis.*

triketopurine (tri″ke-to-pu′rin). Uric acid.

trilabe (tri′lāb) [*tri-* + Gr. *labē* a handle]. A three-pronged instrument for taking calculi from the bladder.

trilafon (tri′lah-fon). Trade mark for preparations of perphenazine.

trilaminar (tri-lam′ĭ-nar). Consisting of three layers.

trilateral (tri-lat′er-al) [*tri-* + L. *latus* side]. Having or pertaining to three sides.

trilaurin (tri-law′rin). A crystalline glyceride, $C_3H_5(OC_{12}H_{23}O)_3$, forming the principal constituent of coconut oil, and found in bayberry oil and palm nut oil.

trilene (tri′lēn). Trade mark for a preparation of trichloroethylene.

trilinolein (tri″lin-o′le-in). A glyceride, $C_3H_5(OC_{18}H_{32}O)_3$, found in linseed oil, hempseed oil, sunflower oil, etc.

trilliin (tril′e-in). A concentration prepared from *Trillium erectum,* a North American plant.

Trillium (tril′e-um). A genus of liliaceous plants. **T. erec′tum,** wake-robin; the rhizome contains trilliin.

trilobate (tri-lo′bāt) [*tri-* + L. *lobus* lobe]. Having three lobes.

trilobectomy (tri″lo-bek′to-me). Excision of three pulmonary lobes, two from one lung and one from the other.

trilobed (tri′lōbd). Trilobate.

trilocular (tri-lok′u-lar) [*tri-* + L. *loculus* cell]. Having three compartments or cells.

trilogy (tril′o-je). A combination of three elements, such as three concurrent defects or symptoms. **t. of Fallot,** a term sometimes applied to the combination of pulmonic stenosis, atrial septal defect, and right ventricular hypertrophy.

trimanual (tri-man′u-al) [*tri-* + L. *manus* hand]. Accomplished by the use of three hands.

Trimastigamoeba (tri-mas″tĭg-ah-me′bah). A form of ameba having three equal flagella in the flagellate stage. *T. philippen′sis* has been obtained in culture from city water.

trimastigote (tri-mas′tĭ-gōt). 1. Having three flagella. 2. A cell having three flagella.

trimenon (tri-me′non) [*tri-* + Gr. *mēn* month + *on* neuter ending]. A period of three months; a trimester.

trimensual (tri-men′su-al). Occurring every three months.

trimeprazine (tri-mep′rah-zēn). Chemical name: 10-(3-dimethylamino-2-methylpropyl)phenothiazine: used as a tranquilizer.

trimercuric (tri″mer-ku′rik). Containing three atoms of bivalent mercury.

trimester (tri-mes′ter). A period of three months.

trimethadione (tri″meth-ah-di′ōn). Chemical name: 3,5,5-trimethyl-2,4-oxazolidinedione: used as an anticonvulsant in petit mal and psychomotor epilepsy.

trimethaphan (tri-meth′ah-fan). Chemical name: d-1,3-dibenzyldecahydro-2-oxo-imidazo[c]thieno-[1,2-α]thiolium: used in ganglionic blockade, and as a hypotensive agent.

trimethidinium (tri-meth″ĭ-din′e-um). Chemical name: d-[N-methyl-N-(γ-trimethylammonium-propyl)]-1-methyl-8,8-dimethyl-3-azabicyclo-[3.2.1]octane: used in ganglionic blockade, and as a hypotensive agent.

trimethobenzamide (tri-meth″o-ben′zah-mīd). Chemical name: N-(dimethylaminoethoxybenzyl)-3,4,5-trimethoxybenzamide: used as an antiemetic.

trimethylamine (tri″meth-il-am′in). A colorless gaseous alkaloid, $(CH_3)_3N$, from beet sugar residue and herring brine. In the body it probably results from the decomposition of choline. It has been used in gout, chorea, and rheumatism. **t. hydrochlorate,** a crystalline salt, which has been used therapeutically for rheumatism and gout.

trimethylxanthine (tri-meth″il-zan′thin). Caffeine.

trimeton (tri′me-ton). Trade mark for preparations of pheniramine maleate.

trimorphous (tri-mor′fus) [*tri-* + Gr. *morphē* form]. Existing in three different forms.

trinegative (tri-neg′ah-tiv). Having three negative valencies.

trineural (tri-nu′ral). Pertaining to three nerves.

trineuric (tri-nu′rik). Pertaining to or having three neurons.

trinitrate (tri-ni′trāt). A nitrate which contains three radicals of nitric acid.

trinitrin (tri-ni′trin). Glyceryl trinitrate.

trinitrocellulose (tri″ni-tro-sel′u-lōs). Pyroxylin.

trinitrocresol (tri″ni-tro-kre′sol). An antiseptic and highly explosive compound, $(NO_2)_3C_6H(CH_3)OH$, formed by the action of concentrated nitric acid on coal tar cresol.

trinitroglycerin (tri″ni-tro-glis′er-in). Glyceryl trinitrate.

trinitroglycerol (tri-ni′tro-glis′er-ol). Glyceryl trinitrate.

trinitrol (tri-ni′trol). Tetranitroerythritol, $C_4H_6(ONO)_4$.

trinitrophenol (tri″ni-tro-fe′nol). A yellow, crystalline substance, $C_6H_2(NO_2)_3OH$, resulting from the action of nitric acid on indigo, salicin, phenol, etc.: used as a dye, a reagent, and a fixing agent, as an explosive. It is also used as a germicide and astringent. Called also *picric acid* and *carbazotic acid*.

trinitrotoluene (tri″ni-tro-tol′u-ēn). A high explosive, $C_6H_2(NO_2)_3CH_3$, obtained by nitrating toluene. Also called TNT.

trinomial (tri-no′me-al) [*tri-* + L. *nomen* name]. Composed of three names or terms.

trinucleate (tri-nu′kle-āt). Having three nuclei.

trinucleotide (tri-nu′kle-o-tīd). A nucleic acid made up of three mononucleotides.

triocephalus (tri″o-sef′ah-lus) [*tri-* + Gr. *kephalē* head]. A fetal monstrosity in which the structures of the mouth, nose, and eyes are wanting, the head being nearly a shapeless mass.

Triodontophorus (tri″o-don-tof′o-rus). A genus of nematode worms of the family Strongylidae. **T. diminu′tus,** a parasite frequently present in monkeys and occasionally found in man.

triolein (tri-o′le-in). Ordinary olein.

trionym (tri′o-nim) [*tri-* + Gr. *onyma* name]. A name made up of three terms.

triophthalmos (tri″of-thal′mos) [*tri-* + Gr. *ophthalmos* eye]. A double-faced monster with three eyes.

triopodymus (tri″o-pod′ĭ-mus) [*tri-* + Gr. *ops* face + *didymos* twin]. A fetal monster having a fused head with three faces.

triorchid (tri-or′kid) [*tri-* + Gr. *orchis* testis]. An individual with three testes.

triorchidism (tri-or′kĭ-dizm). The condition of having three testes.

triorchis (tri-or′kis). Triorchid.

triorchism (tri-or′kizm). Triorchidism.

triose (tri′ōs). A monosaccharide containing three carbon atoms in a molecule.

triotus (tri-o′tus) [*tri-* + Gr. *ous* ear]. An individual with a supernumerary ear.

trioxide (tri-ok′sīd). A compound containing three atoms of oxygen to one of another element.

trioxypurine (tri″ok-se-pu′rin). Uric acid.

tripalmitin (tri-pal′mĭ-tin). Ordinary palmitin.

tripara (trip′ah-rah) [*tri-* + L. *parere* to bring forth, produce]. A woman who has had three pregnancies which resulted in viable offspring. Also written Para III.

triparanol (tri-par′ah-nol). Chemical name: [p-(β-diethylaminolthoxy)phenyl]-1-(p-tolyl)-2-(p-chlorophenyl)ethanol: used to depress the synthesis of cholesterol.

tripelennamine (tri″pel-en′nah-min). Chemical name: N-benzyl-N′,N′-dimethyl-N-2-pyridylethylenediamine: used as an antihistaminic.

tripeptide (tri-pep′tid). A peptide which on hydrolysis yields three amino acids.

triphalangeal (tri″fah-lan′je-al). Pertaining to or characterized by triphalangia.

triphalangia (tri″fah-lan′je-ah). Triphalangism.

triphalangism (tri-fal′an-jizm). The presence of three phalanges in the longitudinal axis of a digit normally composed of only two.

triphasic (tri-fa′zik) [*tri-* + Gr. *phasis* phase]. Triply varied or triply phasic: used in describing the electromotive actions of muscles.

triphenylethylene (tri-fen″il-eth′ĭ-lēn). A synthetic estrogen, $C_{20}H_{16}$ (*alpha*-phenyl-stilbene), not related to naturally occurring estrogens with the phenanthrene nucleus.

triphenylmethane (tri-fen″il-meth′ān). Rosaniline, $CH(C_6H_5)_3$.

Triphleps insidiosus (tri′fleps in-sid″e-o′sus). The flower bug which causes a skin eruption in man.

triphthemia (trif-the′me-ah) [Gr. *tribein* to wear out + *haima* blood + *-ia*]. The retention of waste products in the blood.

Tripier's amputation (trip″e-āz) [Léon *Tripier*, French surgeon, 1842–1891]. See under *amputation*.

triple-angle (trip′′l ang′g′l). Having three angles; Black's term for a dental instrument having three angulations in the shank connecting the handle, or shaft, with the working portion of the instrument, known as the blade, or nib.

triplegia (tri-ple′je-ah) [*tri-* + Gr. *plēgē* stroke]. Paralysis of three of the extremities.

triplet (trip′let). 1. One of three individuals having coextensive gestation periods and produced at the same birth. 2. A combination of three objects or entities occurring or acting together, as three lenses constituting a microscope eyepiece or objective, or three nucleotides in a genetic codon.

triplex (tri′pleks) [Gr. *triploos* triple]. Triple or three-fold.

triploblastic (trip″lo-blas′tik) [Gr. *triploos* triple + *blastos* germ]. Having three germ layers or blastodermic membranes: said of an embryo.

triploid (trip′loid). 1. Pertaining to or characterized by triploidy. 2. An individual or cell having three sets of chromosomes.

triploidy (trip′loi-de). The state of having three sets of chromosomes (3n).

triplokoria (trip″lo-ko′re-ah) [Gr. *triploos* triple + *korē* pupil + *-ia*]. The presence of three pupils in one eye.

triplopia (trip-lo′pe-ah) [Gr. *triploos* triple + *ōpē* sight + *-ia*]. The perception of three images of a single object; triple vision.

tripod (tri′pod) [Gr. *treis* three + *pous* foot]. Anything having three feet or supports. **t. of the Empirics,** the three principles on which the Empirics based their theory of medicine: (1) their own chance observations; (2) learning obtained from contemporaries and predecessors; and, in case of a disease not previously encountered, (3) conclusions based on other diseases which it might resemble. **Haller's t.,** truncus celiacus. **t. of life, vital t.,** the brain, heart, and lungs: regarded as the triple support of life.

tripodia (tri-po′de-ah) [Gr. *treis* three + *pous* foot]. A type of symmelia characterized by the presence of three feet.

tripoli (trip′o-le). A mild abrasive and polishing agent, used in dentistry, derived from certain porous rocks first found near Tripoli.

tripositive (tri-pos′ĭ-tiv). Having three positive valencies.

tripperfaden (trip″er-fah′den) [Ger.]. Gonorrheal threads.

triprolidine (tri-pro′lĭ-dēn). Chemical name: trans-2-[3-(1-pyrrolidinyl)-1-(p-tolyl)propenyl]-pyridine: used as an antihistaminic.

triprosopus (tri″pro-so′pus) [Gr. *treis* three + *prosōpon* face]. A fetal monster having a triple face.

tripsis (trip′sis) [Gr. *tripsis* rubbing]. 1. A trituration; the process of trituration. 2. The act of shampooing or of massage.

triptokoria (trip″to-ko′re-ah). Triplokoria.

tripus (tri′pus) [Gr. *treis* three + *pous* foot]. 1. A tripod. 2. A conjoined twin monster having three feet. **t. hal′leri,** truncus celiacus.

triquetrous (tri-kwe′trus) [L. *triquetrus*]. Triangular; three cornered.

triquetrum (tri-kwe′trum) [L.]. Three cornered. See *os triquetrum.*

triradial, triradiate (tri-ra′de-al, tri-ra′de-āt) [*tri-* + L. *radiatus* rayed]. Having three rays; radiating in three directions.

triradiation (tri″ra-de-a′shun). Radiation in three directions.

trisaccharidase (tri-sak′ah-rĭ-dās). An enzyme which catalyzes the hydrolysis of trisaccharides.

trisaccharide (tri-sak′ah-rid). A carbohydrate, $C_{18}H_{32}O_{16}$, which contains three saccharide groups.

triskaidekaphobia (tris″kĭ-dek″ah-fo′be-ah) [Gr. *triskaideka* thirteen + *phobein* to be affrighted by + *-ia*]. Morbid fear of the number thirteen.

trismic (triz′mik). Of the nature of or pertaining to trismus.

trismoid (triz′moid) [*trismus* + Gr. *eidos* form]. A variety of trismus nascentium, said to be due to pressure on the occiput during birth.

trismus (triz′mus) [Gr. *trismos* grating, grinding]. Motor disturbance of the trigeminal nerve, especially spasm of the masticatory muscles, with difficulty in opening the mouth (lockjaw); a characteristic early symptom of tetanus. **t. nascen′tium,** inability to open the jaws sometimes observed in an infant at birth. **t. neonato′rum,** tetanus of young infants due to infection of the navel. **t. u′teri,** spasmodic contraction of the uterus.

trisnitrate (tris-ni′trāt). Trinitrate.

trisomia (tri-so′me-ah). Trisomy.

trisomic (tri-so′mik). Pertaining to or characterized by trisomy.

trisomy (tri′so-me). The presence of an additional (third) chromosome of one type in an otherwise diploid cell (2n + 1).

trisplanchnic (tri-splangk′nik) [Gr. *treis* three + *splanchna* viscera]. Pertaining to or supplying the three great body cavities and their viscera.

tristearin (tri-ste′ah-rin). Ordinary stearin.

tristichia (tri-stik′e-ah) [Gr. *treis* three + *stichos* row]. The existence of three rows of eyelashes.

tristimania (tris″tĭ-ma′ne-ah) [L. *tristis* sad + Gr. *mania* madness]. Melancholia.

trisubstituted (tri-sub′stĭ-tūt″ed). Having three molecules or atoms replaced by three other molecules or atoms.

trisulcate (tri-sul′kāt). Having three furrows.

trisulfide (tri-sul′fīd). A sulfur compound containing three atoms of sulfur to one of the base.

Trit. Abbreviation for L. *tri′tura,* triturate.

tritane (tri′tān). Triphenylmethane.

tritanope (tri′tah-nōp″). An individual exhibiting tritanopia.

tritanopia (tri″tah-no′pe-ah) [Gr. *tritos* third + *an-* neg. + *ōpē* sight + *-ia*]. A rare and obscure type of defective color vision, characterized by retention of the sensory mechanism for two hues only (red and green) of the normal 4-primary quota, and lacking blue and yellow, with loss of luminance and shift of brightness and hue curves toward the long-wave end of the spectrum. Often associated with drug administration, retinal detachment, or diseases of the nervous system. Formerly called "blue blindness." Cf. the correlative terms *protanopia, deuteranopia,* and *tetartanopia,* in which the color vision deficiency is in the first, second, and fourth primary, respectively.

tritanopic (tri″tah-nop′ik). Pertaining to or characterized by tritanopia.

tritanopsia (tri″tah-nop′se-ah). Tritanopia.

tritiate (trit′e-āt). To treat with tritium.

triticeous (tri-tish′us) [L. *triticeus*]. Resembling a grain of wheat.

triticeum (tri-tis′e-um) [L.]. A nodule in the thyrohyoid ligament. See *cartilago triticea.*

triticin (trit′ĭ-sin). A fructose polysaccharide, $(C_6H_{10}O_5)_n$, from wheat.

Triticum (trit′ĭ-kum) [L.]. A genus of grasses, including wheat. *T. re′pens* (*Agropyrum repens*), or couch grass, is diuretic.

tritium (trit′e-um) [Gr. *tritos* third]. The mass three isotope of hydrogen, ^3H, a radioactive gas obtained by bombardment of beryllium in the cyclotron with deuterium ions. It has a half-life of about 31 years and is used as an indicator or tracer in metabolic studies.

tritocone (tri′to-kōn) [Gr. *tritos* third + *kōnos* cone]. The distobuccal cusp of an upper premolar tooth.

tritoconid (tri″to-ko′nid). The distobuccal cusp of a lower premolar tooth.

tritol (tri′tol). Any emulsion of the extract of filix mas with the diastasic extract of malt.

triton (tri′ton). Trinitrotoluene.

tritopine (tri-to′pin). An alkaloid obtained from opium.

tritotoxin (tri″to-tok′sin). A toxin which unites less easily with the antitoxin than do the toxins of the other two categories. See *prototoxin* and *deuterotoxin.*

tritoxide (trit-ok′sīd). Trioxide.

triturable (trit′u-rah-b′l). Susceptible of being triturated.

triturate (trit′u-rāt). 1. To rub to a powder. 2. A triturated substance.

trituration (trit″u-ra′shun) [L. *tritura* the treading out of corn]. 1. The reduction of solid bodies to a powder by continuous rubbing. 2. A triturated drug, especially one rubbed up with milk sugar.

triturator (trit″u-ra′tor). An apparatus in which substances can be continuously rubbed, as in the process of amalgamating an alloy with mercury.

triturium (tri-tu′re-um). A vessel for separating liquors of different densities.

trivalence (triv′ah-lens). The condition or quality of being trivalent.

trivalent (triv′ah-lent) [*tri-* + L. *valens* powerful]. 1. Uniting with or replacing three hydrogen atoms. 2. Capable of binding three different complements: said of an amboceptor.

trivalve (tri′valv). Having three valves or three blades, as a speculum.

trixenic (tri-zen′ik) [*tri-* + Gr. *xenos* a guest-friend, stranger]. Associated with three species of microorganisms.

trizonal (tri-zo′nal). Arranged in three zones.

trocar (tro′kar) [Fr. *trois quarts* three quarters]. A sharp-pointed instrument used with a cannula for piercing a cavity wall in paracentesis. **Curschmann's t.**, a trocar for puncture in cutaneous edema. **Duchenne's t.**, an instrument for removing small portions of tissues from deep parts for microscopical study. **Durham's t., piloting t.**, a trocar for introducing a jointed tracheostomy tube. **rectal t.**, a curved trocar for tapping the bladder through the rectum.

troch. Abbreviation for *trochiscus.*

trochanter (tro-kan′ter) [L.; Gr. *trochantēr*]. Either of the two processes below the neck of the femur. **greater t.**, t. major. **lesser t.**, t. minor. **t. ma′jor** [N A, B N A], a broad, flat process at the upper end of the lateral surface of the femur, to which several muscles are attached. Called also *greater t.* **t. mi′nor** [N A, B N A], a short conical process projecting medially from the lower part of the posterior border of the base of the neck of the femur. Called also *lesser t.* **rudimentary t.**, t. tertius. **small t.**, t. minor. **t. ter′tius** [N A, B N A], **third t.**, a term applied to the gluteal tuberosity of the femur when it is unusually prominent.

trochanterian (tro″kan-ter′e-an). Trochanteric.

trochanteric (tro″kan-ter′ik). Pertaining to a trochanter.

trochanterplasty (tro-kan′ter-plas″te). Surgical excision of a ridge of bone to form a new femoral neck.

trochantin (tro-kan′tin). Trochanter minor.

trochantinian (tro″kan-tin′e-an). Pertaining to the lesser trochanter.

troche (tro′ke) [Gr. *trochos* a round cake]. A medicated tablet or disk; a lozenge.

trochin (tro′kin) [L. *trochinus*]. Tuberculum minus humeri.

trochiscus (tro-kis′kus), pl. *trochis′chi* [L.; Gr. *trochiskos*, dim. of *trochos*, a small wheel or disk]. A medicated tablet; a troche.

trochiter (trok′ĭ-ter). 1. Trochanter major. 2. Tuberculum majus humeri.

trochiterian (trok″ĭ-te′re-an). Pertaining to the trochiter.

trochlea (trok′le-ah), pl. *troch′leae* [L.; Gr. *trochilia* pulley]. A pulley-shaped part or structure; used as a general term in anatomical nomenclature. **t. fibula′ris calca′nei,** N A alternative for *t. peronealis calcanei.* **t. hu′meri** [N A, B N A], **t. of humerus,** the pulley-like medial portion of the distal end of the humerus for articulation with the semilunar notch of the ulna. **t. labyrin′thi,** cochlea. **muscular t., t. muscula′ris** [N A, B N A], an anatomical part that serves to change the direction of pull of a tendon; it may be fibrous or bony. **t. mus′culi obli′qui superio′ris bul′bi** [N A], **t. mus′culi obli′qui superio′ris oc′uli** [B N A], the fibrocartilaginous pulley near the internal angular process of the frontal bone, through which the tendon of the superior oblique muscle of the eyeball passes. Called also *t. of superior oblique muscle.* **peroneal t. of calcaneus, t. peronea′lis calca′nei** [N A], a small eminence on the lateral surface of the calcaneus, separating the tendons of the peroneus brevis and longus muscles. Called also *processus trochlearis calcanei* [B N A]. **t. phalan′gis digito′rum ma′nus** [B N A], caput phalangis digitorum manus. **t. phalan′gis digito′rum pe′dis** [B N A], caput phalangis digitorum pedis. **t. of superior oblique muscle,** t. musculi obliqui superioris bulbi. **t. ta′li** [N A, B N A], **t. of talus,** the surface of the talus for articulation with the tibia and fibula.

trochlear (trok′le-ar) [L. *trochlearis*]. 1. Of the nature of or resembling a pulley. 2. Pertaining to a trochlea.

trochleariform (trok″le-ar′ĭ-form). Pulley-shaped.

trochlearis (trok″le-a′ris) [L.]. Trochlear.

trochocardia (tro″ko-kar′de-ah) [Gr. *trochos* wheel + *kardia* heart]. Displacement of the heart due to a rotatory movement on its axis.

trochocephalia (tro″ko-se-fa′le-ah) [Gr. *trochos* wheel + *kephalē* head + *-ia*]. A rounded appearance of the head caused by synostosis of the frontal and parietal bones.

trochocephaly (tro″ko-sef′ah-le). Trochocephalia.

trochoid (tro′koid) [Gr. *trochos* wheel + *eidos* form]. Resembling a pivot or a pulley.

trochoides (tro-koi′dēz) [Gr. *trochoeidēs*, from *trochos* wheel + *eidos* form]. Articulatio trochoidea.

trochophore (tro′ko-fōr) [Gr. *trochos* wheel + *phoros* bearing]. The larval form of annelid worms.

trochorizocardia (trok″o-ri″zo-kar′de-ah). Trochocardia combined with horizocardia.

Troglodytella (trog″lo-di-tel′ah). A genus of ciliates species of which occur in the gorilla and chimpanzee.

Troglotrema (trog″lo-tre′mah). A genus of flukes. **T. salmin′cola,** a fluke transmitted to dogs and ranch foxes by the ingestion of infected trout or salmon, and which itself is the vector of an organism causing acute disease in the infected animal.

troilism (troi′lizm) [Fr. *trois* three]. Paraphilia practiced by three persons, by two women and a man, or by two men and a woman.

Troisier's ganglion, sign, syndrome (trwah-ze-āz′) [Charles-Emile *Troisier*, French physician, 1844–1919]. See under the nouns.

troland (tro′land). The retinal illuminance produced by the image of an object the luminance of which is 1 lumen per square meter for an area of the entrance pupil of 1 square millimeter.

Trolard's net, vein (tro-lardz′) [Paulin *Trolard*, French anatomist, 1842–1910]. See under *net* and *vein.*

trolnitrate (trol-ni′trāt). Chemical name: triethanolamine trinitrate: used as a vasodilator.

Tröltsch's corpuscles, recesses, spaces (trel′ches) [Anton Friedrich von *Tröltsch*, German otologist, 1829–1890]. See under *corpuscle* and *recess.*

Trombicula (trom-bik′u-lah). A genus of acarine mites of the family Trombiculidae. **T. akamu′shi,** the kedani mite, whose larvae transmit *Rickettsia tsutsugamushi.* **T. alfreddugè′si,** *Eutrombicula alfreddugèsi.* See also under *chigger.* **T. autumna′lis,** the autumnal chigger of Europe whose larvae cause lesions of the skin in

Trombicula akamushi. (Tanaka.)

man and animals. Formerly called *Leptus autumnalis.* **T. delien'sis,** a species from the Deli district of northeastern Sumatra. It transmits tsutsugamushi disease. **T. holoseri'ceum,** the common harvest mite of Europe. **T. ir'ritans,** *Eutrombicula alfreddugèsi.* **T. mus'cae domes'ticae,** a red acarid parasite on the housefly; also a homeopathic preparation of the same. **T. musca'rum,** *T. muscae domesticae.* **T. tsalsahua'tl,** a species in Mexico which burrows into the skin causing intense itching and painful little ulcers. **T. vandersan'di** is the gonone of New Guinea which burrows into the skin. **T. wichman'ni** is the gonone of Celebes.

trombiculiasis (trom-bik″u-li'ah-sis). Infestation with Trombicula.

Trombiculidae (trom-bik'u-li″de). A family of mites which is cosmopolitan in distribution, ranging from Alaska and Labrador to New Zealand, and from sea level to an altitude of more than 16,000 feet in the Andes. The parasitic larvae of the mites infest vertebrates. Genera of medical significance are *Eutrombicula* and *Trombicula.*

trombidiiasis (trom-bid″e-i'ah-sis). Trombiculiasis.

trombidiosis (trom-bid″e-o'sis). Trombiculiasis.

Trombidium (trom-bid'e-um). A name formerly given a genus of mites, now included in the genus Trombicula.

tromexan (tro-mek'san). Trade mark for a preparation of ethyl biscoumacetate.

Trommer's test (trom'erz) [Karl August *Trommer,* German chemist, 1806–1879]. See under *tests.*

Trömner's sign [Ernest L. O. *Trömner,* German neurologist, born 1868]. Hoffmann's sign, def. 2.

tromomania (trom″o-ma'ne-ah) [Gr. *tromos* trembling + Gr. *mania* madness]. Delirium tremens.

tromophonia (trom″o-fo'ne-ah). A form of dysphonia characterized by a tremulous voice.

trona (tro'nah) [possible anagram of *natron*]. A crude soda salt.

tronothane (tron'o-thān). Trade mark for preparations of pramoxine.

tropate (tro'pāt). A salt of tropic acid.

tropesis (tro-pe'sis) [Gr. *tropos* a turning]. Haekel's term for the tendency to action shown by every substance.

trophectoderm (trof-ek'to-derm) [*tropho-* + *ectoderm*]. The outer layer of cells of the early blastodermic vesicle; the earliest trophoblast.

trophedema (trof″e-de'mah) [*tropho-* + *edema*]. A disease marked by permanent edema of the feet or legs.

trophema (tro-fe'mah) [*tropho-* + Gr. *haima* blood]. The nourishing blood of the mucosa of the uterus.

trophesial, trophesic (tro-fe'ze-al, tro-fe'sik). Pertaining to or characterized by trophesy.

trophesy (trof'e-se). Defective nutrition due to disorder of the trophic nerves.

trophic (trof'ik) [Gr. *trophikos*]. Of or pertaining to nutrition.

-trophic, -trophin (trof'ik, trof'in) [Gr. *trophikos* nourishing]. Word terminations denoting relationship to nutrition.

trophicity (tro-fis'ĭ-te). A trophic function or relation.

trophism (trof'izm). Direct trophic influence.

tropho- (trof'o) [Gr. *trophē* nutrition]. Combining form denoting relationship to food or nourishment.

trophoblast (trof'o-blast) [*tropho-* + Gr. *blastos* germ]. A layer of extra-embryonic ectodermal tissue on the outside of the blastodermic vesicle. It attaches the ovum to the uterine wall and supplies nutrition to the embryo. The inner cellular layer of the trophoblast is called *cytotrophoblast* and its outer syncytial layer *syntrophoblast.*

trophoblastic (trof″o-blas'tik). Pertaining to the trophoblast.

trophoblastoma (trof″o-blas-to'mah). Chorioepithelioma.

trophochromatin (trof″o-kro'mah-tin). Trophochromidia.

trophochromidia (trof″o-kro-mid'e-ah). Chromatin concerned with the nutrition of the cell rather than with reproduction. Cf. *idiochromidia.*

trophocyte (trof'o-sit). A lower type of cell which furnishes nourishment to a higher type of cell of a tissue. Cf. *trophospongium.*

trophoderm (trof'o-derm) [*tropho-* + Gr. *derma* skin]. Trophoblast.

trophodermatoneurosis (trof″o-der″mah-to-nu-ro'sis). Erythredema polyneuropathy.

trophodynamics (trof″o-di-nam'iks). The study of the forces engaged in nutrition.

trophoedema (trof″o-e-de'mah). Trophedema.

tropholecithal (trof″o-les'ĭ-thal). Pertaining to the tropholecithus.

tropholecithus (trof″o-les'ĭ-thus) [*tropho-* + Gr. *lekithos* yolk]. The food yolk of a meroblastic egg.

trophology (tro-fol'o-je). The science of nutrition of the body.

trophon (trof'on). The nutritive non-neural element of the neuron.

trophoneurosis (trof″o-nu-ro'sis). Any functional nervous disease due to the failure of nutrition from defective nerve influence. **disseminated t.,** scleroderma. **facial t.,** facial hemiatrophy. **lingual t.,** progressive hemiatrophy of the tongue. **muscular t.,** trophic alteration of muscular tissue, dependent on nervous derangement. **t. of Romberg,** facial hemiatrophy.

trophoneurotic (trof″o-nu-rot'ik). Pertaining to or of the nature of a trophoneurosis.

trophonosis (trof″o-no'sis) [*tropho-* + Gr. *nosos* disease]. Any disease or disorder due to nutritional causes.

trophonucleus (trof″o-nu'kle-us). Macronucleus.

trophopathia (trof″o-path'e-ah). Trophopathy.

trophopathy (tro-fop'ah-the) [*tropho-* + Gr. *pathos* disease]. Any derangement of the nutrition.

trophoplasm (trof″o-plasm) [*tropho-* + Gr. *plasma* something formed]. The achromatin of a cell: so called because it is supposed to take part in cell nutrition.

trophoplast (trof'o-plast) [*tropho-* + Gr. *plastos* formed]. A granular protoplasmic body; a plastid.

trophospongia (trof″o-spon'je-ah). Plural of *trophospongium.*

trophospongium (trof″o-spon'je-um), pl. *trophospon'gia* [*tropho-* + Gr. *spongion* sponge]. 1. A canalicular network in the cytoplasm of certain cells which was once believed to be instrumental in the circulation of nutritive material. 2. (pl.). The vascular endometrium between the uterine wall and the trophoblast.

trophotaxis (trof″o-tak'sis) [*tropho-* + Gr. *taxis* a drawing up in rank and file]. An orientation movement of a motile organism in response to the stimulus provided by nutritive materials.

trophotherapy (trof″o-ther'ah-pe). Treatment of disease by dietetic measures.

trophotonos (tro-fot'o-nos) [*tropho-* + Gr. *tonos* tension]. A rigid state of the flagella of a micro-organism, resulting from improper nourishment.

trophotropic (trof″o-trop'ik). Pertaining to or characterized by trophotropism.

trophotropism (tro-fot′ro-pizm) [*tropho-* + Gr. *trepein* to turn]. The orientation of cells toward nutritive material; a form of chemotropism in which the stimulus is provided by nutritive substance.

trophozoite (trof″o-zo′it) [*tropho-* + Gr. *zōon* animal]. The active, motile, feeding stage of a protozoan organism, as contrasted with the nonmotile encysted stage. In the malarial parasite, the stage of schizogony between the signet ring stage and the schizont.

tropia (tro′pe-ah) [Gr. *tropē* a turning]. A manifest deviation of an eye from the normal position when both eyes are open and uncovered; strabismus, or squint. See *cyclotropia, esotropia, exotropia, heterotropia, hypertropia,* and *hypotropia.*

-tropic (tro′pik) [Gr. *tropikos* turning]. Word termination denoting turning toward, changing, or tending to turn or change. See *tropism.*

tropical (trop′e-kal) [Gr. *tropikos* turning]. Pertaining to the regions of the earth bounded by the parallels of latitude 23° 27′ north and south of the equator.

tropicopolitan (trop″ĭ-ko-pol′ĭ-tan) [*tropical* + Gr. *polis* a city or a country]. 1. Occurring in all tropical areas. 2. An organism occurring in all tropical regions.

tropidine (trop′ĭ-din). An oily, liquid base, $CH_3.N{:}C_6H_9{:}CH$, with an odor like that of coniine, formed by the dehydration of tropine.

tropine (tro′pin). 1. A crystalline alkaloid, $CH_3.N.C_6H_{10}.CHOH$, with a smell like tobacco, derivable from atropine and from various plants. 2. Opsonin. See also *bacteriotropine.*

tropism (tro′pizm) [Gr. *tropē* a turn, turning]. A growth response in a non-motile organism, elicited by an external stimulus. Such response may be either positive (toward) or negative (away from the stimulus). By extension, used as a word termination affixed to a stem denoting the nature of the stimulus (phototropism) or the material or entity for which an organism or substance shows a special affinity (neurotropism).

tropochrome (tro′po-krōm″) [*tropo-* + Gr. *chrōma* color]. Refusing to stain with mucin stains after formol-bichromate fixation, as applied to certain serous cells of the salivary glands. Cf. *homeochrome.*

tropococaine (trop″o-ko′kān). Tropacocaine.

tropometer (tro-pom′e-ter) [Gr. *tropē* a turning + *metron* measure]. 1. An instrument for measuring the rotation of the eyeball. 2. An instrument for measuring the twist or torsion of a long bone.

tropomyosin (tro″po-mi′o-sin). A protein isolated from the water-insoluble residue of muscle.

tropon (trop′on). A brownish powder prepared from vegetable and animal albumins; nutrient.

trotyl (tro′til). Trinitrotoluene.

trou (troo) [Fr.]. Hole; gap. **t. auscultatoire** (troo″aws-kool″tah-twahr′), auscultatory gap.

trough (trof). A shallow longitudinal depression or channel. **gingival t.,** gingival sulcus. **vestibular t.,** the sulcus formed by reflection of the mucous membrane from the inner surface of the cheeks or lips onto the tissues overlying the alveoli of the teeth.

Trousseau's phenomenon, sign, spot, twitching (troo-sōz′) [Armand *Trousseau,* French physician, 1801–1867]. See under the nouns.

troxidone (trok′sĭ-dōn). Trimethadione.

troy (troi). A system of weights commonly used in England and the United States for expressing quantities of gold and silver. For equivalents see *tables of weights and measures.*

TRU. Abbreviation for *turbidity reducing unit.*

true (troo). Actually existing; not false; real; meeting all the criteria establishing its identity.

Trueta method, technic, treatment (troo-a′tah) [José *Trueta,* Spanish surgeon in England, born 1897]. See under *treatment.*

truncal (trung′kal). Pertaining to the trunk.

truncate (trung′kāt) [L. *truncare, truncatus*]. 1. To amputate; to deprive of limbs. 2. Having the end cut squarely off.

trunci (trung′ki) [L.]. Plural of *truncus.*

truncus (trung′kus), pl. *trun′ci* [L. "trunk"]. The main part, a stem; used in anatomical nomenclature to designate the main part of the body, to which the head and limbs are attached, or a major, undivided and usually short, portion of a nerve or of a blood or lymphatic vessel or other duct. **t. arterio′sus,** an arterial trunk, especially the artery connected with the fetal heart, which gives off the aortic arches and develops into the aortic and pulmonary arteries. **t. arterio′sus, persistent,** an uncommon congenital anomaly, characterized by a single arterial trunk arising from the heart, receiving blood from both ventricles and supplying blood to the coronary, pulmonary, and systemic circulations. **t. brachiocephal′icus** [N A], the first branch of the arch of the aorta, which behind the right sternoclavicular joint divides into the right common carotid and right subclavian arteries, with distribution to the right side of the head and neck and to the right arm; occasionally the lowest thyroid artery arises from this trunk. Called also *arteria anonyma* [B N A], and *brachiocephalic trunk.* **t. bronchomediastina′lis** [N A], either of the two lymphatic vessels draining the pulmonary, bronchopulmonary, tracheobronchial, tracheal, and parasternal lymph nodes: that on the right side into the right lymphatic duct or subclavian vein, and that on the left into the thoracic duct or the subclavian vein. Called also *bronchomediastinal trunk.* **t. bronchomediastina′lis dex′ter** [B N A], the truncus bronchomediastinalis on the right side; separately designated in the earlier nomenclature. **t. celi′acus** [N A], the arterial trunk that arises from the abdominal aorta, gives off the left gastric, common hepatic, and splenic arteries, and supplies the esophagus, stomach, duodenum, spleen, pancreas, liver, and gallbladder. Called also *arteria coeliaca* [B N A], and *celiac trunk.* **t. cor′poris callo′si** [N A, B N A], the main central portion of the corpus callosum as distinguished from the rostrum and the splenium. Called also *trunk of corpus callosum.* **t. costocervica′lis** [N A, B N A], an artery that arises from the back of the subclavian artery, arches backward, and at the neck of the first rib divides into the deep cervical and highest intercostal arteries, thus supplying blood to the structures of the first two intercostal spaces, the vertebral column, the muscles of the back, and the deep neck muscles. Called also *costocervical trunk.* **t. fascic′uli atrioventricula′ris** [N A], the undivided portion of the atrioventricular bundle, from its origin at the atrioventricular node to the point of division into right and left branches at the superior end of the muscular part of the interventricular septum. **t. infe′rior plex′us brachia′lis** [N A], the trunk of the brachial plexus that is formed by the ventral branches of the eighth cervical and first thoracic nerves and lies behind the subclavian artery. Its anterior division becomes the medial fasciculus or cord of the plexus, and its posterior division helps form the posterior fasciculus; modality, general sensory and motor. Called also *inferior trunk of brachial plexus.* **trun′ci intestina′les** [N A], short lymphatic vessels which leave the gastrointestinal tract and participate in formation of the thoracic duct. Called also *intestinal lymphatic trunks.* **t. jugula′ris** [N A, B N A], either of the two vessels draining the deep cervical lymph nodes: on the right side, into the right lymphatic duct or subclavian vein, and on the left side, into the thoracic duct or subclavian vein. Called also *jugular trunk.* **t. linguofacia′lis** [N A], the common trunk by which the facial and lingual arteries often arise from the external carotid artery. Called also *linguofacial trunk.* **trun′ci lumba′les [dex′ter et sinis′ter]** [N A], lymphatic vessels, one on either side, that drain lymph upward from the lumbar lymph nodes and help form the thoracic duct. Called also *lumbar trunks.* **t. lumbosacra'lis** [N A, B N A], a trunk formed by union of the lower division of the ventral branch of the fourth lumbar nerve with the ventral branch of the fifth lumbar nerve. Called also *lumbosacral trunk.* **t. me'dius plex'us brachia'lis** [N A], the trunk of the brachial plexus that is formed by the ventral branch of the seventh cervical nerve. Its anterior division helps form the lateral fasciculus or cord of the plexus, and its posterior division helps form the posterior fasciculus; modality, general sensory and motor. Called also *middle trunk of brachial plexus.* **trun'ci plex'us brachia'lis** [N A], the three trunks of the brachial plexus, arising from the ventral branches of the lower four cervical nerves and the first thoracic nerve near the lateral border of the scalenus anterior muscle; they continue laterally and downward, above and behind the subclavian artery, and near the clavicle form the lateral, medial, and posterior fasciculi or cords of the plexus. See *t. inferior plexus brachialis, t. medius plexus brachialis,* and *t. superior plexus brachialis.* **t. pulmona'lis** [N A], the vessel arising from the conus arteriosus of the right ventricle, extending upward to divide into the right and left pulmonary arteries beneath the arch of the aorta, and conveying unaerated blood toward the lungs. Called also *arteria pulmonalis* [B N A], and *pulmonary trunk.* **t. subcla'vius** [N A, B N A], either of two lymphatic vessels draining the axillary lymph nodes, that on the right into the right lymphatic duct or subclavian vein, that on the left into the thoracic duct or the subclavian vein. Called also *subclavian trunk.* **t. supe'rior plex'us brachia'lis** [N A], the trunk of the brachial plexus that is formed by the ventral branches of the fifth and sixth cervical nerves. Its anterior division helps form the lateral fasciculus or cord of the plexus, its posterior division helps form the posterior fasciculus, and it gives rise directly to the suprascapular and subclavian nerves; modality, general sensory and motor. Called also *superior trunk of brachial plexus.* **t. sympath'icus** [N A, B N A], the double line of ganglia and interconnecting nerves situated to either side of and just in front of the vertebral column. It extends from the base of the skull to the sacrum and is connected with the spinal nerves by communicating branches. Called also *sympathetic trunk.* **t. thyreocervica'lis** [B N A], **t. thyrocervica'lis** [N A], a short artery that arises from the convex side of the subclavian artery just medial to the anterior scalene muscle and at once divides into the inferior thyroid, transverse cervical, and suprascapular arteries, supplying thyroid, neck, and scapular regions. Called also *thyrocervical trunk.* **t. vaga'lis ante'rior** [N A], a nerve trunk formed by fibers from both left and right vagus nerves, collected from the anterior part of the esophageal plexus; it descends through the esophageal opening of the diaphragm to supply branches to the anterior surface of the stomach. Called also *anterior vagal trunk.* **t. vaga'lis poste'rior** [N A], a nerve trunk formed by fibers from both left and right vagus nerves, collected from the posterior part of the esophageal plexus; it descends through the esophageal opening of the diaphragm to supply branches to the posterior surface of the stomach. Called also *posterior vagal trunk.*

Trunecek's sign, symptom (troo'net-seks) [Karel *Trunecek*, physician in Prague, born 1865]. See under *sign.*

trunk (trunk) [L. *truncus* the stem or trunk of a tree]. 1. The main part of the body, to which head and limbs are attached. 2. A major, undivided and usually short, portion of a nerve or of a blood or lymphatic vessel, or other duct. **t. of atrioventricular bundle,** truncus fasciculi atrioventricularis. **basilar t.,** arteria basilaris. **t's of brachial plexus,** trunci plexus brachialis. **brachiocephalic t.,** truncus brachiocephalicus. **bronchomediastinal t.,** truncus bronchomediastinalis. **celiac t.,** truncus celiacus. **t. of corpus callosum,** truncus corporis callosi. **costocervical t.,** truncus costocervicalis. **inferior t. of brachial plexus,** truncus inferior plexus brachialis. **intestinal lymphatic t's,** trunci intestinales. **jugular t.,** truncus jugularis. **linguofacial t.,** truncus linguofacialis. **lumbar t's,** trunci lumbales [dexter et sinister]. **lumbosacral t.,** truncus lumbosacralis. **middle t. of brachial plexus,** truncus medius plexus brachialis. **pulmonary t.,** truncus pulmonalis. **subclavian t.,** truncus subclavius. **superior t. of brachial plexus,** truncus superior plexus brachialis. **sympathetic t.,** truncus sympathicus. **thyrocervical t.,** truncus thyrocervicalis. **vagal t., anterior,** truncus vagalis anterior. **vagal t., posterior,** truncus vagalis posterior.

trusion (troo'zhun) [L. *trudere* to shove]. Malposition of a tooth. **bimaxillary t.,** malposition of the teeth of both the upper and the lower jaw. **bodily t.,** malposition of the entire tooth, crown and root. **coronal t.,** malposition of the crown of a tooth, the root being normally placed. **mandibular t.,** malposition of the mandibular teeth. **maxillary t.,** malposition of the maxillary teeth.

truss (trus). A device for retaining a reduced hernia in its place. **nasal t.,** a trusslike support for fractured nasal bones. **yarn t.,** a trusslike bandage of worsted yarn for the support of inguinal hernia in infants.

truxilline (truks'ĭ-lin). An amorphous alkaloid prepared from coca leaves or made synthetically.

try-in (tri'in). A preliminary insertion of a dental prosthetic appliance to determine its fit and suitability.

trypaflavine (trip"ah-fla'vin). Acriflavine hydrochloride.

trypan-atoxyl (tri"pan-ah-tok'sil). A supposed compound formed by a combination between atoxyl and some albuminous substance in the body of a patient affected with trypanosomiasis.

trypanblau (tri'pan-blaw") [Ger.]. Trypan blue.

trypanid (tri'pan-id). An eruption occurring in trypanosomiasis.

trypanocidal (tri-pan"o-si'dal). Trypanosomicidal.

trypanocide (tri-pan'o-sīd). Trypanosomicide.

trypanocidia (tri"pan-o-si'de-ah). The destruction of trypanosomes.

trypanolysis (tri"pan-ol'ĭ-sis). The destruction of trypanosomes.

trypanolytic (tri"pan-o-lit'ik). Destructive to trypanosomes.

Trypanophis (tri"pan-o'fis). A parasite resembling *Trypanoplasma,* but with a very small kinetonucleus.

Trypanoplasma (tri"pan-o-plaz'mah) [Gr. *trypanon* borer + *plasma* anything formed or molded]. A genus of sporozoan parasites resembling Trypanosoma, but having a posterior, as well as an anterior, flagellum. **T. abram'dis,** a species found in the bream (*Abramis brama*). **T. borrel'li,** a species found in blood of fish. **T. intestina'lis,** a species found in a salt water fish, *Bax boops;* it was the first trypanosome-like organism to be found outside the blood. **T. trut'tae,** a species found in the trout (*Salmo fario*). **T. ventric'uli,** a species found in *Cyclopterus lumpus.*

trypanosan (tri-pan'o-san). A dyestuff used in treating trypanosomiasis.

Trypanosoma (tri"pan-o-so'mah) [Gr. *trypanon* borer + *sōma* body]. A genus of sporozoan parasites found in the blood plasma of man and animals, characterized by the delicate, undulatory membrane attached to the body and whiplike flagellum. Most species live part of their life cycle in insects or other invertebrate hosts, where they undergo remarkable transformations: 1. They are rounded bodies resembling Leishmania. 2. They are elongated, with a flagellum at one end. 3. They have an undulating membrane for half their length like Crithidia. 4. The undulating membrane extends the entire length and they become typical trypanosomes. **T. america'num,** a species infecting cattle in the United States. **T. a'vium,** a parasite 20–70 μ long found in the blood of birds, but apparently not pathogenic. **T. ber'berum,** *T. evansi.* **T. bru'cei** occurs in the disease nagana or tsetse-fly disease of horses and cattle of central Africa. **T. calmet'ii,** a species found in the blood of a domestic fowl in Tonkin. **T. cap'rae,** a form found in goats in Africa; probably the same as *T. vivax.* **T. castella'ni,** *T. gambiense.* **T. cazal'boui,** a species parasitic in the goat in French Guiana and transmitted by the biting fly *Stomoxys bouffardi.* **T. confu'sum,** *T. congolense.* **T. congolen'se,** a species causing Gambian horse sickness in Central Africa. **T. cru'zi,** a species which causes the American form of trypanosomiasis called Chagas' disease. **T. dimor'pha,** a species causing a disease of horses and other domestic animals in Gambia and other parts of Africa. It is transmitted by *Glossina palpalis* and perhaps by other species. **T. equi'num,** the species found in horses suffering from mal de caderas, a disease of central South America. **T. equiper'dum,** the species causing dourine in horses and asses. **T. esco'mili,** a species from Peru somewhat larger than *T. cruzi.* **T. evan'si,** found in the disease surra of mules and horses in India. **T. gambien'se,** found in the cerebrospinal fluid and the blood of man in cases of tropical splenomegaly, sleeping sickness, and various cachexial fevers of warm countries. It is transmitted by the tsetse fly, *Glossina palpalis.* See *African trypanosomiasis,* under *trypanosomiasis.* **T. granulo'sum,** a species parasitic in the eel. Its intermediate host is the leech, *Hemiclepsis marginata.* **T. grus'sei,** a species found in horses and other domestic animals in Africa. **T. guyanen'se,** a species causing a fatal disease of cattle in French Guiana and Venezuela. **T. hip'picum,** the species causing a disease of horses and mules known in Panama as murina de caderas and as derrengadera de caderas. **T. hom'inis,** *T. gambiense.* **T. inopina'tum,** a species parasitic in the frog and transmitted by a leech, *Helobdella algira.* **T. lew'isi,** a species found in the blood of the rat, and transmitted by a second host, the rat flea, *Nosopsyllus fasciatus.* **T. lu'is,** *Treponema pallidum.* **T. macroca'num,** *T. evansi.* **T. melopha'gium,** a nonpathogenic species occurring in sheep. **T. metacyclique,** a small and immature form of *T. granulosum.* **T. montgom'eri,** *T. congolense.* **T. na'num,** a species causing disease in cattle along the White Nile: probably the same as *T. congolense.* **T. nigerien'se,** the form which causes sleeping sickness in Nigeria. It is transmitted by *Glossina tachinoides* and is probably the same as *T. gambiense.* **T. noc'tuae,** a species found in the blood of the little owl, being disseminated by the gnat, *Culex pipiens.* **T. pecau'di,** a species said to cause baleri. **T. rhodesien'se,** a species found in the antelope in Nyassaland in South Africa. It may be transmitted to man by the bite of *Glossina morsitans.* It causes a form of sleeping sickness (kaodzera). **T. rotato'rium,** the type species of the genus, and found in the blood of several species of frogs. **T. rouge'ti,** *T. equiperdum.* **T. san'guinis,** a species discovered by David Gruby in 1843. **T. sim'iae,** a species resembling *T. congolense* but found in dogs. **T. soudanen'se,** a species found in camels which causes tahaga. **T. thei'leri,** a nonpathogenic species found in cattle in South Africa. **T. triato'mae,** a form very similar to *T. cruzi.* **T. uganden'se,** *T. gambiense.* **T. unifor'me,** *T. vivax.* **T. venezuelen'se,** a species causing a disease of horses in Venezuela called "pesteboba" or derrengadera. **T. vi'vax,** a species causing souma in cattle, sheep, and goats throughout tropical Africa.

trypanosomal (tri-pan″o-so′mal). Pertaining to or caused by trypanosomes.

trypanosomatic (tri-pan″o-so-mat′ik). Pertaining to or caused by trypanosomes.

trypanosomatosis (tri-pan″o-so″mah-to′sis). Trypanosomiasis.

trypanosomatotropic (tri-pan″o-so″mah-to-trop′ik). Having a selective affinity for trypanosomes.

trypanosome (tri-pan′o-sōm). An organism of the genus Trypanosoma.

trypanosomiasis (tri-pan″o-so-mi′ah-sis). The state of being infected with protozoa of the genus Trypanosoma; characterized by fever, anemia, and erythema. **African t.,** a disease due to invasion with *Trypanosoma gambiense* or *T. rhodesiense,* and common among the Negroes in tropical Africa. The parasite is conveyed by the bite of the tsetse flies, *Glossina palpalis* and *G. morsitans.* The early stage of the disease (known as trypanosome fever) is ushered in by fever, chills, headache, and vomiting. There are then alternating periods of fever and apyrexia lasting for several months. This is followed by pains in the extremities, enlargement of the lymph glands, and anemia. Later the central nervous system becomes involved, producing *sleeping sickness,* when the patients become depressed, tremulous, lethargic, and somnolent, until finally they sleep all the time, become emaciated, and eventually die. The disease may last for years, but it is always fatal after the nervous system has become involved. It is also known as *African sleeping sickness, African lethargy, nelavan,* and *Negro lethargy.* **American t., Brazilian t.,** Chagas' disease. **Congo t.,** African t. **Cruz t.,** Chagas' disease. **Rhodesian t.,** kaodzera. **South American t.,** Chagas' disease.

trypanosomic (tri-pan″o-so′mik). Pertaining to or infected with trypanosomes.

trypanosomicidal (tri-pan″o-so″mĭ-si′dal). Destructive to trypanosomes.

trypanosomicide (tri-pan″o-so′mĭ-sīd) [*trypanosome* + L. *caedere* to kill]. 1. Destructive to trypanosomes. 2. A substance which destroys trypanosomes.

trypanosomid (tri-pan′o-so-mid). A skin eruption occurring in trypanosomiasis.

Trypanosomonas (tri-pan″o-so-mo′nas). Trypanosoma.

trypanosomosis (tri-pan″o-so-mo′sis). Trypanosomiasis.

trypanotoxyl (try-pan″o-tok′sil). A substance produced by mixing an emulsion of liver with a solution of atoxyl. It is directly toxic to trypanosomes.

Trypanozoon (tri-pan″o-zo′on). Trypanosoma.

trypanroth (tri′pan-roth) [Ger.]. Trypan red.

tryparosan (tri-par′o-san). A preparation formed by introducing a halogen radical (e.g., chlorine) into the parafuchsin molecule: used by injection in trypanosomiasis.

tryparsamide (trip″ars-am′id). Chemical name: sodium N-carbamoyl-methyl-p-aminobenzenearsonate: used as an antitrypanosomal agent.

trypasafrol (tri″pah-saf′rol). One of the safranine group of aniline dyes: believed to be useful in trypanosomiasis.

trypesis (tri-pe′sis) [Gr. *trypēsis*]. Trephination.

Trypocastellanelleae (tri″po-kas-tel″yah-nel′e-e). A type of trypanosomes embracing the genera *Castellanella, Schizotrypanum,* and *Duttonella.*

trypochete (tri′po-kēt). A name given to Döhle's inclusion bodies. See under *body.*

tryponarsyl (tri″po-nar′sil). Tryparsamide.

trypotan (tri′po-tan). Tryparsamide.

trypoxyl (tri-pok′sil). Atoxyl.

trypsase (trip′sās). Trypsin considered as an enzyme or nonorganized ferment.

trypsin (trip′sin) [Gr. *tryein* to rub + pe*psin*]. One of the proteolytic enzymes of the pancreatic secretion, so named by Willy Kühne, in 1874. It is an endoproteinase, acting on peptide linkages containing the carboxyl group of either lysine or arginine. **t. crystallized,** a purified, crystallized preparation from an extract of the pancreas of the ox, *Bos taurus:* used as a proteolytic enzyme in débridement of necrotic wounds and ulcers, abscesses, fistulas, and sinuses, and in treatment of empyema.

trypsinize (trip′sin-īz). To subject to the action of trypsin.

trypsinogen (trip-sin′o-jen) [*trypsin* + Gr. *gennan* to produce]. The crystallizable zymogen occurring in the pancreas, from which trypsin is formed when it comes into contact with enterokinase.

trypsogen (trip′so-jen). Trypsinogen.

tryptase (trip′tās). One of a class of enzymes which split native proteins to peptides in neutral or near neutral solutions.

tryptic (trip″tik). Relating to or produced as a result of digestion by trypsin.

tryptolysis (trip-tol′ĭ-sis) [*tryptone* + Gr. *lysis* dissolution]. The splitting up of tryptone.

tryptolytic (trip″to-lit′ik). Splitting up tryptone; pertaining to the proteolytic properties of trypsin.

tryptone (trip′tōn). Any peptone produced by the digestion of albuminates by trypsin.

tryptonemia (trip″to-ne′me-ah) [*tryptone* + Gr. *haima* blood + *-ia*]. The presence of tryptones in the blood.

tryptophan (trip′to-fān). An amino acid, $C_8H_6N.$-$CH_2.CH.NH_2COOH$, or indole aminopropionic acid, existing in proteins, from which it is set free by tryptic digestion; essential for optimal growth in infants and for nitrogen equilibrium in human adults.

tryptophanase (trip′to-fān-ās). An enzyme that catalyzes the cleavage of tryptophan into indole, pyruvic acid, and ammonia.

tryptophane (trip′to-fān). Tryptophan.

tryptophanemia (trip″to-fān-e′me-ah) [*tryptophan* + Gr. *haima* blood + *-ia*]. The presence of tryptophan in the blood.

tryptophanuria (trip″to-fān-u′re-ah). The presence of tryptophan in the urine.

T.S. Abbreviation for *test solution.*

tsalsahuatl (tsal″sa-whaht″l). See *Trombicula tsalsahuatl.*

tsetse (tset′se). An African fly of the genus *Glossina.*

TSH. Abbreviation for *thyroid-stimulating hormone.*

Tsuga (tsoo′gah). A genus of coniferous trees. **T. canaden′sis,** the hemlock tree, affords Canada pitch.

tsutsugamushi (soot″soo-gah-moosh′e) [Japanese "dangerous bug"]. Scrub typhus.

T.U. Abbreviation for *toxic unit.*

tuamine (too′ah-min). Trade mark for preparations of tuaminoheptane.

tuaminoheptane (tu-am″ĭ-no-hep′tān). Chemical name: 1-methylhexylamine: used as a sympathomimetic agent in congestion of the nasal mucosa.

tuba (tu′bah), pl. *tu′bae* [L. "trumpet"]. An elongated hollow cylindrical organ; used as a general term in anatomical nomenclature. **t. acus′tica, t. auditi′va** [N A], **t. auditi′va [Eusta′chii]** [B N A], a channel, about 36 mm. long, lined with mucous membrane, that establishes communication between the tympanic cavity and the nasopharynx and serves to adjust the pressure of air in the cavity to the external pressure. It comprises a pars ossea, located in the temporal bone, and a pars cartilaginea, ending in the nasopharynx. Called also *auditory tube.* **t. uteri′na** [N A], **t. uteri′na [Fallop′pii]** [B N A], a long slender tube that extends from the upper lateral angle of the uterus to the region of the ovary of the same side. It is attached to the broad ligament by the mesosalpinx, and consists of an ampulla, an infundibulum, an isthmus, two ostia, and a pars uterina. Called also *uterine tube.*

tubadil (too′bah-dil). Trade mark for a preparation of tubocurarine.

tubal (tu′bal). Pertaining to a tube.

tubarine (too′bah-rin). Trade mark for a preparation of tubocurarine.

tubatorsion (tu″bah-tor′shun). Torsion or twisting of the uterine tube.

tubba, tubboe (tub′ah, tub′o). Yaws attacking the soles and palms.

tube (tūb) [L. *tubus*]. An elongated hollow cylindrical organ or instrument. **Abbott-Rawson t.,** a double barrelled gastro-enterostomy tube. **air t.,** any tubular passage of the respiratory apparatus. **auditory t.,** the channel that establishes communication between the tympanic cavity and the nasopharynx. See *tuba auditiva* [N A]. **Bellini's t's,** tubuli renales. **Bellocq's t.** See under *cannula.* **Bochdalek's t's,** cecal cavities connected with the thyroglossal duct, together with which they usually disappear soon after birth. **Bouchut's t's,** a set of tubes for use in the intubation of the larynx. **Bowman's t's, corneal t's,** tubes formed artificially between the lamellae of the cornea in the process of injection. **Buchner's t.,** the outer tube used in Buchner's method of anaerobic cultivation of microorganisms. **Cantor t.,** a mercury-weighted tube for intestinal intubation. **Carrel t.,** a combination of small-bore rubber tubes for conveying the antiseptic solution in the Carrel treatment. **cathode-ray t.,** a vacuum tube with a thin window at the end opposite the cathode to allow the cathode rays to pass outside. **cerebromedullary t.,** neural t. **Chaoul t.,** a tube for x-ray therapy to provide (1) short distance, (2) low voltage, (3) localization to the diseased center, (4) superficial action, (5) fractional dosage, (6) great concentration. **Chaussier's t.,** a trumpet-shaped tube for performing insufflation of the lungs. **collecting t's,** tubuli renales. **Coolidge t.,** a vacuum tube for the generation of roentgen rays in which the cathode consists of a spiral filament of incandescent tungsten, and the anode (the target) of massive tungsten. **corneal t.,** a tubelike passage sometimes seen between the layers of the cornea. **Crookes' t.,** an early form of vacuum tube by the use of which the roentgen rays were discovered. **Debove's t.,** a tube for lavage of the stomach, marked so as to show when it has reached that organ. **Depaul's t.,** a tube for performing insufflation of the lungs. **digestive t.,** canalis alimentarius. **discharge t.,** a vessel of insulating material (usually glass) provided with metal electrodes which is exhausted to a low gas pressure and permits the passage of electricity through the residual gas when a moderately high voltage is applied to the electrodes. **Dominici's t.,** a tube of silver for applying radium emanations which permits the passage of the β and γ rays only. **drainage t.,** a tube used in surgery to facilitate the escape of fluids. **dressed t.,** a rubber drainage tube with a gauze strip wound round it, the whole covered with gutta-percha. **duodenal t.,** a tube intended to be passed into the duodenum. **Durham's t.** 1. [Arthur Edward *Durham*]. A jointed tracheostomy tube. 2. [Herbert Edward *Durham*]. A small inverted test tube used in determining bacterial gas production. **empyema t.,** a rubber tube for draining the pus in cases of empyema. **Esmarch's t's,** tubes used in making roll cultures of bacteria. **esophageal t.,** a soft, flexible tube for lavage of the stomach and forcible feeding. **eustachian t.,** tuba auditiva. **fallopian t.,** tuba uterina. **feeding t.,** a tube for introducing food into the stomach. **fermentation t.,** a U-shaped tube with one arm closed for determining gas production by bacteria. **Ferrein's t's,** the convoluted uriniferous tubules. **fusion t's,** the pair of tubes used in observing and cultivating the power of fusion in eyes affected with heterophoria. **gas t.,** a roentgen-ray tube which depends for its action on the presence of residual gas: the cathode is not heated and the target is usually connected electrically to the anode. **Geissler's t., Geissler-Pluecker t.,** a discharge tube for showing the luminous effects of discharges through rarefied gases. **granulation t.,** a laryngeal intubation tube with a large head which covers any granulations that may have been formed about the wound. **Guisez's t.,** a self-retaining rubber tube for use in cancer of the esophagus. **Henle's looped t's,** tubuli renales contorti. **Hittorf t.,** Crookes' t. **hot-cathode t.,** a vacuum tube in which the cathode is electrically heated to incandescence and in which the stream of electrons depends on the temperature of the cathode. **intubation t.,** a breathing tube introduced in the air passage after tracheostomy or laryngostomy. **Jutte t.,** a form of duodenal tube for irrigation, aspiration, and feeding. **Keidel t.,** a 5 cc. bulb or ampule to which a hypodermic needle is attached by means of a rubber tube. The bulb is evacuated, the whole is sterilized and used for obtaining blood aseptically from a vein. **Kelly's t's,** the proctoscope and sigmoidoscope. **Killian's t's,** tubes for use in removing foreign bodies from the trachea and esophagus. **Kimpton-Brown t.,** a tube for performing indirect transfusion of blood. It is a cylindrical tube, terminating in a fine pipet at the lower end and having near the upper end an arm for the attachment of a simple ball hand pump. The inside of the tube is coated with paraffin to prevent the blood from coagulating. **Kobelt's t's,** the remains of the tubules of the mesonephros in the paroophoron. **Kuhn's t.,** a flexible tube of metal for use in intratracheal anesthesia. **Leiter's t's,** flexible tubes of metal to be coiled about some part of the body: cold water is passed through them so as to reduce the temperature. **Leonard t.,** cathode-ray tube. **Levin t.,** a nasal gastroduodenal catheter. **Lyster's t.,** a glass tube containing calcium hypochlorite for sterilizing water in camps. **McCollum t.,** an apparatus for keeping a patient dry when there is a large amount of drainage from a sinus. **Marten's t.,** a drainage tube with a cross piece near the end to retain the tube in place. **medullary t.,** neural t. **Mett's t's,** small glass tubes filled with coagulated egg white for testing peptic activity. **Miescher's t's.** See under *tubule.* **Miller-Abbott t.,** a double channel intestinal tube for diagnosing and treating obstructive lesions of the small intestine. **Momburg's t.** See under *belt.* **nephrostomy t.,** a tube inserted through the abdominal wall into the pelvis of the kidney, for direct drainage of the urine. **Neuber's t's,** drainage tubes of bone. **neural t.,** the epithelial tube developed from the neural plate and forming the central nervous system of the embryo; called also *medullary t., cerebromedullary t.,* and *neural canal.* **O'Beirne's t.,** a long, flexible tube for injecting fluids into the sigmoid flexure. **O'Dwyer's t.,** an intubation tube. **Olshevsky t.,** a roentgen-ray tube constructed to use only the stronger rays which pass through the target and armoring the rest of the tube. **otopharyngeal t.,** tuba auditiva. **ovarian t's,** groups of cells which grow down and are cut off from the germinal epithelial cells of the ovary. They differentiate into a primary oocyte and a follicular layer. Called also *Pflüger's t's.* **Paul-Mixter t.,** a large-calibered, flanged drainage tube of glass used for temporary intestinal anastomosis. **Pflüger's t's.** 1. The ovarian tubes. 2. The salivary tubes. **pharyngotympanic t.,** tuba auditiva. **pus t's,** pyosalpinx. **Rainey's t's,** Miescher's tubules. **Rehfuss' t.,** a specially designed stomach tube used in making the Rehfuss test. **Roida's t.,** a tube designed for the separation of motile from nonmotile bacteria. They make their way through sand, glass-wool and other obstructions. **roll t.,** a test tube in which liquid agar culture medium is placed, the tube then being tilted and rotated so that the inside of the tube becomes coated with the culture medium. **Ruysch's t.,** a very small tubular opening on the nasal septum, just below and before the nasopalatine foramen: it is a relic of the fetal Jacobson's organ. **Ryle's t.,** a thin rubber tube with an olive-shaped end used in giving a test meal. **safety t.,** a small portion of the upper end of the eustachian tube, which, being slightly open, permits a recoil of air from the tympanum when the drum membrane is suddenly driven in, thus equalizing the pressure in the tympanic cavity from the pharynx. **salivary t's,** the interlobular ducts of the salivary glands. **Schachowa's spiral t's,** tubuli renales. **Sengstaken-Blakemore t.,** a device used for the tamponade of bleeding esophageal varices, consisting of three tubes: one leading to a balloon which is inflated in the stomach, to retain the instrument in place, and compress the vessels around the cardia; one leading to a long narrow balloon by which pressure is exerted against the wall of the esophagus; and the third attached to a suction apparatus for aspirating contents of the stomach. **Southey's t's,** cannulas of small caliber pushed by means of a trocar into the tissues to drain them. **Souttar's t.,** a tube employed in the radon treatment of esophageal cancer. **sputum t.,** a graduated capillary tube for containing sputum to be rotated in the centrifuge. **stomach t.,** a tube for feeding or for washing out the stomach. **T t.,** a self-retaining drainage tube in the shape of a T. **tampon t.,** a piece of stout rubber tubing wound with iodoform gauze. It is used in plugging the rectum to control oozing and at the same time to allow the escape of gas. **test t.,** a tube of thin glass closed at one end: used for various procedures in chemistry and for observing the growth of bacterial cultures. **thoracostomy t.,** a tube inserted through an opening in the chest wall, for application of suction to the pleural cavity: used to facilitate re-expansion of the lung in spontaneous pneumothorax. **tracheostomy t.,** a curved tube to be inserted into the trachea through the opening made in tracheostomy. **uterine t.,** tuba uterina. **vacuum t.,** a glass tube from which the air has been exhausted to a high degree of vacuum. See *Crookes's t.* and *Geissler's t.* **valve t.,** a vacuum tube used to rectify an alternating current. **Veillon t.,** a piece of glass tubing with a rubber cork at one end and a plug of cotton at the other, used in bacterial culture work. **Voltolini's t.,** a tube for keeping open an incision in the tympanic membrane. **Wangensteen t.,** a suction apparatus connected with a duodenal tube for aspirating gas and fluid from the stomach and intestine. **West t.** See *West tube method,* under *method.* **x-ray t.,** a glass vacuum bulb containing two electrodes. Electrons are obtained either from gas in the tube or from a heated cathode. When suitable potential is applied, electrons travel at high velocity from cathode to anode, where they are suddenly arrested, giving rise to x-rays.

tubectomy (tu-bek′to-me). Excision of a portion of the fallopian tube.

tuber (tu′ber), pl. *tubers* or *tu′bera* [L.]. A swelling, protuberance; used as a general term in anatomical nomenclature. See also *tubercle, tuberculum, tuberositas,* and *tuberosity.* **t. annula′re,** pons. **t. ante′rius hypothal′ami,** t. cinereum. **t. calca′nei** [N A, B N A], the posteroinferior projection of the calcaneus that forms the heel. Called also *tuberosity of calcaneus.* **t. cine′reum** [N A, B N A], a small, irregular, unpaired downward projection on the base of the brain from the floor of the third ventricle; it is in front of and between the corpora mamillaria and merges anteriorly into the infundibulum. **t. coch′leae,** promontorium tympani. **eustachian t.,** an eminence on the medial wall of the tympanum, below the vestibular window. **external t. of Henle,** tuberculum mentale mandibulae. **frontal t., t. fronta′le** [N A, B N A], one of the slight rounded prominences on the frontal bone on either side above the eyes, forming the most prominent portions of the forehead. Called also *frontal eminence.* **iliopubic t.,** eminentia iliopubica. **t. ischiad'icum** [N A, B N A], **t. is'chii,** a large elongated mass on the inferior part of the posterior margin of the body of the ischium, to which several muscles are attached. Called also *ischial tuberosity.* **t. maxil'lae** [N A], **t. maxilla're** [B N A], **maxillary t.,** a rounded eminence at the posteroinferior angle of the infratemporal surface of the maxilla. Called also *tuberosity of maxilla.* **mental t.,** tuberculum mentale mandibulae. **omental t. of liver,** t. omentale hepatis. **omental t. of pancreas,** t. omentale pancreatis. **t. omenta'le hep'atis** [N A, B N A], the rounded prominence on the posteroinferior surface of the left lobe of the liver, just cranial to the lesser curvature of the stomach. Called also *omental t. of liver.* **t. omenta'le pancrea'tis** [N A, B N A], a rounded prominence chiefly on the anterior surface of the neck of the pancreas. Called also *omental t. of pancreas.* **papillary t. of liver,** processus papillaris hepatis. **parietal t., t. parieta'le** [N A, B N A], the somewhat laterally bulging prominence just superior to the superior temporal line on the external surface of the parietal bone. **t. ra'dii, t. of radius,** tuberositas radii. **sciatic t.,** t. ischiadicum. **t. val'vulae cerebel'li,** t. vermis. **t. ver'mis** [N A, B N A], the part of the vermis of the cerebellum between the folium vermis and the pyramid. **t. zygomat'icum,** tuberculum articulare ossis temporalis.

tubera (tu'ber-ah) [L.]. Plural of *tuber.*

tubercle (tu'ber-k'l). 1. A nodule, especially a solid elevation of the skin, larger in size than a papule. 2. Any small, rounded nodule produced by the *Mycobacterium tuberculosis.* It is the characteristic lesion of tuberculosis, and consists of a translucent mass, gray in color, made up of small spherical cells which contain giant cells and are surrounded by a layer of spindle-shaped connective tissue cells known as *epithelioid cells.* Called also *gray t.* 3. A nodule, or small eminence, such as a rough, rounded eminence on a bone. Called also *tuberculum* [N A]. **acoustic t.,** area vestibularis. **adductor t. of femur,** tuberculum adductorium femoris. **amygdaloid t. of Macalister,** corpus amygdaloideum. **amygdaloid t. of Schwalbe,** area vestibularis. **anatomical t.,** verruca necrogenica. **t. of anterior scalene muscle,** tuberculum musculi scaleni anterioris. **articular t. of temporal bone,** tuberculum articulare ossis temporalis. **t. of atlas, anterior,** tuberculum anterius atlantis. **t. of atlas, posterior,** tuberculum posterius atlantis. **auricular t.,** tuberculum auriculae. **Babes's t's,** cellular aggregations around degenerated neurons in the medulla oblongata and the spinal ganglia in cases of rabies and other types of encephalitis. **brachial t. of humerus,** processus supracondylaris humeri. **calcaneal t.,** processus lateralis tuberis calcanei. **Carabelli t.** See under *cusp.* **carotid t. of sixth cervical vertebra,** tuberculum caroticum vertebrae cervicalis VI. **caseous t.,** a yellowish mass of cheesy material, thought to represent a typical lesion of tuberculosis that has undergone degeneration. **caudal t. of liver,** processus caudatus hepatis. **cervical t's,** two small eminences on the femur, a *superior* on the upper and anterior part of the neck at its junction with the greater trochanter, and an *inferior* at the junction with the lesser trochanter. **t. of cervical vertebrae, anterior,** tuberculum anterius vertebrarum cervicalium. **t. of cervical vertebrae, posterior,** tuberculum posterius vertebrarum cervicalium. **Chassaignac's t.,** tuberculum caroticum vertebrae cervicalis VI. **cloacal t.,** genital t. **condyloid t.,** an eminence on the condylar process of the mandible for attachment of the lateral ligament of the temporomandibular articulation. **conglomerate t.,** a mass made up of an aggregation of many smaller nodules. **conoid t.,** tuberculum conoideum. **corniculate t.,** tuberculum corniculatum. **t's of crown of tooth,** tubercula coronae dentis. **crude t.,** caseous t. **cuneiform t.,** tuberculum cuneiforme. **darwinian t.,** tuberculum auriculae. **deltoid t.** 1. A prominence on the clavicle for attachment of the deltoid muscle. 2. Tuberositas deltoidea humeri. **dental t's,** tubercula coronae dentis. **dissection t.,** verruca necrogenica. **epiglottic t.,** tuberculum epiglotticum. **Farre's t's.** masses beneath the capsule of the liver, felt on palpation in certain cases of hepatic cancer. **fibrous t.,** a tubercle of bacillary origin which contains connective tissue elements. **t. of fibula, posterior,** apex capitis fibulae. **genial t.,** tuberculum mentale mandibulae. **genital t.,** an eminence in front of the cloaca in the early embryo, which becomes the penis or the clitoris. **Ghon t.,** the primary lesion in tuberculosis of the lungs in children, seen as a bean-shaped shadow in the roentgenogram of the lung. **gracile t.,** tuberculum nuclei gracilis. **gray t.,** the typical lesion of tuberculosis. See *tubercle,* def. 2. 2. Tuberculum cinereum. **greater t. of calcaneus,** processus medialis tuberis calcanei. **greater t. of humerus,** tuberculum majus humeri. **t. of greater multangular bone,** tuberculum ossis trapezii. **hippocampal t.,** an expansion of the hippocampus at its lower end, separating the fimbria from the gyrus dentatus. **His' t.,** a small prominence on the posteroinferior part of the pinna. **t. of humerus,** capitulum humeri. **t. of humerus, anterior, of Meckel,** tuberculum majus humeri. **t. of humerus, anterior, of Weber,** tuberculum minus humeri. **t. of humerus, external,** tuberculum majus humeri. **t. of humerus, internal,** tuberculum minus humeri. **t. of humerus, posterior,** tuberculum majus humeri. **iliopectineal t., iliopubic t.,** eminentia iliopubica. **inferior t. of Humphrey,** processus accessorius vertebrarum lumbalium. **infraglenoid t.,** tuberculum infraglenoidale. **intercondylar t.,** eminentia intercondylaris. **intercondylar t., lateral,** tuberculum intercondylare laterale. **intercondylar t., medial,** tuberculum intercondylare mediale. **intervenous t.,** tuberculum intervenosum. **intravascular t.,** a tubercle in the intima of a blood vessel. **jugular t. of occipital bone,** tuberculum jugulare ossis occipitalis. **labial t.,** tuberculum labii superioris. **lacrimal t.,** papilla lacrimalis. **lesser t. of calcaneus,** processus lateralis tuberis calcanei. **lesser t. of humerus,** tuberculum minus humeri. **Lisfranc's t.,** tuberculum musculi scaleni anterioris. **Lower's t.,** tuberculum intervenosum. **Luschka's t.,** carina urethralis vaginae. **lymphoid t.,** a lesion of tuberculosis consisting of lymphoid cells. **mamillary t. of hypothalamus,** corpus mamillare. **mamillary t. of vertebrae,** processus mamillaris vertebrarum. **marginal t. of zygomatic bone,** tuberculum marginale ossis zygomatici. **mental t.,** tuberculum mentale mandibulae. **mental t., external,** protuberantia mentalis. **mental t. of mandible,** tuberculum mentale mandibulae. **miliary t.,** one of the many minute tubercles formed in many organs in acute miliary tuberculosis. **Montgomery's t's,** greatly enlarged sebaceous glands (Morgagni's tubercles) observed on the surface of the areola of the mammary gland during pregnancy. **Morgagni's t.** 1. Bulbus olfactorius. 2. One of the small nodules on the surface of the areola of the mammary gland produced by the superficially situated large sebaceous glands. **Müller's t.,** a protrusion into the urogenital sinus caused by the downward-growing mesonephric and paramesonephric ducts. **muscular t. of atlas,** tuberculum anterius atlantis. **t. of navicular bone,** tuberculum ossis scaphoidei. **nuchal t.,** the prominence formed by the spinous process of the seventh cervical vertebra. **t. of nucleus cuneatus,** tuberculum nuclei cuneati. **t. of nucleus**

gracilis, tuberculum nuclei gracilis. **obturator t., anterior,** tuberculum obturatorium anterius. **obturator t., posterior,** tuberculum obturatorium posterius. **olfactory t.,** bulbus olfactorius. **papillary t.,** processus papillaris hepatis. **pathologic t.,** verruca necrogenica. **pharyngeal t.,** tuberculum pharyngeum. **plantar t.,** tuberositas ossis metatarsalis I. **t. of posterior process of talus, lateral,** tuberculum laterale processus posterioris tali **t. of posterior process of talus, medial,** tuberculum mediale processus posterioris tali. **postmortem t.,** verruca necrogenica. **pterygoid t.,** a boss on the inner surface of the mandible, below and behind the mylohyoid groove, for attachment of the medial pterygoid muscle. **pubic t. of pubic bone,** tuberculum pubicum ossis pubis. **rabic t's,** Babes's t's. **t. of rib,** tuberculum costae. **t. of Rolando,** tuberculum cinereum. **t. of root of zygoma,** tuberculum articulare ossis temporalis. **t. of Santorini,** tuberculum corniculatum. **scalene t.,** tuberculum musculi scaleni anterioris. **t. of scaphoid bone,** tuberculum ossis scaphoidei. **t. of sella turcica,** tuberculum sellae turcicae. **superior t. of Henle,** tuberculum obturatorium posterius. **superior t. of Humphrey,** processus mamillaris vertebrarum. **supraglenoid t.,** tuberculum supraglenoidalis. **supratragic t.,** tuberculum supratragicum. **t. of thalamus, anterior,** tuberculum anterius thalami. **t. of thalamus, posterior,** pulvinar. **thyroid t., inferior,** tuberculum thyroideum inferius. **thyroid t., superior,** tuberculum thyroideum superius. **t. of tibia,** eminentia intercondylaris. **transverse t. of fourth tarsal bone,** tuberositas ossis cuboidei. **t. of trapezium,** tuberculum ossis trapezii. **trochlear t.,** spina trochlearis. **t. of ulna,** tuberositas ulnae. **t. of upper lip,** tuberculum labii superioris. **t's of vertebra,** three elevations (*superior, inferior,* and *external*) upon the transverse process of the last thoracic vertebra, and represented on the lumbar vertebrae by more or less rudimentary structures. **Wrisberg's t.,** tuberculum cuneiforme. **yellow t.,** caseous t. **t. of zygoma, zygomatic t.,** tuberculum articulare ossis temporalis.

tubercula (tu-ber′ku-lah) [L.]. Plural of *tuberculum.*

tubercular (tu-ber′ku-lar). Of, or pertaining to, or resembling tubercles or nodules.

tuberculase (tu-ber′ku-lās). An extract of tubercle germs used for protective inoculation against tuberculosis.

tuberculated (tu-ber′ku-lāt″ed). Covered with tubercles; affected with tubercle.

tuberculation (tu-ber″ku-la′shun). The development of tubercles; the becoming affected with tubercles.

tuberculid (tu-ber′ku-lid). A papular skin lesion attributed to a state of allergy to tuberculosis. **papulonecrotic t., rosacea-like t.,** tuberculosis papulonecrotica.

tuberculigenous (tu-ber″ku-lij′ĭ-nus) [*tubercle* + Gr. *gennan* to produce]. Causing tuberculosis.

tuberculin (tu-ber′ku-lin). A sterile liquid containing the growth products of, or specific substances extracted from, the tubercle bacillus. The form first prepared (Old Tuberculin) by boiling, filtering, and concentrating a bouillon culture of tubercle bacilli, was put forth as a cure for tuberculosis by Koch in 1890 (Koch's lymph). In various forms tuberculin is used in the diagnosis of tuberculosis infection, especially in children and cattle, and also in the treatment of tuberculosis. The tuberculin test, as commonly applied, consists in the injection of tuberculin under or into the skin; the injection has no effect in nontuberculous subjects, but causes inflammation at the site of the injection in tuberculous subjects. See *tuberculin test,* under *tests.* **A.F.** See *albumose-free t.* and *Old t.* **B.E.,** bacillen emulsion t. **B.F.,** t. bouillon filtrate. **O.T.,** Old t. **P.P.D.,** purified protein derivative; Seibert's tuberculin made from three strains of human tuberculosis grown on a protein-free medium, precipitated, concentrated and subjected to ultrafiltration. **P.T.O.,** Spengler's t. **T.A.,** a preparation obtained from tubercle bacilli by extracting with $\frac{1}{10}$ normal soda solution: much the same as the original tuberculin. **T.A.F.,** albumose-free t. **T.B.E.,** bacillen emulsion t. **T.C.** (*tuberculin contagious*), von Behring's name for tuberculin which is said to be taken up by the cells of the body and there transformed into an integral part of those cells; in this form it is called *TX.* **T.F.,** t. filtrate. **T.O.,** New t. **T.R.,** New t. **albumose-free t.,** tuberculin free from albumose, used for the subcutaneous tuberculin test. **alkaline t.** See *T.A.* **autogenous t.,** autotuberculin. **bacillen emulsion t.,** tubercle cultures are dried, ground, and suspended (1 Gm.) in equal parts of water and glycerol (200 cc.). It differs from New tuberculin in that the germs are not washed nor is the supernatant fluid (T.O.) from the first centrifugalization discarded. Called also *B.E.* **v. Behring's t.** 1. Tuberculase. 2. Tulase. **Béraneck's t.,** tubercle cultures grown on a nonpeptonized, 5 per cent glycerin bouillon are filtered and the germs are extracted in 1 per cent orthophosphoric acid by long-continued shaking. This extract (basiotoxin) is mixed with an equal volume of the filtrate (acidotoxin) for use. **t. bouillon filtrate,** the clear glycerin bouillon in which tubercle cultures have been grown and from which they have been filtered out. It is not heated or concentrated. Called also *Denys' tuberculin* and *B.F.* **Buchner's t.,** tuberculoplasmin. **Calmette's t.,** purified tuberculin, prepared by precipitating old tuberculin with alcohol, washing, dissolving in water, and filtering: used in Calmette's ophthalmoreaction. Called also *t. precipitation* and *T.P.* **Denys' t.,** t. bouillon filtrate. **diagnostic t.,** a tuberculin prepared from selected stock cultures of Old tuberculin by partial concentration and addition of bovine tuberculin; called also *Moro's t.* **diaplyte t.,** Dreyer's vaccine. **Dixon's t.,** a tuberculin prepared by treating living tubercle cultures with ether and extracting in salt solution. **t. filtrate,** a tuberculin preparation made by precipitating and filtering the dissolved precipitate separately. Called also *T.F.* **Hirschfelder's t.,** oxytuberculin. **Klebs' t.** 1. Tuberculocidin. 2. Antiphthisin. 3. Selenin. **Klemperer's t.,** a tuberculin prepared from cultures of bovine tuberculosis. **Koch's t.** See *New t., Old t.* **Maragliano's t.,** a tuberculin containing all the extracts of the tubercle bacillus that are soluble in water. **Maréchal's t.,** a mixture of old tuberculin and guaiacol. **Moro's t.,** diagnostic t. **New t.,** a suspension of the fragments of tubercle germs, freed from all soluble materials and with glycerin added. It is known as tuberculin residue (Rückstand) and is abbreviated to T.R. **Old t.,** the concentrated germ-free culture medium (glycerol bouillon) in which tubercle cultures have grown. The cultures are sterilized by heat and concentrated by evaporation to one tenth their original volume. The germs are filtered out and the filtrate is used. It is a clear brown stable liquid with a characteristic odor. **perisucht t.,** Spengler's t. **purified t.,** Calmette's t. **residual t., t. residue,** the sediment left after centrifugalizing an aqueous extract of triturated tubercle bacilli. **Rosenbach's t.,** tuberculin prepared from cultures which have been infected with *Trichophyton holosericum-album,* which reduces the toxicity of the tubercle bacilli. **v. Ruck's watery extract t.,** tubercle cultures are concentrated in vacuo at 55 C. to one tenth volume and filtered. The filtrate is precipitated with an acid solution of sodium bismuth iodide. Filter, neutralize the filtrate, and filter again. Precipitate the filtrate with enough absolute alcohol to make 90 per cent alcohol, filter, and make a 1 per cent aqueous solution of the dry precipitate. **Seibert's t.** 1. See *P.P.D.* 2. A purified tuberculin (T.O.T.)

used intradermally as a test for tuberculosis. **Selter's t.,** vital t. **Spengler's t.,** a preparation from the bacilli of bovine tuberculosis. **Thamm's t.,** tuberculo-albumin. **vacuum t.,** Old tuberculin reduced in a vacuum to much less than its original volume. **Vaudremer's t.,** tuberculin prepared by macerating it in the ground up mycelia of *Aspergillus fumigatus*, which renders the tuberculin nearly free from toxicity. **vital t.,** a tuberculin prepared by triturating moist attenuated human tubercle bacilli; the preparation contains a few living tubercle bacilli of very slight virulence.

tuberculination (tu-ber″ku-lin-a′shun). Tuberculinization.

tuberculinization (tu-ber″ku-lin″i-za′shun). Treatment by use of tuberculin or the application of the tuberculin test.

tuberculinose (tu-ber′ku-lin″ōs). A modified form of tuberculin.

tuberculinotherapy (tu-ber″ku-lin″o-ther′ah-pe). The therapeutic use of tuberculin.

tuberculinum (tu-ber″ku-li′num) [L.]. Tuberculin. **t. pristi′num,** Old tuberculin. **t. pu′rum,** endotin.

tuberculitis (tu″ber-ku-li′tis) [*tubercle* + *-itis*]. Inflammation of or near a tubercle.

tuberculization (tu-ber″ku-li-za′shun). 1. Treatment with tuberculin or its modifications. 2. The formation of or conversion into tubercles.

tuberculo-albumin (tu-ber″ku-lo-al-bu′min). A preparation very much like tuberculase.

tuberculocele (tu-ber′ku-lo-sēl) [*tubercle* + Gr. *kēlē* tumor]. Tuberculous disease of the testicle.

tuberculocidal (tu-ber″ku-lo-si′dal). Destructive to *Mycobacterium tuberculosis*.

tuberculocide (tu-ber′ku-lo-sīd). An agent which is destructive to *Mycobacterium tuberculosis*.

tuberculocidin (tu-ber″ku-lo-si′din). An albumose derived from tuberculin by treating it with platinum chloride. It is used like tuberculin, but is said to be free from the objectionable characters of the latter.

tuberculoderm (tu-ber′ku-lo-derm). Any tuberculous condition or disease of the skin.

tuberculofibroid (tu-ber″ku-lo-fi′broid). Characterized by tubercle that has undergone a fibroid degeneration.

tuberculofibrosis (tu-ber″ku-lo-fi-bro′sis). Fibroid phthisis.

tuberculoid (tu-ber′ku-loid). Resembling a tubercle or tuberculosis.

tuberculoidin (tu-ber″ku-loi′din). A form of modified tuberculin cleared of its bacilli by treatment with alcohol.

tuberculoma (tu-ber″ku-lo′mah). A tumor-like mass resulting from enlargement of a caseous tubercle. **t. en plaque,** a flat plaque on the surface of the frontoparietal cortex in tuberculous meningo-encephalitis, producing the symptoms of brain tumor.

tuberculomania (tu-ber″ku-lo-ma′ne-ah) [*tuberculosis* + Gr. *mania* madness]. A morbid belief that one is affected with tuberculosis.

tuberculomucin (tu-ber″ku-lo-mu′sin). A substance resembling mucin prepared from old glycerin peptone-bouillon cultures of tubercle bacilli by periodically removing the scum of zooglea for a year: used in tuberculosis of the skin and glands.

tuberculomyces (tu-ber″ku-lom′ĭ-sēz) [*tuberculosis* + Gr. *mykēs* fungus]. A name for the group of bacteria including the *Mycobacterium tuberculosis* and similar bacteria.

tuberculonastin (tu-ber″ku-lo-nas′tin). A fatty substance or lipoid derived from tubercle bacilli; said to produce immunity to tuberculosis when injected. Cf. *nastin*.

tuberculo-opsonic (tu-ber″ku-lo-op-son′ik). Pertaining to the opsonin of tubercle bacilli.

tuberculophobia (tu-ber″ku-lo-fo′be-ah) [*tuberculosis* + Gr. *phobein* to be affrighted by]. Morbid dread of tuberculosis.

tuberculoplasmin (tu-ber″ku-lo-plas′min). A filtered watery solution of the protoplasm of moist living tubercle bacilli extracted by hydraulic pressure.

tuberculoprotein (tu-ber″ku-lo-pro′te-in). Protein derived from the bodies of tubercle bacilli.

tuberculosaccharid (tu-ber″ku-lo-sak′ah-rid). A saccharid isolated from tubercle bacilli.

tuberculosamine (tu-ber″ku-lo-sam′in). An amine occurring in tubercle bacilli.

tuberculosarium (tu-ber″ku-lo-sa′re-um). A sanatorium for the tuberculous.

tuberculosilicosis (tu-ber″ku-lo-sil″ĭ-ko′sis). Silicosis complicated by pulmonary tuberculosis.

tuberculosis (tu-ber″ku-lo′sis). An infectious disease caused by *Mycobacterium tuberculosis*, and characterized by the formation of tubercles in the tissues. These tubercles tend to spread in all directions, more especially in the route of least resistance, and may undergo caseous degeneration. Infection may also be disseminated throughout the body through the lymph vessels and blood vessels. It is attended by symptoms due to the destruction it produces, and varying with the location of the infection. When the infection is not strictly localized, the general symptoms of septic infection are present, such as hectic fever, increasing emaciation, and night-sweats. **acute miliary t.,** an acute form of tuberculosis in which minute tubercles are formed in a number of organs of the body, due to dissemination of the bacilli throughout the body by the blood stream. **adrenal t.,** Addison's disease. **aerogenic t.,** inhalation t. **anthracotic t.,** pneumoconiosis. **attenuated t.,** tuberculosis characterized by gummy and caseous lesions in the skin, with a tendency to cold abscess. **avian t.,** a variety of tuberculosis affecting various birds, including chickens and ducks, caused by *Mycobacterium tuberculosis avium*, and characterized by tubercles consisting principally of epithelioid cells. It may be communicated to other animals and man. **basal t.,** tuberculosis situated in the lower part of the affected lung. **t. of bones and joints,** tuberculosis involving the bones and joints, producing strumous arthritis, or white swelling, and cold abscess. **bovine t.,** an infection of cattle caused by *Mycobacterium bovis*, transmissible to man and other animals. **cerebral t.,** tuberculous meningitis. **cestodic t.,** a disease simulating tuberculosis, but due to excessive infestation with cestode parasites. **chicken t.,** avian tuberculosis occurring in chickens. **t. colliquati′va,** scrofuloderma. **t. cu′tis,** tuberculosis of the skin. **t. cu′tis colliquati′va,** scrofuloderma. **t. cu′tis indurati′va,** a notoriously chronic and recurrent condition occurring most often in young adult females, characteristically on the calves of the legs, with deep subcutaneous nodules or infiltrations gradually rising to the surface, forming blue plaques which become necrotic or resorb without ulceration, leaving an atrophic scar. **t. cu′tis orificia′lis,** a condition occurring in patients with systemic tuberculosis, characterized by the development, about the mucocutaneous junctions and on the skin contiguous to the body orifices, of indolent, round, shallow granulating ulcers, covered with thin crusts. **disseminated t.,** acute miliary t. **fowl t.,** avian tuberculosis occurring in fowl. **hematogenous t.,** infection caused by *Mycobacterium tuberculosis* carried through the blood stream to other organs from the primary site of infection. **hilus t.,** tuberculosis involving the hilus of the lung. **t. indurati′va,** t. cutis indurativa. **inhalation t.,** tuberculosis caused by inspiration of the tubercle bacilli into the lungs. **t. of intestines,** tuberculosis involving the intestines, marked by formation of spreading ulcers, especially of the lymphoid tissue; attended by diarrhea, and sometimes resulting in cicatricial stricture. **t. of kidney and bladder,** tuberculosis involving the urinary tract, attended by hematuria and pyuria. **t. of larynx,** tuberculosis involving the larynx, producing ulceration of the vocal cords and elsewhere on the mucosa, and attended by cough, dyspnea, and hemoptysis. **t. of lungs,** infection of the lungs caused by *Mycobacterium tuberculosis*, marked by the development of cavities in the lungs, with bronchopneumonia or fibroid pneumonia, and attended by dyspnea, cough, expectoration of purulent material, and hemoptysis. **t. lupo'sa,** lupus vulgaris. **t. of lymphatic glands,** scrofula. **miliary t.** See *acute miliary t.* **open t.,** tuberculosis in which there are lesions from which the tubercle bacilli are being discharged out of the body. **t. orificia'lis,** t. cutis orificialis. **t. papulonecrot'ica,** an eruption on the skin of children and young adults with chronic tuberculosis, appearing in successive crops, and consisting of small papules or nodules which undergo necrosis and heal with scarring. Called also *acnitis, acne scrofulosorum, acne agminata, folliclis* and *rosacea-like tuberculid.* **pulmonary t.,** t. of lungs. **t. of serous membranes,** tuberculosis involving the pleura, peritoneum, pericardium, and cerebral meninges, producing inflammation of those structures; it may also involve other organs, as the stomach, heart, or liver. **surgical t.,** tuberculosis which is amenable to treatment by surgical means. **t. ulcero'sa,** t. cutis orificialis. **uveoparotid t.,** uveoparotid fever. **t. verruco'sa, t. verruco'sa cu'tis,** a condition usually resulting from external inoculation of the tubercle bacilli into the skin, but sometimes initiated by systemic infection, with wartlike papules coalescing to form distinctly verrucous patches with an inflammatory, erythematous border. **zoogleic t.,** pseudotuberculosis.

tuberculostatic (tu-ber″ku-lo-stat'ik). Inhibiting the growth of *Mycobacterium tuberculosis.*

tuberculotic (tu-ber″ku-lot'ik). Pertaining to or affected with tuberculosis.

tuberculotoxin (tu-ber″ku-lo-tok'sin). Any toxin of the *Mycobacterium tuberculosis.*

tuberculotropic (tu-ber″ku-lo-tro'pik). Having a special affinity for the tubercle bacillus.

tuberculous (tu-ber'ku-lus). Pertaining to or affected with tuberculosis: tuberculotic; caused by the *Mycobacterium tuberculosis.*

tuberculum (tu-ber'ku-lum), pl. *tuber'cula* [L., dim. of *tuber*]. A nodule, or small eminence; used as a general term in anatomical nomenclature. Called also *tubercle.* **t. acus'ticum,** area vestibularis. **t. adducto'rium fem'oris** [N A], a small projection from the upper part of the medial epicondyle of the femur, to which the tendon of the adductor magnus muscle is attached. Called also *adductor tubercle of femur.* **t. annula're,** pons. **t. ante'rius atlan'tis** [N A, B N A], the conical eminence on the front of the anterior arch of the atlas. Called also *anterior tubercle of atlas.* **t. ante'rius thal'ami** [N A, B N A], the anterior prominent extremity of the thalamus. Called also *anterior tubercle of thalamus.* **t. ante'rius vertebra'rum cervica'lium** [N A, B N A], a tubercle on the anterior part of the extremity of each transverse process of the cervical vertebrae. Called also *anterior tubercle of cervical vertebrae.* **t. arthrit'icum,** a gouty concretion in a joint. **t. articula're os'sis tempora'lis** [N A, B N A], an enlargement of the inferior border of the zygomatic process of the temporal bone, forming the anterior boundary of the mandibular fossa and part of the anterior root of the zygoma; it gives attachment to the lateral ligament of the temporomandibular articulation. Called also *articular tubercle of temporal bone* and *tubercle of root of zygoma.* **t. auric'ulae** [N A], **t. auric'ulae [Darwin'i]** [B N A], a small projection sometimes found on the edge of the helix, and conjectured by some to be a relic of a simioid ancestry. Called also *auricular tubercle.* **t. carot'icum ver'tebrae cervica'lis VI** [N A, B N A], either of the large anterior tubercles of the sixth cervical vertebra. Called also *carotid tubercle of sixth cervical vertebra.* **t. cine'reum.** 1. [B N A] The club-shaped upper end of the posterior portion of the lateral funiculus of the medulla oblongata. Omitted in N A. 2. Tuber cinereum. **t. conoi'deum** [N A], a prominent elevation on the inferior aspect of the lateral part of the clavicle, to which the conoid part of the coracoclavicular ligament is attached. Called also *conoid tubercle.* **t. cornicula'tum** [N A], **t. cornicula'tum [Santorin'i]** [B N A], a rounded eminence near the posterior end of the aryepiglottic fold, behind the cuneiform tubercle, corresponding to the corniculate cartilage. Called also *corniculate tubercle.* **tuber'cula coro'nae den'tis** [N A, B N A], the projections on the crown of a tooth. Called also *dental cusps.* **t. cos'tae** [N A, B N A], a small eminence on the posterior surface of a rib where the neck and body join; it protrudes inferiorly and posteriorly, and bears on its medial part a surface that articulates with the transverse process of the corresponding vertebra. Called also *tubercle of rib.* **t. cunea'tum,** t. nuclei cuneati. **t. cuneifor'me** [N A], **t. cuneifor'me [Wrisber'gi]** [B N A], a rounded eminence in the posterior portion of the aryepiglottic fold, in front of the corniculate tubercle, corresponding to the cuneiform cartilage. Called also *cuneiform tubercle.* **t. doloro'sum,** a painful nodule or tubercle, such as one situated in the subcutaneous tissue near a joint, produced by enlargement of the end of a sensory nerve. **t. ephip'pii,** oliva. **t. epiglot'ticum** [N A, B N A], a backward projection on the lower part of the posterior surface of the epiglottic cartilage. Called also *epiglottic tubercle.* **t. genia'le** t. mentale mandibulae. **t. hypoglos'si,** trigonum nervi hypoglossi. **t. im'par,** a small tubercle in the midline on the floor of the pharynx of the embryo, between the ends of the mandibular and hyoid arches, which is the primordium of the tongue. **t. infraglenoida'le** [N A], a roughened area, just below the glenoid cavity of the scapula, that gives origin to the long head of the triceps muscle. Called also *tuberositas infraglenoidalis* [B N A], and *infraglenoid tubercle.* **t. intercondyla're latera'le** [N A], a lateral spur projecting upward from the intercondylar eminence at the proximal end of the tibia. Called also *t. intercondyloideum laterale* [B N A], and *lateral intercondylar tubercle.* **t. intercondyla're media'le** [N A], a medial spur projecting upward from the intercondylar eminence at the proximal end of the tibia. Called also *t. intercondyloideum mediale* [B N A], and *medial intercondylar tubercle.* **t. intercondyloi'deum,** eminentia intercondylaris. **t. intercondyloi'deum latera'le** [B N A], t. intercondylare laterale. **t. intercondyloi'deum media'le** [B N A], t. intercondylare mediale. **t. interveno'sum** [N A], **t. interveno'sum [Low'eri]** [B N A], a more or less distinct ridge across the inner surface of the right atrium between the openings of the venae cavae. Called also *intervenous tubercle.* **t. jugula're os'sis occipita'lis** [N A, B N A], a smooth eminence overlying the hypoglossal canal on the superior surface of the lateral part of the occipital bone. Called also *jugular tubercle of occipital bone.* **t. la'bii superio'ris** [N A], the slight elevation on the upper lip that marks the lower limit of the philtrum. Called also *tubercle of upper lip.* **t. latera'le proces'sus posterio'ris ta'li** [N A], the lateral eminence of the posterior process of the talus. **t. Low'eri,** t. intervenosum. **t. ma'jus hu'meri** [N A, B N A], a large flattened prominence at the upper end of the lateral surface of the humerus, just lateral to the highest part of the anatomical neck, giving attachment to the infraspinatus, the supraspinatus, and the teres minor muscles. Called also *greater tubercle of humerus.* **t. margina'le os'sis zygomat'ici** [N A], a process on the superior part of the temporal border of the zygomatic bone to which a strong slip of the temporal fascia is attached. Called also *processus* *marginalis ossis zygomatici* [B N A], and *marginal tubercle of zygomatic bone.* **t. media′le proces′sus posterio′ris ta′li** [N A], the medial eminence of the posterior process of the talus. **t. menta′le mandib′ulae** [N A, B N A], a more or less distinct prominence on the inferior border of either side of the mental protuberance of the mandible. Called also *mental tubercle of mandible.* **t. mi′nus hu′meri** [N A, B N A], a distinct prominence at the proximal end of the anterior surface of the humerus, just lateral to the anatomical neck. It gives insertion to the subscapular muscle. Called also *lesser tubercle of humerus.* **t. mus′culi scale′ni anterio′ris** [N A], the tubercle on the cranial surface of the first rib for the insertion of the anterior scalene muscle. Called also *t. scaleni [Lisfranci]* [B N A], and *tubercle of anterior scalene muscle.* **t. nu′clei cunea′ti** [N A], an enlargement of the fasciculus cuneatus in the medulla oblongata just lateral to the tubercle of the nucleus gracilis. Called also *tubercle of nucleus cuneatus.* **t. nu′clei gra′cilis** [N A], an enlargement of the fasciculus gracilis in the medulla oblongata, forming the lower lateral border of the posterior part of the fourth ventricle. Called also *clava medullae oblongatae* [B N A], and *tubercle of nucleus gracilis.* **t. obturato′rium ante′rius** [N A, B N A], a small spur sometimes present on the margin of the obturator foramen, projecting from the superior ramus of the pubis. Called also *anterior obturator tubercle.* **t. obturato′rium poste′rius** [N A, B N A], a small protuberance often present on the margin of the obturator foramen, projecting from the free edge of the acetabular fossa near the junction of the pubis and ischium. Called also *posterior obturator tubercle.* **t. os′sis multan′guli majo′ris** [B N A], t. ossis trapezii. **t. os′sis navicula′ris** [B N A], t. ossis scaphoidei. **t. os′sis scaphoi′dei** [N A], a projection on the volar surface of the scaphoid bone of the wrist, giving attachment to the transverse carpal ligament. Called also *t. ossis navicularis* [B N A], and *tubercle of scaphoid bone.* **t. os′sis trape′zii** [N A], a prominent ridge on the volar surface of the trapezium bone, forming the lateral margin of the groove that transmits the tendon of the flexor carpi radialis muscle. Called also *t. ossis multanguli majoris* [B N A], and *tubercle of trapezium.* **t. pharyn′geum** [N A, B N A], a midline eminence on the inferior surface of the basilar part of the occipital bone, for attachment of the pharynx (superior constrictor and pharyngeal raphe). Called also *pharyngeal tubercle.* **t. poste′rius atlan′tis** [N A, B N A], a variable prominence on the posterior surface of the posterior arch of the atlas, which represents a spinous process and gives attachment to the rectus capitis posterior minor muscle. Called also *posterior tubercle of atlas.* **t. poste′rius thal′ami,** pulvinar. **t. poste′rius vertebra′rum cervica′lium** [N A, B N A], a tubercle on the posterior part of the extremity of a transverse process of a cervical vertebra. Called also *posterior tubercle of cervical vertebrae.* **t. pu′bicum os′sis pu′bis** [N A, B N A], a prominent tubercle situated at the lateral end of the pubic crest and at the medial end of the superior border of the superior ramus of the pubic bone. It is the anterior medial terminal of the obturator crest and of the pecten of the pubic bone. Called also *pubic tubercle of pubic bone.* **t. retroloba′re,** His′ tubercle. **t. Santori′ni,** t. corniculatum. **t. scale′ni [Lisfran′ci]** [B N A], t. musculi scaleni anterioris. **t. seba′ceum,** milium. **t. sel′lae os′sis sphenoida′lis** [B N A], t. sellae turcicae. **t. sel′lae tur′cicae** [N A], a transverse ridge on the upper surface of the body of the sphenoid bone. It is in front of the sella turcica, back of the sulcus chiasmatis, and between the anterior clinoid processes. Called also *tubercle of sella turcica.* **t. sep′ti,** a tubercle or prominence on the upper anterior part of the nasal septum. **t. supraglenoida′le** [N A], a raised roughened area, just above the glenoid cavity of the scapula, that gives attachment to the long head of the biceps muscle of the arm. Called also *tuberositas supraglenoidalis scapulae* [B N A], and *supraglenoid tubercle.* **t. supratra′gicum** [N A, B N A], a small tubercle sometimes seen on the pinna just above the tragus. Called also *supratragic tubercle.* **t. thyreoi′deum infe′rius** [B N A], t. thyroideum inferius. **t. thyreoi′deum supe′rius** [B N A], t. thyroideum superius. **t. thyroi′deum infe′rius** [N A], a more or less distinct tubercle at the inferior end of the oblique line of the thyroid cartilage. Called also *t. thyreoideum inferius* [B N A], and *inferior thyroid tubercle.* **t. thyroi′deum supe′rius** [N A], a more or less distinct tubercle at the superior extremity of the oblique line of the thyroid cartilage. Called also *t. thyreoideum superius* [B N A], and *superior thyroid tubercle.*

tuberin (tu′ber-in). A simple globulin from potatoes.

tuberon (tu′ber-on). An oily ketone from the volatile oil of the plant tuberose.

tuberosis (tu″ber-o′sis). A condition characterized by the development of nodules. **t. cu′tis prurigino′sa,** prurigo nodularis.

tuberositas (tu″ber-os′ĭ-tas), pl. *tuberosita′tes* [L.]. An elevation or protuberance. Called also *tuberosity.* **t. coracoi′dea** [B N A]. See *tuberculum conoideum* and *linea trapezoidea.* **t. cos′tae II** [B N A], t. musculi serrati anterioris. **t. costa′lis clavic′ulae** [B N A], impressio ligamenti costoclavicularis. **t. deltoi′dea hu′meri** [N A, B N A], a rough, triangular elevation, about the middle of the anterolateral border of the shaft of the humerus, for attachment of the deltoid muscle. Called also *deltoid tuberosity of humerus.* **t. fem′oris exter′na,** epicondylus lateralis femoris. **t. fem′oris inter′na,** epicondylus medialis femoris. **t. glu′tea fem′oris** [N A], an elevation on the upper part of the shaft of the femur for attachment of the gluteus maximus muscle. Called also *gluteal tuberosity of femur.* **t. ili′aca** [N A, B N A], a roughened area on the sacropelvic surface of the ilium, between the iliac crest and the auricular surface, for the attachment of muscles and ligaments. Called also *iliac tuberosity.* **t. infraglenoida′lis** [B N A], tuberculum infraglenoidale. **t. masseter′ica** [N A, B N A], an elongated, raised and roughened area on the lateral side of the angle of the mandible, for the insertion of tendinous bundles of the masseter muscles. Called also *masseteric tuberosity.* **t. mus′culi serra′ti anterio′ris** [N A], a roughened, raised area on the second rib that gives attachment to a slip of the anterior serratus muscle. Called also *t. costae II* [B N A], and *tuberosity for serratus anterior muscle.* **t. os′sis cuboi′dei** [N A, B N A], a transverse ridge on the lower surface of the cuboid bone over which the tendon of the peroneus longus muscle plays. Called also *tuberosity of cuboid bone.* **t. os′sis metatarsa′lis I** [N A, B N A], a blunt process projecting downward and laterally from the lower surface of the base of the first metatarsal bone, to which the tendon of the peroneus longus muscle is attached. Called also *tuberosity of first metatarsal bone.* **t. os′sis metatarsa′lis V** [N A, B N A], a large conical protuberance projecting backward and laterally from the base of the fifth metatarsal bone, to which the tendon of the peroneus brevis muscle is attached. Called also *tuberosity of fifth metatarsal bone.* **t. os′sis navicula′ris** [N A, B N A], a rough protuberance on the navicular bone of the foot, projecting downward and medially, and giving attachment to the tendon of the posterior tibial muscle. Called also *tuberosity of navicular bone.* **t. patella′ris,** t. tibiae. **t. phalan′gis dista′lis ma′nus** [N A], a roughened, raised bony mass on the palmar surface of the tip of a distal phalanx of the hand. Called also *t. unguicularis manus* [B N A], and *distal tuberosity of fingers.* **t. phalan′gis dista′lis pe′dis** [N A], a roughened, raised bony mass on the plantar surface of the tip of a distal phalanx of the foot. Called also *t. unguicularis pedis* [B N A], and *distal tuberosity of toes.* **t. pterygoi'dea mandib'ulae** [N A, B N A], a roughened area on the inner side of the angle of the mandible for the insertion of the internal pterygoid muscle. Called also *pterygoid tuberosity of mandible.* **t. ra'dii** [N A, B N A], the tuberosity on the anterior inner surface of the neck of the radius, for the insertion of the tendon of the biceps muscle. Called also *radial tuberosity.* **t. sacra'lis** [N A, B N A], a roughened area on the pars lateralis of the sacrum, on the dorsal surface between the lateral sacral crest and the auricular surface, which gives attachment to the sacrotuberous and sacrospinous ligaments. Called also *sacral tuberosity.* **t. supraglenoida'lis** [B N A], tuberculum supraglenoidale. **t. tib'iae** [N A, B N A], a longitudinally elongated, raised and roughened area on the anterior crest of the tibia, located just distal to the intercondylar eminence, and giving attachment to the patellar ligament. Called also *tuberosity of tibia.* **t. tib'iae exter'na,** condylus lateralis tibiae. **t. tib'iae inter'na,** condylus medialis tibiae. **t. ul'nae** [N A, B N A], a large roughened area on the volar surface of the ulna, located just distal to the coronoid process, and giving attachment to the brachialis muscle. Called also *tuberosity of ulna.* **t. unguicula'ris ma'nus** [B N A], t. phalangis distalis manus. **t. unguicula'ris pe'dis** [B N A], t. phalangis distalis pedis.

tuberositates (tu″ber-os″ĭ-tah'tēs) [L.]. Plural of *tuberositas.*

tuberosity (tu″ber-os'ĭ-te). An elevation or protuberance. Called also *tuberositas.* **t. for anterior serratus muscle,** tuberositas musculi serrati anterioris. **bicipital t.,** tuberositas radii. **t. of calcaneus,** tuber calcanei. **t. of clavicle,** impressio ligamenti costoclavicularis. **coracoid t.** See *tuberculum conoideum* and *linea trapezoidea.* **costal t. of clavicle,** impressio ligamenti costoclavicularis. **t. of cuboid bone,** tuberositas ossis cuboidei. **deltoid t. of humerus,** tuberositas deltoidea humeri. **distal t. of fingers,** tuberositas phalangis distalis manus. **distal t. of toes,** tuberositas phalangis distalis pedis. **t. of femur, external,** epicondylus lateralis femoris. **t. of femur, internal,** epicondylus medialis femoris. **t. of femur, lateral,** epicondylus lateralis femoris. **t. of femur, medial,** epicondylus medialis femoris. **t. of fifth metatarsal bone,** tuberositas ossis metatarsalis V. **t. of first carpal bone,** tuberculum ossis scaphoidei. **t. of first metatarsal bone,** tuberositas ossis metatarsalis I. **t. of fourth tarsal bone,** tuberositas ossis cuboidei. **gluteal t. of femur,** tuberositas glutea femoris. **greater t. of humerus,** tuberculum majus humeri. **t. of greater multangular bone,** tuberculum ossis trapezii. **t's of humerus,** the three elevations on the humerus. See *tuberculum majus humeri, tuberculum minus humeri,* and *tuberositas deltoidea humeri.* **iliac t.,** tuberositas iliaca. **infraglenoid t.,** tuberculum infraglenoidale. **ischial t., t. of ischium,** tuber ischiadicum. **lesser t. of humerus,** tuberculum minus humeri. **malar t.,** the prominence of the zygomatic bone. **masseteric t.,** tuberositas masseterica. **t. of maxilla,** tuber maxillae. **t. of navicular bone,** tuberositas ossis navicularis. **patellar t.,** tuberositas tibiae. **pterygoid t. of mandible,** tuberositas pterygoidea mandibulae. **t. of pubic bone,** tuberculum pubicum ossis pubis. **pyramidal t. of palatine bone,** processus pyramidalis ossis palatini. **radial t., t. of radius,** tuberositas radii. **sacral t.,** tuberositas sacralis. **t. of scaphoid bone.** 1. Tuberculum ossis scaphoidei. 2. Tuberositas ossis navicularis. **scapular t. of Henle,** processus coracoideus scapulae. **t. of second rib, t. for serratus anterior muscle,** tuberositas musculi serrati anterioris. **supraglenoid t.,** tuberculum supraglenoidale. **t. of tibia,** tuberositas tibiae. **t. of tibia, external,** condylus lateralis tibiae. **t. of tibia, internal,** condylus medialis tibiae. **t. of trapezium,** tuberculum ossis trapezii. **t. of ulna,** tuberositas ulnae. **ungual t., unguicular t.** See *tuberositas phalangis distalis manus* and *tuberositas phalangis distalis pedis.*

tuberous (tu'ber-us). Covered with tubers; knobby.

tubiferous (tu-bif'er-us) [L. *tuber* + *ferre* to bear]. Having tubers; tuberous.

tubo-abdominal (tu″bo-ab-dom'ĭ-nal). Pertaining to the oviduct and the abdomen.

tubo-adnexopexy (tu″bo-ad-nek'so-pek″se). The operation of suturing the uterine adnexa in a fixed position.

tubocurarine (tu″bo-ku-rah'rin). An alkaloid isolated from the bark and stems of *Chondodendron tomentosum:* used as a skeletal muscle relaxant. **dimethyl t.,** chemical name: O-methyl-d-tubocurarine: used as a muscle relaxant.

tuboligamentous (tu″bo-lig″ah-men'tus). Pertaining to a uterine tube and a broad ligament.

tubo-ovarian (tu″bo-o-va're-an). Of or pertaining to a uterine tube and ovary.

tubo-ovariotomy (tu″bo-o-va″re-ot'o-me). Excision of the ovaries and uterine tubes.

tubo-ovaritis (tu″bo-o″vah-ri'tis). Salpingo-oophoritis.

tuboperitoneal (tu″bo-per″ĭ-to-ne'al). Pertaining to a uterine tube and the peritoneum.

tuborrhea (tu″bo-re'ah) [*tube* + Gr. *rhoia* flow]. A condition marked by a discharge from the auditory tube.

tubotorsion (tu″bo-tor'shun). A twisting of a tube, especially of the auditory tube.

tubotympanal (tu″bo-tim'pah-nal). Pertaining to the auditory tube and the tympanic cavity.

tubo-uterine (tu″bo-u'ter-in). Pertaining to a uterine tube and the uterus.

tubovaginal (tu″bo-vaj'ĭ-nal). Pertaining to a uterine tube and the vagina.

tubular (tu'bu-lar) [*L. tubularis*]. Shaped like a tube; of or pertaining to a tubule.

tubulature (tu'bu-lah-tūr) [L. *tuba* tube]. The tube of a receiver or retort.

tubule (tu'būl). A small tube. Called also *tubulus.* **Albarran's t's,** small branching tubules in the cervical part of the prostate gland. **Bellinis' t's,** tubuli renales recti. **biliferous t.,** any small channel conveying bile. **caroticotympanic t's,** canaliculi caroticotympanici. **collecting t's,** channels through which fluids pass from the secreting cells. See *tubuli renales recti.* **connecting t's,** channels connecting other tubules, such as the arching portion of a renal tubule that connects the distal convoluted tubule with the straight tubule. **convoluted t's,** channels which follow a tortuous course. See *tubuli renales contorti* and *tubuli seminiferi contorti.* **convoluted t., distal.** See *tubuli renales contorti.* **convoluted t., proximal.** See *tubuli renales contorti.* **dental t's, dentinal t's,** canaliculi dentales. **discharging t's,** channels by which a fluid is discharged from the substance of the gland or organ in which it is secreted. See *tubuli renales recti.* **Ferrein's t's,** the portions of the renal tubules making up the pars radiata of the lobules of the kidney cortex. **galactophorous t's,** lactiferous t's. **Henle's t's,** the straight ascending and descending portions of a renal tubule forming Henle's loop. **Kobelt's t's.** 1. The outer series of tubules in the epoophoron. 2. A similar series of tubules in the paradidymis of the male. **lactiferous t's,** small channels for the passage of milk from the secreting cells in the mammary gland. **mesonephric t's,** the tubules comprising the mesonephros, or temporary kidney of amniotes. **metanephric t's,** the tubules comprising the permanent kidney of amniotes. **Miescher's t's,** large elongated cysts containing the parasites, found in the muscles of subjects infected with sarcosporidia. **paraurethral t's,** ductus paraurethrales. **pronephric t's,** the tubules comprising the primitive kidney of vertebrates, rudimentary in amniotes. **Rainey's t's,** Miescher's t's. **renal t's,** tubuli renales. **renal t's, convoluted,** tubuli renales contorti. **renal t's, straight** 1. Tubuli renales recti. 2. See *Henle's tubule.* **segmental t's,** the tubules of the mesonephros. **seminiferous t's,** channels in the testis in which the spermatozoa develop and through which they leave the gland. See *tubuli seminiferi contorti* and *tubuli seminiferi recti.* **seminiferous t's, convoluted,** tubuli seminiferi contorti. **seminiferous t's, straight,** tubuli seminiferi recti. **Skene's t's,** ductus paraurethrales. **spiral t's,** channels which follow a spiral course. See *tubuli renales contorti.* **straight t's,** channels which follow a comparatively straight course. See *tubuli renales recti* and *tubuli seminiferi recti.* **subtracheal t.,** ductus thyroglossus. **uriniferous t's, uriniparous t's,** channels for the passage of urine. See *tubuli renales.* **vertical t's,** the inner set of tubules in the epoophoron.

tubuli (tu′bu-li) [L.]. Plural of *tubulus.*

tubulization (tu″bu-li-za′shun). Foramitti's method of treating injured nerves by isolating the nerve stump in an absorbable cylinder which serves as a guide for new growth.

tubulocyst (tu′bu-lo-sist). Any cystic dilatation of an obsolete canal or functionless duct.

tubulodermoid (tu″bu-lo-der′moid). A dermoid tumor due to the persistence of a fetal tube.

tubuloracemose (tu″bu-lo-ras′ĕ-mōs). Both tubular and racemose.

tubulorrhexis (tu″bu-lo-rek′sis) [*tubule* + Gr. *rhēxis* a breaking]. Disruption of continuity of kidney tubules, the basement membrane being suddenly interrupted, or disintegrated into fibrils.

tubulosaccular (tu″bu-lo-sak′u-lar). Both tubular and saccular.

tubulous (tu′bu-lus). Containing tubules.

tubulus (tu′bu-lus), pl. *tu′buli* [L., dim. of *tubus*]. A small tube; used as a general term in anatomical nomenclature. Called also *tubule.* **t. bilif′erus,** a channel for conveying bile. See *ductus cysticus.* **tu′buli contor′ti,** convoluted tubules. See *tubuli renales contorti* and *tubuli seminiferi contorti.* **tu′buli rec′ti,** straight tubules. See *tubuli renales recti* and *tubuli seminiferi recti.* **tu′buli rena′les** [N A, B N A], the minute secretory and collecting canals, made up of basement membrane lined with epithelium, that form the substance of the kidneys. Called also *renal tubules.* **tu′buli rena′les contor′ti** [N A, B N A], the convoluted secretory portions of the renal tubules, found in the renal cortex. Called also *convoluted renal tubules.* The *proximal convoluted tubule* begins at the renal corpuscle and is continuous with the descending portion of Henle's loop; after passing back near the point of origin of the tubule, the ascending portion of the loop is continuous with the *distal convoluted tubule.* **tu′buli rena′les rec′ti** [N A, B N A], the excretory or collecting portions of the renal tubules, each of which descends from the distal convoluted tubule through the medulla, joining with others to form a common duct that opens at the apex of a renal papilla. Called also *straight renal tubules.* **tu′buli seminif′eri contor′ti** [N A, B N A], the numerous delicate, contorted canals within each lobule of the testis, from whose epithelial linings the spermatozoa are formed. Called also *convoluted seminiferous tubules.* **tu′buli seminif′eri rec′ti** [N A, B N A], the straight terminal portions of the seminiferous tubules, which form the rete testis. Called also *straight seminiferous tubules.*

tubus (tu′bus), pl. *tu′bi* [L.]. Tube. **t. digesto′rius** [B N A], canalis alimentarius.

Tuerck. See *Türck.*

Tuffier's operation, test (te′fe-āz) [Marin Théodore *Tuffier,* surgeon in Paris, 1857–1929]. See under *operation* and *tests.*

Tuffnell's diet, treatment (tuf′nelz) [Thomas Joliffe *Tuffnell,* English surgeon, 1819–1885]. See under *diet* and *treatment.*

tuft (tuft). A small clump or cluster; a coil. **enamel t's,** groups or bunches of poorly calcified enamel rods extending from the dento-enamel junction through about one third the thickness of the enamel. **hair t's,** groups of several hairs from one follicle, consisting of one main hair and certain secondary hairs. **malpighian t's, renal t's,** glomeruli renis. **synovial t's,** villi synoviales.

tugging (tug′ing). A pulling sensation. **tracheal t.,** a pulling sensation in the trachea, due to aneurysm of the arch of the aorta.

tularemia (too″lah-re′me-ah) [*Tulare* a district in California, where the disease was first described]. A disease of rodents, resembling plague, which is transmitted by the bites of flies, fleas, ticks, and lice, and may be acquired by man through handling of infected animals. It is caused by *Pasteurella tularensis.* In man the disease is marked by the formation of an ulcer at the site of inoculation, followed by inflammation of the lymph glands and the development of severe constitutional symptoms such as headache and other pains, chills and rapid rise of temperature. Also called *deerfly fever, Pahvant Valley plague, rabbit fever, alkali disease* and *Francis' disease.*

tulase (too′lās). Von Behring's fluid, used by him in the treatment of tuberculosis.

tulle gras (tul-grah′) [Fr. "fatty tulle"]. A close-meshed net cut into squares and impregnated with soft paraffin, Peruvian balsam and vegetable oil: used in treating raw surfaces.

tulose (tu′lōs). Tulase.

Tulpius' valve (tul′pe-us) [Nikolaas *Tulpius,* Dutch physician, 1593–1674]. See under *valve.*

tumefacient (tu″me-fa′shent) [L. *tumefaciens*]. Tending to cause or causing a swelling.

tumefaction (tu″me-fak′shun) [L. *tumefactio*]. A swelling; the state of being swollen, or the act of swelling; puffiness; edema.

tumentia (tu-men′she-ah) [L.]. Swelling. **vasomotor t.,** irregular partial swelling of the lower limbs, and sometimes of the arms associated with vasomotor changes.

tumescence (tu-mes′ens). 1. The condition of being tumid or swollen. 2. A swelling.

tumeur (too-mer′) [Fr.]. Tumor. **t. perlée** (too-mer′ per-la′) [Fr. "pearly tumor"], cholesteatoma. **t. pileuse** (too-mer′ pe-luz′) [Fr. "hairy tumor"], trichobezoar.

tumid (tu′mid) [L. *tumidus*]. Swollen or edematous.

tumor (tu′mor) [L., from *tumere* to swell]. **1.** Swelling, one of the cardinal signs of inflammation; morbid enlargement. 2. A neoplasm. A mass of new tissue which persists and grows independently of its surrounding structures, and which has no physiologic use. **Abrikossoff's t., Abrikossov's t.,** myoblastoma. **acoustic nerve t.,** a tumor growing from the sheath of the acoustic nerve at the cerebropontine angle. **acute splenic t.,** a swelling resulting from acute splenitis. **adenoid t.,** adenoma. **adipose t.,** lipoma. **adrenal rest t.,** a tumor thought to arise from adrenal rests. See *masculinovoblastoma.* **t. al′bus,** white swelling; tuberculosis of a bone or joint. **t. al′bus pyo′genes,** a chronic inflammation of gunshot injuries of the bones and joints marked by great swelling of the capsule of the joint and surrounding soft parts, which become converted into a gelatinous, edematous granulation tissue (A. Tietze). **aniline t.,** cancer appearing in workers in the synthetic aniline dye industry. **benign t.,** any tumor not likely to recur after removal; an innocent tumor. **blood t.,** a hematoma; also an aneurysm. **Brenner t.,** a tumor of the ovary whose structure consists of groups of epithelial cells lying in a fibrous connecting tissue stroma. When small the tumor may be solid, resembling fibroma; when large it may appear like a cystadenoma with nodular masses of the tumor (Brenner nodules) in the cyst wall. Called by Brenner *oophoroma folliculare*. **Brooke's t.,** epithelioma adenoides cysticum. **Brown-Pearce t.,** a malignant carcinoma of the skin having very little stroma and an irregular cell arrangement, and metastasizing early. **butyroid t.,** a collection of material in the mammary gland closely resembling butter. **carotid body t.,** a firm round mass at the bifurcation of the common carotid artery, with nests of large polyhedral cells in alveolar or organoid arrangement; usually asymptomatic, but sometimes causing dizziness and nausea or vomiting. **cartilaginous t.,** a chondroma or an enchondroma. **cavernous t.,** cavernoma. **cellular t.,** a tumor made up chiefly of cells in a homogeneous stroma. **chromaffin-cell t.,** pheochromocytoma. **Cock's peculiar t.,** septic ulceration of a neglected sebaceous cyst of the scalp, simulting an epithelioma. **t. col'li,** a tumor in the neck. **colloid t.,** myxoma. **connective-tissue t.,** any tumor developed from some structure of the connective tissue, such as a lipoma, fibroma, glioma, chondroma, or sarcoma. **craniopharyngeal duct t.,** craniopharyngioma. **cystic t.,** one not solid, but more or less hollow. **dermoid t.,** a tumor which contains fatty cutaneous elements, and sometimes hair, nails, etc. **desmoid t.,** a hard fibrous tumor. **dumb-bell t.,** hourglass t. **eiloid t.,** a skin tumor having the look of a coil of intestine. **embryoplastic t.,** one due to the growth of persistent embryo cells. **encysted t.,** a tumor enclosed in a membranous sac. **epithelial t.,** a tumor containing epithelium; an organized tumor. **erectile t.,** one made up of erectile tissue. **Ewing's t.,** a malignant tumor of the bone which always arises in medullary tissue, occurring more often in cylindrical bones, with pain, fever, and leukocytosis as prominent symptoms. **false t.,** one due to extravasations, exudation, echinococcus, or retained sebaceous matter. **fatty t.,** lipoma. **fecal t.,** stercoroma. **fibrocellular t.,** fibroma. **fibroid t.,** fibroma. **fibroplastic t.,** a variety of spindle-celled sarcoma. **fluid t.,** lymphangioma cysticum. **follicular t.,** a sebaceous cyst; a dilated sebaceous follicle. **fungating t.,** a tumor with exuberant granulation. **gelatinous t.,** myxoma. **giant-cell t.,** a tumor containing large numbers of giant cells, especially such a tumor in bone, i.e., benign myeloid sarcoma. **glassblowers' t.,** tumor of the parotid gland occurring as an occupational disease in glassblowers. **glomus t.,** glomangioma. **granulation t.,** a granuloma. **granulosa t., granulosa cell t.,** an ovarian tumor originating in the cells of the primordial membrana granulosa. It is associated with excessive production of estrin inducing endometrial hyperplasia with menorrhagia. Called also *folliculoma* and *oophoroma*. **Grawitz's t's of the kidney,** hypernephroma; the tumors formerly known as adenomas of the kidney, but which Grawitz thought to be an overgrowth of fetal inclusion in the midst of the kidney substance of particles of suprarenal glandular tissue: now considered carcinoma of the renal parenchyma. **Gubler's t.,** a tumor on the back of the wrist in cases of paralysis of the extensors of the hand. **gummy t.,** gumma. **heterologous t.,** one made up of tissue which differs from that in which it grows. **heterotypic t.,** heterologous t. **histioid t.,** one which is formed of a single tissue resembling that of the surrounding parts. **homoiotypic t., homologous t.,** a tumor which resembles the surrounding parts in its structure. **hourglass t.,** a spinal tumor made up of intradural and extradural masses joined by a narrow pedicle passing through an enlarged intervertebral foramen. **Hürthle cell t.,** a tumor arising from and including Hürthle cells of the thyroid gland. **hylic t.,** hyloma. **infiltrating t.,** a tumor which is not clearly marked off from the surrounding tissue. **innocent t.,** benign t. **iron-hard t.,** Reidel's struma. **islet cell t.,** a tumor of the islands of Langerhans. **ivory-like t.,** osteoma eburneum. **Krompecher's t.,** rodent ulcer. **Krukenberg's t.,** a special type of carcinoma of the ovary, usually metastatic from cancer of the gastro-intestinal tract, especially of the stomach. It is characterized by areas of mucoid degeneration and the presence of signet-ring-like cells. Called also *carcinoma mucocellulare* and, by Krukenberg, *fibrosarcoma ovarii mucocellulare carcinomatodes*. **lacteal t.,** a mammary abscess or galactocele. **lepidic t.,** lepidoma. **t. lie'nis,** enlargement of the spleen less in degree than splenomegaly. **limbal t.,** a tumor situated at the margin between the cornea and the conjunctiva. **malignant t.,** one which is likely to progress and eventually destroy life. **march t.,** syndesmitis metatarsea. **margaroid t.,** a cholesteatoma. **migrated t., migratory t.,** a tumor arising from a portion of a primary tumor which has become detached from its original location and fixed in some other place or lies free in a cavity. **mixed t.,** a tumor composed of more than one type of neoplastic tissue; especially "a complex embryonal tumor of local origin, which reproduces the normal development of the tissues and organs of the affected part" (Ewing). **mucous t.,** a myxoma. **muscular t.,** a myoma. **Nélaton's t.,** a dermoid tumor of the wall of the abdomen. **oozing t.,** a rare disease, consisting of a large, flat tumor on one or both labia majora, divided with deep fissures, and discharging a large amount of acrid, offensive fluid. **organoid t.,** a teratoma. **Pancoast's t.,** pulmonary sulcus t. **papillary t.,** a papilloma. **pearl t., pearly t.,** cholesteatoma. **phantom t.,** an abdominal swelling not due to a structural change, but to a neurosis; it is generally due to gaseous distention of the bowels. **potato t.,** a hard nodular tumor of the carotid body. **Pott's puffy t.,** a circumscribed edema of the scalp associated with osteomyelitis of the skull bones. **pseudointraligamentous t.,** a kind of ovarian tumor simulating intraligamentous tumors, but in reality adherent to the posterior surface of the broad ligament. **pulmonary sulcus t.,** one at the apex of the chest, extending outward to destroy the ribs and vertebrae and invading the brachial plexus. Called also *Pancoast's t.* **ranine t.,** ranula. **Rathke's t., Rathke's pouch t.,** craniopharyngioma. **Recklinghausen's t.,** adenoleiomyofibroma of the posterior uterine wall or of the wall of an oviduct. **rind t.,** lepidoma. **Rokitansky's t.,** a kind of dropsy of the graafian follicle, forming a small, pedunculated cyst, and giving the ovary the appearance of a bunch of grapes. **sacrococcygeal t.,** a form of spina bifida containing teratomatous tissue. **sand t.,** psammoma. **Schloffer's t.,** inflammatory swelling of the abdomen after herniotomy or any other abdominal operation. **Schmincke t.,** a lymphoepithelioma originating in Waldeyer's ring of tissue in the nasopharynx and extending through the base of the skull into the cranium to involve the cerebral nerves at the base of the brain. It metastasizes to the cervical lymph nodes, the lungs, abdominal viscera, and the bones. **sebaceous t.,** a cyst formed by the retention of the secretions of a sebaceous gland. **sheath t.,** a tumor of the sheaths of the brain, including meningioma and acoustic nerve tumor. **Spiegler's t's,** multiple benign epitheliomata occurring in the scalp. **Steiner's t's,** Jeanselme's nodules. **stercoral t.,** stercoroma. **superior sulcus t.,** pulmonary sulcus t. **teratoid t.,** teratoma. **theca-cell t.,** thecoma; a fibroid-like tumor of the ovary containing yellow areas of lipoid material derived from theca cells: regarded by some as a form of granulosa-cell tumor. Called also *fibroma thecocellulare xanthomatodes*. **tomato t.,** multiple benign epithelioma of the scalp. **transition t.,** one which recurs after removal and then shows malignant characters. **tridermic t.,** a dermoid cyst derived from the three embryonic layers. **true t.,** any tumor produced by proliferation. **turban t.,** multiple benign epitheliomata of the scalp grouped together so as to cover the entire scalp. **varicose t.,** a swelling of purple color, composed of dilated veins. **vascular t.** 1. An aneurysm. 2. An angioma. 3. A bleeding internal hemorrhoidal growth. **villous t.,** papilloma. **warty cicatricial t.,** a neoplasm which appears in a set of warty growths in parallel lines on the surface of a scar: it often breaks down and becomes what is known as Marjolin's ulcer. **white t.,** chronic tuberculous arthritis. **Wilms' t.,** embryonal carcinosarcoma of the kidney. See under *carcinosarcoma.*

tumoraffin (tu″mor-af′in) [*tumor* + L. *affinis* related]. Having a special affinity for tumor cells; oncotropic.

tumorcidin (tu″mor-si′din). A serum derived from animals that have been treated with injections of gonad substances: used for the prevention of recurrence of malignant tumors after operation.

tumoricidal (tu″mor-ĭ-si′dal). Destructive to cancer cells.

tumorigenesis (tu″mor-ĭ-jen′e-sis). The production of tumors.

tumorigenic (tu″mor-ĭ-jen′ik). Causing or producing tumors.

tumorous (tu′mor-us). Of the nature of a tumor.

tumultus (tu-mul′tus) [L.]. Excessive organic action or motility.

Tunga (tung′gah). A genus of fleas of the family Hectopsyllidae. Five other species of the genus are known, in addition to *T. penetrans,* one of which occurs in Brazil and one in China. **T. pen′etrans,** a species of fleas widely distributed in the tropical regions of America and Africa. The fertilized female burrows into the skin of the feet, often beneath the nail, where it produces intense irritation and sometimes leads to spontaneous amputation of the digit.

tungiasis (tung-gi′ah-sis). Infestation of the skin with *Tunga penetrans.*

tungstate (tung′stāt). A salt of tungstic acid.

tungsten (tung′sten) [Swed. "heavy stone"]. The chemical element of atomic number 74, symbol W, and atomic weight 183.85: used in electric light filaments and in steel alloys to secure hardness.

tunic (tu′nik). A covering or coat. See *tunica.* **Bichat's t.,** tunica intima vasorum. **Bruecke's t.,** tunica nervea of Bruecke. **fibrous t.,** tunica fibrosa. **fibrous t. of eyeball,** tunica fibrosa bulbi. **fibrous t. of liver,** tunica fibrosa hepatis. **mucous t.,** tunica mucosa. **muscular t.,** tunica muscularis. **pharyngeal t., pharyngobasilar t.,** fascia pharyngobasilaris. **proper t.,** tunica propria. **Ruysch's t.,** lamina choriocapillaris. **serous t.,** tunica serosa. **t's of spermatic cord and testis,** tunicae funiculi spermatici et testis.

tunica (tu′nĭ-kah), pl. *tu′nicae* [L.]. A covering or coat; used in anatomical nomenclature as a general term to designate a membrane or other structure covering or lining a body part or organ. Called also *tunic.* **t. abdomina′lis,** the aponeurosis of the abdominal muscles in certain quadrupeds, as the horse. **t. adna′ta oc′uli,** tunica conjunctiva; sometimes applied specifically to the tunica conjunctiva bulbi. **t. adna′ta tes′tis,** lamina parietalis tunicae vaginalis testis. **t. adventi′tia** [N A, B N A], the outer coat of various tubular structures, made up of connective tissue and elastic fibers. **t. adventi′tia duc′tus deferen′tis** [N A, B N A], the adventitious coat of the ductus deferens. **t. adventi′tia esoph′agi** [N A], the adventitious coat of the esophagus. **t. adventi′tia tu′bae uteri′nae** [B N A], tela subserosa tubae uterinae. **t. adventi′tia ure′teris** [N A, B N A], the adventitious coat of the ureter. **t. adventi′tia vaso′rum,** t. externa vasorum. **t. adventi′tia vesic′ulae semina′lis** [N A, B N A], the adventitious coat of the seminal vesicle. **t. albugin′ea** [N A, B N A], a dense, white, fibrous sheath enclosing a part or organ. **t. albugin′ea cor′poris spongio′si** [N A], the dense, white, fibroelastic sheath that encloses the corpus spongiosum of the penis. **t. albugin′ea corpo′rum cavernoso′rum** [N A, B N A], the dense, white, fibroelastic sheath that encloses the corpora cavernosi penis. Its superficial, longitudinal fibers form a tunic surrounding both corpora, and the deep circularly coursing fibers surround them separately, uniting medially to form the septum of the penis. **t. albugin′ea lie′nis** [B N A], t. fibrosa lienis. **t. albugin′ea tes′tis** [N A, B N A], the dense, white, inelastic tissue immediately covering the testis, beneath the visceral layer of the tunica vaginalis. **t. conjuncti′va** [N A], the thin, transparent mucous membrane lining the eyelids and covering the front surface of the eyeball. Called also *conjunctiva* [B N A]. It comprises the tunica conjunctiva bulbi and the tunica conjunctiva palpebrarum. **t. conjuncti′va bul′bi** [N A], **t. conjuncti′va bul′bi oc′uli** [B N A], the portion of the tunica conjunctiva covering the cornea and front part of the sclera, appearing white because of the sclera behind it. Called also *bulbar conjunctiva.* **t. conjuncti′va palpebra′rum** [N A, B N A], the portion of the tunica conjunctiva lining the eyelids, appearing red because of its great vascularity. Called also *palpebral conjunctiva.* **t. dar′tos** [N A, B N A], a layer of smooth muscle fibers situated in the superficial fascia of the scrotum; the deeper fibers help to form the septum of the scrotum. Called also *dartos.* **t. elas′tica inter′na,** t. intima vasorum. **t. ex′terna the′cae follic′uli** [N A, B N A], the external, fibrous layer of the theca folliculi. **t. exter′na vaso′rum** [N A], **t. exter′na vaso′rum [adventi′cia]** [B N A], the outer, fibroelastic coat of a blood vessel. **t. fibro′sa** [N A, B N A], an enveloping fibrous membrane. Called also *fibrous tunic.* **t. fibro′sa bul′bi** [N A], the outer of the three tunics of the eye, comprising the cornea and the sclera. Called also *t. fibrosa oculi* [B N A], and *fibrous tunic of eyeball.* **t. fibro′sa hep′atis** [N A], the fibroelastic layer that surrounds the liver beneath the peritoneum; it is continuous at the hepatic portal with the perivascular fibrous capsule. Called also *fibrous tunic of liver.* **t. fibro′sa lie′nis** [N A], the fibroelastic coat of the spleen. Called also *t. albuginea lienis* [B N A]. **t. fibro′sa oc′uli** [B N A], t. fibrosa bulbi. **t. fibro′sa re′nis** [B N A], capsula fibrosa renis. **tu′nicae funic′uli spermat′ici** [N A, B N A], the coverings of the spermatic cord. See *tunicae funiculi spermatici et testis.* **tu′nicae funic′uli spermat′ici et tes′tis** [N A], the coverings of the spermatic cord and testis, comprising the external spermatic fascia, the cremasteric muscle and fascia, the internal spermatic fascia, and the tunica vaginalis testis. Called also *tunics of spermatic cord and testis.* **t. inter′na bul′bi** [N A], the internal nervous tunic of the eye. See *retina.* **t. inter′na the′cae follic′uli** [N A, B N A], the inner, vascular layer of the theca folliculi. **t. in′tima vaso′rum** [N A, B N A], the inner coat of the blood vessels, made up of endothelial cells surrounded by longitudinal elastic fibers and connective tissue. **t. me′dia vaso′rum** [N A, B N A], the middle coat of the blood vessels, made up of transverse elastic and muscle fibers. **t. muco′sa** [N A, B N A], the mucous membrane lining of various tubular structures, comprising the epithelium, basement membrane, lamina propria mucosae, and lamina muscularis mucosae. Called also *mucous tunic.* **t. muco′sa bronchio′rum** [N A, B N A], the mucous membrane lining the bronchi. **t. muco′sa ca′vi tym′pani** [N A], the mucous membrane covering the walls and much of the contents of the tympanic cavity. Called also *t. mucosa tympanica* [B N A], and *mucous coat of tympanic cavity.* **t. muco′sa co′li** [N A, B N A], the mucous coat of the colon. **t. muco′sa duc′tus deferen′tis** [N A, B N A], the mucous coat of the ductus deferens. **t. muco′sa esoph′agi** [N A], the mucous coat of the esophagus. **t. muco′sa intesti′ni rec′ti** [B N A], t. mucosa recti. **t. muco′sa intesti′ni ten′uis** [N A, B N A], the mucous coat of the small intestine. **t. muco′sa laryn′gis** [N A, B N A], the mucous coat of the larynx. **t. muco′sa lin′guae** [N A, B N A], the mucous membrane covering the tongue. **t. muco′sa na′si** [N A], the mucous membrane lining the nasal cavity. Called also *membrana mucosa nasi* [B N A]. **t. muco′sa o′ris** [N A, B N A], the tunica mucosa of the mouth. **t. muco′sa pharyn′gis** [N A, B N A], the mucous coat of the pharynx. **t. muco′sa rec′ti** [N A], the mucous coat of the rectum. Called also *t. mucosa intestini recti* [B N A]. **t. muco′sa tra′cheae** [N A, B N A], the mucous coat of the trachea. **t. muco′sa tu′bae auditi′vae** [N A, B N A], the mucous membrane lining the auditory tube. **t. muco′sa tu′bae uteri′nae** [N A, B N A], the mucous coat of the uterine tube. **t. muco′sa tympan′ica** [B N A], t. mucosa cavi tympani. **t. muco′sa ure′teris** [N A, B N A], the mucous coat of the ureter. **t. muco′sa ure′thrae femini′nae** [N A], **t. muco′sa ure′thrae mulie′bris** [B N A], the mucous coat of the female urethra. **t. muco′sa u′teri** [N A, B N A], the mucous membrane lining the uterus, the thickness and structure of which vary with the phase of the menstrual cycle. Called also *endometrium*. **t. muco′sa vagi′nae** [N A, B N A], the mucous coat of the vagina. **t. muco′sa ventric′uli** [N A, B N A], the mucous coat of the stomach. **t. muco′sa ves′icae fel′leae** [N A, B N A], the mucous coat of the gallbladder. **t. muco′sa ves′icae urina′riae** [N A, B N A], the mucous coat of the urinary bladder. **t. muco′sa vesic′ulae semina′lis** [N A, B N A], the mucous coat of the seminal vesicle. **t. muscula′ris** [N A, B N A], the muscular coat or layer surrounding the tela submucosa in most portions of the digestive, respiratory, urinary, and genital tracts. Called also *muscular tunic*. **t. muscula′ris bronchio′rum** [N A, B N A], the muscular coat of the bronchi. **t. muscula′ris cer′vicis u′teri** [B N A], the muscular coat of the cervix of the uterus. Omitted in N A. **t. muscula′ris coli** [N A, B N A], the muscular coat of the colon, consisting of layers of longitudinally and circularly coursing fibers. **t. muscula′ris duc′tus deferen′tis** [N A, B N A], the muscular coat of the ductus deferens. **t. muscula′ris esoph′agi** [N A], the muscular coat of the esophagus. **t. muscula′ris intesti′ni rec′ti** [B N A], t. muscularis recti. **t. muscula′ris intesti′ni ten′uis** [N A, B N A], the muscular coat of the small intestine, consisting of an inner circular and an outer longitudinal layer. **t. muscula′ris pharyn′gis** [N A, B N A], the muscular coat of the pharynx, consisting primarily of the pharyngeal constrictor muscles. **t. muscula′ris rec′ti** [N A], the muscular coat of the rectum, consisting of an outer longitudinal and an inner circular layer. Called also *t. muscularis intestini recti* [B N A]. **t. muscula′ris re′nis** [B N A], the muscular coat of the kidney. Omitted in N A. **t. muscula′ris tra′cheae** [N A, B N A], the muscular coat of the trachea. **t. muscula′ris tu′bae uteri′nae** [N A, B N A], the muscular coat of the uterine tube. **t. muscula′ris ure′teris** [N A, B N A], the muscular coat of the ureter. **t. muscula′ris ure′thrae femini′nae** [N A], **t. muscula′ris ure′thrae mulie′bris** [B N A], the muscular coat of the female urethra. **t. muscula′ris u′teri** [N A, B N A], the smooth muscle coat of the uterus, which forms the mass of the organ. Called also *myometrium*. **t. muscula′ris vagi′nae** [N A, B N A], the muscular coat of the vagina. **t. muscula′ris ventric′uli** [N A, B N A], the muscular coat of the stomach, composed of longitudinal, circular, and oblique fibers. **t. muscula′ris ves′icae fel′leae** [N A, B N A], the muscular coat of the gallbladder. **t. muscula′ris ves′icae urina′riae** [N A, B N A], the smooth muscle coat of the urinary bladder. **t. muscula′ris vesic′ulae semina′lis** [N A, B N A], the muscular coat of the seminal vesicle. **t. ner′vea of Bruecke,** the cerebral layer of the retina, exclusive of the rod and cone layer with its fibers and nuclei. **t. pro′pria** [N A, B N A], a general term in anatomical nomenclature for the proper coat or layer of a part, as distinguished from an investing membrane. Called also proper tunic. See also *lamina propria*. **t. pro′pria cer′ebri,** dura mater encephali. **t. pro′pria co′rii** [B N A], stratum reticulare corii. **t. pro′pria tu′buli tes′tis** [B N A], the proper coat of the seminiferous tubules. Omitted in N A. **t. ruyschia′na,** lamina choriocapillaris. **t. sero′sa** [N A, B N A], the membrane lining the external walls of the body cavities and reflected over the exposed surfaces of protruding organs; it consists of mesothelium lying upon a connective tissue layer, and it secretes a watery exudate. Called also *serous tunic*. **t. sero′sa co′li** [N A, B N A], the serous coat of the colon. **t. sero′sa hep′atis** [N A, B N A], the serous coat of the liver. **t. sero′sa intesti′ni ten′uis** [N A, B N A], the serous coat of the small intestine. **t. sero′sa lie′nis** [N A, B N A], the serous coat of the spleen. **t. sero′sa peritone′i** [N A], the serous coat of the peritoneum. **t. sero′sa tes′tis,** lamina visceralis tunicae vaginalis testis. **t. sero′sa tu′bae uteri′nae** [N A, B N A], the serous coat of the uterine tube. **t. sero′sa u′teri** [N A, B N A], the serous coat of the uterus. Called also *perimetrium*. **t. sero′sa ventric′uli** [N A, B N A], the serous coat of the stomach. **t. sero′sa ves′icae fel′leae** [N A, B N A], the serous coat of the gallbladder. **t. sero′sa ves′icae urina′riae** [N A, B N A], the serous coat of the urinary bladder. **t. submuco′sa ure′thrae mulie′bris** [B N A], the submucous coat of the female urethra. Omitted in N A. **tu′nicae tes′tis** [N A, B N A], the coverings of the testis. See *tunicae funiculi spermatici et testis*. **t. u′vea,** t. vasculosa bulbi. **t. vagina′lis commu′nis tes′tis et funic′uli spermat′ici** [B N A], fascia spermatica interna. **t. vagina′lis pro′pria tes′tis** [B N A], **t. vagina′lis tes′tis** [N A], the serous membrane covering the front and sides of the testis and epididymis, composed of a visceral and a parietal layer. **t. vasculo′sa,** a vascular coat, or a layer well supplied with blood vessels. **t. vasculo′sa bul′bi** [N A], **t. vasculo′sa oc′uli** [B N A], the middle, pigmented, vascular tunic of the eyeball, comprising the choroid, the ciliary body, and the iris. Called also *uvea*. **t. vasculo′sa len′tis,** the vascular envelope which encloses and nourishes the developing lens of the fetus; it consists of the *pupillary membrane* in the region of the pupil, the *capsulopupillary membrane* around the edge of the lens, and the *capsular membrane* at the back of the lens.

tunicary (tu′nĭ-ker″e). Pertaining to or possessing a tunic or enveloping membrane.

Tunicata (tu″nĭ-ka′tah) [L. "clothed with a tunic"]. A class of small animals with a saclike body and a leathery tunic. They are intermediate between the invertebrates and true vertebrates.

tunicate (tu′nĭ-kāt). An animal belonging to the class Tunicata.

tunicin (tu′nĭ-sin). A substance resembling cellulose, derivable from certain of the lowest vertebrates, such as the tunicates or ascidians; animal cellulose.

tuning fork. A two-pronged forklike instrument of steel, the prongs of which when struck give off a musical note.

tunnel (tun′el). A passageway of varying length, through a solid body, completely enclosed except for the open ends, permitting entrance and exit. **carpal t.,** the osseofibrous passage for the median nerve and the flexor tendons, formed by the flexor retinaculum and the carpal bones. **Corti's t.,** canal of Corti. **cubital t.,** the opening through which the ulnar nerve passes from its superficial position to its course deep to the muscles just distal to the elbow, the roof being formed by the aponeurosis of the carpi ulnaris muscle and the floor by the medial ligament of the elbow. **flexor t.,** carpal t.

tuntun (tun′tun). Ancylostomiasis.

turacin (tu′rah-sin). A red or crimson pigment, a copper salt of uroporphyrin.

turacoporphyrin (tu″rah-ko-por′fĭ-rin). A derivative from turacin: nearly identical with hematoporphyrin.

turanose (tu′rah-nōs). A disaccharide, $C_{12}H_{22}O_{11}$, obtained by hydrolyzing melazitose.

Turbellaria [tur″be-la′re-ah). The class of planarian worms.

turbid (tur′bid) [L. *turba* a tumult]. Cloudy; showing turbidity.

turbidimeter (tur″bĭ-dim′e-ter). An instrument for measuring turbidity.

turbidimetric (tur″bid-ĭ-met′rik). Performed by the turbidimeter.

turbidimetry (tur″bĭ-dim′e-tre). The measurement of the turbidity of a fluid.

turbidity (tur-bid′ĭ-te). Cloudiness; disturbance of solids (sediment) in a solution, so that it is not clear.

turbinal (tur′bĭ-nal) [L. *turbinalis*, from *turbo* a child's top]. 1. Shaped like a top. 2. A turbinate bone.

turbinate (tur′bĭ-nāt) [L. *turbineus*]. 1. Shaped like a top. 2. A turbinate bone (concha nasalis ossea). **inferior t.,** concha nasalis inferior ossea. **middle t.,** concha nasalis media ossea. **sphenoid t.,** concha sphenoidalis. **superior t.,** concha nasalis superior ossea. **supreme t.,** concha nasalis suprema ossea.

turbinated (tur′bĭ-nāt″ed). Shaped like a top.

turbinectomy (tur″bĭ-nek′to-me) [*turbinate* + Gr. *ektomē* excision]. The surgical removal of a turbinate bone.

turbinotome (tur-bin′o-tōm). A cutting instrument for use in the removal or cutting of a turbinate bone.

turbinotomy (tur″bĭ-not′o-me) [*turbinate* + Gr. *tome* a cutting]. The surgical cutting of a turbinate bone.

Türck's bundle, column, degeneration, trachoma (tĕrks) [Ludwig *Türck*, neurologist and laryngologist in Vienna, 1810–1868]. See under the nouns.

Turck's zone (turks) [Fenton B. *Turck*, New York physician, 1857–1932]. See *zona transformans.*

turgescence (tur-jes′ens) [L. *turgescens* swelling]. The distention or swelling of a part.

turgescent (tur-jes′ent) [L. *turgescens*]. Swelling or beginning to swell.

turgid (tur′jid) [L. *turgidus*]. Swollen and congested.

turgidization (tur″jid-i-za′shun). The creation of turgor in a tissue by the injection of fluid.

turgograph (tur′go-graf). Sphygmomanometer.

turgometer (tur-gom′e-ter) [L. *turgor* swelling + *metrum* measure]. An instrument for measuring the amount of turgescence.

turgor (tur′gor) [L.]. The condition of being turgid; normal or other fullness. **t. vita′lis,** the normal fullness of the blood vessels and capillaries. When the surrounding tissues lose their normal resistance, this turgor increases, and swelling results.

turgoscope (tur′go-skōp). Sphygmomanometer.

turgosphygmoscope (tur″go-sfig′mo-skōp). Sphygmomanometer.

Türk's cell, leukocyte (tĕrks) [Wilhelm *Türk*, Austrian physician, 1871–1916]. See under *leukocyte.*

turmeric (tur′mer-ik). The rhizome of *Curcuma longa*, a plant of South America. Its alkaloid curcumin is a dye and chemical indicator.

turmerol (tur′mer-ol). An oily alcohol derivable from the oil of turmeric; also the oil itself.

Turner's sign (tur′nerz) [George Grey *Turner*, English surgeon, 1877–1951]. See under *sign.*

Turner's sulcus (tur′nerz) [William Aldren *Turner*, British neurologist, born 1864]. See under *sulcus.*

Turner's syndrome (tur′nerz) [Henry Hubert *Turner*, American endocrinologist, born 1892]. See under *syndrome.*

Turner tooth (tur′ner) [Joseph George *Turner*, British dentist, died 1955]. See under *tooth.*

turnera (tur′ner-ah). Damiana.

turnsick, turnsickness (turn′sik, turn′sik-nes). Staggers.

turnsol (turn′sol). Litmus.

turpentine (tur′pen-tīn) [L. *terebinthina*]. The concrete oleoresin obtained from *Pinus palustris* and other species of Pinus. It contains a volatile oil, to which its properties are due, and in which form it is generally used.

turpentole (tur′pen-tōl). A light, purified petroleum spirit.

turricephaly (tur″ĭ-sef′ah-le). Oxycephaly.

turunda (tu-run′dah) [L.]. 1. A surgeon's tent. 2. A suppository.

Turyn's sign (too′rinz) [Felix *Turyn*, Warsaw physician, born 1899]. See under *sign.*

tus. Abbreviation for L. *tus′sis*, a cough.

tusk (tusk). An extremely large tooth projecting beyond the lips.

tussal (tus′al) [L. *tussis* cough]. Pertaining to a cough.

tussicula (tŭ-sik′u-lah) [L., dim. of *tussis* cough]. A slight cough.

tussicular (tŭ-sik′u-lar) [L. *tussicula*]. Of or relating to a cough.

tussiculation (tŭ-sik″u-la′shun). A short, hacking cough.

tussis (tus′is) [L.]. Cough. **t. convul′siva,** pertussis.

tussive (tus′iv). Pertaining to or due to a cough.

tutamen (tu-ta′men), pl. *tutam′ina* [L.]. A protective covering or structure. **tutam′ina cer′ebri** [L. "defenses of the brain"], the hair, scalp, skull, and meninges. **tutam′ina oc′uli** ["defenses of the eye"], the appendages of the eye: the eyelids, lashes, etc. (organa oculi accessoria [N A]).

tutamina (tu-tam′ĭ-nah) [L.]. Plural of *tutamen.*

Tuttle's mask, proctoscope (tut′l′z) [Edward G. *Tuttle*, surgeon in New York, 1857–1913]. See under *mask* and *proctoscope.*

TV. Abbreviation for *tuberculin volutin*, a principle believed to exist in tubercle bacilli.

tween (twēn). Trade mark for a sorbitan polyoxyalkalene derivative: used as an emulsifier and detergent. **t. 80,** trade mark for polysorbate 80.

'tween-brain (twēn′brān). Diencephalon.

twin (twin). One of two offspring produced in the same pregnancy and developed from one ovum or from two ova fertilized at the same time. **acardiac t.,** acardius. **allantoido-angiopagous t's,** twins united by the umbilical vessels only. **binovular t's,** dizygotic t's. **conjoined t's,** a double fetal monster, ranging from two well-developed individuals joined by a superficial connection of varying extent, usually in the frontal, transverse, or sagittal body plane (*symmetrical c. t's*), to those in which only a small part of the body is duplicated or one small and incompletely developed component, the parasite, is attached to a much larger and more fully developed one, the autosite (asymmetrical c. t's). **dichorial t's, dichorionic t's,** dizygotic t's. **dissimilar t's,** dizygotic t's. **dizygotic t's,** two offspring developed from two separate ova fertilized at the same time. Called also *binovular, dichorial, dicho-*

rionic, dissimilar, false, fraternal, heterologous, hetero-ovular, two-egg, and *unlike t's.* **enzygotic t's,** monozygotic t's. **false t's,** dizygotic t's. **fraternal t's,** dizygotic t's. **heterologous t's,** dizygotic t's. **hetero-ovular t's,** dizygotic t's. **identical t's,** monozygotic t's. **monochorial t's, monochorionic t's,** monozygotic t's. **mono-ovular t's,** monozygotic t's. **monozygotic t's,** two offspring developed from one zygote or fertilized ovum. Called also *enzygotic, identical, monochorial, monochorionic, mono-ovular, similar, true,* and *uniovular t's.* **omphalo-angiopagous t's,** allantoido-angiopagous t's. **one-egg t's,** monozygotic t's. **similar t's,** monozygotic t's. **true t's,** monozygotic t's. **two-egg t's,** dizygotic t's. **unequal t's,** twins of which one is incompletely developed. **uniovular t's,** monozygotic t's. **unlike t's,** dizygotic t's.

twinge (twinj). A short, sharp pain.

Twining's pill (twi'ningz) [William *Twining,* British physician in India, 1813–1848]. See under *pill.*

twinning (twin'ing). 1. The production of symmetrical structures or parts by division. 2. The simultaneous intrauterine production of two (or more) embryos. **experimental t.,** embryonic duplication produced by purposeful external intervention. **spontaneous t.,** embryonic duplication without external intervention, as occurs in nature.

twitch (twich). A brief contractile response of a skeletal muscle elicited by a single maximal volley of impulses in the motor neurons supplying it.

twitching (twich'ing). The occurrence of a single contraction or a series of contractions of a muscle. See *twitch.* **fascicular t.,** repetitive brief contraction of large groups of bundles of muscle fibers. **fibrillar t.,** repetitive brief contraction of single bundles of muscle fibers. **Trousseau's t.,** repetitive brief contraction involving muscles of the face.

twitch-up (twich'up). A noose passed through a perforation in a board, used for compressing a part, as the lip of a horse, during slight operations.

Twort's phenomenon (tworts) [Frederick William *Twort,* British bacteriologist, 1877–1950]. See *Twort-d'Herelle phenomenon,* under *phenomenon.*

TX. The symbol for a derivative of TC, prepared by v. Behring. See under *tuberculin.*

Ty. Abbreviation for *type.*

tychastics (ti-kas'tiks) [Gr. *tychē* chance, accident]. The science of industrial accidents.

Tydeus molestus (ti'de-us mo-les'tus). A very small mite, found in Belgium, which attacks man.

tylenol (ti'lĕ-nol). Trade mark for preparations of acetaminophen.

tylion (til'e-on) [Gr. *tyleion* cushion]. The point on the anterior edge of the optic groove in the median line.

tyloma (ti-lo'mah) [Gr. *tylōma*]. A callus or callosity.

Tylophora asthmatica (ti-lof'o-rah az-mat'ĭ-kah) [Gr. *tylos* knot + *pherein* to bear]. An asclepiadaceous plant of South Asia. It is emetic, and is useful in dysentery and asthma.

tylophorine (ti-lof'o-rin). An alkaloid, $C_{24}H_{27}O_4N$, from *Tylophora asthmatica:* emetic and antasthmatic.

tylosis (ti-lo'sis) [Gr. *tylōsis*]. 1. The formation of calluses upon the skin. 2. A callus, or callosity. See *keratosis.* 3. Typical tuberculosis. **t. cilia'ris,** thickening of the eyelids. **t. lin'guae,** leukoplakia buccalis. **t. palma'ris et planta'ris,** keratosis palmaris et plantaris.

tylotic (ti-lot'ik). Pertaining to or affected with tylosis.

tympanal (tim'pah-nal). Pertaining to the tympanic cavity or to the tympanic membrane.

tympanectomy (tim"pah-nek'to-me) [*tympanum* + Gr. *ektomē* excision]. Excision of the tympanic membrane.

tympania (tim-pan'e-ah). Tympanites.

tympanic (tim-pan'ik) [L. *tympanicus*]. 1. Of or pertaining to the tympanum. 2. Bell-like; resonant.

tympanichord (tim-pan'ĭ-kord). Chorda tympani.

tympanichordal (tym"pah-nĭ-kor'dal). Pertaining to chorda tympani.

tympanicity (tim"pah-nis'ĭ-te). A tympanic quality.

tympanion (tim-pan'e-on) [Gr.]. A point at either end of the vertical diameter of the anulus tympanicus. **lower t.,** the lowest point on the anulus tympanicus. **upper t.,** the highest point on the anulus tympanicus.

tympanism (tim'pah-nizm) [Gr. *tympanon* drum]. Distention with gas; tympanites.

tympanites (tim"pah-ni'tēz) [Gr. *tympanitēs,* from *tympanon* drum]. Distention of the abdomen, due to the presence of gas or air in the intestine or in the peritoneal cavity, as in peritonitis and typhoid fever. **uterine t.,** physometra.

tympanitic (tim"pah-nit'ik). 1. Pertaining to or affected with tympanites. 2. Bell-like, or tympanic.

tympanitis (tim"pah-ni'tis). Otitis media.

tympanoacryloplasty (tim"pah-no-ah-kril'o-plas"te). Surgical obliteration of the mastoid cavity by instillation of an acrylic compound.

tympanoeustachian (tim"pah-no-u-sta'ke-an). Pertaining to the tympanic cavity and auditory tube.

tympanohyal (tim"pah-no-hi'al). 1. Pertaining to the tympanum and the hyoid arch. 2. A small bone or cartilage at the base of the styloid process. In early life it becomes a part of the temporal bone.

tympanolabyrinthopexy (tim"pah-no-lab"ĭ-rin'tho-pek"se). Sourdille's operation of uniting a neotympanic system to a labyrinthine fistula for the cure of progressive deafness from otosclerosis.

tympanomalleal (tim"pah-no-mal'e-al). Pertaining to the pars tympanica ossis temporalis and the malleus.

tympanomandibular (tim"pah-no-man-dib'u-lar). Pertaining to the middle ear and the mandible.

tympanomastoiditis (tim"pah-no-mas"toid-i'-tis). Inflammation of the middle ear and the pneumatic cells of the mastoid process.

tympanophonia (tim"pah-no-fo'ne-ah) [*tympanum* + Gr. *phōnē* sound]. Autophony.

tympanoplasty (tim"pah-no-plas'te) [*tympanum* + Gr. *plassein* to form]. Surgical reconstruction of the hearing mechanism of the middle ear, with restoration of the drum membrane to protect the round window from sound pressure, and establishment of ossicular continuity between the tympanic membrane and the oval window. See also *myringoplasty.*

tympanosclerosis (tim"pah-no-skle-ro'sis). A condition characterized by the presence of masses of very hard, dense connective tissue around the auditory ossicles in the tympanic cavity.

tympanosquamosal (tim"pah-no-skwah-mo'-sal). Pertaining to the pars tympanica and pars squamosa of the temporal bone.

tympanostapedial (tim"pah-no-sta-pe'de-al). Pertaining to the tympanum and the stapes.

tympanosympathectomy (tim"pah-no-sim"-pah-thek'to-me). The operation of excising the tympanic plexus for the relief of tinnitus aurium.

tympanotemporal (tim"pah-no-tem'po-ral). Pertaining to the tympanum and the region over the temporal bone.

tympanotomy (tim"pah-not'o-me) [*tympanum* + Gr. *tomē* a cutting]. Surgical puncture of the membrana tympani.

tympanous (tim'pah-nus). Pertaining to or marked by tympanism; distended with gas.

tympanum (tim'pah-num) [L.; Gr. *tympanon* drum]. The cavity of the middle ear, located just medial to the tympanic membrane. Called also *cavum tympani.*

tympany (tim'pah-ne) [Gr. *tympanias*]. 1. Tympanites. 2. A tympanic, or bell-like, percussion note. **bell t.,** a modified tympanitic note heard on percussion of the chest in some cases of pneumothorax. **Skoda's t., skodaic t.,** skodaic resonance. **t. of stomach,** hoven.

Tyndall light, phenomenon (tin'dal) [John *Tyndall,* British physicist, 1820–1893]. See under *light* and *phenomenon.*

tyndallization (tyn″dal-i-za'shun) [John *Tyndall*]. Fractional sterilization.

type (tīp) [L. *typus;* Gr. *typos* mark]. The general or prevailing character of any particular case of disease, person or substance. **allotropic t.,** a personality which tends to be preoccupied with what others do or think or mean. **amyostatic-kinetic t.,** a type of epidemic encephalitis marked by apathy, rigidity, akinesis, slowing of movement and sometimes tremor. **apoplectic t.** See *habitus apoplecticus.* **asthenic t.,** a type of physical constitution: slender, flat in front, long chested, poor muscular development. **athletic t.,** a type of physical constitution, marked by broad shoulders, deep chest, flat abdomen, thick neck, and good muscular development. **Aztec t., bird's head t.** See *microcephalic idiocy,* under *idiocy.* **blood t's.** See *blood type,* under B. **body t.,** the general character of the body structure or constitution. **buffalo t.,** obesity confined to the neck, head, and trunk; seen in pituitary basophilism. **Charcot-Marie-Tooth t.** See *progressive neuropathic (peroneal) muscular atrophy,* under *atrophy.* **cycloid t.** See *syntonic.* **Dejerine t.,** a type of multiple sclerosis involving the pyramidal tract and anterior horns; the amyotrophic lateral sclerosis type. **Dejerine-Landouzy t.,** Landouzy-Dejerine dystrophy. **Duchenne-Aran t.** See *myelopathic muscular atrophy,* under *atrophy.* **Duchenne-Landouzy t.,** Landouzy t. **dysplastic t.,** any body type which differs from the asthenic, the athletic, and the pyknic types. **Eichhorst's t.,** the femorotibial type of progressive muscular atrophy with contraction of the toes. **Erb-Zimmerlin t.,** the juvenile scapular type of primary muscular dystrophy. **Fazio-Londe t.,** the bulbofacial type of familial infantile progressive spinal muscular atrophy. **Hayem's t.,** acute nonsuppurative encephalitis. **Hutchison t.,** adrenal sarcoma in infants with cranial metastases. **Kalmuch t.,** Mongolian idiocy. **koinotropic t.,** the socially adjusted type; the "good mixer." **Kretschmer t's,** types of physique related to personality: the *asthenic* (leptosome) is schizoid; the *pyknic* is cycloid. **Landouzy t., Landouzy-Dejerine t.** See under *dystrophy.* **leg t.,** progressive hereditary muscular atrophy. **Leichtenstern's t.,** encephalitic haemorrhagica. **leptosome t.,** ashthenic type. **Levi-Lorain t.** See *hypophysial infantilism,* under *infantilism.* **Leyden-Moebius t.,** hereditary progressive muscular dystrophy beginning in the pelvic muscles. **Lorain t.,** arrested physical development (infantilism) of pituitary causation. **Nothnagel's t.** See under *acroparesthesia.* **organic reaction t.,** a type of psychosis due to organic disease of the brain. **overactive t.,** a mental make-up characterized by mental and physical aggressiveness and activity, talkativeness and a tendency to exaltation. **Pepper t.,** congenital sarcoma of adrenal and liver in infants. **phthinoid t.,** a body type characterized by a flat, narrow chest. **phthisic t.,** habitus phthisicus. **Putnam t.,** combined spinal sclerosis with pernicious anemia and cachexia. **pyknic t.,** a physical type marked by rounded body, large chest, thick shoulders, broad head, and short neck. **Raymond t. of apoplexy,** ingravescent apoplexy marked by paresthesia of the hand of the side which is going to become paralyzed. **Remak's t.,** paralysis of the extensor muscles of the fingers and wrist. **Runeberg's t.,** progressive pernicious anemia with brief periods of apparent improvement. **scapulohumeral t.,** progressive spinal muscular atrophy beginning in the shoulder. **schizoid t.** See *schizoid.* **Schultze's t.** See under *acroparesthesia.* **seclusive t.,** a mental make-up characterized by quietness, reserve, shyness, secretiveness, and aversion to social contacts. **Simmerlin t.,** Leyden-Moebius t. **sthenic t.,** a type of physical constitution characterized by muscular strength. **Strumpell's t.,** the familial type of lateral spinal sclerosis. **suspicious t.,** a mental make-up characterized by abnormal mistrustfulness and suspicion. **sympatheticotonic t.,** a type of physical constitution characterized by sympathicotonia. **syntonic t.** See *syntonic.* **Tooth's t.,** the familial or hereditary form of progressive muscular atrophy. **unstable t.,** a mental make-up characterized by emotional changeableness. **vagotonic t.,** a physical type characteristic of deficient suprarenal activity: there are slow pulse, low blood pressure, localized sweating, high sugar tolerance, and oculocardiac reflex. **vesanic t.,** insanity due to primary psychiatric disorder and not to any external cause, as injury, poisoning, or disease of some other organ. It includes mania, melancholia, etc. **visual t.,** an individual who depends mainly on sight and whose imagery is mostly visual. **Werdnig-Hoffmann t.** See under *paralysis.* **Wernicke-Mann t.,** partial hemiplegia of the extremities. **Zimmerlin's t.,** hereditary progressive muscular atrophy, beginning in the upper part of the body.

typembryo (tīp-em'bre-o). An embryo in that stage of development at which the characteristics of the type to which it belongs may be seen.

Typhaceae (ti-fa'se-e). A name once proposed for the family including the causative organism of typhoid fever and related forms.

typhase (ti'fās). A ferment or enzyme formed by and capable of lysing the bacillus of typhoid fever.

typhemia (ti-fe'me-ah) [*typhus* + Gr. *haima* blood + *-ia*]. The presence of typhoid bacilli in the blood.

typhia (tif'e-ah). Typhoid fever.

typhic (ti'fik). Pertaining to typhus or typhoid fever.

typhinia (ti-fi'ne-ah). Relapsing fever.

typhization (tif″i-za'shun). Induction of a disease condition by exposure to the poison of typhus.

typhlatonia (tif″lah-to'ne-ah). Typhlatony.

typhlatony (tif-lat'o-ne) [Gr. *typhlon* cecum + *atony*]. Inefficiency of the motor activity of the cecum.

typhlectasis (tif-lek'tah-sis) [Gr. *typhlon* cecum + *ektasis* distention]. Distention of the cecum.

typhlectomy (tif-lek'to-me). Cecectomy.

typhlenteritis (tif″len-ter-i'tis) [Gr. *typhlon* cecum + Gr. *enteron* intestine]. Inflammation of the cecum.

typhlitis (tif-li'tis) [Gr. *typhlon* cecum + *-itis*]. Inflammation of the cecum. The term was formerly used for the condition now called *appendicitis.*

typhlo- (tif'lo). 1. [Gr. *typhlon* cecum]. Combining form denoting relationship to the cecum. 2. [Gr. *typhlos* blind]. Combining form denoting relationship to blindness.

typhloalbuminuria (tif″lo-al-bu″mĭ-nu're-ah). Alimentary albuminuria proceeding from the cecum.

typhlocele (tif'lo-sēl). Cecocele.

typhlocholecystitis (tif″lo-ko″le-sis-ti'tis). Inflammation of the gallbladder accompanied by symptoms of recurrent subacute appendicitis.

Typhlocoelum (tif″lo-se'lum). A genus of trematode parasites. **T. cucumeri'num,** a trematode parasitic in the trachea, esophagus and thoracic cavity of chicks in Brazil.

typhlocolitis (tif″lo-ko-li'tis) [*typhlo-*(1) + *colitis*]. Colitis in the region of the cecum.

typhlodicliditis (tif″lo-dik″lĭ-di′tis) [*typhlo-*(1) + Gr. *diklis* door + *-itis*]. Inflammation of the ileocecal valve.

typhloempyema (tif″lo-em″pi-e′mah) [*typhlo-*(1) + *empyema*]. An abdominal abscess accompanying appendicitis.

typhloenteritis (tif″lo-en″ter-i′tis). Typhlenteritis.

typhlohepatitis (tif″lo-hep″ah-ti′tis). Infectious enterohepatitis of turkeys.

typhlolexia (tif″lo-lek′se-ah) [*typhlo-*(2) + Gr. *lexis* speech + *-ia*]. Word blindness.

typhlolithiasis (tif″lo-lĭ-thi′ah-sis) [*typhlo-*(1) + Gr. *lithos* stone + *-ia*]. The presence of calculi in the cecum.

typhlology (tif-lol′o-je) [*typhlo-*(2) + *-logy*]. The sum of what is known in regard to blindness.

typhlomegaly (tif″lo-meg′ah-le) [*typhlo-*(1) + Gr. *megas* large]. Abnormal enlargement of the cecum.

typhlon (tif′lon) [Gr.]. The cecum.

typhlopexia (tif″lo-pek′se-ah). Typhlopexy.

typhlopexy (tif′lo-pek″se) [*typhlo-*(1) + Gr. *pēxis* fixation]. The operation of fixing the cecum to the abdominal wall for the relief of invagination.

typhloptosis (tif″lo-to′sis) [*typhlo-*(1) + Gr. *ptōsis* falling]. Downward displacement of the cecum.

typhlorrhaphy (tif-lor′ah-fe). Suture of the cecum.

typhlosis (tif-lo′sis) [Gr. *typhlōsis* a making blind]. Blindness.

typhlostenosis (tif″lo-ste-no′sis) [*typhlo-*(1) + Gr. *stenōsis* narrowing]. Contraction of the cecum.

typhlostomy (tif-los′to-me) [*typhlo-*(1) + Gr. *stomoun* to provide with an opening, or mouth]. Colostomy in which the opening is made into the cecum.

typhloteritis (tif″lo-ter-i′tis). Typhlenteritis.

typhlotomy (tif-lot′o-me) [*typhlo-*(1) + Gr. *tomē* a cutting]. Incision of the cecum.

typhlo-ureterostomy (tif″lo-u-re″ter-os′to-me) [*typhlo-*(1) + Gr. *ourētēr* ureter + *stomoun* to provide with an opening, or mouth]. Anastomosis of the ureter to the cecum.

typhobacillosis (ti″fo-bas″ĭ-lo′sis) [*typhus* + *bacillus* + *-osis*]. The symptoms due to poisoning by the toxins of *Salmonella typhosa*. **t. tubercu-lo′sa,** a condition due to tuberculous infection and exhibiting the symptoms of typhoid fever. It is frequently followed by tuberculosis of the viscera or lungs.

typhobacterin (ti″fo-bak′ter-in). Typhoid vaccine.

typhodiphtheria (ti″fo-dif-the′re-ah). The association of typhoid fever and diphtheria.

typhogenic (ti″fo-jen′ik). Causing typhus or typhoid fever.

typhohemia (ti″fo-he′me-ah) [*typhus* + Gr. *haima* blood + *-ia*]. Putrefaction of the blood.

typhoid (ti′foid) [Gr. *typhōdes* like smoke; delirious]. 1. Resembling typhus. 2. Typhoid fever. **abenteric t., ambulatory t., apyretic t.** See *typhoid fever*, under *fever*. **bilious t.,** the icteric variety of relapsing fever; Weil's disease. **cholera t.,** the typhoid state sometimes coming on after the algid stage of cholera. It is occasionally attended by a skin eruption. **fowl t.,** an acute contagious disease of fowls caused by *Shigella gallinarum*. **Manchurian t.,** a disease seen in Manchuria during the Russo-Japanese War, distinct from typhoid, and resembling in its symptoms Brill's disease. **pellagra t.,** pellagra marked by moderate fever with mild delirium. **provocation t.,** typhoid fever that follows and is caused by the administration of typhoid vaccine, the infection occurring during the susceptible or negative phase. **subcontinuous t.,** a form of malarial disease simulating typhoid fever. **walking t.** See *typhoid fever*, under *fever*.

typhoidal (ti-foid′al). Resembling typhoid.

typhoidette (ti″foid-et′). A mild form of typhoid fever.

typhoidin (ti′foi-din). A ten-day culture of a single strain of *Eberthella typhosa* on glycerin broth evaporated to one-tenth volume (Gay and Force, 1914). It is also used in the cutaneous reaction for typhoid fever. See *typhoidin test*, under *tests*.

typholumbricosis (ti″fo-lum″brĭ-ko′sis). A fever resembling typhoid fever in its symptoms, but due to lumbricoid worms such as Ascaris.

typhomalarial (ti″fo-mah-la′re-al). Of malarial origin, but with typhoid symptoms. See under *fever*.

typhomania (ti″fo-ma′ne-ah) [Gr. *typhos* stupor + *mania* madness]. The state of muttering delirium accompanying typhus or typhoid fever, and characteristic of the typhoid state.

typhonia (ti-fo′ne-ah). Typhomania.

Typhonium trilobatum (ti-fo′ne-um tri″lo-ba′-tum) [L.]. An Asiatic plant, highly valued in oriental practice as a polychrest remedy.

typhopaludism (ti″fo-pal′u-dizm). Malarial fever with typhoid symptoms.

typhophor (ti′fo-fōr) [*typhoid* + Gr. *phoros* bearing]. A typhoid carrier. See under *carrier*.

typhopneumonia (ti″fo-nu-mo′ne-ah). Pneumonia complicated with typhoid fever, or pneumonia with symptoms of typhoid.

typhoremittent (ti″fo-re-mit′ent). Remittent and having typhoid symptoms.

typhorubeloid (ti″fo-roo′bĕ-loid). Typhoid fever with an eruption resembling that of measles.

typhose (ti′fōs). Resembling typhoid fever.

typhosepsis ((ti″fo-sep′sis) [Gr. *typhos* stupor + *sēpsis* putrefaction]. The septic poisoning that occurs in typhoid.

typhosis (ti-fo′sis). Any typhus-like affection; the typhoid state.

typhotoxin (ti″fo-tok′sin). A deadly ptomaine, $C_7H_{17}NO_2$, isomeric with gadinin, derived from cultures of typhoid fever bacillus. It causes diarrhea, muscular paralysis, salivation, and dilatation of the pupil.

typhous (ti′fus). Pertaining to or resembling typhus.

typhus (ti′fus) [Gr. *typhos* stupor arising from fever]. Any one of a group of related infectious diseases caused by species of *Rickettsia* and marked by malaise, severe headache, sustained high fever, and a macular or maculopapular eruption which appears from the third to the seventh day. Called also *typhus fever*. See *epidemic t.*, *murine t.*, and *scrub t.* **abdominal t., t. abdomina′lis,** typhoid fever. **amarillic t.,** yellow fever. **benign t.,** Brill's disease. **bovine t.,** cattle plague. **canine t.,** Stuttgart disease. **classic t.,** epidemic t. **collapsing t.,** the im-pyeng of Korea; an infectious typhoid fever. **contagious t. of cattle,** cattle plague. **endemic t.,** murine t. **epidemic t.,** the classic form of typhus, caused by *Rickettsia prowazekii*, which is transmitted from man to man by the louse, *Pediculus humanus* var. *corporis*. **European t.,** epidemic t. **exanthematic t.,** epidemic t. **exanthematic t. of São Paulo,** Rocky Mountain spotted fever. **t. exanthemat′icus, t. exanthematique′, exanthematous t.,** epidemic t. **flea t., flea-borne t.,** murine t. **Gubler-Robin t.,** the renal form of typhus. **t. icteroi′des,** yellow fever. **K T t.,** rural t. **Kenya t.,** a rickettsial disease resembling boutonneuse fever, observed in Kenya. **t. laevis′-simus,** a very mild form of enteric fever. **louse t., louse-borne t.,** epidemic t. **Manchurian t.,** murine t. **Mexican t.,** murine t. **mite-borne t.,** scrub t. **Moscow t.,** murine t. **mouse t.,** an epizootic disease of mice caused by *Salmonella typhimurium*. **murine t.,** an infectious disease clinically similar to epidemic typhus, but caused by *Rickettsia typhi*, which is transmitted from rat to man by the rat flea, *Xenopsylla cheopis*, and by the rat louse, *Polyplax spinulosa*. **petechial t.,** epidemic t. **rat t.,** murine t. **recrudescent t.,** Brill's disease. **t. recur'rens,** relapsing fever. **rückfall t.,** relapsing fever. **rural t.,** a form of scrub typhus seen mostly in outdoor workers. **São Paulo t.,** a disease transmitted by the tick, *Amblyomma cajennense*. **scrub t.,** a self-limited, febrile disease of two weeks' duration, caused by *Rickettsia tsutsugamushi*, transmitted by chiggers, and distributed widely in the Asiatic-Pacific area; characterized by sudden onset of fever with a primary skin lesion (eschar), and development of a rash about the fifth day. **shop t.,** murine t. **t. sid'erans,** typhus in a malignant and quickly fatal form. **Toulon t.,** murine t. **tropical t.,** scrub t. **urban t., W T t.,** a form of scrub typhus seen mostly in indoor workers.

typical (tip'ĭ-kal) [Gr. *typikos*]. Presenting the distinctive features of any type.

typing (tīp'ing). Determination of the type or category to which an individual, object, or other entity belongs. **t. of blood,** classification of the blood with reference to various agglutinins, including M-N, P, Rh-Hr.

typoscope (ti'po-skōp) [Gr. *typos* type + *skopein* to examine]. An instrument to aid amblyopia and cataract patients in reading.

tyramine (ti'rah-mēn). A decarboxylation product of tyrosine, which may be converted to cresol and phenol; closely related structurally to epinephrine and norepinephrine, it has a similar but weaker action: found in decayed animal tissue, ripe cheese, and ergot.

tyrannism (tir'ah-nizm) [Gr. *tyrrhanos* tyrant]. Insane or morbid cruelty.

tyrein (ti're-in). The coagulated casein of milk.

tyremesis (ti-rem'e-sis) [*tyro-* + Gr. *emesis* vomiting]. The caseous vomiting of infants.

tyresin (ti-re'sin). A principle derivable from the venom of serpents and from the juice of mushrooms; it is said to be an antidote for snake poisoning.

tyriasis (tĭ-ri'ah-sis). 1. Elephantiasis. 2. Alopecia.

tyro- (ti'ro) [Gr. *tyros* cheese]. Combining form denoting relationship to cheese.

tyrocidine (ti″ro-si'din). A crystalline antibiotic substance which is the major component of tyrothricin.

Tyrode's solution (ti'rōdz) [Maurice Vejux *Tyrode*, American pharmacologist, 1878–1930]. See under *solution*.

tyrogenous (ti-roj'e-nus) [*tyro-* + Gr. *gennan* to produce]. Originating in cheese.

Tyroglyphus (ti-rog'lĭ-fus) [*tyro-* + Gr. *glyphein* to carve]. A genus of pale, soft-bodied acarids. **T. fari'nae** is the flour mite, which is found in flour mills and granaries. **T. lon'gior,** the species which causes copra itch. **T. si'ro,** the cheese mite; said sometimes to produce gastritis and diarrhea in persons who eat cheese: ova may be found in the stools.

tyroid (ti'roid) [*tyro-* + Gr. *eidos* form]. Caseous; resembling cheese.

tyroleucine (ti″ro-lu'sin). A substance, $C_{14}H_{22}N_2O_4$, from decomposed albumin.

tyroma (ti-ro'mah). A caseous tumor; a new growth or nodule of cheesy material.

tyromatosis (ti″ro-mah-to'sis). A condition characterized by caseous degeneration.

tyrosamine (ti-rōs'ah-mēn). Tyramine.

tyrosiluria (ti″ro-sĭ-lu're-ah). Presence in the urine of metabolites of tyrosine.

tyrosinase (ti-ro'sin-ās). An oxidizing enzyme in animal and plant tissues which catalyzes the oxidation of various phenolic compounds, including tyrosine, into black pigments.

tyrosine (ti-ro'sin). A crystallizable amino acid, *p*-hydroxyphenylalanine, $C_9H_{11}O_3N$, an essential constituent of any diet. It has been found in many organs of the body and appears in the urine in disease conditions, particularly acute yellow atrophy of the liver.

tyrosinosis (ti″ro-sin-o'sis). A condition characterized by a faulty metabolism of tyrosine in which an intermediate product, parahydroxyphenyl pyruvic acid, appears in the urine and gives it an abnormal reducing power.

tyrosinuria (ti″ro-sin-u're-ah) [*tyrosine* + Gr. *ouron* urine + *-ia*]. The presence of tyrosine in urine.

tyrosis (ti-ro'sis). Cheesy degeneration or caseation.

tyrothricin (ti″ro-thri'sin). An antibiotic substance isolated from the soil bacillus *Bacillus brevis*, and consisting principally of two substances, gramicidin and tyrocidine. It is applied locally in 0.05 per cent solution. Called also *Dubos enzyme* or *lysin*.

Tyrothrix (ti'ro-thriks) [*tyro-* + Gr. *thrix* hair]. A genus name once given by Duclaux to certain microorganisms later included in the genera Lactobacillus, Bacillus, or Clostridium.

tyrotoxicon (ti″ro-tok'sĭ-kon). A poisonous crystalline ptomaine, $C_6H_5N.N.OH$, or diazobenzene hydroxide, sometimes occurring in stale milk, cheese, and ice cream. When ingested, it causes vertigo, headache, vomiting, chills, muscular cramps, purging, prostration, and death.

tyrotoxicosis (ti″ro-tok″sĭ-ko'sis). A morbid condition resulting from ingestion of tyrotoxicon.

tyrotoxin (ti″ro-tok'sin). Any toxin developed in cheese or milk by a bacillus.

tyrotoxism (ti″ro-tok'sizm). Poisoning resulting from ingestion of cheese.

tyroxin (ti-rok'sin). One of the derivatives of the decomposition of albumin.

Tyrrell's fascia, hook (tir'elz) [Frederick *Tyrrell*, English anatomist, 1797–1843]. See under *fascia* and *hook*.

Tyson's glands (ti'sunz) [Edward *Tyson*, English physician and anatomist, 1649–1708]. See under *gland*.

tysonian (ti-so'ne-an). Named for Edward *Tyson*.

tysonitis (ti″son-i'tis). Inflammation of Tyson's glands.

tyvid (ti'vid). Trade mark for a preparation of isoniazid.

tyzine (ti'zēn). Trade mark for preparations of tetrahydrozoline hydrochloride.

TZ. Symbol for *tuberculin zymoplastiche*, or the dried residue of the portions of the tubercle bacilli which are soluble in alcohol.

Tzanck cell, test (tsank) [Arnault *Tzanck*, Russian dermatologist in Paris, 1886–1954]. See under *cell* and *tests*.

tzetze (set'se). Tsetse.

U

U. 1. Abbreviation for *unit.* 2. Chemical symbol for *uranium.*

U^{235}. An isotope of uranium of mass number 235.

uarthritis (u″ar-thri′tis). Gout due to excess of uric acid in the system.

uaterium (wah-te′re-um) [Gr. *ous* ear]. A medical preparation for use in the ear.

uberous (u′ber-us). Prolific.

uberty (u′ber-te) [L. *ubertas* fruitfulness]. Fertility.

UBI. Ultraviolet blood irradiation, a treatment involving removal of blood from a patient, exposing it to ultraviolet light and returning it to the patient's circulation.

Ucko's test (oo′kōz) [H. *Ucko*, physician at the Hotel Dieu, Paris]. See under *tests.*

udder (ud′er). The mammary gland of cattle and certain other animals.

Udránszky's test (oo-dran′skēz) [László *Udránszky*, Budapest physiologist, 1862–1914]. See under *tests.*

udruj (ud′ruj). An East Indian medicinal gum.

UFA. Abbreviation for *unesterified fatty acids.*

Uffelmann's test (oof′el-mahnz) [Jules *Uffelmann*, German physician, 1837–1894]. See under *tests.*

Uhlenhuth's test (oo′len-hootz) [Paul *Uhlenhuth*, German bacteriologist, 1870–1957]. See under *tests.*

Uhthoff's sign (oot′hofs) [Wilhelm *Uhthoff*, ophthalmologist in Breslau, 1853–1927]. See under *sign.*

uixi (wik′se). The *Myristica platysperma*, a medicinal plant of South America.

ula (u′lah) [Gr. *oulon* gum]. Gingiva.

ulaganactesis (u-lag″an-ak-te′sis) [Gr. *oulon* gum + *aganaktēsis* irritation]. Irritation or itching of the gums.

ulalgia (u-lal′je-ah) [Gr. *oulon* gum + *algos* pain + *-ia*]. Pain in the gums.

ulatrophia (u″lah-tro′fe-ah). Ulatrophy.

ulatrophy (u-lat′ro-fe) [Gr. *oulon* gum + *atrophy*]. Shrinkage of the gums; gum recession; a form of pericementoclasia marked by a decrease in the bulk of the marginal and cemental gingiva with exposure of the cementum. **afunctional u.,** ulatrophy due to congenital malocclusion. **atrophic u.,** ischemic u. **calcic u.,** ulatrophy that is caused by the presence of salivary concretions. **ischemic u.,** ulatrophy due to atrophy of the gum from deficient vascular nourishment. **traumatic u.,** ulatrophy due to excessive strain, as from nail biting, etc.

ulcer (ul′ser) [L. *ulcus;* Gr. *helkōsis*]. A loss of substance on a cutaneous or mucous surface, causing gradual disintegration and necrosis of the tissues. **Aden u.** 1. A form of oriental sore or Aleppo boil. 2. Tropical ulcer. **adherent u.,** a skin ulcer the base of which adheres to the subcutaneous fascia. **Allingham's u.,** fissure of the anus. **amputating u.,** ulceration which encircles a part and destroys the tissues to the bone. **anamite u.,** an obstinate endemic sore of Indo-China: probably furunculus orientalis. Called also *Cochin-China u.* **anastomotic u.,** ulcer of the jejunum occurring as a complication following gastroenterostomy performed for duodenal ulcer. **Annam u.,** an ulcer endemic in tropical parts of Asia, similar to Aleppo boil. **arrosion u.,** an annoying ulcer of the respiratory tract: usually tuberculous. **arterial u.,** an ulcer of the skin caused by disease of an artery. **atheromatous u.,** a loss of substance in the wall of an artery or in the endocardium, caused by the breaking down of an atheromatous patch or abscess. **atonic u.,** a chronic ulcer with unhealthy granulations. **autochthonous u.,** a chancre. **Bouveret's u.,** an ulcer occurring in typhoid fever in the fauces just above and to the outer side of the tonsil. **callous u.,** indolent u. **carious u.,** a gangrenous sore. **chancroidal u.,** chancroid. **Chiclero u.,** cutaneous leishmaniasis. **chrome u.,** an ulcer produced by chromium or its salts: seen in tanners and others working in chromium. **chronic u.,** indolent u. **chronic undermining u.,** a rare chronic ulceration of the skin in which the margins become undermined and inverted: due to hemolytic streptococcus infection. **Clarke's u.,** corroding ulcer of the neck of the uterus. **Cochin-China u.,** anamite u. **cockscomb u.,** an ulcer with condylomatous outgrowths. **cold u.,** a small noninflammatory ulcer of the extremities, sometimes gangrenous. It is due to imperfect nutrition, and is attended with coldness of the surface. **concealed u.,** destructive inflammation affecting some internal tissue. **constitutional u.,** one that is a local expression of a general disease, such as tuberculosis or pyemia. **corroding u.,** one which spreads by a gangrenous process. **corrosive u.,** gangrenous stomatitis. **crateriform u.,** a conical and swiftly growing epithelioma of the face, having a crater-like ulcer at the apex. **creeping u.,** serpiginous u. **Crombie's u.,** ulcer of the gum in sprue. **Cruveilhier's u.,** simple gastric ulcer. See *ulcus ventriculi.* **Curling's u.,** an ulcer of the duodenum following a severe burn upon the surface of the body. **Cushing's u.,** a peptic ulcer associated with manifest or occult lesions of the central nervous system. **cystoscopic u.,** ulcer of the bladder due to injury by the cystoscope. **decubital u., decubitus u.,** an ulceration caused by prolonged pressure in a patient confined to bed for a long period of time. Called also *decubitus* and *pressure sore.* **dendriform u., dendritic u.,** ulcer of the cornea branching in various directions. **dental u.,** a lesion on the oral mucosa, resulting from trauma inflicted by the teeth, as by biting, or from irritation by a sharp or broken tooth. **Dieulafoy's u.,** a form of acute gastric ulcer with erosions of the mucosa. **diphtheritic u.,** one the surface of which is partly or entirely covered by a diphtheritic membrane. **duodenal u.,** an ulcer resembling gastric ulcer but situated in the duodenum. **Dyak hair u.,** a sharply circumscribed intestinal ulcer in amebiasis, the base of which is formed by fringe-like projections of the more resistant supporting tissues. **elusive u.,** Hunner's u. **endemic u.,** any form of ulcer prevailing in special districts or regions, like furunculus orientalis. **erethistic u.,** irritable u. **Fenwick-Hunner u.,** Hunner's u. **fissurated u.,** a lacerated and ulcerated condition of the cervix uteri. **fissured u.,** a deep and more or less linear form of ulcer. **fistulous u.,** the ulcerated superficial end of a fistula. **follicular u.,** a small ulcer on the mucous membrane having its origin in a lymph follicle. **fungous u.,** one covered by pale, fungous granulations, projecting above the level of the skin. Called also *weak u.* **Gaboon u.,** a variety of tropical ulcer occurring in the French Congo, Africa. **gastric u.,** an ulceration of the mucous lining of the stomach. **girdle u.,** a tuberculous ulcer that spreads along the wall of the intestine in an encircling manner. **gouty u.,** a superficial ulcer occurring over a gouty joint. **gummatous u.,** a broken-down superficial gumma. **gwaliar u.,** furunculus orientalis. **hard u.,** chancre. **healthy u.,** an ulcer which tends to progress toward a cure. It is attended with serous exudation, red, nonprojecting, and painless granulations, and smooth, soft edges. **hemorrhagic u.,** one from which blood occasionally flows. **Hunner's**

u., a lesion occurring in chronic interstitial cystitis, involving all the layers of the bladder wall, and appearing as a small brownish red patch on the mucosa; it tends to heal superficially and is notoriously difficult to detect. **hypopyon u.**, ulcus serpens corneae. **indolent u.**, one with an indurated and elevated edge and a nongranulating base, usually occurring on the leg, and nearly painless. Called also *chronic u.* and *callous u.* **inflamed u.**, one with edematous and painful borders and a purulent discharge. **intractable u.**, an indolent ulcer that resists treatment. **irritable u.**, one of which the surface and surrounding parts are red, tender, and painful. **Jacob's u.**, rodent ulcer; especially that of an eyelid. **Jeddah u.**, tropical u. **jejunal u.**, an ulcer of the jejunum. Such an ulcer developing after gastroenterostomy is called *secondary jejunal u.* **Kocher's dilatation u.**, ulceration occurring in a greatly distended intestine or in the course of ileus. **Kurunegala u.**, pyosis tropica. **Lahore u.**, tropical u. **Lipschütz u.**, ulcus vulvae acutum. **lupoid u.**, a skin ulcer that simulates or resembled lupus. **lymphatic u.**, one with an exudate resembling lymph. **Malabar u.**, tropical u. **Mann-Williamson u.**, progressive peptic ulcer produced in experimental animals by the performance of gastric resection or gastroenterostomy. **marginal u.**, a gastric ulcer in the jejunal mucosa near the site of a gastrojejunal anastomosis. Called also *stoma u.* **Marjolin's u.**, an ulcer seated upon an old cicatrix; it follows the breaking down of warty cicatricial tumors. **menstrual u.**, an ulcer which is the site of vicarious menstruation. **mercurial u.**, an ulcer caused by mercurial poisoning. **Mooren's u.**, rodent ulcer of the cornea. **Mozambique u.**, an endemic ulcer of East Africa: apparently a form of tropical ulcer. **mycotic u.**, an ulcer due to fungus infection. **neurogenic u.**, **neurotrophic u.**, an ulcer caused by nervous disease or by psychic factors. **Parrot's u.**, the ulceration seen in thrush. **Pendinski u.**, tropical u. **penetrating u.**, an ulcerative lesion which involves also the wall or substance of an adjacent organ. **Penjdeh u.**, cutaneous leishmaniasis. **peptic u.**, an ulceration of the mucous membrane of the esophagus, stomach, or duodenum, caused by the action of the acid gastric juice. **perambulating u.**, phagedenic u. **perforating u.**, an ulcer which involves the entire thickness of an organ, as the foot, or the wall of the stomach or intestine, creating an opening on both surfaces. **Persian u.**, tropical u. **phagedenic u.**, one which spreads rapidly and destructively, eating away the tissues, and marked by sloughing particles in the discharge. Called also *perambulating u.* and *sloughing u.* **phlegmonous u.**, inflamed u. **Plaut's u.**, Vincent's angina. **pneumococcus u.**, ulcus serpens corneae. **pudendal u.**, granuloma inguinale. **putrid u.**, hospital gangrene. **ring u.**, fusion of foci of ulceration in the cornea to form a peripheral ring of ulceration. **rodent u.**, carcinomatous or epitheliomatous ulcer which gradually involves and eats away the soft tissues and bones. It is generally seated upon the face. **round u.** 1. A peptic ulcer of the stomach. See *u. ventriculi.* 2. A rapid ulceration of the uterus, probably malignant. **Saemisch's u.**, an infectious and serpiginous ulcer of the cornea. **scorbutic u.**, one due to scurvy. **sea anemone u.**, an intestinal ulcer in amebiasis, with a deep crater and partly necrotic undermined edges which are raised above the level of the surrounding mucosa. **serpiginous u.**, one which moves from place to place, healing in one part and extending in another. **simple u.**, a mild form of ulcer which is neither of septic origin nor the expression of a general disease. **sloughing u.**, phagedenic u. **soft u.**, chancroid. **stasis u.**, ulceration on the lower extremity due to venous stasis or insufficiency. **stercoraceous u.**, stercoral u. **stercoral u.**, an ulcer caused by the pressure of impacted feces; also a fistulous ulcer through which fecal matter escapes. **stoma u.**, **stomal u.**, marginal u. **sublingual u.**, an ulcer on the frenum of the tongue, caused by irritation of the lower incisor teeth. **submucous u.**, Hunner's u.; so called because of the tendency of the lesion to heal superficially. **symptomatic u.**, an ulcer that indicates some general disease. **syphilitic u.**, chancre. **Syriac u.**, diphtheria. **Syrian u.** 1. Diphtheria. 2. Aleppo boil, or cutaneous leishmaniasis. **tanner's u.**, chrome u. **Tashkend u.**, one of the crusted ulcers that are developed in sartian disease, an endemic affection occurring in Tashkend in Asiatic Russia. **toenail u.**, onychia maligna, chiefly of the great toe. **traumatic u.**, one due to a local injury. **trophic u.**, an ulcer due to imperfect nutrition of the part. **trophoneurotic u.**, ulcer due to a nervous disease of central origin. **tropical u.** 1. A chronic sloughing ulcer usually on the lower extremities, of unknown causation and occurring in tropical regions. Called also *ulcus tropicum, tropical phagedena, Aden ulcer, Malabar ulcer, Cochin sore*, and *Nagana sore.* Many other terms of only geographical significance have been applied to tropical ulcer. 2. Cutaneous leishmaniasis. **tuberculous u.**, one due to the bacillus of tuberculosis. **Turkestan u.**, sartian disease; probably cutaneous leishmaniasis. **unhealthy u.**, an ulcer which does not tend to progress to a cure. The term includes *callous u., fungous u.*, and *phagedenic u.* **varicose u.**, one that is due to varicose veins. **venereal u.**, chancroid. **veneroid u.**, a disease marked by the formation of ulcers about the vulvae of women who have not been exposed to venereal disease. The ulcers resemble chancre or chancroid. Called also *Welander's u.* **warty u.**, Marjolin's u. **weak u.**, one with flabby, projecting, fungous granulations; a fungous ulcer. **Welander's u.**, veneroid u. **Yemen u.**, tropical u. **Zambesi u.**, an ulcer endemic among laborers of the Zambesi valley. It occurs on the leg or foot and is not attended with constitutional symptoms. It is caused by the larva of a dipterous fly which burrows into the subcutaneous tissue.

ulcerate (ul'ser-āt) [L. *ulcerare, ulceratus*]. To become affected with ulceration.

ulceration (ul"ser-a'shun) [L. *ulceratio*]. 1. The formation or development of an ulcer. 2. An ulcer. **u. of Daguet**, ulceration of the uvula and other parts of the throat, seen in typhoid fever.

ulcerative (ul'ser-a"tiv). Pertaining to or characterized by ulceration.

ulcerocancer (ul"ser-o-kan'ser). Carcinoma of the stomach following ulcer; malignant ulcer.

ulcerogangrenous (ul"ser-o-gan'grĕ-nus). Characterized by both ulceration and gangrene; pertaining to a gangrenous ulcer.

ulcerogenic (ul"ser-o-jen'ik). Causing ulceration; leading to the production of ulcers.

ulcerogranuloma (ul"ser-o-gran"u-lo'mah). A granuloma developing on an ulcer.

ulceromembranous (ul"ser-o-mem'brah-nus). Characterized by ulceration and by a membranous exudation.

ulcerous (ul'ser-us) [L. *ulcerosus*]. 1. Of the nature of an ulcer. 2. Affected with ulceration.

ulcus (ul'kus), pl. *ul'cera* [L.]. Ulcer. **u. am'bulans**, phagedenic ulcer. **u. ambustifor'me**, a chancroid which resembles a simple excoriation. **u. cancro'sum**, cancerous ulcer. **u. cru'ris**, indolent ulcer of the leg. **u. du'rum**, hard ulcer. **u. ex'edens**, rodent ulcer. **u. hypostat'icum**, an ulcer due to hypostatic congestion. **u. mol'le, u. mol'le cu'tis**, chancroid. **u. pen'etrans**, one that penetrates not into the peritoneal cavity but into an abutting organ. **u. phagedaen'icum corro'dens**, a gangrenous phagedenic ulcer of the vaginal part of the uterus. **u. ro'dens**, rodent ulcer. **u. scorbu'ticum**, an ulcer forming in scurvy. **u. ser'pens**, serpiginous ulcer. **u. ser'pens cor'neae**, a serpiginous ulcer of the cornea; a creeping central suppurative ulcer of the cornea due usually to pneumococcus. Called also *hypopyon ulcer* and *pneumococcus ulcer.* **u. sim'plex,** chancroid. **u. sim'plex vesi'cae,** Hunner's ulcer. **u. syphilit'icum,** a chancre or other syphilitic sore. **u. tropic'um,** tropical ulcer, def. 1. **u. ventric'uli,** gastric ulcer. **u. vul'vae acu'tum,** a rapidly growing ulcer of the vulva, of nonvenereal origin, and always associated with the presence of *Bacillus crassus.* Called also *Lipschütz ulcer.*

ule-. See *ulo-*.

ulectomy (u-lek'to-me) [Gr. *oulē* scar + Gr. *ektomē* excision]. 1. Excision of scar tissue, i.e., in secondary iridectomy. 2. [Gr. *oulon* gum + *ektomē* excision]. Excision of the gingiva; gingivectomy.

ulegyria (u"le-ji're-ah) [Gr. *oulē* scar + *gyrus* + *-ia*]. A condition in which the cerebral gyri are narrow and distorted by scars, resulting from lesions existing in fetal life or early infancy.

ulemorrhagia (u"lem-o-ra'je-ah) [Gr. *oulon* gum + *haimorrhagia* bleeding]. Bleeding or hemorrhage from the gingivae.

ulerythema (u"ler-ĭ-the'mah) [Gr. *oulē* scar + *erythēma* redness]. An erythematous disease of the skin characterized by the formation of cicatrices and by atrophy. **u. acneifor'ma,** a condition characterized by erythema and thickening of the skin about the hair follicles. **u. centrif'ugum,** lupus erythematosus. **u. ophryo'genes,** keratosis pilaris affecting the follicles of the eyebrow hairs, associated with erythema, and often leading to scarring and atrophy. **u. sycosifor'me,** lupoid sycosis.

uletic (u-let'ik). Pertaining to the gums.

uletomy (u-let'o-me) [Gr. *oulē* scar + *tomē* a cutting]. Incision of a cicatrix.

uliginous (u-lij'ĭ-nus) [L. *uliginosus* moist]. Muddy or slimy.

ulitis (u-li'tis) [Gr. *oulon* gum + *-itis*]. Inflammation of the gums; gingivitis. **aphthous u.,** ulitis combined with aphthae. **fungus u.,** ulitis due to presence of a fungus. **interstitial u.,** inflammation of the connective tissue of the gums around the teeth. **mercurial u.,** ulitis due to mercurialism. **scorbutic u.,** ulitis due to scurvy. **ulcerative u.,** ulitis with ulceration.

ullem (ul'em). A kind of dyspepsia occurring in Lapland.

Ullmann's line (ul'manz) [Emerich *Ullmann*, Hungarian surgeon, 1861–1937]. See under *line*.

Ulmus (ul'mus) [L. "elm"]. A genus of ulmaceous trees; the elms. **U. ful'va,** the slippery elm, the inner bark of which is mucilaginous and demulcent.

ulna (ul'nah), pl. *ul'nae* [L. "the arm"]. [N A, B N A] The inner and larger bone of the forearm, on the side opposite that of the thumb. It articulates with the humerus and with the head of the radius at its proximal end; with the radius and bones of the carpus at the distal end.

ulnad (ul'nad). Toward the ulna.

ulnar (ul'nar) [L. *ulnaris*]. Pertaining to the ulna.

ulnare (ul-na're) [L.]. Os triquetrum.

ulnaris (ul-na'ris). Ulnar; in official anatomical nomenclature, designating relationship to the ulna.

ulnen (ul'nen). Pertaining to the ulna alone.

ulnocarpal (ul"no-kar'pal). Pertaining to the ulna and carpus.

ulnoradial (ul"no-ra'de-al). Pertaining to the ulna and radius.

ulo- (u'lo). 1. [Gr. *oulē* scar]. Combining form denoting relationship to a scar, or cicatrix. 2. [Gr. *oulon* gum]. Combining form denoting relationship to the gingivae.

ulocace (u-lok'ah-se) [*ulo-*(2) + Gr. *kakē* badness]. Ulceration of the gingivae.

ulocarcinoma (u"lo-kar"sĭ-no'mah) [*ulo-*(2) + *carcinoma*]. Carcinoma of the gums.

ulodermatitis (u"lo-der"mah-ti'tis) [*ulo-*(1) + *dermatitis*]. Inflammation of the skin, producing scars.

uloglossitis (u"lo-glos-si'tis) [*ulo-*(2) + Gr. *glōssa* tongue + *-itis*]. Inflammation of the gums and the tongue.

uloid (u'loid) [*ulo-*(1) + Gr. *eidos* form]. 1. Resembling a scar, but not due to any lesion of the skin. 2. A spurious cicatrix; a scarlike spot due to a subcutaneous degeneration. It is seen in syphilis and lupus of the skin, and is also called *uloid cicatrix.*

uloncus (u-long'kus) [*ulo-*(2) + Gr. *onkos* mass, tumor]. A swelling or tumor of the gums.

ulorrhagia (u"lo-ra'je-ah) [*ulo-*(2) + Gr. *rhēgnynai* to burst forth]. A sudden or free discharge of blood from the gums.

ulorrhea (u"lo-re'ah) [*ulo-*(2) + Gr. *rhoia* flow]. An oozing of blood from the gums.

ulosis (u-lo'sis). Cicatrization.

ulotic (u-lot'ik). Pertaining to a cicatrix; producing cicatrization.

ulotomy (u-lot'o-me). 1. [Gr. *oulē* scar + *tomē* a cutting]. The cutting or division of scar tissue. 2. [Gr. *oulon* gum + *tomē* a cutting]. Incision of the gingivae.

ulotrichous (u-lot'rĭ-kus) [Gr. *oulotrichos*]. Having crisp curly hair.

ulotripsis (u"lo-trip'sis) [*ulo-*(2) + Gr. *tripsis* rubbing]. Gum revitalization by massage.

ultandren (ul-tan'dren). Trade mark for a preparation of fluoxymesterone.

ultimate (ul'tĭ-māt) [L. *ultimus* last]. The last or farthest; final or most remote.

ultimisternal (ul"tĭ-mĭ-ster'nal). Pertaining to the xiphoid process.

ultimum moriens (ul'tĭ-mum mo're-enz) [L. "last to die"]. 1. The right atrium, said to be the last part of the body to cease moving in death. 2. The upper part of the trapezius muscle.

ult. praes. Abbreviation for L. *ul'timum praescriptus,* last prescribed.

ultra- [L. "beyond"]. A prefix denoting excess.

ultrabrachycephalic (ul"trah-brak"e-se-fal'ik). Having a cephalic index of more than 90.

ultracentrifuge (ul"trah-sen'trĭ-fūj). A centrifuge with an exceedingly high rate of rotation which will separate and sediment the molecules of a substance.

ultradolichocephalic (ul"trah-dol"ĭ-ko-se-fal'ik). Extremely dolichocephalic; having a cephalic index of not more than 64.

ultrafilter (ul"trah-fil'ter). An apparatus for performing ultrafiltration.

ultrafiltration (ul"trah-fil-tra'shun). Filtration under pressure through filters with minute pores: used to separate a substance in colloid solution from its dispersion medium.

ultragaseous (ul"trah-gas'e-us). Having the properties of gas at one millionth of atmospheric pressure. See *radiant matter,* under *matter.*

ultraligation (ul"trah-li-ga'shun). Ligation of a vessel beyond the point of origin of a branch.

ultramicrobe (ul"trah-mi'krōb). An ultramicroscopic microorganism.

ultramicrochemistry (ul"trah-mi"kro-kem'is-tre). The chemical study of materials in extremely minute quantities.

ultramicron (ul"trah-mi'kron). 1. An ultramicroscopical particle less than one fourth of a micron in diameter. 2. An individual element of the dispersed phase of a colloid.

ultramicroscope (ul"trah-mi'kro-skōp). A special darkfield microscope for the examination of particles of colloidal size.

ultramicroscopic (ul"trah-mi"kro-skop'ik). 1. Pertaining to the ultramicroscope. 2. Too small to be seen with an ordinary microscope.

ultramicroscopy (ul"trah-mi-kros'ko-pe). The employment of the ultramicroscope.

ultran (ul′tran). Trade mark for preparations of phenaglycodol.

ultraprophylaxis (ul″trah-pro″fĭ-lak′sis). Prophylaxis directed toward the prevention of diseased or abnormal children by regulation of the marriage of the unfit.

ultraquinine (ul″trah-kwin′in). An alkaloid from cuprea bark. Called also *homoquinine.*

ultra-red (ul″trah-red′). Infrared.

ultrasome (ul′trah-sōm) [*ultra-* + Gr. *sōma* body]. Any body so small that it is beyond the vision even when aided by the most powerful microscope.

ultrasonic (ul″trah-son′ik) [*ultra-* + L. *sonus* sound]. Pertaining to mechanical radiant energy having a frequency beyond the upper limit of perception by the human ear, that is, beyond about 20,000 cycles per second.

ultrasonics (ul″trah-son′iks). That part of the science of acoustics dealing with the frequency range beyond the upper limit of perception by the human ear (beyond 20 kilocycles).

ultrasound (ul′trah-sownd). Mechanical radiant energy (see *sound*), with a frequency greater than 20,000 cycles per second.

ultrastructure (ul′trah-struk″tūr). The arrangement of the smallest elements making up a body; the arrangement of ultramicrons making up a substance.

ultratoxon (ul″trah-tok′son). A toxon of the lowest degree of toxicity.

ultraviolet (ul″trah-vi′o-let). Beyond the violet end of the spectrum: said of rays or radiation between the violet rays and the roentgen rays, that is, with wavelengths between 1800 and 3900 angstroms. They have powerful actinic and chemical properties. **far u.,** ultraviolet radiation of shortest wavelength, between 1800 and 2900 angstroms. **near u.,** that portion of the ultraviolet near the visible spectrum, that is, with wavelengths between 2900 and 3900 angstroms.

ultravirus (ul″trah-vi′rus). An extremely small pathogenic agent. See *filterable virus,* under *virus.*

ultravisible (ul″trah-viz′ĭ-b'l). Ultramicroscopic.

ultromotivity (ul″tro-mo-tiv′ĭ-te). Ability to move spontaneously.

Ultzmann's test (ooltz′mahnz) [Robert *Ultzmann,* German urologist, 1842–1889]. See under *tests.*

ululation (ul″u-la′shun) [L. *ululare* to howl]. The loud crying or wailing of hysterical patients.

umb. Abbreviation for L. *umbilicus.*

umbauzonen (um″bou-zo′nen) [Ger., "rebuilding zones"]. Looser's transformation zones. See under *zone.*

umber (um′ber). A natural earth containing chiefly manganese, iron oxide, and silica: used as a pigment.

Umber's test (um′berz) [Friedrich *Umber,* German physician, 1871–1946]. See under *tests.*

umbilectomy (um″bĭ-lek′to-me) [*umbilicus* + Gr. *ektomē* excision]. Excision of the umbilicus.

umbilical (um-bil′ĭ-kal) [L. *umbilicalis*]. Pertaining to the umbilicus.

umbilicate (um-bil′ĭ-kāt) [L. *umbilicatus*]. Shaped like or resembling the umbilicus.

umbilicated (um-bil′ĭ-kāt″ed). Marked by depressed areas resembling the umbilicus.

umbilication (um″bil-ĭ-ka′shun). A pit or depression resembling the umbilicus.

umbilicus (um″bĭ-li′kus) [L.]. [N A, B N A] The cicatrix marking the site of attachment of the umbilical cord in the fetus. **amniotic u.,** the oval aperture formed by converging amnion folds. **decidual u.,** a small cicatricial mark on the blastocyst during the early part of its stay in the uterus, marking the place of the closure of the decidua capsularis. **posterior u.,** pilonidal sinus.

umbo (um′bo), pl. *umbo′nes* [L. "a boss"]. A round projection; the projecting center of any rounded surface, such as the boss of a shield. **u. membra′nae tym′pani** [N A, B N A], **u. of tympanic membrane,** the slight projection at the center of the outer surface of the tympanic membrane, corresponding to the point of attachment of the tip of the manubrium of the malleus.

umbonate (um′bo-nāt) [L. *umbo* a knob]. Knoblike; button-like; having a button-like, raised center.

umbrascopy (um-bras′ko-pe) [L. *umbra* shade + Gr. *skopein* to examine]. Skiascopy.

unazotized (un-a′zo-tizd). Containing no nitrogen.

unbalance (un-bal′ans). Lack or loss of normal balance.

Uncaria (un-ka′re-ah) [L.]. A genus of rubiaceous tropical plants.

uncia (un′se-ah) [L.]. 1. Ounce. 2. Inch.

unciform (un′sĭ-form) [L. *uncus* hook + *forma* form]. Shaped like a hook.

unciforme (un″sĭ-for′me) [L.]. Hooked. See *os hamatum.*

uncinal (un′sĭ-nal). Uncinate.

Uncinaria (un″sĭ-na′re-ah) [L. *uncus* hook]. A genus of nematode worms. **U. america′na,** *Necator americanus.* **U. duodena′lis,** *Ancylostoma duodenale.* **U. stenoceph′ala,** the fox hookworm, a common cause of hookworm disease in dogs.

uncinariasis (un″sin-ah-ri′ah-sis). The state of being infected with hookworms. See *ancylostomiasis* and *necatoriasis.*

uncinariatic (un″sĭ-na″re-at′ik). Pertaining to or exhibiting uncinariasis.

uncinate (un′sĭ-nāt). Hooked or barred; unciform.

uncinatum (un″sĭ-na′tum) [L.]. Hooked. See *os hamatum.*

uncipressure (un′sĭ-presh″ur) [L. *uncus* hook + *pressura* pressure]. Pressure with a hook to stay hemorrhage.

uncomplemented (un-kom′ple-ment″ed). Not joined with complement, and therefore not active.

unconscious (un-kon′shus). 1. Insensible; incapable of responding to sensory stimuli and of having subjective experiences. 2. In freudian terminology, that part of mental activity which includes primitive or repressed wishes. Since these are concealed from consciousness by the psychic censor, the subject cannot know of them unless they are revealed to him through some psychotherapeutic procedure or as a result of severe emotional strain.

unco-ossified (un″ko-os′ĭ-fīd). Not united into one bone.

uncotomy (ung-kot′o-me) [*uncus* + Gr. *tomē* a cutting]. The production of a circumscribed lesion in the uncus in the treatment of psychotic states.

unction (ungk′shun) [L. *unctio*]. 1. An ointment. 2. The application of an ointment or salve; inunction.

unctuous (ungk′tu-us). Greasy or oily.

uncus (ung′kus) [L. "hook"]. [N A, B N A] The medial protrusion of the anterior part of the parahippocampal gyrus. Called also *u. gyri fornicati, u. gyri hippocampi,* and *u. gyri parahippocampalis.* **u. of hamate bone,** hamulus ossis hamati.

undecane (un′de-kān). A colorless petroleum hydrocarbon, $CH_3(CH_2)_9CH_3$. **u. diamidine,** a compound which cures trypanosome infection in laboratory animals.

undercut (un′der-kut). A side cut made in the wall of a cavity for the purpose of retaining the filling in the tooth.

underhorn (un′der-horn). Cornu inferius ventriculi lateralis.

undernutrition (un″der-nu-trish′un). Improper nutrition due to inadequate food supply or to failure to ingest, assimilate, or utilize any or all of the necessary food elements.

understain (un′der-stān). To stain less deeply than usual.

undertoe (un′der-to). A condition in which the great toe is displaced under the others.

Underwood's disease (un′der-woodz) [Michael *Underwood*, London obstetrician and pediatrist, 1737–1820]. Sclerema neonatorum.

undifferentiation (un″dif-er-en″she-a′shun). Absence of normal differentiation; anaplasia.

undine (un′dīn). A small glass flask for irrigating the eye.

undinism (un′din-izm) [*Undine* a water nymph, from L. *unda* wave]. The association of sexual ideas with water, including urine and urination.

undulant (un′du-lant) [L. *unda* wave]. Characterized by wavelike fluctuations.

undulation (un″du-la′shun) [L. *undulatio*]. A wavelike motion in any medium; a vibration. **jugular u.**, venous pulse. **respiratory u.**, the variation of the blood pressure curve due to respiration.

Undulina (un″du-li′nah). Trypanosoma.

ung. Abbreviation for L. *unguen′tum*, ointment.

ungual (ung′gwal) [L. *unguis* nail]. Pertaining to the nails.

unguent (ung′gwent) [L. *unguentum*]. An ointment, salve, or cerate.

unguentum (ung-gwen′tum) [L.]. Ointment. **u. ac′idi bo′rici,** boric acid ointment. **u. ac′idi undecylen′ici compos′itum,** compound undecylenic acid ointment. **u. aeth′ylis aminobenzoa′tis,** ethyl aminobenzoate ointment. **u. al′bum,** white ointment. **u. a′quae ro′sae,** rose water ointment. **u. a′quae ro′sae petrola′tum,** petrolatum rose water ointment. **u. belladon′nae,** belladonna ointment. **u. calami′nae,** calamine ointment. **u. epinephri′nae bitartra′tis ophthal′micum,** epinephrine bitartrate ophthalmic ointment. **u. fla′vum,** yellow ointment. **u. glycol′is polyethyle′ni,** polyethylene glycol ointment. **u. hydrar′gyri ammonia′ti,** ammoniated mercury ointment. **u. hydrar′gyri biochlo′ridi,** mercury bichloride ointment. **u. hydrar′gyri chlori′di mi′tis,** mild mercurous chloride ointment. **u. hydrar′gyri mi′te,** mild mercurial ointment. **u. hydrar′gyri ox′idi fla′vi,** yellow mercuric oxide ointment. **u. hydrophil′icum,** hydrophilic ointment. **u. ichthammol′lis,** ichthammol ointment. **u. menthol′is compos′itum,** compound methol ointment. **u. nitrofurazo′ni,** nitrofurazone ointment. **u. pi′cis carbo′nis,** coal tar ointment. **u. pi′cis pi′ni,** pine tar ointment. **u. resorcinol′is compos′itum,** compound resorcinol ointment. **u. sulfacetami′di so′dici,** sulfacetamide sodium ointment. **u. sulfu′ris,** sulfur ointment. **u. zin′ci ox′idi,** zinc oxide ointment.

unguiculate (ung-gwik′u-lāt). Provided with claws; resembling a claw.

unguiculus (ung-gwik′u-lus) [L., dim. of *unguis*]. A small nail or claw.

unguinal (ung′gwĭ-nal) [L. *unguis* a nail]. Pertaining to a nail or to the nails; resembling a nail; pertaining to an unguis.

unguis (ung′gwis), pl. *un′gues* [L.] 1. [N A] The horny cutaneous plate on the dorsal surface of the distal end of the terminal phalanx of a finger or toe, made up of flattened epithelial scales developed from the stratum lucidum of the skin. Called also *nail.* 2. A collection of pus in the cornea; an onyx. 3. A nail-like part or structure. **u. incarna′tus,** ingrowing toenail. **u. ventric′uli latera′lis cer′ebri,** calcar avis.

ungula (ung′gu-lah) [L. "hoof," "claw," "talon"]. 1. The hoof of an animal. 2. An instrument for extracting a dead fetus.

ungulate (ung″gu-lāt) [L. *ungula* hoof]. A four-legged mammal in which the digits may be more or less fused and their ends are protected with a horny coating layer, or hoof.

uni- [L. *unus* one]. Prefix meaning *one.*

uni-acral (u″ne-a′kral) [*uni-* + Gr. *akron* extremity]. Pertaining to or affecting only one extremity or limb.

uniarticular (u″ne-ar-tik′u-lar) [*uni-* + L. *articulus* joint]. Pertaining to a single joint.

uniaural (u″ne-aw′ral). Monaural.

uniaxial (u″ne-ak′se-al) [*uni-* + L. *axis* axis]. 1. Having but one axis. 2. Developing in an axial direction only, as, *uniaxial* organism.

unibasal (u″nĭ-ba′sal) [*uni-* + L. *basis* base]. Having only one base.

unicameral (u″nĭ-kam′er-al) [*uni-* + L. *camera* chamber]. Having only one cavity or compartment.

unicellular (u″nĭ-sel′u-lar) [*uni-* + L. *cellula* cell]. Made up of but a single cell.

unicentral (u″nĭ-sen′tral) [*uni-* + L. *centrum* center]. Pertaining to or having a single center.

unicentric (u″nĭ-sen′trik). Unicentral.

uniceps (u″nĭ-seps) [*uni-* + L. *caput* head] Having one head or origin: said of a muscle.

uniceptor (u′nĭ-sep″tor). A ceptor with a single combining group. See *Ehrlich's side-chain theory,* under *theory.*

unicism (u′nĭ-sizm) [L. *unicus* single]. The obsolete opinion that there is but one kind of venereal virus.

unicornous (u″nĭ-kor′nus) [L. *unicornis*]. Having only one horn.

unicuspid (u″nĭ-kus′pid). A tooth with only one cusp.

unicuspidate (u″nĭ-kus′pĭ-dāt). Having only one cusp.

unidirectional (u″nĭ-di-rek′shun-al). Flowing in only one direction.

uniflagellate (u″nĭ-flaj′ĕ-lāt). Having one flagellum.

unifocal (u″nĭ-fo′kal). Arising from or pertaining to a single focus.

uniforate (u″nĭ-fo′rāt) [*uni-* + L. *foratus* pierced]. Having only one opening.

unigeminal (u″nĭ-jem′ĭ-nal) [*uni-* + L. *geminus* twin]. Pertaining to or affecting one twin of a pair.

unigerminal (u″nĭ-jer′mĭ-nal). Pertaining to a single germ.

uniglandular (u″nĭ-glan′du-lar). Pertaining to or affecting only one gland.

unigravida (u″nĭ-grav′ĭ-dah). Primigravida.

unilaminar (u″nĭ-lam′ĭ-nar). Having only one layer.

unilateral (u″ne-lat′er-al) [*uni-* + L. *latus* side]. Affecting but one side.

unilobar (u″ne-lo′bar). Having only one lobe; consisting of a single lobe.

unilocular (u″ne-lok′u-lar) [*uni-* + L. *loculus*]. Having but one loculus or compartment.

unimodal (u″ne-mo′dal). Having only one mode.

uninephrectomized (u-ne-ne-frek′to-mīzd). Having one kidney removed by excision.

uninuclear (u″ne-nu′kle-ar). Pertaining to a single nucleus.

uninucleated (u″ne-nu′kle-āt″ed). Having but one nucleus.

uniocular (u″ne-ok′u-lar) [*uni-* + L. *oculus* eye]. Pertaining to or affecting but one eye.

union (ūn′yun) [L. *unio*]. The process of healing; the renewal of continuity in a broken bone or between the lips of a wound. See *healing.* **faulty u.,** an ununited fracture. **primary u.,** healing by first intention. **vicious u.,** union of the ends of a fractured bone so as to produce deformity.

uniovular (u″ne-ov′u-lar) [*uni-* + L. *ovum* egg]. Arising from one ovum: said of certain twin pregnancies.

unipara (u-nip′ah-rah). Primipara.

uniparental (u″ne-pah-ren′tal). Pertaining to one of the parents only.

uniparous (u-nip′ah-rus) [*uni-* + L. *parere* to bring forth, produce]. 1. Producing only one ovum or offspring at one time. 2. Primiparous.

unipolar (u″ne-po′lar) [*uni-* + L. *polus* pole]. 1. Having but a single pole or process, as a nerve cell. 2. Performed with one electric pole.

unipotency (u″ne-po′ten-se) [L. *unus* one + *potentia* power]. The ability of a part to develop in one manner only, or of a cell to develop into only one type of cell.

unipotent (u-nip′o-tent). Unipotential.

unipotential (u″ne-po-ten′shal) [*uni-* + L. *potens* able]. Capable in one way only: said of cells which have had their fates determined and can give rise to cells of one order only. Cf. *totipotential.*

unirritable (un-ir′ĭ-tah-b′l). Not irritable; not capable of being stimulated.

uniseptate (u″ne-sep′tāt). Having only one septum.

unisexual (u″ne-seks′u-al) [*uni-* + L. *sexus* sex]. Of only one sex; having the sexual organs of one sex only.

unit (u′nit) [L. *unus* one]. 1. A single thing. 2. A quantity assumed as a standard of measurement. 3. A gene. **alexinic u.,** the smallest quantity of alexinic serum required to dissolve a given amount of red blood corpuscles in the presence of an excess of hemolytic serum. **Allen-Doisy u.** See *mouse u.* and *rat u.* **amboceptor u.,** the least quantity of amboceptor with which a definite amount of red blood corpuscles will be dissolved by an excess of complement. **American Drug Manufacturers' Association u.,** one tenth of the Steenbock unit. **Angström u.,** the unit of wavelength of electromagnetic and corpuscular radiations: equal to 10^{-7} mm. Called also *angstrom.* **Ansbacher u.,** a unit of vitamin K dosage. **antigen u.,** the least quantity of antigen which will fix one unit of complement so as to prevent hemolysis. **antitoxic u.,** a unit for expressing the strength of an antitoxin. The unit of diphtheria antitoxin is approximately the amount of antitoxin which will preserve the life of a guinea pig weighing 250 Gm. for at least four days after it is injected subcutaneously with a mixture of 100 times the minimum fatal dose of diphtheria toxin and the antitoxin. Practically, it is the equivalent of a standard unit preserved in Washington. The unit of tetanus antitoxin is approximately ten times the amount of tetanus antitoxin which will preserve the life of a guinea pig weighing 350 Gm. for at least ninety-six hours after the injection of a mixture of 100 minimum lethal doses of tetanus toxin and the antitoxin. The U. S. Public Health Service unit for scarlet fever antitoxin neutralizes 50 skin test doses of scarlet fever toxin. **avena u.,** the amount of auxin which applied to one side of the tip of an oat sprout will cause a curvature of 10 degrees. **Behnken's u.,** a unit of roentgen-ray dosage, being that quantity which, when applied in 1 cc. of air at 18 C. and 760 mm. Hg of pressure, engenders sufficient electric conductivity to equal one electrostatic unit, as measured by the saturation current. **Bodansky u.,** the quantity of phosphatase required to liberate 1 mg. of phosphorus in the form of phosphorus ion in an hour of incubation with a substrate of sodium β-glycerophosphate. **British thermal u.,** the amount of heat necessary to raise the temperature of 1 pound of water from 39°F. to 40°F., abbreviated B.T.U. **cat u.,** that amount of a drug calculated per kilogram of cat which is just sufficient to kill when slowly and continuously injected into the vein (Hatcher). **C. G. S. u.,** any unit in the centimeter-gram-second system. **chlorophyll u.,** a group of about 2000 chlorophyll molecules that participate in the reduction of one molecule of carbon dioxide in photosynthesis. **Clauberg's u.,** a unit of progestin which is essentially one half of a Corner-Allen unit. **clinical u.,** a unit of estrogenic activity equal to approximately one sixth of the international unit. **Collip u.,** a unit of dosage of parathyroid extract: it is one one-hundredth of the amount required to increase by 5 mg. the quantity of calcium in 100 cc. of blood at the end of fifteen hours in a dog of 20 Kg. weight. **Columbia u.,** a unit of bacitracin, being the amount which diluted 1024 times and added to 2 cc. of beef infusion broth will completely inhibit the growth of a stock culture of hemolytic streptococci. **complement u.,** the least quantity of complement which will hemolyze a definite amount of red blood corpuscles in the presence of an amboceptor unit. **Corner-Allen u.,** a unit of progestin dosage. **cortin u.,** the least quantity of cortin per kilogram of body weight which administered daily will maintain an adrenalectomized dog in normal condition for from seven to ten days. **Craw u.,** the amount of veratrum viride which causes cardiac arrest in the crustacean *Daphnia magna.* **u. of current.** See *ampere.* **dental u.,** a single tooth. **digitalis u.,** the activity of 0.1 Gm. of powdered digitalis. **dog u.,** the maximum daily dose of adrenal cortical hormone per kilogram of body weight necessary to keep an adrenalectomized dog in normal condition for from seven to ten days. **electromagnetic u's,** that system of units which is based on the fundamental definition of a unit magnetic pole as one which will repel an exactly similar pole with a force of one dyne when the poles are 1 cm. apart. **electrostatic u's,** that system of units which is based on the fundamental definition of a unit charge as one which will repel a similar charge with a force of one dyne when the two charges are 1 cm. apart. **Felton's u.,** a unit of antipneumococcic serum. **Florey u.,** Oxford u. **u. of force.** See *dyne.* **Hampson u.,** a unit of roentgen-ray dosage; it is one quarter of the erythema dose. **Hanson u.,** a unit of parathyroid extract, being one one-hundredth of the amount required to increase by 1 mg. the amount of calcium in the blood serum of a parathyroidectomized dog weighing 15 Kg. **u. of heat,** the quantity of heat required to raise a kilogram of water 1°C. See *calorie* and *therm.* **hemolytic u.,** the amount of inactivated immune serum which, in the presence of complement, will completely hemolyze 1 cc. of a 5 per cent emulsion of washed red blood corpuscles. **hemorrhagin u.,** the amount of snake venon necessary to produce hemorrhages in the vascular network of a three-day-old chick embryo. **Holzknecht u.,** a unit of roentgen-ray dosage equal to $\frac{1}{5}$ the erythema dose. **immunizing u.** See *antitoxic u.* **international u. of estrogenic activity,** the estrus-producing activity represented in 0.1 microgram of the international standard estrone. **international u. of gonadotrophic activity,** the specific gonadotrophic activity of 0.1 mg. of the standard material preserved at and distributed from the National Institute for Medical Research, Hampstead, London. It is derived from pregnancy urine and it is approximately the amount required to produce cornification of the vaginal epithelium of the immature rat. **international insulin u.,** one twenty-second of a milligram of the pure crystalline product now adopted as the standard. **international u. of male hormone,** the androgenic activity represented in 0.1 milligram of crystalline androsterone. **international u. of penicillin,** the specific penicillin activity contained in 0.6 microgram of the international standard sodium salt of II or G penicillin. **international u. of vitamin A,** activity equivalent to 0.6 gamma (0.0006 mg.) of pure beta-carotene. **international u. of vitamin B,** the activity of 10 mg. of the international standard absorption product. **international u. of vitamin C,** the vitamin C activity of 0.05 mg. of the international standard levo-ascorbic acid. **international u. of vitamin D,** the activity of 1 mg. of the international standard solution of irradiated ergosterol (1 mg. in 10 cc. of olive oil). One mg. given daily to rachitic rats for eight consecutive days should produce a wide calcium line. **Kienböck u.,** a unit of roentgen-ray dosage equal to $\frac{1}{10}$ of the erythema dose. **King u., King-Armstrong u.,** the amount of phosphatase which, when allowed to act upon an excess of disodium phenylphosphate at a pH of 9 for 30 minutes at 37.5°C., will liberate 1 mg. of phenol. **Lf u.,** that amount of diphtheria toxin or toxoid which gives the most rapid flocculation with one standard unit of antitoxin when mixed and incubated *in vitro.* **light u.** See *footcandle.* **lung u.,** all the structures distal to a respiratory bronchiole, including the alveoli and their blood vessels, lymphatics, nerves and connective tissue. **Mache u.,** a German unit for expressing the concentration of radium emanation in solution. It is equivalent to 3.64 eman. **motor u.,** the unit of motor activity formed by a motor nerve cell and its many innervated muscle fibers. **mouse u.,** the least amount of estrus-producing hormone which will cause in a spayed mouse a characteristic change in the vaginal epithelium. **Noon pollen u.,** the activity present in the saline extract from one millionth of a grain of pollen. **Oxford u.,** that amount of penicillin which, when dissolved in 50 cc. of meat extract broth, just inhibits completely a test strain of *Staphylococcus aureus.* **pepsin u.,** a unit for measuring the proportion of pepsin in the gastric juice. **physiologic u.,** micelle. **pigeon u. of vitamin B_1,** the dose of vitamin B_1 which will completely cure a beriberi pigeon for one day. It is 0.0025–0.0035 mg. of vitamin B_1 hydrochloride. **quantum u.** See *Planck's constant,* under *constant.* **rat u.,** the highest dilution of an estrus-producing hormone (estrin) which when given to a mature spayed rat in three injections at four-hour intervals during the first day will produce cornification and desquamation of the vaginal epithelium. **u. of resistance.** See *ohm.* **Schönheyder u.,** a unit of vitamin K dosage. **Sherman u.** (*for vitamin A*). See *Sherman-Munsell u. of vitamin A.* **Sherman u. of vitamin C,** that amount of vitamin C which fed daily will protect a 300-Gm. guinea pig from scurvy for ninety days. **Sherman-Bourquin u. of vitamin B_2,** that amount of riboflavin which fed daily to a standard test rat for eight weeks will give a gain of 3 Gm. a week. **Sherman-Chase u. of vitamin B,** that amount of vitamin B which fed daily to a standard test rat already depleted of its store of vitamin B will produce a gain of 3 Gm. per week during eight weeks. **Sherman-Munsell u. of vitamin A,** that amount of vitamin A which when fed daily just suffices to support a rate of gain of 3 Gm. per week for eight weeks in a standard rat previously depleted of vitamin A. **skin test u.,** that amount of scarlet fever toxin which when injected intradermally gives a positive reaction in susceptible persons and no reaction in unsusceptible or immune persons. A positive reaction is a faint to bright red area measuring as much as 10 mm. in one diameter. **Somogyi u.,** that amount of amylase which will destroy 1.5 mg. of starch in 8 minutes at 37°C. The normal range of the value in blood serum is considered by some to be between 80 and 200 units per 100 ml. **specific smell u.,** the smallest amount in substance in grams per liter which can be determined by odor. **spermatocyte u.,** the smallest amount of tuberculin which will destroy spermatogenesis when injected into the testicle of a guinea pig. **Steenbock u. of vitamin D,** the total amount of vitamin D which will produce a narrow line of calcium deposit in the rachitic metaphyses of the distal ends of the radii and ulnae of standard rachitic rats within ten days. **sudanophobic u.,** the smallest amount of corticotropic hormone which will cause the disappearance of the sudanophobic zone in at least two or three hypophysectomized rats when they are injected morning and evening on eight consecutive days. **Thayer u.,** a unit of vitamin K dosage. **Thayer-Doisy u.,** a unit of vitamin K activity, being equivalent to the activity of 1 μg. of pure vitamin K_1. **toxic u., toxin u.,** the smallest dose of toxin which will kill a guinea pig weighing about 250 Gm. in three to four days. **turbidity reducing u.,** the amount of hyaluronidase which is just sufficient to reduce the turbidity produced by 0.2 mg. of hyaluronate to that produced by 0.1 mg. after addition of acidified horse serum. **uranium u.,** a unit for measuring radioactivity, the activity of uranium being considered as 1. **urotoxic u.,** the smallest quantity of urotoxin which will kill an animal weighing 1 Gm. **U. S. P. u.,** one used in the United States Pharmacopeia in expressing the potency of antibiotic, pharmacodynamic, and endocrine preparations, as well as most of the serums, toxins, vaccines, and related products, corresponding to units established internationally, by the Food and Drug Administration, or by the National Institutes of Health. **vitamin A u.** See *international u. of vitamin A,* and *Sherman-Munsell u. of vitamin A.* **u. of vitamin B_1,** the antineuritic activity of 3 micrograms of the international standard preparation deposited at the National Institute for Medical Research, Hampstead. **vitamin C u.** See *international u. of vitamin C* and *Sherman u. of vitamin C.* **vitamin D u.** See *international u. of vitamin D, Steenbock u. of vitamin D* and *American Drug Manufacturers' Association u. of vitamin D.* **vitamin G u.** See *Sherman-Bourquin u. of vitamin B_2.* **Voegtlin u.,** the amount of contraction produced in the isolated guinea-pig uterus by 0.5 mg. of the standard powdered preparation of the posterior pituitary. **x-ray u.,** Kienböck u.

unitage (u′nit-ij). A statement of the unit quantity in any system of measurement.

unitary (u′nĭ-tăr″e) [L. *unitas* oneness]. Composed of or pertaining to a single unit.

unitensen (u″nĭ-ten′sen). Trade mark for preparations of cryptenamine.

uniterminal (u″nĭ-ter′mĭ-nal). Monoterminal.

unitubercular (u″nĭ-tu-ber′ku-lar). Having one tubercle or cusp: said of a tooth.

univalence (u″nĭ-va′lens). The state or condition of being univalent.

univalent (u″nĭ-va′lent) [*uni-* + L. *valere* to be strong]. Having a valence of one; replacing or combining with one atom of hydrogen or its equivalent.

univitelline (u″nĭ-vi-tel′in). Pertaining to or derived from a single ovum.

unmedullated (un-med′u-lāt″ed). Not possessing a medulla or medullary substance: said of a nerve fiber.

Unna's boot, dermatosis, paste, stain, etc. (oo′nahz) [Paul Gerson *Unna,* dermatologist in Hamburg, 1850–1929]. See under the nouns.

unof. Abbreviation for *unofficial.*

unofficial (un″o-fish′al) [L. *un* not + *official*]. Not authorized by the established dispensatories and formularies.

unorganized (un-or′gan-īzd). Not developed into an organic structure; not having organs.

unorientation (un″o-re-en-tā′shun). Extreme disorder of memory in which the person loses the ideas of place and time; disorientation.

unphysiologic (un″fiz-e-o-loj′ik). Not in harmony with the laws of physiology.

unrest (un-rest′). A state of uneasiness, or restlessness. **peristaltic u.,** a state of disturbed peristalsis of the stomach or intestine.

unsaturated (un-sat′u-rāt″ed). Not saturated: said of (1) a menstruum which has not dissolved as much of the solid as it is capable of doing; (2) an organic compound in which two or more carbon atoms are united by double or triple bonds. They are unsaturated in the sense that various atoms or groups such as Cl, OH, etc., can be added (not substituted) easily at these points.

Unschuld's sign (oon′shooldz) [Paul *Unschuld,* German internist, born 1835]. See under *sign.*

unsex (un-seks′). To deprive of the sex glands, or gonads.

unstriated (un-stri′āt-ed). Having no striations or striae.

Unverricht's disease (oon′fer-ikts) [Heinrich *Unverricht*, German physician, 1853–1912]. Myoclonus epilepsy.

upgrade (up-grād′). To raise to a higher grade or standard.

upsiloid (up′sĭ-loid) [Gr. υ + *eidos* form]. Shaped like the Greek upsilon (υ or Υ). See also *hypsiloid*.

ur-. See *uro-*.

urachal (u′rah-kal). Pertaining to the urachus.

urachovesical (u″rah-ko-ves′ĭ-kal). Pertaining to the urachus and the bladder.

urachus (u′rah-kus) [Gr. *ourachos*]. [N A, B N A] A canal in the fetus that connects the bladder with the allantois; it persists throughout life as a cord (the median umbilical ligament) into which a patent canal extends for one third of the distance to the umbilicus.

uracil (u′rah-sil). A ureide dihydroxypyrimidin, $C_4H_4O_2N_2$, obtained from nucleinic acid. **5-methyl u.** See *thymine*.

uracrasia (u″rah-kra′se-ah) [*ur-* + Gr. *akrasia* bad mixture]. A disordered state of the urine.

uracratia (u″rah-kra′she-ah) [*ur-* + Gr. *akrateia* lack of self control]. Urinary incontinence.

uragogue (u′rah-gog) [*ur-* + Gr. *agōgos* leading]. 1. Increasing urinary secretion; diuretic. 2. An agent that increases secretion of urine.

uramil (u′rah-mil). A crystalline body, $CO(NH.CO)_2CH.NH_2$, or dialuramide, obtainable from uric acid, alloxantin, and other substances.

uranalysis (u″rah-nal′ĭ-sis). Urinalysis.

uran-gallein (u″ran-gal′e-in). A combination of gallein and uranium: used as a stain for elastic tissue.

uranianism (u-ra′ne-an-izm). Uranism.

uranidin (u-ran′ĭ-din). Any one of a group of yellow animal pigments found in sponges, corals, medusae and worms.

uranisco- (u″rah-nis′ko) [Gr. *ouraniskos*, the roof of the mouth]. Combining form denoting relationship to the palate. See also *urano-*.

uraniscochasma (u″rah-nis″ko-kaz′mah) [*uranisco-* + Gr. *chasma* cleft]. Fissure of the palate.

uraniscolalia (u″rah-nis″ko-la′le-ah) [*uranisco-* + Gr. *lalia* talking]. A speech defect due to cleft palate.

uranisconitis (u″rah-nis″ko-ni′tis). Inflammation of the palate.

uraniscoplasty (u″rah-nis′ko-plas″te). Uranoplasty.

uraniscorrhaphy (u″rah-nis-kor′ah-fe) [*uranisco-* + Gr. *rhaphē* seam]. Palatorrhaphy.

uraniscus (u″rah-nis′kus) [Gr. *ouraniskos*, dim. of *ouranos*]. The palate.

uranism (u′rah-nizm) [Gr. *ourania* the heavenly one, one of the epithets of Aphrodite, or Venus, as the patroness of homosexuals]. Homosexuality.

uranium (u-ra′ne-um) [L. *Uranus* a planet]. A hard and heavy radioactive metallic element; symbol, U; atomic number, 92; atomic weight, 238.03; specific gravity, 18.68. Some of its compounds are medicinal. Naturally occurring uranium is composed of three isotopes of mass numbers 234, 235 and 238 respectively. Uranium 235 separated from U 238 breaks up easily, giving up a neutron which joins the nucleus of U 238 to form neptunium, which in turn decays by beta particle emission to form plutonium. Cf. *neptunium* and *plutonium*.

urano- (u′rah-no) [Gr. *ouranos* the roof of the mouth, also the vault of heaven, or sky]. Combining form denoting relationship to the palate; sometimes used in reference to the sky, or heaven.

uranophobia (u″rah-no-fo′be-ah) [*urano-* + Gr. *phobein* to be affrighted by]. Morbid dread of heaven.

uranoplastic (u″rah-no-plas′tik). Pertaining to uranoplasty.

uranoplasty (u′rah-no-plas″te) [*urano-* + Gr. *plassein* to mold]. Plastic surgery of the palate.

uranoplegia (u″rah-no-ple′je-ah) [*urano-* + Gr. *plēge* stroke + *-ia*]. Paralysis of the soft palate.

uranorrhaphy (u″rah-nor′ah-fe) [*urano-* + Gr. *rhaphē* seam]. Palatorrhaphy.

uranoschisis (u″rah-nos′kĭ-sis) [*urano-* + Gr. *schisis* fissure]. Fissure of the palate; cleft palate.

uranoschism (u-ran′o-skizm) [*urano-* + Gr. *schisma* cleft]. Fissure of the palate.

uranostaphyloplasty (u″rah-no-staf′ĭ-lo-plas″-te). A plastic operation for repairing a defect of both the soft and hard palates; palatoplasty.

uranostaphylorrhaphy (u″rah-no-staf″ĭ-lor′-ah-fe) [*urano-* + Gr. *staphylē* uvula + *rhaphē* suture]. Closure of fissure of both the hard and soft palates; palatorrhaphy.

uranostaphyloschisis (u″rah-no-staf″ĭ-los′kĭ-sis). Fissure of both the hard and the soft palate.

uranosteoplasty (u″rah-nos′te-o-plas″te). Uranoplasty.

Uranotaenia (u″rah-no-te′ne-ah). A genus of mosquitoes. **U. sappari′nus,** a species occurring in the eastern United States.

uranyl (u′rah-nil). Uranium dioxide, UO_2. **u. acetate,** a yellow crystalline compound: used in coryza. **u. nitrate,** a greenish-yellow crystalline compound.

urapostema (u″rah-pos-te′mah) [*ur-* + Gr. *apostēma* abscess]. An abscess which contains urine.

uraroma (u″rah-ro′mah) [*ur-* + Gr. *arōma* spice]. The spicy odor of urine.

urarthritis (u″rar-thri′tis). Gouty arthritis.

urase (u′rās). Urease.

urasin (u-ras′in). An enzyme derivable from urea by the action of various bacteria.

urate (u′rāt) [L. *uras*]. Any salt of uric acid. Urates, especially that of sodium, are constituents of the urine, the blood, and of tophi, or calcareous concretions.

uratemia (u″rah-te′me-ah) [*urate* + Gr. *haima* blood + *-ia*]. The presence of urates in the blood.

uratic (u-rat′ik). Pertaining to urates or to gout.

uratohistechia (u″rah-to-his-tek′e-ah) [*urate* + Gr. *histos* tissue + *echein* to hold]. The presence of an excessive amount of urate, urea or uric acid in a tissue.

uratolysis (u″rah-tol′ĭ-sis) [*urate* + Gr. *lysis* dissolution]. The decomposition or splitting up of urates.

uratolytic (u″rah-to-lit′ik). Pertaining to, characterized by, or promoting uratolysis.

uratoma (u″rah-to′mah). A tophus, or concretion made up of urates.

uratosis (u″rah-to′sis). The deposition of crystalline urates in the tissues.

uraturia (u″rah-tu′re-ah) [*urate* + Gr. *ouron* urine + *-ia*]. The presence of an excess of urates in the urine; lithuria.

urazin, urazine (u′rah-zin). A crystalline basic substance, $C_2H_4N_4O_2$, of the tetrazine class, derivable from two molecules of urea.

urazole (u′rah-zōl). A crystalline compound, $(NH.CO)_2NH$, formed by heating urea with hydrazine sulfate.

Urbach-Oppenheim disease (ur″bak op′en-hīm) [Erich *Urbach*, Philadelphia dermatologist, 1893–1946; Maurice *Oppenheim*, Chicago dermatologist, 1876–1949]. Necrobiosis lipoidica diabeticorum.

urceiform (ur-se′ĭ-form) [L. *urceus* pitcher + *forma* shape]. Pitcher-shaped.

urceolate (ur-se′o-lāt). Urceiform.

ur-defense (ur″de-fens′) [Ger. *Ur* ultimate, transcendent + *defense*]. A belief essential to the psychological integrity of the individual. Such beliefs include faith in personal survival, in religious, philosophic, or scientific systems, and in human succorance.

urea (u-re′ah). A white, crystallizable substance, the diamide of carbonic acid, $NH_2CO.NH_2$, from the urine, blood, and lymph. It is the chief nitrogenous constituent of the urine, and is the final product of the decomposition of proteins in the body, being the form under which the nitrogen of the body is given off. It is believed to be formed in the liver out of amino acids and other compounds of ammonia. See also *carbamide.* **diethyl malonyl u.,** barbital. **malo u.,** veronal. **malonyl u.,** barbituric acid. **mesoxalyl u.,** alloxan. **u. quinate, u. salicylate,** urea compounds which are used in gouty conditions. **tartronyl u.,** dialuric acid.

ureagenetic (u-re″ah-je-net′ik) [*urea* + Gr. *gennan* to produce]. Forming or producing urea.

ureal (u′re-al). Pertaining to urea.

ureameter (u″re-am′e-ter) [*urea* + Gr. *metron* measure]. An instrument used in determining the amount of urea present in the urine.

Doremus ureameter.

ureametry (u″re-am′e-tre). The measurement of the urea present in the urine.

ureapoiesis (u-re″ah-poi-e′sis) [*urea* + Gr. *poiein* to make]. The formation of urea.

urease (u′re-ās). A colorless, crystalline globulin that was first extracted by Takeuchi from soy bean. It is also found in mucous urine passed during inflammation of the bladder. It is formed by various microorganisms, and is capable of causing the change of urea into carbon dioxide and ammonia and of hippuric acid into benzoic acid and glycocoll. Called also *urea enzyme* and *urea ferment.*

urecchysis (u-rek′ĭ-sis) [*uro-* + Gr. *ekchysis* a pouring out]. The effusion of urine into the cellular tissue.

Urechites (u-rek′ĭ-tēz). A genus of plants. **U. suberec′ta,** Savannah flower; an apocynaceous plant of tropical America, with poisonous and antipyretic leaves.

urechitin (u-rek′ĭ-tin). A poisonous glycoside, $C_{28}H_{42}O_8 + xH_2O$, from *Urechites suberecta.*

urechitoxin (u-rek″ĭ-tok′sin). A poisonous glycoside, $C_{13}H_{20}O_5$, from *Urechites suberecta.*

urecholine (u″re-ko′lin). Trade mark for preparations of bethanechol.

uredema (u″re-de′mah) [*uro-* + Gr. *oidēma* swelling]. A puffy condition of the tissues caused by infiltration of extravasated urine.

uredo (u-re′do), pl. *ured′ines* [L.]. 1. An itching or burning sensation of the skin. 2. Urticaria.

ureide (u′re-id). A compound of urea and an acid or aldehyde formed by the elimination of water. Those from one molecule of urea, as alloxan, are monoureides; those derived from two, as uric acid, are diureides.

urein (u-re′in). A yellowish, oily substance isolated from the urine, and said to be the principal organic constituent and the true cause of uremia. It has a specific gravity of 1.27, and mixes freely with water and alcohol.

urelcosis (u″rel-ko′sis) [*uro-* + Gr. *helkōsis* ulceration]. 1. Ulceration of the urinary passages. 2. An ulcer due to derangement of the urinary apparatus.

uremia (u-re′me-ah) [Gr. *ouron* urine + *haima* blood + *-ia*]. The presence of urinary constituents in the blood, and the toxic condition produced thereby. It is marked by nausea, vomiting, headache, vertigo, dimness of vision, coma or convulsions, and a urinous odor of the breath and perspiration. It is due to suppression or deficient secretion of the urine from any cause. **azotemic u.,** retention uremia. **convulsive u.,** uremia in which the symptoms are due to spasm of the cerebral arteries or to increase of intracranial tension. **eclamptic u.,** convulsive uremia. **extrarenal u., prerenal u.,** uremia due to inhibition of renal function by disorders not related to the urinary tract. **puerperal u.,** uremic poisoning following childbirth. **retention u.,** uremia due to the retention of urinary nitrogenous substances in the blood.

uremic (u-re′mik). Pertaining to or characterized by uremia.

uremide (u′re-mīd). Any erythematous eruption due to uremic poisoning.

uremigenic (u-re″mĭ-jen′ik). 1. Caused by or due to uremia. 2. Causing uremia.

ureo-. For other words beginning thus, see those beginning *urea-.*

ureolysis (u″re-ol′ĭ-sis) [*urea* + Gr. *lysis* a loosing, setting free]. The disintegration or decomposition of urea into carbon dioxide and ammonia.

ureolytic (u″re-o-lit′ik). Pertaining to, characterized by, or promoting ureolysis.

ureosecretory (u″re-o-se′kre-to-re). Pertaining to the secretion of urea.

ureotelic (u″re-o-tel′ik) [*urea* + Gr. *telikos* belonging to the completion, or end]. Having urea as the chief excretory product of nitrogen metabolism.

uresiesthesis (u-re″se-es-the′sis) [*uresis* + Gr. *aisthēsis* perception + *-ia*]. The normal impulse to pass the urine.

uresis [u-re′sis) [Gr. *ourēsis*]. The passage of urine; urination. Sometimes used as a word termination denoting excretion in the urine of the substance indicated by the stem to which it is affixed, as chloruresis, cupruresis, saluresis.

uret (u′ret). The chemical group CH_2NO.

uretal (u-re′tal). Ureteral.

ureter (u-re′ter) [Gr. *ourētēr*]. [N A, B N A] The fibromuscular tube which conveys the urine from the kidney to the bladder. It begins with the pelvis of the kidney, a funnel-like dilatation, and empties into the base of the bladder, being from 16 to 18 inches long. **ectopic u.,** a ureter which opens elsewhere than in the bladder wall, usually arising from the upper segment of a double kidney, and, in the females, opening in the vestibule, terminal urethra, vagina, cervix, or uterine cavity; in the male it invariably enters the genital or urinary tract above the level of the external sphincter.

ureteral (u-re′ter-al). Pertaining to or used upon the ureter.

ureteralgia (u″re-ter-al′je-ah). Pain in the ureter; neuralgia of the ureter.

ureterectasia (u-re″ter-ek-ta′se-ah). Ureterectasis.

ureterectasis (u-re″ter-ek′tah-sis) [*ureter* + Gr. *ektasis* distention]. Distention of the ureter.

ureterectomy (u″re-ter-ek′to-me) [*ureter* + Gr. *ektomē* excision]. The surgical removal of a ureter or of a part of it.

ureteric (u″re-ter′ik). Ureteral.

ureteritis (u″re-ter-i′tis). Inflammation of a ureter. **u. cys′tica,** ureteritis characterized by the formation of multiple submucosal cysts. **u. glandula′ris,** ureteritis characterized by the conversion of transitional mucosal into cylindrical epithelium, with formation of glandular acini.

uretero- (u-re′ter-o) [Gr. *ourētēr* the duct which conveys urine from the kidney to the bladder]. Combining form denoting relationship to the ureter.

ureterocele (u-re′ter-o-sēl) [*uretero-* + Gr. *kēlē* hernia]. Sacculation of the terminal portion of the ureter into the bladder, as a result of stenosis of the ureteral meatus.

ureterocervical (u-re″ter-o-ser′vĭ-kal). Pertaining to a ureter and to the cervix uteri.

ureterocolostomy (u-re″ter-o-ko-los′to-me) [*ure-*

tero- + Gr. *kōlon* colon + *stomoun* to provide with an opening, or mouth]. Transplantation of the ureter into the colon.

ureterocutaneostomy (u-re″ter-o-ku-ta″ne-os′-to-me). Surgical creation of an opening of the ureter on the skin, permitting drainage of urine directly to the exterior of the body.

ureterocystanastomosis (u-re″ter-o-sis″tah-nas″to-mo′sis). Ureteroneocystostomy.

ureterocystoneostomy (u-re″ter-o-sis″to-ne-os′to-me) [*uretero-* + Gr. *kystis* bladder + *neos* new + *stomoun* to provide with an opening, or mouth]. Ureteroneocystostomy.

ureterocystoscope (u-re″ter-o-sis′to-skōp) [*uretero-* + *cystoscope*]. A cystoscope with an arrangement for catheterizing the ureters.

ureterocystostomy (u-re″ter-o-sis-tos′to-me) [*uretero-* + Gr. *kystis* bladder + *stomoun* to provide with an opening, or mouth]. Ureteroneocystostomy.

ureterodialysis (u-re″ter-o-di-al′ĭ-sis) [*uretero-* + Gr. *dialysis* separation]. Rupture of a ureter.

ureteroduodenal (u-re″ter-o-du″o-de′nal). Pertaining to or communicating with a ureter and the duodenum, as a ureteroduodenal fistula.

uretero-enteric (u-re″ter-o-en-ter′ik). Pertaining to or connecting the ureter and the intestine.

uretero-entero-anastomosis (u-re″ter-o-en″-ter-o-ah-nas″to-mo′sis). Uretero-enterostomy.

uretero-enterostomy (u-re″ter-o-en″ter-os′to-me) [*uretero-* + Gr. *enteron* bowel + *stomoun* to provide with an opening, or mouth]. The operation of forming an anastomosis between a ureter and the intestine.

ureterogram (u-re′ter-o-gram). A radiogram of the ureter.

ureterography (u-re″ter-og′rah-fe) [*uretero-* + Gr. *graphein* to write]. Radiography of the ureter after injection of an opaque medium into the ureter.

uretero-ileostomy (u-re″ter-o-il″e-os′to-me). Anastomosis of the ureters to an isolated loop of the ileum, drained through a stoma on the abdominal wall.

uretero-intestinal (u-re″ter-o-in-tes′tĭ-nal). Pertaining to or connecting the ureter and intestine.

ureterolith (u-re′ter-o-lith) [*uretero-* + Gr. *lithos* stone]. A calculus lodged or formed in a ureter.

ureterolithiasis (u-re″ter-o-lĭ-thi′ah-sis). The formation of a calculus in the ureter.

ureterolithotomy (u-re″ter-o-lĭ-thot′o-me) [*uretero-* + Gr. *lithos* stone + *tomē* a cutting]. The removal of a calculus from the ureter by incision.

ureterolysis (u-re″ter-ol′ĭ-sis) [*uretero-* + Gr. *lysis* dissolution]. 1. Rupture of the ureter. 2. Paralysis of the ureter. 3. The operation of freeing the ureter from adhesions.

ureteroneocystostomy (u-re″ter-o-ne″o-sis-tos′to-me) [*uretero-* + Gr. *neos* new + *kystis* bladder + *stomoun* to provide with an opening, or mouth]. Surgical transplantation of the ureter to a different site in the bladder.

ureteroneopyelostomy (u-re″ter-o-ne″o-pi″e-los′to-me) [*uretero-* + Gr. *neos* new + *pyelos* pelvis + *stomoun* to provide with an opening, or mouth]. An operation for cutting out a stricture of the ureter and inserting the upper end of the lower segment of the ureter through a new aperture into the pelvis of the kidney.

ureteronephrectomy (u-re″ter-o-ne-frek′to-me) [*uretero-* + Gr. *nephros* kidney + *ektomē* excision]. Extirpation of a kidney and its ureter.

ureteropathy (u-re″ter-op′ah-the) [*uretero-* + Gr. *pathos* disease]. Any disease of the ureter.

ureteropelvioneostomy (u-re″ter-o-pel″ve-o-ne-os′to-me). Ureteroneopyelostomy.

ureterophlegma (u-re″ter-o-fleg′mah) [*uretero-* + Gr. *phlegma* phlegm]. The presence of mucus in the ureter.

ureteroplasty (u-re′ter-o-plas″te) [*uretero-* + Gr. *plassein* to form]. Plastic operation upon the ureter for widening a stricture.

ureteroproctostomy (u-re″ter-o-prok-tos′to-me) [*uretero-* + Gr. *prōktos* anus + *stomoun* to provide with an opening, or mouth]. The operation of forming an anastomosis between the ureter and the lower rectum.

ureteropyelitis (u-re″ter-o-pi-ĕ-li′tis) [*uretero-* + Gr. *pyelos* pelvis]. Inflammation of a ureter and of the pelvis of a kidney.

ureteropyelography (u-re″ter-o-pi-ĕ-log′rah-fe). Roentgenography of the ureter and pelvis of the kidney.

ureteropyeloneostomy (u-re″ter-o-pi″ĕ-lo-ne-os′to-me) [*uretero-* + Gr. *pyelos* pelvis + *neos* new + *stomoun* to provide with an opening, or mouth]. Surgical formation of a new passage from the pelvis of a kidney to the ureter.

ureteropyelonephritis (u-re″ter-o-pi″ĕ-lo-ne-fri′tis) [*uretero-* + Gr. *pyelos* pelvis + *nephros* kidney + *-itis*]. Inflammation of the ureter and the pelvis of the kidney.

ureteropyelonephrostomy (u-re″ter-o-pi″ĕ-lo-ne-fros′to-me). Operative anastomosis of the ureter and the pelvis of the kidney.

ureteropyeloplasty (u-re″ter-o-pi′ĕ-lo-plas″te). Any plastic operation on the ureter and renal pelvis.

ureteropyelostomy (u-re″ter-o-pi″ĕ-los′to-me). Ureteropyeloneostomy.

ureteropyosis (u-re″ter-o-pi-o′sis) [*uretero-* + Gr. *pyon* pus + *-osis*]. Suppurative inflammation of the ureter.

ureterorectal (u-re″ter-o-rek′tal). Pertaining to or communicating with a ureter and the rectum, as a ureterorectal fistula.

ureterorectoneostomy (u-re″ter-o-rek″to-ne-os′to-me). Ureteroproctostomy.

ureterorectostomy (u-re″ter-o-rek-tos′to-me). Ureteroproctostomy.

ureterorrhagia (u-re″ter-o-ra′je-ah) [*uretero-* + Gr. *rhēgnynai* to burst forth]. A discharge of blood from the ureter.

ureterorrhaphy (u″re-ter-or′ah-fe) [*uretero-* + Gr. *rhaphē* suture]. The operation of suturing the ureter for fistula.

ureterosigmoidostomy (u-re″ter-o-sig″moid-os′to-me). The operation of implanting the ureter into the sigmoid flexure.

ureterostegnosis (u-re″ter-o-steg-no′sis) [*uretero-* + Gr. *stegnōsis* contraction]. Ureterostenosis.

ureterostenoma (u-re″ter-o-ste-no′mah) [*uretero-* + Gr. *stenōma* stricture]. Ureterostenosis.

ureterostenosis (u-re″ter-o-ste-no′sis) [*uretero-* + Gr. *stenōsis* narrowing]. Stricture of the ureter.

ureterostoma (u″re-ter-os′to-mah) [*uretero-* + Gr. *stoma* mouth]. 1. The vesical orifice of the ureter (ostium ureteris [N A]). 2. A ureteral fistula.

ureterostomosis (u-re″ter-o-sto-mo′sis). Ureterostomy.

ureterostomy (u″re-ter-os′to-me) [*uretero-* + Gr. *stomoun* to provide with an opening, or mouth]. The formation of a permanent fistula through which a ureter may discharge its contents. **cutaneous u.,** the operation of bringing the ureter to the skin through an incision in the iliac region; ureterocutaneostomy.

ureterotomy (u″re-ter-ot′o-me) [*uretero-* + Gr. *tomē* a cutting]. Surgical incision of a ureter.

ureterotrigono-enterostomy (u-re″ter-o-tri-go″no-en″ter-os′to-me). Implantation into the intestine of the ureter with the part of the bladder wall surrounding its termination.

ureterotrigonosigmoidostomy (u-re″ter-o-tri-go″no-sig″moid-os′to-me). Implantation into the sigmoid flexure of the ureter with the part of the bladder wall surrounding its termination.

ureteroureteral (u-re″ter-o-u-re′ter-al). Connecting two parts of the ureter.

ureteroureterostomy (u-re″ter-o-u-re″ter-os′-to-me). End-to-end anastomosis of the two portions of a transected ureter. See also *transureteroureterostomy*.

ureterouterine (u-re″ter-o-u′ter-in). Pertaining to or communicating with a ureter and the uterus.

ureterovaginal (u-re″ter-o-vaj′ĭ-nal). Pertaining to or communicating with a ureter and the vagina.

ureterovesical (u-re″ter-o-ves′ĭ-kal). Pertaining to a ureter and the bladder.

ureterovesicostomy (u-re″ter-o-ves″ĭ-kos′to-me). The operation of reimplanting the ureter at a different site in the bladder wall.

urethan (u′re-thăn). Chemical name: ethyl carbamate: used as a neoplastic suppressant.

urethane (u′re-thăn). Urethan.

urethra (u-re′thrah) [Gr. *ourēthra*]. The membranous canal conveying urine from the bladder to the exterior of the body. **anterior u.,** the portion of the male urethra extending from the bulb to the meatus on the summit of the glans penis, tunneling the corpus spongiosum; it consists of three parts, the bulbous, the pendulous, and the most distal, glandular part. **female u., u. femini′na** [N A], a canal, about 1½ inches long, extending from the neck of the bladder, running above the anterior vaginal wall and piercing the urogenital diaphragm, to reach the urinary meatus. Called also *u. muliebris* [B N A]. **male u., u. masculi′na** [N A], a canal extending from the neck of the bladder to the urinary meatus, measuring 8 or 9 inches in length, and presenting a double curve when the penis is flaccid. It is divided into a *pars prostatica, pars membranacea,* and *pars spongiosa.* Called also *u. virilis* [B N A]. **u. mulie′bris** [B N A], u. feminina. **posterior u.,** the portion of the male urethra, extending from the bladder to the bulb, and consisting of the membranous and prostatic parts. **u. viri′lis** [B N A], u. masculina.

urethral (u-re′thral). Pertaining to the urethra.

urethralgia (u″re-thral′je-ah). Pain in the urethra.

urethrascope (u-re′thrah-skōp). Urethroscope.

urethratresia (u-re″thrah-tre′ze-ah). Imperforation of the urethra.

urethrectomy (u″re-threk′to-me) [*urethra* + Gr. *ektomē* excision]. The surgical removal of the urethra or a part of it.

urethremphraxis (u″re-threm-frak′sis) [*urethra* + Gr. *emphraxis* stoppage]. Obstruction of the urethra.

urethreurynter (u-rēth″roo-rin′ter) [*urethra* + Gr. *eurynein* to make wide]. An instrument for dilating the urethra.

urethrism (u′re-thrizm) [L. *urethrismus*]. Irritability or chronic spasm of the urethra.

urethritis (u″re-thri′tis). Inflammation of the urethra. **u. cys′tica,** inflammation of the urethra, with the formation of multiple submucosal cysts. **u. glandula′ris,** inflammation of the urethra, with conversion of transitional mucosal into cylindrical epithelium, with formation of glandular acini. **gonorrheal u.,** gonorrheal infection of the urethra. **gouty u.,** urethritis due to gout. **u. granulo′sa,** urethritis in which the anterior urethra is filled with granulations. **nonspecific u.,** simple urethritis. **u. orifi′cii exter′ni,** inflammation and ulceration of the external urethral meatus. **u. petrif′icans,** urethritis with the formation of calcareous matter in the urethral wall. **prophylactic u.,** a mild urethritis that sometimes follows irrigations used to prevent venereal infections. **simple u.,** inflammation not due to a specific infection. **specific u.,** that due to infection with the gonococcus. **u. vene′rea,** gonorrhea.

urethro- (u-re′thro) [Gr. *ourēthra* the tube by which urine is discharged from the bladder]. Combining form denoting relationship to the urethra.

urethroblennorrhea (u-re″thro-blen″o-re′ah). A purulent discharge from the urethra.

urethrobulbar (u-re″thro-bul′bar). Pertaining to the urethra and the bulbus penis.

urethrocele (u-re′thro-sēl) [*urethro-* + Gr. *kēlē* tumor]. 1. Prolapse of the female urethra through the meatus urinarius. 2. A diverticulum of the urethral walls encroaching upon the vaginal canal.

urethrocystitis (u-re″thro-sis-ti′tis). Inflammation of the urethra and bladder.

urethrocystogram (u-re″thro-sis′to-gram). A roentgenogram of the urethra and bladder.

urethrocystography (u-re″thro-sis-tog′rah-fe) [*urethro-* + Gr. *kystis* bladder + *graphein* to write]. Roentgenography of the urethra and bladder after the injection of a contrast medium.

urethrocystopexy (u-re″thro-sis′to-pek″se) [*urethro-* + Gr. *kystis* bladder + *pēxis* fixation]. Surgical fixation of the urethrovesical junction, and the area of the bladder just above it, to the back of the pubic bones, for relief of stress incontinence.

urethrodynia (u-re″thro-din′e-ah) [*urethro-* + Gr. *odynē* pain]. Pain in the urethra; urethralgia.

urethrograph (u-re′thro-graf). An instrument for recording graphically the caliber of the urethra.

urethrography (u″re-throg′rah-fe). Roentgenography of the urethra after the injection of an opaque medium.

urethrometer (u″re-throm′e-ter) [*urethro-* + Gr. *metron* measure]. An instrument for measuring the urethra.

urethrometry (u″re-throm′e-tre). 1. Determination of the resistance of various segments of the urethra to retrograde flow of fluid. 2. Measurement of the urethra.

urethropenile (u-re″thro-pe′nīl). Pertaining to the urethra and the penis.

urethroperineal (u-re″thro-per″ĭ-ne′al). Pertaining to or communicating with the urethra and the perineum.

urethroperineoscrotal (u-re″thro-per-in″e-o-skro′tal). Pertaining to the urethra, perineum, and scrotum.

urethropexy (u-re′thro-pek″se) [*urethro-* + Gr. *pēxis* fixation]. Surgical fixation of the urethra to the overlying symphysis pubis and fascia of the rectus abdominis muscle, in correction of stress incontinence in the female.

urethrophraxis (u-re″thro-frak′sis) [*urethro-* + Gr. *phrassein* to stop up]. Obstruction of the urethra.

urethrophyma (u-re″thro-fi′mah) [*urethro-* + Gr. *phyma* growth]. A tumor or growth in the urethra.

urethroplasty (u-re′thro-plas″te) [*urethro-* + Gr. *plassein* to form]. Plastic surgery of the urethra; operative repair of a wound or defect in the urethra.

urethroprostatic (u-re″thro-pros-tat′ik). Pertaining to the urethra and the prostate.

urethrorectal (u-re″thro-rek′tal). Pertaining to or communicating with the urethra and the rectum.

urethrorrhagia (u-re″thro-ra′je-ah) [*urethro-* + Gr. *rhēgnynai* to burst forth]. A flow of blood from the urethra.

urethrorrhaphy (u″re-thror′ah-fe) [*urethro-* + Gr. *rhaphē* seam]. Suturation of the urethra; the closing of a urethral fistula by suture.

urethrorrhea (u-re″thro-re′ah) [*urethro-* + Gr. *rhoia* flow]. An abnormal discharge from the urethra.

urethroscope (u-re′thro-skōp) [*urethro-* + Gr. *skopein* to examine]. An instrument for viewing the interior of the urethra.

urethroscopic (u-re″thro-skop′ik). Pertaining to the urethroscope or urethroscopy.

urethroscopy (u″re-thros′ko-pe) [*urethro-* + Gr. *skopein* to examine]. Visual inspection of the interior of the urethra.

urethroscrotal (u-re″thro-skro′tal). Pertaining

to or communicating with the urethra and scrotum, as a urethroscrotal fistula.

urethrospasm (u-re′thro-spazm) [*urethro-* + Gr. *spasmos* spasm]. Spasm of the muscular tissue of the urethra.

urethrostaxis (u-re″thro-stak′sis) [*urethro-* + Gr. *staxis* dropping]. Oozing of blood from the urethra.

urethrostenosis (u-re″thro-ste-no′sis) [*urethro-* + Gr. *stenōsis* stricture]. Stricture, or stenosis, of the urethra.

urethrostomy (u″re-thros′to-me) [*urethro-* + Gr. *stomoun* to provide with an opening, or mouth]. The formation of a permanent fistula opening into the urethra in cases of incurable stricture.

urethrotome (u-re′thro-tōm). An instrument for cutting a urethral stricture. **Maisonneuve's u.,** a urethrotome in which the knife is concealed until it reaches the stricture, when the knife may be exposed.

urethrotomy (u″re-throt′o-me) [*urethro-* + Gr. *tomē* a cutting]. A cutting operation for curing a stricture of the urethra. It may be performed either externally or internally. *External urethrotomy* consists in opening the urethra from the outside. *Internal urethrotomy* may be performed in two ways, viz.: Incising from before backward, as with the instrument of Maisonneuve; incising from behind forward, as with the urethrotome of S. W. Gross.

urethrovaginal (u-re″thro-vaj′ĭ-nal). Pertaining to or communicating with the urethra and the vagina.

urethrovesical (u-re″thro-ves′ĭ-kal). Pertaining to or communicating with the urethra and the bladder.

uretic (u-ret′ik) [L. *ureticus;* Gr. *ourētikos*]. 1. Pertaining to the urine. 2. Diuretic.

Urginea (ur-jin′e-ah) [L.]. A genus of liliaceous plants. *U. marit′ima* affords squills. See under *Scilla.*

urhidrosis (ur″hid-ro′sis) [*ur-* + Gr. *hidrōs* sweat]. The presence in the sweat of urinous materials, such as uric acid, urea, etc. **u. crystal′lina,** a form in which crystals of uric acid are deposited upon the skin.

-uria (u′re-ah) [Gr. *ouron* urine + *-ia* state]. A word termination denoting a characteristic or constituent of the urine, indicated by the stem to which it is affixed, as oliguria, proteinuria.

urian (u′re-an). Urochrome.

uric (u′rik) [Gr. *ourikos*]. Pertaining to the urine.

uricacidemia (u″rik-as″ĭ-de′me-ah) [*uric* acid + Gr. *haima* blood + *-ia*]. The accumulation of uric acid in the blood. See *lithemia.*

uricaciduria (u″rik-as″ĭ-du′re-ah) [*uric* acid + Gr. *ouron* urine + *-ia*]. Presence in the urine of an excess of uric acid, and the morbid state produced thereby. See *lithemia.*

uricase (u′rĭ-kās). An enzyme found in most of the mammals except man, which catalyzes the complicated transformation of uric acid into allantoin.

uricemia (u″rĭ-se′me-ah). Uricacidemia.

uricocarboxylase (u″rĭ-ko-kar-bok′sĭ-lās). A hypothetical enzyme contained in uricase.

uricocholia (u″rĭ-ko-ko′le-ah) [*uric* acid + Gr. *cholē* bile]. The presence of uric acid in the bile.

uricolysis (u″rĭ-kol′ĭ-sis) [*uric* acid + Gr. *lysis* dissolution]. The splitting up of uric acid or of urates.

uricolytic (u″rĭ-ko-lit′ik). Pertaining to, characterized by, or promoting uricolysis.

uricometer (u″rĭ-kom′e-ter) [*uric* acid + Gr. *metron* measure]. An instrument for measuring the amount of uric acid in the urine. **Ruhemann's u.,** one based on the principle that uric acid will absorb iodine.

urico-oxidase (u″rĭ-ko-ok′sĭ-dās). A hypothetical enzyme contained in uricase.

uricopoiesis (u″rĭ-ko-poi-e′sis). The formation of uric acid.

uricosuria (u″rĭ-ko-su′re-ah). The excretion of uric acid in the urine.

uricosuric (u″rĭ-ko-su′rik). Pertaining to, characterized by, or promoting uricosuria.

uricotelic (u″rĭ-ko-tel′ik) [*uric* acid + Gr. *telikos* belonging to the completion, or end]. Having uric acid as the chief excretory product of nitrogen metabolism.

uricotelism (u″rĭ-ko-te′lizm). The excretion of uric acid as the end product of nitrogen metabolism.

uricoxidase (u″rĭ-kok′si-dās). An enzyme which oxidizes uric acid.

uridin (u′rĭ-din). A pentoside from nucleic acid. On hydrolysis it yields uracil and ribose.

uridrosis (u″rĭ-dro′sis). Urhidrosis.

uriesthesis (u″re-es′the-sis). Uresiesthesis.

urina (u-ri′nah) [L.]. Urine. **u. chy′li, u. ci′bi** ["urine of food"], the urine secreted after a full meal. **u. cruen′ta,** bloody urine. **u. galacto′des,** urine of a milky color. **u. hyster′ica** ["hysterical urine"], urine passed after an attack of hysteria. It is watery and of a pale color. **u. jumento′sa,** cloudy urine. **u. po′tus** ["urine of drink"], urine secreted after copious drinking. **u. san′guinis** ["urine of the blood"], urine passed after a night's rest, and so not influenced by food or drink. **u. spas′tica,** u. hysterica.

urinable (u′rin-ah-b'l). Capable of being excreted in the urine.

urinaccelerator (u″rin-ak-sel′er-a″tor). Musculus bulbocavernosus.

urinacidometer (u″rin-as″ĭ-dom′e-ter). An instrument for estimating the pH of urine.

urinaemia (u″rĭ-ne′me-ah). Uremia.

urinal (u′rĭ-nal) [L. *urinalis* urinary]. A vessel or other receptacle for urine.

urinalysis (u″rĭ-nal′ĭ-sis). Chemical or microscopical analysis of urine.

urinary (u′rĭ-ner″e). Pertaining to the urine; containing or secreting urine.

urinaserum (u-ri″nah-se′rum). Serum from an animal into which has been injected albuminous urine from another animal. The serum will precipitate albuminous urine and pleuritic exudates of an animal of the same species as that from which the injected material was taken. It is used as a test for albumin in the urine.

urinate (u′rĭ-nāt). To void or discharge urine.

urination (u″rĭ-na′shun). The discharge or passage of urine. **precipitant u.,** a sudden and strong desire to urinate. **stuttering u.,** an intermittent flow of urine, due to vesical spasm.

urinative (u′rĭ-na″tiv). Diuretic.

urine (u′rin) [L. *urina;* Gr. *ouron*]. The fluid secreted by the kidneys, stored in the bladder, and discharged by the urethra. Urine, in health, has an amber color, a slight acid reaction, a peculiar odor, and a bitter, saline taste. The average quantity secreted in twenty-four hours in a man in health is about 3 pints, or from 1200 to 1600 cc. Specific gravity, about 1.024, varying from 1.005 to 1.030. One thousand parts of healthy urine contain about 960 parts of water and 40 parts of solid matter, which consists chiefly of urea, 23 parts; sodium chloride, 11 parts; phosphoric acid, 2.3 parts; sulfuric acid, 1.3 parts; uric acid, 0.5 part; also hippuric acid, leukomaines, urobilin, and certain organic salts. The abnormal matters found in the urine in various conditions include acetone, albumin, albumose, bile, blood, cystine, glucose, hemoglobin, fat, pus, spermatozoa, epithelial cells, mucous casts and crystals of sulfanilamide derivatives (crystalluria). **anemic u.,** the urine of anemic persons. **Bence Jones u.** See *Bence Jones protein,* under *protein.* **black u.,** urine colored black by melanin; melanuria. **chylous u.,** urine of a milky color from the presence of chyle or fat; chyluria. **crude u.,** light-colored, watery urine, which deposits little sediment. **diabetic u.,** that which contains an excess of sugar. **dyspeptic u.,** the urine in dyspepsia, frequently containing calcium oxalate crystals. **febrile u.,** strong, odorous, high-colored urine, such as is secreted in fever. **gouty u.,** scanty, high-colored urine containing large quantities of uric acid. **hysterical u.,** watery, light-colored urine secreted in large quantity. **milky u.** See *chyluria.* **nebulous u.,** urine that is cloudy from the presence of earthy phosphates. **nervous u.,** hysterical u. **residual u.,** the urine that remains in the bladder after urination in disease of the bladder and hypertrophy of the prostate.

urinemia (u″rĭ-ne′me-ah) [*urine* + Gr. *haima* blood + *-ia*]. Uremia.

urine-mucoid (u″rin-mu′koid). A mucin-like substance found in the urine.

urineserum (u″rin-se′rum). Urinaserum.

urinidrosis (u″rin-ĭ-dro′sis). Urhidrosis.

uriniferous (u″rĭ-nif′er-us) [*urine* + L. *ferre* to bear]. Transporting or conveying the urine.

urinific (u″rĭ-nif′ik). Uriniparous.

uriniparous (u″rĭ-nip′ah-rus) [*urine* + L. *parere* to produce]. Producing or elaborating urine.

urino- (u′rĭ-no) [L. *urina;* Gr. *ouron*]. Combining form denoting relationship to urine.

urinocryoscopy (u-ri″no-kri-os′ko-pe). Cryoscopy of the urine.

urinogenital (u″rĭ-no-jen′ĭ-tal). Urogenital.

urinogenous (u″rĭ-noj′e-nus). Of urinary origin.

urinoglucosometer (u″rĭ-no-gloo″ko-som′e-ter). An instrument for measuring the glucose in the urine.

urinologist (u″rĭ-nol′o-jist). Urologist.

urinology (u″rĭ-nol′o-je). Urology.

urinoma (u″rĭ-no′mah). A cyst containing urine.

urinometer (u″rĭ-nom′e-ter) [*urino-* + Gr. *metron* measure]. An instrument for determining the specific gravity of the urine.

urinometry (u″rĭ-nom′e-tre). The ascertainment of the specific gravity of the urine.

urinophil (u-ri′no-fil). 1. Urinophilous. 2. A urinophilous organism.

urinophilous (u″rĭ-nof′ĭ-lus) [*urino-* + Gr. *philein* to love]. Having an affinity for urine, as a microorganism which grows best in urine, or an organism (such as a certain South American fish) which invades the urinary meatus of bathers.

urinoscopy (u″rĭ-nos′ko-pe). Uroscopy.

urinous (u′rĭ-nus). Pertaining to the urine; containing elements commonly excreted in the urine.

urinosexual (u″rĭ-no-seks′u-al). Genitourinary.

urinserum (u′rin-se″rum). Urinaserum.

uriposia (u″rĭ-po′ze-ah) [*urine* + Gr. *posis* drinking + *-ia*]. The drinking of urine.

urisolvent (u″rĭ-sol′vent). Dissolving uric acid.

uritis (u-ri′tis) [L. *urere* to burn + *-itis*]. Dermatitis calorica.

uritone (u′rĭ-tōn). Trade mark for preparations of methanamine.

urningism (oor′ning-izm). Uranism.

urnism (oorn′izm). Uranism.

uro-, ur-, urono- [Gr. *ouron* urine]. Combining form denoting relationship to urine, the urinary tract, or urination.

uro-acidimeter (u″ro-as″ĭ-dim′e-ter). An instrument for measuring the acidity of the urine.

uro-ammoniac (u″ro-ah-mo′ne-ak). Containing acid and ammonia.

uroanthelone (u″ro-an′the-lōn). Urogastrone.

uro-azotometer (u″ro-az″o-tom′e-ter). An apparatus for measuring the nitrogenous matter of the urine.

urobilin (u″ro-bi′lin) [*uro-* + L. *bilis* bile]. An amorphous, brownish pigment, $C_{35}H_{44}O_8N_4$, an oxidized form of urobilinogen, found in the feces and sometimes in the urine after standing in the air.

urobilinemia (u″ro-bil″ĭ-ne′me-ah) [*urobilin* + Gr. *haima* blood + *-ia*]. The presence of urobilin in the blood.

urobilinicterus (u″ro-bi″lin-ik′ter-us). A brownish coloration of the skin due to the deposit of urobilin in the tissues.

urobilinogen (u″ro-bi-lin′o-jen) [*urobilin* + Gr. *gennan* to produce]. A colorless compound formed in the intestines by the reduction of bilirubin. Some is excreted in the feces where by oxidation it becomes urobilin; some is reabsorbed, and re-excreted in the bile as bilirubin, or at times in the urine where it may be later oxidized to urobilin.

urobilinogenemia (u″ro-bi-lin″o-je-ne′me-ah). The presence of urobilinogen in the blood.

urobilinogenuria (u″ro-bi-lin″o-je-nu′re-ah). The presence of urobilinogen in the urine.

urobilinoid (u″ro-bil′ĭ-noid). Resembling urobilin.

urobilinoiden (u″ro-bil″ĭ-noi′din). A reduction product of hematin, resembling urobilin, sometimes found in the urine.

urobilinuria (u″ro-bil″ĭ-nu′re-ah) [*urobilin* + Gr. *ouron* urine + *-ia*]. The presence of an excess of urobilin in the urine.

urocanin (u″ro-ka′nin) [*uro-* + L. *canis* dog]. A base, $C_{11}H_{10}N_4O$, derivable from urocaninic acid, $C_{12}H_{12}N_4O_4$, a crystalline substance sometimes occurring in the urine of dogs.

urocele (u′ro-sēl) [*uro-* + Gr. *kēlē* hernia]. Distention of the scrotum with extravasated urine.

urocheras (u-rok′er-as) [*uro-* + Gr. *cheras* gravel]. Uropsammus.

urochezia (u″ro-ke′ze-ah) [*uro-* + Gr. *chezein* to defecate + *-ia*]. The discharge of urine in the feces.

urochrome (u′ro-krōm) [*uro-* + Gr. *chrōma* color]. A yellow, amorphous pigment of the urine, which gives the urine its yellow color.

urochromogen (u″ro-kro′mo-gen). A low oxidation product found in the urine, which on further oxidation becomes urochrome.

urocinetic (u″ro-si-net′ik). Urokinetic.

uroclepsia (u″ro-klep′se-ah) [*uro-* + Gr. *kleptein* to steal]. The unconscious escape of urine.

urocrisia (u″ro-kriz′e-ah) [*uro-* + Gr. *krinein* to judge]. Diagnosis by observing or examining the urine.

urocrisis (u-rok′rĭ-sis) [*uro-* + Gr. *krisis* crisis]. A crisis marked by a free discharge of urine.

urocriterion (u″ro-kri-te′re-on) [*uro-* + Gr. *kritērion* test]. An indication of disease observed in examination of the urine.

urocyanin (u-ro-si′ah-nin) [*uro-* + Gr. *kyanos* blue]. Uroglaucin.

urocyanogen (u″ro-si-an′o-jen) [*uro-* + Gr. *kyanos* blue + *gennan* to produce]. A blue pigment of the urine, especially of that of cholera patients.

urocyanosis (u″ro-si″ah-no′sis) [*uro-* + Gr. *kyanos* blue]. Indicanuria.

urocyst (u′ro-sist) [*uro-* + Gr. *kystis* bladder]. The urinary bladder (vesica urinaria [N A]).

urocystic (u″ro-sis′tik). Pertaining to the urinary bladder.

Urocystis (u″ro-sis′tis). A genus of fungi. **U. trit′ici,** a fungus which causes flag smut of wheat in Australia.

urocystis (u″ro-sis′tis) [L.]. The urinary bladder.

urocystitis (u″ro-sis-ti′tis). Inflammation of the urinary bladder.

urodeum (u″ro-de′um) [*uro-* + Gr. *hodaios* on the way]. The portion of the cloaca into which the ureters and genital ducts empty.

urodialysis (u″ro-di-al′ĭ-sis) [*uro-* + Gr. *dialysis* cessation]. Partial or complete suppression of the urine.

urodochium (u″ro-do′ke-um, u″ro-do-ki′um) [*uro-* + Gr. *docheion* holder]. A urinal.

urodynia (u″ro-din′e-ah) [*uro-* + Gr. *odynē* pain + *-ia*]. Pain accompanying urination.

uroenterone (u″ro-en′ter-ōn). Urogastrone.

uroerythrin (u″ro-er′ĭ-thrin) [*uro-* + Gr. *erythros* red]. A dark reddish coloring matter found in the urine; it gives the red color seen in deposits of urates.

urofuscin (u″ro-fus′in) [*uro-* + L. *fuscus* tawny]. A pigment of the urine which is the precursor of hematoporphyrin.

urofuscohematin (u″ro-fus″ko-hem′ah-tin). A red-brown pigment from the urine in certain diseases.

urogaster (u″ro-gas′ter) [*uro-* + Gr. *gastēr* stomach]. The urinary intestine; a part of the allantoic cavity of the embryo.

urogastrone (u″ro-gas′trōn). An inhibitor of gastric secretion, obtainable from the normal and pregnancy urine of man and other mammals.

urogenital (u″ro-jen′ĭ-tal). Pertaining to the urinary and genital apparatus.

urogenous (u-roj′e-nus) [*uro-* + Gr. *gennan* to produce]. Producing urine; also produced from or in the urine.

uroglaucin (u″ro-glaw′sin) [*uro-* + Gr. *glaukos* green]. Indigo blue occurring in the urine. It is due to oxidation of a colorless chromogen in the urine, and is seen in conditions such as scarlet fever.

Uroglena (u″ro-gle′nah). A genus of free-swimming, flagellate protozoans, which sometimes impart a fishy odor to a water supply.

Uroglenopsis (u″ro-gle-nop′sis). Uroglena.

urogram (u′ro-gram). A roentgenogram of part of the urinary tract.

urography (u-rog′rah-fe). Roentgenography of a part of the urinary tract which has been rendered opaque by some opaque medium. **ascending u.,** retrograde u. **cystoscopic u.,** retrograde urography. **descending u., excretion u., excretory u., intravenous u.,** roentgen examination of the urinary tract after the intravenous injection of an opaque medium that is rapidly excreted in the urine. **oral u.,** urography in which the opaque medium is given by mouth. **retrograde u.,** urography in which the contrast medium is injected into the bladder through the urethra.

urogravimeter (u″ro-grah-vim′e-ter) [*uro-* + L. *gravis* heavy + *metrum* measure]. Urinometer.

urohematin (u″ro-hem′ah-tin). The coloring matter or pigments of the urine: regarded as identical with hematin.

urohematonephrosis (u″ro-hem″ah-to-ne-fro′sis). Distention of the kidney with urine and blood.

urohematoporphyrin (u″ro-hem″ah-to-por′fĭ-rin). Hematoporphyrin derived from the urine.

urohypertensin (u″ro-hi-per-ten′sin). A mixture of bases obtained from the urine, which, when injected into the blood, produces a rise of arterial blood pressure.

urokinase (u″ro-ki′nās). A substance found in the urine of mammals, including man, and of other vertebrates, which activates the fibrinolytic system, acting enzymatically by splitting plasminogen.

urokinetic (u″ro-ki-net′ik) [*uro-* + Gr. *kinēsis* movement]. Caused by a reflex from the urinary organs: said of a form of dyspepsia.

urokymography (u″ro-ki-mog′rah-fe). Kymography applied to study of the urogenital system.

urolagnia (u″ro-lag′ne-ah) [*uro-* + Gr. *lagneia* lust]. A form of paraphilia in which sexual excitement is associated with the sight or thought of urine or urination.

urolith (u′ro-lith) [*uro-* + Gr. *lithos* stone]. A urinary calculus or stone.

urolithiasis (u″ro-lĭ-thi′ah-sis). 1. The formation of urinary calculi. 2. The diseased condition associated with the presence of urinary calculi.

urolithic (u″ro-lith′ik). Pertaining to urinary calculi.

urolithology (u″ro-lĭ-thol′o-je). The sum of knowledge regarding urinary calculi.

urologic, urological (u″ro-loj′ik, u″ro-loj′ĭ-kal). Pertaining to urology.

urologist (u-rol′o-jist). A physician who specializes in urology.

urology (u-rol′o-je). That branch of medicine which concerns itself with the urinary tract in both male and female, and with the genital organs in the male.

urolutein (u″ro-lu′te-in) [*uro-* + L. *luteus* yellow]. A yellow pigment of the urine.

uromancy (u′ro-man″se) [*uro-* + Gr. *manteia* a divination]. Prognosis based on examination of urine.

uromantia (u″ro-man′she-ah). Uromancy.

uromelanin (u″ro-mel′ah-nin) [*uro-* + Gr. *melas* black]. A black pigment, $C_{18}H_{43}N_7O_{10}$, sometimes found in urine. It results from the decomposition of urochrome.

uromelus (u-rom′e-lus) [Gr. *oura* tail + *melos* limb]. A fetal monster with legs fused and a single foot.

urometer (u-rom′e-ter) [*uro-* + Gr. *metron* measure]. Urinometer.

uron (u′ron). Proton.

uroncus (u-rong′kus) [*uro-* + Gr. *onkos* mass]. A swelling containing urine.

Uronema caudatum (u″ro-ne′mah kaw-da′tum). A species of ciliate found in the feces in a case of dysentery.

uronephrosis (u″ro-ne-fro′sis). Abnormal distention of the pelvis and tubules of the kidney with urine.

urono-. See *uro-*.

uronology (u″ro-nol′o-je). Urology.

urononcometry (u″ron-on-kom′e-tre) [*urono-* + Gr. *onkos* mass + *metron* measure]. The measurement of the quantity of urine excreted in twenty-four hours.

uronophile (u-ron′o-fil) [*urono-* + Gr. *philein* to love]. Growing in a medium containing urine: said of a microorganism.

uronoscopy (u″ro-nos′ko-pe). Examination of the urine.

uropathogen (u″ro-path′o-jen). A microorganism which causes diseases of the urinary tract.

uropathy (u-rop′ah-the) [*uro-* + Gr. *pathos* disease]. Any pathologic change in the urinary tract. **obstructive u.,** any pathologic change in the urinary tract due to obstruction.

uropenia (u″ro-pe′ne-ah) [*uro-* + Gr. *penia* poverty]. Deficiency of urine or urinary secretion.

uropepsin (u″ro-pep′sin). A pepsin-like enzyme occurring in the urine.

urophanic (u″ro-fan′ik) [*uro-* + Gr. *phainein* to show]. Appearing in the urine.

urophein (u″ro-fe′in) [*uro-* + Gr. *phaios* gray]. An odoriferous gray pigment of the urine.

urophobia (u″ro-fo′be-ah). Fear of passing the urine.

urophosphometer (u″ro-fos-fom′e-ter). An instrument for measuring the quantity of phosphorus in the urine.

uropittin (u″ro-pit′in) [*uro-* + Gr. *pitta* pitch]. A resinous product, $C_9H_{10}N_2O_3$, of the decomposition of urochrome.

uroplania (u″ro-pla′ne-ah) [*uro-* + Gr. *planē* wandering + *-ia*]. The presence of urine in, or its discharge from, organs not of the urogenital tract.

uropoiesis (u″ro-poi-e′sis) [*uro-* + Gr. *poiein* to make]. The secretion of the urine.

uropoietic (u″ro-poi-et′ik). Pertaining to or concerned in the secretion of the urine.

uroporphyrin (u″ro-por′fĭ-rin). A porphyrin, $C_{40}H_{38}O_{16}N_4$, occurring in the urine.

uroporphyrinogen (u″ro-por″fĭ-rin′o-jen). A reduced, colorless compound, readily giving rise to uroporphyrin by oxidation.

uropsammus (u″ro-sam′us) [*uro-* + Gr. *psammos* sand]. Sediment or gravel in the urine.

uropterin (u-rop′ter-in). A pigment, probably identical with xanthopterin, isolated from human urine.

uropyonephrosis (u″ro-pi″o-ne-fro′sis). The presence of urine and pus in the pelvis of the kidney.

uropyoureter (u″ro-pi″o-u-re′ter) [*uro-* + Gr. *pyon* pus + *oureter* ureter]. A collection of urine and pus in the ureter.

uro-reaction (u″ro-re-ak′shun). See *Malmajde's test*, under *tests*.

urorhythmography (u″ro-rith-mog′rah-fe) [*uro-* + Gr. *rhythmos* rhythm + *graphein* to write]. Graphic registration of the ejaculation of the urine from the ureteral orifices.

urorosein (u″ro-ro′ze-in). Urorrhodin.

uroroseinogen (u″ro-ro″se-in′o-jen). Urorrhodinogen.

urorrhagia (u″ro-ra′je-ah) [*uro-* + Gr. *rhēgnynai* to burst forth]. An excessive flow of urine; diabetes.

urorrhea (u″ro-re′ah) [*uro-* + Gr. *rhoia* flow]. An involuntary discharge of urine; enuresis.

urorrhodin (u″ro-ro′din) [*uro-* + Gr. *rhodon* rose]. A rose-colored pigment found in the urine in typhoid fever, nephritis, pulmonary tuberculosis, and other diseases.

urorrhodinogen (u″ro-ro-din′o-jen) [*urorrhodin* + Gr. *gennan* to produce]. A chromogen in the urine which, on decomposition, yields urorrhodin.

urorubin (u″ro-roo′bin) [*uro-* + L. *ruber* red]. A red pigment derivable from the urine by the action of hydrochloric acid.

urorubinogen (u″ro-roo-bin′o-jen). A chromogen from which urorubin is derived.

urorubrohematin (u″ro-roo″bro-hem′ah-tin) [*uro-* + L. *ruber* red + *hematin*]. A red pigment rarely found in the urine in certain constitutional diseases, as leprosy.

urosaccharometry (u″ro-sak″ah-rom′e-tre). The measurement or estimation of sugar in the urine.

urosacin (u-ro′sa-sin). Urorrhodin.

uroscheocele (u-ros′ke-o-sēl) [*uro-* + Gr. *oscheon* scrotum + *kēlē* tumor]. Urocele.

uroschesis (u-ros′kĕ-sis) [*uro-* + Gr. *schesis* holding]. Retention of the urine.

uroscopic (u″ro-skop′ik). Pertaining to uroscopy.

uroscopy (u-ros′ko-pe) [*uro-* + Gr. *skopein* to examine]. Diagnostic examination of the urine.

uroselectan (u″ro-se-lek′tan). Iopax.

urosemiology (u″ro-se″me-ol′o-je). Diagnostic study of the urine.

urosepsin (u″ro-sep′sin). A septic poison arising from urine in the tissues.

urosepsis (u″ro-sep′sis) [*uro-* + Gr. *sēpsis* decay]. Septic poisoning from the absorption and decomposition of urinary substances in the tissues.

uroseptic (u″ro-sep′tik). Pertaining to or marked by urosepsis.

urosis (u-ro′sis). Any disease of the urinary apparatus.

urospectrin (u″ro-spek′trin) [*uro-* + L. *spectrum* image]. One of the pigments of normal urine; a substance obtainable from certain specimens of urine, allied to hematoporphyrin.

urostalagmometry (u″ro-stal″ag-mom′e-tre). The use of the stalagmometer in the study of the urine.

urostealith (u″ro-ste′ah-lith) [*uro-* + Gr. *stear* fat + *lithos* stone]. A fatty constituent of certain urinary calculi; a urinary calculus having fatty constituents.

urotheobromine (u″ro-the″o-bro′min). Paraxanthine.

urotherapy (u″ro-ther′ah-pe). Treatment by the subcutaneous injection of the patient's urine.

urotoxia (u″ro-tok′se-ah) [*uro-* + Gr. *toxikon* poison]. 1. The toxicity of the urine. 2. The toxic substance of the urine (Bouchard). 3. The unit of the toxicity of the urine or a quantity sufficient to kill 1 kilogram of living substance.

urotoxic (u″ro-tok′sik). Pertaining to the toxic materials of the urine.

urotoxicity (u″ro-toks-is′ĭ-te). The toxic quality of the urine.

urotoxin (u″ro-tok′sin). The toxic or poisonous principle of the urine.

urotoxy (u′ro-tok″se). Urotoxia.

urotropin (u-rot′ro-pin). Trade mark for a preparation of methenamine.

uroureter (u″ro-u-re′ter). Distention of the ureter with urine.

uroxanthin (u″ro-zan′thin) [*uro-* + Gr. *xanthos* yellow]. A yellow pigment of normal urine convertible into indigo blue.

urrhodin (u-ro′din). Urorrhodin.

ursin (ur′sin). Arbutin.

ursone (ur′sōn). A crystallizable triterpene, $C_{30}H_{48}O_3$, from apples, pears, rhododendron, and uva ursi.

Urtica (ur-ti′kah) [L.]. A genus of plants, including the true or typical nettles; plants covered with stinging hairs and secreting a poisonous fluid. **U. dio′ica,** a stinging nettle of temperate regions having stimulant, diuretic, and hemostatic properties; also its homeopathic preparation.

urtica (ur-ti′kah), pl. *urti′cae* [L., "a stinging nettle"]. A wheal or pomphus.

urticant (ur′tĭ-kant). Causing an itching or stinging sensation.

urticaria (ur″tĭ-ka′re-ah) [L. *urtica* stinging nettle + *-ia*]. A vascular reaction of the skin marked by the transient appearance of smooth, slightly elevated patches, which are redder or paler than the surrounding skin and often attended by severe itching. The eruption rarely lasts longer than two days, but may exist in a chronic form. Certain foods (e.g., shellfish) or drugs (e.g. penicillin) may be the exciting cause. **u. bullo′sa,** a rare form of urticaria characterized by the appearance of bullae. **endemic u., u. endem′ica,** a variety caused by certain species of caterpillar, and occurring as an endemic. **epidemic u., u. epidem′ica,** a severe form ascribed to caterpillar poisoning. **u. facti′tia,** dermographia. **giant u., u. gigan′tea,** angioneurotic edema. **u. hemorrhag′ica,** purpura urticans. **u. medicamento′sa,** urticaria caused by the use of a drug. **papular u., u. papulo′sa,** a common condition in temperate parts of the world, usually occurring in children, caused by the bites of fleas, bedbugs, and other insects, and representing a stage in the development of sensitization to them. **u. per′stans,** a form in which the lesions (wheals) persist for long periods. **u. photogen′ica,** a rare form of urticaria thought to be due only to visible light rays, or wavelengths between 4,000 and 5,000 angstroms. **u. pigmento′sa,** an uncommon but highly distinctive dermatosis, usually developing in the first year of life, with the appearance of yellowish or reddish brown macules; rubbing or other trauma to the lesions results in localized pruritus and urticaria. Called also *mastocytosis* and *xanthelasmoidea*. **solar u., u. sola′ris,** urticaria produced by exposure to sunlight. **u. subcuta′nea, subcutaneous u.,** a form resulting from subcutaneous edema.

urticarial (ur″tĭ-ka′re-al). Pertaining to, characterized by, or of the nature of urticaria.

urticariogenic (ur″tĭ-ka″re-o-jen′ik). Causing urticaria.

urticarious (ur″tĭ-ka′re-us). Urticarial.

urticate (ur′tĭ-kāt). 1. Marked by the presence of wheals. 2. To perform urtication.

urtication (ur″tĭ-ka′shun) [L. *urtica* a stinging nettle]. 1. The flogging of a part with green nettles for their revulsive or stimulant effect. 2. A burning sensation as of stinging with nettles. 3. The development or formation of urticaria.

urushiol (u-roo′she-ol). The toxic irritant principle of poison ivy and of various related plants. It is 3-pentadeca dienyl catechol, $C_{15}H_{27}.C_6H_3(OH)_2$.

USAN (u′san) Acronym for *United States Adopted Name,* a non-proprietary designation for any compound used as a drug, established by negotiation between the manufacturer of the compound and a nomenclature committee known as the USAN Council, which is sponsored jointly by the American Medical Association, the American Pharmaceutical Association, and The United States Pharmacopoeial Association, Inc. The term is currently limited to names adopted by the Council since June, 1961. These names will appear as the monograph titles in the official compendia, U.S.P. and N.F., when and if the respective drugs are admitted to either compendium.

Uschinsky's solution (us-chin′skēz) [Nikolaus *Uschinsky,* Leningrad bacteriologist, born 1863]. See under *solution.*

U.S.M.H. Abbreviation for *United States Marine Hospital.*

Usnea barbata (us′ne-ah bar-ba′tah). A large lichen growing on forest trees; also its homeopathic preparation.

U.S.P. The United States Pharmacopeia, a legally recognized compendium of standards for drugs, published by The United States Pharmacopoeial Convention, Inc., and revised periodically. It includes also assays and tests for the determination of strength, quality, and purity.

U.S.P.H.S. Abbreviation for *United States Public Health Service.*

ustilaginism (us″tĭ-laj′ĭ-nizm). A condition resembling ergotism caused by eating maize containing *Ustilago maydis.*

Ustilago (us″tĭ-la′go) [L.]. A genus of moldlike fungi of the order Basidiomycetes, called smuts, parasitic on other plants. **U. hypody′tes,** a fungus thought by some to cause friente. **U. may′dis,** the smut of maize, used like ergot.

ustion (us′chun) [L. *ustio*]. Burning with the actual cautery.

ustulation (us″tu-la′shun) [L. *ustulare* to scorch]. The drying of a moist drug by heat.

ustus (us′tus) [L.]. Burnt; calcined.

usustatus (u-su′sta-tus) [L. *usus* use + *status* position]. The ordinary erect or standing posture usual to an animal.

U.S.V.B. Abbreviation for *United States Veterans' Bureau.*

uta (oo′tah). Naso-oral leishmaniasis.

Ut dict. Abbreviation for L. *ut dic′tum,* as directed.

Utend. Abbreviation for L. *uten′dus,* to be used.

uteralgia (u″ter-al′je-ah). Pain in the uterus; metralgia.

uterectomy (u″ter-ek′to-me). Hysterectomy.

uteri (u′ter-i) [L.]. Plural of *uterus.*

uterine (u′ter-īn) [L. *uterinus*]. Of or pertaining to the uterus.

uterismus (u″ter-iz′mus). Uterine pain.

uteritis (u″ter-i′tis). Inflammation of the uterus; metritis.

uteroabdominal (u″ter-o-ab-dom′ĭ-nal). Pertaining to the uterus and the abdomen.

uterocervical (u″ter-o-ser′vĭ-kal). Pertaining to the uterus and the cervix uteri.

uterodynia (u″ter-o-din′e-ah). Pain in the uterus.

uterofixation (u″ter-o-fik-sa′shun). Hysteropexy.

uterogestation (u″ter-o-jes-ta′shun) [*uterus* + L. *gestatio* a carrying]. 1. Uterine pregnancy; any pregnancy which is not extra-uterine. 2. The full period of time of normal pregnancy.

uterography (u″ter-og′rah-fe). Roentgenography of the uterus.

uterolith (u′ter-o-lith) [*uterus* + Gr. *lithos* stone]. A uterine calculus.

uteromania (u″ter-o-ma′ne-ah). Nymphomania.

uterometer (u″ter-om′e-ter). An instrument for measuring the uterus.

uterometry (u″ter-om′e-tre). Measurement of the uterus.

utero-ovarian (u″ter-o-o-va′re-an). Pertaining to the uterus and ovary.

uteropexy (u′ter-o-pek″se). Hysteropexy.

uteroplacental (u″ter-o-plah-sen′tal). Pertaining to the uterus and the placenta.

uteroplasty (u′ter-o-plas″te). Any plastic operation on the uterus.

uterorectal (u″ter-o-rek′tal). Pertaining to the uterus and rectum, or communicating with the uterine cavity and rectum, as a uterorectal fistula.

uterosacral (u″ter-o-sa′kral). Pertaining to the uterus and the sacrum.

uterosalpingography (u″ter-o-sal″ping-gog′rah-fe). Hysterosalpingography.

uteroscope (u′ter-o-skōp) [*uterus* + Gr. *skopein* to examine]. An instrument for examining the interior of the uterus.

uterothermometry (u″ter-o-ther-mom′e-tre). The measurement of the temperature in the uterus.

uterotomy (u″ter-ot′o-me). Hysterotomy.

uterotonic (u″ter-o-ton′ik). 1. Giving muscular tone to the uterus. 2. An agent which increases the tonus of the uterine muscle.

uterotropic (u″ter-o-trop′ik). Having a special affinity for or exerting its principal influence upon the uterus.

uterotubal (u″ter-o-tu′bal). Pertaining to the uterus and the oviducts.

uterotubography (u″ter-o-tu-bog′rah-fe). Hysterosalpingography.

uterovaginal (u″ter-o-vaj′ĭ-nal). Pertaining to the uterus and the vagina.

uteroventral (u″ter-o-ven′tral). Pertaining to the uterus and the cavity of the abdomen.

uteroverdin (u″ter-o-ver′din). A green pigment, $C_{33}H_{34}N_4OC$, occurring in dog placentae and in the eggs of some birds.

uterovesical (u″ter-o-ves′ĭ-kal). Pertaining to the uterus and the bladder.

uterus (u′ter-us) [L.; Gr. *hystera*]. The hollow muscular organ in female animals which is the abode and the place of nourishment of the embryo and fetus. In the human [N A, B N A], it is a pear-shaped structure, about 3 inches in length, consisting of a body, fundus, isthmus, and cervix. Its cavity opens into the vagina below, and into the uterine tube on either side above. It is supported by direct attachment to the vagina and by indirect attachment to various other nearby pelvic structures. **u. acol′lis,** a uterus in which the vaginal portion is absent. **u. arcua′tus,** a uterus with a depressed fundus. **u. bicor′nis,** a uterus which has two horns, or cornua. **u. bif′oris,** a uterus in which the external os is divided by a septum. **u. bilocula′ris,** a uterus the cavity of which is divided into two parts by a partition. **u. biparti′tus,** u. bilocularis. **cochleate u.,** a small adult uterus with a conical cervix and body which is small, globular, and acutely flexed. **u. cordifor′mis,** a heart-shaped uterus. **Couvelaire u.** See *uteroplacental apoplexy,* under *apoplexy.* **u. didel′phys,** either of two distinct uteri occurring side by side in the same individual. **duplex u., u. du′plex,** a double uterus; normal in marsupial mammals, and rarely seen in the human subject. **fetal u.,** a uterus in which the cervical canal is longer than the cavity of the corpus. **gravid u.,** the pregnant uterus. **u. incudifor′mis,** a uterus bicornis which is broad between the two horns.

u. masculi'nus, utriculus prostaticus. **u. parvicol'lis,** a uterus in which the cervical portion is very small. **pubescent u.,** one which is adult in type but is undeveloped. **u. sep'tus,** u. bilocularis. **u. simplex,** one that is single throughout its length, as in the human. **u. unicor'nis,** one with only one cornu, one lateral half being undeveloped or imperfectly developed.

utricle (u'tre-k'l) [L. *utriculus*]. 1. Any small sac. 2. The larger of the two divisions of the membranous labyrinth. See *utriculus*, def. 2. **prostatic u., urethral u.,** utriculus prostaticus.

utricular (u-trik'u-lar). 1. Pertaining to a utricle. 2. Resembling a bladder.

utriculi (u-trik'u-li) [L.]. Plural of *utriculus*.

utriculitis (u-trik"u-li'tis). Inflammation of the prostatic utricle or of the utricle of the ear.

utriculoplasty (u-trik'u-lo-plas"te). The operation of excising a wedge-shaped piece of the whole thickness of the uterine wall, the two halves remaining being then sutured together so as to form a miniature uterus, or utriculus.

utriculosaccular (u-trik"u-lo-sak'u-lar). Pertaining to the utricle and saccule of the labyrinth.

utriculus (u-trik'u-lus), pl. *utric'uli* [L., dim. of *uter*]. 1. A small sac. 2. [N A, B N A] The larger of the two divisions of the membranous labyrinth, located in the posterosuperior region of the vestibule. It is the major organ of the vestibular system, which gives information about position and movements of the head. Called also *utricle*, and *utriculus vestibuli*. **u. masculi'nus,** u. prostaticus. **u. prostat'icus** [N A, B N A], the remains of the lower part of the paramesonephric duct in the male. It is a small blind pouch arising in the prostatic substance and opening onto the seminal colliculus. Called also *prostatic utricle*. **u. vestib'uli,** utriculus (def. 2).

utriform (u'trĭ-form). Having the shape of a bottle.

uva (u'vah), pl. *u'vae* [L. "grape"]. The raisin; the dried fruit of *Vitis vinifera*, grape vine. **u. pas'sae,** dried grapes or raisins. **u. pas'sae mino'res,** commercial currants; a variety of small raisins. **u. ur'si** [L. "bear's grapes"], the leaves of *Arctostaphylos uva-ursi*, or bear berry, a trailing ericaceous shrub. The leaves contain the glucoside *arbutin*, and are tonic, astringent, diuretic and anthelmintic.

uvea (u've-ah). The iris, ciliary body, and choroid considered together (tunica vasculosa bulbi [N A]).

uveal (u've-al). Pertaining to the uvea.

uveitic (u"ve-it'ik). Pertaining to uveitis.

uveitis (u"ve-i'tis) [*uvea* + *-itis*]. Inflammation of the uvea. **anterior u.,** keratitis involving the front part of the uvea. **Förster's u.,** syphilitic involvement of the entire uvea. **heterochromic u.,** uveitis in which the color of the diseased eye differs from that of the normal one. **sympathetic u.,** uveitis following the same affection in the other eye.

uveoparotid (u"ve-o-pah-rot'id). Affecting the uvea and the parotid gland.

uveoparotitis (u"ve-o-par"o-ti'tis). Uveoparotid fever.

uveoplasty (u've-o-plas"te). Plastic operation of the uvea.

uveoscleritis (u"ve-o-skle-ri'tis). Scleritis resulting from an extension of the inflammation from the uvea to the sclera.

uviform (u'vĭ-form) [L. *uva* grape + *forma* form]. Having the form of a grape.

uviofast (u've-o-fast). Uvioresistant.

uviolize (u've-o-līz). To subject to the action of ultraviolet rays.

uviometer (u"ve-om'e-ter). An instrument for measuring ultraviolet emanation.

uvioresistant (u"ve-o-re-zis'tant). Resistant to or not affected by ultraviolet rays.

uviosensitive (u"ve-o-sen'sĭ-tiv). Sensitive to ultraviolet rays.

uvula (u'vu-lah), pl. *u'vulae* [L. "little grape"]. A pendent, fleshy mass; used as a general term in anatomical terminology. Usually used alone to designate the *uvula palatina*. **bifid u.,** a split uvula. **u. of bladder,** u. vesicae. **u. cerebel'li, u. of cerebellum,** u. vermis. **u. fis'sa,** a forked or split uvula. **Lieutaud's u.,** u. vesicae. **u. palati'na** [N A, B N A], **palatine u.,** the small, fleshy mass hanging from the soft palate above the root of the tongue, composed of the levator and tensor palati muscles and the muscle of the uvula, connective tissue, and mucous membrane. **u. ver'mis** [N A, B N A], the part of the vermis of the cerebellum between the pyramis and the nodulus. Called also *u. of cerebellum*. **u. ves'icae** [N A, B N A], a rounded elevation at the neck of the bladder, formed by convergence of many fibers of the trigonal muscle as they pass through the encircling musculus sphincter vesicae to terminate in the urethra. Called also *u. of bladder*.

uvulaptosis (u"vu-lap-to'sis). Uvuloptosis.

uvular (u'vu-lar). Pertaining to the uvula.

uvularis (u"vu-la'ris) [L.]. Uvular.

uvulatome (u'vu-lah-tōm). Uvulotome.

uvulatomy (u"vu-lat'o-me). Uvulotomy.

uvulectomy (u"vu-lek'to-me) [*uvula* + Gr. *ektomē* excision]. Excision of the uvula.

uvulitis (u"vu-li'tis) [*uvula* + *-itis*]. Inflammation of the uvula.

uvuloptosis (u"vu-lop-to'sis) [*uvula* + Gr. *ptōsis* falling]. Falling of the palate: a relaxed and pendulous condition of the palate; staphyloptosis.

uvulotome (u'vu-lo-tōm). An instrument for cutting the uvula.

uvulotomy (u"vu-lot'o-me) [*uvula* + Gr. *tomē* a cutting]. The operation of cutting off the uvula or a part of it.

uzara (u-zah'rah). The root of an African plant: used by the natives in diarrhea and dysentery.

V

V. 1. Chemical symbol for *vanadium.* 2. Abbreviation for *Vibrio, vision,* and *visual acuity.*

v. Abbreviation for L. *vena* vein, and for *volt.*

V_T. Abbreviation for *tidal volume.*

V.A. Abbreviation for *Veterans Administration.*

Va. Abbreviation for *visual acuity.*

V. and T. Abbreviation for *volume and tension* (of pulse).

vaccigenous (vak-sij′e-nus) [*vaccine* + Gr. *gennan* to produce]. Producing vaccine.

vaccin (vak′sin). Vaccine.

vaccina (vak-si′nah). Vaccinia.

vaccinable (vak-sin′ah-b'l). Susceptible of being successfully vaccinated.

vaccinal (vak′sĭ-nal) [L. *vaccinus*]. 1. Pertaining to vaccinia, to vaccine, or to vaccination. 2. Having protective qualities when used by way of inoculation.

vaccinate (vak′sĭ-nāt). To inject vaccine for the purpose of producing immunity.

vaccination (vak″sĭ-na′shun) [L. *vacca* cow]. The injection of vaccine for the purpose of inducing immunity. Coined originally to apply to the injection of smallpox vaccine, the term has come to mean any immunizing procedure in which vaccine is injected. **smallpox v.,** the application of smallpox vaccine upon the denuded or scarified skin, to produce immunity to smallpox.

vaccinationist (vak″sĭ-na′shun-ist). One who defends the practice of vaccination.

vaccinator (vak′sĭ-na″tor). 1. One who vaccinates. 2. An instrument for use in vaccination.

vaccine (vak′sēn) [L. *vaccinus*]. A suspension of attenuated or killed microorganisms (bacteria, viruses, or rickettsiae), administered for the prevention, amelioration, or treatment of infectious diseases. **anthrax v.,** anthrax cultures attenuated by growing them at 42°C. for varying lengths of time and injected into horses, cattle, sheep, and goats to protect them against anthrax. It is a triple vaccine: No. 1 is the weakest and is given first; Nos. 2 and 3 are progressively stronger and are given after intervals of twelve days. **antirabic v.,** rabies v. **antityphoid v.,** typhoid v. **autogenous v.,** a vaccine prepared from microorganisms which have been freshly isolated from the lesion of the patient who is to be treated with it. **bacterial v.,** a standardized suspension of attenuated or killed bacteria which is injected subcutaneously, intramuscularly or intradermally, to increase the patient's immunity to the organisms injected, or sometimes for pyrogenetic effects in treatment of certain noninfectious diseases. **BCG v.** (bacille Calmette Guérin), a preparation for the prophylactic inoculation of young infants against tuberculosis. It consists of living cultures of bovine tubercle bacilli that have been grown over a period of many years on glycerinated ox bile so that their virulence is greatly reduced. Originally given by mouth, the preparation is now administered subcutaneously. **Calmette's v.,** BCG v. **cholera v.,** a bacterial vaccine prepared in various ways from cultures of the *Vibrio cholerae* and used as a prophylactic. **Cox v.,** a typhus fever vaccine consisting of a suspension of killed epidemic typhus rickettsiae prepared by the yolk-sac culture method. **glycerinated v.,** vaccine material purified by treatment with glycerin. **hydrophobia v.,** rabies v. **measles virus v.,** a preparation derived from the causative virus of rubeola grown in monkey kidney or chick embryo tissue, and inactivated or attenuated: used to produce immunity to naturally occurring rubeola. **mixed v.,** polyvalent v. **mumps v.,** a sterile suspension of mumps virus, grown in embryonated chicken eggs and inactivated by ultraviolet light or formaldehyde: used to produce active immunity against mumps. **pertussis v.,** a sterile bacterial fraction or suspension of killed *Bordetella pertussis* in isotonic sodium chloride solution or other diluent. **plague v.,** a bacterial vaccine made from cultures of *Pasteurella pestis* and used as a prophylactic. **poliomyelitis v., attenuated,** material containing living types of poliomyelitis viruses which presumably have lost their virulence and should be useful in producing immunity against this disease without the risk of paralysis incurred from the natural infection. **polyvalent v.,** a bacterial vaccine prepared from cultures of more than one strain or species of bacteria. **rabies v.,** material prepared from the spinal cords of rabbits killed by subdural injections of fixed virus: used for prevention of rabies in patients infected or contaminated with rabies virus. **Sabin's oral polio v.,** an orally administered vaccine consisting of the three types of live, attenuated polioviruses grown in monkey kidney tissue culture. **Salk v.,** a vaccine containing three types of poliomyelitis virus which, although inactivated with formalin, still retain the capacity to produce resistance against the natural disease. **Sauer's v.,** a pertussis vaccine prepared from freshly isolated strains of *Bordetella pertussis,* used in immunizing children against whooping cough. **Semple v.,** an antirabies vaccine prepared from 4 per cent inoculated rabbit brain treated with 0.5 per cent phenol. **sensitized v.,** a vaccine consisting of bacteria which have been immersed in their specific immune serum. Such a vaccine is believed to cause no negative phase, but only a slight local reaction and to facilitate the antibody formation. Called also *serobacterin.* **smallpox v.,** a preparation of lymph from the vaccinia vesicles of a cow (or of culture virus), used in producing immunity to smallpox. **Sobernheim's v.,** a vaccine consisting of virulent *Bacillus anthracis* mixed with antiserum: used for immunization of cattle against anthrax. **Spencer-Parker v.,** a vaccine for Rocky Mountain spotted fever, prepared from ground infected ticks. **staphylococcus v.,** a bacterial vaccine prepared from one or more strains of staphylococci. **streptococcus v.,** a bacterial vaccine made from cultures of streptococci. **TAB v.,** a polyvalent vaccine containing killed typhoid bacilli, paratyphoid A bacilli, and paratyphoid B bacilli. **triple v.,** a bacterial vaccine prepared from the cultures of three different species of organisms. **tuberculosis v.,** BCG v. **typhoid v.,** a sterile suspension of killed cultures of *Salmonella typhosa* in physiologic salt solution, used as a prophylactic against typhoid fever. **typhoparatyphoid v.,** TAB v. **univalent v.,** a vaccine containing only one variety of organism in pure culture. **Weigl v.,** a typhus fever vaccine prepared by inoculating lice per rectum with rickettsiae and then emulsifying the intestines of the lice in phenolized solution of sodium chloride.

vaccinella (vak″sĭ-nel′ah). A spurious and ineffective form of vaccinia.

vaccinia (vak-sin′e-ah) [L., from *vacca* cow]. A virus disease of cattle. Communicated to man, usually by vaccination, it confers a greater or less degree of immunity against smallpox. See *vaccination.* Called also *cowpox.*

vaccinial (vak-sin′e-al). Pertaining to or characteristic of vaccinia.

vacciniculturist (vak″sĭ-nĭ-kul′tūr-ist). One who raises heifers and uses them for the production of vaccine.

vaccinid (vak′sĭ-nid). The skin manifestations of

vaccination, especially when there are numerous vesicles.

vaccinifer (vak-sin′ĭ-fer) [*vaccine* + L. *ferre* to carry]. The source (individual organism) from which smallpox vaccine is derived.

vacciniform (vak-sin′ĭ-form). Resembling vaccinia.

vaccinin (vak′sĭ-nin). The inoculable principle by which vaccinia is transmitted.

vaccininum (vak″sĭ-ni′num). A homeopathic remedy prepared from vaccine virus.

vacciniola (vak″sĭ-ne-o′lah) [L., dim. of *vaccinia*]. A secondary form of vesicle appearing after vaccination and resembling the rash of smallpox.

vaccinization (vak″sin-i-za′shun). Vaccination persistently repeated until the virus has no perceptible effect.

vaccinogen (vak-sin′o-jen). A source from which vaccine is derived.

vaccinogenous (vak″sĭ-noj′e-nus). Producing vaccine.

vaccinoid (vak′sĭ-noid). Spurious or modified vaccinia.

vaccinophobia (vak″sĭ-no-fo′be-ah) [*vaccine* + Gr. *phobein* to be affrighted by]. Perverse and morbid dread of vaccination.

vaccinostyle (vak-sin′o-stīl). A small lance used in vaccination.

vaccinotherapy (vak″sĭ-no-ther′ah-pe). Therapeutic use of bacterial vaccines.

vaccinum (vak-si′num) [L.]. Vaccine. **v. antityph′icum,** typhoid vaccine. **v. pertus′sis,** pertussis vaccine. **v. pes′tis,** plague vaccine. **v. typho′sum,** typhoid vaccine. **v. typho′sum et paratypho′sum,** TAB vaccine. **v. vaccin′iae, v. vari′olae,** smallpox vaccine.

vacuolar (vak′u-o″lar). Pertaining to a vacuole; characterized by the presence of vacuoles.

vacuolated (vak′u-o-lāt″ed). Pertaining to or characterized by vacuoles.

vacuolation (vak″u-o-la′shun). The process of forming vacuoles; the condition of being vacuolated.

vacuole (vak′u-ōl) [L. *vacuus* empty + *-ole* diminutive ending]. Any small space or cavity formed in the protoplasm of a cell. **air v.** See under *sac*. **contractile v.,** a small cavity containing watery fluid, seen in the protoplasm of certain unicellular organisms. It gradually increases in size and then collapses. Its function is thought to be respiratory or excretory. **food v.,** a small cavity in protozoa containing ingested food particles. **plasmocrine v.,** a small cavity containing crystalloids in a secretory cell. **rhagiocrine v.,** a small cavity containing colloids in a secretory cell. **water v.,** a small drop of water within the protoplasm of a cell.

vacuolization (vak″u-o-li-za′shun). Vacuolation.

vacuome (vak′u-ōm). The system of vacuoles in a cell which stain with neutral red.

vacuum (vak′u-um) [L.]. A space devoid of air or of other gas; a space from which the air has been exhausted. **high v.,** a vacuum in which the attenuation is extreme. **torricellian v.,** the vacuum in a barometric tube.

vadum (va′dum) [L. "a shallow"]. An elevation within a cerebral fissure, rendering it more or less shallow.

vagabondage (vag′ah-bon″dij) [L. *vagare* to ramble]. The habit of wandering about in idleness, a manifestation of psychopathic personality.

vagal (va′gal). Pertaining to the vagus nerve.

vagi (va′gi) [L.]. Plural of *vagus*.

vagina (vah-ji′nah), pl. *vagi′nae* [L.]. 1. A sheath, or sheathlike structure; used as a general term in anatomical nomenclature. 2. [N A, B N A] The canal in the female, extending from the vulva to the cervix uteri, which receives the penis in copulation. **vagi′nae bul′bi** [N A], connective tissues that form the capsule enclosing the posterior part of the eyeball, extending anteriorly to the conjunctival fornix, and continuous with the muscular fascia of the eye. Called also *fascia bulbi [Tenoni]* [B N A], *bulbar fascia*, and *sheaths of eyeball*. **v. carot′ica fas′ciae cervica′lis** [N A], the portion of the cervical fascia that encloses the carotid vessels and vagus nerve. **v. cellulo′sa,** a connective tissue sheath surrounding a body structure. **v. cor′dis,** pericardium. **v. exter′na ner′vi op′tici** [N A], the thick outer sheath of the optic nerve, continuous with the dura mater and connecting it with the sclera. Called also *external sheath of optic nerve*. **v. fem′oris,** fascia lata. **vagi′nae fibro′sae digito′rum ma′nus** [N A], strong, fibrous, semicylindrical sheaths investing the grooved palmar surface of the proximal and middle phalanges of the fingers. Called also *ligamenta vaginalia digitorum manus* [B N A], and *fibrous sheaths of fingers*. **vagi′nae fibro′sae digito′rum pe′dis** [N A], more or less complete fascial sheaths surrounding the phalanges of the toes, for attachment of the tendons and their synovial membranes. Called also *ligamenta vaginalia digitorum pedis* [B N A], and *fibrous sheaths of toes*. **v. fibro′sa ten′dinis** [N A, B N A], the fibrous sheath of a tendon, usually confining it to an osseous groove. **v. inter′na ner′vi op′tici** [N A], the inner sheath of the optic nerve, continuous with the pia mater. Called also *internal sheath of optic nerve*. **v. masculi′na,** utriculus prostaticus. **vagi′nae muco′sae** [B N A], vaginae synoviales. **v. muco′sa intertubercula′ris** [B N A], v. synovialis intertubercularis. **v. muco′sa ten′dinis** [B N A], v. synovialis tendinis. **vagi′nae muco′sae ten′dinum digito′rum pe′dis** [B N A], vaginae synoviales digitorum pedis. **vagi′nae muco′sae ten′dinum flexo′rum ma′nus** [B N A], vaginae synoviales digitorum manus. **v. mulie′bris,** the organ of copulation in the female. See *vagina*, def. 2. **v. mus′culi rec′ti abdo′minis** [N A, B N A], a sheath formed by the aponeuroses of other abdominal muscles, within which the rectus abdominis can move. **vagi′nae ner′vi op′tici** [B N A], the internal and external meningeal sheaths of the optic nerve within the orbit, continuous with the meninges of the brain. See *v. externa nervi optici* and *v. interna nervi optici*. Called also *sheaths of optic nerve*. **v. oc′uli.** See *vaginae bulbi*. **v. pi′li,** a sheath surrounding the root of a hair. See *folliculus pili*. **v. proces′sus styloi′dei** [B N A], a ridge on the lower surface of the temporal bone, partly enclosing the base of the styloid process. Called also *vaginal process of styloid*. Omitted in N A. **vagi′nae synovia′les** [N A], double-layered, fluid-filled sheaths such as those that usually surround tendons running in osseofibrous tunnels. **v. synovia′lis commu′nis musculo′rum flexo′rum** [N A], the common synovial sheath for the flexor tendons as they pass through osteofibrous canals of the fingers. Called also *v. tendinum musculorum flexorum communium manus* [B N A]. **vagi′nae synovia′les digito′rum ma′nus** [N A], the synovial sheaths of the tendons of the fingers. Called also *vaginae mucosae tendinum flexorum manus* [B N A]. **vagi′nae synovia′les digito′rum pe′dis** [N A], the synovial sheaths of the tendons of the toes. Called also *vaginae mucosae tendinum digitorum pedis* [B N A]. **v. synovia′lis intertubercula′ris** [N A], the synovial membrane that surrounds the long head of the biceps brachii muscle as it passes through the intertubercular sulcus. Called also *v. mucosa intertubercularis* [B N A], and *synovial sheath of intertubercular groove*. **v. synovia′lis musculo′rum fibula′rium commu′nis,** N A alternative for *v. synovialis musculorum peroneorum communis*. **v. synovia′lis mus′culi obli′qui superio′ris** [N A], the synovial sheath of the superior oblique muscle, particularly where its tendon passes through the trochlea. Called also *bursa musculi trochlearis* [B N A]. **v. synovia′lis musculo′rum peroneo′rum commu′nis**

[N A], the double tendon sheath for the peroneus longus and peroneus brevis muscles. Called also *v. tendinum musculorum peronaeorum communis* [B N A]. **v. synovia′lis ten′dinis** [N A], a double-layered, fibrous sheath usually found surrounding a tendon running in an osteofibrous canal, with synovial fluid present between the layers. Called also *v. mucosa tendinis* [B N A], and *synovial sheath of tendon.* **vagi′nae synovia′les ten′dinum digito′rum ma′nus** [N A], the tendon sheaths of the long and short flexors of the fingers. Called also *vaginae tendinum digitales manus* [B N A]. **v. synovia′lis ten′dinis mus′culi flexo′ris car′pi radia′lis** [N A], the tendon sheath of the flexor carpi radialis muscle. Called also *bursa musculi flexoris carpi radialis* [B N A]. **v. synovia′lis ten′dinis mus′culi flexo′ris hallu′cis lon′gi** [N A], the tendon sheath of the flexor hallucis longus muscle, extending from the medial malleolus to where it crosses the tendon of the flexor digitorum longus. Called also *v. tendinis musculi flexoris hallucis longi* [B N A]. **v. synovia′lis ten′dinis mus′culi tibia′lis posterio′ris** [N A], the tendon sheath of the tibialis posterior muscle, beginning at the medial malleolus and extending into the foot. Called also *v. tendinis musculi tibialis posterioris* [B N A]. **v. synovia′lis troch′leae,** bursa synovialis trochlearis. **vagi′nae ten′dinum digita′les ma′nus** [B N A], vaginae synoviales tendinum digitorum manus. **vagi′nae ten′dinum digita′les pe′dis** [B N A], **vagi′nae ten′dinum digito′rum pe′dis** [N A], the tendon sheaths of the long and short flexor muscles of the toes, beginning at the heads of the metatarsal bones. **v. ten′dinum musculo′rum abducto′ris lon′gi et extenso′ris bre′vis pol′licis** [N A, B N A], the tendon sheath of the long abductor and short extensor muscles of the thumb. **v. ten′dinum musculo′rum extenso′rum car′pi radia′lium** [N A, B N A], the tendon sheath of the short and long extensor carpi radialis muscles. **v. ten′dinis mus′culi extenso′ris car′pi ulna′ris** [N A, B N A], the tendon sheath of the extensor carpi ulnaris muscle. **v. ten′dinum musculo′rum extenso′ris digito′rum commu′nis et extenso′ris in′dicis** [B N A], **v. ten′dinum musculo′rum extenso′ris digito′rum et extenso′ris in′dicis** [N A], the tendon sheath of the extensor digitorum and extensor indicis muscles. **v. ten′dinis mus′culi extenso′ris dig′iti min′imi** [N A, B N A], the tendon sheath of the extensor digiti minimi muscle. **vagi′nae ten′dinum mus′culi extenso′ris digito′rum pe′dis lon′gi** [N A, B N A], the tendon sheaths of the extensor digitorum longus muscle, running from the cruciate ligament to the intermediate cuneiform bone. **v. ten′dinis mus′culi extenso′ris hal′lucis lon′gi** [N A, B N A], the tendon sheath of the extensor hallucis longus muscle, extending from the cruciate ligament to the dorsal fascia of the foot. **v. ten′dinis mus′culi extenso′ris pol′licis lon′gi** [N A, B N A], the sheath of the extensor pollicis longus tendon. **v. ten′dinis mus′culi fibula′ris lon′gi planta′ris,** N A alternative for *v. tendinis musculi peronei longi plantaris.* **v. ten′dinum musculo′rum flexo′rum commu′nium ma′nus** [B N A], v. synovialis communis musculorum flexorum. **vagi′nae ten′dinum mus′culi flexo′ris digito′rum pe′dis lon′gi** [N A, B N A], the tendon sheaths of the flexor digitorum longus muscle, extending from the medial malleolus to below the navicular bone. **v. ten′dinis mus′culi flexo′ris hallu′cis lon′gi** [B N A], v. synovialis tendinis musculi flexoris hallucis longi. **v. ten′dinis mus′culi flexo′ris pol′licis lon′gi** [N A, B N A], the tendon sheath for the long flexor muscle of the thumb in the wrist and palm. **v. ten′dinum musculo′rum peronaeo′rum commu′nis** [B N A], v. synovialis musculorum peroneorum communis. **v. ten′dinis mus′culi perone′i lon′gi planta′ris** [N A], the tendon sheath of the peroneus longus muscle, beginning in the peroneal groove of the cuboid bone. **v. ten′dinis mus′culi tibia′lis anterio′ris** [N A, B N A], the tendon sheath of the tibialis anterior muscle, extending from the transverse crural ligament to the talonavicular joint. **v. ten′dinis mus′culi tibia′lis posterio′ris** [B N A], v. synovialis tendinis musculi tibialis posterioris. **v. vaso′rum** [N A, B N A], a fibrous sheath that encloses certain arteries, sometimes along with their veins and nerves.

vaginal (vaj′ĭ-nal). 1. Of the nature of a sheath; ensheathing. 2. Pertaining to the vagina. 3. Pertaining to the tunica vaginalis testis.

vaginalectomy (vaj″ĭ-nal-ek′to-me). Vaginectomy.

vaginalitis (vaj″ĭ-nah-li′tis). Inflammation of the tunica vaginalis testis. **plastic v.,** pachyvaginalitis.

vaginapexy (vaj″ĭ-nah-pek′se). Colpopexy.

vaginate (vaj′ĭ-nāt) [L. *vaginatus* sheathed]. Provided with a sheath.

vaginectomy (vaj″ĭ-nek′to-me). 1. Resection of the tunica vaginalis testis. 2. Excision of the vagina.

vaginicoline (vaj″ĭ-nik′o-lin) [L. *vagina* sheath + *colere* to inhabit]. Living in the vagina: descriptive of certain microorganisms.

vaginiperineotomy (vaj″ĭ-nĭ-per″ĭ-ne-ot′o-me). Vaginoperineotomy.

vaginismus (vaj″ĭ-niz′mus) [L.]. Painful spasm of the vagina due to local hyperesthesia. It is distinguished as *superficial* and *deep*, according as the seat is at the entrance of the vagina, or probably in the bulbocavernosus muscle, or in the levator ani muscle. **mental v.,** extreme aversion to coitus on the part of a woman, attended with contraction of the muscles when the act is attempted. **perineal v.,** spasm of the perineal muscles. **posterior v.,** vaginismus caused by spasm of the levator ani muscle. **vulvar v.,** vaginismus caused by spasm of the constrictor vaginae muscle.

vaginitis (vaj″ĭ-ni′tis). 1. Inflammation of the vagina. It is marked by pain and by a purulent leukorrheal discharge. 2. Inflammation of a sheath. **v. adhaesi′va,** senile v. **contagious granular v.,** v. verrucosa. **diphtheritic v.,** diphtheritic inflammation of the vagina. **emphysematous v.,** inflammation of the vagina characterized by the formation of small blebs on the mucous membrane. **glandular v.,** vaginitis limited to the vaginal follicles. **granular v.,** the most common variety, in which the papillae are enlarged and infiltrated with small cells. **papulous v.,** vaginitis showing papules on the vagina and cervix. **senile v.,** vaginitis occurring in old age and marked by the formation of raw patches, which often adhere to apposed surfaces, causing obliteration of the vaginal canal. **v. tes′tis,** perididymitis. **trichomonas v.,** vaginitis produced by Trichomonas. **v. verruco′sa, vesicular v.,** an infectious inflammation of the vagina in cows, prevalent in European countries, and caused by the streptococcus of Ostertag. Called also *colpitis granulosa.*

vaginoabdominal (vaj″ĭ-no-ab-dom′ĭ-nal). Pertaining to the vagina and the abdomen.

vaginocele (vaj′ĭ-no-sēl) [L. *vagina* sheath + Gr. *kēlē* tumor]. Colpocele.

vaginocutaneous (vaj″ĭ-no-ku-ta′ne-us). Pertaining to the vagina and skin, or communicating with the vagina and the cutaneous surface of the body, as a vaginocutaneous fistula.

vaginodynia (vaj″ĭ-no-din′e-ah) [L. *vagina* sheath + Gr. *odynē* pain + *-ia*]. Pain in the vagina.

vaginofixation (vaj″ĭ-no-fiks-a′shun). Colpopexy; suturing of the fundus of the uterus to the vaginal peritoneum in cases of retroflexion. Called also *vaginal hysteropexy.*

vaginogenic (vaj′ĭ-no-jen′ik). Formed in the vagina.

vaginogram (vah-ji′no-gram). A roentgenogram of the vagina.

vaginography (vaj″ĭ-nog′rah-fe). Roentgenography of the vagina.

vaginolabial (vaj″ĭ-no-la′be-al). Pertaining to the vagina and the labia.

vaginometer (vaj″ĭ-nom′e-ter) [*vagina* + Gr. *metron* measure]. An instrument for measuring the length and diameter of the vagina.

vaginomycosis (vaj″ĭ-no-mi-ko′sis) [*vagina* + Gr. *mykēs* fungus]. A disease of the vagina due to a plant growth, chiefly *Leptothrix vaginalis.*

vaginopathy (vaj″ĭ-nop′ah-the) [*vagina* + Gr. *pathos* disease]. Any disease of the vagina.

vaginoperineal (vaj″ĭ-no-per″ĭ-ne′al). Pertaining to the vagina and perineum.

vaginoperineorrhaphy (vaj″ĭ-no-per″ĭ-ne-or′-ah-fe). The operation of suturing the divided or ruptured vagina and perineum.

vaginoperineotomy (vaj′ĭ-no-per″ĭ-ne-ot′o-me). The operation of dividing the vagina and perineum in order to secure enlargement of the vulvovaginal outlet.

vaginoperitoneal (vaj″ĭ-no-per″ĭ-to-ne′al). Pertaining to the vagina and peritoneum.

vaginopexy (vah-ji′no-pek″se) [*vagina* + Gr. *pēxis* fixation]. The operation of suturing the vagina to the abdominal wall in cases of vaginal relaxation.

vaginoplasty (vah-ji′no-plas″te) [*vagina* + Gr. *plassein* to form]. Plastic surgery on the vagina.

vaginoscope (vaj′ĭ-no-skōp) [*vagina* + Gr. *skopein* to examine]. A vaginal speculum.

vaginoscopy (vaj″ĭ-nos′ko-pe) [*vagina* + Gr. *skopein* to examine]. Inspection of the vagina.

vaginotome (vah-ji′no-tōm). An instrument for incision or division of the vagina.

vaginotomy (vaj″ĭ-not′o-me) [*vagina* + Gr. *tomē* a cutting]. Surgical incision of the vaginal wall.

vaginovesical (vaj″ĭ-no-ves′ĭ-kal). Pertaining to the vagina and bladder.

vaginovulvar (vaj″ĭ-no-vul′var). Vulvovaginal.

vagitis (va-gi′tis). Inflammation of the vagus.

vagitus (vah-ji′tus) [L.]. The cry of an infant. **v. uteri′nus,** the crying of a child in the uterus. **v. vagina′lis,** the crying of a child while its head is still within the vagina.

vago-accessorius (va″go-ak″ses-so′re-us) [L.]. The vagus and the cranial root of the accessory nerves regarded as together forming one nerve.

vagoglossopharyngeal (va″go-glos″o-fah-rin′-je-al). Pertaining to the vagus and glossopharyngeal nerves.

vagogram (va′go-gram) [*vagus* + Gr. *gramma* mark]. A tracing showing the electrical variations of the vagus nerve; called also *electrovagogram.*

vagolysis (va-gol′ĭ-sis) [*vagus* + Gr. *lysis* dissolution]. The operation of tearing off the esophageal branches of the vagus from the esophagus for the relief of cardiospasm.

vagomimetic (va″go-mi-met′ik). Having an effect which resembles that produced by vagal stimulation.

vagosplanchnic (va″go-splank′nik). Vagosympathetic.

vagosympathetic (va″go-sim″pah-thet′ik). Pertaining to both the vagus and sympathetic innervation.

vagotomy (va-got′o-me) [*vagus* + Gr. *tomē* a cutting]. Interruption of the impulses carried by the vagus nerve or nerves; so called because it was first performed by surgical methods. **bilateral v.,** transection of the vagus nerve on both sides of the body. **complete v.,** disruption of vagal secretory fibers sufficient to prevent increased flow or acidity of gastric secretion in insulin hypoglycemia. **medical v.,** interruption of the impulses carried by the vagus nerve by administration of suitable drugs. **surgical v.,** interruption of the impulses carried by the vagus nerve by surgical interruption of its fibers. Called also *gastric neurectomy.*

vagotonia (va″go-to′ne-ah) [*vagus* + Gr. *tonos* tension + *-ia*]. Hyperexcitability of the vagus nerve; a condition in which the vagus nerve dominates in the general functioning of the body organs. It is marked by vasomotor instability, constipation, sweating, and involuntary motor spasms with pain.

vagotonic (va″go-ton′ik). Pertaining to or characterized by vagotonia.

vagotonin (va-got′o-nin). A preparation of hormone from the pancreas which increases vagal tone, slows the heart and increases the store of glycogen in the liver.

vagotony (va-got′o-ne). Vagotonia.

vagotrope (va′go-trōp). Vagotropic.

vagotropic (va″go-trop′ik). Having an effect on the vagus nerve.

vagotropism (va-got′ro-pizm) [*vagus* + Gr. *tropos* a turning]. Affinity of a drug or poison for the vagus nerve.

vagovagal (va″go-va′gal). Arising as a result of afferent and efferent impulses which are both mediated through the vagus nerve.

vagrant (va′grant) [L. *vagrans,* from *vagare* to wander]. **1.** Wandering; moving from one place to another. 2. A vagabond.

vagus (va′gus), pl. *va′gi* [L. "wandering"]. Designating the tenth cranial nerve. See *nervus vagus.*

Vahlkampfia (vahl-kamp′fe-ah). A genus of amebae in which there is no flagellate stage of development.

valamin (val′ah-min). The valerian ester of amylene hydrate, $(CH_3)_2.C_2H_5.CO.O.C_5H_9$: hypnotic and sedative.

Valangin's solution (vah-lan′jinz) [Francis J. P. de *Valangin,* London physician, 1725–1805]. Solution of arsenous acid.

valence (va′lens) [L. *valentia* strength]. The numerical measure of the capacity to combine. In chemistry it is an expression of the number of atoms of hydrogen (or its equivalent) which one atom of a chemical element can hold in combination, if negative, or displace in a reaction, if positive. An element is characterized as univalent or monovalent, bivalent or divalent, tervalent or trivalent, multivalent or polyvalent, according to its valence—one, two, three, many, etc. In immunology it is an expression of the number of reactive sites on the surface of the molecules by which homologous antigen and antibody specifically combine. In antigens the number depends upon the size of the molecule (5–6 in ovalbumin of a molecular weight of 40,500, and 30–40 in thyroglobulin with a molecular weight of 650,-000). In the antibody molecule there are usually two (complete antibody), but monovalent (or incomplete) antibody is also formed. **biologic v.,** the combining power of molecules of homologous antigen and antibody.

valency (va′len-se) [L. *valentia*]. 1. Strength; ability. 2. Valence.

Valentin's corpuscles, ganglion (val′en-tēnz) [Gabriel Gustav *Valentin,* German physician, 1810–1883]. See under the nouns.

Valentine's position (val′en-tīnz) [Ferdinand C. *Valentine,* surgeon in New York, 1851–1909]. See under *position.*

valethamate (val-eth′ah-māt). Chemical name: 2-diethylaminoethyl 3-methyl-2-phenylvalerate: used in parasympathetic blockade.

valetudinarian (val″e-tu″dĭ-na′re-an) [L. *valetudinarius* sickly]. An invalid; a feeble person.

valetudinarianism (val″e-tu″dĭ-na′re-an-izm). An infirm or feeble habit of body.

valgus (val′gus) [L.]. Bent outward, twisted; denoting a deformity in which the angulation of the part is away from the midline of the body, such as *talipes valgus.* The term valgus is an adjective and should be used only in connection with the noun it describes, as talipes valgus, genu valgum, coxa valga, etc. Cf. *varus.*

valine (val′in). An amino acid, alpha-amino-isovalerianic acid, $(CH_3)_2.CH.CH(NH_2).COOH$, produced by the digestion or hydrolytic decomposition of proteins: essential for optimal growth in infants and for nitrogen equilibrium in human adults.

vallate (val′āt) [L. *vallatus* walled]. Having a wall or rim; cup-shaped.

vallecula (val-lek′u-lah), pl. *vallec′ulae* [dim. of L. *valles* a hollow]. A depression or furrow; used as a general term in anatomical nomenclature; often used alone to designate the *vallecula epiglottica.* **v. cerebel′li** [N A, B N A], the hollow on the inferior surface of the cerebellum, between the hemispheres, in which rests the medulla oblongata. **v. epiglot′tica** [B N A], a depression between the lateral and median glossoepiglottic folds on each side. Omitted in N A. **v. ova′ta,** fossa vesicae felleae. **v. for petrosal ganglion,** fossula petrosa. **v. syl′vii,** fossa lateralis cerebri. **v. un′guis,** sulcus matricis unguis.

vallecular (vah-lek′u-lar). Pertaining to or affecting a vallecula.

Valleix's points (vahl-lāz′) [François Louis *Valleix,* French physician, 1807–1855]. See under *point.*

vallestril (val-les′tril). Trade mark for a preparation of methallenestril.

valley (val′e). A small hollow. **v. of cerebellum,** vallecula cerebelli.

Valli-Ritter law (val″e-rit′er) [Eusebio *Valli,* Italian physiologist, 1726–1816; Johann Wilhelm *Ritter,* German physicist, 1776–1810]. See *Ritter-Valli law,* under *law.*

vallicepobufagin (vah-lis″ĕ-po-bu′fah-jin). A cardiac poison, $C_{26}H_{38}O_5$, from the skin glands of the toad, *Bufo valliceps.*

vallis (val′is) [L. "valley"]. Vallecula cerebelli.

vallum (val′um), pl. *val′la* [L. "a fortification"]. A mound, or wall. **v. un′guis** [N A, B N A], the fold of skin overlapping the sides and the proximal end of a nail. Called also *wall of nail.*

valmid (val′mid). Trade mark for a preparation of ethinamate.

valonia (vah-lo′ne-ah) [Ital. *vallonia;* Gr. *balanos* acorn]. The acorn cups of *Quercus aegilops:* strongly astringent.

Valsalva's experiment, maneuver, sinus (val-sal′vahz) [Antonio Maria *Valsalva,* an Italian anatomist, 1666–1723]. See under *maneuver* and *sinus.*

Valsuani's disease (val″su-an′ēz) [Emilio *Valsuani,* Italian gynecologist of 19th Century]. See under *disease.*

value (val′u). A measure of worth or efficiency. **acetyl v.,** acetyl number. **acid v.,** acid number. **buffer v.,** the ability of a fluid such as the blood to absorb small amounts of acids or of alkalis without much change in its hydrogen ion concentration. **cryocrit v.,** the per cent volume of sedimented cryoglobulin after centrifuging for 30 minutes, at 3,000 r.p.m. at 4°C., blood which has been kept in a hematocrit tube for three days at 4 to 5°C. **fuel v.,** the potential heat energy of the food. **globular v.,** the percentage of hemoglobin in a red corpuscle. It is represented by a fraction, the numerator of which represents the quantity of hemoglobin and the denominator the amount of red corpuscles. **Hehner's v.,** the percentage of fatty acids that are insoluble in water after saponification of the fat. **liminal v.,** that intensity of a stimulus which produces a just noticeable impression. **saponification v.,** saponification number. **threshold v.,** liminal v. **valence v.,** the number obtained by multiplying the lowering of the freezing point in degrees by the amount of urine in cubic centimeters.

valva (val′vah), pl. *val′vae* [sing. of L. *valvae* folding doors]. [N A] A membranous fold in a canal or passage, which prevents the reflux of the contents passing through it. Called also *valve.* **v. aor′tae** [N A], a valve, composed of three semilunar segments (posterior, right, and left), located at the orifice of the aorta in the left ventricle of the heart. Called also *vulvulae semilunares aortae* [B N A], and *aortic valve.* **v. atrioventricula′ris dex′tra** [N A], the valve between the right atrium and right ventricle of the heart. It is composed of three cusps: anterior, posterior, and septal. Called also *valvula tricuspidalis* [B N A], and *right atrioventricular valve.* **v. atrioventricula′ris sinis′tra** [N A], the valve between the left atrium and left ventricle of the heart. It is composed of two cusps: anterior and posterior. Called also *valvula bicuspidalis* [*mitralis*] [B N A], and *left atrioventricular valve.* **v. ileoceca′lis** [N A], two folds of mucous membrane at the junction of the distal end of the ileum and the large intestine, which function more or less as a valve to prevent backward flow of contents from the cecum into the ileum. It consists of a labium inferior and labium superior. Called also *valvula coli* [B N A], and *ileocecal valve.* **v. mitra′lis,** N A alternative for *v. atrioventricularis sinistra.* **v. tricuspida′lis,** N A alternative for *v. atrioventricularis dextra.* **v. trun′ci pulmona′lis** [N A], a valve, composed of three semilunar segments (anterior, right, and left), located at the orifice of the pulmonary trunk in the right ventricle of the heart. Called also *valvulae semilunares arteriae pulmonalis* [B N A], and *valve of pulmonary trunk.*

valval, valvar (val′val, val′var). Pertaining to a valve.

valvate (val′vāt). Pertaining to or having valves.

valve (valv). A membranous fold in a canal or passage, which prevents the reflux of the contents passing through it. Called also *valva.* **Amussat's v.,** plica spiralis. **anal v's,** valvulae anales. **v. of aorta, aortic v.,** valva aortae. **atrioventricular v., left,** valva atrioventricularis sinistra. **atrioventricular v., right,** valva atrioventricularis dextra. **auriculoventricular v., left,** valva atrioventricularis sinistra. **auriculoventricular v., right,** valva atrioventricularis dextra. **Ball's v's,** valvulae anales. **Bauer v.,** a piece of unglazed porcelain fused into the wall of a gas tube by means of which air can be admitted as needed. **Bauhin's v.,** valva ileocecalis. **Béraud's v.,** a fold of mucous membrane sometimes found at the junction of the lacrimal sac and the nasolacrimal duct. **Bianchi's v.,** the lower termination of the nasolacrimal duct. **bicuspid v.,** valva atrioventricularis sinistra. **Bochdalek's v.,** a fold within the lacrimal duct near the punctum lacrimale. **cardiac v's,** valves that control the flow of blood through and from the heart; they are the atrioventricular, aortic, and pulmonary trunk valves. **caval v.,** valvula venae cavae inferioris. **v. of colon,** valva ileocecalis. **coronary v., v. of coronary sinus,** valvula sinus coronarii. **electric v.,** a vacuum tube having for one electrode a hot filament: employed for rectifying an alternating to a direct current. **eustachian v.,** valvula venae cavae inferioris. **fallopian v.,** valva ileocecalis. **Foltz's v.,** a fold of membrane at the lacrimal canaliculus. **v. of foramen ovale.** 1. Valvula foraminis ovalis [N A, B N A]. 2. The septum primum of the fetal heart. **Gerlach's v.,** valvula processus vermiformis. **Guérin's v.,** valvula fossae navicularis. **Hasner's v.,** plica lacrimalis. **Heister's v.,** plica spiralis. **Hoboken's v's,** foldlike thickenings of the media of the umbilical arteries which protrude into the lumen of the arteries. **Houston's v.,** the middle one of the three transverse folds of mucous membrane in the rectum (plicae transversales recti).

Huschke's v., plica lacrimalis. **hymenal v. of male urethra**, valvula fossae navicularis. **ileocecal v., ileocolic v.**, valva ileocecalis. **v. of inferior vena cava**, valvula venae cavae inferioris. **interauricular v.** 1. Limbus fossae ovalis. 2. Valvula foraminis ovalis, def. 1. **Kerckring's v's**, plicae circulares. **Krause's v.**, Béraud's v. **lymphatic v.**, valvula lymphaticum. **v. of Macalister**, valva ileocecalis. **Mercier's v.**, interureteric ridge. **mitral v.**, valva atrioventricularis sinistra. **Morgagni's v's**, valvulae anales. **v. of navicular fossa**, valvula fossae navicularis. **O'Beirne's v.** See under *sphincter*. **pulmonary v., pulmonary trunk v.**, valva trunci pulmonalis. **pyloric v.**, valvula pylori. **Rosenmüller's v.**, plica lacrimalis. **semilunar v's**, the valves that guard the openings from the left ventricle into the aorta (*valva aortae*) and the pulmonary trunk (*valva trunci pulmonalis*); used also to designate the semilunar segments or cusps composing these valves (valvulae semilunares). **semilunar v's of aorta**, the segments (cusps) composing the valve of the aorta, including the valvula semilunaris dextra aortae, valvula semilunaris posterior aortae, and valvula semilunaris sinistra aortae. **semilunar v's of colon**, plicae semilunares coli. **semilunar v's of Morgagni**, sinus anales. **semilunar v's of pulmonary trunk**, the segments (cusps) composing the valve of the pulmonary trunk, including the valvula semilunaris dextra trunci pulmonalis and valvula semilunaris sinistra trunci pulmonalis. **sigmoid v's of colon**, plicae semilunares coli. **sigmoid v's of pulmonary trunk.** See *semilunar v's of pulmonary trunk*. **spiral v. of cystic duct, spiral v. of Heister**, plica spiralis. **v. of Sylvius**, valvula venae cavae inferioris. **Taillefer's v.**, a fold of the mucous membrane of the nasolacrimal duct near the middle of its course. **Tarinus' v.**, velum medullare posterius. **thebesian v.**, valvula sinus coronarii. **tricuspid v.**, valva atrioventricularis dextra. **v. of Tulpius, v. of Varolius**, valva ileocecalis. **v. of veins**, valvula venosa. **v. of vermiform appendix**, valvula processus vermiformis. **v. of Vieussens, Willis' v.**, velum medullare anterius.

valved (valvd). Having valves; opening by valves.

valveless (valv′les). Without valves.

valviform (val′vĭ-form) [L. *valva* valve + *forma* shape]. Shaped like a valve.

valvotomy (val-vot′o-me) [L. *valva* valve + Gr. *tomē* a cutting]. Incision of a valve, such as valve of the heart, or of Houston's valve of the rectum. **mitral v.**, dilation of the left atrioventricular (mitral) valve, the commissures being split and extended with the finger, with or without the aid of a knife or a mechanical dilator.

valvula (val′vu-lah), pl. *val′vulae* [L., dim. of *valva*]. A small valve; used in B N A as a general term to designate a valve, such as in the heart; in N A its use is restricted to designation of a cusp of the aortic valve or of the valve of the pulmonary trunk, or the valves of the anus, foramen ovale, navicular fossa, coronary sinus, inferior vena cava, or of the lymphatic vessels and veins. **val′vulae ana′les** [N A], archlike folds of mucous membrane connecting the caudal ends of the anal columns. Called also *anal valves*. **v. bicuspida′lis [mitra′lis]** [B N A], valva atrioventricularis sinistra. **v. co′li** [B N A], valva ileocecalis. **val′vulae conniven′tes** [L. "closing valves"], plicae circulares. **v. foram′inis ova′lis.** 1. [N A, B N A] In the adult, a crescentic ridge on the left side of the interatrial septum, representing the edge of what was the septum primum before fusion of the septum. Called also *falx septi* and *valve of foramen ovale*. 2. The septum primum of the fetal heart. **v. fos′sae navicula′ris** [N A, B N A], a fold of mucous membrane occasionally occurring in the roof of the fossa navicularis of the urethra. Called also *valve of navicular fossa*. **v. ileocol′ica**, valva ileocecalis. **v. lymphat′icum** [N A], any one of the usually doubled cusps in the collecting lymphatic vessels, serving to ensure flow in only one direction. Called also *lymphatic valve*. **v. mitra′lis**, valva atrioventricularis sinistra. **v. proces′sus vermifor′mis** [B N A], a fold of mucous membrane at the opening into the cecum of the canal of the vermiform appendix. Omitted in N A. **v. pylo′ri** [B N A], a prominent circular fold of mucous membrane at the pyloric orifice of the stomach. Omitted in N A. **v. semiluna′ris**, a semilunar valve. **v. semiluna′ris ante′rior arte′riae pulmona′lis** [B N A], **v. semiluna′ris ante′rior trun′ci pulmona′lis** [N A], the anterior cusp of the valve of the pulmonary trunk. **val′vulae semiluna′res aor′tae** [B N A], valva aortae. **val′vulae semiluna′res arte′riae pulmona′lis** [B N A], valva trunci pulmonalis. **v. semiluna′ris dex′tra aor′tae** [N A, B N A], the right cusp of the valve of the aorta. **v. semiluna′ris dex′tra arte′riae pulmona′lis** [B N A], **v. semiluna′ris dex′tra trun′ci pulmona′lis** [N A], the right cusp of the valve of the pulmonary trunk. **v. semiluna′ris poste′rior aor′tae** [N A, B N A], the posterior cusp of the valve of the aorta. **v. semiluna′ris sinis′tra aor′tae** [N A, B N A], the left cusp of the valve of the aorta. **v. semiluna′ris sinis′tra arte′riae pulmona′lis** [B N A], **v. semiluna′ris sinis′tra trun′ci pulmona′lis** [N A], the left cusp of the valve of the pulmonary trunk. **v. si′nus corona′rii** [N A], **v. si′nus corona′rii [Thebe′sii]** [B N A], a fold of endocardium along the right margin of the opening of the coronary sinus into the right atrium of the heart. Called also *valve of coronary sinus*. **v. spira′lis [Heis′teri]** [B N A], plica spiralis. **v. tricuspida′lis** [B N A], valva atrioventricularis dextra. **v. vagi′nae**, hymen. **v. ve′nae ca′vae inferio′ris** [N A], **v. ve′nae ca′vae inferio′ris [Eusta′chii]** [B N A], the variably-sized crescentic fold of endocardial and subendocardial tissue that partially guards the opening of the inferior vena cava into the right atrium of the heart. Called also *valve of inferior vena cava*. **v. veno′sa** [N A], any one of the small, cup-shaped valves found in many of the veins, serving to prevent the backflow of blood. Called also *valve of veins*. **v. vestib′uli**, either of the two thin folds bordering the opening of the sinus reuniens into the right auricle of the embryonic heart. They develop into the valves of the inferior vena cava and coronary sinus.

valvulae (val′vu-le) [L.]. Plural of *valvula*.

valvular (val′vu-lar). Pertaining to, affecting, or of the nature of, a valve.

valvulitis (val″vu-li′tis). Inflammation of a valve or valvula, especially a valve of the heart. **rheumatic v.**, endocarditis.

valvuloplasty (val′vu-lo-plas″te). Plastic operation on a valve.

valvulotome (val′vu-lo-tōm). An instrument for cutting a valve.

valvulotomy (val″vu-lot′o-me). Valvotomy.

valyl (val′il). Valerianic acid diethylamide, CH_3-$(CH_2)_3$.CO.N$(C_2H_5)_2$, a liquid with a strong odor: used in hysteria and other nervous disorders.

valylene (val′ĭ-lēn). A hydrocarbon, C_5H_6.

vampire (vam′pīr). A blood-sucking bat, *Desmodus rufus;* also *Diphylla ecaudata*, a bat of similar habits; both South American. Their bites may transmit the virus of rabies to man.

vanadate (van′ah-dāt). Any salt of vanadic acid.

vanadiotherapy (vah-na″de-o-ther′ah-pe). Treatment by vanadium compounds.

vanadium (vah-na′de-um) [*Vanadis*, a Norse deity]. A rare, gray, metallic element; symbol, V; atomic number, 23; atomic weight, 50.942.

vanadiumism (vah-na′de-um-izm). A chronic intoxication caused by absorption of vanadium: seen in workers in that metal or its compounds.

van Buren's disease (van-bu′renz) [William Holme *van Buren*, American surgeon, 1819–1883]. Hardening of the corpora cavernosa.

vancocin (van′ko-sin). Trade mark for a preparation of vancomycin.

vancomycin (van′ko-mi″sin). A substance obtained from strains of *Streptomyces orientalis*, a highly effective antibiotic against gram-positive cocci.

Van de Graaff machine (van de grahf) [Robert J. *van de Graaff*, American physicist, born 1901]. An electrostatic generator of high voltage.

van Deen's test (van dēnz) [Izaak Abramson *van Deen*, Dutch physician, 1804–1869]. See *Deen's test*, under *tests*.

van den Bergh's test (van den bergz′) [A. A. Himans *van den Bergh*, Dutch physician, 1869–1943]. See under *tests*.

van den Velden's test (van den vel′denz) [Reinhardt *van den Velden*, German physician, 1851–1903]. See under *tests*.

van Gehuchten's method (van-ga-hook′tenz) [Arthur *van Gehuchten*, Belgian anatomist, 1861–1915]. See under *method*.

Vanghetti's prosthesis (vahn-get′ēz) [Giuliano *Vanghetti*, Italian surgeon, 1861–1940]. See under *prosthesis*.

van Gieson's stain (van-ge′sonz) [Ira *van Gieson*, New York neuropathologist, 1865–1913]. See *stains, table of*.

van Helmont's mirror (van hel′monts) [Johannes Baptista *van Helmont*, Belgian physician, 1577–1644]. The central tendon of the diaphragm (centrum tendineum [N A]).

van Hook's operation (van hooks′) [Weller *van Hook*, Chicago surgeon, 1862–1933]. Uretero-ureterostomy.

van Hoorne's canal (van hornz) [Jean *van Hoorne*, Dutch anatomist, 1621–1670]. The thoracic duct (ductus thoracicus [N A]).

Vanilla (vah-nil′ah) [L.]. A genus of climbing orchidaceous plants of hot climates. The fruit of *V. planifolia*, of Mexico, are the vanilla beans, which contain vanilla and are used as a flavor and a mild stimulant: said to be aphrodisiac.

vanillal (vah-nil′lal). Ethyl vanillin.

vanillin (vah-nil′in). An aromatic, crystallizable principle, 4-hydroxy-3-methoxybenzaldehyde: used as a flavoring agent. **ethyl v.,** fine white or slightly yellowish crystals, with a taste and odor similar to those of vanilla: used as a flavoring agent for pharmaceuticals.

vanillism (vah-nil′izm). Symptoms of dermatitis, coryza, and malaise seen in those handling raw vanilla and caused by a species of mite.

vanogel (van′o-jel). Trade mark for an aqueous suspension of aluminum hydroxide gel.

Van Slyke's formula, method, test (van-sliks′) [Donald D. *Van Slyke*, American biochemist, born 1883]. See under the nouns.

van't Hoff's law, rule (vant hofs) [Jacobus Hendricus *van't Hoff*, Dutch chemist in Berlin, 1852–1911]. See under *law* and *rule*.

Vanzetti's sign (vahn-tset′ēz) [Tito *Vanzetti*, Italian surgeon, 1809–1888]. See under *sign*.

vapocauterization (va″po-kaw″ter-i-za′shun). Cauterization by means of steam or other hot vapor.

vapor (va′por), pl. *vapo′res, va′pors* [L.]. 1. Steam, gas, or exhalation. 2. (pl.). Hypochondriasis or hysterical depression of spirits.

vaporarium (va″po-rār′e-um) [L.]. An establishment or apparatus for treating certain diseases by the use of vapors.

vaporish (va′por-ish). Splenetic or hysterical.

vaporium (va-po′re-um) [L.]. Vaporarium.

vaporization (va″por-i-za′shun). 1. The conversion of a solid or liquid into a vapor without chemical change. 2. Treatment by vapors.

vaporize (va′por-iz). To convert into vapor or to be transformed into vapor.

vapotherapy (va″po-ther′ah-pe). The therapeutic use of vapor, steam or spray.

Vaquez's disease (vak-āz′) [Louis Henri *Vaquez*, French physician, 1860–1936]. Polycythemia vera.

var. Abbreviation for *variety*.

variable (va′re-ah-b′l) [L. *variare* to change]. 1. Changing from time to time. 2. A quantity or value subject to change; in statistics, one of the separate numerical values from which a curve of variability can be constructed.

variate (va′re-āt). Variable.

variation (va″re-a′shun). Deviation in characters in an individual from those typical of the group to which it belongs; also, deviation in characters of the offspring from those of its parents. **bacterial v.,** microbic dissociation. **continuous v.,** a series of small variations. **impressed v.,** a variation which occurs in response to a particular environmental stimulus. **inborn v.,** one which arises from changes in the germ and not from the somatic cells. **meristic v.,** variation in the number of parts in the offspring.

varication (var″ĭ-ka′shun). 1. The formation of a varix. 2. A varicose condition.

variceal (var″ĭ-se′al). Pertaining to or caused by a varix.

varicella (var″ĭ-sel′ah) [L.]. Chickenpox. **v. gangreno′sa,** a rare form of chickenpox in which the eruption leads to a gangrenous ulceration. Called also *dermatitis gangrenosa infantum*. **v. inocula′ta,** the inoculation of children with a virus from a fresh clear vesicle of chickenpox; usually no general symptoms develop. **pustular v., v. pustulo′sa,** chickenpox in which the eruption develops into furuncles. **vaccination v.,** v. inoculata.

varicellation (var″ĭ-sel-la′shun). Prophylactic inoculation with the virus of varicella.

varicelliform (var″ĭ-sel′ĭ-form). Resembling varicella.

varicellization (var″ĭ-sel-i-za′shun). Varicellation.

varicelloid (var″ĭ-sel′oid) [*varicella* + Gr. *eidos* form]. Resembling varicella.

varices (var′ĭ-sēz) [L.]. Plural of *varix*.

variciform (var-is′ĭ-form) [*varix* + L. *forma* form]. Resembling a varix; varicose.

varico- (var′ĭ-ko) [L. *varix* a varicose vein]. Combining form denoting relationship to a varix, or meaning twisted and swollen.

varicoblepharon (var″ĭ-ko-blef′ah-ron) [*varico-* + Gr. *blepharon* eyelid]. A varicose swelling of the eyelid.

varicocele (var′ĭ-ko-sēl) [*varico-* + Gr. *kēlē* tumor]. A varicose condition of the veins of the pampiniform plexus, forming a swelling that feels like a "bag of worms," appearing bluish through the skin of the scrotum, and accompanied by a constant pulling, dragging, or dull pain in the scrotum. **ovarian v., pelvic v.,** a varicose condition of the veins of the broad ligament. **utero-ovarian v.,** a varicose condition of the veins of the pampiniform plexus of the female.

varicocelectomy (var″ĭ-ko-se-lek′to-me) [*varicocele* + Gr. *ektomē* excision]. The excision of a part of the scrotum and the enlarged veins for varicocele.

varicography (var″ĭ-kog′rah-fe) [*varico-* + Gr. *graphein* to write]. Roentgenological visualization of varicose veins.

varicoid (var′ĭ-koid) [*varico-* + Gr. *eidos* form]. Resembling a varix.

varicole (var′ĭ-kōl). Varicocele.

varicomphalus (var″ĭ-kom′fah-lus) [*varico-* + Gr. *omphalos* navel]. A varicose tumor at the navel.

varicophlebitis (var″ĭ-ko-fle-bi′tis). Latent infection existing in varicose veins.

varicosclerosation (var″ĭ-ko-skle″ro-za′shun).

Treatment of varicose veins by the induction of artificial sclerosis.

varicose (var′ĭ-kōs) [L. *varicosus*]. Of the nature of or pertaining to a varix; unnaturally swollen: said of a vein.

varicosis (var″ĭ-ko′sis) [L.]. A varicose condition of the veins of any part.

varicosity (var″ĭ-kos′ĭ-te). 1. A varicose condition; the quality or fact of being varicose. 2. A varix or varicose vein.

varicotomy (var″ĭ-kot′o-me) [*varico-* + Gr. *tomē* a cutting]. The excision of a varix or of a varicose vein.

varicula (vah-rik′u-lah) [L.]. A varix of the conjunctiva.

varidase (var′ĭ-dās). Trade mark for preparations of streptokinase and streptodornase.

variola (vah-ri′o-lah) [L.]. Smallpox. **v. capri′na,** goatpox. **v. crystal′lina,** chickenpox. **v. inser′ta,** smallpox acquired by inoculation. **v. ma′jor,** a severe form of smallpox, such as hemorrhagic smallpox or malignant smallpox, characterized by a case fatality rate of 25 to 40 per cent. **v. milia′ris,** smallpox with an eruption of small vesicles. **v. mi′nor,** a mild form of smallpox, caused by a virus slightly less virulent for the chick embryo than the virus causing variola major, and distinguished from the latter condition by its much lower fatality rate. **v. mitiga′ta,** v. minor. **v. pemphigo′sa,** smallpox with an eruption of large blebs. **v. siliquo′sa,** smallpox in which the contents of the pustules become absorbed, leaving the walls empty. **v. ve′ra,** simple and unmodified smallpox. **v. verruco′sa,** a variety of smallpox in which the eruption does not pass beyond the papular stage.

variolar (vah-ri′o-lar). Pertaining to smallpox.

Variolaria amara (va″re-o-la′re-ah ah-ma′rah). A febrifugal and anthelmintic lichen of the Old World.

variolate (va′re-o-lāt). 1. Having the nature or appearance of smallpox. 2. To inoculate with smallpox virus.

variolation (va″re-o-la′shun). Inoculation with the virus of unmodified smallpox. **bovine v.,** inoculation of a calf with smallpox.

variolic (var″e-ol′ik). Variolar.

varioliform (va″re-o′lĭ-form). Resembling smallpox.

variolinum (va″re-o-li′num). A homeopathic remedy prepared from the virus of smallpox.

variolization (va″re-o-li-za′shun). Variolation.

varioloid (va′re-o-loid). A modified and mild form of smallpox occurring in a patient who has had a previous attack or has been vaccinated.

variolous (vah-ri′o-lus). Pertaining to or of the nature of smallpox.

variolovaccine (vah-ri″o-lo-vak′sēn). 1. Pertaining to vaccine or bovine variola. 2. A virus obtained by vaccinating the heifer with the virus of smallpox.

variolovaccinia (vah-ri″o-lo-vak-sin′e-ah). Cowpox in the heifer caused by inoculation with smallpox.

varisse (var-is′). A lump on the inner surface of a horse's hind leg.

varix (var′iks), pl. *var′ices* [L.]. An enlarged and tortuous vein, artery, or lymphatic vessel. **anastomotic v.,** a varix composed of intercommunicating channels. **aneurysmal v., aneurysmoid v.,** a form of arteriovenous aneurysm in which the blood flows directly into a neighboring vein without the intervention of a connecting sac. **arterial v.,** a cirsoid aneurysm or varicose artery. **cirsoid v.,** cirsoid aneurysm. **gelatinous v.,** a nodular state of the umbilical cord. **lymph v., v. lymphat′icus,** a soft, lobulated swelling of a lymph node, resulting from obstruction and dilatation of the lymphatic vessels. **papillary v.,** de Morgan's spots.

varnish (var′nish). A solution of a resin or of several resins in a suitable solvent or solvents, applied in a thin layer to form a hard, smooth surface: sometimes used in dentistry. **black v., Burmese v., Martaban v.,** a varnish produced in Burma from *Melanorrhoea usitata*, a terebinthinaceous tree. **Whitehead's v.,** gum benzoin 4 parts, styrax 3 parts, balsam of tolu, 1 part, ether 40 parts, 10 per cent iodoform: used as a dressing seal for wounds.

varolian (vah-ro′le-an). 1. Described by or named for Costanzo *Varolio* (*Varolius*), Italian anatomist and surgeon, 1543–1575. 2. Pertaining to the pons.

varus (va′rus) [L.]. Bent inward; denoting a deformity in which the angulation of the part is toward the midline of the body, such as talipes varus. The term varus is an adjective and should be used only in connection with the noun it describes, as talipes varus, genu varum, coxa vara, etc. Cf. *valgus*.

vas (vas), pl. *va′sa* [L.]. Any canal for carrying a fluid; used in anatomical nomenclature as a general term to designate such channels, especially those carrying blood or lymph. Called also *vessel.* **v. aber′rans.** 1. A blind tubule sometimes connected with the epididymis; it is a vestigial mesonephric tubule. 2. Any anomalous or unusual vessel. **va′sa aberran′tia hep′atis** [B N A], numerous vessels found in the fibrous appendix and in the capsule of the liver. Omitted in N A. **v. aber′rans of Roth.** See *ductuli aberrantes.* **va′sa afferen′tia,** vessels that convey fluid to a structure or part. **v. af′ferens glomer′uli** [N A, B N A], a branch of an interlobular artery that goes to a renal glomerulus. Called also *afferent vessel of glomerulus.* **va′sa afferen′tia lymphoglan′dulae** [B N A], vasa afferentia nodi lymphatici. **va′sa afferen′tia no′di lymphat′ici** [N A], lymphatic vessels that carry lymph to a lymph node, entering through the capsule. **v. anastomot′icum** [N A, B N A], a vessel that serves to interconnect other vessels; such communications are present in the palm of the hand, sole of the foot, base of the brain, and other regions. **va′sa au′ris inter′nae** [N A, B N A], vessels of the internal ear. **va′sa bre′via,** arteriae gastricae breves. **v. capilla′re** [N A, B N A], any one of the minute vessels connecting the arterioles and the venules, forming networks found in nearly all parts of the body. See *capillary* (def. 2). **v. collatera′le** [N A, B N A], a vessel that parallels another vessel, nerve, or other structure. Called also *collateral vessel.* **v. def′erens,** ductus deferens. **va′sa efferen′tia,** vessels that convey fluid away from a structure or part. See *vasa efferentia nodi lymphatici* and *ductuli efferentes testis.* **v. ef′ferens glomer′uli** [N A, B N A], an arteriole that arises from a renal glomerulus, breaking up into capillaries to supply renal tubules. Called also *efferent vessel of glomerulus.* **va′sa efferen′tia lymphoglan′dulae** [B N A], vasa efferentia nodi lymphatici. **va′sa efferen′tia no′di lymphat′ici** [N A], lymphatic vessels that carry lymph away from a lymph node, emerging at the hilus. Called also *efferent vessels of lymph node.* **v. epididym′idis,** ductus epididymidis. **va′sa intesti′ni ten′uis,** arteriae intestinales. **v. lymphat′icum** [N A, B N A], a vessel that conveys lymph; pl. **va′sa lymphat′ica** [N A, B N A], the capillaries, collecting vessels, and trunks which collect lymph from the tissues and through which the lymph passes to reach the blood stream. Called also *lymphatic vessels.* **va′sa lymphat′ica profun′da** [N A, B N A], lymphatic vessels that accompany the deeply placed blood vessels. Called also *deep lymphatic vessels.* **va′sa lymphat′ica superficia′lia** [N A, B N A], lymphatic vessels located under the skin and superficial fascia, in the submucous areolar tissue of the digestive, respiratory, and genitourinary tracts, and in the subserous tissue of the walls of the abdomen and thorax. Called also *superficial lymphatic vessels.* **va′sa nervo′-**

rum, blood vessels supplying the nerves. **va'sa nutri'tia.** See *vasa vasorum.* **va'sa prae'via,** presentation in front of the fetal head in labor of the blood vessels of the umbilical cord where they enter the placenta. **v. prom'inens duc'tus cochlea'ris** [N A, B N A], a small vessel often seen deep to the spiral prominence in the cochlear duct. **va'sa pro'pria of Jungbluth,** vessels situated beneath the amnion of the early embryo. **va'sa rec'ta** [L. "straight vessels"]. See *tubuli renales recti* and *tubuli seminiferi recti.* **va'sa sanguin'ea integumen'ti commu'nis,** the blood vessels of the skin, or common integument. **va'sa sanguin'ea ret'inae** [N A, B N A], the blood vessels of the retina, including all the arterioles, derived from the central artery of the retina, and the venules, which return blood to the central vein. **v. spira'le** [N A], a prominent vessel in the basilar membrane near the osseous spiral lamina. **va'sa vaso'rum** [N A, B N A], the small nutrient arteries and the veins in the walls of the larger blood vessels. **va'sa vortico'sa,** venae vorticosae.

vasa (va'sah) [L.]. Plural of *vas.*

vasal (va'sal). Pertaining to a vas or to a vessel.

vasalgia (vah-sal'je-ah). Pain in vessels.

vasalium (vah-sa'le-um). True vascular tissue, such as is found in closed or vascular organs.

vascular (vas'ku-lar). Pertaining to or full of vessels.

vascularity (vas"ku-lar'ĭ-te). The condition of being vascular.

vascularization (vas"ku-lar-i-za'shun). The process of becoming vascular, or the development of vessels in a part or tissue.

vascularize (vas'ku-lar"iz). To supply with vessels.

vasculature (vas'ku-lah-tūr). The vascular system of the body or any part of it.

vasculitis (vas"ku-li'tis) [L. *vasculum* vessel + *-itis*]. Inflammation of a vessel. **nodular v.,** a name that has been given to the nontuberculous type of erythema induratum.

vasculogenesis (vas"ku-lo-jen'e-sis) [L. *vasculum* vessel + Gr. *genesis* production]. The development of the vascular system.

vasculolymphatic (vas"ku-lo-lim-fat'ik). Pertaining to blood or lymph vessels.

vasculomotor (vas"ku-lo-mo'tor). Vasomotor.

vasculotoxic (vas"ku-lo-tok'sik). Pertaining to or characterized by a deleterious or toxic effect on the vessels of the body.

vasculum (vas'ku-lum), pl. *vas'cula* [L., dim. of *vas*]. A small vessel. **v. aber'rans,** vas aberrans.

vasectomized (vas-ek'to-mizd). Deprived of the ductus deferentes (vasa deferentia).

vasectomy (vas-ek'to-me) [*vas* + Gr. *ektomē* excision]. Surgical removal of the ductus (vas) deferens, or of a portion of it.

vasifactive (vas"ĭ-fak'tiv) [*vas* + L. *facere* to make]. Vasoformative.

vasiform (vas'ĭ-form) [*vas* + L. *forma* form]. Having the appearance of a vessel.

vasitis (vas-i'tis). Inflammation of the ductus (vas) deferens.

vaso- (vas'o) [L. *vas* vessel]. Combining form denoting relationship to a vessel, or duct.

vasoactive (vas"o-ak'tiv). Exerting an effect upon the blood vessels.

vasoconstriction (vas"o-kon-strik'shun). The diminution of the caliber of vessels, especially constriction of arterioles leading to decreased blood flow to a part.

vasoconstrictive (vas"o-kon-strik'tiv). Pertaining to, characterized by, or producing vasoconstriction.

vasoconstrictor (vas"o-kon-strik'tor). 1. Causing constriction of the blood vessels. 2. An agent (motor nerve or chemical compound) that causes constriction of the blood vessels.

vasocorona (vas"o-ko-ro'nah) [*vaso-* + L. *corona* crown]. The arterial vessels which pass radially from the spinal cord to its periphery.

vasodentin (vas"o-den'tin) [*vaso-* + L. *dens* tooth]. Dentin provided with blood vessels.

vasodepression (vas"o-de-presh'un). Vasomotor depression or collapse.

vasodepressor (vas"o-de-pres'sor). 1. Having a depressing effect on the circulation; causing vasomotor depression. 2. An agent that causes vasomotor depression.

vasodilan (vas"o-di'lan). Trade mark for preparations of isoxsuprine hydrochloride.

vasodilatation (vas"o-di-lah-ta'shun). A state of increased caliber of the blood vessels.

vasodilatin (vas"o-di-la'tin). A substance supposed to exist in organic extracts and to cause vascular dilatation.

vasodilation (vas"o-di-la'shun). Dilation of a vessel; especially dilation of arterioles leading to increased blood flow to a part. **reflex v.,** vasodilation occurring as a reflex response to stimuli applied elsewhere, or subsequent to an initial vasoconstrictive response.

vasodilative (vas"o-di'la-tiv). Pertaining to, characterized by, or producing vasodilatation.

vasodilator (vas"o-di-lāt'or). 1. Causing dilation of the blood vessels. 2. An agent (motor nerve or chemical compound) that causes dilation of the blood vessels.

vaso-epididymostomy (vas"o-ep"ĭ-did-ĭ-mos'to-me). Operative formation of a communication between the ductus (vas) deferens and the epididymis.

vasofactive (vas"o-fak'tiv). Vasoformative.

vasoformative (vas"o-for'mah-tiv). Pertaining to or promoting the formation of blood vessels.

vasoganglion (vas"o-gang'gle-on). Any vascular ganglion or rete.

vasography (vas-og'rah-fe) [*vaso-* + Gr. *graphein* to write]. Roentgenography of the blood vessels.

vasohypertonic (vas"o-hi"per-ton'ik). Vasoconstrictor.

vasohypotonic (vas"o-hi"po-ton'ik). Vasodilator.

vasoinert (vas"o-in-ert'). Exerting no effect on the caliber of blood vessels.

vaso-inhibitor (vas"o-in-hib'ĭ-tor). An agent that inhibits the action of the vasomotor nerves.

vaso-inhibitory (vas"o-in-hib'ĭ-tor-e). Hindering the action of the vasomotor nerves.

vasoligation (vas"o-li-ga'shun). Ligation of the ductus (vas) deferens.

vasoligature (vas"o-lig'ah-tūr). Vasoligation.

vasomotion (vas"o-mo'shun) [*vaso-* + L. *motio* movement]. Change in the caliber of a vessel, especially of a blood vessel.

vasomotor (vas-o-mo'tor) [*vaso-* + L. *motor* mover]. 1. Affecting the caliber of a vessel, especially of a blood vessel. 2. Any element or agent that affects the caliber of a blood vessel.

vasomotorial (vas"o-mo-to're-al). 1. Pertaining to the vasomotorium. 2. Pertaining to the change in caliber of a blood vessel.

vasomotoricity (vas"o-mo-tor-is'ĭ-te). The power of producing change in the caliber of blood vessels.

vasomotorium (vas"o-mo-to're-um). The vasomotor system of the body.

vasomotory (vas"o-mo'tor-e). Affecting the caliber of a vessel, especially a blood vessel.

vasoneuropathy (vas"o-nu-rop'ah-the). A combined vascular and neurologic defect, the lesions being caused by simultaneous action of both the vascular and the nervous system, or by the interaction of the two systems.

vasoneurosis (vas"o-nu-ro'sis). Angioneurosis.

vaso-orchidostomy (vas"o-or"kid-os'to-me).

The operation of suturing tubules of the epididymis to the ductus (vas) deferens.

vasoparesis (vas″o-pah-re′sis) [*vaso-* + Gr. *paresis* relaxation]. Partial paralysis of vasomotor nerves.

vasopressin (vas″o-pres′in). One of two hormones formed by the neuronal cells of the hypothalamic nuclei and stored in the posterior lobe of the hypophysis, the other being oxytocin. It stimulates the contraction of the muscular tissue of the capillaries and arterioles, raising the blood pressure. It stimulates contraction of the intestinal musculature and increases peristalsis, and also exerts some influence on the uterus.

vasopressor (vas″o-pres′sor). 1. Stimulating contraction of the muscular tissue of the capillaries and arteries. 2. An agent that stimulates contraction of the muscular tissue of the capillaries and arteries.

vasopuncture (vas′o-punk″tūr). Puncture of the ductus (vas) deferens.

vasoreflex (vas″o-re′flex). A reflex of a blood vessel.

vasorelaxation (vas″o-re-lak-sa′shun). Decrease of vascular pressure.

vasoresection (vas″o-re-sek′shun). Resection of the ductus (vas) deferens.

vasorrhaphy (vas-or′ah-fe). Suture of the ductus (vas) deferens.

vasosection (vas″o-sek′shun) [*vaso-* + L. *sectio* a cutting]. The severing of a vessel or vessels, especially of the ductus deferentes (vasa deferentia).

vasosensory (vas″o-sen′so-re). Supplying sensory filaments to the vessels.

vasospasm (vas′o-spazm). Spasm of the blood vessels, resulting in decrease in their caliber.

vasospastic (vas″o-spas′tik). Angiospastic.

vasostimulant (vas″o-stim′u-lant). Stimulating or arousing vasomotor action.

vasostomy (vas-os′to-me) [*vas* deferens + Gr. *stomoun* to provide with an opening, or mouth]. The operation of forming an opening into the ductus (vas) deferens.

vasothrombin (vas″o-throm′bin) [*vaso-* + *thrombin*]. A fibrin factor similar to leukothrombin, except that it is formed by the endothelial cells, which unites with hepatothrombin to form thrombin.

vasotomy (vas-ot′o-me) [*vaso-* + Gr. *tomē* a cutting]. Incision into or cutting of the ductus (vas) deferens.

vasotonia (vas″o-to′ne-ah) [*vaso-* + Gr. *tonos* tone + *-ia*]. Tone or tension of the vessels.

vasotonic (vas″o-ton′ic). Pertaining to, characterized by, or promoting vasotonia.

vasotribe (vas′o-trīb). Angiotribe.

vasotripsy (vas′o-trip″se). Angiotripsy.

vasotrophic (vas″o-trof′ik) [*vaso-* + Gr. *trophē* nutrition]. Affecting nutrition through the alteration of the caliber of the blood vessels.

vasotropic (vas″o-trop′ik). Tending to act on blood vessels.

vasovagal (vas″o-va′gal). Vascular and vagal: a term applied by Gowers to a syndrome consisting of precordial distress, anxiety, feeling of impending death, nausea, and respiratory difficulty.

vasovasotomy (vas″o-vas-ot′o-me). Anastomosis of the ends of the severed ductus (vas) deferens.

vasovesiculectomy (vas″o-ve-sik″u-lek′to-me). Excision of the ductus (vas) deferens and seminal vesicles.

vasovesiculitis (vas″o-ve-sik″u-li′tis). Inflammation of the ductus deferentes (vasa deferentia) and seminal vesicles.

vasoxyl (vas-ok′sil). Trade mark for preparations of methoxamine hydrochloride.

vastus (vas′tus) [L.]. Great; vast.

Vater's ampulla, corpuscles, papilla (fah′terz) [Abraham *Vater*, German anatomist, 1684–1751]. See under the nouns.

Vater-Pacini corpuscles (fah′ter-pa-se′ne) [Abraham *Vater:* Filippo *Pacini*, Italian anatomist, 1812–1883]. Corpuscula lamellosa.

Vateria (vah-te′re-ah) [named for A. *Vater*]. A genus of Asian trees. **V. in′dica,** an East Indian tree which affords Indian copal, piny varnish, white dammar, or Indian anime: used as a varnish, candle-stuff, and medicine.

Vaughan and Novy's test [Victor C. *Vaughan*, American pathologist, 1851–1929; Frederick G. *Novy*, American bacteriologist, born 1864]. See under *tests*.

vault (vawlt). A domelike or archlike structure. In dentistry, the longest palatal border obtainable through a coronal section of the maxilla. **v. of pharynx,** fornix pharyngis.

V.C. 1. Abbreviation for *vital capacity*. 2. Symbol for *acuity of color vision*.

V-cillin (ve-sil′lin). Trade mark for preparations of penicillin V. See *penicillin phenoxymethyl*.

V.D. Abbreviation for *venereal disease*.

V.D.A. Abbreviation for *visual discriminatory acuity*.

VDEL. Abbreviation for *Venereal Disease Experimental Laboratory*.

V.D.G. Abbreviation for *venereal disease—gonorrhea*.

V.D.H. Abbreviation for *valvular disease of the heart*.

VDM. Abbreviation for *vasodepressor material*, a substance formed by the liver that stimulates secretion of antidiuretic hormone.

VDRL. Abbreviation for *Venereal Disease Research Laboratories*.

V.D.S. Abbreviation for *venereal disease—syphilis*.

vecordia (ve-kor′de-ah) [L. *vecors* without reason]. An old term for a concept of partial insanity. Cf. *vesania*.

vection (vek′shun) [L. *vectio* a carrying]. The carrying of disease germs from an infected person to a well person. It is *circumferential, indirect,* or *mediate* when they are carried by an intermediate host; *direct, immediate,* or *radial* when they are transferred directly from one person to another.

vectis (vek′tis) [L., from *vehere* to carry]. A curved lever for making traction upon the fetal head in labor.

vector (vek′tor) [L. "one who carries," from *vehere* to carry]. A carrier, especially the animal (usually an arthropod) which transfers an infective agent from one host to another. **biological v.,** an anthropod vector in whose body the infecting organism develops or multiplies before becoming infective to the recipient individual. **mechanical v.,** an arthropod vector which transmits an infective organism from one host to another but which is not essential to the life cycle of the parasite.

vectorcardiogram (vek″tor-kar′de-o-gram). A graphic record of the magnitude and direction of the electrical forces of the heart.

vectorcardiography (vek″tor-kar″de-og′rah-fe). Determination of the direction and magnitude of the electrical forces of the heart. **spatial v.,** determination of the electrical forces of the heart as they exist in three dimensional space by placement of three limb leads equidistant from the heart and a fourth lead back of the heart, the positions of the electrodes defining a four-sided pyramid, the base being defined by the three limb leads, and the apex at the back electrode.

vectorial (vek-to′re-al). Pertaining to a vector.

Vedder's medium, sign (ved′erz) [Col. Edward Bright *Vedder*, U. S. Army Surgeon, retired, 1878–1952]. See under *medium* and *sign*.

VEE. Abbreviation for *Venezuelan equine encephalomyelitis*.

vegan (vej′an). An extreme vegetarian who excludes all animal protein from his diet.

veganism (vej′ah-nizm). Strict limitation to a vegetable diet, with exclusion of all protein of animal origin.

vegetable (vej′e-tah-b'l) [L. *vegetabilis* quickening]. 1. Pertaining to or derived from plants. 2. Any plant or species of plant, especially one cultivated as a source of food.

vegetal (vej′e-tal). 1. Pertaining to plants or to a plant. 2. Vegetative.

vegetality (vej″e-tal′ĭ-te). The aggregate of phenomena that are common to plants.

vegetarian (vej″e-tăr′e-an). One whose food is exclusively of vegetable origin.

vegetarianism (vej″e-tăr′e-an-izm). Restriction of the diet to food substances of vegetable origin.

vegetation (vej″e-ta′shun) [L. *vegetatio*]. Any plantlike fungoid neoplasm or growth; a luxuriant fungus-like growth of pathologic tissue. **adenoid v.,** fungus-like growths of lymphoid tissue in the nasopharynx. **bacterial v's,** spongelike growths in the endocardium composed of clot and bacteria. **dendritic v.** 1. The shaggy appearance of a villous cancer. 2. The arachnoidal tufts and villous neoplasms on the pleura and other serous membranes. **verrucous v's,** firm white nodular swellings on the endocardium.

vegetative (vej′e-ta″tiv). 1. Concerned with growth and with nutrition. 2. Functioning involuntarily or unconsciously.

vegeto-alkali (vej″e-to-al′kah-li). An alkaloid.

vegeto-animal (vej″e-to-an′ĭ-mal). Common to plants and animals.

Vehic. Abbreviation for L. *vehiculum,* a vehicle.

vehicle (ve′hĭ-k'l) [L. *vehiculum*]. 1. An excipient. 2. Any medium through which an impulse is propagated.

Veiel's paste (fi′elz) [Theodor P. *Veiel,* German dermatologist, 1848–1923]. See under *paste.*

veil (văl). 1. A covering structure. See *velum.* 2. A caul or piece of the amniotic sac occasionally covering the face of a newborn child. 3. A slight huskiness in the voice of a singer. **Fick's v.** See under *phenomenon.* **Hottentot v.** See under *apron.* **Jackson's v.** See under *membrane.* **posterior v. of soft palate,** velum palatinum. **Sattler's v.** See *Fick's phenomenon.*

Veillon tube (va-yaw′) [Adrien *Veillon,* Paris bacteriologist, 1864–1931]. See under *tube.*

Veillonella (va″yon-el′lah) [Adrien *Veillon*]. A genus of microorganisms of the family Neisseriaceae, order Eubacteriales, made up of minute (0.3–0.4 μ) obligate anaerobic cocci, found as nonpathogenic parasites in the mouth, intestines, and urogenital and respiratory tracts of man and other animals. Six species have been named, *V. alcales'cens, V. discoi'des, V. orbic'ulus, V. par'vula, V. renifor'mis,* and *V. vulvovaginit'idis.*

vein (văn) [L. *vena*]. A vessel through which blood passes from various organs or parts back to the heart. Called also *vena* [N A]. All veins except the pulmonary veins carry dark, venous blood. Veins, like arteries, have three coats, an *inner, middle,* and *outer,* but the coats are not so thick, and they collapse when the vessel is cut. Many veins, especially the superficial, have *valves* formed of reduplications of their lining membrane. **accompanying v.,** vena comitans. **accompanying v. of hypoglossal nerve,** vena comitans nervi hypoglossi. **afferent v's,** veins that carry blood to an organ. **allantoic v's,** paired vessels that accompany the allantois, growing out from the primitive hindgut and entering the body stalk of the early embryo; they fuse later into one vessel, the umbilical vein. **anastomotic v., inferior,** vena anastomotica inferior. **anastomotic v., superior,** vena anastomotica superior. **angular v.,** vena angularis. **anonymous v's,** venae brachiocephalicae [dextra et sinistra]. **antebrachial v., median,** vena mediana antebrachii. **appendicular v.,** vena appendicularis. **v. of aqueduct of vestibule,** vena aqueductus vestibuli. **aqueous v's,** microscopic, blood vessel-like pathways on the surface of the eye, containing aqueous humor or diluted blood and connecting the sinus venosus sclerae (Schlemm's canal) with conjunctival or subconjunctival veins. **arciform v's, arcuate v's of kidney,** venae arcuatae renis. **arterial v.,** truncus pulmonalis. **arterial v. of Soemmering,** vena portae. **ascending v's of Rosenthal,** venae cerebri inferiores. **auditory v's, internal,** venae labyrinthi. **auricular v's, anterior,** venae auriculares anteriores. **auricular v., posterior,** vena auricularis posterior. **axillary v.,** vena axillaris. **azygos v.,** vena azygos. **azygos v., left,** vena hemiazygos. **azygos v., lesser superior,** vena hemiazygos accessoria. **basal v.,** vena basilis. **basilic v.,** vena basilica. **basilic v., median,** vena mediana basilica. **basivertebral v's,** venae basivertebrales. **brachial v's,** venae brachiales. **brachiocephalic v's,** venae brachiocephalicae [dextra et sinistra]. **Breschet's v's,** venae diploicae. **bronchial v's,** venae bronchiales. **Browning's v.,** the upper portion of the inferior anastomotic vein. **v. of bulb of penis,** vena bulbi penis. **v. of bulb of vestibule,** vena bulbi vestibuli. **Burow's v.,** a vessel formed by the two inferior epigastric veins and a branch from the bladder; it joins the portal vein. **v. of canaliculus of cochlea,** vena canaliculi cochleae. **cardiac v's,** venae cordis. **cardiac v's, anterior,** venae cordis anteriores. **cardiac v., great,** vena cordis magna. **cardiac v., middle,** vena cordis media. **cardiac v., small,** vena cordis parva. **cardiac v's, smallest,** venae cordis minimae. **cardinal v's,** embryonic vessels that include the precardinal and postcardinal veins and the ducts of Cuvier (common cardinal veins). **carotid v., external,** vena retromandibularis. **cavernous v's of penis,** venae cavernosae penis. **central v.,** a vein that occupies the axis of an organ. **central v's of hepatic lobules, central v's of liver,** venae centrales hepatis. **central v. of retina,** vena centralis retinae. **central v. of suprarenal gland,** vena centralis glandulae suprarenalis. **cephalic v.,** vena cephalica. **cephalic v., accessory,** vena cephalica accessoria. **cephalic v., median,** vena mediana cephalica. **cerebellar v's, inferior,** venae cerebelli inferiores. **cerebellar v's, superior,** venae cerebelli superiores. **cerebral v's,** venae cerebri. **cerebral v., anterior,** vena cerebri anterior. **cerebral v., great,** vena cerebri magna. **cerebral v's, inferior,** venae cerebri inferiores. **cerebral v's, internal,** venae cerebri internae. **cerebral v., middle, deep,** vena cerebri media profunda. **cerebral v., middle, superficial,** vena cerebri media superficialis. **cerebral v's, superior,** venae cerebri

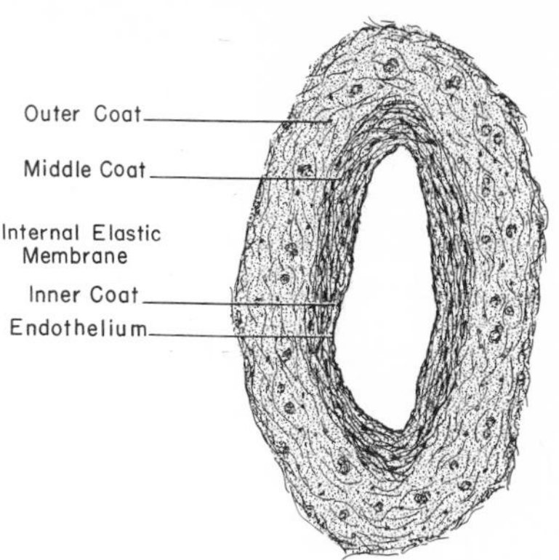

Cross section of vein. (Villee.)

superiores. **cervical v., deep,** vena cervicalis profunda. **cervical v's, transverse,** vena transversae colli. **choroid v.,** vena choroidea. **ciliary v's,** venae ciliares. **circumflex femoral v's, lateral,** venae circumflexae femoris laterales. **circumflex femoral v's, medial,** venae circumflexae femoris mediales. **circumflex iliac v., deep,** vena circumflexa ilium profunda. **circumflex iliac v., superficial,** vena circumflexa ilium superficialis. **v. of cochlear canal,** vena canaliculi cochleae. **colic v., left,** vena colica sinistra. **colic v., middle,** vena colica media. **colic v., right,** vena colica dextra. **conjunctival v's,** venae conjunctivales. **coronary v., left,** vena cordis magna. **costoaxillary v's,** venae costoaxillares. **cubital v., median,** vena mediana cubiti. **cutaneous v.,** vena cutanea. **cutaneous v., ulnar,** vena basilica. **cystic v.,** vena cystica. **deep v's of clitoris,** venae profundae clitoridis. **deep v's of penis,** venae profundae penis. **deep v. of thigh,** vena profunda femoris. **deep v. of tongue,** vena profunda linguae. **digital v's, palmar,** venae digitales palmares. **digital v's, plantar,** venae digitales plantares. **digital v's, of foot, common,** venae digitales communes pedis. **digital v's of foot, dorsal,** venae digitales dorsales pedis. **diploic v's,** venae diploicae. **diploic v., frontal,** vena diploica frontalis. **diploic v., occipital,** vena diploica occipitalis. **diploic v., temporal, anterior,** vena diploica temporalis anterior. **diploic v., temporal, posterior,** vena diploica temporalis posterior. **dorsal v. of clitoris,** vena dorsalis clitoridis. **dorsal v's of clitoris, superficial,** venae dorsales clitoridis superficiales. **dorsal v. of penis,** vena dorsalis penis. **dorsal v's of penis, superficial,** venae dorsales penis superficiales. **dorsal v's of tongue,** venae dorsales linguae. **dorsispinal v's.** See *plexus venosi vertebrales externi* [*anterior et posterior*]. **emissary v.,** one passing through a foramen of the skull and draining blood from a cerebral sinus into a vessel outside the skull. Called also *vena emissaria*. **emissary v., condylar,** vena emissaria condylaris. **emissary v., mastoid,** vena emissaria mastoidea. **emissary v., occipital,** vena emissaria occipitalis. **emissary v., parietal,** vena emissaria parietalis. **emulgent v.,** the portion of the left spermatic vein near its termination in the left renal vein. **epigastric v., inferior,** vena epigastrica inferior. **epigastric v., superficial,** vena epigastrica superficialis. **epigastric v's, superior,** venae epigastricae superiores. **episcleral v's,** venae episclerales. **esophageal v's,** venae esophageae. **ethmoidal v's,** venae ethmoidales. **facial v.,** vena facialis. **facial v., anterior, facial v., common.** See *vena facialis*. **facial v., deep,** vena faciei profunda. **facial v., posterior,** vena retromandibularis. **facial v., transverse,** vena transversa faciei. **femoral v.,** vena femoralis. **femoral v., deep,** vena profunda femoris. **femoropopliteal v.,** vena femoropoplitea. **fibular v's,** venae peroneae. **frontal v's,** venae supratrochleares. **Galen's v's,** vena cerebri interna and vena cerebri magna. **gastric v., left,** vena gastrica sinistra. **gastric v., right,** vena gastrica dextra. **gastric v's, short,** venae gastricae breves. **gastroepiploic v., left,** vena gastroepiploica sinistra. **gastroepiploic v., right,** vena gastroepiploica dextra. **genicular v's,** venae genus. **gluteal v's, inferior,** venae gluteae inferiores. **gluteal v's, superior,** venae gluteae superiores. **hemiazygos v.,** vena hemiazygos. **hemiazygos v., accessory,** vena hemiazygos accessoria. **hemorrhoidal v's, inferior,** venae rectales inferiores. **hemorrhoidal v's, middle,** venae rectales mediae. **hemorrhoidal v., superior,** vena rectalis superior. **hepatic v's,** venae hepaticae. **hypogastric v.,** vena iliaca interna. **hypophyseoportal v's,** a system of venules connecting capillaries in the hypothalamus with sinusoidal capillaries in the anterior lobe of the hypophysis. **ileal v's,** veins draining blood from the ileum. See *venae jejunales et ilei*. **ileocolic v.,** vena ileocolica. **iliac v., common,** vena iliaca communis. **iliac v., external,** vena iliaca externa. **iliac v., internal,** vena iliaca interna. **iliolumbar v.,** vena iliolumbalis. **innominate v's,** venae brachiocephalicae [dextra et sinistra]. **intercapital v's,** venae intercapitales. **intercapitular v's of foot,** venae intercapitulares pedis. **intercapitular v's of hand,** venae intercapitales. **intercostal v's, anterior,** venae intercostales anteriores. **intercostal v., highest,** vena intercostalis suprema. **intercostal v's, posterior, IV–XI,** venae intercostales posteriores [IV–XI]. **intercostal v., superior, left,** vena intercostalis superior sinistra. **intercostal v., superior, right,** vena intercostalis superior dextra. **interlobar v's of kidney,** venae interlobares renis. **interlobular v's of kidney,** venae interlobulares renis. **interlobular v's of liver,** venae interlobulares hepatis. **interosseous v's of foot, dorsal,** venae metatarseae dorsales. **interosseous metacarpal v's, dorsal,** venae metacarpeae dorsales. **intervertebral v.,** vena intervertebralis. **jejunal v's,** veins that drain blood from the jejunum. See *venae jejunales et ilei*. **jugular v., anterior,** vena jugularis anterior. **jugular v., anterior horizontal,** arcus venosus juguli. **jugular v., external,** vena jugularis externa. **jugular v., internal,** vena jugularis interna. **v's of kidney,** venae renis. **Kohlrausch v's,** superficial veins passing from the under surface of the penis to the dorsal vein. **Krukenberg's v's,** venae centrales hepatis. **Labbé's v.,** vena anastomotica superior. **labial v's, anterior,** venae labiales anteriores. **labial v's, inferior,** venae labiales inferiores. **labial v's, posterior,** venae labiales posteriores. **labial v., superior,** vena labialis superior. **v's of labyrinth,** venae labyrinthi. **lacrimal v.,** vena lacrimalis. **laryngeal v., inferior,** vena laryngea inferior. **laryngeal v., superior,** vena laryngea superior. **lingual v.,** vena lingualis. **lingual v., deep,** vena profunda linguae. **lingual v's, dorsal,** venae dorsales linguae. **lumbar v's I and II,** venae lumbales [I et II]. **lumbar v's III and IV,** venae lumbales [III et IV]. **lumbar v., ascending,** vena lumbalis ascendens. **mammary v's, external,** venae costoaxillares. **mammary v., internal.** See *venae thoracicae internae*. **v. of Marshall, Marshall's oblique v.,** vena obliqua atrii sinistri. **masseteric v's,** venae massetericae. **maxillary v's,** venae maxillares. **median v. of elbow,** vena mediana cubiti. **median v. of forearm,** vena mediana antebrachii. **mediastinal v's,** venae mediastinales. **meningeal v's,** venae meningeae. **meningeal v's, middle,** venae meningeae mediae. **mesenteric v., inferior,** vena mesenterica inferior. **mesenteric v., superior,** vena mesenterica superior. **metacarpal v's, dorsal,** venae metacarpeae dorsales. **metacarpal v's, palmar,** venae metacarpeae palmares. **metatarsal v's, dorsal,** venae metatarseae dorsales. **metatarsal v's, plantar,** venae metatarseae plantares. **muscular v's,** venae musculares. **musculophrenic v's,** venae musculophrenicae. **nasal v's, external,** venae nasales externae. **nasofrontal v.,** vena nasofrontalis. **oblique v. of left atrium,** vena obliqua atrii sinistri. **obturator v's,** venae obturatoriae. **occipital v.,** vena occipitalis. **oesophageal v's,** venae esophageae. **omphalomesenteric v's,** vitelline v's. **ophthalmic v., inferior,** vena ophthalmica inferior. **ophthalmic v., superior,** vena ophthalmica superior. **ophthalmomeningeal v.,** vena ophthalmomeningea. **ovarian v., left,** vena ovarica sinistra. **ovarian v., right,** vena ovarica dextra. **palatine v., external,** vena palatina externa. **palpe-**

bral v's, venae palpebrales. **palpebral v's, inferior,** venae palpebrales inferiores. **palpebral v's, superior,** venae palpebrales superiores. **pancreatic v's,** venae pancreaticae. **pancreaticoduodenal v's,** venae pancreaticoduodenales. **paraumbilical v's,** venae paraumbilicales. **parietal v. of Santorini,** vena emissaria parietalis. **parotid v's,** venae parotideae. **parotid v's, anterior,** rami parotidei venae facialis. **parotid v's, posterior,** venae parotideae. **parumbilical v's,** venae paraumbilicales. **perforating v's,** venae perforantes. **pericardiac v's,** venae pericardiacae. **pericardiacophrenic v's,** venae pericardiacophrenicae. **peroneal v's,** venae peroneae. **pharyngeal v's,** venae pharyngeae. **phrenic v's, inferior,** venae phrenicae inferiores. **phrenic v's, superior,** venae pericardiacophrenicae. **popliteal v.,** vena poplitea. **portal v.,** vena portae. **postcardinal v's,** paired vessels in the embryo caudal to the heart. **posterior v. of left ventricle,** vena posterior ventriculi sinistri cordis. **precardinal v's,** paired venous trunks in the embryo cranial to the heart. **prepyloric v.,** vena prepylorica. **primary head v's,** vessels alongside the embryonic brain that continue into the precardinal veins. **v. of pterygoid canal,** vena canalis pterygoidei. **pudendal v's, external,** venae pudendae externae. **pudendal v., internal,** vena pudenda interna. **pulmonary v's,** venae pulmonales. **pulmonary v., inferior, left,** vena pulmonalis inferior sinistra. **pulmonary v., inferior, right,** vena pulmonalis inferior dextra. **pulmonary v., superior, left,** vena pulmonalis superior sinistra. **pulmonary v., superior, right,** vena pulmonalis superior dextra. **pulp v's,** vessels draining the venous sinuses of the spleen. **pyloric v.,** vena gastrica dextra. **radial v's,** venae radiales. **radial v., external, of Soemmering,** vena cephalica accessoria. **ranine v.,** vena sublingualis. **rectal v's, inferior,** venae rectales inferiores. **rectal v's, middle,** venae rectales mediae. **rectal v., superior,** vena rectalis superior. **renal v's,** venae renales. **retromandibular v.,** vena retromandibularis. **Retzius's v's,** veins from the walls of the intestine to the branches of the inferior vena cava. **Rosenthal's v.,** vena basalis. **Ruysch's v's,** venae vorticosae. **sacral v's, lateral,** venae sacrales laterales. **sacral v., middle,** vena sacralis mediana. **salvatella v.,** a small vein of the little finger and dorsum of the hand. **saphenous v., accessory,** vena saphena accessoria. **saphenous v., great,** vena saphena magna. **saphenous v., small,** vena saphena parva. **v's of Sappey,** venae paraumbilicales. **scrotal v's, anterior,** venae scrotales anteriores. **scrotal v's, posterior,** venae scrotales posteriores. **v. of septum pellucidum,** vena septi pellucidi. **sigmoid v's,** venae sigmoideae. **small v. of heart,** vena cordis parva. **spermatic v.,** vena spermatica. **spinal v's,** venae spinales. **spiral v. of modiolus,** vena spiralis modioli. **splenic v.,** vena lienalis. **stellate v's of kidney,** venulae stellatae renis. **Stensen's v's,** venae vorticosae. **sternocleidomastoid v.,** vena sternocleidomastoidea. **striate v.,** vena striata. **stylomastoid v.,** vena stylomastoidea. **subcardinal v's,** paired vessels in the embryo, replacing the postcardinal veins and persisting to some degree as definitive vessels. **subclavian v.,** vena subclavia. **subcostal v.,** vena subcostalis. **subcutaneous v's of abdomen,** venae subcutaneae abdominis. **sublingual v.,** vena sublingualis. **sublobular v's,** tributaries of the hepatic veins that receive the central veins of hepatic lobules. **submental v.,** vena submentalis. **supracardinal v's,** paired vessels in the embryo, developing later than the subcardinal veins and persisting chiefly as the lower segment of the inferior vena cava. **supraorbital v.,** vena supraorbitalis. **suprarenal v., left,** vena suprarenalis sinistra. **suprarenal v., right,** vena suprarenalis dextra. **suprascapular v.,** vena suprascapularis. **supratrochlear v's,** venae supratrochleares. **sylvian v., v. of sylvian fossa,** vena cerebri media superficialis. **temporal v's, deep,** venae temporales profundae. **temporal v., middle,** vena temporalis media. **temporal v's, superficial,** venae temporales superficiales. **temporomandibular articular v's,** venae articulares temporomandibulares. **terminal v.,** vena thalamostriata. **testicular v., left,** vena testicularis sinistra. **testicular v., right,** vena testicularis dextra. **thalamostriate v.,** vena thalamostriata. **thebesian v's, v's of Thebesius,** venae cordis minimae. **thoracic v's, internal,** venae thoracicae internae. **thoracic v., lateral,** vena thoracica lateralis. **thoracoacromial v.,** vena thoracoacromialis. **thoracoepigastric v's,** venae thoracoepigastricae. **thymic v's,** venae thymicae. **thyroid v., inferior,** vena thyroidea inferior. **thyroid v's, middle,** venae thyroideae mediae. **thyroid v., superior,** venae thyroidea superior. **tibial v's, anterior,** venae tibiales anteriores. **tibial v's, posterior,** venae tibiales posteriores. **trabecular v's,** vessels coursing in splenic trabeculae, formed by tributary pulp veins. **tracheal v's,** venae tracheales. **transverse v. of face,** vena transversa faciei. **transverse v's of neck,** venae transversae colli. **Trolard's v.,** vena anastomotica inferior. **tympanic v's,** venae tympanicae. **ulnar v's,** venae ulnares. **umbilical v.,** vena umbicalis. **uterine v's,** venae uterinae. **varicose v.,** a permanently distended and tortuous vein, especially one in the lower extremity. See *varix.* **vertebral v.,** vena vertebralis. **vertebral v., accessory,** vena vertebralis accessoria. **vertebral v., anterior,** vena vertebralis anterior. **vertebral v's, superficial, v's of vertebral column, external.** See *plexus venosi vertebrales externi [anterior et posterior].* **vesalian v.,** an emissary vein connecting the cavernous sinus with the pterygoid venous plexus, sometimes passing through an opening in the great wing of the sphenoid bone. **vesical v's,** venae vesicales. **vestibular v's** venae vestibulares. **vidian v's,** venae canalis pterygoidei. **v's of Vieussens,** venae cordis anteriores. **vitelline v's,** veins that return the blood from the yolk sac to the primitive heart of the early embryo. **vorticose v's,** venae vorticosae.

velacycline (vel″ah-si′klēn). Trade mark for preparations of rolitetracycline.

velamen (ve-la′men) [L. "a covering"]. Any membrane, velum, meninx, or tegument. **v. vul′vae,** Hottentot apron.

velamenta (vel″ah-men′tah) [L.]. Plural of *velamentum.*

velamentous (vel″ah-men′tus) [L. *velamen* veil]. Membranous and pendent; like a veil.

velamentum (vel″ah-men′tum), pl. *velamen′ta* [L.]. Any covering, velum, or envelope. **velamen′ta cer′ebri,** the meninges.

velar (ve′lar). Pertaining to a velum, especially to the velum palatinum.

velban (vel′ban). Trade mark for a preparation of vinblastine sulfate.

veliform (vel′ĭ-form). Velamentous.

Vella's fistula (ve′lahz) [Luigi *Vella,* Italian physiologist, 1825–1886]. See under *fistula.*

vellication (vel″ĭ-ka′shun) [L. *vellicatio*]. A twitching of the muscles.

vellosine (vel-lo′sin). A poisonous alkaloid occurring in yellow crystals, $C_{23}H_{28}N_2O_4$, from the bark of *Geissospermum laeve (vellosii).*

vellus (vel′us) [L. "fleece"]. The fine hair which succeeds the lanugo over most of the body and persists until puberty. **v. oli′vae,** a narrow band of tangential fibers surrounding the olive.

velonoskiascopy (ve″lo-no-ski-as′ko-pe). Skiascopy of shadows made by the movement of a needle held before the patient's pupil.

velopharyngeal (vel″o-fah-rin′je-al). Pertaining to the velum palatinum and pharynx.

velosynthesis (vel″o-sin′the-sis) [L. *velum* veil + Gr. *synthesis* a putting together]. Staphylorrhaphy.

Velpeau's bandage, deformity, hernia, mixture (vel-pōz′) [Alfred Armand Louis Marie *Velpeau*, surgeon in Paris, 1795–1867]. See under the nouns.

velum (ve′lum), pl. *ve′la* [L.]. A covering; used in anatomical nomenclature as a general term to designate a veil or veil-like structure or organ. **artificial v.,** a prosthetic appliance used in correction of fissure of the soft palate. **Baker's v.,** an obturator used in cleft palate. **v. interpos′itum cer′ebri,** tela choroidea ventriculi tertii. **v. interpos′itum rhombenceph′ali,** v. medullare superius. **v. medulla′re ante′rius** [B N A], v. medullare superius. **v. medulla′re infe′rius** [N A], **v. medulla′re poste′rius** [B N A], a thin layer of white substance that forms part of the roof of the fourth ventricle below the fastigium; it is continuous above with the nodulus, on the sides with the pedunculus flocculi and the teniae, and ventrally it is fused with the choroid plexus. Called also *inferior medullary v.* **v. medulla′re supe′rius** [N A], a thin layer of white substance that forms the anterior portion of the roof of the fourth ventricle, extending from the tectal lamina in front to the fastigium behind, and between the superior cerebellar peduncles on the sides. Called also *v. medullare anterius* [B N A], and *superior medullary v.* **medullary v., anterior,** v. medullare superius. **medullary v., inferior, medullary v., posterior,** v. medullare inferius. **medullary v., superior,** v. medullare superius. **nursing v.,** a suitable piece of soft rubber, attached to a handle, that may be held in an infant's mouth to enable it to nurse in spite of a cleft palate. **v. pala′ti,** v. palatinum. **v. palati′num** [N A, B N A], the posterior, downward-extending portion of the soft palate, comprising the uvula and the palatoglossal and palatopharyngeal arches. **v. pen′dulum pala′ti,** v. palatinum. **v. semiluna′re,** v. medullare inferius. **v. of Tarinus,** v. medullare inferius. **v. transver′sum,** a transverse fold of the tela choroidea marking the boundary between the diencephalon and the telencephalon in the embryonic brain.

VEM. Abbreviation for *vasoexciter material.*

vena (ve′nah), pl. *ve′nae* [L.]. [N A, B N A] A vessel that conveys blood to or toward the heart, or one in the wall of the heart itself by which blood is returned to the right atrium. Called also *vein.* For names and description of specific veins see *Table of Venae.*

TABLE OF VENAE

Descriptions of veins are given on N A terms. B N A terms, when different, are cross referred to names used in Nomina Anatomica.

ve′nae advehen′tes, channels in the early embryo that convey blood to the sinusoids of the liver and later become the portal vein.

v. anastomot′ica infe′rior [N A], inferior anastomotic vein: a vein that interconnects the superficial middle cerebral vein and the transverse sinus.

v. anastomot′ica supe′rior [N A], superior anastomotic vein: a vein that interconnects the superficial middle cerebral vein and the sinus.

v. angula′ris [N A, B N A], angular vein: a short vein between the eye and the root of the nose; it is formed by union of the supratrochlear and supraorbital veins and continues inferiorly as the facial vein.

ve′nae anon′ymae dex′tra et sinis′tra [B N A], venae brachiocephalicae [dextra et sinistra].

v. appendicula′ris [N A], appendicular vein: the vena comitans of the appendicular artery; it unites with the anterior and posterior cecal veins to form the ileocolic vein.

v. aqueduc′tus vestib′uli [N A], vein of aqueduct of vestibule: a small vein from the internal ear that passes through the aqueduct of the vestibule and empties into the superior petrosal sinus.

ve′nae arcifor′mes re′nis [B N A], venae arcuatae renis.

ve′nae arcua′tae re′nis [N A], arcuate veins of kidney: a series of complete arches across the bases of the pyramids of the kidneys; they are formed by union of the interlobular veins and the venulae rectae and drain into the interlobar veins. Called also *venae arciformes renis* [B N A].

ve′nae articula′res mandib′ulae [B N A], venae articulares temporomandibulares.

ve′nae articula′res temporomandibula′res [N A], temporomandibular articular veins: small vessels that drain the plexus around the temporomandibular articulation into the retromandibular vein. Called also *venae articulares mandibulae* [B N A].

ve′nae auditi′vae inter′nae [B N A], venae labyrinthi.

ve′nae auricula′res anterio′res [N A, B N A], anterior auricular veins: branches from the anterior part of the pinna that enter the superficial temporal vein.

v. auricula′ris poste′rior [N A, B N A], posterior auricular vein: a vein that begins in a plexus on the side of the head, passes down behind the pinna, and joins with the retromandibular vein to form the external jugular vein.

v. axilla′ris [N A, B N A], axillary vein; the venous trunk of the upper member; it begins at the lower border of the teres major muscle by junction of the basilic and brachial veins, and at the lateral border of the first rib is continuous with the subclavian vein.

v. az′ygos [N A, B N A], azygos vein: an intercepting trunk for the right intercostal veins as well as a connecting branch between the superior and inferior venae cavae: it arises from the ascending lumbar vein, passes up in front of and on the right side of the vertebrae, and empties into the superior vena cava.

v. basa′lis [N A], basal vein: a vein that arises at the anterior perforated substance, passes backward and around the cerebral peduncle, and empties into the internal cerebral vein. Called also *v. basalis* [*Rosenthali*] [B N A].

v. basa′lis [Rosentha′li] [B N A], v. basalis.

v. basil′ica [N A, B N A], basilic vein: the superficial vein that arises from the ulnar side of the dorsal rete of the hand, passes up the forearm and joins with the brachial veins to form the axillary vein.

ve′nae basivertebra′les [N A, B N A], basivertebral veins: venous sinuses in the cancellous tissue of the bodies of the vertebrae, which communicate with the plexus of veins on the anterior surface of the vertebrae and with the anterior internal vertebral plexus.

ve′nae brachia′les [N A, B N A], brachial veins: the venae comitantes of the brachial artery, which join with the basilic vein to form the axillary vein.

ve′nae brachiocephal′icae [dex′tra et sinis′tra] [N A], brachiocephalic veins: the two veins that drain blood from the head, neck, and upper extremities, and unite to form the superior vena cava. Each is formed at the root of the neck by union of the ipsilateral internal jugular and subclavian veins. The right vein (*v. brachiocephalica dextra*) passes almost vertically downward in front of the brachiocephalic artery, and the left vein (*v. brachiocephalica sinistra*) passes from left to right behind the upper part of the sternum. Each vein receives the vertebral, deep cervical, deep thyroid, and internal thoracic veins. The left vein also receives intercostal, thymic, tracheal, esophageal, phrenic, mediastinal, and pericardiac branches, as well as the thoracic duct. The right vein receives the right lymphatic duct. Called also *venae anonymae dextra et sinistra* [B N A].

ve′nae bronchia′les [N A], bronchial veins: vessels that drain blood from the larger subdivisions of the bronchi into the azygos vein on the left, and into the hemiazygos or the superior intercostal vein on the right.

ve′nae bronchia′les anterio′res [B N A], **ve′nae bronchia′les posterio′res** [B N A]. See *venae bronchiales*.

v. bul′bi pe′nis [N A], vein of bulb of penis: a vein in the male draining blood from the bulb of the penis into the internal pudendal vein.

v. bul′bi vestib′uli [N A], vein of bulb of vestibule: a vein in the female draining blood from the bulb of the vestibule into the internal pudendal vein.

v. canalic′uli coch′leae [N A, B N A], vein of cochlear canal: a vein that arises in the cochlea and empties into the superior bulb of the internal jugular vein.

v. cana′lis pterygoi′dei [N A], vein of pterygoid canal: one of the veins that pass through the pterygoid canal and empty into the pterygoid plexus. Called also *v. canalis pterygoidei [Vidii]* [B N A].

v. cana′lis pterygoi′dei [Vid′ii] [B N A], v. canalis pterygoidei.

v. ca′va infe′rior [N A, B N A], inferior v. cava: the venous trunk for the lower extremities and for the pelvic and abdominal viscera; it begins at the level of the fifth lumbar vertebra by union of the common iliac veins, passes upward on the right of the aorta, and empties into the right atrium of the heart.

v. ca′va supe′rior [N A, B N A], superior v. cava: the venous trunk draining blood from the head, neck, upper extremities, and chest; it begins by union of the two brachiocephalic veins, passes directly downward, and empties into the right atrium of the heart.

ve′nae caverno′sae pe′nis [N A, B N A], cavernous veins of penis: veins that return the blood from the corpora cavernosa to the deep veins and the dorsal vein of the penis.

v. centra′lis glan′dulae suprarena′lis [N A, B N A], central vein of suprarenal gland: the large single vein into which the various veins within the substance of the gland empty, and which continues at the hilus as the suprarenal vein.

ve′nae centra′les hep′atis [N A, B N A], central veins of liver: veins in the middle of the hepatic lobules, draining into the hepatic vein.

v. centra′lis ret′inae [N A, B N A], central vein of retina: the vein that is formed by union of the retinal veins; it passes out in the optic nerve to empty into the superior ophthalamic vein.

v. cephal′ica [N A, B N A], cephalic vein: the superficial vein that arises from the radial side of the dorsal rete of the hand, and winds anteriorly to pass along the anterior border of the brachioradialis muscle; above the elbow it ascends along the lateral border of the biceps muscle and opens into the axillary vein.

v. cephal′ica accesso′ria [N A, B N A], accessory cephalic vein: a vein arising from the dorsal rete of the hand, passing up the forearm to join the cephalic vein just above the elbow.

ve′nae cerebel′li inferio′res [N A, B N A], inferior cerebellar veins: rather large veins from the inferior surface of the cerebellum which empty into the transverse, sigmoid, and inferior petrosal sinuses, or into the occipital sinus.

ve′nae cerebel′li superio′res [N A, B N A], superior cerebellar veins: veins from the upper surface of the cerebellum, emptying into the straight sinus and the great cerebral vein, or into the transverse and superior petrosal sinuses.

ve′nae cer′ebri [N A, B N A], cerebral veins: veins that drain blood from the brain.

v. cer′ebri ante′rior [N A], anterior cerebral vein: the vein that accompanies the anterior cerebral artery and joins the basal vein.

ve′nae cer′ebri inferio′res [N A, B N A], inferior cerebral veins: veins that ramify on the base and the inferolateral surface of the brain. Those on the inferior surface of the frontal lobe drain into the inferior sagittal sinus and the cavernous sinus; those on the temporal lobe, into the superior petrosal sinus and the transverse sinus; those on the occipital lobe, into the straight sinus.

ve′nae cer′ebri inter′nae [N A, B N A], internal cerebral veins: two veins that arise at the interventricular foramen by the union of the thalamostriate and the choroid veins; they pass backward through the tela choroidea, collecting blood from the basal nuclei, and unite at the splenium of the corpus callosum to form the great cerebral vein.

v. cer′ebri mag′na [N A], great cerebral vein: a short median trunk, formed by union of the two internal cerebral veins, which curves around the splenium of the corpus callosum and empties into, or is continued as, the straight sinus. Called also *v. cerebri magna [Galeni]* [B N A].

v. cer′ebri mag′na [Gale′ni] [B N A], v. cerebri magna.

v. cer′ebri me′dia [B N A], v. cerebri media superficialis.

v. cer′ebri me′dia profun′da [N A], deep middle cerebral vein: the vein that accompanies the middle cerebral artery in the floor of the lateral sulcus, and joins the basal vein.

v. cer′ebri me′dia superficia′lis [N A], superficial middle cerebral vein: a vein that drains the lateral surface of the cerebrum, follows the lateral cerebral fissure, and empties into the cavernous sinus. Called also *v. cerebri media* [B N A].

ve′nae cer′ebri superio′res [N A, B N A], superior cerebral veins: about twelve veins that drain the superior, lateral, and medial surfaces of the cerebrum toward the longitudinal cerebral fissure, where they open into the superior sagittal sinus.

v. cervica′lis profun′da [N A, B N A], deep cervical vein: a vein that arises from a plexus in the suboccipital triangle, follows the deep cervical artery down the neck, and empties into the vertebral or the brachiocephalic vein.

v. chorioi′dea [B N A], v. choroidea.

v. choroi′dea [N A], choroid vein: the vein that runs along the whole length of the choroid plexus, draining it and the hippocampus, fornix, and corpus callosum; it unites with the thalamostriate vein to form the internal cerebral vein. Called also *v. chorioidea* [B N A].

ve′nae choroi′deae oc′uli, N A alternative for *venae vorticosae*.

ve′nae cilia′res [N A], ciliary veins: veins that arise inside the eyeball by branches from the ciliary muscle and drain into the superior ophthalmic vein. The *anterior ciliary veins* follow the anterior ciliary arteries, and receive branches from the sinus venosus, sclerae, the episcleral veins, and the tunica conjunctiva bulbi. The *posterior ciliary veins* follow the posterior ciliary arteries and empty also into the inferior ophthalmic vein.

ve′nae cilia′res anterio′res [B N A], **ve′nae cilia′res posterio′res** [B N A]. See *venae ciliares*.

ve′nae circumflex′ae fem′oris latera′les [N A, B N A], lateral circumflex femoral veins: venae comitantes of the lateral circumflex femoral artery, emptying into the femoral or the deep femoral vein.

ve′nae circumflex′ae fem′oris media′les [N A, B N A], medial circumflex femoral veins: venae comitantes of the medial circumflex femoral artery, emptying into the femoral or the deep femoral vein.

v. circumflex′a il′ium profun′da [N A, B N A], deep circumflex iliac vein: a common trunk formed from the venae comitantes of the homonymous artery and emptying into the external iliac vein.

v. circumflex′a il′ium superficia′lis [N A, B N A], superficial circumflex iliac vein: a vein that follows the homonymous artery and empties into the great saphenous vein.

v. col′ica dex′tra [N A], right colic vein: a vein that follows the distribution of the right colic artery and empties into the superior mesenteric vein.

v. col′ica me′dia [N A, B N A], middle colic vein: a vein that follows the distribution of the middle colic artery and empties into the superior mesenteric vein.

v. col′ica sinis′tra [N A, B N A], left colic vein: a vein that follows the left colic artery and opens into the inferior mesenteric vein.

v. com′itans [N A, B N A], an accompanying vein. Such veins (venae comitantes), usually two in number, closely accompany their homonymous artery and are found especially among the smaller deep vessels of the extremities.

ve′nae comitan′tes arte′riae femora′lis [B N A], accompanying veins of the femoral artery, which empty into the external iliac vein. Omitted in N A.

v. com′itans ner′vi hypoglos′si [N A, B N A], accompanying vein of hypoglossal nerve: a vessel, formed by union of the vena profunda linguae and the vena sublingualis, that accompanies the hypoglossal nerve. It empties into the facial, lingual, or internal jugular vein.

ve′nae conjunctiva′les [N A], conjunctival veins: small veins that drain blood from the conjunctiva to the superior ophthalmic vein.

ve′nae conjunctiva′les anterio′res [B N A], **ve′nae conjunctiva′les posterio′res** [B N A]. See *venae conjunctivales.*

ve′nae cor′dis [N A, B N A], cardiac veins: the veins of the heart, which drain blood from the various tissues making up the organ.

ve′nae cor′dis anterio′res [N A, B N A], anterior cardiac veins: small vessels from the anterior wall of the right ventricle that empty into the right atrium or join the lesser cardiac vein.

v. cor′dis mag′na [N A, B N A], great cardiac vein: a vein that collects blood from the anterior surface of the ventricles, follows the anterior longitudinal sulcus, and empties into the coronary sinus.

v. cor′dis me′dia [N A, B N A], middle cardiac vein: a vein that collects blood from the diaphragmatic surface of the ventricles, follows the posterior longitudinal sulcus, and empties into the coronary sinus.

ve′nae cor′dis min′imae [N A, B N A], smallest cardiac veins: numerous small veins arising in the muscular walls and draining independently into the cavities of the heart, and most readily seen in the atria; in some cases of coronary artery obstruction they may act as collateral channels.

v. cor′dis par′va [N A, B N A], small cardiac vein: a vein that collects blood from both parts of the right heart, follows the coronary sulcus to the left, and opens into the coronary sinus.

v. corona′ria ventric′uli [B N A]. See *v. gastrica dextra, v. gastrica sinistra,* and *v. prepylorica.*

ve′nae costoaxilla′res [B N A], costoaxillary veins: veins that arise from the areolar venous plexus, anastomose with the upper six or seven posterior intercostal veins, and empty into the axillary vein. Omitted in N A.

v. cuta′nea [N A, B N A], cutaneous vein: one of the small veins that begin in the papillae of the skin, form subpapillary plexuses, and open into the subcutaneous veins.

v. cys′tica [N A, B N A], cystic vein: a small vein that returns the blood from the gallbladder to the right branch of the portal vein, within the substance of the liver.

ve′nae digita′les commu′nes pe′dis [B N A], short veins formed by union of the dorsal digital and the intercapitular veins of the foot. Omitted in N A.

ve′nae digita′les dorsa′les pe′dis [N A], dorsal digital veins of foot: the veins on the dorsal surfaces of the toes that unite in pairs around each cleft to form the dorsal metatarsal veins. Called also *venae digitales pedis dorsales* [B N A].

ve′nae digita′les palma′res [N A], palmar digital veins: the venae comitantes of the proper and common palmar digital arteries, which join the superficial palmar venous arch.

ve′nae digita′les pe′dis dorsa′les [B N A], venae digitales dorsales pedis.

ve′nae digita′les planta′res [N A, B N A], plantar digital veins: veins from the plantar surfaces of the toes which unite at the clefts to form the plantar metatarsal veins of the foot.

ve′nae digita′les vola′res commu′nes [B N A]. See *venae digitales palmares.*

ve′nae digita′les vola′res pro′priae [B N A]. See *venae digitales palmares.*

ve′nae diplo′icae [N A, B N A], diploic veins: veins of the skull, including the frontal, occipital, anterior temporal, and posterior temporal diploic veins, which form sinuses in the cancellous tissue between the laminae of the cranial bones. They send branches to the external and the internal lamina, the periosteum, and the dura mater, and empty in part inside and in part outside the skull.

v. diplo′ica fronta′lis [N A, B N A], frontal diploic vein: a vein that drains the frontal bone, emptying externally into the supraorbital vein or internally into the superior sagittal sinus.

v. diplo′ica occipita′lis [N A, B N A], occipital diploic vein: the largest of the diploic veins, which drains blood from the occipital bone and empties into the occipital vein or the transverse sinus.

v. diplo′ica tempora′lis ante′rior [N A, B N A], anterior temporal diploic vein: a vein that drains the lateral portion of the frontal and the anterior part of the parietal bone, opening internally into the sphenoparietal sinus and externally into a deep temporal vein.

v. diplo′ica tempora′lis poste′rior [N A, B N A], posterior temporal diploic vein: a vein that drains the parietal bone and empties into the transverse sinus.

v. dorsa′lis clitor′idis [N A, B N A], dorsal vein of clitoris: a vein that follows the course of its homonymous artery and opens into the vesical plexus.

ve′nae dorsa′les clitor′idis superficia′les [N A], superficial dorsal veins of clitoris: veins that collect blood subcutaneously from the clitoris and drain into the external pudendal vein.

ve′nae dorsa′les lin′guae [N A, B N A], dorsal lingual veins: veins that unite with a small vena comitans of the lingual artery and join the main lingual trunk.

v. dorsa′lis pe′nis [N A, B N A], dorsal vein of penis: the single vein lying subfascially in the midline of the penis between the dorsal arteries; it begins in small veins around the corona glandis, is joined by the deep veins of the penis as it passes proximally, and passes between the arcuate pubic and transverse perineal ligaments, where it divides into a left and right vein to join the prostatic plexus.

ve′nae dorsa′les pe′nis subcuta′neae [B N A], venae dorsales penis superficiales.

ve′nae dorsa′les pe′nis superficia′les [N A], superficial dorsal veins of penis: veins that collect blood subcutaneously from the penis and drain into the external pudendal vein. Called also *venae dorsales penis subcutaneae* [B N A].

ve'nae duodena'les [B N A], duodenal veins; veins draining blood from the duodenum. Omitted in N A.

v. emissa'ria [N A], emissary vein: one of the small, valveless veins that pass through foramina of the skull, connecting the dural venous sinuses with scalp veins or with deep veins below the base of the skull. Called also *emissarium* [B N A].

v. emissa'ria condyla'ris [N A], condylar emissary vein: a small vein running through the condylar canal of the skull, connecting the sigmoid sinus with the vertebral or the internal jugular vein. Called also *emissarium condyloideum* [B N A].

v. emissa'ria mastoid'ea [N A], mastoid emissary vein: a small vein passing through the mastoid foramen of the skull and connecting the sigmoid sinus with the occipital or the posterior auricular vein. Called also *emissarium mastoideum* [B N A].

v. emissa'ria occipita'lis [N A], occipital emissary vein: an occasional small vein running through a minute foramen in the occipital protuberance of the skull and connecting the confluence of the sinuses with the occipital vein. Called also *emissarium occipitale* [B N A].

v. emissa'ria parieta'lis [N A], parietal emissary vein: a small vein passing through the parietal foramen of the skull and connecting the superior sagittal sinus with the superficial temporal veins. Called also *emissarium parietale* [B N A].

v. epigas'trica infe'rior [N A, B N A], inferior epigastric vein: a vein that accompanies the inferior epigastric artery and opens into the external iliac vein.

v. epigas'trica superficia'lis [N A, B N A], superficial epigastric vein: a vein that follows its homonymous artery and opens into the great saphenous or the femoral vein.

ve'nae epigas'tricae superio'res [N A], superior epigastric veins: the venae comitantes of the superior epigastric artery, which open into the internal thoracic vein.

ve'nae episclera'les [N A, B N A], episcleral veins: the veins that ring the cornea and drain into the vorticose and ciliary veins.

ve'nae esophage'ae [N A], esophageal veins: small vessels that drain blood from the esophagus into the hemiazygos and azygos veins, or into the left brachiocephalic vein.

ve'nae ethmoida'les [N A], ethmoidal veins: veins that follow the anterior and posterior ethmoidal arteries, emerge from the ethmoidal foramina, and empty into the superior ophthalmic vein.

v. ethmoida'lis ante'rior [B N A], **v. ethmoida'lis poste'rior** [B N A]. See *venae ethmoidales.*

v. facia'lis [N A], facial vein; the vein that begins at the medial angle of the eye as the angular vein, descends behind the facial artery, and usually ends in the internal jugular vein; formerly called the *anterior facial vein*, this vessel sometimes joins the retromandibular vein to form a common trunk previously known as the *common facial vein.*

v. facia'lis ante'rior [B N A], **v. facia'lis commu'nis** [B N A]. See *v. facialis.*

v. facia'lis poste'rior [B N A], v. retromandibularis.

v. facie'i profun'da [N A], deep facial vein: a vein draining from the pterygoid plexus to the facial vein.

v. femora'lis [N A, B N A], femoral vein: a vein that lies in the proximal two-thirds of the thigh; it is a direct continuation of the popliteal vein, follows the course of the femoral artery, and at the inguinal ligament becomes the external iliac vein.

v. femoropoplite'a [B N A], femoropopliteal vein: a superficial descending vein draining the lower and back part of the thigh and opening into the small saphenous vein just before it perforates the deep fascia. Omitted in N A.

ve'nae fibula'res, N A alternative for *venae peroneae.*

ve'nae fronta'les [B N A], venae supratrochleares.

ve'nae gas'tricae bre'ves [N A, B N A], short gastric veins: small vessels draining the left portion of the greater curvature of the stomach and emptying into the splenic vein.

v. gas'trica dex'tra [N A], right gastric vein: the vena comitans of the right gastric artery, emptying into the portal vein.

v. gas'trica sinis'tra [N A], left gastric vein: the vena comitans of the left gastric artery, emptying into the portal vein.

v. gastroepiplo'ica dex'tra [N A, B N A], right gastroepiploic vein: a vein that follows the distribution of its homonymous artery and empties into the superior mesenteric vein.

v. gastroepiplo'ica sinis'tra [N A, B N A], left gastroepiploic vein: a vein that follows the distribution of its homonymous artery and empties into the splenic vein.

ve'nae ge'nus [N A], genicular veins: veins accompanying the genicular arteries and draining into the popliteal vein.

ve'nae glu'taeae inferio'res [B N A], venae gluteae inferiores.

ve'nae glu'taeae superio'res [B N A], venae gluteae superiores.

ve'nae glu'teae inferio'res [N A], inferior gluteal veins: venae comitantes of the inferior gluteal artery; they drain the subcutaneous tissue of the back of the thigh and the muscles of the buttock, unite into a single vein after passing through the greater sciatic foramen, and empty into the internal iliac vein.

ve'nae glu'teae superio'res [N A], superior gluteal veins: venae comitantes of the superior gluteal artery; they drain the muscles of the buttock, pass through the greater sciatic foramen, and empty into the internal iliac vein.

ve'nae haemorrhoida'les inferio'res [B N A], venae rectales inferiores.

v. haemorrhoida'lis me'dia [B N A]. See *venae rectales mediae.*

v. haemorrhoida'lis supe'rior [B N A], v. rectalis superior.

v. hemiaz'ygos [N A, B N A], hemiazygos vein: an intercepting trunk for the lower left posterior intercostal veins; it arises from the ascending lumbar vein, passes up on the left side of the vertebrae to the eighth thoracic vertebra, where it may receive the accessory branch, and crosses over the vertebral column to open into the azygos vein.

v. hemiaz'ygos accesso'ria [N A, B N A], accessory hemiazygos vein: the descending intercepting trunk for the upper, often the fourth through the eighth, left posterior intercostal veins. It lies on the left side and at the eighth thoracic vertebra joins the hemiazygos vein or crosses to the right side to join the azygos vein directly; above, it may communicate with the left superior intercostal vein.

ve'nae hepat'icae [N A, B N A], hepatic veins: several veins that receive blood from the central veins of the liver; two or three large vessels in an upper group and six to twenty small veins in a lower group form successively larger vessels which ultimately open into the inferior vena cava on the posterior aspect of the liver.

v. hypogas'trica [B N A], v. iliaca interna.

v. ileocol'ica [N A, B N A], ileocolic vein: a vein that follows the distribution of its homonymous artery and empties into the vena mesenterica superior.

v. ili'aca commu'nis [N A, B N A], common iliac vein: a vein that arises at the sacroiliac articulation by union of the external iliac and the internal iliac vein, and passes upward to the right side of the fifth lumbar vertebra where the two unite to form the inferior vena cava.

v. ili'aca exter'na [N A, B N A], external iliac vein: the continuation of the femoral vein from the inguinal ligament to the sacroiliac articulation, where it joins with the internal iliac vein to form the common iliac vein.

v. ili'aca inter'na [N A], internal iliac vein: a short trunk formed by union of parietal branches; it extends from the greater sciatic notch to the brim of the pelvis, where it joins the external iliac vein to form the common iliac vein. Called also *v. hypogastrica* [B N A].

v. iliolumba'lis [N A, B N A], iliolumbar vein: a vein that follows the distribution of the iliolumbar artery and opens into the internal iliac or the common iliac vein, or it may divide to end in both.

inferior v. cava, v. cava inferior.

ve'nae intercapita'les [N A], intercapital veins: veins at the clefts of the fingers which pass between the heads of the metacarpal bones and establish communication between the dorsal and the palmar venous system of the hand. Called also *venae intercapitulares manus* [B N A].

ve'nae intercapit'ulares ma'nus [B N A], venae intercapitales.

ve'nae intercapitula'res pe'dis [B N A], veins at the clefts of the toes which pass between the heads of the metatarsal bones and establish communication between the dorsal and the plantar venous system. Omitted in N A.

ve'nae intercosta'les [B N A], veins that accompany the intercostal arteries. See *venae intercostales anteriores, venae intercostales posteriores, v. intercostalis superior dextra, v. intercostalis superior sinistra,* and *v. intercostalis suprema.*

ve'nae intercosta'les anterio'res [N A], anterior intercostal veins: the twelve paired venae comitantes of the anterior thoracic arteries, which drain into the internal thoracic veins.

ve'nae intercosta'les posterio'res IV–XI [N A], posterior intercostal veins IV–XI: venae comitantes of posterior intercostal arteries IV to XI, draining on the right side into the azygos vein and on the left side into the hemiazygos or accessory hemiazygos vein.

v. intercosta'lis supe'rior dex'tra [N A], right superior intercostal vein: a common trunk formed by union of the second, third, and sometimes fourth posterior intercostal veins, which drains into the azygos vein.

v. intercosta'lis supe'rior sinis'tra [N A], left superior intercostal vein: the common trunk formed by union of the second, third, and sometimes fourth posterior intercostal veins, which crosses the arch of the aorta and joins the left brachiocephalic vein.

v. intercosta'lis supre'ma [N A, B N A], highest intercostal vein: the first posterior intercostal vein of either side, which passes over the apex of the lung and ends in the brachiocephalic, vertebral, or superior intercostal vein.

ve'nae interloba'res re'nis [N A, B N A], interlobar veins of kidney: veins that drain the venous arcades of the kidney, pass down between the pyramids, and unite to form the renal vein.

ve'nae interlobula'res hep'atis [N A, B N A], interlobular veins of liver: the veins that arise as tributaries of the portal vein between the hepatic lobules.

ve'nae interlobula'res re'nis [N A, B N A], interlobular veins of kidney: veins that collect blood from the capillary network of the cortex and empty into the venous arcades of the kidney.

ve'na intervertebra'lis [N A], intervertebral vein: any one of the veins that drain the vertebral plexuses, passing out through the intervertebral foramina and emptying into the regional veins: in the neck, into the vertebral; in the thorax, the intercostal; in the abdomen, the lumbar; and in the pelvis, the lateral sacral veins.

ve'nae intestina'les [B N A], the veins draining blood from the small intestines (venae jejunales et ilei [N A]).

ve'nae jejuna'les et il'ei [N A], jejunal and ileal veins: veins draining blood from the jejunum and the ileum into the superior mesenteric vein. Called also *venae intestinales* [B N A].

v. jugula'ris ante'rior [N A, B N A], anterior jugular vein: a vein that arises under the chin, passes down the neck, and opens into the external jugular or the subclavian vein or into jugular venous arch.

v. jugula'ris exter'na [N A, B N A], external jugular vein: the vein that begins in the parotid gland behind the angle of the jaw by union of the retromandibular and the posterior auricular vein, passes down the neck, and opens into the subclavian, the internal jugular, or the brachiocephalic vein.

v. jugula'ris inter'na [N A, B N A], internal jugular vein: the vein that begins as the superior bulb in the jugular fossa, draining much of the head and neck; it descends with first the internal carotid and then the common carotid artery in the neck, and joins with the subclavian vein to form the brachiocephalic vein.

ve'nae labia'les anterio'res [N A], anterior labial veins: veins that collect blood from the anterior aspect of the labia and drain into the external pudendal vein. They are homologues of the anterior scrotal veins in the male.

ve'nae labia'les inferio'res [N A], inferior labial veins: veins that drain the region of the lower lip into the facial vein.

ve'nae labia'les posterio'res [N A], posterior labial veins: small branches from the labia which open into the vesical venus plexus. They are homologues of the posterior scrotal veins in the male.

v. labia'lis supe'rior [N A, B N A], superior labial vein: the vein that drains blood from the region of the upper lip into the facial vein.

ve'nae labyrin'thi [N A], veins of labyrinth: several small veins that pass through the internal acoustic meatus from the cochlea into the inferior petrosal or the transverse sinus. Called also *venae auditivae internae* [B N A].

v. lacrima'lis [N A, B N A], lacrimal vein: the vein that drains blood from the lacrimal gland into the superior ophthalmic vein.

v. laryn'gea infe'rior [N A, B N A], inferior laryngeal vein: a vein draining blood from the larynx into the inferior thyroid vein.

v. laryn'gea supe'rior [N A, B N A], superior laryngeal vein: a vein that drains blood from the larynx into the superior thyroid vein.

v. liena'lis [N A, B N A], splenic vein: the vein formed by union of several branches at the hilus of the spleen, passing from left to right to the neck of the pancreas, where it joins the superior mesenteric vein to form the portal vein.

v. lingua'lis [N A, B N A], lingual vein: the deep vein that follows the distribution of the lingual artery and empties into the internal jugular vein.

ve'nae lumba'les [B N A]. See *venae lumbales [I et II]* and *venae lumbales [III et IV]*.

ve'nae lumba'les [I et II] [N A], lumbar veins I and II: venae comitantes of the first and second lumbar arteries, which drain into the ascending lumbar vein and thence into the azygos or hemiazygos vein.

ve'nae lumba'les [III et IV] [N A], lumbar veins III and IV: venae comitantes of the third and fourth lumbar arteries, which usually drain into the inferior vena cava.

v. lumba'lis ascen'dens [N A, B N A], ascending lumbar vein: an ascending intercepting vein for the lumbar veins of either side; it begins in the lateral sacral veins and passes up the spine to the first lumbar vertebra, where by union with the subcostal vein it becomes on the right side the azygos vein, and on the left side, the hemiazygos vein.

v. mamma'ria inter'na [B N A]. See *venae thoracicae internae.*

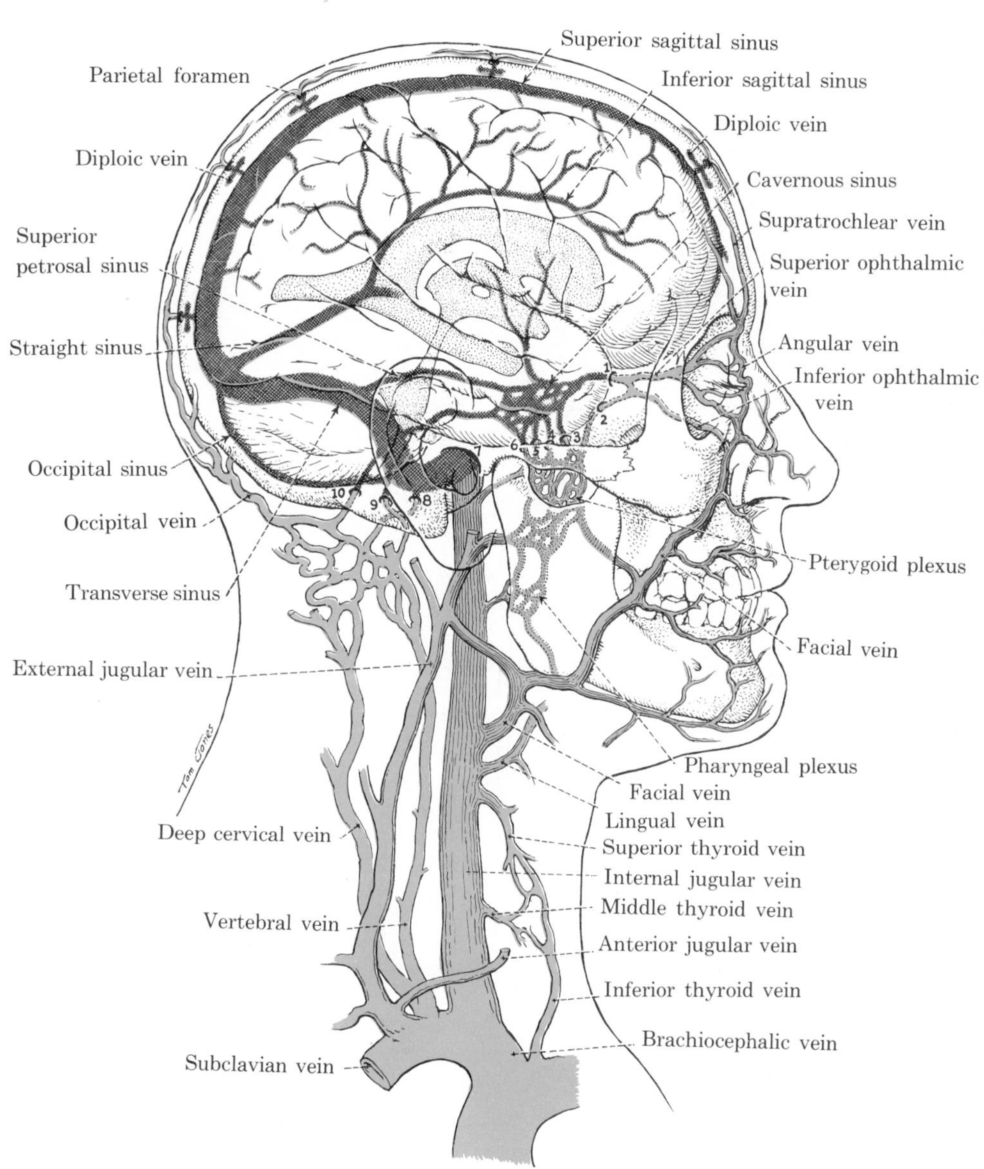

VEINS OF THE HEAD AND NECK
(Modified from Jones and Shepard)

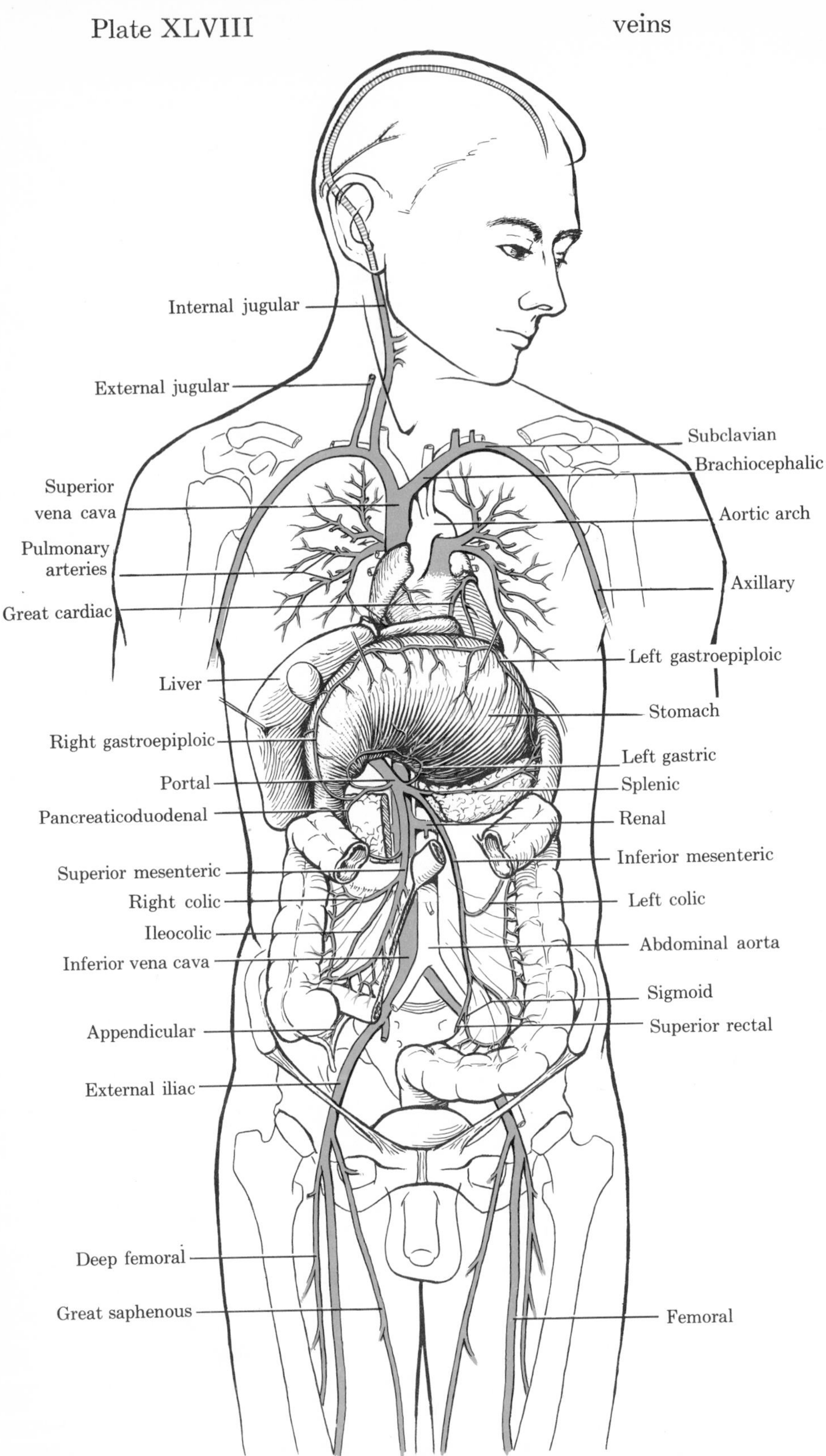

PRINCIPAL VEINS OF THE BODY

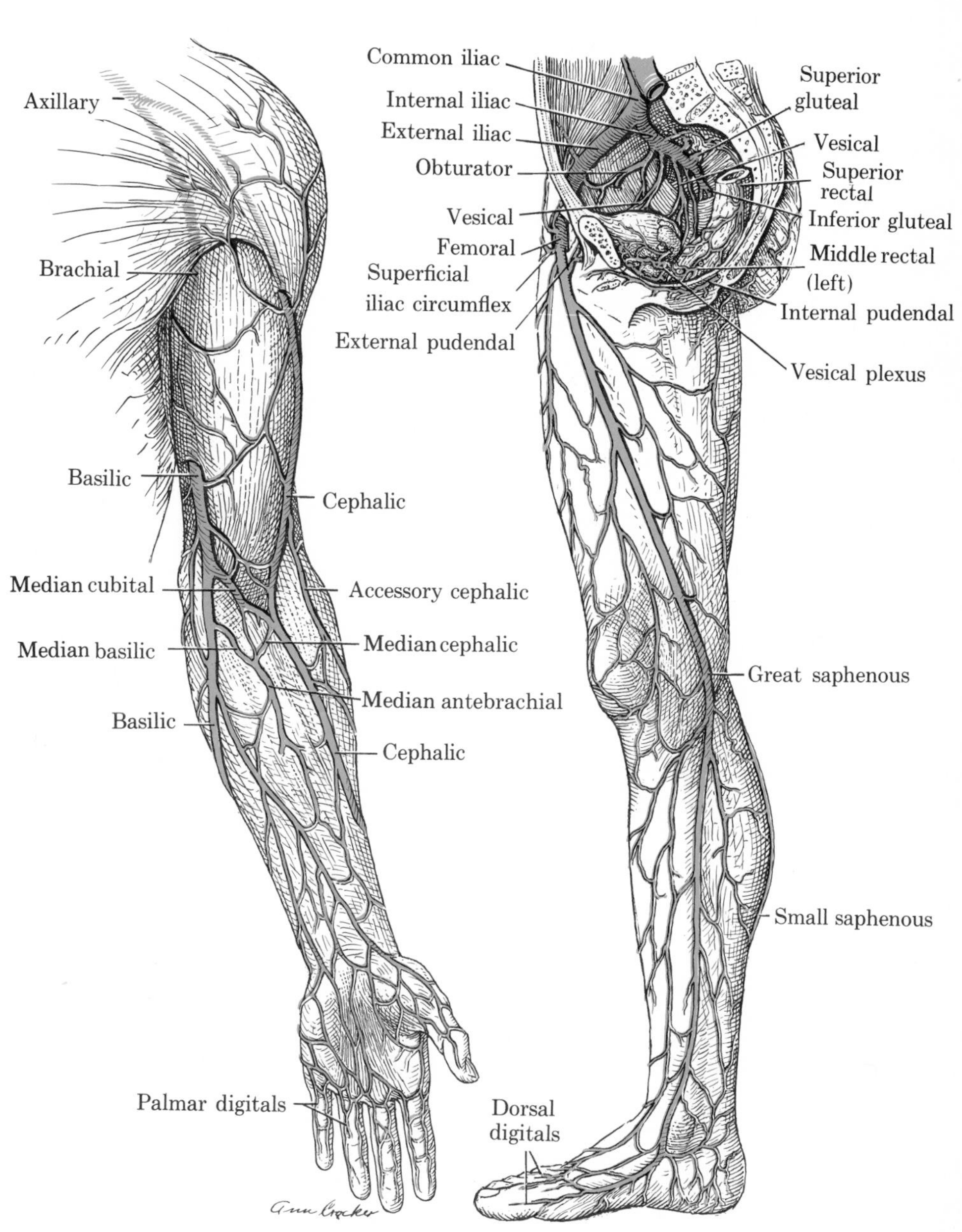

SUPERFICIAL VEINS OF THE EXTREMITIES

ve′nae masseter′icae [B N A], masseteric veins: veins from the masseter muscle that empty into the facial vein. Omitted in N A.

ve′nae maxilla′res [N A], maxillary veins: veins from the pterygoid plexus, usually forming a single short trunk, passing back and uniting with the superficial temporal vein in the parotid gland to form the retromandibular vein.

v. media′na antebra′chii [N A], median antebrachial vein: a vein that arises from a palmar venous plexus and passes up the forearm between the cephalic and the basilic veins to the elbow, where it either joins one of these, bifurcates to join both, or joins the median cubital vein. Called also *v. mediana antibrachii* [B N A].

v. media′na antibra′chii [B N A], v. mediana antebrachii.

v. media′na basil′ica [N A, B N A], median basilic vein: a vein sometimes present as the medial branch, ending in the basilic vein, of a bifurcation of the median antebrachial vein.

v. media′na cephal′ica [N A, B N A], median cephalic vein: a vein sometimes present as the lateral branch, ending in the cephalic vein, formed by bifurcation of the median antebrachial vein.

v. media′na col′li [B N A], median vein of neck: a vein formed when the anterior jugular veins unite as they pass down the neck. Omitted in N A.

v. media′na cu′biti [N A, B N A], median cubital vein: the large connecting branch that arises from the cephalic vein below the elbow and passes obliquely upward over the cubital fossa to join the basilic vein.

ve′nae mediastina′les [N A], mediastinal veins: numerous small branches that drain blood from the anterior mediastinum into the brachiocephalic vein, azygos vein, or the superior vena cava. Called also *venae mediastinales anteriores* [B N A].

ve′nae mediastina′les anterio′res [B N A], venae mediastinales.

ve′nae menin′geae [N A, B N A], meningeal veins: the venae comitantes of the meningeal arteries, which drain the dura mater, communicate with the lateral lacunae, and empty into the regional sinuses and veins.

ve′nae menin′geae me′diae [N A, B N A], middle meningeal veins: the venae comitantes of the middle meningeal artery, which end in the pterygoid venous plexus.

v. mesenter′ica infe′rior [N A, B N A], inferior mesenteric vein: a vein that follows the distribution of its homonymous artery and empties into the splenic vein.

v. mesenter′ica supe′rior [N A, B N A], superior mesenteric vein: a vein that follows the distribution of its homonymous artery and joins with the splenic vein to form the portal vein.

ve′nae metacar′peae dorsa′les [N A, B N A], dorsal metacarpal veins: veins that arise from the union of dorsal veins of adjacent fingers and pass proximally to join in forming the dorsal venous rete of the hand.

ve′nae metacar′peae palma′res [N A], palmar metacarpal veins: the venae comitantes of the palmar metacarpal arteries, which open into the deep palmar venous arch. Called also *venae metacarpeae volares* [B N A].

ve′nae metacar′peae vola′res [B N A], venae metacarpeae palmares.

ve′nae metatar′seae dorsa′les [N A, B N A], dorsal metatarsal veins: veins that are formed by the dorsal digital veins of the toes at the clefts of the toes, joining the dorsal venous arch.

ve′nae metatar′seae planta′res [N A, B N A], plantar metatarsal veins: deep veins of the foot that arise from the plantar digital veins at the clefts of the toes and pass back to open into the plantar venous arch.

ve′nae muscula′res [B N A], muscular veins: veins that drain blood from the levator palpebrae, superior rectus, superior oblique, and medial rectus muscles into the superior ophthalmic vein. Omitted in N A.

ve′nae musculophren′icae [N A], musculophrenic veins: the venae comitantes of the musculophrenic artery, draining blood from parts of the diaphragm and from the wall of the thorax and abdomen.

ve′nae nasa′les exter′nae [N A, B N A], external nasal veins: small ascending branches from the nose that open into the angular and facial veins.

v. nasofronta′lis [N A, B N A], nasofrontal vein: a vein that begins at the supraorbital vein, enters the orbit, and joins the superior ophthalmic vein.

v. obli′qua a′trii sinis′tri [N A], oblique vein of left atrium: a small vein from the left atrium that opens into the coronary sinus. Called also *v. obliqua atrii sinistri* [*Marshalli*] [B N A].

v. obli′qua a′trii sinis′tri [Marshal′li] [B N A], v. obliqua atrii sinistri.

ve′nae obturato′riae [N A, B N A], obturator veins: veins that drain the hip joint and the regional muscles, enter the pelvis through the obturator canal, and empty into the internal iliac or the inferior epigastric vein, or both.

v. occipita′lis [N A, B N A], occipital vein: a vein in the scalp that follows the distribution of the occipital artery and opens under the trapezius muscle into the suboccipital venous plexus; it may continue with the occipital artery and end in the internal jugular vein.

ve′nae oesophage′ae [B N A], venae esophageae.

v. ophthal′mica infe′rior [N A, B N A], inferior ophthalmic vein: a vein formed by confluence of muscular and ciliary branches, and running backward either to join the superior ophthalmic vein or to open directly into the cavernous sinus; it sends a communicating branch through the inferior orbital fissure to join the pterygoid venous plexus.

v. ophthal′mica supe′rior [N A, B N A], superior ophthalmic vein: the vein that begins at the medial angle of the eyelid, where it communicates with the frontal, supraorbital, and angular veins; it follows the distribution of the ophthalmic artery, and may be joined by the inferior ophthalmic vein at the superior orbital fissure before opening into the cavernous sinus.

v. ophthalmomenin′gea [B N A], ophthalmomeningeal vein: a small inferior meningeal vein that opens usually into the superior ophthalmic vein, or occasionally into the superior petrosal sinus. Omitted in N A.

v. ova′rica [B N A]. See *v. ovarica dextra* and *v. ovarica sinistra.*

v. ova′rica dex′tra [N A], right ovarian vein: a vein that drains the pampiniform plexus of the broad ligament on the right into the inferior vena cava.

v. ova′rica sinis′tra [N A], left ovarian vein: a vein that drains the pampiniform plexus of the broad ligament on the left into the left renal vein.

v. palati′na [B N A], v. palatina externa.

v. palati′na exter′na [N A], external palatine vein: the vein that drains blood from the tonsils and the soft palate into the facial vein. Called also *v. palatina* [B N A].

ve′nae palpebra′les [N A, B N A], palpebral veins: small branches from the eyelids that open into the superior ophthalmic vein.

ve′nae palpebra′les inferio′res [N A, B N A], inferior palpebral veins: branches that drain the blood from the lower eyelid into the facial vein.

ve′nae palpebra′les superio′res [N A, B N A], superior palpebral veins: branches that drain the blood from the upper eyelid to the angular vein.

ve′nae pancreat′icae [N A, B N A], pancreatic veins: numerous branches from the pancreas which open into the splenic and the superior mesenteric vein.

ve′nae pancreaticoduodena′les [N A, B N A], pancreaticoduodenal veins: four veins that drain blood from the pancreas and duodenum, closely following the homonymous arteries. A superior and an inferior vein originate from both an anterior and a posterior venous arcade. The anterior superior vein joins the right gastroepiploic vein; the posterior superior vein joins the portal vein. The anterior and posterior inferior veins join, sometimes as one trunk, the uppermost jejunal vein or the superior mesenteric vein.

ve′nae paraumbilica′les [N A], paraumbilical veins: veins that communicate with the portal vein above and descend to the anterior abdominal wall to anastomose with the superior and inferior epigastric and the superior vesical veins in the region of the umbilicus. They form a significant part of the collateral circulation of the portal vein in event of hepatic obstruction. Called also *venae parumbilicales [Sappeyi]* [B N A].

ve′nae parotide′ae [N A], parotid veins: small veins from the parotid gland that open into the superficial temporal vein. Called also *venae parotideae posteriores* [B N A].

ve′nae parotide′ae anterio′res [B N A], rami parotidei venae facialis.

ve′nae parotide′ae posterio′res [B N A], venae parotideae.

ve′nae parumbilica′les [Sap′peyi] [B N A], venae paraumbilicales.

ve′nae perforan′tes [N A], perforating veins: the venae comitantes for the perforating arteries of the thigh, which empty into the deep femoral vein. Called also *venae perforantes femoris* [B N A].

ve′nae perforan′tes fem′oris [B N A], venae perforantes.

ve′nae pericardi′acae [N A, B N A], pericardiac veins: numerous small branches that drain blood from the pericardium into the brachiocephalic, inferior thyroid, and azygos veins, and the superior vena cava.

ve′nae pericardiacophren′icae [N A], pericardiacophrenic veins: small veins that drain blood from the pericardium and diaphragm into the left brachiocephalic vein. Called also *venae phrenicae superiores* [B N A].

ve′nae perone′ae [N A], peroneal veins: the venae comitantes of the peroneal artery, emptying into the posterior tibial vein.

ve′nae pharyn′geae [N A, B N A], pharyngeal veins: veins that drain the pharyngeal plexus and empty into the internal jugular vein.

ve′nae phren′icae inferio′res [N A], inferior phrenic veins: veins that follow the homonymous arteries, the one on the right entering the inferior vena cava, and the one on the left entering the left suprarenal or renal vein or the inferior vena cava.

ve′nae phren′icae superio′res [B N A], venae pericardiacophrenicae.

v. poplite′a [N A], popliteal vein: a vein following the popliteal artery, and formed by union of the venae comitantes of the anterior and posterior tibial arteries; at the adductor hiatus it becomes continuous with the femoral vein.

v. por′tae [N A, B N A], portal vein: a short thick trunk formed by union of the superior mesenteric and the splenic vein behind the neck of the pancreas; it passes upward to the right end of the porta hepatis, where it divides into successively smaller branches, following the branches of the hepatic artery, until it forms a capillary-like system of sinusoids that permeates the entire substance of the liver.

v. poste′rior ventric′uli sinis′tri cor′dis [N A, B N A], posterior vein of left ventricle: the vein that drains blood from the posterior surface of the left ventricle into the coronary sinus.

v. prepylo′rica [N A], prepyloric vein: a vein that accompanies the prepyloric artery, passing upward over the anterior surface of the junction between the pylorus and the duodenum and emptying into the right gastric vein.

ve′nae profun′dae, deeply situated veins.

ve′nae profun′dae clitor′idis [N A, B N A], deep veins of clitoris: small veins of the clitoris that drain into the vesical venous plexus.

v. profun′da fem′oris [N A], deep femoral vein: a vein that follows the distribution of the deep femoral artery and opens into the femoral vein.

v. profun′da lin′guae [N A], deep lingual vein: a vein that drains blood from the deep aspect of the tongue and joins the sublingual vein to form the vena comitans of the hypoglossal nerve.

ve′nae profun′dae pe′nis [N A, B N A], deep veins of penis: veins that follow the distribution of the homonymous artery and empty into the dorsal vein of the penis.

ve′nae puden′dae exter′nae [N A, B N A], external pudendal veins: veins that follow the distribution of the external pudendal artery and open into the great saphenous vein.

v. puden′da inter′na [N A], internal pudendal vein: a vein that follows the course of the internal pudendal artery, and drains into the internal iliac vein.

ve′nae pulmona′les [N A, B N A], pulmonary veins: the four veins, the superior and inferior pulmonary veins of either side, that return aerated blood from the lungs to the left atrium of the heart.

ve′nae pulmona′les dex′trae [B N A]. See *v. pulmonalis inferior dextra* and *v. pulmonalis superior dextra.*

v. pulmona′lis infe′rior dex′tra [N A], right inferior pulmonary vein: the vein that returns blood from the lower lobe of the right lung (from the apical branch and from the common, superior, and inferior basal veins) to the left atrium of the heart.

v. pulmona′lis infe′rior sinis′tra [N A], left inferior pulmonary vein: the vein that returns blood from the lower lobe of the left lung (from the superior apical branch and the common basal vein) to the left atrium of the heart.

ve′nae pulmona′les sinis′trae [B N A]. See *v. pulmonalis inferior sinistra* and *v. pulmonalis superior sinistra.*

v. pulmona′lis supe′rior dex′tra [N A], right superior pulmonary vein: the vein that returns blood from the upper and middle lobes of the right lung (from the apical, anterior, and posterior branches and the middle lobar branch) to the left atrium of the heart.

v. pulmona′lis supe′rior sinis′tra [N A], left superior pulmonary vein: the vein that returns blood from the upper lobe of the left lung (from the apicoposterior, anterior, and lingular branches) to the left atrium of the heart.

ve′nae radia′les [N A, B N A], radial veins: the venae comitantes of the radial artery, which open into the brachial veins.

ve′nae recta′les inferio′res [N A], inferior rectal veins: veins that drain the rectal plexus into the internal pudendal vein. Called also *venae haemorrhoidales inferiores* [B N A].

ve′nae recta′les me′diae [N A], middle rectal veins: veins that drain the rectal plexus and empty into the internal iliac and superior rectal veins.

v. recta′lis supe′rior [N A], superior rectal vein: the vein that drains the upper part of the rectal plexus into the inferior mesenteric vein and thus establishes connection between the portal and the systemic system. Called also *v. haemorrhoidalis superior* [B N A].

ve′nae rena′les [N A, B N A], renal veins: short thick trunks, the one on the left longer than that on the right, that pass from the kidneys to the inferior vena cava.

ve′nae re′nis [N A, B N A], the veins within the kidney, including the *venae interlobares renis, venae arcuatae renis, venae interlobulares renis, venulae rectae renis,* and *venulae stellatae renis.*

v. retromandibula'ris [N A], retromandibular vein: the vein that is formed in the upper part of the parotid gland behind the neck of the mandible by union of the maxillary and superficial temporal veins; it passes downward through the gland, communicates with the facial vein, and emerging from the gland joins with the posterior auricular vein to form the external jugular vein. Called also *v. facialis posterior* [B N A].

ve'nae revehen'tes, channels in the early embryo that convey blood from the sinusoids of the liver to the sinus venosus and later become the hepatic veins.

ve'nae sacra'les latera'les [N A, B N A], lateral sacral veins: veins that follow the homonymous arteries, help to form the lateral sacral plexus, and empty into the internal iliac vein or the superior gluteal veins.

v. sacra'lis me'dia [B N A], v. sacralis mediana.

v. sacra'lis media'na [N A], middle sacral vein: a vein that follows the middle sacral artery and opens into the common iliac vein. Called also *v. sacralis media* [B N A].

v. saphe'na accesso'ria [N A, B N A], accessory saphenous vein: a vein that, when present, drains the medial and posterior superficial parts of the thigh and opens into the great saphenous vein.

v. saphe'na mag'na [N A, B N A], great saphenous vein: the longest vein in the body, extending from the dorsum of the foot to just below the inguinal ligament, where it opens into the femoral vein.

v. saphe'na par'va [N A, B N A], small saphenous vein: the vein that continues the marginal vein from behind the malleolus and passes up the back of the leg to the knee joint, where it opens into the popliteal vein.

ve'nae scrota'les anterio'res [N A, B N A], anterior scrotal veins: veins that collect blood from the anterior aspect of the scrotum and drain into the external pudendal vein.

ve'nae scrota'les posterio'res [N A, B N A], posterior scrotal veins: small branches from the scrotum that open into the vesical venous plexus.

v. sep'ti pellu'cidi [N A, B N A], vein of septum pellucidum: a vein from the septum pellucidum that empties into the thalamostriate vein.

ve'nae sigmoi'deae [N A, B N A], sigmoid veins: veins from the sigmoid colon that empty into the inferior mesenteric vein.

v. spermat'ica [B N A], spermatic vein: the vein that drains blood from the testis and epididymis, forms the pampiniform plexus of the spermatic cord, and accompanies the internal spermatic artery. The vein on the right enters the inferior vena cava; that on the left enters the left renal vein. Omitted in N A.

ve'nae spina'les [N A], spinal veins: anastomosing networks of small veins that drain blood from the spinal cord and its pia mater into the internal vertebral venous plexuses.

ve'nae spina'les exter'nae anterio'res [B N A], small longitudinal veins draining blood from the anterior part of the pia mater of the spinal cord. See *venae spinales.*

ve'nae spina'les exter'nae posterio'res [B N A], small longitudinal veins draining blood from the posterior part of the pia mater of the spinal cord. See *venae spinales.*

ve'nae spina'les inter'nae [B N A], minute veins draining blood from the substance of the spinal cord. See *venae spinales.*

v. spira'lis modi'oli [N A, B N A], spiral vein of modiolus: a small vein in the spiral modiolus, a tributary of the labyrinthine veins.

ve'nae stella'tae re'nis [B N A], venulae stellatae renis.

v. sternocleidomastoi'dea [N A, B N A], sternocleidomastoid vein: a vein that follows the course of the homonymous artery and opens into the internal jugular vein.

v. stria'ta [N A], striate vein: the vein that arises from the anterior perforated substance of the brain and joins the basal vein.

v. stylomastoi'dea [N A, B N A], stylomastoid vein: a vein following the stylomastoid artery and emptying into the retromandibular vein.

v. subcla'via [N A, B N A], subclavian vein: the vein that continues the axillary as the main venous stem of the upper member, follows the subclavian artery, and joins with the internal jugular vein to form the brachiocephalic vein.

v. subcosta'lis [N A], subcostal vein: the vena comitans of the subcostal artery, which joins the ascending lumbar vein to form the azygos or hemiazygos vein, on the right or left side respectively.

ve'nae subcuta'neae abdom'inis [N A, B N A], subcutaneous veins of abdomen: the superficial veins of the abdominal wall.

v. sublingua'lis [N A, B N A], sublingual vein: a vein that follows the sublingual artery and opens into the lingual vein.

v. submenta'lis [N A, B N A], submental vein: a vein that follows the submental artery and opens into the facial vein.

superior v. cava, v. cava superior.

v. supraorbita'lis [N A, B N A], supraorbital vein: the vein that passes down the forehead lateral to the supratrochlear vein, joining it at the root of the nose to form the angular vein.

ve'nae suprarena'les [B N A]. See *v. suprarenalis dextra* and *v. suprarenalis sinistra.*

v. suprarena'lis dex'tra [N A], right suprarenal vein: a vein that drains the right suprarenal gland into the inferior vena cava.

v. suprarena'lis sinis'tra [N A], left suprarenal vein: the vein that returns blood from the left suprarenal gland to the left renal vein.

v. suprascapula'ris [N A], suprascapular vein: the vein that accompanies the homonymous artery (sometimes as two veins that unite), opening usually into the external jugular, or occasionally into the subclavian vein. Called also *v. transversa scapulae* [B N A].

ve'nae supratrochlea'res [N A], supratrochlear veins: two veins, each beginning in a venous plexus high up on the forehead and descending to the root of the nose, where it joins with the supraorbital to form the angular vein. Called also *venae frontales* [B N A].

v. tempora'lis me'dia [N A, B N A], middle temporal vein: the vein that arises in the substance of the temporal muscle and passes down under the fascia to the zygoma, where it breaks through to join the superficial temporal vein.

ve'nae tempora'les profun'dae [N A, B N A], deep temporal veins: veins that drain the deep portions of the temporal muscle and empty into the pterygoid plexus.

ve'nae tempora'les superficia'les [N A, B N A], superficial temporal veins: veins that drain the lateral part of the scalp in the frontal and parietal regions, the tributaries forming a single superficial temporal vein in front of the ear, just above the zygoma. This descending vein receives the middle temporal and transverse facial veins and, entering the parotid gland, unites with the maxillary vein deep to the neck of the mandible to form the retromandibular vein.

v. termina'lis [B N A], v. thalamostriata.

v. testicula'ris [B N A]. See *v. testicularis dextra* and *v. testicularis sinistra.*

v. testicula'ris dex'tra [N A], right testicular vein: a vein that drains the right pampiniform plexus into the inferior vena cava.

v. testicula'ris sinis'tra [N A], left testicular vein: a vein that drains the left pampiniform plexus into the left renal vein.

v. thalamostria'ta [N A], thalamostriate

vein: a vein that collects blood from the corpus striatum and thalamus, and joins with the choroid vein to form the internal cerebral veins. Called also *v. terminalis* [B N A].

v. thoraca'lis latera'lis [B N A], v. thoracica lateralis.

ve'nae thora'cicae inter'nae [N A], internal thoracic veins: two veins formed by junction of the venae comitantes of the internal thoracic artery of either side; each continues along the artery to open into the brachiocephalic vein. Called also (sing.) *v. mammaria interna* [B N A].

v. thora'cica latera'lis [N A], lateral thoracic vein: a large vein accompanying the lateral thoracic artery and draining into the axillary vein. Called also *v. thoracalis lateralis* [B N A].

v. thoracoacromia'lis [N A, B N A], thoracoacromial vein: the vein that follows the homonymous artery and opens into the subclavian vein.

ve'nae thoracoepigas'tricae [N A, B N A], thoracoepigastric veins: long, longitudinal, superficial veins in the anterolateral subcutaneous tissue of the torso, which empty superiorly into the lateral thoracic and inferiorly into the femoral vein.

ve'nae thy'micae [N A, B N A], thymic veins: small branches from the thymus gland that open into the left brachiocephalic vein.

v. thyreoi'dea i'ma [B N A], an occasional vein formed by high junction of the right and left inferior thyroid veins, and emptying usually into the left brachiocephalic vein. Omitted in N A.

ve'nae thyreoi'deae inferio'res [B N A]. See *v. thyroidea inferior.*

ve'nae thyreoi'deae superio'res [B N A]. 1. See *vena thyroidea superior.* 2. Veins draining blood from the upper portion of the thyroid gland into the posterior facial vein. Omitted in N A.

v. thyroi'dea infe'rior [N A], inferior thyroid vein: either of two veins, left and right, that drain the thyroid plexus into the left and right brachiocephalic veins; occasionally they may unite into a common trunk to empty, usually, into the left brachiocephalic vein.

ve'nae thyroi'deae me'diae [N A], middle thyroid veins: veins that drain blood from the thyroid gland into the internal jugular vein.

v. thyroi'dea supe'rior [N A], superior thyroid vein: a vein arising from the upper part of the thyroid gland on either side, opening into the internal jugular vein, occasionally in common with the facial vein.

ve'nae tibia'les anterio'res [N A, B N A], anterior tibial veins: venae comitantes of the anterior tibial artery, which unite with the posterior tibial veins to form the popliteal vein.

ve'nae tibia'les posterio'res [N A, B N A], posterior tibial veins: venae comitantes of the posterior tibial artery, which unite with the anterior tibial veins to form the popliteal vein.

ve'nae trachea'les [N A, B N A], tracheal veins: small branches that drain blood from the trachea into the brachiocephalic vein.

ve'nae transver'sae col'li [N A, B N A], transverse cervical veins: veins that follow the transverse artery of the neck and open into the subclavian vein.

v. transver'sa facie'i [N A, B N A], transverse facial vein: a vein that passes backward with the transverse facial artery just below the zygomatic arch to join the retromandibular vein.

v. transver'sa scap'ulae [B N A], v. suprascapularis.

ve'nae tympan'icae [N A, B N A], tympanic veins: small veins from the tympanic cavity that pass through the petrotympanic fissure, open into the plexus around the temporomandibular articulation, and finally drain into the retromandibular vein.

ve'nae ulna'res [N A, B N A], ulnar veins: the venae comitantes of the ulnar artery, which unite with the radial veins at the elbow to form the brachial veins.

v. umbilica'lis [N A, B N A], umbilical vein: in the early embryo, either of the paired veins that carry blood from the chorion to the sinus venosus and heart; they later fuse and a single vessel persisting in the umbilical cord carries all the blood from the placenta to the ductus venosus of the fetus.

ve'nae uteri'nae [N A, B N A], uterine veins: veins that drain the uterine plexus into the internal iliac veins.

ve'nae vaso'rum, small veins that return blood from the tissues making up the walls of the blood vessels themselves.

v. vertebra'lis [N A, B N A], vertebral vein: a vein that arises from the suboccipital venous plexus, passes with the vertebral artery through the foramina of the transverse processes of the upper six cervical vertebrae, and opens into the brachiocephalic vein.

v. vertebra'lis accesso'ria [N A], accessory vertebral vein: a vein that sometimes arises from a plexus formed around the vertebral artery by the vertebral vein, descends with the vertebral vein, and emerges through the transverse foramen of the seventh cervical vertebra to empty into the brachiocephalic vein.

v. vertebra'lis ante'rior [N A], anterior vertebral vein: a small vein arising from the venous plexus around the transverse processes of the upper cervical vertebrae, and descending to end in the vertebral vein.

ve'nae vesica'les [N A], vesical veins: veins passing from the vesical plexus to the internal iliac vein.

ve'nae vestibula'res [N A, B N A], vestibular veins: branches draining blood from the vestibule into the labyrinthine veins.

ve'nae vortico'sae [N A, B N A], vorticose veins: four veins that pierce the sclera and carry blood from the choroid to the superior ophthalmic vein. Called also *venae choroideae oculi.*

---

venae (ve'ne) [L.]. Plural of *vena.*

venation (ve-na'shun) [L. *vena* vein]. The manner of distribution of the veins of a part.

venectasia (ve″nek-ta'ze-ah). Phlebectasia.

venectomy (ve-nek'to-me). Phlebectomy.

venenation (ven″ĕ-na'shun) [L. *venenum* poison]. Poisoning; a condition of being poisoned.

veneniferous (ven″ĕ-nif'er-us) [L. *venenum* poison + *ferre* to bear]. Carrying poison.

venenific (ven″ĕ-nif'ik) [L. *venenum* poison + *facere* to make]. Forming poison.

Venenosa (ven″ĕ-no'sah) [pl., L. *venenosus* poisonous]. Venomous snakes collectively; Thanatophidia.

venenosalivary (ven″ĕ-no-sal'ĭ-ver″e). Venomosalivary.

venenosity (ven″ĕ-nos'ĭ-te). The condition of being toxic or poisonous.

venenous (ven'ĕ-nus) [L. *venenosus*]. Poisonous or toxic.

venenum (ve-ne'num), pl. *vene'na* [L.]. A poison.

venepuncture (ven'e-punk″tūr). Venipuncture.

venereal (ve-ne're-al) [L. *venereus*]. Due to or propagated by sexual intercourse.

venereologist (ve-ne″re-ol'o-jist). A practitioner who specializes in venereal disease.

venereology (ve-ne″re-ol'o-je). The branch of medicine which deals with venereal disease.

venereophobia (ve-ne″re-o-fo'be-ah) [*venereal* + Gr. *phobein* to be affrighted by]. Morbid dread of venereal infection.

venerology (ven″er-ol'o-je). Venereology.

venerupin (ven″er-oo′pin) [*Venerupis* (L. *veneris*) the Venus shell + *-in,* suffix for chemical compounds]. A toxic substance, believed to be an amine, found in certain Japanese pelecypods which were formerly placed in the genus *Venerupis;* this toxin, the exact chemical nature of which is unknown, is entirely distinct from the mussel poison found in related bivalves.

venery (ven′er-e) [L. *venereus* pertaining to Venus]. Coitus; sexual intercourse.

venesection (ven″e-sek′shun) [L. *vena* vein + *sectio* cutting]. Phlebotomy.

venesuture (ven″e-su′tūr). Phleborrhaphy.

venin-antivenin (ven″in-an″te-ven′in). A mixture of venin and antivenin used as a vaccine to counteract the effect of snake poisons.

veniplex (ven′ĭ-pleks) [L. *vena* vein + *plexus* plexus]. A venous plexus.

venipuncture (ven′ĭ-punk″tūr). Puncture of a vein.

venisection (ven″ĭ-sek′shun). Phlebotomy.

venisuture (ven′ĭ-su″tūr) [L. *vena* vein + *sutura* stitch]. Phleborrhaphy.

veno- (ve′no) [L. *vena* vein]. Combining form denoting relationship to a vein.

veno-auricular (ve″no-aw-rik′u-lar). Pertaining to the vena cava, and the atrium (auricle).

venoclysis (ve-nok′lĭ-sis) [*vena* + Gr. *klysis* injection]. Phleboclysis.

venofibrosis (ve″no-fi-bro′sis). A disease of the veins characterized by hyperplasia of the fibrous connective tissue of the median coat of the vein.

venogram (ve′no-gram). 1. Phlebogram. 2. A venous-pulse tracing.

venography (ve-nog′rah-fe). Phlebography. **intraosseous v.,** roentgenography of the veins after injection of the contrast medium into bone marrow at an appropriate site, such as the iliac crest, ischium, pubic bones, greater trochanter, spinous processes of the vertebrae, or sternum. **portal v.,** portography. **splenic v.,** splenic portography.

venom (ven′um) [L. *venenum* poison]. A poison; especially a toxic substance normally secreted by a serpent, insect, or other animal. **Russell's viper v.,** the venom of the Russell viper, which acts *in vitro* as an intrinsic thromboplastin and is useful in defining deficiencies of blood coagulation factor X. **snake v.,** the poisonous secretion of snakes, containing hemotoxins, hemagglutinins, neurotoxins, leukotoxins, and endotheliotoxins. The venoms of various species have been used as hemostatics. **spider v.,** the venom of a poisonous spider such as *Latrodectus, Atrax, Ctenus,* and *Lycosa.*

venomin (ven′o-min). A substance isolated from the venom of pit vipers: used in the treatment of rheumatoid arthritis.

venomization (ven″um-i-za′shun). Treatment of a substance with snake venom.

venomosalivary (ven″o-mo-sal′ĭ-ver″e). Secreting a poisonous saliva.

venomotor (ve″no-mo′tor). Pertaining to or producing constriction or dilatation of the veins.

venomous (ven′o-mus). Secreting venom; poisonous.

veno-occlusive (ve″no-ŏ-kloo′siv). Pertaining to or characterized by obstruction of the veins.

venoperitoneostomy (ve″no-per″ĭ-to″ne-os′to-me) [*veno-* + *peritoneum* + Gr. *stomoun* to provide with an opening, or mouth]. Anastomosis of the saphenous vein with the peritoneum for permanent drainage of the abdomen in ascites. Called also *Routti's operation.*

venopressor (ve-no-pres″or). Pertaining to venous blood pressure.

venosclerosis (ve″no-skle-ro′sis). Phlebosclerosis.

venose (ve′nōs). Provided with veins.

venosinal (ve″no-si′nal). Pertaining to the venae cavae and the right atrium of the heart.

venosity (ve-nos′ĭ-te). 1. Excess of venous blood in a part. 2. A plentiful supply of blood vessels or of venous blood.

venostasis (ve″no-sta′sis) [*veno-* + Gr. *stasis* stopping]. The checking of the return flow of blood by compressing the veins in the four extremities.

venostat (ve′no-stat). An apparatus for performing venostasis.

venotomy (ve-not′o-me). Phlebotomy.

venous (ve′nus) [L. *venosus*]. Of or pertaining to the veins.

venovenostomy (ve″no-ve-nos′to-me). Phlebophlebostomy.

vent (vent) [Fr. *fente* slit]. 1. Any opening or outlet; especially the anus. 2. An opening that discharges pus. **pulmonic alveolar v's,** interalveolar pores.

venter (ven′ter), pl. *ven′tres* [L. "belly"]. 1. Any belly-shaped part; used in anatomical nomenclature to designate a fleshy contractile part of a muscle. 2. The stomach or belly. 3. The uterus. 4. Any hollowed part or cavity. **v. ante′rior mus′culi digas′trici** [N A, B N A], the shorter belly of the digastric muscle, arising from the digastric fossa on the mandible and extending backward to join the posterior belly through an intermediate tendon attached to the hyoid bone. Called also *anterior belly of digastric muscle.* **v. fronta′lis mus′culi occipitofronta′lis** [N A], the frontal belly of the occipitofrontal muscle, originating from the galea aponeurotica and inserting into the skin of the eyebrows and the root of the nose. Called also *musculus frontalis* [B N A], and *frontal belly of occipitofrontal muscle.* **v. il′ii,** the free (pelvic) portion of the sacropelvic surface of the ilium. **v. i′mus,** the lowermost of the great body cavities, the abdominal cavity (cavum abdominis). **v. infe′rior mus′culi omohyoi′dei** [N A, B N A], the lowermost belly of the omohyoid muscle. **v. me′dius,** the middle of the great body cavities, the thoracic cavity (cavum thoracis). **v. mus′culi** [N A, B N A], the fleshy contractile part of a muscle. Called also *belly of muscle.* **v. occipita′lis mus′culi occipitofronta′lis** [N A], the occipital belly of the occipitofrontal muscle, originating from the highest nuchal line of the occipital bone and inserting into the galea aponeurotica. Called also *musculus occipitalis* [B N A], and *occipital belly of occipitofrontal muscle.* **v. poste′rior mus′culi digas′trici** [N A, B N A], the longer belly of the digastric muscle, arising from the mastoid notch of the temporal bone and extending forward to join the anterior belly through an intermediate tendon attached to the hyoid bone. Called also *posterior belly of digastric muscle.* **v. propen′dens.** 1. Pendulous abdomen. 2. Anteroversion of the uterus. **v. scap′ulae,** fossa subscapularis. **v. supe′rior mus′culi omohyoi′dei** [N A, B N A], the uppermost belly of the omohyoid muscle. **v. supre′mus,** the uppermost of the great body cavities, the cranial cavity.

ventilation (ven″tĭ-la′shun) [L. *ventilatio*]. 1. The process or act of supplying a house or room continuously with fresh air. 2. In physiology, the constant supplying of oxygen through the lungs. 3. In psychiatry, the open discussion of grievances. **downward v.,** that in which the outlets have places lower than those of the inlets. **exhausting v.,** ventilation by means of the exhausting fan or by some other process which withdraws the foul air. **natural v.,** ventilation effected without any special appliance to render it certain. **plenum v.,** the supply of fresh air to a building by fan blowers. **upward v.,** that which introduces air below the place of its withdrawal. **vacuum v.,** that which is effected by the forced extraction of air.

ventouse (vaw-tooz′) [Fr.]. A cupping glass.

ventrad (ven′trad) [L. *venter* belly + *ad* to]. Toward a belly, venter, or ventral aspect.

ventral (ven′tral) [L. *ventralis*]. 1. Pertaining to

the belly or to any venter. 2. Denoting a position more toward the belly surface than some other object of reference; same as *anterior* in human anatomy.

ventralis (ven-tra′lis). Ventral; in official anatomical nomenclature, used to designate a position closer to the belly surface. Cf. *anterior.*

ventralward (ven′tral-ward). Ventrad.

ventri-. See *ventro-.*

ventricle (ven′trĭ-k'l). A small cavity, such as one of the several cavities of the brain, or one of the lower chambers of the heart. Called also *ventriculus.* **aortic v. of heart,** ventriculus sinister cordis. **v. of Arantius.** 1. Cavum septi pellucidi. 2. Fossa rhomboidea. **v's of the brain,** the cavities within the brain, including the two lateral, the third, and the fourth ventricles, and the cavum septi pellucidi. **v. of cord,** canalis centralis medullae spinalis. **Duncan's v., fifth v.,** cavum septi pellucidi. **first v. of cerebrum.** 1. Cavum septi pellucidi. 2. Ventriculus lateralis cerebri. **fourth v. of cerebrum,** an irregularly shaped cavity in the rhombencephalon. See *ventriculus quartus cerebri.* **Galen's v.,** ventriculus laryngis. **v. of heart,** one of the lower pair of cavities, with thick muscular walls, that make up the bulk of the heart. See *ventriculus dexter cordis* and *ventriculus sinister cordis.* **Krause's v.,** ventriculus terminalis medullae spinalis. **v. of larynx,** ventriculus laryngis. **lateral v. of cerebrum,** the space in each hemisphere representing the cavity of the original neural canal. See *ventriculus lateralis cerebri.* **left v. of heart,** ventriculus sinister cordis. **Morgagni's v.,** ventriculus laryngis. **v. of myelon,** canalis centralis medullae spinalis. **pineal v.,** recessus pinealis. **right v. of heart,** ventriculus dexter cordis. **second v. of cerebrum,** ventriculus lateralis cerebri. **sixth v.,** Verga's v. **v. of Sylvius,** cavum septi pellucidi. **terminal v. of spinal cord,** ventriculus terminalis medullae spinalis. **third v. of cerebrum,** a cavity of irregular shape situated between and below the cerebral hemispheres. See *ventriculus tertius cerebri.* **Verga's v.,** an occasional space between the corpus callosum and the fornix. Called also *sixth v.* **Vieussen's v.,** cavum septi pellucidi.

ventricornu (ven″trĭ-kor′nu) [*ventri-* + L. *cornu* horn]. Cornu anterius medullae spinalis.

ventricornual (ven″trĭ-kor′nu-al). Pertaining to the ventricornu.

ventricose (ven′trĭ-kōs). Having an expansion or belly on one side.

ventricular (ven-trik′u-lar). Pertaining to a ventricle.

ventriculitis (ven-trik″u-li′tis). Inflammation of a ventricle, especially of a ventricle of the brain.

ventriculo- (ven-trik′u-lo) [L. *ventriculus,* dim. of *venter* belly]. Combining form denoting relationship to a ventricle, of the heart or brain.

ventriculoatriostomy (ven-trik″u-lo-a″tre-os′to-me). Surgical creation of a passage, by means of subcutaneously placed catheters with a one-way valve, permitting drainage of cerebrospinal fluid from a cerebral ventricle to the right atrium by way of the jugular vein; performed for relief of hydrocephalus.

ventriculocisternostomy (ven-trik″u-lo-sis″ter-nos′to-me). Surgical establishment of a communication between the third ventricle and the cisterna interpeduncularis. See *ventriculostomy.*

ventriculocordectomy (ven-trik″u-lo-kor-dek′to-me). Chevalier Jackson operation for laryngeal stenosis with bilateral recurrent paralysis, done by excising with the punch forceps the entire ventricular floor anterior to the vocal process and antero-external surface of the arytenoid.

ventriculogram (ven-trik′u-lo-gram). A roentgenogram of the cerebral ventricles.

ventriculography (ven-trik″u-log′rah-fe) [*ventriculo* + Gr. *graphein* to write]. 1. Roentgenography of the head following removal of cerebrospinal fluid from the cerebral ventricles and its replacement by air or other contrast medium. 2. Roentgenography of a ventricle of the heart after injection of a contrast medium.

ventriculometry (ven-trik″u-lom′e-tre) [*ventriculo-* + Gr. *metron* measure]. The measurement of the intraventricular (intracranial) pressure.

ventriculomyotomy (ven-trik″u-lo-mi-ot′o-me). Incision of the obstructing muscular band in treatment of subaortic stenosis.

ventriculonector (ven-trik″u-lo-nek′ter) [*ventriculo-* + L. *nector* joiner]. The atrioventricular bundle.

ventriculopuncture (ven-trik′u-lo-punk″tūr). Puncture of a lateral ventricle of the brain by the insertion of a needle.

ventriculoscope (ven-trik′u-lo-skōp). An endoscope for examining the cerebral ventricles and for cauterizing the choroid plexus.

ventriculoscopy (ven-trik″u-los′ko-pe) [*ventriculo-* + Gr. *skopein* to examine]. Direct examination of the cerebral ventricles by means of an endoscope or cystoscope.

ventriculostium (ven-trik″u-los′te-um) [*ventriculo-* + L. *ostium* mouth]. The development of an opening between one of the cerebral ventricles and the external surface of the brain.

ventriculostomy (ven-trik″u-los′to-me) [*ventriculo-* + Gr. *stomoun* to provide with an opening, or mouth]. The operation of establishing a free communication between the floor of the third ventricle and the underlying cisterna interpeduncularis: for the treatment of hydrocephalus.

ventriculosubarachnoid (ven-trik″u-lo-sub″ah-rak′noid). Pertaining to the cerebral ventricles and the subarachnoid spaces.

ventriculotomy (ven-trik″u-lot′o-me) [*ventriculo-* + Gr. *tomē* a cutting]. Incision of a ventricle of the heart, for repair of cardiac defects.

ventriculus (ven-trik′u-lus) [L., dim. of *venter* belly] [N A, B N A]. 1. The musculomembranous expansion of the alimentary canal between esophagus and duodenum. See also *stomach.* 2. A small cavity in an organ. Called also *ventricle.* **v. cor′dis** [N A, B N A], one of the lower pair of cavities, with thick muscular walls, that make up the bulk of the heart. See *v. dexter cordis* and *v. sinister cordis.* Called also *ventricle of heart.* **v. dex′ter cer′ebri,** the ventriculus lateralis cerebri of the right cerebral hemisphere. **v. dex′ter cor′dis** [N A, B N A], the cavity of the heart that propels the blood through the pulmonary trunk and arteries into the lungs. Called also *right ventricle of heart.* **v. laryn′gis** [N A], **v. laryn′gis [Morgagnii]** [B N A], a lateral evagination of mucous membrane between the vocal and vestibular folds, reaching nearly to the angle of the thyroid cartilage. Called also *ventricle of larynx.* **v. latera′lis cer′ebri** [N A, B N A], the space in each hemisphere representing the cavity of the original neural canal; it consists of a pars centralis and three horns—anterior, inferior, and posterior, all of which are filled with fluid. Called also *lateral ventricle of cerebrum.* **v. quar′tus cer′ebri** [N A], an irregularly shaped cavity in the rhombencephalon, dorsal to the medulla oblongata, the pons, and the isthmus, and ventral to the cerebellum. It is continuous with the central canal of the cord below and with the cerebral aqueduct above. Called also *fourth ventricle of cerebrum.* **v. sinis′ter cer′ebri,** the ventriculus lateralis cerebri of the left cerebral hemisphere. **v. sinis′ter cor′dis** [N A, B N A], the cavity of the heart that propels the blood out through the aorta into the systemic arteries. Called also *left ventricle of heart.* **superior colic v.,** Evan's name for the cecum with the ascending colon and part of the transverse colon considered as a chamber (holotyphlon). **v. termina′lis medul′lae spina′lis** [N A, B N A], a saclike expansion of the central canal of the spinal cord within the conus medullaris. Called also *terminal* *ventricle of spinal cord.* **v. ter'tius cer'ebri** [N A, B N A], a cavity of irregular shape situated between and below the cerebral hemispheres; it extends from the corpus callosum above to the infundibulum below and from the pineal body behind to the lamina terminalis in front. Called also *third ventricle of cerebrum.*

ventricumbent (ven″trĭ-kum′bent) [*ventri-* + L. *cumbere* to lie]. Lying upon the belly; prone.

ventriduct (ven′trĭ-dukt) [*ventri-* + L. *ducere* to draw]. To bring or carry ventrad.

ventriduction (ven″trĭ-duk′shun). The act of drawing a part ventrad.

ventrifixation (ven″trĭ-fiks-a′shun). Ventrofixation.

ventrifixure (ven′trĭ-fiks″ūr). Ventrifixation.

ventriflexion (ven″trĭ-flek′shun) [*ventri-* + *flexion*]. Flexion toward the belly.

ventrimesal (ven″trĭ-me′sal). Pertaining to the ventrimeson.

ventrimeson (ven-trim′e-son) [*ventri-* + Gr. *meson* middle]. The middle line on the ventral surface.

ventripyramid (ven″trĭ-pir′ah-mid). Pyramis medullae oblongatae.

ventro-, ventri- (ven′tro, ven′tre) [L. *venter* belly or abdomen]. Combining form denoting relationship to the belly, or to the front (anterior) aspect of the body.

ventrocystorrhaphy (ven″tro-sis-tor′ah-fe). The stitching of a cyst, or of the bladder, to the abdominal wall.

ventrodorsad (ven″tro-dor′sad). From the ventral toward the dorsal aspect.

ventrodorsal (ven″tro-dor′sal). Pertaining to the ventral and dorsal surfaces.

ventrofixation (ven″tro-fiks-a′shun) [*ventro-* + L. *fixare* to fix]. The operation of suspending the retroplaced uterus to the abdominal wall. Cf. *hysteropexy.*

ventrohysteropexy (ven″tro-his′ter-o-pek″se). Ventrofixation of the uterus.

ventro-inguinal (ven″tro-ing′gwĭ-nal). Pertaining to the abdomen and the inguinal region.

ventrolateral (ven″tro-lat′er-al). Both ventral and lateral.

ventromedian (ven″tro-me′de-an). Both ventral and median.

ventromyel (ven″tro-mi′el) [*ventro-* + Gr. *myelos* marrow]. The anterior (ventral) portion of the spinal cord.

ventroposterior (ven″tro-pos-te′re-or). Situated on the lower hinder part of an organ.

ventroptosia (ven″trop-to′se-ah) [*ventro-* + Gr. *ptōsis* falling + *-ia*]. Gastroptosia.

ventroptosis (ven″trop-to′sis). Gastroptosia.

ventroscopy (ven-tros′ko-pe) [*ventro-* + Gr. *skopein* to examine]. Illumination of the abdominal cavity for purposes of examination.

ventrose (ven′trōs) [L. *ventrosus*]. Having a belly-like expansion.

ventrosuspension (ven″tro-sus-pen′shun). Ventrofixation.

ventrotomy (ven-trot′o-me) [*ventro-* + Gr. *tomē* a cutting]. Celiotomy.

ventrovesicofixation (ven″tro-ves″ĭ-ko-fiks-a′shun) [*ventro-* + L. *vesica* bladder + *fixatio* fastening]. The operation of suturing the uterus to the bladder and the abdominal wall.

venturimeter (ven″tu-rim′e-ter) [G. B. *Venturi* (Italian physicist, 1746–1822) + Gr. *metron* measure]. An instrument for measuring the flow of liquids, as of the blood in vessels.

venula (ven′u-lah), pl. *ven′ulae* [L., dim. of *vena*]. [N A, B N A] Any one of the small vessels that collect blood from the capillary plexuses and join to form veins. Called also *venule.* **v. macula′ris infe′rior** [N A, B N A], the inferior venule draining blood from the macula retinae. **v. macula′ris supe′rior** [N A, B N A], the superior venule draining blood from the macula retinae. **v. media′lis ret′inae** [N A], a small branch draining blood from the central region of the retina to the central retinal vein. Called also *v. retinae medialis* [B N A]. **v. nasa′lis ret′inae infe′rior** [N A, B N A], a small vein returning blood from the inferior nasal region of the retina to the central vein. **v. nasa′lis ret′inae supe′rior** [N A, B N A], a small vein returning blood from the superior nasal region of the retina to the central vein. **ven′ulae rec′tae re′nis** [N A, B N A], straight veins from the papillary part of the kidney, emptying into the arcuate veins. Called also *straight venules of kidney.* **v. ret′inae media′lis** [B N A], v. medialis retinae. **ven′ulae stella′tae re′nis** [N A], veins on the surface of the kidney that collect blood from the superficial parts of the cortex and empty into the interlobular veins. Called also *venae stellatae renis* [B N A], and *stellate venules of kidney.* **v. tempora′lis ret′inae infe′rior** [N A, B N A], a small vein returning blood from the inferior temporal region of the retina to the central vein. **v. tempora′lis ret′inae supe′rior** [N A, B N A], a small vein returning blood from the superior temporal region of the retina to the central vein.

venulae (ven′u-le) [L.]. Plural of *venula.*

venular (ven′u-lar). Pertaining to, composed of, or affecting venules.

venule (ven′ūl). Any one of the small vessels that collect blood from the capillary plexuses and join to form veins. Called also *venula* [N A]. **macular v., inferior,** venula macularis inferior. **macular v., superior,** venula macularis superior. **medial v. of retina,** venula medialis retinae. **nasal v. of retina, inferior,** venula nasalis retinae inferior. **nasal v. of retina, superior,** venula nasalis retinae superior. **stellate v's of kidney,** venulae stellatae renis. **straight v's of kidney,** venulae rectae renis. **temporal v. of retina, inferior,** venula temporalis retinae inferior. **temporal v. of retina, superior,** venula temporalis retinae superior.

Veraguth's fold (va′rah-goots) [Otto *Veraguth*, Zurich neurologist, 1870–1940]. See under *fold.*

veralba (ver-al′bah). Trade mark for preparations of protoveratrines A and B.

veratralbine (ver″ah-tral′bin). An alkaloid from veratrine, $C_{36}H_{51}O_{11}N$.

veratria (ve-ra′tre-ah). Veratrine.

veratridine (ve-rat′rĭ-din). One of the alkaloids of veratrine, $C_{37}H_{51}O_{11}N$.

veratrine (ve-ra′trin). A mixture of cevadine, veratridine, and cevine: a drastic emetocathartic.

veratroidine (ver″ah-troi′din). A crystallizable base, $C_{32}H_{53}NO_9$, from *Veratrum album* and *V. viride:* a powerful nerve stimulant and cardiac inhibitor.

Veratrum (ve-ra′trum) [L.]. A genus of poisonous liliaceous plants. **V. al′bum,** white hellebore, has an emetic, errhine, and cathartic rhizome. **V. vir′ide,** green hellebore, has a poisonous rhizome which produces vasodilatation and has been used in hypertension.

verbal (ver′bal) [L. *verbum*]. Consisting of words; pertaining to words or speech.

verbenol (ver-be′nol). A terpene alcohol, $(CH_3)_2$-$C{:}C_6H_6(OH).CH_3$, from *Boswellia carterii.*

verbenone (ver-be′nōn). A terpene ketone, $(CH_3)_2$-$C{:}C_6H_5O.CH_3$, from *Verbena triphylla.*

verbigeration (ver-bij″er-a′shun) [L. *verbigerare* to chatter]. The repetition of meaningless words and sentences.

verbomania (ver″bo-ma′ne-ah) [L. *verba* word + Gr. *mania* madness]. Morbid talkativeness.

Verco's sign (ver′kōz) [Sir Joseph Cooke *Verco*, English physician, 1851–1933]. See under *sign.*

verdigris (ver′dĭ-gris) [Fr., from *vert de Grèce* green of Greece]. A blue, hydrated, basic copper acetate, $(CH_3.COO)_2.Cu.Cu(OH)_2$; astringent.

verdohemin (ver″do-he′min). A compound analogous to hemin, in which one porphyrin ring is open.

verdohemochromogen (ver″do-he″mo-kro′mo-jen). A compound analogous to hemochromogen, in which one porphyrin ring is open.

verdohemoglobin (ver″do-he″mo-glo″bin). A compound analogous to hemoglobin, in which one porphyrin ring is open.

verdoperoxidase (ver″do-per-ok′sĭ-dās) [Fr. *vert* green + *peroxidase*]. An enzyme found in white cells of the body which may be important in defense against germs and poisons.

verdunization (ver″dun-i-za′shun) [*Verdun*, a French city besieged during World War I]. The addition of small amounts of chlorine and potassium permanganate to water for the purpose of sterilizing it.

Verga's groove, ventricle (ver′gahz) [Andrea *Verga*, Italian neurologist, 1811–1895]. See under *groove* and *ventricle*.

verge (verj). A circumference, or ring. **anal v.,** the external or distal boundary of the anal canal; the line where the walls of the anus come in contact during the normal state of apposition.

vergence (ver′jens) [L. *vergere* to be inclined]. A horizontal or vertical turning of one eye as compared with the other. Horizontal vergence may be convergence or divergence; vertical vergence may be infravergence or supravergence.

vergency (ver′jen-se). Vergence.

vergeture (ver′jet-chūr). One of the striae atrophicae cutis.

Verheyen's stars (ver-hi′enz) [Philippe *Verheyen*, Flemish anatomist, 1648–1710]. Venulae stellatae renis.

Verhoeff's operation (ver′hefz) [Frederick Herman *Verhoeff*, American ophthalmologist, born 1874]. See under *operation*.

veriloid (ver′ĭ-loid). Trade mark for a preparation of alkavervir.

verin (ve′rin). A substance, $C_{28}H_{45}NO_8$, from sabadilla.

Vermale's operation (ver-malz′) [Raymond de *Vermale*, French surgeon of the 18th century]. See under *operation*.

vermetoid (ver′mĕ-toid). Wormlike.

vermian (ver′me-an). Pertaining to the vermis of the cerebellum.

Vermicella (ver″mĭ-sel′ah) [L.]. A genus of venomous Australian serpents.

vermicidal (ver″mĭ-si′dal). Destructive to worms.

vermicide (ver′mĭ-sīd) [*vermis* + L. *caedere* to kill]. An anthelmintic drug or medicine destructive to intestinal animal parasites.

vermicular (ver-mik′u-lar) [L. *vermicularis*, from *vermis* worm]. Wormlike in shape or appearance.

vermiculation (ver-mik″u-la′shun) [L. *vermiculatio*, from *vermis* worm]. Peristaltic or wormlike movements, as of the intestine: peristalsis.

vermicule (ver′mĭ-kūl). A wormlike structure. See also *ookinete*.

vermiculose (ver-mik′u-lōs). Vermiculous.

vermiculous (ver-mik′u-lus). 1. Wormlike. 2. Infected with worms.

vermiform (ver′mĭ-form) [L. *vermiformis*, from *vermis* worm + *forma* shape]. Shaped like a worm.

vermifugal (ver-mif′u-gal) [*vermis* + L. *fugare* to put to flight]. Expelling worms or intestinal animal parasites.

vermifuge (ver′mĭ-fūj). An agent that expels worms or intestinal animal parasites; an anthelmintic.

vermilionectomy (ver-mil″yon-ek′to-me). Excision of the vermilion border of the lip, the surgically created defect being resurfaced by advancement of the undermined labial mucosa.

vermin (ver′min) [L. *vermis* worm]. An external animal parasite; animal ectoparasites collectively.

verminal (ver′mĭ-nal). Pertaining or due to worms or vermin.

vermination (ver″mĭ-na′shun) [L. *verminatio*]. Infection with worms or with other vermin.

verminosis (ver″mĭ-no′sis). Infection with worms.

verminotic (ver″mĭ-not′ik). Pertaining to or caused by infection with worms.

verminous (ver′mĭ-nus) [L. *verminosus*]. Pertaining or due to worms.

vermiphobia (ver″mĭ-fo′be-ah) [L. *vermis* worm + Gr. *phobein* to be affrighted by]. Helminthophobia.

vermis (ver′mis) [L.]. A worm or wormlike structure; often used alone to designate the vermis cerebelli. **v. cerebel′li** [N A, B N A], the median part of the cerebellum, between the two hemispheres; it comprises the lingula, lobulus centralis, culmen, declive, folium vermis, tuber vermis, pyramis, uvula, and nodulus. **inferior v.,** the inferior aspect of the vermis cerebelli, from the tuber vermis to the nodulus. **superior v.,** the superior aspect of the vermis cerebelli, from the lingula to the folium vermis.

vermix (ver′miks). Appendix vermiformis.

vermography (ver-mog′rah-fe). Roentgenography of the vermiform appendix.

vernal (ver′nal) [L. *vernalis* of the spring]. Pertaining to or occurring in the spring.

Vernes' test (vārnz) [Arthur *Vernes*, French physician, born 1879]. See under *tests*.

Verneuil's canals, disease, neuroma, operation (ver-na′ēz) [Aristide August *Verneuil*, French surgeon, 1823–1895]. See under the nouns.

vernier (ver′ne-er) [Pierre *Vernier*, French physicist, 1580–1637]. A finely graduated scale accessory to a more coarsely graduated one for measuring fractions of the divisions of the latter.

vernin (ver′nin). A pentoside of adenine found in Vicia seedlings.

vernix (ver′niks) [L.]. Varnish. **v. caseo′sa** ["cheesy varnish"], an unctuous substance composed of sebum and desquamated epithelial cells, which covers the skin of the fetus.

Vernonia anthelmintica (ver-no′ne-ah an″-thel-min′tĭ-kah). A plant called *somraj* in India: anthelmintic.

Verocay bodies (ver′o-ka) [José *Verocay*, Prague pathologist, 1876–1927]. See under *body*.

vérole (va-rōl′) [Fr.]. Syphilis. **v. nerveuse** (va-rōl′ ner-vo͞os′), neurosyphilis.

verruca (ver-rooh′kah), pl. *verru′cae* [L.]. 1. An epidermal tumor of viral origin. Called also *wart*. 2. One of the wartlike elevations developing on the endocardium in various types of endocarditis. **v. acumina′ta,** condyloma acuminatum. **v. digita′ta,** a wart with finger-like excrescences growing from its surface. **v. filifor′mis,** a wart with soft, thin, threadlike projections on its surface. **v. gla′bra,** a wart with a smooth surface. **v. necrogen′ica,** a verrucous growth, occurring usually about the knuckles, or elsewhere on the hands, of those who dissect cadavers or perform autopsies. A form of cutaneous tuberculosis, it is usually a single, hyperkeratotic dull red lesion which persists harmlessly and indefinitely, with little growth. Called also *anatomical, dissection*, or *postmortem tubercle*, or *anatomical, necrogenic, postmortem*, or *prosector's wart*. **v. perua′na, v. peruvia′na,** verruga peruana. **v. pla′na, v. pla′na juveni′lis,** a small, smooth, slightly raised wart sometimes occurring in great numbers, on the face, neck, back of the hands, wrists, and knees; seen most frequently in children, these growths occur also in adults. **v. planta′ris,** a viral epidermal tumor on the sole of the foot. **v. seborrhe′ica,** seborrheic keratosis. **v. seni′lis,** senile keratosis. **v. sim′plex,** a simple raised epidermal tumor of viral origin. **v. tuberculo′sa,** v. necrogenica. **v. vulga′ris,** a designation once given the common viral epidermal tumor of the skin.

verrucae (vĕ-roo′se) [L.]. Plural of *verruca.*

verruciform (vĕ-roo′sĭ-form) [L. *verruca* wart + *forma* form]. Resembling or shaped like a verruca, or wart.

verrucose (ver′o͝o-kōs) [L. *verrucosus*]. Warty; covered with warts, or verrucae.

verrucosis (ver″o͝o-ko′sis). A condition marked by the presence of multiple warts, or verrucae.

verrucous (ver′o͝o-kus). Verrucose.

verruga (ver-roo′gah) [Sp.]. Verruca, or wart. **v. peruana,** one of the characteristic hemangioma-like tumors or nodules which are sometimes the first manifestations of bartonellosis, or Carrion's disease.

versicolor (ver-sik′o-lor) [L. *vertere* to turn + *color* color]. Variegated; changing color.

version (ver-zhun) [L. *versio*]. Change of direction. In obstetrics, change of the polarity of the fetus with reference to the body of the mother, in order to convert an abnormal or relatively abnormal relation into a normal or relatively normal relation. **abdominal v.,** external v. **bimanual v.,** version done by combined external and internal manipulation, the cervix being open enough to admit the hand. **bipolar v.,** version done by purely external manipulation or by combined internal and external manipulation. **Braxton Hicks' v.,** Hicks' v. **cephalic v.,** version in which the fetal head is brought down into the maternal pelvis. **combined v.,** version done by both external and internal manipulation. **external v.,** manipulation of the fetal body by force applied through the abdominal wall of the mother. **Hicks' v.,** version done by combined external and internal manipulation, the cervix being dilated only enough to admit two fingers. **pelvic v.,** version done by manipulating the buttocks of the fetus. **podalic v.,** version in which the legs of the fetus are brought down into the maternal pelvis. **Potter v.,** podalic version in head presentation when the cervix is fully effaced and dilated. **spontaneous v.,** conversion of an abnormal position of the fetus into a normal or relatively normal one, occurring without the aid of manipulation. **Wigand's v.** (external), conversion of a transverse presentation into a cephalic presentation. **Wright's v.,** cephalic version in transverse presentation when the cervix is completely dilated, or nearly so.

vertebra (ver′te-brah), pl. *ver′tebrae* [L.]. Any one of the thirty-three bones of the spinal column (columna vertebralis), comprising the seven *cervical,* twelve *thoracic,* five *lumbar,* five *sacral,* and four *coccygeal* vertebrae. **abdominal vertebrae,** vertebrae lumbales. **basilar v.,** the lowest or last of the lumbar vertebrae. **caudal vertebrae, caudate vertebrae,** vertebrae coccygeae. **cervical vertebrae, ver′tebrae cervica′les** [N A, B N A], the upper seven vertebrae, constituting the skeleton of the neck. **ver′tebrae coccyg′eae** [N A, B N A], **coccygeal vertebrae,** the lowest segments of the vertebral column, comprising three to five rudimentary vertebrae which form the coccyx. **ver′tebrae col′li,** vertebrae cervicales. **cranial v.,** the segments of the skull and facial bones, by some regarded as modified vertebrae. **v. denta′ta,** the second cervical vertebra, or axis. **dorsal vertebrae,** vertebrae thoracicae. **false vertebrae,** the sacral and coccygeal vertebrae. **ver′tebrae lumba′les** [N A, B N A], **lumbar vertebrae,** the five vertebrae between the thoracic vertebrae and the sacrum. **v. mag′num,** os sacrum. **odontoid v.,** the second cervical vertebra, or axis. **v. pla′na,** a condition of spondylitis in which the body of the vertebra is reduced to a sclerotic disk. **v. prom′inens** [N A, B N A], **prominent v.,** the seventh cervical vertebra; so called because of the length of its spinous process. **sacral vertebrae, ver′tebrae sacra′les** [N A, B N A], the vertebrae below the lumbar vertebrae (usually five in number), which normally fuse to form the sacrum. **sternal v.,** sternebra. **terminal v., great,** os sacrum. **ver′tebrae thoraca′les** [B N A], **thoracic vertebrae,** vertebrae thoracicae. **ver′tebrae thora′cicae** [N A], the vertebrae, usually twelve in number, situated between the cervical and the lumbar

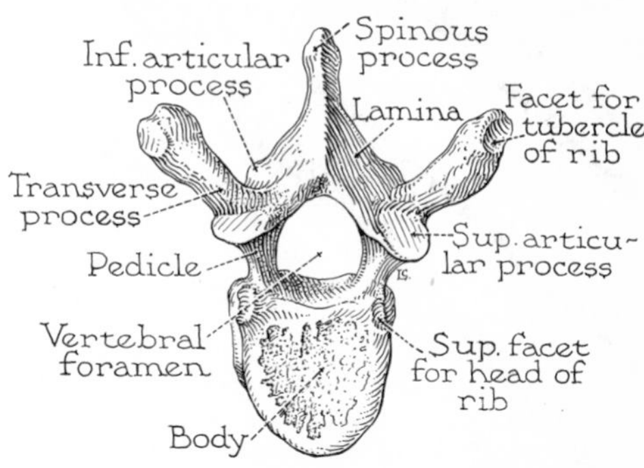

Typical (sixth) thoracic vertebra viewed from above. (King & Showers.)

vertebrae, giving attachment to the ribs and forming part of the posterior wall of the thorax. Called also *vertebrae thoracales* [B N A], and *thoracic vertebrae.* **tricuspid v.,** the sixth cervical vertebra of quadrupeds. **true vertebrae,** the vertebrae that normally remain unfused throughout life, that is, the cervical, thoracic, and lumbar vertebrae.

vertebrae (ver′te-bre) [L.]. Plural of *vertebra.*

vertebral (ver′te-bral) [L. *vertebralis*]. Of or pertaining to a vertebra.

vertebrarium (ver″te-bra′re-um) [L.]. The vertebral column.

vertebrarterial (ver″te-brar-te′re-al). Pertaining to the vertebral artery.

Vertebrata (ver″te-bra′tah). A division of the animal kingdom comprising all animals that have a vertebral column, and including mammals, birds, reptiles, and fishes.

vertebrate (ver′te-brāt) [L. *vertebratus*]. 1. Having a vertebral column. 2. An animal having a vertebral column.

vertebrated (ver′te-brāt″ed). Made up of joints resembling the vertebrae.

vertebrectomy (ver″te-brek′to-me) [*vertebro-* + Gr. *ektomē* excision]. Excision of a vertebra.

vertebro- (ver′te-bro) [L. *vertebra,* from *vertere* to turn]. Combining form denoting relationship to a vertebra, or to the vertebral column.

vertebro-arterial (ver″te-bro-ar-te′re-al). Vertebrarterial.

vertebrochondral (ver″te-bro-kon′dral). Pertaining to a vertebra and a costal cartilage.

vertebrocostal (ver″te-bro-kos′tal) [*vertebro-* + L. *costa* rib]. Pertaining to a vertebra and a rib.

vertebrodidymus (ver″te-bro-did′ĭ-mus) [*vertebro-* + Gr. *didymos* twin]. A twin monster united in the region of the spinal column.

vertebrodymus (ver″te-brod′ĭ-mus). Vertebrodidymus.

vertebrofemoral (ver″te-bro-fem′or-al). Relating to the vertebrae and the femur.

vertebro-iliac (ver″te-bro-il′e-ak). Pertaining to the vertebrae and the ilium.

vertebromammary (ver″te-bro-mam′er-e). Pertaining to or extending between the vertebral and mammary aspects of the chest.

vertebrosacral (ver″te-bro-sa′kral). Pertaining to the vertebrae and the sacrum.

vertebrosternal (ver″te-bro-ster′nal). Pertaining to the vertebrae and the sternum.

vertex (ver′teks), pl. *ver′tices* [L.]. 1. A summit or top; used as a general term in anatomical nomenclature. Sometimes used alone to designate the top of the head (*vertex cranii*). 2. Vortex. **v. of bony cranium,** v. cranii ossei. **v. cor′dis,** vortex cordis. **v. of cornea, v. cor′neae** [N A, B N A], the central, thinner portion of the cornea. **v. cra′nii** [N A, B N A], the top or crown of the head. **v. cra′nii os′sei** [N A, B N A], the highest point of the skull; although its position varies somewhat in different skulls, it is generally located on the sagittal suture, usually near the midpoint of the suture. Called also *v. of bony cranium.* **v. of urinary bladder, v. vesi′cae urina′riae** [B N A], apex vesicae urinariae.

vertical (ver-tĭ-kal). 1. Perpendicular to the plane of the horizon. 2. Relating to the vertex.

verticalis (ver″tĭ-ka′lis) [L.]. Vertical, or perpendicular to the plane of the horizon; in official anatomical nomenclature the term is used in reference to structures with the body in the anatomical, that is, the upright, position.

verticillate (ver-tis′ĭ-lāt) [L. *vertex* a whorl]. Arranged in the form of a whorl.

Verticillium (ver″tĭ-sil′e-um). A genus of mold. **V. gra′phii,** a mold sometimes occurring in otitis externa.

verticine (ver′tĭ-sin). A crystalline alkaloid, $C_{19}H_{33}O_2N$, from *Fritillaria verticillata.*

verticomental (ver″tĭ-ko-men′tal). Pertaining to the vertex and the chin.

vertiginous (ver-tij′ĭ-nus) [L. *vertiginosus*]. Pertaining to or affected with vertigo.

vertigo (ver′tĭ-go, ver-ti′go) [L. *vertigo*]. A hallucination of movement; a sensation as if the external world were revolving around the patient (*objective vertigo*) or as if he himself were revolving in space (*subjective vertigo*). The term is sometimes erroneously used as a synonym for dizziness. Vertigo may result from disease of the inner ear (Meniere's syndrome), from cardiac, gastric, or ocular disorders, from some peripheral irritations (as laryngeal vertigo), as a precursor of an epileptic fit, in hysteria, from toxemias (as Bright's disease), from organic brain disease, and from unrecognized causes (essential vertigo). **v. ab au′re lae′so,** Meniere's syndrome. **v. ab stom′acho lae′so,** stomachal v. **angiopathic v.,** vertigo due to arteriosclerosis of the cerebral vessels. **apoplectic v.,** scotodinia. **arteriosclerotic v.,** angiopathic v. **auditory v., aural v.,** Meniere's syndrome. **cardiac v.,** vertigo due to some chronic disease of the heart. **cardiovascular v.,** vertigo due to sclerosis of the blood vessels and heart. **cerebral v.,** that which is due to some brain disease. **encephalic v.,** a sensation of movement of tissues within the skull, as of the brain turning over and over, or round and round. **endemic paralytic v.,** Gerlier's disease. **epidemic v.,** an epidemic condition characterized chiefly by vertigo but with some nausea and vomiting. See *epidemic nausea,* under *nausea.* **epileptic v.,** that which attends or follows an epileptic attack. **essential v.,** a vertigo, often severe, but of no discoverable cause; probably due to some disease or lesion in a brain center. **galvanic v.,** voltaic v. **gastric v.,** a form associated with disease or disorder of the stomach. **height v.,** dizziness felt on looking down from a high location. **horizontal v.,** that which comes on when a person lies down. **hysterical v.,** vertigo associated with hysterical symptoms, often of a bizarre form. **labyrinthine v.,** a form associated with disease of the labyrinth of the ear. **laryngeal v.,** tussive syncope. **lateral v.,** that which is caused by rapidly passing a row of similar objects, as a fence or series of pillars. **lithemic v.,** that which is associated with gout and lithemia. **mechanical v.,** vertigo due to long-continued turning or vibration of the body, as in seasickness. **neurasthenic v.,** a subjective form of vertiginous sensation associated with neurasthenia. **nocturnal v.,** a sensation of falling occurring as the subject is going to sleep. **objective v.,** a form in which the objects seen by the patient seem to be moving around him. **ocular v.,** a form due to eye disease, especially to paralysis of or lack of balance in the eye muscles. **oleander v.,** a variety said to be caused by the administration of oleander. **organic v.,** vertigo which is due to brain disease or to locomotor ataxia. **paralyzing v.,** Gerlier's disease. **peripheral v.,** vertigo due to irritation in some part distant from the brain. **riders' v.,** a form of mechanical vertigo produced by riding in cars. **rotary v., rotatory v.,** vertigo in which there is a definite feeling of rotation. **sham-movement v.,** vertigo attended by a sensation as if objects were circling around the body. **smokers' v.,** vertigo occurring as a result of excessive smoking. **special sense v.,** aural or ocular vertigo. **stomachal v.,** vertigo due to disorder of the digestive system. **subjective v.,** that in which the patient seems to himself to be turning round and round. **systematic v.,** rotary v. **tenebric v.,** scotodinia. **toxemic v., toxic v.,** a form of vertigo which results from poisoning, alcoholism, uremia, or lithemia. **vertical v.,** that which is caused by looking up or down at a distant object. **villous v.,** that which is caused by a functional derangement of the liver. **voltaic v.,** an inclination of the head toward the shoulder on the side of the positive pole when a galvanic current is applied to the vestibular fibers of the eighth nerve.

vertigraphy (ver-tig′rah-fe) [L. *vertigo* a whirling + Gr. *graphein* to write]. See *body section roentgenography,* under *roentgenography.*

verumontanitis (ve″ru-mon″tah-ni′tis). Inflammation of the verumontanum (colliculus seminalis).

verumontanum (ve″ru-mon-ta′num) [L. "mountain ridge"]. Colliculus seminalis.

Ves. Abbreviation for L. *vesi′ca,* the bladder.

vesalian (ve-sa′le-an). Named in honor of Andreas *Vesalius.*

vesalianum (ve-sa″le-a′num) [Andreas *Vesalius*]. A name applied to several sesamoid bones: one on the outer border of the foot between the cuboid and fifth metatarsal bone, and one (sometimes more) in the tendon of origin of the gastrocnemius muscle.

Vesalius (ve-sa′le-us), Andreas (1514–1564). Flemish anatomist and physician, who was the most eminent anatomist of the 16th century. His great work on anatomy (1543), entitled *De humani corporis fabrica libri septem* (Seven Books on the Structure of the Human Body), is said to be "one of the most remarkable known to science," and "one of the most noble and magnificent volumes in the history of printing" (Saunders & O'Malley).

vesania (ve-sa′ne-ah) [L.]. An old term for full-fledged mental disorder, marked by the four stages of mania, melancholia, paranoia, and dementia. Cf. *vecordia.*

vesanic (ve-san′ik). Pertaining to or exhibiting vesania.

Vesic. Abbreviation for L. *vesic′ula, vesicato′rium,* a blister.

vesica (ve-si′kah), pl. *vesi′cae* [L.]. A membranous sac or receptacle for a secretion; used as a general term in anatomical nomenclature. Called also *bladder.* **v. fel′lea** [N A, B N A], the pear-shaped reservoir for the bile on the posteroinferior surface of the lines between the right and quadrate lobes. Called also *gallbladder.* **v. prostat′ica,** utriculus prostaticus. **v. urina′ria** [N A, B N A], the musculomembranous sac, situated in the anterior part of the pelvic cavity, that serves as a reservoir for urine. Called also *urinary bladder.*

vesicae (ve-si′ke) [L.]. Plural of *vesica.*

vesical (ves′ĭ-kal). Pertaining to the bladder.

vesicant (ves′ĭ-kant) [L. *vesica* blister]. 1. Causing blisters; blistering. 2. A blistering drug or agent.

vesication (ves″ĭ-ka′shun). 1. The process of blistering. 2. A blistered spot or surface.

vesicatory (ves′ĭ-kah-tor″e) [L. *vesicare* to blister]. Vesicant.

vesicle (ves′ĭ-k'l) [L. *vesicula*, dim. of *vesica* bladder]. 1. A small bladder or sac containing liquid. Called also *vesicula*. 2. A small blister; a small circumscribed elevation of the epidermis containing a serous liquid. **acoustic v.**, auditory v. **air v.**, an air cell, vacuole or saccule of the lung tissue. **allantoic v.**, the internal hollow portion of the allantois. **amniocardiac v's**, fissures in the mesoderm of the early embryo representing the paired primordia of the pericardial sac and the heart. **archoplasmic v.**, a sac developed from the attraction sphere of a spermatid and growing into the sheath of the tail of the spermatozoon. **Ascherson's v's**, small vesicles formed by shaking together oil and liquid albumin. They consist of drops of oil enclosed in a layer of albumin. **auditory v.**, a detached ovoid sac formed by closure of the auditory pit, in embryonic development of the internal ear. **Baer's v.**, the vesicular ovarian follicle (graafian follicle) of the ovary with its contained ovum. **blastodermic v.**, the blastocyst. **brain v's**, the five divisions of the closed neural tube in the developing embryo, including, in craniocaudal sequence, the telencephalon, diencephalon, mesencephalon, metencephalon, and myelencephalon. **brain v's, primary**, the three earliest subdivisions of the embryonic neural tube, including the prosencephalon, mesencephalon, and rhombencephalon. **brain v's, secondary**, the four brain vesicles formed by specialization of the prosencephalon (the telencephalon and diencephalon) and of the rhombencephalon (the metencephalon and myelencephalon) in later embryonic development. **cephalic v's, cerebral v's**, brain v's. **cervical v.**, a temporary sac in the cervical region of the embryo formed by the closing off of the cervical sinus. **chorionic v.**, the mammalian chorion. **compound v.**, a vesicle on the skin containing more than one chamber or compartment. **encephalic v's**, brain v's. **germinal v.**, the nucleus of an unripe ovum. **graafian v's**, folliculi ovarici vesiculosi. **lens v.**, a vesicle formed from the lens pit of the embryo and developing into the crystalline lens. Called also *lens sac*. **Malpighi's v's**, alveoli pulmonis. **Naboth's v's**, nabothian follicles. **ocular v.**, vesicula ophthalmica. **olfactory v.**, the vesicle in the embryo which later develops into the olfactory bulb and tract. **ophthalmic v.**, **optic v.**, vesicula ophthalmica. **otic v.**, auditory v. **pituitary v.**, Rathke's pouch. **prostatic v.**, utriculus prostaticus. **pulmonary v's**, alveoli pulmonis. **Purkinje's v.**, germinal v. **seminal v.**, vesicula seminalis. **sense v.**, the vesicular primordium of a sense organ in the embryo. **simple v.**, a vesicle on the skin having a single chamber or compartment. **spermatic v.**, **false**, utriculus prostaticus. **umbilical v.**, that part of the yolk sac which is outside the body of the embryo, being joined with it by means of the umbilical or vitelline duct.

vesico- (ves′ĭ-ko) [L. *vesica* bladder]. Combining form denoting relationship to the bladder, or to a blister.

vesicoabdominal (ves″ĭ-ko-ab-dom′ĭ-nal). Pertaining to the urinary bladder and abdomen, or communicating with the bladder and an abdominal viscus, as a vesicoabdominal fistula.

vesicocavernous (ves″ĭ-ko-kav′er-nus). Both vesicular and cavernous.

vesicocele (ves′ĭ-ko-sēl) [*vesico-* + Gr. *kēlē* hernia]. Hernial protrusion of the bladder.

vesicocervical (ves″ĭ-ko-ser′vĭ-kal) [*vesico-* + L. *cervix* neck]. Pertaining to the urinary bladder and the cervix uteri, or communicating with the bladder and the cervical canal, as a vesicocervical fistula.

vesicoclysis (ves″ĭ-kok′lĭ-sis) [*vesico-* + Gr. *klysis* washing]. The injection of a fluid into the urinary bladder.

vesicocolonic (ves″ĭ-ko-ko-lon′ik). Pertaining to or communicating with the urinary bladder and colon, as a vesicocolonic fistula.

vesicoenteric (ves″ĭ-ko-en-ter′ik). Vesicointestinal.

vesicofixation (ves″ĭ-ko-fiks-a′shun). 1. The stitching of the uterus to the urinary bladder. 2. The surgical fixation of the urinary bladder; cystopexy.

vesicointestinal (ves″ĭ-ko-in-tes′tĭ-nal). Pertaining to or communicating with the urinary bladder and intestine, as a vesicointestinal fistula.

vesicoperineal (ves″ĭ-ko-per″ĭ-ne′al). Pertaining to or communicating with the urinary bladder and perineum, as a vesicoperineal fistula.

vesicoprostatic (ves″ĭ-ko-pros-tat′ik). Pertaining to the urinary bladder and the prostate.

vesicopubic (ves″ĭ-ko-pu′bik). Pertaining to the urinary bladder and the pubes.

vesicopustule (ves″ĭ-ko-pus′tūl). A vesicle which is developing into a pustule.

vesicorectal (ves″ĭ-ko-rek′tal). Pertaining to the urinary bladder and the rectum.

vesicorenal (ves″ĭ-ko-re′nal). Pertaining to the urinary bladder and the kidney.

vesicosigmoid (ves″ĭ-ko-sig′moid). Pertaining to the urinary bladder and sigmoid flexure.

vesicosigmoidostomy (ves″ĭ-ko-sig″moi-dos′to-me) [L. *vesica* bladder + *sigmoid* + Gr. *stomoun* to provide with an opening or mouth]. The operation of making a permanent communication between the urinary bladder and sigmoid flexure.

vesicospinal (ves″ĭ-ko-spi′nal). Pertaining to the urinary bladder and the spine.

vesicotomy (ves″ĭ-kot′o-me) [L. *vesica* bladder + Gr. *tomē* a cutting]. Incision of the urinary bladder; cystotomy.

vesicoumbilical (ves″ĭ-ko-um-bil′ĭ-kal). Pertaining to the umbilicus and the urinary bladder.

vesicourachal (ves″ĭ-ko-u′rah-kal). Pertaining to the urinary bladder and the urachus.

vesicoureteral (ves″ĭ-ko-u-re′ter-al). Pertaining to or communicating with the urinary bladder and the ureter.

vesicourethral (ves″ĭ-ko-u-re′thral). Pertaining to or communicating with the urinary bladder and the urethra.

vesicouterine (ves″ĭ-ko-u′ter-in). Pertaining to or communicating with the urinary bladder and the uterus.

vesicouterovaginal (ves″ĭ-ko-u″ter-o-vaj′ĭ-nal). Pertaining to or communicating with the urinary bladder, uterus, and vagina.

vesicovaginal (ves″ĭ-ko-vaj′ĭ-nal). Pertaining to or communicating with the urinary bladder and vagina.

vesicovaginorectal (ves″ĭ-ko-vaj″ĭ-no-rek′tal). Pertaining to or communicating with the urinary bladder, vagina, and rectum.

vesicula (ve-sik′u-lah), pl. *vesic′ulae* [L., dim. of *vesica*]. A small bladder or sac containing liquid; used as a general term in anatomical nomenclature. Called also *vesicle*. **v. bi′lis, v. fel′lea**, vesica fellea. **v. germinati′va**, germinal vesicle. **vesic′ulae graafia′nae**, folliculi ovarici vesiculosi. **vesic′ulae nabo′thi**, nabothian follices. **v. ophthal′mica** [N A, B N A], an evagination developing on either side of the forebrain of the early embryo, from which the percipient parts of the eye are formed. Called also *optic vesicle*. **v. prolig′era**, a secondary or daughter cyst produced by budding from a cysticercus cyst. **v. prostat′ica**, utriculus prostaticus. **vesic′ulae pulmona′les**, alveoli pulmonis. **v. semina′lis** [N A, B N A], either of the paired, sacculated pouches attached to the posterior part of the urinary bladder; the duct of each joins the ipsilateral ductus deferens to form the ejaculatory duct. Called also *seminal vesicle.* **v. sero'sa,** chorion.

vesiculae (ve-sik'u-le) [L.]. Plural of *vesicula.*

vesicular (ve-sik'u-lar) [L. *vesicula* a little bladder]. 1. Composed of or relating to small, saclike bodies. 2. Pertaining to or made up of vesicles on the skin.

vesiculase (ve-sik'u-lās). A ferment from the prostate gland which coagulates semen.

vesiculated (ve-sik'u-lāt"ed). Marked by the presence of vesicles.

vesiculation (ve-sik"u-la'shun). The presence or formation of vesicles.

vesiculectomy (ve-sik"u-lek'to-me) [*vesicle* + Gr. *ektomē* excision]. Excision of a vesicle, especially the seminal vesicle.

vesiculiform (ve-sik'u-lĭ-form) [*vesicle* + L. *forma* form]. Shaped like a vesicle.

vesiculitis (ve-sik"u-li'tis). Inflammation of a vesicle, especially of a seminal vesicle. **seminal v.,** inflammation of a seminal vesicle.

vesiculobronchial (ve-sik"u-lo-brong'ke-al). Both vesicular and bronchial; bronchovesicular.

vesiculocavernous (ve-sik"u-lo-kav'er-nus). Both vesicular and cavernous.

vesiculogram (ve-sik'u-lo-gram). A roentgenogram of the seminal vesicles.

vesiculography (ve-sik"u-log'rah-fe). Roentgenography of the seminal vesicles.

vesiculopapular (ve-sik"u-lo-pap'u-lar). Pertaining to or characterized by vesicles and papules.

vesiculopustular (ve-sik"u-lo-pus'tu-lar). Consisting of or pertaining to vesicles and pustules.

vesiculose (ve-sik'u-lōs). Vesicular.

vesiculotomy (ve-sik"u-lot'o-me) [*vesicle* + Gr. *tomē* a cutting]. Incision of a vesicle. **seminal v.,** the operation of exposing and opening the seminal vesicles.

vesiculotubular (ve-sik"u-lo-tu'bu-lar). Having both a vesicular and a tubular quality.

vesiculotympanic (ve-sik"u-lo-tim-pan'ik). Having both a vesicular and tympanic quality.

vesiglandin (ves"ĭ-glan'din). A substance similar to prostaglandin but found in monkeys.

Vespa crabro (ves'pah kra'bro). A common wasp of Europe, from which a homeopathic preparation is derived.

vespajus (ves-pa'jus). Suppurative inflammation of the hairy part of the scalp.

vesperal (ves'per-al) [L. *vespera* evening]. Pertaining to or occurring in the evening.

vesprin (ves'prin). Trade mark for preparations of triflupromazine.

vessel (ves'el). Any channel for carrying a fluid, such as the blood or lymph. Called also *vas.* **absorbent v's,** lymphatic vessels. **afferent v. of glomerulus,** vas afferens glomeruli. **afferent v's of lymph node,** vasa afferentia nodi lymphatici. **anastomotic v.,** vas anastomoticum. **arterioluminal v's,** small branches of coronary arterioles that lie near the endocardium, and after a short course open directly into the lumen of the heart. **arteriosinusoidal v's,** small branches of coronary arterioles that soon break up into sinusoids that lie between bundles or individual muscle fibers of the heart. **bile v.,** one of the vessels in the liver which conduct bile. **blood v.,** one of the vessels conveying the blood, and comprising the arteries, capillaries, and veins. **chyliferous v's,** lymphatic vessels transporting chyle from the intestinal villi to the thoracic duct. **collateral v.** 1. A vessel that parallels another vessel, nerve, or other structure (vas collaterale [N A]). 2. A vessel important in establishing and maintaining a collateral circulation. **efferent v. of glomerulus,** vas efferens glomeruli. **efferent v's of lymph node,** vasa efferentia nodi lymphatici. **hemorrhoidal v's,** veins of the rectum which have become dilated and swollen. **Jungbluth's v's,** vasa propria of Jungbluth. **lacteal v's,** lymphatic capillaries in the villi of the small intestine, which take up emulsified fat (chyle) from the intestinal contents. **lymphatic v's,** the capillaries, collecting vessels, and trunks that collect lymph from the tissues and carry it to the blood stream. Called also *vasa lymphatica* [N A]. **lymphatic v's, deep,** vasa lymphatica profunda. **lymphatic v's, superficial,** vasa lymphatica superficialia. **nutrient v's,** vessels that supply nutritive elements to special tissues, such as arteries entering the substance of bone, or supplying walls of the blood vessels themselves.

vessicnon, vessignon (ves'ik-non, ves"ēn-yaw) [Fr.]. A tumor within the synovial membrane of a joint, especially of the hock of a horse. Called also *wind gall.*

vestibula (ves-tib'u-lah) [L.]. Plural of *vestibulum.*

vestibular (ves-tib'u-lar). Pertaining to a vestibule.

vestibule (ves'tĭ-būl). A space or cavity at the entrance to a canal. Called also *vestibulum* [N A]. **v. of aorta,** a small space within the left ventricle at the root of the aorta. **buccal v.,** that portion of the vestibule of the mouth which lies between the cheeks and the teeth and gingivae, or the residual alveolar ridges. **v. of ear,** an oval cavity in the middle of the bony labyrinth. See *vestibulum auris* [N A]. **Gibson's v.,** v. of aorta. **labial v.,** that portion of the vestibule of the mouth which lies between the lips and the teeth and gingivae, or residual alveolar ridges. **v. of larynx,** vestibulum laryngis. **v. of mouth,** that portion of the oral cavity bounded on the one side by the teeth and gingivae, or the residual alveolar ridges, and on the other side by the lips (*labial v.*) and cheeks (*buccal v.*). Called also *vestibulum oris* [N A]. **v. of nose,** vestibulum nasi. **v. of omental bursa,** vestibulum bursae omentalis. **v. of pharynx,** the fauces, or the oropharynx. **Sibson's v.,** v. of aorta. **v. of vagina, v. of vulva,** vestibulum vaginae.

vestibuloplasty (ves-tib'u-lo-plas"te). The surgical modification of the gingival–mucous membrane relationships in the vestibule of the mouth, including deepening of the vestibular trough, repositioning of the frenum or muscle attachments, and broadening of the zone of attached gingiva, after periodontal treatment.

vestibulotomy (ves-tib"u-lot'o-me) [*vestibule* + Gr. *tomē* a cutting]. Surgical opening of the vestibule of the inner ear.

vestibulo-urethral (ves-tib"u-lo-u-re'thral). Pertaining to the vestibulum vaginae and to the urethra.

vestibulum (ves-tib'u-lum), pl. *vestib'ula* [L.]. A space or cavity at the entrance to a canal; used as a general term in anatomical nomenclature. Called also *vestibule.* **v. au'ris** [N A, B N A], an oval cavity in the middle of the bony labyrinth, communicating in front with the cochlea and behind with the semicircular canals, and containing the sacculus and utriculus. Called also *vestibule of ear.* **v. bur'sae omenta'lis** [N A, B N A], that part of the omental bursa dorsal to the lesser omentum and adjacent to the epiploic foramen. Called also *vestibule of omental bursa.* **v. glot'tidis,** v. laryngis. **v. laryn'gis** [N A, B N A], the portion of the laryngeal cavity above the vestibular folds. Called also *vestibule of larynx.* **v. na'si** [N A, B N A], the anterior part of the nasal cavity situated just inferior to the nares and limited posteriorly by the limen nasi. Called also *vestibule of nose.* **v. o'ris** [N A, B N A], the part of the oral cavity exterior to the teeth. See *vestibule of mouth.* **v. vagi'nae** [N A, B N A], the space between the labia minora into which the urethra and vagina open. Called also *vestibule of vagina.*

vestige (ves'tij). The remnant of a structure which functioned in a previous stage of species or individual development. Called also *vestigium.* **coccygeal v.,** the remnant of the caudal end of the neural tube. **v. of vaginal process,** vestigium processus vaginalis.

vestigia (ves-tij′e-ah) [L.]. Plural of *vestigium.*

vestigial (ves-tij′e-al). Of the nature of a vestige, trace, or relic; rudimentary.

vestigium (ves-tij′e-um), pl. *vestig′ia* [L. "a trace"]. The remnant of a structure which functioned in a previous stage of species or individual development; used in N A to designate the degenerating remains of any structure which served as a functioning entity in the embryo or fetus. Called also *vestige.* **v. proces′sus vagina′lis** [N A], a band of connective tissue in the spermatic cord which is that vestige of the processus vaginalis. Called also *rudimentum processus vaginalis* [B N A], and *vestige of vaginal process.*

vesuvin (ve-su′vin). Bismarck brown.

veta (va′tah) [Sp.]. Mountain sickness of the Andes.

veterinarian (vet″er-ĭ-nar′e-an). One who practices veterinary medicine.

veterinary (vet′er-ĭ-nar″e) [L. *veterinarius*]. 1. Pertaining to domestic animals and their diseases. 2. A veterinarian.

V.F. Abbreviation for *vocal fremitus.*

V.f. Abbreviation for *field of vision.*

VIA. Abbreviation for *virus inactivating agent,* an agent present in the serous secretion of the nose which inactivates the influenza and certain other viruses.

via (vi′ah), pl. *vi′ae* [L.]. A way or passage. **vi′ae natura′les,** the natural passages of the body. **pri′mae vi′ae,** canalis alimentarius. **secun′dae vi′ae,** the lacteals and blood vessels.

viability (vi″ah-bil′ĭ-te). Ability to live after birth.

viable (vi′ah-b′l). Capable of living; especially said of a fetus that has reached such a stage of development that it can live outside of the uterus.

viadril (vi′ah-dril). Trade mark for a preparation of hydroxydione sodium.

viae (vi′e) [L.]. Plural of *via.*

vial (vi′al) [Gr. *phialē*]. A small bottle.

vib. Abbreviation for *vibration.*

vibesate (vi′bĕ-sāt). A modified polyvinyl plastic applied topically as a spray, to form an occlusive dressing for surgical wounds and other surface lesions.

vibex (vi′beks), pl. *vibi′ces* [L. *vibix* mark of a blow]. A narrow linear mark or streak; a linear subcutaneous effusion of blood.

vibices (vĭ-bi′sēz) [L.]. Plural of *vibex.*

vibratile (vi′brah-til) [L. *vibratilis*]. Having an oscillatory motion; swaying or moving to and fro.

vibration (vi-bra′shun) [L. *vibratio,* from *vibrare* to shake]. 1. A rapid movement to and fro; oscillation. 2. The shaking of the body as a therapeutic measure. 3. A form of massage. **photoelectric v.,** a change in the position of the visual cells, and a series of photo-electric movements in the rods and cones under the influence of light.

vibrative (vib′rah-tiv). A consonantal sound like that of *r,* produced by so forcing the breath that the margins of a narrow portion of the respiratory canal are made to vibrate, the nasal cavity being shut off.

vibratode (vi′brah-tōd). The instrument or appliance at the end of a vibratory appliance by which the vibrations are applied to the body.

vibrator (vi′bra-tor). An instrument used in the mechanical treatment of disease.

vibratory (vi′brah-tor″e) [L. *vibratorius*]. Vibrating or causing vibration.

Vibrio (vib′re-o). A genus of microorganisms of the family Spirillaceae, suborder Pseudomonadineae, order Pseudomonadales, made up of short, slightly curved, actively motile gram-negative rods, occurring singly and occasionally found end-to-end. The 34 species described include the cholera and El Tor vibrios pathogenic for man, agents of specific disease in lower animals, and paracholera or cholera-like water vibrios (non-agglutinating, or NAG, vibrios). See also *vibrio.* **V. chol′erae, V. chol′erae-asiat′icae,** *V. comma.* **V. co′li,** the etiologic agent of swine dysentery. **V. com′ma,** the etiologic agent of Asiatic cholera in man; characterized as non-hemolytic (Greig test) and the somatic antigen of vibrio O group I. It may occur in one of three serological types, the distribution of which has no epidemiological significance. **V. danu′bicus.** See *paracholera vibrios.* **V. fe′tus,** the etiologic agent of abortion in pregnant cattle, sheep, and goats, and of an essentially symptomless infection in the males; not pathogenic for man. **V. fink′leri,** *V. proteus.* **V. ghin′da.** See *paracholera vibrios.* **V. jeju′ni,** the etiologic agent of a diarrheal disease in cows and calves. **V. leonar′dii,** a species causing disease in insects, such as the wax moth and the European corn borer. **V. massau′ah.** See *paracholera vibrios.* **V. metchniko′vii,** a microorganism pathogenic for chickens, pigeons, and other animals, producing an epidemic, cholera-like disease. **V. ni′ger,** a species found frequently in man in certain pathologic conditions, such as purulent otitis, mastoiditis, or pulmonary gangrene. **V. phosphores′cens,** a phosphorescent microorganism isolated from the intestinal contents of patients with cholera and other gastrointestinal infections. **V. pis′cium,** the etiologic agent of an epidemic disease of carp and other fish. **V. pro′teus,** a microorganism isolated from the feces of patients with a mild diarrheal disease. **V. sep′ticus.** 1. *Vibrio comma.* 2. *Clostridium septicum.* **V. tyrog′enus,** a curved, rod-shaped organism, somewhat smaller and more slender than *V. comma,* isolated from cheese.

vibrio (vib′re-o), pl. *vib′rios* or *vibrio′nes.* An organism of the genus Vibrio, or other spiral motile organism. **Celebes v.,** an El Tor vibrio which is immunologically identical with the cholera vibrio, and is the cause of choleriform enteritis. **cholera v.,** the etiologic agent of classic (Asiatic) cholera, *Vibrio comma.* **El Tor v's,** cholera-like vibrios first isolated at the Tor Quarantine Station from man; some are identical immunologically with the cholera vibrio but are differentiated as hemolytic by the Greig test, and are prevalent in the Western Pacific area where they produce endemic and epidemic cholera-like disease. **NAG v's, non-agglutinating v's,** non-pathogenic paracholera vibrios, unrelated to the cholera vibrio O antigenic group. **paracholera v's,** microorganisms closely similar to *Vibrio comma,* but differing from it immunologically and having variable pathogenic properties. Many such organisms isolated from water and from the feces of individuals with mild diarrheal disease have been designated by the name of the place of their discovery, as *V. danu′bicus, V. ghin′da,* and *V. massau′ah.*

vibriocidal (vib″re-o-si′dal). Destructive to organisms of the genus Vibrio, especially *V. comma.*

vibrion (ve″bre-on′) [Fr.]. A vibrio, or spiral motile organism. **v. septique** (ve″bre-on′ sep-tēk′), *Clostridium septicum.*

vibriones (vib″re-o′nēz). Plural of *vibrio.*

vibrissa (vi-bris′sah), pl. *vibris′sae* [L.]. 1. A long coarse hair, such as those occurring about the nose (muzzle) of an animal, as of the dog or cat. 2. (pl. **vibris′sae** [N A, B N A]) The hairs growing in the vestibular region of the nasal cavity.

vibrissae (vi-bris′se) [L.]. Plural of *vibrissa.*

vibrocardiogram (vi″bro-kar′de-o-gram). A tracing of the vibrations of the heart sounds made by an apparatus consisting of a microphone actuating a cathode ray.

vibrolode (vi′bro-lōd). Vibratode.

vibromasseur (vib″ro-mah-sūr′) [Fr.]. An instrument used in vibratory massage of the ear.

vibrometer (vi-brom′e-ter)) [L. *vibrare* to quiver + *metrum* measure]. A device used in the treatment of deafness due to deposits of plastic material or inspissated mucus: it acts by producing vibrations which tend to break up adhesions.

vibrophone (vib′ro-fōn) [L. *vibrare* to quiver + Gr. *phōne* sound]. An instrument similar to a vibrometer, and used for the same purpose.

vibrotherapeutics (vi″bro-ther″ah-pu′tiks) [L. *vibrare* to shake + *therapeutics*]. The therapeutic use of vibratory appliances.

Viburnum (vi-bur′num) [L.]. A genus of caprifoliaceous trees and shrubs. **V. op′ulus,** or cranberry tree, the dried bark of which has been used as an antispasmodic and uterine sedative. **V. prunifo′lium,** black haw, the dried bark of the root or stem of which has been used as a uterine sedative.

vicarious (vi-kar′e-us) [L. *vicarius*]. Acting in the place of another or of something else; occurring in an abnormal situation.

vice (vis) [L. *vitium*]. 1. A blemish, defect, or imperfection. 2. Depravity; immorality.

vicho (ve′cho). A vernacular Peruvian name for dysentery, the protrusion of the rectum being attributed to the presence of an insect (vicho).

Vicia (vish′e-ah). A genus of herbs including the vetch and broad bean. **V. fa′ba (fa′va),** a species whose beans or pollen contain a component that is capable of causing hemolysis in susceptible individuals. Called also *fava, fava bean,* and *broad bean.*

vicianose (vis′e-ah-nōs). A disaccharide, $C_{11}H_{20}O_{10}$, which on hydrolysis yields glucose and arabinose.

vicilin (vi′sĭ-lin). A globulin from lentils and other legumes.

vicine (vi′sin). A white crystalline glycoside, $C_{10}H_{16}N_4O_8$, found in *Vicia sativa* and other species of vetch. It is a mononucleoside and on hydrolysis yields divicin and dextrose.

vicious (vish′us) [L. *vitio′sus*]. 1. Faulty or defective; malformed. 2. Depraved; refractory or unruly.

Vicq d'Azyr's bundle (vēk dah-zērz′) [Félix *Vicq d'Azyr,* a French anatomist, 1748–1794]. Fasciculus mamillothalamicus.

Vidal's disease, treatment (ve-dahlz′) [Emilie *Vidal,* dermatologist in Paris, 1825–1893]. See under *disease* and *treatment.*

Vidal's operation (ve-dahlz′) [Auguste Théodore *Vidal* de Cassis, French surgeon, 1803–1856]. See under *operation.*

videognosis (vid″e-og-no′sis) [(*video-,* from L. *videre* to see + dia*gnosis*]. Diagnosis based on the interpretation of roentgenograms transmitted by television technics to a radiologic center.

vidian artery, canal, nerve (vid′e-an) [Guido Guidi (L. *Vidius*), Italian physician, 1500–1569]. See under the nouns.

Vierordt's hemotachometer (fēr′orts) [Karl *Vierordt,* German clinician, 1818–1884]. An instrument for measuring the velocity of the blood flow.

Vieussens' annulus, ansa, ring, valve (ve-uh-sahz′) [Raymond de *Vieussens,* French anatomist, 1641–1715]. See under *annulus, ansa,* and *valve.*

vigilambulism (vij″il-am′bu-lizm). A state resembling somnambulism, but not occurring in sleep; double or multiple personality.

vigilance (vij′ĭ-lans) [L. *vigilantia*]. Morbid wakefulness; watchfulness.

vigintinormal (vi-jin″tĭ-nor′mal) [L. *viginti* twenty + *norma* rule]. Having one twentieth of what is normal.

Vignal's cells (vēn-yahlz′) [Guillaume *Vignal,* French physiologist, 1852–1893]. See under *cell.*

vignin (vig′nin). A protein from the cow pea.

vigor (vig′or) [L. *vigere* to flourish]. A combination of attributes of living organisms which expresses itself in rapid growth, high fertility and fecundity, large size, and long life. **hybrid v.,** heterosis.

Vigouroux's sign (vēg″oo-rōōz′) [Auguste *Vigouroux,* a French neurologist of the 19th century]. See under *sign.*

Villard's button (ve-larz′) [Eugêne *Villard,* surgeon in Lyons, born 1868]. See under *button.*

Villaret's syndrome (ve-lar-āz′) [Maurice *Villaret,* French neurologist, 1877–1946]. See under *syndrome.*

Villarsia nymphaeoides (vil-lar′ze-ah nim″fe-oi′dēz). An old world gentianaceous plant: antiscorbutic.

Villemin's theory (vēl-maz′) [Jean Antoine *Villemin,* French surgeon, 1827–1892]. See under *theory.*

villi (vil′i) [L.]. Plural of *villus.*

villiferous (vil-lif′er-us). Having or bearing villi.

villikinin (vil-lik′ĭ-nin) [*villi* + Gr. *kinein* to move]. A hormone produced by action of hydrochloric acid on the mucous membrane of the duodenum, which accelerates any movement of the villi of the small intestine.

villioma (vil″e-o′mah). Villoma.

villitis (vil-li′tis) [*villi* + *-itis*]. Inflammation of the villous tissue of the coronet and of the plantar substance of a horse's foot.

villoma (vil-lo′mah). A villous tumor, chiefly of the rectum.

villose (vil-lōs′) [L. *villosus*]. Shaggy with soft hairs; covered with villi.

villositis (vil″o-si′tis). A bacterial disease characterized by alterations in the villi of the placenta.

villosity (vil-los′ĭ-te). 1. The condition of being covered with villi. 2. A villus.

villous (vil′us). Villose.

villus (vil′lus), pl. *vil′li* [L. "tuft of hair"]. A small vascular process or protrusion, especially such a protrusion from the free surface of a membrane; used as a general term in anatomical nomenclature. **amniotic v.,** one of the irregular, flat, opaque areas of imperfect skin on the amnion near the distal end of the umbilical cord. **anchoring v.,** a chorionic villus that attaches to the decidua basalis. **arachnoid villi,** granulationes arachnoideales. **chorionic v.,** one of the threadlike projections growing in tufts on the external surface of the chorion. **free v.,** a chorionic villus that projects into the intervillous space. **intestinal villi, vil′li intestina′les** [N A, B N A], the multitudinous threadlike projections that cover the surface of the mucosa of the small intestine. **lingual villi,** papillae filiformes. **Luschka's villi,** granulationes arachnoideales. **pericardial v.,** one of the threadlike projections on the free surface of the pericardium. **pleural villi, vil′li pleura′les** [B N A], the shaggy appendages on the surface of the pleura near the costomediastinal sinus. Omitted in N A. **primary v.,** one of the earliest chorionic villi, composed of trophoblast only.

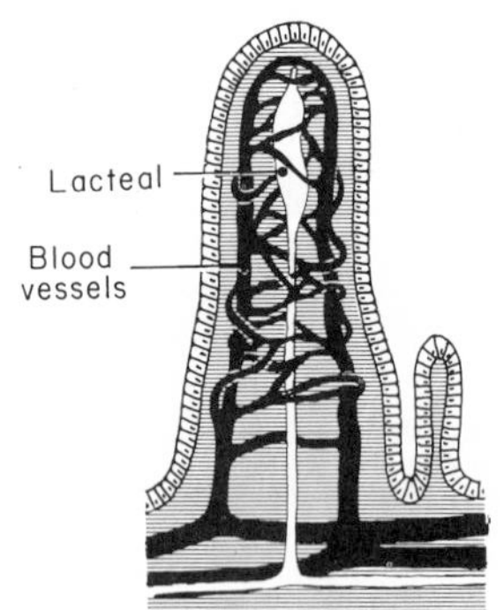

Intestinal villus. (Routh.)

secondary v., one of the definitive type of chorionic villi, having a core of connective tissue and vessels. **villi of small intestine,** villi intestinales. **synovial villi, vil′li synovia′les** [N A, B N A], slender projections of the synovial membrane from its free inner surface into the joint cavity.

villusectomy (vil″us-ek′to-me). Synovectomy; excision of a synovial villus.

vin. Abbreviation for L. *vi′num,* wine.

vinactane (vin-ak′tān). Trade mark for a preparation of viomycin.

vinbarbital (vin-bar′bĭ-tal). Chemical name: 5-ethyl-5-(1-methyl-1-butenyl) barbituric acid: used as a central nervous system depressant.

vinblastine (vin-blas′tēn). An alkaloid extracted from *Vinca rosea:* used as a neoplastic depressant.

Vinca minor (vin′kah mi′nor). An apocynaceous plant, lesser periwinkle, which is the source of a homeopathic preparation.

Vincent's angina, infection, organisms (vin′sents) [Henri *Vincent,* physician in Paris, 1862–1950]. See *necrotizing ulcerative gingivitis,* and under *organism.*

vincula (ving′ku-lah) [L.]. Plural of *vinculum.*

vinculum (ving′ku-lum), pl. *vin′cula* [L.]. A band or bandlike structure. **v. bre′ve** [N A], either of two fan-shaped expansions near the ends of the flexor tendons of a finger, one connecting the superficial tendon to the proximal interphalangeal joint and the other connecting the deep tendon to the intermediate interphalangeal joint. **v. lin′guae,** frenulum linguae. **vin′cula lin′gulae cerebel′li** [B N A], lateral prolongations of the lingula of the cerebellum. Omitted in N A. **v. lon′gum** [N A], either of two independent pairs of slender bands in each finger, one connecting the deep flexor tendon to the superficial tendon after the latter becomes subjacent, and the other connecting the superficial tendon to the proximal phalanx. **vin′cula ten′dinum digito′rum ma′nus** [N A, B N A], small vascular bands that connect the tendons of the flexor digitorum profundus and flexor digitorum superficialis muscles to the phalanges and interphalangeal articulations of the hand. The tendon blood supply is also carried in them. See *v. breve* and *v. longum.* Called also *vincula of tendons of fingers.* **vin′cula ten′dinum digito′rum pe′dis** [N A], bands connecting the tendons of the flexor digitorum longus and flexor digitorum brevis muscles to the phalanges and interphalangeal articulations of the foot. They are similar to the vincula found in the hand. Called also *vincula of tendons of toes.*

vinegar (vin′e-gar) [Fr. *vinaigre* sour wine]. 1. A weak and impure dilution of acetic acid; especially a sour liquid consisting chiefly of acetic acid, formed by the fermentation of cider, wine, etc., or by the distillation of wood. 2. A medicinal solution of a drug in dilute acetic acid.

vinegaroon (vin″e-gah-ro͞on′). The whip-tailed scorpion, *Thelyphonus giganteus,* so called because it produces an irritating excretion which has an odor resembling that of vinegar.

vinethene (vin′ĕ-thēn). Trade mark for vinyl ether.

vinic (vi′nik) [L. *vinum* wine]. Pertaining to wine.

vinine (vin′in). An alkaloid, $C_{19}H_{26}O_4N$, from *Vinca pubescens.*

vinometer (vi-nom′e-ter) [L. *vinum* wine + L. *metrum* measure]. An instrument for estimating the percentage of alcohol in wine.

vinous (vi′nus) [L. *vinosus,* from *vinum* wine]. Pertaining to, or containing, wine.

Vinson's syndrome [Porter P. *Vinson,* American surgeon, born 1890]. See *Plummer-Vinson syndrome,* under *syndrome.*

vinum (vi′num), gen. *vi′ni* [L.]. Wine.

vinyl (vi′nil). The univalent group, $CH_2{:}CH$—, from vinyl alcohol. **v. acetate,** a vinyl group to which the monovalent radical CH_3COO— is attached, the monomer which polymerizes to polyvinyl acetate. **v. benzene,** styrene. **v. chloride,** a vinyl group to which an atom of chlorine is attached, $CH_2.CHCl$, the monomer which polymerizes to polyvinyl chloride.

viocid (vi′o-sid). Methylrosaniline.

viocin (vi′o-sin). Trade mark for a preparation of viomycin sulfate.

vioform (vi′o-form). Trade mark for preparations of iodochlorhydroxyquin.

Viola (vi′o-lah) [L.]. A genus of plants: the violets and pansies. **V. odora′ta,** a sweet-scented violet of Europe and Asia; also its homeopathic preparation. **V. tri′color** is emetic.

Violaquercitrin (vi-o″lah-kwer′sĭ-trin). Rutin.

violescent (vi″o-les′ent). Somewhat violet in color.

violet (vi′o-let). 1. The hue seen in the most refracted end of the spectrum. 2. A violet-colored dye. **afridol v.,** a benzopurpurine dye which has a urea linkage. $CO[NH.C_6H_4N_2.(NH_2)C_{10}H_3\text{-}(SO_2ONa)_2OH]_2$. **amethyst v.,** a tetra-ethyl-pheno-safranine used in triple staining, $(C_2H_5)_2\text{-}N.C_6H_3.N_2Cl(C_6H_5).C_6H_3.N(C_2H_5)_2$. **aniline v.,** methylrosaniline chloride. **v. 7 B or C,** methylrosaniline chloride. **chrom v.,** a tricarboxyl derivative of pararosolic acid, $COONa.C_6H_3(O)\text{-}C[C_6H_3(OH)COONa]_2$. **cresyl v., cresylecht v.,** a rare dye which has been used in pathologic staining. **crystal v., v. G, gentian v., hexamethyl v.,** methylrosaniline. **Hoffmann's v., iodine v.,** dahlia. **iris v.,** amethyst v. **Lauth's v.,** thionine hydrochloride. **methyl v.,** gentian v. **methylene v.,** one of the constituents of polychrome methylene blue, $(CH_3)_2N.C_6H_3(SN)CH_3{:}O$. **neutral v.,** a dye resembling neutral red, but more violet in color, $(CH_3)_2N.C_6H_3.N_2.C_6H_2.(NH_2.HCl).NH.C_6H_4.N\text{-}(CH_3)_2$. **Paris v., pentamethyl v.,** gentian v. **visual v.,** a photosensitive violet-colored pigment of the retinal cones which is closely related to rhodopsin.

violin (vi′o-lin). The active principle of several species of violet: its properties are much like those of emetine.

viomycin (vi′o-mi″sin). An antibiotic substance produced by *Streptomyces puniceus:* used as a tuberculostatic.

viosterol (vi-os′ter-ol). Calciferol.

viper (vi′per). A snake of the genus *Vipera.* **pit v.,** any one of a group of venomous snakes having a depression or pit between the nostril and the eye. They include the rattlesnake, copperhead, water moccasin and fer-de-lance. **Russell's v.,** the daboia, a venomous snake of Southeastern Asia. See under *venom.*

viraginity (vi″rah-jin′ĭ-te) [L. *virago* a manlike woman]. A condition in which a woman has the sexual feelings and mentality of a man.

viral (vi′ral). Pertaining to, caused by or of the nature of virus.

Virales (vi-ra′lēz). A taxonomic order of class Microtatobiotes made up of etiologic agents of disease in bacteria, animals, and plants, characterized by small size and usually by ability to pass filters which normally retain bacteria, by multiplication only in the presence of living cells, and by mutation which results in the production of new strains. Further formal classification, however, has been abandoned. See under *virus.*

Virchow's angle, disease, line, etc. (vĕr′kōz) [Rudolf *Virchow,* German pathologist, 1821–1902]. See under the nouns.

viremia (vi-re′me-ah). The presence of viruses in the blood.

virgin (vir′jin) [L. *virgo*]. A woman or girl who has not had sexual intercourse.

virginal (vir′jĭ-nal). Pertaining to a virgin or to virginity.

virginity (vir-jin′ĭ-te) [L. *virginitas*]. Maidenhood; the condition of being a virgin.

virginium (vir-jin′e-um). A former name of the element francium.

viricidal (vir″ĭ-si′dal). Virucidal.

viricide (vir′ĭ-sīd). Virucide.

viridin (vi-rid′in). 1. An oily principle, $C_{12}H_{19}N$, distilled from bone oil and from coal tar. 2. Jervine.

viridobufagin (vir″ĭ-do-bu′fah-jin). A cardiac poison, $C_{23}H_{34}O_5$, from the skin glands of the toad, *Bufo viridis.*

virile (vir′il) [L. *virilis*]. 1. Peculiar to men or the male sex. 2. Possessing masculine traits, especially copulative power.

virilescence (vir″ĭ-les′ens). The development of male secondary sex characters in the female.

virilia (vi-ril′e-ah) [L.]. The male generative organs.

viriligenic (vir″ĭ-li-jen′ik). Promoting virility or promoting male characteristics.

virilism (vir′ĭ-lizm) [L. *virilis* masculine]. 1. Masculinity; the development of masculine physical and mental traits in the female. 2. Hermaphrodism in which the subject is a female, but has male external genitals. **adrenal v.,** virilism due to adrenal changes developed after puberty. In it the adult body regresses toward the masculine type. **prosopopilary v.,** virilism marked by growth of hair on the face.

virility (vi-ril′ĭ-te) [L. *virilitas,* from *vir* man]. Possession of the normal primary sex characters in one of the male sex.

virilization (vir″ĭ-li-za′shun). The induction or development of male secondary sex characters, especially the induction of such changes in the female, including enlargement of the clitoris, growth of facial and body hair, development of a hairline typical of the male forehead, stimulation of secretion and proliferation of the sebaceous glands (often with acne), and deepening of the voice.

viripotent (vi-rip′o-tent) [L. *viripotens; vir* man + *potens* able]. 1. Sexually mature: said of a male. 2. Marriageable or nubile: said of the female.

virogenetic (vi″ro-je-net′ik). Having a viral origin; caused by a virus.

viroid (vi′roid). A general term for any biological specific used in immunization.

virologist (vi-rol′o-jist). A specialist in virology.

virology (vi-rol′o-je). That branch of microbiology which is concerned with viruses and virus diseases.

viropexis (vi″ro-pek′sis) [*virus* + Gr. *pēxis* fixation]. The fixation of virus.

virose (vi′rōs) [L. *virosus,* from *virus* poison]. Having poisonous qualities.

virosis (vi-ro′sis), pl. *viro′ses.* A disease caused by a virus.

virous (vi′rus). Virose.

virtual (vir′tu-al) [L. *virtus* strength]. Appearing to be present, but not really so; having efficacy without a material substratum. See *focus.*

virucidal (vir″u-si′dal). Capable of neutralizing or destroying a virus.

virucide (vir′u-sīd). An agent which neutralizes or destroys a virus.

virulence (vir′u-lens) [L. *virulen′tia,* from *virus* poison]. The degree of pathogenicity of a microorganism as indicated by case fatality rates and/or its ability to invade the tissues of the host. It is measured experimentally by the median lethal dose (LD_{50}) or median effective dose (ED_{50}). By extension, the competence of any infectious agent to produce pathologic effects.

virulent (vir′u-lent) [L. *virulentus,* from *virus* poison]. Pertaining to or characterized by virulence; exceedingly pathogenic, noxious, or deleterious.

virulicidal (vir″u-lis′ĭ-dal). Destructive of virulence; capable of destroying the deleterious potency of a virus or other noxious agent.

viruliferous (vir″u-lif′er-us) [L. *virus* poison + *ferre* to bear]. Conveying or producing a virus or other noxious agent.

virulin (vir′u-lin). Rosenow's term for substances formed by pathogenic bacteria that facilitate invasion of the host tissue and dissemination of the infectious agent within the body. Cf. *aggressin.*

viruria (vīr-u′re-ah). The presence of viruses in the urine.

virus (vi′rus) [L.]. One of a group of minute infectious agents, with certain exceptions (e.g., poxviruses, psittacosis group) not resolved in the light microscope, and characterized by a lack of independent metabolism and by the ability to replicate only within living host cells. They range from 200–300 mμ to 15 mμ in size and are morphologically heterogeneous, occurring as rod-shaped, spherical or polyhedral, and tadpole-shaped forms; masses of the spherical or polyhedral forms may be made up of orderly arrays, to give a crystalline structure. The individual particle, or elementary body, consists of nucleic acid, DNA or RNA, but not both, contained within a protein coat, which may be multilayered. They are customarily separated into three sub-groups on the basis of host specificity, namely bacterial viruses, animal viruses, and plant viruses. They are also classified as to their origin (e.g., reoviruses), mode of transmission (arbor viruses, tick-borne viruses), or the manifestations they produce (polioviruses, polyoma viruses, poxviruses). They are sometimes named for the geographical location in which they were first isolated (e.g., Coxsackie virus). **animal v's,** viruses that produce diseases of man and other animals. **v. anima′tum,** a living animal poison. **arbor v's** (*ar*thropod-*bor*ne), a group of viruses, including the causative agents of yellow fever, viral encephalitides, and certain febrile infections, such as dengue, which are transmitted to man by various mosquitoes and ticks; those transmitted by ticks are often considered in a separate category (tick-borne viruses). **attenuated v.,** one whose pathogenicity has been reduced by serial animal passage or by other means. **Australian X disease v.,** Murray Valley encephalitis v. **B. v.,** a virus isolated from the central nervous system of a laboratory worker who died of ascending myelitis with visceral necrosis after being bit on the hand by an apparently normal monkey; presumed to be the cause of a natural infection in monkeys. **bacterial v.,** a virus capable of producing transmissible lysis of bacteria; the virus particle attaches to the bacterial cell wall and viral nucleoprotein enters the cell, resulting in the synthesis of virus and its liberation on physical disruption of the cell. Bacterial viruses are usually specific for bacterial species, but they may be strain specific or may infect more than one species of bacteria. **Brunhilde v.,** the prototype strain of poliovirus type 1. **Bunyamwera v.,** an arbor virus causing mild febrile disease in Uganda. **Bwamba fever v.,** an arbor virus causing mild febrile disease in Uganda. **C v.,** Coxsackie v. **CA v.** (*c*roup-*a*ssociated), parainfluenza 2 virus. **Cache Valley v.,** an arbor virus found in Utah, Brazil, and Trinidad; related to the Bunyamwera group of viruses. **California v.,** a virus isolated in California in 1943 from species of mosquitoes; capable of causing disease in laboratory animals and the probable cause of fatal encephalitis in an infant. **Chikungunya v.,** an arbor virus found in Tanganyika as the etiological agent of an epidemic dengue-like disease; closely related to Semliki Forest virus. **Coe v.,** Coxsackie virus type A21. **Colorado tick fever v.,** a tick-borne virus causing a febrile disease in the Rocky Mountain regions of the United States. **coryza v.** See *coryzavirus.* **Coxsackie v.,** one of a heterogeneous group of enteroviruses producing, in man, a disease resembling poliomyelitis, but without paralysis; separable into two groups: A, producing degenerative lesions of striated muscle and B, producing leptomeningitis in infant mice. A number of different serotypes have also been identified. **croup-associated v.,** parain-

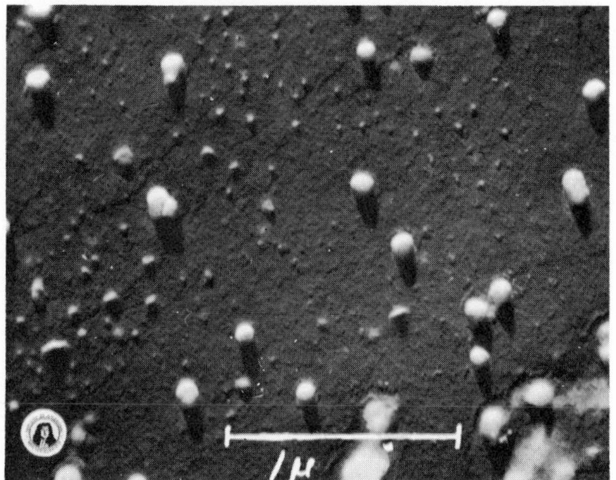

Influenza virus. (Williams and Wyckoff, S.A.B. LS-136.)

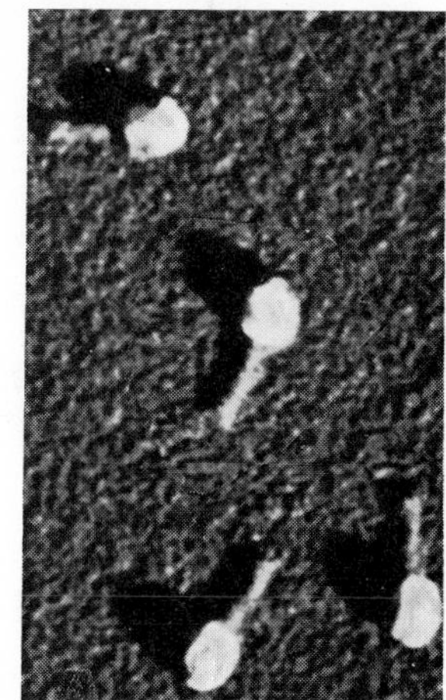

Bacteriophage (T_2) of *Escherichia coli*. (Williams and Frazer, Virology, vol. 2.)

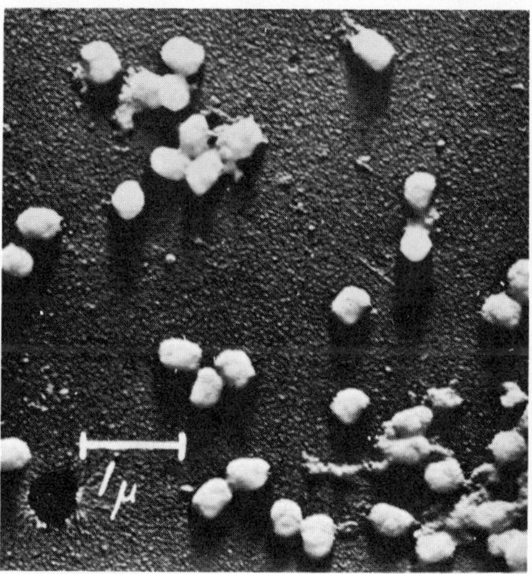

Vaccinia virus. (G. G. Sharp, S.A.B. LS-142.)

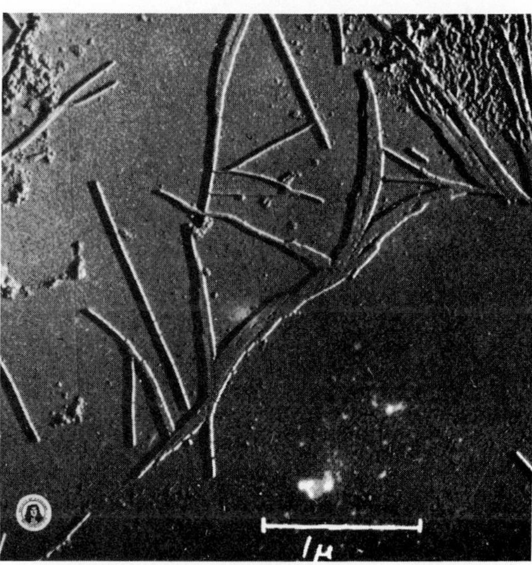

Tobacco mosaic virus. (Williams and Wyckoff, S.A.B. LS-135.)

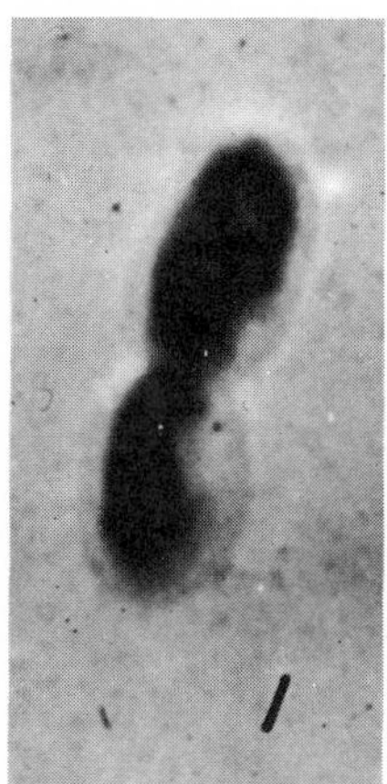

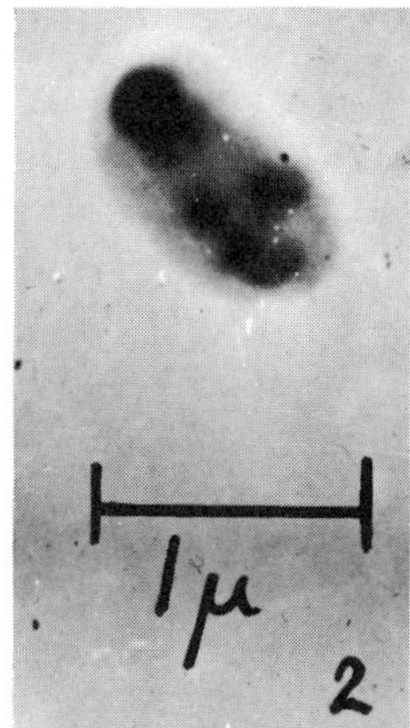

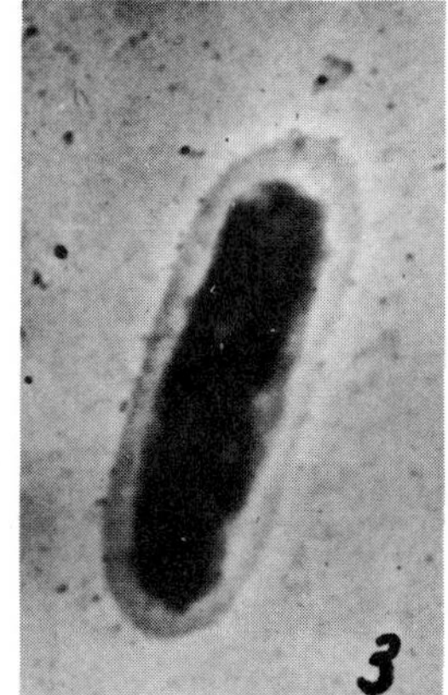

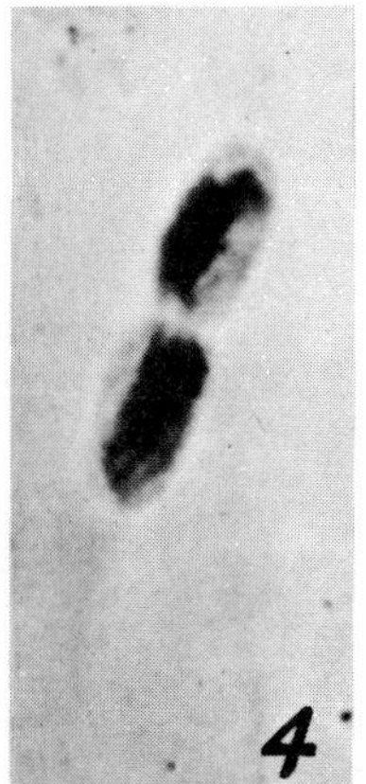

Rickettsiae: *1*, epidemic typhus fever; *2*, endemic typhus fever; *3*, Rocky Mountain spotted fever; *4*, American Q fever. (Plotz, Smadel, Anderson, and Chambers, S.A.B. LS-25.)

ELECTRON MICROGRAPHS OF VIRUSES AND RICKETTSIAE

fluenza 2 virus. **cytomegalic inclusion disease v.** See *cytomegalovirus.* **dengue v.,** the etiological agent of dengue, existing as two immunological types, designated 1 and 2, and related to other arthropod-borne viruses. **ECBO v.** (*e*nteric *c*ytopathogenic *b*ovine *o*rphan), an enteric orphan virus isolated from cattle. **ECDO v.** (*e*nteric *c*ytopathogenic *d*og *o*rphan), an enteric orphan virus isolated from dogs. **ECHO v.** (*e*nteric *c*ytopathogenic *h*uman *o*rphan), an enteric orphan virus isolated from man, separable into several serotypes, certain of which are associated with aseptic meningitis. **ECHO 28 v.,** a virus isolated from patients with mild respiratory disease, pathogenic for man but not for the conventional laboratory animals, including the suckling mouse and monkey by the intracerebral route. **ECMO v.** (*e*nteric *c*ytopathogenic *m*onkey *o*rphan), an enteric orphan virus isolated from monkeys. **ECSO v.** (*e*nteric *c*ytopathogenic *s*wine *o*rphan), an enteric orphan virus isolated from swine. **EEE v.,** Eastern equine encephalomyelitis v. See under *equine encephalomyelitis v.* **EMC v.,** encephalomyocarditis v. **encephalomyocarditis v.,** an arbor virus found in Africa, South America, and elsewhere, which causes mild aseptic meningitis and a non-paralytic poliomyelitis-like disease; represented by four strains which appear to be substantially identical in immunological and other respects. **enteric v.,** enterovirus. **enteric orphan v's,** viruses isolated from the intestinal tract of man and various other animals, called orphan viruses because they are often not specifically associated with illness; they include such viruses isolated from cattle (ECBO viruses), dogs (ECDO viruses), man (ECHO viruses), monkeys (ECMO viruses), and swine (ECSO viruses). **epidemic keratoconjunctivitis v.,** adenovirus type 8. **equine encephalomyelitis v.,** one of a group of viruses causing encephalomyelitis in horses, mules, and man, with a reservoir of infection in birds, and transmitted by mosquitoes. The group includes *Eastern equine encephalomyelitis virus,* the cause of equine encephalomyelitis in a region extending from New Hampshire to Texas, and as far west as Wisconsin; *Venezuelan equine encephalomyelitis virus,* the cause of equine encephalomyelitis in Venezuela and various other South American countries; and *Western equine encephalomyelitis virus,* the cause of equine encephalomyelitis in the United States west of the Mississippi, transmitted primarily by *Culex tarsalis.* **filterable v.,** a name formerly applied to a pathogenic agent capable of passing filters that retain bacteria. **v. fixé, fixed v.,** rabies virus whose virulence has been increased by serial animal passage and remains fixed during further transmission; used for inoculating animals from which rabies vaccine is prepared. **Guaroa v.,** an arbor virus isolated in Colombia from the blood of patients with a febrile disease; a member of the Bunyamwera group of viruses. **hemadsorption v., type 1 (HA1),** parainfluenza 3 virus. **hemadsorption v., type 2 (HA2),** a parainfluenza 1 virus isolated from children with febrile respiratory disease. **hepatitis v.,** the etiological agent of viral hepatitis. Two types are recognized: *hepatitis virus A,* the agent causing infectious hepatitis, acquired by parenteral inoculation or ingestion, and *hepatitis virus B,* the agent causing serum hepatitis, transmitted by inadequately sterilized syringes and needles, or through infectious blood plasma, or certain blood products. **herpangina v.,** one of the viruses of the Coxsackie A group, causing a febrile disease, usually of children, characterized by small herpes-like lesions on the soft palate or in the faucial area. **herpes v.** See *herpesvirus.* **Ilheus v.,** an arbor virus first isolated in Brazil; related to St. Louis encephalitis virus, Japanese B encephalitis virus, and West Nile virus. **inclusion conjunctivitis v.,** the agent causing inclusion conjunctivitis, related to the trachoma, ornithosis, and lymphogranuloma viruses; harbored in the human genitourinary tract, where it causes infection which is asymptomatic or of minor significance, it may be transmitted to eyes of the newborn, or of obstetricians and gynecologists. **insect v's,** viruses capable of causing disease in insects. **Japanese B encephalitis v.,** the causative agent of Japanese B encephalitis, closely similar to the various agents causing the different types of equine encephalomyelitis and St. Louis encephalitis, but having a wider range of pathogenicity for experimental animals. **JH v.,** ECHO 28 v. **Junin v.,** an arbor virus causing febrile hemorrhagic disease in Argentina. **Kumba v.,** a virus isolated from mosquitoes in the Kumba region of West Africa; antigenically identical with the Semliki Forest virus. **Kyasanur Forest disease v.,** a tick-borne virus found in native monkeys in the Kyasanur Forest in Mysore, India, and the cause of a highly fatal disease in man; closely related to the Russian spring-summer encephalitis virus. **Lansing v.,** the prototype strain of poliovirus type 2. **latent v.,** masked v. **Leon v.,** the prototype strain of poliovirus type 3. **louping ill v.,** the tick-borne agent causing louping ill of sheep, which is transmissible to man; closely related to Russian spring-summer encephalitis virus. **Lunyo v.,** a neurotropic variant of Rift Valley fever virus. **lymphogranuloma venereum v.,** the etiological agent of lymphogranuloma venereum; related to the ornithosis viruses. **masked v.,** a virus which ordinarily occurs in a non-infective state and is demonstrable by indirect methods which activate it, such as blind passage in experimental animals. **Mayaro v.,** an arbor virus found in Trinidad and Brazil as an etiological agent of febrile disease; closely related to and possibly identical with Semliki Forest virus. **Mengo v.,** an encephalomyocarditis virus isolated originally in 1948 from a captive monkey in Uganda and later from mosquitoes and a mongoose of the same area; identified also as the cause of an epizootic disease of swine in Panama. **Murray Valley encephalitis v.,** a variant of Japanese B encephalitis virus causing encephalitis in Australia and New Guinea. **Newcastle disease v.,** a virus causing disease in chickens and occasionally in man; related to the influenza viruses. **O'nyong-nyong v.,** an arbor virus found in Uganda and Kenya as the etiological agent of an epidemic febrile, dengue-like disease. **ornithosis v.,** one of a group of agents, including the psittacosis virus, transmissible to man from birds; related to certain pneumonitis viruses. **Oropouche v.,** an arbor virus isolated from a patient with febrile disease in Trinidad; related to the Simbu virus. **orphan v's,** viruses which have been isolated in tissue culture but have not been found specifically associated with any illness. Such are the enteric orphan viruses. **pappataci fever v.,** the etiological agent of phlebotomus (pappataci) fever, transmitted by Phlebotomus, and occurring as two serotypes, the Naples and Sicilian types. **parainfluenza v.,** one of a group of viruses isolated from patients with upper respiratory tract disease of varying severity. Parainfluenza viruses are separated into three groups: *parainfluenza 1 v.,* comprising two immunologically related but not identical viruses, *Sendai virus* and *hemadsorption type 2* (*HA2*) *virus; parainfluenza 2 v.,* a virus isolated from patients with acute laryngotracheobronchitis; and *parainfluenza 3 v.,* isolated from patients with acute febrile respiratory disease, and originally described as hemadsorption type 1 (HA1) virus. **parrot v.,** psittacosis v. **pharyngoconjunctival fever v.,** adenovirus type 3. **plant v's,** viruses that produce diseases of higher plants. **pneumonitis v.,** the etiological agent of pneumonitis; the agents causing human, feline, and mouse pneumonitis are related to those causing ornithosis, psittacosis, and lymphogranuloma venereum. They and other similar agents have been provisionally classified together under the genus name Miyagasvanella, in the family Rickettsiales. **poliomyelitis v.** See *poliovirus.* **polyoma v.,** a virus producing neoplastic disease in mice and hamsters. **Powassan v.,** a tick-borne virus isolated from a fatal case of encephalitis in Ontario, Canada; closely related to Russian spring-summer encephalitis virus. **pox v.** See *poxvirus.* **psittacosis v.,** a name given the etiological agent of an infection acquired from parrots (psittacosis), now recognized as being closely related to, if not identical with, ornithosis virus. **rabies v.,** the etiological agent of rabies, one of the most neurotropic of the viruses. **respiratory syncytial v.,** a virus isolated from children with bronchopneumonia and bronchitis, characteristically causing syncytium formation in tissue culture; first isolated from chimpanzees with symptoms of respiratory disease. **Rift Valley fever v.,** the etiological agent of Rift Valley fever in South Africa, transmitted by blood-sucking arthropods which feed at night. **RS v.,** respiratory syncytial v. **Russian spring-summer encephalitis v.,** a tick-borne virus which causes spring-summer encephalitis in Russia and Central Europe. **St. Louis encephalitis v.,** the etiological agent of St. Louis encephalitis, with a distribution similar to that of western equine encephalomyelitis virus, but differing from it immunologically. **salivary gland v.,** cytomegalovirus. **Semliki Forest v.,** an arbor virus isolated from mosquitoes of the Semliki Forest of western Uganda, which is pathogenic for laboratory animals and man. **Sendai v.,** a parainfluenza 1 virus, the etiological agent of a highly fatal epidemic pneumonitis of newborn infants in Japan; related to the mumps virus. **Simbu v.,** a virus isolated from a species of mosquitoes (*Aedes circumluteolis*) in Africa. **simian v's,** viruses that have been recovered from monkeys; they belong to many different groups, including adenoviruses, Coxsackie viruses, ECHO viruses, reoviruses, and others. **Sindbis v.,** an arbor virus first isolated from mosquitoes in the Sindbis district of northern Egypt, capable of causing infection in experimental animals. **street v.,** Pasteur's name for rabies virus derived from a dog with a naturally acquired case of the disease. **Teschen v.,** the etiological agent of encephalomyelitis in swine (Teschen disease). **Theiler's v.,** the etiological agent of a spontaneous encephalomyelitis of mice; it resembles human polioviruses but is immunologically distinct from them. **tick-borne v's,** viruses that are transmitted by ticks. **trachoma v.,** the etiological agent of trachoma; related to the ornithosis and lymphogranuloma venereum viruses. **2060 v.,** ECHO 28 v. **Uganda S v.,** an arbor virus causing mild febrile disease in certain areas in Africa, and very common in Nigeria. **unorganized v.,** any poisonous substance developed within the body. **Uruma v.,** an arbor virus causing epidemic febrile disease in Colombia. **vaccine v., v. vaccin'icum,** material from the pustules of vaccinia in healthy vaccinated animals which has been rubbed up in a mortar with glycerin to form a permanent suspension. **VEE v.,** Venezuelan equine encephalomyelitis v. See under *equine encephalomyelitis v.* **WEE v.,** Western equine encephalomyelitis v. See under *equine encephalomyelitis v.* **Wesselsbron v.,** an arbor virus repeatedly isolated in South Africa from mosquitoes and from sheep and man, in whom it causes a mild febrile disease. **West Nile v.,** an arbor virus causing mild but widespread human disease in Africa; related to Japanese encephalitis B virus and St. Louis encephalitis virus.

virusemia (vi″rus-e′me-ah). Viremia.

virustatic (vir″u-stat′ik) [*virus* + Gr. *statikos* bringing to a standstill]. Checking the growth or multiplication of viruses.

vis (vis), pl. *vi′res* [L.]. Force; energy. **v. a fron′te,** force exerted from the front; applied to a factor affecting venous blood pressure, which includes resistance to flow on the part of the veins themselves, and the resistance of the heart. **v. a lat′ere,** force from the side; applied to a factor affecting venous blood pressure, comprising the external influences and including contractility of the veins, pressure by skeletal muscle and other tissues, and pressure resulting from respiratory movements. **v. a par′te interio′re,** force from within; applied to a factor affecting venous blood pressure, a consequence of blood volume versus vascular volume. **v. a ter′go,** force exerted from the back; applied to a factor affecting venous blood pressure, arising from the impulse imparted to the blood stream by the beat of the heart. **v. conserva′trix,** the natural power of the organism to resist injury and disease. **v. formati′va,** energy manifesting itself in the formation of new tissue to replace that which has been destroyed. **v. in si′tu,** power or force inherent in a particular tissue. **v. medica′trix natu′rae,** the healing power of nature; the natural curative power inherent in the organism. **v. vi′tae, v. vita′lis,** the vital, or life, force.

viscera (vis′er-ah) [L.]. Plural of *viscus.*

viscerad (vis′er-ad). Toward the viscera.

visceral (vis′er-al) [L. *visceralis,* from *viscus* a viscus]. Pertaining to a viscus.

visceralgia (vis′er-al′je-ah) [L. *viscus* viscus + Gr. *algos* pain + *-ia*]. Pain in the viscera or in any bodily organ.

visceralism (vis′er-al-izm). The opinion that the viscera are the principal seats of disease.

viscerimotor (vis″er-ĭ-mo′tor) [L. *viscus* viscus + *motor* mover]. Conveying motor impulses to a viscus.

viscero- (vis′er-o) [L. *viscus,* pl. *viscera*]. Combining form denoting relationship to the organs (viscera) of the body.

viscerocranium (vis″er-o-kra′ne-um). That part of the skull which is derived from the branchial arches.

viscerography (vis″er-og′rah-fe). Roentgenography of the viscera.

viscero-inhibitory (vis″er-o-in-hib′ĭ-tor″e). Inhibiting the essential movements of any viscus or organ.

visceromotor (vis″er-o-mo′tor). Concerned in the essential movements of the viscera.

visceroparietal (vis″er-o-pah-ri′ĕ-tal). Pertaining to the viscera and the abdominal wall.

visceroperitoneal (vis″er-o-per″ĭ-to-ne′al). Pertaining to the viscera and the peritoneum.

visceropleural (vis″er-o-ploor′al). Pertaining to the viscera and the pleura.

visceroptosis (vis″er-op-to′sis) [L. *viscus* viscus + Gr. *ptōsis* fall]. Splanchnoptosis.

viscerosensory (vis″er-o-sen′so-re). Pertaining to sensation in the viscera.

visceroskeletal (vis″er-o-skel′e-tal). Pertaining to the visceral skeleton.

viscerosomatic (vis″er-o-so-mat′ik). Pertaining to the viscera and body.

viscerotome (vis′er-o-tōm). 1. An instrument designed for obtaining specimens of liver tissue from cadavers by simple puncture. 2. An area on an abdominal viscus which is supplied with afferent nerve fibers by a single posterior root.

viscerotomy (vis″er-ot′o-me) [*viscero-* + Gr. *tomē* a cutting]. Incision of an organ, especially postmortem excision of a portion of the liver.

Viscerotomy Service (vis″er-ot′o-me ser′vis). An organization, legalized in some tropical countries, to promote the systematic collection of specimens of the liver from persons dying after an illness of short duration, and the examination of these specimens in an effort to reveal silent foci of yellow fever.

viscerotonia (vis″er-o-to′ne-ah). A group of traits characterized by general relaxation; love of comfort, sociability, and conviviality; and gluttony for food, people, and affection.

viscerotrophic (vis″er-o-trof′ik). Trophic and dependent upon the viscera.

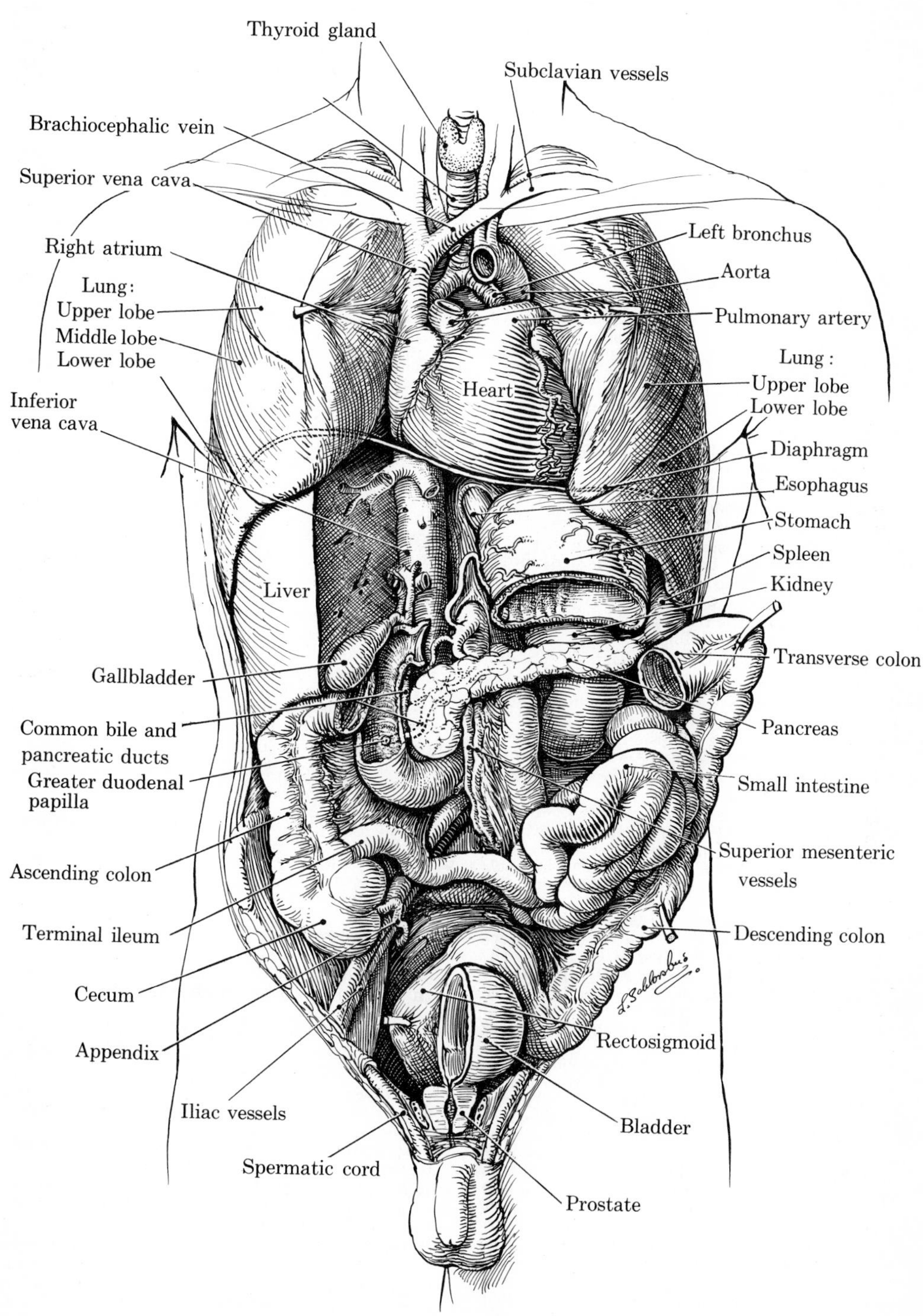

THORACIC AND ABDOMINAL VISCERA

viscerotropic (vis″er-o-trop′ik) [*viscero-* + Gr. *tropos* a turning]. Primarily attacking the viscera; having a predilection for the abdominal or thoracic viscera.

viscid (vis′id) [L. *viscidus*]. Glutinous or sticky.

viscidity (vĭ-sid′ĭ-te). The quality of being viscid.

viscin (vis′in) [L. *viscum* mistletoe]. A glutinous principle obtainable from mistletoe.

viscogel (vis′ko-jel). A gel which on melting gives a sol of high viscosity. Cf. *liquogel.*

viscometer (vis-kom′e-ter). Viscosimeter.

viscometry (vis-kom′e-tre). Viscosimetry.

viscosaccharase (vis″ko-sak′ah-rās). An enzyme which catalyzes the synthesis of dextran and levan from sucrose.

viscose (vis′kōs). 1. A glutinous product of the viscous fermentation of dextrose or of invertin. 2. Viscous.

viscosimeter (vis″ko-sim′e-ter). An apparatus used in determination of the viscosity of a substance. **Stormer v.,** an apparatus for determining viscosity by measurement of the time required, under controlled conditions, for a definite number of revolutions of a rotating cylinder immersed in the substance to be tested.

viscosimetry (vis″ko-sim′e-tre). The measurement of the viscosity of a substance.

viscosity (vis-kos′ĭ-te). A physical property of a substance that is dependent on the friction of its component molecules as they slide by one another.

viscous (vis′kus) [L. *viscosus*]. Characterized by a high degree of friction between component molecules as they slide by each other.

viscus (vis′kus), pl. *vis′cera* [L.]. Any large interior organ in any one of the three great cavities of the body, especially in the abdomen.

visibility (viz″ĭ-bil′ĭ-te) [L. *visibilitas*]. The quality of being visible.

visible (viz′ĭ-b′l) [L. *visibilis*]. Capable of being seen; perceptible by the sight.

visile (viz′il). Pertaining to vision; recalling most readily impression of vision. A term applied to a type of individual who uses chiefly the sense of sight.

vision (vizh′un) [L. *visio, videre* to see]. 1. The act or faculty of seeing; sight. 2. An apparition; a subjective sensation of vision not elicited by actual visual stimuli. 3. Visual acuity; symbol, V. **achromatic v.,** a condition in which the entire solar spectrum is seen as colorless, that is, in bands of grays; it occurs in two types, cone and rod, with and without loss of central foveal function. **binocular v.,** the use of both eyes together without diplopia. **central v.,** that which is elicited by stimuli impinging directly on the macula retinae. **chromatic v.,** chromatopsia. **day v.,** visual perception in the daylight, or under conditions of bright illumination. See also *light adaptation.* **dichromatic v.,** a condition in which color perception is restricted to a pair of primaries, either blue and yellow or (rarely) red and green, the entire visible spectrum appearing either in various degrees of vividness and brightness of the effective color pair or the missing colors appearing as grays. The 150 hues discriminable in normal vision are reduced to two, with slight differences in saturation and brilliance doing duty for the varied hues. **direct v.,** central v. **double v.,** diplopia. **facial v.,** the power of judging of the distance, direction, etc., of objects in one's environment by the sensation felt in the skin of the face. **finger v.,** the alleged ability to perceive colors and receive other sensations ordinarily elicited by visual stimuli, as a result of stimuli received through the skin of the fingertips. **fovial v.,** central v. **half v.,** hemianopia. **halo v.,** perception of a colored halo about a light source, one of the symptoms of glaucoma. **haploscopic v.,** stereoscopic v. **indirect v.,** peripheral v. **iridescent v.,** halo v. **monocular v.,** vision with one eye. **multiple v.,** polyopia. **night v.,** visual perception in the darkness of night, or under conditions of reduced illumination. See also *dark adaptation.* **v. nul,** the existence of scotomas in the field of vision of which the patient is not aware. **v. obscure,** the existence of scotomas in the field of vision of which the patient is aware. **oscillating v.,** oscillopsia. **peripheral v.,** that which is elicited by stimuli falling on areas of the retina distant from the macula. **photopic v.,** day v. **Pick's v.,** a visual condition in which objects lose their normal horizontal-vertical alignment and converge toward or diverge from one another. **pseudoscopic v.,** the reverse of stereoscopic vision, an object appearing not as a solid body, but as a hollow one. **rainbow v.,** halo v. **rod v.,** vision in which the cones of the retina play little or no part, as in scotopic vision. **scoterythrous v.,** a form of anomalous color vision in which there is failure of perception of wavelengths at the red end of the spectrum. **scotopic v.,** night v. **shaft v.,** tunnel v. **solid v., stereoscopic v.,** perception of the relief of objects or of their depth; vision in which objects are perceived as having three dimensions, and not merely as two-dimensional pictures. **tunnel v.,** a condition characterized by great reduction in the visual field, as though the subject were looking through a long tunnel. **twilight v.,** night v. **word v.,** the ability to perceive printed or written words.

visual (vizh′u-al) [L. *visualis*, from *videre* to see]. 1. Pertaining to vision or sight. 2. A person in whom the visual centers are predominant in memory and learning.

visualization (vizh″u-al-i-za′shun). The act of viewing, or of achieving a complete visual impression of an object. **double contrast v.** See *mucosal relief roentgenography*, under *roentgenography.*

visualize (vizh′u-al-īz). 1. To achieve a complete view of. 2. To picture in the mind.

visuo-auditory (vizh″u-o-aw′dĭ-tor″e). Pertaining to both sight and hearing; stimulating both the visual and the auditory center.

visuognosis (vizh″u-og-no′sis) [L. *visus* sight + Gr. *gnōsis* knowledge]. The recognition and interpretation of visual impressions.

visuometer (vizh″u-om′e-ter) [L. *visus* sight + *metrum* measure]. An instrument for measuring the range of vision.

visuopsychic (vizh″u-o-si′kik). Visual and psychic; a term applied to that area of the cerebral cortex concerned in the judgment of visual sensations.

visuosensory (vizh″u-o-sen′sor-e). Pertaining to the perception of stimuli giving rise to visual impressions.

vita (vi′tah) [L.]. Life. **v. sexua′lis,** the sexual life.

vitaglass (vi′tah-glas) [L. *vita* life + *glass*]. A quartz-containing glass which transmits the ultraviolet portion of sunlight.

vitagonist (vi-tag′o-nist). A vitamin antagonist; a substance that produces deficiency of a given vitamin.

vitagraph (vi′tah-graf). A variety of chronophotograph.

vital (vi′tal) [L. *vitalis*, from *vita* life]. 1. Necessary to, or pertaining to life. 2. (pl.). The parts and organs necessary to life.

vitaletiscope (vi″tal-et′ĭ-skōp). A variety of chronophotograph.

Vitali's test (ve-tal′ēz) [Dioscoride *Vitali*, Italian physician, 1832–1917]. See under *tests.*

vitalism (vi′tal-izm) [L. *vita* life]. The theory that biological activities are directed by a supernatural force.

vitalist (vi′tal-ist). A believer in vitalism.

vitalistic (vi″tal-is′tik). Pertaining to vitalism.

vitality (vi-tal′ĭ-te). 1. The life principle. 2. The condition of being alive.

vitalize (vi′tal-iz). To give life to.

vitamer (vi′tah-mer). Any one of a number of compounds that possess a given vitamin activity, i.e., that act to overcome a given vitamin deficiency in one or another organism, plant or animal. Thus, there are biotin vitamers, niacin vitamers, thiamine vitamers, pyridoxin vitamers, A vitamers, D vitamers, K vitamers, etc. (Dean Burk).

vitameter (vi-tam′e-ter). An instrument for assaying vitamins.

vitamin (vi′tah-min) [L. *vita* life + *amine*]. A general term for a number of unrelated organic substances that occur in many foods in small amounts and that are necessary for the normal metabolic functioning of the body. They may be water-soluble, or fat-soluble. See *Table of Vitamins.* **anticanitic v.,** a substance that counteracts or prevents graying of the hair. See *para-aminobenzoic acid.* **antihemorrhagic v.,** a substance that counteracts a hemorrhagic tendency. See *vitamin K* in *Table of Vitamins.* **anti-infection v.,** one that is useful in preventing infection. See *vitamin A* in *Table of Vitamins.* **antineuritic v.,** thiamine. **antipellagra v.,** nicotinic acid. **antiscorbutic v.,** ascorbic acid. **antisterility v.,** a substance that promotes fertility. See *vitamin E* in *Table of Vitamins.* **antixerophthalmic v.,** a substance that counteracts xerophthalmia. See *vitamin A* in *Table of Vitamins.* **fertility v.,** a substance that promotes fertility. See *vitamin A* in *Table of Vitamins.* **permeability v.,** a substance necessary to insure integrity of the capillary walls. See *vitamin P,* in *Table of Vitamins.*

TABLE OF VITAMINS

Individual vitamins are listed here under their different designations (letters and subscript numbers or letters), with description or cross reference to name of the specific compound.

v. A, an unsaturated aliphatic alcohol, $(CH_3)_3$-C_6H_6.CH:CH.C(CH_3):CH.CH:CH.C(CH_3):CH.-CH_2OH. Deficiency in the diet causes (*a*) inadequate production and regeneration of the visual purple with resulting night blindness and (*b*) disturbances in the epithelial tissue resulting in keratomalacia, xerophthalmia and lessened resistance to infections through the epithelial surfaces. Vitamin A is present in the liver oils of the cod and other fish, in butter, egg yolk, cheese, and liver as well as in tomatoes and many other vegetable foods in most of which it exists as carotene.

v. A_1, a form of vitamin A found in the eye tissues of marine fishes.

v. A_2, a compound with properties similar to those of vitamin A but with a different absorption spectrum in the ultraviolet: it is found in the livers of fresh water fish.

v. B, a member of the vitamin B complex.

v. B complex, a group of water-soluble substances including thiamine, riboflavin, nicotinic acid (niacin), nicotinamide (niacin amide, nicotinic acid amide), the vitamin B_6 group (pyridoxine, pyridoxal, pyridoxamine, alpha pyracin, beta pyracin), biotin, pantothenic acid, folic acid, possibly para-aminobenzoic acid, inositol, vitamin B_{12}, and possibly choline. Nicotinic acid and nicotinamide are also known, together, as the pellagra-preventing factor, P.-P. factor, or antipellagra factor.

v. B_1, thiamine.

v. B_2, riboflavin.

v. B_3, nicotinamide.

v. B_4, a water-soluble factor from yeast that prevents a specific paralysis in rats and chicks.

v. B_5, a factor necessary to maintain growth in rats and weight in pigeons.

v. B_6, pyridoxine.

v. B_8, adenylic acid.

v. B_{10}, v. B_{11}, names that have been applied to compounds allied to folic acid which have an influence on feathering and on growth in chicks.

v. B_{12}, cyanocobalamin.

v. B_{14}, a compound isolated from urine; said to check the reproduction of cancer cells and to act as an antipernicious anemia factor.

v. B_{15}, pangamic acid.

v. B_c, folic acid.

v. B_c conjugate, folic acid.

v. B_t, a vitamin necessary for the nutrition of the meal worm, *Tenebrio molitor.*

v. B_x, para-aminobenzoic acid.

v. C, ascorbic acid.

v. D, any one of several related sterols which have antirachitic properties. They may be produced artificially by the irradiation of ergosterol and a few related sterols. See *ergosterol.* Deficiency of vitamin D tends to cause rickets in children and osteomalacia and osteoporosis in adults. It is present in the liver oils of various fish, in butter and egg yolk and is produced in the body on exposure to sunlight.

v. D_1, a term formerly applied to an impure mixture of calciferol with another sterol.

v. D_2, calciferol.

v. D_3, an antirachitic factor occurring naturally in cod liver oil or prepared by activation of 7-dehydrocholesterol.

v. E, a vitamin necessary in the diet of rats to insure reproduction. Chemically it is alpha-tocopherol, one of three tocopherols (alpha, beta and gamma) occurring in wheat germ oil, cereals, egg yolk and beef liver. It is also prepared synthetically. It has been administered in the treatment of amyotrophic lateral sclerosis and other degenerative diseases.

v. F, a name given to the fatty acids, linoleic, linolenic, and arachidonic acids.

v. G, riboflavin.

v. H, biotin.

v. H′, para-aminobenzoic acid.

v. J, a vitamin which is apparently necessary for development in guinea pigs.

v. K, a compound which promotes clotting of the blood by increasing the synthesis of prothrombin by the liver. It occurs naturally in alfalfa, spinach, cabbage, putrefied fish meal, hog-liver fat, egg yolk, hempseed. Vitamin K and its synthetic analogues have an antihemorrhagic activity with a specific effect on prothrombin deficiency. They are used in obstructive jaundice, in hemorrhagic states associated with intestinal diseases and with disease of the liver, in the hypoprothrombinemia of the newborn, administered parenterally to the infant or to the mother during labor.

v. K_1, phytonadione.

v. K_3, menadione.

v. L, a factor necessary for lactation in rats. L_1 is found in beef-liver extract, L_2 in yeast.

v. M, folic acid.

v. P, the flavone factor in lemon juice (citrin), and Hungarian red pepper, deficiency of which causes increased permeability of capillary walls: possibly a mixture of flavones, eriodictyol and hesperidin.

v. R, a vitamin necessary for proper development of chicks.

v. S, a vitamin necessary for proper development of chicks.

v. V, a vitamin concerned in the development of chicks.

v. X, a name formerly given to vitamin P.

vitaminogenic (vi-tam″ĭ-no-jen′ik). Caused by or due to vitamin.

vitaminoid (vi′tah-min-oid). Resembling vitamin.

vitaminology (vi″tah-min-ol′o-je). The study of vitamins.

vitaminoscope (vi″tah-min′o-skōp) [*vitamin* + Gr. *skopein* to examine]. An instrument for measuring the time required for recovery from glare as an indication of the vitamin A reserve of the body.

vitanition (vi″tan-ish′un). Nutritional disorder due to vitamin deficiency.

vitascope (vi′tah-skōp) [L. *vita* life + Gr. *skopein* to examine]. An instrument for use in the study of animal movements.

vitascopic (vi″tah-skop′ik). Pertaining to the vitascope.

Vitel. Abbreviation for L. *vitel′lus*, yolk.

vitellarium (vit″ĕ-lăr′e-um). An accessory genital gland found in tapeworms which secretes the yolk or albumin for the fertilized egg. Called also *vitelline gland*.

vitellary (vit′ĕ-lăr″e). Pertaining to the vitellus, or yolk.

vitellase (vi-tel′ās). An enzyme from various microorganisms which coagulates egg yolk.

vitellicle (vi-tel′ĭ-k′l) [L. *vitellus* yolk]. The yolk sac.

vitellin (vi-tel′in) [L. *vitellus* yolk]. A simple protein resembling a globulin in all respects except that it cannot be precipitated from its solution with sodium chloride. It includes ordinary vitellin and crystallin. Ordinary vitallin (ovovitellin) is derived from the yolk of eggs, in which it exists in combination with lecithin.

vitelline (vi-tel′in) [L. *vitellus* yolk]. Resembling or pertaining to the yolk of an egg or ovum.

vitellogenesis (vi″tel-o-jen′e-sis). Production of yolk.

vitellolutein (vi″tel-o-lu′te-in) [L. *vitellus* yolk + *luteus* yellow]. A yellow pigment obtainable from lutein.

vitellorubin (vi″tel-o-ru′bin) [L. *vitellus* yolk + *ruber* red]. 1. A reddish pigment obtainable from lutein. 2. Crustaceorubin.

vitellose (vi-tel′ōs). A form of proteose derived from vitellin.

vitellus (vi-tel′us) [L.]. The yolk of an egg, or of an ovum.

vitiatin (vi-ti′ah-tin). A compound sometimes occurring in the urine along with creatine and creatinine. It is a homologue of choline.

vitiation (vish″e-a′shun) [L. *vitiatio*]. Impairment of efficiency; the perversion of any process so as to render it faulty or ineffective.

vitiligines (vit″ĭ-lij′ĭ-nēz) [pl. of *vitiligo*]. Depigmented areas of the skin, as those occurring in vitiligo, or the whitened lines of striae atrophicae.

vitiliginous (vit″ĭ-lij′ĭ-nus). Relating to or affected with vitiligo.

vitiligo (vit″ĭ-li′go) [L.]. An idiopathic condition characterized by failure of the skin to form melanin, with patches of depigmentation often having a hyperpigmented border, and often enlarging slowly. Called also *piebald skin* and *leukoderma*. **v. cap′itis, Celsus′ v.,** alopecia areata. **circumnervic v.,** leukoderma acquisitum centrifugum. **v. i′ridis,** depigmentation of the iris. **perinevic v.,** vitiligo appearing around a nevus.

vitiligoidea (vit″ĭ-li-goi′de-ah). Xanthoma. **v. pla′num, v. tubero′sum,** essential xanthoma.

Vitis (vi′tis) [L.]. A genus of plants including various species of grape or grape vine. **V. carno′sa,** an Asiatic species of grape: in India the seeds and roots are used in medicine. **V. latifo′lia,** an East Indian grape vine affording detergent, alterative, and soothing medicines. **V. vinif′era,** a species affording most of the more valuable varieties of cultivated and wine-producing grapes.

vitium (vish′e-um), pl. *vit′ia* [L.]. Fault, defect. **v. conformatio′nis,** a defect in shape; a malformation. **v. cor′dis,** an organic heart defect. **v. pri′mae formatio′nis,** a developmental anomaly.

vitochemical (vi″to-kem′ĭ-kal). Organic; pertaining to organic chemistry.

vitodynamic (vi″to-di-nam′ik). Biodynamic.

vit. ov. sol. Abbreviation for L. *vitel′lo o′vi solu′tus*, dissolved in yolk of egg.

vitreocapsulitis (vit″re-o-kap″su-li′tis) [L. *vitreus* glassy + *capsula* capsule + *-itis*]. Inflammation of the capsule enclosing the vitreous; hyalitis.

vitreodentin (vit″re-o-den′tin) [L. *vitreus* glassy + *dentin*]. An unusually hard and glasslike form of dentin.

Vitreoscillaceae (vit″re-os″sil-la′se-e). A family of Schizomycetes (order Beggiatoales), made up of saprophytic microorganisms, found in decaying organic matter, occurring in colorless trichomes of varying flexibility, which show a gliding motion when attached to a substrate. It includes three genera, *Bactoscil′la*, *Microscil′la*, and *Vitreoscil′la*.

vitreous (vit′re-us) [L. *vitreus* glassy]. Glasslike or hyaline; often used alone to designate the vitreous body of the eye (corpus vitreum [N A]).

vitreum (vit′re-um). The vitreous body of the eye (corpus vitreum [N A]).

vitrina (vĭ-tri′nah) [L. *vitrum* glass]. A translucent or glassy material. **v. audito′ria, v. au′ris,** endolympha. **v. ocula′ris, v. oc′uli,** corpus vitreum.

vitriol (vit′re-ol) [L. *vitriolum*]. Any crystalline sulfate. **blue v.,** copper sulfate, $CuSO_4$. **elixir of v.,** aromatic sulfuric acid. **green v.,** iron sulfate or copperas, Fe_2SO_4. **oil of v.,** sulfuric acid. **white v., zinc v.,** zinc sulfate.

vitriolated (vit′re-o-lāt″ed). Containing vitriol; containing sulfuric acid.

vitropression (vit″ro-presh′un). Production of anemia of the skin by pressing on it with a slip of glass in order to detect abnormal discolorations of the skin other than that produced by hyperemia.

vitrum (vit′rum) [L.]. Glass.

vitular (vit′u-lar) [L. *vitulus* calf]. Pertaining to a calf, or to calving.

vitulary (vit′u-ler″e). Vitular.

vituline (vit′u-lĭn). Pertaining to or derived from a calf.

vives (vīvz). Chronic inflammation of the submaxillary glands of the horse.

vivi- (viv′e) [L. *vivus* alive]. Combining form meaning alive or denoting relationship to life.

vividialysis (viv″ĭ-di-al′ĭ-sis). Removal by dialysis through a living membrane (the peritoneum). Cf. *peritoneal lavage*, under *lavage*.

vividiffusion (viv″ĭ-dĭ-fu′zhun). Removal of diffusible substances from the circulating blood of living animals by dialysis, performed by the continuous passage of the blood from an artery through a system of tubes made of celloidin immersed in saline solution, and its return to a vein, thus yielding by dialysis certain of its constituents to the fluid surrounding the tubes.

vivification (viv″ĭ-fi-ka′shun) [L. *vivificatio*, from *vivus* living + *facere* to make]. The conversion of lifeless into living protein matter in the process of assimilation.

viviparity (viv″ĭ-par′ĭ-te). The quality of being viviparous.

viviparous (vi-vip′ah-rus) [*vivi-* + L. *parere* to bring forth, produce]. Bearing living young which derive nutrition directly from the maternal organism through a special organ, the placenta, which is an outgrowth of the embryo.

vivipation (viv″ĭ-pa′shun). The form of reproduction in which the embryo develops within and derives nutrition directly from the maternal organism.

viviperception (viv″ĭ-per-sep′shun). The study of the vital processes of the living organism.

vivisection (viv″ĭ-sek′shun). The performance of surgical procedures upon living animals for purposes of research.

vivisectionist (viv″ĭ-sek′shun-ist). One who practices or defends vivisection.

vivosphere (vi′vo-sfēr) [L. *vivus* alive + *atmosphere*]. The region between the atmosphere above and the petrosphere below, in which life is found most abundantly.

Vleminckx solution (vlem′inks) [Jean Francois *Vleminckx*, Belgian physician, 1800-1876]. Lime sulfurated solution.

V.M. Abbreviation for *voltmeter*.

vocal (vo′kal) [L. *vocalis*, from *vox* voice]. Pertaining to the voice.

Voegtlin's unit (vegt′lin) [Carl *Voegtlin*, American pharmacologist, 1879–1960]. See under *unit*.

Voge's test (vo′jēz) [C. I. B. *Voge*, British physician]. See under *tests*.

Voges-Proskauer reaction [O. *Voges*, German physician; Bernhard *Proskauer*, German hygienist, 1851–1915]. See under *reaction*.

Vogt's angle (fōgts) [Karl *Vogt*, German naturalist and physiologist, 1817–1895]. See under *angle*.

Vogt's disease, syndrome (fōgts) [Oskar *Vogt*, German neurologist, 1870–1959]. See under *disease* and *syndrome*.

Vogt's point (fōgts) [Paul Frederick Emmanuel *Vogt*, surgeon in Greifswald, 1847–1885]. See under *point*.

Vogt-Hueter point (fōgt-he′ter) [P. F. E. *Vogt;* Karl *Hueter*, German surgeon, 1838–1882]. See *Vogt's point*, under *point*.

voice (vois) [L. *vox* voice]. A sound produced by the speech organs and uttered by the mouth. **amphoric v.,** cavernous v. **cavernous v.,** a hollow sound heard on auscultation when the patient speaks. It indicates a cavity in the lung or a dilated bronchus. **eunuchoid v.,** a high falsetto voice in a man, resembling that of a eunuch or a woman. **whispered v.,** the transmission of a whisper to the auscultating ear, heard in pulmonary consolidation.

void (void). To cast out as waste matter.

Voigt's lines (voits) [Christian August *Voigt*, Austrian anatomist, 1809–1890]. See under *line*.

Voillemier's point (vwal-me-āz′) [Léon Clémont *Voillemier*, French urologist]. See under *point*.

Voit's nucleus (foits) [Carl von *Voit*, physiologist in Munich, 1831–1908]. See under *nucleus*.

voix (vwah) [Fr.]. Voice. **v. de polichinelle** (vwah″dĕ-pol″ish-ĭ-nel′) [Fr. "voice of Punch"], a variety of egophony.

vol. Abbreviation for *volume*.

vola (vo′lah) [L.]. A concave or hollow surface. **v. ma′nus** [B N A], the hollow of the hand (palma manus [N A]). **v. pe′dis,** the hollow of the foot (planta pedis [N A]).

volar (vo′lar). Pertaining to the palm or sole; indicating the flexor surface of the forearm, wrist, or hand.

volardorsal (vo″lar-dor′sal). From the volar to the dorsal surface.

volaris (vo-la′ris). Palmar; in B N A terminology, designating relationship to the palm of the hand.

volatile (vol′ah-til) [L. *volatilis*, from *volare* to fly]. Tending to evaporate rapidly.

volatilization (vol″ah-til-i-za′shun). The conversion into vapor or gas without chemical change.

volatilize (vol′ah-til-īz). To convert into vapor.

volatilizer (vol′ah-til-īz″er). An apparatus for producing volatilization.

vole (vōl). A mouselike rodent of the genus *Microtus*. The field vole of Great Britain is affected by a disease resembling tuberculosis, being caused by *Mycobacterium muris*, formerly called the *vole bacillus*. From this organism has been prepared a vaccine for use in tuberculosis of man and cattle.

Volhard's solution (fōl′harts) [J. *Volhard*, German chemist, 1834–1910]. See under *solution*.

Volhard's test (fōl′harts) [Franz *Volhard*, German internist, 1872–1950]. See under *tests*.

volition (vo-lish′un) [L. *velle* to will]. The act or power of willing.

volitional (vo-lish′un-al). Pertaining to the will.

Volkmann's canal, membrane (fōlk′mahnz) [Alfred Wilhelm *Volkmann*, German physiologist, 1800–1877]. See under the nouns.

Volkmann's contracture, deformity, operation, splint, spoon (flōk′mahnz) [Richard von *Volkmann*, German surgeon, 1830–1889]. See under the nouns.

volley (vol′e). A rhythmical succession of muscular twitches artificially induced; the aggregate of nerve impulses set up by a single stimulus. **antidromic v.,** the back-fire excitation traveling centrad through the anterior root during the reflex arc.

volsella (vol-sel′ah) [L.]. Vulsella.

volt (vōlt) [Alessandro *Volta*, Italian physiologist and physicist, 1745–1827]. The unit of electromotive force in the M.K.S. system of measurement, being the force necessary to cause one ampere of current to flow against one ohm of resistance. **electron v.,** the energy acquired by an electron when accelerated by a potential of one volt, being equivalent to 3.82×10^{-20} gram-calories, or 1.6×10^{-12} ergs.

voltage (vōl′tij). Electromotive force measured in volts.

voltagramme (vōl′tah-gram). A kind of faradic battery giving a nearly continuous current.

voltaic (vol-ta′ik). Pertaining to galvanism.

voltaism (vol′tah-izm). Galvanism.

voltaization (vol″tah-i-za′shun). Continued or discontinuous electrization with a current of relatively large quantity under medium or feeble tension.

voltammeter (vōlt-am′me-ter). An instrument for measuring both volts and amperes.

voltampere (vōlt-am′pēr). The product of multiplying a volt by a milliampere.

voltmeter (vōlt′me-ter). An instrument for measuring electromotive force in volts.

Voltolini's disease, tube (vol″to-le′nēz) [Frederic Edward Rudolf *Voltolini*, rhinologist and otologist in Breslau, 1819–1889]. See under *disease* and *tube*.

volume (vol′ūm). The measure of the quantity of a substance. **atomic v.,** the value obtained by dividing the atomic weight of an element by its specific gravity in the solid condition. **blood v.,** the total quantity of blood in the body: expressed in liters or in liters per kilogram of body weight. **circulation v., v. of circulation,** the amount of blood pumped through the lungs and out to all the organs of the body by the heart: expressed in liters of blood flow per minute. **expiratory reserve v.,** the maximal amount of gas that can be expired from the end-expiratory level. Abbreviated ERV. **inspiratory reserve v.,** the maximal amount of gas that can be inspired from the end-inspiratory position. Abbreviated IRV. **minute v.** 1. (*Of the blood.*) The total flow of blood through the heart per minute. 2. (*Of air.*) The total volume of air breathed per minute. **packed-cell v.,** the volume of the blood corpuscles in a centrifuged sample of blood. **residual v.,** the amount of gas remaining in the lung at the end of a maximal expiration. Abbreviated RV. **stroke v.,** the amount of blood ejected from each ventricle at each beat of the heart. **tidal v.,** the amount of gas passing into and out of the lungs in each respiratory cycle. Abbreviated VT.

volumebolometer (vol″ūm-bo-lom′e-ter). Volumesphygmobolometer.

volumenometer (vol″ūm-nom′e-ter). Volumometer.

volumesphygmobolometer (vol″ūm-sfig″mo-bo-lom′e-ter). Sahli apparatus for measuring the pulse volume. Called also *volumebolometer.*

volumetric (vol″u-met′rik) [*volume* + *metric*]. Pertaining to or accomplished by measurement in volumes.

volumette (vol″u-met′). An instrument for delivering repeatedly quantities of fluid in accurate predetermined amounts.

volumination (vol″u-mĭ-na′shun). The swelling of the bodies of bacteria produced by blood serum. Normal serum produces a certain amount of swelling, but immune serum produces much more.

volumometer (vol″u-mom′e-ter) [*volume* + Gr. *metron* measure]. An instrument for measuring volume or changes in volume.

voluntary (vol′un-tār″e) [L. *voluntas* will]. Accomplished in accordance with the will.

voluntomotory (vo″lun-to-mo′tor-e) [L. *voluntas* will + *motor* mover]. Subject to voluntary motor influence.

volute (vo-lūt′). Rolled up.

volutin (vo-lu′tin). Bacterial nucleoprotein occurring as cytoplasmic granules (metachromatic granules) having a marked affinity for basic dyes.

volvulate (vol′vu-lāt) [L. *volvere* to twist round]. To twist or form a knot (volvulus).

volvulosis (vol″vu-lo′sis). Infestation with the worm *Onchocerca volvulus,* which produces cutaneous or subcutaneous fibrous tumors.

volvulus (vol′vu-lus) [L. *volvere* to twist round]. Intestinal obstruction due to a knotting and twisting of the bowel. **v. neonato′rum,** volvulus occurring in the newborn.

vomer (vo′mer) [L. "plowshare"]. [N A, B N A] The unpaired flat bone that forms the inferior and posterior part of the nasal septum.

vomerine (vo′mer-in). Of or pertaining to the vomer.

vomerobasilar (vo″mer-o-bas′ĭ-lar). Pertaining to the vomer and to the basilar portion of the cranium.

vomeronasal (vo″mer-o-na′sal). Pertaining to the vomer and the nasal bone.

vomica (vom′ĭ-kah), pl. *vom′icae* [L. "abscess"). 1. The profuse and sudden expectoration of pus and putrescent matter. 2. An abnormal cavity in an organ, especially in the lung, caused by suppuration and the breaking down of tissue.

vomicose (vom′ĭ-kōs). Full of ulcers; ulcerous.

vomit (vom′it) [L. *vomitare*]. 1. To cast up from the stomach by the mouth. 2. Matter cast up from the stomach; vomited matter. 3. An emetic. **Barcoo v.,** vomiting and nausea, with bulimia, affecting persons in southern Australia. **bilious v.,** vomited matter stained with bile. **black v.,** blackish matter consisting of blood which has been acted upon by the gastric juice, cast up from the stomach in yellow fever and other conditions in which blood collects in the stomach. **bloody v.,** vomit containing blood. **coffee-ground v.,** the bloody vomit of malignant disease of the stomach. It consists of broken-down blood mixed with stomach contents.

vomiting (vom′it-ing). The forcible expulsion of the contents of the stomach through the mouth. **cerebral v.,** spontaneous vomiting without nausea, frequently seen in intracranial disease. **cyclic v.,** vomiting recurring at irregular intervals: called also *periodic v.* and *recurrent v.* **dry v.,** nausea with attempts at vomiting, but with the ejection of nothing but gas. **fecal v.,** stercoraceous v. **hyperacid v.,** gastroxynsis. **hysterical v.,** vomiting accompanying an attack of hysteria. **incoercible v.,** vomiting that cannot be controlled. **nervous v.,** vomiting as a symptom of gastric neurosis. **periodic v.,** cyclic v. **pernicious v.,** vomiting in pregnancy, so severe as to threaten the life of the mother. **v. of pregnancy,** vomiting occurring in pregnancy, especially the early morning vomiting common in that condition. **projectile v.,** vomiting in which the vomitus is ejected with force. **recurrent v.,** cyclic v. **stercoraceous v.,** the vomiting of fecal matter. It is seen in intestinal obstruction, appendicitis, etc.

vomitive (vom′ĭ-tiv). Emetic.

vomito (vom′ĭ-to) [Sp.]. Vomit. **v. negro** (vom′ĭ-to na′gro) [Sp.]. 1. Black vomit. 2. Yellow fever.

vomitory (vom′ĭ-tor″e). An emetic.

vomiturition (vom″it-u-rish′un). Repeated ineffectual attempts at vomiting; retching.

vomitus (vom′ĭ-tus) [L.]. 1. Vomiting. 2. Matter vomited. **v. cruen′tus,** bloody vomit. **v. matuti′nus,** the morning vomiting of chronic gastric catarrh.

von Behring. See *Behring.*

von Bezold. See *Bezold.*

von Graefe. See *Graefe.*

von Haller. See *Haller.*

von Hippel. See *Hippel.*

von Jaksch. See *Jaksch.*

von Langenbeck. See *Langenbeck.*

von Leyden. See *Leyden.*

von Mikulicz. See *Mikulicz.*

von Recklinghausen. See *Recklinghausen.*

von Wahl. See *Wahl.*

vonulo (von′u-lo). A bronchial disease occurring in west Africa, and marked by severe pains in the chest, usually under the sternum, and occasionally under the shoulder blades.

Voorhees' bag (voor′ēz) [James Ditmars *Voorhees,* obstetrician in New York, 1869–1929]. See under *bag.*

Voronoff's operation (vo′ro-nofs) [Serge *Voronoff,* Russian physician in Paris, born 1866]. See under *operation.*

vortex (vor′teks), pl. *vor′tices* [L. "whirl"]. A whorled arrangement, design, or pattern, as of muscle fibers, or of the ridges or hairs on the skin; used as a general term in anatomical nomenclature. **coccygeal v., v. coccyg′eus** [B N A], a spiral arrangement of hairs over the region of the coccyx. Omitted in N A. **v. cor′dis** [N A, B N A], **v. of heart,** the whorled arrangement of muscle fibers at the apex, in the left ventricle of the heart, through which the more superficial fibers pass to the interior of the left ventricle toward the base. **v. len′tis,** a spiral figure on the surface of the lens of the eye produced by the concentric arrangement of the fibers composing it. **vor′tices pilo′rum** [N A, B N A], whorled patterns of hair growth on the body, as that on the crown of the head.

Vorticella (vor″tĭ-sel′ah). A genus of ciliate protozoans, often found in feces, urine, nasal mucus, etc.

v. o. s. Abbreviation for L. *vitel′lo o′vi solu′tus,* dissolved in yolk of egg.

Vossius lenticular ring (vos′e-us) [Adolf *Vossius,* German ophthalmologist, 1855–1925]. See under *ring.*

voussure (voo-ser′) [Fr. "arch," "curve"]. A bulging of the precordium due to hypertrophy and dilatation of the heart during childhood.

vox (voks), pl. *vo′ces* [L.]. Voice. **v. choler′ica,** the peculiar suppressed voice of true cholera.

voyeur (voi-yer′). A person who practices voyeurism.

voyeurism (voi′yer-izm). A form of paraphilia in which sexual gratification is derived from looking at another's genital organs.

V.R. Abbreviation for *vocal resonance.*

V.S. Abbreviation for *volumetric solution.*

Vs. Abbreviation for L. *venaesec′tio,* venisection.

v.s. Abbreviation for *vibration seconds,* the unit of measurement of sound waves.

Vs.B. Abbreviation for L. *venaesec′tio bra′chii,* bleeding in the arm.

V.T. Abbreviation for *vacuum tuberculin.*

vuerometer (vu″er-om′e-ter) [Fr. *vue* sight + Gr. *metron* measure]. An instrument for measuring the distance between the eyes.

vulcanite (vul′kan-it). Vulcanized caoutchouc or India rubber, formerly used as a base for artificial dentures.

vulcanize (vul′kah-niz). To subject caoutchouc, in the presence of sulfur, to heat and high steam pressure, producing a flexible or hard rubber, as desired.

vulgaris (vul-ga′ris) [L.]. Ordinary; common.

vulnerability (vul″ner-ah-bil′ĭ-te). Susceptibility to injury or to contagion.

vulnerant (vul′ner-ant). 1. Inflicting injury or causing a wound. 2. An agent which causes injury.

vulnerary (vul′ner-er″e) [L. *vulnerarius*, from *vulnus* wound]. 1. Pertaining to or healing wounds. 2. An agent that heals wounds.

vulnerate (vul′ner-āt) [L. *vulnerare*]. To wound.

vulnus (vul′nus), pl. *vul′nera* [L.]. A wound.

Vulpian's atrophy, law, reaction (vul′pe-anz) [Edme Felix Alfred *Vulpian*, French physician, 1826–1887]. See under the nouns.

vulpis (vul′pis) [L.]. Genitive of L. *vul′pes* fox. **v. fel,** the bile or gall of the fox, or its homeopathic preparation. **v. he′par,** the liver of the fox, or its homeopathic preparation. **v. pul′mo,** the lung of the fox, or its homeopathic preparation.

vulsella, vulsellum (vul-sel′ah, vul-sel′um) [L.]. A forceps with clawlike hooks at the extremity of each blade.

vulva (vul′vah) [L.]. The region of the external genital organs of the female, including the labia majora, labia minora, mons pubis, clitoris, perineum, and vestibule of the vagina. Called also *pudendum femininum* [N A]. **v. cer′ebri,** an opening into the third ventricle of the brain, below the column of the fornix. **v. clau′sa, v. coni′vens,** a vulva in which the labia majora are plump and closed. **fused v.,** synechia vulvae. **v. hi′ans,** a vulva in which the labia majora are flaccid and gaping.

vulval, vulvar (vul′val, vul′var). Pertaining to the vulva.

vulvectomy (vul-vek′to-me). Excision of the vulva.

vulvismus (vul-viz′mus). Vaginismus.

vulvitis (vul-vi′tis) [*vulva* + *-itis*]. Inflammation of the vulva. **v. blenorrha′gica,** a mucopurulent discharge from the mucous membrane of the vulva, usually resulting from gonorrheal infection. **creamy v.,** vulvitis with a white thick exudate covering the inflamed mucosa. **diabetic v.,** vulvitis occurring in diabetes. **diphtheric v., diphtheritic v.,** vulvitis with the formation of a false membrane. **eczematiform v.,** vulvitis marked by the formation of vesicular pustules. **follicular v.,** inflammation of the follicles of the vulva. **leukoplakic v.,** kraurosis vulvae. **pseudoleukoplakic v.,** vulvitis in which the mucosa is whitish and opaque, resembling leukoplakia. **ulcerative v.,** a form with ulceration, pain, and lymphangitis.

vulvocrural (vul-vo-kroo′ral). Pertaining to the vulva and the thigh.

vulvopathy (vul-vop′ah-the) [*vulva* + Gr. *pathos* disease]. Any disease of the vulva.

vulvorectal (vul″vo-rek′tal). Pertaining to or communicating with the vulva and rectum, as a vulvorectal fistula.

vulvo-uterine (vul″vo-u′ter-in). Pertaining to the vulva and uterus.

vulvovaginal (vul″vo-vaj′ĭ-nal). Pertaining to the vulva and vagina.

vulvovaginitis (vul″vo-vaj″ĭ-ni′tis). Inflammation of the vulva and vagina, or of the vulvovaginal glands.

vv. Abbreviation for L. *ve′nae* (veins).

V.W. Abbreviation for *vessel wall.*

W

W. 1. Chemical symbol for *tungsten.* 2. Abbreviation for *wehnelt*, a unit of hardness roentgen rays.

w. Abbreviation for *watt.*

Wachendorf's membrane (vahk′en-dorfs) [Eberhard Jacob *Wachendorf*, German anatomist of the 18th century]. See under *membrane.*

Wachsmuth's mixture (vahks′moots) [Hans *Wachsmuth*, German neurologist, born 1872]. See under *mixture.*

wagaga (wah-gag′ah). Fiji name for filariasis.

Wagner's corpuscles, spot (vahg′nerz) [Rudolf *Wagner*, German physiologist, 1805–1864]. See under *corpuscle* and *spot.*

Wagner's disease (vahg′nerz) [Ernst Lebrecht *Wagner*, Leipzig pathologist, 1829–1888]. Colloid milium.

Wagner's hammer (vahg′nerz) [Johann Philip *Wagner*, German physicist, 1799–1879]. See under *hammer.*

Wagner's operation (vahg′nerz) [Wilhelm *Wagner*, German surgeon, 1848–1900]. See under *operation.*

Wagner's theory (vahg′nerz) [Moritz *Wagner*, German scientist, 1813–1887]. See *migration theory*, under *theory.*

Wagner-Jauregg treatment (vahg′ner-yow′-reg) [Julius *Wagner-Jauregg*, Austrian neuropsychiatrist, 1857–1940, noted for his research on cretinism and for treatment of dementia paralytica by malarial infection; winner of the Nobel prize for medicine in 1927]. See under *treatment.*

wagnerism (vahg′ner-izm). Inoculation with malarial organisms in the asexual cycle.

Wagstaffe's fracture (wag′stafs) [William Warwick *Wagstaffe*, English surgeon, 1843–1910]. See under *fracture.*

Wahl's sign (vahlz′) [Eduard von *Wahl*, German surgeon, 1833–1890]. See under *sign.*

wakamba (wa-kam′bah). An African arrow poison.

wakefulness (wāk′ful-nes). A state marked by indisposition to sleep: sleeplessness.

Waksman (waks′man), Selman A. Russian microbiologist in the United States, born 1888, noted for his research in the field of antibiotics; winner of the Nobel prize in medicine and physiology for 1952.

Walcher's position (vahl′kerz) [Gustav Adolf *Walcher*, gynecologist in Stuttgart, 1856–1935]. See under *position.*

Walcheren fever (vahl′ka-ren) [*Walcheren*, a region in Holland]. Severe malaria endemic in Holland.

Waldenburg's apparatus (vahl′den-boorgz) [Louis *Waldenburg*, German physician, 1837–1881]. See under *apparatus.*

Waldenström's disease (vahl′den-stremz) [Johan Henning *Waldenström*, orthopedic surgeon in Stockholm, born 1877]. Osteochondrosis of the capitular epiphysis.

Waldeyer's fossa, glands, layer, ring, sul-

cus, etc. (vahl′di-erz) [Wilhelm von *Waldeyer*, anatomist in Berlin, 1836–1921]. See under the nouns.

wale (wāl). Wheal.

walk (wok). 1. To move on foot. 2. The manner in which one moves on foot. See also *gait* and *walking*.

walking (wok′ing). Progressing on foot, or the manner in which one moves on foot. **camel's w.,** dromedary gait. **heel w.,** a gait marked by walking on the heels to avoid the pain of pressure upon the hyperalgesic soles of the feet in cases of peripheral neuritis. **kangaroo w.,** walking on all fours with the palms of the hands on the floor and the knees held as stiffly as possible; employed in the management of puerperal retroversions of the uterus. **moon w.,** sleep walking on moonlit nights. **sleep w.,** somnambulism.

wall (wawl). The limiting structure of a space, as of the chest, abdomen, or uterus, or of a definitive mass of material. For official names of specific walls of various anatomical structures, see under *paries*. **axial w.,** in a cavity involving an axial surface of a tooth, that wall which lies nearest the pulp (parallel with the long axis of the tooth). **cavity w.,** a plane surface of a tooth cavity prepared to receive a restoration, being named for the surface which it faces, or parallels, as buccal, distal, incisal, labial, lingual, mesial, occlusal; depending on the situation of the cavity there are also axial, gingival, pulpal, and subpulpal walls. **cell w.,** a structure outside of and protecting the cell membrane, present in all plant cells (composed chiefly of cellulose) and in many bacteria and other types of cells. **germ w.,** a ringlike thickening around the blastoderm of the bird, consisting of the advancing boundary zone at its margin. **gingival w.,** in a cavity involving an axial surface of a tooth, that wall which is nearest the gingiva. **nail w.,** vallum unguis. **parietal w.,** somatopleure. **periotic w.,** the wall of the otic vesicle. **pulpal w.,** in a cavity involving the occlusal or incisal surface of a tooth, that wall which overlies the pulp. **splanchnic w.,** splanchnopleure. **subpulpal w.,** the exposed inner surface of the pulp chamber of a tooth after the pulp has been removed.

Wallenberg's syndrome (vahl′en-bergz) [Adolf *Wallenberg*, German physician, 1862–1949]. See under *syndrome*.

wallerian degeneration, law (wahl-le′re-an) [Augustus Volney *Waller*, English physician, 1816–1870]. See under *degeneration* and *law*.

walleye (wahl′i). 1. Leukoma of the cornea. 2. Divergent strabismus.

Wallhauser and Whitehead's method [A. *Wallhauser;* J. M. *Whitehead*, American physicians]. The use of an autogenous gland filtrate in treating Hodgkin's disease.

wall-plate (wahl′plāt). An electrical apparatus for giving off a current of low tension and low voltage.

Walter's test (vahl′terz) [Friedrich Karl *Walter*, Bremen neurologist, born 1881]. See under *tests*.

Walthard's cell rests, inclusions, islets [Max *Walthard*, Swiss gynecologist, 1867–1933]. See under *islet*.

Walther's ducts, ganglion, ligament, etc. (vahl′terz) [August Friedrich *Walther*, German anatomist, 1688–1746]. See under the nouns.

wambles (wahm′b′lz). Milk sickness.

wandering (wahn′der-ing). Moving about freely; abnormally movable; too loosely attached. **mind w.,** reverie, day dreaming and similar states. **w. of a tooth,** displacement of a tooth due to destruction of the periodontal membrane by resorption or to absence of an adjacent tooth in the dental arch.

Wang's test (wangz) [*Wang* Chung Tik, Chinese physician, 1889–1931]. See under *tests*.

Wangensteen apparatus, suction, tube (wan′gen-stēn) [Owen H. *Wangensteen*, American surgeon, born 1898]. See under *tube*.

Wanner's symptom (vahn′erz) [Friedrich *Wanner*, Munich otologist, born 1870]. See under *symptom*.

Wanscher's mask (vahn′sherz) [Oscar *Wanscher*, Danish physician, 1846–1906]. A mask for ether anesthesia.

warbles (war′b′lz). See *Hypoderma*. **ox w.,** larvae of flies of the genus Hypoderma (*H. bovis* and *H. lineatum*) which infest cattle of the Northern Hemisphere.

Warburg's coenzyme, respiratory enzyme (war′boorgs) [Otto Heinrich *Warburg*, German physiological chemist, born 1883, noted for his research on the chemistry of respiration and on enzymes; winner of the Nobel prize for medicine and physiology in 1931]. See *triphosphopyridine nucleotide*, under *nucleotide*, and see under *enzyme*.

ward (ward). A large room in a hospital for the accommodation of several patients. **isolation w.,** a hospital ward for the isolation of persons having or suspected of having an infectious disease. **psychopathic w.,** a ward in a general hospital for temporary reception of psychiatric patients.

Wardrop's disease, operation (war′drops) [James *Wardrop*, English surgeon, 1782–1869]. See under *disease* and *operation*.

warfarin (war′far-in) [named for *Wisconsin Alumni Research Foundation*]. An anticoagulant compound, 3-(α-acetonylbenzyl)-4-hydroxycoumarin.

Waring's method, system (wār′ings) [George Edward *Waring*, American sanitarian, 1833–1898]. A method of sewage disposal by subsurface irrigation.

Warren's fat columns (war′enz) [John Collins *Warren*, Boston surgeon, 1778–1856]. See *fat columns*, under *column*.

wart (wort) [L. *verruca*]. An epidermal tumor of viral origin. Called also *verruca*. **anatomical w.,** verruca necrogenica. **cattle w.,** a condition of viral origin in cattle, characterized by development of nodular tumors, usually on the head, neck, and shoulders, and often on the udder. **fig w.,** condyloma acuminatum. **filiform w.,** verruca filiformis. **fugitive w.,** a form seen on the hands of young persons and generally not persistent. **Hassal-Henle w's,** hyaline excrescences in the periphery of Descemet's membrane occurring with advancing age; comparable to the so-called drusen in Bruch's membrane. **moist w.,** condyloma acuminatum. **mosaic w.,** an irregularly shaped lesion on the sole of the foot, with a granular surface, formed by an aggregation of contiguous plantar warts. **mother w.,** an epidermal tumor which seems to give rise to other similar growths. **necrogenic w.,** verruca necrogenica. **peruvian w.,** verruga peruana. **pitch w's,** epidermal tumors occurring in individuals who work in gas, tar, pitch, or various oils derived from coal. **plantar w.,** verruca plantaris. **pointed w.,** condyloma acuminatum. **postmortem w., prosector's w.,** verruca necrogenica. **seborrheic w.,** seborrheic keratosis. **seed w.,** a small wart apparently caused by inoculation from a larger one. **senile w.,** senile keratosis. **soot w.,** chimneysweeps' cancer. **telangiectatic w.,** angiokeratoma. **tuberculous w.,** verruca necrogenica. **venereal w.,** condyloma acuminatum.

Wartenberg's disease, phenomenon, sign, symptom (wor′ten-bergz) [Robert *Wartenberg*, American neurologist, 1887–1956]. See under the nouns.

Warthin's sign (wor′thinz) [Aldred Scott *Warthin*, American pathologist, 1866–1931]. See under *sign*.

wash (wosh). A lotion; a solution to be applied to mucous membrane or skin. **eye w.,** collyrium.

Wasielewskia (was″e-el-u′ske-ah). A form of amebae which acquire and lose flagella. *W. gru′beri* has been obtained in cultures from diarrheic stools.

Waskia (was′ke-ah). A name for the genus *Embadomonas.*

wasp (wosp) [L. *vespa*]. Any stinging hymenopterous insect of the family Vespidae, of which the genus Vespa is the type. Wasp-venom is employed in homeopathic practice.

wasserhelle (vos′er-hel″lĕ). [Ger. "water-clear"]. See *water-clear cells,* under *cell.*

Wassermann reaction, test (wos′er-man) [August Paul von *Wassermann,* bacteriologist in Berlin, 1866–1925]. See under *reaction.*

Wassermann-fast (wos′er-man fast). Showing a persistent positive Wassermann reaction despite antisyphilitic treatment.

Wassilieff's disease (was-sil′e-efs) [Nikolai Porfiryevich *Wassilieff,* Russian physician, born 1861]. Weil's disease.

waste (wāst). 1. Gradual loss, decay, or diminution of bulk. 2. Useless and effete material, unfit for further use within the organism. 3. To pine away or dwindle. **phonetic w. of the breath,** a too rapid expiratory act, due to paralysis of a lateral crico-arytenoid muscle.

waster (wās′ter). An ox or cow affected with tuberculosis.

water (wah′ter). 1. A tasteless, odorless, colorless liquid, $(H_2O)_n$, used as the standard of specific gravity and of specific heat. It freezes at 32°F. (0°C.) and boils at 212°F. (100°C.). It is present in all organic tissues and in many other substances. 2. Aromatic water. The waters for which official standards are promulgated include anise w., camphor w., chloroform w., cinnamon w., fennel w., hamamelis w., orange flower w., peppermint w., rose w., stronger rose w., spearmint w., and wintergreen w. **ammonia w.,** diluted ammonia solution. **ammonia w., stronger,** strong ammonia solution. **aromatic w.,** a solution, usually saturated, of a volatile oil or other aromatic or volatile substance in purified water, prepared by distillation or solution. **bound w.,** that portion of the water in body tissues which is attached more tenaciously to the colloids and is therefore more difficult to release from the tissue than the free water. **capillary w.,** the water contained in the soil above the water table of the ground water. **carbon dioxide-free w.,** purified water which has been boiled vigorously for 5 minutes or more and protected from absorption of carbon dioxide from the atmosphere while it is cooling. **w. of combustion,** metabolic w. **w. of crystallization,** that which is an ingredient of many salts, imparting to them a crystalline form. **distilled w.,** water which has been purified by distillation. **egg w.,** water containing fertilizin exuded from the ripe eggs of sea urchins and other aquatic animals, by which the spermatozoa are agglutinated. **fish w.,** an extract of fish used in preparing bacteriologic culture mediums. **free w.,** that portion of the water in body tissues which is not closely bound by attachment to the colloids. **Goulard's w.,** diluted lead subacetate solution. **ground w.,** the water which lies in the depth of soils, being carried along under ground over impervious strata. **hamamelis w.,** an astringent solution prepared by maceration in water of cut dormant twigs of *Hamamelis virginiana.* **hard w.,** water that contains salts of calcium or magnesium, which resist the action of soap, so that it does not readily form lather. **heavy w.,** a compound analogous to water, but containing deuterium, the mass two isotope of hydrogen, the formula being D_2O or $H^2{}_2O$. It differs from ordinary water in having a higher freezing point (3.8°C.) and boiling point (101.4°C.), and in the fact that it is incapable of supporting life. Called also *deuterium oxide.* **Hiss' serum w.** See *serum w.* **w. for injection,** water for parenteral use, prepared by distillation, and meeting certain standards as to sterility and clarity. **lead w.,** diluted lead subacetate solution. **lime w.,** calcium hydroxide solution. **metabolic w.,** water in the body derived from metabolism of a food element such as starch, glucose, or fat. Called also *w. of combustion.* **mineral w.,** water containing mineral salts in solution in sufficient quantity to give it special properties and taste. **peptone w.** See under *culture medium.* **potable w.,** water that is suitable for drinking purposes. **purified w.,** water obtained by distillation or de-ionization, used for pharmaceutical or other purposes requiring a mineral-free water. **saline w.,** a water which contains neutral salts. **serum w.,** a mixture of blood serum and distilled water, with sugar and indicator added: used in preparing bacteriological culture mediums. **soft w.,** water that contains little or no mineral matter. **witch-hazel w.,** hamamelis water.

water-bite (wah′ter-bīt″). See *trench foot,* under *foot.*

water-borne (wah′ter-born″). Propagated by contaminated drinking water: said of diseases.

waterbrain (wah′ter-brān). A disease of sheep marked by a staggering gait.

Waterhouse-Friderichsen syndrome (wah′ter-hous frid″er-ik′sen) [Rupert *Waterhouse,* British physician, 1873–1958; Carl *Friderichsen,* Danish physician, born 1886]. See under *syndrome.*

waters (wah′terz). A popular name for the liquor amnii.

watershed (wah′ter-shed). A ridge which directs drainage toward either side. **abdominal w's,** the ridges formed in the supine position by the forward projection of the lumbar vertebrae and the projecting brim of the pelvis, causing free effusions to gravitate into the lumbar fossae and pelvis.

Watkins' operation (wot′kinz) [Thomas James *Watkins,* gynecologist in Chicago, 1863–1925]. See under *operation.*

Watson (wot′son), James Dewey. United States geneticist, born 1928; co-winner, with Maurice Wilkins and Francis Crick, of the Nobel prize in medicine and physiology for 1962, for the discovery of the molecular structure of deoxyribonucleic acid.

Watson-Schwartz test (wot′son-shwarts) [Cecil J. *Watson,* American physician, born 1901; Samuel *Schwartz,* American physician, born 1916]. See under *tests.*

Watsonius watsoni (wot-so′ne-us wot-so′ni) [Malcolm *Watson,* British physician, 1873–1955]. A pear-shaped amphistome trematode found in a case of diarrhea in Africa. Called also *Amphistoma watsoni.*

watt (wot) [after James *Watt,* 1736–1819]. A unit of electric power, being the work done at the rate of 1 joule per second. It is equivalent to a current of 1 ampere under a pressure of 1 volt.

wattage (wot′ij). The power output or consumption of an electrical device expressed in watts.

watt-hour (wot′our). A unit of electrical work or energy, equal to the wattage multiplied by the time in hours.

wattmeter (wot′me-ter). An instrument for measuring electric activity in watts.

wave (wāv). A uniformly advancing disturbance in which the parts moved undergo a double oscillation. **alpha w's,** waves in the electroencephalogram which have a frequency of 8 to 13 per second. **anacrotic w., anadicrotic w.** See under *pulse.* **arterial w.,** a wave in the phlebogram of the jugular vein, due to a shock transmitted to the vein by a pulsation of the carotid artery. **beta w's,** waves in the electroencephalogram, which have a frequency of 18 to 30 per second. **brain w's,** the fluctuations of electrical potential in the brain, as recorded by electroencephalography. See *alpha, beta, delta,* and *theta w's.* Some observers distinguish three types of waves: (1) *trains,* which correspond to alpha waves; (2) *spindles,* short series with a frequency of 14 per second; and (3) *random w's,* irregular changes of potential with no fixed frequency which appear at the beginning of sleep. **catacrotic**

w., catadicrotic w. See under *pulse.* **contraction w.,** the wave of progression of the contraction in a muscle from the point of stimulation; also the graphic representation of a contracting muscle. **delta w's,** waves in the electroencephalogram which have a frequency of ½ to 3 per second. **dicrotic w.** 1. The second or smaller ascending wave in the descending line of the sphygmogram. 2. Recoil wave. **electromagnetic w's,** the entire series of ethereal waves which are similar in character, and which move with the velocity of light, but which vary enormously in wavelength. The unbroken series is known from the hertzian waves used in radio transmission which may be miles in length (one mile equals 1.6×10^5 cm.) through heat and light, the ultraviolet, roentgen rays, and the gamma rays of radium to the cosmic rays, the wavelength of which may be as short as 0.0004 of an Angström unit (4×10^{-12} cm.). **Erb's w's,** undulations in a muscle stimulated by a moderately powerful constant current: sometimes seen in myotonia congenita. **excitation w.,** an electric wave flowing from a muscle just previous to its contraction. **F w's,** a series of rapid vibratory waves that take the place of the waves in the venous pulse in auricular fibrillation. **fibrillary w's,** small irregular waves which replace the P wave of the electrocardiogram in auricular fibrillation. **hertzian w's,** electromagnetic waves resembling light waves, but having greater wavelength; they are used in wireless telegraphy. **light w's,** the waves in the ether which produce sensations in the retina. See *light.* **longitudinal w.,** one in which the oscillatory motion is parallel to the direction of propagation of the wave. **menstrual w.,** the cyclic changes in the pelvic organs which culminate in menstruation. **oscillation w.,** a secondary pulse wave due to the inertia of the vessel wall. **outflow remainder w.,** overflow w. **overflow w.,** the part of the descending portion of the sphygmographic tracing that intervenes between the apex of the curve and the secondary elevation, and corresponds to the overflow of the ventricles. **P w.,** the first upward deflection in the electrocardiogram. See *electrocardiogram.* **papillary w., percussion w.,** the chief ascending portion of a sphygmographic tracing. **peridicrotic w.,** overflow w. **phrenic w.** See *diaphragm phenomenon,* under *phenomenon.* **predicrotic w.,** a small rise in the pulse wave preceding the dicrotic wave. **pulse w.,** the elevation of the pulse felt by the finger or shown graphically in the curve recorded by the sphygmograph. **Q w.,** the initial downward deflection in the depolarization complex of the ventricular musculature. **random w's,** See *brain w's.* **recoil w.,** the second of the two principal waves of a dicrotic pulse, due to the reflected impulse of the closure of the aortic valves. **respiratory w.,** a wave in the curve of blood pressure, rising during inspiration and falling during expiration. **short w.,** a wave having a wavelength of 60 meters or less. **sonic w's,** audible sound waves which under certain conditions may be destructive to microorganisms. **Stephenson's w.,** menstrual w. **stimulus w.,** the wave which passes along a muscle as a result of a stimulus applied at a certain point. **supersonic w's,** a term applied to waves similar to ordinary sound waves but of frequencies from 200,000 to 1,500,000 cycles per second. They are highly destructive to some organisms and some chemical substances. **T w.** See *electrocardiogram.* **theta w's,** waves in the electroencephalogram which have a frequency of 4 to 7 per second. **tidal w.,** the sphygmographic wave next after the percussion wave; the second elevation of the sphygmographic tracing between the percussion wave and the dicrotic elevation. It is believed to be caused by the afflux of blood in systole. **transverse w.,** one in which the oscillatory motion is perpendicular to the direction of propagation of the wave. **Traube-Hering w's,** rhythmical rises and falls in the arterial pressure, due to rhythmical activity of the vasoconstrictor center. **tricrotic w.,** a third wave in the sphygmographic curve in addition to the tidal and dicrotic waves, occurring during systole. **ultrashort w.,** an electromagnetic wave of wavelength of less than 10 meters. Also called *microwave.* **ultrasonic w's,** waves similar to sound waves but of such high frequency that the human ear does not perceive them as sound. **vasomotor w.,** a fluctuation in the quantity of blood supplied to some part. **ventricular w.,** the part of the tracing of the venous pulse between the auricular and ventricular depressions.

wavelength (wāv′length). The distance between the top of one wave and the identical phase of the succeeding one. **minimum w.,** the shortest wavelength in an x-ray spectrum.

wax (waks) [L. *cera*]. A plastic substance deposited by insects or obtained from plants. Waxes are esters of various fatty acids with higher, usually monohydric alcohols. The wax of pharmacy is principally *beeswax,* the material of which honeycomb is made. It consists chiefly of cerin and myricin and is used in making ointments, cerates, etc. In its natural state it is yellow (*yellow w.*), but in bleaching it becomes white (*white w.*). See also *cera.* **bayberry w.,** bayberry tallow. **bone w.** See *Mosetig-Moorhof bone w.* **boxing w.,** wax used for boxing impressions for dental prostheses. **candelilla w.,** a wax obtained from *Euphorbia antisyphilitica* and used as a substitute for beeswax. **carnauba w.,** a wax largely obtained from *Copernic′ia cerif′era,* a palm of South America. **casting w.,** a compound of various waxes, having controlled properties of thermal expansion and contraction, which is used in making patterns for metal castings for dental prostheses. **Chinese w.,** a hard white wax of insect origin, procured from *Frax′inus chinen′sis,* a tree of China; also a similar wax from *Ligus′trum mad′ra.* **ear w.,** cerumen. **earth w.,** ceresin. **grave w.,** adipocere. **Horsley's w.,** a mixture of wax, petrolatum, and phenol: used for packing small bone cavities, as in the bones of the skull, and for controlling bleeding from them. **inlay w.,** wax used in preparation of the pattern from which a dental inlay is cast, the main ingredient generally being paraffin, with other natural substances from mineral or vegetable sources. **Japan w.,** a fat from the fruit of *Myri′ca cerif′era* and other species of the same genus. **Mosetig-Moorhof bone w.,** a preparation for filling sterile bone cavities. It consists of equal parts of spermaceti and oil of sesame, which are sterilized in a water bath. To 60 parts of this is added 40 parts of iodoform. **myrtle w.,** bayberry tallow. **ocuba w.,** a wax obtained from *Myrist′ica oc′uba,* a South American tree. **palm w.** 1. Carnauba wax. 2. A wax from *Cerox′ylon andic′ola,* a South American palm. **tubercle bacillus w.,** a complex phosphatide extracted from *Mycobac′terium tuberculosis.* **vegetable w.,** a waxy substance, resembling beeswax, derived from various vegetable sources. **white w.,** the bleached, purified wax from the honeycomb of the bee, *Apis mellifera,* used as an ingredient in several ointments. **yellow w.,** the purified wax from the honeycomb of the bee; called also *cera flava* and *beeswax.*

waxing (wak′sing). The shaping of a wax pattern or the wax base of a trial denture into the contours desired. Spoken of also as *waxing up.*

waxy (wak′se). Resembling wax.

W.B.C. Abbreviation for *white blood cell* and *white blood [cell] count.*

wean (wēn). To discontinue the breast feeding of an infant, with substitution of other feeding habits.

weanling (wēn′ling). 1. Newly changed to nourishment other than breast feeding. 2. An animal newly changed to other forms of nourishment than breast feeding.

weasand (we′zand). The trachea.

webbed (webd). Connected by a membrane.

weber (web′er). Coulomb.

Weber's corpuscles, glands, organ (va′berz) [Moritz Ignatz *Weber*, German anatomist, 1795–1875]. See under the nouns.

Weber's disease (web′erz) [Frederick Parkes *Weber*, British physician, 1863–1962]. Localized epidermolysis bullosa.

Weber's douche (va′berz) [Theodor *Weber*, German physician, 1829–1914]. A nasal douche.

Weber's law, paradox, test (va′berz) [Ernest Heinrich *Weber*, German anatomist and physiologist, 1795–1878]. See under the nouns.

Weber's syndrome (web′erz) [Sir Hermann David *Weber*, London physician, 1824–1918]. See under *syndrome*.

Weber's test (va′berz) [Friedrich Eugen *Weber*, German otologist, 1832–1891]. See under *tests*.

Weber-Christian disease (web′er-kris′chan) [F. P. *Weber;* Henry A. *Christian*, born 1876]. Nodular nonsuppurative panniculitis.

Webster's operation (web′sterz) [John Clarence *Webster*, American gynecologist, 1863–1950]. See under *operation*.

Webster's test (web′sterz) [John *Webster*, London chemist, 1878–1927]. See under *tests*.

WEE. Abbreviation for *western equine encephalomyelitis*.

Weeks' bacillus (wēks) [John Elmer *Weeks*, New York ophthalmologist, 1853–1949]. *Haemophilus aegyptius*.

Wegner's disease, sign (veg′nerz) [Friedrich Rudolf Georg *Wegner*, German pathologist, born 1843]. See under *disease* and *sign*.

wehnelt (va′nelt). The unit of hardness or penetrating ability of roentgen rays.

Wehnelt's interrupter (va′nelts) [Arthur *Wehnelt*, Berlin physicist, born 1871]. A device for making rapid interruptions in an electric current.

Weichardt's antikenotoxin (vi′karts) [Wolfgang *Weichardt*, German pathologist, 1875–1945]. See *antikenotoxin*.

Weichbrodt's reaction (vīk′brōts) [Raphael *Weichbrodt*, Frankfurt neurologist, born 1886]. See under *reaction*.

Weidel's test (vi′delz) [Hugo *Weidel*, Austrian chemist, 1849–1899]. See under *tests*.

Weigert's law, method, stain (vi′gerts) [Karl *Weigert*, German pathologist, 1843–1904]. See under *law*, and *stains, table of*.

weight (wāt). Heaviness; the degree to which a body is drawn toward the earth by gravity. **apothecaries' w.,** a system of weights used in compounding prescriptions based on the grain (equivalent 64.8 mg.). Its units are the scruple (20 grains), dram (3 scruples), ounce (8 drams), and pound (12 ounces). **atomic w.,** the weight of an atom of a substance as compared with the weight of an atom of oxygen which is taken as 16. **avoirdupois w.,** the system of weight commonly used for ordinary commodities in English-speaking countries. Its units are the dram (27.344 grains), ounce (16 drams), and pound (16 ounces). **combining w.,** the relative weight, compared with that of hydrogen (which is considered as 1), of an element that enters into combination with other elements. **equivalent w.,** the weight in grams of a substance which is equivalent in a chemical reaction to 1.008 Gm. of hydrogen. **gram molecular w.,** the molecular weight of a substance expressed in grams. **molecular w.,** the weight of a molecule of a substance as compared with that of hydrogen; it is equal to the sum of the weights of its constituent atoms. **troy w.,** a system of weights used by jewelers for gold and precious stones.

weights and measures. See *tables of weights and measures*.

Weil's basal layer, zone (vīlz) [L. A. *Weil*, German dentist of the 19th century]. See under *layer*.

Weil's disease, syndrome (vīlz) [Adolf *Weil*, physician in Wiesbaden, 1848–1916]. See under *disease* and *syndrome*.

Weil's stain (wīlz) [Arthur *Weil*, American neuropathologist, born 1887]. See *stains, table of*.

Weil's test (wīlz) [Richard *Weil*, New York physician, 1876–1917]. See under *tests*.

Weil-Felix reaction (vīl-fa′liks) [Edmund *Weil*, German physician in Prague, 1880–1922; Arthur *Felix*, Prague bacteriologist, 1887–1956]. See under *reaction*.

Weill's sign (vĕlz) [Edmond *Weill*, French pediatrician, 1859–1924]. See under *sign*.

Weinberg's reaction, test (vīn′bergz) [Michel *Weinberg*, French pathologist, 1868–1940]. See under *test*.

Weinmannia (win-man′e-ah). A genus of saxifragaceous plants with an astringent medicinal bark.

Weinstein's test (wīn′stīnz) [Julius William *Weinstein*, New York physician, 1873–1923]. See under *tests*.

Weir Mitchell treatment (wēr-mich′el). See *Mitchell*, and under *treatment*.

Weir's operation (wērz) [Robert Fulton *Weir*, New York surgeon, 1838–1927]. Appendicostomy.

Weisbach's angle (vīs′bahks) [Albin *Weisbach*, Austrian anthropologist of the 19th century]. See under *angle*.

Weisman's test (wīs′manz) [Abner I. *Weisman*, New York obstetrician, born 1907]. See under *tests*.

weismannism (wīs′man-izm) [August *Weismann*, German biologist, 1834–1914]. The doctrine of the noninheritance of acquired characters.

Weiss's reflex (vīs′ez) [Leopold *Weiss*, Austrian oculist, 1848–1901]. See under *reflex*.

Weiss's sign (vīs′ez) [Nathan *Weiss*, physician in Vienna, 1851–1883]. See under *sign*.

Weiss's test (vīs′ez) [Moriz *Weiss*, Vienna physician]. See under *tests*.

Weitbrecht's foramen, ligament (vīt′brekts) [Josias *Weitbrecht*, German anatomist in Petrograd, 1702–1747]. See under *foramen* and *ligament*.

Welander's ulcer (val′an-derz) [Edvard Wilhelm *Welander*, physician in Stockholm, 1840–1917]. See under *ulcer*.

Welch's bacillus (welch′ez) [William Henry *Welch*, pathologist in Baltimore, 1850–1934]. *Clostridium perfringens*.

well (wel). A vessel or space for containing fluid. **atrial w.,** an adjuvant device used during surgical repair of atrial septal defects. Attached to the right atrial wall, it permits blood to rise within it while the surgeon explores and repairs the defect below the surface of the blood. **Gross's atrial w.,** a large rubber truncated cone, about 15 cm. high, 13 cm. in diameter at the top and 4 cm. at the bottom, attached to the right atrial wall, during cardiac surgery, to help contain the blood.

Weller (wel′ler), Thomas H. United States physician and parasitologist, born 1915; co-winner, with John F. Enders and Frederick C. Robbins, of the Nobel prize in medicine and physiology for 1954, for the discovery that poliomyelitis viruses multiply in human tissue.

Wells' facies (welz) [Sir Thomas Spencer *Wells*, English gynecologist, 1818–1897]. See under *facies*.

Weltmann's reaction, test (velt′manz) [Oskar *Weltmann*, Austrian internist, 1885–1934]. See under *tests*.

weltmerism (welt′mer-izm) [Sidney A. *Weltmer*]. A system of suggestive treatment aiming to bring the body and mind into harmony.

wen (wen). A sebaceous cyst.

Wenckebach's disease, period, sign (ven′kĕ-bahks) [Karel Frederik *Wenckebach*, Dutch

TABLES OF WEIGHTS AND MEASURES

MEASURES OF MASS

Avoirdupois Weight

GRAINS	DRAMS	OUNCES	POUNDS	METRIC EQUIVALENTS, GRAMS
1	0.0366	0.0023	0.00014	0.0647989
27.34	1	0.0625	0.0039	1.772
437.5	16	1	0.0625	28.350
7000	256	16	1	453.5924277

Apothecaries' Weight

GRAINS	SCRUPLES (℈)	DRAMS (ʒ)	OUNCES (℥)	POUNDS (℔.)	METRIC EQUIVALENTS, GRAMS
1	0.05	0.0167	0.0021	0.00017	0.0647989
20	1	0.333	0.042	0.0035	1.296
60	3	1	0.125	0.0104	3.888
480	24	8	1	0.0833	31.103
5760	288	96	12	1	373.24177

Metric Weight

MICRO-GRAM	MILLI-GRAM	CENTI-GRAM	DECI-GRAM	GRAM	DECA-GRAM	HECTO-GRAM	KILO-GRAM	METRIC TON	EQUIVALENTS	
									Avoirdupois	Apothecaries'
1	...	...	...	...	...	..	...	...	0.000015 grains	
10^3	1	...	...	...	...	...	...	...	0.015432 grains	
10^4	10	1	...	...	...	...	...	...	0.154323 grains	
10^5	100	10	1	...	...	...	...	...	1.543235 grains	
10^6	1000	100	10	1	...	...	...	...	15.432356 grains	
10^7	10^4	1000	100	10	1	...	...	...	5.6438 dr.	7.7162 scr.
10^8	10^5	10^4	1000	100	10	1	...	...	3.527 oz.	3.215 oz.
10^9	10^6	10^5	10^4	1000	100	10	1	...	2.2046 lb.	2.6792 lb.
10^{12}	10^9	10^8	10^7	10^6	10^5	10^4	1000	1	2204.6223 lb.	2679.2285 lb.

Troy Weight

GRAINS	PENNYWEIGHTS	OUNCES	POUNDS	METRIC EQUIVALENTS, GRAMS
1	0.042	0.002	0.00017	0.0647989
24	1	0.05	0.0042	1.555
480	20	1	0.083	31.103
5760	240	12	1	373.24177

MEASURES OF CAPACITY

Apothecaries' (Wine) Measure

MINIMS	FLUID DRAMS	FLUID OUNCES	GILLS	PINTS	QUARTS	GALLONS	EQUIVALENTS		
							CUBIC INCHES	MILLILITERS	CUBIC CENTIMETERS
1	0.0166	0.002	0.0005	0.00013	.....	.....	0.00376	0.06161	0.06161
60	1	0.125	0.0312	0.0078	0.0039	.....	0.22558	3.6966	3.6967
480	8	1	0.25	0.0625	0.0312	0.0078	1.80468	29.5729	29.5737
1920	32	4	1	0.25	0.125	0.0312	7.21875	118.2915	118.2948
7680	128	16	4	1	0.5	0.125	28.875	473.167	473.179
15360	256	32	8	2	1	0.25	57.75	946.333	946.358
61440	1024	128	32	8	4	1	231	3785.332	3785.434

METRIC MEASURE

MICRO-LITER	MILLI-LITER	CENTI-LITER	DECI-LITER	LITER	DEKA-LITER	HECTO-LITER	KILO-LITER	MYRIA-LITER	EQUIVALENTS (APOTHECARIES' FLUID)
1	...	...	...	...	...	...	...	...	0.01623108 min.
10^3	1	...	...	...	...	...	...	...	16.23 min.
10^4	10	1	...	...	...	...	...	...	2.7 fl.dr.
10^5	100	10	1	...	...	...	...	...	3.38 fl.oz.
10^6	10^3	100	10	1	...	...	...	...	2.11 pts.
10^7	10^4	10^3	100	10	1	...	...	...	2.64 gal.
10^8	10^5	10^4	10^3	100	10	1	...	...	26.418 gals.
10^9	10^6	10^5	10^4	10^3	100	10	1	...	264.18 gals.
10^{10}	10^7	10^6	10^5	10^4	10^3	100	10	1	2641.8 gals.

1 liter = 2.113363738 pints (Apothecaries).

MEASURES OF LENGTH

METRIC MEASURE

MI-CRON	MILLI-METER	CENTI-METER	DECI-METER	METER	DEKA-METER	HECTO-METER	KILO-METER	MYRIA-METER	MEGA-METER	EQUIVALENTS
1	0.001	10^{-4}	...	...	...	...	...	...	...	0.000039 inch
10^3	1	10^{-1}	...	...	...	...	...	...	...	0.03937 inch
10^4	10	1	...	...	...	...	...	...	...	0.3937 inch
10^5	100	10	1	...	...	...	...	...	...	3.937 inch
10^6	1000	100	10	1	...	...	...	...	...	39.37 inch
10^7	10^4	1000	100	10	1	...	...	...	...	10.9361 yards
10^8	10^5	10^4	1000	100	10	1	...	...	...	109.3612 yards
10^9	10^6	10^5	10^4	1000	1000	10	1	...	...	1093.6121 yards
10^{10}	10^7	10^6	10^5	10^4	1000	100	10	1	...	6.2137 miles
10^{12}	10^9	10^8	10^7	10^6	10^5	10^4	1000	100	1	621.370 miles

CONVERSION TABLES

AVOIRDUPOIS—METRIC WEIGHT

OUNCES	GRAMS	OUNCES	GRAMS	POUNDS	GRAMS	KILOGRAMS
1/16	1.772	7	198.447	1 (16 oz.)	453.59	
1/8	3.544	8	226.796	2	907.18	
1/4	7.088	9	255.146	3	1360.78	1.36
1/2	14.175	10	283.495	4	1814.37	1.81
1	28.350	11	311.845	5	2267.96	2.27
2	56.699	12	340.194	6	2721.55	2.72
3	85.049	13	368.544	7	3175.15	3.18
4	113.398	14	396.893	8	3628.74	3.63
5	141.748	15	425.243	9	4082.33	4.08
6	170.097	16 (1 lb.)	453.59	10	4535.92	4.54

METRIC—AVOIRDUPOIS WEIGHT

GRAMS	OUNCES	GRAMS	OUNCES	GRAMS	POUNDS
0.001 (1 mg.)	0.000035274	1	0.035274	1000 (1 kg.)	2.2046

TABLES OF WEIGHTS AND MEASURES (*Continued*)

Apothecaries'—Metric Weight

GRAINS	GRAMS	GRAINS	GRAMS
1/150	0.0004	2/5	0.03
1/120	0.0005	1/2	0.032
1/100	0.0006	3/5	0.04
1/90	0.0007	2/3	0.043
1/80	0.0008	3/4	0.05
1/64	0.001	7/8	0.057
1/60	0.0011	1	0.065
1/50	0.0013	1 1/2	0.097(0.1)
1/48	0.0014	2	0.12
1/40	0.0016	3	0.20
1/36	0.0018	4	0.24
1/32	0.002	5	0.30
1/30	0.0022	6	0.40
1/25	0.0026	7	0.45
1/20	0.003	8	0.50
1/16	0.004	9	0.60
1/12	0.005	10	0.65
1/10	0.006	15	1.00
1/9	0.007	20 (1 ℈)	1.30
1/8	0.008	30	2.00
1/7	0.009		
1/6	0.01		
1/5	0.013		
1/4	0.016		
1/3	0.02		

SCRUPLES	GRAMS
1	1.296(1.3)
2	2.592(2.6)
3 (1 ʒ)	3.888(3.9)

DRAMS	GRAMS
1	3.888
2	7.776
3	11.664
4	15.552
5	19.440
6	23.328
7	27.216
8 (1 ℥)	31.103

OUNCES	GRAMS
1	31.103
2	62.207
3	93.310
4	124.414
5	155.517
6	186.621
7	217.724
8	248.828
9	279.931
10	311.035
11	342.138
12 (1 ℔.)	373.242

Metric—Apothecaries' Weight

MILLIGRAMS	GRAINS	GRAMS	GRAINS	GRAMS	EQUIVALENTS
1	0.015432	0.1	1.5432	10	2.572 drams
2	0.030864	0.2	3.0864	15	3.858 "
3	0.046296	0.3	4.6296	20	5.144 "
4	0.061728	0.4	6.1728	25	6.430 "
5	0.077160	0.5	7.7160	30	7.716 "
6	0.092592	0.6	9.2592	40	1.286 oz.
7	0.108024	0.7	10.8024	45	1.447 "
8	0.123456	0.8	12.3456	50	1.607 "
9	0.138888	0.9	13.8888	100	3.215 "
10	0.154320	1.0	15.4320	200	6.430 "
15	0.231480	1.5	23.1480	300	9.644 "
20	0.308640	2.0	30.8640	400	12.859 "
25	0.385800	2.5	38.5800	500	1.34 lb.
30	0.462960	3.0	46.2960	600	1.61 "
35	0.540120	3.5	54.0120	700	1.88 "
40	0.617280	4.0	61.728	800	2.14 "
45	0.694440	4.5	69.444	900	2.41 "
50	0.771600	5.0	77.162	1000	2.68 "
100	1.543240	10.0	154.324		

Apothecaries'—Metric Liquid Measure

MINIMS	MILLILITERS	FLUID DRAMS	MILLILITERS	FLUID OUNCES	MILLILITERS
1	0.06	1	3.70	1	29.57
2	0.12	2	7.39	2	59.15
3	0.19	3	11.09	3	88.72
4	0.25	4	14.79	4	118.29
5	0.31	5	18.48	5	147.87
10	0.62	6	22.18	6	177.44
15	0.92	7	25.88	7	207.01
20	1.23	8 (1 fl.oz.)	29.57	8	236.58
25	1.54			9	266.16
30	1.85			10	295.73
35	2.16			11	325.30
40	2.46			12	354.88
45	2.77			13	384.45
50	3.08			14	414.02
55	3.39			15	443.59
60 (1 fl.dr.)	3.70			16 (1 pt.)	473.17
				32 (1 qt.)	946.33
				128 (1 gal.)	3785.32

METRIC—APOTHECARIES' LIQUID MEASURE

MILLILITERS	MINIMS	MILLILITERS	FLUID DRAMS	MILLILITERS	FLUID OUNCES
1	16.231	5	1.35	30	1.01
2	32.5	10	2.71	40	1.35
3	48.7	15	4.06	50	1.69
4	64.9	20	5.4	500	16.91
5	81.1	25	6.76	1000 (1 L.)	33.815
		30	7.1		

TABLE OF METRIC DOSES WITH APPROXIMATE APOTHECARY EQUIVALENTS

These *approximate* dose equivalents represent the quantities usually prescribed, under identical conditions, by physicians using, respectively, the metric system or the apothecary system of weights and measures. In labeling dosage forms in both the metric and the apothecary systems, if one is the approximate equivalent of the other, the approximate figure shall be enclosed in parentheses.

When prepared dosage forms such as tablets, capsules, pills, etc., are prescribed in the metric system, the pharmacist may dispense the corresponding *approximate* equivalent in the apothecary system, and vice versa, as indicated in the following table.

For the conversion of specific quantities in converting pharmaceutical formulas, exact equivalents must be used. In the compounding of prescriptions, the exact equivalents, rounded to three significant figures, should be used.

LIQUID MEASURE		LIQUID MEASURE	
METRIC	APPROXIMATE APOTHECARY EQUIVALENTS	METRIC	APPROXIMATE APOTHECARY EQUIVALENTS
1000 ml.	1 quart	3 ml.	45 minims
750 ml.	1 1/2 pints	2 ml.	30 minims
500 ml.	1 pint	1 ml.	15 minims
250 ml.	8 fluid ounces	0.75 ml.	12 minims
200 ml.	7 fluid ounces	0.6 ml.	10 minims
100 ml.	3 1/2 fluid ounces	0.5 ml.	8 minims
50 ml.	1 3/4 fluid ounces	0.3 ml.	5 minims
30 ml.	1 fluid ounce	0.25 ml.	4 minims
15 ml.	4 fluid drams	0.2 ml.	3 minims
10 ml.	2 1/2 fluid drams	0.1 ml.	1 1/2 minims
8 ml.	2 fluid drams	0.06 ml.	1 minim
5 ml.	1 1/4 fluid drams	0.05 ml.	3/4 minim
4 ml.	1 fluid dram	0.03 ml.	1/2 minim

WEIGHT		WEIGHT	
METRIC	APPROXIMATE APOTHECARY EQUIVALENTS	METRIC	APPROXIMATE APOTHECARY EQUIVALENTS
30 Gm.	1 ounce	30 mg.	1/2 grain
15 Gm.	4 drams	25 mg.	3/8 grain
10 Gm.	2 1/2 drams	20 mg.	1/3 grain
7.5 Gm.	2 drams	15 mg.	1/4 grain
6 Gm.	90 grains	12 mg.	1/5 grain
5 Gm.	75 grains	10 mg.	1/6 grain
4 Gm.	60 grains (1 dram)	8 mg.	1/8 grain
3 Gm.	45 grains	6 mg.	1/10 grain
2 Gm.	30 grains (1/2 dram)	5 mg.	1/12 grain
1.5 Gm.	22 grains	4 mg.	1/15 grain
1 Gm.	15 grains	3 mg.	1/20 grain
0.75 Gm.	12 grains	2 mg.	1/30 grain
0.6 Gm.	10 grains	1.5 mg.	1/40 grain
0.5 Gm.	7 1/2 grains	1.2 mg.	1/50 grain
0.4 Gm.	6 grains	1 mg.	1/60 grain
0.3 Gm.	5 grains	0.8 mg.	1/80 grain
0.25 Gm.	4 grains	0.6 mg.	1/100 grain
0.2 Gm.	3 grains	0.5 mg.	1/120 grain
0.15 Gm.	2 1/2 grains	0.4 mg.	1/150 grain
0.12 Gm.	2 grains	0.3 mg.	1/200 grain
0.1 Gm.	1 1/2 grains	0.25 mg.	1/250 grain
75 mg.	1 1/4 grains	0.2 mg.	1/300 grain
60 mg.	1 grain	0.15 mg.	1/400 grain
50 mg.	3/4 grain	0.12 mg.	1/500 grain
40 mg.	2/3 grain	0.1 mg.	1/600 grain

NOTE—A milliliter (ml.) is the approximate equivalent of a cubic centimeter (cc.).

The above *approximate* dose equivalents have been adopted by the Pharmacopeia, National Formulary and New and Nonofficial Drugs, and these dose equivalents have the approval of the federal Food and Drug Administration.

internist in Vienna, 1864–1940]. See under the nouns.

Wender's test (ven′derz) [Neumann *Wender*, Austrian chemist]. See under *tests.*

Wenzell's test (wen′zelz) [William Theodore *Wenzell*, American physician, born 1829]. See under *tests.*

Werdnig-Hoffmann paralysis, type (verd′-nig-hof′man) [Guido *Werdnig*, Austrian neurologist; Ernst *Hoffmann*, German neurologist, born 1868]. See under *paralysis.*

Werlhof's disease (verl′hofs) [Paul Gottlieb *Werlhof*, German physician, 1699–1767]. Thrombopenic purpura.

Werneking's commissure (ver′nĕ-kingz) [Friedrich Christian Gregor *Werneking*, German anatomist, 1798–1835]. See under *commissure.*

Werner-His disease (ver′ner-his′) [Heinrich *Werner*, German physician, born 1874; William *His*, Jr., German physician, 1863–1934]. Trench fever.

Wernicke's aphasia, center, disease, fissure, sign, etc. (ver′nĭ-kez) [Karl *Wernicke*, German neurologist, 1848–1905]. See under the nouns.

Wernicke-Mann type (ver′nĭ-kĕ-mahn) [Karl *Wernicke;* Ludwig *Mann*, German neurologist, born 1866]. See under *type.*

Wertheim's ointment (ver′tīmz) [Gustav *Wertheim*, physician in Vienna, 1822–1888]. See under *ointment.*

Wertheim's operation (ver′tīmz) [Ernst *Wertheim*, gynecologist in Vienna, 1864–1920]. See under *operation.*

Wertheim-Schauta operation (ver′tīm-show′-tah) [Ernst *Wertheim;* Friedrich *Schauta*, Vienna gynecologist; 1849–1919]. See under *operation.*

Westberg's disease, space (vest′bergz) [Friedrich *Westberg*, German physician of the 19th century]. See under *disease* and *space.*

Westphal's contraction, nucleus, sign (vest′fahls) [Carl Friedrich Otto *Westphal*, German neurologist, 1833–1890]. See under the nouns.

Westphal's pupillary reflex (vest′fahlz) [Alexander Karl Otto *Westphal*, German neurologist, 1863–1941]. See under *reflex.*

Westphal-Piltz phenomenon, reflex (vest′-fahl-pilts′) [A. K. O. *Westphal;* Jan *Piltz*, Austrian neurologist, 1871–1930]. See under *phenomenon* and *reflex.*

Westphal-Strümpell neurosis, pseudosclerosis (vest′fahl-strim′p′l) [C. F. O. *Westphal;* Adolf von *Strümpell*, physician in Leipzig, 1853–1925]. See under *pseudosclerosis.*

wet-nurse (wet′nurs). A woman who nurses the child of another at her own breast.

wet-scald (wet′skahld). Eczema in sheep.

Wetzel's grid (wet′selz) [Norman Carl *Wetzel*, Cleveland pediatrician, born 1897]. See under *grid.*

Wetzel's test (vet′selz) [Georg *Wetzel*, German anatomist, born 1871]. See under *tests.*

Weyl's test (vīlz) [Theodor *Weyl*, German chemist 1851–1913]. See under *tests.*

Wharton's duct, jelly (hwar′tunz) [Thomas *Wharton*, English physician and anatomist, 1614–1673]. See under *duct* and *jelly.*

whartonitis (hwar″ton-i′tis). Inflammation of Wharton's duct.

wheal (hwēl). A smooth, slightly elevated area on the body surface, which is redder or paler than the surrounding skin; it is often attended with severe itching, and is usually evanescent. It is the typical lesion of urticaria, the dermal evidence of allergy, and in sensitive persons may be provoked by irritation of the skin.

wheat (hwēt). The plant *Triticum vulgare* and its cereal grain.

wheatmeal (hwēt′mēl). Eighty-five per cent extracted wheat flour. **National w.** (British), wheatmeal to which calcium carbonate has been added at the rate of 14 ounces to every 280 pounds of flour.

Wheatstone's bridge (hwēt′stōnz) [Charles *Wheatstone*, English physicist, 1802–1875]. See under *bridge.*

Wheelhouse's operation (hwēl′hows-ez) [Claudius Galen *Wheelhouse*, English surgeon of the 19th century]. Urethrotomy.

wheeze (hwēz). A whistling sound made in breathing. **asthmatoid w.,** a sound similar to the wheezing heard when the ear is placed close to the mouth of an asthmatic; heard in cases of foreign body in the trachea or bronchus. Called also *Jackson's sign.*

whelk (hwelk). A wheal, or other raised lesion on the skin.

whey (hwa). The thin serum of milk remaining after the curd and cream have been removed. **alum w.,** a whey prepared by boiling milk with a piece of alum and removing the curd by straining. **litmus w., Petruschky's litmus w.,** whey colored with litmus to a deep purplish-red color. **wine w.,** a preparation of milk coagulated with white wine, strained from the curd, and sweetened with sugar.

Whipple's disease (hwip′elz) [George Hoyt *Whipple*, American pathologist, born 1878; co-winner, with George R. Minot and William P. Murphy, of the Nobel prize in medicine and physiology for 1934]. See *lipophagia granulomatosis* and *lipodystrophy, intestinal.*

Whipple's operation (hwip′elz) [Allen O. *Whipple*, American surgeon, born 1881]. Radical excision of the ampulla of Vater.

whipworm (hwip′werm). *Trichuris trichiura.*

whirlbone (hwirl′bōn). 1. The patella, rotula, or kneecap. 2. The head of the femur (caput femoris [N A]).

whisper (hwis′per). A soft, low, sibilant breathing sound produced by the unvoiced passage of the breath through the glottis.

whistle (hwis′el). 1. A shrill musical sound produced by the forcing of air or steam against a thin edge or into a cavity. 2. A device or apparatus which produces a whistling sound. **Edelmann-Galton w.,** a modification of Galton's whistle for testing acuity of hearing. **Galton's w.,** a metallic whistle used in testing the sense of hearing. **Sahli's w.,** a sound resembling whistling heard in the abdomen and caused by flatus passing an intestinal stenosis.

White (hwīt), Charles (1728–1813). English surgeon and obstetrician, whose *Treatise on the Management of Pregnant and Lying-in Women* (1773) antedated the work of Semmelweis in its appeal for surgical cleanliness to combat puerperal fever.

white (hwīt). Of the color of snow; reflecting all the rays of the spectrum; the opposite of black. **Spanish w.,** bismuth subnitrate. **visual w.,** a colorless, noncarotinoid substance that results from the action of light on retinene.

White's disease (hwīts) [James C. *White*, dermatologist in Boston, 1833–1916]. Keratosis follicularis.

White's operation (hwīts) [J. William *White*, Philadelphia surgeon, 1850–1916]. See under *operation.*

whitecomb (hwīt′kōm). Comb disease.

Whitehead's operation, varnish (hwīt′hedz) [Walter *Whitehead*, English surgeon, 1840–1913]. See under *operation* and *varnish.*

whiteleg (hwīt′leg). Phlegmasia alba dolens.

whitepox (hwīt′poks). Variola minor.

Whitfield's ointment (hwit′fēldz) [Arthur *Whitfield*, British dermatologist, 1868–1946]. Benzoic and salicylic acid ointment.

whitlow (hwit′lo). A felon. **melanotic w.,** a malignant tumor of the nail bed characterized by the formation of melanotic tissue about the nail border and under the nail. **thecal w.,** suppurative tenosynovitis of the terminal phalanx of a finger.

Whitman's operation (hwit′mahnz) [Royal *Whitman*, New York orthopedic surgeon, 1857–1946]. See under *operation*.

Whitmore's disease, fever (hwit′mōrz) [Major Alfred *Whitmore*, of the Indian Medical Service]. Melioidosis.

W.H.O. Abbreviation for *World Health Organization*.

whoop (ho͞op). The sonorous and convulsive inspiration of whooping cough.

whooping cough (ho͞op′ing kawf). An infectious disease characterized by catarrh of the respiratory tract and peculiar paroxysms of cough, ending in a prolonged crowing or whooping respiration. After an incubation period of about two weeks the *catarrhal stage* begins, with slight fever, sneezing, running at the nose, and a dry cough. In a week or two the *paroxysmal stage* begins, with the characteristic paroxysmal cough. This consists of a deep inspiration, followed by a series of quick, short coughs, continuing until the air is expelled from the lungs. During the paroxysm the face becomes cyanosed, the eyes injected, and the veins distended. The cough frequently induces vomiting, and, in severe cases, epistaxis or other hemorrhage. The close of the paroxysm is marked by a long-drawn, shrill, whooping inspiration, due to spasmodic closure of the glottis. The number of paroxysms varies from ten or twelve to forty of fifty in twenty-four hours. This stage lasts from three to four weeks, and is followed by the *stage of decline*, during which the paroxysms grow less frequent and less violent, and finally cease. The disease is most frequently met in children, is much more prevalent in cold weather, and is very contagious. *Bordetella* (*Hemophilus*) *pertussis* is etiologically associated with the disease. Also called *pertussis*.

whorl (hworl). A spiral turn or twist, such as one of the turns of the cochlea of the ear, the arrangement of muscle fibers in the heart (*vortex*), or a spiral arrangement of the ridges apparent in a finger print. **bone w.,** an enostosis. **lens w.,** the peculiar bowed appearance presented by the marginal portion of the lens in meridional sections.

Whytt's disease (hwits) [Robert *Whytt*, Scotch physician, 1714–1766]. See under *disease*.

Wichmann's asthma (vik′mahnz) [Johann Ernst *Wichmann*, German physician, 1740–1802]. Laryngismus stridulus.

Wickersheimer's fluid (vik′er-shi″merz) [J. *Wickersheimer*, anatomist in Berlin, 1832–1896]. See under *fluid*.

Wickham's striae (wik′amz) [Louis-Frédéric *Wickham*, Paris dermatologist, 1861–1913]. See under *stria*.

Widal reaction, test (ve-dahl′) [Fernand *Widal*, French physician, 1862–1929]. See under *reaction* and *tests*.

Wigand's maneuver (ve′gants) [Just. Heinrich *Wigand*, German gynecologist, 1766–1817]. See under *maneuver*.

Wildbolz reaction (vilt′bōlts) [Hans *Wildbolz*, Swiss urologist, 1873–1940]. See under *reaction*.

Wilde's cord, incision, etc. (wīldz) [Sir William Robert Wills *Wilde*, Irish surgeon, 1815–1876]. See under the nouns.

Wilder's diet (wīl′derz) [Russell Morse *Wilder*, Sr., American physician, 1885–1959]. See under *diet*.

Wilder's law of initial value (wīl′derz) [Joseph *Wilder*, neuropsychiatrist in New York, born 1895]. See under *law*.

Wilder's sign (wīl′derz) [William Hamlin *Wilder*, ophthalmologist in Chicago, 1860–1935]. See under *sign*.

Wildermuth's ear (vil′der-moots) [Hermann A. *Wildermuth*, alienist in Stuttgart, 1852–1907]. See under *ear*.

Wilkins (wil′kinz), Maurice. English biochemist, born 1916; co-winner, with Francis Crick and James Dewey Watson, of the Nobel prize in medicine and physiology for 1962, for the discovery of the molecular structure of deoxyribonucleic acid.

Wilks' disease (wilks) [Sir Samuel *Wilks*, English physician, 1824–1911]. See under *disease*.

Willan's lepra (wil′anz) [Robert *Willan*, English physician, 1757–1812]. Psoriasis.

Willems' treatment (wil′emz) [Charles *Willems*, Belgian surgeon]. See under *treatment*.

Willett forceps (wil′et) [J. Abernethy *Willett*, London obstetrician, died 1932]. See under *forceps*.

Willia (wil′e-ah). A genus of fungi. *W. anom′ala*, a species parasitic in man.

Williams' sign, tracheal tone (wil′yamz) [Charles J. B. *Williams*, English physician, 1805–1889]. See under *sign*, def. 1.

Williamson's sign (wil′yam-sunz) [Oliver K. *Williamson*, London physician]. See under *sign*.

Williamson's test (wil′yam-sunz) [Richard Thomas *Williamson*, English physician]. See under *tests*.

williasis (wil-li′ah-sis). Infection with fungi of the genus Willia.

Willis' circle, cords (wil′is) [Thomas *Willis*, English anatomist and physician, 1621–1675]. See under *circle* and *cord*.

Wilms' tumor (vilmz) [Marx *Wilms*, German surgeon, 1867–1918]. Embryonal carcinosarcoma of the kidney.

wilpo (wil′po). Trade mark for a preparation of phenyl tertiary butylamine hydrochloride.

Wilson's disease (wil′sunz). 1. [Samuel Alex. Kinnier *Wilson*, English neurologist, 1878–1936]. Progressive lenticular degeneration. 2. [William James Erasmus *Wilson*, English dermatologist, 1809–1884]. Dermatitis exfoliativa.

Wilson's muscle (wil′sunz) [James *Wilson*, English surgeon, 1765–1821]. Musculus sphincter urethrae.

Wilson's test (wil′sunz) [Karl Miller *Wilson*, American gynecologist, born 1885]. See under *tests*.

Wimshurst machine (wimz′hurst) [James *Wimshurst*, English engineer, 1832–1903]. A machine for the development of static current.

Winckel's disease (ving′kelz) [Franz Ch. W. von *Winckel*, gynecologist in Munich, 1837–1911]. See under *disease*.

windage (win′dij). An internal lesion caused by compression of the air by a passing missile.

windburn (wind′burn). Injury to the skin caused by excessive exposure to wind.

windchill (wind′chil). Loss of heat from bodies subjected to wind.

windgall (wind′gawl). A soft swelling in the region of the fetlock joint of a horse.

windlass, Spanish (wind′las). An improvised tourniquet consisting of a handkerchief tied around a part and twisted by a stick passed under it.

window (win′do) [L. *fenestra*]. A circumscribed opening in a plane surface. **aortic w.,** a transparent region below the aortic arch formed by the bifurcation of the trachea, visible in the left anterior oblique roentgenogram of the heart and adjacent vessels. **oval w.,** fenestra vestibuli. **round w.,** fenestra cochleae.

windowing (win′do-ing). Surgical creation of an opening in the cortex of a bone.

windpipe (wind′pīp). The trachea.

windpuff (wind′puf). A swelling just below the fetlock joint of a horse, caused by a collection of synovial fluid between the tendons of the leg.

windstroke (wind′strōk). Acute spinal paralysis of a horse.

wind-sucking (wind′suk-ing). Cribbing.

wineglass (wīn′glas). A measure approximately equal to 2 fluid ounces.

wing (wing) [L. *ala*]. 1. The modified anterior appendage of birds, which is the organ of aerial flight. 2. A structure or part resembling the wing of a bird. Called also *ala*. **ash-like w.,** trigonum nervi vagi. **great w. of sphenoid bone, greater w. of sphenoid bone,** ala major ossis sphenoidalis. **w. of ilium,** ala ossis ilii. **w's of Ingrassias,** w's of sphenoid bone. **lateral w. of sacrum,** pars lateralis ossis sacri. **lateral w. of sphenoid bone,** ala major ossis sphenoidalis. **lesser w. of sphenoid bone,** ala minor ossis sphenoidalis. **major w. of sphenoid bone,** ala major ossis sphenoidalis. **minor w. of sphenoid bone,** ala minor ossis sphenoidalis. **w. of nose,** ala nasi. **orbital w. of sphenoid bone, small w. of sphenoid bone,** ala minor ossis sphenoidalis. **w's of sphenoid bone,** the laterally projecting processes of the sphenoid bone. See *ala major ossis sphenoidalis* and *ala minor ossis sphenoidalis*. **superior w. of sphenoid bone,** ala minor ossis sphenoidalis. **temporal w. of sphenoid bone,** ala major ossis sphenoidalis. **w. of vomer,** ala vomeris.

Winiwarter's operation (vin′ĭ-var″terz) [Alexander von *Winiwarter*, German surgeon, 1848–1917]. See under *operation*.

Winkelman's disease (wing′k′l-manz) [Nathaniel W. *Winkelman*, Philadelphia neurologist, 1891–1956]. Progressive pallidal degeneration.

winking (wingk′ing). Quick closing and opening of the eyelids. **jaw w.,** involuntary closing movements of the eyelid occasionally associated with movements of the jaw.

Winkler's disease (vink′lerz) [Max *Winkler*, Swiss physician, 1875–1952]. Chondrodermatitis nodularis chronica helicis.

Winslow's foramen, ligament, stars, etc. (winz′lōz) [Jacob Benignus *Winslow*, anatomist in Paris, 1669–1760]. See under the nouns.

winstrol (win′strol). Trade mark for a preparation of stanozolol.

Winterbottom's sign, symptom (win′ter-bot″umz) [Thomas Masterman *Winterbottom*, English physician, 1764–1859]. See under *sign*.

Winternitz's sound, test (vin′ter-nits″ez) [Wilhelm *Winternitz*, physician in Vienna, 1835–1917]. See under *sound* and *tests*.

Wintrich's sign (vin′triks) [Anton *Wintrich*, German physician, 1812–1882]. See under *sign*.

wire (wīr). 1. A long, circular, flexible structure of metal, used in surgery and dentistry. 2. To insert wires into a body structure, as into a broken bone to immobilize the fragments, or into an aneurysm to promote the formation of clots. **arch w.,** wire applied around the dental arch: used in correcting irregularities of the teeth. **Kirschner w.,** a steel wire for skeletal transfixion of fractured bones and for obtaining skeletal traction in fractures. It is inserted through the soft parts and the bone and held tight in a clamp.

wireworm (wīr′werm). *Haemonchus contortus*.

Wirsung's canal, duct (vēr′soongz) [Johann Georg *Wirsung*, German physician, 1600–1643]. Ductus pancreaticus.

Wishart test (wish′art) [Mary B. *Wishart*]. See under *tests*.

Wistaria (wis-ta′re-ah) [Caspar *Wistar*, American anatomist, 1760–1818]. A genus of woody vines with blue, purple, or white flowers. **W. chinen′sis,** the Chinese wistaria, with showy purple flowers.

withers (with′erz). The top of the shoulders of the horse. **fistulous w.,** a name applied to a condition occurring in horses after a dual infection of the supraspinous bursa by Brucella and Actinomyces, leading to distention and sometimes to rupture of the bursa, with suppuration.

witkop (wit′kop). A noncontagious favus-like disease of the scalp, marked by confluent crusts which give the appearance of a white skull cap, affecting syphilitic natives in South Africa: called also *dikwakwadi*.

Witzel's operation (vit′selz) [Friedrich Oskar *Witzel*, German surgeon, 1856–1925]. See under *operation*.

witzelsucht (vit′sel-zo͝okt) [Ger.]. A mental condition marked by the making of poor jokes and puns and the telling of pointless stories, at which the patient himself is intensely amused.

W.L. Abbreviation for *wavelength*.

Wladimiroff's operation (vlad″ĭ-mer′ofs) [Russian surgeon, 1837–1903]. See under *operation*.

Wohlfahrtia (vōl-fahr′te-ah). A genus of flies. **W. magnif′ica,** a flesh fly of Russia. Its larvae may occur in wounds of man and animals. **W. meige′nii, W. vig′il,** species which produce cutaneous myiasis in man in the United States.

Wohlgemuth's test (vōl′ge-moots) [Julius *Wohlgemuth*, German physician]. See under *tests*.

Woillez's disease (vwah-lāz′) [Eugène Joseph *Woillez*, French physician, 1811–1882]. See under *disease*.

Wolbachia (wol-bak′e-ah) [Simeon Burt *Wolbach*, American physician, 1880–1954]. A genus of microorganisms of the tribe Wolbachieae, family Rickettsiaceae, order Rickettsiales; nine species of these rickettsia-like microorganisms have been described, none of which is pathogenic for mammals.

Wolbachieae (wol″bah-ki′e-e) [S. B. *Wolbach*]. A tribe of the family Rickettsiaceae, order Rickettsiales, class Microtatobiotes, made up of rickettsia-like organisms occurring symbiotically or parasitically within the cells of arthropod hosts. Many organisms previously classified in the genus Rickettsia have been assigned to this tribe, which includes three genera, *Rickettsiella*, *Symbiotes*, and *Wolbachia*.

Woldman's test (wold′manz) [Edward Elbert *Woldman*, American physician, born 1897]. See under *tests*.

Wolfe's graft (woolfs) [John Reisberg *Wolfe*, Scotch ophthalmologist, 1824–1904]. See under *graft*.

Wolfenden's position (wol′fen-denz) [Richard Norris *Wolfenden*, British laryngologist of the 19th century]. See under *position*.

Wolff's law (volfs) [Julius *Wolff*, German anatomist, 1836–1902]. See under *law*.

Wolff-Eisner reaction (volf īz′ner) [Alfred *Wolf-Eisner*, German serologist, 1877–1948]. See under *reaction*.

Wolff-Parkinson-White syndrome [Louis *Wolff*, American cardiologist, born 1898; Sir John *Parkinson*, British physician, born 1885; Paul D. *White*, American cardiologist, born 1886]. See under *syndrome*.

wolffian (woolf′e-an). Described by Kaspar Friedrich *Wolff*, German anatomist and embryologist, 1733–1794. See under *body*, *cyst*, and *duct*.

Wölfler's operation, sign, suture (vel′flerz) [Anton *Wölfler*, surgeon in Prague, 1850–1917]. See under the nouns.

wolfram (wool′fram). Tungsten.

wolframium (wolf-ra′me-um) [L. "wolfram"]. Tungsten.

Wolfring's glands (vōlf′ringz) [Emilij Franzevic von *Wolfring*, Polish ophthalmologist, 1832–1906]. See under *gland*.

Wollaston's doublet (wool′as-tonz) [William Hyde *Wollaston*, English physician, 1766–1828]. See under *doublet*.

womb (wo͞om). The uterus.

Wood's filter, glass, light (woodz) [Robert Williams *Wood*, American physicist, born 1868]. See under *filter*.

Woodbridge treatment (wood′brij) [John Eliot *Woodbridge*, American physician, 1845–1901]. See under *treatment*.

Woodyatt's pump (wood′yats) [Rollin Turner *Woodyatt,* American physician, 1878–1953]. See under *pump.*

wool (wool). The hair of sheep and lambs; by extension applied to any material existing as fine threads. **collodion w.,** pyroxylin. **gut w.,** catgut shredded into fine fibers. **styptic w.,** wool impregnated with ferric chloride. **synthetic w.,** thin fibers spun from a synthetic material, such as the precipitate of milk casein.

Woolner's tip (wool′nerz) [Thomas *Woolner,* English sculptor and poet, 1826–1892]. Tuberculum auriculae.

worm (werm) [L. *vermis*]. 1. Any member of the invertebrate group *Vermes.* 2. Any anatomical structure resembling a worm. See *vermis.* 3. The spiral tube of a distilling apparatus. **beef w.,** a burrowing parasite, *Dermatobia noxialis,* of tropical America. It infests man and domestic animals. **bilharzia w.,** Schistosoma. **bladder w.,** a cysticercus; bladder worms exist in various parenchymatous tissues of a host; being then transferred to the stomach of another host, they develop into tapeworms. **blinding w.,** *Onchocerca caecutiens.* **case w.,** Echinococcus. **cayor w.,** Ochromyia. **w. of cerebellum,** vermis cerebelli. **dragon w.,** *Dracunculus medinensis.* **eel w.,** Ascaris. **eye w.,** *Loa loa.* **flat w.,** Platyhelminthes. **fluke w.** See *fluke.* **guinea w.,** *Dracunculus medinensis.* **heart w.,** *Dirofilaria immitis.* **lung w.,** a nematode parasite that invades the lungs. See *Metastrongylus apri.* **macaco w.,** the larva of *Dermatobia noxialis,* of South America, which burrows under the skin of man and animals. **maw w.,** Ascaris. **meal w.,** *Asopia farinalis.* **Medina w.,** *Dracunculus medinensis.* **mosquito w.,** the maggot of Dermatobia. **palisade w.,** *Strongylus equinus.* **pork w.,** *Trichinella spiralis.* **serpent w.,** *Dracunculus medinensis.* **spiny-headed w.,** Acanthocephala. **stomach w.,** a small, threadlike worm, *Haemonchus contortus,* infesting the fourth stomach of sheep, and producing weakness, wasting, and death. **thorn-headed w.,** Acanthocephala. **tongue w.** See *Linguatula* and *Porocephalus.* **travelling w.,** the larva of *Hermetia illucens.* **trichina w.,** Trichina.

wormian bone (wer′me-an) [Olaus *Worm,* Danish anatomist, 1588–1654]. See under *bone.*

Wormley's test (worm′lēz) [Theodore G. *Wormley,* Philadelphia chemist, 1826–1897]. See under *tests.*

Worm-Müller's test (vorm-mil′erz) [Jacob *Worm-Müller,* Norwegian physician, 1834–1889]. See under *tests.*

Woulfe's bottle (woolfs) [Peter *Woulfe,* English chemist, 1727–1803]. See under *bottle.*

wound (wo͞ond) [L. *vulnus*]. An injury to the body caused by physical means, with disruption of the normal continuity of body structures. **aseptic w.,** one which is not infected with pathogenic germs. **blowing w.,** open pneumothorax. **bullet w.,** one made by a bullet. **contused w.,** a wound in which the skin is unbroken. **gunshot w.,** a wound produced by a projectile from a gun. **gutter w.,** a glancing wound which produces a furrow or groove on the wounded part. **incised w.,** one caused by a cutting instrument. **lacerated w.,** one in which the tissues are torn. **nonpenetrating w.,** one in which there is no disruption of the body integument, the force being transmitted to subcutaneous tissues or viscera. **open w.,** one that has a free outward opening. **penetrating w.,** one in which the skin is disrupted, with entrance of the agent causing the wound into subcutaneous tissues or viscera. **perforating w.,** one in which the skin is disrupted with passage of the agent causing the wound through subcutaneous tissues and viscera, creating also a wound of exit. **poisoned w.,** one into which septic matter has been introduced. **puncture w.,** one made by a pointed instrument. **septic w.,** one that is infected with pathogenic germs. **seton w.,** a perforating wound, the entrance and exit of which are on the same side of the part. **subcutaneous w.,** one in which there is only a very small opening in the skin. **sucking w.,** traumatopneic w. **summer w's.** See *esponja* and *habronemiasis.* **tangential w.,** a glancing wound producing a lesion on one side of the wounded part. **traumatopneic w.,** a penetrating wound of the chest in which air is drawn in and out.

W.P. Abbreviation for *working point.*

W.R. Abbreviation for *Wassermann reaction.*

wreath (rēth). An encircling structure, resembling a circlet of flowers or leaves such as may be worn about the head. **daughter w.,** the amphiaster as viewed from its surface. **hippocratic w.,** the sparse peripheral rim of scalp hair which is the ultimate stage of male pattern alopecia.

Wreden's sign (vra′denz) [Robert Robertovich *Wreden,* otologist in Petrograd, 1837–1893]. See under *sign.*

Wright's syndrome (rītz) [Irving S. *Wright,* New York physician, born 1901]. See under *syndrome.*

wrightine (ri′tin). Conessine.

Wrisberg's cartilage, ganglion, nerve, etc. (ris′bergz) [Heinrich August *Wrisberg,* German anatomist, 1739–1808]. See under the nouns.

wrist (rist). The region of the articulation between the forearm and hand, or the corresponding part in the thoracic limb of a quadruped. **tennis w.,** tenovaginitis of the tendons of the wrist in tennis players.

wristdrop (rist′drop). A condition resulting from paralysis of the extensor muscles of the hand and fingers.

writing (rīt′ing). The inscription of letters or other symbols, and of words, phrases and sentences, usually on paper, so that they may be perceived by the eyes or, by the blind, through the fingertips. **automatic w.,** writing that is done more or less independently of the volition of the writer. **dextrad w.,** writing that progresses from left to right. **mirror w., specular w.,** writing in which the right and left relationships of letters and words are reversed, as if seen in a mirror. **sinistrad w.,** writing that progresses from right to left.

wryneck (ri′nek). Torticollis.

wt. Abbreviation for *weight.*

Wuchereria (voo″ker-e′re-ah) [Otto *Wucherer,* German physician in Brazil, 1820–1873]. A genus of white threadlike roundworms indigenous in various countries of warmer regions of the world. **W. bancrof′ti** is a white threadlike worm which causes elephantiasis, lymphangitis, and chyluria by interfering with the lymphatic circulation. The immature forms or microfilariae (*Microfilaria bancrofti*) are found in the circulating blood, especially at night, and are carried by Culex and other mosquitoes. **W. ma′layi,** a species occurring in India, China and Malaya and causing symptoms closely resembling those caused by *W. bancrofti.*

wuchereriasis (voo-ker″e-ri′ah-sis). Infestation with worms of the genus *Wuchereria.*

Wunderlich's curve (voon′der-liks) [Carl Reinhold *Wunderlich,* German physician, 1815–1877]. See under *curve.*

Wundt's tetanus (voonts) [Wilhelm *Wundt,* German physiologist, 1832–1920]. See under *tetanus.*

wurras (wur′as). Waras.

Wurster's test (vurs′terz) [Casimir *Wurster,* Dresden chemist, 1854–1913]. See under *tests.*

wyamine (wi′ah-min). Trade mark for preparations of mephentermine.

wycillin (wi-sil′lin). Trade mark for a preparation of penicillin G procaine.

wydase (wi′dās). Trade mark for preparations of hyaluronidase for injection.

Wyeomyia (we″o-mi′yah). A genus of culicine mosquitoes.

Wyeth's method, operation (wi′eths) [John Allan *Wyeth*, surgeon in New York, 1845–1922]. See under *method* and *operation*.

Wyethia (wi-e′the-ah). A genus of plants. **W. helenioi′des,** a composite-flowered herb of California; also a homeopathic preparation of same.

Wylie's drain, operation (wi′lēz) [W. Gill *Wylie*, gynecologist in New York, 1848–1923]. See under *drain* and *operation*.

Wysler's suture (vis′lerz) [F. *Wysler*, German surgeon]. See under *suture*.

X

X. 1. The homeopathic symbol for the decimal scale of potencies. 2. Abbreviation for *Kienbock's unit* of x-ray dosage.

xanchromatic (zan″kro-mat′ik). Xanthochromatic.

xanthate (zan′thāt). Any salt of xanthic acid.

xanthein (zan′the-in). A yellow coloring matter of plants, insoluble in alcohol, but soluble in water.

xanthelasma (zan″thel-az′mah) [*xantho-* + Gr. *elasma* plate]. A form of xanthoma affecting the eyelids and characterized by soft yellowish spots or plaques: called also *xanthelasma palpebrarum*.

xanthelasmatosis (zan″thel-az″mah-to′sis). Xanthomatosis.

xanthelasmoidea (zan″thel-az-moi′de-ah) [*xanthelasma* + Gr. *eidos* form]. Urticaria pigmentosa.

xanthematin (zan-them′ah-tin). A yellow, bitter substance derivable from hematin.

xanthemia (zan-the′me-ah) [*xantho-* + Gr. *haima* blood + *-ia*]. Presence of yellow coloring matter in the blood; carotinemia.

xanthene (zan′thēn). The compound, $(C_6H_4)_2$-(O)CH_2, or dibenzpyran, from which the xanthene dyes and indicators are derived.

xanthic (zan′thik). 1. Yellow. 2. Pertaining to xanthine.

xanthide (zan′thīd). Any compound of xanthogen.

xanthin (zan′thin). A yellow pigment obtained from yellow flowers.

xanthine (zan′thēn) [Gr. *xanthos* yellow: named from the yellow color of its nitrate]. A white, amorphous base, 2,6-dioxypurine, $C_5H_4N_4O_2$, from most of the body tissues and fluids, urinary calculi, and certain plants. It is formed by the oxidation of hypoxanthine and may be oxidized to uric acid. It is insoluble in cold water, but freely soluble in dilute acid and alkaline solutions. It possesses stimulant properties to muscle tissue, especially that of the heart. **dimethyl x.,** theobromine. **methyl x.,** heteroxanthine. **trimethyl x.,** caffeine.

xanthinin (zan′thĭ-nin). A white, crystalline substance, $C_4H_3N_3O_2$, formed by heating ammonium thionurate.

xanthinoxidase (zan″thin-ok′sĭ-dās). An enzyme which oxidizes xanthine and hypoxanthine into uric acid.

xanthinuria (zan″thin-u′re-ah) [*xanthine* + Gr. *ouron* urine]. Excess of xanthine in the urine.

xanthiuria (zan″the-u′re-ah). Xanthinuria.

xantho- (zan′tho) [Gr. *xanthos* yellow]. Combining form meaning yellow.

xanthochroia (zan″tho-kroi′ah) [*xantho-* + Gr. *chroia* skin]. Yellowish discoloration caused by changes in the pigmentary layer of the skin.

xanthochromatic (zan″tho-kro-mat′ik). Having a yellow color.

xanthochromia (zan″tho-kro′me-ah) [*xantho-* + Gr. *chrōma* color + *-ia*]. Any yellowish discoloration, as of the skin or of the spinal fluid.

xanthochromic (zan″tho-kro′mik). 1. Having a yellow color. 2. Pertaining to xanthochromia.

xanthochroous (zan-thok′ro-us) [Gr. *xanthochroos*]. Having a yellowish complexion.

Xanthochymus pictorius (zan-thok′ĭ-mus pikto′re-us). An East Indian plant called *thaikal:* it affords a purgative extract resembling cambogia.

xanthocreatine (zan″tho-kre′ah-tin). Xanthocreatinine.

xanthocreatinine (zan″tho-kre-at′ĭ-nin). A poisonous leukomaine, $C_5H_{10}N_4O$, occurring in muscle tissue. It resembles creatinine, and appears in the form of yellow crystals.

xanthocyanopsia (zan″tho-si″ah-nop′se-ah) [*xantho-* + Gr. *kyanos* blue + *opsis* vision + *-ia*]. Ability to discern yellow and blue tints, but not red or green.

xanthocystine (zan″tho-sis′tin). A substance found in tubercles from a dead body.

xanthocyte (zan′tho-sīt). A cell that contains yellow pigment.

xanthoderm (zan′tho-derm) [*xantho-* + Gr. *derma* skin]. A person belonging to a yellow race.

xanthoderma, xanthodermia (zan″tho-der-mah, zan″tho-der′me-ah) [*xantho-* + Gr. *derma* skin]. A yellow coloration of the skin.

xanthodontous (zan″tho-don′tus) [*xantho-* + Gr. *odous* tooth]. Having yellowish teeth.

xanthofibroma thecocellulare (zan″tho-fi-bro′mah the″ko-sel″u-lah′re). Luteoma.

xanthogen (zan′tho-jen) [*xantho-* + Gr. *gennan* to produce]. A coloring matter of vegetables, producing a yellow color with alkalis.

xanthoglobulin (xan″tho-glob′u-lin). A yellow pigment from the liver and pancreas.

xanthogranuloma (zan″tho-gran″u-lo′mah). A tumor having the histologic characteristics of both granuloma and xanthoma.

xanthogranulomatosis (zan″tho-gran″u-lo″-mah-to′sis). The Hand-Christian-Schüller form of xanthomatosis in which the lipid deposits are granulomatous and occur chiefly in the tissues about the skull.

xanthokreatinine (zan″tho-kre-at′ĭ-nin). Xanthocreatinine.

xanthokyanopy (zan″tho-ki-an′o-pe). Xanthocyanopsia.

xanthoma (zan-tho′mah). A condition characterized by the presence of small, flat plaques of a yellow color in the skin, due to deposits of lipids. Microscopically the lesions show light cells with foamy protoplasm (foam cells, or xanthoma cells). **craniohypophysial x.,** Hand-Schüller-Christian disease. **diabetic x., x. diabetico′rum,** a skin disease associated with diabetes mellitus, and marked by the formation of reddish, solid patches, larger than those of xanthoma. The patches sometimes have a yellow spot at the top. **x. dissemina′tum,** xanthoma distributed throughout the body in the tendon sheaths, periosteum or viscera as well as on the skin. **essential x.,** a heredofamilial form of xanthoma in which the lipid deposits consist largely of cholesterol and its esters. **x. mul′tiplex,** that which is distributed over the whole body, including the serous and mucous membranes. **x. palpebra′rum,** xanthoma that affects the eyelids; xanthelasma. **x. pla′num,** a disease attended with the formation of smooth, neoplastic plates in the skin. **primary x.,** essential x. **x. tubero'sum, x. tubero'sum mul'tiplex,** a form of infiltration lipidosis attended with the formation of neoplastic nodules upon the skin, chiefly of the palms, soles, and extensor surfaces of the extremities.

xanthomatosis (zan"tho-mah-to'sis). An accumulation of an excess of lipids in the body due to disturbance of lipid metabolism and marked by the formation of fatty tumors in various parts and sometimes by profound effects on bodily health. **x. bul'bi,** fatty degeneration of the cornea. **chronic idiopathic x.,** Hand-Schüller-Christian disease. **x. generalisa'ta os'sium,** lipid granulomatosis of the bones. **x. i'ridis,** the formation of yellow patches in the discolored iris of an eye blinded as the result of protracted iritis or glaucoma.

xanthomatous (zan-tho'mah-tus). Pertaining to or of the nature of xanthoma.

Xanthomonas (zan"tho-mo'nas). A genus of microorganisms of the family Pseudomonadaceae, suborder Pseudomonadineae, order Pseudomonadales, occurring as monotrichous cells producing a yellow pigment, the type species being *X. hyacin'thi.* Most of the 60 described species, as well as many of the 14 species provisionally included, are pathogenic for plants.

xanthomycin (zan"tho-mi'sin). A yellow antibiotic from cultures of a streptomyces.

xanthomyeloma (zan"tho-mi"ĕ-lo'mah). Xanthosarcoma.

xanthone (zan'thōn). 1. Xanthene ketone, CO:-$(C_6H_4)_2$:O, a derivative of xanthine. 2. Brometone.

xanthophane (zan'tho-fān). A yellow pigment from the retina.

xanthophore (zan'tho-fōr) [*xantho-* + Gr. *phoros* bearing]. A chromatophore of cold-blooded animals containing granules of yellow-red pigment: called also *lipophore.*

xanthophose (zan'tho-fōz) [*xantho-* + Gr. *phōs* light]. Any yellow or yellowish phose.

xanthophyll (zan'tho-fil) [*xantho-* + Gr. *phyllon* leaf]. The yellow coloring-matter of plants, the 3,3-dihydroxy alpha-carotene, $C_{40}H_{56}O_2$, occurring along with carotene in green leaves, grass and other vegetable matter.

xanthopia (zan-tho'pe-ah). Xanthopsia.

xanthopicrite (zan"tho-pik'rīt). Berberine.

xanthoplasty (zan'tho-plas"te) [*xantho-* + Gr. *plassein* to form]. Xanthoderma.

xanthoproteic (zan"tho-pro-te'ik). Pertaining to xanthoprotein.

xanthoprotein (zan"tho-pro'te-in). An orange pigment produced by heating proteins with nitric acid.

xanthopsia (zan-thop'se-ah) [*xantho-* + Gr. *opsis* vision + *-ia*]. A form of chromatopsia in which objects looked at appear yellow.

xanthopsin (zan-thop'sin). A conjugated protein, the prosthetic group of which is retinene, a product of visual purple through bleaching by light.

xanthopsis (zan-thop'sis) [*xantho-* + Gr. *opsis* appearance]. A yellow pigment or pigmentation in cancers.

xanthopsydracia (zan-thop"si-dra'she-ah) [*xantho-* + Gr. *psydrax* pustule]. The occurrence on the skin of small yellow pustules.

xanthopterin (zan-thop'ter-in) [*xanto-* + Gr. *pteron* wing]. A yellow pigment, $C_{19}H_{18}O_6N_6$, from the integument of wasps and hornets and from butterfly wings, which has some hematopoietic activity in anemic animals. It has been suggested that the pterin is part of the folic acid molecule. See *pterin.*

xanthopuccine (zan"tho-puk'sin) [*xantho-* + *puccoon,* Algonquin name for plants used as pigments]. An alkaloid from *Hydrastis canadensis.*

xanthorhamnin (zan"tho-ram'nin). A yellow glycoside, $C_{34}H_{42}O_{20}$, from the fruit of several species of *Rhamnus.*

Xanthorrhiza (zan-tho-ri'zah) [*xantho-* + Gr. *rhiza* root]. A genus of herbs. **X. apiifo'lia,** a North American shrub, called yellowroot: the root and wood are bitter and tonic.

xanthorubin (zan"tho-ru'bin). Xantorubin.

xanthosarcoma (zan"tho-sar-ko'mah). Giant celled sarcoma of tendon sheaths and aponeuroses containing xanthoma cells and regarded as a phase of xanthomatosis. Called also *xanthomyeloma.*

xanthosine (zan'tho-sīn). A nucleoside, xanthine-9-ribofuranoside, $C_{10}H_{12}O_6N_4$, which on hydrolysis yields xanthine and ribose.

xanthosis (zan-tho'sis). A yellowish discoloration; degeneration with yellowish pigmentation. **x. cu'tis,** yellowish or orange-colored pigmentation of the skin, without involvement of the sclera, often following excessive consumption of carotene-rich foods. **x. diabet'ica,** a yellowish appearance of the skin of diabetics attributed to an excess of lipochromes in the blood. **x. of septum nasi,** yellow pigmentation of the mucous membrane of the nose, due to degeneration of the blood after hemorrhage.

xanthotoxin (zan"tho-tok'sin). A ketone, $C_{12}H_8$-O_4, found in the fruit of *Fagara xanthoxyloides.*

xanthous (zan'thus). Yellow or yellowish.

xanthuria (zan-thu're-ah) [*xanthine* + Gr. *ouron* urine + *-ia*]. Excess of xanthine in the urine.

xanthydrol (zant-hi'drol). A compound, $C_{13}H_{10}O_2$, or diphenyleneoxycarbinol.

xanthyl (zan'thil). The monovalent radical $C_{13}H_9O$.

xanthylic (zan-thil'ik). Pertaining to xanthine.

xantorubin (zan"to-roo'bin). A yellow pigment found in the blood serum after hepatectomy.

Xe. Chemical symbol for *xenon.*

xenembole (zen-em'bo-le) [*xeno-* + Gr. *embolē* insertion]. The introduction of foreign substances into the system.

xenenthesis (zen"en-the'sis) [*xeno-* + Gr. *enthesis* putting in]. Xenembole.

xenia (ze'ne-ah) [Gr. "a friendly relation between two foreigners"]. The appearance in the endosperm (seed) resulting from cross-pollination of dominant characters inherited from the male (pollen) plant.

xeno- (zen'o) [Gr. *xenos* a guest-friend; any stranger or foreigner]. Combining form meaning strange, or denoting relationship to foreign material.

xenodiagnosis (zen"o-di-ag-no'sis) [*xeno-* + *diagnosis*]. Diagnosis by means of finding, in the feces of clean laboratory-bred bugs fed on the patient, the infective forms of the organism causing the disease: used in the early stages of Chagas' disease.

xenodochia (zen"o-do'ke-ah). Medieval hospitals for poor and infirm pilgrims.

xenogenesis (zen"o-jen'e-sis). 1. Alternation of generation; heterogenesis. 2. The production of offspring unlike either parent.

xenogenous (zen-oj'e-nus) [*xeno-* + Gr. *gennan* to produce]. 1. Caused by a foreign body, or originating outside the organism. 2. Formed or developed in the host: a term applied to toxins formed by the action of stimuli on the cells of the host.

xenology (ze-nol'o-je). The science of the relations of parasites to their hosts.

xenomenia (zen"o-me'ne-ah) [*xeno-* + Gr. *mēniaia* menses]. Vicarious menstruation.

xenon (ze'non) [Gr. *xenos* stranger]. An inert gaseous element found in the atmosphere; atomic number, 54; atomic weight, 131.30; symbol, Xe.

xenoparasite (zen"o-par'ah-sīt). An organism not usually parasitic on the host, but which becomes so because of a weakened condition of the host.

xenophobia (zen″o-fo′be-ah) [*xeno-* + Gr. *phobein* to be affrighted by + *-ia*]. Morbid dread of strangers.

xenophonia (zen″o-fo′ne-ah) [*xeno-* + Gr. *phōnē* voice + *-ia*]. Alteration of the accent and intonation of a person's speech.

xenophthalmia (zen″of-thal′me-ah) [*xeno-* + Gr. *ophthalmia* ophthalmia]. Traumatic conjunctivitis.

Xenopsylla (zen″op-sil′ah) [*xeno-* + Gr. *psylla* flea]. A genus of fleas. *X. as′tia*, a rat flea of India which may transmit plague. *X. brasilien′sis*, a rat flea of southern India, Africa and South America, a transmitter of bubonic plague. *X. cheo′pis*, a rat flea of India and of the coast of the United States, which transmits plague and murine typhus. *X. hawaiien′sis* transmits a plague of field rats in the Hawaiian Islands.

Xenopus (zen′o-pus). A genus of amphibians. **X. lae′vis,** the South African clawed toad. See *xenopus test*, under *tests*.

xenorexia (zen″o-rek′se-ah) [*xeno-* + *orexis* appetite + *-ia*]. A perversion of appetite leading to the repeated swallowing of foreign bodies not ordinarily ingested.

xenyl (zen′il). The univalent chemical group, $C_6H_5.C_6H_4—$.

xeransis (ze-ran′sis) [Gr. *xēransis*]. A drying up; loss of moisture.

xerantic (ze-ran′tik). Causing dryness; siccative.

xeraphium (ze-raf′e-um). A drying powder.

xerasia (ze-ra′se-ah). A disease of the hair in which it becomes dry and dusty.

xero- (ze′ro) [Gr. *xēros* dry]. Combining form meaning dry, or denoting relationship to dryness.

xerocheilia (ze″ro-ki′le-ah) [*xero-* + Gr. *cheilos* lip + *-ia*]. Dryness of the lips, a form of simple cheilitis.

xerocollyrium (ze″ro-ko-lir′e-um) [*xero-* + Gr. *kollyrion* collyrium]. A dry collyrium; an eye salve.

xeroderma (ze″ro-der′mah) [*xero-* + Gr. *derma* skin]. A disease marked by roughness and dryness of the skin; especially a disease resembling ichthyosis, and marked by a dry, rough, discolored state of the skin, with the formation of a scaly desquamation. **follicular x.,** keratosis pilaris. **x. of Kaposi,** x. pigmentosum. **x. pigmento′sum,** a rare and fatal disease which is characterized by brown spots and ulcers of the skin, with muscular and cutaneous atrophy and telangiectasis. Called also *atrophoderma pigmentosum*, *Kaposi's disease*, and *melanosis lenticularis progressiva*.

xerodermatic (ze″ro-der-mat′ik). Pertaining to or of the nature of xeroderma.

xerodermia (ze″ro-der′me-ah). Xeroderma.

xerodermosteosis (ze″ro-derm-os″te-o′sis) [*xero-* + Gr. *derma* skin + *osteon* bone + *-osis*]. A mucocutaneous syndrome resulting from deficiency of glandular secretions, with dryness of the ocular, buccal, nasal, bronchial, digestive, and genito-anal mucosa, dryness and ichthyotic state of the skin, severe derangement of dental and osteo-articular calcification of the chronic rheumatic type producing progressive deformity, and various systemic manifestations.

xerogel (ze′ro-jel). A gel containing little liquid. Cf. *lyogel*.

xeroma (ze-ro′mah). An abnormally dry condition of the conjunctiva; xerophthalmia.

xeromenia (ze″ro-me′ne-ah) [*xero-* + Gr. *mēniaia* menses]. A condition in which the bodily symptoms of menstruation occur without any flow.

xeromycteria (ze″ro-mik-te′re-ah) [*xero-* + Gr. *myktēr* nose]. Dryness of the nasal mucous membrane.

xerophagia (ze″ro-fa′je-ah) [*xero-* + Gr. *phagein* to eat]. The eating of dry food.

xerophagy (ze-rof′ah-je). Xerophagia.

xerophobia (ze″ro-fo′be-ah). Inhibition of saliva flow because of fear, anger, or excitement.

xerophthalmia (ze″rof-thal′me-ah) [*xero-* + Gr. *ophthalmos* eye + *-ia*]. Conjunctivitis with atrophy and no liquid discharge, producing an abnormally dry and lusterless condition of the eyeball. It is due to a deficiency of vitamin A.

xerophthalmus (ze″rof-thal′mus). Xerophthalmia.

xeroradiography (ze″ro-ra″de-og′rah-fe). A dry, totally photoelectric process for recording x-ray images, using metal plates coated with a semiconductor, such as selenium.

xerosis (ze-ro′sis) [Gr. *xērosis*]. Abnormal dryness, as of the eye or skin. **x. conjuncti′vae,** xerophthalmia. **x. cu′tis,** asteatosis cutis. **x. parenchymato′sus,** xerophthalmia due to trachoma. **x. superficia′lis,** xerophthalmia due to abnormal exposure of the eyeball to the air.

xerostomia (ze″ro-sto′me-ah) [*xero-* + Gr. *stoma* mouth + *-ia*]. Dryness of the mouth from lack of the normal secretion.

xerotes (zer′o-tēz) [Gr. *xērotēs*]. Dryness.

xerotic (ze-rot′ik). Characterized by xerosis or dryness.

xerotocia (ze″ro-to′se-ah) [*xero-* + Gr. *tokos* labor + *-ia*]. Dry labor.

xerotripsis (ze″ro-trip′sis) [*xero-* + Gr. *tripsis* friction]. Dry friction.

Ximenia (zi-me′ne-ah). A genus of African olacineous trees: the drupes of some species are edible and aromatic.

xiphi- (zif′e). See *xipho-*.

xiphin (zif′in). A protamine from the sperm of the sword fish, *Xiphias gladius*.

xiphisternal (zif″e-ster′nal). Pertaining to the xiphisternum.

xiphisternum (zif″e-ster′num) [*xiphi-* + Gr. *sternon* sternum]. The xiphoid process (processus xiphoideus [N A]).

xipho-, xiphi- (zif′o, zif′e) [Gr. *xiphos* sword]. Combining form denoting relationship to the xiphoid process.

xiphocostal (zif″o-kos′tal) [*xipho-* + L. *costa* rib]. Pertaining to the xiphoid process and the ribs.

xiphodidymus (zif″o-did′ĭ-mus) [*xipho-* + Gr. *didymos* twin]. Xiphopagus.

xiphodymus (zi-fod′ĭ-mus). Xiphopagus.

xiphodynia (zif″o-din′e-ah) [*xipho-* + Gr. *odynē* pain + *-ia*]. Pain in the xiphoid process.

xiphoid (zi′foid) [*xipho-* + Gr. *eidos* form]. 1. Shaped like a sword. 2. The xiphoid process (processus xiphoideus [N A]).

xiphoiditis (zif″oid-i′tis). Inflammation of the xiphoid process.

xiphopagotomy (zi-fop″ah-got′o-me). Surgical separation of conjoined twins fused in the region of the xiphoid process.

xiphopagus (zi-fop′ah-gus) [*xipho-* + Gr. *pagos* thing fixed]. Symmetrical conjoined twins fused in the region of the xiphoid process.

xylanthrax (zi-lan′thraks). Charcoal.

xylem (zi′lem) [Gr. *xylon* wood]. The woody portion of a vascular bundle of plant tissue as contrasted with the *phloem*.

xylene (zi′lēn). 1. Dimethylbenzene; an antiseptic hydrocarbon, $C_6H_4(CH_3)_2$, from methyl alcohol or coal tar: used in microscopy as a solvent and clarifier. 2. A group of hydrocarbons of the benzene series.

xylenin (zi-le′nin). A poison like etherin, chloroformin, and benzenin, extractable by xylene from tubercle bacilli. Called also *xylenobacillin*.

xylenobacillin (zi-le″no-bah-sil′in). Xylenin.

xylenol (zi′lĕ-nol). Any one of a series of colorless, crystalline substances, $(CH_3)_2C_6H_3OH$, resembling phenol. **x. salicylate,** a white powder, $OH.C_6H_4.CO.O.C_6H_3(CH_3)_2$: antirheumatic.

xylidine (zi′lĭ-din). A compound, dimethyl aniline, $(CH_3)_2C_6H_3.NH_2$: used as a dye and for blending gasoline.

xylindein (zi-lin′de-in). A crystalline dye, $C_{34}H_{26}O_{11}$, from the wood of *Peziza*.

xylitol (zi′lĭ-tol). An alcohol, $CH_2OH(CHOH)_3CH_2OH$, from xylose.

xylitone (zi′lĭ-tōn). An oil, $C_{12}H_{18}O$, formed by treating acetone with hydrochloric acid.

xylo- (zi′lo) [Gr. *xylon* wood]. Combining form denoting relationship to wood.

xylocaine (zi′lo-kān). Trade mark for preparations of lidocaine.

xylogen (zi′lo-jen). Lignin.

xyloidin (zi-loid′in) [*xylo-* + Gr. *eidos* form]. A white, explosive substance, $C_6H_9(NO_2)O_5$, prepared from starch by the action of nitric acid.

xyloketose (zi″lo-ke′tōs). A pentose sugar, $CH_2OH(CHOH)_2CO.CH_2OH$, which has been found in urine.

xyloketosuria (zi″lo-ke″to-su′re-ah). The presence of an excess of xyloketose (pentose) in the urine; essential pentosuria.

xylol (zi′lol) [Gr. *xylon* wood]. Xylene.

xyloma (zi-lo′mah). A woody tumor on a tree or plant.

xylometazoline (zi″lo-met″ah-zo′lēn). Chemical name: 2(4-tert-butyl-2,6-dimethylbenzyl)-2-imidazoline: used as a nasal decongestant.

xylonite (zi′lo-nīt). A substance which resembles celluloid manufactured from pyroxylin.

xylopyranose (zi″lo-pi′rah-nōs). Xylose.

xylosazone (zi-lo′sa-zōn). The phenyl-osazone of xylose. It is isomeric with arabinosazone.

xylose (zi′lōs). Wood sugar; a pentose, $CH_2OH(CHOH)_3CHO$, obtained from beechwood, jute, etc., and sometimes found in the urine.

xyloside (zi-lo-sīd). An ester of xylose.

xylosidoglucose (zi″lo-sid″o-gloo′kōs). Primverose.

xylosuria (zi″lo-su′re-ah). Presence of xylose in the urine.

xylotherapy (zi″lo-ther′ah-pe) [*xylo-* + Gr. *therapeia* treatment]. Medical treatment by the application of certain woods to the body.

xylyl (zi′lil). The hydrocarbon radicle, $CH_3C_6H_4CH_2$. **x. bromide,** benzyl bromide. **x. chloride,** a compound, $CH_3.C_6H_4.CH_2Cl$.

xylylene-diamine (zi″lil-ēn-di-am′in). One of a group of compounds, $C_6H_4(CH_2.NH_2)_2$: used in making dye colors.

xyphoid (zi′foid). Xiphoid.

xysma (zis′mah) [Gr. "that which is scraped or shaved off"]. A material, like bits of membrane, seen in the stools of diarrhea.

xyster (zis′ter) [Gr. *xystēr* a scraper]. A surgeon's file or raspatory.

xystos (zis′tos) [Gr. *xystos* scraped]. Scraped lint.

Y

Y. Chemical symbol for *yttrium*.

yahourth (yah′oort). Yogurt.

yard (yard). 1. A unit of linear measure, three feet or 36 inches, being the equivalent of 0.9144 meter. 2. The penis.

yatobyo (yah″to-bi′yo) [Japanese *ya* wild, or field + *to* rabbit, or hare + *byo* disease]. Tularemia.

yaw (yaw). A lesion of yaws (q.v.). **guinea corn y.,** a lesion of yaws which resembles a grain of maize. **mother y.,** the initial cutaneous lesion of yaws. **ringworm y.,** a circular or ring-shaped lesion of yaws.

yawey (yaw′e). Affected with yaws.

yawning (yawn′ing). A deep, involuntary inspiration with the mouth open, often accompanied by the act of stretching; also called *pandiculation*.

yaws (yawz). An infection caused by *Treponema pertenue*, occurring in hot regions and marked by raspberry-like excrescences on the face, hands, and feet, and around the external genitals. The lesions may run together in fungus-like masses, may form pustules, or may become ulcerated. Called also *frambesia, pian, parangi,* and *bouba*. **bush y.,** cutaneous leishmaniasis. **crab y.,** yaws characterized by hyperkeratosis with fissuring and ulceration of the soles of the feet, and less commonly involving the palms of the hands.

Ya Yan Tzu. The Chinese species of the plant *Brucea:* its seeds are used in treating amebic dysentery.

Yb. Chemical symbol for *ytterbium*.

yeast (yēst). The common name of Saccharomyces, a genus of ascomycetous fungi, used for leavening bread, for producing alcoholic fermentation, and to some extent as remedial agents. Some yeasts are pathogenic for man. **brewer's y.,** yeast obtained as a by-product in the brewing of beer. See *dried yeast*. **dried y.,** the dry cells of any suitable strain of *Saccharomyces cerevisiae*, used as a natural source of protein and B-complex vitamins.

yeki (ya′ke) [Japanese]. Bubonic plague.

yellow (yel′o). One of the primary colors of wavelength of approximately 575.5 millimicrons. **acid y.,** fast y. **acid y. D.,** tropeolin OO. **acridinium y.,** the dimethyl derivative of acriflavine, $CH(NH_2.C_6H_5.CH_3)_2N(CH_3)Cl$. **alizarin y.,** an indicator used in the determination of hydrogen ion concentration with a pH range of 10.1–12.1. **brilliant y.,** an indicator used in determining hydrogen ion concentration of 6–8. **butter y.,** dimethyl-amino-azo-benzene. **canary y.,** auramine. **chrome y.,** lead chromate, $PbCrO_4$: used in stains and paints. **corallin y.,** the sodium salt of rosolic acid. **fast y.,** a yellow, acid azo dye, $(N.C_6H_4.SO_2ONa)_2NH_2$: used in staining bone. **imperial y.,** aurantia. **king's y.,** orpiment. **Manchester y., Martius y.,** a poisonous, yellow, azo dye, $C_6H_5(NO_2)_2OH$: used as a stain and in the preparation of light filters. **metanil y., metaniline y. (extra),** an indicator used in the determination of hydrogen ion concentration, with a pH range of 1.2–2.3. **naphthol y.,** Manchester y. **nitrazine y.,** an indicator used in distinguishing between acid and base solutions of low concentration. **Philadelphia y.,** phosphin. **pyoktanin y.,** auramine. **visual y.,** xanthopsin.

Yeo's treatment (ye′ōz) [Isaac Burney *Yeo*, London physician, 1835–1914]. See under *treatment*.

yerba (yer′bah) [Sp.]. Herb. **y. santa** (yer′bah sahn′tah) [Sp. "sacred herb"], eriodictyon.

yerbine (yer′bin). An alkaloid from *Ilex paraguayensis*, resembling caffeine.

Yerkes-Bridges test (yer′kēz-brij′ez) [Robert M. *Yerkes*, Boston psychiatrist, 1876–1956; James W. *Bridges*, Canadian psychiatrist, born 1885]. See under *tests*.

yerli (yer′le). A fine quality of Turkish opium.

Yersin's serum (yer′sinz) [Alexandre John Emile *Yersin*, Swiss bacteriologist in Paris, 1863–1943]. See under *serum*.

-yl [Gr. *hylē* matter or substance]. A chemical suffix signifying a radical, particularly a univalent hydrocarbon radical.

ylang-ylang (e″lahng-e′lahng). A tree of the

Malayan Islands, *Cananga odorata:* its flowers afford a fragrant volatile oil.

-ylene. A suffix used in chemistry to denote a bivalent hydrocarbon radical.

yochubio (yo-chu′be-o). Scrub typhus.

yodoxin (yo-dok′sin). Trade mark for preparations of diiodohydroxyquin.

yogurt (yo′goort). A form of curdled milk, produced by fermentation with organisms of the genus Lactobacillus.

yoke (yōk). A connecting structure; a depression or ridge connecting two structures. Called also *jugum.* **alveolar y's of mandible,** juga alveolaria mandibulae. **alveolar y's of maxilla,** juga alveolaria maxillae. **cerebral y's of bones of cranium,** juga cerebralia ossium cranii. **sphenoidal y.,** jugum sphenoidale.

yolk (yōk) [L. *vitellus*]. 1. The nutrient part of the ovum. 2. Crude wool fat or suint. **accessory y.,** the portion of the yolk that serves for the nutrition of the formative portion. **egg y.,** the yellow portion of the egg of a bird. **formative y.,** that part of the ovum from which the embryo is developed. **nutritive y.,** accessory y.

Young's operation (yungz) [Hugh H. *Young,* Baltimore urologist, 1870–1945]. See under *operation.*

Young's rule (yungz) [Thomas *Young,* English physician, physicist, mathematician, and philologist, 1773–1829, the "father of physiologic optics"]. See under *rule.*

Young-Helmholtz theory (yung-helm′hōlts) [Thomas *Young;* H. L. F. *Helmholtz,* German physician, 1821–1894]. See under *theory.*

yperite (i′per-īt). Dichlorodiethyl sulfide.

ypsiliform (ip-sil′ĭ-form). Upsiloid.

ypsiloid (ip′sĭ-loid). Upsiloid.

y.s. Abbreviation for *yellow spot* of the retina.

ytterbium (ĭ-ter′be-um) [from *Ytterby,* in Sweden]. A very rare metal; symbol, Yb; atomic number, 70; atomic weight, 173.04.

yttrium (it′re-um) [from *Ytterby,* in Sweden]. A very rare metal, allied to cerium; symbol, Y; atomic number, 39; atomic weight, 88.905.

yukon (u′kon) [*Yukawa,* Japanese physicist]. See *barytron.*

Yvon's coefficient, test (e′vonz) [Paul *Yvon,* French physician, 1848–1913]. See under the nouns.

Yzquierdo's bacillus (iz″ke-er′dōz) [Vicente *Yzquierdo,* histologist in Santiago, Chile]. A microorganism thought to be the cause of verruga peruana, or Carrión's disease.

Z

Z. Abbreviation for Ger. *Zuckung,* contraction.

z. Symbol for *atomic number.*

zacatilla (zak″ah-tēl′yah) [Sp.]. The choicest quality of cochineal.

zactane (zak′tān). Trade mark for a preparation of ethoheptazine citrate.

Zagari's disease (zah-gah′rēz) [Giuseppe *Zagari,* Italian physician (Naples), 1863–1946]. Xerostomia.

Zahn's lines, ribs (zahnz) [Friedrich Wilhelm *Zahn,* German pathologist, 1845–1904]. See under *line.*

zaire (zi′ra). An epidemic form of cholera occurring in Portugal.

Zambrini's ptyaloreaction (zam-bre′nēz) [A. R. *Zambrini,* Argentine physician]. See under *ptyaloreaction.*

zanchol (zan′kol). Trade mark for a preparation of florantyrone.

Zander apparatus (zan′der) [Jonas Gustav Wilhelm *Zander,* Swedish physician, 1835–1920]. See under *apparatus.*

Zang's space (zangz) [Christoph Bonifacius *Zang,* German surgeon, 1772–1835]. Fossa supraclavicularis minor.

Zangemeister's test (zan″gĕ-mīs′terz) [Wilhelm *Zangemeister,* German gynecologist, 1871–1930]. See under *tests.*

Zappert's chamber (tsap′erts) [Julius *Zappert,* physician in Vienna, born 1867]. See under *chamber.*

zaranthan (zah-ran′than) [Heb.]. A hardening of the breast.

zarontin (zah-ron′tin). Trade mark for a preparation of ethosuximide.

Zaufal's sign (tsow′fahlz) [Emanuel *Zaufal,* Prague rhinologist, 1837–1910]. Saddle nose.

Zea (ze′ah) [L.]. A genus of large grasses of which *Zea mays,* our ordinary corn or maize, is the only species.

zearin (ze′ah-rin). A colorless substance, $C_{52}H_{88}O_4$, from various lichens.

zeaxanthin (ze″ah-zan′thin) [*zea* + Gr. *xanthos* yellow]. A carotinoid, $C_{40}H_{56}O_2$, from yellow corn, egg yolk and *Fucus vesiculosus.*

zedoary (zed′o-a″re) [L. *zedoaria*]. The rhizome of *Curcuma zedoaria,* a plant of India, which resembles ginger.

Zeeman effect (tse′man) [Pieter *Zeeman,* Dutch physicist, 1865–1943]. See under *effect.*

zein (ze′in). A soft, yellowish prolamin obtainable from maize.

zeinolysis (ze″in-ol′ĭ-sis) [*zein* + Gr. *lysis* dissolution]. The decomposition or splitting up of zein.

zeinolytic (ze″in-o-lit′ik). Pertaining to, characterized by, or promoting zeinolysis.

zeiosis (zi-o′sis) [Gr. *zeiein* to boil, seethe + *-osis*]. Bubbling or blebbing activity, giving the appearance of boiling in slow motion, observed at the periphery of cells cultured in artificial media.

zeiotic (zi-ot′ik). Pertaining to or characterized by zeiosis.

zeisian gland, sty (zi′se-an) [Edward *Zeis,* Dresden ophthalmologist, 1807–1868]. See under *gland* and *sty.*

zeism (ze′izm) [L. *zea* maize]. A condition attributed to excessive use of maize in the diet.

zeismus (ze-is′mus). Zeism.

zeistic (ze-is′tik). Pertaining to maize.

Zeller's test, treatment (zel′erz) [O. *Zeller,* German physician]. See under *tests* and *treatment.*

zelotypia (ze″lo-tip′e-ah) [Gr. *zēlos* zeal + *typtein* to strike + *-ia*]. 1. Morbid or insane zeal. 2. Morbid jealousy.

Zenker's crystals, degeneration, diverticulum, etc. (zeng′kerz) [Friedrich Albert *Zenker,* German pathologist, 1825–1898]. See under the nouns.

Zenker's fixative, fluid, solution (zeng′kerz) [Konrad *Zenker,* German histologist, died 1894]. See under *fixative.*

zenkerism (zeng′ker-izm) [F. A. *Zenker*]. Zenker's degeneration of muscular tissue. See under *degeneration.*

zenkerize (zeng′ker-īs) [K. *Zenker*]. To treat with Zenker's fixative.

zeolite (ze′o-lit). A hydrated double silicate; probably the active constituent in permutit.

zeoscope (ze′o-skōp) [Gr. *zeein* to boil, seethe + *skopein* to examine]. An apparatus for determining the alcoholic strength of a liquid by means of its boiling point.

zephiran (zef′ĭ-ran). Trade mark for preparations of benzalkonium.

zero (ze′ro) [Ital. "naught"]. The point on a thermometer scale at which the graduation begins. The zero of the Celsius (centigrade) and Réamur temperature scales is the ice point; that of the Fahrenheit scale is 32 degrees below the ice point. **absolute z.,** the lowest possible temperature, designated as 0 on the Kelvin or Rankine scale; by definition this is equivalent to −273.15°C. or −459.67°F. **limes z.** See *Lo dose,* under *dose.* **physiologic z.,** the temperature at which a thermal stimulus ceases to cause a sensation.

zerumbet (ze-rum′bet) [East Indian]. A spice or drug, the dried rhizome of *Zingiber zerumbet:* now little used.

zestocausis (zes″to-kaw′sis) [Gr. *zestos* boiling hot + *kausis* burning]. The therapeutic application of a tube containing superheated steam.

zestocautery (zes″to-kaw′ter-e). A tube or appliance used in zestocausis.

ziega (ze-a′gah). A kind of curd made by treating milk with rennet and afterward with acetic acid.

Ziegler's operation (zēg′lerz) [S. Louis *Ziegler,* ophthalmologist in Philadelphia, 1861–1925]. See under *operation.*

Ziehen's test (ze′henz) [Georg Theodor *Ziehen,* German neurologist, born 1862]. See under *tests.*

Ziehen-Oppenheim disease (ze′hen-op′en-hīm) [Georg Theodor *Ziehen;* Herman *Oppenheim,* German neurologist, 1858–1919]. Dystonia musculorum deformans.

Ziehl-Neelsen's method (zēl-nēl′senz) [Franz *Ziehl,* German bacteriologist, 1857–1926; Friederich Karl Adolf *Neelsen,* 1854–1894]. See *stains, table of.*

Ziemssen's motor points, treatment (zēm′senz) [Hugo Wilhelm von *Ziemssen,* physician in Munich, 1829–1902]. See under *point* and *treatment.*

zimb (zimb). A fly of the genus *Pangonia,* found in Ethiopia: exceedingly annoying to man and animals.

Zimmerlin's type (zim′er-linz) [Franz *Zimmerlin,* Swiss physician, 1858–1932]. See under *type.*

Zimmermann's arch, corpuscle (zim′er-mahnz) [Karl Wilhelm *Zimmermann,* German histologist, 1861–1935]. See under *arch* and *corpuscle.*

zinc (zingk) [L. *zin′cum*]. A blue-white metal, many of whose salts are used in medicine: symbol, Zn; atomic number, 30; atomic weight, 65.37. Its salts are often poisonous, when absorbed by the system, producing a chronic poisoning resembling that caused by lead. **z. acetate,** a salt, $Zn(C_2H_3O_2)_2.2H_2O$: produced by the reaction of zinc oxide with acetic acid: used as an astringent solution in ophthalmia, and an irrigation in gonorrhea. **z. carbonate,** a salt, $2ZnCO_3.3Zn(OH)_2$: used as a dusting powder or in the form of a cerate. **z. chloride,** a white, or nearly white, odorless cystalline powder, $ZnCl_2$: used as an astringent. **z. gelatin,** a preparation containing gelatin, zinc oxide, and glycerin: used as a supportive and protective application in ulcers and varicose eczema. **granulated z.,** a granular form of zinc, made by pouring molten zinc, in a thin stream, into a vessel of cold water. **z. hydroxide,** a white powder, $Zn(OH)_2$, an ingredient of medicinal zinc peroxide. **z. iodide,** a white, granular powder, ZnI_2: astringent and caustic. **z. oxide,** a fine, odorless powder, ZnO: used as an astringent and protective. **z. permanganate,** a salt, $Zn(MnO_4)_2.6H_2O$, in violet crystals: antiseptic, sometimes used in urethritis. **z. peroxide,** a white to yellowish white odorless powder, ZnO_2: used in pharmaceuticals. **z. peroxide, medicinal,** a mixture of zinc peroxide, zinc carbonate, and zinc hydroxide: used as a local anti-infective and oxidant. **z. phenolsulfonate,** a colorless, crystalline salt, $(HO.C_6H_4.SO_3)_2Zn.8H_2O$: used as an astringent. **z. salicylate,** a salt in colorless crystals, $(C_7H_5O_3)_2Zn.3H_2O$, antiseptic: used in skin diseases, etc. **z. stearate,** a compound of zinc with variable proportions of stearic acid and palmitic acid, containing 12.5 to 14.0 per cent of zinc oxide: used as a dusting powder. **z. sulfate,** a colorless, crystalline substance, $ZnSO_4.7H_2O$: used as an ophthalmic astringent. **z. sulfocarbolate,** z. phenolsulfonate. **z. undecylenate,** a fine, white powder, $[CH_2{:}CH(CH_2)_8COO]_2Zn$: fungistatic. **white z.,** z. oxide.

zincalism (zingk′al-izm). Chronic zinc poisoning.

zincative (zingk′ah-tiv). Electrically negative, i.e., like the zinc in a Daniell cell.

zinciferous (zingk-if′er-us). Containing zinc.

zincoid (zing′koid) [L. *zincum* + Gr. *eidos* form]. The platinum (or other metallic) plate which is connected with a copper plate in the voltaic circuit. It is called *zincoid* because it takes the place of the zinc in the voltaic circuit.

zincum (zing′kum), gen. *zin′ci* [L.]. Zinc.

Zinn's artery, circlet, corona, ligament, membrane, zonule (zinz) [Johann Gottfried *Zinn,* German anatomist, 1727–1759]. See under the nouns.

Zinsser inconsistency (zin′ser) [Hans *Zinsser,* American bacteriologist, 1878–1940]. Lack of parallelism between local and systemic anaphylactic symptomatology.

zipp (zip). A paste made by grinding together 1 part of zinc oxide, 2 parts of iodoform and 2 to 3 parts of liquid paraffin. It is applied to wounds to facilitate healing.

zirconium (zir-ko′ne-um). A rather rare metallic element; symbol, Zr; atomic number, 40; atomic weight, 91.22; chiefly obtained from a mineral called zircon. **z. dioxide,** a heavy white powder, ZrO_2, used as a radiopaque medium in roentgenography of the digestive tract, and in an ointment for treating poison ivy dermatitis. **z. oxide,** z. dioxide.

zisp (zisp). A modified form of zipp in which zinc peroxide is used in place of zinc oxide.

Zn. Chemical symbol for zinc.

$ZnSO_4$. Zinc sulfate.

zoacanthosis (zo″ak-an-tho′sis). Any dermatitis caused by the retention of animal structures, such as bristles, stings, hairs, etc.

zoamylin (zo-am′ĭ-lin). Glycogen.

zoanthropic (zo″an-throp′ik). Pertaining to or characterized by zoanthropy.

zoanthropy (zo-an′thro-pe) [Gr. *zōon* animal + *anthrōpos* man]. The abnormal belief of a patient that he has become a beast.

zoescope (zo′ĕ-skōp) [Gr. *zōē* life + *skopein* to examine]. Stroboscope.

zoetic (zo-et′ik) [Gr. *zōē* life]. Pertaining to life.

zoetrope (zo′ĕ-trōp) [Gr. *zōē* life + *trepein* to turn]. An apparatus which affords pictures of objects apparently moving as in life.

zoiatrics (zo″e-at′riks) [Gr. *zōon* animal + *iatrikē* surgery, medicine]. Veterinary medicine.

zoic (zo′ik) [Gr. *zōikos* of or proper to animals]. Pertaining to or characterized by animal life.

Zollinger-Ellison syndrome (zol′lin-jer-el′lĭ-son) [Robert M. *Zollinger,* American physician, born 1903; Edwin H. *Ellison,* American physician, born 1918]. See under *syndrome.*

Zöllner's lines (zel′nerz) [Johann Carl Friedrich *Zöllner,* German physicist, 1834–1882]. See under *line.*

zomidin (zo′mĭ-din) [Gr. *zōmos* broth]. A constituent of meat extract.

zomotherapy (zo″mo-ther′ah-pe) [Gr. *zōmos*

broth + *therapeia* service done to the sick]. The treatment of disease by muscle plasma, meat juice, or by meat diet.

zona (zo′nah), pl. *zo′nae* [L. "a girdle"]. 1. An encircling region or area; used in anatomical nomenclature to designate any area with specific boundary or characteristics. Called also *zone*. 2. Herpes zoster. **z. arcua′ta,** canal of Corti. **z. cartilagin′ea,** limbus laminae spiralis osseae. **z. cilia′ris,** ciliary zone. **z. cor′nea un′guis,** stratum corneum unguis. **z. denticula′ta,** the inner zone of the lamina basilaris ductus cochlearis with the limbus of the osseous spiral lamina. **z. dermat′ica,** an elevation of thick skin around the protruding mass in spina bifida. **z. epitheliosero′sa,** an area of membranous tissue inside the zona dermatica. **z. facia′lis,** herpes zoster of the face. **z. fascicula′ta,** the thick middle layer of the cortex of the suprarenal gland. **z. gangliona′ris,** a mass of ganglion tissue on the pars cochlearis nervi octavi. **z. germinati′vum un′guis,** stratum germinativum unguis. **z. glomerulo′sa,** the thin outer layer of the cortex of the suprarenal gland, which is contiguous with the capsule. **z. granulo′sa,** cumulus oophorus. **z. hemorrhoida′lis** [N A], that part of the anal canal extending from the anal valves to the anus and containing the rectal venous plexus. Called also *annulus haemorrhoidalis* [B N A], and *hemorrhoidal zone*. **z. ig′nia,** herpes zoster. **z. incer′ta,** a mixture of gray and white substance between the nucleus subthalamicus and the dorsal layer of white substance of the hypothalamus. **z. ophthal′mica,** herpetic infection of the cornea. **z. orbicula′ris articulatio′nis cox′ae** [N A, B N A], circular fibers of the articular capsule of the hip joint which form a ring around the neck of the femur; they are especially prominent at the inferior and posterior part of the capsule. Called also *orbicular zone of hip joint*. **z. pectina′ta,** the outer part of the lamina basilaris ductus cochlearis running from the rods of Corti to the spiral ligament. **z. pellu′cida,** a transparent, non-cellular, secreted layer surrounding an ovum. **z. perfora′ta,** the inner portion of the lamina basilaris ductus cochlearis. **z. radia′ta,** a zona pellucida exhibiting conspicuous radial striations. **z. reticula′ris,** the inner layer of the cortex of the suprarenal gland, consisting of cells arranged as clearly anastomosing cords, and abutting on the medulla. **z. rolan′dica,** the motor area of the cerebral cortex. **z. serpigino′sa,** herpes zoster. **z. spongio′sa,** apex cornus posterioris medullae spinalis. **z. stria′ta,** a zona pellucida exhibiting conspicuous striations. **z. tec′ta,** canal of Corti. **zo′nae tendino′sae cor′dis,** anuli fibrosi cordis. **z. transfor′mans,** the connective-tissue layer of the intestinal wall where bacteria penetrating from the intestine are destroyed. **z. Valsal′vae,** lamina basilaris ductus cochlearis. **z. vasculo′sa,** a region in the supramastoid fossa containing many foramina for the passage of blood vessels. **z. Web′eri,** z. orbicularis articulationis coxae.

zonae (zo′ne) [L.]. Plural of *zona*.

zonal (zo′nal) [L. *zona′lis*]. Of the nature of a zone.

zonary (zo′ner-e). Zonal.

Zondek-Aschheim test (tson′dek-ash′hīm). See *Aschheim-Zondek*, and under *tests*.

zone (zōn) [Gr. *zōnē* a belt, girdle]. An encircling region or area; by extension any area with specific characteristics or boundary. Called also *zona*. **abdominal z's,** three zones into which the surface of the abdomen is divided by transverse lines. These zones are the *subcostal* or *epigastric*—that above the subcostal line; the *mesogastric*—that between the subcostal and intertubercular lines; and the *hypogastric*—that below the intertubercular line. **z. of alarm,** the upper internal portion of the supraspinous fossa, which represents the area of extreme projection of the apex of the lung where the earliest signs of tuberculous infection are to be sought. **androgenic z.,** the provisional cortex of the embryonic suprarenal gland, which is possessed of certain testicular hormonal functions. **anelectrotonic z.,** polar z. **apical z.,** a narrow area along the gingivae over the apexes of the roots of the teeth. **arcuate z.,** canal of Corti. **biokinetic z.,** the range of temperatures within which the living cell carries on its life activities, lying approximately between 10 and 45°C. **border z.,** a zone at the boundary of two contiguous structures, as that where the trophoblast and the endometrium meet. **cervi′cal z.,** that third of the coronal zone which is nearest the necks of the teeth. **Charcot's z.,** hysterogenic z. **ciliary z.,** the outer of the two regions into which the anterior surface of the iris is divided by the angular line. Cf. *pupillary z.* **comfort z.,** an environmental temperature between 13 and 21°C. (55–70°F.) with a humidity of 30 to 55 per cent. **contact point z.,** the middle third of the coronal zone of the teeth between the occlusal zone and the cervical zone. **cornuradicular z.,** the outer part of the fasciculus cuneatus medullae spinalis. **coronal z.,** the vertical surface (labial and buccal) of a crown of a tooth, divided horizontally into three areas, the occlusal zone, the contact point zone, and the cervical zone. **Cozzolino's z.,** fissula ante fenestram. **denticulate z.,** zona denticulata. **dentofacial z.,** the region of the face overlying the teeth and the alveolar processes of the jaws. **Dierk's z.** See under *layer*. **z's of discontinuity,** zones of varying optic density, seen with the slit lamp, in the lens of the eye; these zones are formed at particular periods in the prenatal development of the lens. **dolorogenic z.,** an area stimulation of which produces pain, or excites an attack of neuralgia. **dorsal z. of His,** the smaller upper thickening of the dorsal portion of the embryonic spinal cord projecting into the central canal; from it are developed the cerebral hemispheres and the thalami. **entry z.,** the area of the spinal cord where the dorsal spinal roots enter. **ependymal z.** See under *layer*. **epigastric z.** See *abdominal z's*. **epileptogenic z., epileptogenous z.,** an area stimulation of which may bring on an epileptic attack. **equivalence z.,** that dilution of the antigen, in a precipitin test, at which precipitation of the serum takes place. **erogenous z., erotogenic z.,** a portion of the body stimulation of which produces erotic excitation; such are the genitals, urethra, lips, anus, and breasts. **extravisual z.,** that part of the dioptric surfaces and mediums outside the visual zone, which is practically incapable of accurately focusing light. **fascicular z.,** zona fasciculata. **germinative z. of epidermis,** the portion of the epidermis comprising the stratum basale and stratum spinosum. **germinative z. of nail,** stratum germinativum unguis. **gingival z.,** the zone of the teeth extending along the gingivae between the apical and the cervical zone. **glomerular z.,** zona glomerulosa. **Head's z's,** areas of cutaneous sensitiveness associated with diseases of the viscera; called also *z's of hyperalgesia*. **hemorrhoidal z.,** zona hemorrhoidalis. **His's z's,** four thickenings which run the entire length of the embryonic spinal cord. **horny z. of epidermis,** that portion of the epidermis comprising the stratum corneum, stratum lucidum, and stratum granulosum. **horny z. of nail,** stratum corneum unguis. **z's of hyperalgesia,** Head's z's. **hyperesthetic z.,** a region of the body surface marked by abnormal sensibility. **hypnogenic z., hypnogenous z.,** an area of the body on which pressure will characteristically induce sleep. **hypogastric z.** See *abdominal z's*. **hysterogenic z., hysterogenous z.,** a region of the body on which pressure may elicit a hysterial attack. **inhibition z.** See *prozone*. **intermediate z.,** that portion of the field of vision which lies between the fifteenth and forty-fifth concentric circles. **interpalpebral z.,** the part of the cornea not covered by the eyelids when the eye is open. **language z.,** the word center of the cerebral cortex. **z. of large pyramids,** the deepest but one of the four zones in the cortex of the cerebrum. **lenticular z.,** an area of the cerebrum bounded anteriorly by the white substance of the inferior frontal gyrus, posteriorly by Wernicke's area, externally by the insula, and internally by the wall of the third ventricle; it comprises the external capsule, the lenticular and caudate nuclei, the anterior and posterior segments of the internal capsule, and the thalamus. **Lissauer's marginal z.,** a bridge of white substance between the apex of the posterior horn and the periphery of the spinal cord. **Looser's transformation z's,** dark lines seen on roentgenograms of bones, thought to represent pathological healing phases of fatigue fractures occurring in certain bone diseases. **mantle z.** See under *layer*. **marginal z.** 1. Boundary zone. 2. Marginal layer. **median root z.,** oval fasciculus. **mesogastric z.** See *abdominal z's.* **motor z.,** an area of the cortex of the brain which, when electrically stimulated, causes contraction of voluntary muscles. **nephrogenic z.,** the subcapsular layer of the kidney. **neutral z.,** the potential space between the lips and cheeks on one side and the tongue on the other, natural or artificial teeth in this zone being subject to equal and opposite forces from the surrounding musculature. **neutral z. of His,** a thickening of the dorsal portion of the embryonic spinal cord projecting into the central canal. **Nitabuch z.** See under *stria.* **nuclear z.,** vortex lentis. **Obersteiner-Redlich z.** See under *area.* **occlusal z.,** that third of the coronal zone of the teeth which is nearest the occlusal plane. **orbicular z. of hip joint,** zona orbicularis articulationis coxae. **z. of oval nuclei,** a narrow band of sustentacular cells with oval nuclei in the olfactory mucosa. **pectinate z.,** zona pectinata. **pellucid z.,** zona pellucida. **peripolar z.,** the region surrounding a polar zone. **placental z.,** the surface of the uterus to which the placenta is attached. **polar z.,** the region immediately around an electrode applied to the body. **z. of polymorphous cells,** the innermost or deepest of the four zones of the cerebral cortex. **proagglutinoid z.,** prozone. **pupillary z.,** the inner of the two regions into which the anterior surface of the iris is divided by the angular line. Cf. *ciliary z.* **reticular z.,** zona reticularis. **Rolando's z.,** the motor area of the cerebral cortex. **root z.,** that part of the white substance of the spinal cord which is connected with the anterior and posterior nerve roots. **z. of round nuclei,** a broad band of olfactory cells with round nuclei in the olfactory mucosa. **rugae z.,** rugae area. **segmental z.,** a zone of undifferentiated mesoderm between somites already formed and the primitive knot, from which additional somites will be produced. **z. of small pyramids,** the layer next beneath the superficial zone in the cerebral cortex. **subcostal z.** See *abdominal z's.* **sudanophobic z.,** a broad zone of cells which appears in the adrenal cortex of rats following hypophysectomy, and which does not stain with Sudan. **superficial z.,** the outermost of the four layers of cortical cells of the cerebrum. **tendinous z's of heart,** anuli fibrosi cordis. **transformation z.,** zona transformans. **transition z., transitional z.,** the circle in the equator of the lens of the eye in which epithelial fibers are developed into lens fibers. **transparent z.** See *transparent dentin,* under *dentin.* **trigger z.,** dolorogenic z. **Turck's z.,** zona transformans. **umbau z's** [Ger.], Looser's transformation z's. **Valsalva's z.,** lamina basilaris ductus cochlearis. **vascular z.,** zona vasculosa. **visual z.,** that part of the dioptric surfaces and mediums around an optic axis in which there is practically no aberration of light rays. **Weber's z.,** zona orbicularis articulationis coxae. **Weil's basal z.** See under *layer.* **Wernicke's z.** See under *center.* **Westphal's z.,** a zone of the posterior gray column of the spinal cord in the lumbar region: said to contain the exodic fibers concerned in the patellar reflex. **X z.,** androgenic z. **z. of Zinn,** zonula ciliaris.

zonesthesia (zo″nes-the′ze-ah) [Gr. *zōnē* girdle + *aisthēsis* perception + *-ia*]. A sensation of constriction, as by a girdle.

zonifugal (zo-nif′u-gal) [L. *zona* zone + *fugere* to flee from]. Passing outward from any area or region.

zoning (zōn′ing). The occurrence of a stronger fixation of complement in a lesser amount of suspected serum.

zonipetal (zo-nip′ĕ-tal) [L. *zona* zone + *petere* to seek]. Passing from outside into any area or region.

zonula (zōn′u-lah), pl. *zon′ulae* [L., dim. of zona]. A small zone, or zonula. **z. cilia′ris** [N A], **z. cilia′ris [Zin′nii]** [B N A], a system of fibers extending between the ciliary body and the equator of the lens, holding the lens in place. Called also *ciliary zonule.*

zonulae (zon′u-le) [L.]. Plural of *zonula.*

zonular (zon′u-lar). Pertaining to a zonule.

zonule (zōn′ul). A small zone. Called also *zonula.* **ciliary z., z. of Zinn,** zonula ciliaris.

zonulitis (zōn″u-li′tis). Inflammation of the ciliary zonule.

zonulolysis (zon″u-lol′ĭ-sis) [*zonule* + Gr. *lysis* dissolution]. Dissolution of the zonule of Zinn (zonula ciliaris) in surgery, by means of enzymes, such as alpha-chymotrypsin.

zonulotomy (zon″u-lot′o-me) [*zonule* + Gr. *tomē* a cutting]. Incision of the ciliary zonule.

zonulysis (zon″u-li′sis). Zonulolysis.

zoo- [Gr. *zōon* animal]. Combining form denoting relationship to an animal.

zoo-agglutinin (zo″o-ah-gloo′tĭ-nin). A substance in animal poisons having the power of agglutinating red blood corpuscles.

zooamylon (zo″o-am′ĭ-lon) [*zoo-* + Gr. *amylon* starch]. Animal starch; glycogen.

zoo-anaphylactogen (zo″o-an″ah-fi-lak′to-jen). Zoosensitinogen.

zoobiology (zo″o-bi-ol′o-je) [*zoo-* + Gr. *bios* life + *-logy*]. The biology of animals.

zoobiotism (zo″o-bi′o-tizm). Biotics.

zooblast (zo′o-blast) [*zoo-* + Gr. *blastos* germ]. An animal cell.

zoochemical (zo″o-kem′ĭ-kal). Pertaining to zoochemistry.

zoochemistry (zo″o-kem′is-tre). The study of the chemical reactions occurring in animal tissues.

zoocyst (zo′o-sist). A protozoan cyst.

zoodermic (zo″o-der′mik) [*zoo-* + Gr. *derma* skin]. Performed with the skin of an animal; said of skin grafting in which the grafts are from the skin of an animal.

zoodetritus (zo″o-de-tri′tus). Detritus produced by the disintegration and decomposition of animal organisms.

zoodynamic (zo″o-di-nam′ik). Pertaining to zoodynamics.

zoodynamics (zo″o-di-nam′iks) [*zoo-* + Gr. *dynamis* power]. Animal physiology.

zooerastia (zo″o-e-ras′te-ah) [*zoo-* + Gr. *erastēs* lover]. Sexual intercourse with an animal.

zoofulvin (zo″o-ful′vin). A yellow pigment from the feathers of certain birds.

zoogenesis (zo″o-jen′e-sis). Zoogeny.

zoogenous (zo-oj′e-nus). 1. Acquired from animals. 2. Viviparous.

zoogeny (zo-oj′e-ne) [*zoo-* + Gr. *gennan* to produce]. The development and evolution of animals.

zoogeography (zo″o-je-og′rah-fe). The study of the distribution of animal life on the earth.

zooglea (zo″o-gle′ah) [*zoo-* + Gr. *gloios* gum]. A colony of bacteria embedded in a gelatinous matrix.

zoogleic (zo″o-gle′ik). Pertaining to or characterized by the presence of zooglea.

Zoogloea (zo″o-gle′ah). A genus of microorganisms of the family Pseudomonadaceae, suborder Pseudomonadineae, order Pseudomonadales, occurring as rod-shaped cells embedded in a gelatinous matrix. It includes two species, *Z. filipen′dula* and *Z. rami′gera.*

zoogloea (zo″o-gle′ah). Zooglea.

zoogloeic (zo″o-gle′ik). Zoogleic.

zoogonous (zo-og′o-nus). Viviparous.

zoogony (zo-og′o-ne) [*zoo-* + Gr. *gonē* offspring]. The production of living young from within the body.

zoograft (zo′o-graft). A graft of tissue from an animal; a zooplastic graft.

zoografting (zo′o-graft″ing). The grafting of an animal tissue upon the human body.

zoography (zo-og′rah-fe) [*zoo-* + Gr. *graphein* to write]. A treatise on animals.

zoohormone (zo″o-hor′mōn). An animal hormone.

zooid (zo′oid) [*zoo-* + Gr. *eidos* form]. **1.** Resembling an animal. 2. An object or form which resembles an animal. 3. One of the individuals in a united colony of animals.

zookinase (zo″o-kin′ās). A naturally occurring activator of autolytic activity in a cell.

zoolagnia (zo″o-lag′ne-ah) [*zoo-* + Gr. *lagneia* lust]. Sexual attraction toward animals.

zoology (zo-ol′o-je) [*zoo-* + Gr. *logos* treatise]. The biology of animals; the sum of what is known regarding animals. **experimental z.,** the study of animals by means of experiments performed upon them.

zoomania (zo″o-ma′ne-ah) [*zoo-* + Gr. *mania* madness]. A morbid love of animals.

zoomylus (zo-om′ĭ-lus). A dermoid cyst.

zoonerythrin (zo″on-er′ĭ-thrin) [*zoo-* + Gr. *erythros* red]. Crustaceorubin.

zoonite (zo′o-nīt). A cerebrospinal metamere.

zoonomy (zo-on′o-me) [*zoo-* + Gr. *nomos* law]. Zoobiology.

zoonoses (zo″o-no′sēz). Plural of *zoonosis.*

zoonosis (zo″o-no′sis), pl. *zoono′ses* [*zoo-* + Gr. *nosos* disease]. A disease of animals that may secondarily be transmitted to man.

zoonosology (zo″o-no-sol′o-je) [*zoo-* + Gr. *nosos* disease + *logos* treatise]. The classification of diseases of animals.

zoonotic (zo″o-not′ik). 1. Pertaining to zoonosis. 2. Due to animal parasites: said of certain diseases.

zooparasite (zo″o-par′ah-sīt). Any animal parasite.

zooparasitic (zo″o-par″ah-sit′ik). Pertaining to or produced by zooparasites.

zoopathology (zo″o-pah-thol′o-je). Animal pathology; the study of the diseases of animals.

zooperal (zo-op′er-al). Pertaining to zoopery.

zoopery (zo-op′er-e) [*zoo-* + Gr. *peiran* to experiment.] The performing of experiments on animals.

zoophagous (zo-of′ah-gus) [*zoo-* + Gr. *phagein* to eat]. Subsisting upon animal food.

zoopharmacology (zo″o-fahr″mah-kol′o-je). Veterinary pharmacology.

zoopharmacy (zo-o-fahr′mah-se). Veterinary pharmacy.

zoophile (zo′o-fīl) [*zoo-* + Gr. *philein* to love]. 1. Zoophilic. 2. An antivivisectionist.

zoophilic (zo″o-fil′ik). Preferring animals to man: said of certain mosquitoes. Cf. *anthropophilic.*

zoophilism (zo-of′ĭ-lizm). 1. Fondness for animals; opposition to vivisection. 2. The state of being zoophilic. **erotic z.,** sexual pleasure experienced in the fondling of animals.

zoophilous (zo-of′ĭ-lus). Zoophilic.

zoophobia (zo″o-fo′be-ah) [*zoo-* + Gr. *phobein* to be affrighted by]. Abnormal dread of animals.

zoophysiology (zo″o-fiz″e-ol′o-je). Animal physiology.

zoophyte (zo′o-fīt) [*zoo-* + Gr. *phyton* plant]. Any plantlike animal, such as sponges or hydroids.

zooplankton (zo″o-plank′ton) [*zoo-* + Gr. *planktos* wandering]. The minute animal organisms which, with those of the vegetable kingdom, make up the plankton of natural waters.

zooplasty (zo′o-plast″te) [*zoo-* + Gr. *plassein* to form]. Zoografting.

zooprecipitin (zo″o-pre-sip′ĭ-tin). A precipitin obtained by injections of protein substances of animal origin.

zooprophylaxis (zo″o-pro″fĭ-lak′sis). **1.** Prophylaxis applied to animals; veterinary prophylaxis. 2. Protecting man from the bites of mosquitoes by providing cattle or other animals for the mosquitoes to feed on.

zoopsia (zo-op′se-ah) [*zoo-* + Gr. *opsis* vision + *-ia*]. A hallucination in which the patient thinks he sees animals.

zoopsychology (zo″o-si-kol′o-je). Animal psychology.

zoosadism (zo″o-sa′dizm). Sadism directed toward animals.

zooscopy (zo-os′ko-pe) [*zoo-* + Gr. *skopein* to view]. 1. Zoopsia. 2. The scientific study or observation of animals.

zoosensitinogen (zo″o-sen″sĭ-tin′o-jen). A protein substance of animal origin capable of producing anaphylaxis. Called also *zoo-anaphylactogen.*

zoosis (zo-o′sis) [*zoo-* + *-osis*]. Any disease due to animal agents.

zoosmosis (zo″os-mo′sis) [Gr. *zōē life* + *osmosis*]. The passage of living protoplasm from the blood vessels into the tissues.

zoosperm (zo′o-sperm) [*zoo-* + Gr. *sperma* seed]. Spermatozoon.

zoospermia (zo″o-sper′me-ah). The presence of live spermatozoa in the ejaculated semen.

zoospore (zo′o-spōr). See *spore.*

zoosteroid (zo″o-ste′roid). Any steroid of animal origin.

zoosterol (zo″o-ste′rol). Any sterol of animal origin.

zootechnics (zo″o-tek′niks) [*zoo-* + Gr. *technē* art]. The art of breeding, keeping, and handling animals in domestication or captivity.

zootherapeutics (zo″o-ther-ah-pu′tiks) [*zoo-* + Gr. *therapeutikos* inclined to take care of]. The science and art of the treatment of diseases in animals.

zootherapy (zo″o-ther′ah-pe). Veterinary medicine.

zootic (zo-ot′ik). Pertaining to the lower animals. Cf. *demic.*

zootomist (zo-ot′o-mist). A dissector of animals.

zootomy (zo-ot′o-me) [*zoo-* + Gr. *tomē* a cutting]. 1. The dissection of animals. 2. The anatomy of animals.

zootoxin (zo″o-tok′sin) [*zoo-* + Gr. *toxikon* poison]. A toxic substance of animal origin, such as the venoms of snakes, spiders, and scorpions.

zootrophic (zo″o-trof′ik) [*zoo-* + Gr. *trophē* nutrition]. Pertaining to the nutrition of animals.

zootrophotoxism (zo″o-trof″o-tok′sizm) [*zoo-* + Gr. *trophē* nutrition + *toxikon* poison]. Poisoning with animal foods.

zooxanthine (zo″oks-an′thēn). A red pigment from the feathers of certain birds.

Zopfius (zop′fe-us). A former genus of bacteria, now named *Kurthia.* **Z. zenk′eri,** *Kurthia zenkeri.*

zoster (zos′ter) [Gr. *zōstēr*]. A girdle, or encircling structure or pattern. See *herpes zoster.*

Zostera marina (zos′ter-ah mah-ri′nah). Seawrack or eelgrass, a marine plant.

zosteriform (zos-ter′ĭ-form). Resembling herpes zoster.

zosteroid (zos′ter-oid). Resembling herpes zoster.

zoxazolamine (zok″sah-zol′ah-mēn). Chemical name: 2-amino-5-chlorobenzoxazole: used as a skeletal muscle relaxant and uricosuric agent.

Z-plasty (ze-plas′te). A plastic operation for the relaxation of contractures, in which a Z-shaped incision is made, the middle bar of the Z being over the contracted scar, and the triangular flaps rotated so that their apices cross the line of contracture.

Zr. Chemical symbol for *zirconium.*

Zsigmondy's gold number method (sig-mon′dēz) [Richard *Zsigmondy,* chemist in Göttingen, 1865–1929, the inventor of the ultramicroscope]. Lange's test. See under *tests.*

Zuberella (zu″ber-el′ah). A genus of gram-negative anaerobic bacteria.

zuckergussdarm (tsook′er-goos″darm) [Ger. "sugar-ice skin"]. Peritonitis chronica fibrosa encapsulans.

zuckergussleber (tsook′er-goos″la-ber) [Ger. "sugar-ice liver"]. Chronic perihepatitis characterized by a thickened whitish capsule.

Zuckerkandl's body, convolution, organs, etc. (tsook′er-kan″d′lz) [Emil *Zuckerkandl,* German anatomist, 1849–1910]. See under the nouns.

Zünd-Burguet apparatus (zint-boor-ga′). Electrophonoide.

zwetschgen-wasser (tsvetsh′gen-vos″er) [Ger. "plum-water"]. A cordial or liquor prepared in Germany from prunes.

zwieback (tsve′bak). Pieces of bread made of rich dough and heated in the oven until they are deep yellow in color.

zwischenkörper (tsvish′en-ker″per) [Ger.]. Amboceptor.

zwischenscheibe (tsvish′en-shi″bĕ) [Ger.]. Krause's membrane.

zwitterion (tsvit′er-i″on). An ion that is charged both positively and negatively.

zwölffingerdarm (tsvelf-fing′ger-darm) [Ger. *zwölf* twelve + *finger* finger + *darm* bowel]. The duodenum.

zygadenine (zi-gad′ĕ-nin). A crystalline alkaloid, $C_{39}H_{63}NO_{10}$, from *Zygadenus intermedius.*

zygal (zi′gal) [Gr. *zygon* yoke]. Shaped like a yoke.

zygapophyseal (zi″gah-po-fiz′e-al). Pertaining to a zygapophysis.

zygapophysis (zi″gah-pof′ĭ-sis), pl. *zygapoph′yses.* An articular process of a vertebra. See *processus articularis inferior vertebrarum* and *processus articularis superior vertebrarum.*

zygia (zij′e-ah). Plural of *zygion.*

zygion (zij′e-on), pl. *zygia* [Gr.]. An anthropometric landmark, being the most laterally situated point on either zygomatic arch.

zygo- (zi′go) [Gr. *zygon* yoke]. Combining form meaning yoked or joined, or denoting relationship to a junction.

Zygocotyle ceratosa (zi″go-ko′tĭ-le ser″ah-to′sah). A trematode parasitic in the intestine of ducks in North America.

zygocyte (zi′go-sīt). See *zygote.*

zygodactyly (zi″go-dak′tĭ-le) [*zygo-* + Gr. *daktylos* finger]. A term sometimes used to designate simple syndactyly, as distinguished from syndactyly in which there is bony fusion between the phalanges of the digits involved; usually occurring in the hand between the third and fourth digits, and in the foot between the fourth and fifth.

zygoite (zi′go-īt). An organism formed by zygosis; a zygote.

zygoma (zi-go′mah) [Gr. *zygōma* bolt or bar]. The zygomatic process of the temporal bone.

zygomatic (zi″go-mat′ik). Pertaining to the zygoma.

zygomaticofacial (zi″go-mat″ĭ-ko-fa′shal). Pertaining to the zygoma and the face.

zygomaticofrontal (zi″go-mat″ĭ-ko-fron′tal). Pertaining to the zygoma and the frontal bone.

zygomaticomaxillary (zi″go-mat″ĭ-ko-mak′sĭ-ler″e). Pertaining to the zygoma and the maxilla.

zygomatico-orbital (zi″go-mat″ĭ-ko-or′bĭ-tal). Pertaining to the zygoma and the orbit.

zygomaticosphenoid (zi″go-mat″ĭ-ko-sfe′noid). Pertaining to the zygoma and the sphenoid bone.

zygomaticotemporal (zi″go-mat″ĭ-ko-tem′poral). Pertaining to the zygoma and the temporal bone.

zygomaxillare (zi″go-mak′sĭ-la″re) [L.]. A craniometric point at the lower end of the zygomatic suture.

zygomaxillary (zi″go-mak′sĭ-ler″e). Pertaining to the zygoma and the maxilla.

zygomycetes (zi″go-mi-se′tēz). A group of phycomycetic fungi, including some of the molds.

zygon (zi′gon) [Gr.]. The bar or stem connecting the two branches of a zygal fissure.

zygoneure (zi′go-nūr) [*zygo-* + Gr. *neuron* nerve]. A nerve cell connected with other nerve cells.

zygoplast (zi′go-plast) [*zygo-* + Gr. *plassein* to form]. A body connected with the nucleus and giving rise to the flagellum in certain protozoa.

zygosis (zi-go′sis) [Gr. *zygōsis* a balancing]. The sexual union of two unicellular organisms.

zygosity (zi-gos′ĭ-te) [Gr. *zygon* yoke + *-ity* state or condition]. The condition relating to conjugation, or to the zygote, as (*a*) the state of a cell or individual in regard to the alleles determining a specific character, whether identical (homozygosity) or different (heterozygosity); or (*b*), in the case of twins, whether developing from one zygote (monozygosity) or two (dizygosity). Often used as a word termination affixed to a root descriptive of the condition.

zygosperm (zi′go-sperm). Zygospore.

zygosphere (zi′go-sfēr). A gamete which unites with another to form a zygospore.

zygospore (zi′go-spōr). A spore formed by the conjugation of two cells (gametes) which are morphologically identical and do not show any sexual differentiation. See *spore.*

zygostyle (zi′go-stīl). The last coccygeal vertebra.

zygote (zi′gōt) [Gr. *zygōtos* yoked together]. 1. The cell resulting from the fusion of two gametes; the fertilized ovum. 2. The individual developing from a cell formed by the union of two gametes. **duplex z.,** one possessing two identical genes for a given dominant character. **multiplex z.,** one possessing no gene for a given dominant character. **simplex z.,** one possessing only one gene for a given dominant character.

zygotene (zi′go-tēn). Amphitene.

zygotic (zi-got′ik). Pertaining to a zygote.

zygotoblast (zi-go′to-blast) [*zygote* + Gr. *blastos* germ]. Sporozoite.

zygotomere (zi-go′to-mēr) [*zygote* + Gr. *meros* part]. Sporoblast.

zylonite (zi′lo-nīt) [Gr. *xylon* wood]. Xylonite.

zymad (zi′mad). The organism of a zymotic or infectious disease.

zymase (zi′mās). 1. An enzyme. 2. A microzyme. 3. The intracellular enzyme of yeast by which alcoholic fermentation is produced; called also *Buchner's z.*

zymasis (zi′mah-sis). The excretion of the active substance of yeast by hydraulic pressure.

zyme (zīm) [Gr. *zymē* ferment]. 1. An enzyme. 2. Any pathogenic agent that produces a zymotic disease.

zymetology (zi″mĕ-tol′o-je). Zymology.

zymic (zi′mik). Pertaining to organized ferments.

zymin (zi′min). 1. A pancreatic extract prepared for therapeutic use. 2. Zyme.

zymo- (zi′mo) [Gr. *zymē* ferment]. Combining form denoting relationship to an enzyme, or to fermentation.

Zymobacterium (zi″mo-bak-te′re-um) [Gr. *zymē* leaven + *baktērion* little rod]. A genus of microorganisms of the family Propionibacteriaceae, order Eubacteriales, non–spore-forming, anaerobic to microaerophilic, gram-positive bacilli, nonpathogenic but occurring as parasites in the intestinal tract.

zymochemistry (zi″mo-kem′is-tre). The chemistry of fermentation.

zymocyte (zi′mo-sīt). An organism which causes fermentation.

zymoexcitator (zi″mo-ek′si-ta″tor). Any substance which serves to convert zymogens into their enzymes. Cf. *kinase*.

zymoexciter (zi″mo-ek-si′ter). Zymoexcitator.

zymogen (zi′mo-jen) [*zymo-* + Gr. *gennan* to produce]. An inactive precursor that is converted to active enzyme by the action of acid, another enzyme, or by other means. Called also *proenzyme*. **lab z.,** a proenzyme in the stomach that is transformed into lab ferment by acids of the gastric juice.

zymogenesis (zi″mo-jen′e-sis). The formation of an enzyme from a zymogen.

zymogenic (zi″mo-jen′ik). 1. Causing a fermentation. 2. Pertaining to a fermentation.

zymogenous (zi-moj′e-nus). Zymogenic.

zymogic (zi-moj′ik). Zymogenic.

zymogram (zi′mo-gram). A graphic representation of enzymatically active components separated electrophoretically.

zymohexase (zi″mo-hek′sās). An enzyme which catalyzes the splitting of fructose 1,6-diphosphate into dihydroxy acetone phosphate and phosphoglyceric aldehyde; said to be increased in tumor-bearing animals.

zymohexose (zi″mo-hek′sōs). A monosaccharide which ferments easily.

zymohydrolysis (zi″mo-hi-drol′ĭ-sis). Zymolysis.

zymoid (zi′moid) [*zymo-* + Gr. *eidos* form]. 1. Any poison derived from a decaying tissue. 2. A ferment or enzyme which has lost its power of decomposing the substratum, but not its power of uniting with it.

zymolite (zi′mo-līt). Substrate.

zymologic (zi″mo-loj′ik). Pertaining to zymology.

zymologist (zi-mol′o-jist). A specialist in the science of zymology.

zymology (zi-mol′o-je) [*zymo-* + Gr. *logos* treatise]. The sum of knowledge regarding fermentation.

zymolysis (zi-mol′ĭ-sis) [*zymo-* + Gr. *lysis* dissolution]. Fermentation or digestion by means of an enzyme.

zymolyte (zi′mo-līt). Substrate.

zymolytic (zi″mo-lit′ik). Pertaining to, characterized by, or promoting zymolysis.

zymome (zi′mōm). Microzyme.

zymometer (zi-mom′e-ter) [*zymo-* + Gr. *metron* measure]. Zymosimeter.

Zymomonas (zi″mo-mo′nas). A genus of microorganisms of the family Pseudomonadaceae, suborder Pseudomonadineae, order Pseudomonadales, occurring as rod-shaped or ellipsoidal cells in fermenting beverages. It includes two species, *Z. anaero′bia* and *Z. mo′bilis*.

Zymonema (zi″mo-ne′mah) [*zymo-* + Gr. *nēma* thread]. A genus of fungi of the family Eramascaceae. **Z. al′bicans,** *Endomyces albicans*. **Z. capsula′tum, Z. dermatit′idis, Z. gilchris′ti,** *Blastomyces dermatitidis*. **Z. farcimino′sum,** a species causing epizootic lymphangitis in horses.

zymonematosis (zi″mo-nem″ah-to′sis). Infestation with fungi of the genus Zymonema.

zymophore (zi′mo-fōr) [*zymo-* + Gr. *phoros* bearing]. The group of atoms in the molecule of an enzyme which is responsible for its specific effect.

zymophorous (zi-mof′o-rus). Pertaining to the zymophore; responsible for the specific action of an enzyme.

zymophosphate (zi″mo-fos′fāt). Hexosephosphoric acid occurring in yeast.

zymophyte (zi′mo-fīt) [*zymo-* + Gr. *phyton* plant]. A bacterium that causes fermentation.

zymoplasm (zi′mo-plazm). Thrombase.

zymoplastic (zi″mo-plas′tik) [*zymo-* + Gr. *plassein* to form]. Ferment forming.

zymoprotein (zi″mo-pro′te-in). Any one of a class of proteins having catalytic powers. They include catalase, chymase, papain, pepsin, peroxidase and urease.

zymosan (zi′mo-san). A mixture of lipids, polysaccharides, proteins, and ash, of variable concentration, derived from the cell walls, or the entire cell, of yeast, commonly *Saccharomyces cerevisiae*.

zymoscope (zi′mo-skōp) [*zymo-* + Gr. *skopein* to examine]. An apparatus for determining the zymotic power of yeast.

zymose (zi′mōs). Invertin.

zymosimeter, zymosiometer (zi″mo-sim′e-ter, zi-mo″se-om′e-ter). An instrument for measuring the degree of fermentation.

zymosis (zi-mo′sis) [Gr. *zymōsis* fermentation]. 1. Fermentation. 2. The development of any zymotic disease; the propagation and development of an infectious disease, known by the growth of bacteria and their products. 3. Any infectious or contagious disease. **z. gas′trica,** a condition marked by the formation of organic acids in the stomach, due to the action of yeasts.

zymosterol (zi-mos′ter-ol). Mycosterol; a sterol occurring in fungi and molds.

zymosthenic (zi″mos-then′ik) [*zymo-* + Gr. *sthenos* strength]. Increasing the activity of an enzyme.

zymotechnic (zi″mo-tek′nik). Zymurgy.

zymotechnique (zi″mo-tek-nēk′). Zymurgy.

zymotechny (zi″mo-tek′ne) [*zymo-* + Gr. *technē* art]. Zymurgy.

zymotic (zi-mot′ik). 1. Caused by or pertaining to zymosis. 2. A zymotic disease.

zymurgy (zi′mer-je) [Gr. *zymē* leaven + *ergon* work]. The art of brewing, distilling, and wine-making; the branch of chemistry that deals with the commercial application of fermentation.

zytase (zi′tās). An enzyme which changes xylan to xylose.

Zz. Abbreviation for L. *zin′giber*, ginger.

Z. Z.′ Z.″ Increasing degrees of contraction.